The Heath Anthology of American Literature

The Heath Anthology of American Literature

FOURTH EDITION

Volume 2

Paul Lauter
Trinity College
General Editor

Richard Yarborough
University of California, Los Angeles
Associate General Editor

Jackson Bryer
University of Maryland

Anne Goodwyn Jones
University of Florida

King-Kok Cheung
University of California, Los Angeles

Wendy Martin
Claremont Graduate University

Charles Molesworth
Queens College, City University of New York

Raymund Paredes
University of California, Los Angeles

Ivy T. Schweitzer
Dartmouth College

Linda Wagner-Martin
University of North Carolina, Chapel Hill

Andrew O. Wiget
New Mexico State University

Sandra A. Zagarell
Oberlin College

John Alberti
Northern Kentucky University
Editor, Instructor's Guide

James Kyung-Jin Lee
The University of Texas at Austin
Associate Editor

Randall Bass
Georgetown University
Electronic Resources Editor

Lois Leveen
Reed College
Electronic Resources Editor

Edward Maloney
Georgetown University
Electronic Resources Editor

Houghton Mifflin Company
Boston New York

Editor in Chief: Patricia A. Coryell
Sponsoring Editor: Michael Gillespie
Development Editor: Janet Edmonds
Senior Project Editor: Kathryn Dinovo
Senior Cover Design Coordinator: Deborah Azerrad Savona
Manufacturing Manager: Florence Cadran
Marketing Manager: Cindy Graff Cohen

Cover image: Furedi, Lily (b. 1901). *Subway*, 1934. Oil on canvas. Smithsonian American Art Museum, Washington, D.C./Art Resource, N.Y.

Printed in the U.S.A.

Library of Congress Control Number: 2001087561

ISBN: 0-618-10920-X

3 4 5 6 7 8 9-DOC-05 04 03

CONTENTS

PREFACE

When *The Heath Anthology of American Literature* first came out in 1989, it was both a symbol and a tool. It symbolized the desire among many teachers, critics, and students to study the full range of the literatures produced in America rather than the very limited number of works that had come to be known as the "literary canon." And it provided a tool, in the form of a diverse collection of literary works, for broadening our view of the authors and texts worth reading and thinking about. The *Heath,* as it has come to be called, challenged all of us to respond to earlier movements for social change that had asked of our classrooms, our curricula, and our textbooks questions like "Where are the minorities?" and "Where are the women?" And once these voices began to be heard, new questions arose, like "What differences did difference make?" and "How would our understanding of *all* American culture be transformed by their inclusion in the cultural conversation?"

In the years since, most anthologies of American literature followed our lead in diversifying the scope of what constituted "American literature," moving away from the idea that the culture of this nation could adequately be represented by eight or twelve or even forty American authors. And most courses in American literature today have come to include an expansive selection of writers that would have been unthinkable even twenty years ago. In many respects, then, the "question of the canon," as it came to be called, has been resolved: it is now widely agreed that the writers and the works you will find in these volumes constitute meaningful parts of that vast panorama of mountains, hills, and valleys, baffling forests and dry arroyos, city boulevards and village lanes, that we call "American literature."

That *was* the story of the *Heath.* What *is* its story today, in the second decade of its existence, as well as in a new century?

Today's *Heath* maintains its emphasis on the multiple origins and histories of the cultures of the United States and on the need to see literary works in relation to the particular historical circumstances in which they appeared, were circulated, and read. But we are increasingly interested in the ongoing conversations among these cultures; how they engage with and influence one another; whether (as Bartolomeo Vanzetti put it) some voices "must speak loudly to be heard" while others "have only to whisper and even be silent to be understood"; and how these conversations have come to define America as plural, complex, heterogeneous—a chorus, perhaps, rather than a melting pot. We have reorganized much of Volume 1 and added a number of texts (for example, those about Spanish America and the Southwest) in order to portray more fully the emergence of the varied cultures of the United States. Readers will find what we believe to be more historically coherent and usable presentations of the cultures of Native America, New Spain, New England, the Middle Atlantic, and the South. At the same time, we have emphasized works that illustrate how the borders between these cultures were, and have remained, places of political and cultural tension but also permeable, open to interaction and change. We have striven not only to clarify regional and cultural differences but to offer more of a hemispheric view, while maintaining the focus necessary to most courses on the literatures of what is now the United States. We think these reconfigurations open opportunities to think differently about how national identities are constructed, not only in the past but in today's global city—national identities that have been constituted sometimes in ways that have engaged admiration and hope, sometimes by "designs of darkness to appall," to ring a change on Frost's memorable line.

The new *Heath* also is fashioned to raise a number of questions increasingly on the agenda of literary and cultural study. These include the fundamental issue of what defines "the literary"; how, indeed whether, it might be distinguished from other forms of writing; and what we mean when we talk of the *aesthetic* value of a work. We have therefore widened the range of genres included in the anthology, for example, by adding novels (*The Scarlet Letter* in Volume 1 and *The Awakening* in Volume 2), extending our inclusion of popular cultural forms like songs, and offering a full repertoire of the variety of compositions used to construct a "republic of letters," especially during the first four hundred years of the advent of European writing technologies in the Americas. We also have looked hard at works (as some of the alterations in Volume 2 will illustrate) to ask about the changing ways in which certain literary texts challenge and attract readers' responses while others strike us as "weary, stale, flat, and unprofitable."

To say this another way, the initial idea of the *Heath* was to promote and enable the inclusion in literature courses of the diverse voices of America and the variety of issues to which they spoke. That goal, though not always implemented in practice, has, in our view, been generally accepted in principle across the profession. It seems time, therefore, to listen more fully to the timbre and tone, the music and the dream, of these voices themselves. We continue to believe that some works are better seen in the context of the historical specificity that certain thematic groupings preserve, and we have therefore, for example, retained units like that in the Early Nineteenth Century section on "Literature and 'The Woman Question.'" Still, we believe the more flexible organizational formats of this edition will better serve teachers as well as students.

The construction of an anthology, like that of a syllabus, is of course an ongoing struggle, a process of discussion, alteration, success, compromise, and "visions and revisions" that many classroom moments will revise. We continue to invite the participation in these processes of all users of these books—students, teachers, critics, even the newspaper columnists who periodically pronounce upon the *Heath*. In the preface to the first edition we quoted Emerson to the effect that "each new age requires a new confession." Perhaps in a speeded-up electronic dispensation the phrase should be "each new year." However that might be, these books will continue to change, continue to respond to altered cultural and aesthetic imperatives. Still, we remain committed to certain core values: preserving the complex connections between historical realities and the literary works that emerge within them; extending what remains the greatest diversity of coverage in any American literature textbook; and sustaining this work as a participatory and democratic experiment of a community of scholars, students, and teachers.

Specific features of this, the Fourth Edition of the *Heath Anthology of American Literature,* include:

Colonial Period to 1700

Changes in this section reflect the growing interest among scholars of early American and New World studies in literature not originally in English and its impact upon the predominately English literatures of North America. These changes also reflect a growing consensus that while the literature and culture of New England and colonial English Puritanism were major influences in the shaping of American literature and of U.S. national identity, they were neither homogeneous nor the only influences that students should study. We have made our Native American offerings more broadly representative, and we have carried forward the effort to place them more fully in relation to European American literary texts and cultural movements.

The most significant change occurs in the subsection formerly entitled "Cultures in Contact," which has been reorganized along regional lines to suggest the development and facilitate the comparison of *different* imperial agendas. The subsection now includes the writings from the subsection called "Voices from Anglo-America" in the third edition. In this new arrangement, the subsection on New Spain brings together all of the selections from Spanish expeditions and settlements across the continent and now includes selections from the important mid-seventeenth-century woman writer, Sor Juana Inés de la Cruz.

The next new subsection, on New France, includes a selection from the *Jesuit Relation* of Father Isaac Jogues. A new subsection on the Chesapeake region highlights the exploration of the southeastern coast and includes material by Nathaniel Bacon on the important popular rebellion of 1676, and a ballad by a young felon transported to Virginia, which gives more insight into the lives of the servant and criminal classes forced to supply much-needed labor to the southern colonies. The subsection on New England now includes additional material from Mary Rowlandson's captivity narrative and some new texts—such as portions of Thomas Shepard's *Autobiography*—that suggest the diversity of genres and strains within New England Puritanism.

Eighteenth Century

The selections in this section of the anthology have been reorganized to suggest a hemispheric rather than a strictly British American perspective on revolution and nationalism. We have also expanded the selections by important women writers in this period. The first new subsection, "Settlement and Religion," includes several writers new to the *Heath:* for example, Louis Armand de Lom d'Arce, Baron de Lahontan, one of the most influential chroniclers of New France and an important source of Native American ethnography for Anglo-American writers in this period. Francisco Palou has been moved into this subsection, providing insight into the Spanish missionary movement in California. The selection of eighteenth-century poetry has been expanded to include the important woman writer Susanna Wright, selections from Margaretta Bleecker Faugère's work that presage early-nineteenth-century poetic trends, new selections from William Dawson and Thomas Godfrey, including an excerpt from the first blank-verse tragedy written in North America, and Canto 1 of Sarah Wentworth Morton's influential narrative poem, *Ouâbi.*

The renamed subsection "Voices of Revolution and Nationalism" includes selections from Handsome Lake on Native American movements; a new set of selections from the work of Mercy Otis Warren, including the complete version, fully annotated, of her satiric play, *The Group;* and excerpts from the political writing of Toussaint L'Overture. The final subsection in this period, renamed "Contested Visions, American Voices," includes expanded selections from J. Hector St. Jean de Crèvecoeur and added selections from Ann Eliza Bleecker, including excerpts from *The History of Maria Kittle.*

Early Nineteenth Century: 1800–1865

The early-nineteenth-century period has been largely reorganized. Major subsections emphasize literary and social developments in the differing geographical and cultural communities that came to constitute the United States: Native America, Spanish America, New England, and the South. Here we can see texts and writers in dialogue with one another as well as the somewhat differing social and political issues that help characterize these cultural communities.

At the same time, we have retained sections that teachers have found useful for the classroom, particularly those on "The Woman Question" and on the development of poetry. The fiction section has been reorganized into a single, chronological unit to capture a sense of its evolution over the sixty years or so encompassed by this part of Volume 1.

Late Nineteenth Century: 1865–1910

Changes in this section reflect conceptual shifts that more effectively expand the literary scope of the *Heath Anthology* beyond New England. These changes emphasize the way the literature of the late nineteenth century participated in—and helped articulate—the productive ferment of the post–Civil War national project of remaking America.

We have changed the name of the subsection "Regional Voices, National Voices" to "Nation, Regions, Borders." The Late Nineteenth Century section now begins with this subsection rather than "Developments in Women's Writing." We have rearranged the former's contents to highlight work from the South (especially New Orleans) and to accentuate the issue of miscegenation, one central focus of the racial anxieties of the era. We also have included border literature, moving the *corridos* to this subsection and complementing them with the work of the "border" novelist María Amparo Ruiz de Burton.

Keeping questions about the nation and the debates that occurred around them in the foreground, we followed this subsection with "Critical Visions of Postbellum America" and then with "Developments in Women's Writing." Harding Davis's "Life in the Iron-Mills" has been moved to Volume 1, owing to its year of publication, genre, and style.

The last subsection, formerly entitled "New Explorations of 'An American Self,'" is now called "The Making of 'Americans.'" The change in title and content reflects our understanding that "America" was in flux geographically as well as culturally and that its expansion was a matter of intense debate outside its borders as well as within and along them. We have moved José Martí's' "Our America" to this section; it concludes the Late Nineteenth Century section of the *Heath.*

The Modern Period: 1910–1945

The strength of the Modern Period selections is that the canonical authors and works—Eliot's "The Waste Land," Faulkner's fiction, Frost's poetry, and so forth—can be read alongside lesser known writers like H. L. Mencken, Randolph Bourne, Alain Locke (and others from the New Negro Renaissance, such as George Samuel Schuyler and Nella Larsen). This combination of the well-known with the lesser known has been one of the *Heath*'s major innovations, and it is well exemplified in the Modern Period.

Thus changes to this section in the fourth edition are relatively few. We substituted two Fitzgerald stories for the one in the previous edition, we changed the Faulkner selection somewhat by introducing one of his more artistically demanding stories. We added a selection from one of the voices of anti-modernism, H. L. Mencken, to better represent the South. The Gertrude Stein selections were recast to include both well-known and lesser known works.

The Contemporary Period: 1945 to the Present

The variety, and therefore representativeness, of the contemporary section has been further increased by the addition of new authors. Among them are Dorothy Allison, Sherman Alexie, Jack Kerouac, Frank Chin, Jessica Hagedorn, Mario Suárez, Richard Rodriguez, Lawson Fusao Inada, Yusef Komunyakaa, James Merrill, Kimiko Hahn, and Karen Yamashita.

New and existing selections have been reorganized and grouped into a "Beat Movement" subsection, a "New Communities, New Identities, New Energies" subsection that now includes Amiri Baraka's *The Dutchman,* and a Vietnam section that includes fiction by Tim O'Brien and poetry by Robert Bly.

A number of selections have been changed, and an essay by Audre Lorde has also been added to the subsection on "Postmodernity and Difference."

Some Words of Thanks and of Remembrance

A number of scholars who are no longer members of the editorial board contributed substantially to and wrote significant materials adapted for this, as well as previous, editions of the *Heath Anthology.* We want to acknowledge the very great contributions of Carla Mulford, who was the editor of the early sections of Volume 1 for the first three editions of this anthology. The late Elaine Hedges likewise served as editor for the Late Nineteenth–Early Twentieth Century section of Volume 2 for the first three editions, and the late Amy Ling provided guidance for a number of the introductions and headnotes as well as critiques of many parts of the book. We have tried to adapt their work with appropriate regard for their authorship and for the ongoing work of freshly understanding American culture, of which the *Heath Anthology* is one major product.

We also wish to acknowledge the contributions of other scholars who have, for periods of time, served on the editorial board and who, in a number of cases, wrote materials now incorporated into the text. These include Juan Bruce-Novoa, and Paula Gunn Allen. In addition, Paul Smith, the sponsoring editor of the first three editions of the *Heath Anthology,* at D. C. Heath and at Houghton Mifflin, effectively served as a full and active member of the editorial board; these books would not exist without his work and support.

A number of young scholars have worked with the editorial board members to bring this edition of the *Heath* to publication. Without their insights and their hard work, we would not have been able to complete the complex tasks involved in changing and refreshing this edition. They include Danielle Hinrichs, Claremont Graduate University; Sonnet Retman, Deborah Banner, and Grace Park, UCLA; Juanita Davis, Oberlin College; and Kelly Reames, University of North Carolina–Chapel Hill. Dean Clayton Koppes of Oberlin College and Raymund Paredes of UCLA provided generous support for this work.

We wish to take special note of the work of the new members of the editorial board: Ivy Schweitzer, Dartmouth College, who has had final responsibility for the early periods; Sandra A. Zagarell, Oberlin College, who has had final responsibility for the late nineteenth–early twentieth century period; and King-Kok Cheung, UCLA and the University of Hong Kong, who with James Kyung-Jin Lee, University of Texas, Austin, has had final responsibility for the Asian American selections.

One of the most important innovations connected with this edition of the *Heath Anthology* has been the enormous expansion of the materials available on the website for the anthology: http://college.hmco.com/english/heath. Those responsible for the development of the electronic materials are Randy Bass and Eddie Maloney, Georgetown University, and Lois Leveen, Reed College. John Alberti, Northern Kentucky University, has continued to edit the instructor's guide and, in that capacity, has contributed significantly both to the evolution of the website and to the work of the editorial board.

We are indebted to our reviewers, who offered us insights into necessary and desirable changes for this edition. They were Maryam Barrie, Washtenaw Community College; Sarah E. Chinn, Trinity College; Judith Cortellini, Lincoln College; Robert DeMott, Ohio University; Donald Gilzinger, Suffolk Community College; Neill Matheson, University of South Alabama; Douglas J. McMillan, East Carolina University; Thomas Moore, University of Maryland; Virgil W. Norris, Park College; Lisa Hammond Rashley, University of South Carolina, Lancaster; Shelley Reid, Austin College; Elaine J. Roberts, Judson College; Larry Severeid, College of Eastern Utah; John Allen Shearer, Jr., Geneva College; Suzanne Shepard, SUNY/Broome County Community College; Amy Smith, Hilbert College; Walter Squire, University of Tennessee; Marcy L. Tanter, Tarleton State University.

We want to extend our thanks to all of the contributing editors who devoted their time and scholarship to headnotes, choices of texts, and teaching materials. For the current edition they include: Jesse Alemán, University of New Mexico; Paula Bernat Bennett, Southern Illinois University, Carbondale; Renée L. Bergland, Simmons College; Cynthia Butos, Trinity College; Juliana Chang, Santa Clara University; Allan Chavkin, Southwest Texas State University; Amanda J. Cobb, New Mexico State University; Sharon L. Dean, Rivier College; Elizabeth Maddock Dillon, Yale

University; Joanne Dobson, Fordham University; Michael J. Drexler, Brown University; Hugh English, City University of New York; Allison Giffen, New Mexico State University; Susan Clair Imbarrato, Minnesota State University, Moorhead; Gregory S. Jackson, University of Arizona; Rose Yalon Kamel, University of Sciences in Philadelphia; Karen L. Kilcup, University of North Carolina–Greensboro; Daniel Y. Kim, Brown University; Walter K. Lew, UCLA; Cliff Lewis, University of Massachusetts, Lowell; Genny Lim, New College of California; Derek C. Maus, University of North Carolina–Chapel Hill; Meredith L. McGill, Rutgers University; Keith D. Miller, Arizona State University; Kelly Reames; Thelma Shinn Richard, Arizona State University; Douglas C. Sackman, University of Puget Sound; Thomas Scanlan, Ohio University; Gary Scharnhorst, University of New Mexico; Bethany Ridgway Schneider, Oberlin College; Ronnie Theisz, Black Hills State University; George Uba, California State University, Northridge; Judy Yung.

We also want to thank those who contributed to this as well as to earlier editions of this work: Thomas P. Adler, Purdue University; Elizabeth Ammons, Tufts University; William L. Andrews, University of Kansas; Frances R. Aparicio, University of Michigan; Elaine Sargent Apthorp, San Jose State University; Evelyn Avery, Towson State University; Liahna Babener, Montana State University; Barbara A. Bardes, Loyola University of Chicago; Helen Barolini; Marleen Barr, Virginia Polytechnic Institute and State University; Sam S. Baskett, Michigan State University; Rosalie Murphy Baum, University of South Florida; Herman Beavers, University of Pennsylvania; Eileen T. Bender, Indiana University at Bloomington; Carol Marie Bensick, University of California, Riverside; David Bergman, Towson State University; Susan L. Blake, Lafayette College; Michael Boccia, Tufts University; Robert H. Brinkmeyer, Jr., University of Mississippi; Carol A. Burns, Southern Illinois University Press; John F. Callahan, Lewis and Clark College; Jane Campbell, Purdue University, Calumet; Jean Ferguson Carr, University of Pittsburgh; Allan Chavkin, Southwest Texas State University; Beverly Lyon Clark, Wheaton College; C. B. Clark, Oklahoma City University; Arthur B. Coffin, Montana State University; the late Constance Coiner, State University of New York at Binghamton; James W. Coleman, University of North Carolina at Chapel Hill; Martha E. Cook, Longwood College; Angelo Costanzo, Shippensburg University; Patti Cowell, Colorado State University; John W. Crowley, Syracuse University; Sister Martha Curry, Wayne State University; Walter C. Daniel, University of Missouri–Columbia; Cathy N. Davidson, Duke University; Jane Krause DeMouy; Dorothy L. Denniston, Brown University; Kathryn Zabelle Derounian-Stodola, University of Arkansas at Little Rock; Margaret Dickie, University of Georgia; Raymond F. Dolle, Indiana State University; Sheila Hurst Donnelly, Orange County Community College; Carole K. Doreski, Daniel Webster College; Sally Ann Drucker, North Carolina State University; Arlene A. Elder, University of Cincinnati; Everett Emerson, University of North Carolina at Chapel Hill; Bernard F. Engel, Michigan State University; Betsy Erkkila, University of Pennsylvania; Lillian Faderman, California State University–Fresno; Charles Fanning, Southern Illinois University; Robert M. Farnsworth, University of Missouri–Kansas City; Laraine Fergenson, City University of New York, Bronx Community College; Judith Fetterley, State University of New York at Albany; Joseph Fichtelberg, Hofstra University; Lucy M. Freibert, University of Louisville; George S. Friedman, Towson State University; Susan Stanford Friedman, University of Wisconsin–Madison; Albert Furtwangler,

Mount Allison University; Diana Hume George, Pennsylvania State University at Erie—Behrend College; Leah Blatt Glasser, Mount Holyoke College; Wendell P. Glick, University of Minnesota; William Goldhurst, University of Florida; Rita K. Gollin, State University of New York College at Geneseo; Suzanne Gossett, Loyola University of Chicago; Philip Gould, DePaul University; Maryemma Graham, University of Kansas; Theodora Rapp Graham, Pennsylvania State University–Harrisburg; Robert M. Greenberg, Temple University; Barry Gross, Michigan State University; James Guimond, Rider College; Minrose C. Gwin, University of New Mexico; Alfred Habegger, University of Kansas; Joan F. Hallisey, Regis College; Jeffrey A. Hammond, St. Mary's College of Maryland; Earl N. Harbert, Northeastern University; Sharon M. Harris, Texas Christian University; Trudier Harris, University of North Carolina–Chapel Hill; Ellen Louise Hart, University of California, Santa Cruz; William L. Hedges, Goucher College; Joan D. Hedrick, Trinity College; Allison Heisch, San Jose State University; Robert Hemenway, University of Kentucky; Kristin Herzog, University of Massachusetts, Lowell; Donald R. Hettinga, Calvin College; Hilary W. Holladay, Independent Scholars Association of the North Carolina Triangle at Chapel Hill; Elvin Holt, Southwest Texas State University; Kenneth Alan Hovey, University of Texas at San Antonio; Akasha (Gloria) Hull, University of California, Santa Cruz; James M. Hutchisson, The Citadel; Paul Jones, University of North Carolina–Chapel Hill; Joyce Ann Joyce, Temple University; Nancy Carol Joyner, Western Carolina University; Rose Yalow Kamel, University of Sciences in Philadelphia; Carolyn L. Karcher, Temple University; Janet Kaufman, University of Iowa; Richard S. Kennedy, Temple University; Carol Farley Kessler, Pennsylvania State University; Elizabeth L. Keyser, Hollins University; Elaine H. Kim, University of California, Berkeley; Michael Kreyling, Vanderbilt University; Him Mark Lai; David M. Larson, Cleveland State University; Estella Lauter, University of Wisconsin–Green Bay; Barry Leeds, Central Connecticut State University; George S. Lensing, University of North Carolina–Chapel Hill; James A. Levernier, University of Arkansas at Little Rock; Cliff Lewis, University of Massachusetts at Lowell; Patricia Liggins-Hill, University of San Francisco; Shirley Geok-lin Lim, University of California at Santa Barbara; John Lowe, Louisiana State University; Juanita Luna-Lawhn, San Antonio College; Joseph Mancini, Jr., George Washington University; Daniel Marder, University of Tulsa; Robert A. Martin; Deborah E. McDowell, University of Virginia; Joseph R. McElrath, Florida State University; Peggy McIntosh, Wellesley College Center for Research on Women; Nellie Y. McKay, University of Wisconsin–Madison; D. H. Melhem, Union for Experimenting Colleges and Universities; Michael J. Mendelsohn, University of Tampa; Gabriel Miller, Rutgers University; James A. Miller, George Washington University; Jeanne-Marie A. Miller, Howard University; Keith D. Miller, Arizona State University; Arthenia J. Bates Millican; James S. Moy, University of Wisconsin–Madison; Joel Myerson, University of South Carolina; Cary Nelson, University of Illinois at Urbana–Champaign; Margaret F. Nelson, Oklahoma State University; Charles H. Nichols, Brown University Professor Emeritus; Vera Norwood, University of New Mexico; Michael O'Brien, Miami University; Margaret Anne O'Connor, University of North Carolina–Chapel Hill; Genaro M. Padilla, University of California, Berkeley; Linda Pannill, Transylvania University; James W. Parins, University of Arkansas at Little Rock; Vivian M. Patraka, Bowling Green State University; John J. Patton, Atlantic Cape

Community College; James Robert Payne, New Mexico State University; Richard Pearce, Wheaton College; Michael W. Peplow, Western International University; Ronald Primeau, Central Michigan University; John Purdy, Western Washington University; Jennifer L. Randisi, University of California, Berkeley; Geoffrey Rans, University of Western Ontario; Julius Rowan Raper, University of North Carolina at Chapel Hill; John M. Reilly, Howard University; Phillip M. Richards, Colgate University; Marilyn Richardson; Evelyn Hoard Roberts, Saint Louis Community College at Meramec; James A. Robinson, University of Maryland; William H. Robinson, Rhode Island College; Kenneth M. Roemer, University of Texas at Arlington; Judith Roman-Royer, Indiana University East; Nicholas D. Rombes, Jr., Pennsylvania State University; Lora Romero, Stanford University; Robert C. Rosen, William Paterson University; Deborah S. Rosenfelt, University of Maryland; Karen E. Rowe, University of California, Los Angeles; A. LaVonne Brown Ruoff, University of Illinois at Chicago, Professor Emerita; Roshni Rustomji-Kerns, Stanford University; Doreen Alvarez Saar, Drexel University; Enrique Sacerio-Garí, Bryn Mawr College; Ramón Saldívar, Stanford University; Sonia Saldívar-Hull, University of California, Los Angeles; George J. Searles, Mohawk Valley Community College; Cynthia Secor, HERS, Mid America at the University of Denver; David S. Shields, The Citadel; Thelma J. Shinn, Arizona State University; Frank C. Shuffelton, University of Rochester; Peggy Skaggs, Angelo State University; Beth Helen Stickney, City University of New York; Catharine R. Stimpson, New York University; Janis P. Stout, Texas A & M University; Claudia Tate, Princeton University; John Edgar Tidwell, University of Kansas; Eleanor Q. Tignor, City University of New York, La Guardia Community College; Jane Tompkins, Duke University; Steven C. Tracy; Eleanor W. Traylor, Howard University; Richard Tuerk, Texas A&M University–Commerce; Bonnie TuSmith, Northeastern University; Paula Uruburu, Hofstra University; Donald Vanouse, State University of New York College at Oswego; Daniel Walden, Pennsylvania State University; Arthur E. Waterman, Georgia State University; Sybil Weir, San Jose State University; Judith Wellman, State University of New York College at Oswego; James L. W. West III, Pennsylvania State University; Thomas R. Whitaker, Yale University; Barbara A. White, University of New Hampshire; Margaret B. Wilkerson, University of California, Berkeley; Kenny J. Williams, Duke University; Marcellette G. Williams, Michigan State University; James C. Wilson, University of Cincinnati; Norma Clark Wilson, University of South Dakota; Amy E. Winans, Susquehanna University; Kate H. Winter, State University of New York at Albany; Frederick Woodard, University of Iowa; Jean Fagan Yellin, Pace University; Amy Marie Yerkes, Johns Hopkins University; Judith Yung, University of California, Santa Cruz.

Finally, we wish to acknowledge the hard work of our editors and other staff members at Houghton Mifflin. They have included Suzanne Phelps-Weir, Michael Gillespie, and in particular our most indefatigable cheerleader, supporter, and general factotum, Janet Edmonds.

LATE NINETEENTH CENTURY 1865–1910

ON May 1, 1893, a city spread out over a thousand acres along Lake Michigan officially opened its doors to the first of some twenty-seven and a half million people, equal to well over a third of the United States population at the time, who would visit it in the brief six months of its existence. Resplendent with white buildings designed in the classical style, whose peristyles, porticoes, and colonnades shone in the sun and in the reflected light of canals and lagoons, and at night were illuminated by thousands of electric light bulbs, this spectacle was the World's Columbia Exposition, otherwise known as the Chicago World's Fair and, most familiarly, the "White City." The largest international world's fair ever held until that time, built at a cost that today would translate into well over three hundred million dollars, it was the United States' and the world's celebration of the "discovery" of the Americas by Columbus four hundred years before. Its central core of buildings was a marvel of coordinated planning by architects, sculptors, painters, landscape gardeners, and engineers, who in less than two and a half years had transformed an area of swamp and sand into one of terraced parks, broad boulevards, and monumental buildings. Although officially commemorating the arrival of Europeans on the continent, and including exhibits from countries throughout the world, the Fair was above all a spectacular statement of the United States' material and technological might on the eve of the twentieth century.

By 1893 just about all of the elements we identify with modern America were in place: large-scale industry and advanced technology, densely inhabited urban areas, concentrations of capital in banks, businesses, and corporations, nationwide systems of transportation and print communication, and a heterogeneous population of diverse races, classes, and ethnic groups. It was a nation that looked and was radically different from the cluster of states, primarily agrarian and increasingly riven by sectional strife, that had existed only forty years before. The launching of the Spanish-American War five years after the Fair solidified the final element, imperialistic power, that would characterize the nation in the twentieth century.

A sense of being at a historic divide, looking both back and ahead, animated the speeches given at the Fair's dedication ceremonies (held in October 1892 to mark the official date of Columbus's arrival). The opening oration swept through four hundred years of history to review Columbus's voyages, the struggles of Spain, England, and France for control of the newly discovered territories, the rise of the young American republic, and its darkest moment of threatened disunion during the years of the Civil War. That threat averted, the nation's post-war history was cast as one of steadily increasing political and material power and progress. Under the benign rule of a strong Constitution, with "the curse of slavery . . . gone," and with its mills, mines, and forests producing their incomparable wealth, the United States had arrived at the moment of the Fair, when it could "bask in the sunshine of . . . prosperity and happiness," and proudly "bid a welcome to the world."

This mood of confidence and optimism would be shattered just five days after the Fair opened, when the stock market plunged, inaugurating a four-year depression, one of the worst the nation had ever experienced. If the Fair was proof of American progress, the Panic of 1893 revealed part of the price that progress exacted. What then did the Columbian Exposition show, not just about America's official perception of itself but about American realities? In its harmonies but also in its contradictions and disjunctions, both in what it included and what it ignored, the Fair tells us much about the nature of American life at the turn into the twentieth century.

For the many writers who visited the Fair and speculated about it, two impressions dominated: the esthetic unity of its central core of buildings, and the awesome sense of power conveyed by its sheer size and its massive displays of technology. For William Dean Howells, one of the country's most respected and successful authors, the two impressions ideally conjoined. The Fair to him was a grand altruistic gesture. To create it, capitalists had placed themselves in the hands of artists, and "for once" American businessmen and entrepreneurs had put aside "their pitiless economic struggle, their habitual warfare" to come together in a mighty "work of peace." Howells's hopeful vision, voiced in *A Traveler from Altruria* (1894) by a visitor from a Utopian land, was one of America's money and technology put in the service of civic virtue, the nation's vast natural resources and manufactured products used for the welfare of all rather than the profit of the few. The Fair's architecture held not only esthetic but spiritual promise.

Less sanguine was Henry Adams, for whom the Fair marked a crucial moment in that ongoing enterprise of educating himself to which he devoted his life. For him the Fair's architecture was imitative and derivative—"imported Beaux Arts"—and the Fair itself, despite any idealistic impulses in its genesis, was an "industrial, speculative growth." Like Howells, Adams was looking for some principle of meaning in American life, some way of making sense out of what seemed to be the chaos of forces, political, economic, and scientific, that had been unleashed in the post-Civil War period. He looked behind the white facades for answers. Inside the buildings "education ran riot" amidst displays of telephone and telegraph apparatus, steam engines, multiple drill presses, cable-laying devices, electric motors, transformers, convertors, and generators. The dynamo—the generator producing the electric current that powered and drove so much of the machinery and made possible the Fair's dazzling displays of incandescent lighting—became his symbol of the driving force in American life. It "gave to history a new phase," but one that Adams could not measure by the republican standards he had inherited from his presidential forebears, John and John Quincy Adams. If "Chicago asked for the first time the question whether the American people knew where they were driving," the answer was not easily arrived at. Adams feared that the uncontrolled application of new scientific discoveries would outpace and vitiate republican ideals.

Adams and Howells had focused on two aspects of the dramatic changes the United States had undergone in the second half of the nineteenth century. The very existence of the Fair testified to one of these: that by the 1890s the United States had become an urban nation. The Fair City (and it was a city, with its own transportation, sewage, police, and governmental systems) was the product of the entrepreneurial drive of Chicago, which had successfully outmaneuvered New York to get it, and Chicago in turn was the most dramatic example of post-war urban development. Little more than a fur-trapping village of about 350 people in 1830, by 1880 it had become a city of half a million people; within another ten years it had doubled its size, so that by the time of the Fair, it was the second largest city in the nation, with a population of over one million. The largest, New York, had also grown at a phenomenal rate: by 1900 it would contain almost three and a half million people. Other midwestern cities—Detroit, Columbus, Milwaukee, Minneapolis, and St. Paul—saw their populations double and triple in the post-war decades, while on the west coast Los Angeles went from eleven thousand inhabitants in 1880 to five times that number twenty years later. From being for over 150 years characteristically a nation of rural dwellers, the United States had within a few short decades become distinctively urbanized. Although at the end of the nineteenth century forty percent of the American population was still rural, the trend to urbanization was irreversible.

Occurring with such rapidity, this growth had taken place with little or none of the civic planning that Howells admired in the White City. Real American cities, he knew, were the result of "the straggling and shapeless accretion of accident." At their strongest and most vivid—again Chicago was a case in point—they manifested the nation's immense new business and commercial energy, as in the iron and steel skyscrapers of Chicago's architects Louis Sullivan, John Wellborn Root, and William LeBaron Jenney. At their worst—and the worst was widespread—they were places where what housing reformer Jacob Riis in 1890 called "the other half" lived—places of slums and overcrowding, of dirt and noise, lack of sanitation and disease, poverty, child labor, prostitution, violence, and crime. The Fair City officially ignored these urban realities, its white facades implicitly denying that not far away lay the Chicago slums, where settlement worker Jane Addams's Hull House was located among tenements crowded with Irish, Polish, Czech, Russian Jewish, and Italian immigrants, and that also within striking distance was the Union Stockyard, with its four hundred square miles of malodorous cattle pens and runways, which would be the subject of Upton Sinclair's exposé of the meat-packing industry in his novel *The Jungle* in 1906.

The Fair's much-vaunted whiteness was also a symbol of the intensified dominance in the 1890s of white Anglo-Saxon Protestantism in a nation in which African Americans, Native Americans, Mexican Americans, and other racial, ethnic, and religious groups were becoming increasingly apparent. Over the protests of some black leaders, the nation's eight to nine million African Americans were allowed no representation at the Fair's opening ceremonies, and no blacks were appointed to positions of authority on any of the Fair's various governing commissions. Frederick Douglass, present as commissioner from Haiti, not a representative of the United States, termed the Fair "a whited sepulcher." Journalist and anti-lynching activist Ida B. Wells-Barnett published a pamphlet, to which Douglass contributed a chapter, exposing the white supremacy that lay behind "The Reason Why the Colored American Is Not in the World's Columbia Exposition" and detailing African Americans' contributions to the United States. Other racial and ethnic groups also were excluded from the United States as the Fair represented it. Indian writer Simon Pokagon called attention to the absence of official Native American representation through his pamphlet "Red Man's Greeting." Printed on birch bark and distributed at the event, it reminded fair-goers that the exposition, and the entire city of Chicago, were built on land taken from Indians and never paid for.

The only way the Fair did officially recognize racial and ethnic variety was as something foreign to the United States. South of the main buildings, on the mile-long stretch called the Midway Plaisance, in shops, restaurants, tent shows, and miniature villages, three thousand entertainers and vendors from ethnic cultures throughout the world sold their wares, displayed native costumes, and performed dances and other ceremonies. "[O]dd bits of tribes and nationalities from every quarter of the globe" was the description in the official history of the Fair. Although the Irish Village, Japanese Bazaar, Javanese Village, German Village, and several other re-creations of "foreign" villages drew many visitors, among the greatest attractions were the Dahomey Village and the Arab section, with its "Street in Cairo," "Algerian Village," and "Persian Palace of Eros." Viewing indigenous music and dance, including "dancing girls" from Egypt and elsewhere, as spectacles, many American visitors who prized their nation's supposed homogeneity and propriety exoticized—and savored—difference as something outside U.S. borders. Professor F. W. Putnam, a Harvard professor and the Fair's "Chief of the Department of Ethnography," produced a book of portraits of the "different types of men and women" on display at the Midway Plaisance. In the introduction he captured the way the Fair's very architecture affirmed its fundamental assumption that non-Western peoples were quaint and non-developed, in stark contrast to the progressive modernity of the United States. Extolling the "Great Ferris Wheel" that rose in the midst of the Midway, Putnam characterized the elevated view it gave fair-goers of the Midway as at one and the same time physical and cultural: a monument to technology that embodied the superior position from which the world's most "advanced" country could survey and comprehend other cultures. "Our own crowning achievement in mechanics . . . arising in the midst of this magic gathering," he proclaimed, "enabled us to view this mimic world as from another planet, and to look down upon an enchanted land filled with happy folk."

But if the Midway in effect pinioned Jews, Arabs, Africans, and others within late-century Western ideas about the stratification of the races and peoples of the world, the Fair also became an occasion for some from supposedly "backward" countries and cultures to convey their own views of themselves—and of American culture. From September 11 to September 27, a related event, the World Parliament of Religions, was held in downtown Chicago. Featuring close to two hundred speakers representing twelve major religions, the Parliament provided a forum for various Protestant denominations and also one allowing some representative Buddhists and Hindus to explain their religions to the nearly 150,000 spectators who attended. But American Protestant control of the Parliament was quickly unsettled as Asian speakers galvanized attendees and the press with their faith, their profound knowledge of both their own religions and Christianity, and their attacks on Christian missionaries' lack of concern about the poverty they encountered and their cooperation with colonialism. Several Asian delegates developed enthusiastic American followings, among them Swami Vivekananda, a charismatic Hindu speaker from Calcutta. Vivekananda, an ascetic, combined religion and nationalism in a powerful repudiation of Western stereotypes of Asian men as effeminate, as Carrie Tirado Bramen explains. The Hindi-based form of celibate, virile, and self-disciplined masculinity he promoted was, in his representation of it, far superior to the sexually active, unrestrained masculinity of Western men.

Swami Vivekananda and others developed an especially large following among the American women who were the majority of the Parliament's attendees. The women's enthusiasm for the Asian religious leaders expressed a commitment to independence of thought and spiritual life that constituted one way in which many American women were beginning to assert their independence. The Fair itself officially recognized that American women were becoming less identified with domesticity and increasingly more visible as a public force. It included them in the Fair's planning to an extent unprecedented at any previous exposition, and it allotted them a "Women's Building" with its own board of managers, which housed an international display of women's achievement in art and industry. The board's chair, Mrs. Potter Palmer of Chicago, observed in her opening address that "Even more than the discovery of Columbus, which we are gathered together to celebrate, is the fact that the general government has just discovered women." Indeed, the forty-five-year-long campaign for women's political and legal rights was bearing some fruit: in the year of the Fair, Colorado became the first state to grant the vote to women, though the suffrage movement's full success came only with the passage of the Nineteenth Amendment in 1920. But American women, as represented by the Fair, were white: African American women were kept off the board of managers despite their repeated requests for representation, and exhibits in the Women's Building included very little by or about African American women. In response to black women's pressure, however, six black women, including activist/suffragist Frances E. W. Harper and educator Anna Julia Cooper, were eventually invited to speak about African American women's circumstances and achievements at the World's Congress of Representative Women.

The energies white women were displaying at the end of the century fascinated Henry Adams, who wondered if here might be a force as significant for the nation's future as that of science and technology. But technology made the strongest statement at the Fair, visible evidence that the overriding feature of American life, on which the cities depended for their existence and that explained their growth, was the unprecedented industrialization the nation had undergone since the end of the Civil War. Among the most important buildings at the Fair were those devoted to Manufactures, Mechanic Arts, Transportation, and Electricity, and by far the largest and most impressive of these was the Manufactures Building. In the Fair's official history the Manufactures Building was described, in the quantitative terms Americans love to use to measure greatness, as three times the size of St. Peter's Church in Rome, four times that of the Roman Colosseum, and big enough that six baseball games could be played on its floor at once or the entire Russian army mobilized inside it. To create such a structure, the powerful forces of the United States economy and industrial machine had been marshaled.

Chief among these was the railway system. The decades before the Civil War had seen the development of steam power and the locomotive, making possible the extensive network of railroads that crisscrossed the country by the 1890s, joining all states and sections and creating national markets for agricultural produce and manufactured goods. Fruits and vegetables from California, cattle from Texas, corn from Iowa, lumber from Minnesota, cotton from Georgia and Alabama, coal from West Virginia, iron from Pennsylvania could all be shipped to processing and manufacturing centers, often located in cities. Chicago's extraordinary growth, in fact, was due to its location at the intersection of several major railroad lines that brought to it the agricultural and mineral wealth of the Midwest and that led in turn to the development of its grain, lumber, meat-packing, steel, and railroad equipment industries. By 1890 the United States had nearly half the railroad mileage in the world, and that mileage represented one-sixth of the nation's estimated wealth.

Before the Civil War, the railroads had helped to open up the Midwest, and in the post-war period they carried settlers to the Great Plains of the Dakotas, western

Kansas, and Nebraska, which had been bypassed by earlier pioneers eager to reach the gold fields of California and the fertile acreage of Oregon's Willamette Valley. Now, tens of thousands of families moved on to the Plains, pushing the Native American inhabitants off their lands. The use on the Plains of expensive machinery—harvesters, tractors, and binders—led farmers to increase the size of their holdings. Although the small family farm that Jefferson had celebrated as the locus of the American ideal of independent self-sufficiency continued to exist, the new trend toward farming as a large-scale, mechanized operation meant that agriculture, too, had entered the modern age. The Chicago World's Fair had been the occasion, at the World's Congress Auxiliary held in conjunction with it, for the delivery of Frederick Jackson Turner's paper "The Significance of the Frontier in American History," with its thesis that the existence of the frontier, as an area of free land beyond the line of settlement, had helped determine the national character and national ideals. Now, Turner announced, there was no more open land, and the frontier no longer existed.

Turner celebrated the experience of the frontier as fostering democratic institutions, but the new world of business and industry of which the railroads were both symbol and cause seemed in the post-war decades to make a mockery of many of them. The burgeoning industrial economy had entailed enormous cost in the waste and misuse of both material and moral resources. For example, the railroad companies did not hesitate to use intimidation and cutthroat competition to destroy rival lines, or discriminatory rates and rebates to lure customers. Their practices were condoned by a federal government eager to push forward America's industrial expansion and by public officials not averse to reaping from that expansion their own private gain. Whereas the Civil War had demanded both massive, coordinated planning in the use of material resources and intense moral commitment and sacrifice, the post-war period saw general acceptance of a laissez-faire policy under which business, through its enormous economic power, was able to exert often corrupting pressure on government. One particularly notorious scandal erupted in 1872, when the Credit Mobilier, a construction company set up by promoters of the Union Pacific to build the transcontinental railroad at immense profit to themselves, was discovered to have bribed members of Congress and the vice president. The same year saw the conviction of "Boss" (William Marcey) Tweed, head of the infamous Tweed Ring in New York, which for years had systematically plundered the city treasury of from 75 to 200 million dollars. The period from the 1870s to the 1890s was marked by corruption—bribery, graft, vote- and office-selling, the spoils system—at every government level, from the federal administration and Congress to the local city ward politician. "The Gilded Age," Mark Twain called it, capturing in the novel of that title (co-written with Charles Dudley Warner in 1873) its fever of unrestrained speculation and get-rich-quick schemes, its glitter and fraudulence.

Like the railroads, other businesses and industries also consolidated on a national scale. This concentration of vast resources in the hands of a few constituted one of the most drastic changes from the pre-war period. No longer an economy of small shops, local craftsmen, and artisans, nor of primarily small- or medium-sized companies producing manufactured goods, the post-war economy was characterized by the growth of giant corporations, monopolies, and trusts, such as Rockefeller's Standard Oil and Carnegie's United States Steel. Such enterprises employed hundreds and in some cases thousands of workers, whose traditional skills were increasingly replaced by the new machinery and who were reduced, through techniques devised by "scientific management," to performing small, unskilled, repetitive tasks. The lives of workers were

> "I cheat my boys every chance I get. I want to make 'em sharp. I trade with the boys and skin 'em and I just beat 'em every time I can. I want to make 'em sharp."
>
> John D. Rockefeller

increasingly separated by such experiences, often by language and religion as well, and of course by wealth, from those of company managers and owners.

For with the formation of giant corporations and trusts went the making of gigantic fortunes. By 1890 one percent of American families owned over twenty-five percent of the nation's wealth. By 1893 there were over four thousand millionaires in the United States—not an inconsiderable number at a time when $700 was a comfortable, if modest, annual income. And the millionaires, or plutocrats, flaunted their wealth, spending it conspicuously, as the sociologist Thorstein Veblen satirically observed in his anatomy of the rich, *The Theory of the Leisure Class* (1899). They built mansions that imitated French chateaux, English castles, and Italian Renaissance palaces, bought up the art works of Europe, and, by heavily dowering their daughters, purchased titles of nobility; they also threw parties costing thousands of dollars for their friends, their horses, and their dogs. Business, *big* business, was the order of the day, and the fortunes reaped from it were justified by an ideology that drew upon the old Protestant ethic of the virtuousness of industry and of the acquisition of wealth as proof of God's favor, and also on the new social thinking, derived from Darwin's biological theories of human evolution, which defended what sociologist Herbert Spencer termed "the survival of the fittest." George F. Baer in 1902 argued that "God in His infinite wisdom has given the control of the property interests of the country" to businessmen, and the imperialist mentality that lay behind his words had also found expression in the Chicago Fair's opening dedicatory speech. Congratulating the Fair's designers and engineers, the speaker observed that "the earth and all it contains have been subservient to your will." A dramatic proof of the power of American big business occurred in the same year as the Fair, when American sugar growers in Hawaii, aided by United States gunboats and marines, overthrew the Hawaiian government, an event that led to the annexation of Hawaii five years later during the Spanish-American War.

By 1893, then, industrialization in the form of immense, privately owned corporations and trusts had established itself, and monopoly capitalism had become the American economic mode. Thus for Henry Adams 1893 meant not just the Chicago Exposition but the repeal of the Sherman Silver Purchase Act, a blow to the nation's debtor farmers who had wanted silver coinage in order to increase the money supply and relieve the burden of their debt, and a victory for the gold standard. Adams himself had favored silver, being "against State Street, banks, capitalism altogether," and he saw the year 1893 as symbolically marking the consolidation of power in the capitalist class. Not the farmers who supplied the raw materials nor the urban workers who supplied the physical labor and skills that ran the industrial machine, but the machine's owners—capitalists, industrialists, and bankers—would dominate in political power and significantly determine the nation's future course.

Publishing and Writing

Seen in terms of its production and distribution, literature had also become big business by the 1890s. Like telephones, tractors, or sewing machines, books and

> I say that you ought to get rich, and it is your duty to get rich. How many of my pious brethren say to me, "Do you, a Christian minister, spend your time going up and down the country advising young people to get rich, to get money?" "Yes, of course I do." They say, "Isn't that awful! Why don't you preach the gospel instead of preaching about man's making money?" "Because to make money honestly is to preach the gospel. That is the reason. The men who get rich may be the most honest men you find in the community."
>
> Russell H. Conwell, *Acres of Diamonds,* 1888

magazines were being produced on a national scale. Even before the Civil War, publishing had begun to assume many of its modern characteristics, and the post-war period saw the process accelerated. In the early decades of the nineteenth century, as in the eighteenth, publishing was still primarily local. Village printers and small shops produced newspapers, schoolbooks, religious tracts, and modest editions of novels or collections of poetry with a limited range of distribution. But by 1860 large publishing houses located in the cities could reach national markets by way of the railroads, and books and magazines could be produced more rapidly and cheaply with the new technology of steam-powered rotary presses, multiple presses, and binding machinery. National best-sellers were already a phenomenon in the 1850s, as novels of domestic realism by women writers found a growing audience among the wives and daughters of the emerging middle class. (At the beginning of the post-war period in 1866, when the nation's population was thirty-six million, one such novel, Augusta Jane Evans's *St. Elmo,* reputedly reached a readership of one million in the year of its publication alone.) The steady increase in literacy in these years, with the development of a system of free public grade and high schools, kept expanding the market for printed reading matter. And publishers in turn both catered to and helped create that market, becoming increasingly aggressive in distributing and advertising their wares. Indeed, large-circulation periodical publishers found that in selling literature, especially by widely known authors, they were also able to sell the products of their advertisers, on whom they increasingly depended for revenues.

One should in fact talk of multiple markets and of different, if also often overlapping, audiences for literature. The technology of mass production and distribution meant both that something approaching a uniform national print culture was possible and also that specialized audiences could be profitably cultivated. The period therefore saw greater uniformity in what people read, but also the development of many specialized markets. The largest audience was probably that created and served by the "story papers"—newspapers that printed romance and adventure stories in serial installments—and by the new "dime novels" that first appeared in 1860 and quickly reached circulations in the millions. Cheaper than the average novel that sold for twenty-five cents, these books, produced by Erastus Beadle and his many imitators, were like today's paperback romance novels, quickly written by a stable of writers employed by the publisher and with new titles appearing almost weekly. Read by the young and the new working class in the cities, they offered larger-than-life, simpler-than-life heroes and heroines. At a time when the frontier was closing and urban congestion was the reality of many readers' lives, they depicted stereotypically rugged and self-

WORK

Work, work, my boy, be not afraid;
Look labor boldly in the face;
Take up the hammer or the spade,
And blush not for your humble place.

There's glory in the shuttle's song;
There's triumph in the anvil's stroke;
There's merit in the brave and strong,
Who dig the mine or fell the oak.

Eliza Cook from *McGuffey's Fifth Eclectic Reader,* 1879 edition

reliant frontiersmen and cowboys, who in their victories over stereotypically savage and treacherous Indians provided readers with the contours of a mythic American past, with elements of adventure, heroism, and spatial freedom. Later, detective stories set in the city offered new heroes in recognition of the new urban world, including its crime and violence. Consonant with the underlying mythos of individualism and self-reliance of the dime novels were the over one hundred novels produced from the 1860s through the 1890s by Horatio Alger. Their titles—*Risen from the Ranks, Strive and Succeed, Struggling Upward*—were catchy labels for their packaged messages of success achieved through a combination of industriousness, middle-class morality, and luck. That virtue and hard work brought success was a message also conveyed by the maxims and uplifting literary excerpts of the McGuffey readers, over one hundred million of which were used in the schools between 1836 and 1890 and which, like the dime novels and the Alger stories, functioned as an important part of the acculturation process for millions of immigrants, introducing them to the values of white Protestant culture.

Yet at the same time, the publishing industry reflected the growing diversity of the American population. The cultures of the many peoples who comprised the nation found outlets in the approximately 1,200 foreign language periodicals that were in existence by 1896, serving immigrant groups from the Germans and Scandinavians to the Czechs and Poles, Spanish and Italians. Groups like the Germans and Scandinavians, who maintained strong connections with the old country, published works in their native languages and translated others into English. By establishing strong cultural institutions to sustain them and to aid in the translation of works into English, they both retained and modified their native cultures. In addition, there were by 1896 over 150 African American magazines and newspapers, a well-developed periodical press established by American Indians and publishing their works, newspapers in the Southwest that circulated local and international news as well as the folk songs of Mexican Americans, and several weeklies publishing news and poetry in Chinese.

On yet another level were the literary magazines—*Atlantic Monthly, Harper's Monthly,* and *Scribner's Monthly* (later the *Century*)—with an influence far greater than the modest circulations of some of them might suggest. It was in these magazines that much of the exciting and important literature of the period appeared. Mark Twain, Henry James, Stephen Crane, Charles Chesnutt, Paul Laurence Dunbar, Hamlin Garland, George Washington

Cable, Sarah Orne Jewett, Mary E. Wilkins Freeman, and Abraham Cahan all published in their pages. At the center of that magazine establishment was William Dean Howells, whose career was a graph of the post-war publishing industry. Through the editorial positions he held on two of the most important magazines, Howells advanced the careers of all of those writers, disseminated his own work, and pressed his advocacy of realism as the form that literature should take.

Assistant editor and then editor in the 1860s and 1870s of the prestigious *Atlantic Monthly* in Boston, Howells moved to New York in the 1880s, signalling the shift of literary power to that metropolis. For the next thirty-five years he was associated with *Harper's Monthly,* and the literary criticism, book reviews, and social commentary with which he filled his *Atlantic* and *Harper's* editorial columns comprised the most sustained body of commentary on the post-war literary scene. When in 1892 Howells signed an agreement to write for Edward Bok's *Ladies' Home Journal,* he was still abreast of the time, for Bok's magazine heralded the advent of a new era in periodical journalism: that of the lower-priced, mass-circulated commercial magazine heavily dependent on advertising for its revenues. By then the great days of the literary magazines were ending, and a new era in American publishing had begun.

Like any label, "realism," used to describe the literature Howells wrote and encouraged others to write, obscures differences among writers to whom it is collectively applied; but it also serves to suggest certain common features of what became the distinctive form of prose fiction in the second half of the nineteenth century. Realism was the response of writers to the sweeping economic, social, and political changes of post-war life; to the recognized need to capture, report, and interpret the world of the developing cities and the declining rural regions. In order to convey the nature of an urban world of speeded-up tempos, crowded spaces, new kinds of work, and new mixtures of people, or to capture before they totally disappeared the landscapes and speech patterns, habits, and manners of the nation's rural areas, such conventions of pre-war romance fiction as its often leisurely narrative pace, use of allegory and symbolism, and frequent focus on the exceptional individual no longer seemed appropriate. Rather, realists like Howells emphasized situations and characters drawn from ordinary, everyday life, and the use of authentic American speech and dialogue rather than authorial comment as primary narrative mode.

On the simplest level, realism was a matter of faithfulness to the surfaces of American life, and in its interest in accuracy it reflected the rise of science and, by the end of the nineteenth century, the social sciences, as a source of empirically derived truth, an interest that was also manifest in everything from the spate of investigative journalism to the popular fascination with the Kodak camera, invented in 1888. But literature of course is never merely a photograph or a mirror that passively reflects external reality; like all imaginative writing, works of realism were the unique products of their authors' individual perspectives conveyed through and shaped by language, literary conventions, and the literary traditions that writers inherited. For Howells and Henry James, this last included Hawthorne, especially his concern with moral ambiguities, and the tradition of domestic realistic fiction developed by pre-war women writers, with its interest in manners and behavior. These were as important as the French and Russian realist writers such as Balzac and Turgenev who initially helped provide Howells with his esthetic of realism, and whom he introduced to the American reading public.

Three novels that appeared in 1885 (all in the pages of *Century* magazine) suggest something of the range of realistic writing. Howells's *The Rise of Silas*

Lapham was the story of a self-made American businessman encountering social situations and moral dilemmas for which his rural upbringing had scarcely prepared him. James's *The Bostonians* dealt (however ambivalently) with what James saw as the most salient feature of post-war life—the changing status of women, their greater public and political visibility. And Mark Twain's *Adventures of Huckleberry Finn,* although it takes place in rural and small-town mid-America before the Civil War, dealt with issues crucial in the post-war period—racial and class divisions, the fragility of the family as an institution, social hypocrisy and pretension, violence and crime. Among them, these three novels engaged issues central to American life in the last half of the nineteenth century: the effects of the new business economy on individual lives, the changing relationship between the sexes, and the intensification of white supremacy after the Civil War.

The 1880s were the height of realism, which could capaciously embrace everything from Twain's disreputable runaway, Huck, with his ungrammatical speech and fear of "sivilization," to Howells's decent but puzzled average Americans, to the heightened consciousness and psychological acuities of the characters who inhabited James's country houses and drawing rooms. Meanwhile the term "realism" also encompassed the explorations of new subject matter and the perspectives of a host of other writers: the accounts of mill and factory life of Rebecca Harding Davis, Elizabeth Stuart Phelps, and Upton Sinclair; Paul Laurence Dunbar's stories of black life during and after Reconstruction; Charles Chesnutt's black dialect tales and stories of the color line and racist violence; Kate Chopin's examinations of marriage, female sexuality, and racial relations; Hamlin Garland's and Mary E. Wilkins Freeman's studies of the depradations and resilience of rural life in the Midwest and New England; Abraham Cahan's fictions of New York Jewish ghetto life. Much of this work, given its regional focus, has been subsumed under the labels "local color" or "regional" writing—labels that at best call attention to its distinguishing concern with locale and culture, but that at worst have implied minor status for its authors. As Eric Sundquist has noted, the term "realist" has tended to be reserved for those in or nearest the seats of power in the cities, while those at a remove—midwesterners and southerners, blacks, women, immigrants—have been categorized as regionalists or local colorists. That a great deal of post–Civil War literature was regionalist in origin and emphasis should not be overlooked; regionalism was an important defining characteristic of the period's writing. In face of the increasing homogeneity and standardization of life attendant on mass production and mass distribution of goods and entertainment, interest in preserving local and regional folkways and traditions that were in imminent danger of being lost was widespread. Further, as Richard Brodhead has suggested, such writing appealed to middle-class readers as a kind of cultural tourism. It complemented the development of the vacation industry in places like rural New England and Florida. Such interests helped open markets for the stories and sketches of northern New England written by Sarah Orne Jewett and by Freeman. Indeed, throughout the post-war period numerous authors would be closely identified with the particular areas they chose to treat: Jack London with the Pacific Coast and Alaska, Cable and Chopin with Louisiana, and Twain, of course, with the Mississippi.

The city was also a region, a new space whose contours and contents were being imaginatively mapped. But as Howells continued to explore this new urban space from the mid-1880s through the 1890s, he found it harder to accommodate it to his version of realism, which had always carried with it a democratic, egalitarian faith in "the large cheerful average of health and

> Men were nothings, mere animalcules, mere ephemerides that fluttered and fell and were forgotten between dawn and dusk. Vanamee had said there was no death. But for one second Presley could go one step further. Men were naught, death was naught, life was naught; FORCE only existed—FORCE that brought men into the world, FORCE that crowded them out of it to make way for the succeeding generation, FORCE that made the wheat grow, FORCE that garnered it from the soil to give place to the succeeding crop.
>
> Frank Norris
> *The Octopus,* 1901

success and happy life." The "average" he had implicitly equated with the middle class; by 1890, however, the industrial working class far outnumbered the middle class (by 1915 the poor would be sixty-five percent of the population), and the circumstances of their lives, their relative helplessness against the massed might of the industrial machine, began to make a mockery of one of realism's prevailing tenets—the belief in the free moral agency of the individual, the capacity, despite adverse or countervailing pressures, to exercise choice and to a significant extent determine one's own fate that had distinguished a Silas Lapham, a Huck Finn, and the heroes and heroines of James's fictions, and that had given to the great novels of realism their pivotal dramatic moments. Choice began to seem less operative than chance, as the very titles of Howells's New York novels of 1890 and 1893, *A Hazard of New Fortunes* and *The World of Chance,* recognized, and his middle-class protagonist and alter-ego, Basil March, found himself increasingly bewildered and alienated by a city he had, twenty years earlier, fondly and comfortably embraced. Increasing strife between capital and labor, which would climax in 1894 with the killing of scores of workers during the Pullman strike in Chicago, led one journalist that year to proclaim that "probably . . . in no civilized country in this century, not actually in the throes of war or open insurrection, has society been so disorganized . . . never was human life held so cheap."

As the 1890s advanced, realism darkened its hues, and a new literature by a younger generation emerged with a distinctively new emphasis. "Naturalism" is the term used to describe the fiction, or a dominant element in it, of writers like Stephen Crane, Jack London, Frank Norris, Theodore Dreiser, Paul Laurence Dunbar, and others, where environmental forces, whether of nature or of the city, outweigh or overwhelm human agency, the individual can exert little or no control over determining events, and the world is at worst hostile, at best indifferent to humankind. Crane's "The Open Boat" pits puny human beings against a natural force—the sea—that mocks their efforts to survive. And in Dreiser's *Sister Carrie,* personal success or failure is as much a matter of accident as of ability and will, as individuals often helplessly rise or fall within the surging, anonymous urban mass. Influenced by Darwinian ideas on the importance of environment in shaping human life and by other forms of scientific determinism, such naturalistic fiction also took issue with popular notions of heroism, including heroic interpretations of the Civil War, which had become mythologized in the fiction of southern writers and through articles on heroic battles and generals in the popular press. In *The Red Badge of Courage* or a story like "A Mystery of Heroism," Crane adopts a point of view more akin to that of the second half of the twentieth century, where courage, in the words of Michael Herr on the Vietnam War, is "only undifferentiated energy cut loose by the intensity of the moment." And Ambrose Bierce's short story "Chickamauga" exposed the vainglory of war by pitting a child's pretend-heroics against scenes of actual and meaningless slaughter. By the turn of the century Crane's ironies and Bierce's cynicism were matched by the increasingly dark, even nihilistic, views of Mark Twain, whose "The War Prayer" (1905), *The Mysterious Stranger,* and other writings toward the end of his life betrayed a bitterness rooted not only in personal disappointments and family tragedies but also in disgust at the United States' growing imperialistic stance, a bitterness anticipated in the dark doubts about human goodness that had threaded their way through the idyllicism of *Huckleberry Finn.*

Such dark views of human nature and human possibility, however, ultimately comprise only one strand in the totality of post-Civil War realistic fiction, a body of writing that offered America a rich diversity of narrative views of its landscapes and cityscapes, its people, their actions and their feelings. The second half of the nineteenth century was above all an age of narrative prose, in which the short story and the novel arrived at maturity as literary forms, reaching out to include whole new areas of subject matter, acquiring increased formal sophistication and linguistic suppleness, and providing a legacy that twentieth-century writers would inherit and develop.

Recent scholarly judgments of the poetry produced in the late nineteenth century have generally not been favorable. The early 1890s saw the deaths of most of the well-known (and long-lived) poets who had been part of the dominant New England tradition of literature at mid-century. James Russell Lowell, John Greenleaf Whittier, and Oliver Wendell Holmes all died between 1891 and 1894, although their portraits would continue to hang on schoolroom walls into the early decades of the twentieth century as the tradition they represented became enshrined as the nation's "official" culture. They would become part of what the philosopher George Santayana in 1911 called "the genteel tradition"—a literature of uplift and refinement written by latter-day New Englanders in emulation of its Transcendental past but increasingly distant from the realities of American experience and the new sources of its intellectual vitality. Walt Whitman, whose poetry had radically challenged that of the "schoolroom poets," died in 1892, and no new generation of poets had by then emerged to assume his mantle, although Edwin Arlington Robinson, working in isolation, and Paul Laurence Dunbar, writing in both black vernacular and mainstream English, were harbingers of things to come, as were several women poets whose substantial body of work in the post-war period has only recently begun to be systematically examined. The early 1890s did see the first published editions of Emily Dickinson's poems, which Stephen Crane read and to which his own poetry bears interesting if coincidental resemblance. The clipped, laconic verses that Crane produced toward the end of his short life, as well as the imagist lyrics published in the 1890s by women poets, anticipated, in their ironies and understatements, one dominant mood and style of the modernists who would inaugurate a great new age of American poetry after 1912, and who would find in Dickinson and Whitman their eminent precursors.

That the period produced few poets whose work has stood the test of time should not, however, obscure the fact that this was a flush time for the writers of verse. The explosive growth of periodicals and newspapers of all kinds in the last two decades of the nineteenth century created countless new outlets for poetry, and some actually paid for what they published. In fact, poetry was in demand everywhere, from local papers to highbrow national magazines, and the need produced both professional and amateur poets. Much of this poetry falls into two general categories: mainstream verse in conventional English and what came to be termed "dialect poetry," an important development that paralleled the "local color" movement in fiction and is just beginning to receive scholarly attention as a many-faceted cultural phenomenon. On the surface, it represented attempts to render in verse the vernacular ethnic speech of everyday Americans, and there is dialect poetry allegedly written in the voices of blacks, Chinese, Jews, Irish, Germans, rural whites, and others. Much of it was little better than doggerel, however, and it was frequently produced by writers who were not members of the groups whose language habits they were often caricaturing. Indeed, much dialect verse followed predictable formulas that had little to do with how people spoke, and it served to ridicule groups viewed as outsiders in a manner similar to that of the minstrel shows in which white men in blackface impersonated African Americans. In this way, dialect poetry reflects the complex cultural tensions resulting from the new racial and ethnic social interactions that immigration from abroad and the internal migration of certain groups spawned.

Dialect verse was exceedingly popular and, in fact, provided a medium for two men who were among the country's first poets to make their livings largely with their pens: James Whitcomb Riley and Paul Laurence Dunbar. The former wrote verse in Hoosier dialect (that of white midwestern farming folk); the latter was celebrated for his verse in southern African American dialect—though he, too, produced some Hoosier dialect poetry. While constrained by the limited conventions of dialect verse, Riley and Dunbar, along with other ambitious writers, often transcended the restrictions of the form to produce works of complexity, subtlety, and rich humanity. Dunbar, for example, produced dialect poems that actually subverted, usually through humor, the problematic cultural and racial assumptions that most writers of black dialect took for granted. In an important way, these more accomplished dialect poets can be seen as carrying on, even if indirectly, the groundbreaking work of poets who, like Whitman, were committed to making verse out of the plain speech of plain American folk. Thus they played an important, though still not sufficiently appreciated, role in preparing the literary terrain for the modernist poetic innovators who appeared in the years just before and after World War I.

Circumstances and Literary Achievements of Women

The single most significant fact about women, especially white, middle-class women, as a group in the post-war period was their visibility, as they increasingly moved beyond domestic discourse to lay claim to the public world. The extent to which these women became the subject of attention by male writers in the period is one index to the changes taking place in their situation and status. In Daisy Miller, Isabel Archer of *The Portrait of a Lady,* and a host of other fresh, young heroines, Henry James created "the American girl," a type of the modern in her independent adventurousness. And in *The Bostonians,* as suggested earlier, he directly addressed the implications of the new public roles women were assuming. Howells offered a portrait of the new professional woman in *Dr. Breen's Practice* and in Marcia Gaylord of *A Modern Instance* a woman, rare in fiction in the 1880s, of strong sexual feeling. Henry Adams wrote two novels with strong female heroines, exploring his sense of women as a potentially vital new force, and other novelists, such as Robert Herrick, would devote significant portions of their careers to studying the new, emancipated woman.

But if the appearance of such characters was an encouraging sign, their fictional

> The woman had been set free. . . . One had but to pass a week in Florida, or on any of a hundred huge ocean steamers, or walk through the Place Vendome, or join a party of Cook's tourists to Jerusalem, to see that the woman had been set free. . . . Behind them, in every city, town and farm-house, were myriads of new types,—or type-writers,—telephone and telegraph-girls, shopclerks, factory hands, running into millions on millions, and, as classes, unknown to themselves as to historians. . . . all these new women had been created since 1840; all were to show their meaning before 1940.
>
> Henry Adams, *The Education of Henry Adams*

fates were not. Most often they were contained within the conventions of the traditional romantic plot, punished rather than rewarded for their forays into the world by endings that offered only a choice between a confining marriage and death—witness to their authors' ambivalence about the new freedoms women were assuming. And older attitudes toward women also persisted: woman as civilizing agent who censors man's freedom, in *Huckleberry Finn* or Crane's "The Bride Comes to Yellow Sky," or woman as helpless victim, in Crane's narrative of a young girl driven to prostitution, *Maggie: a Girl of the Streets.* Hamlin Garland approached women with much more sympathy, but his female characters were also often victims—the overworked and defeated women of isolated, impoverished midwestern farms.

Collectively, women writers told a more varied and complex story about the realities of their lives, lives that were responding to and shaped by new circumstances. Among the most important changes affecting women as a group in the second half of the nineteenth century were the increased educational and employment opportunities available to them, and their increasing involvement in political and reform activity. The pre-war period had seen higher education begin to open up for women, and the momentum quickened in the post-war period as the public midwestern land grant colleges admitted more women (partly due to the dearth of males as a result of the Civil War) and as private women's colleges were established. The period saw the establishment of such elite eastern institutions as Vassar, Smith, Wellesley, Bryn Mawr, and Barnard. Although serving only a limited (and privileged) group, their success nevertheless importantly demonstrated that women could be the intellectual equals of men, thus countering the still prevalent belief in women's intellectual inferiority. (A new source of resistance to women's education did arise when influential medical practitioners warned that women's development of their brains would sap reproductive and maternal energy.) Although racism operated to curtail educational opportunities, black women were attending the new coeducational and single-sex institutions established after the war, such as Howard University and Spelman College. From these and other schools came women, many of them with post-graduate training as well, who by the end of the century composed a class of professional and intellectual leaders in education, in the women's club movement, in medicine, and in the new area of work spawned by the needs of the cities—social work, including settlement house work.

Meanwhile an expanding economy and rapid population growth were creating other forms of employment that drew ever larger numbers of women into the paid labor force. The new commercial and business world demanded higher levels of literacy of its workers, and as public elementary and high school education spread throughout the states women were enlisted as teachers. (They could be paid less than men, and the work was seen as a suitable extension of their child-rearing capacities.) In addition, women, especially middle- and lower-middle-class white women, began entering the new business world directly, as department store clerks, telephone and telegraph operators, and "typewriters," as the earliest workers on that newly invented machine were called. Mostly young and unmarried, with incomes of their own, dressed in the slim (if still long) skirts and trim shirtwaists that had replaced the bustled and flounced, heavily layered and cumbersome clothing of earlier decades, these women were one of the more visible manifestations of the "new woman," as the economically and socially emancipated woman at the turn of the century came to be described. Such emancipations were limited for all women, however, and sharply limited by race. As a group, women were routinely paid less than men, and only sixteen percent were in clerical, trade, or professional positions. Black women were largely confined to agricultural and domestic work, northern immigrant women to domestic work and factory labor. Many of the latter worked in the sweatshops of New York and other cities, where unsanitary and unsafe working conditions led to disasters like the Triangle Shirtwaist Company fire in 1910, in which 146 women lost their lives. Such disasters, together with the organization of unions in the clothing and other "light" industries, eventually led to successful agitation for industrial reform in hours, wages, and working conditions.

Labor legislation was but one of many reform activities in which women were involved by the turn of the century, when they were an important part of the progressive movement, helping to secure not only improved working conditions but better housing, sanitation, recreational and educational facilities for the industrial class, and when they were working within the international peace movement and the suffrage movement. The woman's rights movement, the longest organized reform movement in United States history, officially dated from the Seneca Falls Convention of 1848. In abeyance during the Civil War, it resumed its work for women's rights in the post-war years and moved into a period of new activism in the 1880s and 1890s, launching state and national campaigns for women's suffrage and steadily increasing the number of its adherents. The period also saw the founding, in 1874, of what would become the largest women's organization in the world, the Woman's Christian Temperance Union. Initially created to deal with the high degree of alcoholism in the country at the time—a condition that especially affected married women, who often still lacked legal rights to their own property and wages and were dependent on husbands for their support—the W.C.T.U. under the charismatic leadership of Frances Willard adopted a broad reform agenda that included not only temperance legislation but advocacy of the eight-hour workday, child care centers for working mothers, prison reform, and suffrage.

The woman's club movement that began in the 1870s and spread rapidly among both white and black women was by the end of the century yet another major agency through which significant numbers of women were working to educate themselves and to improve social conditions. Indeed, for black women, who were excluded on account of their race from many of the movements in which white women were active, the club movement was a crucial means of fostering racial uplift and forging connections among African Americans across the nation. It also provided the means of mounting activist responses to the racist portrayals of black women as sexually uncontrolled that pervaded both the scientific and the popular media at the time. In 1895, for instance, the National Federation of Afro-American Women formed as a direct result of a piece by a white journalist contending that black women were impure.

The quest for full legal, economic, and social equality for women would still need to be pursued in the twentieth century, and racism would remain a persistent obstacle for women of color. But by 1900, white women of the middle and upper classes had made significant strides. The prevailing ideology of the pre-war decades that had idealized the "true woman" as domestic and maternal had been largely replaced by the image of the "new woman," whose educational level, social mobility, relative economic self-sufficiency, and, by the time of World War I, greater sexual freedom, had released her from much of her earlier dependency.

Post-Civil War fiction by women reflected and responded to these broad social changes. By the 1870s women had a record of more than a half-century of substantial achievement in prose fiction; some women had established themselves as best-selling authors; some had initiated directions that realistic writing would take. In the post-war period, women writers carried further themes introduced by women before the war, and they introduced new themes and concerns. For example, women authors pioneered in writing about the conditions of industrial factory life. As early as 1861 Rebecca Harding Davis published a grim, unflinching narrative of the dehumanizing conditions of work in the iron mills of West Virginia; in 1873 Elizabeth Stuart Phelps published *The Silent Partner,* an account of the lives of the "hands" in New England textile factories and of one woman's efforts to bridge the gap between the propertied and the working classes. Work—especially the kinds available to women—became a paramount subject in the post-war decades. It was the central concern of Louisa May Alcott's novel *Work* (1873), which explored some of the options—as a domestic, a governess, a seamstress, an actress, a Civil War nurse—available to working and middle-class women in the period just preceding and immediately following the Civil War. Stemming from the pre-war women's literary tradition of domestic realism, Alcott's novel focused on her heroine's pursuit of her own autonomy, the development of a strong and independent sense of self, to which rewarding work was seen as essential. This search for self-fulfilling work was seemingly encouraged by increased acceptance of women's aspirations and talents, but it was often in conflict with society's and women's own expectations and desires for marriage and motherhood. Some version of this conflict underlay a series of important post-war fictions by writers from Rebecca Harding Davis, Elizabeth Stuart Phelps, and Charlotte Perkins Gilman to Frances Ellen Watkins Harper, Pauline Hopkins, Kate Chopin, and Mary Austin.

Such fictions frequently took the romance plot beyond its conventional ending to explore the realities of women's lives after marriage, with a new emphasis on the conflicts their heroines experienced. Davis produced a number of stories in which women characters are torn by ambivalence as they try to balance their own needs for creative expression and self-fulfillment against their families' needs. In Phelps's *The Story of Avis,* the heroine's artistic talent wastes away under the incessant demands of the daily domestic routine, and in *Dr. Zay* the question of whether marriage and the heroine's medical practice are compatible is left unanswered. In Gilman's "The Yellow Wall-Paper" and Chopin's *The Awakening,* two radical nineteenth-century fictional critiques of the effects of marriage and motherhood upon middle-class white women, those institutions ultimately destroy the artist-heroines. Despite living in an age of greater economic and sexual freedom for women, Mary Austin in the early twentieth century still experienced the same conflict, which she dealt with in her autobiography, *Earth Horizon,* and her semi-autobiographical novel, *A Woman of Genius.*

Gilman's, Chopin's and Austin's frank analyses of marriage and motherhood as harmful to women's continuing development brought them censure—Chopin, for instance, wrote little after the storm of criticism that greeted *The Awakening.* Nevertheless their works, which by the 1890s were supported by a growing body of feminist criticism of women's role and status in society, were a logical culmination of themes introduced by pre-war women writers, who had examined the stresses for women of marriage and family life, the authoritarian roles of fathers and husbands, and women's need to develop an independent sense of self while still acknowledging the claims of others and women's ties to their families. Pre-war writers, by contrast, had often embraced the primacy of the values that marriage and family ideally fostered: the role women had as wives and mothers in advancing values of cooperation, connection, and responsibility to others. They saw such values, transferred to the public world, as potentially transformative, challenging and even replacing the competitiveness and materialism of capitalism. Their vision, rooted in antebellum domestic ideology, was inherited at the end of the century by Sarah Orne Jewett. Jewett's *The Country of the Pointed Firs* and "The Foreigner" depict communities of women where ties of friendship and respect for nature create the basis for living (a vision that Charlotte Perkins Gilman would also offer in her Utopian fiction *Herland* [1915]). But Jewett's world of rural New England was nonetheless a world in economic decline, a region existing on the edges of the industrial world, and the note she struck was elegiac. Even as she wrote in the 1890s a new cult of masculinity was emerging partly in reaction to women's increased visibility—exemplified in the big game hunting of Theodore Roosevelt, the adventurous journalism of Rebecca Harding Davis's son Richard, the popularity of Owen Wister's novel of the West, *The Virginian* (1902), and America's imperialist expansion. Though similarly situated in declining New England rural regions, women in the stories of Mary E. Wilkins Freeman often cultivate domestic life for their own self-sustenance and even pleasure. The sometimes stark confrontations with male power and the wresting of small but suggestive victories by some of Freeman's women also testify to continuing, unresolved problems of gender conflict.

Circumstances and Literary Achievements of African Americans

In the post-war period, literature by African American writers drew upon and reflected crucial realities in their lives. The most critical event, of course, had been the abolition of slavery. With the passage of the Thirteenth Amendment to the Constitution in 1865, four million black people were freed, and with emancipation came Reconstruction—the federal government's radical attempt to restructure the South. The brief period of Reconstruction (1867–77) saw massive economic rehabilitation, the greatest black participation in local, state, and national politics before the late twentieth century, and the education of a quarter of a million black people. This last was effected especially through the efforts of the Freedman's Bureau, which established some four thousand schools staffed by black and white teachers from the North who went to the South to teach the former slaves. In the hopeful years immediately following the end of the Civil War, many important southern black colleges and universities were also established. Between 1866 and 1868 alone Fisk, Morehouse, Howard, and Atlanta Universities and Talladega College were founded, as well as Hampton Institute, where the

> The nation was rushing forward with giant strides toward colossal wealth and world-dominion, before the exigencies of which mere abstract ethical theories must not be permitted to stand. The same argument that justified the conquest of an inferior nation could not be denied to those who sought the suppression of an inferior race. In the South, an obscure jealousy of the negro's progress, an obscure fear of the very equality so contemptuously denied, furnished a rich soil for successful agitation. Statistics of crime, ingeniously manipulated, were made to present a fearful showing against the negro. Vital statistics were made to prove that he had degenerated from an imaginary standard of physical excellence which had existed under the benign influence of slavery. Constant lynchings emphasized his impotence, and bred everywhere a growing contempt for his rights.
>
> *The Marrow of Tradition*
> Charles W. Chestnut (1901)

young, ambitious Booker T. Washington arrived in 1872, having walked and begged rides to cover the long distance from his West Virginia home.

But the decade of reform ended when federal troops were withdrawn from the southern states in 1877. Abandoned by the Supreme Court and the Republican party, southern blacks were disenfranchised in the ensuing decades; by 1910 all eleven of the states of the former Confederacy had effectively abolished black voting rights. In addition, newly passed "Jim Crow" laws established segregation in everything from public transportation and schools to drinking fountains. Meanwhile, the Civil War had not fully dismantled the plantation system of large landholdings, and some sixty percent of southern land was owned by ten percent of whites, with the result that freed blacks, as well as poor whites, soon found themselves forced into sharecropping or tenant farming. By 1900 over three-quarters of the southern black population were tenant farmers, with black women working in the fields beside black men, as they had in the days of slavery, or hiring themselves out as domestic workers in white houses.

In these post-Reconstruction years, both illegal and legal methods of constraint and intimidation increased. Beginning with the Ku Klux Klan, first organized in 1866, white vigilante groups launched systematic campaigns of terror and violence. In the two years between 1868 and 1870, thousands of blacks were killed and tens of thousands driven from their homes, and such violence continued throughout the post-war decades. Lynchings, which often entailed torture and being burned alive, escalated in the latter part of the century. At least thirty-five hundred occurred between 1885 and 1910, with the alleged rape of white women by black men constituting the most frequent rationalization. Nor was such intimidation and violence confined to the South. Segregation and race riots occurred in the North as well. So virulent were attacks on the black community between 1880 and 1900 that the period has been described as "the nadir" of the free black experience.

The attacks were not only physical. Mental and psychological violence was done by the widespread propagation of negative racial stereotypes. Stereotypes are one window on relations between minority groups and the dominant culture. As cultural prescriptions for behavior, postbellum racist stereotypes denigrated blacks, limited their perceived possibilities, and denied them opportunities. The post-war period saw attacks especially on blacks' morality: men depicted as animalistic rapists and women as "Jezebels," promiscuous and lascivious. Also harmful were the stereotypes, perpetuated through such popular cultural forms as minstrel shows, of the happy darky, the loyal, self-sacrificing Mammy, and the superstitious, lazy, country folk—images that, among other purposes, served to rationalize the economic exploitation of blacks as field and domestic workers. The stereotypes were further bolstered by pseudo-scientific studies produced by white historians, sociologists, and anthropologists that appeared in the wake of Darwin's theory of evolution, claiming that blacks were nonhuman—a different species than whites—and likely doomed to extinction. And retrogressionist arguments also appeared, asserting that, once freed from the discipline of slavery, blacks had deteriorated. Such ideas—and similar ones existed to explain the alleged inferiority of women, Native Americans, Mexican Americans, Asian Americans, and the new immigrants from southern and eastern Europe—fed into and in turn were exacerbated by the imperialist and colonizing mentality that solidified in the late nineteenth century with the Spanish-American War, the annexation of Puerto Rico, Hawaii, and the Philippines, and America's growing role as a world power.

In addition, such stereotypes played a crucial role in the nostalgic depiction of pre-war life that came to be known as the "plantation tradition" of writing. Produced mainly by southern white writers like Thomas Nelson Page, this literature mythologized the South as a noble, well-ordered patriarchal world run by kindly masters and inhabited by contented slaves. The grimmer underside of such depictions emerged in the pro-Ku Klux Klan novels of Thomas Dixon, whose *The Clansman* inspired one of the most important silent movies of the newly developing film industry, D. W. Griffith's *The Birth of a Nation* (1915). Other white southern writers, however, produced thoughtful, sensitive portrayals of black individuals as part of their interest in exploring both the strengths and the stresses of a multicultural society. The Louisiana writers George Washington Cable and Kate Chopin wrote of the Creoles, Acadians, blacks, whites (Anglo-Americans), and those of mixed blood in their region, exposing in the process the false idealization of the antebellum South and reflecting on the actualities of racial mixing and the light it cast on white claims to racial purity. And the Georgia writer Joel Chandler Harris, through his collections of black dialect tales and creation of the character Uncle Remus, offered to white audiences sympathetic though patronizing and often distorted readings of black slave culture.

For black writers the post-war decades provided increased publishing opportunities and a larger readership. As black literacy increased, so too did the number of newspapers and magazines addressing them as an audience, among them the *Colored American Magazine.* Many black writers published as well in the pages of the major nationally circulated journals like the *Atlantic Monthly, Harper's,* and *McClure's.* But the new opportunities were accompanied by constraints. Although the post-war period saw growing interest in reclaiming and preserving slave culture, especially the spirituals and work songs that had been the slaves' major expressive outlets, the association in the public mind of dialect and vernacular language with comic ignorance and inferiority posed a dilemma for the black writer who wanted to transcribe the racial experience in the language of the rural black masses. Like others of his generation, Paul Laurence Dunbar, one of the most popular poets in the post-war period, faced what Marcus Cunliffe has called the "double burden of racial and linguistic definition." Throughout his career Dunbar wrote both in the vernacular and in the more formal and conventional language of late-nineteenth-century genteel poetry, but influential whites like Howells wanted him to produce only "dialect" literature. The agonized debates he conducted with himself over the use of folk language and art forms would be repeated by other black writers in the years of the Harlem Renaissance before black vernacular became fully acceptable in literature. Meanwhile, Charles Chesnutt, consciously trying to undermine racist preconceptions, used dialect to create the sly ironies of his conjure tales, where the ex-slave narrator, Uncle Julius, drawing upon the rich oral traditions of his race, scores victories over his white listeners. Through the interactive play of black and white voices Chesnutt explored and exposed the inequitable power relationships in both pre- and post-Civil War society.

White mainstream literary conventions and audience expectations also posed serious obstacles for black women writers. Chesnutt might ironically declare that "the object of my writings would not be so much the elevation of the colored people as the elevation of the whites," but post-war novelists like Pauline Hopkins and Frances Harper, whose *Iola LeRoy* in 1892 culminated a distinguished career as writer and reformer that stretched back to the pre-Civil War period, saw their mission very explicitly as one of "racial uplift"—that of improving not just the public image but the self-image of blacks, and especially of black women, for whom the Jezebel stereotype, which blamed them for the sexual exploitation they suffered, was especially pernicious. Some heroines in *Iola LeRoy* and in Hopkins's novels, including her most important work, *Contending Forces* (1900), are pale-skinned and light-haired—physical features associated with racial and moral superiority. In creating black heroines who were thus often physically indistinguishable from whites, Harper and Hopkins do reveal the power of reigning middle-class white cultural standards, but their work is centered primarily in issues crucial to black women: family stability, education and finding worthwhile employment, sexual exploitation, the advancement of African American community, racial pride. By the late nineteenth century, with the growth of a substantial black middle class, especially though not exclusively in the North, African American professional women, often working through their extensive network of women's clubs and organizations, were a significant force for racial progress. Educator Anna Julia Cooper, whose feminist essays, *A Voice from the South,* appeared in 1892, proclaimed that the status of black women would be a crucial determinant of the condition of the entire race. Only the black woman can say, Cooper asserted, that "when and where I enter, in the quiet, undisputed dignity of my womanhood, without violence and without suing or special patronage, then and there the whole *Negro race enters with me.*"

By the turn of the century the terms on which blacks could or should enter into white mainstream society were in fact the subject of extensive and ongoing debate, crystallized in the opposing positions of Booker T. Washington and W.E.B. Du Bois. The dominant black political leader at the end of the nineteenth century, Washington argued for conciliating and accommodating to the white world. His famous Atlanta Exposition Speech in 1895, while promoting black pride and extolling self-help, urged blacks to eschew any hopes for social equality with whites and to limit their expectations for legal and economic advancement as well. By the turn of the century a vocal younger generation was demanding a more militant posture, refusing to be defined as a separate underclass. Du Bois's rejoinder to Washington, *The Souls of Black Folk* (1903), articulated his demand not only for civil rights for blacks but for the right to equal participation in higher education and liberal learning. By the beginning of the twentieth century, in poetry, fiction, and non-fictional prose, African American writers had established the terms for many of the major issues that the rest of the century would continue to confront.

Circumstances and Literary Achievements of Native Americans

During the four decades following the Civil War, the Native Americans suffered social discontinuity on a larger scale and to a greater degree than ever before or since, as white American society penetrated and firmly rooted itself in even the remotest interior of the trans-Mississippi West. War, confinement to reservations, and the resulting poverty, disease, and dispossession through fraud contributed to many white Americans' belief that the Indians were casualties of the sweep of the Caucasian (abetted by Western technology) across the face of the continent, and that they were destined to vanish, losers in the struggle for the fittest survivors. Opposed to this view were those well-meaning reformers who believed that with certain adjustments in their way of life, the American Indians could be saved. Thus during this period assimilation became the watchword, and federal policy drifted slowly from one of trying to defeat the Native Americans in warfare to attempting to make them over in white America's image. To do so required drastic changes in the Indians' relation to the land, new directions in their education, and a revolution in their way of life, all of which bore significantly on literary production among Native Americans.

To obtain the "proper" relation between Indian and land, the federal government had to undo its former policy of removal, which involved settling tribes in the Indian Territory (now Oklahoma). Both before the Civil War and in the twenty years after it, removal had chilling and sometimes devastating effects on individual and tribal life, including sharp rises in mortality rates. It was not, however, until after the forced march of the Poncas in 1877 from Dakota Territory to Indian Territory that any substantial sentiment rose against the policy. This shift in public attitude was due in significant measure to the efforts of a small group of writers, both Native American and white, who shaped the new public awareness of the effects of removal and contributed significantly to the development of an Indian policy reform movement that culminated in a major step toward assimilation—the General Allotment Act of 1887, or Dawes Act.

The first protest literature emerged from the Omaha Ponca Committee and the people they attracted. Consisting of Standing Bear (Ponca), Susette La Flesche (Omaha), her brother Francis La Flesche, and journalist Thomas H. Tibbles, the committee toured the East in 1879 and 1880, lecturing to inform the public about the dire effects of the Poncas' march. Capturing the public's attention, they won the support of reform and religious groups and of writers such as the aging Henry Wadsworth Longfellow, Oliver Wendell Holmes, and Helen Hunt Jackson, who took the Indians' situation to the periodical press. In 1881 Jackson published *A Century of Dishonor,* an indictment of federal Indian policy and an important step in the movement for reform. The book that captured the public imagination, however, and became the Native Americans' *Uncle Tom's Cabin,* was Jackson's popular novel, *Ramona* (1885). In the dispossession of Alisandro's people from their rancheria, readers found the archetype of dispossession of all Native American peoples in the past.

The General Allotment Act of 1887 dissolved collective tribal title to the land and allotted plots to individual Indians, who received deeds just as their Euro-American counterparts did throughout the country. The balance of unallotted land, which was always sizeable, was put up for sale, with the proceeds to be held in trust for the Indian tribes by the U.S. government. Allotted Native Americans also became citizens, subject to state laws and liable to taxation. The idea that private property would serve as an effective engine of democracy was an old one. The nation's agrarian founders had believed that the best life was that of the yeoman farmer, and ownership of land had figured prominently in the definition of the good citizen. In transferring the idea to Indian tribes, however, reformers ran roughshod over tribal traditions of collective land use; they also failed to consider the Indians' lack of operating capital and modern agricultural skills, the poor quality of much Indian land, and the lack of sufficient legal knowledge among the tribes to prevent them from losing their land. They also failed to calculate the scale of white American land hunger. Reactionary elements and land-hungry railroads had supported the General Allotment Act for their own reasons. They viewed Indian reservation land as a vast resource waiting to be exploited by the forces of expansionist capitalism. By 1887, Native Americans had lost all but 150 million acres of their aboriginal three-billion-acre landhold. By 1934, when the General Allotment Act was repealed, only 48 million acres, less than 1.5 percent of aboriginal America, still remained in Indian hands.

The goal of assimilation into mainstream society was pursued not just by disrupting the Indians' communal land base and thus undermining tribal sovereignty and self-determination, but by an educational policy that also separated individuals from their tribal heritage and customs. On the reservations, education was mainly mission based, giving the Native Americans instruction in Christian dogma and basic skills. In 1878, the government began a policy of off-reservation education by creating a number of boarding schools far from the reservations. Students were taken from their homes for a number of years, given Christian instruction, discouraged from speaking their native languages or following traditional practices, and provided with vocational training in the trades. The assumption underlying this plan was that the educated students could not return to the reservation and feel satisfied with conditions there. Rather, they were to enter mainstream America, participate in its economic system, and share its goods. Hamlin Garland and others, including the Santee Sioux writer Charles A. Eastman, believed that the transition would be easier if, like the immigrants arriving from abroad, the Indians' names were "Americanized." In the early twentieth century, Eastman, funded by the U.S. government, assigned Anglicized names to the Sioux.

Much literary production by Indians in this period was in some way a response to these efforts at assimilation. Susette La Flesche initially believed that individual land ownership and citizenship were the only means by which Native Americans could protect themselves; later she became disillusioned and concluded that the American economic system favored the rich over the poor, no matter what their color. Her brother, Francis, however, remained faithful to his early views, while also using his knowledge of traditional Indian life in writing autobiographical works, stories, legends, and a libretto for an opera. Although Charles A. Eastman found it difficult to reconcile the Christian faith he had embraced as a teenager and the Army's massacre of the Indians at Wounded Knee, he continued in his Christianity and also championed Indian culture. In the face of growing evidence that full participation in American society was not possible for American Indians, writers such as Zitkala-Sa, who had early embraced white America's ways, became embittered, professed their "paganism," and began a revival of interest in American Indian cultures. Her work, and that of others in her generation, led directly to the reforms in the 1920s and 1930s that attempted to arrest many of the devastating effects of allotment and recognized the value of cultural pluralism.

Representing another development in American Indian writing are those authors from tribes in the Indian Territory (especially the Cherokees, Choctaws, and Creeks) that had been there for many years before the Civil War. Having reestablished themselves as constitutional nations following removal in the 1830s and 1840s, they had developed systems of public education, embraced modern farming and ranching techniques, and were, in most respects, on the road to assimilation well before the U.S. government promoted assimilation. The educated populations in those tribes were well read in mainstream American literature, and from their ranks came a number of writers who, by the end of the nineteenth century, were adept in the rhetoric and conventions of that literature. By the late 1870s, the Cherokees, for instance, had established libraries, reading circles, and debating societies, and they subscribed to the popular magazines from the states, gaining access to the poetry and fiction of mainstream American writers. In their local newspapers appeared works by writers such as Mark Twain, Josh Billings, and Joel Chandler Harris. Cherokee writers such as D. W. C. Duncan (Tooquastee), John T. Adair, D. J. Brown, and John Oskison carried on the literary tradition begun by pre-Civil War Cherokees, including Elias Boudinot and John Rollin Ridge.

Literary activity also flourished elsewhere in the Indian Territory. Writers like Carrie Le Flore followed pre-Civil War Choctaw authors such as Israel Folsom and George Harkins. In the Creek Nation, writers James Roan Gregory, Charles Gibson, and Alexander Posey emerged, as did William Jones among the Sac and Fox and Bertrand N. O. Walker (Hen-toh) among the Wyandots.

Many Indian writers responded to literary movements in mainstream America. Dialect and humor became favorite forms of expression for writers such as Alexander Posey and, later, Will Rogers (Cherokee), and lesser-known writers contributed pieces to local publications after the fashion of Billings and other popular literary comedians. Posey created dialect poetry from his Indian background just as Paul Laurence Dunbar and Frances Ellen Watkins Harper did from their African American one. Walker wrote animal stories in the manner of Harris's Uncle Remus stories, and Posey, Jones, and Oskison produced a number of stories in the tradition of the regional writers.

Through the efforts of the Indian Territory writers, the La Flesches, Zitkala-Sa, and Eastman from the Great Plains, or Sarah Winnemucca of the Northern Paiutes, Indian literature began to find a national market. Autobiographies were of special interest, dealing as they did with the problem of a double identity that members of other ethnic groups were struggling with at the turn of the century, as the question of what it meant to be an "American" gained new urgency in a time both of increasing cultural diversity and of pressures to conform to mainstream ways. Simultaneously, the sharply increased interest in compilations of Indian oral traditions and tribal lore indicated a growing awareness of the impending loss of indigenous cultural life. Indian writers by the end of the century had laid a solid foundation on which twentieth-century American Indian literature could build. In turn, the critical attention that has been given to contemporary Indian writing has resulted in the rediscovery of many of the pre-World War I writers who are now finding a place in American literature.

Circumstances and Literary Achievements of Mexican Americans

For the Mexican Americans of the Southwest, the fifty years after 1865 comprised a period during which their traditions and literature evolved into a distinctive culture and body of expression. The Treaty of Guadalupe Hidalgo, which ended the Mexican War in 1848, transformed Spanish-speaking peoples from California to New Mexico into Americans only in a political sense, and a generation passed before they began to delineate their new geocultural realities. The literary instruments that Mexican Americans employed were mostly familiar ones: historical and personal narratives, stories, poems, and various folkloric forms such as the folktale, the legend, and the *corrido,* a type of Mexican ballad. As yet, the novel had made only an occasional appearance.

Aside from the question of Americanization, the issues that gripped the attention of writers in more populous regions of the United States—urbanization, technological innovation, the entrenchment of industrial capitalism—were regarded with considerably less enthusiasm in the Mexican American Southwest, which remained, defiantly, a place apart. Its heritage was unique among all the regions of the United States, a *mestizo* blend of Spanish, Indian, and, finally, Mexican traditions that contrasted vividly with the English traits of the dominant culture. Additionally, the primary religious influence was Catholic, not Protestant. For many Mexican Americans in the last third of the nineteenth century, the fountainheads of mainstream American culture and politics—Boston, New York, Philadelphia, and Washington—seemed remote if not irrelevant. What was decidedly neither remote nor irrelevant was the physical presence of the *gringos,* arriving in the Southwest in ever larger numbers, presumably to take the Mexican Americans' land and to demolish their culture.

Among American ethnic groups, Mexican Americans occupied a curious position, being neither immigrants—the United States, after all, had absorbed them—nor a minority in many of the southwestern communities they inhabited. Mexican Americans took pride in the fact that they could trace a longer history in North America than Anglo-Americans: Juan de Oñate had established a permanent settlement in northern New Mexico along the Rio Grande in 1598, nine years before the founding of Jamestown and twenty-two years before Plymouth. Another factor that separated Mexican Americans from other ethnic groups was the proximity of their homeland. The United States and Mexico shared a border that stretched some two thousand miles from the Pacific to the Gulf of Mexico, and most Mexican Americans lived within easy traveling distance; many lived on or near the border itself. While ethnic Europeans mourned the decline of their traditional cultures far away from their homelands, Mexican Americans had easy access to theirs.

Their long presence in the Southwest and their enduring cultural vitality and pride help to explain the vehemence with which Mexican Americans responded to the many Anglo-Americans who came into the region with little respect for the natives and little interest in cultural accommodation. Numerous historical and personal narratives appeared to denounce the arrogant and bigoted *gringos.* Not surprisingly, many of the fiercest condemnations came from once-wealthy and prominent landowners who had lost the most to the acquisitive Anglos. In addition to Mariano Vallejo and Juan Seguín, (represented in Vol. 1 of this anthology), writers of such works included Ignacio Sepúlveda, Juan Bautista Alvarado, Juan Bandini, and María Arparo Ruiz de Burton.

Even as they denounced the Anglo interlopers, Mexican Americans recognized that their world had changed and would change still more. Here, then, were the components of a distinctive Mexican American sensibility: ethnic pride and a powerful sense of history and endurance forged within the dynamics of the border.

In the late nineteenth century, easily the most popular literary form among

Mexican Americans was poetry, much of which appeared in the hundreds of Spanish-language newspapers that proliferated in the Southwest. Much of the poetry was lyrical, generally in the prevailing Spanish and Latin American styles, but a great deal was political, treating such issues as the quality of education available for Mexican Americans, the necessity of learning English, and land grant disputes. A particularly explosive issue debated in verse was the Spanish-American War of 1898. Some poets encouraged their readers to support the war effort as a show of patriotism; others maintained that the United States had done nothing to deserve Mexican American loyalty. Much of the newspaper poetry was anonymous; as a body of work it provides valuable insights into the collective consciousness of the Mexican American community.

The production of conventional literary works increased steadily toward the end of the nineteenth century and beyond, but folkloric forms continued to dominate Mexican American expression. The *corrido* ballad tradition matured around the turn of the century and thrived long thereafter. The *corrido* proved to be the perfect expressive vehicle for preserving the Mexican American version of cultural conflict with the Anglo. *Corridos* were composed—usually anonymously—and sung across the Southwest, attaining epic proportions in the lower border regions of Texas. Here, in an environment of intense conflict with the Anglo community and true trans-culturalism, the "border Mexicans" celebrated the exploits of such figures as Gregorio Cortez and Jacinto Treviño, common men who stood up to Anglo injustice with, as the saying went, pistols in their hands.

Although Mexican American literary works, including the narratives of Miguel Otero and Andrew García, occasionally appeared in English, Spanish remained the primary language of expression in both conventional and folkloric forms until well into the twentieth century. Indeed, Mexican American Spanish had become a distinctive oral and literary idiom, incorporating English words and phrases and creating new expressions from both standard Spanish and English.

Circumstances and Literary Achievements of Asian Americans

By the turn of the century, Asian Americans constituted a comparatively small percentage of the population of the United States. Out of a total of fourteen million immigrant arrivals between 1860 and 1900, less than half a million were of Asian descent. Of this number, Chinese immigrants comprised roughly 260,000 but experienced discrimination out of all proportion to their modest numerical presence. Indeed, in the post-Civil War period, Sinophobia became widespread, and cities, states, and the national government passed repressive legislation. The Chinese had been the primary labor force in the building of the transcontinental railroad east from Sacramento, doing the backbreaking and dangerous work of tunneling through the Sierra Nevada and Rocky Mountains. With the railroad's completion in 1869, however, they found themselves barred from other occupations, a situation that worsened throughout the 1870s, when a nationwide depression led to a scarcity of jobs. In California, they were largely confined to cooking, laundry, and domestic work; elsewhere, employers' exploitation of them as strikebreakers exacerbated hostility against them. Designed primarily to increase contributions, accounts of missionaries working in China that described the Chinese as "heathens living in darkness" served to encourage feelings of distrust and disgust among whites. By the late nineteenth century, the Chinese were contributing to American society in a variety of fields, including innovations in the

Florida citrus fruit and the California wine industries; nonetheless, the prevalent stereotype saw them as "coolies," slant-eyed and idolatrous.

From the 1870s on, local and state laws in California limited not only the employment of Chinese but also their freedom to engage in their own cultural practices. Violence against them also escalated, with over a thousand killed and innumerable others driven from their homes between 1871 and 1886 in California, Washington, Wyoming, and Colorado. The repression peaked in 1882 with the passage of the Chinese Exclusion Act, which banned the entry of all Chinese except for a few diplomats, students, teachers, merchants, and tourists. Further legislation in 1888 voided Certificates of Return, leaving twenty thousand Chinese stranded outside the United States with useless reentry permits.

Compared to the antipathy directed toward the Chinese, mainstream American attitudes toward Japanese immigrants were relatively benign for a time. Modest immigration flows, coupled with Japan's military power (manifested by its victories over China in 1872 and 1895 and over Russia in 1905), helped prevent anti-Chinese sentiment from spilling into violence and discrimination against Japanese. Still, the Gentleman's Agreement of 1908, which limited but did not completely bar Japanese immigration, portended greater restrictions on Japanese as the United States became increasingly isolationist and as racist social theory continued to fuel segregationist domestic policies.

The status of Koreans in the United States in the early twentieth century was tied closely to Japan's imperialistic drive to control Korea, which it made a protectorate in 1905 before formal annexation occurred in 1910. Upon becoming subjects of the Japanese emperor, the roughly eight thousand Koreans in the United States were directly affected by the Gentleman's Agreement. The loss of their sovereignty generated considerable nationalist sentiment among them, and in 1905 Koreans in Hawaii sent a letter to President Theodore Roosevelt asking for American intervention

THE NEW COLOSSUS

Not like the brazen giant of Greek fame,
With conquering limbs astride from land to land;
Here at our sea-washed, sunset gates shall stand
A mighty woman with a torch, whose flame
Is the imprisoned lightning, and her name
Mother of Exiles. From her beacon-hand
Glows world-wide welcome; her mild eyes command
The air-bridged harbor that twin cities frame.
"Keep, ancient lands, your storied pomp!" cries she
With silent lips. "Give me your tired, your poor,
Your huddled masses yearning to breathe free,
The wretched refuse of your teeming shore.
Send these, the homeless, tempest-tost to me,
I lift my lamp beside the golden door!"

Emma Lazarus
1883

in the wake of the Japanese takeover of Korea. This political appeal was but one manifestation of what was to be a vibrant independence movement among Koreans in this country.

That few Asian American writers of this period came to the notice of mainstream readers should not cause us to overlook the plentiful material produced by every Asian group in the United States. Much of the writing by Koreans consisted of tracts, pamphlets, and sermons in Korean. It would take another generation for authors like Younghill Kang during the 1930s to begin expressing in English some of the aforementioned political sentiments that marked the Korean American community.

Filipino literary expression was marked by a strong nationalist strain as well, with exiles from the Philippines such as Felipe Agoncillo, Sixto Lopez, and Galicano Apacible writing to dispel American colonialist stereotypes of their people and to prove Filipino competence. Although these authors generally did not write for or about the several thousand Filipino workers in the United States, their nationalist fervor would inspire the next (the "manong") generation to focus attention on the experiences of this group.

In the late nineteenth and early twentieth centuries, native Hawaiian cultural workers (including the overthrown Queen Liliuokalani) composed poems and songs that quietly but defiantly expressed resentment against continental U.S. missionary and business interests intent on expropriating Hawaii's resources and lands. The lyrics of "*Kaulana na Pua,*" for instance, exhort the children of Hawaii to remain loyal to the land in the face of the "evil-hearted messenger" with his "greedy document of extortion"; but because the song was sung in Hawaiian, its protest statement went unrecognized by the colonizers even as it spread among the colonized. Such expressions of protest would persist throughout the islands and even inspire writers on the mainland in the twentieth century.

The best-known early Asian American authors were Edith and Winnifred Eaton. The Canada-raised daughters of a Chinese mother and an English father, both adopted pen names that reflected the ethnic identities they chose to assume. Under the Chinese pseudonym Sui Sin Far, Edith Eaton too up the cause of the much-maligned Chinese in short stories and articles that she published in the major magazines of the day, thereby becoming the first Chinese American to write in their defense. Winnifred Eaton, in contrast, chose a Japanese-sounding name, Onoto Watanna, under which between 1899 and 1925 she published hundreds of stories and nearly a score of novels, mostly set in Japan. Exquisitely printed on paper decorated with Asian motifs, her novels were widely popular, conforming as they did to the racial and sexual stereotypes of her time: her Japanese men are noble and martial, her young Japanese women shy and charming. During a period when nearly half the states had laws against miscegenation, the popularity of Winnifred Eaton's books was not diminished by the interracial relationships they portrayed. Romance between American or English men and Japanese or Eurasian women was acceptable within the stereotypes; romance between Asian men and white women would not have been. It is Edith Eaton, meanwhile, who laid a groundwork for twentieth-century Asian American literature by dramatizing the discrimination experienced by Chinese Americans, including the agonies suffered by those involved in Chinese-Caucasian marriages that predated the anti-miscegenation laws. Furthermore, in presenting in her autobiographical work a sense of her own split identity as a person living in two cultures but feeling at home in neither, she began that exploration of a dual heritage that later Asian American writers would reaffirm, challenge, or revise in their own contexts.

Immigration, Urban Conditions, and Reform

If the need to balance the claim's of one's ethnic or racial heritage against those of the dominant culture was an imperative for African Americans, American Indians, Mexican Americans, and Asian Americans, so too at the turn of the century it became the paramount literary subject for the first generation of writers to emerge from among those called the "new immigrants," the southern and eastern Europeans who entered the United States in unprecedented numbers in the decades after the Civil War. Before 1860 most immigrants had come from Great Britain, Ireland, Germany, and Scandinavia, and while their entry was steady it was not overwhelming: five million had arrived in the forty years between 1820 and 1860. The next forty years, however, saw fourteen million new arrivals to the United States, the vast majority of whom came from Italy and Poland, Russia, Austria, Turkey, Greece, and Syria. Heavily Catholic or Jewish and non-English-speaking, they settled primarily in the cities of the Northeast and Midwest, where they frequently took the least skilled industrial jobs and were viewed by the native-born and by earlier arrivals with apprehension and distrust. Their sheer numbers radically altered the ethnic composition of the nation, and their different

UNGUARDED GATES

Wide open and unguarded stand our gates
And through them presses a wild, motley throng—
Men from the Volga and the Tartar steppes,
Featureless figures of the Hoang-Ho,
Malayan, Scythian, Teuton, Kelt, and Slav,
Flying the Old World's poverty and scorn;
These bringing with them unknown gods and rites,
Those, tiger passions, here to stretch their claws.
In the street and alley what strange tongues are loud,
Accents of menace alien to our air,
Voices that once the Tower of Babel knew!

O Liberty, white Goddess! is it well
To leave the gates unguarded? On thy breast
Fold Sorrow's children, soothe the hurts of hate,
Lift the down-trodden, but with hands of steel
Stay those who to thy sacred portals come
To waste the gifts of freedom. Have a care
Lest from thy brow the clustered stars be torn
And trampled in the dust. For so of old
The thronging Goth and Vandal trampled Rome,
And where the temples of the Caesars stood
The lean wolf unmolested made her lair.

Thomas Bailey Aldrich
1894

manners and customs, modes of dress, and religious observances were seen as threatening and disruptive to Anglo-Saxon hegemony and power. Reaction to the new immigrants took the form of expressed fears of race suicide or a dilution of "American" racial stock, which led after World War I to major legislation restricting immigration into the country.

Increased cultural diversity created increased pressure to conform, and as with American Indians, assimilation was the prescribed goal. The idea of the United States as a melting pot in which ethnic and racial differences would be dissolved into a common identity prevailed, and by the end of the century that common identity was being consciously defined as based on spoken and written English and on Anglo-Saxon cultural values. And as with the Indians, education was an essential mechanism for accomplishing the process. The public school, as Mary Antin declared, was to be "the immigrant child's road to Americanization."

The ways in which the new immigrants responded to the expectations of their newly adopted country differed from those of other minority groups, primarily because, unlike blacks, who were brought to America forcibly, or American Indians and Mexican Americans, who first inhabited the land and were then subjugated by white settlers, the new immigrants largely chose to come. True, they came because conditions at home were often intolerable—wars, religious and political persecutions, crop failures and famines, overpopulation and unemployment—but they came, like Abraham Cahan in 1882 or Mary Antin's father in 1892, because they saw America as a land of economic opportunity and political freedom. The terms on which they struck their bargains with the new land, the conflicts they experienced, the accommodations they made, therefore, bore the marks of their own unique situations.

Some immigrant groups, such as the Jews and the Germans, brought with them traditions of literacy and often cultural networks and institutions. Others, such as southern Italians, Poles, and many Irish, came from peasant stock with well-developed oral but not written literary traditions. Among the new arrivals, Jewish immigrants took quickly to print, and their autobiographies and novels expressed the eagerness to assimilate that distinguished the new immigrants as a whole from most of the other American minority populations. The immediate popularity of Mary Antin's autobiography, *The Promised Land,* which appeared in 1912 after having first been serialized in the *Atlantic Monthly,* was to a significant extent due to the glowing portrait it presented of the acculturation process. Antin was eager to exchange her "hateful homemade European costume" for "real American machine-made garments" and her "impossible" Hebrew name, "Maryashe," for "Mary." But her truly transformative experience came when she was enrolled in the public school—a moment of supreme fulfillment for her father as well, who through his children thus vicariously "took possession of America." More problematic was the experience recorded in the novels of Abraham Cahan, which assessed the emotional and spiritual cost of economic success for his immigrant heroes, a price paid in a sense of self-division and even self-betrayal by the sundering of family, religious, and class bonds. Like most Jewish immigrants from eastern Europe, the titular hero of *Yekl* lives both in the Old World with its biblical and Talmudic roots and values and in the New World of hustle and competition. The claims of the Old World, and of his own former self, he is "neither willing to banish from his memory nor able to reconcile with the actualities of his American present." The tensions that begin to surface in *Yekl* are more fully exposed in Cahan's *The Rise of David Levinsky* (1917), a classic rendition of the immigrant experience. Levinsky's rise to business success as a cloak manufacturer can be compared to that of Howells's Silas Lapham thirty years earlier, as a measure of the more acute degree of personal and cultural dislocation, and of the increased precariousness of the self, given the greater estrangement between one's cultural origins and one's new social and economic goals.

Antin's autobiography and Cahan's novels recognize that the success of some is built on the deprivation of others—Antin's older sister, Frieda, who must work in a factory if the younger children are to be educated; the fellow tailors whom Levinsky abandons when he rises above their ranks. For the mass of the new immigrants, the good fortune of an Antin or a Cahan was elusive, and the nightmare side of their American success dream was powerfully captured by socialist writer Upton Sinclair, whose hero Jurgis in *The Jungle* (1906) is also an immigrant, for whom Chicago initially holds the promise that Boston held for Antin or New York for Yekl and Levinsky. But Jurgis's life, both as factory worker and as husband, father, and provider for his extended ethnic family, becomes a series of brutalizing defeats, as the impersonal workings of the industrial economy crush, one by one, all of his hopes and efforts to rise.

Based on actual investigation of the filthy working conditions and contaminated products of the Chicago meat-packing industry, Sinclair's novel was one instance of the "muckraking" literature that appeared in the 1890s and early 1900s—journalistic exposés intended to underscore and bring to public attention the plight of groups like the factory workers, and the business and government practices that were often responsible for their plight. Such exposés, often first appearing in the new mass circulation magazines such as *McClure's* and *Cosmopolitan* and later published as books, included Ida Tarbell's articles on Standard Oil, Jacob Riis's on the conditions of New York city tenements, and Lincoln Steffens's on graft and corruption in municipal governments. In turn they were a part of what had become by the turn of the century a groundswell of social protest writing that also included, for example, Ray Stannard Baker's and Charles W. Chesnutt's on race riots and Ida B. Wells's on lynching. Such writing was indicative of the ever-deepening concern of writers, social workers, sociologists, economists, and social philosophers over the destructive effects both for social stability and democratic ideals of the unregulated growth and periodic breakdowns of the industrial economy and of the inequities inherent in America's social and economic structures. This extensive literature of social protest, which took the form of novels, journalistic articles, and book-length scholarly analyses, addressed major social problems and offered programs for change that ranged from Utopian visions of radically restructured societies to remedies that would alleviate specific social ills.

One of the distinguishing features of realistic fiction throughout the post-war period, of course, was its awareness of and concern for the effects of the industrial economy on individual lives, social groups, and regional cultures. Indeed, much of the fiction (as well as nonfiction) of the post-Civil War period that seems most alive to us today is that dealing with the social dislocations created by America's overwhelming material progress, and such writing is often informed, at least implicitly, by a protest impulse. Often, therefore, writers crossed the line—an arbitrary one at best—between esthetic and political intent to produce narratives, like *The Jungle,* with a deliberate "message." Hamlin Garland, for example, always the advocate of the midwestern farmer, responded to their worsening conditions in the early 1890s—falling crop prices exacerbated by often exorbitant railroad freight and bank loan rates—by writing novels that argued for specific legislative reforms, including the single tax on land that Henry George had proposed in *Progress and Poverty* in 1879, and other legislative remedies advocated by the Populist party, formed in the early 1890s in response to agrarian and labor needs. And in *The Octopus* (1901) Frank Norris exposed the railroads' immense power over the farmers. Other writers used the genre of the Utopian novel as a vehicle for their visions of transformed societies based on principles of social justice. The most famous and influential of these was Edward Bellamy's *Looking Backward* (1888), the first Utopia of the industrial age, which depicted the United States in the year 2000 as a nation where government ownership of the means of production and the rational, "scientific" rule of a managerial class guaranteed economic equality and happiness for all citizens. Bellamy's work, which was still selling as many as ten thousand copies a week in the early 1890s, inspired a host of successors—several hundred Utopian fictions appeared between the 1880s and the early 1900s, including Howells's *A Traveler from Altruria,* a work that, like Bellamy's, envisioned a socialist state. Many Utopias by women, including Charlotte Perkins Gilman's *Herland* (1915), addressed crucial issues of women's continuing subordination, which male writers were likely to ignore.

On balance, however, it was the conditions of urban life and of the industrial workers that increasingly catalyzed writers and reformers and that led to the outpouring of social protest literature, as well as to direct political action. The periodic breakdowns of the economy that resulted from uncontrolled industrial growth affected all groups, including farmers and the middle class; however, they had their most dramatic, because most visible and most violent, impact on the working class in the congested cities. The severe and prolonged depressions that began in 1873 and again in 1893 were especially devastating, leading to massive unemployment; in 1894 the situation reached crisis proportions, with twenty percent of the labor force out of work. With the formation of the Knights of Labor and later the Industrial Workers of the World and the American Federation of Labor, the post-war period saw the steady growth of the trade union movement, which, however, reached only a portion of workers and met with widespread employer resistance. Labor dissatisfaction therefore took the form of strikes, which management countered with armed force and violence. The extremity of the conflict between capital and labor can be read in the fact that between 1881 and 1905 the nation witnessed over thirty-six thousand strikes involving some six million workers. The Chicago Fair was bracketed by two of the most notorious: the Homestead Strike in 1892, which broke the organizing efforts of the iron and steel workers, and the Pullman strike in Chicago in 1894, in which scores of striking workers were killed when state militia and federal troops were called in and the American Railway Union, led by Eugene V. Debs, was broken. It was the specter of such industrial violence, already apparent in the 1880s, and the fear of social chaos, that had led Bellamy to conceive his Utopia, where state control of the industrial machine precludes the potential anarchy of free enterprise.

Efforts to implement social change peaked in the Progressive Era, the period from the 1890s until the eve of World War I, which saw the first nationwide reform movement in modern history, when calls for social justice issued in a flood from the nation's presses. To the exposés of the muckrakers were added the investigative studies and documented reports of social workers and sociologists calling attention to the social ills of capitalism: the uneven and unplanned growth of the cities with their rapid influx of population, which had led to hastily built tenement housing with its attendant problems of lack of sanitation, overcrowding, dirt and noise; the existence of a working class, and heavily immigrant, population dependent on an inadequate weekly wage and vulnerable to the erratic shifts in a profit-oriented mar-

> The golf links lie so near the mill
> That almost every day
> The laboring children can look out
> And see the men at play.
>
> Sarah N. Cleghorn

ket economy; the resulting poverty that led to long working hours, child labor, prostitution, and crime; the rule of corrupt party bosses that blocked reform. The settlement house movement, described in Chicagoan Jane Addams's *Twenty Years at Hull House* (1910) and exemplified in the work of reformers like Lillian Wald and Vida Scudder, had since the 1880s attempted to rectify some of the worst living and employment problems of the urban poor and to acculturate the poor to middle-class values. Their efforts contributed to the passage of local, state, and federal laws regulating the hours and working conditions of women and children, providing workers' compensation, and improving living, educational, and recreational facilities in urban slums and ghettoes.

Such laws, the first significant body of reform legislation in the nation's history, represented a major, indeed a profound, shift in national attitudes from those that had prevailed earlier, in the heyday of unrestrained industrial growth. Then, the ideology of Social Darwinism, as purveyed by writers like William Graham Sumner, had justified a hands-off approach to economic development, arguing that social, like biological, evolution was governed by natural laws that should not be interfered with. The literature of social protest constituted a strong collective rejoinder to that ideology, and the reform legislation was official recognition of the need for greater governmental involvement and responsibility, for legislative controls and for social planning, if American society was to fulfill its democratic promise. Essentially the work of middle-class reformers, the progressive movement functioned to repair some of the damage done by a capitalist system while containing resistance to capitalism, which remained intact despite a briefly successful challenge from socialists, who mounted a series of political campaigns and in 1912 garnered 900,000 votes for Eugene V. Debs as presidential candidate and elected socialist mayors in thirty-three cities.

Some socialist tendencies colored progressive reform thought, including that of the Social Gospel movement that spread inside liberal Protestantism in the 1880s and 1890s. Dedicated to improving society through the application of Christian ethical precepts, emphasizing morality rather than theology, and social rather than individual redemption, the Social Gospel movement included writers like economist Richard T. Ely, whose arguments appeared in *Social Aspects of Christianity* in 1889, ministers like Walter Rauschenbusch, who offered a form of Christian socialism in *Christianity and the Social Crisis* (1907) and *Christianizing the Social Order* (1912), and popularizers like Congregational minister Charles M. Sheldon, who wrote one of the nation's most popular novels, *In His Steps* (1897), in which urban residents reform a city by asking "what would Jesus do" and acting accordingly. Social Gospel thinking also influenced William Dean Howells, who was increasingly concerned in the mid-1880s with issues of poverty and labor unrest. *The Minister's Charge* (1886) is the story of a clergyman who realizes the need for changed clerical attitudes and broader involvement in issues of social justice and reform.

In the Social Gospel movement, religion remained a viable force in American life, and it continued to be a source of spiritual strength and cultural cohesion for blacks. But generally, the influence of religion, specifically the Protestantism on which the nation had been founded and that had provided a common set of values and assumptions for over 250 years, waned in the post-war period, a time when scientifically derived empirical findings replaced biblical revelation as the source of truth. Darwin's *On the Origin of Species* (1859), which undermined belief in the possibility of a separate creation of the human species by God, dealt religion a powerful blow, and indeed the Social Gospel movement can be seen as an effort to regain for ministers some of the status that science was steadily eroding.

But the age was a secular one, and intellectual authority increasingly passed to scientists, social scientists, and other university-trained and -based scholars and philosophers, as professionalization replaced the genteel amateurism of earlier New England cultural leaders. The very American philosophy of pragmatism, invented and expounded by William James in the final decades of the century and further developed by John Dewey in the twentieth, was an effort to provide the country with a philosophy that responded to new social complexities while retaining the traditional American belief in individualism: recognizing the constrictions of environment and circumstance on human life, pragmatism nonetheless argued for the ameliorative power of human agency to effect constructive change. Other schools of thought, however, which would gain increased currency in the years after World War I, offered less sanguine outlooks. The ideas of Marx and Freud, brewed in the ferment of nineteenth-century Europe, would constitute major intellectual shifts in the twentieth. Both served to accelerate the undermining of traditional ideas regarding the development and organization of society, and individual psychological and moral development as well; and both reinforced the widespread tendency toward a determinist view of individual and social life. As the twentieth century began to take shape in the years before World War I, these and other powerful new intellectual developments would drastically alter the cultural landscape.

Elaine Hedges

James Kyung-Jin Lee

Richard Yarborough

Sandra A. Zagarell

Nation, Regions, Borders

If the end of the Civil War brought a new sense of national unity to the United States, the new economic and technological developments in the post-war period were making unification a reality. Transcontinental railroads, the telephone and telegraph, the mass production and distribution of printed materials, and the standardized consumer products dispensed by large corporations were linking all parts of the country geographically and creating, with national markets, certain uniformities of taste and opinion as well. Before the war the United States had been more sectional than national in orientation: a collection of regions—South, North, Midwest, Southwest, West—and of locales within those regions, each with its different and distinguishing customs, manners, and linguistic traits. In the post-war period the perceived need for a national identity prompted calls for a national literature, one that would capture and express distinctively "American" characteristics. Although such calls had been voiced earlier—almost, indeed, as soon as the United States had come into being in 1786—they now were vigorously renewed, and as prose fiction came more and more to dominate the literary scene, the call was especially for "the Great American Novel."

Much post-war fiction, including that of William Dean Howells and Henry James, was affected by and often a conscious response to such expectations. Howells's well-known statement that "the smiling aspects of life are the most American" conveyed his belief (one he later modified) in the appropriateness of certain kinds of subject matter and certain treatments of it as indexes of the nature of American life. The very title, *The American,* that James gave to his novel about a businessman (with the revealing name of Christopher Newman), as well as his portrayals of the "new American girl" in *Daisy Miller* and other works, indicated his interest in identifying representative national types. Other novelists, including Harold Frederic, Robert Herrick, and Frank Norris, wrote novels that ambitiously, if not always successfully, tried to capture and dramatize what they saw as major national political, social, and economic developments.

Yet if one were to ask which post-Civil War novel seems today most typically "American," the answer might well be *Adventures of Huckleberry Finn,* a work whose enduring vitality is surely attributable in large part to its richly grounded and vividly evoked localisms of manners, customs, character types, and dialects. For the reality of America has always been, to a significant degree, its extraordinary diversity—of regions, and of ethnic and racial groups; and a truly "national" literature, in the final analysis, must be one that honors such diversity. Howells himself understood this fact: he encouraged ethnic and regional writers, and in his own novels he scrupulously recorded the stories of easterners, southerners, and westerners, the upper, middle, and working classes, and the new immigrant population, so that his various works become, as Jay Martin has said, "chapters of the Great American Novel."

The interest in creating a national literature, therefore, was paralleled by an interest in producing writing that was notably local or regional in emphasis, and much post-Civil War fiction is characterized by its attention to distinguishing features of speech, behavior, and landscape—the cultural geography—of specific and seemingly out-of-the-way places. The growth of a new, well-to-do, and more traveled audience for fiction helps explain the post-Civil War flowering both of the international novel such as Henry James wrote and of regional fiction. In addition, the theory of realism, with its belief that good writing is rooted in closely observed particulars, also encouraged regional writing, as did the widespread awareness that the very economic and political forces that were uniting the nation were thereby eroding sectional and local differences. Much regional literature, therefore, had a historical as well as an esthetic impulse. George Washington Cable's stories of prewar New Orleans and Alexander Posey's verse commemorations of Creek and Cherokee leaders capture and record ways of life that were disappearing or had already disappeared.

Such endangered local ways of life are often pitted, in the era's fiction, against others more powerful or dominant, and much regional writing derives its plots and dramatic interest from the clash of disparate and often conflicting cultures: rural and urban in Garland's "Up the Coulé," for instance; frontier West and settled East in Crane's "The Bride Comes to Yellow Sky"; Christian and Creek in Oskison's "The Story of Old Harjo"; and southern black and northern white in Chesnutt's "The Goophered Grapevine." These cultural contrasts were often embodied not just in plot and characters but in language as well. Dialects—speech patterns indigenous to particular locales—may be played off against standard or literary English to dramatize differences of outlook and values.

Even as the regionalist play of voices expressed differences and tensions between local cultures and a national identity, areas of the Southwest that had been part of Mexico until 1848 saw the emergence of a literature reflecting the particular linguistic, cultural, political, and economic struggles of the border. Both oral and written, mainly in Spanish but sometimes in English, this literature included the *corrido,* a vivid ballad form specific to the border, which expressed the resilience, hardships, and dangers of the lives of ordinary Mexican Americans. It also included an extensive Mexican American autobiographical literature, retrospective in nature, in which writers like the patrician Mariano C. Vallejo recorded personal pasts interwoven with the much-mourned era when they were still Mexican, and when many of them were wealthy landowners. In yet another form, the novel, María Amparo Ruiz de Burton attempted to influence the future of the border by reflecting on its past and present. Her *The Squatter and the Don* sought to marshal appreciation for the cosmopolitanism and integrity of the *californios* (Mexican feudal property-holders) and to mobilize public opinion against the U.S. trend toward national consolidation.

In the prominence it accords to language itself, Mexican American literature of the border displays a certain similarity to a development prominent in more mainstream writing: the crafting of a style closer than most antebellum writing to the actual rhythms of American speech. This was an important aspect of the democratizing tendency of much of the nation's literature and here, too, *Huckleberry Finn* was of major importance. In it, Twain fashioned Huck's vernacular speech into a supple instrument for conveying moral seriousness and emotional complexity. Such use of language was also part of the growing emphasis on self-conscious artistry that distinguished prose fiction in this period. Writers, especially Henry James, attended more deliberately to the techniques of composing and crafting artful narratives. An emphasis on scenic presentation and an absence of intrusive authorial comment distinguishes much post-war fiction, as does the use of carefully controlled points of view. In such stories as Chesnutt's "The Passing of Grandison," Crane's "The Open Boat," and Bierce's "Chickamauga" the reader is often confined inside the mind of a single character, limited to that individual's understanding of events, with the result that truth, or ultimate meaning, becomes relative and often problematic. This retreat from the use of an omniscient point of view suggests a skepticism of authority and of inherited certitudes; what is often conveyed is a sense that both truth and morality are subjective, dependent upon particular experiences and upon perspectives that may be allied with class, race, and gender differences.

In turn, such formal devices are used to convey both new subject matter and more candid treatments of subject matter. Chopin's nonjudgmental depictions of women's sexuality, Crane's skepticism, and Bierce's cynicism about war point the way, by the end of the century, toward the greater candidness and increased formal experimentation that would mark the literature of the twentieth century.

Elaine Hedges
Towson State University
Sandra A. Zagarell
Oberlin College

African American Folktales

Folktales provide a radical illustration of the principle that fictions are not the fixed texts that printed pages imply but interactions between authors and audiences, who bring to the meeting their own social and individual experiences. The printed texts of the folktales below are themselves products of a complex network of interactions. Though the process of collection, publication, and now selection gives them the appearance of a fixed identity, they are actually only moments in a continuous process of invention, adaptation, and performance—cupfuls dipped out of a river.

What goes into a published folktale? The structural elements of folktales are traditional tale types and motifs widespread in world folklore and classified by folklorists. The motifs of African American folktales come from both African and European tradition. Over time, storytellers have selected and adapted them to reflect their own social experience. For example, in European variants of the popular tale "Dividing Souls," here represented by John Blackamore's individualized "Old Boss Wants into Heaven," the two watchers are typically a parson and a sexton, but in most African American variants, they are a crippled master and the slave who carries him. The motif of the dependent master frightened into running on his own two feet becomes a metaphor for the unwarranted economic dependency of white on black in slavery. Blackamore's highly developed and pointed version of this tale calls attention to another component of the folktale, the individual storyteller's insight and imagination.

An oral story also involves interaction between the storyteller and the audience. The printed story, however, is the product of a different interaction, that between the storyteller and the folklore collector, who is at least to some extent an outsider to the folk group. Conventions of how to represent the folk storytelling situation and acknowledge the role of the collector have changed over the years. Early folklore popularizers often embedded the tales in a fictional framework and retold them in heightened language. "Brer Coon Gets His Meat" provides an example of exaggerated dialect as well as the mimicry and music of folk delivery. Zora Neale Hurston's "John Calls on the Lord" seems to reflect collaboration between storyteller and collector; here John addresses "the Lord" in language that Hurston, the daughter of a black lay preacher, had heard all her life and repeated with relish in her fiction. In the 1930s, Federal Writers Project teams collecting the reminiscences of the last generation of former slaves attempted to portray accurately the relationship between informants and collectors by describing the communities they visited, identifying individual informants, and recording their own role in eliciting the stories. They set the standard that subsequent collectors, notably Richard M. Dorson, have developed.

We cannot be sure to what extent collectors rather than storytellers have determined the history of the African American folktale repertoire. There is little doubt that the animal tales were told during slavery. But tales of the contest of wits between the black man and the white first appear in collections between 1915 and 1919, and only gradually develop in the 1930s and 1940s into the cycle of episodes in the perpetual battle between John the unsubmissive slave and his Old Marster. Whether former slaves withheld these stories for fifty years after Emancipation, or early collectors intent on animal stories failed to seek them out, or they developed in the twentieth century as a commentary on the perpetuation of inequality, we don't know. What the published record does show is that, while African American folk narrative comes out of slavery, it is not an artifact of the slave period but a living tradition. In the twentieth century, as the selections below reflect, African American folktales became increasingly politically pointed and were adapted to the rhythms and concerns of an increasingly urban folk. Perhaps the clearest testimony to the continuing vitality of African American folk narrative is its importance in the fiction of such writers as Charles Chesnutt, Zora Neale Hurston, Langston Hughes, Ralph Ellison, and Toni Morrison.

The tales in this section have been chosen to represent some of the most commonly collected tales and a variety of narrative styles and collection principles. For more tales (including genres such as ghost stories and preacher jokes not included here), see the collections from which these are taken.

Susan L. Blake
Lafayette College

PRIMARY WORKS

In addition to the sources identified in the notes to the tales, see Bruce Jackson, *"Get Your Ass in the Water and Swim like Me": Narrative Poetry from Black Oral Tradition,* 1974; Daryl Cumber Dance, *Shuckin' and Jivin': Folklore from Contemporary Black Americans,* 1978; Roger D. Abrahams, *Afro-American Folktales: Stories from Black Traditions in the New World,* 1985; Linda Goss and Marian E. Barnes, *Talk That Talk: An Anthology of African-American Storytelling,* 1989.

Animal Tales

When Brer Deer and Brer Terrapin Runned a Race[1]

Brer Deer and Brer Terrapin was a-courting of Mr. Coon's daughter. Brer Deer was a peart chap, and have the airs of the quality, no put-on bigoty ways; Brer Deer am a right sure 'nough gentleman, that he is. Well, old Brer Terrapin am a poor, slow, old man; all the creeters wonder how the gal can smile on hisself when Mr. Deer flying round her, but them what knows tells how, when old man Terrapin lay hisself out, he have a mighty taking way with the gals, and the gals in the old times mighty like the gals these here times, and ain't got no sense nohow.

Well, old man Coon he favor Brer Deer, and he powerful set again Brer Terrapin, and he fault him to the gals constant; but the more Brer Coon fault Brer Terrapin, the more the hard-headed gal giggle and cut her eye when Brer Terrapin come 'bout; and old Brer Coon, he just nigh 'bout outdone with her foolishness, and he say he gwine set down on the fooling.

So he say, Brer Coon did, how Brer Deer and Brer Terrapin shall run a seven-mile race, and the one what get there first shall surely have the gal, 'cause he feel that sure in he mind, Brer Coon do, that Brer Deer nat'rally bound to outrun poor old Brer Terrapin.

But I tell you, sah, when old Brer Terrapin pull he head in he house, and shut up all the doors, and just give himself to study, when he do that there way, the old man ain't just dozing away the time. Don't you mind, sah, he have a mighty bright eye, Brer Terrapin have, sah.

Well, Brer Terrapin, he say he run the race, if he can run in the water, 'cause he 'low he mighty slow on the foots. And Brer Deer and Brer Coon, they talk it over to theyselves, and they 'low Brer Deer mighty slow in the water, and so they set the race 'long the river bank. Brer Deer, he gwine run seven miles on the bank, and Brer Terrapin, he gwine run 'long the shore in the water, and he say every mile he gwine raise he head out the water and say, "Oho! here I is."

Den Brer Deer and Brer Coon laugh to burst theyselves, 'cause they lay out for Brer Terrapin done pass the first mile, Brer Deer done win the race.

Well, sah, Brer Terrapin he have six brothers, and he set one in the water every mile, and he set one in the water at the starting-place, and the old man, he set hisself in the water at the seven-mile post. O my, massa, dat old Brer Terrapin, he got a head on hisself, he surely have.

Well, Brer Coon and Brer Deer, they come down to the water, and they see Brer Terrapin out there in the water, an' Brer Coon, he place Brer Deer, and tell him hold on till he get hisself there, 'cause he bound to see the end of the race. So he get on the horse and whip up, and directly Brer Deer and Brer Terrapin start out, and when

[1]Emma Backus, "Animal Tales from North Carolina," *Journal of American Folk-Lore* 11(1898):284–85.

Brer Deer come to the first milestone he stick his head out the water, and he say, "Oho, here I is!" and Brer Deer, he just set to faster, 'cause he know Brer Terrapin mighty short-winded, but when he git to the two-mile post, sure 'nough, there Brer Terrapin stick he head out and say, "Oho, here I is!" and Brer Deer, he that astonished he nigh 'bout break down, but he set to and do he best, and when he come to the three-mile post, 'fore God if there ain't Brer Terrapin's head come out the water, and he just holler out, "Oho, here I is!"

But Brer Deer he push on, and every mile that there bodacious old Brer Terrapin. Well, when Brer Deer come a-puffing and a-blowing up to the last-most post, and Brer Coon set there on the horse, and just 'fore Brer Deer come up, if there ain't sure 'nough old Brer Terrapin, just where he done been waiting all the time, and just 'fore Brer Deer fotch round *the* bend, he just stick up he head and say, "Oho, Brer Deer, here I is for yourself!"

But Brer Terrapin never tell the gals 'bout his management, and how he get there that soon.

1898

Why Mr. Dog Runs Brer Rabbit[2]

One morning, Mr. Buzzard he say he stomach just hungry for some fish, and he tell Mrs. Buzzard he think he go down to the branch, and catch some for breakfast. So he take he basket, and he sail along till he come to the branch.

He fish right smart, and by sun up he have he basket plum full. But Mr. Buzzard am a powerful greedy man, and he say to hisself, he did, I just catch one more. But while he done gone for this last one, Brer Rabbit he came along, clipity, clipity, and when he see basket plum full of fine whitefish he stop, and he say, "I 'clare to goodness, the old woman just gwine on up to the cabin, 'cause they got nothing for to fry for breakfast. I wonder what she think of this yer fish," and so he put the basket on he head, Brer Rabbit did, and make off to the cabin.

Direc'ly he meet up with Mr. Dog, and he ax him where he been fishing that early in the day, and Brer Rabbit he say how he done sot on the log 'longside of the branch, and let he tail hang in the water and catch all the fish, and he done tell Mr. Dog, the old rascal did, that he tail mighty short for the work, but that Mr. Dog's tail just the right sort for fishing.

So Mr. Dog, he teeth just ache for them whitefish, and he go set on the log and hang he tail in the water, and it mighty cold for he tail, and the fish don't bite, but he mouth just set for them fish, and so he just sot dar, and it turn that cold that when he feel he gin up, sure's you born, Mr. Dog, he tail froze fast in the branch, and he call he chillens, and they come and break the ice.

And then, to be sure, he start off to settle Ole Brer Rabbit, and he get on he track and he run the poor ole man to beat all, and directly he sight him he run him round and round the woods and holler, "Hallelujah! hallelujah!" and the puppies come on behind, and they holler, "Glory! glory!" and they make such a fuss, all the creeters

[2]Emma Backus, "Tales of the Rabbit from Georgia Negroes," *Journal of American Folk-Lore* 12 (1899):112–13.

in the woods, they run to see what the matter. Well, sah, from that day, Mr. Dog he run Brer Rabbit, and when they just get gwine on the swing in the big woods, you can hear ole Ben dar just letting hisself out, "Hallelujah! hallelujah!" and them pups just gwine "Glory! glory!" and it surely am the sound what has the music dar, it surely has the music dar.

1899

How Sandy Got His Meat[3]

Brer Rabbit an Brer Coon wuz fishermuns. Brer Rabbit fished fur fish an Brer Coon fished fur f-r-o-g-s.

Arter while de frogs all got so wile Brer Coon couldent ketch em, an he hadn't hab no meat to his house an de chilluns wuz hongry an de ole oman beat em ober de haid wid de broom.

Brer Coon felt mighty bad an he went off down de rode wid he head down wundering what he gwine do. Des den ole Brer Rabbit wuz er skippin down de rode an he seed Brer Coon wuz worried an throwed up his years an say-ed:

"Mornin, Brer Coon."

"Mornin, Brer Rabbit."

"How is yer copperrosity segashuatin, Brer Coon?"

"Porely, Brer Rabbit, porely. De frogs haz all got so wile I caint ketch em an I aint got no meat to my house an de ole oman is mad an de chilluns hongry. Brer Rabbit, I'se got to hab help. Sumthin' haz got to be dun."

Old Brer Rabbit look away crost de ruver long time; den he scratch hiz year wid his hind foot, an say:

"I'll tole ye whut we do Brer Coon. We'll git eber one of dem frogs. You go down on de san bar an lie down an play des lack you wuz d-a-i-d. Don't yer mobe. Be jes as still, jest lack you wuz d-a-i-d."

Ole Brer Coon mosied on down to de ruver. De frogs hear-ed em er comin an de ole big frog say-ed:

"Yer better look er roun. Yer better look er roun. Yer better look er round."

Nother ole frog say-ed:

"Knee deep, knee deep, knee deep."

An "ker-chug" all de frogs went in de water.

But Ole Brer Coon lide down on de san an stretched out jest lack he wuz d-a-i-d. De flies got all ober em, but he never moobe. De sun shine hot, but he never moobe; he lie still jest lack he wuz d-a-i-d.

Drectly Ole Brer Rabbit cum er runnin tru de woods an out on de san bar an put his years up high an hollered out:

"Hay, de Ole Coon is d-a-i-d."

De ole big frog out in de ruver say-ed:

"I don't bleve it, I don't bleve it, I don't bleve it." And all de littul frogs roun de edge say-ed:

"I don't bleve it, I don't bleve it, I don't bleve it."

[3]A.W. Eddins, in *Round the Levee,* ed. Stith Thompson, Publications of the Texas Folk-Lore Society 1 (Austin: Texas Folk-Lore Society, 1916): 47–49.

But de ole coon play jes lack he's d-a-i-d an all de frogs cum up out of de ruver an set er roun whare de ole coon lay.

Jes den Brer Rabbit wink his eye an say-ed:

"I'll tell yer what I'de do, Brer Frogs. I'de berry Old Sandy, berry em so deep he never could scratch out."

Den all de frogs gun to dig out de san, dig out de san from under de ole coon. When de had dug er great deep hole wid de ole coon in de middle of it, de frogs all got tired an de ole frog say-ed:

"Deep er nough,—deep er nough,—deep er nough."

An all de littul frogs say-ed:

"Deep er nough,—deep er nough,—deep er nough."

Ole Brer Rabbit was er takin er littul nap in der sun, and he woke up an say-ed:

"Kin you jump out?"

De ole big frog look up to de top of de hole an say-ed:

"Yes I kin. Yes I kin. Yes I kin."

An de littul frogs say-ed:

"Yes I kin. Yes I kin. Yes I kin."

Ole Brer Rabbit tole em:

"Dig it deeper."

Den all de frogs went to wuk an dug er great deep hole way down inside de san wid Old Brer Coon right in de middle jest lack he wuz d-a-i-d. De frogs wuz er gittin putty tired an de ole big frog sung out loud:—

"Deep er nough. Deep er nough. Deep er nough."

An all de littul frogs sung out too:—

"Deep er nough. Deep er nough. Deep er nough."

An Ole Brer Rabbit woke up er gin an axed em:—

"Kin yer jump out?"

"I bleve I kin. I bleve I kin. I bleve I kin."

Ole Brer Rabbit look down in de hole agin an say-ed:—

"Dig dat hole deeper."

Den all de frogs gin to wuk throwin out san, throwin out san, clear till most sun down and dey had er great deep hole way, way down in de san, wid de ole coon layin right in de middle. De frogs wuz plum clean tired out and de ole big frog say-ed:—

"Deep er nough. Deep er nough. Deep er nough."

An all de littul frogs say-ed:—

"Deep er nough. Deep er nough. Deep er nough."

Ole Brer Rabbit peeped down in de hole agin and say:—

"Kin yer jump out?"

An de ole frog say:—

"No I caint. No I caint. No I caint."

An all de littul frogs say:—

"No I caint. No I caint. No I caint."

Den Ole Brer Rabbit jump up right quick an holler out:—

"RISE UP SANDY AN GIT YOUR MEAT."

An Brer Coon had meat fer sepper dat nite.

1916

Who Ate Up the Butter?[4]

All the animals was farming a crop together. And they bought a pound of butter—they was in cahoots, all chipped in equally. So the next day they all goes to the field to work. All at once Brother Rabbit says, "Heya." All of them quits working, ask, "What is it, Brother Rabbit?"

"It's my wife, she's calling me, I ain't got time to fool with her." All of them together say, "Well you better go on, Brother Rabbit, and see what it is she wants." Off he goes to the house to see what his wife wants.

Twenty minutes he was back. They say, "What did your wife want, Brother Rabbit?" "Well she got a new baby up there." So they slapped Brother Rabbit on the back, said "Good, good. You named him yet?" "Yes, I named him Quarter Gone."

So they begin to work again. About thirty minutes more Brother Rabbit begins to holler again, "What do you want?" They say, "What was that, who you talking to?" "That was my wife, didn't you hear her calling?" "Well, you better go see what she wants." The Rabbit said, "I'm working, I haven't got time to fool with her." They said, "You'd better go on, Brother Rabbit."

So he goes on to the house to see what she wants. In about twenty more minutes he was back again. "What's the trouble this time, Brother Rabbit, what did your wife want?" "Same thing, another baby." They all said, "Good, good, what was it?" Said, "It was a boy." "What did you name him?" Said, "Oh, Half Gone." Said, "That sure is a pretty name." So he goes back hard to work.

After a while he hollers again, "Oooh, I ain't studying about you." They said, "What you hollering about, what you studying about, we ain't seed no one. Who was it?" "It was my wife." (She'd been calling him all morning.) "Well, why don't you go on Brother Rabbit, and see what she wants." "No, we'll never get nothing done if I just keep running to the house; no, I'm not going." The animals said, "That's all right, Brother Rabbit, it's only a little time, we don't mind, go on."

So Brother Rabbit goes on to the house. Well, he was there about forty minutes this time. "Brother Rabbit, what was your trouble this time?" "My wife had twins." "Good, good, good." They just rejoiced over it. "You'll have to set 'em up when we go to town this time." He said, "Well, the reason I was gone so long I was studying what to name those two twins so it would sound nearly alike." They asked, "What did you name them, Brother Rabbit?" They'd never heard tell of twins before, or of the rabbit having four. "Three Quarters Gone and All Gone." They insist on "Let's go see 'em." He says, "Well, we'll just work on till noon, then we'll have plenty of time, no need to hurry."

So he sent Brother Terrapin into the house to get some water. Well, he drank the water. Then he wanted a match, he wanted a smoke bad. So he said to Brother Deer, "Brother Terrapin is too slow, you run up there and bring those matches." Told Brother Fox, "You run on and drive the horses to the barn, we think we're going to plow this evening. We'll be home 'gainst you get there." So he taken off to drive the horses. When Brother Fox got out of sight good, Brother Rabbit said, "Well, we'll go." So they had to go slow, 'cause Brother Terrapin poked along, and they all walked together with him.

[4]Told by J. D. Suggs, in Richard M. Dorson, *American Negro Folktales* (Greenwich, CT: Fawcett, 1967): 68–71. Dorson collected the tales in this volume in Arkansas, Mississippi, and Michigan in 1952 and 1953.

When they got to the house, Brother Fox was sitting on the front porch waiting for them. He said, "Mens, I sure is hungry, let's wash up and get in the kitchen."

In a few seconds, they was all washed up and in the kitchen they'd go. Brother Rabbit was the first one in there; he says, "Well, where's the butter? The butter's all gone!" *(Loud)* The first one they accused was Brother Rabbit. "Remember when he came by the house to see about his wife and them babies?"

He says, "No, I didn't even think about the butter. Now listen, you remember more than me come to the house, Brother Terrapin and Brother Deer and Brother Fox, and I'd be afraid to 'cuse them, for I know I didn't and I wouldn't say they did. But I got a plan and we can soon find out who done it, I or him or whom."

They all agreed to hear about Brother Rabbit's plan—they was confused and mad and forgot about being hungry, and said, "His plan always did work."

Now Brother Rabbit told them, "We'll make a big log heap and set fire to it, and run and jump, and the one that falls in it, he ate the butter." So they made the log heap and put the fire in it. The fire begins to burn and smoke, smoke and burn. "All right, we're ready to jump."

They were all lined up. Brother Deer taken the first jump. Brother Rabbit said, "Well, Brother Terrapin, guess I better take the next one." He done jump. Terrapin was waiting for the wind to turn. He was so short he knew he couldn't jump far. The wind started blowing the smoke down to the ground, on both sides of the log heap. So Brother Terrapin said, "Well, I guess it's my jump." He ran around the heap and turned somersault on the other side. Brother Rabbit and Brother Deer were looking way up in the smoke to see the others coming over; they weren't looking low, and thought he had jumped over. They said, "Well, Brother Terrapin he made it."

So all the rest of them they jumped it clear, Brother Fox, and Brother Bear, and that made everybody on the other side. "Well, Brother Deer, it's your jump again." So the three they jump over again, and only Brother Bear and Brother Terrapin is left. Brother Terrapin says, "Step here, Brother Bear, before you jump." Said, "I hear you can jump high across that fire, cross your legs and pull your teat out and show it to 'em (his back teat), stop in space, and then jump from there onto the other side. I don't know if you can, I only heard it." Brother Bear says, "O, yes I can." So Brother Terrapin was glad he was making that deal, for he didn't know if the smoke would be in his favor going back.

The Bear says, "Stand back, Mr. Terrapin, let me jump first this time, you can see this." *(Deep, gruff)* The Bear backed further, further than ever to get speed up to stop and cross his legs. He calls out, "Here goes Brother Bear," and takes off. In the middle he tries to cross his leg, and down he went, into the fire. Brother Rabbit said, "Push the fire on him, push the fire on him." *(Excited)* "He's the one that eat the butter." So all of them go to the end, and begin to shove the chunks on Brother Bear. They all give Brother Rabbit credit for being the smart one to find the guilty fellow what eat the butter.

None of them ever thought Brother Bear was the only one never went to the house. Just like in a law case many men are convicted from showing evidence against them where there isn't any. They get a smart lawyer to show you was there when you wasn't there at all, trap you with his questions, get you convicted and behind the bars. Then they say, "He's a smart lawyer."

1967

Fox and Rabbit in the Well[5]

The Fox was after the Rabbit to kill him. So Ber Fox was about to catch Brother Rabbit. There was a well down in the flat between the two hills. It had two water buckets, one on each end of the rope. When you let one down, you'd be pulling one bucket of water up. Brother Rabbit jumped in the bucket was up. Down he went, the other bucket come up. The moon was shining right in the well. It looked like a round hoop of cheese. Ber Rabbit didn't know how he was goin' git back up after he was down there. He commenced hollering for Mr. Fox to come here quick.

Mr. Fox goes up to the well and looked down in there, says "What you want, Brother Rabbit?"

"See this big old hoop of cheese I got down in here?"

Says "Man, it sure is good."

Ber Fox says, "How did you get down in there?"

Says "Git in that bucket up there," says "That's the way I come down." Mr. Fox jumped in that bucket was up, Brother Rabbit jumped in the one was down. Down goes Mr. Fox, up come Brother Rabbit. Brother Rabbit passed Brother Fox. "Hey Brother Fox, this the way the world goes, some going and some coming."

My sister'd been watching round that well and she left a bar of soap. I stepped on it, and I skated on back home.[6]

1967

The Signifying Monkey[7]

Deep down in the jungle so they say
There's a signifying motherfucker down the way.
There hadn't been no disturbin' in the jungle for quite a bit,
For up jumped the monkey in the tree one day and laughed,
"I guess I'll start some shit."
Now the lion come through the jungle one peaceful day,
When the signifying monkey stopped him and this what he started
    to say.
He said, "Mr. Lion," he said, "A bad-assed motherfucker down
    your way."
He said, "Yeah! The way he talks about your folks is a certain
    shame.
I even heard him curse when he mentioned your grandmother's
    name."

[5]Suggs, Dorson 97–98.
[6]A formulaic closing.
[7]Roger D. Abrahams, *Deep Down in the Jungle: Negro Narrative Folklore from the Streets of Philadelphia* (Hatboro, PA: Folklore Associates, 1964): 149–51. This variant of "The Signifying Monkey" is a toast, a narrative poem improvised in performance from a store of themes, conventions, and formulas. Other common toast subjects are the badman Stackolee and the sinking of the Titanic.

The lion's tail shot back like a forty-four,
When he went down the jungle in all uproar.
He was pushing over mountains, knocking down trees.
In the middle of a pass he met an ape.
He said, "I ought to beat your ass just to get in shape."
He met the elephant in the shade of a tree.
"Come on long-eared motherfucker, it's gonna be you and me."
Now the elephant looked up out the corner of his eye,
Said, "Go on bird-shit, fight somebody your size."
Then the lion jumped back and made a hell of a pass.
The elephant side-stepped and kicked him dead on his ass.
Now he knocked in his teeth, fucked-up his eye,
Kicked in his ribs, tied-up his face,
Tied his tail in knots, stretched his tail out of place.
Now they fought all that night, half the next day.
I'll be damned if I can see how the lion got away.
When they was fussing and fighting, lion came back through the
jungle more dead than alive,
When the monkey started some more of that signifying jive.
He said, "Damn, Mr. Lion, you went through here yesterday, the
jungle rung.
Now you come back today, damn near hung."
He said, "Now you come by here when me and my wife trying to
get a little bit,
T' tell me that 'I rule' shit."
He said, "Shut up, motherfucker, you better not roar
'Cause I'll come down there and kick your ass some more."
The monkey started getting panicked and jumped up and down,
When his feet slipped and his ass hit the ground.
Like a bolt of lightning, a stripe of white heat,
The lion was on the monkey with all four feet.
The monkey looked up with a tear in his eyes,
He said, "Please, Mr. Lion, I apologize."
He said, "You lemme get my head out the sand
Ass out the grass, I'll fight you like a natural man."
The lion jumped back and squared for a fight.
The motherfucking monkey jumped clear out of sight.
He said, "Yeah, you had me down, you had me last,
But you left me free, now you can still kiss my ass."
Again he started getting panicked and jumping up and down.
His feet slipped and his ass hit the ground.
Like a bolt of lightning, stripe of white heat,
Once more the lion was on the monkey with all four feet.
Monkey looked up again with tears in his eyes.
He said, "Please, Mr. Lion, I apologize."
Lion said, "Ain't gonna be no apologizing.

I'ma put an end to his motherfucking signifying."
Now when you go through the jungle, there's a tombstone so they
say,
"Here the Signifying Monkey lay,
Who got kicked in the nose, fucked-up in the eyes,
Stomped in the ribs, kicked in the face,
Drove backwards to his ass-hole, knocked his neck out of place."
That's what I say.

"Kid"
1964

Memories of Slavery

Malitis[1]

. . . I remember Mammy told me about one master who almost starved his slaves. Mighty stingy, I reckon he was.

Some of them slaves was so poorly thin they ribs would kinda rustle against each other like corn stalks a-drying in the hot winds. But they gets even one hog-killing time, and it was funny, too, Mammy said.

They was seven hogs, fat and ready for fall hog-killing time. Just the day before Old Master told off they was to be killed, something happened to all them porkers. One of the field boys found them and come a-telling the master: "The hogs is all died, now they won't be any meats for the winter."

When the master gets to where at the hogs is laying, they's a lot of Negroes standing round looking sorrow-eyed at the wasted meat. The master asks: "What's the illness with 'em?"

"Malitis," they tells him, and they acts like they don't want to touch the hogs. Master says to dress them anyway for they ain't no more meat on the place.

He says to keep all the meat for the slave families, but that's because he's afraid to eat it hisself account of the hogs' got malitis.

"Don't you all know what is malitis?" Mammy would ask the children when she was telling of the seven fat hogs and seventy lean slaves. And she would laugh, remembering how they fooled Old Master so's to get all them good meats.

"One of the strongest Negroes got up early in the morning," Mammy would explain, "long 'fore the rising horn called the slaves from their cabins. He skitted to the hog pen with a heavy mallet in his hand. When he tapped Mister Hog 'tween the eyes

[1]Told by Mrs. Josie Jordan, in B. A. Botkin, ed., *Lay My Burden Down: A Folk History of Slavery* (Chicago: U of Chicago P, 1945): 4–5. This volume contains excerpts from the Slave Narrative Collection of the Federal Writers' Project, collected during the 1930s.

with that mallet, 'malitis' set in mighty quick, but it was a uncommon 'disease,' even with hungry Negroes around all the time."

1945

The Flying Africans[2]

A.

Prince [Sneed] proved to be an interesting talker, much of his knowledge having been gleaned from conversations by the fireside with his grandfather. The following narrative was still fresh in his memory:

"Muh gran say ole man Waldburg down on St. Catherine own some slabes wut wuzn climatize an he wuk um hahd an one day dey wuz hoein in duh fiel an duh dribuh come out an two ub um wuz unuh a tree in duh shade, an duh hoes wuz wukin by demsef. Duh dribuh say 'Wut dis?' an dey say, 'Kum buba yali kum buba tambe, Kum kunka yali kum kunka tambe,' quick like. Den dey rise off duh groun an fly away. Nobody ebuh see um no mo. Some say dey fly back tuh Africa. Muh gran see dat wid he own eye."

B.

We asked the old man [Wallace Quatermain] if he remembered any slaves that were real Africans.

"Sho I membuhs lots ub um. Ain I sees plenty ub um? I membuhs one boatload uh seben aw eight wut come down frum Savannah. Dat wuz jis a lill befo duh waw. Robbie McQueen wuz African an Katie an ole man Jacob King, dey's all African. I membuhs um all. Ole man King he lib till he ole, lib till I hep bury um. But yuh caahn unduhstan much wut deze people say. Dey caahn unduhstan yo talk an you caahn unduhstan dey talk. Dey go 'quack, quack, quack,' jis as fas as a hawse kin run, an muh pa say, 'Ain no good tuh lissen tuh um.' Dey git long all right but yuh know dey wuz a lot ub um wut ain stay down yuh."

Did he mean the Ibos[3] on St. Simons who walked into the water?

"No, ma'am, I ain mean dem. Ain yuh heah bout um? Well, at dat time Mr. Blue he wuz duh obuhseeuh an Mr. Blue put um in duh fiel, but he couldn do nuttn wid um. Dey gabble, gabble, gabble, an nobody couldn unduhstan um an dey didn know how tuh wuk right. Mr. Blue he go down one mawnin wid a long whip fuh tuh whip um good."

"Mr. Blue was a hard overseer?" we asked.

[2]Two of more than two dozen variants recorded in *Drums and Shadows: Survival Studies among the Georgia Coastal Negroes* (Athens: U of Georgia P, 1940): 78–79, 150–51.

[3]A group of slaves from the Ibo tribe refused to submit to slavery. Led by their chief and singing tribal songs, they walked into the water and were drowned at a point on Dunbar Creek later named Ebo (Ibo) Landing. [Note in original.]

"No, ma'am, he ain hahd, he jis caahn make um unduhstan. Dey's foolish actin. He got tuh whip um, Mr. Blue, he ain hab no choice. Anyways, he whip um good an dey gits tuhgedduh an stick duh hoe in duh fiel an den say 'quack, quack, quack,' an dey riz up in duh sky an tun hesef intuh buzzuds an fly right back tuh Africa."

At this, we exclaimed and showed our astonishment.

"Wut, you ain heah bout um? Ebrybody know bout um. Dey sho lef duh hoe stannin in duh fiel an dey riz right up an fly right back tuh Africa."

Had Wallace actually seen this happen, we asked.

"No, ma'am, I ain seen um. I bin tuh Skidaway, but I knowd plenty wut did see um, plenty wut wuz right deah in duh fiel wid um an seen duh hoe wut dey lef stickin up attuh dey done fly way."

1940

Conjure Stories

Two Tales from Eatonville, Florida[1]

A.

Aunt Judy Cox was Old Man Massey's rival. She thought so anyway. Massey laughed at the very thought, but things finally got critical. She began to boast about being able to "throw back" his work on him. They had quit speaking.

One evening before sundown, Aunt Judy went fishing. That was something strange. She never fished. But she made her grandchildren fix her up a bait pole and a trout pole and set out to Blue Sink alone.

When it got good and dark and she did not come home, her folks got bothered about her. Then one of the village men said he had heard a woman cry out as he passed along the road near the lake. So they went to look for her.

They found her lying in the lake in shallow water having a hard time holding her old neck above the water for so long a time. She couldn't get up. So they lifted her and carried her home. A large alligator was lying beside her, but dived away when the lantern flashed in his face.

Aunt Judy said that she hadn't wanted to go fishing to begin with, but that something had commanded her to go. She couldn't help herself. She had fished until the sun got very low; she started to come home, but somehow she couldn't, even though she was afraid to be down on the lake after dark. Furthermore, she was afraid to walk home when she couldn't see well for fear of snakes. *But she couldn't leave the lake.* When it was finally dark, she said some force struck her like lightning and threw her

[1]Zora Neale Hurston, "Hoodoo in America: Conjure Stories," *Journal of American Folk-Lore* 44 (1931):404–05.

into the water. She screamed and called for help, holding her head above the water by supporting the upper part of her body with her hands.

Then the whole surface of the lake lit up with a dull blue light with a red path across it, and Old Man Massey walked to her upon the lake and thousands upon thousands of alligators swam along on each side of him as he walked down this red path of light to where she was and spoke.

"Hush!" he commanded. "Be quiet, or I'll make an end of you right now."

She hushed. She was too scared to move her tongue. Then he asked her: "Where is all that power you make out you got? I brought you to the lake and made you stay here till I got ready for you. I throwed you in, and you can't come out till I say so. When you acknowledge to yourself that I am your top-superior, then you can come out the water. I got to go about my business, but I'm going to leave a watchman, and the first time you holler he'll tear you to pieces. The minute you change your mind—I'll send help to you."

He vanished and the big 'gator slid up beside her. She didn't know how long she had been in the water, but it seemed hours. But she made up her mind to give up root-working all together before she was rescued. The doctor from Orlando said that she had had a stroke. She recovered to the point where she crept about her yard and garden, but she never did any more "work".

B.

But Aunt Judy was not unsung. The people had not forgotten how she fixed Horace Carter.

Horace was a husband eternally searching for love outside his home. He spent every cent he could rake and scrape on his clothes, on hair pomades and walking sticks, and the like.

When he brutally impressed his wife with the fact that there was nothing, absolutely nothing she could do about it, she said to him one Sunday in desperation: "Horace, if you don't mind your ways I'm going to take your case to Aunt Judy."

He laughed. "Tell her, sell her; turn her up and smell her." He went on about his business.

She did tell Aunt Judy and it is said she laid a hearing on Mr. Horace. He had a new suit in the post office. (It is customary to order clothes C.O.D. from mail-order houses, and they remain in the post office until paid out.) He was bragging about how swell he would look in it. An out-of-town girl was coming over the first Sunday after he got his suit out to help him switch it around. That was the next Sunday after he had laughed at his wife and Aunt Judy.

So he got his suit out. He had a hat, shoes and everything to match.

He put the suit on and strolled over to the depot to meet the train, but before it came he took sick. He seemed to be vomiting so violently that it was running out of his nose as well as his mouth. His clothes were ruined and a great swarm of flies followed him. Before he could reach home, it was discovered that he was defecating through his mouth and nose. This kept up, off and on, for six months. He couldn't tell when it would start, nor stop. Se he kept himself hidden most of the time.

Aunt Judy said, "The dirty puppy! I'll show him how to talk under *my* clothes! Turn me up and smell me, hunh? I'll turn *him* up, and they'll sho smell him."

They say he paid her to take it off him after a while.

1931

John and Old Marster

Master Disguised[1]

Was his mahster's chicken-raiser. Mahster trust him. His mahster went away, so he give a big party. Mahster changed his clothes and blacked his face. Came an' knocked at de do'. John came to de do', said, "Whatshyer want here?" Mahster said, "Ise looking for Mister Johnson's plantation. Ise got lost." John said, "Come in heah, make yourself sca'se, too. Sit down here, eat dis. I'll show you where to go. I wantshyer to get out of heah, too." Mahster went home. Nex' day Mahster call him: "John, what did you steal my chicken fo'?"—"Mahster, let me tell you dishyere one t'ing. I done saw in de Bible dat de man had to reab whey he labor. Mahster, I done labor raisin' dose chickens."

1919

The Diviner[2]

The body-servant of a white man, Mr. Crum, he went out one night to see his girl, and took his master's horse. On his way home he turned the horse loose in the woods and walked home, so his master wouldn' know he had that horse. Next morning his master went to the stable, the horse wasn't there. He called John and told him about it. John said next morning at four o'clock the horse would come at the gate. Next morning at four o'clock John called his master. The horse was at the gate. "Yes, I told you so." Mr. Crum went to one of his neighbors, and said he had one of the smartest niggers in the country, could tell anything, do anything. The neighbor's name was Simmons, and Simmons said he bet he could do something he couldn't tell. He went out and caught a coon, and dug a hole and put in the coon, and a barrel over the hole. And they bet a thousand dollars against a thousand dollars, he couldn't tell what was under that barrel. Mr. Crum said he was going to give the negro his freedom if he could tell, and he'd beat him if he couldn't tell. He got his cards and threw 'em down, spit on his sticks, threw them down, made a cross-mark in his hand, picked up his cards, threw a stick and then a card. Now he made a motion with his body, raised himself up, picked up his cards and sticks, scratched the back of his head, and said,

[1]Portia Smiley, "Folk-Lore from Virginia, South Carolina, Georgia, Alabama, and Florida," *Journal of American Folk-Lore* 32 (1919):362.
[2]Smiley 370.

"Marstah, you got dis here coon at las'!" Mr. Simmons kicked over the barrel with an oath, and the coon jumped out.[3]

1919

Massa and the Bear[4]

During slavery time, you know, Ole Massa had a nigger named John and he was a faithful nigger and Ole Massa lakted John a lot too.

One day Ole Massa sent for John and tole him, says: "John, somebody is stealin' my corn out de field. Every mornin' when I go out I see where they done carried off some mo' of my roastin' ears. I want you to set in de corn patch tonight and ketch whoever it is."

So John said all right and he went and hid in de field.

Pretty soon he heard somethin' breakin' corn. So John sneaked up behind him wid a short stick in his hand and hollered: "Now, break another ear of Ole Massa's corn and see what *Ah'll* do to you."

John thought it was a man all dis time, but it was a bear wid his arms full of roastin' ears. He throwed down de corn and grabbed John. And him and dat bear!

John, after while got loose and got de bear by the tail wid de bear tryin' to git to him all de time. So they run around in a circle all night long. John was so tired. But he couldn't let go of de bear's tail, do de bear would grab him in de back.

After a stretch they quit runnin' and walked. John swingin' on to de bear's tail and de bear's nose 'bout to touch him in de back.

Daybreak, Ole Massa come out to see 'bout John and he seen John and de bear walkin' 'round in de ring. So he run up and says: "Lemme take holt of 'im, John, whilst you run git help!"

John says: "All right, Massa. Now you run in quick and grab 'im just so."

Ole Massa run and grabbed holt of de bear's tail and said: "Now, John you make haste to git somebody to help us."

John staggered off and set down on de grass and went to fanning hisself wid his hat.

Ole Massa was havin' plenty trouble wid dat bear and he looked over and see John settin' on de grass and he hollered:

"John, you better g'wan git help or else I'm gwinter turn dis bear aloose!"

John says: "Turn 'im loose, then. Dat's whut Ah tried to do all night long but Ah couldn't."

1935

Baby in the Crib[5]

John stole a pig from Old Marsa. He was on his way home with him and his Old Marsa seen him. After John got home he looked out and seen his Old Marsa coming

[4]Hurston, *Mules* 100–01.

[5]Told by E. L. Smith, Dorson 138.

down to the house. So he put this pig in a cradle they used to rock the babies in in them days (some people called them cribs), and he covered him up. When his Old Marster come in John was sitting there rocking him.

Old Marster says, "What's the matter with the baby, John?" "The baby got the measles." "I want to see him." John said, "Well you can't; the doctor said if you uncover him the measles will go back in on him and kill him." So his Old Marster said, "It doesn't matter; I want to see him, John." He reached down to uncover him.

John said, "If that baby is turned to a pig now, don't blame me."

1967

John Steals a Pig and a Sheep[6]

Old Marster had some sheep, and a fellow named John living on the place, a tenant there, he got hungry and he stole the meat from Old Boss. Then he got tired of the sheep meat and stole him a pig. Old Marster come down night after he stole the pig, to get him to play a piece on the banjo. Old Marster knocked on the door, when John had just got through putting the pig away. So Old Marster come in and say, "Play me a piece on the banjo." John started to pick a piece on the banjo; while he's playing he looked around and sees a pig's foot sticking out, so he sings, "Push that pig's foot further back under the bed." (He was talking to his wife.)

When he got tired of that pig meat he turned around and killed him another sheep. So he went back down to the barn and told Old Marster, "Another sheep dead, can't I have him?" Old Marster give him that sheep and he took that one home and ate it up. That made two that Old Marster had given him, so Old Marster got a watch out for him. John killed another one and went and told Old Marster again that a sheep had died. Old Marster told him, "You killed that sheep. What did you kill my sheep for?" John says, "Old Marster, I'll tell you; I won't let nobody's sheep bite me."

1967

Talking Bones[7]

They used to carry the slaves out in the woods and leave them there, if they killed them—just like dead animals. There wasn't any burying then. It used to be a secret, between one plantation and another, when they beat up their hands and carried them off.

So John was walking out in the woods and seed a skeleton. He says: "This looks like a human. I wonder what he's doing out here." And the skeleton said, "Tongue is the cause of my being here." So John ran back to Old Marster and said, "The skeleton at the edge of the woods is talking." Old Marster didn't believe him and went to see. And a great many people came too. They said, "Make the bones talk." But the skeleton wouldn't talk. So they beat John to death, and left him there. And then the bones talked. They said, "Tongue brought us here, and tongue brought you here."

1967

[6]Told by Ray Brooks, Dorson 138–39.

[7]Told by Beulah Tate, Dorson 147–48.

Old Boss Wants into Heaven[8]

Old Boss he was a big plantation owner, but he was paralyzed and he couldn't even walk. So every time he was ready to move he'd call Mac up, to carry him around on his back and push him around in his wheel chair. This was back in slavery times, and Mac was his servant, his slave. Old Boss had a whole lot of slaves working for him, but Mac was the main attraction.

Every time the Boss had Mac carry him on his back, Mac figured he was being done wrong, since Boss had a wheel chair. He got to talking to himself about it out loud: "O Lord, these days ain't going to be much longer; God almighty going to call us all in." Then he wouldn't have to carry Old Boss around no more, 'cause he'd be flying around with angels in heaven, and Old Boss'd be down in hell burning with brimstone. Quite a few times the Boss heard him say it; so finally he asked him what did he mean by that remark.

Mac tells him, "You-all know what the Good Book says?" So the Boss says: "What do you mean by that? If anybody's going to Heaven I'm going, because I got all the money I can use, I got a lot of land, I got all the slaves I want to work the land, so I got everything I need to get to Heaven."

"That's just how come you ain't going to Heaven," Mac answers. "The Good Book says so." But Old Boss he really thought because he had all the land and all the money and all the slaves he was fixed straight, that was all he needed. Mac was kind of afraid to speak up any more, being a slave, you know. He just said, "That's all right Boss, you'll see," and kind of walked off from him.

Old Boss couldn't sleep that night. He tried to brush it off his mind but it kept coming on back to him, what Mac had told him. Finally he decided that Mac didn't know what he was talking about, that he was an ignorant slave and didn't know no more than what he (Old Boss) said: "I'll give you a forty-acre farm and a team of mules, if you accept about what work to do." Finally he went on to sleep. Early next morning Mac gets up and starts about his chores. Boss heard him singing.

Soon I will be up in Heaven with the angels,
Having a good time enjoying eternal life.

So that thought kind of hit Old Boss again—he wanted to know how could a slave go to heaven, and he himself being rich and going to hell. That kind of lay on his mind all day. That was Saturday. Sunday morning Mac gets up singing another song. He got on his clean overalls, and a clean shirt, and he gave himself a shave with one of the Boss's old razors—he was barefooted even on Sunday, but he was still happy; he was going to church. The song he was singing was:

I'm going to the mourning bench this morning,
And praise my master up above.

Boss knew they had a church, but he'd never heard a song like that before; so he got curious. He gets his wheel chair, and kind of sneaks on down to the church where they were having the meeting. So when he got there service had already begun. The preacher is up in the pulpit asking did anybody want anything explained to them. Mac raised his hand to let the preacher know he had a question. So he told him about

[8]Told by John Blackamore, Dorson 158–61.

his discussion with Old Boss. Since he could not read, he asked the preacher to explain it to him. The preacher gets his textbook, and gives Mac the book and the chapter and the verse, and then he read it to him. (Some of them could read and some of 'em could not.) So he read, "It's easier for a camel to go through the eye of a needle than it is for a rich man to go to Heaven." (In the meantime Old Boss is outside the window listening, taking it all in.) So he says, "Sisters and Brothers, there only two places to go after you die, and that is Heaven or Hell. And since Old Boss can't go to Heaven, there's no other place for him to go but to Hell."

Old Boss heard enough then. He wheels his chair on back home, he sets down on the porch, and calls his wife to bring him the Bible. He remembered the book and the chapter and the verse and he wanted to see if they knew what they were talking about. When he turns to the page, he found there in big red letters just what the preacher had read. That kind of worried him; he felt uneasy all day Sunday. Mac was away so he couldn't talk to him. Night came; still no Mac. So he decided to set up and wait for him.

On the way home from church Mac had to pass a graveyard. This being Sunday night, a couple of fellows had gone into Old Boss's cornfield and had stole a sack of corn. They went in to get two sacks of corn, but when they heard Mac coming they thought it might be Old Boss, and jumped over the fence into the graveyard. In getting over the fence they dropped a couple of ears. Mac heard them and that kind of scared him, because he thought they was hants, and so he hid behind a big tombstone.

One of the fellows said, "Well, since we didn't get but one sackful we're going to have to divide it." Mac didn't know what they were talking about, so he sat and listened. The two fellows started counting the corn. They figured they didn't have time to count all the ears together and then separate them; so they started counting off, "One for you and one for me." And they kept that up for quite a while.

Mac said, "O Lord, Judgment Day done come. I better go tell the Boss." So he struck out to running. When he gets to the house Old Boss is sitting on the porch smoking his pipe uneasily. Boss was glad to see Mac, and kind of scared for him too, 'cause he was running so hard. Before he could ask Mac how to get to Heaven, Mac fell upon the porch, almost out of breath. "I told you Judgment Day would be soon here; I sure told you!"

Old Boss says: "Well calm yourself. Tell me what this is all about." Mac tells him, "God and the Devil is down there in the graveyard separating the souls." Old Boss doesn't believe it. "Well, that couldn't be true, you know you're just lying." So Mac tells him, "Well if you think I am lying, I'll take you down there and prove it to you."

So he carries Old Boss down to the graveyard on his back. When Old Boss gets there he hears him counting, "One for you and one for me." So he wants to get a closer look; he wants to see what God and the Devil look like. It was dark out there, and the two fellows had moved around to the other side of the fence, where they'd dropped the corn. But when Old Boss gets around there he can't make out who it was because each of them had a great white cotton sack; that was all he could see, that cotton sack. Mac says, "See Boss, I told you so, they're down there sacking up souls." So one of the guys said, "Well, one for you and one for me." T'other pointed over to the fence where they had dropped the two ears, and he said, "There's two over there by the fence—you can have the big one and I'll take the little one."

Old Boss didn't want to hear no more. Mac was scared too. In fact Mac was too scared to move; he froze there in his tracks for a minute. Since Mac wasn't moving fast enough to carry Old Boss, Old Boss jumped down and run. And Mac looked around to see what had happened to Old Boss. Old Boss was out of sight. He figured 'cause Old Boss couldn't walk they must have sacked him up. So Mac run for Old Boss's house to tell Old Missy what happened. When he gets to the house he falls on the porch again, calling Old Missy.

Old Boss come out, without his wheel chair. Mac went to tell him what had happened to Old Boss. Then he realized it was Old Boss he was talking to. He froze again, so Old Boss asked him, "What happened after you left?" Mac told him, and asked Old Boss what happened to him. Boss said, "Well, you weren't moving fast enough; so I decided I'd come on without you." And he's been walking ever since.

Then Old Boss gave all his slaves an equal share in his kingdom that he had already built. He didn't want to get caught in that predicament no more.

1967

Samuel Langhorne Clemens (Mark Twain) 1835–1910

Samuel L. Clemens, best known as Mark Twain, is at the same time revered as a classic American writer and one of the most popular—in his own lifetime and at present, in the United States and abroad. Born in Missouri, he was brought up in the Mississippi River town of Hannibal, which, as St. Petersburg, was to provide the setting for *Tom Sawyer* and the early chapters of *Huckleberry Finn.* When his father died in young Sam's eleventh year, he left school and went to work for a printing shop. Soon he was attracted to the possibility of writing, and as early as his sixteenth year he published a piece in a Boston magazine. After four years of travel as a journeyman printer, he determined to become a riverboat pilot. How he learned the piloting skills and what they meant to him as a writer he later recounted, memorably, in "Old Times on the Mississippi," which was incorporated into *Life on the Mississippi.* He continued to write as an avocation.

When the Civil War put an end to piloting, Clemens served briefly in an unorganized Confederate unit, then headed west with his brother, who had been appointed secretary for the Nevada Territory. There Clemens tried to strike it rich as a miner. In time, his lack of success drove him back to writing, and he became a reporter for the Virginia City *Territorial Enterprise.* There he began the use of the river leadsman's cry "Mark Twain" (two fathoms of water, just deep enough for a steamboat to pass) as a pen name for his humorous writings. In 1864 he moved to California, where he continued writing both as a journalist and as the creator of humorous sketches. He became a satirist who saw as his target pretentious gentility. In 1865 his first famous piece, "Jim Smiley and His Jumping Frog," appeared in a New York periodical. He also began a secondary career as a lecturer. In time he was to become a truly public personality.

After an assignment in Hawaii he went to New York, writing regularly for a San Francisco newspaper. A turning point in his life came when he traveled in 1867 on an excursion to the Mediterranean and the Holy Land. Afterwards he made a book by putting together in revised form the letters he sent back for newspaper publication:

the result was *The Innocents Abroad,* which was a popular success. In it Mark Twain presents himself as an iconoclastic critic of all forms of conventionality, from American reverence for things European to its opposite, our national sense of superiority to the decayed civilization of Europe. The book was sold, as were many of the author's subsequent books, by subscription agents who worked mostly in small towns. His next book was *Roughing It,* which recounted in somewhat fictionalized form his western adventures. Mark Twain, the good-natured humorist, was now a highly popular author, even among those he had satirized in *The Innocents Abroad,* the American bourgeoisie.

In 1870 Clemens married Olivia Langdon, the daughter of a wealthy coal merchant from Elmira, New York. Clemens had become socially ambitious, and he and his wife settled in Hartford, Connecticut, where their "Gilded Age" lifestyle (to use the term that the writer himself coined in the title of his 1873 novel co-authored with Charles Dudley Warner) led to their building the mansion that is today a major tourist attraction. The Clemenses had three daughters, and the family became notably genteel. Nonetheless, "Mark Twain" identified himself as an irreverent skeptic, the enemy of both genteel hypocrisy and the public and private corruption that he attacked in *The Gilded Age* (1873).

The situation that Mark Twain was in often made him feel uncomfortable. Did his marriage and his Hartford lifestyle mean that he had "sold out"? Something inside him felt a strong sense of rebellion, most fully illustrated by *Adventures of Huckleberry Finn,* in which he speaks through an outsider, the son of the town drunk. In "The Facts Concerning the Recent Carnival of Crime in Connecticut," written before *Huck Finn,* he found a way to protest that was socially acceptable because it was funny. Here, as in *Huckleberry Finn,* Mark Twain focuses on the power of conscience. After writing this highly amusing account of his personal situation, he had the satisfaction of reading it to the Monday Evening Club of Hartford, whose distinguished members were lawyers, clergymen, and political leaders. "The Carnival of Crime" belongs to the now established psychological genre of the dopplegänger, in which a ghostly double haunts its fleshly counterpart.

In 1874 Mark Twain recorded the story of a former slave's adventures in his moving report of Auntie Cord's "True Story." He was deeply attracted to African American culture, folk beliefs, and music. This interest led to his recalling his memories of his own childhood in the pre-Civil War South. At first he used a genteel narrator, as in *Tom Sawyer.* A charming account of village life on the banks of the Mississippi River, the novel should also be seen as a highly critical view of the violence and self-deception underlying the idyllic St. Petersburg, where both Tom Sawyer and Huckleberry Finn live. In addition, it prepares the reader for Mark Twain's later return to Huck in his masterpiece, *Huckleberry Finn.*

As both a critic of sentimental, genteel values—the elevation of children and women, for example, as cultural ideals—and also a candidate for gentility, the author was pulled two ways throughout most of the rest of his career. He was both a proper family man and a humorist and satirist out of the West. Often he did not know what to write about. In the early 1880s he was at the same time composing two entirely different books: the historical novel *The Prince and the Pauper,* which he dedicated to his "well mannered and amiable" daughters and by means of which he had hoped to prove himself to be an author that the genteel could approve of, and *Huckleberry Finn,* whose central figure is an outcast. *Huck Finn,* his masterpiece, is idyll, epic, picaresque, and satire. It is especially admired for its comedy, though Huck, the superb narrator, quite lacks a sense of humor.

Huck's great problem is to reconcile his adherence to social norms, particularly those associated with slavery's definition of the black as chattel, with what his heart tells him. The conflict centers on his experiences with Jim, whose humanity he has to learn to respect, for it is denied by what Huck has been taught. *Huckleberry Finn* is an attack on racism and on the exaltation of property values over human values. It is also a celebration of freedom. Despite the weakness of the last chapters, the book ends powerfully, as it demonstrates, in Roy Pearce's words, "the absolute incompatibility of the sort of self" Huck is and "the sort of world in which he tries so hard to live."

Why is *Huckleberry Finn* by far Mark Twain's most popular book? One answer is that his deepest feelings found an outlet in it. Through his mouthpiece Huck he could free himself for a time from the inhibitions of the culture that one whole side of him had chosen to embrace. Through Huck the novelist who had chosen to be civilized escapes more completely and out of greater need than young Sam Clemens ever had. The exhilaration that the author felt is the energy behind the book.

Huck's voice helped define what truly *American* literature was to be. The appealing vernacular speech prepared the way for the acceptance of African American voices, as Ralph Ellison has observed. Indeed, both black and white writers have come to recognize that the use of the vernacular liberates American literature from genteel strictures. Ernest Hemingway proclaimed, "All modern American literature comes from one book by Mark Twain called *Huckleberry Finn.*"

In the late 1880s Clemens turned away to a large extent from writing and gave much of his energy to business. For a time he was successful enough that he thought he could become very rich, but the typesetting machine in which he invested heavily and the publishing company that he created both eventually failed. He was able to produce during these years the powerful *A Connecticut Yankee in King Arthur's Court,* which mixes romance and social and political satire. The objects of the satire are, in the author's words, "unjust laws, the power of the rich and dependence and oppression of the poor."

In the 1890s the Clemens family lived abroad—chiefly in England and Austria. One of the notable works of these years is *Pudd'nhead Wilson,* a compelling exploration of racism that is linked to the writer's longstanding interest in twins. Mark Twain's 1895 trip around the world, described in his *Following the Equator,* opened his eyes to American imperialism and increased his sensitivity to world affairs. As a result he wrote many short works, especially in the early years of the century, that reflect his new enlightenment, for example, "The War Prayer" (1905), an ironic attack on chauvinism. During the last years of his life, Mark Twain was much celebrated; his honors included an honorary doctorate from Oxford University. He saw himself more and more as a philosopher, and his later works, many left incomplete at the time of his death, show him to be a pessimist and a determinist. The best of these are "The Chronicle of Young Satan" (1898–1900) and "Letters from the Earth" (1909). Both were published long after Clemens's death. Despite the fact that he told the story of his life only very incompletely and in fragments, his great lifelong work is his autobiography. It includes a masterful account of his youth.

Mark Twain's most serious philosophical statement is his extended dialogue between an old man and a young man entitled *What Is Man?* There he argues that every creature "is moved, directed, COMMANDED, by *exterior* influences—solely" and "will always do the thing which will bring him the *most* mental comfort." The author had some copies of the work printed but did not reveal his authorship because he assumed that his name would be identified only with humorous writing.

Closely associated with Mark Twain's "philosophical" writings are his pessimistic ones, written about the same time.

Many of these are not intended to be amusing. Why Twain felt as he did is explained by his clergyman friend Joseph Twichell, who described Mark Twain's outlook in these words: "He was ever profoundly affected with the feeling of the pathos of life. Contemplating its heritage of inevitable pain and tears, he would question if to anyone it was a good gift."

For many years after Mark Twain's death, his literary executor and biographer, Albert B. Paine, sought to keep before the public an image of Mark Twain as an avuncular, accessible humorist, almost a Santa Claus with a cigar and a collection of one-liners. From our vantage point today, however, he appears to be a highly complex, even contradictory personality, quite different from what both Paine and the author himself wished the world to suppose. There is much that is unattractive about the man and his career: he failed to practice what he preached, and he was too much concerned with what would sell, too ready to frame his creative impulses in terms that would either please or shock his audience. He had little ability to judge his own work: he had little confidence in the work that became *Huckleberry Finn,* for instance, and he might have left it incomplete, like some of his posthumous works that have recently been published. Perhaps because of these contradictions, he was a compelling literary personality, a great humorist, an effective satirist, and a writer who tells much about America, warts and all.

Everett Emerson
University of North Carolina at Chapel Hill

PRIMARY WORKS

The Innocents Abroad, 1869; *Roughing It,* 1872; *The Adventures of Tom Sawyer,* 1876; *A Tramp Abroad,* 1880; *The Prince and the Pauper,* 1882; *Life on the Mississippi,* 1883; *Adventures of Huckleberry Finn,* 1885; *A Connecticut Yankee in King Arthur's Court,* 1889; *The Tragedy of Pudd'nhead Wilson and the Comedy of Those Extraordinary Twins,* 1894; *Personal Recollections of Joan of Arc,* 1896; *Following the Equator,* 1897; *Autobiography,* 1924; *Mark Twain in Eruption: Hitherto Unpublished Pages about Men and Events,* 1940; *The Mysterious Stranger Manuscripts,* 1969; *What Is Man? and Other Philosophical Writings,* 1973; *Letters,* 1988–; *The Oxford Mark Twain,* 29 vols., Shelley Fisher Fishkin, gen. ed., 1997.

Jim Smiley and His Jumping Frog[1]

Mr. A. Ward.

Dear Sir:—Well, I called on good-natured, garrulous old Simon Wheeler, and I inquired after your friend Leonidas W. Smiley, as you requested me to do, and I hereunto append the result. If you can get any information out of it you are cordially

[1]In 1865, while living in California, Mark Twain sent "Jim Smiley and His Jumping Frog" to the comic writer Artemus Ward, who had asked for a sketch for a book he was putting together. But because it arrived too late, it was published elsewhere, in the *New York Saturday Press* on November 18, 1865. Told by two narrators, Mark Twain and Simon Wheeler, the ironic sketch allows readers to feel superior to Wheeler, but ultimately they find that they have been taken in. The story of the jumping frog made Mark Twain famous because it was copied repeatedly by other publications. Later the author revised the sketch substantially and gave it a new name, "The Celebrated Jumping Frog of Calaveras County," when he included it in his *Sketches, New and Old* (1875).

welcome to it. I have a lurking suspicion that your Leonidas W. Smiley is a myth—that you never knew such a personage, and that you only conjectured that if I asked old Wheeler about him it would remind him of his infamous *Jim* Smiley, and he would go to work and bore me nearly to death with some infernal reminiscence of him as long and tedious as it should be useless to me. If that was your design, Mr. Ward, it will gratify you to know that it succeeded.

I found Simon Wheeler dozing comfortably by the barroom stove of the little old dilapidated tavern in the ancient mining camp of Boomerang, and I noticed that he was fat and bald-headed, and had an expression of winning gentleness and simplicity upon his tranquil countenance. He roused up and gave me good-day. I told him a friend of mine had commissioned me to make some inquiries about a cherished companion of his boyhood named Leonidas W. Smiley—Rev. Leonidas W. Smiley—a young minister of the gospel, who he had heard was at one time a resident of this village of Boomerang. I added that if Mr. Wheeler could tell me anything about this Rev. Leonidas W. Smiley, I would feel under many obligations to him.

Simon Wheeler backed me into a corner and blockaded me there with his chair—and then sat down and reeled off the monotonous narrative which follows this paragraph. He never smiled, he never frowned, he never changed his voice from the quiet, gently-flowing key to which he turned the initial sentence, he never betrayed the slightest suspicion of enthusiasm—but all through the interminable narrative there ran a vein of impressive earnestness and sincerity, which showed me plainly that so far from his imagining that there was anything ridiculous or funny about his story, he regarded it as a really important matter, and admired its two heroes as men of transcendent genius in finesse. To me, the spectacle of a man drifting serenely along through such a queer yarn without ever smiling was exquisitely absurd. As I said before, I asked him to tell me what he knew of Rev. Leonidas W. Smiley, and he replied as follows. I let him go on in his own way, and never interrupted him once:

There was a feller here once by the name of *Jim* Smiley, in the winter of '49—or maybe it was the spring of '50—I don't recollect exactly, some how, though what makes me think it was one or the other is because I remember the big flume wasn't finished when he first come to the camp; but anyway, he was the curiosest man about always betting on anything that turned up you ever see, if he could get anybody to bet on the other side, and if he couldn't he'd change sides—any way that suited the other man would suit *him*—any way just so's he got a bet, *he* was satisfied. But still, he was lucky—uncommon lucky; he most always come out winner. He was always ready and laying for a chance; there couldn't be no solitry thing mentioned but what that feller'd offer to bet on it—and take any side you please, as I was just telling you: if there was a horse race, you'd find him flush or you find him busted at the end of it; if there was a dog-fight, he'd bet on it; if there was a cat-fight, he'd bet on it; if there was a chicken-fight, he'd bet on it; why if there was two birds setting on a fence, he would bet you which one would fly first—or if there was a camp-meeting he would be there reglar to bet on parson Walker, which he judged to be the best exhorter about here, and so he was, too, and a good man; if he even see a straddle-bug start to go any wheres, he would bet you how long it would take him to get wherever he was going to, and if you took him up he would foller that straddle-bug to Mexico but what he would find out where he was bound for and how long he was on the road. Lots of the boys here has seen that Smiley and can tell you about him. Why, it never made no difference to *him*—he would bet on *anything*—the dangdest feller. Parson Walker's wife laid very sick, once, for a good while, and it seemed as if they warn't going to save her; but one morning he come in and Smiley asked him how she was, and he said she was considerable better—thank the Lord for his inf'nit mercy—and coming on so smart that with the blessing of Providence she'd get well yet—and Smiley, before he thought, says, "Well, I'll resk two-and-a-half that she don't, anyway."

Thish-yer Smiley had a mare—the boys called her the fifteen-minute nag, but that was only in fun, you know, because, of course, she was faster than that—and he used to win money on that horse, for all she was so slow and always had the asthma, or the distemper, or the consumption, or something of that kind. They used to give her two or three hundred yards' start, and then pass her under way; but always at the fag-end of the race she'd get excited and desperate-like, and come cavorting and spraddling up, and scattering her legs around limber, sometimes in the air, and sometimes out to one side amongst the fences, and kicking up m-o-r-e dust, and raising m-o-r-e racket with her coughing and sneezing and blowing her nose—and always fetch up at the stand just about a neck ahead, as near as you could cipher it down.

And he had a little small bull-pup, that to look at him you'd think he warn't worth a cent, but to set around and look ornery, and lay for a chance to steal something. But as soon as money was up on him he was a different dog—his under-jaw'd begin to stick out like the for'castle of a steamboat, and his teeth would uncover, and shine savage like the furnaces. And a dog might tackle him, and bully-rag him, and bite him, and throw him over his shoulder two or three times, and Andrew Jackson—which was the name of the pup—Andrew Jackson would never let on but what he was satisfied, and hadn't expected nothing else—and the bets being doubled and doubled on the other side all the time, till the money was all up—and then all of a sudden he would grab that other dog just by the joint of his hind legs and freeze to it—not chaw, you understand, but only just grip and hang on till they throwed up the sponge, if it was a year. Smiley always came out winner on that pup till he harnessed a dog once that didn't have no hind legs, because they'd been sawed off in a circular saw, and when the thing had gone along far enough, and the money was all up, and he came to make a snatch for his pet holt, he saw in a minute how he'd been imposed on, and how the other dog had him in the door, so to speak, and he 'peared surprised, and then he looked sorter discouraged like, and didn't try no more to win the fight, and so he got shucked out bad. He gave Smiley a look as much as to say his heart was broke, and it was *his* fault, for putting up a dog that hadn't no hind legs for him to take holt of, which was his main dependence in a fight, and then he limped off a piece, and laid down and died. It was a good pup, was that Andrew Jackson, and would have made a name for hisself if he'd lived, for the stuff was in him, and he had genius—I know it, because he hadn't had no opportunities to speak of, and it don't stand to reason that a dog could make such a fight as he could under them circumstances, if he hadn't no talent. It always makes me feel sorry when I think of that last fight of his'on, and the way it turned out.

Well, thish-yer Smiley had rat-terriers and chicken cocks, and tom-cats, and all them kind of things, till you couldn't rest, and you couldn't fetch nothing for him to bet on but he'd match you. He ketched a frog one day and took him home and said he cal'lated to educate him; and so he never done nothing for three months but set in his back yard and learn that frog to jump. And you bet you he *did* learn him, too. He'd give him a little hunch behind, and the next minute you'd see that frog whirling in the air like a doughnut—see him turn one summerset, or maybe a couple, if he got a good start, and come down flat-footed and all right, like a cat. He got him up so in the matter of ketching flies, and kept him in practice so constant, that he'd nail a fly every time as far as he could see him. Smiley said all a frog wanted was education, and he could do most anything—and I believe him. Why, I've seen him set Dan'l Webster down here on this floor—Dan'l Webster was the name of the frog—and sing out, "Flies! Dan'l, flies," and quicker'n you could wink, he'd spring straight up, and snake a fly off'n the counter there, and flop down on the floor again as solid as a gob of mud, and fall to scratching the side of his head with his hind foot as indifferent as if he hadn't no idea he'd done any more'n any frog might do. You never see a frog so modest and straightfor'ard as he was, for all he was so gifted. And when it come to fair-and-square jumping on a dead level, he could get over more ground at one straddle than any animal of his breed you ever see. Jumping on a dead level was his strong suit, you understand, and when it come to that, Smiley would ante up money on him as long as he had a red. Smiley was monstrous proud of his frog, and well he might be, for fellers that had travelled and ben everywheres all said he laid over any frog that ever *they* see.

Well, Smiley kept the beast in a little lattice box, and he used to fetch him down town sometimes and lay for a bet. One day a feller—a stranger in the camp, he was—come across him with his box, and says:

"What might it be that you've got in the box?"

And Smiley says, sorter indifferent like, "It might be a parrot, or it might be a canary, maybe, but it ain't—it's only just a frog."

And the feller took it, and looked at it careful, and turned it round this way and that, and says, "H'm—so 'tis. Well, what's *he* good for?"

"Well," Smiley says, easy and careless, "He's good enough for *one* thing I should judge—he can out-jump ary frog in Calaveras county."

The feller took the box again, and took another long, particular look, and give it back to Smiley and says, very deliberate, "Well—I don't see no points about that frog that's any better'n any other frog."

"Maybe you don't," Smiley says. "Maybe you understand frogs, and maybe you don't understand 'em; maybe you've had experience, and maybe you ain't only a amature, as it were. Anyways, I've got *my* opinion, and I'll resk forty dollars that he can outjump ary frog in Calaveras county."

And the feller studied a minute, and then says, kinder sad, like, "Well—I'm only a stranger here, and I ain't got no frog—but if I had a frog I'd bet you."

And then Smiley says, "That's all right—that's all right—if you'll hold my box a minute I'll go and get you a frog;" and so the feller took the box, and put up his forty dollars along with Smiley's, and set down to wait.

So he set there a good while thinking and thinking to hisself, and then he got the frog out and prized his mouth open and took a teaspoon and filled him full of quail-shot—filled him pretty near up to his chin—and set him on the floor. Smiley he went out to the swamp and slopped around in the mud for a long time, and finally he ketched a frog and fetched him in and give him to this feller and says:

"Now if you're ready, set him alongside of Dan'l, with his fore-paws just even with Dan'ls, and I'll give the word." Then he says, "one—two—three—jump!" and him and the feller touched up the frogs from behind, and the new frog hopped off lively, but Dan'l give a heave, and hysted up his shoulders—so—like a Frenchman, but it wasn't no use—he couldn't budge; he was planted as solid as a anvil, and he couldn't no more stir than if he was anchored out. Smiley was a good deal surprised, and he was disgusted too, but he didn't have no idea what the matter was, of course.

The feller took the money and started away, and when he was going out at the door he sorter jerked his thumb over his shoulder—this way—at Dan'l, and says again, very deliberate, "Well—*I* don't see no points about that frog that's any better'n any other frog."

Smiley he stood scratching his head and looking down at Dan'l a long time, and at last he says, "I do wonder what in the nation that frog throwed off for—I wonder if there ain't something the matter with him—he 'pears to look mighty baggy, somehow"—and he ketched Dan'l by the nap of the neck, and lifted him up and says, "Why blame my cats if he don't weigh five pound"—and turned him upside down, and he belched out about a double-handful of shot. And then he see how it was, and he was the maddest man—he set the frog down and took out after that feller, but he never ketched him. And——

[Here Simon Wheeler heard his name called from the front-yard, and got up to go and see what was wanted.] And turning to me as he moved away, he said: "Just sit where you are, stranger, and rest easy—I ain't going to be gone a second."

But by your leave, I did not think that a continuation of the history of the enterprising vagabond Jim Smiley would be likely to afford me much information concerning the Rev. Leonidas W. Smiley, and so I started away.

At the door I met the sociable Wheeler returning, and he buttonholed me and recommenced:

"Well, thish-yer Smiley had a yaller one-eyed cow that didn't have no tail only just a short stump like a bannanner and——"

"O, curse Smiley and his afflicted cow!" I muttered, good-naturedly, and bidding the old gentleman good-day, I departed.

Yours, truly
Mark Twain

1865

Goldsmith's Friend Abroad Again[1]

[Note.—No experience is set down in the following letters which had to be invented. Fancy is not needed to give variety to the history of a Chinaman's sojourn in America. Plain fact is amply sufficient.]

Letter I

Shanghai, 18—

Dear Ching-Foo: It is all settled, and I am to leave my oppressed and overburdened native land and cross the sea to that noble realm where all are free and all equal, and none reviled or abused—America! America, whose precious privilege it is to call herself the Land of the Free and the Home of the Brave. We and all that are about us here look over the waves longingly, contrasting the privations of this our birthplace with the opulent comfort of that happy refuge. We know how America has welcomed the Germans and the Frenchmen and the stricken and sorrowing Irish, and we know how she has given them bread and work and liberty, and how grateful they are. And we know that America stands ready to welcome all other oppressed peoples and offer her abundance to all that come, without asking what their nationality is, or their creed or color. And, without being told it, we know that the foreign sufferers she has rescued from oppression and starvation are the most eager of her children to welcome us, because, having suffered themselves, they know what suffering is, and having been generously succored, they long to be generous to other unfortunates and thus show that magnanimity is not wasted upon them.

Ah Song Hi

Letter II

At Sea, 18—

Dear Ching-Foo: We are far away at sea now, on our way to the beautiful Land of the Free and Home of the Brave. We shall soon be where all men are alike, and where sorrow is not known.

The good American who hired me to go to his country is to pay me $12 a month, which is immense wages, you know—twenty times as much as one gets in China. My passage in the ship is a very large sum—indeed, it is a fortune—and this I must pay myself eventually, but I am allowed ample time to make it good

[1]In 1870 Samuel Clemens married Olivia Langdon. They made their first home in Buffalo, New York, where Clemens divided his time between working for a newspaper and writing for a magazine, the *Galaxy.* He drew on his California memories to compose for the magazine a series of imaginary letters that appeared to be written by a Chinese immigrant whose American experiences are uniformly painful. The title indicates that the author was following the example of Oliver Goldsmith's "Citizen of the World" letters.

to my employer in, he advancing it now. For a mere form, I have turned over my wife, my boy, and my two daughters to my employer's partner for security for the payment of the ship fare. But my employer says they are in no danger of being sold, for he knows I will be faithful to him, and that is the main security.

I thought I would have twelve dollars to begin life with in America, but the American Consul took two of them for making a certificate that I was shipped on the steamer. He has no right to do more than charge the ship two dollars for *one* certificate for the *ship,* with the number of her Chinese passengers set down in it; but he chooses to force a certificate upon each and every Chinaman and put the two dollars in his pocket. As 1,300 of my countrymen are in this vessel, the Consul received $2,600 for certificates. My employer tells me that the Government at Washington know of this fraud, and are so bitterly opposed to the existence of such a wrong that they tried hard to have the extor—— the fee, I mean, legalized by the last Congress[2] but as the bill did not pass, the Consul will have to take the fee dishonestly until next Congress makes it legitimate. It is a great and good and noble country, and hates all forms of vice and chicanery.

We are in that part of the vessel always reserved for my countrymen. It is called the steerage. It is kept for us, my employer says, because it is not subject to changes of temperature and dangerous drafts of air. It is only another instance of the loving unselfishness of the Americans for all unfortunate foreigners. The steerage is a little crowded, and rather warm and close, but no doubt it is best for us that it should be so.

Yesterday our people got to quarrelling among themselves, and the captain turned a volume of hot steam upon a mass of them and scalded eighty or ninety of them more or less severely. Flakes and ribbons of skin came off some of them. There was wild shrieking and struggling while the vapor enveloped the great throng, and so some who were not scalded got trampled upon and hurt. We do not complain, for my employer says this is the usual way of quieting disturbances on board the ship, and that it is done in the cabins among the Americans every day or two.

Congratulate me, Ching-Foo! In ten days more I shall step upon the shore of America, and be received by her great-hearted people; and I shall straighten myself up and feel that I am a free man among freemen.

Ah Song Hi

Letter III

San Francisco, 18—

Dear Ching-Foo: I stepped ashore jubilant! I wanted to dance, shout, sing, worship the generous Land of the Free and Home of the Brave. But as I walked from the gang-plank a man in a gray uniform[3] kicked me violently behind and told me to look out—so my employer translated it. As I turned, another officer of the same kind struck me with a short club and also instructed me to look out. I was about to take hold of my end of the pole which had mine and Hong-Wo's basket and things suspended from it, when a third officer hit me with his club to signify that I was to drop it, and then kicked me to signify that he was satisfied

[2]Pacific and Mediterranean steamship bills. [3]Policeman.

with my promptness. Another person came now, and searched all through our basket and bundles, emptying everything out on the dirty wharf. Then this person and another searched us all over. They found a little package of opium sewed into the artificial part of Hong-Wo's queue, and they took that, and also they made him prisoner and handed him over to an officer, who marched him away. They took his luggage, too, because of his crime, and as our luggage was so mixed together that they could not tell mine from his, they took it all. When I offered to help divide it, they kicked me and desired me to look out.

Having now no baggage and no companion, I told my employer that if he was willing, I would walk about a little and see the city and the people until he needed me. I did not like to seem disappointed with my reception in the good land of refuge for the oppressed, and so I looked and spoke as cheerily as I could. But he said, wait a minute—I must be vaccinated to prevent my taking the small-pox. I smiled and said I had already had the small-pox, as he could see by the marks, and so I need not wait to be "vaccinated," as he called it. But he said it was the law, and I must be vaccinated anyhow. The doctor would never let me pass, for the law obliged him to vaccinate all Chinamen and charge them *ten dollars apiece* for it, and I might be sure that no doctor who would be the servant of that law would let a fee slip through his fingers to accommodate any absurd fool who had seen fit to have the disease in some other country. And presently the doctor came and did his work and took my last penny—my ten dollars which were the hard savings of nearly a year and a half of labor and privation. Ah, if the law-makers had only known there were plenty of doctors in the city glad of a chance to vaccinate people for a dollar or two, they would never have put the price up so high against a poor friendless Irish, or Italian, or Chinese pauper fleeing to the good land to escape hunger and hard times.

Ah Song Hi

Letter IV

San Francisco, 18—

Dear Ching-Foo: I have been here about a month now, and am learning a little of the language every day. My employer was disappointed in the matter of hiring us out to service on the plantations in the far eastern portion of this continent. His enterprise was a failure, and so he set us all free, merely taking measures to secure to himself the repayment of the passage money which he paid for us. We are to make this good to him out of the first moneys we earn here. He says it is sixty dollars apiece.

We were thus set free about two weeks after we reached here. We had been massed together in some small houses up to that time, waiting. I walked forth to seek my fortune. I was to begin life a stranger in a strange land, without a friend, or a penny, or any clothes but those I had on my back. I had not any advantage on my side in the world—not one, except good health and the lack of any necessity to waste any time or anxiety on the watching of my baggage. No, I forget. I reflected that I had one prodigious advantage over paupers in other lands—I was in America! I was in the heaven-provided refuge of the oppressed and the forsaken!

Just as that comforting thought passed through my mind, some young men set a fierce dog on me. I tried to defend myself, but could do nothing. I retreated to the recess of a closed doorway, and there the dog had me at his mercy, flying at my throat and face or any part of my body that presented itself. I shrieked for help, but the young men only jeered and laughed. Two men in gray uniforms (policemen is their official title) looked on for a minute and then walked leisurely away. But a man stopped them and brought them back and told them it was a shame to leave me in such distress. Then the two policemen beat off the dog with small clubs, and a comfort it was to be rid of him, though I was just rags and blood from head to foot. The man who brought the policemen asked the young men why they abused me in that way, and they said they didn't want any of his meddling. And they said to him:

"This Ching divil comes till Ameriky to take the bread out o' dacent intilligent white men's mouths, and whin they try to defind their rights there's a dale o' fuss made about it."

They began to threaten my benefactor, and as he saw no friendliness in the faces that had gathered meanwhile, he went on his way. He got many a curse when he was gone. The policemen now told me I was under arrest and must go with them. I asked one of them what wrong I had done to any one that I should be arrested, and he only struck me with his club and ordered me to "hold my yop." With a jeering crowd of street boys and loafers at my heels, I was taken up an alley and into a stone-paved dungeon which had large cells all down one side of it, with iron gates to them. I stood up by a desk while a man behind it wrote down certain things about me on a slate. One of my captors said:

"Enter a charge against this Chinaman of being disorderly and disturbing the peace."

I attempted to say a word, but he said:

"Silence! Now ye had better go slow, my good fellow. This is two or three times you've tried to get off some of your d—d insolence. Lip won't do here. You've *got* to simmer down, and if you don't take to it paceable we'll see if we can't make you. Fat's your name?"

"Ah Song Hi."

"*Alias* what?"

I said I did not understand, and he said what he wanted was my *true* name, for he guessed I picked up this one since I stole my last chickens. They all laughed loudly at that.

Then they searched me. They found nothing, of course. They seemed very angry and asked who I supposed would "go my bail or pay my fine." When they explained these things to me, I said I had done nobody any harm, and why should I need to have bail or pay a fine? Both of them kicked me and warned me that I would find it to my advantage to try and be as civil as convenient. I protested that I had not meant anything disrespectful. Then one of them took me to one side and said:

"Now look here, Johnny, it's no use you playing softy wid us. We mane business, ye know; and the sooner ye put us on the scent of a V, the asier ye'll save yerself from a dale of trouble. Ye can't get out o' this for anny less. Who's your frinds?"

I told him I had not a single friend in all the land of America, and that I was far from home and help, and very poor. And I begged him to let me go.

He gathered the slack of my blouse collar in his grip and jerked and shoved and hauled at me across the dungeon, and then unlocking an iron cell-gate thrust me in with a kick and said:

"Rot there, ye furrin spawn, till ye lairn that there's no room in America for the likes of ye or your nation."

Ah Song Hi

Letter V

San Francisco, 18—

Dear Ching-Foo: You will remember that I had just been thrust violently into a cell in the city prison when I wrote last. I stumbled and fell on some one. I got a blow and a curse; and on top of these a kick or two and a shove. In a second or two it was plain that I was in a nest of prisoners and was being "passed around"—for the instant I was knocked out of the way of one I fell on the head or heels of another and was promptly ejected, only to land on a third prisoner and get a new contribution of kicks and curses and a new destination. I brought up at last in an unoccupied corner, very much battered and bruised and sore, but glad enough to be let alone for a little while. I was on the flagstones, for there was no furniture in the den except a long, broad board, or combination of boards, like a barn door, and this bed was accommodating five or six persons, and that was its full capacity. They lay stretched side by side, snoring—when not fighting. One end of the board was four inches higher than the other, and so the slant answered for a pillow. There were no blankets, and the night was a little chilly; the nights are always a little chilly in San Francisco, though never severely cold. The board was a deal more comfortable than the stones, and occasionally some flag-stone plebeian like me would try to creep to a place on it; and then the aristocrats would hammer him good and make him think a flag pavement was a nice enough place after all.

I lay quiet in my corner, stroking my bruises and listening to the revelations the prisoners made to each other—and to me—for some that were near me talked to me a good deal. I had long had an idea that Americans, being free, had no need of prisons, which are a contrivance of despots for keeping restless patriots out of mischief. So I was considerably surprised to find out my mistake.

Ours was a big general cell, it seemed, for the temporary accommodation of all comers whose crimes were trifling. Among us there were two Americans, two "Greasers" (Mexicans), a Frenchman, a German, four Irishmen, a Chilenean (and, in the next cell, only separated from us by a grating, two women), all drunk, and all more or less noisy; and as night fell and advanced, they grew more and more discontented and disorderly, occasionally shaking the prison bars and glaring through them at the slowly pacing officer, and cursing him with all their hearts. The two women were nearly middle-aged, and they had only had enough liquor to stimulate instead of stupefy them. Consequently they would fondle and kiss each other for some minutes, and then fall to fighting and keep it up till they were just two grotesque tangles of rags and blood and tumbled hair. Then they would rest awhile, and pant and swear. While they were affectionate, they always spoke of each other as "ladies," but while they were fighting "strumpet" was the mildest name they could think of—and they could only make that do by tacking some sounding profanity to it. In their last fight, which was toward midnight, one of them bit off the other's finger, and then the officer interfered and put the "Greaser" into the "dark cell" to answer for it—because the woman that did it laid it on him, and the other woman did not deny it because, as she said afterward, she "wanted another crack at the huzzy when her finger quit hurting," and so she did not want her removed. By this time those two women had mutilated each other's clothes to that extent that there was not sufficient left to cover their nakedness. I found that one of these creatures had spent nine years in the county jail, and that the other one had spent about four or five years in the same place. They had done it from choice. As soon as they were discharged from captivity they would go straight and get drunk, and then steal some trifling thing while an officer was observing them. That would entitle them to another two months in jail, and there they would occupy clean, airy apartments, and have good food in plenty, and being at no expense at all, they could make shirts for the clothiers at half a dollar apiece and thus keep themselves in smoking tobacco and such other luxuries as they wanted. When the two months were up, they would go just as straight as they could walk to Mother Leonard's and get drunk; and from there to Kearney street and steal something; and thence to this city prison, and next day back to the old quarters in the county jail again. One of them had really kept this up for nine years and the other four or five, and both said they meant to end their days in that prison. Finally, both these creatures fell upon me while I was dozing with my head against their grating, and battered me considerably, because they discovered that I was a Chinaman, and they said I was "a bloody interlopin' loafer come from the divil's own country to take the bread out of dacent people's mouths and put down the wages for work whin it was all a Christian could do to kape body and sowl together as it was." "Loafer" means one who will not work.

Ah Song Hi

Letter VI

San Francisco, 18—

Dear Ching-Foo: To continue—the two women became reconciled to each other again through the common bond of interest and sympathy created between them by pounding me in partnership, and when they had finished me they fell to embracing each other again and swearing more eternal affection like that which had subsisted between them all the evening, barring occasional interruptions. They agreed to swear the finger-biting on the Greaser in open court, and get him sent to the penitentiary for the crime of mayhem.

Another of our company was a boy of fourteen who had been watched for some time by officers and teachers, and repeatedly detected in enticing young girls from the public schools to the lodgings of gentlemen down town. He had been furnished with lures in the form of pictures and books of a peculiar kind, and these he had distributed among his clients. There were likenesses of fifteen of these young girls on exhibition (only to prominent citizens and persons in authority, it was said, though most people came to get a sight) at the police headquarters, but no punishment at all was to be inflicted on the poor little misses. The boy was afterward sent into captivity at the House of Correction for some months, and there was a strong disposition to punish the gentlemen who had employed the boy to entice the girls, but as that could not be done without making public the names of those gentlemen and thus injuring them socially, the idea was finally given up.

There was also in our cell that night a photographer (a kind of artist who makes likenesses of people with a machine), who had been for some time patching the pictured heads of well-known and respectable young ladies to the nude, pictured bodies of another class of women; then from this patched creation he would make photographs and sell them privately at high prices to rowdies and blackguards, averring that these, the best young ladies of the city, had hired him to take their likenesses in that unclad condition. What a lecture the police judge read that photographer when he was convicted! He told him his crime was little less than an outrage. He abused that photographer till he almost made him sink through the floor, and then he fined him a hundred dollars. And he told him he might consider himself lucky that he didn't fine him a hundred and twenty-five dollars. They are awfully severe on crime here.

About two or two and a half hours after midnight, of that first experience of mine in the city prison, such of us as were dozing were awakened by a noise of beating and dragging and groaning, and in a little while a man was pushed into our den with a "There, d—n you, soak there a spell!"—and then the gate was closed and the officers went away again. The man who was thrust among us fell limp and helpless by the grating, but as nobody could reach him with a kick without the trouble of hitching along toward him or getting fairly up to deliver it, our people only grumbled at him, and cursed him, and called him insulting names—for misery and hardship do not make their victims gentle or charitable toward each other. But as he neither tried humbly to conciliate our people nor swore back at them, his unnatural conduct created surprise, and several of the party crawled to him where he lay in the dim light that came through the grating, and examined into his case. His head was very bloody and his wits were gone. After about an hour, he sat up and stared around; then his eyes grew more natural and he began to tell how that he was going along with a bag on his shoulder and a brace of policemen ordered him to stop, which he did not do—was chased and caught, beaten ferociously about the head on the way to the prison and after arrival there, and finally thrown into our den like a dog. And in a few seconds he sank down again and grew flighty of speech. One of our people was at last penetrated with something vaguely akin to compassion, may be, for he looked out through the gratings at the guardian officer pacing to and fro, and said:

"Say, Mickey, this shrimp's goin' to die."

"Stop your noise!" was all the answer he got. But presently our man tried it again. He drew himself to the gratings, grasping them with his hands, and looking out through them, sat waiting till the officer was passing once more, and then said:

"Sweetness, you'd better mind your eye, now, because you beats have killed this cuss. You've busted his head and he'll pass in his checks before sun-up. You better go for a doctor, now, you bet you had."

The officer delivered a sudden rap on our man's knuckles with his club, that sent him scampering and howling among the sleeping forms on the flagstones, and an answering burst of laughter came from the half dozen policemen idling about the railed desk in the middle of the dungeon.

But there was a putting of heads together out there presently, and a conversing in low voices, which seemed to show that our man's talk had made an impression; and presently an officer went away in a hurry, and shortly came back with a person who entered our cell and felt the bruised man's pulse and threw the glare of a lantern on his drawn face, striped with blood, and his glassy eyes, fixed and vacant. The doctor examined the man's broken head also, and presently said:

"If you'd called me an hour ago I might have saved this man, may be—too late now."

Then he walked out into the dungeon and the officers surrounded him, and they kept up a low and earnest buzzing of conversation for fifteen minutes, I should think, and then the doctor took his departure from the prison. Several of the officers now came in and worked a little with the wounded man, but toward daylight he died.

It was the longest, longest night! And when the daylight came filtering reluctantly into the dungeon at last, it was the gravest, dreariest, saddest daylight! And yet, when an officer by and by turned off the sickly yellow gas flame, and immediately the gray of dawn became fresh and white, there was a lifting of my spirits that acknowledged and believed that the night *was* gone, and straightway I fell to stretching my sore limbs, and looking about me with a grateful sense of relief and a returning interest in life. About me lay evidences that what seemed now a feverish dream and a nightmare was the memory of a reality instead. For on the boards lay four frowsy, ragged, bearded vagabonds, snoring—one turned end-for-end and resting an unclean foot, in a ruined stocking, on the hairy breast of a neighbor; the young boy was uneasy, and lay moaning in his sleep; other forms lay half revealed and half concealed about the floor; in the furthest corner the gray light fell upon a sheet, whose elevations and depressions indicated the places of the dead man's face and feet and folded hands; and through the dividing bars one could discern the almost nude forms of the two exiles from the county jail twined together in a drunken embrace, and sodden with sleep.

By and by all the animals in all the cages awoke, and stretched themselves, and exchanged a few cuffs and curses, and then began to clamor for breakfast. Breakfast was brought in at last—bread and beefsteak on tin plates, and black coffee in tin cups, and no grabbing allowed. And after several dreary hours of waiting, after this, we were all marched out into the dungeon and joined there by all manner of vagrants and vagabonds, of all shades and colors and nationalities, from the other cells and cages of the place; and pretty soon our whole menagerie was marched up stairs and locked fast behind a high railing in a dirty room with a dirty audience in it. And this audience stared at us, and at a man seated on high behind what they call a pulpit in this country, and at some clerks and other officials seated below him—and waited. This was the police court.

The court opened. Pretty soon I was compelled to notice that a culprit's nationality made for or against him in this court. Overwhelming proofs were necessary to convict an Irishman of crime, and even then his punishment amounted to little; Frenchmen, Spaniards, and Italians had strict and unprejudiced justice meted out to them, in exact accordance with the evidence; negroes were promptly punished, when there was the slightest preponderance of testimony against them; but Chinamen were punished *always,* apparently. Now this gave me some uneasiness, I confess. I knew that this state of things must of necessity be accidental, because in this country all men were free and equal, and one person could not take to himself an advantage not accorded to all other individuals. I knew that, and yet in spite of it I was uneasy.

And I grew still more uneasy, when I found that any succored and befriended refugee from Ireland or elsewhere could stand up before that judge and swear away the life or liberty or character of a refugee from China; but that by the law of the land *the Chinaman could not testify against the Irishman.*[5] I was really and truly uneasy, but still my faith in the universal liberty that America accords and defends, and my deep veneration for the land that offered all distressed outcasts a home and protection, was strong within me, and I said to myself that it would all come out right yet.

Ah Song Hi

Letter VII

San Francisco, 18—

Dear Ching Foo: I was glad enough when my case came up. An hour's experience had made me as tired of the police court as of the dungeon. I was not uneasy about the result of the trial, but on the contrary felt that as soon as the large auditory of Americans present should hear how that the rowdies had set the dogs on me when I was going peacefully along the street, and how, when I was all torn and bleeding, the officers arrested *me* and put me in jail and let the rowdies go free, the gallant hatred of oppression which is part of the very flesh and blood of every American would be stirred to its utmost, and I should be instantly set at liberty. In truth I began to fear for the other side. There in full view stood the ruffians who had misused me, and I began to fear that in the first burst of generous anger occasioned by the revealment of what they had done, they might be harshly handled, and possibly even banished the country as having dishonored her and being no longer worthy to remain upon her sacred soil.

The official interpreter of the court asked my name, and then spoke it aloud so that all could hear. Supposing that all was now ready, I cleared my throat and began—in Chinese, because of my imperfect English:

"Hear, O high and mighty mandarin, and believe! As I went about my peaceful business in the street, behold certain men set a dog on me, and——"

"Silence!"

It was the judge that spoke. The interpreter whispered to me that I must keep

[4]A California law prohibited Chinese, African Americans, and Native Americans from providing testimony in court cases.

perfectly still. He said that no statement would be received from me—I must only talk through my lawyer.

I had no lawyer. In the early morning a police court lawyer (termed, in the higher circles of society, a "shyster") had come into our den in the prison and offered his services to me, but I had been obliged to go without them because I could not pay in advance or give security. I told the interpreter how the matter stood. He said I must take my chances on the witnesses then. I glanced around, and my failing confidence revived.

"Call those four Chinamen yonder," I said. "They saw it all. I remember their faces perfectly. They will prove that the white men set the dog on me when I was not harming them."

"That won't work," said he. "In this country white men can testify against Chinamen all they want to, but *Chinamen ain't allowed to testify against white men!*"

What a chill went through me! And then I felt the indignant blood rise to my cheek at this libel upon the Home of the Oppressed, where all men are free and equal—perfectly equal—perfectly free and perfectly equal. I despised this Chinese-speaking Spaniard for his mean slander on the land that was sheltering and feeding him. I sorely wanted to sear his eyes with that sentence from the great and good American Declaration of Independence which we have copied in letters of gold in China and keep hung up over our family altars and in our temples—I mean the one about all men being created free and equal.

But woe is me, Ching Foo, the man was right. He was right, after all. There were my witnesses, but I could not use them. But now came a new hope. I saw my white friend come in, and I felt that he had come there purposely to help me. I may almost say I knew it. So I grew easier. He passed near enough to me to say under his breath, "Don't be afraid," and then I had no more fear. But presently the rowdies recognized him and began to scowl at him in no friendly way, and to make threatening signs at him. The two officers that arrested me fixed their eyes steadily on his; he bore it well, but gave in presently, and dropped his eyes. They still gazed at his eyebrows, and every time he raised his eyes he encountered their winkless stare—until after a minute or two he ceased to lift his head at all. The judge had been giving some instructions privately to some one for a little while, but now he was ready to resume business. Then the trial so unspeakably important to me, and freighted with such prodigious consequence to my wife and children, began, progressed, ended, was recorded in the books, noted down by the newspaper reporters, and *forgotten* by everybody but me—all in the little space of two minutes!

"Ah Song Hi, Chinaman. Officers O'Flannigan and O'Flaherty, witnesses. Come forward. Officer O'Flannigan."

OFFICER: "He was making a disturbance in Kearny street."

JUDGE: "Any witnesses on the other side?"

No response. The white friend raised his eyes—encountered Officer O'Flaherty's—blushed a little—got up and left the court-room, avoiding all glances and not taking his own from the floor.

JUDGE: "Give him five dollars or ten days."

In my desolation there was a glad surprise in the words; but it passed away when I found that he only meant that I was to be fined five dollars or imprisoned ten days longer in default of it.

There were twelve or fifteen Chinamen in our crowd of prisoners, charged with all manner of little thefts and misdemeanors, and their cases were quickly disposed of, as a general thing. When the charge came from a policeman or other white man, he made his statement and that was the end of it, unless the Chinaman's lawyer could find some white person to testify in his client's behalf; for, neither the accused Chinaman nor his countrymen being allowed to say anything, the statement of the officers or other white person was amply sufficient to convict. So, as I said, the Chinamen's cases were quickly disposed of, and fines and imprisonment promptly distributed among them. In one or two of the cases the charges against Chinamen were brought by Chinamen themselves, and in those cases Chinamen testified against Chinamen, through the interpreter; but the fixed rule of the court being that the *preponderance* of testimony in such cases should determine the prisoner's guilt or innocence, and there being nothing very binding about an oath administered to the lower orders of our people without the ancient solemnity of cutting off a chicken's head and burning some yellow paper at the same time, the interested parties naturally drum up a cloud of witnesses who are cheerfully willing to give evidence without ever knowing anything about the matter in hand. The judge has a custom of rattling through with as much of this testimony as his patience will stand, and then shutting off the rest and striking an average.

By noon all the business of the court was finished, and then several of us who had not fared well were remanded to prison; the judge went home; the lawyers, and officers, and spectators departed their several ways, and left the uncomely courtroom to silence, solitude, and Stiggers, the newspaper reporter, which latter would now write up his items (said an ancient Chinaman to me), in the which he would praise all the policemen indiscriminately and abuse the Chinamen and dead people.

Ah Song Hi

October and November 1870 and January 1871

A True Story[1]

Repeated Word for Word as I Heard It

It was summer-time, and twilight. We were sitting on the porch of the farmhouse, on the summit of the hill, and "Aunt Rachel" was sitting respectfully below our level, on the steps—for she was our servant, and colored. She was a mighty frame and stature; she was sixty years old, but her eye was undimmed and her strength unabated. She was a cheerful, hearty soul, and it was no more trouble for her to laugh than it is for a bird to sing. She was under fire now, as usual when the day was done. That is to say, she was being chaffed without mercy, and was enjoying it. She would let off peal after peal of laughter, and then sit with her face in her hands and shake with throes of

[1]This was the first piece that Mark Twain published in the *Atlantic Monthly*. It records the painful experiences of the cook at Quarry Farm in Elmira, New York, where the Clemenses summered. According to the author's letter to W. D. Howells, the editor and soon to become his close friend, it was reproduced as he heard it from "Auntie Cord" in the summer of 1874, "not altered, except to begin at the beginning, instead of the middle, as she did—and travelled both ways."

enjoyment which she could no longer get breath enough to express. At such a moment as this a thought occurred to me, and I said:

"Aunt Rachel, how is it that you've lived sixty years and never had any trouble?"

She stopped quaking. She paused, and there was a moment of silence. She turned her face over her shoulder toward me, and said, without even a smile in her voice:

"Misto C—, is you in 'arnest?"

It surprised me a good deal; and it sobered my manner and my speech, too. I said: "Why, I thought—that is, I meant—why, you *can't* have had any trouble. I've never heard you sigh, and never seen your eye when there wasn't a laugh in it."

She faced fairly around now, and was full of earnestness.

"Has I had any trouble? Misto C—, I's gwyne to tell you, den I leave it to you. I was bawn down 'mongst de slaves; I knows all 'bout slavery, 'case I ben one of 'em my own se'f. Well, sah, my ole man—dat's my husban'—he was lovin' an kind to me, jist as kind as you is to yo' own wife. An' we had chil'en—seven chil'en—an' we loved dem chil'en just de same as you loves yo' chil'en. Dey was black, but de Lord can't make no chil'en so black but what dey mother loves 'em an' wouldn't give 'em up, no, not for anything dat's in dis whole world.

"Well, sah, I was raised in ole Fo'ginny, but my mother she was raised in Maryland; an' my *souls!* she was turrible when she'd git started! My *lan'!* but she'd make de fur fly! When she'd git into dem tantrums, she always had one word dat she said. She'd straighten herse'f up an' put her fists in her hips an' say, 'I want you to understan' dat I wa'n't bawn in the mash to be fool' by trash! I's one o' de ole Blue Hen's Chickens, I is!' 'ca'se, you see, dat's what folks dat's bawn in Maryland calls deyselves, an' dey's proud of it. Well, dat was her word. I don't ever forgit it, beca'se she said it so much, an' beca'se she said it one day when my little Henry tore his wris' awful, and most busted his head, right up at de top of his forehead, an' de niggers didn't fly aroun' fas' enough to 'tend to him. An' when dey talk' back at her, she up an' she says, 'Look-a-heah!' she says, 'I want you niggers to understan' dat I wa'n't bawn in de mash to be fool' by trash! I's one o' de ole Blue Hen's Chickens, *I* is!' an' den she clar' dat kitchen an' bandage' up de chile herse'f. So I says dat word, too, when I's riled.

"Well, bymeby my ole mistis say she's broke, an' she got to sell all de niggers on de place. An' when I heah dat dey gwyne to sell us all off at oction in Richmon', oh, de good gracious! I know what dat mean!"

Aunt Rachel had gradually risen, while she warmed to her subject, and now she towered above us, black against the stars.

"Dey put chains on us an' put us on a stan' as high as dis po'ch—twenty foot high—an' all de people stood aroun', crowds an' crowds. An' dey'd come up dah an' look at us all roun', an' squeeze our arm, an' make us git up an' walk, an' den say, 'Dis one too ole,' or 'Dis one lame,' or 'Dis one don't 'mount to much.' An' dey sole my ole man, an' took him away, an' dey begin to sell my chil'en an' take *dem* away, an' I begin to cry; an' de man say, 'Shet up yo' damn blubberin',' an' hit me on de mouf wid his han'. An' when de las' one was gone but my little Henry, I grab' *him* clost up to my breas' so, an' I ris up an' says, 'You sha'n't take him away,' I says; 'I'll kill de man dat tetches him!' I says. But my little Henry whisper an' say, 'I gwyne to run away, an' den I work an' buy yo' freedom.' Oh, bless de chile, he always so good! But dey got him—dey got him, de men did; but I took and tear de clo'es mos' off of 'em an' beat 'em over de head wid my chain; an' *dey* give it to *me,* too, but I didn't mine dat.

"Well, dah was my ole man gone, an' all my chil'en, all my seven chil'en—an' six of 'em I hain't set eyes on ag'in to this day, an' dat's twenty-two years ago las' Easter. De man dat bought me b'long' in Newbern, an' he took me dah. Well, bymeby de years roll on an' de waw come. My marster he was a Confedrit colonel, an' I was his family's cook. So when de Unions took dat town, dey all run away an' lef' me all by myse'f wid de other niggers in dat mons'us big house. So de big Union officers move in dah, an' dey ask me would I cook for *dem.* 'Lord bless you,' says I, 'dat's what I's *for.*'

"Dey wa'n't no small-fry officers, mine you, dey was de biggest dey *is*; an' de way dey made dem sojers mosey roun'! De Gen'l he tole me to boss dat kitchen; an' he say, 'If anybody come meddlin' wid you, you just make 'em walk chalk; don't you be afeared,' he say; 'you's 'mong frens now.'

"Well, I thinks to myse'f, if my little Henry ever got a chance to run away, he'd make to de Norf, o' course. So one day I comes in dah whar de big officers was, in de parlor, an' I drops a kurtchy, so, an' I up an' tole 'em 'bout my Henry, dey a-listenin' to my troubles jist de same as if I was white folks; an' I says, 'What I come for is be-ca'se if he got away and got up Norf whar you gemmen comes from, you might 'a' seen him, maybe, an' could tell me so as I could fine him ag'in; he was very little, an' he had a sk-yar on his lef' wris' an' at de top of his forehead.' Den dey look mournful, an' de Gen'l says, 'How long sence you los' him?' an' I say, 'Thirteen year.' Den de Gen'l say, 'He wouldn't be little no mo' now—he's a man!'

"I never thought o' dat befo'! He was only dat little feller to *me* yit. I never thought 'bout him growin' up an' bein' big. But I see it den. None o' de gemmen had run acrost him, so dey couldn't do nothin' for me. But all dat time, do' *I* didn't know it, my Henry *was* run off to de Norf, years an' years, an' he was a barber, too, an' worked for hisse'f. An' bymeby, when de waw come he ups an' he says: 'I's done bar-berin',' he says, 'I's gwyne to fine my ole mammy, less'n she's dead.' So he sole out an' went to whar dey was recruitin', an' hired hisse'f out to de colonel for his servant; an' den he went all froo de battles everywhah, huntin' for his ole mammy; yes, in-deedy, he'd hire to fust one officer an' den another, tell he'd ransacked de whole Souf; but you see *I* didn't know nuffin 'bout *dis.* How was *I* gwyne to know it?

"Well, one night we had a big sojer ball; de sojers dah at Newbern was always havin' balls an' carryin' on. Dey had 'em in my kitchen, heaps o' times, 'ca'se it was so big. Mine you, I was *down* on sich doin's; beca'se my place was wid de officers, an' it rasp me to have dem common sojers cavortin' roun' my kitchen like dat. But I al-way' stood aroun' an' kep' things straight, I did; an' sometimes dey'd git my dander up, an' den I'd make 'em clar dat kitchen, mine I *tell* you!

"Well, one night—it was a Friday night—dey comes a whole platoon f'm a *nig-ger* ridgment dat was on guard at de house—de house was headquarters, you know—an' den I was just a-*bilin'!* Mad? I was just a-*boomin'!* I swelled aroun', an' swelled aroun'; I just was a-itchin' for 'em to do somefin for to start me. *An'* dey was a-waltzin' an' a-dancin'! *my!* but dey was havin' a time! an' I jist a-swellin' an' a-swellin' up! Pooty soon, 'long comes *sich* a spruce young nigger a-sailin' down de room wid a yaller wench roun' de wais'; an' roun' an' roun' an' roun' dey went, enough to make a body drunk to look at 'em; an' when dey got abreas' o' me, dey went to kin' o' balancin' aroun' fust on one leg an' den on t'other, an' smilin' at my big red turban, an' makin' fun, an' I ups an' says '*Git* along wid you!—rubbage!' De young man's face kin' o' changed, all of a sudden, for 'bout a second, but den he went to smilin' ag'in, same as he was befo'. Well, 'bout dis time, in comes some niggers dat played music and b'long' to de ban', an' dey *never* could git along widout puttin' on airs. An' de very fust air dey put on dat night, I lit into 'em! Dey laughed, an' dat made me wuss. De res' o' de niggers got to laughin', an' den my soul *alive* but I was hot! My eye was just ablazin'! I jist straightened myself up so—jist as I is now, plum to de ceilin' mos'—an' I digs my fists into my hips, an' I says, 'Look-a-heah!' I says, 'I want you niggers to understan' dat I wa'n't bawn in de mash to be fool' by trash! I's one o' de ole Blue Hen's Chickens, *I* is!' an' den I see dat young man stan' a-starin' an' stiff, lookin' kin' o' up at de ceilin' like he fo'got somefin, an' couldn't 'member it no mo'. Well, I jist march' on dem niggers—so lookin' like a gen'l—an' dey jist cave' away befo' me an' out at de do'. An as dis young man was a-goin' out, I heah him say to another nigger, 'Jim,' he says, 'you go 'long an' tell de cap'n I be on han' 'bout eight o'clock in de mawnin'; dey's somefin on my mine,' he says; 'I don't sleep no mo' dis night. You go 'long,' he says, 'an' leave me by my own se'f.'

"Dis was 'bout one o'clock in de mawnin'. Well, 'bout seven, I was up an' on han', gittin' de officers' breakfast. I was a-stoppin' down by de stove—just so, same as if yo' foot was de stove—an' I'd opened de stove do' wid my right han'—so, pushin' it back, just as I pushes yo' foot—an' I'd jist got de pan o' hot biscuits in my han' an' was 'bout to raise up, when I see a black face come aroun' under mine, an' de eyes alookin' up into mine, just as I's a-lookin' up close under yo' face now; an' I just stopped *right dah,* an' never budged! jist gazed an' gazed so; an' de pan begin to tremble, an' all of a sudden I *knowed!* De pan drop' on de flo' an' I grab his lef han' an' shove back his sleeve—jist so, as I's doin' to you—an' den I goes for his forehead an' push de hair back so, an' 'Boy!' I says, 'if you ain't my Henry, what is you doin' wid dis welt on yo' wris' an' dat sk-yar on yo' forehead? De Lord God ob heaven be praise', I got my own ag'in!'

"Oh no, Misto C—, *I* hain't had no trouble. An' no *joy!*"

1874

The Man That Corrupted Hadleyburg[1]

I

It was many years ago. Hadleyburg was the most honest and upright town in all the region round about it. It had kept that reputation unsmirched during three generations, and was prouder of it than of any other of its possessions. It was so proud of it, and so anxious to insure its perpetuation, that it began to teach the principles of honest dealing to its babies in the cradle, and made the like teachings the staple of their culture thenceforward through all the years devoted to their education. Also, throughout the formative years temptations were kept out of the way of the young

[1]After two decades of living well, in Hartford and in Elmira, New York, the Clemenses suffered from considerable financial need. Thereafter for a decade they felt obliged to reside in Europe, where living expenses were much lower. In 1898 while they were in Austria, Mark Twain produced an elaborately plotted story, "The Man That Corrupted Hadleyburg." Focusing clinically on Mary and Edward Richards, the story tells how they are corrupted by greed, suffer from moral degeneration, then finally experience self-recrimination that destroys them.

people, so that their honesty could have every chance to harden and solidify, and became a part of their very bone. The neighboring towns were jealous of this honorable supremacy and affected to sneer at Hadleyburg's pride in it and call it vanity; but all the same they were obliged to acknowledge that Hadleyburg was in reality an incorruptible town; and if pressed they would also acknowledge that the mere fact that a young man hailed from Hadleyburg was all the recommendation he needed when he went forth from his natal town to seek for responsible employment.

But at last, in the drift of time, Hadleyburg had the ill luck to offend a passing stranger—possibly without knowing it, certainly without caring, for Hadleyburg was sufficient unto itself, and cared not a rap for strangers or their opinions. Still, it would have been well to make an exception in this one's case, for he was a bitter man and revengeful. All through his wanderings during a whole year he kept his injury in mind, and gave all his leisure moments to trying to invent a compensating satisfaction for it. He contrived many plans, and all of them were good, but none of them was quite sweeping enough; the poorest of them would hurt a great many individuals, but what he wanted was a plan which would comprehend the entire town, and not let so much as one person escape unhurt. At last he had a fortunate idea, and when it fell into his brain it lit up his whole head with an evil joy. He began to form a plan at once, saying to himself, "That is the thing to do—I will corrupt the town."

Six months later he went to Hadleyburg, and arrived in a buggy at the house of the old cashier of the bank about ten at night. He got a sack out of the buggy, shouldered it, and staggered with it through the cottage yard, and knocked at the door. A woman's voice said "Come in," and he entered, and set his sack behind the stove in the parlor, saying politely to the old lady who sat reading the *Missionary Herald* by the lamp:

"Pray keep your seat, madam, I will not disturb you. There—now it is pretty well concealed; one would hardly know it was there. Can I see your husband a moment, madam?"

No, he was gone to Brixton, and might not return before morning.

"Very well, madam, it is no matter. I merely wanted to leave that sack in his care, to be delivered to the rightful owner when he shall be found. I am a stranger; he does not know me; I am merely passing through the town to-night to discharge a matter which has been long in my mind. My errand is now completed, and I go pleased and a little proud, and you will never see me again. There is a paper attached to the sack which will explain everything. Goodnight, madam."

The old lady was afraid of the mysterious big stranger, and was glad to see him go. But her curiosity was roused, and she went straight to the sack and brought away the paper. It began as follows:

"TO BE PUBLISHED; or, the right man sought out by private inquiry—either will answer. This sack contains gold coin weighing a hundred and sixty pounds four ounces—"

"Mercy on us, and the door is not locked!"

Mrs. Richards flew to it all in a tremble and locked it, then pulled down the window-shades and stood frightened, worried, and wondering if there was anything else she could do toward making herself and the money more safe. She listened awhile for burglars, then surrendered to curiosity and went back to the lamp and finished reading the paper:

"I am a foreigner, and am presently going back to my own country, to remain there permanently. I am grateful to America for what I have received at her hands during my long stay

under her flag; and to one of her citizens—a citizen of Hadleyburg—I am especially grateful for a great kindness done me a year or two ago. Two great kindnesses, in fact. I will explain. I was a gambler. I say I WAS. *I was a ruined gambler. I arrived in this village at night, hungry and without a penny. I asked for help—in the dark; I was ashamed to beg in the light. I begged of the right man. He gave me twenty dollars—that is to say, he gave me life, as I considered it. He also gave me fortune; for out of that money I have made myself rich at the gaming-table. And finally, a remark which he made to me has remained with me to this day, and has at last conquered me; and in conquering has saved the remnant of my morals: I shall gamble no more. Now I have no idea who that man was, but I want him found, and I want him to have this money, to give away, throw away, or keep, as he pleases. It is merely my way of testifying my gratitude to him. If I could stay, I would find him myself; but no matter, he will be found. This is an honest town, an incorruptible town, and I know I can trust it without fear. This man can be identified by the remark which he made to me; I feel persuaded that he will remember it.*

"And now my plan is this: If you prefer to conduct the inquiry privately, do so. Tell the contents of this present writing to any one who is likely to be the right man. If he shall answer, 'I am the man; the remark I made was so-and-so,' apply the test—to wit: open the sack, and in it you will find a sealed envelope containing that remark. If the remark mentioned by the candidate tallies with it, give him the money, and ask no further questions, for he is certainly the right man.

"But if you shall prefer a public inquiry, then publish this present writing in the local paper—with these instructions added, to wit: Thirty days from now, let the candidate appear at the town-hall at eight in the evening (Friday), and hand his remark, in a sealed envelope, to the Rev. Mr. Burgess (if he will be kind enough to act): and let Mr. Burgess there and then destroy the seals of the sack, open it, and see if the remark is correct; if correct, let the money be delivered, with my sincere gratitude, to my benefactor thus identified."

Mrs. Richards sat down, gently quivering with excitement, and was soon lost in thinkings—after this pattern: "What a strange thing it is! . . . And what a fortune for that kind man who set his bread afloat upon the waters! . . . If it had only been my husband that did it!—for we are so poor, so old and poor! . . ." Then, with a sigh—"But it was not my Edward; no, it was not he that gave a stranger twenty dollars. It is a pity too; I see it now. . . ." Then, with a shudder—"But it is *gambler*'s money! the wages of sin; we couldn't take it; we couldn't touch it. I don't like to be near it; it seems a defilement." She moved to a farther chair. . . . "I wish Edward would come, and take it to the bank; a burglar might come at any moment; it is dreadful to be here all alone with it."

At eleven Mr. Richards arrived, and while his wife was saying, "I am *so* glad you've come!" he was saying, "I'm so tired—tired clear out; it is dreadful to be poor, and have to make these dismal journeys at my time of life. Always at the grind, grind, grind, on a salary—another man's slave, and he sitting at home in his slippers, rich and comfortable."

"I am so sorry for you, Edward, you know that; but be comforted; we have our livelihood; we have our good name—"

"Yes, Mary, and that is everything. Don't mind my talk—it's just a moment's irritation and doesn't mean anything. Kiss me—there, it's all gone now, and I am not complaining any more. What have you been getting? What's in the sack?"

Then his wife told him the great secret. It dazed him for a moment; then he said:

"It weighs a hundred and sixty pounds? Why, Mary, it's for-ty thou-sand dollars—think of it—a whole fortune! Not ten men in this village are worth that much. Give me the paper."

He skimmed through it and said:

"Isn't it an adventure! Why, it's a romance; it's like the impossible things one reads about in books, and never sees in life." He was well stirred up now; cheerful, even gleeful. He tapped his old wife on the cheek, and said, humorously, "Why, we're rich, Mary, rich; all we've got to do is to bury the money and burn the papers. If the gambler ever comes to inquire, we'll merely look coldly upon him and say: 'What is this nonsense you are talking? We have never heard of you and your sack of gold before;' and then he would look foolish, and—"

"And in the mean time, while you are running on with your jokes, the money is still here, and it is fast getting along toward burglar-time."

"True. Very well, what shall we do—make the inquiry private? No, not that; it would spoil the romance. The public method is better. Think what a noise it will make! And it will make all the other towns jealous; for no stranger would trust such a thing to any town but Hadleyburg, and they know it. It's a great card for us. I must get to the printing office now, or I shall be too late."

"But stop—stop—don't leave me here alone with it, Edward!"

But he was gone. For only a little while, however. Not far from his own house he met the editor-proprietor of the paper, and gave him the document, and said, "Here is a good thing for you, Cox—put it in."

"It may be too late, Mr. Richards, but I'll see."

At home again he and his wife sat down to talk the charming mystery over; they were in no condition for sleep. The first question was, Who could the citizen have been who gave the stranger the twenty dollars? It seemed a simple one; both answered it in the same breath—

"Barclay Goodson."

"Yes," said Richards, "he could have done it, and it would have been like him, but there's not another in the town."

"Everybody will grant that, Edward—grant it privately, anyway. For six months, now, the village has been its own proper self once more—honest, narrow, self-righteous, and stingy."

"It is what he always called it, to the day of his death—said it right out publicly, too."

"Yes, and he was hated for it."

"Oh, of course; but he didn't care. I reckon he was the best-hated man among us, except the Reverend Burgess."

"Well, Burgess deserves it—he will never get another congregation here. Mean as the town is, it knows how to estimate *him.* Edward, doesn't it seem odd that the stranger should appoint Burgess to deliver the money?"

"Well, yes—it does. That is—that is—"

"Why so much that-*is*-ing? Would *you* select him?"

"Mary, maybe the stranger knows him better than this village does."

"Much *that* would help Burgess!"

The husband seemed perplexed for an answer; the wife kept a steady eye upon him, and waited. Finally Richards said, with the hesitancy of one who is making a statement which is likely to encounter doubt,

"Mary, Burgess is not a bad man."

His wife was certainly surprised.

"Nonsense!" she exclaimed.

"He is not a bad man. I know. The whole of his unpopularity had its foundation in that one thing—the thing that made so much noise."

"That 'one thing,' indeed! As if that 'one thing' wasn't enough, all by itself."

"Plenty. Plenty. Only he wasn't guilty of it."

"How you talk! Not guilty of it! Everybody knows he *was* guilty."

"Mary, I give you my word—he was innocent."

"I can't believe it, and I don't. How do you know?"

"It is a confession. I am ashamed, but I will make it. I was the only man who knew he was innocent. I could have saved him, and—well, you know how the town was wrought up—I hadn't the pluck to do it. It would have turned everybody against me. I felt mean, ever so mean; but I didn't dare; I hadn't the manliness to face that."

Mary looked troubled, and for a while was silent. Then she said, stammeringly:

"I—I didn't think it would have done for you to—to—One mustn't—er—public opinion—one has to be so careful—so—" It was a difficult road, and she got mired; but after a little she got started again. "It was a great pity, but—Why, we couldn't afford it, Edward—we couldn't indeed. Oh, I wouldn't have had you do it for anything!"

"It would have lost us the good-will of so many people, Mary; and then—and then—"

"What troubles me now is, what *he* thinks of us, Edward."

"He? *He* doesn't suspect that I could have saved him."

"Oh," exclaimed the wife, in a tone of relief, "I am glad of that. As long as he doesn't know that you could have saved him, he—he—well, that makes it a great deal better. Why, I might have known he didn't know, because he is always trying to be friendly with us, as little encouragement as we give him. More than once people have twitted me with it. There's the Wilsons, and the Wilcoxes, and the Harknesses, they take a mean pleasure in saying, '*Your friend* Burgess,' because they know it pesters me. I wish he wouldn't persist in liking us so; I can't think why he keeps it up."

"I can explain it. It's another confession. When the thing was new and hot, and the town made a plan to ride him on a rail, my conscience hurt me so that I couldn't stand it, and I went privately and gave him notice, and he got out of the town and staid out till it was safe to come back."

"Edward! If the town had found it out—"

"*Don't!* It scares me yet, to think of it. I repented of it the minute it was done; and I was even afraid to tell you, lest your face might betray it to somebody. I didn't sleep any that night, for worrying. But after a few days I saw that no one was going to suspect me, and after that I got to feeling glad I did it. And I feel glad yet, Mary—glad through and through."

"So do I, now, for it would have been a dreadful way to treat him. Yes, I'm glad; for really you did owe him that, you know. But Edward, suppose it should come out yet, some day!"

"It won't."

"Why?"

"Because everybody thinks it was Goodson."

"Of course they would!"

"Certainly. And of course *he* didn't care. They persuaded poor old Sawlsberry to go and charge it on him, and he went blustering over there and did it. Goodson looked him over, like as if he was hunting for a place on him that he could despise the most, then he says, 'So you are the Committee of Inquiry, are you?' Sawlsberry said that was about what he was. 'Hm. Do they require particulars, or do you reckon a kind of a *general* answer will do?' 'If they require particulars, I will come back, Mr. Goodson; I will take the general answer first.' 'Very well, then, tell them to go to hell—I reckon that's general enough. And I'll give you some advice, Sawlsberry; when you come back for the particulars, fetch a basket to carry the relics of yourself home in.'"

"Just like Goodson; it's got all the marks. He had only one vanity; he thought he could give advice better than any other person."

"It settled the business, and saved us, Mary. The subject was dropped."

"Bless you, I'm not doubting *that.*"

Then they took up the gold-sack mystery again, with strong interest. Soon the conversation began to suffer breaks—interruptions caused by absorbed thinkings. The breaks grew more and more frequent. At last Richards lost himself wholly in thought. He sat long, gazing vacantly at the floor, and by-and-by he began to punctuate his thoughts with little nervous movements of his hands that seemed to indicate vexation. Meantime his wife too had relapsed into a thoughtful silence, and her movements were beginning to show a troubled discomfort. Finally Richards got up and strode aimlessly about the room, ploughing his hands through his hair, much as a somnambulist might do who was having a bad dream. Then he seemed to arrive at a definite purpose; and without a word he put on his hat and passed quickly out of the house. His wife sat brooding, with a drawn face, and did not seem to be aware that she was alone. Now and then she murmured, "Lead us not into t. . . . but—but—we are so poor, so poor! . . . Lead us not into. . . . Ah, who would be hurt by it?—and no one would ever know. . . . Lead us. . . ." The voice died out in mumblings. After a little she glanced up and muttered in a half-frightened, half-glad way—

"He is gone! But, oh dear, he may be too late—too late. . . . Maybe not—maybe there is still time." She rose and stood thinking, nervously clasping and unclasping her hands. A slight shudder shook her frame, and she said, out of a dry throat, "God forgive me—it's awful to think such things—but. . . . Lord, how we are made—how strangely we are made!"

She turned the light low, and slipped stealthily over and kneeled down by the sack and felt of its ridgy sides with her hands, and fondled them lovingly; and there was a gloating light in her poor old eyes. She fell into fits of absence; and came half out of them at times to mutter, "If we had only waited!—oh, if we had only waited a little, and not been in such a hurry!"

Meantime Cox had gone home from his office and told his wife all about the strange thing that had happened, and they had talked it over eagerly, and guessed that the late Goodson was the only man in the town who could have helped a suffering stranger with so noble a sum as twenty dollars. Then there was a pause, and the two became thoughtful and silent. And by-and-by nervous and fidgety. At last the wife said, as if to herself,

"Nobody knows this secret but the Richardses . . . and us . . . nobody."

The husband came out of his thinkings with a slight start, and gazed wistfully at his wife, whose face was becoming very pale; then he hesitatingly rose, and glanced furtively at his hat, then at his wife—a sort of mute inquiry. Mrs. Cox swallowed once or twice, with her hand at her throat, then in place of speech she nodded her head. In a moment she was alone, and mumbling to herself.

And now Richards and Cox were hurrying through the deserted streets, from opposite directions. They met, panting, at the foot of the printing-office stairs; by the night-light where they read each other's face. Cox whispered,

"Nobody knows about this but us?"

The whispered answer was,

"Not a soul—on honor, not a soul!"

"If it isn't too late to—"

The men were starting up-stairs; at this moment they were overtaken by a boy, and Cox asked,

"Is that you, Johnny?"

"Yes, sir."

"You needn't ship the early mail—nor *any* mail; wait till I tell you."

"It's already gone, sir."

"Gone?" It had the sound of an unspeakable disappointment in it.

"Yes, sir. Time-table for Brixton and all the towns beyond changed to-day, sir—had to get the papers in twenty minutes earlier than common. I had to rush; if I had been two minutes later—"

The men turned and walked slowly away, not waiting to hear the rest. Neither of them spoke during ten minutes; the Cox said, in a vexed tone,

"What possessed you to be in such a hurry, *I* can't make out."

The answer was humble enough:

"I see it now, but somehow I never thought, you know, until it was too late. But the next time—"

"Next time be hanged! It won't come in a thousand years."

Then the friends separated without a good-night, and dragged themselves home with the gait of mortally stricken men. At their homes their wives sprang up with an eager "Well?"—then saw the answer with their eyes and sank down sorrowing, without waiting for it to come in words. In both houses a discussion followed of a heated sort—a new thing; there had been discussions before, but not heated ones, not ungentle ones. The discussions to-night were a sort of seeming plagiarisms of each other. Mrs. Richards said,

"If you had only waited, Edward—if you had only stopped to think; but no, you must run straight to the printing-office and spread it all over the world."

"It *said* publish it."

"That is nothing; it also said do it privately, if you liked. There, now—is that true, or not?"

"Why, yes—yes, it is true; but when I thought what a stir it would make, and what a compliment it was to Hadleyburg that a stranger should trust it so—"

"Oh, certainly, I know all that; but if you had only stopped to think, you would have seen that you *couldn't* find the right man, because he is in his grave, and hasn't left chick nor child nor relation behind him; and as long as the money went to somebody that awfully needed it, and nobody would be hurt by it, and—and—"

She broke down, crying. Her husband tried to think of some comforting thing to say, and presently came out with this:

"But after all, Mary, it must be for the best—it *must* be; we know that. And we must remember that it was so ordered—"

"Ordered! Oh, everything's *ordered,* when a person has to find some way out when he has been stupid. Just the same, it was *ordered* that the money should come to us in this special way, and it was you that must take it on yourself to go meddling with the designs of Providence—and who gave you the right? It was wicked, that is what it was—just blasphemous presumption, and no more becoming to a meek and humble professor of—"

"But, Mary, you know how we have been trained all our lives long, like the whole village, till it is absolutely second nature to us to stop not a single moment to think when there's an honest thing to be done—"

"Oh, I know it, I know it—it's been one everlasting training and training and training in honesty—honesty shielded, from the very cradle, against every possible temptation, and so it's *artificial* honesty, and weak as water when temptation comes, as we have seen this night. God knows I never had shade nor shadow of a doubt of my petrified and indestructible honesty until now—and now, under the very first big and real temptation, I—Edward, it is my belief that this town's honesty is as rotten as mine is; as rotten as yours is. It is a mean town, a hard, stingy town, and hasn't a virtue in the world but this honesty it is so celebrated for and so conceited about; and so help me, I do believe that if ever the day comes that its honesty falls under great temptation, its grand reputation will go to ruin like a house of cards. There, now, I've made confession, and I feel better; I am a humbug, and I've been one all my life, without knowing it. Let no man call me honest again—I will not have it."

"I—well, Mary, I feel a good deal as you do; I certainly do. It seems strange, too, so strange. I never could have believed it—never."

A long silence followed; both were sunk in thought. At last the wife looked up and said,

"I know what you are thinking, Edward."

Richards had the embarrassed look of a person who is caught.

"I am ashamed to confess it, Mary, but—"

"It's no matter, Edward, I was thinking the same question myself."

"I hope so. State it."

"You were thinking, if a body could only guess out *what the remark was* that Goodson made to the stranger."

"It's perfectly true. I feel guilty and ashamed. And you?"

"I'm past it. Let us make a pallet here; we've got to stand watch till the bank vault opens in the morning and admits the sack. . . . Oh, dear, oh, dear—if we hadn't made the mistake!"

The pallet was made, and Mary said:

"The open sesame—what could it have been? I do wonder what that remark could have been? But come; we will get to bed now."

"And sleep?"

"No; think."

"Yes, think."

By this time the Coxes too had completed their spat and their reconciliation, and were turning in—to think, to think, and toss, and fret, and worry over what the remark could possibly have been which Goodson made to the stranded derelict: that golden remark; that remark worth forty thousand dollars, cash.

The reason that the village telegraph-office was open later than usual that night was this: The foreman of Cox's paper was the local representative of the Associated Press. One might say its honorary representative, for it wasn't four times a year that he could furnish thirty words that would be accepted. But this time it was different. His despatch stating what he had caught got an instant answer:

Send the whole thing—all the details—twelve hundred words.

A colossal order! The foreman filled the bill; and he was the proudest man in the State. By breakfast-time the next morning the name of Hadleyburg the Incorruptible was on every lip in America, from Montreal to the Gulf, from the glaciers of Alaska to the orange-groves of Florida; and millions and millions of people were discussing the stranger and his money-sack, and wondering if the right man would be found, and hoping some more news about the matter would come soon—right away.

II

Hadleyburg village woke up world-celebrated—astonished—happy—vain. Vain beyond imagination. Its nineteen principal citizens and their wives went about shaking hands with each other, and beaming, and smiling, and congratulating, and saying *this* thing adds a new word to the dictionary—*Hadleyburg,* synonym for *incorruptible*—destined to live in dictionaries forever! And the minor and unimportant citizens and their wives went around acting in much the same way. Everybody ran to the bank to see the gold-sack; and before noon grieved and envious crowds began to flock in from Brixton and all neighboring towns; and that afternoon and next day reporters began to arrive from everywhere to verify the sack and its history and write the whole thing up anew, and make dashing free-hand pictures of the sack, and of Richards's house, and the bank, and the Presbyterian church, and the Baptist church, and the public square, and the town-hall where the test would be applied and the money delivered; and damnable portraits of the Richardses, and Pinkerton the banker, and Cox, and the foreman, and Reverend Burgess, and the postmaster—and even of Jack Halliday, who was the loafing, good-natured, no-account, irreverent fisherman, hunter, boys' friend, stray-dogs' friend, typical "Sam Lawson" of the town. The little mean, smirking, oily Pinkerton showed the sack to all comers, and rubbed his sleek palms together pleasantly, and enlarged upon the town's fine old reputation for honesty and upon this wonderful endorsement of it, and hoped and believed that the example would now spread far and wide over the American world, and be epoch-making in the matter of moral regeneration. And so on, and so on.

By the end of a week things had quieted down again; the wild intoxication of pride and joy had sobered to a soft, sweet, silent delight—a sort of deep, nameless, unutterable content. All faces bore a look of peaceful, holy happiness.

Then a change came. It was a gradual change: so gradual that its beginnings were hardly noticed; maybe were not noticed at all, except by Jack Halliday, who always noticed everything; and always made fun of it, too, no matter what it was. He began to throw out chaffing remarks about people not looking quite so happy as they did a day or two ago; and next he claimed that the new aspect was deepening to positive sadness; next, that it was taking on a sick look; and finally he said that everybody was become so moody, thoughtful, and absent-minded that he could rob the meanest man in town of a cent out of the bottom of his breeches pocket and not disturb his revery.

At this stage—or at about this stage—a saying like this was dropped at bedtime—with a sigh, usually—by the head of each of the nineteen principal households:

"Ah, what *could* have been the remark that Goodson made!"

And straightway—with a shudder—came this, from the man's wife:

"Oh, *don't!* What horrible thing are you mulling in your mind? Put it away from you, for God's sake!"

But that question was wrung from those men again the next night—and got the same retort. But weaker.

And the third night the men uttered the question yet again—with anguish, and absently. This time—and the following night—the wives fidgeted feebly, and tried to say something. But didn't.

And the night after that they found their tongues and responded—longingly,

"Oh, if we *could* only guess!"

Halliday's comments grew daily more and more sparklingly disagreeable and disparaging. He went diligently about, laughing at the town, individually and in mass. But his laugh was the only one left in the village: it fell upon a hollow and mournful vacancy and emptiness. Not even a smile was findable anywhere; Halliday carried a cigar-box around on a tripod, playing that it was a camera, and halted all passers and aimed the thing and said, "Ready!—now look pleasant, please," but not even this capital joke could surprise the dreary faces into any softening.

So three weeks passed—one week was left. It was Saturday evening—after supper. Instead of the aforetime Saturday-evening flutter and bustle and shopping and larking, the streets were empty and desolate. Richards and his old wife sat apart in their little parlor—miserable and thinking. This was become their evening habit now: the life-long habit which had preceded it, of reading, knitting, and contented chat, or receiving or paying neighborly calls, was dead and gone and forgotten, ages ago—two or three weeks ago; nobody talked now, nobody read, nobody visited—the whole village sat at home, sighing, worrying, silent. Trying to guess out that remark.

The postman left a letter. Richards glanced listlessly, at the superscription and the post-mark—unfamiliar, both—and tossed the letter on the table and resumed his might-have-beens and his hopeless dull miseries where he had left them off. Two or three hours later his wife got wearily up and was going away to bed without a good-night—custom now—but she stopped near the letter and eyed it awhile with a dead interest, then broke it open, and began to skim it over. Richards, sitting there with his chair tilted back against the wall and his chin between his knees, heard something fall. It was his wife. He sprang to her side, but she cried out:

"Leave me alone, I am too happy. Read the letter—read it!"

He did. He devoured it, his brain reeling. The letter was from a distant State, and it said:

"I am a stranger to you, but no matter: I have something to tell. I have just arrived home from Mexico, and learned about that episode. Of course you do not know who made that remark, but I know, and I am the only person living who does know. It was GOODSON. *I knew him well, many years ago. I passed through your village that very night, and was his guest till the midnight train came along. I overheard him make that remark to the stranger in the dark—it was in Hale Alley. He and I talked of it the rest of the way home, and while smoking in his house. He mentioned many of your villagers in the course of his talk—most of them in a very uncomplimentary way, but two or three favorably: among these latter yourself. I say 'favorably'—nothing stronger. I remember his saying he did not actually* LIKE *any person in the town—not one; but that you—I* THINK *he said you—am almost sure—had done him a very great service once, possibly without knowing the full value of it, and he wished he had a fortune, he would leave it to you when he died, and a curse apiece for the rest of the citizens. Now, then, if it was you that did him that service, you are his legitimate*

heir, and entitled to the sack of gold. I know that I can trust to your honor and honesty, for in a citizen of Hadleyburg these virtues are an unfailing inheritance, and so I am going to reveal to you the remark, well satisfied that if you are not the right man you will seek and find the right one and see that poor Goodson's debt of gratitude for the service referred to is paid. This is the remark: 'YOU ARE FAR FROM BEING A BAD MAN: GO, AND REFORM.'

"Howard L. Stephenson."

"Oh, Edward, the money is ours, and I am so grateful, *oh,* so grateful—kiss me, dear, it's forever since we kissed—and we needed it so—the money—and now you are free of Pinkerton and his bank, and nobody's slave any more; it seems to me I could fly for joy."

It was a happy half-hour that the couple spent there on the settee caressing each other; it was the old days come again—days that had begun with their courtship and lasted without a break till the stranger brought the deadly money. By-and-by the wife said:

"Oh, Edward, how lucky it was you did him that grand service, poor Goodson! I never liked him, but I love him now. And it was fine and beautiful of you never to mention it or brag about it." Then, with a touch of reproach, "But you ought to have told *me,* Edward, you ought to have told your wife, you know."

"Well, I—er—well, Mary, you see—"

"Now stop hemming and hawing, and tell me about it, Edward. I always loved you, and now I'm proud of you. Everybody believes there was only one good generous soul in this village, and now it turns out that you—Edward, why don't you tell me?"

"Well—er—er—Why, Mary, I can't!"

"You *can't? Why* can't you?"

"You see, he—well, he—he made me promise I wouldn't."

The wife looked him over, and said, very slowly,

"Made—you—promise? Edward, what do you tell me that for?"

"Mary, do you think I would lie?"

She was troubled and silent for a moment, then she laid her hand within his and said:

"No . . . no. We have wandered far enough from our bearings—God spare us that! In all your life you have never uttered a lie. But now—now that the foundations of things seem to be crumbling from under us, we—we—" She lost her voice for a moment, then said, brokenly, "Lead us not into temptation . . . I think you made the promise, Edward. Let it rest so. Let us keep away from that ground. Now—that is all gone by; let us be happy again; it is no time for clouds."

Edward found it something of an effort to comply, for his mind kept wandering—trying to remember what the service was that he had done Goodson.

The couple lay awake the most of the night, Mary happy and busy, Edward busy, but not so happy. Mary was planning what she would do with the money. Edward was trying to recall that service. At first his conscience was sore on account of the lie he had told Mary—if it was a lie. After much reflection—suppose it *was* a lie? What then? Was it such a great matter? Aren't we always *acting* lies? Then why not *tell* them? Look at Mary—look what she had done. While he was hurrying off on his honest errand, what was she doing? Lamenting because the papers hadn't been destroyed and the money kept! Is theft better than lying?

That point lost its sting—the lie dropped into the background and left comfort behind it. The next point came to the front: *had* he rendered that service? Well, here was Goodson's own evidence as reported in Stephenson's letter; there could be no better evidence than that—it was even *proof* that he had rendered it. Of course. So that point was settled. . . . No, not quite. He recalled with a wince that this unknown Mr. Stephenson was just a trifle unsure as to whether the performer of it was Richards or some other—and, oh dear, he had put Richards on his honor! He must himself decide whither that money must go—and Mr. Stephenson was not doubting that if he was the wrong man he would go honorably and find the right one. Oh, it was odious to put a man in such a situation—ah, why couldn't Stephenson have left out that doubt! What did he want to intrude that for?

Further reflection. How did it happen that *Richards's* name remained in Stephenson's mind as indicating the right man, and not some other man's name? That looked good. Yes, that looked very good. In fact, it went on looking better and better, straight along—until by-and-by it grew into positive *proof.* And then Richards put the matter at once out of his mind, for he had a private instinct that a proof once established is better left so.

He was feeling reasonably comfortable now, but there was still one other detail that kept pushing itself on his notice: of course he had done that service—that was settled; but what *was* that service? He must recall it—he would not go to sleep till he had recalled it; it would make his peace of mind perfect. And so he thought and thought. He thought of a dozen things—possible services, even probable services—but none of them seemed adequate, none of them seemed large enough, none of them seemed worth the money—worth the fortune Goodson had wished he could leave in his will. And besides, he couldn't remember having done them, anyway. Now, then—now, then—what *kind* of a service would it be that would make a man so inordinately grateful? Ah—the saving of his soul! That must be it. Yes, he could remember, now, how he once set himself the task of converting Goodson, and labored at it as much as—he was going to say three months; but upon closer examination it shrunk to a month, then to a week, then to a day, then to nothing. Yes, he remembered now, and with unwelcome vividness, that Goodson had told him to go to thunder and mind his own business—*he* wasn't hankering to follow Hadleyburg to heaven!

So that solution was a failure—he hadn't saved Goodson's soul. Richards was discouraged. Then after a little came another idea: had he saved Goodson's property? No, that wouldn't do—he hadn't any. His life? That is it! Of course. Why, he might have thought of it before. This time he was on the right track, sure. His imagination-mill was hard at work in a minute, now.

Thereafter during a stretch of two exhausting hours he was busy saving Goodson's life. He saved it in all kinds of difficult and perilous ways. In every case he got it saved satisfactorily up to a certain point; then, just as he was beginning to get well persuaded that it had really happened, a troublesome detail would turn up which made the whole thing impossible. As in the matter of drowning, for instance. In that case he had swum out and tugged Goodson ashore in an unconscious state with a great crowd looking on and applauding, but when he had got it all thought out and was just beginning to remember all about it a whole swarm of disqualifying details arrived on the ground: the town would have known of the circumstance, Mary would have known of it, it would glare like a limelight in his own memory instead of being an inconspicuous service which he had possibly rendered "without knowing its full value." And at this point he remembered that he couldn't swim, anyway.

Ah—*there* was a point which he had been overlooking from the start; it had to be a service which he had rendered "possibly without knowing the full value of it."

Why, really, that ought to be an easy hunt—much easier than those others. And sure enough, by-and-by he found it. Goodson, years and years ago, came near marrying a very sweet and pretty girl named Nancy Hewitt, but in some way or other the match had been broken off; the girl died, Goodson remained a bachelor, and by-and-by became a soured one and a frank despiser of the human species. Soon after the girl's death the village found out, or thought it had found out, that she carried a spoonful of negro blood in her veins. Richards worked at these details a good while, and in the end he thought he remembered things concerning them which must have gotten mislaid in his memory through long neglect. He seemed to dimly remember that it was *he* that found out about the negro blood; that it was he that told the village; that the village told Goodson where they got it; that he thus saved Goodson from marrying the tainted girl; that he had done him this great service "without knowing the full value of it," in fact without knowing that he *was* doing it; but that Goodson knew the value of it, and what a narrow escape he had had, and so went to his grave grateful to his benefactor and wishing he had a fortune to leave him. It was all clear and simple now, and the more he went over it the more luminous and certain it grew; and at last, when he nestled to sleep satisfied and happy, he remembered the whole thing just as if it had been yesterday. In fact, he dimly remembered Goodson's *telling* him his gratitude once. Meantime Mary had spent six thousand dollars on a new house for herself and a pair of slippers for her pastor, and then had fallen peacefully to rest.

That same Saturday evening the postman had delivered a letter to each of the other principal citizens—nineteen letters in all. No two of the envelopes were alike, and no two of the superscriptions were in the same hand, but the letters inside were just like each other in every detail but one. They were exact copies of the letter received by Richards—handwriting and all—and were all signed by Stephenson, but in place of Richards's name each receiver's own name appeared.

All night long eighteen principal citizens did what their caste-brother Richards was doing at the same time—they put in their energies trying to remember what notable service it was that they had unconsciously done Barclay Goodson. In no case was it a holiday job; still they succeeded.

And while they were at this work, which was difficult, their wives put in the night spending the money, which was easy. During that one night the nineteen wives spent an average of seven thousand dollars each out of the forty thousand in the sack—a hundred and thirty-three thousand altogether.

Next day there was a surprise for Jack Halliday. He noticed that the faces of the nineteen chief citizens and their wives bore that expression of peaceful and holy happiness again. He could not understand it, neither was he able to invent any remarks about it that could damage it or disturb it. And so it was his turn to be dissatisfied with life. His private guesses at the reasons for the happiness failed in all instances, upon examination. When he met Mrs. Wilcox and noticed the placid ecstasy in her face, he said to himself, "Her cat has had kittens"—and went and asked the cook; it was not so; the cook had detected the happiness, but did not know the cause. When Halliday found the duplicate ecstasy in the face of "Shadbelly" Billson (village nickname), he was sure some neighbor of Billson's had broken his leg, but inquiry showed that this had not happened. The subdued ecstasy in Gregory Yates's face could mean but one thing—he was a mother-in-law short; it was another mistake. "And Pinkerton—Pinkerton—he has collected ten cents that he thought he was going to lose." And so on, and so on. In some cases the guesses had to remain in doubt, in the others they proved distinct errors. In the end Halliday said to himself, "Anyway it foots up that there's nineteen Hadleyburg families temporarily in heaven: I don't know how it happened; I only know Providence is off duty to-day."

An architect and builder from the next State had lately ventured to set up a small business in this unpromising village, and his sign had now been hanging out a week. Not a customer yet; he was a discouraged man, and sorry he had come. But his weather changed suddenly now. First one and then another chief citizen's wife said to him privately:

"Come to my house Monday week—but say nothing about it for the present. We think of building."

He got eleven invitations that day. That night he wrote his daughter and broke off her match with her student. He said she could marry a mile higher than that.

Pinkerton the banker and two or three other well-to-do men planned country-seats—but waited. That kind don't count their chickens until they are hatched.

The Wilsons devised a grand new thing—a fancy-dress ball. They made no actual promises, but told all their acquaintanceship in confidence that they were thinking the matter over and thought they should give it"—"and if we do, you will be invited, of course." People were surprised, and said, one to another, "Why, they are crazy, those poor Wilsons, they can't afford it." Several among the nineteen said privately to their husbands, "It is a good idea, we will keep still till their cheap thing is over, then *we* will give one that will make it sick."

The days drifted along, and the bill of future squanderings rose higher and higher, wilder and wilder, more and more foolish and reckless. It began to look as if every member of the nineteen would not only spend his whole forty thousand dollars before receiving-day, but be actually in debt by the time he got the money. In some cases light-headed people did not stop with planning to spend, they really spent—on credit. They bought land, mortgages, farms, speculative stocks, fine clothes, horses, and various other things, paid down the bonus, and made themselves liable for the rest—at ten days. Presently the sober second thought came, and Halliday noticed that a ghastly anxiety was beginning to show up in a good many faces. Again he was puzzled, and didn't know what to make of it. "The Wilcox kittens aren't dead, for they weren't born; nobody's broken a leg; there's no shrinkage in mother-in-laws; *nothing* has happened—it is an insolvable mystery."

There was another puzzled man, too—the Rev. Mr. Burgess. For days, wherever he went, people seemed to follow him or to be watching out for him; and if he ever found himself in a retired spot, a member of the nineteen would be sure to appear, thrust an envelope privately into his hand, whisper "To be opened at the town-hall Friday evening," then vanish away like a guilty thing. He was expecting that there might be one claimant for the sack—doubtful, however, Goodson being dead—but it never occurred to him that all this crowd might be claimants. When the great Friday came at last, he found that he had nineteen envelopes.

III

The town-hall had never looked finer. The platform at the end of it was backed by a showy draping of flags; at intervals along the walls were festoons of flags; the gallery fronts were clothed in flags; the supporting columns were swathed in flags; all this was to impress the stranger, for he would be there in considerable force, and in a large degree he would be connected with the press. The house was full. The 412 fixed seats were occupied; also the 68 extra chairs which had been packed into the aisles; the steps of the platform were occupied; some distinguished strangers were given seats on the platform; at the horseshoe of tables which fenced the front and sides of the platform sat a strong force of special correspondents who had come from everywhere. It was the best-dressed house the town had ever produced. There were some tolerably expensive toilets there, and in several cases the ladies who wore them had the look of being unfamiliar with that kind of clothes. At least the town thought they had that look, but the notion could have arisen from the town's knowledge of the fact that these ladies had never inhabited such clothes before.

The gold-sack stood on a little table at the front of the platform where all the house could see it. The bulk of the house gazed at it with a burning interest, a mouth-watering interest, a wistful and pathetic interest; a minority of nineteen couples gazed at it tenderly, lovingly, proprietarily, and the male half of this minority kept saying over to themselves the moving little impromptu speeches of thankfulness for the audience's applause and congratulations which they were presently going to get up and deliver. Every now and then one of these got a piece of paper out of his vest pocket and privately glanced at it to refresh his memory.

Of course there was a buzz of conversation going on—there always is, but at last when the Rev. Mr. Burgess rose and laid his hand on the sack he could hear his microbes gnaw, the place was so still. He related the curious history of the sack, then went on to speak in warm terms of Hadleyburg's old and well-earned reputation for spotless honesty, and of the town's just pride in this reputation. He said that this reputation was a treasure of priceless value; that under Providence its value had now become inestimably enhanced, for the recent episode had spread this fame far and wide, and thus had focussed the eyes of the American world upon this village, and made its name for all time, as he hoped and believed, a synonym for commercial incorruptibility. [*Applause.*] "And who is to be the guardian of this noble treasure—the community as a whole? No! The responsibility is individual, not communal. From this day forth each and every one of you is in his own person its special guardian, and individually responsible that no harm shall come to it. Do you—does each of you—accept this great trust? [*Tumultuous assent.*] Then all is well. Transmit it to your children and to your children's children. To-day your purity is beyond reproach—see to it that it shall remain so. To-day there is not a person in your community who could be beguiled to touch a penny not his own—see to it that you abide in this grace. [*"We will! we will!"*] This is not the place to make comparisons between ourselves and other communities—some of them ungracious toward us; they have their ways, we have ours; let us be content. [*Applause.*] I am done. Under my hand, my friends, rests a stranger's eloquent recognition of what we are: through him the world will always henceforth know what we are. We do not know who he is, but in your name I utter your gratitude, and ask you to raise your voices in indorsement."

The house rose in a body and made the walls quake with the thunders of its thankfulness for the space of a long minute. Then it sat down, and Mr. Burgess took an envelope out of his pocket. The house held its breath while he slit the envelope open and took from it a slip of paper. He read its contents—slowly and impressively—the audience listening with tranced attention to this magic document, each of whose words stood for an ingot of gold:

"'*The remark which I made to the distressed stranger was this: "You are very far from being a bad man: go, and reform."*'" Then he continued:

"We shall know in a moment now whether the remark here quoted corresponds with the one concealed in the sack; and if that shall prove to be so—and it undoubtedly will—this sack of gold belongs to a fellow-citizen who will henceforth stand before the nation as the symbol of the special virtue which has made our town famous throughout the land—Mr. Billson!"

The house had gotten itself all ready to burst into the proper tornado of applause; but instead of doing it, it seemed stricken with a paralysis; there was a deep hush for a moment or two, then a wave of whispered murmurs swept the place—of about this tenor: "*Billson!* oh, come, this is *too* thin! Twenty dollars to a stranger—or *anybody—Billson!* Tell it to the marines!" And now at this point the house caught its breath all of a sudden, in a new access of astonishment, for it discovered that whereas in one part of the hall Deacon Billson was standing up with his head meekly bowed, in another part of it Lawyer Wilson was doing the same. There was a wondering silence now for a while. Everybody was puzzled, and nineteen couples were surprised and indignant.

Billson and Wilson turned and stared at each other. Billson asked, bitingly.

"Why do *you* rise, Mr. Wilson?"

"Because I have a right to. Perhaps you will be good enough to explain to the house why *you* rise?

"With great pleasure. Because I wrote that paper."

"It is an impudent falsity! I wrote it myself."

It was Burgess's turn to be paralyzed. He stood looking vacantly at first one of the men and then the other, and did not seem to know what to do. The house was stupefied. Lawyer Wilson spoke up, now, and said,

"I ask the Chair to read the name signed to that paper."

That brought the Chair to itself, and it read out the name,

"'John Wharton *Billson.*'"

"There!" shouted Billson, "what have you got to say for yourself, now? And what kind of apology are you going to make to me and to this insulted house for the imposture which you have attempted to play here?"

"No apologies are due, sir; and as for the rest of it, I publicly charge you with pilfering my note from Mr. Burgess and substituting a copy of it signed with your own name. There is no other way by which you could have gotten hold of the test-remark; I alone, of living men, possessed the secret of its wording."

There was likely to be a sandalous state of things if this went on; everybody noticed with distress that the short-hand scribes were scribbling like mad; many people were crying "Chair, Chair! Order! order!" Burgess rapped with his gavel, and said:

"Let us not forget the proprieties due. There has evidently been a mistake somewhere, but surely that is all. If Mr. Wilson gave me an envelope—and I remember now that he did—I still have it."

He took one out of his pocket, opened it, glanced at it, looked surprised and worried, and stood silent a few moments. Then he waved his hand in a wandering and mechanical way, and made an effort or two to say something, then gave it up, despondently. Several voices cried out:

"Read it! read it! What is it?"

So he began in a dazed and sleep-walker fashion:

"*'The remark which I made to the unhappy stranger was this: "You are far from being a bad man.* [The house gazed at him, marvelling.] *Go, and reform."'* [*Murmurs:* "Amazing! what can this mean?"] This one," said the Chair, "is signed Thurlow G. Wilson."

"There!" cried Wilson. "I reckon that settles it! I knew perfectly well my note was purloined."

"Purloined!" retorted Billson. "I'll let you know that neither you nor any man of your kidney must venture to—"

THE CHAIR: "Order, gentlemen, order! Take your seats, both of you, please."

They obeyed, shaking their heads and grumbling angrily. The house was profoundly puzzled; it did not know what to do with this curious emergency. Presently Thompson got up. Thompson was the hatter. He would have liked to be a Nineteener; but such was not for him; his stock of hats was not considerable enough for the position. He said:

"Mr. Chairman, if I may be permitted to make a suggestion, can both of these gentlemen be right? I put it to you, sir, can both have happened to say the very same words to the stranger? It seems to me—"

The tanner got up and interrupted him. The tanner was a disgruntled man; he believed himself entitled to be a Nineteener, but he couldn't get recognition. It made him a little unpleasant in his ways and speech. Said he:

"Sho, *that's* not the point! *That* could happen—twice in a hundred years—but not the other thing. *Neither* of them gave the twenty dollars!" [*A ripple of applause.*]

BILLSON: "*I* did!"

WILSON: "*I* did!"

Then each accused the other of pilfering.

THE CHAIR: "Order! Sit down, if you please—both of you. Neither of the notes has been out of my possession at any moment."

A VOICE: "Good—that settles *that!*"

THE TANNER: "Mr. Chairman, one thing is now plain: one of these men has been eavesdropping under the other one's bed, and filching family secrets. If it is not unparliamentary to suggest it, I will remark that both are equal to it. [THE CHAIR: "Order! order!"] I withdraw the remark, sir, and will confine myself to suggesting that *if* one of them has overheard the other reveal the test-remark to his wife, we shall catch him now."

A VOICE: "How?"

THE TANNER: "Easily. The two have not quoted the remark in exactly the same words. You would have noticed that, if there hadn't been a considerable stretch of time and an exciting quarrel inserted between the two readings."

A VOICE: "Name the difference."

THE TANNER: "The word *very* is in Billson's note, and not in the other."

MANY VOICES: "That's so—he's right!"

THE TANNER: "And so, if the Chair will examine the test-remark in the sack, we shall know which of these two frauds—[THE CHAIR: "Order!"]—which of these two adventurers—[The Chair: "Order! order!"]—which of these two gentlemen—[*laughter and applause*]—is entitled to wear the belt as being the first dishonest blatherskite ever bred in this town—which he has dishonored, and which will be a sultry place for him from now out!" [*Vigorous applause.*]

Many Voices: "Open it!—open the sack!"

Mr. Burgess made a slit in the sack, slid his hand in and brought out an envelope. In it were a couple of folded notes. He said:

"One of these is marked, 'Not to be examined until all written communications which have been addressed to the Chair—if any—shall have been read.' The other is marked *'The Test.'* Allow me. It is worded—to wit:

"'I do not require that the first half of all the remark which was made to me by my benefactor shall be quoted with exactness, for it was not striking, and could be forgotten; but its closing fifteen words are quite striking, and I think easily rememberable; unless *these* shall be accurately reproduced, let the applicant be regarded as an imposter. My benefactor began by saying he seldom gave advice to any one, but that it always bore the hall-mark of high value when he did give it. Then he said this—and it has never faded from my memory: *"You are far from being a bad man—"'"*

Fifty Voices: "That settles it—the money's Wilson's! Wilson! Wilson! Speech! Speech!"

People jumped up and crowded around Wilson, wringing his hand and congratulating fervently—meantime the Chair was hammering with the gavel and shouting:

"Order, gentlemen! Order! Order! Let me finish reading, please." When quiet was restored, the reading was resumed as follows:

*"'"Go, and reform—or, mark my words—some day, for your sins, you will die and go to hell or Hadleyburg—*TRY AND MAKE IT THE FORMER.*"'"*

A ghastly silence followed. First an angry cloud began to settle darkly upon the faces of the citizenship; after a pause the cloud began to rise, and a tickled expression tried to take its place; tried so hard that it was only kept under with great and painful difficulty; the reporters, the Brixtonites, and other strangers bent their heads down and shielded their faces with their hands, and managed to hold in by main strength and heroic courtesy. At this most inopportune time burst upon the stillness the roar of a solitary voice—Jack Halliday's:

"*That's* got the hall-mark on it!"

Then the house let go, strangers and all. Even Mr. Burgess's gravity broke down presently, then the audience considered itself officially absolved from all restraint, and it made the most of its privilege. It was a good long laugh, and a tempestuously whole-hearted one, but it ceased at last—long enough for Mr. Burgess to try to resume, and for the people to get their eyes partially wiped; then it broke out again; and afterward yet again; then at last Burgess was able to get out these serious words:

"It is useless to try to disguise the fact—we find ourselves in the presence of a matter of grave import. It involves the honor of your town, it strikes at the town's good name. The difference of a single word between the test-remarks offered by Mr. Wilson and Mr. Billson was itself a serious thing, since it indicated that one of the other of these gentlemen had committed a theft—"

The two men were sitting limp, nerveless, crushed; but at these words both were electrified into movement, and started to get up—

"Sit down!" said the Chair, sharply, and they obeyed. "That, as I have said, was a serious thing. And it was—but for only one of them. But the matter has become graver; for the honor of *both* is now in formidable peril. Shall I go even further, and say in inextricable peril? *Both* left out the crucial fifteen words." He paused. During several moments he allowed the pervading stillness to gather and deepen its impressive effects, then added: "There would seem to be but one way whereby this could happen. I ask these gentlemen—Was there *collusion?—agreement?*"

A low murmur sifted through the house; its import was, "He's got them both."

Billson was not used to emergencies; he sat in a helpless collapse. But Wilson was a lawyer. He struggled to his feet, pale and worried, and said:

"I ask the indulgence of the house while I explain this most painful matter. I am sorry to say what I am about to say, since it must inflict irreparable injury upon Mr. Billson, whom I have always esteemed and respected until now, and in whose invulnerability to temptation I entirely believed—as did you all. But for the preservation of my own honor I must speak—and with frankness. I confess with shame—and I now beseech your pardon for it—that I said to the ruined stranger all of the words contained in the test-remark, including the disparaging fifteen. [*Sensation.*] When the late publication was made I recalled them, and I resolved to claim the sack of coin, for by every right I was entitled to it. Now I will ask you to consider this point, and weigh it well: that stranger's gratitude to me that night knew no bounds; he said himself that he could find no words for it that were adequate, and that if he should ever be able he would repay me a thousandfold. Now, then, I ask you this: could I expect—could I believe—could I even remotely imagine—that, feeling as he did, he would do so ungrateful a thing as to add those quite unnecessary fifteen words to his test?—set a trap for me?—expose me as a slanderer of my own town before my own people assembled in a public hall? It was preposterous; it was impossible. His test would contain only the kindly opening clause of my remark. Of that I had no shadow of doubt. You would have thought as I did. You would not have expected a base betrayal from one whom you had befriended and against whom you had committed no offence. And so, with perfect confidence, perfect trust, I wrote on a piece of paper the opening words—ending with 'Go, and reform,'—and signed it. When I was about to put it in an envelope I was called into my back office, and without thinking I left the paper lying open on my desk." He stopped, turned his head slowly toward Billson, waited a moment, then added: "I ask you to note this: when I returned, a little later, Mr. Billson was retiring by my street door." [*Sensation.*]

In a moment Billson was on his feet shouting:

"It's a lie! It's an infamous lie!"

THE CHAIR: "Be seated, sir! Mr. Wilson has the floor."

Billson's friends pulled him into his seat and quieted him, and Wilson went on:

"Those are the simple facts. My note was now lying in a different place on the table from where I had left it. I noticed that, but attached no importance to it, thinking a draught had blown it there. That Mr. Billson would read a private paper was a thing which could not occur to me; he was an honorable man, and he would be above that. If you will allow me to say it, I think his extra word *'very'* stands explained; it is attributable to a defect of memory. I was the only man in the world who could furnish here any detail of the test-mark—by *honorable* means. I have finished."

There is nothing in the world like a persuasive speech to fuddle the mental apparatus and upset the convictions and debauch the emotions of an audience not practised in the tricks and delusions of oratory. Wilson sat down victorious. The house submerged him in tides of approving applause; friends swarmed to him and shook him by the hand and congratulated him, and Billson was shouted down and not allowed to say a word. The Chair hammered and hammered with its gavel, and kept shouting,

"But let us proceed, gentlemen, let us proceed!"

At last there was a measurable degree of quiet, and the hatter said,

"But what is there to proceed with, sir, but to deliver the money?"

VOICES: "That's it! That's it! Come forward, Wilson!"

THE HATTER: "I move three cheers for Mr. Wilson, Symbol of the special virtue which—"

The cheers burst forth before he could finish; and in the midst of them—and in the midst of the clamor of the gavel also—some enthusiasts mounted Wilson on a big friend's shoulder and were going to fetch him in triumph to the platform. The Chair's voice now rose above the noise—

"Order! To your places! You forget that there is still a document to be read." When quiet had been restored he took up the document, and was going to read it, but laid it down again, saying, "I forgot; this is not to be read until all written communications received by me have first been read." He took an envelope out of his pocket, removed its enclosure, glanced at it—seemed astonished—held it out and gazed at it—stared at it.

Twenty or thirty voices cried out:

"What is it? Read it! read it!"

And he did—slowly, and wondering:

"'The remark which I made to the stranger—[VOICES: "Hello! how's this?"]—was this: "You are far from being a bad man. [VOICES: "Great Scott!"] Go, and reform."' [VOICE: "Oh, saw my leg off!"] Signed by Mr. Pinkerton the banker."

The pandemonium of delight which turned itself loose now was of a sort to make the judicious weep. Those whose withers were unwrung laughed till the tears ran down; the reporters, in throes of laughter, set down disordered pot-hooks which would never in the world be decipherable; and a sleeping dog jumped up, scared out of its wits, and barked itself crazy at the turmoil. All manner of cries were scattered through the din: "We're getting rich—*two* Symbols of Incorruptibility!—without counting Billson!" "*Three!*—count Shadbelly in—we can't have too many!" "All right—Billson's elected!" "Alas, poor Wilson—victim of *two* thieves!"

A POWERFUL VOICE: "Silence! The Chair's fished up something more out of its pocket."

VOICES: "Hurrah! Is it something fresh? Read it! read! read!"

THE CHAIR [*reading*]: "'The remark which I made,' etc. 'You are far from being a bad man. Go,' etc. Signed, 'Gregory Yates.'"

TORNADO OF VOICES: "Four Symbols!" "'Rah for Yates!" "Fish again!"

The house was in a roaring humor now, and ready to get all the fun out of the occasion that might be in it. Several Nineteeners, looking pale and distressed, got up and began to work their way toward the aisles, but a score of shouts went up:

"The doors, the doors—close the doors; no Incorruptible shall leave this place! Sit down, everybody!"

The mandate was obeyed.

"Fish again! Read! read!"

The Chair fished again, and once more the familiar words began to fall from its lips—"'You are far from being a bad man—'"

"Name! name! What's his name?"

"'L. Ingoldsby Sargent.'"

"Five elected! Pile up the Symbols! Go on, go on!"

"'You are far from being a bad—'"

"Name! name!"

"'Nicholas Whitworth.'"

"Hooray! hooray! it's a symbolical day!"

Somebody wailed in, and began to sing this rhyme (leaving out "it's") to the lovely "Mikado" tune of "When a man's afraid of a beautiful maid"; the audience joined in, with joy; then, just in time, somebody contributed another line—

"And don't you this forget—"

The house roared it out. A third line was at once furnished—

"Corruptibles far from Hadleyburg are—"

The house roared that one too. As the last note died, Jack Halliday's voice rose high and clear, freighted with a final line—

"But the Symbols are here, you bet!"

That was sung, with booming enthusiasm. Then the happy house started in at the beginning and sang the four lines through twice, with immense swing and dash, and finished up with a crashing three-times-three and a tiger for "Hadleyburg the Incorruptible and all Symbols of it which we shall find worthy to receive the hall-mark to-night."

Then the shoutings at the Chair began again, all over the place:

"Go on! go on! Read! read some more! Read all you've got!"

"That's it—go on! We are winning eternal celebrity."

A dozen men got up now and began to protest. They said that this farce was the work of some abandoned joker, and was an insult to the whole community. Without a doubt these signatures were all forgeries—

"Sit down! sit down! Shut up! You are confessing. We'll find *your* names in the lot."

"Mr. Chairman, how many of those envelopes have you got?"

The Chair counted.

"Together with those that have been already examined, there are nineteen."

A storm of derisive applause broke out.

"Perhaps they all contain the secret. I move that you open them all and read every signature that is attached to a note of that sort—and read also the first eight words of the note."

"Second that motion!"

It was put and carried—uproariously. Then poor old Richards got up, and his wife rose and stood at his side. Her head was bent down, so that none might see that she was crying. Her husband gave her his arm, and so supporting her, he began to speak in a quavering voice:

"My friends, you have known us two—Mary and me—all our lives, and I think you have liked us and respected us—"

The Chair interrupted him:

"Allow me. It is quite true—that which you are saying, Mr. Richards; this town *does* know you two; it *does* like you; it *does* respect you; more—it honors you and *loves* you—"

Halliday's voice rang out:

"That's the hall-marked truth, too! If the Chair is right, let the house speak up and say it. Rise! Now, then—hip! hip! hip—all together!"

The house rose in mass, faced toward the old couple eagerly, filled the air with a snow-storm of waving handkerchiefs, and delivered the cheers with all its affectionate heart.

The Chair then continued:

"What I was going to say is this: We know your good heart, Mr. Richards, but this is not a time for the exercise of charity toward offenders. [Shouts of "Right right!"] I see your generous purpose in your face, but I cannot allow you to plead for these men—"

"But I was going to—"

"Please take your seat, Mr. Richards. We must examine the rest of these notes—simple fairness to the men who have already been exposed requires this. As soon as that has been done—I give you my word for this—you shall be heard."

MANY VOICES: "Right!—the Chair is right—no interruption can be permitted at this stage! Go on!—the names! the names!—according to the terms of the motion!"

The old couple sat reluctantly down, and the husband whispered to the wife, "It is pitifully hard to have to wait; the shame will be greater than ever when they find we were only going to plead for *ourselves.*"

Straightway the jollity broke loose again with the reading of the names.

" 'You are far from being a bad man—' Signature, 'Robert J. Titmarsh.'

" 'You are far from being a bad man—' Signature, 'Eliphalet Weeks.'

" 'You are far from being a bad man—' Signature, 'Oscar B. Wilder.' "

At this point the house lit upon the idea of taking the eight words out of the Chairman's hands. He was not unthankful for that. Thenceforward he held up each note in its turn, and waited. The house droned out the eight words in a massed and measured and musical deep volume of sound (with a daringly close resemblance to a well-known church chant)—" 'You are f-a-r from being a b-a-a-a-d man.' " Then the Chair said, "Signature, 'Archibald Wilcox.'" And so on, and so on, name after name, and everybody had an increasingly and gloriously good time except the wretched Nineteen. Now and then, when a particularly shining name was called, the house made the Chair wait while it chanted the whole of the test-remark from the beginning to the closing words. "And go to hell or Hadleyburg—try and make it the for-or-m-e-r!" and in these special cases they added a grand and agonized and imposing "A-a-a-a-*men!*"

The list dwindled, dwindled, dwindled, poor old Richards keeping tally of the count, wincing when a name resembling his own was pronounced, and waiting in miserable suspense for the time to come when it would be his humiliating privilege to rise with Mary and finish his plea, which he was intending to word thus: ". . . for until now we have never done any wrong thing, but have gone our humble way unreproached. We are very poor, we are old, and have no chick nor child to help us; we were sorely tempted, and we fell. It was my purpose when I got up before to make confession and beg that my name might not be read out in this public place, for it seemed to us that we could not bear it; but I was prevented. It was just; it was our place to suffer with the rest. It has been hard for us. It is the first time we have ever heard our name fall from any one's lips—sullied. Be merciful—for the sake of the better days; make our shame as light to bear as in your charity you can." At this point in his revery Mary nudged him, perceiving that his mind was absent. The house was chanting, "You are f-a-r," etc.

"Be ready," Mary whispered. "Your name comes now; he has read eighteen."

The chant ended.

"Next! next! next!" came volleying from all over the house.

Burgess put his hand into his pocket. The old couple, trembling, began to rise. Burgess fumbled a moment, then said,

"I find I have read them all."

Faint with joy and surprise, the couple sank into their seats, and Mary whispered.

"Oh, bless God, we are saved!—he has lost ours—I wouldn't give this for a hundred of those sacks!"

The house burst out with its "Mikado" travesty, and sang it three times with ever-increasing enthusiasm, rising to its feet when it reached for the third time the closing line—

"But the Symbols are here, you bet!"

and finishing up with cheers and a tiger for "Hadleyburg purity and our eighteen immortal representatives of it."

Then Wingate, the saddler, got up and proposed cheers "for the cleanest man in town, the one solitary important citizen in it who didn't try to steal that money—Edward Richards."

They were given with great and moving heartiness; then somebody proposed that Richards "be elected sole Guardian and Symbol of the now Sacred Hadleyburg Tradition, with power and right to stand up and look the whole sarcastic world in the face."

Passed, by acclamation; then they sang the "Mikado" again, and ended it with,

"And there's *one* Symbol left, you bet!"

There was a pause; then—

A VOICE: "Now, then, who's to get the sack?"

THE TANNER *(with bitter sarcasm)*: "That's easy. The money has to be divided among the eighteen Incorruptibles. They gave the suffering stranger twenty dollars apiece—and that remark—each in his turn—it took twenty-two minutes for the procession to move past. Staked the stranger—total contribution, $360. All they want is just the loan back—and interest—forty thousand dollars altogether."

MANY VOICES [*derisively*]: "That's it Divvy! divvy! Be kind to the poor—don't keep them waiting!"

THE CHAIR: "Order! I now offer the stranger's remaining document. It says: 'If no claimant shall appear [*grand chorus of groans*], I desire that you open the sack and count out the money to the principal citizens of your town, they to take it in trust [*cries of "Oh! Oh! Oh!"*], and use it in such ways as to them shall seem best for the propagation and preservation of your community's noble reputation for incorruptible honesty [*more cries*]—a reputation to which their names and their efforts will add a new and far-reaching lustre.' [*Enthusiastic outburst of sarcastic applause.*] That seems to be all. No—here is a postscript:

"'P.S.—CITIZENS OF HADLEYBURG: There *is* no test-remark—nobody made one. [*Great sensation*] There wasn't any pauper stranger, nor any twenty-dollar contribution, nor any accompanying benediction and compliment—these are all inventions. [*General buzz and hum of astonishment and delight.*] Allow me to tell my story—it will take but a word or two. I passed through your town at a certain time, and received a deep offence which I had not earned. Any other man would have been content to kill one or two of you and call it square, but to me that would have been a trivial revenge, and inadequate; for the dead do not *suffer.* Besides, I could not kill you all—and, anyway, made as I am, even that would not have satisfied me. I wanted to damage every man in the place, and every woman—and not in their bodies or in their estate, but in the vanity—the place where feeble and foolish people are most vulnerable. So I disguised myself and came back and studied you. You were easy game. You had an old and lofty reputation for honesty, and naturally you were proud of it—it was your treasure of treasures, the very apple of your eye. As soon as I found out that you carefully and vigilantly kept yourselves and your children *out of temptation,* I knew how to proceed. Why, you simple creatures, the weakest of all weak thing is a virtue which has not been tested in the fire. I laid a plan, and gathered a list of names. My project was to corrupt Hadleyburg the Incorruptible. My idea was to make liars and thieves of nearly half a hundred smirchless men and women who had never in their lives uttered a lie or stolen a penny. I was afraid of Goodson. He was neither born nor reared in Hadleyburg. I was afraid that if I started to operate my scheme by getting my letter laid before you, you would say to yourselves, "Goodson is the only man among us who would give away twenty dollars to a poor devil"—and then you might not bite at my bait. But Heaven took Goodson; then I knew I was safe, and I set my trap and baited it. It may be that I shall not catch all the men to whom I mailed the pretended test secret, but I shall catch the most of them, if I know Hadleyburg nature. [*Voices.* "Right—he got every last one of them."] I believe they will even steal ostensible *gamble*-money, rather than miss, poor, tempted, and mistrained fellows. I am hoping to eternally and everlastingly squelch your vanity and give Hadleyburg a new renown—one that will *stick*—and spread far. If I have succeeded, open the sack and summon the Committee on Propagation and Preservation of the Hadleyburg Reputation.'"

A CYCLONE OF VOICES: "Open it! Open it! The Eighteen to the front! Committee on Propagation of the Tradition! Forward—the Incorruptibles!"

The chair ripped the sack wide, and gathered up a handful of bright, broad yellow coins, shook them together, then examined them—

"Friends, they are only gilded disks of lead!"

There was a crashing outbreak of delight over this news, and when the noise had subsided, the tanner called out:

"By right of apparent seniority in this business, Mr. Wilson is Chairman of the Committee on Propagation of the Tradition. I suggested that he step forward on behalf of his pals, and receive in trust the money."

A HUNDRED VOICES: "Wilson! Wilson! Wilson! Speech! Speech!"
WILSON: [*in a voice trembling with anger*]. "You will allow me to say, and without apologies for my language, *damn* the money!"
A VOICE: "Oh, and him a Baptist!"
A VOICE: "Seventeen Symbols left! Step up, gentlemen, and assume your trust!"

There was a pause—no response.

THE SADDLER: "Mr. Chairman, we've got *one* clean man left, anyway, out of the late aristocracy; and he needs money, and deserves it. I move that you appoint Jack Halliday to get up there and auction off that sack of gilt twenty-dollar pieces, and give the result to the right man—the man whom Hadleyburg delights to honor—Edward Richards."

This was received with great enthusiasm, the dog taking a hand again; the saddler started the bids at a dollar, the Brixton folk and Barnum's representative fought hard for it, the people cheered every jump that the bids made, the excitement climbed moment by moment higher and higher, the bidders got on their mettle and grew steadily more and more daring, more and more determined, the jumps went from a dollar up to five, then to ten, then to twenty, then fifty, then to a hundred, then—

At the beginning of the auction Richards whispered in distress to his wife: "Oh, Mary, can we allow it? It—it—you see, it is an honor-reward, a testimonial to purity of character, and—and—can we allow it? Hadn't I better get up and—Oh, Mary, what ought we to do?—what do you think we—" [*Halliday's voice, "Fifteen I'm bid!—fifteen for the sack!—twenty!—ah, thanks!—thirty—thanks again! Thirty, thirty, thirty—do I hear forty?—forty it is! Keep the ball rolling, gentlemen, keep it rolling!—fifty!—thanks noble Roman!—going at fifty, fifty, fifty!—seventy!—ninety!—splendid!—a hundred!—pile it up, pile it up!—hundred and twenty—forty!—just in time!—hundred and fifty;—*TWO *hundred!—superb! Do I hear two h—thanks!—two hundred and fifty!—"*]

"It is another temptation, Edward—I'm all in a tremble—but, oh, we've escaped *one* temptation, and that ought to warn us, to—[*"Six did I hear?—thanks!—six fifty, six f—*SEVEN *hundred!"*] And yet, Edward, when you think—nobody susp—[*"Eight hundred dollars!—hurrah!—make it nine!—Mr. Parsons, did I hear you say—thanks!—nine!—this noble sack of virgin lead going at only nine hundred dollars, gilding and all—come! do I hear—a thousand!—gratefully yours!—did some one say eleven?—a sack which is going to be the most celebrated in the whole Uni—"*] Oh, Edward" (beginning to sob), "we are *so* poor!—but—but—do as you think best—do as you think best."

Edward fell—that is, he sat still; sat with a conscience which was not satisfied, but which was overpowered by circumstances.

Meantime a stranger, who looked like an amateur detective gotten up as an impossible English earl, had been watching the evening's proceedings with manifest interest, and with a contented expression in his face; and he had been privately commenting to himself. He was now soliloquizing somewhat like this: "None of the Eighteen are bidding; that is not satisfactory; I must change that—the dramatic unities require it; they must buy the sack they tried to steal; they must pay a heavy price, too—some of them are rich. And another thing, when I make a mistake in Hadleyburg nature the man that puts that error upon me is entitled to a high honorarium, and some one must pay it. This poor old Richards has brought my judgment to shame; he is an honest man:—I don't understand it, but I acknowledge it. Yes, he saw my deuces *and* with a straight flush, and by rights the pot is his. And it shall be a jack-pot, too, if I can manage it. He disappointed me, but let that pass."

He was watching the bidding. At a thousand, the market broke; the prices tumbled swiftly. He waited—and still watched. One competitor dropped out; then another, and another. He put in a bid or two, now. When the bids had sunk to ten dollars, he added a five; some one raised him a three; he waited a moment, then flung in a fifty-dollar jump, and the sack was his—at $1282. The house broke out in cheers—then stopped; for he was on his feet, and had lifted his hand. He began to speak.

"I desire to say a word, and ask a favor. I am a speculator in rarities, and I have dealings with persons interested in numismatics all over the world. I can make a profit on this purchase, just as it stands; but there is a way, if I can get your approval, whereby I can make every one of these leaden twenty-dollar pieces worth its face in gold, and perhaps more. Grant me that approval, and I will give part of my gains to your Mr. Richards, whose invulnerable probity you have so justly and so cordially recognized to-night; his share will be ten thousand dollars, and I will hand him the money to-morrow. [*Great applause from the house.* But the "invulnerable probity" made the Richardses blush prettily; however, it went for modesty, and did no harm.] If you will pass my proposition by a good majority—I would like a two-thirds vote—I will regard that as the town's consent, and that is all I ask. Rarities are always helped by any device which will rouse curiosity and compel remark. Now if I may have your permission to stamp upon the faces of each of these ostensible coins the names of the eighteen gentlemen who—"

Nine-tenths of the audience were on their feet in a moment—dog and all—and the proposition was carried with a whirlwind of approving applause and laughter.

They sat down, and all the Symbols except "Dr." Clay Harkness, got up, violently protesting against the proposed outrage, and threatening to—

"I beg you not to threaten me," said the stranger, calmly. "I know my legal rights, and am not accustomed to being frightened at bluster." [*Applause.*] He sat down. "Dr." Harkness saw an opportunity here. He was one of the two very rich men of the place, and Pinkerton was the other. Harkness was proprietor of a mint; that is to say, a popular patent medicine. He was running for the Legislature on one ticket, and Pinkerton on the other. It was a close race and a hot one, and getting hotter every day. Both had strong appetites for money; each had bought a great tract of land, with a purpose; there was going to be a new railway, and each wanted to be in the Legislature and help locate the route to his own advantage; a single vote might make the decision, and with it two or three fortunes. The stake was large, and Harkness was a daring speculator. He was sitting close to the stranger. He leaned over while one or another of the other Symbols was entertaining the house with protests and appeals, and asked, in a whisper,

"What is your price for the sack?"

"Forty thousand dollars."

"I'll give you twenty."

"No."

"Twenty-five."

"No."

"Say thirty."

"The price is forty thousand dollars; not a penny less."

"All right, I'll give it. I will come to the hotel at ten in the morning. I don't want it known; will see you privately."

"Very good." Then the stranger got up and said to the house:

"I find it late. The speeches of these gentlemen are not without merit, not without interest, not without grace; yet if I may be excused I will take my leave. I thank you for the great favor which you have shown me in granting my petition. I ask the Chair to keep the sack for me until to-morrow, and to hand these three five-hundred-dollar notes to Mr. Richards." They were passed up to the Chair. "At nine I will call for the sack, and at eleven will deliver the rest of the ten thousand to Mr. Richards in person, at his home. Good-night."

Then he slipped out, and left the audience making a vast noise, which was composed of a mixture of cheers, the "Mikado" song, dog-disapproval, and the chant. "You are f-a-r from being a b-a-a-d man—a-a-a-a-men!"

IV

At home the Richardses had to endure congratulations and compliments until midnight. Then they were left to themselves. They looked a little sad, and they sat silent and thinking. Finally Mary sighed and said,

"Do you think we are to blame, Edward—*much* to blame?" and her eyes wandered to the accusing triplet of big bank-notes lying on the table, where the congratulators had been gloating over them and reverently fingered them. Edward did not answer at once; then he brought out a sigh, and said hesitatingly:

"We—we couldn't help it, Mary. It—well, it was ordered. *All* things are."

Mary glanced up and looked at him steadily; but he didn't return the look. Presently she said:

"I thought congratulations and praises always tasted good. But—it seems to me, now—Edward?"

"Well?"

"Are you going to stay in the bank?"

"N-no."

"Resign?"

"In the morning—by note."

"It does seem best."

Richards bowed his head in his hands and muttered:

"Before, I was not afraid to let oceans of people's money pour through my hands, but—Mary, I am so tired, so tired—"

"We will go to bed."

At nine in the morning the stranger called for the sack and took it to the hotel in a cab. At ten Harkness had a talk with him privately. The stranger asked for and got five checks on a metropolitan bank—drawn to "Bearer,"—four for $1,500 each, and one for $34,000. He put the former in his pocketbook, and the remainder, representing $38,500, he put in an envelope, and with these he added a note, which he wrote after Harkness was gone. At eleven he called at the Richards house and knocked. Mrs. Richards peeped through the shutters, then went and received the envelope, and the stranger disappeared without a word. She came back flushed and a little unsteady on her legs, and gasped out:

"I am sure I recognized him! Last night it seemed to me that maybe I had seen him somewhere before."

"He is the man that brought the sack here?"

"I am almost sure of it."

"Then he is the ostensible Stephenson too, and sold every important citizen in this town with his bogus secret. Now if he has sent checks instead of money, we are sold too, after we thought we had escaped. I was beginning to feel fairly comfortable once more, after my night's rest, but the look of that envelope makes me sick. It isn't fat enough; $8500 in even the largest bank-notes makes more bulk than that."

"Edward, why do you object to checks?"

"Checks signed by Stephenson! I am resigned to take the $8500 if it could come in bank-notes—for it does seem that it was so ordered, Mary—but I have never had much courage, and I have not the pluck to try to market a check signed with that disastrous name. It would be a trap. That man tried to catch me; we escaped somehow or other; and now he is trying a new way. If it is checks—"

"Oh, Edward, it is *too* bad!" and she held up the checks and began to cry.

"Put them in the fire! quick! we mustn't be tempted. It is a trick to make the world laugh at *us,* along with the rest, and—Give them to *me,* since you can't do it!" He snatched them and tried to hold his grip till he could get to the stove; but he was human, he was a cashier, and he stopped a moment to make sure of the signature. Then he came near to fainting.

"Fan me, Mary, fan me! They are the same as gold!"

"Oh, how lovely, Edward! Why?"

"Signed by Harkness. What can the mystery of that be, Mary?"

"Edward, do you think—"

"Look here—look at this! Fifteen—fifteen—fifteen—thirty-four. Thirty-eight thousand five hundred! Mary, the sack isn't worth twelve dollars, and Harkness—apparently—has paid about par for it."

"And does it all come to us, do you think—instead of the ten thousand?"

"Why, it looks like it. And the checks are made to 'Bearer,' too."

"Is that good, Edward? What is it for?"

"A hint to collect them at some distant bank, I reckon. Perhaps Harkness doesn't want the matter known. What is that—a note?"

"Yes. It was with the checks."

It was in the "Stephenson" handwriting, but there was no signature. It said:

"I am a disappointed man. Your honesty is beyond the reach of temptation. I had a different idea about it, but I wronged you in that, and I beg pardon, and do it sincerely. I honor you—and that is sincere, too. This town is not worthy to kiss the hem of your garment. Dear sir, I made a square bet with myself that there were nineteen debauchable men in your self-righteous community. I have lost. Take the whole pot, you are entitled to it."

Richards drew a deep sigh, and said:

"It seems written with fire—it burns so. Mary—I am miserable again."

"I, too. Ah, dear, I wish—"

"To think, Mary——he *believes* in me."

"Oh, don't Edward—I can't bear it."

"If those beautiful words were deserved, Mary—and God knows I believed I deserved them once—I think I could give the forty thousand dollars for them. And I would put that paper away, as representing more than gold and jewels, and keep it always. But now— We could not live in the shadow of its accusing presence, Mary."

He put it in the fire.

A messenger arrived and delivered an envelope. Richards took from it a note and read it; it was from Burgess.

"You saved me, in a difficult time. I saved you last night. It was at cost of a lie, but I made the sacrifice freely, and out of a grateful heart. None in this village knows so well as I know how brave and good and noble you are. At bottom you cannot respect me, knowing as you do of that matter of which I am accused, and by the general voice condemned; but I beg that you will at least believe that I am a grateful man; it will help me to bear my burden.
[Signed] "BURGESS."

"Saved, once more. And on such terms!" He put the note in the fire. "I—I wish I were dead, Mary, I wish I were out of it all."

"Oh, these are bitter, bitter days, Edward. The stabs, through their very generosity, are so deep—and they come so fast!"

Three days before the election each of two thousand voters suddenly found himself in possession of a prized momento—one of the renowned bogus double-eagles. Around one of its faces was stamped these words: "THE REMARK I MADE TO THE POOR STRANGER WAS—" Around the other face was stamped these "GO, AND REFORM. [SIGNED] PINKERTON." Thus the entire remaining refuse of the renowned joke was emptied upon a single head, and with calamitous effect. It revived the recent vast laugh and concentrated it upon Pinkerton; and Harkness's election was a walk-over.

Within twenty-four hours after the Richardses had received their checks their consciences were quieting down, discouraged; the old couple were learning to reconcile themselves to the sin which they had committed. But they were to learn, now, that a sin takes on new and real terrors when there seems a chance that it is going to be found out. This gives it a fresh and most substantial and important aspect. At church the morning sermon was of the usual pattern; it was the same old things said in the same old way; they had heard them a thousand times and found them innocuous, next to meaningless, and easy to sleep under; but now it was different: the sermon seemed to bristle with accusations; it seemed aimed straight and specially at people who were concealing deadly sins. After church they got away from the mob of congratulators as soon as they could and hurried homeward, chilled to the bone as they did not know what—vague, shadowy, indefinite fears. And by chance they caught a glimpse of Mr. Burgess as he turned a corner. He paid no attention to their nod of recognition! He hadn't seen it; but they did not know that. What could his conduct mean? It might mean—it might mean—oh, a dozen dreadful things. Was it possible that he knew that Richards could have cleared him of guilt in that bygone time, and had been silently waiting for a chance to even up accounts? At home, in their distress they got to imagining that their servant might have been in the next room listening when Richards revealed the secret to his wife that he knew of Burgess's innocence; next Richards began to imagine that he had heard the swish of a gown in there at that time; next, he was sure he *had* heard it. They would call Sarah in, on a pretext, and watch her face: if she had been betraying them to Mr. Burgess, it would show in her manner. They asked her some questions—questions which were so random and incoherent and seemingly purposeless that the girl felt sure that the old people's minds had been affected by their sudden good fortune; the sharp and watchful gaze which they bent upon her frightened her, and that completed the business. She blushed, she became nervous and confused, and to the old people these were plain signs of guilt—guilt of some fearful sort or other—without doubt she was a spy and a traitor. When they were alone again they began to piece many unrelated things together and get horrible results out of the combination. When things had got about to the worst, Richards was delivered of a sudden gasp, and his wife asked,

"Oh, what is it?—what is it?"

"The note—Burgess's note! Its language was sarcastic, I see it now." He quoted: "'At bottom you cannot respect me, *knowing* as you do, of *that matter* of which I am accused'—oh, it is perfectly plain, now, God help me! He knows that I know! You see the ingenuity of the phrasing. It was a trap—and like a fool, I walked into it. And Mary—?"

"Oh, it is dreadful—I know what you are going to say—he didn't return your transcript of the pretended test-remark."

"No—kept it to destroy us with. Mary, he has exposed us to some already. I know it—I know it well. I saw it in a dozen faces after church. Ah, he wouldn't answer our nod of recognition—*he* knew what he had been doing!"

In the night the doctor was called. The news went around in the morning that the old couple were rather seriously ill—prostrated by the exhausting excitement growing out of their great windfall, the congratulations, and the late hours, the doctor said. The town was sincerely distressed; for these old people were about all it had left to be proud of now.

Two days later the news was worse. The old couple were delirious, and were doing strange things. By witness of the nurses, Richards had exhibited checks—for \$8,500? No—for an amazing sum—\$38,500! What could be the explanation of this gigantic piece of luck?

The following day the nurses had more news—and wonderful. They had concluded to hide the checks, lest harm come to them; but when they searched they were gone from under the patient's pillow—vanished away. The patient said:

"Let the pillow alone; what do you want?"

"We thought it best that the checks—"

"You will never see them again—they are destroyed. They came from Satan. I saw the hell-brand on them, and I knew they were sent to betray me to sin." Then he fell to gabbling strange and dreadful things which were not clearly understandable, and which the doctor admonished them to keep to themselves.

Richards was right; the checks were never seen again.

A nurse must have talked in her sleep, for within two days the forbidden gabblings were the property of the town; and they were of a surprising sort. They seemed to indicate that Richards had been a claimant for the sack himself, and that Burgess had concealed that fact and then maliciously betrayed it.

Burgess was taxed with this and stoutly denied it. And he said it was not fair to attach weight to the chatter of a sick old man who was out of his mind. Still, suspicion was in the air, and there was much talk.

After a day or two it was reported that Mrs. Richards's delirious deliveries were getting to be duplicates of her husband's. Suspicion flamed up into conviction now, and the town's pride in the purity of its one undiscredited important citizen began to dim down and flicker toward extinction.

Six days passed, then came more news. The old couple were dying. Richards's mind cleared in his latest hour, and he sent for Burgess. Burgess said:

"Let the room be cleared. I think he wishes to say something in privacy."

"No!" said Richards; "I want witnesses. I want you all to hear my confession, so that I may die a man, and not a dog. I was clean—artificially—like the rest; and like the rest I fell when temptation came. I signed a lie, and claimed the miserable sack. Mr. Burgess remembered that I had done him a service, and in gratitude (and ignorance) he suppressed my claim and saved me. You know the thing that was charged against Burgess years ago. My testimony, and mine alone, could have cleared him, and I was a coward, and left him to suffer disgrace—"

"No—no—Mr. Richards, you—"

"My servant betrayed my secret to him—"

"No one has betrayed anything to me—"

—"and then he did a natural and justifiable thing, he repented of the saving kindness which he had done me, and he *exposed* me—as I deserved—"

"Never!—I make oath—"

"Out of my heart I forgive him."

Burgess's impassioned protestations fell upon deaf ears; the dying man passed away without knowing that once more he had done poor Burgess a wrong. The old wife died that night.

The last of the sacred Nineteen had fallen a prey to the fiendish sack; the town was stripped the last rag of its ancient glory. Its mourning was not showy, but it was deep.

By act of the Legislature—upon prayer and petition—Hadleyburg was allowed to change its name to (never mind what—I will not give it away), and leave one word out of the motto that for many generations had graced the town's official seal.

It is an honest town once more, and the man will have to rise early that catches it napping again.

1899, 1900

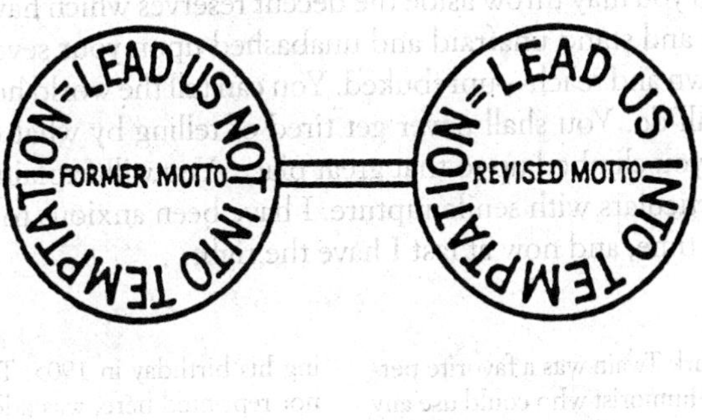

from Seventieth Birthday Dinner Speech[1]

Mark Twain's Seventieth Birthday Dinner, Delmonico's, New York

. . . I have had a great many birthdays in my time. I remember the first one very well, and I always think of it with indignation; everything was so crude, unesthetic, primeval. Nothing like this at all. No proper appreciative preparation made; nothing really ready. Now, for a person born with high and delicate instincts—why, even the cradle wasn't white-washed—nothing ready at all. I hadn't any hair, I hadn't any teeth, I hadn't any clothes, I had to go to my first banquet just like that. Well, everybody came swarming in. It was the merest little bit of a village—hardly that, just a little hamlet, in the backwoods of Missouri, where nothing ever happened, and the people were all interested, and they all came; they looked me over to see if there was anything fresh in my line. Why, nothing ever happened in that village—I—why, I was the only thing that had really happened there for months and months; and although I say it myself that shouldn't, I came the nearest to being a real event that had happened in that village in more than two years. Well, those people came, they came with that curiosity which is so provincial, with that frankness which also is so provincial, and they examined me all around and gave their opinion. Nobody asked them, and I shouldn't have minded if anybody had paid me a compliment, but nobody did. Their opinions were all just green with prejudice, and I feel those opinions to this day. Well, I stood that as long as—well, you know I was born courteous, and I stood it to the limit. I stood it an hour, and then the worm turned. I was the worm; it was my turn to turn, and I turned. I knew very well the strength of my position; I knew that I was the only spotlessly pure and innocent person in that whole town, and I came out and said so. And they could not say a word. It was so true. They blushed; they were embarrassed. Well, that was the first after-dinner speech I ever made. I think it was after dinner.

It's a long stretch between that first birthday speech and this one. That was my cradle song, and this is my swan song, I suppose. I am used to swan songs; I have sung them several times.

This is my seventieth birthday, and I wonder if you all rise to the size of that proposition, realizing all the significance of that phrase, seventieth birthday.

The seventieth birthday! It is the time of life when you arrive at a new and awful dignity; when you may throw aside the decent reserves which have oppressed you for a generation and stand unafraid and unabashed upon your seven-terraced summit and look down and teach—unrebuked. You can tell the world how you got there. It is what they all do. You shall never get tired of telling by what delicate arts and deep moralities you climbed up to that great place. You will explain the process and dwell on the particulars with senile rapture. I have been anxious to explain my own system this long time, and now at last I have the right.

[1]In his own day, Mark Twain was a favorite personality, a colorful humorist who could use any public occasion to entertain his audience. Here is how he entertained a large gathering celebrating his birthday in 1905. The first paragraph, not reprinted here, was addressed to the man who introduced him.

I have achieved my seventy years in the usual way: by sticking strictly to a scheme of life which would kill anybody else. It sounds like an exaggeration, but that is really the common rule for attaining to old age. When we examine the program of any of these garrulous old people we always find that the habits which have preserved them would have decayed us; that the way of life which enabled them to live upon the property of their heirs so long, as Mr. Choate says, would have put us out of commission ahead of time. I will offer here, as a sound maxim, this: That we can't reach old age by another man's road.

I will now teach, offering my way of life to whomsoever desires to commit suicide by the scheme which has enabled me to beat the doctor and the hangman for seventy years. Some of the details may sound untrue, but they are not. I am not here to deceive; I am here to teach.

We have no permanent habits until we are forty. Then they begin to harden, presently they petrify, then business begins. Since forty I have been regular about going to bed and getting up—and that is one of the main things. I have made it a rule to go to bed when there wasn't anybody left to sit up with; and I have made it a rule to get up when I had to. This has resulted in an unswerving regularity of irregularity. It has saved me sound, but it would injure another person.

In the matter of diet—which is another main thing—I have been persistently strict in sticking to the things which didn't agree with me until one or the other of us got the best of it. Until lately I got the best of it myself. But last spring I stopped frolicking with mince pie after midnight; up to then I had always believed it wasn't loaded. For thirty years I have taken coffee and bread at eight in the morning, and no bite nor sup until seven-thirty in the evening. Eleven hours. That is all right for me, and is wholesome, because I have never had a headache in my life, but headachy people would not reach seventy comfortably by that road, and they would be foolish to try it. And I wish to urge upon you this—which I think is wisdom—that if you find you can't make seventy by any but an uncomfortable road, don't you go. When they take off the Pullman and retire you to the rancid smoker, put on your things, count your checks, and get out at the first way station where there's a cemetery.

I have made it a rule never to smoke more than one cigar at a time. I have no other restriction as regards smoking. I do not know just when I began to smoke, I only know that it was in my father's lifetime, and that I was discreet. He passed from this life early in 1847, when I was a shade past eleven; ever since then I have smoked publicly. As an example to others, and not that I care for moderation myself, it has always been my rule never to smoke when asleep, and never to refrain when awake. It is a good rule. I mean, for me; but some of you know quite well that it wouldn't answer for everybody that's trying to get to be seventy.

I smoke in bed until I have to go to sleep. I wake up in the night, sometimes once, sometimes twice, sometimes three times, and I never waste any of these opportunities to smoke. This habit is so old and dear and precious to me that I would feel as you, sir, would feel if you should lose the only moral you've got—meaning the chairman—if you've got one; I am making no charges. I will grant, here, that I have stopped smoking now and then, for a few months at a time, but it was not on principle, it was only to show off; it was to pulverize those critics who said I was a slave to my habits and couldn't break my bonds.

Today it is all of sixty years since I began to smoke the limit. I have never bought cigars with life belts around them. I early found that those were too expensive for me. I have always bought cheap cigars—reasonably cheap, at any rate. Sixty years ago they cost me four dollars a barrel, but my taste has improved, latterly, and I pay seven now. Six or seven. Seven, I think. Yes, it's seven. But that includes the barrel. I often have smoking parties at my house; but the people that come have always just taken the pledge. I wonder why that is?

As for drinking, I have no rule about that. When the others drink I like to help; otherwise I remain dry, by habit and preference. This dryness does not hurt me, but it could easily hurt you, because you are different. You let it alone.

Since I was seven years old I have seldom taken a dose of medicine, and have still seldomer needed one. But up to seven I lived exclusively on allopathic medicines. Not that I needed them, for I don't think I did; it was for economy; my father took a drug store for a debt, and it made cod liver oil cheaper than other breakfast foods. We had nine barrels of it, and it lasted me seven years. Then I was weaned. The rest of the family had to get along with rhubarb and ipecac and such things, because I was the pet. I was the first Standard Oil Trust. I had it all. By the time the drug store was exhausted my health was established and there has never been much the matter with me since. But you know very well it would be foolish for the average child to start for seventy on that basis. It happened to be just the thing for me, but that was merely an accident; it couldn't happen again in a century.

I have never taken any exercise, except sleeping and resting, and I never intend to take any. Exercise is loathsome. And it cannot be any benefit when you are tired; and I was always tired. But let another person try my way, and see where he will come out.

I desire now to repeat and emphasize that maxim: We can't reach old age by another man's road. My habits protect my life but they would assassinate you.

I have lived a severely moral life. But it would be a mistake for other people to try that, or for me to recommend it. Very few would succeed: you have to have a perfectly colossal stock of morals; and you can't get them on a margin; you have to have the whole thing, and put them in your box. Morals are an acquirement—like music, like a foreign language, like piety, poker, paralysis—no man is born with them. I wasn't myself, I started poor. I hadn't a single moral. There is hardly a man in this house that is poorer than I was then. Yes, I started like that—the world before me, not a moral in the slot. Not even an insurance moral. I can remember the first one I ever got. I can remember the landscape, the weather, the—I can remember how everything looked. It was an old moral, an old secondhand moral, all out of repair, and didn't fit, anyway. But if you are careful with a thing like that, and keep it in a dry place, and save it for processions, and chautauquas, and World's Fairs, and so on, and disinfect it now and then, and give it a fresh coat of whitewash once in a while, you will be surprised to see how well she will last and how long she will keep sweet, or at least inoffensive. When I got that mouldy old moral, she had stopped growing, because she hadn't any exercise; but I worked her hard. I worked her Sundays and all. Under this cultivation she waxed in might and stature beyond belief, and served me well and was my pride and joy for sixty-three years; then she got to associating with insurance presidents, and lost flesh and character, and was a sorrow to look at and no longer competent for business. She was a great loss to me. Yet not all loss. I sold her—ah, pathetic skeleton, as she was—I sold her to Leopold, the pirate King of Belgium; he sold her to our Metropolitan Museum, and it was very glad to get her, for, without a rag on, she stands fifty-seven feet long and sixteen feet high, and they think she's a brontosaur. Well, she looks it. They believe it will take nineteen geological periods to breed her match.

Morals are of inestimable value, for every man is born crammed with sin microbes, and the only thing that can extirpate these sin microbes is morals. Now you take a sterilized Christian—I mean, you take *the* sterilized Christian, for there's only one. Dear sir, I wish you wouldn't look at me like that.

Threescore years and ten!

It is the Scriptural statute of limitations. After that, you owe no active duties; for you the strenuous life is over. You are a time-expired man, to use Kipling's military phrase. You have served your term, well or less well, and you are mustered out. You are become an honorary member of the republic, you are emancipated, compulsions are not for you, nor any bugle call but "lights out." You pay the timeworn duty bills if you choose, or decline if you prefer—and without prejudice—for they are not legally collectible.

The previous engagement plea, which in forty years has cost you so many twinges, you can lay aside forever; on this side of the grave you will never need it again. If you shrink at thought of night, and winter, and the late homecoming from the banquet and the lights and the laughter through the deserted streets—a desolation which would not remind you now, as for a generation it did, that your friends are sleeping, and you must creep in a-tiptoe and not disturb them, but would only remind you that you need not tiptoe, you can never disturb them more—if you shrink at thought of these things, you need only reply, "Your invitation honors me, and pleases me because you still keep me in your remembrance, but I am seventy; seventy, and would nestle in the chimney corner, and smoke my pipe, and read my book, and take my rest, wishing you well in all affection, and that when you in your turn shall arrive at pier No. 70 you may step aboard your waiting ship with a reconciled spirit, and lay your course toward the sinking sun with a contented heart."

1905

The War Prayer[1]

It was a time of great and exalting excitement. The country was up in arms, the war was on, in every breast burned the holy fire of patriotism; the drums were beating, the bands playing, the toy pistols popping, the bunched firecrackers hissing and spluttering; on every hand and far down the receding and fading spread of roofs and balconies a fluttering wilderness of flags flashed in the sun; daily the young volunteers marched down the wide avenue gay and fine in their new uniforms, the proud fathers and mothers and sisters and sweethearts cheering them with voices choked with happy emotion as they swung by; nightly the packed mass meetings listened,

[1]In 1905, Mark Twain submitted this piece to *Harper's Bazaar.* When it was rejected as being unsuitable for a woman's magazine, he left it unpublished. It first appeared in 1923, thirteen years after the author's death.

panting, to patriot oratory which stirred the deepest deeps of their hearts, and which they interrupted at briefest intervals with cyclones of applause, the tears running down their cheeks the while; in the churches the pastors preached devotion to flag and country, and invoked the God of Battles, beseeching His aid in our good cause in outpouring of fervid eloquence which moved every listener. It was indeed a glad and gracious time, and the half dozen rash spirits that ventured to disapprove of the war and cast a doubt upon its righteousness straightway got such a stern and angry warning that for their personal safety's sake they quickly shrank out of sight and offended no more in that way.

Sunday morning came—next day the battalions would leave for the front; the church was filled; the volunteers were there, their young faces alight with martial dreams—visions of the stern advance, the gathering momentum, the rushing charge, the flashing sabers, the flight of the foe, the tumult, the enveloping smoke, the fierce pursuit, and surrender!—then home from the war, bronzed heroes, welcomed, adored, submerged in golden seas of glory! With the volunteers sat their dear ones, proud, happy, and envied by the neighbors and friends who had no sons and brothers to send forth to the field of honor, there to win for the flag, or, failing, die the noblest of noble deaths. The service proceeded; a war chapter from the Old Testament was read; the first prayer was said; it was followed by an organ burst that shook the building, and with one impulse the house rose, with glowing eyes and beating hearts, and poured out that tremendous invocation—

> "God the all-terrible! Thou who ordainest,
> Thunder thy clarion and lightning thy sword!"

Then came the "long" prayer. None could remember the like of it for passionate pleading and moving and beautiful language. The burden of its supplication was, that an ever-merciful and benignant Father of us all would watch over our noble young soldiers, and aid, comfort, and encourage them in their patriotic work; bless them, shield them in the day of battle and the hour of peril, bear them in His mighty hand, make them strong and confident, invincible in the bloody onset; help them to crush the foe, grant to them and to their flag and country imperishable honor and glory—

An aged stranger entered and moved with slow and noiseless step up the main aisle, his eyes fixed upon the minister, his long body clothed in a robe that reached to his feet, his head bare, his white hair descending in a frothy cataract to his shoulders, his seamy face unnaturally pale, pale even to ghastliness. With all eyes following him and wondering, he made his silent way; without pausing, he ascended to the preacher's side and stood there, waiting. With shut lids the preacher, unconscious of his presence, continued his moving prayer, and at last finished it with the words, uttered in fervent appeal, "Bless our arms, grant us the victory, O Lord our God, Father and Protector of our land and flag!"

The stranger touched his arm, motioned him to step aside—which the startled minister did—and took his place. During some moments he surveyed the spellbound audience with solemn eyes, in which burned an uncanny light; then in a deep voice he said:

"I come from the Throne—bearing a message from Almighty God!" The words smote the house with a shock; if the stranger perceived it he gave no attention. "He has heard the prayer of His servant your shepherd, and will grant it if such shall be your desire after I, His messenger, shall have explained to you its import—that is to say, its full import. For it is like unto many of the prayers of men, in that it asks for more than he who utters it is aware of—except he pause and think.

"God's servant and yours has prayed his prayer. Has he paused and taken thought? Is it one prayer? No, it is two—one uttered, the other not. Both have reached the ear of Him Who heareth all supplications, the spoken and the unspoken. Ponder this—keep it in mind. If you would beseech a blessing upon yourself, beware! lest without intent you invoke a curse upon a neighbor at the same time. If you pray for the blessing of rain upon your crop which needs it, by that act you are possibly praying for a curse upon some neighbor's crop which may not need rain and can be injured by it.

"You have heard your servant's prayer—the uttered part of it. I am commissioned of God to put into words the other part of it—that part which the pastor—and also you in your hearts—fervently prayed silently. And ignorantly and unthinkingly? God grant that it was so! You heard these words: 'Grant us the victory, O Lord our God!' That is sufficient. The *whole* of the uttered prayer is compact into those pregnant words. Elaborations were not necessary. When you have prayed for victory you have prayed for many unmentioned results which follow victory—*must* follow it, cannot help but follow it. Upon the listening spirit of God the Father fell also the unspoken part of the prayer. He commandeth me to put it into words. Listen!

"O Lord our Father, our young patriots, idols of our hearts, go forth to battle—be Thou near them! With them—in spirit—we also go forth from the sweet peace of our beloved firesides to smite the foe. O Lord our God, help us to tear their soldiers to bloody shreds with our shells; help us to cover their smiling fields with the pale forms of their patriot dead; help us to drown the thunder of the guns with the shrieks of their wounded, writhing in pain; help us to lay waste their humble homes with a hurricane of fire; help us to wring the hearts of their unoffending widows with unavailing grief; help us to turn them out roofless with their little children to wander unfriended the wastes of their desolated land in rags and hunger and thirst, sports of the sun flames of summer and the icy winds of winter, broken in spirit, worn with travail, imploring Thee for the refuge of the grave and denied it—for our sakes who adore Thee, Lord, blast their hopes, blight their lives, protract their bitter pilgrimage, make heavy their steps, water their way with their tears, stain the white snow with the blood of their wounded feet! We ask it, in the spirit of love, or Him Who is the Source of Love, and Who is the ever-faithful refuge and friend of all that are sore beset and seek His aid with humble and contrite hearts. Amen."

(After a pause.) "Ye have prayed it; if ye still desire it, speak! The messenger of the Most High waits."

It was believed afterward that the man was a lunatic, because there was no sense in what he said.

1905

Joel Chandler Harris 1848–1908

The conflicts between the values of the Old and New South were vividly illustrated in the journalistic and literary career of Joel Chandler Harris.

Born in Eatonton, Putnam County, Georgia, in 1848, Harris was the son of a poor white mother and an Irish day laborer who deserted his family shortly after Harris's birth. His mother supported the family through her work as a seamstress, but at thirteen Harris set out on his own, becoming an apprentice to Joseph Addison Turner, who published a newspaper on his plantation, Turnwold. It was from the slaves on this plantation, in the twilight of the Old South, that Harris first heard the African American folktales that were to make him famous.

Following the Civil War he worked on other newspapers in New Orleans and throughout Georgia, culminating in 1876 in his appointment to the editorial staff of the Atlanta *Constitution.* The *Constitution* was run by Henry Woodfin Grady (1850–1889), Georgia's most enthusiastic promoter of the "New South," an industrialized, urbanized, "Yankeefied" society totally reconciled to its restoration to the Union. Harris too was a believer in both sectional reconciliation and the commercial development of the region, and he produced numerous editorials supporting Grady's vision. In addition, however, he fulfilled a quite different assignment for the paper as he returned to the world of his youth in the retelling of the slave stories through a black character called Uncle Remus. Modeled after some of the slaves he had encountered at Turnwold, Uncle Remus in the earliest sketches was presented in an urban setting and used to express harsh critiques of the ex-slaves, particularly those who sought political power and formal education. This character evolved into the Remus with whom contemporary readers are familiar: the gentle old man who transfixes a little white boy night after night with stories about small, seemingly defenseless animals whose cunning outwits stronger but less intelligent beasts.

Reprinted in newspapers throughout the nation, the Uncle Remus stories were an immediate success, appealing to a reading public already receptive to the image of the antebellum South as an idyllic land where master and slave lived in harmony and older slaves considered the master's children their own. In 1880 Harris published his first collection, *Uncle Remus: His Songs and Sayings,* followed in 1883 by *Nights With Uncle Remus.* There were several collections of Uncle Remus stories during Harris's lifetime, of which the first, with the classic Tar Baby story, is probably the best. As the demand for more stories intensified, he was hard-pressed to come up with them and had to turn to the recollections of others; inevitably these later stories lacked the immediacy and vividness of those in the 1880 edition.

Harris was not unaware of the psychological implications of the stories he retold; he knew why the slaves, with few or no means at hand for effective physical resistance, celebrated the successes of weak but clever creatures like Brer Tarrypin and Brer Rabbit over the stronger but slower Brer Fox, Brer Bear, and Brer Wolf. He never told the stories to his own children, because in so many of them the punishments doled out to the smaller creatures' enemies (boiling, skinning alive, and burning) are so brutal. Nonetheless, in essays and rare public appearances he persisted in depicting the African American as gentle, compassionate, and eager for reconciliation with whites.

Harris became prolific in the 1880s and 1890s, producing such short story collections as *Mingo and Other Sketches in Black and White* (1884) and *Free Joe, and Other Georgia Sketches* (1887). He also wrote several novels and a collection of sketches built around a poor white homespun philosopher called Uncle Billy Sanders. But it was for Uncle Remus that Harris was destined to be best remembered, and the release of a full-length Walt Disney motion picture, *Song of the South,* in 1946 introduced new generations to a set of characters who appear assured of a permanent place in American folklore.

A shy, self-effacing man, Harris thought of himself as a "cornfield journalist" whose chief contribution was as compiler rather than creator. But his picturesque recollections and his marvelous ear for dialect have won him well-deserved praise. Harris unquestionably sentimentalized the lives of slaves in his sketches, and even in "Free Joe," where he reveals an awareness of the cruel side of race relations in the antebellum South, he has written a story that many critics see as supporting mainstream southern claims that blacks were better off in slavery. In judging Harris's work, however, we must recall that he was writing at a time when the South's most virulent spokespeople, in literature and in politics, were painting for a gullible public a picture of African Americans as vicious and bestial. Whatever his deficiencies in bridging the gap between races, Harris's nostalgic black portraits did serve to awaken white readers to the richness of African American folklore, a treasure they would have otherwise not encountered.

George Friedman
Towson State University

PRIMARY WORKS

Uncle Remus: His Songs and His Sayings, 1880; *Mingo, and Other Sketches in Black and White,* 1884; *Free Joe, and Other Georgian Sketches,* 1887; *Gabriel Tolliver: A Story of Reconstruction,* 1902; *The Complete Tales of Uncle Remus,* 1955.

from Uncle Remus: His Songs and His Sayings

II The Wonderful Tar-Baby Story

"Didn't the fox *never* catch the rabbit, Uncle Remus?" asked the little boy the next evening. "He come mighty nigh it, honey, sho's you bawn—Brer Fox did. One day atter Brer[1] Rabbit fool 'im wid dat calamus root, Brer Fox went ter wuk en got 'im some tar, en mix it wid some turkentime, en fix up a contrapshun wat he call a Tar-Baby, en he tuck dish yer Tar-Baby en he sot 'er in de big road, en den he lay off in de bushes fer ter see wat de news wuz gwineter be. En he didn't hatter wait long, nudder, kaze[2] bimeby[3] here come Brer Rabbit pacin' down de road—lippity-clippity, clippity-lippity—dez ez sassy ez a jay-bird. Brer Fox, he lay low. Brer Rabbit come prancin' 'long twel he spy de Tar-Baby, en den he fotch up on his behime legs like he wuz 'stonished. De Tar-Baby, she sot dar, she did, en Brer Fox, he lay low.

"'Mawnin'!' sez Brer Rabbit, sezee—'nice wedder dis mawnin',' sezee.

"Tar-Baby ain't sayin' nuthin', en Brer Fox, he lay low.

"'How duz yo' sym'tums seem ter segashuate?'[4] sez Brer Rabbit, sezee.

[1]Brother; used in the same way members of a church congregation refer to each other.

[2]Because.

[3]By and by.

[4]*I.e.,* how are you feeling today?

"Brer Fox, he wink his eye slow, en lay low, en de Tar-Baby, she ain't sayin' nuthin'.

"'How you come on, den? Is you deaf?' sez Brer Rabbit, sezee. 'Kaze if you is, I kin holler louder,' sezee.

"Tar-Baby stay still, en Brer Fox, he lay low.

"'Youer stuck up, dat's w'at you is,' says Brer Rabbit, sezee, 'en I'm gwineter kyore you, dat's w'at I'm a gwineter do,' sezee.

"Brer Fox, he sorter chuckle in his stummuck, he did, but Tar-Baby ain't sayin' nuthin'.

"'I'm gwineter larn you howter talk ter 'specttubble fokes ef hit's de las' ack,' sez Brer Rabbit, sezee. 'Ef you don't take off dat hat en tell me howdy, I'm gwineter bus' you wide open,' sezee.

"Tar-Baby stay still, en Brer Fox, he lay low.

"Brer Rabbit keep on axin' 'im, en de Tar-Baby, she keep on sayin' nuthin', twel present'y Brer Rabbit draw back wid his fis', he did, en blip he tuck 'er side er de head. Right dar's whar he broke his merlasses jug. His fis' stuck, en he can't pull loose. De tar hilt 'im. But Tar-Baby, she stay still, en Brer Fox, he lay low.

"'Ef you don't lemme loose, I'll knock you agin,' sez Brer Rabbit, sezee, en wid dat he fotch 'er a wipe wid de udder han', en dat stuck. Tar-Baby, she ain't sayin' nuthin', en Brer Fox, he lay low.

"'Tu'n me loose, fo' I kick de natal stuffin' outen you,' sez Brer Rabbit, sezee, but de Tar-Baby, she ain't sayin' nuthin'. She des hilt on, en den Brer Rabbit lose de use er his feet in de same way. Brer Fox, he lay low. Den Brer Rabbit squall out dat ef de Tar-Baby don't tu'n 'im loose he butt 'er cranksided. En den he butted, en his head got stuck. Den Brer Fox, he sa'ntered fort', lookin' des ez innercent ez wunner yo' mammy's mockin'-birds.

"'Howdy, Brer Rabbit,' sez Brer Fox, sezee. 'You look sorter stuck up dis mawnin',' sezee, en den he rolled on de groun', en laft en laft twel he couldn't laff no mo'. 'I speck you'll take dinner wid me dis time, Brer Rabbit. I done laid in some calamus root, en I ain't gwineter take no skuse,' sez Brer Fox, sezee."

Here Uncle Remus paused, and drew a two-pound yam out of the ashes.

"Did the fox eat the rabbit?" asked the little boy to whom the story had been told.

"Dat's all de fur de tale goes," replied the old man. "He mout, en den agin he mountent. Some say Jedge B'ar come 'long en loosed 'im—some say he didn't. I hear Miss Sally callin'. You better run 'long."

IV *How Mr. Rabbit Was Too Sharp for Mr. Fox*

"Uncle Remus," said the little boy one evening, when he had found the old man with little or nothing to do, "did the fox kill and eat the rabbit when he caught him with the Tar-Baby?"

"Law, honey, ain't I tell you 'bout dat?" replied the old darkey, chuckling slyly. "I 'clar ter grashus I ought er tole you dat, but ole man Nod wuz ridin' on my eyeleds 'twel a leetle mo'n I'd a dis'member'd my own name, en den on to dat here come yo' mammy hollerin' atter you.

"W'at I tell you w'en I fus' begin? I tole you Brer Rabbit wuz a monstus soon beas'; leas'ways dat's w'at I laid out fer ter tell you. Well, den, honey, don't you go en make no udder kalkalashuns, kaze in dem days Brer Rabbit en his fambly wuz at de head er de gang w'en enny racket wuz on han', en dar dey stayed. 'Fo' you begins fer ter wipe yo' eyes 'bout Brer Rabbit, you wait en see whar'bouts Brer Rabbit gwineter fetch up at. But dat's needer yer ner dar.

"W'en Brer Fox fine Brer Rabbit mixt up wid de Tar-Baby, he feel mighty good, en he roll on de groun' en laff. Bimeby he up'n say, sezee:

" 'Well, I speck I got you dis time, Brer Rabbit,' sezee; 'maybe I ain't, but I speck I is. You been runnin' roun' here sassin' atter me a mighty long time, but I speck you done come ter de een' er de row. You bin cuttin' up yo' capers en bouncin' 'roun' in dis naberhood ontwel you come ter b'leeve yo'se'f de boss er de whole gang. En den youer allers some'rs whar you got no bizness,' sez Brer Fox, sezee. 'Who ax you fer ter come en strike up a 'quaintence wid dish yer Tar-Baby? En who stuck you up dar whar you iz? Nobody in de roun' worril. You des tuck en jam yo'se'f on dat Tar-Baby widout waitin' fer enny invite,' sez Brer Fox, sezee, 'en dar you is, en dar you'll stay twel I fixes up a bresh-pile and fires her up, kaze I'm gwineter bobbycue you dis day, sho,' sez Brer Fox, sezee.

"Den Brer Rabbit talk mighty 'umble.

" 'I don't keer w'at you do wid me, Brer Fox,' sezee, 'so you don't fling me in dat brier-patch. Roas' me, Brer Fox,' sezee, 'but don't fling me in dat brier-patch,' sezee.

" 'Hit's so much trouble fer ter kindle a fire,' sez Brer Fox, sezee, 'dat I speck I'll hatter hang you,' sezee.

" 'Hang me des ez high ez you please, Brer Fox,' sez Brer Rabbit, sezee, 'but do fer de Lord's sake don't fling me in that brier-patch,' sezee.

" 'I ain't got no string,' sez Brer Fox, sezee, 'en now I speck I'll hatter drown you,' sezee.

" 'Drown me des ez deep ez you please, Brer Fox,' sez Brer Rabbit, sezee, 'but do don't fling me in dat brier-patch,' sezee.

" 'Dey ain't no water nigh,' sez Brer Fox, sezee, 'en now I speck I'll hatter skin you,' sezee.

" 'Skin me, Brer Fox,' sez Brer Rabbit, sezee, 'snatch out my eyeballs, t'ar out my years by de roots, en cut off my legs,' sezee, 'but do please, Brer Fox, don't fling me in dat brier-patch,' sezee.

"Co'se Brer Fox wanter hurt Brer Rabbit bad ez he kin, so he cotch 'im by de behime legs en slung 'im right in de middle er de brier-patch. Dar was a considerbul flutter whar Brer Rabbit struck de bushes, en Brer Fox sorter hang 'roun' fer ter see w'at wuz gwineter happen. Bimeby he hear somebody call 'im, en way up de hill he see Brer Rabbit settin' cross-legged on a chinkapin log koamin' de pitch outen his har wid a chip. Den Brer Fox know dat he bin swop off mighty bad. Brer Rabbit wuz bleedzed[1] fer ter fling back some er his sass, en he holler out:

" 'Bred en bawn in a brier-patch, Brer Fox—bred en bawn in a brier-patch!' en wid dat he skip out des ez lively ez a cricket in de embers."

1880

[1]Obliged.

from Free Joe, and Other Georgian Sketches

Free Joe and the Rest of the World

The name of Free Joe strikes humorously upon the ear of memory. It is impossible to say why, for he was the humblest, the simplest, and the most serious of all God's living creatures, sadly lacking in all those elements that suggest the humorous. It is certain, moreover, that in 1850 the sober-minded citizens of the little Georgian village of Hillsborough were not inclined to take a humorous view of Free Joe, and neither his name nor his presence provoked a smile. He was a black atom, drifting hither and thither without an owner, blown about by all the winds of circumstance, and given over to shiftlessness.

The problems of one generation are the paradoxes of a succeeding one, particularly if war, or some such incident, intervenes to clarify the atmosphere and strengthen the understanding. Thus, in 1850, Free Joe represented not only a problem of large concern, but, in the watchful eyes of Hillsborough, he was the embodiment of that vague and mysterious danger that seemed to be forever lurking on the outskirts of slavery, ready to sound a shrill and ghostly signal in the impenetrable swamps, and steal forth under the midnight stars to murder, rapine, and pillage,—a danger always threatening, and yet never assuming shape; intangible, and yet real; impossible, and yet not improbable. Across the serene and smiling front of safety, the pale outlines of the awful shadow of insurrection sometimes fell. With this invisible panorama as a background, it was natural that the figure of Free Joe, simple and humble as it was, should assume undue proportions. Go where he would, do what he might, he could not escape the finger of observation and the kindling eye of suspicion. His lightest words were noted, his slightest actions marked.

Under all the circumstances it was natural that his peculiar condition should reflect itself in his habits and manners. The slaves laughed loudly day by day, but Free Joe rarely laughed. The slaves sang at their work and danced at their frolics, but no one ever heard Free Joe sing or saw him dance. There was something painfully plaintive and appealing in his attitude, something touching in his anxiety to please. He was of the friendliest nature, and seemed to be delighted when he could amuse the little children who had made a playground of the public square. At times he would please them by making his little dog Dan perform all sorts of curious tricks, or he would tell them quaint stories of the beasts of the field and birds of the air; and frequently he was coaxed into relating the story of his own freedom. That story was brief, but tragical.

In the year of our Lord 1840, when a negro-speculator of a sportive turn of mind reached the little village of Hillsborough on his way to the Mississippi region, with a caravan of likely negroes of both sexes, he found much to interest him. In that day and at that time there were a number of young men in the village who had not bound themselves over to repentance for the various misdeeds of the flesh. To these young men the negro-speculator (Major Frampton was his name) proceeded to address himself. He was a Virginian, he declared; and, to prove the statement, he referred all the festively inclined young men of Hillsborough to a barrel of peach-brandy in one of his covered wagons. In the minds of these young men there was less doubt in regard to the age and quality of the brandy than there was in regard to the negro-trader's birthplace. Major Frampton might or might not have been born in the Old Dominion,—that was a matter for consideration and inquiry,—but there could be no question as to the mellow pungency of the peach-brandy.

In his own estimation, Major Frampton was one of the most accomplished of men. He had summered at the Virginia Springs; he had been to Philadelphia, to Washington, to Richmond, to Lynchburg, and to Charleston, and had accumulated a great deal of experience which he found useful. Hillsborough was hid in the woods of Middle Georgia, and its general aspect of innocence impressed him. He looked on the young men who had shown their readiness to test his peach-brandy, as overgrown country boys who needed to be introduced to some of the arts and sciences he had at his command. Thereupon the major pitched his tents, figuratively speaking, and became, for the time being, a part and parcel of the innocence that characterized Hillsborough. A wiser man would doubtless have made the same mistake.

The little village possessed advantages that seemed to be providentially arranged to fit the various enterprises that Major Frampton had in view. There was the auction-block in front of the stuccoed court-house, if he desired to dispose of a few of his negroes; there was a quarter-track, laid out to his hand and in excellent order, if he chose to enjoy the pleasures of horse-racing; there were secluded pine thickets within easy reach, if he desired to indulge in the exciting pastime of cock-fighting; and various lonely and unoccupied rooms in the second story of the tavern, if he cared to challenge the chances of dice or cards.

Major Frampton tried them all with varying luck, until he began his famous game of poker with Judge Alfred Wellington, a stately gentleman with a flowing white beard and mild blue eyes that gave him the appearance of a benevolent patriarch. The history of the game in which Major Frampton and Judge Alfred Wellington took part is something more than a tradition in Hillsborough, for there are still living three or four men who sat around the table and watched its progress. It is said that at various stages of the game Major Frampton would destroy the cards with which they were playing, and send for a new pack, but the result was always the same. The mild blue eyes of Judge Wellington, with few exceptions, continued to overlook "hands" that were invincible—a habit they had acquired during a long and arduous course of training from Saratoga to New Orleans. Major Frampton lost his money, his horses, his wagons, and all his negroes but one, his body-servant. When his misfortune had reached this limit, the major adjourned the game. The sun was shining brightly, and all nature was cheerful. It is said that the major also seemed to be cheerful. However this may be, he visited the courthouse, and executed the papers that gave his body-servant his freedom. This being done, Major Frampton sauntered into a convenient pine thicket, and blew out his brains.

The negro thus freed came to be known as Free Joe. Compelled, under the law, to choose a guardian, he chose Judge Wellington, chiefly because his wife Lucinda was among the negroes won from Major Frampton. For several years Free Joe had what may be called a jovial time. His wife Lucinda was well provided for, and he found it a comparatively easy matter to provide for himself; so that, taking all the circumstances into consideration, it is not matter for astonishment that he became somewhat shiftless.

When Judge Wellington died, Free Joe's troubles began. The judge's negroes, including Lucinda, went to his half-brother, a man named Calderwood, who was a hard master and a rough customer generally,—a man of many eccentricities of mind and character. His neighbors had a habit of alluding to him as "Old Spite"; and the name seemed to fit him so completely, that he was known far and near as "Spite" Calderwood. He probably enjoyed the distinction the name gave him, at any rate, he never resented it, and it was not often that he missed an opportunity to show that he deserved it. Calderwood's place was two or three miles from the village of Hillsborough, and Free Joe visited his wife twice a week, Wednesday and Saturday nights.

One Sunday he was sitting in front of Lucinda's cabin, when Calderwood happened to pass that way.

"Howdy, marster?" said Free Joe, taking off his hat.

"Who are you?" exclaimed Calderwood abruptly, halting and staring at the negro.

"I'm name' Joe, marster. I'm Lucindy's ole man."

"Who do you belong to?"

"Marse John Evans is my gyardeen, marster."

"Big name—gyardeen. Show your pass."

Free Joe produced that document, and Calderwood read it aloud slowly, as if he found it difficult to get at the meaning:

"*To whom it may concern: This is to certify that the boy Joe Frampton has my permission to visit his wife Lucinda.*"

This was dated at Hillsborough, and signed "*John W. Evans.*"

Calderwood read it twice, and then looked at Free Joe, elevating his eyebrows, and showing his discolored teeth.

"Some mighty big words in that there. Evans own this place, I reckon. When's he comin' down to take hold?"

Free Joe fumbled with his hat. He was badly frightened.

"Lucindy says she speck you wouldn't min' my comin', long ez I behave, marster."

Calderwood tore the pass in pieces and flung it away.

"Don't want no free niggers 'round here," he exclaimed. "There's the big road. It'll carry you to town. Don't let me catch you here no more. Now, mind what I tell you."

Free Joe presented a shabby spectacle as he moved off with his little dog Dan slinking at his heels. It should be said in behalf of Dan, however, that his bristles were up, and that he looked back and growled. It may be that the dog had the advantage of insignificance, but it is difficult to conceive how a dog bold enough to raise his bristles under Calderwood's very eyes could be as insignificant as Free Joe. But both the negro and his little dog seemed to give a new and more dismal aspect to forlornness as they turned into the road and went toward Hillsborough.

After this incident Free Joe appeared to have clearer ideas concerning his peculiar condition. He realized the fact that though he was free he was more helpless than any slave. Having no owner, every man was his master. He knew that he was the object of suspicion, and therefore all his slender resources (ah! how pitifully slender they were!) were devoted to winning, not kindness and appreciation, but toleration; all his efforts were in the direction of mitigating the circumstances that tended to make his condition so much worse than that of the negroes around him,—negroes who had friends because they had masters.

So far as his own race was concerned, Free Joe was an exile. If the slaves secretly envied him his freedom (which is to be doubted, considering his miserable condition), they openly despised him, and lost no opportunity to treat him with contumely. Perhaps this was in some measure the result of the attitude which Free Joe chose to maintain toward them. No doubt his instinct taught him that to hold himself aloof from the slaves would be to invite from the whites the toleration which he coveted, and without which even his miserable condition would be rendered more miserable still.

His greatest trouble was the fact that he was not allowed to visit his wife; but he soon found a way out of this difficulty. After he had been ordered away from the Calderwood place, he was in the habit of wandering as far in that direction as prudence would permit. Near the Calderwood place, but not on Calderwood's land, lived an old man named Micajah Staley and his sister Becky Staley. These people were old and very poor. Old Micajah had a palsied arm and hand; but, in spite of this, he managed to earn a precarious living with his turning-lathe.

When he was a slave Free Joe would have scorned these representatives of a class known as poor white trash, but now he found them sympathetic and helpful in various ways. From the back door of their cabin he could hear the Calderwood negroes singing at night, and he sometimes fancied he could distinguish Lucinda's shrill treble rising above the other voices. A large poplar grew in the woods some distance from the Staley cabin, and at the foot of this tree Free Joe would sit for hours with his face turned toward Calderwood's. His little dog Dan would curl up in the leaves near by, and the two seemed to be as comfortable as possible.

One Saturday afternoon Free Joe, sitting at the foot of this friendly poplar, fell asleep. How long he slept, he could not tell; but when he awoke little Dan was licking his face, the moon was shining brightly, and Lucinda his wife stood before him laughing. The dog, seeing that Free Joe was asleep, had grown somewhat impatient, and he concluded to make an excursion to the Calderwood place on his own account. Lucinda was inclined to give the incident a twist in the direction of superstition.

"I'uz settin' down front er de fireplace," she said, "cookin' me some meat, w'en all of a sudden I year sumpin at de do'—scratch, scratch. I tuck'n tu'n de meat over, en make out I aint year it. Bimeby it come dar 'gin—scratch, scratch. I up en open de do', I did, en, bless de Lord! dar wuz little Dan, en it look like ter me dat his ribs done grow tergeer. I gin 'im some bread, en den, w'en he start out, I tuck'n foller 'im, kaze, I say ter myse'f, maybe my nigger man mought be some'rs 'roun'. Dat ar little dog got sense, mon."

Free Joe laughed and dropped his hand lightly on Dan's head. For a long time after that he had no difficulty in seeing his wife. He had only to sit by the poplar-tree until little Dan could run and fetch her. But after a while the other negroes discovered that Lucinda was meeting Free Joe in the woods, and information of the fact soon reached Calderwood's ears. Calderwood was what is called a man of action. He said nothing; but one day he put Lucinda in his buggy, and carried her to Macon, sixty miles away. He carried her to Macon, and came back without her; and nobody in or around Hillsborough, or in that section, ever saw her again.

For many a night after that Free Joe sat in the woods and waited. Little Dan would run merrily off and be gone a long time, but he always came back without Lucinda. This happened over and over again. The "willis-whistlers"[1] would call and call, like phantom huntsmen wandering on a far-off shore; the screech-owl would shake and shiver in the depths of the woods; the night-hawks, sweeping by on noiseless wings, would snap their beaks as though they enjoyed the huge joke of which Free Joe and little Dan were the victims; and the whip-poor-wills would cry to each other through the gloom. Each night seemed to be lonelier than the preceding, but Free Joe's patience was proof against loneliness. There came a time, however, when little Dan refused to go after Lucinda. When Free Joe motioned him in the direction of the Calderwood place, he would simply move about uneasily and whine; then he would curl up in the leaves and make himself comfortable.

One night, instead of going to the poplar-tree to wait for Lucinda, Free Joe went to the Staley cabin, and, in order to make his welcome good, as he expressed it, he carried with him an armful of fat-pine splinters. Miss Becky Staley had a great reputation in those parts as a fortune-teller, and the schoolgirls, as well as older people, often tested her powers in this direction, some in jest and some in earnest. Free Joe placed his humble offering of light-wood in the chimney-corner, and then seated himself on the steps, dropping his hat on the ground outside.

"Miss Becky," he said presently, "whar in de name er gracious you reckon Lucindy is?"

"Well, the Lord he'p the nigger!" exclaimed Miss Becky, in a tone that seemed to reproduce, by some curious agreement of sight with sound, her general aspect of peakedness. "Well, the Lord he'p the nigger! haint you been a-seein' her all this blessed time? She's over at old Spite Calderwood's, if she's anywheres, I reckon."

"No'm, dat I aint, Miss Becky. I aint seen Lucindy in now gwine on mighty nigh a mont'."

"Well, it haint a-gwine to hurt you," said Miss Becky, somewhat sharply. "In my day an' time it wuz allers took to be a bad sign when niggers got to honeyin' 'roun' an' gwine on."

"Yessum," said Free Joe, cheerfully assenting to the proposition—"yessum, dat's so, but me an' my ole 'oman, we 'uz raise tergeer, en dey aint bin many days w'en we 'uz 'way fum one 'n'er like we is now."

"Maybe she's up an' took up wi' some un else," said Micajah Staley from the corner. "You know what the sayin' is, 'New master, new nigger.'"

"Dat's so, dat's de sayin', but tain't wid my ole 'oman like 'tis wid yuther niggers. Me en her wuz des natally raise up tergeer. Dey's lots likelier niggers dan w'at I is," said Free Joe, viewing his shabbiness with a critical eye, "but I knows Lucindy mos' good ez I does little Dan dar—dat I does."

There was no reply to this, and Free Joe continued,

"Miss Becky, I wish you please, ma'am, take en run yo' kyards en see sump'n n'er 'bout Lucindy; kaze ef she sick, I'm gwine dar. Dey ken take en take me up en gimme a stroppin', but I'm gwine dar."

Miss Becky got her cards, but first she picked up a cup, in the bottom of which

[1]The willet, a bird with a loud whistle.

were some coffee-grounds. These she whirled slowly round and round, ending finally by turning the cup upside down on the hearth and allowing it to remain in that position.

"I'll turn the cup first," said Miss Becky, "and then I'll run the cards and see what they say."

As she shuffled the cards the fire on the hearth burned low, and in its fitful light the gray-haired, thin-featured woman seemed to deserve the weird reputation which rumor and gossip had given her. She shuffled the cards for some moments, gazing intently in the dying fire; then, throwing a piece of pine on the coals, she made three divisions of the pack, disposing them about in her lap. Then she took the first pile, ran the cards slowly through her fingers, and studied them carefully. To the first she added the second pile. The study of these was evidently not satisfactory. She said nothing, but frowned heavily; and the frown deepened as she added the rest of the cards until the entire fifty-two had passed in review before her. Though she frowned, she seemed to be deeply interested. Without changing the relative position of the cards, she ran them all over again. Then she threw a larger piece of pine on the fire, shuffled the cards afresh, divided them into three piles, and subjected them to the same careful and critical examination.

"I can't tell the day when I've seed the cards run this a-way," she said after a while. "What is an' what aint, I'll never tell you; but I know what the cards sez."

"W'at does dey say, Miss Becky?" the negro inquired, in a tone the solemnity of which was heightened by its eagerness.

"They er runnin' quare.[2] These here that I'm a-lookin' at," said Miss Becky, "they stan' for the past. Them there, they er the present; and the t'others, they er the future. Here's a bundle,"—tapping the ace of clubs with her thumb,—"an' here's a journey as plain as the nose on a man's face. Here's Lucinda"—

"Whar she, Miss Becky?"

"Here she is—the queen of spades."

Free Joe grinned. The idea seemed to please him immensely.

"Well, well, well!" he exclaimed. "Ef dat don't beat my time! De queen er spades! W'en Lucindy year dat hit'll tickle 'er, sho'!"

Miss Becky continued to run the cards back and forth through her fingers.

"Here's a bundle an' a journey, and here's Lucinda. An' here's ole Spite Calderwood."

She held the cards toward the negro and touched the king of clubs.

"De Lord he'p my soul!" exclaimed Free Joe with a chuckle. "De faver's dar.[3] Yesser, dat's him! W'at de matter 'long wid all un um, Miss Becky?"

The old woman added the second pile of cards to the first, and then the third, still running them through her fingers slowly and critically. By this time the piece of pine in the fireplace had wrapped itself in a mantle of flame illuminating the cabin and throwing into strange relief the figure of Miss Becky as she sat studying the cards. She frowned ominously at the cards and mumbled a few words to herself. Then she dropped her hands in her lap and gazed once more into the fire. Her

[2]Queer.

[3]*I.e.,* It looks like him.

shadow danced and capered on the wall and floor behind her, as if, looking over her shoulder into the future, it could behold a rare spectacle. After a while she picked up the cup that had been turned on the hearth. The coffee-grounds, shaken around, presented what seemed to be a most intricate map.

"Here's the journey," said Miss Becky, presently; "here's the big road, here's rivers to cross, here's the bundle to tote." She paused and sighed. "They haint no names writ here, an' what it all means I'll never tell you. Cajy, I wish you'd be so good as to han' me my pipe."

"I haint no hand wi' the kyards," said Cajy, as he handed the pipe, "but I reckon I can patch out your misinformation, Becky, bekaze the other day, whiles I was a-finishin' up Mizzers Perdue's rollin'-pin, I hearn a rattlin' in the road. I looked out, an' Spite Calderwood was a-drivin' by in his buggy an' thar sot Lucinda by him. It'd in-about drapt out er my min'."

Free Joe sat on the door-sill and fumbled at his hat, flinging it from one hand to the other.

"You aint see um gwine back, is you, Mars Cajy?" he asked after a while.

"Ef they went back by this road," said Mr. Staley, with the air of one who is accustomed to weigh well his words, "it must 'a' bin endurin' of the time whiles I was asleep, bekaze I haint bin no furder from my shop than to yon bed."

"Well, sir!" exclaimed Free Joe in an awed tone, which Mr. Staley seemed to regard as a tribute to his extraordinary powers of statement.

"Ef it's my beliefs you want," continued the old man, "I'll pitch 'em at you fair and free. My beliefs is that Spite Calderwood is gone an' took Lucindy outen the county. Bless your heart and soul! when Spite Calderwood meets the Old Boy[4] in the road they'll be a turrible scuffle. You mark what I tell you."

Free Joe, still fumbling with his hat, rose and leaned against the doorfacing. He seemed to be embarrassed. Presently he said,

"I speck I better be gittin' 'long. Nex' time I see Lucindy, I'm gwine tell 'er w'at Miss Becky say 'bout de queen er spades—dat I is. Ef dat don't tickle 'er, dey ain't no nigger 'oman never bin tickle'."

He paused a moment, as though waiting for some remark or comment, some confirmation of misfortune, or, at the very least, some endorsement of his suggestion that Lucinda would be greatly pleased to know that she had figured as the queen of spades; but neither Miss Becky nor her brother said any thing.

"One minnit ridin' in the buggy 'longside er Mars Spite, en de nex' highfalutin' 'roun' playin' de queen er spades. Mon, deze yer nigger gals gittin' up in de pictur's; dey sholy is."

With a brief "Good-night, Miss Becky, Mars Cajy," Free Joe went out into the darkness, followed by little Dan. He made his way to the poplar, where Lucinda had been in the habit of meeting him, and sat down. He sat there a long time; he sat there until little Dan, growing restless, trotted off in the direction of the Calderwood place. Dozing against the poplar, in the gray dawn of the morning Free Joe heard Spite Calderwood's fox-hounds in full cry a mile away.

[4]The devil.

"Shoo!" he exclaimed, scratching his head, and laughing to himself, "dem ar dogs is des a-warmin' dat old fox up."

But it was Dan the hounds were after, and the little dog came back no more. Free Joe waited and waited, until he grew tired of waiting. He went back the next night and waited, and for many nights thereafter. His waiting was in vain, and yet he never regarded it as in vain. Careless and shabby as he was, Free Joe was thoughtful enough to have his theory. He was convinced that little Dan had found Lucinda, and that some night when the moon was shining brightly through the trees, the dog would rouse him from his dreams as he sat sleeping at the foot of the poplar-tree, and he would open his eyes and behold Lucinda standing over him, laughing merrily as of old; and then he thought what fun they would have about the queen of spades.

How many long nights Free Joe waited at the foot of the poplar-tree for Lucinda and little Dan, no one can ever know. He kept no account of them, and they were not recorded by Micajah Staley nor by Miss Becky. The season ran into summer and then into fall. One night he went to the Staley cabin, cut the two old people an armful of wood, and seated himself on the door-steps, where he rested. He was always thankful—and proud, as it seemed—when Miss Becky gave him a cup of coffee, which she was sometimes thoughtful enough to do. He was especially thankful on this particular night.

"You er still layin' off for to strike up wi' Lucindy out thar in the woods, I reckon," said Micajah Staley, smiling grimly. The situation was not without its humorous aspects.

"Oh, dey er comin', Mars Cajy, dey er comin', sho," Free Joe replied. "I boun' you dey'll come; en w'en dey does come, I'll des take en fetch um yer, whar you kin see um wid your own eyes, you en Miss Becky."

"No," said Mr. Staley, with a quick and emphatic gesture of disapproval. "Don't! don't fetch 'em anywheres. Stay right wi' 'em as long as may be."

Free Joe chuckled, and slipped away into the night, while the two old people sat gazing in the fire. Finally Micajah spoke.

"Look at that nigger; look at 'im. He's pine-blank as happy now as a killdee[5] by a mill-race. You can't 'faze 'em. I'd in-about give up my t'other hand ef I could stan' flat-footed, an' grin at trouble like that there nigger."

"Niggers is niggers," said Miss Becky, smiling grimly, "an' you can't rub it out; yit I lay I've seed a heap of white people lots meaner'n Free Joe. He grins,—an' that's nigger,—but I've ketched his under jaw a-trimblin' when Lucindy's name uz brung up. An' I tell you," she went on, bridling up a little, and speaking with almost fierce emphasis, "the Old Boy's done sharpened his claws for Spite Calderwood. You'll see it."

"Me, Rebecca?" said Mr. Staley, hugging his palsied arm; "me? I hope not."

"Well, you'll know it then," said Miss Becky, laughing heartily at her brother's look of alarm.

[5]The killdeer.

The next morning Micajah Staley had occasion to go into the woods after a piece of timber. He saw Free Joe sitting at the foot of the poplar, and the sight vexed him somewhat.

"Git up from there," he cried, "an' go an' arn your livin'. A mighty purty pass it's come to, when great big buck niggers can lie a-snorin' in the woods all day, when t'other folks is got to be up an' a-gwine. Git up from there!"

Receiving no response, Mr. Staley went to Free Joe, and shook him by the shoulder; but the negro made no response. He was dead. His hat was off, his head was bent, and a smile was on his face. It was as if he had bowed and smiled when death stood before him, humble to the last. His clothes were ragged; his hands were rough and callous; his shoes were literally tied together with strings; he was shabby in the extreme. A passer-by, glancing at him, could have no idea that such a humble creature had been summoned as a witness before the Lord God of Hosts.

1887

Charles Waddell Chesnutt 1858–1932

Charles W. Chesnutt was born in Cleveland, Ohio, the son of free blacks who had emigrated from Fayetteville, N.C. When he was eight years old, his parents returned to Fayetteville, where Charles worked in the family grocery store and attended a school founded by the Freedmen's Bureau. Financial necessity required that he begin a teaching career while still a teenager. By 1880 he had become principal of the Fayetteville State Normal School for Negroes. Seeking broader economic opportunity and a chance to hone the literary skills that he had begun to develop in his private journals, Chesnutt moved to the North in 1883, settling his family in Cleveland in 1884. There he passed the state bar examination and founded his own court-reporting firm. His business success and prominence in civic affairs made him one of Cleveland's most respected citizens.

"The Goophered Grapevine" was Chesnutt's first nationally recognized work of fiction. Written in black dialect and set in the Old South, "The Goophered Grapevine" appeared to be another contribution to the popular "plantation literature" of late-nineteenth-century America, in which slavery and the plantation system of the antebellum South were sentimentalized. But this story, like all of Chesnutt's "conjure" tales, displayed an unusually intimate knowledge of black southern folk culture and an appreciation of the importance of voodoo practices to the slave community. The teller of the conjure tales, Uncle Julius, is also a unique figure in southern plantation literature, a former slave who recalls the past not to celebrate it but to exploit white people's sentimentality about it. The publication of "The Goophered Grapevine" marked the first time that a short story by an African American had appeared in the prestigious *Atlantic Monthly.* After subsequent tales in this vein were accepted by other magazines, Chesnutt reached an agreement with Houghton Mifflin to publish his first work of fiction, *The Conjure Woman,* a collection of stories. Its reception was positive enough to convince the Boston firm to publish a second collection of Chesnutt's short fiction, *The Wife of His Youth and Other Stories of the Color Line.* This volume treated a broader range of southern and northern racial experience than any previous delineator of black American life in literature had attempted. Typical of Chesnutt's interest in life on the color line in the North is "A Matter of Principle," a satiric study of racial prejudice within the light-skinned, aspiring black middle class of Cleveland. "The Passing of Grandison" debunks the myth of the faithful slave retainer of the Old South, revealing beneath the mask of the docile slave a crafty and determined individual much more committed to the welfare of his family and himself than to his supposedly beloved master.

Chesnutt's short story collections provided his entering wedge into the world of professional authorship. In 1900 Houghton Mifflin published his first novel, *The House Behind the Cedars,* the story of two African Americans who pass for white in the post-war South. The novel testifies to Chesnutt's sensitivity to the psychological and social dilemmas that faced persons of mixed blood. His second novel, *The Marrow of Tradition,* is based on the Wilmington, N.C., racial massacre of 1898. Hoping to create the *Uncle Tom's Cabin* of his generation, Chesnutt wrote into his book a plea for racial justice that impressed the noted critic William Dean Howells and roused considerable controversy among reviewers. But when *The Marrow of Tradition* did not sell widely, Chesnutt was forced to give up the effort he began two years earlier to support his family as a man of letters. His final novel appeared in 1905. *The Colonel's Dream* portrays an idealist's attempt to uplift a North Carolina town mired in economic depression and social injustice. The tragic outcome of the Colonel's program did not appeal to the few reviewers who commented on the novel.

During the later years of his life Chesnutt continued to write and publish occasional short stories, but he was largely eclipsed in the 1920s by the writers of the New Negro Renaissance. Nevertheless, he was awarded the Spingarn Medal in 1928 by the National Association for the Advancement of Colored People for his pioneering literary efforts on behalf of the African American struggle. In the last twenty-five years Chesnutt has been recognized as a major innovator in the tradition of African American fiction. He showed his literary successors new ways of writing about black folk culture in the South and the embryonic black middle class in the North. His fiction participated in the deromanticizing of southern life that made possible a realistic literary tradition in the South. Perhaps most important, he recognized the genuinely comic potential of the black writer as manipulator of and ironic commentator on the myths and presumptions of the mainstream American reader.

William L. Andrews
University of North Carolina–Chapel Hill

PRIMARY WORKS

The Conjure Woman, 1899; *The Wife of His Youth and Other Stories of the Color Line,* 1899; *The House Behind the Cedars,* 1900; *The Marrow of Tradition,* 1901; *The Colonel's Dream,* 1905; *Mandy Oxendine,* 1997; *Paul Marchand,* 1999; *The Quarry,* 1999; *Essays and Speeches,* 1999.

The Goophered Grapevine

Some years ago my wife was in poor health, and our family doctor, in whose skill and honesty I had implicit confidence, advised a change of climate. I shared, from an unprofessional standpoint, his opinion that the raw winds, the chill rains, and the violent changes of temperature that characterized the winters in the region of the Great

Lakes tended to aggravate my wife's difficulty, and would undoubtedly shorten her life if she remained exposed to them. The doctor's advice was that we seek, not a temporary place of sojourn, but a permanent residence, in a warmer and more equable climate. I was engaged at the time in grape-culture in northern Ohio, and, as I liked the business and had given it much study, I decided to look for some other locality suitable for carrying it on. I thought of sunny France, of sleepy Spain, of Southern California, but there were objections to them all. It occurred to me that I might find what I wanted in some one of our own Southern States. It was a sufficient time after the war for conditions in the South to have become somewhat settled; and I was enough of a pioneer to start a new industry, if I could not find a place where grape-culture had been tried. I wrote to a cousin who had gone into the turpentine business in central North Carolina. He assured me, in response to my inquiries, that no better place could be found in the South than the State and neighborhood where he lived; the climate was perfect for health, and, in conjunction with the soil, ideal for grape-culture; labor was cheap, and land could be bought for a mere song. He gave us a cordial invitation to come and visit him while we looked into the matter. We accepted the invitation, and after several days of leisurely travel, the last hundred miles of which were up a river on a sidewheel steamer, we reached our destination, a quaint old town, which I shall call Patesville, because, for one reason, that is not its name. There was a red brick market-house in the public square, with a tall tower, which held a four-faced clock that struck the hours, and from which there pealed out a curfew at nine o'clock. There were two or three hotels, a court-house, a jail, stores, offices, and all the appurtenances of a county seat and a commercial emporium; for while Patesville numbered only four or five thousand inhabitants, of all shades of complexion, it was one of the principal towns in North Carolina, and had a considerable trade in cotton and naval stores. This business activity was not immediately apparent to my unaccustomed eyes. Indeed, when I first saw the town, there brooded over it a calm that seemed almost sabbatic in its restfulness, though I learned later on that underneath its somnolent exterior the deeper currents of life—love and hatred, joy and despair, ambition and avarice, faith and friendship—flowed not less steadily than in livelier latitudes.

We found the weather delightful at that season, the end of summer, and were hospitably entertained. Our host was a man of means and evidently regarded our visit as a pleasure, and we were therefore correspondingly at our ease, and in a position to act with the coolness of judgment desirable in making so radical a change in our lives. My cousin placed a horse and buggy at our disposal, and himself acted as our guide until I became somewhat familiar with the country.

I found that grape-culture, while it had never been carried on to any great extent, was not entirely unknown in the neighborhood. Several planters thereabouts had attempted it on a commercial scale, in former years, with greater or less success; but like most Southern industries, it had felt the blight of war and had fallen into desuetude.

I went several times to look at a place that I thought might suit me. It was a plantation of considerable extent, that had formerly belonged to a wealthy man by the name of McAdoo. The estate had been for years involved in litigation between disputing heirs, during which period shiftless cultivation had well-nigh exhausted the soil. There had been a vineyard of some extent on the place, but it had not been attended to since the war, and had lapsed into utter neglect. The vines—here partly supported by decayed and broken-down trellises, there twining themselves among the branches of the slender saplings which had sprung up among them—grew in wild and unpruned luxuriance, and the few scattered grapes they bore were the undisputed prey of the first comer. The site was admirably adapted to grape-raising; the soil, with a little attention, could not have been better; and with the native grape, the luscious scuppernong, as my main reliance in the beginning, I felt sure that I could introduce and cultivate successfully a number of other varieties.

One day I went over with my wife to show her the place. We drove out of the town over a long wooden bridge that spanned a spreading mill-pond, passed the long whitewashed fence surrounding the county fair-ground, and struck into a road so sandy that the horse's feet sank to the fetlocks. Our route lay partly up hill and partly down, for we were in the sand-hill county; we drove past cultivated farms, and then by abandoned fields grown up in scrub-oak and short-leaved pine, and once or twice through the solemn aisles of the virgin forest, where the tall pines, well-nigh meeting over the narrow road, shut out the sun, and wrapped us in cloistral solitude. Once, at a cross-roads, I was in doubt as to the turn to take, and we sat there waiting ten minutes—we had already caught some of the native infection of restfulness—for some human being to come along, who could direct us on our way. At length a little negro girl appeared, walking straight as an arrow, with a piggin[1] full of water on her head. After a little patient investigation, necessary to overcome the child's shyness, we learned what we wished to know, and at the end of about five miles from the town reached our destination.

We drove between a pair of decayed gateposts—the gate itself had long since disappeared—and up a straight sandy lane, between two lines of rotting rail fence, partly concealed by jimsonweeds and briers, to the open space where a dwelling-house had once stood, evidently a spacious mansion, if we might judge from the ruined chimneys that were still standing, and the brick pillars on which the sills rested. The house itself, we had been informed, had fallen a victim to the fortunes of war.

We alighted from the buggy, walked about the yard for a while, and then wandered off into the adjoining vineyard. Upon Annie's complaining of weariness I led the way back to the yard, where a pine log, lying under a spreading elm, afforded a shady though somewhat hard seat. One end of the log was already occupied by a venerable-looking colored man. He held on his knees a hat full of grapes, over which he was smacking his lips with great gusto, and a pile of grape-skins near him indicated that the performance was no new thing. We approached him at an angle from the rear, and were close to him before he perceived us. He respectfully rose as we drew near, and was moving away, when I begged him to keep his seat.

"Don't let us disturb you," I said. "There is plenty of room for us all."

He resumed his seat with somewhat of embarrassment. While he had been standing, I had observed that he was a tall man, and, though slightly bowed by the weight of years, apparently quite vigorous. He was not entirely black, and this fact, together with the quality of his hair, which was about six inches long and very bushy, except on the top of his head, where he was quite bald, suggested a slight strain of

[1]A wooden pail.

other than negro blood. There was a shrewdness in his eyes, too, which was not altogether African, and which, as we afterwards learned from experience, was indicative of a corresponding shrewdness in his character. He went on eating the grapes, but did not seem to enjoy himself quite so well as he had apparently done before he became aware of our presence.

"Do you live around here?" I asked, anxious to put him at his ease.

"Yas, suh. I lives des ober yander, behine de nex' san'-hill, on de Lumberton plank-road."

"Do you know anything about the time when this vineyard was cultivated?"

"Lawd bless you, suh, I knows all about it. Dey ain' na'er a man in dis settlement w'at won' tell you ole Julius McAdoo 'uz bawn en raise' on dis yer same plantation. Is you de Norv'n gemman w'at 's gwine ter buy de ole vimya'd?"

"I am looking at it," I replied; "but I don't know that I shall care to buy unless I can be reasonably sure of making something out of it."

"Well, suh, you is a stranger ter me, en I is a stranger ter you, en we is bofe strangers ter one anudder, but 'f I 'uz in yo' place, I wouldn' buy dis vimya'd."

"Why not?" I asked.

"Well, I dunno whe'r you b'lieves in cunj'in' er not,—some er de w'ite folks don't, er says dey don't,—but de truf er de matter is dat dis yer ole vimya'd is goophered."

"Is what?" I asked, not grasping the meaning of this unfamiliar word.

"Is goophered,—cunju'd, bewitch'."

He imparted this information with such solemn earnestness, and with such an air of confidential mystery, that I felt somewhat interested, while Annie was evidently much impressed, and drew closer to me.

"How do you know it is bewitched?" I asked.

"I wouldn' spec' fer you ter b'lieve me 'less you know all 'bout de fac's. But ef you en young miss dere doan' min' lis'nin' ter a ole nigger run on a minute er two w'ile you er restin', I kin 'splain to you how it all happen'."

We assured him that we would be glad to hear how it all happened, and he began to tell us. At first the current of his memory—or imagination—seemed somewhat sluggish; but as his embarrassment wore off, his language flowed more freely, and the story acquired perspective and coherence. As he became more and more absorbed in the narrative, his eyes assumed a dreamy expression, and he seemed to lose sight of his auditors, and to be living over again in monologue his life on the old plantation.

"Ole Mars Dugal' McAdoo," he began, "bought dis place long many years befo' de wah, en I 'member well w'en he sot out all dis yer part er de plantation in scuppernon's. De vimes growed monst'us fas', en Mars Dugal' made a thousan' gallon er scuppernon' wine eve'y year.

"Now, ef dey's an'thing a nigger lub, nex' ter 'possum, en chick'n, en wattermillyums, it's scuppernon's. Dey ain' nuffin dat kin stan' up side'n de scuppernon' fer sweetness; sugar ain't a suckumstance ter scuppernon'. W'en de season is nigh 'bout ober, en de grapes begin ter swivel up des a little wid de wrinkles er ole age,—w'en de skin git sof' en brown,—den de scuppernon' make you smack yo' lip en roll yo' eye en wush fer mo'; so I reckon it ain' very 'stonishin' dat niggers lub scuppernon'.

"Dey wuz a sight er niggers in de naberhood er de vimya'd. Dere wuz ole Mars Henry Brayboy's niggers, en ole Mars Jeems McLean's niggers, en Mars Dugal's own niggers; den dey wuz a settlement er free niggers en po' buckrahs[2] down by de Wim'l'ton Road, en Mars Dugal' had de only vimya'd in de naberhood. I reckon it ain' so much so nowadays, but befo' de wah, in slab'ry times, a nigger didn' mine goin' fi' er ten mile in a night, w'en dey wuz sump'n good ter eat at de yuther een'.

"So atter a w'ile Mars Dugal' begin ter miss his scuppernon's. Co'se he 'cuse' de niggers er it, but dey all 'nied it ter de las'. Mars Dugal' sot spring guns en steel traps, en he en de oberseah sot up nights once't er twice't, tel one night Mars Dugal'—he 'uz a monst'us keerless man—got his leg shot full er cow-peas. But somehow er nudder dey could n' nebber ketch none er de niggers. I dunner how it happen, but it happen des like I tell you, en de grapes kep' on a-goin' des de same.

"But bimeby ole Mars Dugal' fix' up a plan ter stop it. Dey wuz a cunjuh 'oman livin' down 'mongs' de free niggers on de Wim'l'ton Road, en all de darkies fum Rockfish ter Beaver Crick wuz feared er her. She would wuk de mos' powerfulles' kin' er goopher,—could make people hab fits, er rheumatiz, er make 'em des dwinel away en die; en dey say she went out ridin' de niggers at night, fer she wuz a witch 'sides bein' a cunjuh 'oman. Mars Dugal' hearn 'bout Aun' Peggy's doin's, en begun ter 'flect whe'r er no he couldn' git her ter he'p him keep de niggers off'n de grape vimes. One day in de spring er de year, ole miss pack' up a basket er chick'n en poun'-cake, en a bottle er scuppernon' wine, en Mars Dugal' tuk it in his buggy en driv ober ter Aun' Peggy's cabin. He tuk de basket in, en had a long talk wid Aun' Peggy.

"De nex' day Aun' Peggy come up ter de vimya'd. De niggers seed her slippin' 'round', en dey soon foun' out what she 'uz doin' dere. Mars Dugal' had hi'ed her ter goopher de grapevimes. She sa'ntered 'roun' 'mongs' de vimes, en tuk a leaf fum dis one, en a grape-hull fum dat one, en a grape-seed fum anudder one; en den a little twig fum here, en a little pinch er dirt fum dere,—en put it all in a big black bottle, wid a snake's toof en a speckle' hen's gall en some ha'rs fum a black cat's tail, en den fill' de bottle wid scuppernon' wine. W'en she got de goopher all ready en fix', she tuk 'n went out in de woods en buried it under de root uv a red oak tree, en den come back en tole one er de niggers she done goopher de grapevimes, en a'er a nigger w'at eat dem grapes 'ud be sho ter die inside'n twel' mont's.

"Atter dat de niggers let de scuppernon's 'lone, en Mars Dugal' didn' hab no 'casion ter fine no mo' fault; en de season wuz mos' gone, w'en a strange gemman stop at de plantation one night ter see Mars Dugal' on some business; en his coachman, seein' de scuppernon's growin' so nice en sweet, slip 'roun' behine de smokehouse, en et all de scuppernon's he could hole. Nobody didn' notice it at de time, but dat night, on de way home, de gemman's hoss runned away en kill' de coachman. W'en we hearn de noos, Aun' Lucy, de cook, she up'n say she seed de strange nigger eat'n' er de scuppernon's behine de smokehouse; en den we knowed de goopher had b'en er wukkin'. Den one er de nigger chilluns runned away fum de quarters one day, en got in de scuppernon's, en died de nex' week. W'ite folks say he die' er de fevuh, but de niggers knowed it wuz de goopher. So you k'n be sho de darkies didn' hab much ter do wid dem scuppernon' vimes.

"W'en de scuppernon' season 'uz ober fer dat year, Mars Dugal' foun' he had made fifteen hund'ed gallon er wine; en one er de niggers hearn him laffin' wid de

[2]Whites regarded as of the lowest class by blacks.

oberseah fit ter kill, en sayin' dem fifteen hund'ed gallon er wine wuz monst'us good intrus' on de ten dollars he laid out on de vimya'd. So I 'low ez he paid Aun' Peggy ten dollars fer to goopher de grapevimes.

"De goopher didn' wuk no mo' tel de nex' summer, w'en 'long to'ds de middle er de season one er de fiel' han's died; en ez dat lef' Mars Dugal' sho't er han's, he went off ter town fer ter buy anudder. He fotch de noo nigger home wid 'im. He wuz er ole nigger, er de color er a gingy-cake, en ball ez a hoss-apple on de top er his head. He wuz a peart ole nigger, do', en could do a big day's wuk.

"Now it happen dat one er de niggers on de nex' plantation, one er ole Mars Henry Brayboy's niggers, had runned away de day befo', en tuk ter de swamp, en ole Mars Dugal' en some er de yuther nabor w'ite folks had gone out wid dere guns en dere dogs fer ter he'p 'em hunt fer de nigger; en de han's on our own plantation wuz all so flusterated dat we fuhgot ter tell de noo han' 'bout de goopher on de scuppernon' vimes. Co'se he smell de grapes en see de vimes, an atter dahk de fus' thing he done wuz ter slip off ter de grapevimes 'dout sayin' nuffin ter nobody. Nex' mawnin' he tole some er de niggers 'bout de fine bait er scuppernon' he et de night befo'.

"W'en dey tole 'im 'bout de goopher on de grapevimes, he 'uz dat tarrified dat he turn pale, en look des like he gwine ter die right in his tracks. De oberseah come up en axed w'at 'uz de matter; en w'en dey tole 'im Henry be'n eatin' er de scuppernon's, en got de goopher on 'im, he gin Henry a big drink er w'iskey, en 'low dat de nex' rainy day he take 'im ober ter Aun' Peggy's, en see ef she wouldn' take de goopher off'n him, seein' ez he didn' know nuffin erbout it tel he done et de grapes.

"Sho nuff, it rain de nex' day, en de oberseah went ober ter Aun' Peggy's wid Henry. En Aun' Peggy say dat bein' ez Henry didn' know 'bout de goopher, en et de grapes in ign'ance er de conseq'ences, she reckon she mought be able fer ter take de goopher of'n him. So she fotch out er bottle wid some cunjuh medicine in it, en po'd some out in a go'd fer Henry ter drink. He manage ter git it down; he say it tas'e like whiskey wid sump'n bitter in it. She 'lowed dat 'ud keep de goopher off'n him tel de spring; but w'en de sap begin ter rise in de grapevimes he ha' ter come en see her ag'in, en she tell him w'at e's ter do.

"Nex' spring, w'en de sap commence' ter rise in de scuppernon' vime, Henry tuk a ham one night. Whar'd he git de ham? *I* doan know; dey wa'n't no hams on de plantation 'cep'n' w'at 'uz in de smoke-house, but *I* never see Henry 'bout de smokehouse. But ez I wuz a-sayin', he tuk de ham ober ter Aun' Peggy's; en Aun' Peggy tole 'im dat w'en Mars Dugal' begin ter prune de grapevimes, he mus' go en take 'n scrape off de sap whar it ooze out'n de cut een's er de vimes, en 'n'int his ball head wid it; en ef he do dat once't a year de goopher wouldn' wuk agin 'im long ez he done it. En bein' ez he fotch her de ham, she fix' it so he kin eat all de scuppernon' he want.

"So Henry 'n'int his head wid de sap out'n de big grapevime des ha'fway 'twix' de quarters en de big house, en de goopher nebber wuk again him dat summer. But de beatenes' thing you eber see happen ter Henry. Up ter dat time he wuz ez ball ez a sweeten' 'tater, but des ez soon ez de young leaves begun ter come out on de grapevimes, de ha'r begun ter grow out on Henry's head, en by de middle er de summer he had de bigges' head er ha'r on de plantation. Befo' dat, Henry had tol'able good ha'r 'roun' de aidges, but soon ez de young grapes begun ter come, Henry's ha'r begun to quirl all up in little balls, des like dis yer reg'lar grapy ha'r, en by de time de grapes got ripe his head look des like a bunch er grapes. Combin' it didn' do no good; he wuk at it ha'f de night wid er Jim Crow,[3] en think he git it straighten' out, but in de mawnin' de grapes 'ud be dere des de same. So he gin it up, en tried ter keep de grapes down by havin' his ha'r cut sho't.

"But dat wa'n't de quares' thing 'bout de goopher. When Henry come ter de plantation, he wuz gittin' a little ole an stiff in de j'ints. But dat summer he got des ez spry en libely ez any young nigger on de plantation; fac', he got so biggity dat Mars Jackson, de oberseah, ha' ter th'eaten ter whip 'im, ef he didn' stop cuttin' up his didos en behave hisse'f. But de mos' cur'ouses' thing happen' in de fall, when de sap begin ter go down in de grapevimes. Fus', when de grapes 'uz gethered, de knots begun ter straighten out'n Henry's ha'r; en w'en de leaves begin ter fall, Henry's ha'r 'mence' ter drap out; en when de vimes 'uz bar', Henry's head wuz baller 'n it wuz in de spring, en he begin ter git ole en stiff in de j'ints ag'in, en paid no mo' 'tention ter de gals dyoin' er de whole winter. En nex' spring, w'en he rub de sap on ag'in, he got young ag'in, en so soopl en libely dat none er de young niggers on de plantation couldn' jump, ner dance, ner hoe ez much cotton ez Henry. But in de fall er de year his grapes 'mence' ter straighten out, en his j'ints ter git stiff, en his ha'r drap off, en de rheumatiz begin ter wrastle wid 'im.

"Now, ef you 'd 'a' knowed ole Mars Dugal' McAdoo, you'd 'a' knowed dat it ha' ter be a mighty rainy day when he couldn' fine sump'n fer his niggers ter do, en it ha' ter be a mighty little hole he couldn' crawl thoo, en ha' ter be a monst'us cloudy night when a dollar git by him in de dahkness; en w'en he see how Henry git young in de spring en ole in de fall, he 'lowed ter hisse'f ez how he could make mo' money out'n Henry dan by wukkin' him in de cotton-fiel'. 'Long de nex' spring, atter de sap 'mence' ter rise, en Henry 'n'int 'is head en sta'ted fer ter git young en soopl, Mars Dugal' up 'n tuk Henry ter town, en sole 'im fer fifteen hunder' dollars. Co'se de man w'at bought Henry didn' know nuffin 'bout de goopher, en Mars Dugal' didn' see no 'casion fer ter tell 'im. Long to'ds de fall, w'en de sap went down, Henry begin ter git ole ag'in same ez yuzhal, en his noo marster begin ter git skeered les'n he gwine ter lose his fifteen-hunder'-dollar nigger. He sent fer a mighty fine doctor, but de med'cine didn' 'pear ter do no good; de goopher had a good holt. Henry tole de doctor 'bout de goopher, but de doctor des laff at 'im.

"One day in de winter Mars Dugal' went ter town, en wuz santerin' 'long de Main Street, when who should he meet but Henry's noo marster. Dey said 'Hoddy,' en Mars Dugal' ax 'im ter hab a seegyar; en atter dey run on awhile 'bout de craps en de weather, Mars Dugal' ax 'im, sorter keerless, like ez ef he des thought of it,—

"'How you like de nigger I sole you las' spring?'

"Henry's marster shuck his head en knock de ashes off'n his seegyar.

"'Spec' I made a bad bahgin when I bought dat nigger. Henry done good wuk all de summer, but sence de fall set in he 'pears ter be sorter pinin' away. Dey ain' nuffin pertickler de matter wid 'im—leastways de doctor say so—'cep'n' a tech er de rheumatiz; but his ha'r is all fell out, en ef he don't pick up his strenk mighty soon, I spec' I'm gwine ter lose 'im.'

[3] "A small card, resembling a currycomb in construction, and used by negroes in the rural districts instead of a comb." [Chesnutt's note.]

"Dey smoked on awhile, en bimeby ole mars say, 'Well, a bahgin 's a bahgin, but you en me is good fren's, en I doan wan' ter see you lose all de money you paid fer dat nigger; en ef w'at you say is so, en I ain't 'sputin' it, he ain't wuf much now. I 'spec's you wukked him too ha'd dis summer, er e'se de swamps down here don't agree wid de san'-hill nigger. So you des lemme know, en ef he gits any wusser I'll be willin' ter gib yer five hund'ed dollars fer 'im, en take my chances on his livin'.'

"Sho 'nuff, when Henry begun ter draw up wid de rheumatiz en it look like he gwine ter die fer sho, his noo marster sen' fer Mars Dugal', en Mars Dugal' gin him what he promus, en brung Henry home ag'in. He tuk good keer uv 'im dyoin' er de winter,—give 'im w'iskey ter rub his rheumatiz, en terbacker ter smoke, en all he want ter eat,—'caze a nigger w'at he could make a thousan' dollars a year off'n didn' grow on eve'y huckleberry bush.

"Nex' spring, w'en de sap ris en Henry's ha'r commence' ter sprout, Mars Dugal' sole 'im ag'in, down in Robeson County dis time; en he kep' dat sellin' business up fer five year er mo'. Henry nebber say nuffin 'bout de goopher ter his noo marsters, 'caze he know he gwine ter be tuk good keer uv de nex' winter, w'en Mars Dugal' buy him back. En Mars Dugal' made 'nuff money off'n Henry ter buy anudder plantation ober on Beaver Crick.

"But 'long 'bout de een' er dat five year dey come a stranger ter stop at de plantation. De fus' day he 'uz dere he went out wid Mars Dugal' en spent all de mawnin' lookin' ober de vimya'd, en atter dinner dey spent all de evenin' playing' kya'ds. De niggers soon 'skiver' dat he wuz a Yankee, en dat he come down ter Norf C'lina fer ter l'arn de w'ite folks how to raise grapes en make wine. He promus Mars Dugal' he c'd make de grapevimes b'ar twice't ez many grapes, en dat de noo winepress he wuz a-sellin' would make mo' d'n twice't ez many gallons er wine. En ole Mars Dugal' des drunk it all in, des 'peared ter be bewitch' wid dat Yankee. W'en de darkies see dat Yankee runnin' 'roun' de vimya'd en diggin' under de grapevimes, dey shuk dere heads, en 'lowed dat dey feared Mars Dugal' losin' his min'. Mars Dugal' had all de dirt dug away fum under de roots er all de scuppernon' vimes, an' let 'em stan' dat away fer a week er mo'. Den dat Yankee made de niggers fix up a mixtry er lime en ashes en manyo, en po' it 'roun' de roots er de grapevimes. Den he 'vise Mars Dugal' fer ter trim de vimes close't, en Mars Dugal' tuck 'n done eve'ything de Yankee tole him ter do. Dyoin' all er dis time, mind yer, dis yer Yankee wuz libbin' off'n de fat er de lan', at de big house, en playin' kya'ds wid Mars Dugal' eve'y night; en dey say Mars Dugal' los' mo'n a thousan' dollars dyoin' er de week dat Yankee wuz a-ruinin' de grapevimes.

"W'en de sap ris nex' spring, ole Henry 'n'inted his head ez yuzhal, en his ha'r 'mence' ter grow des de same ez it done eve'y year. De scuppernon' vimes growed monst's fas', en de leaves wuz greener en thicker dan dey eber be'n dyoin' my remem'b'ance; en Henry's ha'r growed out thicker dan eber, en he 'peared ter git younger 'n younger, en soopler 'n soopler; en seein' ez he wuz sho't er han's dat spring, havin' tuk in consid'able noo groun', Mars Dugal' 'cluded he wouldn' sell Henry 'tel he git de crap in en de cotton chop'. So he kep' Henry on de plantation.

"But 'long 'bout time fer de grapes ter come on de scuppernon' vimes, dey 'peared ter come a change ober 'em; de leaves withered en swivel' up, en de young grapes turn' yaller, en bimeby eve'ybody on de plantation could see dat de whole vimya'd wuz dyin'. Mars Dugal' tuk 'n water de vimes en done all he could, but 't wa'n' no use: dat Yankee had done bus' de watermillyum. One time de vimes picked up a bit, en Mars Dugal' 'lowed dey wuz gwine ter come out ag'in; but dat Yankee done dug too close under de roots, en prune de branches too close ter de vime, en all dat lime en ashes done burn' de life out'n de vimes, en dey des kep' a-with'in' en a-swivelin'.

"All dis time de goopher wuz a-wukkin'. When de vimes sta'ted ter wither, Henry 'mence' ter complain er his rheumatiz; en when de leaves begin ter dry up, his ha'r 'mence' ter drap out. When de vimes fresh' up a bit, Henry'd git peart ag'in, en when de vimes wither' ag'in, Henry'd git ole ag'in, en des kep' gittin' mo' en mo' fitten fer nuffin; he des pined away, en pined away, en fine'ly tuk ter his cabin; en when de big vimes whar he got de sap ter 'n'int his head withered en turned yaller en died, Henry died too,—des went out sorter like a cannel. Dey didn't 'pear ter be nuffin de matter wid 'im, 'cep'n' de rheumatiz, but his strenk des dwinel' away 'tel he didn' hab ernuff lef' ter draw his bref. De goopher had got de under holt, en th'owed Henry dat time fer good en all.

"Mars Dugal' tuk on might'ly 'bout losin' his vimes en his nigger in de same year; en he swo' dat ef he could git holt er dat Yankee he'd wear 'im ter a frazzle, en den chaw up de frazzle; en he'd done it, too, for Mars Dugal' 'uz a monst'us brash man w'en he once git started. He sot de vimya'd out ober ag'in, but it wuz th'ee er fo' year befo' de vimes got ter b'arin' any scuppernon's.

"W'en de wah broke out, Mars Dugal' raise' a comp'ny, en went off ter fight de Yankees. He say he wuz mighty glad dat wah come, en he des want ter kill a Yankee fer eve'y dollar he los' 'long er dat grape-raisin' Yankee. En I 'spec' he would 'a' done it, too, ef de Yankees hadn' s'picioned sump'n, en killed him fus'. Atter de s'render ole miss move' ter town, de niggers all scattered 'way fum de plantation, en de vimya'd ain' be'n cultervated sence."

"Is that story true?" asked Annie doubtfully, but seriously, as the old man concluded his narrative.

"It's des ez true ez I'm a-settin' here, miss. Dey's a easy way ter prove it: I kin lead de way right ter Henry's grave ober yander in de plantation buryin'-groun'. En I tell yer w'at, marster, I wouldn' 'vise you to buy dis yer ole vimya'd, 'caze de goopher's on it yit, en dey ain' no tellin' w'en it's gwine ter crap out."

"But I thought you said all the old vines died."

"Dey did 'pear ter die, but a few un 'em come out ag'in, en is mixed in 'mongs' de yuthers. I ain' skeered ter eat de grapes, 'caze I knows de old vimes fum de noo ones; but wid strangers dey ain' no tellin' w'at mought happen. I wouldn' 'vise yer ter buy dis vimya'd."

I bought the vineyard, nervertheless, and it has been for a long time in a thriving condition, and is often referred to by the local press as a striking illustration of the opportunities open to Northern capital in the development of Southern industries. The luscious scuppernong holds first rank among our grapes, though we cultivate a great many other varieties, and our income from grapes packed and shipped to the Northern markets is quite considerable. I have not noticed any developments of the goopher in the vineyard, although I have a mild suspicion that our colored assistants do not suffer from want of grapes during the season.

I found, when I bought the vineyard, that Uncle Julius had occupied a cabin on the place for many years, and derived a respectable revenue from the product of the neglected grapevines. This, doubtless, accounted for his advice to me not to buy the vineyard, though whether it inspired the goopher story I am unable to state. I believe, however, that the wages I paid him for his services as coachman, for I gave him employment in that capacity, were more than an equivalent for anything he lost by the sale of the vineyard.

1899

Po' Sandy

On the northeast corner of my vineyard in central North Carolina, and fronting on the Lumberton plank-road, there stood a small frame house, of the simplest construction. It was built of pine lumber, and contained but one room, to which one window gave light and one door admission. Its weather-beaten sides revealed a virgin innocence of paint. Against one end of the house, and occupying half its width, there stood a huge brick chimney: the crumbling mortar had left large cracks between the bricks; the bricks themselves had begun to scale off in large flakes, leaving the chimney sprinkled with unsightly blotches. These evidences of decay were but partially concealed by a creeping vine, which extended its slender branches hither and thither in an ambitious but futile attempt to cover the whole chimney. The wooden shutter, which had once protected the unglazed window, had fallen from its hinges, and lay rotting in the rank grass and jimsonweeds beneath. This building, I learned when I bought the place, had been used as a schoolhouse for several years prior to the breaking out of the war, since which time it had remained unoccupied, save when some stray cow or vagrant hog had sought shelter within its walls from the chill rains and nipping winds of winter.

One day my wife requested me to build her a new kitchen. The house erected by us, when we first came to live upon the vineyard, contained a very conveniently arranged kitchen; but for some occult reason my wife wanted a kitchen in the back yard, apart from the dwelling-house, after the usual Southern fashion. Of course I had to build it.

To save expense, I decided to tear down the old schoolhouse, and use the lumber, which was in a good state of preservation, in the construction of the new kitchen. Before demolishing the old house, however, I made an estimate of the amount of material contained in it, and found that I would have to buy several hundred feet of lumber additional, in order to build the new kitchen according to my wife's plan.

One morning old Julius McAdoo, our colored coachman, harnessed the gray mare to the rockaway,[1] and drove my wife and me over to the sawmill from which I meant to order the new lumber. We drove down the long lane which led from our house to the plank-road; following the plank-road for about a mile, we turned into a road running through the forest and across the swamp to the sawmill beyond. Our carriage jolted over the half-rotted corduroy road[2] which traversed the swamp, and then climbed the long hill leading to the sawmill. When we reached the mill, the fore-

[1]A four-wheeled carriage with two seats and a standing top.

[2]Made of logs laid together transversely.

man had gone over to a neighboring farmhouse, probably to smoke or gossip, and we were compelled to await his return before we could transact our business. We remained seated in the carriage, a few rods from the mill, and watched the leisurely movements of the mill-hands. We had not waited long before a huge pine log was placed in position, the machinery of the mill was set in motion, and the circular saw began to eat its way through the log, with a loud whir which resounded throughout the vicinity of the mill. The sound rose and fell in a sort of rhythmic cadence, which, heard from where we sat, was not unpleasing, and not loud enough to prevent conversation. When the saw started on its second journey through the log, Julius observed, in a lugubrious tone, and with a perceptible shudder:—

"Ugh! but dat des do cuddle my blood!"

"What's the matter, Uncle Julius?" inquired my wife, who is of a very sympathetic turn of mind. "Does the noise affect your nerves?"

"No, Mis' Annie," replied the ole man, with emotion, "I ain' narvous; but dat saw, a-cuttin' en grindin' thoo dat stick er timber, en moanin', en groanin,' en sweekin', kyars my 'memb'ance back ter ole times, en 'min's me er po' Sandy." The pathetic intonation with which he lengthened out the "po' Sandy" touched a responsive chord in our own hearts.

"And who was poor Sandy?" asked my wife, who takes a deep interest in the stories of plantation life which she hears from the lips of the older colored people. Some of these stories are quaintly humorous; others wildly extravagant, revealing the Oriental cast of the negro's imagination; while others, poured freely into the sympathetic ear of a Northern-bred woman, disclose many a tragic incident of the darker side of slavery.

"Sandy," said Julius, in reply to my wife's question, "was a nigger w'at useter b'long ter old Mars Marrabo McSwayne. Mars Marrabo's place wuz on de yuther side'n de swamp, right nex' ter yo' place. Sandy wuz a monst'us good nigger, en could do so many things erbout a plantation, en alluz 'ten' ter his wuk so well, dat w'en Mars Marrabo's chilluns growed up en married off, dey all un 'em wanted dey daddy fer ter gin 'em Sandy fer a weddin' present. But Mars Marrabo knowed de res' wouldn' be satisfied ef he gin Sandy ter a'er one un 'em; so w'en dey wuz all done married, he fix it by 'lowin' one er his chilluns ter take Sandy fer a mont' er so, en den ernudder for a mont' er so, en so on dat erway tel dey had all had 'im de same lenk er time; en den dey would all take him roun' ag'in, 'cep'n' oncet in a w'ile w'en Mars Marrabo would len' 'im ter some er his yuther kinfolks 'roun' de country, w'en dey wuz short er han's; tel bimeby it got so Sandy didn' hardly knowed whar he wuz gwine ter stay fum one week's een' ter de yuther.

"One time w'en Sandy wuz lent out ez yushal, a spekilater come erlong wid a lot er niggers, en Mars Marrabo swap' Sandy's wife off fer a noo 'oman. W'en Sandy come back, Mars Marrabo gin 'im a dollar, en 'lowed he wuz monst'us sorry fer ter break up de fambly, but de spekilater had gin 'im big boot,[3] en times wuz hard en money skase, en so he wuz bleedst ter make de trade. Sandy tuk on some 'bout losin' his wife, but he soon seed dey want no use cryin' ober spilt merlasses; en bein' ez he lacked de looks er de noo 'oman, he tuk up wid her atter she'd be'n on de plantation a mont' er so.

[3]Special, unexpected value.

"Sandy en his noo wife got on mighty well tergedder, en de niggers all 'mence' ter talk about how lovin' dey wuz. W'en Tenie wuz tuk sick oncet, Sandy useter set up all night wid 'er, en den go ter wuk in de mawnin' des lack he had his reg'lar sleep; en Tenie would 'a' done anythin' in de worl' for her Sandy.

"Sandy en Tenie hadn' be'n libbin' tergedder fer mo' d'n two mont's befo' Mars Marrabo's old uncle, w'at libbed down in Robeson County, sent up ter fin' out ef Mars Marrabo couldn' len' 'im er hire 'im a good han' fer a mont' er so. Sandy's marster wuz one er dese yer easy-gwine folks w'at wanter please eve'ybody, en he says yas, he could len' 'im Sandy. En Mars Marrabo tol' Sandy fer ter git ready ter go down ter Robeson nex' day, fer ter stay a mont' er so.

"It wuz monst'us hard on Sandy fer ter take 'im 'way fum Tenie. It wuz so fur down ter Robeson dat he didn' hab no chance er comin' back ter see her tel de time wuz up; he would n' 'a' mine comin' ten er fifteen mile at night ter see Tenie, but Mars Marrabo's uncle's plantation wuz mo' d'n forty mile off. Sandy wuz mighty sad en cas' down atter w'at Mars Marrabo tol' 'im, en he says ter Tenie, sezee:—

"'I'm gittin' monst'us ti'ed er dish yer gwine roun' so much. Here I is lent ter Mars Jeems dis mont', en I got ter do so-en-so; en ter Mars Archie de nex' mont', en I got ter do so-en-so; den I got ter go ter Miss Jinnie's: en hit 's Sandy dis en Sandy dat, en Sandy yer en Sandy dere, tel it 'pears ter me I ain' got no home, ner no marster, ner no mistiss, ner no nuffin. I can't eben keep a wife: my yuther ole 'oman wuz sol' away widout my gittin' a chance fer ter tell her good-by; en now I got ter go off en leab you, Tenie, en I dunno whe'r I'm eber gwine ter see you ag'in er no. I wisht I wuz a tree, er a stump, er a rock, er sump'n w'at could stay on de plantation fer a w'ile.'

"Atter Sandy got thoo talkin', Tenie didn' say naer word, but des sot dere by de fier, studyin' en studyin'. Bimeby she up'n' says:—

"'Sandy, is I eber tol' you I wuz a cunjuh 'oman?'

"Co'se Sandy hadn' ebber dremp' er nuffin lack dat, en he made a great 'miration w'en he hear w'at Tenie say. Bimeby Tenie went on:—

"'I ain't goophered nobody, ner done no cunjuh wuk, fer fifteen year er mo'; en w'en I got religion I made up my mine I wouldn' wuk no mo' goopher. But dey is some things I doan b'lieve it's no sin fer ter do; en ef you doan wanter be sent roun' fum pillar ter pos', en ef you doan wanter go down ter Robeson, I kin fix things so you won't haf ter. Ef you'll des say de word, I kin turn you ter w'ateber you wanter be, en you kin stay right whar you wanter, ez long ez you mineter.'

"Sandy say he doan keer; he's willin' fer ter do anythin' fer ter stay close ter Tenie. Den Tenie ax 'im ef he doan wanter be turnt inter a rabbit.

"Sandy say, 'No, de dogs mought git atter me.'

"'Shill I turn you ter a wolf?' sez Tenie.

"'No, eve'ybody's skeered er a wolf, en I doan want nobody ter be skeered er me.'

"'Shill I turn you ter a mawkin'-bird?'

"'No, a hawk mought ketch me. I wanter be turnt inter sump'n w'at'll stay in one place.'

"'I kin turn you ter a tree,' sez Tenie. 'You won't hab no mouf ner years, but I kin turn you back oncet in a w'ile, so you kin git sump'n ter eat, en hear w'at's gwine on.'

"Well, Sandy say dat'll do. En so Tenie tuk 'im down by de aidge er de swamp, not fur fum de quarters, en turnt 'im inter a big pine-tree, en sot 'im out 'mongs' some yuther trees. En de nex' mawnin', ez some er de fiel' han's wuz gwine long dere, dey seed a tree w'at dey didn' 'member er habbin' seed befo'; it wuz monst'us quare, en dey wuz bleedst ter 'low dat dey hadn' 'membered right, er e'se one er de saplin's had be'n growin' monst'us fas'.

"W'en Mars Marrabo 'skiver' dat Sandy wuz gone, he 'lowed Sandy had runned away. He got de dogs out, but de las' place dey could track Sandy ter wuz de foot er dat pine-tree. En dere de dogs stood en barked, en bayed, en pawed at de tree, en tried ter climb up on it; en w'en dey wuz tuk roun' thoo de swamp ter look fer de scent, dey broke loose en made fer dat tree ag'in. It wuz de beatenis' thing de w'ite folks eber hearn of, en Mars Marrabo 'lowed dat Sandy must 'a' clim' up on de tree en jump' off on a mule er sump'n, en rid fur ernuff fer ter spile de scent. Mars Marrabo wanted ter 'cuse some er de yuther niggers er heppin' Sandy off, but dey all 'nied it ter de las'; en eve'ybody knowed Tenie sot too much sto' by Sandy fer ter he'p 'im run away whar she couldn' nebber see 'im no mo'.

"W'en Sandy had be'n gone long ernuff fer folks ter think he done got clean away, Tenie useter go down ter de woods at night en turn 'im back, en den dey'd slip up ter de cabin en set by de fire en talk. But dey ha' ter be monst'us keerful, er e'se somebody would 'a' seed 'em, en dat would 'a' spile' de whole thing; so Tenie alluz turnt Sandy back in de mawnin' early, befo' anybody wuz a-stirrin'.

"But Sandy didn' git erlong widout his trials en tribberlations. One day a woodpecker come erlong en 'mence' ter peck at de tree; en de nex' time Sandy wuz turnt back he had a little roun' hole in his arm, des lack a sharp stick be'n stuck in it. Atter dat Tenie sot a sparrer-hawk fer ter watch de tree; en w'en de woodpecker come erlong nex' mawnin' fer ter finish his nes', he got gobble' up mos' 'fo' he stuck his bill in de bark.

"Nudder time, Mars Marrabo sent a nigger out in de woods fer ter chop tuppentime boxes. De man chop a box in dish yer tree, en hack' de bark up two er th'ee feet, fer ter let de tuppentime run. De nex' time Sandy wuz turnt back he had a big skyar on his lef' leg, des lack it be'n skunt; en it tuk Tenie nigh 'bout all night fer ter fix a mixtry ter kyo it up. Atter dat, Tenie sot a hawnet fer ter watch de tree; en w'en de nigger come back ag'in fer ter cut ernudder box on de yuther side'n de tree, de hawnet stung 'im so hard dat de ax slip en cut his foot nigh 'bout off.

"W'en Tenie see so many things happenin' ter de tree, she 'cluded she'd ha' ter turn Sandy ter sump'n e'se; en atter studyin' de matter ober, en talkin' wid Sandy one ebenin', she made up her mine fer ter fix up a goopher mixtry w'at would turn herse'f en Sandy ter foxes, er sump'n, so dey could run away en go some'rs whar dey could be free en lib lack w'ite folks.

"But dey ain' no tellin' w'at 's gwine ter happen in dis worl'. Tenie had got de night sot fer her en Sandy ter run away, w'en dat ve'y day one er Mars Marrabo's sons rid up ter de big house in his buggy, en say his wife wuz monst'us sick, en he want his mammy ter len' 'im a 'oman fer ter nuss his wife. Tenie's mistiss say sen' Tenie; she wuz a good nuss. Young mars wuz in a tarrible hurry fer ter git back home. Tenie wuz washin' at de big house dat day, en her mistiss say she should go right 'long wid her young marster. Tenie tried ter make some 'scuse fer ter git away en hide 'tel night, w'en she would have eve'ything fix' up fer her en Sandy; she say she wanter go ter her cabin fer ter git her bonnet. Her mistiss say it doan matter 'bout de bonnet; her head-hankcher wuz good ernuff. Den Tenie say she wanter git her bes' frock; her mistiss say no, she doan need no mo' frock, en w'en dat one got dirty she could git a clean one whar she wuz gwine. So Tenie had ter git in de buggy en go 'long wid young Mars Dunkin ter his plantation, w'ich wuz mo' d'n twenty mile away; en dey wa'n't no chance er her seein' Sandy no mo' 'tel she come back home. De po' gal felt monst'us bad 'bout de way things wuz gwine on, en she knowed Sandy mus' be a wond'rin' why she didn' come en turn 'im back no mo'.

"W'iles Tenie wuz away nussin' young Mars Dunkin's wife, Mars Marrabo tuk a notion fer ter buil' 'im a noo kitchen; en bein' ez he had lots er timber on his place, be begun ter look 'roun' fer a tree ter hab de lumber sawed out'n. En I dunno how it come to be so, but he happen fer ter hit on de ve'y tree w'at Sandy wuz turnt inter. Tenie wuz gone, en dey wa'n't nobody ner nuffin fer ter watch de tree.

"De two men w'at cut de tree down say dey nebber had sech a time wid a tree befo': dey axes would glansh off, en didn' 'pear ter make no prōgress thoo de wood; en of all de creakin', en shakin', en wobblin' you eber see, dat tree done it w'en it commence' ter fall. It wuz de beatenis' thing!

"W'en dey got de tree all trim' up, dey chain it up ter a timber waggin, en start fer de sawmill. But dey had a hard time gittin' de log dere: fus' dey got stuck in de mud w'en dey wuz gwine crosst de swamp, en it wuz two er th'ee hours befo' dey could git out. W'en dey start' on ag'in, de chain kep' a-comin' loose, en dey had ter keep a-stoppin' en a-stoppin' fer ter hitch de log up ag'in. W'en dey commence' ter climb de hill ter de sawmill, de log broke loose, en roll down de hill en in 'mongs' de trees, en hit tuk nigh 'bout half a day mo' ter git it haul' up ter de sawmill.

"De nex' mawnin' atter de dey de tree wuz haul' ter de sawmill, Tenie come home. W'en she got back ter her cabin, de fus' thing she done wuz ter run down ter de woods en see how Sandy wuz gittin' on. W'en she seed de stump standin' dere, wid de sap runnin' out'n it, en de limbs layin' scattered roun', she nigh 'bout went out'n her min'. She run ter her cabin, en got her goopher mixtry, en den follered de track er de timber waggin ter de sawmill. She knowed Sandy couldn' lib mo' d'n a minute er so ef she turnt him back, fer he wuz all chop' up so he'd 'a' be'n bleedst ter die. But she wanted ter turn 'im back long ernuff fer ter 'splain ter 'im dat she hadn' went off a-purpose, en lef' 'im ter be chop' down en sawed up. She didn' want Sandy ter die wid no hard feelin's to'ds her.

"De han's at de sawmill had des got de big log on de kerridge, en wuz startin' up de saw, w'en dey seed a 'oman runnin' up de hill, all out er bref, cryin' en gwine on des lack she wuz plumb 'stracted. It wuz Tenie; she come right inter de mill, en th'owed herse'f on de log, right in front er de saw, a-hollerin' en cryin' ter her Sandy ter fergib her, en not ter think hard er her, fer it wa'n't no fault er hern. Den Tenie 'membered de tree didn' hab no years, en she wuz gittin' ready fer ter wuk her goopher mixtry so ez ter turn Sandy back, w'en de mill-hands kotch holt er her en tied her arms wid a rope, en fasten' her to one er de posts in de sawmill; en den dey started de saw up ag'in, en cut de log up inter bo'ds en scantlin's right befo' her eyes. But it wuz mighty hard wuk; fer of all de sweekin', en moanin', en groanin', dat log done it w'iles de saw wuz a-cuttin' thoo it. De saw wuz one er dese yer oletimey, up-en-down saws, en hit tuk longer dem days ter saw a log 'en it do now. Dey greased de saw, but dat didn' stop de fuss; hit kep' right on, tel fin'ly dey got de log all sawed up.

"W'en de oberseah w'at run de sawmill come fum breakfas', de han's up en tell him 'bout de crazy 'oman—ez dey s'posed she wuz—w'at had come runnin' in de sawmill, a-hollerin' en gwine on, en tried ter th'ow herse'f befo' de saw. En de oberseah sent two er th'ee er de han's fer ter take Tenie back ter her marster's plantation.

"Tenie 'peared ter be out'n her min' fer a long time, en her marster ha' ter lock her up in de smoke-'ouse 'tel she got ober her spells. Mars Marrabo wuz monst'us mad, en hit would 'a' made yo' flesh crawl fer ter hear him cuss, 'caze he say de spekilater w'at he got Tenie fum had fooled 'im by wukkin' a crazy 'oman off on him. W'iles Tenie wuz lock up in de smoke-'ouse, Mars Marrabo tuk 'n' haul de lumber fum de sawmill, en put up his noo kitchen.

"W'en Tenie got quiet' down, so she could be 'lowed ter go 'roun' de plantation, she up'n' tole her marster all erbout Sandy en de pine-tree; en w'en Mars Marrabo hearn it, he 'lowed she wuz de wuss 'stracted nigger he eber hearn of. He did n' know w'at ter do wid Tenie: fus' he thought he'd put her in de po'-house; but fin'ly, seein' ez she didn' do no harm ter nobody ner nuffin, but des went 'roun' moanin', en groanin', en shakin' her head, he 'cluded ter let her stay on de plantation en nuss de little nigger chilluns w'en dey mammies wuz ter wuk in de cotton-fiel'.

"De noo kitchen Mars Marrabo buil' wuzn' much use, fer it hadn' be'n put up long befo' de niggers 'mence' ter notice quare things erbout it. Dey could hear sump'n moanin' en groanin' 'bout de kitchen in de night-time, en w'en de win' would blow dey could hear sump'n a-hollerin' en sweekin' lack it wuz in great pain en sufferin'. En it got so atter a w'ile dat it wuz all Mars Marrabo's wife could do ter git a 'oman ter stay in de kitchen in de daytime long ernuff ter do de cookin'; en dey wa'n't naer nigger on de plantation w'at wouldn' rudder take forty dan ter go 'bout dat kitchen atter dark,—dat is, 'cep'n' Tenie; she didn' 'pear ter min' de ha'nts.[4] She useter slip 'roun' at night, en set on de kitchen steps, en lean up agin de do'-jamb, en run on ter herse'f wid some kine er foolishness w'at nobody couldn' make out; fer Mars Marrabo had th'eaten' ter sen' her off'n de plantation ef she say anything ter any er de yuther niggers 'bout de pine-tree. But somehow er 'nudder de niggers foun' out all erbout it, en dey all knowed de kitchen wuz ha'nted by Sandy's sperrit. En bimeby hit got so Mars Marrabo's wife herse'f wuz skeered ter go out in de yard atter dark.

"W'en it come ter dat, Mars Marrabo tuk en to' de kitchen down, en use' de lumber fer ter buil' dat ole school'ouse w'at you er talkin' 'bout pullin' down. De school'ouse wuzn' use' 'cep'n' in de daytime, en on dark nights folks gwine 'long de road would hear quare soun's en see quare things. Po' ole Tenie useter go down dere at night, en wander 'roun' de school'ouse; en de niggers all 'lowed she went fer ter talk wid Sandy's sperrit. En one winter mawnin', w'en one er de boys went ter school early fer ter start de fire, w'at should he fin' but po' ole Tenie, layin' on de flo', stiff, en col', en dead. Dere didn' 'pear ter be nuffin pertickler de matter wid her,—she had des grieve' herse'f ter def fer her Sandy. Mars Marrabo did n' shed no tears. He thought Tenie wuz crazy, en dey wa'n't no tellin' w'at she mought do nex'; en dey ain' much room in dis worl' fer crazy w'ite folks, let 'lone a crazy nigger.

"Hit wa'n't long atter dat befo' Mars Marrabo sol' a piece er his track er lan' ter Mars Dugal' McAdoo,—*my* ole marster,—en dat's how de ole school'ouse happen to

[4]Ghosts.

be on yo' place. W'en de wah broke out, de school stop', en de ole school'ouse be'n stannin' empty ever sence,—dat is, 'cep'n' fer de ha'nts. En folks sez dat de ole school'ouse, er any yuther house w'at got any er dat lumber in it w'at wuz sawed out'n de tree w'at Sandy wuz turnt inter, is gwine ter be ha'nted tel de las' piece er plank is rotted en crumble' inter dus'."

Annie had listened to this gruesome narrative with strained attention.

"What a system it was," she exclaimed, when Julius had finished, "under which such things were possible!"

"What things?" I asked, in amazement. "Are you seriously considering the possibility of a man's being turned into a tree?"

"Oh, no," she replied quickly, "not that;" and then she murmured absently, and with a dim look in her fine eyes, "Poor Tenie!"

We ordered the lumber, and returned home. That night, after we had gone to bed, and my wife had to all appearances been sound asleep for half an hour, she startled me out of an incipient doze by exclaiming suddenly,—

"John, I don't believe I want my new kitchen built out of the lumber in that old schoolhouse."

"You wouldn't for a moment allow yourself," I replied, with some asperity, "to be influenced by that absurdly impossible yarn which Julius was spinning to-day?"

"I know the story is absurd," she replied dreamily, "and I am not so silly as to believe it. But I don't think I should ever be able to take any pleasure in that kitchen if it were built out of that lumber. Besides, I think the kitchen would look better and last longer if the lumber were all new."

Of course she had her way. I bought the new lumber, though not without grumbling. A week or two later I was called away from home on business. On my return, after an absence of several days, my wife remarked to me,—

"John, there has been a split in the Sandy Run Colored Baptist Church, on the temperance question. About half the members have come out from the main body, and set up for themselves. Uncle Julius is one of the seceders, and he came to me yesterday and asked if they might not hold their meetings in the old schoolhouse for the present."

"I hope you didn't let the old rascal have it," I returned, with some warmth. I had just received a bill for the new lumber I had bought.

"Well," she replied, "I couldn't refuse him the use of the house for so good a purpose."

"And I'll venture to say," I continued, "that you subscribed something toward the support of the new church?"

She did not attempt to deny it.

"What are they going to do about the ghost?" I asked, somewhat curious to know how Julius would get around this obstacle.

"Oh," replied Annie, "Uncle Julius says that ghosts never disturb religious worship, but that if Sandy's spirit *should* happen to stray into meeting by mistake, no doubt the preaching would do it good."

1899

The Wife of His Youth

I

Mr. Ryder was going to give a ball. There were several reasons why this was an opportune time for such an event.

Mr. Ryder might aptly be called the dean of the Blue Veins. The original Blue Veins were a little society of colored persons organized in a certain Northern city shortly after the war. Its purpose was to establish and maintain correct social standards among a people whose social condition presented almost unlimited room for improvement. By accident, combined perhaps with some natural affinity, the society consisted of individuals who were, generally speaking, more white than black. Some envious outsider made the suggestion that no one was eligible for membership who was not white enough to show blue veins. The suggestion was readily adopted by those who were not of the favored few, and since that time the society, though possessing a longer and more pretentious name, had been known far and wide as the "Blue Vein Society," and its members as the "Blue Veins."

The Blue Veins did not allow that any such requirement existed for admission to their circle, but, on the contrary, declared that character and culture were the only things considered; and that if most of their members were light-colored, it was because such persons, as a rule, had had better opportunities to qualify themselves for membership. Opinions differed, too, as to the usefulness of the society. There were those who had been known to assail it violently as a glaring example of the very prejudice from which the colored race had suffered most; and later, when such critics had succeeded in getting on the inside, they had been heard to maintain with zeal and earnestness that the society was a life-boat, an anchor, a bulwark and a shield,—a pillar of cloud by day and of fire by night, to guide their people through the social wilderness. Another alleged prerequisite for Blue Vein membership was that of free birth; and while there was really no such requirement, it is doubtless true that very few of the members would have been unable to meet it if there had been. If there were one or two of the older members who had come up from the South and from slavery, their history presented enough romantic circumstances to rob their servile origin of its grosser aspects.

While there were no such tests of eligibility, it is true that the Blue Veins had their notions on these subjects, and that not all of them were equally liberal in regard to the things they collectively disclaimed. Mr. Ryder was one of the most conservative. Though he had not been among the founders of the society, but had come in some years later, his genius for social leadership was such that he had speedily become its recognized adviser and head, the custodian of its standards, and the preserver of its traditions. He shaped its social policy, was active in providing for its entertainment, and when the interest fell off, as it sometimes did, he fanned the embers until they burst again into a cheerful flame.

There were still other reasons for his popularity. While he was not as white as some of the Blue Veins, his appearance was such as to confer distinction upon them. His features were of a refined type, his hair was almost straight; he was always neatly dressed; his manners were irreproachable, and his morals above suspicion. He had come to Groveland a young man, and obtaining employment in the office of a railroad company as messenger had in time worked himself up to the position of stationery clerk, having charge of the distribution of the office supplies for the whole company. Although the lack of early training had hindered the orderly development of a naturally fine mind, it had not prevented him from doing a great deal of reading or from forming decidedly literary tastes. Poetry was his passion. He could repeat whole pages of the great English poets; and if his pronunciation was sometimes faulty, his eye, his voice, his gestures, would respond to the changing sentiment with a precision that revealed a poetic soul and disarmed criticism. He was economical, and had saved money; he owned and occupied a very comfortable house on a respectable street. His residence was handsomely furnished, containing among other things a good library, especially rich in poetry, a piano, and some choice engravings. He generally shared his house with some young couple, who looked after his wants and were company for him; for Mr. Ryder was a single man. In the early days of his connection with the Blue Veins he had been regarded as quite a catch, and young ladies and their mothers had manœuvred with much ingenuity to capture him. Not, however, until Mrs. Molly Dixon visited Groveland had any woman ever made him wish to change his condition to that of a married man.

Mrs. Dixon had come to Groveland from Washington in the spring, and before the summer was over she had won Mr. Ryder's heart. She possessed many attractive qualities. She was much younger than he; in fact, he was old enough to have been her father, though no one knew exactly how old he was. She was whiter than he, and better educated. She had moved in the best colored society of the country, at Washington, and had taught in the schools of that city. Such a superior person had been eagerly welcomed to the Blue Vein Society, and had taken a leading part in its activities. Mr. Ryder had at first been attracted by her charms of person, for she was very good looking and not over twenty-five; then by her refined manners and the vivacity of her wit. Her husband had been a government clerk, and at his death had left a considerable life insurance. She was visiting friends in Groveland, and, finding the town and the people to her liking, had prolonged her stay indefinitely. She had not seemed displeased at Mr. Ryder's attentions, but on the contrary had given him every proper encouragement; indeed, a younger and less cautious man would long since have spoken. But he had made up his mind, and had only to determine the time when he would ask her to be his wife. He decided to give a ball in her honor, and at some time during the evening of the ball to offer her his heart and hand. He had no special fears about the outcome, but, with a little touch of romance, he wanted the surroundings to be in harmony with his own feelings when he should have received the answer he expected.

Mr. Ryder resolved that this ball should mark an epoch in the social history of Groveland. He knew, of course,—no one could know better,—the entertainments that had taken place in past years, and what must be done to surpass them. His ball must be worthy of the lady in whose honor it was to be given, and must, by the quality of its guests, set an example for the future. He had observed of late a growing liberality, almost a laxity, in social matters, even among members of his own set, and had several times been forced to meet in a social way persons whose complexions and callings in life were hardly up to the standard which he considered proper for the society to maintain. He had a theory of his own.

"I have no race prejudice," he would say, "but we people of mixed blood are ground between the upper and the nether millstone. Our fate lies between absorption by the white race and extinction in the black. The one does n't want us yet, but may take us in time. The other would welcome us, but it would be for us a backward step. 'With malice towards none, with charity for all,'[1] we must do the best we can for ourselves and those who are to follow us. Self-preservation is the first law of nature."

His ball would serve by its exclusiveness to counteract leveling tendencies, and his marriage with Mrs. Dixon would help to further the upward process of absorption he had been wishing and waiting for.

II

The ball was to take place on Friday night. The house had been put in order, the carpets covered with canvas, the halls and stairs decorated with palms and potted plants; and in the afternoon Mr. Ryder sat on his front porch, which the shade of a vine running up over a wire netting made a cool and pleasant lounging place. He expected to respond to the toast "The Ladies" at the supper, and from a volume of Tennyson—his favorite poet—was fortifying himself with apt quotations. The volume was open at "A Dream of Fair Women." His eyes fell on these lines, and he read them aloud to judge better of their effect:—

> At length I saw a lady within call,
> Stiller than chisell'd marble, standing there;
> A daughter of the gods, divinely tall,
> And most divinely fair.[2]

He marked the verse, and turning the page read the stanza beginning,—

> O sweet pale Margaret,
> O rare pale Margaret.[3]

He weighed the passage a moment, and decided that it would not do. Mrs. Dixon was the palest lady he expected at the ball, and she was of a rather ruddy complexion, and of lively disposition and buxom build. So he ran over the leaves until his eye rested on the description of Queen Guinevere:—

> She seem'd a part of joyous Spring:
> A gown of grass-green silk she wore,
> Buckled with golden clasps before;
> A light-green tuft of plumes she bore
> Closed in a golden ring.
> . . . .
> She look'd so lovely, as she sway'd
> The rein with dainty finger-tips,

[1]Abraham Lincoln, Second Inaugural Address (March 4, 1865). The full citation is, "With malice towards none, with charity for all, with firmness in the right, as God gives us to see."

[2]Alfred Lord Tennyson (1809–1892), "A Dream of Fair Women" (1832), stanza xxii, lines 85–88.

[3]Tennyson, "Margaret" (1833), lines 1–2.

A man had given all other bliss,
And all his worldly worth for this,
To waste his whole heart in one kiss
Upon her perfect lips.[4]

As Mr. Ryder murmured these words audibly, with an appreciative thrill, he heard the latch of his gate click, and a light foot-fall sounding on the steps. He turned his head, and saw a woman standing before his door.

She was a little woman, not five feet tall, and proportioned to her height. Although she stood erect, and looked around her with very bright and restless eyes, she seemed quite old; for her face was crossed and recrossed with a hundred wrinkles, and around the edges of her bonnet could be seen protruding here and there a tuft of short gray wool. She wore a blue calico gown of ancient cut, a little red shawl fastened around her shoulders with an old-fashioned brass brooch, and a large bonnet profusely ornamented with faded red and yellow artificial flowers. And she was very black,—so black that her toothless gums, revealed when she opened her mouth to speak, were not red, but blue. She looked like a bit of the old plantation life, summoned up from the past by the wave of a magician's wand, as the poet's fancy had called into being the gracious shapes of which Mr. Ryder had just been reading.

He rose from his chair and came over to where she stood.

"Good-afternoon, madam," he said.

"Good-evenin', suh," she answered, ducking suddenly with a quaint curtsy. Her voice was shrill and piping, but softened somewhat by age. "Is dis yere whar Mistuh Ryduh lib, suh?" she asked, looking around her doubtfully, and glancing into the open windows, through which some of the preparations for the evening were visible.

"Yes," he replied, with an air of kindly patronage, unconsciously flattered by her manner, "I am Mr. Ryder. Did you want to see me?"

"Yas, suh, ef I ain't 'sturbin' of you too much."

"Not at all. Have a seat over here behind the vine, where it is cool. What can I do for you?"

"'Scuse me, suh," she continued, when she had sat down on the edge of a chair, "'scuse me, suh, I 's lookin' for my husban'. I heerd you wuz a big man an' had libbed heah a long time, an' I 'lowed you would n't min' ef I 'd come roun' an' ax you ef you'd ever heerd of a merlatter man by de name er Sam Taylor 'quirin' roun' in de chu'ches ermongs' de people fer his wife 'Liza Jane?"

Mr. Ryder seemed to think for a moment.

"There used to be many such cases right after the war," he said, "but it has been so long that I have forgotten them. There are very few now. But tell me your story, and it may refresh my memory."

She sat back farther in her chair so as to be more comfortable, and folded her withered hands in her lap.

"My name's 'Liza," she began, "'Liza Jane. W'en I wuz young I us'ter b'long ter Marse Bob Smif, down in old Missoura. I wuz bawn down dere. W'en I wuz a gal I wuz married ter a man named Jim. But Jim died, an' after dat I married a merlatter

[4] Tennyson, "Sir Lancelot and Queen Guinevere" (1842), lines 23–27, 40–45.

man named Sam Taylor. Sam wuz free-bawn, but his mammy and daddy died, an' de w'ite folks 'prenticed him ter my marster fer ter work fer 'im 'tel he wuz growed up. Sam worked in de fiel', an' I wuz de cook. One day Ma'y Ann, ole miss's maid, came rushin' out ter de kitchen, an' says she, ''Liza Jane, ole marse gwine sell yo' Sam down de ribber.'

"'Go way f'm yere,' says I; 'my husban' 's free!'

"'Don' make no diff'ence. I heerd ole marse tell ole miss he wuz gwine take yo' Sam 'way wid 'im ter-morrow, fer he needed money, an' he knowed whar he could git a t'ousan' dollars fer Sam an' no questions axed.'

"W'en Sam come home f'm de fiel' dat night, I tole him 'bout ole marse gwine steal 'im, an' Sam run erway. His time wuz mos' up, an' he swo' dat w'en he wuz twenty-one he would come back an' he'p me run erway, er else save up de money ter buy my freedom. An' I know he'd 'a' done it, fer he thought a heap er me, Sam did. But w'en he come back he did n' find me, fer I wuz n' dere. Ole marse had heerd dat I warned Sam, so he had me whip' an' sol' down de ribber.

"Den de wah broke out, an' w'en it wuz ober de cullud folks wuz scattered. I went back ter de ole home; but Sam wuz n' dere, an' I could n' l'arn nuffin' 'bout 'im. But I knowed he'd be'n dere to look fer me an' had n' foun' me, an' had gone erway ter hunt fer me.

"I 's be'n lookin' fer 'im eber sence," she added simply, as though twenty-five years were but a couple of weeks, "an' I knows he 's be'n lookin' fer me. Fer he sot a heap er sto' by me, Sam did, an' I know he 's be'n huntin' fer me all dese years,—'less'n he 's be'n sick er sump'n, so he could n' work, er out'n his head, so he could n' 'member his promise. I went back down de ribber, fer I 'lowed he'd gone down dere lookin' fer me. I 's be'n ter Noo Orleens, an' Atlanty, an' Chalreston, an' Richmon'; an' w'en I'd be'n all ober de Souf I come ter de Norf. Fer I knows I'll fin' 'im some er dese days," she added softly, "er he 'll fin' me, an' den we 'll bofe be as happy in freedom as we wuz in de ole days befo' de wah." A smile stole over her withered countenance as she paused a moment, and her bright eyes softened into a faraway look.

This was the substance of the old woman's story. She had wandered a little here and there. Mr. Ryder was looking at her curiously when she finished.

"How have you lived all these years?" he asked.

"Cookin', suh. I 's a good cook. Does you know anybody w'at needs a good cook, suh? I 's stoppin' wid a cullud fam'ly roun' de corner yonder 'tel I kin git a place."

"Do you really expect to find your husband? He may be dead long ago."

She shook her head emphatically. "Oh no, he ain' dead. De signs an' de tokens tells me. I dremp three nights runnin' on'y dis las' week dat I foun' him."

"He may have married another woman. Your slave marriage would not have prevented him, for you never lived with him after the war, and without that your marriage does n't count."

"Would n' make no diff'ence wid Sam. He would n' marry no yuther 'ooman 'tel he foun' out 'bout me. I knows it," she added. "Sump'n 's be'n tellin' me all dese years dat I 's gwine fin' Sam 'fo' I dies."

"Perhaps he's outgrown you, and climbed up in the world where he would n't care to have you find him."

"No, indeed, suh," she replied, "Sam ain' dat kin' er man. He wuz good ter me,

Sam wuz, but he wuz n' much good ter nobody e'se, fer he wuz one er de triflin'es' han's on de plantation. I 'spec's ter haf ter suppo't 'im w'en I fin' 'im, fer he nebber would work 'less'n he had ter. But den he wuz free, an' he did n' git no pay fer his work, an' I don' blame 'im much. Mebbe he's done better sence he run erway, but I ain' 'spectin' much."

"You may have passed him on the street a hundred times during the twenty-five years, and not have known him; time works great changes."

She smiled incredulously. "I'd know 'im 'mong's a hund'ed men. Fer dey wuz n' no yuther merlatter man like my man Sam, an' I could n' be mistook. I 's toted his picture roun' wid me twenty-five years."

"May I see it?" asked Mr. Ryder. "It might help me to remember whether I have seen the original."

As she drew a small parcel from her bosom he saw that it was fastened to a string that went around her neck. Removing several wrappers, she brought to light an old-fashioned daguerreotype in a black case. He looked long and intently at the portrait. It was faded with time, but the features were still distinct, and it was easy to see what manner of man it had represented.

He closed the case, and with a slow movement handed it back to her.

"I don't know of any man in town who goes by that name," he said, "nor have I heard of any one making such inquiries. But if you will leave me your address, I will give the matter some attention, and if I find out anything I will let you know."

She gave him the number of a house in the neighborhood, and went away, after thanking him warmly.

He wrote the address on the fly-leaf of the volume of Tennyson, and, when she had gone, rose to his feet and stood looking after her curiously. As she walked down the street with mincing step, he saw several persons whom she passed turn and look back at her with a smile of kindly amusement. When she had turned the corner, he went upstairs to his bedroom, and stood for a long time before the mirror of his dressing-case, gazing thoughtfully at the reflection of his own face.

III

At eight o'clock the ballroom was a blaze of light and the guests had begun to assemble; for there was a literary programme and some routine business of the society to be gone through with before the dancing. A black servant in evening dress waited at the door and directed the guests to the dressing-rooms.

The occasion was long memorable among the colored people of the city; not alone for the dress and display, but for the high average of intelligence and culture that distinguished the gathering as a whole. There were a number of school-teachers, several young doctors, three or four lawyers, some professional singers, an editor, a lieutenant in the United States army spending his furlough in the city, and others in various polite callings; these were colored, though most of them would not have attracted even a casual glance because of any marked difference from white people. Most of the ladies were in evening costume, and dress coats and dancing pumps were the rule among the men. A band of string music, stationed in an alcove behind a row of palms, played popular airs while the guests were gathering.

The dancing began at half past nine. At eleven o'clock supper was served. Mr. Ryder had left the ballroom some little time before the intermission, but reappeared at the supper-table. The spread was worthy of the occasion, and the guests did full justice to it. When the coffee had been served, the toast-master, Mr. Solomon Sadler, rapped the order. He made a brief introductory speech, complimenting host and guests, and then presented in their order the toasts of the evening. They were responded to with a very fair display of after-dinner wit.

"The last toast," said the toast-master, when he reached the end of the list, "is one which must appeal to us all. There is no one of us of the sterner sex who is not at some time dependent upon woman,—in infancy for protection, in manhood for companionship, in old age for care and comforting. Our good host has been trying to live alone, but the fair faces I see around me to-night prove that he too is largely dependent upon the gentler sex for most that makes life worth living,—the society and love of friends,—and rumor is at fault if he does not soon yield entire subjection to one of them. Mr. Ryder will now respond to the toast,—The Ladies."

There was a pensive look in Mr. Ryder's eyes as he took the floor and adjusted the eye-glasses. He began by speaking of woman as the gift of Heaven to man, and after some general observations on the relations of the sexes he said: "But perhaps the quality which most distinguishes woman is her fidelity and devotion to those she loves. History is full of examples, but has recorded none more striking than one which only to-day came under my notice."

He then related, simply but effectively, the story told by his visitor of the afternoon. He gave it in the same soft dialect, which came readily to his lips, while the company listened attentively and sympathetically. For the story had awakened a responsive thrill in many hearts. There were some present who had seen, and others who had heard their fathers and grandfathers tell, the wrongs and sufferings of this past generation, and all them still felt, in their darker moments, the shadow hanging over them. Mr. Ryder went on:—

"Such devotion and confidence are rare even among women. There are many who would have searched a year, some who would have waited five years, a few who might have hoped ten years; but for twenty-five years this woman has retained her affection for and her faith in a man she has not seen or heard of in all that time.

"She came to me to-day in the hope that I might be able to help her find this long-lost husband. And when she was gone I gave my fancy rein, and imagined a case I will put to you.

"Suppose that this husband, soon after his escape, had learned that his wife had been sold away, and that such inquiries as he could make brought no information of her whereabouts. Suppose that he was young, and she much older than he; that he was light, and she was black; that their marriage was a slave marriage, and legally binding only if they chose to make it so after the war. Suppose, too, that he made his way to the North, as some of us have done, and there, where he had larger opportunities, had improved them, and had in the course of all these years grown to be as different from the ignorant boy who ran away from fear of slavery as the day is from the night. Suppose, even, that he had qualified himself, by industry, by thrift, and by study, to win the friendship and be considered worthy the society of such people as these I see around me to-night, gracing my board and filling my heart with gladness; for I am old enough to remember the day when such a gathering would not have been possible in this land. Suppose, too, that, as the years went by, this man's memory of the past grew more and more indistinct, until at last it was rarely, except in his dreams, that any image of this bygone period rose before his mind. And then suppose that accident should bring to his knowledge the fact that the wife of his youth, the wife he had left behind him,—not one who had walked by his side and kept pace with him in his upward struggle, but one upon whom advancing years and a laborious life had set their mark,—was alive and seeking him, but that he was absolutely safe from recognition or discovery, unless he chose to reveal himself. My friends, what would the man do? I will presume that he was one who loved honor, and tried to deal justly with all men. I will even carry the case further, and suppose that perhaps he had set his heart upon another, whom he had hoped to call his own. What would he do, or rather what ought he to do, in such a crisis of a lifetime?

"It seemed to me that he might hesitate, and I imagined that I was an old friend, a near friend, and that he had come to me for advice; and I argued the case with him. I tried to discuss it impartially. After we had looked upon the matter from every point of view, I said to him, in words that we all know:—

> This above all: to thine own self be true,
> And it must follow, as the night the day,
> Thou canst not then be false to any man.[5]

Then, finally, I put the question to him, 'Shall you acknowledge her?'

"And now, ladies and gentlemen, friends and companions, I ask you, what should he have done?"

There was something in Mr. Ryder's voice that stirred the hearts of those who sat around him. It suggested more than mere sympathy with an imaginary situation; it seemed rather in the nature of a personal appeal. It was observed, too, that his look rested more especially upon Mrs. Dixon, with a mingled expression of renunciation and inquiry.

She had listened, with parted lips and streaming eyes. She was the first to speak: "He should have acknowledged her."

"Yes," they all echoed, "he should have acknowledged her."

"My friends and companions," responded Mr. Ryder. "I thank you, one and all. It is the answer I expected, for I knew your hearts."

He turned and walked toward the closed door of an adjoining room, while every eye followed him in wondering curiosity. He came back in a moment, leading by the hand his visitor of the afternoon, who stood startled and trembling at the sudden plunge into this scene of brilliant gayety. She was neatly dressed in gray, and wore the white cap of an elderly woman.

"Ladies and gentlemen," he said, "this is the woman, and I am the man, whose story I have told you. Permit me to introduce to you the wife of my youth."

1898

[5]William Shakespeare (1564–1616), *Hamlet,* act 1, scene 3, lines 78–80.

The Passing of Grandison

I

When it is said that it was done to please a woman, there ought perhaps to be enough said to explain anything; for what a man will not do to please a woman is yet to be discovered. Nevertheless, it might be well to state a few preliminary facts to make it clear why young Dick Owens tried to run one of his father's negro men off to Canada.

In the early fifties, when the growth of anti-slavery sentiment and the constant drain of fugitive slaves into the North had so alarmed the slaveholders of the border States as to lead to the passage of the Fugitive Slave Law,[1] a young white man from Ohio, moved by compassion for the sufferings of a certain bondman who happened to have a "hard master," essayed to help the slave to freedom. The attempt was discovered and frustrated; the abductor was tried and convicted for slave-stealing, and sentenced to a term of imprisonment in the penitentiary. His death, after the expiration of only a small part of the sentence, from cholera contracted while nursing stricken fellow prisoners, lent to the case a melancholy interest that made it famous in anti-slavery annals.

Dick Owens had attended the trial. He was a youth of about twenty-two, intelligent, handsome, and amiable, but extremely indolent, in a graceful and gentlemanly way; or, as old Judge Fenderson put it more than once, he was lazy as the Devil,—a mere figure of speech, of course, and not one that did justice to the Enemy of Mankind. When asked why he never did anything serious, Dick would good-naturedly reply, with a well-modulated drawl, that he didn't have to. His father was rich; there was but one other child, an unmarried daughter, who because of poor health would probably never marry, and Dick was therefore heir presumptive to a large estate. Wealth or social position he did not need to seek, for he was born to both. Charity Lomax had shamed him into studying law, but notwithstanding an hour or so a day spent at old Judge Fenderson's office, he did not make remarkable headway in his legal studies.

"What Dick needs," said the judge, who was fond of tropes, as became a scholar, and of horses, as was befitting a Kentuckian, "is the whip of necessity, or the spur of ambition. If he had either, he would soon need the snaffle to hold him back."

But all Dick required, in fact, to prompt him to the most remarkable thing he accomplished before he was twenty-five, was a mere suggestion from Charity Lomax. The story was never really known to but two persons until after the war, when it came out because it was a good story and there was no particular reason for its concealment.

Young Owens had attended the trial of this slave-stealer, or martyr,—either or both,—and, when it was over, had gone to call on Charity Lomax, and, while they sat on the veranda after sundown, had told her all about the trial. He was a good talker, as his career in later years disclosed, and described the proceedings very graphically.

"I confess," he admitted, "that while my principles were against the prisoner, my

[1]Enacted by congress as part of the Compromise of 1850, the Fugitive Slave Law provided for the return of escaped slaves in the North to their southern owners.

sympathies were on his side. It appeared that he was of good family, and that he had an old father and mother, respectable people, dependent upon him for support and comfort in their declining years. He had been led into the matter by pity for a negro whose master ought to have been run out of the county long ago for abusing his slaves. If it had been merely a question of old Sam Briggs's negro, nobody would have cared anything about it. But father and the rest of them stood on the principle of the thing, and told the judge so, and the fellow was sentenced to three years in the penitentiary."

Miss Lomax had listened with lively interest.

"I've always hated old Sam Briggs," she said emphatically, "ever since the time he broke a negro's leg with a piece of cordwood. When I hear of a cruel deed it makes the Quaker blood that came from my grandmother assert itself. Personally I wish that all Sam Briggs's negroes would run away. As for the young man, I regard him as a hero. He dared something for humanity. I could love a man who would take such chances for the sake of others."

"Could you love me, Charity, if I did something heroic?"

"You never will, Dick. You're too lazy for any use. You'll never do anything harder than playing cards or fox-hunting."

"Oh, come now, sweetheart! I've been courting you for a year, and it's the hardest work imaginable. Are you never going to love me?" he pleaded.

His hand sought hers, but she drew it back beyond his reach.

"I'll never love you, Dick Owens, until you have done something. When that time comes, I'll think about it."

"But it takes so long to do anything worth mentioning, and I don't want to wait. One must read two years to become a lawyer, and work five more to make a reputation. We shall both be gray by then."

"Oh, I don't know," she rejoined. "It doesn't require a lifetime for a man to prove that he is a man. This one did something, or at least tried to."

"Well, I'm willing to attempt as much as any other man. What do you want me to do, sweetheart? Give me a test."

"Oh, dear me!" said Charity, "I don't care what you *do,* so you do *something.* Really, come to think of it, why should I care whether you do anything or not?"

"I'm sure I don't know why you should, Charity," rejoined Dick humbly, "for I'm aware that I'm not worthy of it."

"Except that I do hate," she added, relenting slightly, "to see a really clever man so utterly lazy and good for nothing."

"Thank you, my dear; a word of praise from you has sharpened my wits already. I have an idea! Will you love me if *I* run a negro off to Canada?"

"What nonsense!" said Charity scornfully. "You must be losing your wits. Steal another man's slave, indeed, while your father owns a hundred!"

"Oh, there'll be no trouble about that," responded Dick lightly; "I'll run off one of the old man's; we've got too many anyway. It may not be quite as difficult as the other man found it, but it will be just as unlawful, and will demonstrate what I am capable of."

"Seeing's believing," replied Charity. "Of course, what you are talking about now is merely absurd. I'm going away for three weeks, to visit my aunt in Tennessee.

If you're able to tell me, when I return, that you've done something to prove your quality, I'll—well, you may come and tell me about it."

II

Young Owens got up about nine o'clock next morning, and while making his toilet put some questions to his personal attendant, a rather bright looking young mulatto of about his own age.

"Tom," said Dick.

"Yas, Mars Dick," responded the servant.

"I'm going on a trip North. Would you like to go with me?"

Now, if there was anything that Tom would have liked to make, it was a trip North. It was something he had long contemplated in the abstract, but had never been able to muster up sufficient courage to attempt in the concrete. He was prudent enough, however, to dissemble his feelings.

"I wouldn't min' it, Mars Dick, ez long ez you'd take keer er me an' fetch me home all right."

Tom's eyes belied his words, however, and his young master felt well assured that Tom needed only a good opportunity to make him run away. Having a comfortable home, and a dismal prospect in case of failure, Tom was not likely to take any desperate chances; but young Owens was satisfied that in a free State but little persuasion would be required to lead Tom astray. With a very logical and characteristic desire to gain his end with the least necessary expenditure of effort, he decided to take Tom with him, if his father did not object.

Colonel Owens had left the house when Dick went to breakfast, so Dick did not see his father till luncheon.

"Father," he remarked casually to the colonel, over the fried chicken, "I'm feeling a trifle run down. I imagine my health would be improved somewhat by a little travel and change of scene."

"Why don't you take a trip North?" suggested his father. The colonel added to paternal affection a considerable respect for his son as the heir of a large estate. He himself had been "raised" in comparative poverty, and had laid the foundations of his fortune by hard work; and while he despised the ladder by which he had climbed, he could not entirely forget it, and unconsciously manifested, in his intercourse with his son, some of the poor man's deference toward the wealthy and well-born.

"I think I'll adopt your suggestion, sir," replied the son, "and run up to New York; and after I've been there awhile I may go on to Boston for a week or so. I've never been there, you know."

"There are some matters you can talk over with my factor in New York," rejoined the colonel, "and while you are up there among the Yankees, I hope you'll keep your eyes and ears open to find out what the rascally abolitionists are saying and doing. They're becoming altogether too active for our comfort, and entirely too many ungrateful niggers are running away. I hope the conviction of that fellow yesterday may discourage the rest of the breed. I'd just like to catch any one trying to run off one of my darkeys. He'd get short shrift; I don't think any Court would have a chance to try him."

"They are a pestiferous lot," assented Dick, "and dangerous to our institutions. But say, father, if I go North I shall want to take Tom with me."

Now, the colonel, while a very indulgent father, had pronounced views on the subject of negroes, having studied them, as he often said, for a great many years, and, as he asserted oftener still, understanding them perfectly. It is scarcely worth while to say, either, that he valued more highly than if he had inherited them the slaves he had toiled and schemed for.

"I don't think it safe to take Tom up North," he declared, with promptness and decision. "He's a good enough boy, but too smart to trust among those low-down abolitionists. I strongly suspect him of having learned to read, though I can't imagine how. I saw him with a newspaper the other day, and while he pretended to be looking at a woodcut, I'm almost sure he was reading the paper. I think it by no means safe to take him."

Dick did not insist, because he knew it was useless. The colonel would have obliged his son in any other matter, but his negroes were the outward and visible sign of his wealth and station, and therefore sacred to him.

"Whom do you think it safe to take?" asked Dick. "I suppose I'll have to have a body-servant."

"What's the matter with Grandison?" suggested the colonel. "He's handy enough, and I reckon we can trust him. He's too fond of good eating, to risk losing his regular meals; besides, he's sweet on your mother's maid, Betty, and I've promised to let 'em get married before long. I'll have Grandison up, and we'll talk to him. Here, you boy Jack," called the colonel to a yellow youth in the next room who was catching flies and pulling their wings off to pass the time, "go down to the barn and tell Grandison to come here."

"Grandison," said the colonel, when the negro stood before him, hat in hand.

"Yas, marster."

"Haven't I always treated you right?"

"Yas, marster."

"Haven't you always got all you wanted to eat?"

"Yas, marster."

"And as much whiskey and tobacco as was good for you, Grandison?"

"Y-a-s, marster."

"I should just like to know, Grandison, whether you don't think yourself a great deal better off than those poor free negroes down by the plank road, with no kind master to look after them and no mistress to give them medicine when they're sick and—and"—

"Well, I sh'd jes' reckon I is better off, suh, dan dem low-down free niggers, suh! Ef anybody ax 'em who dey b'long ter, dey has ter say nobody, er e'se lie erbout it. Anybody ax me who I b'longs ter, I ain' got no 'casion ter be shame' ter tell 'em, no, suh, 'deed I ain', suh!"

The colonel was beaming. This was true gratitude, and his feudal heart thrilled at such appreciative homage. What cold-blooded, heartless monsters they were who would break up this blissful relationship of kindly protection on the one hand, of wise subordination and loyal dependence on the other! The colonel always became indignant at the mere thought of such wickedness.

"Grandison," the colonel continued, "your young master Dick is going North for a few weeks, and I am thinking of letting him take you along. I shall send you on this trip, Grandison, in order that you may take care of your young master. He will need some one to wait on him, and no one can ever do it so well as one of the boys brought up with him on the old plantation. I am going to trust him in your hands, and I'm sure you'll do your duty faithfully, and bring him back home safe and sound—to old Kentucky."

Grandison grinned. "Oh yas, marster, I'll take keer er young Mars Dick."

"I want to warn you, though, Grandison," continued the colonel impressively, "against these cussed abolitionists, who try to entice servants from their comfortable homes and their indulgent masters, from the blue skies, the green fields, and the warm sunlight of their southern home, and send them away off yonder to Canada, a dreary country, where the woods are full of wildcats and wolves and bears, where the snow lies up to the eaves of the houses for six months of the year, and the cold is so severe that it freezes your breath and curdles your blood; and where, when runaway niggers get sick and can't work, they are turned out to starve and die, unloved and uncared for. I reckon, Grandison, that you have too much sense to permit yourself to be led astray by any such foolish and wicked people."

"'Deed, suh, I wouldn' low none er dem cussed, low-down abolitioners ter come nigh me, suh. I'd—I'd—would I be 'lowed ter hit 'em, suh?"

"Certainly, Grandison," replied the colonel, chuckling, "hit 'em as hard as you can. I reckon they'd rather like it. Begad, I believe they would! It would serve 'em right to be hit by a nigger!"

"Er ef I didn't hit 'em, suh," continued Grandison reflectively, "I'd tell Mars Dick, en *he'd* fix 'em. He'd smash de face off'n 'em, suh, I jes' knows he would."

"Oh yes, Grandison, your young master will protect you. You need fear no harm while he is near."

"Dey won't try ter steal me, will dey, marster?" asked the negro, with sudden alarm.

"I don't know, Grandison," replied the colonel, lighting a fresh cigar. "They're a desperate set of lunatics, and there's no telling what they may resort to. But if you stick close to your young master, and remember always that he is your best friend, and understands your real needs, and has your true interests at heart, and if you will be careful to avoid strangers who try to talk to you, you'll stand a fair chance of getting back to your home and your friends. And if you please your master Dick, he'll buy you a present, and a string of beads for Betty to wear when you and she get married in the fall."

"Thanky, marster, thanky, suh," replied Grandison, oozing gratitude at every pore; "you is a good marster, to be sho', suh; yas, 'deed you is. You kin jes' bet me and Mars Dick gwine git 'long jes' lack I wuz own boy ter Mars Dick. En it won't be my fault ef he don' want me fer his boy all de time, w'en we come back home ag'in."

"All right, Grandison, you may go now. You needn't work any more to-day, and here's a piece of tobacco for you off my own plug."

"Thanky, marster, thanky, marster! You is de bes' marster any nigger ever had in dis worl'." And Grandison bowed and scraped and disappeared round the corner, his jaws closing around a large section of the colonel's best tobacco.

"You may take Grandison," said the colonel to his son. "I allow he's abolitionist-proof."

III

Richard Owens, Esq., and servant, from Kentucky, registered at the fashionable New York hostelry for Southerners in those days, a hotel where an atmosphere congenial to Southern institutions was sedulously maintained. But there were negro waiters in the dining-room, and mulatto bell-boys, and Dick had no doubt that Grandison, with the native gregariousness and garrulousness of his race, would foregather and palaver with them sooner or later, and Dick hoped that they would speedily inoculate him with the virus of freedom. For it was not Dick's intention to say anything to his servant about his plan to free him, for obvious reasons. To mention one of them, if Grandison should go away, and by legal process be recaptured, his young master's part in the matter would doubtless become known, which would be embarrassing to Dick, to say the least. If, on the other hand, he should merely give Grandison sufficient latitude, he had no doubt he would eventually lose him. For while not exactly skeptical about Grandison's perfervid loyalty, Dick had been a somewhat keen observer of human nature, in his own indolent way, and based his expectations upon the force of the example and argument that his servant could scarcely fail to encounter. Grandison should have a fair chance to become free by his own initiative; if it should become necessary to adopt other measures to get rid of him, it would be time enough to act when the necessity arose; and Dick Owens was not the youth to take needless trouble.

The young master renewed some acquaintances and made others, and spent a week or two very pleasantly in the best society of the metropolis, easily accessible to a wealthy, well-bred young Southerner, with proper introductions. Young women smiled on him, and young men of convivial habits pressed their hospitalities; but the memory of Charity's sweet, strong face and clear blue eyes made him proof against the blandishments of the one sex and the persuasions of the other. Meanwhile he kept Grandison supplied with pocket-money, and left him mainly to his own devices. Every night when Dick came in he hoped he might have to wait upon himself, and every morning he looked forward with pleasure to the prospect of making his toilet unaided. His hopes, however, were doomed to disappointment, for every night when he came in Grandison was on hand with a bootjack, and a nightcap mixed for his young master as the colonel had taught him to mix it, and every morning Grandison appeared with his master's boots blacked and his clothes brushed, and laid his linen out for the day.

"Grandison," said Dick one morning, after finishing his toilet, "this is the chance of your life to go around among your own people and see how they live. Have you met any of them?"

"Yas, suh, I's seen some of 'em. But I don' keer nuffin fer 'em, suh. Dey're diffe'nt f'm de niggers down ou' way. Dey 'lows dey're free, but dey ain' got sense 'nuff ter know dey ain' half as well off as dey would be down Souf, whar dey'd be 'preciated."

When two weeks had passed without any apparent effect of evil example upon Grandison, Dick resolved to go on to Boston, where he thought the atmosphere might prove more favorable to his ends. After he had been at the Revere House for a day or two without losing Grandison, he decided upon slightly different tactics.

Having ascertained from a city directory the addresses of several well-known abolitionists, he wrote them each a letter something like this:—

> DEAR FRIEND AND BROTHER:—
>
> *A wicked slaveholder from Kentucky, stopping at the Revere House, has dared to insult the liberty-loving people of Boston by bringing his slave into their midst. Shall this be tolerated? Or shall steps be taken in the name of liberty to rescue a fellow-man from bondage? For obvious reasons I can only sign myself,*
>
> A FRIEND OF HUMANITY.

That his letter might have an opportunity to prove effective, Dick made it a point to send Grandison away from the hotel on various errands. On one of these occasions Dick watched him for quite a distance down the street. Grandison had scarcely left the hotel when a long-haired, sharp-featured man came out behind him, followed him, soon overtook him, and kept along beside him until they turned the next corner. Dick's hopes were roused by this spectacle, but sank correspondingly when Grandison returned to the hotel. As Grandison said nothing about the encounter, Dick hoped there might be some self-consciousness behind this unexpected reticence, the results of which might develop later on.

But Grandison was on hand again when his master came back to the hotel at night, and was in attendance again in the morning, with hot water, to assist at his master's toilet. Dick sent him on further errands from day to day, and upon one occasion came squarely up to him—inadvertently of course—while Grandison was engaged in conversation with a young white man in clerical garb. When Grandison saw Dick approaching, he edged away from the preacher and hastened toward his master, with a very evident expression of relief upon his countenance.

"Mars Dick," he said, "dese yer abolitioners is jes' pesterin' de life out er me tryin' ter git me ter run away. I don' pay no 'tention ter 'em, but dey riles me so sometimes dat I'm feared I'll hit some of 'em some er dese days, an' dat mought git me inter trouble. I ain' said nuffin' ter you 'bout it, Mars Dick, fer I didn' wanter 'sturb yo' min'; but I don' like it, suh; no, suh, I don'! Is we gwine back home 'fo' long, Mars Dick?"

"We'll be going back soon enough," replied Dick somewhat shortly, while he inwardly cursed the stupidity of a slave who could be free and would not, and registered a secret vow that if he were unable to get rid of Grandison without assassinating him, and were therefore compelled to take him back to Kentucky, he would see that Grandison got a taste of an article of slavery that would make him regret his wasted opportunities. Meanwhile he determined to tempt his servant yet more strongly.

"Grandison," he said next morning, "I'm going away for a day or two, but I shall leave you here. I shall lock up a hundred dollars in this drawer and give you the key. If you need any of it, use it and enjoy yourself,—spend it all if you like,—for this is probably the last chance you'll have for some time to be in a free State, and you'd better enjoy your liberty while you may."

When he came back a couple of days later and found the faithful Grandison at his post, and the hundred dollars intact, Dick felt seriously annoyed. His vexation was increased by the fact that he could not express his feelings adequately. He did not even scold Grandison; how could he, indeed, find fault with one who so sensibly recognized his true place in the economy of civilization, and kept it with such touching fidelity?

"I can't say a thing to him," groaned Dick. "He deserves a leather medal, made out of his own hide tanned. I reckon I'll write to father and let him know what a model servant he has given me."

He wrote his father a letter which made the colonel swell with pride and pleasure. "I really think," the colonel observed to one of his friends, "that Dick ought to have the nigger interviewed by the Boston papers, so that they may see how contented and happy our darkeys really are."

Dick also wrote a long letter to Charity Lomax, in which he said, among many other things, that if she knew how hard he was working, and under what difficulties, to accomplish something serious for her sake, she would no longer keep him in suspense, but overwhelm him with love and admiration.

Having thus exhausted without result the more obvious methods of getting rid of Grandison, and diplomacy having also proved a failure, Dick was forced to consider more radical measures. Of course he might run away himself, and abandon Grandison, but this would be merely to leave him in the United States, where he was still a slave, and where, with his notions of loyalty, he would speedily be reclaimed. It was necessary, in order to accomplish the purpose of his trip to the North, to leave Grandison permanently in Canada, where he would be legally free.

"I might extend my trip to Canada," he reflected, "but that would be too palpable. I have it! I'll visit Niagara Falls on the way home, and lose him on the Canadian side. When he once realizes that he is actually free, I'll warrant that he'll stay."

So the next day saw them westward bound, and in due course of time, by the somewhat slow conveyances of the period, they found themselves at Niagara. Dick walked and drove about the Falls for several days, taking Grandison along with him on most occasions. One morning they stood on the Canadian side, watching the wild whirl of the waters below them.

"Grandison," said Dick, raising his voice above the roar of the cataract, "do you know where you are now?"

"I's wid you, Mars Dick; dat's all I keers."

"You are now in Canada, Grandison, where your people go when they run away from their masters. If you wished, Grandison, you might walk away from me this very minute, and I could not lay my hand upon you to take you back."

Grandison looked around uneasily.

"Let's go back ober de ribber, Mars Dick. I's feared I'll lose you ovuh heah, an' den I won' hab no marster, an' won't nebber be able to git back home no mo'."

Discouraged, but not yet hopeless, Dick said, a few minutes later,—

"Grandison, I'm going up the road a bit, to the inn over yonder. You stay here until I return. I'll not be gone a great while."

Grandison's eyes opened wide and he looked somewhat fearful.

"Is dey any er dem dadblasted abolitioners roun' heah, Mars Dick?"

"I don't imagine that there are," replied his master, hoping there might be. "But I'm not afraid of *your* running away, Grandison. I only wish I were," he added to himself.

Dick walked leisurely down the road to where the whitewashed inn, built of stone, with true British solidity, loomed up through the trees by the roadside. Arrived there he ordered a glass of ale and a sandwich, and took a seat at a table by a window, from which he could see Grandison in the distance. For a while he hoped that the seed he had sown might have fallen on fertile ground, and that Grandison, relieved from the restraining power of a master's eye, and finding himself in a free country, might get up and walk away; but the hope was vain, for Grandison remained faithfully at his post, awaiting his master's return. He had seated himself on a broad flat stone, and, turning his eyes away from the grand and awe-inspiring spectacle that lay close at hand, was looking anxiously toward the inn where his master sat cursing his ill-timed fidelity.

By and by a girl came into the room to serve his order, and Dick very naturally glanced at her; and as she was young and pretty and remained in attendance, it was some minutes before he looked for Grandison. When he did so his faithful servant had disappeared.

To pay his reckoning and go away without the change was a matter quickly accomplished. Retracing his footsteps toward the Falls, he saw, to his great disgust, as he approached the spot where he had left Grandison, the familiar form of his servant stretched out on the ground, his face to the sun, his mouth open, sleeping the time away, oblivious alike to the grandeur of the scenery, the thunderous roar of the cataract, or the insidious voice of sentiment.

"Grandison," soliloquized his master, as he stood gazing down at his ebony encumbrance, "I do not deserve to be an American citizen; I ought not to have the advantages I possess over you; and I certainly am not worthy of Charity Lomax, if I am not smart enough to get rid of you. I have an idea! You shall yet be free, and I will be the instrument of your deliverance. Sleep on, faithful and affectionate servitor, and dream of the blue grass and the bright skies of old Kentucky, for it is only in your dreams that you will ever see them again!"

Dick retraced his footsteps towards the inn. The young woman chanced to look out of the window and saw the handsome young gentleman she had waited on a few minutes before, standing in the road a short distance away, apparently engaged in earnest conversation with a colored man employed as hostler for the inn. She thought she saw something pass from the white man to the other, but at that moment her duties called her away from the window, and when she looked out again the young gentleman had disappeared, and the hostler, with two other young men of the neighborhood, one white and one colored, were walking rapidly towards the Falls.

IV

Dick made the journey homeward alone, and as rapidly as the conveyances of the day would permit. As he drew near home his conduct in going back without Grandison took on a more serious aspect than it had borne at any previous time, and although he had prepared the colonel by a letter sent several days ahead, there was still the prospect of a bad quarter of an hour with him; not, indeed, that his father would upbraid him, but he was likely to make searching inquiries. And notwithstanding the vein of quiet recklessness that had carried Dick through his preposterous scheme, he was a very poor liar, having rarely had occasion or inclination to tell anything but the truth. Any reluctance to meet his father was more than offset, however, by a stronger force drawing him homeward, for Charity Lomax must long since have returned from her visit to her aunt in Tennessee.

Dick got off easier than he had expected. He told a straight story, and a truthful one, so far as it went.

The colonel raged at first, but rage soon subsided into anger, and anger moderated into annoyance, and annoyance into a sort of garrulous sense of injury. The colonel thought he had been hardly used; he had trusted this negro, and he had broken faith. Yet, after all, he did not blame Grandison so much as he did the abolitionists, who were undoubtedly at the bottom of it.

As for Charity Lomax, Dick told her, privately of course, that he had run his father's man, Grandison, off to Canada, and left him there.

"Oh, Dick," she had said with shuddering alarm, "what have you done? If they knew it they'd send you to the penitentiary, like they did that Yankee."

"But they don't know it," he had replied seriously; adding, with an injured tone, "you don't seem to appreciate my heroism like you did that of the Yankee; perhaps it's because I wasn't caught and sent to the penitentiary. I thought you wanted me to do it."

"Why, Dick Owens!" she exclaimed. "You know I never dreamed of any such outrageous proceeding.

"But I presume I'll have to marry you," she concluded, after some insistence on Dick's part, "if only to take care of you. You are too reckless for anything; and a man who goes chasing all over the North, being entertained by New York and Boston society and having negroes to throw away, needs some one to look after him."

"It's a most remarkable thing," replied Dick fervently, "that your views correspond exactly with my profoundest convictions. It proves beyond question that we were made for one another."

They were married three weeks later. As each of them had just returned from a journey, they spent their honeymoon at home.

A week after the wedding they were seated, one afternoon, on the piazza of the colonel's house, where Dick had taken his bride, when a negro from the yard ran down the lane and threw open the big gate for the colonel's buggy to enter. The colonel was not alone. Beside him, ragged and travel-stained, bowed with weariness, and upon his face a haggard look that told of hardship and privation, sat the lost Grandison.

The colonel alighted at the steps.

"Take the lines, Tom," he said to the man who had opened the gate, "and drive round to the barn. Help Grandison down,—poor devil, he's so stiff he can hardly move!—and get a tub of water and wash him and rub him down, and feed him, and give him a big drink of whiskey, and then let him come round and see his young master and his new mistress."

The colonel's face wore an expression compounded of joy and indignation,—joy at the restoration of a valuable piece of property; indignation for reasons he proceeded to state.

"It's astounding, the depths of depravity the human heart is capable of! I was coming along the road three miles away, when I heard some one call me from the roadside. I pulled up the mare, and who should come out of the woods but Grandison. The poor nigger could hardly crawl along, with the help of a broken limb. I was never more astonished in my life. You could have knocked me down with a feather. He seemed pretty far gone,—he could hardly talk above a whisper,—and I had to give him a mouthful of whiskey to brace him up so he could tell his story. It's just as I thought from the beginning, Dick; Grandison had no notion of running away; he knew when he was well off, and where his friends were. All the persuasions of abolition liars and runaway niggers did not move him. But the desperation of those fanatics knew no bounds; their guilty consciences gave them no rest. They got the notion somehow that Grandison belonged to a nigger-catcher, and had been brought North as a spy to help capture ungrateful runaway servants. They actually kidnaped him—just think of it!—and gagged him and bound him and threw him rudely into a wagon, and carried him into the gloomy depths of a Canadian forest, and locked him in a lonely hut, and fed him on bread and water for three weeks. One of the scoundrels wanted to kill him, and persuaded the others that it ought to be done; but they got to quarreling about how they should do it, and before they had their minds made up Grandison escaped, and, keeping his back steadily to the North Star, made his way, after suffering incredible hardships, back to the old plantation, back to his master, his friends, and his home. Why, it's as good as one of Scott's novels![2] Mr. Simms[3] or some other one of our Southern authors ought to write it up."

"Don't you think, sir," suggested Dick, who had calmly smoked his cigar throughout the colonel's animated recital, "that that kidnaping yarn sounds a little improbable? Isn't there some more likely explanation?"

"Nonsense, Dick; it's the gospel truth! Those infernal abolitionists are capable of anything—everything! Just think of their locking the poor, faithful nigger up, beating him, kicking him, depriving him of his liberty, keeping him on bread and water for three long, lonesome weeks, and he all the time pining for the old plantation!"

There were almost tears in the colonel's eyes at the picture of Grandison's sufferings that he conjured up. Dick still professed to be slightly skeptical, and met Charity's severely questioning eye with bland unconsciousness.

The colonel killed the fatted calf for Grandison, and for two or three weeks the returned wanderer's life was a slave's dream of pleasure. His fame spread throughout the county, and the colonel gave him a permanent place among the house servants, where he could always have him conveniently at hand to relate his adventures to admiring visitors.

About three weeks after Grandison's return the colonel's faith in sable humanity was rudely shaken, and its foundations almost broken up. He came near losing his belief in the fidelity of the negro to his master,—the servile virtue most highly prized and most sedulously cultivated by the colonel and his kind. One Monday morning Grandison was missing. And not only Grandison, but his wife, Betty the maid; his

[2]Sir Walter Scott (1771–1832), immensely popular British historical novelist in both the United States and Great Britain.

[3]William Gilmore Simms (1806–1870), perhaps the antebellum South's most admired author, glorified the history and aristocratic traditions of his region in novels, magazines, histories, and biographies centering on his native South Carolina.

mother, aunt Eunice; his father, uncle Ike; his brothers, Tom and John, and his little sister Elsie, were likewise absent from the plantation; and a hurried search and inquiry in the neighborhood resulted in no information as to their whereabouts. So much valuable property could not be lost without an effort to recover it, and the wholesale nature of the transaction carried consternation to the hearts of those whose ledgers were chiefly bound in black. Extremely energetic measures were taken by the colonel and his friends. The fugitives were traced, and followed from point to point, on their northward run through Ohio. Several times the hunters were close upon their heels, but the magnitude of the escaping party begot unusual vigilance on the part of those who sympathized with the fugitives, and strangely enough, the underground railroad seemed to have had its tracks cleared and signals set for this particular train. Once, twice, the colonel thought he had them, but they slipped through his fingers.

One last glimpse he caught of his vanishing property, as he stood, accompanied by a United States marshal, on a wharf at a port on the south shore of Lake Erie. On the stern of a small steamboat which was receding rapidly from the wharf, with her nose pointing toward Canada, there stood a group of familiar dark faces, and the look they cast backward was not one of longing for the fleshpots of Egypt.[4] The colonel saw Grandison point him out to one of the crew of the vessel, who waved his hand derisively toward the colonel. The latter shook his fist impotently—and the incident was closed.

1899

Paul Laurence Dunbar 1872–1906

Paul Laurence Dunbar achieved nationwide fame for his dialect poetry depicting a romanticized plantation life of southern blacks. Born in Dayton, Ohio, to former Kentucky slaves, the sickly child was fascinated by his mother's stories and by tales of his father's experience as a Union soldier during the Civil War. He early exhibited an interest in writing, and before he completed high school, a few of his pieces had been published in local newspapers. They already manifested the late-nineteenth-century romantic strains and sentimental elements that were to become characteristic of his mature work.

Upon graduation, Dunbar could find work only as an elevator operator at four dollars per week. However, he continued to read widely and began to write fiction. Selling his first story, "The Tenderfoot," to the Kellogg Syndicate of Chicago for six dollars made him realize the commercial potential of authorship. There followed a series of lucky coincidences including the printing of *Oak and Ivy* with the help of Orville and Wilbur Wright (close friends from his school days) as well as an invitation to join the Western Association of Writers when the organization met in Dayton.

With the promised opening of the World's Columbian Exposition in 1893, Dunbar went to Chicago to seek work and met several outstanding blacks, including

[4]See Exodus 16:2–3.

Frederick Douglass, who, as Consul General to the Republic of Haiti, hired Dunbar in the Haitian Pavilion. Dunbar's experience in Chicago led to lasting friendships and resulted in his "Columbian Ode," by far the best—albeit the least known—of the many poems written for that occasion. When the Exposition ended, Dunbar returned to Dayton and his job as elevator operator. Shortly thereafter, the noted actor James A. Herne publicly recited a Dunbar poem and was instrumental in introducing the poet's work to William Dean Howells, who reviewed *Majors and Minors* in *Harper's Weekly* (June 27, 1896) and persuaded Dodd, Mead to publish Dunbar's third volume of verse.

Lyrics of Lowly Life appeared with the now-famous introduction by Howells. Claiming that Dunbar "is the first black man" to express "the life of the Negro aesthetically and...lyrically," the influential critic provided a testimony that led to Dunbar's celebrity. By the time he was twenty-four, with three books to his credit, he had received the acclaim that few writers achieve in a lifetime.

Despite Dunbar's success, he was criticized as a supporter of negative racial stereotypes. If James Weldon Johnson's record of a late conversation is accurate, Dunbar was saddened that many critics and much of his public wanted nothing more than dialect pieces from him. Some of this self-reproach undoubtedly found its way into "The Poet," which begins: "He sang of life, serenely sweet,/With, now and then, a deeper note," and ends with the realization "But, ah, the world, it turned to praise/A jingle in a broken tongue." That some of these "jingles in a broken tongue" were to become famous for the wrong reasons is unfortunate. Many, including Howells and later critics, overlooked the fact that while Dunbar used the plantation tradition, he was not particularly adept at producing an authentic black speech pattern—relying instead upon Hoosier dialect like that popularized by James Whitcomb Riley.

Because Dunbar is so closely associated with tales and poems of southern life, other aspects of his work have been overlooked. He devoted a great deal of creative energy to "raceless" verse and stories: his earliest published tales, "The Tenderfoot" and "Little Billy," are westerns; his first novel, *The Uncalled,* is set in the Midwest and is a sentimental work whose action is not dependent upon the race of the characters. Dunbar recognized that racial problems were not regional; and like other nineteenth-century romantics, he believed that life could not flourish in an urban setting. Thus, despite the negative portrait of the South in *The Sport of the Gods,* the North—represented by New York City—does not provide an adequate alternative.

The Strength of Gideon and Other Stories, composed of twenty narratives that range from plantation tales to realistic portrayals of contemporary life, is one of Dunbar's best short story collections. In some, the imagined loyalty of ex-slaves is treated both tenderly and sarcastically; others examine the hostility of the northern environment and the shortcomings of urban life. The tales of Reconstruction, set in a time when blacks were attempting to become part of the body politic, remain pertinent today. Perhaps nowhere is the indifference of the white political structure more poignantly presented than in "Mr. Cornelius Johnson, Office-Seeker."

Like such diverse personalities as Frederick Douglass, W.E.B. DuBois, and Booker T. Washington, who dealt in their respective ways with America's racial problems, Dunbar used his talents to write "protest" pieces in essay form. Among his most perceptive analyses of American society, which also reflect the range of his concerns, are "The Race Question Discussed" (*Toledo Journal,* December 11, 1898), "Is Negro Education for the Negro Hopeless?" (*Philadelphia Times,* June 10, 1900), and "The Fourth of July and Race Outrages:

Paul Laurence Dunbar's Bitter Satire on Independence Day" (*New York Times,* July 10, 1903).

Dunbar's non-dialect verse has received little attention in recent years, much of it outdated by its sentimentality and didacticism. There are, however, moments of innovation and poetic insight to indicate that Dunbar was more than just an imitative versifier. Moreover, much of his poetry reflects the protest elements seen in his essays. There are, for example, poems in praise of such figures as Harriet Beecher Stowe, Alexander Crummell, and Booker T. Washington. And upon the death of Frederick Douglass in 1895, Dunbar—who had formed an unusually strong bond with the older man—paid homage to the man who had become a legend.

The growing unhappiness of Dunbar resulted in an uncharacteristic pessimism that was undoubtedly caused in part by his short-lived marriage to Alice Moore and in part by his painful illness—now recognized as tuberculosis. Toward the end of his life, as he longed for the day when people would be judged by their work rather than by the color of their skin, he began to understand the mirage-like quality of the American dream.

Kenny J. Williams
Duke University

PRIMARY WORKS

Oak and Ivy, 1893; *Majors and Minors,* 1896; *Lyrics of Lowly Life,* 1896; *Folks from Dixie,* 1898; *The Uncalled,* 1898; *Lyrics of the Hearthside,* 1899; *The Strength of Gideon and Other Stories,* 1900; *The Love of Landry,* 1900; *The Fanatics,* 1901; *The Sport of the Gods,* 1902; *Lyrics of Love and Laughter,* 1903; *In Old Plantation Days,* 1903; *The Heart of Happy Hollow,* 1904; *Lyrics of Sunshine and Shadow,* 1905.

Mr. Cornelius Johnson, Office-Seeker

It was a beautiful day in balmy May and the sun shone pleasantly on Mr. Cornelius Johnson's very spruce Prince Albert suit of grey as he alighted from the train in Washington. He cast his eyes about him, and then gave a sigh of relief and satisfaction as he took his bag from the porter and started for the gate. As he went along, he looked with splendid complacency upon the less fortunate mortals who were streaming out of the day coaches. It was a Pullman sleeper on which he had come in. Out on the pavement he hailed a cab, and giving the driver the address of a hotel, stepped in and was rolled away. Be it said that he had cautiously inquired about the hotel first and found that he could be accommodated there.

As he leaned back in the vehicle and allowed his eyes to roam over the streets, there was an air of distinct prosperity about him. It was in evidence from the tips of his ample patent-leather shoes to the crown of the soft felt hat that sat rakishly upon his head. His entrance into Washington had been long premeditated, and he had got himself up accordingly.

It was not such an imposing structure as he had fondly imagined, before which the cab stopped and set Mr. Johnson down. But then he reflected that it was about the only house where he could find accommodation at all, and he was content. In Alabama one learns to be philosophical. It is good to be philosophical in a place where the proprietor of a café fumbles vaguely around in the region of his hip pocket and insinuates that he doesn't want one's custom. But the visitor's ardor was not cooled for all that. He signed the register with a flourish, and bestowed a liberal fee upon the shabby boy who carried his bag to his room.

"Look here, boy," he said, "I am expecting some callers soon. If they come, just send them right up to my room. You take good care of me and look sharp when I ring and you'll not lose anything."

Mr. Cornelius Johnson always spoke in a large and important tone. He said the simplest thing with an air so impressive as to give it the character of a pronouncement. Indeed, his voice naturally was round, mellifluous and persuasive. He carried himself always as if he were passing under his own triumphal arch. Perhaps, more than anything else, it was these qualities of speech and bearing that had made him invaluable on the stump in the recent campaign in Alabama. Whatever it was that held the secret of his power, the man and principles for which he had labored triumphed, and he had come to Washington to reap his reward. He had been assured that his services would not be forgotten, and it was no intention of his that they should be.

After a while he left his room and went out, returning later with several gentlemen from the South and a Washington man. There is some freemasonry among these office-seekers in Washington that throws them inevitably together. The men with whom he returned were such characters as the press would designate as "old wheelhorses" or "pillars of the party." They all adjourned to the bar, where they had something at their host's expense. Then they repaired to his room, whence for the ensuing two hours the bell and the bell-boy were kept briskly going.

The gentleman from Alabama was in his glory. His gestures as he held forth were those of a gracious and condescending prince. It was his first visit to the city, and he said to the Washington man: "I tell you, sir, you've got a mighty fine town here. Of course, there's no opportunity for anything like local pride, because it's the outsiders, or the whole country, rather, that makes it what it is, but that's nothing. It's a fine town, and I'm right sorry that I can't stay longer."

"How long do you expect to be with us, Professor?" inquired Col. Mason, the horse who had bent his force to the party wheel in the Georgia ruts.

"Oh, about ten days, I reckon, at the furthest. I want to spend some time sightseeing. I'll drop in on the Congressman from my district tomorrow, and call a little later on the President."

"Uh, huh!" said Col. Mason. He had been in the city for some time.

"Yes, sir, I want to get through with my little matter and get back home. I'm not asking for much, and I don't anticipate any trouble in securing what I desire. You see, it's just like this, there's no way for them to refuse us. And if any one deserves the good things at the hands of the administration, who more than we old campaigners, who have been helping the party through its fights from the time that we had our first votes?"

"Who, indeed?" said the Washington man.

"I tell you, gentlemen, the administration is no fool. It knows that we hold the colored vote down there in our vest pockets and it ain't going to turn us down."

"No, of course not, but sometimes there are delays——"

"Delays, to be sure, where a man doesn't know how to go about the matter. The thing to do, is to go right to the centre of authority at once. Don't you see?"

"Certainly, certainly," chorused the other gentlemen.

Before going, the Washington man suggested that the newcomer join them that evening and see something of society at the capital. "You know," he said, "that outside of New Orleans, Washington is the only town in the country that has any colored society to speak of, and I feel that you distinguished men from different sections of the country owe it to our people that they should be allowed to see you. It would be an inspiration to them."

So the matter was settled, and promptly at 8:30 o'clock Mr. Cornelius Johnson joined his friends at the door of his hotel. The grey Prince Albert was scrupulously buttoned about his form, and a shiny top hat replaced the felt of the afternoon. Thus clad, he went forth into society, where he need be followed only long enough to note the magnificence of his manners and the enthusiasm of his reception when he was introduced as Prof. Cornelius Johnson, of Alabama, in a tone which insinuated that he was the only really great man his state had produced.

It might also be stated as an effect of this excursion into Vanity Fair, that when he woke the next morning he was in some doubt as to whether he should visit his Congressman or send for that individual to call upon him. He had felt the subtle flattery of attention from that section of colored society which imitates—only imitates, it is true, but better than any other, copies—the kindnesses and cruelties, the niceties and deceits, of its white prototype. And for the time, like a man in a fog, he had lost his sense of proportion and perspective. But habit finally triumphed, and he called upon the Congressman, only to be met by an under-secretary who told him that his superior was too busy to see him that morning.

"But——"

"Too busy," repeated the secretary.

Mr. Johnson drew himself up and said: "Tell Congressman Barker that Mr. Johnson, Mr. Cornelius Johnson, of Alabama, desires to see him. I think he will see me."

"Well, I can take your message," said the clerk, doggedly, "but I tell you now it won't do you any good. He won't see any one."

But, in a few moments an inner door opened, and the young man came out followed by the desired one. Mr. Johnson couldn't resist the temptation to let his eyes rest on the underling in a momentary glance of triumph as Congressman Barker hurried up to him, saying: "Why, why, Cornelius, how'do? how'do? Ah, you came about that little matter, didn't you? Well, well, I haven't forgotten you; I haven't forgotten you."

The colored man opened his mouth to speak, but the other checked him and went on: "I'm sorry, but I'm in a great hurry now. I'm compelled to leave town today, much against my will, but I shall be back in a week; come around and see me then. Always glad to see you, you know. Sorry I'm so busy now; good-morning, good-morning."

Mr. Johnson allowed himself to be guided politely, but decidedly, to the door. The triumph died out of his face as the reluctant good-morning fell from his lips. As he walked away, he tried to look upon the matter philosophically. He tried to reason with himself—to prove to his own consciousness that the Congressman was very busy and could not give the time that morning. He wanted to make himself believe that he had not been slighted or treated with scant ceremony. But, try as he would, he continued to feel an obstinate, nasty sting that would not let him rest, nor forget his reception. His pride was hurt. The thought came to him to go at once to the President, but he had experience enough to know that such a visit would be vain until he had seen the dispenser of patronage for his district. Thus, there was nothing for him to do but to wait the necessary week. A whole week! His brow knitted as he thought of it.

In the course of these cogitations, his walk brought him to his hotel, where he found his friends of the night before awaiting him. He tried to put on a cheerful face. But his disappointment and humiliation showed through his smile, as the hollows and bones through the skin of a cadaver.

"Well, what luck?" asked Col. Mason, cheerfully.

"Are we to congratulate you?" put in Mr. Perry.

"Not yet, not yet, gentlemen. I have not seen the President yet. The fact is—ahem—my Congressman is out of town."

He was not used to evasions of this kind, and he stammered slightly and his yellow face turned brick-red with shame.

"It is most annoying," he went on, "most annoying. Mr. Barker won't be back for a week, and I don't want to call on the President until I have had a talk with him."

"Certainly not," said Col. Mason, blandly. "There will be delays." This was not his first pilgrimage to Mecca.

Mr. Johnson looked at him gratefully. "Oh, yes; of course, delays," he assented; "most natural. Have something."

At the end of the appointed time, the office-seeker went again to see the Congressman. This time he was admitted without question, and got the chance to state his wants. But somehow, there seemed to be innumerable obstacles in the way. There were certain other men whose wishes had to be consulted; the leader of one of the party factions, who, for the sake of harmony, had to be appeased. Of course, Mr. Johnson's worth was fully recognized, and he would be rewarded according to his deserts. His interests would be looked after. He should drop in again in a day or two. It took time, of course, it took time.

Mr. Johnson left the office unnerved by his disappointment. He had thought it would be easy to come up to Washington, claim and get what he wanted, and, after a glance at the town, hurry back to his home and his honors. It had all seemed so easy—before election; but now——

A vague doubt began to creep into his mind that turned him sick at heart. He knew how they had treated Davis, of Louisiana. He had heard how they had once kept Brotherton, of Texas—a man who had spent all his life in the service of his party—waiting clear through a whole administration, at the end of which the opposite party had come into power. All the stories of disappointment and disaster that he had ever heard came back to him, and he began to wonder if some one of these things was going to happen to him.

Every other day for the next two weeks, he called upon Barker, but always with the same result. Nothing was clear yet, until one day the bland legislator told him that considerations of expediency had compelled them to give the place he was asking for to another man.

"But what am I to do?" asked the helpless man.

"Oh, you just bide your time. I'll look out for you. Never fear."

Until now, Johnson had ignored the gentle hints of his friend, Col. Mason, about a boarding-house being more convenient than a hotel. Now, he asked him if there was a room vacant where he was staying, and finding that there was, he had his things moved thither at once. He felt the change keenly, and although no one really paid any attention to it, he believed that all Washington must have seen it, and hailed it as the first step in his degradation.

For a while the two together made occasional excursions to a glittering palace down the street, but when the money had grown lower and lower Col. Mason had the knack of bringing "a little something" to their rooms without a loss of dignity. In fact, it was in these hours with the old man, over a pipe and a bit of something, that Johnson was most nearly cheerful. Hitch after hitch had occurred in his plans, and day after day he had come home unsuccessful and discouraged. The crowning disappointment, though, came when, after a long session that lasted even up into the hot days of summer, Congress adjourned and his one hope went away. Johnson saw him just before his departure, and listened ruefully as he said: "I tell you, Cornelius, now, you'd better go on home, get back to your business and come again next year. The clouds of battle will be somewhat dispelled by then and we can see clearer what to do. It was too early this year. We were too near the fight still, and there were party wounds to be bound up and little factional sores that had to be healed. But next year, Cornelius, next year we'll see what we can do for you."

His constituent did not tell him that even if his pride would let him go back home a disappointed applicant, he had not the means wherewith to go. He did not tell him that he was trying to keep up appearances and hide the truth from his wife, who, with their two children, waited and hoped for him at home.

When he went home that night, Col. Mason saw instantly that things had gone wrong with him. But here the tact and delicacy of the old politician came uppermost and, without trying to draw his story from him—for he already divined the situation too well—he sat for a long time telling the younger man stories of the ups and downs of men whom he had known in his long and active life.

They were stories of hardship, deprivation and discouragement. But the old man told them ever with the touch of cheeriness and the note of humor that took away the ghastly hopelessness of some of the pictures. He told them with such feeling and sympathy that Johnson was moved to frankness and told him his own pitiful tale.

Now that he had some one to whom he could open his heart, Johnson himself was no less willing to look the matter in the face, and even during the long summer days, when he had begun to live upon his wardrobe, piece by piece, he still kept up; although some of his pomposity went, along with the Prince Albert coat and the shiny hat. He now wore a shiny coat, and less showy head-gear. For a couple of weeks, too, he disappeared, and as he returned with some money, it was fair to presume that he had been at work somewhere, but he could not stay away from the city long.

It was nearing the middle of autumn when Col. Mason came home to their rooms one day to find his colleague more disheartened and depressed than he had ever seen him before. He was lying with his head upon his folded arm, and when he looked up there were traces of tears upon his face.

"Why, why, what's the matter now?" asked the old man. "No bad news, I hope."

"Nothing worse than I should have expected," was the choking answer. "It's a letter from my wife. She's sick and one of the babies is down, but"—his voice broke—"she tells me to stay and fight it out. My God, Mason, I could stand it if she whined or accused me or begged me to come home, but her patient, long-suffering bravery breaks me all up."

Col. Mason stood up and folded his arms across his big chest. "She's a brave little woman," he said, gravely. "I wish her husband was as brave a man." Johnson raised his head and arms from the table where they were sprawled, as the old man went on: "The hard conditions of life in our race have taught our women a patience and fortitude which the women of no other race have ever displayed. They have taught the men less, and I am sorry, very sorry. The thing, that as much as anything else, made the blacks such excellent soldiers in the civil war was their patient endurance of hardship. The softer education of more prosperous days seems to have weakened this quality. The man who quails or weakens in this fight of ours against adverse circumstances would have quailed before—no, he would have run from an enemy on the field."

"Why, Mason, your mood inspires me. I feel as if I could go forth to battle cheerfully." For the moment, Johnson's old pomposity had returned to him, but in the next, a wave of despondency bore it down. "But that's just it; a body feels as if he could fight if he only had something to fight. But here you strike out and hit—nothing. It's only a contest with time. It's waiting—waiting—waiting!"

"In this case, waiting is fighting."

"Well, even that granted, it matters not how grand his cause, the soldier needs his rations."

"Forage," shot forth the answer like a command.

"Ah, Mason, that's well enough in good country; but the army of office-seekers has devastated Washington. It has left a track as bare as lay behind Sherman's troopers." Johnson rose more cheerfully. "I'm going to the telegraph office," he said as he went out.

A few days after this, he was again in the best of spirits, for there was money in his pocket.

"What have you been doing?" asked Mr. Toliver.

His friend laughed like a boy. "Something very imprudent, I'm sure you will say. I've mortgaged my little place down home. It did not bring much, but I had to have money for the wife and the children, and to keep me until Congress assembles; then I believe that everything will be all right."

Col. Mason's brow clouded and he sighed.

On the reassembling of the two Houses, Congressman Barker was one of the first men in his seat. Mr. Cornelius Johnson went to see him soon.

"What, you here already, Cornelius?" asked the legislator.

"I haven't been away," was the answer.

"Well, you've got the hang-on, and that's what an officer-seeker needs. Well, I'll attend to your matter among the very first. I'll visit the President in a day or two."

The listener's heart throbbed hard. After all his waiting, triumph was his at last.

He went home walking on air, and Col. Mason rejoiced with him. In a few days came word from Barker: "Your appointment was sent in to-day. I'll rush it through on the other side. Come up to-morrow afternoon."

Cornelius and Mr. Toliver hugged each other.

"It came just in time," said the younger man; "the last of my money was about gone, and I should have had to begin paying off that mortgage with no prospect of ever doing it."

The two had suffered together, and it was fitting that they should be together to receive the news of the long-desired happiness; so arm in arm they sauntered down to the Congressman's office about five o'clock the next afternoon. In honor of the occasion, Mr. Johnson had spent his last dollar in redeeming the grey Prince Albert and the shiny hat. A smile flashed across Barker's face as he noted the change.

"Well, Cornelius," he said, "I'm glad to see you still prosperous-looking, for there were some alleged irregularities in your methods down in Alabama, and the Senate has refused to confirm you. I did all I could for you, but——"

The rest of the sentence was lost, as Col. Mason's arms received his friend's fainting form.

"Poor devil!" said the Congressman. "I should have broken it more gently."

Somehow Col. Mason got him home and to bed, where for nine weeks he lay wasting under a complete nervous give-down. The little wife and the children came up to nurse him, and the woman's ready industry helped him to such creature comforts as his sickness demanded. Never once did she murmur; never once did her faith in him waver. And when he was well enough to be moved back, it was money that she had earned, increased by what Col. Mason, in his generosity of spirit, took from his own narrow means, that paid their second-class fare back to the South.

During the fever-fits of his illness, the wasted politician first begged piteously that they would not send him home unplaced, and then he would break out in the most extravagant and pompous boasts about his position, his Congressman and his influence. When he came to himself, he was silent, morose, and bitter. Only once did he melt. It was when he held Col. Mason's hand and bade him good-bye. Then the tears came into his eyes, and what he would have said was lost among his broken words.

As he stood upon the platform of the car as it moved out, and gazed at the white dome and feathery spires of the city, growing into grey indefiniteness, he ground his teeth, and raising his spent hand, shook it at the receding view. "Damn you! damn you!" he cried. "Damn your deceit, your fair cruelties; damn you, you hard, white liar!"

1899

from Lyrics of Lowly Life

Frederick Douglass

A hush is over all the teeming lists,
 And there is pause, a breath-space in the strife;
A spirit brave has passed beyond the mists
 And vapors that obscure the sun of life.
And Ethiopia, with bosom torn,
Laments the passing of her noblest born.

She weeps for him a mother's burning tears—
 She loved him with a mother's deepest love.
He was her champion thro' direful years,
 And held her weal all other ends above.

When Bondage held her bleeding in the dust,
He raised her up and whispered, "Hope and Trust."

For her his voice, a fearless clarion, rung
That broke in warning on the ears of men;
For her the strong bow of his power he strung,
And sent his arrows to the very den
Where grim Oppression held his bloody place
And gloated o'er the mis'ries of a race.

And he was no soft-tongued apologist;
He spoke straightforward, fearlessly uncowed;
The sunlight of his truth dispelled the mist,
And set in bold relief each dark-hued cloud;
To sin and crime he gave their proper hue,
And hurled at evil what was evil's due.

Through good and ill report he cleaved his way
Right onward, with his face set toward the heights,
Nor feared to face the foeman's dread array,—
The lash of scorn, the sting of petty spites.
He dared the lightning in the lightning's track,
And answered thunder with his thunder back.

When men maligned him, and their torrent wrath
In furious imprecations o'er him broke,
He kept his counsel as he kept his path;
'T was for his race, not for himself, he spoke.
He knew the import of his Master's call,
And felt himself too mighty to be small.

No miser in the good he held was he,—
His kindness followed his horizon's rim.
His heart, his talents, and his hands were free
To all who truly needed aught of him.
Where poverty and ignorance were rife,
He gave his bounty as he gave his life.

The place and cause that first aroused his might
Still proved its power until his latest day.
In Freedom's lists and for the aid of Right
Still in the foremost rank he waged the fray;
Wrong lived; his occupation was not gone.
He died in action with his armor on!

We weep for him, but we have touched his hand,
And felt the magic of his presence nigh,

The current that he sent throughout the land,
The kindling spirit of his battle-cry.
O'er all that holds us we shall triumph yet,
And place our banner where his hopes were set!

Oh, Douglass, thou hast passed beyond the shore,
But still thy voice is ringing o'er the gale!
Thou'st taught thy race how high her hopes may soar,
And bade her seek the heights, nor faint, nor fail.
She will not fail, she heeds thy stirring cry,
She knows thy guardian spirit will be nigh,
And, rising from beneath the chast'ning rod,
She stretches out her bleeding hands to God!

1896

An Ante-Bellum Sermon

We is gathahed hyeah, my brothahs,
In dis howlin' wildaness,
Fu' to speak some words of comfo't
To each othah in distress.
An' we chooses fu' ouah subjic'
Dis—we'll 'splain it by an' by;
"An' de Lawd said, 'Moses, Moses,'
An' de man said, 'Hyeah am I.'"

Now ole Pher'oh, down in Egypt,
Was de wuss man evah bo'n,
An' he had de Hebrew chillun
Down dah wukin' in his co'n;
'T well de Lawd got tiahed o' his foolin',
An' sez he: "I'll let him know—
Look hyeah, Moses, go tell Pher'oh
Fu' to let dem chillun go."

"An' ef he refuse to do it,
I will make him rue de houah,
Fu' I'll empty down on Egypt
All de vials of my powah."
Yes, he did—an' Pher'oh's ahmy
Was n't wuth a ha'f a dime;
Fu' de Lawd will he'p his chillun,
You kin trust him evah time.

An' yo' enemies may 'sail you
In de back an' in de front;

But de Lawd is all aroun' you,
  Fu' to ba' de battle's brunt.
  Dey kin fo'ge yo' chains an' shackles
F'om de mountains to de sea;
  But de Lawd will sen' some Moses
  Fu' to set his chillun free.

An' de lan' shall hyeah his thundah,
  Lak a blas' f'om Gab'el's ho'n,
Fu' de Lawd of hosts is mighty
  When he girds his ahmor on.
But fu' feah some one mistakes me,
  I will pause right hyeah to say,
  Dat I'm still a-preachin' ancient,
I ain't talkin' 'bout to-day.

But I tell you, fellah christuns,
  Things 'll happen mighty strange;
Now, de Lawd done dis fu' Isrul,
  An' his ways don't nevah change,
An' de love he showed to Isrul
  Was n't all on Isrul spent;
Now don't run an' tell yo' mastahs
  Dat I's preachin' discontent.

'Cause I is n't; I'se a-judgin'
  Bible people by deir ac's;
I'se a-givin' you de Scriptuah,
  I'se a-handin' you de fac's.
Cose ole Pher'oh b'lieved in slav'ry,
  But de Lawd he let him see,
Dat de people he put bref in,—
  Evah mothah's son was free.

An' dahs othahs thinks lak Pher'oh,
  But dey calls de Scriptuah liar,
Fu' de Bible says "a servant
  Is a-worthy of his hire."
An' you cain't git roun' nor thoo dat,
  An' you cain't git ovah it,
Fu' whatevah place you git in,
  Dis hyeah Bible too 'll fit.

So you see de Lawd's intention,
  Evah sence de worl' began,
Was dat His almighty freedom
  Should belong to evah man,

But I think it would be bettah,
Ef I'd pause agin to say,
Dat I'm talkin' 'bout ouah freedom
In a Bibleistic way.

But de Moses is a-comin',
An' he's comin', suah and fas'
We kin hyeah his feet a-trompin',
We kin hyeah his trumpit blas'.
But I want to wa'n you people,
Don't you git too brigity;
An' don't you git to braggin'
'Bout dese things, you wait an' see.

But when Moses wif his powah
Comes an' sets us chillun free,
We will praise de gracious Mastah
Dat has gin us liberty;
An' we'll shout ouah halleluyahs,
On dat mighty reck'nin' day,
When we'se reco'nised ez citiz'—
Huh uh! Chillun, let us pray!

1896

We Wear the Mask

We wear the mask that grins and lies,
It hides our cheeks and shades our eyes,—
This debt we pay to human guile;
With torn and bleeding hearts we smile,
And mouth with myriad subtleties.

Why should the world be over-wise,
In counting all our tears and sighs?
Nay, let them only see us, while
We wear the mask.

We smile, but, O great Christ, our cries
To thee from tortured souls arise.
We sing, but oh the clay is vile
Beneath our feet, and long the mile;
But let the world dream otherwise,
We wear the mask!

1896

When Malindy Sings

G'way an' quit dat noise, Miss Lucy—
  Put dat music book away;
What's de use to keep on tryin'?
  Ef you practise twell you're gray,
You cain't sta't no notes a-flyin'
  Lak de ones dat rants and rings
F'om de kitchen to de big woods
  When Malindy sings.

You ain't got de nachel o'gans
  Fu' to make de soun' come right,
You ain't got de tu'ns an' twistin's
  Fu' to make it sweet an' light.
Tell you one thing now, Miss Lucy,
  An' I'm tellin' you fu' true,
When hit comes to raal right singin',
  'T ain't no easy thing to do.

Easy 'nough fu' folks to hollah,
  Lookin' at de lines an' dots,
When dey ain't no one kin sence it,
  An' de chune comes in, in spots;
But fu' real melojous music,
  Dat jes' strikes yo' hea't and clings,
Jes' you stan' an' listen wif me
  When Malindy sings.

Ain't you nevah hyeahd Malindy?
  Blessed soul, tek up de cross!
Look hyeah, ain't you jokin', honey?
  Well, you don't know whut you los'.
Y' ought to hyeah dat gal a-wa'blin',
  Robins, la'ks, an' all dem things,
Heish dey moufs an' hides dey faces
  When Malindy sings.

Fiddlin' man jes' stop his fiddlin',
  Lay his fiddle on de she'f;
Mockin'-bird quit tryin' to whistle,
  'Cause he jes' so shamed hisse'f.
Folks a-playin' on de banjo
  Draps dey fingahs on de strings—
Bless yo' soul—fu'gits to move 'em,
  When Malindy sings.

She jes' spreads huh mouf and hollahs,
"Come to Jesus," twell you hyeah
Sinnahs' tremblin' steps and voices,
Timid-lak a-drawin' neah;
Den she tu'ns to "Rock of Ages,"
Simply to de cross she clings,
An' you fin' yo' teahs a-drappin'
When Malindy sings.

Who dat says dat humble praises
Wif de Master nevah counts?
Heish yo' mouf, I hyeah dat music,
Ez hit rises up an' mounts—
Floatin' by de hills an' valleys,
Way above dis buryin' sod,
Ez hit makes its way in glory
To de very gates of God!

Oh, hit's sweetah dan de music
Of an edicated band;
An' hit's dearah dan de battle's
Song o' triumph in de lan'.
It seems holier dan evenin'
When de solemn chu'ch bell rings,
Ez I sit an' ca'mly listen
While Malindy sings.

Towsah, stop dat ba'kin', hyeah me!
Mandy, mek dat chile keep still;
Don't you hyeah de echoes callin'
F'om de valley to de hill?
Let me listen, I can hyeah it,
Th'oo de bresh of angel's wings,
Sof' an' sweet, "Swing Low, Sweet Chariot,"
Ez Malindy sings.

1896

from Lyrics of the Hearthside

Sympathy

I know what the caged bird feels, alas!
When the sun is bright on the upland slopes;
When the wind stirs soft through the springing grass,

And the river flows like a stream of glass;
When the first bird sings and the first bud opes,
And the faint perfume from its chalice steals—
I know what the caged bird feels!

I know why the caged bird beats his wing
Till its blood is red on the cruel bars;
For he must fly back to his perch and cling
When he fain would be on the bough a-swing;
And a pain still throbs in the old, old scars
And they pulse again with a keener sting—
I know why he beats his wing!

I know why the caged bird sings, ah me,
When his wing is bruised and his bosom sore,—
When he beats his bars and he would be free;
It is not a carol of joy or glee,
But a prayer that he sends from his heart's deep core,
But a plea, that upward to Heaven he flings—
I know why the caged bird sings!

1899

George Washington Cable 1844–1925

In his early novels and stories, George Washington Cable gave us perhaps our most memorable view of the drama of multicultural Louisiana in the nineteenth century, especially of New Orleans Creole life. Born in New Orleans in 1844, Cable was of New England Puritan background on his mother's side and of a Virginia slaveholding family of German descent on his father's side. Upon the death of his father, Cable had to leave school at age fourteen to take a job at the New Orleans customhouse. At nineteen, during the Civil War, Cable enlisted in the Fourth Mississippi Cavalry, little knowing that he was providing himself with an experience that would form the basis of one of his most popular novels. After the war Cable obtained a position as a surveyor of the Atchafalaya River levees, contracted malaria, and was incapacitated for two years. Taking advantage of the enforced "leisure," he began writing and started to contribute a column to the New Orleans *Picayune.* In 1869 Cable married Louise Bartlett, with whom he was to have five children. As he established a home in New Orleans, he worked as bookkeeper for a cotton firm after a brief stint as a newspaper reporter.

Although he had had to forgo formal education, Cable enjoyed private study, often rising early for reading and writing before work. He mastered French and loved to peruse the old New Orleans city records in that language, thereby developing a store of knowledge and lore which he soon began to transmute into fictional narratives. Cable achieved national attention with the publication of his story "'Sieur George" in *Scribner's Monthly* in 1873. Within the next three years *Scribner's Monthly* would publish "Belles Demoiselles Plantation," "'Tite Poulette," "Madame Délicieuse," "Jean-ah Poquelin," and other stories, which were collected in *Old Creole Days* (1879). On the basis of these stories, Cable gained a national reputation as an important local color realist, adept at suggesting language and character of the varied groups of his region.

Following serial publication in *Scribner's,* Cable's novel *The Grandissimes* appeared as a book in 1880. A short novel, *Madame Delphine,* was published in the following year. Both novels vividly depict dramatic aspects of Creole life in pre-Civil War New Orleans, including black-white relations and problems stemming from the exploitation of African Americans. In spite of complaints of Creole readers that his representation of their community amounted to caricature, Cable's first three books brought him enough success that he could give up his clerical position and devote himself full time to writing.

At the high point of his career Cable turned his attention to polemical themes. *Dr. Sevier,* a novel dealing with the need for prison reform, was published in 1884, the year that Cable's exposé "The Convict Lease System in the Southern States" appeared in *Century Magazine.* With Creole New Orleans resentful of its portrayal by Cable and with white southerners in general angered by his writings about injustice toward blacks, Cable found the Northeast, which he enjoyed on several trips, more and more congenial. In 1885 he moved his family to Northampton, Mass., where he would be closer to publishers and to friends like Mark Twain, with whom he had recently conducted a successful reading tour.

Noteworthy among Cable's publications after his move north are *The Negro Question* and *John March, Southerner,* a novel of an aristocratic southerner's attempt to transcend limitations of family and regional background. *The Cavalier* (1901), a popularly successful novel for which he drew on his Civil War experience, marks Cable's turn toward a more romantic type of fiction in the latter part of his career. His work at this stage has been criticized for sometimes being excessively tailored to demands of genteel editors and readers. Yet all in all, it can be said that with his unflinching representation of moral dimensions of interethnic relations, his imaginative understanding of the impact of the past on the present, and his aesthetic sensitivity to exotic aspects of his region, Cable helped prepare the ground for William Faulkner, Eudora Welty, Flannery O'Connor, and other modern southern writers.

James Robert Payne
New Mexico State University

PRIMARY WORKS

Old Creole Days, 1879; *The Grandissimes,* 1880, rev. 1883; *Madame Delphine,* 1881; *Dr. Sevier,* 1884; *John March, Southerner,* 1894; *The Negro Question,* ed. Arlin Turner, 1958.

'Tite Poulette[1]

Kristian Koppig[2] was a rosy-faced, beardless young Dutchman. He was one of that army of gentlemen who, after the purchase of Louisiana, swarmed from all parts of the commercial world, over the mountains of Franco-Spanish exclusiveness, like the

[1]French: "little chick."

[2]Dutch: "headstrong, stubborn."

Goths over the Pyrenees,[3] and settled down in New Orleans to pick up their fortunes, with the diligence of hungry pigeons. He may have been a German; the distinction was too fine for Creole haste and disrelish.

He made his home in a room with one dormer window looking out, and somewhat down, upon a building opposite, which still stands, flush with the street, a century old. Its big, round-arched windows in a long, second-story row, are walled up, and two or three from time to time have had smaller windows let into them again, with odd little latticed peep-holes in their batten shutters. This had already been done when Kristian Koppig first began to look at them from his solitary, dormer window.

All the features of the building lead me to guess that it is a remnant of the old Spanish Barracks,[4] whose extensive structure fell by government sale into private hands a long time ago. At the end toward the swamp a great, oriental-looking passage is left, with an arched entrance, and a pair of ponderous wooden doors. You look at it, and almost see Count O'Reilly's[5] artillery come bumping and trundling out, and dash around into the ancient Plaza to bang away at King St. Charles's birthday.[6]

I do not know who lives there now. You might stand about on the opposite *banquette*[7] for weeks and never find out. I suppose it is a residence, for it does not look like one. That is the rule in that region.

In the good old times of duels, and bagatelle-clubs,[8] and theatre-balls,[9] and Cayetano's circus,[10] Kristian Koppig rooming as described, there lived in the portion of this house, partly overhanging the archway, a palish handsome woman, by the name—or going by the name—of Madame John. You would hardly have thought of her being "colored." Though fading, she was still of very attractive countenance, fine, rather severe features, nearly straight hair carefully kept, and that vivid black eye so peculiar to her kind. Her smile, which came and went with her talk, was sweet and exceedingly intelligent; and something told you, as you looked at her, that she was one who had had to learn a great deal in this troublesome life.

[3]In the fifth century A.D., the Visigoths, a Germanic tribe, crossed the mountain range of the Pyrenees to invade the land that is now Spain. The Visigoths ruled Spain until the Moors conquered them in the eighth century.

[4]Residence of the Spanish army. Colonized by France in 1682, Louisiana was ceded to Spain and England in 1763, when New Orleans became the capital of Spanish Louisiana. The French and Creole residents' frequently violent rebellion against Spanish rule required the constant presence of Spanish troops in the city.

[5]Irish-born Alexander O'Reilly (1722–1794), nicknamed "Bloody O'Reilly," the Spanish army officer who defeated the Creole revolt against the first Spanish governor of Louisiana. O'Reilly became governor in 1769 and was made a count in 1771.

[6]November 4 or 5, feast day of St. Charles Borromeo, Catholic saint who cared for the sick and is invoked against the plague.

[7]Brick sidewalk.

[8]*Bagatelle* was a table game similar to pool or billards, popular in Europe at the turn of the nineteenth century.

[9]In 1805, the St. Philip Street Theatre became the first home of New Orlean's so-called quadroon balls or octoroon balls, famous dancing parties limited to white men and free women of mixed race. (See note 11.)

[10]The Cuban Cayetano Mariotini directed one of the first multi-act touring circuses in North America. He established a base in New Orleans in the early 1800s. Cayetano went bankrupt in 1816 when the theater he built failed; he had to sign over his performing horses and his slave William to creditors.

"But!"—the Creole lads in the street would say—"her daughter!" and there would be lifting of arms, wringing of fingers, rolling of eyes, rounding of mouths, gaspings and clasping of hands. "So beautiful, beautiful, beautiful! White?—white like a water lily! White—like a magnolia!"

Applause would follow, and invocation of all the saints to witness.

And she could sing.

"Sing?" (disdainfully)—"if a mocking-bird can *sing!* Ha!"

They could not tell just how old she was; they "would give her about seventeen."

Mother and daughter were very fond. The neighbors could hear them call each other pet names, and see them sitting together, sewing, talking happily to each other in the unceasing French way, and see them go out and come in together on their little tasks and errands. "'Tite Poulette," the daughter was called; she never went out alone.

And who was this Madame John?

"Why, you know!—she was"—said the wig-maker at the corner to Kristian Koppig—"I'll tell you. You know?—she was"—and the rest atomized off in a rasping whisper. She was the best yellow-fever nurse in a thousand yards round; but that is not what the wig-maker said.

A block nearer the river stands a house altogether different from the remnant of old barracks. It is of frame, with a deep front gallery over which the roof extends. It has become a den of Italians, who sell fuel by daylight, and by night are up to no telling what extent of deviltry. This was once the home of a gay gentleman, whose first name happened to be John. He was a member of the Good Children Social Club. As his parents lived with him, his wife would, according to custom, have been called Madame John, but he had no wife. His father died, then his mother; last of all, himself. As he is about to be off, in comes Madame John, with 'Tite Poulette, then an infant, on her arm.

"Zalli," said he, "I am going."

She bowed her head, and wept.

"You have been very faithful to me, Zalli."

She wept on.

"Nobody to take care of you now, Zalli."

Zalli only went on weeping.

"I want to give you this house, Zalli; it is for you and the little one."

An hour after, amid the sobs of Madame John, she and the "little one" inherited the house, such as it was. With the fatal caution which characterizes ignorance, she sold the property and placed the proceeds in a bank, which made haste to fail. She put on widow's weeds, and wore them still when 'Tite Poulette "had seventeen," as the frantic lads would say.

How they did chatter over her. Quiet Kristian Koppig had never seen the like. He wrote to his mother, and told her so. A pretty fellow at the corner would suddenly double himself up with beckoning to a knot of chums; these would hasten up; recruits would come in from two or three other directions; as they reached the corner their countenances would quickly assume a genteel severity, and presently, with her mother, 'Tite Poulette would pass—tall, straight, lithe, her great black eyes made tender by their sweeping lashes, the faintest tint of color in her Southern cheek, her form all grace, her carriage a wonder of simple dignity.

The instant she was gone every tongue was let slip on the marvel of her beauty;

but, though theirs were only the loose New Orleans morals of over fifty years ago, their unleashed tongues never had attempted any greater liberty than to take up the pet name, 'Tite Poulette. And yet the mother was soon to be, as we shall discover, a paid dancer at the *Salle de Condé*.

To Zalli, of course, as to all "quadroon[11] ladies," the festivities of the Conde-street ball-room were familiar of old. There, in the happy days when dear Monsieur John was young, and the eighteenth century old, she had often repaired under guard of her mother—dead now, alas!—and Monsieur John would slip away from the dull play and dry society of Théâtre d'Orléans,[12] and come around with his crowd of elegant friends; and through the long sweet hours of the ball she had danced, and laughed, and coquetted under her satin mask, even to the baffling and tormenting of that prince of gentlemen, dear Monsieur John himself. No man of questionable blood dare set his foot within the door. Many noble gentlemen were pleased to dance with her. Colonel De —— and General La ——: city councilmen and officers from the Government House. There were no paid dancers then. Every thing was decorously conducted indeed! Every girl's mother was there, and the more discreet always left before there was too much drinking. Yes, it was gay, gay!—but sometimes dangerous. Ha! More times than a few had Monsieur John knocked down some long-haired and long-knifed rowdy, and kicked the breath out of him for looking saucily at her; but that was like him, he was so brave and kind;—and he is gone!

There was no room for widow's weeds there. So when she put these on, her glittering eyes never again looked through her pink and white mask, and she was glad of it; for never, never in her life had they so looked for anybody but her dear Monsieur John, and now he was in heaven—so the priest said—and she was a sick-nurse.

Living was hard work; and, as Madame John had been brought up tenderly, and had done what she could to rear her daughter in the same mistaken way, with, of course, no more education than the ladies in society got, they knew nothing beyond a little music and embroidery. They struggled as they could, faintly; now giving a few private dancing lessons, now dressing hair, but ever beat back by the steady detestation of their imperious patronesses; and, by and by, for want of that priceless worldly grace known among the flippant as "money-sense," these two poor children, born of misfortune and the complacent badness of the times, began to be in want.

Kristian Koppig noticed from his dormer window one day a man standing at the big archway opposite, and clanking the brass knocker on the wicket that was in one of the doors. He was a smooth man, with his hair parted in the middle, and his cigarette poised on a tiny gold holder. He waited a moment, politely cursed the dust, knocked again, threw his slender sword-cane under his arm, and wiped the inside of his hat with his handkerchief.

Madame John held a parley with him at the wicket. 'Tite Poulette was nowhere seen. He stood at the gate while Madame John went up-stairs. Kristian Koppig knew him. He knew him as one knows a snake. He was the manager of the *Salle de Condé*. Presently Madame John returned with a little bundle, and they hurried off together.

And now what did this mean? Why, by any one of ordinary acuteness the matter was easily understood, but, to tell the truth, Kristian Koppig was a trifle dull,

[11]Legal term for a person with one-fourth black ancestry. *Octoroon* (see note 9) means that the person's ancestry is one-eighth black.

[12]Opera house patronized by elite white Creole society.

and got the idea at once that some damage was being planned against 'Tite Poulette. It made the gentle Dutchman miserable not to be minding his own business, and yet—

"But the woman certainly will not attempt"—said he to himself—"no, no! she cannot." Not being able to guess what he meant, I cannot say whether she could or not. I know that next day Kristian Koppig, glancing eagerly over the "*Ami des Lois,*"[13] read an advertisement which he had always before skipped with a frown. It was headed, "*Salle de Condé,*" and, being interpreted, signified that a new dance was to be introduced, the *Danse de Chinois,*[14] and that *a young lady* would follow it with the famous "*Danse du Shawl.*"[15]

It was the Sabbath. The young man watched the opposite window steadily and painfully from early in the afternoon until the moon shone bright; and from the time the moon shone bright until Madame John!—joy!—Madame John! And not 'Tite Poulette, stepped through the wicket, much dressed and well muffled and hurried off toward the *Rue Condé.* Madame John was the "young lady;" and the young man's mind, glad to return to its own unimpassioned affairs, relapsed into quietude.

Madame John danced beautifully. It had to be done. It brought some pay, and pay was bread; and every Sunday evening, with a touch here and there of paint and powder, the mother danced the dance of the shawl, the daughter remaining at home alone.

Kirstian Koppig, simple, slow-thinking young Dutchman, never noticing that he staid at home with his window darkened for the very purpose, would see her come to her window and look out with a little wild, alarmed look in her magnificent eyes, and go and come again, and again, until the mother, like a storm-driven bird, came panting home.

Two or three months went by.

One night, on the mother's return, Kristian Koppig coming to his room nearly at the same moment, there was much earnest conversation, which he could see, but not hear.

"'Tite Poulette," said Madame John, "you are seventeen."

"True, Maman."

"Ah! My child, I see not how you are to meet the future." The voice trembled plaintively.

"But how, Maman?"

"Ah! you are not like others; no fortune, no pleasure, no friend."

"Maman!"

"No, no;—I thank God for it; I am glad you are not; but you will be lonely, lonely, all your poor life long. There is no place in this world for us poor women. I wish that we were either white or black!"—and the tears, two "shining ones," stood in the poor quadroon's eyes.

The daughter stoop up, her eyes flashing.

[13]French: "Friend of the Laws," a New Orleans evening newspaper published from 1809 to 1834.

[14]French: "Chinese Dance."

[15]French: "Dance of the Shawl," an erotic dance in which a woman removes some or all of her clothing but remains hidden behind artfully maneuvered shawls or veils. The dance of the shawl was popular in the late nineteenth century when Cable was writing, not during the earlier period in which the story is set.

"God made us, Maman," she said with a gentle, but stately smile.

"Ha!" said the mother, her keen glance darting through her tears, "Sin made *me,* yes."

"No," said 'Tite Poulette, "God made us. He made us just as we are; not more white, not more black."

"He made you, truly!" said Zalli. "You are so beautiful; I believe it well." She reached and drew the fair form to a kneeling posture. "My sweet, white daughter!"

Now the tears were in the girl's eyes. "And could I be whiter than I am?" she asked.

"Oh, no, no! 'Tite Poulette," cried the other; "but if we were only *real white!*—both of us; so that some gentleman might come to see me and say 'Madame John, I want your pretty little chick. She is so beautiful. I want to take her home. She is so good—I want her to be my wife.' Oh, my child, my child, to see that I would give my life—I would give my soul! Only you should take me along to be your servant. I walked behind two young men to-night; they were coming home from their office; presently they began to talk about you."

'Tite Poulette's eyes flashed fire.

"No, my child, they spoke only the best things. One laughed a little at times and kept saying 'Beware!' but the other—I prayed the Virgin to bless him, he spoke such kind and noble words. Such gentle pity; such a holy heart! 'May God defend her,' he said, *cherie;*[16] he said, 'May God defend her, for I see no help for her.' The other one laughed and left him. He stopped in the door right across the street. Ah, my child, do you blush? Is that something to bring the rose to your cheek? Many fine gentlemen at the ball ask me often, 'How is your daughter, Madame John?'"

The daughter's face was thrown into the mother's lap, not so well satisfied, now, with God's handiwork. Ah, how she wept! Sob, sob, sob; gasps and sighs and stifled ejaculations, her small right hand clinched and beating on her mother's knee; and the mother weeping over her.

Kristian Koppig shut his window. Nothing but a generous heart and a Dutchman's phlegm could have done so at that moment. And even thou, Kristian Koppig!———for the window closed very slowly.

He wrote to his mother, thus:

"In this wicked city, I see none so fair as the poor girl who lives opposite me, and who, alas! though so fair, is one of those whom the taint of caste has cursed. She lives a lonely, innocent life in the midst of corruption, like the lilies I find here in the marshes, and I have great pity for her. 'God defend her,' I said to-night to a fellow clerk, 'I see no help for her.' I know there is a natural, and I think proper, horror of mixed blood (excuse the mention, sweet mother), and I feel it, too; and yet if she were in Holland to-day, not one of a hundred suitors would detect the hidden blemish."

In such strain this young man wrote on trying to demonstrate the utter impossibility of his ever loving the loveable unfortunate, until the midnight tolling of the cathedral clock sent him to bed.

About the same hour Zalli and 'Tite Poulette were kissing good-night.

"'Tite Poulette, I want you to promise me one thing."

[16]French: "sweetheart."

"Well, Maman?"

"If any gentleman should ever love you and ask you to marry,—not knowing, you know,—promise me you will not tell him you are not white."

"It can never be," said 'Tite Poulette.

"But if it should," said Madame John pleadingly.

"And break the law?"[17] asked 'Tite Poulette, impatiently.

"But the law is unjust," said the mother.

"But it is the law!"

"But you will not, dearie, will you?"

"I would surely tell him!" said the daughter.

When Zalli, for some cause, went next morning to the window, she started.

"'Tite Poulette!"—she called softly without moving. The daughter came. The young man, whose idea of propriety had actuated him to this display, was sitting in the dormer window, reading. Mother and daughter bent a steady gaze at each other. It meant in French, "If he saw us last night!"—

"Ah! dear," said the mother, her face beaming with fun—

"What can it be, Maman?"

"He speaks—oh! ha, ha!—he speaks—such miserable French!"

It came to pass one morning at early dawn that Zalli and 'Tite Poulette, going to mass, passed a café, just as—who should be coming out but Monsieur, the manager of the *Salle de Condé*. He had not yet gone to bed. Monsieur was astonished. He had a Frenchman's eye for the beautiful, and certainly there the beautiful was. He had heard of Madame John's daughter, and had hoped once to see her, but did not; but could this be she?

They disappeared within the cathedral. A sudden pang of piety moved him; he followed. 'Tite Poulette was already kneeling in the aisle. Zalli, still in the vestibule, was just taking her hand from the font of holy-water.

"Madame John," whispered the manager.

She courtesied.

"Madame John, that young lady—is she your daughter?"

"She—she—is my daughter," said Zalli, with somewhat of alarm in her face, which the manager misinterpreted.

"I think not, Madame John." He shook his head, smiling as one too wise to be fooled.

"Yes, Monsieur, she is my daughter."

"O no, Madame John, it is only make-believe, I think."

"I swear she is, Monsieur de la Rue."[18]

"Is that possible?" pretending to waver, but convinced in his heart of hearts, by Zalli's alarm, that she was lying. "But how? Why does she not come to our ball-room with you?"

[17]In 1724, Louis XV of France applied to Louisiana the Code Noir, or Black Code, a series of laws forbidding intermarriage and concubinage between whites and people of color. Although the Code Noir remained in effect throughout Spanish and American possessions, white Louisianans ignored strictures against concubinage, often maintaining separate households for their black mistresses and mixed-race children.

[18]French: "man of the street."

Zalli, trying to get away from him, shrugged and smiled. "Each to his taste, Monsieur; it pleases her not."

She was escaping, but he followed one step more. "I shall come to see you, Madame John."

She whirled and attacked him with her eyes. "Monsieur must not give himself the trouble!" she said, the eyes at the same time adding, "Dare to come!" She turned again, and knelt to her devotions. The manager dipped in the font, crossed himself, and departed.

Several weeks went by, and M. de la Rue had not accepted the fierce challenge of Madame John's eyes. One or two Sunday nights she had succeeded in avoiding him, though fulfilling her engagement in the *Salle;* but by and by pay-day,—a Saturday,—came round, and though the pay was ready, she was loath to go up to Monsieur's little office.

It was an afternoon in May. Madame John came to her own room, and, with a sigh, sank into a chair. Her eyes were wet.

"Did you go to his office, dear mother?" asked 'Tite Poulette.

"I could not," she answered, dropping her face in her hands.

"Maman, he has seen me at the window!"

"While I was gone?" cried the mother.

"He passed on the other side of the street. He looked up purposely, and saw me." The speaker's cheeks were burning red.

Zalli wrung her hands.

"It is nothing, mother; do not go near him."

"But the pay, my child."

"The pay matters not."

"But he will bring it here; he wants the chance."

That was the trouble, sure enough.

About this time Kristian Koppig lost his position in the German importing house where, he had fondly told his mother, he was indispensable.

"Summer was coming on," the senior said, "and you see our young men are almost idle. Yes, our engagement *was* for a year, but ah—we could not foresee"—etc., etc., "besides" (attempting a parting flattery), "your father is a rich gentleman, and you can afford to take the summer easy. If we can ever be of any service to you," etc., etc.

So the young Dutchman spent the afternoons at his dormer window reading and glancing down at the little casement opposite, where a small, rude shelf had lately been put out, holding a row of cigar-boxes with wretched little botanical specimens in them trying to die. 'Tite Poulette was their gardener; and it was odd to see,—dry weather or wet—how many waterings per day those plants could take. She never looked up from her task; but I know she performed it with that unacknowledged pleasure which all girls love and deny, that of being looked upon by noble eyes.

On this peculiar Saturday afternoon in May, Kristian Koppig had been witness of the distressful scene over the way. It occurred to 'Tite Poulette that such might be the case, and she stepped to the casement to shut it. As she did so, the marvellous delicacy of Kristian Koppig moved him to draw in one of his shutters. Both young heads came out at one moment, while at the same instant—

"Rap, rap, rap, rap, rap!" clanked the knocker on the wicket. The black eyes of the maiden and the blue over the way, from looking into each other for the first time in life, glanced down to the arched doorway upon Monsieur the manager. Then the black eyes disappeared within, and Kristian Koppig thought again, and re-opening his shutter, stood up at the window prepared to become a bold spectator of what might follow.

But for a moment nothing followed.

"Trouble over there," thought the rosy Dutchman, and waited. The manager waited too, rubbing his hat and brushing his clothes with the tips of his kidded fingers.

"They do not wish to see him," slowly concluded the spectator.

"Rap, rap, rap, rap, rap!" quoth the knocker, and M. de la Rue looked up around at the windows opposite and noticed the handsome young Dutchman looking at him.

"Dutch!" said the manager softly, between his teeth.

"He is staring at me," said Kristian Koppig to himself;—"but then I am staring at him, which accounts for it."

A long pause, and then another long rapping.

"They want him to go away," thought Koppig.

"Knock hard!" suggested a street youngster, standing by.

"Rap, rap"—The manager had no sooner recommenced than several neighbors looked out of doors and windows.

"Very bad," thought our Dutchman; "somebody should make him go off. I wonder what they will do."

The manager stepped into the street, looked up at the closed window, returned to the knocker, and stood with it in his hand.

"They are all gone out, Monsieur," said the street youngster.

"You lie!" said the cynosure of neighboring eyes.

"Ah!" thought Kristian Koppig; "I will go down and ask him"—Here his thoughts lost outline; he was only convinced that he had somewhat to say to him, and turned to go down stairs. In going he became a little vexed with himself because he could not help hurrying. He noticed, too, that his arm holding the stair-rail trembled in a silly way, whereas he was perfectly calm. Precisely as he reached the street-door the manager raised the knocker; but the latch clicked and the wicket was drawn slightly ajar.

Inside could just be descried Madame John. The manager bowed, smiled, talked, talked on, held money in his hand, bowed, smiled, talked on, flourished the money, smiled, bowed, talked on and plainly persisted in some intention to which Madame John was steadfastly opposed.

The window above, too,—it was Kristian Koppig who noticed that,—opened a wee bit, like the shell of a terrapin.[19] Presently the manager lifted his foot and put forward an arm, as though he would enter the gate by pushing, but as quick as gunpowder it clapped—in his face!

You could hear the fleeing feet of Zalli pounding up the staircase.

As the panting mother re-entered her room, "See, Maman," said 'Tite Poulette, peeping at the window, "the young gentleman from over the way has crossed!"

"Holy Mary bless him!" said the mother.

[19]A kind of turtle.

"I will go over," thought Kristian Koppig, "and ask him kindly if he is not making a mistake."

"What are they doing, dear?" asked the mother, with clasped hands.

"They are talking; the young man is tranquil, but 'Sieur de la Rue is very angry," whispered the daughter; and just then—pang! came a sharp, keen sound rattling up the walls on either side of the narrow way, and "Aha!" and laughter and clapping of female hands from two or three windows.

"Oh! what a slap!" cried the girl, half in fright, half in glee, jerking herself back from the casement simultaneously with the report. But the "ahas" and laughter, and clapping of feminine hands, which still continued, came from another cause. 'Tite Poulette's rapid action had struck the slender cord that held up an end of her hanging garden, and the whole rank of cigar-boxes slid from their place, turned gracefully over as they shot through the air, and emptied themselves plump upon the head of the slapped manager. Breathless, dirty, pale as whitewash, he gasped a threat to be heard from again, and, getting round the corner as quick as he could walk, left Kristian Koppig, standing motionless, the most astonished man in that street.

"Kristian Koppig, Kristian Koppig," said Greatheart to himself, slowly dragging up-stairs, "what a mischief you have done. One poor woman certainly to be robbed of her bitter wages, and another—so lovely!—put to the burning shame of being the subject of a street brawl! What will this silly neighborhood say? 'Has the gentleman a heart as well as a hand?' 'Is it jealousy?'" There he paused, afraid himself to answer the supposed query; and then—"Oh! Kristian Koppig, you have been such a dunce!" "And I cannot apologize to them. Who in this street would carry my note, and not wink and grin over it with low surmises? I cannot even make restitution. Money? They would not dare receive it. Oh! Kristian Koppig, why *did* you not mind your own business? Is she any thing to you? Do you love her? *Of course not!* Oh!—such a dunce!"

The reader will eagerly admit that however faulty this young man's course of reasoning, his conclusion was correct. For mark what he did.

He went to his room, which was already growing dark, shut his window, lighted his big Dutch lamp, and sat down to write. "Something *must* be done," said he aloud, taking up his pen; "I will be calm and cool; I will be distant and brief; but—I shall have to be kind or I may offend. Ah! I shall have to write in French; I forgot that; I write it so poorly, dunce that I am, when all my brothers and sisters speak it so well." He got out his French dictionary. Two hours slipped by. He made a new pen, washed and refilled his inkstand, mended his "abominable!" chair, and after two hours more made another attempt, and another failure. "My head aches," said he, and lay down on his couch, the better to frame his phrases.

He was awakened by the Sabbath sunlight. The bells of the Cathedral and the Ursulines' chapel[20] were ringing for high mass, and mocking-bird, perching on a chimney-top above Madame John's rooms, was carolling, whistling, mewing, chirping,

[20]The French Quarter convent of the Ursuline nuns, a Roman Catholic order housed in the oldest building in Louisiana and devoted to educating young women.

screaming, and trilling with the ecstasy of a whole May in his throat. "Oh! sleepy Kristian Koppig," was the young man's first thought, "—such a dance!"

Madame John and daughter did not go to mass. The morning wore away, and their casement remained closed. "They are offended," said Kristian Koppig, leaving the house, and wandering up to the little Protestant affair known as Christ Church.

"No, possibly they are not," he said, returning and finding the shutters thrown back.

By a sad accident, which mortified him extremely, he happened to see, late in the afternoon,—hardly conscious that he was looking across the street,—that Madame John was—dressing. Could it be that she was going to the *Salle de Condé?* He rushed to his table, and began to write.

He had guessed aright. The wages were too precious to be lost. The manager had written her a note. He begged to assure her that he was a gentleman of the clearest cut. If he had made a mistake the previous afternoon, he was glad no unfortunate result had followed except his having been assaulted by a ruffian; that the *Danse du Shawl* was promised in his advertisement, and he hoped Madame John (whose wages were in hand waiting for her) would not fail to assist as usual. Lastly, and delicately put, he expressed his conviction that Mademoiselle was wise and discreet in declining to entertain gentlemen at her home.

So, against much beseeching on the part of 'Tite Poulette, Madame John was going to the ball-room. "Maybe I can discover what 'Sieur de la Rue is planning against Monsieur over the way," she said, knowing certainly the slap would not be forgiven; and the daughter, though tremblingly, at once withdrew her objections.

The heavy young Dutchman, now thoroughly electrified, was writing like mad. He wrote and tore up, wrote and tore up, lighted his lamp, started again, and at last signed his name. A letter by a Dutchman in French!—what can be made of it in English? We will see:

> Madame and Mademoiselle:
>
> A stranger, seeking not to be acquainted, but seeing and admiring all days the goodness and high honor, begs to be pardoned of them for the mistakes, alas! of yesterday, and to make reparation and satisfaction in destroying the ornaments of the window, as well as the loss of compensation from Monsieur the manager, with the enclosed bill of the *Banque de la Louisiane*[21] for fifty dollars ($50). And, hoping they will seeing what he is meaning, remains, respectfully,
>
> Kristian Koppig
>
> P.S.—Madame must not go to the ball.

He must bear the missive himself. He must speak in French. What should the words be? A moment of study—he has it, and is off down the long three-story stair-

[21] A New Orleans bank, the first American bank founded in the Louisiana Territory after the Louisiana Purchase (1803).

way. At the same moment Madame John stepped from the wicket, and glided off to the *Salle de Condé,* a trifle late.

"I shall see Madame John, of course," thought the young man, crushing a hope, and rattled the knocker. 'Tite Poulette sprang up from praying for her mother's safety. "What has she forgotten?" she asked herself, and hastened down. The wicket opened. The two innocents were stunned.

"Aw—aw"—said the pretty Dutchman, "aw,"—blurted out something in virgin Dutch, . . . handed her the letter, and hurried down street.

"Alas! what have I done?" said the poor girl, bending over her candle, and bursting into tears that fell on the unopened letter. "And what shall I do? It may be wrong to open it—and worse not to." Like her sex, she took the benefit of the doubt, and intensified her perplexity and misery by reading and misconstruing the all but unintelligible contents. What then? Not only sobs and sighs, but moaning and beating of little fists together, and outcries of soul-felt agony stifled against the bedside, and temples pressed into knitted palms, because of one who "sought *not to be* acquainted," but offered money—money!—in pity to a poor—shame on her for saying that!—a poor *nigresse.*[22]

And now our self-confessed dolt turned back from a half-hour's walk, concluding there might be an answer to his note. "Surely Madame John will appear this time." He knocked. The shutter stirred above, and something white came fluttering wildly down like a shot dove. It was his own letter containing the fifty-dollar bill. He bounded to the wicket, and softly but eagerly knocked again.

"Go away," said a trembling voice from above.

"Madame John?" said he; but the window closed, and he heard a step, the same step on the stair. Step, step, every step one step deeper into his heart. 'Tite Poulette came to the closed door.

"What will you?" said the voice within.

"I—I—don't wish to see you. I wish to see Madame John."

"I must pray Monsieur to go away. My mother is at the *Salle de Condé.*"

"At the ball!" Kristian Koppig strayed off, repeating the words for want of definite thought. All at once it occurred to him that at the ball he could make Madame John's acquaintance with impunity. "Was it courting sin to go?" By no means; he should, most likely, save a woman from trouble, and help the poor in their distress.

Behold Kristian Koppig standing on the floor of the *Salle de Condé.* A large hall, a blaze of lamps, a bewildering flutter of fans and floating robes, strains of music, columns of gay promenaders, a long row of turbaned mothers lining either wall, gentlemen of the portlier sort filling the recesses of the windows, whirling waltzers gliding here and there—smiles and grace, smiles and grace; all fair, orderly, elegant, bewitching. A young Creole's laugh mayhap a little loud, and—truly there were many sword-canes.[23] But neither grace nor foulness satisfied the eye of the zealous young Dutchman.

Suddenly a muffled woman passed him, leaning on a gentleman's arm. It looked like—it must be, Madame John. Speak quick, Kristian Koppig; do not stop to notice the man!

"Madame John"—bowing—"I am your neighbor, Kristian Koppig."

[22]French: "negress," a black woman.

[23]Blades concealed in sheaths designed to resemble walking canes, so that the carrier appears unarmed.

Madame John bows low, and smiles—a ball-room smile, but is frightened, and her escort,—the manager,—drops her hand and slips away.

"Ah! Monsieur," she whispers excitedly, "you will be killed if you stay here a moment. Are you armed? No. Take this." She tried to slip a dirk into his hands, but he would not have it.

"Oh, my dear young man, go! Go quickly!" she pleaded, glancing furtively down the hall.

"I wish you not to dance," said the young man.

"I have danced already; I am going home. Come; be quick! we will go together." She thrust her arm through his, and they hastened into the street. When a square had been passed there came a sound of men running behind them.

"Run, Monsieur, run!" she cried, trying to drag him; but Monsieur Dutchman would not.

"*Run,* Monsieur! Oh, my God! it is 'Sieur"—

"*That* for yesterday!" cried the manager, striking fiercely with his cane. Kristian Koppig's fist rolled him in the dirt.

"*That* for 'Tite Poulette!" cried another man dealing the Dutchman a terrible blow from behind.

"And *that* for me!" hissed a third, thrusting at him with something bright.

"*That* for yesterday!" screamed the manager, bounding like a tiger; "That!" "THAT!" "Ha!"

Then Kristian Koppig knew that he was stabbed.

"That!" and "That!" and "That!" and the poor Dutchman struck wildly here and there, grasped the air, shut his eyes, staggered, reeled, fell, rose half up, fell again for good, and they were kicking him and jumping on him. All at once they scampered. Zalli had found the night-watch.

"Buz-z-z-z!" went a rattle. "Buz-z-z-z!" went another.

"Pick him up."

"Is he alive?"

"Can't tell; hold him steady; lead the way, misses."

"He's bleeding all over my breeches."

"This way—here—around this corner."

"This way now—only two squares more."

"Here we are."

"Rap-rap-rap!" on the old brass knocker. Curses on the narrow wicket, more on the dark archway, more still on the twisting stairs.

Up at last and into the room.

"Easy, easy, push this under his head! never mind his boots!"

So he lies—on 'Tite Poulette's own bed.

The watch are gone. They pause under the corner lamp to count profits;—a single bill—*Banque de la Louisiane,* fifty dollars. Providence is kind—tolerably so. Break it at the "Guillaume Tell."[24] "But did you ever hear any one scream like that girl did?"

[24] A French ship that, presumably, required no proof of identity upon changing large sums of money.

And there lies the young Dutch neighbor. His money will not flutter back to him this time; nor will any voice behind a gate "beg Monsieur to go away." O, Woman!—that knows no enemy so terrible as man! Come nigh, poor Woman, you have nothing to fear. Lay your strange, electric touch upon the chilly flesh; it strikes no eager mischief along the fainting veins. Look your sweet looks upon the grimy face, and tenderly lay back the locks from the congested brows; no wicked misinterpretation lurks to bite your kindness. Be motherly, be sisterly, fear nought. Go, watch him by night; you may sleep at his feet and he will not stir. Yet his lives, and shall live—may live to forget you, who knows? But for all that, be gentle and watchful; be womanlike, we ask no more; and God reward you!

Even while it was taking all the two women's strength to hold the door against Death, the sick man himself laid a grief upon them.

"Mother," he said to Madame John, quite a master of French in his delirium, "dear mother, fear not; trust your boy; fear nothing. I will not marry 'Tite Poulette; I cannot. She is fair, dear mother, but ah! she is not—don't you know, mother? don't you know? The race! the race! Don't you know that she is jet black. Isn't it?"

The poor nurse nodded "Yes," and gave a sleeping draught; but before the patient quite slept he started once and stared.

"Take her away,"—waving his hand—"take your beauty away. She is jet white. Who could take a jet white wife? O, no, no, no, no!"

Next morning his brain was right.

"Madame," he weakly whispered, "I was delirious last night?"

Zalli shrugged. "Only a very, very, wee, wee trifle of a bit."

"And did I say something wrong or—foolish?"

"O, no, no," she replied; "you only clasped your hands, so, and prayed, prayed all the time to the dear Virgin."

"To the virgin?" asked the Dutchman, smiling incredulously.

"And St. Joseph—yes, indeed," she insisted; "you may strike me dead."

And so, for politeness' sake, he tried to credit the invention, but grew suspicious instead.

Hard was the battle against death. Nurses are sometimes amazons, and such were these. Through the long, enervating summer, the contest lasted; but when at last the cool airs of October came stealing in at the bedside like long-banished little children, Kristian Koppig rose upon his elbow and smiled them a welcome.

The physician, blessed man, was kind beyond measure; but said some inexplicable things, which Zalli tried in vain to make him speak in an undertone. "If I knew Monsieur John?" he said, "certainly! Why, we were chums at school. And he left you so much as that, Madame John? Ah! my old friend John, always noble! And you had it all in that naughty bank? Ah, well, Madame John, it matters little. No, I shall not tell 'Tite Poulette. Adieu."

And another time:—"If I will let you tell me something? With pleasure, Madame John. No, and not tell anybody, Madame John. No, Madame, not even 'Tite Poulette. What?"—a long whistle—"is that pos-si-ble?—and Monsieur John knew it?—encouraged it?—eh, well, eh, well!—But—can I believe you, Madame John? Oh! you have Monsieur John's sworn statement. Ah! very good, truly, but—you *say* you have it; but where is it? Ah! to-mor-row!" a sceptical shrug. "Pardon me, Madame John, I think perhaps, *perhaps* you are telling the truth.

"If I think you did right? Certainly! What nature keeps back, accident sometimes gives, Madame John; either is God's will. Don't cry. 'Stealing from the dead?' No! It was giving, yes! They are thanking you in heaven, Madame John."

Kristian Koppig, lying awake, but motionless and with closed eyes, hears in part, and, fancying he understands, rejoices with silent intensity. When the doctor is gone he calls Zalli.

"I give you a great deal of trouble, eh, Madame John?"

"No, no; you are no trouble at all. Had you the yellow fever—ah! then!"

She rolled her eyes to signify the superlative character of the tribulations attending yellow fever.

"I had a lady and gentleman once—a Spanish lady and gentleman, just off the ship; both sick at once with the fever—delirious—could not tell their names. Nobody to help me but sometimes Monsieur John! I never had such a time,—never before, never since—as that time. Four days and nights this head touched not a pillow."

"And they died!" said Kristian Koppig.

"The third night the gentleman went. Poor Señor! 'Sieur John,—he did not know the harm,—gave him some coffee and toast! The fourth night it rained and turned cool, and just before day the poor lady"—

"Died!" said Koppig.

Zalli dropped her arms listlessly into her lap and her eyes ran brimful.

"And left an infant!" said the Dutchman, ready to shout with exultation.

"Ah! no, Monsieur," said Zalli.

The invalid's heart sank like a stone.

"Madame John,"—his voice was all in a tremor,—"tell me the truth. Is 'Tite Poulette your own child?"

"Ah-h-h, ha! ha! What foolishness! Of course she is my child!" And Madame gave vent to a true Frenchwoman's laugh.

It was too much for the sick man. In the pitiful weakness of his shattered nerves he turned his face into his pillow and wept like a child. Zalli passed into the next room to hide her emotion.

"Maman, dear Maman," said 'Tite Poulette, who had overheard nothing, but only saw the tears.

"Ah! my child, my child, my task—my task is too great—too great for me. Let me go now—another time. Go and watch at his bedside."

"But, Maman,"—for 'Tite Poulette was frightened,—"he needs no care now."

"Nay, but go, my child; I wish to be alone."

The maiden stole in with averted eyes and tiptoed to the window—*that window.* The patient, already a man again, gazed at her till she could feel the gaze. He turned his eyes from her a moment to gather resolution. And now, stout heart, farewell; a word or two of friendly parting—nothing more.

"'Tite Poulette."

The slender figure at the window turned and came to the bedside.

"I believe I owe my life to you," he said.

She looked down meekly, the color rising in her cheek.

"I must arrange to be moved across the street tomorrow, on a litter."

She did not stir or speak.

"And I must now thank you, sweet nurse, for your care. Sweet nurse! Sweet nurse!"

She shook her head in protestation.

"Heaven bless you, 'Tite Poulette!"

Her face sank lower.

"God has made you very beautiful, 'Tite Poulette!"

She stirred not. He reached, and gently took her little hand, and as he drew her one step nearer, a tear fell from her long lashes. From the next room, Zalli, with a face of agonized suspense, gazed upon the pair, undiscovered. The young man lifted the hand to lay it upon his lips, when, with a mild, firm force, it was drawn away, yet still rested in his own upon the bedside, like some weak thing snared, that could only not get free.

"Thou wilt not have my love, 'Tite Poulette?"

No answer.

"Thou wilt not, beautiful?"

"Cannot!" was all that she could utter, and upon their clasped hands the tears ran down.

"Thou wrong'st me, 'Tite Poulette. Thou dost not trust me; thou fearest the kiss may loosen the hands. But I tell thee nay. I have struggled hard, even to this hour, against Love, but I yield me now; I yield; I am his unconditioned prisoner forever. God forbid that I ask aught but that you will be my wife."

Still the maiden moved not, looked not up, only rained down tears.

"Shall it not be, 'Tite Poulette?" He tried in vain to draw her.

"'Tite Poulette?" So tenderly he called? And then she spoke.

"It is against the law."

"It is not!" cried Zalli, seizing her round the waist and dragging her forward. "Take her! she is thine. I have robbed God long enough. Here are the sworn papers—here! Take her; she is as white as snow—so! Take her, kiss her; Mary be praised! I never had a child—she is the Spaniard's daughter!"

1874, 1879

Grace King 1852–1932

Grace King called herself a "southern woman of letters." Persistent assumptions about southern women might suggest that she was a living oxymoron. But King's life and work have offered recent critics the opportunity to tease out some of the enormous complexities of privilege and oppression in the American South.

Robert Bush's anthology (1973) and biography (1983) have brought recognition to Grace King after decades of oblivion. Bush identifies King's as "the patrician voice" of the post-Civil War South, a voice that spoke for southern tradition against Reconstruction's devastation. Yet her work is polyvocal. She wrote, most crucially, as a woman in a patriarchal literary establishment, a fact that contradicted the very conventions of race, class, and language that she otherwise represented. As a woman whose most honest relationships were with other women, she both manipulated and criticized men's power. As a woman writer, she refused to "just rip the story open and insert a love story!" as advised by Thomas Nelson Page. As a white woman, she wrote about blacks from conflicting positions of racism and identification. She experienced poverty after the Civil War when her family moved to a working-class neighborhood in New Orleans, yet she never identified herself as other than patrician. She defended the South yet befriended writers and feminists in the North. And as a bilingual Protestant writer, equally fluent in French and English, she wrote from a position of "other" about the Roman Catholic Creoles. Thus, though frequently indirectly and perhaps unwittingly, she challenged the very tradition for which she spoke. What difference, if any, such indirect challenges make to a dominant ideology is one of the questions raised by her work.

Grace King was born in New Orleans in 1852. She spent most of her life in New Orleans. After the war, her father slowly rebuilt his law practice; it was a great victory for the King children when, in middle age, they were able in 1904 to own a house that fit the family image. King never married; she lived with her (also unmarried) sisters and traveled widely and independently after gaining fame as a writer. Her brand of "local color" struck the right note for late-nineteenth-century American readers.

In 1885, King wrote her first story, "Monsieur Motte," which appeared in the *New Princeton Review.* She wrote it in a state of pique at the popularity of George Washington Cable's representations of New Orleans, particularly his sympathetic portrayals of the oppression of blacks. When Richard Watson Gilder, editor of *Century,* asked her, "Why do not some of you write better?" she sat down to write a story about a black woman's devotion to her young white mistress, suggesting the traditional southern view of "good darkies." Yet she also wrote about the agony of Marcelite's internalized racism. The popularity of "Monsieur Motte" led her to complete three more sections and make it into a novel. The social connections King made in New Orleans with visiting members of the northern literary establishment such as Julia Ward Howe, Richard Watson Gilder, and Charles Dudley Warner gave her a professional entrée. Visiting the enclave of writers in Hartford, Connecticut, she became Olivia Clemens's confidante and befriended the feminist Isabella Hooker. And in Paris she befriended Madame Blanc (who published as "Th. Bentzon"), a pupil of George Sand. Her work as well as her person circulated nationally and internationally.

Early in her career King focused on short fiction, of which one story is included here. "The Little Convent Girl" appeared in *Balcony Stories,* a collection that took its title from the habit of New Orleans women to sit on their balconies and tell tales. "The Little Convent Girl" is a good example of the ways in which questions of gender and race become entwined in the South with issues of identity. After publishing another collection of stories, *Tales of a Time and Place,* King moved next to writing histories, appropriating a traditionally public, "masculine" genre for *New Orleans: The Place and the People* and *Stories from Louisiana History.* During the teens, she returned to fiction; she spent years composing what some consider her masterpiece, *The Pleasant Ways of St. Medard.* A "novel" set during Reconstruction, it is arguably an early modernist text in its experimental structure. King's last novel, *La Dame de Sainte Hermine,* appeared in 1924; her autobiography, *Memories of a Southern Woman of Letters,* appeared in the year of her death, 1932.

Anne Jones
University of Florida

PRIMARY WORKS

Monsieur Motte, 1888; *Tales of a Time and Place,* 1892; *Balcony Stories,* 1893; *New Orleans: The Place and the People,* 1895; *Stories from Louisiana History,* 1905; *The Pleasant Ways of St. Medard,* 1916; *La Dame de Sainte Hermine,* 1924; *Memories of a Southern Woman of Letters,* 1932; *Grace King of New Orleans: A Selection of Her Writings,* ed. Robert Bush, 1973.

The Little Convent Girl

She was coming down on the boat from Cincinnati, the little convent girl. Two sisters had brought her aboard. They gave her in charge of the captain, got her a state-room, saw that the new little trunk was put in it, hung the new little satchel up on the wall, showed her how to bolt the door at night, shook hands with her for good-by (good-bys have really no significance for sisters), and left her there. After a while the bells all rang, and the boat, in the awkward elephantine fashion of boats, got into midstream. The chambermaid found her sitting on the chair in the state-room where the sisters had left her, and showed her how to sit on a chair in the saloon. And there she sat until the captain came and hunted her up for supper. She could not do anything of herself; she had to be initiated into everything by some one else.

She was known on the boat only as "the little convent girl." Her name, of course, was registered in the clerk's office, but on a steamboat no one thinks of consulting the clerk's ledger. It is always the little widow, the fat madam, the tall colonel, the parson, etc. The captain, who pronounced by the letter, always called her the little con-*vent* girl. She was the beau-ideal of the little convent girl. She never raised her eyes except when spoken to. Of course she never spoke first, even to the chambermaid, and when she did speak it was in the wee, shy, furtive voice one might imagine a just-budding violet to have; and she walked with such soft, easy, carefully calculated steps that one naturally felt the penalties that must have secured them—penalties dictated by a black code of deportment.

She was dressed in deep mourning. Her black straw hat was trimmed with stiff new crape, and her stiff new bombazine dress had crape collar and cuffs. She wore her hair in two long plaits fastened around her head tight and fast. Her hair had a strong inclination to curl, but that had been taken out of it as austerely as the noise out of her footfalls. Her hair was as black as her dress; her eyes, when one saw them, seemed blacker than either, on account of the bluishness of the white surrounding the pupil. Her eyelashes were almost as thick as the black veil which the sisters had fastened around her hat with an extra pin the very last thing before leaving. She had a round little face, and a tiny pointed chin; her mouth was slightly protuberant from the teeth, over which she tried to keep her lips well shut, the effort giving them a pathetic little forced expression. Her complexion was sallow, a pale sallow, the complexion of a brunette bleached in darkened rooms. The only color about her was a blue taffeta ribbon from which a large silver medal of the Virgin hung over the place where a breastpin should have been. She was so little, so little, although she was eighteen, as the sisters told the captain; otherwise they would not have permitted her to travel all the way to New Orleans alone.

Unless the captain or the clerk remembered to fetch her out in front, she would sit all day in the cabin, in the same place, crocheting lace, her spool of thread and box of patterns in her lap, on the handkerchief spread to save her new dress. Never leaning back—oh, no! always straight and stiff, as if the conventual back board were there within call. She would eat only convent fare at first, notwithstanding the importunities of the waiters, and the jocularities of the captain, and particularly of the clerk. Every one knows the fund of humor possessed by a steamboat clerk, and what a field for display the table at meal-times affords. On Friday she fasted rigidly, and she never began to eat, nor finished, without a little Latin movement of the lips and a sign of the cross. And always at six o'clock of the evening she remembered the angelus, although there was no church bell to remind her of it.

She was in mourning for her father, the sisters told the captain, and she was going to New Orleans to her mother. She had not seen her mother since she was an infant, on account of some disagreement between the parents, in consequence of which the father had brought her to Cincinnati and placed her in the convent. There she had been for twelve years, only going to her father for vacations and holidays. So long as the father lived he would never let the child have any communication with her mother. Now that he was dead all that was changed, and the first thing the girl herself wanted to do was to go to her mother.

The mother superior had arranged it all with the mother of the girl, who was to come personally to the boat in New Orleans, and receive her child from the captain, presenting a letter from the mother superior, a facsimile of which the sisters gave the captain.

It is a long voyage from Cincinnati to New Orleans, the rivers doing their best to make it interminable, embroidering themselves *ad libitum* all over the country. Every five miles, and sometimes oftener, the boat would stop to put off or take on freight, if not both. The little convent girl, sitting in the cabin, had her terrible frights at first from the hideous noises attendant on these landings—the whistles, the ringings of the bells, the running to and fro, the shouting. Every time she thought it was shipwreck, death, judgment, purgatory; and her sins! her sins! She would drop her crochet, and clutch her prayer-beads from her pocket, and relax the constraint over her lips, which would go to rattling off prayers with the velocity of a relaxed windlass. That was at first, before the captain took to fetching her out in front to see the boat make a landing. Then she got to liking it so much that she would stay all day just where the captain put her, going inside only for her meals. She forgot herself at times so much that she would draw her chair a little closer to the railing, and put up her veil, actually, to see better. No one ever usurped her place, quite in front, or intruded upon her either with word or look; for every one learned to know her shyness, and began to feel a personal interest in her, and all wanted the little convent girl to see everything that she possibly could.

And it was worth seeing—the balancing and *chasséeing* and waltzing of the cumbersome old boat to make a landing. It seemed to be always attended with the difficulty and the improbability of a new enterprise; and the relief when it did sidle up anywhere within rope's-throw of the spot aimed at! And the roustabout throwing the rope from the perilous end of the dangling gang-plank! And the dangling roustabouts hanging like drops of water from it—dropping sometimes twenty feet to the land, and not infrequently into the river itself. And then what a rolling of barrels, and shouldering of sacks, and singing of Jim Crow songs, and pacing of Jim Crow steps; and black skins glistening through torn shirts, and white teeth gleaming through red lips, and laughing, and talking and—bewildering! entrancing! Surely the little convent girl in her convent walls never dreamed of so much unpunished noise and movement in the world!

The first time she heard the mate—it must have been like the first time woman ever heard man—curse and swear, she turned pale, and ran quickly, quickly into the saloon, and—came out again? No, indeed! not with all the soul she had to save, and all the other sins on her conscience. She shook her head resolutely, and was not seen in her chair on deck again until the captain not only reassured her, but guaranteed his reassurance. And after that, whenever the boat was about to make a landing, the mate would first glance up to the guards, and if the little convent girl were sitting there he would change his invective to sarcasm, and politely request the colored gentlemen not to hurry themselves—on no account whatever; to take their time about shoving out the plank; to send the rope ashore by post office—write him when it got there; begging them not to strain their backs; calling them mister, colonel, major, general, prince, and your royal highness, which was vastly amusing. At night, however, or when the little convent girl was not there, language flowed in its natural curve, the mate swearing like a pagan to make up for lost time.

The captain forgot himself one day: it was when the boat ran aground in the most unexpected manner and place, and he went to work to express his opinion, as only steamboat captains can, of the pilot, mate, engineer, crew, boat, river, country, and the world in general, ringing the bell, first to back, then to head, shouting himself hoarser than his own whistle—when he chanced to see the little black figure hurrying through the chaos on the deck; and the captain stuck as fast aground in midstream as the boat had done.

In the evening the little convent girl would be taken on the upper deck, and there was such confusion, going up, in keeping the black skirts down over the stiff white petticoats; and, coming down, such blushing when suspicion would cross the unprepared face that a rim of white stocking might be visible; and the thin feet, laced so tightly in the glossy new leather boots, would cling to each successive round as if they could never, never make another venture; and then one boot would (there is but that word) hesitate out, and feel and feel around, and have such a pause of helpless agony as if indeed the next step must have been wilfully removed, or was nowhere to be found on the wide, wide earth.

It was a miracle that the pilot ever got her up into the pilot-house; but pilots have a lonely time, and do not hesitate even at miracles when there is a chance for company. He would place a box for her to climb to the tall bench behind the wheel, and he would arrange the cushions, and open a window here to let in air, and shut one there to cut off a draft, as if there could be no tenderer consideration in life for him than her comfort. And he would talk of the river to her, explain the chart, pointing out eddies, whirlpools, shoals, depths, new beds, old beds, cut-offs, caving banks, and making banks, as exquisitely and respectfully as if she had been the River Commission.

It was his opinion that there was as great a river as the Mississippi flowing directly under it—an underself of a river, as much a counterpart of the other as the second story of a house is of the first; in fact, he said they were navigating through the upper story. Whirlpools were holes in the floor of the upper river, so to speak; eddies were rifts and cracks. And deep under the earth, hurrying toward the subterranean stream, were other streams, small and great, but all deep, hurrying to and from that great mother-stream underneath, just as the small and great overground streams hurry to and from their mother Mississippi. It was almost more than the little convent girl could take in: at least such was the expression of her eyes; for they opened as all eyes have to open at pilot stories. And he knew as much of astronomy as he did of hydrology, could call the stars by name, and define the shapes of the constellations; and she, who had studied astronomy at the convent, was charmed to find that it was all true what she had learned. It was in the pilot-house, one night, that she forgot herself for the first time in her life, and stayed up until after nine o'clock at night. Although she appeared almost intoxicated at the wild pleasure, she was immediately overwhelmed at the wickedness of it, and observed much more rigidity of conduct thereafter. The engineer, the boiler-men, the firemen, the stokers, they all knew when the little convent girl was up in the pilot-house: the speaking-tube became so mild and gentle.

With all the delays of river and boat, however, there is an end to the journey from Cincinnati to New Orleans. The latter city, which at one time to the impatient seemed at the terminus of the never, began, all of a sudden, one day to make its nearingness felt; and from that period every other interest paled before the interest in the imminence of arrival into port, and the whole boat was seized with a panic of preparation, the little convent girl with the others. Although so immaculate was she in person and effects that she might have been struck with a landing, as some good people might be struck with death, at any moment without fear of results, her trunk was packed and repacked, her satchel arranged and rearranged, and, the last day, her hair was brushed and plaited and smoothed over and over again until the very last glimmer of a curl disappeared. Her dress was whisked, as if for microscopic inspection; her face was washed; and her finger-nails were scrubbed with the hard convent nail-brush, until the disciplined little tips ached with a pristine soreness. And still there were hours to wait, and still the boat added up delays. But she arrived at last, after all, with not more than the usual and expected difference between the actual and the advertised time of arrival.

There was extra blowing and extra ringing, shouting, commanding, rushing up the gangway and rushing down the gangway. The clerks, sitting behind tables on the first deck, were plied, in the twinkling of an eye, with estimates, receipts, charges, countercharges, claims, reclaims, demands, questions, accusations, threats, all at topmost voices. None but steamboat clerks could have stood it. And there were throngs composed of individuals every one of whom wanted to see the captain first and at once; and those who could not get to him shouted over the heads of the others; and as usual he lost his temper and politeness, and began to do what he termed "hustle."

"Captain! Captain!" a voice called him to where a hand plucked his sleeve, and a letter was thrust toward him. "The cross, and the name of the convent." He recognized the envelop of the mother superior. He read the duplicate of the letter given by the sisters. He looked at the woman—the mother—casually, then again and again.

The little convent girl saw him coming, leading some one toward her. She rose. The captain took her hand first, before the other greeting. "Good-by, my dear," he said. He tried to add something else, but seemed undetermined what. "Be a good little girl—" It was evidently all he could think of. Nodding to the woman behind him, he turned on his heel, and left.

One of the deck-hands was sent to fetch her trunk. He walked out behind them, through the cabin, and the crowd on deck, down the stairs, and out the gangway. The little convent girl and her mother went with hands tightly clasped. She did not turn her eyes to the right or left, or once (what all passengers do) look backward at the boat which, however slowly, had carried her surely over dangers that she wot not of. All looked at her as she passed. All wanted to say good-by to the little convent girl, to see the mother who had been deprived of her so long. Some expressed surprise in a whistle; some in other ways. All exclaimed audibly, or to themselves, "Colored!"

It takes about a month to make the round trip from New Orleans to Cincinnati and back, counting five days' stoppage in New Orleans. It was a month to a day when the steamboat came puffing and blowing up to the wharf again, like a stout dowager after too long a walk; and the same scene of confusion was enacted, as it had been enacted twelve times a year at almost the same wharf for twenty years; and the same calm, a death calmness by contrast, followed as usual the next morning.

The decks were quiet and clean; one cargo had just been delivered, part of another stood ready on the levee to be shipped. The captain was there waiting for his business to begin, the clerk was in his office getting his books ready, the voice of the mate could be heard below, mustering the old crew out and a new crew in; for if steamboat crews have a single principle,—and there are those who deny them any,—it is never to ship twice in succession on the same boat. It was too early yet for any but roustabouts, marketers, and church-goers; so early that even the river was still partly mist-covered; only in places could the swift, dark current be seen rolling swiftly along.

"Captain!" A hand plucked at his elbow, as if not confident that the mere calling would secure attention. The captain turned. The mother of the little convent girl stood there, and she held the little convent girl by the hand. "I have brought her to see you," the woman said. "You were so kind—and she is so quiet, so still, all the time, I thought it would do her a pleasure."

She spoke with an accent, and with embarrassment; otherwise one would have said that she was bold and assured enough.

"She don't go nowhere, she don't do nothing but make her crochet and her prayers, so I thought I would bring her for a little visit of 'How d' ye do' to you."

There was, perhaps, some inflection in the woman's voice that might have made known, or at least awakened, the suspicion of some latent hope or intention, had the captain's ear been fine enough to detect it. There might have been something in the little convent girl's face, had his eye been more sensitive,—a trifle paler, maybe, the lips a little tighter drawn, the blue ribbon a shade faded. He may have noticed that, but—And the visit of "How d' ye do" came to an end.

They walked down the stairway, the woman in front, the little convent girl—her hand released to shake hands with the captain—following, across the bared deck, out to the gangway, to the middle of it. No one was looking, no one saw more than a flutter of white petticoats, a show of white stockings, as the little convent girl went under the water.

The roustabout dived, as the roustabouts always do, after the drowning, even at the risk of their good-for-nothing lives. The mate himself jumped overboard; but she had gone down in a whirlpool. Perhaps, as the pilot had told her whirlpools always did, it may have carried her through to the underground river, to that vast, hidden, dark Mississippi that flows beneath the one we see; for her body was never seen again.

1893

Alice Dunbar-Nelson 1875–1935

The most striking feature of Alice Dunbar-Nelson's work is the way that it contrives to treat serious, even radical, social concerns while adhering on the surface to conventional forms and modes of expression. For her as for many other African American writers of her generation, race was a particularly vexed (and vexing) issue—one which she skillfully elided in her life and writings.

Dunbar-Nelson was personally acquainted with cultural ambiguity, being born of mixed African, Native American, and white ancestry into the Creole society of postbellum New Orleans. There she shone as a beautiful and promising young woman from whom much was expected. After her graduation from Straight College (now Dilliard University) in 1892 and four years teaching elementary school, she went north, where she continued her education and taught public and mission school in New York City. On March 8, 1898, after a storybook courtship, she married the famous black poet Paul Laurence Dunbar. Plagued from the beginning by temperamental clashes, her family's disapproval, and his medically related alcohol and drug addiction, the union did not last long. They separated in 1902, four years before Dunbar died. However brief, her relationship with him exposed her to the world of professional authorship.

From 1902 to 1920, she taught English and was an administrator at Howard High School, in Wilmington, Delaware. Later, she was instructor and parole officer at the Industrial School for Colored Girls (1924–1928) and executive secretary of the American Friends Inter-Racial Peace Committee (1928–1931). Despite the fact that she was light-skinned enough to pass for white and privately harbored some negativity about darker-skinned, less educated or refined blacks, Dunbar-Nelson worked assiduously for racial causes. She headed the 1922 Delaware Anti-Lynching Crusaders and, with her husband Robert J. Nelson (whom she married in 1916), co-edited and published the Wilmington *Advocate,* a newspaper that challenged vested racist and capitalist interests. Because she was also a feminist, many of her activities centered on women. She was particularly prominent in the social and cultural projects of the Federation of Colored Women's Clubs and in political party organizing among black women.

A strong individual with a sense of her own worth, Dunbar-Nelson sought recognition through her writing. She published her first book, *Violets,* when she was barely twenty years old and until her death at age sixty produced poems, volumes of short stories, a few plays and pageants, and three unpublished novels. However, some of her most significant writing was done in non-canonical forms. The newspaper columns which she wrote between 1926 and 1930 are informational and linguistic treasures. Her diary (1921, 1926–1931) likewise possesses artistic merit while revealing her complex life and times. Speeches and essays in black journals and anthologies round out the body of her work.

Dunbar-Nelson devoted most of her literary attention to her short stories. They were regularly published in such popular magazines as *Leslie's Weekly* and *The Mirror.* Her turn-of-the-century short stories confounded the reading public's expectations that black fictional characters conform to plantation and minstrel stereotypes. That helps explain why most of her work "has no characteristics peculiar to her race," as one reviewer in 1900 put it. Thus, Dunbar-Nelson achieved her renown as a "local colorist" who penned charming sketches of the Louisiana Creole.

The subtext of her work tells a different story. "Sister Josepha" (which appeared in *The Goodness of St. Rocque*), seems to be just another romantically sad convent tale slightly distinguished by its Old World New Orleans ambience and French patois. In reality, it is a remarkable exploration of the "heavy door" of illegitimacy, racism, sexism, female vulnerability, traditional religion, and forced confinement. Dunbar-Nelson wrote a few fictional pieces that deal more explicitly with the cultural confusion of the black Creole and with racism in general. However, because these serious works were not nearly as marketable as her airier tales (finding outlets only in publications such as *Southern Workman* and *Crisis*), she tended to reserve her overtly race-conscious statements for her non-belletristic writings. In a story like "Sister Josepha," the reader must tread surreptitiously with Dunbar-Nelson beyond the safe and acceptable into more personally and socially sensitive areas.

Gloria T. Hull
University of California at Santa Cruz

PRIMARY WORKS

Violets and Other Tales, 1895, *The Goodness of St. Rocque and Other Stories,* 1899, in *The Works of Alice Dunbar-Nelson,* 3 vols., ed. Gloria T. Hull, 1988; *The Diary of Alice Dunbar-Nelson,* ed. Gloria T. Hull, 1984.

Sister Josepha

Sister Josepha told her beads mechanically, her fingers numb with the accustomed exercise. The little organ creaked a dismal "O Salutaris,"[1] and she still knelt on the floor, her white-bonneted head nodding suspiciously. The Mother Superior gave a sharp glance at the tired figure; then, as a sudden lurch forward brought the little sister back to consciousness, Mother's eyes relaxed into a genuine smile.

The bell tolled the end of vespers, and the sombre-robed nuns filed out of the chapel to go about their evening duties. Little Sister Josepha's work was to attend to the household lamps, but there must have been as much oil spilled upon the table tonight as was put in the vessels. The small brown hands trembled so that most of the wicks were trimmed with points at one corner which caused them to smoke that night.

"Oh, cher Seigneur,"[2] she sighed, giving an impatient polish to a refractory chimney, "it is wicked and sinful, I know, but I am so tired. I can't be happy and sing any more. It doesn't seem right for le bon Dieu[3] to have me all cooped up here with nothing to see but stray visitors, and always the same old work, teaching those mean little girls to sew, and washing and filling the same old lamps. Pah!" And she polished the chimney with a sudden vigorous jerk which threatened destruction.

They were rebellious prayers that the red mouth murmured that night, and a restless figure that tossed on the hard dormitory bed. Sister Dominica called from her couch to know if Sister Josepha were ill.

"No," was the somewhat short reponse; then a muttered, "Why can't they let me alone for a minute? That pale-eyed Sister Dominica never sleeps; that's why she is so ugly."

[1]Opening words of "O Salutaris Hostia," "Oh, Saving Host," the hymn to the Blessed Sacrament consecrated outside of Mass.

[2]French: "dear Lord."

[3]French: "the good Lord/God."

About fifteen years before this night some one had brought to the orphan asylum connected with this convent, du Sacre Coeur, a round, dimpled bit of three-year-old humanity, who regarded the world from a pair of gravely twinkling black eyes, and only took a chubby thumb out of a rosy mouth long enough to answer in monosyllabic French. It was a child without an identity; there was but one name that any one seemed to know, and that, too, was vague,—Camille.

She grew up with the rest of the waifs; scraps of French and American civilization thrown together to develop a seemingly inconsistent miniature world. Mademoiselle Camille was a queen among them, a pretty little tyrant who ruled the children and dominated the more timid sisters in charge.

One day an awakening came. When she was fifteen, and almost fully ripened into a glorious tropical beauty of the type that matures early, some visitors to the convent were fascinated by her and asked the Mother Superior to give the girl into their keeping.

Camille fled like a frightened fawn into the yard, and was only unearthed with some difficulty from behind a group of palms. Sulky and pouting, she was led into the parlour, picking at her blue pinafore like a spoiled infant.

"The lady and gentleman wish you to go home with them, Camille," said the Mother Superior, in the language of the convent. Her voice was kind and gentle apparently; but the child, accustomed to its various inflections, detected a steely ring behind its softness, like the proverbial iron hand in the velvet glove.

"You must understand, madame," continued Mother, in stilted English, "that we never force children from us. We are ever glad to place them in comfortable—how you say that?—quarters—maisons—homes—bien! But we will not make them go if they do not wish."

Camille stole a glance at her would-be guardians, and decided instantly, impulsively, finally. The woman suited her; but the man! It was doubtless intuition of the quick, vivacious sort which belonged to her blood that served her. Untutored in worldly knowledge, she could not divine the meaning of the pronounced leers and admiration of her physical charms which gleamed in the man's face, but she knew it made her feel creepy, and stoutly refused to go.

Next day Camille was summoned from a task to the Mother Superior's parlour. The other girls gazed with envy upon her as she dashed down the courtyard with impetuous movement. Camille, they decided crossly, received too much notice. It was Camille this, Camille that; she was pretty, it was to be expected. Even Father Ray lingered longer in his blessing when his hands pressed her silky black hair.

As she entered the parlour, a strange chill swept over the girl. The room was not an unaccustomed one, for she had swept it many times, but to-day the stiff black chairs, the dismal crucifixes, the gleaming whiteness of the walls, even the cheap lithograph of the Madonna which Camille had always regarded as a perfect specimen of art, seemed cold and mean.

"Camille, ma chere,"[4] said Mother, "I am extremely displeased with you. Why did you not wish to go with Monsieur and Madame Lafaye yesterday?"

[4]French: "my dear."

The girl uncrossed her hands from her bosom, and spread them out in a deprecating gesture.

"Mais, ma mere,[5] I was afraid."

Mother's face grew stern. "No foolishness now," she exclaimed.

"It is not foolishness, ma mere; I could not help it, but that man looked at me so funny, I felt all cold chills down my back. Oh, dear Mother, I love the convent and the sisters so, I just want to stay and be a sister too, may I?"

And thus it was that Camille took the white veil at sixteen years. Now that the period of novitiate was over, it was just beginning to dawn upon her that she had made a mistake.

"Maybe it would have been better had I gone with the funny-looking lady and gentleman," she mused bitterly one night. "Oh, Seigneur, I'm so tired and impatient; it's so dull here, and, dear God, I'm so young."

There was no help for it. One must arise in the morning, and help in the refectory with the stupid Sister Francesca, and go about one's duties with a prayerful mien, and not even let a sigh escape when one's head ached with the eternal telling of beads.

A great fete day was coming, and an atmosphere of preparation and mild excitement pervaded the brown walls of the convent like a delicate aroma. The old Cathedral around the corner had stood a hundred years, and all the city was rising to do honour to its age and time-softened beauty. There would be a service, oh, but such a one! with two Cardinals, and Archbishops and Bishops, and all the accompanying glitter of soldiers and orchestras. The little sisters of the Convent du Sacre Coeur clasped their hands in anticipation of the holy joy. Sister Josepha curled her lip, she was so tired of churchly pleasures.

The day came, a gold and blue spring day, when the air hung heavy with the scent of roses and magnolias, and the sunbeams fairly laughed as they kissed the houses. The old Cathedral stood gray and solemn, and the flowers in Jackson Square smiled cheery birthday greetings across the way. The crowd around the door surged and pressed and pushed in its eagerness to get within. Ribbons stretched across the banquette were of no avail to repress it, and important ushers with cardinal colours could do little more.

The Sacred Heart sisters filed slowly in at the side door, creating a momentary flutter as they paced reverently to their seats, guarding the blue-bonneted orphans. Sister Josepha, determined to see as much of the world as she could, kept her big black eyes opened wide, as the church rapidly filled with the fashionably dressed, perfumed, rustling, and self-conscious throng.

Her heart beat quickly. The rebellious thoughts that will arise in the most philosophical of us surged in her small heavily gowned bosom. For her were the gray things, the neutral tinted skies, the ugly garb, the coarse meats; for them the rainbow, the ethereal airiness of earthly joys, the bonbons and glacés of the world. Sister Josepha did not know that the rainbow is elusive, and its colours but the illumination of tears; she had never been told that earthly ethereality is necessarily ephemeral,

[5]French: "But, mother."

nor that bonbons and glaces, whether of the palate or of the soul, nauseate and pall upon the taste. Dear God, forgive her, for she bent with contrite tears over her worn rosary, and glanced no more at the worldly glitter of femininity.

The sunbeams streamed through the high windows in purple and crimson lights upon a veritable fugue of colour. Within the seats, crush upon crush of spring millinery; within the aisles erect lines of gold-braided, gold-buttoned military. Upon the altar, broad sweeps of golden robes, great dashes of crimson skirts, mitres and gleaming crosses, the soft neutral hue of rich lace vestments; the tender heads of childhood in picturesque attire; the proud, golden magnificence of the domed altar with its weighting mass of lilies and wide-eyed roses, and the long candles that sparkled their yellow star points above the reverent throng within the altar rails.

The soft baritone of the Cardinal intoned a single phrase in the suspended silence. The censer took up the note in its delicate clink clink, as it swung to and fro in the hands of a fair-haired child. Then the organ, pausing an instant in a deep, mellow, long-drawn note, burst suddenly into a magnificent strain, and the choir sang forth, "Kyrie Eleison, Christe Eleison."[6] One voice, flute-like, piercing, sweet, rang high over the rest. Sister Josepha heard and trembled, as she buried her face in her hands, and let her tears fall, like other beads, through her rosary.

It was when the final word of the service had been intoned, the last peal of the exit march had died away, that she looked up meekly, to encounter a pair of youthful brown eyes gazing pityingly upon her. That was all she remembered for a moment, that the eyes were youthful and handsome and tender. Later, she saw that they were placed in a rather beautiful boyish face, surmounted by waves of brown hair, curling and soft, and that the head was set on a pair of shoulders decked in military uniform. Then the brown eyes marched away with the rest of the rear guard, and the white-bonneted sisters filed out the side door, through the narrow court, back into the brown convent.

That night Sister Josepha tossed more than usual on her hard bed, and clasped her fingers often in prayer to quell the wickedness in her heart. Turn where she would, pray as she might, there was ever a pair of tender, pitying brown eyes, haunting her persistently. The squeaky organ at vespers intoned the clank of military accoutrements to her ears, the white bonnets of the sisters about her faded into mists of curling brown hair. Briefly, Sister Josepha was in love.

The days went on pretty much as before, save for the one little heart that beat rebelliously now and then, though it tried so hard to be submissive. There was the morning work in the refectory, the stupid little girls to teach sewing, and the insatiable lamps that were so greedy for oil. And always the tender, boyish brown eyes, that looked so sorrowfully at the fragile, beautiful little sister, haunting, following, pleading.

Perchance, had Sister Josepha been in the world, the eyes would have been an incident. But in this home of self-repression and retrospection, it was a life-story. The eyes had gone their way, doubtless forgetting the little sister they pitied; but the little sister?

[6]"Lord, have mercy, Christ, have mercy," penitential prayer used at the beginning of the liturgy.

The days glided into weeks, the weeks into months. Thoughts of escape had come to Sister Josepha, to flee into the world, to merge in the great city where recognition was impossible, and, working her way like the rest of humanity, perchance encounter the eyes again.

It was all planned and ready. She would wait until some morning when the little band of black-robed sisters wended their way to mass at the Cathedral. When it was time to file out the side-door into the courtway, she would linger at prayers, then slip out another door, and unseen glide up Chartres Street to Canal, and once there, mingle in the throng that filled the wide thoroughfare. Beyond this first plan she could think no further. Penniless, garbed, and shaven though she would be, other difficulties never presented themselves to her. She would rely on the mercies of the world to help her escape from this torturing life of inertia. It seemed easy now that the first step of decision had been taken.

The Saturday night before the final day had come, and she lay feverishly nervous in her narrow little bed, wondering with wide-eyed fear at the morrow. Pale-eyed Sister Dominica and Sister Francesca were whispering together in the dark silence, and Sister Josepha's ears pricked up as she heard her name.

"She is not well, poor child," said Francesca. "I fear the life is too confining."

"It is best for her," was the reply. "You know, sister, how hard it would be for her in the world, with no name but Camille, no friends, and her beauty; and then—"

Sister Josepha heard no more, for her heart beating tumultously in her bosom drowned the rest. Like the rush of the bitter salt tide over a drowning man clinging to a spar, came the complete submerging of her hopes of another life. No name but Camille, that was true; no nationality, for she could never tell from whom or whence she came; no friends, and a beauty that not even an ungainly bonnet and shaven head could hide. In a flash she realised the deception of the life she would lead, and the cruel self-torture of wonder at her own identity. Already, as if in anticipation of the world's questionings, she was asking herself, "Who am I? What am I?"

The next morning the sisters du Sacre Coeur filed into the Cathedral at High Mass, and bent devout knees at the general confession. "Confiteor Deo omnipotenti,"[7] murmured the priest; and tremblingly one little sister followed the words, "Je confesse a Dieu, tout puissant—que j'ai beaucoup peche par pensees—c'est ma faute—c'est ma faute—c'est ma tres grande faute."

The organ pealed forth as mass ended, the throng slowly filed out, and the sisters paced through the courtway back into the brown convent walls. One paused at the entrance, and gazed with swift longing eyes in the direction of narrow, squalid Chartres Street, then, with a gulping sob, followed the rest, and vanished behind the heavy door.

1899

[7]"I confess to God Almighty." The priest begins, in Latin, the formulaic prayer traditionally used to initiate confession. It is taken up in French which translates: "I confess to God Almighty—that I have gravely sinned in my thoughts—it is my fault—it is my fault—it is my most grievous fault."

Ghost Dance Songs

In 1871, Congress terminated the U.S. policy of making treaties with Native American tribes as sovereign nations, thus making the tribes subject to the will of Congress and the administrative rulings of the president. The pace of Anglo-American expansion and expropriation of Indian lands quickened, culminating within a decade in the destruction of the vast buffalo herds and the forcible confinement of many tribes to unproductive reservation land, where starvation threatened their lives and acculturation threatened their traditional cultures with extinction. The response of many Native American societies to threats to their way of life was a powerful apocalyptic dream of a future time when enemies would be overthrown and the world returned to the divine order established in the beginning.

The Ghost Dance, the most dramatic and widespread manifestation of this phenomenon, began when the Paiute prophet Wovoka experienced such a vision. He prophesied that the crow would bring whirlwinds and earthquakes to cleanse the earth and destroy the white invaders, and that the Indian dead (the "ghosts") and the slaughtered buffalo would return to reclaim the land. The vision and the trance-inducing round dance and songs accompanying it spread like wildfire among reservation communities from California to the Dakotas.

Among the Sioux, facing a desperate struggle for both physical and cultural survival, the Ghost Dance became especially powerful, catching up men like Sitting Bull in its fervor and persuading others of their invulnerability to the white man's bullets. Fear swept over whites living on and near the Pine Ridge Reservation in South Dakota, provoking confrontations. In 1890, when Sitting Bull was killed while being arrested, others like Big Foot and his band saw no future and left the reservation. They made it into the Dakota Badlands as far as a place called Wounded Knee, where members of the U.S. cavalry armed with machine guns surrounded and searched them for weapons. A few shots were heard, then many from the machine guns. When silence settled, around 200 Native American men, women, and children were dead, and so was the hope awakened by Wovoka's dream. The Ghost Dance songs that follow should be read with the account of Charles Eastman, a Dakota trained in medicine, who returned to the Pine Ridge Reservation in time to witness the calamity at Wounded Knee.

Andrew O. Wiget
New Mexico State University

PRIMARY SOURCES

James Mooney, *The Ghost Dance Religion and Sioux Outbreak of 1890.* Fourteenth Annual Report of the Bureau of American Ethnology, Pt. 2. Washington: GPO, 1893.

Ghost Dance Songs

I

My children,[1] when at first I liked the whites,
My children, when at first I liked the whites,
I gave them fruits,
I gave them fruits.

II

Father, have pity on me,
Father, have pity on me;
I am crying for thirst,
I am crying for thirst;
All is gone—I have nothing to eat.
All is gone—I have nothing to eat.

III

My son, let me grasp your hand,
My son, let me grasp your hand,
Says the father,
Says the father.
You shall live,
You shall live,
Says the father,
Says the father.
I bring you a pipe,[2]
I bring you a pipe,
Says the father,
Says the father.
By means of it you shall live,
By means of it you shall live,
Says the father,
Says the father.

[1]The songs are sung as a dialogue, with the Sun ("Our Father") addressing the Indians ("my children").
[2]*I.e.,* "a vision." The pipe was smoked to put one in prayerful contact with the sacred. Here "a pipe" functions as symbol for the vision which smoking the pipe would induce.

IV

My children, my children,
I take pity on those who have been taught,
I take pity on those who have been taught,
Because they push on hard,
Because they push on hard.
Says our father,
Says our father.

V

The whole world is coming,
A nation is coming, a nation is coming,
The Eagle has brought the message to the tribe.
The father says so, the father says so.
Over the whole earth they are coming.
The buffalo are coming, the buffalo are coming.
The Crow has brought the message to his tribe,
The father says so, the father says so.

VI

The spirit host is advancing, they say,
The spirit host is advancing, they say,
They are coming with the buffalo, they say,
They are coming with the buffalo, they say.
They are coming with the new earth, they say,
They are coming with the new earth, they say.

VII

He' yoho' ho! He' yoho' ho![3]
The yellow-hide, the white skin
I have now put him aside—
I have now put him aside—
I have no more sympathy with him,
I have no more sympathy with him,
He' yoho' ho! he' yoho' ho!

[3]The words are vocables, with no referential significance.

VIII

I' yehe! my children—*Uhi 'yeye 'heye!*
I' yehe! my children—*Uhi 'yeye 'heye!*
I' yehe! we have rendered them desolate—*Eye' ae 'yuhe' yu!*
I' yehe! we have rendered them desolate—*Eye' ae 'yuhe' yu!*
The whites are crazy—*Ahe 'yuhe' yu!*

1893

Alexander Lawrence Posey (Creek) 1873–1908

Alexander Posey's life was cut short on May 27, 1908. At the age of thirty-five, the Creek writer drowned while crossing the flooded Oktahutche River. It was barely a year since Indian Territory and the tribal governments within it had been dissolved. Born in the Creek Nation, Posey died in the brand-new state of Oklahoma. The end of tribal governments and the advent of statehood were long, bitterly contested transitions. As a poet, politician, and political satirist, Posey had a strong and complicated voice in the deliberations.

Often called a "progressivist" because he believed that native peoples needed at least partially to assimilate to white culture in order to survive, Posey criticized "traditionalists," calling them "pull back" Indians who couldn't possibly survive in the imminent future. Nevertheless, he respected older Creeks who remembered another way of life. Posey has been somewhat reviled among Creeks for his participation in the bureaucracy surrounding the dissolution of tribal government and for his subsequent activities as a real estate speculator in formerly tribal land. But he is recognized as having penned some of the most cogent and long-sighted critiques of both that bureaucracy and the greed for Indian land. Posey lived during a complicated period of change for the Creek Nation, and his motivations were never simple. They are still difficult to decipher, perhaps because they are so often couched in humor.

Posey's mother was half Creek and half Chickasaw. Because she was from the tribal town of Tuskegee and Creek clan membership follows matrilineal lines, Posey himself was a Wind Clan member of Tuskegee. Although Posey's father was born to white parents, he called himself Creek. He was raised in the Creek Nation from the time he was orphaned, he spoke Creek fluently, and he was a member of the Broken Arrow tribal town. Young Alexander spoke only Creek; when he was fourteen, his father insisted that he speak English and punished him if he spoke in his native language. From that time, Posey received a formal education, including three years at Bacone Indian University in Muskogee. His mixed-blood status, his estrangement from the Creek language, and his education fostered his ambivalence toward Creek traditionalism; this ambivalence separated him from his own culture but gave him a powerful critical voice within it.

Posey began writing while a student at Bacone. Influenced by the conventional English forms he studied in school, Posey's poetry pays homage to Whittier, Longfellow, Kipling, and Tennyson. Naturalists who wrote in English, like Thoreau and John Burroughs, also influenced the aspiring Creek poet. A lover of nature, Posey was passionately attached to the Tulledega Hills, where he spent his childhood. Not satisfied with the English language's abilities to translate Creek experience, Posey tried to replicate in his English poetry the rhythms and cadences of the musical Creek language. His poetry achieved moderate success, regularly appearing in Indian Territory publications. In 1900 and 1901, a few poems appeared in publications in the East and Midwest.

Soon after leaving school, Posey became involved in Creek politics. His leadership skills, intelligence, and personal charm proved highly useful to the struggling Creek Nation. Elected to the Creek National Council at age twenty-two, he would continue his political involvement until his death. By the turn of the century his interest in poetry had waned, and in 1902 he started a career as a journalist, setting the stage for his most effective writing. As owner and editor of the *Eufaula (Okla.) Indian Journal,* Posey achieved national prominence in the United States for establishing the first Indian-published daily newspaper. More important, he was recognized for comic letters written by his fictional persona, Fus Fixico (Heartless Bird), which he printed in the *Indian Journal* as substitutes for editorials. A full-blooded Creek, Fus Fixico wrote to the paper about his everyday life or sent in transcriptions of speeches that he had heard the Creek medicine man Hotgun deliver to an audience of other old men—Kono Harjo, Tookpafka Micco, and Wolf Warrior. The monologues are in dialect and achieve a wickedly satirical perspective on Creek culture and politics.

Sometimes read as expressions of nostalgia for a vanishing way of life, the Fus Fixico letters are also cogent political commentary aimed at influencing Indian Territory, Oklahoma, and United States politics. Across the years when Posey wrote and published the Fus Fixico letters, politics in Indian Territory was a veritable Gordian knot. The Curtis Act of 1898, which decreed that Indian land held in common by tribal governments be broken up and alloted in small portions to individual tribal members, was being implemented, and debates about statehood were raging. Not only were native peoples ambivalent about statehood, but there was a very real possibility that Oklahoma would be admitted as two states—one white, one Indian. Posey was a strong advocate of the two-state proposal and was secretary at the 1905 convention to organize Sequoyah, the proposed Indian state. The Fus Fixico letters, written from 1902 to 1908, satirized every aspect of the debate. Posey was frequently approached by U.S. newspaper syndicates that wanted to publish his Fus Fixico letters nationally. He refused permission. His political satires were intended for Indian Territory readers, and he knew that their dialect and humor would suffer in translation for a national audience that knew little of the intricacies of Indian Territory politics.

Dialect literature was hugely popular at the turn of the twentieth century. Posey's father liked to tell stories in black dialect, and Alexander Posey's favorite poet was Robert Burns, famous for his Scottish dialect poems. Posey read the dialect literatures of poet James Whitcomb Riley and Paul Laurence Dunbar and dialect humorists such as Josh Billings and Max Adler. But he was doing far more than simply catering to U.S. national taste. He switched from poetry to dialect writing as he became more politically active, and his dialect writings represent Creek life more effectively than does his poetry. Though his characters speak Creek English, the dialect writings are representations of Creek oral culture. Posey had no patience for writers who wrote dialect simply because it was fashionable: "Those cigar store Indian dialect stories . . . will fool no one who has lived 'six months in the precinct.' Like the wooden aborigine, they are the product of a white man's factory, and bear no resemblance to the real article."

Posey was mourned throughout the Indian Territory after his premature death. He remains a complicated figure in Creek culture, remembered with mingled respect and suspicion. Two years after his death, his wife collected and published much of his poetry, but his Fus Fixico letters remained uncollected until the 1990s.

Bethany Ridgway Schneider
Oberlin College

PRIMARY WORKS

Edward Everett Dale, ed., "The Journal of Alexander Lawrence Posey, January 1 to September 4, 1897," *Chronicles of Oklahoma* 45 (Winter 1967–1968); Minnie Posey, ed., *The Poems of Alexander Lawrence Posey,* 1910; Daniel F. Littlefield, Jr. and Carol A. Petter Hunter, eds., *The Fus Fixico Letters,* 1993.

Ode to Sequoyah[1]

The names of Waitie and Boudinot—[2]
  The valiant warrior and gifted sage—
And other Cherokees, may be forgot,
  But thy name shall descend to every age;
The mysteries enshrouding Cadmus' name[3]
Cannot obscure thy claim to fame.

The people's language cannot perish—nay,
  When from the face of this great continent
  Inevitable doom hath swept away
The last memorial—the last fragment
  Of tribes,—some scholar learned shall pore
Upon thy letters, seeking ancient lore.

Some bard shall lift a voice in praise of thee,
  In moving numbers tell the world how men
Scoffed thee, hissed thee, charged with lunacy![4]
  And who could not give 'nough honor when
At length, in spite of jeers, of want and need,
Thy genius shaped a dream into a deed.

[1]Sequoyah, or George Guess, was the well-known inventor of the Cherokee syllabary. This poetic tribute appeared in *Twin Territories* (Muskogee) in 1899. (All footnotes by Daniel F. Littlefield, Jr.)

[2]Stand Watie (1806–1871), a leader of the Treaty Party of Cherokees, had favored removal of the Cherokees from the Southeast to the West. Watie, who reached the rank of general during the Civil War, was reputedly the last Confederate general to surrender. Elias Boudinot (ca. 1802–1839), Watie's brother and likewise a leader of the Treaty Party, was educated at Cornwall, Connecticut, and edited the *Cherokee Phoenix,* the Cherokee national newspaper. He was assassinated in 1839 because of his pro-removal stand. Some of his work appears in Volume 1.

[3]In Greek mythology, Cadmus introduced the alphabet to Greece.

[4]Sequoyah was thought by many of his fellow tribesmen to be mad because of the strange characters he scratched out during his work on the Cherokee syllabary.

By cloud-capped summits in the boundless west,
Or mighty river rolling to the sea,
Where'er thy footsteps led thee on that quest,
Unknown, rest thee, illustrious Cherokee![5]

1899

Hotgun on the Death of Yadeka Harjo

"Well so," Hotgun[1] he say,
"My ol'-time frien', Yadeka Harjo,[2] he
Was died the other day,
An' they was no ol'-timer left but me.

"Hotulk Emathla he
Was go to be good Injin long time 'go,
An' Woxie Harjoche
Been dead ten years or twenty, maybe so.

All had to die at las';
I live long time, but now my days was few;
'Fore long poke-weeds[3] an' grass
Be growin' all aroun' my grave-house,[4] too."

Wolf Warrior he listen close,
An' Kono Harjo pay close 'tention, too;
Tookpafka Micco he almos'
Let his pipe go out a time or two.

1908

[5]The site of Sequoyah's burial is unknown. He left the Cherokee Nation in search of some of his tribesmen who had chosen to go to Mexico rather than to remove to the Indian Territory. He disappeared, and an official inquiry by the Cherokees failed to determine what happened to him.

[1]Hotgun, whose Indian name was Mitchka Hiyah, was described by Posey as "A philosopher, carpenter, blacksmith, fiddler, clockmaker, worker in metals and a maker of medicines." He is the central figure in Posey's Fus Fixico letters. The other characters of the poem were either real persons or were based on real persons. Hotulk Emathla (Edward Bullet), for instance, had been well known in Creek political affairs and, as principal chief in 1895, appointed Posey superintendent of the Creek Orphan Asylum. Tookpafka Micco, Wolf Warrior, and Kono Harjo, like Hotgun, appear as characters in the Fus Fixico letters.

[2]Yadeka Harjo, of Hickory Ground Town, whom Posey knew personally, was a well-known figure in the Creek Nation. He was supposedly past ninety when he died. Posey first attempted to pay tribute to the old man in a Fus Fixico letter, but gave that up and wrote this poem, which appeared in the *Eufaula (Okla.) Indian Journal* on January 24, 1908. It was often reprinted.

[3]Pokeweed is the common name of *Phytolacca americana.*

[4]During Posey's lifetime, as now, it was common for traditional Creeks to build small, low-roofed houses over graves.

Fus Fixico's Letter Number 44
Eufaula [Creek Nation] Tribune

April 29, 1904

[The Creeks and other tribes in Indian Territory had been exempted from the provisions of the General Allotment Act (1887). Congress had established the Dawes Commission in 1893 to negotiate allotment agreements with the tribes and, that failing, had passed the Curtis Act (1898), which forced the tribes to negotiate. By 1904 the common title to tribal land had been nullified and allotment was well under way. Though at first the Indians' titles to their allotments were protected by restrictions from sale, Congress soon provided for the removal of those restrictions under certain circumstances. Land brokers quickly seized their opportunities and established title or claims to thousands of acres through outright purchase or a system of leasing. Graft became commonplace because of the vagueness of the law. What were known as "old-time" or "conservative" Creeks—like Hotgun and his friends in the letter below—had difficulty adjusting to not only the changing pattern in land tenure but also the crass commercialism of modern society. As they sit around the fire and converse about their affairs, they conclude that grafters are there to stay and that the Indians must learn to live with them. Though Hotgun and his friends are philosophically at odds with the materialism of the new society, they recognize the Indians' complicity in the changes taking place through the sale of their land and the wasteful spending of the proceeds. The mild satire in their analysis of current affairs is typical of the Fus Fixico letters.]

"Well, so," Hotgun he say, "the Injin he sell land and sell land, and the white man he give whiskey and give whiskey and put his arm around the Injin's neck and they was good friends like two Elks out for a time."

"Well, maybe so," Tookpafka Micco he say, "the white man was cut it out when the Injun was all in."

Then Hotgun he make the smoke b'il out a his pipe good and answer Tookpafka Micco, "Well, so the Injin was had to go up against it to learn and, maybe so, after while he catch on, same like the white man and go to Mexico and bunco the greaser."[1]

Then Hotgun he take another puff and go on and say, "Well, so like I start to say history was repeat itself. The Injin he sell his land in the old country (Alabama) and he sell his land in Injin Territory and was had a good time out here like back there in olden times. But back in old country he was live different, 'cause he was sit on a long

[1]Not only some Creeks but members of the other Indian Territory nations often discussed emigration to Mexico as an alternative to accepting the changes taking place in their societies.

chair like a fence rail—but he was no mugwump.[2] Now the Injin was sit on a chair that was had fore legs and hind legs too, like a oxen, and also a cushion soft like moss. He was got civilized and called the old chair a bench. He wear a white shirt now and black clothes and shoes that was look like a ripe musk melon.[3] Then he was buy bon bons for his papoose and drop-stitch stockings[4] for his squaw and part his name in the middle, J. Little Bear.

"Then the white man he tell the Injin, 'Well so your wagon was out of date and you better buy you a fine buggy; or, maybe so, a fine surrey.' The Injin he grunt and say, 'Well, so let's see um.' Then the white man he say, 'Well, so I sell it cheap like stealing it—sell it to Injun the fine buggy and harness and all for hundred and fifty dollars. That was cheap, 'cause Injun he was sell land and got it lots a money and was out of date riding on two horse wagon.' Then the Injin he look at fine buggy a long time and make good judgment and buy um. His little pony mare team look mighty weak and woolly and got colt, but they was pulled the fine buggy home all right. Then when the Injin was got home he was put the fine buggy under a tree to look at like fine painting."

(Tookpafka Micco and Wolf Warrior and Kono Harjo they was look in the fire and spit in the ashes and pay close attention like they was interested.)

Then Hotgun he go on and say, "Well, maybe so about three years from now the starch was go out a the Injin's white shirt and make it limber like a dish rag, and his black suit was fade like the last rose a summer and his breeches was get slack like a gunny sack,[5] and his big toe was stick through his tan shoes like a snag in Deep Fork,[6] and his fine buggy was tied together with bailing wire[7] and his old fillies was made good crow bait pulling the fine buggy to stomp dances." Then, Hotgun he go on and say, "Maybe so the Injin was awakened up to his sense a duty and earn his bread by the sweat a his brow like a good republican or maybe so a democrat."

And Tookpafka Micco he say, "Well, maybe so he be a middle of a the roader."

Then Hotgun he say, "Well, so they was only two sides to a clapboard and it's the same way in politics. The Injin couldn't cut any ice or raise any sofky sitting on top a the rail looking at the crabgrass."[8]

(Then Tookpafka Micco and Wolf Warrior and Kono Harjo they was grunt and spit in the ashes again and say, "Well, so we vote it straight.")

1904

[2]The Creeks had signed a treaty in 1832, relinquishing their land title in Alabama and agreeing to remove to Indian Territory. The mugwumps were Republican reformers who supported the Democrats in 1884 and helped elect Grover Cleveland president. Hotgun's comparison of the traditional Creek split-log bench to a rail fence suggests the mugwumps were engaged in political fence sitting, which he urges his friends to avoid at the end of the letter.

[3]Tan shoes were in fashion.

[4]Machine-knitted stockings in which patterns were created by dropping stitches at intervals.

[5]*I.e.,* a sack made of coarse jute.

[6]*I.e.,* a tree stump or limb visible above the surface of the water in the Deep Fork River, a tributary of the North Fork of the Canadian River, which formed the southern boundary of the Creek Nation.

[7]Baling (not *bailing*) wire was used to tie bales of hay produced by mechanical balers.

[8]Sofky was white corn raised by the Creeks; also the name of a favorite drink made by cooking the pulverized corn in lye water. Crabgrass (*Digitaria sanguinalis*) was particularly bothersome to farmers.

John Milton Oskison (Cherokee) 1874–1947

John Oskison was born at Vinita in the Cherokee Nation, to a Cherokee mother and a white father. He began his college career at Willie Halsell College in his hometown; one of his classmates was the future movie-star cowboy Will Rogers, who became his lifelong friend. Leaving Indian Territory, Oskison embarked upon an exclusive education, finishing his B.A. at Stanford in 1898, then going to Harvard to study literature. He had already written for Cherokee Nation publications and for the Stanford magazine *Sequoia,* but Oskison's career as a writer took off while he was at Harvard. In 1899 he submitted his short story "Only the Master Shall Praise," which borrowed its title from Rudyard Kipling, to the *Century* magazine competition for college graduates. Oskison won the coveted prize, which brought him to national attention, and he embarked upon a long, flourishing career as a writer.

As an adult, Oskison was removed from Cherokee and other Native American populations by both geography and education. He drew upon his childhood in the Cherokee Nation for his material; his regionalist stories are set in Indian Territory and reproduce the cultural idiosyncracies and dialects of the many people who struggled to make the Territory their own. Published in the early years of the twentieth century, his short stories brought to national attention the particular culture and the peculiar conflicts that characterized Indian Territory in the last days before native governments were dissolved and the state of Oklahoma was created in their place. Oskison had a keen eye for the painful ironies that often surface in cultural conflict; his stories are populated with a miscellany of full and mixed-blood Cherokees as well as white cowboys, outlaws, ministers, and missionaries. His tales of Indian Territory, such as "The Problem of Old Harjo," "The Fall of King Chris," and "When the Grass Grew Long," were widely published in national magazines such as *Century, North American Review* and *McClure's.* In spite of his success, Oskison didn't continue writing short stories. Beginning in 1903, he devoted his time to journalism, which he pursued until 1912. Across those years he edited a daily newspaper, wrote for the *Saturday Evening Post,* and climbed the editorial ladder at *Colliers,* ending up as financial editor. His writings on finance were syndicated in several publications, and he was often called upon to write about Indian affairs.

The First World War interrupted Oskison's peaceful professional progression. He served with the American Expeditionary Force in Europe, and upon his return to the United States he began a third writing career, this time as a novelist. Again, he turned to the now long-gone Indian Territory for inspiration. *Wild Harvest* and *Black Jack Davy,* the two novels he published in the 1920s, concern white heroes. They evoke the desperate and ruthless mood that pervaded the final years of native government in Indian Territory; Oskison condemns the greed of both whites and mixed-bloods who took advantage of the chaos to line their own pockets. In 1929—an ironic year in which to publish the biography of a rich man—Oskison produced *A Texas Titan,* which told the story of Sam Houston. During the Great Depression, Oskison turned his eyes again to native subject matter, publishing *Brothers Three,* a novel that traces the tragedy of mixed-blood siblings who give up a traditional relationship to the land in order to pursue the American dream of individual wealth. Although Oskison's novels are not as appreciated as his shorter, earlier works, they round out a lifework concerned with the problems of mixed-race people struggling to make sense of a homeland and politics that were changing more quickly than their own abilities to adapt. In 1938, Oskison published *Tecumseh and His Times,* a biography of the Shawnee leader who led a confederacy of Native American nations to resist white encroachments on land and sovereignty. That biography was Oskison's last completed work. When he died in 1947, he was at work on an autobiography.

Bethany Ridgway Schneider
Oberlin College

PRIMARY WORKS

Wild Harvest; A Novel of Transition Days in Oklahoma, 1925; *Black Jack Davy,* 1926; *A Texas Titan: The Story of Sam Houston,* 1929; *Brothers Three,* 1935; *Tecumseh and His Times: The Story of a Great Indian,* 1938.

The Problem of Old Harjo[1]

The Spirit of the Lord had descended upon old Harjo.[2] From the new missionary, just out from New York, he had learned that he was a sinner. The fire in the new missionary's eyes and her gracious appeal had convinced old Harjo that this was the time to repent and be saved. He was very much in earnest, and he assured Miss Evans that he wanted to be baptized and received into the church at once. Miss Evans was enthusiastic and went to Mrs. Rowell with the news. It was Mrs. Rowell who had said that it was no use to try to convert the older Indians, and she, after fifteen years of work in Indian Territory missions, should have known. Miss Evans was pardonably proud of her conquest.

"Old Harjo converted!" exclaimed Mrs. Rowell. "Dear Miss Evans, do you know that old Harjo has two wives?"[3] To the older woman it was as if some one had said to her "Madame, the Sultan of Turkey wishes to teach one of your mission Sabbath school classes."

"But," protested the younger woman, "he is really sincere, and—"

"Then ask him," Mrs. Rowell interrupted a bit sternly, "if he will put away one of his wives. Ask him, before he comes into the presence of the Lord, if he is willing to conform to the laws of the country in which he lives, the country that guarantees his idle existence. Miss Evans, your work is not even begun." No one who knew Mrs. Rowell would say that she lacked sincerity and patriotism. Her own cousin was an earnest crusader against Mormonism, and had gathered a goodly share of that wagonload of protests that the Senate had been asked to read when it was considering

[1]From *Southern Workman,* 36 (April, 1907), 235–241. (All footnotes by Daniel F. Littlefield, Jr.)

[2]Harjo is a well-known Creek family name.

[3]Plural marriages were common and sometimes obligatory in Creek culture. If not obligatory, subsequent marriages required the consent of the first wife, such as 'Liza gives Harjo later in the story.

whether a certain statesman of Utah should be allowed to represent his state at Washington.[4]

In her practical, tactful way, Mrs. Rowell had kept clear of such embarrassments. At first, she had written letters of indignant protest to the Indian Office against the toleration of bigamy amongst the tribes. A wise inspector had been sent to the mission, and this man had pointed out that it was better to ignore certain things, "deplorable, to be sure," than to attempt to make over the habits of the old men. Of course, the young Indians would not be permitted to take more than one wife each.

So Mrs. Rowell had discreetly limited her missionary efforts to the young, and had exercised toward the old and bigamous only that strict charity which even a hopeless sinner might claim.

Miss Evans, it was to be regretted, had only the vaguest notions about "expediency;" so weak on matters of doctrine was she that the news that Harjo was living with two wives didn't startle her. She was young and possessed of but one enthusiasm—that for saving souls.

"I suppose," she ventured, "that old Harjo *must* put away one wife before he can join the church?"

"There can be no question about it, Miss Evans."

"Then I shall have to ask him to do it." Miss Evans regretted the necessity for forcing this sacrifice, but had no doubt that the Indian would make it in order to accept the gift of salvation which she was commissioned to bear to him.

Harjo lived in a "double" log cabin[5] three miles from the mission. His ten acres of corn had been gathered into its fence-rail crib; four hogs that were to furnish his winter's bacon had been brought in from the woods and penned conveniently near to the crib;[6] out in a corner of the garden, a fat mound of dirt rose where the crop of turnips and potatoes had been buried against the corrupting frost; and in the hayloft of his log stable were stored many pumpkins, dried corn, onions (suspended in bunches from the rafters) and the varied forage that Mrs. Harjo number one and Mrs. Harjo number two had thriftily provided. Three cows, three young heifers, two colts, and two patient, capable mares bore the Harjo brand, a fantastic "**H-I**" that the old man had designed. Materially, Harjo was solvent; and if the Government had ever come to his aid he could not recall the date.

This attempt to rehabilitate old Harjo morally, Miss Evans felt, was not one to be made at the mission; it should be undertaken in the Creek's own home where the evidences of his sin should confront him as she explained.

[4]Polygamy (more specifically polygyny) among the Mormons had been an issue of public debate for many years. Congress had used it as a means of delaying statehood for Utah and had refused to seat or attempted to exclude a number of elected members because of polygamy or Mormonism. Congress passed legislation outlawing the practice, and in 1890, Wilford Woodruff, president of the Church of Jesus Christ of Latter-day Saints, issued a proclamation that called for abandonment of the practice by church members. It persisted, however, and in 1900 Brigham H. Roberts, a Democrat, was excluded from the House for polygamy, and in 1907, probably the case Oskison alludes to here, Reed Smoot, a Republican, was admitted to the Senate after an attempt to exclude him on a charge of "Mormonism."

[5]*I.e.,* two cabins joined by a covered breezeway.

[6]In Indian Territory days, when the Indian tribes owned the land in common, the people let their livestock run at large on the public domain and penned them in order to fatten them for slaughter.

When Miss Evans rode up to the block in front of Harjo's cabin, the old Indian came out, slowly and with a broadening smile of welcome on his face. A clean gray flannel shirt had taken the place of the white collarless garment, with crackling stiff bosom, that he had worn to the mission meetings. Comfortable, well-patched moccasins had been substituted for creaking boots, and brown corduroys, belted in at the waist, for tight black trousers. His abundant gray hair fell down on his shoulders. In his eyes, clear and large and black, glowed the light of true hospitality. Miss Evans thought of the patriarchs as she saw him lead her horse out to the stable; thus Abraham might have looked and lived.

"Harjo," began Miss Evans before following the old man to the covered passageway between the disconnected cabins, "is it true that you have two wives?" Her tone was neither stern nor accusatory. The Creek had heard that question before, from scandalized missionaries and perplexed registry clerks when he went to Muscogee to enroll himself and his family in one of the many "final" records ordered to be made by the Government preparatory to dividing the Creek lands among the individual citizens.[7]

For answer, Harjo called, first into the cabin that was used as a kitchen and then, in a loud, clear voice, toward the small field, where Miss Evans saw a flock of half-grown turkeys running about in the corn stubble. From the kitchen emerged a tall, thin Indian woman of fifty-five, with a red handkerchief bound severely over her head. She spoke to Miss Evans and sat down in the passageway. Presently, a clear, sweet voice was heard in the field; a stout, handsome woman, about the same age as the other, climbed the rail fence and came up to the house. She, also, greeted Miss Evans briefly. Then she carried a tin basin to the well near by, where she filled it to the brim. Setting it down on the horse block, she rolled back her sleeves, tucked in the collar of her gray blouse, and plunged her face in the water. In a minute she came out of the kitchen freshened and smiling. 'Liza Harjo had been pulling dried bean stalks at one end of the field, and it was dirty work. At last old Harjo turned to Miss Evans and said, "These two my wife—this one 'Liza, this one Jennie."

It was done with simple dignity. Miss Evans bowed and stammered. Three pairs of eyes were turned upon her in patient, courteous inquiry.

It was hard to state the case. The old man was so evidently proud of his women, and so flattered by Miss Evans' interest in them, that he would find it hard to understand. Still, it had to be done, and Miss Evans took the plunge.

"Harjo, you want to come into our church?" The old man's face lighted.

"Oh, yes, I would come to Jesus, please, my friend."

"Do you know, Harjo, that the Lord commanded that one man should mate with but one woman? The question was stated again in simpler terms, and the Indian replied, "Me know that now, my friend. Long time ago"—Harjo plainly meant the

[7]Present-day Muskogee, Oklahoma, was in the eastern Creek Nation and was the site of the Indian agency where much official business was conducted. A last (or "final") roll of tribal members was made preparatory to dissolution of the tribal title to the land, and each tribal member was given what was purported to be an equal share of the land to which he had personal title.

whole period previous to his conversion—"me did not know. The Lord Jesus did not speak to me in that time and so I was blind. I do what blind man do."

"Harjo, you must have only one wife when you come into our church. Can't you give up one of these women?" Miss Evans glanced at the two, sitting by with smiles of polite interest on their faces, understanding nothing. They had not shared Harjo's enthusiasm either for the white man's God or his language.

"Give up my wife?" A sly smile stole over his face. He leaned closer to Miss Evans. "You tell me, my friend, which one I give up." He glanced from 'Liza to Jennie as if to weigh their attractions, and the two rewarded him with their pleasantest smiles. "You tell me which one," he urged.

"Why, Harjo, how can I tell you!" Miss Evans had little sense of humor; she had taken the old man seriously.

"Then," Harjo sighed, continuing the comedy, for surely the missionary was jesting with him, "'Liza and Jennie must say." He talked to the Indian women for a time, and they laughed heartily. 'Liza, pointing to the other, shook her head. At length Harjo explained, "My friend, they cannot say. Jennie, she would run a race to see which one stay, but 'Liza, she say no, she is fat and cannot run."

Miss Evans comprehended at last. She flushed angrily, and protested, "Harjo, you are making a mock of a sacred subject; I cannot allow you to talk like this."

"But did you not speak in fun, my friend?" Harjo queried, sobering. "Surely you have just said what your friend, the white woman at the mission (he meant Mrs. Rowell) would say, and you do not mean what you say."

"Yes, Harjo, I mean it. It is true that Mrs. Rowell raised the point first, but I agree with her. The church cannot be defiled by receiving a bigamist into its membership." Harjo saw that the young woman was serious, distressingly serious. He was silent for a long time, but at last he raised his head and spoke quietly, "It is not good to talk like that if it is not in fun."

He rose and went to the stable. As he led Miss Evans' horse up to the block it was champing a mouthful of corn, the last of a generous portion that Harjo had put before it. The Indian held the bridle and waited for Miss Evans to mount. She was embarrassed, humiliated, angry. It was absurd to be dismissed in this way by—"by an ignorant old bigamist!" Then the humor of it burst upon her, and its human aspect. In her anxiety concerning the spiritual welfare of the sinner Harjo, she had insulted the man Harjo. She began to understand why Mrs. Rowell had said that the old Indians were hopeless.

"Harjo," she begged, coming out of the passageway, "please forgive me. I do not want you to give up one of your wives. Just tell me why you took them."

"I will tell you that, my friend." The old Creek looped the reins over his arm and sat down on the block. "For thirty years Jennie has lived with me as my wife. She is of the Bear people,[8] and she came to me when I was thirty-five and she was twenty-five. She could not come before, for her mother was old, very old, and Jennie, she stay with her and feed her.

[8]*I.e.,* belongs to the Bear Clan of the Muscogee (Creek) people. The Creeks had more known clans than any other tribe. As indicated below, 'Liza belonged to the Crow Clan.

"So, when I was thirty years old I took 'Liza for my woman. She is of the Crow people. She help me make this little farm here when there was no farm for many miles around.

"Well, five years 'Liza and me, we live here and work hard. But there was no child. Then the old mother of Jennie she died, and Jennie got no family left in this part of the country. So 'Liza say to me, 'Why don't you take Jennie in here?' I say, 'You don't care?' and she say, 'No, maybe we have children here then.' But we have no children—never have children. We do not like that, but God He would not let it be. So, we have lived here thirty years very happy. Only just now you make me sad."

"Harjo," cried Miss Evans, "forget what I said. Forget that you wanted to join the church." For a young mission worker with a single purpose always before her, Miss Evans was saying a strange thing. Yet she couldn't help saying it; all of her zeal seemed to have been dissipated by a simple statement of the old man.

"I cannot forget to love Jesus, and I want to be saved." Old Harjo spoke with solemn earnestness. The situation was distracting. On one side stood a convert eager for the protection of the church, asking only that he be allowed to fulfill the obligations of humanity and on the other stood the church, represented by Mrs. Rowell, that set an impossible condition on receiving old Harjo to itself. Miss Evans wanted to cry; prayer, she felt, would be entirely inadequate as a means of expression.

"Oh! Harjo," she cried out, "I don't know what to do. I must think it over and talk with Mrs. Rowell again."

But Mrs. Rowell could suggest no way out; Miss Evans' talk with her only gave the older woman another opportunity to preach the folly of wasting time on the old and "unreasonable" Indians. Certainly the church could not listen even to a hint of a compromise in this case. If Harjo wanted to be saved there was one way and only one—unless—

"Is either of the two women old? I mean, so old that she is—an—"

"Not at all," answered Miss Evans. "They're both strong and—yes, happy. I think they will outlive Harjo."

"Can't you appeal to one of the women to go away? I dare say we could provide for her." Miss Evans, incongruously, remembered Jennie's jesting proposal to race for the right to stay with Harjo. What could the mission provide as a substitute for the little home that 'Liza had helped to create there in the edge of the woods? What other home would satisfy Jennie?

"Mrs. Rowell, are you sure that we ought to try to take one of Harjo's women from him? I'm not sure that it would in the least advance morality amongst the tribe, but I'm certain that it would make three gentle people unhappy for the rest of their lives."

"You may be right, Miss Evans." Mrs. Rowell was not seeking to create unhappiness, for enough of it inevitably came to be pictured in the little mission building. "You may be right," she repeated, "but it is a grevious misfortune that old Harjo should wish to unite with the church."

No one was more regular in his attendance at the mission meetings than old Harjo. Sitting well forward, he was always in plain view of Miss Evans at the organ. Before the service began, and after it was over, the old man greeted the young woman. There was never a spoken question, but in the Creek's eyes was always a mute inquiry.

Once Miss Evans ventured to write to her old pastor in New York, and explain her trouble. This was what he wrote in reply: "I am surprised that you are troubled, for I should have expected you to rejoice, as I do, over this new and wonderful evidence of the Lord's reforming power. Though the church cannot receive the old man so long as he is confessedly a bigamist and violator of his country's just laws, you should be greatly strengthened in your work through bringing him to desire salvation."

"Oh! it's easy to talk when you're free from responsibility!" cried out Miss Evans. "But I woke him up to a desire for this water of salvation that he cannot take. I have seen Harjo's home, and I know how cruel and useless it would be to urge him to give up what he loves—for he does love those two women who have spent half their lives and more with him. What, what can be done!"

Month after month, as old Harjo continued to occupy his seat in the mission meetings, with that mute appeal in his eyes and a persistent light of hope on his face, Miss Evans repeated the question, "What can be done?" If she was sometimes tempted to say to the old man, "Stop worrying about your soul; you'll get to Heaven as surely as any of us," there was always Mrs. Rowell to remind her that she was not a Mormon missionary. She could not run away from her perplexity. If she should secure a transfer to another station, she felt that Harjo would give up coming to the meetings, and in his despair become a positive influence for evil amongst his people. Mrs. Rowell would not waste her energy on an obstinate old man. No, Harjo was her creation, her impossible convert, and throughout the years, until death—the great solvent which is not always a solvent—came to one of them, would continue to haunt her.

And meanwhile, what?

1907

Corridos

The *corrido* is perhaps the most important expressive form for the Mexican Americans of the Southwest during the period from 1865 to 1915. The *corrido* (from *correr,* the Spanish verb to run) is a fast-paced narrative ballad whose roots may be traced to the romances of medieval Spain. In colonizing what is now the American Southwest, the Spaniards carried their musical traditions with them and these flourished, simultaneously preserving old songs and themes and adapting to the particular circumstances of life in the New World. Of the various Spanish musical traditions that prospered in the Southwest—the *copla,* the *danza,* and the *décima* for example—the *corrido* stands out, in terms of quantity, persistence, and historical and cultural interest. Countless *corridos* emerged in the Southwest, generally composed anonymously and transmitted by word of mouth to commemorate events and experiences of sometimes epic proportions. As the distinguished folklorist Américo Paredes has shown, the *corrido* thrived particularly in circumstances of cultural conflict; in the Southwest this often meant between Mexican American and Anglo-American.

As a distinct ballad form, the *corrido* first appeared in Mexico in the mid-nineteenth century and began to emerge in the American Southwest soon thereafter, most conspicuously in the border regions of south Texas where Mexican and Mexican American cultures were virtually indistinguishable.

"Kiansis," the oldest of the *corridos* presented here, dates from the 1860s (a more precise date of origin is impossible for such an anonymous song) when cattle drives from Texas to Kansas were conducted regularly, more often than not with Mexican American as well as Anglo cowboys. "Kiansis," like virtually all *corridos* including the others printed here, was composed in Spanish and is presented in translation without any attempt to preserve its original rhythm or other poetic qualities. Notice that "Kiansis" depicts the sometimes fierce rivalry between Mexican American and Anglo-American cowboys. In their songs, Mexican Americans liked to point out that ranching in the Southwest was essentially a Mexican institution that Anglos had later claimed as their own.

"Gregorio Cortez" and "Jacinto Trevino" are probably the best known of Mexican American *corridos*, again dealing with episodes of conflict between a Mexican American and Anglos, in this case Texas Rangers. These two ballads date from the early 1900s and feature violent conflict. Gregorio Cortez, an ordinary rancher and farmer, shoots the "major sheriff" in defense of his brother and then flees for the Mexican border, knowing he'll not receive justice in a Texas court. He skillfully eludes his hundreds of pursuers but finally surrenders when he realizes that other Mexican Americans are being punished in retribution. "Jacinto Trevino" presents a similar scenario: a fight breaks out in a south Texas saloon, the Texas Rangers come to arrest Trevino and he backs them down, finally making his way to safety. Both *corridos* present admittedly biased versions of Mexican American/Anglo conflict but also provide a necessary counterbalance to the conventional and better-known accounts of Texas Ranger heroics in American folklore and popular culture.

Like the *corridos* noted above, "El Hijo Desobediente" (The Disobedient Son) is from Texas but this time focuses not on a broad cultural issue but a family matter. Considered one of the greatest of all ballads from along the south Texas border, "El Hijo Desobediente" poignantly relates the tragedy of a young man trapped in his excessive masculinity.

The final two *corridos* are of rather recent origin, demonstrating that the *corrido* tradition is still active. "Recordando al Presidente" ("Remembering the President") was composed by Willie López of McAllen, Texas to commemorate John F. Kennedy, the first Catholic president, who was widely admired in the Mexican American community. The "*Corrido* de César Chávez" is notable for several reasons. It focuses on the work of one of the great contemporary Mexican American heroes, César Chávez, who dedicated his career to fighting for decent working and living conditions for farm workers. Secondly, this ballad was composed and recorded by Lalo Guerrero, one of the most gifted and influential of contemporary Mexican American musicians. Both of the contemporary *corridos* are of known authorship and have been sold commercially, indicating the adaptability of this musical form to contemporary circumstances.

Raymund Paredes
University of California at Los Angeles

PRIMARY WORKS

Américo Paredes, comp. *A Texas-Mexican Cancionero: Folksongs of the Lower Border,* 1976.

Kiansis I

["Kiansis I" is sung in a slow, reflective tempo, most often by one singer alone and frequently without guitar accompaniment. The rhythm is not the usual *one*-two-three strum used for the *corrido.* It is more of a three-*one*-two-three-*one* rhythm similar to the *colombiana* or *yucateca* strums. "Kiansis II" has a straight *corrido* rhythm. It is more often sung by two voices, with guitar accompaniment. It is a *canción de grito,* the type you would expect to hear at cantinas as well as at ranchos.]

Cuando salimos pa' Kiansis
con una grande partida,
¡ah, qué camino tan largo!
no contaba con mi vida.

Nos decía el caporal,
como queriendo llorar:
—Allá va la novillada,
no me la dejen pasar.—

¡Ah, qué caballo tan bueno!
todo se le iba en correr,
¡y, ah, qué fuerte aguacerazo!
no contabe yo en volver.

Unos pedían cigarro,
otros pedían que comer,
y el caporal nos decía:
—Sea por Dios, qué hemos de hacer.—

En el charco de Palomas
se cortó un novillo bragado,
y el caporal lo lazó
en su caballo melado.

Avísenle al caporal
que un vaquero se mató,
en las trancas del corral
nomás la cuera dejó.

Llegamos al Río Salado
y nos tiramos a nado,
decía un americano:
—Esos hombres ya se ahogaron.—

Pues qué pensaría ese hombre
que venimos a esp'rimentar,

si somos del Río Grande,
de los buenos pa'nadar.

Y le dimos vista a Kiansis,
y nos dice el caporal:
—Ora sí somos de vida,
ya vamos a hacer corral.—

Y de vuelta en San Antonio
compramos buenos sombreros,
y aquí se acaban cantando
versos de los aventureros.

Kansas I

When we left for Kansas with a great herd of cattle,
ah, what a long trail it was! I was not sure I would survive.

The *caporal* would tell us, as if he was going to cry,
"Watch out for that bunch of steers; don't let them get past you."

Ah, what a good horse I had! He did nothing but gallop.
And, ah, what a violent cloudburst! I was not sure I would come back.

Some of us asked for cigarettes, others wanted something to eat;
and the *caporal* would tell us, "So be it, it can't be helped."

By the pond at Palomas a vicious steer left the herd.
and the *caporal* lassoed it on his honey-colored horse.

Go tell the *caporal* that a vaquero has been killed;
all he left was his leather jacket hanging on the rails of the corral.

We got to the Salado River, and we swam our horses across;
an American was saying, "Those men are as good as drowned."

I wonder what the man thought, that we came to learn, perhaps;
why, we're from the Rio Grande, where the good swimmers are from.

And then Kansas came in sight, and the *caporal* tells us,
"We have finally made it, we'll soon have them in the corral."

Back again in San Antonio, we all bought ourselves good hats,
and this is the end of the singing of the stanzas about the trail
drivers.

1976

Gregorio Cortez

["Gregorio Cortez" is sung a bit more slowly than the average *corrido,* with the basses on the guitar strongly accented.]

En el condado de El Carmen
miren lo que ha sucedido,
murió el Cherife Mayor,
quedando Román herido.

En el condado de El Carmen
tal desgracia sucedió,
murió el Cherife Mayor,
no saben quién lo mató.

Se anduvieron informando
como media hora después,
supieron que el malhechor
era Gregorio Cortez.

Ya insortaron a Cortez
por toditito el estado,
que vivo o muerto se aprehenda
porque a varios ha matado.

Decía Gregorio Cortez
con su pistola en la mano:
—No siento haberlo matado,
lo que siento es a mi hermano.—

Decía Gregorio Cortez
con su alma muy encendida:
—No siento haberlo matado,
la defensa es permitida.—

Venían los americanos
más blancos que una amapola,
de miedo que le tenían
a Cortez con su pistola.

Decían los americanos,
decían con timidez:
—Vamos a seguir la huella
que el malhechor es Cortez.—

Soltaron los perros jaunes
pa' que siguieran la huella,
pero alcanzar a Cortez
era seguir a una estrella.

Tiró con rumbo a Gonzales
sin ninguna timidez:
—Síganme, rinches cobardes,
yo soy Gregorio Cortez.—

Se fue de Belmont al rancho,
lo alcanzaron a rodear,
poquitos más de trescientos,
y allí les brincó el corral.

Cuando les brincó el corral,
según lo que aquí se dice,
se agarraron a balazos
y les mató otro cherife.

Decía Gregorio Cortez
con su pistola en la mano:
—No corran, rinches cobardes,
con un solo mexicano.—

Salió Gregorio Cortez,
salió con rumbo a Laredo,
no lo quisieron seguir
porque le tuvieron miedo.

Decía Gregorio Cortez:
—¿Pa' qué se valen de planes?
No me pueden agarrar
ni con esos perros jaunes.—

Decían los americanos:
—Si lo alcanzamos ¿qué hacemos?
Si le entramos por derecho
muy poquitos volveremos.—

Allá por El Encinal,
según lo que aquí se dice,

le formaron un corral
y les mató otro cherife.

Decía Gregorio Cortez
echando muchos balazos:
—Me he escapado de aguaceros,
contimás de nublinazos.—

Ya se encontró a un mexicano,
le dice con altivez:
—Platícame qué hay de nuevo,
yo soy Gregorio Cortez.

—Dicen que por culpa mía
han matado mucha gente,
pues ya me voy a entregar
porque eso no es conveniente.—

Cortez le dice a Jesús:
—Ora sí lo vas a ver,
anda diles a los rinches
que me vengan a aprehender.—

Venían todos los rinches,
venían que hasta volaban,
porque se iban a ganar
diez mil pesos que les daban.

Cuando rodearon la casa
Cortez se les presentó:
—Por la buena sí me llevan
porque de otro modo no.—

Decía el Cherife Mayor
como queriendo llorar:
—Cortez, entrega tus armas,
no te vamos a matar.—

Decía Gregorio Cortez,
les gritaba en alta voz:
—Mis armas no las entrego
hasta estar en calaboz'.—

Decía Gregorio Cortez,
decía en su voz divina:
—Mis armas no las entrego
hasta estar en bartolina.—

Ya agarraron a Cortez,
ya terminó la cuestión,
la pobre de su familia
lo lleva en el corazón.

Ya con ésta me despido
a la sombra de un ciprés,
aquí se acaba el corrido
de don Gregorio Cortez.

Gregorio Cortez

In the county of El Carmen, look what has happened;
the Major Sheriff is dead, leaving Román badly wounded.

In the county of El Carmen such a tragedy took place:
the Major Sheriff is dead; no one knows who killed him.

They went around asking questions about half an hour afterward;
they found out that the wrongdoer had been Gregorio Cortez.

Now they have outlawed Cortez throughout the whole of the state;
let him be taken, dead or alive, for he has killed several men.

Then said Gregorio Cortez, with his pistol in his hand,
"I don't regret having killed him; what I regret is my brother's death."

Then said Gregorio Cortez, with his soul aflame,
"I don't regret having killed him; self-defense is permitted."

The Americans were coming; they were whiter than a poppy
from the fear that they had of Cortez and his pistol.

Then the Americans said, and they said it fearfully,
"Come, let us follow the trail, for the wrongdoer is Cortez."

They let loose the bloodhounds so they could follow the trail,
but trying to overtake Cortez was like following a star.

He struck out for Gonzales, without showing any fear:
"Follow me, cowardly *rinches;* I am Gregorio Cortez."

From Belmont he went to the ranch, where they succeeded in surrounding him,
quite a few more than three hundred, but he jumped out of their corral.

When he jumped out of their corral, according to what is said here,
they got into a gunfight, and he killed them another sheriff.

Then said Gregorio Cortez, with his pistol in his hand,
"Don't run, you cowardly *rinches,* from a single Mexican."

Gregorio Cortez went out, he went out toward Laredo;
they would not follow him because they were afraid of him.

Then said Gregorio Cortez, "What is the use of your scheming?
You cannot catch me, even with those bloodhounds."

Then said the Americans, "If we catch up with him, what shall we do?
If we fight him man to man, very few of us will return."

Way over near El Encinal, according to what is said here,
they made him a corral, and he killed them another sheriff.

Then said Gregorio Cortez, shooting out a lot of bullets,
"I have weathered thunderstorms; this little mist doesn't bother me."

Now he has met a Mexican; he says to him haughtily,
"Tell me the news; I am Gregorio Cortez.

"They say that because of me many people have been killed;
so now I will surrender, because such things are not right."

Cortez says to Jesús, "At last you are going to see it;
go and tell the *rinches* that they can come and arrest me."

All the *rinches* were coming, so fast that they almost flew,
because they were going to get the ten thousand dollars that were offered.

When they surrounded the house, Cortez appeared before them:
"You will take me if I'm willing but not any other way."

Then said the Major Sheriff, as if he was going to cry,
"Cortez, hand over your weapons; we do not want to kill you."

Then said Gregorio Cortez, shouting to them in a loud voice,
"I won't surrender my weapons until I am in a cell."

Then said Gregorio Cortez, speaking in his godlike voice,
"I won't surrender my weapons until I'm inside a jail."

Now they have taken Cortez, and now the matter is ended;
his poor family are keeping him in their hearts.

Now with this I say farewell in the shade of a cypress;
this is the end of the ballad of Don Gregorio Cortez.

1976

Jacinto Treviño

Ya con ésta van tres veces
que se ha visto lo bonito,
la primera fue en Macalen,
en Brónsvil y en San Benito.

Y en la cantina de Bekar
se agarraron a balazos,
por dondequiera saltaban
botellas hechas pedazos.

Esa cantina de Bekar
al momento quedó sola,
nomás Jacinto Treviño
de carabina y pistola.

—Entrenle, rinches cobardes,
que el pleito no es con un niño,
querían concocer su padre,
¡yo soy Jacinto Treviño!

—Entrenle, rinches cobardes,
validos de la ocasión,
no van a comer pan blanco
con tajadas de jamón.—

Decía el Rinche Mayor,
como era un americano:
—¡Ah, qué Jacinto tan hombre,
no niega el ser mexicano!—

Decía Jacinto Treviño
que se moría de la risa:
—A mí me hacen los ojales,
los puños de la camisa.—

Decía Jacinto Treviño,
abrochándose un zapato:
—Aquí traigo más cartuchos
pa' divertirnos un rato.—

Decía Jacinto Treviño,
con su pistola en la mano:
No corran, rinches cobardes,
con un solo mexicano.—

Decía Jacinto Treviño:
—Yo ya me vo' a retirar,
me voy para Río Grande
y allá los voy a esperar.—

Decía Jacinto Treviño,
al bajar una bajada:
—¡Ay, qué rinches tan cobardes,
que no me haigan hecho nada!—

Decía Jacinto Treviño,
andando en Nuevo Laredo:
—Yo soy Jacinto Treviño,
nacido en Montemorelos.—

Ya con ésta me despido
aquí a presencia de todos,
yo soy Jacinto Treviño,
vecino de Matamoros.

Jacinto Treviño

With this it will be three times that remarkable things have happened;
the first time was in McAllen, then in Brownsville and San Benito.

They had a shoot-out at Baker's saloon;
broken bottles were popping all over the place.

Baker's saloon was immediately deserted;
only Jacinto Treviño remained, with his rifle and his pistol.

"Come on, you cowardly *rinches,* you're not playing games with a
child.
You wanted to meet your father? I am Jacinto Treviño!

"Come on, you cowardly *rinches,* you always like to take the
advantage;
this is not like eating white bread with slices of ham."

The chief of the *rinches* said, even though he was an American,
"Ah, what a brave man is Jacinto; you can see he is a Mexican!"

Then said Jacinto Treviño, who was dying of laughter,
"All you're good for is to make the buttonholes and the cuffs on
my shirt."

Then said Jacinto Treviño, as he was tying his shoe,
"I have more cartridges here, so we can amuse ourselves a while."

Then said Jacinto Treviño, with his pistol in his hand,
"Don't run, you cowardly *rinches,* from a single Mexican."

Then said Jacinto Treviño, "I am going to retire.
I'm going to Rio Grande City, and I will wait for you there."

Then said Jacinto Treviño, as he came down an incline,
"Ah, what a cowardly bunch of *rinches;* they didn't do anything to
me!"

Then said Jacinto Treviño, when he was in Nuevo Laredo,
"I am Jacinto Treviño, born in Montemorelos."

Now with this I say farewell, here in everybody's presence;
I am Jacinto Treviño, a citizen of Matamoros.

1976

El Hijo Desobediente

Un domingo estando herrando
se encontraron dos mancebos,
echando mano a los fieros
como queriendo pelear;
cuando se estaban peleando
pues llegó su padre de uno:
—Hijo de mi corazón,
ya no pelees con ninguno.—

—Quítese de aquí mi padre
que estoy más bravo que un león
no vaya a sacar la espada
y la parta el corazón.—
—Hijo de mi corazón,
por lo que acabas de hablar
antes de que raye el sol
la vida te han de quitar.—

—Lo que le pido a mi padre
que no me entierre en sagrado,
que me entierre en tierra bruta
donde me trille el ganado,
con una mano de fuera
y un papel sobre-dorado,
con un letrero que diga,
"Felipe fue desdichado."

—La vaquilla colorada,
hace un año que nació.
ahi se la dejo a mi padre
por la crianza que me dió;
los tres caballos que tengo,
ahi se los dejo a los pobres
para que digan en vida,
"Felipe, Dios te perdone."—

Bajaron el toro prieto,
que nunca lo habían bajado,
pero ora si ya bajó
revuelto con el ganado;
ya con ésta me despido
por la estrella del oriente,
y aquí se acaba el corrido
de El Hijo Desobediente.

The Disobedient Son

On a Sunday during branding
Two young cowboys did meet,
Each going for his steel
Each looking to fight;
As they were fighting
The father of one arrived:
—My beloved son
Do not fight with anyone.—

—Get away from here, my father
I feel more fierce than a lion,
For I may draw my knife
To split your heart in two.—
—My beloved son,
Because of what you have said
Before the next sunrise
Your life will be taken away.—

—I only ask of my father
Do not bury me in sacred ground,
Bury me in brute earth
Where the stock may trample me
With one hand out of the grave
And a gilded paper,
With an epitaph that reads
"Felipe was an ill-fated man."

The red yearling
Born a year ago,
I leave to my father
My upbringing to him I owe;
My three stallions
I leave to the poor
So that they may say
"May God forgive you, Felipe."

They brought the black bull down,
Never before brought down,
But now the bull has come down
With the rest of the stock;
Now with this I say farewell
Guided by the eastern star
This ends the ballad
Of the disobedient son.

Recordando al Presidente

by Willie López

Los latinoaméricanos de esta tierra
recordamos con tristeza al Presidente:
en los tiempos de la paz y de la guerra
estuviste defendiendo al continente.

En la guerra fuiste siempre buen soldado,
en la paz fuiste un honrado presidente,
un gran hombre de todos appreciado,
un demócrata sincero y muy valiente.

John F. [efe] Kennedy tu recuerdo vivirá,
que Dios te tenga con el allí en la gloria,
te lloramos los de aquí, te sintieron los de allá,
ya tu nombre escrito está en el mundo y en la historia.

Teniendo Cuba muchas armas peligrosas,
a los rusos les hablaste muy en serio,
desafiando los peligros y otras cosas
y salvando de la muerte al hemisferio.

Mexicanos, de acá somos residentes,
y por pochos nos distinguen los demas,
te quisimos como a pocos presidentes,
pues pensamos como tú, ¡viva la paz!

John F. [efe] Kennedy tu recuerdo vivirá,
que Dios te tenga con el allí en la gloria,
te lloramos los de aquí, te sintieron los de allá,
ya tu nombre escrito está en el mundo y en la historia.

Remembering the President

by Willie López

We Latin Americans of this country,
With sadness we remember the President,
In times of war and peace
You were defending the continent.

In the war you were always a good soldier,
In peace you were an honorable president,
A great man esteemed by all,
A sincere and brave democrat.

John F. Kennedy your memory will live,
May God have you with him in his glory,
We weep for you here and others grieve for you
elsewhere,
Now your name is inscribed in the world and in history.

When Cuba had many dangerous arms,
You spoke very seriously to the Russians,
Facing dangers and other things
And saving the hemisphere from death.

Mexicans here [in Texas] we are citizens,
And others [Mexicans] call us *pochos,*[1]
We loved you as we have loved few presidents,
And we believed as you, long live peace!

John F. Kennedy your memory will live,
May God have you with him in his glory,
We weep for you here and others grieve for you
elsewhere,
Now your name is inscribed in the world and in history.

Corrido de César Chávez

Detente mi corazón,
En el pecho no me cabe
El regocijo y orgullo
Al cantarle a César Chávez.

Inspiración de mi gente,
Protector del campesino
El es un gran mexicano
Ese sería su destino.

[1]Slang term for an Americanized Mexican.

De muy humildes principios
Organizaste a la gente;
Y a los hacendados ricos
Te paraste frente a frente.

Injustamente te acusan
Que intentaste usar violencia
Ayunaste veinticinco días
Pa' probar tu inocencia.

En el estandarte que lleva
Mi Virgen de Guadalupe,
En tu incesante labor
De bendiciones te tuve.

A los venticinco días
El ayuno terminó
En el parque de Delano
Una misa celebró.

Junto con ocho mil almas
Bobby Kennedy asistió;
Admiración y cariño
Nuestra gente le brindó.

Vuela de aquí de me seno,
Paloma, vete a Delano;
Y por si acaso no sabes
Allí vive César Chávez.

Ballad of César Chávez[1]

Stop, my heart,
In my breast there is no room
For the joy and pride
Of singing of César Chávez.

Inspiration of my people,
Protector of the farm worker,
He is a great Mexican;
This would be his destiny.

[1]Head of the United Farm Workers, 1965–1993.

From very humble beginnings
You organized your people;
And against the rich ranchers
You stood face to face.

Unjustly they accuse you
Of intending to use violence.
You fasted for twenty-five days
In order to prove your innocence.

On the standard that carries
My Virgin of Guadalupe,
In whose presence you came to worship,
I esteemed you with my praise.

After twenty-five days
The fast ended;
In the park in Delano
A mass was celebrated.

Together with eight thousand souls
Bobby Kennedy attended;
Admiration and affection
Our people offered him a toast.

Fly from my breast,
Dove, go to Delano;
And if perhaps you don't know,
There lives César Chávez.

María Amparo Ruiz de Burton 1832–1895

The life and writings of María Amparo Ruiz de Burton—the first known Mexican American to write two novels in English—demonstrate the historical contradictions of Mexican American identity. Born in 1832 to an elite, land-holding family in Loreto, Baja California, Mexico, she died destitute in Chicago in 1895. She witnessed the 1846 U.S. invasion of La Paz, Baja California, at the start of the Mexican War; and three years later she married the captain of the invading army, Henry S. Burton, a West Point graduate from Connecticut. She attended the 1861 inauguration of President Lincoln and successfully petitioned him to promote Burton to the rank of colonel; but after the Civil War she had private talks with Varina Davis, wife of the Confederacy's ex-president, and the two women denounced the Yankees. Fluent in English and Spanish, she penned copious letters, wrote a play based on the Spanish classic *Don Quixote* and two novels that openly critiqued northeastern materialism and portrayed California's land-holding Mexicans as a genteel, white population wrongfully displaced in the United States by racism and corrupt politics. No wonder it took over one hundred years for her life and novels to emerge from obscurity—they challenge traditional American and Mexican American literary histories.

When the Treaty of Guadalupe Hidalgo (1848) ended the Mexican War, the United States gained upper California, along with extensive southwestern territory, but left lower (Baja) California to Mexico. Captain Burton arranged to have over four hundred friendly Mexicans transported north to Monterey, California, granting them full rights of U.S. citizenship as guaranteed by the treaty. María was one of those who made the trip. By most accounts, she and the captain were in love. She was Catholic and he Protestant, and their marriage seemed to signal a happy union between California's Mexican landholding gentry, known as *californios,* and the upstart Yankee invaders. In 1852, the Burtons moved to San Diego. Henry took command of the army post there and purchased property on Rancho Jamul, a large Mexican land grant that would figure heavily in María's later misfortunes. While she raised their daughter Nellie and two years later gave birth to son Henry Halleck, she and her husband enjoyed an aristocratic way of life.

The Civil War brought an end to the Burtons' California romance. The family moved east in 1859, living in Rhode Island, New York, Washington, D.C., and Virginia. While Burton's war heroics were winning him a promotion to the rank of brigadier general, she was taking in Yankee culture with a skeptical eye. "And it is also necessary that you come for a visit, to stay a winter in Washington and see what a great humbug is this Yankie [sic] nation," she wrote to her friend and fellow *californio,* Mariano G. Vallejo; "A humbug so methodical and well supported that they even almost believe it." Her stay in the East lasted a decade; in 1869 she returned to California a widowed mother of two after General Burton died of malarial fever. The "Maid of Monterey," as she was once remembered in a romantic California ballad, spent the rest of her life fighting the realities of economic hardship, unscrupulous land litigation, and the social dislocation that had already devastated many *californios.*

She returned to find parts of her Rancho Jamul property sold off to pay her husband's debts; she also found fifteen American squatters, each claiming a 160-acre homestead on the Jamul property. In 1851, Congress had passed the California Land Act, which, contrary to the 1848 treaty, considered all Mexican land grants public domain and available for resettlement until a federal Land Commission could verify the legitimacy of land titles. Verification required long legal battles that forced Ruiz de Burton and other *californios* to mortgage their land to lawyers and judges to pay the legal fees needed to confirm their titles. At one point, Ruiz de Burton wrote her own legal briefs because she could not afford a lawyer. An enterprising woman, she planted castor beans on the rancho, considered using it for a water reservoir, and started a short-lived cement company, all to generate income beyond the meager widow's pension she was receiving from the U.S. government. Rival claimants to Jamul kept the title tied up in court long after Ruiz de Burton's death. She never regained the Jamul property and even discovered she never had rights to a tract in Ensenada that she had inherited from her grandfather.

Her personal experiences, legal frustrations, and financial straits led her to a literary career. In 1872, she published *Who Would Have Thought It?,* a biting satire of northeastern culture based in part on her ten-year stay on the east coast. Set during the Civil War and Reconstruction but including significant events in the Southwest during the Mexican War, the novel—published in Philadelphia—exposes Yankee hypocrisy and the shortcomings of liberal democracy. While Lola Medina, a wealthy Mexican American born in Indian captivity, faces the overt racism of her adopted New England family, the novel's narrator provides a critique of unprincipled Yankee politics. Yet *Who Would Have Thought It?* challenges the Northeast's anglocentrism, not by disputing it but by insisting that upper-class Mexicans should be recognized as white. "[I]t happens that this child has no more Indian or Negro blood than you or I have," Lola's adoptive father explains to his family; she is white.

Ruiz de Burton's second novel, *The Squatter and the Don* (1885), turns on the same challenge. In the selection reprinted here, the aristocratic Don Mariano proposes a plan that rests on cheap Indian labor to benefit himself and the Anglo squatters who have settled on his ranch. The scene exhibits the novel's reliance on racial and ethnic caricature. It features genteel white Mexicans; vulgar and myopic Anglo squatters; sympathetic, business-minded Yankees; a younger generation of settlers whose attraction to the Don's daughters provides the novel's hope for social reconciliation, and nameless Indian laborers whose presence reminds us that a colonial hierarchy existed in California long before the arrival of American squatters. Although the novel reflects Ruiz de Burton's legal troubles with squatters on Rancho Jamul, its strongest critique is directed at the corruption of the U.S. government, which it traces to the confluence of capitalism and democracy. Squatters and *californios* alike fall victim to railroad barons who bribe state legislators for control of California property. Even the romance between Mercedes Alamar, the Don's daughter, and Clarence Darrell, a squatter's son, cannot prevent both families from being displaced from their homesteads. Their marriage signals a happy ending for the lovers but does not stop the railroad magnates—Stanford, Huntington, Crocker, and Hopkins—from profiting from California land at the expense of both Anglos and *californios.*

Ruiz de Burton works within many established literary traditions. She follows the historical romance tradition set by contemporary British, French, Spanish, and Mexican writers, but she also incorporates American modes of realism and naturalism later made popular by writers such as Theodore Dreiser and Frank Norris. As a Mexican American female novelist, however, her identity remained marginal. She published her first novel as "Mrs. Henry S. Burton" and her second one anonymously as "C. Loyal," an abbreviated form of *Ciudadano Leal,* "Loyal Citizen," a conventional method of closing official letters in nineteenth-century Mexico that Ruiz de Burton uses ironically to demonstrate her Mexican loyalties and signal her criticism of the corruption of American political ideals. She covers themes central to Mexican American history—Anglo-Mexican cultural clashes, disputes over land, and problems of racial identity—but values aristocratic *californios,* who have more in common with their Anglo counterparts than with working-class Mexican Americans. Her novels thus complicate history by leveling scathing critiques of U.S. colonialism not because it excludes *californios,* dispossessing them of their land and livelihood, but because it does not view them as white and extend class mobility to them.

Jesse Alemán
University of New Mexico

PRIMARY WORKS

Who Would Have Thought It?, ed. Rosaura Sánchez and Beatrice Pita (1872; Houston: Arte Público, 1995); *The Squatter and the Don,* ed. Rosaura Sánchez and Beatrice Pita, 2nd ed. (1885; Houston: Arte Público, 1997); *Don Quixote de la Mancha* (San Francisco: J. H. Carmany, 1876). María Amparo Ruiz de Burton's letters and documents can be found in the Bancroft Collection at the Berkeley Library of the University of California at Berkeley; Mission Santa Barbara in Santa Barbara, California; the Huntington Library in San Marino, California; and the San Diego Historical Society in San Diego, California.

from The Squatter and the Don

Chapter V The Don in His Broad Acres

"The one great principle of English law"—Charles Dickens says, "is to make business for itself. There is no other principle distinctly, certainly and consistently maintained through all its narrow turnings. Viewed by this light, it becomes a coherent scheme . . . and not the monstrous maze the laity are apt to think it. Let them but once clearly perceive that its grand principle is to make business for itself at their expense, and surely they will cease to grumble."[1]

The one great principle of American law is very much the same; our lawgivers keep giving us laws and then enacting others to explain them. The lawyers find plenty of occupation, but what becomes of the laity?

"No. 189. *An Act to ascertain and settle the private land claims in the State of California,*" says the book.[2]

And by a sad subversion of purposes, all the private land titles became *unsettled.* It ought to have been said, "An Act to *unsettle* land titles, and to upset the rights of the Spanish population of the State of California."

It thus became not only necessary for the Spanish people to present their titles for revision, and litigate to maintain them (in case of anyone contesting their validity, should the least irregularity be discovered, and others covet their possession), but to maintain them against the government before several tribunals; for the

[1]The quotation is from *Bleak House* (1852–1853). Based on an actual case, Dickens's novel recounts the property dispute between Jarndyce and Jarndyce. While the case is tied up in the legal fog of the Chancery court, characters stake their lives on the pending decision, but when the court finally names the heirs to the Jarndyce fortune, all of it has been eaten up by court costs. The novel's third-person narrator provides a satirical criticism of the legal quagmire while a romance between two characters offers a sense of hope but no resolution to England's social and political ills.

[2]The 1851 Land Law. Three years after the Treaty of Guadalupe Hidalgo granted citizenship rights to Mexicans remaining in the United States, Congress passed the California Land Act, which established a lengthy process for confirming Spanish and Mexican land titles. Claimants had to prove to the Board of Land Commissions that their title was legitimate; if the title could not be verified, the land became public domain and open for resettlement. Even if the title was verified, attorneys or settlers could appeal the case to the U.S. Supreme Court, and squatters were permitted to remain on the disputed land while the Mexican claimant paid the property taxes and compensated the squatters for property improvements. Because it took an average of seventeen years to confirm a land title in California, many land-owning Mexicans had to mortgage their property to American businessmen and lawyers to pay legal fees.

government, besides making its own laws, *appeals to itself* as against the landowners, after their titles might have been *approved.* But this benign Act says (in "Sec. II"), "That the Commissioners, the District and Supreme Courts, in deciding on the validity of any claim, shall be governed by the treaty of Guadalupe Hidalgo; the law of nations; the laws, usages, and customs of the government *from which the claim is derived;* the principles of equity, and the decisions of the Supreme Court of the United States, etc., etc."

Thus the government washes its hands clean, liberally providing plenty of tribunals, plenty of crooked turnings through which to scourge the wretched landowners.

Don Mariano had been for some years under the lash of the maternal government, whom he had found a cruel stepmother, indeed.

As it was arranged with Clarence, the meeting would take place that day on the broad piazza of John Gasbang's house, this being the most central point in the rancho.

The heads of families all came—the male heads, be it understood—as the squatters did not make any pretense to regard female opinion with any more respect than other men.

All the benches and chairs that the house contained, with the exception of Mrs. Gasbang's sewing rocker, had been brought to the porch, which was quite roomy and airy.

At ten minutes before two, all the settlers were there, that is to say, all the old men, with their elder sons.

Clarence, Romeo, Tom and Jack sat together in a corner, conversing in low tones, while Gasbang was entertaining his guests with some broad anecdotes, which brought forth peals of laughter.

At five minutes to two, Señor Alamar, accompanied by Mr. Mechlin, arrived in a buggy; his two sons followed on horseback.

Clarence had time to look at them leisurely while they dismounted and tied their horses to a hitching post.

"They are gentlemen, no doubt," observed Clarence.

"You bet they are," Romeo coincided. Evidently he admired and liked them.

"How much the boys look like the old man," Tom said.

"They look like Englishmen," was Clarence's next observation.

"Yes, particularly Victoriano; he is so light he looks more like a German, I think," said Romeo.

"I think Gabriel is very handsome," Tom said, "only of late he seems always so sad or thoughtful."

"That won't do for a man who is to marry soon," said Romeo. "I think he has always been rather reserved. He has only a cold salutation to give, while Victoriano will be laughing and talking to everybody. But, perhaps, you are right, and he is changed. I think he is less reconciled than others, to have us settlers helping outselves to what they consider their land. He certainly was far more talkative four or five years ago. I used to work with them in ploughing and harvesting time, and both boys and the Don were always very kind to me, and I can't help liking them."

"The ladies, though, ain't so affable. They are very proud," said Tom; "they walk like queens."

"They didn't seem proud to me, but I never spoke to them," said Romeo.

Gasbang went forward to meet his guests, and all came into the porch.

"Good afternoon, gentlemen," said Don Mariano to the settlers, lifting his hat and bowing. His sons and Mr. Mechlin did the same. Clarence arose, and so did the other young men with him, returning their salutation. The elder Darrell, Pittikin and Hughes followed this example; the other settlers nodded only, and remained sitting with their hats on, looking with affected indifference at the trees beyond.

"I thank you for your courtesy in complying with my request to have this meeting," he said. Some nodded, others grinned and winked, others smiled silently.

"Take this chair, Señor, and you, Mr. Mechlin, take this one. They are the best in my establishment," said Gasbang. "The young gentlemen will find seats somewhere on the benches."

Clarence came forward and offered three chairs. Mr. Mechlin took his arm and presented him to the Alamars.

"I take pleasure in making your acquaintance, and I hope to have the opportunity to thank you for your kind cooperation more appropriately afterward," said Don Mariano. His sons shook hands with Clarence cordially and accepted the proffered chairs.

Don Mariano excused himself for not speaking English more fluently.

"If you don't understand me I will repeat my words until I make my meaning clear, but I hope you will ask me to repeat them; or perhaps, some one of these young gentlemen will do me the kindness to be my interpreter," said he.

"Romeo talks Spanish; he can interpret for you," said Victoriano.

"You talk English better," Romeo proudly replied, thinking he could tell his wife that the Don had asked him to be his interpreter.

"Perhaps Mr. Clarence Darrell would do me the favor," said Don Mariano.

"You speak very good English, Señor. We understand you perfectly. You do not require an interpreter," Clarence said.

"That is so; you speak very well," said Mr. Mechlin.

Gasbang and Pittikin added: "Certainly, we understand him very well."

"You are very kind," said the Don, smiling, "and I will try to be brief, and not detain you long."

"We have all the afternoon," said Hughes.

"That's so; we ain't in a hurry," said several.

"Only let us out in time to bring the milch cows home, before night comes on," said old Miller dryly.

"Exactly, we want to look after our cows, too," said the Don laughing.

All saw the fine irony of the rejoinder and laughed heartily. Miller scratched his ear as if he had felt the retort there, knowing well that, with the exception of Mathews and Gasbang, he had killed and *"corralled"* more of the Don's cattle than any other settler.

"Speaking about cows brings us at once to the object of this meeting"—Don Mariano, still smiling, went on saying: "You know that I have lost many, and that it is natural I should wish to save those I have left. To do this, and yet not ask that you give up your claims, I have one or two propositions to make you. The reason why you have taken up land here is because you want homes. You want to make money. Isn't that the reason? Money! money!"

"That's it, exactly," said many voices, and all laughed.

"Well, I can show you how you may keep your home and make more money than you can by your present methods, while at the same time I also save my cattle. That little point, you know, I must keep in view."

All laughed again.

"To fence your fields, you have said, is too expensive, particularly as the rainy seasons are too uncertain to base upon them any calculations for getting crops to pay for fencing. I believe this is what most of you say; is it not?"

"We could have raised better crops if your cattle hadn't damaged them," said Mathews.[3]

"I beg to differ; but supposing that you are right, do you think you could be sure of good crops if you killed all my stock, or if I took them all away to the mountains? No, most assuredly. The rainy season would still be irregular and unreliable, I think. Yes, I may say, I feel sure, it is a mistake to try to make San Diego County a grain-producing county. It is not so, and I feel certain it never will be, to any great extent. This county is, and has been and will be always, a good grazing county—one of the best counties for cattle-raising on this coast, and the very best for fruit-raising on the face of the earth. God intended it should be. Why, then, not devote your time, your labor and your money to raising vineyards, fruits and cattle, instead of trusting to the uncertain rains to give you grain crops?"

"It takes a long time to get fruit trees to bearing. What are we to do for a living in the meantime?" asked Miller.

"Begin raising cattle—that will support you," the Don replied.

"Where is the capital to buy cattle with?" Gasbang asked.

"You don't require any more capital than you already have. I can let each of you have a number of cows to begin with, and give you four or five years' time to pay me. So you see, it will be with the increase of these cattle you will pay, for I shall charge you no interest."

"What do you expect us to do in return? To give back to you our homesteads?" asked Hughes.

"No, sir; I have said, and repeat again, you will retain your homesteads."

"And will you stop contesting our claims?" asked Mathews.

"I will, and will give each one a quit-claim deed."

"You will not fight our claims, but you don't want us to plant grain on our land," said Gasbang.

"You can plant grain, if you like, but to do so you must fence your land; so, as you all say, that fencing is expensive, I suggest your fencing orchards and vineyards only, but no grain fields—I mean large fields."

[3]The point of contention here is the "No Fence Law," a state constitutional amendment that exempted several counties, including San Diego, from California's otherwise strict fencing statutes. Residents of San Diego County were not required to build lawful fences as defined by the state, but the county did enforce state laws on animal trespassing. If an animal trespassed onto private property, the landowner could corral the animal and hold its owner liable for twice the amount of property damage done by the wayward animal. Neither state nor local laws permitted property owners to kill trespassing animals.

"Pshaw! I knew there was to be something behind all that display of generosity," muttered Mathews.

Don Mariano reddened with a thrill of annoyance, but quietly answered:

"You are too good business men to suppose that I should not reserve some slight advantage for myself, when I am willing you should have many more yourselves. All I want to do is to save the few cattle I have left. I am willing to quit-claim to you the land you have taken, and give you cattle to begin the stock business, and all I ask you in return is to put a fence around whatever land you wish to cultivate, so that my cattle cannot go in there. So I say, plant vineyards, plant olives, figs, oranges; make wines and oil and raisins; export olives and dried and canned fruits. I had some very fine California canned fruit sent to me from San Francisco. Why could we not can fruits as well, or better? Our olives are splendid—the same our figs, oranges, apricots, and truly all semitropical fruits are of a superior quality. When this fact becomes generally known, I feel very sure that San Diego Couny will be selected for fruit and grape-growing. In two years grape vines begin to bear; the same with figs, peaches and other fruits. At three years old they bear quite well, and all without irrigation. So you would not have to wait so very long to begin getting a return from your labor and capital. Moreover, an orchard of forty acres or vineyard of twenty will pay better after three years' growth than one hundred and sixty acres of wheat or barley in good seasons, and more than three hundred acres of any grain in moderately good seasons, one thousand acres in bad seasons. You can easily fence twenty or forty or sixty acres for a vineyard or orchard, but not so easily fence a field of one hundred and sixty, and the grain crop would be uncertain, depending on the rains, but not so the trees, for you can irrigate them, and after the trees are rooted that is not required."[4]

"Where is the water to irrigate?" asked Miller.

"The water is in the sea now, for there we let it go every year; but if we were sensible, judicious men, we would not let it go to waste—we would save it. This rancho has many deep ravines which bring water from hills and sierras. These ravines all open into the valleys and run like so many little rivers in the rainy season. By converting these ravines into reservoirs we could have more water than would be needed for irrigating the fruit trees on the foothills. In the low valleys no irrigation would be needed. If we all join forces to put up dams across the most convenient of the ravines, we will have splendid reservoirs.[5] I will defray half the expense if you will get together and stand the other half. Believe me, it will be a great godsend to have a thriving, fruit-growing business in our county. To have the cultivated land well fenced, and the remainder left out for grazing. Then there would not be so many thousands upon thousands of useless acres as now have to be. For every ten acres of cultivated land (not fenced) there are ten thousand, yes, twenty thousand, entirely idle, useless. Why? Because those ten acres of growing grain must be protected, and the cattle

[4]The Don's plan indicates his eagerness to profit from the changes in California, and it demonstrates Ruiz de Burton's exceptional foresight. Southern California's agricultural industry eventually followed the development the Don outlines here.

[5]The Don seems to be describing Ruiz de Burton's own 1873 plans to establish a waterworks on Rancho Jamul and create a reservoir for San Diego. She enlisted the aid of George Davidson, a friend and professor at Berkeley, who deemed Rancho Jamul an ideal location for a reservoir that would provide water for nearly 100,000 people. But lack of capital and investors thwarted her plans.

which don't know the 'no fence law,' follow their inclination to go and eat the green grass. Then they are *"corralled"* or killed. Is it not a pity to kill the poor dumb brutes, because we can't make them understand the law, and see the wisdom of our Sacramento legislators who enacted it? And is it not a pity to impoverish our county by making the bulk of its land useless? The foolishness of letting all of the rainfall go to waste is an old time folly with us. Still, in old times, we had at least the good excuse that we raised all the fruits we needed for our use, and there was no market for any more. But we were not then, as now, guilty of the folly of making the land useless. We raised cattle and sold hides and tallow every year, and made money. When gold was discovered, we drove our stock north, got a good price for it, and made money. But now no money will be made by anybody out of cattle, if they are to be destroyed, and no money made out of land, for the grazing will be useless when there will be no stock left to eat it. Thus, the county will have no cattle, and the crops be always uncertain. Believe me, in years to come, you will see that the county was impoverished by the 'no fence law,' unless we try to save our county, in spite of foolish legislation. If our wise legislators could enact a law obliging rain to come, so that we could have better chances to raise grain, then there would be some show of excuse for the 'no fence law,' perhaps. I say PERHAPS, because, in my humble opinion, we ought to prefer cattle raising and fruit growing for our county. We should make these our speciality."

"I think it would be much more foolish to trust a few cows to make out a living while trees grow," said Miller, "than to the seasons to give us grain crops."

"No, sir; because cattle are sure to increase, if they are not killed, and you could make cheese and butter, and sell your steers every year, while trees grow. You have been seven years a settler on this rancho. In these seven years you have raised two good crops; three poor, or only middling, and two, no crops at all."

"Yes, because your cattle destroyed them," said Mathews.

"No, sir; my cattle were not all over California; but the bad seasons were, and only in few places, moderately good crops were harvested; in the southern counties none at all. We had rains enough to get sufficiently good grazing, but not to raise grain."

"I think you are right about the uncertainty of our seasons, and I think a good dairy always pays well, also a good orchard and vineyard," said Darrell. "But the question is, whether we can adopt some feasible plan to put your idea into practice."

"Yes, how many cows will you let us have?" asked Hager.

"I will divide with you. Next week I shall have my *rodeo.* We can see then the number of cattle I have left. We shall count them. I shall take half, the other half you divide pro rata, each head of a family taking a proportionate number of cattle."

"That is fair," Darrell said.

"I don't want any cattle. I ain't no *vaquero* to go *busquering* around and *lassoing* cattle.[6] I'll *lasso* myself; what do I know about whirling a *lariat*?" said Mathews.

[6] *Vaquero* is Spanish for "cowboy"; *busquering* is an Anglicization of the Spanish verb *buscar,* "to look for." Throughout this section, Ruiz de Burton uses language to mark the difference in cultural and social status between the squatters and the Don. The squatters speak a vernacular English; the Don's English is impeccable, despite his initial statement that he speaks it poorly.

"Then don't take cattle. You can raise fruit trees and vineyards," said Darrell.

"Yes, and starve meantime," Mathews replied.

"You will not have to be a *vaquero.* I don't go *busquering* around *lassoing,* unless I wish to do so," said the Don. "You can hire an Indian boy to do that part. They know how to handle *la reata* and *echar el lazo*[7] to perfection. You will not starve, either, for if you wish, you can make butter and cheese enough to help to pay expenses. I think this State ought to make and export as good cheese as it now imports, and some day people will see it, and do it, too. Thus, with the produce of your dairies at first, and afterward with your fruits, you will do far better than with grain crops, and not work as hard. Let the northern counties raise grain, while we raise fruits and make wine, butter and cheese. You must not forget, either, that every year you can sell a number of cattle, besides keeping as many milch cows as you need."

"Where can we sell our cattle?" asked Hancock.

"Cattle-buyers will come to buy from you. But if you prefer it, you can drive your stock north yourselves, and make a good profit. Since 1850, I have sent nine times droves of cattle to the northern counties, and made a handsome profit every time. The first time we took stock north was in '50; I took nearly six thousand head—three thousand were mine—and the others belonged to my brothers. We lost very few, and sold at a good price—all the way from eighteen dollars to twenty five dollars per head. About five hundred of mine I sold as high as thirty dollars per head. I made sixty thousand dollars by this operation. Then out of the next lot I made twenty seven thousand dollars. Then I made twenty two thousand, and so on, until my tame cows began to disappear, as you all know. In four years after my cows began to get shot, my cattle decreased more than half. Now I don't think I have many more than three thousand head. So you cannot blame me for wishing to save these few. But believe me, the plan I propose will be as beneficial to you as to me, and also to the entire county, for as soon as it is shown that we can make a success of the industries I propose, others will follow our example."

"If you have only three thousand head, you can't spare many to us, and it will hardly be worth while to stop planting crops to get a few cows," said Gasbang.

"I think I will be able to spare five hundred or six hundred cows. I don't know how many I have left."

"We will buy from somebody else, if we want more," said Darrell. "We won't want many to begin with; it will be something of an experiment for some of us."

"For all of us here. Perhaps you understand *vaquering,*[8] we don't," said Hancock; all laughed.

"Then fence your claim and plant grain," Darrell retorted.

"I am not so big a fool as to spend money in fences. The 'no fence law' is better than all the best fences," Mathews said.

"But what if you make more money by following other laws that are more just, more rational?" said the Don.

[7]Spanish: "the rope" and "to lasso."

[8]Hancock combines the Spanish word for "cowboy" with an English verb ending to create *cowboying,* "to perform the work of cowboys." The bilingual exchanges between the squatters and the Don undermine an enduring myth about the American West. Cowboy culture is not an American tradition but a Mexican one, with help from hired Indian laborers.

"The 'no fence law' is rational enough for me," said Miller.

"And so say I," said Mathews.

"And I," said Gasbang.

Hughes nodded approvingly, but he was too much of a hypocrite to commit himself in words.

"We did not come to discuss the 'no fence law,' but only to propose something that will put more money in your pockets than killing dumb beasts," said Mr. Mechlin.

"Then propose something practicable," said Mathews.

"I think what has been proposed is practicable enough," Darrell said.

"Certainly it is," Mr. Mechlin added.

"I don't see it," said Mathews.

"Nor I, either," added Gasbang.

"Nor I, neither," said Hughes.

"Well, gentlemen," said Don Mariano, rising, "I shall leave you now; you know my views, and you perhaps prefer to discuss them, and discuss your own among yourselves, and not in my presence. Take your time, and when you come to a final decision let me know. Perhaps I can advance the money to those of you who do not have it ready to purchase fencing lumber, I shall charge no interest, and give you plenty of time to pay."

"I will do that, Señor Alamar," Clarence said; "if the settlers agree to fence their lands, I will advance the money to them to put up their fences."

"Yes, and if our crops fail, we will be in debt to the ears, with a chain around our necks," Mathews growled.

"I thought you said that if it were not for my cattle, your crops would not have failed," said Don Mariano, smiling.

"I said so, and it is so. But you see, that was before we had the 'no fence law,'" answered he, grinning.

Don Mariano shook hands with Clarence, whom he invited to call at his house—this invitation Clarence accepted with warm thanks—and, followed by his sons and his friend Mr. Mechlin, Don Mariano took his leave, bowing to the settlers, who nodded and grinned in return.

"I suppose you, too, think the 'no fence law' iniquitous, as you appear to favor the aristocracy," said Gasbang to Clarence.

"It is worse than that; it is stupid. Now it kills the cattle, afterwards it will kill the county," Clarence answered.

"Shall we plant no wheat, because the Spaniards want to raise cattle?" Mathews asked.

"Plant wheat, if you can do so without killing cattle. But do not destroy the larger industry with the smaller. If, as the Don very properly says, this is a grazing county, no legislation can change it. So it would be wiser to make laws to suit the county, and not expect that the county will change its character to suit absurd laws," Clarence replied.

1885

William Dean Howells 1837–1920

The most influential American novelist, editor, and critic of his generation, W. D. Howells was at the center of American literary culture for over fifty years. Born and raised in frontier Ohio, Howells was also one of the first important western writers to emigrate to the publishing centers of the East. Largely self-educated, he visited New England in July 1860 and met Nathaniel Hawthorne, Ralph Waldo Emerson, Henry David Thoreau, and other luminaries. As he later reminisced, Hawthorne gave him a note to pass to Emerson: "I find this young man worthy." And while hosting Howells at dinner at the Parker House, James T. Fields said to James Russell Lowell, "this is something like the apostolic succession; this is the laying on of hands." Later in the same year, Howells published a campaign biography of Abraham Lincoln, and after Lincoln's election he was rewarded with an appointment as U.S. consul in Venice. There he wrote the essays collected in his first major book, *Venetian Life* (1866). Settling in Boston the same year, he became the assistant editor of the redoubtable *Atlantic Monthly,* the most important magazine in America, and upon the retirement of Fields in 1871 Howells became its editor, a position he held for the next ten years. In this office he became a dominant critical voice, an arbiter of taste and fashion, and a champion of literary realism or "the truthful treatment of material."

For Howells, realism was a democratic movement in the arts, a focus on the normal and commonplace, distinct from romanticism or "romanticistic" fiction with its emphasis on the more ideal, bizarre, sentimental, or aristocratic. In a word, he promoted such writers as Henry James and Mark Twain and criticized others such as Sir Walter Scott and William Makepeace Thackeray. He urged readers to apply this singular test to any work of the imagination: "Is it true?—true to the motives, the impulses, the principles that shape the life of actual men and women?" He was profoundly moved in the late 1880s by Leo Tolstoy's ideas about nonviolence and economic equality. The Russian realist "has not influenced me in aesthetics only, but in ethics, too," he explained, "so that I can never again see life in the way I saw it before I knew him." Howells summarized his notion of moral complicity in his novel *The Minister's Charge* (1886). No one "sinned or suffered to himself alone," a character remarks. "If a community was corrupt, if an age was immoral, it was not because of the vicious, but the virtuous who fancied themselves indifferent spectators." Faithful to such principles in his life as well as in his art, Howells flirted with socialism and inveighed against imperialism, as in his story "Editha" (1905), a satire of a young woman who challenges her weak-willed lover to win glorious honors in battle.

Nowhere were Howells's democratic ethics more apparent than in his courageous but ill-fated defense of the Haymarket anarchists. On May 4, 1886, after a wave of labor strikes in Chicago in favor of an eight-hour workday, a policeman was killed, and seven others were mortally wounded by a bomb of unknown origin thrown during a rally in Haymarket Square organized by anarchists to protest police brutality. Eight anarchists were arrested, though none was identified as the bomb-thrower, and tried for murder. All were found guilty on August 20 and seven of them sentenced to hang. Howells fairly believed they had been railroaded. After the Supreme Court of Illinois denied their appeal on November 2, he resolved to take a stand on their behalf. On November 4 he sent a letter to the editor of the *New York Tribune* in which he urged readers to petition the governor of Illinois to commute the anarchists' sentences. The letter appeared in the newspaper on November 6 under the banner "Clemency for the Anarchists/A Letter from W. D. Howells." Howells stood virtually alone on behalf of the doomed men and became the target of public scorn. Even his friends refused to help. As Lowell wrote him, "I thought those Chicago ruffians well hanged," though he "honored your [Howells's] courage in saying what you did about them." After one of the men committed suicide and the sentences of two others were commuted to life in prison, the other four anarchists were executed on August 11. The next day Howells wrote a second letter to the *Tribune* entitled "A Word for the Dead," though it was not published in the paper and probably was never sent. However, Howells expressed similar views in his portrayal of the German socialist Lindau in *A Hazard of New Fortunes* (1890), the novel many critics consider his best. In 1893, the new governor of Illinois pardoned the three surviving anarchists, vindicating Howells's position.

Theodore Dreiser once compared Howells to a sentry "on the watch tower, straining for a first glimpse of approaching genius." As an editor of the *Atlantic* for fifteen years and later as the contributor of the "Editor's Study" and "Editor's Easy Chair" series to *Harper's,* Howells befriended and promoted the careers of such writers as James, Twain, Bret Harte, Sarah Orne Jewett, Mary E. Wilkins (later Freeman), Frank Norris, Charles W. Chesnutt, John W. De Forest, Paul Laurence Dunbar, Hamlin Garland, Edith Wharton, Charlotte Perkins Gilman, Abraham Cahan, and Stephen Crane. Such selections from Howells's late critical writing as his reviews of Wilkins's stories in 1891 and Chesnutt's stories in 1900 and his introduction to Dunbar's *Lyrics of Lowly Life* (1896) illustrate his sponsorship of women writers and writers of color. (Howells also endorsed women's suffrage and was one of the founding members of the NAACP in 1909.)

Known late in life as "the Dean of American letters," Howells was the first president of the American Academy of Arts and Letters and served in that office for thirteen years before his death. Though he became a favorite target of such iconoclasts as H. L. Mencken and Sinclair Lewis for whom he seemed to epitomize Victorian gentility, he deserves better from his critics. Frank Norris dismissed realism as "the drama of a broken teacup," but as practiced by Howells it both affirmed and subtly questioned bourgeois values. While he once asserted that the "smiling aspects of life" are the "more truly American," Howells was neither snob nor prig but an influential literary theorist, a prolific author, and a courageous spokesman for unpopular, progressive, and occasionally radical causes.

Gary Scharnhorst
University of New Mexico

PRIMARY WORKS

A Foregone Conclusion, 1875; *A Modern Instance,* 1882; *The Rise of Silas Lapham,* 1885; *Indian Summer,* 1886; *The Minister's Charge,* 1886; *A Hazard of New Fortunes,* 1890; *Criticism and Fiction,* 1891; *An Imperative Duty,* 1892; *A Traveler from Altruria,* 1894; *The Landlord at Lion's Head,* 1897; *Literary Friends and Acquaintance,* 1900; *My Mark Twain,* 1910; *A Selected Edition of W. D. Howells,* 1968–; *Selected Letters of W. D. Howells,* 1979–1983.

from Suburban Sketches

Scene

On that loveliest autumn morning, the swollen tide had spread over all the russet levels, and gleamed in the sunlight a mile away. As the contributor moved onward down the street, luminous on either hand with crimsoning and yellowing maples, he was so filled with the tender serenity of the scene, as not to be troubled by the spectacle of small Irish houses standing miserably about on the flats ankle deep, as it were, in little pools of the tide, or to be aware at first, of a strange stir of people upon the streets: a fluttering to and fro and lively encounter and separation of groups of bareheaded women, a flying of children through the broken fences of the neighborhood, and across the vacant lots on which the insulted sign-boards forbade them to trespass; a sluggish movement of men through all, and a pause of different vehicles along the sidewalks. When a sense of these facts had penetrated his enjoyment, he asked a matron whose snowy arms, freshly taken from the wash-tub, were folded across a mighty chest, "What is the matter?"

"A girl drowned herself, sir-r-r, over there on the flats, last Saturday, and they're looking for her."

"It was the best thing she could do," said another matron grimly.

Upon this answer that literary soul fell at once to patching himself up a romantic story for the suicide, after the pitiful fashion of this fiction-ridden age, when we must relate everything we see to something we have read. He was the less to blame for it, because he could not help it; but certainly he is not to be praised for his associations with the tragic fact brought to his notice. Nothing could have been more trite or obvious, and he felt his intellectual poverty so keenly that he might almost have believed his discomfort a sympathy for the girl who had drowned herself last Saturday. But of course, this could not be, for he had but lately been thinking what a very tiresome figure to the imagination the Fallen Woman had become. As a fact of Christian civilization, she was a spectacle to wring one's heart, he owned; but he wished she were well out of the romances, and it really seemed a fatality that she should be the principal personage of this little scene. The preparation for it, whatever it was to be, was so deliberate, and the reality had so slight relation to the French roofs and modern improvements of the comfortable Charlesbridge[1] which he knew, that he could not consider himself other than as a spectator awaiting some entertainment, with a faint inclination to be critical.

In the mean time there passed through the motley crowd, not so much a cry as a sensation of "They've found her, they've found her!" and then the one terrible picturesque fact, "She was standing upright!"

Upon this there was wilder and wilder clamor among the people, dropping by degrees and almost dying away, before a flight of boys came down the street with the tidings, "They are bringing her—bringing her in a wagon."

[1]Cambridge, Massachusetts, across the Charles River from Boston.

The contributor knew that she whom they were bringing in the wagon, had had the poetry of love to her dismal and otherwise squalid death; but the history was of fancy, not of fact in his mind. Of course, he reflected, her lot must have been obscure and hard; the aspect of those concerned about her death implied that. But of her hopes and her fears, who could tell him anything? To be sure he could imagine the lovers, and how they first met, and where, and who he was that was doomed to work her shame and death; but here his fancy came upon something coarse and common: a man of her own race and grade, handsome after that manner of beauty which is so much more hateful than ugliness is; or, worse still, another kind of man whose deceit must have been subtler and wickeder; but whatever the person, a presence defiant of sympathy or even interest, and simply horrible. Then there were the details of the affair, in great degree common to all love affairs, and not varying so widely in any condition of life; for the passion which is so rich and infinite to those within its charm, is apt to seem a little tedious and monotonous in its character, and poor in resources to the cold looker-on.

Then, finally, there was the crazy purpose and its fulfillment: the headlong plunge from bank or bridge; the eddy, and the bubbles on the current that calmed itself above the suicide; the tide that rose and stretched itself abroad in the sunshine, carrying hither and thither the burden with which it knew not what to do; the arrest, as by some ghastly caprice of fate, of the dead girl, in that upright posture, in which she should meet the quest for her, as it were defiantly.

And now they were bringing her in a wagon.

Involuntarily all stood aside, and waited till the funeral car, which they saw, should come up toward them through the long vista of the maple-shaded street, a noiseless riot stirring the legs and arms of the boys into frantic demonstration, while the women remained quiet with arms folded or akimbo. Before and behind the wagon, driven slowly, went a guard of ragged urchins, while on the raised seat above sat two Americans, unperturbed by anything, and concerned merely with the business of the affair.

The vehicle was a grocer's cart which had perhaps been pressed into the service; and inevitably the contributor thought of Zenobia, and of Miles Coverdale's[2] belief that if she could have foreboded all the *post-mortem* ugliness and grotesqueness of suicide, she never would have drowned herself. This girl, too, had doubtless had her own ideas of the effect that her death was to make, her conviction that it was to wring one heart, at least, and to strike awe and pity to every other; and her woman's soul must have been shocked from death could she have known in what a ghastly comedy the body she put off was to play a part.

In the bottom of the cart lay something long and straight and terrible, covered with a red shawl that drooped over the end of the wagon; and on this thing were piled the baskets in which the grocers had delivered their orders for sugar and flour,

[2]In chapter 27 of Nathaniel Hawthorne's *The Blithedale Romance* (1852), the narrator Miles Coverdale helps recover the body of the feminist Zenobia, who drowned herself. "Being the woman that she was," he remarks, "could Zenobia have foreseen all these ugly circumstances of death, how ill it would become her," she "would not more have committed the dreadful act, than have exhibited herself to a public assembly in a badly-fitted garment."

and coffee and tea. As the cart jolted through their lines, the boys could no longer be restrained; they broke out with wild yells, and danced madly about it, while the red shawl hanging from the rigid feet nodded to their frantic mirth; and the sun dropped its light through the maples and shone bright upon the flooded flats.

1871

from The Editor's Study

Nevertheless, we are in hopes that the communistic era in taste foreshadowed by Burke[1] is approaching, and that it will occur within the lives of men now overawed by the foolish old superstition that literature and art are anything but the expression of life, and are to be judged by any other test than that of their fidelity to it. The time is coming, we trust, when each new author, each new artist, will be considered, not in his proportion to any other author or artist, but in his relation to the human nature, known to us all, which it is his privilege, his high duty, to interpret. "The true standard of the artist is in every man's power," already as Burke says; Michelangelo's[2] "light of the piazza," the glance of the common eye, is and always was the best light on a statue; Goethe's[3] "boys and blackbirds" have in all ages been the real connoisseurs of berries; but hitherto the mass of common men have been afraid to apply their own simplicity, naturalness, and honesty to the appreciation of the beautiful. They have always cast about for the instruction of some one who professed to know better, and who browbeat wholesome common-sense into the self-distrust that ends in sophistication. They have fallen generally to the worst of this bad species, and have been "amused and misled" (how pretty that quaint old use of *amuse* is!) "by the false lights" of critical vanity and self-righteousness. They have been taught to compare what they see and what they read, not with the things that they have observed and known, but with the things that some other artist or writer has done. Especially if they have themselves the artistic impulse in any direction they are taught to form themselves, not upon life, but upon the masters who became masters only by forming themselves upon life. The seeds of death are planted in them, and they can produce only the still-born, the academic. They are not told to take their work into the public square and see if it seems true to the chance passer, but to test it by the work of the very men who refused and decried any other test of their own work. The young writer who attempts to report the phrase and carriage of every-day life, who tries to tell just how he has heard men talk and seen them look, is made to feel guilty of something low and unworthy by the stupid people who would like to have him show how

[1]Edmund Burke (1729–1797), British statesman and political essayist.

[2]Michelangelo (1475–1564), Italian artist, one of the greatest figures of the Italian Renaissance.

[3]Johann Wolfgang von Goethe (1749–1832), German poet, novelist, and playwright.

Shakespeare's men talked and looked, or Scott's, or Thackeray's, or Balzac's, or Hawthorne's, or Dickens's;[4] he is instructed to idealize his personages, that is, to take the life-likeness out of them, and put the literary-likeness into them. He is approached in the spirit of the wretched pedantry into which learning, much or little, always decays when it withdraws itself and stands apart from experience in an attitude of imagined superiority, and which would say with the same confidence to the scientist: "I see that you are looking at a grasshopper there which you have found in the grass, and I suppose you intend to describe it. Now don't waste your time and sin against culture in *that* way. I've got a grasshopper here, which has been evolved at considerable pains and expense out of the grasshopper in general; in fact, it's a type. It's made up of wire and card-board, very prettily painted in a conventional tint, and it's perfectly indestructible. It isn't very much like a real grasshopper, but it's a great deal nicer, and it's served to represent the notion of a grasshopper ever since man emerged from barbarism. You may say that it's artificial. Well, it *is* artificial: but then it's ideal too; and what you want to do is to cultivate the ideal. You'll find the books full of my kind of grasshopper, and scarcely a trace of yours in any of them. The thing that you are proposing to do is commonplace; but if you say that it isn't commonplace, for the very reason that it hasn't been done before, you'll have to admit that it's photographic."

As we said, we hope the time is coming when not only the artist, but the common, average man, who always "has the standard of the arts in his power," will have also the courage to apply it, and will reject the ideal grasshopper wherever he finds it, in science, in literature, in art, because it is not "simple, natural, and honest," because it is not like a real grasshopper. But we will own that we think the time is yet far off, and that the people who have been brought up on the ideal grasshopper, the heroic grasshopper, the impassioned grasshopper, the self-devoted, adventureful, good old romantic card-board grasshopper, must die out before the simple, honest, and natural grasshopper can have a fair field.

1887

from Criticism and Fiction

I am not sure that the Americans have not brought the short story nearer perfection in the all-round sense than almost any other people, and for reasons very simple and near at hand. It might be argued from the national hurry and impatience that it was a literary form peculiarly adapted to the American temperament, but I suspect that its extraordinary development among us is owing much more to more tangible facts. The success of American magazines, which is nothing less than prodigious, is only commensurate with their excellence. Their sort of success is not only from the

[4]William Shakespeare (1564–1616); Sir Walter Scott (1771–1832); William Makepeace Thackeray (1811–1863); Honoré de Balzac (1799–1850); Nathaniel Hawthorne (1804–1864); Charles Dickens (1812–1870)—all eminent men of letters.

courage to decide what ought to please, but from the knowledge of what does please; and it is probable that, aside from the pictures, it is the short stories which please the readers of our best magazines. The serial novels they must have, of course; but rather more of course they must have short stories, and by operation of the law of supply and demand, the short stories, abundant in quantity and excellent in quality, are forthcoming because they are wanted. By another operation of the same law, which political economists have more recently taken account of, the demand follows the supply, and short stories are sought for because there is a proven ability to furnish them, and people read them willingly because they are usually very good. The art of writing them is now so disciplined and diffused with us that there is no lack either for the magazines or for the newspaper "syndicates" which deal in them almost to the exclusion of the serials. In other countries the feuilleton[1] of the journals is a novel continued from day to day, but with us the papers, whether daily or weekly, now more rarely print novels, whether they get them at first hand from the writers, as a great many do, or through the syndicates, which purvey a vast variety of literary wares, chiefly for the Sunday editions of the city journals. In the country papers the short story takes the place of the chapters of a serial which used to be given.

An interesting fact in regard to the different varieties of the short story among us is that the sketches and studies by the women seem faithfuler and more realistic than those of the men, in proportion to their number. Their tendency is more distinctly in that direction, and there is a solidity, an honest observation, in the work of such women as Mrs. Cooke, Miss Murfree, Miss Wilkins and Miss Jewett,[2] which often leaves little to be desired. I should, upon the whole, be disposed to rank American short stories only below those of such Russian writers as I have read, and I should praise rather than blame their free use of our different local parlances, or "dialects," as people call them. I like this because I hope that our inherited English may be constantly freshened and revived from the native sources which our literary decentralization will help to keep open, and I will own that as I turn over novels coming from Philadelphia, from New Mexico, from Boston, from Tennessee, from rural New England, from New York, every local flavor of diction gives me courage and pleasure. M. Alphonse Daudet, in a conversation which Mr. H. H. Boyesen has set down in a recently recorded interview with him, said, in speaking of Tourguéneff.[3] "What a luxury it must be to have a great big untrodden barbaric language to wade into! We poor fellows who work in the language of an old civilization, we may sit and chisel our little verbal felicities, only to find in the end that it is a borrowed jewel we are polishing. The crown of jewels of our French tongue have passed through the hands of so many generations of monarchs that it seems like presumption on the part of any late-born pretender to attempt to wear them."

[1]The literary section of a newspaper or magazine.

[2]Rose Terry Cooke (1827–1892); Mary Noailles Murfree (a.k.a. Charles Egbert Craddock) (1850–1922); Mary E. Wilkins Freeman (1852–1930); Sarah Orne Jewett (1849–1909).

[3]M. Alphonse Daudet (1840–1897), French writer; Hjalmar Hjorth Boyesen (1848–1895), a prolific American magazinist; Ivan Tourguéneff or Turgenev (1818–1883), Russian novelist.

This grief is, of course, a little whimsical, yet it has a certain measure of reason in it, and the same regret has been more seriously expressed by the Italian poet Aleardi:[4]

> Muse of an aged people, in the eve
> Of fading civilization, I was born.
> . . . . Oh, fortunate,
> My sisters, who in the heroic dawn
> Of races sung! To them did destiny give
> The virgin fire and chaste ingenuousness
> Of their land's speech; and, reverenced, their hands
> Ran over potent strings.

It will never do to allow that we are at such a desperate pass in English, but something of this divine despair we may feel too in thinking of "the spacious times of great Elizabeth,"[5] when the poets were trying the stops of the young language, and thrilling with the surprises of their own music. We may comfort ourselves, however, unless we prefer a luxury of grief, by remembering that no language is ever old on the lips of those who speak it, no matter how decrepit it drops from the pen. We have only to leave our studies, editorial and other, and go into the shops and fields to find the "spacious times" again; and from the beginning Realism, before she had put on her capital letter, had divined this near-at-hand truth along with the rest. Mr. Lowell,[6] almost the greatest and finest realist who ever wrought in verse, showed us that Elizabeth was still Queen where he heard Yankee farmers talk. One need not invite slang into the company of its betters, though perhaps slang has been dropping its "s" and becoming language ever since the world began, and is certainly sometimes delightful and forcible beyond the reach of the dictionary. I would not have any one go about for new words, but if one of them came aptly, not to reject its help. For our novelists to try to write Americanly, from any motive, would be a dismal error, but being born Americans, I would have them use "Americanisms" whenever these serve their turn; and when their characters speak, I should like to hear them speak true American, with all the varying Tennessean, Philadelphian, Bostonian, and New York accents. If we bother ourselves to write what the critics imagine to be "English," we shall be priggish and artificial, and still more so if we make our Americans talk "English." There is also this serious disadvantage about "English," that if we wrote the best "English" in the world, probably the English themselves would not know it, or, if they did, certainly would not own it. It has always been supposed by grammarians and purists that a language can be kept as they find it; but languages, while they live, are perpetually changing. God apparently meant them for the common people—whom Lincoln believed God liked because he had made so many of them; and the common people will use them freely as they use other gifts of God. On their lips our continental English will differ more and more from the insular English, and I believe that this is not deplorable, but desirable.

[4]Gaetano Aleardi (1812–1878), Italian poet and politician.

[5]Alfred Lord Tennyson, "A Dream of Fair Women" (1832): "Dan Chaucer, the first warbler, whose sweet breath/Preluded those melodious bursts that fill/the spacious times of great Elizabeth."

[6]James Russell Lowell (1819–1891), American poet.

In fine, I would have our American novelists be as American as they unconsciously can. Matthew Arnold[7] complained that he found no "distinction" in our life, and I would gladly persuade all artists intending greatness in any kind among us that the recognition of the fact pointed out by Mr. Arnold ought to be a source of inspiration to them, and not discouragement. We have been now some hundred years building up a state on the affirmation of the essential equality of men in their rights and duties, and whether we have been right or wrong the gods have taken us at our word, and have responded to us with a civilization in which there is no "distinction" perceptible to the eye that loves and values it. Such beauty and such grandeur as we have is common beauty, common grandeur, or the beauty and grandeur in which the quality of solidarity so prevails that neither distinguishes itself to the disadvantage of anything else. It seems to me that these conditions invite the artist to the study and the appreciation of the common, and to the portrayal in every art of those finer and higher aspects which unite rather than sever humanity, if he would thrive in our new order of things. The talent that is robust enough to front the every-day world and catch the charm of its work-worn, care-worn, brave, kindly face, need not fear the encounter, though it seems terrible to the sort nurtured in the superstition of the romantic, the bizarre, the heroic, the distinguished, as the things alone worthy of painting or carving or writing. The arts must become democratic, and then we shall have the expression of America in art; and the reproach which Mr. Arnold was half right in making us shall have no justice in it any longer; we shall be "distinguished."

1891

Letters to the Editor of the *New York Tribune*

4 November 1887, Dansville, New York,
to the Editor of the *New York Tribune*

Sir:[1]

As I have petitioned the Governor of Illinois to commute the death penalty of the Anarchists to imprisonment, and have also personally written him in their behalf, I ask your leave to express here the hope that those who are inclined to do either will not lose faith in themselves because the Supreme Court has denied the condemned a writ of error. That court simply affirmed the legality of the forms under which the Chicago court proceeded; it did not affirm the propriety of trying for murder men fairly indictable for conspiracy alone; and it by no means approved the principle of punishing them because of their frantic opinions, for a crime which they were not shown to have committed. The justice or injustice of their sentence was not before the

[7]Matthew Arnold (1822–1888), English poet and critic.

[1]Whitelaw Reid (1837–1912), editor-in-chief of the *New York Tribune* from 1872 to 1905.

highest tribunal of our law, and unhappily could not be got there. That question must remain for history, which judges the judgment of courts, to deal with; and I, for one, cannot doubt what the decision of history will be.

But the worst is still for a very few days reparable; the men sentenced to death are still alive, and their lives may be finally saved through the clemency of the Governor, whose prerogative is now the supreme law in their case.[2] I conjure all those who believe that it would be either injustice or impolicy to put them to death, to join in urging him by petition, by letter, through the press, and from the pulpit and the platform, to use his power, in the only direction where power can never be misused, for the mitigation of their punishment.

William Dean Howells

Dansville, N.Y., Nov. 4, 1887

12 November 1887, Dansville, New York,
to the Editor of the *New York Tribune*

To the Editor of The Tribune:

I have borne with what patience I must, during the past fortnight, to be called by the Tribune, day after day imbecile and bad citizen, with the others who desired mercy for the men killed yesterday at Chicago, in conformity with our still barbarous law. I now ask you to have a little patience with me.

It seems, of course, almost a pity to mix a note of regret with the hymn of thanksgiving for blood going up from thousands of newspapers all over the land this morning; but I reflect that though I write amidst this joyful noise, my letter cannot reach the public before Monday at the earliest, and cannot therefore be regarded as an indecent interruption of the *Te Deum.*

By that time journalism will not have ceased, but history will have at least begun. All over the world where civilized men can think and feel, they are even now asking themselves, For what, really, did those four men die so bravely? Why did one other die so inexorably? Next week the journalistic theory that they died so because they were desperate murderers will have grown even more insufficient than it is now for the minds and hearts of dispassionate inquirers, and history will make the answer to which she must adhere for all time, *They died, in the prime of the freest Republic the world has ever known, for their opinions' sake.*

It is useless to deny this truth, to cover it up, to turn our backs upon it, to frown it down, or sneer it down. We have committed an atrocious and irreparable wrong. We have been undergoing one of those spasms of paroxysmal righteousness to which our Anglo-Saxon race is peculiarly subject, and in which, let us hope, we are not more responsible for our actions than the victim of *petit mal.*[3] Otherwise, we could not forgive ourselves; and I say we, because this deed has apparently been done with the approval of the whole nation.

[2]Richard J. Oglesby (1824–1899) commuted to life in prison the sentences of two of the convicted men.

[3]A type of epilepsy.

The dead men who now accuse us of the suicidal violence in which they perished, would be alive to-day, if one thousandth part of the means employed to compass their death had been used by the people to inquire into the question of their guilt; for, under the forms of law, their trial has not been a trial by justice, but a trial by passion, by terror, by prejudice, by hate, by newspaper.

To the minority who asked mercy for them because they had made this inquiry (but who were hooted at in your columns as ignorant sentimentalists and cowards) the whole business of their conviction, except for the hideous end attained, might seem a colossal piece of that American humor, so much admired by the English for its grotesque surprises in material and proportion. But perhaps the wildest of our humorists could not have conceived of a joke so monstrous as the conviction of seven men for a murderous conspiracy which they carried into effect while one was at home playing cards with his family, another was addressing a meeting five miles away, another was present with his wife and little children, two others had made pacific speeches, and not one, except on the testimony of a single, notoriously untruthful witness,[4] was proven to have had anything to do with throwing the Haymarket bomb, or to have even remotely instigated the act. It remained for a poetic brain to imagine this, and bring its dream yesterday to homicidal realization.

I mean the brain of Mr. State's Attorney Grinnell,[5] who has shown gifts of imagination that would perhaps fit him better for the functions of a romantic novelist than for the duties of official advocate in a free commonwealth.

It was apparently inconveivable to him that it was the civic duty as well as the sacred privilege of such an officer to seek the truth concerning the accused rather than to seek their destruction. He brought into court the blood-curdling banners of the Anarchists, and unfurled them before the eyes of a jury on which eight or nine men had owned themselves prejudiced against Anarchists before the law delivered the lives of these Anarchists into their hands. He appealed to the already heated passions of the jury; he said the seven were no more guilty than a thousand other men in Chicago, but he told them that if they would hang the seven men before them the other nine hundred and ninety-three equally guilty contrivers of bombs would not explode them in the bosom of the impartial jurymen's families and Society would be saved.

If he proved absolutely nothing against the Anarchists worthy of death, it cannot be denied that he at least posed successfully as a Savior of Society—the rôle once filled by the late Emperor of the French, (on the famous 2d December)[6] with great effect against the Socialists of his day. He was, throughout, the expression of the worst passions of the better classes, their fear, their hate, their resentment, which I do not find so much better than the worst passions of the worst classes that I can altogether respect them. He did not show that any of the accused threw the bomb, or had anything to do with

[4]A painter named Harry Gilmer had testified that the anarchist August Spies supplied the match that lit the bomb.

[5]Julius S. Grinnell, the prosecuting attorney.

[6]Louis Napoleon Bonaparte (1803–1873) remained president of France by ordering the army to take power on December 2, 1851.

throwing it; but he got them convicted of murder all the same. Spies was convicted of murder partly because he conspired against Society with men some of whom he was not on speaking terms with. Among the crimes for which Parsons was convicted of murder was quoting in his paper General Sheridan's belief that a dynamite bomb might kill a regiment of soldiers; and the Supreme Court of Illinois, reviewing the testimony, located him at two points, a block apart, when the bomb was thrown, and found him doubly privy to the act upon this bold topographical conception.

But Mr. Grinnell does not deserve all the honor—if it is an honor—of bringing the Anarchists to their death. He was ably seconded by Judge Gary,[7] whose interpretation of the law against murder, to make it do the work of the law against conspiracy, is a masterpiece of its kind; though perhaps even this is surpassed by his recommendation of Fielden and Schwab to the Governor's mercy because (it is like the logic of a "Bab Ballad")[8] they were pretty-behaved when brought up for sentence. It had indeed been proved, as proof went in that amusingly credulous court, that Fielden was the very man who gave the signal for throwing the bomb; but Judge Gary contributes to the science of jurisprudence the novel principle that if you are pretty-behaved when asked to say why you should not be hung for a crime of which you know your innocence, you ought afterwards to have your sentence commuted. He himself was not always pretty-behaved. When he asked Parsons that comical question, and Parsons entered upon his reasons, he refused to let him pause for a moment's refreshment while delivering his long protest, and thought it good taste and good feeling to sneer at him for reading extracts from the newspapers. Perhaps it was so; or perhaps the judge was tired—the prosecution had been reading whole files of newspapers.

When he said that the seven were no more guilty than a thousand other Anarchists, Mr. Grinnell was counting for Chicago alone; but he could doubtless have figured up ten thousand men equally guilty, upon the same medieval principle, if he took in the whole country. Seven is rather a small percentage, though seven is a mystical number, and he may have thought it had peculiar properties for that reason; but it always struck me as much too few, or wholly too many, according as the men accused did or did not do murder. With his love of poetic justice, (I will call it melodramatic justice if the word poetic seems too strong) I rather wonder that Mr. Grinnell did not at least want the men's families hanged; but since he did not ask this, I do not see why he could not have satisfied himself with having the seven Anarchists hanged in effigy. Possibly if Parsons, believing that he could suffer no wrong in an American court, had not come back and voluntarily given himself up after having made good his escape,[9] Mr. Grinnell would have demanded that sort of expiation for him.

But this is mere conjecture, and I have wished to deal with facts. One of these is that we had a political execution in Chicago yesterday. The sooner we

[7]Judge Joseph E. Gary (1821–1906) of the Cooke County Superior Court.

[8]A nonsense song.

[9]Parsons escaped to Wisconsin after the bombing, then surrendered to authorities in Chicago six weeks later.

realize this, the better for us. By such a perversion of law as brought the Anarchists to their doom, William Lloyd Garrison who published a paper denouncing the constitution as a compact with hell and a covenant with death, and every week stirred up the blacks and their friends throughout the country to abhor the social system of the South, could have been sent to the gallows if a slave had killed his masters.[10] Emerson, Parker, and Howe, Giddings and Wade, Sumner and Greeley,[11] and all who encouraged the war against slavery in Kansas, and the New England philanthropists[12] who supplied the Free State men with Sharp's rifles could have been held "morally responsible," and made to pay with their persons, when John Brown took seven Missourians out of their beds and shot them. Wendell Phillips, and Thoreau, and the other literary men whose sympathy inflamed Brown to homicidal insurrection at Harper's Ferry, could have been put to death with the same justice that consigned the Anarchists to the gallows in Chicago. The American law yesterday was made to do a deed beside which the treatment of William O'Brien by British law for the like offence, is caressing tenderness.[13]

But the men are dead. They are with God, as the simple, devout old phrase goes; or if the scientific spirit of the age does not consent to this idea, I will say that they are at least not with the newspapers. They are where, as men your words cannot hurt, nor mine help them more. But as memories, they are not beyond the reach of either, and I protest against any farther attempt to defame them. They were no vulgar or selfish murderers. However they came by their craze against society it was not through hate of the rich so much as love of the poor. Let both rich and poor remember this, and do them this piece of justice at least.

I dread the Anarchy of the Courts, but I have never been afraid of the prevalence of the dead Anarchists' doctrine, because that must always remain to plain common sense, unthinkable; and I am not afraid of any acts of revenge from their fellow conspirators because I believe they never were part of any conspiracy. I have no doubt that Judge Gary will live long to enjoy the reward upon which he has already entered in his re-election. I have no question either as to the safety of Mr. State's Attorney Grinnell, and I hope he has not suffered too keenly from the failure to realize his poetical ideal in the number of the Anarchists finally hanged. He himself helped to reduce it to four; perhaps he will yet wish that none had died.

W. D. Howells

Dansville, Nov. 12, 1887

[10] In his abolitionist paper, the *Liberator,* Garrison (1805–1879) had described the U.S. Constitution as a "covenant with hell" because it sanctioned slavery.

[11] Ralph Waldo Emerson (1803–1882), Theodore Parker (1810–1860), Samuel G. Howe (1801–1876), Joshua R. Giddings (1795–1864), Benjamin Franklin Wade (1800–1878), William Sumner (1811–1874), and Horace Greeley (1811–1872) were all outspoken in their opposition to slavery.

[12] The "secret six" New Englanders who supported militant abolitionists such as John Brown were Parker, Howe, Thomas Wentworth Higginson (1823–1911), Gerrit Smith (1799–1874), F. B. Sanborn (1831–1917), and George L. Stearns (1809–1867).

[13] William O'Brien had been convicted in British courts of sedition and sentenced to ninety days in jail for a speech he had delivered in Ireland.

Mary E. Wilkins's[1] Short Stories

To turn from this great world of *Gentlemen*, to the small, lowly sphere where Miss Wilkins's humble folk have their being, is a vast change, but there is a kind of consolation in it. Here at least are real interests, passions, ambitions; and yonder there do not seem to be any. The scenes of *A New England Nun and Other Stories* are laid in that land of little village houses which the author of *A Humble Romance* has made her own. The record never strays beyond; there is hardly a person in the dramas who does not work for a living; the tragedies and comedies are those of the simplest and commonest people, who speak a crabbed Yankee through their noses, and whose dress and address would be alike shocking to *Gentlemen*. Still they may be borne with, at least in the hands of an artist such as Miss Wilkins has shown herself to be. We are not sure that there is anything better in this volume than in her first; we note the same powers, the same weaknesses; the never-erring eye, the sometimes mistaken fancy. The figures are drawn with the same exquisitely satisfying veracity; but about half the time we doubt whether they would do what they are shown doing. We have a lurking fear at moments that Miss Wilkins would like to write entirely romantic stories about these honest people of hers; but her own love of truth and her perfect knowledge of such life as theirs forbid her actually to do this. There is apparently a conflict of purposes in her sketches which gives her art an undecided effect, or a divided effect, as in certain of them where we make the acquaintance of her characters in their village of little houses, and lose it in the No Man's Land of exaggerated action and conventional emotion. In the interest of her art, which is so perfectly satisfying in the service of reality, it could almost be wished that she might once write a thoroughly romantic story, and wreak in it all the impulses she has in that direction. Then perhaps she might return to the right exercise of a gift which is one of the most precious in fiction. But perhaps this could not happen; perhaps the Study is itself romantic in imagining such a thing. It may be that we shall always have to content ourselves with now a story of the real and unreal mixed, and now one of unmixed reality, such as Miss Wilkins alone can give us. At any rate her future is not in the keeping of criticism, to shape or to direct. Who can forecast the course of such a talent? Not even the talent itself; and what we must be grateful for is what it has already given us in the two volumes of tales, which are as good in their way as anything ever done amongst us; that is, among any people. In form they instinctively approach that of the best work everywhere in the fine detail of the handling; but in spirit they are distinctively ours. The humor is American, and they are almost all humorously imagined, with a sort of direct reference to the facts of the usual rustic American experience. The life of the human heart, its affections, its hopes, its fears, however these mask themselves from low to high, or high to low, is always the same, in every time and land; but in each it has a special physiognomy. What our artist has done is to catch the American look of life, so that if her miniatures remain to other ages they shall know just the expression of that vast average of Americans who do the hard

[1]Mary E. Wilkins, later Freeman (1852–1930), New England regionalist writer.

work of the country, and live narrowly on their small earnings and savings. If there is no gayety in that look, it is because the face of hard work is always sober, and because the consciousness of merciless fortuities and inexorable responsibilities comes early and stays late with our people.

1891

Paul Laurence Dunbar

I think I should scarcely trouble the reader with a special appeal in behalf of this book, if it had not specially appealed to me for reasons apart from the author's race, origin, and condition. The world is too old now, and I find myself too much of its mood, to care for the work of a poet because he is black, because his father and mother were slaves, because he was, before and after he began to write poems, an elevator-boy. These facts would certainly attract me to him as a man, if I knew him to have a literary ambition, but when it came to his literary art, I must judge it irrespective of these facts, and enjoy or endure it for what it was in itself.

It seems to me that this was my experience with the poetry of Paul Laurence Dunbar when I found it in another form, and in justice to him I cannot wish that it should be otherwise with his readers here. Still, it will legitimately interest those who like to know the causes, or, if these may not be known, the sources, of things, to learn that the father and mother of the first poet of his race in our language were negroes without admixture of white blood. The father escaped from slavery in Kentucky to freedom in Canada, while there was still no hope of freedom otherwise; but the mother was freed by the events of the civil war, and came North to Ohio, where their son was born at Dayton, and grew up with such chances and mischances for mental training as everywhere befall the children of the poor. He has told me that his father picked up the trade of a plasterer, and when he had taught himself to read, loved chiefly to read history. The boy's mother shared his passion for literature, with a special love of poetry, and after the father died she struggled on in more than the poverty she had shared with him. She could value the faculty which her son showed first in prose sketches and attempts at fiction, and she was proud of the praise and kindness they won him among the people of the town, where he has never been without the warmest and kindest friends.

In fact, from every part of Ohio and from several cities of the adjoining States, there came letters in cordial appreciation of the critical recognition which it was my pleasure no less than my duty to offer Paul Dunbar's work in another place.[1] It seemed to me a happy omen for him that so many people who had known him, or known of him, were glad of a stranger's good word; and it was gratifying to see that at home he was esteemed for the things he had done rather than because as the son of negro slaves he had done them. If a prophet is often without honor in his own

[1]Howells had reviewed Dunbar's *Majors and Minors* in *Harper's Weekly* for June 27, 1896.

country, it surely is nothing against him when he has it. In this case it deprived me of the glory of a discoverer; but that is sometimes a barren joy, and I am always willing to forego it.

What struck me in reading Mr. Dunbar's poetry was what had already struck his friends in Ohio and Indiana, in Kentucky and Illinois. They had felt, as I felt, that however gifted his race had proven itself in music, in oratory, in several of the other arts, here was the first intance of an American negro who had evinced innate distinction in literature. In my criticism of his book I had alleged Dumas in France, and I had forgetfully failed to allege the far greater Pushkin in Russia;[2] but these were both mulattoes, who might have been supposed to derive their qualities from white blood vastly more artistic than ours, and who were the creatures of an environment more favorable to their literary development. So far as I could remember, Paul Dunbar was the only man of pure African blood and of American civilization to feel the negro life æsthetically and express it lyrically. It seemed to me that this had come to its most modern consciousness in him, and that his brilliant and unique achievement was to have studied the American negro objectively, and to have represented him as he found him to be, with humor, with sympathy, and yet with what the reader must instinctively feel to be entire truthfulness. I said that a race which had come to this effect in any member of it, had attained civilization in him, and I permitted myself the imaginative prophecy that the hostilities and the prejudices which had so long constrained his race were destined to vanish in the arts; that these were to be the final proof that God had made of one blood all nations of men. I thought his merits positive and not comparative; and I held that if his black poems had been written by a white man, I should not have found them less admirable. I accepted them as an evidence of the essential unity of the human race, which does not think or feel black in one and white in another, but humanly in all.

Yet it appeared to me then, and it appears to me now, that there is a precious difference of temperament between the races which it would be a great pity ever to lose, and that this is best preserved and most charmingly suggested by Mr. Dunbar in those pieces of his where he studies the moods and traits of his race in its own accent of our English. We call such pieces dialect pieces for want of some closer phrase, but they are really not dialect so much as delightful personal attempts and failures for the written and spoken language. In nothing is his essentially refined and delicate art so well shown as in these pieces, which, as I ventured to say, describe the range between appetite and emotion, with certain lifts far beyond and above it, which is the range of the race. He reveals in these a finely ironical perception of the negro's limitations, with a tenderness for them which I think so very rare as to be almost quite new. I should say, perhaps, that it was this humorous quality which Mr. Dunbar had added to our literature, and it would be this which would most distinguish him, now and hereafter. It is something that one feels in nearly all the dialect pieces; and I hope that in the present collection he has kept all of these in his earlier volume, and added others to them. But the contents of this book are wholly of his own choosing, and I do

[2]Alexandre Dumas, or Dumas *père* (the father) (1802–1870), French novelist and playwright; Alexander Pushkin (1799–1837), Russian poet.

not know how much or little he may have preferred the poems in literary English. Some of these I thought very good, and even more than very good, but not distinctively his contribution to the body of American poetry. What I mean is that several people might have written them; but I do not know any one else at present who could quite have written the dialect pieces. These are divinations and reports of what passes in the hearts and minds of a lowly people whose poetry had hitherto been inarticulately expressed in music, but now finds, for the first time in our tongue, literary interpretation of a very artistic completeness.

I say the event is interesting, but how important it shall be can be determined only by Mr. Dunbar's future performance. I cannot undertake to prophesy concerning this; but if he should do nothing more than he has done, I should feel that he had made the strongest claim for the negro in English literature that the negro has yet made. He has at least produced something that, however we may critically disagree about it, we cannot well refuse to enjoy; in more than one piece he has produced a work of art.

1896

Mr. Charles W. Chesnutt's Stories

The critical reader of the story called The Wife of his Youth, which appeared in these pages two years ago, must have noticed uncommon traits in what was altogether a remarkable piece of work. The first was the novelty of the material; for the writer dealt not only with people who were not white, but with people who were not black enough to contrast grotesquely with white people,—who in fact were of that near approach to the ordinary American in race and color which leaves, at the last degree, every one but the connoisseur in doubt whether they are Anglo-Saxon or Anglo-African. Quite as striking as this novelty of the material was the author's thorough mastery of it, and his unerring knowledge of the life he had chosen in its peculiar racial characteristics. But above all, the story was notable for the passionless handling of a phase of our common life which is tense with potential tragedy; for the attitude, almost ironical, in which the artist observes the play of contesting emotions in the drama under his eyes; and for his apparently reluctant, apparently helpless consent to let the spectator know his real feeling in the matter. Any one accustomed to study methods in fiction, to distinguish between good and bad art, to feel the joy which the delicate skill possible only from a love of truth can give, must have known a high pleasure in the quiet self-restraint of the performance; and such a reader would probably have decided that the social situation in the piece was studied wholly from the outside, by an observer with special opportunities for knowing it, who was, as it were, surprised into final sympathy.

Now, however, it is known that the author of this story is of negro blood,—diluted, indeed, in such measure that if he did not admit this descent few would imagine it, but still quite of that middle world which lies next, though wholly outside, our own. Since his first story appeared he has contributed several others to these pages, and he now makes a showing palpable to criticism in a volume called The Wife of his

Youth, and Other Stories of the Color Line; a volume of Southern sketches called The Conjure Woman; and a short life of Frederick Douglass, in the Beacon Series of biographies. The last is a simple, solid, straight piece of work, not remarkable above many other biographical studies by people entirely white, and yet important as the work of a man not entirely white treating of a great man of his inalienable race. But the volumes of fiction *are* remarkable above many, above most short stories by people entirely white, and would be worthy of unusual notice if they were not the work of a man not entirely white.

It is not from their racial interest that we could first wish to speak of them, though that must have a very great and very just claim upon the critic. It is much more simply and directly, as works of art, that they make their appeal, and we must allow the force of this quite independently of the other interest. Yet it cannot always be allowed. There are times in each of the stories of the first volume when the simplicity lapses, and the effect is as of a weak and uninstructed touch. There are other times when the attitude, severely impartial and studiously aloof, accuses itself of a little pompousness. There are still other times when the literature is a little too ornate for beauty, and the diction is journalistic, reporteristic. But it is right to add that these are the exceptional times, and that for far the greatest part Mr. Chesnutt seems to know quite as well what he wants to do in a given case as Maupassant,[1] or Tourguénief, or Mr. James, or Miss Jewett, or Miss Wilkins, in other given cases, and has done it with an art of kindred quiet and force. He belongs, in other words, to the good school, the only school, all aberrations from nature being so much truancy and anarchy. He sees his people very clearly, very justly, and he shows them as he sees them, leaving the reader to divine the depth of his feeling for them. He touches all the stops, and with equal delicacy in stories of real tragedy and comedy and pathos, so that it would be hard to say which is the finest in such admirably rendered effects as The Web of Circumstance, The Bouquet, and Uncle Wellington's Wives. In some others the comedy degenerates into satire, with a look in the reader's direction which the author's friend must deplore.

As these stories are of our own time and country, and as there is not a swashbuckler of the seventeenth century, or a sentimentalist of this, or a princess of an imaginary kingdom, in any of them, they will possibly not reach half a million readers in six months, but in twelve months possibly more readers will remember them than if they had reached the half million. They are new and fresh and strong, as life always is, and fable never is; and the stories of The Conjure Woman have a wild, indigenous poetry, the creation of sincere and original imagination, which is imparted with a tender humorousness and a very artistic reticence. As far as his race is concerned, or his sixteenth part of a race, it does not greatly matter whether Mr. Chesnutt invented their motives, or found them, as he feigns, among his distant cousins of the Southern cabins. In either case, the wonder of their beauty is the same; and whatever is primitive and sylvan or campestral in the reader's heart is touched by the spells thrown on the simple black lives in these enchanting tales. Character, the most precious thing in fiction, is as faithfully portrayed against the poetic background as in the setting of the Stories of the Color Line.

[1]Guy de Maupassant (1850–1893), French novelist.

Yet these stories, after all, are Mr. Chesnutt's most important work, whether we consider them merely as realistic fiction, apart from their author, or as studies of that middle world of which he is naturally and voluntarily a citizen. We had known the nethermost world of the grotesque and comical negro and the terrible and tragic negro through the white observer on the outside, and black character in its lyrical moods we had known from such an inside witness as Mr. Paul Dunbar; but it had remained for Mr. Chesnutt to acquaint us with those regions where the paler shades dwell as hopelessly, with relation to ourselves, as the blackest negro. He has not shown the dwellers there as very different from ourselves. They have within their own circles the same social ambitions and prejudices; they intrigue and truckle and crawl, and are snobs, like ourselves, both of the snobs that snub and the snobs that are snubbed. We may choose to think them droll in their parody of pure white society, but perhaps it would be wiser to recognize that they are like us because they are of our blood by more than a half, or three quarters, or nine tenths. It is not, in such cases, their negro blood that characterizes them; but it is their negro blood that excludes them, and that will imaginably fortify them and exalt them. Bound in that sad solidarity from which there is no hope of entrance into polite white society for them, they may create a civilization of their own, which need not lack the highest quality. They need not be ashamed of the race from which they have sprung, and whose exile they share; for in many of the arts it has already shown, during a single generation of freedom, gifts which slavery apparently only obscured. With Mr. Booker Washington the first American orator of our time,[2] fresh upon the time of Frederick Douglass; with Mr. Dunbar among the truest of our poets; with Mr. Tanner, a black American, among the only three Americans from whom the French government ever bought a picture,[3] Mr. Chesnutt may well be willing to own his color.

But that is his personal affair. Our own more universal interest in him arises from the more than promise he has given in a department of literature where Americans hold the foremost place. In this there is, happily, no color line; and if he has it in him to go forward on the way which he has traced for himself, to be true to life as he has known it, to deny himself the glories of the cheap success which awaits the charlatan in fiction, one of the places at the top is open to him. He has sounded a fresh note, boldly, not blatantly, and he has won the ear of the more intelligent public.

1900

Editha

The air was thick with the war feeling,[1] like the electricity of a storm which has not yet burst. Editha sat looking out into the hot spring afternoon, with her lips parted, and panting with the intensity of the question whether she could let him go. She had

[2]Booker T. Washington (1856–1915), the principal of Tuskegee Institute in Alabama.

[3]Henry Ossawa Tanner (1859–1937), American painter.

[1]Howells apparently alludes to the then-recent Spanish-American War of 1898, which he opposed.

decided that she could not let him stay, when she saw him at the end of the still leafless avenue, making slowly up toward the house, with his head down, and his figure relaxed. She ran impatiently out on the veranda, to the edge of the steps, and imperatively demanded greater haste of him with her will before she called aloud to him, "George!"

He had quickened his pace in mystical response to her mystical urgence, before he could have heard her; now he looked up and answered, "Well?"

"Oh, how united we are!" she exulted, and then she swooped down the steps to him. "What is it?" she cried.

"It's war," he said, and he pulled her up to him, and kissed her.

She kissed him back intensely, but irrelevantly, as to their passion, and uttered from deep in her throat, "How glorious!"

"It's war," he repeated, without consenting to her sense of it; and she did not know just what to think at first. She never knew what to think of him; that made his mystery, his charm. All through their courtship, which was contemporaneous with the growth of the war feeling, she had been puzzled by his want of seriousness about it. He seemed to despise it even more than he abhorred it. She could have understood his abhorring any sort of bloodshed; that would have been a survival of his old life when he thought he would be a minister, and before he changed and took up the law. But making light of a cause so high and noble seemed to show a want of earnestness at the core of his being. Not but that she felt herself able to cope with a congenital defect of that sort, and make his love for her save him from himself. Now perhaps the miracle was already wrought in him. In the presence of the tremendous fact that he announced, all triviality seemed to have gone out of him; she began to feel that. He sank down on the top step, and wiped his forehead with her handkerchief, while she poured out upon him her question of the origin and authenticity of his news.

All the while, in her duplex emotioning, she was aware that now at the very beginning she must put a guard upon herself against urging him, by any word or act, to take the part that her whole soul willed him to take, for the completion of her ideal of him. He was very nearly perfect as he was, and he must be allowed to perfect himself. But he was peculiar, and he might very well be reasoned out of his peculiarity. Before her reasoning went her emotioning: her nature pulling upon his nature, her womanhood upon his manhood, without her knowing the means she was using to the end she was willing. She had always supposed that the man who won her would have done something to win her; she did not know what, but something. George Gearson had simply asked her for her love, on the way home from a concert, and she gave her love to him, without, as it were, thinking. But now, it flashed upon her, if he could do something worthy to *have* won her—be a hero, *her* hero—it would be even better than if he had done it before asking her; it would be grander. Besides, she had believed in the war from the beginning.

"But don't you see, dearest," she said, "that it wouldn't have come to this, if it hadn't been in the order of Providence? And I call any war glorious that is for the liberation of people who have been struggling for years against the cruelest oppression. Don't you think so too?"

"I suppose so," he returned, languidly. "But war! Is it glorious to break the peace of the world?"

"That ignoble peace! It was no peace at all, with that crime and shame at our very gates." She was conscious of parroting the current phrases of the newspapers, but it was no time to pick and choose her words. She must sacrifice anything to the high ideal she had for him, and after a good deal of rapid argument she ended with the climax: "But now it doesn't matter about the how or why. Since the war has come, all that is gone. There are no two sides, any more. There is nothing now but our country."

He sat with his eyes closed and his head leant back against the veranda, and he said with a vague smile, as if musing aloud, "Our country—right or wrong."

"Yes, right or wrong!" she returned fervidly. "I'll go and get you some lemonade." She rose rustling, and whisked away; when she came back with two tall glasses of clouded liquid, on a tray, and the ice clucking in them, he still sat as she left him, and she said as if there had been no interruption: "But there is no question of wrong in this case. I call it a sacred war. A war for liberty, and humanity, if ever there was one. And I know you will see it just as I do, yet."

He took half the lemonade at a gulp, and he answered as he set the glass down: "I know you always have the highest ideal. When I differ from you, I ought to doubt myself."

A generous sob rose in Editha's throat for the humility of a man, so very nearly perfect, who was willing to put himself below her.

Besides, she felt, more subliminally, that he was never so near slipping through her fingers as when he took that meek way.

"You shall not say that! Only, for once I happen to be right." She seized his hand in her two hands, and poured her soul from her eyes into his. "Don't you think so?" she entreated him.

He released his hand and drank the rest of his lemonade, and she added, "Have mine, too," but he shook his head in answering, "I've no business to think so, unless I act so, too."

Her heart stopped a beat before it pulsed on with leaps that she felt in her neck. She had noticed that strange thing in men; they seemed to feel bound to do what they believed, and not think a thing was finished when they said it, as girls did. She knew what was in his mind, but she pretended not, and she said, "Oh, I am not sure," and then faltered.

He went on as if to himself without apparently heeding her, "There's only one way of proving one's faith in a thing like this."

She could not say that she understood, but she did understand.

He went on again. "If I believed—if I felt as you do about this war—Do you wish me to feel as you do?"

Now she was really not sure; so she said, "George, I don't know what you mean."

He seemed to muse away from her as before. "There is a sort of fascination in it. I suppose that at the bottom of his heart every man would like at times to have his courage tested; to see how he would act."

"How can you talk in that ghastly way!"

"It *is* rather morbid. Still, that's what it comes to, unless you're swept away by ambition, or driven by conviction. I haven't the conviction or the ambition, and the other thing is what it comes to with me. I ought to have been a preacher, after all;

then I couldn't have asked it of myself, as I must, now I'm a lawyer. And you believe it's a holy war, Editha?" he suddenly addressed her. "Or, I know you do! But you wish me to believe so, too?"

She hardly knew whether he was mocking or not, in the ironical way he always had with her plainer mind. But the only thing was to be outspoken with him.

"George, I wish you to believe whatever you think is true, at any and every cost. If I've tried to talk you into anything, I take it all back."

"Oh, I know that, Editha. I know how sincere you are, and how—I wish I had your undoubting spirit! I'll think it over; I'd like to believe as you do. But I don't, now; I don't, indeed. It isn't this war alone; though this seems peculiarly wanton and needless; but it's every war—so stupid; it makes me sick. Why shouldn't this thing have been settled reasonably?"

"Because," she said, very throatily again, "God meant it to be war."

"You think it was God? Yes, I suppose that is what people will say."

"Do you suppose it would have been war if God hadn't meant it?"

"I don't know. Sometimes it seems as if God had put this world into men's keeping to work it as they pleased."

"Now, George, that is blasphemy."

"Well, I won't blaspheme. I'll try to believe in your pocket Providence," he said, and then he rose to go.

"Why don't you stay to dinner?" Dinner at Balcom's Works was at one o'clock.

"I'll come back to supper, if you'll let me. Perhaps I shall bring you a convert."

"Well, you may come back, on that condition."

"All right. If I don't come, you'll understand."

He went away without kissing her, and she felt it a suspension of their engagement. It all interested her intensely; she was undergoing a tremendous experience, and she was being equal to it. While she stood looking after him, her mother came out through one of the long windows, on to the veranda, with a catlike softness and vagueness.

"Why didn't he stay to dinner?"

"Because—because—war has been declared," Editha pronounced, without turning.

Her mother said, "Oh, my!" and then said nothing more until she had sat down in one of the large Shaker chairs, and rocked herself for some time. Then she closed whatever tacit passage of thought there had been in her mind with the spoken words, "Well, I hope *he* won't go."

"And *I* hope he *will,*" the girl said, and confronted her mother with a stormy exaltation that would have frightened any creature less unimpressionable than a cat.

Her mother rocked herself again for an interval of cogitation. What she arrived at in speech was, "Well, I guess you've done a wicked thing, Editha Balcom."

The girl said, as she passed indoors through the same window her mother had come out by, "I haven't done anything—yet."

In her room, she put together all her letters and gifts from Gearson, down to the withered petals of the first flower he had offered, with that timidity of his veiled in that irony of his. In the heart of the packet she enshrined her engagement ring which she had restored to the pretty box he had brought it her in. Then she sat down, if not calmly yet strongly, and wrote:

"George: I understood—when you left me. But I think we had better emphasize your meaning that if we cannot be one in everything we had better be one in nothing. So I am sending these things for your keeping till you have made up your mind.

"I shall always love you, and therefore I shall never marry any one else. But the man I marry must love his country first of all, and be able to say to me,

> 'I could not love thee, dear, so much,
> Loved I not honor more,'[2]

"There is no honor above America with me. In this great hour there is no other honor.

"Your heart will make my words clear to you. I had never expected to say so much, but it has come upon me that I must say the utmost.

Editha."

She thought she had worded her letter well, worded it in a way that could not be bettered; all had been implied and nothing expressed.

She had it ready to send with the packet she had tied with red, white, and blue ribbon, when it occurred to her that she was not just to him, that she was not giving him a fair chance. He had said he would go and think it over, and she was not waiting. She was pushing, threatening, compelling. That was not a woman's part. She must have him free, free, free. She could not accept for her country or herself a forced sacrifice.

In writing her letter she had satisfied the impulse from which it sprang; she could well afford to wait till he had thought it over. She put the packet and the letter by, and rested serene in the consciousness of having done what was laid upon her by her love itself to do, and yet used patience, mercy, justice.

She had her reward. Gearson did not come to tea, but she had given him till morning, when, late at night there came up from the village the sound of a fife and drum with a tumult of voices, in shouting, singing, and laughing. The noise drew nearer and nearer; it reached the street end of the avenue; there it silenced itself, and one voice, the voice she knew best, rose over the silence. It fell; the air was filled with cheers; the fife and drum struck up, with the shouting, singing, and laughing again, but now retreating; and a single figure came hurrying up the avenue.

She ran down to meet her lover and clung to him. He was very gay, and he put his arm round her with a boisterous laugh. "Well, you must call me Captain, now; or Cap, if you prefer; that's what the boys call me. Yes, we've had a meeting at the town hall, and everybody has volunteered; and they selected me for captain, and I'm going to the war, the big war, the glorious war, the holy war ordained by the pocket Providence that blesses butchery. Come along; let's tell the whole family about it. Call them from their downy beds, father, mother, Aunt Hitty, and all the folks!"

[2]Editha cites the final lines of "To Lucasta, Going to the Wars," by Richard Lovelace (1618–1658).

But when they mounted the veranda steps he did not wait for a larger audience; he poured the story out upon Editha alone.

"There was a lot of speaking, and then some of the fools set up a shout for me. It was all going one way, and I thought it would be a good joke to sprinkle a little cold water on them. But you can't do that with a crowd that adores you. The first thing I knew I was sprinkling hell-fire on them. 'Cry havoc, and let slip the dogs of war.'[3] That was the style. Now that it had come to the fight, there were no two parties; there was one country, and the thing was to fight the fight to a finish as quick as possible. I suggested volunteering then and there, and I wrote my name first of all on the roster. Then they elected me—that's all. I wish I had some ice-water!"

She left him walking up and down the veranda, while she ran for the ice-pitcher and a goblet, and when she came back he was still walking up and down, shouting the story he had told her to her father and mother, who had come out more sketchily dressed than they commonly were by day. He drank goblet after goblet of the ice-water without noticing who was giving it, and kept on talking, and laughing through his talk wildly. "It's astonishing," he said, "how well the worse reason looks when you try to make it appear the better. Why, I believe I was the first convert to the war in that crowd to-night! I never thought I should like to kill a man; but now, I shouldn't care; and the smokeless powder lets you see the man drop that you kill. It's all for the country! What a thing it is to have a country that *can't* be wrong, but if it is, is right anyway!"

Editha had a great, vital thought, an inspiration. She set down the ice-pitcher on the veranda floor, and ran up-stairs and got the letter she had written him. When at last he noisily bade her father and mother, "Well, good night. I forgot I woke you up; I sha'n't want any sleep myself," she followed him down the avenue to the gate. There, after the whirling words that seemed to fly away from her thoughts and refuse to serve them, she made a last effort to solemnize the moment that seemed so crazy, and pressed the letter she had written upon him.

"What's this?" he said, "Want me to mail it?"

"No, no. It's for you. I wrote it after you went this morning. Keep it—keep it—and read it sometime—" She thought, and then her inspiration came: "Read it if ever you doubt what you've done, or fear that I regret your having done it. Read it after you've started."

They strained each other in embraces that seemed as ineffective as their words, and he kissed her face with quick, hot breaths that were so unlike him, that made her feel as if she had lost her old lover and found a stranger in his place. The stranger said, "What a gorgeous flower you are, with your red hair, and your blue eyes that look black now, and your face with the color painted out by the white moonshine! Let me hold you under my chin, to see whether I love blood, you tiger-lily!" Then he laughed Gearson's laugh, and released her, scared and giddy. Within her willfulness she had been frightened by a sense of subtler force in him, and mystically mastered as she had never been before.

She ran all the way back to the house, and mounted the steps panting. Her

[3]George quotes Mark Anton in Shakespeare's *Julius Caesar,* act 2, scene 1, line 273.

mother and father were talking of the great affair. Her mother said: "Wa'n't Mr. Gearson in rather of an excited state of mind? Didn't you think he acted curious?"

"Well, not for a man who'd just been elected captain and had to set'em up for the whole of Company A," her father chuckled back.

"What in the world do you mean, Mr. Balcom? Oh! There's Editha!" She offered to follow the girl indoors.

"Don't come, mother!" Editha called, vanishing.

Mrs. Balcom remained to reproach her husband. "I don't see much of anything to laugh at."

"Well, it's catching. Caught it from Gearson. I guess it won't be much of a war, and I guess Gearson don't think so, either. The other fellows will back down as soon as they see we mean it. I wouldn't lose any sleep over it. I'm going back to bed, myself."

Gearson came again next afternoon, looking pale, and rather sick, but quite himself, even to his languid irony. "I guess I'd better tell you, Editha, that I consecrated myself to your god of battles last night by pouring too many libations to him down my own throat. But I'm all right, now. One has to carry off the excitement, somehow."

"Promise me," she commanded, "that you'll never touch it again!"

"What! Not let the cannikin clink? Not let the soldier drink? Well, I promise."

"You don't belong to yourself now; you don't even belong to *me*. You belong to your country, and you have a sacred charge to keep yourself strong and well for your country's sake. I have been thinking, thinking all night and all day long."

"You look as if you had been crying a little, too," he said with his queer smile.

"That's all past. I've been thinking, and worshipping *you*. Don't you suppose I know all that you've been through, to come to this? I've followed you every step from your old theories and opinions."

"Well, you've had a long row to hoe."

"And I know you've done this from the highest motives—"

"Oh, there won't be much pettifogging to do till this cruel war is—"

"And you haven't simply done it for my sake. I couldn't respect you if you had."

"Well, then we'll say I haven't. A man that hasn't got his own respect intact wants the respect of all the other people he can corner. But we won't go into that. I'm in for the thing now, and we've got to face our future. My idea is that this isn't going to be a very protracted struggle; we shall just scare the enemy to death before it comes to a fight at all. But we must provide for contingencies, Editha. If anything happens to me—"

"Oh, George!" She clung to him sobbing.

"I don't want you to feel foolishly bound to my memory. I should hate that, wherever I happened to be."

"I am yours, for time and eternity—time and eternity." She liked the words; they satisfied her famine for phrases.

"Well, say eternity; that's all right; but time's another thing; and I'm talking about time. But there is something! My mother! If anything happens—"

She winced, and he laughed. "You're not the bold soldier-girl of yesterday!" Then he sobered. "If anything happens, I want you to help my mother out. She won't like my doing this thing. She brought me up to think war a fool thing as well as a bad thing. My father was in the civil war; all through it; lost his arm in it." She thrilled with the sense of the arm round her; what if that should be lost? He laughed as if divining her: "Oh, it doesn't run in the family, as far as a I know!" Then he added, gravely, "He came home with misgivings about war, and they grew on him. I guess he and mother agreed between them that I was to be brought up in his final mind about it; but that was before my time. I only knew him from my mother's report of him and his opinions; I don't know whether they were hers first; but they were hers last. This will be a blow to her. I shall have to write and tell her—"

He stopped, and she asked, "Would you like me to write too, George?"

"I don't believe that would do. No, I'll do the writing. She'll understand a little if I say that I thought the way to minimize it was to make war on the largest possible scale at once—that I felt I must have been helping on the war somehow if I hadn't helped keep it from coming, and I knew I hadn't; when it came, I had no right to stay out of it."

Whether his sophistries satisfied him or not, they satisfied her. She clung to his breast, and whispered, with closed eyes and quivering lips, "Yes, yes, yes!"

"But if anything should happen, you might go to her, and see what you could do for her. You know? It's rather far off; she can't leave her chair—"

"Oh, I'll go, if it's the ends of the earth! But nothing will happen! Nothing *can!* I—"

She felt herself lifted with his rising, and Gearson was saying, with his arm still round her, to her father: "Well, we're off at once, Mr. Balcom. We're to be formally accepted at the capital, and then bunched up with the rest somehow, and sent into camp somewhere, and got to the front as soon as possible. We all want to be in the van, of course; we're the first company to report to the Governor. I came to tell Editha, but I hadn't got round to it."

She saw him again for a moment at the capital, in the station, just before the train started southward with his regiment. He looked well, in his uniform, and very soldierly, but somehow girlish, too, with his clean-shaven face and slim figure. The manly eyes and the strong voice satisfied her, and his preoccupation with some unexpected details of duty flattered her. Other girls were weeping and bemoaning themselves, but she felt a sort of noble distinction in the abstraction, the almost unconsciousness, with which they parted. Only at the last moment he said, "Don't forget my mother. It mayn't be such a walk-over as I supposed," and he laughed at the notion.

He waved his hand to her, as the train moved off—she knew it among a score of hands that were waved to other girls from the platform of the car, for it held a letter which she knew was hers. Then he went inside the car to read it, doubtless, and she did not see him again. But she felt safe for him through the strength of what she called her love. What she called her God, always speaking the name in a deep voice and with the implication of a mutual understanding, would watch over him and keep him and bring him back to her. If with an empty sleeve, then he should have three arms instead of two, for both of hers should be his for life. She did not see, though, why she should always be thinking of the arm his father had lost.

There were not many letters from him, but they were such as she could have wished, and she put her whole strength into making hers such as she imagined he could have wished, glorifying and supporting him. She wrote to his mother glorifying him as their hero, but the brief answer she got was merely to the effect that Mrs. Gearson was not well enough to write herself, and thanking her for her letter by the hand of some one who called herself "Yrs truly, Mrs. W.J. Andrews."

Editha determined not to be hurt, but to write again quite as if the answer had been all she expected. But before it seemed as if she could have written, there came news of the first skirmish, and in the list of the killed which was telegraphed as a trifling loss on our side, was Gearson's name. There was a frantic time of trying to make out that it might be, must be, some other Gearson; but the name, and the company and the regiment, and the State were too definitely given.

Then there was a lapse into depths out of which it seemed as if she never could rise again; then a lift into clouds far above all grief, black clouds, that blotted out the sun, but where she soared with him, with George, George! She had the fever that she expected of herself, but she did not die in it; she was not even delirious, and it did not last long. When she was well enough to leave her bed, her one thought was of George's mother, of his strangely worded wish that she should go to her and see what she could do for her. In the exaltation of the duty laid upon her—it buoyed her up instead of burdening her—she rapidly recovered.

Her father went with her on the long railroad journey from northern New York to western Iowa; he had business out at Davenport, and he said he could just as well go then as any other time; and he went with her to the little country town where George's mother lived in a little house on the edge of illimitable corn-fields, under trees pushed to a top of the rolling prairie. George's father had settled there after the civil war, as so many other old soldiers had done; but they were Eastern people, and Editha fancied touches of the East in the June rose overhanging the front door, and the garden with early summer flowers stretching from the gate of the paling fence.

It was very low inside the house, and so dim, with the closed blinds, that they could scarcely see one another: Editha tall and black in her crapes which filled the air with the smell of their dyes; her father standing decorously apart with his hat on his forearm, as at funerals; a woman rested in a deep armchair, and the woman who had let the strangers in stood behind the chair.

The seated woman turned her head round and up, and asked the woman behind her chair, "*Who* did you say?"

Editha, if she had done what she expected of herself, would have gone down on her knees at the feet of the seated figure and said, "I am George's Editha," for answer.

But instead of her own voice she heard that other woman's voice, saying, "Well, I don't know as I *did* get the name just right. I guess I'll have to make a little more light in here," and she went and pushed two of the shutters ajar.

Then Editha's father said in his public will-now-address-a-few-remarks tone, "My name is Balcom, ma'am; Junius H. Balcom, of Balcom's Works, New York; my daughter—"

"Oh!" The seated woman broke in, with a powerful voice, the voice that always surprised Editha from Gearson's slender frame. "Let me see you! Stand round where the light can strike on your face," and Editha dumbly obeyed. "So, you're Editha Balcom," she sighed.

"Yes," Editha said, more like a culprit than a comforter.

"What did you come for?" Mrs. Gearson asked.

Editha's face quivered, and her knees shook. "I came—because—because George—" She could go no farther.

"Yes," the mother said, "he told me he had asked you to come if he got killed. You didn't expect that, I suppose, when you sent him."

"I would rather have died myself than done it!" Editha said with more truth in her deep voice than she ordinarily found in it. "I tried to leave him free—"

"Yes, that letter of yours, that came back with his other things, left him free."

Editha saw now where George's irony came from.

"It was not to be read before—unless—until—I told him so," she faltered.

"Of course, he wouldn't read a letter of yours, under the circumstances, till he thought you wanted him to. Been sick?" the woman abruptly demanded.

"Very sick," Editha said, with self-pity.

"Daughter's life," her father interposed, "was almost despaired of, at one time."

Mrs. Gearson gave him no heed. "I suppose you would have been glad to die, such a brave person as you! I don't believe *he* was glad to die. He was always a timid boy, that way; he was afraid of a good many things; but if he was afraid he did what he made up his mind to. I suppose he made up his mind to go, but I knew what it cost him, by what it cost me when I heard of it. I had been through *one* war before. When you sent him you didn't expect he would get killed?"

The voice seemed to compassionate Editha, and it was time. "No," she huskily murmured.

"No, girls don't; women don't, when they give their men up to their country. They think they'll come marching back, somehow, just as gay as they went, or if it's an empty sleeve, or even an empty pantaloon, it's all the more glory, and they're so much the prouder of them, poor things."

The tears began to run down Editha's face; she had not wept till then; but it was now such a relief to be understood that the tears came.

"No, you didn't expect him to get killed," Mrs. Gearson repeated in a voice which was startlingly like Gearson's again. "You just expected him to kill some one else, some of those foreigners, that weren't there because they had any say about it, but because they had to be there, poor wretches—conscripts, or whatever they call 'em. You thought it would be all right for my George, *your* George, to kill the sons of those miserable mothers and the husbands of those girls that you would never see the faces of." The woman lifted her powerful voice in a psalmlike note. "I thank my God he didn't live to do it! I thank my God they killed him first, and that he ain't livin' with their blood on his hands!" She dropped her eyes which she had raised with her voice, and glared at Editha. "What you got that black on for?" She lifted herself by her powerful arms so high that her helpless body seemed to hang limp its full length. "Take it off, take it off, before I tear it from your back!"

The lady who was passing the summer near Balcom's Works was sketching Editha's beauty, which lent itself wonderfully to the effects of a colorist. It had come to that confidence which is rather apt to grow between artist and sitter, and Editha had told her everything.

"To think of your having such a tragedy in your life!" the lady said. She added:

"I suppose there are people who feel that way about war. But when you consider the good this war had done—how much it has done for the country! I can't understand such people, for my part. And when you had come all the way out there to console her—got up out of a sick bed! Well!"

"I think," Editha said, magnanimously, "she wasn't quite in her right mind; and so did papa."

"Yes," the lady said, looking at Editha's lips in nature and then at her lips in art, and giving an empirical touch to them in the picture. "But how dreadful of her! How perfectly—excuse me—how *vulgar!*"

A light broke upon Editha in the darkness which she felt had been without a gleam of brightness for weeks and months. The mystery that had bewildered her was solved by the word; and from that moment she rose from grovelling in shame and self-pity, and began to live again in the ideal.

1905

Henry James 1843–1916

With his lifelong productivity, his saturation in the world of contemporary fiction, including his knowledge of British and French literature, his attentiveness to style and technique, his rejection of America in favor of the Old World, and his coolness toward democratic aspirations and reforms, Henry James stands alone among nineteenth-century United States writers. The first writer in English to see the high artistic potential of the novel as a form, he was also the first to produce a distinguished body of critical analysis of fiction—his own as well as others'. His fiction has attracted many sophisticated readers, who generally regard him as a master craftsman and renowned critic of American culture; but his work has also attracted negative comment because of its distance from common life. His best work, which includes *Daisy Miller* and "The Beast in the Jungle," offers shrewd insights into human psychology, including a penetrating interrogation of his own aloofness.

Born in New York City, James was named after his father, an independently wealthy thinker who obsessively devised and promoted his own theological system. James, Sr. emphasized the role of suffering, submission, and rebirth in human life, and he insisted on a conservative view of marriage and the difference between the sexes. "Woman," he preached, was not truly a person but a "form of personal affection," and her mission was to redeem man from his natural egotism and brutality. His self-effacing wife, Mary, devoted herself to him and to their five children. According to most reports, the Jameses enjoyed extremely close and intense relationships among themselves. But their family life also had an oppressive aspect, and although Henry, Jr. wrote about it with great affection, he eventually moved to England partly to escape it.

James's two younger brothers fought in the Union Army, one of them participating in the charge on Fort Wagner, South Carolina, that inspired Robert Lowell's great poem "For the Union Dead." His one sister, Alice, though gifted, was incapacitated by depression and rage, partly because of the restrictions imposed on her as a woman. William, the eldest son, bright, aggressive, and adventurous, had an extraordinary influence on Henry, who tried throughout boyhood to catch up with him. William became a pioneering psychologist and the world-renowned philosopher of pragmatism.

The Jameses were educated by a series of governesses and tutors and in private and public schools in America and Europe. As a boy, Henry was fascinated by the European spectacle, especially by the obvious distinctions between social classes and the display of leisurely aristocratic civilization. The most valuable part of his education came from the fiction writers, esteemed as well as popular, he devoured on his own—Hawthorne, Balzac, George Sand, Turgenev, George Eliot, and many others. Later, a professional writer himself, he often rewrote what he'd read. Biographer Leon Edel has shown that when James wrote his famous ghost story, "The Turn of the Screw," he made use of a sensational novel first serialized when he was eleven. In writing *The Portrait of a Lady* he reworked a story-line common in women's novels of the 1860s and 1870s, the story of the independent-minded heroine who enters a marriage that proves unbearable. But James's resolution of the heroine's predicament was founded less on fictional models than on his father's conservative theories of women and marriage.

It was by writing for the major American magazines of his day, in his early twenties, that James got started in his career. When he was twenty-six he crossed the Atlantic for a fifteen-month sojourn in England, Switzerland, and Italy. This, his first independent foray away from home, resulted in "A Passionate Pilgrim" (1871), his best story until then. Like the later "Madame de Mauves" (1874), the story tells of an American abroad burdened by an enraptured but deceptive vision of the European past. In 1875, at thirty-two, James permanently moved to the Old World and in the next few years wrote a number of moderately realistic novels that contrast the American and European social orders—*Roderick Hudson* (1875), *The American* (1877), and *The Portrait of a Lady* (1881). The American protagonists of these works are noble, intrepid, and full of dangerous illusions about the complex European order. James concentrated on the international scene to get at the peculiarities of American character, to design spectacular moral dramas involving the innocent and the experienced.

James's realistic period ran from about 1875 to 1889. During this time, James, who was a prolific and innovative essayist on the subject of the novel itself, wrote one of his best essays, "The Art of Fiction" (1884). In this piece, he treats the novel as an art form worthy of serious discussion and criticism. Speaking from his position as an active practitioner, he focuses on problems of craft and execution. As a realist writer, James claims that "the only reason for the existence of a novel is that it does attempt to represent life." In this way, he conceives of the novelist's undertaking as similar to that of the historian. Beyond the requirements that a writer proceed from a working idea, his or her donnée, and that the novel "be interesting," he dismisses any notion of a set of rules necessary for successful writing. In his estimation, rules impede the novelist's imagination. A fine example of James's theory at work is *Daisy Miller: A Study,* a short novel about an expatriate's effort to understand and deal with a charming, independent, but uninformed heroine who poses a strong challenge to conservative manners. In the end, the story's emphasis is not so much on social portraiture as on the tragic effects of class distinction.

James wrote few novels set in the United States. One, *Washington Square* (1880), tells of a stolid young woman's victimization by a tyrannical father and an opportunistic lover. Like James's best work of this period, this short novel combines social realism with psychological exploration of a set of oppressive relationships. *The Bostonians* (1886), an ambitious novel with a substantial set of characters, represents what James saw as the conflicting commercial and idealistic strains of postbellum American society. His focus was on the lives of contemporary women—on the movement to grant women the vote and even more on the supposed decline of gender differences and sexual attraction. Writing with insight, condescension, and hostility, James set forth a conservative, biting critique of democratic culture.

In the 1890s, with demand for his fiction declining, James unsuccessfully tried his hand at writing popular, money-making plays for the British stage. During the final years of the century he produced a series of difficult fictions unlike anything previously written—*The Spoils of Poynton* (1897), *What Maisie Knew* (1897), *The Turn of the Screw* (1898), and *The Awkward Age* (1899). His protagonists in these works were females, often immature, and their lives entailed deep difficulties and frustrations and a conspicuous element of sexual innuendo. *What Maisie Knew,* the best of these works, tells of a young girl who is neglected by most of the adult world beginning with her divorced parents. But the narrative focuses less on her victimization than on her resistance, her passionate effort to understand the queer adult order and to operate in it.

Leon Edel has argued that in novels like *Maisie,* James was privately reworking his own traumas and that this labor made possible his formidably polished late novels—*The Wings of the Dove* (1902), *The Ambassadors* (1903), and *The Golden Bowl* (1904). Like the international novels James had written in his first maturity, these introduced a rather innocent American hero or heroine into a circle of cosmopolitans. But in these later works, there was no question of social realism. Instead, James deployed a labyrinthine style, the artful use of imagery and symbolism, and systematically restricted points of view in order to focus with hypnotic concentration on what had been his essential subject all along—the struggle to make sense of ambiguous and corrupting social situations. For many readers these late James novels constitute formal literary perfection, the kind of art that shows supreme stylistic discrimination and structural control. For others they seem too remote from human life.

"The Beast in the Jungle" (1903) may well represent James's late manner at its best. Like the much earlier *Daisy Miller* it tells of love frustrated by a certain masculine aloofness. The cold reserve each work looks at so critically may, indeed, be the author's own coldness—in which case that coldness produced its greatest writing precisely by criticizing itself.

Alfred Habegger

PRIMARY WORKS

The Novels and Tales of Henry James (New York Edition), 26 vols., 1907–1917; Magbool Aziz, *The Tales of Henry James,* 8 vols. (projected), 1973–; Leon Edel and Mark Wilson, eds., *Literary Criticism,* 2 vols., 1984; Leon Edel and Lyall H. Powers, eds., *The Complete Notebooks of Henry James,* 1987; David Bromwich and John Hollander, eds., *Complete Stories 1892–1898,* 1996; Ignas K. Skrupskelis and Elizabeth M. Berkeley, eds., *William and Henry James: Selected Letters,* 1997.

Daisy Miller: A Study

I

At the little town of Vevey, in Switzerland, there is a particularly comfortable hotel. There are, indeed, many hotels; for the entertainment of tourists is the business of the place, which, as many travellers will remember, is seated upon the edge of a remarkably blue lake—a lake that it behoves every tourist to visit. The shore of the lake presents an unbroken array of establishments of this order, of every category, from the "grand hotel" of the newest fashion, with a chalk-white front, a hundred balconies, and a dozen flags flying from its roof, to the little Swiss *pension*[1] of an elder day, with its name inscribed in German-looking lettering upon a pink or yellow wall, and an awkward summer-house in the angle of the garden. One of the hotels at Vevey, however, is famous, even classical, being distinguished from many of its upstart neighbours by an air both of luxury and of maturity. In this region, in the month of June, American travellers are extremely numerous; it may be said, indeed, that Vevey assumes at this period some of the characteristics of an American watering-place. There are sights and sounds which evoke a vision, an echo, of Newport and Saratoga.[2] There is a flitting hither and thither of "stylish" young girls, a rustling of muslin flounces, a rattle of dance-music in the morning hours, a sound of high-pitched voices at all times. You receive an impression of these things at the excellent inn of the "Trois Couronnes,"[3] and are transported in fancy to the Ocean House or to Congress Hall.[4] But at the "Trois Couronnes," it must be added, there are other features that are much at variance with these suggestions: neat German waiters, who look like secretaries of legation; Russian princesses sitting in the garden; little Polish boys walking about, held by the hand, with their governors; a view of the snowy crest of the Dent du Midi[5] and the picturesque towers of the Castle of Chillon.

I hardly know whether it was the analogies or the differences that were uppermost in the mind of a young American, who, two or three years ago, sat in the garden of the "Trois Couronnes," looking about him, rather idly, at some of the graceful objects I have mentioned. It was a beautiful summer morning, and in whatever fashion the young American looked at things, they must have seemed to him charming. He had come from Geneva the day before, by the little steamer, to see his aunt, who was staying at the hotel—Geneva having been for a long time his place of residence. But his aunt had a headache—his aunt had almost always a headache—and now she was shut up in her room, smelling camphor, so that he was at liberty to wander about. He was some seven-and-twenty years of age; when his friends spoke of him, they usually said that he was at Geneva, "studying." When his enemies spoke of him they said—but, after all, he had no enemies; he was an extremely amiable fellow, and universally liked. What I should say is, simply, that when cer-

[1]European boarding-house.
[2]Upper-class resort towns in Rhode Island and New York respectively.
[3]French: "Three Crowns."
[4]Hotels in Newport and Saratoga.
[5]Swiss mountain peak visible from Vevey.

tain persons spoke of him they affirmed that the reason of his spending so much time at Geneva was that he was extremely devoted to a lady who lived there—a foreign lady—a person older than himself. Very few Americans—indeed I think none—had ever seen this lady, about whom there were some singular stories. But Winterbourne had an old attachment for the little metropolis of Calvinism; he had been put to school there as a boy, and he had afterwards gone to college there—circumstances which had led to his forming a great many youthful friendships. Many of these he had kept, and they were a source of great satisfaction to him.

After knocking at his aunt's door and learning that she was indisposed, he had taken a walk about the town, and then he had come in to his breakfast. He had now finished his breakfast; but he was drinking a small cup of coffee, which had been served to him on a little table in the garden by one of the waiters who looked like an *attaché*.[6] At last he finished his coffee and lit a cigarette. Presently a small boy came walking along the path—an urchin of nine or ten. The child, who was diminutive for his years, had an aged expression of countenance, a pale complexion, and sharp little features. He was dressed in knickerbockers, with red stockings, which displayed his poor little spindleshanks; he also wore a brilliant red cravat. He carried in his hand a long alpenstock, the sharp point of which he thrust into everything that he approached—the flower-beds, the garden-benches, the trains of the ladies' dresses. In front of Winterbourne he paused, looking at him with a pair of bright, penetrating little eyes.

"Will you give me a lump of sugar?" he asked, in a sharp, hard little voice—a voice immature, and yet, somehow, not young.

Winterbourne glanced at the small table near him, on which his coffee-service rested, and saw that several morsels of sugar remained. "Yes, you may take one," he answered; "but I don't think sugar is good for little boys."

This little boy stepped forward and carefully selected three of the coveted fragments, two of which he buried in the pocket of his knickerbockers, depositing the other as promptly in another place. He poked his alpenstock, lance-fashion, into Winterbourne's bench, and tried to crack the lump of sugar with his teeth.

"Oh, blazes; it's har-r-d!" he exclaimed, pronouncing the adjective in a peculiar manner.

Winterbourne had immediately perceived that he might have the honour of claiming him as a fellow-countryman. "Take care you don't hurt your teeth," he said, paternally.

"I haven't got any teeth to hurt. They have all come out. I have only got seven teeth. My mother counted them last night, and one came out right afterwards. She said she'd slap me if any more came out. I can't help it. It's this old Europe. It's the climate that makes them come out. In America they didn't come out. It's these hotels."

Winterbourne was much amused. "If you eat three lumps of sugar, your mother will certainly slap you," he said.

[6]Member of a diplomatic staff.

"She's got to give me some candy, then," rejoined his young interlocutor. "I can't get any candy here—any American candy. American candy's the best candy."

"And are American little boys the best little boys?" asked Winterbourne.

"I don't know. I'm an American boy," said the child.

"I see you are one of the best!" laughed Winterbourne.

"Are you an American man?" pursued this vivacious infant. And then, on Winterbourne's affirmative reply—"American men are the best," he declared.

His companion thanked him for the compliment; and the child, who had now got astride of his alpenstock, stood looking about him, while he attacked a second lump of sugar. Winterbourne wondered if he himself had been like this in his infancy, for he had been brought to Europe at about this age.

"Here comes my sister!" cried the child, in a moment. "She's an American girl."

Winterbourne looked along the path and saw a beautiful young lady advancing. "American girls are the best girls," he said, cheerfully, to his young companion.

"My sister ain't the best!" the child declared. "She's always blowing at me."

"I imagine that is your fault, not hers," said Winterbourne. The young lady meanwhile had drawn near. She was dressed in white muslin, with a hundred frills and flounces, and knots of pale-coloured ribbon. She was bare-headed; but she balanced in her hand a large parasol, with a deep border of embroidery; and she was strikingly, admirably pretty. "How pretty they are!" thought Winterbourne, straightening himself in his seat, as if he were prepared to rise.

The young lady paused in front of his bench, near the parapet of the garden, which overlooked the lake. The little boy had now converted his alpenstock into a vaulting-pole, by the aid of which he was springing about in the gravel, and kicking it up not a little.

"Randolph," said the young lady, "what *are* you doing?"

"I'm going up the Alps," replied Randolph. "This is the way!" And he gave another little jump, scattering the pebbles about Winterbourne's ears.

"That's the way they come down," said Winterbourne.

"He's an American man!" cried Randolph, in his little hard voice.

The young lady gave no heed to this announcement, but looked straight at her brother. "Well, I guess you had better be quiet," she simply observed.

It seemed to Winterbourne that he had been in a manner presented. He got up and stepped slowly towards the young girl, throwing away his cigarette. "This little boy and I have made acquaintance," he said, with great civility. In Geneva, as he had been perfectly aware, a young man was not at liberty to speak to a young unmarried lady except under certain rarely-occurring conditions; but here at Vevey, what conditions could be better than these?—a pretty American girl coming and standing in front of you in a garden. This pretty American girl, however, on hearing Winterbourne's observation, simply glanced at him; she then turned her head and looked over the parapet, at the lake and the opposite mountains. He wondered whether he had gone too far; but he decided that he must advance farther, rather than retreat. While he was thinking of something else to say, the young lady turned to the little boy again.

"I should like to know where you got that pole," she said.

"I bought it!" responded Randolph.

"You don't mean to say you're going to take it to Italy."

"Yes, I am going to take it to Italy!" the child declared.

The young girl glanced over the front of her dress, and smoothed out a knot or two of ribbon. Then she rested her eyes upon the prospect again. "Well, I guess you had better leave it somewhere," she said, after a moment.

"Are you going to Italy?" Winterbourne inquired, in a tone of great respect.

The young lady glanced at him again. "Yes, sir," she replied. And she said nothing more.

"Are you—a—going over the Simplon?"[7] Winterbourne pursued, a little embarrassed.

"I don't know," she said. "I suppose it's some mountain. Randolph, what mountain are we going over?"

"Going where?" the child demanded.

"To Italy," Winterbourne explained.

"I don't know," said Randolph. "I don't want to go to Italy. I want to go to America."

"Oh, Italy is a beautiful place!" rejoined the young man.

"Can you get candy there?" Randolph loudly inquired.

"I hope not," said his sister. "I guess you have had enough candy, and mother thinks so too."

"I haven't had any for ever so long—for a hundred weeks!" cried the boy, still jumping about.

The young lady inspected her flounces and smoothed her ribbons again; and Winterbourne presently risked an observation upon the beauty of the view. He was ceasing to be embarrassed, for he had begun to perceive that she was not in the least embarrassed herself. There had not been the slightest alteration in her charming complexion; she was evidently neither offended nor fluttered. If she looked another way when he spoke to her, and seemed not particularly to hear him, this was simply her habit, her manner. Yet, as he talked a little more, and pointed out some of the objects of interest in the view, with which she appeared quite unacquainted, she gradually gave him more of the benefit of her glance; and then he saw that this glance was perfectly direct and unshrinking. It was not, however, what would have been called an immodest glance, for the young girl's eyes were singularly honest and fresh. They were wonderfully pretty eyes; and, indeed, Winterbourne had not seen for a long time anything prettier than his fair countrywoman's various features—her complexion, her nose, her ears, her teeth. He had a great relish for feminine beauty; he was addicted to observing and analysing it; and as regards this young lady's face he made several observations. It was not at all insipid, but it was not exactly expressive; and though it was eminently delicate Winterbourne mentally accused it—very forgivingly—of a want of finish. He thought it very possible that Master Randolph's sister was a coquette; he was sure she had a spirit of her own; but in her bright, sweet, superficial little visage there was no mockery, no irony. Before long it became obvious that she was much disposed towards conversation. She told him that they were going to Rome for the winter—she and her mother and Randolph. She asked him if he was a "real American;" she wouldn't have taken him for one; he seemed more like a

[7]Mountain pass between Switzerland and Italy.

German—this was said after a little hesitation, especially when he spoke. Winterbourne, laughing, answered that he had met Germans who spoke like Americans; but that he had not, so far as he remembered, met an American who spoke like a German. Then he asked her if she would not be more comfortable in sitting upon the bench which he had just quitted. She answered that she liked standing up and walking about; but she presently sat down. She told him she was from New York State—"if you know where that is." Winterbourne learned more about her by catching hold of her small, slippery brother and making him stand a few minutes by his side.

"Tell me your name, my boy," he said.

"Randolph C. Miller," said the boy, sharply. "And I'll tell you her name;" and he levelled his alpenstock at his sister.

"You had better wait till you are asked!" said this young lady, calmly.

"I should like very much to know your name," said Winterbourne.

"Her name is Daisy Miller!" cried the child. "But that isn't her real name; that isn't her name on her cards."

"It's a pity you haven't got one of my cards!" said Miss Miller.

"Her real name is Annie P. Miller," the boy went on.

"Ask him *his* name," said his sister, indicating Winterbourne.

But on this point Randolph seemed perfectly indifferent; he continued to supply information with regard to his own family. "My father's name is Ezra B. Miller," he announced. "My father ain't in Europe; my father's in a better place than Europe."

Winterbourne imagined for a moment that this was the manner in which the child had been taught to intimate that Mr. Miller had been removed to the sphere of celestial rewards. But Randolph immediately added, "My father's in Schenectady. He's got a big business. My father's rich, you bet."

"Well!" ejaculated Miss Miller, lowering her parasol and looking at the embroidered border. Winterbourne presently released the child, who departed, dragging his alpenstock along the path. "He doesn't like Europe," said the young girl. "He wants to go back."

"To Schenectady, you mean?"

"Yes; he wants to go right home. He hasn't got any boys here. There is one boy here, but he always goes round with a teacher; they won't let him play."

"And your brother hasn't any teacher?" Winterbourne inquired.

"Mother thought of getting him one, to travel round with us. There was a lady told her of a very good teacher; an American lady—perhaps you know her—Mrs. Sanders. I think she came from Boston. She told her of this teacher, and we thought of getting him to travel round with us. But Randolph said he didn't want a teacher travelling round with us. He said he wouldn't have lessons when he was in the cars. And we *are* in the cars about half the time. There was an English lady we met in the cars—I think her name was Miss Featherstone; perhaps you know her. She wanted to know why I didn't give Randolph lessons—give him "instruction," she called it. I guess he could give me more instruction than I could give him. He's very smart."

"Yes," said Winterbourne; "he seems very smart."

"Mother's going to get a teacher for him as soon as we get to Italy. Can you get good teachers in Italy?"

"Very good, I should think," said Winterbourne.

"Or else she's going to find some school. He ought to learn some more. He's only nine. He's going to college." And in this way Miss Miller continued to converse upon the affairs of her family, and upon other topics. She sat there with her extremely pretty hands, ornamented with very brilliant rings, folded in her lap, and with her pretty eyes now resting upon those of Winterbourne, now wandering over the garden, the people who passed by, and the beautiful view. She talked to Winterbourne as if she had known him a long time. He found it very pleasant. It was many years since he had heard a young girl talk so much. It might have been said of this unknown young lady, who had come and sat down beside him upon a bench, that she chattered. She was very quiet, she sat in a charming tranquil attitude; but her lips and her eyes were constantly moving. She had a soft, slender, agreeable voice, and her tone was decidedly sociable. She gave Winterbourne a history of her movements and intentions, and those of her mother and brother, in Europe, and enumerated, in particular, the various hotels at which they had stopped. "That English lady in the cars," she said—"Miss Featherstone—asked me if we didn't all live in hotels in America. I told her I had never been in so many hotels in my life as since I came to Europe. I have never seen so many—it's nothing but hotels." But Miss Miller did not make this remark with a querulous accent; she appeared to be in the best humour with everything. She declared that the hotels were very good, when once you got used to their ways, and that Europe was perfectly sweet. She was not disappointed—not a bit. Perhaps it was because she had heard so much about it before. She had ever so many intimate friends that had been there ever so many times. And then she had had ever so many dresses and things from Paris. Whenever she put on a Paris dress she felt as if she were in Europe.

"It was a kind of a wishing-cap," said Winterbourne.

"Yes," said Miss Miller, without examining this analogy; "it always made me wish I was here. But I needn't have done that for dresses. I am sure they send all the pretty ones to America; you see the most frightful things here. The only thing I don't like," she proceeded, "is the society. There isn't any society; or, if there is, I don't know where it keeps itself. Do you? I suppose there is some society somewhere, but I haven't seen anything of it. I'm very fond of society, and I have always had a great deal of it. I don't mean only in Schenectady, but in New York. I used to go to New York every winter. In New York I had lots of society. Last winter I had seventeen dinners given me; and three of them were by gentlemen," added Daisy Miller. "I have more friends in New York than in Schenectady—more gentlemen friends; and more young lady friends too," she resumed in a moment. She paused again for an instant; she was looking at Winterbourne with all her prettiness in her lively eyes and in her light, slightly monotonous smile. "I have always had," she said, "a great deal of gentlemen's society."

Poor Winterbourne was amused, perplexed, and decidedly charmed. He had never yet heard a young girl express herself in just this fashion; never, at least, save in cases where to say such things seemed a kind of demonstrative evidence of a certain laxity of deportment. And yet was he to accuse Miss Daisy Miller of actual or potential *inconduite,*[8] as they said at Geneva? He felt that he had lived at Geneva so long

[8]French: misconduct.

that he had lost a good deal; he had become dishabituated to the American tone. Never, indeed, since he had grown old enough to appreciate things, had he encountered a young American girl of so pronounced a type as this. Certainly she was very charming; but how deucedly sociable! Was she simply a pretty girl from New York State—were they all like that, the pretty girls who had a good deal of gentlemen's society? Or was she also a designing, an audacious, an unscrupulous young person? Winterbourne had lost his instinct in this matter, and his reason could not help him. Miss Daisy Miller looked extremely innocent. Some people had told him that, after all, American girls were exceedingly innocent; and others had told him that, after all, they were not. He was inclined to think Miss Daisy Miller was a flirt—a pretty American flirt. He had never, as yet, had any relations with young ladies of this category. He had known, here in Europe, two or three women—persons older than Miss Daisy Miller, and provided, for respectability's sake, with husbands—who were great coquettes—dangerous, terrible women, with whom one's relations were liable to take a serious turn. But this young girl was not a coquette in that sense; she was very unsophisticated; she was only a pretty American flirt. Winterbourne was almost grateful for having found the formula that applied to Miss Daisy Miller. He leaned back in his seat; he remarked to himself that she had the most charming nose he had ever seen; he wondered what were the regular conditions and limitations of one's intercourse with a pretty American flirt. It presently became apparent that he was on the way to learn.

"Have you been to that old castle?" asked the young girl, pointing with her parasol to the far-gleaming walls of the Château de Chillon.

"Yes, formerly, more than once," said Winterbourne. "You too, I suppose, have seen it?"

"No; we haven't been there. I want to go there dreadfully. Of course I mean to go there. I wouldn't go away from here without having seen that old castle."

"It's a very pretty excursion," said Winterbourne, "and very easy to make. You can drive, you know, or you can go by the little steamer."

"You can go in the cars,"[9] said Miss Miller.

"Yes; you can go in the cars," Winterbourne assented.

"Our courier says they take you right up to the castle," the young girl continued. "We were going last week; but my mother gave out. She suffers dreadfully from dyspepsia. She said she couldn't go. Randolph wouldn't go either; he says he doesn't think much of old castles. But I guess we'll go this week, if we can get Randolph."

"Your brother is not interested in ancient monuments?" Winterbourne inquired, smiling.

"He says he don't care much about old castles. He's only nine. He wants to stay at the hotel. Mother's afraid to leave him alone, and the courier won't stay with him; so we haven't been to many places. But it will be too bad if we don't go up there." And Miss Miller pointed again at the Château de Chillon.

"I should think it might be arranged," said Winterbourne. "Couldn't you get some one to stay—for the afternoon—with Randolph?"

[9] *I.e.,* by rail.

Miss Miller looked at him a moment; and then, very placidly—"I wish *you* would stay with him!" she said.

Winterbourne hesitated a moment. "I would much rather go to Chillon with you."

"With me?" asked the young girl, with the same placidity.

She didn't rise, blushing, as a young girl at Geneva would have done; and yet Winterbourne, conscious that he had been very bold, thought it possible she was offended. "With your mother," he answered very respectfully.

But it seemed that both his audacity and his respect were lost upon Miss Daisy Miller. "I guess my mother won't go, after all," she said. "She don't like to ride round in the afternoon. But did you really mean what you said just now; that you would like to go up there?"

"Most earnestly," Winterbourne declared.

"Then we may arrange it. If mother will stay with Randolph, I guess Eugenio will."

"Eugenio?" the young man inquired.

"Eugenio's our courier. He doesn't like to stay with Randolph; he's the most fastidious man I ever saw. But he's a splendid courier. I guess he'll stay at home with Randolph if mother does, and then we can go to the castle."

Winterbourne reflected for an instant as lucidly as possible—"we" could only mean Miss Daisy Miller and himself. This programme seemed almost too agreeable for credence; he felt as if he ought to kiss the young lady's hand. Possibly he would have done so—and quite spoiled the project; but at this moment another person—presumably Eugenio—appeared. A tall, handsome man, with superb whiskers, wearing a velvet morning-coat and a brilliant watch-chain, approached Miss Miller, looking sharply at her companion. "Oh, Eugenio!" said Miss Miller, with the friendliest accent.

Eugenio had looked at Winterbourne from head to foot; he now bowed gravely to the young lady. "I have the honour to inform mademoiselle that luncheon is upon the table."

Miss Miller slowly rose. "See here, Eugenio," she said. "I'm going to that old castle, any way."

"To the Château de Chillon, mademoiselle?" the courier inquired. "Mademoiselle has made arrangements?" he added, in a tone which struck Winterbourne as very impertinent.

Eugenio's tone apparently threw, even to Miss Miller's own apprehension, a slightly ironical light upon the young girl's situation. She turned to Winterbourne, blushing a little—a very little. "You won't back out?" she said.

"I shall not be happy till we go!" he protested.

"And you are staying in this hotel?" she went on. "And you are really an American?"

The courier stood looking at Winterbourne, offensively. The young man, at least, thought his manner of looking an offence to Miss Miller; it conveyed an imputation that she "picked up" acquaintances. "I shall have the honour of presenting to you a person who will tell you all about me," he said smiling, and referring to his aunt.

"Oh, well, we'll go some day," said Miss Miller. And she gave him a smile and turned away. She put up her parasol and walked back to the inn beside Eugenio.

Winterbourne stood looking after her; and as she moved away, drawing her muslin furbelows over the gravel, said to himself that she had the *tournure*[10] of a princess.

II

He had, however, engaged to do more than proved feasible, in promising to present his aunt, Mrs. Costello, to Miss Daisy Miller. As soon as the former lady had got better of her headache he waited upon her in her apartment; and, after the proper inquiries in regard to her health, he asked her if she had observed, in the hotel, an American family—a mamma, a daughter, and a little boy.

"And a courier?" said Mrs. Costello. "Oh, yes, I have observed them. Seen them—heard them—and kept out of their way." Mrs. Costello was a widow with a fortune; a person of much distinction, who frequently intimated that, if she were not so dreadfully liable to sick-headaches, she would probably have left a deeper impress upon her time. She had a long pale face, a high nose, and a great deal of very striking white hair, which she wore in large puffs and *rouleaux*[11] over the top of her head. She had two sons married in New York, and another who was now in Europe. This young man was amusing himself at Homburg,[12] and, though he was on his travels, was rarely perceived to visit any particular city at the moment selected by his mother for her own appearance there. Her nephew, who had come up to Vevey expressly to see her, was therefore more attentive than those who, as she said, were nearer to her. He had imbibed at Geneva the idea that one must always be attentive to one's aunt. Mrs. Costello had not seen him for many years, and she was greatly pleased with him, manifesting her approbation by initiating him into many of the secrets of that social sway which, as she gave him to understand, she exerted in the American capital. She admitted that she was very exclusive; but, if he were acquainted with New York, he would see that one had to be. And her picture of the minutely hierarchical constitution of the society of that city, which she presented to him in many different lights, was, to Winterbourne's imagination, almost oppressively striking.

He immediately perceived, from her tone, that Miss Daisy Miller's place in the social scale was low. "I am afraid you don't approve of them," he said.

"They are very common," Mrs. Costello declared. "They are the sort of Americans that one does one's duty by not—not accepting."

"Ah, you don't accept them?" said the young man.

"I can't, my dear Frederick. I would if I could, but I can't."

"The young girl is very pretty," said Winterbourne, in a moment.

"Of course she's pretty. But she is very common."

"I see what you mean, of course," said Winterbourne, after another pause.

"She has that charming look that they all have," his aunt resumed. "I can't think where they pick it up; and she dresses in perfection—no, you don't know how well she dresses. I can't think where they get their taste."

"But, my dear aunt, she is not, after all, a Comanche savage."

[10] French: figure, bearing.
[11] French: rolls.
[12] German resort famed for its curative waters and (before 1872) its casino.

"She is a young lady," said Mrs. Costello, "who has an intimacy with her mamma's courier?"

"An intimacy with the courier?" the young man demanded.

"Oh, the mother is just as bad! They treat the courier like a familiar friend—like a gentleman. I shouldn't wonder if he dines with them. Very likely they have never seen a man with such good manners, such fine clothes, so like a gentleman. He probably corresponds to the young lady's idea of a Count. He sits with them in the garden, in the evening. I think he smokes."

Winterbourne listened with interest to these disclosures; they helped him to make up his mind about Miss Daisy. Evidently she was rather wild. "Well," he said, "I am not a courier, and yet she was very charming to me."

"You had better have said at first," said Mrs. Costello with dignity, "that you had made her acquaintance."

"We simply met in the garden, and we talked a bit."

"*Tout bonnement!*[13] And pray what did you say?"

"I said I should take the liberty of introducing her to my admirable aunt."

"I am much obliged to you."

"It was to guarantee my respectability," said Winterbourne.

"And pray who is to guarantee hers?"

"Ah, you are cruel!" said the young man. "She's a very nice girl."

"You don't say that as if you believed it," Mrs. Costello observed.

"She is completely uncultivated," Winterbourne went on. "But she is wonderfully pretty, and, in short, she is very nice. To prove that I believe it, I am going to take her to the Château de Chillon."

"You two are going off there together? I should say it proved just the contrary. How long had you known her, may I ask, when this interesting project was formed? You haven't been twenty-four hours in the house."

"I had known her half-an-hour!" said Winterbourne, smiling.

"Dear me!" cried Mrs. Costello. "What a dreadful girl!"

Her nephew was silent for some moments. "You really think, then," he began, earnestly, and with a desire for trustworthy information—"you really think that——" But he paused again.

"Think what, sir?" said his aunt.

"That she is the sort of young lady who expects a man—sooner or later—to carry her off?"

"I haven't the least idea what such young ladies expect a man to do. But I really think that you had better not meddle with little American girls that are uncultivated, as you call them. You have lived too long out of the country. You will be sure to make some great mistake. You are too innocent."

"My dear aunt, I am not so innocent," said Winterbourne, smiling and curling his moustache.

"You are too guilty, then!"

Winterbourne continued to curl his moustache, meditatively. "You won't let the poor girl know you then?" he asked at last.

[13]French: As simply as that!

"Is it literally true that she is going to the Château de Chillon with you?"

"I think that she fully intends it."

"Then, my dear Frederick," said Mrs. Costello, "I must decline the honour of her acquaintance. I am an old woman, but I am not too old—thank Heaven—to be shocked!"

"But don't they all do these things—the young girls in America?" Winterbourne inquired.

Mrs. Costello stared a moment. "I should like to see my granddaughters do them!" she declared, grimly.

This seemed to throw some light upon the matter, for Winterbourne remembered to have heard that his pretty cousins in New York were "tremendous flirts." If, therefore, Miss Daisy Miller exceeded the liberal license allowed to these young ladies, it was probable that anything might be expected of her. Winterbourne was impatient to see her again, and he was vexed with himself that, by instinct, he should not appreciate her justly.

Though he was impatient to see her, he hardly knew what he should say to her about his aunt's refusal to become acquainted with her; but he discovered, promptly enough, that with Miss Daisy Miller there was no great need of walking on tiptoe. He found her that evening in the garden, wandering about in the warm starlight, like an indolent sylph, and swinging to and fro the largest fan he had ever beheld. It was ten o'clock. He had dined with his aunt, had been sitting with her since dinner, and had just taken leave of her till the morrow. Miss Daisy Miller seemed very glad to see him; she declared it was the longest evening she had ever passed.

"Have you been all alone?" he asked.

"I have been walking round with mother. But mother gets tired walking round," she answered.

"Has she gone to bed?"

"No; she doesn't like to go to bed," said the young girl. "She doesn't sleep—not three hours. She says she doesn't know how she lives. She's dreadfully nervous. I guess she sleeps more than she thinks. She's gone somewhere after Randolph; she wants to try to get him to go to bed. He doesn't like to go to bed."

"Let us hope she will persuade him," observed Winterbourne.

"She will talk to him all she can; but he doesn't like her to talk to him," said Miss Daisy, opening her fan. "She's going to try to get Eugenio to talk to him. But he isn't afraid of Eugenio. Eugenio's a splendid courier, but he can't make much impression on Randolph! I don't believe he'll go to bed before eleven." It appeared that Randolph's vigil was in fact triumphantly prolonged, for Winterbourne strolled about with the young girl for some time without meeting her mother. "I have been looking round for that lady you want to introduce me to," his companion resumed. "She's your aunt." Then, on Winterbourne's admitting the fact, and expressing some curiosity as to how she had learned it, she said she had heard all about Mrs. Costello from the chambermaid. She was very quiet and very *comme il faut,*[14] she wore white puffs; she spoke to no one, and she never dined at the *table d'hôte.*[15] Every two days

[14]French: correct, proper.

[15]French: common table for hotel guests.

she had a headache. "I think that's a lovely description, headache and all!" said Miss Daisy, chattering along in her thin, gay voice. "I want to know her ever so much. I know just what *your* aunt would be; I know I should like her. She would be very exclusive. I like a lady to be exclusive; I'm dying to be exclusive myself. Well, we *are* exclusive, mother and I. We don't speak to every one—or they don't speak to us. I suppose it's about the same thing. Any way, I shall be ever so glad to know your aunt."

Winterbourne was embarrassed. "She would be most happy," he said; "but I am afraid those headaches will interfere."

The young girl looked at him through the dusk. "But I suppose she doesn't have a headache every day," she said, sympathetically.

Winterbourne was silent a moment. "She tells me she does," he answered at last—not knowing what to say.

Miss Daisy Miller stopped and stood looking at him. Her prettiness was still visible in the darkness; she was opening and closing her enormous fan. "She doesn't want to know me!" she said, suddenly. "Why don't you say so? You needn't be afraid. I'm not afraid!" And she gave a little laugh.

Winterbourne fancied there was a tremor in her voice; he was touched, shocked, mortified by it. "My dear young lady," he protested, "she knows no one. It's her wretched health."

The young girl walked on a few steps, laughing still. "You needn't be afraid," she repeated. "Why should she want to know me?" Then she paused again; she was close to the parapet of the garden, and in front of her was the starlit lake. There was a vague sheen upon its surface, and in the distance were dimly-seen mountain forms. Daisy Miller looked out upon the mysterious prospect, and then she gave another little laugh. "Gracious! she *is* exclusive!" she said. Winterbourne wondered whether she was seriously wounded, and for a moment almost wished that her sense of injury might be such as to make it becoming in him to attempt to reassure and comfort her. He had a pleasant sense that she would be very approachable for consolatory purposes. He felt then, for the instant, quite ready to sacrifice his aunt, conversationally; to admit that she was a proud, rude woman, and to declare that they needn't mind her. But before he had time to commit himself to this perilous mixture of gallantry and impiety, the young lady, resuming her walk, gave an exclamation in quite another tone. "Well; here's mother! I guess she hasn't got Randolph to go to bed." The figure of a lady appeared, at a distance, very indistinct in the darkness, and advancing with a slow and wavering movement. Suddenly it seemed to pause.

"Are you sure it is your mother? Can you distinguish her in this thick dusk?" Winterbourne asked.

"Well!" cried Miss Daisy Miller, with a laugh, "I guess I know my own mother. And when she has got on my shawl, too! She is always wearing my things."

The lady in question, ceasing to advance, hovered vaguely about the spot at which she had checked her steps.

"I am afraid your mother doesn't see you," said Winterbourne. "Or perhaps," he added—thinking, with Miss Miller, the joke permissible—"perhaps she feels guilty about your shawl."

"Oh, it's a fearful old thing!" the young girl replied, serenely. "I told her she could wear it. She won't come here, because she sees you."

"Ah, then," said Winterbourne, "I had better leave you."

"Oh no; come on!" urged Miss Daisy Miller.

"I'm afraid your mother doesn't approve of my walking with you."

Miss Miller gave him a serious glance. "It isn't for me; it's for you—that is, it's for *her.* Well; I don't know who it's for! But mother doesn't like any of my gentlemen friends. She's right down timid. She always makes a fuss if I introduce a gentleman. But I *do* introduce them—almost always. If I didn't introduce my gentlemen friends to mother," the young girl added, in her little soft, flat monotone, "I shouldn't think I was natural."

"To introduce me," said Winterbourne, "you must know my name." And he proceeded to pronounce it.

"Oh, dear; I can't say all that!" said his companion, with a laugh. But by this time they had come up to Mrs. Miller, who, as they drew near, walked to the parapet of the garden and leaned upon it, looking intently at the lake and turning her back upon them. "Mother!" said the young girl, in a tone of decision. Upon this the elder lady turned round. "Mr. Winterbourne," said Miss Daisy Miller, introducing the young man very frankly and prettily. "Common," she was, as Mrs. Costello had pronounced her; yet it was a wonder to Winterbourne that, with her commonness, she had a singularly delicate grace.

Her mother was a small, spare, light person, with a wandering eye, a very exiguous nose, and a large forehead, decorated with a certain amount of thin, much-frizzled hair. Like her daughter, Mrs. Miller was dressed with extreme elegance; she had enormous diamonds in her ears. So far as Winterbourne could observe, she gave him no greeting—she certainly was not looking at him. Daisy was near her, pulling her shawl straight. "What are you doing, poking round here?" this young lady inquired; but by no means with that harshness of accent which her choice of words may imply.

"I don't know," said her mother, turning towards the lake again.

"I shouldn't think you'd want that shawl!" Daisy exclaimed.

"Well—I do!" her mother answered, with a little laugh.

"Did you get Randolph to go to bed?" asked the young girl.

"No; I couldn't induce him," said Mrs. Miller, very gently. "He wants to talk to the waiter. He likes to talk to that waiter."

"I was telling Mr. Winterbourne," the young girl went on; and to the young man's ear her tone might have indicated that she had been uttering his name all her life.

"Oh, yes!" said Winterbourne; "I have the pleasure of knowing your son."

Randolph's mamma was silent; she turned her attention to the lake. But at last she spoke. "Well, I don't see how he lives!"

"Anyhow, it isn't so bad as it was at Dover,"[16] said Daisy Miller.

"And what occurred at Dover?" Winterbourne asked.

"He wouldn't go to bed at all. I guess he sat up all night—in the public parlour. He wasn't in bed at twelve o'clock: I know that."

"It was half-past twelve," declared Mrs. Miller, with mild emphasis.

"Does he sleep much during the day?" Winterbourne demanded.

[16]English coastal town, point of departure for France.

"I guess he doesn't sleep much," Daisy rejoined.

"I wish he would!" said her mother. "It seems as if he couldn't."

"I think he's real tiresome," Daisy pursued.

Then, for some moments, there was silence. "Well, Daisy Miller," said the elder lady, presently, "I shouldn't think you'd want to talk against your own brother!"

"Well, he *is* tiresome, mother," said Daisy, quite without the asperity of a retort.

"He's only nine," urged Mrs. Miller.

"Well, he wouldn't go to that castle," said the young girl. "I'm going there with Mr. Winterbourne."

To this announcement, very placidly made, Daisy's mamma offered no response. Winterbourne took for granted that she deeply disapproved of the projected excursion; but he said to himself that she was a simple, easily-managed person, and that a few deferential protestations would take the edge from her displeasure. "Yes," he began; "your daughter has kindly allowed me the honour of being her guide."

Mrs. Miller's wandering eyes attached themselves, with a sort of appealing air, to Daisy, who, however, strolled a few steps farther, gently humming to herself. "I presume you will go in the cars," said her mother.

"Yes; or in the boat," said Winterbourne.

"Well, of course, I don't know," Mrs. Miller rejoined. "I have never been to that castle."

"It is a pity you shouldn't go," said Winterbourne, beginning to feel reassured as to her opposition. And yet he was quite prepared to find that, as a matter of course, she meant to accompany her daughter.

"We've been thinking ever so much about going," she pursued; "but it seems as if we couldn't. Of course Daisy—she wants to go round. But there's a lady here—I don't know her name—she says she shouldn't think we'd want to go to see castles *here*; she should think we'd want to wait till we got to Italy. It seems as if there would be so many there," continued Mrs. Miller, with an air of increasing confidence. "Of course, we only want to see the principal ones. We visited several in England," she presently added.

"Ah, yes! in England there are beautiful castles," said Winterbourne. "But Chillon, here, is very well worth seeing."

"Well, if Daisy feels up to it——," said Mrs. Miller, in a tone impregnated with a sense of the magnitude of the enterprise. "It seems as if there was nothing she wouldn't undertake."

"Oh, I think she'll enjoy it!" Winterbourne declared. And he desired more and more to make it a certainty that he was to have the privilege of a *tête-à-tête* with the young lady, who was still strolling along in front of them, softly vocalising. "You are not disposed, madam," he inquired, "to undertake it yourself?"

Daisy's mother looked at him, an instant, askance, and then walked forward in silence. Then—"I guess she had better go alone," she said, simply.

Winterbourne observed to himself that this was a very different type of maternity from that of the vigilant matrons who massed themselves in the forefront of social intercourse in the dark old city at the other end of the lake. But his meditations were interrupted by hearing his name very distinctly pronounced by Mrs. Miller's unprotected daughter.

"Mr. Winterbourne!" murmured Daisy.

"Mademoiselle!" said the young man.

"Don't you want to take me out in a boat?"

"At present?" he asked.

"Of course!" said Daisy.

"Well, Annie Miller!" exclaimed her mother.

"I beg you, madam, to let her go," said Winterbourne, ardently; for he had never yet enjoyed the sensation of guiding through the summer starlight a skiff freighted with a fresh and beautiful young girl.

"I shouldn't think she'd want to," said her mother. "I should think she'd rather go indoors."

"I'm sure Mr. Winterbourne wants to take me," Daisy declared. "He's so awfully devoted!"

"I will row you over to Chillon, in the starlight."

"I don't believe it!" said Daisy.

"Well!" ejaculated the elder lady again.

"You haven't spoken to me for half-an-hour," her daughter went on.

"I have been having some very pleasant conversation with your mother," said Winterbourne.

"Well; I want you to take me out in a boat!" Daisy repeated. They had all stopped, and she had turned round and was looking at Winterbourne. Her face wore a charming smile, her pretty eyes were gleaming, she was swinging her great fan about. No; it's impossible to be prettier than that, thought Winterbourne.

"There are half-a-dozen boats moored at that landing-place," he said, pointing to certain steps which descended from the garden to the lake. "If you will do me the honour to accept my arm, we will go and select one of them."

Daisy stood there smiling; she threw back her head and gave a little light laugh. "I like a gentleman to be formal!" she declared.

"I assure you it's a formal offer."

"I was bound I would make you say something," Daisy went on.

"You see it's not very difficult," said Winterbourne. "But I am afraid you are chaffing me."

"I think not, sir," remarked Mrs. Miller, very gently.

"Do, then, let me give you a row," he said to the young girl.

"It's quite lovely, the way you say that!" cried Daisy.

"It will be still more lovely to do it."

"Yes, it would be lovely!" said Daisy. But she made no movement to accompany him; she only stood there laughing.

"I should think you had better find out what time it is," interposed her mother.

"It is eleven o'clock, madam," said a voice, with a foreign accent, out of the neighbouring darkness; and Winterbourne, turning, perceived the florid personage who was in attendance upon the two ladies. He had apparently just approached.

"Oh, Eugenio," said Daisy, "I am going out in a boat!"

Eugenio bowed. "At eleven o'clock, mademoiselle?"

"I am going with Mr. Winterbourne. This very minute."

"Do tell her she can't," said Mrs. Miller to the courier.

"I think you had better not go out in a boat, mademoiselle," Eugenio declared.

Winterbourne wished to Heaven this pretty girl were not so familiar with her courier; but he said nothing.

"I suppose you don't think it's proper!" Daisy exclaimed. "Eugenio doesn't think anything's proper."

"I am at your service," said Winterbourne.

"Does mademoiselle propose to go alone?" asked Eugenio of Mrs. Miller.

"Oh, no; with this gentleman!" answered Daisy's mamma.

The courier looked for a moment at Winterbourne—the latter thought he was smiling—and then, solemnly, with a bow, "As mademoiselle pleases!" he said.

"Oh, I hoped you would make a fuss!" said Daisy. "I don't care to go now."

"I myself shall make a fuss if you don't go," said Winterbourne.

"That's all I want—a little fuss!" And the young girl began to laugh again.

"Mr. Randolph has gone to bed!" the courier announced, frigidly.

"Oh, Daisy; now we can go!" said Mrs. Miller.

Daisy turned away from Winterbourne, looking at him, smiling and fanning herself. "Good night," she said; "I hope you are disappointed, or disgusted, or something!"

He looked at her, taking the hand she offered him. "I am puzzled," he answered.

"Well; I hope it won't keep you awake!" she said, very smartly; and, under the escort of the privileged Eugenio, the two ladies passed towards the house.

Winterbourne stood looking after them; he was indeed puzzled. He lingered beside the lake for a quarter of an hour, turning over the mystery of the young girl's sudden familiarities and caprices. But the only very definite conclusion he came to was that he should enjoy deucedly "going off" with her somewhere.

Two days afterwards he went off with her to the Castle of Chillon. He waited for her in the large hall of the hotel, where the couriers, the servants, the foreign tourists were lounging about and staring. It was not the place he would have chosen, but she had appointed it. She came tripping downstairs, buttoning her long gloves, squeezing her folded parasol against her pretty figure, dressed in the perfection of a soberly elegant travelling-costume. Winterbourne was a man of imagination and, as our ancestors used to say, of sensibility; as he looked at her dress and, on the great staircase, her little rapid, confiding step, he felt as if there were something romantic going forward. He could have believed he was going to elope with her. He passed out with her among all the idle people that were assembled there; they were all looking at her very hard; she had begun to chatter as soon as she joined him. Winterbourne's preference had been that they should be conveyed to Chillon in a carriage; but she expressed a lively wish to go in the little steamer; she declared that she had a passion for steamboats. There was always such a lovely breeze upon the water, and you saw such lots of people. The sail was not long, but Winterbourne's companion found time to say a great many things. To the young man himself their little excursion was so much of an escapade—an adventure—that, even allowing for her habitual sense of freedom, he had some expectation of seeing her regard it in the same way. But it must be confessed that, in this particular, he was disappointed. Daisy Miller was extremely animated, she was in charming spirits; but she was apparently not at all excited; she was not fluttered; she avoided neither his eyes nor those of any one else; she blushed neither when she looked at him nor when she saw that people were looking at her.

People continued to look at her a great deal, and Winterbourne took much satisfaction in his pretty companion's distinguished air. He had been a little afraid that she would talk loud, laugh overmuch, and even, perhaps, desire to move about the boat a good deal. But he quite forgot his fears; he sat smiling, with his eyes upon her face, while, without moving from her place, she delivered herself of a great number of original reflections. It was the most charming garrulity he had ever heard. He had assented to the idea that she was "common;" but was she so, after all, or was he simply getting used to her commonness? Her conversation was chiefly of what metaphysicians term the objective cast; but every now and then it took a subjective turn.

"What on *earth* are you so grave about?" she suddenly demanded, fixing her agreeable eyes upon Winterbourne's.

"Am I grave?" he asked. "I had an idea I was grinning from ear to ear."

"You look as if you were taking me to a funeral. If that's a grin, your ears are very near together."

"Should you like me to dance a hornpipe on the deck?"

"Pray do, and I'll carry round your hat. It will pay the expenses of our journey."

"I never was better pleased in my life," murmured Winterbourne.

She looked at him a moment, and then burst into a little laugh. "I like to make you say those things! You're a queer mixture!"

In the castle, after they had landed, the subjective element decidedly prevailed. Daisy tripped about the vaulted chambers, rustled her skirts in the corkscrew staircases, flirted back with a pretty little cry and a shudder from the edge of the *oubliettes,*[17] and turned a singularly well-shaped ear to everything that Winterbourne told her about the place. But he saw that she cared very little for feudal antiquities, and that the dusky traditions of Chillon made but a slight impression upon her. They had the good fortune to have been able to walk about without other companionship than that of the custodian; and Winterbourne arranged with this functionary that they should not be hurried—that they should linger and pause wherever they chose. The custodian interpreted the bargain generously—Winterbourne, on his side, had been generous—and ended by leaving them quite to themselves. Miss Miller's observations were not remarkable for logical consistency; for anything she wanted to say she was sure to find a pretext. She found a great many pretexts in the rugged embrasures of Chillon for asking Winterbourne sudden questions about himself—his family, his previous history, his tastes, his habits, his intentions—and for supplying information upon corresponding points in her own personality. Of her own tastes, habits and intentions Miss Miller was prepared to give the most definite, and indeed the most favourable, account.

"Well; I hope you know enough!" she said to her companion, after he had told her the history of the unhappy Bonivard.[18] "I never saw a man that knew so much!" The history of Bonivard had evidently, as they say, gone into one ear and out of the other. But Daisy went on to say that she wished Winterbourne would travel with

[17]French: dungeons opening beneath the floor.

[18]A leader of the Genevan resistance against foreign domination, imprisoned in the Castle of Chillon 1532–1536. Byron's famous poem, "The Prisoner of Chillon" (1816), gave nineteenth-century readers an exaggerated image of Bonivard's sufferings.

them and "go round" with them; they might know something, in that case. "Don't you want to come and teach Randolph?" she asked. Winterbourne said that nothing could possibly please him so much; but that he had unfortunately other occupations. "Other occupations? I don't believe it!" said Miss Daisy. "What do you mean? You are not in business." The young man admitted that he was not in business; but he had engagements which, even within a day or two, would force him to go back to Geneva. "Oh, bother!" she said, "I don't believe it!" and she began to talk about something else. But a few moments later, when he was pointing out to her the pretty design of an antique fireplace, she broke out irrelevantly, "You don't mean to say you are going back to Geneva?"

"It is a melancholy fact that I shall have to return to Geneva to-morrow."

"Well, Mr. Winterbourne," said Daisy; "I think you're horrid!"

"Oh, don't say such dreadful things!" said Winterbourne—"just at the last."

"The last!" cried the young girl; "I call it the first. I have half a mind to leave you here and go straight back to the hotel alone." And for the next ten minutes she did nothing but call him horrid. Poor Winterbourne was fairly bewildered; no young lady had as yet done him the honour to be so agitated by the announcement of his movements. His companion, after this, ceased to pay any attention to the curiosities of Chillon or the beauties of the lake; she opened fire upon the mysterious charmer in Geneva, whom she appeared to have instantly taken it for granted that he was hurrying back to see. How did Miss Daisy Miller know that there was a charmer in Geneva? Winterbourne, who denied the existence of such a person, was quite unable to discover; and he was divided between amazement at the rapidity of her induction and amusement at the frankness of her *persiflage.*[19] She seemed to him, in all this, an extraordinary mixture of innocence and crudity. "Does she never allow you more than three days at a time?" asked Daisy, ironically. "Doesn't she give you a vacation in summer? There's no one so hard worked but they can get leave to go off somewhere at this season. I suppose, if you stay another day, she'll come after you in the boat. Do wait over till Friday, and I will go down to the landing to see her arrive!" Winterbourne began to think he had been wrong to feel disappointed in the temper in which the young lady had embarked. If he had missed the personal accent, the personal accent was now making its appearance. It sounded very distinctly, at last, in her telling him she would stop "teasing" him if he would promise her solemnly to come down to Rome in the winter.

"That's not a difficult promise to make," said Winterbourne. "My aunt has taken an apartment in Rome for the winter, and has already asked me to come and see her."

"I don't want you to come for your aunt," said Daisy; "I want you to come for me." And this was the only allusion that the young man was ever to hear her make to his invidious kinswoman. He declared that, at any rate, he would certainly come. After this Daisy stopped teasing. Winterbourne took a carriage, and they drove back to Vevey in the dusk; the young girl was very quiet.

In the evening Winterbourne mentioned to Mrs. Costello that he had spent the afternoon at Chillon, with Miss Daisy Miller.

"The Americans—of the courier?" asked this lady.

[19]Raillery, banter.

"Ah, happily," said Winterbourne, "the courier stayed at home."

"She went with you all alone?"

"All alone."

Mrs. Costello sniffed a little at her smelling-bottle. "And that," she exclaimed, "is the young person you wanted me to know!"

III

Winterbourne, who had returned to Geneva the day after his excursion to Chillon, went to Rome towards the end of January. His aunt had been established there for several weeks, and he had received a couple of letters from her. "Those people you were so devoted to last summer at Vevey have turned up here, courier and all," she wrote. "They seem to have made several acquaintances, but the courier continues to be the most *intime.*[20] The young lady, however, is also very intimate with some third-rate Italians, with whom she rackets about in a way that makes much talk. Bring me that pretty novel of Cherbuliez's—'Paule Méré'[21]—and don't come later than the 23rd."

In the natural course of events, Winterbourne, on arriving in Rome, would presently have ascertained Mrs. Miller's address at the American banker's and have gone to pay his compliments to Miss Daisy. "After what happened at Vevey I certainly think I may call upon them," he said to Mrs. Costello.

"If, after what happens—at Vevey and everywhere—you desire to keep up the acquaintance, you are very welcome. Of course a man may know every one. Men are welcome to the privilege!"

"Pray what is it that happens—here, for instance?" Winterbourne demanded.

"The girl goes about alone with her foreigners. As to what happens farther, you must apply elsewhere for information. She has picked up half-a-dozen of the regular Roman fortune-hunters, and she takes them about to people's houses. When she comes to a party she brings with her a gentleman with a good deal of manner and a wonderful moustache."

"And where is the mother?"

"I haven't the least idea. They are very dreadful people."

Winterbourne meditated a moment. "They are very ignorant—very innocent only. Depend upon it they are not bad."

"They are hopelessly vulgar," said Mrs. Costello. "Whether or not being hopelessly vulgar is being 'bad' is a question for the metaphysicians. They are bad enough to dislike, at any rate; and for this short life that is quite enough."

The news that Daisy Miller was surrounded by half-a-dozen wonderful moustaches checked Winterbourne's impulse to go straightway to see her. He had perhaps not definitely flattered himself that he had made an ineffaceable impression upon her heart, but he was annoyed at hearing of a state of affairs so little in harmony with an image that had lately flitted in and out of his own meditations; the image of a very

[20]French: familiar, confidential, intimate.

[21]This 1864 novel by a popular Swiss-French novelist told of a spontaneous young woman who runs afoul of the rigid social code of Geneva.

pretty girl looking out of an old Roman window and asking herself urgently when Mr. Winterbourne would arrive. If, however, he determined to wait a little before reminding Miss Miller of his claims to her consideration, he went very soon to call upon two or three other friends. One of these friends was an American lady who had spent several winters at Geneva, where she had placed her children at school. She was a very accomplished woman and she lived in the Via Gregoriana.[22] Winterbourne found her in a little crimson drawing-room, on a third-floor; the room was filled with southern sunshine. He had not been there ten minutes when the servant came in, announcing "Madame Mila!" This announcement was presently followed by the entrance of little Randolph Miller, who stopped in the middle of the room and stood staring at Winterbourne. An instant later his pretty sister crossed the threshold; and then, after a considerable interval, Mrs. Miller slowly advanced.

"I know you!" said Randolph.

"I'm sure you know a great many things," exclaimed Winterbourne, taking him by the hand. "How is your education coming on?"

Daisy was exchanging greetings very prettily with her hostess; but when she heard Winterbourne's voice she quickly turned her head. "Well, I declare!" she said.

"I told you I should come, you know," Winterbourne rejoined, smiling.

"Well—I didn't believe it," said Miss Daisy.

"I am much obliged to you," laughed the young man.

"You might have come to see me!" said Daisy.

"I arrived only yesterday."

"I don't believe that!" the young girl declared.

Winterbourne turned with a protesting smile to her mother; but this lady evaded his glance, and seating herself, fixed her eyes upon her son. "We've got a bigger place than this," said Randolph. "It's all gold on the walls."

Mrs. Miller turned uneasily in her chair. "I told you if I were to bring you, you would say something!" she murmured.

"I told *you*!" Randolph exclaimed. "I tell *you,* sir!" he added jocosely, giving Winterbourne a thump on the knee. "It *is* bigger, too!"

Daisy had entered upon a lively conversation with her hostess; Winterbourne judged it becoming to address a few words to her mother. "I hope you have been well since we parted at Vevey," he said.

Mrs. Miller now certainly looked at him—at his chin. "Not very well, sir," she answered.

"She's got the dyspepsia," said Randolph. "I've got it too. Father's got it. I've got it worst!"

This announcement, instead of embarrassing Mrs. Miller, seemed to relieve her. "I suffer from the liver," she said. "I think it's this climate; it's less bracing than Schenectady, especially in the winter season. I don't know whether you know we reside at Schenectady. I was saying to Daisy that I certainly hadn't found any one like Dr. Davis, and I didn't believe I should. Oh, at Schenectady, he stands first; they think everything of him. He has so much to do, and yet there was nothing he wouldn't do

[22]A fashionable street near the Spanish Steps, the center of Rome's English quarter.

for me. He said he never saw anything like my dyspepsia, but he was bound to cure it. I'm sure there was nothing he wouldn't try. He was just going to try something new when we came off. Mr. Miller wanted Daisy to see Europe for herself. But I wrote to Mr. Miller that it seems as if I couldn't get on without Dr. Davis. At Schenectady he stands at the very top; and there's a great deal of sickness there, too. It affects my sleep."

Winterbourne had a good deal of pathological gossip with Dr. Davis's patient, during which Daisy chattered unremittingly to her own companion. The young man asked Mrs. Miller how she was pleased with Rome. "Well, I must say I am disappointed," she answered. "We had heard so much about it; I suppose we had heard too much. But we couldn't help that. We had been led to expect something different."

"Ah, wait a little, and you will become very fond of it," said Winterbourne.

"I hate it worse and worse every day!" cried Randolph.

"You are like the infant Hannibal,"[23] said Winterbourne.

"No, I ain't!" Randolph declared, at a venture.

"You are not much like an infant," said his mother. "But we have seen places," she resumed, "that I should put a long way before Rome." And in reply to Winterbourne's interrogation, "There's Zurich," she observed; "I think Zurich is lovely; and we hadn't heard half so much about it."

"The best place we've seen is the City of Richmond!" said Randolph.

"He means the ship," his mother explained. "We crossed in that ship. Randolph had a good time on the City of Richmond."

"It's the best place I've seen," the child repeated. "Only it was turned the wrong way."

"Well, we've got to turn the right way some time," said Mrs. Miller, with a little laugh. Winterbourne expressed the hope that her daughter at least found some gratification in Rome, and she declared that Daisy was quite carried away. "It's on account of the society—the society's splendid. She goes round everywhere; she has made a great number of acquaintances. Of course she goes round more than I do. I must say they have been very sociable; they have taken her right in. And then she knows a great many gentlemen. Oh, she thinks there's nothing like Rome. Of course, it's a great deal pleasanter for a young lady if she knows plenty of gentlemen."

By this time Daisy had turned her attention again to Winterbourne. "I've been telling Mrs. Walker how mean you were!" the young girl announced.

"And what is the evidence you have offered?" asked Winterbourne, rather annoyed at Miss Miller's want of appreciation of the zeal of an admirer who on his way down to Rome had stopped neither at Bologna nor at Florence, simply because of a certain sentimental impatience. He remembered that a cynical compatriot had once told him that American women—the pretty ones, and this gave a largeness to the axiom—were at once the most exacting in the world and the least endowed with a sense of indebtedness.

"Why, you were awfully mean at Vevey," said Daisy. "You wouldn't do anything. You wouldn't stay there when I asked you."

[23]Carthaginian general, 247–183 B.C., trained from early childhood to seek vengeance against Rome.

"My dearest young lady," cried Winterbourne, with eloquence, "have I come all the way to Rome to encounter your reproaches?"

"Just hear him say that!" said Daisy to her hostess, giving a twist to a bow on this lady's dress. "Did you ever hear anything so quaint?"

"So quaint, my dear?" murmured Mrs. Walker, in the tone of a partisan of Winterbourne.

"Well, I don't know," said Daisy, fingering Mrs. Walker's ribbons. "Mrs. Walker, I want to tell you something."

"Motherr," interposed Randolph, with his rough ends to his words, "I tell you you've got to go. Eugenio'll raise something!"[24]

"I'm not afraid of Eugenio," said Daisy, with a toss of her head. "Look here, Mrs. Walker," she went on, "you know I'm coming to your party."

"I am delighted to hear it."

"I've got a lovely dress."

"I am very sure of that."

"But I want to ask a favour—permission to bring a friend."

"I shall be happy to see any of your friends," said Mrs. Walker, turning with a smile to Mrs. Miller.

"Oh, they are not my friends," answered Daisy's mamma, smiling shyly, in her own fashion. "I never spoke to them!"

"It's an intimate friend of mine—Mr. Giovanelli," said Daisy, without a tremor in her clear little voice or a shadow on her brilliant little face.

Mrs. Walker was silent a moment, she gave a rapid glance at Winterbourne. "I shall be glad to see Mr. Giovanelli," she then said.

"He's an Italian," Daisy pursued, with the prettiest serenity. "He's a great friend of mine—he's the handsomest man in the world—except Mr. Winterbourne! He knows plenty of Italians, but he wants to know some Americans. He thinks ever so much of Americans. He's tremendously clever. He's perfectly lovely!"

It was settled that this brilliant personage should be brought to Mrs. Walker's party, and then Mrs. Miller prepared to take her leave. "I guess we'll go back to the hotel," she said.

"You may go back to the hotel, mother, but I'm going to take a walk," said Daisy.

"She's going to walk with Mr. Giovanelli," Randolph proclaimed.

"I am going to the Pincio,"[25] said Daisy, smiling.

"Alone, my dear—at this hour?" Mrs. Walker asked. The afternoon was drawing to a close—it was the hour for the throng of carriages and of contemplative pedestrians. "I don't think it's safe, my dear," said Mrs. Walker.

"Neither do I," subjoined Mrs. Miller. "You'll get the fever as sure as you live. Remember what Dr. Davis told you!"

"Give her some medicine before she goes," said Randolph.

The company had risen to its feet; Daisy, still showing her pretty teeth, bent over and kissed her hostess. "Mrs. Walker, you are too perfect," she said. "I'm not going alone; I am going to meet a friend."

[24] *I.e.,* raise hell.

[25] An elevated terrace laid out in gardens, walks, and driveways, much frequented for the afternoon promenade.

"Your friend won't keep you from getting the fever,"[26] Mrs. Miller observed.

"Is it Mr. Giovanelli?" asked the hostess.

Winterbourne was watching the young girl; at this question his attention quickened. She stood there smiling and smoothing her bonnet-ribbons; she glanced at Winterbourne. Then, while she glanced and smiled, she answered without a shade of hesitation, "Mr. Giovanelli—the beautiful Giovanelli."

"My dear young friend," said Mrs. Walker, taking her hand, pleadingly, "don't walk off to the Pincio at this hour to meet a beautiful Italian."

"Well, he speaks English," said Mrs. Miller.

"Gracious me!" Daisy exclaimed, "I don't want to do anything improper. There's an easy way to settle it." She continued to glance at Winterbourne. "The Pincio is only a hundred yards distant, and if Mr. Winterbourne were as polite as he pretends he would offer to walk with me!"

Winterbourne's politeness hastened to affirm itself, and the young girl gave him gracious leave to accompany her. They passed down-stairs before her mother, and at the door Winterbourne perceived Mrs. Miller's carriage drawn up, with the ornamental courier whose acquaintance he had made at Vevey seated within. "Good-bye, Eugenio!" cried Daisy, "I'm going to take a walk." The distance from the Via Gregoriana to the beautiful garden at the other end of the Pincian Hill is, in fact, rapidly traversed. As the day was splendid, however, and the concourse of vehicles, walkers, and loungers numerous, the young Americans found their progress much delayed. This fact was highly agreeable to Winterbourne, in spite of his consciousness of his singular situation. The slow-moving, idly-gazing Roman crowd bestowed much attention upon the extremely pretty young foreign lady who was passing through it upon his arm; and he wondered what on earth had been in Daisy's mind when she proposed to expose herself, unattended, to its appreciation. His own mission, to her sense, apparently, was to consign her to the hands of Mr. Giovanelli; but Winterbourne, at once annoyed and gratified, resolved that he would do no such thing.

"Why haven't you been to see me?" asked Daisy. "You can't get out of that."

"I have had the honour of telling you that I have only just stepped out of the train."

"You must have stayed in the train a good while after it stopped!" cried the young girl, with her little laugh. "I suppose you were asleep. You have had time to go to see Mrs. Walker."

"I knew Mrs. Walker—" Winterbourne began to explain.

"I knew where you knew her. You knew her at Geneva. She told me so. Well, you knew me at Vevey. That's just as good. So you ought to have come." She asked him no other question than this; she began to prattle about her own affairs. "We've got splendid rooms at the hotel; Eugenio says they're the best rooms in Rome. We are going to stay all winter—if we don't die of the fever; and I guess we'll stay then. It's a great deal nicer than I thought; I thought it would be fearfully quiet; I was sure it would be awfully poky. I was sure we should be going round all the time with one of those dreadful old men that explain about the pictures and things. But we only

[26]Roman fever, malaria.

had about a week of that, and now I'm enjoying myself. I know ever so many people, and they are all so charming. The society's extremely select. There are all kinds—English, and Germans, and Italians. I think I like the English best. I like their style of conversation. But there are some lovely Americans. I never saw anything so hospitable. There's something or other every day. There's not much dancing; but I must say I never thought dancing was everything. I was always fond of conversation. I guess I shall have plenty at Mrs. Walker's—her rooms are so small." When they had passed the gate of the Pincian Gardens, Miss Miller began to wonder where Mr. Giovanelli might be. "We had better go straight to that place in front," she said, "where you look at the view."

"I certainly shall not help you to find him," Winterbourne declared.

"Then I shall find him without you," said Miss Daisy.

"You certainly won't leave me!" cried Winterbourne.

She burst into her little laugh. "Are you afraid you'll get lost—or run over? But there's Giovanelli, leaning against that tree. He's staring at the women in the carriages: did you ever see anything so cool?"

Winterbourne perceived at some distance a little man standing with folded arms, nursing his cane. He had a handsome face, an artfully poised hat, a glass in one eye and a nosegay in his button-hole. Winterbourne looked at him a moment and then said, "Do you mean to speak to that man?"

"Do I mean to speak to him? Why, you don't suppose I mean to communicate by signs?"

"Pray understand, then," said Winterbourne, "that I intend to remain with you."

Daisy stopped and looked at him, without a sign of troubled consciousness in her face; with nothing but the presence of her charming eyes and her happy dimples. "Well, she's a cool one!" thought the young man.

"I don't like the way you say that," said Daisy. "It's too imperious."

"I beg your pardon if I say it wrong. The main point is to give you an idea of my meaning."

The young girl looked at him more gravely, but with eyes that were prettier than ever. "I have never allowed a gentleman to dictate to me, or to interfere with anything I do."

"I think you have made a mistake," said Winterbourne. "You should sometimes listen to a gentleman—the right one?"

Daisy began to laugh again. "I do nothing but listen to gentlemen!" she exclaimed. "Tell me if Mr. Giovanelli is the right one?"

The gentleman with the nosegay in his bosom had now perceived our two friends, and was approaching the young girl with obsequious rapidity. He bowed to Winterbourne as well as to the latter's companion; he had a brilliant smile, an intelligent eye; Winterbourne thought him not a bad-looking fellow. But he nevertheless said to Daisy—"No, he's not the right one."

Daisy evidently had a natural talent for performing introductions; she mentioned the name of each of her companions to the other. She strolled along with one of them on each side of her; Mr. Giovanelli, who spoke English very cleverly—Winterbourne afterwards learned that he had practised the idiom upon a great many American heiresses—addressed her a great deal of very polite nonsense; he was extremely urbane, and the young American, who said nothing, reflected upon that profundity of Italian cleverness which enables people to appear more gracious in proportion as they are more acutely disappointed. Giovanelli, of course, had counted upon something more intimate; he had not bargained for a party of three. But he kept his temper in a manner which suggested far-stretching intentions. Winterbourne flattered himself that he had taken his measure. "He is not a gentleman," said the young American; "he is only a clever imitation of one. He is a music-master, or a penny-a-liner, or a third-rate artist. Damn his good looks!" Mr. Giovanelli had certainly a very pretty face; but Winterbourne felt a superior indignation at his own lovely fellow-country-woman's not knowing the difference between a spurious gentleman and a real one. Giovanelli chattered and jested and made himself wonderfully agreeable. It was true that if he was an imitation the imitation was very skilful. "Nevertheless," Winterbourne said to himself, "a nice girl ought to know!" And then he came back to the question whether this was in fact a nice girl. Would a nice girl—even allowing for her being a little American flirt—make a rendezvous with a presumably low-lived foreigner? The rendezvous in this case, indeed, had been in broad daylight, and in the most crowded corner of Rome; but was it not impossible to regard the choice of these circumstances as a proof of extreme cynicism? Singular though it may seem, Winterbourne was vexed that the young girl, in joining her *amoroso,*[27] should not appear more impatient of his own company, and he was vexed because of his inclination. It was impossible to regard her as a perfectly well-conducted young lady; she was wanting in a certain indispensable delicacy. It would therefore simplify matters greatly to be able to treat her as the object of one of those sentiments which are called by romancers "lawless passions." That she should seem to wish to get rid of him would help him to think more lightly of her, and to be able to think more lightly of her would make her much less perplexing. But Daisy, on this occasion, continued to present herself as an inscrutable combination of audacity and innocence.

She had been walking some quarter of an hour, attended by her two cavaliers, and responding in a tone of very childish gaiety, as it seemed to Winterbourne, to the pretty speeches of Mr. Giovanelli, when a carriage that had detached itself from the revolving train drew up beside the path. At the same moment Winterbourne perceived that his friend Mrs. Walker—the lady whose house he had lately left—was seated in the vehicle and was beckoning to him. Leaving Miss Miller's side, he hastened to obey her summons. Mrs. Walker was flushed; she wore an excited air. "It is really too dreadful," she said. "That girl must not do this sort of thing. She must not walk here with you two men. Fifty people have noticed her."

Winterbourne raised his eyebrows. "I think it's a pity to make too much fuss about it."

"It's a pity to let the girl ruin herself!"

"She is very innocent," said Winterbourne.

"She's very crazy!" cried Mrs. Walker. "Did you ever see anything so imbecile as her mother? After you had all left me, just now, I could not sit still for thinking of it.

[27]Italian: admirer, suitor.

It seemed too pitiful, not even to attempt to save her. I ordered the carriage and put on my bonnet, and came here as quickly as possible. Thank heaven I have found you!"

"What do you propose to do with us?" asked Winterbourne, smiling.

"To ask her to get in, to drive her about here for half-an-hour, so that the world may see she is not running absolutely wild, and then to take her safely home."

"I don't think it's a very happy thought," said Winterbourne; "but you can try."

Mrs. Walker tried. The young man went in pursuit of Miss Miller, who had simply nodded and smiled at his interlocutrix in the carriage and had gone her way with her own companion. Daisy, on learning that Mrs. Walker wished to speak to her, retraced her steps with a perfect good grace and with Mr. Giovanelli at her side. She declared that she was delighted to have a chance to present this gentleman to Mrs. Walker. She immediately achieved the introduction, and declared that she had never in her life seen anything so lovely as Mrs. Walker's carriage-rug.

"I am glad you admire it," said this lady, smiling sweetly. "Will you get in and let me put it over you?"

"Oh, no, thank you," said Daisy. "I shall admire it much more as I see you driving round with it."

"Do get in and drive with me," said Mrs. Walker.

"That would be charming, but it's so enchanting just as I am!" and Daisy gave a brilliant glance at the gentlemen on either side of her.

"It may be enchanting, dear child, but it is not the custom here," urged Mrs. Walker, leaning forward in her victoria[28] with her hands devoutly clasped.

"Well, it ought to be, then!" said Daisy. "If I didn't walk I should expire."

"You should walk with your mother, dear," cried the lady from Geneva, losing patience.

"With my mother dear!" exclaimed the young girl. Winterbourne saw that she scented interference. "My mother never walked ten steps in her life. And then, you know," she added with a laugh, "I am more than five years old."

"You are old enough to be more reasonable. You are old enough, dear Miss Miller, to be talked about."

Daisy looked at Mrs. Walker, smiling intensely. "Talked about? What do you mean?"

"Come into my carriage and I will tell you."

Daisy turned her quickened glance again from one of the gentlemen beside her to the other. Mr. Giovanelli was bowing to and fro, rubbing down his gloves and laughing very agreeably; Winterbourne thought it a most unpleasant scene. "I don't think I want to know what you mean," said Daisy presently. "I don't think I should like it."

Winterbourne wished that Mrs. Walker would tuck in her carriage-rug and drive away; but this lady did not enjoy being defied, as she afterwards told him. "Should you prefer being thought a very reckless girl?" she demanded.

"Gracious me!" exclaimed Daisy. She looked again at Mr. Giovanelli, then she turned to Winterbourne. There was a little pink flush in her cheek; she was

[28]Four-wheeled pleasure carriage for two.

tremendously pretty. "Does Mr. Winterbourne think," she asked slowly, smiling, throwing back her head and glancing at him from head to foot, "that—to save my reputation—I ought to get into the carriage?"

Winterbourne coloured; for an instant he hesitated greatly. It seemed so strange to hear her speak that way of her "reputation." But he himself, in fact, must speak in accordance with gallantry. The finest gallantry, here, was simply to tell her the truth; and the truth, for Winterbourne, as the few indications I have been able to give have made him known to the reader, was that Daisy Miller should take Mrs. Walker's advice. He looked at her exquisite prettiness; and then he said very gently, "I think you should get into the carriage."

Daisy gave a violent laugh. "I never heard anything so stiff! If this is improper, Mrs. Walker," she pursued, "then I am all improper, and you must give me up. Good-bye; I hope you'll have a lovely ride!" and, with Mr. Giovanelli, who made a triumphantly obsequious salute, she turned away.

Mrs. Walker sat looking after her, and there were tears in Mrs. Walker's eyes. "Get in here, sir," she said to Winterbourne, indicating the place beside her. The young man answered that he felt bound to accompany Miss Miller; whereupon Mrs. Walker declared that if he refused her this favour she would never speak to him again. She was evidently in earnest. Winterbourne overtook Daisy and her companion and, offering the young girl his hand, told her that Mrs. Walker had made an imperious claim upon his society. He expected that in answer she would say something rather free, something to commit herself still farther to that "recklessness" from which Mrs. Walker had so charitably endeavoured to dissuade her. But she only shook his hand, hardly looking at him, while Mr. Giovanelli bade him farewell with a too emphatic flourish of the hat.

Winterbourne was not in the best possible humour as he took his seat in Mrs. Walker's victoria. "That was not clever of you," he said candidly, while the vehicle mingled again with the throng of carriages.

"In such a case," his companion answered, "I don't wish to be clever, I wish to be *earnest!*"

"Well, your earnestness has only offended her and put her off."

"It has happened very well," said Mrs. Walker. "If she is so perfectly determined to compromise herself, the sooner one knows it the better; one can act accordingly."

"I suspect she meant no harm," Winterbourne rejoined.

"So I thought a month ago. But she has been going too far."

"What has she been doing?"

"Everything that is not done here. Flirting with any man she could pick up; sitting in corners with mysterious Italians; dancing all the evening with the same partners; receiving visits at eleven o'clock at night. Her mother goes away when visitors come."

"But her brother," said Winterbourne, laughing, "sits up till midnight."

"He must be edified by what he sees. I'm told that at their hotel every one is talking about her, and that a smile goes round among the servants when a gentleman comes and asks for Miss Miller."

"The servants be hanged!" said Winterbourne angrily. "The poor girl's only fault," he presently added, "is that she is very uncultivated."

"She is naturally indelicate," Mrs. Walker declared. "Take that example this morning. How long had you known her at Vevey?"

"A couple of days."

"Fancy, then, her making it a personal matter that you should have left the place!"

Winterbourne was silent for some moments; then he said, "I suspect, Mrs. Walker, that you and I have lived too long at Geneva!" And he added a request that she should inform him with what particular design she had made him enter her carriage.

"I wished to beg you to cease your relations with Miss Miller—not to flirt with her—to give her no farther opportunity to expose herself—to let her alone, in short."

"I'm afraid I can't do that," said Winterbourne. "I like her extremely."

"All the more reason that you shouldn't help her to make a scandal."

"There shall be nothing scandalous in my attentions to her."

"There certainly will be in the way she takes them. But I have said what I had on my conscience," Mrs. Walker pursued. "If you wish to rejoin the young lady I will put you down. Here, by-the-way, you have a chance."

The carriage was traversing that part of the Pincian Garden which overhangs the wall of Rome and overlooks the beautiful Villa Borghese.[29] It is bordered by a large parapet, near which there are several seats. One of the seats, at a distance, was occupied by a gentleman and a lady, towards whom Mrs. Walker gave a toss of her head. At the same moment these persons rose and walked towards the parapet. Winterbourne had asked the coachman to stop; he now descended from the carriage. His companion looked at him a moment in silence; then, while he raised his hat, she drove majestically away. Winterbourne stood there; he had turned his eyes towards Daisy and her cavalier. They evidently saw no one; they were too deeply occupied with each other. When they reached the low garden-wall they stood a moment looking off at the great flat-topped pine-clusters of the Villa Borghese; then Giovanelli seated himself familiarly upon the broad ledge of the wall. The western sun in the opposite sky sent out a brilliant shaft through a couple of cloud-bars; whereupon Daisy's companion took her parasol out of her hands and opened it. She came a little nearer and he held the parasol over her; then, still holding it, he let it rest upon her shoulder, so that both of their heads were hidden from Winterbourne. This young man lingered a moment, then he began to walk. But he walked—not towards the couple with the parasol; towards the residence of his aunt, Mrs. Costello.

IV

He flattered himself on the following day that there was no smiling among the servants when he, at least, asked for Mrs. Miller at her hotel. This lady and her daughter, however, were not at home; and on the next day after, repeating his visit, Winterbourne again had the misfortune not to find them. Mrs. Walker's party took place

[29]The Borghese mansion/museum and its large wooded park.

on the evening of the third day, and in spite of the frigidity of his last interview with the hostess Winterbourne was among the guests. Mrs. Walker was one of those American ladies who, while residing abroad, make a point, in their own phrase, of studying European society; and she had on this occasion collected several specimens of her diversely-born fellow-mortals to serve, as it were, as text-books. When Winterbourne arrived Daisy Miller was not there; but in a few moments he saw her mother come in alone, very shyly and ruefully. Mrs. Miller's hair, above her exposed-looking temples, was more frizzled than ever. As she approached Mrs. Walker, Winterbourne also drew near.

"You see I've come all alone," said poor Mrs. Miller. "I'm so frightened; I don't know what to do; it's the first time I've ever been to a party alone—especially in this country. I wanted to bring Randolph or Eugenio, or some one, but Daisy just pushed me off by myself. I ain't used to going round alone."

"And does not your daughter intend to favour us with her society?" demanded Mrs. Walker, impressively.

"Well, Daisy's all dressed," said Mrs. Miller, with that accent of the dispassionate, if not of the philosophic, historian with which she always recorded the current incidents of her daughter's career. "She got dressed on purpose before dinner. But she's got a friend of hers there; that gentleman—the Italian—that she wanted to bring. They've got going at the piano; it seems as if they couldn't leave off. Mr. Giovanelli sings splendidly. But I guess they'll come before very long," concluded Mrs. Miller hopefully.

"I'm sorry she should come—in that way," said Mrs. Walker.

"Well, I told her that there was no use in her getting dressed before dinner if she was going to wait three hours," responded Daisy's mamma. "I didn't see the use of her putting on such a dress as that to sit round with Mr. Giovanelli."

"This is most horrible!" said Mrs. Walker, turning away and addressing herself to Winterbourne. "*Elle s'affiche.*[30] It's her revenge for my having ventured to remonstrate with her. When she comes I shall not speak to her."

Daisy came after eleven o'clock, but she was not, on such an occasion, a young lady to wait to be spoken to. She rustled forward in radiant loveliness, smiling and chattering, carrying a large bouquet and attended by Mr. Giovanelli. Every one stopped talking, and turned and looked at her. She came straight to Mrs. Walker. "I'm afraid you thought I never was coming, so I sent mother off to tell you. I wanted to make Mr. Giovanelli practise some things before he came; you know he sings beautifully, and I want you to ask him to sing. This is Mr. Giovanelli; you know I introduced him to you; he's got the most lovely voice and he knows the most charming set of songs. I made him go over them this evening, on purpose; we had the greatest time at the hotel." Of all this Daisy delivered herself with the sweetest, brightest audibleness, looking now at her hostess and now round the room, while she gave a series of little pats, round her shoulders, to the edges of her dress. "Is there any one I know?" she asked.

"I think every one knows you!" said Mrs. Walker pregnantly, and she gave a very cursory greeting to Mr. Giovanelli. This gentleman bore himself gallantly. He smiled

[30]French: She is making a spectacle of herself.

and bowed and showed his white teeth, he curled his moustaches and rolled his eyes, and performed all the proper functions of a handsome Italian at an evening party. He sang, very prettily, half-a-dozen songs, though Mrs. Walker afterwards declared that she had been quite unable to find out who asked him. It was apparently not Daisy who had given him his orders. Daisy sat at a distance from the piano, and though she had publicly, as it were, professed a high admiration for his singing, talked, not inaudibly, while it was going on.

"It's a pity these rooms are so small; we can't dance," she said to Winterbourne, as if she had seen him five minutes before.

"I am not sorry we can't dance," Winterbourne answered; "I don't dance."

"Of course you don't dance; you're too stiff," said Miss Daisy. "I hope you enjoyed your drive with Mrs. Walker."

"No, I didn't enjoy it; I preferred walking with you."

"We paired off, that was much better," said Daisy. "But did you ever hear anything so cool as Mrs. Walker's wanting me to get into her carriage and drop poor Mr. Giovanelli; and under the pretext that it was proper? People have different ideas! It would have been most unkind; he had been talking about that walk for ten days."

"He should not have talked about it at all," said Winterbourne; "he would never have proposed to a young lady of this country to walk about the streets with him."

"About the streets?" cried Daisy, with her pretty stare. "Where then would he have proposed to her to walk? The Pincio is not the streets, either; and I, thank goodness, am not a young lady of this country. The young ladies of this country have a dreadfully poky time of it, so far as I can learn; I don't see why I should change my habits for *them*."

"I am afraid your habits are those of a flirt," said Winterbourne gravely.

"Of course they are," she cried, giving him her little smiling stare again. "I'm a fearful, frightful flirt! Did you ever hear of a nice girl that was not? But I suppose you will tell me now that I am not a nice girl."

"You're a very nice girl, but I wish you would flirt with me, and me only," said Winterbourne.

"Ah! thank you, thank you very much; you are the last man I should think of flirting with. As I have had the pleasure of informing you, you are too stiff."

"You say that too often," said Winterbourne.

Daisy gave a delighted laugh. "If I could have the sweet hope of making you angry, I would say it again."

"Don't do that; when I am angry I'm stiffer than ever. But if you won't flirt with me, do cease at least to flirt with your friend at the piano; they don't understand that sort of thing here."

"I thought they understood nothing else!" exclaimed Daisy.

"Not in young unmarried women."

"It seems to me much more proper in young unmarried women than in old married ones," Daisy declared.

"Well," said Winterbourne, "when you deal with natives you must go by the custom of the place. Flirting is a purely American custom; it doesn't exist here. So when you show yourself in public with Mr. Giovanelli and without your mother——"

"Gracious! poor mother!" interposed Daisy.

"Though you may be flirting, Mr. Giovanelli is not; he means something else."

"He isn't preaching, at any rate," said Daisy with vivacity. "And if you want very much to know, we are neither of us flirting; we are too good friends for that; we are very intimate friends."

"Ah!" rejoined Winterbourne, "if you are in love with each other it is another affair."

She had allowed him up to this point to talk so frankly that he had no expectation of shocking her by this ejaculation; but she immediately got up, blushing visibly, and leaving him to exclaim mentally that little American flirts were the queerest creatures in the world. "Mr. Giovanelli, at least," she said, giving her interlocutor a single glance, "never says such very disagreeable things to me."

Winterbourne was bewildered; he stood staring. Mr. Giovanelli had finished singing; he left the piano and came over to Daisy. "Won't you come into the other room and have some tea?" he asked, bending before her with his decorative smile.

Daisy turned to Winterbourne, beginning to smile again. He was still more perplexed, for this inconsequent smile made nothing clear, though it seemed to prove, indeed, that she had a sweetness and softness that reverted instinctively to the pardon of offences. "It has never occurred to Mr. Winterbourne to offer me any tea," she said, with her little tormenting manner.

"I have offered you advice," Winterbourne rejoined.

"I prefer weak tea!" cried Daisy, and she went off with the brilliant Giovanelli. She sat with him in the adjoining room, in the embrasure of the window, for the rest of the evening. There was an interesting performance at the piano, but neither of these young people gave heed to it. When Daisy came to take leave of Mrs. Walker, this lady conscientiously repaired the weakness of which she had been guilty at the moment of the young girl's arrival. She turned her back straight upon Miss Miller and left her to depart with what grace she might. Winterbourne was standing near the door; he saw it all. Daisy turned very pale and looked at her mother, but Mrs. Miller was humbly unconscious of any violation of the usual social forms. She appeared, indeed, to have felt an incongruous impulse to draw attention to her own striking observance of them. "Good night, Mrs. Walker," she said; "we've had a beautiful evening. You see if I let Daisy come to parties without me, I don't want her to go away without me." Daisy turned away, looking with a pale, grave face at the circle near the door; Winterbourne saw that, for the first moment, she was too much shocked and puzzled even for indignation. He on his side was greatly touched.

"That was very cruel," he said to Mrs. Walker.

"She never enters my drawing-room again," replied his hostess.

Since Winterbourne was not to meet her in Mrs. Walker's drawing-room, he went as often as possible to Mrs. Miller's hotel. The ladies were rarely at home, but when he found them the devoted Giovanelli was always present. Very often the polished little Roman was in the drawing-room with Daisy alone, Mrs. Miller being apparently constantly of the opinion that discretion is the better part of surveillance.[31] Winterbourne noted, at first with surprise, that Daisy on these occasions was never embarrassed or annoyed by his own entrance; but he very presently began to feel that

[31]A variation on Falstaff's statement in Henry IV, Part I, that "the better part of valour is discretion."

she had no more surprises for him; the unexpected in her behaviour was the only thing to expect. She showed no displeasure at her *tête-à-tête* with Giovanelli being interrupted; she could chatter as freshly and freely with two gentlemen as with one; there was always in her conversation, the same odd mixture of audacity and puerility. Winterbourne remarked to himself that if she was seriously interested in Giovanelli it was very singular that she should not take more trouble to preserve the sanctity of their interviews, and he liked her the more for her innocent-looking indifference and her apparently inexhaustible good humour. He could hardly have said why, but she seemed to him a girl who would never be jealous. At the risk of exciting a somewhat derisive smile on the reader's part, I may affirm that with regard to the women who had hitherto interested him it very often seemed to Winterbourne among the possibilities that, given certain contingencies, he should be afraid—literally afraid—of these ladies. He had a pleasant sense that he should never be afraid of Daisy Miller. It must be added that this sentiment was not altogether flattering to Daisy; it was part of his conviction, or rather of his apprehension, that she would prove a very light young person.

But she was evidently very much interested in Giovanelli. She looked at him whenever he spoke; she was perpetually telling him to do this and to do that; she was constantly "chaffing" and abusing him. She appeared completely to have forgotten that Winterbourne had said anything to displease her at Mrs. Walker's little party. One Sunday afternoon, having gone to St. Peter's[32] with his aunt, Winterbourne perceived Daisy strolling about the great church in company with the inevitable Giovanelli. Presently he pointed out the young girl and her cavalier to Mrs. Costello. This lady looked at them a moment through her eyeglass, and then she said:

"That's what makes you so pensive in these days, eh?"

"I had not the least idea I was pensive," said the young man.

"You are very much pre-occupied, you are thinking of something."

"And what is it," he asked, "that you accuse me of thinking of?"

"Of that young lady's—Miss Baker's, Miss Chandler's—what's her name?—Miss Miller's intrigue with that little barber's block."

"Do you call it an intrigue," Winterbourne asked—"an affair that goes on with such peculiar publicity?"

"That's their folly," said Mrs. Costello, "it's not their merit."

"No," rejoined Winterbourne, with something of that pensiveness to which his aunt had alluded. "I don't believe that there is anything to be called an intrigue."

"I have heard a dozen people speak of it; they say she is quite carried away by him."

"They are certainly very intimate," said Winterbourne.

Mrs. Costello inspected the young couple again with her optical instrument. "He is very handsome. One easily sees how it is. She thinks him the most elegant man in the world, the finest gentleman. She has never seen anything like him; he is better even than the courier. It was the courier probably who introduced him, and if he

[32]The Papal church, the largest and most imposing in Christendom.

succeeds in marrying the young lady, the courier will come in for a magnificent commission."

"I don't believe she thinks of marrying him," said Winterbourne, "and I don't believe he hopes to marry her."

"You may be very sure she thinks of nothing. She goes on from day to day, from hour to hour, as they did in the Golden Age. I can imagine nothing more vulgar. And at the same time," added Mrs. Costello, "depend upon it that she may tell you any moment that she is 'engaged.'"

"I think that is more than Giovanelli expects," said Winterbourne.

"Who is Giovanelli?"

"The little Italian. I have asked questions about him and learned something. He is apparently a perfectly respectable little man. I believe he is in a small way a *cavaliere avvocato.*[33] But he doesn't move in what are called the first circles. I think it is really not absolutely impossible that the courier introduced him. He is evidently immensely charmed with Miss Miller. If she thinks him the finest gentleman in the world, he, on his side, has never found himself in personal contact with such splendour, such opulence, such expensiveness, as this young lady's. And then she must seem to him wonderfully pretty and interesting. I rather doubt whether he dreams of marrying her. That must appear to him too impossible a piece of luck. He has nothing but his handsome face to offer, and there is a substantial Mr. Miller in that mysterious land of dollars. Giovanelli knows that he hasn't a title to offer. If he were only a count or a *marchese!*[34] He must wonder at his luck at the way they have taken him up."

"He accounts for it by his handsome face, and thinks Miss Miller a young lady *qui se passe ses fantaisies!*[35]" said Mrs. Costello.

"It is very true," Winterbourne pursued, "that Daisy and her mamma have not yet risen to that stage of—what shall I call it?—of culture, at which the idea of catching a count or a *marchese* begins. I believe that they are intellectually incapable of that conception."

"Ah! but the *cavaliere* can't believe it," said Mrs. Costello.

Of the observation excited by Daisy's "intrigue," Winterbourne gathered that day at St. Peter's sufficient evidence. A dozen of the American colonists in Rome came to talk with Mrs. Costello, who sat on a little portable stool at the base of one of the great pilasters. The vesper-service was going forward in splendid chants and organ-tones in the adjacent choir, and meanwhile, between Mrs. Costello and her friends, there was a great deal said about poor little Miss Miller's going really "too far." Winterbourne was not pleased with what he heard; but when, coming out upon the great steps of the church, he saw Daisy, who had emerged before him, get into an open cab with her accomplice and roll away through the cynical streets of Rome, he could not deny to himself that she was going very far indeed. He felt very sorry for her—not exactly that he believed that she had completely lost her head, but because it was painful to hear so much that was pretty and undefended and natural assigned to a vulgar place among the categories of disorder. He made an attempt after this to

[33]A lawyer given an honorary knighthood (the lowest noble ranking) by the Italian government.

[34]Italian: marquis.

[35]French: who indulges her whims.

give a hint to Mrs. Miller. He met one day in the Corso[36] a friend—a tourist like himself—who had just come out of the Doria Palace,[37] where he had been walking through the beautiful gallery. His friend talked for a moment about the superb portrait of Innocent X. by Velasquez, which hangs in one of the cabinets of the palace, and then said, "And in the same cabinet, by-the-way, I had the pleasure of contemplating a picture of a different kind—that pretty American girl whom you pointed out to me last week." In answer to Winterbourne's inquiries, his friend narrated that the pretty American girl—prettier than ever—was seated with a companion in the secluded nook in which the great papal portrait is enshrined.

"Who was her companion?" asked Winterbourne.

"A little Italian with a bouquet in his button-hole. The girl is delightfully pretty, but I thought I understood from you the other day that she was a young lady *du meilleur monde.*"[38]

"So she is!" answered Winterbourne; and having assured himself that his informant had seen Daisy and her companion but five minutes before, he jumped into a cab and went to call on Mrs. Miller. She was at home; but she apologised to him for receiving him in Daisy's absence.

"She's gone out somewhere with Mr. Giovanelli," said Mrs. Miller. "She's always going round with Mr. Giovanelli."

"I have noticed that they are very intimate," Winterbourne observed.

"Oh! it seems as if they couldn't live without each other!" said Mrs. Miller. "Well, he's a real gentleman, anyhow. I keep telling Daisy she's engaged!"

"And what does Daisy say?"

"Oh, she says she isn't engaged. But she might as well be!" this impartial parent resumed. "She goes on as if she was. But I've made Mr. Giovanelli promise to tell me, if *she* doesn't. I should want to write to Mr. Miller about it—shouldn't you?"

Winterbourne replied that he certainly should; and the state of mind of Daisy's mamma struck him as so unprecedented in the annals of parental vigilance that he gave up as utterly irrelevant the attempt to place her upon her guard.

After this Daisy was never at home, and Winterbourne ceased to meet her at the houses of their common acquaintance, because, as he perceived, these shrewd people had quite made up their minds that she was going too far. They ceased to invite her, and they intimated that they desired to express to observant Europeans the great truth that, though Miss Daisy Miller was a young American lady, her behaviour was not representative—was regarded by her compatriots as abnormal. Winterbourne wondered how she felt about all the cold shoulders that were turned towards her, and sometimes it annoyed him to suspect that she did not feel at all. He said to himself that she was too light and childish, too uncultivated and unreasoning, too provincial, to have reflected upon her ostracism or even to have perceived it. Then at other moments he believed that she carried about in her elegant and irresponsible little organism a defiant, passionate, perfectly observant consciousness of the impression she produced. He asked himself whether Daisy's defiance came from the consciousness

[36]"The finest street in Rome," according to Hare's *Walks in Rome.*

[37]Famed for its picture gallery. The painting of Pope Innocent X by the seventeenth-century Spanish painter Velasquez is still exhibited in a small room.

[38]French: of good society.

of innocence or from her being, essentially, a young person of the reckless class. It must be admitted that holding oneself to a belief in Daisy's "innocence" came to seem to Winterbourne more and more a matter of fine-spun gallantry. As I have already had occasion to relate, he was angry at finding himself reduced to chopping logic about this young lady; he was vexed at his want of instinctive certitude as to how far her eccentricities were generic, national, and how far they were personal. From either view of them he had somehow missed her, and now it was too late. She was "carried away" by Mr. Giovanelli.

A few days after his brief interview with her mother, he encountered her in that beautiful abode of flowering desolation known as the Palace of the Caesars. The early Roman spring had filled the air with bloom and perfume, and the rugged surface of the Palatine[39] was muffled with tender verdure. Daisy was strolling along the top of one of those great mounds of ruin that are embanked with mossy marble and paved with monumental inscriptions. It seemed to him that Rome had never been so lovely as just then. He stood looking off at the enchanting harmony of line and colour that remotely encircles the city, inhaling the softly humid odours and feeling the freshness of the year and the antiquity of the place reaffirm themselves in mysterious interfusion. It seemed to him also that Daisy had never looked so pretty; but this had been an observation of his whenever he met her. Giovanelli was at her side, and Giovanelli, too, wore an aspect of even unwonted brilliancy.

"Well," said Daisy, "I should think you would be lonesome!"

"Lonesome?" asked Winterbourne.

"You are always going round by yourself. Can't you get any one to walk with you?"

"I am not so fortunate," said Winterbourne, "as your companion."

Giovanelli, from the first, had treated Winterbourne with distinguished politeness; he listened with a deferential air to his remarks; he laughed, punctiliously, at his pleasantries; he seemed disposed to testify to his belief that Winterbourne was a superior young man. He carried himself in no degree like a jealous wooer; he had obviously a great deal of tact; he had no objection to your expecting a little humility of him. It even seemed to Winterbourne at times that Giovanelli would find a certain mental relief in being able to have a private understanding with him—to say to him, as an intelligent man, that, bless you, *he* knew how extraordinary was this young lady, and didn't flatter himself with delusive—or at least *too* delusive—hopes of matrimony and dollars. On this occasion he strolled away from his companion to pluck a sprig of almond blossom, which he carefully arranged in his button-hole.

"I know why you say that," said Daisy, watching Giovanelli. "Because you think I go round too much with *him!*" And she nodded at her attendant.

"Every one thinks so—if you care to know," said Winterbourne.

"Of course I care to know!" Daisy exclaimed seriously. "But I don't believe it. They are only pretending to be shocked. They don't really care a straw what I do. Besides, I don't go round so much."

"I think you will find they do care. They will show it—disagreeably."

[39]Numerous Roman emperors had their official residences on this hill.

Daisy looked at him a moment. "How—disagreeably?"

"Haven't you noticed anything?" Winterbourne asked.

"I have noticed you. But I noticed you were as stiff as an umbrella the first time I saw you."

"You will find I am not so stiff as several others," said Winterbourne, smiling.

"How shall I find it?"

"By going to see the others."

"What will they do to me?"

"They will give you the cold shoulder. Do you know what that means?"

Daisy was looking at him intently; she began to colour. "Do you mean as Mrs. Walker did the other night?"

"Exactly!" said Winterbourne.

She looked away at Giovanelli, who was decorating himself with his almond-blossom. Then looking back at Winterbourne—"I shouldn't think you would let people be so unkind!" she said.

"How can I help it?" he asked.

"I should think you would say something."

"I do say something;" and he paused a moment. "I say that your mother tells me that she believes you are engaged."

"Well, she does," said Daisy very simply.

Winterbourne began to laugh. "And does Randolph believe it?" he asked.

"I guess Randolph doesn't believe anything," said Daisy. Randolph's scepticism excited Winterbourne to farther hilarity, and he observed that Giovanelli was coming back to them. Daisy, observing it too, addressed herself again to her countryman. "Since you have mentioned it," she said, "I *am* engaged." . . . Winterbourne looked at her; he had stopped laughing. "You don't believe it!" she added.

He was silent a moment; and then, "Yes, I believe it!" he said.

"Oh, no, you don't," she answered. "Well, then—I am not!"

The young girl and her cicerone were on their way to the gate of the enclosure, so that Winterbourne, who had but lately entered, presently took leave of them. A week afterwards he went to dine at a beautiful villa on the Cælian Hill,[40] and, on arriving, dismissed his hired vehicle. The evening was charming, and he promised himself the satisfaction of walking home beneath the Arch of Constantine[41] and past the vaguely-lighted monuments of the Forum.[42] There was a waning moon in the sky, and her radiance was not brilliant, but she was veiled in a thin cloud-curtain which seemed to diffuse and equalise it. When, on his return from the villa (it was eleven o'clock), Winterbourne approached the dusky circle of the Colosseum,[43] it occurred to him, as a lover of the picturesque, that the interior, in the pale moonshine, would be well worth a glance. He turned aside and walked to one of the empty arches, near

[40]The Coelian Hill, sparsely inhabited in the 1870s, was known for its views and quiet walks.

[41]Erected in the fourth century to celebrate a military victory by the first Christian emperor.

[42]The heart of ancient Rome, site of the senate and various temples and memorials.

[43]The great amphitheater where gladiators fought and Christians were martyred. James pictures it as it was before 1872, when the large cross was removed and the arena excavated.

which, as he observed, an open carriage—one of the little Roman street-cabs—was stationed. Then he passed in among the cavernous shadows of the great structure, and emerged upon the clear and silent arena. The place had never seemed to him more impressive. One-half of the gigantic circus was in deep shade; the other was sleeping in the luminous dusk. As he stood there he began to murmur Byron's famous lines, out of "Manfred;"[44] but before he had finished his quotation he remembered that if nocturnal meditations in the Colosseum are recommended by the poets, they are deprecated by the doctors. The historic atmosphere was there, certainly; but the historic atmosphere, scientifically considered, was no better than a villainous miasma. Winterbourne walked to the middle of the arena, to take a more general glance, intending thereafter to make a hasty retreat. The great cross in the centre was covered with shadow; it was only as he drew near it that he made it out distinctly. Then he saw that two persons were stationed upon the low steps which formed its base. One of these was a woman, seated; her companion was standing in front of her.

Presently the sound of the woman's voice came to him distinctly in the warm night-air. "Well, he looks at us as one of the old lions or tigers may have looked at the Christian martyrs!" These were the words he heard, in the familiar accent of Miss Daisy Miller.

"Let us hope he is not very hungry," responded the ingenious Giovanelli. "He will have to take me first; you will serve for dessert!"

Winterbourne stopped, with a sort of horror; and, it must be added, with a sort of relief. It was as if a sudden illumination had been flashed upon the ambiguity of Daisy's behaviour and the riddle had become easy to read. She was a young lady whom a gentleman need no longer be at pains to respect. He stood there looking at her—looking at her companion, and not reflecting that though he saw them vaguely, he himself must have been more brightly visible. He felt angry with himself that he had bothered so much about the right way of regarding Miss Daisy Miller. Then, as he was going to advance again, he checked himself; not from the fear that he was doing her injustice, but from a sense of the danger of appearing unbecomingly exhilarated by this sudden revulsion from cautious criticism. He turned away towards the entrance of the place; but as he did so he heard Daisy speak again.

"Why, it was Mr. Winterbourne! He saw me—and he cuts me!"

What a clever little reprobate she was, and how smartly she played an injured innocence! But he wouldn't cut her. Winterbourne came forward again, and went towards the great cross. Daisy had got up; Giovanelli lifted his hat. Winterbourne had now begun to think simply of the craziness, from a sanitary point of view, of a delicate young girl lounging away the evening in this nest of malaria. What if she *were* a clever little reprobate? that was no reason for her dying of the *perniciosa*.[45] "How long have you been here?" he asked, almost brutally.

Daisy, lovely in the flattering moonlight, looked at him a moment. Then—"All the evening," she answered gently. . . . "I never saw anything so pretty."

[44]". . . upon such a night
I stood within the Coliseum's wall,
Midst the chief relics of almighty Rome."
Manfred, III, iv, 9–11

[45]*I.e.,* malaria.

"I am afraid," said Winterbourne, "that you will not think Roman fever very pretty. This is the way people catch it. I wonder," he added, turning to Giovanelli, "that you, a native Roman, should countenance such a terrible indiscretion."

"Ah," said the handsome native, "for myself, I am not afraid."

"Neither am I—for you! I am speaking for this young lady."

Giovanelli lifted his well-shaped eyebrows and showed his brilliant teeth. But he took Winterbourne's rebuke with docility. "I told the Signorina[46] it was a grave indiscretion; but when was the Signorina ever prudent?"

"I never was sick, and I don't mean to be!" the Signorina declared. "I don't look like much, but I'm healthy! I was bound to see the Colosseum by moonlight; I shouldn't have wanted to go home without that; and we have had the most beautiful time, haven't we, Mr. Giovanelli? If there has been any danger, Eugenio can give me some pills. He has got some splendid pills."

"I should advise you," said Winterbourne, "to drive home as fast as possible and take one!"

"What you say is very wise," Giovanelli rejoined. "I will go and make sure the carriage is at hand." And he went forward rapidly.

Daisy followed with Winterbourne. He kept looking at her; she seemed not in the least embarrassed. Winterbourne said nothing; Daisy chattered about the beauty of the place. "Well, I *have* seen the Colosseum by moonlight!" she exclaimed. "That's one good thing." Then, noticing Winterbourne's silence, she asked him why he didn't speak. He made no answer; he only began to laugh. They passed under one of the dark archways; Giovanelli was in front with the carriage. Here Daisy stopped a moment, looking at the young American. "*Did* you believe I was engaged the other day?" she asked.

"It doesn't matter what I believed the other day," said Winterbourne, still laughing.

"Well, what do you believe now?"

"I believe that it makes very little difference whether you are engaged or not!"

He felt the young girl's pretty eyes fixed upon him through the thick gloom of the archway; she was apparently going to answer. But Giovanelli hurried her forward. "Quick, quick," he said; "if we get in by midnight we are quite safe."

Daisy took her seat in the carriage, and the fortunate Italian placed himself beside her. "Don't forget Eugenio's pills!" said Winterbourne, as he lifted his hat.

"I don't care," said Daisy, in a little strange tone, "whether I have Roman fever or not!" Upon this the cab-driver cracked his whip, and they rolled away over the desultory patches of the antique pavement.

Winterbourne—to do him justice, as it were—mentioned to no one that he had encountered Miss Miller, at midnight, in the Colosseum with a gentleman; but nevertheless, a couple of days later, the fact of her having been there under these circumstances was known to every member of the little American circle, and commented accordingly. Winterbourne reflected that they had of course known it at the hotel, and that, after Daisy's return, there had been an exchange of jokes between the porter and the cab-driver. But the young man was conscious at the same moment that

[46]The Miss, the young lady.

it had ceased to be a matter of serious regret to him that the little American flirt should be "talked about" by low-minded menials. These people, a day or two later, had serious information to give: the little American flirt was alarmingly ill. Winterbourne, when the rumour came to him, immediately went to the hotel for more news. He found that two or three charitable friends had preceded him, and that they were being entertained in Mrs. Miller's salon by Randolph.

"It's going round at night," said Randolph—"that's what made her sick. She's always going round at night. I shouldn't think she'd want to—it's so plaguey dark. You can't see anything here at night, except when there's a moon. In America there's always a moon!" Mrs. Miller was invisible; she was now, at least, giving her daughter the advantage of her society. It was evident that Daisy was dangerously ill.

Winterbourne went often to ask for news of her, and once he saw Mrs. Miller, who, though deeply alarmed, was—rather to his surprise—perfectly composed, and, as it appeared, a most efficient and judicious nurse. She talked a good deal about Dr. Davis, but Winterbourne paid her the compliment of saying to himself that she was not, after all, such a monstrous goose. "Daisy spoke of you the other day," she said to him. "Half the time she doesn't know what she's saying, but that time I think she did. She gave me a message; she told me to tell you. She told me to tell you that she never was engaged to that handsome Italian. I am sure I am very glad; Mr. Giovanelli hasn't been near us since she was taken ill. I thought he was so much of a gentleman; but I don't call that very polite! A lady told me that he was afraid I was angry with him for taking Daisy round at night. Well, so I am; but I suppose he knows I'm a lady. I would scorn to scold him. Any way, she says she's not engaged. I don't know why she wanted you to know; but she said to me three times—'Mind you tell Mr. Winterbourne.' And then she told me to ask if you remembered the time you went to that castle, in Switzerland. But I said I wouldn't give any such messages as that. Only, if she is not engaged, I'm sure I'm glad to know it."

But, as Winterbourne had said, it mattered very little. A week after this the poor girl died; it had been a terrible case of the fever. Daisy's grave was in the little Protestant cemetery, in an angle of the wall of imperial Rome, beneath the cypresses and the thick spring-flowers. Winterbourne stood there beside it, with a number of other mourners; a number larger than the scandal excited by the young lady's career would have led you to expect. Near him stood Giovanelli, who came nearer still before Winterbourne turned away. Giovanelli was very pale; on this occasion he had no flower in his button-hole; he seemed to wish to say something. At last he said, "She was the most beautiful young lady I ever saw, and the most amiable." And then he added in a moment, "And she was the most innocent."

Winterbourne looked at him, and presently repeated his words, "And the most innocent?"

"The most innocent!"

Winterbourne felt sore and angry. "Why the devil," he asked, "did you take her to that fatal place?"

Mr. Giovanelli's urbanity was apparently imperturbable. He looked on the ground a moment, and then he said, "For myself, I had no fear; and she wanted to go."

"That was no reason!" Winterbourne declared.

The subtle Roman again dropped his eyes. "If she had lived, I should have got nothing. She would never have married me, I am sure."

"She would never have married you?"

"For a moment I hoped so. But no. I am sure."

Winterbourne listened to him; he stood staring at the raw protuberance among the April daisies. When he turned away again Mr. Giovanelli, with his light slow step, had retired.

Winterbourne almost immediately left Rome; but the following summer he again met his aunt, Mrs. Costello, at Vevey. Mrs. Costello was fond of Vevey. In the interval Winterbourne had often thought of Daisy Miller and her mystifying manners. One day he spoke of her to his aunt—said it was on his conscience that he had done her injustice.

"I am sure I don't know," said Mrs. Costello. "How did your injustice affect her?"

"She sent me a message before her death which I didn't understand at the time. But I have understood it since. She would have appreciated one's esteem."

"Is that a modest way," asked Mrs. Costello, "of saying that she would have reciprocated one's affection?"

Winterbourne offered no answer to this question; but he presently said, "You were right in that remark that you made last summer. I was booked to make a mistake. I have lived too long in foreign parts."

Nevertheless, he went back to live at Geneva, whence there continue to come the most contradictory accounts of his motives of sojourn: a report that he is "studying" hard—an intimation that he is much interested in a very clever foreign lady.

1879

The Art of Fiction

I should not have affixed so comprehensive a title to these few remarks, necessarily wanting in any completeness upon a subject the full consideration of which would carry us far, did I not seem to discover a pretext for my temerity in the interesting pamphlet lately published under this name by Mr. Walter Besant.[1] Mr Besant's lecture at the Royal Institution—the original form of his pamphlet—appears to indicate that many persons are interested in the art of fiction, and are not indifferent to such remarks, as those who practise it may attempt to make about it. I am therefore anxious not to lose the benefit of this favourable association, and to edge in a few words under cover of the attention which Mr. Besant is sure to have excited. There is something very encouraging in his having put into form certain of his ideas on the mystery of story-telling.

[1]Sir Walter Besant (1836–1901), English novelist known for his romantic style and his concern for social causes.

It is a proof of life and curiosity—curiosity on the part of the brotherhood of novelists as well as on the part of their readers. Only a short time ago it might have been supposed that the English novel was not what the French call *discutable.*[2] It had no air of having a theory, a conviction, a consciousness of itself behind it—of being the expression of an artistic faith, the result of choice and comparison. I do not say it was necessarily the worse for that: it would take much more courage than I possess to intimate that the form of the novel as Dickens[3] and Thackeray[4] (for instance) saw it had any taint of incompleteness. It was, however, *naïf* (if I may help myself out with another French word); and evidently if it be destined to suffer in any way for having lost its *naïveté* it has now an idea of making sure of the corresponding advantages. During the period I have alluded to there was a comfortable, good-humoured feeling abroad that a novel is a novel, as a pudding is a pudding, and that our only business with it could be to swallow it. But within a year or two, for some reason or other, there have been signs of returning animation—the era of discussion would appear to have been to a certain extent opened. Art lives upon discussion, upon experiment, upon curiosity, upon variety of attempt, upon the exchange of views and the comparison of standpoints; and there is a presumption that those times when no one has anything particular to say about it, and has no reason to give for practice or preference, though they may be times of honour, are not times of development—are times, possibly even, a little of dulness. The successful application of any art is a delightful spectacle, but the theory too is interesting; and though there is a great deal of the latter without the former I suspect there has never been a genuine success that has not had a latent core of conviction. Discussion, suggestion, formulation, these things are fertilising when they are frank and sincere. Mr. Besant has set an excellent example in saying what he thinks, for his part, about the way in which fiction should be written, as well as about the way in which it should be published; for his view of the "art," carried on into an appendix, covers that too. Other labourers in the same field will doubtless take up the argument, they will give it the light of their experience, and the effect will surely be to make our interest in the novel a little more what it had for some time threatened to fail to be—a serious, active, inquiring interest, under protection of which this delightful study may, in moments of confidence, venture to say a little more what it thinks of itself.

It must take itself seriously for the public to take it so. The old superstition about fiction being "wicked" has doubtless died out in England; but the spirit of it lingers in a certain oblique regard directed toward any story which does not more or less admit that it is only a joke. Even the most jocular novel feels in some degree the weight of the proscription that was formerly directed against literary levity: the jocularity does not always succeed in passing for orthodoxy. It is still expected, though perhaps people are ashamed to say it, that a production which is after all only a "make-believe" (for what else is a "story"?) shall be in some degree apologetic—shall renounce the

[2]French: questionable.

[3]Charles Dickens (1812–1870), the most popular English novelist of the nineteenth century, wrote prolifically about all levels of British society employing a variety of literary modes from the sensational and the dramatic to the sentimental.

[4]William Makepeace Thackeray (1811–1863), satiric Victorian novelist.

pretension of attempting really to represent life. This, of course, any sensible, wide-awake story declines to do, for it quickly perceives that the tolerance granted to it on such a condition is only an attempt to stifle it disguised in the form of generosity. The old evangelical hostility to the novel, which was as explicit as it was narrow, and which regarded it as little less favourable to our immortal part than a stage-play, was in reality far less insulting. The only reason for the existence of a novel is that it does attempt to represent life. When it relinquishes this attempt, the same attempt that we see on the canvas of the painter, it will have arrived at a very strange pass. It is not expected of the picture that it will make itself humble in order to be forgiven; and the analogy between the art of the painter and the art of the novelist is, so far as I am able to see, complete. Their inspiration is the same, their process (allowing for the different quality of the vehicle), is the same, their success is the same. They may learn from each other, they may explain and sustain each other. Their cause is the same, and the honour of one is the honour of another. The Mahometans[5] think a picture an unholy thing, but it is a long time since any Christian did, and it is therefore the more odd that in the Christian mind the traces (dissimulated though they may be) of a suspicion of the sister art should linger to this day. The only effectual way to lay it to rest is to emphasise the analogy to which I just alluded—to insist on the fact that as the picture is reality, so the novel is history. That is the only general description (which does it justice) that we may give of the novel. But history also is allowed to represent life; it is not, any more than painting, expected to apologise. The subject-matter of fiction is stored up likewise in documents and records, and if it will not give itself away, as they say in California, it must speak with assurance, with the tone of the historian. Certain accomplished novelists have a habit of giving themselves away which must often bring tears to the eyes of people who take their fiction seriously. I was lately struck, in reading over many pages of Anthony Trollope,[6] with his want of discretion in this particular. In a digression, a parenthesis or an aside, he concedes to the reader that he and this trusting friend are only "making believe." He admits that the events he narrates have not really happened, and that he can give his narrative any turn the reader may like best. Such a betrayal of a sacred office seems to me, I confess, a terrible crime; it is what I mean by the attitude of apology, and it shocks me every whit as much in Trollope as it would have shocked me in Gibbon[7] or Macaulay.[8] It implies that the novelist is less occupied in looking for the truth (the truth, of course I mean, that he assumes, the premises that we must grant him, whatever they may be), than the historian, and in doing so it deprives him at a stroke of all his standing-room. To represent and illustrate the past, the actions of men, is the task of either writer, and the only difference that I can see is, in proportion as he succeeds, to the honour of the novelist, consisting as it does in his having more difficulty in collecting his evidence, which is so far from being purely literary. It seems to me to give him a great character, the fact that he has at once so much in common with the philosopher and the painter; this double analogy is a magnificent heritage.

[5]Muslims.

[6]English novelist noted for the verisimilitude of his Victorian fiction (1815–1882).

[7]Edward Gibbon (1737–1794), English historian.

[8]Thomas Babbington Macaulay (1800–1859), English historian, author, and politician.

It is of all this evidently that Mr. Besant is full when he insists upon the fact that fiction is one of the *fine* arts, deserving in its turn of all the honours and emoluments that have hitherto been reserved for the successful profession of music, poetry, painting, architecture. It is impossible to insist too much on so important a truth, and the place that Mr. Besant demands for the work of the novelist may be represented, a trifle less abstractly, by saying that he demands not only that it shall be reputed artistic, but that it shall be reputed very artistic indeed. It is excellent that he should have struck this note, for his doing so indicates that there was need of it, that his proposition may be to many people a novelty. One rubs one's eyes at the thought; but the rest of Mr. Besant's essay confirms the revelation. I suspect in truth that it would be possible to confirm it still further, and that one would not be far wrong in saying that in addition to the people to whom it has never occurred that a novel ought to be artistic, there are a great many others who, if this principle were urged upon them, would be filled with an indefinable mistrust. They would find it diffucult to explain their repugnance, but it would operate strongly to put them on their guard. "Art," in our Protestant communities, where so many things have got so strangely twisted about, is supposed in certain circles to have some vaguely injurious effect upon those who make it an important consideration, who let it weigh in the balance. It is assumed to be opposed in some mysterious manner to morality, to amusement, to instruction. When it is embodied in the work of the painter (the sculptor is another affair!) you know what it is: it stands there before you, in the honesty of pink and green and a gilt frame; you can see the worst of it at a glance, and you can be on your guard. But when it is introduced into literature it becomes more insidious—there is danger of its hurting you before you know it. Literature should be either instructive or amusing, and there is in many minds an impression that these artistic preoccupations, the search for form, contribute to neither end, interfere indeed with both. They are too frivolous to be edifying, and too serious to be diverting; and they are moreover priggish and paradoxical and superfluous. That, I think, represents the manner in which the latent thought of many people who read novels as an exercise in skipping would explain itself if it were to become articulate. They would argue, of course, that a novel ought to be "good," but they would interpret this term in a fashion of their own, which indeed would vary considerably from one critic to another. One would say that being good means representing virtuous and aspiring characters, placed in prominent positions; another would say that it depends on a "happy ending," on a distribution at the last of prizes, pensions, husbands, wives, babies, millions, appended paragraphs, and cheerful remarks. Another still would say that it means being full of incident and movement, so that we shall wish to jump ahead, to see who was the mysterious stranger, and if the stolen will was ever found, and shall not be distracted from this pleasure by any tiresome analysis or "description." But they would all agree that the "artistic" idea would spoil some of their fun. One would hold it accountable for all the description, another would see it revealed in the absence of sympathy. Its hostility to a happy ending would be evident, and it might even in some cases render any ending at all impossible. The "ending" of a novel is, for many persons, like that of a good dinner, a course of dessert and ices, and the artist in fiction is regarded as a sort of meddlesome doctor who forbids agreeable aftertastes. It is therefore true that this conception of Mr. Besant's of the novel as a superior form encounters not only a negative but a positive indifference. It matters little that as a work of art it should really be as little or as much of its essence to supply happy endings, sympathetic characters, and an objective tone, as if it were a work of mechanics: the association of ideas, however incongruous, might easily be too much for it if an eloquent voice were not sometimes raised to call attention to the fact that it is at once as free and as serious a branch of literature as any other.

Certainly this might sometimes be doubted in presence of the enormous number of works of fiction that appeal to the credulity of our generation, for it might easily seem that there could be no great character in a commodity so quickly and easily produced. It must be admitted that good novels are much compromised by bad ones, and that the field at large suffers discredit from overcrowding. I think, however, that this injury is only superficial, and that the superabundance of written fiction proves nothing against the principle itself. It has been vulgarised, like all other kinds of literature, like everything else to-day, and it has proved more than some kinds accessible to vulgarisation. But there is as much difference as there ever was between a good novel and a bad one: the bad is swept with all the daubed canvases and spoiled marble into some unvisited limbo, or infinite rubbish-yard beneath the back-windows of the world, and the good subsists and emits its light and stimulates our desire for perfection. As I shall take the liberty of making but a single criticism of Mr. Besant, whose tone is so full of the love of his art, I may as well have done with it at once. He seems to me to mistake in attempting to say so definitely beforehand what sort of an affair the good novel will be. To indicate the danger of such an error as that has been the purpose of these few pages; to suggest that certain traditions on the subject, applied *a priori,* have already had much to answer for, and that the good health of an art which undertakes so immediately to reproduce life must demand that it be perfectly free. It lives upon exercise, and the very meaning of exercise is freedom. The only obligation to which in advance we may hold a novel, without incurring the accusation of being arbitrary, is that it be interesting. That general responsibility rests upon it, but it is the only one I can think of. The ways in which it is at liberty to accomplish this result (of interesting us) strike me as innumerable, and such as can only suffer from being marked out or fenced in by prescription. They are as various as the temperament of man, and they are successful in proportion as they reveal a particular mind, different from others. A novel is in its broadest definition a personal, a direct impression of life; that, to begin with, constitutes its value, which is greater or less according to the intensity of the impression. But there will be no intensity at all, and therefore no value, unless there is freedom to feel and say. The tracing of a line to be followed, of a tone to be taken, of a form to be filled out, is a limitation of that freedom and a suppression of the very thing that we are most curious about. The form, it seems to me, is to be appreciated after the fact: then the author's choice has been made, his standard has been indicated; then we can follow lines and directions and compare tones and resemblances. Then in a word we can enjoy one of the most charming of pleasures, we can estimate quality, we can apply the test of execution. The execution belongs to the author alone; it is what is most personal to him, and we measure him by that. The advantage, the luxury, as well as the torment and responsibility of the novelist, is that there is no limit to what he may attempt as an executant—no limit to his possible experiments, efforts, discoveries, successes. Here it is especially that he works, step by step, like his brother of the brush, of whom we may always say that he has painted his picture in a manner best known to himself. His manner is his secret, not necessarily a jealous one. He cannot disclose it as a general thing if he would; he would be at a loss to teach it to others. I say this with a due recollection of having insisted on the community of method of the artist who paints a picture and the artist who writes a novel. The painter *is* able to teach the rudiments of his practice, and it is possible, from the study of good work (granted the aptitude), both to learn how to paint and to learn how to write. Yet it remains true, without injury to the *rapprochement,*[9] that the literary artist would be obliged to say to his pupil much more than the other, "Ah, well, you must do it as you can!" It is a question of degree, a matter of delicacy. If there are exact sciences, there are also exact arts, and the grammar of painting is so much more definite that it makes the difference.

I ought to add, however, that if Mr. Besant says at the beginning of his essay that the "laws of fiction may be laid down and taught with as much precision and exactness as the laws of harmony, perspective, and proportion," he mitigates what might appear to be an extravagance by applying his remark to "general" laws, and by expressing most of these rules in a manner with which it would certainly be unaccommodating to disagree. That the novelist must write from his experience, that his "characters must be real and such as might be met with in actual life;" that "a young lady brought up in a quiet country village should avoid descriptions of garrison life," and "a writer whose friends and personal experiences belong to the lower middle-class should carefully avoid introducing his characters into society," that one should enter one's notes in a common-place book;[10] that one's figures should be clear in outline; that making them clear by some trick of speech or of carriage is a bad method, and "describing them at length" is a worse one; that English Fiction should have a "conscious moral purpose;" that "it is almost impossible to estimate too highly the value of careful workmanship—that is, of style;" that "the most important point of all is the story," that "the story is everything": these are principles with most of which it is surely impossible not to sympathise. That remark about the lower middle-class writer and his knowing his place is perhaps rather chilling; but for the rest I should find it difficult to dissent from any one of these recommendations. At the same time, I should find it difficult positively to assent to them, with the exception, perhaps, of the injunction as to entering one's notes in a common-place book. They scarcely seem to me to have the quality that Mr. Besant attributes to the rules of the novelist—the "precision and exactness" of "the laws of harmony, perspective, and proportion." They are suggestive, they are even inspiring, but they are not exact, though they are doubtless as much so as the case admits of: which is a proof of that liberty of interpretation for which I just contended. For the value of these different injunctions—so beautiful and so vague—is wholly in the meaning one attaches to them. The characters, the situation, which strike one as real will be those that touch and interest one most, but the measure of reality is very difficult to fix. The reality of Don Quixote[11] or of Mr. Micawber[12] is a very delicate shade; it is a reality so coloured by

[9]French: accord.

[10]A book in which quotations, poems, extracts, comments, and so on are recorded for future use.

[11]Protagonist of Miguel de Cervantes's romance *Don Quixote de la Mancha* (1605), who lived according to chivalrous but impractical ideals.

[12]Wilkins Micawber, a character in Charles Dickens's *David Copperfield,* known for his good heart and erratic temperament.

the author's vision that, vivid as it may be, one would hesitate to propose it as a model: one would expose one's self to some very embarrassing questions on the part of a pupil. It goes without saying that you will not write a good novel unless you possess the sense of reality; but it will be difficult to give you a recipe for calling that sense into being. Humanity is immense, and reality has a myriad forms; the most one can affirm is that some of the flowers of fiction have the odour of it, and others have not; as for telling you in advance how your nosegay should be composed, that is another affair. It is equally excellent and inconclusive to say that one must write from experience; to our supposititious aspirant such a declaration might savour of mockery. What kind of experience is intended, and where does it begin and end? Experience is never limited, and it is never complete; it is an immense sensibility, a kind of huge spider-web of the finest silken threads suspended in the chamber of consciousness, and catching every air-borne particle in its tissue. It is the very atmosphere of the mind; and when the mind is imaginative—much more when it happens to be that of a man of genius—it takes to itself the faintest hints of life, it converts the very pulses of the air into revelations. The young lady living in a village has only to be a damsel upon whom nothing is lost to make it quite unfair (as it seems to me) to declare to her that she shall have nothing to say about the military. Greater miracles have been seen than that, imagination assisting, she should speak the truth about some of these gentlemen. I remember an English novelist, a woman of genius, telling me that she was much commended for the impression she had managed to give in one of her tales of the nature and way of life of the French Protestant youth. She had been asked where she learned so much about this recondite being, she had been congratulated on her peculiar opportunities. These opportunities consisted in her having once, in Paris, as she ascended a staircase, passed an open door where, in the household of a *pasteur,*[13] some of the young Protestants were seated at table round a finished meal. The glimpse made a picture; it lasted only a moment, but that moment was experience. She had got her direct personal impression, and she turned out her type. She knew what youth was, and what Protestantism; she also had the advantage of having seen what it was to be French, so that she converted these ideas into a concrete image and produced a reality. Above all, however, she was blessed with the faculty which when you give it an inch takes an ell, and which for the artist is a much greater source of strength than any accident of residence or of place in the social scale. The power to guess the unseen from the seen, to trace the implication of things, to judge the whole piece by the pattern, the condition of feeling life in general so completely that you are well on your way to knowing any particular corner of it—this cluster of gifts may almost be said to constitute experience, and they occur in country and in town, and in the most differing stages of education. If experience consists of impressions, it may be said that impressions *are* experience, just as (have we not seen it?) they are the very air we breathe. Therefore, if I should certainly say to a novice, "Write from experience and experience only," I should feel that this was rather a tantalising monition if I were not careful immediately to add, "Try to be one of the people on whom nothing is lost!"

[13]French: minister, priest.

I am far from intending by this to minimise the importance of exactness—of truth of detail. One can speak best from one's own taste, and I may therefore venture to say that the air of reality (solidity of specification) seems to me to be the supreme virtue of a novel—the merit on which all its other merits (including that conscious moral purpose of which Mr. Besant speaks) helplessly and submissively depend. If it be not there they are all as nothing, and if these be there, they owe their effect to the success with which the author has produced the illusions of life. The cultivation of this success, the study of this exquisite process, form, to my taste, the beginning and the end of the art of the novelist. They are his inspiration, his despair, his reward, his torment, his delight. It is here in very truth that he competes with life; it is here that he competes with his brother the painter in *his* attempt to render the look of things, the look that conveys their meaning, to catch the colour, the relief, the expression, the surface, the substance of the human spectacle. It is in regard to this that Mr. Besant is well inspired when he bids him take notes. He cannot possibly take too many, he cannot possibly take enough. All life solicits him, and to "render" the simplest surface, to produce the most momentary illusion, is a very complicated business. His case would be easier, and the rule would be more exact, if Mr. Besant had been able to tell him what notes to take. But this, I fear, he can never learn in any manual; it is the business of his life. He has to take a great many in order to select a few, he has to work them up as he can, and even the guides and philosophers who might have most to say to him must leave him alone when it comes to the application of precepts, as we leave the painter in communion with his palette. That his characters "must be clear in outline," as Mr. Besant says—he feels that down to his boots; but how he shall make them so is a secret between his good angel and himself. It would be absurdly simple if he could be taught that a great deal of "description" would make them so, or that on the contrary the absence of description and the cultivation of dialogue, or the absence of dialogue and the multiplication of "incident," would rescue him from his difficulties. Nothing, for instance, is more possible than that he be of a turn of mind for which this odd, literal opposition of description and dialogue, incident and description, has little meaning and light. People often talk of these things as if they had a kind of internecine[14] distinctness, instead of melting into each other at every breath, and being intimately associated parts of one general effort of expression. I cannot imagine composition existing in a series of blocks, nor conceive, in any novel worth discussing at all, of a passage of dialogue that is not in its intention descriptive, a touch of truth of any sort that does not partake of the nature of incident, or an incident that derives its interest from any other source than the general and only source of the success of a work of art—that of being illustrative. A novel is a living thing, all one and continuous, like any other organism, and in proportion as it lives will it be found, I think, that in each of the parts there is something of each of the other parts. The critic who over the close texture of a finished work shall pretend to trace a geography of items will mark some frontiers as artificial, I fear, as any that have been known to history. There is an old-fashioned distinction betwen the novel of character and the novel of incident which must have cost many a smile to the intending fabulist who was keen about his work. It appears to me as little to the point

[14]Mutually destructive.

as the equally celebrated distinction between the novel and the romance—to answer as little to any reality. There are bad novels and good novels, as there are bad pictures and good pictures; but that is the only distinction in which I see any meaning, and I can as little imagine speaking of a novel of character as I can imagine speaking of a picture of character. When one says picture one says of character, when one says novel one says of incident, and the terms may be transposed at will. What is character but the determination of incident? What is incident but the illustration of character? What is either a picture or a novel that is *not* of character? What else do we seek in it and find in it? It is an incident for a woman to stand up with her hand resting on a table and look out at you in a certain way; or if it be not an incident I think it will be hard to say what it is. At the same time it is an expression of character. If you say you don't see it (character in *that—allons donc!*),[15] this is exactly what the artist who has reasons of his own for thinking he *does* see it undertakes to show you. When a young man makes up his mind that he has not faith enough after all to enter the church as he intended, that is an incident, though you may not hurry to the end of the chapter to see whether perhaps he doesn't change once more. I do not say that these are extraordinary or startling incidents. I do not pretend to estimate the degree of interest proceeding from them, for this will depend upon the skill of the painter. It sounds almost puerile to say that some incidents are intrinsically much more important than others, and I need not take this precaution after having professed my sympathy for the major ones in remarking that the only classification of the novel that I can understand is into that which has life and that which has it not.

The novel and the romance, the novel of incident and that of character—these clumsy separations appear to me to have been made by critics and readers for their own convenience, and to help them out of some of their occasional queer predicaments, but to have little reality or interest for the producer, from whose point of view it is of course that we are attempting to consider the art of fiction. The case is the same with another shadowy category which Mr. Besant apparently is disposed to set up—that of the "modern English novel"; unless indeed it be that in this matter he has fallen into an accidental confusion of standpoints. It is not quite clear whether he intends the remarks in which he alludes to it to be didactic or historical. It is as difficult to suppose a person intending to write a modern English as to suppose him writing an ancient English novel: that is a label which begs the question. One writes the novel, one paints the picture, of one's language and of one's time, and calling it modern English will not, alas! make the difficult task any easier. No more, unfortunately, will calling this or that work of one's fellow-artist a romance—unless it be, of course, simply for the pleasantness of the thing, as for instance when Hawthorne[16] gave this heading to his story of *Blithedale*. The French, who have brought the theory of fiction to remarkable completeness, have but one name for the novel, and have not attempted smaller things in it, that I can see, for that. I can think of no obligation to which the "romancer" would not be held equally with the novelist; the standard of execution is equally high for each. Of course it is of execution that we are talking—that being the only point of a novel that is open to contention. This is perhaps too often lost sight of, only to produce interminable confusions and cross-purposes.

[15]French: come on!

[16]Nathaniel Hawthorne (1804–1864), antebellum American writer known for romance fiction set mainly in New England.

We must grant the artist his subject, his idea, his *donnée*:[17] our criticism is applied only to what he makes of it. Naturally I do not mean that we are bound to like it or find it interesting: in case we do not our course is perfectly simple—to let it alone. We may believe that of a certain idea even the most sincere novelist can make nothing at all, and the event may perfectly justify our belief; but the failure will have been a failure to execute, and it is in the execution that the fatal weakness is recorded. If we pretend to respect the artist at all, we must allow him his freedom of choice, in the face, in particular cases, of innumerable presumptions that the choice will not fructify. Art derives a considerable part of its beneficial exercise from flying in the face of presumptions, and some of the most interesting experiments of which it is capable are hidden in the bosom of common things. Gustave Flaubert[18] has written a story about the devotion of a servant-girl to a parrot, and the production, highly finished as it is, cannot on the whole be called a success. We are perfectly free to find it flat, but I think it might have been interesting; and I, for my part, am extremely glad he should have written it; it is a contribution to our knowledge of what can be done—or what cannot. Ivan Turgénieff[19] has written a tale about a deaf and dumb serf and a lap-dog, and the thing is touching, loving, a little masterpiece. He struck the note of life where Gustave Flaubert missed it—he flew in the face of a presumption and achieved a victory.

Nothing, of course, will ever take the place of the good old fashion of "liking" a work of art or not liking it: the most improved criticism will not abolish that primitive, that ultimate test. I mention this to guard myself from the accusation of intimating that the idea, the subject, of a novel or a picture, does not matter. It matters, to my sense, in the highest degree, and if I might put up a prayer it would be that artists should select none but the richest. Some, as I have already hastened to admit, are much more remunerative than others, and it would be a world happily arranged in which persons intending to treat them should be exempt from confusions and mistakes. This fortunate condition will arrive only, I fear, on the same day that critics become purged from error. Meanwhile, I repeat, we do not judge the artist with fairness unless we say to him, "Oh, I grant you your starting-point, because if I did not I should seem to prescribe to you, and heaven forbid I should take that responsibility. If I pretend to tell you what you must not take, you will call upon me to tell you then what you must take; in which case I shall be prettily caught. Moreover, it isn't till I have accepted your data that I can begin to measure you. I have the standard, the pitch; I have no right to tamper with your flute and then criticise your music. Of course I may not care for your idea at all; I may think it silly, or stale, or unclean; in which case I wash my hands of you altogether. I may content myself with believing that you will not have succeeded in being interesting, but I shall, of course, not attempt to demonstrate it, and you will be as indifferent to me as I am to you. I needn't remind you that there are all sorts of tastes: who can know it better? Some people, for excellent reasons, don't like to read about carpenters; others, for reasons

[17]French: literally, "given"; refers to the autonomy of a writer's material and standpoint.

[18]French novelist noted for his realist fiction and artistry (1821–1880).

[19]Ivan Sergeevich Turgenieff (Turgenev) (1818–1883), Russian realist novelist recognized for his engagement with social and political issues.

even better, don't like to read about courtesans. Many object to Americans. Others (I believe they are mainly editors and publishers) won't look at Italians. Some readers don't like quiet subjects; others don't like bustling ones. Some enjoy a complete illusion, others the consciousness of large concessions. They choose their novels accordingly, and if they don't care about your idea they won't, *a fortiori,*[20] care about your treatment."

So that it comes back very quickly, as I have said, to the liking: in spite of M. Zola,[21] who reasons less powerfully than he represents, and who will not reconcile himself to this absoluteness of taste, thinking that there are certain things that people ought to like, and that they can be made to like. I am quite at a loss to imagine anything (at any rate in this matter of fiction) that people *ought* to like or to dislike. Selection will be sure to take care of itself, for it has a constant motive behind it. That motive is simply experience. As people feel life, so they will feel the art that is most closely related to it. This closeness of relation is what we should never forget in talking of the effort of the novel. Many people speak of it as a factitious, artificial form, a product of ingenuity, the business of which is to alter and arrange the things that surround us, to translate them into conventional, traditional moulds. This, however, is a view of the matter which carries us but a very short way, condemns the art to an eternal repetition of a few familiar *clichés,* cuts short its development, and leads us straight up to a dead wall. Catching the very note and trick, the strange irregular rhythm of life, that is the attempt whose strenuous force keeps Fiction upon her feet. In proportion as in what she offers us we see life *without* rearrangement do we feel that we are touching the truth; in proportion as we see it *with* rearrangement do we feel that we are being put off with a substitute, a compromise and convention. It is not uncommon to hear an extraordinary assurance of remark in regard to this matter of rearranging, which is often spoken of as if it were the last word of art. Mr. Besant seems to me in danger of falling into the great error with his rather unguarded talk about "selection." Art is essentially selection, but it is a selection whose main care is to be typical, to be inclusive. For many people art means rose-coloured window-panes and selection means picking a bouquet for Mrs. Grundy.[22] They will tell you glibly that artistic considerations have nothing to do with the disagreeable, with the ugly; they will rattle off shallow commonplaces about the province of art and the limits of art till you are moved to some wonder in return as to the province and the limits of ignorance. It appears to me that no one can ever have made a seriously artistic attempt without becoming conscious of an immense increase—a kind of revelation—of freedom. One perceives in that case—by the light of a heavenly ray—that the province of art is all life, all feeling, all observation, all vision. As Mr. Besant so justly intimates, it is all experience. That is a sufficient answer to those who maintain that it must not touch the sad things of life, who stick into its divine unconscious bosom little prohibitory inscriptions on the end of sticks, such as we see in public gardens—"It is forbidden to walk on the grass; it is forbidden to touch the flowers; it is not allowed to introduce dogs or to remain after dark; it is requested to keep to the right." The young aspirant in the line of fiction whom we continue to imagine will do

[20]Latin: all the more so.

[21]Émile Zola (1840–1902), French novelist noted for his naturalistic novels.

[22]A narrow-minded or priggish person (after a character by the same name featured in *Speed the Plough* [1798], a play by Thomas Morton).

nothing without taste, for in that case his freedom would be of little use to him; but the first advantage of his taste will be to reveal to him the absurdity of the little sticks and tickets. If he have taste, I must add, of course he will have ingenuity, and my disrespectful reference to that quality just now was not meant to imply that it is useless in fiction. But it is only a secondary aid; the first is a capacity for receiving straight impressions.

Mr. Besant has some remarks on the question of "the story" which I shall not attempt to criticise, though they seem to me to contain a singular ambiguity, because I do not think I understand them. I cannot see what is meant by talking as if there were a part of a novel which is the story and part of it which for mystical reasons is not—unless indeed the distinction be made in a sense in which it is difficult to suppose that any one should attempt to convey anything. "The story," if it represents anything, represents the subject, the idea, the *donnée* of the novel; and there is surely no "school"—Mr. Besant speaks of a school—which urges that a novel should be all treatment and no subject. There must assuredly be something to treat; every school is intimately conscious of that. This sense of the story being the idea, the starting-point, of the novel, is the only one that I see in which it can be spoken of as something different from its organic whole; and since in proportion as the work is successful the idea permeates and penetrates it, informs and animates it, so that every word and every punctuation-point contribute directly to the expression, in that proportion do we lose our sense of the story being a blade which may be drawn more or less out of its sheath. The story and the novel, the idea and the form, are the needle and thread, and I never heard of a guild of tailors who recommended the use of the thread without the needle, or the needle without the thread. Mr. Besant is not the only critic who may be observed to have spoken as if there were certain things in life which constitute stories, and certain others which do not. I find the same odd implication in an entertaining article in the *Pall Mall Gazette*[23] devoted, as it happens, to Mr. Besant's lecture. "The story is the thing!" says this graceful writer, as if with a tone of opposition to some other idea. I should think it was, as every painter who, as the time for "sending in" his picture looms in the distance, finds himself still in quest of a subject—as every belated artist not fixed about his theme will heartily agree. There are some subjects which speak to us and others which do not, but he would be a clever man who should undertake to give a rule—an index expurgatorius—by which the story and the no-story should be known apart. It is impossible (to me at least) to imagine any such rule which shall not be altogether arbitrary. The writer in the *Pall Mall* opposes the delightful (as I suppose) novel of *Margot la Balafrée* to certain tales in which "Bostonian nymphs" appear to have "rejected English dukes for psychological reasons." I am not acquainted with the romance just designated, and can scarcely forgive the *Pall Mall* critic for not mentioning the name of the author, but the title appears to refer to a lady who may have received a scar in some heroic adventure. I am inconsolable at not being acquainted with this episode, but am utterly at a loss to see why it is a story when the rejection (or acceptance) of a duke is not, and why a reason, psychological or other, is not a subject when a cicatrix is. They are all patricles of the multitudinous life with which the novel deals, and surely no dogma which pretends to make it lawful to touch the one and unlawful to touch the

[23] A liberal London "penny paper."

other will stand for a moment on its feet. It is the special picture that must stand or fall, according as it seem to possess truth or to lack it. Mr. Besant does not, to my sense, light up the subject by intimating that a story must, under penalty of not being a story, consist of "adventures." Why of adventures more than of green spectacles? He mentions a category of impossible things, and among them he places "fiction without adventure." Why without adventure, more than without matrimony, or celibacy, or parturition, or cholera, or hydrophaty, or Jansenism?[24] This seems to me to bring the novel back to the hapless little *rôle* of being an artificial, ingenious thing—bring it down from its large, free character of an immense and exquisite correspondence with life. And what *is* adventure, when it comes to that, and by what sign is the listening pupil to recognize it? It is an adventure—an immense one—for me to write this little article; and for a Bostonian nymph to reject an English duke is an adventure only less stirring, I should say, than for an English duke to be rejected by a Bostonian nymph. I see dramas within dramas in that, and innumerable points of view. A psychological reason is, to my imagination, an object adorably pictorial; to catch the tint of its complexion—I feel as if that idea might inspire one to Titianesque[25] efforts. There are few things more exciting to me, in short, than a psychological reason, and yet, I protest, the novel seems to me the most magnificent form of art. I have just been reading, at the same time, the delightful story of *Treasure Island,* by Mr. Robert Louis Stevenson[26] and, in a manner less consecutive, the last tale from M. Edmond de Goncourt,[27] which is entitled *Chérie.* One of these works treats of murders, mysteries, islands of dreadful renown, hairbreadth escapes, miraculous coincidences and buried doubloons. The other treats of a little French girl who lived in a fine house in Paris, and died of wounded sensibility because no one would marry her. I call *Treasure Island* delightful, because it appears to me to have succeeded wonderfully in what it attempts; and I venture to bestow no epithet upon *Chérie,* which strikes me as having failed deplorably in what it attempts—that is in tracing the development of the moral consciousness of a child. But one of these productions strikes me as exactly as much of a novel as the other, and as having a "story" quite as much. The moral consciousness of a child is as much a part of life as the islands of the Spanish Main, and the one sort of geography seems to me to have those "surprises" of which Mr. Besant speaks quite as much as the other. For myself (since it comes back in the last resort, as I say, to the preference of the individual), the picture of the child's experience has the advantage that I can at successive steps (an immense luxury, near to the "sensual pleasure" of which Mr. Besant's critic in the *Pall Mall* speaks) say Yes or No, as it may be, to what the artist puts before me. I have been a child in fact, but I have been on a quest for a buried treasure only in supposition, and it is a simple accident that with M. de Goncourt I should have for the most part to say No. With George Eliot,[28] when she painted that country with a far other intelligence, I always said Yes.

[24]A religious doctrine based upon the predestinarian teachings of Cornelis Jansen (1585–1638), a Dutch Roman Catholic theologian.

[25]After Titian (Italian name Tiziano Vecellio), the Venetian painter (1490–1576).

[26]Scottish novelist, essayist, and poet known for his adventure tales and thrillers (1850–1894).

[27]French art critic, novelist, and historian (1822–1896).

[28]George Eliot (pseudonym of Mary Ann Evans, 1819–1880), English novelist noted for the great depth and intellectual range of her realist novels.

The most interesting part of Mr. Besant's lecture is unfortunately the briefest passage—his very cursory allusion to the "conscious moral purpose" of the novel. Here again it is not very clear whether he be recording a fact or laying down a principle; it is a great pity that in the latter case he should not have developed his idea. This branch of the subject is of immense importance, and Mr. Besant's few words point to considerations of the widest reach, not to be lightly disposed of. He will have treated the art of fiction but superficially who is not prepared to go every inch of the way that these considerations will carry him. It is for this reason that at the beginning of these remarks I was careful to notify the reader that my reflections on so large a theme have no pretension to be exhaustive. Like Mr. Besant, I have left the question of the morality of the novel till the last, and at the last I find I have used up my space. It is a question surrounded with difficulties, as witness the very first that meets us, in the form of a definite question, on the threshold. Vagueness, in such a discussion, is fatal, and what is the meaning of your morality and your conscious moral purpose? Will you not define your terms and explain how (a novel being a picture) a picture can be either moral or immoral? You wish to paint a moral picture or carve a moral statue: will you not tell us how you would set about it? We are discussing the Art of Fiction; questions of art are questions (in the widest sense) of execution; questions of morality are quite another affair, and will you not let us see how it is that you find it so easy to mix them up? These things are so clear to Mr. Besant that he has deduced from them a law which he sees embodied in English Fiction, and which is "a truly admirable thing and a great cause for congratulation." It is a great cause for congratulation indeed when such thorny problems become as smooth as silk. I may add that in so far as Mr. Besant perceives that in point of fact English Fiction has addressed itself preponderantly to these delicate questions he will appear to many people to have made a vain discovery. They will have been positively struck, on the contrary, with the moral timidity of the usual English novelist; with his (or with her) aversion to face the difficulties with which on every side the treatment of reality bristles. He is apt to be extremely shy (whereas the picture that Mr. Besant draws is a picture of boldness), and the sign of his work, for the most part, is a cautious silence on certain subjects. In the English novel (by which of course I mean the American as well), more than in any other, there is a traditional difference between that which people know and that which they agree to admit that they know, that which they see and that which they speak of, that which they feel to be a part of life and that which they allow to enter into literature. There is the great difference, in short, between what they talk of in conversation and what they talk of in print. The essence of moral energy is to survey the whole field, and I should directly reverse Mr. Besant's remark and say not that the English novel has a purpose, but that it has a diffidence. To what degree a purpose in a work of art is a source of corruption I shall not attempt to inquire; the one that seems to me least dangerous is the purpose of making a perfect work. As for our novel, I may say lastly on this score that as we find it in England today it strikes me as addressed in a large degree to "young people," and that this in itself constitutes a presumption that it will be rather shy. There are certain things which it is generally agreed not to discuss, not even to mention, before young people. That is very well, but the absence of discussion is not a symptom of the moral passion. The purpose of the English novel—"a truly admirable thing, and a great cause for congratulation"—strikes me therefore as rather negative.

There is one point at which the moral sense and the artistic sense lie very near together; that is in the light of the very obvious truth that the deepest quality of a work of art will always be the quality of the mind of the producer. In proportion as that intelligence is fine will the novel, the picture, the statue partake of the substance of beauty and truth. To be constituted of such elements is, to my vision, to have purpose enough. No good novel will ever proceed from a superficial mind; that seems to me an axiom which, for the artist in fiction, will cover all needful moral ground: if the youthful aspirant take it to heart it will illuminate for him many of the mysteries of "purpose." There are many other useful things that might be said to him, but I have come to the end of my article, and can only touch them as I pass. The critic in the *Pall Mall Gazette,* whom I have already quoted, draws attention to the danger, in speaking of the art of fiction, of generalising. The danger that he has in mind is rather, I imagine, that of particularising, for there are some comprehensive remarks which, in addition to those embodied in Mr. Besant's suggestive lecture, might without fear of misleading him be addressed to the ingenuous student. I should remind him first of the magnificence of the form that is open to him, which offers to sight so few restrictions and such innumerable opportunities. The other arts, in comparison, appear confined and hampered; the various conditions under which they are exercised are so rigid and definite. But the only condition that I can think of attaching to the composition of the novel is, as I have already said, that it be sincere. This freedom is a splendid privilege, and the first lesson of the young novelist is to learn to be worthy of it. "Enjoy it as it deserves," I should say to him; "take possession of it, explore it to its utmost extent, publish it, rejoice in it. All life belongs to you, and do not listen either to those who would shut you up into corners of it and tell you that it is only here and there that art inhabits, or to those who would persuade you that this heavenly messenger wings her way outside of life altogether, breathing a superfine air, and turning away her head from the truth of things. There is no impression of life, no manner of seeing it and feeling it, to which the plan of the novelist may not offer a place; you have only to remember that talents so dissimilar as those of Alexandre Dumas[29] and Jane Austen,[30] Charles Dickens and Gustave Flaubert have worked in this field with equal glory. Do not think too much about optimism and pessimism; try and catch the colour of life itself. In France to-day we see a prodigious effort (that of Emile Zola, to whose solid and serious work no explorer of the capacity of the novel can allude without respect), we see an extraordinary effort vitiated by a spirit of pessimism on a narrow basis. M. Zola is magnificent, but he strikes an English reader as ignorant; he has an air of working in the dark; if he had as much light as energy, his results would be of the highest value. As for the aberrations of a shallow optimism, the ground (of English fiction especially) is strewn with their brittle particles as with broken glass. If you must indulge in conclusions, let them have the taste of a wide knowledge. Remember that your first duty is to be as complete as possible—to make as perfect a work. Be generous and delicate and pursue the prize."

1884

[29]Either Alexandre Dumas, the father (1802–1870), or Alexandre Dumas, the son (1824–1895), both French novelists and playwrights.

[30]English novelist recognized for her witty novels of middle-class mores and manners (1775–1817).

The Beast in the Jungle

I

What determined the speech that startled him in the course of their encounter scarcely matters, being probably but some words spoken by himself quite without intention—spoken as they lingered and slowly moved together after their renewal of acquaintance. He had been conveyed by friends an hour or two before to the house at which she was staying; the party of visitors at the other house, of whom he was one, and thanks to whom it was his theory, as always, that he was lost in the crowd, had been invited over to luncheon. There had been after luncheon much dispersal, all in the interest of the original motive, a view of Weatherend itself and the fine things, intrinsic features, pictures, heirlooms, treasures of all the arts, that made the place almost famous; and the great rooms were so numerous that guests could wander at their will, hang back from the principal group and in cases where they took such matters with the last seriousness give themselves up to mysterious appreciations and measurements. There were persons to be observed, singly or in couples, bending toward objects in out-of-the-way corners with their hands on their knees and their heads nodding quite as with the emphasis of an excited sense of smell. When they were two they either mingled their sounds of ecstasy or melted into silences of even deeper import, so that there were aspects of the occasion that gave it for Marcher much the air of the "look round," previous to a sale highly advertised, that excites or quenches, as may be, the dream of acquisition. The dream of acquisition at Weatherend would have had to be wild indeed, and John Marcher found himself, among such suggestions, disconcerted almost equally by the presence of those who knew too much and by that of those who knew nothing. The great rooms caused so much poetry and history to press upon him that he needed some straying apart to feel in a proper relation with them, though this impulse was not, as happened, like the gloating of some of his companions, to be compared to the movements of a dog sniffing a cupboard. It had an issue promptly enough in a direction that was not to have been calculated.

It led, briefly, in the course of the October afternoon, to his closer meeting with May Bartram, whose face, a reminder, yet not quite a remembrance, as they sat much separated at a very long table, had begun merely by troubling him rather pleasantly. It affected him as the sequel of something of which he had lost the beginning. He knew it, and for the time quite welcomed it, as a continuation, but didn't know what it continued, which was an interest or an amusement the greater as he was also somehow aware—yet without a direct sign from her—that the young woman herself hadn't lost the thread. She hadn't lost it, but she wouldn't give it back to him, he saw, without some putting forth of his hand for it; and he not only saw that, but saw several things more, things odd enough in the light of the fact that at the moment some accident of grouping brought them face to face he was still merely fumbling with the idea that any contact between them in the past would have had no importance. If it had had no importance he scarcely knew why his actual impression of her should so seem to have so much; the answer to which, however, was that in such a life as they all appeared to be leading for the moment one could but take things as they came. He was satisfied, without in the least being able to say why, that this young lady might roughly have ranked in the house as a poor relation; satisfied also that she was not there on a brief visit, but was more or less a part of the establishment—almost a working, a remunerated part. Didn't she enjoy at periods a protection that she paid for by helping, among other services, to show the place and explain it, deal with the tiresome people, answer questions about the dates of the building, the styles of the furniture, the authorship of the pictures, the favourite haunts of the ghost? It wasn't that she looked as if you could have given her shillings—it was impossible to look less so. Yet when she finally drifted toward him, distinctly handsome, though ever so much older—older than when he had seen her before—it might have been as an effect of her guessing that he had, within the couple of hours, devoted more imagination to her than to all the others put together, and had thereby penetrated to a kind of truth that the others were too stupid for. She *was* there on harder terms than any one; she was there as a consequence of things suffered, one way and another, in the interval of years; and she remembered him very much as she was remembered—only a good deal better.

By the time they at last thus came to speech they were alone in one of the rooms—remarkable for a fine portrait over the chimney-place—out of which their friends had passed, and the charm of it was that even before they had spoken they had practically arranged with each other to stay behind for talk. The charm, happily, was in other things too—partly in there being scarce a spot at Weatherend without something to stay behind for. It was in the way the autumn day looked into the high windows as it waned; the way the red light, breaking at the close from under a low sombre sky, reached out in a long shaft and played over old wainscots, old tapestry, old gold, old colour. It was most of all perhaps in the way she came to him as if, since she had been turned on to deal with the simpler sort, he might, should he choose to keep the whole thing down, just take her mild attention for a part of her general business. As soon as he heard her voice, however, the gap was filled up and the missing link supplied; the slight irony he divined in her attitude lost its advantage. He almost jumped at it to get there before her. "I met you years and years ago in Rome. I remember all about it." She confessed to disappointment—she had been so sure he didn't; and to prove how well he did he began to pour forth the particular recollections that popped up as he called for them. Her face and her voice, all at his service now, worked the miracle—the impression operating like the torch of a lamplighter who touches into flame, one by one, a long row of gas-jets. Marcher flattered himself the illumination was brilliant, yet he was really still more pleased on her showing him, with amusement, that in his haste to make everything right he had got most things rather wrong. It hadn't been at Rome—it had been at Naples; and it hadn't been eight years before—it had been more nearly ten. She hadn't been, either, with her uncle and aunt, but with her mother and her brother; in addition to which it was not with the Pembles *he* had been, but with the Boyers, coming down in their company from Rome—a point on which she insisted, a little to his confusion, and as to which she had her evidence in hand. The Boyers she had known, but didn't know the Pembles, though she had heard of them, and it was the people he was with who had made them acquainted. The incident of the thunderstorm that had raged round them with such violence as to drive them for refuge into an excavation—this incident had not occurred at the Palace of the Caesars, but at Pompeii,[1] on an occasion when they had been present there at an important find.

He accepted her amendments, he enjoyed her corrections, though the moral of them was, she pointed out, that he *really* didn't remember the least thing about her; and he only felt it as a drawback that when all was made strictly historic there didn't appear much of anything left. They lingered together still, she neglecting her office—for from the moment he was so clever she had no proper right to him—and both neglecting the house, just waiting as to see if a memory or two more wouldn't again breathe on them. It hadn't taken them many minutes, after all, to put down on the table, like the cards of a pack, those that constituted their respective hands; only what came out was that the pack was unfortunately not perfect—that the past, invoked, invited, encouraged, could give them, naturally, no more than it had. It had made them anciently meet—her at twenty, him at twenty-five; but nothing was so strange, they seemed to say to each other, as that, while so occupied, it hadn't done a little more for them. They looked at each other as with the feeling of an occasion missed; the present would have been so much better if the other, in the far distance, in the foreign land, hadn't been so stupidly meagre. There weren't apparently, all counted, more than a dozen little old things that had succeeded in coming to pass between them; trivialities of youth, simplicities of freshness, stupidities of ignorance, small possible germs, but too deeply buried—too deeply (didn't it seem?) to sprout after so many years. Marcher could only feel he ought to have rendered her some service—saved her from a capsized boat in the Bay or at least recovered her dressing-bag, filched from her cab in the streets of Naples by a lazzarone[2] with a stiletto. Or it would have been nice if he could have been taken with fever all alone at his hotel, and she could have come to look after him, to write to his people, to drive him out in convalescence. *Then* they would be in possession of the something or other that their actual show seemed to lack. It yet somehow presented itself, this show, as too good to be spoiled; so that they were reduced for a few minutes more to wondering a little helplessly why—since they seemed to know a certain number of the same people—their reunion had been so long averted. They didn't use that name for it, but their delay from minute to minute to join the others was a kind of confession that they didn't quite want it to be a failure. Their attempted supposition of reasons for their not having met but showed how little they knew of each other. There came in fact a moment when Marcher felt a positive pang. It was vain to pretend she was an old friend, for all the communities were wanting, in spite of which it was as an old friend that he saw she would have suited him. He had new ones enough—was surrounded with them for instance on the stage of the other house; as a new one he probably wouldn't have so much as noticed her. He would have liked to invent something, get her to make-believe with him that some passage of a romantic or critical kind *had* originally occurred. He was really almost reaching out in imagination—as against time—for something that would do, and saying to himself that if it didn't

[1]*I.e.,* had not occurred in Rome but in nearby, Naples.

[2]Italian: beggar, loafer.

come this sketch of a fresh start would show for quite awkwardly bungled. They would separate, and now for no second or no third chance. They would have tried and not succeeded. Then it was, just at the turn, as he afterwards made it out to himself, that, everything else failing, she herself decided to take up the case and, as it were, save the situation. He felt as soon as she spoke that she had been consciously keeping back what she said and hoping to get on without it; a scruple in her that immensely touched him when, by the end of three or four minutes more, he was able to measure it. What she brought out, at any rate, quite cleared the air and supplied the link—the link it was so odd he should frivolously have managed to lose.

"You know you told me something I've never forgotten and that again and again has made me think of you since; it was that tremendously hot day when we went to Sorrento,[3] across the bay, for the breeze. What I allude to was what you said to me, on the way back, as we sat under the awning of the boat enjoying the cool. Have you forgotten?"

He had forgotten and was even more surprised than ashamed. But the great thing was that he saw in this no vulgar reminder of any "sweet" speech. The vanity of women had long memories, but she was making no claim on him of a compliment or a mistake. With another woman, a totally different one, he might have feared the recall possibly even some imbecile "offer." So, in having to say that he had indeed forgotten, he was conscious rather of a loss than of a gain; he already saw an interest in the matter of her mention. "I try to think—but I give it up. Yet I remember the Sorrento day."

"I'm not very sure you do," May Bartram after a moment said; "and I'm not very sure I ought to want you to. It's dreadful to bring a person back at any time to what he was ten years before. If you've lived away from it," she smiled, "so much the better."

"Ah if *you* haven't why should I?" he asked.

"Lived away, you mean, from what I myself was?"

"From what *I* was. I was of course an ass," Marcher went on; "but I would rather know from you just the sort of ass I was than—from the moment you have something in your mind—not know anything."

Still, however, she hesitated. "But if you've completely ceased to be that sort—?"

"Why I can then all the more bear to know. Besides, perhaps I haven't."

"Perhaps. Yet if you haven't," she added, "I should suppose you'd remember. Not indeed that *I* in the least connect with my impression the invidious name you use. If I had only thought you foolish," she explained, "the thing I speak of wouldn't so have remained with me. It was about yourself." She waited as if it might come to him; but as, only meeting her eyes in wonder, he gave no sign, she burnt her ships. "Has it ever happened?"

Then it was that, while he continued to stare, a light broke for him and the blood slowly came to his face, which began to burn with recognition. "Do you mean I told you—?" But he faltered, lest what came to him shouldn't be right, lest he should only give himself away.

[3]This cool, picturesque town on the Bay of Naples was a favored summer resort.

"It was something about yourself that it was natural one shouldn't forget—that is if one remembered you at all. That's why I ask you," she smiled, "if the thing you then spoke of has ever come to pass?"

Oh then he saw, but he was lost in wonder and found himself embarrassed. This, he also saw, made her sorry for him, as if her allusion had been a mistake. It took him but a moment, however, to feel it hadn't been, much as it had been a surprise. After the first little shock of it her knowledge on the contrary began, even if rather strangely, to taste sweet to him. She was the only other person in the world then who would have it, and she had had it all these years, while the fact of his having so breathed his secret had unaccountably faded from him. No wonder they couldn't have met as if nothing had happened. "I judge," he finally said, "that I know what you mean. Only I had strangely enough lost any sense of having taken you so far into my confidence."

"Is it because you've taken so many others as well?"

"I've taken nobody. Not a creature since then."

"So that I'm the only person who knows?"

"The only person in the world."

"Well," she quickly replied, "I myself have never spoken. I've never, never repeated of you what you told me." She looked at him so that he perfectly believed her. Their eyes met over it in such a way that he was without a doubt. "And I never will."

She spoke with an earnestness that, as if almost excessive, put him at ease about her possible derision. Somehow the whole question was a new luxury to him—that is from the moment she was in possession. If she didn't take the sarcastic view she clearly took the sympathetic, and that was what he had had, in all the long time, from no one whomsoever. What he felt was that he couldn't at present have begun to tell her, and yet could profit perhaps exquisitely by the accident of having done so of old. "Please don't then. We're just right as it is."

"Oh I am," she laughed, "if you are!" To which she added: "Then you do still feel in the same way?"

It was impossible he shouldn't take to himself that she was really interested, though it all kept coming as perfect surprise. He had thought of himself so long as abominably alone, and lo he wasn't alone a bit. He hadn't been, it appeared, for an hour—since those moments on the Sorrento boat. It was *she* who had been, he seemed to see as he looked at her—she who had been made so by the graceless fact of his lapse of fidelity. To tell her what he had told her—what had it been but to ask something of her? something that she had given, in her charity, without his having, by a remembrance, by a return of the spirit, failing another encounter, so much as thanked her. What he had asked of her had been simply at first not to laugh at him. She had beautifully not done so for ten years, and she was not doing so now. So he had endless gratitude to make up. Only for that he must see just how he had figured to her. "What, exactly, was the account I gave—?"

"Of the way you did feel? Well, it was very simple. You said you had had from your earliest time, as the deepest thing within you, the sense of being kept for something rare and strange, possibly prodigious and terrible, that was sooner or later to happen to you, that you had in your bones the foreboding and the conviction of, and that would perhaps overwhelm you."

"Do you call that very simple?" John Marcher asked.

She thought a moment. "It was perhaps because I seemed, as you spoke, to understand it."

"You do understand it?" he eagerly asked.

Again she kept her kind eyes on him. "You still have the belief?"

"Oh!" he exclaimed helplessly. There was too much to say.

"Whatever it's to be," she clearly made out, "it hasn't yet come."

He shook his head in complete surrender now. "It hasn't yet come. Only, you know, it isn't anything I'm to *do,* to achieve in the world, to be distinguished or admired for. I'm not such an ass as *that.* It would be much better, no doubt, if I were."

"It's to be something you're merely to suffer?"

"Well, say to wait for—to have to meet, to face, to see suddenly break out in my life; possibly destroying all further consciousness, possibly annihilating me; possibly, on the other hand, only altering everything, striking at the root of all my world and leaving me to the consequences, however they shape themselves."

She took this in, but the light in her eyes continued for him not to be that of mockery. "Isn't what you describe perhaps but the expectation—or at any rate the sense of danger, familiar to so many people—of falling in love?"

John Marcher wondered. "Did you ask me that before?"

"No—I wasn't so free-and-easy then. But it's what strikes me now."

"Of course," he said after a moment, "it strikes you. Of course it strikes *me.* Of course what's in store for me may be no more than that. The only thing is," he went on, "that I think if it had been that I should by this time know."

"Do you mean because you've *been* in love?" And then as he but looked at her in silence: "You've been in love, and it hasn't meant such a cataclysm, hasn't proved the great affair?"

"Here I am, you see. It hasn't been overwhelming."

"Then it hasn't been love," said May Bartram.

"Well, I at least thought it was. I took it for that—I've taken it till now. It was agreeable, it was delightful, it was miserable," he explained. "But it wasn't strange. It wasn't what *my* affair's to be."

"You want something all to yourself—something that nobody else knows or *has* known?"

"It isn't a question of what I 'want'—God knows I don't want anything. It's only a question of the apprehension that haunts me—that I live with day by day."

He said this so lucidly and consistently that he could see it further impose itself. If she hadn't been interested before she'd have been interested now. "Is it a sense of coming violence?"

Evidently now too again he liked to talk of it. "I don't think of it as—when it does come—necessarily violent. I only think of it as natural and as of course above all unmistakeable. I think of it simply as *the* thing. *The* thing will of itself appear natural."

"Then how will it appear strange?"

Marcher bethought himself. "It won't—to *me.*"

"To whom then?"

"Well," he replied, smiling at last, "say to you."

"Oh then I'm to be present?"

"Why you *are* present—since you know."

"I see." She turned it over. "But I mean at the catastrophe."

At this, for a minute, their lightness gave way to their gravity; it was as if the long look they exchanged held them together. "It will only depend on yourself—if you'll watch with me."

"Are you afraid?" she asked.

"Don't leave me *now*," he went on.

"Are you afraid?" she repeated.

"Do you think me simply out of my mind?" he pursued instead of answering. "Do I merely strike you as a harmless lunatic?"

"No," said May Bartram. "I understand you. I believe you."

"You mean you feel how my obsession—poor old thing!—may correspond to some possible reality?"

"To some possible reality."

"Then you *will* watch with me?"

She hesitated, then for the third time put her question. "Are you afraid?"

"Did I tell you I was—at Naples?"

"No, you said nothing about it."

"Then I don't know. And I should *like* to know," said John Marcher. "You'll tell me yourself whether you think so. If you'll watch with me you'll see."

"Very good then." They had been moving by this time across the room, and at the door, before passing out, they paused as for the full wind-up of their understanding. "I'll watch with you," said May Bartram.

II

The fact that she "knew"—knew and yet neither chaffed him nor betrayed him—had in a short time begun to constitute between them a goodly bond, which became more marked when, within the year that followed their afternoon at Weatherend, the opportunities for meeting multiplied. The event that thus promoted these occasions was the death of the ancient lady her great-aunt, under whose wing, since losing her mother, she had to such an extent found shelter, and who, though but the widowed mother of the new successor to the property, had succeeded—thanks to a high tone and a high temper—in not forfeiting the supreme position at the great house. The deposition of this personage arrived but with her death, which, followed by many changes, made in particular a difference for the young woman in whom Marcher's expert attention had recognised from the first a dependent with a pride that might ache though it didn't bristle. Nothing for a long time had made him easier than the thought that the aching must have been much soothed by Miss Bartram's now finding herself able to set up a small home in London. She had acquired property, to an amount that made that luxury just possible, under her aunt's extremely complicated will, and when the whole matter began to be straightened out, which indeed took time, she let him know that the happy issue was at last in view. He had seen her again before that day, both because she had more than once accompanied the ancient lady to town and because he had paid another visit to the friends who so conveniently made of Weatherend one of the charms of their own hospitality. These friends had taken him back there; he had achieved there again with Miss Bartram some quiet detachment; and he had in London succeeded in persuading her to more than one brief absence from her aunt. They went together, on these latter occasions, to the National Gallery and the South Kensington Museum, where, among vivid reminders, they talked of Italy at large—not now attempting to recover, as at first, the taste of their youth and their ignorance. That recovery, the first day at Weatherend, had served its purpose well, had given them quite enough; so that they were, to Marcher's sense, no longer hovering about the headwaters of their stream, but had felt their boat pushed sharply off and down the current.

They were literally afloat together; for our gentleman this was marked, quite as marked as that the fortunate cause of it was just the buried treasure of her knowledge. He had with his own hands dug up this little hoard, brought to light—that is to within reach of the dim day constituted by their discretions and privacies—the object of value the hiding-place of which he had, after putting it into the ground himself, so strangely, so long forgotten. The rare luck of his having again just stumbled on the spot made him indifferent to any other question; he would doubtless have devoted more time to the odd accident of his lapse of memory if he hadn't been moved to devote so much to the sweetness, the comfort, as he felt, for the future, that this accident itself had helped to keep fresh. It had never entered into his plan that any one should "know," and mainly for the reason that it wasn't in him to tell any one. That would have been impossible, for nothing but the amusement of a cold world would have waited on it. Since, however, a mysterious fate had opened his mouth betimes, in spite of him, he would count that a compensation and profit by it to the utmost. That the right person *should* know tempered the asperity of his secret more even than his shyness had permitted him to imagine; and May Bartram was clearly right, because—well, because there she was. Her knowledge simply settled it; he would have been sure enough by this time had she been wrong. There was that in his situation, no doubt, that disposed him too much to see her as a mere confidant, taking all her light for him from the fact—the fact only—of her interest in his predicament; from her mercy, sympathy, seriousness, her consent not to regard him as the funniest of the funny. Aware, in fine, that her price for him was just in her giving him this constant sense of his being admirably spared, he was careful to remember that she had also a life of her own, with things that might happen to *her,* things that in friendship one should likewise take account of. Something fairly remarkable came to pass with him, for that matter, in this connexion—something represented by a certain passage of his consciousness, in the suddenest way, from one extreme to the other.

He had thought himself, so long as nobody knew, the most disinterested person in the world, carrying his concentrated burden, his perpetual suspense, ever so quietly, holding his tongue about it, giving others no glimpse of it nor of its effect upon his life, asking of them no allowance and only making on his side all those that were asked. He hadn't disturbed people with the queerness of their having to know a haunted man, though he had had moments of rather special temptation on hearing them say they were forsooth "unsettled." If they were as unsettled as he was—he who had never been settled for an hour in his life—they would know what it meant. Yet it wasn't, all the same, for him to make them, and he listened to them civilly enough. This was why he had such good—though possibly such rather colourless—manners; this was why, above all, he could regard himself, in a greedy world, as decently—as in fact perhaps even a little sublimely—unselfish. Our point is accordingly that he valued this character quite sufficiently to measure his present danger of letting it lapse, against which he promised himself to be much on his guard. He was quite ready, none the less, to be selfish just a little, since surely no more charming occasion for it had come to him. "Just a little," in a word, was just as much as Miss Bartram, taking one day with another, would let him. He never would be in the least coercive, and would keep well before him the lines on which consideration for her—the very highest—ought to proceed. He would thoroughly establish the heads under which her affairs, her requirements, her peculiarities—he went so far as to give them the latitude of that name—would come into their intercourse. All this naturally was a sign of how much he took the intercourse itself for granted. There was nothing more to be done about *that*. It simply existed; had sprung into being with her first penetrating question to him in the autumn light there at Weatherend. The real form it should have taken on the basis that stood out large was the form of their marrying. But the devil in this was that the very basis itself put marrying out of the question. His conviction, his apprehension, his obsession, in short, wasn't a privilege he could invite a woman to share; and that consequence of it was precisely what was the matter with him. Something or other lay in wait for him, amid the twists and the turns of the months and the years, like a crouching beast in the jungle. It signified little whether the crouching beast were destined to slay him or to be slain. The definite point was the inevitable spring of the creature; and the definite lesson from that was that a man of feeling didn't cause himself to be accompanied by a lady on a tiger-hunt. Such was the image under which he had ended by figuring his life.

They had at first, none the less, in the scattered hours spent together, made no allusion to that view of it; which was a sign he was handsomely alert to give that he didn't expect, that he in fact didn't care, always to be talking about it. Such a feature in one's outlook was really like a hump on one's back. The difference it made every minute of the day existed quite independently of discussion. One discussed of course *like* a hunchback, for there was always, if nothing else, the hunchback face. That remained, and she was watching him; but people watched best, as a general thing, in silence, so that such would be predominantly the manner of their vigil. Yet he didn't want, at the same time, to be tense and solemn; tense and solemn was what he imagined he too much showed for with other people. The thing to be, with the one person who knew, was easy and natural—to make the reference rather than be seeming to avoid it, to avoid it rather than be seeming to make it, and to keep it, in any case, familiar, facetious even, rather than pedantic and portentous. Some such consideration as the latter was doubtless in his mind for instance when he wrote pleasantly to Miss Bartram that perhaps the great thing he had so long felt as in the lap of the gods was no more than this circumstance, which touched him so nearly, of her acquiring a house in London. It was the first allusion they had yet again made, needing any other hitherto so little; but when she replied, after having given him the news, that she was by no means satisfied with such a trifle as the climax to so special a suspense, she almost set him wondering if she hadn't even a larger conception of singularity for him than he had for himself. He was at all events destined to become aware little by little, as time went by, that she was all the while looking at his life, judging it, measuring it, in the light of the thing she knew, which grew to be at last, with the consecration of the years, never mentioned between them save as "the real truth" about him. That had always been his own form of reference to it, but she adopted the form so quietly that, looking back at the end of a period, he knew there was no moment at which it was traceable that she had, as he might say, got inside his idea, or exchanged the attitude of beautifully indulging for that of still more beautifully believing him.

It was always open to him to accuse her of seeing him but as the most harmless of maniacs, and this, in the long run—since it covered so much ground—was his easiest description of their friendship. He had a screw loose for her, but she liked him in spite of it and was practically, against the rest of the world, his kind wise keeper, unremunerated but fairly amused and, in the absence of other near ties, not disreputably occupied. The rest of the world of course thought him queer, but she, she only, knew how, and above all why, queer; which was precisely what enabled her to dispose the concealing veil in the right folds. She took his gaiety from him—since it had to pass with them for gaiety—as she took everything else; but she certainly so far justified by her unerring touch his finer sense of the degree to which he had ended by convincing her. *She* at least never spoke of the secret of his life except as "the real truth about you," and she had in fact a wonderful way of making it seem, as such, the secret of her own life too. That was in fine how he so constantly felt her as allowing for him; he couldn't on the whole call it anything else. He allowed for himself, but she, exactly, allowed still more; partly because, better placed for a sight of the matter, she traced his unhappy perversion through reaches of its course into which he could scarce follow it. He knew how he felt, but, besides knowing that, she knew how he *looked* as well; he knew each of the things of importance he was insidiously kept from doing, but she could add up the amount they made, understand how much, with a lighter weight on his spirit, he might have done, and thereby establish how, clever as he was, he fell short. Above all she was in the secret of the difference between the forms he went through—those of his little office under Government, those of caring for his modest patrimony, for his library, for his garden in the country, for the people in London whose invitations he accepted and repaid—and the detachment that reigned beneath them and that made of all behaviour, all that could in the least be called behaviour, a long act of dissimulation. What it had come to was that he wore a mask painted with the social simper, out of the eye-holes of which there looked eyes of an expression not in the least matching the other features. This the stupid world, even after years, had never more than half-discovered. It was only May Bartram who had, and she achieved, by an art indescribable, the feat of at once—or perhaps it was only alternately—meeting the eyes from in front and mingling her own vision, as from over his shoulder, with their peep through the apertures.

So while they grew older together she did watch with him, and so she let this association give shape and colour to her own existence. Beneath *her* forms as well detachment had learned to sit, and behaviour had become for her, in the social sense, a false account of herself. There was but one account of her that would have been true all the while and that she could give straight to nobody, least of all to John Marcher. Her whole attitude was a virtual statement, but the perception of that only seemed called to take its place for him as one of the many things necessarily crowded out of his consciousness. If she had moreover, like himself, to make sacrifices to their real truth, it was to be granted that her compensation might have affected her as more prompt and more natural. They had long periods, in this London time, during which, when they were together, a stranger might have listened to them without in the least pricking up his ears; on the other hand the real truth was equally liable at any moment to rise to the surface, and the auditor would then have wondered indeed what they were talking about. They had from an early hour made up their mind that society was, luckily, unintelligent, and the margin allowed them by this had fairly become one of their commonplaces. Yet there were still moments when the situation turned almost fresh—usually under the effect of some expression drawn from herself. Her expressions doubtless repeated themselves, but her intervals were generous. "What saves us, you know, is that we answer so completely to so usual an appearance: that of the man and woman whose friendship has become such a daily habit—or almost—as to be at last indispensable." That for instance was a remark she had frequently enough had occasion to make, though she had given it at different times different developments. What we are especially concerned with is the turn it happened to take from her one afternoon when he had come to see her in honour of her birthday. This anniversary had fallen on a Sunday, at a season of thick fog and general outward gloom; but he had brought her his customary offering, having known her now long enough to have established a hundred small traditions. It was one of his proofs to himself, the present he made her on her birthday, that he hadn't sunk into real selfishness. It was mostly nothing more than a small trinket, but it was always fine of its kind, and he was regularly careful to pay for it more than he thought he could afford. "Our habit saves you at least, don't you see? because it makes you, after all, for the vulgar, indistinguishable from other men. What's the most inveterate mark of men in general? Why the capacity to spend endless time with dull women—to spend it I won't say without being bored, but without minding that they are, without being driven off at a tangent by it; which comes to the same thing. I'm your dull woman, a part of the daily bread for which you pray at church. That covers your tracks more than anything."

"And what covers yours?" asked Marcher, whom his dull woman could mostly to this extent amuse. "I see of course what you mean by your saving me, in this way and that, so far as other people are concerned—I've seen it all along. Only what is it that saves *you?* I often think, you know, of that."

She looked as if she sometimes thought of that too, but rather in a different way. "Where other people, you mean, are concerned?"

"Well, you're really so in with me, you know—as a sort of result of my being so in with yourself. I mean of my having such an immense regard for you, being so tremendously mindful of all you've done for me. I sometimes ask myself if it's quite fair. Fair I mean to have so involved and—since one may say it—interested you. I almost feel as if you hadn't really had time to do anything else."

"Anything else but be interested?" she asked. "Ah what else does one ever want to be? If I've been 'watching' with you, as we long ago agreed I was to do, watching's always in itself an absorption."

"Oh certainly," John Marcher said, "if you hadn't had your curiosity—! Only doesn't it sometimes come to you as time goes on that your curiosity isn't being particularly repaid?"

May Bartram had a pause. "Do you ask that, by any chance, because you feel at all that yours isn't? I mean because you have to wait so long."

Oh he understood what she meant! "For the thing to happen that never does happen? For the beast to jump out? No, I'm just where I was about it. It isn't a matter as to which I can *choose,* I can decide for a change. It isn't one as to which there *can* be a change. It's in the lap of the gods. One's in the hands of one's law—there one is. As to the form the law will take, the way it will operate, that's its own affair."

"Yes," Miss Bartram replied; "of course one's fate's coming, of course it *has* come in its own form and its own way, all the while. Only, you know, the form and the way in your case were to have been—well, something so exceptional and, as one may say, so particularly *your* own."

Something in this made him look at her with suspicion. "You say 'were to *have* been,' as if in your heart you had begun to doubt."

"Oh!" she vaguely protested.

"As if you believed," he went on, "that nothing will now take place."

She shook her head slowly but rather inscrutably. "You're far from my thought."

He continued to look at her. "What then is the matter with you?"

"Well," she said after another wait, "the matter with me is simply that I'm more sure than ever my curiosity, as you call it, will be but too well repaid."

They were frankly grave now; he had got up from his seat, had turned once more about the little drawing-room to which, year after year, he brought his inevitable topic; in which he had, as he might have said, tasted their intimate community with every sauce, where every object was as familiar to him as the things of his own house and the very carpets were worn with his fitful walk very much as the desks in old counting-houses are worn by the elbows of generations of clerks. The generations of his nervous moods had been at work there, and the place was the written history of his whole middle life. Under the impression of what his friend had just said he knew himself, for some reason, more aware of these things; which made him, after a moment, stop again before her. "Is it possibly that you've grown afraid?"

"Afraid?" He thought, as she repeated the word, that his question had made her, a little, change colour; so that, lest he should have touched on a truth, he explained very kindly: "You remember that that was what you asked *me* long ago—that first day at Weatherend."

"Oh yes, and you told me you didn't know—that I was to see for myself. We've said little about it since, even in so long a time."

"Precisely," Marcher interposed—"quite as if it were too delicate a matter for us to make free with. Quite as if we might find, on pressure, that I *am* afraid. For then," he said, "we shouldn't, should we? quite know what to do."

She had for the time no answer to this question. "There have been days when I thought you were. Only, of course," she added, "there have been days when we have thought almost anything."

"Everything. Oh!" Marcher softly groaned as with a gasp, half-spent, at the face, more uncovered just then than it had been for a long while, of the imagination always with them. It had always had its incalculable moments of glaring out, quite as with the very eyes of the very Beast, and, used as he was to them, they could still draw from him the tribute of a sigh that rose from the depths of his being. All they had thought, first and last, rolled over him; the past seemed to have been reduced to mere barren speculation. This in fact was what the place had just struck him as so full of—the simplification of everything but the state of suspense. That remained only by seeming to hang in the void surrounding it. Even his original fear, if fear it had been, had lost itself in the desert. "I judge, however," he continued, "that you see I'm not afraid now."

"What I see, as I make it out, is that you've achieved something almost unprecedented in the way of getting used to danger. Living with it so long and so closely you've lost your sense of it; you know it's there, but you're indifferent, and you cease even, as of old, to have to whistle in the dark. Considering what the danger is," May Bartram wound up, "I'm bound to say I don't think your attitude could well be surpassed."

John Marcher faintly smiled. "It's heroic?"

"Certainly—call it that."

It was what he would have liked indeed to call it. "I *am* then a man of courage?"

"That's what you were to show me."

He still, however, wondered. "But doesn't the man of courage know what he's afraid of—or *not* afraid of? I don't know *that,* you see. I don't focus it. I can't name it. I only know I'm exposed."

"Yes, but exposed—how shall I say?—so directly. So intimately. That's surely enough."

"Enough to make you feel then—as what we may call the end and the upshot of our watch—that I'm not afraid?"

"You're not afraid. But it isn't," she said, "the end of our watch. That is it isn't the end of yours. You've everything still to see."

"Then why haven't *you?*" he asked. He had had, all along, to-day, the sense of her keeping something back, and he still had it. As this was his first impression of that it quite made a date. The case was the more marked as she didn't at first answer; which in turn made him go on. "You know something I don't." Then his voice, for that of a man of courage, trembled a little. "You know what's to happen." Her silence, with the face she showed, was almost a confession—it made him sure. "You know, and you're afraid to tell me. It's so bad that you're afraid I'll find out."

All this might be true, for she did look as if, unexpectedly to her, he had crossed some mystic line that she had secretly drawn round her. Yet she might, after all, not have worried; and the real climax was that he himself, at all events, needn't. "You'll never find out."

III

It was all to have made, none the less, as I have said, a date; which came out in the fact that again and again, even after long intervals, other things that passed between them wore in relation to this hour but the character of recalls and results. Its immediate effect had been indeed rather to lighten insistence—almost to provoke a reaction; as if their topic had dropped by its own weight and as if moreover, for that matter, Marcher had been visited by one of his occasional warnings against egotism. He had kept up, he felt, and very decently on the whole, his consciousness of the importance of not being selfish, and it was true that he had never sinned in that direction without promptly enough trying to press the scales the other way. He often repaired his fault, the season permitting, by inviting his friend to accompany him to the opera; and it not infrequently thus happened that, to show he didn't wish her to have but one sort of food for her mind, he was the cause of her appearing there with him a dozen nights in the month. It even happened that, seeing her home at such times, he occasionally went in with her to finish, as he called it, the evening, and, the better to make his point, sat down to the frugal but always careful little supper that awaited his pleasure. His point was made, he thought, by his not eternally insisting with her on himself; made for instance, at such hours, when it befell that, her piano at hand and each of them familiar with it, they went over passages of the opera together. It chanced to be on one of these occasions, however, that he reminded her of her not having answered a certain question he had put to her during the talk that had taken place between them on her last birthday. "What is it that saves *you?*"—saved her, he meant, from that appearance of variation from the usual human type. If he had practically escaped remark, as she pretended, by doing, in the most important particular, what most men do—find the answer to life in patching up an alliance of a sort with a woman no better than himself—how had she escaped it, and how could the alliance, such as it was, since they must suppose it had been more or less noticed, have failed to make her rather positively talked about?

"I never said," May Bartram replied, "that it hadn't made me a good deal talked about."

"Ah well then you're not 'saved.'"

"It hasn't been a question for me. If you've had your woman I've had," she said, "my man."

"And you mean that makes you all right?"

Oh it was always as if there were so much to say! "I don't know why it shouldn't make me—humanly, which is what we're speaking of—as right as it makes you."

"I see," Marcher returned. "'Humanly,' no doubt, as showing that you're living for something. Not, that is, just for me and my secret."

May Bartram smiled. "I don't pretend it exactly shows that I'm not living for you. It's my intimacy with you that's in question."

He laughed as he saw what she meant. "Yes, but since, as you say, I'm only, so far as people make out, ordinary, you're—aren't you?—no more than ordinary either. You help me to pass for a man like another. So if I *am,* as I understand you, you're not compromised. Is that it?"

She had another of her waits, but she spoke clearly enough. "That's it. It's all that concerns me—to help you to pass for a man like another."

He was careful to acknowledge the remark handsomely. "How kind, how beautiful, you are to me! How shall I ever repay you?"

She had her last grave pause, as if there might be a choice of ways. But she chose. "By going on as you are."

It was into this going on as he was that they relapsed, and really for so long a time that the day inevitably came for a further sounding of their depths. These depths, constantly bridged over by a structure firm enough in spite of its lightness and of its occasional oscillation in the somewhat vertiginous air, invited on occasion, in the interest of their nerves, a dropping of the plummet and a measurement of the abyss. A difference had been made moreover, once for all, by the fact that she had all the while not appeared to feel the need of rebutting his charge of an idea within her that she didn't dare to express—a charge uttered just before one of the fullest of their later discussions ended. It had come up for him then that she "knew" something and that what she knew was bad—too bad to tell him. When he had spoken of it as visibly so bad that she was afraid he might find it out, her reply had left the matter too equivocal to be let alone and yet, for Marcher's special sensibility, almost too formidable again to touch. He circled about it at a distance that alternately narrowed and widened and that still wasn't much affected by the consciousness in him that there was nothing she could "know," after all, any better than he did. She had no source of knowledge he hadn't equally—except of course that she might have finer nerves. That was what women had where they were interested; they made out things, where people were concerned, that the people often couldn't have made out for themselves. Their nerves, their sensibility, their imagination, were conductors and revealers, and the beauty of May Bartram was in particular that she had given herself so to his case. He felt in these days what, oddly enough, he had never felt before, the growth of a dread of losing her by some catastrophe—some catastrophe that yet wouldn't at all be *the* catastrophe: partly because she had almost of a sudden begun to strike him as more useful to him than ever yet, and partly by reason of an appearance of uncertainty in her health, coincident and equally new. It was characteristic of the inner detachment he had hitherto so successfully cultivated and to which our whole account of him is a reference, it was characteristic that his complications, such as they were, had never yet seemed so as at this crisis to thicken about him, even to the point of making him ask himself if he were, by any chance, of a truth, within sight or sound, within touch or reach, within the immediate jurisdiction, of the thing that waited.

When the day came, as come it had to, that his friend confessed to him her fear of a deep disorder in her blood, he felt somehow the shadow of a change and the chill of a shock. He immediately began to imagine aggravations and disasters, and above all to think of her peril as the direct menace for himself of personal privation. This indeed gave him one of those partial recoveries of equanimity that were agreeable to him—it showed him that what was still first in his mind was the loss she herself might suffer. "What if she should have to die before knowing, before seeing—?" It would have been brutal, in the early stages of her trouble, to put that question to her; but it had immediately sounded for him to his own concern, and the possibility was what most made him sorry for her. If she did "know," moreover, in the sense of her having had some—what should he think?—mystical irresistible light, this would make the matter not better, but worse, inasmuch as her original adoption of his own curiosity had quite become the basis of her life. She had been living to see what would *be* to be seen, and it would quite lacerate her to have to give up before the accomplishment of the vision. These reflexions, as I say, quickened his generosity; yet, make them as he might, he saw himself, with the lapse of the period, more and more disconcerted. It lapsed for him with a strange steady sweep, and the oddest oddity was that it gave him, independently of the threat of much inconvenience, almost the only positive surprise his career, if career it could be called, had yet offered him. She kept the house as she had never done; he had to go to her to see her—she could meet him nowhere now, though there was scarce a corner of their loved old London in which she hadn't in the past, at one time or another, done so; and he found her always seated by her fire in the deep old-fashioned chair she was less and less able to leave. He had been struck one day, after an absence exceeding his usual measure, with her suddenly looking much older to him than he had ever thought of her being; then he recognised that the suddenness was all on his side—he had just simply and suddenly noticed. She looked older because inevitably, after so many years, she *was* old, or almost;

which was of course true in still greater measure of her companion. If she was old, or almost, John Marcher assuredly was, and yet it was her showing of the lesson, not his own, that brought the truth home to him. His surprises began here; when once they had begun they multiplied; they came rather with a rush: it was as if, in the oddest way in the world, they had all been kept back, sown in a thick cluster, for the late afternoon of life, the time at which for people in general the unexpected has died out.

One of them was that he should have caught himself—for he *had* so done—*really* wondering if the great accident would take form now as nothing more than his being condemned to see this charming woman, this admirable friend, pass away from him. He had never so unreservedly qualified her as while confronted in thought with such a possibility; in spite of which there was small doubt for him that as an answer to his long riddle the mere effacement of even so fine a feature of his situation would be an abject anti-climax. It would represent, as connected with his past attitude, a drop of dignity under the shadow of which his existence could only become the most grotesque of failures. He had been far from holding it a failure—long as he had waited for the appearance that was to make it a success. He had waited for quite another thing, not for such a thing as that. The breath of his good faith came short, however, as he recognised how long he had waited, or how long at least his companion had. That she, at all events, might be recorded as having waited in vain—this affected him sharply, and all the more because of his at first having done little more than amuse himself with the idea. It grew more grave as the gravity of her condition grew, and the state of mind it produced in him, which he himself ended by watching as if it had been some definite disfigurement of his outer person, may pass for another of his surprises. This conjoined itself still with another, the really stupefying consciousness of a question that he would have allowed to shape itself had he dared. What did everything mean—what, that is, did *she* mean, she and her vain waiting and her probable death and the soundless admonition of it all—unless that, at this time of day, it was simply, it was overwhelmingly too late? He had never at any stage of his queer consciousness admitted the whisper of such a correction; he had never till within these last few months been so false to his conviction as not to hold that what was to come to him had time, whether *he* struck himself as having it or not. That at last, at last, he certainly hadn't it, to speak of, or had it but in the scantiest measure—such, soon enough, as things went with him, became the inference with which his old obsession had to reckon: and this it was not helped to do by the more and more confirmed appearance that the great vagueness casting the long shadow in which he had lived had, to attest itself, almost no margin left. Since it was in Time that he was to have met his fate, so it was in Time that his fate was to have acted; and as he waked up to the sense of no longer being young, which was exactly the sense of being stale, just as that, in turn, was the sense of being weak, he waked up to another matter beside. It all hung together; they were subject, he and the great vagueness, to an equal and indivisible law. When the possibilities themselves had accordingly turned stale, when the secret of the gods had grown faint, had perhaps even quite evaporated, that, and that only, was failure. It wouldn't have been failure to be bankrupt, dishonoured, pilloried, hanged; it was failure not to be anything. And so, in the dark valley into which his path had taken its unlooked-for twist, he wondered not a little as he groped. He didn't care what awful crash might overtake him, with what ignominy or what monstrosity he might yet be associated—since he wasn't after all too utterly old to suffer—if it would only be decently proportionate to the posture he had kept, all his life, in the threatened presence of it. He had but one desire left—that he shouldn't have been "sold."

IV

Then it was that, one afternoon, while the spring of the year was young and new she met all in her own way his frankest betrayal of these alarms. He had gone in late to see her, but evening hadn't settled and she was presented to him in that long fresh light of waning April days which affects us often with a sadness sharper than the greyest hours of autumn. The week had been warm, the spring was supposed to have begun early, and May Bartram sat, for the first time in the year, without a fire; a fact that, to Marcher's sense, gave the scene of which she formed part a smooth and ultimate look, an air of knowing, in its immaculate order and cold meaningless cheer, that it would never see a fire again. Her own aspect—he could scarce have said why—intensified this note. Almost as white as wax, with the marks and signs in her face as numerous and as fine as if they had been etched by a needle, with soft white draperies relieved by a faded green scarf on the delicate tone of which the years had further refined, she was the picture of a serene and exquisite but impenetrable sphinx, whose head, or indeed all whose person, might have been powdered with silver. She was a sphinx, yet with her white petals and green fronds she might have been a lily too—only an artificial lily, wonderfully imitated and constantly kept, without dust or stain, though not exempt from a slight droop and a complexity of faint creases, under some clear glass bell. The perfection of household care, of high polish and finish, always reigned in her rooms, but they now looked most as if everything had been wound up, tucked in, put away, so that she might sit with folded hands and with nothing more to do. She was "out of it," to Marcher's vision; her work was over; she communicated with him as across some gulf or from some island of rest that she had already reached, and it made him feel strangely abandoned. Was it—or rather wasn't it—that if for so long she had been watching with him the answer to their question must have swum into her ken and taken on its name, so that her occupation was verily gone? He had as much as charged her with this in saying to her, many months before, that she even then knew something she was keeping from him. It was a point he had never since ventured to press, vaguely fearing as he did that it might become a difference, perhaps a disagreement, between them. He had in this later time turned nervous, which was what he in all the other years had never been; and the oddity was that his nervousness should have waited till he had begun to doubt, should have held off so long as he was sure. There was something, it seemed to him, that the wrong word would bring down on his head, something that would so at least ease off his tension. But he wanted not to speak the wrong word; that would make everything ugly. He wanted the knowledge he lacked to drop on him; if drop it could, by its own august weight. If she was to forsake him it was surely for her to take leave. This was why he didn't directly ask her again what she knew; but it was also why, approaching the matter from another side, he said to her in the course of his visit: "What do you regard as the very worst that at this time of day *can* happen to me?"

He had asked her that in the past often enough; they had, with the odd irregular rhythm of their intensities and avoidances, exchanged ideas about it and then had seen the ideas washed away by cool intervals, washed like figures traced in sea-sand. It had ever been the mark of their talk that the oldest allusions in it required but a little dismissal and reaction to come out again, sounding for the hour as new. She could thus at present meet his enquiry quite freshly and patiently. "Oh yes, I've repeatedly thought, only it always seemed to me of old that I couldn't quite make up my mind. I thought of dreadful things, between which it was difficult to choose; and so must you have done."

"Rather! I feel now as if I had scarce done anything else. I appear to myself to have spent my life in thinking of nothing *but* dreadful things. A great many of them I've at different times named to you, but there were others I couldn't name."

"They were too, too dreadful?"

"Too, too dreadful—some of them."

She looked at him a minute, and there came to him as he met it an inconsequent sense that her eyes, when one got their full clearness, were still as beautiful as they had been in youth, only beautiful with a strange cold light—a light that somehow was a part of the effect, if it wasn't rather a part of the cause, of the pale hard sweetness of the season and the hour. "And yet," she said at last, "there are horrors we've mentioned."

It deepened the strangeness to see her, as such a figure in such a picture, talk of "horrors," but she was to do in a few minutes something stranger yet—though even of this he was to take the full measure but afterwards—and the note of it already trembled. It was, for the matter of that, one of the signs that her eyes were having again the high flicker of their prime. He had to admit, however, what she said. "Oh yes, there were times when we did go far." He caught himself in the act of speaking as if it all were over. Well, he wished it were; and the consummation depended for him clearly more and more on his friend.

But she had now a soft smile. "Oh far—!"

It was oddly ironic. "Do you mean you're prepared to go further?"

She was frail and ancient and charming as she continued to look at him, yet it was rather as if she had lost the thread. "Do you consider that we went far?"

"Why I thought it the point you were just making—that we *had* looked most things in the face."

"Including each other?" She still smiled. "But you're quite right. We've had together great imaginations, often great fears; but some of them have been unspoken."

"Then the worst—we haven't faced that. I *could* face it, I believe, if I knew what you think it. I feel," he explained, "as if I had lost my power to conceive such things." And he wondered if he looked as blank as he sounded. "It's spent."

"Then why do you assume," she asked, "that mine isn't?"

"Because you've given me signs to the contrary. It isn't a question for you of conceiving, imagining, comparing. It isn't a question now of choosing." At last he came out with it. "You know something I don't. You've shown me that before."

These last words had affected her, he made out in a moment, exceedingly, and she spoke with firmness. "I've shown you, my dear, nothing."

He shook his head. "You can't hide it."

"Oh, oh!" May Bartram sounded over what she couldn't hide. It was almost a smothered groan.

"You admitted it months ago, when I spoke of it to you as of something you were afraid I should find out. Your answer was that I couldn't, that I wouldn't, and I don't pretend I have. But you had something therefore in mind, and I now see how it must have been, how it still is, the possibility that, of all possibilities, has settled itself for you as the worst. This," he went on, "is why I appeal to you. I'm only afraid of ignorance to-day—I'm not afraid of knowledge." And then as for a while she said nothing: "What makes me sure is that I see in your face and feel here, in this air and amid these appearances, that you're out of it. You've done. You've had your experience. You leave me to my fate."

Well, she listened, motionless and white in her chair, as on a decision to be made, so that her manner was fairly an avowal, though still, with a small fine inner stiffness, an imperfect surrender. "It *would* be the worst," she finally let herself say. "I mean the thing I've never said."

It hushed him a moment. "More monstrous than all the monstrosities we've named?"

"More monstrous. Isn't that what you sufficiently express," she asked, "in calling it the worst?"

Marcher thought. "Assuredly—if you mean, as I do, something that includes all the loss and all the shame that are thinkable."

"It would if it *should* happen," said May Bartram. "What we're speaking of, remember, is only my idea."

"It's your belief," Marcher returned. "That's enough for me. I feel your beliefs are right. Therefore if, having this one, you give me no more light on it, you abandon me."

"No, no!" she repeated. "I'm with you—don't you see?—still." And as to make it more vivid to him she rose from her chair—a movement she seldom risked in these days—and showed herself, all draped and all soft, in her fairness and slimness. "I haven't forsaken you."

It was really, in its effort against weakness, a generous assurance, and had the success of the impulse not, happily, been great, it would have touched him to pain more than to pleasure. But the cold charm in her eyes had spread, as she hovered before him, to all the rest of her person, so that it was for the minute almost a recovery of youth. He couldn't pity her for that; he could only take her as she showed—as capable even yet of helping him. It was as if, at the same time, her light might at any instant go out; wherefore he must make the most of it. There passed before him with intensity the three or four things he wanted most to know; but the question that came of itself to his lips really covered the others. "Then tell me if I shall consciously suffer."

She promptly shook her head. "Never!"

It confirmed the authority he imputed to her, and it produced on him an extraordinary effect. "Well, what's better than that? Do you call that the worst?"

"You think nothing is better?" she asked.

She seemed to mean something so special that he again sharply wondered, though still with the dawn of a prospect of relief. "Why not, if one doesn't *know?*" After which, as their eyes, over his question, met in a silence, the dawn deepened and something to his purpose came prodigiously out of her very face. His own, as he took it in, suddenly flushed to the forehead, and he gasped with the force of a perception to which, on the instant, everything fitted. The sound of his gasp filled the air; then he became articulate. "I see—if I don't suffer!"

In her own look, however, was doubt. "You see what?"

"Why what you mean—what you've always meant."

She again shook her head. "What I mean isn't what I've always meant. It's different."

"It's something new?"

She hung back from it a little. "Something new. It's not what you think. I see what you think."

His divination drew breath then; only her correction might be wrong. "It isn't that I *am* a blockhead?" he asked between faintness and grimness. "It isn't that it's all a mistake?"

"A mistake?" she pityingly echoed. *That* possibility, for her, he saw, would be monstrous; and if she guaranteed him the immunity from pain it would accordingly not be what she had in mind. "Oh no," she declared; "it's nothing of that sort. You've been right."

Yet he couldn't help asking himself if she weren't, thus pressed, speaking but to save him. It seemed to him he should be most in a hole if his history should prove all a platitude. "Are you telling me the truth, so that I shan't have been a bigger idiot than I can bear to know? I *haven't* lived with a vain imagination, in the most besotted illusion? I haven't waited but to see the door shut in my face?"

She shook her head again. "However the case stands *that* isn't the truth. Whatever the reality, it *is* a reality. The door isn't shut. The door's open," said May Bartram.

"Then something's to come?"

She waited once again, always with her cold sweet eyes on him. "It's never too late." She had, with her gliding step, diminished the distance between them, and she stood nearer to him, close to him, a minute, as if still charged with the unspoken. Her movement might have been for some finer emphasis of what she was at once hesitating and deciding to say. He had been standing by the chimney-piece, fireless and sparely adorned, a small perfect old French clock and two morsels of rosy Dresden constituting all its furniture; and her hand grasped the shelf while she kept him waiting, grasped it a little as for support and encouragement. She only kept him waiting, however; that is he only waited. It had become suddenly, from her movement and attitude, beautiful and vivid to him that she had something more to give him; her wasted face delicately shone with it—it glittered almost as with the white lustre of silver in her expression. She was right, incontestably, for what he saw in her face was the truth, and strangely, without consequence, while their talk of it as dreadful was still in the air, she appeared to present it as inordinately soft. This, prompting bewilderment, made him but gape the more gratefully for her revelation, so that they continued for some minutes silent, her face shining at him, her contact imponderably pressing, and his stare all kind but all expectant. The end, none the less, was that what he had expected failed to come to him. Something else took place instead, which seemed to consist at first in the mere closing of her eyes. She gave way at the same instant to a slow fine shudder, and though he remained staring—though he stared in fact but the harder—turned off and regained her chair. It was the end of what she had been intending, but it left him thinking only of that.

"Well, you don't say—?"

She had touched in her passage a bell near the chimney and had sunk back strangely pale. "I'm afraid I'm too ill."

"Too ill to tell me?" It sprang up sharp to him, and almost to his lips, the fear she might die without giving him light. He checked himself in time from so expressing his question, but she answered as if she had heard the words.

"Don't you know—now?"

"'Now'—?" She had spoken as if some difference had been made within the moment. But her maid, quickly obedient to her bell, was already with them. "I know nothing." And he was afterwards to say to himself that he must have spoken with odious impatience, such an impatience as to show that, supremely disconcerted, he washed his hands of the whole question.

"Oh!" said May Bartram.

"Are you in pain?" he asked as the woman went to her.

"No," said May Bartram.

Her maid, who had put an arm round her as if to take her to her room, fixed on him eyes that appealingly contradicted her; in spite of which, however, he showed once more his mystification. "What then has happened?"

She was once more, with her companion's help, on her feet, and, feeling withdrawal imposed on him, he had blankly found his hat and gloves and had reached the door. Yet he waited for her answer. "What *was* to," she said.

V

He came back the next day, but she was then unable to see him, and as it was literally the first time this had occurred in the long stretch of their acquaintance he turned away, defeated and sore, almost angry—or feeling at least that such a break in their custom was really the beginning of the end—and wandered alone with his thoughts, especially with the one he was least able to keep down. She was dying and he would lose her; she was dying and his life would end. He stopped in the Park, into which he had passed, and stared before him at his recurrent doubt. Away from her the doubt pressed again; in her presence he had believed her, but as he felt his forlornness he threw himself into the explanation that, nearest at hand, had most of a miserable warmth for him and least of a cold torment. She had deceived him to save him—to put him off with something in which he should be able to rest. What could the thing that was to happen to him be, after all, but just this thing that had begun to happen? Her dying, her death, his consequent solitude—*that* was what he had figured as the Beast in the Jungle, that was what had been in the lap of the gods. He had had her word for it as he left her—what else on earth could she have meant? It wasn't a thing of a monstrous order; not a fate rare and distinguished; not a stroke of fortune that overwhelmed and immortalised; it had only the stamp of the common doom. But poor Marcher at this hour judged the common doom sufficient. It would serve his turn, and even as the consummation of infinite waiting he would bend his pride to accept it. He sat down on a bench in the twilight. He hadn't been a fool. Something had *been,* as she had said, to come. Before he rose indeed it had quite struck him that the final fact really matched with the long avenue through which he had had to reach it. As sharing his suspense and as giving herself all, giving her life, to bring it to an end, she had come with him every step of the way. He had lived by her aid, and to leave her behind would be cruelly, damnably to miss her. What could be more overwhelming than that?

Well, he was to know within the week, for though she kept him a while at bay, left him restless and wretched during a series of days on each of which he asked about her only again to have to turn away, she ended his trial by receiving him where she had always received him. Yet she had been brought out at some hazard into the presence of so many of the things that were, consciously, vainly, half their past, and there was scant service left in the gentleness of her mere desire, all too visible, to check his obsession and wind up his long trouble. That was clearly what she wanted, the one thing more for her own peace while she could still put out her hand. He was so affected by her state that, once seated by her chair, he was moved to let everything go; it was she herself therefore who brought him back, took up again, before she dismissed him, her last word of the other time. She showed how she wished to leave their business in order. "I'm not sure you understood. You've nothing to wait for more. It *has* come."

Oh how he looked at her! "Really?"

"Really."

"The thing that, as you said, *was* to?"

"The thing that we began in our youth to watch for."

Face to face with her once more he believed her; it was a claim to which he had so abjectly little to oppose. "You mean that it has come as a positive definite occurrence, with a name and a date?"

"Positive. Definite. I don't know about the 'name,' but oh with a date!"

He found himself again too helplessly at sea. "But come in the night—come and passed me by?"

May Bartram had her strange faint smile. "Oh no, it hasn't passed you by!"

"But if I haven't been aware of it and it hasn't touched me—?"

"Ah your not being aware of it"—and she seemed to hesitate an instant to deal with this—"your not being aware of it is the strangeness *in* the strangeness. It's the wonder *of* the wonder." She spoke as with the softness almost of a sick child, yet now at last, at the end of all, with the perfect straightness of a sibyl. She visibly knew that she knew, and the effect on him was of something co-ordinate, in its high character, with the law that had ruled him. It was the true voice of the law; so on her lips would the law itself have sounded. "It *has* touched you," she went on. "It has done its office. It has made you all its own."

"So utterly without my knowing it?"

"So utterly without your knowing it." His hand, as he leaned to her, was on the arm of her chair, and, dimly smiling always now, she placed her own on it. "It's enough if *I* know it."

"Oh!" he confusedly breathed, as she herself of late so often had done.

"What I long ago said is true. You'll never know now, and I think you ought to be content. You've *had* it," said May Bartram.

"But had what?"

"Why what was to have marked you out. The proof of your law. It has acted. I'm too glad," she then bravely added, "to have been able to see what it's *not*."

He continued to attach his eyes to her, and with the sense that it was all beyond him, and that *she* was too, he would still have sharply challenged her hadn't he so felt it an abuse of her weakness to do more than take devoutly what she gave him, take it hushed as to a revelation. If he did speak, it was out of the foreknowledge of his loneliness to come. "If you're glad of what it's 'not' it might then have been worse?"

She turned her eyes away, she looked straight before her; with which after a moment: "Well, you know our fears."

He wondered. "It's something then we never feared?"

On this slowly she turned to him. "Did we ever dream, with all our dreams, that we should sit and talk of it thus?"

He tried for a little to make out that they had; but it was as if their dreams, numberless enough, were in solution in some thick cold mist through which thought lost itself. "It might have been that we couldn't talk?"

"Well"—she did her best for him—"not from this side. This, you see," she said, "is the *other* side."

"I think," poor Marcher returned, "that all sides are the same to me." Then, however, as she gently shook her head in correction: "We mightn't, as it were, have got across—?"

"To where we are—no. We're *here*"—she made her weak emphasis.

"And much good does it do us!" was her friend's frank comment.

"It does us the good it can. It does us the good that *it* isn't here. It's past. It's behind," said May Bartram. "Before—" but her voice dropped.

He had got up, not to tire her, but it was hard to combat his yearning. She after all told him nothing but that his light had failed—which he knew well enough without her. "Before—?" he blankly echoed.

"Before, you see, it was always to *come.* That kept it present."

"Oh I don't care what comes now! Besides," Marcher added, "it seems to me I liked it better present, as you say, than I can like it absent with *your* absence."

"Oh mine!"—and her pale hands made light of it.

"With the absence of everything." He had a dreadful sense of standing there before her for—so far as anything but this proved, this bottomless drop was concerned—the last time of their life. It rested on him with a weight he felt he could scarce bear, and this weight it apparently was that still pressed out what remained in him of speakable protest. "I believe you; but I can't begin to pretend I understand. *Nothing,* for me, is past; nothing *will* pass till I pass myself, which I pray my stars may be as soon as possible. Say, however," he added, "that I've eaten my cake, as you contend, to the last crumb—how can the thing I've never felt at all be the thing I was marked out to feel?"

She met him perhaps less directly, but she met him unperturbed. "You take your 'feelings' for granted. You were to suffer your fate. That was not necessarily to know it."

"How in the world—when what is such knowledge but suffering?"

She looked up at him a while in silence. "No—you don't understand."

"I suffer," said John Marcher.

"Don't, don't!"

"How can I help at least *that?*"

"Don't!" May Bartram repeated.

She spoke it in a tone so special, in spite of her weakness, that he stared an instant—stared as if some light, hitherto hidden, had shimmered across his vision. Darkness again closed over it, but the gleam had already become for him an idea. "Because I haven't the right—?"

"Don't *know*—when you needn't," she mercifully urged. "You needn't—for we shouldn't."

"Shouldn't?" If he could but know what she meant!

"No—it's too much."

"Too much?" he still asked but, with a mystification that was the next moment of a sudden to give way. Her words, if they meant something, affected him in this light—the light also of her wasted face—as meaning *all,* and the sense of what knowledge had been for herself came over him with a rush which broke through into a question. "Is it of that then you're dying?"

She but watched him, gravely at first, as to see, with this, where he was, and she might have seen something or feared something that moved her sympathy. "I would live for you still—if I could." Her eyes closed for a little, as if, withdrawn into herself, she were for a last time trying. "But I can't!" she said as she raised them again to take leave of him.

She couldn't indeed, as but too promptly and sharply appeared, and he had no vision of her after this that was anything but darkness and doom. They had parted for ever in that strange talk; access to her chamber of pain, rigidly guarded, was almost wholly forbidden him; he was feeling now moreover, in the face of doctors, nurses, the two or three relatives attracted doubtless by the presumption of what she had to "leave," how few were the rights, as they were called in such cases, that he had to put forward, and how odd it might even seem that their intimacy shouldn't have given him more of them. The stupidest fourth cousin had more, even though she had been nothing in such a person's life. She had been a feature of features in *his,* for what else was it to have been so indispensable? Strange beyond saying were the ways of existence, baffling for him the anomaly of his lack, as he felt it to be, of producible claim. A woman might have been, as it were, everything to him, and it might yet present him in no connexion that any one seemed held to recognise. If this was the case in these closing weeks it was the case more sharply on the occasion of the last offices rendered, in the great grey London cemetery, to what had been mortal, to what had been precious, in his friend. The concourse at her grave was not numerous, but he saw himself treated as scarce more nearly concerned with it than if there had been a thousand others. He was in short from this moment face to face with the fact that he was to profit extraordinarily little by the interest May Bartram had taken in him. He couldn't quite have said what he expected, but he hadn't surely expected this approach to a double privation. Not only had her interest failed him, but he seemed to feel himself unattended—and for a reason he couldn't seize—by the distinction, the dignity, the propriety, if nothing else, of the man markedly bereaved. It was as if in the view of society he had not *been* markedly bereaved, as if there still failed some sign or proof of it, and as if none the less his character could never be affirmed nor the deficiency ever made up. There were moments as the weeks went by when he would have liked, by some almost aggressive act, to take his stand on the intimacy of his loss, in order that it *might* be questioned and his retort, to the relief of his spirit, so recorded; but the moments of an irritation more helpless followed fast on these, the moments during which, turning things over with a good conscience but with a bare horizon, he found himself wondering if he oughtn't to have begun, so to speak, further back.

He found himself wondering indeed at many things, and this last speculation had others to keep it company. What could he have done, after all, in her lifetime, without giving them both, as it were, away? He couldn't have made known she was watching him, for that would have published the superstition of the Beast. This was what closed his mouth now—now that the Jungle had been threshed to vacancy and that the Beast had stolen away. It sounded too foolish and too flat; the difference for him in this particular, the extinction in his life of the element of suspense, was such as in fact to surprise him. He could scarce have said what the effect resembled; the abrupt cessation, the positive prohibition, of music perhaps, more than anything else, in some place all adjusted and all accustomed to sonority and to attention. If he could at any rate have conceived lifting the veil from his image at some moment of the past (what had he done, after all, if not lift it to *her?*) so to do this to-day, to talk to people at large of the Jungle cleared and confide to them that he now felt it as safe, would have been not only to see them listen as to a goodwife's tale, but really to hear himself tell one. What it presently came to in truth was that poor Marcher waded through his beaten grass, where no life stirred, where no breath sounded, where no evil eye seemed to gleam from a possible lair, very much as if vaguely looking for the Beast, and still more as if acutely missing it. He walked about in an existence that had grown strangely more spacious, and, stopping fitfully in places where the undergrowth of life struck him as closer, asked himself yearningly, wondered secretly and sorely, if it would have lurked here or there. It would have at all events *sprung;* what was at least complete was his belief in the truth itself of the assurance given him. The change from his old sense to his new was absolute and final: what was to happen *had* so absolutely and finally happened that he was as little able to know a fear for his future as to know a hope; so absent in short was any question of anything still to come. He was to live entirely with the other question, that of his unidentified past, that of his having to see his fortune impenetrably muffled and masked.

The torment of this vision became then his occupation; he couldn't perhaps have consented to live but for the possibility of guessing. She had told him, his friend, not to guess; she had forbidden him, so far as he might, to know, and she had even in a sort denied the power in him to learn: which were so many things, precisely, to deprive him of rest. It wasn't that he wanted, he argued for fairness, that anything past and done should repeat itself; it was only that he shouldn't, as an anticlimax, have been taken sleeping so sound as not to be able to win back by an effort of thought the lost stuff of consciousness. He declared to himself at moments that he would either win it back or have done with consciousness for ever; he made this idea his one motive in fine, made it so much his passion that none other, to compare with it, seemed ever to have touched him. The lost stuff of consciousness became thus for him as a strayed or stolen child to an unappeasable father; he hunted it up and down very much as if he were knocking at doors and enquiring of the police. This was the spirit in which, inevitably, he set himself to travel; he started on a journey that was to be as long as he could make it; it danced before him that, as the other side of the globe couldn't possibly have less to say to him, it might, by a possibility of suggestion, have more. Before he quitted London, however, he made a pilgrimage to May Bartram's grave, took his way to it through the endless avenues of the grim suburban metropolis, sought it out in the wilderness of tombs, and, though he had come but for the renewal of the act of farewell, found himself, when he had at last stood by it, beguiled into long intensities. He stood for an hour, powerless to turn away and yet powerless to penetrate the darkness of death; fixing with his eyes her inscribed name and date, beating his forehead against the fact of the secret they kept, drawing his breath, while he waited, as if some sense would in pity of him rise from the stones. He kneeled on the stones, however, in vain; they kept what they concealed; and if the face of the tomb did become a face for him it was because her two names became a pair of eyes that didn't know him. He gave them a last long look, but no palest light broke.

VI

He stayed away, after this, for a year; he visited the depths of Asia, spending himself on scenes of romantic interest, of superlative sanctity; but what was present to him everywhere was that for a man who had known what *he* had known the world was vulgar and vain. The state of mind in which he had lived for so many years shone out to him, in reflexion, as a light that coloured and refined, a light beside which the glow of the East was garish cheap and thin. The terrible truth was that he had lost—with everything else—a distinction as well; the things he saw couldn't help being common when he had become common to look at them. He was simply now one of them himself—he was in the dust, without a peg for the sense of difference; and there were hours when, before the temples of gods and the sepulchres of kings, his spirit turned for nobleness of association to the barely discriminated slab in the London suburb. That had become for him, and more intensely with time and distance, his one witness of a past glory. It was all that was left to him for proof or pride, yet the past glories of Pharaohs were nothing to him as he thought of it. Small wonder then that he came back to it on the morrow of his return. He was drawn there this time as irresistibly as the other, yet with a confidence, almost, that was doubtless the effect of the many months that had elapsed. He had lived, in spite of himself, into his change of feeling, and in wandering over the earth had wandered, as might be said, from the circumference to the centre of his desert. He had settled to his safety and accepted perforce his extinction; figuring to himself, with some colour, in the likeness of certain little old men he remembered to have seen, of whom, all meagre and wizened as they might look, it was related that they had in their time fought twenty duels or been loved by ten princesses. They indeed had been wondrous for others while he was but wondrous for himself; which, however, was exactly the cause of his haste to renew the wonder by getting back, as he might put it, into his own presence. That had quickened his steps and checked his delay. If his visit was prompt it was because he had been separated so long from the part of himself that alone he now valued.

It's accordingly not false to say that he reached his goal with a certain elation and stood there again with a certain assurance. The creature beneath the sod *knew* of his rare experience, so that, strangely now, the place had lost for him its mere blankness of expression. It met him in mildness—not, as before, in mockery; it wore for him the air of conscious greeting that we find, after absence, in things that have closely belonged to us and which seem to confess of themselves to the connexion. The plot of ground, the graven tablet, the tended flowers affected him so as belonging to him that he resembled for the hour a contented landlord reviewing a piece of property. Whatever had happened—well, had happened. He had not come back this time with the vanity of that question, his former worrying "What, *what?*" now practically so spent. Yet he would none the less never again so cut himself off from the spot; he would come back to it every month, for if he did nothing else by its aid he at least held up his head. It thus grew for him, in the oddest way, a positive resource; he carried out his idea of periodical returns, which took their place at last among the most inveterate of his habits. What it all amounted to, oddly enough, was that in his finally so simplified world this garden of death gave him the few square feet of earth on which he could still most live. It was as if, being nothing anywhere else for any one, nothing even for himself, he were just everything here, and if not for a crowd of witnesses or indeed for any witness but John Marcher, then by clear right of the register that he could scan like an open page. The open page was the tomb of his friend, and *there* were the facts of the past, there the truth of his life, there the backward reaches in which he could lose himself. He did this from time to time with such effect that he seemed to wander through the old years with his hand in the arm of a companion who was, in the most extraordinary manner, his other, his younger self; and to wander, which was more extraordinary yet, round and round a third presence—not wandering she, but stationary, still, whose eyes, turning with his revolution, never ceased to follow him, and whose seat was his point, so to speak, of orientation. Thus in short he settled to live—feeding all on the sense that he once *had* lived, and dependent on it not alone for a support but for an identity.

It sufficed him in its way for months and the year elapsed; it would doubtless even have carried him further but for an accident, superficially slight, which moved him, quite in another direction, with a force beyond any of his impressions of Egypt or of India. It was a thing of the merest chance—the turn, as he afterwards felt, of a hair, though he was indeed to live to believe that if light hadn't come to him in this particular fashion it would still have come in another. He was to live to believe this, I say, though he was not to live, I may not less definitely mention, to do much else. We allow him at any rate the benefit of the conviction, struggling up for him at the end, that, whatever might have happened or not happened, he would have come round of himself to the light. The incident of an autumn day had put the match to the train laid from of old by his misery. With the light before him he knew that even of late his ache had only been smothered. It was strangely drugged, but it throbbed; at the touch it began to bleed. And the touch, in the event, was the face of a fellow mortal. This face, one grey afternoon when the leaves were thick in the alleys, looked into Marcher's own, at the cemetery, with an expression like the cut of a blade. He felt it, that is, so deep down that he winced at the steady thrust. The person who so mutely assaulted him was a figure he had noticed, on reaching his own goal, absorbed by a grave a short distance away, a grave apparently fresh, so that the emotion of the visitor would probably match it for frankness. This fact alone forbade further attention, though during the time he stayed he remained vaguely conscious of his neighbour, a middle-aged man apparently, in mourning, whose bowed back, among the clustered monuments and mortuary yews, was constantly presented. Marcher's theory that these were elements in contact with which he himself revived, had suffered, on this occasion, it may be granted, a marked, an excessive check. The autumn day was dire for him as none had recently been, and he rested with a heaviness he had not yet known on the low stone table that bore May Bartram's name. He rested without power to move, as if some spring in him, some spell vouchsafed, had suddenly been broken for ever. If he could have done that moment as he wanted he would simply have stretched himself on the slab that was ready to take him, treating it as a place prepared to receive his last sleep. What in all the wide world had he now to keep awake for? He stared before him with the question, and it was then that, as one of the cemetery walks passed near him, he caught the shock of the face.

His neighbour at the other grave had withdrawn, as he himself, with force enough in him, would have done by now, and was advancing along the path on his way to one of the gates. This brought him close, and his pace was slow, so that—and all the more as there was a kind of hunger in his look—the two men were for a minute directly confronted. Marcher knew him at once for one of the deeply stricken—a perception so sharp that nothing else in the picture comparatively lived, neither his dress, his age, nor his presumable character and class; nothing lived but the deep ravage of the features he showed. He *showed* them—that was the point; he was moved, as he passed, by some impulse that was either a signal for sympathy or, more possibly, a challenge to an opposed sorrow. He might already have been aware of our friend, might at some previous hour have noticed in him the smooth habit of the scene, with which the state of his own senses so scantly consorted, and might thereby have been stirred as by an overt discord. What Marcher was at all events conscious of was in the first place that the imaged of scarred passion presented to him was conscious too—of something that profaned the air; and in the second that, roused, startled, shocked, he was yet the next moment looking after it, as it went, with envy. The most extraordinary thing that had happened to him—though he had given that name to other matters as well—took place, after his immediate vague stare, as a consequence of this impression. The stranger passed, but the raw glare of his grief remained, making our friend wonder in pity what wrong, what wound it expressed, what injury not to be healed. What had the man *had,* to make him by the loss of it so bleed and yet live?

Something—and this reached him with a pang—that *he,* John Marcher, hadn't; the proof of which was precisely John Marcher's arid end. No passion had ever touched him, for this was what passion meant; he had survived and maundered and pined, but where had been *his* deep ravage? The extraordinary thing we speak of was the sudden rush of the result of this question. The sight that had just met his eyes named to him, as in letters of quick flame, something he had utterly, insanely missed, and what he had missed made these things a train of fire, made them mark themselves in an anguish of inward throbs. He had seen *outside* of his life, not learned it within, the way a woman was mourned when she had been loved for herself: such was the force of his conviction of the meaning of the stranger's face, which still flared for him as a smoky torch. It hadn't come to him, the knowledge, on the wings of experience; it had brushed him, jostled him, upset him, with the disrespect of chance, the insolence of accident. Now that the illumination had begun, however, it blazed to the zenith, and what he presently stood there gazing at was the sounded void of his life. He gazed, he drew breath, in pain; he turned in his dismay, and, turning, he had before him in sharper incision than ever the open page of his story. The name on the table smote him as the passage of his neighbour had done, and what it said to him, full in the face, was that *she* was what he had missed. This was the awful thought, the answer to all the past, the vision at the dread clearness of which he grew as cold as the stone beneath him. Everything fell together, confessed, explained, overwhelmed; leaving him most of all stupefied at the blindness he had cherished. The fate he had been marked for he had met with a vengeance—he had emptied the cup to the lees; he had been the man of his time, *the* man, to whom nothing on earth was to have happened. That was the rare stroke—that was his visitation. So he saw it, as we say, in pale horror, while the pieces fitted and fitted. So *she* had seen it while he didn't, and so she served at this hour to drive the truth home. It was the truth, vivid and monstrous, that all the while he had waited the wait was itself his portion. This the companion of his vigil had at a given moment made out, and she had then offered him the chance to baffle his doom. One's doom, however, was never baffled, and on the day she told him his own had come down she had seen him but stupidly stare at the escape she offered him.

The escape would have been to love her; then, *then* he would have lived. *She* had lived—who could say now with what passion?—since she had loved him for himself; whereas he had never thought of her (ah how it hugely glared at him!) but in the chill of his egotism and the light of her use. Her spoken words came back to him—the chain stretched and stretched. The Beast had lurked indeed, and the Beast, at its hour, had sprung; it had sprung in that twilight of the cold April when, pale, ill, wasted, but all beautiful, and perhaps even then recoverable, she had risen from her chair to stand before him and let him imaginably guess. It had sprung as he didn't guess; it had sprung as she hopelessly turned from him, and the mark, by the time he left her, had fallen where it *was* to fall. He had justified his fear and achieved his fate; he had failed, with the last exactitude, of all he was to fail of; and a moan now rose to his lips as he remembered she had prayed he mightn't know. This horror of waking—*this* was knowledge, knowledge under the breath of which the very tears in his eyes seemed to freeze. Through them, none the less, he tried to fix it and hold it; he kept it there before him so that he might feel the pain. That at least, belated and bitter, had something of the taste of life. But the bitterness suddenly sickened him, and it was as if, horribly, he saw, in the truth, in the cruelty of his image, what had been appointed and done. He saw the Jungle of his life and saw the lurking Beast; then, while he looked, perceived it, as by a stir of the air, rise, huge and hideous, for the leap that was to settle him. His eyes darkened—it was close; and, instinctively turning, in his hallucination, to avoid it, he flung himself, face down, on the tomb.

1903

Kate Chopin 1851–1904

Critics hardly knew what to do about the work of Kate Chopin, author of some of the boldest and best stories written in America before 1960. Hers were nineteenth-century stories exploring all sorts of taboo subjects—miscegenation, divorce, and even female sexuality.

The daughter of Thomas and Eliza (Faris) O'Flaherty, Chopin grew up in a wealthy Roman Catholic family in St. Louis. She graduated from the Academy of the Sacred Heart in 1868 and on June 9, 1870, married Oscar Chopin, a French Creole businessman from Louisiana. During the next nine years, Chopin bore six children and fulfilled heavy social obligations as the wife of a seemingly successful New Orleans cotton broker. But in 1879 Oscar's business failed and the family moved from New Orleans to Cloutierville, where they operated a plantation store and a farm owned by Oscar's family. On December 10, 1882, Oscar died, leaving Kate a thirty-two-year-old widow with six children and limited financial resources. In 1884 she moved her family back to St. Louis, where she lived the rest of her life.

In 1889, already thirty-nine years old, Chopin began writing poetry and fiction. Only a decade later, she had published twenty poems, ninety-five short stories, two novels, one play, and eight essays of literary criticism. Her fiction is, without question, her best work. She set most of her stories in late-nineteenth-century Louisiana, and she portrayed characters from all social classes of her time and place—aristocratic Creoles, middle- and lower-class Acadians and "Americans," mulattoes, and blacks. Her stories explore relationships among these various classes and, especially, relationships between men and women.

In 1889, Chopin published her first two stories, "Wiser Than a God" and "A Point at Issue," both focusing on what would prove to be her favorite theme—the inherent conflict between the traditional requirement that a wife form her life around her husband's and a woman's need for discrete personhood, a conflict that in Chopin's stories often prevents a woman from having both a happy marriage and a life of her own. These first stories lack finesse; but they introduce the central conflict of her last important work, the novel *The Awakening.*

Her first novel, *At Fault* (1890), features an unusually strong woman as protagonist and dares to introduce two topics then considered daring: divorce and alchoholism. The boldness that would end her literary career nine years later was already apparent, though little noted because the novel attracted almost no attention.

Chopin's first stories were published in local periodicals in the St. Louis and New Orleans areas, but in 1890 she placed children's stories in two important eastern magazines. Though most noted today for her feminist themes, Chopin also wrote many outstanding children's stories, such as "Loka" and "Odalie Misses Mass." Two published volumes of her collected stories, *Bayou Folk* and *A Night in Acadie,* and a still-unpublished collection, "A Vocation and a Voice," contain several fine children's stories in addition to those that illustrate her most mature themes.

A number of Chopin's adult stories, including "Athénaïse," "A Pair of Silk Stockings," "The Story of an Hour," and *The Awakening,* feature wives and mothers who feel enslaved. But she also created women who experience complete fulfillment in marriage, as Mentine does in "A Visit to Avoyelles"; and she portrays others who come to realize the emptiness of a self-sufficient life without husband and children, as does Mamzelle Aurélie in "Regret."

Chopin dared to treat miscegenation in "Désirée's Baby" and to portray the tragic life of a slave under even the kindest of mistresses in "La Belle Zoraïde." "A Vocation and a Voice," the title story of her unpublished collection, illustrates the writer's awareness that men as well as women face identity crises and conflicts between selfhood and sexual attraction.

In Chopin's masterpiece, *The Awakening,* we encounter a husband beset by the "man-instinct of possession" and a woman who discovers that she needs to be a person as well as a wife and mother. The novel evoked outrage from critics, readers, and library censors primarily because Chopin allowed the protagonist, Edna Pontellier, to take control of her own life without criticizing her for doing so.

For many years, twentieth-century critics dismissed Chopin as a local color writer. But after her *Complete Works* became available, this viewpoint became untenable, and critics began attempting to place Chopin's works in their proper place in the canon of American literature. The influence of Hawthorne, Whitman, Henry James, and especially Maupassant on Chopin's work has been documented. Elements of romanticism, Transcendentalism, realism, and naturalism have been noted, thus placing Chopin squarely in the mainstream of nineteenth-century literary currents. Per Seyersted, in particular, shows that Chopin's works hold kinship with twentieth-century existentialism. And numerous critics have claimed that Chopin's fiction prophesied twentieth-century feminism. Chopin not only used but also transcended the works of those who preceded her. She found her own unique voice and expanded the possibilities for all who might follow.

Peggy Skaggs
Angelo State University

PRIMARY WORKS

At Fault, 1890; *Bayou Folk,* 1894; *A Night in Acadie,* 1897; *The Awakening,* 1899; *The Complete Works,* ed. Per Seyersted, 1969; *A Kate Chopin Miscellany,* ed. Per Seyersted and Emily Toth, 1979.

Désirée's Baby

As the day was pleasant, Madame Valmondé drove over to L'Abri to see Désirée and the baby.

It made her laugh to think of Désirée with a baby. Why, it seemed but yesterday that Désirée was little more than a baby herself; when Monsieur in riding through the gateway of Valmondé had found her lying asleep in the shadow of the big stone pillar.

The little one awoke in his arms and began to cry for "Dada." That was as much as she could do or say. Some people thought she might have strayed there of her own accord, for she was of the toddling age. The prevailing belief was that she had been purposely left by a party of Texans, whose canvas-covered wagon, late in the day, had crossed the ferry that Coton Maïs kept, just below the plantation. In time Madame Valmondé abandoned every speculation but the one that Désirée had been sent to her by a beneficent Providence to be the child of her affection, seeing that she was without child of the flesh. For the girl grew to be beautiful and gentle, affectionate and sincere,—the idol of Valmondé.

It was no wonder, when she stood one day against the stone pillar in whose shadow she had lain asleep, eighteen years before, that Armand Aubigny riding by and seeing her there, had fallen in love with her. That was the way all the Aubignys fell in love, as if struck by a pistol shot. The wonder was that he had not loved her before; for he had known her since his father brought him home from Paris, a boy of eight, after his mother died there. The passion that awoke in him that day, when he saw her at the gate, swept along like an avalanche, or like a prairie fire, or like anything that drives headlong over all obstacles.

Monsieur Valmondé grew practical and wanted things well considered: that is, the girl's obscure origin. Armand looked into her eyes and did not care. He was reminded that she was nameless. What did it matter about a name when he could give her one of the oldest and proudest in Louisiana? He ordered the *corbeille*[1] from Paris, and contained himself with what patience he could until it arrived; then they were married.

Madame Valmondé had not seen Désirée and the baby for four weeks. When she reached L'Abri she shuddered at the first sight of it, as she always did. It was a sad looking place, which for many years had not known the gentle presence of a mistress, old Monsieur Aubigny having married and buried his wife in France, and she having loved her own land too well ever to leave it. The roof came down steep and black like a cowl, reaching out beyond the wide galleries that encircled the yellow stuccoed house. Big, solemn oaks grew close to it, and their thick-leaved, far-reaching branches shadowed it like a pall. Young Aubigny's rule was a strict one, too, and under it his negroes had forgotten how to be gay, as they had been during the old master's easy-going and indulgent lifetime.

The young mother was recovering slowly, and lay full length, in her soft white muslins and laces, upon a couch. The baby was beside her, upon her arm, where he had fallen asleep, at her breast. The yellow nurse woman sat beside a window fanning herself.

Madame Valmondé bent her portly figure over Désirée and kissed her, holding her an instant tenderly in her arms. Then she turned to the child.

"This is not the baby!" she exclaimed, in startled tones. French was the language spoken at Valmondé in those days.

"I knew you would be astonished," laughed Désirée, "at the way he has grown. The little *cochon de lait!*[2] Look at his legs, mamma, and his hands and fingernails,—real finger-nails. Zandrine had to cut them this morning. Isn't it true, Zandrine?"

The woman bowed her turbaned head majestically, "Mais si,[3] Madame."

"And the way he cries," went on Désirée, "is deafening. Armand heard him the other day as far away as La Blanche's cabin."

Madame Valmondé had never removed her eyes from the child. She lifted it and walked with it over to the window that was lightest. She scanned the baby narrowly, then looked as searchingly at Zandrine, whose face was turned to gaze across the fields.

[1]Wedding presents.
[2]Suckling pig.
[3]Yes, indeed!

"Yes, the child has grown, has changed," said Madame Valmondé, slowly, as she replaced it beside its mother. "What does Armand say?"

Désirée's face became suffused with a glow that was happiness itself.

"Oh, Armand is the proudest father in the parish, I believe, chiefly because it is a boy, to bear his name; though he says not,—that he would have loved a girl as well. But I know it isn't true. I know he says that to please me. And mamma," she added, drawing Madame Valmondé's head down to her, and speaking in a whisper, "he hasn't punished one of them—not one of them—since baby is born. Even Négrillon, who pretended to have burnt his leg that he might rest from work—he only laughed, and said Négrillon was a great scamp. Oh, mamma, I'm so happy; it frightens me."

What Désirée said was true. Marriage, and later the birth of his son had softened Armand Aubigny's imperious and exacting nature greatly. This was what made the gentle Désirée so happy, for she loved him desperately. When he frowned she trembled, but loved him. When he smiled, she asked no greater blessing of God. But Armand's dark, handsome face had not often been disfigured by frowns since the day he fell in love with her.

When the baby was about three months old, Désirée awoke one day to the conviction that there was something in the air menacing her peace. It was at first too subtle to grasp. It had only been a disquieting suggestion; an air of mystery among the blacks; unexpected visits from far-off neighbors who could hardly account for their coming. Then a strange, an awful change in her husband's manner, which she dared not ask him to explain. When he spoke to her, it was with averted eyes, from which the old love-light seemed to have gone out. He absented himself from home; and when there, avoided her presence and that of her child, without excuse. And the very spirit of Satan seemed suddenly to take hold of him in his dealings with the slaves. Désirée was miserable enough to die.

She sat in her room, one hot afternoon, in her *peignoir,*[4] listlessly drawing through her fingers the strands of her long, silky brown hair that hung about her shoulders. The baby, half naked, lay asleep upon her own great mahogany bed, that was like a sumptuous throne, with its satin-lined half-canopy. One of La Blanche's little quadroon boys—half naked too—stood fanning the child slowly with a fan of peacock feathers. Désirée's eyes had been fixed absently and sadly upon the baby, while she was striving to penetrate the threatening mist that she felt closing about her. She looked from her child to the boy who stood beside him, and back again; over and over. "Ah!" It was a cry that she could not help; which she was not conscious of having uttered. The blood turned like ice in her veins, and a clammy moisture gathered upon her face.

She tried to speak to the little quadroon boy; but no sound would come, at first. When he heard his name uttered, he looked up, and his mistress was pointing to the door. He laid aside the great, soft fan, and obediently stole away, over the polished floor, on his bare tiptoes.

She stayed motionless, with gaze riveted upon her child, and her face the picture of fright.

[4]A lady's loose dressing gown.

Presently her husband entered the room, and without noticing her, went to a table and began to search among some papers which covered it.

"Armand," she called to him, in a voice which must have stabbed him, if he was human. But he did not notice. "Armand," she said again. Then she rose and tottered towards him. "Armand," she panted once more, clutching his arm, "look at our child. What does it mean? tell me."

He coldly but gently loosened her fingers from about his arm and thrust the hand away from him. "Tell me what it means!" she cried despairingly.

"It means," he answered lightly, "that the child is not white; it means that you are not white."

A quick conception of all that this accusation meant for her nerved her with unwonted courage to deny it. "It is a lie; it is not true, I am white! Look at my hair, it is brown; and my eyes are gray, Armand, you know they are gray. And my skin is fair," seizing his wrist. "Look at my hand; whiter than yours, Armand," she laughed hysterically.

"As white as La Blanche's," he returned cruelly; and went away leaving her alone with their child.

When she could hold a pen in her hand, she sent a despairing letter to Madame Valmondé.

"My mother, they tell me I am not white. Armand has told me I am not white. For God's sake tell them it is not true. You must know it is not true. I shall die. I must die. I cannot be so unhappy, and live."

The answer that came was as brief:

"My own Désirée: Come home to Valmondé; back to your mother who loves you. Come with your child."

When the letter reached Désirée she went with it to her husband's study, and laid it open upon the desk before which he sat. She was like a stone image; silent, white, motionless after she placed it there.

In silence he ran his cold eyes over the written words. He said nothing. "Shall I go, Armand?" she asked in tones sharp with agonized suspense.

"Yes, go."

"Do you want me to go."

"Yes, I want you to go."

He thought Almighty God had dealt cruelly and unjustly with him; and felt, somehow, that he was paying Him back in kind when he stabbed thus into his wife's soul. Moreover he no longer loved her, because of the unconscious injury she had brought upon his home and his name.

She turned away like one stunned by a blow, and walked slowly towards the door, hoping he would call her back.

"Good-by, Armand," she moaned.

He did not answer her. That was his last blow at fate.

Désirée went in search of her child. Zandrine was pacing the sombre gallery with it. She took the little one from the nurse's arms with no word of explanation, and descending the steps, walked away, under the live-oak branches.

It was an October afternoon; the sun was just sinking. Out in the still fields the negroes were picking cotton.

Désirée had not changed the thin white garment nor the slippers which she wore. Her hair was uncovered and the sun's rays brought a golden gleam from its brown meshes. She did not take the broad, beaten road which led to the far-off plantation of Valmondé. She walked across a deserted field, where the stubble bruised her tender feet, so delicately shod, and tore her thin gown to shreds.

She disappeared among the reeds and willows that grew thick along the banks of the deep, sluggish bayou; and she did not come back again.

Some weeks later there was a curious scene enacted at L'Abri. In the centre of the smoothly swept back yard was a great bonfire. Armand Aubigny sat in the wide hallway that commanded a view of the spectacle; and it was he who dealt out to a half dozen negroes the material which kept this fire ablaze.

A graceful cradle of willow, with all its dainty furbishings, was laid upon the pyre, which had already been fed with the richness of a priceless *layette.*[5] Then there were silk gowns, and velvet and satin ones added to these; laces, too, and embroideries; bonnets and gloves; for the *corbeille* had been of rare quality.

The last thing to go was a tiny bundle of letters; innocent little scribblings that Désirée had sent to him during the days of their espousal. There was the remnant of one back in the drawer from which he took them. But it was not Désirée's; it was part of an old letter from his mother to his father. He read it. She was thanking God for the blessing of her husband's love:—

"But, above all," she wrote, "night and day, I thank the good God for having so arranged our lives that our dear Armand will never know that his mother, who adores him, belongs to the race that is cursed with the brand of slavery."

1892

The Awakening

I

A green and yellow parrot, which hung in a cage outside the door, kept repeating over and over:

"*Allez vous-en! Allez vous-en! Sapristi!*[1] That's all right!"

He could speak a little Spanish, and also a language which nobody understood, unless it was the mocking-bird that hung on the other side of the door, whistling his fluty notes out upon the breeze with maddening persistence.

Mr. Pontellier, unable to read his newspaper with any degree of comfort, arose with an expression and an exclamation of disgust. He walked down the gallery and across the narrow "bridges" which connected the Lebrun cottages one with the other. He had been seated before the door of the main house. The parrot and the

[5]A complete outfit for a newborn baby, including clothes, bedding, and accessories.

[1]French: "Go away! Go away! Heavens!"

mocking-bird were the property of Madame Lebrun, and they had the right to make all the noise they wished. Mr. Pontellier had the privilege of quitting their society when they ceased to be entertaining.

He stopped before the door of his own cottage, which was the fourth one from the main building and next to the last. Seating himself in a wicker rocker which was there, he once more applied himself to the task of reading the newspaper. The day was Sunday; the paper was a day old. The Sunday papers had not yet reached Grand Isle.[2] He was already acquainted with the market reports, and he glanced restlessly over the editorials and bits of news which he had not had time to read before quitting New Orleans the day before.

Mr. Pontellier wore eye-glasses. He was a man of forty, of medium height and rather slender build; he stooped a little. His hair was brown and straight, parted on one side. His beard was neatly and closely trimmed.

Once in a while he withdrew his glance from the newspaper and looked about him. There was more noise than ever over at the house. The main building was called "the house," to distinguish it from the cottages. The chattering and whistling birds were still at it. Two young girls, the Farival twins, were playing a duet from "Zampa"[3] upon the piano. Madame Lebrun was bustling in and out, giving orders in a high key to a yard-boy whenever she got inside the house, and directions in an equally high voice to a dining-room servant whenever she got outside. She was a fresh, pretty woman, clad always in white with elbow sleeves. Her starched skirts crinkled as she came and went. Farther down, before one of the cottages, a lady in black was walking demurely up and down, telling her beads.[4] A good many persons of the *pension*[5] had gone over to the *Chênière Caminada*[6] in Beaudelet's lugger[7] to hear mass. Some young people were out under the water-oaks playing croquet. Mr. Pontellier's two children were there—sturdy little fellows of four and five. A quadroon[8] nurse followed them about with a far-away, meditative air.

Mr. Pontellier finally lit a cigar and began to smoke, letting the paper drag idly from his hand. He fixed his gaze upon a white sunshade that was advancing at snail's pace from the beach. He could see it plainly between the gaunt trunks of the water-oaks and across the stretch of yellow camomile. The gulf looked far away, melting hazily into the blue of the horizon. The sunshade continued to approach slowly. Beneath its pink-lined shelter were his wife, Mrs. Pontellier, and young Robert Lebrun. When they reached the cottage, the two seated themselves with some appearance of fatigue upon the upper step of the porch, facing each other, each leaning against a supporting post.

"What folly! to bathe at such an hour in such heat!" exclaimed Mr. Pontellier. He himself had taken a plunge at daylight. That was why the morning seemed long to him.

[2] A popular resort island south of Louisiana.

[3] A romantic opera (1831) by Louis Hérold.

[4] The act of manipulating a string of beads to count out the recitation of a series of prayers.

[5] French: boarding house.

[6] Another coastal island between Grande Isle and Louisiana.

[7] A nearby island.

[8] A person of one-quarter black ancestry; thus, someone whose grandparent is African American.

"You are burnt beyond recognition," he added, looking at his wife as one looks at a valuable piece of personal property which has suffered some damage. She held up her hands, strong, shapely hands, and surveyed them critically drawing up her lawn sleeves above the wrists. Looking at them reminded her of her rings, which she had given to her husband before leaving for the beach. She silently reached out to him, and he, understanding, took the rings from his vest pocket and dropped them into her open palm. She slipped them upon her fingers; then clasping her knees, she looked across at Robert and began to laugh. The rings sparkled upon her fingers. He sent back an answering smile.

"What is it?" asked Pontellier, looking lazily and amused from one to the other. It was some utter nonsense; some adventure out there in the water, and they both tried to relate it at once. It did not seem half so amusing when told. They realized this, and so did Mr. Pontellier. He yawned and stretched himself. Then he got up, saying he had half a mind to go over to Klein's hotel[9] and play a game of billiards.

"Come go along, Lebrun," he proposed to Robert. But Robert admitted quite frankly that he preferred to stay where he was and talk to Mrs. Pontellier.

"Well, send him about his business when he bores you, Edna," instructed her husband as he prepared to leave.

"Here, take the umbrella," she exclaimed, holding it out to him. He accepted the sunshade, and lifting it over his head descended the steps and walked away.

"Coming back to dinner?" his wife called after him. He halted a moment and shrugged his shoulders. He felt in his vest pocket; there was a ten-dollar bill there. He did not know; perhaps he would return for the early dinner and perhaps he would not. It all depended upon the company which he found over at Klein's and the size of "the game." He did not say this, but she understood it, and laughed, nodding good-by to him.

Both children wanted to follow their father when they saw him starting out. He kissed them and promised to bring them back bonbons and peanuts.

II

Mrs. Pontellier's eyes were quick and bright; they were a yellowish brown, about the color of her hair. She had a way of turning them swiftly upon an object and holding them there as if lost in some inward maze of contemplation or thought.

Her eyebrows were a shade darker than her hair. They were thick and almost horizontal, emphasizing the depth of her eyes. She was rather handsome than beautiful. Her face was captivating by reason of a certain frankness of expression and a contradictory subtle play of features. Her manner was engaging.

Robert rolled a cigarette. He smoked cigarettes because he could not afford cigars, he said. He had a cigar in his pocket which Mr. Pontellier had presented him with, and he was saving it for his after-dinner smoke.

This seemed quite proper and natural on his part. In coloring he was not unlike his companion. A clean-shaved face made the resemblance more pronounced than it

[9]A popular resort hotel.

would otherwise have been. There rested no shadow of care upon his open countenance. His eyes gathered in and reflected the light and languor of the summer day.

Mrs. Pontellier reached over for a palmleaf fan that lay on the porch and began to fan herself, while Robert sent between his lips light puffs from his cigarette. They chatted incessantly: about the things around them; their amusing adventure out in the water—it had again assumed its entertaining aspect; about the wind, the trees, the people who had gone to the *Chênière;* about the children playing croquet under the oaks, and the Farival twins, who were now performing the overture to "The Poet and the Peasant."[10]

Robert talked a good deal about himself. He was very young, and did not know any better. Mrs. Pontellier talked a little about herself for the same reason. Each was interested in what the other said. Robert spoke of his intention to go to Mexico in the autumn, where fortune awaited him. He was always intending to go to Mexico, but some way never got there. Meanwhile he held on to his modest position in a mercantile house in New Orleans, where an equal familiarity with English, French and Spanish gave him no small value as a clerk and correspondent.

He was spending his summer vacation, as he always did, with his mother at Grand Isle. In former times, before Robert could remember, "the house" had been a summer luxury of the Lebruns. Now, flanked by its dozen or more cottages, which were always filled with exclusive visitors from the "*Quartier Français,*"[11] it enabled Madame Lebrun to maintain the easy and comfortable existence which appeared to be her birthright.

Mrs. Pontellier talked about her father's Mississippi plantation and her girlhood home in the old Kentucky blue-grass country. She was an American woman, with a small infusion of French which seemed to have been lost in dilution. She read a letter from her sister, who was away in the East, and who had engaged herself to be married. Robert was interested, and wanted to know what manner of girls the sisters were, what the father was like, and how long the mother had been dead.

When Mrs. Pontellier folded the letter it was time for her to dress for the early dinner.

"I see Léonce isn't coming back," she said, with a glance in the direction whence her husband had disappeared. Robert supposed he was not, as there were a good many New Orleans club men over at Klein's.

When Mrs. Pontellier left him to enter her room, the young man descended the steps and strolled over toward the croquet players, where, during the half-hour before dinner, he amused himself with the little Pontellier children, who were very fond of him.

[10]A comic operetta by Franz Von Suppé (1819–1895).

[11]The French Quarter, New Orleans's oldest neighborhood, settled by the French in the early eighteenth century.

III

It was eleven o'clock that night when Mr. Pontellier returned from Klein's hotel. He was in an excellent humor, in high spirits, and very talkative. His entrance awoke his wife, who was in bed and fast asleep when he came in. He talked to her while he undressed, telling her anecdotes and bits of news and gossip that he had gathered during the day. From his trousers pockets he took a fistful of crumpled bank notes and a good deal of silver coin, which he piled on the bureau indiscriminately with keys, knife, handkerchief, and whatever else happened to be in his pockets. She was overcome with sleep, and answered him with little half utterances.

He thought it very discouraging that his wife, who was the sole object of his existence, evinced so little interest in things which concerned him and valued so little his conversation.

Mr. Pontellier had forgotten the bonbons and peanuts for the boys. Notwithstanding he loved them very much, and went into the adjoining room where they slept to take a look at them and make sure that they were resting comfortably. The result of his investigation was far from satisfactory. He turned and shifted the youngsters about in bed. One of them began to kick and talk about a basket full of crabs.

Mr. Pontellier returned to his wife with the information that Raoul had a high fever and needed looking after. Then he lit a cigar and went and sat near the open door to smoke it.

Mrs. Pontellier was quite sure Raoul had no fever. He had gone to bed perfectly well, she said, and nothing had ailed him all day. Mr. Pontellier was too well acquainted with fever symptoms to be mistaken. He assured her the child was consuming at that moment in the next room.

He reproached his wife with her inattention, her habitual neglect of the children. If it was not a mother's place to look after children, whose on earth was it? He himself had his hands full with his brokerage business. He could not be in two places at once; making a living for his family on the street, and staying at home to see that no harm befell them. He talked in a monotonous, insistent way.

Mrs. Pontellier sprang out of bed and went into the next room. She soon came back and sat on the edge of the bed, leaning her head down on the pillow. She said nothing, and refused to answer her husband when he questioned her. When his cigar was smoked out he went to bed, and in half a minute he was fast asleep.

Mrs. Pontellier was by that time thoroughly awake. She began to cry a little, and wiped her eyes on the sleeve of her *peignoir.*[12] Blowing out the candle, which her husband had left burning, she slipped her bare feet into a pair of satin *mules* at the foot of the bed and went out on the porch, where she sat down in the wicker chair and began to rock gently to and fro.

It was then past midnight. The cottages were all dark. A single faint light gleamed out from the hallway of the house. There was no sound abroad except the hooting of an old owl in the top of a water-oak, and the everlasting voice of the sea, that was not uplifted at that soft hour. It broke like a mournful lullaby upon the night.

[12]French: robe.

The tears came so fast to Mrs. Pontellier's eyes that the damp sleeve of her *peignoir* no longer served to dry them. She was holding the back of her chair with one hand; her loose sleeve had slipped almost to the shoulder of her uplifted arm. Turning, she thrust her face, steaming and wet, into the bend of her arm, and she went on crying there, not caring any longer to dry her face, her eyes, her arms. She could not have told why she was crying. Such experiences as the foregoing were not uncommon in her married life. They seemed never before to have weighed much against the abundance of her husband's kindness and a uniform devotion which had come to be tacit and self-understood.

An indescribable oppression, which seemed to generate in some unfamiliar part of her consciousness, filled her whole being with a vague anguish. It was like a shadow, like a mist passing across her soul's summer day. It was strange and unfamiliar; it was a mood. She did not sit there inwardly upbraiding her husband, lamenting at Fate, which had directed her footsteps to the path which they had taken. She was just having a good cry all to herself. The mosquitoes made merry over her, biting her firm, round arms and nipping at her bare insteps.

The little stinging, buzzing imps succeeded in dispelling a mood which might have held her there in the darkness half a night longer.

The following morning Mr. Pontellier was up in good time to take the rockaway[13] which was to convey him to the steamer at the wharf. He was returning to the city to his business, and they would not see him again at the Island till the coming Saturday. He had regained his composure, which seemed to have been somewhat impaired the night before. He was eager to be gone, as he looked forward to a lively week in Carondelet Street.[14]

Mr. Pontellier gave his wife half the money which he had brought away from Klein's hotel the evening before. She liked money as well as most women, and accepted it with no little satisfaction.

"It will buy a handsome wedding present for Sister Janet!" she exclaimed, smoothing out the bills as she counted them one by one.

"Oh! we'll treat Sister Janet better than that, my dear," he laughed, as he prepared to kiss her good-by.

The boys were tumbling about, clinging to his legs, imploring that numerous things be brought back to them. Mr. Pontellier was a great favorite, and ladies, men, children, even nurses, were always on hand to say good-by to him. His wife stood smiling and waving, the boys shouting, as he disappeared in the old rockaway down the sandy road.

A few days later a box arrived for Mrs. Pontellier from New Orleans. It was from her husband. It was filled with *friandises,*[15] with luscious and toothsome bits—the finest of fruits, *patés,*[16] a rare bottle or two, delicious syrups, and bonbons in abundance.

Mrs. Pontellier was always very generous with the contents of such a box; she was quite used to receiving them when away from home. The *patés* and fruit were

[13]A carriage.

[14]New Orleans's center for commercial exchange.

[15]French: candy.

[16]French: pastries.

brought to the dining-room; the bonbons were passed around. And the ladies, selecting with dainty and discriminating fingers and a little greedily, all declared that Mr. Pontellier was the best husband in the world. Mrs. Pontellier was forced to admit that she knew of none better.

IV

It would have been a difficult matter for Mr. Pontellier to define to his own satisfaction or any one else's wherein his wife failed in her duty toward their children. It was something which he felt rather than perceived, and he never voiced the feeling without subsequent regret and ample atonement.

If one of the little Pontellier boys took a tumble whilst at play, he was not apt to rush crying to his mother's arms for comfort; he would more likely pick himself up, wipe the water out of his eyes and the sand out of his mouth, and go on playing. Tots as they were, they pulled together and stood their ground in childish battles with doubled fists and uplifted voices, which usually prevailed against the other mother-tots. The quadroon nurse was looked upon as a huge encumbrance, only good to button up waists and panties and to brush and part hair; since it seemed to be a law of society that hair must be parted and brushed.

In short, Mrs. Pontellier was not a mother-woman. The mother-women seemed to prevail that summer at Grand Isle. It was easy to know them, fluttering about with extended, protecting wings when any harm, real or imaginary, threatened their precious brood. They were women who idolized their children, worshiped their husbands, and esteemed it a holy privilege to efface themselves as individuals and grow wings as ministering angels.

Many of them were delicious in the rôle; one of them was the embodiment of every womanly grace and charm. If her husband did not adore her, he was a brute, deserving of death by slow torture. Her name was Adèle Ratignolle. There are no words to describe her save the old ones that have served so often to picture the bygone heroine of romance and the fair lady of our dreams. There was nothing subtle or hidden about her charms; her beauty was all there, flaming and apparent: the spun-gold hair that comb nor confining pin could restrain; the blue eyes that were like nothing but sapphires; two lips that pouted, that were so red one could only think of cherries or some other delicious crimson fruit in looking at them. She was growing a little stout, but it did not seem to detract an iota from the grace of every step, pose, gesture. One would not have wanted her white neck a mite less full or her beautiful arms more slender. Never were hands more exquisite than hers, and it was a joy to look at them when she threaded her needle or adjusted her gold thimble to her taper middle finger as she sewed away on the little night-drawers or fashioned a bodice or a bib.

Madame Ratignolle was very fond of Mrs. Pontellier, and often she took her sewing and went over to sit with her in the afternoons. She was sitting there the afternoon of the day the box arrived from New Orleans. She had possession of the rocker, and she was busily engaged in sewing upon a diminutive pair of night-drawers.

She had brought the pattern of the drawers for Mrs. Pontellier to cut out—a marvel of construction, fashioned to enclose a baby's body so effectually that only two small eyes might look out from the garment, like an Eskimo's. They were designed for winter wear, when treacherous drafts came down chimneys and insidious currents of deadly cold found their way through key-holes.

Mrs. Pontellier's mind was quite at rest concerning the present material needs of her children, and she could not see the use of anticipating and making winter night garments the subject of her summer meditations. But she did not want to appear unamiable and uninterested, so she had brought forth newspapers which she spread upon the floor of the gallery, and under Madame Ratignolle's directions she had cut a pattern of the impervious garment.

Robert was there, seated as he had been the Sunday before, and Mrs. Pontellier also occupied her former position on the upper step, leaning listlessly against the post. Beside her was a box of bonbons, which she held out at intervals to Madame Ratignolle.

That lady seemed at a loss to make a selection, but finally settled upon a stick of nugat, wondering if it were not too rich; whether it could possibly hurt her. Madame Ratignolle had been married seven years. About every two years she had a baby. At that time she had three babies, and was beginning to think of a fourth one. She was always talking about her "condition." Her "condition" was in no way apparent, and no one would have known a thing about it but for her persistence in making it the subject of conversation.

Robert started to reassure her, asserting that he had known a lady who had subsisted upon nugat during the entire—but seeing the color mount into Mrs. Pontellier's face he checked himself and changed the subject.

Mrs. Pontellier, though she had married a Creole,[17] was not thoroughly at home in the society of Creoles; never before had she been thrown so intimately among them. There were only Creoles that summer at Lebrun's. They all knew each other, and felt like one large family, among whom existed the most amicable relations. A characteristic which distinguished them and which impressed Mrs. Pontellier most forcibly was their entire absence of prudery. Their freedom of expression was at first incomprehensible to her, though she had no difficulty in reconciling it with a lofty chastity which in the Creole woman seems to be inborn and unmistakable.

Never would Edna Pontellier forget the shock with which she heard Madame Ratignolle relating to old Monsieur Farival the harrowing story of one of her *accouchements,*[18] withholding no intimate detail. She was growing accustomed to like shocks, but she could not keep the mounting color back from her cheeks. Oftener than once her coming had interrupted the droll story with which Robert was entertaining some amused group of married women.

A book had gone the rounds of the *pension.* When it came her turn to read it, she did so with profound astonishment. She felt moved to read the book in secret and solitude, though none of the others had done so—to hide it from view at the sound of approaching footsteps. It was openly criticised and freely discussed at table. Mrs. Pontellier gave over being astonished, and concluded that wonders would never cease.

[17]In Chopin's usage, aristocrats of French and Spanish ancestry.

[18]French: childbirths.

V

They formed a congenial group sitting there that summer afternoon—Madame Ratignolle sewing away, often stopping to relate a story or incident with much expressive gesture of her perfect hands; Robert and Mrs. Pontellier sitting idle, exchanging occasional words, glances or smiles which indicated a certain advanced stage of intimacy and *camaraderie*.

He had lived in her shadow during the past month. No one thought anything of it. Many had predicted that Robert would devote himself to Mrs. Pontellier when he arrived. Since the age of fifteen, which was eleven years before, Robert each summer at Grand Isle had constituted himself the devoted attendant of some fair dame or damsel. Sometimes it was a young girl, again a widow; but as often as not it was some interesting married woman.

For two consecutive seasons he lived in the sunlight of Mademoiselle Duvigné's presence. But she died between summers; then Robert posed as an inconsolable, prostrating himself at the feet of Madame Ratignolle for whatever crumbs of sympathy and comfort she might be pleased to vouchsafe.

Mrs. Pontellier liked to sit and gaze at her fair companion as she might look upon a faultless Madonna.

"Could any one fathom the cruelty beneath that fair exterior?" murmured Robert. She knew that I adored her once, and she let me adore her. It was 'Robert, come; go; stand up; sit down; do this; do that; see if the baby sleeps; my thimble, please, that I left God knows where. Come and read Daude[19] to me while I sew.'"

"*Par exemple!*[20] I never had to ask. You were always there under my feet, like a troublesome cat."

"You mean like an adoring dog. And just as soon as Ratignolle appeared on the scene, then it *was* like a dog. *'Passez! Adieu! Allez vous-en!'*"[21]

"Perhaps I feared to make Alphonse jealous," she interjoined, with excessive naïveté. That made them all laugh. The right hand jealous of the left! The heart jealous of the soul! But for that matter, the Creole husband is never jealous; with him the gangrene passion is one which has become dwarfed by disuse.

Meanwhile Robert, addressing Mrs. Pontellier, continued to tell of his one time hopeless passion for Madame Ratignolle; of sleepless nights, of consuming flames till the very sea sizzled when he took his daily plunge. While the lady at the needle kept up a little running, contemptuous comment:

"Blagueur—farceur—gros bête, va!"[22]

He never assumed this serio-comic tone when alone with Mrs. Pontellier. She never knew precisely what to make of it; at that moment it was impossible for her to guess how much of it was jest and what proportion was earnest. It was understood that he had often spoken words of love to Madame Ratignolle, without any thought of being taken seriously. Mrs. Pontellier was glad he had not assumed a similar rôle toward herself. It would have been unacceptable and annoying.

[19]Alphonse Daudet (1840–1897), French novelist noted for his naturalism.
[20]French: "For God's sake!"
[21]French: "Go on! Goodbye! Go away!"
[22]French: "Joker—mischief-maker—fool, come off it!"

Mrs. Pontellier had brought her sketching materials, which she sometimes dabbled with in an unprofessional way. She liked the dabbling. She felt in it satisfaction of a kind which no other employment afforded her.

She had long wished to try herself on Madame Ratignolle. Never had that lady seemed a more tempting subject than at that moment, seated there like some sensuous Madonna, with the gleam of the fading day enriching her splendid color.

Robert crossed over and seated himself upon the step below Mrs. Pontellier, that he might watch her work. She handled her brushes with a certain ease and freedom which came, not from long and close acquaintance with them, but from a natural aptitude. Robert followed her work with close attention, giving forth little ejaculatory expressions of appreciation in French, which he addressed to Madame Ratignolle.

"Mais ce n'est pas mal! Elle s'y connait, elle a de la force, oui."[23]

During his oblivious attention he once quietly rested his head against Mrs. Pontellier's arm. As gently she repulsed him. Once again he repeated the offense. She could not but believe it to be thoughtlessness on his part; yet that was no reason she should submit to it. She did not remonstrate, except again to repulse him quietly but firmly. He offered no apology.

The picture completed bore no resemblance to Madame Ratignolle. She was greatly disappointed to find that it did not look like her. But it was a fair enough piece of work, and in many respects satisfying.

Mrs. Pontellier evidently did not think so. After surveying the sketch critically she drew a broad smudge of paint across its surface, and crumpled the paper between her hands.

The youngsters came tumbling up the steps, the quadroon following at the respectful distance which they required her to observe. Mrs. Pontellier made them carry her paints and things into the house. She sought to detain them for a little talk and some pleasantry. But they were greatly in earnest. They had only come to investigate the contents of the bonbon box. They accepted without murmuring what she chose to give them, each holding out two chubby hands scoop-like, in the vain hope that they might be filled; and then away they went.

The sun was low in the west, and the breeze soft and languorous that came up from the south, charged with the seductive odor of the sea. Children, freshly befurbelowed were gathering for their games under the oaks. Their voices were high and penetrating.

Madame Ratignolle folded her sewing, placing thimble, scissors and thread all neatly together in the roll, which she pinned securely. She complained of faintness. Mrs. Pontellier flew for the cologne water and a fan. She bathed Madame Ratignolle's face with cologne, while Robert plied the fan with unnecessary vigor.

The spell was soon over, and Mrs. Pontellier could not help wondering if there were not a little imagination responsible for its origin, for the rose tint had never faded from her friend's face.

She stood watching the fair woman walk down the long line of galleries with the grace and majesty which queens are sometimes supposed to possess. Her little ones

[23]French: "Not bad at all! She knows what she is doing, she has talent!"

ran to meet her. Two of them clung about her white skirts, the third she took from its nurse and with a thousand endearments bore it along in her own fond, encircling arms. Though, as everybody well knew, the doctor had forbidden her to lift so much as a pin!

"Are you going bathing?" asked Robert of Mrs. Pontellier. It was not so much a question as a reminder.

"Oh, no," she answered, with a tone of indecision. "I'm tired; I think not." Her glance wandered from his face away toward the Gulf, whose sonorous murmur reached her like a loving but imperative entreaty.

"Oh, come!" he insisted. "You mustn't miss your bath. Come on. The water must be delicious; it will not hurt you. Come."

He reached up for her big, rough straw hat that hung on a peg outside the door, and put it on her head. They descended the steps, and walked away together toward the beach. The sun was low in the west and the breeze was soft and warm.

VI

Edna Pontellier could not have told why, wishing to go to the beach with Robert, she should in the first place have declined, and in the second place have followed in obedience to one of the two contradictory impulses which impelled her.

A certain light was beginning to dawn dimly within her,—the light which, showing the way, forbids it.

At that early period it served but to bewilder her. It moved her to dreams, to thoughtfulness, to the shadowy anguish which had overcome her the midnight when she had abandoned herself to tears.

In short, Mrs. Pontellier was beginning to realize her position in the universe as a human being, and to recognize her relations as an individual to the world within and about her. This may seem like a ponderous weight of wisdom to descend upon the soul of a young woman of twenty-eight—perhaps more wisdom than the Holy Ghost is usually pleased to vouchsafe to any woman.

But the beginning of things, of a world especially, is necessarily vague, tangled, chaotic, and exceedingly disturbing. How few of us ever emerge from such beginning! How many souls perish in its tumult!

The voice of the sea is seductive; never ceasing, whispering, clamoring, murmuring, inviting the soul to wander for a spell in abysses of solitude; to lose itself in mazes of inward contemplation.

The voice of the sea speaks to the soul. The touch of the sea is sensuous, enfolding the body in its soft, close embrace.

VII

Mrs. Pontellier was not a woman given to confidences, a characteristic hitherto contrary to her nature. Even as a child she had lived her own small life all within herself. At a very early period she had apprehended instinctively the dual life—that outward existence which conforms, the inward life which questions.

That summer at Grand Isle she began to loosen a little the mantle of reserve that had always enveloped her. There may have been—there must have been—influences, both subtle and apparent, working in their several ways to induce her to do this; but the most obvious was the influence of Adèle Ratignolle. The excessive physical charm of the Creole had first attracted her, for Edna had a sensuous susceptibility to beauty. Then the candor of the woman's whole existence, which every one might read, and which formed so striking a contrast to her own habitual reserve—this might have furnished a link. Who can tell what metals the gods use in forging the subtle bond which we call sympathy, which we might as well call love.

The two women went away one morning to the beach together, arm in arm, under the huge white sunshade. Edna had prevailed upon Madame Ratignolle to leave the children behind, though she could not induce her to relinquish a diminutive roll of needlework, which Adèle begged to be allowed to slip into the depths of her pocket. In some unaccountable way they had escaped from Robert.

The walk to the beach was no inconsiderable one, consisting as it did of a long, sandy path, upon which a sporadic and tangled growth that bordered it on either side made frequent and unexpected inroads. There were acres of yellow camomile reaching out on either hand. Further away still, vegetable gardens abounded, with frequent small plantations of orange or lemon trees intervening. The dark green clusters glistened from afar in the sun.

The women were both of goodly height, Madame Ratignolle possessing the more feminine and matronly figure. The charm of Edna Pontellier's physique stole insensibly upon you. The lines of her body were long, clean and symmetrical; it was a body which occasionally fell into splendid poses; there was no suggestion of the trim, stereotyped fashion-plate about it. A casual and indiscriminating observer, in passing, might not cast a second glance upon the figure. But with more feeling and discernment he would have recognized the noble beauty of its modeling, and the graceful severity of poise and movement, which made Edna Pontellier different from the crowd.

She wore a cool muslin that morning—white, with a waving vertical line of brown running through it; also a white linen collar and the big straw hat which she had taken from the peg outside the door. The hat rested any way on her yellow-brown hair, that waved a little, was heavy, and clung close to her head.

Madame Ratignolle, more careful of her complexion, had twined a gauze veil about her head. She wore dogskin gloves, with gauntlets that protected her wrists. She was dressed in pure white, with a fluffiness of ruffles that became her. The draperies and fluttering things which she wore suited her rich, luxuriant beauty as a greater severity of line could not have done.

There were a number of bath-houses along the beach, of rough but solid construction, built with small, protecting galleries facing the water. Each house consisted of two compartments, and each family at Lebrun's possessed a compartment for itself, fitted out with all the essential paraphernalia of the bath and whatever other conveniences the owners might desire. The two women had no intention of bathing; they had just strolled down to the beach for a walk and to be alone and near the water. The Pontellier and Ratignolle compartments adjoined one another under the same roof.

Mrs. Pontellier had brought down her key through force of habit. Unlocking the door of her bath-room she went inside, and soon emerged, bringing a rug, which she spread upon the floor of the gallery, and two huge hair pillows covered with crash, which she placed against the front of the building.

The two seated themselves there in the shade of the porch, side by side, with their backs against the pillows and their feet extended. Madame Ratignolle removed her veil, wiped her face with a rather delicate handkerchief, and fanned herself with the fan which she always carried suspended somewhere about her person by a long, narrow ribbon. Edna removed her collar and opened her dress at the throat. She took the fan from Madame Ratignolle and began to fan both herself and her companion. It was very warm, and for a while they did nothing but exchange remarks about the heat, the sun, the glare. But there was a breeze blowing, a choppy stiff wind that whipped the water into froth. It fluttered the skirts of the two women and kept them for a while engaged in adjusting, readjusting, tucking in, securing hair-pins and hat-pins. A few persons were sporting some distance away in the water. The beach was very still of human sound at that hour. The lady in black was reading her morning devotions on the porch of a neighboring bath-house. Two young lovers were exchanging their hearts' yearnings beneath the children's tent, which they had found unoccupied.

Edna Pontellier, casting her eyes about had finally kept them at rest upon the sea. The day was clear and carried the gaze out as far as the blue sky went; there were a few white clouds suspended idly over the horizon. A lateen sail was visible in the direction of Cat Island, and others to the south seemed almost motionless in the far distance.

"Of whom—of what are you thinking?" asked Adèle of her companion, whose countenance she had been watching with a little amused attention, arrested by the absorbed expression which seemed to have seized and fixed every feature into a statuesque repose.

"Nothing," returned Mrs. Pontellier, with a start, adding at once: "How stupid! But it seems to me it is the reply we make instinctively to such a question. Let me see," she went on, throwing back her head and narrowing her fine eyes till they shone like two vivid points of light. "Let me see. I was really not conscious of thinking of anything, but perhaps I can retrace my thoughts."

"Oh! never mind!" laughed Madame Ratignolle. "I am not quite so exacting. I will let you off this time. It is really too hot to think, especially to think about thinking."

"But for the fun of it," persisted Edna. "First of all, the sight of the water stretching so far away, those motionless sails against the blue sky, made a delicious picture that I just wanted to sit and look at. The hot wind beating in my face made me think—without any connection that I can trace—of a summer day in Kentucky, of a meadow that seemed as big as the ocean to the very little girl walking through the grass, which was higher than her waist. She threw out her arms as if swimming when she walked, beating the tall grass as one strikes out in the water. Oh, I see the connection now!"

"Where were you going that day in Kentucky, walking through the grass?"

"I don't remember now. I was just walking diagonally across a big field. My sunbonnet obstructed the view. I could see only the stretch of green before me, and I felt as if I must walk on forever, without coming to the end of it. I don't remember whether I was frightened or pleased. I must have been entertained.

"Likely as not it was Sunday," she laughed; "and I was running away from prayers, from the Presbyterian service, read in a spirit of gloom by my father that chills me yet to think of."

"And have you been running away from prayers ever since, *ma chère?*"[24] asked Madame Ratignolle, amused.

"No! oh, no!" Edna hastened to say. "I was a little unthinking child in those days, just following a misleading impulse without question. On the contrary, during one period of my life religion took a firm hold upon me; after I was twelve and until—until—why, I suppose until now, though I never thought much about it—just driven along by habit. But do you know," she broke off, turning her quick eyes upon Madame Ratignolle and leaning forward a little so as to bring her face quite close to that of her companion, "sometimes I feel this summer as if I were walking through the green meadow again; idly, aimlessly, unthinking and unguided."

Madame Ratignolle laid her hand over that of Mrs. Pontellier, which was near her. Seeing that the hand was not withdrawn, she clasped it firmly and warmly. She even stroked it a little, fondly, with the other hand, murmuring in an undertone, "*Pauvre chérie.*"[25]

The action was at first a little confusing to Edna, but she soon lent herself readily to the Creole's gentle caress. She was not accustomed to an outward and spoken expression of affection, either in herself or in others. She and her younger sister, Janet, had quarreled a good deal through force of unfortunate habit. Her older sister, Margaret, was matronly and dignified, probably from having assumed matronly and house-wifely responsibilities too early in life, their mother having died when they were quite young. Margaret was not effusive; she was practical. Edna had had an occasional girl friend, but whether accidentally or not, they seemed to have been all of one type—the self-contained. She never realized that the reserve of her own character had much, perhaps everything, to do with this. Her most intimate friend at school had been one of rather exceptional intellectual gifts, who wrote fine-sounding essays, which Edna admired and strove to imitate; and with her she talked and glowed over the English classics, and sometimes held religious and political controversies.

Edna often wondered at one propensity which sometimes had inwardly disturbed her without causing any outward show or manifestation on her part. At a very early age—perhaps it was when she traversed the ocean of waving grass—she remembered that she had been passionately enamored of a dignified and sad-eyed cavalry officer who visited her father in Kentucky. She could not leave his presence when he was there, nor remove her eyes from his face, which was something like Napoleon's, with a lock of black hair falling across the forehead. But the cavalry officer melted imperceptibly out of her existence.

At another time her affections were deeply engaged by a young gentleman who visited a lady on a neighboring plantation. It was after they went to Mississippi to live. The young man was engaged to be married to the young lady, and they sometimes called upon Margaret, driving over of afternoons in a buggy. Edna was a little miss, just merging into her teens; and the realization that she herself was nothing,

[24]French: "my dear."
[25]French: "Poor dear."

meadow—freedom

nothing, nothing to the engaged young man was a bitter affliction to her. But he, too, went the way of dreams.

She was a grown young woman when she was overtaken by what she supposed to be the climax of her fate. It was when the face and figure of a great tragedian[26] began to haunt her imagination and stir her senses. The persistence of the infatuation lent it an aspect of genuineness. The hopelessness of it colored it with the lofty tones of a great passion.

The picture of the tragedian stood enframed upon her desk. Any one may possess the portrait of a tragedian without exciting suspicion or comment. (This was a sinister reflection which she cherished.) In the presence of others she expressed admiration for his exalted gifts, as she handed the photograph around and dwelt upon the fidelity of the likeness. When alone she sometimes picked it up and kissed the cold glass passionately.

Her marriage to Léonce Pontellier was purely an accident, in this respect resembling many other marriages which masquerade as the decrees of Fate. It was in the midst of her secret great passion that she met him. He fell in love, as men are in the habit of doing, and pressed his suit with an earnestness and an ardor which left nothing to be desired. He pleased her; his absolute devotion flattered her. She fancied there was a sympathy of thought and taste between them, in which fancy she was mistaken. Add to this the violent opposition of her father and her sister Margaret to her marriage with a Catholic, and we need seek no further for the motives which led her to accept Monsieur Pontellier for her husband.

The acme of bliss, which would have been a marriage with the tragedian, was not for her in this world. As the devoted wife of a man who worshiped her, she felt she would take her place with a certain dignity in the world of reality, closing the portals forever behind her upon the realm of romance and dreams.

But it was not long before the tragedian had gone to join the cavalry officer and the engaged young man and a few others; and Edna found herself face to face with the realities. She grew fond of her husband, realizing with some unaccountable satisfaction that no trace of passion or excessive and fictitious warmth colored her affection, thereby threatening its dissolution.

She was fond of her children in an uneven, impulsive way. She would sometimes gather them passionately to her heart; she would sometimes forget them. The year before they had spent part of the summer with their grandmother Pontellier in Iberville. Feeling secure regarding their happiness and welfare, she did not miss them except with an occasional intense longing. Their absence was a sort of relief, though she did not admit this, even to herself. It seemed to free her of a responsibility which she had blindly assumed and for which Fate had not fitted her.

Edna did not reveal so much as all this to Madame Ratignolle that summer day when they sat with faces turned to the sea. But a good part of it escaped her. She had put her head down on Madame Ratignolle's shoulder. She was flushed and felt intoxicated with the sound of her own voice and the unaccustomed taste of candor. It muddled her like wine, or like a first breath of freedom.

There was the sound of approaching voices. It was Robert, surrounded by a

[26]Actor.

troop of children, searching for them. The two little Pontelliers were with him, and he carried Madame Ratignolle's little girl in his arms. There were other children beside, and two nursemaids followed, looking disagreeable and resigned.

The women at once rose and began to shake out their draperies and relax their muscles. Mrs. Pontellier threw the cushions and rug into the bath-house. The children all scampered off to the awning, and they stood there in a line, gazing upon the intruding lovers, still exchanging their vows and sighs. The lovers got up, with only a silent protest, and walked slowly away somewhere else.

The children possessed themselves of the tent, and Mrs. Pontellier went over to join them.

Madame Ratignolle begged Robert to accompany her to the house; she complained of cramp in her limbs and stiffness of the joints. She leaned draggingly upon his arm as they walked.

VIII

"Do me a favor, Robert," spoke the pretty woman at his side, almost as soon as she and Robert had started on their slow, homeward way. She looked up in his face, leaning on his arm beneath the encircling shadow of the umbrella which he had lifted.

"Granted; as many as you like," he returned, glancing down into her eyes that were full of thoughtfulness and some speculation.

"I only ask for one; let Mrs. Pontellier alone."

"*Tiens!*" he exclaimed, with a sudden, boyish laugh. "*Voilà que Madame Ratignolle est jalouse!*"[27]

"Nonsense! I'm in earnest; I mean what I say. Let Mrs. Pontellier alone."

"Why?" he asked; himself growing serious at his companion's solicitation.

"She is not one of us; she is not like us. She might make the unfortunate blunder of taking you seriously."

His face flushed with annoyance, and taking off his soft hat he began to beat it impatiently against his leg as he walked. "Why shouldn't she take me seriously?" he demanded sharply. "Am I a comedian, a clown, a jack-in-the-box? Why shouldn't she? You Creoles! I have no patience with you! Am I always to be regarded as a feature of an amusing programme? I hope Mrs. Pontellier does take me seriously. I hope she has discernment enough to find in me something besides the *blagueur.* If I thought there was any doubt—"

"Oh, enough, Robert!" she broke into his heated outburst. "You are not thinking of what you are saying. You speak with about as little reflection as we might expect from one of those children down there playing in the sand. If your attentions to any married women here were ever offered with any intention of being convincing, you would not be the gentleman we all know you to be, and you would be unfit to associate with the wives and daughters of the people who trust you."

Madame Ratignolle had spoken what she believed to be the law and the gospel. The young man shrugged his shoulders impatiently.

[27]French: "So! Madame Ratignolle is jealous!"

"Oh! well! That isn't it," slamming his hat down vehemently upon his head. "You ought to feel that such things are not flattering to say to a fellow."

"Should our whole intercourse consist of an exchange of compliments? *Ma foi!*"[28]

"It isn't pleasant to have a woman tell you—" he went on, unheedingly, but breaking off suddenly: "Now if I were like Arobin—you remember Alcée Arobin and that story of the consul's wife at Biloxi?"[29] And he related the story of Alcée Arobin and the consul's wife; and another about the tenor of the French Opera, who received letters which should never have been written; and still other stories, grave and gay, till Mrs. Pontellier and her possible propensity for taking young men seriously was apparently forgotten.

Madame Ratignolle, when they had regained her cottage, went in to take the hour's rest which she considered helpful. Before leaving her, Robert begged her pardon for the impatience—he called it rudeness—with which he had received her well-meant caution.

"You made one mistake, Adèle," he said, with a light smile; "there is no earthly possibility of Mrs. Pontellier ever taking me seriously. You should have warned me against taking myself seriously. Your advice might then have carried some weight and given me subject for some reflection. *Au revoir.*[30] But you look tired," he added, solicitously. "Would you like a cup of bouillon? Shall I stir you a toddy? Let me mix you a toddy with a drop of Angostura."

She acceded to the suggestion of bouillon, which was grateful and acceptable. He went himself to the kitchen, which was a building apart from the cottages and lying to the rear of the house. And he himself brought her the golden-brown bouillon, in a dainty Sèvres cup, with a flaky cracker or two on the saucer.

She thrust a bare, white arm from the curtain which shielded her open door, and received the cup from his hands. She told him he was a *bon garçon,*[31] and she meant it. Robert thanked her and turned away toward "the house."

The lovers were just entering the grounds of the *pension*. They were leaning toward each other as the water-oaks bent from the sea. There was not a particle of earth beneath their feet. Their heads might have been turned upside-down, so absolutely did they tread upon blue ether. The lady in black, creeping behind them, looked a trifle paler and more jaded than usual. There was no sign of Mrs. Pontellier and the children. Robert scanned the distance for any such apparition. They would doubtless remain away till the dinner hour. The young man ascended to his mother's room. It was situated at the top of the house, made up of odd angles and a queer, sloping ceiling. Two broad dormer windows looked out toward the Gulf, and as far across it as a man's eye might reach. The furnishings of the room were light, cool, and practical.

Madame Lebrun was busily engaged at the sewing-machine. A little black girl sat on the floor, and with her hands worked the treadle of the machine. The Creole woman does not take any chances which may be avoided of imperiling her health.

Robert went over and seated himself on the broad sill of one of the dormer windows. He took a book from his pocket and began energetically to read it, judging by

[28]French: "For heaven's sake!"
[29]A resort on the coast of Mississippi.
[30]French: "Goodbye."
[31]French: a good boy.

the precision and frequency with which he turned the leaves. The sewing-machine made a resounding clatter in the room; it was of a ponderous, by-gone make. In the lulls, Robert and his mother exchanged bits of desultory conversation.

"Where is Mrs. Pontellier?"

"Down at the beach with the children."

"I promised to lend her the Goncourt.[32] Don't forget to take it down when you go; it's there on the bookshelf over the small table." Clatter, clatter, clatter, bang! for the next five or eight minutes.

"Where is Victor going with the rockaway?"

"The rockaway? Victor?"

"Yes; down there in front. He seems to be getting ready to drive away somewhere."

"Call him." Clatter, clatter!

Robert uttered a shrill, piercing whistle which might have been heard back at the wharf.

"He won't look up."

Madame Lebrun flew to the window. She called "Victor!" She waved a handkerchief and called again. The young fellow below got into the vehicle and started the horse off at a gallop.

Madame Lebrun went back to the machine, crimson with annoyance. Victor was the younger son and brother—a *tête montée,*[33] with a temper which invited violence and a will which no ax could break.

"Whenever you say the word I'm ready to thrash any amount of reason into him that he's able to hold."

"If your father had only lived!" Clatter, clatter, clatter, clatter, bang! It was a fixed belief with Madame Lebrun that the conduct of the universe and all things pertaining thereto would have been manifestly of a more intelligent and higher order had not Monsieur Lebrun been removed to other spheres during the early years of their married life.

"What do you hear from Montel?" Montel was a middle-aged gentleman whose vain ambition and desire for the past twenty years had been to fill the void which Monsieur Lebrun's taking off had left in the Lebrun household. Clatter, clatter, bang, clatter!

"I have a letter somewhere," looking in the machine drawer and finding the letter in the bottom of the work-basket. "He says to tell you he will be in Vera Cruz the beginning of next month"—clatter, clatter!—"and if you still have the intention of joining him"—bang! clatter, clatter, bang!

"Why didn't you tell me so before, mother? You know I wanted—" Clatter, clatter, clatter!

"Do you see Mrs. Pontellier starting back with the children? She will be in late to luncheon again. She never starts to get ready for luncheon till the last minute." Clatter, clatter! "Where are you going?"

"Where did you say the Goncourt was?"

[32]A novel by Edward Goncourt (1822–1896), a French realist.

[33]French: an impulsive character.

IX

Every light in the hall was ablaze; every lamp turned as high as it could be without smoking the chimney or threatening explosion. The lamps were fixed at intervals against the wall, encircling the whole room. Some one had gathered orange and lemon branches and with these fashioned graceful festoons between. The dark green of the branches stood out and glistened against the white muslin curtains which draped the windows, and which puffed, floated, and flapped at the capricious will of a stiff breeze that swept up from the Gulf.

It was Saturday night a few weeks after the intimate conversation held between Robert and Madame Ratignolle on their way from the beach. An unusual number of husbands, fathers, and friends had come down to stay over Sunday; and they were being suitably entertained by their families, with the material help of Madame Lebrun. The dining tables had all been removed to one end of the hall, and the chairs ranged about in rows and in clusters. Each little family group had had its say and exchanged its domestic gossip earlier in the evening. There was now an apparent disposition to relax; to widen the circle of confidences and give a more general tone to the conversation.

Many of the children had been permitted to sit up beyond their usual bedtime. A small band of them were lying on their stomachs on the floor looking at the colored sheets of the comic papers which Mr. Pontellier had brought down. The little Pontellier boys were permitting them to do so, and making their authority felt.

Music, dancing, and a recitation or two were the entertainments furnished, or rather, offered. But there was nothing systematic about the programme, no appearance of prearrangement nor even premeditation.

At an early hour in the evening the Farival twins were prevailed upon to play the piano. They were girls of fourteen, always clad in the Virgin's colors, blue and white, having been dedicated to the Blessed Virgin at their baptism. They played a duet from "Zampa," and at the earnest solicitation of every one present followed it with the overture to "The Poet and the Peasant."

"Allez vous-en! Sapristi!" shrieked the parrot outside the door. He was the only being present who possessed sufficient candor to admit that he was not listening to these gracious performances for the first time that summer. Old Monsieur Farival, grandfather of the twins, grew indignant over the interruption, and insisted upon having the bird removed and consigned to regions of darkness. Victor Lebrun objected; and his decrees were as immutable as those of Fate. The parrot fortunately offered no further interruption to the entertainment, the whole venom of his nature apparently having been cherished up and hurled against the twins in that one impetuous outburst.

Later a young brother and sister gave recitations, which every one present had heard many times at winter evening entertainments in the city.

A little girl performed a skirt dance in the center of the floor. The mother played her accompaniments and at the same time watched her daughter with greedy admiration and nervous apprehension. She need have had no apprehension. The child was mistress of the situation. She had been properly dressed for the occasion in black tulle and black silk tights. Her little neck and arms were bare, and her hair, artificially crimped, stood out like fluffy black plumes over her head. Her poses were full of grace, and her little black-shod toes twinkled as they shot out and upward with a rapidity and suddenness which were bewildering.

But there was no reason why every one should not dance. Madame Ratignolle could not, so it was she who gaily consented to play for the others. She played very well, keeping excellent waltz time and infusing an expression into the strains which was indeed inspiring. She was keeping up her music on account of the children, she said; because she and her husband both considered it a means of brightening the home and making it attractive.

Almost every one danced but the twins, who could not be induced to separate during the brief period when one or the other should be whirling around the room in the arms of a man. They might have danced together, but they did not think of it.

The children were sent to bed. Some went submissively; others with shrieks and protests as they were dragged away. They had been permitted to sit up till after the ice-cream, which naturally marked the limit of human indulgence.

The ice-cream was passed around with cake—gold and silver cake arranged on platters in alternate slices; it had been made and frozen during the afternoon back of the kitchen by two black women, under the supervision of Victor. It was pronounced a great success—excellent if it had only contained a little less vanilla or a little more sugar, if it had been frozen a degree harder, and if the salt might have been kept out of portions of it. Victor was proud of his achievement, and went about recommending it and urging every one to partake of it to excess.

After Mrs. Pontellier had danced twice with her husband, once with Robert, and once with Monsieur Ratignolle, who was thin and tall and swayed like a reed in the wind when he danced, she went out on the gallery and seated herself on the low window-sill, where she commanded a view of all that went on in the hall and could look out toward the Gulf. There was a soft effulgence in the east. The moon was coming up, and its mystic shimmer was casting a million lights across the distant, restless water.

"Would you like to hear Mademoiselle Reisz play?" asked Robert, coming out on the porch where she was. Of course Edna would like to hear Mademoiselle Reisz play; but she feared it would be useless to entreat her.

"I'll ask her," he said. "I'll tell her that you want to hear her. She likes you. She will come." He turned and hurried away to one of the far cottages, where Mademoiselle Reisz was shuffling away. She was dragging a chair in and out of her room, and at intervals objecting to the crying of a baby, which a nurse in the adjoining cottage was endeavoring to put to sleep. She was a disagreeable little woman, no longer young, who had quarreled with almost every one, owing to a temper which was self-assertive and a disposition to trample upon the rights of others. Robert prevailed upon her without any too great difficulty.

She entered the hall with him during a lull in the dance. She made an awkward, imperious little bow as she went in. She was a homely woman, with a small weazened face and body and eyes that glowed. She had absolutely no taste in dress, and wore a batch of rusty black lace with a bunch of artificial violets pinned to the side of her hair.

"Ask Mrs. Pontellier what she would like to hear me play," she requested of Robert. She sat perfectly still before the piano, not touching the keys, while Robert carried her message to Edna at the window. A general air of surprise and genuine satisfaction fell upon every one as they saw the pianist enter. There was a settling down, and a prevailing air of expectancy everywhere. Edna was a trifle embarrassed at being thus signaled out for the imperious little woman's favor. She would not dare to choose, and begged that Mademoiselle Reisz would please herself in her selections.

Edna was what she herself called very fond of music. Musical strains, well rendered, had a way of evoking pictures in her mind. She sometimes liked to sit in the room of mornings when Madame Ratignolle played or practiced. One piece which that lady played Edna had entitled "Solitude." It was a short, plaintive, minor strain. The name of the piece was something else, but she called it "Solitude." When she heard it there came before her imagination the figure of a man standing beside a desolate rock on the seashore. He was naked. His attitude was one of hopeless resignation as he looked toward a distant bird winging its flight away from him.

Another piece called to her mind a dainty young woman clad in an Empire gown, taking mincing dancing steps as she came down a long avenue between tall hedges. Again, another reminded her of children at play, and still another of nothing on earth but a demure lady stroking a cat.

The very first chords which Mademoiselle Reisz struck upon the piano sent a keen tremor down Mrs. Pontellier's spinal column. It was not the first time she had heard an artist at the piano. Perhaps it was the first time she was ready, perhaps the first time her being was tempered to take an impress of the abiding truth.

She waited for the material pictures which she thought would gather and blaze before her imagination. She waited in vain. She saw no pictures of solitude, of hope, of longing, or of despair. But the very passions themselves were aroused within her soul, swaying it, lashing it, as the waves daily beat upon her splendid body. She trembled, she was choking, and the tears blinded her.

Mademoiselle had finished. She arose, and bowing her stiff, lofty bow, she went away, stopping for neither thanks nor applause. As she passed along the gallery she patted Edna upon the shoulder.

"Well, how did you like my music?" she asked. The young woman was unable to answer; she pressed the hand of the pianist convulsively. Mademoiselle Reisz perceived her agitation and even her tears. She patted her again upon the shoulder as she said:

"You are the only one worth playing for. Those others? Bah!" and she went shuffling and sidling on down the gallery toward her room.

But she was mistaken about "those others." Her playing had aroused a fever of enthusiasm. "What passion!" "What an artist!" "I have always said no one could play Chopin[34] like Mademoiselle Reisz!" "That last prelude! Bon Dieu! It shakes a man!"

It was growing late, and there was a general disposition to disband. But some one, perhaps it was Robert, thought of a bath at that mystic hour and under that mystic moon.

[34]Frederic Francois Chopin (1810–1849), Polish composer and pianist of the early Romantic period.

X

At all events Robert proposed it, and there was not a dissenting voice. There was not one but was ready to follow when he led the way. He did not lead the way, however, he directed the way; and he himself loitered behind with the lovers, who had betrayed a disposition to linger and hold themselves apart. He walked between them, whether with malicious or mischievous intent was not wholly clear, even to himself.

The Pontelliers and Ratignolles walked ahead; the women leaning upon the arms of their husbands. Edna could hear Robert's voice behind them, and could sometimes hear what he said. She wondered why he did not join them. It was unlike him not to. Of late he had sometimes held away from her for an entire day, redoubling his devotion upon the next and the next, as though to make up for hours that had been lost. She missed him the days when some pretext served to take him away from her, just as one misses the sun on a cloudy day without having thought much about the sun when it was shining.

The people walked in little groups toward the beach. They talked and laughed; some of them sang. There was a band playing down at Klein's hotel, and the strains reached them faintly, tempered by the distance. There were strange, rare odors abroad—a tangle of the sea smell and of weeds and damp, new-plowed earth, mingled with the heavy perfume of a field of white blossoms somewhere near. But the night sat lightly upon the sea and the land. There was no weight of darkness; there were no shadows. The white light of the moon had fallen upon the world like the mystery and the softness of sleep.

Most of them walked into the water as though into a native element. The sea was quiet now, and swelled lazily in broad billows that melted into one another and did not break except upon the beach in little foamy crests that coiled back like slow, white serpents.

Edna had attempted all summer to learn to swim. She had received instructions from both the men and women; in some instances from the children. Robert had pursued a system of lessons almost daily; and he was nearly at the point of discouragement in realizing the futility of his efforts. A certain ungovernable dread hung about her when in the water, unless there was a hand near by that might reach out and reassure her.

But that night she was like the little tottering, stumbling, clutching child, who of a sudden realizes it powers, and walks for the first time alone, boldly and with overconfidence. She could have shouted for joy. She did shout for joy, as with a sweeping stroke or two she lifted her body to the surface of the water.

A feeling of exultation overtook her, as if some power of significant import had been given her soul. She grew daring and reckless, overestimating her strength. She wanted to swim far out, where no woman had swum before.

Her unlooked-for achievement was the subject of wonder, applause, and admiration. Each one congratulated himself that his special teachings had accomplished this desired end.

"How easy it is!" she thought. "It is nothing," she said aloud; "why did I not discover before that it was nothing. Think of the time I have lost splashing about like a baby!" She would not join the groups in their sports and bouts, but intoxicated with her newly conquered power, she swam out alone.

She turned her face seaward to gather in an impression of space and solitude, which the vast expanse of water, meeting and melting with the moonlit sky, conveyed to her excited fancy. As she swam she seemed to be reaching out for the unlimited in which to lose herself.

Once she turned and looked toward the shore, toward the people she had left there. She had not gone any great distance—that is, what would have been a great distance for an experienced swimmer. But to her unaccustomed vision the stretch of water behind her assumed the aspect of a barrier which her unaided strength would never be able to overcome.

A quick vision of death smote her soul, and for a second of time appalled and enfeebled her senses. But by an effort she rallied her staggering faculties and managed to regain the land.

She made no mention of her encounter with death and her flash of terror, except to say to her husband, "I thought I should have perished out there alone."

"You were not so very far, my dear; I was watching you," he told her.

Edna went at once to the bath-house, and she had put on her dry clothes and was ready to return home before the others had left the water. She started to walk away alone. They all called to her and shouted to her. She waved a dissenting hand, and went on, paying no further heed to their renewed cries which sought to detain her.

"Sometimes I am tempted to think that Mrs. Pontellier is capricious" said Madame Lebrun, who was amusing herself immensely and feared that Edna's abrupt departure might put an end to the pleasure.

"I know she is," assented Mr. Pontellier; "sometimes, not often."

Edna had not traversed a quarter of the distance on her way home before she was overtaken by Robert.

"Did you think I was afraid?" she asked him, without a shade of annoyance.

"No; I knew you weren't afraid."

"Then why did you come? Why didn't you stay out there with the others?"

"I never thought of it."

"Thought of what?"

"Of anything. What difference does it make?"

"I'm very tired," she uttered, complainingly.

"I know you are."

"You don't know anything about it. Why should you know? I never was so exhausted in my life. But it isn't unpleasant. A thousand emotions have swept through me to-night. I don't comprehend half of them. Don't mind what I'm saying; I am just thinking aloud. I wonder if I shall ever be stirred again as Mademoiselle Reisz's playing moved me to-night. I wonder if any night on earth will ever again be like this one. It is like a night in a dream. The people about me are like some uncanny, half-human beings. There must be spirits abroad to-night."

"There are," whispered Robert. "Didn't you know this was the twenty-eighth of August?"

"The twenty-eighth of August?"

"Yes. On the twenty-eighth of August, at the hour of midnight, and if the moon is shining—the moon must be shining—a spirit that has haunted these shores for ages rises up from the Gulf. With its own penetrating vision the spirit seeks some one mortal worthy to hold him company, worthy of being exalted for a few hours into realms of the semi-celestials. His search has always hitherto been fruitless, and he has sunk back, disheartened, into the sea. But tonight he found Mrs. Pontellier. Perhaps he will never wholly release her from the spell. Perhaps she will never again suffer a poor, unworthy earthling to walk in the shadow of her divine presence."

"Don't banter me," she said, wounded at what appeared to be his flippancy. He did not mind the entreaty, but the tone with its delicate note of pathos was like a reproach. He could not explain; he could not tell her that he had penetrated her mood and understood. He said nothing except to offer her his arm, for, by her own admission, she was exhausted. She had been walking alone with her arms hanging limp, letting her white skirts trail along the dewy path. She took his arm, but she did not lean upon it. She let her hand lie listlessly, as though her thoughts were elsewhere—somewhere in advance of her body, and she was striving to overtake them.

Robert assisted her into the hammock which swung from the post before her door out to the trunk of a tree.

"Will you stay out here and wait for Mr. Pontellier?" he asked.

"I'll stay out here. Good-night."

"Shall I get you a pillow?"

"There's one here," she said, feeling about, for they were in the shadow.

"It must be soiled; the children have been tumbling it about."

"No matter." And having discovered the pillow, she adjusted it beneath her head. She extended herself in the hammock with a deep breath of relief. She was not a supercilious or an over-dainty woman. She was not much given to reclining in the hammock, and when she did so it was with no cat-like suggestion of voluptuous ease, but with a beneficent repose which seemed to invade her whole body.

"Shall I stay with you till Mr. Pontellier comes?" asked Robert, seating himself on the outer edge of one of the steps and taking hold of the hammock rope which was fastened to the post.

"If you wish. Don't swing the hammock. Will you get my white shawl which I left on the window-sill over at the house?"

"Are you chilly?"

"No; but I shall be presently."

"Presently?" he laughed. "Do you know what time it is? How long are you going to stay out here?"

"I don't know. Will you get the shawl?"

"Of course I will," he said, rising. He went over to the house, walking along the grass. She watched his figure pass in and out of the strips of moonlight. It was past midnight. It was very quiet.

When he returned with the shawl she took it and kept it in her hand. She did not put it around her.

"Did you say I should stay till Mr. Pontellier came back?"

"I said you might if you wished to."

He seated himself again and rolled a cigarette, which he smoked in silence. Neither did Mrs. Pontellier speak. No multitude of words could have been more significant than those moments of silence, or more pregnant with the first-felt throbbings of desire.

When the voices of the bathers were heard approaching, Robert said good-night. She did not answer him. He thought she was asleep. Again she watched his figure pass in and out of the strips of moonlight as he walked away.

XI

"What are you doing out here, Edna? I thought I should find you in bed," said her husband, when he discovered her lying there. He had walked up with Madame Lebrun and left her at the house. His wife did not reply.

"Are you asleep?" he asked, bending down close to look at her.

"No." Her eyes gleamed bright and intense, with no sleepy shadows, as they looked into his.

"Do you know it is past one o'clock? Come on," and he mounted the steps and went into their room.

"Edna!" called Mr. Pontellier from within, after a few moments had gone by.

"Don't wait for me," she answered. He thrust his head through the door.

"You will take cold out there," he said, irritably. "What folly is this? Why don't you come in?"

"It isn't cold; I have my shawl."

"The mosquitoes will devour you."

"There are no mosquitoes."

She heard him moving about the room; every sound indicating impatience and irritation. Another time she would have gone in at his request. She would, through habit, have yielded to his desire; not with any sense of submission or obedience to his compelling wishes, but unthinkingly, as we walk, move, sit, stand, go through the daily treadmill of the life which has been portioned out to us.

"Edna, dear, are you not coming in soon?" he asked again, this time fondly, with a note of entreaty.

"No; I am going to stay out here."

"This is more than folly," he blurted out. "I can't permit you to stay out there all night. You must come in the house instantly."

With a writhing motion she settled herself more securely in the hammock. She perceived that her will had blazed up, stubborn and resistant. She could not at that moment have done other than denied and resisted. She wondered if her husband had ever spoken to her like that before, and if she had submitted to his command. Of course she had; she remembered that she had. But she could not realize why or how she should have yielded, feeling as she then did.

"Léonce, go to bed," she said. "I mean to stay out here. I don't wish to go in, and I don't intend to. Don't speak to me like that again; I shall not answer you."

Mr. Pontellier had prepared for bed, but he slipped on an extra garment. He opened a bottle of wine, of which he kept a small and select supply in a buffet of his own. He drank a glass of the wine and went out on the gallery and offered a glass to his wife. She did not wish any. He drew up the rocker, hoisted his slippered feet on the rail, and proceeded to smoke a cigar. He smoked two cigars; then he went inside and drank another glass of wine. Mrs. Pontellier again declined to accept a glass when it was offered to her. Mr. Pontellier once more seated himself with elevated feet, and after a reasonable interval of time smoked some more cigars.

Edna began to feel like one who awakens gradually out of a dream, a delicious, grotesque, impossible dream, to feel again the realities pressing into her soul. The physical need for sleep began to overtake her; the exuberance which had sustained and exalted her spirit left her helpless and yielding to the conditions which crowded her in.

The stillest hour of the night had come, the hour before dawn, when the world seems to hold its breath. The moon hung low, and had turned from silver to copper in the sleeping sky. The old owl no longer hooted, and the water-oaks had ceased to moan as they bent their heads.

Edna arose, cramped from lying so long and still in the hammock. She tottered up the steps, clutching feebly at the post before passing into the house.

"Are you coming in, Léonce?" she asked, turning her face toward her husband.

"Yes, dear," he answered, with a glance following a misty puff of smoke. "Just as soon as I have finished my cigar."

XII

She slept but a few hours. They were troubled and feverish hours, disturbed with dreams that were intangible, that eluded her, leaving only an impression upon her half-awakened senses of something unattainable. She was up and dressed in the cool of the early morning. The air was invigorating and steadied somewhat her faculties. However, she was not seeking refreshment or help from any source, either external or from within. She was blindly following whatever impulse moved her, as if she had placed herself in alien hands for direction, and freed her soul of responsibility.

Most of the people at that early hour were still in bed and asleep. A few, who intended to go over to the *Chênière* for mass, were moving about. The lovers, who had laid their plans the night before, were already strolling toward the wharf. The lady in black, with her Sunday prayer book, velvet and gold-clasped, and her Sunday silver beads, was following them at no great distance. Old Monsieur Farival was up, and was more than half inclined to do anything that suggested itself. He put on his big straw hat, and taking his umbrella from the stand in the hall, followed the lady in black, never overtaking her.

The little negro girl who worked Madame Lebrun's sewing-machine was sweeping the galleries with long, absent-minded strokes of the broom. Edna sent her up into the house to awaken Robert.

"Tell him I am going to the *Chênière.* The boat is ready; tell him to hurry."

He had soon joined her. She had never sent for him before. She had never asked for him. She had never seemed to want him before. She did not appear conscious that she had done anything unusual in commanding his presence. He was apparently equally unconscious of anything extraordinary in the situation. But his face was suffused with a quiet glow when he met her.

They went together back to the kitchen to drink coffee. There was no time to wait for any nicety of service. They stood outside the window and the cook passed them their coffee and a roll, which they drank and ate from the window-sill. Edna said it tasted good. She had not thought of coffee nor of anything. He told her he had often noticed that she lacked forethought.

"Wasn't it enough to think of going to the *Chênière* and waking you up?" she laughed. "Do I have to think of everything?—as Léonce says when he's in a bad humor. I don't blame him; he'd never be in a bad humor if it weren't for me."

They took a short cut across the sands. At a distance they could see the curious procession moving toward the wharf—the lovers, shoulder to shoulder, creeping; the lady in black, gaining steadily upon them; old Monsieur Farival, losing ground inch by inch, and a young barefooted Spanish girl, with a red kerchief on her head and a basket on her arm, bringing up the rear.

Robert knew the girl, and he talked to her a little in the boat. No one present understood what they said. Her name was Mariequita. She had a round, sly, piquant face and pretty black eyes. Her hands were small, and she kept them folded over the handle of her basket. Her feet were broad and coarse. She did not strive to hide them. Edna looked at her feet, and noticed the sand and slime between her brown toes.

Beaudelet grumbled because Mariequita was there, taking up so much room. In reality he was annoyed at having old Monsieur Farival, who considered himself the better sailor of the two. But he would not quarrel with so old a man as Monsieur Farival, so he quarreled with Mariequita. The girl was deprecatory at one moment, appealing to Robert. She was saucy the next, moving her head up and down, making "eyes" at Robert and making "mouths" at Beaudelet.

The lovers were all alone. They saw nothing, they heard nothing. The lady in black was counting her beads for the third time. Old Monsieur Farival talked incessantly of what he knew about handling a boat, and of what Beaudelet did not know on the same subject.

Edna liked it all. She looked Mariequita up and down, from her ugly brown toes to her pretty black eyes, and back again.

"Why does she look at me like that?" inquired the girl of Robert.

"Maybe she thinks you are pretty. Shall I ask her?"

"No. Is she your sweetheart?"

"She's a married lady, and has two children."

"Oh! well! Francisco ran away with Sylvano's wife, who had four children. They took all his money and one of the children and stole his boat."

"Shut up!"

"Does she understand?"

"Oh, hush!"

"Are those two married over there—leaning on each other?"

"Of course not," laughed Robert.

"Of course not," echoed Mariequita, with a serious, confirmatory bob of the head.

The sun was high up and beginning to bite. The swift breeze seemed to Edna to bury the sting of it into the pores of her face and hands. Robert held his umbrella over her.

As they went cutting sidewise through the water, the sails bellied taut, with the wind filling and overflowing them. Old Monsieur Farival laughed sardonically at something as he looked at the sails, and Beaudelet swore at the old man under his breath.

Sailing across the bay to the *Chênière Caminada,* Edna felt as if she were being borne away from some anchorage which had held her fast, whose chains had been loosening—had snapped the night before when the mystic spirit was abroad, leaving her free to drift whithersoever she chose to set her sails. Robert spoke to her incessantly; he no longer noticed Mariequita. The girl had shrimps in her bamboo basket. They were covered with Spanish moss. She beat the moss down impatiently, and muttered to herself sullenly.

"Let us go to Grande Terre[35] to-morrow?" said Robert in a low voice.

"What shall we do there?"

"Climb up the hill to the old fort and look at the little wriggling gold snakes, and watch the lizards sun themselves."

She gazed away toward Grande Terre and thought she would like to be alone there with Robert, in the sun, listening to the ocean's roar and watching the slimy lizards writhe in and out among the ruins of the old fort.

"And the next day or the next we can sail to the Bayou Brulow,"[36] he went on.

"What shall we do there?"

"Anything—cast bait for fish."

"No; we'll go back to Grande Terre. Let the fish alone."

"We'll go wherever you like," he said. "I'll have Tonie come over and help me patch and trim my boat. We shall not need Beaudelet nor any one. Are you afraid of the pirogue?"[37]

"Oh, no."

"Then I'll take you some night in the pirogue when the moon shines. Maybe your Gulf spirit will whisper to you in which of these islands the treasures are hidden—direct you to the very spot, perhaps."

"And in a day we should be rich!" she laughed. "I'd give it all to you, the pirate gold and every bit of treasure we could dig up. I think you would know how to spend it. Pirate gold isn't a thing to be hoarded or utilized. It is something to squander and throw to the four winds, for the fun of seeing the golden specks fly."

"We'd share it, and scatter it together," he said. His face flushed.

They all went together up to the quaint little Gothic church of Our Lady of Lourdes, gleaming all brown and yellow with paint in the sun's glare.

Only Beaudelet remained behind, tinkering at his boat, and Mariequita walked away with her basket of shrimps, casting a look of childish ill-humor and reproach at Robert from the corner of her eye.

XIII

A feeling of oppression and drowsiness overcame Edna during the service. Her head began to ache, and the lights on the altar swayed before her eyes, Another time she might have made an effort to regain her composure; but her one thought was to quit the stifling atmosphere of the church and reach the open air. She arose, climbing over Robert's feet with a muttered apology. Old Monsieur Farival, flurried, curious, stood up, but upon seeing that Robert had followed Mrs. Pontellier, he sank back into his seat. He whispered an anxious inquiry of the lady in black, who did not notice him or reply, but kept her eyes fastened upon the pages of her velvet prayerbook.

"I felt giddy and almost overcome," Edna said, lifting her hands instinctively to her head and pushing her straw hat up from her forehead. "I couldn't have stayed

[35]An island near Grand Isle.

[36]A village near Grande Isle built upon a platform in the bayou.

[37]A boat similar to a canoe.

through the service." They were outside in the shadow of the church. Robert was full of solicitude.

"It was folly to have thought of going in the first place, let alone staying. Come over to Madame Antoine's; you can rest there." He took her arm and led her away, looking anxiously and continuously down into her face,

How still it was, with only the voice of the sea whispering through the reeds that grew in the salt-water pools! The long line of little gray, weather-beaten houses nestled peacefully among the orange trees. It must always have been God's day on that low, drowsy island, Edna thought. They stopped, leaning over a jagged fence made of sea-drift, to ask for water. A youth, a mild-faced Acadian,[38] was drawing water from the cistern, which was nothing more than a rusty buoy, with an opening on one side, sunk in the ground. The water which the youth handed to them in a tin pail was not cold to taste, but it was cool to her heated face, and it greatly revived and refreshed her.

Madame Antoine's cot was at the far end of the village. She welcomed them with all the native hospitality, as she would have opened her door to let the sunlight in. She was fat, and walked heavily and clumsily across the floor. She could speak no English, but when Robert made her understand that the lady who accompanied him was ill and desired to rest, she was all eagerness to make Edna feel at home and to dispose of her comfortably.

The whole place was immaculately clean, and the big, four-posted bed, snow-white, invited one to repose. It stood in a small side room which looked out across a narrow grass plot toward the shed, where there was a disabled boat lying keel upward.

Madame Antoine had not gone to mass. Her son Tonie had, but she supposed he would soon be back, and she invited Robert to be seated and wait for him. But he went and sat outside the door and smoked. Madame Antoine busied herself in the large front room preparing dinner. She was boiling mullets[39] over a few red coals in the huge fireplace.

Edna, left alone in the little side room, loosened her clothes, removing the greater part of them. She bathed her face, her neck and arms in the basin that stood between the windows. She took off her shoes and stockings and stretched herself in the very center of the high, white bed. How luxurious it felt to rest thus in a strange, quaint bed, with its sweet country odor of laurel lingering about the sheets and mattress! She stretched her strong limbs that ached a little. She ran her fingers through her loosened hair for a while. She looked at her round arms as she held them straight up and rubbed them one after the other, observing closely, as if it were something she saw for the first time, the fine, firm quality and texture of her flesh. She clasped her hands easily above her head, and it was thus she fell asleep.

She slept lightly at first, half awake and drowsily attentive to the things about her. She could hear Madame Antoine's heavy, scraping tread as she walked back and forth on the sanded floor. Some chickens were clucking outside the windows, scratching for bits of gravel in the grass. Later she half heard the voices of Robert and Tonie talking under the shed. She did not stir. Even her eyelids rested numb and heavily over her sleepy eyes. The voices went on—Tonie's slow, Acadian drawl,

[38]A person of French Canadian descent.

[39]An edible spiny-finned fish.

Robert's quick, soft, smooth French. She understood French imperfectly unless directly addressed, and the voices were only part of the other drowsy, muffled sounds lulling her senses.

When Edna awoke it was with the conviction that she had slept long and soundly. The voices were hushed under the shed. Madame Antoine's step was no longer to be heard in the adjoining room. Even the chickens had gone elsewhere to scratch and cluck. The mosquito bar was drawn over her; the old woman had come in while she slept and let down the bar. Edna arose quietly from the bed, and looking between the curtains of the window, she saw by the slanting rays of the sun that the afternoon was far advanced. Robert was out there under the shed, reclining in the shade against the sloping keel of the overturned boat. He was reading from a book. Tonie was no longer with him. She wondered what had become of the rest of the party. She peeped out at him two or three times as she stood washing herself in the little basin between the windows.

Madame Antoine had laid some coarse, clean towels upon a chair, and had placed a box of *poudre de riz*[40] within easy reach. Edna dabbed the powder upon her nose and cheeks as she looked at herself closely in the little distorted mirror which hung on the wall above the basin. Her eyes were bright and wide awake and her face glowed.

When she had completed her toilet she walked into the adjoining room. She was very hungry. No one was there. But there was a cloth spread upon the table that stood against the wall, and a cover was laid for one, with a crusty brown loaf and a bottle of wine beside the plate. Edna bit a piece from the brown loaf, tearing it with her strong, white teeth. She poured some of the wine into the glass and drank it down. Then she went softly out of doors, and plucking an orange from the low-hanging bough of a tree, threw it at Robert, who did not know she was awake and up.

An illumination broke over his whole face when he saw her and joined her under the orange tree.

"How many years have I slept?" she inquired. "The whole island seems changed. A new race of beings must have sprung up, leaving only you and me as past relics. How many ages ago did Madame Antoine and Tonie die? and when did our people from Grand Isle disappear from the earth?"

He familiarly adjusted a ruffle upon her shoulder.

"You have slept precisely one hundred years. I was left here to guard your slumbers; and for one hundred years I have been out under the shed reading a book. The only evil I couldn't prevent was to keep a broiled fowl from drying up."

"If it had turned to stone, still will I eat it," said Edna, moving with him into the house. "But really, what has become of Monsieur Farival and the others?"

"Gone hours ago. When they found that you were sleeping they thought it best not to awake you. Any way, I wouldn't have let them. What was I here for?"

"I wonder if Léonce will be uneasy!" she speculated, as she seated herself at table.

"Of course not; he knows you are with me," Robert replied, as he busied himself among sundry pans and covered dishes which had been left standing on the hearth.

[40]French: a cosmetic powder made of rice.

"Where are Madame Antoine and her son?" asked Edna.

"Gone to Vespers,[41] and to visit some friends, I believe. I am to take you back in Tonie's boat whenever you are ready to go."

He stirred the smoldering ashes till the broiled fowl began to sizzle afresh. He served her with no mean repast, dripping the coffee anew and sharing it with her. Madame Antoine had cooked little else than the mullets, but while Edna slept Robert had foraged the island. He was childishly gratified to discover her appetite, and to see the relish with which she ate the food which he had procured for her.

"Shall we go right away?" she asked, after draining her glass and brushing together the crumbs of the crusty loaf.

"The sun isn't as low as it will be in two hours," he answered.

"The sun will be gone in two hours."

"Well, let it go; who cares!"

They waited a good while under the orange trees, till Madame Antoine came back, panting, waddling, with a thousand apologies to explain her absence. Tonie did not dare to return. He was shy, and would not willingly face any woman except his mother.

It was very pleasant to stay there under the orange trees, while the sun dipped lower and lower, turning the western sky to flaming copper and gold. The shadows lengthened and crept out like stealthy, grotesque monsters across the grass.

Edna and Robert both sat upon the ground—that is, he lay upon the ground beside her, occasionally picking at the hem of her muslin gown.

Madame Antoine seated her fat body, broad and squat, upon a bench beside the door. She had been talking all the afternoon, and had wound herself up to the story-telling pitch.

And what stories she told them! But twice in her life she had left the *Chênière Caminada,* and then for the briefest span. All her years she had squatted and waddled there upon the island, gathering legends of the Bartarians[42] and the sea. The night came on, with the moon to lighten it. Edna could hear the whispering voices of dead men and the click of muffled gold.

When she and Robert stepped into Tonie's boat, with the red lateen sail, misty spirit forms were prowling in the shadows and among the reeds, and upon the water were phantom ships, speeding to cover.

XIV

The youngest boy, Etienne, had been very naughty, Madame Ratignolle said, as she delivered him into the hands of his mother. He had been unwilling to go to bed and had made a scene; whereupon she had taken charge of him and pacified him as well as she could. Raoul had been in bed and asleep for two hours.

[41]Evening prayer.

[42]The pirates who plundered the region of Barataria Bay.

The youngster was in his long white nightgown, that kept tripping him up as Madame Ratignolle led him along by the hand. With the other chubby fist he rubbed his eyes, which were heavy with sleep and ill humor. Edna took him in her arms, and seating herself in the rocker, began to coddle and caress him, calling him all manner of tender names, soothing him to sleep.

It was not more than nine o'clock. No one had yet gone to bed but the children.

Léonce had been very uneasy at first, Madame Ratignolle said, and had wanted to start at once for the *Chênière.* But Monsieur Farival had assured him that his wife was only overcome with sleep and fatigue, that Tonie would bring her safely back later in the day; and he had thus been dissuaded from crossing the bay. He had gone over to Klein's, looking up some cotton broker whom he wished to see in regard to securities, exchanges, stocks, bonds, or something of the sort, Madame Ratignolle did not remember what. He said he would not remain away late. She herself was suffering from heat and oppression, she said. She carried a bottle of salts and a large fan. She would not consent to remain with Edna, for Monsieur Ratignolle was alone, and he detested above all things to be left alone.

When Etienne had fallen asleep Edna bore him into the back room, and Robert went and lifted the mosquito bar that she might lay the child comfortably in his bed. The quadroon had vanished. When they emerged from the cottage Robert bade Edna goodnight.

"Do you know we have been together the whole livelong day, Robert—since early this morning?" she said at parting.

"All but the hundred years when you were sleeping. Good-night."

He pressed her hand and went away in the direction of the beach. He did not join any of the others, but walked alone toward the Gulf.

Edna stayed outside, awaiting her husband's return. She had no desire to sleep or to retire; nor did she feel like going over to sit with the Ratignolles, or to join Madame Lebrun and a group whose animated voices reached her as they sat in conversation before the house. She let her mind wander back over her stay at Grand Isle; and she tried to discover wherein this summer had been different from any and every other summer of her life. She could only realize that she herself—her present self—was in some way different from the other self. That she was seeing with different eyes and making the acquaintance of new conditions in herself that colored and changed her environment, she did not yet suspect.

She wondered why Robert had gone away and left her. It did not occur to her to think he might have grown tired of being with her the livelong day. She was not tired, and she felt that he was not. She regretted that he had gone. It was so much more natural to have him stay, when he was not absolutely required to leave her.

As Edna waited for her husband she sang low a little song that Robert had sung as they crossed the bay. It began with "Ah! *Si tu savais,*" and every verse ended with "*si tu savais.*"[43]

Robert's voice was not pretentious. It was musical and true. The voice, the notes, the whole refrain haunted her memory.

[43]"Couldst Thou but Know," a refrain from a song of the same name written by Michael William Balfe (1808–1870), an Irish composer and baritone.

XV

When Edna entered the dining-room one evening a little late, as was her habit, an unusually animated conversation seemed to be going on. Several persons were talking at once, and Victor's voice was predominating, even over that of his mother. Edna had returned late from her bath, had dressed in some haste, and her face was flushed. Her head, set off by her dainty white gown, suggested a rich, rare blossom. She took her seat at table between old Monsieur Farival and Madame Ratignolle.

As she seated herself and was about to begin to eat her soup, which had been served when she entered the room, several persons informed her simultaneously that Robert was going to Mexico. She laid her spoon down and looked about her bewildered. He had been with her, reading to her all the morning, and had never even mentioned such a place as Mexico. She had not seen him during the afternoon; she had heard some one say he was at the house, upstairs with his mother. This she had thought nothing of, though she was surprised when he did not join her later in the afternoon, when she went down to the beach.

She looked across at him, where he sat beside Madame Lebrun, who presided. Edna's face was a blank picture of bewilderment, which she never thought of disguising. He lifted his eyebrows with the pretext of a smile as he returned her glance. He looked embarrassed and uneasy.

"When is he going?" she asked of everybody in general, as if Robert were not there to answer for himself.

"To-night!" "This very evening!" "Did you ever!" "What possesses him!" were some of the replies she gathered, uttered simultaneously in French and English.

"Impossible!" she exclaimed. "How can a person start off from Grand Isle to Mexico at a moment's notice, as if he were going over to Klein's or to the wharf or down to the beach?"

"I said all along I was going to Mexico; I've been saying so for years!" cried Robert, in an excited and irritable tone, with the air of a man defending himself against a swarm of stinging insects.

Madame Lebrun knocked on the table with her knife handle.

"Please let Robert explain why he is going, and why he is going to-night," she called out. "Really, this table is getting to be more and more like Bedlam[44] every day, with everybody talking at once. Sometimes—I hope God will forgive me—but positively sometimes I wish Victor would lose the power of speech."

Victor laughed sardonically as he thanked his mother for her holy wish, of which he failed to see the benefit to anybody, except that it might afford her a more ample opportunity and license to talk herself.

Monsieur Farival thought that Victor should have been taken out in mid-ocean in his earliest youth and drowned. Victor thought there would be more logic in thus disposing of old people with an established claim for making themselves universally obnoxious. Madame Lebrun grew a trifle hysterical; Robert called his brother some sharp, hard names.

"There's nothing much to explain, mother," he said; though he explained, nev-

[44]An insane asylum.

ertheless—looking chiefly at Edna—that he could only meet the gentleman whom he intended to join at Vera Cruz by taking such and such a steamer, which left New Orleans on such a day; that Beaudelet was going out with his lugger-load of vegetables that night, which gave him an opportunity of reaching the city and making his vessel in time.

"But when did you make up your mind to all this?" demanded Monsieur Farival.

"This afternoon," returned Robert, with a shade of annoyance.

"At what time this afternoon?" persisted the old gentleman, with nagging determination, as if he were cross-questioning a criminal in a court of justice.

"At four o'clock this afternoon, Monsieur Farival," Robert replied, in a high voice and with a lofty air, which reminded Edna of some gentleman on the stage.

She had forced herself to eat most of her soup, and now she was picking the flaky bits of a *court bouillon*[45] with her fork.

The lovers were profiting by the general conversation on Mexico to speak in whispers of matters which they rightly considered were interesting to no one but themselves. The lady in black had once received a pair of prayer-beads of curious workmanship from Mexico, with very special indulgence attached to them, but she had never been able to ascertain whether the indulgence extended outside the Mexican border. Father Fochel of the Cathedral had attempted to explain it; but he had not done so to her satisfaction. And she begged that Robert would interest himself, and discover, if possible, whether she was entitled to the indulgence accompanying the remarkably curious Mexican prayer-beads.

Madame Ratignolle hoped that Robert would exercise extreme caution in dealing with the Mexicans, who, she considered, were a treacherous people, unscrupulous and revengeful. She trusted she did them no injustice in thus condemning them as a race. She had known personally but one Mexican, who made and sold excellent tamales, and whom she would have trusted implicitly, so softspoken was he. One day he was arrested for stabbing his wife. She never knew whether he had been hanged or not.

Victor had grown hilarious, and was attempting to tell an anecdote about a Mexican girl who served chocolate one winter in a restaurant in Dauphine Street.[46] No one would listen to him but old Monsieur Farival, who went into convulsions over the droll story.

Edna wondered if they had all gone mad, to be talking and clamoring at that rate. She herself could think of nothing to say about Mexico or the Mexicans.

"At what time do you leave?" she asked Robert.

"At ten," he told her. "Beaudelet wants to wait for the moon."

"Are you all ready to go?"

"Quite ready. I shall only take a handbag, and shall pack my trunk in the city."

He turned to answer some question put to him by his mother, and Edna, having finished her black coffee, left the table.

She went directly to her room. The little cottage was close and stuffy after leaving the outer air. But she did not mind; there appeared to be a hundred different things demanding her attention indoors. She began to set the toilet-stand to rights,

[45]French: fish broth.

[46]A street located in the French Quarter.

grumbling at the negligence of the quadroon, who was in the adjoining room putting the children to bed. She gathered together stray garments that were hanging on the backs of chairs, and put each where it belonged in closet or bureau drawer. She changed her gown for a more comfortable and commodious wrapper. She rearranged her hair, combing and brushing it with unusual energy. Then she went in and assisted the quadroon in getting the boys to bed.

They were very playful and inclined to talk—to do anything but lie quiet and go to sleep. Edna sent the quadroon away to her supper and told her she need not return. Then she sat and told the children a story. Instead of soothing it excited them, and added to their wakefulness. She left them in heated argument, speculating about the conclusion of the tale which their mother promised to finish the following night.

The little black girl came in to say that Madame Lebrun would like to have Mrs. Pontellier go and sit with them over at the house till Mr. Robert went away. Edna returned answer that she had already undressed, that she did not feel quite well, but perhaps she would go over to the house later. She started to dress again, and got as far advanced as to remove her *peignoir.* But changing her mind once more she resumed the *peignoir,* and went outside and sat down before her door. She was overheated and irritable, and fanned herself energetically for a while. Madame Ratignolle came down to discover what was the matter.

"All that noise and confusion at the table must have upset me," replied Edna, "and moreover, I hate shocks and surprises. The idea of Robert starting off in such a ridiculously sudden and dramatic way! As if it were a matter of life and death! Never saying a word about it all morning when he was with me."

"Yes," agreed Madame Ratignolle. "I think it was showing us all—you especially—very little consideration. It wouldn't have surprised me in any of the others; those Lebruns are all given to heroics. But I must say I should never have expected such a thing from Robert. Are you not coming down? Come on, dear, it doesn't look friendly."

"No," said Edna, a little sullenly. "I can't go to the trouble of dressing again; I don't feel like it."

"You needn't dress; you look all right; fasten a belt around your waist. Just look at me!"

"No," persisted Edna; "but you go on. Madame Lebrun might be offended if we both stayed away."

Madame Ratignolle kissed Edna good-night, and went away, being in truth rather desirous of joining in the general and animated conversation which was still in progress concerning Mexico and the Mexicans.

Somewhat later Robert came up, carrying his hand-bag.

"Aren't you feeling well?" he asked,

"Oh, well enough. Are you going right away?"

He lit a match and looked at his watch. "In twenty minutes," he said. The sudden and brief flare of the match emphasized the darkness for a while. He sat down upon a stool which the children had left out on the porch.

"Get a chair," said Edna.

"This will do," he replied. He put on his soft hat and nervously took it off again, and wiping his face with his handkerchief, complained of the heat.

"Take the fan," said Edna, offering it to him.

"Oh, no! Thank you. It does no good; you have to stop fanning some time, and feel all the more uncomfortable afterward."

"That's one of the ridiculous things which men always say. I have never known one to speak otherwise of fanning. How long will you be gone?"

"Forever, perhaps. I don't know. It depends upon a good many things."

"Well, in case it shouldn't be forever, how long will it be?"

"I don't know."

"This seems to me perfectly preposterous and uncalled for. I don't like it. I don't understand your motive for silence and mystery, never saying a word to me about it this morning." He remained silent, not offering to defend himself. He only said, after a moment:

"Don't part from me in an ill-humor. I never knew you to be out of patience with me before."

"I don't want to part in any ill-humor," she said. "But can't you understand? I've grown used to seeing you, to having you with me all the time, and your action seems unfriendly, even unkind. You don't even offer an excuse for it. Why, I was planning to be together, thinking of how pleasant it would be to see you in the city next winter."

"So was I," he blurted. "Perhaps that's the—" He stood up suddenly and held out his hand. "Good-by, my dear Mrs. Pontellier; good-by. You won't—I hope you won't completely forget me." She clung to his hand, striving to detain him.

"Write to me when you get there, won't you, Robert?" she entreated.

"I will, thank you. Good-by."

How unlike Robert! The merest acquaintance would have said something more emphatic than "I will, thank you; good-by," to such a request.

He had evidently already taken leave of the people over at the house, for he descended the steps and went to join Beaudelet, who was out there with an oar across his shoulder waiting for Robert. They walked away in the darkness. She could only hear Beaudelet's voice; Robert had apparently not even spoken a word of greeting to his companion.

Edna bit her handkerchief convulsively, striving to hold back and to hide, even from herself as she would have hidden from another, the emotion which was troubling—tearing—her. Her eyes were brimming with tears.

For the first time she recognized anew the symptoms of infatuation which she felt incipiently as a child, as a girl in her earliest teens, and later as a young woman. The recognition did not lessen the reality, the poignancy of the revelation by any suggestion or promise of instability. The past was nothing to her; offered no lesson which she was willing to heed. The future was a mystery which she never attempted to penetrate. The present alone was significant; was hers, to torture her as it was doing then with the biting conviction that she had lost that which she had held, that she had been denied that which her impassioned, newly awakened being demanded.

XVI

"Do you miss your friend greatly?" asked Mademoiselle Reisz one morning as she came creeping up behind Edna, who had just left her cottage on her way to the beach. She spent much of her time in the water since she had acquired finally the art of swimming. As their stay at Grand Isle drew near its close, she felt that she could not give too much time to a diversion which afforded her the only real pleasurable moments that she knew. When Mademoiselle Reisz came and touched her upon the shoulder and spoke to her, the woman seemed to echo the thought which was ever in Edna's mind; or, better, the feeling which constantly possessed her.

Robert's going had some way taken the brightness, the color, the meaning out of everything. The conditions of her life were in no way changed, but her whole existence was dulled, like a faded garment which seems to be no longer worth wearing. She sought him everywhere—in others whom she induced to talk about him. She went up in the mornings to Madame Lebrun's room, braving the clatter of the old sewing-machine. She sat there and chatted at intervals as Robert had done. She gazed around the room at the pictures and photographs hanging upon the wall, and discovered in some corner an old family album, which she examined with the keenest interest, appealing to Madame Lebrun for enlightenment concerning the many figures and faces which she discovered between its pages.

There was a picture of Madame Lebrun with Robert as a baby, seated in her lap, a round-faced infant with a fist in his mouth. The eyes alone in the baby suggested the man. And that was he also in kilts, at the age of five, wearing long curls and holding a whip in his hand. It made Edna laugh, and she laughed, too, at the portrait in his first long trousers; while another interested her, taken when he left for college, looking thin, long-faced, with eyes full of fire, ambition and great intentions. But there was no recent picture, none which suggested the Robert who had gone away five days ago, leaving a void and wilderness behind him.

"Oh, Robert stopped having his pictures taken when he had to pay for them himself! He found wiser use for his money, he says," explained Madame Lebrun. She had a letter from him, written before he left New Orleans. Edna wished to see the letter, and Madame Lebrun told her to look for it either on the table or the dresser, or perhaps it was on the mantelpiece.

The letter was on the bookshelf. It possessed the greatest interest and attraction for Edna; the envelope, its size and shape, the postmark, the handwriting. She examined every detail of the outside before opening it. There were only a few lines, setting forth that he would leave the city that afternoon, that he had packed his trunk in good shape, that he was well, and sent her his love and begged to be affectionately remembered to all. There was no special message to Edna except a postscript saying that if Mrs. Pontellier desired to finish the book which he had been reading to her, his mother would find it in his room, among other books there on the table. Edna experienced a pang of jealousy because he had written to his mother rather than to her.

Every one seemed to take for granted that she missed him. Even her husband, when he came down the Saturday following Robert's departure, expressed regret that he had gone.

"How do you get on without him, Edna?" he asked.

"It's very dull without him," she admitted. Mr. Pontellier had seen Robert in the city, and Edna asked him a dozen questions or more. Where had they met? On Carondelet Street, in the morning. They had gone "in" and had a drink and a cigar together. What had they talked about? Chiefly about his prospects in Mexico, which

Mr. Pontellier thought were promising. How did he look? How did he seem—grave, or gay, or how? Quite cheerful, and wholly taken up with the idea of his trip, which Mr. Pontellier found altogether natural in a young fellow about to seek fortune and adventure in a strange, queer country.

Edna tapped her foot impatiently, and wondered why the children persisted in playing in the sun when they might be under the trees. She went down and led them out of the sun, scolding the quadroon for not being more attentive.

It did not strike her as in the least grotesque that she should be making of Robert the object of conversation and leading her husband to speak of him. The sentiment which she entertained for Robert in no way resembled that which she felt for her husband, or had ever felt, or ever expected to feel. She had all her life long been accustomed to harbor thoughts and emotions which never voiced themselves. They had never taken the form of struggles. They belonged to her and were her own, and she entertained the conviction that she had a right to them and that they concerned no one but herself. Edna had once told Madame Ratignolle that she would never sacrifice herself for her children, or for any one. Then had followed a rather heated argument; the two women did not appear to understand each other or to be talking the same language. Edna tried to appease her friend, to explain.

"I would give up the unessential; I would give my money, I would give my life for my children; but I wouldn't give myself. I can't make it more clear; it's only something which I am beginning to comprehend, which is revealing itself to me."

"I don't know what you would call the essential, or what you mean by the unessential," said Madame Ratignolle, cheerfully; "but a woman who would give her life for her children could do no more than that—your Bible tells you so. I'm sure I couldn't do more than that."

"Oh, yes you could!" laughed Edna.

She was not surprised at Mademoiselle Reisz's question the morning that lady, following her to the beach, tapped her on the shoulder and asked if she did not greatly miss her young friend.

"Oh, good morning, Mademoiselle; it is you? Why, of course I miss Robert. Are you going down to bathe?"

"Why should I go down to bathe at the very end of the season when I haven't been in the surf all summer?" replied the woman, disagreeably.

"I beg your pardon," offered Edna, in some embarrassment, for she should have remembered that Mademoiselle Reisz's avoidance of the water had furnished a theme for much pleasantry. Some among them thought it was on account of her false hair, or the dread of getting the violets wet, while others attributed it to the natural aversion for water sometimes believed to accompany the artistic temperament. Mademoiselle offered Edna some chocolates in a paper bag, which she took from her pocket, by way of showing that she bore no ill feeling. She habitually ate chocolates for their sustaining quality; they contained much nutriment in small compass, she said. They saved her from starvation, as Madame Lebrun's table was utterly impossible; and no one save so impertinent a woman as Madame Lebrun could think of offering such food to people and requiring them to pay for it.

"She must feel very lonely without her son," said Edna, desiring to change the subject. "Her favorite son, too. It must have been quite hard to let him go."

Mademoiselle laughed maliciously.

"Her favorite son! Oh, dear! Who could have been imposing such a tale upon you? Aline Lebrun lives for Victor, and for Victor alone. She has spoiled him into the worthless creature he is. She worships him and the ground he walks on. Robert is very well in a way, to give up all the money he can earn to the family, and keep the barest pittance for himself. Favorite son, indeed! I miss the poor fellow myself, my dear. I liked to see him and to hear him about the place—the only Lebrun who is worth a pinch of salt. He comes to see me often in the city. I like to play to him. That Victor! hanging would be too good for him. It's a wonder Robert hasn't beaten him to death long ago."

"I thought he had great patience with his brother," offered Edna, glad to be talking about Robert, no matter what was said.

"Oh! he thrashed him well enough a year or two ago," said Mademoiselle. "It was about a Spanish girl, whom Victor considered that he had some sort of claim upon. He met Robert one day talking to the girl, or walking with her, or bathing with her, or carrying her basket—I don't remember what;—and he became so insulting and abusive that Robert gave him a thrashing on the spot that has kept him comparatively in order for a good while. It's about time he was getting another."

"Was her name Mariequita?" asked Edna.

"Mariequita—yes, that was it; Mariequita. I had forgotten. Oh, she's a sly one, and a bad one, that Mariequita!"

Edna looked down at Mademoiselle Reisz and wondered how she could have listened to her venom so long. For some reason she felt depressed, almost unhappy. She had not intended to go into the water; but she donned her bathing suit, and left Mademoiselle alone, seated under the shade of the children's tent. The water was growing cooler as the season advanced. Edna plunged and swam about with an abandon that thrilled and invigorated her. She remained a long time in the water, half hoping that Mademoiselle Reisz would not wait for her.

But Mademoiselle waited. She was very amiable during the walk back, and raved much over Edna's appearance in her bathing suit. She talked about music. She hoped that Edna would go to see her in the city, and wrote her address with the stub of a pencil on a piece of card which she found in her pocket.

"When do you leave?" asked Edna.

"Next Monday; and you?"

"The following week," answered Edna, adding, "It has been a pleasant summer, hasn't it, Mademoiselle?"

"Well," agreed Mademoiselle Reiz, with a shrug, "rather pleasant, if it hadn't been for the mosquitoes and the Farival twins."

XVII

The Pontelliers possessed a very charming home on Esplanade Street[47] in New Orleans. It was a large, double cottage, with a broad front veranda, whose round, fluted columns supported the sloping roof. The house was painted a dazzling white; the

[47]A street in New Orleans's most elite neighborhood.

outside shutters, or jalousies, were green. In the yard, which was kept scrupulously neat, were flowers and plants of every description which flourishes in South Louisiana. Within doors the appointments were perfect after the conventional type. The softest carpets and rugs covered the floors; rich and tasteful draperies hung at doors and windows. There were paintings, selected with judgment and discrimination, upon the walls. The cut glass, the silver, the heavy damask which daily appeared upon the table were the envy of many women whose husbands were less generous than Mr. Pontellier.

Mr. Pontellier was very fond of walking about his house examining its various appointments and details, to see that nothing was amiss. He greatly valued his possessions, chiefly because they were his, and derived genuine pleasure from contemplating a painting, a statuette, a rare lace curtain—no matter what—after he had bought it and placed it among his household gods.

On Tuesday afternoons—Tuesday being Mrs. Pontellier's reception day[48]—there was a constant stream of callers—women who came in carriages or in the street cars, or walked when the air was soft and distance permitted. A light-colored mulatto boy, in dress coat and bearing a diminutive silver tray for the reception of cards, admitted them. A maid, in white fluted cap, offered the callers liqueur, coffee, or chocolate, as they might desire. Mrs. Pontellier, attired in a handsome reception gown, remained in the drawing-room the entire afternoon receiving her visitors. Men sometimes called in the evening with their wives.

This had been the programme which Mrs. Pontellier had religiously followed since her marriage, six years before. Certain evenings during the week she and her husband attended the opera or sometimes the play.

Mr. Pontellier left his home in the mornings between nine and ten o'clock, and rarely returned before half-past six or seven in the evening—dinner being served at half-past seven.

He and his wife seated themselves at table on Tuesday evening, a few weeks after their return from Grand Isle. They were alone together. The boys were being put to bed; the patter of their bare, escaping feet could be heard occasionally, as well as the pursuing voice of the quadroon, lifted in mild protest and entreaty. Mrs. Pontellier did not wear her usual Tuesday reception gown; she was in ordinary house dress. Mr. Pontellier, who was observant about such things, noticed it, as he served the soup and handed it to the boy in waiting.

"Tired out, Edna? Whom did you have? Many callers?" he asked. He tasted his soup and began to season it with pepper, salt, vinegar, mustard—everything within reach.

"There were a good many," replied Edna, who was eating her soup with evident satisfaction. "I found their cards when I got home; I was out."

"Out!" exclaimed her husband, with something like genuine consternation in his voice as he laid down the vinegar cruet and looked at her through his glasses. "Why, what could have taken you out on Tuesday? What did you have to do?"

"Nothing. I simply felt like going out, and I went out."

[48]Women of the upper class were expected to receive visitors on one designated day of the week.

"Well, I hope you left some suitable excuse," said her husband, somewhat appeased, as he added a dash of cayenne pepper to the soup.

"No, I left no excuse. I told Joe to say I was out, that was all."

"Why, my dear, I should think you'd understand by this time that people don't do such things; we've got to observe *les convenances*[49] if we ever expect to get on and keep up with the procession. If you felt that you had to leave home this afternoon, you should have left some suitable explanation for your absence.

"This soup is really impossible; it's strange that woman hasn't learned yet to make a decent soup. Any free-lunch stand in town serves a better one. Was Mrs. Belthrop here?"

"Bring the tray with the cards, Joe. I don't remember who was here."

The boy retired and returned after a moment, bringing the tiny silver tray, which was covered with ladies' visiting cards. He handed it to Mrs. Pontellier.

"Give it to Mr. Pontellier," she said.

Joe offered the tray to Mr. Pontellier, and removed the soup.

Mr. Pontellier scanned the names of his wife's callers, reading some of them aloud, with comments as he read.

"'The Misses Delasidas.' I worked a big deal in futures[50] for their father this morning; nice girls; it's time they were getting married. 'Mrs. Belthrop.' I tell you what it is, Edna; you can't afford to snub Mrs. Belthrop. Why, Belthrop could buy and sell us ten times over. His business is worth a good, round sum to me. You'd better write her a note. 'Mrs. James Highcamp.' Hugh! the less you have to do with Mrs. Highcamp, the better. 'Madame Laforcé.' Came all the way from Carrolton, too, poor old soul. 'Miss Wiggs,' 'Mrs. Eleanor Boltons.'" He pushed the cards aside.

"Mercy!" exclaimed Edna, who had been fuming. "Why are you taking the thing so seriously and making such a fuss over it?"

"I'm not making any fuss over it. But it's just such seeming trifles that we've got to take seriously; such things count."

The fish was scorched. Mr. Pontellier would not touch it. Edna said she did not mind a little scorched taste. The roast was in some way not to his fancy, and he did not like the manner in which the vegetables were served.

"It seems to me," he said, "we spend money enough in this house to procure at least one meal a day which a man could eat and retain his self-respect."

"You used to think the cook was a treasure," returned Edna, indifferently.

"Perhaps she was when she first came; but cooks are only human. They need looking after, like any other class of persons that you employ. Suppose I didn't look after the clerks in my office, just let them run things their own way; they'd soon make a nice mess of me and my business."

"Where are you going?" asked Edna, seeing that her husband arose from table without having eaten a morsel except a taste of the highly-seasoned soup.

"I'm going to get my dinner at the club. Good night." He went into the hall, took his hat and stick from the stand, and left the house.

[49]French: social conventions.

[50]A contract for a specific commodity bought or sold for delivery at a future date.

She was somewhat familiar with such scenes. They had often made her very unhappy. On a few previous occasions she had been completely deprived of any desire to finish her dinner. Sometimes she had gone into the kitchen to administer a tardy rebuke to the cook. Once she went to her room and studied the cookbook during an entire evening, finally writing out a menu for the week, which left her harassed with a feeling that, after all, she had accomplished no good that was worth the name.

But that evening Edna finished her dinner alone, with forced deliberation. Her face was flushed and her eyes flamed with some inward fire that lighted them. After finishing her dinner she went to her room, having instructed the boy to tell any other callers that she was indisposed.

It was a large, beautiful room, rich and picturesque in the soft, dim light which the maid had turned low. She went and stood at an open window and looked out upon the deep tangle of the garden below. All the mystery and witchery of the night seemed to have gathered there amid the perfumes and the dusky and tortuous outlines of flowers and foliage. She was seeking herself and finding herself in just such sweet, half-darkness which met her moods. But the voices were not soothing that came to her from the darkness and the sky above and the stars. They jeered and sounded mournful notes without promise, devoid even of hope. She turned back into the room and began to walk to and fro down its whole length, without stopping, without resting. She carried in her hands a thin handkerchief, which she tore into ribbons, rolled into a ball, and flung from her. Once she stopped, and taking off her wedding ring, flung it upon the carpet. When she saw it lying there, she stamped her heel upon it, striving to crush it. But her small boot heel did not make an indenture, not a mark upon the little glittering circlet.

In a sweeping passion she seized a glass vase from the table and flung it upon the tiles of the hearth. She wanted to destroy something. The crash and clatter were what she wanted to hear.

A maid, alarmed at the din of breaking glass, entered the room to discover what was the matter.

"A vase fell upon the hearth," said Edna. "Never mind; leave it till morning."

"Oh! you might get some of the glass in your feet, ma'am," insisted the young woman, picking up bits of the broken vase that were scattered upon the carpet. "And here's your ring, ma'am, under the chair."

Edna held out her hand, and taking the ring, slipped it upon her finger.

XVIII

The following morning Mr. Pontellier, upon leaving for his office, asked Edna if she would not meet him in town in order to look at some new fixtures for the library.

"I hardly think we need new fixtures, Léonce. Don't let us get anything new; you are too extravagant. I don't believe you ever think of saving or putting by."

"The way to become rich is to make money, my dear Edna, not to save it," he said. He regretted that she did not feel inclined to go with him and select new fixtures. He kissed her good-by, and told her she was not looking well and must take care of herself. She was unusually pale and very quiet.

She stood on the front veranda as he quitted the house, and absently picked a few sprays of jessamine[51] that grew upon a trellis near by. She inhaled the odor of the blossoms and thrust them into the bosom of her white morning gown. The boys were dragging along the banquette[52] a small "express wagon," which they had filled with blocks and sticks. The quadroon was following them with little quick steps, having assumed a fictitious animation and alacrity for the occasion. A fruit vender was crying his wares in the street.

Edna looked straight before her with a self-absorbed expression upon her face. She felt no interest in anything about her. The street, the children, the fruit vender, the flowers growing there under her eyes, were all part and parcel of an alien world which had suddenly become antagonistic.

She went back into the house. She had thought of speaking to the cook concerning her blunders of the previous night; but Mr. Pontellier had saved her that disagreeable mission, for which she was so poorly fitted. Mr. Pontellier's arguments were usually convincing with those whom he employed. He left home feeling quite sure that he and Edna would sit down that evening, and possibly a few subsequent evenings, to a dinner deserving of the name.

Edna spent an hour or two in looking over some of her old sketches. She could see their shortcomings and defects, which were glaring in her eyes. She tried to work a little, but found she was not in the humor. Finally she gathered together a few of the sketches—those which she considered the least discreditable; and she carried them with her when, a little later, she dressed and left the house. She looked handsome and distinguished in her street gown. The tan of the seashore had left her face, and her forehead was smooth, white, and polished beneath her heavy, yellow-brown hair. There were a few freckles on her face, and a small, dark mole near the under lip and one on the temple, half-hidden in her hair.

As Edna walked along the street she was thinking of Robert. She was still under the spell of her infatuation. She had tried to forget him, realizing the inutility of remembering. But the thought of him was like an obsession, ever pressing itself upon her. It was not that she dwelt upon details of their acquaintance, or recalled in any special or peculiar way his personality; it was his being, his existence, which dominated her thought, fading sometimes as if it would melt into the mist of the forgotten, reviving again with an intensity which filled her with an incomprehensible longing.

Edna was on her way to Madame Ratignolle's. Their intimacy, begun at Grand Isle, had not declined, and they had seen each other with some frequency since their return to the city. The Ratignolles lived at no great distance from Edna's home, on the corner of a side street, where Monsieur Ratignolle owned and conducted a drug store which enjoyed a steady and prosperous trade. His father had been in the business before him, and Monsieur Ratignolle stood well in the community and bore an enviable reputation for integrity and clear-headedness. His family lived in commodious apartments over the store, having an entrance on the side within the *porte cochère*.[53] There was something which Edna thought very French, very foreign,

[51]French: jasmine.
[52]French: sidewalk.
[53]French: carriage entrance.

about their whole manner of living. In the large and pleasant salon which extended across the width of the house, the Ratignolles entertained their friends once a fortnight with a *soirée musicale,*[54] sometimes diversified by card-playing. There was a friend who played upon the cello. One brought his flute and another his violin, while there were some who sang and a number who performed upon the piano with various degrees of taste and agility. The Ratignolles' *soirées musicales* were widely known, and it was considered a privilege to be invited to them.

Edna found her friend engaged in assorting the clothes which had returned that morning from the laundry. She at once abandoned her occupation upon seeing Edna, who had been ushered without ceremony into her presence.

"'Cité can do it as well as I; it is really her business," she explained to Edna, who apologized for interrupting her. And she summoned a young black woman, whom she instructed, in French, to be very careful in checking off the list which she handed her. She told her to notice particularly if a fine linen handkerchief of Monsieur Ratignolle's, which was missing last week, had been returned; and to be sure to set to one side such pieces as required mending and darning.

Then placing an arm around Edna's waist, she led her to the front of the house, to the salon, where it was cool and sweet with the odor of great roses that stood upon the hearth in jars.

Madame Ratignolle looked more beautiful than ever there at home, in a negligé which left her arms almost wholly bare and exposed the rich, melting curves of her white throat.

"Perhaps I shall be able to paint your picture some day," said Edna with a smile when they were seated. She produced the roll of sketches and started to unfold them. "I believe I ought to work again. I feel as if I wanted to be doing something. What do you think of them? Do you think it worth while to take it up again and study some more? I might study for a while with Laidpore."

She knew that Madame Ratignolle's opinion in such a matter would be next to valueless, that she herself had not alone decided, but determined; but she sought the words and praise and encouragement that would help her to put heart into her venture.

"Your talent is immense, dear!"

"Nonsense!" Protested Edna, well pleased.

"Immense, I tell you," persisted Madame Ratignolle, surveying the sketches one by one, at close range, then holding them at arm's length, narrowing her eyes, and dropping her head on one side. "Surely, this Bavarian peasant is worthy of framing; and this basket of apples! never have I seen anything more lifelike. One might almost be tempted to reach out a hand and take one."

Edna could not control a feeling which bordered upon complacency at her friend's praise, even realizing, as she did, its true worth. She retained a few of the sketches, and gave all the rest to Madame Ratignolle, who appreciated the gift far beyond its value and proudly exhibited the pictures to her husband when he came up from the store a little later for his midday dinner.

Mr. Ratignolle was one of those men who are called the salt of the earth. His

[54]French: an evening of music.

cheerfulness was unbounded, and it was matched by his goodness of heart, his broad charity, and common sense. He and his wife spoke English with an accent which was only discernible through its un-English emphasis and a certain carefulness and deliberation. Edna's husband spoke English with no accent whatever. The Ratignolles understood each other perfectly. If ever the fusion of two human beings into one has been accomplished on this sphere it was surely in their union.

As Edna seated herself at table with them she thought, "Better a dinner of herbs,"[55] though it did not take her long to discover that was no dinner of herbs, but a delicious repast, simple, choice, and in every way satisfying.

Monsieur Ratignolle was delighted to see her, though he found her looking not so well as at Grand Isle, and he advised a tonic. He talked a good deal on various topics, a little politics, some city news and neighborhood gossip. He spoke with an animation and earnestness that gave an exaggerated importance to every syllable he uttered. His wife was keenly interested in everything he said, laying down her fork the better to listen, chiming in, taking the words out of his mouth.

Edna felt depressed rather than soothed after leaving them. The little glimpse of domestic harmony which had been offered her, gave her no regret, no longing. It was not a condition of life which fitted her, and she could see in it but an appalling and hopeless ennui. She was moved by a kind of commiseration for Madame Ratignolle,—a pity for that colorless existence which never uplifted its possessor beyond the region of blind contentment, in which no moment of anguish ever visited her soul, in which she would never have the taste of life's delirium. Edna vaguely wondered what she meant by "life's delirium." It had crossed her thought like some unsought, extraneous impression.

XIX

Edna could not help but think that it was very foolish, very childish, to have stamped upon her wedding ring and smashed the crystal vase upon the tiles. She was visited by no more outbursts, moving her to such futile expedients. She began to do as she liked and to feel as she liked. She completely abandoned her Tuesdays at home, and did not return the visits of those who had called upon her. She made no ineffectual efforts to conduct her household *en bonne ménagère,*[56] going and coming as it suited her fancy, and, so far as she was able, lending herself to any passing caprice.

Mr. Pontellier had been a rather courteous husband so long as he met a certain tacit submissiveness in his wife. But her new and unexpected line of conduct completely bewildered him. It shocked him. Then her absolute disregard for her duties as a wife angered him. When Mr. Pontellier became rude, Edna grew insolent. She had resolved never to take another step backward.

"It seems to me the utmost folly for a woman at the head of a household, and the mother of children, to spend in an atelier[57] days which would be better employed contriving for the comfort of her family."

[55]Allusion to Proverbs 15:17: "Better is a dinner of herbs where love is, than a stalled ox and hatred therewith."

[56]French: as a good housewife.

[57]French: studio.

"I feel like painting," answered Edna. "Perhaps I shan't always feel like it."

"Then in God's name paint! but don't let the family go to the devil. There's Madame Ratignolle; because she keeps up her music, she doesn't let everything else go to chaos. And she's more of a musician than you are a painter."

"She isn't a musician, and I'm not a painter. It isn't on account of painting that I let things go."

"On account of what, then?"

"Oh! I don't know. Let me alone; you bother me."

It sometimes entered Mr. Pontellier's mind to wonder if his wife were not growing a little unbalanced mentally. He could see plainly that she was not herself. That is, he could not see that she was becoming herself and daily casting aside that fictitious self which we assume like a garment with which to appear before the world.

Her husband let her alone as she requested, and went away to his office. Edna went up to her atelier—a bright room in the top of the house. She was working with great energy and interest, without accomplishing anything, however, which satisfied her even in the smallest degree. For a time she had the whole household enrolled in the service of art. The boys posed for her. They thought it amusing at first, but the occupation soon lost its attractiveness when they discovered that it was not a game arranged especially for their entertainment. The quadroon sat for hours before Edna's palette, patient as a savage, while the housemaid took charge of the children, and the drawing-room went undusted. But the house-maid, too, served her term as model when Edna perceived that the young woman's back and shoulders were molded on classic lines, and that her hair, loosened from its confining cap, became an inspiration. While Edna worked she sometimes sang low the little air, "Ah! *si tu savais!*"

It moved her with recollections. She could hear again the ripple of the water, the flapping sail. She could see the glint of the moon upon the bay, and could feel the soft, gusty beating of the hot south wind. A subtle current of desire passed through her body, weakening her hold upon the brushes and making her eyes burn.

There were days when she was very happy without knowing why. She was happy to be alive and breathing, when her whole being seemed to be one with the sunlight, the color, the odors, the luxuriant warmth of some perfect Southern day. She liked then to wander alone into strange and unfamiliar places. She discovered many a sunny, sleepy corner, fashioned to dream in. And she found it good to dream and to be alone and unmolested.

There were days when she was unhappy, she did not know why,—when it did not seem worth while to be glad or sorry, to be alive or dead; when life appeared to her like a grotesque pandemonium and humanity like worms struggling blindly toward inevitable annihilation. She could not work on such a day, nor weave fancies to stir her pulses and warm her blood.

XX

It was during such a mood that Edna hunted up Mademoiselle Reisz. She had not forgotten the rather disagreeable impression left upon her by their last interview; but she nevertheless felt a desire to see her—above all, to listen while she played upon the piano. Quite early in the afternoon she started upon her quest for the pianist. Unfortunately she had mislaid or lost Mademoiselle Reisz's card, and looking up her address in the city directory, she found that the woman lived on Bienvilles Street,[58] some distance away. The directory which fell into her hands was a year or more old, however, and upon reaching the number indicated, Edna discovered that the house was occupied by a respectable family of mulattoes who had *chambres garnies*[59] to let. They had been living there for six months, and knew absolutely nothing of a Mademoiselle Reisz. In fact, they knew nothing of any of their neighbors; their lodgers were all people of the highest distinction, they assured Edna. She did not linger to discuss class distinctions with Madame Pouponne, but hastened to a neighboring grocery store, feeling sure that Mademoiselle would have left her address with the proprietor.

He knew Mademoiselle Reisz a good deal better than he wanted to know her, he informed his questioner. In truth, he did not want to know her at all, anything concerning her—the most disagreeable and unpopular woman who ever lived in Bienville Street. He thanked heaven she had left the neighborhood, and was equally thankful that he did not know where she had gone.

Edna's desire to see Mademoiselle Reisz had increased tenfold since these unlooked-for obstacles had arisen to thwart it. She was wondering who could give her the information she sought, when it suddenly occurred to her that Madame Lebrun would be the one most likely to do so. She knew it was useless to ask Madame Ratignolle, who was on the most distant terms with the musician, and preferred to know nothing concerning her. She had once been almost as emphatic in expressing herself upon the subject as the corner grocer.

Edna knew that Madame Lebrun had returned to the city, for it was the middle of November. And she also knew where the Lebruns lived, on Chartres Street.

Their home from the outside looked like a prison, with iron bars before the door and lower windows. The iron bars were a relic of the old *régime,*[60] and no one had ever thought of dislodging them. At the side was a high fence enclosing the garden. A gate or door opening upon the street was locked. Edna rang the bell at this side garden gate, and stood upon the banquette, waiting to be admitted.

It was Victor who opened the gate for her. A black woman, wiping her hands upon her apron, was close at his heels. Before she saw them Edna could hear them in altercation, the woman—plainly an anomaly—claiming the right to be allowed to perform her duties, one of which was to answer the bell.

Victor was surprised and delighted to see Mrs. Pontellier, and he made no attempt to conceal either his astonishment or his delight. He was a dark-browed, good-looking youngster of nineteen, greatly resembling his mother, but with ten times her impetuosity. He instructed the black woman to go at once and inform Madame Lebrun that Mrs. Pontellier desired to see her. The woman grumbled a refusal to do part of her duty when she had not been permitted to do it all, and started back to her interrupted task of weeding the garden. Whereupon Victor administered a rebuke in the form of a volley of abuse, which owing to its rapidity and incoherence, was all but

[58]A street near New Orleans's shipyards.
[59]French: furnished rooms.
[60]The Spanish regime (1766–1803).

incomprehensible to Edna. Whatever it was, the rebuke was convincing, for the woman dropped her hoe and went mumbling into the house.

Edna did not wish to enter. It was very pleasant there on the side porch, where there were chairs, a wicker lounge, and a small table. She seated herself, for she was tired from her long tramp; and she began to rock gently and smooth out the folds of her silk parasol. Victor drew up his chair beside her. He at once explained that the black woman's offensive conduct was all due to imperfect training, as he was not there to take her in hand. He had only come up from the island the morning before, and expected to return next day. He stayed all winter at the island; he lived there, and kept the place in order and got things ready for the summer visitors.

But a man needed occasional relaxation, he informed Mrs. Pontellier, and every now and again he drummed up a pretext to bring him to the city. My! but he had had a time of it the evening before! He wouldn't want his mother to know, and he began to talk in a whisper. He was scintillant with recollections. Of course, he couldn't think of telling Mrs. Pontellier all about it, she being a woman and not comprehending such things. But it all began with a girl peeping and smiling at him through the shutters as he passed by. Oh! but she was a beauty! Certainly he smiled back, and went up and talked to her. Mrs. Pontellier did not know him if she supposed he was one to let an opportunity like that escape him. Despite herself, the youngster amused her. She must have betrayed in her look some degree of interest or entertainment. The boy grew more daring, and Mrs. Pontellier might have found herself, in a little while, listening to a highly colored story but for the timely appearance of Madame Lebrun.

That lady was still clad in white, according to her custom of the summer. Her eyes beamed an effusive welcome. Would not Mrs. Pontellier go inside? Would she partake of some refreshment? Why had she not been there before? How was that dear Mr. Pontellier and how were those sweet children? Has Mrs. Pontellier ever known such a warm November?

Victor went and reclined on the wicker lounge behind his mother's chair, where he commanded a view of Edna's face. He had taken her parasol from her hands while he spoke to her, and he now lifted it and twirled it above him as he lay on his back. When Madame Lebrun complained that it was *so* dull coming back to the city; that she saw *so* few people now; that even Victor, when he came up from the island for a day or two, had *so* much to occupy him and engage his time; then it was that the youth went into contortions on the lounge and winked mischievously at Edna. She somehow felt like a confederate in crime, and tried to look severe and disapproving.

There had been but two letters from Robert, with little in them, they told her. Victor said it was really not worth while to go inside for the letters, when his mother entreated him to go in search of them. He remembered the contents, which in truth he rattled off very glibly when put to the test.

One letter was written from Vera Cruz and the other from the City of Mexico. He had met Montel, who was doing everything toward his advancement. So far, the financial situation was no improvement over the one he had left in New Orleans, but of course the prospects were vastly better. He wrote of the City of Mexico, the buildings, the people and their habits, the conditions of life which he found there. He sent his love to the family. He inclosed a check to his mother, and hoped she would affectionately remember him to all his friends. That was about the substance of the two letters. Edna felt that if there had been a message for her, she would have received it. The despondent frame of mind in which she had left home began again to overtake her, and she remembered that she wished to find Mademoiselle Reisz.

Madame Lebrun knew where Mademoiselle Reisz lived. She gave Edna the address, regretting that she would not consent to stay and spend the remainder of the afternoon, and pay a visit to Mademoiselle Reisz some other day. The afternoon was already well advanced.

Victor escorted her out upon the banquette, lifted her parasol, and held it over her while he walked to the car with her. He entreated her to bear in mind that the disclosures of the afternoon were strictly confidential. She laughed and bantered him a little, remembering too late that she should have been dignified and reserved.

"How handsome Mrs. Pontellier looked!" said Madame Lebrun to her son.

"Ravishing!" he admitted. "The city atmosphere has improved her. Some way she doesn't seem like the same woman."

XXI

Some people contended that the reason Mademoiselle Reisz always chose apartments up under the roof was to discourage the approach of beggars, peddlars and callers. There were plenty of windows in her little front room. They were for the most part dingy, but as they were nearly always open it did not make so much difference. They often admitted into the room a good deal of smoke and soot; but at the same time all the light and air that there was came through them. From her windows could be seen the crescent of the river, the masts of ships and the big chimneys of the Mississippi steamers. A magnificent piano crowded the apartment. In the next room she slept, and in the third and last she harbored a gasoline stove on which she cooked her meals when disinclined to descend to the neighboring restaurant. It was there also that she ate, keeping her belongings in a rare old buffet, dingy and battered from a hundred years of use.

When Edna knocked at Mademoiselle Reisz's front room door and entered, she discovered that person standing beside the window, engaged in mending or patching an old prunella gaiter.[61] The little musician laughed all over when she saw Edna. Her laugh consisted of a contortion of the face and all the muscles of the body. She seemed strikingly homely, standing there in the afternoon light. She still wore the shabby lace and the artificial bunch of violets on the side of her head.

"So you remembered me at last," said Mademoiselle. "I had said to myself, 'Ah, bah! she will never come.'"

"Did you want me to come?" asked Edna with a smile.

"I had not thought much about it," answered Mademoiselle. The two had seated themselves on a little bumpy sofa which stood against the wall. "I am glad, however, that you came. I have the water boiling back there, and was just about to make some coffee. You will drink a cup with me. And how is *la belle dame?*[62] Always handsome!

[61]A shoe with a twill upper section.
[62]French: "my beautiful friend."

always healthy! always contented!" She took Edna's hand between her strong wiry fingers, holding it loosely without warmth, and executing a sort of double theme upon the back and palm.

"Yes," she went on; "I sometimes thought: 'She will never come. She promised as those women in society always do, without meaning it. She will not come.' For I really don't believe you like me, Mrs. Pontellier."

"I don't know whether I like you or not," replied Edna, gazing down at the little woman with a quizzical look.

The candor of Mrs. Pontellier's admission greatly pleased Mademoiselle Reisz. She expressed her gratification by repairing forthwith to the region of the gasoline stove and rewarding her guest with the promised cup of coffee. The coffee and the biscuit accompanying it proved very acceptable to Edna, who had declined refreshment at Madame Lebrun's and was now beginning to feel hungry. Mademoiselle set the tray which she brought in upon a small table near at hand, and seated herself once again on the lumpy sofa.

"I have had a letter from your friend," she remarked, as she poured a little cream into Edna's cup and handed it to her.

"My friend?"

"Yes, your friend Robert. He wrote to me from the City of Mexico."

"Wrote to *you*?" repeated Edna in amazement, stirring her coffee absently.

"Yes, to me. Why not? Don't stir all the warmth out of your coffee; drink it. Though the letter might as well have been sent to you; it was nothing but Mrs. Pontellier from beginning to end."

"Let me see it," requested the young woman, entreatingly.

"No; a letter concerns no one but the person who writes it and the one to whom it is written."

"Haven't you just said it concerned me from beginning to end?"

"It was written about you, not to you. 'Have you seen Mrs. Pontellier? How is she looking?' he asks. 'As Mrs. Pontellier says,' or 'as Mrs. Pontellier once said!' 'If Mrs. Pontellier should call upon you, play for her that Impromptu of Chopin's, my favorite. I heard it here a day or two ago, but not as you play it. I should like to know how it affects her,' and so on, as if he supposed we were constantly in each other's society."

"Let me see the letter."

"Oh, no."

"Have you answered it?"

"No."

"Let me see the letter."

"No, and again, no."

"Then play the Impromptu for me."

"It is growing late; what time do you have to be home?"

"Time doesn't concern me. Your question seems a little rude. Play the Impromptu."

"But you have told me nothing of yourself. What are you doing?"

"Painting!" laughed Edna. "I am becoming an artist. Think of it!"

"Ah! an artist! You have pretensions, Madame."

"Why pretensions? Do you think I could not become an artist?"

"I do not know you well enough to say. I do not know your talent or your temperament. To be an artist includes much; one must possess many gifts—absolute gifts—which have not been acquired by one's own effort. And, moreover, to succeed, the artist must possess the courageous soul."

"What do you mean by the courageous soul?"

"Courageous, *ma foi!* The brave soul. The soul that dares and defies."

"Show me the letter and play for me the Impromptu. You see that I have persistence. Does that quality count for anything in art?"

"It counts with a foolish old woman whom you have captivated," replied Mademoiselle, with her wriggling laugh.

The letter was right there at hand in the drawer of the little table upon which Edna had just placed her coffee cup. Mademoiselle opened the drawer and drew forth the letter, the topmost one. She placed it in Edna's hands, and without further comment arose and went to the piano.

Mademoiselle played a soft interlude. It was an improvisation. She sat low at the instrument, and the lines of her body settled into ungraceful curves and angles that gave it an appearance of deformity. Gradually and imperceptibly the interlude melted into the soft opening minor chords of the Chopin Impromptu.

Edna did not know when the Impromptu began or ended. She sat in the sofa corner reading Robert's letter by the fading light. Mademoiselle had glided from the Chopin into the quivering lovenotes of Isolde's song,[63] and back again to the Impromptu with its soulful and poignant longing.

The shadows deepened in the little room. The music grew strange and fantastic—turbulent, insistent, plaintive and soft with entreaty. The shadows grew deeper. The music filled the room. It floated out upon the night, over the housetops, the crescent of the river, losing itself in the silence of the upper air.

Edna was sobbing, just as she had wept one midnight at Grand Isle when strange, new voices awoke in her. She arose in some agitation to take her departure. "May I come again, Mademoiselle?" she asked at the threshold.

"Come whenever you feel like it. Be careful; the stairs and landings are dark; don't stumble."

Mademoiselle reëntered and lit a candle. Robert's letter was on the floor. She stooped and picked it up. It was crumpled and damp with tears. Mademoiselle smoothed the letter out, restored it to the envelope, and replaced it in the table drawer.

XXII

One morning on his way into town Mr. Pontellier stopped at the house of his old friend and family physician, Doctor Mandelet. The Doctor was a semi-retired physician, resting, as the saying is, upon his laurels. He bore a reputation for wisdom

[63] Refers to German composer Richard Wagner's (1813–1883) tragic opera *Tristan and Isolde* (1865); in particular, to the song "Liebestod" ("Love-death"), which Isolde sings as she dies in her dead lover's arms.

rather than skill—leaving the active practice of medicine to his assistants and younger contemporaries—and was much sought for in matters of consultation. A few families, united to him by bonds of friendship, he still attended when they required the services of a physician. The Pontelliers were among these.

Mr. Pontellier found the Doctor reading at the open window of his study. His house stood rather far back from the street, in the center of a delightful garden, so that it was quiet and peaceful at the old gentleman's study window. He was a great reader. He stared up disapprovingly over his eye-glasses as Mr. Pontellier entered, wondering who had the temerity to disturb him at that hour of the morning.

"Ah, Pontellier! Not sick, I hope. Come and have a seat. What news do you bring this morning?" He was quite portly, with a profusion of gray hair, and small blue eyes which age had robbed of much of their brightness but none of their penetration.

"Oh! I'm never sick, Doctor. You know that I come of tough fiber—of that old Creole race of Pontelliers that dry up and finally blow away. I came to consult—no, not precisely to consult—to talk to you about Edna. I don't know what ails her."

"Madame Pontellier not well?" marveled the Doctor. "Why, I saw her—I think it was a week ago—walking along Canal Street, the picture of health, it seemed to me."

"Yes, yes; she seems quite well," said Mr. Pontellier, leaning forward and whirling his stick between his two hands; "but she doesn't act well. She's odd, she's not like herself. I can't make her out, and I thought perhaps you'd help me."

"How does she act?" inquired the doctor.

"Well, it isn't easy to explain," said Mr. Pontellier, throwing himself back in his chair. "She lets the housekeeping go to the dickens."

"Well, well; women are not all alike, my dear Pontellier. We've got to consider—"

"I know that; I told you I couldn't explain. Her whole attitude—toward me and everybody and everything—has changed. You know I have a quick temper, but I don't want to quarrel or be rude to a woman, especially my wife; yet I'm driven to it, and feel like ten thousand devils after I've made a fool of myself. She's making it devilishly uncomfortable for me," he went on nervously. "She's got some sort of notion in her head concerning the eternal rights of women; and—you understand—we meet in the morning at the breakfast table."

The old gentleman lifted his shaggy eyebrows, protruded his thick nether lip, and tapped the arms of his chair with his cushioned finger-tips.

"What have you been doing to her, Pontellier?"

"Doing! *Parbleu!*"[64]

"Has she," asked the Doctor, with a smile, "has she been associating of late with a circle of pseudo-intellectual women—super-spiritual superior beings? My wife has been telling me about them."

"That's the trouble," broke in Mr. Pontellier, "she hasn't been associating with any one. She has abandoned her Tuesdays at home, has thrown over all her acquaintances, and goes tramping about by herself, moping in the street-cars, getting in after dark. I tell you she's peculiar. I don't like it; I feel a little worried over it."

[64]French: "Good Lord!"

This was a new aspect for the Doctor. "Nothing hereditary?" he asked, seriously. "Nothing peculiar about her family antecedents, is there?"

"Oh, no, indeed! She comes of sound old Presbyterian Kentucky stock. The old gentleman, her father, I have heard, used to atone for his week-day sins with his Sunday devotions. I know for a fact, that his race horses literally ran away with the prettiest bit of Kentucky farming land I ever laid eyes upon. Margaret—you know Margaret—she has all the Presbyterianism undiluted. And the youngest is something of a vixen. By the way, she gets married in a couple of weeks from now."

"Send your wife up to the wedding," exclaimed the Doctor, foreseeing a happy solution. "Let her stay among her own people for a while; it will do her good."

"That's what I want her to do. She won't go to the marriage. She says a wedding is one of the most lamentable spectacles on earth. Nice thing for a woman to say to her husband!" exclaimed Mr. Pontellier, fuming anew at the recollection.

"Pontellier," said the Doctor, after a moment's reflection, "let your wife alone for a while. Don't bother her, and don't let her bother you. Woman, my dear friend, is a very peculiar and delicate organism—a sensitive and highly organized woman, such as I know Mrs. Pontellier to be, is especially peculiar. It would require an inspired psychologist to deal successfully with them. And when ordinary fellows like you and me attempt to cope with their idiosyncrasies the result is bungling. Most women are moody and whimsical. This is some passing whim of your wife, due to some cause or causes which you and I needn't try to fathom. But it will pass happily over, especially if you let her alone. Send her around to see me."

"Oh! I couldn't do that; there'd be no reason for it," objected Mr. Pontellier.

"Then I'll go around and see her," said the Doctor. "I'll drop in to dinner some evening *en bon ami*."[65]

"Do! by all means," urged Mr. Pontellier. "What evening will you come? Say Thursday. Will you come Thursday?" he asked, rising to take his leave.

"Very well; Thursday. My wife may possibly have some engagement for me Thursday. In case she has, I shall let you know. Otherwise, you may expect me."

Mr. Pontellier turned before leaving to say:

"I am going to New York on business very soon. I have a big scheme on hand, and want to be on the field proper to pull the ropes and handle the ribbons.[66] We'll let you in on the inside if you say so, Doctor," he laughed.

"No, I thank you, my dear sir," returned the Doctor. "I leave such ventures to you younger men with the fever of life still in your blood."

"What I wanted to say," continued Mr. Pontellier, with his hand on the knob; "I may have to be absent a good while. Would you advise me to take Edna along?"

"By all means, if she wishes to go. If not, leave her here. Don't contradict her. The mood will pass, I assure you. It may take a month, two, three months—possibly longer, but it will pass; have patience."

"Well, good-by, *à jeudi*,"[67] said Mr. Pontellier, as he let himself out.

The Doctor would have liked during the course of conversation to ask, "Is there any man in the case?" but he knew his Creole too well to make such a blunder as that.

[65]French: "as a friend."
[66]To be in charge.
[67]French: "until Thursday."

He did not resume his book immediately, but sat for a while meditatively looking out into the garden.

XXIII

Edna's father was in the city, and had been with them several days. She was not very warmly or deeply attached to him, but they had certain tastes in common, and when together they were companionable. His coming was in the nature of a welcome disturbance; it seemed to furnish a new direction for her emotions.

He had come to purchase a wedding gift for his daughter, Janet, and an outfit for himself in which he might make a creditable appearance at her marriage. Mr. Pontellier had selected the bridal gift, as every one immediately connected with him always deferred to his taste in such matters. And his suggestions on the question of dress—which too often assumes the nature of a problem—were of inestimable value to his father-in-law. But for the past few days the old gentleman had been upon Edna's hands, and in his society she was becoming acquainted with a new set of sensations. He had been a colonel in the Confederate army, and still maintained, with the title, the military bearing which had always accompanied it. His hair and mustache were white and silky, emphasizing the rugged bronze of his face. He was tall and thin, and wore his coats padded, which gave a fictitious breadth and depth to his shoulders and chest. Edna and her father looked very distinguished together, and excited a good deal of notice during their perambulations. Upon his arrival she began by introducing him to her atelier and making a sketch of him. He took the whole matter very seriously. If her talent had been ten-fold greater than it was, it would not have surprised him, convinced as he was that he had bequeathed to all of his daughters the germs of a masterful capability, which only depended upon their own efforts to be directed toward successful achievement.

Before her pencil he sat rigid and unflinching, as he had faced the cannon's mouth in days gone by. He resented the intrusion of the children, who gaped with wondering eyes at him, sitting so stiff up there in their mother's bright atelier. When they drew near he motioned them away with an expressive action of the foot, loath to disturb the fixed lines of his countenance, his arms, or his rigid shoulders.

Edna, anxious to entertain him, invited Mademoiselle Reisz to meet him, having promised him a treat in her piano playing; but Mademoiselle declined the invitation. So together they attended a *soirée musicale* at the Ratignolle's. Monsieur and Madame Ratignolle made much of the Colonel, installing him as the guest of honor and engaging him at once to dine with them the following Sunday, or any day which he might select. Madame coquetted with him in the most captivating and naive manner, with eyes, gestures, and a profusion of compliments, till the Colonel's old head felt thirty years younger on his padded shoulders. Edna marveled, not comprehending. She herself was almost devoid of coquetry.

There were one or two men whom she observed at the *soirée musicale;* but she would never have felt moved to any kittenish display to attract their notice—to any feline or feminine wiles to express herself toward them. Their personality attracted her in an agreeable way. Her fancy selected them, and she was glad when a lull in the music gave them an opportunity to meet her and talk with her. Often on the street the glance of strange eyes had lingered in her memory, and sometimes had disturbed her.

Mr. Pontellier did not attend these *soirées musicales.* He considered them *bourgeois,*[68] and found more diversion at the club. To Madame Ratignolle he said the music dispensed at her *soirées* was too "heavy," too far beyond his untrained comprehension. His excuse flattered her. But she disapproved of Mr. Pontellier's club, and she was frank enough to tell Edna so.

"It's a pity Mr. Pontellier doesn't stay home more in the evenings. I think you would be more—well, if you don't mind my saying it—more united, if he did."

"Oh! dear no!" said Edna, with a blank look in her eyes. "What should I do if he stayed home? We wouldn't have anything to say to each other."

She had not much of anything to say to her father, for that matter; but he did not antagonize her. She discovered that he interested her, though she realized that he might not interest her long; and for the first time in her life she felt as if she were thoroughly acquainted with him. He kept her busy serving him and ministering to his wants. It amused her to do so. She would not permit a servant or one of the children to do anything for him which she might do herself. Her husband noticed, and thought it was the expression of a deep filial attachment which he had never suspected.

The Colonel drank numerous "toddies" during the course of the day, which left him, however, imperturbed. He was an expert at concocting strong drinks. He had even invented some, to which he had given fantastic names, and for whose manufacture he required diverse ingredients that it devolved upon Edna to procure for him.

When Doctor Mandelet dined with the Pontelliers on Thursday he could discern in Mrs. Pontellier no trace of that morbid condition which her husband had reported to him. She was excited and in a manner radiant. She and her father had been to the race course, and their thoughts when they seated themselves at table were still occupied with the events of the afternoon, and their talk was still of the track. The Doctor had not kept pace with turf affairs. He had certain recollections of racing in what he called "the good old times" when the Lecompte stables[69] flourished, and he drew upon this fund of memories so that he might not be left out and seem wholly devoid of the modern spirit. But he failed to impose upon the Colonel, and was even far from impressing him with this trumped-up knowledge of bygone days. Edna had staked her father on his last venture, with the most gratifying results to both of them. Besides, they had met some very charming people, according to the Colonel's impressions. Mrs. Mortimer Merriman and Mrs. James Highcamp, who were there with Alcée Arobin, had joined them and had enlivened the hours in a fashion that warmed him to think of.

Mr. Pontellier himself had no particular leaning toward horseracing, and was even rather inclined to discourage it as a pastime, especially when he considered the fate of that blue-grass farm in Kentucky. He endeavored, in a general way, to express

[68]French: middle-class, boorish.

[69]These stables were integral to the races that were so popular in New Orleans during the antebellum period.

a particular disapproval, and only succeeded in arousing the ire and opposition of his father-in-law. A pretty dispute followed, in which Edna warmly espoused her father's cause and the Doctor remained neutral.

He observed his hostess attentively from under his shaggy brows, and noted a subtle change which had transformed her from the listless woman he had known into a being who, for the moment, seemed palpitant with the forces of life. Her speech was warm and energetic. There was no repression in her glance or gesture. She reminded him of some beautiful, sleek animal waking up in the sun.

The dinner was excellent. The claret was warm and the champagne was cold, and under their beneficent influence the threatened unpleasantness melted and vanished with the fumes of the wine.

Mr. Pontellier warmed up and grew reminiscent. He told some amusing plantation experiences, recollections of old Iberville and his youth, when he hunted 'possum in company with some friendly darky; thrashed the pecan trees, shot the grosbec,[70] and roamed the woods and fields in mischievous idleness.

The Colonel, with little sense of humor and of the fitness of things, related a somber episode of those dark and bitter days, in which he had acted a conspicuous part and always formed a central figure. Nor was the Doctor happier in his selection, when he told the old, ever new and curious story of the waning of a woman's love, seeking strange, new channels, only to return to its legitimate source after days of fierce unrest. It was one of the many little human documents which had been unfolded to him during his long career as a physician. The story did not seem especially to impress Edna. She had one of her own to tell, of a woman who paddled away with her lover one night in a pirogue and never came back. They were lost amid the Baratarian Islands, and no one ever heard of them or found trace of them from that day to this. It was a pure invention. She said that Madame Antoine had related it to her. That, also, was an invention. Perhaps it was a dream she had had. But every glowing word seemed real to those who listened. They could feel the hot breath of the Southern night; they could hear the long sweep of the pirogue through the glistening moonlit water, the beating of birds' wings, rising startled from among the reeds in the salt-water pools; they could see the faces of the lovers, pale, close together, rapt in oblivious forgetfulness, drifting into the unknown.

The champagne was cold, and its subtle fumes played fantastic tricks with Edna's memory that night.

Outside, away from the glow of the fire and the soft lamplight, the night was chill and murky. The Doctor doubled his old-fashioned cloak across his breast as he strode home through the darkness. He knew his fellow-creatures better than most men; knew that inner life which so seldom unfolds itself to unanointed eyes. He was sorry he had accepted Pontellier's invitation. He was growing old, and beginning to need rest and an imperturbed spirit. He did not want the secrets of other lives thrust upon him.

"I hope it isn't Arobin," he muttered to himself as he walked. "I hope to heaven it isn't Alcée Arobin."

[70]French: a game bird with a large beak.

XXIV

Edna and her father had a warm, and almost violent dispute upon the subject of her refusal to attend her sister's wedding. Mr. Pontellier declined to interfere, to interpose either his influence or his authority. He was following Doctor Mandelet's advice, and letting her do as she liked. The Colonel reproached his daughter for her lack of filial kindness and respect, her want of sisterly affection and womanly consideration. His arguments were labored and unconvincing. He doubted if Janet would accept any excuse—forgetting that Edna had offered none. He doubted if Janet would ever speak to her again, and he was sure Margaret would not.

Edna was glad to be rid of her father when he finally took himself off with his wedding garments and his bridal gifts, with his padded shoulders, his Bible reading, his "toddies" and ponderous oaths.

Mr. Pontellier followed him closely. He meant to stop at the wedding on his way to New York and endeavor by every means which money and love could devise to atone somewhat for Edna's incomprehensible action.

"You are too lenient, too lenient by far, Léonce," asserted the Colonel. "Authority, coercion are what is needed. Put your foot down good and hard; the only way to manage a wife. Take my word for it."

The Colonel was perhaps unaware that he had coerced his own wife into her grave. Mr. Pontellier had a vague suspicion of it which he thought it needless to mention at that late day.

Edna was not so consciously gratified at her husband's leaving home as she had been over the departure of her father. As the day approached when he was to leave her for a comparatively long stay, she grew melting and affectionate, remembering his many acts of consideration and his repeated expressions of an ardent attachment. She was solicitous about his health and his welfare. She bustled around, looking after his clothing, thinking about heavy underwear, quite as Madame Ratignolle would have done under similar circumstances. She cried when he went away, calling him her dear, good friend, and she was quite certain she would grow lonely before very long and go to join him in New York.

But after all, a radiant peace settled upon her when she at last found herself alone. Even the children were gone. Old Madame Pontellier had come herself and carried them off to Iberville with their quadroon. The old madame did not venture to say she was afraid they would be neglected during Léonce's absence; she hardly ventured to think so. She was hungry for them—even a little fierce in her attachment. She did not want them to be wholly "children of the pavement," she always said when begging to have them for a space. She wished them to know the country, with its streams, its fields, its woods, its freedom, so delicious to the young. She wished them to taste something of the life their father had lived and known and loved when he, too, was a little child.

When Edna was at last alone, she breathed a big, genuine sigh of relief. A feeling that was unfamiliar but very delicious came over her. She walked all through the house, from one room to another, as if inspecting it for the first time. She tried the various chairs and lounges, as if she had never sat and reclined upon them before. And she perambulated around the outside of the house, investigating, looking to see if windows and shutters were secure and in order. The flowers were like new acquaintances; she approached them in a familiar spirit, and made herself at home among them. The garden walks were damp, and Edna called to the maid to bring out her rubber sandals. And there she stayed, and stooped, digging around the plants, trimming, picking dead, dry leaves. The children's little dog came out, interfering, getting in her way. She scolded him, laughing at him, played with him. The garden smelled so good and looked so pretty in the afternoon sunlight. Edna plucked all the bright flowers she could find, and went into the house with them, she and the little dog.

Even the kitchen assumed a sudden interesting character which she had never before perceived. She went in to give directions to the cook, to say that the butcher would have to bring much less meat, that they would require only half their usual quantity of bread, of milk and groceries. She told the cook that she herself would be greatly occupied during Mr. Pontellier's absence, and she begged her to take all thought and responsibility of the larder upon her own shoulders.

That night Edna dined alone. The candelabra, with a few candles in the center of the table, gave all the light she needed. Outside the circle of light in which she sat, the large dining-room looked solemn and shadowy. The cook, placed upon her mettle, served a delicious repast—a luscious tenderloin broiled à point. The wine tasted good; the marron glacé[71] seemed to be just what she wanted. It was so pleasant, too, to dine in a comfortable peignoir.

She thought a little sentimentally about Léonce and the children, and wondered what they were doing. As she gave a dainty scrap or two to the doggie, she talked intimately to him about Etienne and Raoul. He was beside himself with astonishment and delight over these companionable advances, and showed his appreciation by his little quick, snappy barks and a lively agitation.

Then Edna sat in the library after dinner and read Emerson[72] until she grew sleepy. She realized that she had neglected her reading, and determined to start anew upon a course of improving studies, now that her time was completely her own to do with as she liked.

After a refreshing bath, Edna went to bed. And as she snuggled comfortably beneath the eiderdown a sense of restfulness invaded her, such as she had not known before.

XXV

When the weather was dark and cloudy Edna could not work. She needed the sun to mellow and temper her mood to the sticking point. She had reached a stage when she seemed to be no longer feeling her way, working, when in the humor, with sureness and ease. And being devoid of ambition, and striving not toward accomplishment, she drew satisfaction from the work in itself.

On rainy or melancholy days Edna went out and sought the society of the friends she had made at Grand Isle. Or else she stayed indoors and nursed a mood with

[71]French: chestnuts glazed with sugar.

[72]Ralph Waldo Emerson (1803–1882), American philosopher in the forefront of the Transcendental movement.

which she was becoming too familiar for her own comfort and peace of mind. It was not despair; but it seemed to her as if life were passing by, leaving its promise broken and unfulfilled. Yet there were other days when she listened, was led on and deceived by fresh promises which her youth held out to her.

She went again to the races, and again. Alcée Arobin and Mrs. Highcamp called for her one bright afternoon in Arobin's drag.[73] Mrs. Highcamp was a worldly but unaffected, intelligent, slim, tall blonde woman in the forties, with an indifferent manner and blue eyes that stared. She had a daughter who served her as a pretext for cultivating the society of young men of fashion. Alcée Arobin was one of them. He was a familiar figure at the race course, the opera, the fashionable clubs. There was a perpetual smile in his eyes, which seldom failed to awaken a corresponding cheerfulness in any one who looked into them and listened to his good-humored voice. His manner was quiet, and at times a little insolent. He possessed a good figure, a pleasing face, not overburdened with depth of thought or feeling; and his dress was that of the conventional man of fashion.

He admired Edna extravagantly, after meeting her at the races with her father. He had met her before on other occasions, but she had seemed to him unapproachable until that day. It was at his instigation that Mrs. Highcamp called to ask her to go with them to the Jockey Club[74] to witness the turf event of the season.

There were possibly a few track men out there who knew the race horse as well as Edna, but there was certainly none who knew it better. She sat between her two companions as one having authority to speak. She laughed at Arobin's pretensions, and deplored Mrs. Highcamp's ignorance. The race horse was a friend and intimate associate of her childhood. The atmosphere of the stables and the breath of the blue grass paddock revived in her memory and lingered in her nostrils. She did not perceive that she was talking like her father as the sleek geldings ambled in review before them. She played for very high stakes, and fortune favored her. The fever of the game flamed in her cheeks and eyes, and it got into her blood and into her brain like an intoxicant. People turned their heads to look at her, and more than one lent an attentive ear to her utterances, hoping thereby to secure the elusive but ever-desired "tip." Arobin caught the contagion of excitement which drew him to Edna like a magnet. Mrs. Highcamp remained, as usual, unmoved, with her indifferent stare and uplifted eyebrows.

Edna stayed and dined with Mrs. Highcamp upon being urged to do so. Arobin, also remained and sent away his drag.

The dinner was quiet and uninteresting, save for the cheerful efforts of Arobin to enliven things. Mrs. Highcamp deplored the absence of her daughter from the races, and tried to convey to her what she had missed by going to the "Dante[75] reading" instead of joining them. The girl held a geranium leaf up to her nose and said nothing, but looked knowing and noncommittal. Mr. Highcamp was a plain, baldheaded man, who only talked under compulsion. He was unresponsive. Mrs. Highcamp was full of delicate courtesy and consideration toward her husband. She addressed most of her conversation to him at table. They sat in the library after dinner

[73]A coach.
[74]A local elite club.
[75]Dante Alighieri (1265–1321), Italian poet and author of *The Divine Comedy*.

and read the evening papers together under the drop-light;[76] while the younger people went into the drawing-room near by and talked. Miss Highcamp played some selections from Grieg upon the piano. She seemed to have apprehended all of the composer's coldness and none of his poetry. While Edna listened she could not help wondering if she had lost her taste for music.

When the time came for her to go home, Mr. Highcamp grunted a lame offer to escort her, looking down at his slippered feet with tactless concern. It was Arobin who took her home. The car ride was long, and it was late when they reached Esplanade Street. Arobin asked permission to enter for a second to light his cigarette—his match safe[77] was empty. He filled his match safe, but did not light his cigarette until he left her, after she had expressed her willingness to go to the races with him again.

Edna was neither tired nor sleepy. She was hungry again, for the Highcamp dinner, though of excellent quality, had lacked abundance. She rummaged in the larder and brought forth a slice of "Gruyère"[78] and some crackers. She opened a bottle of beer which she found in the ice-box. Edna felt extremely restless and excited. She vacantly hummed a fantastic tune as she poked at the wood embers on the hearth and munched a cracker.

She wanted something to happen—something, anything; she did not know what. She regretted that she had not made Arobin stay a half hour to talk over the horses with her. She counted the money she had won. But there was nothing else to do, so she went to bed, and tossed there for hours in a sort of monotonous agitation.

In the middle of the night she remembered that she had forgotten to write her regular letter to her husband; and she decided to do so next day and tell him about her afternoon at the Jockey Club. She lay wide awake composing a letter which was nothing like the one which she wrote next day. When the maid awoke her in the morning Edna was dreaming of Mr. Highcamp playing the piano at the entrance of a music store on Canal Street, while his wife was saying to Alcée Arobin, as they boarded an Esplanade Street car:

"What a pity that so much talent has been neglected! but I must go."

When, a few days later, Alcée Arobin again called for Edna in his drag, Mrs. Highcamp was not with him. He said they would pick her up. But as that lady had not been apprised of his intention of picking her up, she was not at home. The daughter was just leaving the house to attend the meeting of a branch Folk Lore Society, and regretted that she could not accompany them. Arobin appeared nonplused, and asked Edna if there were any one else she cared to ask.

She did not deem it worth while to go in search of any of the fashionable acquaintances from whom she had withdrawn herself. She thought of Madame Ratignolle, but knew that her fair friend did not leave the house, except to take a languid walk around the block with her husband after nightfall. Mademoiselle Reisz would have laughed at such a request from Edna. Madame Lebrun might have enjoyed the outing, but for some reason Edna did not want her. So they went alone, she and Arobin.

[76]A gas lamp. [78]A type of cheese.
[77]A box designed to contain friction matches.

The afternoon was intensely interesting to her. The excitement came back upon her like a remittent fever. Her talk grew familiar and confidential. It was no labor to become intimate with Arobin. His manner invited easy confidence. The preliminary stage of becoming acquainted was one which he always endeavored to ignore when a pretty and engaging woman was concerned.

He stayed and dined with Edna. He stayed and sat beside the wood fire. They laughed and talked; and before it was time to go he was telling her how different life might have been if he had known her years before. With ingenuous frankness he spoke of what a wicked, ill-disciplined boy he had been, and impulsively drew up his cuff to exhibit upon his wrist the scar from a saber cut which he had received in a duel outside of Paris when he was nineteen. She touched his hand as she scanned the red cicatrice on the inside of his white wrist. A quick impulse that was somewhat spasmodic impelled her fingers to close in a sort of clutch upon his hand. He felt the pressure of her pointed nails in the flesh of his palm.

She arose hastily and walked toward the mantel.

"The sight of a wound or scar always agitates and sickens me," she said. "I shouldn't have looked at it."

"I beg your pardon," he entreated, following her; "it never occurred to me that it might be repulsive."

He stood close to her, and the effrontery in his eyes repelled the old, vanishing self in her, yet drew all her awakening sensuousness. He saw enough in her face to impel him to take her hand and hold it while he said his lingering good night.

"Will you go to the races again?" he asked.

"No," she said. "I've had enough of the races. I don't want to lose all the money I've won, and I've got to work when the weather is bright, instead of—"

"Yes; work; to be sure. You promised to show me your work. What morning may I come up to your atelier? To-morrow?"

"No!"

"Day after?"

"No, no."

"Oh, please don't refuse me! I know something of such things. I might help you with a stray suggestion or two."

"No. Good night. Why don't you go after you have said good night? I don't like you," she went on in a high, excited pitch, attempting to draw away her hand. She felt that her words lacked dignity and sincerity, and she knew that he felt it.

"I'm sorry you don't like me. I'm sorry I offended you. How have I offended you? What have I done? Can't you forgive me?" And he bent and pressed his lips upon her hand as if he wished never more to withdraw them.

"Mr. Arobin," she complained, "I'm greatly upset by the excitement of the afternoon; I'm not myself. My manner must have misled you in some way. I wish you to go, please." She spoke in a monotonous, dull tone. He took his hat from the table, and stood with eyes turned from her, looking into the dying fire. For a moment or two he kept an impressive silence.

"Your manner has not misled me, Mrs. Pontellier," he said finally. "My own emotions have done that. I couldn't help it. When I'm near you, how could I help it? Don't think anything of it, don't bother, please. You see, I go when you command me. If you wish me to stay away, I shall do so. If you let me come back, I—oh! you will let me come back?"

He cast one appealing glance at her, to which she made no response. Alcée Arobin's manner was so genuine that it often deceived even himself.

Edna did not care or think whether it were genuine or not. When she was alone she looked mechanically at the back of her hand which he had kissed so warmly. Then she leaned her head down on the mantelpiece. She felt somewhat like a woman who in a moment of passion is betrayed into an act of infidelity, and realizes the significance of the act without being wholly awakened from its glamour. The thought was passing vaguely through her mind, "What would he think?"

She did not mean her husband; she was thinking of Robert Lebrun. Her husband seemed to her now like a person whom she had married without love as an excuse.

She lit a candle and went up to her room. Alcée Arobin was absolutely nothing to her. Yet his presence, his manners, the warmth of his glances, and above all the touch of his lips upon her hand had acted like a narcotic upon her.

She slept a languorous sleep, interwoven with vanishing dreams.

XXVI

Alcée Arobin wrote Edna an elaborate note of apology, palpitant with sincerity. It embarrassed her; for in a cooler, quieter moment it appeared to her absurd that she should have taken his action so seriously, so dramatically. She felt sure that the significance of the whole occurrence had lain in her own self-consciousness. If she ignored his note it would give undue importance to a trivial affair. If she replied to it in a serious spirit it would still leave in his mind the impression that she had in a susceptible moment yielded to his influence. After all, it was no great matter to have one's hand kissed. She was provoked at his having written the apology. She answered in as light and bantering a spirit as she fancied it deserved, and said she would be glad to have him look in upon her at work whenever he felt the inclination and his business gave him the opportunity.

He responded at once by presenting himself at her home with all his disarming naïveté. And then there was scarcely a day which followed that she did not see him or was not reminded of him. He was prolific in pretexts. His attitude became one of good-humored subservience and tacit adoration. He was ready at all times to submit to her moods, which were as often kind as they were cold. She grew accustomed to him. They became intimate and friendly by imperceptible degrees, and then by leaps. He sometimes talked in a way that astonished her at first and brought the crimson into her face; in a way that pleased her at last, appealing to the animalism that stirred impatiently within her.

There was nothing which so quieted the turmoil of Edna's senses as a visit to Mademoiselle Reisz. It was then, in the presence of that personality which was offensive to her, that the woman, by her divine art, seemed to reach Edna's spirit and set it free.

It was misty, with heavy, lowering atmosphere, one afternoon, when Edna climbed the stairs to the pianist's apartments under the roof. Her clothes were dripping with moisture. She felt chilled and pinched as she entered the room. Mademoiselle was poking at a rusty stove that smoked a little and warmed the room indifferently. She was endeavoring to heat a pot of chocolate on the stove. The room looked cheerless and dingy to Edna as she entered. A bust of Beethoven, covered with a hood of dust, scowled at her from the Mantelpiece.

"Ah! here comes the sunlight!" exclaimed Mademoiselle, rising from her knees before the stove. "Now it will be warm and bright enough; I can let the fire alone."

She closed the stove door with a bang, and approaching, assisted in removing Edna's dripping mackintosh.

"You are cold; you look miserable. The chocolate will soon be hot. But would you rather have a taste of brandy? I have scarcely touched the bottle which you brought me for my cold." A piece of red flannel was wrapped around Mademoiselle's throat; a stiff neck compelled her to hold her head on one side.

"I will take some brandy," said Edna, shivering as she removed her gloves and overshoes. She drank the liquor from the glass as a man would have done. Then flinging herself upon the uncomfortable sofa she said, "Mademoiselle, I am going to move away from my house on Esplanade Street."

"Ah!" ejaculated the musician, neither surprised nor especially interested. Nothing ever seemed to astonish her very much. She was endeavoring to adjust the bunch of violets which had become loose from its fastening in her hair. Edna drew her down upon the sofa, and taking a pin from her own hair, secured the shabby artificial flowers in their accustomed place.

"Aren't you astonished?"

"Passably. Where are you going? To New York? to Iberville? to your father in Mississippi? where?"

"Just two steps away," laughed Edna, "in a little four-room house around the corner. It looks so cozy, so inviting and restful, whenever I pass by; and it's for rent. I'm tired looking after that big house. It never seemed like mine, anyway—like home. It's too much trouble. I have to keep too many servants. I am tired bothering with them.

"That is not your true reason, *ma belle.* There is no use in telling me lies. I don't know your reason, but you have not told me the truth." Edna did not protest or endeavor to justify herself.

"The house, the money that provides for it, are not mine. Isn't that enough reason?"

"They are your husband's," returned Mademoiselle, with a shrug and a malicious elevation of the eyebrows.

"Oh! I see there is no deceiving you. Then let me tell you: It is a caprice. I have a little money of my own from my mother's estate, which my father sends me by driblets. I won a large sum this winter on the races, and I am beginning to sell my sketches. Laidpore is more and more pleased with my work; he says it grows in force and individuality. I cannot judge of that myself, but I feel that I have gained in ease and confidence. However, as I said, I have sold a good many through Laidpore. I can live in the tiny house for little or nothing, with one servant. Old Celestine, who works occasionally for me, says she will come stay with me and do my work. I know I shall like it, like the feeling of freedom and independence."

"What does your husband say?"

"I have not told him yet. I only thought of it this morning. He will think I am demented, no doubt. Perhaps you think so."

Mademoiselle shook her head slowly. "Your reason is not yet clear to me," she said.

Neither was it quite clear to Edna herself; but it unfolded itself as she sat for a while in silence. Instinct had prompted her to put away her husband's bounty in casting off her allegiance. She did not know how it would be when he returned. There would have to be an understanding, an explanation. Conditions would some way adjust themselves, she felt; but whatever came, she had resolved never again to belong to another than herself.

"I shall give a grand dinner before I leave the old house!" Edna exclaimed. "You will have to come to it, Mademoiselle. I will give you everything that you like to eat and to drink. We shall sing and laugh and be merry for once." And she uttered a sigh that came from the very depths of her being.

If Mademoiselle happened to have received a letter from Robert during the interval of Edna's visits, she would give her the letter unsolicited. And she would seat herself at the piano and play as her humor prompted her while the young woman read the letter.

The little stove was roaring; it was red-hot, and the chocolate in the tin sizzled and sputtered. Edna went forward and opened the stove door, and Mademoiselle rising, took a letter from under the bust of Beethoven and handed it to Edna.

"Another! so soon!" she exclaimed, her eyes filled with delight. "Tell me, Mademoiselle, does he know that I see his letters?"

"Never in the world! He would be angry and would never write to me again if he thought so. Does he write to you? Never a line. Does he send you a message? Never a word. It is because he loves you, poor fool, and is trying to forget you, since you are not free to listen to him or to belong to him."

"Why do you show me his letters, then?"

"Haven't you begged for them? Can I refuse you anything? Oh! you cannot deceive me," and Mademoiselle approached her beloved instrument and began to play. Edna did not at once read the letter. She sat holding it in her hand, while the music penetrated her whole being like an effulgence, warming and brightening the dark places of her soul. It prepared her for joy and exultation.

"Oh!" she exclaimed, letting the letter fall to the floor. "Why did you not tell me?" She went and grasped Mademoiselle's hands up from the keys. "Oh! unkind! malicious! Why did you not tell me?"

"That he was coming back? No great news, *ma foi.*[79] I wonder he did not come long ago."

"But when, when?" cried Edna, impatiently. "He does not say when."

"He says 'very soon.' You know as much about it as I do; it is all in the letter."

"But why? Why is he coming? Oh, if I thought—" and she snatched the letter from the floor and turned the pages this way and that way, looking for the reason, which was left untold.

"If I were young and in love with a man," said Mademoiselle, turning on the stool and pressing her wiry hands between her knees as she looked down at Edna, who sat on the floor holding the letter, "it seems to me he would have to be some *grand esprit;* a man with lofty aims and ability to reach them; one who stood high enough to attract the notice of his fellow-men. It seems to me if I were young and in love I should never deem a man of ordinary caliber worthy of my devotion."

[79]French: "in fact.

"Now it is you who are telling lies and seeking to deceive me, Mademoiselle; or else you have never been in love, and know nothing about it. Why," went on Edna, clasping her knees and looking up into Mademoiselle's twisted face, "do you suppose a woman knows why she loves? Does she select? Does she say to herself: 'Go to! Here is a distinguished statesman with presidential possibilities; I shall proceed to fall in love with him.' Or, 'I shall set my heart upon this musician, whose fame is on every tongue?' Or, 'This financier, who controls the world's money markets?'"

"You are purposely misunderstanding me, *ma reine.*[80] Are you in love with Robert?"

"Yes," said Edna. It was the first time she had admitted it, and a glow overspread her face, blotching it with red spots.

"Why?" asked her companion. "Why do you love him when you ought not to?"

Edna, with a motion or two, dragged herself on her knees before Mademoiselle Reisz, who took the glowing face between her two hands.

"Why? Because his hair is brown and grows away from his temples; because he opens and shuts his eyes, and his nose is a little out of drawing; because he has two lips and a square chin, and a little finger which he can't straighten from having played baseball too energetically in his youth. Because—"

"Because you do, in short," laughed Mademoiselle. "What will you do when he comes back?" she asked.

"Do? Nothing, except feel glad and happy to be alive."

She was already glad and happy to be alive at the mere thought of his return. The murky, lowering sky, which had depressed her a few hours before, seemed bracing and invigorating as she splashed through the streets on her way home.

She stopped at a confectioner's and ordered a huge box of bonbons for the children in Iberville. She slipped a card in the box, on which she scribbled a tender message and sent an abundance of kisses.

Before dinner in the evening Edna wrote a charming letter to her husband, telling him of her intention to move for a while into the little house around the block, and to give a farewell dinner before leaving, regretting that he was not there to share it, to help her out with the menu and assist her in entertaining the guests. Her letter was brilliant and brimming with cheerfulness.

XXVII

"What is the matter with you?" asked Arobin that evening. "I never found you in such a happy mood." Edna was tired by that time, and was reclining on the lounge before the fire.

"Don't you know the weather prophet has told us we shall see the sun pretty soon?"

"Well, that ought to be reason enough," he acquiesced. "You wouldn't give me another if I sat here all night imploring you." He sat close to her on a low tabouret,

[80]French: "my queen" or "my lovely."

and as he spoke his fingers lightly touched the hair that fell a little over her forehead. She liked the touch of his fingers through her hair, and closed her eyes sensitively.

"One of these days," she said, "I'm going to pull myself together for a while and think—try to determine what character of a woman I am; for, candidly I don't know. By all the codes which I am acquainted with, I am a devilishly wicked specimen of the sex. But some way I can't convince myself that I am. I must think about it."

"Don't. What's the use? Why should you bother thinking about it when I can tell you what manner of woman you are." His fingers strayed occasionally down to her warm, smooth cheeks and firm chin, which was growing a little full and double.

"Oh, yes! You will tell me that I am adorable; everything that is captivating. Spare yourself the effort."

"No; I shan't tell you anything of the sort, though I shouldn't be lying if I did."

"Do you know Mademoiselle Reisz?" she asked irrelevantly.

"The pianist? I know her by sight. I've heard her play."

"She says queer things sometimes in a bantering way that you don't notice at the time and you find yourself thinking about afterward."

"For instance?"

"Well, for instance, when I left her today, she put her arms around me and felt my shoulder blades, to see if my wings were strong, she said. 'The bird that would soar above the level plain of tradition and prejudice must have strong wings. It is a sad spectacle to see the weaklings bruised, exhausted, fluttering back to earth.'"

"Whither would you soar?"

"I'm not thinking of any extraordinary flights. I only half comprehend her."

"I've heard she's partially demented," said Arobin.

"She seems to me wonderfully sane," Edna replied.

"I'm told she's extremely disagreeable and unpleasant. Why have you introduced her at a moment when I desired to talk of you?"

"Oh! talk of me if you like," cried Edna, clasping her hands beneath her head; "but let me think of something else while you do."

"I'm jealous of your thoughts to-night. They're making you a little kinder than usual; but some way I feel as if they were wandering, as if they were not here with me." She only looked at him and smiled. His eyes were very near. He leaned upon the lounge with an arm extended across her, while the other hand still rested upon her hair. They continued silently to look into each other's eyes. When he leaned forward and kissed her, she clasped his head, holding his lips to hers.

It was the first kiss of her life to which her nature had really responded. It was a flaming torch that kindled desire.

XXVIII

Edna cried a little that night after Arobin left her. It was only one phase of the multitudinous emotions which had assailed her. There was with her an overwhelming feeling of irresponsibility. There was the shock of the unexpected and the unaccustomed. There was her husband's reproach looking at her from the external things around her which he had provided for her external existence. There was Robert's reproach making itself felt by a quicker, fiercer, more overpowering love, which had awakened within her toward him. Above all, there was understanding. She felt as if a mist had been lifted from her eyes, enabling her to look upon and comprehend the significance of life, that monster made up of beauty and brutality. But among the conflicting sensations which assailed her, there was neither shame nor remorse. There was a dull pang of regret because it was not the kiss of love which had inflamed her, because it was not love which had held this cup of life to her lips.

XXIX

Without even waiting for an answer from her husband regarding his opinion or wishes in the matter, Edna hastened her preparations for quitting her home on Esplanade Street and moving into the little house around the block. A feverish anxiety attended her every action in that direction. There was no moment of deliberation, no interval of repose between the thought and its fulfillment. Early upon the morning following those hours passed in Arobin's society, Edna set about securing her new abode and hurrying her arrangements for occupying it. Within the precincts of her home she felt like one who has entered and lingered within the portals of some forbidden temple in which a thousand muffled voices bade her begone.

Whatever was her own in the house, everything which she had acquired aside from her husband's bounty, she caused to be transported to the other house, supplying simple and meager deficiencies from her own resources.

Arobin found her with rolled sleeves, working in company with the house-maid when he looked in during the afternoon. She was splendid and robust, and had never appeared handsomer than in the old blue gown, with a red silk handkerchief knotted at random around her head to protect her hair from the dust. She was mounted upon a high step-ladder, unhooking a picture from the wall when he entered. He had found the front door open, and had followed his ring by walking in unceremoniously.

"Come down!" he said. "Do you want to kill yourself?" She greeted him with affected carelessness, and appeared absorbed in her occupation.

If he had expected to find her languishing, reproachful, or indulging in sentimental tears, he must have been greatly surprised.

He was no doubt prepared for any emergency, ready for any one of the foregoing attitudes, just as he bent himself easily and naturally to the situation which confronted him.

"Please come down," he insisted, holding the ladder and looking up at her.

"No," she answered; "Ellen is afraid to mount the ladder. Joe is working over at the 'pigeon house'—that's the name Ellen gives it, because it's so small and looks like a pigeon house[81]—and some one has to do this."

Arobin pulled off his coat, and expressed himself ready and willing to tempt fate in her place. Ellen brought him one of her dustcaps, and went into contortions of mirth, which she found it impossible to control, when she saw him put it on before the mirror as grotesquely as he could. Edna herself could not refrain from smiling

[81]A dove-cote; a house for domesticated pigeons.

when she fastened it at his request. So it was he who in turn mounted the ladder, unhooking pictures and curtains, and dislodging ornaments as Edna directed. When he had finished he took off his dust-cap and went out to wash his hands.

Edna was sitting on the tabouret,[82] idly brushing the tips of a feather duster along the carpet when he came in again.

"Is there anything more you will let me do?" he asked.

"That is all," she answered. "Ellen can manage the rest." She kept the young woman occupied in the drawing-room, unwilling to be left alone with Arobin.

"What about the dinner?" he asked; "the grand event, the *coup d'état?*"

"It will be day after to-morrow. Why do you call it the '*coup d'état?*' Oh! it will be very fine; all my best of everything—crystal, silver and gold, Sèvres, flowers, music, and champagne to swim in. I'll let Léonce pay the bills. I wonder what he'll say when he sees the bills."

"And you ask me why I call it a *coup d'état?*" Arobin had put on his coat, and he stood before her and asked if his cravat[83] was plumb. She told him it was, looking no higher than the tip of his collar.

"When do you go to the 'pigeon house?'—with all due acknowledgment to Ellen."

"Day after to-morrow, after the dinner. I shall sleep there."

"Ellen, will you very kindly get me a glass of water?" asked Arobin. "The dust in the curtains, if you will pardon me for hinting such a thing, has parched my throat to a crisp."

"While Ellen gets the water," said Edna, rising, "I will say good-by and let you go. I must get rid of this grime, and I have a million things to do and think of."

"When shall I see you?" asked Arobin, seeking to detain her, the maid having left the room.

"At the dinner, of course. You are invited."

"Not before?—not to-night or to-morrow morning or to-morrow noon or night? or the day after morning or noon? Can't you see yourself, without my telling you, what an eternity it is?"

He had followed her into the hall and to the foot of the stairway, looking up at her as she mounted with her face half turned to him.

"Not an instant sooner," she said. But she laughed and looked at him with eyes that at once gave him courage to wait and made it torture to wait.

XXX

Though Edna had spoken of the dinner as a very grand affair, it was in truth a very small affair and very select, in so much as the guests invited were few and were selected with discrimination. She had counted upon an even dozen seating themselves at her round mahogany board, forgetting for the moment that Madame Ratignolle was to the last degree *souffrante*[84] and unpresentable, and not foreseeing that

[82]French: stool.
[83]A necktie or scarf
[84]French: ill.

Madame Lebrun would send a thousand regrets at the last moment. So there were only ten, after all, which made a cozy, comfortable number.

There were Mr. and Mrs. Merriman, a pretty, vivacious little woman in the thirties; her husband, a jovial fellow, something of a shallow pate,[85] who laughed a good deal at other people's witticisms, and had thereby made himself extremely popular. Mrs. Highcamp had accompanied them. Of course, there was Alcée Arobin; and Mademoiselle Reisz had consented to come. Edna had sent her a fresh bunch of violets with black lace trimmings for her hair. Monsieur Ratignolle brought himself and his wife's excuses. Victor Lebrun, who happened to be in the city, bent upon relaxation, had accepted with alacrity. There was a Miss Mayblunt, no longer in her teens, who looked at the world through lorgnettes[86] and with the keenest interest. It was thought and said that she was intellectual; it was suspected of her that she wrote under a *nom de guerre.*[87] She had come with a gentleman by the name of Gouvernail, connected with one of the daily papers, of whom nothing special could be said, except that he was observant and seemed quiet and inoffensive. Edna herself made the tenth, and at half-past eight they seated themselves at table, Arobin and Monsieur Ratignolle on either side of their hostess.

Mrs. Highcamp sat between Arobin and Victor Lebrun. Then came Mrs. Merriman, Mr. Gouvernail, Miss Mayblunt, Mr. Merriman, and Mademoiselle Reisz next to Monsieur Ratignolle.

There was something extremely gorgeous about the appearance of the table, an effect of splendor conveyed by a cover of pale yellow satin under strips of lace-work. There were wax candles in massive brass candelabra, burning softly under yellow silk shades; full, fragrant roses, yellow and red, abounded. There were silver and gold, as she had said there would be, and crystal which glittered like the gems which the women wore.

The ordinary stiff dining chairs had been discarded for the occasion and replaced by the most commodious and luxurious which could be collected throughout the house. Mademoiselle Reisz, being exceedingly diminutive, was elevated upon cushions, as small children are sometimes hoisted at table upon bulky volumes.

"'Something new, Edna?" exclaimed Miss Mayblunt, with lorgnette directed toward a magnificent cluster of diamonds that sparkled, that almost sputtered, in Edna's hair, just over the center of her forehead.

"Quite new; 'brand' new, in fact; a present from my husband. It arrived this morning from New York. I may as well admit that this is my birthday, and that I am twenty-nine. In good time I expect you to drink my health. Meanwhile, I shall ask you to begin with this cocktail, composed—would you say 'composed?'" with an appeal to Miss Mayblunt—"composed by my father in honor of Sister Janet's wedding."

Before each guest stood a tiny glass that looked and sparkled like a garnet gem.

"Then, all things considered," spoke Arobin, "it might not be amiss to start out by drinking the Colonel's health in the cocktail which he composed, on the birthday of the most charming of women—the daughter whom he invented."

[85]A clown.
[86]Eyeglasses attached to a handle.
[87]French: pseudonym.

Mr. Merriman's laugh at this sally was such a genuine outburst and so contagious that it started the dinner with an agreeable swing that never slackened.

Miss Mayblunt begged to be allowed to keep her cocktail untouched before her, just to look at. The color was marvelous! She could compare it to nothing she had ever seen, and the garnet lights which it emitted were unspeakably rare. She pronounced the Colonel an artist, and stuck to it.

Monsieur Ratignolle was prepared to take things seriously; the *mets,* the *entremets,*[88] the service, the decorations, even the people. He looked up from his pompono and inquired of Arobin if he were related to the gentleman of that name who formed one of the firm of Laitner and Arobin, lawyers. The young man admitted that Laitner was a warm personal friend, who permitted Arobin's name to decorate the firm's letterheads and to appear upon a shingle that graced Perdido Street.

"There are so many inquisitive people and institutions abounding," said Arobin, "that one is really forced as a matter of convenience these days to assume the virtue of an occupation if he has it not."

Monsieur Ratignolle stared a little, and turned to ask Mademoiselle Reisz if she considered the symphony concerts up to the standard which had been set the previous winter. Mademoiselle Reisz answered Monsieur Ratignolle in French, which Edna thought a little rude, under the circumstances, but characteristic. Mademoiselle had only disagreeable things to say of the symphony concerts, and insulting remarks to make of all the musicians of New Orleans, singly and collectively. All her interest seemed to be centered upon the delicacies placed before her.

Mr. Merriman said that Mr. Arobin's remark about inquisitive people reminded him of a man from Waco[89] the other day at the St. Charles Hotel—but as Mr. Merriman's stories were always lame and lacking point, his wife seldom permitted him to complete them. She interrupted him to ask if he remembered the name of the author whose book she had bought the week before to send to a friend in Geneva. She was talking "books" with Mr. Gouvernail and trying to draw from him his opinion upon current literary topics. Her husband told the story of the Waco man privately to Miss Mayblunt, who pretended to be greatly amused and to think it extremely clever.

Mrs. Highcamp hung with languid but unaffected interest upon the warm and impetuous volubility of her left-hand neighbor, Victor Lebrun. Her attention was never for a moment withdrawn from him after seating herself at table; and when he turned to Mrs. Merriman, who was prettier and more vivacious than Mrs. Highcamp, she waited with easy indifference for an opportunity to reclaim his attention. There was the occasional sound of music, of mandolins, sufficiently removed to be an agreeable accompaniment rather than an interruption to the conversation. Outside the soft, monotonous splash of a fountain could be heard; the sound penetrated into the room with the heavy odor of jessamine that came through the open windows.

The golden shimmer of Edna's satin gown spread in rich folds on either side of her. There was a soft fall of lace encircling her shoulders. It was the color of her skin, without the glow, the myriad living tints that one may sometimes discover in vibrant flesh. There was something in her attitude, in her whole appearance when she leaned

[88]French: the main and side dishes.
[89]Waco, Texas.

her head against the high-backed chair and spread her arms, which suggested the regal woman, the one who rules, who looks on, who stands alone.

But as she sat there amid her guests, she felt the old ennui overtaking her; the hopelessness which so often assailed her, which came upon her like an obsession, like something extraneous, independent of volition. It was something which announced itself; a chill breath that seemed to issue from some vast cavern wherein discords wailed. There came over her the acute longing which always summoned into her spiritual vision the presence of the beloved one, overpowering her at once with a sense of the unattainable.

The moments glided on, while a feeling of good fellowship passed around the circle like a mystic cord, holding and binding these people together with jest and laughter. Monsieur Ratignolle was the first to break the pleasant charm. At ten o'clock he excused himself. Madame Ratignolle was waiting for him at home. She was *bien souffrante*[90] and she was filled with vague dread, which only her husband's presence could allay.

Mademoiselle Reisz arose with Monsieur Ratignolle, who offered to escort her to the car. She had eaten well; she had tasted the good, rich wines, and they must have turned her head, for she bowed pleasantly to all as she withdrew from table. She kissed Edna upon the shoulder, and whispered: "*Bonne nuit, ma reine; soyez sage.*"[91] She had been a little bewildered upon rising, or rather, descending from her cushions, and Monsieur Ratignolle gallantly took her arm and led her away.

Mrs. Highcamp was weaving a garland of roses, yellow and red. When she had finished the garland, she laid it lightly upon Victor's black curls. He was reclining far back in the luxurious chair, holding a glass of champagne to the light.

As if a magician's wand had touched him, the garland of roses transformed him into a vision of Oriental beauty. His cheeks were the color of crushed grapes, and his dusky eyes glowed with a languishing fire.

"*Sapristi!*" exclaimed Arobin.

But Mrs. Highcamp had one more touch to add to the picture. She took from the back of her chair a white silken scarf, with which she had covered her shoulders in the early part of the evening. She draped it across the boy in graceful folds, and in a way to conceal his black, conventional evening dress. He did not seem to mind what she did to him, only smiled, showing a faint gleam of white teeth, while he continued to gaze with narrowing eyes at the light through his glass of champagne.

"Oh! to be able to paint in color rather than in words!" exclaimed Miss Mayblunt, losing herself in a rhapsodic dream as she looked at him.

> "'There was a graven image of Desire
> Painted with red blood on a ground of gold.'"[92]

murmured Gouvernail, under his breath.

The effect of the wine upon Victor was, to change his accustomed volubility into silence. He seemed to have abandoned himself to a reverie, and to be seeing pleasing visions in the amber bead.

[90]French: very ill.
[91]French: "Good night, my love; be good."
[92]An excerpt from the sonnet "A Cameo," by A. C. Swinburne (1837–1909).

"Sing," entreated Mrs. Highcamp. "Won't you sing to us?"

"Let him alone," said Arobin.

"He's posing," offered Mr. Merriman; "let him have it out."

"I believe he's paralyzed," laughed Mrs. Merriman. And leaning over the youth's chair, she took the glass from his hand and held it to his lips. He sipped the wine slowly, and when he had drained the glass she laid it upon the table and wiped his lips with her little filmy handkerchief.

"Yes, I'll sing for you," he said, turning in his chair toward Mrs. Highcamp. He clasped his hands behind his head, and looking up at the ceiling began to hum a little, trying his voice like a musician tuning an instrument. Then, looking at Edna, he began to sing:

"Ah! si tu savais!"

"Stop!" she cried, "don't sing that. I don't want you to sing it," and she laid her glass so impetuously and blindly upon the table as to shatter it against a caraffe. The wine spilled over Arobin's legs and some of it trickled down upon Mrs. Highcamp's black gauze gown. Victor had lost all idea of courtesy, or else he thought his hostess was not in earnest, for he laughed and went on:

"Ah! si tu savais
Ce que tes yeux me disent"—

"Oh! you mustn't! you mustn't," exclaimed Edna, and pushing back her chair she got up, and going behind him placed her hand over his mouth. He kissed the soft palm that pressed upon his lips.

"No, no, I won't, Mrs. Pontellier. I didn't know you meant it," looking up at her with caressing eyes. The touch of his lips was like a pleasing sting to her hand. She lifted the garland of roses from his head and flung it across the room.

"Come, Victor; you've posed long enough. Give Mrs. Highcamp her scarf."

Mrs. Highcamp undraped the scarf from about him with her own hands. Miss Mayblunt and Mr. Gouvernail suddenly conceived the notion that it was time to say good night. And Mr. and Mrs. Merriman wondered how it could be so late.

Before parting from Victor, Mrs. Highcamp invited him to call upon her daughter, who she knew would be charmed to meet him and talk French and sing French songs with him. Victor expressed his desire and intention to call upon Miss Highcamp at the first opportunity which presented itself. He asked if Arobin were going his way. Arobin was not.

The mandolin players had long since stolen away. A profound stillness had fallen upon the broad, beautiful street. The voices of Edna's disbanding guests jarred like a discordant note upon the quiet harmony of the night.

XXXI

"Well?" questioned Arobin, who had remained with Edna after the others had departed.

"Well," she reiterated, and stood up, stretching her arms, and feeling the need to relax her muscles after having been so long seated.

"What next?" he asked.

"The servants are all gone. They left when the musicians did. I have dismissed them. The house has to be closed and locked, and I shall trot around to the pigeon house, and shall send Celestine over in the morning to straighten things up."

He looked around, and began to turn out some of the lights.

"What about upstairs?" he inquired.

"I think it is all right; but there may be a window or two unlatched. We had better look; you might take a candle and see. And bring me my wrap and hat on the foot of the bed in the middle room."

He went up with the light, and Edna began closing doors and windows. She hated to shut in the smoke and the fumes of the wine. Arobin found her cape and hat, which he brought down and helped her to put on.

When everything was secured and the lights put out, they left through the front door, Arobin locking it and taking the key, which he carried for Edna. He helped her down the steps.

"Will you have a spray of jessamine?" he asked, breaking off a few blossoms as he passed.

"No; I don't want anything."

She seemed disheartened, and had nothing to say. She took his arm, which he offered her, holding up the weight of her satin train with the other hand. She looked down, noticing the black line of his leg moving in and out so close to her against the yellow shimmer of her gown. There was the whistle of a railway train somewhere in the distance, and the midnight bells were ringing. They met no one in their short walk.

The "pigeon-house" stood behind a locked gate, and a shallow *parterre*[93] that had been somewhat neglected. There was a small front porch, upon which a long window and the front door opened. The door opened directly into the parlor; there was no side entry. Back in the yard was a room for servants, in which old Celestine had been ensconced.

Edna had left a lamp burning low upon the table. She had succeeded in making the room look habitable and homelike. There were some books on the table and a lounge near at hand. On the floor was a fresh matting, covered with a rug or two; and on the walls hung a few tasteful pictures. But the room was filled with flowers. These were a surprise to her. Arobin had sent them, and had had Celestine distribute them during Edna's absence. Her bedroom was adjoining, and across a small passage were the dining-room and kitchen.

Edna seated herself with every appearance of discomfort.

"Are you tired?" he asked.

"Yes, and chilled, and miserable. I feel as if I had been wound up to a certain pitch—too tight—and something inside of me had snapped." She rested her head against the table upon her bare arm.

"You want to rest," he said, "and to be quiet. I'll go; I'll leave you and let you rest."

"Yes," she replied.

[93]French: garden.

He stood up beside her and smoothed her hair with his soft, magnetic hand. His touch conveyed to her a certain physical comfort. She could have fallen quietly asleep there if he had continued to pass his hand over her hair. He brushed the hair upward from the nape of her neck.

"I hope you will feel better and happier in the morning," he said. "You have tried to do too much in the past few days. The dinner was the last straw; you might have dispensed with it."

"Yes," she admitted; "it was stupid."

"No, it was delightful; but it has worn you out." His hand had strayed to her beautiful shoulders, and he could feel the response of her flesh to his touch. He seated himself beside her and kissed her lightly upon the shoulder.

"I thought you were going away," she said, in an uneven voice.

"I am, after I have said good night."

"Good night," she murmured.

He did not answer, except to continue to caress her. He did not say good night until she had become supple to his gentle, seductive entreaties.

XXXII

When Mr. Pontellier learned of his wife's intention to abandon her home and take up her residence elsewhere, he immediately wrote her a letter of unqualified disapproval and remonstrance. She had given reasons which he was unwilling to acknowledge as adequate. He hoped she had not acted upon her rash impulse; and he begged her to consider first, foremost, and above all else, what people would say. He was not dreaming of scandal when he uttered this warning; that was a thing which would never have entered into his mind to consider in connection with his wife's name or his own. He was simply thinking of his financial integrity. It might get noised about that the Pontelliers had met with reverses, and were forced to conduct their *ménage*[94] on a humbler scale than heretofore. It might do incalculable mischief to his business prospects.

But remembering Edna's whimsical turn of mind of late, and foreseeing that she had immediately acted upon her impetuous determination, he grasped the situation with his usual promptness and handled it with his well-known business tact and cleverness.

The same mail which brought to Edna his letter of disapproval carried instructions—the most minute instructions—to a well-known architect concerning the remodeling of his home, changes which he had long contemplated, and which he desired carried forward during his temporary absence.

Expert and reliable packers and movers were engaged to convey the furniture, carpets, pictures—everything movable, in short—to places of security. And in an incredibly short time the Pontellier house was turned over to the artisans. There was to be an addition—a small snuggery;[95] there was to be frescoing, and hardwood flooring was to be put into such rooms as had not yet been subjected to this improvement.

[94]French: household.
[95]A small, comfortable room.

Furthermore, in one of the daily papers appeared a brief notice to the effect that Mr. and Mrs. Pontellier were contemplating a summer sojourn abroad, and that their handsome residence on Esplanade Street was undergoing sumptuous alterations, and would not be ready for occupancy until their return. Mr. Pontellier had saved appearances!

Edna admired the skill of his maneuver, and avoided any occasion to balk his intentions. When the situation as set forth by Mr. Pontellier was accepted and taken for granted, she was apparently satisfied that it should be so.

The pigeon-house pleased her. It at once assumed the intimate character of a home, while she herself invested it with a charm which it reflected like a warm glow. There was with her a feeling of having descended in the social scale, with a corresponding sense of having risen in the spiritual. Every step which she took toward relieving herself from obligations added to her strength and expansion as an individual. She began to look with her own eyes; to see and to apprehend the deeper undercurrents of life. No longer was she content to "feed upon opinion" when her own soul had invited her.

After a little while, a few days, in fact, Edna went up and spent a week with her children in Iberville. They were delicious February days, with all the summer's promise hovering in the air.

How glad she was to see the children! She wept for very pleasure when she felt their little arms clasping her; their hard, ruddy cheeks pressed against her own glowing cheeks. She looked into their faces with hungry eyes that could not be satisfied with looking. And what stories they had to tell their mother! About the pigs, the cows, the mules! About riding to the mill behind Gluglu; fishing back in the lake with their Uncle Jasper; picking pecans with Lidie's little black brood, and hauling chips in their express wagon. It was a thousand times more fun to haul real chips for old lame Susie's real fire than to drag painted blocks along the banquette on Esplanade Street!

She went with them herself to see the pigs and the cows, to look at the darkies laying the cane, to thrash the pecan trees, and catch fish in the back lake. She lived with them a whole week long, giving them all of herself, and gathering and filling herself with their young existence. They listened, breathless, when she told them the house in Esplanade Street was crowded with workmen, hammering, nailing, sawing, and filling the place with clatter. They wanted to know where their bed was; what had been done with their rocking-horse; and where did Joe sleep, and where had Ellen gone, and the cook? But, above all, they were fired with a desire to see the little house around the block. Was there any place to play? Were there any boys next door? Raoul, with pessimistic foreboding, was convinced that there were only girls next door. Where would they sleep, and where would papa sleep? She told them the fairies would fix it all right.

The old Madame was charmed with Edna's visit, and showered all manner of delicate attentions upon her. She was delighted to know that the Esplanade Street house was in a dismantled condition. It gave her the promise and pretext to keep the children indefinitely.

It was with a wrench and a pang that Edna left her children. She carried away with her the sound of their voices and the touch of their checks. All along the journey homeward their presence lingered with her like the memory of a delicious song.

But by the time she had regained the city the song no longer echoed in her soul. She was again alone.

XXXIII

It happened sometimes when Edna went to see Mademoiselle Reisz that the little musician was absent, giving a lesson or making some small necessary household purchase. The key was always left in a secret hiding-place in the entry, which Edna knew. If Mademoiselle happened to be away, Edna would usually enter and wait for her return.

When she knocked at Mademoiselle Reisz's door one afternoon there was no response; so unlocking the door, as usual, she entered and found the apartment deserted, as she had expected. Her day had been quite filled up, and it was for a rest, for a refuge, and to talk about Robert, that she sought out her friend.

She had worked at her canvas—a young Italian character study—all the morning, completing the work without the model; but there had been many interruptions, some incident to her modest housekeeping, and others of a social nature.

Madame Ratignolle had dragged herself over, avoiding the too public thoroughfares, she said. She complained that Edna had neglected her much of late. Besides, she was consumed with curiosity to see the little house and the manner in which it was conducted. She wanted to hear all about the dinner party; Monsieur Ratignolle had left so early. What had happened after he left? The champagne and grapes which Edna sent over were *too* delicious. She had so little appetite; they had refreshed and toned her stomach. Where on earth was she going to put Mr. Pontellier in that little house, and the boys? And then she made Edna promise to go to her when her hour of trial overtook her.

"At any time—any time of the day or night, dear," Edna assured her.

Before leaving Madame Ratignolle said:

"In some way you seem to me like a child, Edna. You seem to act without a certain amount of reflection which is necessary in this life. That is the reason I want to say you mustn't mind if I advise you to be a little careful while you are living here alone. Why don't you have some one come and stay with you? Wouldn't Mademoiselle Reisz come?"

"No; she wouldn't wish to come, and I shouldn't want her always with me."

"Well, the reason—you know how evil-minded the world is—some one was talking of Alcée Arobin visiting you. Of course, it wouldn't matter if Mr. Arobin had not such a dreadful reputation. Monsieur Ratignolle was telling me that his attentions alone are considered enough to ruin a woman's name."

"Does he boast of his successes?" asked Edna, indifferently, squinting at her picture.

"No, I think not. I believe he is a decent fellow as far as that goes. But his character is so well known among the men. I shan't be able to come back and see you; it was very, very imprudent today."

"Mind the step!" cried Edna.

"Don't neglect me," entreated Madame Ratignolle; "and don't mind what I said about Arobin, or having some one to stay with you."

"Of course not," Edna laughed. "You may say anything you like to me." They kissed each other good-bye. Madame Ratignolle had not far to go, and Edna stood on the porch a while watching her walk down the street.

Then in the afternoon Mrs. Merriman and Mrs. Highcamp had made their "party call." Edna felt that they might have dispensed with the formality. They had also come to invite her to play *vingt-et-un*[96] one evening at Mrs. Merriman's. She was asked to go early, to dinner, and Mr. Merriman or Mr. Arobin would take her home. Edna accepted in a half-hearted way. She sometimes felt very tired of Mrs. Highcamp and Mrs. Merriman.

Late in the afternoon she sought refuge with Mademoiselle Reisz, and stayed there alone, waiting for her, feeling a kind of repose invade her with the very atmosphere of the shabby, unpretentious little room.

Edna sat at the window, which looked out over the house-tops and across the river. The window frame was filled with pots of flowers, and she sat and picked the dry leaves from a rose geranium. The day was warm, and the breeze which blew from the river was very pleasant. She removed her hat and laid it on the piano. She went on picking the leaves and digging around the plants with her hat pin. Once she thought she heard Mademoiselle Reisz approaching. But it was a young black girl, who came in, bringing a small bundle of laundry, which she deposited in the adjoining room, and went away.

Edna seated herself at the piano, and softly picked out with one hand the bars of a piece of music which lay open before her. A half-hour went by. There was the occasional sound of people going and coming in the lower hall. She was growing interested in her occupation of picking out the aria, when there was a second rap at the door. She vaguely wondered what these people did when they found Mademoiselle's door locked.

"Come in," she called, turning her face toward the door. And this time it was Robert Lebrun who presented himself. She attempted to rise; she could not have done so without betraying the agitation which mastered her at sight of him, so she fell back upon the stool, only exclaiming, "Why, Robert!"

He came and clasped her hand, seemingly without knowing what he was saying or doing.

"Mrs. Pontellier! How do you happen—oh! how well you look! Is Mademoiselle Reisz not here? I never expected to see you."

"When did you come back?" asked Edna in an unsteady voice, wiping her face with her handkerchief. She seemed ill at ease on the piano stool, and he begged her to take the chair by the window. She did so, mechanically, while he seated himself on the stool.

"I returned day before yesterday," he answered, while he leaned his arm on the keys, bringing forth a crash of discordant sound.

"Day before yesterday!" she repeated, aloud; and went on thinking to herself, "day before yesterday," in a sort of an uncomprehending way. She had pictured him seeking her at the very first hour, and he had lived under the same sky since day be-

[96]French: twenty-one, a card game.

fore yesterday; while only by accident had he stumbled upon her. Mademoiselle must have lied when she said, "Poor fool, he loves you."

"Day before yesterday," she repeated, breaking off a spray of Mademoiselle's geranium; "then if you had not met me here to-day you wouldn't—when—that is, didn't you mean to come and see me?"

"Of course, I should have gone to see you. There have been so many things—" he turned the leaves of Mademoiselle's music nervously. "I started in at once yesterday with the old firm. After all there is as much chance for me here as there was there—that is, I might find it profitable some day. The Mexicans were not very congenial."

So he had come back because the Mexicans were not congenial; because business was as profitable here as there; because of any reason, and not because he cared to be near her. She remembered the day she sat on the floor, turning the pages of his letter, seeking the reason which was left untold.

She had not noticed how he looked—only feeling his presence; but she turned deliberately and observed him. After all, he had been absent but a few months, and was not changed. His hair—the color of hers—waved back from his temples in the same way as before. His skin was not more burned than it had been at Grand Isle. She found in his eyes, when he looked at her for one silent moment, the same tender caress, with an added warmth and entreaty which had not been there before—the same glance which had penetrated to the sleeping places of her soul and awakened them.

A hundred times Edna had pictured Robert's return, and imagined their first meeting. It was usually at her home, whither he had sought her out at once. She always fancied him expressing or betraying in some way his love for her. And here, the reality was that they sat ten feet apart, she at the window, crushing geranium leaves in her hand and smelling them, he twirling around on the piano stool, saying:

"I was very much surprised to hear of Mr. Pontellier's absence; it's a wonder Mademoiselle Reisz did not tell me; and your moving—mother told me yesterday. I should think you would have gone to New York with him, or to Iberville with the children, rather than be bothered here with housekeeping. And you are going abroad, too, I hear. We shan't have you at Grand Isle next summer, it won't seem—do you see much of Mademoiselle Reisz? She often spoke of you in the few letters she wrote."

"Do you remember that you promised to write to me when you went away?" A flush overspread his whole face.

"I couldn't believe that my letters would be of any interest to you."

"That is an excuse; it isn't the truth." Edna reached for her hat on the piano. She adjusted it, sticking the hat pin through the heavy coil of hair with some deliberation.

"Are you not going to wait for Mademoiselle Reisz?" asked Robert.

"No; I have found when she is absent this long, she is liable not to come back till late." She drew on her gloves, and Robert picked up his hat.

"Won't you wait for her?" asked Edna.

"Not if you think she will not be back till late," adding, as if suddenly aware of some discourtesy in his speech, "and I should miss the pleasure of walking home with you." Edna locked the door and put the key back in its hiding-place.

They went together, picking their way across muddy streets and sidewalks encumbered with the cheap display of small tradesmen. Part of the distance they rode in the car, and after disembarking, passed the Pontellier mansion, which looked broken and half torn asunder. Robert had never known the house, and looked at it with interest.

"I never knew you in your home," he remarked.

"I am glad you did not."

"Why?" She did not answer. They went on around the corner, and it seemed as if her dreams were coming true after all, when he followed her into the little house.

"You must stay and dine with me, Robert. You see I am all alone, and it is so long since I have seen you. There is so much I want to ask you."

She took off her hat and gloves. He stood irresolute, making some excuse about his mother who expected him; he even muttered something about an engagement. She struck a match and lit the lamp on the table; it was growing dusk. When he saw her face in the lamplight, looking pained, with all the soft lines gone out of it, he threw his hat aside and seated himself.

"Oh! you know I want to stay if you will let me!" he exclaimed. All the softness came back. She laughed, and went and put her hand on his shoulder.

"This is the first moment you have seemed like the old Robert. I'll go tell Celestine." She hurried away to tell Celestine to set an extra place. She even sent her off in search of some added delicacy which she had not thought of for herself. And she recommended great care in dripping the coffee and having the omelet done to a proper turn.

When she reëntered, Robert was turning over magazines, sketches, and things that lay upon the table in great disorder. He picked up a photograph, and exclaimed: "Alcée Arobin! What on earth is his picture doing here?"

"I tried to make a sketch of his head one day," answered Edna, "and he thought the photograph might help me. It was at the other house. I thought it had been left there. I must have packed it up with my drawing materials."

"I should think you would give it back to him if you have finished with it."

"Oh! I have a great many such photographs. I never think of returning them. They don't amount to anything." Robert kept on looking at the picture.

"It seems to me—do you think his head worth drawing? Is he a friend of Mr. Pontellier's? You never said you knew him."

"He isn't a friend of Mr. Pontellier's; he's a friend of mine. I always knew him—that is, it is only of late that I know him pretty well. But I'd rather talk about you, and know what you have been seeing and doing and feeling out there in Mexico." Robert threw aside the picture.

"I've been seeing the waves and the white beach of Grand Isle; the quiet, grassy street of the *Chênière;* the old fort at Grande Terre. I've been working like a machine, and feeling like a lost soul. There was nothing interesting."

She leaned her head upon her hand to shade her eyes from the light.

"And what have you been seeing and doing and feeling all these days?" he asked.

"I've been seeing the waves and the white beach of Grand Isle; the quiet, grassy street of the *Chênière Caminada;* the old sunny fort at Grande Terre. I've been working with little more comprehension than a machine, and still feeling like a lost soul. There was nothing interesting."

"Mrs. Pontellier, you are cruel," he said, with feeling, closing his eyes and resting his head back in his chair. They remained in silence till old Celestine announced dinner.

XXXIV

The dining-room was very small. Edna's round mahogany would have almost filled it. As it was there was but a step or two from the little table to the kitchen, to the mantel, the small buffet, and the side door that opened out on the narrow brick-paved yard.

A certain degree of ceremony settled upon them with the announcement of dinner. There was no return to personalities. Robert related incidents of his sojourn in Mexico, and Edna talked of events likely to interest him, which had occurred during his absence. The dinner was of ordinary quality, except for the few delicacies which she had sent out to purchase. Old Celestine, with a bandana *tignon*[97] twisted about her head, hobbled in and out, taking a personal interest in everything; and she lingered occasionally to talk patois[98] with Robert, whom she had known as a boy.

He went out to a neighboring cigar stand to purchase cigarette papers, and when he came back he found that Celestine had served the black coffee in the parlor.

"Perhaps I shouldn't have come back," he said, "When you are tired of me, tell me to go."

"You never tire me. You must have forgotten the hours and hours at Grand Isle in which we grew accustomed to each other and used to being together."

"I have forgotten nothing at Grand Isle," he said, not looking at her, but rolling a cigarette. His tobacco pouch, which he laid upon the table, was a fantastic embroidered silk affair, evidently the handiwork of a woman.

"You used to carry your tobacco in a rubber pouch," said Edna, picking up the pouch and examining the needlework.

"Yes; it was lost."

"Where did you buy this one? In Mexico?"

"It was given to me by a Vera Cruz girl; they are very generous," he replied, striking a match and lighting his cigarette.

"They are very handsome, I suppose, those Mexican women; very picturesque, with their black eyes and their lace scarfs."

"Some are; others are hideous. Just as you find women everywhere."

"What was she like—the one who gave you the pouch? You must have known her very well."

"She was very ordinary. She wasn't of the slightest importance. I knew her well enough."

"Did you visit at her house? Was it interesting? I should like to know and hear about the people you met, and the impressions they made on you."

"There are some people who leave impressions not so lasting as the imprint of an oar upon the water."

97 A hair "bun."

98 A provincial or local dialect that blends several languages; in this case, a dialect spoken by Acadian descendents that combines French, English, Spanish, German, and Native American words and phrases.

"Was she such a one?"

"It would be ungenerous for me to admit that she was of that order and kind." He thrust the pouch back in his pocket, as if to put away the subject with the trifle which had brought it up.

Arobin dropped in with a message from Mrs. Merriman, to say that the card party was postponed on account of the illness of one of her children.

"How do you do, Arobin?" said Robert, rising from the obscurity

"Oh! Lebrun. To be sure! I heard yesterday you were back. How did they treat you down in Mexique?"

"Fairly well."

"But not well enough to keep you there. Stunning girls, though, in Mexico. I thought I should never get away from Vera Cruz when I was down there a couple of years ago."

"Did they embroider slippers and tobacco pouches and hat-bands and things for you?" asked Edna.

"Oh! my! no! I didn't get so deep in their regard. I fear they made more impression on me than I made on them."

"You, were less fortunate than Robert, then."

"I am always less fortunate than Robert. Has he been imparting tender confidences?"

"I've been imposing myself long enough," said Robert, rising, and shaking hands with Edna. "Please convey my regards to Mr. Pontellier when you write."

He shook hands with Arobin and went away.

"Fine fellow, that Lebrun," said Arobin when Robert had gone. "I never heard you speak of him."

"I knew him last summer at Grand Isle," she replied. "Here is that photograph of yours. Don't you want it?"

"What do I want with it? Throw it away." She threw it back on the table.

"I'm not going to Mrs. Merriman's," she said. "If you see her, tell her so. But perhaps I had better write. I think I shall write now, and say that I am sorry her child is sick, and tell her not to count on me."

"It would be a good scheme," acquiesced Arobin. "I don't blame you; stupid lot!"

Edna opened the blotter, and having procured paper and pen, began to write the note. Arobin lit a cigar and read the evening paper, which he had in his pocket.

"What is the date?" she asked. He told her.

"Will you mail this for me when you go out?"

"Certainly." He read to her little bits out of the newspaper, while she straightened things on the table.

"What do you want to do?" he asked, throwing aside the paper. "Do you want to go out for a walk or a drive or anything? It would be a fine night to drive."

"No; I don't want to do anything but just be quiet. You go away and amuse yourself. Don't stay."

"I'll go away if I must; but I shan't amuse myself. You know that I only live when I am near you."

He stood up to bid her good night.

"Is that one of the things you always say to women?"

"I have said it before, but I don't think I ever came so near meaning it," he answered with a smile. There were no warm lights in her eyes; only a dreamy, absent look.

"Good night. I adore you. Sleep well," he said, and he kissed her hand and went away.

She stayed alone in a kind of reverie—a sort of stupor. Step by step she lived over every instant of the time she had been with Robert after he had entered Mademoiselle Reisz's door. She recalled his words, his looks. How few and meager they had been for her hungry heart! A vision—a transcendently seductive vision of a Mexican girl arose before her. She writhed with a jealous pang. She wondered when he would come back. He had not said he would come back. She had been with him, had heard his voice and touched his hand. But some way he had seemed nearer to her off there in Mexico.

XXXV

The morning was full of sunlight and hope. Edna could see before her no denial—only the promise of excessive joy. She lay in bed awake, with bright eyes full of speculation. "He loves you, poor fool." If she could but get that conviction firmly fixed in her mind, what mattered about the rest? She felt she had been childish and unwise the night before in giving herself over to despondency. She recapitulated the motives which no doubt explained Robert's reserve. They were not insurmountable; they would not hold if he really loved her; they could not hold against her own passion, which he must come to realize in time. She pictured him going to his business that morning. She even saw how he was dressed; how he walked down one street, and turned the corner of another; saw him bending over his desk, talking to people who entered the office, going to his lunch, and perhaps watching for her on the street. He would come to her in the afternoon or evening, sit and roll his cigarette, talk a little, and go away as he had done the night before. But how delicious it would be to have him there with her! She would have no regrets, nor seek to penetrate his reserve if he still chose to wear it.

Edna ate her breakfast only half dressed. The maid brought her a delicious printed scrawl from Raoul, expressing his love, asking her to send him some bonbons, and telling her they had found that morning ten tiny white pigs all lying in a row beside Lidie's big white pig.

A letter also came from her husband, saying he hoped to be back early in March, and then they would get ready for that journey abroad which he had promised her so long, which he felt now fully able to afford; he felt able to travel as people should, without any thought of small economies—thanks to his recent speculations in Wall Street.

Much to her surprise she received a note from Arobin, written at midnight from the club. It was to say good morning to her, to hope that she had slept well, to assure her of his devotion, which he trusted she in some faintest manner returned.

All these letters were pleasing to her. She answered the children in a cheerful frame of mind, promising them bonbons, and congratulating them upon their happy find of the little pigs.

She answered her husband with friendly evasiveness,—not with any fixed design to mislead him, only because all sense of reality had gone out of her life; she had abandoned herself to Fate, and awaited the consequences with indifference.

To Arobin's note she made no reply. She put it under Celestine's stove-lid.

Edna worked several hours with much spirit. She saw no one but a picture dealer, who asked her if it were true that she was going abroad to study in Paris.

She said possibly she might, and he negotiated with her for some Parisian studies to reach him in time for the holiday trade in December.

Robert did not come that day. She was keenly disappointed. He did not come the following day, nor the next. Each morning she awoke with hope, and each night she was a prey to despondency. She was tempted to seek him out. But far from yielding to the impulse, she avoided any occasion which might throw her in his way. She did not go to Mademoiselle Reisz's nor pass by Madame Lebrun's, as she might have done if he had still been in Mexico.

When Arobin, one night, urged her to drive with him, she went—out to the lake, on the Shell Road. His horses were full of mettle, and even a little unmanageable. She liked the rapid gait at which they spun along, and the quick, sharp sound of the horses' hoofs on the hard road. They did not stop anywhere to eat or to drink. Arobin was not needlessly imprudent. But they ate and they drank when they regained Edna's little dining-room—which was comparatively early in the evening.

It was late when he left her. It was getting to be more than a passing whim with Arobin to see her and be with her. He had detected the latent sensuality, which unfolded under his delicate sense of her nature's requirements like a torpid, torrid, sensitive blossom.

There was no despondency when she fell asleep that night; nor was there hope when she awoke in the morning.

XXXVI

There was a garden out in the suburbs; a small, leafy corner, with a few green tables under the orange trees. An old cat slept all day on the stone step in the sun, and an old *mulatresse*[99] slept her idle hours away in her chair at the open window, till some one happened to knock on one of the green tables. She had milk and cream cheese to sell, and bread and butter. There was no one who could make such excellent coffee or fry a chicken so golden brown as she.

The place was too modest to attract the attention of people of fashion, and so quiet as to have escaped the notice of those in search of pleasure and dissipation. Edna had discovered it accidentally one day when the high-board gate stood ajar. She caught sight of a little green table, blotched with the checkered sunlight that filtered through the quivering leaves overhead. Within she had found the slumbering *mulatresse,* the drowsy cat, and a glass of milk which reminded her of the milk she had tasted in Iberville.

She often stopped there during her perambulations; sometimes taking a book

[99]Woman of mixed racial origin.

with her, and sitting an hour or two under the trees when she found the place deserted. Once or twice she took a quiet dinner there alone, having instructed Celestine beforehand to prepare no dinner at home. It was the last place in the city where she would have expected to meet any one she knew.

Still she was not astonished when, as she was partaking of a modest dinner late in the afternoon, looking into an open book, stroking the cat, which had made friends with her—she was not greatly astonished to see Robert come in at the tall garden gate.

"I am destined to see you only by accident," she said, shoving the cat off the chair beside her. He was surprised, ill at ease, almost embarrassed at meeting her thus so unexpectedly.

"Do you come here often?" he asked.

"I almost live here," she said.

"I used to drop in very often for a cup of Catiche's good coffee. This is the first time since I came back."

"She'll bring you a plate, and you will share my dinner. There's always enough for two—even three." Edna had intended to be indifferent and as reserved as he when she met him; she had reached the determination by a laborious train of reasoning, incident to one of her despondent moods. But her resolve melted when she saw him before her, seated there beside her in the little garden, as if a designing Providence had led him into her path.

"Why have you kept away from me, Robert?" she asked, closing the book that lay open upon the table.

"Why are you so personal, Mrs. Pontellier? Why do you force me to idiotic subterfuges?" he exclaimed with sudden warmth. "I suppose there's no use telling you I've been very busy, or that I've been sick, or that I've been to see you and not found you at home. Please let me off with any one of these excuses."

"You are the embodiment of selfishness," she said. "You save yourself something—I don't know what—but there is some selfish motive, and in sparing yourself you never consider for a moment what I think, or how I feel your neglect and indifference. I suppose this is what you would call unwomanly; but I have got into a habit of expressing myself. It doesn't matter to me, and you may think me unwomanly if you like."

"No; I only think you cruel, as I said the other day. Maybe not intentionally cruel; but you seem to be forcing me into disclosures which can result in nothing; as if you would have me bare a wound for the pleasure of looking at it, without the intention or power of healing it."

"I'm spoiling your dinner, Robert; never mind what I say. You haven't eaten a morsel."

"I only came in for a cup of coffee." His sensitive face was all disfigured with excitement.

"Isn't this a delightful place?" she remarked. "I am so glad it has never actually been discovered. It is so quiet, so sweet, here. Do you notice there is scarcely a sound to be heard? It's so out of the way; and a good walk from the car. However, I don't mind walking. I always feel so sorry for women who don't like to walk; they miss so much—so many rare little glimpses of life; and we women learn so little of life on the whole.

"Catiche's coffee is always hot. I don't know how she manages it, here in the open air. Celestine's coffee gets cold bringing it from the kitchen to the dining-room. Three lumps! How can you drink it so sweet? Take some of the cress with your chop; it's so biting and crisp. Then there's the advantage of being able to smoke with your coffee out here. Now, in the city—aren't you going to smoke?"

"After a while," he said, laying a cigar on the table.

"Who gave it to you?" she laughed.

"I bought it. I suppose I'm getting reckless; I bought a whole box." She was determined not to be personal again and make him uncomfortable.

The cat made friends with him, and climbed into his lap when he smoked his cigar. He stroked her silky fur, and talked a little about her. He looked at Edna's book, which he had read; and he told her the end, to save her the trouble of wading through it, he said.

Again he accompanied her back to her home; and it was after dusk when they reached the little "pigeon-house." She did not ask him to remain, which he was grateful for, as it permitted him to stay without the discomfort of blundering through an excuse which he had no intention of considering. He helped her to light the lamp; then she went into her room to take off her hat and to bathe her face and hands.

When she came back Robert was not examining the pictures and magazines as before; he sat off in the shadow, leaning his head back on the chair as if in a reverie. Edna lingered a moment beside the table, arranging the books there. Then she went across the room to where he sat. She bent over the arm of his chair and called his name.

"Robert," she said, "are you asleep?"

"No," he answered, looking up at her.

She leaned over and kissed him—a soft, cool, delicate kiss, whose voluptuous sting penetrated his whole being—then she moved away from him. He followed, and took her in his arms, just holding her close to him. She put her hand up to his face and pressed his cheek against her own. The action was full of love and tenderness. He sought her lips again. Then he drew her down upon the sofa beside him and held her hand in both of his.

"Now you know," he said, "now you know what I have been fighting against since last summer at Grand Isle; what drove me away and drove me back again."

"Why have you been fighting against it?" she asked. Her face glowed with soft lights.

"Why? Because you were not free; you were Léonce Pontellier's wife. I couldn't help loving you if you were ten times his wife; but so long as I went away from you and kept away I could help telling you so." She put her free hand up to his shoulder, and then against his cheek, rubbing it softly. He kissed her again. His face was warm and flushed.

"There in Mexico I was thinking of you all the time, and longing for you."

"But not writing to me," she interrupted.

"Something put into my head that you cared for me; and I lost my senses. I forgot everything but a wild dream of your some way becoming my wife."

"Your wife!"

"Religion, loyalty, everything would give way if only you cared."

"Then you must have forgotten that I was Léonce Pontellier's wife."

"Oh! I was demented, dreaming of wild, impossible things, recalling men who had set their wives free, we have heard of such things."

"Yes, we have heard of such things."

"I came back full of vague, mad intentions. And when I got here—"

"When you got here you never came near me!" She was still caressing his cheek.

"I realized what a cur I was to dream of such a thing, even if you had been willing."

She took his face between her hands and looked into it as if she would never withdraw her eyes more. She kissed him on the forehead, the eyes, the cheeks, and the lips.

"You have been a very, very foolish boy, wasting your time dreaming of impossible things when you speak of Mr. Pontellier setting me free! I am no longer one of Mr. Pontellier's possessions to dispose of or not. I give myself where I choose. If he were to say, 'Here, Robert, take her and be happy; she is yours,' I should laugh at you both."

His face grew a little white. "What do you mean?" he asked.

There was a knock at the door. Old Celestine came in to say that Madame Ratignolle's servant had come around the back way with a message that Madame had been taken sick and begged Mrs. Pontellier to go to her immediately.

"Yes, yes," said Edna, rising; "I promised. Tell her yes—to wait for me. I'll go back with her."

"Let me walk over with you," offered Robert.

"No," she said; "I will go with the servant." She went into her room to put on her hat, and when she came in again she sat once more upon the sofa beside him. He had not stirred. She put her arms about his neck.

"Good-by, my sweet Robert. Tell me good-by." He kissed her with a degree of passion which had not before entered into his caress, and strained her to him.

"I love you," she whispered, "only you; no one but you. It was you who awoke me last summer out of a life-long, stupid dream. Oh! you have made me so unhappy with your indifference. Oh! I have suffered, suffered! Now you are here we shall love each other, my Robert. We shall be everything to each other. Nothing else in the world is of any consequence. I must go to my friend; but you will wait for me? No matter how late; you will wait for me, Robert?"

"Don't go; don't go! Oh! Edna, stay with me," he pleaded. "Why should you go? Stay with me, stay with me."

"I shall come back as soon as I can; I shall find you here." She buried her face in his neck, and said good-by again. Her seductive voice, together with his great love for her, had enthralled his senses, had deprived him of every impulse but the longing to hold her and keep her.

XXXVII

Edna looked in at the drug store. Monsieur Ratignolle was putting up a mixture himself, very carefully, dropping a red liquid into a tiny glass. He was grateful to Edna for having come; her presence would be a comfort to his wife. Madame Ratignolle's sister, who had always been with her at such trying times, had not been able to come up from the plantation, and Adèle had been inconsolable until Mrs. Pontellier so kindly promised to come to her. The nurse had been with them at night for the past week, as she lived a great distance away. And Dr. Mandelet had been coming and going all the afternoon. They were then looking for him any moment.

Edna hastened upstairs by a private stairway that led from the rear of the store to the apartments above. The children were all sleeping in a back room. Madame Ratignolle was in the salon, whither she had strayed in her suffering impatience. She sat on the sofa, clad in an ample white *peignoir,* holding a handkerchief tight in her hand with a nervous clutch. Her face was drawn and pinched, her sweet blue eyes haggard and unnatural. All her beautiful hair had been drawn back and plaited. It lay in a long braid on the sofa pillow, coiled like a golden serpent. The nurse, a comfortable looking *Griffe*[100] woman in white apron and cap, was urging her to return to her bedroom.

"There is no use, there is no use," she said at once to Edna. "We must get rid of Mandelet; he is getting too old and careless. He said he would be here at half-past seven; now it must be eight. See what time it is, Joséphine."

The woman was possessed of a cheerful nature, and refused to take any situation too seriously, especially a situation with which she was so familiar. She urged Madame to have courage and patience. But Madame only set her teeth hard into her under lip, and Edna saw the sweat gather in beads on her white forehead. After a moment or two she uttered a profound sigh and wiped her face with the handkerchief rolled in a ball. She appeared exhausted. The nurse gave her a fresh handkerchief, sprinkled with cologne water.

"This is too much!" she cried. "Mandelet ought to be killed! Where is Alphonse? Is it possible I am to be abandoned like this—neglected by every one?"

"Neglected, indeed!" exclaimed the nurse. Wasn't she there? And here was Mrs. Pontellier leaving, no doubt, a pleasant evening at home to devote to her? And wasn't Monsieur Ratignolle coming that very instant through the hall? And Joséphine was quite sure she had heard Doctor Mandelet's coupé. Yes, there it was, down at the door.

Adèle consented to go back to her room. She sat on the edge of a little low couch next to her bed.

Doctor Mandelet paid no attention to Madame Ratignolle's upbraidings. He was accustomed to them at such times, and was too well convinced of her loyalty to doubt it.

He was glad to see Edna, and wanted her to go with him into the salon and entertain him. But Madame Ratignolle would not consent that Edna should leave her for an instant. Between agonizing moments, she chatted a little, and said it took her mind off her sufferings.

Edna began to feel uneasy. She was seized with a vague dread. Her own like experiences seemed far away, unreal, and only half remembered. She recalled faintly an ecstasy of pain, the heavy odor of chloroform, a stupor which had deadened sensation, and an awakening to find a little new life to which she had given being, added to the great unnumbered multitude of souls that come and go.

She began to wish she had not come; her presence was not necessary. She might

[100]Descendent of a mulatto and an African American or Native American.

have invented a pretext for staying away; she might even invent a pretext now for going. But Edna did not go. With an inward agony, with a flaming, outspoken revolt against the ways of Nature, she witnessed the scene [of] torture.

She was still stunned and speechless with emotion when later she leaned over her friend to kiss her and softly say good-by. Adèle, pressing her check, whispered in an exhausted voice: "Think of the children, Edna. Oh think of the children! Remember them!"

XXXVIII

Edna still felt dazed when she got outside in the open air. The Doctor's coupé had returned for him and stood before the *porte cochère*. She did not wish to enter the coupé, and told Doctor Mandelet she would walk; she was not afraid, and would go alone. He directed his carriage to meet him at Mrs. Pontellier's, and he started to walk home with her.

Up—away up, over the narrow street between the tall houses, the stars were blazing. The air was mild and caressing, but cool with the breath of spring and the night. They walked slowly, the Doctor with a heavy, measured tread and his hands behind him; Edna, in an absent-minded way, as she had walked one night at Grand Isle, as if her thoughts had gone ahead of her and she was striving to overtake them.

"You shouldn't have been there, Mrs. Pontellier," he said. "That was no place for you. Adèle is full of whims at such times. There were a dozen women she might have had with her, unimpressionable women. I felt that it was cruel, cruel. You shouldn't have gone."

"Oh, well!" she answered, indifferently. "I don't know that it matters after all. One has to think of the children some time or other; the sooner the better."

"When is Léonce coming back?"

"Quite soon. Some time in March."

"And you are going abroad?"

"Perhaps—no, I am not going. I'm not going to be forced into doing things. I don't want to go abroad. I want to be let alone. Nobody has any right—except children, perhaps—and even then, it seems to me—or it did seem—" She felt that her speech was voicing the incoherency of her thoughts, and stopped abruptly.

"The trouble is," sighed the Doctor, grasping her meaning intuitively, "that youth is given up to illusions. It seems to be a provision of Nature; a decoy to secure mothers for the race. And Nature takes no account of moral consequences, of arbitrary conditions which we create, and which we feel obliged to maintain at any cost."

"Yes," she said. "The years that are gone seem like dreams—if one might go on sleeping and dreaming—but to wake up and find—oh! well! perhaps it is better to wake up after all, even to suffer, rather than to remain a dupe to illusions all one's life."

"It seems to me, my dear child," said the Doctor at parting, holding her hand, "you seem to me to be in trouble. I am not going to ask for your confidence. I will only say that if ever you feel moved to give it to me, perhaps I might help you. I know I would understand, and I tell you there are not many who would—not many, my dear."

"Some way I don't feel moved to speak of things that trouble me. Don't think I am ungrateful or that I don't appreciate your sympathy. There are periods of despondency and suffering which take possession of me. But I don't want anything but my own way. That is wanting a good deal, of course, when you have to trample upon the lives, the hearts, the prejudices of others—but no matter—still, I shouldn't want to trample upon the little lives. Oh! I don't know what I'm saying, Doctor. Good night. Don't blame me for anything."

"Yes, I will blame you if you don't come and see me soon. We will talk of things you never have dreamt of talking about before. It will do us both good. I don't want you to blame yourself, whatever comes. Good night, my child."

She let herself in at the gate, but instead of entering she sat upon the step of the porch. The night was quiet and soothing. All the tearing emotion of the last few hours seemed to fall away from her like a somber, uncomfortable garment, which she had but to loosen to be rid of. She went back to that hour before Adèle had sent for her; and her senses kindled afresh in thinking of Robert's words, the pressure of his arms, and the feeling of his lips upon her own. She could picture at that moment no greater bliss on earth than possession of the beloved one. His expression of love had already given him to her in part. When she thought that he was there at hand, waiting for her, she grew numb with the intoxication of expectancy. It was so late; he would be asleep perhaps. She would awaken him with a kiss. She hoped he would be asleep that she might arouse him with her caresses.

Still, she remembered Adèle's voice whispering, "Think of the children; think of them." She meant to think of them; that determination had driven into her soul like a death wound—but not tonight. To-morrow would be time to think of everything.

Robert was not waiting for her in the little parlor. He was nowhere at hand. The house was empty. But he had scrawled on a piece of paper that lay in the lamplight: "I love you. Good-by—because I love you."

Edna grew faint when she read the words. She went and sat on the sofa. Then she stretched herself out there, never uttering a sound. She did not sleep. She did not go to bed. The lamp sputtered and went out. She was still awake in the morning, when Celestine unlocked the kitchen door and came in to light the fire.

XXXIX

Victor, with hammer and nails and scraps of scantling, was patching a corner of one of the galleries. Mariequita sat near by, dangling her legs, watching him work, and handing him nails from the tool-box. The sun was beating down upon them. The girl had covered her head with her apron folded into a square pad. They had been talking for an hour or more. She was never tired of hearing Victor describe the dinner at Mrs. Pontellier's. He exaggerated every detail, making it appear a veritable Lucillean[101] feast. The flowers were in tubs, he said. The champagne was quaffed[102] from huge golden goblets. Venus rising from the foam[103] could have presented no more entrancing a spectacle than Mrs. Pontellier, blazing with beauty and diamonds at the head of the board, while the other women were all of them youthful houris[104] possessed of incomparable charms.

[101]After the famously lavish banquets of Lucius Licinius Lucullus, a first-century Roman general.

[102]To drink deeply.

[103]The goddess of love and beauty, counterpart to the Greek Aphrodite.

[104]Nymphs.

She got it into her head that Victor was in love with Mrs. Pontellier, and he gave her evasive answers, framed so as to confirm her belief. She grew sullen and cried a little, threatening to go off and leave him to his fine ladies. There were a dozen men crazy about her at the *Chênière;* and since it was the fashion to be in love with married people, why, she could run away any time she liked to New Orleans with Célina's husband.

Célina's husband was a fool, a coward, and a pig, and to prove it to her, Victor intended to hammer his head into a jelly the next time he encountered him. This assurance was very consoling to Mariequita. She dried her eyes, and grew cheerful at the prospect.

They were still talking of the dinner and the allurements of city life when Mrs. Pontellier herself slipped around the corner of the house. The two youngsters stayed dumb with amazement before what they considered to be an apparition. But it was really she in flesh and blood, looking tired and a little travel-stained.

"I walked up from the wharf," she said, "and heard the hammering. I supposed it was you, mending the porch. It's a good thing. I was always tripping over those loose planks last summer. How dreary and deserted everything looks!"

It took Victor some little time to comprehend that she had come in Beaudelet's lugger, that she had come alone, and for no purpose but to rest.

"There's nothing fixed up yet, you see. I'll give you my room; it's the only place."

"Any corner will do," she assured him.

"And if you can stand Philomel's cooking," he went on, "though I might try to get her mother while you are here. Do you think she would come?" turning to Mariequita.

Mariequita thought that perhaps Philomel's mother might come for a few days, and money enough.

Beholding Mrs. Pontellier make her appearance, the girl had at once suspected a lovers' rendezvous. But Victor's astonishment was so genuine, and Mrs. Pontellier's indifference so apparent, that the disturbing notion did not lodge long in her brain. She contemplated with the greatest interest this woman who gave the most sumptuous dinners in America, and who had all the men in New Orleans at her feet.

"What time will you have dinner?" asked Edna. "I'm very hungry; but don't get anything extra."

"I'll have it ready in little or no time," he said, bustling and packing away his tools. "You may go to my room to brush up and rest yourself. Mariequita will show you."

"Thank you," said Edna. "But, do you know, I have a notion to go down to the beach and take a good wash and even a little swim, before dinner?"

"The water is too cold!" they both exclaimed. "Don't think of it."

"Well, I might go down and try—dip my toes in. Why, it seems to me the sun is hot enough to have warmed the very depths of the ocean. Could you get me a couple of towels? I'd better go right away, so as to be back in time. It would be a little too chilly if I waited till this afternoon."

Mariequita ran over to Victor's room, and returned with some towels, which she gave to Edna.

"I hope you have fish for dinner," said Edna, as she started to walk away; "but don't do anything extra if you haven't."

"Run and find Philomel's mother," Victor instructed the girl. "I'll go to the kitchen and see what I can do. By Gimminy! Women have no consideration! She might have sent me word."

Edna walked on down to the beach rather mechanically, not noticing anything special except that the sun was hot. She was not dwelling upon any particular train of thought. She had done all the thinking which was necessary after Robert went away, when she lay awake upon the sofa till morning.

She had said over and over to herself: "To-day it is Arobin; to-morrow it will be some one else. It makes no difference to me, it doesn't matter about Léonce Pontellier—but Raoul and Etienne!" She understood now clearly what she had meant long ago when she said to Adèle Ratignolle that she would give up the unessential, but she would never sacrifice herself for her children.

Despondency had come upon her there in the wakeful night, and had never lifted. There was no one thing in the world that she desired. There was no human being whom she wanted near her except Robert; and she even realized that the day would come when he, too, and the thought of him would melt out of her existence, leaving her alone. The children appeared before her like antagonists who had overcome her; who had overpowered and sought to drag her into the soul's slavery for the rest of her days. But she knew a way to elude them. She was not thinking of these things when she walked down to the beach.

The water of the Gulf stretched out before her, gleaming with the million lights of the sun. The voice of the sea is seductive, never ceasing, whispering, clamoring, murmuring, inviting the soul to wander in abysses of solitude. All along the white beach, up and down, there was no living thing in sight. A bird with a broken wing was beating the air above, reeling, fluttering, circling disabled down, down to the water.

Edna had found her old bathing suit still hanging, faded, upon its accustomed peg.

She put it on, leaving her clothing in the bath-house. But when she was there beside the sea, absolutely alone, she cast the unpleasant, pricking garments from her, and for the first time in her life she stood naked in the open air, at the mercy of the sun, the breeze that beat upon her, and the waves that invited her.

How strange and awful it seemed to stand naked under the sky! how delicious! She felt like some new-born creature, opening its eyes in a familiar world that it had never known.

The foamy wavelets curled up to her white feet, and coiled like serpents about her ankles. She walked out. The water was chill, but she walked on. The water was deep, but she lifted her white body and reached out with a long, sweeping stroke. The touch of the sea is sensuous, enfolding the body in its soft, close embrace.

She went on and on. She remembered the night she swam far out, and recalled the terror that seized her at the fear of being unable to regain the shore. She did not look back now, but went on and on, thinking of the blue-grass meadow that she had traversed when a little child, believing that it had no beginning and no end.

Her arms and legs were growing tired.

She thought of Léonce and the children. They were a part of her life. But they need not have thought that they could possess her, body and soul. How Mademoiselle Reisz would have laughed, perhaps sneered, if she knew! "And you call yourself an artist! What pretensions, Madame! The artist must possess the courageous soul that dares and defies."

Exhaustion was pressing upon and over-powering her.

"Good-by—because, I love you." He did not know; he did not understand. He would never understand. Perhaps Doctor Mandelet would have understood if she had seen him—but it was too late; the shore was far behind her, and her strength was gone.

She looked into the distance, and the old terror flamed up for an instant, then sank again. Edna heard her father's voice and her sister Margaret's. She heard the barking of an old dog that was chained to the sycamore tree. The spurs of the cavalry officer clanged as he walked across the porch. There was the hum of bees, and the musky odor of pinks filled the air.

1899

Ambrose Bierce 1842–1914(?)

Perhaps the most striking aspect of Ambrose Bierce's life is the mystery of his death. In 1913, when he was over seventy years of age, Bierce decided to tour Mexico in order to meet the revolutionary Pancho Villa, and understand firsthand the civil war in progress there. He realized he would probably never return from that war-torn country. His last letter was dated December 26, 1913. After that, his whereabouts are simply unknown, although the contemporary Mexican writer Carlos Fuentes insists that one still hears stories about "an old gringo" wandering the Mexican countryside. In spirit, Bierce certainly haunts the South American literary landscape: major writers such as Jorge Luis Borges, Julio Cortázar, and Fuentes have all been influenced and intrigued by his work and his life.

Bierce was tenth of the thirteen children of Laura Sherwood and Marcus Aurelius Bierce, poor farmers in southeastern Ohio who believed in the western dream of expansion. The family moved in 1846 to a farm outside of Warsaw, Indiana, but did not achieve prosperity there either. Bierce early evinced a keen literary imagination and a nonconformist temperament. While still in school, he worked on *The Northern Indianan,* an anti-slavery newspaper.

In 1861, at the age of eighteen, he enlisted in the Ninth Indiana Infantry. Bierce performed a number of notable acts of bravery during his war years, including carrying a wounded comrade off a battlefield. The soldier died, and Bierce had his first taste of ambivalent heroism. Similarly, occupying the staff position of topographical engineer, Bierce surveyed some of the most famous—and bloodiest—battles of the Civil War, including those at Shiloh, Chickamauga, Lookout Mountain, and Missionary Ridge.

After the war, Bierce traveled for nearly seven years, trying his hand at different careers, and only in 1871 did he publish his first short story, "The Haunted Valley." On Christmas Day of the same year, he married Mollie Day. The couple lived first in San Rafael, California, and then, the following year, moved to London where Bierce wrote satirical pieces for *Fun* and *Figaro.*

Bierce returned to America in 1875. He settled in San Francisco with his wife and their three children and forged a career as a short story writer and one of the best-known journalists of his age. Unwilling to compromise his principles or tone down his scathing criticisms of those he thought to be unscrupulous or merely pompous, he was known as "bitter Bierce" and "the wickedest man in San Francisco" and seemed to enjoy both titles.

Although his personal life was not happy—he separated from his wife and experienced the tragic deaths of both of his sons—Bierce enjoyed the respect of a number of his contemporaries. He pioneered a number of important literary techniques, including a fluid, sometimes surrealistic prose style, the use of stream of consciousness, and the exploration of the subjectivity of time. In his stories he is particularly preoccupied with the human capacity for self-deception. Whether writing ghost stories or war tales, he often portrays characters who destroy themselves by their unwillingness to examine their own assumptions. "Chickamauga," in particular, is one of the most graphic anti-war stories in American literature. A fictional experimentalist, Ambrose Bierce nonetheless remained a moral writer who believed that the reader might learn from the lessons that his characters typically learn too late.

Cathy N. Davidson
Duke University

PRIMARY WORKS

Tales of Soldiers and Civilians, 1892; *Black Beetles in Amber,* 1892; *Can Such Things Be?,* 1893; *Fantastic Fables,* 1899; *The Cynic's Word Book,* 1906; *The Collected Works of Ambrose Bierce,* 12 vols., 1909–12.

Chickamauga[1]

One sunny autumn afternoon a child strayed away from its rude home in a small field and entered a forest unobserved. It was happy in a new sense of freedom from control, happy in the opportunity of exploration and adventure; for this child's spirit, in bodies of its ancestors, had for thousands of years been trained to memorable feats of discovery and conquest—victories in battles whose critical moments were centuries, whose victors' camps were cities of hewn stone. From the cradle of its race it had conquered its way through two continents and passing a great sea had penetrated a third, there to be born to war and dominion as a heritage.

The child was a boy aged about six years, the son of a poor planter. In his younger manhood the father had been a soldier, had fought against naked savages and followed the flag of his country into the capital of a civilized race to the far South. In the peaceful life of a planter the warrior-fire survived; once kindled, it is never extinguished. The man loved military books and pictures and the boy had understood enough to make himself a wooden sword, though even the eye of his father would hardly have known it for what it was. This weapon he now bore bravely, as became the son of an heroic race, and pausing now and again in the sunny spaces of the

[1]The Battle of Chickamauga Creek took place in Georgia on September 19–20, 1863. Casualties in the first four hours of battle ran to over fifty percent on both sides. There were nearly 40,000 casualties in all, making it one of the most confusing and deadly battles of the Civil War.

forest assumed, with some exaggeration, the postures of aggression and defense that he had been taught by the engraver's art. Made reckless by the ease with which he overcame invisible foes attempting to stay his advance, he committed the common enough military error of pushing the pursuit to a dangerous extreme, until he found himself upon the margin of a wide but shallow brook, whose rapid waters barred his direct advance against the flying foe that had crossed with illogical ease. But the intrepid victor was not to be baffled; the spirit of the race which had passed the great sea burned unconquerable in that small breast and would not be denied. Finding a place where some bowlders in the bed of the stream lay but a step or a leap apart, he made his way across and fell again upon the rear-guard of his imaginary foe, putting all to the sword.

Now that the battle had been won, prudence required that he withdraw to his base of operations. Alas; like many a mightier conquerer, and like one, the mightiest, he could not

> curb the lust for war,
> Nor learn that tempted Fate will leave the loftiest star.[2]

Advancing from the bank of the creek he suddenly found himself confronted with a new and more formidable enemy: in the path that he was following, sat, bolt upright, with ears erect and paws suspended before it, a rabbit. With a startled cry the child turned and fled, he knew not in what direction, calling with inarticulate cries for his mother, weeping, stumbling, his tender skin cruelly torn by brambles, his little heart beating hard with terror—breathless, blind with tears—lost in the forest! Then, for more than an hour, he wandered with erring feet through the tangled undergrowth, till at last, overcome by fatigue, he lay down in a narrow space between two rocks, within a few yards of the stream and still grasping his toy sword, no longer a weapon but a companion, sobbed himself to sleep. The wood birds sang merrily above his head; the squirrels, whisking their bravery of tail, ran barking from tree to tree, unconscious of the pity of it, and somewhere far away was a strange, muffled thunder, as if the partridges were drumming in celebration of nature's victory over the son of her immemorial enslavers. And back at the little plantation, where white men and black were hastily searching the fields and hedges in alarm, a mother's heart was breaking for her missing child.

Hours passed, and then the little sleeper rose to his feet. The chill of the evening was in his limbs, the fear of the gloom in his heart. But he had rested, and he no longer wept. With some blind instinct which impelled to action he struggled through the undergrowth about him and came to a more open ground—on his right the brook, to the left a gentle acclivity studded with infrequent trees; over all, the gathering gloom of twilight. A thin, ghostly mist rose along the water. It frightened and repelled him; instead of recrossing, in the direction whence he had come, he turned his back upon it, and went forward toward the dark inclosing wood. Suddenly he saw before him a strange moving object which he took to be some large animal—a

[2]From *Childe Harold's Pilgrimage* by Lord Byron. Byron's "conqueror" is Napoleon.

dog, a pig—he could not name it; perhaps it was a bear. He had seen pictures of bears, but knew of nothing to their discredit and had vaguely wished to meet one. But something in form or movement of this object—something in the awkwardness of its approach—told him that it was not a bear, and curiosity was stayed by fear. He stood still and as it came slowly on gained courage every moment, for he saw that at least it had not the long, menacing ears of the rabbit. Possibly his impressionable mind was half conscious of something familiar in its shambling, awkward gait. Before it had approached near enough to resolve his doubts he saw that it was followed by another and another. To right and to left were many more; the whole open space about him was alive with them—all moving toward the brook.

They were men. They crept upon their hands and knees. They used their hands only, dragging their legs. They used their knees only, their arms hanging idle at their sides. They strove to rise to their feet, but fell prone in the attempt. They did nothing naturally, and nothing alike, save only to advance foot by foot in the same direction. Singly, in pairs and in little groups, they came on through the gloom, some halting now and again while others crept slowly past them, then resuming their movement. They came by dozens and by hundreds; as far on either hand as one could see in the deepening gloom they extended, and the black wood behind them appeared to be inexhaustible. The very ground seemed in motion toward the creek. Occasionally one who had paused did not again go on, but lay motionless. He was dead. Some, pausing, made strange gestures with their hands, erected their arms and lowered them again, clasped their heads; spread their palms upward, as men are sometimes seen to do in public prayer.

Not all of this did the child note; it is what would have been noted by an elder observer; he saw little but that these were men, yet crept like babes. Being men, they were not terrible, though unfamiliarly clad. He moved among them freely, going from one to another and peering into their faces with childish curiosity. All their faces were singularly white and many were streaked and gouted with red. Something in this—something too, perhaps, in their grotesque attitudes and movements—reminded him of the painted clown whom he had seen last summer in the circus, and he laughed as he watched them. But on and ever on they crept, these maimed and bleeding men, as heedless as he of the dramatic contrast between his laughter and their own ghastly gravity. To him it was a merry spectacle. He had seen his father's negroes creep upon their hands and knees for his amusement—had ridden them so, "making believe" they were his horses. He now approached one of these crawling figures from behind and with an agile movement mounted it astride. The man sank upon his breast, recovered, flung the small boy fiercely to the ground as an unbroken colt might have done, then turned upon him a face that lacked a lower jaw—from the upper teeth to the throat was a great red gap fringed with hanging shreds of flesh and splinters of bone. The unnatural prominence of nose, the absence of chin, the fierce eyes, gave this man the appearance of a great bird of prey crimsoned in throat and breast by the blood of its quarry. The man rose to his knees, the child to his feet. The man shook his fist at the child; the child, terrified at last, ran to a tree near by, got upon the farther side of it and took a more serious view of the situation. And so the clumsy multitude dragged itself slowly and painfully along in hideous pantomime—moved forward down the slope like a swarm of great black beetles, with never a sound of going—in silence profound, absolute.

Instead of darkening, the haunted landscape began to brighten. Through the belt of trees beyond the brook shone a strange red light, the trunks and branches of the trees making a black lacework against it. It struck the creeping figures and gave them monstrous shadows, which caricatured their movements on the lit grass. It fell upon their faces, touching their whiteness with a ruddy tinge, accentuating the stains with which so many of them were freaked and maculated. It sparkled on buttons and bits of metal in their clothing. Instinctively the child turned toward the growing splendor and moved down the slope with his horrible companions; in a few moments had passed the foremost of the throng—not much of a feat, considering his advantages. He placed himself in the lead, his wooden sword still in hand, and solemnly directed the march, conforming his pace to theirs and occasionally turning as if to see that his forces did not straggle. Surely such a leader never before had such a following.

Scattered about upon the ground now slowly narrowing by the encroachment of this awful march to water, were certain articles to which, in the leader's mind, were coupled no significant associations: an occasional blanket, tightly rolled lengthwise, doubled and the ends bound together with a string; a heavy knapsack here, and there a broken rifle—such things, in short, as are found in the rear of retreating troops, the "spoor" of men flying from their hunters. Everywhere near the creek, which here had a margin of lowland, the earth was trodden into mud by the feet of men and horses. An observer of better experience in the use of his eyes would have noticed that these footprints pointed in both directions; the ground had been twice passed over—in advance and in retreat. A few hours before, these desperate, stricken men, with their more fortunate and now distant comrades, had penetrated the forest in thousands. Their successive battalions, breaking into swarms and reforming in lines, had passed the child on every side—had almost trodden on him as he slept. The rustle and murmur of their march had not awakened him. Almost within a stone's throw of where he lay they had fought a battle; but all unheard by him were the roar of the musketry, the shock of the cannon, "the thunder of the captains and the shouting."[3] He had slept through it all, grasping his little wooden sword with perhaps a tighter clutch in unconscious sympathy with his martial environment, but as heedless of the grandeur of the struggle as the dead who had died to make the glory.

The fire beyond the belt of woods on the farther side of the creek, reflected to earth from the canopy of its own smoke, was now suffusing the whole landscape. It transformed the sinuous line of mist to the vapor of gold. The water gleamed with dashes of red, and red, too, were many of the stones protruding above the surface. But that was blood; the less desperately wounded had stained them in crossing. On them, too, the child now crossed with eager steps; he was going to the fire. As he stood upon the farther bank he turned about to look at the companions of his march. The advance was arriving at the creek. The stronger had already drawn themselves to the brink and plunged their faces into the flood. Three or four who lay without motion appeared to have no heads. At this the child's eyes expanded with wonder;

[3]Job 39:25. "He saith among the trumpets, Ha, ha! and he smelleth the battle afar off, the thunder of the captains, and the shouting."

even his hospitable understanding could not accept a phenomenon implying such vitality as that. After slaking their thirst these men had not the strength to back away from the water, nor to keep their heads above it. They were drowned. In rear of these, the open spaces of the forest showed the leader as many formless figures of his grim command as at first; but not nearly so many were in motion. He waved his cap for their encouragement and smilingly pointed with his weapon in the direction of the guiding light—a pillar of fire to this strange exodus.[4]

Confident of the fidelity of his forces, he now entered the belt of woods, passed through it easily in the red illumination, climbed a fence, ran across a field, turning now and again to coquet with his responsive shadow, and so approached the blazing ruin of a dwelling. Desolation everywhere! In all the wide glare not a living thing was visible. He cared nothing for that; the spectacle pleased, and he danced with glee in imitation of the wavering flames. He ran about, collecting fuel, but every object that he found was too heavy for him to cast in from the distance to which the heat limited his approach. In despair he flung in his sword—a surrender to the superior forces of nature. His military career was at an end.

Shifting his position, his eyes fell upon some outbuildings which had an oddly familiar appearance, as if he had dreamed of them. He stood considering them with wonder, when suddenly the entire plantation, with its inclosing forest, seemed to turn as if upon a pivot. His little world swung half around; the points of the compass were reversed. He recognized the blazing building as his own home!

For a moment he stood stupefied by the power of the revelation, then ran with stumbling feet, making a half-circuit of the ruin. There, conspicuous in the light of the conflagration, lay the dead body of a woman—the white face turned upward, the hands thrown out and clutched full of grass, the clothing deranged, the long dark hair in tangles and full of clotted blood. The greater part of the forehead was torn away, and from the jagged hole the brain protruded, overflowing the temple, a frothy mass of gray, crowned with clusters of crimson bubbles—the work of a shell.

The child moved his little hands, making wild, uncertain gestures. He uttered a series of inarticulate and indescribable cries—something between the chattering of an ape and the gobbling of a turkey—a startling, soulless, unholy sound, the language of a devil. The child was a deaf mute.

Then he stood motionless, with quivering lips, looking down upon the wreck.

1889

Hamlin Garland 1860–1940

Hannibal Hamlin Garland's childhood and youth epitomize the late nineteenth-century American westering movement he would represent in fiction and autobiography. Born on a farm in Wisconsin, Garland moved with his family to successive farming locations in Minnesota and Iowa, a movement spurred by his father's restless drive for new land and a fresh start. Garland's lifelong sensitivity to the situation of

[4]Exodus 13:21. During the flight from Egypt, God led the Israelites with a pillar of fire lighting the night.

women appears to have stemmed from his view of his mother's suffering and hardship in attempting to establish a home on these farms on the raw prairie. In 1876 the family was settled in Osage, Iowa, where Garland enrolled in the Cedar Valley Seminary. Following his graduation in 1881 and a trip east with his brother, Garland returned to the West to stake a claim in the Dakota Territory, where his family was now settled.

Garland's growing dissatisfaction with what he took to be the bleakness of upper-midwestern farm life together with his fresh, favorable impressions of the more settled and established East crystallized in 1884 with a decision to move to Boston to pursue further education and to attempt to establish a career. Working on his own at the Boston Public Library, Garland studied widely, from the poetry of Walt Whitman to the evolutionary philosophy of Charles Darwin and Herbert Spencer. His reading of Henry George's economic theories convinced Garland that radical reform of the tax system was needed to bring justice to working farmers in relation to the land owners, an idea that informed much of his subsequent fiction.

Gradually establishing himself, Garland obtained a teaching position at the Boston School of Oratory, gave lectures on literature, and started to write about the prairie life that was engraved upon his memory. Visits to his parents in 1887 and 1888 renewed those memories and stimulated a series of stories that were collected with the title *Main-Travelled Roads* (1891). These stories, including "Up the Coulé," "The Return of a Private," and "Under the Lion's Paw," are unsparing in their depiction of harsh realities of midwestern farm life and are especially noteworthy for their knowledgeable portrayal of the lives of farm women and of the need for economic reform. William Dean Howells, a central figure in American letters, hailed *Main-Travelled Roads* as a strong contribution to the movement toward realism in literature. *Prairie Folks* (1893) collects more of Garland's early stories of farm life and, with *Main-Travelled Roads,* represents the best of Garland's short fiction. In 1892 Garland followed up his successful short stories with the publication of three novels of strongly polemical bent: *Jason Edwards: Average Man,* which expounds the tax theories of Henry George; *A Spoil of Office,* an exposé of political corruption and exploration of possibilities of reform along Populist Party lines; and *A Member of the Third House,* a depiction of the influence of the railroad monopoly on a state legislature. Garland's career as novelist climaxed in 1895 with the publication of *Rose of Dutcher's Coolly,* which presents, in a sense, a female alter ego to Garland. Like Garland, Rose, born on a farm, wearies of the monotony of farm life and dreams of escape through establishing herself as an author. When Rose leaves the farm, her guilt toward her father, left behind, recalls themes of guilt felt by the departing young in relation to farm families that we see in "Up the Coulé" and elsewhere in Garland's fiction and autobiography. With marriage, Rose and her husband pledge to live as equals, a relationship Garland explicitly sought with the artist Zulime Taft, whom he married in 1899.

In essays collected in *Crumbling Idols* (1894) Garland gave his theory of the literary realism, or "Veritism" as he called it, that he championed in the earlier part of his career. In the mid-1890s, with an eye to attracting a larger readership Garland turned to the production of romantic adventure stories. One of the better of these later novels, *The Captain of the Gray-Horse Troop* (1902), deals with the abuse of American Indians by cattlemen. Garland's knowledgeable interest in American Indians, based on his travels to Indian reservations, is also strongly apparent in stories collected in his late *Book of the American Indian* (1923), a work meriting wider attention.

Garland's literary career yielded a final, rich harvest with the publication of his autobiographies. *A Son of the Middle Border* (1917), a recognized classic American personal narrative, was followed by the sequel *A Daughter of the Middle Border* (1921), which was awarded the Pulitzer Prize. Subsequent autobiographical works (some semi-fictionalized), including *Trail-Makers of the Middle Border* (1926) and *Back-Trailers from the Middle Border* (1928), though perhaps lacking the power of the first two, remain a lasting and rich resource for students of American life and literary history.

James Robert Payne
New Mexico State University

PRIMARY WORKS

Main-Travelled Roads, 1891; *Jason Edwards,* 1892; *Crumbling Idols,* 1894; *Rose of Dutcher's Coolly,* 1895, ed. Donald Pizer, 1969; *A Son of the Middle Border,* 1917; *The Book of the American Indian,* 1923; *Hamlin Garland's Diary,* ed. Donald Pizer, 1968.

Up the Coulé[1]

A Story of Wisconsin

"Keep the main-travelled road up the Coolly—it's the second house after crossin' the crick."

The ride from Milwaukee to the Mississippi is a fine ride at any time, superb in summer. To lean back in a reclining-chair and whirl away in a breezy July day, past lakes, groves of oak, past fields of barley being reaped, past hay-fields, where the heavy grass is toppling before the swift sickle, is a panorama of delight, a road full of delicious surprises, where down a sudden vista lakes open, or a distant wooded hill looms darkly blue, or swift streams, foaming deep down the solid rock, send whiffs of cool breezes in at the window.

It has majesty, breadth. The farming has nothing apparently petty about it. All seems vigorous, youthful, and prosperous. Mr. Howard McLane in his chair let his newspaper fall on his lap, and gazed out upon it with dreaming eyes. It had a certain mysterious glamour to him; the lakes were cooler and brighter to his eye, the greens fresher, and the grain more golden than to any one else, for he was coming back to it all after an absence of ten years. It was, besides, *his* West. He still took pride in being a Western man.

His mind all day flew ahead of the train to the little town far on toward the Mississippi, where he had spent his boyhood and youth. As the train passed the Wisconsin River, with its curiously carved cliffs, its cold, dark, swift-swirling water eat-

[1]A valley or ravine often with a stream at the bottom. Among Garland's various spellings are *coule, coulé,* and *coolly.*

ing slowly under cedar-clothed banks, Howard began to feel curious little movements of the heart, like a lover as he nears his sweetheart.

The hills changed in character, growing more intimately recognizable. They rose higher as the train left the ridge and passed down into the Black River valley, and specifically into the La Crosse valley.[2] They ceased to have any hint of upheavals of rock, and became simply parts of the ancient level left standing after the water had practically given up its post-glacial, scooping action.

It was about six o'clock as he caught sight of the dear broken line of hills on which his baby eyes had looked thirty-five years ago. A few minutes later and the train drew up at the grimy little station set in at the hillside, and, giving him just time to leap off, plunged on again toward the West. Howard felt a ridiculous weakness in his legs as he stepped out upon the broiling hot splintery planks of the station and faced the few idlers lounging about. He simply stood and gazed with the same intensity and absorption one of the idlers might show standing before the Brooklyn Bridge.

The town caught and held his eyes first. How poor and dull and sleepy and squalid it seemed! The one main street ended at the hillside at his left, and stretched away to the north, between two rows of the usual village stores, unrelieved by a tree or a touch of beauty. An unpaved street, drab-colored, miserable, rotting wooden buildings, with the inevitable battlements—the same, only worse, was the town.

The same, only more beautiful still, was the majestic amphitheatre of green wooded hills that circled the horizon, and toward which he lifted his eyes. He thrilled at the sight.

"Glorious!" he cried involuntarily.

Accustomed to the White Mountains, to the Alleghanies,[3] he had wondered if these hills would retain their old-time charm. They did. He took off his hat to them as he stood there. Richly wooded, with gently-sloping green sides, rising to massive square or rounded tops with dim vistas, they glowed down upon the squalid town, gracious, lofty in their greeting, immortal in their vivid and delicate beauty.

He was a goodly figure of a man as he stood there beside his valise. Portly, erect, handsomely dressed, and with something unusually winning in his brown mustache and blue eyes, something scholarly suggested by the pinch-nose glasses, something strong in the repose of the head. He smiled as he saw how unchanged was the grouping of the old loafers on the salt-barrels and nail-kegs. He recognized most of them—a little dirtier, a little more bent, and a little grayer.

They sat in the same attitudes, spat tobacco with the same calm delight, and joked each other, breaking into short and sudden fits of laughter, and pounded each other on the back, just as when he was a student at the La Crosse Seminary, and going to and fro daily on the train.

They ruminated on him as he passed, speculating in a perfectly audible way upon his business.

"Looks like a drummer."

"No, he ain't no drummer. See them Boston glasses?"

[2]In western Wisconsin.

[3]Both the White Mountains, in northern New Hampshire and southwestern Maine, and the Allegheinies, extending from northern Pennsylvania to southwestern Virginia, are parts of the Appalachian system.

"That's so. Guess he's a teacher."

"Looks like a moneyed cuss."

"Bos'n, I *guess.*"

He knew the one who spoke last—Freeme Cole, a man who was the fighting wonder of Howard's boyhood, now degenerated into a stoop-shouldered, faded, garrulous, and quarrelsome old man. Yet there was something epic in the old man's stories, something enthralling in the dramatic power of recital.

Over by the blacksmith shop the usual game of "quaits"[4] was in progress, and the drug-clerk on the corner was chasing a crony with the squirt-pump, with which he was about to wash the windows. A few teams stood ankle-deep in the mud, tied to the fantastically-gnawed pine pillars of the wooden awnings. A man on a load of hay was "jawing" with the attendant of the platform scales, who stood below, pad and pencil in hand.

"Hit 'im! hit 'im! Jump off and knock 'im!" suggested a bystander, jovially.

Howard knew the voice.

"Talk's cheap. Takes money t' buy whiskey," he said, when the man on the load repeated his threat of getting off and whipping the scales-man.

"You're William McTurg," Howard said, coming up to him.

"I am, sir," replied the soft-voiced giant, turning and looking down on the stranger, with an amused twinkle in his deep brown eyes. He stood as erect as an Indian, though his hair and beard were white.

"I'm Howard McLane."

"Ye begin t' look it," said McTurg, removing his right hand from his pocket. "How are yeh?"

"I'm first-rate. How's mother and Grant?"

"Saw 'im ploughing corn as I came down. Guess he's all right. Want a boost?"

"Well, yes. Are you down with a team?"

"Yep. 'Bout goin' home. Climb right in. That's my rig, right there," nodding at a sleek bay colt hitched in a covered buggy. "Heave y'r grip under the seat."

They climbed into the seat after William had lowered the buggy-top and unhitched the horse from the post. The loafers were mildly curious. Guessed Bill had got hooked onto by a lightnin'-rod peddler, or somethin' o' that kind.

"Want to go by river, or 'round by the hills?"

"Hills, I guess."

The whole matter began to seem trivial, as if he had only been away for a month or two.

William McTurg was a man little given to talk. Even the coming back of a nephew did not cause any flow of questions or reminiscences. They rode in silence. He sat a little bent forward, the lines held carelessly in his hands, his great leonine head swaying to and fro with the movement of the buggy.

As they passed familiar spots, the younger man broke the silence with a question.

"That's old man McElvaine's place, ain't it?"

"Yep."

[4]A ring toss game.

"Old man living?"

"I *guess* he is. Husk more corn 'n any man he c'n hire."

In the edge of the village they passed an open lot on the left, marked with circus-rings of different eras.

"There's the old ball-ground. Do they have circuses on it just the same as ever?"

"Just the same."

"What fun that field calls up! The games of ball we used to have! Do you play yet?"

"Sometimes. Can't stoop so well as I used to." He smiled a little. "Too much fat."

It all swept back upon Howard in a flood of names and faces and sights and sounds; something sweet and stirring somehow, though it had little of aesthetic charm at the time. They were passing along lanes now, between superb fields of corn, wherein ploughmen were at work. Kingbirds flew from post to post ahead of them; the insects called from the grass. The valley slowly outspread below them. The workmen in the fields were "turning out" for the night. They all had a word of chaff with McTurg.

Over the western wall of the circling amphitheatre the sun was setting. A few scattering clouds were drifting on the west wing, their shadows sliding down the green and purpled slopes. The dazzling sunlight flamed along the luscious velvety grass, and shot amid the rounded, distant purple peaks, and streamed in bars of gold and crimson across the blue mist of the narrower upper Coulés.

The heart of the young man swelled with pleasure almost like pain, and the eyes of the silent older man took on a far-off, dreaming look, as he gazed at the scene which had repeated itself a thousand times in his life, but of whose beauty he never spoke.

Far down to the left was the break in the wall, through which the river ran, on its way to join the Mississippi. As they climbed slowly among the hills, the valley they had left grew still more beautiful, as the squalor of the little town was hid by the dusk of distance. Both men were silent for a long time. Howard knew the peculiarities of his companion too well to make any remarks or ask any questions, and besides it was a genuine pleasure to ride with one who could feel that silence was the only speech amid such splendors.

Once they passed a little brook singing in a mournfully sweet way its eternal song over its pebbles. It called back to Howard the days when he and Grant, his younger brother, had fished in this little brook for trout, with trousers rolled above the knee and wrecks of hats upon their heads.

"Any trout left?" he asked.

"Not many. Little fellers." Finding the silence broken, William asked the first question since he met Howard. "Less see: you're a show feller now? B'long to a troupe?"

"Yes, yes; I'm an actor."

"Pay much?"

"Pretty well."

That seemed to end William's curiosity about the matter.

"Ah, there's our old house, ain't it?" Howard broke out, pointing to one of the houses farther up the Coulé. It'll be a surprise to them, won't it?"

"Yep; only they don't live there."

"What! They don't!"

"No."

"Who does?"

"Dutchman."

Howard was silent for some moments. "Who lives on the Dunlap place?"

"'Nother Dutchman."

"Where's Grant living, anyhow?"

"Farther up the Coolly."

"Well, then I'd better get out here, hadn't I?"

"Oh, I'll drive yeh up."

"No, I'd rather walk."

The sun had set, and the Coulé was getting dusk when Howard got out of McTurg's carriage, and set off up the winding lane toward his brother's house. He walked slowly to absorb the coolness and fragrance and color of the hour. The katydids sang a rhythmic song of welcome to him. Fireflies were in the grass. A whippoorwill in the deep of the wood was calling weirdly, and an occasional nighthawk, flying high gave his grating shriek, or hollow boom, suggestive and resounding.

He had been wonderfully successful, and yet had carried into his success as a dramatic author as well as actor a certain puritanism that made him a paradox to his fellows. He was one of those actors who are always in luck, and the best of it was he kept and made use of his luck. Jovial as he appeared, he was inflexible as granite against drink and tobacco. He retained through it all a certain freshness of enjoyment that made him one of the best companions in the profession; and now as he walked on, the hour and the place appealed to him with great power. It seemed to sweep away the life that came between.

How close it all was to him, after all! In his restless life, surrounded by the glare of electric lights, painted canvas, hot colors, creak of machinery, mock trees, stones, and brooks, he had not lost but gained appreciation for the coolness, quiet and low tones, the shyness of the wood and field.

In the farm-house ahead of him a light was shining as he peered ahead, and his heart gave another painful movement. His brother was awaiting him there, and his mother, whom he had not seen for ten years and who had grown unable to write. And when Grant wrote, which had been more and more seldom of late, his letters had been cold and curt.

He began to feel that in the pleasure and excitement of his life he had grown away from his mother and brother. Each summer he had said, "Well, now I'll go home *this* year sure." But a new play to be produced, or a yachting trip, or a tour of Europe, had put the home-coming off; and now it was with a distinct consciousness of neglect of duty that he walked up to the fence and looked into the yard, where William had told him his brother lived.

It was humble enough—a small white house, story-and-a-half structure, with a wing, set in the midst of a few locust-trees; a small drab-colored barn, with a sagging ridge-pole; a barnyard full of mud, in which a few cows were standing, fighting the flies and waiting to be milked. An old man was pumping water at the well; the pigs were squealing from a pen near by; a child was crying.

Instantly the beautiful, peaceful valley was forgotten. A sickening chill struck into Howard's soul as he looked at it all. In the dim light he could see a figure milking a cow. Leaving his valise at the gate, he entered, and walked up to the old man, who had finished pumping and was about to go to feed the hogs.

"Good-evening," Howard began. "Does Mr. Grant McLane live here?"

"Yes, sir, he does. He's right over there milkin'."

"I'll go over there an—"

"Don't b'lieve I would. It's darn muddy over there. It's been turrible rainy. He'll be done in a minute, anyway."

"Very well; I'll wait."

As he waited, he could hear a woman's fretful voice, and the impatient jerk and jar of kitchen things, indicative of ill-temper or worry. The longer he stood absorbing this farm-scene, with all its sordidness, dulness, triviality, and its endless drudgeries, the lower his heart sank. All the joy of the home-coming was gone, when the figure arose from the cow and approached the gate, and put the pail of milk down on the platform by the pump.

"Good-evening," said Howard, out of the dusk.

Grant stared a moment. "Good-evening."

Howard knew the voice, though it was older and deeper and more sullen. "Don't you know me, Grant? I am Howard."

The man approached him, gazing intently at his face. "You are?" after a pause. "Well, I'm glad to see yeh, but I can't shake hands. That damned cow had laid down in the mud."

They stood and looked at each other. Howard's cuffs, collar, and shirt, alien in their elegance, showed through the dusk, and a glint of light shot out from the jewel of his necktie, as the light from the house caught it at the right angle. As they gazed in silence at each other, Howard divined something of the hard, bitter feeling which came into Grant's heart, as he stood there, ragged, ankle-deep in muck, his sleeves rolled up, a shapeless old straw hat on his head.

The gleam of Howard's white hands angered him. When he spoke, it was in a hard, gruff tone, full of rebellion.

"Well, go in the house and set down. I'll be in soon's I strain the milk and wash the dirt off my hands."

"But mother—"

"She's 'round somewhere. Just knock on the door under the porch round there."

Howard went slowly around the corner of the house, past a vilely smelling rain-barrel, toward the west. A gray-haired woman was sitting in a rocking-chair on the porch, her hands in her lap, her eyes fixed on the faintly yellow sky, against which the hills stood dim purple silhouettes, and the locust-trees were etched as fine as lace. There was sorrow, resignation, and a sort of dumb despair in her attitude.

Howard stood, his throat swelling till it seemed as if he would suffocate. This was his mother—the woman who bore him, the being who had taken her life in her hand for him; and he, in his excited and pleasurable life, had neglected her!

He stepped into the faint light before her. She turned and looked at him without fear. "Mother!" he said. She uttered one little, breathing, gasping cry, called his name, rose, and stood still. He bounded up the steps and took her in his arms.

"Mother! Dear old mother!"

In the silence, almost painful, which followed, an angry woman's voice could be heard inside: "I don't care. I ain't goin' to wear myself out fer him. He c'n eat out here with us, or else—"

Mrs. McLane began speaking. "Oh, I've longed to see yeh, Howard. I was afraid you wouldn't come till—too late."

"What do you mean, mother? Ain't you well?"

"I don't seem to be able to do much now 'cept sit around and knit a little. I tried to pick some berries the other day, and I got so dizzy I had to give it up."

"You mustn't work. You *needn't* work. Why didn't you write to me how you were?" Howard asked in an agony of remorse.

"Well, we felt as if you probably had all you could do to take care of yourself."

"Are you married, Howard?"

"No, mother; and there ain't any excuse for me—not a bit," he said, dropping back into her colloquialisms. "I'm ashamed when I think of how long it's been since I saw you. I could have come."

"It don't matter now," she interrupted gently. "It's the way things go. Our boys grow up and leave us."

"Well, come in to supper," said Grant's ungracious voice from the doorway. "Come, mother."

Mrs. McLane moved with difficulty. Howard sprang to her aid, and leaning on his arm she went through the little sitting-room, which was unlighted, out into the kitchen, where the supper-table stood near the cook-stove.

"How, this is my wife," said Grant, in a cold, peculiar tone.

Howard bowed toward a remarkably handsome young woman, on whose forehead was a scowl, which did not change as she looked at him and the old lady.

"Set down, anywhere," was the young woman's cordial invitation.

Howard sat down next his mother, and facing the wife, who had a small, fretful child in her arms. At Howard's left was the old man, Lewis. The supper was spread upon a gay-colored oilcloth, and consisted of a pan of milk, set in the midst, with bowls at each plate. Beside the pan was a dipper and a large plate of bread, and at one end of the table was a dish of fine honey.

A boy of about fourteen leaned upon the table, his bent shoulders making him look like an old man. His hickory shirt, like that of Grant, was still wet with sweat, and discolored here and there with grease, or green from grass. His hair, freshly wet and combed, was smoothed away from his face, and shone in the light of the kerosene lamp. As he ate, he stared at Howard, as if he would make an inventory of each thread of the visitor's clothing.

"Did I look like that at his age?" thought Howard.

"You see we live jest about the same's ever," said Grant, as they began eating, speaking with a grim, almost challenging inflection.

The two brothers studied each other curiously, as they talked of neighborhood scenes. Howard seemed incredibly elegant and handsome to them all, with his rich, soft clothing, his spotless linen, and his exquisite enunciation and ease of speech. He had always been "smooth-spoken," and he had become "elegantly persuasive," as his friends said of him, and it was a large factor in his success.

Every detail of the kitchen, the heat, the flies buzzing aloft, the poor furniture, the dress of the people—all smote him like the lash of a wire whip. His brother was a man of great character. He could see that now. His deep-set, gray eyes and rugged face showed at thirty a man of great natural ability. He had more of the Scotch in his face than Howard, and he looked much older.

He was dressed, like the old man and the boy, in a checked shirt without vest. His suspenders, once gay-colored, had given most of their color to his shirt, and had marked irregular broad bands of pink and brown and green over his shoulders. His hair was uncombed, merely pushed away from his face. He wore a mustache only, though his face was covered with a week's growth of beard. His face was rather gaunt, and was brown as leather.

Howard could not eat much. He was disturbed by his mother's strange silence and oppression, and sickened by the long-drawn gasps with which the old man ate his bread and milk, and by the way the boy ate. He had his knife gripped tightly in his fist, knuckles up, and was scooping honey upon his bread.

The baby, having ceased to be afraid, was curious, gazing silently at the stranger.

"Hello, little one! Come and see your uncle. Eh? Course 'e will," cooed Howard in the attempt to escape the depressing atmosphere. The little one listened to his inflections as a kitten does, and at last lifted its arms in sign of surrender.

The mother's face cleared up a little. "I declare, she wants to go to you."

"Course she does. Dogs and kittens always come to me when I call 'em. Why shouldn't my own niece come?"

He took the little one and began walking up and down the kitchen with her, while she pulled at his beard and nose. "I ought to have you, my lady, in my new comedy. You'd bring down the house."

"You don't mean to say you put babies on the stage, Howard," said his mother in surprise.

"Oh, yes. Domestic comedy must have a baby these days."

"Well, that's another way of makin' a livin', sure," said Grant. The baby had cleared the atmosphere a little. "I s'pose you fellers make a pile of money."

"Sometimes we make a thousand a week; oftener we don't."

"A thousand dollars!" They all stared.

"A thousand dollars sometimes, and then lose it all the next week in another town. The dramatic business is a good deal like gambling—you take your chances."

"I wish you weren't in it, Howard. I don't like to have my son—"

"I wish I was in somethin' that paid better'n farmin'. Anything under God's heavens is better'n farmin'," said Grant.

"No, I ain't laid up much," Howard went on, as if explaining why he hadn't helped them. "Costs me a good deal to live, and I need about ten thousand dollars leeway to work on. I've made a good living, but I—I ain't made any money."

Grant looked at him, darkly meditative.

Howard went on:

"How'd ye come to sell the old farm? I was in hopes—"

"How'd we come to sell it?" said Grant with terrible bitterness. "We had something on it that didn't leave anything to sell. You probably don't remember anything about it, but there was a mortgage on it that eat us up in just four years by the almanac. 'Most killed mother to leave it. We wrote to you for money, but I don't s'-pose you remember *that.*"

"No, you didn't."

"Yes, I did."

"When was it? I don't—why, it's—I never received it. It must have been that summer I went with Rob Manning to Europe." Howard put the baby down and faced his brother. "Why, Grant, you didn't think I refused to help?"

"Well, it looked that way. We never heard a word from yeh all summer, and when y' did write, it was all about yerself'n plays 'n things we didn't know anything about. I swore to God I'd never write to you again, and I won't."

"But, good heavens! I never got it."

"Suppose you didn't. You might of known we were poor as Job's off-ox.[5] Everybody is that earns a living. We fellers on the farm have to earn a livin' for ourselves and you fellers that don't work. I don't blame yeh. I'd do it if I could."

"Grant, don't talk so! Howard didn't realize—"

"I tell yeh I don't blame 'im. Only I don't want him to come the brotherly business over me, after livin' as he has—that's all." There was a bitter accusation in the man's voice.

Howard leaped to his feet, his face twitching. "By God, I'll go back to-morrow morning!" he threatened.

"Go, an' be damned! I don't care what yeh do," Grant growled, rising and going out.

"Boys," called the mother, piteously, "it's terrible to see you quarrel."

"But I'm not to blame, mother," cried Howard in a sickness that made him white as chalk. "The man is a savage. I came home to help you all, not to quarrel."

"Grant's got one o' his fits on," said the young wife, speaking for the first time. "Don't pay any attention to him. He'll be all right in the morning."

"If it wasn't for you, mother, I'd leave now, and never see that savage again."

He lashed himself up and down in the room, in horrible disgust and hate of his brother and of this home in his heart. He remembered his tender anticipations of the home-coming with a kind of self-pity and disgust. This was his greeting!

He went to bed, to toss about on the hard, straw-filled mattress in the stuffy little best room. Tossing, writhing under the bludgeoning of his brother's accusing inflections, a dozen times he said, with a half-articulate snarl:

"He can go to hell! I'll not try to do anything more for him. I don't care if he *is* my brother; he has no right to jump on me like that. On the night of my return, too. My God! he is a brute, a savage!"

He thought of the presents in his trunk and valise which he couldn't show to him that night, after what had been said. He had intended to have such a happy evening of it, such a tender reunion! It was to be so bright and cheery!

In the midst of his cursings, his hot indignation, would come visions of himself in his own modest rooms. He seemed to be yawning and stretching in his beautiful

[5]The Old Testament figure Job traditionally possesses qualities of poverty and patience. With reference to a team of oxen, the *off-ox* would be the one on the far side, the one of less use.

bed, the sun shining in, his books, foils, pictures around him, to say good-morning and tempt him to rise, while the squat little clock on the mantel struck eleven warningly.

He could see the olive walls, the unique copper-and-crimson arabesque frieze (his own selection), and the delicate draperies; an open grate full of glowing coals, to temper the sea-winds; and in the midst of it, between a landscape by Enneking and an Indian in a canoe in a cañon, by Brush, he saw a sombre landscape by a master greater than Millet,[6] a melancholy subject, treated with pitiless fidelity.

A farm in the valley! Over the mountains swept jagged, gray, angry, sprawling clouds, sending a freezing, thin drizzle of rain, as they passed, upon a man following a plough. The horses had a sullen and weary look, and their manes and tails streamed sidewise in the blast. The ploughman clad in a ragged gray coat, with uncouth, muddy boots upon his feet, walked with his head inclined towards the sleet, to shield his face from the cold and sting of it. The soil rolled away, black and sticky and with a dull sheen upon it. Near by, a boy with tears on his cheeks was watching cattle, a dog seated near, his back to the gale.

As he looked at this picture, his heart softened. He looked down at the sleeve of his soft and fleecy night-shirt, at his white, rounded arm, muscular yet fine as a woman's, and when he looked for the picture it was gone. Then came again the assertive odor of stagnant air, laden with camphor; he felt the springless bed under him, and caught dimly a few soap-advertising lithographs on the walls. He thought of his brother, in his still more inhospitable bedroom, disturbed by the child, condemned to rise at five o'clock and begin another day's pitiless labor. His heart shrank and quivered, and the tears started to his eyes.

"I forgive him, poor fellow! He's not to blame."

II

He woke, however, with a dull, languid pulse, and an oppressive melancholy on his heart. He looked around the little room, clean enough, but oh, how poor! how barren! Cold plaster walls, a cheap wash-stand, a wash-set of three pieces, with a blue band around each; the windows, rectangular, and fitted with fantastic green shades.

Outside he could hear the bees humming. Chickens were merrily moving about. Cow-bells far up the road were sounding irregularly. A jay came by and yelled an insolent reveille, and Howard sat up. He could hear nothing in the house but the rattle of pans on the back side of the kitchen. He looked at his watch and saw it was half-past seven. His brother was in the field by this time, after milking, currying the horses, and eating breakfast—had been at work two hours and a half.

He dressed himself hurriedly in a négligé shirt with a windsor scarf, light-colored, serviceable trousers with a belt, russet shoes and a tennis hat—a knock-about costume, he considered. His mother, good soul, thought it a special suit put on for her benefit, and admired it through her glasses.

[6]John Joseph Enneking (1841–1916), American painter noted for landscapes; George de Forest Brush (1855–1941), American painter of American Indian subjects; Jean François Millet (1814–1875), French painter known for realistic portrayal of peasant life.

He kissed her with a bright smile, nodded at Laura the young wife, and tossed the baby, all in a breath, and with the manner as he himself saw, of the returned captain in the war-dramas of the day.

"Been to breakfast?" He frowned reproachfully. "Why didn't you call me? I wanted to get up, just as I used to, at sunrise."

"We thought you was tired, and so we didn't—"

"Tired! Just wait till you see me help Grant pitch hay or something. Hasn't finished his haying, has he?"

"No, I guess not. He will to-day if it don't rain again."

"Well, breakfast is all ready—Howard," said Laura, hesitating a little on his name.

"Good! I am ready for it. Bacon and eggs, as I'm a jay![7] Just what I was wanting. I was saying to myself: 'Now if they'll only get bacon and eggs and hot biscuits and honey—' Oh, say, mother, I heard the bees humming this morning; same noise they used to make when I was a boy, exactly. Must be the same bees.— Hey, you young rascal! come here and have some breakfast with your uncle."

"I never saw her take to any one so quick," Laura smiled. Howard noticed her in particular for the first time. She had on a clean calico dress and a gingham apron, and she looked strong and fresh and handsome. Her head was intellectual, her eyes full of power. She seemed anxious to remove the impression of her unpleasant looks and words the night before. Indeed it would have been hard to resist Howard's sunny good-nature.

The baby laughed and crowed. The old mother could not take her dim eyes off the face of her son, but sat smiling at him as he ate and rattled on. When he rose from the table at last, after eating heartily and praising it all, he said, with a smile:

"Well, now I'll just telephone down to the express and have my trunk brought up. I've got a few little things in there you'll enjoy seeing. But this fellow," indicating the baby, "I didn't take into account. But never mind; Uncle How'll make that all right."

"You ain't goin' to lay it up agin Grant, be you, my son?" Mrs. McLane faltered, as they went out into the best room.

"Of course not! He didn't mean it. Now can't you send word down and have my trunk brought up? Or shall I have to walk down?"

"I guess I'll see somebody goin' down," said Laura.

"All right. Now for the hay-field," he smiled, and went out into the glorious morning.

The circling hills the same, yet not the same as at night. A cooler, tenderer, more subdued cloak of color upon them. Far down the valley a cool, deep, impalpable, blue mist lay, under which one divined the river ran, under its elms and basswoods and wild grapevines. On the shaven slopes of the hills cattle and sheep were feeding, their cries and bells coming to the ear with a sweet suggestiveness. There was something immemorial in the sunny slopes dotted with red and brown and gray cattle.

Walking toward the haymakers, Howard felt a twinge of pain and distrust. Would he ignore it all and smile—

[7]A country person.

He stopped short. He had not seen Grant smile in so long—he couldn't quite see him smiling. He had been cold and bitter for years. When he came up to them, Grant was pitching on; the old man was loading, and the boy was raking after.

"Good-morning," Howard cried cheerily. The old man nodded, the boy stared. Grant growled something, without looking up. These "finical" things of saying good-morning and good-night are not much practised in such homes as Grant McLane's.

"Need some help? I'm ready to take a hand. Got on my regimentals this morning."

Grant looked at him a moment.

"You look like it."

"Gimme a hold on that fork, and I'll show you. I'm not so soft as I look, now you bet."

He laid hold upon the fork in Grant's hands, who released it sullenly and stood back sneering. Howard stuck the fork into the pile in the old way, threw his left hand to the end of the polished handle, brought it down into the hollow of his thigh, and laid out his strength till the handle bent like a bow. "Oop she rises!" he called laughingly, as the whole pile began slowly to rise, and finally rolled upon the high load.

"Oh, I ain't forgot how to do it," he laughed, as he looked around at the boy, who was studying the jacket and hat with a devouring gaze.

Grant was studying him too, but not in admiration.

"I shouldn't say you had," said the old man, tugging at the forkful.

"Mighty funny to come out here and do a little of this. But if you had to come here and do it all the while, you wouldn't look so white and soft in the hands," Grant said, as they moved on to another pile. "Give me that fork. You'll be spoiling your fine clothes."

"Oh, these don't matter. They're made for this kind of thing."

"Oh, are they? I guess I'll dress in that kind of a rig. What did that shirt cost? I need one."

"Six dollars a pair; but then it's old."

"And them pants," he pursued; "they cost six dollars too, didn't they?"

Howard's face darkened. He saw his brother's purpose. He resented it. "They cost fifteen dollars, if you want to know, and the shoes cost six-fifty. This ring on my cravat cost sixty dollars and the suit I had on last night cost eighty-five. My suits are made by Breckstein, on Fifth Avenue and Twentieth Street, if you want to patronize him," he ended brutally, spurred on by the sneer in his brother's eyes. "I'll introduce you."

"Good idea," said Grant, with a forced, mocking smile. "I need just such a get-up for haying and corn-ploughing. Singular I never thought of it. Now my pants cost eighty-five cents, s'penders fifteen, hat twenty, shoes one-fifty; stockin's I don't bother about."

He had his brother at a disadvantage, and he grew fluent and caustic as he went on, almost changing places with Howard, who took the rake out of the boy's hands and followed, raking up the scatterings.

"Singular we fellers here are discontented and mulish, ain't it? Singular we don't believe your letters when you write, sayin', 'I just about make a live of it'? Singular we think the country's goin' to hell, we fellers, in a two-dollar suit, wadin' around in the mud or sweatin' around in the hay-field, while you fellers lay around New York and smoke and wear good clothes and toady to millionaires?"

Howard threw down the rake and folded his arms. "My God! you're enough to make a man forget the same mother bore us!"

"I guess it wouldn't take much to make you forget that. You ain't put much thought on me nor her for ten years."

The old man cackled, the boy grinned, and Howard, sick and weak with anger and sorrow, turned away and walked down toward the brook. He had tried once more to get near his brother, and had failed. Oh, God! how miserably, pitiably! The hot blood gushed all over him as he thought of the shame and disgrace of it.

He, a man associating with poets, artists, sought after by brilliant women, accustomed to deference even from such people, to be sneered at, outfaced, shamed, shoved aside, by a man in a stained hickory shirt and patched overalls, and that man his brother! He lay down on the bright grass, with the sheep all around him, and writhed and groaned with the agony and despair of it.

And worst of all, underneath it was a consciousness that Grant was right in distrusting him. He *had* neglected him; he *had* said, "I guess they're getting along all right." He had put them behind him when the invitation to spend summer on the Mediterranean or in the Adirondacks,[8] came.

"What can I do? What can I do?" he groaned.

The sheep nibbled the grass near him, the jays called pertly, "Shame, shame," a quail piped somewhere on the hillside, and the brook sung a soft, soothing melody that took away at last the sharp edge of his pain, and he sat up and gazed down the valley, bright with the sun and apparently filled with happy and prosperous people.

Suddenly a thought seized him. He stood up so suddenly the sheep fled in affright. He leaped the brook, crossed the flat, and began searching in the bushes on the hillside. "Hurrah!" he said, with a smile.

He had found an old road which he used to travel when a boy—a road that skirted the edge of the valley, now grown up to brush, but still passable for footmen. As he ran lightly along down the beautiful path, under oaks and hickories, past masses of poison-ivy, under hanging grapevines, through clumps of splendid hazelnut bushes loaded with great sticky, rough, green burs, his heart threw off part of its load.

How it all came back to him! How many days, when the autumn sun burned the frost off the bushes, had he gathered hazel-nuts here with his boy and girl friends—Hugh and Shelley McTurg, Rome Sawyer, Orrin McIlvaine, and the rest! What had become of them all? How he had forgotten them!

This thought stopped him again, and he fell into a deep muse, leaning against an oak-tree and gazing into the vast fleckless space above. The thrilling, inscrutable mystery of life fell upon him like a blinding light. Why was he living in the crush and thunder and mental unrest of a great city, while his companions, seemingly his equals, in powers, were milking cows, making butter, and growing corn and wheat in the silence and drear monotony of the farm?

His boyish sweethearts! their names came back to his ear now, with a dull, sweet sound as of faint bells. He saw their faces, their pink sunbonnets tipped back upon

[8]Mountains in northeastern New York.

their necks, their brown ankles flying with the swift action of the scurrying partridge. His eyes softened; he took off his hat. The sound of the wind and the leaves moved him almost to tears.

A woodpecker gave a shrill, high-keyed, sustained cry. "Ki, ki, ki!" and he started from his revery, the dapples of sun and shade falling upon his lithe figure as he hurried on down the path.

He came at last to a field of corn that ran to the very wall of a large weather-beaten house, the sight of which made his breathing quicker. It was the place where he was born. The mystery of his life began there. In the branches of those poplar and hickory trees he had swung and sung in the rushing breeze, fearless as a squirrel. Here was the brook where, like a larger Kildee, he with Grant had waded after craw-fish, or had stolen upon some wary trout, rough-cut pole in hand.

Seeing someone in the garden, he went down along the corn-row through the rustling ranks of green leaves. An old woman was picking berries, a squat and shape-less figure.

"Good-morning," he called cheerily.

"Morgen,"[9] she said, looking up at him with a startled and very red face. She was German in every line of her body.

"Ich bin Herr McLane,"[10] he said, after a pause.

"So?"[11] she replied, with a questioning inflection.

"Yah; ich bin Herr Grant's Bruder."[12]

"Ach, so!"[13] she said, with a downward inflection. "Ich no spick Inglish. No spick Inglis."

"Ich bin durstig,"[14] he said. Leaving her pans, she went with him to the house, which was what he wanted to see.

"Ich bin hier geboren."[15]

"Ach, so!" She recognized the little bit of sentiment, and said some sentences in German whose general meaning was sympathy. She took him to the cool cellar where the spring had been trained to run into a tank containing pans of cream and milk, she gave him a cool draught from a large tin cup, and then at his request they went upstairs. The house was the same, but somehow seemed cold and empty. It was clean and sweet, but it had so little evidence of being lived in. The old part, which was built of logs, was used as best room, and modelled after the best rooms of the neighbor-ing Yankee homes, only it was emptier, without the cabinet organ and the rag-carpet and the chromos.[16]

The old fireplace was bricked up and plastered—the fireplace beside which in the far-off days he had lain on winter nights, to hear his uncles tell tales of hunting, or to hear them play the violin, great dreaming giants that they were.

The old woman went out and left him sitting there, the centre of a swarm of memories coming and going like so many ghostly birds and butterflies.

[9]German: "Morning."
[10]German: "I am Mr. McLane."
[11]German: "Indeed?"
[12]Howard's German: "Yes; I am Mr. Grant's brother."
[13]German: "Oh, I see!"
[14]German: "I am thirsty."
[15]Howard's German: "I was born here."
[16]Short form of *chromolithographs,* pictures printed in colors from lithographic stones or plates.

A curious heartache and listlessness, a nerveless mood came on him. What was it worth, anyhow—success? Struggle, strife, trampling on some one else. His play crowding out some other poor fellow's hope. The hawk eats the partridge, the partridge eats the flies and bugs, the bugs eat each other and the hawk, when he in his turn is shot by man. So, in the world of business, the life of one man seemed to him to be drawn from the life of another man, each success to spring from other failures.

He was like a man from whom all motives had been withdrawn. He was sick, sick to the heart. Oh, to be a boy again! An ignorant baby, pleased with a block and string, with no knowledge and no care of the great unknown! To lay his head again on his mother's bosom and rest! To watch the flames on the hearth!—

Why not? Was not that the very thing to do? To buy back the old farm? It would cripple him a little for the next season, but he could do it. Think of it! To see his mother back in the old home, with the fireplace restored, the old furniture in the sitting-room around her, and fine new things in the parlor!

His spirits rose again. Grant couldn't stand out when he brought to him a deed of the farm. Surely his debt would be cancelled when he had seen them all back in the wide old kitchen. He began to plan and to dream. He went to the windows, and looked out on the yard to see how much it had changed.

He'd build a new barn, and buy them a new carriage. His heart glowed again, and his lips softened into their usual feminine grace—lips a little full and falling easily into curves.

The old German woman came in at length, bringing some cakes and a bowl of milk, smiling broadly and hospitably as she waddled forward.

"Ach! Goot!" he said, smacking his lips over the pleasant draught.

"Wo ist ihre goot mann?"[17] he inquired, ready for business.

III

When Grant came in at noon Mrs. McLane met him at the door, with a tender smile on her face.

"Where's Howard, Grant?"

"I don't know," he replied in a tone that implied "I don't care."

The dim eyes clouded with quick tears.

"Ain't you seen him?"

"Not since nine o'clock."

"Where d'you think he is?"

"I tell yeh I don't know. He'll take care of himself; don't worry."

He flung off his hat and plunged into the washbasin. His shirt was wet with sweat and covered with dust of the hay and fragments of leaves. He splashed his burning face with the water, paying no further attention to his mother. She spoke again, very gently, in reproof:

[17]Howard's German: "Where is your good husband?"

"Grant, why do you stand out against Howard so?"

"I don't stand out against him," he replied harshly, pausing with the towel in his hands. His eyes were hard and piercing. "But if he expects me to gush over his coming back, he's fooled, that's all. He's left us to paddle our own canoe all this while, and, so far as *I'm* concerned, he can leave us alone hereafter. He looked out for his precious hide mighty well, and now he comes back here to play big-gun and pat us on the head. I don't propose to let him come that over me."

Mrs. McLane knew too well the temper of her son to say any more, but she inquired about Howard of the old hired man.

"He went off down the valley. He 'n' Grant had s'm *words,* and he pulled out down toward the old farm. That's the last I see of 'im."

Laura took Howard's part at the table. "Pity you can't be decent," she said, brutally direct as usual. "You treat Howard as if he was a—a—I do' know what."

"Will you let me alone?"

"No, I won't. If you think I'm going to set by an' agree to your bullyraggin[18] him, you're mistaken. It's a shame! You're mad 'cause he's succeeded and you ain't. He ain't to blame for his brains. If you and I'd had any, we'd 'a 'succeeded too. It ain't our fault and it ain't his; so what's the use?"

There was a look came into Grant's face that the wife knew. It meant bitter and terrible silence. He ate his dinner without another word.

It was beginning to cloud up. A thin, whitish, all-pervasive vapor which meant rain was dimming the sky, and he forced his hands to their utmost during the afternoon in order to get most of the down hay in before the rain came. He was pitching hay up into the barn when Howard came by just before one o'clock.

It was windless there. The sun fell through the white mist with undiminished fury, and the fragrant hay sent up a breath that was hot as an oven-draught. Grant was a powerful man, and there was something majestic in his action as he rolled the huge flakes of hay through the door. The sweat poured from his face like rain, and he was forced to draw his dripping sleeve across his face to clear away the blinding sweat that poured into his eyes.

Howard stood and looked at him in silence, remembering how often he had worked there in that furnace-heat, his muscles quivering, cold chills running over his flesh, red shadows dancing before his eyes.

His mother met him at the door, anxiously, but smiled as she saw his pleasant face and cheerful eyes.

"You're a little late, m' son."

Howard spent most of the afternoon sitting with his mother on the porch, or under the trees, lying sprawled out like a boy, resting at times with sweet forgetfulness of the whole world, but feeling a dull pain whenever he remembered the stern, silent man pitching hay in the hot sun on the torrid side of the barn.

His mother did not say anything about the quarrel; she feared to reopen it. She talked mainly of old times in a gentle monotone of reminiscence, while he listened, looking up into her patient face.

[18] Bullying.

The heat slowly lessened as the sun sank down toward the dun clouds rising like a more distant and majestic line of mountains beyond the western hills. The sound of cow-bells came irregularly to the ear, and the voices and sounds of the haying-fields had a jocund, thrilling effect on the ear of the city-dweller.

He was very tender. Everything conspired to make him simple, direct, and honest.

"Mother, if you'll only forgive me for staying away so long, I'll surely come to see you every summer."

She had nothing to forgive. She was so glad to have him there at her feet—her great, handsome, successful boy! She could only love him and enjoy him every moment of the precious days. If Grant would only reconcile himself to Howard! That was the great thorn in her flesh.

Howard told her how he had succeeded.

"It was luck, mother. First I met Cooke, and he introduced me to Jake Saulsman of Chicago. Jake asked me to go to New York with him, and—I don't know why—took a fancy to me some way. He introduced me to a lot of the fellows in New York, and they all helped me along. I did nothing to merit it. Everybody helps me. Anybody can succeed in that way."

The doting mother thought it not at all strange that they all helped him.

At the supper-table Grant was gloomily silent, ignoring Howard completely. Mrs. McLane sat and grieved silently, not daring to say a word in protest. Laura and the baby tried to amuse Howard, and under cover of their talk the meal was eaten.

The boy fascinated Howard. He "sawed wood"[19] with a rapidity and uninterruptedness which gave alarm. He had the air of coaling up for a long voyage.

"At that age," Howard thought, "I must have gripped my knife in my right hand so, and poured my tea into my saucer so. I must have buttered and bit into a huge slice of bread just so, and chewed at it with a smacking sound in just that way. I must have gone to the length of scooping up honey with my knife-blade."

It was magically, mystically beautiful over all this squalor and toil and bitterness, from five till seven—a moving hour. Again the falling sun streamed in broad banners across the valleys; again the blue mist lay far down the Coulé over the river; the cattle called from the hills in the moistening, sonorous air; the bells came in a pleasant tangle of sound; the air pulsed with the deepening chorus of katydids and other nocturnal singers.

Sweet and deep as the very springs of his life was all this to the soul of the elder brother; but in the midst of it, the younger man, in ill-smelling clothes and great boots that chafed his feet, went out to milk the cows—on whose legs the flies and mosquitoes swarmed, bloated with blood,—to sit by the hot side of the cow and be lashed with her tail as she tried frantically to keep the savage insects from eating her raw.

"The poet who writes of milking the cows does it from the hammock, looking on," Howard soliloquized, as he watched the old man Lewis racing around the filthy

[19]To focus on one's own business; here, of course, on the business of eating.

yard after one of the young heifers that had kicked over the pail in her agony with the flies and was unwilling to stand still and be eaten alive.

"So, *so!* you beast!" roared the old man, as he finally cornered the shrinking, nearly frantic creature.

"Don't you want to look at the garden?" asked Mrs. McLane of Howard; and they went out among the vegetables and berries.

The bees were coming home heavily laden and crawling slowly into the hives. The level, red light streamed through the trees, blazed along the grass, and lighted a few old-fashioned flowers into red and gold flame. It was beautiful, and Howard looked at it through his half-shut eyes as the painters do, and turned away with a sigh at the sound of blows where the wet and grimy men were assailing the frantic cows.

"There's Wesley with your trunk," Mrs. McLane said, recalling him to himself.

Wesley helped him carry the trunk in, and waved off thanks.

"Oh, that's all right," he said; and Howard knew the Western man too well to press the matter of pay.

As he went in an hour later and stood by the trunk, the dull ache came back into his heart. How he had failed! It seemed like a bitter mockery now to show his gifts.

Grant had come in from his work, and with his feet released from his chafing boots, in his wet shirt and milk-splashed overalls, sat at the kitchen table reading a newspaper which he held close to a small kerosene lamp. He paid no attention to any one. His attitude, curiously like his father's, was perfectly definite to Howard. It meant that from that time forward there were to be no words of any sort between them. It meant that they were no longer brothers, not even acquaintances. "How inexorable that face!" thought Howard.

He turned sick with disgust and despair, and would have closed his trunk without showing any of the presents, only for the childish expectancy of his mother and Laura.

"Here's something for you, mother," he said, assuming a cheerful voice, as he took a fold of fine silk from the trunk and held it up. "All the way from Paris."

He laid it on his mother's lap and stooped and kissed her, and then turned hastily away to hide the tears that came to his own eyes as he saw her keen pleasure.

"And here's a parasol for Laura. I don't know how I came to have that in here. And here's General Grant's[20] autobiography for his namesake," he said, with an effort at carelessness, and waited to hear Grant rise.

"Grant, won't you come in?" asked his mother, quaveringly.

Grant did not reply nor move. Laura took the handsome volumes out and laid them beside him on the table. He simply pushed them one side and went on with his reading.

Again that horrible anger swept hot as flame over Howard. He could have cursed him. His hands shook as he handed out other presents to his mother and Laura and the baby. He tried to joke.

"I didn't know how old the baby was, so she'll have to grow to some of these things."

[20]General Ulysses S. Grant (1822–1885), commander-in-chief of the U.S. Army in the Civil War, became the 18th U.S. President (1869–1877).

But the pleasure was all gone for him and for the rest. His heart swelled almost to a feeling of pain as he looked at his mother. There she sat with the presents in her lap. The shining silk came too late for her. It threw into appalling relief her age, her poverty, her work-weary frame. "My God!" he almost cried aloud, "how little it would have taken to lighten her life!"

Upon this moment, when it seemed as if he could endure no more, came the smooth voice of William McTurg:

"Hello, folkses!"

"Hello, Uncle Bill! Come in."

"That's what we came for," laughed a woman's voice.

"Is that you, Rose?" asked Laura.

"It's me—Rose," replied the laughing girl, as she bounced into the room and greeted everybody in a breathless sort of way.

"You don't mean little Rosy?"

"Big Rosy now," said William.

Howard looked at the handsome girl and smiled, saying in a nasal sort of tone, "Wal, wal! Rosy, how you've growed since I saw yeh!"

"Oh, look at all this purple and fine linen! Am I left out?"

Rose was a large girl of twenty-five or there-abouts, and was called an old maid. She radiated good-nature from every line of her buxom self. Her black eyes were full of drollery, and she was on the best of terms with Howard at once. She had been a teacher, but that did not prevent her from assuming a peculiar directness of speech. Of course they talked about old friends.

"Where's Rachel?" Howard inquired. Her smile faded away.

"Shellie married Orrin McIlvaine. They're way out in Dakota. Shellie's havin' a hard row of stumps."

There was a little silence.

"And Tommy?"

"Gone West. Most all the boys have gone West. That's the reason there's so many old maids."

"You don't mean to say—"

"I don't *need* to say—I'm an old maid. Lots of the girls are."

"It don't pay to marry these days."

"Are you married?"

"Not *yet.*" His eyes lighted up again in a humorous way.

"Not yet! That's good! That's the way old maids all talk."

"You don't mean to tell me that no young fellow comes prowling around—"

"Oh, a young Dutchman or Norwegian once in a while. Nobody that counts. Fact is, we're getting like Boston—four women to one man; and when you consider that we're getting more particular each year, the outlook is—well, it's dreadful!"

"It certainly is."

"Marriage is a failure these days for most of us. We can't live on the farm, and can't get a living in the city, and there we are." She laid her hand on his arm. "I declare, Howard, you're the same boy you used to be. I ain't a bit afraid of you, for all your success."

"And you're the same girl? No, I can't say that. It seems to me you've grown more than I have—I don't mean physically, I mean mentally," he explained, as he saw her smile in the defensive way a fleshy girl has, alert to ward off a joke.

They were in the midst of talk. Howard telling one of his funny stories, when a wagon clattered up to the door, and merry voices called loudly:

"Whoa, there, Sampson!"

"Hullo, the house!"

Rose looked at her father with a smile in her black eyes exactly like his. They went to the door.

"Hullo! What's wanted?"

"Grant McLane live here?"

"Yup. Right here."

A moment later there came a laughing, chatting squad of women to the door. Mrs. McLane and Laura stared at each other in amazement. Grant went out-doors.

Rose stood at the door as if she were hostess.

"Come in, Nettie. Glad to see yeh—glad to see yeh! Mrs. McIlvaine, come right in! Take a seat. Make yerself to home, *do!* And Mrs. Peavey! Wal, I never! This must be a surprise-party. Well, I swan! How many more o' ye air they?"

All was confusion, merriment, hand-shakings as Rose introduced them in her roguish way.

"Folks, this is Mr. Howard McLane of New York. He's an actor, but it hain't spoiled him a bit as *I* can see. How, this is Nettie McIlvaine—Wilson that was."

Howard shook hands with Nettie, a tall, plain girl with prominent teeth.

"This is Ma McIlvaine."

"She looks just the same," said Howard, shaking her hand and feeling how hard and work-worn it was.

And so amid bustle, chatter, and invitations "to lay off y'r things an' stay awhile," the women got disposed about the room at last. Those that had rocking-chairs rocked vigorously to and fro to hide their embarrassment. They all talked in loud voices.

Howard felt nervous under this furtive scrutiny. He wished his clothes didn't look so confoundedly dressy. Why didn't he have sense enough to go and buy a fifteen-dollar suit of diagonals for every-day wear.

Rose was the life of the party. Her tongue rattled on in the most delightful way.

"It's all Rose an' Bill's doin's," Mrs. McIlvaine explained. "They told us to come over an' pick up anybody we see on the road. So we did."

Howard winced a little at her familiarity of tone. He couldn't help it for the life of him.

"Well, I wanted to come to-night because I'm going away next week, and I wanted to see how he'd act at a surprise-party again," Rose explained.

"Married, I s'pose," said Mrs. McIlvaine, abruptly.

"No, not yet."

"Good land! Why, y' mus' be thirty-five, How. Must 'a' dis'p'inted y'r mam not to have a young 'un to call 'er granny."

The men came clumping in, talking about haying and horses. Some of the older ones Howard knew and greeted, but the younger ones were mainly too much changed. They were all very ill at ease. Most of them were in compromise dress—

something lying between working "rig" and Sunday dress. Most of them had on clean shirts and paper collars, and wore their Sunday coats (thick woollen garments) over rough trousers. All of them crossed their legs at once, and most of them sought the wall and leaned back perilously upon the hind legs of their chairs, eyeing Howard slowly.

For the first few minutes the presents were the subjects of conversation. The women especially spent a good deal of talk upon them.

Howard found himself forced to taking the initiative, so he inquired about the crops and about the farms.

"I see you don't plough the hills as we used to. And reap! *What* a job it ust to be. It makes the hills more beautiful to have them covered with smooth grass and cattle."

There was only dead silence to this touching upon the idea of beauty.

"I s'pose it pays reasonably."

"Not enough to kill," said one of the younger men. "You c'n see that by the houses we live in—that is, most of us. A few that came in early an' got land cheap, like McIlvaine, here—he got a lift that the rest of us can't get."

"I'm a free-trader,[21] myself," said one young fellow, blushing and looking away as Howard turned and said cheerily:

"So 'm I."

The rest seemed to feel that this was a tabooed subject—a subject to be talked out of doors, where one could prance about and yell and do justice to it.

Grant sat silently in the kitchen doorway, not saying a word, not looking at his brother.

"Well, I don't never use hot vinegar for mine," Mrs. McIlvaine was heard to say. "I jest use hot water, an' I rinse 'em out good, and set 'em bottom-side up in the sun. I do' know but what hot vinegar *would* be more cleansin'."

Rose had the younger folks in a giggle with a droll telling of a joke on herself.

"How'd y' stop 'em from laffin'?"

"I let 'em laugh. Oh, my school is a disgrace—so one director says. But I like to see children laugh. It broadens their cheeks."

"Yes, that's all hand-work." Laura was showing the baby's Sunday clothes.

"Goodness Peter! How do you find time to do so much?"

"I take time."

Howard, being the lion of the evening, tried his best to be agreeable. He kept near his mother, because it afforded her so much pride and satisfaction, and because he was obliged to keep away from Grant, who had begun to talk to the men. Howard talked mainly about their affairs, but still was forced more and more into talking of life in the city. As he told of the theatre and the concerts, a sudden change fell upon them; they grew sober, and he felt deep down in the hearts of these people a melancholy which was expressed only elusively with little tones or sighs. Their gayety was fitful.

They were hungry for the world, for art—these young people. Discontented and yet hardly daring to acknowledge it; indeed, few of them could have made definite

[21]Many western farmers at the time of the story were advocates of free trade, or limitations on tariffs, which they believed artificially increased the prices of many items they required.

statement of their dissatisfaction. The older people felt it less. They practically said, with a sigh of pathetic resignation:

"Well, I don't expect ever to see these things *now*."

A casual observer would have said, "What a pleasant bucolic—this little surprise-party of welcome!" But Howard with his native ear and eye had no such pleasing illusion. He knew too well these suggestions of despair and bitterness. He knew that, like the smile of the slave, this cheerfulness was self-defence; deep down was another self.

Seeing Grant talking with a group of men over by the kitchen door, he crossed over slowly and stood listening. Wesley Cosgrove—a tall, raw-boned young fellow with a grave, almost tragic face—was saying:

"Of course I ain't. Who is? A man that's satisfied to live as we do is a fool."

"The worst of it is," said Grant, without seeing Howard, "a man can't get out of it during his lifetime, and *I* don't know that he'll have any chance in the next—the speculator'll be there ahead of us."

The rest laughed, but Grant went on grimly:

"Ten years ago Wess, here, could have got land in Dakota pretty easy, but now it's about all a feller's life's worth to try it. I tell you things seem shuttin' down on us fellers."

"Plenty o' land to rent?" suggested some one.

"Yes, in terms that skin a man alive. More than that, farmin' ain't so free a life as it used to be. This cattle-raisin' and butter-makin' makes a nigger of a man. Binds him right down to the grindstone, and he gets nothin' out of it—that's what rubs it in. He simply wallers around in the manure for somebody else. I'd like to know what a man's life is worth who lives as we do? How much higher is it than the lives the niggers used to live?"

These brutally bald words made Howard thrill with emotion like some great tragic poem. A silence fell on the group.

"That's the God's truth, Grant," said young Cosgrove, after a pause.

"A man like me is helpless," Grant was saying. "Just like a fly in a pan of molasses. There ain't any escape for him. The more he tears around the more liable he is to rip his legs off."

"What can he do?"

"Nothin'."

The men listened in silence.

"Oh come, don't talk politics all night!" cried Rose, breaking in. "Come, let's have a dance. Where's that fiddle?"

"Fiddle!" cried Howard, glad of a chance to laugh. "Well, now! Bring out that fiddle. Is it William's?"

"Yes, pap's old fiddle."

"O Gosh! he don't want to hear me play," protested William. "He's heard s' many fiddlers."

"Fiddlers! I've heard a thousand violinists, but not fiddlers. Come, give us 'Honest John.'"

William took the fiddle in his work-calloused and crooked hands and began tuning it. The group at the kitchen door turned to listen, their faces lighting up a little. Rose tried to get a set on the floor.

"Oh, good land!" said some. "We're all tuckered out. What makes you so anxious?"

"She wants a chance to dance with the New Yorker."

"That's it exactly," Rose admitted.

"Wal, if you'd churned and mopped and cooked for hayin' hands as I have today, you wouldn't be so full o' nonsense."

"Oh, bother! Life's short. Come quick, get Bettie out. Come, Wess, never mind your hobby-horse."

By incredible exertion she got a set on the floor, and William got the fiddle in tune. Howard looked across at Wesley, and thought the change in him splendidly dramatic. His face had lighted up into a kind of deprecating, boyish smile. Rose could do anything with him.

William played some of the old tunes that had a thousand associated memories in Howard's brain, memories of harvest-moons, of melon-feasts, and of clear, cold winter nights. As he danced, his eyes filled with a tender, luminous light. He came closer to them all than he had been able to do before. Grant had gone out into the kitchen.

After two or three sets had been danced, the company took seats and could not be stirred again. So Laura and Rose disappeared for a few moments, and returning, served strawberries and cream, which Laura said she "just happened to have in the house."

And then William played again. His fingers, now grown more supple, brought out clearer, firmer tones. As he played, silence fell on these people. The magic of music sobered every face; the women looked older and more care-worn, the men slouched sullenly in their chairs, or leaned back against the wall.

It seemed to Howard as if the spirit of tragedy had entered this house. Music had always been William's unconscious expression of his unsatisfied desires. He was never melancholy except when he played. Then his eyes grew sombre, his drooping face full of shadows.

He played on slowly, softly, wailing Scotch tunes and mournful Irish songs. He seemed to find in the songs of these people, and especially in a wild, sweet, low-keyed negro song, some expression for his indefinable inner melancholy.

He played on, forgetful of everybody, his long beard sweeping the violin, his toil-worn hands marvellously obedient to his will.

At last he stopped, looked up with a faint, deprecating smile, and said with a sigh:

"Well, folkses, time to go home."

The going was quiet. Not much laughing. Howard stood at the door and said good-night to them all, his heart very tender.

"Come and see us," they said.

"I will," he replied cordially. "I'll try and get around to see everybody, and talk over old times, before I go back."

After the wagons had driven out of the yard, Howard turned and put his arm about his mother's neck.

"Tired?"

"A little."

"Well, now good-night. I'm going for a little stroll."

His brain was too active to sleep. He kissed his mother good-night, and went out into the road, his hat in his hand, the cool, moist wind on his hair.

It was very dark, the stars being partly hidden by a thin vapor. On each side the hills rose, every line familiar as the face of an old friend. A whippoorwill called occasionally from the hillside, and the spasmodic jangle of a bell now and then told of some cow's battle with the mosquitoes.

As he walked, he pondered upon the tragedy he had re-discovered in these people's lives. Out here under the inexorable spaces of the sky, a deep distaste of his own life took possession of him. He felt like giving it all up. He thought of the infinite tragedy of these lives which the world loves to call "peaceful and pastoral." His mind went out in the aim to help them. What could he do to make life better worth living? Nothing. They must live and die practically as he saw them to-night.

And yet he knew this was a mood, and that in a few hours the love and the habit of life would come back upon him and upon them; that he would go back to the city in a few days; that these people would live on and make the best of it.

"*I'll* make the best of it," he said at last, and his thought came back to his mother and Grant.

IV

The next day was a rainy day; not a shower, but a steady rain—an unusual thing in mid-summer in the West. A cold, dismal day in the fireless, colorless farm-houses. It came to Howard in that peculiar reaction which surely comes during a visit of this character, when thought is a weariness, when the visitor longs for his own familiar walls and pictures and books, and longs to meet his friends, feeling at the same time the tragedy of life which makes friends nearer and more congenial than blood-relations.

Howard ate his breakfast alone, save Baby and Laura, its mother, going about the room. Baby and mother alike insisted on feeding him to death. Already dyspeptic pangs were setting in.

"Now ain't there something more I can—"

"Good heavens! No!" he cried in dismay. "I'm likely to die of dyspepsia now. This honey and milk, and these delicious hot biscuits—"

"I'm afraid it ain't much like the breakfasts you have in the city."

"Well, no, it ain't," he confessed. "But this is the kind a man needs when he lives in the open air."

She sat down opposite him, with her elbows on the table, her chin in her palm, her eyes full of shadows.

"I'd like to go to a city once. I never saw a town bigger'n Lumberville. I've never seen a play, but I've read of 'em in the magazines. It must be wonderful; they say they have wharves and real ships coming up to the wharf, and people getting off and on. How do they do it?"

"Oh, that's too long a story to tell. It's a lot of machinery and paint and canvas. If I told you how it was done, you wouldn't enjoy it so well when you come on and see it."

"Do you ever expect to see *me* in New York?"

"Why, yes. Why not? I expect Grant to come on and bring you all some day, especially Tonikins here. Tonikins, you hear, sir? I expect you to come on you' forf birfday, sure." He tried thus to stop the woman's gloomy confidence.

"I hate farm-life," she went on with a bitter inflection. "It's nothing but fret, fret and work the whole time, never going any place, never seeing anybody but a lot of neighbors just as big fools as you are. I spend my time fighting flies and washing dishes and churning. I'm sick of it all."

Howard was silent. What could he say to such an indictment? The ceiling swarmed with flies which the cold rain had driven to seek the warmth of the kitchen. The gray rain was falling with a dreary sound outside, and down the kitchen stovepipe an occasional drop fell on the stove with a hissing, angry sound.

The young wife went on with a deeper note:

"I lived in Lumberville two years, going to school, and I know a little something of what city life is. If I was a man, I bet I wouldn't wear my life out on a farm, as Grant does. I'd get away and I'd do something. I wouldn't care what, but I'd get away."

There was a certain volcanic energy back of all the woman said, that made Howard feel she'd make the attempt. She didn't know that the struggle for a place to stand on this planet was eating the heart and soul out of men and women in the city, just as in the country. But he could say nothing. If he had said in conventional phrase, sitting there in his soft clothing, "We must make the best of it all," the woman could justly have thrown the dish-cloth in his face. He could say nothing.

"I was a fool for ever marrying," she went on, while the baby pushed a chair across the room. "I made a decent living teaching, I was free to come and go, my money was my own. Now I'm tied right down to a churn or a dish-pan, I never have a cent of my own. *He*'s growlin' round half the time, and there's no chance of his ever being different."

She stopped with a bitter sob in her throat. She forgot she was talking to her husband's brother. She was conscious only of his sympathy.

As if a great black cloud had settled down upon him, Howard felt it all—the horror, hopelessness, immanent tragedy of it all. The glory of nature, the bounty and splendor of the sky, only made it the more benumbing. He thought of a sentence Millet once wrote:

"I see very well the aureole of the dandelions, and the sun also, far down there behind the hills, flinging his glory upon the clouds. But not alone that—I see in the plains the smoke of the tired horses at the plough, or, on a stony-hearted spot of ground, a back-broken man trying to raise himself upright for a moment to breathe. The tragedy is surrounded by glories—that is no invention of mine."[22]

Howard arose abruptly and went back to his little bedroom, where he walked up and down the floor till he was calm enough to write, and then he sat down and poured it all out to "Dearest Margaret," and his first sentence was this:

"If it were not for you (just to let you know the mood I'm in)—if it were not *for*

[22]The quotation is adapted from a letter from Millet to the art historian Alfred Sensier. A somewhat different, fuller version of Millet's letter appears in Alfred Sensier, *Jean-François Millet: Peasant and Painter,* trans. Helena de Kay, 1880, 157–158.

you, and I had the world in my hands, I'd crush it like a puffball; evil so predominates, suffering is so universal and persistent, happiness so fleeting and so infrequent."

He wrote on for two hours, and by the time he had sealed and directed several letters he felt calmer, but still terribly depressed. The rain was still falling, sweeping down from the half-seen hills, wreathing the wooded peaks with a gray garment of mist, and filling the valley with a whitish cloud.

It fell around the house drearily. It ran down into the tubs placed to catch it, dripped from the mossy pump, and drummed on the upturned milk-pails, and upon the brown and yellow beehives under the maple-trees. The chickens seemed depressed, but the irrepressible bluejay screamed amid it all, with the same insolent spirit, his plumage untarnished by the wet. The barnyard showed a horrible mixture of mud and mire, through which Howard caught glimpses of the men, slumping to and fro without more additional protection than a ragged coat and a shapeless felt hat.

In the sitting-room where his mother sat sewing there was not an ornament, save the etching he had brought. The clock stood on a small shelf, its dial so much defaced that one could not tell the time of day; and when it struck, it was with noticeably disproportionate deliberation, as if it wished to correct any mistake into which the family might have fallen by reason of its illegible dial.

The paper on the walls showed the first concession of the Puritans to the Spirit of Beauty, and was made up of a heterogeneous mixture of flowers of unheard-of shapes and colors, arranged in four different ways along the wall. There were no books, no music, and only a few newspapers in sight—a bare, blank, cold, drab-colored shelter from the rain, not a home. Nothing cosey, nothing heart-warming; a grim and horrible shed.

"What are they doing? It can't be they're at work such a day as this," Howard said, standing at the window.

"They find plenty to do, even on rainy days," answered his mother. "Grant always has some job to set the men at. It's the only way to live."

"I'll go out and see them." He turned suddenly. "Mother, why should Grant treat me so? Have I deserved it?"

Mrs. McLane sighed in pathetic hopelessness. "I don't know, Howard. I'm worried about Grant. He gets more an' more down-hearted an' gloomy every day. Seems if he'd go crazy. He don't care how he looks any more, won't dress up on Sunday. Days an' days he'll go aroun' not sayin' a word. I was in hopes you could help him, Howard."

"My coming seems to have had an opposite effect. He hasn't spoken a word to me, except when he had to, since I came. Mother, what do you say to going home with me to New York?"

"Oh, I couldn't do that!" she cried in terror. "I couldn't live in a big city—never!"

"There speaks the truly rural mind," smiled Howard at his mother, who was looking up at him through her glasses with a pathetic forlornness which sobered him again. "Why, mother, you could live in Orange, New Jersey, or out in Connecticut, and be just as lonesome as you are here. You wouldn't need to live in the city. I could see you then every day or two."

"Well, I couldn't leave Grant an' the baby, anyway," she replied, not realizing how one could live in New Jersey and do business daily in New York.

"Well, then, how would you like to go back into the old house?" he said, facing her.

The patient hands fell to the lap, the dim eyes fixed in searching glance on his face. There was a wistful cry in the voice.

"Oh, Howard! Do you mean—"

He came and sat down by her, and put his arm about her and hugged her hard. "I mean, you dear, good, patient, work-weary old mother, I'm going to buy back the old farm and put you in it."

There was no refuge for her now except in tears, and she put up her thin, trembling old hands about his neck, and cried in that easy, placid, restful way age has.

Howard could not speak. His throat ached with remorse and pity. He saw his forgetfulness of them all once more without relief,—the black thing it was!

"There, there mother, don't cry!" he said, torn with anguish by her tears. Measured by man's tearlessness, her weeping seemed terrible to him. "I didn't realize how things were going here. It was all my fault—or, at least, most of it. Grant's letter didn't reach me. I thought you were still on the old farm. But no matter; it's all over now. Come, don't cry any more, mother dear. I'm going to take care of you now."

It had been years since the poor, lonely woman had felt such warmth of love. Her sons had been like her husband, chary of expressing their affection; and like most Puritan families, there was little of caressing among them. Sitting there with the rain on the roof and driving through the trees, they planned getting back into the old house. Howard's plan seemed to her full of splendor and audacity. She began to understand his power and wealth now, as he put it into concrete form before her.

"I wish I could eat Thanksgiving dinner there with you," he said at last, "but it can't be thought of. However, I'll have you all in there before I go home. I'm going out now and tell Grant. Now don't worry any more; I'm going to fix it all up with him, sure." He gave her a parting hug.

Laura advised him not to attempt to get to the barn; but as he persisted in going, she hunted up an old rubber coat for him. "You'll mire down and spoil your shoes," she said, glancing at his neat calf gaiters.

"Darn the difference!" he laughed in his old way. "Besides, I've got rubbers."

"Better go round by the fence," she advised, as he stepped out into the pouring rain.

How wretchedly familiar it all was! The miry cow-yard, with the hollow trampled out around the horse-trough, the disconsolate hens standing under the wagons and sheds, a pig wallowing across its sty, and for atmosphere the desolate, falling rain. It was so familiar he felt a pang of the old rebellious despair which seized him on such days in his boyhood.

Catching up courage, he stepped out on the grass, opened the gate and entered the barnyard. A narrow ribbon of turf ran around the fence, on which he could walk by clinging with one hand to the rough boards. In this way he slowly made his way around the periphery, and came at last to the open barn-door without much harm.

It was a desolate interior. In the open floorway Grant, seated upon a half-bushel, was mending a harness. The old man was holding the trace in his hard brown hands; the boy was lying on a wisp of hay. It was a small barn, and poor at that. There was a bad smell, as of dead rats, about it, and the rain fell through the shingles here and there. To the right, and below, the horses stood, looking up with their calm and beautiful eyes, in which the whole scene was idealized.

Grant looked up an instant and then went on with his work.

"Did yeh wade through?" grinned Lewis, exposing his broken teeth.

"No, I kinder circumambiated the pond." He sat down on the little tool-box near Grant. "Your barn is a good deal like that in 'The Arkansas Traveller.' Needs a new roof, Grant." His voice had a pleasant sound, full of the tenderness of the scene through which he had just been. "In fact, you need a new barn."

"I need a good many things more'n I'll ever get," Grant replied shortly.

"How long did you say you'd been on this farm?"

"Three years this fall."

"I don't s'pose you've been able to think of buying— Now hold on, Grant," he cried, as Grant threw his head back. "For God's sake, don't get mad again! Wait till you see what I'm driving at."

"I don't see what you're drivin' at, and I don't care. All I want you to do is to let us alone. That ought to be easy enough for you."

"I tell you, I didn't get your letter. I didn't know you'd lost the old farm." Howard was determined not to quarrel. "I didn't suppose—"

"You might 'a' come to see."

"Well, I'll admit that. All I can say in excuse is that since I got to managing plays I've kept looking ahead to making a big hit and getting a barrel of money—just as the old miners used to hope and watch. Besides, you don't understand how much pressure there is on me. A hundred different people pulling and hauling to have me go here or go there, or do this or do that. When it isn't yachting, it's canoeing, or—"

He stopped. His heart gave a painful throb, and a shiver ran through him. Again he saw his life, so rich, so bright, so free, set over against the routine life in the little low kitchen, the barren sitting-room, and this still more horrible barn. Why should his brother sit there in wet and grimy clothing mending a broken trace, while he enjoyed all the light and civilization of the age?

He looked at Grant's fine figure, his great strong face; recalled his deep, stern, masterful voice. "Am I so much superior to him? Have not circumstances made me and destroyed him?"

"Grant, for God's sake, don't sit there like that! I'll admit I've been negligent and careless. I can't understand it all myself. But let me do something for you now. I've sent to New York for five thousand dollars. I've got terms on the old farm. Let me see you all back there once more before I return."

"I don't want any of your charity."

"It ain't charity. It's only justice to you." He rose. "Come now, let's get at an understanding, Grant. I can't go on this way. I can't go back to New York and leave you here like this."

Grant rose too. "I tell you, I don't ask your help. You can't fix this thing up with money. If you've got more brains 'n I have, why it's all right. I ain't got any right to take anything that I don't earn."

"But you don't get what you do earn. It ain't your fault. I begin to see it now. Being the oldest, I had the best chance. I was going to town to school while you were ploughing and husking corn. Of course I thought you'd be going soon, yourself. I had three years the start of you. If you'd been in my place, *you* might have met a man like Cooke, *you* might have gone to New York and have been where I am."

"Well, it can't be helped now. So drop it."

"But it must be!" Howard said, pacing about, his hands in his coat-pockets. Grant had stopped work, and was gloomily looking out of the door at a pig nosing in the mud for stray grains of wheat at the granary door:

"Good God! I see it all now," Howard burst out in an impassioned tone. "I went ahead with *my* education, got *my* start in life, then father died, and you took up his burdens. Circumstances made me and crushed you. That's all there is about that. Luck made me and cheated you. It ain't right."

His voice faltered. Both men were now oblivious of their companions and of the scene. Both were thinking of the days when they both planned great things in the way of an education, two ambitious, dreamful boys.

"I used to think of you, Grant, when I pulled out Monday morning in my best suit—cost fifteen dollars in those days." He smiled a little at the recollection. "While you in overalls and an old 'wammus'[23] was going out into the field to plough, or husk corn in the mud. It made me feel uneasy, but, as I said, I kept saying to myself, 'His turn'll come in a year or two.' But it didn't."

His voice choked. He walked to the door, stood a moment, came back. His eyes were full of tears.

"I tell you, old man, many a time in my boarding-house down to the city, when I thought of the jolly times I was having, my heart hurt me. But I said: 'It's no use to cry. Better go on and do the best you can, and then help them afterwards. There'll only be one more miserable member of the family if you stay at home.' Besides, it seemed right to me to have first chance. But I never thought you'd be shut off, Grant. If I had, I never would have gone on. Come, old man, I want you to believe that." His voice was very tender now and almost humble.

"I don't know as I blame yeh for that, How," said Grant, slowly. It was the first time he had called Howard by his boyish nickname. His voice was softer, too, and higher in key. But he looked steadily away.

"I went to New York. People liked my work. I was very successful, Grant; more successful than you realize. I could have helped you at any time. There's no use lying about it. And I ought to have done it; but some way—it's no excuse, I don't mean it for an excuse, only an explanation—some way I got in with the boys. I don't mean I was a drinker and all that. But I bought pictures and kept a horse and a yacht, and of course I had to pay my share of all expeditions, and—oh, what's the use!"

He broke off, turned, and threw his open palms out toward his brother, as if throwing aside the last attempt at an excuse.

"I *did* neglect you, and it's a damned shame! and I ask your forgiveness. Come, old man!"

He held out his hand, and Grant slowly approached and took it. There was a little silence. Then Howard went on, his voice trembling, the tears on his face.

"I want you to let me help you, old man. That's the way to forgive me. Will you?"

[23]Loose-fitting work jacket.

"Yes, if you can help me."

Howard squeezed his hand. "That's right, old man. Now you make me a boy again. Course I can help you. I've got ten—"

"I don't mean that, How." Grant's voice was very grave. "Money can't give me a chance now."

"What do you mean?"

"I mean life ain't worth very much to me. I'm too old to take a new start. I'm a dead failure. I've come to the conclusion that life's a failure for ninety-nine per cent of us. You can't help me now. It's too late."

The two men stood there, face to face, hands clasped, the one fair-skinned, full-lipped, handsome in his neat suit; the other tragic, sombre in his softened mood, his large, long, rugged Scotch face bronzed with sun and scarred with wrinkles that had histories, like sabre-cuts on a veteran, the record of his battles.

1891

Stephen Crane 1871–1900

With the publication of his Civil War novel, *The Red Badge of Courage* (1895), when he was twenty-four years old, Stephen Crane became famous in the United States and England. Less than five years later he was dead of tuberculosis. In his brief life, however, he had published five novels, two volumes of poetry, and over three hundred sketches, reports, and short stories. His writings significantly enriched the subject matter of American literature, and his craftsmanship influenced both poetry and prose in the twentieth century.

Crane was born in Newark, New Jersey, the fourteenth child of Jonathan Townley Crane, a Methodist minister, and Mary Helen Peck Crane, who was herself descended from a long line of Methodist clergy. The family moved frequently, and Crane's formal education included brief stays at Pennington Seminary, Lafayette College, Claverack College, and Syracuse University. At Claverack, a military school, he gained the rank of adjutant and may have had experiences that contributed to his later success in writing about war, the subject for which he became famous. In 1891 Crane left Syracuse to work as a journalist in New York City, where he lived in a community of struggling artists and medical students that he depicted, some years later, in his novel of manners, *The Third Violet* (1897). Most important, during this period he published *Maggie: A Girl of the Streets* (1893), a powerful portrayal of the blighted, poverty-stricken lives of the Bowery. Although few copies were sold, the book led to Crane's friendships with two of the leading figures in American literary realism, Hamlin Garland and William Dean Howells, both of whom publicly praised the book.

Crane's interest in the powerful role of environment in shaping character and determining lives derived both from the ideas of Charles Darwin and from his work as a journalist. While still in his teens he had written articles for the Asbury Park, New Jersey, newspaper and worked as a part-time stringer for the *New York Tribune.* During his years in New York City he wrote many works about city life that reflected his interest in extreme environments. The sketches, "An Experiment in Misery" and "An Experiment in Luxury"

(1894), in which he described living in a flophouse and in a millionaire's mansion, recorded the effects of these experiences on his own consciousness. As experiments in perception, they anticipated the subjective "new journalism" of the 1960s, such as Norman Mailer's *Armies of the Night.*

Crane's interest in environmental determinism links him to late-nineteenth-century naturalistic writers such as Frank Norris, Jack London, and Theodore Dreiser, but he avoids their often heavy factual documentation; instead, he usually defines his characters with sharply focused comments and vivid images. Such compression and imagery and an intense concern with color have led numerous critics to see in his writing a literary parallel to impressionist painting. Crane is comparable to both naturalists and impressionists in his desire to shock readers with new and often disturbing ideas and perceptions. For example, he rejected the conventionalities of small-town life that he had known as a child (about which he would write in *Whilomville Stories,* 1900) and the intense religious piety of his parents. He seems, when quite young, to have developed skepticism about "the lake of fire and other sideshows" of conventional Christianity.

In his poetry, collected in *The Black Riders and Other Lines* (1895) and *War Is Kind* (1900), he often aims rebukes at conventional piety while also revealing his preoccupation with questions that parallel the concerns of religion. Experimental in form, unconventional in rhyme, and brief often to the point of being cryptic, Crane's poems in some ways foreshadowed the *vers libre* of the early twentieth century and also bear resemblance to the koans of Zen Buddhist religious practice. When published, their brevity was comparable to that of Emily Dickinson's poems, but to a large degree they were unlike any poems written previously in the United States.

Crane's Civil War writings are imaginative reconstructions of events that took place before he was born. Historical writings and conversations with veterans contributed to his understanding of the war, but such sources do not fully explain his powerful rendering of the young recruit, Henry Fleming, and his consciousness in *The Red Badge of Courage* or equally powerful passages in "A Mystery of Heroism" (1895) and other works. The Civil War seems to have been an unusually provocative stimulus for Crane's imagination, enabling him to envision emotional and psychological struggles in nearly hallucinatory detail. For example, his intuition enabled him to be among the first writers to describe the effect of the modern bullet upon the soldier's perception of space in landscape.

Scholars have sometimes argued that Crane wrote best from his imagination and simply exhausted himself pursuing facts in the Bowery, the West, and the battlefields of Greece and Cuba. But Crane sought such experience. In 1895, in the first flush of success of *The Red Badge of Courage,* he traveled in the American West and in Mexico. Later he expressed a desire to go to Alaska and to the Transvaal to report on the Boers. In 1897 he tried to slip into Cuba to observe the guerrilla insurgency. Later that same year he traveled to Europe to report the Greco-Turkish war. The reports he wrote in these instances are uneven, but at their best they are vivid and thoughtful journalism. Most important, Crane drew upon these experiences for some of his most successful short stories, most notably "The Bride Comes to Yellow Sky" (1898), "The Blue Hotel" (1898), and "Death and the Child" (1898). Although his strenuous travel adventures may have shortened his life, they also provided him with the material for some of his most probing fictions.

"The Open Boat" (1898), the story that many critics believe is Crane's best piece of work, is a remarkable fusion of his respect for the power of the external world and his intense concern with the mysterious inner world of emotions and fantasies. The story derives directly from his experience in a dinghy adrift at sea for thirty hours after the sinking of the *Commodore,* a steamship illegally bound for Cuba shortly before the Spanish-American War. In exploring the developing consciousness of the narrator, his growing awareness of nature, and his deepening relationships to other human beings, the story measures the vastness of human loneliness and defines a brotherhood of those who have encountered the sea. "The Open Boat" balances cosmic uncertainties with glimpses of human achievements in awareness, cooperation, and courage.

After his ordeal at sea, Crane was nursed back to health by Cora Taylor, the proprietor of a house of assignation in Jacksonville, Florida, whom he had met shortly before the ill-fated *Commodore* left port. They traveled together to Greece and then to England, where, early in 1898, they moved into an ancient manor house in Sussex, with the writers Henry James and Joseph Conrad for neighbors. Brede House was an extravagant distraction for Crane; nevertheless, during his period there he produced a substantial amount of work, including poems, stories, a novel (*Active Service*), and part of a historical romance (*The O'Ruddy*). Much of this work shows his continuing fascination with the behavior of individuals under the pressure of extreme situations.

Crane seems to have first learned he was tubercular when he tried to enlist in the army in 1897 to go to Cuba. It appears he did little to regain his health. When he became very ill in April 1900, Cora took him in desperation to a sanitorium in the Black Forest in Germany, where he died on June 5.

Donald Vanouse
State University of New York
(College at Oswego)

PRIMARY WORKS

Maggie: A Girl of the Streets (1893), A Facsimile of the First Edition, ed. Donald Pizer, 1968; *The Works of Stephen Crane,* 12 vols., ed. Fredson Bowers, 1969–76; *The Correspondence of Stephen Crane,* 2 vols., ed. Stanley Wertheim and Paul Sorrentino, 1987.

A Mystery of Heroism

A Detail of an American Battle

The dark uniforms of the men were so coated with dust from the incessant wrestling of the two armies that the regiment almost seemed a part of the clay bank which shielded them from the shells. On the top of the hill a battery was arguing in tremendous roars with some other guns and to the eye of the infantry, the artillerymen, the guns, the caissons, the horses, were distinctly outlined upon the blue sky. When a piece was fired a red streak as round as a log flashed low in the heavens, like a monstrous bolt of lightning. The men of the battery wore white duck trousers, which somehow emphasized their legs, and when they ran and crowded in little groups at the bidding of the shouting officers, it was more impressive than usual to the infantry.

Fred Collins of A Company was saying: "Thunder, I wisht I had a drink. Ain't there any water round here?" Then somebody yelled: "There goes th' bugler!"

As the eyes of half of the regiment swept in one machine-like movement there was an instant's picture of a horse in a great convulsive leap of a death wound and a rider leaning back with a crooked arm and spread fingers before his face. On the ground was the crimson terror of an exploding shell, with fibres of flame that seemed like lances. A glittering bugle swung clear of the rider's back as fell headlong the horse and the man. In the air was an odor as from a conflagration.

Sometimes they of the infantry looked down at a fair little meadow which spread at their feet. Its long, green grass was rippling gently in a breeze. Beyond it was the grey form of a house half torn to pieces by shells and by the busy axes of soldiers who had pursued firewood. The line of an old fence was now dimly marked by long weeds and by an occasional post. A shell had blown the well-house to fragments. Little lines of grey smoke ribboning upward from some embers indicated the place where had stood the barn.

From beyond a curtain of green woods there came the sound of some stupendous scuffle as if two animals of the size of islands were fighting. At a distance there were occasional appearances of swift-moving men, horses, batteries, flags, and, with the crashing of infantry volleys were heard, often, wild and frenzied cheers. In the midst of it all, Smith and Ferguson, two privates of A Company, were engaged in a heated discussion, which involved the greatest questions of the national existence.

The battery on the hill presently engaged in a frightful duel. The white legs of the gunners scampered this way and that way and the officers redoubled their shouts. The guns, with their demeanors of stolidity and courage, were typical of something infinitely self-possessed in this clamor of death that swirled around the hill.

One of the "swing" team was suddenly smitten quivering to the ground and his maddened brethren dragged his torn body in their struggle to escape from this turmoil and danger. A young soldier astride one of the leaders swore and fumed in his saddle and furiously jerked at the bridle. An officer screamed out an order so violently that his voice broke and ended the sentence in a falsetto shriek.

The leading company of the infantry regiment was somewhat exposed and the colonel ordered it moved more fully under the shelter of the hill. There was the clank of steel against steel.

A lieutenant of the battery rode down and passed them, holding his right arm carefully in his left hand. And it was as if this arm was not at all a part of him, but belonged to another man. His sober and reflective charger went slowly. The officer's face was grimy and perspiring and his uniform was tousled as if he had been in direct grapple with an enemy. He smiled grimly when the men stared at him. He turned his horse toward the meadow.

Collins of A Company said: "I wisht I had a drink. I bet there's water in that there ol' well yonder!"

"Yes; but how you goin' to git it?"

For the little meadow which intervened was now suffering a terrible onslaught of shells. Its green and beautiful calm had vanished utterly. Brown earth was being flung in monstrous handfuls. And there was a massacre of the young blades of grass.

They were being torn, burned, obliterated. Some curious fortune of the battle had made this gentle little meadow the object of the red hate of the shells and each one as it exploded seemed like an imprecation in the face of a maiden.

The wounded officer who was riding across this expanse said to himself: "Why, they couldn't shoot any harder if the whole army was massed here!"

A shell struck the grey ruins of the house and as, after the roar, the shattered wall fell in fragments, there was a noise which resembled the flapping of shutters during a wild gale of winter. Indeed the infantry paused in the shelter of the bank, appeared as men standing upon a shore contemplating a madness of the sea. The angel of calamity had under its glance the battery upon the hill. Fewer white-legged men labored about the guns. A shell had smitten one of the pieces and after the flare, the smoke, the dust, the wrath of this blow was gone, it was possible to see white legs stretched horizontally upon the ground. And at that interval to the rear, where it is the business of battery horses to stand with their noses to the fight awaiting the command to drag their guns out of the destruction or into it or wheresoever these incomprehensible humans demanded with whip and spur—in this line of passive and dumb spectators, whose fluttering hearts yet would not let them forget the iron laws of man's control of them—in this rank of brute-soldiers there had been relentless and hideous carnage. From the ruck of bleeding and prostrate horses, the men of the infantry could see one animal raising its stricken body with its fore-legs and turning its nose with mystic and profound eloquence toward the sky.

Some comrades joked Collins about his thirst. "Well, if yeh want a drink so bad, why don't yeh go git it?"

"Well, I will in a minnet if yeh don't shut up."

A lieutenant of artillery floundered his horse straight down the hill with as great concern as if it were level ground. As he galloped past the colonel of the infantry, he threw up his hand in swift salute. "We've got to get out of that," he roared angrily. He was a black-bearded officer, and his eyes, which resembled beads, sparkled like those of an insane man. His jumping horse sped along the column of infantry.

The fat major standing carelessly with his sword held horizontally behind him and with his legs far apart, looked after the receding horseman and laughed. "He wants to get back with orders pretty quick or there'll be no batt'ry left," he observed.

The wise young captain of the second company hazarded to the lieutenant colonel that the enemy's infantry would probably soon attack the hill, and the lieutenant colonel snubbed him.

A private in one of the rear companies looked out over the meadow and then turned to a companion and said: "Look there, Jim." It was the wounded officer from the battery, who some time before had started to ride across the meadow, supporting his right arm carefully with his left hand. This man had encountered a shell apparently at a time when no one perceived him and he could now be seen lying face downward with a stirruped foot stretched across the body of his dead horse. A leg of the charger extended slantingly upward precisely as stiff as a stake. Around this motionless pair the shells still howled.

There was a quarrel in A Company. Collins was shaking his fist in the faces of some laughing comrades. "Dern yeh! I ain't afraid t'go. If yeh say much, I will go!"

"Of course, yeh will! Yeh'll run through that there medder, won't yeh?"

Collins said, in a terrible voice: "You see, now!" At this ominous threat his comrades broke into renewed jeers.

Collins gave them a dark scowl and went to find his captain. The latter was conversing with the colonel of the regiment.

"Captain," said Collins, saluting and standing at attention. In those days all trousers bagged at the knees. "Captain, I want t' git permission to go git some water from that there well over yonder!"

The colonel and the captain swung about simultaneously and stared across the meadow. The captain laughed. "You must be pretty thirsty, Collins?"

"Yes, sir; I am."

"Well—ah," said the captain. After a moment he asked: "Can't you wait?"

"No, sir."

The colonel was watching Collins's face. "Look here, my lad," he said, in a pious sort of a voice. "Look here, my lad." Collins was not a lad. "Don't you think that's taking pretty big risks for a little drink of water?"

"I dunno," said Collins, uncomfortably. Some of the resentment toward his companions, which perhaps had forced him into this affair, was beginning to fade. "I dunno wether 'tis."

The colonel and the captain contemplated him for a time.

"Well," said the captain finally.

"Well," said the colonel, "if you want to go, why go."

Collins saluted. "Much obliged t' yeh."

As he moved away the colonel called after him. "Take some of the other boys' canteens with you an' hurry back now."

"Yes, sir. I will."

The colonel and the captain looked at each other then, for it had suddenly occurred that they could not for the life of them tell whether Collins wanted to go or whether he did not.

They turned to regard Collins and as they perceived him surrounded by gesticulating comrades the colonel said: "Well, by thunder! I guess he's going."

Collins appeared as a man dreaming. In the midst of the questions, the advice, the warnings, all the excited talk of his company mates, he maintained a curious silence.

They were very busy in preparing him for his ordeal. When they inspected him carefully it was somewhat like the examination that grooms give a horse before a race; and they were amazed, staggered by the whole affair. Their astonishment found vent in strange repetitions.

"Are yeh sure a-goin'?" they demanded again and again.

"Certainly I am," cried Collins, at last furiously.

He strode sullenly away from them. He was swinging five or six canteens by their cords. It seemed that his cap would not remain firmly on his head, and often he reached and pulled it down over his brow.

There was a general movement in the compact column. The long animal-like thing moved slightly. Its four hundred eyes were turned upon the figure of Collins.

"Well, sir, if that ain't th' derndest thing. I never thought Fred Collins had the blood in him for that kind of business."

"What's he goin' to do, anyhow?"

"He's goin' to that well there after water."

"We ain't dyin' of thirst, are we? That's foolishness."

"Well, somebody put him up to it an' he's doin' it."

"Say, he must be a desperate cuss."

When Collins faced the meadow and walked away from the regiment he was vaguely conscious that a chasm, the deep valley of all prides, was suddenly between him and his comrades. It was provisional, but the provision was that he return as a victor. He had blindly been led by quaint emotions and laid himself under an obligation to walk squarely up to the face of death.

But he was not sure that he wished to make a retraction even if he could do so without shame. As a matter of truth he was sure of very little. He was mainly surprised.

It seemed to him supernaturally strange that he had allowed his mind to maneuver his body into such a situation. He understood that it might be called dramatically great.

However, he had no full appreciation of anything excepting that he was actually conscious of being dazed. He could feel his dulled mind groping after the form and color of this incident.

Too, he wondered why he did not feel some keen agony of fear cutting his sense like a knife. He wondered at this because human expression had said loudly for centuries that men should feel afraid of certain things and that all men who did not feel this fear were phenomena, heroes.

He was then a hero. He suffered that disappointment which we would all have if we discovered that we were ourselves capable of those deeds which we most admire in history and legend. This, then, was a hero. After all, heroes were not much.

No, it could not be true. He was not a hero. Heroes had no shames in their lives and, as for him, he remembered borrowing fifteen dollars from a friend and promising to pay it back the next day, and then avoiding that friend for ten months. When at home his mother had aroused him for the early labor of his life on the farm, it had often been his fashion to be irritable, childish, diabolical, and his mother had died since he had come to the war.

He saw that in this matter of the well, the canteens, the shells, he was an intruder in the land of fine deeds.

He was now about thirty paces from his comrades. The regiment had just turned its many faces toward him.

From the forest of terrific noises there suddenly emerged a little uneven line of men. They fired fiercely and rapidly at distant foliage on which appeared little puffs of white smoke. The spatter of skirmish firing was added to the thunder of the guns on the hill. The little line of men ran forward. A color-sergeant fell flat with his flag as if he had slipped on ice. There was hoarse cheering from this distant field.

Collins suddenly felt that two demon fingers were pressed into his ears. He could see nothing but flying arrows, flaming red. He lurched from the shock of this explosion, but he made a mad rush for the house, which he viewed as a man submerged to the neck in a boiling surf might view the shore. In the air, little pieces of shell howled and the earthquake explosions drove him insane with the menace of their roar. As he ran the canteens knocked together with a rhythmical tinkling.

As he neared the house each detail of the scene became vivid to him. He was aware of some bricks of the vanished chimney lying on the sod. There was a door which hung by one hinge.

Rifle bullets called forth by the insistent skirmishers came from the far-off bank of foliage. They mingled with the shells and the pieces of shells until the air was torn in all directions by hootings, yells, howls. The sky was full of fiends who directed all their wild rage at his head.

When he came to the well he flung himself face downward and peered into its darkness. There were furtive silver glintings some feet from the surface. He grabbed one of the canteens and, unfastening its cap, swung it down by the cord. The water flowed slowly in with an indolent gurgle.

And now as he lay with his face turned away he was suddenly smitten with the terror. It came upon his heart like the grasp of claws. All the power faded from his muscles. For an instant he was no more than a dead man.

The canteen filled with a maddening slowness in the manner of all bottles. Presently he recovered his strength and addressed a screaming oath to it. He leaned over until it seemed as if he intended to try to push water into it with his hands. His eyes as he gazed down into the well shone like two pieces of metal and in their expression was a great appeal and a great curse. The stupid water derided him.

There was the blaring thunder of a shell. Crimson light shone through the swift-boiling smoke and made a pink reflection on part of the wall of the well. Collins jerked out his arm and canteen with the same motion that a man would use in withdrawing his head from a furnace.

He scrambled erect and glared and hesitated. On the ground near him lay the old well bucket, with a length of rusty chain. He lowered it swiftly into the well. The bucket struck the water and then turning lazily over, sank. When, with hand reaching tremblingly over hand, he hauled it out, it knocked often against the walls of the well and spilled some of its contents.

In running with a filled bucket, a man can adopt but one kind of gait. So through this terrible field over which screamed practical angels of death Collins ran in the manner of a farmer chased out of a dairy by a bull.

His face went staring white with anticipation—anticipation of a blow that would whirl him around and down. He would fall as he had seen other men fall, the life knocked out of them so suddenly that their knees were no more quick to touch the ground than their heads. He saw the long blue line of the regiment, but his comrades were standing looking at him from the edge of an impossible star. He was aware of some deep wheel ruts and hoof prints in the sod beneath his feet.

The artillery officer who had fallen in this meadow had been making groans in the teeth of the tempest of sound. These futile cries, wrenched from him by his agony, were heard only by shells, bullets. When wild-eyed Collins came running, this officer raised himself. His face contorted and blanched from pain, he was about to utter some great beseeching cry. But suddenly his face straightened and he called: "Say, young man, give me a drink of water, will you?"

Collins had no room amid his emotions for surprise. He was mad from the threats of destruction.

"I can't," he screamed, and in this reply was a full description of his quaking apprehension. His cap was gone and his hair was riotous. His clothes made it appear that he had been dragged over the ground by the heels. He ran on.

The officer's head sank down and one elbow crooked. His foot in its brass-bound stirrup still stretched over the body of his horse and the other leg was under the steed.

But Collins turned. He came dashing back. His face had now turned grey and in his eyes was all terror. "Here it is! Here it is!"

The officer was as a man gone in drink. His arm bended like a twig. His head drooped as if his neck was of willow. He was sinking to the ground, to lie face downward.

Collins grabbed him by the shoulder. "Here it is. Here's your drink. Turn over! Turn over, man, for God's sake!"

With Collins hauling at his shoulder, the officer twisted his body and fell with his face turned toward that region where lived the unspeakable noises of the swirling missiles. There was the faintest shadow of a smile on his lips as he looked at Collins. He gave a sigh, a little primitive breath like that from a child.

Collins tried to hold the bucket steadily, but his shaking hands caused the water to splash all over the face of the dying man. Then he jerked it away and ran on.

The regiment gave him a welcoming roar. The grimed faces were wrinkled in laughter.

His captain waved the bucket away. "Give it to the men!"

The two genial, sky-larking young lieutenants were the first to gain possession of it. They played over it in their fashion.

When one tried to drink the other teasingly knocked his elbow. "Don't, Billie! You'll make me spill it," said the one. The other laughed.

Suddenly there was an oath, the thud of wood on the ground, and a swift murmur of astonishment from the ranks. The two lieutenants glared at each other. The bucket lay on the ground empty.

1895

The Open Boat

A Tale Intended to Be After the Fact Being the Experience of Four Men from the Sunk Steamer Commodore

I

None of them knew the color of the sky. Their eyes glanced level, and were fastened upon the waves that swept toward them. These waves were of the hue of slate, save for the tops, which were of foaming white, and all of the men knew the colors of the sea. The horizon narrowed and widened, and dipped and rose, and at all times its edge was jagged with waves that seemed thrust up in points like rocks.

Many a man ought to have a bath-tub larger than the boat which here rode upon the sea. These waves were most wrongfully and barbarously abrupt and tall, and each froth-top was a problem in small boat navigation.

The cook squatted in the bottom and looked with both eyes at the six inches of gunwale which separated him from the ocean. His sleeves were rolled over his fat forearms, and the two flaps of his unbuttoned vest dangled as he bent to bail out the boat. Often he said: "Gawd! That was a narrow clip." As he remarked it he invariably gazed eastward over the broken sea.

The oiler, steering with one of the two oars in the boat, sometimes raised himself suddenly to keep clear of water that swirled in over the stern. It was a thin little oar and it seemed often ready to snap.

The correspondent, pulling at the other oar, watched the waves and wondered why he was there.

The injured captain, lying in the bow, was at this time buried in that profound dejection and indifference which comes, temporarily at least, to even the bravest and most enduring when, willy nilly, the firm fails, the army loses, the ship goes down. The mind of the master of a vessel is rooted deep in the timbers of her, though he command for a day or a decade, and this captain had on him the stern impression of a scene in the grays of dawn of seven turned faces, and later a stump of a top-mast with a white ball on it that slashed to and fro at the waves, went low and lower, and down. Thereafter there was something strange in his voice. Although steady, it was deep with mourning, and of a quality beyond oration or tears.

"Keep'er a little more south, Billie," said he.

"'A little more south,' sir," said the oiler in the stern.

A seat in this boat was not unlike a seat upon a bucking broncho, and, by the same token, a broncho is not much smaller. The craft pranced and reared, and plunged like an animal. As each wave came, and she rose for it, she seemed like a horse making at a fence outrageously high. The manner of her scramble over these walls of water is a mystic thing, and, moreover, at the top of them were ordinarily these problems in white water, the foam racing down from the summit of each wave, requiring a new leap, and a leap from the air. Then, after scornfully bumping a crest, she would slide, and race, and splash down a long incline and arrive bobbing and nodding in front of the next menace.

A singular disadvantage of the sea lies in the fact that after successfully surmounting one wave you discover that there is another behind it just as important and just as nervously anxious to do something effective in the way of swamping boats. In a ten-foot dingey one can get an idea of the resources of the sea in the line of waves that is not probable to the average experience, which is never at sea in a dingey. As each slaty wall of water approached, it shut all else from the view of the men in the boat, and it was not difficult to imagine that this particular wave was the final outburst of the ocean, the last effort of the grim water. There was a terrible grace in the move of the waves, and they came in silence, save for the snarling of the crests.

In the wan light, the faces of the men must have been gray. Their eyes must have glinted in strange ways as they gazed steadily astern. Viewed from a balcony, the whole thing would doubtlessly have been weirdly picturesque. But the men in the boat had no time to see it, and if they had had leisure there were other things to occupy their minds. The sun swung steadily up the sky, and they knew it was broad day because the color of the sea changed from slate to emerald-green, streaked with amber lights, and the foam was like tumbling snow. The process of the breaking day was unknown to them. They were aware only of this effect upon the color of the waves that rolled toward them.

In disjointed sentences the cook and the correspondent argued as to the difference between a life-saving station and a house of refuge. The cook had said: "There's a house of refuge just north of the Mosquito Inlet Light, and as soon as they see us, they'll come off in their boat and pick us up."

"As soon as who see us?" said the correspondent.

"The crew," said the cook.

"Houses of refuge don't have crews," said the correspondent. "As I understand them, they are only places where clothes and grub are stored for the benefit of shipwrecked people. They don't carry crews."

"Oh, yes, they do," said the cook.

"No, they don't," said the correspondent.

"Well, we're not there yet, anyhow," said the oiler, in the stern.

"Well," said the cook, "perhaps it's not a house of refuge that I'm thinking of as being near Mosquito Inlet Light. Perhaps it's a life-saving station."

"We're not there yet," said the oiler, in the stern.

II

As the boat bounced from the top of each wave, the wind tore through the hair of the hatless men, and as the craft plopped her stern down again the spray slashed past them. The crest of each of these waves was a hill, from the top of which the men surveyed, for a moment, a broad tumultuous expanse; shining and wind-riven. It was probably splendid. It was probably glorious, this play of the free sea, wild with lights of emerald and white and amber.

"Bully good thing it's an on-shore wind," said the cook. "If not, where would we be? Wouldn't have a show."

"That's right," said the correspondent.

The busy oiler nodded his assent.

Then the captain, in the bow, chuckled in a way that expressed humor, contempt, tragedy, all in one. "Do you think we've got much of a show, now, boys?" said he.

Whereupon the three were silent, save for a trifle of hemming and hawing. To express any particular optimism at this time they felt to be childish and stupid, but they all doubtless possessed this sense of the situation in their mind. A young man thinks doggedly at such times. On the other hand, the ethics of their condition was decidedly against any open suggestion of hopelessness. So they were silent.

"Oh, well," said the captain, soothing his children, "we'll get ashore all right."

But there was that in his tone which made them think, so the oiler quoth:

"Yes! If this wind holds!"

The cook was bailing: "Yes! If we don't catch hell in the surf."

Canton flannel gulls flew near and far. Sometimes they sat down on the sea, near patches of brown sea-weed that rolled over the waves with a movement like carpets on a line in a gale. The birds sat comfortably in groups, and they were envied by some in the dingey, for the wrath of the sea was no more to them than it was to a covey of prairie chickens a thousand miles inland. Often they came very close and stared at the men with black beadlike eyes. At these times they were uncanny and sinister in their unblinking scrutiny, and the men hooted angrily at them, telling them to be gone. One came, and evidently decided to alight on the top of the captain's head. The bird flew parallel to the boat and did not circle, but made short sidelong jumps in the air in chicken-fashion. His black eyes were wistfully fixed upon the captain's head. "Ugly brute," said the oiler to the bird. "You look as if you were made with a jack-knife." The cook and the correspondent swore darkly at the creature. The captain naturally wished to knock it away with the end of the heavy painter,[1] but he did not dare do it, because anything resembling an emphatic gesture would have capsized this freighted boat, and so with his open hand, the captain gently and carefully waved the gull away. After it had been discouraged from the pursuit the captain breathed easier on account of his hair, and others breathed easier because the bird struck their minds at this time as being somehow grewsome and ominous.

In the meantime the oiler and the correspondent rowed. And also they rowed.

They sat together in the same seat, and each rowed an oar. Then the oiler took both oars; then the correspondent took both oars; then the oiler; then the correspondent. They rowed and they rowed. The very ticklish part of the business was when the time came for the reclining one in the stern to take his turn at the oars. By the very last star of truth, it is easier to steal eggs from under a hen than it was to change seats in the dingey. First the man in the stern slid his hand along the thwart and moved with care, as if he were of Sèvres.[2] Then the man in the rowing seat slid his hand along the other thwart. It was all done with the most extraordinary care. As the two sidled past each other, the whole party kept watchful eyes on the coming wave, and the captain cried: "Look out now! Steady there!"

The brown mats of sea-weed that appeared from time to time were like islands, bits of earth. They were travelling, apparently, neither one way nor the other. They were, to all intents, stationary. They informed the men in the boat that it was making progress slowly toward the land.

The captain, rearing cautiously in the bow, after the dingey soared on a great swell, said that he had seen the lighthouse at Mosquito Inlet. Presently the cook remarked that he had seen it. The correspondent was at the oars, then, and for some reason he too wished to look at the lighthouse, but his back was toward the far shore and the waves were important, and for some time he could not seize an opportunity to turn his head. But at last there came a wave more gentle than the others, and when at the crest of it he swiftly scoured the western horizon.

"See it?" said the captain.

[1]A rope attached to the bow used for tying up a boat.

[2]A delicate porcelain made in Sèvres, France.

"No," said the correspondent, slowly, "I didn't see anything."

"Look again," said the captain. He pointed. "It's exactly in that direction."

At the top of another wave, the correspondent did as he was bid, and this time his eyes chanced on a small still thing on the edge of the swaying horizon. It was precisely like the point of a pin. It took an anxious eye to find a lighthouse so tiny.

"Think we'll make it, captain?"

"If this wind holds and the boat don't swamp, we can't do much else," said the captain.

The little boat, lifted by each towering sea, and splashed viciously by the crests, made progress that in the absence of seaweed was not apparent to those in her. She seemed just a wee thing wallowing, miraculously, top-up, at the mercy of five oceans. Occasionally, a great spread of water, like white flames, swarmed into her.

"Bail her, cook," said the captain, serenely.

"All right, captain," said the cheerful cook.

III

It would be difficult to describe the subtle brotherhood of men that was here established on the seas. No one said that it was so. No one mentioned it. But it dwelt in the boat, and each man felt it warm him. They were a captain, an oiler, a cook, and a correspondent, and they were friends, friends in a more curiously ironbound degree than may be common. The hurt captain, lying against the waterjar in the bow, spoke always in a low voice and calmly, but he could never command a more ready and swiftly obedient crew than the motley three of the dingey. It was more than a mere recognition of what was best for the common safety. There was surely in it a quality that was personal and heartfelt. And after this devotion to the commander of the boat there was this comradeship that the correspondent, for instance, who had been taught to be cynical of men, knew even at the time was the best experience of his life. But no one said that it was so. No one mentioned it.

"I wish we had a sail," remarked the captain. "We might try my overcoat on the end of an oar and give you two boys a chance to rest." So the cook and the correspondent held the mast and spread wide the overcoat. The oiler steered, and the little boat made good way with her new rig. Sometimes the oiler had to scull sharply to keep a sea from breaking into the boat, but otherwise sailing was a success.

Meanwhile the light-house had been growing slowly larger. It had now almost assumed color, and appeared like a little gray shadow on the sky. The man at the oars could not be prevented from turning his head rather often to try for a glimpse of this little gray shadow.

At last, from the top of each wave the men in the tossing boat could see land. Even as the light-house was an upright shadow on the sky, this land seemed but a long black shadow on the sea. It certainly was thinner than paper. "We must be about opposite New Smyrna," said the cook, who had coasted this shore often in schooners. "Captain, by the way, I believe they abandoned that life-saving station there about a year ago."

"Did they?" said the captain.

The wind slowly died away. The cook and the correspondent were not now obliged to slave in order to hold high the oar. But the waves continued their old impetuous swooping at the dingey, and the little craft, no longer under way, struggled woundily over them. The oiler or the correspondent took the oars again.

Shipwrecks are *apropos* of nothing. If men could only train for them and have them occur when the men had reached pink condition, there would be less drowning at sea. Of the four in the dingey none had slept any time worth mentioning for two days and two nights previous to embarking in the dingey, and in the excitement of clambering about the deck of a foundering ship they had also forgotten to eat heartily.

For these reasons, and for others, neither the oiler nor the correspondent was fond of rowing at this time. The correspondent wondered ingenuously how in the name of all that was sane could there be people who thought it amusing to row a boat. It was not an amusement; it was a diabolical punishment, and even a genius of mental aberrations could never conclude that it was anything but a horror to the muscles and a crime against the back. He mentioned to the boat in general how the amusement of rowing struck him, and the weary-faced oiler smiled in full sympathy. Previously to the foundering, by the way, the oiler had worked doublewatch in the engine-room of the ship.

"Take her easy, now, boys," said the captain. "Don't spend yourselves. If we have to run a surf you'll need all your strength, because we'll sure have to swim for it. Take your time."

Slowly the land arose from the sea. From a black line it became a line of black and a line of white, trees, and sand. Finally, the captain said that he could make out a house on the shore. "That's the house of refuge, sure," said the cook. "They'll see us before long, and come out after us."

The distant light-house reared high. "The keeper ought to be able to make us out now, if he's looking through a glass," said the captain. "He'll notify the life-saving people."

"None of those other boats could have got ashore to give word of the wreck," said the oiler, in a low voice. "Else the life-boat would be out hunting us."

Slowly and beautifully the land loomed out of the sea. The wind came again. It had veered from the northeast to the southeast. Finally, a new sound struck the ears of the men in the boat. It was the low thunder of the surf on the shore. "We'll never be able to make the light-house now," said the captain. "Swing her head a little more north, Billie," said the captain.

"'A little more north,' sir," said the oiler.

Whereupon the little boat turned her nose once more down the wind, and all but the oarsman watched the shore grow. Under the influence of this expansion doubt and direful apprehension was leaving the minds of the men. The management of the boat was still most absorbing, but it could not prevent a quiet cheerfulness. In an hour, perhaps, they would be ashore.

Their back-bones had become thoroughly used to balancing in the boat and they now rode this wild colt of a dingey like circus men. The correspondent thought that he had been drenched to the skin, but happening to feel in the top pocket of his coat, he found therein eight cigars. Four of them were soaked with sea-water; four were perfectly scatheless. After a search, somebody produced three dry matches, and thereupon the four waifs rode in their little boat, and with an assurance of an impending rescue shining in their eyes, puffed at the big cigars and judged well and ill of all men. Everybody took a drink of water.

IV

"Cook," remarked the captain, "there don't seem to be any signs of life about your house of refuge."

"No," replied the cook. "Funny they don't see us!"

A broad stretch of lowly coast lay before the eyes of the men. It was of low dunes topped with dark vegetation. The roar of the surf was plain, and sometimes they could see the white lip of a wave as it spun up the beach. A tiny house was blocked out black upon the sky. Southward, the slim light-house lifted its little gray length.

Tide, wind, and waves were swinging the dingey northward. "Funny they don't see us," said the men.

The surf's roar was here dulled, but its tone was, nevertheless, thunderous and mighty. As the boat swam over the great rollers, the men sat listening to this roar.

"We'll swamp sure," said everybody.

It is fair to say here that there was not a life-saving station within twenty miles in either direction, but the men did not know this fact and in consequence they made dark and opprobrious remarks concerning the eyesight of the nation's life-savers. Four scowling men sat in the dingey and surpassed records in the invention of epithets.

"Funny they don't see us."

The light-heartedness of a former time had completely faded. To their sharpened minds it was easy to conjure pictures of all kinds of incompetency and blindness and, indeed, cowardice. There was the shore of the populous land, and it was bitter and bitter to them that from it came no sign.

"Well," said the captain, ultimately, "I suppose we'll have to make a try for ourselves. If we stay out here too long, we'll none of us have strength left to swim after the boat swamps."

And so the oiler, who was at the oars, turned the boat straight for the shore. There was a sudden tightening of muscles. There was some thinking.

"If we don't all get ashore—" said the captain. "If we don't all get ashore, I suppose you fellows know where to send news of my finish?"

They then briefly exchanged some addresses and admonitions. As for the reflections of the men, there was a great deal of rage in them. Perchance they might be formulated thus: "If I am going to be drowned—if I am going to be drowned—if I am going to be drowned, why, in the name of the seven mad gods who rule the sea, was I allowed to come thus far and contemplate sand and trees? Was I brought here merely to have my nose dragged away as I was about to nibble the sacred cheese of life? It is preposterous. If this old ninny-woman, Fate, cannot do better than this, she should be deprived of the management of men's fortunes. She is an old hen who knows not her intention. If she has decided to drown me, why did she not do it in the beginning and save me all this trouble. The whole affair is absurd. . . . But, no, she cannot mean to drown me. She dare not drown me. She cannot drown me. Not after all this work." Afterward the man might have had an impulse to shake his fist at the clouds: "Just you drown me, now, and then hear what I call you!"

The billows that came at this time were more formidable. They seemed always just about to break and roll over the little boat in a turmoil of foam. There was a preparatory and long growl in the speech of them. No mind unused to the sea would have concluded that the dingey could ascend these sheer heights in time. The shore was still afar. The oiler was a wily surfman. "Boys," he said, swiftly, "she won't live three minutes more and we're too far out to swim. Shall I take her to sea again, captain?"

"Yes! Go ahead!" said the captain.

This oiler, by a series of quick miracles, and fast and steady oarsmanship, turned the boat in the middle of the surf and took her safely to sea again.

There was a considerable silence as the boat bumped over the furrowed sea to deeper water. Then somebody in gloom spoke. "Well, anyhow, they must have seen us from the shore by now."

The gulls went in slanting flight up the wind toward the gray desolate east. A squall, marked by dingy clouds, and clouds brick-red, like smoke from a burning building, appeared from the southeast.

"What do you think of those life-saving people? Ain't they peaches?"

"Funny they haven't seen us."

"Maybe they think we're out here for sport! Maybe they think we're fishin'. Maybe they think we're damned fools."

It was a long afternoon. A changed tide tried to force them southward, but wind and wave said northward. Far ahead, where coast-line, sea, and sky formed their mighty angle, there were little dots which seemed to indicate a city on the shore.

"St. Augustine?"

The captain shook his head. "Too near Mosquito Inlet."

And the oiler rowed, and then the correspondent rowed. Then the oiler rowed. It was a weary business. The human back can become the seat of more aches and pains than are registered in books for the composite anatomy of a regiment. It is a limited area, but it can become the theatre of innumerable muscular conflicts, tangles, wrenches, knots, and other comforts.

"Did you ever like to row, Billie?" asked the correspondent.

"No," said the oiler. "Hang it."

When one exchanged the rowing-seat for a place in the bottom of the boat, he suffered a bodily depression that caused him to be careless of everything save an obligation to wiggle one finger. There was cold sea-water swashing to and fro in the boat, and he lay in it. His head, pillowed on a thwart, was within an inch of the swirl of a wave crest, and sometimes a particularly obstreperous sea came in-board and drenched him once more. But these matters did not annoy him. It is almost certain that if the boat had capsized he would have tumbled comfortably out upon the ocean as if he felt sure that it was a great soft mattress.

"Look! There's a man on the shore!"

"Where?"

"There! See 'im? See 'im?"

"Yes, sure! He's walking along."

"Now he's stopped. Look! He's facing us!"

"He's waving at us!"

"So he is! By thunder!"

"Ah, now, we're all right! Now we're all right! There'll be a boat out here for us in half an hour."

"He's going on. He's running. He's going up to that house there."

The remote beach seemed lower than the sea, and it required a searching glance to discern the little black figure. The captain saw a floating stick and they rowed to it. A bath-towel was by some weird chance in the boat, and, tying this on the stick, the captain waved it. The oarsman did not dare turn his head, so he was obliged to ask questions.

"What's he doing now?"

"He's standing still again. He's looking, I think. . . . There he goes again. Toward the house. . . . Now he's stopped again."

"Is he waving at us?"

"No, not now! he was, though."

"Look! There comes another man!"

"He's running."

"Look at him go, would you."

"Why, he's on a bicycle. Now he's met the other man. They're both waving at us. Look!"

"There comes something up the beach."

"What the devil is that thing?"

"Why, it looks like a boat."

"Why, certainly it's a boat."

"No, it's on wheels."

"Yes, so it is. Well, that must be the life-boat. They drag them along shore on a wagon."

"That's the life-boat, sure."

"No, by—, it's—it's an omnibus."

"I tell you it's a life-boat."

"It is not! It's an omnibus. I can see it plain. See? One of these big hotel omnibuses."

"By thunder, you're right. It's an omnibus, sure as fate. What do you suppose they are doing with an omnibus? Maybe they are going around collecting the life-crew, hey?"

"That's it, likely. Look! There's a fellow waving a little black flag. He's standing on the steps of the omnibus. There come those other two fellows. Now they're all talking together. Look at the fellow with the flag. Maybe he ain't waving it."

"That ain't a flag, is it? That's his coat. Why, certainly, that's his coat."

"So it is. It's his coat. He's taken it off and is waving it around his head. But would you look at him swing it."

"Oh, say, there isn't any life-saving station there. That's just a winter resort hotel omnibus that has brought over some of the boarders to see us drown."

"What's that idiot with the coat mean? What's he signaling, anyhow?"

"It looks as if he were trying to tell us to go north. There must be a life-saving station up there."

"No! He thinks we're fishing. Just giving us a merry hand. See? Ah, there, Willie."

"Well, I wish I could make something out of those signals. What do you suppose he means?"

"He don't mean anything. He's just playing."

"Well, if he'd just signal us to try the surf again, or to go to sea and wait, or go north, or go south, or go to hell—there would be some reason in it. But look at him. He just stands there and keeps his coat revolving like a wheel. The ass!"

"There come more people."

"Now there's quite a mob. Look! Isn't that a boat?"

"Where? Oh, I see where you mean. No, that's no boat."

"That fellow is still waving his coat."

"He must think we like to see him do that. Why don't he quit it. It don't mean anything."

"I don't know. I think he is trying to make us go north. It must be that there's a life-saving station there somewhere."

"Say, he ain't tired yet. Look at 'im wave."

"Wonder how long he can keep that up. He's been revolving his coat ever since he caught sight of us. He's an idiot. Why aren't they getting men to bring a boat out. A fishing boat—one of those big yawls—could come out here all right. Why don't he do something?"

"Oh, it's all right, now."

"They'll have a boat out here for us in less than no time, now that they've seen us."

A faint yellow tone came into the sky over the low land. The shadows on the sea slowly deepened. The wind bore coldness with it, and the men began to shiver.

"Holy smoke!" said one, allowing his voice to express his impious mood, "if we keep on monkeying out here! If we've got to flounder out here all night!"

"Oh, we'll never have to stay here all night! Don't you worry. They've seen us now, and it won't be long before they'll come chasing out after us."

The shore grew dusky. The man waving a coat blended gradually into this gloom, and it swallowed in the same manner the omnibus and the group of people. The spray, when it dashed uproariously over the side, made the voyagers shrink and swear like men who were being branded.

"I'd like to catch the chump who waved the coat. I feel like soaking him one, just for luck."

"Why? What did he do?"

"Oh, nothing, but then he seemed so damned cheerful."

In the meantime the oiler rowed, and then the correspondent rowed, and then the oiler rowed. Gray-faced and bowed forward, they mechanically, turn by turn, plied the leaden oars. The form of the light-house had vanished from the southern horizon, but finally a pale star appeared, just lifting from the sea. The streaked saffron in the west passed before the all-merging darkness, and the sea to the east was black. The land had vanished, and was expressed only by the low and drear thunder of the surf.

"If I am going to be drowned—if I am going to be drowned—if I am going to be drowned, why, in the name of the seven mad gods, who rule the sea, was I allowed to come thus far and contemplate sand and trees? Was I brought here merely to have my nose dragged away as I was about to nibble the sacred cheese of life?"

The patient captain, drooped over the water-jar, was sometimes obliged to speak to the oarsman.

"Keep her head up! Keep her head up!"

"'Keep her head up,' sir." The voices were weary and low.

This was surely a quiet evening. All save the oarsman lay heavily and listlessly in the boat's bottom. As for him, his eyes were just capable of noting the tall black waves that swept forward in a most sinister silence, save for an occasional subdued growl of a crest.

The cook's head was on a thwart, and he looked without interest at the water under his nose. He was deep in other scenes. Finally he spoke. "Billie," he murmured, dreamfully, "what kind of pie do you like best?"

V

"Pie," said the oiler and the correspondent, agitatedly. "Don't talk about those things, blast you!"

"Well," said the cook, "I was just thinking about ham sandwiches, and—"

A night on the sea in an open boat is a long night. As darkness settled finally, the shine of the light, lifting from the sea in the south, changed to full gold. On the northern horizon a new light appeared, a small bluish gleam on the edge of the waters. These two lights were the furniture of the world. Otherwise there was nothing but waves.

Two men huddled in the stern, and distances were so magnificent in the dingey that the rower was enabled to keep his feet partly warmed by thrusting them under his companions. Their legs indeed extended far under the rowing-seat until they touched the feet of the captain forward. Sometimes, despite the efforts of the tired oarsman, a wave came piling into the boat, an icy wave of the night, and the chilling water soaked them anew. They would twist their bodies for a moment and groan, and sleep the dead sleep once more, while the water in the boat gurgled about them as the craft rocked.

The plan of the oiler and the correspondent was for one to row until he lost the ability, and then arouse the other from his sea-water couch in the bottom of the boat.

The oiler plied the oars until his head drooped forward, and the overpowering sleep blinded him. And he rowed yet afterward. Then he touched a man in the bottom of the boat, and called his name. "Will you spell me for a little while?" he said, meekly.

"Sure, Billie," said the correspondent, awakening and dragging himself to a sitting position. They exchanged places carefully, and the oiler, cuddling down in the sea-water at the cook's side, seemed to go to sleep instantly.

The particular violence of the sea had ceased. The waves came without snarling. The obligation of the man at the oars was to keep the boat headed so that the tilt of the rollers would not capsize her, and to preserve her from filling when the crests rushed past. The black waves were silent and hard to be seen in the darkness. Often one was almost upon the boat before the oarsman was aware.

In a low voice the correspondent addressed the captain. He was not sure that the captain was awake, although this iron man seemed to be always awake. "Captain, shall I keep her making for that light north, sir?"

The same steady voice answered him. "Yes. Keep it about two points off the port bow."

The cook had tied a life-belt around himself in order to get even the warmth which this clumsy cork contrivance could donate, and he seemed almost stove-like when a rower, whose teeth invariably chattered wildly as soon as he ceased his labor, dropped down to sleep.

The correspondent, as he rowed, looked down at the two men sleeping under foot. The cook's arm was around the oiler's shoulders, and, with their fragmentary clothing and haggard faces, they were the babes of the sea, a grotesque rendering of the old babes in the wood.

Later he must have grown stupid at his work, for suddenly there was a growling of water, and a crest came with a roar and a swash into the boat, and it was a wonder that it did not set the cook afloat in his life-belt. The cook continued to sleep, but the oiler sat up, blinking his eyes and shaking with the new cold.

"Oh, I'm awful sorry, Billie," said the correspondent, contritely.

"That's all right, old boy," said the oiler, and lay down again and was asleep.

Presently it seemed that even the captain dozed, and the correspondent thought that he was the one man afloat on all the oceans. The wind had a voice as it came over the waves, and it was sadder than the end.

There was a long, loud swishing astern of the boat, and a gleaming trail of phosphorescence, like blue flame, was furrowed on the black waters. It might have been made by a monstrous knife.

Then there came a stillness, while the correspondent breathed with the open mouth and looked at the sea.

Suddenly there was another swish and another long flash of bluish light, and this time it was alongside the boat, and might almost have been reached with an oar. The correspondent saw an enormous fin speed like a shadow through the water, hurling the crystalline spray and leaving the long glowing trail.

The correspondent looked over his shoulder at the captain. His face was hidden, and he seemed to be asleep. He looked at the babes of the sea. They certainly were asleep. So, being bereft of sympathy, he leaned a little way to one side and swore softly into the sea.

But the thing did not then leave the vicinity of the boat. Ahead or astern, on one side or the other, at intervals long or short, fled the long sparkling streak, and there was to be heard the whiroo of the dark fin. The speed and power of the thing was greatly to be admired. It cut the water like a gigantic and keen projectile.

The presence of this biding thing did not affect the man with the same horror that it would if he had been a picnicker. He simply looked at the sea dully and swore in an undertone.

Nevertheless, it is true that he did not wish to be alone with the thing. He wished one of his companions to awaken by chance and keep him company with it. But the captain hung motionless over the water-jar and the oiler and the cook in the bottom of the boat were plunged in slumber.

VI

"If I am going to be drowned—if I am going to be drowned—if I am going to be drowned, why, in the name of the seven mad gods, who rule the sea, was I allowed to come thus far and contemplate sand and trees?"

During this dismal night, it may be remarked that a man would conclude that it was really the intention of the seven mad gods to drown him, despite the abominable injustice of it. For it was certainly an abominable injustice to drown a man who had worked so hard, so hard. The man felt it would be a crime most unnatural. Other people had drowned at sea since galleys swarmed with painted sails, but still——

When it occurs to a man that nature does not regard him as important, and that she feels she would not maim the universe by disposing of him, he at first wishes to throw bricks at the temple, and he hates deeply the fact that there are no bricks and no temples. Any visible expression of nature would surely be pelleted with his jeers.

Then, if there be no tangible thing to hoot he feels, perhaps, the desire to confront a personification and indulge in pleas, bowed to one knee, and with hands supplicant, saying: "Yes, but I love myself."

A high cold star on a winter's night is the word he feels that she says to him. Thereafter he knows the pathos of his situation.

The men in the dingey had not discussed these matters, but each had, no doubt, reflected upon them in silence and according to his mind. There was seldom any expression upon their faces save the general one of complete weariness. Speech was devoted to the business of the boat.

To chime the notes of his emotion, a verse mysteriously entered the correspondent's head. He had even forgotten that he had forgotten this verse, but it suddenly was in his mind.

> A soldier of the Legion lay dying in Algiers,
> There was lack of woman's nursing, there was dearth of woman's tears;
> But a comrade stood beside him, and he took that comrade's hand
> And he said: "I shall never see my own, my native land."[3]

In his childhood, the correspondent had been made acquainted with the fact that a soldier of the Legion lay dying in Algiers, but he had never regarded the fact as important. Myriads of his school-fellows had informed him of the soldier's plight, but the dinning had naturally ended by making him perfectly indifferent. He had never considered it his affair that a soldier of the Legion lay dying in Algiers, nor had it appeared to him as a matter for sorrow. It was less to him than breaking of a pencil's point.

Now, however, it quaintly came to him as a human, living thing. It was no longer merely a picture of a few throes in the breast of a poet, meanwhile drinking tea and warming his feet at the grate; it was an actuality—stern, mournful, and fine.

The correspondent plainly saw the soldier. He lay on the sand with his feet out

[3]Crane has skillfully condensed the lines of "Bingen on the Rhine" (1883) by Caroline E. S. Norton.

straight and still. While his pale left hand was upon his chest in an attempt to thwart the going of his life, the blood came between his fingers. In the far Algerian distance, a city of low square forms was set against a sky that was faint with the last sunset hues. The correspondent, plying the oars and dreaming of the slow and slower movements of the lips of the soldier, was moved by a profound and perfectly impersonal comprehension. He was sorry for the soldier of the Legion who lay dying in Algiers.

The thing which had followed the boat and waited had evidently grown bored at the delay. There was no longer to be heard the slash of the cut-water, and there was no longer the flame of the long trail. The light in the north still glimmered, but it was apparently no nearer to the boat. Sometimes the boom of the surf rang in the correspondent's ears, and he turned the craft seaward then and rowed harder. Southward, someone had evidently built a watch-fire on the beach. It was too low and too far to be seen, but it made a shimmering, roseate reflection upon the bluff back of it, and this could be discerned from the boat. The wind came stronger, and sometimes a wave suddenly raged out like a mountain-cat and there was to be seen the sheen and sparkle of a broken crest.

The captain, in the bow, moved on his water-jar and sat erect. "Pretty long night," he observed to the correspondent. He looked at the shore. "Those life-saving people take their time."

"Did you see that shark playing around?"

"Yes, I saw him. He was a big fellow, all right."

"Wish I had known you were awake."

Later the correspondent spoke into the bottom of the boat.

"Billie!" There was a slow and gradual disentanglement. "Billie, will you spell me?"

"Sure," said the oiler.

As soon as the correspondent touched the cold comfortable sea-water in the bottom of the boat, and had huddled close to the cook's life-belt he was deep in sleep, despite the fact that his teeth played all the popular airs. This sleep was so good to him that it was but a moment before he heard a voice call his name in a tone that demonstrated the last stages of exhaustion. "Will you spell me?"

"Sure, Billie."

The light in the north had mysteriously vanished, but the correspondent took his course from the wide-awake captain.

Later in the night they took the boat farther out to sea, and the captain directed the cook to take one oar at the stern and keep the boat facing the seas. He was to call out if he should hear the thunder of the surf. This plan enabled the oiler and the correspondent to get respite together. "We'll give those boys a chance to get into shape again," said the captain. They curled down and, after a few preliminary chatterings and trembles, slept once more the dead sleep. Neither knew they had bequeathed to the cook the company of another shark, or perhaps the same shark.

As the boat caroused on the waves, spray occasionally bumped over the side and gave them a fresh soaking, but this had no power to break their repose. The ominous slash of the wind and the water affected them as it would have affected mummies.

"Boys," said the cook, with the notes of every reluctance in his voice, "she's drifted in pretty close. I guess one of you had better take her to sea again." The correspondent, aroused, heard the crash of the toppled crests.

As he was rowing, the captain gave him some whiskey and water, and this steadied the chills out of him. "If I ever get ashore and anybody shows me even a photograph of an oar—"

At last there was a short conversation.

"Billie. . . . Billie, will you spell me?"

"Sure," said the oiler.

VII

When the correspondent again opened his eyes, the sea and the sky were each of the gray hue of the dawning. Later, carmine and gold was painted upon the waters. The morning appeared finally, in its splendor, with a sky of pure blue, and the sunlight flamed on the tips of the waves.

On the distant dunes were set many little black cottages, and a tall white windmill reared above them. No man, nor dog, nor bicycle appeared on the beach. The cottages might have formed a deserted village.

The voyagers scanned the shore. A conference was held in the boat. "Well," said the captain, "if no help is coming, we might better try to run through the surf right away. If we stay out here much longer we will be too weak to do anything for ourselves at all." The others silently acquiesced in this reasoning. The boat was headed for the beach. The correspondent wondered if none ever ascended the tall windtower, and if then they never looked seaward. This tower was a giant, standing with its back to the plight of the ants. It represented in a degree, to the correspondent, the serenity of nature amid the struggles of the individual—nature in the wind, and nature in the vision of men. She did not seem cruel to him then, nor beneficent, nor treacherous, nor wise. But she was indifferent, flatly indifferent. It is, perhaps, plausible that a man in this situation, impressed with the unconcern of the universe, should see the innumerable flaws of his life and have them taste wickedly in his mind and wish for another chance. A distinction between right and wrong seems absurdly clear to him, then, in this new ignorance of the grave-edge, and he understands that if he were given another opportunity he would mend his conduct and his words, and be better and brighter during an introduction, or at a tea.

"Now, boys," said the captain, "she is going to swamp sure. All we can do is to work her in as far as possible, and then when she swamps, pile out and scramble for the beach. Keep cool now and don't jump until she swamps sure."

The oiler took the oars. Over his shoulders he scanned the surf. "Captain," he said, "I think I'd better bring her about, and keep her head-on to the seas and back her in."

"All right, Billie," said the captain. "Back her in." The oiler swung the boat then and, seated in the stern, the cook and the correspondent were obliged to look over their shoulders to contemplate the lonely and indifferent shore.

The monstrous inshore rollers heaved the boat high until the men were again enabled to see the white sheets of water scudding up the slanted beach. "We won't get in very close," said the captain. Each time a man could wrest his attention from the rollers, he turned his glance toward the shore, and in the expression of the eyes during this contemplation there was a singular quality. The correspondent, observing the others, knew that they were not afraid, but the full meaning of their glances was shrouded.

As for himself, he was too tired to grapple fundamentally with the fact. He tried to coerce his mind into thinking of it, but the mind was dominated at this time by the muscles, and the muscles said they did not care. It merely occurred to him that if he should drown it would be a shame.

There were no hurried words, no pallor, no plain agitation. The men simply looked at the shore. "Now, remember to get well clear of the boat when you jump," said the captain.

Seaward the crest of a roller suddenly fell with a thunderous crash, and the long white comber came roaring down upon the boat.

"Steady now," said the captain. The men were silent. They turned their eyes from the shore to the comber and waited. The boat slid up the incline, leaped at the furious top, bounced over it, and swung down the long back of the waves. Some water had been shipped and the cook bailed it out.

But the next crest crashed also. The tumbling boiling flood of white water caught the boat and whirled it almost perpendicular. Water swarmed in from all sides. The correspondent had his hands on the gunwale at this time, and when the water entered at that place he swiftly withdrew his fingers, as if he objected to wetting them.

The little boat, drunken with this weight of water, reeled and snuggled deeper into the sea.

"Bail her out, cook! Bail her out," said the captain.

"All right, captain," said the cook.

"Now, boys, the next one will do for us, sure," said the oiler. "Mind to jump clear of the boat."

The third wave moved forward, huge, furious, implacable. It fairly swallowed the dingey, and almost simultaneously the men tumbled into the sea. A piece of life-belt had lain in the bottom of the boat, and as the correspondent went overboard he held this to his chest with his left hand.

The January water was icy, and he reflected immediately that it was colder than he had expected to find it off the coast of Florida. This appeared to his dazed mind as a fact important enough to be noted at the time. The coldness of the water was said; it was tragic. This fact was somehow mixed and confused with his opinion of his own situation that it seemed almost a proper reason for tears. The water was cold.

When he came to the surface he was conscious of little but the noisy water. Afterward he saw his companions in the sea. The oiler was ahead in the race. He was swimming strongly and rapidly. Off to the correspondent's left, the cook's great white and corked back bulged out of the water, and in the rear the captain was hanging with his one good hand to the keel of the overturned dingey.

There is a certain immovable quality to a shore, and the correspondent wondered at it amid the confusion of the sea.

It seemed also very attractive, but the correspondent knew that it was a long journey, and he paddled leisurely. The piece of life-preserver lay under him, and sometimes he whirled down the incline of a wave as if he were on a hand-sled.

But finally he arrived at a place in the sea where travel was beset with difficulty. He did not pause swimming to inquire what manner of current had caught him, but there his progress ceased. The shore was set before him like a bit of scenery on a stage, and he looked at it and understood with his eyes each detail of it.

As the cook passed, much farther to the left, the captain was calling to him, "Turn over on your back, cook! Turn over on your back and use the oar."

"All right, sir." The cook turned on his back, and, paddling with an oar, went ahead as if he were a canoe.

Presently the boat also passed to the left of the correspondent with the captain clinging with one hand to the keel. He would have appeared like a man raising himself to look over a board fence, if it were not for the extraordinary gymnastics of the boat. The correspondent marvelled that the captain could still hold to it.

They passed on, nearer to shore—the oiler, the cook, the captain—and following them went the water-jar, bouncing gayly over the seas.

The correspondent remained in the grip of this strange new enemy—a current. The shore, with its white slope of sand and its green bluff, topped with little silent cottages, was spread like a picture before him. It was very near to him then, but he was impressed as one who in a gallery looks at a scene from Brittany or Algiers.

He thought: "I am going to drown? Can it be possible? Can it be possible? Can it be possible? Perhaps an individual must consider his own death to be the final phenomenon of nature.

But later a wave perhaps whirled him out of this small deadly current, for he found suddenly that he could again make progress toward the shore. Later still, he was aware that the captain, clinging with one hand to the keel of the dingey, had his face turned away from the shore and toward him, and was calling his name. "Come to the boat! Come to the boat!"

In his struggle to reach the captain and the boat, he reflected that when one gets properly wearied, drowning must really be a comfortable arrangement, a cessation of hostilities accompanied by a large degree of relief, and he was glad of it, for the main thing in his mind for some moments had been horror of the temporary agony. He did not wish to be hurt.

Presently he saw a man running along the shore. He was undressing with most remarkable speed. Coat, trousers, shirt, everything flew magically off him.

"Come to the boat," called the captain.

"All right, captain." As the correspondent paddled, he saw the captain let himself down to bottom and leave the boat. Then the correspondent performed his one little marvel of the voyage. A large wave caught him and flung him with ease and supreme speed completely over the boat and far beyond it. It struck him even then as an event in gymnastics, and a true miracle of the sea. An overturned boat in the surf is not a plaything to a swimming man.

The correspondent arrived in water that reached only to his waist, but his condition did not enable him to stand for more than a moment. Each wave knocked him into a heap, and the under-tow pulled at him.

Then he saw the man who had been running and undressing, and undressing and running, come bounding into the water. He dragged ashore the cook, and then waded toward the captain, but the captain waved him away, and sent him to the correspondent. He was naked, naked as a tree in winter, but a halo was about his head, and he shone like a saint. He gave a strong pull, and a long drag, and a bully heave at the correspondent's hand. The correspondent, schooled in the minor formulae, said: "Thanks, old man." But suddenly the man cried: "What's that?" He pointed a swift finger. The correspondent said: "Go."

In the shallows, face downward, lay the oiler. His forehead touched sand that was periodically, between each wave, clear of the sea.

The correspondent did not know all that transpired afterward. When he achieved safe ground he fell, striking the sand with each particular part of his body. It was as if he had dropped from a roof, but the thud was grateful to him.

It seems that instantly the beach was populated with men with blankets, clothes, and flasks, and women with coffee-pots and all the remedies sacred to their minds. The welcome of the land to the men from the sea was warm and generous, but a still and dripping shape was carried slowly up the beach, and the land's welcome for it could only be the different and sinister hospitality of the grave.

When it came night, the white waves paced to and fro in the moonlight, and the wind brought the sound of the great sea's voice to the men on shore, and they felt that they could then be interpreters.

1897

The Bride Comes to Yellow Sky

I

The great Pullman was whirling onward with such dignity of motion that a glance from the window seemed simply to prove that the plains of Texas were pouring eastward. Vast flats of green grass, dull-hued spaces of mesquite and cactus, little groups of frame houses, woods of light and tender trees, all were sweeping into the east, sweeping over the horizon, a precipice.

A newly married pair had boarded this coach at San Antonio. The man's face was reddened from many days in the wind and sun, and a direct result of his new black clothes was that his brick-colored hands were constantly performing in a most conscious fashion. From time to time he looked down respectfully at his attire. He sat with a hand on each knee, like a man waiting in a barber's shop. The glances he devoted to other passengers were furtive and shy.

The bride was not pretty, nor was she very young. She wore a dress of blue cashmere, with small reservations of velvet here and there and with steel buttons abounding. She continually twisted her head to regard her puff sleeves, very stiff, straight, and high. They embarrassed her. It was quite apparent that she had cooked, and that she expected to cook, dutifully. The blushes caused by the careless scrutiny of some passengers as she had entered the car were strange to see upon this plain, under-class countenance, which was drawn in placid, almost emotionless lines.

They were evidently very happy. "Ever been in a parlor-car before?" he asked, smiling with delight.

"No," she answered. "I never was. It's fine, ain't it?"

"Great! And then after a while we'll go forward to the diner and get a big lay-out. Finest meal in the world. Charge a dollar."

"Oh, do they?" cried the bride. "Charge a dollar? Why, that's too much—for us—ain't it, Jack?"

"Not this trip, anyhow," he answered bravely. "We're going to go the whole thing."

Later, he explained to her about the trains. "You see, it's a thousand miles from one end of Texas to the other, and this train runs right across it and never stops but four times." He had the pride of an owner. He pointed out to her the dazzling fittings of the coach, and in truth her eyes opened wider as she contemplated the sea-green figured velvet, the shining brass, silver, and glass, the wood that gleamed as darkly brilliant as the surface of a pool of oil. At one end a bronze figure sturdily held a support for a separated chamber, and at convenient places on the ceiling were frescoes in olive and silver.

To the minds of the pair, their surroundings reflected the glory of their marriage that morning in San Antonio. This was the environment of their new estate, and the man's face in particular beamed with an elation that made him appear ridiculous to the negro porter. This individual at times surveyed them from afar with an amused and superior grin. On other occasions he bullied them with skill in ways that did not make it exactly plain to them that they were being bullied. He subtly used all the manners of the most unconquerable kind of snobbery. He oppressed them, but of this oppression they had small knowledge, and they speedily forgot that infrequently a number of travelers covered them with stares of derisive enjoyment. Historically there was supposed to be something infinitely humorous in their situation.

"We are due in Yellow Sky at 3.42," he said, looking tenderly into her eyes.

"Oh, are we?" she said, as if she had not been aware of it. To evince surprise at her husband's statement was part of her wifely amiability. She took from a pocket a little silver watch, and as she held it before her and stared at it with a frown of attention, the new husband's face shone.

"I bought it in San Anton' from a friend of mine," he told her gleefully.

"It's seventeen minutes past twelve," she said, looking up at him with a kind of shy and clumsy coquetry. A passenger, noting this play, grew excessively sardonic, and winked at himself in one of the numerous mirrors.

At last they went to the dining-car. Two rows of negro waiters, in glowing white suits, surveyed their entrance with the interest and also the equanimity of men who had been forewarned. The pair fell to the lot of a waiter who happened to feel pleasure in steering them through their meal. He viewed them with the manner of a fatherly pilot, his countenance radiant with benevolence. The patronage, entwined with the ordinary deference, was not plain to them. And yet, as they returned to their coach, they showed in their faces a sense of escape.

To the left, miles down a long purple slope, was a little ribbon of mist where moved the keening Rio Grande. The train was approaching it at an angle, and the apex was Yellow Sky. Presently it was apparent that, as the distance from Yellow Sky grew shorter, the husband became commensurately restless. His brick-red hands were more insistent in their prominence. Occasionally he was even rather absent-minded and far-away when the bride leaned forward and addressed him.

As a matter of truth, Jack Potter was beginning to find the shadow of a deed weigh upon him like a leaden slab. He, the town marshal of Yellow Sky, a man known, liked, and feared in his corner, a prominent person, had gone to San Antonio to meet a girl he believed he loved, and there, after the usual prayers, had actually induced her to marry him, without consulting Yellow Sky for any part of the transaction. He was now bringing his bride before an innocent and unsuspecting community.

Of course, people in Yellow Sky married as it pleased them, in accordance with a general custom; but such was Potter's thought of his duty to his friends, or of their idea of his duty, or of an unspoken form which does not control men in these matters, that he felt he was heinous. He had committed an extraordinary crime. Face to face with this girl in San Antonio, and spurred by his sharp impulse, he had gone headlong over all the social hedges. At San Antonio he was like a man hidden in the dark. A knife to sever any friendly duty, any form, was easy to his hand in that remote city. But the hour of Yellow Sky, the hour of daylight, was approaching.

He knew full well that his marriage was an important thing to his town. It could only be exceeded by the burning of the new hotel. His friends could not forgive him. Frequently he had reflected on the advisability of telling them by telegraph, but a new cowardice had been upon him. He feared to do it. And now the train was hurrying him toward a scene of amazement, glee, and reproach. He glanced out of the window at the line of haze swinging slowly in towards the train.

Yellow Sky had a kind of brass band, which played painfully, to the delight of the populace. He laughed without heart as he thought of it. If the citizens could dream of his prospective arrival with his bride, they would parade the band at the station and escort them, amid cheers and laughing congratulations, to his adobe home.

He resolved that he would use all the devices of speed and plains-craft in making the journey from the station to his house. Once within that safe citadel, he could issue some sort of a vocal bulletin, and then not go among the citizens until they had time to wear off a little of their enthusiasm.

The bride looked anxiously at him. "What's worrying you, Jack?"

He laughed again, "I'm not worrying, girl. I'm only thinking of Yellow Sky."

She flushed in comprehension.

A sense of mutual guilt invaded their minds and developed a finer tenderness. They looked at each other with eyes softly aglow. But Potter often laughed the same nervous laugh. The flush upon the bride's face seemed quite permanent.

The traitor to the feelings of Yellow Sky narrowly watched the speeding landscape. "We're nearly there," he said.

Presently the porter came and announced the proximity of Potter's home. He held a brush in his hand and, with all his airy superiority gone, he brushed Potter's new clothes as the latter slowly turned this way and that way. Potter fumbled out a coin and gave it to the porter, as he had seen others do. It was a heavy and muscle-bound business, as that of a man shoeing his first horse.

The porter took their bag, and as the train began to slow they moved forward to the hooded platform of the car. Presently the two engines and their long string of coaches rushed into the station of Yellow Sky.

"They have to take water here," said Potter, from a constricted throat and in mournful cadence, as one announcing death. Before the train stopped, his eye had swept the length of the platform, and he was glad and astonished to see there was none upon it but the station-agent, who, with a slightly hurried and anxious air, was walking toward the water-tanks. When the train had halted, the porter alighted first and placed in position a little temporary step.

"Come on, girl," said Potter hoarsely. As he helped her down they each laughed on a false note. He took the bag from the negro, and bade his wife cling to his arm. As they slunk rapidly away, his hang-dog glance perceived that they were unloading the two trunks, and also that the station-agent far ahead near the baggage-car had turned and was running toward him, making gestures. He laughed, and groaned as he laughed, when he noted the first effect of his marital bliss upon Yellow Sky. He gripped his wife's arm firmly to his side, and they fled. Behind them the porter stood chuckling fatuously.

II

The California Express on the Southern Railway was due at Yellow Sky in twenty-one minutes. There were six men at the bar of the "Weary Gentleman" saloon. One was a drummer who talked a great deal and rapidly; three were Texans who did not care to talk at that time; and two were Mexican sheep-herders who did not talk as a general practice in the "Weary Gentleman" saloon. The barkeeper's dog lay on the board walk that crossed in front of the door. His head was on his paws, and he glanced drowsily here and there with the constant vigilance of a dog that is kicked on occasion. Across the sandy street were some vivid green grass plots, so wonderful in appearance amid the sands that burned near them in a blazing sun that they caused a doubt in the mind. They exactly resembled the grass mats used to represent lawns on the stage. At the cooler end of the railway station a man without a coat sat in a tilted chair and smoked his pipe. The fresh-cut bank of the Rio Grande circled near the town, and there could be seen beyond it a great, plum-colored plain of mesquite.

Save for the busy drummer and his companions in the saloon, Yellow Sky was dozing. The new-comer leaned gracefully upon the bar, and recited many tales with the confidence of a bard who has come upon a new field.

"——and at the moment that the old man fell down stairs with the bureau in his arms, the old woman was coming up with two scuttles of coal, and, of course—"

The drummer's tale was interrupted by a young man who suddenly appeared in the open door. He cried: "Scratchy Wilson's drunk, and has turned loose with both hands." The two Mexicans at once set down their glasses and faded out of the rear entrance of the saloon.

The drummer, innocent and jocular, answered: "All right, old man. S'pose he has. Come in and have a drink, anyhow."

But the information had made such an obvious cleft in every skull in the room that the drummer was obliged to see its importance. All had become instantly solemn. "Say," said he, mystified, "what is this?" His three companions made the introductory gesture of eloquent speech, but the young man at the door forestalled them.

"It means, my friend," he answered, as he came into the saloon, "that for the next two hours this town won't be a health resort."

The barkeeper went to the door and locked and barred it. Reaching out of the window, he pulled in heavy wooden shutters and barred them. Immediately a solemn, chapel-like gloom was upon the place. The drummer was looking from one to another.

"But, say," he cried, "what is this, anyhow? You don't mean there is going to be a gun-fight?"

"Don't know whether there'll be a fight or not," answered one man grimly. "But there'll be some shootin'—some good shootin'."

The young man who had warned them waved his hand. "Oh, there'll be a fight fast enough, if anyone wants it. Anybody can get a fight out there in the street. There's a fight just waiting."

The drummer seemed to be swayed between the interest of a foreigner and a perception of personal danger.

"What did you say his name was?" he asked.

"Scratchy Wilson," they answered in chorus.

"And will he kill anybody? What are you going to do? Does this happen often? Does he rampage around like this once a week or so? Can he break in that door?"

"No, he can't break down that door," replied the barkeeper. "He's tried it three times. But when he comes you'd better lay down on the floor, stranger. He's dead sure to shoot at it, and a bullet may come through."

Thereafter the drummer kept a strict eye upon the door. The time had not yet been called for him to hug the floor, but, as a minor precaution, he sidled near to the wall. "Will he kill anybody?" he said again.

The men laughed low and scornfully at the question.

"He's out to shoot, and he's out for trouble. Don't see any good in experimentin' with him."

"But what do you do in a case like this? What do you do?"

A man responded: "Why, he and Jack Potter—"

"But," in chorus, the other men interrupted, "Jack Potter's in San Anton'."

"Well, who is he? What's he got to do with it?"

"Oh, he's the town marshal. He goes out and fights Scratchy when he gets on one of these tears."

"Wow," said the drummer, mopping his brow. "Nice job he's got."

The voices had toned away to mere whisperings. The drummer wished to ask further questions which were born of an increasing anxiety and bewilderment; but when he attempted them, the men merely looked at him in irritation and motioned him to remain silent. A tense waiting hush was upon them. In the deep shadows of the room their eyes shone as they listened for sounds from the street. One man made three gestures at the barkeeper, and the latter, moving like a ghost, handed him a glass and a bottle. The man poured a full glass of whisky, and set down the bottle noiselessly. He gulped the whisky in a swallow, and turned again toward the door in immovable silence. The drummer saw that the barkeeper, without a sound, had taken a Winchester from beneath the bar. Later he saw this individual beckoning to him, so he tiptoed across the room.

"You better come with me back of the bar."

"No, thanks," said the drummer, perspiring. "I'd rather be where I can make a break for the back door."

Whereupon the man of bottles made a kindly but peremptory gesture. The drummer obeyed it, and finding himself seated on a box with his head below the level of the bar, balm was laid upon his soul at sight of various zinc and copper fittings that bore a resemblance to armorplate. The barkeeper took a seat comfortably upon an adjacent box.

"You see," he whispered, "this here Scratchy Wilson is a wonder with a gun—a perfect wonder—and when he goes on the war trail, we hunt our holes—naturally. He's about the last one of the old gang that used to hang out along the river here. He's a terror when he's drunk. When he's sober he's all right—kind of simple—wouldn't hurt a fly—nicest fellow in town. But when he's drunk—whoo!"

There were periods of stillness. "I wish Jack Potter was back from San Anton'," said the barkeeper. "He shot Wilson up once—in the leg—and he would sail in and pull out the kinks in this thing."

Presently they heard from a distance the sound of a shot, followed by three wild yowls. It instantly removed a bond from the men in the darkened saloon. There was a shuffling of feet. They looked at each other. "Here he comes," they said.

III

A man in a maroon-colored flannel shirt, which had been purchased for purposes of decoration and made, principally, by some Jewish women on the east side of New York, rounded a corner and walked into the middle of the main street of Yellow Sky. In either hand the man held a long, heavy, blue-black revolver. Often he yelled, and these cries rang through a semblance of a deserted village, shrilly flying over the roofs in a volume that seemed to have no relation to the ordinary vocal strength of a man. It was as if the surrounding stillness formed the arch of a tomb over him. These cries of ferocious challenge rang against walls of silence. And his boots had red tops with gilded imprints, of the kind beloved in winter by little sledding boys on the hillsides of New England.

The man's face flamed in a rage begot of whisky. His eyes, rolling and yet keen for ambush, hunted the still doorways and windows. He walked with the creeping movement of the midnight cat. As it occurred to him, he roared menacing information. The long revolvers in his hands were as easy as straws; they were moved with an electric swiftness. The little fingers of each hand played sometimes in a musician's way. Plain from the low collar of the shirt, the cords of his neck straightened and sank, straightened and sank, as passion moved him. The only sounds were his terrible invitations. The calm adobes preserved their demeanor at the passing of this small thing in the middle of the street.

There was no offer of fight; no offer of fight. The man called to the sky. There were no attractions. He bellowed and fumed and swayed his revolvers here and everywhere.

The dog of the barkeeper of the "Weary Gentleman" saloon had not appreciated the advance of events. He yet lay dozing in front of his master's door. At sight of the dog, the man paused and raised his revolver humorously. At sight of the man, the dog sprang up and walked diagonally away, with a sullen head, and growling. The man yelled, and the dog broke into a gallop. As it was about to enter an alley, there was a loud noise, a whistling, and something spat the ground directly before it. The dog screamed, and, wheeling in terror, galloped headlong in a new direction. Again there was a noise, a whistling, and sand was kicked viciously before it. Fear-stricken, the dog turned and flurried like an animal in a pen. The man stood laughing, his weapons at his hips.

Ultimately the man was attracted by the closed door of the "Weary Gentleman" saloon. He went to it, and hammering with a revolver, demanded drink.

The door remaining imperturbable, he picked up a bit of paper from the walk and nailed it to the framework with a knife. He then turned his back contemptuously upon this popular resort, and walking to the opposite side of the street, and spinning there on his heel quickly and lithely, fired at the bit of paper. He missed it by a half inch. He swore at himself, and went away. Later, he comfortably fusilladed the windows of his most intimate friend. The man was playing with this town. It was a toy for him.

But still there was no offer of fight. The name of Jack Potter, his ancient antagonist, entered his mind, and he concluded that it would be a glad thing if he should go to Potter's house and by bombardment induce him to come out and fight. He moved in the direction of his desire, chanting Apache scalp-music.

When he arrived at it, Potter's house presented the same still front as had the other adobes. Taking up a strategic position, the man howled a challenge. But this house regarded him as might a great stone god. It gave no sign. After a decent wait, the man howled further challenges, mingling with them wonderful epithets.

Presently there came the spectacle of a man churning himself into deepest rage over the immobility of a house. He fumed at it as the winter wind attacks a prairie cabin in the North. To the distance there should have gone the sound of a tumult like the fighting of 200 Mexicans. As necessity bade him, he paused for breath or to reload his revolvers.

IV

Potter and his bride walked sheepishly and with speed. Sometimes they laughed together shamefacedly and low.

"Next corner, dear," he said finally.

They put forth the efforts of a pair walking bowed against a strong wind. Potter was about to raise a finger to point the first appearance of the new home when, as they circled the corner, they came face to face with a man in a maroon-colored shirt who was feverishly pushing cartridges into a large revolver. Upon the instant the man dropped his revolver to the ground, and, like lightning, whipped another from its holster. The second weapon was aimed at the bridegroom's chest.

There was a silence. Potter's mouth seemed to be merely a grave for his tongue. He exhibited an instinct to at once loosen his arm from the woman's grip, and he dropped the bag to the sand. As for the bride, her face had gone as yellow as old cloth. She was a slave to hideous rites gazing at the apparitional snake.

The two men faced each other at a distance of three paces. He of the revolver smiled with a new and quiet ferocity.

"Tried to sneak up on me," he said. "Tried to sneak up on me!" His eyes grew more baleful. As Potter made a slight movement, the man thrust his revolver venomously forward. "No, don't you do it, Jack Potter. Don't you move a finger toward a gun just yet. Don't you move an eyelash. The time has come for me to settle with you, and I'm goin' to do it my own way and loaf along with no interferin'. So if you don't want a gun bent on you, just mind what I tell you."

Potter looked at his enemy. "I ain't got a gun on me, Scratchy," he said. "Honest, I ain't." He was stiffening and steadying, but yet somewhere at the back of his mind a vision of the Pullman floated, the sea-green figured velvet, the shining brass, silver, and glass, the wood that gleamed as darkly brilliant as the surface of a pool of oil—all the glory of the marriage, the environment of the new estate. "You know I fight when it comes to fighting, Scratchy Wilson, but I ain't got a gun on me. You'll have to do all the shootin' yourself."

His enemy's face went livid. He stepped forward and lashed his weapon to and fro before Potter's chest. "Don't you tell me you ain't got no gun on you, you whelp. Don't tell me no lie like that. There ain't a man in Texas ever seen you without no gun. Don't take me for no kid." His eyes blazed with light, and his throat worked like a pump.

"I ain't takin' you for no kid," answered Potter. His heels had not moved an inch backward. "I'm takin' you for a——fool. I tell you I ain't got a gun, and I ain't. If you're goin' to shoot me up, you better begin now. You'll never get a chance like this again."

So much enforced reasoning had told on Wilson's rage. He was calmer. "If you ain't got a gun, why ain't you got a gun?" he sneered. "Been to Sunday-school?"

"I ain't got a gun because I've just come from San Anton' with my wife. I'm married," said Potter. "And if I'd thought there was going to be any galoots like you prowling around when I brought my wife home, I'd had a gun, and don't you forget it."

"Married!" said Scratchy, not at all comprehending.

"Yes, married. I'm married," said Potter distinctly.

"Married?" said Scratchy. Seemingly for the first time he saw the drooping, drowning woman at the other man's side. "No!" he said. He was like a creature allowed a glimpse of another world. He moved a pace backward, and his arm with the revolver dropped to his side. "Is this the lady?" he asked.

"Yes, this is the lady," answered Potter.

There was another period of silence.

"Well," said Wilson at last, slowly, "I s'pose it's all off now."

"It's all off if you say so, Scratchy. You know I didn't make the trouble." Potter lifted his valise.

"Well, I 'low it's off, Jack," said Wilson. He was looking at the ground. "Married!" He was not a student of chivalry; it was merely that in the presence of this foreign condition he was a simple child of the earlier plains. He picked up his starboard revolver, and placing both weapons in their holsters, he went away. His feet made funnel-shaped tracks in the heavy sand.

1898

from The Black Riders and Other Lines[1]

God Lay Dead in Heaven

God lay dead in Heaven;
Angels sang the hymn of the end;
Purple winds went moaning,
Their wings drip-dripping
With blood
That fell upon the earth.
It, groaning thing,
Turned black and sank.
Then from the far caverns
Of dead sins
Came monsters, livid with desire.
They fought,
Wrangled over the world,
A morsel.
But of all sadness this was sad,—
A woman's arms tried to shield
The head of a sleeping man
From the jaws of the final beast.

1895

from War Is Kind

Do Not Weep, Maiden, For War Is Kind

Do not weep, maiden, for war is kind.
Because your lover threw wild hands toward the sky
And the affrighted steed ran on alone,
Do not weep.
War is kind.

[1]In the two volumes of verse which he published, Crane chose to omit titles for individual poems. Poems in *The Black Riders and Other Lines* were identified by roman numerals at the beginning of each poem. The decision to omit titles for individual poems reflects Crane's desire to present his innovative writing in an appropriately *avant garde* format. (Here the editors have included first lines as titles for reference purposes.)

Hoarse, booming drums of the regiment
Little souls who thirst for fight,
These men were born to drill and die
The unexplained glory flies above them
Great is the battle-god, great, and his kingdom—
A field where a thousand corpses lie.

Do not weep, babe, for war is kind.
Because your father tumbled in the yellow trenches,
Raged at his breast, gulped and died,
Do not weep.
War is kind.

Swift, blazing flag of the regiment
Eagle with crest of red and gold,
These men were born to drill and die
Point for them the virtue of slaughter
Make plain to them the excellence of killing
And a field where a thousand corpses lie.

Mother whose heart hung humble as a button
On the bright splendid shroud of your son,
Do not weep.
War is kind.

1896

The Impact of a Dollar Upon the Heart

The impact of a dollar upon the heart
Smiles warm red light
Sweeping from the hearth rosily upon the white table,
With the hanging cool velvet shadows
Moving softly upon the door.
The impact of a million dollars
Is a crash of flunkeys
And yawning emblems of Persia
Cheeked against oak, France and a sabre,
The outcry of old Beauty
Whored by pimping merchants
To submission before wine and chatter.
Silly rich peasants stamp the carpets of men,
Dead men who dreamed fragrance and light
Into their woof, their lives;
The rug of an honest bear

Under the feet of a cryptic slave
Who speaks always of baubles
Forgetting place, multitude, work and state,
Champing and mouthing of hats
Making ratful squeak of hats,
Hats.

1898

A Man Said to the Universe

A man said to the universe:
"Sir, I exist!"
"However," replied the universe,
"The fact has not created in me
"A sense of obligation."

1899

A Newspaper Is a Collection of Half-Injustices

A newspaper is a collection of half-injustices
Which, bawled by boys from mile to mile,
Spreads its curious opinion
To a million merciful and sneering men,
While families cuddle the joys of the fireside
When spurred by tale of dire lone agony.
A newspaper is a court
Where every one is kindly and unfairly tried
By a squalor of honest men.
A newspaper is a market
Where wisdom sells its freedom
And melons are crowned by the crowd.
A newspaper is a game
Where his error scores the player victory
While another's skill wins death.
A newspaper is a symbol;
It is fetless life's chronicle,
A collection of loud tales
Concentrating eternal stupidities,
That in remote ages lived unhaltered,
Roaming through a fenceless world.

1899

There Was a Man with Tongue of Wood

There was a man with tongue of wood
Who essayed to sing
And in truth it was lamentable
But there was one who heard
The clip-clapper of this tongue of wood
And knew what the man
Wished to sing
And with that the singer was content.

1899

from Uncollected Poems

Chant You Loud of Punishments

Chant you loud of punishments,
Of the twisting of the heart's poor strings
Of the crash of the lightning's fierce revenge.

Then sing I of the supple-souled men
And the strong, strong gods
That shall meet in times hereafter
And the amaze of the gods
At the strength of the men.
—The strong, strong gods—
—And the supple-souled men—

1929

Jack London 1876–1916

Jack London was born in San Francisco to Flora Wellman, a young unmarried woman who had run away from her Ohio family. His father was probably William Chaney, an itinerant astrologer, who left London's mother when he learned of her pregnancy. London was adopted and raised in Oakland and its environs by the man his mother soon after married, John London. The Londons were never able to establish themselves securely; alternating hard work with spiritualism and get-rich-quick schemes, they struggled to maintain a precarious lower-middle-class respectability.

During his adolescence, London held a variety of manual jobs, dropped out of high school, shipped out on a sealing vessel, apprenticed himself as an electrician, and became a tramp. While he was on the road, he was imprisoned in the Erie County Penitentiary for vagrancy. The "unspeakable" brutalities he witnessed in his thirty days in prison awakened him to the reality of his downward class mobility. He saw a vision of the "Social Pit," and of himself slipping further and further into it. The contradictions of his life and writings are suggested in his responses: in rapid succession he returned to high school, fled to the Alaskan Gold Rush, embraced socialism, and determined to become a writer.

Longing for stability and roots, London seized upon writing as a ticket to a secure middle-class identity. At a time when novelists like Henry James were becoming self-conscious about their profession and articulating a privileged culture around their activity, London approached writing as a working-class trade; he apprenticed himself to the popular magazines and learned their formulas. In 1899 he broke into print in the *Overland Monthly* with his Alaskan stories. They brought him immediate success and are among the finest he ever wrote. London's first novel, *A Daughter of the Snows* (1902), was a commercial and critical failure, but *The Call of the Wild* (1903) brought him national fame at the age of twenty-six. As myth, adventure story, and lyrical transformation of his working-class experiences, it remains his most fully realized work. Success was accompanied by sharp disillusionment, reflected in the pessimism and contradictions of *The Sea-Wolf* (1904) and the dissolution of his short-lived marriage to Bessie Maddern. By the willpower that marked his attempt to pull himself out of the Social Pit, London pulled himself out of his depression, married Charmian Kittredge, and wrote a total of fifty-one volumes before he died at the age of forty. In addition to many novels and volumes of short stories, including tales of the South Seas, he wrote political essays and a journalistic exposé of the East End of London (*The People of the Abyss,* 1903), covered the Russo-Japanese War, and published several autobiographical volumes (*The Road,* 1907, and *John Barleycorn,* 1913). Both participant in and observer of the American dream, London in his most powerful work articulated the longings and contradictions at its heart. These are movingly depicted in his autobiographical novel, *Martin Eden* (1909), which chronicles in vivid detail his own struggle to become a writer and his disillusionment with success. At the time of his death he was in poor health, his body marked by the strenuous life he had sometimes glorified in his fiction. He died of a self-administered overdose of morphine, which he was taking to counter the pain of nephritis, a side effect of his alcoholism.

Joan D. Hedrick
Trinity College

PRIMARY WORKS

The Call of the Wild, 1903 [1998]; *The People of the Abyss,* 1903; *The Sea-Wolf,* 1904; *The Road,* 1907; *The Iron Heel,* 1908; *Martin Eden,* 1909; *The Valley of the Moon,* 1913 [1999]; *John Barleycorn,* 1913 [1998]; *Novels, Stories and Social Writings,* ed. Donald Pizer, 2 vols., 1982; *The Letters of Jack London*, ed. Earle Labor et al., 3 vols., 1988; *The Complete Short Stories of Jack London,* ed. Earle Labor et al., 1993; *No Mentor but Myself: A Collection of Articles, Essays, Reviews, and Letters on Writing and Writers,* ed. Dale L. Walker and Jeanne Campbell Reesman, 1999.

South of the Slot

Old San Francisco, which is the San Francisco of only the other day, the day before the Earthquake, was divided midway by the Slot. The Slot was an iron crack that ran along the center of Market street, and from the Slot arose the burr of the ceaseless, endless cable that was hitched at will to the cars it dragged up and down. In truth, there were two slots, but in the quick grammar of the West time was saved by calling them, and much more that they stood for, "The Slot." North of the Slot were the theaters, hotels, and shopping district, the banks and the staid, respectable business houses. South of the Slot were the factories, slums, laundries, machine-shops, boiler works, and the abodes of the working class.

The Slot was the metaphor that expressed the class cleavage of Society, and no man crossed this metaphor, back and forth, more successfully than Freddie Drummond. He made a practice of living in both worlds, and in both worlds he lived signally well. Freddie Drummond was a professor in the Sociology Department of the University of California, and it was as a professor of sociology that he first crossed over the Slot, lived for six months in the great labor-ghetto, and wrote "The Unskilled Laborer"—a book that was hailed everywhere as an able contribution to the literature of progress, and as a splendid reply to the literature of discontent. Politically and economically it was nothing if not orthodox. Presidents of great railway systems bought whole editions of it to give to their employees. The Manufacturers' Association alone distributed fifty thousand copies of it. In a way, it was almost as immoral as the far-famed and notorious "Message to Garcia,"[1] while in its pernicious preachment of thrift and content it ran "Mrs. Wiggs of the Cabbage Patch"[2] a close second.

At first, Freddie Drummond found it monstrously difficult to get along among the working people. He was not used to their ways, and they certainly were not used to his. They were suspicious. He had no antecedents. He could talk of no previous jobs. His hands were soft. His extraordinary politeness was ominous. His first idea of the rôle he would play was that of a free and independent American who chose to work with his hands and no explanations given. But it wouldn't do, as he quickly discovered. At the beginning they accepted him, very provisionally, as a freak. A little later, as he began to know his way about better, he insensibly drifted into the rôle that would work—namely, he was a man who had seen better days, very much better days, but who was down in his luck, though, to be sure, only temporarily.

He learned many things, and generalized much and often erroneously, all of which can be found in the pages of "The Unskilled Laborer." He saved himself, however, after the sane and conservative manner of his kind, by labeling his generalizations as "tentative." One of his first experiences was in the great Wilmax Cannery,

[1]A didactic essay by Elbert Hubbard (1856–1915) preaching to employees the virtues of obedience and efficiency.

[2]One of the most popular novels by Alice Caldwell Hegan Rice (1870–1942), *Mrs. Wiggs of the Cabbage Patch* (1901), features a widow whose husband has died of drink. She sustains herself and her many children with the refrain, "Everything in the world comes right if we jes' wait long enough."

where he was put on piece-work making small packing cases. A box factory supplied the parts, and all Freddie Drummond had to do was to fit the parts into a form and drive in the wire nails with a light hammer.

It was not skilled labor, but it was piece-work. The ordinary laborers in the cannery got a dollar and a half per day. Freddie Drummond found the other men on the same job with him jogging along and earning a dollar and seventy-five cents a day. By the third day he was able to earn the same. But he was ambitious. He did not care to jog along and, being unusually able and fit, on the fourth day earned two dollars. The next day, having keyed himself up to an exhausting high-tension, he earned two dollars and a half. His fellow workers favored him with scowls and black looks, and made remarks, slangily witty and which he did not understand, about sucking up to the boss and pace-making and holding her down when the rains set in. He was astonished at their malingering on piece-work, generalized about the inherent laziness of the unskilled laborer, and proceeded next day to hammer out three dollars' worth of boxes.

And that night, coming out of the cannery, he was interviewed by his fellow workmen, who were very angry and incoherently slangy. He failed to comprehend the motive behind their action. The action itself was strenuous. When he refused to ease down his pace and bleated about freedom of contract, independent Americanism, and the dignity of toil, they proceeded to spoil his pace-making ability. It was a fierce battle, for Drummond was a large man and an athlete, but the crowd finally jumped on his ribs, walked on his face, and stamped on his fingers, so that it was only after lying in bed for a week that he was able to get up and look for another job. All of which is duly narrated in that first book of his, in the chapter entitled "The Tyranny of Labor."

A little later, in another department of the Wilmax Cannery, lumping as a fruit-distributor among the women, he essayed to carry two boxes of fruit at a time, and was promptly reproached by the other fruit-lumpers. It was palpable malingering; but he was there, he decided, not to change conditions, but to observe. So he lumped one box thereafter, and so well did he study the art of shirking that he wrote a special chapter on it, with the last several paragraphs devoted to tentative generalizations.

In those six months he worked at many jobs and developed into a very good imitation of a genuine worker. He was a natural linguist, and he kept notebooks, making a scientific study of the workers' slang or argot, until he could talk quite intelligibly. This language also enabled him more intimately to follow their mental processes, and thereby to gather much data for a projected chapter in some future book which he planned to entitle "Synthesis of Working-Class Psychology."

Before he arose to the surface from that first plunge into the underworld he discovered that he was a good actor and demonstrated the plasticity of his nature. He was himself astonished at his own fluidity. Once having mastered the language and conquered numerous fastidious qualms, he found that he could flow into any nook of working-class life and fit it so snugly as to feel comfortably at home. As he said, in the preface to his second book, "The Toiler," he endeavored really to know the working people, and the only possible way to achieve this was to work beside them, eat their food, sleep in their beds, be amused with their amusements, think their thoughts, and feel their feelings.

He was not a deep thinker. He had no faith in new theories. All his norms and criteria were conventional. His Thesis, on the French Revolution, was noteworthy in college annals, not merely for its painstaking and voluminous accuracy, but for the fact that it was the dryest, deadest, most formal, and most orthodox screed ever written on the subject. He was a very reserved man, and his natural inhibition was large in quantity and steel-like in quality. He had but few friends. He was too undemonstrative, too frigid. He had no vices, nor had anyone ever discovered any temptations. Tobacco he detested, beer he abhorred, and he was never known to drink anything stronger than an occasional light wine at dinner.

When a freshman he had been baptized "Ice-Box" by his warmer-blooded fellows. As a member of the faculty he was known as "Cold-Storage." He had but one grief, and that was "Freddie." He had earned it when he played full-back on the 'Varsity eleven, and his formal soul had never succeeded in living it down. "Freddie" he would ever be, expect officially, and through nightmare vistas he looked into a future when his world would speak of him as "Old Freddie."

For he was very young to be a Doctor of Sociology, only twenty-seven, and he looked younger. In appearance and atmosphere he was a strapping big college man, smooth-faced and easy-mannered, clean and simple and wholesome, with a known record of being a splendid athlete and an implied vast possession of cold culture of the inhibited sort. He never talked shop out of class and committee rooms, except later on, when his books showered him with distasteful public notice and he yielded to the extent of reading occasional papers before certain literary and economic societies.

He did everything right—too right; and in dress and comportment was inevitably correct. Not that he was a dandy. Far from it. He was a college man, in dress and carriage as like as a pea to the type that of late years is being so generously turned out of our institutions of higher learning. His handshake was satisfyingly strong and stiff. His blue eyes were coldly blue and convincingly sincere. His voice, firm and masculine, clean and crisp of enunciation, was pleasant to the ear. The one drawback to Freddie Drummond was his inhibition. He never unbent. In his football days, the higher the tension of the game, the cooler he grew. He was noted as a boxer, but he was regarded as an automaton, with the inhuman precision of a machine judging distance and timing blows, guarding, blocking, and stalling. He was rarely punished himself, while he rarely punished an opponent. He was too clever and too controlled to permit himself to put a pound more weight into a punch than he intended. With him it was a matter of exercise. It kept him fit.

As time went by, Freddie Drummond found himself more frequently crossing the Slot and losing himself in South of Market. His summer and winter holidays were spent there, and, whether it was a week or a week-end, he found the time spent there to be valuable and enjoyable. And there was so much material to be gathered. His third book, "Mass and Master," became a text-book in the American universities; and almost before he knew it, he was at work on a fourth one, "The Fallacy of the Inefficient."

Somewhere in his make-up there was a strange twist or quirk. Perhaps it was a recoil from his environment and training, or from the tempered seed of his ancestors, who had been bookmen generation preceding generation; but at any rate, he found enjoyment in being down in the working-class world. In his own world he was "Cold-Storage," but down below he was "Big" Bill Totts, who could drink and smoke, and slang and fight, and be an all-around favorite. Everybody liked Bill, and more than one working girl made love to him. At first he had been merely a good actor, but as time went on, simulation became second nature. He no longer played a part, and he loved sausages, sausages and bacon, than which, in his own proper sphere, there was nothing more loathsome in the way of food.

From doing the thing for the need's sake, he came to doing the thing for the thing's sake. He found himself regretting as the time drew near for him to go back to his lecture-room and his inhibition. And he often found himself waiting with anticipation for the dreamy time to pass when he could cross the Slot and cut loose and play the devil. He was not wicked, but as "Big" Bill Totts he did a myriad things that Freddie Drummond would never have been permitted to do. Moreover, Freddie Drummond never would have wanted to do them. That was the strangest part of his discovery. Freddie Drummond and Bill Totts were two totally different creatures. The desires and tastes and impulses of each ran counter to the other's. Bill Totts could shirk at a job with clear conscience, while Freddie Drummond condemned shirking as vicious, criminal, and un-American, and devoted whole chapters to condemnation of the vice. Freddie Drummond did not care for dancing, but Bill Totts never missed the nights at the various dancing clubs, such as The Magnolia, The Western Star, and The Elite; while he won a massive silver cup, standing thirty inches high, for being the best-sustained character at the Butchers and Meat Workers' annual grand masked ball. And Bill Totts liked the girls and the girls liked him, while Freddie Drummond enjoyed playing the ascetic in this particular, was open in his opposition to equal suffrage, and cynically bitter in his secret condemnation of coeducation.

Freddie Drummond changed his manners with his dress, and without effort. When he entered the obscure little room used for his transformation scenes, he carried himself just a bit too stiffly. He was too erect, his shoulders were an inch too far back, while his face was grave, almost harsh, and practically expressionless. But when he emerged in Bill Totts's clothes he was another creature. Bill Totts did not slouch, but somehow his whole form limbered up and became graceful. The very sound of the voice was changed, and the laugh was loud and hearty, while loose speech and an occasional oath were as a matter of course on his lips. Also, Bill Totts was a trifle inclined to late hours, and at times, in saloons, to be good-naturedly bellicose with other workmen. Then, too, at Sunday picnics or when coming home from the show, either arm betrayed a practiced familiarity in stealing around girls' waists, while he displayed a wit keen and delightful in the flirtatious badinage that was expected of a good fellow in his class.

So thoroughly was Bill Totts himself, so thoroughly a workman, a genuine denizen of South of the Slot, that he was as class-conscious as the average of his kind, and his hatred for a scab even exceeded that of the average loyal union man. During the Water Front Strike, Freddie Drummond was somehow able to stand apart from the unique combination, and, coldly critical, watch Bill Totts hilariously slug scab longshoremen. For Bill Totts was a dues-paying member of the Longshoremen Union and had a right to be indignant with the usurpers of his job. "Big" Bill Totts was so very big, and so very able, that it was "Big" Bill to the front when trouble was brewing. From acting outraged feelings, Freddie Drummond, in the rôle of his other self, came to experience genuine outrage, and it was only when he returned to the classic atmosphere of the university that he was able, sanely and conservatively, to generalize upon his underworld experiences and put them down on paper as a trained sociologist should. That Bill Totts lacked the perspective to raise him above class-consciousness, Freddie Drummond clearly saw. But Bill Totts could not see it. When he saw a scab taking his job away, he saw red at the same time, and little else did he see. It was Freddie Drummond, irreproachably clothed and comported, seated at his study desk or facing his class in "Sociology 17," who saw Bill Totts, and all around Bill Totts, and all around the whole scab and union-labor problem and its relation to the economic welfare of the United States in the struggle for the world market. Bill Totts really wasn't able to see beyond the next meal and the prize-fight the following night at the Gaiety Athletic Club.

It was while gathering material for "Women and Work" that Freddie received his first warning of the danger he was in. He was too successful at living in both worlds. This strange dualism he had developed was after all very unstable, and, as he sat in his study and meditated, he saw that it could not endure. It was really a transition stage, and if he persisted he saw that he would inevitably have to drop one world or the other. He could not continue in both. And as he looked at the row of volumes that graced the upper shelf of his revolving book-case, his volumes, beginning with his Thesis and ending with "Women and Work," he decided that that was the world he would hold to and stick by. Bill Totts had served his purpose, but he had become a too dangerous accomplice. Bill Totts would have to cease.

Freddie Drummond's fright was due to Mary Condon, President of the International Glove Workers' Union No. 974. He had seen her, first, from the spectators' gallery, at the annual convention of the Northwest Federation of Labor, and he had seen her through Bill Totts' eyes, and that individual had been most favorably impressed by her. She was not Freddie Drummond's sort at all. What if she were a royal-bodied woman, graceful and sinewy as a panther, with amazing black eyes that could fill with fire or laughter-love, as the mood might dictate? He detested women with a too exuberant vitality and a lack of . . . well, of inhibition. Freddie Drummond accepted the doctrine of evolution because it was quite universally accepted by college men, and he flatly believed that man had climbed up the ladder of life out of the weltering muck and mess of lower and monstrous organic things. But he was a trifle ashamed of this genealogy, and preferred not to think of it. Wherefore, probably, he practiced his iron inhibition and preached it to others, and preferred women of his own type, who could shake free of this bestial and regrettable ancestral line and by discipline and control emphasize the wideness of the gulf that separated them from what their dim forbears had been.

Bill Totts had none of these considerations. He had liked Mary Condon from the moment his eyes first rested on her in the convention hall, and he had made it a point, then and there, to find out who she was. The next time he met her, and quite by accident, was when he was driving an express wagon for Pat Morrissey. It was in a lodging house in Mission Street, where he had been called to take a trunk into storage. The landlady's daughter had called him and led him to the little bedroom, the occupant of which, a glove-maker, had just been removed to hospital. But Bill did not know this. He stooped, up-ended the trunk, which was a large one, got it on his shoulder, and struggled to his feet with his back toward the open door. At that moment he heard a woman's voice.

"Belong to the union?" was the question asked.

"Aw, what's it to you?" he retorted. "Run along now, an' git outa my way. I wanta turn round."

The next he knew, big as he was, he was whirled half around and sent reeling backward, the trunk overbalancing him, till he fetched up with a crash against the wall. He started to swear, but at the same instant found himself looking into Mary Condon's flashing, angry eyes.

"Of course I b'long to the union," he said. "I was only kiddin' you."

"Where's your card?" she demanded in business-like tones.

"In my pocket. But I can't git it out now. This trunk's too damn heavy. Come on down to the wagon an' I'll show it to you."

"Put that trunk down," was the command.

"What for? I got a card, I'm tellin' you."

"Put it down, that's all. No scab's going to handle that trunk. You ought to be ashamed of yourself, you big coward, scabbing on honest men. Why don't you join the union and be a man?"

Mary Condon's color had left her face, and it was apparent that she was in a rage.

"To think of a big man like you turning traitor to his class. I suppose you're aching to join the militia for a chance to shoot down union drivers the next strike. You may belong to the militia already, for that matter. You're the sort—"

"Hold on, now, that's too much!" Bill dropped the trunk to the floor with a bang, straightened up, and thrust his hand into his inside coat pocket. "I told you I was only kiddin'. There, look at that."

It was a union card properly enough.

"All right, take it along," Mary Condon said. "And the next time don't kid."

Her face relaxed as she noticed the ease with which he got the big trunk to his shoulder, and her eyes glowed as they glanced over the graceful massiveness of the man. But Bill did not see that. He was too busy with the trunk.

The next time he saw Mary Condon was during the Laundry Strike. The Laundry Workers, but recently organized, were green at the business, and had petitioned Mary Condon to engineer the strike. Freddie Drummond had had an inkling of what was coming, and had sent Bill Totts to join the union and investigate. Bill's job was in the wash-room, and the men had been called out first, that morning, in order to stiffen the courage of the girls; and Bill chanced to be near the door to the mangle-room when Mary Condon started to enter. The superintendent, who was both large and stout, barred her way. He wasn't going to have his girls called out, and he'd teach her a lesson to mind her own business. And as Mary tried to squeeze past him he thrust her back with a fat hand on her shoulder. She glanced around and saw Bill.

"Here you, Mr. Totts," she called. "Lend a hand. I want to get in."

Bill experienced a startle of warm surprise. She had remembered his name from his union card. The next moment the superintendent had been plucked from the doorway raving about rights under the law, and the girls were deserting their machines. During the rest of that short and successful strike, Bill constituted himself Mary Condon's henchman and messenger, and when it was over returned to the University to be Freddie Drummond and to wonder what Bill Totts could see in such a woman.

Freddie Drummond was entirely safe, but Bill had fallen in love. There was no getting away from the fact of it, and it was this fact that had given Freddie Drummond his warning. Well, he had done his work, and his adventures could cease. There was no need for him to cross the Slot again. All but the last three chapters of his latest, "Labor Tactics and Strategy," was finished, and he had sufficient material on hand adequately to supply those chapters.

Another conclusion he arrived at, was that in order to sheet-anchor himself as Freddie Drummond, closer ties and relations in his own social nook were necessary. It was time that he was married, anyway, and he was fully aware that if Freddie Drummond didn't get married, Bill Totts assuredly would, and the complications were too awful to contemplate. And so, enters Catherine Van Vorst. She was a college woman herself, and her father, the one wealthy member of the faculty, was the head of the Philosophy Department as well. It would be a wise marriage from every standpoint, Freddie Drummond concluded when the engagement was consummated and announced. In appearance cold and reserved, aristocratic and wholesomely conservative, Catherine Van Vorst, though warm in her way, possessed an inhibition equal to Drummond's.

All seemed well with him, but Freddie Drummond could not quite shake off the call of the underworld, the lure of the free and open, of the unhampered, irresponsible life South of the Slot. As the time of his marriage approached, he felt that he had indeed sowed wild oats, and he felt, moreover, what a good thing it would be if he could have but one wild fling more, play the good fellow and the wastrel one last time, re he settled down to gray lecture-rooms and sober matrimony. And, further to tempt him, the very last chapter of "Labor Tactics and Strategy" remained unwritten for lack of a trifle more of essential data which he had neglected to gather.

So Freddie Drummond went down for the last time as Bill Totts, got his data, and, unfortunately, encountered Mary Condon. Once more installed in his study, it was not a pleasant thing to look back upon. It made his warning doubly imperative. Bill Totts had behaved abominably. Not only had he met Mary Condon at the Central Labor Council, but he had stopped in at a chop-house with her, on the way home, and treated her to oysters. And before they parted at her door, his arms had been about her, and he had kissed her on the lips and kissed her repeatedly. And her last words in his ear, words uttered softly with a catchy sob in the throat that was nothing more nor less than a love cry, were "Bill . . . dear, dear Bill."

Freddie Drummond shuddered at the recollection. He saw the pit yawning for him. He was not by nature a polygamist, and he was appalled at the possibilities of the situation. It would have to be put an end to, and it would end in one only of two ways: either he must become wholly Bill Totts and be married to Mary Condon, or he must remain wholly Freddie Drummond and be married to Catherine Van Vorst. Otherwise, his conduct would be beneath contempt and horrible.

In the several months that followed, San Francisco was torn with labor strife. The unions and the employers' associations had locked horns with a determination that looked as if they intended to settle the matter, one way or the other, for all time. But Freddie Drummond corrected proofs, lectured classes, and did not budge. He devoted himself to Catherine Van Vorst, and day by day found more to respect and admire in her—nay, even to love in her. The Street Car Strike tempted him, but not so severely as he would have expected; and the great Meat Strike came on and left him cold. The ghost of Bill Totts had been successfully laid, and Freddie Drummond with rejuvenescent zeal tackled a brochure, long-planned, on the topic of "diminishing returns."

The wedding was two weeks off, when, one afternoon, in San Francisco, Catherine Van Vorst picked him up and whisked him away to see a Boys' Club, recently instituted by the settlement workers with whom she was interested. It was her brother's machine, but they were alone with the exception of the chauffeur. At the junction with Kearny Street, Market and Geary Streets intersect like the sides of a sharp-angled letter "V." They, in the auto, were coming down Market with the intention of negotiating the sharp apex and going up Geary. But they did not know what was coming down Geary, timed by fate to meet them at the apex. While aware from the papers that the Meat Strike was on and that it was an exceedingly bitter one, all thought of it at that moment was farthest from Freddie Drummond's mind. Was he not seated beside Catherine? And, besides, he was carefully expositing to her his views on settlement work—views that Bill Totts' adventures had played a part in formulating.

Coming down Geary Street were six meat wagons. Beside each scab driver sat a policeman. Front and rear, and along each side of this procession, marched a protecting escort of one hundred police. Behind the police rear guard, at a respectful distance, was an orderly but vociferous mob, several blocks in length, that congested the street from sidewalk to sidewalk. The Beef Trust was making an effort to supply the hotels, and, incidentally, to begin the breaking of the strike. The St. Francis had already been supplied, at a cost of many broken windows and broken heads, and the expedition was marching to the relief of the Palace Hotel.

All unwitting, Drummond sat beside Catherine, talking settlement work, as the auto, honking methodically and dodging traffic, swung in a wide curve to get around the apex. A big coal wagon, loaded with lump coal and drawn by four huge horses, just debouching from Kearny Street as though to turn down Market, blocked their way. The driver of the wagon seemed undecided, and the chauffeur, running slow but disregarding some shouted warning from the crossing policemen, swerved the auto to the left, violating the traffic rules, in order to pass in front of the wagon.

At that moment Freddie Drummond discontinued his conversation. Nor did he resume it again, for the situation was developing with the rapidity of a transformation scene. He heard the roar of the mob at the rear, and caught a glimpse of the helmeted police and the lurching meat wagons. At the same moment, laying on his whip and standing up to his task, the coal driver rushed horses and wagon squarely in front of the advancing procession, pulled the horses up sharply, and put on the big brake. Then he made his lines fast to the brake-handle and sat down with the air of one who had stopped to stay. The auto had been brought to a stop, too, by his big panting leaders which had jammed against it.

Before the chauffeur could back clear, an old Irishman, driving a rickety express wagon and lashing his one horse to a gallop, had locked wheels with the auto. Drummond recognized both horse and wagon, for he had driven them often himself. The Irishman was Pat Morrissey. On the other side a brewery wagon was locking with the coal wagon, and an east-bound Kearny-Street car, wildly clanging its gong, the motorman shouting defiance at the crossing policeman, was dashing forward to complete the blockade. And wagon after wagon was locking and blocking and adding to the confusion. The meat wagons halted. The police were trapped. The roar at the rear increased as the mob came on to the attack, while the vanguard of the police charged the obstructing wagons.

"We're in for it," Drummond remarked coolly to Catherine.

"Yes," she nodded, with equal coolness. "What savages they are."

His admiration for her doubled on itself. She was indeed his sort. He would have been satisfied with her even if she had screamed and clung to him, but this—this was magnificent. She sat in that storm center as calmly as if it had been no more than a block of carriages at the opera.

The police were struggling to clear a passage. The driver of the coal wagon, a big man in shirt sleeves, lighted a pipe and sat smoking. He glanced down complacently at a captain of police who was raving and cursing at him, and his only acknowledgment was a shrug of the shoulders. From the rear arose the rat-tat-tat of clubs on heads and a pandemonium of cursing, yelling, and shouting. A violent accession of noise proclaimed that the mob had broken through and was dragging a scab from a wagon. The police captain reinforced from his vanguard, and the mob at the rear was repelled. Meanwhile, window after window in the high office building on the right had been opened, and the class-conscious clerks were raining a shower of office furniture down on the heads of police and scabs. Waste-baskets, ink-bottles, paper-weights, typewriters—anything and everything that came to hand was filling the air.

A policeman, under orders from his captain, clambered to the lofty seat of the coal wagon to arrest the driver. And the driver, rising leisurely and peacefully to meet him, suddenly crumpled him in his arms and threw him down on top of the captain. The driver was a young giant, and when he climbed on top his load and poised a lump of coal in both hands, a policeman, who was just scaling the wagon from the side, let go and dropped back to earth. The captain ordered half a dozen of his men to take the wagon. The teamster, scrambling over the load from side to side, beat them down with huge lumps of coal.

The crowd on the sidewalks and the teamsters on the locked wagons roared encouragement and their own delight. The motorman, smashing helmets with his controller bar, was beaten into insensibility and dragged from his platform. The captain of police, beside himself at the repulse of his men, led the next assault on the coal wagon. A score of police were swarming up the tall-sided fortress. But the teamster multiplied himself. At times there were six or eight policemen rolling on the pavement and under the wagon. Engaged in repulsing an attack on the rear end of his fortress, the teamster turned about to see the captain just in the act of stepping on to the seat from the front end. He was still in the air and in most unstable equilibrium, when the teamster hurled a thirty-pound lump of coal. It caught the captain fairly on the chest, and he went over backward, striking on a wheeler's back, tumbling on to the ground, and jamming against the rear wheel of the auto.

Catherine thought he was dead, but he picked himself up and charged back. She reached out her gloved hand and patted the flank of the snorting, quivering horse. But Drummond did not notice the action. He had eyes for nothing save the battle of the coal wagon, while somewhere in his complicated psychology, one Bill Totts was heaving and straining in an effort to come to life. Drummond believed in law and order and the maintenance of the established, but this riotous savage within him would have none of it. Then, if ever, did Freddie Drummond call upon his iron inhibition to save him. But it is written that the house divided against itself must fall. And Freddie Drummond found that he had divided all the will and force of him with Bill Totts, and between them the entity that constituted the pair of them was being wrenched in twain.

Freddie Drummond sat in the auto, quite composed, alongside Catherine Van Vorst; but looking out of Freddie Drummond's eyes was Bill Totts, and somewhere behind those eyes, battling for the control of their mutual body, were Freddie Drummond, the sane and conservative sociologist, and Bill Totts, the class-conscious and bellicose union workingman. It was Bill Totts, looking out of those eyes, who saw the inevitable end of the battle on the coal wagon. He saw a policeman gain the top of the load, a second, and a third. They lurched clumsily on the loose footing, but their long riot-clubs were out and swinging. One blow caught the teamster on the head. A second he dodged, receiving it on the shoulder. For him the game was plainly up. He dashed in suddenly, clutched two policemen in his arms, and hurled himself a prisoner to the pavement, his hold never relaxing on his two captors.

Catherine Van Vorst was sick and faint at sight of the blood and brutal fighting. But her qualms were vanquished by the sensational and most unexpected happening that followed. The man beside her emitted an unearthly and uncultured yell and rose to his feet. She saw him spring over the front seat, leap to the broad rump of the wheeler, and from there gain the wagon. His onslaught was like a whirlwind. Before the bewildered officer on top the load could guess the errand of this conventionally clad but excited-seeming gentleman, he was the recipient of a punch that arched him back through the air to the pavement. A kick in the face led an ascending policeman to follow his example. A rush of three more gained the top and locked with Bill Totts in a gigantic clinch, during which his scalp was opened up by a club, and coat, vest, and half his starched shirt were torn from him. But the three policemen were flung wide and far, and Bill Totts, raining down lumps of coal, held the fort.

The captain led gallantly to the attack, but was bowled over by a chunk of coal that burst on his head in black baptism. The need of the police was to break the blockade in front before the mob could break in at the rear, and Bill Totts' need was to hold the wagon till the mob did break through. So the battle of the coal went on.

The crowd had recognized its champion. "Big" Bill, as usual, had come to the front, and Catherine Van Vorst was bewildered by the cries of "Bill! O you Bill!" that arose on every hand. Pat Morrissey, on his wagon seat, was jumping and screaming in an ecstasy, "Eat 'em, Bill! Eat 'em! Eat 'em alive!" From the sidewalk she heard a woman's voice cry out, "Look out, Bill—front end!" Bill took the warning and with well-directed coal cleaned the front end of the wagon of assailants. Catherine Van Vorst turned her head and saw on the curb of the sidewalk a woman with vivid coloring and flashing black eyes who was staring with all her soul at the man who had been Freddie Drummond a few minutes before.

The windows of the office building became vociferous with applause. A fresh shower of office chairs and filing cabinets descended. The mob had broken through on one side the line of wagons, and was advancing, each segregated policeman the center of a fighting group. The scabs were torn from their seats, the traces of the horses cut, and the frightened animals put in flight. Many policemen crawled under the coal wagon for safety, while the loose horses, with here and there a policeman on their backs or struggling at their heads to hold them, surged across the sidewalk opposite the jam and broke into Market Street.

Catherine Van Vorst heard the woman's voice calling in warning. She was back on the curb again, and crying out:

"Beat it, Bill! Now's your time! Beat it!"

The police for the moment had been swept away. Bill Totts leaped to the pavement and made his way to the woman on the sidewalk. Catherine Van Vorst saw her throw her arms around him and kiss him on the lips; and Catherine Van Vorst watched him curiously as he went on down the sidewalk, one arm around the woman, both talking and laughing, and he with a volubility and abandon she could never have dreamed possible.

The police were back again and clearing the jam while waiting for reinforcements and new drivers and horses. The mob had done its work and was scattering, and Catherine Van Vorst, still watching, could see the man she had known as Freddie Drummond. He towered a head above the crowd. His arm was still about the woman. And she in the motorcar, watching, saw the pair cross Market Street, cross the Slot, and disappear down Third Street into the labor ghetto.

In the years that followed no more lectures were given in the University of California by one Freddie Drummond, and no more books on economics and the labor question appeared over the name of Frederick A. Drummond. On the other hand there arose a new labor leader, William Totts by name. He it was who married Mary Condon, President of the International Glove Workers' Union No. 974; and he it was who called the notorious Cooks and Waiters' Strike, which, before its successful termination, brought out with it scores of other unions, among which, of the more remotely allied, were the Chicken Pickers and the Undertakers.

1909

Critical Visions of Postbellum America

In varying degrees all writing reflects and responds to its time and place, emerges out of a cultural context that animates and helps to shape it. The line between writings that seem less governed by their immediate historical circumstances and those that adhere more closely to the issues and occasions of their origins is never hard and fast, and examples of writings that represent their authors' reactions to specific issues or historical events can be found elsewhere in this post-Civil War section. The works in this unit have in common their engagement, usually direct and often urgent, with clearly identifiable political, social, and economic problems that confronted America in the post-war decades. All are written out of a desire to inform and to persuade, in most cases to convince their audience of the wrongness of a situation, the rightness of a cause; many of them are intended not only to arouse feeling and compel conviction but to influence behavior and encourage action. In this last respect they show their authors' belief in the power of language to help create social and political change.

The issues these writings deal with, all still very real today, range from the injustices experienced by minority racial and ethnic groups to the problem of inequality between the sexes, from poverty and industrial pollution to the threats posed by the growing power of science. Their authors employ a variety of literary forms, from speech, sketch, essay, and autobiography to poem, short story, and novel; and they use the literary conventions, the rhetorical and stylistic possibilities of those forms, to evoke both intellectual and emotional response. Their styles repay examination, as revealing some of the ways in which language can be used for persuasion and advocacy. The spare speech of Standing Bear achieves its force through its emotional restraint as he describes the theft of Indian lands; it contrasts dramatically with the heavily charged prose of Upton Sinclair, who invokes a barrage of detail in order to arouse horror and disgust at industrial conditions. Marietta Holley uses dialect and irreverent, deflating humor to call attention to women's continued lack of political rights, as Frances Ellen Watkins Harper uses it to argue for both voting rights and education for black women, and Finley Peter Dunne uses it to satirize end-of-the-century chauvinism. Henry Adams, by contrast, uses distanced, self-mocking ironies to convey his sense of the helplessness of the individual in a world governed by impersonal scientific forces.

Writings that describe and protest injustice usually stem from a belief in the possibility of improvement, and many of these texts either imply or explicitly convey their authors' visions and dreams of constructive change. Authors like Holley and Sinclair saw their writings as instrumental in the political campaigns for, respectively, women's suffrage and socialism. Charlotte Perkins Gilman's short story "Turned" envisions a new sisterhood among women. Anna Julia Cooper's essays are motivated not only by anger at racial injustice but by a belief in racial progress. All such hopeful and resilient visions are counterpointed by Henry Adams's more skeptical and somber one, of a twentieth-century America where human agency may not be able to constrain the destructive potential of new scientific forces. Taken together, these writings reveal some of the major hopes and apprehensions about the American future that were finding expression at the turn into the twentieth century and would continue to find expression into our own time.

Elaine Hedges
Towson State University

Standing Bear (Machunazha; Ponca) 1829–1908

The heritage of eloquence in Native American oral tradition reflects the notion that selected individuals possess the gifts of thought, language, and moral courage to lead us to recognize the underlying meaning of human existence. Thus, life experience, historical circumstance, personal character, and oral rhetorical skill combine to allow speakers to share with their audience a moment of authentic understanding, the momentary recognition of the confluence of real events and their verbal interpretation.

The Ponca people of north-central Nebraska and south-central South Dakota, centered on the Niobrara River of Nebraska, established a record of peaceful relations with their non-Indian neighbors and with the U.S. government. Having entered into four previous treaties with the United States, the Poncas nevertheless were callously deprived of their homeland in a treaty in which they were not even a participant. In the Fort Laramie Treaty of 1868 with the bands of the Lakota (Western Sioux), the U.S. government inexplicably and carelessly granted the ancestral Ponca homelands to the Lakota as part of the Great Sioux Reservation. Then, fearing warfare between the two tribal nations, government representatives unilaterally determined that the Poncas should be removed to Indian Territory, present-day Oklahoma.

In May 1877, the Poncas were forcibly removed to Baxter Springs in eastern Oklahoma and then to Ponca City in north-central Oklahoma. In the Ponca version of the Trail of Tears, eight chiefs were selected to visit Indian Territory to select a new homeland. Upon seeing their choices, the chiefs expressed their dissatisfaction and requested to be allowed to return to their northern home. Although denied permission, they defiantly made the 500-mile trip back to their homeland. In spite of all their appeals, E. C. Kemble, U.S. Indian inspector, ordered the Ponca removal, which concluded on July 29, 1878. As a result of climatic difficulties, exposure, and poor nutrition, only 681 Poncas arrived in Indian Territory, having lost one-third of their number along the way.

The tribulations of the Poncas crested as the death of Chief Standing Bear's son was linked with the son's request to be buried in the Niobrara homeland. In the winter of 1879, Chief Standing Bear and sixty-six Poncas set out from Indian Territory for Nebraska. Taken into custody by General George Crook, Standing Bear and his people were able to attract public attention with the assistance of *Omaha Daily Herald* assistant editor Thomas Henry Tibbles, who was committed to the principle of "equality of all men before the law." With help from two prominent attorneys, Tibbles was able to assist Standing Bear in obtaining a writ of habeas corpus in the court of federal judge Elmer S. Dundy, who ruled in *Standing Bear et al. v. Crook* in favor of Standing Bear, in effect declaring that "an Indian is a person within the meaning of the laws of the United States." By thus invoking the protection of the Fourteenth Amendment of the United States Constitution, Standing Bear's small band was able to prevent its return to Indian Territory. As a result of this decision, Standing Bear and the members of his party were released, and their legal possession of their reservation was subsequently affirmed by Judge Dundy.

Among the notables taking up the cause of the injustices imposed upon the Poncas was Helen Hunt Jackson, who attacked Secretary of the Interior Carl Schurz and his policies regarding Indian nations. In 1881 she published *A Century of Dishonor,* which condemned federal policy toward Native American people. In response to public pressure, a U.S. Senate commission in its report to President Rutherford B. Hayes in 1881 determined that the Poncas should be allowed to remain on their lands in Nebraska with every member who so desired receiving an allotment on the "old Dakota Reservation." Poncas who chose to remain in the north became known as Northern Ponca; so-called Southern Ponca remained in Indian Territory. Because of the allotment policy of 1887, most northern Ponca land was lost to non-Indian ownership in the decades that followed.

In another period of detrimental federal policy after the 1950s, in April 1962, Senator Frank Church of Idaho introduced a bill terminating the Northern Ponca band's federal trust relationship. On September 5, 1962, Congress passed Public Law 870-629, in effect terminating the Ponca Tribe of Nebraska. Today, the Northern Poncas are engaged in an effort to restore their federal recognition as a tribe. In May 1989, the Northern Ponca Restoration Committee initiated an ongoing effort to restore federal recognition to the Northern Poncas.

In his statement to the presidential commission in January 1881, Standing Bear intended to move his audience through the organization of his thoughts and the power of his language (in translation) to share the Poncas' view of their treatment by the U.S. government. Although Standing Bear's words were translated by David Le Clair, a Ponca, in the presence of James Owen Dorsey, a well-known non-Indian ethnographer and linguist, the quality of the translation, as of other Native American texts, continues to be of some concern. Nevertheless, Standing Bear's abilities as a public speaker are evident. He begins by establishing his goodwill toward the audience—a common practice of Native American orators—and then his credibility in relation to God. Using another common device of tribal spokesmen, he traces the pertinent history of his people in the body of his statement, making appropriate references to previous speakers, speaking directly and humbly from a personal point of view with repeated rhetorical questions. His conclusion presents the issues at hand and appeals for justice and fair treatment for his people.

Standing Bear and his band were allowed to move back to their old lands and received allotments there in 1890. He often went to visit his Southern Ponca relatives in Indian Territory. He died in 1908.

R. D. Theisz
Black Hills State University

PRIMARY WORK

Speech to the Ponca Commission, 1881.

What I Am Going to Tell You Here Will Take Me Until Dark[1]

I do not think we have made this day, but I think that God has caused it, and my heart is glad to see you all here. Why should I tell you a different word? I have told to God my troubles, and why should I deceive Him?[2] I have told my troubles to Him. Whatever God does is good, I think; even if a thing happens which may not suit us or which may be unfortunate, still God causes it, I think. If a man gets by accident or puts himself into a bad place, or gets frightened, he remembers God and asks Him to help him. You have seen that land, my friends. God made us there,[3] my friends, and He made you, too, but I have been very weak. You have driven me from the East to this place, and I have been here two thousand years or more.[4]

I don't know how it came about that I encountered misfortunes. My friends, they spoke of carrying me away. I was unwilling. My friends, if you took me away from this land it would be very hard for me. I wish to die in this land. I wish to be an old man here. As I was unwilling, they fastened me and made a prisoner of me and carried me to the fort.[5] When I came back, the soldiers came with their guns and bayonets; they aimed their guns at us, and our people and our children were crying. This was a very different thing that was done to me; I had hoped the Great Father had not done this thing to me—forcing me to leave this land. They took me and carried me without stopping; they traveled all day until night came, and they carried me down to Baxter Springs——.[6]

——I reached that place,[7] and that while I was there fully 150 of my people died. The land was truly bad, and so I came back again. One of the employees of the President—a commissioner—came to see me, and I said to him: "I am going back to my own land. I have never given it to you—I have never sold it to you. You have not paid me for it. I am going back to my own land. The lawyers, ministers, and those who are with them—those who control the land, and God Himself, if He desire it—all will help me." I came back, and there was some talk about this affair; they took pity on me, just as you here take pity on me, and there was a suit brought about it in the

[1]Standing Bear's talk appeared in *Senate Executive Document 30* of the third session of the Forty-sixth Congress (p. 31). The occasion was a January 1881 session of a presidential commission sent to Nebraska to take testimony concerning the Ponca removal. Standing Bear's speech was translated by David Le Clair, a Ponca. [All footnotes by Daniel F. Littlefield, Jr.]

[2]General George Crook had asked Standing Bear for his account of the removal but asked him to be brief, saying rather impatiently that he had heard the story before. Standing Bear's question is the chief's way of politely asserting the truth of his statement.

[3]*I.e.,* to the east.

[4]Such use of the first person is common in Indian oratory. It indicates that the speaker does not distinguish himself from his people, past or present.

[5]Fort Randall, South Dakota.

[6]In southeastern Kansas. The removal plan called for settling the Poncas on Quapaw lands just south of Baxter Springs in Indian Territory because the Quapaws were a cognate tribe with the Omaha, Ponca, Osage, and Kansa, having similar language, tribal organization, and religion.

[7]*I.e.,* Indian Territory.

courts, and the affair was settled, and I came back successful.[8] Some of my people have gone to my Great Father in Washington. Are they there now?——[9]

——My friends, I haven't got much brain, but you whites have a great deal of brain. The Indians do not know much, but the Great Father has caused you to come to look into our affairs. I refer to this land, not knowing about it. The Indians are ignorant about it. When they went from Indian Territory to sell their lands they didn't know all about it, and the Great Father should have told them correctly. Which of the Great Fathers was it? He should have released me—let me alone. Was it the Secretary of the Interior? What I am going to tell you here will take me until dark. Since I got from the Territory up to this time I have not wished to give even a part of it to the Great Father. Though he were to give me a million dollars I would not give him the land. Even if the Great Father should wish to buy a part of the land from me the Indians up the river would hear of it and would be unwilling. My friends, I have been in your lands—to Omaha, Chicago, New York, Boston, Philadelphia, Washington, all these cities, and I've been to the Dakotas, and they've given me my land back——[10]

——I wish to take back my own people from the Indian Territory. I wish them to live. I hadn't heard what you've done with regard to them. If the Secretary is sick or foolish, I hope you'll act as physicians and heal him—I mean the one who speaks German.[11] If one man cheats another, tries to make sport of him, or to kill him, and the other party finds out his danger, he don't have anything more to do with him—he lets him go to one side. I refer to the land. When they went to the Great Father to sell the land, which land did they mean? They live in Indian Territory. Did they want to sell that land or to sell this where I live, and which is mine? One thing I forgot. The land in which you dwell, my friends, is your own. Who would come from another quarter to take it away from you? Your land is your own, and so are your things, and you wouldn't like anybody to come and try to take them away from you. If men want to trade, they say, How much do you want for that piece of property? What price do you put upon it? But nothing of that kind was said; they came and took me away without saying a word.

1881

[8]Standing Bear refers to the famous case of *Standing Bear et al. v. Crook,* which said that an Indian is a person under the laws of the United States.

[9]Standing Bear refers to a delegation of the Indian Territory Poncas that had gone to Washington to air their concerns. General Crook's response to Standing Bear's question was that the delegation had returned to the Indian Territory.

[10]In the previous summer the Dakotas had attended a grand council of the Sioux, at which Spotted Trail told his people that they must return the disputed land to the Poncas. As one of the major reasons for removing the Poncas, the United States officials had argued that war between the Poncas and the Sioux was inevitable.

[11]Secretary of the Interior Carl Schurz had publicly defended the government's removal policy and had charged that Standing Bear and his entourage were simply troublemakers during their speaking tour of the east in 1879 and 1880.

Charles Alexander Eastman (Sioux) 1858–1939

What's in a name? In the case of Charles Eastman, a complicated story of cross cultural relations. Born in 1858, he was given the name Hakadah ("Pitiful Last"), because his mother soon died. Raised in the culture of the Santee Sioux, at the age of four he was given a new name, Ohiyesa ("The Winner"), after his village won a game of lacrosse. Eastman was in more ways than one a champion, but he would also face more than his share of losses.

Tensions between encroaching whites and Indians in Minnesota were mounting, and the failure of the U.S. government to adhere to its treaty obligations created a desperate situation. In 1862 some Sioux rebelled, killing a number of settlers. When the U.S. Army put down the insurrection, some three hundred Sioux were imprisoned and sentenced to die—including Eastman's father, Many Lightnings. His uncle and grandmother escaped with other Santee into the "deep woods" of Canada. His uncle gave Ohiyesa a warrior's education, preparing him to take revenge.

But in 1873 Ohiyesa's father reappeared, as if back from the dead. Abraham Lincoln had commuted his sentence to a term in prison, where he had converted to Christianity. The elder Eastman now read the Bible and took up the plow, following a model that reformers had advocated for hunting-and-gathering Indians. To symbolize the change, he adopted the last name of his deceased wife Mary Eastman, whose father was a white soldier. He expected his son to follow in his footsteps along this new path, and thus Ohiyesa journeyed with him to his farm in South Dakota and was there christened Charles Eastman.

Eastman began his cultural re-education by going to a nearby missionary-run school, where he soon excelled. Reversing the westward route of manifest destiny, he then traveled ever eastward from school to school—Beloit in Wisconsin, Knox in Illinois, Dartmouth in New Hampshire, and finally Boston University, where he earned a medical degree in 1890. He was then ready to go back to the West to serve his people at the Pine Ridge Agency in South Dakota, where he became known as the "white doctor who is an Indian."

In 1890, the Ghost Dance religion was spreading among the Sioux. Following the vision of the prophet Wovoka, some Sioux believed that if the Ghost Dance was performed, whites would vanish, the buffalo would return, and Indian land, life, and culture would be restored. Attempting to quell this millenarian movement, the army ended up massacring approximately 200 men, women, and children at Wounded Knee. Although Eastman had adopted much of what the white world offered, the sight of so many brutalized bodies shattered the idea that white society represented only light and progress.

Many reformers of his day clung to this idea and tried to convince both Native Americans and whites that native cultures were inferior and backward. They espoused a "Kill the Indian and save the man" philosophy, believing that the only way Indians could survive in modern America was to wash their hands of the old ways and completely assimilate. Reformers often held up educated Native Americans like Eastman as confirmation of their views. While Eastman's life proved that American Indians could succeed on the white man's terms, he himself insisted that Native American culture was valuable in its own right and, further, that it had much to offer modern America. While the missionaries believed that Christianity would civilize the "savage," Eastman held that Indians could educate white Americans on how to become truly civilized and spiritual. His motto could have been "Save the Indian and save the American."

Interestingly, he found a receptive audience among white Americans. As the country stepped up the pace of industrialization, many people became unsettled in the increasingly urbanized landscape. Seeking a kind of therapy for the anxieties of the machine age, many turned to Native Americans to try to reconnect with nature and recover a soul seemingly being exhausted by smokestack America.

Much of what Eastman wrote responded to this desire. His wife, Elaine Goodale, a poet and writer whom he had met at Pine Ridge in 1890 when she was serving as a supervisor of Indian education, encouraged his literary efforts. In 1902, in *Indian Boyhood,* he told the story of the years before his introduction to white education. With the editorial help of his wife he wrote several other popular works, becoming a leading light in the Boy Scout movement and lecturing widely. In books such as *The Soul of an Indian* (1911) and his autobiographical *From Deep Woods to Civilization* (1916), Eastman acted as a spokesperson, explaining Native American culture to white America. In the process of explaining, though, he was also creating, for, as he well knew, there was no single Indian culture. Eastman was helping forge a pan-Indian identity that could both command the respect of whites and offer a vantage point from which to criticize the materialism and other drawbacks of mainstream American culture. The traditional ways and wisdom he celebrated were thus reinvented for a new audience, a new time, and a new purpose.

Eastman's legacy is perhaps best illustrated by the work he did between 1903 and 1909 to standardize the family names of the Sioux. This project involved more than simple translation from Lakota into English, because the Sioux followed a different cultural logic in their naming than did the dominant society. Eastman had to negotiate between two cultures in order to create a synthesis that was somehow true to both sides. This was the sort of challenge Eastman faced his whole life; and because he met this particular one, his people gave him a new and most appropriate appellation: Name Giver. Through his writing and other work, Eastman made a name both for himself and for Indian people at a time when they otherwise might have been deleted from the rolls of the nation.

Douglas C. Sackman
University of Puget Sound

PRIMARY WORKS

Indian Boyhood, 1902; *Red Hunters and the Animal People,* 1904; *Old Indian Days,* 1907; *Wigwam Evenings* (with Elaine Goodale Eastman), 1909; *The Soul of the Indian,* 1911; *Indian Child Life,* 1913; *Indian Scout Talks,* 1914; *The Indian To-Day,* 1915; *From the Deep Woods to Civilization,* 1916; *Indian Heroes and Great Chieftains,* 1918.

from The Soul of the Indian

I The Great Mystery[1]

The original attitude of the American Indian toward the Eternal, the "Great Mystery" that surrounds and embraces us, was as simple as it was exalted. To him it was the supreme conception, bringing with it the fullest measure of joy and satisfaction possible in this life.

[1]In subsequent chapters, Eastman describes the family's role in religious training, the social reinforcement of religious views through ritual and ceremony, the nurturing of morality in Indian society, the role of oral tradition in religion, and Indian concepts regarding the spirit world. [All footnotes by Daniel F. Littlefield, Jr.]

The worship of the "Great Mystery" was silent, solitary, free from all self-seeking. It was silent, because all speech is of necessity feeble and imperfect; therefore the souls of my ancestors ascended to God in wordless adoration. It was solitary, because they believed that He is nearer to us in solitude, and there were no priests authorized to come between a man and his Maker. None might exhort or confess or in any way meddle with the religious experience of another. Among us all men were created sons of God and stood erect, as conscious of their divinity. Our faith might not be formulated in creeds, nor forced upon any who were unwilling to receive it; hence there was no preaching, proselyting, nor persecution, neither were there any scoffers or atheists.

There were no temples or shrines among us save those of nature. Being a natural man, the Indian was intensely poetical. He would deem it sacrilege to build a house for Him who may be met face to face in the mysterious, shadowy aisles of the primeval forest, or on the sunlit bosom of virgin prairies, upon dizzy spires and pinnacles of naked rock, and yonder in the jeweled vault of the night sky! He who enrobes Himself in filmy veils of cloud, there on the rim of the visible world where our Great-Grandfather Sun kindles his evening camp-fire, He who rides upon the rigorous wind of the north, or breathes forth His spirit upon aromatic southern airs, whose warcanoe is launched upon majestic rivers and inland seas—He needs no lesser cathedral!

That solitary communion with the Unseen which was the highest expression of our religious life is partly described in the word *hambeday,* literally "mysterious feeling," which has been variously translated "fasting" and "dreaming." It may better be interpreted as "consciousness of the divine."

The first *hambeday,* or religious retreat, marked an epoch in the life of the youth, which may be compared to that of confirmation or conversion in Christian experience. Having first prepared himself by means of the purifying vapor-bath, and cast off as far as possible all human or fleshly influences, the young man sought out the noblest height, the most commanding summit in all the surrounding region. Knowing that God sets no value upon material things, he took with him no offerings or sacrifices other than symbolic objects, such as paints and tobacco. Wishing to appear before Him in all humility, he wore no clothing save his moccasins and breech-clout. At the solemn hour of sunrise or sunset he took up his position, overlooking the glories of earth and facing the "Great Mystery," and there he remained, naked, erect, silent, and motionless, exposed to the elements and forces of His arming, for a night and a day to two days and nights, but rarely longer. Sometimes he would chant a hymn without words, or offer the ceremonial "filled pipe." In this holy trance or ecstasy the Indian mystic found his highest happiness and the motive power of his existence.

When he returned to the camp, he must remain at a distance until he had again entered the vapor-bath and prepared himself for intercourse with his fellows. Of the vision or sign vouchsafed to him he did not speak, unless it had included some commission which must be publicly fulfilled. Sometimes an old man, standing upon the brink of eternity, might reveal to a chosen few the oracle of his long-past youth.

The native American has been generally despised by his white conquerors for his poverty and simplicity. They forget, perhaps, that his religion forbade the accumulation of wealth and the enjoyment of luxury. To him, as to other single-minded men in every age and race, from Diogenes to the brothers of Saint Francis, from the Montanists to the Shakers,[2] the love of possessions has appeared a snare, and the burdens of a complex society a source of needless peril and temptation. Furthermore, it was the rule of his life to share the fruits of his skill and success with his less fortunate brothers. Thus he kept his spirit free from the clog of pride, cupidity, or envy, and carried out, as he believed, the divine decree—a matter profoundly important to him.

It was not, then, wholly from ignorance or improvidence that he failed to establish permanent towns and to develop a material civilization. To the untutored sage, the concentration of population was the prolific mother of all evils, moral no less than physical. He argued that food is good, while surfeit kills; that love is good, but lust destroys; and not less dreaded than the pestilence following upon crowded and unsanitary dwellings was the loss of spiritual power inseparable from too close contact with one's fellow-men. All who have lived much out of doors know that there is a magnetic and nervous force that accumulates in solitude and that is quickly dissipated by life in a crowd; and even his enemies have recognized the fact that for a certain innate power and self-poise, wholly independent of circumstances, the American Indian is unsurpassed among men.

The red man divided mind into two parts,—the spiritual mind and the physical mind. The first is pure spirit, concerned only with the essence of things, and it was this he sought to strengthen by spiritual prayer, during which the body is subdued by fasting and hardship. In this type of prayer there was no beseeching of favor or help. All matters of personal or selfish concern, as success in hunting or warfare, relief from sickness, or the sparing of a beloved life, were definitely relegated to the plane of the lower or material mind, and all ceremonies, charms, or incantations designed to secure a benefit or to avert a danger, were recognized as emanating from the physical self.

The rites of this physical worship, again, were wholly symbolic, and the Indian no more worshiped the Sun than the Christian adores the Cross. The Sun and the Earth, by an obvious parable, holding scarcely more of poetic metaphor than of scientific truth, were in his view the parents of all organic life. From the Sun, as the universal father, proceeds the quickening principle in nature, and in the patient and fruitful womb of our mother, the Earth, are hidden embryos of plants and men. Therefore our reverence and love for them was really an imaginative extension of our love for our immediate parents, and with this sentiment of filial piety was joined a willingness to appeal to them, as to a father, for such good gifts as we may desire. This is the material or physical prayer.

The elements and majestic forces in nature, Lightning, Wind, Water, Fire, and Frost, were regarded with awe as spiritual powers, but always secondary and intermediate in character. We believed that the spirit pervades all creation and that every creature possesses a soul in some degree, though not necessarily a soul conscious of

[2]Diogenes of Sinope (c. 400–c. 325 B.C.), as an exile in Athens, lived in poverty and believed that happiness resulted from satisfaction of one's natural needs as easily and cheaply as possible and that any natural act was decent and honorable. The doctrine of poverty espoused by St. Francis of Assisi was practiced by the Franciscan friars he founded in 1209. Montanism, based on the apocalyptic teachings of Montanus of Phrygia (who lived sometime in the second century), was characterized by asceticism, zeal, and anti-institutionalism in the Church. Shakers grew out of the Quaker revival in England in 1747. In America, after 1774, they formed communal societies in which property was held in common.

itself. The tree, the waterfall, the grizzly bear, each is an embodied Force, and as such an object of reverence.

The Indian loved to come into sympathy and spiritual communion with his brothers of the animal kingdom, whose inarticulate souls had for him something of the sinless purity that we attribute to the innocent and irresponsible child. He had faith in their instincts, as in a mysterious wisdom given from above; and while he humbly accepted the supposedly voluntary sacrifice of their bodies to preserve his own, he paid homage to their spirits in prescribed prayers and offerings.

In every religion there is an element of the supernatural, varying with the influence of pure reason over its devotees. The Indian was a logical and clear thinker upon matters within the scope of his understanding, but he had not yet charted the vast field of nature or expressed her wonders in terms of science. With his limited knowledge of cause and effect, he saw miracles on every hand,—the miracle of life in seed and egg, the miracle of death in lightning flash and in the swelling deep! Nothing of the marvelous could astonish him; as that a beast should speak, or the sun stand still. The virgin birth would appear scarcely more miraculous than is the birth of every child that comes into the world, or the miracle of the loaves and fishes excite more wonder than the harvest that springs from a single ear of corn.

Who may condemn his superstition? Surely not the devout Catholic, or even Protestant missionary, who teaches Bible miracles as literal fact! The logical man must either deny all miracles or none, and our American Indian myths and hero stories are perhaps, in themselves, quite as credible as those of the Hebrews of old. If we are of the modern type of mind, that sees in natural law a majesty and grandeur far more impressive than any solitary infraction of it could possibly be, let us not forget that, after all, science has not explained everything. We have still to face the ultimate miracle,—the origin and principle of life! Here is the supreme mystery that is the essence of worship, without which there can be no religion, and in the presence of this mystery our attitude cannot be very unlike that of the natural philosopher, who beholds with awe the Divine in all creation.

It is simple truth that the Indian did not, so long as his native philosophy held sway over his mind, either envy or desire to imitate the splendid achievements of the white man. In his own thought he rose superior to them! He scorned them, even as a lofty spirit absorbed in its stern task rejects the soft beds, the luxurious food, the pleasure-worshiping dalliance of a rich neighbor. It was clear to him that virtue and happiness are independent of these things, if not incompatible with them.

There was undoubtedly much in primitive Christianity to appeal to this man, and Jesus' hard sayings to the rich and about the rich would have been entirely comprehensible to him. Yet the religion that is preached in our churches and practiced by our congregations, with its element of display and self-aggrandizement, its active proselytism, and its open contempt of all religions but its own, was for a long time extremely repellent. To his simple mind, the professionalism of the pulpit, the paid exhorter, the moneyed church, was an unspiritual and unedifying thing, and it was not until his spirit was broken and his moral and physical constitution undermined by trade, conquest, and strong drink, that Christian missionaries obtained any real hold upon him. Strange as it may seem, it is true that the proud pagan in his secret soul despised the good men who came to convert and to enlighten him!

Nor were its publicity and its Phariseeism the only elements in the alien religion that offended the red man. To him, it appeared shocking and almost incredible that there were among this people who claimed superiority many irreligious, who did not even pretend to profess the national faith. Not only did they not profess it, but they stooped so low as to insult their God with profane and sacrilegious speech! In our own tongue His name was not spoken aloud, even with utmost reverence, much less lightly or irreverently.

More than this, even in those white men who professed religion we found much inconsistency of conduct. They spoke much of spiritual things, while seeking only the material. They bought and sold everything: time, labor, personal independence, the love of woman, and even the ministrations of their holy faith! The lust for money, power, and conquest so characteristic of the Anglo-Saxon race did not escape moral condemnation at the hands of his untutored judge, nor did he fail to contrast this conspicuous trait of the dominant race with the spirit of the meek and lowly Jesus.

He might in time come to recognize that the drunkards and licentious among white men, with whom he too frequently came in contact, were condemned by the white man's religion as well, and must not be held to discredit it. But it was not so easy to overlook or to excuse national bad faith. When distinguished emissaries from the Father at Washington, some of them ministers of the gospel and even bishops, came to the Indian nations, and pledged to them in solemn treaty the national honor, with prayer and mention of their God; and when such treaties, so made, were promptly and shamelessly broken, is it strange that the action should arouse not only anger, but contempt? The historians of the white race admit that the Indian was never the first to repudiate his oath.

It is my personal belief, after thirty-five years' experience of it, that there is no such thing as "Christian civilization." I believe that Christianity and modern civilization are opposed and irreconcilable, and that the spirit of Christianity and of our ancient religion is essentially the same.

1911

from From the Deep Woods to Civilization

VII The Ghost Dance War[1]

A religious craze such as that of 1890–91 was a thing foreign to the Indian philosophy.[2] I recalled that a hundred years before, on the overthrow of the Algonquin nations, a somewhat similar faith was evolved by the astute Delaware prophet, brother

[1]In earlier chapters, Eastman describes his life as a student at Santee Normal Training School, Dartmouth College, and Boston University Medical School. Subsequent chapters relate his career as a government physician, as a lecturer and writer, and as a leader in the Indian Y.M.C.A. His final chapter contains his estimation of how well Indians have fared in the assimilation process.

[2]The Ghost Dance and the messianic religion with which it was associated. See headnote to *Ghost Dance Songs*.

to Tecumseh.[3] It meant that the last hope of race entity had departed, and my people were groping blindly after spiritual relief in their bewilderment and misery. I believe that the first prophets of the "Red Christ" were innocent enough and that the people generally were sincere, but there were doubtless some who went into it for self-advertisement, and who introduced new and fantastic features to attract the crowd.[4]

The ghost dancers had gradually concentrated on the Medicine Root creek and the edge of the "Bad Lands,"[5] and they were still further isolated by a new order from the agent, calling in all those who had not adhered to the new religion.[6] Several thousand of these "friendlies" were soon encamped on the White Clay creek, close by the agency.[7] It was near the middle of December, with weather unusually mild for that season. The dancers held that there would be no snow so long as their rites continued.

An Indian called Little[8] had been guilty of some minor offense on the reservation and had hitherto evaded arrest. Suddenly he appeared at the agency on an issue day, for the express purpose, as it seemed, of defying the authorities. The assembly room of the Indian police, used also as a council room, opened out of my dispensary[9] and on this particular morning a council was in progress. I heard some loud talking, but was too busy to pay particular attention, though my assistant had gone in to listen to the speeches. Suddenly the place was in an uproar, and George[10] burst into the inner office, crying excitedly "Look out for yourself, friend! They are going to fight!"

I went around to see what was going on. A crowd had gathered just outside the council room, and the police were surrounded by wild Indians with guns and drawn knives in their hands. "Hurry up with them!" one shouted, while another held his stone war-club over a policeman's head. The attempt to arrest Little had met with a stubborn resistance.

At this critical moment, a fine-looking Indian in citizen's clothes faced the excited throng, and spoke in a clear, steady, almost sarcastic voice.

[3] Tenskwatawa rose to prominence in 1805 when, in a vision, the Master of Life announced to him a new mode of action, which his people must take in order to regain divine favor. They must reject witchcraft and the white man's whiskey, dress, and technology, and Indian women must no longer marry whites. Only when they returned to their former life ways would they find the happiness that they had known in aboriginal days. Tenskwatawa's teachings, like Wovoka's, were a response to the cultural discontinuity that came with white contact. Tenskwatawa and Tecumseh were Shawnees, not Delawares as Eastman says.

[4] Eastman may refer here to the trances common among dancers and their belief that bullets could not penetrate the Ghost Dance shirts they wore.

[5] An area of rough, broken land just off the reservation, about fifty miles northwest of the Pine Ridge agency, South Dakota.

[6] Agency officials, Washington bureaucrats, and military officers considered the Ghost Dance movement a serious threat to their authority and control over the Indians. As Eastman indicates below, the excitement at the time of the so-called Ghost Dance War was heightened by political differences among the Indians, personal ambitions, and real grievances against the federal government.

[7] The agency was located near the Nebraska border, southwest of the Wounded Knee massacre site.

[8] Little had been arrested and brought to the agency, but had been rescued by his friends a few weeks earlier.

[9] Eastman had been appointed government physician at Pine Ridge only weeks earlier, after graduation from medical school at Boston University.

[10] Perhaps George Sword, captain of the agency's Indian police squad.

"Stop! Think! What are you going to do? Kill these men of our own race? Then what? Kill all these helpless white men, women and children? And what then? What will these brave words, brave deeds lead to in the end? How long can you hold out? Your country is surrounded with a network of railroads; thousands of white soldiers will be here within three days. What ammunition have you? what provisions? What will become of your families? Think, think, my brothers! this is a child's madness."

It was the "friendly" chief, American Horse,[11] and it seems to me as I recall the incident that this man's voice had almost magic power. It is likely that he saved us all from massacre, for the murder of the police, who represented the authority of the Government, would surely have been followed by a general massacre. It is a fact that those Indians who upheld the agent were in quite as much danger from their wilder brethren as were the whites, indeed it was said that the feeling against them was even stronger. Jack Red Cloud, son of the chief,[12] thrust the muzzle of a cocked revolver almost into the face of American Horse. "It is you and your kind," he shouted, "who have brought us to this pass!" That brave man never flinched. Ignoring his rash accuser, he quietly reentered the office; the door closed behind him; the mob dispersed, and for the moment the danger seemed over.

I scarcely knew at the time, but gradually learned afterward, that the Sioux had many grievances and causes for profound discontent, which lay back of and were more or less closely related to the ghost dance craze and the prevailing restlessness and excitement. Rations had been cut from time to time; the people were insufficiently fed, and their protests and appeals were disregarded. Never was more ruthless fraud and graft practiced upon a defenseless people than upon these poor natives by the politicians! Never were there more worthless "scraps of paper" anywhere in the world than many of the Indian treaties and Government documents! Sickness was prevalent and the death rate alarming, especially among the children. Trouble from all these causes had for some time been developing, but might have been checked by humane and conciliatory measures. The "Messiah craze" in itself was scarcely a source of danger, and one might almost as well call upon the army to suppress Billy Sunday[13] and his hysterical followers. Other tribes than the Sioux who adopted the new religion were let alone, and the craze died a natural death in the course of a few months.

Among the leaders of the malcontents at this time were Jack Red Cloud, No Water, He Dog, Four Bears, Yellow Bear, and Kicking Bear.[14] Friendly leaders included

[11]American Horse, an Oglala, had signed a treaty in 1887 by which the Sioux reservation was reduced by one half. Objections to the treaty added to the discontent of the Ghost Dance adherents and led them to their so-called "hostile" state in 1890. American Horse worked to resolve differences and to convince the "hostiles" to relent.

[12]Red Cloud (1822–1909), an Oglala, had been one of the most famous and powerful chiefs and since 1867 had been on peaceful terms with the United States. Old and partially blind, he took no part in the events of 1890. Jack Red Cloud was one of the Ghost Dancers who had earlier been induced to leave the Bad Lands and come to the agency.

[13]William Ashley Sunday (1862–1935), a well-known American evangelist.

[14]No Water's camp on the White River near Pine Ridge was the site of much Ghost Dance activity. In 1891, He Dog served as one of the Sioux delegates to Washington, sent to try to resolve tribal differences. Kicking Bear, from the Cheyenne River reservation, was a Ghost Dance priest who had organized the first dance at Sitting Bull's camp on the Standing Rock reservation. Four Bears and Yellow Bear have not been identified.

American Horse, Young Man Afraid of His Horses, Bad Wound, Three Stars.[15] There was still another set whose attitude was not clearly defined, and among these men was Red Cloud, the greatest of them all. He who had led his people so brilliantly and with such remarkable results, both in battle and diplomacy, was now an old man of over seventy years, living in a frame house which had been built for him within a half mile of the agency. He would come to council, but said little or nothing. No one knew exactly where he stood, but it seemed that he was broken in spirit as in body and convinced of the hopelessness of his people's cause.

It was Red Cloud who asked the historic question, at a great council held in the Black Hills region with a Government commission, and after good Bishop Whipple[16] had finished the invocation, "Which God is our brother praying to now? Is it the same God whom they have twice deceived, when they made treaties with us which they afterward broke?"

Early in the morning after the attempted arrest of Little, George rushed into my quarters and awakened me. "Come quick!" he shouted, "the soldiers are here!" I looked along the White Clay creek toward the little railroad town of Rushville, Nebraska, twenty-five miles away, and just as the sun rose above the knife-edged ridges black with stunted pine, I perceived a moving cloud of dust that marked the trail of the Ninth Cavalry. There was instant commotion among the camps of friendly Indians. Many women and children were coming in to the agency for refuge, evidently fearing that the dreaded soldiers might attack their villages by mistake. Some who had not heard of their impending arrival hurried to the offices to ask what it meant. I assured those who appealed to me that the troops were here only to preserve order, but their suspicions were not easily allayed.

As the cavalry came nearer, we saw that they were colored troopers, wearing buffalo overcoats and muskrat caps; the Indians with their quick wit called them "buffalo soldiers." They halted, and established their temporary camp in the open space before the agency enclosure. The news had already gone out through the length and breadth of the reservation, and the wildest rumors were in circulation. Indian scouts might be seen upon every hill top, closely watching the military encampment.

At this juncture came the startling news from Fort Yates, some two hundred and fifty miles to the north of us, that Sitting Bull had been killed by Indian police while resisting arrest, and a number of his men with him, as well as several of the police. We next heard that the remnant of his band had fled in our direction, and soon afterward, that they had been joined by Big Foot's band from the western part of Cheyenne River agency, which lay directly in their road.[17] United States troops continued to gather at strategic points, and of course the press seized upon the opportunity to enlarge upon the strained situation and predict an "Indian uprising." The

[15] Young Man Afraid of His Horses, an Oglala, had made his reputation in the wars of the 1860s but, like Red Cloud, had lived peaceably since 1867 and counseled peace during the crisis. Bad Wound and Three Stars have not been identified.

[16] Episcopal Bishop Henry Benjamin Whipple.

[17] After Sitting Bull's death, the Hunkpapa Ghost Dancers fled from the Standing Rock reservation. The group Eastman refers to fled to the camp of Big Foot, a Minneconjou. Big Foot, gravely ill, yet considered dangerous by the authorities, started with his people toward the Pine Ridge reservation, where he hoped to find refuge.

reporters were among us, and managed to secure much "news" that no one else ever heard of. Border towns were fortified and cowboys and militia gathered in readiness to protect them against the "red devils." Certain classes of the frontier population industriously fomented the excitement for what there was in it for them, since much money is apt to be spent at such times. As for the poor Indians, they were quite as badly scared as the whites and perhaps with more reason.

General Brooke[18] undertook negotiations with the ghost dancers, and finally induced them to come within reach. They camped on a flat about a mile north of us and in full view, while the more tractable bands were still gathered on the south and west. The large boarding school had locked its doors and succeeded in holding its hundreds of Indian children, partly for their own sakes, and partly as hostages for the good behavior of their fathers. At the agency were now gathered all the government employees and their families, except such as had taken flight, together with traders, missionaries, and ranchmen, army officers, and newspaper men. It was a conglomerate population.

During this time of grave anxiety and nervous tension, the cooler heads among us went about our business, and still refused to believe in the tragic possibility of an Indian war. It may be imagined that I was more than busy, though I had not such long distances to cover, for since many Indians accustomed to comfortable log houses were compelled to pass the winter in tents, there was even more sickness than usual. I had access and welcome to the camps of all the various groups and factions, a privilege shared by my good friend Father Jutz,[19] the Catholic missionary, who was completely trusted by his people.

Three days later, we learned that Big Foot's band of ghost dancers from the Cheyenne river reservation north of us was approaching the agency, and that Major Whiteside[20] was in command of troops with orders to intercept them.

Late that afternoon, the Seventh Cavalry under Colonel Forsythe[21] was called to the saddle and rode off toward Wounded Knee creek, eighteen miles away. Father Craft,[22] a Catholic priest with some Indian blood, who knew Sitting Bull and his people, followed an hour or so later, and I was much inclined to go too, but my fiancée[23] pointed out that my duty lay rather at home with our Indians, and I stayed.

The morning of December 29th was sunny and pleasant. We were all straining our ears toward Wounded Knee, and about the middle of the forenoon we distinctly heard the reports of the Hotchkiss guns. Two hours later, a rider was seen approaching at full speed, and in a few minutes he had dismounted from his exhausted

[18]General J. R. Brooke, commander of the troops sent to Pine Ridge.

[19]Father John Jutz.

[20]Major Samuel Whiteside, with a detachment of the Seventh Cavalry, intercepted Big Foot on December 28 and convinced him to encamp for the night at Wounded Knee.

[21]Colonel James W. Forsyth, commander of the Seventh Cavalry, joined Whiteside at Wounded Knee on the night of December 28.

[22]Father Craft was at the massacre and was wounded.

[23]Elaine Goodale, who had taught for a number of years on the Great Sioux Reservation, was then superintendent for Indian education in the Dakotas. She and Eastman married in 1891. In later years, an author in her own right, she encouraged Eastman to write and lecture and collaborated with him on many works. The extent of her influence on his writing may never be known, but it was certainly great.

horse and handed his message to General Brooke's orderly. The Indians were watching their own messenger, who ran on foot along the northern ridges and carried the news to the so-called "hostile" camp. It was said that he delivered his message at almost the same time as the mounted officer.

The resulting confusion and excitement was unmistakable. The white teepees disappeared as if by magic and soon the caravans were in motion, going toward the natural fortress of the "Bad Lands." In the "friendly" camp there was almost as much turmoil, and crowds of frightened women and children poured into the agency. Big Foot's band had been wiped out by the troops, and reprisals were naturally looked for. The enclosure was not barricaded in any way and we had but a small detachment of troops for our protection. Sentinels were placed, and machine guns trained on the various approaches.

A few hot-headed young braves fired on the sentinels and wounded two of them. The Indian police began to answer by shooting at several braves who were apparently about to set fire to some of the outlying buildings. Every married employee was seeking a place of safety for his family, the interpreter among them. Just then General Brooke ran out into the open, shouting at the top of his voice to the police: "Stop, stop! Doctor, tell them they must not fire until ordered!" I did so, as the bullets whistled by us, and the General's coolness perhaps saved all our lives, for we were in no position to repel a large attacking force. Since we did not reply, the scattered shots soon ceased, but the situation remained critical for several days and nights.

My office was full of refugees. I called one of my good friends aside and asked him to saddle my two horses and stay by them. "When general fighting begins, take them to Miss Goodale and see her to the railroad if you can," I told him. Then I went over to the rectory. Mrs. Cook refused to go without her husband,[24] and Miss Goodale would not leave while there was a chance of being of service. The house was crowded with terrified people, most of them Christian Indians, whom our friends were doing their best to pacify.

At dusk, the Seventh Cavalry returned with their twenty-five dead and I believe thirty-four wounded, most of them by their own comrades, who had encircled the Indians, while few of the latter had guns.[25] A majority of the thirty or more Indian wounded were women and children, including babies in arms. As there were not tents enough for all, Mr. Cook offered us the mission chapel, in which the Christmas tree still stood, for a temporary hospital. We tore out the pews and covered the floor with hay and quilts. There we laid the poor creatures side by side in rows, and the night was devoted to caring for them as best we could. Many were frightfully torn by pieces of shells, and the suffering was terrible. General Brooke placed me in charge and I had to do nearly all the work, for although the army surgeons were more than ready to help as soon as their own men had been cared for, the tortured Indians

[24]The Reverend Charles Smith Cook, an Oglala, was an 1881 graduate of Trinity College and had studied theology at Seabury Divinity School. He was ordained and served as a teacher and minister on the Pine Ridge reservation. Cook died in 1892.

[25]The few Indians who had weapons had been disarmed, except one, when the firing commenced.

would scarcely allow a man in uniform to touch them. Mrs. Cook, Miss Goodale, and several of Mr. Cook's Indian helpers acted as volunteer nurses. In spite of all our efforts, we lost the greater part of them, but a few recovered, including several children who had lost all their relatives and who were adopted into kind Christian families.

On the day following the Wounded Knee massacre there was a blizzard, in the midst of which I was ordered out with several Indian police, to look for a policeman who was reported to have been wounded and left some two miles from the agency. We did not find him. This was the only time during the whole affair that I carried a weapon; a friend lent me a revolver which I put in my overcoat pocket, and it was lost on the ride. On the third day it cleared, and the ground was covered with an inch or two of fresh snow. We had feared that some of the Indian wounded might have been left on the field, and a number of us volunteered to go and see. I was placed in charge of the expedition of about a hundred civilians, ten or fifteen of whom were white men. We were supplied with wagons in which to convey any of whom we might find still alive. Of course a photographer and several reporters were of the party.

Fully three miles from the scene of the massacre we found the body of a woman completely covered with a blanket of snow, and from this point on we found them scattered along as they had been relentlessly hunted down and slaughtered while fleeing for their lives. Some of our people discovered relatives or friends among the dead, and there was much wailing and mourning. When we reached the spot where the Indian camp had stood, among the fragments of burned tents and other belongings we saw the frozen bodies lying close together or piled one upon another. I counted eighty bodies of men who had been in the council and who were almost as helpless as the women and babes when the deadly fire began, for nearly all their guns had been taken from them. A reckless and desperate young Indian fired the first shot when the search for weapons was well under way,[26] and immediately the troops opened fire from all sides, killing not only unarmed men, women, and children, but their own comrades who stood opposite them, for the camp was entirely surrounded.

It took all of my nerve to keep my composure in the face of this spectacle, and of the excitement and grief of my Indian companions, nearly every one of whom was crying aloud or singing his death song. The white men became very nervous, but I set them to examining and uncovering every body to see if one were living. Although they had been lying untended in the snow and cold for two days and nights, a number had survived. Among them I found a baby of about a year old warmly wrapped and entirely unhurt. I brought her in, and she was afterward adopted and educated by an army officer. One man who was severely wounded begged me to fill his pipe. When we brought him into the chapel he was welcomed by his wife and daughters with cries of joy, but he died a day or two later.

Under a wagon I discovered an old woman, totally blind and entirely helpless. A few had managed to crawl away to some place of shelter, and we found in a log store near by several who were badly hurt and others who had died after reaching there. After we had dispatched several wagon loads to the agency, we observed groups of warriors watching us from adjacent buttes; probably friends of the victims

[26]The young man who fired the first shot was Black Coyote, alleged to have been deaf.

who had come there for the same purpose as ourselves. A majority of our party, fearing an attack, insisted that some one ride back to the agency for an escort of soldiers, and as mine was the best horse, it fell to me to go. I covered the eighteen miles in quick time and was not interfered with in any way, although if the Indians had meant mischief they could easily have picked me off from any of the ravines and gulches.

All this was a severe ordeal for one who had so lately put all his faith in the Christian love and lofty ideals of the white man. Yet I passed no hasty judgment, and was thankful that I might be of some service and relieve even a small part of the suffering. An appeal published in a Boston paper brought us liberal supplies of much needed clothing, and linen for dressings. We worked on. Bishop Hare of South Dakota[27] visited us, and was overcome by faintness when he entered his mission chapel, thus transformed into a rude hospital.

After some days of extreme tension, and weeks of anxiety, the "hostiles," so called, were at last induced to come in and submit to a general disarmament. Father Jutz, the Catholic missionary, had gone bravely among them and used all his influence toward a peaceful settlement. The troops were all recalled and took part in a grand review before General Miles,[28] no doubt intended to impress the Indians with their superior force.

1916

Sarah Winnemucca (Thocmetony; Paiute) c. 1844–1891

Born about 1844 near Humboldt Lake in what is now northwestern Nevada, the daughter of a respected Paiute leader, Sarah Winnemucca (Thocmetony, or Shell Flower) would become one of the principal voices for Indian rights in the late nineteenth century. Although she spent part of her youth in the company of whites as well as Indians, Winnemucca was largely self-educated, fluent in three Indian languages as well as English and Spanish. In a period of extreme upheaval during white incursions on traditional Northern Paiute lands in present-day western Nevada, northern California, and southeastern Oregon, she consistently sought to advance the well-being of her people in the face of daunting personal hardship.

Her major publication, *Life Among the Piutes: Their Wrongs and Claims,* encompasses the first encounters of Paiutes with whites, described in the selection below; the Bannock Indian War of 1878; and the accomplishment of her father's dream, the establishment of a reservation on some of the Paiutes' ancestral lands, in 1889. Winnemucca's remarkable story is complex in both content and form, combining elements of history, autobiography, myth, sentimental appeal, humor, adventure, political tract, and oratory. Reflecting her experiences as a translator for the U.S. Army, an advocate for the Paiutes in Washington, a popular stage performer, and an innovative teacher and school reformer, the volume also seeks to educate white readers

[27]Bishop W. D. Hare, long-time Episcopal missionary bishop among the Sioux.

[28]General Nelson A. Miles, commander of the Army Department of the Missouri, who had ordered the arrest of Sitting Bull.

about her people. Winnemucca depicts a civilized tribe that deserves whites' sympathy and support. Willing to risk her livelihood and even her life, she gives outspoken testimony against the wrongs committed by reservation agents, whose corruption outraged not only Sarah but many sympathetic observers. She also reveals the efforts of governmental representatives and elected officials to prevent her from lecturing and garnering support for her cause.

One surprise to many contemporary readers may be her praise of the U.S. Army, whose commanding officers often proved to be much more honest and compassionate than government-appointed reservation agents, who were sometimes only nominal Christians. Winnemucca reserves some of her most intense attacks for the latter, who not only profited from government supplies meant for the Indians but regularly permitted their charges to freeze and starve to death. Her fiery stance inspired her to tell one agent to his face that "hell is full of just such Christians as you are."

Negotiating between two worlds was never easy, and Sarah was often placed in a precarious position with her own people by the false promises of white officials as well as by her own goal of assimilation. Her difficulties were also intensified by gender. A favorite claim of detractors—and one leveled at many women reformers of the time—was that she was promiscuous. This charge is ironic in view of the sexual abuse of Indian women by white men that Winnemucca describes in the selection below, abuse so prevalent and unrelenting that she affirms, "the mothers are afraid to have more children, for fear they shall have daughters, who are not safe even in their mother's presence." At least two of the wars that Sarah describes in her book were initiated by such abuse.

After suffering many frustrations and bitter disappointments at the hands of the government and its agents, Winnemucca finally decided that she could best serve her people by opening an Indian-run school. With the financial and emotional support of formidable Boston reformer Elizabeth Palmer Peabody and her sister Mary Mann (also the editor of Life Among the Piutes), Sarah founded, managed, and taught at the Peabody Indian School for nearly four years. In contrast to government-run schools, her school not only practiced bilingualism, it also affirmed Paiute values and traditions. During these last few years before her early death, Winnemucca suffered from ill health brought on by long-term physical hardship, as well as from the emotional stresses due to her last marriage to the improvident Lewis Hopkins, who frequently gambled away her hard-won earnings. Winnemucca amply deserves the renewed recognition she is beginning to receive, and we can place her securely in Native American literary and activist traditions begun by William Apess and continued in the late nineteenth and early twentieth centuries by Zitkala-Sa, Alice Callahan, and Mourning Dove.

Karen Kilcup
University of North Carolina at Greensboro

PRIMARY WORKS

Life Among the Piutes: Their Wrongs and Claims, 1883.

from Life Among the Piutes

Chapter I
First Meeting of Piutes and Whites

I was born somewhere near 1844, but am not sure of the precise time. I was a very small child when the first white people came into our country. They came like a lion, yes, like a roaring lion, and have continued so ever since, and I have never forgotten their first coming. My people were scattered at that time over nearly all the territory now known as Nevada. My grandfather was chief of the entire Piute nation, and was camped near Humboldt Lake, with a small portion of his tribe, when a party travelling eastward from California was seen coming. When the news was brought to my grandfather, he asked what they looked like? When told that they had hair on their faces, and were white, he jumped up and clasped his hands together, and cried aloud,—

"My white brothers,—my long-looked for white brothers have come at last!"

He immediately gathered some of his leading men, and went to the place where the party had gone into camp. Arriving near them, he was commanded to halt in a manner that was readily understood without an interpreter. Grandpa at once made signs of friendship by throwing down his robe and throwing up his arms to show them he had no weapons; but in vain,—they kept him at a distance. He knew not what to do. He had expected so much pleasure in welcoming his white brothers to the best in the land, that after looking at them sorrowfully for a little while, he came away quite unhappy. But he would not give them up so easily. He took some of his most trustworthy men and followed them day after day, camping near them at night, and travelling in sight of them by day, hoping in this way to gain their confidence. But he was disappointed, poor dear old soul!

I can imagine his feelings, for I have drank deeply from the same cup. When I think of my past life, and the bitter trials I have endured, I can scarcely believe I live, and yet I do; and, with the help of Him who notes the sparrow's fall, I mean to fight for my down-trodden race while life lasts.

Seeing they would not trust him, my grandfather left them, saying, "Perhaps they will come again next year." Then he summoned his whole people, and told them this tradition:—

"In the beginning of the world there were only four, two girls and two boys. Our forefather and mother were only two, and we are their children. You all know that a great while ago there was a happy family in this world. One girl and one boy were dark and the others were white. For a time they got along together without quarrelling, but soon they disagreed, and there was trouble. They were cross to one another and fought, and our parents were very much grieved. They prayed that their children might learn better, but it did not do any good; and afterwards the whole household was made so unhappy that the father and mother saw that they must separate their children; and then our father took the dark boy and girl, and the white boy and girl, and asked them, 'Why are you so cruel to each other?' They hung down their heads, and would not speak. They were ashamed. He said to them, 'Have I not been kind to you all, and given you everything your hearts wished for? You do not have to hunt and kill your own game to live upon. You see, my dear children, I have power to call whatsoever kind of game we want to eat; and I also have the power to separate my dear children, if they are not good to each other.' So he separated his children by a word. He said, 'Depart from each other, you cruel children;—go across the mighty ocean and do not seek each other's lives.'

"So the light girl and boy disappeared by that one word, and their parents saw them no more, and they were grieved, although they knew their children were happy. And by-and-by the dark children grew into a large nation; and we believe it is the one we belong to, and that the nation that sprung from the white children will some time send some one to meet us and heal all the old trouble. Now, the white people we saw a few days ago must certainly be our white brothers, and I want to welcome them. I want to love them as I love all of you. But they would not let me; they were afraid. But they will come again, and I want you one and all to promise that, should I not live to welcome them myself, you will not hurt a hair on their heads, but welcome them as I tried to do."[1]

How good of him to try and heal the wound, and how vain were his efforts! My people had never seen a white man, and yet they existed, and were a strong race. The people promised as he wished, and they all went back to their work.

The next year came a great emigration,[2] and camped near Humboldt Lake. The name of the man in charge of the trains was Captain Johnson, and they stayed three days to rest their horses, as they had a long journey before them without water. During their stay my grandfather and some of his people called upon them, and they all shook hands, and when our white brothers were going away they gave my grandfather a white tin plate. Oh, what a time they had over that beautiful gift,—it was so bright! They say that after they left, my grandfather called for all his people to come together, and he then showed them the beautiful gift which he had received from his white brothers. Everybody was so pleased; nothing like it was ever seen in our country before. My grandfather thought so much of it that he bored holes in it and fastened it on his head, and wore it as a hat. He held it in as much admiration as my white sisters hold their diamond rings or a sealskin jacket. So that winter they talked of nothing but their white brothers. The following spring there came great news down the Humboldt River, saying that there were some more of the white brothers coming, and there was something among them that was burning all in a blaze. My grandfather asked them what it was like. They told him it looked like a man; it had legs and hands and a head, but the head had quit burning, and it was left quite black. There was the greatest excitement among my people everywhere about the men in a blazing fire. They were excited because they did not know there were any people in the world but the two,—that is, the Indians and the whites; they thought that was all of us in the beginning of the world, and, of course, we did not know where the others had come from, and we don't know yet. Ha! ha! oh, what a laughable thing that was! It was two negroes wearing red shirts!

The third year more emigrants came, and that summer Captain Fremont, who is now General Fremont.

[1]This story represents a selective retelling of a popular Paiute tradition, the quarreling children. Captain Truckee chooses to emphasize the last section of the story and thus positive relations among whites and Indians; he deemphasizes the opening section that would identify the whites as cannibals. The latter is implied later in Winnemucca's narrative when the mothers bury their children alive.

[2]Of white settlers.

My grandfather met him, and they were soon friends. They met just where the railroad crosses Truckee River, now called Wadsworth, Nevada. Captain Fremont gave my grandfather the name of Captain Truckee, and he also called the river after him. Truckee is an Indian word, it means *all right,* or *very well.* A party of twelve of my people went to California with Captain Fremont. I do not know just how long they were gone.

During the time my grandfather was away in California, where he staid till after the Mexican war, there was a girl-baby born in our family. I can just remember it. It must have been in spring, because everything was green. I was away playing with some other children when my mother called me to come to her. So I ran to her. She then asked me to sit down, which I did. She then handed me some beautiful beads, and asked me if I would like to buy something with them. I said:—

"Yes, mother,—some pine nuts."

My mother said:—

"Would you like something else you can love and play with? Would you like to have a little sister?" I said,—

"Yes, dear mother, a little, little sister; not like my sister Mary, for she won't let me play with her. She leaves me and goes with big girls to play;" and then my mother wanted to know if I would give my pretty beads for the little sister.

Just then the baby let out such a cry it frightened me; and I jumped up and cried so that my mother took me in her arms, and said it was a little sister for me, and not to be afraid. This is all I can remember about it.

When my grandfather went to California he helped Captain Fremont fight the Mexicans. When he came back he told the people what a beautiful country California was. Only eleven returned home, one having died on the way back.

They spoke to their people in the English language, which was very strange to them all.

Captain Truckee, my grandfather, was very proud of it, indeed. They all brought guns with them. My grandfather would sit down with us for hours, and would say over and over again, "Goodee gun, goodee, goodee gun, heap shoot." They also brought some of the soldiers' clothes with all their brass buttons, and my people were very much astonished to see the clothes, and all that time they were peaceable toward their white brothers. They had learned to love them, and they hoped more of them would come. Then my people were less barbarous than they are nowadays.

That same fall, after my grandfather came home, he told my father to take charge of his people and hold the tribe, as he was going back to California with as many of his people as he could get to go with him. So my father took his place as Chief of the Piutes, and had it as long as he lived. Then my grandfather started back to California again with about thirty families. That same fall, very late, the emigrants kept coming. It was this time that our white brothers first came amongst us. They could not get over the mountains, so they had to live with us. It was on Carson River, where the great Carson City stands now. You call my people bloodseeking. My people did not seek to kill them, nor did they steal their horses,—no, no, far from it. During the winter my people helped them. They gave them such as they had to eat. They did not hold out their hands and say:—

"You can't have anything to eat unless you pay me." No,—no such word was used by us savages at that time; and the persons I am speaking of are living yet; they could speak for us if they choose to do so.

The following spring, before my grandfather returned home, there was a great excitement among my people on account of fearful news coming from different tribes, that the people whom they called their white brothers were killing everybody that came in their way, and all the Indian tribes had gone into the mountains to save their lives. So my father told all his people to go into the mountains and hunt and lay up food for the coming winter. Then we all went into the mountains. There was a fearful story they told us children. Our mothers told us that the whites were killing everybody and eating them. So we were all afraid of them. Every dust that we could see blowing in the valleys we would say it was the white people. In the late fall my father told his people to go to the rivers and fish, and we all went to Humboldt River, and the women went to work gathering wild seed, which they grind between the rocks. The stones are round, big enough to hold in the hands. The women did this when they got back, and when they had gathered all they could they put it in one place and covered it with grass, and then over the grass mud. After it is covered it looks like an Indian wigwam.

Oh, what a fright we all got one morning to hear some white people were coming. Every one ran as best they could. My poor mother was left with my little sister and me. Oh, I never can forget it. My poor mother was carrying my little sister on her back, and trying to make me run; but I was so frightened I could not move my feet, and while my poor mother was trying to get me along my aunt overtook us, and she said to my mother: "Let us bury our girls, or we shall be killed and eaten up." So they went to work and buried us, and told us if we heard any noise not to cry out, for if we did they would surely kill us and eat us. So our mothers buried me and my cousin, planted sage bushes over our faces to keep the sun from burning them, and there we were left all day.

Oh, can any one imagine my feelings *buried alive,* thinking every minute that I was to be unburied and eaten up by the people that my grandfather loved so much? With my heart throbbing, and not daring to breathe, we lay there all day. It seemed that the night would never come. Thanks be to God! the night came at last. Oh, how I cried and said: "Oh, father, have you forgotten me? Are you never coming for me?" I cried so I thought my very heartstrings would break.

At last we heard some whispering. We did not dare to whisper to each other, so we lay still. I could hear their footsteps coming nearer and nearer. I thought my heart was coming right out of my mouth. Then I heard my mother say, "'T is right here!" Oh, can any one in this world ever imagine what were my feelings when I was dug up by my poor mother and father? My cousin and I were once more happy in our mothers' and fathers' care, and we were taken to where all the rest were.

I was once buried alive; but my second burial shall be for ever, where no father or mother will come and dig me up. It shall not be with throbbing heart that I shall listen for coming footsteps. I shall be in the sweet rest of peace,—I, the chieftain's weary daughter.

Well, while we were in the mountains hiding, the people that my grandfather called our white brothers came along to where our winter supplies were. They set everything we had left on fire. It was a fearful sight. It was all we had for the winter, and it was all burnt during that night. My father took some of his men during the night to try and save some of it, but they could not; it had burnt down before they got there.

These were the last white men that came along that fall. My people talked fearfully that winter about those they called our white brothers. My people said they had something like awful thunder and lightning, and with that they killed everything that came in their way.

This whole band of white people perished in the mountains, for it was too late to cross them. We could have saved them, only my people were afraid of them. We never knew who they were, or where they came from. So, poor things, they must have suffered fearfully, for they all starved there. The snow was too deep.

[Soon after these events, Sarah's father has a powerful and prophetic dream about the impending violence of white settlers, and members of the tribe are deeply troubled. Captain Truckee, on the other hand, maintains a vision of peaceful coexistence and white benevolence, even following the murder of one of Sarah's uncles. Shortly afterward, Sarah's grandfather persuades part of his band of Paiutes to go to California, and he insists that his daughter (Tuboitonie, Sarah's mother), Sarah, and her sisters accompany him. In spite of Tuboitonie's pleas, Sarah's father is left behind as the leader of another band. The journey is perilous because of potential white and Mexican hostility, although Captain Truckee manages to negotiate successfully with the former and to gain assistance along the way. Sarah is particularly afraid of the white settlers, who, with their beards and light eyes, seem like the owls in a frightening Paiute myth. She loses this fear when a kind and gentle white woman nurses her through a painful illness that youthful Sarah attributes to "poisoned sugar-bread" (cake), but that is actually a severe case of poison oak. Soon after this episode, they arrive at the ranch of Hiram Scott and Jacob Bonsal, where the men of Captain Truckee's group have been hired to work.]

One of my grandpa's friends was named Scott, and the other Bonsal. After we got there, his friend killed beef for him and his people. We stayed there some time. Then grandpa told us that he had taken charge of Mr. Scott's cattle and horses, and he was going to take them all up the mountains to take care of them for his brothers. He wanted my uncles and their families and my mother and her two sons and three daughters to stay where they were; that is, he told his dear daughter that he wanted her two sons to take care of a few horses and cows that would be left. My mother began to cry, and said,—

"Oh, father, don't leave us here! My children might get sick, and there would be no one to speak for us; or something else might happen." He again said, "I don't think my brothers will do anything that is wrong to you and your children." Then my mother asked my grandfather if he would take my sister with him. My poor mother felt that her daughter was unsafe, for she was young and very good-looking.

"I would like to take her along," he said, "but I want her to learn how to work and cook. Scott and Bonsal say they will take the very best care of you and the children. It is not as if I was going to leave you here really alone; your brothers will be with you." So we staid. Two men owned the ferry, and they had a great deal of money. So my brothers took care of their horses and cows all winter, and they paid them well for their work. But, oh, what trouble we had for a while! The men whom my grandpa called his brothers would come into our camp and ask my mother to give our sister to them. They would come in at night, and we would all scream and cry; but that would not stop them. My sister, and mother, and my uncles all cried and said, "Oh, why did we come? Oh, we shall surely all be killed some night." My uncles and brothers would not dare to say a word, for fear they would be shot down. So we used to go away every night after dark and hide, and come back to our camp every morning. One night we were getting ready to go, and there came five men. The fire was out; we could see two men come into the tent and shut off the postles outside. My uncles and my brothers made such a noise! I don't know what happened; when I woke I asked my mother if they had killed my sister. She said, "We are all safe here. Don't cry."

"Where are we, mother?"

"We are in a boarding-house."

"Are my uncles killed?"

"No, dear, they are all near here too.

I said, "Sister, where are you? I want to come to you."

She said, "Come on."

I laid down, but I could not sleep. I could hear my poor sister's heart beat. Early the next morning we got up and went down stairs, for it was upstairs where we slept. There were a great many in the room. When we came down, my mother said, "We will go outside."

My sister said, "There is no outlet to the house. We can't get out."

Mother looked round and said, "No, we cannot get out." I as usual began to cry. My poor sister! I ran to her, I saw tears in her eyes. I heard some one speak close to my mother. I looked round and saw Mr. Scott holding the door open. Mother said, "Children, come."

He went out with us and pointed to our camp, and shook his head, and motioned to mother to go into a little house where they were cooking. He took my hand in his, and said the same words that I had learned, "Poor little girl." I could see by his looks that he pitied me, so I was not afraid of him. We went in and sat down on the floor. Oh, what pretty things met my eyes. I was looking all round the room, and I saw beautiful white cups, and every beautiful thing on something high and long, and around it some things that were red.

I said to my sister, "Do you know what those are?" for she had been to the house before with my brothers. She said, "That high thing is what they use when eating, and the white cups are what they drink hot water from, and the red things you see is what they sit upon when they are eating." There was one now near us, and I thought if I could sit upon it I should be so happy! I said to my mother, "Can I sit on that one?" She said, "No, they would whip you." I did not say any more, but sat looking at the beautiful red chair. By-and-by the white woman went out, and I wished in my heart I could go and sit upon it while she was gone. Then she came in with her little child in her arms. As she came in she went right to the very chair I wanted to sit in so badly, and set her child in it. I looked up to my mother, and said, "Will she get a whipping?"

"No, dear, it belongs to her father."

So I said no more. Pretty soon a man came in. She said something to him, and he went out, and in a little while they all came in and sat round that high thing, as I called it. That was the table. It was all very strange to me, and they were drinking the hot water as they ate. I thought it was indeed hot water. After they got through, they all went out again, but Mr. Scott staid and talked to the woman and the man a long time. Then the woman fixed five places and the men went out and brought in my brothers, and kept talking to them. My brother said, "Come and sit here, and you, sister, sit there." But as soon as I sat down in the beautiful chair I began to look at the pretty picture on the back of the chair. "Dear, sit nice and eat, or the white woman will whip you," my mother said. I was quiet, but did not eat much. I tasted the black hot water; I did not like it. It was coffee that we called hot water. After we had done, brother said, "Mother, come outside; I want to talk to you." So we all went out. Brother said, "Mother, Mr. Scott wants us all to stay here. He says you and sister are to wash dishes, and learn all kinds of work. We are to stay here all the time and sleep upstairs, and the white woman is going to teach my sister how to sew. I think, dear mother, we had better stay, because grandpa said so, and our father Scott will take good care of us. He is going up into the mountains to see how grandpa is getting along, and he says he will take my uncles with him." All the time brother was talking, my mother and sister were crying. I did not cry, for I wanted to stay so that I could sit in the beautiful red chairs. Mother said,—

"Dear son, you know if we stay here sister will be taken from us by the bad white man. I would rather see her die than see her heart full of fear every night."

"Yes, dear mother, we love our dear sister, and if you say so we will go to papa."

"Yes, dear son, let us go and tell him what his white brothers are doing to us."

"Then I will go and tell Mr. Scott we want to go to our papa." He was gone some time, and at last came back.

"Mother," he says, "we can't go,—that is, brother and I must stay;—but you and sister can go if you wish to."

"Oh no, my dear children, how can I go and leave you here? Oh, how can that bad man keep you from going? You are not his children. How dare he say you cannot go with your mother? He is not your father; he is nothing but a bad white man, and he dares to say you cannot go. Your own father did not say you should not come with me. Oh, had my dear husband said those words I would not have been here to-day, and see my dear children suffer from day to day. Oh, if your father only knew how his children were suffering, I know he would kill that white man who tried to take your sister. I cannot see for my life why my father calls them his white brothers. They are not people; they have no thought, no mind, no love. They are beasts, or they would know I, a lone woman, am here with them. They tried to take my girl from me and abuse her before my eyes and yours too, and oh, you must go too."

"Oh, mother, here he comes!"

My mother got up. She held out her two hands to him, and cried out,—

"Oh, good father, don't keep my children from me. If you have a heart in you, give them back to me. Let me take them to their good father, where they can be cared for."

We all cried to see our poor mother pleading for us. Mother held on to him until he gave some signs of letting her sons go with her; then he nodded his head,—they might go. My poor mother's crying was turned into joy, and we were all glad. The wagon was got ready,—we were to ride in it. Oh, how I jumped about because I was going to ride in it! I ran up to sister, and said,—

"Ain't you glad we are going to ride in that beautiful red house?" I called it house. My sister said,—

"Not I, dear sister, for I hate everything that belongs to the white dogs. I would rather walk all the way; oh, I hate them so badly!"

When everything was got ready, we got into the red house, as we called the wagon. I soon got tired of riding in the red house and went to sleep. Nothing happened during the day, and after awhile mother told us not to say a word about why we left, for grandpa might get mad with us. So we got to our people, and grandpa ran out to meet us. We were all glad to see him. The white man staid all night, and went home the next day. After he left us my grandpa called my brothers to him.

"Now, my dear little boys, I have something to tell you that will make you happy. Our good father (he did not say my white brother, but he said our good father) has left something with me to give you, and he also told me that he had given you some money for your work. He says you are all good boys, and he likes you very much; and he told me to give you three horses apiece, which makes six in all, and he wants you and your brother to go back and to go on with the same work, and he will pay you well for it. He is to come back in three days; then if you want to go with him you can."

Brother said, "Will mother and sisters go too?"

"No, they will stay with me." My brothers were so happy over their horses.

Now, my dear reader, there is no word so endearing as the word father, and that is why we call all good people father or mother; no matter who it is,—negro, white man, or Indian, and the same with the women. Grandpa talked to my mother a long time, but I did not hear what he said to her, as I went off to play with the other children. But the first thing I knew the white man came and staid four days. Then all the horses were got up, and he saw them all, and the cattle also. I could see my poor mother and sister crying now and then, but I did not know what for. So one morning the man was going away, and I saw mother getting my brothers' horses ready too. I ran to my mother, and said, "Mother, what makes you cry so?" Grandpa was talking to her. He said, "They will not be hurt; they will have quite a number of horses by the time we are ready to go back to our home again."

I knew then that my brothers were going back with this man. Oh, then I began to cry, and said everything that was bad to them. I threw myself down upon the ground.

"Oh, brothers, I will never see them any more. They will kill them, I know. Oh, you naughty, naughty grandpa, you want my poor brothers to be killed by the bad men. You don't know what they do to us. Oh, mother, run,—bring them back again!"

Oh, how we missed our brothers for a long time. We did not see them for a long time, but the men came now and then. They never brought my brothers with them. After they went away, grandpa would come in with his rag friend[3] in hand and say to mother, "My friend here says my boys are all right, not sick."

My mother said, "Father, why can you not have them come and see us sometimes?"

[3]A written introduction and testimonial given to Captain Truckee by Captain Fremont for his help in the war against Mexico. Captain Truckee regards the letter as a pledge of friendship between whites and Paiutes.

"Dear daughter, we will get ready to go home. It is time now that the snow is off the mountains. In ten days more we will go, and we will get the children as we go by."

Oh, how happy everybody was! Everybody was singing here and there, getting beautiful dresses made, and before we started we had a thanksgiving dance. The day we were to start we partook of the first gathering of food for that summer. So that morning everybody prayed, and sang songs, and danced, and ate before starting. It was all so nice, and everybody was so happy because they were going to see their dear country and the dear ones at home. Grandpa took all the horses belonging to the white men. After we got home the horses were put into the corral for all night, and the two white men counted their horses the next morning. They gave my grandpa eight horses for his work, and two or three horses each to some of the people. To my two brothers they gave sixteen horses and some money, and after we all got our horses, grandpa said to his people,—

"Now, my children, you see that what I have told you about my white brothers is true. You see we have not worked very much, and they have given us all horses. Don't you see they are good people?"

All that time, neither my uncles nor my mother had told what the white men did while we were left all alone.

So the day was set for starting. It was to be in five days. We had been there three days when we saw the very men who were so bad to us. Yes, they were talking to grandpa. Mother said to sister,—

"They are talking about us. You see they are looking this way."

Sister said, "Oh, mother, I hope grandpa will not do such a wicked thing as to give me to those bad men."

Oh, how my heart beat! I saw grandpa shake his head, and he looked mad with them. He came away and left them standing there. From that day my grandma took my sister under her care, and we got along nicely.

Then we started for our home, and after traveling some time we arrived at the head of Carson River. There we met some of our people, and they told us some very bad news, indeed, which made us all cry. They said almost all the tribe had died off, and if one of a family got sick it was a sure thing that the whole family would die. He said the white men had poisoned the Humboldt River, and our people had drank the water and died off.[4] Grandpa said,—

"Is my son dead?"

"No, he has been in the mountains all the time, and all who have been there are all right."

The men said a great many of our relations had died off.

We staid there all night, and the next day our hair was all cut off.[5] My sister and my mother had such beautiful hair!

So grandpa said to the man,—

"Go and tell our people we are coming. Send them to each other, and tell my son to come to meet us."

[4]From typhus.

[5]Hair was cut off as a sign of mourning.

So we went on our journey, and after travelling three days more we came to a place called Genoa, on the west side of Carson River, at the very place where I had first seen a white man. A saw-mill and a grist-mill were there, and five more houses. We camped in the very same place where we did before. We staid there a long time waiting for my father to come to meet us. At last my cousin rode into our camp one evening, and said my father was coming with many of his people. We heard them as they came nearer and nearer; they were all crying, and then we cried too, and as they got off their horses they fell into each other's arms, like so many little children, and cried as if their hearts would break, and told what they had suffered since we went away, and how our people had died off. As soon as one would get sick he would drink water and die right off. Every one of them was in mourning also, and they talked over the sad things which had happened to them during the time we were away. One and all said that the river must have been poisoned by the white people, because that they had prayed, and our spirit-doctors had tried to cure the sick; they too died while they were trying to cure them. After they had told grandpa all, he got angry and said,—

"My dear children, I am heartily sorry to hear your sad story; but I cannot and will not believe my white brothers would do such a thing. Oh, my dear children, do not think so badly of our white fathers, for if they had poisoned the river, why, my dear children, they too would have died when they drank of the water. It is this, my dear children, it must be some fearful disease or sickness unknown to us, and therefore, my dear children, don't blame our brothers. The whole tribe have called me their father, and I have loved you all as my dear children, and those who have died are happy in the Spirit-land, though we mourn their loss here on earth. I know my grandchildren and daughters and brothers are in that happy bright Spirit-land, and I shall soon see them there. Some of you may live a long time yet, and don't let your hearts work against your white fathers; if you do, you will not get along. You see they are already here in our land; here they are all along the river, and we must let our brothers live with us. We cannot tell them to go away. I know your good hearts. I know you won't say *kill them.* Surely you all know that they are human. Their lives are just as dear to them as ours to us. It is a very sad thing indeed to have to lose so many of our dear ones; but maybe it was to be. We can do nothing but mourn for their loss." He went on to say,—

"My dear children, you all know the tradition says: 'Weep not for your dead; but sing and be joyful, for the soul is happy in the Spirit-land.' But it is natural for man or woman to weep, because it relieves our hearts to weep together, and we all feel better afterwards."

Every one hung their heads while grandpa talked on. Now and then one could hear some of them cry out, just as the Methodists cry out at their meetings; and grandpa said a great many beautiful things to his people. He talked so long, I for one wished he would stop, so I could go and throw myself into my father's arms, and tell him what the white people were. At last he stopped, and we all ran to our father and threw our arms around his neck, and cried for joy; and then mother came with little sister. Papa took her in his arms, and mother put her hand in his bosom, and we all wept together, because mother had lost two sisters, and their husbands, and all their children but one girl; and thus passed away the day. Grandpa had gone off during our meeting with father, and prayer was offered, and every one washed their face, and were waiting for something else. Pretty soon grandpa came, and said: "This is my friend," holding up his paper in his hand. "Does it look as if it could talk and ask for anything? Yet it does. It can ask for something to eat for me and my people. Yet, it is nothing but a rag. Oh, wonderful things my white brothers can do. I have taken it down to them, and it has asked for sacks of flour for us to eat. Come, we will go and get them," So the men went down and got the flour. Grandpa took his son down to see the white men, and by-and-by we saw them coming back. They had given my father a red blanket and a red shirt.

Marietta Holley (pseud. "Josiah Allen's Wife") 1836–1926

In her lifetime, Marietta Holley's popularity rivaled that of Mark Twain, to whom she was often compared. Humorist and inventor of the first female comic protagonist of significance in American literature, Holley published twenty-four books between 1873 and 1914. Prior to Holley's work, American humorists had been primarily male, in the tradition of the "literary comedians" and of Down East and southwestern humor. Two women—Ann Stephens and Frances Whitcher—had preceded Holley as humorists, and in developing her own literary manner Holley drew upon their techniques and subject matter as well as those of masculine traditions. For much of her style she depended on the upcountry dialect, proverbs and maxims, and extravagant images that were the stuff of the Down East "cracker-barrel philosophers." To the native idiom of New York State's north country, where she was born and lived, she added other devices of the humor traditions: anticlimax, misquoted Scripture, puns, malapropisms, mixed metaphors, comic similes, and language reversals such as "foremothers."

In addition, she chronicled the homely events and hard work that set the rhythm of life for country women as the local color writers of New England did. Like Stowe, Jewett, and Freeman, Holley re-created the voices and manners peculiar to her fictive landscape, in this case Jones-ville, New York. Taking the notion of home-centeredness and the plot and character conventions that the domestic novelists had used, Holley turned it to her own purposes by showing the failure of gentility to provide a safe, satisfying life for women, and she melded three American literary traditions in a way no other writer had: the attention to regional detail of the local colorists merges with the conventions of the domestic novelists and with the vernacular comedy developed by earlier humorists.

Holley used humor for a new end: to make accessible and palatable the ideals of the temperance and suffrage movements. Whereas the earlier comedians had made the woman—particularly the woman's rights advocate—the butt of their comedy, Holley created characters of both genders who embodied the absurdities of anti-suffrage and intemperance. Her early work was enormously popular with a wide audience, including reformers such as Susan B. Anthony and Frances Willard, who sought her support. Holley was often invited to address audiences, including the U.S. Congress, but because of her intense shyness and a slight speech impediment, she always declined. "Samantha Allen, Josiah Allen's Wife," spoke for her.

Holley was the last of seven children born into a farm family in southern Jefferson County, New York. When her three older brothers left the small farm to make their fortunes in the West after their father's death in the 1860s, Holley was left to help support the family by selling handicrafts and giving music lessons. Her education in the rural district school ended when she was fourteen because there was not enough money, but she continued a program of reading and self-directed study with a neighbor.

At an early age she began writing verses with accompanying illustrations, although she maintained secrecy about all her writing until 1857, when she began publishing poetry in the local newspaper under a pseudonym. Soon her fiction, including some in Yorker dialect, was appearing in popular magazines. In 1872 she boldly sent a few sketches to Mark Twain's publisher. He immediately commissioned her to write a novel in the style of the vernacular humorists, and the career of "Josiah Allen's Wife" was launched. Holley used several pseudonyms during her public career, but none served her so long or well as "Samantha."

Her first "Samantha" book, *My Opinions and Betsey Bobbet's* (1873), was immediately successful. It established the characters of Samantha Smith Allen, her foolish husband Josiah Allen, and the spinster Betsey Bobbet. In that work, Holley adopted the pattern that dominated the remaining books: Samantha is presented with a problem that requires her to travel outside the confines of rural Jonesville; she takes with her a rustic sensibility and common sense that points out the absurdity of much of life in eastern America, especially politics and genteel society. Seven of Holley's novels were commissioned books about places or events as they might be viewed through Samantha's spectacles. Ironically, Holley rarely traveled, writing most of these books entirely from maps and guidebooks. She barely left the precincts of her farm home until her first trip when she was forty-five years old, preferring instead to live quietly among the people of her county. She led a circumscribed and singular life, avoiding publicity and glamor. Settled in a mansion built to replace her father's farmhouse, she lived quietly until her death at nearly ninety years.

Her conversion to the Baptist faith led to a lifelong concern with piety and spirituality that, yoked with her feminism, informed most of her adult writing.

In all her fiction, including the travel books, Holley took on nearly every reform women agitated for. Temperance was Samantha's concern in most of Holley's fiction, but it was the central issue in *Sweet Cicely: Josiah Allen as a Politician* (1885), her most accomplished and well-crafted book, showing her at her best with rustic and dialect humor and the temperance and domestic novel genres. Her most commercially successful book, *Samantha at Sara-toga* (1887), followed with its criticism of dress and morals. Her concern with women's subordinate status within the established churches, especially the refusal of the 1888 Methodist Conference to seat duly elected women delegates, was developed in *Samantha Among the Brethren* (1890). As her legacy to literature, Holley left the traditional threads of American humor woven into a tough and bristly new strand.

Kate H. Winter
State University of New York at Albany

PRIMARY WORKS

My Opinions and Betsey Bobbet's, 1873; *Sweet Cicely,* 1885; *Samantha at Saratoga or Flirtin' with Fashion,* 1887; *Samantha Among the Brethren,* 1890; *Samantha on the Race Problem,* 1892.

from Samantha Among the Brethren

Chapter XIX

Couldn't help a-me-thinkin' to myself several times. It duz seem to me that there hain't a question a-comin' up before that Conference that is harder to tackle than this plasterin' and the conundrum that is up before us Jonesville wimmen how to raise 300 dollars out of nuthin', and to make peace in a meetin' house where anarky is now rainin' down.

But I only thought these thoughts to myself, fur I knew every women there wuz peacible and law abidin' and there wuzn't one of 'em but what would ruther fall offen her barell than go agin the rules of the Methodist Meetin' House.

Yes, I tried to curb down my rebellous thoughts, and did, pretty much all the time.

And good land! we worked so hard that we hadn't time to tackle very curius and peculier thoughts, them that wuz dretful strainin' and wearin' on the mind. Not of our own accord we didn't, fur we had to just nip in and work the hull durin' time.

And then we all knew how deathly opposed our pardners wuz to our takin' any public part in meetin' house matters or mountin' rostrums, and that thought quelled us down a sight.

Of course when these subjects wuz brung up before us, and turned round and round in front of our eyes, why we had to look at 'em and be rousted up by 'em more or less. It was Nater.[1]

And Josiah not havin' anything to do evenin's only to set and look at the ceilin'. Every single night when I would go home from the meetin' house, Josiah would tackle me on it, on the danger of allowin' wimmen to ventur out of her spear in Meetin' House matters, and specially the Conference.

It begin to set in New York the very day we tackled the meetin' in Jonesville with a extra grip.

So's I can truly say, the Meetin' House wuz on me day and night. For workin' on it es I did, all day long, and Josiah a-talkin' abut it till bed time, and I a-dreamin' abut it a sight, that, and the Conference.

Truly, if I couldn't set on the Conference, the Conference sot on me, from mornin' till night, and from night till mornin'.

I spoze it wuz Josiah's skairful talk that brung it onto me, it wuz brung on nite mairs mostly, in the nite time.

He would talk *very* skairful, and what he called deep, and repeat pages of Casper Keeler's arguments, and they would appear to me (drawed also by nite mairs) every page on 'em lookin' fairly lurid.

I suffered.

Josiah would set with the *World*[2] and other papers in his hand, a-perusin' of 'em,

[1]Nature.

[2]The New York World, a contemporary newspaper.

while I would be a-washin' up my dishes, and the very minute I would get 'em done and my sleeves rolled down, he would tackle me, and often he wouldn't wait for me to get my work done up, or even supper got, but would begin on me as I filled up my tea kettle, and keep up a stiddy drizzle of argument till bed time, and as I say, when he left off, the nite mairs would begin.

I suffered beyond tellin' almost.

The secont night of my arjuous labors on the meetin' house, he began wild and eloquent about wimmen bein' on Conferences, and mountin' rostrums. And sez he, "That is suthin' that we Methodist men can't stand."

And I, havin' stood up on a barell all day a-scrapin' the ceilin', and not bein' recuperated yet from the skairtness and dizziness of my day's work, I sez to him:

"Is rostrums much higher than them barells we have to stand on to the meetin' house?"

And Josiah said, "it wuz suthin' altogether different." And he assured me agin,

"That in any modest, unpretendin' way the Methodist Church wuz willin' to accept wimmen's work. It wuzn't aginst the Discipline. And that is why," sez he, "that wimmen have all through the ages been allowed to do most all the hard work in the church—such as raisin' money for church work—earnin' money in all sorts of ways to carry on the different kinds of charity work connected with it—teachin' the children, nursin' the sick, carryin' on hospital work, etc., etc. But," sez he, "this is fur, fur different from gettin' up on a rostrum, or tryin' to set on a Conference. Why," sez he, in a haughty tone, "I should think they'd know without havin' to be told that laymen don't mean women."

Sez I, "Them very laymen that are tryin' to keep wimmen out of the Conference wouldn't have got in themselves if it hadn't been for wimmen's votes. If they can legally vote for men to get in why can't men vote for them?"

"That is the pint," sez Josiah, "that is the very pint I have been tryin' to explain to you. Wimmen can help men to office, but men can't help wimmen; that is law, that is statesmanship. I have been a-tryin' to explain it to you that the word laymen *always* means woman when she can help men in any way, but *not* when he can help her, or in any other sense."

Sez I, "It seemed to mean wimmen when Metilda Henn wuz turned out of the meetin' house."

"Oh, yes," sez Josiah in a reasonin' tone, "the word laymen always means wimmen when it is used in a punishin' and condemnatory sense, or in the case of work and so fourth, but when it comes to settin' up in high places, or drawin' sallerys, or anything else difficult, it alweys means men."

Sez I, in a very dry axent, "Then the word man, when it is used in church matters, always means wimmen, so fur as scrubbin' is concerned, and drowdgin' round?"

"Yes," sez Josiah haughtily. "And it always means men in the higher and more difficult matters of decidin' questions, drawin' sallerys, settin' on Conferences, etc. It has long been settled to be so," sez he.

"Who settled it?" sez I.

"Why the men, of course," sez he. "The men have always made the rules of the churches, and translated the Bibles, and everying else that is difficult," sez he. Sez I, in fearful dry axents, almost husky ones, "It seems to take quite a knack to know jest when the word laymen means men and when it means wimmen."

"That is so," sez Josiah. "It takes a man's mind to grapple with it; wimmen's minds are too weak to tackle it. It is jest as it is with the word 'men' in the Declaration of Independence. Now that word 'men', in that Declaration, means men some of the time, and some of the time men and wimmen both. It means both sexes when it relates to punishment, taxin' property, obeyin' the laws strictly, etc., etc., and then it goes right on the very next minute and means men only, as to wit, namely, votin', takin' charge of public matters, makin' laws, etc.

"I tell you it takes deep minds to foller on and see jest to a hair where the division is made. It takes statesmanship.

"Now take that claws, 'All men are born free and equal.'

"Now half of that means men, and the other half men and wimmen. Now to understand them words perfect you have got to divide the tex. 'Men are born.' That means men and wimmen both—men and wimmen are both born, nobody can dispute that. Then comes the next claws, 'Free and equal.' Now that means men only—anybody with one eye can see that.

"Then the claws, 'True government consists.' That means men and wimmen both—consists—of course the government consists of men and wimmen, 'twould be a fool who would dispute that. 'In the consent of the governed.' That means men alone. Do you see, Samantha?" sez he.

I kep' my eye fixed on the tea kettle, fer I stood with my tea-pot in hand waitin' for it to bile—"I see a great deal, Josiah Allen."

"Wall," sez he, "I am glad on't. Now to sum it up," sez he, with some the mean of a preacher—or, ruther, a exhauster—"to sum the matter all up, the words 'bretheren,' 'laymen,' etc., always means wimmen so fur as this: punishment for all offenses, strict obedience to the rules of the church, work of any kind and all kinds, raisin' money, givin' money all that is possible, teachin' in the Sabbath school, gettin' up missionary and charitable societies, carryin' on the same with no help from the male sect leavin' that sect free to look after their half of the meanin' of the word—sallerys, office, makin' the laws that bind both of the sexes, rulin' things generally, translatin' Bibles to suit their own idees, preachin' at 'em, etc., etc. Do you see, Samantha?" sez he, proudly and loftily.

"Yes," sez I, as I filled up my tea-pot, for the water had at last biled. "Yes, I see."

And I spoze he thought he had convinced me, for he acted high headeder and haughtier for as much as an hour and a half. And I didn't say anything to break it up, for I see he had stated it jest as he and all his sect looked at it, and good land! I couldn't convince the hull male sect if I tried—clergymen, statesmen and all—so I didn't try, and I wuz truly beat out with my day's work, and I didn't drop more than one idee more, I simply dropped this remark es I poured out his tea and put some good cream into it—I merely sez:

"There is three times es many wimmen in the meetin' house es there is men."

"Yes," sez he, "that is one of the pints I have been explainin' to you," and then he went on agin real high headed, and skairt, about the old ground, of the willingness of the meetin' house to shelter wimmen in its folds, and how much they needed gaurdin' and guidin', and about their delicacy of frame, and how unfitted they wuz to tackle anything hard, and what a grief it wuz to the male sect to see 'em a-tryin' to set on Conferences or mount rostrums, etc., etc.

And I didn't try to break up his argument, but simply repeated the question I had put to him—for es I said before, I wuz tired, and skairt, and giddy yet from my hard labor and my great and hazardus elevatin'; I had not, es you may say, recovered yet from my recuperation, and so I sez agin them words—

"Is rostrums much higher than them barells to stand on?"

And Josiah said agin, "it wuz suthin' entirely different;" he said barells and rostrums wuz so fur apart that you couldn't look at both on 'em in one day hardly, let alone a minute. And he went on once more with a long argument full of Bible quotations and everything.

And I wuz too tuckered out to say much more. But I did contend for it to the last, that I didn't believe a rostrum would be any more tottlin' and skairful a place than the barell I had been a-standin' on all day, nor the work I'd do on it any harder than the scrapin' of the ceilin' of that meetin' house.

And I don't believe it would, I stand jest as firm on it to-day as I did then.

1890

Frances Ellen Watkins Harper 1825–1911

Frances Ellen Watkins Harper's career spanned the critical period in American history from abolition to women's suffrage, and she cared deeply about both. Harper frequently centered her writing on political issues and, conversely, incorporated her literary work into her speeches on political topics. She is one of the premier artist activists—or activist artists—in American literary history.

An only child born to free parents in Baltimore, Maryland, Frances Ellen Watkins was orphaned at three and raised by her aunt and uncle, whose school she attended. She worked as a domestic in her teens; moved to Ohio in 1850, where she taught at Union Seminary near Columbus; moved again in the 1850s to York, Pennsylvania, where she became active in abolition work; and traveled throughout New England before the Civil War giving antislavery speeches and being hired by the Anti-Slavery Society of Maine as their official speaker. In 1860 she married a widowed farmer, Fenton Harper, in Ohio and had one daughter. When her husband died in 1864, she returned east and resumed her life of full-time speaking and writing.

Frances Harper was extolled as a brilliant and moving public lecturer who used no notes and often talked for two hours at a time. Though proud of the effect she had on audiences—Harper declared in the early 1870s, "both white and colored come out to hear me, and I have very fine meetings"—Harper experienced bigotry. She knew that many of her white listeners found it virtually impossible to believe that a black woman could be articulate and rational. She wrote to a friend in 1871, "I don't know but that you would laugh if you were to hear some of the remarks that my lectures call forth: 'She is a man,' again 'She is not colored, she is painted.'"

In addition to her speeches, which unfortunately have not survived because she normally did not read from prepared texts, Harper's poetry won her acclaim as the most popular and best-known black poet in the United States between Phillis Wheatley and Paul Laurence Dunbar. She published at least four volumes of poetry as an adult, reissuing several of them in slightly varying editions, and her poems also appeared in periodicals. Often concentrating on slavery before the Civil War, her poetry during the second half of the nineteenth century took up anti-lynching, women's rights, temperance, white racism, Christianity, black history and community issues, patriotism, and various historical and biblical themes. She followed the popular aesthetic of her time, writing poetry that directly and unabashedly appeals to readers' emotions. Also she used formal devises such as rhyme, meter, and stanza formation in regular, even predictable, ways that foster audience accessibility and powerful oral presentation, both of which were especially important in a period when most poetry was written to be heard and verse was frequently committed to memory. As an innovator, Harper was one of the pioneers of dialect verse and as such an important figure in the history of realism in American literature.

As a writer of fiction, Harper is recognized as the author of what is thought to be the first short story published by a black person in the United States, "The Two Offers" (1859); and she wrote three serialized short novels, *Minnie's Sacrifice* (1869), *Sowing and Reaping* (1876–1877), and *Trial and Triumph* (1888–1889). Her best-known novel, *Iola Leroy; or Shadows Uplifted,* published in 1892, was for many years regarded as the first full-length novel by an African American woman. Though it was not the first, its stature in American literary history is considerable because of the book's ambitiousness and accomplishment.

The life chosen by Frances Ellen Harper was not easy. Often her work placed her in danger, traveling alone in the South to speak out against lynching and discrimination. Also, her life must have been lonely at times, and by her own account often it was filled with hardship (summer nights spent in windowless cabins, winter nights in unheated rooms). In addition, in her commitment to the primarily female issues of temperance and women's suffrage she had the bitter experience of many black women in America of suffering the racism of white women who argued for their own equality but treated black women as inferiors and ignored the horror of lynching. Undaunted, Harper persisted in linking the issues of lynching and women's suffrage at every opportunity, pronouncing at the World's Congress of Representative Women in 1893, for example, that lynchers—white men—should be denied the franchise as women—all women—gained it. Yet she had hope, declaring at this historic Congress: "Through weary, wasting years men have destroyed, dashed in pieces, and overthrown, but today we stand on the threshold of woman's era; and woman's work is grandly constructive. In her hands are possibilities whose use or abuse must tell upon the political life of the nation, and send their influence for good or evil across the track of unborn ages."

At the age of eighty-six Harper died of heart disease in Philadelphia and was buried in Eden Cemetery.

Elizabeth Ammons
Tufts University

PRIMARY WORKS

Poems on Miscellaneous Subjects, 1854; "The Two Offers," 1859 (short story); *Sketches of Southern Life,* 1872 (poems); *Iola Leroy; or Shadows Uplifted,* 1892 (novel); *The Martyr of Alabama and Other Poems,* 1894; *Complete Poems of Frances E. W. Harper,* Maryemma Graham, ed., 1988; *A Brighter Day Coming: A Frances Ellen Watkins Harper Reader,* Frances Smith Foster, ed., 1990; *Three Rediscovered Novels by Frances E. W. Harper,* Frances Smith Foster, ed., 1994.

Aunt Chloe's Politics

Of course, I don't know very much
About these politics,
But I think that some who run 'em,
Do mighty ugly tricks.

I've seen 'em honey-fugle round,
And talk so awful sweet,
That you'd think them full of kindness,
As an egg is full of meat.

Now I don't believe in looking
Honest people in the face,
And saying when you're doing wrong,
That "I haven't sold my race."

When we want to school our children,
If the money isn't there,
Whether black or white have took it,[1]
The loss we all must share.

And this buying up each other
Is something worse than mean,[2]
Though I thinks a heap of voting,[3]
I go for voting clean.

1872

Learning to Read

Very soon the Yankee teachers
Came down and set up school;
But, oh! how the Rebs did hate it,—
It was agin' their rule.

[1]One of the major issues in the South was whether or not public funds should be expended on the education of children, black or white. In some cases, black politicians had been accused, rightly or wrongly, of diverting such funds to their own or other uses.

[2]The period about which Aunt Chloe is speaking was notable for political corruption. New York's "Boss" Tweed had been exposed in 1871 and the Credit Mobilier scandal broke in 1872.

[3]While it would be almost half a century before the Woman's Suffrage amendment to the Constitution would pass, in 1872 the idea of women's voting did not seem so remote. The amendment had first been introduced into Congress in 1868 and had been given considerable visibility in 1871 by Victoria Woodhull's Congressional testimony. Women had gone to the polls in Wyoming and Utah in 1870 and in 1871. In 1872, after women had tried to vote in ten states and the District of Columbia, Susan B. Anthony had tried to cast her ballot in the presidential election.

Our masters always tried to hide
Book learning from our eyes;
Knowledge didn't agree with slavery—
'Twould make us all too wise.

But some of us would try to steal
A little from the book,
And put the words together,
And learn by hook or crook.

I remember Uncle Caldwell,
Who took pot liquor fat
And greased the pages of his book,
And hid it in his hat.

And had his master ever seen
The leaves upon his head,
He'd have thought them greasy papers,
But nothing to be read.

And there was Mr. Turner's Ben,
Who heard the children spell,
And picked the words right up by heart,
And learned to read 'em well.

Well, the Northern folks kept sending
The Yankee teachers down;
And they stood right up and helped us,
Though Rebs did sneer and frown.

And I longed to read my Bible,
For precious words it said;
But when I begun to learn it,
Folks just shook their heads,

And said there is no use trying,
Oh! Chloe, you're too late;
But as I was rising sixty,
I had no time to wait.

So I got a pair of glasses,
And straight to work I went,
And never stopped till I could read
The hymns and Testament.

Then I got a little cabin—
A place to call my own—
And I felt as independent
As the queen upon her throne.

1873

The Martyr of Alabama

[The following news item appeared in the newspapers throughout the country, issue of December 27th, 1894:

"Tim Thompson, a little negro boy, was asked to dance for the amusement of some white toughs. He refused, saying he was a church member. One of the men knocked him down with a club and then danced upon his prostrate form. He then shot the boy in the hip. The boy is dead; his murderer is still at large."][1]

He lifted up his pleading eyes,
And scanned each cruel face,
Where cold and brutal cowardice
Had left its evil trace.

It was when tender memories
Round Beth'lem's manger lay,
And mothers told their little ones
Of Jesu's natal day.

And of the Magi from the East
Who came their gifts to bring,
And bow in rev'rence at the feet
Of Salem's new-born King.

And how the herald angels sang
The choral song of peace,
That war should close his wrathful lips,
And strife and carnage cease.

At such an hour men well may hush
Their discord and their strife,
And o'er that manger clasp their hands
With gifts to brighten life.

Alas! that in our favored land,
That cruelty and crime
Should cast their shadows o'er a day,
The fairest pearl of time.

A dark-browed boy had drawn anear
A band of savage men,

[1]This text in brackets following the title appeared in the original publication.

Just as a hapless lamb might stray
  Into a tiger's den.

Cruel and dull, they saw in him
  For sport an evil chance,
And then demanded of the child
  To give to them a dance.

"Come dance for us," the rough men said;
  "I can't," the child replied,
"I cannot for the dear Lord's sake,
  Who for my sins once died."

Tho' they were strong and he was weak,
  He wouldn't his Lord deny.
His life lay in their cruel hands,
  But he for Christ could die.

Heard they aright? Did that brave child
  Their mandates dare resist?
Did he against their stern commands
  Have courage to resist?

Then recklessly a man (?) arose,
  And dealt a fearful blow.
He crushed the portals of that life,
  And laid the brave child low.

And trampled on his prostrate form,
  As on a broken toy;
Then danced with careless, brutal feet,
  Upon the murdered boy.

Christians! behold that martyred child!
  His blood cries from the ground;
Before the sleepless eye of God,
  He shows each gaping wound.

Oh! Church of Christ arise! arise!
  Lest crimson stain thy hand,
When God shall inquisition make
  For blood shed in the land.

Take sackcloth of the darkest hue,
  And shroud the pulpits round;
Servants of him who cannot lie
  Sit mourning on the ground.

Let holy horror blanch each brow,
  Pale every cheek with fears,
And rocks and stones, if ye could speak,
  Ye well might melt to tears.

Through every fane send forth a cry,
  Of sorrow and regret,
Nor in an hour of careless ease
  Thy brother's wrongs forget.

Veil not thine eyes, nor close thy lips,
  Nor speak with bated breath;
This evil shall not always last,—
  The end of it is death.

Avert the doom that crime must bring
  Upon a guilty land;
Strong in the strength that God supplies,
  For truth and justice stand.

For Christless men, with reckless hands,
  Are sowing round thy path
The tempests wild that yet shall break
  In whirlwinds of God's wrath.

1895

A Double Standard

Do you blame me that I loved him?
  If when standing all alone
I cried for bread a careless world
  Pressed to my lips a stone.

Do you blame me that I loved him,
  That my heart beat glad and free,
When he told me in the sweetest tones
  He loved but only me?

Can you blame me that I did not see
  Beneath his burning kiss
The serpent's wiles, nor even hear
  The deadly adder hiss?

Can you blame me that my heart grew cold
That the tempted, tempter turned;
When he was feted and caressed
And I was coldly spurned?

Would you blame him, when you draw from me
Your dainty robes aside,
If he with gilded baits should claim
Your fairest as his bride?

Would you blame the world if it should press
On him a civic crown;
And see me struggling in the depth
Then harshly press me down?

Crime has no sex and yet to-day
I wear the brand of shame;
Whilst he amid the gay and proud
Still bears an honored name.

Can you blame me if I've learned to think
Your hate of vice a sham,
When you so coldly crushed me down
And then excused the man?

Would you blame me if to-morrow
The coroner should say,
A wretched girl, outcast, forlorn,
Has thrown her life away?

Yes, blame me for my downward course,
But oh! remember well,
Within your homes you press the hand
That led me down to hell.

I'm glad God's ways are not our ways,
He does not see as man;
Within His love I know there's room
For those whom others ban.

I think before His great white throne,
His throne of spotless light,
That whited sepulchres shall wear
The hue of endless night.

That I who fell, and he who sinned,
Shall reap as we have sown;

That each the burden of his loss
  Must bear and bear alone.

No golden weights can turn the scale
  Of justice in His sight;
And what is wrong in woman's life
  In man's cannot be right.

1895

Songs for the People

Let me make the songs for the people,
  Songs for the old and young;
Songs to stir like a battle-cry
  Wherever they are sung.

Not for the clashing of sabres,
  For carnage nor for strife;
But songs to thrill the hearts of men
  With more abundant life.

Let me make the songs for the weary,
  Amid life's fever and fret,
Till hearts shall relax their tension,
  And careworn brows forget.

Let me sing for little children,
  Before their footsteps stray,
Sweet anthems of love and duty,
  To float o'er life's highway.

I would sing for the poor and aged,
  When shadows dim their sight;
Of the bright and restful mansions,
  Where there shall be no night.

Our world, so worn and weary,
  Needs music, pure and strong,
To hush the jangle and discords
  Of sorrow, pain, and wrong.

Music to soothe all its sorrow,
  Till war and crime shall cease;

And the hearts of men grown tender
Girdle the world with peace.

1895

Woman's Political Future

If before sin had cast its deepest shadows or sorrow had distilled its bitterest tears, it was true that it was not good for man to be alone, it is no less true, since the shadows have deepened and life's sorrows have increased, that the world has need of all the spiritual aid that woman can give for the social advancement and moral development of the human race. The tendency of the present age, with its restlessness, religious upheavals, failures, blunders, and crimes, is toward broader freedom, an increase of knowledge, the emancipation of thought, and a recognition of the brotherhood of man; in this movement woman, as the companion of man, must be a sharer. So close is the bond between man and woman that you can not raise one without lifting the other. The world can not move without woman's sharing in the movement, and to help give a right impetus to that movement is woman's highest privilege.

If the fifteenth century discovered America to the Old World, the nineteenth is discovering woman to herself. Little did Columbus imagine, when the New World broke upon his vision like a lovely gem in the coronet of the universe, the glorious possibilities of a land where the sun should be our engraver, the winged lightning our messenger, and steam our beast of burden. But as mind is more than matter, and the highest ideal always the true real, so to woman comes the opportunity to strive for richer and grander discoveries than ever gladdened the eye of the Genoese mariner.

Not the opportunity of discovering new worlds, but that of filling this old world with fairer and higher aims than the greed of gold and the lust of power, is hers. Through weary, wasting years men have destroyed, dashed in pieces, and overthrown, but to-day we stand on the threshold of woman's era, and woman's work is grandly constructive. In her hand are possibilities whose use or abuse must tell upon the political life of the nation, and send their influence for good or evil across the track of unborn ages.

As the saffron tints and crimson flushes of morn herald the coming day, so the social and political advancement which woman has already gained bears the promise of the rising of the full-orbed sun of emancipation. The result will be not to make home less happy, but society more holy; yet I do not think the mere extension of the ballot a panacea for all the ills of our national life. What we need to-day is not simply more voters, but better voters. To-day there are red-handed men in our republic, who walk unwhipped of justice, who richly deserve to exchange the ballot of the freeman for the wristlets of the felon; brutal and cowardly men, who torture, burn, and lynch their fellow-men, men whose defenselessness should be their best defense and their weakness an ensign of protection. More than the changing of institutions we need the development of a national conscience, and the upbuilding of national character. Men may boast of the aristocracy of blood, may glory in the aristocracy of talent, and be proud of the aristocracy of wealth, but there is one aristocracy which must ever outrank them all, and that is the aristocracy of character; and it is the women of a country who help to mold its character, and to influence if not determine its destiny; and in the political future of our nation woman will not have done what she could if she does not endeavor to have our republic stand foremost among the nations of the earth, wearing sobriety as a crown and righteousness as a garment and a girdle. In coming into her political estate woman will find a mass of illiteracy to be dispelled. If knowledge is power, ignorance is also power. The power that educates wickedness may manipulate and dash against the pillars of any state when they are undermined and honeycombed by injustice.

I envy neither the heart nor the head of any legislator who has been born to an inheritance of privileges, who has behind him ages of education, dominion, civilization, and Christianity, if he stands opposed to the passage of a national education bill, whose purpose is to secure education to the children of those who were born under the shadow of institutions which made it a crime to read.

To-day women hold in their hands influence and opportunity, and with these they have already opened doors which have been closed to others. By opening doors of labor woman has become a rival claimant for at least some of the wealth monopolized by her stronger brother. In the home she is the priestess, in society the queen, in literature she is a power, in legislative halls law-makers have responded to her appeals, and for her sake have humanized and liberalized their laws. The press has felt the impress of her hand. In the pews of the church she constitutes the majority; the pulpit has welcomed her, and in the school she has the blessed privilege of teaching children and youth. To her is apparently coming the added responsibility of political power; and what she now possesses should only be the means of preparing her to use the coming power for the glory of God and the good of mankind; for power without righteousness is one of the most dangerous forces in the world.

Political life in our country has plowed in muddy channels, and needs the infusion of clearer and cleaner waters. I am not sure that women are naturally so much better than men that they will clear the stream by the virtue of their womanhood; it is not through sex but through character that the best influence of women upon the life of the nation must be exerted.

I do not believe in unrestricted and universal suffrage for either men or women. I believe in moral and educational tests. I do not believe that the most ignorant and brutal man is better prepared to add value to the strength and durability of the government than the most cultured, upright, and intelligent woman. I do not think that willful ignorance should swamp earnest intelligence at the ballot box, nor that educated wickedness, violence, and fraud should cancel the votes of honest men. The unsteady hands of a drunkard can not cast the ballot of a freeman. The hands of lynchers are too red with blood to determine the political character of the government for even four short years. The ballot in the hands of woman means power added to influence. How well she will use that power I can not foretell. Great evils stare us in the face that need to be throttled by the combined power of an upright manhood and an enlightened womanhood; and I know that no nation can gain its full measure of enlightenment and happiness if one-half of it is free and the other half is fettered. China compressed the feet of her women and thereby retarded the steps of her men. The elements of a nation's weakness must ever be found at the hearthstone.

More than the increase of wealth, the power of armies, and the strength of fleets is the need of good homes, of good fathers, and good mothers.

The life of a Roman citizen was in danger in ancient Palestine, and men had bound themselves with a vow that they would eat nothing until they had killed the Apostle Paul. Pagan Rome threw around that imperiled life a bulwark of living clay consisting of four hundred and seventy human hearts, and Paul was saved.[1] Surely the life of the humblest American citizen should be as well protected in America as that of a Roman citizen was in heathen Rome. A wrong done to the weak should be an insult to the strong. Woman coming into her kingdom will find enthroned three great evils, for whose overthrow she should be as strong in a love of justice and humanity as the warrior is in his might. She will find intemperance sending its flood of shame, and death, and sorrow to the homes of men, a fretting leprosy in our politics, and a blighting curse in our social life; the social evil sending to our streets women whose laughter is sadder than their tears, who slide from the paths of sin and shame to the friendly shelter of the grave; and lawlessness enacting in our republic deeds over which angels might weep, if heaven knows sympathy.

How can any woman send petitions to Russia against the horrors of Siberian prisons if, ages after the Inquisition has ceased to devise its tortures, she has not done all she could by influence, tongue, and pen to keep men from making bonfires of the bodies of real or supposed criminals?

O women of America! into your hands God has pressed one of the sublimest opportunities that ever came into the hands of the women of any race or people. It is yours to create a healthy public sentiment; to demand justice, simple justice, as the right of every race; to brand with everlasting infamy the lawless and brutal cowardice that lynches, burns, and tortures your own countrymen.

To grapple with the evils which threaten to undermine the strength of the nation and to lay magazines to powder under the cribs of future generations is no child's play.

Let the hearts of the women of the world respond to the song of the herald angels of peace on earth and good will to men. Let them throb as one heart unified by the grand and holy purpose of uplifting the human race, and humanity will breathe freer, and the world grow brighter. With such a purpose Eden would spring up in our path, and Paradise be around our way.

1894

[1]This is a somewhat romanticized version of the biblical story (Acts 24) in which the Apostle Paul is rescued from enemies who have sworn to kill him. His rescuers are four hundred and seventy soldiers sent to defend him because he was a Roman citizen.

Anna Julia Cooper 1858?–1964

Born in North Carolina to a slave named Hannah Stanley Haywood and Haywood's white master, Anna Julia Cooper rose from these unpromising beginnings to establish herself as one of the leading black scholars and teachers of her day. Her remarkable career in education began quite early, when at nine she was offered a scholarship to attend St. Augustine's Normal School, an institution founded to train teachers for service among the ex-slaves. Cooper stayed there for roughly fourteen years, eventually joining the school's faculty. It was while teaching at St. Augustine's that she married George Cooper, a Bahamas-born Greek instructor. In September 1879, however, her husband died, and Cooper remained single for the remainder of her life.

In 1881 Cooper entered Oberlin College, graduating in 1884 with two other black women, one of whom, Mary Church (Terrell), would gain considerable celebrity as an important activist of the time. After teaching briefly at Wilberforce, Cooper returned to St. Augustine's in 1885. In 1887, she received a master's degree in mathematics from Oberlin and then moved to Washington, D.C., where she began a long and at times stormy tenure at the distinguished Washington Colored High School, also known as the M Street School. Cooper became principal there in 1902.

The 1890s constituted an especially productive period for Cooper. In June 1892, she helped to organize the Colored Woman's League of Washington, D.C.; the following year, she and two other black leaders, Fannie Barrier Williams and Fannie Jackson Coppin, addressed the Women's Congress in Chicago, convened during the Columbian Exposition held in that city. Cooper spoke on "The Needs and the Status of Black Women." In 1895, she played an active role in the first meeting of the National Conference of Colored Women; and in 1900 she traveled to London, where she participated in the Pan-African Conference along with W.E.B. Du Bois. Cooper also helped edit *The Southland,* a magazine founded in 1890 by Joseph C. Price, the head of Livingstone College in North Carolina. More importantly, Cooper published *A Voice from the South: By a Black Woman of the South* in 1892, a collection of essays in which she addresses a wide range of issues concerning black women at the end of the nineteenth century.

The conceptual core of *A Voice from the South* is Cooper's contention that "the fundamental agency under God in the regeneration, the re-training of the race, as well as the ground work and starting point of its progress upward, must be the *black woman.*" Or, as Cooper put it, "Only the BLACK WOMAN can say 'when and where I enter, in the quiet, undisputed dignity of my womanhood, without violence and without suing or special patronage, then and there the whole *Negro race enters with me.*'" The dominant position that Cooper accords the black woman in her vision of racial progress reflects, in part, the influence of nineteenth-century bourgeois ideals of "true womanhood," which assumed that women constituted the moral center of a society. At the same time, Cooper consistently argued for the unique position of black women in a male-dominated, racist society, contending that they brought to bear on contemporary problems an invaluable perspective forged in the crucible of multiple and intersecting oppressions. Therefore, the full development of their talents—especially through formal education, Cooper argued—would be of inestimable value not just to women or blacks generally but to the nation as a whole. It also follows that no one could or should speak for the black woman; to Cooper, it was critical that the black woman's voice be raised on her own behalf.

By the mid-1890s, Cooper had come to be recognized as an important member of the black intelligentsia. She was active in the Bethel Literary and Historical Association in Washington, D.C., and she even received an invitation to join the American Negro Academy, the previously male-only organization of such leading black thinkers as W.E.B. Du Bois, Francis Grimke, Alexander Crummell, and Carter Woodson. Cooper's distinguished record as a scholar and teacher, however, did not protect her from scandal. She became embroiled in 1904 in what became known as the "M Street School controversy." Under fire for allegedly condoning smoking and drinking by her students and morally questionable behavior by her teachers, she herself was the target of rumors linking her romantically with a member of the school's faculty whom she happened to have raised in her house. Despite the support of many local blacks, Cooper was dismissed in 1906. After teaching in Missouri, she returned in 1910 to the M Street School (known as Paul Laurence Dunbar High School after 1916), where she worked until her retirement in 1930.

The remainder of Cooper's life was marked by academic achievement and commitment to ensuring the welfare of the black community through education and social service organizations. After studying at Columbia University, Cooper earned a Ph.D. in French from the University of Paris in 1925 despite extraordinary obstacles, including lack of support from her employers. In so doing, Cooper (then in her mid-sixties) became only the fourth black American woman to receive a doctorate. During this time, she continued her efforts to improve conditions within the local black community as well, taking a leadership role in the Colored Settlement House in Washington, D.C., and in the local Colored Young Women's Christian Association. This involvement culminated in 1930 in her accepting the presidency of Frelinghuysen University, a school founded in 1917 to serve black Washington, D.C., residents (especially working people) who might otherwise have little access to higher education. At one point, in an attempt to save the school, Cooper moved its operations into her home. Anna Julia Cooper's educational and community activities continued to the end of her life, one as long and rich and full of dedicated service to her race as that of her far-better-known contemporary W.E.B. Du Bois, whom she outlived by six months.

Richard Yarborough
University of California at Los Angeles

PRIMARY WORKS
A Voice from the South, 1892.

from A Voice from the South

Our Raison D'être[1]

In the clash and clatter of our American Conflict, it has been said that the South remains Silent. Like the Sphinx[2] she inspires vociferous disputation, but herself takes

[1]French; reason for being, rationale.
[2]In Greek mythology, a creature with a lion's body and woman's head that asked travelers a riddle and devoured them if they answered it incorrectly.

little part in the noisy controversy. One muffled strain in the Silent South, a jarring chord and a vague and uncomprehended cadenza has been and still is the Negro. And of that muffled chord, the one mute and voiceless note has been the sadly expectant Black Woman,

> An infant crying in the night,
> An infant crying for the light;
> And with *no language—but a cry.*[3]

The colored man's inheritance and apportionment is still the sombre crux, the perplexing *cul de sac*[4] of the nation,—the dumb skeleton in the closet provoking ceaseless harangues, indeed, but little understood and seldom consulted. Attorneys for the plaintiff and attorneys for the defendant, with bungling *gaucherie*[5] have analyzed and dissected, theorized and synthesized with sublime ignorance or pathetic misapprehension of counsel from the black client. One important witness has not yet been heard from. The summing up of the evidence deposed, and the charge to the jury have been made—but no word from the Black Woman.

It is because I believe the American people to be conscientiously committed to a fair trial and ungarbled evidence, and because I feel it essential to a perfect understanding and an equitable verdict that truth from *each* standpoint be presented at the bar,—that this little Voice has been added to the already full chorus. The "other side" has not been represented by one who "lives there." And not many can more sensibly realize and more accurately tell the weight and the fret of the "long dull pain" than the open-eyed but hitherto voiceless Black Woman of America.

The feverish agitation, the perfervid energy, the busy objectivity of the more turbulent life of our men serves, it may be, at once to cloud or color their vision somewhat, and as well to relieve the smart and deaden the pain for them. Their voice is in consequence not always temperate and calm, and at the same time radically corrective and sanatory. At any rate, as our Caucasian barristers are not to blame if they cannot *quite* put themselves in the dark man's place, neither should the dark man be wholly expected fully and adequately to reproduce the exact Voice of the Black Woman.

Delicately sensitive at every pore to social atmospheric conditions, her calorimeter may well be studied in the interest of accuracy and fairness in diagnosing what is often conceded to be a "puzzling" case. If these broken utterances can in any way help to a clearer vision and a truer pulse-beat in studying our Nation's Problem, this Voice by a Black Woman of the South will not have been raised in vain.

Tawawa Chimney Corner,
Sept. 17, 1892

[3]Alfred, Lord Tennyson, "In Memoriam A. H. H.," LIV. Cooper has added the dash and italics.

[4]French; dead end.

[5]French; awkwardness.

Woman Versus the Indian

In the National Woman's Council convened at Washington in February 1891, among a number of thoughtful and suggestive papers read by eminent women, was one by the Rev. Anna Shaw,[6] bearing the above title.

That Miss Shaw is broad and just and liberal in principal is proved beyond contradiction. Her noble generosity and womanly firmness are unimpeachable. The unwavering stand taken by herself and Miss Anthony[7] in the subsequent color ripple in Wimodaughsis ought to be sufficient to allay forever any doubts as to the pure gold of these two women.

Of Wimodaughsis (which, being interpreted for the uninitiated, is a woman's culture club whose name is made up of the first few letters of the four words wives, mothers, daughters, and sisters) Miss Shaw is president, and a lady from the Blue Grass State *was* secretary.

Pandora's box is opened in the ideal harmony of this modern Eden without an Adam when a colored lady, a teacher in one of our schools, applies for admission to its privileges and opportunities.

The Kentucky secretary, a lady zealous in good works and one who, I can't help imagining, belongs to that estimable class who daily thank the Lord that He made the earth that they may have the job of superintending its rotations, and who really would like to help "elevate" the colored people (in her own way of course and so long as they understand their places) is filled with grief and horror that any persons of Negro extraction should aspire to learn type-writing or languages or to enjoy any other advantages offered in the sacred halls of Wimodaughsis. Indeed, she had not calculated that there were any wives, mothers, daughters, and sisters, except white ones; and she is really convinced that *Whimodaughsis* would sound just as well, and then it need mean just *white mothers, daughters and sisters.* In fact, so far as there is anything in a name, nothing would be lost by omitting for the sake of euphony, from this unique mosaic, the letters that represent wives. *Whiwimodaughsis* might be a little startling, and on the whole wives would better yield to white; since clearly all women are not wives, while surely all wives are daughters. The daughters therefore could represent the wives and this immaculate assembly for propagating liberal and progressive ideas and disseminating a broad and humanizing culture might be spared the painful possibility of the sight of a black man coming in the future to escort from an evening class this solitary cream-colored applicant. Accordingly the Kentucky secretary took the cream-colored applicant aside, and, with emotions befitting such an epochmaking crisis, told her, "as kindly as she could," that colored people were not admitted to the classes, at the same time refunding the money which said cream-colored applicant had paid for lessons in type-writing.

When this little incident came to the knowledge of Miss Shaw, she said firmly and emphatically, NO. As a minister of the gospel and as a Christian woman, she could not lend her influence to such unreasonable and uncharitable discrimination;

[6]Anna Shaw (1847–1919), American minister, physician, and activist in the women's suffrage and temperance movements.

[7]Susan B. Anthony (1820–1906), American leader of the women's suffrage and temperance movements.

and she must resign the honor of president of Wimodaughsis if persons were to be proscribed solely on account of their color.

To the honor of the board of managers, be it said, they sustained Miss Shaw; and the Kentucky secretary, and those whom she succeeded in inoculating with her prejudices, resigned.

'Twas only a ripple,—some bewailing of lost opportunity on the part of those who could not or would not seize God's opportunity for broadening and enlarging their own souls—and then the work flowed on as before.

Susan B. Anthony and Anna Shaw are evidently too noble to be held in thrall by the provincialisms of women who seem never to have breathed the atmosphere beyond the confines of their grandfathers' plantations. It is only from the broad plateau of light and love that one can see petty prejudice and narrow priggishness in their true perspective; and it is on this high ground, as I sincerely believe, these two grand women stand.

As leaders in the woman's movement of today, they have need of clearness of vision as well as firmness of soul in adjusting recalcitrant forces, and wheeling into line the thousand and one none-such, never-to-be-modified, won't-be-dictated-to banners of their somewhat mottled array.

The black woman and the southern woman, I imagine, often get them into the predicament of the befuddled man who had to take singly across a stream a bag of corn, a fox and a goose. There was no one to help, and to leave the goose with the fox was death—with the corn, destruction. To re-christen the animals, the lion could not be induced to lie down with the lamb unless the lamb would take the inside berth.

The black woman appreciates the situation and can even sympathize with the actors in the serio-comic dilemma.

But, may it not be that, as women, the very lessons which seem hardest to master now, are possibly the ones most essential for our promotion to a higher grade of work?

We assume to be leaders of thought and guardians of society. Our country's manners and morals are under our tutoring. Our standards are law in our several little worlds. However tenaciously men may guard some prerogatives, they are our willing slaves in that sphere which they have always conceded to be woman's. Here, no one dares demur when her fiat has gone forth. The man would be mad who presumed, however inexplicable and past finding out any reason for her action might be, to attempt to open a door in her kingdom officially closed and regally sealed by her.

The American woman of to-day not only gives tone directly to her immediate world, but her tiniest pulsation ripples out and out, down and down, till the outermost circles and the deepest layers of society feel the vibrations. It is pre-eminently an age of organizations. The "leading woman," the preacher, the reformer, the organizer "enthuses" her lieutenants and captains, the literary women, the thinking women, the strong, earnest, irresistible women; these in turn touch their myriads of church clubs, social clubs, culture clubs, pleasure clubs and charitable clubs, till the same lecture has been duly administered to every married man in the land (not to speak of sons and brothers) from the President in the White House to the stone-splitter of the ditches. And so woman's lightest whisper is heard as in

Dionysius'[8] ear, by quick relays and endless reproductions, through every recess and cavern as well as on every hilltop and mountain in her vast domain. And her mandates are obeyed. When she says "thumbs up," woe to the luckless thumb that falters in its rising. They may be little things, the amenities of life, the little nothings which cost nothing and come to nothing, and yet can make a sentient being so comfortable or so miserable in this life, the oil of social machinery, which we call the courtesies of life, all are under the magic key of woman's permit.

The American woman then is responsible for American manners. Not merely the right ascension and declination of the satellites of her own drawing room; but the rising and the setting of the pestilential or life-giving orbs which seem to wander afar in space, all are governed almost wholly through her magnetic polarity. The atmosphere of street cars and parks and boulevards, of cafes and hotels and steamboats is charged and surcharged with her sentiments and restrictions. Shop girls and serving maids, cashiers and accountant clerks, scribblers and drummers, whether wage earner, salaried toiler, or proprietress, whether laboring to instruct minds, to save souls, to delight fancies, or to win bread,—the working women of America in whatever station or calling they may be found, are subjects, officers, or rulers of a strong centralized government, and bound together by a system of codes and countersigns, which, though unwritten, forms a network of perfect subordination and unquestioning obedience as marvelous as that of the Jesuits. At the head and center in this regime stands the Leading Woman in the principality. The one talismanic word that plays along the wires from palace to cook-shop, from imperial Congress to the distant plain, is *Caste.* With all her vaunted independence, the American woman of to-day is as fearful of losing caste as a Brahmin in India. That is the law under which she lives, the precepts which she binds as frontlets between her eyes and writes on the door-posts of her homes, the lesson which she instils into her children with their first baby breakfasts, the injunction she lays upon husband and lover with direst penalties attached.

The queen of the drawing room is absolute ruler under this law. Her pose gives the cue. The microscopic angle at which her pencilled brows are elevated, signifies who may be recognized and who are beyond the pale. The delicate intimation is, quick as electricity, telegraphed down. Like the wonderful transformation in the House that Jack Built (or regions thereabouts) when the rat began to gnaw the rope, the rope to hang the butcher, the butcher to kill the ox, the ox to drink the water, the water to quench the fire, the fire to burn the stick, the stick to beat the dog, and the dog to worry the cat, and on, and on, and on,—when miladi[9] causes the inner arch over her matchless orbs to ascend the merest trifle, *presto*! the Miss at the notions counter grows curt and pert, the dress goods clerk becomes indifferent and taciturn, hotel waiters and ticket dispensers look the other way, the Irish street laborer snarles and scowls, conductors, policemen and park superintendents jostle and push and threaten, and society suddenly seems transformed into a band of organized adders, snapping, and striking and hissing just because they like it on general principles. The tune set by the head singer, sung through all keys and registers, with all qualities of tone,—the smooth, flowing, and gentle, the creaking, whizzing, grating, screeching,

[8]Greek soldier and tyrant of Syracuse (405–367 B.C.). Not to be confused with the Greek god Dionysus.

[9]A woman regarded as having fashionable or expensive tastes.

growling—according to ability, taste, and temperament of the singers. Another application of like master, like man. In this case, like mistress, like nation.

It was the good fortune of the Black Wo[man] of the South to spend some weeks, not long since, in a land over which floated the Union Jack. The Stars and Stripes were not the only familiar experiences missed. A uniform, matter-of-fact courtesy, a genial kindliness, quick perception of opportunities for rendering any little manly assistance, a readiness to give information to strangers,—a hospitable, thawing-out atmosphere everywhere—in shops and waiting rooms, on cars and in the streets, actually seemed to her chilled little soul to transform the commonest boor in the service of the public into one of nature's noblemen, and when the old whipped-cur feeling was taken up and analyzed she could hardly tell whether it consisted mostly of self pity for her own wounded sensibilities, or of shame for her country and mortification that her countrymen offered such an unfavorable contrast.

Some American girls, I noticed recently, in search of novelty and adventure, were taking an extended trip through our country unattended by gentleman friends; their wish was to write up for a periodical or lecture the ease and facility, the comfort and safety of American travel, even for the weak and unprotected, under our well-nigh perfect railroad systems and our gentlemanly and efficient corps of officials and public servants. I have some material I could furnish these young ladies, though possibly it might not be just on the side they wish to have illuminated. The Black Woman of the South has to do considerable travelling in this country, often unattended. She thinks she is quiet and unobtrusive in her manner, simple and inconspicuous in her dress, and can see no reason why in any chance assemblage of *ladies,* or even a promiscuous gathering of ordinarily well-bred and dignified individuals, she should be signaled out for any marked consideration. And yet she has seen these same "gentlemanly and efficient" railroad conductors, when their cars had stopped at stations having no raised platforms, making it necessary for passengers to take the long and trying leap from the car step to the ground or step on the narrow little stool placed under by the conductor, after standing at their posts and handing woman after woman from the steps to the stool, thence to the ground, or else relieving her of satchels and bags and enabling her to make the descent easily, deliberately fold their arms and turn round when the Black Woman's turn came to alight—bearing her satchel, and bearing besides another unnamable burden inside the heaving bosom and tightly compressed lips. The feeling of slighted womanhood is unlike every other emotion of the soul. Happily for the human family, it is unknown to many and indescribable to all. Its poignancy, compared with which even Juno's *spretae injuria formae*[10] is earthly and vulgar, is holier than that of jealousy, deeper than indignation, tenderer than rage. Its first impulse of wrathful protest and proud self vindication is checked and shamed by the consciousness that self assertion would outrage still further the same delicate instinct. Were there a brutal attitude of hate or of ferocious attack, the feminine response of fear or repulsion is simple and spontaneous. But when the keen sting comes through the finer sensibilities, from a hand which, by all known traditions and ideals of propriety, should have been trained to reverence and respect

[10]Latin: Virgil, *Aeneid*, I, 26: "the wrong offered her slighted beauty" by the Judgment of Paris. Spoken by Juno, queen of the gods.

them, the condemnation of man's inhumanity to woman is increased and embittered by the knowledge of personal identity with a race of beings so fallen.

I purposely forbear to mention instances of personal violence to colored women travelling in less civilized sections of our country, where women have been forcibly ejected from cars, thrown out of seats, their garments rudely torn, their person wantonly and cruelly injured. America is large and must for some time yet endure its out-of-the-way jungles of barbarism as Africa its uncultivated tracts of marsh and malaria. There are murderers and thieves and villains in both London and Paris. Humanity from the first has had its vultures and sharks, and representatives of the fraternity who prey upon mankind may be expected no less in America than elsewhere. That this virulence breaks out most readily and commonly against colored persons in this country, is due of course to the fact that they are, generally speaking, weak and can be imposed upon with impunity. Bullies are always cowards at heart and may be credited with a pretty safe instinct in scenting their prey. Besides, society, where it has not exactly said to its dogs "s-s-sik him!" has at least engaged to be looking in another direction or studying the rivers on Mars. It is not of the dogs and their doings, but of society holding the leash that I shall speak. It is those subtile exhalations of atmospheric odors for which woman is accountable, the indefinable, unplaceable aroma which seems to exude from the very pores in her finger tips like the delicate sachet so dexterously hidden and concealed in her linens; the essence of her teaching, guessed rather than read, so adroitly is the lettering and wording manipulated; it is the undertones of the picture laid finely on by woman's own practiced hand, the reflection of the lights and shadows on her own brow; it is, in a word, the reputation of our nation for general politeness and good manners and of our fellow citizens to be somewhat more than cads or snobs that shall engage our present study. There can be no true test of national courtesy without travel. Impressions and conclusions based on provincial traits and characteristics can thus be modified and generalized. Moreover, the weaker and less influential the experimenter, the more exact and scientific the deductions. Courtesy "for revenue only" is not politeness, but diplomacy. Any rough can assume civilty toward those of "his set," and does not hesitate to carry it even to servility toward those in whom he recognizes a possible patron or his master in power, wealth, rank, or influence. But, as the chemist prefers distilled H_2O in testing solutions to avoid complications and unwarranted reactions, so the Black Woman holds that her femininity linked with the impossibility of popular affinity or unexpected attraction through position and influence in her case makes her a touchstone of American courtesy exceptionally pure and singularly free from extraneous modifiers. The man who is courteous to her is so, not because of anything he hopes or fears or sees, but because *he is a gentleman.*

I would eliminate also from the discussion all uncharitable reflections upon the orderly execution of laws existing in certain states of this Union, requiring persons known to be colored to ride in one car, and persons supposed to be white in another. A good citizen may use his influence to have existing laws and statutes changed or modified, but a public servant must not be blamed for obeying orders. A railroad conductor is not asked to dictate measures, nor to make and pass laws. His bread and butter are conditioned on his managing his part of the machinery as he is told to do. If, therefore, I found myself in that compartment of a train designated by the sovereign law of the state for presumable Caucasians, and for colored persons only when traveling in the capacity of nurses and maids, should a conductor inform me, as a gentleman might, that I had made a mistake, and offer to show me the proper car for black ladies; I might wonder at the expensive arrangements of the company and of the state in providing special and separate accommodations for the transportation of the various hues of humanity, but I certainly could not take it as a want of courtesy on the conductor's part that he gave the information. It is true, public sentiment precedes and begets all laws, good or bad; and on the ground I have taken, our women are to be credited largely as teachers and moulders of public sentiment. But when a law has passed and received the sanction of the land, there is nothing for our officials to do but enforce it till repealed; and I for one, as a loyal American citizen, will give those officials cheerful support and ready sympathy in the discharge of their duty. But when a great burly six feet of masculinity with sloping shoulders and unkempt beard swaggers in, and, throwing a roll of tobacco into one corner of his jaw, growls out at me over the paper I am reading, "Here gurl," (I am past thirty) "you better git out 'n dis kyar 'f yer don't, I'll put yer out,"—my mental annotation is *Here's an American citizen who has been badly trained. He is sadly lacking in both 'sweetness' and 'light'*; and when in the same section of our enlightened and progressive country, I see from the car window, working on private estates, convicts from the state penitentiary, among them squads of boys from fourteen to eighteen years of age in a chain-gang, their feet chained together and heavy blocks attached—not in 1850, but in 1890, '91 and '92, I make a note on the flyleaf of my memorandum, *The women in this section should organize a Society for the Prevention of Cruelty to Human Beings, and disseminate civilizing tracts, and send throughout the region apostles of anti-barbarism for the propagation of humane and enlightened ideas.* And when farther on in the same section our train stops at a dilapidated station, rendered yet more unsightly by dozens of loafers with their hands in their pockets while a productive soil and inviting climate beckon in vain to industry; and when, looking a little more closely, I see two dingy little rooms with "FOR LADIES" swinging over one and "FOR COLORED PEOPLE" over the other; while wondering under which head I come, I notice a little way off the only hotel proprietor of the place whittling a pine stick as he sits with one leg thrown across an empty goods box; and as my eye falls on a sample room next door which seems to be driving the only wide-awake and popular business of the commonwealth, I cannot help ejaculating under my breath, "What a field for the missionary woman." I know that if by any fatality I should be obliged to lie over at that station, and, driven by hunger, should be compelled to seek refreshments or the bare necessaries of life at the only public accommodation in the town, that same stick-whittler would coolly inform me, without looking up from his pine splinter, "We doan uccommodate no niggers hyur." And yet we are so scandalized at Russia's barbarity and cruelty to the Jews! We pay a man a thousand dollars a night just to make us weep, by a recital of such heathenish inhumanity as is practiced on Slavonic soil. . . .

Now, am I right in holding the American Woman responsible? Is it true that the exponents of woman's advancement, the leaders in woman's thought, the preachers and teachers of all woman's reforms, can teach this nation to be courteous, to be pitiful, having compassion one of another, not rendering evil for inoffensiveness, and railing in proportion to the improbability of being struck back; but contrariwise, being *all* of one mind, to love as brethren?

I think so.

It may require some heroic measures, and like all revolutions will call for a determined front and a courageous, unwavering, stalwart heart on the part of the leaders of the reform.

The "*all*" will inevitably stick in the throat of the Southern woman. She must be allowed, please, to except the 'darkey' from the 'all'; it is too bitter a pill with black people in it. You must get the Revised Version to put it, "*love all white people* as brethren." She really could not enter any society on earth, or in heaven above, or in—the waters under the earth, on such unpalatable conditions.

The Black Woman has tried to understand the Southern woman's difficulties; to put herself in her place, and to be as fair, as charitable, and as free from prejudice in judging her antipathies, as she would have others in regard to her own. She has honestly weighed the apparently sincere excuse, "But you must remember that these people were once our slaves"; and that other, "But civility towards the Negroes will bring us on *social equality* with them."

These are the two bugbears; or rather, the two humbugbears: for, though each is founded on a most glaring fallacy, one would think they were words to conjure with, so potent and irresistible is their spell as an argument at the North as well as in the South.

One of the most singular facts about the unwritten history of this country is the consummate ability with which Southern influence, Southern ideas and Southern ideals, have from the very beginning even up to the present day, dictated to and domineered over the brain and sinew of this nation. Without wealth, without education, without inventions, arts, sciences, or industries, without well-nigh every one of the progressive ideas and impulses which have made this country great, prosperous and happy, personally indolent and practically stupid, poor in everything but bluster and self-esteem, the Southerner has nevertheless with Italian finesse and exquisite skill, uniformly and invariably, so manipulated Northern sentiment as to succeed sooner or later in carrying his point and shaping the policy of this government to suit his purposes. Indeed, the Southerner is a magnificent manager of men, a born educator. For two hundred and fifty years he trained to his hand a people whom he made absolutely his own, in body, mind, and sensibility. He so insinuated differences and distinctions among them, that their personal attachment for him was stronger than for their own brethren and fellow sufferers. He made it a crime for two or three of them to be gathered together in Christ's name without a white man's supervision, and a felony for one to teach them to read even the Word of Life; and yet they would defend his interest with their life blood; his smile was their happiness, a pat on the shoulder from him their reward. The slightest difference among themselves in condition, circumstances, opportunities, became barriers of jealousy and disunion. He sowed his blood broadcast among them, then pitted mulatto against black, bond against free, house slave against plantation slave, even the slave of one clan against like slave of another clan; till, wholly oblivious of their ability for mutual succor and defense, all became centers of myriad systems of repellent forces, having but one sentiment in common, and that their entire subjection to that master hand.

And he not only managed the black man, he also hoodwinked the white man, the tourist and investigator who visited his lordly estates. The slaves were doing well, in fact couldn't be happier,—plenty to eat, plenty to drink, comfortably housed and clothed—they wouldn't be free if they could; in short, in his broad brimmed plantation hat and easy aristocratic smoking gown, he made you think him a veritable patriarch in the midst of a lazy, well fed, good natured, over-indulged tenantry.

Then, too, the South represented blood—not red blood, but blue blood. The difference is in the length of the stream and your distance from its source. If your own father was a pirate, a robber, a murderer, his hands are dyed in red blood, and you don't say very much about it. But if your great great great grandfather's grandfather stole and pillaged and slew, and you can prove it, your blood has become blue and you are at great pains to establish the relationship. So the South had neither silver nor gold, but she had blood; and she paraded it with so much gusto that the substantial little Puritan maidens of the North, who had been making bread and canning currants and not thinking of blood the least bit, began to hunt up the records of the Mayflower to see if some of the passengers thereon could not claim the honor of having been one of William the Conqueror's brigands, when he killed the last of the Saxon kings and, red-handed, stole his crown and his lands. Thus the ideal from out the Southland brooded over the nation and we sing less lustily than of yore

> Kind hearts are more than coronets
> And simple faith than Norman blood.[11]

In politics, the two great forces, commerce and empire, which would otherwise have shaped the destiny of the country, have been made to pander and cater to Southern notions. "Cotton is King" meant the South must be allowed to dictate or there would be no fun. Every statesman from 1830 to 1860 exhausted his genius in persuasion and compromises to smooth out her ruffled temper and gratify her petulant demands. But like a sullen younger sister, the South has pouted and sulked and cried: "I won't play with you now; so there!" and the big brother at the North has coaxed and compromised and given in, and—ended by letting her have her way. Until 1860 she had as her pet an institution which it was death by the law to say anything about, except that it was divinely instituted, inaugurated by Noah, sanctioned by Abraham, approved by Paul, and just ideally perfect in every way. And when, to preserve the autonomy of the family arrangements, in '61, '62 and '63, it became necessary for the big brother to administer a little wholesome correction and set the obstreperous Miss vigorously down in her seat again, she assumed such an air of injured innocence, and melted away so lugubriously, the big brother has done nothing since but try to sweeten and pacify and laugh her back into a companionable frame of mind.

Father Lincoln did all he could to get her to repent of her petulance and behave herself. He even promised she might keep her pet, so disagreeable to all the neighbors and hurtful even to herself, and might manage it at home to suit herself, if she would only listen to reason and be just tolerably nice. But, no—she was going to leave and set up for herself; she didn't propose to be meddled with; and so, of course, she had to be spanked. Just a little at first—didn't mean to hurt, merely to teach her who was who. But she grew so ugly, and kicked and fought and scratched so outrageously, and seemed so determined to smash up the whole business, the head of the

[11] Alfred, Lord Tennyson, "Lady Clara Vere de Vere," 11. 55–56.

family got red in the face, and said: "Well, now, he couldn't have any more of that foolishness. Arabella must just behave herself or take the consequences." And after the spanking, Arabella sniffed and whimpered and pouted, and the big brother bit his lip, looked half ashamed, and said: "Well, I didn't want to hurt you. You needn't feel so awfully bad about it, I only did it for your good. You know I wouldn't do anything to displease you if I could help it; but you would insist on making the row, and so I just had to. Now, there—there—let's be friends!" and he put his great strong arms about her and just dared anybody to refer to that little unpleasantness—he'd show them a thing or two. Still Arabella sulked,—till the rest of the family decided she might just keep her pets, and manage her own affairs and nobody should interfere.

So now, if one intimates that some clauses of the Constitution are a dead letter at the South and that only the name and support of that pet institution are changed while the fact and essence, minus the expense and responsibility, remain, he is quickly told to mind his own business and informed that he is waving the bloody shirt.[12] . . .

. . . Not even the chance traveller from England or Scotland escapes. The arch-manipulator takes him under his special watchcare and training, uses up his stock arguments and gives object lessons with his choicest specimens of Negro depravity and worthlessness; takes him through what, in New York, would be called "the slums," and would predicate there nothing but the duty of enlightened Christians to send out their light and emulate their Master's aggressive labors of love; but in Georgia is denominated "our terrible problem, which people of the North so little understand, yet vouchsafe so much gratuitous advice about." With an injured air he shows the stupendous and atrocious mistake of reasoning about these people as if they were just ordinary human beings, and amenable to the tenets of the Gospel; and not long after the inoculation begins to work, you hear this old-time friend of the oppressed delivering himself something after this fashion: "Ah, well, the South must be left to manage the Negro. She is most directly concerned and must understand her problem better than outsiders. We must not meddle. We must be very careful not to widen the breaches. The Negro is not worth a feud between brothers and sisters."

Lately a great national and international movement characteristic of this age and country, a movement based on the inherent right of every soul to its own highest development, I mean the movement making for Woman's full, free, and complete emancipation, has, after much courting, obtained the gracious smile of the Southern woman—I beg her pardon—the Southern *lady.*

She represents blood, and of course could not be expected to leave that out; and firstly and foremostly she must not, in any organization she may deign to grace with her presence, be asked to associate with "these people who were once her slaves."

Now the Southern woman (I may be pardoned, being one myself) was never renowned for her reasoning powers, and it is not surprising that just a little picking will make her logic fall to pieces even here.

In the first place she imagines that because her grandfather had slaves who were black, all the blacks in the world of every shade and tint were once in the position of

[12] A post-Civil War expression referring to attempts to perpetuate sectional hostility between North and South in order to gain political advantage.

her slaves. This is as bad as the Irishman who was about to kill a peaceable Jew in the streets of Cork,—having just learned that Jews slew his Redeemer. The black race constitutes one-seventh the known population of the globe; and there are representatives of it here as elsewhere who were never in bondage at any time to any man,—whose blood is as blue and lineage as noble as any, even that of the white lady of the South. That her slaves were black and she despises her slaves, should no more argue antipathy to all dark people and peoples, than that Guiteau,[13] an assassin, was white, and I hate assassins, should make me hate all persons more or less white. The objection shows a want of clear discrimination.

The second fallacy in the objection grows out of the use of an ambiguous middle, as the logicians would call it, or assigning a double signification to the term "*Social equality.*"

Civility to the Negro implies social equality. I am opposed to *associating* with dark persons on terms of social equality. Therefore, I abrogate civility to the Negro. This is like

Light is opposed to darkness.
Feathers are light.
Ergo, Feathers are opposed to darkness.

The "social equality" implied by civility to the Negro is a very different thing from forced association with him socially. Indeed it seems to me that the mere application of a little cold common sense would show that uncongenial social environments could by no means be forced on any one. I do not, and cannot be made to associate with all dark persons, simply on the ground that I am dark; and I presume the Southern lady can imagine some whose faces are white, with whom she would no sooner think of chatting unreservedly than, were it possible, with a veritable 'darkey.' Such things must and will always be left to individual election. No law, human or divine, can legislate for or against them. Like seeks like; and I am sure with the Southern lady's antipathies at their present temperature, she might enter ten thousand organizations besprinkled with colored women without being any more deflected by them than by the proximity of a stone. The social equality scare then is all humbug, conscious or unconscious, I know not which. And were it not too bitter a thought to utter here, I might add that the overtures for forced association in the past history of these two races were not made by the manacled black man, nor by *the silent and suffering black woman!*

When I seek food in a public café or apply for first-class accommodations on a railway train, I do so because my physical necessities are identical with those of other human beings of like constitution and temperament, and crave satisfaction. I go because I want food, or I want comfort—not because I want association with those who frequent these places; and I can see no more "social equality" in buying lunch at the same restaurant, or riding in a common car, than there is in paying for dry goods at the same counter or walking on the same street.

The social equality which means forced or unbidden association would be as much deprecated and as strenuously opposed by the circle in which I move as by the most hide-bound Southerner in the land. Indeed I have been more than once an-

[13]The assassin of President James Garfield.

noyed by the inquisitive white interviewer, who, with spectacles on nose and pencil and note-book in hand, comes to get some "points" about "*your people.*" My "people" are just like other people—indeed, too like for their own good. They hate, they love, they attract and repel, they climb or they grovel, struggle or drift, aspire or despair, endure in hope or curse in vexation, exactly like all the rest of unregenerate humanity. Their likes and dislikes are as strong; their antipathies—and prejudices too I fear, are as pronounced as you will find anywhere; and the entrance to the inner sanctuary of their homes and hearts is as jealously guarded against profane intrusion.

What the dark man wants then is merely to live his own life, in his own world, with his own chosen companions, in whatever of comfort, luxury, or emoluments his talent or his money can in an impartial market secure. Has he wealth, he does not want to be forced into inconvenient or unsanitary sections of cities to buy a home and rear his family. Has he art, he does not want to be cabined and cribbed into emulation with the few who merely happen to have his complexion. His talent aspires to study without proscription the masters of all ages and to rub against the broadest and fullest movements of his own day.

Has he religion, he does not want to be made to feel that there is a white Christ and a black Christ, a white Heaven and a black Heaven, a white Gospel and a black Gospel,—but the one ideal of perfect manhood and womanhood, the one universal longing for development and growth, the one desire for being, and being better, the one great yearning, aspiring, outreaching, in all the heartthrobs of humanity in whatever race or clime.

A recent episode in the Corcoran art gallery at the American capital is to the point. A colored woman who had shown marked ability in drawing and coloring, was advised by her teacher, himself an artist of no mean rank, to apply for admission to the Corcoran school in order to study the models and to secure other advantages connected with the organization. She accordingly sent a written application accompanied by specimens of her drawings, the usual *modus operandi* in securing admission.

The drawings were examined by the best critics and pronounced excellent, and a ticket of admission was immediately issued together with a highly complimentary reference to her work.

The next day my friend, congratulating her country and herself that at least in the republic of art no caste existed, presented her ticket of admission *in propria persona.*[14] There was a little preliminary side play in Delsarte[15] pantomine,—aghast—incredulity—wonder; then the superintendent told her in plain unartistic English that of course he had not dreamed a colored person could do such work, and had he suspected the truth he would never have issued the ticket of admission; that, to be right frank, the ticket would have to be cancelled,—she could under no condition be admitted to the studio.

Can it be possible that even art in America is to be tainted by this shrivelling caste spirit? If so, what are we coming to? Can any one conceive a Shakespeare, a Michael Angelo, or a Beethoven putting away any fact of simple merit because the

[14]Latin; literally in her own person, i.e., physically.

[15]French musician and teacher.

thought, or the suggestion, or the creation emanated from a soul with an unpleasing exterior? . . .

. . . No true artist can allow himself to be narrowed and provincialized by deliberately shutting out any class of facts or subjects through prejudice against externals. And American art, American science, American literature can never be founded in truth, the universal beauty; can never learn to speak a language intelligible in all climes and for all ages, till this paralyzing grip of caste prejudice is loosened from its vitals, and the healthy sympathetic eye is taught to look out on the great universe as holding no favorites and no black beasts, but bearing in each plainest or loveliest feature the handwriting of its God.

And this is why, as it appears to me, woman in her lately acquired vantage ground for speaking an earnest helpful word, can do this country no deeper and truer and more lasting good than by bending all her energies to thus broadening, humanizing, and civilizing her native land.

"Except ye become as little children" is not a pious precept, but an inexorable law of the universe. God's kingdoms are all sealed to the seedy, moss-grown mind of self-satisfied maturity. Only the little child in spirit, the simple, receptive, educable mind can enter. Preconceived notions, blinding prejudices, and shrivelling antipathies must be wiped out, and the cultivable soul made a *tabula rasa*[16] for whatever lesson great Nature has to teach.

This, too, is why I conceive the subject to have been unfortunately worded which was chosen by Miss Shaw at the Woman's Council and which stands at the head of this chapter.

Miss Shaw is one of the most powerful of our leaders, and we feel her voice should give no uncertain note. Woman should not, even by inference, or for the sake of argument, seem to disparage what is weak. For woman's cause is the cause of the weak; and when all the weak shall have received their due consideration, then woman will have her "rights," and the Indian will have his rights, and the Negro will have his rights, and all the strong will have learned at last to deal justly, to love mercy, and to walk humbly; and our fair land will have been taught the secret of universal courtesy which is after all nothing but the art, the science, and the religion of regarding one's neighbor as one's self, and to do for him as we would, were conditions swapped, that he do for us.

It cannot seem less than a blunder, whenever the exponents of a great reform or the harbingers of a noble advance in thought and effort allow themselves to seem distorted by a narrow view of their own aims and principles. All prejudices, whether of race, sect or sex, class pride and caste distinctions are the belittling inheritance and badge of snobs and prigs.

The philosophic mind sees that its own "rights" are the rights of humanity. That in the universe of God nothing trivial is or mean; and the recognition it seeks is not through the robber and wild beast adjustment of the survival of the bullies but through the universal application ultimately of the Golden Rule. . . .

The cause of freedom is not the cause of a race or a sect, a party or a class,—it is the cause of human kind, the very birthright of humanity. Now unless we are greatly mistaken the Reform of our day, known as the Woman's Movement, is essentially

[16]Latin; blank slate.

such an embodiment, if its pioneers could only realize it, of the universal good. And specially important is it that there be no confusion of ideas among its leaders as to its scope and universality. All mists must be cleared from the eyes of woman if she is to be a teacher of morals and manners: the former strikes its roots in the individual and its training and pruning may be accomplished by classes; but the latter is to lubricate the joints and minimize the friction of society, and it is important and fundamental that there be no chromatic or other aberration when the teacher is settling the point, "Who is my neighbor?"

It is not the intelligent woman vs. the ignorant woman; nor the white woman vs. the black, the brown, and the red,—it is not even the cause of woman vs. man. Nay, 'tis woman's strongest vindication for speaking that *the world needs to hear her voice.* It would be subversive of every human interest that the cry of one-half the human family be stifled. Woman in stepping from the pedestal of statue-like inactivity in the domestic shrine, and daring to think and move and speak,—to undertake to help shape, mold, and direct the thought of her age, is merely completing the circle of the world's vision. Hers is every interest that has lacked an interpreter and a defender. Her cause is linked with that of every agony that has been dumb—every wrong that needs a voice.

It is no fault of man's that he has not been able to see truth from her standpoint. It does credit both to his head and heart that no greater mistakes have been committed or even wrongs perpetrated while she sat making tatting and snipping paper flowers. Man's own innate chivalry and the mutual interdependence of their interests have insured his treating her cause, in the main at least, as his own. And he is pardonably surprised and even a little chagrined, perhaps, to find his legislation not considered "perfectly lovely" in every respect. But in any case his work is only impoverished by her remaining dumb. The world has had to limp along with the wobbling gait and one-sided hesitancy of a man with one eye. Suddenly the bandage is removed from the other eye and the whole body is filled with light. It sees a circle where before it saw a segment. The darkened eye restored, every member rejoices with it.

What a travesty of its case for this eye to become plaintiff in a suit, *Eye vs. Foot.* "There is that dull clod, the foot, allowed to roam at will, free and untrammelled; while I, the source and medium of light, brilliant and beautiful, am fettered in darkness and doomed to desuetude." The great burly black man, ignorant and gross and depraved, is allowed to vote; while the franchise is withheld from the intelligent and refined, the pure-minded and lofty souled white woman. Even the untamed and untamable Indian of the prairie, who can answer nothing but 'ugh' to great economic and civic questions, is thought by some worthy to wield the ballot which is still denied the Puritan maid and the first lady of Virginia.

Is not this hitching our wagon to something much lower than a star? Is not woman's cause broader, and deeper, and grander, than a blue stocking debate or an aristocratic pink tea? Why should woman become plaintiff in a suit versus the Indian, or the Negro or any other race or class who have been crushed under the iron heel of Anglo-Saxon power and selfishness? If the Indian has been wronged and cheated by the puissance of this American government, it is woman's mission to plead with her country to cease to do evil and to pay its honest debts. If the Negro has been deceitfully cajoled or inhumanly cuffed according to selfish expediency or capricious antipathy, let it be woman's mission to plead that he be met as a man and honestly given half the road. If woman's own happiness has been ignored or misunderstood in our country's legislating for bread winners, for rum sellers, for property holders, for the family relations, for any or all the interests that touch her vitally, let her rest her plea, not on Indian inferiority, nor on Negro depravity, but on the obligation of legislators to do for her as they would have others do for them were relations reversed. Let her try to teach her country that every interest in this world is entitled at least to a respectful hearing, that every sentiency is worthy of its own gratification, that a helpless cause should not be trampled down, nor a bruised reed broken; and when the right of the individual is made sacred, when the image of God in human form, whether in marble or in clay, whether in alabaster or in ebony, is consecrated and inviolable, when men have been taught to look beneath the rags and grime, the pomp and pageantry of mere circumstance and have regard unto the celestial kernel uncontaminated at the core,—when race, color, sex, condition, are realized to be the accidents, not the substance of life, and consequently as not obscuring or modifying the inalienable title to life, liberty, and pursuit of happiness,—then is mastered the science of politeness, the art of courteous contact, which is naught but the practical application of the principle of benevolence, the back bone and marrow of all religion; then woman's lesson is taught and woman's cause is won—not the white woman nor the black woman nor the red woman, but the cause of every man or woman who has writhed silently under a mighty wrong. The pleading of the American woman for the right and the opportunity to employ the American method of influencing the disposal to be made of herself, her property, her children in civil, economic, or domestic relations is thus seen to be based on a principle as broad as the human race and as old as human society. Her wrongs are thus indissolubly linked with all undefended woe, all helpless suffering, and the plenitude of her "rights" will mean the final triumph of all right over might, the supremacy of the moral forces of reason and justice and love in the government of the nation.

God hasten the day.

1892

Charlotte Perkins Gilman 1860–1935

Considered the leading intellectual in the woman's movement from the 1890s to 1920, Charlotte Perkins Gilman was widely known both in the United States and abroad for her incisive studies of woman's role and status in society. By the time of her death in 1935, all of her books were out of print, and in the intervening decades her ideas were largely forgotten. Since the 1970s her writings have been rediscovered—both the sociological analyses that made her popular in her own time, and her less widely known fiction, especially her short story "The Yellow Wall-Paper," regarded today as a classic of nineteenth-century literature.

Gilman was born in Hartford, Connecticut in 1860 to Mary Westcott and Frederick Beecher Perkins; her childhood was a difficult one. Her father (through whom she was related to the famous Beecher clan, including Harriet Beecher Stowe) abandoned his family shortly after Charlotte's birth, and she, her mother, and brother moved constantly, often barely skirting poverty. Determined to be self-supporting, Gilman studied art and earned her living by teaching and by designing greeting cards. In 1884, after much hesitation—some of it due to her apprehension about the difficulties a woman faced in attempting to combine marriage and motherhood with professional work—she married a fellow artist, Charles Stetson. When the birth of a daughter a year after her marriage was followed by a severe depression, Gilman consulted the prominent nerve specialist Dr. S. Weir Mitchell and underwent his famous "rest cure"—a regimen of total bed rest, confinement, and isolation. Once at home, she attempted to follow Mitchell's advice: to devote herself to domestic work and her child and "never touch pen, brush, or pencil as long as you live." It drove her, she said, to the brink of "utter mental ruin." A trial separation from her husband and a trip to California restored her health, and eventually she and Stetson were amicably divorced. Gilman's second marriage, to a first cousin, George Houghton Gilman, in 1900, was deeply satisfying and endured until his death in 1934, a year before her own.

Establishing herself in California, Gilman began to write and lecture on suffrage and woman's rights, and on the social reforms advocated by the Nationalist clubs inspired by Edward Bellamy's Utopian novel *Looking Backward* (1888). In 1892 she published "The Yellow Wall-Paper." Based on her experience with Dr. Mitchell, it is an indictment of nineteenth-century medical attitudes toward women as well as a subtle analysis of the power politics of marriage. Rejected by the prestigious *Atlantic Monthly,* whose editor found it too personally distressing to publish, it appeared instead in the less widely circulated *New England Magazine.*

It was for her sociological studies, however, that Gilman became best known in her own lifetime. In 1898 she published *Women and Economics,* her comprehensive analysis of women's past and present subordination in society. An ambitious blend of history, sociology, anthropology, and psychology, it was Gilman's important contribution to the newly developing social sciences. Gilman's major thesis was that women's economic dependence inside marriage, their unpaid and therefore undervalued work in the home, determines their subordinate status. Her solution was to remove "women's work," and women themselves, from the home and to professionalize and socialize domestic work. Abolishing the sexual division of labor would free women to pursue work in the public world and become more productive members of society.

Women and Economics brought Gilman immediate fame. In the decades that followed she enjoyed an international reputation, lecturing extensively in the United States and abroad. She continued to develop her social analyses in a series of books, including *The Home* (1904), *Human Work* (1904), and *The Man-Made World* (1911), and in a magazine, *The Forerunner,* that she published from 1910 to 1916 and for which she wrote all the copy—articles, editorials, poems, short stories, and serialized novels—the equivalent, she estimated, of twenty-eight books in seven years. The total included three Utopian novels that presented ideal societies based on her reform principles. In one of these, *Herland* (1915), a Utopia of women without men, she wittily exposed American society's arbitrary assignment of "masculine" and "feminine" sex roles and behavioral traits. *Herland* is a society governed by principles of nurturing, in which children, raised collectively by trained specialists, are the most valuable resource.

In addition to "The Yellow Wall-Paper" Gilman wrote over two hundred short stories, most of them for *The Forerunner.* "Turned" is an example of this fiction, written to dramatize and offer solutions for the inequities in women's lives that Gilman's nonfiction works analyzed. "Turned" forthrightly treats marital infidelity, and its "solution" is as provocative as it is unexpected.

Elaine Hedges
late of Towson State University

PRIMARY WORKS

"The Yellow Wall-Paper," 1892; *Women and Economics* 1898; *Forerunner,* vols. 1–7, 1901–1916; *The Man-Made World,* 1911; *The Living of Charlotte Perkins Gilman: An Autobiography,* 1935; Barbara H. Solomon, ed., *"Herland" and Selected Stories by Charlotte Perkins Gilman,* 1992; Denise D. Knight, ed., *"The Yellow Wall-Paper" and Selected Stories of Charlotte Perkins Gilman,* 1994; idem, *The Diaries of Charlotte Perkins Gilman,* 2 vols., 1994; idem, *The Later Poetry of Charlotte Perkins Gilman,* 1996.

The Yellow Wall-Paper

It is very seldom that mere ordinary people like John and myself secure ancestral halls for the summer.

A colonial mansion, a hereditary estate, I would say a haunted house, and reach the height of romantic felicity—but that would be asking too much of fate!

Still I will proudly declare that there is something queer about it.

Else, why should it be let so cheaply? And why have stood so long untenanted?

John laughs at me, of course, but one expects that in marriage.

John is practical in the extreme. He has no patience with faith, an intense horror of superstition, and he scoffs openly at any talk of things not to be felt and seen and put down in figures.

John is a physician, and *perhaps*—(I would not say it to a living soul, of course, but this is dead paper and a great relief to my mind—) *perhaps* that is one reason I do not get well faster.

You see he does not believe I am sick!

And what can one do?

If a physician of high standing, and one's own husband, assures friends and relatives that there is really nothing the matter with one but temporary nervous depression—a slight hysterical tendency[1]—what is one to do?

My brother is also a physician, and also of high standing, and he says the same thing.

So I take phosphates or phosphites—whichever it is, and tonics, and journeys, and air, and exercise, and am absolutely forbidden to "work" until I am well again.

Personally, I disagree with their ideas.

Personally, I believe that congenial work, with excitement and change, would do me good.

But what is one to do?

I did write for a while in spite of them; but it *does* exhaust me a good deal—having to be so sly about it, or else meet with heavy opposition.

I sometimes fancy that in my condition if I had less opposition and more society and stimulus—but John says the very worst thing I can do is to think about my condition, and I confess it always makes me feel bad.

So I will let it alone and talk about the house.

[1]Women's emotional problems from anxiety and depression to fatigue and nervousness were described as "hysteria" at this time.

The most beautiful place! It is quite alone, standing well back from the road, quite three miles from the village. It makes me think of English places that you read about, for there are hedges and walls and gates that lock, and lots of separate little houses for the gardeners and people.

There is a *delicious* garden! I never saw such a garden—large and shady, full of box-bordered paths, and lined with long grape-covered arbors with seats under them.

There were greenhouses, too, but they are all broken now.

There was some legal trouble, I believe, something about the heirs and coheirs; anyhow, the place has been empty for years.

That spoils my ghostliness, I am afraid, but I don't care—there is something strange about the house—I can feel it.

I even said so to John one moonlight evening, but he said what I felt was a *draught,* and shut the window.

I get unreasonably angry with John sometimes. I'm sure I never used to be so sensitive. I think it is due to this nervous condition.

But John says if I feel so, I shall neglect proper self-control; so I take pains to control myself—before him, at least, and that makes me very tired.

I don't like our room a bit. I wanted one downstairs that opened on the piazza and had roses all over the window, and such pretty old-fashioned chintz hangings! but John would not hear of it.

He said there was only one window and not room for two beds, and no near room for him if he took another.

He is very careful and loving, and hardly lets me stir without special direction.

I have a schedule prescription for each hour in the day; he takes all care from me, and so I feel basely ungrateful not to value it more.

He said we came here solely on my account, that I was to have perfect rest and all the air I could get. "Your exercise depends on your strength, my dear," said he, "and your food somewhat on your appetite; but air you can absorb all the time." So we took the nursery at the top of the house.

It is a big, airy room, the whole floor nearly, with windows that look all ways, and air and sunshine galore. It was nursery first and then playroom and gymnasium, I should judge; for the windows are barred for little children, and there are rings and things in the walls.

The paint and paper look as if a boys' school had used it. It is stripped off—the paper—in great patches all around the head of my bed, about as far as I can reach, and in a great place on the other side of the room low down. I never saw a worse paper in my life.

One of those sprawling flamboyant patterns committing every artistic sin.

It is dull enough to confuse the eye in following, pronounced enough to constantly irritate and provoke study, and when you follow the lame uncertain curves for a little distance they suddenly commit suicide—plunge off at outrageous angles, destroy themselves in unheard of contradictions.

The color is repellant, almost revolting; a smouldering unclean yellow, strangely faded by the slow-turning sunlight.

It is a dull yet lurid orange in some places, a sickly sulphur tint in others.

No wonder the children hated it! I should hate it myself if I had to live in this room long.

There comes John, and I must put this away,—he hates to have me write a word.

* * * * * *

We have been here two weeks, and I haven't felt like writing before, since that first day.

I am sitting by the window now, up in this atrocious nursery, and there is nothing to hinder my writing as much as I please, save lack of strength.

John is away all day, and even some nights when his cases are serious.

I am glad my case is not serious!

But these nervous troubles are dreadfully depressing.

John does not know how much I really suffer. He knows there is no *reason* to suffer, and that satisfies him.

Of course it is only nervousness. It does weigh on me so not to do my duty in any way!

I meant to be such a help to John, such a real rest and comfort, and here I am a comparative burden already!

Nobody would believe what an effort it is to do what little I am able,—to dress and entertain, and order things.

It is fortunate Mary is so good with the baby. Such a dear baby!

And yet I *cannot* be with him, it makes me so nervous.

I suppose John never was nervous in his life. He laughs at me so about this wall-paper!

At first he meant to repaper the room, but afterwards he said that I was letting it get the better of me, and that nothing was worse for a nervous patient than to give way to such fancies.

He said that after the wall-paper was changed it would be the heavy bedstead, and then the barred windows, and then that gate at the head of the stairs, and so on.

"You know the place is doing you good," he said, "and really, dear, I don't care to renovate the house just for a three months' rental."

"Then do let us go downstairs," I said, "there are such pretty rooms there."

Then he took me in his arms and called me a blessed little goose, and said he would go down cellar, if I wished, and have it whitewashed into the bargain.

But he is right enough about the beds and windows and things.

It is an airy and comfortable room as any one need wish, and, of course, I would not be so silly as to make him uncomfortable just for a whim.

I'm really getting quite fond of the big room, all but that horrid paper.

Out of one window I can see the garden, those mysterious deep-shaded arbors, the riotous old-fashioned flowers, and bushes and gnarly trees.

Out of another I get a lovely view of the bay and a little private wharf belonging to the estate. There is a beautiful shaded lane that runs down there from the house. I always fancy I see people walking in these numerous paths and arbors, but John has cautioned me not to give way to fancy in the least. He says that with my imaginative power and habit of story-making, a nervous weakness like mine is sure to lead to all manner of excited fancies, and that I ought to use my will and good sense to check the tendency. So I try.

I think sometimes that if I were only well enough to write a little it would relieve the press of ideas and rest me.

But I find I get pretty tired when I try.

It is so discouraging not to have any advice and companionship about my work. When I get really well, John says we will ask cousin Henry and Julia down for a long visit; but he says he would as soon put fireworks in my pillow-case as to let me have those stimulating people about now.

I wish I could get well faster.

But I must not think about that. This paper looks to me as if it *knew* what a vicious influence it had!

There is a recurrent spot where the pattern lolls like a broken neck and two bulbous eyes stare at you upside down.

I get positively angry with the impertinence of it and the everlastingness. Up and down and sideways they crawl, and those absurd, unblinking eyes are everywhere. There is one place where two breadths didn't match, and the eyes go all up and down the line, one a little higher than the other.

I never saw so much expression in an inanimate thing before, and we all know how much expression they have! I used to lie awake as a child and get more entertainment and terror out of blank walls and plain furniture than most children could find in a toy-store.

I remember what a kindly wink the knobs of our big, old bureau used to have, and there was one chair that always seemed like a strong friend.

I used to feel that if any of the other things looked too fierce I could always hop into that chair and be safe.

The furniture in this room is no worse than inharmonious, however, for we had to bring it all from downstairs. I suppose when this was used as a playroom they had to take the nursery things out, and no wonder! I never saw such ravages as the children have made here.

The wall-paper, as I said before, is torn off in spots, and it sticketh closer than a brother—they must have had perseverance as well as hatred.

Then the floor is scratched and gouged and splintered, the plaster itself is dug out here and there, and this great heavy bed which is all we found in the room, looks as if it had been through the wars.

But I don't mind it a bit—only the paper.

There comes John's sister. Such a dear girl as she is, and so careful of me! I must not let her find me writing.

She is a perfect and enthusiastic housekeeper, and hopes for no better profession. I verily believe she thinks it is the writing which made me sick!

But I can write when she is out, and see her a long way off from these windows.

There is one that commands the road, a lovely shaded winding road, and one that just looks off over the country. A lovely country, too, full of great elms and velvet meadows.

This wallpaper has a kind of subpattern in a different shade, a particularly irritating one, for you can only see it in certain lights, and not clearly then.

But in the places where it isn't faded and where the sun is just so—I can see a strange, provoking, formless sort of figure, that seems to skulk about behind that silly and conspicuous front design.

There's sister on the stairs!

* * * * * *

Well, the Fourth of July is over! The people are all gone and I am tired out. John thought it might do me good to see a little company, so we just had mother and Nellie and the children down for a week.

Of course I didn't do a thing. Jennie sees to everything now.

But it tired me all the same.

John says if I don't pick up faster he shall send me to Weir Mitchell[2] in the fall.

But I don't want to go there at all. I had a friend who was in his hands once, and she says he is just like John and my brother, only more so!

Besides, it is such an undertaking to go so far.

I don't feel as if it was worth while to turn my hand over for anything, and I'm getting dreadfully fretful and querulous.

I cry at nothing, and cry most of the time.

Of course I don't when John is here, or anybody else, but when I am alone.

And I am alone a good deal just now. John is kept in town very often by serious cases, and Jennie is good and lets me alone when I want her to.

So I walk a little in the garden or down that lovely lane, sit on the porch under the roses, and lie down up here a good deal.

I'm getting really fond of the room in spite of the wallpaper. Perhaps *because* of the wall-paper.

It dwells in my mind so!

I lie here on this great immovable bed—it is nailed down, I believe—and follow that pattern about by the hour. It is as good as gymnastics, I assure you. I start, we'll say, at the bottom, down in the corner over there where it has not been touched, and I determine for the thousandth time that I *will* follow that pointless pattern to some sort of a conclusion.

I know a little of the principle of design, and I know this thing was not arranged on any laws of radiation, or alternation, or repetition, or symmetry, or anything else that I ever heard of.

It is repeated, of course, by the breadths, but not otherwise.

Looked at in one way each breadth stands alone, the bloated curves and flourishes—a kind of "debased Romanesque"[3] with *delirium tremens*—go waddling up and down in isolated columns of fatuity.

But, on the other hand, they connect diagonally, and the sprawling outlines run off in great slanting waves of optic horror, like a lot of wallowing seaweeds in full chase.

The whole thing goes horizontally, too, at least it seems so, and I exhaust myself in trying to distinguish the order of its going in that direction.

They have used a horizontal breadth for a frieze, and that adds wonderfully to the confusion.

There is one end of the room where it is almost intact, and there, when the crosslights fade and the low sun shines directly upon it, I can almost fancy radiation after all,—the interminable grotesques seem to form around a common centre and rush off in headlong plunges of equal distraction.

It makes me tired to follow it. I will take a nap I guess.

[2]Dr. S. Weir Mitchell (1829–1914), whose celebrated "rest cure" for "hysteria" Gilman had undergone.

[3]A style of architecture with profuse ornamentation.

* * * * * *

I don't know why I should write this.

I don't want to.

I don't feel able.

And I know John would think it absurd. But I *must* say what I feel and think in some way—it is such a relief!

But the effort is getting to be greater than the relief.

But the effort is getting to be greater than the relief.

Half the time now I am awfully lazy, and lie down ever so much.

John says I mustn't lose my strength, and has me take cod liver oil and lots of tonics and things, to say nothing of ale and wine and rare meat.

Dear John! He loves me very dearly, and hates to have me sick. I tried to have a real earnest reasonable talk with him the other day, and tell him how I wish he would let me go and make a visit to Cousin Henry and Julia.

But he said I wasn't able to go, nor able to stand it after I got there; and I did not make out a very good case for myself, for I was crying before I had finished.

It is getting to be a great effort for me to think straight. Just this nervous weakness I suppose.

And dear John gathered me up in his arms, and just carried me upstairs and laid me on the bed, and sat by me and read to me till it tired my head.

He said I was his darling and his comfort and all he had, and that I must take care of myself for his sake, and keep well.

He says no one but myself can help me out of it, that I must use my will and self-control and not let any silly fancies run away with me.

There's one comfort, the baby is well and happy, and does not have to occupy this nursery with the horrid wallpaper.

If we had not used it, that blessed child would have! What a fortunate escape! Why, I wouldn't have a child of mine, an impressionable little thing, live in such a room for worlds.

I never thought of it before, but it is lucky that John kept me here after all, I can stand it so much easier than a baby, you see.

Of course I never mention it to them any more—I am too wise,—but I keep watch of it all the same.

There are things in that paper that nobody knows but me, or ever will.

Behind that outside pattern the dim shapes get clearer every day.

It is always the same shape, only very numerous.

And it is like a woman stooping down and creeping about behind that pattern. I don't like it a bit. I wonder—I begin to think—I wish John would take me away from here!

* * * * * *

It is so hard to talk with John about my case, because he is so wise, and because he loves me so.

But I tried it last night.

It was moonlight. The moon shines in all around just as the sun does.

I hate to see it sometimes, it creeps so slowly, and always comes in by one window or another.

John was asleep and I hated to waken him, so I kept still and watched the moonlight on that undulating wallpaper till I felt creepy.

The faint figure behind seemed to shake the pattern, just as if she wanted to get out.

I got up softly and went to feel and see if the paper *did* move, and when I came back John was awake.

"What is it, little girl?" he said. "Don't go walking about like that—you'll get cold."

I thought it was a good time to talk, so I told him that I really was not gaining here, and that I wished he would take me away.

"Why, darling!" said he, "our lease will be up in three weeks, and I can't see how to leave before.

"The repairs are not done at home, and I cannot possibly leave town just now. Of course if you were in any danger, I could and would, but you really are better, dear, whether you can see it or not. I am a doctor, dear, and I know. You are gaining flesh and color, your appetite is better, I feel really much easier about you."

"I don't weigh a bit more," said I, "nor as much; and my appetite may be better in the evening when you are here, but it is worse in the morning when you are away!"

"Bless her little heart!" said he with a big hug, "she shall be as sick as she pleases! But now let's improve the shining hours[4] by going to sleep, and talk about it in the morning!"

"And you won't go away?" I asked gloomily.

"Why, how can I, dear? It is only three weeks more and then we will take a nice little trip of a few days while Jennie is getting the house ready. Really dear you are better!"

"Better in body perhaps—" I began, and stopped short, for he sat up straight and looked at me with such a stern, reproachful look that I could not say another word.

"My darling," said he, "I beg of you, for my sake and for our child's sake, as well as for your own, that you will never for one instant let that idea enter your mind! There is nothing so dangerous, so fascinating, to a temperament like yours. It is a false and foolish fancy. Can you not trust me as a physician when I tell you so?"

So of course I said no more on that score, and we went to sleep before long. He thought I was asleep first, but I wasn't, and lay there for hours trying to decide whether that front pattern and the back pattern really did move together or separately.

* * * * * *

On a pattern like this, by daylight, there is a lack of sequence, a defiance of law, that is a constant irritant to a normal mind.

The color is hideous enough, and unreliable enough, and infuriating enough, but the pattern is torturing.

[4]From a poem by Isaac Watts (1674–1748), "Against Idleness and Mischief," containing the lines: How doth the little busy bee/Improve each shining hour,/ And gather honey all the day/ From every opening flower!

You think you have mastered it, but just as you get well underway in following, it turns a back-somersault and there you are. It slaps you in the face, knocks you down, and tramples upon you. It is like a bad dream.

The outside pattern is a florid arabesque, reminding one of a fungus. If you can imagine a toadstool in joints, an interminable string of toadstools, budding and sprouting in endless convolutions—why, that is something like it.

That is, sometimes!

There is one marked peculiarity about this paper, a thing nobody seems to notice but myself, and that is that it changes as the light changes.

When the sun shoots in through the east window—I always watch for that first long, straight ray—it changes so quickly that I never can quite believe it.

That is why I watch it always.

By moonlight—the moon shines in all night when there is a moon—I wouldn't know it was the same paper.

At night in any kind of light, in twilight, candlelight, lamplight, and worst of all by moonlight, it becomes bars! The outside pattern I mean, and the woman behind it is as plain as can be.

I didn't realize for a long time what the thing was that showed behind, that dim sub-pattern, but now I am quite sure it is a woman.

By daylight she is subdued, quiet. I fancy it is the pattern that keeps her so still. It is so puzzling. It keeps me quiet by the hour.

I lie down ever so much now. John says it is good for me, and to sleep all I can.

Indeed he started the habit by making me lie down for an hour after each meal.

It is a very bad habit I am convinced, for you see I don't sleep.

And that cultivates deceit, for I don't tell them I'm awake—O no!

The fact is I am getting a little afraid of John.

He seems very queer sometimes, and even Jennie has an inexplicable look.

It strikes me occasionally, just as a scientific hypothesis,—that perhaps it is the paper!

I have watched John when he did not know I was looking, and come into the room suddenly on the most innocent excuses, and I've caught him several times *looking at the paper!* And Jennie too. I caught Jennie with her hand on it once.

She didn't know I was in the room, and when I asked her in a quiet, a very quiet voice, with the most restrained manner possible, what she was doing with the paper—she turned around as if she had been caught stealing, and looked quite angry—asked me why I should frighten her so!

Then she said that the paper stained everything it touched, that she had found yellow smooches on all my clothes and John's, and she wished we would be more careful!

Did not that sound innocent? But I know she was studying that pattern, and I am determined that nobody shall find it out but myself!

* * * * * *

Life is very much more exciting now than it used to be. You see I have something more to expect, to look forward to, to watch. I really do eat better, and am more quiet than I was.

John is so pleased to see me improve! He laughed a little the other day, and said I seemed to be flourishing in spite of my wall-paper.

I turned it off with a laugh. I had no intention of telling him it was *because* of the wall-paper—he would make fun of me. He might even want to take me away.

I don't want to leave now until I have found it out. There is a week more, and I think that will be enough.

* * * * * *

I'm feeling ever so much better! I don't sleep much at night, for it is so interesting to watch developments; but I sleep a good deal in the daytime.

In the daytime it is tiresome and perplexing.

There are always new shoots on the fungus, and new shades of yellow all over it. I cannot keep count of them, though I have tried conscientiously.

It is the strangest yellow, that wall-paper! It makes me think of all the yellow things I ever saw—not beautiful ones like buttercups, but old foul, bad yellow things.

But there is something else about that paper—the smell! I noticed it the moment we came into the room, but with so much air and sun it was not bad. Now we have had a week of fog and rain, and whether the windows are open or not, the smell is here.

It creeps all over the house.

I find it hovering in the dining-room, skulking in the parlor, hiding in the hall, lying in wait for me on the stairs.

It gets into my hair.

Even when I go to ride, if I turn my head suddenly and surprise it—there is that smell!

Such a peculiar odor, too! I have spent hours in trying to analyze it, to find what it smelled like.

It is not bad—at first, and very gentle, but quite the subtlest, most enduring odor I ever met.

In this damp weather it is awful, I wake up in the night and find it hanging over me.

It used to disturb me at first. I thought seriously of burning the house—to reach the smell.

But now I am used to it. The only thing I can think of that it is like is the *color* of the paper! A yellow smell.

There is a very funny mark on this wall, low down, near the mopboard. A streak that runs round the room. It goes behind every piece of furniture, except the bed, a long, straight, even *smooch,* as if it had been rubbed over and over.

I wonder how it was done and who did it, and what they did it for. Round and round and round—round and round and round—it makes me dizzy!

* * * * * *

I really have discovered something at last.

Through watching so much at night, when it changes so, I have finally found out.

The front pattern *does* move—and no wonder! The woman behind shakes it!

Sometimes I think there are a great many women behind, and sometimes only one, and she crawls around fast, and her crawling shakes it all over.

Then in the very bright spots she keeps still, and in the very shady spots she just takes hold of the bars and shakes them hard.

And she is all the time trying to climb through. But nobody could climb through that pattern—it strangles so; I think that is why it has so many heads.

They get through, and then the pattern strangles them off and turns them upside down, and makes their eyes white!

If those heads were covered or taken off it would not be half so bad.

* * * * * *

I think that woman gets out in the daytime!

And I'll tell you why—privately—I've seen her!

I can see her out of every one of my windows!

It is the same woman, I know, for she is always creeping, and most women do not creep by daylight.

I see her in that long shaded lane, creeping up and down. I see her in those dark grape arbors, creeping all around the garden.

I see her on that long road under the trees, creeping along, and when a carriage comes she hides under the blackberry vines.

I don't blame her a bit. It must be very humiliating to be caught creeping by daylight!

I always lock the door when I creep by daylight. I can't do it at night, for I know John would suspect something at once.

And John is so queer now, that I don't want to irritate him. I wish he would take another room! Besides, I don't want anybody to get that woman out at night but myself.

I often wonder if I could see her out of all the windows at once.

But, turn as fast as I can, I can only see out of one at one time.

And though I always see her, she *may* be able to creep faster than I can turn!

I have watched her sometimes away off in the open country, creeping as fast as a cloud shadow in a high wind.

* * * * * *

If only that top pattern could be gotten off from the under one! I mean to try it, little by little.

I have found out another funny thing, but I shan't tell it this time! It does not do to trust people too much.

There are only two more days to get this paper off, and I believe John is beginning to notice. I don't like the look in his eyes.

And I heard him ask Jennie a lot of professional questions about me. She had a very good report to give.

She said I slept a good deal in the daytime.

John knows I don't sleep very well at night, for all I'm so quiet!

He asked me all sorts of questions, too, and pretended to be very loving and kind.

As if I couldn't see through him!

Still, I don't wonder he acts so, sleeping under this paper for three months.

It only interests me, but I feel sure John and Jennie are secretly affected by it.

* * * * *

Hurrah! This is the last day, but it is enough. John to stay in town over night, and won't be out until this evening.

Jennie wanted to sleep with me—the sly thing! but I told her I should undoubtedly rest better for a night all alone.

That was clever, for really I wasn't alone a bit! As soon as it was moonlight and that poor thing began to crawl and shake the pattern, I got up and ran to help her.

I pulled and she shook, I shook and she pulled, and before morning we had peeled off yards of that paper.

A strip about as high as my head and half around the room.

And then when the sun came and that awful pattern began to laugh at me, I declared I would finish it to-day!

We go away to-morrow, and they are moving all my furniture down again to leave things as they were before.

Jennie looked at the wall in amazement, but I told her merrily that I did it out of pure spite at the vicious thing.

She laughed and said she wouldn't mind doing it herself, but I must not get tired.

How she betrayed herself that time!

But I am here, and no person touches this paper but me,—not *alive!*

She tried to get me out of the room—it was too patent! But I said it was so quiet and empty and clean now that I believed I would lie down again and sleep all I could; and not to wake me even for dinner—I would call when I woke.

So now she is gone, and the servants are gone, and the things are gone, and there is nothing left but that great bedstead nailed down, with the canvas mattress we found on it.

We shall sleep downstairs to-night, and take the boat home to-morrow.

I quite enjoy the room, now it is bare again.

How those children did tear about here!

This bedstead is fairly gnawed!

But I must get to work.

I have locked the door and thrown the key down into the front path.

I don't want to go out, and I don't want to have anybody come in, till John comes.

I want to astonish him.

I've got a rope up here that even Jennie did not find. If that woman does get out, and tries to get away, I can tie her!

But I forgot I could not reach far without anything to stand on!

This bed will *not* move!

I tried to lift and push it until I was lame, and then I got so angry I bit off a little piece at one corner—but it hurt my teeth.

Then I peeled off all the paper I could reach standing on the floor. It sticks horribly and the pattern just enjoys it! All those strangled heads and bulbous eyes and waddling fungus growths just shriek with derision!

I am getting angry enough to do something desperate. To jump out of the window would be admirable exercise, but the bars are too strong even to try.

Besides I wouldn't do it. Of course not. I know well enough that a step like that is improper and might be misconstrued.

I don't like to *look* out of the windows even—there are so many of those creeping women, and they creep so fast.

I wonder if they all come out of that wall-paper as I did?

But I am securely fastened now by my well-hidden rope—you don't get *me* out in the road there!

I suppose I shall have to get back behind the pattern when it comes night, and that is hard!

It is so pleasant to be out in this great room and creep around as I please!

I don't want to go outside. I won't, even if Jennie asks me to.

For outside you have to creep on the ground, and everything is green instead of yellow.

But here I can creep smoothly on the floor, and my shoulder just fits in that long smooch around the wall, so I cannot lose my way.

Why there's John at the door!

It is no use, young man, you can't open it!

How he does call and pound!

Now he's crying for an axe.

It would be a shame to break down that beautiful door!

"John dear!" said I in the gentlest voice, "the key is down by the front steps, under a plantain leaf!"

That silenced him for a few moments.

Then he said—very quietly indeed, "Open the door, my darling!"

"I can't," said I. "The key is down by the front door under a plantain leaf!"

And then I said it again, several times, very gently and slowly, and said it so often that he had to go and see, and he got it of course, and came in. He stopped short by the door.

"What is the matter?" he cried. "For God's sake, what are you doing!"

I kept on creeping just the same, but I looked at him over my shoulder.

["I've got out at last," said I, "in spite of you and Jane.[5] And I've pulled off most of the paper, so you can't put me back!"]

Now why should that man have fainted? But he did, and right across my path by the wall, so that I had to creep over him every time!

1892

Turned

In her soft-carpeted, thick-curtained, richly furnished chamber, Mrs. Marroner lay sobbing on the wide, soft bed.

She sobbed bitterly, chokingly, despairingly; her shoulders heaved and shook

[5]Presumably another name for Jennie.

convulsively; her hands were tight-clenched; she had forgotten her elaborate dress, the more elaborate bedcover; forgotten her dignity, her self-control, her pride. In her mind was an overwhelming, unbelievable horror, an immeasurable loss, a turbulent, struggling mass of emotion.

In her reserved, superior, Boston-bred life she had never dreamed that it would be possible for her to feel so many things at once, and with such trampling intensity.

She tried to cool her feelings into thoughts; to stiffen them into words; to control herself—and could not. It brought vaguely to her mind an awful moment in the breakers at York Beach, one summer in girlhood, when she had been swimming under water and could not find the top.

* * *

In her uncarpeted, thin-curtained, poorly furnished chamber on the top floor, Gerta Petersen lay sobbing on the narrow, hard bed.

She was of larger frame than her mistress, grandly built and strong; but all her proud young womanhood was prostrate, now, convulsed with agony, dissolved in tears. She did not try to control herself. She wept for two.

* * *

If Mrs. Marroner suffered more from the wreck and ruin of a longer love—perhaps a deeper one; if her tastes were finer, her ideals loftier; if she bore the pangs of bitter jealousy and outraged pride, Gerta had personal shame to meet, a hopeless future, and a looming present which filled her with unreasoning terror.

She had come like a meek young goddess into that perfectly ordered house, strong, beautiful, full of good will and eager obedience, but ignorant and childish—a girl of eighteen.

Mr. Marroner had frankly admired her, and so had his wife. They discussed her visible perfections and as visible limitations with that perfect confidence which they had so long enjoyed. Mrs. Marroner was not a jealous woman. She had never been jealous in her life—till now.

Gerta had stayed and learned their ways. They had both been fond of her. Even the cook was fond of her. She was what is called "willing," was unusually teachable and plastic; and Mrs. Marroner, with her early habits of giving instruction, tried to educate her somewhat.

"I never saw anyone so docile," Mrs. Marroner had often commented. "It is perfection in a servant, but almost a defect in character. She is so helpless and confiding."

She was precisely that; a tall, rosy-cheeked baby; rich womanhood without, helpless infancy within. Her braided wealth of dead-gold hair, her grave blue eyes, her mighty shoulders, and long, firmly moulded limbs seemed those of a primal earth spirit; but she was only an ignorant child, with a child's weakness.

When Mr. Marroner had to go abroad for his firm, unwillingly, hating to leave his wife, he had told her he felt quite safe to leave her in Gerta's hands—she would take care of her.

"Be good to your mistress, Gerta," he told the girl that last morning at breakfast. "I leave her to you to take care of. I shall be back in a month at latest."

Then he turned, smiling, to his wife. "And you must take care of Gerta, too," he said. "I expect you'll have her ready for college when I get back."

This was seven months ago. Business had delayed him from week to week, from month to month. He wrote to his wife, long, loving, frequent letters; deeply regretting the delay, explaining how necessary, how profitable it was; congratulating her on the wide resources she had; her well-filled, well-balanced mind; her many interests.

"If I should be eliminated from your scheme of things, by any of those 'acts of God' mentioned on the tickets, I do not feel that you would be an utter wreck," he said. "That is very comforting to me. Your life is so rich and wide that no one loss, even a great one, would wholly cripple you. But nothing of the sort is likely to happen, and I shall be home again in three weeks—if this thing gets settled. And you will be looking so lovely, with that eager light in your eyes and the changing flush I know so well—and love so well! My dear wife! We shall have to have a new honeymoon—other moons come every month, why shouldn't the mellifluous kind?"

He often asked after "little Gerta," sometimes enclosed a picture postcard to her, joked his wife about her laborious efforts to educate "the child"; was so loving and merry and wise——.

All this was racing through Mrs. Marroner's mind as she lay there with the broad, hemstitched border of fine linen sheeting crushed and twisted in one hand, and the other holding a sodden handkerchief.

She had tried to teach Gerta, and had grown to love the patient, sweet-natured child, in spite of her dullness. At work with her hands, she was clever, if not quick, and could keep small accounts from week to week. But to the woman who held a Ph.D., who had been on the faculty of a college, it was like baby-tending.

Perhaps having no babies of her own made her love the big child the more, though the years between them were but fifteen.

To the girl she seemed quite old, of course; and her young heart was full of grateful affection for the patient care which made her feel so much at home in this new land.

And then she had noticed a shadow on the girl's bright face. She looked nervous, anxious, worried. When the bell rang she seemed startled, and would rush hurriedly to the door. Her peals of frank laughter no longer rose from the area gate as she stood talking with the always admiring tradesmen.

Mrs. Marroner had labored long to teach her more reserve with men, and flattered herself that her words were at last effective. She suspected the girl of homesickness; which was denied. She suspected her of illness, which was denied also. At last she suspected her of something which could not be denied.

For a long time she refused to believe it, waiting. Then she had to believe it, but schooled herself to patience and understanding. "The poor child," she said. "She is here without a mother—she is so foolish and yielding—I must not be too stern with her." And she tried to win the girl's confidence with wise, kind words.

But Gerta had literally thrown herself at her feet and begged her with streaming tears not to turn her away. She would admit nothing, explain nothing; but frantically promised to work for Mrs. Marroner as long as she lived—if only she would keep her.

Revolving the problem carefully in her mind, Mrs. Marroner thought she would keep her, at least for the present. She tried to repress her sense of ingratitude in one she had so sincerely tried to help, and the cold, contemptuous anger she had always felt for such weakness.

"The thing to do now," she said to herself, "is to see her through this safely. The child's life should not be hurt any more than is unavoidable. I will ask Dr. Bleet about it—what a comfort a woman doctor is! I'll stand by the poor, foolish thing till it's over, and then get her back to Sweden somehow with her baby. How they do come where they are not wanted—and don't come where they are wanted!" And Mrs. Marroner, sitting alone in the quiet, spacious beauty of the house, almost envied Gerta.

Then came the deluge.

She had sent the girl out for needed air toward dark. The late mail came; she took it in herself. One letter for her—her husband's letter. She knew the postmark, the stamp, the kind of typewriting. She impulsively kissed it in the dim hall. No one would suspect Mrs. Marroner of kissing her husband's letters—but she did, often.

She looked over the others. One was for Gerta, and not from Sweden. It looked precisely like her own. This struck her as a little odd, but Mr. Marroner had several times sent messages and cards to the girl. She laid the letter on the hall table and took hers to her room.

"My poor child," it began. What letter of hers had been sad enough to warrant that?

"I am deeply concerned at the news you send." What news to so concern him had she written? "You must bear it bravely, little girl. I shall be home soon, and will take care of you, of course. I hope there is no immediate anxiety—you do not say. Here is money, in case you need it. I expect to get home in a month at latest. If you have to go, be sure to leave your address at my office. Cheer up—be brave—I will take care of you."

The letter was typewritten, which was not unusual. It was unsigned, which was unusual. It enclosed an American bill—fifty dollars. It did not seem in the least like any letter she had ever had from her husband, or any letter she could imagine him writing. But a strange, cold feeling was creeping over her, like a flood rising around a house.

She utterly refused to admit the ideas which began to bob and push about outside her mind, and to force themselves in. Yet under the pressure of these repudiated thoughts she went downstairs and brought up the other letter—the letter to Gerta. She laid them side by side on a smooth dark space on the table; marched to the piano and played, with stern precision, refusing to think, till the girl came back. When she came in, Mrs. Marroner rose quietly and came to the table. "Here is a letter for you," she said.

The girl stepped forward eagerly, saw the two lying together there, hesitated, and looked at her mistress.

"Take yours, Gerta. Open it, please."

The girl turned frightened eyes upon her.

"I want you to read it, here," said Mrs. Marroner.

"Oh, ma'am——No! Please don't make me!"

"Why not?"

There seemed to be no reason at hand, and Gerta flushed more deeply and opened her letter. It was long; it was evidently puzzling to her; it began "My dear wife." She read it slowly.

"Are you sure it is your letter?" asked Mrs. Marroner. "Is not this one yours? Is not that one—mine?"

She held out the other letter to her.

"It is a mistake," Mrs. Marroner went on, with a hard quietness. She had lost her social bearings somehow; lost her usual keen sense of the proper thing to do. This was not life, this was a nightmare.

"Do you not see? Your letter was put in my envelope and my letter was put in your envelope. Now we understand it."

But poor Gerta had no antechamber to her mind; no trained forces to preserve order while agony entered. The thing swept over her, resistless, overwhelming. She cowered before the outraged wrath she expected; and from some hidden cavern that wrath arose and swept over her in pale flame.

"Go and pack your trunk," said Mrs. Marroner. "You will leave my house to-night. Here is your money."

She laid down the fifty-dollar bill. She put with it a month's wages. She had no shadow of pity for those anguished eyes, those tears which she heard drop on the floor.

"Go to your room and pack," said Mrs. Marroner. And Gerta, always obedient, went.

Then Mrs. Marroner went to hers, and spent a time she never counted, lying on her face on the bed.

But the training of the twenty-eight years which had elapsed before her marriage; the life at college, both as student and teacher; the independent growth which she had made, formed a very different background for grief from that in Gerta's mind.

After a while Mrs. Marroner arose. She administered to herself a hot bath, a cold shower, a vigorous rubbing. "Now I can think," she said.

First she regretted the sentence of instant banishment. She went upstairs to see if it had been carried out. Poor Gerta! The tempest of her agony had worked itself out at last as in a child, and left her sleeping, the pillow wet, the lips still grieving, a big sob shuddering itself off now and then.

Mrs. Marroner stood and watched her, and as she watched she considered the helpless sweetness of the face; the defenseless, unformed character; the docility and habit of obedience which made her so attractive—and so easily a victim. Also she thought of the mighty force which had swept over her; of the great process now working itself out through her; of how pitiful and futile seemed any resistance she might have made.

She softly returned to her own room, made up a little fire, and sat by it, ignoring her feelings now, as she had before ignored her thoughts.

Here were two women and a man. One woman was a wife; loving, trusting, affectionate. One was a servant; loving, trusting, affectionate: a young girl, an exile, a dependent; grateful for any kindness; untrained, uneducated, childish. She ought, of course, to have resisted temptation; but Mrs. Marroner was wise enough to know how difficult temptation is to recognize when it comes in the guise of friendship and from a source one does not suspect.

Gerta might have done better in resisting the grocer's clerk; had, indeed, with Mrs. Marroner's advice, resisted several. But where respect was due, how could she criticize? Where obedience was due, how could she refuse—with ignorance to hold her blinded—until too late?

As the older, wiser woman forced herself to understand and extenuate the girl's misdeed and foresee her ruined future, a new feeling rose in her heart, strong, clear, and overmastering; a sense of measureless condemnation for the man who had done this thing. He knew. He understood. He could fully foresee and measure the consequences of his act. He appreciated to the full the innocence, the ignorance, the grateful affection, the habitual docility, of which he deliberately took advantage.

Mrs. Marroner rose to icy peaks of intellectual apprehension, from which her hours of frantic pain seemed far indeed removed. He had done this thing under the same roof with her—his wife. He had not frankly loved the younger woman, broken with his wife, made a new marriage. That would have been heart-break pure and simple. This was something else.

That letter, that wretched, cold, carefully guarded, unsigned letter: that bill—far safer than a check—these did not speak of affection. Some men can love two women at one time. This was not love.

Mrs. Marroner's sense of pity and outrage for herself, the wife, now spread suddenly into a perception of pity and outrage for the girl. All that splendid, clean young beauty, the hope of a happy life, with marriage and motherhood; honorable independence, even—these were nothing to that man. For his own pleasure he had chosen to rob her of her life's best joys.

He would "take care of her" said the letter? How? In what capacity?

And then, sweeping over both her feelings for herself, the wife, and Gerta, his victim, came a new flood, which literally lifted her to her feet. She rose and walked, her head held high. "This is the sin of man against woman," she said. "The offense is against womanhood. Against motherhood. Against—the child."

She stopped.

The child. His child. That, too, he sacrificed and injured—doomed to degradation.

Mrs. Marroner came of stern New England stock. She was not a Calvinist, hardly even a Unitarian, but the iron of Calvinism was in her soul: of that grim faith which held that most people had to be damned "for the glory of God."

Generations of ancestors who both preached and practiced stood behind her; people whose lives had been sternly moulded to their highest moments of religious conviction. In sweeping bursts of feeling they achieved "conviction," and afterward they lived and died according to that conviction.

When Mr. Marroner reached home, a few weeks later, following his letters too soon to expect an answer to either, he saw no wife upon the pier, though he had cabled; and found the house closed darkly. He let himself in with his latch-key, and stole softly upstairs, to surprise his wife.

No wife was there.

He rang the bell. No servant answered it.

He turned up light after light; searched the house from top to bottom; it was utterly empty. The kitchen wore a clean, bald, unsympathetic aspect. He left it and slowly mounted the stair, completely dazed. The whole house was clean, in perfect order, wholly vacant.

One thing he felt perfectly sure of—she knew.

Yet was he sure? He must not assume too much. She might have been ill. She might have died. He started to his feet. No, they would have cabled him. He sat down again.

For any such change, if she had wanted him to know, she would have written. Perhaps she had, and he, returning so suddenly, had missed the letter. The thought was some comfort. It must be so. He turned to the telephone, and again hesitated. If she had found out—if she had gone—utterly gone, without a word—should he announce it himself to friends and family?

He walked the floor; he searched everywhere for some letter, some word of explanation. Again and again he went to the telephone—and always stopped. He could not bear to ask: "Do you know where my wife is?"

The harmonious, beautiful rooms reminded him in a dumb, helpless way of her; like the remote smile on the face of the dead. He put out the lights; could not bear the darkness; turned them all on again.

It was a long night—

In the morning he went early to the office. In the accumulated mail was no letter from her. No one seemed to know of anything unusual. A friend asked after his wife—"Pretty glad to see you, I guess?" He answered evasively.

About eleven a man came to see him; John Hill, her lawyer. Her cousin, too. Mr. Marroner had never liked him. He liked him less now, for Mr. Hill merely handed him a letter, remarked, "I was requested to deliver this to you personally," and departed, looking like a person who is called on to kill something offensive.

"I have gone. I will care for Gerta. Good-bye. Marion."

That was all. There was no date, no address, no postmark; nothing but that.

In his anxiety and distress he had fairly forgotten Gerta and all that. Her name aroused in him a sense of rage. She had come between him and his wife. She had taken his wife from him. That was the way he felt.

At first he said nothing, did nothing; lived on alone in his house, taking meals where he chose. When people asked him about his wife he said she was traveling—for her health. He would not have it in the newspapers. Then, as time passed, as no enlightenment came to him, he resolved not to bear it any longer, and employed detectives. They blamed him for not having put them on the track earlier, but set to work, urged to the utmost secrecy.

What to him had been so blank a wall of mystery seemed not to embarrass them in the least. They made careful inquiries as to her "past," found where she had studied, where taught, and on what lines; that she had some little money of her own, that her doctor was Josephine L. Bleet, M.D., and many other bits of information.

As a result of careful and prolonged work, they finally told him that she had resumed teaching under one of her old professors; lived quietly, and apparently kept boarders; giving him town, street, and number, as if it were a matter of no difficulty whatever.

He had returned in early spring. It was autumn before he found her.

A quiet college town in the hills, a broad, shady street, a pleasant house standing in its own lawn, with trees and flowers about it. He had the address in his hand, and the number showed clear on the white gate. He walked up the straight gravel path and rang the bell. An elderly servant opened the door.

"Does Mrs. Marroner live here?"

"No, sir."

"This is number twenty-eight?"

"Yes, sir."

"Who does live here?"

"Miss Wheeling, sir."

Ah! Her maiden name. They had told him, but he had forgotten.

He stepped inside. "I would like to see her," he said.

He was ushered into a still parlor, cool and sweet with the scent of flowers, the flowers she had always loved best. It almost brought tears to his eyes. All their years of happiness rose in his mind again; the exquisite beginnings; the days of eager longing before she was really his; the deep, still beauty of her love.

Surely she would forgive him—she must forgive him. He would humble himself; he would tell her of his honest remorse—his absolute determination to be a different man.

Through the wide doorway there came in to him two women. One like a tall Madonna, bearing a baby in her arms:

Marion, calm, steady, definitely impersonal; nothing but a clear pallor to hint of inner stress.

Gerta, holding the child as a bulwark, with a new intelligence in her face, and her blue, adoring eyes fixed on her friend—not upon him.

He looked from one to the other dumbly.

And the woman who had been his wife asked quietly:

"What have you to say to us?"

1911

Finley Peter Dunne 1867–1936

Born to Irish immigrants on Chicago's West Side in 1867, Finley Peter Dunne began a career as a newspaperman in the city in 1884. After working on six different dailies, he settled in as the precocious editorial chair at the *Chicago Evening Post* in 1892. There, he imagined himself into the character of Martin Dooley, whose 750-word monologues (delivered to genial politician John McKenna or long-suffering millworker Malachi Hennessy) became a Chicago tradition. The last in a series of dialect experiments by his creator, Mr. Dooley succeeded Dunne's Colonel Malachi McNeery, a fictional downtown Chicago barkeeper who had become a popular *Post* feature during the World's Fair of 1893. Unlike the cosmopolitan McNeery, Mr. Dooley was placed on Chicago's South Side, in the Irish working-class neighborhood known as Bridgeport.

Between 1893 and 1900, when Dunne moved on to New York and a different sort of career as a satirist of our national life, some 300 Dooley pieces appeared in Chicago newspapers. Taken together, they form a coherent body of work, in which a vivid, detailed world comes into existence—that of Bridgeport, a self-contained immigrant culture with its own set of customs and ceremonies, and a social structure rooted in family, geography, and occupation.

The Chicago Dooley pieces contain

valuable chunks of social history and pioneering contributions to the development of literary realism in America. Dunne takes the late-nineteenth-century journalistic phenomenon of urban local color and extends it, through his feeling for place and community, to evoke Bridgeport as the most solidly realized ethnic neighborhood in nineteenth-century American literature. He takes the realist's faith in the common man as literary subject and creates sympathetic, dignified, even heroic characters, plausibly placed in a working-class immigrant neighborhood. And finally, place, community, and character are all embodied in the vernacular voice of a sixty-year-old, smiling public-house man, the first such dialect voice to transcend the stereotypes of "stage-Irish" ethnic humor. Throughout the 1890s, Mr. Dooley gave Chicagoans a weekly example of the potential for serious fiction of common speech and everyday life. In his way, Dunne was as much a trailblazer into the American city as a setting for literature as Theodore Dreiser or Stephen Crane. Actually, he adds a dimension lacking in the work of both of these better known writers. Unlike those archetypal lost souls in the alien city, Dreiser's Carrie Meeber and Crane's Maggie, Mr. Dooley is relatively comfortable in Bridgeport. He proves that the city can be a home.

Dunne's career took a sharp turn in 1898, when Mr. Dooley's satirical coverage of the Spanish-American War brought him to the attention of readers outside Chicago. Beginning with his scoop of "Cousin George" Dewey's victory at Manila, Mr. Dooley's reports of military and political bungling during the "splendid little war" were widely reprinted, and national syndication soon followed. By the time Dunne moved to New York in 1900, Mr. Dooley was the most popular figure in American journalism. From this point until World War I, Dunne's gadfly mind ranged over the spectrum of newsworthy events and characters, both national and international: from Teddy Roosevelt's health fads to Andrew Carnegie's passion for libraries; from the invariable silliness of politics to society doings at Newport; from the Boer and Boxer Rebellions abroad to the so-called Negro, Indian, and immigration problems in the United States.

Mr. Dooley's perspective was consistently skeptical and critical. The salutary effect of most pieces was the exposure of affectation and hypocrisy through undercutting humor and common sense. The most frequently quoted Dooleyisms indicate this thrust. Teddy Roosevelt's egocentric account of the Rough Riders is retitled, "Alone in Cuba." The rationale of American imperialists becomes "Hands acrost th' sea an' into somewan else's pocket." High Court solemnity is undercut with a memorable phrase: "America follows th' flag, but th' Supreme Court follows th' illiction returns." A fanatic is defined as "a man that does what he thinks th' Lord wud do if He knew th' facts iv th' case." Although he joined Ida Tarbell and Lincoln Steffens in taking over the *American Magazine* in 1906, Dunne was not himself a progressive reformer. He viewed the world as irrevocably fallen and unimprovable, and many Dooley pieces reflect their author's tendency toward fatalism. More pronounced in the early Chicago work than in the lighter national commentary, Dunne's darker side may be explained by his roots in the oppressed, colonized culture of Ireland and his journalist's education into the harsh realities of nineteenth-century urban life.

The pieces in this selection represent both Dunne's Chicago work—his pioneering realistic sketches of an urban ethnic community—and his national phase, which includes some of the best social and political commentary ever written in America.

Charles Fanning
Southern Illinois University at Carbondale

PRIMARY WORKS

Mr. Dooley in Peace and in War, 1898; *Mr. Dooley in the Hearts of His Countrymen,* 1899; *Mr. Dooley's Philosophy,* 1900; *Mr. Dooley's Opinions,* 1901; *Observations by Mr. Dooley,* 1902; *Dissertations by Mr. Dooley,* 1906; *Mr. Dooley Says,* 1910; *Mr. Dooley on Making a Will and Other Necessary Evils,* 1919; *Mr. Dooley and the Chicago Irish,* ed. Charles Fanning, 1987.

The Wanderers

[Mr. Dooley's version of the archetypal crossing narrative balances humor and pathos in a memorable short piece, a prose poem of the trauma of immigration by sea.

Dunne attempts to render Mr. Dooley's Irish brogue or accent by spelling words phonetically. Here is a brief key to some words he uses that may confuse a contemporary American reader: *iv* = of; *dure* = door; *sthrapping* = strapping; *dhrink* = drink; *say* = sea; *aise* = ease; *ivry* = every; *on'y* = only.]

"Poor la-ads, poor la-ads," said Mr. Dooley, putting aside his newspaper and rubbing his glasses. "'Tis a hard lot theirs, thim that go down into th' say in ships, as Shakespeare says. Ye niver see a storm on th' ocean? Iv coorse ye didn't. How cud ye, ye that was born away fr'm home? But I have, Jawn. May th' saints save me fr'm another! I come over in th' bowels iv a big crazy balloon iv a propeller, like wan iv thim ye see hooked up to Dempsey's dock, loaded with lumber an' slabs an' Swedes. We watched th' little ol' island fadin' away behind us, with th' sun sthrikin' th' white house-tops iv Queenstown[1] an' lightin' up th' chimbleys iv Martin Hogan's liquor store. Not wan iv us but had left near all we loved behind, an' sare a chance that we'd iver spoon th' stirabout out iv th' pot above th' ol' peat fire again. Yes, by dad, there was wan,—a lad fr'm th' County Roscommon.[2] Divvle th' tear he shed. But, whin we had parted fr'm land, he turns to me, an' says, 'Well, we're on our way,' he says. 'We are that,' says I. 'No chanst f'r thim to turn around an' go back,' he says. 'Divvle th' fut,' says I. 'Thin,' he says, raisin' his voice, 'to 'ell with th' Prince iv Wales,'[3] he says. 'To 'ell with him' he says.

"An' that was th' last we see of sky or sun f'r six days. That night come up th' divvle's own storm. Th' waves tore an' walloped th' ol' boat, an' th' wind howled, an' ye cud hear th' machinery snortin' beyant. Murther, but I was sick. Wan time th' ship 'd be settin' on its tail, another it'd be standin' on its head, thin rollin' over cow-like on th' side; an' ivry time it lurched me stummick lurched with it, an' I was tore an' rint an' racked till, if death come, it 'd found me willin'. An' th' Roscommon man,—glory be, but he was disthressed. He set on th' flure, with his hands on his belt an' his face

[1]Harbor village outside Cork City from which emigrant ships embarked. Original name was Cobh; renamed by the British in honor of Queen Victoria. Now called Cobh again.

[2]Irish county in the west midlands.

[3]Member of British royal family, traditionally heir to the throne.

as white as stone, an' rocked to an' fro. 'Ahoo,' he says, 'ahoo, but me insides has torn loose,' he says, 'an' are tumblin' around,' he says. 'Say a pather an' avy,'[4] says I, I was that mad f'r th' big bosthoon[5] f'r his blatherin' on th' flure. 'Say a pather an' avy,' I says; 'f'r ye're near to death's dure, avick.[6]' 'Am I?' says he, raising up. 'Thin,' he says, 'to 'ell with the whole rile fam'ly,' he says. Oh, he was a rebel!

"Through th' storm there was a babby cryin'. 'Twas a little wan, no more thin a year ol'; an' 'twas owned be a Tipp'rary man[7] who come fr'm near Clonmel,[8] a poor, weak, scarey-lookin' little divvle that lost his wife, an' see th' bailiff walk off with th' cow, an' thin see him come back again with th' process servers. An' so he was comin' over with th' babby, an' bein' mother an' father to it. He'd rock it be th' hour on his knees, an' talk dam nonsense to it, an' sing it songs, 'Aha, 'twas there I met a maiden down be th' tanyard side,' an' 'Th' Wicklow Mountaineer,' an' 'Th' Rambler fr'm Clare,' an' 'O'Donnel Aboo,'[9] croonin' thim in th' little babby's ears, an' payin' no attintion to th' poorin' thunder above his head, day an' night, day an' night, poor soul. An' th' babby cryin' out his heart, an' him settin' there with his eyes as red as his hair, an' makin' no kick, poor soul.

"But wan day th' ship settled down steady, an' ragin' stummicks with it; an' th' Roscommon man shakes himself, an' says, 'to 'ell with th' Prince iv Wales an' th' Dook iv Edinboroo,'[10] an' goes out. An' near all th' steerage followed; f'r th' storm had done its worst, an' gone on to throuble those that come afther, an' may th' divvle go with it. 'Twill be rest f'r that little Tipp'rary man; f'r th' waves was r-runnin' low an' peaceful, an' th' babby have sthopped cryin'.

"He had been settin' on a stool, but he come over to me. 'Th' storm,' says I, 'is over.' 'Yis,' says he, ''tis over.' ''Twas wild while it lasted,' says I. 'Ye may say so,' says he. 'Well, please Gawd,' says I, 'that it left none worse off thin us.' 'It blew ill f'r some an' aise f'r others,' says he. 'Th' babby is gone.'

"An' so it was, Jawn, f'r all his rockin' an' singin'. An' in th' avnin' they burried it over th' side into th' say, an' th' little Tipp'rary man wint up an' see thim do it. He see thim do it."

1895

The Popularity of Firemen

[A Chicago fire-fighting tragedy prompted this piece which opens with Mr. Dooley naming the four firemen who had died the day before in a downtown factory and warehouse blaze.]

[4]A Pater Noster (Our Father) and an Ave Maria (Hail Mary).
[5]A blunderer (Irish).
[6]My son (Irish).
[7]A man from County Tipperary in the southeast of Ireland.
[8]A town in County Tipperary.
[9]Traditional Irish songs.
[10]Member of British royalty.

"O'Donnell, Sherrick, Downs, Prendergast," Mr. Dooley repeated slowly. "Poor la-ads. Poor la-ads. Plaze Gawd, they wint to th' long home like thrue min. 'Tis good to read th' names, Jawn. Thanks be, we're not all in th' council.

"I knowed a man be th' name iv Clancy wanst, Jawn. He was fr'm th' County May-o,[1] but a good man f'r all that; an' whin he'd growed to be a big, sthrappin' fellow, he wint on to th' fire departmint. They'se an Irishman 'r two on th' fire departmint an' in th' army, too, Jawn, though ye'd think be hearin' some talk they was all runnin' prim'ries an' thryin' to be cinthral comitymen.[2] So ye wud. Ye niver hear iv thim on'y whin they die; an' thin, murther, what funerals they have!

"Well, this Clancy wint on th' fire departmint, an' they give him a place in thruck twinty-three. All th' r-road was proud iv him, an' faith he was proud iv himsilf. He r-rode free on th' sthreet ca-ars, an' was th' champeen handball player f'r miles around. Ye shud see him goin' down th' sthreet, with his blue shirt an' his blue coat with th' buttons on it, an' his cap on his ear. But ne'er a cap or coat'd he wear whin they was a fire. He might be shiv'rin' be th' stove in th' ingine house with a buffalo robe over his head; but, whin th' gong sthruck, 'twas off with coat an' cap an' buffalo robe, an' out come me brave Clancy, bare-headed an' bare hand, dhrivin' with wan line an' spillin' th' hose cart on wan wheel at ivry jump iv th' horse. Did anny wan iver see a fireman with his coat on or a polisman with his off? Why, wanst, whin Clancy was standin' up f'r Grogan's eighth,[3] his son come runnin' in to tell him they was a fire in Vogel's packin' house. He dhropped th' kid at Father Kelly's feet, an' whipped off his long coat an' wint tearin' f'r th' dure, kickin' over th' poorbox an' buttin' ol' Mis' O'Neill that'd come in to say th' stations. 'Twas lucky 'twas wan iv th' Grogans. They're a fine family f'r falls. Jawn Grogan was wurrukin' on th' top iv Metzri an' O'Connell's brewery wanst, with a man be th' name iv Dorsey. He slipped an' fell wan hundherd feet. Whin they come to see if he was dead, he got up, an' says he: 'Lave me at him.' 'At who?' says they. 'He's deliryous,' they says. 'At Dorsey,' says Grogan. 'He thripped me.' So it didn't hurt Grogan's eighth to fall four 'r five feet.

"Well, Clancy wint to fires an' fires. Whin th' big organ facthry burnt, he carrid th' hose up to th' fourth story an' was squirtin' whin th' walls fell. They dug him out with pick an' shovel, an' he come up fr'm th' brick an' boards an' saluted th' chief. 'Clancy,' says th' chief, 'ye betther go over an' get a dhrink.' He did so, Jawn. I heerd it. An' Clancy was that proud!

"Whin th' Hogan flats on Halsted Sthreet[4] took fire, they got all th' people out but wan; an' she was a woman asleep on th' fourth flure. 'Who'll go up?' says Bill Musham. 'Sure, sir,' says Clancy. 'I'll go'; an' up he wint. His captain was a man be th' name iv O'Connell, fr'm th' County Kerry;[5] an' he had his fut on th' ladder whin Clancy started. Well, th' good man wint into th' smoke, with his wife faintin' down below. 'He'll be kilt,' says his brother. 'Ye don't know him,' says Bill Musham. An' sure enough, whin ivry wan'd give him up, out comes me brave Clancy, as black as a Turk, with th' girl in his arms. Th' others wint up like monkeys, but he shtud wavin'

[1]Irish county on the west coast.

[2]Central committeeman; an important post in the ward system of city government.

[3]Being a godfather at a new child's baptism in Church.

[4]A major north-south Chicago street and one of the main streets in the Bridgeport neighborhood.

[5]Irish county on the southwest coast.

thim off, an' come down th' ladder face forward. 'Where'd ye larn that?' says Bill Musham. 'I seen a man do it at th' Lyceem[6] whin I was a kid,' says Clancy. 'Was it all right?' 'I'll have ye up before th' ol' man,' says Bill Musham. 'I'll teach ye to come down a laddher as if ye was in a quadhrille, ye horse-stealin', ham-sthringin' May-o man,' he says. But he didn't. Clancy wint over to see his wife. 'O Mike,' says she, ''twas fine,' she says. 'But why d'ye take th' risk?' she says. 'Did ye see th' captain?' he says with a scowl. 'He wanted to go. Did ye think I'd follow a Kerry man with all th' ward lukkin' on?' he says.

"Well, so he wint dhrivin' th' hose-cart on wan wheel, an' jumpin' whin he heerd a man so much as hit a glass to make it ring. All th' people looked up to him, an' th' kids followed him down th' sthreet; an' 'twas th' gr-reatest priv'lige f'r anny wan f'r to play dominos with him near th' joker. But about a year ago he come in to see me, an' says he, 'Well, I'm goin' to quit.' 'Why,' says I, 'ye'er a young man yet,' I says. 'Faith,' he says, 'look at me hair,' he says,—'young heart, ol' head. I've been at it these twinty year, an' th' good woman's wantin' to see more iv me thin blowin' into a saucer iv coffee,' he says. 'I'm goin' to quit,' he says, 'on'y I want to see wan more good fire,' he says. 'A rale good ol' hot wan,' he says, 'with th' win' blowin' f'r it an' a good dhraft in th' ilivator-shaft, an' about two stories, with pitcher-frames an' gasoline an' excelsior, an' to hear th' chief yellin': "Play 'way, sivinteen. What th' hell an' damnation are ye standin' aroun' with that pipe f'r? Is this a fire 'r a dam livin' pitcher? I'll break ivry man iv eighteen, four, six, an' chem'cal five to-morrah mornin' befure breakfast." Oh,' he says, bringin' his fist down, 'wan more, an' I'll quit.'

"An' he did, Jawn. Th' day th' Carpenter Brothers' box factory burnt. 'Twas wan iv thim big, fine-lookin' buildings that pious men built out iv celluloid an' plasther iv Paris. An' Clancy was wan iv th' men undher whin th' wall fell. I seen thim bringin' him home; an' th' little woman met him at th' dure, rumplin' her apron in her hands."

1895

The Piano in the Parlor

[In 1890 Edward Harrigan produced a popular musical, *Reilly and the Four Hundred,* about the social pretensions of the "lace curtain" Irish of the new middle class. The show's hit song applies to this Dooley piece: "There's an organ in the parlor, to give the house a tone,/ And you're welcome every evening at Maggie Murphy's home." Here the family conflict between traditional Irish music and tonier classical music indicates the gulf between old and new ways.]

"Ol' man Donahue bought Molly a pianny las' week," Mr. Dooley said in the course of his conversation with Mr. McKenna. "She'd been takin' lessons fr'm a Dutchman

[6]Lyceum; a hall in which public performances are presented.

down th' sthreet, an' they say she can play as aisy with her hands crossed as she can with wan finger. She's been whalin' away iver since, an' Donahue is dhrinkin' again.

"Ye see th' other night some iv th' la-ads wint over f'r to see whether they cud smash his table in a frindly game iv forty-fives. I don't know what possessed Donahue. He niver asked his frinds into the parlor befure. They used to set in th' dining-room; an', whin Mrs. Donahue coughed at iliven o'clock, they'd toddle out th' side dure with their hats in their hands. But this here night, whether 'twas that Donahue had taken on a tub or two too much or not, he asked thim all in th' front room, where Mrs. Donahue was settin' with Molly. 'I've brought me frinds,' he says, 'f'r to hear Molly take a fall out iv th' music-box,' he says. 'Let me have ye'er hat, Mike,' he says. 'Ye'll not feel it whin ye go out,' he says.

"At anny other time Mrs. Donahue'd give him th' marble heart. But they wasn't a man in th' party that had a pianny to his name, an' she knew they'd be throuble whin they wint home an' tould about it. ''Tis a melodjious insthrument,' says she. 'I cud sit here be the hour an' listen to Bootoven and Choochooski,'[1] she says.

"'What did thim write?' says Cassidy. 'Chunes,'[2] says Donahue, 'chunes. Molly,' he says, 'fetch 'er th' wallop to make th' gintlemen feel good,' he says. 'What'll it be, la-ads?' 'D'ye know "The Rambler fr'm Clare"?'[3] says Slavin. 'No,' says Molly. 'It goes like this,' says Slavin. 'A-ah, din yadden, yooden a-yadden, arrah yadden ay-a.' 'I dinnaw it,' says th' girl. ''Tis a low chune, annyhow,' says Mrs. Donahue. 'Misther Slavin ividintly thinks he's at a polis picnic,' she says. 'I'll have no come-all-ye's in this house,' she says. 'Molly, give us a few ba-ars fr'm Wagner.'[4] 'What Wagner's that?' says Flanagan. 'No wan ye know,' says Donahue; 'he's a German musician.' 'Thim Germans is hot people f'r music,' says Cassidy. 'I knowed wan that cud play th' "Wacht am Rhine"[5] on a pair iv cymbals,' he says. 'Whisht!' says Donahue. 'Give th' girl a chanst.'

"Slavin tol' me about it. He says he niver heerd th' like in his born days. He says she fetched th' pianny two or three wallops that made Cassidy jump out iv his chair, an' Cassidy has charge iv th' steam whistle at th' quarry at that. She wint at it as though she had a gredge at it. First 'twas wan hand an' thin th' other, thin both hands, knuckles down; an' it looked, says Slavin, as if she was goin' to leap into th' middle iv it with both feet, whin Donahue jumps up. 'Hol' on!' he says. 'That's not a rented pianny, ye daft girl,' he says. 'Why, pap-pah,' says Molly, 'what d'ye mean?' she says. 'That's Wagner,' she says. ''Tis th' music iv th' future,' she says. 'Yes,' says Donahue, 'but I don't want me hell on earth. I can wait f'r it,' he says, 'with th' kind permission iv Mrs. Donahue,' he says. 'Play us th' "Wicklow Mountaineer,"'[6] he says, 'an' threat th' masheen kindly,' he says. 'She'll play no "Wicklow Mountaineer,"' says Mrs. Donahue. 'If ye want to hear that kind iv chune, ye can go down to Finucane's Hall,'[7] she says, 'an' call in Crowley, th' blind piper,' she says. 'Molly,' she says, 'give us wan iv thim Choochooski things,' she says. 'They're so ginteel.'

[1]Beethoven and Tchaikovsky, composers.
[2]Tunes (dialect).
[3]Traditional Irish song.
[4]Richard Wagner, German composer (1813–1883).
[5]Popular German patriotic anthem.
[6]Traditional Irish song.
[7]A real hall in the Bridgeport neighborhood where many public meetings were held. Owned by the Finucane family.

"With that Donahue rose up. 'Come on,' says he. 'This is no place f'r us,' he says. Slavin, with th' politeness iv a man who's gettin' even, turns at th' dure. 'I'm sorry I can't remain,' he says. 'I think th' wurruld an' all iv Choochooski,' he says. 'Me brother used to play his chunes,' he says,—'me brother Mike, that run th' grip ca-ar,' he says. 'But there's wan thing missin' fr'm Molly's playin',' he says. 'And what may that be?' says Mrs. Donahue. 'An ax,' says Slavin, backin' out.

"So Donahue has took to dhrink."

1895

Immigration

[Senator Henry Cabot Lodge was a vocal advocate of immigration restrictions. As a first step in this direction, he proposed a literacy test for immigrants as early as 1896.]

"Well, I see Congress has got to wurruk again," said Mr. Dooley.

"The Lord save us fr'm harm," said Mr. Hennessy.

"Yes, sir," said Mr. Dooley, "Congress has got to wurruk again, an' manny things that seems important to a Congressman 'll be brought up befure thim. 'Tis sthrange that what's a big thing to a man in Wash'nton, Hinnissy, don't seem much account to me. Divvle a bit do I care whether they dig th' Nicaragoon Canal[1] or cross th' Isthmus in a balloon; or whether th' Monroe docthrine[2] is enfoorced or whether it ain't; or whether th' thrusts is abolished as Teddy Rosenfelt wud like to have thim or encouraged to go on with their neefaryous but magnificent entherprises as th' Prisidint wud like; or whether th' water is poured into th' ditches to reclaim th' arid lands iv th' West or th' money f'r thim to fertilize th' arid pocket-books iv th' conthractors; or whether th' Injun is threated like a depindant an' miserable thribesman or like a free an' indepindant dog; or whether we restore th' merchant marine to th' ocean or whether we lave it to restore itsilf. None iv these here questions inthrests me, an' be me I mane you an' be you I mane ivrybody. What we want to know is, ar-re we goin' to have coal enough in th' hod whin th' cold snap comes; will th' plumbin' hold out, an' will th' job last.

"But they'se wan question that Congress is goin' to take up that you an' me are intherested in. As a pilgrim father that missed th' first boats, I must raise me claryon voice again' th' invasion iv this fair land be th' paupers an' arnychists iv effete Europe. Ye bet I must—because I'm here first. 'Twas diff'rent whin I was dashed high on th' stern an' rockbound coast. In thim days America was th' refuge iv th' oppressed iv all

[1] In 1901 a U.S. Canal Commission decided that a route through Nicaragua was the most practical. In 1903, the route through the Isthmus of Panama was chosen instead. Work on the Panama Canal began in 1905.

[2] President James Monroe in 1823 declared U.S. opposition to European political interference in the Americas.

th' wurruld. They cud come over here an' do a good job iv oppressin' thimsilves. As I told ye I come a little late. Th' Rosenfelts an' th' Lodges[3] bate me be at laste a boat lenth, an' be th' time I got here they was stern an' rockbound thimsilves. So I got a gloryous rayciption as soon as I was towed off th' rocks. Th' stars an' sthripes whispered a welcome in th' breeze an' a shovel was thrust into me hand an' I was pushed into a sthreet excyvatin' as though I'd been born here. Th' pilgrim father who bossed th' job was a fine ol' puritan be th' name iv Doherty, who come over in th' Mayflower about th' time iv th' potato rot in Wexford, an' he made me think they was a hole in th' breakwather iv th' haven iv refuge an' some iv th' wash iv th' seas iv opprission had got through. He was a stern an' rockbound la-ad himsilf, but I was a good hand at loose stones an' wan day—but I'll tell ye about that another time.

"Annyhow, I was rayceived with open arms that sometimes ended in a clinch. I was afraid I wasn't goin' to assimilate with th' airlyer pilgrim fathers an' th' instichoochions iv th' counthry, but I soon found that a long swing iv th' pick made me as good as another man an' it didn't require a gr-reat intellect, or sometimes anny at all, to vote th' dimmycrat ticket, an' befure I was here a month, I felt enough like a native born American to burn a witch. Wanst in a while a mob iv intilligint collajeens, whose grandfathers had bate me to th' dock, wud take a shy at me Pathrick's Day procission[4] or burn down wan iv me churches, but they got tired iv that befure long; 'twas too much like wurruk.

"But as I tell ye, Hinnissy, 'tis diff'rent now. I don't know why 'tis diff'rent but 'tis diff'rent. 'Tis time we put our back again' th' open dure an' keep out th' savage horde. If that cousin iv ye'ers expects to cross, he'd betther tear f'r th' ship. In a few minyits th' gates 'll be down an' whin th' oppressed wurruld comes hikin' acrost to th' haven iv refuge, they'll do well to put a couplin' pin undher their hats, f'r th' Goddess iv Liberty 'll meet thim at th' dock with an axe in her hand. Congress is goin' to fix it. Me frind Shaughnessy says so. He was in yisterdah an' says he: "Tis time we done something to make th' immigration laws sthronger,' says he. 'Thrue f'r ye, Miles Standish,'[5] says I; 'but what wud ye do?' 'I'd keep out th' offscourin's iv Europe,' says he. 'Wud ye go back?' says I. 'Have ye'er joke,' says he. "Tis not so seeryus as it was befure ye come,' says I. 'But what ar-re th' immygrants doin' that's roonous to us?' I says. 'Well,' says he, 'they're arnychists,'[6] he says; 'they don't assymilate with th' counthry,' he says. 'Maybe th' counthry's digestion has gone wrong fr'm too much rich food,' says I; 'perhaps now if we'd lave off thryin' to digest Rockyfellar an' thry a simple diet like Schwartzmeister, we wudden't feel th' effects iv our vittels,' I says. 'Maybe if we'd season th' immygrants a little or cook thim thurly, they'd go down betther,' I says.

"'They're arnychists, like Parsons,'[7] he says. 'He wud've been an immygrant if

[3]Powerful Massachusetts political family. Henry Cabot Lodge (1850–1924) was a U.S. Senator during this period who supported immigration restriction.

[4]Oppose the St. Patrick's Day parade by force.

[5]A military and political leader of the 1620 Pilgrim settlement at Plymouth, Massachusetts.

[6]Anarchists. A late nineteenth-century movement holding the belief that the political state should be abolished and that society should be governed by voluntary groups. The movement's violent wing came to the fore in the 1886 Haymarket Square bombing in Chicago and in the 1901 assassination of President William McKinley.

[7]Albert Parsons, American anarchist, hanged for his role in the Haymarket bombing in which seven policemen died.

Texas hadn't been admitted to th' Union,' I says. 'Or Snolgosh,'[8] he says. 'Has Mitchigan seceded?' I says. 'Or Gittoo,'[9] he says. 'Who come fr'm th' effete monarchies iv Chicago, west iv Ashland Av'noo,'[10] I says. 'Or what's-his-name, Wilkes Booth,'[11] he says. 'I don't know what he was—maybe a Boolgharyen,' says I. 'Well, annyhow,' says he, 'they're th' scum iv th' earth.' 'They may be that,' says I; 'but we used to think they was th' cream iv civilization,' I says. 'They're off th' top annyhow. I wanst believed 'twas th' best men iv Europe come here, th' la-ads that was too sthrong and indepindant to be kicked around be a boorgomasther at home an' wanted to dig out f'r a place where they cud get a chanst to make their way to th' money. I see their sons fightin' into politics an' their daughters tachin' young American idee how to shoot too high in th' public school, an' I thought they was all right. But I see I was wrong. Thim boys out there towin' wan heavy foot afther th' other to th' rowlin' mills is all arnychists. There's warrants out f'r all names endin' in 'inski, an' I think I'll board up me windows, f'r,' I says, 'if immygrants is as dangerous to this counthry as ye an' I an' other pilgrim fathers believe they are, they'se enough iv thim sneaked in already to make us aborigines about as infloointial as the prohibition vote in th' Twinty-ninth Ward.[12] They'll dash again' our stern an' rock-bound coast till they bust it,' says I.

"'But I ain't so much afraid as ye ar-re. I'm not afraid iv me father an' I'm not afraid iv mesilf. An' I'm not afraid iv Schwartzmeister's father or Hinnery Cabin Lodge's grandfather. We all come over th' same way, an' if me ancestors were not what Hogan calls rigicides, 'twas not because they were not ready an' willin', on'y a king niver come their way. I don't believe in killin' kings, mesilf. I niver wud've sawed th' block off that curly-headed potintate that I see in th' pitchers down town, but, be hivins, Presarved Codfish Shaughnessy,[13] if we'd begun a few years ago shuttin' out folks that wudden't mind handin' a bomb to a king, they wudden't be enough people in Mattsachoosetts to make a quorum f'r th' Anti-Impeeryal S'ciety,' says I. 'But what wud ye do with th' offscourin' iv Europe?' says he. 'I'd scour thim some more,' says I.

"An' so th' meetin' iv th' Plymouth Rock Assocyation come to an end. But if ye wud like to get it together, Deacon Hinnissy, to discuss th' immygration question, I'll sind out a hurry call f'r Schwartzmeister[14] an' Mulcahey an' Ignacio Sbarbaro an' Nels Larsen an' Petrus Gooldvink, an' we 'll gather to-night at Fanneilnoviski Hall[15] at th' corner iv Sheridan an' Sigel shtreets. All th' pilgrim fathers is rayquested f'r to bring interpreters."

"Well," said Mr. Hennessy, "divvle th' bit I care, on'y I'm here first, an' I ought to have th' right to keep th' bus fr'm bein' overcrowded."

[8]Leon Czolgosz, anarchist and the assassin of President McKinley in September, 1901.

[9]Charles J. Guiteau, a disappointed office-seeker who fatally wounded President James A. Garfield in July, 1881.

[10]Ashland Avenue, a major Chicago north-south street.

[11]John Wilkes-Booth, assassin of President Abraham Lincoln in 1865.

[12]Voters in favor of the amendment prohibiting sale of alcoholic beverages.

[13]A playful juxtaposition of parodic W.A.S.P. names with an Irish last name.

[14]A mix of names illustrating the ethnic diversity of Chicago.

[15]Connotes the Europeanization of Faneuil Hall, the Boston cradle of liberty.

"Well," said Mr. Dooley, "as a pilgrim father on me gran' nephew's side, I don't know but ye're right. An' they'se wan sure way to keep thim out."

"What's that?" asked Mr. Hennessy.

"Teach thim all about our instichoochions befure they come," said Mr. Dooley.

1902

Upton Sinclair 1878–1968

A savage indictment of wage slavery and of the unsanitary and harrowing conditions in the Chicago meatpacking industry, as well as a call for socialism as the only means by which to end the exploitation of the working class in an industrial society, Upton Sinclair's *The Jungle* has been one of the most widely read of American novels. In its own day it was responsible for federal legislation to correct some of the worst abuses in the meatpacking industry, and since then, widely translated, it has offered an image of America that other cultures have found profoundly significant.

Sinclair was born in Baltimore and raised in New York City, where he attended City College of New York and Columbia University. Before he was twenty he had begun supporting himself by selling juvenile fiction to various magazines and newspapers, and by 1900 he had given up his academic study to become a full-time writer. His first four novels were sentimental and immature, but in 1904 he published *Manassas,* a neo-abolitionist novel about the Civil War that marked an important step in Sinclair's development as a writer—his shift to the historical novel. In the summer of 1904 Sinclair became an official member of the Socialist Party of America, then in the decade of its greatest success. Later that same year Fred D. Warren, the editor of *Appeal to Reason,* a weekly socialist journal published in Kansas, challenged Sinclair to write a novel dealing with contemporary wage slavery as opposed to the antebellum slavery he had written about in *Manassas.* Sinclair accepted the challenge, and a $500 offer for the serial rights to his new novel, then traveled to the stockyards of Chicago, where he lived for seven weeks in November and December of 1904 while he investigated the conditions of the men and women who lived and worked in Packingtown. When *The Jungle* was released in book form on January 25, 1906, its impact was immediate. Meat sales sharply declined, and President Theodore Roosevelt, after inviting Sinclair to the White House, ordered an investigation of the meatpacking industry that in turn led Congress to pass the Beef Inspection Act and the nation's first Pure Food and Drug Act. Ironically, readers of the novel tended to focus on the vivid, often gruesome descriptions of the meatpacking industry rather than on the plea for socialism that Sinclair included in his final chapters. "I aimed at the public's heart, and by accident hit it in the stomach," Sinclair observed. This, despite the fact that Sinclair cut the original version of the novel, which had appeared in serial form in a socialist journal in 1905, by one-third in order to make it more palatable to a mass audience.

The Jungle follows the shifting fortunes of Jurgis Rudkus and his family, Lithuanian peasants who immigrate to Chicago and find employment in Packingtown. The novel describes the horrifying working conditions in the industries in Packingtown and the family's gradual disintegration, including Jurgis's imprisonment for attacking a man who seduces his wife, the family's loss of their house, the deaths of Jurgis's wife and son, and his own impoverished and hopeless drifting from city to city. In the novel's final chapters, however, Sinclair introduces Jurgis to socialism, and through his involvement with the socialist movement Jurgis becomes a "new man," who finds himself at long last "delivered from the thralldom of despair." The famous last line of *The Jungle*—"CHICAGO WILL BE OURS!"—refers to the widespread socialist gains in the 1904 elections.

The Jungle's flaws are obvious; it is openly didactic; its plot is melodramatic; its characters often lack psychological complexity; and its style is heavy and redundant with detail. However, as a muckraking novel that documented and exposed working conditions in the Chicago stockyards, and as a political novel that illustrated the industrial exploitation of immigrants like the Rudkus family, *The Jungle* possesses a raw emotional power that is undiminished in the ninety years since its publication. Sinclair's other major novels, all written in the form he referred to as the "contemporary historical novel," possess the same strengths and weaknesses as *The Jungle*. *King Coal* (1917) concerns the Colorado mine wars of 1913–1914; *Oil* (1927) the Teapot Dome Scandal; and *Boston* (1928) the Sacco and Vanzetti executions. His "Lanny Budd" series, 1940–1949, for one volume of which he won the Pulitzer Prize in 1946, was his personal interpretation of the two World Wars. The historical fictions of later American writers, especially John Steinbeck and John Dos Passos, show the influence of Sinclair.

Throughout his long career, Sinclair remained a passionate critic of the social and political inequities of modern capitalism. His political efforts often extended outside the realm of literature, as, for instance, when in 1906 he founded Helicon Hall, an experiment in cooperative living, and when in 1934 he ran as the Democratic candidate for governor of California on his EPIC ("End Poverty in California") platform. By the time Sinclair died in 1968 at the age of ninety, he had published over fifty novels and twenty books of nonfiction.

James C. Wilson
University of Cincinnati

PRIMARY WORKS

The Jungle, 1906; *King Coal,* 1917; *The Profits of Religion,* 1918; *The Brass Check: A Study of American Journalism,* 1919; *Oil,* 1927; *Boston,* 1928.

from The Jungle

from Chapter II

Jurgis[1] talked lightly about work, because he was young. They told him stories about the breaking down of men, there in the stockyards of Chicago,[2] and of what had happened to them afterwards—stories to make your flesh creep, but Jurgis would only

[1]Jurgis Rudkus and his wife, Ona Lukoszaite, are young Lithuanian immigrants who have moved with their families to Chicago. Jurgis (pronounced *Yoorghis*), the central character in *The Jungle,* has found work in the stockyards of Chicago.

[2]Located on the south side of Chicago, the stockyards (founded 1865) include some of the largest slaughterhouses and meat-processing facilities in the world.

laugh. He had only been there four months, and he was young, and a giant besides. There was too much health in him. He could not even imagine how it would feel to be beaten. "That is well enough for men like you," he would say, "*silpnas,* puny fellows—but my back is broad."

Jurgis was like a boy, a boy from the country. He was the sort of man the bosses like to get hold of, the sort they make it a grievance they cannot get hold of. When he was told to go to a certain place, he would go there on the run. When he had nothing to do for the moment, he would stand round fidgeting, dancing, with the overflow of energy that was in him. If he were working in a line of men, the line always moved too slowly for him, and you could pick him out by his impatience and restlessness. That was why he had been picked out on one important occasion; for Jurgis had stood outside of Brown and Company's "Central Time Station" not more than half an hour, the second day of his arrival in Chicago, before he had been beckoned by one of the bosses. Of this he was very proud, and it made him more disposed than ever to laugh at the pessimists. In vain would they all tell him that there were men in that crowd from which he had been chosen who had stood there a month—yes, many months—and not been chosen yet. "Yes," he would say, "but what sort of men? Broken-down tramps and good-for-nothings, fellows who have spent all their money drinking, and want to get more for it. Do you want me to believe that with these arms"—and he would clench his fists and hold them up in the air, so that you might see the rolling muscles—"that with these arms people will ever let me starve?"

"It is plain," they would answer to this, "that you have come from the country, and from very far in the country." And this was the fact, for Jurgis had never seen a city, and scarcely even a fair-sized town, until he had set out to make his fortune in the world and earn his right to Ona. His father, and his father's father before him, and as many ancestors back as legend could go, had lived in that part of Lithuania known as *Brelovicz,* the Imperial Forest.[3] This is a great tract of a hundred thousand acres, which from time immemorial has been a hunting preserve of the nobility. There are a very few peasants settled in it, holding title from ancient times; and one of these was Antanas Rudkus, who had been reared himself, and had reared his children in turn, upon half a dozen acres of cleared land in the midst of a wilderness. There had been one son besides Jurgis, and one sister. The former had been drafted into the army; that had been over ten years ago, but since that day nothing had ever been heard of him. The sister was married, and her husband had bought the place when old Antanas had decided to go with his son.

It was nearly a year and a half ago that Jurgis had met Ona, at a horse-fair a hundred miles from home. Jurgis had never expected to get married—he had laughed at it as a foolish trap for a man to walk into; but here, without ever having spoken a word to her, with no more than the exchange of half a dozen smiles, he found himself, purple in the face with embarrassment and terror, asking her parents to sell her to him for his wife—and offering his father's two horses he had been sent to the fair to sell. But Ona's father proved as a rock—the girl was yet a child, and he was a rich man, and his daughter was not to be had in that way. So Jurgis went home with a heavy heart, and that spring and summer toiled and tried hard to forget. In the fall,

[3]Apparently in the southeastern, heavily forested part of Lithuania. Located on the Baltic Sea just north of Poland, Lithuania was one of the component republics of the U.S.S.R. from 1940 to 1990. Lithuania has been an independent nation since March, 1990.

after the harvest was over, he saw that it would not do, and tramped the full fortnight's journey that lay between him and Ona.

He found an unexpected state of affairs—for the girl's father had died, and his estate was tied up with creditors; Jurgis's heart leaped as he realized that now the prize was within his reach. There was Elzbieta Lukoszaite, Teta, or Aunt, as they called her, Ona's stepmother, and there were her six children, of all ages. There was also her brother Jonas, a dried-up little man who had worked upon the farm. They were people of great consequence, as it seemed to Jurgis, fresh out of the woods; Ona knew how to read, and knew many other things that he did not know; and now the farm had been sold, and the whole family was adrift—all they owned in the world being about seven hundred roubles, which is half as many dollars. They would have had three times that, but it had gone to court, and the judge had decided against them, and it had cost the balance to get him to change his decision.

Ona might have married and left them, but she would not, for she loved Teta Elzbieta. It was Jonas who suggested that they all go to America, where a friend of his had gotten rich. He would work, for his part, and the women would work, and some of the children, doubtless—they would live somehow. Jurgis, too, had heard of America. That was a country where, they said, a man might earn three roubles a day; and Jurgis figured what three roubles a day would mean, with prices as they were where he lived, and decided forthwith that he would go to America and marry, and be a rich man in the bargain. In that country, rich or poor, a man was free, it was said; he did not have to go into the army, he did not have to pay out his money to rascally officials,—he might do as he pleased, and count himself as good as any other man. So America was a place of which lovers and young people dreamed. If one could only manage to get the price of a passage, he could count his troubles at an end.

It was arranged that they should leave the following spring, and meantime Jurgis sold himself to a contractor for a certain time, and tramped nearly four hundred miles from home with a gang of men to work upon a railroad in Smolensk.[4] This was a fearful experience, with filth and bad food and cruelty and overwork; but Jurgis stood it and came out in fine trim, and with eighty roubles sewed up in his coat. He did not drink or fight, because he was thinking all the time of Ona; and for the rest, he was a quiet, steady man, who did what he was told to, did not lose this temper often, and when he did lose it made the offender anxious that he should not lose it again. When they paid him off he dodged the company gamblers and dramshops, and so they tried to kill him; but he escaped, and tramped it home, working at odd jobs, and sleeping always with one eye open.

So in the summer time they had all set out for America. At the last moment there joined them Marija Berczynskas, who was a cousin of Ona's. Marija was an orphan, and had worked since childhood for a rich farmer of Vilna, who beat her regularly. It was only at the age of twenty that it had occurred to Marija to try her strength, when she had risen up and nearly murdered the man, and then come away.

There were twelve in all in the party, five adults and six children—and Ona, who was a little of both. They had a hard time on the passage; there was an agent who helped them, but he proved a scoundrel, and got them into a trap with some

[4]A city about 220 miles southwest of Moscow. One of Russia's oldest cities, Smolensk is a port on the Dnieper River and an important railroad junction and distribution point for the region's agricultural products.

officials, and cost them a good deal of their precious money, which they clung to with such horrible fear. This happened to them again in New York—for, of course, they knew nothing about the country, and had no one to tell them, and it was easy for a man in a blue uniform to lead them away, and to take them to a hotel and keep them there, and make them pay enormous charges to get away. The law says that the rate-card shall be on the door of a hotel, but it does not say that it shall be in Lithuanian.

It was in the stockyards that Jonas's friend had gotten rich, and so to Chicago the party was bound. They knew that one word, Chicago,—and that was all they needed to know, at least, until they reached the city. Then, tumbled out of the cars without ceremony, they were no better off than before; they stood staring down the vista of Dearborn Street, with its big black buildings towering in the distance, unable to realize that they had arrived, and why, when they said "Chicago," people no longer pointed in some direction, but instead looked perplexed, or laughed, or went on without paying any attention. They were pitiable in their helplessness; above all things they stood in deadly terror of any sort of person in official uniform, and so whenever they saw a policeman they would cross the street and hurry by. For the whole of the first day they wandered about in the midst of deafening confusion, utterly lost; and it was only at night that, cowering in the doorway of a house, they were finally discovered and taken by a policeman to the station. In the morning an interpreter was found, and they were taken and put upon a car, and taught a new word—"stockyards." Their delight at discovering that they were to get out of this adventure without losing another share of their possessions, it would not be possible to describe.

They sat and stared out of the window. They were on a street which seemed to run on forever, mile after mile—thirty-four of them, if they had known it—and each side of it one uninterrupted row of wretched little two-story frame buildings. Down every side street they could see, it was the same,—never a hill and never a hollow, but always the same endless vista of ugly and dirty little wooden buildings. Here and there would be a bridge crossing a filthy creek, with hard-baked mud shores and dingy sheds and docks along it; here and there would be a railroad crossing, with a tangle of switches, and locomotives puffing, and rattling freight-cars filing by; here and there would be a great factory, a dingy building with innumerable windows in it, and immense volumes of smoke pouring from the chimneys, darkening the air above and making filthy the earth beneath. But after each of these interruptions, the desolate procession would begin again—the procession of dreary little buildings.

A full hour before the party reached the city they had begun to note the perplexing changes in the atmosphere. It grew darker all the time, and upon the earth the grass seemed to grow less green. Every minute, as the train sped on, the colors of things became dingier; the fields were grown parched and yellow, the landscape hideous and bare. And along with the thickening smoke they began to notice another circumstance, a strange, pungent odor. They were not sure that it was unpleasant, this odor; some might have called it sickening, but their taste in odors was not developed, and they were only sure that it was curious. Now, sitting in the trolley car, they realized that they were on their way to the home of it—that they had travelled all the way from Lithuania to it. It was now no longer something far-off and faint, that you caught in whiffs; you could literally taste it, as well as smell it—you could take hold of it, almost, and examine it at your leisure. They were divided in their opinions about it. It was an elemental odor, raw and crude; it was rich, almost rancid, sensual, and strong. There were some who drank it in as if it were an intoxicant; there were others who put their handkerchiefs to their faces. The new emigrants were still tasting it, lost in wonder, when suddenly the car came to a halt, and the door was flung open, and a voice shouted—"Stockyards!"

They were left standing upon the corner, staring; down a side street there were two rows of brick houses, and between them a vista: half a dozen chimneys, tall as the tallest of buildings, touching the very sky—and leaping from them half a dozen columns of smoke, thick, oily, and black as night. It might have come from the centre of the world, this smoke, where the fires of the ages still smoulder. It came as if self-impelled, driving all before it, a perpetual explosion. It was inexhaustible; one stared, waiting to see it stop, but still the great streams rolled out. They spread in vast clouds overhead, writhing, curling; then, uniting in one giant river, they streamed away down the sky, stretching a black pall as far as the eye could reach.

Then the party became aware of another strange thing. This, too, like the odor, was a thing elemental; it was a sound, a sound made up of ten thousand little sounds. You scarcely noticed it at first—it sunk into your consciousness, a vague disturbance, a trouble. It was like the murmuring of the bees in the spring, the whisperings of the forest; it suggested endless activity, the rumblings of a world in motion. It was only by an effort that one could realize that it was made by animals, that it was the distant lowing of ten thousand cattle, the distant grunting of ten thousand swine.

They would have liked to follow it up, but, alas, they had no time for adventures just then. The policeman on the corner was beginning to watch them; and so, as usual, they started up the street. Scarcely had they gone a block, however, before Jonas was heard to give a cry, and began pointing excitedly across the street. Before they could gather the meaning of his breathless ejaculations he had bounded away, and they saw him enter a shop, over which was a sign: "J. Szedvilas, Delicatessen." When he came out again it was in company with a very stout gentleman in shirt sleeves and an apron, clasping Jonas by both hands and laughing hilariously. Then Teta Elzbieta recollected suddenly that Szedvilas had been the name of the mythical friend who had made his fortune in America. To find that he had been making it in the delicatessen business was an extraordinary piece of good fortune at this juncture; though it was well on in the morning, they had not breakfasted, and the children were beginning to whimper.

Thus was the happy ending of a woeful voyage. The two families literally fell upon each other's necks—for it had been years since Jokubas Szedvilas had met a man from his part of Lithuania. Before half the day they were lifelong friends. Jokubas understood all the pitfalls of this new world, and could explain all of its mysteries; he could tell them the things they ought to have done in the different emergencies—and what was still more to the point, he could tell them what to do now. He would take them to poni Aniele, who kept a boarding-house the other side of the yards; old Mrs. Jukniene, he explained, had not what one would call choice accommodations, but they might do for the moment. To this Teta Elzbieta hastened to respond that nothing could be too cheap to suit them just then; for they were quite terrified over the sums they had had to expend. A very few days of practical experience in this land of high wages had been sufficient to make clear to them the cruel fact that it was also a land of high prices, and that in it the poor man was almost as poor as in any other corner of the earth; and so there vanished in a night all the wonderful dreams of wealth that had been haunting Jurgis. What had made the discovery all the more painful was that they were spending, at American prices, money which they had earned at home rates of wages—and so were really being cheated by the world! The last two days they had all but starved themselves—it made them quite sick to pay prices that the railroad people asked them for food.

Yet, when they saw the home of the Widow Jukniene they could not but recoil, even so. In all their journey they had seen nothing so bad as this. Poni Aniele had a four-room flat in one of that wilderness of two-story frame tenements that lie "back of the yards." There were four such flats in each building, and each of the four was a "boarding-house" for the occupancy of foreigners—Lithuanians, Poles, Slovaks, or Bohemians. Some of these places were kept by private persons, some were coöperative. There would be an average of half a dozen boarders to each room—sometimes there were thirteen or fourteen to one room, fifty or sixty to a flat. Each one of the occupants furnished his own accommodations—that is, a mattress and some bedding. The mattresses would be spread upon the floor in rows—and there would be nothing else in the place except a stove. It was by no means unusual for two men to own the same mattress in common, one working by day and using it by night, and the other at night and using it in the daytime. Very frequently a lodging-house keeper would rent the same beds to double shifts of men.

Mrs. Jukniene was a wizened-up little woman, with a wrinkled face. Her home was unthinkably filthy; you could not enter by the front door at all, owing to the mattresses, and when you tried to go up the backstairs you found that she had walled up most of the porch with old boards to make a place to keep her chickens. It was a standing jest of the boarders that Aniele cleaned house by letting the chickens loose in the rooms. Undoubtedly this did keep down the vermin, but it seemed probable, in view of all the circumstances, that the old lady regarded it rather as feeding the chickens than as cleaning the rooms. The truth was that she had definitely given up the idea of cleaning anything, under pressure of an attack of rheumatism, which had kept her doubled up in one corner of her room for over a week; during which time eleven of her boarders, heavily in her debt, had concluded to try their chances of employment in Kansas City. This was July, and the fields were green. One never saw the fields, nor any green thing whatever, in Packingtown;[5] but one could go out on the road and "hobo it," as the men phrased it, and see the country, and have a long rest, and an easy time riding on the freight cars. . . .

from Chapter IX

. . . Jurgis heard of these things little by little, in the gossip of those who were obliged to perpetrate them. It seemed as if every time you met a person from a new department, you heard of new swindles and new crimes. There was, for instance, a Lithuanian who was a cattle-butcher for the plant where Marija had worked, which killed

[5]The area surrounding the stockyards on the south side of Chicago.

meat for canning only; and to hear this man describe the animals which came to his place would have been worth while for a Dante[6] or a Zola.[7] It seemed that they must have agencies all over the country, to hunt out old and crippled and diseased cattle to be canned. There were cattle which had been fed on "whiskey malt," the refuse of the breweries, and had become what the men called "steerly"—which means covered with boils. It was a nasty job killing these, for when you plunged your knife into them they would burst and splash foul-smelling stuff into your face; and when a man's sleeves were smeared with blood, and his hands steeped in it, how was he ever to wipe his face, or to clear his eyes so that he could see? It was stuff such as this that made the "embalmed beef" that had killed several times as many United States soldiers as all the bullets of the Spaniards;[8] only the army beef, besides, was not fresh canned, it was old stuff that had been lying for years in the cellars.

Then one Sunday evening, Jurgis sat puffing his pipe by the kitchen stove, and talking with an old fellow whom Jonas had introduced, and who worked in the canning-rooms at Durham's; and so Jurgis learned a few things about the great and only Durham canned goods, which had become a national institution. They were regular alchemists at Durham's; they advertised a mushroom-catsup, and the men who made it did not know what a mushroom looked like. They advertised "potted chicken,"—and it was like the boarding-house soup of the comic papers, through which a chicken had walked with rubbers on. Perhaps they had a secret process for making chickens chemically—who knows? said Jurgis's friend; the things that went into the mixture were tripe, and the fat of pork, and beef suet, and hearts of beef, and finally the waste ends of veal, when they had any. They put these up in several grades, and sold them at several prices; but the contents of the cans all came out of the same hopper. And then there was "potted game" and "potted grouse," "potted ham," and "devilled ham"—de-vyled, as the men called it. "De-vyled" ham was made out of the waste ends of smoked beef that were too small to be sliced by the machines; and also tripe, dyed with chemicals so that it would not show white; and trimmings of hams and corned beef; and potatoes, skins and all; and finally the hard cartilaginous gullets of beef, after the tongues had been cut out. All this ingenious mixture was ground up and flavored with spices to make it taste like something. Anybody who could invent a new imitation had been sure of a fortune from old Durham, said Jurgis's informant; but it was hard to think of anything new in a place where so many sharp wits had been at work for so long; where men welcomed tuberculosis in the cattle they were feeding, because it made them fatten more quickly; and where they bought up all the old rancid butter left over in the grocery-stores of a continent, and "oxidized" it by a forced-air process, to take away the odor, rechurned it with skim-milk, and sold it in bricks in the cities! Up to a year or two ago it had been the custom to kill horses in the yards—ostensibly for fertilizer; but after long agitation

[6]Dante Alighieri, Italian poet, 1265–1321. Author of the *Divine Comedy.* The reference here is to the *Inferno,* the first of three parts of the *Divine Comedy,* in which the poet is conducted by the spirit of the poet Virgil through the 24 great circles of Hell on the first stage of his journey toward God.

[7]Emile Zola, French novelist, 1840–1902. With such novels as *Nana* (1880) and *Germinal* (1885), Zola became the leading exponent of French Naturalism. Zola was famous for his journalistic, ostensibly scientific rendering of social milieu, based on minute and often sordid details. Like Sinclair, Zola was an ardent social reformer.

[8]The Spanish-American War, 1898.

the newspapers had been able to make the public realize that the horses were being canned. Now it was against the law to kill horses in Packingtown, and the law was really complied with—for the present, at any rate. Any day, however, one might see sharp-horned and shaggy-haired creatures running with the sheep—and yet what a job you would have to get the public to believe that a good part of what it buys for lamb and mutton is really goat's flesh!

There was another interesting set of statistics that a person might have gathered in Packingtown—those of the various afflictions of the workers. When Jurgis had first inspected the packing-plants with Szedvilas, he had marvelled while he listened to the tale of all the things that were made out of the carcasses of animals, and of all the lesser industries that were maintained there; now he found that each one of these lesser industries was a separate little inferno, in its way as horrible as the killing-beds, the source and fountain of them all. The workers in each of them had their own peculiar diseases. And the wandering visitor might be sceptical about all the swindles, but he could not be sceptical about these, for the worker bore the evidence of them about on his own person—generally he had only to hold out his hand.

There were the men in the pickle-rooms, for instance, where old Antanas had gotten his death; scarce a one of these that had not some spot of horror on his person. Let a man so much as scrape his finger pushing a truck in the pickle-rooms, and he might have a sore that would put him out of the world; all the joints in his fingers might be eaten by the acid, one by one. Of the butchers and floorsmen, the beef-boners and trimmers, and all those who used knives, you could scarcely find a person who had the use of his thumb; time and time again the base of it had been slashed, till it was a mere lump of flesh against which the man pressed the knife to hold it. The hands of these men would be criss-crossed with cuts, until you could no longer pretend to count them or to trace them. They would have no nails,—they had worn them off pulling hides; their knuckles were swollen so that their fingers spread out like a fan. There were men who worked in the cooking-rooms, in the midst of steam and sickening odors, by artificial light; in these rooms the germs of tuberculosis might live for two years, but the supply was renewed every hour. There were the beef-luggers, who carried two-hundred-pound quarters into the refrigerator-cars; a fearful kind of work, that began at four o'clock in the morning, and that wore out the most powerful men in a few years. There were those who worked in the chilling-rooms, and whose special disease was rheumatism; the time-limit that a man could work in the chilling-rooms was said to be five years. There were the wool-pluckers, whose hands went to pieces even sooner than the hands of the pickle-men; for the pelts of the sheep had to be painted with acid to loosen the wool, and then the pluckers had to pull out this wool with their bare hands, till the acid had eaten their fingers off. There were those who made the tins for the canned-meat; and their hands, too, were a maze of cuts, and each cut represented a chance for blood-poisoning. Some worked at the stamping-machines, and it was seldom that one could work long there at the pace that was set, and not give out and forget himself, and have a part of his hand chopped off. There were the "hoisters," as they were called, whose task it was to press the lever which lifted the dead cattle off the floor. They ran along upon a rafter, peering down through the damp and the steam; and as old Durham's architects had not built the killing-room for the convenience of the hoisters, at every few feet they would have to stoop under a beam, say four feet above the one they ran on; which got them into the habit of stooping, so that in a few years they would be walking like chimpanzees. Worst of any, however, were the fertilizer-men, and those served in the cooking-rooms. These people could not be shown to the visitor,—for the odor of a fertilizer-man would scare any ordinary visitor at a hundred yards, and as for the other men, who worked in tank-rooms full of steam, and in some of which there were open vats near the level of the floor, their peculiar trouble was that they fell into the vats; and when they were fished out, there was never enough of them left to be worth exhibiting,—sometimes they would be overlooked for days, till all but the bones of them had gone out to the world as Durham's Pure Leaf Lard! . . .

from Chapter XI

. . . A time of peril on the killing-beds when a steer broke loose. Sometimes, in the haste of speeding-up, they would dump one of the animals out on the floor before it was fully stunned, and it would get upon its feet and run amuck. Then there would be a yell of warning—the men would drop everything and dash for the nearest pillar, slipping here and there on the floor, and tumbling over each other. This was bad enough in the summer, when a man could see; in winter-time it was enough to make your hair stand up, for the room would be so full of steam that you could not make anything out five feet in front of you. To be sure, the steer was generally blind and frantic, and not especially bent on hurting any one; but think of the chances of running upon a knife, while nearly every man had one in his hand! And then, to cap the climax, the floor-boss would come rushing up with a rifle and begin blazing away!

It was in one of these mêlées that Jurgis fell into his trap. That is the only word to describe it; it was so cruel, and so utterly not to be foreseen. At first he hardly noticed it, it was such a slight accident—simply that in leaping out of the way he turned his ankle. There was a twinge of pain, but Jurgis was used to pain, and did not coddle himself. When he came to walk home, however, he realized that it was hurting him a great deal; and in the morning his ankle was swollen out nearly double its size, and he could not get his foot into his shoe. Still, even then, he did nothing more than swear a little, and wrapped his foot in old rags, and hobbled out to take the car. It chanced to be a rush day at Durham's, and all the long morning he limped about with his aching foot; by noon-time the pain was so great that it made him faint, and after a couple of hours in the afternoon he was fairly beaten, and had to tell the boss. They sent for the company doctor, and he examined the foot and told Jurgis to go home to bed, adding that he had probably laid himself up for months by his folly. The injury was not one that Durham and Company could be held responsible for, and so that was all there was to it, so far as the doctor was concerned.

Jurgis got home somehow, scarcely able to see for the pain, and with an awful terror in his soul. Elzbieta helped him into bed and bandaged his injured foot with cold water, and tried hard not to let him see her dismay; when the rest came home at night she met them outside and told them, and they, too, put on a cheerful face, saying it would only be for a week or two, and that they would pull him through.

When they had gotten him to sleep, however, they sat by the kitchen fire and talked it over in frightened whispers. They were in for a siege, that was plainly to be seen. Jurgis had only about sixty dollars in the bank, and the slack season was upon them. Both Jonas and Marija might soon be earning no more than enough to pay their board, and besides that there were only the wages of Ona and the pittance of the little boy. There was the rent to pay, and still some on the furniture; there was the insurance just due, and every month there was sack after sack of coal. It was January, midwinter, an awful time to have to face privation. Deep snows would come again, and who would carry Ona to her work now? She might lose her place—she was almost certain to lose it. And then little Stanislovas[9] began to whimper—who would take care of him?

It was dreadful that an accident of this sort, that no man can help, should have meant such suffering. The bitterness of it was the daily food and drink of Jurgis. It was of no use for them to try to deceive him; he knew as much about the situation as they did, and he knew that the family might literally starve to death. The worry of fairly ate him up—he began to look haggard the first two or three days of it. In truth, it was almost maddening for a strong man like him, a fighter, to have to lie there helpless on his back. It was for all the world the old story of Prometheus[10] bound. As Jurgis lay on his bed, hour after hour, there came to him emotions that he had never known before. Before this he had met life with a welcome—it had its trials, but none that a man could not face. But now, in the night-time, when he lay tossing about, there would come stalking into his chamber a grisly phantom, the sight of which made his flesh curl and his hair to bristle up. It was like seeing the world fall away from underneath his feet; like plunging down into a bottomless abyss, into yawning caverns of despair. It might be true, then, after all, what others had told him about life, that the best powers of a man might not be equal to it! It might be true that, strive as he would,. toil as he would, he might fail, and go down and be destroyed! The thought of this was like an icy hand at his heart; the thought that here, in this ghastly home of all horror, he and all those who were dear to him might lie and perish of starvation and cold, and there would be no ear to hear their cry, no hand to help them! It was true, it was true,—that here in this huge city, with its stores of heaped-up wealth, human creatures might be hunted down and destroyed by the wild-beast powers of nature, just as truly as ever they were in the days of the cave men! . . .

from Chapter XII

. . . The latter part of April Jurgis went to see the doctor, and was given a bandage to lace about his ankle, and told that he might go back to work. It needed more than the permission of the doctor, however, for when he showed up on the killing-floor of Brown's, he was told by the foreman that it had not been possible to keep his job for him. Jurgis knew that this meant simply that the foreman had found some one else to do the work as well and did not want to bother to make a change. He stood in the

[9]Son of Teta Elzbieta, Ona's stepmother.

[10]Greek Titan, the son of Iapetus and Clymene, who stole fire from heaven, for which crime Zeus ordered him chained to a rock on Mount Caucasus where a vulture fed daily on his liver.

doorway, looking mournfully on, seeing his friends and companions at work, and feeling like an outcast. Then he went out and took his place with the mob of the unemployed.

This time, however, Jurgis did not have the same fine confidence, nor the same reason for it. He was no longer the finest-looking man in the throng, and the bosses no longer made for him; he was thin and haggard, and his clothes were seedy, and he looked miserable. And there were hundreds who looked and felt just like him, and who had been wandering about Packingtown for months begging for work. This was a critical time in Jurgis's life, and if he had been a weaker man he would have gone the way the rest did. Those out-of-work wretches would stand about the packing-houses every morning till the police drove them away, and then they would scatter among the saloons. Very few of them had the nerve to face the rebuffs that they would encounter by trying to get into the buildings to interview the bosses; if they did not get a chance in the morning, there would be nothing to do but hang about the saloons the rest of the day and night. Jurgis was saved from all this—partly, to be sure, because it was pleasant weather, and there was no need to be indoors; but mainly because he carried with him always the pitiful little face of his wife. He must get work, he told himself, fighting the battle with despair every hour of the day. He must get work! He must have a place again and some money saved up, before the next winter came.

But there was no work for him. He sought out all the members of his union—Jurgis had stuck to the union through all this—and begged them to speak a word for him. He went to every one he knew, asking for a chance, there or anywhere. He wandered all day through the buildings; and in a week or two, when he had been all over the yards, and into every room to which he had access, and learned that there was not a job anywhere, he persuaded himself that there might have been a change in the places he had first visited, and began the round all over; till finally the watchmen and the "spotters" of the companies came to know him by sight and to order him out with threats. Then there was nothing more for him to do but go with the crowd in the morning, and keep in the front row and look eager, and when he failed, go back home, and play with little Kotrina[11] and the baby.[12]

The peculiar bitterness of all this was that Jurgis saw so plainly the meaning of it. In the beginning he had been fresh and strong, and he had gotten a job the first day; but now he was second-hand, a damaged article, so to speak, and they did not want him. They had got the best out of him,—they had worn him out, with their speeding-up and their carelessness, and now they had thrown him away! And Jurgis would make the acquaintance of others of these unemployed men and find that they had all had the same experience. There were some, of course, who had wandered in from other places, who had been ground up in other mills; there were others who were out from their own fault—some, for instance, who had not been able to stand the awful grind without drink. The vast majority, however, were simply the worn-out parts of the great merciless packing-machine; they had toiled there, and kept up with the pace, some of them for ten or twenty years, until finally the time had come when they could not keep up with it any more. Some had been frankly told that they were too old, that a sprier man was needed; others had given occasion, by some act of carelessness or in-

[11]Daughter of Teta Elzbieta, Ona's stepmother. [12]Jurgis and Ona's infant son.

competence; with most, however, the occasion had been the same as with Jurgis. They had been overworked and underfed so long, and finally some disease had laid them on their backs; or they had cut themselves, and had blood-poisoning, or met with some other accident. When a man came back after that, he would get his place back only by the courtesy of the boss. To this there was no exception, save when the accident was one for which the firm was liable; in that case they would send a slippery lawyer to see him, first to try to get him to sign away his claims, but if he was too smart for that, to promise him that he and his should always be provided with work. This promise they would keep, strictly and to the letter—for two years. Two years was the "statute of limitations," and after that the victim could not sue.

What happened to a man after any of these things, all depended upon the circumstances. If he were of the highly skilled workers, he would probably have enough saved up to tide him over. The best-paid men, the "splitters," made fifty cents an hour, which would be five or six dollars a day in the rush seasons, and one or two in the dullest. A man could live and save on that; but then there were only half a dozen splitters in each place, and one of them that Jurgis knew had a family of twenty-two children, all hoping to grow up to be splitters like their father. For an unskilled man, who made ten dollars a week in the rush seasons and five in the dull, it all depended upon his age and the number he had dependent upon him. An unmarried man could save, if he did not drink, and if he was absolutely selfish—that is, if he paid no heed to the demands of his old parents, or of his little brothers and sisters, or of any other relatives he might have, as well as of the members of his union, and his chums, and the people who might be starving to death next door. . . .

from Chapter XIV

With one member trimming beef in a cannery, and another working in a sausage factory, the family had a first-hand knowledge of the great majority of Packingtown swindles. For it was the custom, as they found, whenever meat was so spoiled that it could not be used for anything else, either to can it or else to chop it up into sausage. With what had been told them by Jonas, who had worked in the pickle-rooms, they could now study the whole of the spoiled-meat industry on the inside, and read a new and grim meaning into that old Packingtown jest,—that they use everything of the pig except the squeal.

Jonas had told them how the meat that was taken out of pickle would often be found sour, and how they would rub it up with soda to take away the smell, and sell it to be eaten on free-lunch counters; also of all the miracles of chemistry which they performed, giving to any sort of meat, fresh or salted, whole or chopped, any color and any flavor and any odor they chose. In the pickling of hams they had an ingenious apparatus, by which they saved time and increased the capacity of the plant—a machine consisting of a hollow needle attached to a pump; by plunging this needle into the meat and working with his foot, a man could fill a ham with pickle in a few seconds. And yet, in spite of this, there would be hams found spoiled, some of them with an odor so bad that a man could hardly bear to be in the room with them. To pump into these the packers had a second and much stronger pickle which destroyed the odor—a process known to the workers as "giving them thirty per cent." Also, after the hams had been smoked, there would be found some that had gone to the bad. Formerly these had been sold as "Number Three Grade," but later on some ingenious person had hit upon a new device, and now they would extract the bone, about which the bad part generally lay, and insert in the hole a white-hot iron. After this invention there was no longer Number One, Two and Three Grade—there was only Number One Grade. The packers were always originating such schemes—they had what they called "boneless hams," which were all the odds and ends of pork stuffed into casings; and "California hams," which were the shoulders, with big knuckle-joints, and nearly all the meat cut out; and fancy "skinned hams," which were made of the oldest hogs, whose skins were so heavy and coarse that no one would buy them—that is, until they had been cooked and chopped fine and labelled "head cheese"!

It was only when the whole ham was spoiled that it came into the department of Elzbieta. Cut up by the two-thousand-revolutions-a-minute flyers, and mixed with half a ton of other meat, no odor that ever was in a ham could make any difference. There was never the least attention paid to what was cut up for sausage; there would come all the way back from Europe old sausage that had been rejected, and that was mouldy and white—it would be dosed with borax and glycerine, and dumped into the hoppers, and made over again for home consumption. There would be meat that had tumbled out on the floor, in the dirt and sawdust, where the workers had tramped and spit uncounted billions of consumption germs. There would be meat stored in great piles in rooms; and the water from leaky roofs would drip over it, and thousands of rats would race about on it. It was too dark in these storage places to see well, but a man could run his hand over these piles of meat and sweep off handfuls of the dried dung of rats. These rats were nuisances, and the packers would put poisoned bread out for them; they would die, and then rats, bread, and meat would go into the hoppers together. This is no fairy story and no joke; the meat would be shovelled into carts, and the man who did the shovelling would not trouble to lift out a rat even when he saw one—there were things that went into the sausage in comparison with which a poisoned rat was a tidbit. There was no place for the men to wash their hands before they ate dinner, and so they made a practice of washing them in the water that was to be ladled into the sausage. There were the butt-ends of smoked meat, and the scraps of corned beef, and all the odds and ends of the waste of the plants, that would be dumped into old barrels in the cellar and left there. Under the system of rigid economy which the packers enforced, there were some jobs that it only paid to do once in a long time, and among these was the cleaning out of the waste-barrels. Every spring they did it; and in the barrels would be dirt and rust and old nails and stale water—and cart load after cart load of it would be taken up and dumped into the hoppers with fresh meat, and sent out to the public's breakfast. Some of it they would make into "smoked" sausage—but as the smoking took time, and was therefore expensive, they would call upon their chemistry department, and preserve it with borax and color it with gelatine to make it brown. All of their sausage came out of the same bowl, but when they came to wrap it they would stamp some of it "special," and for this they would charge two cents more a pound.

Such were the new surroundings in which Elzbieta was placed, and such was the work she was compelled to do. It was stupefying, brutalizing work; it left her no time to think, no strength for anything. She was part of the machine she tended, and every faculty that was not needed for the machine was doomed to be crushed out of existence. There was only one mercy about the cruel grind—that it gave her the gift of insensibility. Little by little she sank into a torpor—she fell silent. She would meet Jurgis and Ona in the evening, and the three would walk home together, often without saying a word. Ona, too, was falling into a habit of silence—Ona, who had once gone about singing like a bird. She was sick and miserable, and often she would barely have strength enough to drag herself home. And there they would eat what they had to eat, and afterwards, because there was only their misery to talk of, they would crawl into bed and fall into a stupor and never stir until it was time to get up again, and dress by candle-light, and go back to the machines. They were so numbed that they did not even suffer from hunger, now; only the children continued to fret when the food ran short.

Yet the soul of Ona was not dead—the souls of none of them were dead, but only sleeping; and now and then they would waken, and these were cruel times. The gates of memory would roll open—old joys would stretch out their arms to them, old hopes and dreams would call to them, and they would stir beneath the burden that lay upon them, and feel its forever immeasurable weight. They could not even cry out beneath it; but anguish would seize them, more dreadful than the agony of death. It was a thing scarcely to be spoken—a thing never spoken by all the world, that will not know its own defeat.

They were beaten; they had lost the game, they were swept aside. It was not less tragic because it was so sordid, because that it had to do with wages and grocery bills and rents. They had dreamed of freedom; of a chance to look about them and learn something; to be decent and clean, to see their child grow up to be strong. And now it was all gone—it would never be! They had played the game and they had lost. Six years more of toil they had to face before they could expect the least respite, the cessation of the payments upon the house; and how cruelly certain it was that they could never stand six years of such a life as they were living! They were lost, they were going down—and there was no deliverance for them, no hope; for all the help it gave them the vast city in which they lived might have been an ocean waste, a wilderness, a desert, a tomb. So often this mood would come to Ona, in the night-time, when something wakened her; she would lie, afraid of the beating of her own heart, fronting the blood-red eyes of the old primeval terror of life. Once she cried aloud, and woke Jurgis, who was tired and cross. After that she learned to weep silently—their moods so seldom came together now! It was as if their hopes were buried in separate graves. . . .

1906

Henry Adams 1838–1918

At his birth Henry Brooks Adams, the grandson and great-grandson of American presidents, entered a privileged world. Along with his political name he also inherited a special responsibility: to bear witness, through writing, to the complexity of life. Today Adams owes his popular reputation to a single record of that kind, *The*

Education of Henry Adams, which won a Pulitzer Prize in 1919. Yet over a long and productive career as a writer, he also produced a substantial body of essays, biographies, novels, letters, and histories, which largely reward our attention.

Adams's earliest publications, dating from his undergraduate years at Harvard University, from 1854 to 1858, pointed directions for his later work. As he wrote of men, architecture, and books, the young Adams testified to the high seriousness of his concern for human experience as a field of lifelong investigation. Yet he knew his preparation to be incomplete. After graduation and a tour of Europe first he settled in Germany, where he mastered German historical method, the most rigorous type of scholarship available at the time. Then, at the behest of his father, Charles Francis Adams, elected to Congress in 1860, Henry moved to Washington to serve as a private secretary (and as a secret correspondent for the *Boston Daily Advertiser*). In 1861 Henry went to London, spending the years of the Civil War there while his father served as President Lincoln's Minister to the Court of St. James's. From this diplomatic outpost the son wrote letters, dispatches, and essays, honing his thoughts on politics, history, science, and English and American culture—in writings that display the intellectual skills of a critic.

Back in Washington after the war, Adams enlisted his literary talents in the service of political reform, writing essays and reviews in support of such causes as the establishment of the federal civil service system. But the disillusionment caused by the administration of President Ulysses Grant and the growing corruption of American politics quickly foreclosed Adams's personal interest in political service. In 1870 he returned to Boston and Harvard, to begin a joint career as a teacher of history and editor of the prestigious *North American Review.* By 1872 he had married Marian "Clover" Hooper, whose suicide in 1885 Adams would come to regard as the end of his life in the world. During the 1870s, he also introduced German historical techniques, including the use of original documentary sources and the seminar method, into graduate studies at Harvard.

Adams's own research focused on the medieval period in Europe and on medieval women in various early civilizations. This special interest led him, in December 1876, to deliver a seminal public address on "The Primitive Rights of Women." Later, he would investigate the situation of contemporary American women in two novels, *Democracy* (1880) and *Esther* (1884). Neither book proposed a solution to the practical problems of being a woman in nineteenth-century America, but both were sympathetic in recognizing how their lack of control over circumstance handicapped women and reduced their effectiveness in human activities. Already, Adams was approaching his far more ambitious theory of feminine force—the important hypothesis developed in his two most celebrated works, *Mont-Saint-Michel and Chartres* and *The Education of Henry Adams.* In both, Adams drew upon his long study of ancient and modern, "primitive" and "civilized" societies, to conclude that, on the basis of all historical evidence, women—rather than men—represented both the highest standard of moral behavior and the greatest source of human energy. In the figure of the Virgin, for example, woman had exercised her power by inspiring the building of a great cathedral at Chartres. In his own time, however, Adams saw the force of the Virgin superseded by new scientific forces, symbolized by the modern dynamo. History, in Adams's view, traced the path between the two.

Long before he fixed on the technology of the dynamo and the scientific laws that explained its operation as a way of interpreting human history, Adams had considered the possibilities of a more conventional history—as a narrative of events that emphasized the roles played by great men. His classic nine-volume *History of the United States during the Administrations of Thomas Jefferson and James Madison* (1888–1891) used Germanic scholarly methods to examine American life from 1800 to 1816. It failed, however, to locate any convenient key in the American past that could be used predictively—to lay out an American future. Increasingly as he grew older, and as the closing chapters of *The Education* reveal, Adams sought to find such a key, in history, literature, science, and personal experience. But he never succeeded, at least to his own satisfaction.

Mont-Saint-Michel and Chartres (which was privately printed in 1904 and published in 1913) was less an attempt to write conventional history than a compelling invitation to sample the joys of medieval life, including medieval architecture, in which the Virgin is a unifying force. As autobiography, *The Education of Henry Adams* (privately printed in 1907 and published in 1918 after the author's death) is also unconventional—in its use of the third person point of view and its complete silence about Adams's wife and married life. *The Education* tells Adams's story as both unique and representative. As a member of a presidential family his experience was special. But as a man living at a time when the eighteenth-century qualities of civic virtue and service (which had made the Adams name) no longer seem useful, a time that offered the individual only marginal control over the impersonal forces at work in the world, Adams treats his failure as typical. Modern science and technology have brought unforeseen results, and Adams, lacking sufficient explanation, has been reduced to the same diminutive role played by the nineteenth-century woman. Unless his readers, alive in the twentieth and twenty-first centuries, can learn to educate themselves more efficiently, Adams argues, their later experience will be no better than his.

Earl N. Harbert
Independent scholar/editor

PRIMARY WORKS

The Life of Albert Gallatin, 1879; *Democracy: An American Novel* (anon.) 1880, 1882; *John Randolph,* 1882, rev. 1883; *Esther: A Novel* (as Frances Snow Compton) 1884, 1885; *History of the United States of America During the Administrations of Thomas Jefferson and James Madison,* 1884, 1885, 1888, 1889, 1890, 1891; *Historical Essays,* 1891; *Mont-Saint-Michel and Chartres* (anon.) 1904, rev. 1912, 1913, 1914; *The Education of Henry Adams,* 1907, 1918, 1919; *Sketches for the North American Review* (ed. Edward Chalfant), 1986.

from Mont-Saint-Michel and Chartres

Chapter VI The Virgin of Chartres

[Henry Adams's *Mont-Saint-Michel and Chartres* drew from his deep appreciation of medieval culture, especially of the vital role that the Virgin Mary played in religious belief and practice. The book is structured as a tour of medieval France, expertly guided by its author. Along the route the two most memorable points of interest are the impressive fortress abbey, Mont-Saint-Michel, just off the coast of France, and the beautiful cathedral at Chartres, fifty-five miles from Paris. As Chapter VI illustrates, Adams uses his own vast knowledge to encourage the reader's understanding of complexity and power in medieval life. The distant past, in this author's view, should not be considered inferior to the present.]

We must take ten minutes to accustom our eyes to the light, and we had better use them to seek the reason why we come to Chartres rather than to Rheims or Amiens or Bourges,[1] for the cathedral that fills our ideal. The truth is, there are several reasons; there generally are, for doing the things we like; and after you have studied Chartres to the ground, and got your reasons settled, you will never find an antiquarian to agree with you; the architects will probably listen to you with contempt; and even these excellent priests, whose kindness is great, whose patience is heavenly, and whose good opinion you would so gladly gain, will turn from you with pain, if not with horror. The Gothic is singular in this; one seems easily at home in the Renaissance; one is not too strange in the Byzantine; as for the Roman, it is ourselves; and we could walk blindfolded through every chink and cranny of the Greek mind; all these styles[2] seem modern, when we come close to them; but the Gothic gets away. No two men think alike about it, and no woman agrees with either man. The Church itself never agreed about it, and the architects agree even less than the priests. To most minds it casts too many shadows; it wraps itself in mystery; and when people talk of mystery, they commonly mean fear. To others, the Gothic seems hoary with age and decrepitude, and its shadows mean death. What is curious to watch is the fanatical conviction of the Gothic enthusiast, to whom the twelfth century means exuberant youth, the eternal child of Wordsworth, over whom its immortality broods like the day; it is so simple and yet so complicated; it sees so much and so little; it loves so many toys and cares for so few necessities; its youth is so young, its age so old, and its youthful yearning for old thought is so disconcerting, like the mysterious senility of the baby that—

> Deaf and silent, reads the eternal deep,
> Haunted forever by the eternal mind.[3]

One need not take it more seriously than one takes the baby itself. Our amusement is to play with it, and to catch its meaning in its smile; and whatever Chartres may be now, when young it was a smile. To the Church, no doubt, its cathedral here has a fixed and administrative meaning, which is the same as that of every other bishop's seat and with which we have nothing whatever to do. To us, it is a child's fancy; a toy-house to please the Queen of Heaven,—to please her so much that she would be happy in it,—to charm her till she smiled.

The Queen Mother was as majestic as you like; she was absolute; she could be stern; she was not above being angry; but she was still a woman, who loved grace, beauty, ornament,—her toilette, robes, jewels;—who considered the arrangements of her palace with attention, and liked both light and colour; who kept a keen eye on her Court, and exacted prompt and willing obedience from king and archbishops as

[1]French cities in which cathedrals are located.
[2]Adams refers to various historical styles of architecture.
[3]From "Ode: Intimations of Immortality from Recollections of Early Childhood" (VIII) by William Wordsworth (1770–1852).

well as from beggars and drunken priests. She protected her friends and punished her enemies. She required space, beyond what was known in the Courts of kings, because she was liable at all times to have ten thousand people begging her for favours—mostly inconsistent with law—and deaf to refusal. She was extremely sensitive to neglect, to disagreeable impressions, to want of intelligence in her surroundings. She was the greatest artist, as she was the greatest philosopher and musician and theologist, that ever lived on earth, except her Son, Who, at Chartres, is still an Infant under her guardianship. Her taste was infallible; her silence eternally final. This church was built for her in this spirit of simple-minded, practical, utilitarian faith,—in this singleness of thought, exactly as a little girl sets up a doll-house for her favourite blonde doll. Unless you can go back to your dolls, you are out of place here. If you can go back to them, and get rid of one small hour of the weight of custom, you shall see Chartres in glory.

The palaces of earthly queens were hovels compared with these palaces of the Queen of Heaven at Chartres, Paris, Laon, Noyon, Rheims, Amiens, Rouen, Bayeux, Coutances,—a list that might be stretched into a volume. The nearest approach we have made to a palace was the Merveille at Mont-Saint-Michel, but no Queen had a palace equal to that. The Merveille was built, or designed, about the year 1200; toward the year 1500, Louis XI built a great castle at Loches in Touraine, and there Queen Anne de Bretagne had apartments which still exist, and which we will visit. At Blois you shall see the residence which served for Catherine de Medicis till her death in 1589. Anne de Bretagne was trebly queen, and Catherine de Medicis took her standard of comfort from the luxury of Florence. At Versailles you can see the apartments which the queens of the Bourbon line occupied through their century of magnificence. All put together, and then trebled in importance, could not rival the splendour of any single cathedral dedicated to Queen Mary in the thirteenth century; and of them all, Chartres was built to be peculiarly and exceptionally her delight.

One has grown so used to this sort of loose comparison, this reckless waste of words, that one no longer adopts an idea unless it is driven in with hammers of statistics and columns of figures. With the irritating demand for literal exactness and perfectly straight lines which lights up every truly American eye, you will certainly ask when this exaltation of Mary began, and unless you get the dates, you will doubt the facts. It is your own fault if they are tiresome; you might easily read them all in the "Iconographie de la Sainte Vierge," by M. Rohault de Fleury, published in 1878. You can start at Byzantium with the Empress Helena in 326, or with the Council of Ephesus in 431. You will find the Virgin acting as the patron saint of Constantinople and of the Imperial residence, under as many names as Artemis or Aphrodite had borne. As Godmother (Θeomhthr), Deipara (Θetokoς), Pathfinder ('Odohghtria), she was the chief favourite of the Eastern Empire, and her picture was carried at the head of every procession and hung on the wall of every hut and hovel, as it is still wherever the Greek Church goes. In the year 610, when Heraclius sailed from Carthage to dethrone Phocas at Constantinople, his ships carried the image of the Virgin at their mastheads.[4] In 1143, just before the flèche on the Chartres clocher was begun, the Basileus[5] John Comnenus died, and so devoted was he to the Virgin that, on a tri-

[4]Adams traces early appearances of the Virgin in pre-medieval history, beginning with Byzantium and concluding just before Chartres was begun, before the spire (flèche) on the tower (clocher) was started.

[5]King.

umphal entry into Constantinople, he put the image of the Mother of God in his chariot, while he himself walked. In the Western Church the Virgin had always been highly honoured, but it was not until the crusades that she began to overshadow the Trinity itself. Then her miracles became more frequent and her shrines more frequented, so that Chartres, soon after 1100, was rich enough to build its western portal with Byzantine splendour. A proof of the new outburst can be read in the story of Citeaux. For us, Citeaux means Saint Bernard, who joined the Order[6] in 1112, and in 1115 founded his Abbey of Clairvaux in the territory of Troyes. In him, the religious emotion of the half-century between the first and second crusades (1095–1145) centred as in no one else. He was a French precursor of Saint Francis of Assisi who lived a century later. If we were to plunge into the story of Citeaux and Saint Bernard we should never escape, for Saint Bernard incarnates what we are trying to understand, and his mind is further from us than the architecture. You would lose hold of everything actual, if you could comprehend in its contradictions the strange mixture of passion and caution, the austerity, the self-abandonment, the vehemence, the restraint, the love, the hate, the miracles, and the scepticism of Saint Bernard. The Cistercian Order, which was founded in 1098, from the first put all its churches under the special protection of the Virgin, and Saint Bernard in his time was regarded as the apple of the Virgin's eye. Tradition as old as the twelfth century, which long afterwards gave to Murillo[7] the subject of a famous painting, told that once, when he was reciting before her statue the "Ave Maris Stella,"[8] and came to the words, "Monstra te esse Matrem,"[9] the image, pressing its breast, dropped on the lips of her servant three drops of the milk which had nourished the Saviour. The same miracle, in various forms, was told of many other persons, both saints and sinners; but it made so much impression on the mind of the age that, in the fourteenth century, Dante, seeking in Paradise[10] for some official introduction to the foot of the Throne, found no intercessor with the Queen of Heaven more potent than Saint Bernard. You can still read Bernard's hymns to the Virgin, and even his sermons, if you like. To him she was the great mediator. In the eyes of a culpable humanity, Christ was too sublime, too terrible, too just, but not even the weakest human frailty could fear to approach his Mother. Her attribute was humility; her love and pity were infinite. "Let him deny your mercy who can say that he has ever asked it in vain."

Saint Bernard was emotional and to a certain degree mystical, like Adam de Saint-Victor, whose hymns were equally famous, but the emotional saints and mystical poets were not by any means allowed to establish exclusive rights to the Virgin's favour. Abélard was as devoted as they were, and wrote hymns as well. Philosophy claimed her, and Albert the Great, the head of scholasticism, the teacher of Thomas Aquinas, decided in her favour the question: "Whether the Blessed Virgin possessed perfectly the seven liberal arts." The Church at Chartres had decided it a hundred years before by putting the seven liberal arts next her throne, with Aristotle himself to witness; but Albertus[11] gave the reason: "I hold that she did, for it is written, 'Wisdom has built herself a house, and has sculptured seven columns.' That house is the

[6]A group of monks.
[7]Bartolomé Murillo (1617–1682), a Spanish painter of religious subjects.
[8]"Hail, Star of the Sea."
[9]"Show thou art the Mother."
[10]Dante Alighieri (1265–1321), Italian poet who wrote about Paradise in *The Divine Comedy.*
[11]Adams uses these early spokesmen of religion and philosophy to demonstrate widespread interest in the Virgin.

blessed Virgin; the seven columns are the seven liberal arts. Mary, therefore, had perfect mastery of science." Naturally she had also perfect mastery of economics, and most of her great churches were built in economic centres. The guilds were, if possible, more devoted to her than the monks; the bourgeoisie of Paris, Rouen, Amiens, Laon, spent money by millions to gain her favour. Most surprising of all, the great military class was perhaps the most vociferous. Of all inappropriate haunts for the gentle, courteous, pitying Mary, a field of battle seems to be the worst, if not distinctly blasphemous; yet the greatest French warriors insisted on her leading them into battle, and in the actual mêlée when men were killing each other, on every battlefield in Europe, for at least five hundred years, Mary was present, leading both sides. The battle-cry of the famous Constable du Guesclin was "Notre- Dame-Guesclin"; "Notre-Dame-Coucy" was the cry of the great Sires de Coucy; "Notre-Dame-Auxerre"; "Notre-Dame-Sancerre"; "Notre-Dame-Hainault"; "Notre-Dame-Gueldres"; "Notre-Dame-Bourbon"; "Notre-Dame-Bearn";—all well-known battle-cries. The King's own battle at one time cried, "Notre-Dame-Saint-Denis-Montjoie"; the Dukes of Burgundy cried, "Notre-Dame-Bourgogne"; and even the soldiers of the Pope were said to cry, "Notre-Dame-Saint-Pierre."

The measure of this devotion, which proves to any religious American mind, beyond possible cavil, its serious and practical reality, is the money it cost. According to statistics, in the single century between 1170 and 1270, the French built eighty cathedrals and nearly five hundred churches of the cathedral class, which would have cost, according to an estimate made in 1840, more than five thousand millions to replace. Five thousand million francs is a thousand million dollars, and this covered only the great churches of a single century. The same scale of expenditure had been going on since the year 1000, and almost every parish in France had rebuilt its church in stone; to this day France is strewn with the ruins of this architecture, and yet the still preserved churches of the eleventh and twelfth centuries, among the churches that belong to the Romanesque and Transition period, are numbered by hundreds until they reach well into the thousands. The share of this capital which was—if one may use a commercial figure—invested in the Virgin cannot be fixed, any more than the total sum given to religious objects between 1000 and 1300; but in a spiritual and artistic sense, it was almost the whole, and expressed an intensity of conviction never again reached by any passion, whether of religion, of loyalty, of patriotism, or of wealth; perhaps never even parallelled by any single economic effort, except in war. Nearly every great church of the twelfth and thirteenth centuries belonged to Mary, until in France one asks for the church of Notre Dame as though it meant cathedral; but, not satisfied with this, she contracted the habit of requiring in all churches a chapel of her own, called in English the "Lady Chapel," which was apt to be as large as the church but was always meant to be handsomer; and there, behind the high altar, in her own private apartment, Mary sat, receiving her innumerable suppliants, and ready at any moment to step up upon the high altar itself to support the tottering authority of the local saint.

Expenditure like this rests invariably on an economic idea. Just as the French of the nineteenth century invested their surplus capital in a railway system in the belief that they would make money by it in this life, in the thirteenth they trusted their money to the Queen of Heaven because of their belief in her power to repay it with interest in the life to come. The investment was based on the power of Mary as Queen rather than on any orthodox Church conception of the Virgin's legitimate station. Papal Rome never greatly loved Byzantine empresses or French queens. The Virgin of Chartres was never wholly sympathetic to the Roman Curia.[12] To this day the Church writers—like the Abbé Bulteau or M. Rohault de Fleury—are singularly shy of the true Virgin of majesty, whether at Chartres or at Byzantium or wherever she is seen. The fathers Martin and Cahier at Bourges alone left her true value. Had the Church controlled her, the Virgin would perhaps have remained prostrate at the foot of the Cross. Dragged by a Byzantine Court, backed by popular insistence and impelled by overpowering self-interest, the Church accepted the Virgin throned and crowned, seated by Christ, the Judge throned and crowned; but even this did not wholly satisfy the French of the thirteenth century who seemed bent on absorbing Christ in His Mother, and making the Mother the Church, and Christ the Symbol.

The Church had crowned and enthroned her almost from the beginning, and could not have dethroned her if it would. In all Christian art—sculpture or mosaic, painting or poetry—the Virgin's rank was expressly asserted. Saint Bernard, like John Comnenus, and probably at the same time (1120–40), chanted hymns to the Virgin as Queen:—

O Salutaris Virgo Stella Maris Generans prolem, Æquitatis solem, Lucis auctorem, Retinens pudorem, Suscipe laudem!	O saviour Virgin, Star of Sea, Who bore for child the Son of Justice, The source of Light, Virgin always Hear our praise!
Celi Regina Per quam medicina Datur aegrotis, Gratia devotis, Gaudium molstis, Mundo lux cœlestis, Spesque salutis;	Queen of Heaven who have given Medicine to the sick, Grace to the devout, Joy to the sad, Heaven's light to the world And hope of salvation;
Aula regalis, Virgo specialis, Posce medelam Nobis et tutelam, Suscipe vota, Precibusque cuncta Pelle molesta!	Court royal, Virgin typical, Grant us cure and guard, Accept our vows, and by prayers Drive all griefs away!

As the lyrical poet of the twelfth century, Adam de Saint-Victor seems to have held rank higher if possible than that of Saint Bernard, and his hymns on the Virgin are certainly quite as emphatic an assertion of her majesty:—

Imperatrix supernorum! Superatrix infernorum! Eligenda via cœli, Retinenda spe fideli, Separatos a te longe Revocatos ad te junge Tuorum collegio!	Empress of the highest, Mistress over the lowest, Chosen path of Heaven, Held fast by faithful hope, Those separated from you far, Recalled to you, unite In your fold!

To delight in the childish jingle of the mediaeval Latin is a sign of a futile mind, no doubt, and I beg pardon of you and of the Church for wasting your precious summer day on poetry which was regarded as mystical in its age and which now sounds

[12]The administrative organization of the Catholic Church.

like a nursery rhyme; but a verse or two of Adam's hymn on the Assumption of the Virgin completes the record of her rank, and goes to complete also the documentary proof of her majesty at Chartres:—

Salve, Mater Salvatoris!	Mother of our Saviour, hail!
Vas electum! Vas honoris!	Chosen vessel! Sacred Grail!
Vas coelestis Gratiæ!	Font of celestial grace!
Ab æterno Vas provisum!	From eternity forethought!
Vas insigne! Vas excisum	By the hand of Wisdom wrought!
Manu sapientiæ!	Precious, faultless Vase!
Salve, Mater pietatis,	Hail, Mother of Divinity!
Et totius Trinitatis	Hail, Temple of the Trinity!
Nobile Triclinium!	Home of the Triune God!
Verbi tamen incarnati	In whom the Incarnate Word hath birth,
Speciale majestati	The King! to whom you gave on earth
Præparans hospitium!	Imperial abode.
O Maria! Stella maris!	Oh, Maria! Constellation!
Dignitate singularis,	Inspiration! Elevation!
Super omnes ordinaris	Rule and Law and Ordination
Ordines cœlestium!	Of the angels' host!
In supremo sita poli	Highest height of God's Creation,
Nos commenda tuæ proli,	Pray your Son's commiseration,
Ne terrores sive doli	Lest, by fear or fraud, salvation
Nos supplantent hostium!	For our souls be lost!

Constantly—one might better say at once, officially, she was addressed in these terms of supreme majesty: "Imperatrix supernorum!" "Cœli Regina!" "Aula regalis!"[13] but the twelfth century seemed determined to carry the idea out to its logical conclusion in defiance of dogma. Not only was the Son absorbed in the Mother, or represented as under her guardianship, but the Father fared no better, and the Holy Ghost followed. The poets regarded the Virgin as the "Templum Trinitatis"; "totius Trinitatis nobile Triclinium." She was the refectory of the Trinity—the "Triclinium"—because the refectory was the largest room and contained the whole of the members, and was divided in three parts by two rows of columns. She was the "Templum Trinitatis," the Church itself, with its triple aisle. The Trinity was absorbed in her.

This is a delicate subject in the Church, and you must feel it with delicacy, without brutally insisting on its necessary contradictions. All theology and all philosophy are full of contradictions quite as flagrant and far less sympathetic. This particular variety of religious faith is simply human, and has made its appearance in one form or another in nearly all religions; but though the twelfth century carried it to an extreme, and at Chartres you see it in its most charming expression, we have got always to make allowances for what was going on beneath the surface in men's minds, consciously or unconsciously, and for the latent scepticism which lurks behind all faith.

[13] "Empress of the highest," "Queen of Heaven," "Regal Power."

The Church itself never quite accepted the full claims of what was called Mariolatry. One may be sure, too, that the bourgeois capitalist and the student of the schools, each from his own point of view, watched the Virgin with anxious interest. The bourgeois had put an enormous share of his capital into what was in fact an economical speculation, not unlike the South Sea Scheme,[14] or the railway system of our own time; except that in one case the energy was devoted to shortening the road to Heaven; in the other, to shortening the road to Paris; but no serious schoolman could have felt entirely convinced that God would enter into a business partnership with man, to establish a sort of joint-stock society for altering the operation of divine and universal laws. The bourgeois cared little for the philosophical doubt if the economical result proved to be good, but he watched this result with his usual practical sagacity, and required an experience of only about three generations (1200–1300) to satisfy himself that relics were not certain in their effects; that the Saints were not always able or willing to help; that Mary herself could not certainly be bought or bribed; that prayer without money seemed to be quite as efficacious as prayer with money; and that neither the road to Heaven nor Heaven itself had been made surer or brought nearer by an investment of capital which amounted to the best part of the wealth of France. Economically speaking, he became satisfied that his enormous money-investment had proved to be an almost total loss, and the reaction on his mind was as violent as the emotion. For three hundred years it prostrated France. The efforts of the bourgeoisie and the peasantry to recover their property, so far as it was recoverable, have lasted to the present day and we had best take care not to get mixed in those passions.

If you are to get the full enjoyment of Chartres, you must, for the time, believe in Mary as Bernard and Adam did, and feel her presence as the architects did, in every stone they placed, and every touch they chiselled. You must try first to rid your mind of the traditional idea that the Gothic is an intentional expression of religious gloom. The necessity for light was the motive of the Gothic architects. They needed light and always more light, until they sacrificed safety and common sense in trying to get it. They converted their walls into windows, raised their vaults, diminished their piers, until their churches could no longer stand. You will see the limits at Beauvais; at Chartres we have not got so far, but even here, in places where the Virgin wanted it,—as above the high altar,—the architect has taken all the light there was to take. For the same reason, fenestration[15] became the most important part of the Gothic architect's work, and at Chartres was uncommonly interesting because the architect was obliged to design a new system, which should at the same time satisfy the laws of construction and the taste and imagination of Mary. No doubt the first command of the Queen of Heaven was for light, but the second, at least equally imperative, was for colour. Any earthly queen, even though she were not Byzantine in taste, loved colour; and the truest of queens—the only true Queen of Queens—had richer and finer taste in colour than the queens of fifty earthly kingdoms, as you will see when we come to the immense effort to gratify her in the glass of her windows. Illusion for illusion,—granting for the moment that Mary was an illusion,—the Virgin

[14]Between 1711 and 1720 a giant financial speculation involving South Sea trade dominated London gossip. Investments experienced the extremes of boom and bust during this period.

[15]The placement of windows and doors in a structure.

Mother in this instance repaid to her worshippers a larger return for their money than the capitalist has ever been able to get, at least in this world, from any other illusion of wealth which he has tried to make a source of pleasure and profit.

The next point on which Mary evidently insisted was the arrangement for her private apartments, the apse, as distinguished from her throne-room, the choir; both being quite distinct from the hall, or reception-room of the public, which was the nave with its enlargements in the transepts. This arrangement marks the distinction between churches built as shrines for the deity and churches built as halls of worship for the public. The difference is chiefly in the apse, and the apse of Chartres is the most interesting of all apses from this point of view.

The Virgin required chiefly these three things, or, if you like, these four: space, light, convenience; and colour decoration to unite and harmonize the whole. This concerns the interior; on the exterior she required statuary, and the only complete system of decorative sculpture that existed seems to belong to her churches:—Paris, Rheims, Amiens, and Chartres. Mary required all this magnificence at Chartres for herself alone, not for the public. As far as one can see into the spirit of the builders, Chartres was exclusively intended for the Virgin, as the Temple of Abydos[16] was intended for Osiris. The wants of man, beyond a mere roof-cover, and perhaps space to some degree, enter to no very great extent into the problem of Chartres. Man came to render homage or to ask favours. The Queen received him in her palace, where she alone was at home, and alone gave commands.

The artist's second thought was to exclude from his work everything that could displease Mary; and since Mary differed from living queens only in infinitely greater majesty and refinement, the artist could admit only what pleased the actual taste of the great ladies who dictated taste at the Courts of France and England, which surrounded the little Court of the Counts of Chartres. What they were—these women of the twelfth and thirteenth centuries—we shall have to see or seek in other directions; but Chartres is perhaps the most magnificent and permanent monument they left of their taste, and we can begin here with learning certain things which they were not.

In the first place, they were not in the least vague, dreamy, or mystical in a modern sense;—far from it! They seemed anxious only to throw the mysteries into a blaze of light; not so much physical, perhaps,—since they, like all women, liked moderate shadow for their toilettes,—but luminous in the sense of faith. There is nothing about Chartres that you would think mystical, who know your Lohengrin, Siegfried, and Parsifal.[17] If you care to make a study of the whole literature of the subject, read M. Mâle's "Art Religieux du XIIIe Siècle en France," and use it for a guide-book. Here you need only note how symbolic and how simple the sculpture is, on the portals and porches. Even what seems a grotesque or an abstract idea is no more than the simplest child's personification. On the walls you may have noticed the *Ane qui vielle,*—the ass playing the lyre; and on all the old churches you can see "bestiaries," as they were called, of fabulous animals, symbolic or not; but the symbolism is as simple as the realism of the oxen at Laon. It gave play to the artist in his effort for variety of decoration, and it amused the people,—probably the Virgin also was not above

[16]An ancient Egyptian city near the Nile River.
[17]Three legendary heroes, the subjects of operas by the German composer Richard Wagner.

being amused;—now and then it seems about to suggest what you would call an esoteric meaning, that is to say, a meaning which each one of us can consider private property reserved for our own amusement, and from which the public is excluded; yet, in truth, in the Virgin's churches the public is never excluded, but invited. The Virgin even had the additional charm of the public that she was popularly supposed to have no very marked fancy for priests as such; she was a queen, a woman, and a mother, functions, all, which priests could not perform. Accordingly, she seems to have had little taste for mysteries of any sort, and even the symbols that seem most mysterious were clear to every old peasant-woman in her church. The most pleasing and promising of them all is the woman's figure you saw on the front of the cathedral in Paris; her eyes bandaged; her head bent down; her crown falling; without cloak or royal robe; holding in her hand a guidon or banner with its staff broken in more than one place. On the opposite pier stands another woman, with royal mantle, erect and commanding. The symbol is so graceful that one is quite eager to know its meaning; but every child in the Middle Ages would have instantly told you that the woman with the falling crown meant only the Jewish Synagogue, as the one with the royal robe meant the Church of Christ.

Another matter for which the female taste seemed not much to care was theology in the metaphysical sense. Mary troubled herself little about theology except when she retired into the south transept with Pierre de Dreux.[18] Even there one finds little said about the Trinity, always the most metaphysical subtlety of the Church. Indeed, you might find much amusement here in searching the cathedral for any distinct expression at all of the Trinity as a dogma recognized by Mary. One cannot take seriously the idea that the three doors, the three portals, and the three aisles express the Trinity, because, in the first place, there was no rule about it; churches might have what portals and aisles they pleased; both Paris and Bourges have five; the doors themselves are not allotted to the three members of the Trinity, nor are the portals; while another more serious objection is that the side doors and aisles are not of equal importance with the central, but mere adjuncts and dependencies, so that the architect who had misled the ignorant public in accepting so black a heresy would have deserved the stake, and would probably have gone to it. Even this suggestion of Trinity is wanting in the transepts, which have only one aisle, and in the choir, which has five, as well as five or seven chapels, and, as far as an ignorant mind can penetrate, no triplets whatever. Occasionally, no doubt, you will discover in some sculpture or window, a symbol of the Trinity, but this discovery itself amounts to an admission of its absence as a controlling idea, for the ordinary worshipper must have been at least as blind as we are, and to him, as to us, it would have seemed a wholly subordinate detail. Even if the Trinity, too, is anywhere expressed, you will hardly find here an attempt to explain its metaphysical meaning—not even a mystic triangle.

The church is wholly given up to the Mother and the Son. The Father seldom appears; the Holy Ghost still more rarely. At least, this is the impression made on an ordinary visitor who has no motive to be orthodox; and it must have been the same with the thirteenth-century worshipper who came here with his mind absorbed in the perfections of Mary. Chartres represents, not the Trinity, but the identity of the Mother

[18]A Duke of Brittany who built the south porch of Chartres.

and Son. The Son represents the Trinity, which is thus absorbed in the Mother. The idea is not orthodox, but this is no affair of ours. The Church watches over its own.

The Virgin's wants and tastes, positive and negative, ought now to be clear enough to enable you to feel the artist's sincerity in trying to satisfy them; but first you have still to convince yourselves of the people's sincerity in employing the artists. This point is the easiest of all, for the evidence is express. In the year 1145 when the old flèche was begun,—the year before Saint Bernard preached the second crusade at Vézelay,—Abbot Haimon, of Saint-Pierre-sur-Dives in Normandy, wrote to the monks of Tutbury Abbey in England a famous letter to tell of the great work which the Virgin was doing in France and which began at the Church of Chartres. "Hujus sacræ institutionis ritus apud Carnotensem, ecclesiam est inchoatus."[19] From Chartres it had spread through Normandy, where it produced among other things the beautiful spire which we saw at Saint-Pierre-sur-Dives. "Postremo per totam fere Normanniam longe lateque convaluit ac loca per singula Matri misericordiæ dicata præcipue occupavit."[20] The movement affected especially the places devoted to Mary, but ran through all Normandy, far and wide. Of all Mary's miracles, the best attested, next to the preservation of her church, is the building of it; not so much because it surprises us as because it surprised even more the people of the time and the men who were its instruments. Such deep popular movements are always surprising, and at Chartres the miracle seems to have occurred three times, coinciding more or less with the dates of the crusades, and taking the organization of a crusade, as Archbishop Hugo of Rouen described it in a letter to Bishop Thierry of Amiens. The most interesting part of this letter is the evident astonishment of the writer, who might be talking to us to-day, so modern is he:—

> *The inhabitants of Chartres have combined to aid in the construction of their church by transporting the materials; our Lord has rewarded their humble zeal by miracles which have roused the Normans to imitate the piety of their neighbours. . . . Since then the faithful of our diocese and of other neighbouring regions have formed associations for the same object; they admit no one into their company unless he has been to confession, has renounced enmities and revenges, and has reconciled himself with his enemies. That done, they elect a chief, under whose direction they conduct their waggons in silence and with humility.*

The quarries at Berchères-l'Evêque are about five miles from Chartres. The stone is excessively hard, and was cut in blocks of considerable size, as you can see for yourselves; blocks which required great effort to transport and lay in place. The work was done with feverish rapidity, as it still shows, but it is the solidist building of the age, and without a sign of weakness yet. The Abbot told, with more surprise than pride, of the spirit which was built into the cathedral with the stone:—

> *Who has ever seen!—Who has ever heard tell, in times past, that powerful princes of the world, that men brought up in honour and in wealth, that nobles, men*

[19]"This holy institutional work was begun at the church of Chartres."

[20]"Finally it became established far and wide through almost all Normandy, and especially it took hold in certain places dedicated to the Mother of Mercy."

and women, have bent their proud and haughty necks to the harness of carts, and that, like beasts of burden, they have dragged to the abode of Christ these waggons, loaded with wines, grains, oil, stone, wood, and all that is necessary for the wants of life, or for the construction of the church? But while they draw these burdens, there is one thing admirable to observe; it is that often when a thousand persons and more are attached to the chariots,—so great is the difficulty,—yet they march in such silence that not a murmur is heard, and truly if one did not see the thing with one's eyes, one might believe that among such a multitude there was hardly a person present. When they halt on the road, nothing is heard but the confession of sins, and pure and suppliant prayer to God to obtain pardon. At the voice of the priests who exhort their hearts to peace, they forget all hatred, discord is thrown far aside, debts are remitted, the unity of hearts is established. But if any one is so far advanced in evil as to be unwilling to pardon an offender, or if he rejects the counsel of the priest who has piously advised him, his offering is instantly thrown from the wagon as impure, and he himself ignominiously and shamefully excluded from the society of the holy. There one sees the priests who preside over each chariot exhort every one to penitence, to confession of faults, to the resolution of better life! There one sees old people, young people, little children, calling on the Lord with a suppliant voice, and uttering to Him, from the depth of the heart, sobs and sighs with words of glory and praise! After the people, warned by the sound of trumpets and the sight of banners, have resumed their road, the march is made with such ease that no obstacle can retard it. . . . When they have reached the church they arrange the wagons about it like a spiritual camp, and during the whole night they celebrate the watch by hymns and canticles. On each waggon they light tapers and lamps; they place there the infirm and sick, and bring them the precious relics of the Saints for their relief. Afterwards the priests and clerics close the ceremony by processions which the people follow with devout heart, imploring the clemency of the Lord and of his Blessed Mother for the recovery of the sick.

Of course, the Virgin was actually and constantly present during all this labour, and gave her assistance to it, about you would get no light on the architecture from listening to an account of her miracles, nor do they heighten the effect of popular faith. Without the conviction of her personal presence, men would not have been inspired; but, to us, it is rather the inspiration of the art which proves the Virgin's presence, and we can better see the conviction of it in the work than in the words. Every day, as the work went on, the Virgin was present, directing the architects, and it is this direction that we are going to study, if you have now got a realizing sense of what it meant. Without this sense, the church is dead. Most persons of a deeply religious nature would tell you emphatically that nine churches out of ten actually were dead-born, after the thirteenth century, and that church architecture became a pure matter of mechanism and mathematics; but that is a question for you to decide when you come to it; and the pleasure consists not in seeing the death, but in feeling the life.

Now let us look about!

1904

from The Education of Henry Adams

Chapter XXV The Dynamo and the Virgin

[In *The Education of Henry Adams* the author organizes a perceptive commentary on his own times around the facts of his autobiography. Unlike many other autobiographers, however, Adams always resists frank revelation; he does not bare his soul to the reader. His individual experience, distanced through his use of the third person, becomes a sample used to measure the results of human evolution, as Adams compares and contrasts his own life and time with the distant past. That connection between present and past becomes explicit in the very title of Chapter XXV of the *Education,* where both the dynamo and the Virgin share the representative value of force or energy sufficient to get work done in the world. By placing them side by side Adams suggests that the religious faith of the medieval past has been replaced by the forces of modern science and industry, as seen in the electrical power that the dynamo can generate.]

Until the Great Exposition of 1900 closed its doors in November, Adams haunted it, aching to absorb knowledge, and helpless to find it.[1] He would have liked to know how much of it could have been grasped by the best-informed man in the world. While he was thus meditating chaos, Langley came by, and showed it to him. At Langley's[2] behest, the Exhibition dropped its superfluous rags and stripped itself to the skin, for Langley knew what to study, and why, and how; while Adams might as well have stood outside in the night, staring at the Milky Way. Yet Langley said nothing new, and taught nothing that one might not have learned from Lord Bacon, three hundred years before; but though one should have known the "Advancement of Science"[3] as well as one knew the "Comedy of Errors,"[4] the literary knowledge counted for nothing until some teacher should show how to apply it. Bacon took a vast deal of trouble in teaching King James I and his subjects, American or other, towards the year 1620, that true science was the development or economy of forces; yet an elderly American in 1900 knew neither the formula nor the forces; or even so much as to say to himself that his historical business in the Exposition concerned only the economies of developments of force since 1893, when he began the study at Chicago.[5]

Nothing in education is so astonishing as the amount of ignorance it accumulates in the form of inert facts. Adams had looked at most of the accumulations of art in the storehouses called Art Museums; yet he did not know how to look at the art exhibits of 1900. He had studied Karl Marx and his doctrines of history with profound attention, yet he could not apply them at Paris. Langley, with the ease of a great master of experiment, threw out of the field every exhibit that did not reveal a

[1]The Paris Exposition opened on April 15, 1900, and lasted for seven months.

[2]Samuel Pierpont Langley (1834–1906), astronomer and pioneer in aerodynamical experiments. A friend and mentor to Adams.

[3]Adams may have mistaken the title of Francis Bacon's *The Advancement of Learning* (1605).

[4]A play by Shakespeare.

[5]The World's Columbian Exposition held at Chicago in 1893.

new application of force, and naturally threw out, to begin with, almost the whole art exhibit. Equally, he ignored almost the whole industrial exhibit. He led his pupil directly to the forces. His chief interest was in new motors to make his airship feasible, and he taught Adams the astonishing complexities of the new Daimler motor, and of the automobile, which, since 1893, had become a nightmare at a hundred kilometres an hour, almost as destructive as the electric tram which was only ten years older; and threatening to become as terrible as the locomotive steam-engine itself, which was almost exactly Adams's own age.

Then he showed his scholar the great hall of dynamos, and explained how little he knew about electricity or force of any kind, even of his own special sun, which spouted heat in inconceivable volume, but which, as far as he knew, might spout less or more, at any time, for all the certainty he felt in it. To him, the dynamo itself was but an ingenious channel for conveying somewhere the heat latent in a few tons of poor coal hidden in a dirty engine-house carefully kept out of sight; but to Adams the dynamo became a symbol of infinity. As he grew accustomed to the great gallery of machines, he began to feel the forty-foot dynamos as a moral force, much as the early Christians felt the Cross. The planet itself seemed less impressive, in its old-fashioned, deliberate, annual or daily revolution, than this huge wheel, revolving within arm's-length at some vertiginous speed, and barely murmuring—scarcely humming an audible warning to stand a hair's-breadth further for respect of power—while it would not wake the baby lying close against its frame. Before the end, one began to pray to it; inherited instinct taught the natural expression of man before silent and infinite force. Among the thousand symbols of ultimate energy, the dynamo was not so human as some, but it was the most expressive.

Yet the dynamo, next to the steam-engine, was the most familiar of exhibits. For Adams's objects its value lay chiefly in its occult mechanism. Between the dynamo in the gallery of machines and the engine-house outside, the break of continuity amounted to abysmal fracture for a historian's objects. No more relation could he discover between the steam and the electric current than between the Cross and the cathedral. The forces were interchangeable if not reversible, but he could see only an absolute *fiat* in electricity as in faith. Langley could not help him. Indeed, Langley seemed to be worried by the same trouble, for he constantly repeated that the new forces were anarchical, and especially that he was not responsible for the new rays, that were little short of parricidal in their wicked spirit towards science. His own rays, with which he had doubled the solar spectrum, were altogether harmless and beneficent; but Radium denied its God—or, what was to Langley the same thing, denied the truths of his Science. The force was wholly new.

A historian who asked only to learn enough to be as futile as Langley or Kelvin,[6] made rapid progress under this teaching, and mixed himself up in the tangle of ideas until he achieved a sort of Paradise of ignorance vastly consoling to his fatigued senses. He wrapped himself in vibrations and rays which were new, and he would have hugged Marconi and Branly[7] had he met them, as he hugged the dynamo; while he lost his arithmetic in trying to figure out the equation between the discoveries and

[6]Lord Kelvin (1824–1907), famous British scientist.

[7]Guglielmo Marconi (1834–1937) and Edouard Branly (1846–1940), played important roles in the development of radio and the understanding of sound waves.

the economies of force. The economies, like the discoveries, were absolute, supersensual, occult; incapable of expression in horse-power. What mathematical equivalent could he suggest as the value of a Branly coherer? Frozen air, or the electric furnace, had some scale of measurement, no doubt, if somebody could invent a thermometer adequate to the purpose; but X-rays had played no part whatever in man's consciousness, and the atom itself had figured only as a fiction of thought. In these seven years man had translated himself into a new universe which had no common scale of measurement with the old. He had entered a supersensual world, in which he could measure nothing except by chance collisions of movements imperceptible to his senses, perhaps even imperceptible to his instruments, but perceptible to each other, and so to some known ray at the end of the scale. Langley seemed prepared for anything, even for an indeterminable number of universes interfused—physics stark mad in metaphysics.

Historians undertake to arrange sequences,—called stories, or histories—assuming in silence a relation of cause and effect. These assumptions, hidden in the depths of dusty libraries, have been astounding, but commonly unconscious and childlike; so much so, that if any captious critic were to drag them to light, historians would probably reply, with one voice, that they had never supposed themselves required to know what they were talking about. Adams, for one, had toiled in vain to find out what he meant. He had even published a dozen volumes of American history for no other purpose than to satisfy himself whether, by the severest process of stating, with the least possible comment, such facts as seemed sure, in such order as seemed rigorously consequent, he could fix for a familiar moment a necessary sequence of human movement. The result had satisfied him as little as at Harvard College. Where he saw sequence, other men saw something quite different, and no one saw the same unit of measure. He cared little about his experiments and less about his statesmen, who seemed to him quite as ignorant as himself and, as a rule, no more honest; but he insisted on a relation of sequence, and if he could not reach it by one method, he would try as many methods as science knew. Satisfied that the sequence of men led to nothing and that the sequence of their society could lead no further, while the mere sequence of time was artificial, and the sequence of thought was chaos, he turned at last to the sequence of force; and thus it happened that, after ten years' pursuit, he found himself lying in the Gallery of Machines at the Great Exposition of 1900, his historical neck broken by the sudden irruption of forces totally new.

Since no one else showed much concern, an elderly person without other cares had no need to betray alarm. The year 1900 was not the first to upset schoolmasters. Copernicus and Galileo[8] had broken many professional necks about 1600; Columbus had stood the world on its head towards 1500; but the nearest approach to the revolution of 1900 was that of 310, when Constantine set up the Cross.[9] The rays that Langley disowned, as well as those which he fathered, were occult, supersensual, irrational; they were a revelation of mysterious energy like that of the Cross; they were

[8]Copernicus (1473–1543) and Galileo (1564–1642), astronomers who helped to establish belief in the sun, rather than the earth, as the center of the universe.

[9]Adams treats 310 as the beginning of Christianity in the Roman Empire under Constantine I.

what, in terms of mediaeval science, were called immediate modes of the divine substance.

The historian was thus reduced to his last resources. Clearly if he was bound to reduce all these forces to a common value, this common value could have no measure but that of their attraction on his own mind. He must treat them as they had been felt; as convertible, reversible, interchangeable attractions on thought. He made up his mind to venture it; he would risk translating rays into faith. Such a reversible process would vastly amuse a chemist, but the chemist could not deny that he, or some of his fellow physicists, could feel the force of both. When Adams was a boy in Boston, the best chemist in the place had probably never heard of Venus except by way of scandal, or of the Virgin except as idolatry; neither had he heard of dynamos or automobiles or radium; yet his mind was ready to feel the force of all, though the rays were unborn and the women were dead.

Here opened another totally new education, which promised to be by far the most hazardous of all. The knife-edge along which he must crawl, like Sir Lancelot[10] in the twelfth century, divided two kingdoms of force which had nothing in common but attraction. They were as different as a magnet is from gravitation, supposing one knew what a magnet was, or gravitation, or love. The force of the Virgin was still felt at Lourdes, and seemed to be as potent as X-rays; but in America neither Venus nor Virgin ever had value as force—at most as sentiment. No American had ever been truly afraid of either.

This problem in dynamics gravely perplexed an American historian. The Woman had once been supreme; in France she still seemed potent, not merely as a sentiment, but as a force. Why was she unknown in America? For evidently America was ashamed of her, and she was ashamed of herself, otherwise they would not have strewn fig-leaves so profusely all over her. When she was a true force, she was ignorant of fig-leaves, but the monthly-magazine-made American female had not a feature that would have been recognized by Adam.[11] The trait was notorious, and often humorous, but any one brought up among Puritans knew that sex was sin. In any previous age, sex was strength. Neither art nor beauty was needed. Every one, even among Puritans, knew that neither Diana of the Ephesians[12] nor any of the Oriental goddesses was worshipped for her beauty. She was goddess because of her force; she was the animated dynamo; she was reproduction—the greatest and most mysterious of all energies; all she needed was to be fecund. Singularly enough, not one of Adams's many schools of education had ever drawn his attention to the opening lines of Lucretius, though they were perhaps the finest in all Latin literature, where the poet invoked Venus exactly as Dante invoked the Virgin:—

> "Quae quoniam rerum naturam *sola* gubernas."[13]

The Venus of Epicurean philosophy survived in the Virgin of the Schools:—

[10]A legendary hero of chivalric tales.

[11]In "Genesis," after the Fall, Eve and Adam covered their genitals with fig leaves, as a sign of shame. Popular ("monthly-magazine") literature especially avoided dealing with sexuality.

[12]Goddess of the moon and of the hunt.

[13]From *De Rerum Natura,* "Since you [Venus] alone govern the nature of things."

"Donna, sei tanto grande, e tanto vali,
Che qual vuol grazia, e a te non ricorre,
Sua disianza vuol volar senz' ali."[14]

All this was to American thought as though it had never existed. The true American knew something of the facts, but nothing of the feelings; he read the letter, but he never felt the law. Before this historical chasm, a mind like that of Adams felt itself helpless; he turned from the Virgin to the Dynamo as though he were a Branly coherer. On one side, at the Louvre and at Chartres, as he knew by the record of work actually done and still before his eyes, was the highest energy ever known to man, the creator of four-fifths of his noblest art, exercising vastly more attraction over the human mind than all the steam-engines and dynamos ever dreamed of; and yet this energy was unknown to the American mind. An American Virgin would never dare command; an American Venus would never dare exist.

The question, which to any plain American of the nineteenth century seemed as remote as it did to Adams, drew him almost violently to study, once it was posed; and on this point Langleys were as useless as though they were Herbert Spencers[15] or dynamos. The idea survived only as art. There one turned as naturally as though the artist were himself a woman. Adams began to ponder, asking himself whether he knew of any American artist who had ever insisted on the power of sex, as every classic had always done; but he could think only of Walt Whitman; Bret Harte, as far as the magazines would let him venture; and one or two painters, for the fleshtones. All the rest had used sex for sentiment, never for force; to them, Eve was a tender flower, and Herodias[16] an un-feminine horror. American art, like the American language and American education, was as far as possible sexless. Society regarded this victory over sex as its greatest triumph, and the historian readily admitted it, since the moral issue, for the moment, did not concern one who was studying the relations of unmoral force. He cared nothing for the sex of the dynamo until he could measure its energy.

Vaguely seeking a clue, he wandered through the art exhibit, and, in his stroll, stopped almost every day before St. Gaudens's General Sherman,[17] which had been given the central post of honor. St. Gaudens himself was in Paris, putting on the work his usual interminable last touches, and listening to the usual contradictory suggestions of brother sculptors. Of all the American artists who gave to American art whatever life it breathed in the seventies, St. Gaudens was perhaps the most sympathetic, but certainly the most inarticulate. General Grant or Don Cameron[18] had scarcely less instinct of rhetoric than he. All the others—the Hunts, Richardson, John La Farge, Stanford White—were exuberant; only St. Gaudens could never discuss or dilate on an emotion, or suggest artistic arguments for giving to his work the forms that he felt. He never laid down the law, or affected the despot, or became bru-

[14]From Dante, *Divine Comedy* ("Paradiso"), "Lady [Virgin Mary], thou art so great and hast such worth, that if there be one who would have grace yet who has not betaken himself to thee, his longing seeketh to fly without wings."

[15]Herbert Spencer (1820–1903), popularizer of Darwinism in England and America.

[16]King Herod's wife, who ordered that John the Baptist be slain.

[17]A statue by Augustus Saint-Gaudens (1848–1907), now located in Central Park, New York City. It was then in Paris.

[18]James Donald Cameron (1833–1918), U.S. Senator and Secretary of War under President Grant.

talized like Whistler by the brutalities of his world. He required no incense; he was no egoist; his simplicity of thought was excessive; he could not imitate, or give any form but his own to the creations of his hand. No one felt more strongly than he the strength of other men, but the idea that they could affect him never stirred an image in his mind.

This summer his health was poor and his spirits were low. For such a temper, Adams was not the best companion, since his own gaiety was not *folle;*[19] but he risked going now and then to the studio on Mont Parnasse to draw him out for a stroll in the Bois de Boulogne,[20] or dinner as pleased his moods, and in return St. Gaudens sometimes let Adams go about in his company.

Once St. Gaudens took him down to Amiens, with a party of Frenchmen, to see the cathedral. Not until they found themselves actually studying the sculpture of the western portal, did it dawn on Adams's mind that, for his purposes, St. Gaudens on that spot had more interest to him than the cathedral itself. Great men before great monuments express great truths, provided they are not taken too solemnly. Adams never tired of quoting the supreme phrase of his idol Gibbon, before the Gothic cathedrals: "I darted a contemptuous look on the stately monuments of superstition." Even in the footnotes of his history, Gibbon had never inserted a bit of humor more human than this, and one would have paid largely for a photograph of the fat little historian, on the background of Notre Dame of Amiens, trying to persuade his readers—perhaps himself—that he was darting a contemptuous look on the stately monument, for which he felt in fact the respect which every man of his vast study and active mind always feels before objects worthy of it; but besides the humor, one felt also the relation. Gibbon ignored the Virgin, because in 1789 religious monuments were out of fashion. In 1900 his remark sounded fresh and simple as the green fields to ears that had heard a hundred years of other remarks, mostly no more fresh and certainly less simple. Without malice, one might find it more instructive than a whole lecture of Ruskin. One sees what one brings, and at that moment Gibbon brought the French Revolution. Ruskin brought reaction against the Revolution. St. Gaudens had passed beyond all. He liked the stately monuments much more than he liked Gibbon or Ruskin;[21] he loved their dignity; their unity; their scale; their lines; their lights and shadows; their decorative sculpture; but he was even less conscious than they of the force that created it all—the Virgin, the Woman—by whose genius "the stately monuments of superstition" were built, through which she was expressed. He would have seen more meaning in Isis[22] with the cow's horns, at Edfoo, who expressed the same thought. The art remained, but the energy was lost even upon the artist.

Yet in mind and person St. Gaudens was a survivor of the 1500s; he bore the stamp of the Renaissance, and should have carried an image of the Virgin round his neck, or stuck in his hat, like Louis XI. In mere time he was a lost soul that had strayed by chance into the twentieth century, and forgotten where it came from. He

[19]"Wild" or "mad."

[20]Mont Parnasse and the Bois de Boulogne are well-known sections of Paris.

[21]John Ruskin (1819–1900), English critic of art and architecture.

[22]Adams had seen a statue of the goddess Isis during a trip along the Nile River, at Edfu (or "Edfoo") in Egypt.

writhed and cursed at his ignorance, much as Adams did at his own, but in the opposite sense. St. Gaudens was a child of Benvenuto Cellini,[23] smothered in an American cradle. Adams was a quintessence of Boston, devoured by curiosity to think like Benvenuto. St. Gaudens's art was starved from birth, and Adams's instinct was blighted from babyhood. Each had but half of a nature, and when they came together before the Virgin of Amiens they ought both to have felt in her the force that made them one; but it was not so. To Adams she became more than ever a channel of force; to St. Gaudens she remained as before a channel of taste.

For a symbol of power, St. Gaudens instinctively preferred the horse, as was plain in his horse and Victory of the Sherman monument. Doubtless Sherman also felt it so. The attitude was so American that, for at least forty years, Adams had never realized that any other could be in sound taste. How many years had he taken to admit a notion of what Michael Angelo and Rubens were driving at? He could not say; but he knew that only since 1895 had he begun to feel the Virgin or Venus as force, and not everywhere even so. At Chartres—perhaps at Lourdes—possibly at Cnidos if one could still find there the divinely naked Aphrodite of Praxiteles[24]—but otherwise one must look for force to the goddesses of Indian mythology. The idea died out long ago in the German and English stock. St. Gaudens at Amiens was hardly less sensitive to the force of the female energy than Matthew Arnold at the Grande Chartreuse.[25] Neither of them felt goddesses as power—only as reflected emotion, human expression, beauty, purity, taste, scarcely even as sympathy. They felt a railway train as power; yet they, and all other artists, constantly complained that the power embodied in a railway train could never be embodied in art. All the steam in the world could not, like the Virgin, build Chartres.

Yet in mechanics, whatever the mechanicians might think, both energies acted as interchangeable forces on man, and by action on man all known force may be measured. Indeed, few men of science measured force in any other way. After once admitting that a straight line was the shortest distance between two points, no serious mathematician cared to deny anything that suited his convenience, and rejected no symbol, unproved or unproveable, that helped him to accomplish work. The symbol was force, as a compass-needle or a triangle was force, as the mechanist might prove by losing it, and nothing could be gained by ignoring their value. Symbol or energy, the Virgin had acted as the greatest force the Western world ever felt, and had drawn man's activities to herself more strongly than any other power, natural or supernatural, had ever done; the historian's business was to follow the track of the energy; to find where it came from and where it went to; its complex source and shifting channels; its values, equivalents, conversions. It could scarcely be more complex than radium; it could hardly be deflected, diverted, polarized, absorbed more perplexingly than other radiant matter. Adams knew nothing about any of them, but as a mathematical problem of influence on human progress, though all were occult, all reacted on his mind, and he rather inclined to think the Virgin easiest to handle.

The pursuit turned out to be long and tortuous, leading at last into the vast

[23]Cellini (1500–1571) was an Italian artist who wrote a famous autobiography.

[24]A Greek sculptor (4th century B.C.) who created a famous statue of Venus (Aphrodite).

[25]Arnold (1822–1888) wrote "Stanzas from the Grande Chartreuse," an English poem about the loss of medieval religious faith.

forests of scholastic science. From Zeno to Descartes, hand in hand with Thomas Aquinas, Montaigne, and Pascal, one stumbled as stupidly as though one were still a German student of 1860.[26] Only with the instinct of despair could one force one's self into this old thicket of ignorance after having been repulsed at a score of entrances more promising and more popular. Thus far, no path had led anywhere, unless perhaps to an exceedingly modest living. Forty-five years of study had proved to be quite futile for the pursuit of power; one controlled no more force in 1900 than in 1850, although the amount of force controlled by society had enormously increased. The secret of education still hid itself somewhere behind ignorance, and one fumbled over it as feebly as ever. In such labyrinths, the staff is a force almost more necessary than the legs; the pen becomes a sort of blind-man's dog, to keep him from falling into the gutters. The pen works for itself, and acts like a hand, modelling the plastic material over and over again to the form that suits it best. The form is never arbitrary, but is a sort of growth like crystallization, as any artist knows too well; for often the pencil or pen runs into side-paths and shapelessness, loses its relations, stops or is bogged. Then it has to return on its trail, and recover, if it can, its line of force. The result of a year's work depends more on what is struck out than on what is left in; on the sequence of the main lines of thought, than on their play or variety. Compelled once more to lean heavily on this support, Adams covered more thousands of pages with figures as formal as though they were algebra, laboriously striking out, altering, burning, experimenting, until the year had expired, the Exposition had long been closed, and winter drawing to its end, before he sailed from Cherbourg, on January 19, 1901, for home.

1907

[26]Adams refers to his study of Greek, medieval, and seventeenth- and eighteenth-century philosophers, and his studies in Germany, 1858–1860.

Developments in Women's Writing

Although women writers are present in all parts of this anthology, we group some of them here in order to underscore what had become, by the second half of the nineteenth century, a major literary development: their participation in professional authorship in ever-increasing numbers and their forging, as a result, distinctive traditions of prose fiction. Well before the Civil War—indeed from the 1820s on—stories, sketches, and novels by women were providing the primary reading matter for the growing, and largely female, reading audience. Women wrote most of the bestsellers in the pre-war period, and their success encouraged others, who turned to writing both out of a need for self-expression and because it offered one of the more remunerative ways available to them of earning a living. The prose writings in this section, ranging from spiritual autobiography to historical tale and ghost story, from pastoral idyll to realistic and naturalistic prose fiction, suggest the rich diversity of forms within which black and white women as well as Native American women, Mexican American women, and others were writing by the second half of the century.

One important continuity between pre- and post-war women writers is to be found in the traditions of domestic realism, well developed by the 1850s, which post-war writers inherited, extended, and modified. Much post-war narrative, that is to say, focuses on women's daily lives presented in recognizable social, domestic, or natural settings. Often the stories engage the question—crucial in pre-war fiction and of even greater urgency in this new time of accelerated social and economic change—of the possibilities for, and the impediments to, female self-development, autonomy, and creative expression. It is no coincidence that many of the narratives in this section explicitly or implicitly deal with a woman's need to find her own voice. Being able to sing literally saves the life of Harriet Prescott Spofford's heroine; Julia Foote's spiritual well-being is intimately tied to her freedom to speak in public; in Sarah Orne Jewett's "A White Heron" the words that Sylvy can choose to utter to the hunter or withhold from him will determine her future and that of her natural world; out-arguing her minister marks a crucial moment in the successful revolt of "mother" in Mary E. Wilkins Freeman's "The Revolt of 'Mother.'" By contrast, the woman writer in Constance Fenimore Woolson's story is engaged in a losing struggle to get her own unique voice and vision into print. Whatever the circumstances, these are stories of women actively seeking self-definition and self-determination, encountering in their searches the barriers raised by race and class, by conventional views of woman's proper place, by social institutions, and by male power. Their stories thus become the ground from which their authors can critique and challenge the social, economic, political, literary, and religious arrangements and inequalities of American life.

For some authors, a female culture, celebrated in pre-war fiction, still offers nourishing and sustaining values. In Jewett's "The Foreigner," for example, female friendships provide emotional support and understanding. Such a female network was in fact a significant aspect of the professional lives of a number of the white women authors included in this unit. Spofford, Freeman, and Jewett were part of a group of women writers that also included Harriet Beecher Stowe, Catharine Sedgwick, Lydia Maria Child, Rose Terry Cooke, Rebecca Harding Davis, Alice French, and Celia Thaxter (many of whom are represented in Volume 1 of this anthology). For over four decades they found in the Boston home of Annie Adams Fields (1834–1915) a center for a rich, shared, intellectual, social, and emotional life. Wife and literary adviser to James T. Fields, who was editor of the *Atlantic Monthly* and partner in the prestigious publishing firm of Ticknor and Fields, Annie Fields was instrumental as author, editor, and hostess in advancing the careers of many women writers. Her friendship with Sarah Orne Jewett became the most important relationship in both of their lives in the years following James Fields's death in 1881.

But while some authors celebrate the continued viability of a female culture, the narratives included here also reveal women's growing restiveness inside institutions such as marriage and the church that had once fostered that culture. Although still operating within a Christian framework, authors like Foote and Freeman question in differing degrees the church's treatment of women and the poor; and the Christ-like behavior of the male protagonists in some of Pauline Hopkins's stories, though attesting to a continuing tradition of spirituality within the African American community, operates also as bitterly ironic comment on the pervasive racism in post-Civil War society. For such characters as Freeman's widow Magoun, Woolson's "Miss Grief," or Hopkins's Gentleman Jim, defeat and even death are the outcome of unequal struggles with class, race, and gender barriers. The implications of these more somber renderings would also be pursued by other women writers, such as Charlotte Perkins Gilman, Kate Chopin, Frances Ellen Watkins Harper, and Edith Wharton, in the 1880s and 1890s and into the twentieth century.

Although the major literary achievements of both male and female writers in the post-war period were in prose, whose reportorial possibilities seemed better suited to conveying the complexities of social and economic change, poetry continued to be written, a significant amount of it by women. Even more than their prose narratives, however, nineteenth-century women's poetry—especially that written after the Civil War—has been largely overlooked until recently. As this poetry now begins to be rediscovered and systematically examined, it reveals an unexpected richness and diversity of theme and style. The sampling included in this section shows women from a broad range of ethnic and racial groups and regions using lyric, narrative, and dramatic verse forms, often in new and unorthodox ways, to explore a variety of both personal and public concerns, from marriage, love, and sexuality to religion and politics. By the 1890s, indeed, their short, finely crafted and often ironic verses were anticipating the new poetry that would be an important part of the modernist movement in the early twentieth century.

Elaine Hedges
late of Towson State University

Julia A. J. Foote 1823–1900

Julia A. J. Foote's autobiography, *A Brand Plucked from the Fire* (1879), is representative of a large number of similar texts published by nineteenth-century black and white women who believed that Christianity had made them the spiritual equals of men and hence equally authorized to lead the church. Her belief in the androgyny of the Christian spirit and her refusal to defer to husband or minister when her own intuitive sense of personal authority was at stake mark Foote's autobiographical work as an important early expression of the American feminist literary tradition.

Foote was born in Schenectady, New York, the daughter of former slaves. Her parents were strongly committed to Methodism and to the education of their children. Because Schenectady's schools were segregated, Foote's parents hired her out as a domestic servant to a white family who used their influence to place her in a country school outside the city. Here, between the ages of ten and twelve, Julia Foote received the only formal education of her life. Despite the fact that her teenage years were devoted to the care of her younger siblings, she read considerably, especially in the Bible, and attended many church meetings. When she was fifteen, she had a profound conversion experience and joined an African Methodist Episcopal church in Albany, New York. Three years later she married George Foote, a sailor, and moved with him to Boston.

Having no children, Foote devoted a great deal of her time to informal evangelistic work in her community, in which she testified to her belief in the doctrine of "sanctification." The controversial idea that a Christian could be sanctified—totally freed from sin and empowered to lead a life of spiritual perfection—had been under debate in Methodist circles for decades. Advocates of sanctification and perfectionism became leaders in the rise of "holiness" movements in evangelical denominations in the United States during the mid- and late-nineteenth century. Foote's belief that she herself had been sanctified by the Holy Spirit contributed to her growing conviction that her destiny was to become a preacher. George Foote was skeptical about his wife's religious beliefs and attempted to curb her public activities; when she resisted his arguments, he drifted out of her life.

Foote knew that a woman who claimed a divine calling to the ministry challenged Christian tradition and American social prejudice. Women were not expected to assume public leadership positions, nor were they allowed to speak, except under restrictions, in most Christian churches. Yet Foote could neither deny her conscience nor shirk the work that she felt had been given her to do. When the minister of her church in Boston refused her access to his pulpit and threatened to expel her from the congregation, she refused to be daunted. She took her case to higher denominational authorities, and when she received no support from them, she set out on an independent preaching career.

In the mid-1840s she evangelized the upstate New York region, often accompanied or invited by ministers of the A.M.E. church. By 1850 she had crossed the Allegheny Mountains in search of new converts in Ohio and Michigan. She participated in the holiness revivals that swept the Midwest during the 1870s and later became a missionary in the A.M.E. Zion church. During the last decade of her life, she became the first woman to be ordained a deacon and the second woman to hold the office of elder in her denomination. Although her autobiography attacks racism and other social abuses, it is the subordination of women, especially in the spiritual realm, and her desire to inspire faith in her Christian sisters that endow her story with its distinctive voice and intensity.

William L. Andrews
University of North Carolina–Chapel Hill

PRIMARY WORKS

William L. Andrews, ed., *Sisters of the Spirit: Three Black Women's Autobiographies of the Nineteenth Century,* 1986.

from A Brand Plucked from the Fire

Chapter XVII My Call to Preach the Gospel

For months I had been moved upon to exhort and pray with the people, in my visits from house to house; and in meetings my whole soul seemed drawn out for the salvation of souls. The love of Christ in me was not limited. Some of my mistaken friends said I was too forward, but a desire to work for the Master, and to promote the glory of his kingdom in the salvation of souls, was food to my poor soul.

When called of God, on a particular occasion, to a definite work, I said, "No, Lord, not me." Day by day I was more impressed that God would have me work in his vineyard. I thought it could not be that I was called to preach—I, so weak and ignorant. Still, I knew all things were possible with God, even to confounding the wise by the foolish things of this earth. Yet in me there was a shrinking.

I took all my doubts and fears to the Lord in prayer, when, what seemed to be an angel, made his appearance. In his hand was a scroll, on which were these words: "Thee have I chosen to preach my Gospel without delay." The moment my eyes saw it, it appeared to be printed on my heart. The angel was gone in an instant, and I, in agony, cried out, "Lord, I cannot do it!" It was eleven o'clock in the morning, yet everything grew dark as night. The darkness was so great that I feared to stir.

At last "Mam" Riley[1] entered. As she did so, the room grew lighter, and I arose from my knees. My heart was so heavy I scarce could speak. Dear "Mam" Riley saw my distress, and soon left me.

From that day my appetite failed me and sleep fled from my eyes. I seemed as one tormented. I prayed, but felt no better. I belonged to a band of sisters whom I loved dearly, and to them I partially opened my mind. One of them seemed to understand my case at once, and advised me to do as God had bid me, or I would never be happy here or hereafter. But it seemed too hard—I could not give up and obey.

One night as I lay weeping and beseeching the dear Lord to remove this burden from me, there appeared the same angel that came to me before, and on his breast were these words: "You are lost unless you obey God's righteous commands." I saw the writing, and that was enough. I covered my head and awoke my husband, who had returned a few days before. He asked me why I trembled so, but I had not power to answer him. I remained in that condition until morning, when I tried to arise and go about my usual duties, but was too ill. Then my husband called a physician, who prescribed medicine, but it did me no good.

I had always been opposed to the preaching of women, and had spoken against it, though, I acknowledge, without foundation. This rose before me like a mountain, and when I thought of the difficulties they had to encounter, both from professors and non-professors, I shrank back and cried, "Lord, I cannot go!"

The trouble my heavenly Father has had to keep me out of the fire that is never quenched, he alone knoweth. My husband and friends said I would die or go crazy

[1]A close friend and confidante of Foote's in Boston.

if something favorable did not take place soon. I expected to die and be lost, knowing I had been enlightened and had tasted the heavenly gift. I read again and again the sixth chapter of Hebrews.[2]

Chapter XIX Public Effort—Excommunication

From this time the opposition to my lifework commenced, instigated by the minister, Mr. Beman.[3] Many in the church were anxious to have me preach in the hall, where our meetings were held at that time, and were not a little astonished at the minister's cool treatment of me. At length two of the trustees got some of the elder sisters to call on the minister and ask him to let me preach. His answer was: "No; she can't preach her holiness stuff here, and I am astonished that you should ask it of me." The sisters said he seemed to be in quite a rage, although he said he was not angry.

There being no meeting of the society on Monday evening, a brother in the church opened his house to me, that I might preach, which displeased Mr. Beman very much. He appointed a committee to wait upon the brother and sister who had opened their doors to me, to tell them they must not allow any more meetings of that kind, and that they must abide by the rules of the church, making them believe they would be excommunicated if they disobeyed him. I happened to be present at this interview, and the committee remonstrated with me for the course I had taken. I told them my business was with the Lord, and wherever I found a door opened I intended to go in and work for my Master.

There was another meeting appointed at the same place, which I, of course, attended; after which the meetings were stopped for that time, though I held many more there after these people had withdrawn from Mr. Beman's church.

I then held meetings in my own house; whereat the minister told the members that if they attended them he would deal with them, for they were breaking the rules of the church. When he found that I continued the meetings, and that the Lord was blessing my feeble efforts, he sent a committee of two to ask me if I considered myself a member of his church. I told them I did, and should continue to do so until I had done something worthy of dismembership.

At this, Mr. Beman sent another committee with a note, asking me to meet him with the committee, which I did. He asked me a number of questions, nearly all of which I have forgotten. One, however, I do remember: he asked if I was willing to comply with the rules of the discipline. To this I answered: "Not if the discipline prohibits me from doing what God has bidden me to do; I fear God more than man." Similar questions were asked and answered in the same manner. The committee said what they wished to say, and then told me I could go home. When I reached the door,

[2] In this chapter Paul the Apostle urges his readers to remember God as "a sure and steadfast anchor of the soul" and to shun all forms of apostasy or disobedience to God's commands.

[3] Soon after Foote's experience of having been divinely called to preach, Rev. Jehiel C. Beman, pastor of the African Methodist Episcopal Zion church of Boston, informed her of his doubts about the authenticity of her call.

I turned and said: "I now shake off the dust of my feet as a witness against you [Mark 6:11; Luke 9:5]. See to it that this meeting does not rise in judgment against you."

The next evening, one of the committee came to me and told me that I was no longer a member of the church, because I had violated the rules of the discipline by preaching.

When this action became known, the people wondered how any one could be excommunicated for trying to do good. I did not say much, and my friends simply said I had done nothing but hold meetings. Others, anxious to know the particulars, asked the minister what the trouble was. He told them he had given me the privilege of speaking or preaching as long as I chose, but that he could not give me the right to use the pulpit, and that I was not satisfied with any other place. Also, that I had appointed meeting on the evening of his meetings, which was a thing no member had a right to do. For these reasons he said he had turned me out of the church.

Now, if the people who repeated this to me told the truth—and I have no doubt but they did—Mr. Beman told an actual falsehood. I had never asked for his pulpit, but had told him and others, repeatedly, that I did not care where I stood—any corner of the hall would do. To which Mr. Beman had answered: "You cannot have any place in the hall." Then I said: "I'll preach in a private house." He answered me: "No, not in this place; I am stationed over all Boston." He was determined I should not preach in the city of Boston. To cover up his deceptive, unrighteous course toward me, he told the above falsehoods.

From his statements, many erroneous stories concerning me gained credence with a large number of people. At that time, I thought it my duty as well as privilege to address a letter to the Conference, which I took to them in person, stating all the facts. At the same time I told them it was not in the power of Mr. Beman, or any one else, to truthfully bring anything against my moral or religious character—that my only offence was in trying to preach the Gospel of Christ—and that I cherished no ill feelings toward Mr. Beman or any one else, but that I desired the Conference to give the case an impartial hearing, and then give me a written statement expressive of their opinion. I also said I considered myself a member of the Conference, and should do so until they said I was not, and gave me their reasons, that I might let the world know what my offence had been.

My letter was slightingly noticed, and then thrown under the table. Why should they notice it? It was only the grievance of a woman, and there was no justice meted out to women in those days. Even ministers of Christ did not feel that women had any rights which they were bound to respect.[4]

Chapter XX Women in the Gospel

Thirty years ago[5] there could scarcely a person be found, in the churches, to sympathize with any one who talked of Holiness. But, in my simplicity, I did think that a

[4]A parody of the language of the Supreme Court's Dred Scott decision of 1857, in which Chief Justice Roger B. Taney stated that black Americans "had no rights which the white man was bound to respect."

[5]1850.

body of Christian ministers would understand my case and judge righteously. I was, however, disappointed.

It is no little thing to feel that every man's hand is against us, and ours against every man, as seemed to be the case with me at this time; yet how precious, if Jesus but be with us. In this severe trial I had constant access to God, and a clear consciousness that he heard me; yet I did not seem to have that plenitude of the Spirit that I had before. I realized most keenly that the closer the communion that may have existed, the keener the suffering of the slightest departure from God. Unbroken communion can only be retained by a constant application of the blood which cleanseth.

Though I did not wish to pain any one, neither could I please any one only as I was led by the Holy Spirit. I saw, as never before, that the best men were liable to err, and that the only safe way was to fall on Christ, even though censure and reproach fell upon me for obeying his voice. Man's opinion weighed nothing with me, for my commission was from heaven, and my reward was with the Most High.

I could not believe that it was a short-lived impulse or spasmodic influence that impelled me to preach. I read that on the day of Pentecost[6] was the Scripture fulfilled as found in Joel ii. 28, 29; and it certainly will not be denied that women as well as men were at the time filled with the Holy Ghost, because it is expressly stated that women were among those who continued in prayer and supplication, waiting for the fulfillment of the promise. Women and men are classed together, and if the power to preach the Gospel is short-lived and spasmodic in the case of women, it must be equally so in that of men; and if women have lost the gift of prophecy, so have men.

We are sometimes told that if a woman pretends to a Divine call, and thereon grounds the right to plead the cause of a crucified Redeemer in public, she will be believed when she shows credentials from heaven; that is, when she works a miracle. If it be necessary to prove one's right to preach the Gospel, I ask of my brethren to show me their credentials, or I can not believe in the propriety of their ministry.

But the Bible puts an end to this strife when it says: "There is neither male nor female in Christ Jesus" [Gal. 3:28]. Philip had four daughters that prophesied, or preached. Paul called Priscilla, as well as Aquila, his "helper," or, as in the Greek, his "fellow-laborer." Rom. xv. 3; 2 Cor. viii. 23; Phil. ii. 5; 1 Thess. iii. 2. The same word, which, in our common translation, is now rendered a "servant of the church," in speaking of Phebe (Rom. xix. 1.), is rendered "minister" when applied to Tychicus. Eph. vi. 21. When Paul said, "Help those women who labor with me in the Gospel," he certainly meant that they did more than to pour out tea. In the eleventh chapter of First Corinthians Paul gives directions, to men and women, how they should appear when they prophesy or pray in public assemblies; and he defines prophesying to be speaking to edification, exhortation and comfort.

I may further remark that the conduct of holy women is recorded in Scripture as an example to others of their sex. And in the early ages of Christianity many women were happy and glorious in martyrdom. How nobly, how heroically, too, in

[6]According to Acts 2, on the day of Pentecost (Greek for *fifty*), which took place fifty days after Christ's Resurrection, the Holy Spirit descended on Jesus' disciples in the form of tongues of fire.

later ages, have women suffered persecution and death for the name of the LordJesus.

In looking over these facts, I could see no miracle wrought for those women more than in myself.

Though opposed, I went forth laboring for God, and he owned and blessed my labors, and has done so wherever I have been until this day. And while I walk obediently, I know he will, though hell may rage and vent its spite.

1879

Louisa May Alcott 1832–1888

Louisa May Alcott is best known for her children's novel *Little Women* (1868), but there are almost three hundred works in the Alcott canon. In much of this writing Alcott, who never married, ostensibly proposes that women's true work is found in marriage and family, yet her journals and letters illustrate the dichotomy between her own life and her fictional world. Compared with the lives of many of her heroines and contemporaries, Alcott's life was atypical.

Louisa was born in 1832 to Abigail May (Abba) and Amos Bronson Alcott. Her parents were closely tied to many important philosophical and social issues of the day—Transcendentalism, abolition, women's suffrage, and educational reform. Close family friends, including Emerson, Thoreau, Hawthorne, Margaret Fuller, and William Garrison, composed a virtual *Who's Who* of the time. Although the Alcott girls were exposed to great ideas and surrounded by books, the family was impoverished and often moved like vagabonds to smaller and smaller quarters, a consequence of Bronson's inability to provide financial support reliably. Louisa's impractical father was determined to implement his experimental teaching methods, but his efforts met with little success. After the dismal failure of his Utopian experiment in communal living at Fruitlands in 1843–1844, parodied in Louisa's "Transcendental Wild Oats" (1873), the task of supporting the family largely fell to Abba, with help from her relatives and from Emerson. In 1858, the Alcotts purchased Orchard House in Concord, Massachusetts, with the help of Emerson and Abba's relatives, but the family struggled financially until Louisa's success with *Little Women* in 1868. At this time Louisa supplanted her father in the "unwomanly" role of family provider. Named "Duty's Faithful Child" by him, Louisa helped to support her family by repeatedly working at jobs she disliked—teacher, seamstress, and maid. These experiences became the raw material for much of her writing.

Alcott published her first work, a poem, in 1851, but not until the 1860s did she find success. Before the publication of *Little Women,* she had over eighty works published in periodicals as diverse as the prestigious *Atlantic Monthly* and the sensationalist *Frank Leslie's Illustrated Newspaper.* Searching for her literary form while trying to support her family, she wrote poetry, fairy tales, short stories, domestic sketches, melodramatic plays, gothic thrillers, adult novels, and Civil War stories. Beginning in 1863 with the anonymous publication of "Pauline's Passion and Punishment," she wrote secret thrillers for several popular newspapers for five years. She clearly enjoyed writing these stories and told a reporter that her "natural ambition is for the lurid style," but she believed that it was not "natural" for a woman to write plays and stories full of bloodshed and for wronged women aggressively seeking revenge.

Alcott also did not want to be identified with the popular "scribbling" ladies of her time; she wanted to be identified with the great writers she had known since childhood. To that end, during the early 1860s, she worked on two adult novels, *Moods* (1864; revised edition 1882) and *Work* (1873), in which she struggled to define for women a role that relieved them of the rigid code of behavior prescribed in nineteenth-century New England. In these novels, she strove for a realistic middle ground between the heroines' vengeful disregard for convention found in her thrillers and the adherence to the idea of proper "True Womanhood" proposed in much of the popular literature of the day. In a radical departure for young women in nineteenth-century New England, both novels emphasize the growth their heroines must undergo to become intellectually and emotionally independent. In Alcott's vision of womanhood, only when a woman can stand alone and is not dependent on a man for fulfillment is she capable of finding happiness, whether married or not. Alcott had great difficulty in finding a publisher for *Moods,* and when it was originally published in 1864, it received generally poor reviews. Devastated, she wrote in her journal, "My next book shall have no *ideas* in it, only facts, and the people shall be as ordinary as possible." In 1882, after she had attained wealth and fame—as well as influence with publishers, who begged for her work—she revised and reissued *Moods.* Her perseverance with it testifies to her desire for recognition for work other than her literature for children.

One acceptable outlet for Alcott's need for independence and relief from family duties occurred during the Civil War. An avid abolitionist like her parents, Alcott was determined to join the nursing service, and although single women were not usually allowed to participate, her family and friends used their considerable influence to help her gain a post. In December 1862, she left for the Union Hotel Hospital in Georgetown. The work was grueling, conditions were deplorable, and after only a month Alcott contracted a severe case of typhoid fever and had to be taken home to Concord. Although the treatment she received caused lifelong health problems, her war experience provided ideas for three anti-slavery stories published in 1863–1864: "M. L.," "My Contraband," and "An Hour." In these stories, published under her own name, Alcott broke with convention by creating heroines who reverse gender roles by acting to save men. She also tacitly supported inter-racial marriage, a sharp break with most abolitionist thinking.

Although Alcott found satisfaction in writing these stories, as she did her secret thrillers, she was still seeking a more reliable genre that would allow her to earn the money her family desperately needed. Again, the Civil War provided material. During her short stint as a nurse, she wrote letters to friends and family, and when her health improved, her family encouraged her to edit them for publication. Although she wasn't enthusiastic about the project, to her delight, *Hospital Sketches* (1863) was warmly received. This volume was significant to her writing career because she discovered a formula for realistic fiction that she would use later in much of her writing for young people, beginning with the loosely autobiographical March family of *Little Women.* She based the characters and some events on the lives of her family and friends but created an idealized family who enjoyed the stability her own early years lacked. In a period when middle-class fathers typically left home each day to work, her father's unconventional example of allowing his wife, daughters, and friends to support him would have been as difficult for readers to understand as it was for

Louisa to accept. The universality of the characters and events she created and her emphasis on the importance of family, strong moral values, and shared social responsibilities help to explain why *Little Women* was an instant bestseller in 1868 and remains popular.

Cynthia Butos
Trinity College

PRIMARY WORKS

Hospital Sketches, 1863; *Moods,* 1864 (rev. ed. 1882); *Little Women,* 1868–1869; *Little Men,* 1871; *Work: A Story of Experience,* 1873; *Transcendental Wild Oats,* 1873; *A Modern Mephistopheles,* 1877; *Jo's Boys,* 1886; Joel Myerson, Daniel Shealy, and Madeleine B. Stern, eds., *The Selected Letters,* 1987, *The Journals,* 1989; *Selected Fiction,* 1990.

My Contraband[1]

Doctor Franck came in as I sat sewing up the rents in an old shirt, that Tom might go tidily to his grave. New shirts were needed for the living, and there was no wife or mother to "dress him handsome when he went to meet the Lord," as one woman said, describing the fine funeral she had pinched herself to give her son.

"Miss Dane, I'm in a quandary," began the Doctor, with that expression of countenance which says as plainly as words, "I want to ask a favor, but I wish you'd save me the trouble."

"Can I help you out of it?"

"Faith! I don't like to propose it, but you certainly can, if you please."

"Then name it, I beg."

"You see a Reb[2] has just been brought in crazy with typhoid; a bad case every way; a drunken, rascally little captain somebody took the trouble to capture, but whom nobody wants to take the trouble to cure. The wards are full, the ladies worked to death, and willing to be for our own boys, but rather slow to risk their lives for a Reb. Now, you've had the fever, you like queer patients, your mate will see to your ward for a while, and I will find you a good attendant. The fellow won't last long, I fancy; but he can't die without some sort of care, you know. I've put him in the fourth story of the west wing, away from the rest. It is airy, quiet, and comfortable there. I'm on that ward, and will do my best for you in every way. Now, then, will you go?"

"Of course I will, out of perversity, if not common charity; for some of these people think that because I'm an abolitionist I am also a heathen, and I should rather like to show them that, though I cannot quite love my enemies, I am willing to take care of them."

[1]Originally published as "The Brothers" in the *Atlantic Monthly* (November 1863). Reprinted as "My Contraband," Alcott's preferred title, in *Hospital Sketches and Camp and Fireside Stories* (1869). During the Civil War, "contraband" referred to a black slave who escaped to or was brought within Union lines.

[2]During the Civil War, Union supporters referred to Confederate soldiers as "reb" or "rebel."

"Very good; I thought you'd go; and speaking of abolition reminds me that you can have a contraband for servant, if you like. It is that fine mulatto fellow who was found burying his rebel master after the fight, and, being badly cut over the head, our boys brought him along. Will you have him?"

"By all means,—for I'll stand to my guns on that point, as on the other; these black boys are far more faithful and handy than some of the white scamps given me to serve, instead of being served by. But is this man well enough?"

"Yes, for that sort of work, and I think you'll like him. He must have been a handsome fellow before he got his face slashed; not much darker than myself; his master's son, I dare say, and the white blood makes him rather high and haughty about some things. He was in a bad way when he came in, but vowed he'd die in the street rather than turn in with the black fellows below; so I put him up in the west wing, to be out of the way, and he's seen to the captain all the morning. When can you go up?"

"As soon as Tom is laid out, Skinner moved, Haywood washed, Marble dressed, Charley rubbed, Downs taken up, Upham laid down, and the whole forty fed."

We both laughed, though the Doctor was on his way to the dead-house and I held a shroud on my lap. But in a hospital one learns that cheerfulness is one's salvation; for, in an atmosphere of suffering and death, heaviness of heart would soon paralyze usefulness of hand, if the blessed gift of smiles had been denied us.

In an hour I took possession of my new charge, finding a dissipated-looking boy of nineteen or twenty raving in the solitary little room, with no one near him but the contraband in the room adjoining. Feeling decidedly more interest in the black man than in the white, yet remembering the Doctor's hint of his being "high and haughty," I glanced furtively at him as I scattered chloride of lime about the room to purify the air, and settled matters to suit myself. I had seen many contrabands, but never one so attractive as this. All colored men are called "boys," even if their heads are white; this boy was five-and-twenty at least, strong-limbed and manly, and had the look of one who never had been cowed by abuse or worn with oppressive labor. He sat on his bed doing nothing; no book, no pipe, no pen or paper anywhere appeared, yet anything less indolent or listless than his attitude and expression I never saw. Erect he sat, with a hand on either knee, and eyes fixed on the bare wall opposite, so rapt in some absorbing thought as to be unconscious of my presence, though the door stood wide open and my movements were by no means noiseless. His face was half averted, but I instantly approved the Doctor's taste, for the profile which I saw possessed all the attributes of comeliness belonging to his mixed race. He was more quadroon[3] than mulatto, with Saxon features, Spanish complexion darkened by exposure, color in lips and cheek, waving hair, and an eye full of the passionate melancholy which in such men always seems to utter a mute protest against the broken law that doomed them at their birth. What could he be thinking of? The sick boy cursed and raved, I rustled to and fro, steps passed the door, bells rang, and the steady rumble of army-wagons came up from the street, still he never stirred. I had seen colored people in what they call "the black sulks," when, for days, they neither smiled nor spoke, and scarcely ate. But this was something more than that; for the

[3]A person of one-quarter black ancestry.

man was not dully brooding over some small grievance; he seemed to see an all-absorbing fact or fancy recorded on the wall, which was a blank to me. I wondered if it were some deep wrong or sorrow, kept alive by memory and impotent regret; if he mourned for the dead master to whom he had been faithful to the end; or if the liberty now his were robbed of half its sweetness by the knowledge that some one near and dear to him still languished in the hell from which he had escaped. My heart quite warmed to him at that idea; I wanted to know and comfort him; and, following the impulse of the moment, I went in and touched him on the shoulder.

In an instant the man vanished and the slave appeared. Freedom was too new a boon to have wrought its blessed changes yet; and as he started up, with his hand at his temple, and an obsequious "Yes, Missis," any romance that had gathered round him fled away, leaving the saddest of all sad facts in living guise before me. Not only did the manhood seem to die out of him, but the comeliness that first attracted me; for, as he turned, I saw the ghastly wound that had laid open cheek and forehead. Being partly healed, it was no longer bandaged, but held together with strips of that transparent plaster which I never see without a shiver, and swift recollections of the scenes with which it is associated in my mind. Part of his black hair had been shorn away, and one eye was nearly closed; pain so distorted, and the cruel sabre-cut so marred that portion of his face, that, when I saw it, I felt as if a fine medal had been suddenly reversed, showing me a far more striking type of human suffering and wrong than Michael Angelo's bronze prisoner.[4] By one of those inexplicable processes that often teach us how little we understand ourselves, my purpose was suddenly changed; and, though I went in to offer comfort as a friend, I merely gave an order as a mistress.

"Will you open these windows? this man needs more air."

He obeyed at once, and, as he slowly urged up the unruly sash, the handsome profile was again turned toward me, and again I was possessed by my first impression so strongly that I involuntarily said,—

"Thank you."

Perhaps it was fancy, but I thought that in the look of mingled surprise and something like reproach which he gave me, there was also a trace of grateful pleasure. But he said, in that tone of spiritless humility these poor souls learn so soon,—

"I isn't a white man, Missis, I'se a contraband."

"Yes, I know it; but a contraband is a free man, and I heartily congratulate you."

He liked that; his face shone, he squared his shoulders, lifted his head, and looked me full in the eye with a brisk,—

"Thank ye, Missis; anything more to do fer yer?"

"Doctor Franck thought you would help me with this man, as there are many patients and few nurses or attendants. Have you had the fever?"

"No, Missis."

"They should have thought of that when they put him here; wounds and fevers should not be together. I'll try to get you moved."

He laughed a sudden laugh: if he had been a white man, I should have called it

[4]Michelangelo (1475–1564), Italian artist. Alcott seems to be referring to one of the six statues of slaves that he created in marble, not bronze.

scornful; as he was a few shades darker than myself, I suppose it must be considered an insolent, or at least an unmannerly one.

"It don't matter, Missis. I'd rather be up here with the fever than down with those niggers; and there isn't no other place fer me."

Poor fellow! that was true. No ward in all the hospital would take him in to lie side by side with the most miserable white wreck there. Like the bat in Æsop's fable, he belonged to neither race; and the pride of one and the helplessness of the other, kept him hovering alone in the twilight a great sin has brought to over-shadow the whole land.

"You shall stay, then; for I would far rather have you than my lazy Jack. But are you well and strong enough?"

"I guess I'll do, Missis."

He spoke with a passive sort of acquiescence,—as if it did not much matter if he were not able, and no one would particularly rejoice if he were.

"Yes, I think you will. By what name shall I call you?"

"Bob, Missis."

Every woman has her pet whim; one of mine was to teach the men self-respect by treating them respectfully. Tom, Dick, and Harry would pass, when lads rejoiced in those familiar abbreviations; but to address men often old enough to be my father in that style did not suit my old-fashioned ideas of propriety. This "Bob" would never die; I should have found it as easy to call the chaplain "Gus" as my tragical-looking contraband by a title so strongly associated with the tail of a kite.

"What is your other name?" I asked. "I like to call my attendants by their last names rather than by their first."

"I'se got no other, Missis; we has our master's names, or do without. Mine's dead, and I won't have anything of his 'bout me."

"Well, I'll call you Robert, then, and you may fill this pitcher for me, if you will be so kind."

He went; but, through all the tame obedience years of servitude had taught him, I could see that the proud spirit his father gave him was not yet subdued, for the look and gesture with which he repudiated his master's name was a more effective declaration of independence than any Fourth-of-July orator could have prepared.

We spent a curious week together. Robert seldom left his room, except upon my errands; and I was a prisoner all day, often all night, by the bedside of the rebel. The fever burned itself rapidly away, for there seemed little vitality to feed it in the feeble frame of this old young man, whose life had been none of the most righteous, judging from the revelations made by his unconscious lips; since more than once Robert authoritatively silenced him, when my gentler hushings were of no avail, and blasphemous wanderings or ribald camp-songs made my cheeks burn and Robert's face assume an aspect of disgust. The captain was a gentleman in the world's eye, but the contraband was the gentleman in mine;—I was a fanatic, and that accounts for such depravity of taste, I hope. I never asked Robert of himself, feeling that somewhere there was a spot still too sore to bear the lightest touch; but, from his language, manner, and intelligence, I inferred that his color had procured for him the few advantages within the reach of a quick-witted, kindly-treated slave. Silent, grave, and thoughtful, but most serviceable, was my contraband; glad of the books I brought him, faithful in the performance of the duties I assigned to him, grateful for the friendliness I could not but feel and show toward him. Often I longed to ask what purpose was so visibly altering his aspect with such daily deepening gloom. But I never dared, and no one else had either time or desire to pry into the past of this specimen of one branch of the chivalrous "F.F.Vs."[5]

On the seventh night, Dr. Franck suggested that it would be well for some one, besides the general watchman of the ward, to be with the captain, as it might be his last. Although the greater part of the two preceding nights had been spent there, of course I offered to remain,—for there is a strange fascination in these scenes, which renders one careless of fatigue and unconscious of fear until the crisis is past.

"Give him water as long as he can drink, and if he drops into a natural sleep, it may save him. I'll look in at midnight, when some change will probably take place. Nothing but sleep or a miracle will keep him now. Good-night."

Away went the Doctor; and, devouring a whole mouthful of grapes, I lowered the lamp, wet the captain's head, and sat down on a hard stool to begin my watch. The captain lay with his hot, haggard face turned toward me, filling the air with his poisonous breath, and feebly muttering, with lips and tongue so parched that the sanest speech would have been difficult to understand. Robert was stretched on his bed in the inner room, the door of which stood ajar, that a fresh draught from his open window might carry the fever-fumes away through mine. I could just see a long, dark figure, with the lighter outline of a face, and, having little else to do just then, I fell to thinking of this curious contraband, who evidently prized his freedom highly, yet seemed in no haste to enjoy it. Dr. Franck had offered to send him on to safer quarters, but he had said, "No, thank yer, sir, not yet," and then had gone away to fall into one of those black moods of his, which began to disturb me, because I had no power to lighten them. As I sat listening to the clocks from the steeples all about us, I amused myself with planning Robert's future, as I often did my own, and had dealt out to him a generous hand of trumps wherewith to play this game of life which hitherto had gone so cruelly against him, when a harsh choked voice called,—

"Lucy!"

It was the captain, and some new terror seemed to have gifted him with momentary strength.

"Yes, here's Lucy," I answered, hoping that by following the fancy I might quiet him,—for his face was damp with the clammy moisture, and his frame shaken with the nervous tremor that so often precedes death. His dull eye fixed upon me, dilating with a bewildered look of incredulity and wrath, till he broke out fiercely,—

"That's a lie! she's dead,—and so's Bob, damn him!"

Finding speech a failure, I began to sing the quiet tune that had often soothed delirium like this; but hardly had the line,—

See gentle patience smile on pain,

passed my lips, when he clutched me by the wrist, whispering like one in mortal fear,—

"Hush! she used to sing that way to Bob, but she never would to me. I swore I'd

[5]First Families of Virginia.

whip the devil out of her, and I did; but you know before she cut her throat she said she'd haunt me, and there she is!"

He pointed behind me with an aspect of such pale dismay, that I involuntarily glanced over my shoulder and started as if I had seen a veritable ghost; for, peering from the gloom of that inner room, I saw a shadowy face, with dark hair all about it, and a glimpse of scarlet at the throat. An instant showed me that it was only Robert leaning from his bed's foot, wrapped in a gray army-blanket, with his red shirt just visible above it, and his long hair disordered by sleep. But what a strange expression was on his face! The unmarred side was toward me, fixed and motionless as when I first observed it,—less absorbed now, but more intent. His eye glittered, his lips were apart like one who listened with every sense, and his whole aspect reminded me of a hound to which some wind had brought the scent of unsuspected prey.

"Do you know him, Robert? Does he mean you?"

"Laws, no, Missis; they all own half-a-dozen Bobs; but hearin' my name woke me, that's all."

He spoke quite naturally, and lay down again, while I returned to my charge, thinking that this paroxysm was probably his last. But by another hour I perceived a hopeful change; for the tremor had subsided, the cold dew was gone, his breathing was more regular, and Sleep, the healer, had descended to save or take him gently away. Doctor Franck looked in at midnight, bade me keep all cool and quiet, and not fail to administer a certain draught as soon as the captain woke. Very much relieved, I laid my head on my arms, uncomfortably folded on the little table, and fancied I was about to perform one of the feats which practice renders possible,—"sleeping with one eye open," as we say: a half-and-half doze, for all senses sleep but that of hearing; the faintest murmur, sigh, or motion will break it, and give one back one's wits much brightened by the brief permission to "stand at ease." On this night the experiment was a failure, for previous vigils, confinement, and much care had rendered naps a dangerous indulgence. Having roused half-a-dozen times in an hour to find all quiet, I dropped my heavy head on my arms, and, drowsily resolving to look up again in fifteen minutes, fell fast asleep.

The striking of a deep-voiced clock awoke me with a start. "That is one," thought I; but, to my dismay, two more strokes followed, and in remorseful haste I sprang up to see what harm my long oblivion had done. A strong hand put me back into my seat, and held me there. It was Robert. The instant my eye met his my heart began to beat, and all along my nerves tingled that electric flash which foretells a danger that we cannot see. He was very pale, his mouth grim, and both eyes full of sombre fire; for even the wounded one was open now, all the more sinister for the deep scar above and below. But his touch was steady, his voice quiet, as he said,—

"Sit still, Missis; I won't hurt yer, nor scare yer, ef I can help it, but yer waked too soon."

"Let me go, Robert,—the captain is stirring,—I must give him something."

"No, Missis, yer can't stir an inch. Look here!"

Holding me with one hand, with the other he took up the glass in which I had left the draught, and showed me it was empty.

"Has he taken it?" I asked, more and more bewildered.

"I flung it out o' winder, Missis; he'll have to do without."

"But why, Robert? why did you do it?"

"Kase I hate him!"

Impossible to doubt the truth of that; his whole face showed it, as he spoke through his set teeth, and launched a fiery glance at the unconscious captain. I could only hold my breath and stare blankly at him, wondering what mad act was coming next. I suppose I shook and turned white, as women have a foolish habit of doing when sudden danger daunts them; for Robert released my arm, sat down upon the bedside just in front of me, and said, with the ominous quietude that made me cold to see and hear,—

"Don't yer be frightened, Missis; don't try to run away, fer the door's locked and the key in my pocket; don't yer cry out, fer yer'd have to scream a long while, with my hand on yer mouth, 'efore yer was heard. Be still, an' I'll tell yer what I'm gwine to do."

"Lord help us! he has taken the fever in some sudden, violent way, and is out of his head. I must humor him till some one comes"; in pursuance of which swift determination, I tried to say, quite composedly,—

"I will be still and hear you; but open the window. Why did you shut it?"

"I'm sorry I can't do it, Missis; but yer'd jump out, or call, if I did, an' I'm not ready yet. I shut it to make yer sleep, an' heat would do it quicker'n anything else I could do."

The captain moved, and feebly muttered, "Water!" Instinctively I rose to give it to him, but the heavy hand came down upon my shoulder, and in the same decided tone Robert said,—

"The water went with the physic; let him call."

"Do let me go to him! he'll die without care!"

"I mean he shall;—don't yer meddle, if yer please, Missis."

In spite of his quiet tone and respectful manner, I saw murder in his eyes, and turned faint with fear; yet the fear excited me, and, hardly knowing what I did, I seized the hands that had seized me, crying,—

"No, no; you shall not kill him! It is base to hurt a helpless man. Why do you hate him? He is not your master."

"He's my brother."

I felt that answer from head to foot, and seemed to fathom what was coming, with a prescience vague, but unmistakable. One appeal was left to me, and I made it.

"Robert, tell me what it means? Do not commit a crime and make me accessory to it. There is a better way of righting wrong than by violence;—let me help you find it."

My voice trembled as I spoke, and I heard the frightened flutter of my heart; so did he, and if any little act of mine had ever won affection or respect from him, the memory of it served me then. He looked down, and seemed to put some question to himself; whatever it was, the answer was in my favor, for when his eyes rose again, they were gloomy, but not desperate.

"I *will* tell yer, Missis; but mind, this makes no difference; the boy is mine. I'll give the Lord a chance to take him fust: if He don't, I shall."

"Oh, no! remember he is your brother."

An unwise speech; I felt it as it passed my lips, for a black frown gathered on Robert's face, and his strong hands closed with an ugly sort of grip. But he did not touch the poor soul gasping there behind him, and seemed content to let the slow suffocation of that stifling room end his frail life.

"I'm not like to forgit dat, Missis, when I've been thinkin' of it all this week. I knew him when they fetched him in, an' would 'a' done it long 'fore this, but I wanted to ask where Lucy was; he knows,—he told tonight,—an' now he's done for."

"Who is Lucy?" I asked hurriedly, intent on keeping his mind busy with any thought but murder.

With one of the swift transitions of a mixed temperament like this, at my question Robert's deep eyes filled, the clenched hands were spread before his face, and all I heard were the broken words,—

"My wife,—he took her—"

In that instant every thought of fear was swallowed up in burning indignation for the wrong, and a perfect passion of pity for the desperate man so tempted to avenge an injury for which there seemed no redress but this. He was no longer slave nor contraband, no drop of black blood marred him in my sight, but an infinite compassion yearned to save, to help, to comfort him. Words seemed so powerless I offered none, only put my hand on his poor head, wounded, homeless, bowed down with grief for which I had no cure, and softly smoothed the long, neglected hair, pitifully wondering the while where was the wife who must have loved this tender-hearted man so well.

The captain moaned again, and faintly whispered, "Air!" but I never stirred. God forgive me! just then I hated him only as a woman thinking of a sister woman's wrong could hate. Robert looked up; his eyes were dry again, his mouth grim. I saw that, said, "Tell me more," and he did; for sympathy is a gift the poorest may give, the proudest stoop to receive.

"Yer see, Missis, his father,—I might say ours, ef I warn't ashamed of both of 'em,—his father died two years ago, an' left us all to Marster Ned,—that's him here, eighteen then. He always hated me, I looked so like old Marster: he don't,—only the light skin an' hair. Old Marster was kind to all of us, me 'specially, an' bought Lucy off the next plantation down there in South Car'lina, when he found I liked her. I married her, all I could; it warn't much, but we was true to one another till Marster Ned come home a year after an' made hell fer both of us. He sent my old mother to be used up in his rice-swamp in Georgy; he found me with my pretty Lucy, an' though young Miss cried, an' I prayed to him on my knees, an' Lucy ran away, he wouldn't have no mercy; he brought her back, an'—took her."

"Oh, what did you do?" I cried, hot with helpless pain and passion.

How the man's outraged heart sent the blood flaming up into his face and deepened the tones of his impetuous voice, as he stretched his arm across the bed, saying, with a terribly expressive gesture,—

"I half murdered him, an' to-night I'll finish."

"Yes, yes,—but go on now; what came next?"

He gave me a look that showed no white man could have felt a deeper degradation in remembering and confessing these last acts of brotherly oppression.

"They whipped me till I couldn't stand, an' they sold me further South. Yer thought I was a white man once,—look here!"

With a sudden wrench he tore the shirt from neck to waist, and on his strong, brown shoulders showed me furrows deeply ploughed, wounds which, though healed, were ghastlier to me than any in that house. I could not speak to him, and, with the pathetic dignity a great grief lends the humblest sufferer, he ended his brief tragedy by simply saying,—

"That's all, Missis. I'se never seen her since, an' now I never shall in this world,—maybe not in t'other."

"But, Robert, why think her dead? The captain was wandering when he said those sad things; perhaps he will retract them when he is sane. Don't despair; don't give up yet."

"No, Missis, I'spect he's right; she was too proud to bear that long. It's like her to kill herself. I told her to, if there was no other way; an' she always minded me, Lucy did. My poor girl! Oh, it warn't right! No, by God, it warn't!"

As the memory of this bitter wrong, this double bereavement, burned in his sore heart, the devil that lurks in every strong man's blood leaped up; he put his hand upon his brother's throat, and, watching the white face before him, muttered low between his teeth,—

"I'm lettin' him go too easy; there's no pain in this; we a'n't even yet. I wish he knew me. Marster Ned! it's Bob; where's Lucy?"

From the captain's lips there came a long faint sigh, and nothing but a flutter of the eyelids showed that he still lived. A strange stillness filled the room as the elder brother held the younger's life suspended in his hand, while wavering between a dim hope and a deadly hate. In the whirl of thoughts that went on in my brain, only one was clear enough to act upon. I must prevent murder, if I could,—but how? What could I do up there alone, locked in with a dying man and a lunatic?—for any mind yielded utterly to any unrighteous impulse is mad while the impulse rules it. Strength I had not, nor much courage, neither time nor wit for strategem, and chance only could bring me help before it was too late. But one weapon I possessed,—a tongue,—often a woman's best defence; and sympathy, stronger than fear, gave me power to use it. What I said Heaven only knows, but surely Heaven helped me; words burned on my lips, tears streamed from my eyes, and some good angel prompted me to use the one name that had power to arrest my hearer's hand and touch his heart. For at that moment I heartily believed that Lucy lived, and this earnest faith roused in him a like belief.

He listened with the lowering look of one in whom brute instinct was sovereign for the time,—a look that makes the noblest countenance base. He was but a man,—a poor, untaught, outcast, outraged man. Life had few joys for him; the world offered him no honors, no success, no home, no love. What future would this crime mar? and why should he deny himself that sweet, yet bitter morsel called revenge? How many white men, with all New England's freedom, culture, Christianity, would not have felt as he felt then? Should I have reproached him for a human anguish, a human longing for redress, all now left him from the ruin of his few poor hopes? Who had taught him that self-control, self-sacrifice, are attributes that make men masters of the earth, and lift them nearer heaven? Should I have urged the beauty of forgiveness, the duty of devout submission? He had no religion, for he was no saintly "Uncle Tom," and Slavery's black shadow seemed to darken all the world to him, and shut out God. Should I have warned him of penalties, of judgments, and the potency of law? What did he know of justice, or the mercy that should temper that stern virtue, when every law, human and divine, had been broken on his hearthstone? Should I have tried to touch him by appeals to filial duty, to brotherly love? How had his appeals been answered? What memories had father and brother stored up in his heart to plead for either now? No,—all those influences, those associations, would have proved worse than useless, had I been calm enough to try them. I was not; but instinct, subtler than reason, showed me the one safe clue by which to lead this troubled soul from the labyrinth in which it groped and nearly fell. When I paused, breathless, Robert turned to me, asking, as if human assurances could strengthen his faith in Divine Omnipotence,—

"Do you believe, if I let Marster Ned live, the Lord will give me back my Lucy?"

"As surely as there is a Lord, you will find her here or in the beautiful hereafter, where there is no black or white, no master and no slave."

He took his hand from his brother's throat, lifted his eyes from my face to the wintry sky beyond, as if searching for that blessed country, happier even than the happy North. Alas, it was the darkest hour before the dawn!—there was no star above, no light below but the pale glimmer of the lamp that showed the brother who had made him desolate. Like a blind man who believes there is a sun, yet cannot see it, he shook his head, let his arms drop nervelessly upon his knees, and sat there dumbly asking that question which many a soul whose faith is firmer fixed than his has asked in hours less dark than this,—"Where is God?" I saw the tide had turned, and strenuously tried to keep this rudderless life-boat from slipping back into the whirlpool wherein it had been so nearly lost.

"I have listened to you, Robert; now hear me, and heed what I say, because my heart is full of pity for you, full of hope for your future, and a desire to help you now. I want you to go away from here, from the temptation of this place, and the sad thoughts that haunt it. You have conquered yourself once, and I honor you for it, because, the harder the battle, the more glorious the victory; but it is safer to put a greater distance between you and this man. I will write you letters, give you money, and send you to good old Massachusetts to begin your new life a freeman,—yes, and a happy man; for when the captain is himself again, I will learn where Lucy is, and move heaven and earth to find and give her back to you. Will you do this, Robert?"

Slowly, very slowly, the answer came; for the purpose of a week, perhaps a year, was hard to relinquish in an hour.

"Yes, Missis, I will."

"Good! Now you are the man I thought you, and I'll work for you with all my heart. You need sleep, my poor fellow; go, and try to forget. The captain is alive, and as yet you are spared that sin. No, don't look there; I'll care for him. Come, Robert, for Lucy's sake."

Thank Heaven for the immortality of love! for when all other means of salvation failed, a spark of this vital fire softened the man's iron will, until a woman's hand could bend it. He let me take from him the key, let me draw him gently away, and lead him to the solitude which now was the most healing balm I could bestow. Once in his little room, he fell down on his bed and lay there, as if spent with the sharpest conflict of his life. I slipped the bolt across his door, and unlocked my own, flung up the window, steadied myself with a breath of air, then rushed to Doctor Franck. He came; and till dawn we worked together, saving one brother's life, and taking earnest thought how best to secure the other's liberty. When the sun came up as blithely as if it shone only upon happy homes, the Doctor went to Robert. For an hour I heard the murmur of their voices; once I caught the sound of heavy sobs, and for a time a reverent hush, as if in the silence that good man were ministering to soul as well as body. When he departed he took Robert with him, pausing to tell me he should get him off as soon as possible, but not before we met again.

Nothing more was seen of them all day; another surgeon came to see the captain, and another attendant came to fill the empty place. I tried to rest, but could not, with the thought of poor Lucy tugging at my heart, and was soon back at my post again, anxiously hoping that my contraband had not been too hastily spirited away. Just as night fell there came a tap, and, opening, I saw Robert literally "clothed, and in his right mind." The Doctor had replaced the ragged suit with tidy garments, and no trace of that tempestuous night remained but deeper lines upon the forehead, and the docile look of a repentant child. He did not cross the threshold, did not offer me his hand,—only took off his cap, saying, with a traitorous falter in his voice,—

"God bless yer, Missis! I'm gwine."

I put out both my hands, and held his fast.

"Good-by, Robert! Keep up good heart, and when I come home to Massachusetts we'll meet in a happier place than this. Are you quite ready, quite comfortable for your journey?"

"Yes, Missis, yes; the Doctor's fixed everything; I'se gwine with a friend of his; my papers are all right, an' I'm as happy as I can be till I find"——

He stopped there; then went on, with a glance into the room,—

"I'm glad I didn't do it, an' I thank yer, Missis, fer hinderin' me,—thank yer hearty; but I'm afraid I hate him jest the same."

Of course he did; and so did I; for these faulty hearts of ours cannot turn perfect in a night, but need frost and fire, wind and rain, to ripen and make them ready for the great harvest-home. Wishing to divert his mind, I put my poor mite into his hand, and, remembering the magic of a certain little book, I gave him mine, on whose dark cover whitely shone the Virgin Mother and the Child, the grand history of whose life the book contained. The money went into Robert's pocket with a grateful murmur, the book into his bosom, with a long look and a tremulous—

"I never saw *my* baby, Missis."

I broke down then; and though my eyes were too dim to see, I felt the touch of lips upon my hands, heard the sound of departing feet, and knew my contraband was gone.

When one feels an intense dislike, the less one says about the subject of it the better; therefore I shall merely record that the captain lived,—in time was exchanged; and that, whoever the other party was, I am convinced the Government got the best of the bargain. But long before this occurred, I had fulfilled my promise to Robert; for as soon as my patient recovered strength of memory enough to make his answer trustworthy, I asked, without any circumlocution,—

"Captain Fairfax, where is Lucy?"

And too feeble to be angry, surprised, or insincere, he straightway answered,—

"Dead, Miss Dane."

"And she killed herself when you sold Bob?"

"How the devil did you know that?" he muttered, with an expression half-remorseful, half-amazed; but I was satisfied, and said no more.

Of course this went to Robert, waiting far away there in a lonely home,—waiting, working, hoping for his Lucy. It almost broke my heart to do it; but delay was weak, deceit was wicked; so I sent the heavy tidings, and very soon the answer came,—only three lines; but I felt that the sustaining power of the man's life was gone.

"I tort I'd never see her any more; I'm glad to know she's out of trouble. I thank yer, Missis; an' if they let us, I'll fight fer yer till I'm killed, which I hope will be 'fore long."

Six months later he had his wish, and kept his word.

Every one knows the story of the attack on Fort Wagner;[6] but we should not tire yet of recalling how our Fifty-Fourth, spent with three sleepless nights, a day's fast, and a march under the July sun, stormed the fort as night fell, facing death in many shapes, following their brave leaders through a fiery rain of shot and shell, fighting valiantly for "God and Governor Andrew,"—how the regiment that went into action seven hundred strong, came out having had nearly half its number captured, killed, or wounded, leaving their young commander to be buried, like a chief of earlier times, with his body-guard around him, faithful to the death. Surely, the insult turns to honor, and the wide grave needs no monument but the heroism that consecrates it in our sight; surely, the hearts that held him nearest, see through their tears a noble victory in the seeming sad defeat; and surely, God's benediction was bestowed, when this loyal soul answered, as Death called the roll, "Lord, here am I, with the brothers Thou hast given me!"

The future must show how well that fight was fought; for though Fort Wagner once defied us, public prejudice is down; and through the cannon-smoke of that black night, the manhood of the colored race shines before many eyes that would not see, rings in many ears that would not hear, wins many hearts that would not hitherto believe.

When the news came that we were needed, there was none so glad as I to leave teaching contrabands, the new work I had taken up, and go to nurse "our boys," as my dusky flock so proudly called the wounded of the Fifty-Fourth. Feeling more satisfaction, as I assumed my big apron and turned up my cuffs, than if dressing for the President's levee, I fell to work in Hospital No. 10 at Beaufort. The scene was most familiar, and yet strange; for only dark faces looked up at me from the pallets so thickly laid along the floor, and I missed the sharp accent of my Yankee boys in the slower, softer voices calling cheerily to one another, or answering my questions with a stout, "We'll never give it up, Missis, till the last Reb's dead," or, "If our people's free, we can afford to die."

Passing from bed to bed, intent on making one pair of hands do the work of three, at least, I gradually washed, fed, and bandaged my way down the long line of sable heroes, and coming to the very last, found that he was my contraband. So old, so worn, so deathly weak and wan, I never should have known him but for the deep scar on his cheek. That side lay uppermost, and caught my eye at once; but even then I doubted, such an awful change had come upon him, when, turning to the ticket just above his head, I saw the name, "Robert Dane." That both assured and touched me, for, remembering that he had no name, I knew that he had taken mine. I longed for him to speak to me, to tell how he had fared since I lost sight of him, and let me perform some little service for him in return for many he had done for me; but he

[6] In July 1863, Union forces assaulted Fort Wagner as part of the siege of Charleston, S.C., a battle the Union eventually won. The 54th Massachusetts Infantry, the first all-black regiment from the North, was created largely due to the efforts of abolitionist John Albion Andrew, governor of Massachusetts from 1860 to 1866.

seemed asleep; and as I stood re-living that strange night again, a bright lad, who lay next to him softly waving an old fan across both beds, looked up and said,—

"I guess you know him, Missis?"

"You are right. Do you?"

"As much as any one was able to, Missis."

"Why do you say 'was,' as if the man were dead and gone?"

"I s'pose because I know he'll have to go. He's got a bad jab in the breast, an' is bleedin' inside, the Doctor says. He don't suffer any, only gets weaker 'n' weaker every minute. I've been fannin' him this long while, an' he's talked a little; but he don't know me now, so he's most gone, I guess."

There was so much sorrow and affection in the boy's face, that I remembered something, and asked, with redoubled interest,—

"Are you the one that brought him off? I was told about a boy who nearly lost his life in saving that of his mate."

I dare say the young fellow blushed, as any modest lad might have done; I could not see it, but I heard the chuckle of satisfaction that escaped him, as he glanced from his shattered arm and bandaged side to the pale figure opposite.

"Lord, Missis, that's nothin'; we boys always stan' by one another, an' I warn't goin' to leave him to be tormented any more by them cussed Rebs. He's been a slave once, though he don't look half so much like it as me, an' I was born in Boston."

He did not; for the speaker was as black as the ace of spades,—being a sturdy specimen, the knave of clubs would perhaps be a fitter representative,—but the dark freeman looked at the white slave with the pitiful, yet puzzled expression I have so often seen on the faces of our wisest men, when his tangled question of Slavery presented itself, asking to be cut or patiently undone.

"Tell me what you know of this man; for, even if he were awake, he is too weak to talk."

"I never saw him till I joined the regiment, an' no one 'peared to have got much out of him. He was a shut-up sort of feller, an' didn't seem to care for anything but gettin' at the Rebs. Some say he was the fust man of us that enlisted; I know he fretted till we were off, an' when we pitched into old Wagner, he fought like the devil."

"Were you with him when he was wounded? How was it?"

"Yes, Missis. There was somethin' queer about it; for he 'peared to know the chap that killed him, an' the chap knew him. I don't dare to ask, but rather guess one owned the other some time; for, when they clinched, the chap sung out, 'Bob!' an' Dane, 'Marster Ned!'—then they went at it."

I sat down suddenly, for the old anger and compassion struggled in my heart, and I both longed and feared to hear what was to follow.

"You see, when the Colonel,—Lord keep an' send him back to us!—it a'n't certain yet, you know, Missis, though it's two days ago we lost him,—well, when the Colonel shouted, 'Rush on, boys, rush on!' Dane tore away as if he was goin' to take the fort alone; I was next him, an' kept close as we went through the ditch an' up the wall. Hi! warn't that a rusher!" and the boy flung up his well arm with a whoop, as if the mere memory of that stirring moment came over him in a gust of irrepressible excitement.

"Were you afraid?" I said, asking the question women often put, and receiving the answer they seldom fail to get.

"No, Missis!"—emphasis on the "missis"—"I never thought of anything but the damn' Rebs, that scalp, slash, an' cut our ears off, when they git us. I was bound to let daylight into one of 'em at least, an' I did. Hope he liked it!"

"It is evident that you did. Now go on about Robert, for I should be at work."

"He was one of the fust up; I was just behind, an' though the whole thing happened in a minute, I remember how it was, for all I was yellin' an' knockin' round like mad. Just where we were, some sort of an officer was wavin' his sword an' cheerin' on his men; Dane saw him by a big flash that come by; he flung away his gun, give a leap, an' went at that feller as if he was Jeff, Beauregard, an' Lee, all in one. I scrabbled after as quick as I could, but was only up in time to see him git the sword straight through him an' drop into the ditch. You needn't ask what I did next, Missis, for I don't quite know myself; all I'm clear about is, that I managed somehow to pitch that Reb into the fort as dead as Moses, git hold of Dane, an' bring him off. Poor old feller! we said we went in to live or die; he said he went in to die, an' he's done it."

I had been intently watching the excited speaker; but as he regretfully added those last words I turned again, and Robert's eyes met mine,—those melancholy eyes, so full of an intelligence that proved he had heard, remembered, and reflected with that preternatural power which often outlives all other faculties. He knew me, yet gave no greeting; was glad to see a woman's face, yet had no smile wherewith to welcome it; felt that he was dying, yet uttered no farewell. He was too far across the river to return or linger now; departing thought, strength, breath, were spent in one grateful look, one murmur of submission to the last pang he could ever feel. His lips moved, and, bending to them, a whisper chilled my cheek, as it shaped the broken words,—

"I'd 'a' done it,—but it's better so,—I'm satisfied."

Ah! well he might be,—for, as he turned his face from the shadow of the life that was, the sunshine of the life to be touched it with a beautiful content, and in the drawing of a breath my contraband found wife and home, eternal liberty and God.

1863

Harriet Prescott Spofford 1835–1921

Despite her long career and impressive list of publications, Harriet Prescott Spofford has been neglected by anthologists. To overlook this writer who challenged stereotypical depictions of women while blending the colors of romance with the realities of her New England environment is to shortchange our literary history.

Like the majority of women writers of her time, Spofford turned to authorship out of financial need. When barely in her twenties she began writing to help support her parents and younger siblings. Although some anonymous stories were published in Boston family story-papers, she never acknowledged these earliest moneymaking ventures. Her literary career officially began with the publication of the short story "In a Cellar" in the February 1859 issue of the *Atlantic Monthly* and continued throughout her marriage to Richard S. Spofford, Jr. until her last collection, *The Elder's People,* which appeared in 1920, the year before her death.

During a writing career that spanned more than sixty years in two centuries, Spofford published continuously in periodicals, offering short stories, serialized novels, poetry, and articles—much of it still uncollected—for adults and children. Her first book was a romance called *Sir Rohan's Ghost* (1860), but Spofford's short stories would soon outweigh her other writings in lasting importance. She published *The Amber Gods* (1863), her first short-story collection, and two book-length romances before she married on December 19, 1865. In *The Amber Gods,* "Circumstance," "Knitting Sale-Socks," and "The South Breaker" offered the realistic dialect and the social and economic realities of the rural and small-town New England life that she knew best.

"'Circumstance,'" which first appeared in the *Atlantic Monthly* in May 1860 and was later included in W. D. Howells's collection, *The Great Modern American Stories* (1921), is a fine example of Spofford's realism. Based on a true incident in her family history, "'Circumstance'" is nonetheless startlingly unusual. It impressed Emily Dickinson as "the only thing I ever read in my life that I didn't think I could have imagined myself!" Spofford's gift is to treat the sensational or implicitly "romantic" event realistically: a very real wife and mother draws on the art of her life—the hymns and lullabies and folk tunes she has sung—to placate a wild beast and defend herself against death.

In other stories of women's lives Spofford rebuked the prevalent nineteenth-century stereotypes that divided women into good and bad, angels and whores. The title story of her first collection, "The Amber Gods," presented one such pair: the passionate Yone and the patient Lu. Each is defined by the jewelry she wears—"pagan" amber beads or "light" and "limpid" aquamarine. (Spofford asserted in her nonfiction *Art Decoration Applied to Furniture* (1878) that styles reflect the people who adopt them, a tactic she frequently used in her own fiction.) Yone and Lu foreshadow pairs of contrasting women in later Spofford stories who remind us that they are but two possible sides of one woman. Frequently also in Spofford's fiction male characters must learn to appreciate individual differences among women. Men know *woman,* not *women,* Spofford suggests in the story "The Composite Wife" in *A Scarlet Poppy and Other Stories;* when Mr. Chipperley plans to take a fourth wife, he sees her as a composite of the other three.

A Scarlet Poppy did not appear until 1894, but the years between 1863 and 1898 were filled with other writings. In her 1935 study of Spofford, Elizabeth K. Halbeisen identifies eight books and at least 374 works published in periodicals during that period. The works collected in *A Scarlet Poppy* are light satire, quite different from the more somber collection *Old Madame and Other Tragedies* (1900). Spofford's days in Washington with her husband provide the basis for the sentimental stories in *Old Washington* (1906), and her final collection, often considered her best, *The Elder's People* (1920), returns to New England. The dry humor, the New England realities, the believable dialect, and the restraint with which she individualizes each character earned Spofford high praise.

Spofford expresses the sisterhood of women in her final collection in a story called "A Village Dressmaker." In this tale of self-sacrifice, the dressmaker Susanna gives the wedding gown she made for herself to Rowena Mayhew, who is marrying the man they both loved. Spofford's women face the realistic necessities of life, live with the limited perceptions of their men, and triumph through the art they create (songs, quilts, and dresses that only a widened perspective recognizes as true art forms) and the choices they willingly make. Spofford always finds the vermilion and azure threads woven into the duns and grays of the New England life and women she knew so well.

Thelma Shinn Richard
Arizona State University

PRIMARY WORKS

The Amber Gods and Other Stories, 1863; *A Scarlet Poppy and Other Stories,* 1894; *Old Madame and Other Tragedies,* 1900; *Old Washington,* 1906; *The Elder's People,* 1920.

Circumstance

She had remained, during all that day, with a sick neighbor,—those eastern wilds of Maine in that epoch frequently making neighbors and miles synonymous,—and so busy had she been with care and sympathy that she did not at first observe the approaching night. But finally the level rays, reddening the snow, threw their gleam upon the wall, and, hastily donning cloak and hood, she bade her friends farewell and sallied forth on her return. Home lay some three miles distant, across a copse, a meadow, and a piece of woods,—the woods being a fringe on the skirts of the great forests that stretch far away into the North. That home was one of a dozen log-houses lying a few furlongs apart from each other, with their half-cleared demesnes separating them at the rear from a wilderness untrodden save by stealthy native or deadly panther tribes.

She was in a nowise exalted frame of spirit,—on the contrary, rather depressed by the pain she had witnessed and the fatigue she had endured; but in certain temperaments such a condition throws open the mental pores, so to speak, and renders one receptive of every influence. Through the little copse she walked slowly, with her cloak folded about her, lingering to imbibe the sense of shelter, the sunset filtered in purple through the mist of woven spray and twig, the companionship of growth not sufficiently dense to band against her, the sweet homefeeling of a young and tender wintry wood. It was therefore just on the edge of the evening that she emerged from the place and began to cross the meadowland. At one hand lay the forest to which her path wound; at the other the evening star hung over a tide of failing orange that slowly slipped down the earth's broad side to sadden other hemispheres with sweet regret. Walking rapidly now, and with her eyes wide-open, she distinctly saw in the air before her what was not there a moment ago, a winding-sheet,—cold, white, and ghastly, waved by the likeness of four wan hands,—that rose with a long inflation, and fell in rigid folds, while a voice, shaping itself from the hollowness above, spectral and melancholy, sighed,—"The Lord have mercy on the people! The Lord have mercy on the people!" Three times the sheet with its corpse-covering outline waved beneath the pale hands, and the voice, awful in its solemn and mysterious depth, sighed, "The Lord have mercy on the people!" Then all was gone, the place was clear again, the gray sky was obstructed by no deathly blot; she looked about her, shook her shoulders decidedly, and, pulling on her hood, went forward once more.

She might have been a little frightened by such an apparition, if she had led a life of less reality than frontier settlers are apt to lead; but dealing with hard fact does not engender a flimsy habit of mind, and this woman was too sincere and earnest in her character, and too happy in her situation, to be thrown by antagonism, merely, upon superstitious fancies and chimeras of the second-sight. She did not even believe herself subject to an hallucination, but smiled simply, a little vexed that her thought could have framed such a glamour from the day's occurrences, and not sorry to lift the bough of the warder of the woods and enter and disappear in their sombre path. If she had been imaginative, she would have hesitated at her first step into a region whose dangers were not visionary; but I suppose that the thought of a little child at home would conquer that propensity in the most habituated. So, biting a bit of spicy birch, she went along. Now and then she came to a gap where the trees had been partially felled, and here she found that the lingering twilight was explained by that peculiar and perhaps electric film which sometimes sheathes the sky in diffused light for many hours before a brilliant aurora. Suddenly, a swift shadow, like the fabulous flying-dragon, writhed through the air before her, and she felt herself instantly seized and borne aloft. It was that wild beast—the most savage and serpentine and subtle and fearless of our latitudes—known by hunters as the Indian Devil, and he held her in his clutches on the broad floor of a swinging fir-bough. His long sharp claws were caught in her clothing, he worried them sagaciously a little, then, finding that ineffectual to free them, he commenced licking her bare arm with his rasping tongue and pouring over her the wide streams of his hot, foetid breath. So quick had this flashing action been that the woman had had no time for alarm; moreover, she was not of the screaming kind: but now, as she felt him endeavoring to disentangle his claws, and the horrid sense of her fate smote her, and she saw instinctively the fierce plunge of those weapons, the long strips of living flesh torn from her bones, the agony, the quivering disgust, itself a worse agony,—while by her side, and holding her in his great lithe embrace, the monster crouched, his white tusks whetting and gnashing, his eyes glaring through all the darkness like balls of red fire,—a shriek, that rang in every forest hollow, that startled every winter-housed thing, that stirred and woke the least needle of the tasselled pines, tore through her lips. A moment afterward, the beast left the arm, once white, now crimson, and looked up alertly.

She did not think at this instant to call upon God. She called upon her husband. It seemed to her that she had but one friend in the world; that was he; and again the cry, loud, clear, prolonged, echoed through the woods. It was not the shriek that disturbed the creature at his relish; he was not born in the woods to be scared of an owl, you know; what then? It must have been the echo, most musical, most resonant, repeated and yet repeated, dying with long sighs of sweet sound, vibrated from rock to river and back again from depth to depth of cave and cliff. Her thought flew after it; she knew, that, even if her husband heard it, he yet could not reach her in time; she saw that while the beast listened he would not gnaw,—and this she *felt* directly, when the rough, sharp, and multiplied stings of his tongue retouched her arm. Again her lips opened by instinct, but the sound that issued thence came by reason. She had heard that music charmed wild beasts,—just this point between life and death intensified every faculty,—and when she opened her lips the third time, it was not for shrieking, but for singing.

A little thread of melody stole out, a rill of tremulous motion; it was the cradle-song with which she rocked her baby;—how could she sing that? And then she remembered the baby sleeping rosily on the long settee before the fire,—the father cleaning his gun, with one foot on the green wooden rundle,—the merry light from the chimney dancing out and through the room, on the rafters of the ceiling with their tassels of onions and herbs, on the log walls painted with lichens and festooned with apples, on the king's-arm slung across the shelf with the old pirate's-cutlass, on the snow-pile of the bed, and on the great brass clock,—dancing, too, and lingering on the baby, with his fringed-gentian eyes, his chubby fists clenched on the pillow, and his fine breezy hair fanning with the motion of his father's foot. All this struck her in one, and made a sob of her breath, and she ceased.

Immediately the long red tongue thrust forth again. Before it touched, a song sprang to her lips, a wild sea-song, such as some sailor might be singing far out on trackless blue water that night, the shrouds whistling with frost and the sheets glued in ice,—a song with the wind in its burden and the spray in its chorus. The monster raised his head and flared the fiery eyeballs upon her, then fretted the imprisoned claws a moment and was quiet; only the breath like the vapor from some hell-pit still swathed her. Her voice, at first faint and fearful, gradually lost its quaver, grew under her control and subject to her modulation; it rose on long swells, it fell in subtile cadences, now and then its tones pealed out like bells from distant belfries on fresh sonorous mornings. She sung the song through, and, wondering lest his name of Indian Devil were not his true name, and if he would not detect her, she repeated it. Once or twice now, indeed, the beast stirred uneasily, turned, and made the bough sway at his movement. As she ended, he snapped his jaws together, and tore away the fettered member, curling it under him with a snarl,—when she burst into the gayest reel that ever answered a fiddle-bow. How many a time she had heard her husband play it on the homely fiddle made by himself from birch and cherrywood! how many a time she had seen it danced on the floor of their one room, to the patter of wooden clogs and the rustle of homespun petticoat! how many a time she had danced it herself!—and did she not remember once, as they joined clasps for eight-hands-round, how it had lent its gay, bright measure to her life? And here she was singing it alone, in the forest, at midnight, to a wild beast! As she sent her voice trilling up and down its quick oscillations between joy and pain, the creature who grasped her uncurled his paw and scratched the bark from the bough; she must vary the spell; and her voice spun leaping along the projecting points of tune of a hornpipe. Still singing, she felt herself twisted about with a low growl and a lifting of the red lip from the glittering teeth; she broke the hornpipe's thread, and commenced unravelling a lighter, livelier thing, an Irish jig. Up and down and round about her voice flew, the beast threw back his head so that the diabolical face fronted hers, and the torrent of his breath prepared her for his feast as the anaconda slimes his prey. Franticly she darted from tune to tune; his restless movements followed her. She tired herself with dancing and vivid national airs, growing feverish and singing spasmodically as she felt her horrid tomb yawning wider. Touching in this manner all the slogan and keen clan cries, the beast moved again, but only to lay the disengaged paw across her with heavy satisfaction. She did not dare to pause; through the clear cold air, the frosty starlight, she sang. If there were yet any tremor in the tone, it was not fear,—she had learned the secret of sound at last; nor could it be chill,—far too high a fever throbbed her pulses; it was nothing but the thought of the log-house and of what might be passing within it. She fancied the baby stirring in his sleep and moving his pretty lips,—her husband rising and opening the door, looking out after her, and wondering at her absence. She fancied the light pouring through the chink and then shut in again with all the safety and comfort and joy, her husband taking down the fiddle and playing lightly with his head inclined, playing while she sang, while she sang for her life to an Indian Devil. Then she knew he was fumbling for and finding some shining fragment and scoring it down the yellowing hair, and unconsciously her voice forsook the wild wartunes and drifted into the half-gay, half-melancholy Rosin the Bow.

Suddenly she woke pierced with a pang, and the daggered tooth penetrating her flesh;—dreaming of safety, she had ceased singing and lost it. The beast had regained the use of all his limbs, and now, standing and raising his back, bristling and foaming, with sounds that would have been like hisses but for their deep and fearful sonority, he withdrew step by step toward the trunk of the tree, still with his flaming balls upon her. She was all at once free, on one end of the bough, twenty feet from the ground. She did not measure the distance, but rose to drop herself down, careless of any death, so that it were not this. Instantly, as if he scanned her thoughts, the creature bounded forward with a yell and caught her again in his dreadful hold. It might be that he was not greatly famished; for, as she suddenly flung up her voice again, he settled himself composedly on the bough, still clasping her with invincible pressure to his rough, ravenous breast, and listening in a fascination to the sad, strange U-la-lu that now moaned forth in loud, hollow tones above him. He half closed his eyes, and sleepily reopened and shut them again.

What rending pains were close at hand! Death! and what a death! worse than any other that is to be named! Water, be it cold or warm, that which buoys up blue icefields, or which bathes tropical coasts with currents of balmy bliss, is yet a gentle conqueror, kisses as it kills, and draws you down gently through darkening fathoms to its heart. Death at the sword is the festival of trumpet and bugle and banner, with glory ringing out around you and distant hearts thrilling through yours. No gnawing disease can bring such hideous end as this; for that is a fiend bred of your own flesh, and this—is it a fiend, this living lump of appetites? What dread comes with the thought of perishing in flames! but fire, let it leap and hiss never so hotly, is something too remote, too alien, to inspire us with such loathly horror as a wild beast; if it have a life, that life is too utterly beyond our comprehension. Fire is not half ourselves; as it devours, arouses neither hatred nor disgust; is not to be known by the strength of our lower natures let loose; does not drip our blood into our faces with foaming chaps, nor mouth nor slaver above us with vitality. Let us be ended by fire, and we are ashes, for the winds to bear, the leaves to cover; let us be ended by wild beasts, and the base, cursed thing howls with us forever through the forest. All this she felt as she charmed him, and what force it lent to her song God knows. If her voice should fail! If the damp and cold should give her any fatal hoarseness! If all the silent powers of the forest did not conspire to help her! The dark, hollow night rose indifferently over her; the wide, cold air breathed rudely past her, lifted her wet hair and blew it down again; the great boughs swung with a ponderous strength, now and then clashed their iron lengths together and shook off a sparkle of icy spears or some long-lain weight of snow from their heavy shadows. The green depths were utterly cold and silent and stern. These beautiful haunts that all the summer were hers and rejoiced to share with her their bounty, these heavens that had yielded their largess, these stems that had thrust their blossoms into her hands, all these friends of three moons ago forgot her now and knew her no longer.

Feeling her desolation, wild, melancholy, forsaken songs rose thereon from that frightful aerie,—weeping, wailing tunes, that sob among the people from age to age, and overflow with otherwise unexpressed sadness,—all rude, mournful ballads,—old tearful strains, that Shakespeare heard the vagrants sing, and that rise and fall like the wind and tide,—sailor-songs, to be heard only in lone mid-watches beneath the moon and stars,—ghastly rhyming romances, such as that famous one of the Lady Margaret, when

"She slipped on her gown of green
A piece below the knee,—
And 't was all a long cold winter's night
A dead corse followed she."

Still the beast lay with closed eyes, yet never relaxing his grasp. Once a half-whine of enjoyment escaped him,—he fawned his fearful head upon her; once he scored her cheek with his tongue—savage caresses that hurt like wounds. How weary she was! and yet how terribly awake! How fuller and fuller of dismay grew the knowledge that she was only prolonging her anguish and playing with death! How appalling the thought that with her voice ceased her existence! Yet she could not sing forever; her throat was dry and hard; her very breath was a pain; her mouth was hotter than any desert-worn pilgrim's;—if she could but drop upon her burning tongue one atom of the ice that glittered about her!—but both of her arms were pinioned in the giant's vice. She remembered the winding-sheet, and for the first time in her life shivered with spiritual fear. Was it hers? She asked herself, as she sang, what sins she had committed, what life she had led, to find her punishment so soon and in these pangs,—and then she sought eagerly for some reason why her husband was not up and abroad to find her. He failed her,—her one sole hope in life; and without being aware of it, her voice forsook the songs of suffering and sorrow for old Covenanting hymns,—hymns with which her mother had lulled her, which the class-leader pitched in the chimney-corners,—grand and sweet Methodist hymns, brimming with melody and with all fantastic involutions of tune to suit that ecstatic worship,—hymns full of the beauty of holiness, steadfast, relying, sanctified by the salvation they had lent to those in worse extremity than hers,—for they had found themselves in the grasp of hell, while she was but in the jaws of death. Out of this strange music, peculiar to one character of faith, and than which there is none more beautiful in its degree nor owning a more potent sway of sound, her voice soared into the glorified chants of churches. What to her was death by cold or famine or wild beasts? "Though He slay me, yet will I trust in him," she sang. High and clear through the frore[1] fair night, the level moonbeams splintering in the wood, the scarce glints of stars in the shadowy roof of branches, these sacred anthems rose,—rose as a hope from despair, as some snowy spray of flower-bells from blackest mould. Was she not in God's hands? Did not the world swing at his will? If this were in his great plan of providence, was it not best, and should she not accept it?

"He is the Lord our God; his judgments are in all the earth."

[1]Frosty, cold.

Oh, sublime faith of our fathers, where utter self-sacrifice alone was true love, the fragrance of whose unrequired subjection was pleasanter than that of golden censers swung in purple-vapored chancels!

Never ceasing in the rhythm of her thoughts, articulated in music as they thronged, the memory of her first communion flashed over her. Again she was in that distant place on that sweet spring morning. Again the congregation rustled out, and the few remained, and she trembled to find herself among them. How well she remembered the devout, quiet faces, too accustomed to the sacred feast to glow with their inner joy! how well the snowy linen at the altar, the silver vessels slowly and silently shifting! and as the cup approached and passed, how the sense of delicious perfume stole in and heightened the transport of her prayer, and she had seemed, looking up through the windows where the sky soared blue in constant freshness, to feel all heaven's balms dripping from the portals, and to scent the lilies of eternal peace! Perhaps another would not have felt so much ecstasy as satisfaction on that occasion; but it is a true, if a later disciple, who has said, "The Lord bestoweth his blessings there, where he findeth the vessels empty."

"And does it need the walls of a church to renew my communion?" she asked. "Does not every moment stand a temple four-square to God? And in that morning, with its buoyant sunlight, was I any dearer to the Heart of the World than now?—'My beloved is mine, and I am his,'" she sang over and over again, with all varied inflection and profuse tune. How gently all the winter-wrapt things bent toward her then! into what relation with her had they grown! how this common dependence was the spell of their intimacy! how at one with Nature had she become! how all the night and the silence and the forest seemed to hold its breath, and to send its soul up to God in her singing! It was no longer despondency, that singing. It was neither prayer nor petition. She had left imploring, "How long wilt thou forget me, O Lord? Lighten mine eyes, lest I sleep the sleep of death! For in death there is no remembrance of thee,"—with countless other such fragments of supplication. She cried rather, "Yea, though I walk through the valley of the shadow of death, I will fear no evil: for thou art with me; thy rod and thy staff, they comfort me,"—and lingered, and repeated, and sang again, "I shall be satisfied, when I awake, with thy likeness."

Then she thought of the Great Deliverance, when he drew her up out of many waters, and the flashing old psalm pealed forth triumphantly:—

"The Lord descended from above,
 and bow'd the heavens hie:
And underneath his feet he cast
 the darknesse of the skie.
On cherubs and on cherubins
 full royally he road:
And on the wings of all the winds
 came flying all abroad."

She forgot how recently, and with what a strange pity for her own shapeless form that was to be, she had quaintly sung,—

"O lovely appearance of death!
What sight upon earth is so fair?
Not all the gay pageants that breathe,
Can with a dead body compare!"

She remembered instead,—"In thy presence is fulness of joy; at thy right hand there are pleasures forevermore. God will redeem my soul from the power of the grave: for he shall receive me. He will swallow up death in victory." Not once now did she say, "Lord, how long wilt thou look on; rescue my soul from their destructions, my darling from the lions,"—for she knew that the young lions roar after their prey and seek their meat from God. "O Lord, thou preservest man and beast!" she said.

She had no comfort or consolation in this season, such as sustained the Christian martyrs in the amphitheatre. She was not dying for her faith; there were no palms in heaven for her to wave; but how many a time had she declared,—"I had rather be a doorkeeper in the house of my God, than to dwell in the tents of wickedness!" And as the broad rays here and there broke through the dense covert of shade and lay in rivers of lustre on crystal sheathing and frozen fretting of trunk and limb and on the great spaces of refraction, they builded up visibly that house, the shining city on the hill, and singing, "Beautiful for situation, the joy of the whole earth, is Mount Zion, on the sides of the North, the city of the Great King," her vision climbed to that higher picture where the angel shows the dazzling thing, the holy Jerusalem descending out of heaven from God, with its splendid battlements and gates of pearls, and its foundations, the eleventh a jacinth, the twelfth an amethyst,—with its great white throne, and the rainbow round about it, in sight like unto an emerald: "And there shall be no night there,—for the Lord God giveth them light," she sang.

What whisper of dawn now rustled through the wilderness? How the night was passing? And still the beast crouched upon the bough, changing only the posture of his head, that again he might command her with those charmed eyes;—half their fire was gone; she could almost have released herself from his custody; yet, had she stirred, no one knows what malevolent instinct might have dominated anew. But of that she did not dream; long ago stripped of any expectation, she was experiencing in her divine rapture how mystically true it is that "he that dwelleth in the secret place of the Most High shall abide under the shadow of the Almighty."

Slow clarion cries now wound from the distance as the cocks caught the intelligence of day and re-echoed it faintly from farm to farm,—sleepy sentinels of night, sounding the foe's invasion, and translating that dim intuition to ringing notes of warning. Still she chanted on. A remote crash of brushwood told of some other beast on his depredations, or some night-belated traveller groping his way through the narrow path. Still she chanted on. The far, faint echoes of the chanticleers died into distance, the crashing of the branches grew nearer. No wild beast that, but a man's step,—a man's form in the moonlight, stalwart and strong,—on one arm slept a little child, in the other hand he held his gun. Still she chanted on.

Perhaps, when her husband last looked forth, he was half ashamed to find what a fear he felt for her. He knew she would never leave the child so long but for some direst need,—and yet he may have laughed at himself, as he lifted and wrapped it with awkward care, and, loading his gun and strapping on his horn, opened the door again and closed it behind him, going out and plunging into the darkness and dangers of the forest. He was more singularly alarmed than he would have been willing to acknowledge; as he had sat with his bow hovering over the strings, he had half believed to hear her voice mingling gayly with the instrument, till he paused and listened if she were not about to lift the latch and enter. As he drew nearer the heart of the forest, that intimation of melody seemed to grow more actual, to take body and breath, to come and go on long swells and ebbs of the night-breeze, to increase with tune and words, till a strange shrill singing grew ever clearer, and, as he stepped into an open space of moonbeams, far up in the branches, rocked by the wind, and singing, "How beautiful upon the mountains are the feet of him that bringeth good tidings, that publisheth peace," he saw his wife,—his wife,—but, great God in heaven! how? Some mad exclamation escaped him, but without diverting her. The child knew the singing voice, though never heard before in that unearthly key, and turned toward it through the veiling dreams. With a celerity almost instantaneous, it lay, in the twinkling of an eye, on the ground at the father's feet, while his gun was raised to his shoulder and levelled at the monster covering his wife with shaggy form and flaming gaze,—his wife so ghastly white, so rigid, so stained with blood, her eyes so fixedly bent above, and her lips, that had indurated into the chiselled pallor of marble, parted only with that flood of solemn song.

I do not know if it were the mother-instinct that for a moment lowered her eyes,—those eyes, so lately riveted on heaven, now suddenly seeing all life-long bliss possible. A thrill of joy pierced and shivered through her like a weapon, her voice trembled in its course, her glance lost its steady strength, fever-flushes chased each other over her face, yet she never once ceased chanting. She was quite aware, that, if her husband shot now, the ball must pierce her body before reaching any vital part of the beast,—and yet better that death, by his hand, than the other. But this her husband also knew, and he remained motionless, just covering the creature with the sight. He dared not fire, lest some wound not mortal should break the spell exercised by her voice, and the beast, enraged with pain, should rend her in atoms; moreover, the light was too uncertain for his aim. So he waited. Now and then he examined his gun to see if the damp were injuring its charge, now and then he wiped the great drops from his forehead. Again the cocks crowed with the passing hour,—the last time they were heard on that night. Cheerful home sound then, how full of safety and all comfort and rest it seemed! what sweet morning incidents of sparkling fire and sunshine, of gay household bustle, shining dresser, and cooing baby, of steaming cattle in the yard, and brimming milk-pails at the door! what pleasant voices! what laughter! what security! and here—

Now, as she sang on in the slow, endless, infinite moments, the fervent vision of God's peace was gone. Just as the grave had lost its sting, she was snatched back again to the arms of earthly hope. In vain she tried to sing, "There remaineth a rest for the people of God,"—her eyes trembled on her husband's, and she could only think of him, and of the child, and of happiness that yet might be, but with what a dreadful gulf of doubt between! She shuddered now in the suspense; all calm forsook her; she was tortured with dissolving heats or frozen with icy blasts; her face contracted, growing small and pinched; her voice was hoarse and sharp,—every tone cut like a knife,—the notes became heavy to lift,—withheld by some hostile pressure,—impossible. One gasp, a convulsive effort, and there was silence,—she had lost her voice.

The beast made a sluggish movement,—stretched and fawned like one awaking,—then, as if he would have yet more of the enchantment, stirred her slightly with his muzzle. As he did so, a sidelong hint of the man standing below with the raised gun smote him; he sprung round furiously, and, seizing his prey, was about to leap into some unknown airy den of the topmost branches now waving to the slow dawn.

The late moon had rounded through the sky so that her gleam at last fell full upon the bough with fairy frosting; the wintry morning light did not yet penetrate the gloom. The woman, suspended in mid-air an instant, cast only one agonized glance beneath,—but across and through it, ere the lids could fall, shot a withering sheet of flame,—a rifle-crack, half-heard, was lost in the terrible yell of desperation that bounded after it and filled her ears with savage echoes, and in the wide arc of some eternal descent she was falling;—but the beast fell under her.

I think that the moment following must have been too sacred for us, and perhaps the three have no special interest again till they issue from the shadows of the wilderness upon the white hills that skirt their home. The father carries the child hushed again into slumber, the mother follows with no such feeble step as might be anticipated. It is not time for reaction,—the tension not yet relaxed, the nerves still vibrant, she seems to herself like some one newly made; the night was a dream; the present stamped upon her in deep satisfaction, neither weighed nor compared with the past; if she has the careful tricks of former habit, it is as an automaton; and as they slowly climb the steep under the clear gray vault and the paling morning star, and as she stops to gather a spray of the red-rose berries or a feathery tuft of dead grasses for the chimney-piece of the log-house, or a handful of brown cones for the child's play,—of these quiet, happy folk you would scarcely dream how lately they had stolen from under the banner and encampment of the great King Death. The husband proceeds a step or two in advance; the wife lingers over a singular footprint in the snow, stoops and examines it, then looks up with a hurried word. Her husband stands alone on the hill, his arms folded across the babe, his gun fallen,—stands defined as a silhouette against the pallid sky. What is there in their home, lying below and yellowing in the light, to fix him with such a stare? She springs to his side. There is no home there. The log-house, the barns, the neighboring farms, the fences, are all blotted out and mingled in one smoking ruin. Desolation and death were indeed there, and beneficence and life in the forest. Tomahawk and scalping-knife, descending during that night, had left behind them only this work of their accomplished hatred and one subtle foot-print in the snow.

For the rest,—the world was all before them, where to choose.[2]

1860

Constance Fenimore Woolson 1840–1894

On February 12, 1882, Constance Fenimore Woolson wrote to Henry James, "Death is not terrible to me. . . . To me it is only a release; and if, at any time, you should hear that I had died, always be sure that I was quite willing, and even glad, to go. I do'nt [*sic*] think this is a morbid feeling, because it is accompanied by a very strong belief, that, while we *are* here, we should do our very best, and be as courageous and work as hard, as we possibly can." A dozen years later, Woolson's body

[2]Concluding lines of John Milton's *Paradise Lost* (1667) describing Adam and Eve's departure from the Garden of Eden.

lay on the pavement beneath a window of her Venice apartment. Ill from influenza, or possibly a condition she knew to be more serious, plagued by bouts of depression that she had inherited from her father, isolated from society by increasing deafness, disconnected from the places in the United States that she knew and loved, Woolson jumped from her rented rooms on the second floor of the Casa Semeticolo. She had just completed, but not yet seen through publication, her fourth novel, *Horace Chase,* in which she had imagined a similar death for one of her characters, though she has that character rescued at the last moment from the window ledge he has mounted in the delirium of illness.

Given the drama of her death, it is easy to read Woolson as the poor, suffering artist who, as her friend John Hay put it, "had not as much happiness as a convict." She never knew three of her sisters, who died in a scarlet fever epidemic within a month of her birth. She probably did not even visit their graves behind the Universalist Church in Claremont, New Hampshire, because after their deaths her family quickly left the Woolson roots in Claremont to settle in Cleveland, Ohio. In Cleveland, she watched her mother grieve over the death of another daughter in infancy and grieved with her when the two older Woolson daughters died shortly after their marriages. When her father died in 1869, Woolson left Cleveland for St. Augustine, Florida, where she, her mother, and her one living sister, who was widowed with a young daughter to raise, could live more cheaply. For the next ten years, they used this oldest city in the United States as a base for travels throughout the Reconstruction South. They maintained contact with the youngest child in the family, the only son, but the letters that mention him are fraught with justifiable worry about this troubled young man who died under mysterious circumstances in California in 1883. When Woolson's mother died in 1879, Woolson moved again, this time to Europe where she lived, occasionally in England, more often in Florence and Venice, until her death on January 24, 1894.

But to paint Woolson as a suffering artist debilitated by the deaths in her family and by unrequited love—she has been dismissed by biographer Leon Edel as a spinster in love with Henry James—is to miss the strength reflected in her remarks to James that "while we *are* here, we should do our very best, and be as courageous and work as hard, as we possibly can." In a nineteenth century that had created an ideal of physical weakness, even invalidism, for many women of her class, including Henry James's sister, Alice, Woolson embraced physical activity, especially rowing and walking. From childhood on, she traveled to remote or distant places: to Mackinac Island, Michigan; to the Blue Ridge Mountains and coastal regions of the South; to Mentone, Egypt, and Corfu. Drawing on her powers of close observation developed in an education that included the study of geology and botany, she directed her gaze both to her natural surroundings and to the customs of the people she encountered. She wrote travel sketches, poems, and a children's novel (*The Old Stone House* under the pseudonym Anne March in 1872), as well as a novella, four novels, and more than fifty short stories that appeared in the major literary magazines of the nineteenth century.

Woolson published "'Miss Grief'" in *Lippincott's Magazine* in May 1880. This publication date places it near the middle of her career, and to notice what is missing in the story tells us much about that career and about the careers of many women writers in the nineteenth century. Woolson uses her story to show how publishers, and thus readers, miss the names of women writers who write in a different voice. She raises questions about the pressure to satisfy publishers in order to find an audience and to make money, about the dangers of refusing to revise, about the anxiety of influence in the face of more successful writers, and about the way writing that has not been championed by publishers and readers disappears.

"'Miss Grief,'" more than any other of Woolson's best stories, was missed—perhaps even suppressed—by the very publishers it indicts because they did not collect it in either of her two posthumous volumes of Italian short stories, though its setting in Rome makes it eligible. Ironically, to read it now as reflective of Woolson's relationship with Henry James or as representative of her entire body of work is to miss the depth and range that Woolson showed in a successful twenty-five-year career. The story is only one of many she wrote about artist figures and about Americans living in Europe, and, in some ways, it is atypical even of these artist stories. Alone in her fiction, it omits the centrality of setting, perhaps because Woolson had not been in Europe long enough to observe its landscape and to incorporate that landscape as an essential part of her characters' lives as she does in her stories about the Great Lakes and the Reconstruction South and as she would do later in her European stories. Nor does it contain any of her caustic humor, perhaps again because she had not been in Europe long enough to observe the people from whose language and mannerisms she creates her satire. Although "'Miss Grief'" misses the fullness of Woolson's career, it nevertheless tells us much about the unsaid and the unsayable in the lives of people who lived in the nineteenth century, particularly women artists.

After Woolson's death, Henry James helped her sister sort through her belongings. Scholars believe that he burned many of her letters at this time, and, indeed, precious little remains from which to construct a life of Woolson. An anecdote circulates that James tried to drown Woolson's black silk dresses in a Venice canal, but that, refusing to sink, the dresses rose like black balloons surrounding him in his rented gondola. Happily, like those black dresses, Woolson's name, nearly submerged by the literary canon, has refused to drown, but has begun to rise again for readers in the twenty-first century to enjoy.

Sharon L. Dean
Rivier College

PRIMARY WORKS

Castle Nowhere: Lake-Country Sketches, 1875; *Rodman the Keeper: Southern Sketches,* 1880; *Anne,* 1882; *For the Major,* 1883; *East Angels,* 1886; *Jupiter Lights,* 1889; *Horace Chase,* 1894; *The Front Yard and Other Italian Stories,* 1895; *Dorothy and Other Italian Stories,* 1896; Jay B. Hubbell, "Some New Letters of Constance Fenimore Woolson," *New England Quarterly* 14 (1941): 715–35; Alice Hall Petry, ed., "'Always Your Attached Friend': The Unpublished Letters of Constance Fenimore Woolson to John and Clara Hay," *Books at Brown* (1982–83): 11–108.

Miss Grief

"A conceited fool" is a not uncommon expression. Now, I know that I am not a fool, but I also know that I am conceited. But, candidly, can it be helped if one happens to be young, well and strong, passably good-looking, with some money that one has inherited and more that one has earned—in all, enough to make life comfortable—and if upon this foundation rests also the pleasant superstructure of a literary success? The success is deserved, I think: certainly it was not lightly gained. Yet even with this I fully appreciate its rarity. Thus, I find myself very well entertained in life: I have all I wish in the way of society, and a deep, although of course carefully concealed, satisfaction in my own little fame; which fame I foster by a gentle system of non-interference. I know that I am spoken of as "that quiet young fellow who writes those delightful little studies of society, you know;" and I live up to that definition.

A year ago I was in Rome, and enjoying life particularly. There was a large number of my acquaintances there, both American and English, and no day passed without its invitation. Of course I understood it: it is seldom that you find a literary man who is good-tempered, well-dressed, sufficiently provided with money, and amiably obedient to all the rules and requirements of "society." "When found, make a note of it;"[1] and the note was generally an invitation.

One evening, upon returning to my lodgings, my man Simpson informed me that a person had called in the afternoon, and upon learning that I was absent had left not a card, but her name—"Miss Grief." The title lingered—Miss Grief! "Grief has not so far visited me here," I said to myself, dismissing Simpson and seeking my little balcony for a final smoke, "and she shall not now. I shall take care to be 'not at home' to her if she continues to call." And then I fell to thinking of Ethelind[2] Abercrombie, in whose society I had spent that and many evenings: they were golden thoughts.

The next day there was an excursion: it was late when I reached my rooms, and again Simpson informed me that Miss Grief had called.

"Is she coming continuously?" I said, half to myself.

"Yes, sir: she mentioned that she should call again."

"How does she look?"

"Well, sir, a lady, but not so prosperous as she was, I should say," answered Simpson discreetly.

"Young?"

"No, sir."

"Alone?"

"A maid with her, sir."

But once outside in my little high-up balcony with my cigar, I again forgot Miss Grief and whatever she might represent. Who would not forget in that moonlight, with Ethelind Abercrombie's face to remember?

The stranger came a third time, and I was absent: then she let two days pass, and began again. It grew to be a regular dialogue between Simpson and myself when I came in at night: "Grief today?"

"Yes, sir."

"What time?"

"Four, sir."

[1]The line comes from *Dombey and Son* by Charles Dickens (1812–1870). Woolson's reference to this novel is apt because it concerns an industrialist whose son dies, leaving him with a less-valued daughter.

[2]When "'Miss Grief'" appeared in *Stories by American Authors* (1884), the name Ethelind was changed to Isabel. Whether Woolson initiated or approved the change is unclear. Several reprints have incorrectly identified the name Isabel as appearing in the original *Lippincott*'s publication and most scholars have referred to this character as Isabel rather than as Ethelind.

"Happy the man," I thought, "who can keep her confined to a particular hour!"

But I should not have treated my visitor so cavalierly if I had not felt sure that she was eccentric and unconventional—qualities extremely tiresome in a woman no longer young or attractive, and without money to gild them over. If she were not eccentric she would not have persisted in coming to my door day after day in this silent way, without stating her errand, leaving a note or presenting her credentials in any shape. I made up my mind that she had something to sell—a bit of carving or some intaglio[3] supposed to be antique. It was known that I had a fancy for oddities. I said to myself, "She has read or heard of my 'Old Gold' story or else 'The Buried God,' and she thinks me an idealizing ignoramus upon whom she can impose. Her sepulchral name is at least not Italian: probably she is a sharp country-woman of mine, turning by means of aesthetic lies an honest penny when she can."

She had called seven times during a period of two weeks without seeing me, when one day I happened to be at home in the afternoon, owing to a pouring rain and a fit of doubt concerning Miss Abercrombie. For I had constructed a careful theory of that young lady's characteristics in my own mind, and she had lived up to it delightfully until the previous evening, when with one word she had blown it to atoms and taken flight, leaving me standing, as it were, on a desolate shore, with nothing but a handful of mistaken inductions wherewith to console myself. I do not know a more exasperating frame of mind, at least for a constructor of theories. I could not write, and so I took up a French novel (I model myself a little on Balzac).[4] I had been turning over its pages but a few moments when Simpson knocked, and, entering softly, said, with just a shadow of a smile on his well-trained face, "Miss Grief." I briefly consigned Miss Grief to all the Furies,[5] and then, as he still lingered—perhaps not knowing where they resided—I asked where the visitor was.

"Outside, sir—in the hall. I told her I would see if you were at home."

"She must be unpleasantly wet if she had no carriage."

"No carriage, sir: they always come on foot. I think she *is* a little damp, sir."

"Well, let her in, but I don't want the maid. I may as well see her now, I suppose, and end the affair."

"Yes, sir."

I did not put down my book. My visitor should have a hearing, but not much more: she had sacrificed her womanly claims by her persistent attacks upon my door. Presently Simpson ushered her in. "Miss Grief," he said, and then went out, closing the curtain behind him.

A woman—yes, a lady—but shabby, unattractive and more than middle-aged.

I rose, bowed slightly, and then dropped into my chair again, still keeping the book in my hand. "Miss Grief?" I said interrogatively as I indicated a seat with my eyebrows.

"Not Grief," she answered—"Crief: my name is Crief."

She sat down, and I saw that she held a small flat box.

"Not carving, then," I thought—"probably old lace, something that belonged to

[3]A design engraved in metal or stone.

[4]Honoré de Balzac (1799–1850) was known for his novels about French society.

[5]In Greek mythology, the Furies were winged women who represented vengeance.

Tullia[6] or Lucrezia Borgia."[7] But as she did not speak I found myself obliged to begin: "You have been here, I think, once or twice before?"

"Seven times: this is the eighth."

A silence.

"I am often out: indeed, I may say that I am never in," I remarked carelessly.

"Yes: you have many friends."

"Who will perhaps buy old lace," I mentally added. But this time I too remained silent: why should I trouble myself to draw her out? She had sought me: let her advance her idea, whatever it was, now that entrance was gained.

But Miss Grief (I preferred to call her so) did not look as though she could advance anything: her black gown, damp with rain, seemed to retreat fearfully to her thin self, while her thin self retreated as far as possible from me, from the chair, from everything. Her eyes were cast down: an old-fashioned lace veil with a heavy border shaded her face. She looked at the floor, and I looked at her.

I grew a little impatient, but I made up my mind that I would continue silent and see how long a time she would consider necessary to give due effect to her little pantomime. Comedy? Or was it tragedy? I suppose full five minutes passed thus in our double silence; and that is a long time when two persons are sitting opposite each other alone in a small still room.

At last my visitor, without raising her eyes, said slowly, "You are very happy, are you not, with youth, health, friends, riches, fame?"

It was a singular beginning. Her voice was clear, low and very sweet as she thus enumerated my advantages one by one in a list. I was attracted by it, but repelled by her words, which seemed to me flattery both dull and bold.

"Thanks," I said, "for your kindness, but I fear it is undeserved. I seldom discuss myself even when with my friends."

"I am your friend," replied Miss Grief. Then, after a moment, she added slowly, "I have read every word you have written."

I curled the edges of my book indifferently: I am not a fop,[8] I hope, but—others have said the same.

"What is more, I know much of it by heart," continued my visitor. "Wait: I will show you;" and then, without pause, she began to repeat something of mine word for word, just as I had written it. On she went, and I—listened. I intended interrupting her after a moment, but I did not, because she was reciting so well, and also because I felt a desire gaining upon me to see what she would make of a certain conversation which I knew was coming—a conversation between two of my characters which was, to say the least, sphinx-like,[9] and somewhat incandescent also. What won me a little, too, was the fact that the scene she was reciting (it was hardly more than that, although called a story) was secretly my favorite among all the sketches from my

[6]In Roman legend, Tullia murdered her husband and married her brother-in-law. He then murdered her father so that he could be king; she drove over her father's body in her chariot.

[7]Lucrezia Borgia (1480–1519) belonged to a notoriously cruel Italian family.

[8]A fool.

[9]The Sphinx, part lion and part woman, kept Thebes under her power until Oedipus solved a riddle that asked what goes on four legs in the morning, two in the afternoon, and three in the evening (mankind). Hence, to be sphinxlike is to be enigmatic or mysterious.

pen with which a gracious public had been favored. I never said so, but it was; and I had always felt a wondering annoyance that the aforesaid public, while kindly praising beyond their worth other attempts of mine, had never noticed the higher purpose of this little shaft, aimed not at the balconies and lighted windows of society, but straight up toward the distant stars. So she went on, and presently reached the conversation: my two people began to talk. She had raised her eyes now, and was looking at me soberly as she gave the words of the woman, quiet, gentle, cold, and the replies of the man, bitter, hot and scathing. Her very voice changed, and took, although always sweetly, the different tones required, while no point of meaning, however small, no breath of delicate emphasis which I had meant, but which the dull types could not give, escaped appreciative and full, almost overfull, recognition which startled me. For she had understood me—understood me almost better than I had understood myself. It seemed to me that while I had labored to interpret partially a psychological riddle, she, coming after, had comprehended its bearings better than I had, although confining herself strictly to my own words and emphasis. The scene ended (and it ended rather suddenly), she dropped her eyes, and moved her hand nervously to and fro over the box she held: her gloves were old and shabby, her hands small.

I was secretly much surprised by what I had heard, but my ill-humor was deep-seated that day, and I still felt sure, besides, that the box contained something that I was expected to buy.

"You recite remarkably well," I said carelessly, "and I am much flattered also by your appreciation of my efforts. But it is not, I presume, to that alone that I owe the pleasure of this visit?"

"Yes," she answered, still looking down, "it is, for if you had not written that scene I should not have sought you. Your other sketches are interiors—exquisitely painted and delicately finished, but of small scope. *This* is a sketch in a few bold, masterly lines—work of entirely different spirit and purpose."

I was nettled by her insight. "You have bestowed so much of your kind attention upon me that I feel your debtor," I said, conventionally. "It may be that there is something I can do for you—connected, possibly, with that box?"

It was a little impertinent, but it was true, for she answered, "Yes."

I smiled, but her eyes were cast down and she did not see the smile.

"What I have to show you is a manuscript," she said after a pause which I did not break: "it is a drama. I thought that perhaps you would read it."

"An authoress! This is worse than old lace," I said to myself in dismay.—Then, aloud, "My opinion would be worth nothing, Miss Crief."

"Not in a business way, I know. But it might be—an assistance personally." Her voice had sunk to a whisper: outside, the rain was pouring steadily down. She was a very depressing object to me as she sat there with her box.

"I hardly think I have the time at present—" I began.

She had raised her eyes and was looking at me: then, when I paused, she rose and came suddenly toward my chair. "Yes, you will read it," she said with her hand on my arm—"you will read it. Look at this room; look at yourself; look at all you have. Then look at me, and have pity."

I had risen, for she held my arm and her damp skirt was brushing my knees.

Her large dark eyes looked intently into mine as she went on: "I have no shame in asking. Why should I have? It is my last endeavor, but a calm and well-considered one. If you refuse I shall go away, knowing that Fate has willed it so. And I shall be content."

"She is mad," I thought. But she did not look so and she had spoken quietly, even gently.—"Sit down," I said, moving away from her. I felt as if I had been magnetized, but it was only the nearness of her eyes to mine, and their intensity. I drew forward a chair, but she remained standing.

"I cannot," she said in the same sweet, gentle tone, "unless you promise."

"Very well, I promise; only sit down."

As I took her arm to lead her to the chair I perceived that she was trembling, but her face continued unmoved.

"You do not, of course, wish me to look at your manuscript now?" I said, temporizing: "it would be much better to leave it. Give me your address, and I will return it to you with my written opinion; although, I repeat, the latter will be of no use to you. It is the opinion of an editor or publisher that you want."

"It shall be as you please. And I will go in a moment," said Miss Grief, pressing her palms together, as if trying to control the tremor that had seized her slight frame.

She looked so pallid that I thought of offering her a glass of wine: then I remembered that if I did it might be a bait to bring her there again, and this I was desirous to prevent. She rose while the thought was passing through my mind. Her pasteboard box lay on the chair she had first occupied: she took it, wrote an address on the cover, laid it down, and then, bowing with a little air of formality, drew her black shawl around her shoulders and turned toward the door.

I followed, after touching the bell. "You will hear from me by letter," I said.

Simpson opened the door, and I caught a glimpse of the maid, who was waiting in the anteroom. She was an old woman, shorter than her mistress, equally thin, and dressed like her in rusty black. As the door opened she turned toward it a pair of small, dim blue eyes with a look of furtive suspense. Simpson dropped the curtain, shutting me into the inner room: he had no intention of allowing me to accompany my visitor farther. But I had the curiosity to go to a bay-window in an angle from whence I could command the street-door, and presently I saw them issue forth in the rain and walk away side by side, the mistress, being the taller, holding the umbrella: probably there was not much difference in rank between persons so poor and forlorn as these.

It grew dark. I was invited out for the evening, and I knew that if I went I should meet Miss Abercrombie. I said to myself that I would not go. I got out my paper for writing, I made my preparations for a quiet evening at home with myself; but it was of no use. It all ended slavishly in my going. At the last allowable moment I presented myself, and—as a punishment for my vacillation, I suppose—I never passed a more disagreeable evening. I drove homeward in a vixenish temper: it was foggy without, and very foggy within. What Ethelind really was, now that she had broken through my elaborately-built theories, I was not able to decide. There was, to tell the truth, a certain young Englishman— But that is apart from this story.

I reached home, went up to my rooms and had a supper. It was to console myself: I am obliged to console myself scientifically once in a while. I was walking up and down afterward, smoking and feeling somewhat better, when my eye fell upon the pasteboard box. I took it up: on the cover was written an address which showed that my visitor must have walked a long distance in order to see me: "A. Crief."—"A Grief," I thought; "and so she is. I positively believe she has brought all this trouble upon me: she has the evil eye." I took out the manuscript and looked at it. It was in the form of a little volume, and clearly written: on the cover was the word "Armor" in German text,[10] and underneath a pen-and-ink sketch of a helmet, breastplate and shield.

"Grief certainly needs armor," I said to myself, sitting down by the table and turning over the pages. "I may as well look over the thing now: I could not be in a worse mood." And then I began to read.

Early the next morning Simpson took a note from me to the given address, returning with the following reply: "No; I prefer to come to you; at four; A. CRIEF." These words, with their three semicolons, were written in pencil upon a piece of coarse printing-paper, but the handwriting was as clear and delicate as that of the manuscript in ink.

"What sort of a place was it, Simpson?"

"Very poor, sir, but I did not go all the way up. The elder person came down, sir, took the note, and requested me to wait where I was."

"You had no chance, then, to make inquiries?" I said, knowing full well that he had emptied the entire neighborhood of any information it might possess concerning these two lodgers.

"Well, sir, you know how these foreigners will talk, whether one wants to hear or not. But it seems that these two persons have been there but a few weeks: they live alone, and are uncommonly silent and reserved. The people around there call them something that signifies 'the Madames American, thin and dumb.'"

At four the "Madames American" arrived: it was raining again, and they came on foot under their old umbrella. The maid waited in the anteroom, and Miss Grief was ushered into my bachelor's parlor, which was library and dining-room in one. I had thought that I should meet her with great deference, but she looked so forlorn that my deference changed to pity. It was the woman that impressed me then, more than the writer—the fragile, nerveless body more than the inspired mind. For it was inspired: I had sat up half the night over her drama, and had felt thrilled through and through more than once by its earnestness, passion and power.

No one could have been more surprised than I was to find myself thus enthusiastic. I thought I had outgrown that sort of thing. And one would have supposed, too (I myself should have supposed so the day before), that the faults of the drama, which were many and prominent, would have chilled any liking I might have felt, I being a writer myself, and therefore critical; for writers are as apt to make much of the "how," rather than the "what," as painters, who, it is well known, prefer an exquisitely rendered representation of a commonplace theme to an imperfectly executed picture of even the most striking subject. But in this case, on the contrary, the scattered rays of splendor in Miss Grief's drama had made me forget the dark spots, which were numerous and disfiguring; or, rather, the splendor had made me anxious to have the spots removed. And this also was a philanthropic state very unusual for me. Regarding unsuccessful writers my motto had been "Vae victis!"[11]

My visitor took a seat and folded her hands: I could see, in spite of her quiet

[10]A gothic-style typeface.
[11]Woe to the vanquished.

manner, that she was in breathless suspense. It seemed so pitiful that she should be trembling there before me—a woman so much older than I was, a woman who possessed the divine spark of genius, which I was by no means sure, in spite of my success, had been granted to me—that I felt as if I ought to go down on my knees before her and entreat her to take her proper place of supremacy at once. But there! one does not go down on one's knees combustively, as it were, before a woman over fifty, plain in feature, thin, dejected and ill-dressed. I contented myself with taking her hands (in their miserable old gloves) in mine, while I said cordially "Miss Crief, your drama seems to me full of original power. It has roused my enthusiasm: I sat up half the night reading it."

The hands I held shook, but something (perhaps a shame for having evaded the knees business) made me tighten my hold and bestow upon her also a reassuring smile. She looked at me for a moment, and then, suddenly and noiselessly, tears rose and rolled down her cheeks. I dropped her hands and retreated. I had not thought her tearful: on the contrary, her voice and face had seemed rigidly controlled. But now here she was bending herself over the side of the chair with her head resting on her arms, not sobbing aloud, but her whole frame shaken by the strength of her emotion. I rushed for a glass of wine: I pressed her to take it. I did not quite know what to do, but, putting myself in her place, I decided to praise the drama; and praise it I did. I do not know when I have used so many adjectives. She raised her head and began to wipe her eyes.

"Do take the wine," I said, interrupting myself in my cataract of language.

"I dare not," she answered: then added humbly, "that is, unless you have a biscuit here or a bit of bread."

I found some biscuit: she ate two, and then slowly drank the wine while I resumed my verbal Niagara. Under its influence—and that of the wine too, perhaps—she began to show new life. It was not that she looked radiant—she could not—but simply that she looked warm. I now perceived what had been the principal discomfort of her appearance heretofore: it was that she had looked all the time as if suffering from cold.

At last I could think of nothing more to say, and stopped. I really admired the drama, but I thought I had exerted myself sufficiently as an anti-hysteric, and that adjectives enough, for the present at least, had been administered. She had put down her empty wine-glass, and was resting her hands on the broad cushioned arms of her chair with a sort of expanded content.

"You must pardon my tears," she said, smiling: "it was the revulsion of feeling. My life was at a low ebb: if your sentence had been against me it would have been my end."

"Your end?"

"Yes, the end of my life: I should have destroyed myself."

"Then you would have been a weak as well as wicked woman," I said in a tone of disgust: I do hate sensationalism.

"Oh no, you know nothing about it. I should have destroyed only this poor worn tenement of clay. But I can well understand how *you* would look upon it. Regarding the desirableness of life the prince and the beggar may have different opinions.—We will say no more of it, but talk of the drama instead." As she spoke the word "drama" a triumphant brightness came into her eyes.

I took the manuscript from a drawer and sat down beside her. "I suppose you know that there are faults," I said, expecting ready acquiescence.

"I was not aware that there were any," was her gentle reply.

Here was a beginning! After all my interest in her—and, I may say under the circumstances, my kindness—she received me in this way! However, my belief in her genius was too sincere to be altered by her whimsies; so I persevered. "Let us go over it together," I said. "Shall I read it to you, or will you read it to me?"

"I will not read it, but recite it."

"That will never do: you will recite it so well that we shall see only the good points, and what we have to concern ourselves with now is the bad ones."

"I will recite it," she repeated.

"Look here, Miss Crief," I said bluntly, "for what purpose did you come to me? Certainly not merely to recite: I am no stage-manager. In plain English, was it not your idea that I might help you in obtaining a publisher?"

"Yes, yes," she answered, looking at me apprehensively, all her old manner returning.

I followed up my advantage, opened the little paper volume and began. I first took the drama line by line, and spoke of the faults of expression and structure: then I turned back and touched upon two or three glaring impossibilities in the plot. "Your absorbed interest in the motive of the whole no doubt made you forget these blemishes," I said apologetically.

But, to my surprise, I found that she did not see the blemishes—that she appreciated nothing I had said, comprehended nothing. Such unaccountable obtuseness puzzled me. I began again, going over the whole with even greater minuteness and care. I worked hard: the perspiration stood in beads upon my forehead as I struggled with her—what shall I call it—obstinacy? But it was not exactly obstinacy. She simply could not see the faults of her own work, any more than a blind man can see the smoke that dims a patch of blue sky. When I had finished my task the second time she still remained as gently impassive as before. I leaned back in my chair exhausted and looked at her.

Even then she did not seem to comprehend (whether she agreed with it or not) what I must be thinking. "It is such a heaven to me that you like it!" she murmured dreamily, breaking the silence. Then, with more animation, "And *now* you will let me recite it?"

I was too weary to oppose her: she threw aside her shawl and bonnet, and, standing in the centre of the room, began.

And she carried me along with her: all the strong passages were doubly strong when spoken, and the faults, which seemed nothing to her, were made by her earnestness to seem nothing to me, at least for that moment. When it was ended she stood looking at me with a triumphant smile.

"Yes," I said, "I like it, and you see that I do. But I like it because my taste is peculiar. To me originality and force are everything—perhaps because I have them not to any marked degree myself—but the world at large will not overlook as I do your absolutely barbarous shortcomings on account of them. Will you trust me to go over the drama and correct it at my pleasure?" This was a vast deal for me to offer: I was surprised at myself.

"No," she answered softly, still smiling. "There shall not be so much as a comma altered." Then she sat down and fell into a reverie as though she were alone.

"Have you written anything else?" I said after a while, when I had become tired of the silence.

"Yes."

"Can I see it? Or is it *them*?"

"It is *them*. Yes, you can see all."

"I will call upon you for the purpose."

"No, you must not," she said, coming back to the present nervously: "I prefer to come to you."

At this moment Simpson entered to light the room, and busied himself rather longer than was necessary over the task. When he finally went out I saw that my visitor's manner had sunk into its former depression: the presence of the servant seemed to have chilled her.

"When did you say I might come?" I repeated, ignoring her refusal.

"I did not say it. It would be impossible."

"Well, then, when will you come here?" There was, I fear, a trace of fatigue in my tone.

"At your good pleasure, sir," she answered humbly.

My chivalry was touched by this: after all, she was a woman. "Come to-morrow," I said. "By the way, come and dine with me then: why not?" I was curious to see what she would reply.

"Why not, indeed? Yes, I will come. I am forty-three: I might have been your mother."

This was not quite true, as I am over thirty; but I look young, while she—Well, I had thought her over fifty. "I can hardly call you 'mother,' but then we might compromise upon 'aunt,'" I said, laughing. "Aunt what?"

"My name is Aaronna,"[12] she gravely answered. "My father was much disappointed that I was not a boy, and gave me as nearly as possible the name he had prepared—Aaron."

"Then come and dine with me to-morrow, and bring with you the other manuscripts, Aaronna," I said, amused at the quaint sound of the name. On the whole, I did not like "aunt."

"I will come," she answered.

It was twilight and still raining, but she refused all offers of escort or carriage, departing with her maid, as she had come, under the brown umbrella.

The next day we had the dinner. Simpson was astonished—and more than astonished, grieved—when I told him that he was to dine with the maid; but he could not complain in words, since my own guest, the mistress, was hardly more attractive. When our preparations were complete I could not help laughing: the two prim little tables, one in the parlor and one in the anteroom, and Simpson disapprovingly going back and forth between them, were irresistible.

I greeted my guest hilariously when she arrived, and, fortunately, her manner

[12]Cheryl Torsney reads the name Aaronna as a feminization of the biblical Aaron. The first of Israel's high priests and the brother of Moses, Aaron wore armorlike clothing and served as an intermediary with God. In Torsney's interpretation, Woolson uses the meagerly clothed Aaronna to predict a time when female artists will overturn patriarchal traditions and assert their own powerful voices. See Exodus:28–29.

was not quite so depressed as usual: I could never have accorded myself with a tearful mood. I had thought that perhaps she would make, for the occasion, some change in her attire: I have never known a woman who had not some scrap of finery, however small, in reserve for that unexpected occasion of which she is ever dreaming. But no: Miss Grief wore the same black gown, unadored and unaltered. I was glad that there was no rain that day, so that the skirt did not at least look so damp and rheumatic.

She ate quietly, almost furtively, yet with a good appetite, and she did not refuse the wine. Then, when the meal was over and Simpson had removed the dishes, I asked for the new manuscripts. She gave me an old green copybook filled with short poems, and a prose sketch by itself: I lit a cigar and sat down at my desk to look them over.

"Perhaps you will try a cigarette?" I suggested, more for amusement than anything else, for there was not a shade of Bohemianism about her: her whole appearance was puritanical.

"I have not yet succeeded in learning to smoke."

"You have tried?" I said, turning around.

"Yes: Serena[13] and I tried, but we did not succeed."

"Serena is your maid?"

"She lives with me."

I was seized with inward laughter, and began hastily to look over her manuscripts with my back toward her, so that she might not see it. A vision had risen before me of those two forlorn women, alone in their room with locked doors, patiently trying to acquire the smoker's art.

But my attention was soon absorbed by the papers before me. Such a fantastic collection of words, lines and epithets I had never before seen, or even in dreams imagined. In truth, they were like the work of dreams: they were *Kubla Khan,*[14] only more so. Here and there was radiance like the flash of a diamond, but each poem, almost each verse and line, was marred by some fault or lack which seemed wilful perversity, like the work of an evil sprite. It was like a case of jeweller's wares set before you, with each ring unfinished, each bracelet too large or too small for its purpose, each breastpin without its fastening, each necklace purposely broken. I turned the pages, marvelling. When about half an hour had passed, and I was leaning back for a moment to light another cigar, I glanced toward my visitor. She was behind me, in an easy-chair before my small fire, and she was—fast asleep! In the relaxation of her unconsciousness I was struck anew by the poverty her appearance expressed: her feet were visible, and I saw the miserable worn old shoes which hitherto she had kept concealed.

After looking at her for a moment I returned to my task and took up the prose

[13]Woolson changes this name to Martha at the end of the story. Cheryl Torsney equates Martha with the biblical Martha (Luke 10:39–42; John 11:21–27), the sister of Lazarus, who works at household tasks while her sister Mary listens to the words of Jesus. Torsney reads the narrator as a Jesus figure who does not deserve to be heard and who does not perform an act of resurrection as the biblical Jesus does with Lazarus.

[14]A poem by Samuel Taylor Coleridge (1772–1834) that he claimed came from a dream vision.

story: in prose she must be more reasonable. She was less fantastic perhaps, but hardly more reasonable. The story was that of a profligate and commonplace man forced by two of his friends, in order not to break the heart of a dying girl who loves him, to live up to a high imaginary ideal of himself which her pure but mistaken mind has formed. He has a handsome face and sweet voice, and repeats what they tell him. Her long, slow decline and happy death, and his own inward ennui and profound weariness of the rôle he has to play, made the vivid points of the story. So far, well enough, but here was the trouble: through the whole narrative moved another character, a physician of tender heart and exquisite mercy, who practised murder as a fine art, and was regarded (by the author) as a second Messiah! This was monstrous. I read it through twice, and threw it down: then, fatigued, I turned round and leaned back, waiting for her to wake. I could see her profile against the dark hue of the easy-chair.

Presently she seemed to feel my gaze, for she stirred, then opened her eyes. "I have been asleep," she said, rising hurriedly.

"No harm in that, Aaronna."

But she was deeply embarrassed and troubled, much more so than the occasion required; so much so, indeed, that I turned the conversation back upon the manuscripts as a diversion. "I cannot stand that doctor of yours," I said, indicating the prose story: "no one would. You must cut him out."

Her self-possession returned as if by magic. "Certainly not," she answered haughtily.

"Oh, if you do not care—I had labored under the impression that you were anxious these things should find a purchaser."

"I am, I am," she said, her manner changing to deep humility with wonderful rapidity. With such alternations of feeling as this sweeping over her like great waves, no wonder she was old before her time.

"Then you must take out that doctor."

"I am willing, but do not know how," she answered, pressing her hands together helplessly. "In my mind he belongs to the story so closely that he cannot be separated from it."

Here Simpson entered, bringing a note for me: it was a line from Mrs. Abercrombie inviting me for that evening—an unexpected gathering, and therefore likely to be all the more agreeable. My heart bounded in spite of me: I forgot Miss Grief and her manuscripts for the moment as completely as though they had never existed. But, bodily, being still in the same room with her, her speech brought me back to the present.

"You have had good news?" she said.

"Oh no, nothing especial—merely an invitation."

"But good news also," she repeated. "And now, as for me, I must go."

Not supposing that she would stay much later in any case, I had that morning ordered a carriage to come for her at about that hour. I told her this. She made no reply beyond putting on her bonnet and shawl.

"You will hear from me soon," I said: "I shall do all I can for you."

She had reached the door, but before opening it she stopped, turned and extended her hand. "You are good," she said: "I give you thanks. Do not think me ungrateful or envious. It is only that you are young, and I am so—so old." Then she opened the door and passed through the anteroom without pause, her maid accompanying her and Simpson with gladness lighting the way. They were gone. I dressed hastily and went out—to continue my studies in psychology.

Time passed: I was busy, amused and perhaps a little excited (sometimes psychology is delightful). But, although much occupied with my own affairs, I did not altogether neglect my self-imposed task regarding Miss Grief. I began by sending her prose story to a friend, the editor of a monthly magazine, with a letter making a strong plea for its admittance. It should have a chance first on its own merits. Then I forwarded the drama to a publisher, also an acquaintance, a man with a taste for phantasms and a soul above mere common popularity, as his own coffers knew to their cost. This done, I waited with conscience clear.

Four weeks passed. During this waiting period I heard nothing from Miss Grief. At last one morning came a letter from my editor. "The story has force, but I cannot stand that doctor," he wrote. "Let her cut him out, and I might print it." Just what I myself had said. The package lay there on my table, travelworn and grimed: a returned manuscript is, I think, the most melancholy object on earth. I decided to wait, before writing to Aaronna, until the second letter was received. A week later it came. "Armor" was declined. The publisher had been "impressed" by the power displayed in certain passages, but the "impossibilities of the plot" rendered it "unavailable for publication"—in fact, would "bury it in ridicule" if brought before the public, a public "lamentably" fond of amusement, "seeking it, undaunted, even in the cannon's mouth." I doubt if he knew himself what he meant. But one thing, at any rate, was clear: "Armor" was declined.

Now, I am, as I have remarked before, a little obstinate. I was determined that Miss Grief's work should be received. I would alter and improve it myself, without letting her know: the end justified the means. Surely the sieve of my own good taste, whose mesh had been pronounced so fine and delicate, would serve for two. I began, and utterly failed.

I set to work first upon "Armor." I amended, altered, left out, put in, pieced, condensed, lengthened: I did my best, and all to no avail. I could not succeed in completing anything that satisfied me, or that approached, in truth, Miss Grief's own work just as it stood. I suppose I went over that manuscript twenty times: I covered sheets of paper with my copies. But the obstinate drama refused to be corrected: as it was it must stand or fall.

Wearied and annoyed, I threw it aside and took up the prose story: that would be easier. But, to my surprise, I found that that apparently gentle "doctor" would not out: he was so closely interwoven with every part of the tale that to take him out was like taking out one especial figure in a carpet: that is impossible unless you unravel the whole. At last I did unravel the whole, and then the story was no longer good, or Aaronna's: it was weak, and mine. All this took time, for of course I had much to do in connection with my own life and tasks. But, although slowly and at my leisure, I really did try my best as regarded Miss Grief, and without success. I was forced at last to make up my mind that either my own powers were not equal to the task, or else that her perversities were as essential a part of her work as her inspirations, and not to be separated from it. Once during this period I showed two of the short poems to Ethelind, withholding of course the writer's name. "They were written by a woman," I explained.

"Her mind must have been disordered, poor thing!" Ethelind said in her gentle way when she returned them—"at least, judging by these. They are hopelessly mixed and vague."

Now, they were not vague so much as vast. But I knew that I could not make Ethelind comprehend it, and (so complex a creature is man) I do not know that I wanted her to comprehend it. These were the only ones in the whole collection that I would have shown her, and I was rather glad that she did not like even these. Not that poor Aaronna's poems were evil: they were simply unrestrained, large, vast, like the skies or the wind. Ethelind was bounded on all sides, like a violet in a garden-bed. And I liked her so.

One afternoon, about the time when I was beginning to see that I could not "improve" Miss Grief, I came upon the maid. I was driving, and she had stopped on the crossing to let the carriage pass. I recognized her at a glance (by her general forlornness), and called to the driver to stop. "How is Miss Crief?" I said. "I have been intending to write to her for some time."

"And your note, when it comes," answered the old woman on the crosswalk fiercely, "she shall not see."

"What?"

"I say she shall not see it. Your patronizing face shows that you have no good news, and you shall not rack and stab her any more on *this* earth, please God, while I have authority."

"Who has racked or stabbed her, Serena?"

"Serena, indeed! Rubbish! I'm no Serena: I'm her aunt. And as to who has racked and stabbed her, I say you, *you*—YOU literary men!" She had put her old head inside my carriage, and flung out these words at me in a shrill, menacing tone. "But she shall die in peace in spite of you," she continued. "Vampires! you take her ideas and fatten on them, and leave her to starve. You know you do—*you* who have had her poor manuscripts these months and months!"

"Is she ill?" I asked in real concern, gathering that much at least from the incoherent tirade.

"She is dying," answered the desolate old creature, her voice softening and her dim eyes filling with tears.

"Oh, I trust not. Perhaps something can be done. Can I help you in any way?"

"In all ways if you would," she said, breaking down and beginning to sob weakly, with her head resting on the sill of the carriage-window. "Oh, what have we not been through together, we two! Piece by piece I have sold all."

I am good-hearted enough, but I do not like to have old women weeping across my carriage-door. I suggested, therefore, that she should come inside and let me take her home. Her shabby old skirt was soon beside me, and, following her directions, the driver turned toward one of the most wretched quarters of the city, the abode of poverty, crowded and unclean. Here, in a large bare chamber up many flights of stairs, I found Miss Grief.

As I entered I was startled: I thought she was dead. There seemed no life present until she opened her eyes, and even then they rested upon us vaguely, as though she did not know who we were. But as I approached a sudden light came into them: she recognized me, and this sudden animation, this return of the soul to the windows of the almost deserted body, was the most wonderful thing I ever saw. "You have good news of the drama?" she whispered as I bent over her: "tell me. I *know* you have good news."

What was I to answer? Pray, what would you have answered, puritan?

"Yes, I have good news, Aaronna," I said. "The drama will appear." (And who knows? Perhaps it will in some other world.)

She smiled, and her now brilliant eyes did not leave my face.

"He knows I'm your aunt: I told him," said the old woman, coming to the bedside.

"Did you?" whispered Miss Grief, still gazing at me with a smile. "Then please, dear Aunt Martha, give me something to eat."

Aunt Martha hurried across the room, and I followed her. "It's the first time she's asked for food in weeks," she said in a husky tone.

She opened a cupboard-door vaguely, but I could see nothing within. "What have you for her?" I asked with some impatience, although in a low voice.

"Please God, nothing!" answered the poor old woman, hiding her reply and her tears behind the broad cupboard-door. "I was going out to get a little something when I met you."

"Good Heavens! is it money you need? Here, take this and send; or go yourself in the carriage waiting below."

She hurried out breathless, and I went back to the bedside, much disturbed by what I had seen and heard. But Miss Grief's eyes were full of life, and as I sat down beside her she whispered earnestly, "Tell me."

And I did tell her—a romance invented for the occasion. I venture to say that none of my published sketches could compare with it. As for the lie involved, it will stand among my few good deeds, I know, at the judgment-bar.

And she was satisfied. "I have never known what it was," she whispered, "to be fully happy until now." She closed her eyes, and when the lids fell I again thought that she had passed away. But no, there was still pulsation in her small, thin wrist. As she perceived my touch she smiled. "Yes, I am happy," she said again, although without audible sound.

The old aunt returned: food was prepared, and she took some. I myself went out after wine that should be rich and pure. She rallied a little, but I did not leave her: her eyes dwelt upon me and compelled me to stay, or rather my conscience compelled me. It was a damp night, and I had a little fire made. The wine, fruit, flowers and candles I had ordered made the bare place for the time being bright and fragrant. Aunt Martha dozed in her chair from sheer fatigue—she had watched many nights—but Miss Grief was awake, and I sat beside her.

"I make you my executor," she murmured, "as to the drama. But my other manuscripts place, when I am gone, under my head, and let them be buried with me. They are not many—those you have and these. See!"

I followed her gesture, and saw under her pillows the edges of two more copybooks like the one I had. "Do not look at them—my poor dead children!" she said tenderly. "Let them depart with me—unread, as I have been."

Later she whispered, "Did you wonder why I came to you? It was the contrast. You were young—strong—rich—praised—loved—successful: all that I was not. I wanted to look at you—and imagine how it would feel. You had success—but I had the greater power. Tell me: did I not have it?"

"Yes, Aaronna."

"It is all in the past now. But I am satisfied."

After another pause she said with a faint smile, "Do you remember when I fell asleep in your parlor? It was the good and rich food. It was so long since I had had food like that!"

I took her hand and held it, conscience-stricken, but now she hardly seemed to perceive my touch. "And the smoking?" she whispered. "Do you remember how you laughed? I saw it. But I had heard that smoking soothed—that one was no longer tired and hungry—with a cigar."

In little whispers of this sort, separated by long rests and pauses, the night passed. Once she asked if her aunt was asleep, and when I answered in the affirmative she said, "Help her to return home—to America: the drama will pay for it. I ought never to have brought her away."

I promised, and she resumed her bright-eyed silence.

I think she did not speak again. Toward morning the change came, and soon after sunrise, with her old aunt kneeling by her side, she passed away.

All was arranged as she had wished. Her manuscripts, covered with violets, formed her pillow. No one followed her to the grave save her aunt and myself: I thought she would prefer it so. Her name was not "Crief," after all, but "Moncrief:" I saw it written out by Aunt Martha for the coffinplate, as follows: "Aaronna Moncrief, aged forty-three years two months and eight days."

I never knew more of her history than is written here. If there was more that I might have learned, it remained unlearned, for I did not ask.

And the drama? I keep it here in this locked case. I could have had it published at my own expense, but I think that now she knows its faults herself, and would not like it.

I keep it, and once in a while I read it over—not as a *memento mori*[15] exactly, but rather as a memento of my own good-fortune, for which I should continually give thanks. The want of one grain made all her work void, and that one grain was given to me. She, with the greater power, failed—I, with the less, succeeded. But no praise is due to me for that. When I die "Armor" is to be destroyed unread: not even Ethelind is to see it. For women will misunderstand each other; and, dear and precious to me as my sweet wife is, I could not bear that she or any one should cast so much as a thought of scorn upon the memory of the writer, upon my poor dead, "unavailable," unaccepted "Miss Grief."

1880

[15]A reminder of death.

Sarah Orne Jewett 1849–1909

Named for her paternal grandfather and grandmother, Theodora Sarah Orne Jewett was the second of three girls born to Theodore Herman and Caroline Frances Perry Jewett in the New England village of South Berwick, Maine. Descending on both sides from pre-Revolutionary families that had built up comfortable incomes from shipbuilding and seafaring, she was the daughter and granddaughter of physicians. As a child Jewett wished to become a doctor herself. Poor health thwarted that ambition even as it encouraged her close relationship with her father, who took her with him on medical calls to build up her strength. These trips through rural and small-town Maine provided her, by her own account, with material for her writing throughout her career.

Upon graduation from Berwick Academy in 1865, Jewett began writing short fiction. She also published poetry, literature for children, and two novels, one of which, *A Country Doctor,* shows a young woman choosing to become a physician rather than marry. But her true gift was short narrative. As she wrote to Horace Scudder, the assistant editor of the *Atlantic Monthly,* in 1873: "But I don't believe I could write a long story as you and Mr. Howells advise me in this last letter. . . . The story would have no plot." She explained: "I could write you entertaining letters perhaps, from some desirable house where I was in most charming company, but I couldn't make a story about it," and she ended by lamenting: "What shall be done with such a girl? For I wish to keep on writing, and to do the very best I can."

Partly a pose (many of Jewett's stories would have expertly crafted conventional plots), this protest probably reflects resistance to the kind of conventional plotting found in most high-culture, white, Western, masculine fiction. She often experimented with narrative forms that do not follow predictable linear patterns. For example, the sketch, a genre developed primarily though not exclusively by women during the nineteenth century, provided a short flexible structure that encourages realistic depiction of specific environments, moods, relationships, customs, and characters without requiring pronounced protagonist/antagonist plotting and closure.

Fascinated throughout her career with relationships among women, Jewett grounded her personal life in close friendships with women, the most important of which was her long relationship with Annie Fields, a woman prominent and powerful in her own right in the Boston literary and publishing world. The two women's commitment to each other began in the early 1880s, shortly after the death of Fields's husband, the publisher James Fields, and became the strongest bond in the author's adult life. Fields and Jewett traveled widely in Europe and the eastern United States and lived a large part of every year together, dividing their time between Boston and the New England shore (the remainder of the year Jewett lived in her family home in South Berwick). The Fields/Jewett household on Charles Street in the Back Bay in Boston served as an important literary center where well-known figures in the publishing world, from Howells in the 1880s to Cather in the early 1900s, visited and gathered.

Jewett connected two generations of women writers. She counted among her influences Harriet Beecher Stowe, whose New England fiction she greatly admired, and she figured prominently in the tradition of women realists and regionalists active in the second half of the nineteenth century: Rose Terry Cooke, Celia Thaxter, Mary E. Wilkins Freeman, Alice Brown, Elizabeth Stuart Phelps. At the turn of the century writers as different as Kate Chopin and Willa Cather, and probably Alice

Dunbar-Nelson, looked to Jewett as a model. (Edith Wharton did as well, though she chose to call attention to her independence from Jewett rather than her affinity with her.) Cather acknowledged a strong debt to Jewett, who told her to devote herself full-time to writing fiction. Cather gratefully dedicated her first novel about a heroine, *O Pioneers!* (1913), to Jewett and said in 1925 that *The Country of the Pointed Firs* ranked with *The Scarlet Letter* and *Huckleberry Finn* as an American classic.

Toward the end of her career, Jewett fused brilliantly her interests in rural community, female friendship, the making of art, and the structure of narrative in *The Country of the Pointed Firs.* These concerns also shape "A White Heron" (1881), probably Jewett's best-known individual story, and "The Foreigner," whose main character, Almira Todd, is central in *The Country of the Pointed Firs* as well.

"A White Heron" dramatizes the clash of competing sets of values in late-nineteenth-century industrial America: urban/rural, scientific/empathic, masculine/feminine. A story of female initiation (or, actually, anti-initiation), it offers a highly critical perspective on heterosexual romantic love and attraction in modern Western culture. "The Foreigner," written after *The Country of the Pointed Firs,* comes out of Jewett's lifelong interest in the occult and extra-sensory communication. Played out against a violent "natural" backdrop, its themes of mother-daughter love and sororal bonds suggest her faith in the healing power of female friendship and her vision of an alternative world—woman-centered, enduring, cooperative—outside and removed from mainstream, masculine America. In both these stories, race is a covert but key issue, as evidenced by the obsession with whiteness in the former and the West Indies connection in the latter.

In 1901 Bowdoin College conferred on Sarah Orne Jewett the degree of Litt.D., making her the first woman to receive that honor from the college. Eight years later, following a stroke, she died in South Berwick in the house in which she had been born.

Elizabeth Ammons
Tufts University

PRIMARY WORKS

Deephaven, 1877; *A Country Doctor,* 1884; *A White Heron and Other Stories,* 1886; *The Country of the Pointed Firs,* 1896; *The Tory Lover,* 1901.

A White Heron

I

The woods were already filled with shadows one June evening, just before eight o'-clock, though a bright sunset still glimmered faintly among the trunks of the trees. A little girl was driving home her cow, a plodding, dilatory, provoking creature in her behavior, but a valued companion for all that. They were going away from whatever light there was, and striking deep into the woods, but their feet were familiar with the path, and it was no matter whether their eyes could see it or not.

There was hardly a night the summer through when the old cow could be found waiting at the pasture bars; on the contrary, it was her greatest pleasure to hide herself away among the huckleberry bushes, and though she wore a loud bell she had made the discovery that if one stood perfectly still it would not ring. So Sylvia had to hunt for her until she found her, and call Co'! Co'! with never an answering Moo, until her childish patience was quite spent. If the creature had not given good milk and plenty of it, the case would have seemed very different to her owners. Besides, Sylvia had all the time there was, and very little use to make of it. Sometimes in pleasant weather it was a consolation to look upon the cow's pranks as an intelligent attempt to play hide and seek, and as the child had no playmates she lent herself to this amusement with a good deal of zest. Though this chase had been so long that the wary animal herself had given an unusual signal of her whereabouts, Sylvia had only laughed when she came upon Mistress Moolly at the swampside, and urged her affectionately homeward with a twig of birch leaves. The old cow was not inclined to wander farther, she even turned in the right direction for once as they left the pasture, and stepped along the road at a good pace. She was quite ready to be milked now, and seldom stopped to browse. Sylvia wondered what her grandmother would say because they were so late. It was a great while since she had left home at half-past five o'clock, but everybody knew the difficulty of making this errand a short one. Mrs. Tilley had chased the hornéd torment too many summer evenings herself to blame any one else for lingering, and was only thankful as she waited that she had Sylvia, nowadays, to give such valuable assistance. The good woman suspected that Sylvia loitered occasionally on her own account; there never was such a child for straying about out-of-doors since the world was made! Everybody said that it was a good change for a little maid who had tried to grow for eight years in a crowded manufacturing town, but, as for Sylvia herself, it seemed as if she never had been alive at all before she came to live at the farm. She thought often with wistful compassion of a wretched geranium that belonged to a town neighbor.

"'Afraid of folks,'" old Mrs. Tilley said to herself, with a smile, after she had made the unlikely choice of Sylvia from her daughter's houseful of children, and was returning to the farm. "'Afraid of folks,' they said! I guess she won't be troubled no great with 'em up to the old place!" When they reached the door of the lonely house and stopped to unlock it, and the cat came to purr loudly, and rub against them, a deserted pussy, indeed, but fat with young robins, Sylvia whispered that this was a beautiful place to live in, and she never should wish to go home.

The companions followed the shady woodroad, the cow taking slow steps and the child very fast ones. The cow stopped long at the brook to drink, as if the pasture were not half a swamp, and Sylvia stood still and waited, letting her bare feet cool themselves in the shoal water, while the great twilight moths struck softly against her. She waded on through the brook as the cow moved away, and listened to the thrushes with a heart that beat fast with pleasure. There was a stirring in the great boughs overhead. They were full of little birds and beasts that seemed to be wide awake, and going about their world, or else saying good-night to each other in sleepy twitters. Sylvia herself felt sleepy as she walked along. However, it was not much farther to the house, and the air was soft and sweet. She was not often in the woods so late as this, and it made her feel as if she were a part of the gray shadows and the moving leaves. She was just thinking how long it seemed since she first came to the farm a year ago, and wondering if everything went on in the noisy town just the same as when she was there; the thought of the great red-faced boy who used to chase and frighten her made her hurry along the path to escape from the shadow of the trees.

Suddenly this little woods-girl is horror-stricken to hear a clear whistle not very far away. Not a bird's-whistle, which would have a sort of friendliness, but a boy's whistle, determined, and somewhat aggressive. Sylvia left the cow to whatever sad fate might await her, and stepped discreetly aside into the bushes, but she was just too late. The enemy had discovered her, and called out in a very cheerful and persuasive tone, "Halloa, little girl, how far is it to the road?" and trembling Sylvia answered almost inaudibly, "A good ways."

She did not dare to look boldly at the tall young man, who carried a gun over his shoulder, but she came out of her bush and again followed the cow, while he walked alongside.

"I have been hunting for some birds," the stranger said kindly, "and I have lost my way, and need a friend very much. Don't be afraid," he added gallantly. "Speak up and tell me what your name is, and whether you think I can spend the night at your house, and go out gunning early in the morning."

Sylvia was more alarmed than before. Would not her grandmother consider her much to blame? But who could have foreseen such an accident as this? It did not seem to be her fault, and she hung her head as if the stem of it were broken, but managed to answer "Sylvy," with much effort when her companion again asked her name.

Mrs. Tilley was standing in the doorway when the trio came into view. The cow gave a loud moo by way of explanation.

"Yes, you'd better speak up for yourself, you old trial! Where'd she tucked herself away this time, Sylvy?" But Sylvia kept an awed silence; she knew by instinct that her grandmother did not comprehend the gravity of the situation. She must be mistaking the stranger for one of the farmer-lads of the region.

The young man stood his gun beside the door, and dropped a lumpy game-bag beside it; then he bade Mrs. Tilley good-evening, and repeated his wayfarer's story, and asked if he could have a night's lodging.

"Put me anywhere you like," he said. "I must be off early in the morning, before day; but I am very hungry, indeed. You can give me some milk at any rate, that's plain."

"Dear sakes, yes," responded the hostess, whose long slumbering hospitality seemed to be easily awakened. "You might fare better if you went out to the main road a mile or so, but you're welcome to what we've got. I'll milk right off, and you make yourself at home. You can sleep on husks or feathers," she proffered graciously. "I raised them all myself. There's good pasturing for geese just below here towards the ma'sh. Now step round and set a plate for the gentleman, Sylvy!" And Sylvia promptly stepped. She was glad to have something to do, and she was hungry herself.

It was a surprise to find so clean and comfortable a little dwelling in this New England wilderness. The young man had known the horrors of its most primitive housekeeping, and the dreary squalor of that level of society which does not rebel at the companionship of hens. This was the best thrift of an old-fashioned farmstead, though on such a small scale that it seemed like a hermitage. He listened eagerly to the old woman's quaint talk, he watched Sylvia's pale face and shining gray eyes with ever growing enthusiasm, and insisted that this was the best supper he had eaten for a month, and afterward the new-made friends sat down in the door-way together while the moon came up.

Soon it would be berry-time, and Sylvia was a great help at picking. The cow was a good milker, though a plaguy thing to keep track of, the hostess gossiped frankly, adding presently that she had buried four children, so Sylvia's mother, and a son (who might be dead) in California were all the children she had left. "Dan, my boy, was a great hand to go gunning," she explained sadly. "I never wanted for pa'tridges or gray squer'ls while he was to home. He's been a great wand'rer, I expect, and he's no hand to write letters. There, I don't blame him, I'd ha' seen the world myself if it had been so I could."

"Sylvy takes after him," the grandmother continued affectionately, after a minute's pause. "There ain't a foot o' ground she don't know her way over, and the wild creaturs counts her one o' themselves. Squer'ls she'll tame to come an' feed right out o' her hands, and all sorts o' birds. Last winter she got the jaybirds to bangeing[1] here, and I believe she'd 'a' scanted herself of her own meals to have plenty to throw out amongst 'em, if I had n't kep' watch. Anything but crows, I tell her, I'm willin' to help support—though Dan he had a tamed one o' them that did seem to have reason same as folks. It was round here a good spell after he went away. Dan an' his father they did n't hitch,—but he never held up his head ag'in after Dan had dared him an' gone off."

The guest did not notice this hint of family sorrows in his eager interest in something else.

"So Sylvy knows all about birds, does she?" he exclaimed, as he looked round at the little girl who sat, very demure but increasingly sleepy, in the moonlight. "I am making a collection of birds myself. I have been at it ever since I was a boy." (Mrs. Tilley smiled.) "There are two or three very rare ones I have been hunting for these five years. I mean to get them on my own ground if they can be found."

"Do you cage 'em up?" asked Mrs. Tilley doubtfully, in response to this enthusiastic announcement.

"Oh no, they're stuffed and preserved, dozens and dozens of them," said the ornithologist, "and I have shot or snared every one myself. I caught a glimpse of a white heron a few miles from here on Saturday, and I have followed it in this direction. They have never been found in this district at all. The little white heron, it is," and he turned again to look at Sylvia with the hope of discovering that the rare bird was one of her acquaintances.

But Sylvia was watching a hop-toad in the narrow footpath.

"You would know the heron if you saw it," the stranger continued eagerly. "A queer tall white bird with soft feathers and long thin legs. And it would have a nest perhaps in the top of a high tree, made of sticks, something like a hawk's nest."

Sylvia's heart gave a wild beat; she knew that strange white bird, and had once stolen softly near where it stood in some bright green swamp grass, away over at the other side of the woods. There was an open place where the sunshine always seemed

[1]Bangeing is a New England term for loafing or lounging about.

strangely yellow and hot, where tall, nodding rushes grew, and her grandmother had warned her that she might sink in the soft black mud underneath and never be heard of more. Not far beyond were the salt marshes just this side the sea itself, which Sylvia wondered and dreamed much about, but never had seen, whose great voice could sometimes be heard above the noise of the woods on stormy nights.

"I can't think of anything I should like so much as to find that heron's nest," the handsome stranger was saying. "I would give ten dollars to anybody who could show it to me," he added desperately, "and I mean to spend my whole vacation hunting for it if need be. Perhaps it was only migrating, or had been chased out of its own region by some bird of prey."

Mrs. Tilley gave amazed attention to all this, but Sylvia still watched the toad, not divining, as she might have done at some calmer time, that the creature wished to get to its hole under the door-step, and was much hindered by the unusual spectators at that hour of the evening. No amount of thought, that night, could decide how many wished-for treasures the ten dollars, so lightly spoken of, would buy.

The next day the young sportsman hovered about the woods, and Sylvia kept him company, having lost her first fear of the friendly lad, who proved to be most kind and sympathetic. He told her many things about the birds and what they knew and where they lived and what they did with themselves. And he gave her a jack-knife, which she thought as great a treasure as if she were a desert-islander. All day long he did not once make her troubled or afraid except when he brought down some unsuspecting singing creature from its bough. Sylvia would have liked him vastly better without his gun; she could not understand why he killed the very birds he seemed to like so much. But as the day waned, Sylvia still watched the young man with loving admiration. She had never seen anybody so charming and delightful; the woman's heart, asleep in the child, was vaguely thrilled by a dream of love. Some premonition of that great power stirred and swayed these young creatures who traversed the solemn woodlands with soft-footed silent care. They stopped to listen to a bird's song; they pressed forward again eagerly, parting the branches—speaking to each other rarely and in whispers; the young man going first and Sylvia following, fascinated, a few steps behind, with her gray eyes dark with excitement.

She grieved because the longed-for white heron was elusive, but she did not lead the guest, she only followed, and there was no such thing as speaking first. The sound of her own unquestioned voice would have terrified her—it was hard enough to answer yes or no when there was need of that. At last evening began to fall, and they drove the cow home together, and Sylvia smiled with pleasure when they came to the place where she heard the whistle and was afraid only the night before.

II

Half a mile from home, at the farther edge of the woods, where the land was highest, a great pine-tree stood, the last of its generation. Whether it was left for a boundary mark, or for what reason, no one could say; the wood-choppers who had felled its mates were dead and gone long ago, and a whole forest of sturdy trees, pines and oaks and maples, had grown again. But the stately head of this old pine towered above them all and made a landmark for sea and shore miles and miles away. Sylvia knew it well. She had always believed that whoever climbed to the top of it could see the ocean; and the little girl had often laid her hand on the great rough trunk and looked up wistfully at those dark boughs that the wind always stirred, no matter how hot and still the air might be below. Now she thought of the tree with a new excitement, for why, if one climbed it at break of day could not one see all the world, and easily discover from whence the white heron flew, and mark the place, and find the hidden nest?

What a spirit of adventure, what wild ambition! What fancied triumph and delight and glory for the later morning when she could make known the secret! It was almost too real and too great for the childish heart to bear.

All night the door of the little house stood open and the whippoorwills came and sang upon the very step. The young sportsman and his old hostess were sound asleep, but Sylvia's great design kept her broad awake and watching. She forgot to think of sleep. The short summer night seemed as long as the winter darkness, and at last when the whippoorwills ceased, and she was afraid the morning would after all come too soon, she stole out of the house and followed the pasture path through the woods, hastening toward the open ground beyond, listening with a sense of comfort and companionship to the drowsy twitter of a half-awakened bird, whose perch she had jarred in passing. Alas, if the great wave of human interest which flooded for the first time this dull little life should sweep away the satisfactions of an existence heart to heart with nature and the dumb life of the forest!

There was the huge tree asleep yet in the paling moonlight, and small and silly Sylvia began with utmost bravery to mount to the top of it, with tingling, eager blood coursing the channels of her whole frame, with her bare feet and fingers, that pinched and held like bird's claws to the monstrous ladder reaching up, up, almost to the sky itself. First she must mount the white oak tree that grew alongside, where she was almost lost among the dark branches and the green leaves heavy and wet with dew; a bird fluttered off its nest, and a red squirrel ran to and fro and scolded pettishly at the harmless housebreaker. Sylvia felt her way easily. She had often climbed there, and knew that higher still one of the oak's upper branches chafed against the pine trunk, just where its lower boughs were set close together. There, when she made the dangerous pass from one tree to the other, the great enterprise would really begin.

She crept out along the swaying oak limb at last, and took the daring step across into the old pine-tree. The way was harder than she thought; she must reach far and hold fast, the sharp dry twigs caught and held her and scratched her like angry talons, the pitch made her thin little fingers clumsy and stiff as she went round and round the tree's great stem, higher and higher upward. The sparrows and robins in the woods below were beginning to wake and twitter to the dawn, yet it seemed much lighter there aloft in the pine-tree, and the child knew she must hurry if her project were to be of any use.

The tree seemed to lengthen itself out as she went up, and to reach farther and farther upward. It was like a great main-mast to the voyaging earth; it must truly have been amazed that morning through all its ponderous frame as it felt this determined spark of human spirit wending its way from higher branch to branch. Who knows how steadily the least twigs held themselves to advantage this light, weak creature on her way! The old pine must have loved his new dependent. More than all the hawks,

animal-like

her connection w/ nature

and bats, and moths, and even the sweet voiced thrushes, was the brave, beating heart of the solitary gray-eyed child. And the tree stood still and frowned away the winds that June morning while the dawn grew bright in the east.

Sylvia's face was like a pale star, if one had seen it from the ground, when the last thorny bough was past, and she stood trembling and tired but wholly triumphant, high in the treetop. Yes, there was the sea with the dawning sun making a golden dazzle over it, and toward that glorious east flew two hawks with slow-moving pinions. How low they looked in the air from that height when one had only seen them before far up, and dark against the blue sky. Their gray feathers were as soft as moths; they seemed only a little way from the tree, and Sylvia felt as if she too could go flying away among the clouds. Westward, the woodlands and farms reached miles and miles into the distance; here and there were church steeples, and white villages, truly it was a vast and awesome world!

The birds sang louder and louder. At last the sun came up bewilderingly bright. Sylvia could see the white sails of ships out at sea, and the clouds that were purple and rose-colored and yellow at first began to fade away. Where was the white heron's nest in the sea of green branches, and was this wonderful sight and pageant of the world the only reward for having climbed to such a giddy height? Now look down again, Sylvia, where the green marsh is set among the shining birches and dark hemlocks; there where you saw the white heron once you will see him again; look, look! a white spot of him like a single floating feather comes up from the dead hemlock and grows larger, and rises, and comes close at last, and goes by the landmark pine with steady sweep of wing and outstretched slender neck and crested head. And wait! wait! do not move a foot or a finger, little girl, do not send an arrow of light and consciousness from your two eager eyes, for the heron has perched on a pine bough not far beyond yours, and cries back to his mate on the nest and plumes his feathers for the new day!

The child gives a long sigh a minute later when a company of shouting cat-birds comes also to the tree, and vexed by their fluttering and lawlessness the solemn heron goes away. She knows his secret now, the wild, light, slender bird that floats and wavers, and goes back like an arrow presently to his home in the green world beneath. Then Sylvia, well satisfied, makes her perilous way down again, not daring to look far below the branch she stands on, ready to cry sometimes because her fingers ache and her lamed feet slip. Wondering over and over again what the stranger would say to her, and what he would think when she told him how to find his way straight to the heron's nest.

"Sylvy, Sylvy!" called the busy old grandmother again and again, but nobody answered, and the small husk bed was empty and Sylvia had disappeared.

The guest waked from a dream, and remembering his day's pleasure hurried to dress himself that might it sooner begin. He was sure from the way the shy little girl looked once or twice yesterday that she had at least seen the white heron, and now she must really be made to tell. Here she comes now, paler than ever, and her worn old frock is torn and tattered, and smeared with pine pitch. The grandmother and the sportsman stand in the door together and question her, and the splendid moment has come to speak of the dead hemlock-tree by the green marsh.

But Sylvia does not speak after all, though the old grandmother fretfully rebukes her, and the young man's kind, appealing eyes are looking straight in her own. He can make them rich with money; he has promised it, and they are poor now. He is so well worth making happy, and he waits to hear the story she can tell.

No, she must keep silence! What is it that suddenly forbids her and makes her dumb? Has she been nine years growing and now, when the great world for the first time puts out a hand to her, must she thrust it aside for a bird's sake? The murmur of the pine's green branches is in her ears, she remembers how the white heron came flying through the golden air and how they watched the sea and the morning together, and Sylvia cannot speak; she cannot tell the heron's secret and give its life away.

Dear loyalty, that suffered a sharp pang as the guest went away disappointed later in the day, that could have served and followed him and loved him as a dog loves! Many a night Sylvia heard the echo of his whistle haunting the pasture path as she came home with the loitering cow. She forgot even her sorrow at the sharp report of his gun and the sight of thrushes and sparrows dropping silent to the ground, their songs hushed and their pretty feathers stained and wet with blood. Were the birds better friends than their hunter might have been,—who can tell? Whatever treasures were lost to her, woodlands and summer-time, remember! Bring your gifts and graces and tell your secrets to this lonely country child!

1886

The Foreigner

I

One evening, at the end of August, in Dunnet Landing, I heard Mrs. Todd's firm footstep crossing the small front entry outside my door, and her conventional cough which served as a herald's trumpet, or a plain New England knock, in the harmony of our fellowship.

"Oh, please come in!" I cried, for it had been so still in the house that I supposed my friend and hostess had gone to see one of her neighbors. The first cold northeasterly storm of the season was blowing hard outside. Now and then there was a dash of great raindrops and a flick of wet lilac leaves against the window, but I could hear that the sea was already stirred to its dark depths, and the great rollers were coming in heavily against the shore. One might well believe that Summer was coming to a sad end that night, in the darkness and rain and sudden access of autumnal cold. It seemed as if there must be danger offshore among the outer islands.

"Oh, there!" exclaimed Mrs. Todd, as she entered. "I know nothing ain't ever happened out to Green Island since the world began, but I always do worry about mother in these great gales. You know those tidal waves occur sometimes down to the West Indies, and I get dwellin' on 'em so I can't set still in my chair, nor knit a common row to a stocking. William might get mooning, out in his small bo't, and not observe how the sea was making, an' meet with some accident. Yes, I thought I'd come in and set with you if you wa'n't busy. No, I never feel any concern about 'em in winter 'cause then they're prepared, and all ashore and everything snug. William ought to keep help, as I tell him; yes, he ought to keep help."

I hastened to reassure my anxious guest by saying that Elijah Tilley had told me in the afternoon, when I came along the shore past the fish houses, that Johnny Bowden and the Captain were out at Green Island; he had seen them beating up the bay, and thought they must have put into Burnt Island cove, but one of the lobstermen brought word later that he saw them hauling out at Green Island as he came by, and Captain Bowden pointed ashore and shook his head to say that he did not mean to try to get in. "The old Miranda just managed it, but she will have to stay at home a day or two and put new patches in her sail," I ended, not without pride in so much circumstantial evidence.

Mrs. Todd was alert in a moment. "Then they'll all have a very pleasant evening," she assured me, apparently dismissing all fears of tidal waves and other seagoing disasters. "I was urging Alick Bowden to go ashore some day and see mother before cold weather. He's her own nephew; she sets a great deal by him. And Johnny's a great chum o' William's; don't you know the first day we had Johnny out 'long of us, he took an' give William his money to keep for him that he'd been a savin', and William showed it to me an' was so affected I thought he was goin' to shed tears? 'T was a dollar an' eighty cents; yes, they'll have a beautiful evenin' all together, and like's not the sea'll be flat as a doorstep come morning."

I had drawn a large wooden rocking-chair before the fire, and Mrs. Todd was sitting there jogging herself a little, knitting fast, and wonderfully placid of countenance. There came a fresh gust of wind and rain, and we could feel the small wooden house rock and hear it creak as if it were a ship at sea.

"Lord, hear the great breakers!" exclaimed Mrs. Todd. "How they pound!—there, there! I always run of an idea that the sea knows anger these nights and gets full o' fight. I can hear the rote o' them old black ledges way down the thoroughfare. Calls up all those stormy verses in the Book o' Psalms; David he knew how old seagoin' folks have to quake at the heart."

I thought as I had never thought before of such anxieties. The families of sailors and coastwise adventurers by sea must always be worrying about somebody, this side of the world or the other. There was hardly one of Mrs. Todd's elder acquaintances, men or women, who had not at some time or other made a sea voyage, and there was often no news until the voyagers themselves came back to bring it.

"There's a roaring high overhead, and a roaring in the deep sea," said Mrs. Todd solemnly, "and they battle together nights like this. No, I could n't sleep; some women folks always goes right to bed an' to sleep, so's to forget, but 't aint my way. Well, it's a blessin' we don't all feel alike; there's hardly any of our folks at sea to worry about, nowadays, but I can't help my feelin's, an' I got thinking of mother all alone, if William had happened to be out lobsterin' and could n't make the cove gettin' back."

"They will have a pleasant evening," I repeated. "Captain Bowden is the best of good company."

"Mother'll make him some pancakes for his supper, like's not," said Mrs. Todd, clicking her knitting needles and giving a pull at her yarn. Just then the old cat pushed open the unlatched door and came straight toward her mistress's lap. She was regarded severely as she stepped about and turned on the broad expanse, and then made herself into a round cushion of fur, but was not openly admonished. There was another great blast of wind overhead, and a puff of smoke came down the chimney.

"This makes me think o' the night Mis' Cap'n Tolland died," said Mrs. Todd, half to herself. "Folks used to say these gales only blew when somebody's a-dyin', or the devil was a-comin' for his own, but the worst man I ever knew died a real pretty mornin' in June."

"You have never told me any ghost stories," said I; and such was the gloomy weather and the influence of the night that I was instantly filled with reluctance to have this suggestion followed. I had not chosen the best of moments; just before I spoke we had begun to feel as cheerful as possible. Mrs. Todd glanced doubtfully at the cat and then at me, with a strange absent look, and I was really afraid that she was going to tell me something that would haunt my thoughts on every dark stormy night as long as I lived.

"Never mind now; tell me to-morrow by daylight, Mrs. Todd," I hastened to say, but she still looked at me full of doubt and deliberation.

"Ghost stories!" she answered. "Yes, I don't know but I've heard a plenty of 'em first an' last. I was just sayin' to myself that this is like the night Mis' Cap'n Tolland died. 'T was the great line storm in September all of thirty, or maybe forty, year ago. I ain't one that keeps much account o' time."

"Tolland? That's a name I have never heard in Dunnet," I said.

"Then you have n't looked well about the old part o' the buryin' ground, no'theast corner," replied Mrs. Todd. "All their women folks lies there; the sea's got most o' the men. They were a known family o' shipmasters in early times. Mother had a mate, Ellen Tolland, that she mourns to this day; died right in her bloom with quick consumption, but the rest o' that family was all boys but one, and older than she, an' they lived hard seafarin' lives an' all died hard. They were called very smart seamen. I've heard that when the youngest went into one o' the old shippin' houses in Boston, the head o' the firm called out to him: 'Did you say Tolland from Dunnet? That's recommendation enough for any vessel!' There was some o' them old shipmasters as tough as iron, an' they had the name o' usin' their crews very severe, but there wa'n't a man that would n't rather sign with 'em an' take his chances, than with the slack ones that did n't know how to meet accidents."

II

There was so long a pause, and Mrs. Todd still looked so absent-minded, that I was afraid she and the cat were growing drowsy together before the fire, and I should have no reminiscences at all. The wind struck the house again, so that we both started in our chairs and Mrs. Todd gave a curious, startled look at me. The cat lifted her head and listened too, in the silence that followed, while after the wind sank we were more conscious than ever of the awful roar of the sea. The house jarred now and then, in a strange, disturbing way.

"Yes, they'll have a beautiful evening out to the island," said Mrs. Todd again; but she did not say it gayly. I had not seen her before in her weaker moments.

"Who was Mrs. Captain Tolland?" I asked eagerly, to change the current of our thoughts.

"I never knew her maiden name; if I ever heard it, I've gone an' forgot; 't would mean nothing to me," answered Mrs. Todd.

"She was a foreigner, an' he met with her out in the Island o' Jamaica. They said she'd been left a widow with property. Land knows what become of it; she was French born, an' her first husband was a Portugee, or somethin'."

I kept silence now, a poor and insufficient question being worse than none.

"Cap'n John Tolland was the least smartest of any of 'em, but he was full smart enough, an' commanded a good brig at the time, in the sugar trade; he'd taken out a cargo o' pine lumber to the islands from somewheres up the river, an' had been loadin' for home in the port o' Kingston, an' had gone ashore that afternoon for his papers, an' remained afterwards 'long of three friends o' his, all shipmasters. They was havin' their suppers together in a tavern; 't was late in the evenin' an' they was more lively than usual, an' felt boyish; and ever opposite was another house full o' company, real bright and pleasant lookin', with a lot o' lights, an' they heard somebody singin' very pretty to a guitar. They wa'n't in no go-to-meetin' condition, an' one of 'em, he slapped the table an' said, 'Le' 's go over an' hear that lady sing!' an' over they all went, good honest sailors, but three sheets in the wind, and stepped in as if they was invited, an' made their bows inside the door, an' asked if they could hear the music; they were all respectable well-dressed men. They saw the woman that had the guitar, an' there was a company a-listenin', regular highbinders[1] all of 'em; an' there was a long table all spread out with big candlesticks like little trees o' light, and a sight o' glass an' silver ware; an' part o' the men was young officers in uniform, an' the colored folks was steppin' round servin' 'em, an' they had the lady singin'. 'T was a wasteful scene, an' a loud talkin' company, an' though they was three sheets in the wind themselves there wa'n't one o' them cap'ns but had sense to perceive it. The others had pushed back their chairs, an' their decanters an' glasses was standin' thick about, an' they was teasin' the one that was singin' as if they'd just got her in to amuse 'em. But they quieted down; one o' the young officers had beautiful manners, an' invited the four cap'ns to join 'em, very polite; 't was a kind of public house, and after they 'd all heard another song, he come to consult with 'em whether they would n't git up and dance a hornpipe or somethin' to the lady's music.

"They was all elderly men an' shipmasters, and owned property; two of 'em was church members in good standin'," continued Mrs. Todd loftily, "an' they would n't lend theirselves to no such kick-shows as that, an' spite o' bein' three sheets in the wind, as I have once observed; they waved aside the tumblers of wine the young officer was pourin' out for 'em so freehanded, and said they should rather be excused. An' when they all rose, still very dignified, as I've been well informed, and made their partin' bows and was goin' out, them young sports got round 'em an' tried to prevent 'em, and they had to push an' strive considerable, but out they come.

[1]The Highbinders were a gang of vagabonds in New York City in the early 1800s; the term came to refer to any ruffian or swindler.

There was this Cap'n Tolland and two Cap'n Bowdens, and the fourth was my own father." (Mrs. Todd spoke slowly, as if to impress the value of her authority.) "Two of them was very religious, upright men, but they would have their night off sometimes, all o' them old-fashioned cap'ns, when they was free of business and ready to leave port.

"An' they went back to their tavern an' got their bills paid, an' set down kind o' mad with everybody by the front windows, mistrusting some o' their tavern charges, like's not, by that time, an' when they got tempered down, they watched the house over across, where the party was.

"There was a kind of a grove o' trees between the house an' the road, an' they heard the guitar a-goin' an' a-stoppin' short by turns, and pretty soon somebody began to screech, an' they saw a white dress come runnin' out through the bushes, an' tumbled over each other in their haste to offer help; an' out she come, with the guitar, cryin' into the street, and they just walked off four square with her amongst 'em, down toward the wharves where they felt more to home. They could n't make out at first what 't was she spoke,—Cap'n Lorenzo Bowden was well acquainted in Havre an' Bordeaux, an' spoke a poor quality o' French, an' she knew a little mite o' English, but not much; and they come somehow or other to discern that she was in real distress. Her husband and her children had died o' yellow fever; they 'd all come up to Kingston from one o' the far Wind'ard Islands to get passage on a steamer to France, an' a negro had stole their money off her husband while he lay sick o' the fever, an' she had been befriended some, but the folks that knew about her had died too; it had been a dreadful run o' the fever that season, an' she fell at last to playin' an' singin' for hire, and for what money they'd throw to her round them harbor houses.

"'T was a real hard case, an' when them cap'ns made out about it, there wa'n't one that meant to take leave without helpin' of her. They was pretty mellow, an' whatever they might lack o' prudence they more 'n made up with charity: they did n't want to see nobody abused, an' she was sort of a pretty woman, an' they stopped in the street then an' there an' drew lots who should take her aboard, bein' all bound home. An' the lot fell to Cap'n Jonathan Bowden who did act discouraged; his vessel had but small accommodations, though he could stow a big freight, an' she was a dreadful slow sailer through bein' square as a box, an' his first wife, that was livin' then, was a dreadful jealous woman. He threw himself right onto the mercy o' Cap'n Tolland."

Mrs. Todd indulged herself for a short time in a season of calm reflection.

"I always thought they 'd have done better, and more reasonable, to give her some money to pay her passage home to France, or wherever she may have wanted to go," she continued.

I nodded and looked for the rest of the story.

"Father told mother," said Mrs. Todd confidentially, "that Cap'n Jonathan Bowden an' Cap'n John Tolland had both taken a little more than usual; I would n't have you think, either, that they both was n't the best o' men, an' they was solemn as owls, and argued the matter between 'em, an' waved aside the other two when they tried to put their oars in. An' spite o' Cap'n Tolland's bein' a settled old bachelor they fixed it that he was to take the prize on his brig; she was a fast sailer, and there was a good spare cabin or two where he'd sometimes carried passengers, but he'd filled 'em with bags o' sugar on his own account an' was loaded very heavy beside. He said he'd shift the sugar an' get along somehow, an' the last the other three cap'ns saw of the party was Cap'n John handing the lady into his bo't, guitar and all, an' off they all set tow'ds their ships with their men rowin' 'em in the bright moonlight down to Port Royal where the anchorage was, an' where they all lay, goin' out with the tide an' mornin' wind at break o' day. An' the others thought they heard music of the guitar, two o' the bo'ts kept well together, but it may have come from another source."

"Well; and then?" I asked eagerly after a pause. Mrs. Todd was almost laughing aloud over her knitting and nodding emphatically. We had forgotten all about the noise of the wind and sea.

"Lord bless you! he come sailing into Portland with his sugar, all in good time, an' they stepped right afore a justice o' the peace, and Cap'n John Tolland come paradin' home to Dunnet Landin' a married man. He owned one o' them thin, narrow-lookin' houses with one room each side o' the front door, and two slim black spruces spindlin' up against the front windows to make it gloomy inside. There was no horse nor cattle of course, though he owned pasture land, an' you could see rifts o' light right through the barn as you drove by. And there was a good excellent kitchen, but his sister reigned over that; she had a right to two rooms, and took the kitchen an' a bedroom that led out of it; an' bein' given no rights in the kitchen had angered the cap'n so they were n't on no kind o' speakin' terms. He preferred his old brig for comfort, but now and then, between voyages, he'd come home for a few days, just to show he was master over his part o' the house, and show Eliza she could n't commit no trespass.

"They stayed a little while; 't was pretty spring weather, an' I used to see Cap'n John rollin' by with his arms full o' bundles from the store, lookin' as pleased and important as a boy; an' then they went right off to sea again, an' was gone a good many months. Next time he left her to live there alone, after they'd stopped at home together some weeks, an' they said she suffered from bein' at sea, but some said that the owners would n't have a woman aboard. 'T was before father was lost on that last voyage of his, an' he and mother went up once or twice to see them. Father said there wa'n't a mite o' harm in her, but somehow or other a sight o' prejudice arose; it may have been caused by the remarks of Eliza an' her feelin's tow'ds her brother. Even my mother had no regard for Eliza Tolland. But mother asked the cap'n's wife to come with her one evenin' to a social circle that was down to the meetin'-house vestry, so she'd get acquainted a little, an' she appeared very pretty until they started to have some singin' to the melodeon. Mari' Harris an' one o' the younger Caplin girls undertook to sing a duet, an' they sort o' flatted, an' she put her hands right up to her ears, and give a little squeal, an' went quick as could be an' give 'em the right notes, for she could read the music like plain print, an' made 'em try it over again. She was real willin' an' pleasant, but that did n't suit, an' she made faces when they got it wrong. An' then there fell a dead calm, an' we was all settin' round prim as dishes, an' my mother, that never expects ill feelin', asked her if she would n't sing somethin', an' up she got,—poor creatur', it all seems so different to me now,—an' sung a lovely little song standin' in the floor; it seemed to have something gay about it that kept a-repeatin', an' nobody could help keepin' time, an' all of a sudden she looked round at the tables and caught up a tin plate that somebody 'd fetched a Washin'ton pie in, an' she begun to drum on it with her fingers like one o' them tambourines, an' went right on singin' faster an' faster, and next minute she begun to dance a little pretty dance between the verses, just as light and pleasant as a child. You could n't help seein' how pretty 't was; we all got to trottin' a foot, an' some o' the men clapped their hands quite loud, a-keepin' time, 't was so catchin', an' seemed so natural to her. There wa'n't one of 'em but enjoyed it; she just tried to do her part, an' some urged her on, till she stopped with a little twirl of her skirts an' went to her place again by mother. And I can see mother now, reachin' over an' smilin' an' pattin' her hand.

"But next day there was an awful scandal goin' in the parish, an' Mari' Harris reproached my mother to her face, an' I never wanted to see her since, but I've had to a good many times. I said Mis' Tolland did n't intend no impropriety,—I reminded her of David's dancin' before the Lord; but she said such a man as David never would have thought o' dancin' right there in the Orthodox vestry, and she felt I spoke with irreverence.

"And next Sunday Mis' Tolland come walkin' into our meeting, but I must say she acted like a cat in a strange garret, and went right out down the aisle with her head in air, from the pew Deacon Caplin had showed her into. 'T was just in the beginning of the long prayer. I wish she'd stayed through, whatever her reasons were. Whether she'd expected somethin' different, or misunderstood some o' the pastor's remarks, or what 't was, I don't really feel able to explain, but she kind o' declared war, at least folks thought so, an' war 't was from that time. I see she was cryin', or had been, as she passed by me; perhaps bein' in meetin' was what had power to make her feel homesick and strange.

"Cap'n John Tolland was away fittin' out; that next week he come home to see her and say farewell. He was lost with his ship in the Straits of Malacca, and she lived there alone in the old house a few months longer till she died. He left her well off; 't was said he hid his money about the house and she knew where 't was. Oh, I expect you've heard that story told over an' over twenty times, since you've been here at the Landin'?"

"Never one word," I insisted.

"It was a good while ago," explained Mrs. Todd, with reassurance. "Yes, it all happened a great while ago."

III

At this moment, with a sudden flaw of the wind, some wet twigs outside blew against the window panes and made a noise like a distressed creature trying to get in. I started with sudden fear, and so did the cat, but Mrs. Todd knitted away and did not even look over her shoulder.

"She was a good-looking woman; yes, I always thought Mis' Tolland was good-looking, though she had, as was reasonable, a sort of foreign cast, and she spoke very broken English, no better than a child. She was always at work about her house, or settin' at a front window with her sewing; she was a beautiful hand to embroider. Sometimes, summer evenings, when the windows was open, she'd set an' drum on her guitar, but I don't know as I ever heard her sing but once after the cap'n went away. She appeared very happy about havin' him, and took on dreadful at partin' when he was down here on the wharf, going back to Portland by boat to take ship for that last v'y'ge. He acted kind of ashamed, Cap'n John did; folks about here ain't so much accustomed to show their feelings. The whistle had blown an' they was waitin' for him to get aboard, an' he was put to it to know what to do and treated her very affectionate in spite of all impatience; but mother happened to be there and she went an' spoke, and I remember what a comfort she seemed to be. Mis' Tolland clung to her then, and she would n't give a glance after the boat when it had started, though the captain was very eager a-wavin' to her. She wanted mother to come home with her an' would n't let go her hand, and mother had just come in to stop all night with me an' had plenty o' time ashore, which did n't always happen, so they walked off together, an' 't was some considerable time before she got back.

"'I want you to neighbor with that poor lonesome creatur',' says mother to me, lookin' reproachful. 'She's a stranger in a strange land,' says mother. 'I want you to make her have a sense that somebody feels kind to her.'

"'Why, since that time she flaunted out o' meetin', folks have felt she liked other ways better 'n our'n,' says I. I was provoked, because I'd had a nice supper ready, an' mother 'd let it wait so long 't was spoiled. 'I hope you'll like your supper!' I told her. I was dreadful ashamed afterward of speakin' so to mother.

"'What consequence is my supper?' says she to me; mother can be very stern,—'or your comfort or mine, beside letting a foreign person an' a stranger feel so desolate; she's done the best a woman could do in her lonesome place, and she asks nothing of anybody except a little common kindness. Think if 't was you in a foreign land!'

"And mother set down to drink her tea, an' I set down humbled enough over by the wall to wait till she finished. An' I did think it all over, an' next day I never said nothin', but I put on my bonnet, and went to see Mis' Cap'n Tolland, if 't was only for mother's sake. 'T was about three quarters of a mile up the road here, beyond the schoolhouse. I forgot to tell you that the cap'n had bought out his sister's right at three or four times what 't was worth, to save trouble, so they'd got clear o' her, an' I went round into the side yard sort o' friendly an' sociable, rather than stop an' deal with the knocker an' the front door. It looked so pleasant an' pretty I was glad I come; she had set a little table for supper, though 't was still early, with a white cloth on it, right out under an old apple tree close by the house. I noticed 't was same as with me at home, there was only one plate. She was just coming out with a dish; you could n't see the door nor the table from the road.

"In the few weeks she'd been there she 'd got some bloomin' pinks an' other flowers next the doorstep. Somehow it looked as if she'd known how to make it homelike for the cap'n. She asked me to set down; she was very polite, but she looked very mournful, and I spoke of mother, an' she put down her dish and caught holt o' me with both hands an' said my mother was an angel. When I see the tears in her eyes 't was all right between us, and we were always friendly after that, and mother had us come out and make a little visit that summer; but she come a foreigner and she went a foreigner, and never was anything but a stranger among our folks. She taught me a sight o' things about herbs I never knew before nor since; she was well acquainted with the virtues o' plants. She'd act awful secret about some things too, an' used to work charms for herself sometimes, an' some o' the neighbors told to an' fro after she died that they knew enough not to provoke her, but 't was all nonsense; 't is the believin' in such things that causes 'em to be any harm, an' so I told 'em," confided Mrs. Todd contemptuously. "That first night I stopped to tea with her she'd cooked some eggs with some herb or other sprinkled all through, and 't was she that first led me to discern mushrooms; an' she went right down on her knees in my garden here when she saw I had my different officious herbs. Yes, 't was she that learned me the proper use o' parsley too; she was a beautiful cook."

Mrs. Todd stopped talking, and rose, putting the cat gently in the chair, while she went away to get another stick of apple-tree wood. It was not an evening when one wished to let the fire go down, and we had a splendid bank of bright coals. I had always wondered where Mrs. Todd had got such an unusual knowledge of cookery, of the varieties of mushrooms, and the use of sorrel as a vegetable, and other blessings of that sort. I had long ago learned that she could vary her omelettes like a child of France, which was indeed a surprise in Dunnet Landing.

IV

All these revelations were of the deepest interest, and I was ready with a question as soon as Mrs. Todd came in and had well settled the fire and herself and the cat again.

"I wonder why she never went back to France, after she was left alone?"

"She come here from the French islands," explained Mrs. Todd. "I asked her once about her folks, an' she said they were all dead; 't was the fever took 'em. She made this her home, lonesome as 't was; she told me she had n't been in France since she was 'so small,' and measured me off a child o' six. She'd lived right out in the country before, so that part wa'n't unusual to her. Oh yes, there was something very strange about her, and she had n't been brought up in high circles nor nothing o' that kind. I think she'd been really pleased to have the cap'n marry her an' give her a good home, after all she'd passed through, and leave her free with his money an' all that. An' she got over bein' so strange-looking to me after a while, but 't was a very singular expression: she wore a fixed smile that wa'n't a smile; there wa'n't no light behind it, same 's a lamp can't shine if it ain't lit. I don't know just how to express it, 't was a sort of made countenance."

One could not help thinking of Sir Philip Sidney's phrase, "A made countenance, between simpering and smiling."

"She took it hard, havin' the captain go off on that last voyage," Mrs. Todd went on. "She said somethin' told her when they was partin' that he would never come back. He was lucky to speak a home-bound ship this side o' the Cape o' Good Hope, an' got a chance to send her a letter, an' that cheered her up. You often felt as if you was dealin' with a child's mind, for all she had so much information that other folks had n't. I was a sight younger than I be now, and she made me imagine new things, and I got interested watchin' her an' findin' out what she had to say, but you could n't get to no affectionateness with her. I used to blame me sometimes; we used to be real good comrades goin' off for an afternoon, but I never give her a kiss till the day she laid in her coffin and it come to my heart there wa'n't no one else to do it."

"And Captain Tolland died," I suggested after a while.

"Yes, the cap'n was lost," said Mrs. Todd, "and of course word did n't come for a good while after it happened. The letter come from the owners to my uncle, Cap'n Lorenzo Bowden, who was in charge of Cap'n Tolland's affairs at home, and he come right up for me an' said I must go with him to the house. I had known what it was to be a widow, myself, for near a year, an' there was plenty o' widow women along this coast that the sea had made desolate, but I never saw a heart break as I did then.

"'T was this way: we walked together along the road, me an' uncle Lorenzo. You know how it leads straight from just above the schoolhouse to the brook bridge, and their house was just this side o' the brook bridge on the left hand; the cellar's there now, and a couple or three good-sized gray birches growin' in it. And when we come near enough I saw that the best room, this way, where she most never set, was all lighted up, and the curtains up so that the light shone bright down the road, and as we walked, those lights would dazzle and dazzle in my eyes, and I could hear the guitar a-goin', an' she was singin'. She heard our steps with her quick ears and come running to the door with her eyes a-shinin', an' all that set look gone out of her face, an' begun to talk French, gay as a bird, an' shook hands and behaved very pretty an' girlish, sayin' 't was her fête day.[2] I did n't know what she meant then. And she had gone an' put a wreath o' flowers on her hair an' wore a handsome gold chain that the cap'n had given her; an' there she was, poor creatur', makin' believe have a party all alone in her best room; 't was prim enough to discourage a person, with too many chairs set close to the walls, just as the cap'n's mother had left it, but she had put sort o' long garlands on the walls, droopin' very graceful, and a sight of green boughs in the corners, till it looked lovely, and all lit up with a lot o' candles."

"Oh dear!" I sighed. "Oh, Mrs. Todd, what did you do?"

"She beheld our countenances," answered Mrs. Todd solemnly. "I expect they was telling everything plain enough, but Cap'n Lorenzo spoke the sad words to her as if he had been her father; and she wavered a minute and then over she went on the floor before we could catch hold of her, and then we tried to bring her to herself and failed, and at last we carried her upstairs, an' I told uncle to run down and put out the lights, and then go fast as he could for Mrs. Begg, being very experienced in sickness, an' he so did. I got off her clothes and her poor wreath, and I cried as I done it. We both stayed there that night, and the doctor said 't was a shock when he come in the morning; he'd been over to Black Island an' had to stay all night with a very sick child."

"You said that she lived alone some time after the news came," I reminded Mrs. Todd then.

"Oh yes, dear," answered my friend sadly, "but it wa'n't what you'd call livin'; no, it was only dyin', though at a snail's pace. She never went out again those few months, but for a while she could manage to get about the house a little, and do what was needed, an' I never let two days go by without seein' her or hearin' from her. She never took much notice as I came an' went except to answer if I asked her anything. Mother was the one who gave her the only comfort."

"What was that?" I asked softly.

"She said that anybody in such trouble ought to see their minister, mother did,

[2]In France, one's fête day is the day which the Roman Catholic Church has assigned as the festival of the saint who bears one's first name. This day is often celebrated in preference to one's birthday.

and one day she spoke to Mis' Tolland, and found that the poor soul had been believin' all the time that there were n't any priests here. We'd come to know she was a Catholic by her beads and all, and that had set some narrow minds against her. And mother explained it just as she would to a child; and uncle Lorenzo sent word right off somewheres up river by a packet that was bound up the bay, and the first o' the week a priest come by the boat, an' uncle Lorenzo was on the wharf 'tendin' to some business; so they just come up for me, and I walked with him to show him the house. He was a kind-hearted old man; he looked so benevolent an' fatherly I could ha' stopped an' told him my own troubles; yes, I was satisfied when I first saw his face, an' when poor Mis' Tolland beheld him enter the room, she went right down on her knees and clasped her hands together to him as if he 'd come to save her life, and he lifted her up and blessed her, an' I left 'em together, and slipped out into the open field and walked there in sight so if they needed to call me, and I had my own thoughts. At last I saw him at the door; he had to catch the return boat. I meant to walk back with him and offer him some supper, but he said no, and said he was comin' again if needed, and signed me to go into the house to her, and shook his head in a way that meant he understood everything. I can see him now; he walked with a cane, rather tired and feeble; I wished somebody would come along, so's to carry him down to the shore.

"Mis' Tolland looked up at me with a new look when I went in, an' she even took hold o' my hand and kept it. He had put some oil on her forehead, but nothing anybody could do would keep her alive very long; 't was his medicine for the soul rather 'n the body. I helped her to bed, and next morning she could n't get up to dress her, and that was Monday, and she began to fail, and 't was Friday night she died." (Mrs. Todd spoke with unusual haste and lack of detail.) "Mrs. Begg and I watched with her, and made everything nice and proper, and after all the ill will there was a good number gathered to the funeral. 'T was in Reverend Mr. Bascom's day, and he done very well in his prayer, considering he could n't fill in with mentioning all the near connections by name as was his habit. He spoke very feeling about her being a stranger and twice widowed, and all he said about her being reared among the heathen was to observe that there might be roads leadin' up to the New Jerusalem from various points. I says to myself that I guessed quite a number must ha' reached there that wa'n't able to set out from Dunnet Landin'!"

Mrs. Todd gave an odd little laugh as she bent toward the firelight to pick up a dropped stitch in her knitting, and then I heard a heartfelt sigh.

"'T was most forty years ago," she said; "most everybody's gone a'ready that was there that day."

V

Suddenly Mrs. Todd gave an energetic shrug of her shoulders, and a quick look at me, and I saw that the sails of her narrative were filled with a fresh breeze.

"Uncle Lorenzo, Cap'n Bowden that I have referred to"—

"Certainly!" I agreed with eager expectation.

"He was the one that had been left in charge of Cap'n John Tolland's affairs, and had now come to be of unforeseen importance.

"Mrs. Begg an' I had stayed in the house both before an' after Mis' Tolland's decease, and she was now in haste to be gone, having affairs to call her home; but uncle come to me as the exercises was beginning, and said he thought I'd better remain at the house while they went to the buryin' ground. I could n't understand his reasons, an' I felt disappointed, bein' as near to her as most anybody; 't was rough weather, so mother could n't get in, and did n't even hear Mis' Tolland was gone till next day. I just nodded to satisfy him, 't wa'n't no time to discuss anything. Uncle seemed flustered; he'd gone out deep-sea fishin' the day she died, and the storm I told you of rose very sudden, so they got blown off way down the coast beyond Monhegan, and he'd just got back in time to dress himself and come.

"I set there in the house after I'd watched her away down the straight road far 's I could see from the door; 't was a little short walkin' funeral an' a cloudy sky, so everything looked dull an' gray, an' it crawled along all in one piece, same 's walking funerals do, an' I wondered how it ever come to the Lord's mind to let her begin down among them gay islands all heat and sun, and end up here among the rocks with a north wind blowin'. 'T was a gale that begun the afternoon before she died, and had kept blowin' off an' on ever since. I'd thought more than once how glad I should be to get home an' out o' sound o' them black spruces a-beatin' an' scratchin' at the front windows.

"I set to work pretty soon to put the chairs back, an' set outdoors some that was borrowed, an' I went out in the kitchen, an' I made up a good fire in case somebody come an' wanted a cup o' tea; but I did n't expect any one to travel way back to the house unless 't was uncle Lorenzo. 'T was growin' so chilly that I fetched some kindlin' wood and made fires in both the fore rooms. Then I set down an' begun to feel as usual, and I got my knittin' out of a drawer. You can't be sorry for a poor creatur' that's come to the end o' all her troubles; my only discomfort was I thought I'd ought to feel worse at losin' her than I did; I was younger then than I be now. And as I set there, I begun to hear some long notes o' dronin' music from upstairs that chilled me to the bone."

Mrs. Todd gave a hasty glance at me.

"Quick 's I could gather me, I went right upstairs to see what 't was," she added eagerly, "an' 't was just what I might ha' known. She'd always kept her guitar hangin' right against the wall in her room; 't was tied by a blue ribbon, and there was a window left wide open; the wind was veerin' a good deal, an' it slanted in and searched the room. The strings was jarrin' yet.

"'T was growin' pretty late in the afternoon, an' I begun to feel lonesome as I should n't now, and I was disappointed at having to stay there, the more I thought it over, but after a while I saw Cap'n Lorenzo polin' back up the road all alone, and when he come nearer I could see he had a bundle under his arm and had shifted his best black clothes for his every-day ones. I run out and put some tea into the teapot and set it back on the stove to draw, an' when he come in I reached down a little jug o' spirits,—Cap'n Tolland had left his house well provisioned as if his wife was goin' to put to sea same's himself, an' there she'd gone an' left it. There was some cake that Mis' Begg an' I had made the day before. I thought that uncle an' me had a good right to the funeral supper, even if there wa'n't any one to join us. I was lookin' forward to my cup o' tea; 't was beautiful tea out of a green lacquered chest that I 've got now."

"You must have felt very tired," said I, eagerly listening.

"I was 'most beat out, with watchin' an' tendin' and all," answered Mrs. Todd, with as much sympathy in her voice as if she were speaking of another person. "But I called out to uncle as he came in, 'Well, I expect it's all over now, an' we 've all done what we could. I thought we'd better have some tea or somethin' before we go home. Come right out in the kitchen, sir,' says I, never thinking but we only had to let the fires out and lock up everything safe an' eat our refreshment, an' go home.

"'I want both of us to stop here tonight,' says uncle, looking at me very important.

"'Oh, what for?' says I, kind o' fretful.

"'I've got my proper reasons,' says uncle. 'I'll see you well satisfied, Almira. Your tongue ain't so easy-goin' as some o' the women folks, an' there's property here to take charge of that you don't know nothin' at all about.'

"'What do you mean?' says I.

"'Cap'n Tolland acquainted me with his affairs; he had n't no sort o' confidence in nobody but me an' his wife, after he was tricked into signin' that Portland note, an' lost money. An' she did n't know nothin' about business; but what he didn't take to sea to be sunk with him he's hid somewhere in this house. I expect Mis' Tolland may have told you where she kept things?' said uncle.

"I see he was dependin' a good deal on my answer," said Mrs. Todd, "but I had to disappoint him; no, she had never said nothin' to me.

"'Well, then, we 've got to make a search,' says he, with considerable relish; but he was all tired and worked up, and we set down to the table, an' he had somethin', an' I took my desired cup o' tea, and then I begun to feel more interested.

"'Where you goin' to look first?' says I, but he give me a short look an' made no answer, and begun to mix me a very small portion out of the jug, in another glass. I took it to please him; he said I looked tired, speakin' real fatherly, and I did feel better for it, and we set talkin' a few minutes, an' then he started for the cellar, carrying an old ship's lantern he fetched out o' the stairway an' lit.

"'What are you lookin' for, some kind of a chist?' I inquired, and he said yes. All of a sudden it come to me to ask who was the heirs; Eliza Tolland, Cap'n John's own sister, had never demeaned herself to come near the funeral, and uncle Lorenzo faced right about and begun to laugh, sort o' pleased. I thought queer of it; 't wa'n't what he'd taken, which would be nothin' to an old weathered sailor like him.

"'Who's the heir?' says I the second time.

"'Why, it's *you,* Almiry,' says he; and I was so took aback I set right down on the turn o' the cellar stairs.

"'Yes 't is,' said uncle Lorenzo. 'I'm glad of it too. Some thought she did n't have no sense but foreign sense, an' a poor stock o' that, but she said you was friendly to her, an' one day after she got news of Tolland's death, an' I had fetched up his will that left everything to her, she said she was goin' to make a writin', so's you could have things after she was gone, an' she give five hundred to me for bein' executor. Square Pease fixed up the paper, an' she signed it; it's all accordin' to law.' There, I begun to cry," said Mrs. Todd; "I could n't help it. I wished I had her back again to do somethin' for, an' to make her know I felt sisterly to her more 'n I'd ever showed, an' it come over me 't was all too late, an' I cried the more, till uncle showed impatience, an' I got up an' stumbled along down cellar with my apern to my eyes the greater part of the time.

"'I'm goin' to have a clean search,' says he; 'you hold the light.' An' I held it, and he rummaged in the arches an' under the stairs, an' over in some old closet where he reached out bottles an' stone jugs an' canted some kags an' one or two casks, an' chuckled well when he heard there was somethin' inside,—but there wa'n't nothin' to find but things usual in a cellar, an' then the old lantern was givin' out an' we come away.

"'He spoke to me of a chist, Cap'n Tolland did,' says uncle in a whisper. 'He said a good sound chist was as safe a bank as there was, an' I beat him out of such nonsense, 'count o' fire an' other risks,' 'There's no chist in the rooms above,' says I; 'no, uncle, there ain't no sea-chist, for I've been here long enough to see what there was to be seen.' Yet he would n't feel contented till he'd mounted up into the toploft; 't was one o' them single, hip-roofed houses that don't give proper accommodation for a real garret, like Cap'n Littlepage's down here at the Landin'. There was broken furniture and rubbish, an' he let down a terrible sight o' dust into the front entry, but sure enough there was n't no chist. I had it all to sweep up next day.

"'He must have took it away to sea,' says I to the cap'n, an' even then he did n't want to agree, but we was both beat out. I told him where I'd always seen Mis' Tolland get her money from, and we found much as a hundred dollars there in an old red morocco wallet. Cap'n John had been gone a good while a'ready, and she had spent what she needed. 'T was in an old desk o' his in the settin' room that we found the wallet."

"At the last minute he may have taken his money to sea," I suggested.

"Oh yes," agreed Mrs. Todd. "He did take considerable to make his venture to bring home, as was customary, an' that was drowned with him as uncle agreed; but he had other property in shipping, and a thousand dollars invested in Portland in a cordage shop, but 't was about the time shipping begun to decay, and the cordage shop failed, and in the end I wa'n't so rich as I thought I was goin' to be for those few minutes on the cellar stairs. There was an auction that accumulated something. Old Mis' Tolland, the cap'n's mother, had heired some good furniture from a sister: there was above thirty chairs in all, and they 're apt to sell well. I got over a thousand dollars when we come to settle up, and I made uncle take his five hundred; he was getting along in years and had met with losses in navigation, and he left it back to me when he died, so I had a real good lift. It all lays in the bank over to Rockland, and I draw my interest fall an' spring, with the little Mr. Todd was to leave me; but that's kind o' sacred money; 't was earnt and saved with the hope o' youth, an' I'm very particular what I spend it for. Oh yes, what with ownin' my house, I've been enabled to get along very well, with prudence!" said Mrs. Todd contentedly.

"But there was the house and land," I asked,—"what became of that part of the property?"

Mrs. Todd looked into the fire, and a shadow of disapproval flitted over her face.

"Poor old uncle!" she said, "he got childish about the matter. I was hoping to sell at first, and I had an offer, but he always run of an idea that there was more money hid away, and kept wanting me to delay; an' he used to go up there all alone and search, and dig in the cellar, empty an' bleak as 't was in winter weather or any time. An' he'd come and tell me he'd dreamed he found gold behind a stone in the cellar wall, or somethin'. And one night we all see the light o' fire up that way, an' the whole Landin' took the road, and run to look, and the Tolland property was all in a light blaze. I expect the old gentleman had dropped fire about; he said he'd been up there to see if everything was safe in the afternoon. As for the land, 't was so poor that everybody used to have a joke that the Tolland boys preferred to farm the sea instead. It's 'most all grown up to bushes now, where it ain't poor water grass in the low places. There's some upland that has a pretty view, after you cross the brook bridge. Years an' years after she died, there was some o' her flowers used to come up an' bloom in the door garden. I brought two or three that was unusual down here; they always come up and remind me of her, constant as the spring. But I never did want to fetch home that guitar, some way or 'nother; I would n't let it go at the auction, either. It was hangin' right there in the house when the fire took place. I've got some o' her other little things scattered about the house: that picture on the mantelpiece belonged to her."

I had often wondered where such a picture had come from, and why Mrs. Todd had chosen it; it was a French print of the statue of the Empress Josephine[3] in the Savane at old Fort Royal, in Martinique.

VI

Mrs. Todd drew her chair closer to mine; she held the cat and her knitting with one hand as she moved, but the cat was so warm and so sound asleep that she only stretched a lazy paw in spite of what must have felt like a slight earthquake. Mrs. Todd began to speak almost in a whisper.

"I ain't told you all," she continued; "no, I have n't spoken of all to but very few. The way it came was this," she said solemnly, and then stopped to listen to the wind, and sat for a moment in deferential silence, as if she waited for the wind to speak first. The cat suddenly lifted her head with quick excitement and gleaming eyes, and her mistress was leaning forward toward the fire with an arm laid on either knee, as if they were consulting the glowing coals for some augury. Mrs. Todd looked like an old prophetess as she sat there with the firelight shining on her strong face; she was posed for some great painter. The woman with the cat was as unconscious and as mysterious as any sibyl of the Sistine Chapel.[4]

"There, that's the last struggle o' the gale," said Mrs. Todd, nodding her head with impressive certainty and still looking into the bright embers of the fire. "You'll see!" She gave me another quick glance, and spoke in a low tone as if we might be overheard.

"'T was such a gale as this the night Mis' Tolland died. She appeared more comfortable first o' the evenin'; and Mrs. Begg was more spent than I, bein' older, and a beautiful nurse that was the first to see and think of everything, but perfectly quiet an' never asked a useless question. You remember her funeral when you first come

[3]The Empress Josephine (1763–1814) was the wife of Napoleon Bonaparte and Empress of France. She was often considered the epitome of foreign elegance and extravagance.

[4]The ceiling of the Sistine Chapel in Rome, painted by Michelangelo, is ringed by sibyls, prophetesses of the pagan religion of Greece and Rome.

to the Landing? And she consented to goin' an' havin' a good sleep while she could, and left me one o' those good little pewter lamps that burnt whale oil an' made plenty o' light in the room, but not too bright to be disturbin'.

"Poor Mis' Tolland had been distressed the night before, an' all that day, but as night come on she grew more and more easy, an' was layin' there asleep; 't was like settin' by any sleepin' person, and I had none but usual thoughts. When the wind lulled and the rain, I could hear the seas, though more distant than this, and I don' know's I observed any other sound than what the weather made; 't was a very solemn feelin' night. I set close by the bed; there was times she looked to find somebody when she was awake. The light was on her face, so I could see her plain; there was always time when she wore a look that made her seem a stranger you'd never set eyes on before. I did think what a world it was that her an' me should have come together so, and she have nobody but Dunnet Landin' folks about her in her extremity. 'You're one o' the stray ones, poor creatur',' I said. I remember those very words passin' through my mind, but I saw reason to be glad she had some comforts, and did n't lack friends at the last, though she'd seen misery an' pain. I was glad she was quiet; all day she'd been restless, and we could n't understand what she wanted from her French speech. We had the window open to give her air, an' now an' then a gust would strike that guitar that was on the wall and set it swinging by the blue ribbon, and soundin' as if somebody begun to play it. I come near takin' it down, but you never know what'll fret a sick person an' put 'em on the rack, an' that guitar was one o' the few things she'd brought with her."

I nodded assent, and Mrs. Todd spoke still lower.

"I set there close by the bed; I'd been through a good deal for some days back, and I thought I might's well be droppin' asleep too, bein' a quick person to wake. She looked to me as if she might last a day longer, certain, now she'd got more comfortable, but I was real tired, an' sort o' cramped as watchers will get, an' a fretful feeling begun to creep over me such as they often do have. If you give way, there ain't no support for the sick person; they can't count on no composure o' their own. Mis' Tolland moved then, a little restless, an' I forgot me quick enough, an' begun to hum out a little part of a hymn tune just to make her feel everything was as usual an' not wake up into a poor uncertainty. All of a sudden she set right up in bed with her eyes wide open, an' I stood an' put my arm behind her; she had n't moved like that for days. And she reached out both her arms toward the door, an' I looked the way she was lookin', an' I see some one was standin' there against the dark. No, 't wa'n't Mis' Begg; 't was somebody a good deal shorter than Mis' Begg. The lamplight struck across the room between us. I could n't tell the shape, but 't was a woman's dark face lookin' right at us; 't wa'n't but an instant I could see. I felt dreadful cold, and my head begun to swim; I thought the light went out; 't wa'n't but an instant, as I say, an' when my sight come back I could n't see nothing there. I was one that did n't know what it was to faint away, no matter what happened; time was I felt above it in others, but 't was somethin' that made poor human natur' quail. I saw very plain while I could see; 't was a pleasant enough face, shaped somethin' like Mis' Tolland's, and a kind of expectin' look.

"No, I don't expect I was asleep," Mrs. Todd assured me quietly, after a moment's pause, though I had not spoken. She gave a heavy sigh before she went on. I could see that the recollection moved her in the deepest way.

"I suppose if I had n't been so spent an' quavery with long watchin', I might have kept my head an' observed much better," she added humbly; "but I see all I could bear. I did try to act calm, an' I laid Mis' Tolland down on her pillow, an' I was a-shakin' as I done it. All she did was to look up to me so satisfied and sort o' questioning, an' I looked back to her.

"'You saw her, did n't you?' she says to me, speakin' perfectly reasonable. ' 'T is my mother,' she says again, very feeble, but lookin' straight up at me, kind of surprised with the pleasure, and smiling as if she saw I was overcome, an' would have said more if she could, but we had hold of hands. I see then her change was comin', but I did n't call Mis' Begg, nor make no uproar. I felt calm then, an' lifted to somethin' different as I never was since. She opened her eyes just as she was goin'—

"'You saw her, did n't you?' she said the second time, an' I says, *'Yes, dear, I did; you ain't never goin' to feel strange an' lonesome no more.'* An' then in a few quiet minutes 't was all over. I felt they'd gone away together. No, I wa'n't alarmed afterward; 't was just that one moment I could n't live under, but I never called it beyond reason I should see the other watcher. I saw plain enough there was somebody there with me in the room.

VII

"'T was just such a night as this Mis' Tolland died," repeated Mrs. Todd, returning to her usual tone and leaning back comfortably in her chair as she took up her knitting. "'T was just such a night as this. I've told the circumstances to but very few; but I don't call it beyond reason. When folks is goin' 't is all natural, and only common things can jar upon the mind. You know plain enough there's somethin' beyond this world; the doors stand wide open. 'There's somethin' of us that must still live on, we've got to join both worlds together an' live in one but for the other. The doctor said that to me one day, an' I never could forget it; he said 't was in one o' his old doctor's books.'"

We sat together in silence in the warm little room; the rain dropped heavily from the eaves, and the sea still roared, but the high wind had done blowing. We heard the far complaining fog horn of a steamer up the Bay.

"There goes the Boston boat out, pretty near on time," said Mrs. Todd with satisfaction. "Sometimes these late August storms 'll sound a good deal worse than they really be. I do hate to hear the poor steamers callin' when they're bewildered in thick nights in winter, comin' on the coast. Yes, there goes the boat; they 'll find it rough at sea, but the storm 's all over."

1900

Mary E. Wilkins Freeman 1852–1930

The postbellum appeal of regional fiction coincided with three aspects of Mary E. Wilkins Freeman's life and circumstances: her deep appreciation of the people and culture of rural New England, her extraordinary skill as a writer, and her continuing need to write to support herself financially. Attuned by necessity to what she termed her stories' "selling qualities" and widely acclaimed for her literary art, she produced fifteen volumes of highly accomplished short stories, as well as some fifty uncollected stories and prose essays, fourteen novels, three plays, three volumes of poetry, and eight children's books, all centering primarily on the aspirations, quiet accomplishments, bids for independence, and circumscribed conditions of farmers, workers, and the poor (especially women) in New England and the middle states.

Born in Randolph, Massachusetts, and brought up there and in Brattleboro, Vermont, Mary Ella Wilkins observed the irreversible erosion of her parents' economic circumstances, circumstances that reflected the post-Civil War decline of the Massachusetts shoe industry and of small farming. Even though her delicate health and her mother's protectiveness tended to restrict her to indoor activities, many of which focused on orthodox Congregationalist religious functions, nothing could shelter her from the family's economic exigencies. When she was fifteen, her father, Warren, gave up house carpentry in Massachusetts and tried to make a go of it with a Brattleboro dry-goods store. Mary graduated from Brattleboro High School in 1870 and spent what seems to have been an uncomfortable year at Mount Holyoke Female Seminary. But her father's business failed, her closest friend moved away, her efforts to teach were unsuccessful, her younger sister died, and ultimately her mother, Eleanor, was forced, when Mary was twenty-five, to enter service in the household of the Reverend Thomas Pickman Tyler. The family's move into the Tyler home may particularly have troubled Mary because her love for Tyler's son, Hanson, was not reciprocated. Four years passed before Mary could sell her first piece of writing, a children's ballad entitled "The Beggar King," and thus help to relieve the family's economic plight. The beginnings of success came too late for her mother, however, for in 1880 Eleanor Wilkins had suddenly died. Perhaps to memorialize her mother's care and affection, Mary adopted as her own the middle name Eleanor.

Within two years, Mary Eleanor began to sell not only juvenile but adult fiction, publishing among other works a prize story, "A Shadow Family," in a Boston newspaper and "Two Old Lovers" in *Harper's Bazaar.* A few years more and she was recognized as a significant writer and a mainstay for the publishing firm of Harper and Brothers, which issued her first collection, *A Humble Romance and Other Stories,* in 1887. Her father did not live to share that pleasure; when he died in 1883, Mary Eleanor Wilkins moved back to Randolph, taking up residence in the farm family of her childhood friend, Mary Wales. There, in the seclusion of the second-floor room of the Wales homestead—where she continued to live for twenty years—and protected by Mary's care from household chores and her own nightmares, she wrote stories and novels steadily, often working ten hours a day. "Writing," she later said, "is very hard work . . . although nobody among the laboring ranks, or the resting ranks, thinks authors labor."

If writing was for her a labor of survival, it was also a labor of love. Her detailed explorations of women's interior lives and of female relationships frequently pivot on the power of the weak—though sometimes on the greater power of privilege as well. Many of her stories, including "A New England Nun," one of her most famous, explore unmarried women's secret enjoyment of the control spinsterhood gave them over their own lives: their relishing of their independence from blundering suitors and arbitrary husbands. Some also highlight such women's repudiation of judgmental ministers. Always a writer of extraordinary nuance, Freeman also illuminated unmarried women's yearning for what one of her characters calls "a real home of my own and a husband and children in it." Her fiction's contemporary force also stems from its highlighting of other enduring tensions, including the ongoing, intricate relationship between an America that was modernizing and the culture and economy of rural New England. Freeman did not flinch from portraying the depredations that modernization had wrought upon rural New England, but she also showed the region to be possessed of strength and endurance, and her portrayals of rural life often suggest ways in which country life existed in subtle relation to modernity, not apart from it. Even "The Revolt of 'Mother,'" which seems at a far remove from contemporary concerns, revolves around a mother's enactment of her responsibility for her family's well-being, something of general concern when the story was published.

Submitting to the need for a "real home," Mary E. Wilkins married when she was forty-nine. Her hesitation is apparent; although she met Dr. Charles Freeman in 1892, she did not marry him until 1902. By then, she was well known as a writer of what were called "local color" stories. Marriage meant uprooting: she moved from Randolph, the locale of so much of her work, to Metuchen, New Jersey, where, she said, "I have not a blessed thing to write about," though she did compose some stories about the people in her new environment and continued to write about rural New England. The marriage was not a success. Her husband, though initially supportive, proved to be an alcoholic and pushed her to write ever more for the income to sustain his habit. He was institutionalized a number of times before they legally separated in 1922.

Whatever the impact of the move and the marriage on her work, or on her own inner life, her reputation and financial success were sustained through the 1920s. In 1908 she won the *New York Herald*'s trans-Atlantic novel-writing contest with *The Shoulders of Atlas,* and she participated with William Dean Howells, Henry James, Elizabeth Stuart Phelps, and others in writing a "cooperative" novel, *The Whole Family.* In 1926 she was awarded the William Dean Howells Gold Medal for Fiction by the American Academy of Letters, and later that year she and Edith Wharton became the first women inducted into the National Institute of Arts and Letters. When informed that the Institute might be divided on the question of admitting women, Freeman wrote with characteristic wryness that she could "very readily see that many would object." But the bronze doors of the Academy still carry the inscription "Dedicated to the Memory of Mary E. Wilkins Freeman and the Women Writers of America."

Leah Blatt Glasser
Mount Holyoke College

Sandra A. Zagarell
Oberlin College

PRIMARY WORKS

A Humble Romance and Other Stories, 1887; *A New England Nun and Other Stories,* 1891; *Pembroke,* 1894; *By the Light of the Soul,* 1906; "The Girl Who Wants to Write: Things to Do and Avoid," *Harper's Bazaar* (June 1913), 272; *The Infant Sphinx: Collected Letters of Mary E. Wilkins Freeman,* ed. Brent L. Kendrick, 1985; *The Uncollected Stories of Mary Wilkins Freeman,* ed. Mary Reichardt, 1992; *Mary E. Wilkins Freeman Reader,* ed. Mary Reichardt, 1997; *A New England Nun and Other Stories,* ed. Sandra A. Zagarell, 2000.

A New England Nun

It was late in the afternoon, and the light was waning. There was a difference in the look of the tree shadows out in the yard. Somewhere in the distance cows were lowing and a little bell was tinkling; now and then a farm-wagon tilted by, and the dust flew; some blue-shirted laborers with shovels over their shoulders plodded past; little swarms of flies were dancing up and down before the peoples' faces in the soft air. There seemed to be a gentle stir arising over everything for the mere sake of subsidence—a very premonition of rest and hush and night.

This soft diurnal commotion was over Louisa Ellis also. She had been peacefully sewing at her sitting-room window all the afternoon. Now she quilted her needle carefully into her work, which she folded precisely, and laid in a basket with her thimble and thread and scissors. Louisa Ellis could not remember that ever in her life she had mislaid one of these little feminine appurtenances, which had become, from long use and constant association, a very part of her personality.

Louisa tied a green apron round her waist, and got out a flat straw hat with a green ribbon. Then she went into the garden with a little blue crockery bowl, to pick some currants for her tea. After the currants were picked she sat on the back door-step and stemmed them, collecting the stems carefully in her apron, and afterwards throwing them into the hen-coop. She looked sharply at the grass beside the step to see if any had fallen there.

Louisa was slow and still in her movements; it took her a long time to prepare her tea; but when ready it was set forth with as much grace as if she had been a veritable guest to her own self. The little square table stood exactly in the centre of the kitchen, and was covered with a starched linen cloth whose border pattern of flowers glistened. Louisa had a damask napkin on her tea-tray, where were arranged a cut-glass tumbler full of teaspoons, a silver cream-pitcher, a china sugar-bowl, and one pink china cup and saucer. Louisa used china every day—something which none of her neighbors did. They whispered about it among themselves. Their daily tables were laid with common crockery, their sets of best china stayed in the parlor closet, and Louisa Ellis was no richer nor better bred than they. Still she would use the china. She had for her supper a glass dish full of sugared currants, a plate of little cakes, and one of light white biscuits. Also a leaf or two of lettuce, which she cut up daintily. Louisa was very fond of lettuce, which she raised to perfection in her little garden. She ate quite heartily, though in a delicate, pecking way; it seemed almost surprising that any considerable bulk of the food should vanish.

After tea she filled a plate with nicely baked thin corn-cakes, and carried them out into the back-yard.

"Caesar!" she called. "Caesar! Caesar!"

There was a little rush, and the clank of a chain, and a large yellow-and-white dog appeared at the door of his tiny hut, which was half hidden among the tall grasses and flowers. Louisa patted him and gave him the corn-cakes. Then she returned to the house and washed the tea-things, polishing the china carefully. The twilight had deepened; the chorus of the frogs floated in at the open window wonderfully loud and shrill, and once in a while a long sharp drone from a tree-toad pierced it. Louisa took off her green gingham apron, disclosing a shorter one of pink and white print. She lighted her lamp, and sat down again with her sewing.

In about half an hour Joe Dagget came. She heard his heavy step on the walk, and rose and took off her pink-and-white apron. Under that was still another—white linen with a little cambric edging on the bottom; that was Louisa's company apron. She never wore it without her calico sewing apron over it unless she had a guest. She had barely folded the pink and white one with methodical haste and laid it in a table drawer when the door opened and Joe Dagget entered.

He seemed to fill up the whole room. A little yellow canary that had been asleep in his green cage at the south window woke up and fluttered wildly, beating his little yellow wings against the wires. He always did so when Joe Dagget came into the room.

"Good-evening," said Louisa. She extended her hand with a kind of solemn cordiality.

"Good-evening, Louisa," returned the man, in a loud voice.

She placed a chair for him, and they sat facing each other, with the table between them. He sat bolt-upright, toeing out his heavy feet squarely, glancing with a good-humored uneasiness around the room. She sat gently erect, folding her slender hands in her white-linen lap.

"Been a pleasant day," remarked Dagget.

"Real pleasant," Louisa assented, softly. "Have you been haying?" she asked, after a little while.

"Yes, I've been haying all day, down in the ten-acre lot. Pretty hot work."

"It must be."

"Yes, it's pretty hot work in the sun."

"Is your mother well to-day?"

"Yes, mother's pretty well."

"I suppose Lily Dyer's with her now?"

Dagget colored. "Yes, she's with her," he answered, slowly.

He was not very young, but there was a boyish look about his large face. Louisa was not quite as old as he, her face was fairer and smoother, but she gave people the impression of being older.

"I suppose she's a good deal of help to your mother," she said, further.

"I guess she is; I don't know how mother'd get along without her," said Dagget, with a sort of embarrassed warmth.

"She looks like a real capable girl. She's pretty-looking too," remarked Louisa.

"Yes, she is pretty fair looking."

Presently Dagget began fingering the books on the table. There was a square red autograph album, and a Young Lady's Gift-Book[1] which had belonged to Louisa's mother. He took them up one after the other and opened them; then laid them down again, the album on the Gift-Book.

Louisa kept eyeing them with mild uneasiness. Finally she rose and changed the

[1]*Young Lady's Gift-Book: A Common-Place Book of Prose and Poetry* (Providence, R.I., 1836) or a similar anthology of writing intended for young women.

position of the books, putting the album underneath. That was the way they had been arranged in the first place.

Dagget gave an awkward little laugh. "Now what difference did it make which book was on top?" said he.

Louisa looked at him with a deprecating smile. "I always keep them that way," murmured she.

"You do beat everything," said Dagget, trying to laugh again. His large face was flushed.

He remained about an hour longer, then rose to take leave. Going out, he stumbled over a rug, and trying to recover himself, hit Louisa's work-basket on the table and knocked it on the floor.

He looked at Louisa, then at the rolling spools; he ducked himself awkwardly toward them, but she stopped him. "Never mind," said she; "I'll pick them up after you're gone."

She spoke with a mild stiffness. Either she was a little disturbed, or his nervousness affected her, and made her seem constrained in her effort to reassure him.

When Joe Dagget was outside he drew in the sweet evening air with a sigh, and felt much as an innocent and perfectly well-intentioned bear might after his exit from a china shop.

Louisa, on her part, felt much as the kind-hearted, long-suffering owner of the china shop might have done after the exit of the bear.

She tied on the pink, then the green apron, picked up all the scattered treasures and replaced them in her work-basket, and straightened the rug. Then she set the lamp on the floor, and began sharply examining the carpet. She even rubbed her fingers over it, and looked at them.

"He's tracked in a good deal of dust," she murmured. "I thought he must have."

Louisa got a dust-pan and brush, and swept Joe Dagget's track carefully.

If he could have known it, it would have increased his perplexity and uneasiness, although it would not have disturbed his loyalty in the least. He came twice a week to see Louisa Ellis, and every time, sitting there in her delicately sweet room, he felt as if surrounded by a hedge of lace. He was afraid to stir lest he should put a clumsy foot or hand through the fairy web, and he had always the consciousness that Louisa was watching fearfully lest he should.

Still the lace and Louisa commanded perforce his perfect respect and patience and loyalty. They were to be married in a month, after a singular courtship which had lasted for a matter of fifteen years. For fourteen out of the fifteen years the two had not once seen each other, and they had seldom exchanged letters. Joe had been all those years in Australia, where he had gone to make his fortune, and where he had stayed until he made it. He would have stayed fifty years if it had taken so long, and come home feeble and tottering, or never come home at all, to marry Louisa.

But the fortune had been made in the fourteen years, and he had come home now to marry the woman who had been patiently and unquestioningly waiting for him all that time.

Shortly after they were engaged he had announced to Louisa his determination to strike out into new fields, and secure a competency before they should be married. She had listened and assented with the sweet serenity which never failed her, not even when her lover set forth on that long and uncertain journey. Joe, buoyed up as he was by his sturdy determination, broke down a little at the last, but Louisa kissed him with a mild blush, and said good-by.

"It won't be for long," poor Joe had said, huskily; but it was for fourteen years.

In that length of time much had happened. Louisa's mother and brother had died, and she was all alone in the world. But greatest happening of all—a subtle happening which both were too simple to understand—Louisa's feet had turned into a path, smooth maybe under a calm, serene sky, but so straight and unswerving that it could only meet a check at her grave, and so narrow that there was no room for any one at her side.

Louisa's first emotion when Joe Dagget came home (he had not apprised her of his coming) was consternation, although she would not admit it to herself, and he never dreamed of it. Fifteen years ago she had been in love with him—at least she considered herself to be. Just at that time, gently acquiescing with and falling into the natural drift of girlhood, she had seen marriage ahead as a reasonable feature and a probable desirability of life. She had listened with calm docility to her mother's views upon the subject. Her mother was remarkable for her cool sense and sweet, even temperament. She talked wisely to her daughter when Joe Dagget presented himself, and Louisa accepted him with no hesitation. He was the first lover she had ever had.

She had been faithful to him all these years. She had never dreamed of the possibility of marrying any one else. Her life, especially for the last seven years, had been full of a pleasant peace, she had never felt discontented nor impatient over her lover's absence; still she had always looked forward to his return and their marriage as the inevitable conclusion of things. However, she had fallen into a way of placing it so far in the future that it was almost equal to placing it over the boundaries of another life.

When Joe came she had been expecting him, and expecting to be married for fourteen years, but she was as much surprised and taken aback as if she had never thought of it.

Joe's consternation came later. He eyed Louisa with an instant confirmation of his old admiration. She had changed but little. She still kept her pretty manner and soft grace, and was, he considered, every whit as attractive as ever. As for himself, his stent was done; he had turned his face away from fortune-seeking, and the old winds of romance whistled as loud and sweet as ever through his ears. All the song which he had been wont to hear in them was Louisa; he had for a long time a loyal belief that he heard it still, but finally it seemed to him that although the winds sang always that one song, it had another name. But for Louisa the wind had never more than murmured; now it had gone down, and everything was still. She listened for a little while with half-wistful attention; then she turned quietly away and went to work on her wedding clothes.

Joe had made some extensive and quite magnificent alterations to his house. It was the old homestead; the newly-married couple would live there, for Joe could not desert his mother, who refused to leave her old home. So Louisa must leave hers. Every morning, rising and going about among her neat maidenly possessions, she felt as one looking her last upon the faces of dear friends. It was true that in a measure she could take them with her, but, robbed of their old environments, they would appear in such new guises that they would almost cease to be themselves. Then there were some peculiar features of her happy solitary life which she would probably be obliged to relinquish altogether. Sterner tasks than these graceful but half-needless ones would probably devolve upon her. There would be a large house to care for; there would be company to entertain; there would be Joe's rigorous and feeble old mother to wait upon; and it would be contrary to all thrifty village traditions for her to keep more than one servant. Louisa had a little still, and she used to occupy herself pleasantly in summer weather with distilling the sweet and aromatic essences from roses and peppermint and spearmint. By-and-by her still must be laid away. Her store of essences was already considerable, and there would be no time for her to distil for the mere pleasure of it. Then Joe's mother would think it foolishness; she had already hinted her opinion in the matter. Louisa dearly loved to sew a linen seam, not always for use, but for the simple, mild pleasure which she took in it. She would have been loath to confess how more than once she had ripped a seam for the mere delight of sewing it together again. Sitting at her window during long sweet afternoons, drawing her needle gently through the dainty fabric, she was peace itself. But there was small chance of such foolish comfort in the future. Joe's mother, domineering, shrewd old matron that she was even in her old age, and very likely even Joe himself, with his honest masculine rudeness, would laugh and frown down all these pretty but senseless old maiden ways.

Louisa had almost the enthusiasm of an artist over the mere order and cleanliness of her solitary home. She had throbs of genuine triumph at the sight of the window-panes which she had polished until they shone like jewels. She gloated gently over her orderly bureau-drawers, with their exquisitely folded contents redolent with lavender and sweet clover and very purity. Could she be sure of the endurance of even this? She had visions, so startling that she half repudiated them as indelicate, of coarse masculine belongings strewn about in endless litter; of dust and disorder arising necessarily from a coarse masculine presence in the midst of all this delicate harmony.

Among her forebodings of disturbance, not the least was with regard to Caesar. Caesar was a veritable hermit of a dog. For the greater part of his life he had dwelt in his secluded hut, shut out from the society of his kind and all innocent canine joys. Never had Caesar since his early youth watched at a woodchuck's hole; never had he known the delights of a stray bone at a neighbor's kitchen door. And it was all on account of a sin committed when hardly out of his puppyhood. No one knew the possible depth of remorse of which this mild-visaged, altogether innocent-looking old dog might be capable; but whether or not he had encountered remorse, he had encountered a full measure of righteous retribution. Old Caesar seldom lifted up his voice in a growl or a bark; he was fat and sleepy; there were yellow rings which looked like spectacles around his dim old eyes; but there was a neighbor who bore on his hand the imprint of several of Caesar's sharp white youthful teeth, and for that he had lived at the end of a chain, all alone in a little hut, for fourteen years. The neighbor, who was choleric and smarting with the pain of his wound, had demanded either Caesar's death or complete ostracism. So Louisa's brother, to whom the dog had belonged, had built him his little kennel and tied him up. It was now fourteen years since, in a flood of youthful spirits, he had inflicted that memorable bite, and with the exception of short excursions, always at the end of the chain, under the strict guardianship of his master or Louisa, the old dog had remained a close prisoner. It is doubtful if, with his limited ambition, he took much pride in the fact, but it is certain that he was possessed of considerable cheap fame. He was regarded by all the children in the village and by many adults as a very monster of ferocity. St. George's dragon[2] could hardly have surpassed in evil repute Louisa Ellis's old yellow dog. Mothers charged their children with solemn emphasis not to go too near to him, and the children listened and believed greedily, with a fascinated appetite for terror, and ran by Louisa's house stealthily, with many sidelong and backward glances at the terrible dog. If perchance he sounded a hoarse bark, there was a panic. Wayfarers chancing into Louisa's yard eyed him with respect, and inquired if the chain were stout. Caesar at large might have seemed a very ordinary dog, and excited no comment whatever; chained, his reputation overshadowed him, so that he lost his own proper outlines and looked darkly vague and enormous. Joe Dagget, however, with his good-humored sense and shrewdness, saw him as he was. He strode valiantly up to him and patted him on the head, in spite of Louisa's soft clamor of warning, and even attempted to set him loose. Louisa grew so alarmed that he desisted, but kept announcing his opinion in the matter quite forcibly at intervals. "There ain't a better-natured dog in town," he would say, "and it's downright cruel to keep him tied up there. Some day I'm going to take him out."

Louisa had very little hope he would not, one of these days, when their interests and possessions should be more completely fused in one. She pictured to herself Caesar on the rampage through the quiet and unguarded village. She saw innocent children bleeding in his path. She was herself very fond of the old dog, because he had belonged to her dead brother, and he was always very gentle with her; still she had great faith in his ferocity. She always warned people not to go too near him. She fed him on ascetic fare of corn-mush and cakes, and never fired his dangerous temper with heating and sanguinary diet of flesh and bones. Louisa looked at the old dog munching his simple fare, and thought of her approaching marriage and trembled. Still no anticipation of disorder and confusion in lieu of sweet peace and harmony, no forebodings of Caesar on the rampage, no wild fluttering of her little yellow canary, were sufficient to turn her a hair's-breadth. Joe Dagget had been fond of her and working for her all these years. It was not for her, whatever came to pass, to prove untrue and break his heart. She put the exquisite little stitches into her wedding-garments, and time went on until it was only a week before her wedding-day. It was a Tuesday evening, and the wedding was to be a week from Wednesday.

There was a full moon that night. About nine o'clock Louisa strolled down the road a little way. There were harvest-fields on either hand, bordered by low stone walls. Luxuriant clumps of bushes grew beside the wall, and trees—wild cherry and old apple-trees—at intervals. Presently Louisa sat down on the wall and looked about her with mildly sorrowful reflectiveness. Tall shrubs of blueberry and meadow-sweet, all woven together and tangled with blackberry vines and horsebriers, shut her in on either side. She had a little clear space between them. Opposite her, on the other side of the road, was a spreading tree; the moon shone between its boughs, and the leaves twinkled like silver. The road was bespread with a beautiful shifting dapple of silver and shadow; the air was full of a mysterious sweetness. "I wonder if it's

[2]Dragon slain by St. George, patron saint of England.

wild grapes?" murmured Louisa. She sat there some time. She was just thinking of rising, when she heard footsteps and low voices, and remained quiet. It was a lonely place, and she felt a little timid. She thought she would keep still in the shadow and let the persons, whoever they might be, pass her.

But just before they reached her the voices ceased, and the footsteps. She understood that their owners had also found seats upon the stone wall. She was wondering if she could not steal away unobserved, when the voice broke the stillness. It was Joe Dagget's. She sat still and listened.

The voice was announced by a loud sigh, which was as familiar as itself. "Well," said Dagget, "you've made up your mind, then, I suppose?"

"Yes," returned another voice; "I'm going day after to-morrow."

"That's Lily Dyer," thought Louisa to herself. The voice embodied itself in her mind. She saw a girl tall and full-figured, with a firm, fair face, looking fairer and firmer in the moonlight, her strong yellow hair braided in a close knot. A girl full of a calm, rustic strength and bloom, with a masterful way which might have beseemed a princess. Lily Dyer was a favorite with the village folk; she had just the qualities to arouse the admiration. She was good and handsome and smart. Louisa had often heard her praises sounded.

"Well," said Joe Dagget. "I ain't got a word to say."

"I don't know what you could say," returned Lily Dyer.

"Not a word to say," repeated Joe, drawing out the words heavily. Then there was a silence. "I ain't sorry," he began at last, "that that happened yesterday—that we kind of let on how we felt to each other. I guess it's just as well we knew. Of course I can't do anything different. I'm going right on an' get married next week. I ain't going back on a woman that's waited for me fourteen years, an' break her heart."

"If you should jilt her to-morrow, I wouldn't have you," spoke up the girl, with sudden vehemence.

"Well, I ain't going to give you the chance," said he; "but I don't believe you would, either."

"You'd see I wouldn't. Honor's honor, an' right's right. An' I'd never think anything of any man that went against 'em for me or any other girl; you'd find that out, Joe Dagget."

"Well, you'll find out fast enough that I ain't going against 'em for you or any other girl," returned he. Their voices sounded almost as if they were angry with each other. Louisa was listening eagerly.

"I'm sorry you feel as if you must go away," said Joe, "but I don't know but it's best."

"Of course it's best. I hope you and I have got common-sense."

"Well, I suppose you're right." Suddenly Joe's voice got an undertone of tenderness. "Say, Lily," said he, "I'll get along well enough myself, but I can't bear to think—You don't suppose you're going to fret much over it?"

"I guess you'll find out I sha'n't fret much over a married man."

"Well, I hope you won't—I hope you won't, Lily. God knows I do. And—I hope—one of these days—you'll—come across somebody else—"

"I don't see any reason why I shouldn't." Suddenly her tone changed. She spoke in a sweet, clear voice, so loud that she could have been heard across the street. "No, Joe Dagget," said she, "I'll never marry any other man as long as I live. I've got good sense, an' I ain't going to break my heart nor make a fool of myself; but I'm never going to be married, you can be sure of that. I ain't that sort of a girl to feel this way twice."

Louisa heard an exclamation and a soft commotion behind the bushes; then Lily spoke again,—the voice sounded as if she had risen. "This must be put a stop to," said she. "We've stayed here long enough. I'm going home."

Louisa sat there in a daze, listening to their retreating steps. After a while she got up and slunk softly home herself. The next day she did her housework methodically; that was as much a matter of course as breathing; but she did not sew on her wedding-clothes. She sat at her window and meditated. In the evening Joe came. Louisa Ellis had never known that she had any diplomacy in her, but when she came to look for it that night she found it, although meek of its kind, among her little feminine weapons. Even now she could hardly believe that she had heard aright, and that she would not do Joe a terrible injury should she break her troth-plight. She wanted to sound him without betraying too soon her own inclinations in the matter. She did it successfully, and they finally came to an understanding; but it was a difficult thing, for he was as afraid of betraying himself as she.

She never mentioned Lily Dyer. She simply said that while she had no cause of complaint against him, she had lived so long in one way that she shrank from making a change.

"Well, I never shrank, Louisa," said Dagget. "I'm going to be honest enough to say that I think maybe it's better this way; but if you'd wanted to keep on, I'd have stuck to you till my dying day. I hope you know that."

"Yes, I do," said she.

That night she and Joe parted more tenderly than they had done for a long time. Standing in the door, holding each other's hands, a last great wave of regretful memory swept over them.

"Well, this ain't the way we've thought it was all going to end, is it, Louisa?" said Joe.

She shook her head. There was a little quiver on her placid face.

"You let me know if there's ever anything I can do for you," said he. "I ain't ever going to forget you, Louisa." Then he kissed her, and went down the path.

Louisa, all alone by herself that night, wept a little, she hardly knew why; but the next morning, on waking, she felt like a queen who, after fearing lest her domain be wrested away from her, sees it firmly insured in her possession.

Now the tall weeds and grasses might cluster around Caesar's little hermit hut, the snow might fall on its roof year in and year out, but he never would go on a rampage through the unguarded village. Now the little canary might turn itself into a peaceful yellow ball night after night, and have no need to wake and flutter with wild terror against its bars. Louisa could sew linen seams, and distil roses, and dust and polish and fold away in lavender, as long as she listed. That afternoon she sat with her needle-work at the window, and felt fairly steeped in peace. Lily Dyer, tall and erect and blooming, went past; but she felt no qualm. If Louisa Ellis had sold her birthright she did not know it, the taste of the pottage was so delicious, and had been her sole satisfaction for so long. Serenity and placid narrowness had become to her as the birthright itself. She gazed ahead through a long reach of future days strung together like pearls in a rosary, every one like the others, and all smooth and flawless and innocent, and her heart went up in thankfulness. Outside was the fervid summer afternoon; the air was filled with the sounds of the busy harvest of men and birds and bees; there were halloos, metallic clatterings, sweet calls, and long hummings. Louisa sat, prayerfully numbering her days, like an uncloistered nun.

1887

The Revolt of "Mother"

"Father!"

"What is it?"

"What are them men diggin' over there in the field for?"

There was a sudden dropping and enlarging of the lower part of the old man's face, as if some heavy weight had settled therein; he shut his mouth tight, and went on harnessing the great bay mare. He hustled the collar on to her neck with a jerk.

"Father!"

The old man slapped the saddle upon the mare's back.

"Look here, father, I want to know what them men are diggin' over in the field for, an' I'm goin' to know."

"I wish you'd go into the house, mother, an' 'tend to your own affairs," the old man said then. He ran his words together, and his speech was almost as inarticulate as a growl.

But the woman understood; it was her most native tongue. "I ain't goin' into the house till you tell me what them men are doin' over there in the field," said she.

Then she stood waiting. She was a small woman, short and straight-waisted like a child in her brown cotton gown. Her forehead was mild and benevolent between the smooth curves of gray hair; there were meek downward lines about her nose and mouth; but her eyes, fixed upon the old man, looked as if the meekness had been the result of her own will, never of the will of another.

They were in the barn, standing before the wide open doors. The spring air, full of the smell of growing grass and unseen blossoms, came in their faces. The deep yard in front was littered with farm wagons and piles of wood; on the edges, close to the fence and the house, the grass was a vivid green, and there were some dandelions.

The old man glanced doggedly at his wife as he tightened the last buckles on the harness. She looked as immovable to him as one of the rocks in his pasture-land, bound to the earth with generations of blackberry vines. He slapped the reins over the horse, and started forth from the barn.

"Father!" said she.

The old man pulled up. "What is it?"

"I want to know what them men are diggin' over there in that field for."

"They're diggin' a cellar, I s'pose, if you've got to know."

"A cellar for what?"

"A barn."

"A barn? You ain't goin' to build a barn over there where we was goin' to have a house, father?"

The old man said not another word. He hurried the horse into the farm wagon, and clattered out of the yard, jouncing as sturdily on his seat as a boy.

The woman stood a moment looking after him, then she went out of the barn across a corner of the yard to the house. The house, standing at right angles with the great barn and a long reach of sheds and out-buildings, was infinitesimal compared with them. It was scarcely as commodious for people as the little boxes under the barn eaves were for doves.

A pretty girl's face, pink and delicate as a flower, was looking out of one of the house windows. She was watching three men who were digging over in the field which bounded the yard near the road line. She turned quietly when the woman entered.

"What are they digging for, mother?" said she. "Did he tell you?"

"They're diggin' for—a cellar for a new barn."

"Oh, mother, he ain't going to build another barn?"

"That's what he says."

A boy stood before the kitchen glass combing his hair. He combed slowly and painstakingly, arranging his brown hair in a smooth hillock over his forehead. He did not seem to pay any attention to the conversation.

"Sammy, did you know father was going to build a new barn?" asked the girl.

The boy combed assiduously.

"Sammy!"

He turned, and showed a face like his father's under his smooth crest of hair. "Yes, I s'pose I did," he said, reluctantly.

"How long have you known it?" asked his mother.

"'Bout three months, I guess."

"Why didn't you tell of it?"

"Didn't think 'twould do no good."

"I don't see what father wants another barn for," said the girl, in her sweet, slow voice. She turned again to the window, and stared out at the digging men in the field. Her tender, sweet face was full of a gentle distress. Her forehead was as bald and innocent as a baby's, with the light hair strained back from it in a row of curl-papers. She was quite large, but her soft curves did not look as if they covered muscles.

Her mother looked sternly at the boy. "Is he goin' to buy more cows?" said she.

The boy did not reply; he was tying his shoes.

"Sammy, I want you to tell me if he's goin' to buy more cows."

"I s'pose he is."

"How many?"

"Four, I guess."

His mother said nothing more. She went into the pantry, and there was a clatter of dishes. The boy got his cap from a nail behind the door, took an old arithmetic from the shelf, and started for school. He was lightly built, but clumsy. He went out of the yard with a curious spring in the hips, that made his loose homemade jacket tilt up in the rear.

The girl went to the sink, and began to wash the dishes that were piled up there. Her mother came promptly out of the pantry, and shoved her aside. "You wipe 'em," said she; "I'll wash. There's a good many this mornin'."

The mother plunged her hands vigorously into the water, the girl wiped the plates slowly and dreamily. "Mother," said she, "don't you think it's too bad father's going to build that new barn, much as we need a decent house to live in?"

Her mother scrubbed a dish fiercely. "You ain't found out yet we're women-folks, Nanny Penn," said she. "You ain't seen enough of men-folks yet to. One of these days you'll find it out, an' then you'll know that we know only what men-folks think we do, so far as any use of it goes, an' how we'd ought to reckon men-folks in with Providence, an' not complain of what they do any more than we do of the weather."

"I don't care; I don't believe George is anything like that, anyhow," said Nanny. Her delicate face flushed pink, her lips pouted softly, as if she were going to cry.

"You wait an' see. I guess George Eastman ain't no better than other men. You hadn't ought to judge father, though. He can't help it, 'cause he don't look at things jest the way we do. An' we've been pretty comfortable here, after all. The roof don't leak—ain't never but once—that's one thing. Father's kept it shingled right up."

"I do wish we had a parlor."

"I guess it won't hurt George Eastman any to come to see you in a nice clean kitchen. I guess a good many girls don't have as good a place as this. Nobody's ever heard me complain."

"I ain't complained either, mother."

"Well, I don't think you'd better, a good father an' a good home as you've got. S'pose your father made you go out an' work for your livin'? Lots of girls have to that ain't no stronger an' better able to than you be."

Sarah Penn washed the frying-pan with a conclusive air. She scrubbed the outside of it as faithfully as the inside. She was a masterly keeper of her box of a house. Her one living-room never seemed to have in it any of the dust which the friction of life with inanimate matter produces. She swept, and there seemed to be no dirt to go before the broom; she cleaned, and one could see no difference. She was like an artist so perfect that he has apparently no art. To-day she got out a mixing bowl and a board, and rolled some pies, and there was no more flour upon her than upon her daughter who was doing finer work. Nanny was to be married in the fall, and she was sewing on some white cambric and embroidery. She sewed industriously while her mother cooked, her soft milk-white hands and wrists showed whiter than her delicate work.

"We must have the stove moved out in the shed before long," said Mrs. Penn. "Talk about not havin' things, it's been a real blessin' to be able to put a stove up in that shed in hot weather. Father did one good thing when he fixed that stove-pipe out there."

Sarah Penn's face as she rolled her pies had that expression of meek vigor which might have characterized one of the New Testament saints. She was making mince-pies. Her husband, Adoniram Penn, liked them better than any other kind. She baked twice a week. Adoniram often liked a piece of pie between meals. She hurried this morning. It had been later than usual when she began, and she wanted to have a pie baked for dinner. However deep a resentment she might be forced to hold against her husband, she would never fail in sedulous attention to his wants.

Nobility of character manifests itself at loop-holes when it is not provided with large doors. Sarah Penn's showed itself to-day in flaky dishes of pastry. So she made the pies faithfully, while across the table she could see, when she glanced up from her work, the sight that rankled in her patient and steadfast soul—the digging of the cellar of the new barn in the place where Adoniram forty years ago had promised her their new house should stand.

The pies were done for dinner. Adoniram and Sammy were home a few minutes after twelve o'clock. The dinner was eaten with serious haste. There was never much conversation at the table in the Penn family. Adoniram asked a blessing, and they ate promptly, then rose up and went about their work.

Sammy went back to school, taking soft sly lopes out of the yard like a rabbit. He wanted a game of marbles before school, and feared his father would give him some chores to do. Adoniram hastened to the door and called after him, but he was out of sight.

"I don't see what you let him go for, mother," said he. "I wanted him to help me unload that wood."

Adoniram went to work out in the yard unloading wood from the wagon. Sarah put away the dinner dishes, while Nanny took down her curl-papers and changed her dress. She was going down to the store to buy some more embroidery and thread.

When Nanny was gone, Mrs. Penn went to the door. "Father!" she called.

"Well, what is it!"

"I want to see you jest a minute, father."

"I can't leave this wood nohow. I've got to git it unloaded an' go for a load of gravel afore two o'clock. Sammy had ought to helped me. You hadn't ought to let him go to school so early."

"I want to see you jest a minute."

"I tell ye I can't, nohow, mother."

"Father, you come here." Sarah Penn stood in the door like a queen; she held her head as if it bore a crown; there was the patience which makes authority royal in her voice. Adoniram went.

Mrs. Penn led the way into the kitchen, and pointed to a chair. "Sit down, father," said she; "I've got somethin' I want to say to you."

He sat down heavily; his face was quite stolid, but he looked at her with restive eyes. "Well, what is it, mother?"

"I want to know what you're buildin' that new barn for, father?"

"I ain't got nothin' to say about it."

"It can't be you think you need another barn?"

"I tell ye I ain't got nothin' to say about it, mother; an' I ain't goin' to say nothin'."

"Be you goin' to buy more cows?"

Adoniram did not reply; he shut his mouth tight.

"I know you be, as well as I want to. Now, father, look here"—Sarah Penn had not sat down; she stood before her husband in the humble fashion of a Scripture woman—"I'm goin' to talk real plain to you; I never have sence I married you, but I'm goin' to now. I ain't never complained, an' I ain't goin' to complain now, but I'm goin' to talk plain. You see this room here, father; you look at it well. You see there ain't no carpet on the floor, an' you see the paper is all dirty, an' droppin' off the walls. We ain't had no new paper on it for ten year, an' then I put it on myself, an' it didn't cost but ninepence a roll. You see this room, father; it's all the one

I've had to work in an' eat in an' sit in sence we was married. There ain't another woman in the whole town whose husband ain't got half the means you have but what's got better. It's all the room Nanny's got to have her company in; an' there ain't one of her mates but what's got better, an' their fathers not so able as hers is. It's all the room she'll have to be married in. What would you have thought, father, if we had had our weddin' in a room no better than this? I was married in my mother's parlor, with a carpet on the floor, an' stuffed furniture, an' a mahogany card-table. An' this is all the room my daughter will have to be married in. Look here, father!"

Sarah Penn went across the room as though it were a tragic stage. She flung open a door and disclosed a tiny bedroom, only large enough for a bed and bureau, with a path between. "There, father," said she—"there's all the room I've had to sleep in forty year. All my children were born there—the two that died, an' the two that's livin'. I was sick with a fever there."

She stepped to another door and opened it. It led into the small, ill-lighted pantry. "Here," said she, "is all the buttery I've got—every place I've got for my dishes, to set away my victuals in, an' to keep my milk-pans in. Father, I've been takin' care of the milk of six cows in this place, an' now you're goin' to build a new barn, an' keep more cows, an' give me more to do in it."

She threw open another door. A narrow crooked flight of stairs wound upward from it. "There, father," said she, "I want you to look at the stairs that go up to them two unfinished chambers that are all the places our son an' daughter have had to sleep in all their lives. There ain't a prettier girl in town nor a more ladylike one than Nanny, an' that's the place she has to sleep in. It ain't so good as your horse's stall; it ain't so warm an' tight."

Sarah Penn went back and stood before her husband. "Now, father," said she, "I want to know if you think you're doin' right an' accordin' to what you profess. Here, when we was married, forty year ago, you promised me faithful that we should have a new house built in that lot over in the field before the year was out. You said you had money enough, an' you wouldn't ask me to live in no such place as this. It is forty year now, an' you've been makin' more money, an' I've been savin' of it for you ever since, an' you ain't built no house yet. You've built sheds an' cow-houses an' one new barn, an' now you're goin' to build another. Father, I want to know if you think it's right. You're lodgin' your dumb beasts better than you are your own flesh an' blood. I want to know if you think it's right."

"I ain't got nothin' to say."

"You can't say nothin' without ownin' it ain't right, father. An' there's another thing—I ain't complained; I've got along forty year, an' I s'pose I should forty more, if it wa'n't for that—if we don't have another house. Nanny she can't live with us after she's married. She'll have to go somewheres else to live away from us, an' it don't seem as if I could have it so, noways, father. She wa'n't ever strong. She's got considerable color, but there wa'n't ever any backbone to her. I've always took the heft of everything off her, an' she ain't fit to keep house an' do everything herself. She'll be all worn out inside of a year. Think of her doin' all the washin' an' ironin' an' bakin' with them soft white hands an' arms, an' sweepin'! I can't have it so, noways, father."

Mrs. Penn's face was burning; her mild eyes gleamed. She had pleaded her little cause like a Webster;[1] she had ranged from severity to pathos; but her opponent employed that obstinate silence which makes eloquence futile with mocking echoes. Adoniram arose clumsily.

"Father, ain't you got nothin' to say?" said Mrs. Penn.

"I've got to go off after that load of gravel. I can't stan' here talkin' all day."

"Father, won't you think it over, an' have a house built there instead of a barn?"

"I ain't got nothin' to say."

Adoniram shuffled out. Mrs. Penn went into her bedroom. When she came out, her eyes were red. She had a roll of unbleached cotton cloth. She spread it out on the kitchen table, and began cutting out some shirts for her husband. The men over in the field had a team to help them this afternoon; she could hear their halloos. She had a scanty pattern for the shirts; she had to plan and piece the sleeves.

Nanny came home with her embroidery, and sat down with her needlework. She had taken down her curl-papers, and there was a soft roll of fair hair like an aureole over her forehead; her face was as delicately fine and clear as porcelain. Suddenly she looked up, and the tender red flamed all over her face and neck. "Mother," said she.

"What say?"

"I've been thinking—I don't see how we're goin' to have any—wedding in this room. I'd be ashamed to have his folks come if we didn't have anybody else."

"Mebbe we can have some new paper before then; I can put it on. I guess you won't have no call to be ashamed of your belongin's."

"We might have the wedding in the new barn," said Nanny, with gentle pettishness. "Why, mother, what makes you look so?"

Mrs. Penn had started, and was staring at her with a curious expression. She turned again to her work, and spread out a pattern carefully on the cloth. "Nothin'," said she.

Presently Adoniram clattered out of the yard in his two-wheeled dump cart, standing as proudly upright as a Roman charioteer. Mrs. Penn opened the door and stood there a minute looking out; the halloos of the men sounded louder.

It seemed to her all through the spring months that she heard nothing but the halloos and the noises of saws and hammers. The new barn grew fast. It was a fine edifice for this little village. Men came on pleasant Sundays, in their meeting suits and clean shirt bosoms, and stood around it admiringly. Mrs. Penn did not speak of it, and Adoniram did not mention it to her, although sometimes, upon a return from inspecting it, he bore himself with injured dignity.

"It's a strange thing how your mother feels about the new barn," he said, confidentially, to Sammy one day.

Sammy only grunted after an odd fashion for a boy; he had learned it from his father.

The barn was all completed ready for use by the third week in July. Adoniram had planned to move his stock in on Wednesday; on Tuesday he received a letter

[1]Daniel Webster, Congressman and famous nineteenth-century orator.

which changed his plans. He came in with it early in the morning. "Sammy's been to the post-office," said he, "an' I've got a letter from Hiram." Hiram was Mrs. Penn's brother, who lived in Vermont.

"Well," said Mrs. Penn, "what does he say about the folks?"

"I guess they're all right. He says he thinks if I come up country right off there's a chance to buy jest the kind of a horse I want." He stared reflectively out of the window at the new barn.

Mrs. Penn was making pies. She went on clapping the rolling-pin into the crust, although she was very pale, and her heart beat loudly.

"I dun' know but what I'd better go," said Adoniram. "I hate to go off jest now, right in the midst of hayin', but the ten-acre lot's cut, an' I guess Rufus an' the others can git along without me three or four days. I can't get a horse round here to suit me, nohow, an' I've got to have another for all that wood-haulin' in the fall. I told Hiram to watch out, an' if he got wind of a good horse to let me know. I guess I'd better go."

"I'll get out your clean shirt an' collar," said Mrs. Penn calmly.

She laid out Adoniram's Sunday suit and his clean clothes on the bed in the little bedroom. She got his shaving-water and razor ready. At last she buttoned on his collar and fastened his black cravat.

Adoniram never wore his collar and cravat except on extra occasions. He held his head high, with a rasped dignity. When he was all ready, with his coat and hat brushed, and a lunch of pie and cheese in a paper bag, he hesitated on the threshold of the door. He looked at his wife, and his manner was defiantly apologetic. "*If* them cows come to-day, Sammy can drive 'em into the new barn," said he; "an' when they bring the hay up, they can pitch it in there."

"Well," replied Mrs. Penn.

Adoniram set his shaven face ahead and started. When he had cleared the doorstep, he turned and looked back with a kind of nervous solemnity. "I shall be back by Saturday if nothin' happens," said he.

"Do be careful, father," returned his wife.

She stood in the door with Nanny at her elbow and watched him out of sight. Her eyes had a strange, doubtful expression in them; her peaceful forehead was contracted. She went in, and about her baking again. Nanny sat sewing. Her wedding-day was drawing nearer, and she was getting pale and thin with her steady sewing. Her mother kept glancing at her.

"Have you got that pain in your side this mornin'?" she asked.

"A little."

Mrs. Penn's face, as she worked, changed, her perplexed forehead smoothed, her eyes were steady, her lips firmly set. She formed a maxim for herself, although incoherently with her unlettered thoughts. "Unsolicited opportunities are the guide-posts of the Lord to the new roads of life," she repeated in effect, and she made up her mind to her course of action.

"S'posin' I *had* wrote to Hiram," she muttered once, when she was in the pantry—"s'posin' I had wrote, an' asked him if he knew of any horse? But I didn't, an' father's goin' wa'n't none of my doin'. It looks like a providence." Her voice rang out quite loud at the last.

"What you talkin' about, mother?" called Nanny.

"Nothin'."

Mrs. Penn hurried her baking; at eleven o'clock it was all done. The load of hay from the west field came slowly down the cart track, and drew up at the new barn. Mrs. Penn ran out. "Stop!" she screamed—"stop!"

The men stopped and looked; Sammy upreared from the top of the load, and stared at his mother.

"Stop!" she cried out again. "Don't you put the hay in that barn; put it in the old one."

"Why, he said to put it in here," returned one of the hay-makers, wonderingly. He was a young man, a neighbor's son, whom Adoniram hired by the year to help on the farm.

"Don't you put the hay in the new barn; there's room enough in the old one, ain't there?" said Mrs. Penn.

"Room enough," returned the hired man, in his thick, rustic tones. "Didn't need the new barn, nohow, far as room's concerned. Well, I s'pose he changed his mind." He took hold of the horses' bridles.

Mrs. Penn went back to the house. Soon the kitchen windows were darkened, and a fragrance like warm honey came into the room.

Nanny laid down her work. "I thought father wanted them to put the hay into the new barn?" she said, wonderingly.

"It's all right," replied her mother.

Sammy slid down from the load of hay, and came in to see if dinner was ready.

"I ain't goin' to get a regular dinner to-day, as long as father's gone," said his mother. "I've let the fire go out. You can have some bread an' milk an' pie. I thought we could get along." She set out some bowls of milk, some bread and a pie on the kitchen table. "You'd better eat your dinner now," said she. "You might jest as well get through with it. I want you to help me afterward."

Nanny and Sammy stared at each other. There was something strange in their mother's manner. Mrs. Penn did not eat anything herself. She went into the pantry, and they heard her moving dishes while they ate. Presently she came out with a pile of plates. She got the clothes-basket out of the shed, and packed them in it. Nanny and Sammy watched. She brought out cups and saucers, and put them in with the plates.

"What you goin' to do, mother?" inquired Nanny, in a timid voice. A sense of something unusual made her tremble, as if it were a ghost. Sammy rolled his eyes over his pie.

"You'll see what I'm goin' to do," replied Mrs. Penn. "If you're through, Nanny, I want you to go up-stairs an' pack up your things; an' I want you, Sammy, to help me take down the bed in the bedroom."

"Oh, mother, what for?" gasped Nanny.

"You'll see."

During the next few hours a feat was performed by this simple, pious New England mother which was equal in its way to Wolfe's storming of the Heights of Abraham.[2] It took no more genius and audacity of bravery for Wolfe to cheer his won-

[2]James Wolfe, a British general, scored a decisive victory against Quebec in the Seven Years War (1756–1763). Since the bluffs were considered unscalable, his was a very daring and heroic exploit.

dering soldiers up those steep precipices, under the sleeping eyes of the enemy, than for Sarah Penn, at the head of her children, to move all their little household goods into the new barn while her husband was away.

Nanny and Sammy followed their mother's instructions without a murmur; indeed, they were overawed. There is a certain uncanny and superhuman quality about all such purely original undertakings as their mother's was to them. Nanny went back and forth with her light loads, and Sammy tugged with sober energy.

At five o'clock in the afternoon the little house in which the Penns had lived for forty years had emptied itself into the new barn.

Every builder builds somewhat for unknown purposes, and is in a measure a prophet. The architect of Adoniram Penn's barn, while he designed it for the comfort of four-footed animals, had planned better than he knew for the comfort of humans. Sarah Penn saw at a glance its possibilities. These great box-stalls, with quilts hung before them, would make better bedrooms than the one she had occupied for forty years, and there was a tight carriage-room. The harness-room, with its chimney and shelves, would make a kitchen of her dreams. The great middle space would make a parlor, by-and-by, fit for a palace. Up-stairs there was as much room as down. With partitions and windows, what a house would there be! Sarah looked at the row of stanchions before the allotted space for cows, and reflected that she would have her front entry there.

At six o'clock the stove was up in the harness-room, the kettle was boiling, and the table set for tea. It looked almost as home-like as the abandoned house across the yard had ever done. The young hired man milked, and Sarah directed him calmly to bring the milk to the new barn. He came gaping, dropping little blots of foam from the brimming pails on the grass. Before the next morning he had spread the story of Adoniram Penn's wife moving into the new barn all over the little village. Men assembled in the store and talked it over, women with shawls over their heads scuttled into each other's houses before their work was done. Any deviation from the ordinary course of life in this quiet town was enough to stop all progress in it. Everybody paused to look at the staid, independent figure on the side track. There was a difference of opinion with regard to her. Some held her to be insane; some, of a lawless and rebellious spirit.

Friday the minister went to see her. It was in the forenoon, and she was at the barn door shelling pease for dinner. She looked up and returned his salutation with dignity, then she went on with her work. She did not invite him in. The saintly expression of her face remained fixed, but there was an angry flush over it.

The minister stood awkwardly before her, and talked. She handled the pease as if they were bullets. At last she looked up, and her eyes showed the spirit that her meek front had covered for a lifetime.

"There ain't no use talkin', Mr. Hersey," said she. "I've thought it all over an' over, an' I believe I'm doin' what's right. I've made it the subject of prayer, an' it's betwixt me an' the Lord an' Adoniram. There ain't no call for nobody else to worry about it."

"Well, of course, if you have brought it to the Lord in prayer, and feel satisfied that you are doing right, Mrs. Penn," said the minister, helplessly. His thin gray-bearded face was pathetic. He was a sickly man; his youthful confidence had cooled; he had to scourge himself up to some of his pastoral duties as relentlessly as a Catholic ascetic, and then he was prostrated by the smart.

"I think it's right jest as much as I think it was right for our forefathers to come over from the old country 'cause they didn't have what belonged to 'em," said Mrs. Penn. She arose. The barn threshold might have been Plymouth Rock from her bearing. "I don't doubt you mean well, Mr. Hersey," said she, "but there are things people hadn't ought to interfere with. I've been a member of the church for over forty year. I've got my own mind an' my own feet, an' I'm goin' to think my own thoughts an' go my own ways, an' nobody but the Lord is goin' to dictate to me unless I've a mind to have him. Won't you come in an' set down? How is Mis' Hersey?"

"She is well, I thank you," replied the minister. He added some more perplexed apologetic remarks; then he retreated.

He could expound the intricacies of every character study in the Scriptures, he was competent to grasp the Pilgrim Fathers and all historical innovators, but Sarah Penn was beyond him. He could deal with primal cases, but parallel ones worsted him. But, after all, although it was aside from his province, he wondered more how Adoniram Penn would deal with his wife than how the Lord would. Everybody shared the wonder. When Adoniram's four new cows arrived, Sarah ordered three to be put in the old barn, the other in the house shed where the cooking-stove had stood. That added to the excitement. It was whispered that all four cows were domiciled in the house.

Towards sunset on Saturday, when Adoniram was expected home, there was a knot of men in the road near the new barn. The hired man had milked, but he still hung around the premises. Sarah Penn had supper all ready. There were brown-bread and baked beans and a custard pie; it was the supper Adoniram loved on a Saturday night. She had a clean calico, and she bore herself imperturbably. Nanny and Sammy kept close at her heels. Their eyes were large, and Nanny was full of nervous tremors. Still there was to them more pleasant excitement than anything else. An inborn confidence in their mother over their father asserted itself.

Sammy looked out of the harness-room window. "There he is," he announced, in an awed whisper. He and Nanny peeped around the casing. Mrs. Penn kept on about her work. The children watched Adoniram leave the new horse standing in the drive while he went to the house door. It was fastened. Then he went around to the shed. That door was seldom locked, even when the family was away. The thought how her father would be confronted by the cow flashed upon Nanny. There was a hysterical sob in her throat. Adoniram emerged from the shed and stood looking about in a dazed fashion. His lips moved; he was saying something, but they could not hear what it was. The hired man was peeping around a corner of the old barn, but nobody saw him.

Adoniram took the new horse by the bridle and led him across the yard to the new barn. Nanny and Sammy slunk close to their mother. The barn doors rolled back, and there stood Adoniram, with the long mild face of the great Canadian farm horse looking over his shoulder.

Nanny kept behind her mother, but Sammy stepped suddenly forward, and stood in front of her.

Adoniram stared at the group. "What on airth you all down here for?" said he. "What's the matter over to the house?"

"We've come here to live, father," said Sammy. His shrill voice quavered out bravely.

"What"—Adoniram sniffed—"what is it smells like cookin'?" said he. He stepped forward and looked in the open door of the harness-room. Then he turned to his wife. His old bristling face was pale and frightened. "What on airth does this mean, mother?" he gasped.

"You come in here, father," said Sarah. She led the way into the harness-room and shut the door. "Now, father," said she, "you needn't be scared. I ain't crazy. There ain't nothin' to be upset over. But we've come here to live, an' we're goin' to live here. We've got jest as good a right here as new horses an' cows. The house wa'n't fit for us to live in any longer, an' I made up my mind I wa'n't goin' to stay there. I've done my duty by you forty year, an' I'm goin' to do it now; but I'm goin' to live here. You've got to put in some windows and partitions; an' you'll have to buy some furniture."

"Why, mother!" the old man gasped.

"You'd better take your coat off an' get washed—there's the wash-basin—an' then we'll have supper."

"Why, mother!"

Sammy went past the window, leading the new horse to the old barn. The old man saw him, and shook his head speechlessly. He tried to take off his coat, but his arms seemed to lack the power. His wife helped him. She poured some water into the tin basin, and put in a piece of soap. She got the comb and brush, and smoothed his thin gray hair after he had washed. Then she put the beans, hot bread, and tea on the table. Sammy came in, and the family drew up. Adoniram sat looking dazedly at his plate, and they waited.

"Ain't you goin' to ask a blessin', father?" said Sarah.

And the old man bent his head and mumbled.

All through the meal he stopped eating at intervals, and stared furtively at his wife; but he ate well. The home food tasted good to him, and his old frame was too sturdily healthy to be affected by his mind. But after supper he went out, and sat down on the step of the smaller door at the right of the barn, through which he had meant his Jerseys to pass in stately file, but which Sarah designed for her front house door, and he leaned his head on his hands.

After the supper dishes were cleared away and the milk-pans washed, Sarah went out to him. The twilight was deepening. There was a clear green glow in the sky. Before them stretched the smooth level of field; in the distance was a cluster of haystacks like the huts of a village; the air was very cool and calm and sweet. The landscape might have been an ideal one of peace.

Sarah bent over and touched her husband on one of his thin, sinewy shoulders. "Father!"

The old man's shoulders heaved: he was weeping.

"Why, don't do so, father," said Sarah.

"I'll—put up the—partitions, an'—everything you—want, mother."

Sarah put her apron up to her face; she was overcome by her own triumph.

Adoniram was like a fortress whose walls had no active resistance, and went down the instant the right besieging tools were used. "Why, mother," he said, hoarsely, "I hadn't no idee you was so set on't as all this comes to."

1891

Old Woman Magoun

The hamlet of Barry's Ford is situated in a sort of high valley among the mountains. Below it the hills lie in moveless curves like a petrified ocean; above it they rise in green-cresting waves which never break. It is *Barry's* Ford because at one time the Barry family was the most important in the place; and *Ford* because just at the beginning of the hamlet the little turbulent Barry River is fordable. There is, however, now a rude bridge across the river.

Old Woman Magoun was largely instrumental in bringing the bridge to pass. She haunted the miserable little grocery, wherein whiskey and hands of tobacco were the most salient features of the stock in trade, and she talked much. She would elbow herself into the midst of a knot of idlers and talk.

"That bridge ought to be built this very summer," said Old Woman Magoun. She spread her strong arms like wings, and sent the loafers, half laughing, half angry, flying in every direction. "If I were a *man,*" said she, "I'd go out this very minute and lay the fust log. If I were a passel of lazy men layin' round, I'd start up for once in my life, I would." The men cowered visibly—all except Nelson Barry; he swore under his breath and strode over to the counter.

Old Woman Magoun looked after him majestically. "You can cuss all you want to, Nelson Barry," said she; "I ain't afraid of you. I don't expect you to lay ary log of the bridge, but I'm goin' to have it built this very summer." She did. The weakness of the masculine element in Barry's Ford was laid low before such strenuous feminine assertion.

Old Woman Magoun and some other women planned a treat—two sucking pigs, and pies, and sweet cake—for a reward after the bridge should be finished. They even viewed leniently the increased consumption of ardent spirits.

"It seems queer to me," Old Woman Magoun said to Sally Jinks, "that men can't do nothin' without havin' to drink and chew to keep their sperits up. Lord! I've worked all my life and never done nuther."

"Men is different," said Sally Jinks.

"Yes, they be," assented Old Woman Magoun, with open contempt.

The two women sat on a bench in front of Old Woman Magoun's house, and little Lily Barry, her granddaughter, sat holding her doll on a small mossy stone near by. From where they sat they could see the men at work on the new bridge. It was the last day of the work.

Lily clasped her doll—a poor old rag thing—close to her childish bosom, like a little mother, and her face, round which curled her long yellow hair, was fixed upon the men at work. Little Lily had never been allowed to run with the other children of Barry's Ford. Her grandmother had taught her everything she knew—which was not much, but tending at least to a certain measure of spiritual growth—for she, as it were, poured the goodness of her own soul into this little receptive vase of another. Lily was firmly grounded in her knowledge that it was wrong to lie or steal or disobey her grandmother. She had also learned that one should be very industrious. It was seldom that Lily sat idly holding her doll-baby, but this was a holiday because of the bridge. She looked only a child, although she was nearly fourteen; her mother had been married at sixteen. That is, Old Woman Magoun said that her daughter, Lily's mother, had married at sixteen; there had been rumors, but no one had dared openly gainsay the old woman. She said that her daughter had married Nelson Barry, and he had deserted her. She had lived in her mother's house, and Lily had been born there, and she had died when the baby was only a week old. Lily's father, Nelson Barry, was the fairly dangerous degenerate of a good old family. Nelson's father before him had been bad. He was now the last of the family, with the exception of a sister of feeble intellect, with whom he lived in the old Barry house. He was a middle-aged man, still handsome. The shiftless population of Barry's Ford looked up to him as to an evil deity. They wondered how Old Woman Magoun dared brave him as she did. But Old Woman Magoun had within her a mighty sense of reliance upon herself as being on the right track in the midst of a maze of evil, which gave her courage. Nelson Barry had manifested no interest whatever in his daughter. Lily seldom saw her father. She did not often go to the store which was his favorite haunt. Her grandmother took care that she should not do so.

However, that afternoon she departed from her usual custom and sent Lily to the store.

She came in from the kitchen, whither she had been to baste the roasting pig. "There's no use talkin'," said she, "I've got to have some more salt. I've jest used the very last I had to dredge over that pig. I've got to go to the store."

Sally Jinks looked at Lily. "Why don't you send her?" she asked.

Old Woman Magoun gazed irresolutely at the girl. She was herself very tired. It did not seem to her that she could drag herself up the dusty hill to the store. She glanced with covert resentment at Sally Jinks. She thought that she might offer to go. But Sally Jinks said again, "Why don't you let her go?" and looked with a languid eye at Lily holding her doll on the stone.

Lily was watching the men at work on the bridge, with her childish delight in a spectacle of any kind, when her grandmother addressed her.

"Guess I'll let you go down to the store an' git some salt, Lily," said she.

The girl turned uncomprehending eyes upon her grandmother at the sound of her voice. She had been filled with one of the innocent reveries of childhood. Lily had in her the making of an artist or a poet. Her prolonged childhood went to prove it, and also her retrospective eyes, as clear and blue as blue light itself, which seemed to see past all that she looked upon. She had not come of the old Barry family for nothing. The best of the strain was in her, along with the splendid stanchness in humble lines which she had acquired from her grandmother.

"Put on your hat," said Old Woman Magoun; "the sun is hot, and you might git a headache." She called the girl to her, and put back the shower of fair curls under the rubber band which confined the hat. She gave Lily some money, and watched her knot it into a corner of her little cotton handkerchief. "Be careful you don't lose it," said she, "and don't stop to talk to anybody, for I am in a hurry for that salt. Of course, if anybody speaks to you answer them polite, and then come right along."

Lily started, her pocket-handkerchief weighted with the small silver dangling from one hand, and her rag doll carried over her shoulder like a baby. The absurd travesty of a face peeped forth from Lily's yellow curls. Sally Jinks looked after her with a sniff.

"She ain't goin' to carry that rag doll to the store?" said she.

"She likes to," replied Old Woman Magoun, in a half-shamed yet defiantly extenuating voice.

"Some girls at her age is thinkin' about beaux instead of rag dolls," said Sally Jinks.

The grandmother bristled, "Lily ain't big nor old for her age," said she. "I ain't in any hurry to have her git married. She ain't none too strong."

"She's got a good color," said Sally Jinks. She was crocheting white cotton lace, making her thick fingers fly. She really knew how to do scarcely anything except to crochet that coarse lace; somehow her heavy brain or her fingers had mastered that.

"I know she's got a beautiful color," replied Old Woman Magoun, with an odd mixture of pride and anxiety, "but it comes an' goes."

"I've heard that was a bad sign," remarked Sally Jinks, loosening some thread from her spool.

"Yes, it is," said the grandmother. "She's nothin' but a baby, though she's quicker than most to learn."

Lily Barry went on her way to the store. She was clad in a scanty short frock of blue cotton; her hat was tipped back, forming an oval frame for her innocent face. She was very small, and walked like a child, with the clap-clap of little feet of babyhood. She might have been considered, from her looks, under ten.

Presently she heard footsteps behind her; she turned around a little timidly to see who was coming. When she saw a handsome, well-dressed man, she felt reassured. The man came alongside and glanced down carelessly at first, then his look deepened. He smiled, and Lily saw he was very handsome indeed, and that his smile was not only reassuring but wonderfully sweet and compelling.

"Well, little one," said the man, "where are you bound, you and your dolly?"

"I am going to the store to buy some salt for grandma," replied Lily, in her sweet treble. She looked up in the man's face, and he fairly started at the revelation of its innocent beauty. He regulated his pace by hers, and the two went on together. The man did not speak again at once. Lily kept glancing timidly up at him, and every time that she did so the man smiled and her confidence increased. Presently when the man's hand grasped her little childish one hanging by her side, she felt a complete trust in him. Then she smiled up at him. She felt glad that this nice man had come along, for just here the road was lonely.

After a while the man spoke. "What is your name, little one?" he asked, caressingly.

"Lily Barry."

The man started. "What is your father's name?"

"Nelson Barry," replied Lily.

The man whistled. "Is your mother dead?"

"Yes, sir."

"How old are you, my dear?"

"Fourteen," replied Lily.

The man looked at her with surprise. "As old as that?"

Lily suddenly shrank from the man. She could not have told why. She pulled her little hand from his, and he let it go with no remonstrance. She clasped both her arms around her rag doll, in order that her hand should not be free for him to grasp again.

She walked a little farther away from the man, and he looked amused.

"You still play with your doll?" he said, in a soft voice.

"Yes, sir," replied Lily. She quickened her pace and reached the store.

When Lily entered the store, Hiram Gates, the owner, was behind the counter. The only man besides in the store was Nelson Barry. He sat tipping his chair back against the wall; he was half asleep, and his handsome face was bristling with a beard of several days' growth and darkly flushed. He opened his eyes when Lily entered, the strange man following. He brought his chair down on all fours, and he looked at the man—not noticing Lily at all—with a look compounded of defiance and uneasiness.

"Hullo, Jim!" he said.

"Hullo, old man!" returned the stranger.

Lily went over to the counter and asked for the salt, in her pretty little voice. When she had paid for it and was crossing the store, Nelson Barry was on his feet.

"Well, how are you, Lily? It is Lily, isn't it?" he said.

"Yes, sir," replied Lily, faintly.

Her father bent down and, for the first time in her life, kissed her, and the whiskey odor of his breath came into her face.

Lily involuntarily started, and shrank away from him. Then she rubbed her mouth violently with her little cotton handkerchief, which she held gathered up with the rag doll.

"Damn it all! I believe she is afraid of me," said Nelson Barry, in a thick voice.

"Looks a little like it," said the other man, laughing.

"It's that damned old woman," said Nelson Barry. Then he smiled again at Lily. "I didn't know what a pretty little daughter I was blessed with," said he, and he softly stroked Lily's pink cheek under her hat.

Now Lily did not shrink from him. Hereditary instincts and nature itself were asserting themselves in the child's innocent, receptive breast.

Nelson Barry looked curiously at Lily. "How old are you, anyway, child?" he asked.

"I'll be fourteen in September," replied Lily.

"But you still play with your doll?" said Barry, laughing kindly down at her.

Lily hugged her doll more tightly, in spite of her father's kind voice. "Yes, sir," she replied.

Nelson glanced across at some glass jars filled with sticks of candy. "See here, little Lily, do you like candy?" said he.

"Yes, sir."

"Wait a minute."

Lily waited while her father went over to the counter. Soon he returned with a package of the candy.

"I don't see how you are going to carry so much," he said, smiling. "Suppose you throw away your doll?"

Lily gazed at her father and hugged the doll tightly, and there was all at once in the child's expression something mature. It became the reproach of a woman. Nelson's face sobered.

"Oh, it's all right, Lily," he said; "keep your doll. Here, I guess you can carry this candy under your arm."

Lily could not resist the candy. She obeyed Nelson's instructions for carrying it, and left the store laden. The two men also left, and walked in the opposite direction, talking busily.

When Lily reached home, her grandmother, who was watching for her, spied at once the package of candy.

"What's that?" she asked, sharply.

"My father gave it to me," answered Lily, in a faltering voice. Sally regarded her with something like alertness.

"Your father?"

"Yes, ma'am."

"Where did you see him?"

"In the store."

"He gave you this candy?"

"Yes, ma'am."

"What did he say?"

"He asked me how old I was, and—"

"And what?"

"I don't know," replied Lily; and it really seemed to her that she did not know, she was so frightened and bewildered by it all, and, more than anything else, by her grandmother's face as she questioned her.

Old Woman Magoun's face was that of one upon whom a long-anticipated blow had fallen. Sally Jinks gazed at her with a sort of stupid alarm.

Old Woman Magoun continued to gaze at her grandchild with that look of terrible solicitude, as if she saw the girl in the clutch of a tiger. "You can't remember what else he said?" she asked, fiercely, and the child began to whimper softly.

"No, ma'am," she sobbed. "I—don't know, and—"

"And what? Answer me."

"There was another man there. A real handsome man."

"Did he speak to you?" asked Old Woman Magoun.

"Yes ma'am; he walked along with me a piece," confessed Lily, with a sob of terror and bewilderment.

"What did *he* say to you?" asked Old Woman Magoun, with a sort of despair.

Lily told, in her little, faltering, frightened voice, all of the conversation which she could recall. It sounded harmless enough, but the look of the realization of a long-expected blow never left her grandmother's face.

The sun was getting low, and the bridge was nearing completion. Soon the workmen would be crowding into the cabin for their promised supper. There became visible in the distance, far up the road, the heavily plodding figure of another woman who had agreed to come and help. Old Woman Magoun turned again to Lily.

"You go right up-stairs to your own chamber now," said she.

"Good land! ain't you goin' to let that poor child stay up and see the fun?" said Sally Jinks.

"You jest mind your own business," said Old Woman Magoun, forcibly, and Sally Jinks shrank. "You go right up there now, Lily," said the grandmother, in a softer tone, "and grandma will bring you up a nice plate of supper."

"When be you goin' to let that girl grow up?" asked Sally Jinks, when Lily had disappeared.

"She'll grow up in the Lord's good time," replied Old Woman Magoun, and there was in her voice something both sad and threatening. Sally Jinks again shrank a little.

Soon the workmen came flocking noisily into the house. Old Woman Magoun and her two helpers served the bountiful supper. Most of the men had drunk as much as, and more than, was good for them, and Old Woman Magoun had stipulated that there was to be no drinking of anything except coffee during supper.

"I'll git you as good a meal as I know how," she said, "but if I see ary one of you drinkin' a drop, I'll run you all out. If you want anything to drink, you can go up to the store afterward. That's the place for you to go to, if you've got to make hogs of yourselves. I ain't goin' to have no hogs in my house."

Old Woman Magoun was implicitly obeyed. She had a curious authority over most people when she chose to exercise it. When the supper was in full swing, she quietly stole up-stairs and carried some food to Lily. She found the girl, with the rag doll in her arms, crouching by the window in her little rocking-chair—a relic of her infancy, which she still used.

"What a noise they are makin', grandma!" she said, in a terrified whisper, as her grandmother placed the plate before her on a chair.

"They've 'most all of 'em been drinkin'. They air a passel of hogs," replied the old woman.

"Is the man that was with—with my father down there?" asked Lily, in a timid fashion. Then she fairly cowered before the look in her grandmother's eyes.

"No, he ain't; and what's more, he never will be down there if I can help it," said Old Woman Magoun, in a fierce whisper. "I know who he is. They can't cheat me. He's one of them Willises—that family the Barrys married into. They're worse than the Barrys, ef they *have* got money. Eat your supper, and put him out of your mind, child."

It was after Lily was asleep, when Old Woman Magoun was alone, clearing away her supper dishes, that Lily's father came. The door was closed, and he knocked, and the old woman knew at once who was there. The sound of that knock meant as much to her as the whir of a bomb to the defender of a fortress. She opened the door, and Nelson Barry stood there.

"Good-evening, Mrs. Magoun," he said.

Old Woman Magoun stood before him, filling up the doorway with her firm bulk.

"Good-evening, Mrs. Magoun," said Nelson Barry again.

"I ain't got no time to waste," replied the old woman, harshly. "I've got my supper dishes to clean up after them men."

She stood there and looked at him as she might have looked at a rebellious animal which she was trying to tame. The man laughed.

"It's no use," said he. "You know me of old. No human being can turn me from my way when I am once started in it. You may as well let me come in."

Old Woman Magoun entered the house, and Barry followed her.

Barry began without any preface. "Where is the child?" asked he.

"Up-stairs. She has gone to bed."

"She goes to bed early."

"Children ought to," returned the old woman, polishing a plate.

Barry laughed. "You are keeping her a child a long while," he remarked, in a soft voice which had a sting in it.

"She *is* a child," returned the old woman, defiantly.

"Her mother was only three years older when Lily was born."

The old woman made a sudden motion toward the man which seemed fairly menacing. Then she turned again to her dish-washing.

"I want her," said Barry.

"You can't have her," replied the old woman, in a still stern voice.

"I don't see how you can help yourself. You have always acknowledged that she was my child."

The old woman continued her task, but her strong back heaved. Barry regarded her with an entirely pitiless expression.

"I am going to have the girl, that is the long and short of it," he said, "and it is for her best good, too. You are a fool, or you would see it."

"Her best good?" muttered the old woman.

"Yes, her best good. What are you going to do with her, anyway? The girl is a beauty, and almost a woman grown, although you try to make out that she is a baby. You can't live forever."

"The Lord will take care of her," replied the old woman, and again she turned and faced him, and her expression was that of a prophetess.

"Very well, let Him," said Barry, easily. "All the same I'm going to have her, and I tell you it is for her best good. Jim Willis saw her this afternoon, and—"

Old Woman Magoun looked at him. "Jim Willis!" she fairly shrieked.

"Well, what of it?"

"One of them Willises!" repeated the old woman, and this time her voice was thick. It seemed almost as if she were stricken with paralysis. She did not enunciate clearly.

The man shrank a little. "Now what is the need of your making such a fuss?" he said. "I will take her, and Isabel will look out for her."

"Your half-witted sister?" said Old Woman Magoun.

"Yes, my half-witted sister. She knows more than you think."

"More wickedness."

"Perhaps. Well, a knowledge of evil is a useful thing. How are you going to avoid evil if you don't know what it is like? My sister and I will take care of my daughter."

The old woman continued to look at the man, but his eyes never fell. Suddenly her gaze grew inconceivably keen. It was as if she saw through all externals.

"I know what it is!" she cried. "You have been playing cards and you lost, and this is the way you will pay him."

Then the man's face reddened, and he swore under his breath.

"Oh, my God!" said the old woman; and she really spoke with her eyes aloft as if addressing something outside of them both. Then she turned again to her dish-washing.

The man cast a dogged look at her back. "Well, there is no use talking. I have made up my mind," said he, "and you know me and what that means. I am going to have the girl."

"When?" said the old woman, without turning around.

"Well, I am willing to give you a week. Put her clothes in good order before she comes."

The old woman made no reply. She continued washing dishes. She even handled them so carefully that they did not rattle.

"You understand," said Barry. "Have her ready a week from to-day."

"Yes," said Old Woman Magoun, "I understand."

Nelson Barry, going up the mountain road, reflected that Old Woman Magoun had a strong character, that she understood much better than her sex in general the futility of withstanding the inevitable.

"Well," he said to Jim Willis when he reached home, "the old woman did not make such a fuss as I expected."

"Are you going to have the girl?"

"Yes; a week from to-day. Look here, Jim; you've got to stick to your promise."

"All right," said Willis. "Go you one better."

The two were playing at cards in the old parlor, once magnificent, now squalid, of the Barry house. Isabel, the half-witted sister, entered, bringing some glasses on a tray. She had learned with her feeble intellect some tricks, like a dog. One of them was the mixing of sundry drinks. She set the tray on a little stand near the two men, and watched them with her silly simper.

"Clear out now and go to bed," her brother said to her, and she obeyed.

Early the next morning Old Woman Magoun went up to Lily's little sleeping-chamber, and watched her a second as she lay asleep, with her yellow locks spread over the pillow. Then she spoke. "Lily," said she—"Lily, wake up. I am going to Greenham across the new bridge, and you can go with me."

Lily immediately sat up in bed and smiled at her grandmother. Her eyes were still misty, but the light of awakening was in them.

"Get right up," said the old woman. "You can wear your new dress if you want to."

Lily gurgled with pleasure like a baby. "And my new hat?" asked she.

"I don't care."

Old Woman Magoun and Lily started for Greenham before Barry Ford, which kept late hours, was fairly awake. It was three miles to Greenham. The old woman said that, since the horse was a little lame, they would walk. It was a beautiful morning, with a diamond radiance of dew over everything. Her grandmother had curled Lily's hair more punctiliously than usual. The little face peeped like a rose out of two rows of golden spirals. Lily wore her new muslin dress with a pink sash, and her best hat of a fine white straw trimmed with a wreath of rosebuds; also the neatest black open-work stockings and pretty shoes. She even had white cotton gloves. When they set out, the old, heavily stepping woman, in her black gown and cape and bonnet, looked down at the little pink fluttering figure. Her face was full of the tenderest love and admiration, and yet there was something terrible about it. They crossed the new bridge—a primitive structure built of logs in a slovenly fashion. Old Woman Magoun pointed to a gap.

"Jest see that," said she. "That's the way men work."

"Men ain't very nice, be they?" said Lily, in her sweet little voice.

"No, they ain't, take them all together," replied her grandmother.

"That man that walked to the store with me was nicer than some, I guess," Lily said, in a wishful fashion. Her grandmother reached down and took the child's hand in its small cotton glove. "You hurt me, holding my hand so tight," Lily said presently, in a deprecatory little voice.

The old woman loosened her grasp. "Grandma didn't know how tight she was holding your hand," said she. "She wouldn't hurt you for nothin', except it was to save your life, or somethin' like that." She spoke with an undertone of tremendous meaning which the girl was too childish to grasp. They walked along the country road. Just before they reached Greenham they passed a stone wall overgrown with blackberry-vines, and, an unusual thing in that vicinity, a lusty spread of deadly nightshade full of berries.

"Those berries look good to eat, grandma," Lily said.

At that instant the old woman's face became something terrible to see. "You can't have any now," she said, and hurried Lily along.

"They look real nice," said Lily.

When they reached Greenham, Old Woman Magoun took her way straight to the most pretentious house there, the residence of the lawyer, whose name was Mason. Old Woman Magoun bade Lily wait in the yard for a few moments, and Lily ventured to seat herself on a bench beneath an oak-tree; then she watched with some wonder her grandmother enter the lawyer's office door at the right of the house. Presently the lawyer's wife came out and spoke to Lily under the tree. She had in her hand a little tray containing a plate of cake, a glass of milk, and an early apple. She spoke very kindly to Lily; she even kissed her, and offered her the tray of refreshments, which Lily accepted gratefully. She sat eating, with Mrs. Mason watching her, when Old Woman Magoun came out of the lawyer's office with a ghastly face.

"What are you eatin'?" she asked Lily, sharply. "Is that a sour apple?"

"I thought she might be hungry," said the lawyer's wife, with loving, melancholy eyes upon the girl.

Lily had almost finished the apple. "It's real sour, but I like it; it's real nice, grandma," she said.

"You ain't been drinkin' milk with a sour apple?"

"It was real nice milk, grandma."

"You ought never to have drunk milk and eat a sour apple," said her grandmother. "Your stomach was all out of order this mornin', an' sour apples and milk is always apt to hurt anybody."

"I don't know but they are," Mrs. Mason said, apologetically, as she stood on the green lawn with her lavender muslin sweeping around her. "I am real sorry, Mrs. Magoun. I ought to have thought. Let me get some soda for her."

"Soda never agrees with her," replied the old woman, in a harsh voice. "Come," she said to Lily, "it's time we were goin' home."

After Lily and her grandmother had disappeared down the road, Lawyer Mason came out of his office and joined his wife, who had seated herself on the bench beneath the tree. She was idle, and her face wore the expression of those who review joys forever past. She had lost a little girl, her only child, years ago, and her husband always knew when she was thinking about her. Lawyer Mason looked older than his wife; he had a dry, shrewd, slightly one-sided face.

"What do you think, Maria?" he said. "That old woman came to me with the most pressing entreaty to adopt that little girl."

"She is a beautiful little girl," said Mrs. Mason, in a slightly husky voice.

"Yes, she is a pretty child," assented the lawyer, looking pityingly at his wife; "but it is out of the question, my dear. Adopting a child is a serious measure, and in this case a child who comes from Barry's Ford."

"But the grandmother seems a very good woman," said Mrs. Mason.

"I rather think she is. I never heard a word against her. But the father! No, Maria, we cannot take a child with Barry blood in her veins. The stock has run out; it is vitiated physically and morally. It won't do, my dear."

"Her grandmother had her dressed up as pretty as a little girl could be," said Mrs. Mason, and this time the tears welled into her faithful, wistful eyes.

"Well, we can't help that," said the lawyer, as he went back to his office.

Old Woman Magoun and Lily returned, going slowly along the road to Barry's Ford. When they came to the stone wall where the blackberry-vines and the deadly nightshade grew, Lily said she was tired, and asked if she could not sit down for a few minutes. The strange look on her grandmother's face had deepened. Now and then Lily glanced at her and had a feeling as if she were looking at a stranger.

"Yes, you can set down if you want to," said Old Woman Magoun, deeply and harshly.

Lily started and looked at her, as if to make sure that is was her grandmother who spoke. Then she sat down on a stone which was comparatively free of the vines.

"Ain't you goin' to set down, grandma?" Lily asked, timidly.

"No; I don't want to get into that mess," replied her grandmother. "I ain't tired. I'll stand here."

Lily sat still; her delicate little face was flushed with heat. She extended her tiny feet in her best shoes and gazed at them. "My shoes are all over dust," said she.

"It will brush off," said her grandmother, still in that strange voice.

Lily looked around. An elm-tree in the field behind her cast a spray of branches over her head; a little cool puff of wind came on her face. She gazed at the low mountains on the horizon, in the midst of which she lived, and she sighed, for no reason that she knew. She began idly picking at the blackberry-vines; there were no berries on them; then she put her little fingers on the berries of the deadly nightshade: "These look like nice berries," she said.

Old Woman Magoun, standing stiff and straight in the road, said nothing.

"They look good to eat," said Lily.

Old Woman Magoun still said nothing, but she looked up into the ineffable blue of the sky, over which spread at intervals great white clouds shaped like wings.

Lily picked some of the deadly nightshade berries and ate them. "Why, they are real sweet," said she. "They are nice." She picked some more and ate them.

Presently her grandmother spoke. "Come," she said, "it is time we were going. I guess you have set long enough."

Lily was still eating the berries when she slipped down from the wall and followed her grandmother obediently up the road.

Before they reached home, Lily complained of being very thirsty. She stopped and made a little cup of a leaf and drank long at a mountain brook. "I am dreadful dry, but it hurts me to swallow," she said to her grandmother when she stopped drinking and joined the old woman waiting for her in the road. Her grandmother's face seemed strangely dim to her. She took hold of Lily's hand as they went on. "My stomach burns," said Lily, presently. "I want some more water."

"There is another brook a little farther on," said Old Woman Magoun, in a dull voice.

When they reached that brook, Lily stopped and drank again, but she whimpered a little over her difficulty in swallowing. "My stomach burns, too," she said, walking on, "and my throat is so dry, grandma." Old Woman Magoun held Lily's hand more tightly. "You hurt me holding my hand so tight, grandma," said Lily, looking up at her grandmother, whose face she seemed to see through a mist, and the old woman loosened her grasp.

When at last they reached home, Lily was very ill. Old Woman Magoun put her on her own bed in the little bedroom out of the kitchen. Lily lay there and moaned, and Sally Jinks came in.

"Why, what ails her?" she asked. "She looks feverish."

Lily unexpectedly answered for herself. "I ate some sour apples and drank some milk," she moaned.

"Sour apples and milk are dreadful apt to hurt anybody," said Sally Jinks. She told several people on her way home that Old Woman Magoun was dreadful careless to let Lily eat such things.

Meanwhile Lily grew worse. She suffered cruelly from the burning in her stomach, the vertigo, and the deadly nausea. "I am so sick, I am so sick, grandma," she kept moaning. She could no longer see her grandmother as she bent over her, but she could hear her talk.

Old Woman Magoun talked as Lily had never heard her talk before, as nobody had ever heard her talk before. She spoke from the depths of her soul; her voice was as tender as the coo of a dove, and it was grand and exalted. "You'll feel better very soon, little Lily," said she.

"I am so sick, grandma."

"You will feel better very soon, and then—"

"I am sick."

"You shall go to a beautiful place."

Lily moaned.

"You shall go to a beautiful place," the old woman went on.

"Where?" asked Lily, groping feebly with her cold little hands. Then she moaned again.

"A beautiful place, where the flowers grow tall."

"What color? Oh, grandma, I am so sick."

"A blue color," replied the old woman. Blue was Lily's favorite color. "A beautiful blue color, and as tall as your knees, and the flowers always stay there, and they never fade."

"Not if you pick them, grandma? Oh!"

"No, not if you pick them; they never fade, and they are so sweet you can smell them a mile off; and there are birds that sing, and all the roads have gold stones in them, and the stone walls are made of gold."

"Like the ring grandpa gave you? I am so sick, grandma."

"Yes, gold like that. And all the houses are built of silver and gold, and the people all have wings, so when they get tired walking they can fly, and—"

"I am so sick, grandma."

"And all the dolls are alive," said Old Woman Magoun. "Dolls like yours can run, and talk, and love you back again."

Lily had her poor old rag doll in bed with her, clasped close to her agonized little heart. She tried very hard with her eyes, whose pupils were so dilated they looked black, to see her grandmother's face when she said that, but she could not. "It is dark," she moaned, feebly.

"There where you are going it is always light," said the grandmother, "and the commonest things shine like that breastpin Mrs. Lawyer Mason had on to-day."

Lily moaned pitifully, and said something incoherent. Delirium was commencing. Presently she sat straight up in bed and raved; but even then her grandmother's wonderful compelling voice had an influence over her.

"You will come to a gate with all the colors of the rainbow," said her grandmother; "and it will open, and you will go right in and walk up the gold street, and cross the field where the blue flowers come up to your knees, until you find your mother, and she will take you home where you are going to live. She has a little white room all ready for you, white curtains at the windows, and a little white looking-glass, and when you look in it you will see—"

"What will I see? I am so sick, grandma."

"You will see a face like yours, only it's an angel's; and there will be a little white bed, and you can lay down an' rest."

"Won't I be sick, grandma?" asked Lily. Then she moaned and babbled wildly, although she seemed to understand through it all what her grandmother said.

"No, you will never be sick anymore. Talkin' about sickness won't mean anything to you."

It continued. Lily talked on wildly and her grandmother's great voice of soothing never ceased, until the child fell into a deep sleep, or what resembled sleep; but she lay stiffly in that sleep, and a candle flashed before her eyes made no impression on them.

Then it was that Nelson Barry came. Jim Willis waited outside the door. When Nelson entered he found Old Woman Magoun on her knees beside the bed, weeping with dry eyes and a might of agony which fairly shook Nelson Barry, the degenerate of a fine old race.

"Is she sick?" he asked, in a hushed voice.

Old Woman Magoun gave another terrible sob, which sounded like the gasp of one dying.

"Sally Jinks said that Lily was sick from eating milk and sour apples," said Barry, in a tremulous voice. "I remember that her mother was very sick once from eating them."

Lily lay still, and her grandmother on her knees shook with her terrible sobs.

Suddenly Nelson Barry started. "I guess I had better go to Greenham for a doctor if she's as bad as that," he said. He went close to the bed and looked at the sick child. He gave a great start. Then he felt of her hands and reached down under the bedclothes for her little feet. "Her hands and feet are like ice," he cried out. "Good God! why didn't you send for some one—for me—before? Why, she's dying; she's almost gone!"

Barry rushed out and spoke to Jim Willis, who turned pale and came in and stood by the bedside.

"She's almost gone," he said, in a hushed whisper.

"There's no use going for the doctor, she'd be dead before he got here," said Nelson, and he stood regarding the passing child with a strange, sad face—unutterably sad, because of his incapability of the truest sadness.

"Poor little thing, she's past suffering, anyhow," said the other man, and his own face also was sad with a puzzled, mystified sadness.

Lily died that night. There was quite a commotion in Barry's Ford until after the funeral, it was all so sudden, and then everything went on as usual. Old Woman Magoun continued to live as she had done before. She supported herself by the produce of her tiny farm; she was very industrious, but people said that she was a trifle touched, since every time she went over the log bridge with her eggs or her garden vegetables to sell in Greenham, she carried with her, as one might have carried an infant, Lily's old rag doll.

1909

Pauline Elizabeth Hopkins 1859–1930

Pauline Elizabeth Hopkins was one of several pioneering post-Reconstruction black writers whose fiction sharpened awareness of political and racial issues central to African Americans at the turn of the twentieth century. Born in Portland, Maine, Hopkins moved to Boston with her parents, William and Sarah Allen Hopkins, during her childhood. Always possessing a strong desire to write, she won her first award at fifteen for an essay in a contest sponsored by the escaped slave, abolitionist, and novelist William Wells Brown (*Clotelle,* 1853). After graduating from Girls High School in Boston, she began to pursue a dual career in writing and theater; at the age of twenty, she composed and produced a musical drama entitled *Slaves' Escape: or the Underground Railroad.* Hopkins played a central character in this production, and subsequent theatrical performances led to her fame as "Boston's Favorite Soprano." Eventually, she left the stage to become a stenographer and public lecturer so that she might better support herself as a writer.

In her lifetime Hopkins produced four novels, a novella, a play, several short stories, and numerous works of nonfiction. *Contending Forces: A Romance Illustrative of Negro Life North and South,* published by the Colored Co-operative Publishing Company in 1900 and her most famous novel, is an ambitious story about several generations of a black family from their pre-Civil War Caribbean and North Carolina origins to their later life in the North. The narrative dramatizes essential American historical realities: slavery, Klan violence and lynching, hidden inter-racial blood lines, post-Reconstruction voting disenfranchisement, and job discrimination against blacks. What sets Hopkins apart from her male contemporaries is her outrage at black women's victimization, their sexual exploitation by white men. Hopkins had also to contend with the color prejudice in American society that exalted an ideal of beauty based on Anglo-Saxon features, fair skin, and light hair. In "A Dash for Liberty" Susan has extremely fair skin "veined by her master's blood," signaling the rape of black women during slavery at the same time as it suggests physical attractiveness. Susan's appearance exemplifies the cultural contradictions in which post-Civil War black writers were often caught in their efforts, as Hopkins described hers in the preface to *Contending Forces,* "to raise the stigma of degradation from the race."

A large part of the interest and significance of Hopkins's work lies in her use of popular fictional techniques to convey her political perspectives. She uses both the romance form and the conventions of domestic realism, juxtaposing imperiled heroines, concupiscent villains, and tragic misunderstandings with serene domestic scenes celebrating the pleasures of homemaking, marriage, love, and motherhood. Coincidence, a device that earmarks romance, is a central fixture in Hopkins's fiction, underscoring her efforts to point out the remarkable events—in her words "all the fire and romance"—in African American history. Hopkins's choice of the romance form places her in the tradition of African American writers initiated by Harriet Wilson's *Our Nig* in 1859 and continued by Hopkins's contemporaries Frances Ellen Watkins Harper, Amelia Johnson, and Emma Dunham Kelley. Her feminist insistence on women's instrumentality in history and her desire to empower her characters to regard themselves as actors rather than victims anticipates recent African American novelists such as Toni Morrison and Alice Walker.

The themes and fictional strategies of *Contending Forces* appear also in many of Hopkins's other works. "General Washington: A Christmas Story" portrays a homeless child who joins a street gang in the absence of family. Published in 1900, this piece suggests the timelessness of supposedly contemporary social problems such as domestic violence, homelessness, and gang activity. Like Hopkins's other fiction, this story fiercely argues against racism and classism even as it provides hope through the character Fairy, demonstrating that children can point the way toward racial harmony. Once again, Hopkins employs romance elements—an orphaned protagonist, an extreme coincidence, and a reprehensible character who redeems himself in the end.

Similar romance devices emerge in "As the Lord Lives, He Is One of Our Mother's Children." As in other nineteenth- and early twentieth-century American fiction, the plot hinges on an African American passing for white, a choice rendered dramatically necessary in this story by the racist legal system. Hopkins intertwines other historical realities, such as lynching, with notions of heroism and spiritual redemption. Gentleman Jim typifies Hopkins's characters, standing for African American courage and self-sacrifice. In all of her works Hopkins repeatedly asserts the need for racial equality.

Most of Hopkins's work, including three of her novels, was published in the *Colored American Magazine.* Established in 1900 as a forum for African American literary talent and the only monthly magazine of its sort at the time, the *Colored American Magazine* was a forerunner of present-day magazines addressed to black audiences. Hopkins was a founding staff member and one of its powerful editorial forces, working not only to showcase African American creative efforts but to strengthen racial solidarity. Both in her writings and in her editorial work she pursued the goals to which other post-Civil War black writers were also committed: furthering pride in African American history and creating respect for the intelligence and dignity of the race.

Jane Campbell
Purdue University, Calumet

PRIMARY WORKS

Contending Forces: A Romance Illustrative of Negro Life North and South, 1900, reprint 1988; *The Magazine Novels: Hagar's Daughter, A Story of Southern Caste Prejudice,* 1902; *Winona: A Tale of Negro Life in the South and Southwest,* 1902; *Of One Blood, or, the Hidden Self,* 1903, reprint 1988; *Short Fiction by Black Women: 1900–1920* [reprints of most stories], 1991; "Pauline Elizabeth Hopkins," in *The Roots of African-American Drama: A Collection of Early Plays, 1858–1938,* ed. Leo Hamalian and Robert Latham, 1991.

A Dash for Liberty

[Founded on an article written by Col. T. W. Higginson, for the *Atlantic Monthly,* June 1861.]

"So, Madison, you are bound to try it?"

"Yes, sir," was the respectful reply.

There was silence between the two men for a space, and Mr. Dickson drove his horse to the end of the furrow he was making and returned slowly to the starting point, and the sombre figure awaiting him.

"Do I not pay you enough, and treat you well?" asked the farmer as he halted.

"Yes, sir."

"Then why not stay here and let well enough alone?"

"Liberty is worth nothing to me while my wife is a slave."

"We will manage to get her to you in a year or two."

The man smiled and sadly shook his head. "A year or two would mean forever, situated as we are, Mr. Dickson. It is hard for you to understand; you white men are all alike where you are called upon to judge a Negro's heart," he continued bitterly. "Imagine yourself in my place; how would you feel? The relentless heel of oppression in the States will have ground my rights as a husband into the dust, and have driven Susan to despair in that time. A white man may take up arms to defend a bit of property; but a black man has no right to his wife, his liberty or his life against his master! This makes me low-spirited, Mr. Dickson, and I have determined to return to Virginia for my wife. My feelings are centred in the idea of liberty," and as he spoke he stretched his arms toward the deep blue of the Canadian sky in a magnificent gesture. Then with a deep-drawn breath that inflated his mighty chest, he repeated the word: "Liberty! I think of it by day and dream of it by night; and I shall only taste it in all its sweetness when Susan shares it with me."

Madison was an unmixed African, of grand physique, and one of the handsomest of his race. His dignified, calm and unaffected bearing marked him as a leader among his fellows. His features bore the stamp of genius. His firm step and piercing eye attracted the attention of all who met him. He had arrived in Canada along with many other fugitives during the year 1840, and being a strong, able-bodied man, and a willing worker, had sought and obtained employment on Mr. Dickson's farm.

After Madison's words, Mr. Dickson stood for some time in meditative silence.

"Madison," he said at length, "there's desperate blood in your veins, and if you get back there and are captured, you'll do desperate deeds."

"Well, put yourself in my place: I shall be there single-handed. I have a wife whom I love, and whom I will protect. I hate slavery, I hate the laws that make my country a nursery for it. Must I be denied the right of aggressive defense against those who would overpower and crush me by superior force?"

"I understand you fully, Madison; it is not your defense but your rashness that I fear. Promise me that you will be discreet, and not begin an attack." Madison hesitated. Such a promise seemed to him like surrendering a part of those individual rights for which he panted. Mr. Dickson waited. Presently the Negro said significantly: "I promise not to be indiscreet."

There were tears in the eyes of the kind-hearted farmer as he pressed Madison's hand.

"God speed and keep you and the wife you love; may she prove worthy."

In a few days Madison received the wages due him, and armed with tiny saws and files to cut a way to liberty, if captured, turned his face toward the South.

It was late in the fall of 1840 when Madison found himself again at home in the fair Virginia State. The land was blossoming into ripe maturity, and the smiling fields lay waiting for the harvester.

The fugitive, unable to travel in the open day, had hidden himself for three weeks in the shadow of the friendly forest near his old home, filled with hope and fear, unable to obtain any information about the wife he hoped to rescue from slavery. After weary days and nights, he had reached the most perilous part of his mission. Tonight there would be no moon and the clouds threatened a storm; to his listening ears the rising wind bore the sound of laughter and singing. He drew back into the deepest shadow. The words came distinctly to his ears as the singers neared his hiding place.

> All dem purty gals will be dar,
>   Shuck dat corn before you eat.
> Dey will fix it fer us rare,
>   Shuck dat corn before you eat.
> I know dat supper will be big,
>   Shuck dat corn before you eat.
> I think I smell a fine roast pig,
>   Shuck dat corn before you eat.
> Stuff dat coon an' bake him down,
> I spec some niggers dar from town.
>   Shuck dat corn before you eat.
> Please cook dat turkey nice an' brown.
> By de side of dat turkey I'll be foun',
>   Shuck dat corn before you eat.

"Don't talk about dat turkey; he'll be gone before we git dar."

"He's talkin', ain't he?"

"Las' time I shucked corn, turkey was de toughes' meat I eat fer many a day; you's got to have teef sharp lak a saw to eat it."

"S'pose you ain't got no teef, den what you gwine ter do?"

"Why ef you ain't got no teef you muss gum it!"

"Ha, ha, ha!"

Madison glided in and out among the trees, listening until he was sure that it was a gang going to a corn-shucking, and he resolved to join it, and get, if possible, some news of Susan. He came out upon the highway, and as the company reached his hiding place, he fell into the ranks and joined in the singing. The darkness hid his identity from the company while he learned from their conversation the important events of the day.

On they marched by the light of weird, flaring pine knots, singing their merry cadences, in which the noble minor strains habitual to Negro music, sounded the depths of sadness, glancing off in majestic harmony, that touched the very gates of paradise in suppliant prayer.

It was close to midnight; the stars had disappeared and a steady rain was falling when, by a circuitous route, Madison reached the mansion where he had learned that his wife was still living. There were lights in the windows. Mirth at the great house kept company with mirth at the quarters.

The fugitive stole noiselessly under the fragrant magnolia trees and paused, asking himself what he should do next. As he stood there he heard the hoof-beats of the mounted patrol, far in the distance, die into silence. Cautiously he drew near the house and crept around to the rear of the building directly beneath the window of his wife's sleeping closet. He swung himself up and tried it; it yielded to his touch. Softly he raised the sash, and softly he crept into the room. His foot struck against an object and swept it to the floor. It fell with a loud crash. In an instant the door opened. There was a rush of feet, and Madison stood at bay. The house was aroused; lights were brought.

"I knowed 'twas him!" cried the overseer in triumph. "I heern him a-gettin' in the window, but I kept dark till he knocked my gun down; then I grabbed him! I knowed this room'd trap him ef we was patient about it."

Madison shook his captor off and backed against the wall. His grasp tightened on the club in his hand; his nerves were like steel, his eyes flashed fire.

"Don't kill him," shouted Judge Johnson, as the overseer's pistol gleamed in the light. "Five hundred dollars for him alive!"

With a crash, Madison's club descended on the head of the nearest man; again, and yet again, he whirled it around, doing frightful execution each time it fell. Three of the men who had responded to the overseer's cry for help were on the ground, and he himself was sore from many wounds before, weakened by loss of blood, Madison finally succumbed.

The brig "Creole" lay at the Richmond dock taking on her cargo of tobacco, hemp, flax and slaves. The sky was cloudless, and the blue waters rippled but slightly under the faint breeze. There was on board the confusion incident to departure. In the hold and on deck men were hurrying to and fro, busy and excited, making the final preparations for the voyage. The slaves came aboard in two gangs: first the men, chained like cattle, were marched to their quarters in the hold; then came the women to whom more freedom was allowed.

In spite of the blue sky and the bright sunlight that silvered the water the scene was indescribably depressing and sad. The procession of gloomy-faced men and weeping women seemed to be descending into a living grave.

The captain and the first mate were standing together at the head of the gangway as the women stepped aboard. Most were very plain and bore the marks of servitude, a few were neat and attractive in appearances; but one was a woman whose great beauty immediately attracted attention; she was an octoroon.[1] It was a tradition

[1]An archaic term for someone whose great-grandparent is African American. Susan is thus one-eighth African American.

that her grandfather had served in the Revolutionary War, as well as in both Houses of Congress. That was nothing, however, at a time when the blood of the proudest F. F. V.'s was freely mingled with that of the African slaves on their plantations. Who wonders that Virginia has produced great men of color from among the exbondsmen, or, that illustrious black men proudly point to Virginia as a birthplace? Posterity rises to the plane that their ancestors bequeath, and the most refined, the wealthiest and the most intellectual whites of that proud State have not hesitated to amalgamate with the Negro.

"What a beauty!" exclaimed the captain as the line of women paused a moment opposite him.

"Yes," said the overseer in charge of the gang. "She's as fine a piece of flesh as I have had in trade for many a day."

"What's the price?" demanded the captain.

"Oh, way up. Two or three thousand. She's a lady's maid, well-educated, and can sing and dance. We'll get it in New Orleans. Like to buy?"

"You don't suit my pile," was the reply, as his eyes followed the retreating form of the handsome octoroon. "Give her a cabin to herself; she ought not to herd with the rest," he continued, turning to the mate.

He turned with a meaning laugh to execute the order.

The "Creole" proceeded slowly on her way towards New Orleans. In the men's cabin, Madison Monroe lay chained to the floor and heavily ironed. But from the first moment on board ship he had been busily engaged in selecting men who could be trusted in the dash for liberty that he was determined to make. The miniature files and saws which he still wore concealed in his clothing were faithfully used in the darkness of night. The man was at peace, although he had caught no glimpse of the dearly loved Susan. When the body suffers greatly, the strain upon the heart becomes less tense, and a welcome calmness had stolen over the prisoner's soul.

On the ninth day out the brig encountered a rough sea, and most of the slaves were sick, and therefore not watched with very great vigilance. This was the time for action, and it was planned that they should rise that night. Night came on; the first watch was summoned; the wind was blowing high. Along the narrow passageway that separated the men's quarters from the women's, a man was creeping.

The octoroon lay upon the floor of her cabin, apparently sleeping, when a shadow darkened the door, and the captain stepped into the room, casting bold glances at the reclining figure. Profound silence reigned. One might have fancied one's self on a deserted vessel, but for the sound of an occasional footstep on the deck above, and the murmur of voices in the opposite hold.

She lay stretched at full length with her head resting upon her arm, a position that displayed to the best advantage the perfect symmetry of her superb figure; the dim light of a lantern played upon the long black ringlets, finely-chiselled mouth and well-rounded chin, upon the marbled skin veined by her master's blood,—representative of two races, to which did she belong?

For a moment the man gazed at her in silence; then casting a glance around him, he dropped upon one knee and kissed the sleeping woman full upon the mouth.

With a shriek the startled sleeper sprang to her feet. The woman's heart stood still with horror; she recognized the intruder as she dashed his face aside with both hands.

"None of that, my beauty," growled the man, as he reeled back with an oath, and then flung himself forward and threw his arm about her slender waist. "Why did you think you had a private cabin, and all the delicacies of the season? Not to behave like a young catamount, I warrant you."

The passion of terror and desperation lent the girl such strength that the man was forced to relax his hold slightly. Quick as a flash, she struck him a stinging blow across the eyes, and as he staggered back, she sprang out of the doorway, making for the deck with the evident intention of going overboard.

"God have mercy!" broke from her lips as she passed the men's cabin, closely followed by the captain.

"Hold on, girl; we'll protect you!" shouted Madison, and he stooped, seized the heavy padlock which fastened the iron ring that encircled his ankle to the iron bar, and stiffening the muscles, wrenched the fastening apart, and hurled it with all his force straight at the captain's head.

His aim was correct. The padlock hit the captain not far from the left temple. The blow stunned him. In a moment Madison was upon him and had seized his weapons, another moment served to handcuff the unconscious man.

"If the fire of Heaven were in my hands, I would throw it at these cowardly whites. Follow me: it is liberty or death!" he shouted as he rushed for the quarter-deck. Eighteen others followed him, all of whom seized whatever they could wield as weapons.

The crew were all on deck; the three passengers were seated on the companion smoking. The appearance of the slaves all at once completely surprised the whites.

So swift were Madison's movements that at first the officers made no attempt to use their weapons; but this was only for an instant. One of the passengers drew his pistol, fired, and killed one of the blacks. The next moment he lay dead upon the deck from a blow with a piece of a capstan bar in Madison's hand. The fight then became general, passengers and crew taking part.

The first and second mates were stretched out upon the deck with a single blow each. The sailors ran up the rigging for safety, and in short time Madison was master of the "Creole."

After his accomplices had covered the slaver's deck, the intrepid leader forbade the shedding of more blood. The sailors came down to the deck, and their wounds were dressed. All the prisoners were heavily ironed and well guarded except the mate, who was to navigate the vessel; with a musket doubly charged pointed at his breast, he was made to swear to take the brig into a British port.

By one splendid and heroic stroke, the daring Madison had not only gained his own liberty, but that of one hundred and thirty-four others.

The next morning all the slaves who were still fettered, were released, and the cook was ordered to prepare the best breakfast that the stores would permit; this was to be a fête in honor of the success of the revolt and as a surprise to the females, whom the men had not yet seen.

As the women filed into the captain's cabin, where the meal was served, weeping, singing and shouting over their deliverance, the beautiful octoroon with one wild, half-frantic cry of joy sprang towards the gallant leader.

"Madison!"

"My God! Susan! My wife!"

She was locked to his breast; she clung to him convulsively. Unnerved at last by the revulsion to more than relief and ecstacy, she broke into wild sobs, while the astonished company closed around them with loud hurrahs.

Madison's cup of joy was filled to the brim. He clasped her to him in silence, and humbly thanked Heaven for its blessing and mercy.

The next morning the "Creole" landed at Nassau, New Providence, where the slaves were offered protection and hospitality.

Every act of oppression is a weapon for the oppressed. Right is a dangerous instrument; woe to us if our enemy wields it.

1901

As the Lord Lives, He Is One of Our Mother's Children

It was Saturday afternoon in a large Western town, and the Rev. Septimus Stevens sat in his study writing down the headings for his Sunday sermon. It was slow work; somehow the words would not flow with their usual ease, although his brain was teeming with ideas. He had written for his heading at the top of the sheet these words for a text: "As I live, he is one of our mother's children." It was to be a great effort on the Negro question, and the reverend gentleman, with his New England training, was in full sympathy with his subject. He had jotted down a few headings under it, when he came to a full stop; his mind simply refused to work. Finally, with a sigh, he opened the compartment in his desk where his sermons were packed and began turning over those old creations in search of something suitable for the morrow.

Suddenly the whistles in all directions began to blow wildly. The Rev. Septimus hurried to the window, threw it open and leaned out, anxious to learn the cause of the wild clamor. Could it be another of the terrible "cave-ins," that were the terror of every mining district? Men were pouring out of the mines as fast as they could come up. The crowds which surged through the streets night and day were rushing to meet them. Hundreds of policemen were about; each corner was guarded by a squad commanded by a sergeant. The police and the mob were evidently working together. Tramp, tramp, on they rushed; down the serpentine boulevard for nearly two miles they went swelling like an angry torrent. In front of the open window where stood the white-faced clergyman they paused. A man mounted the empty barrel and harangued the crowd: "I am from Dover City, gentlemen, and I have come here today to assist you in teaching the blacks a lesson. I have killed a nigger before," he yelled, "and in revenge of the wrong wrought upon you and yours I am willing to kill again. The only way you can teach these niggers a lesson is to go to the jail and lynch these men as an object lesson. String them up! That is the only thing to do. Kill them, string them up, lynch them! I will lead you. On to the prison and lynch Jones and Wilson, the black fiends!" With a hoarse shout, in which were mingled cries like the screams of enraged hyenas and the snarls of tigers, they rushed on.

Nora, the cook, burst open the study door, pale as a sheet, and dropped at the minister's feet. "Mother of God!" she cried, "and is it the end of the wurruld?"

On the maddened men rushed from north, south, east and west, armed with everything from a brick to a horse-pistol. In the melee a man was shot down. Somebody planted a long knife in the body of a little black newsboy for no apparent reason. Every now and then a Negro would be overwhelmed somewhere on the outskirts of the crowd and left beaten to a pulp. Then they reached the jail and battered in the door.

The solitary watcher at the window tried to move, but could not; terror had stricken his very soul, and his white lips moved in articulate prayer. The crowd surged back. In the midst was only one man; for some reason, the other was missing. A rope was knotted about his neck—charged with murder, himself about to be murdered. The hands which drew the rope were too swift, and, half-strangled, the victim fell. The crowd halted, lifted him up, loosened the rope and let the wretch breathe.

He was a grand man—physically—black as ebony, tall, straight, deep-chested, every fibre full of that life so soon to be quenched. Lucifer, just about to be cast out of heaven, could not have thrown around a glance of more scornful pride. What might not such a man have been, if—but it was too late. "Run fair, boys," said the prisoner, calmly, "run fair! You keep up your end of the rope and I'll keep up mine."

The crowd moved a little more slowly, and the minister saw the tall form "keeping up" its end without a tremor of hesitation. As they neared the telegraph pole, with its outstretched arm, the watcher summoned up his lost strength, grasped the curtain and pulled it down to shut out the dreadful sight. Then came a moment of ominous silence. The man of God sank upon his knees to pray for the passing soul. A thousand-voiced cry of brutal triumph arose in cheers for the work that had been done, and curses and imprecations, and they who had hunted a man out of life hurried off to hunt for gold.

To and fro on the white curtain swung the black silhouette of what had been a man.

For months the minister heard in the silence of the night phantom echoes of those frightful voices, and awoke, shuddering, from some dream whose vista was closed by that black figure swinging in the air.

About a month after this happening, the rector was returning from a miner's cabin in the mountains where a child lay dying. The child haunted him; he thought of his own motherless boy, and a fountain of pity overflowed in his heart. He had dismounted and was walking along the road to the ford at the creek which just here cut the path fairly in two.

The storm of the previous night had refreshed all nature and had brought out the rugged beauty of the landscape in all its grandeur. The sun had withdrawn his last dazzling rays from the eastern highlands upon which the lone traveler gazed, and now they were fast veiling themselves in purple night shadows that rendered them momentarily more grand and mysterious. The man of God stood a moment with uncovered head repeating aloud some lines from a great Russian poet:

"O Thou eternal One! whose presence bright
All space doth occupy, all motion guide;
Unchanged through time's all devastating flight;
Thou only God! There is no God beside
Being above all beings, Mighty One!
Whom none can comprehend and none explore."

Another moment passed in silent reverence of the All-Wonderful, before he turned to remount his horse and enter the waters of the creek. The creek was very much swollen and he found it hard to keep the ford. Just as he was midway the stream he saw something lying half in the water on the other bank. Approaching nearer he discovered it to be a man, apparently unconscious. Again dismounting, he tied his horse to a sapling, and went up to the inert figure, ready, like the Samaritan of old, to succor the wayside fallen. The man opened his deep-set eyes and looked at him keenly. He was gaunt, haggard and despairing, and soaking wet.

"Well, my man, what is the matter?" Rev. Mr. Stevens had a very direct way of going at things.

"Nothing," was the sullen response.

"Can't I help you? You seem ill. Why are you lying in the water?"

"I must have fainted and fallen in the creek," replied the man, answering the last question first. "I've tramped from Colorado hunting for work. I'm penniless, have no home, haven't had much to eat for a week, and now I've got a touch of your d—— mountain fever." He shivered as if with a chill, and smiled faintly.

The man, from his speech, was well educated, and in spite of his pitiful situation, had an air of good breeding, barring his profanity.

"What's your name?" asked Stevens, glancing him over sharply as he knelt beside the man and deftly felt his pulse and laid a cool hand on the fevered brow.

"Stone—George Stone."

Stevens got up. "Well, Stone, try to get on my horse and I'll take you to the rectory. My housekeeper and I together will manage to make you more comfortable."

So it happened that George Stone became a guest at the parsonage, and later, sexton of the church. In that gold-mining region, where new people came and went constantly and new excitements were things of everyday occurrence, and new faces as plenty as old ones, nobody asked or cared where the new sexton came from. He did his work quietly and thoroughly, and quite won Nora's heart by his handy ways about the house. He had a room under the eaves, and seemed thankful and content. Little Flip, the rector's son, took a special liking to him, and he, on his side, worshipped the golden-haired child and was never tired of playing with him and inventing things for his amusement.

"The reverend sets a heap by the boy," he said to Nora one day in reply to her accusation that he spoiled the boy and there was no living with him since Stone's advent. "He won't let me thank him for what he's done for me, but he can't keep me from loving the child."

One day in September, while passing along the street, Rev. Stevens had his attention called to a flaming poster on the side of a fence by the remarks of a crowd of men near him. He turned and read it:

$1,500 REWARD!

"The above reward will be paid for information leading to the arrest of 'Gentleman Jim,' charged with complicity in the murder of Jerry Mason. This nigger is six feet, three inches tall, weight one hundred and sixty pounds. He escaped from jail when his pal was lynched two months ago by a citizen's committee. It is thought that he is in the mountains, etc. He is well educated, and might be taken for a white man. Wore, when last seen, blue jumper and overalls and cowhide boots."

He read it the second time, and he was dimly conscious of seeing, like a vision in the brain, a man playing about the parsonage with little Flip.

"I knowed him. I worked a spell with him over in Lone Tree Gulch before he got down on his luck," spoke a man at his side who was reading the poster with him. "Jones and him was two of the smartest and peaceablest niggers I ever seed. But Jerry Mason kinder sot on 'em both; never could tell why, only some white men can't 'bide a nigger eny mo' than a dog can a cat; it's a natural antiperthy. I'm free to say the niggers seemed harmless, but you can't tell what a man'll do when his blood's up."

He turned to the speaker. "What will happen if they catch him?"

"Lynch him sure; there's been a lot of trouble over there lately. I wouldn't give a toss-up for him if they get their hands on him once more."

Rev. Stevens pushed his way through the crowd, and went slowly down the street to the church. He found Stone there sweeping and dusting. Saying that he wanted to speak with him, he led the way to the study. Facing around upon him suddenly, Stevens said, gravely: "I want you to tell me the truth. Is your real name 'Stone,' and are you a Negro?"

A shudder passed over Stone's strong frame, then he answered, while his eyes never left the troubled face before him, "I am a Negro, and my name is not Stone."

"You said that you had tramped from Colorado."

"I hadn't. I was hiding in the woods; I had been there a month ago. I lied to you."

"Is it all a lie?"

Stone hesitated, and then said: "I was meaning to tell you the first night, but somehow I couldn't. I was afraid you'd turn me out; and I was sick and miserable—"

"Tell me the truth now."

"I will; I'll tell you the God's truth."

He leaned his hand on the back of a chair to steady himself; he was trembling violently. "I came out West from Wilmington, North Carolina, Jones and I together. We were both college men and chums from childhood. All our savings were in the business we had at home when the leading men of the town conceived the idea of driving the Negroes out, and the Wilmington tragedy began.[1] Jones was unmarried, but I lost wife and children that night—burned to death when the mob fired our home. When we got out here we took up claims in the mountains. They were a rough crowd after we struck pay dirt, but Jones and I kept to ourselves and got along all right until Mason joined the crowd. He was from Wilmington; knew us, and took delight in tormenting us. He was a fighting man, but we wouldn't let him push us into trouble."

"You didn't quarrel with him, then?"

The minister gazed at Stone keenly. He seemed a man to trust. "Yes, I did. We didn't want trouble, but we couldn't let Mason rob us. We three had hot words before a big crowd; that was all there was to it that night. In the morning, Mason lay dead upon our claim. He'd been shot by some one. My partner and I were arrested, brought to this city and lodged in the jail over there. Jones was lynched! God, can I ever forget that hooting, yelling crowd, and the terrible fight to get away! Somehow I did it—you know the rest."

"Stone, there's a reward for you, and a description of you as you were the night I found you."

[1]A massacre of African Americans in Wilmington, North Carolina, in 1898.

Gentleman Jim's face was ashy. "I'll never be taken alive. They'll kill me for what I never did!"

"Not unless I speak. I am in sore doubt what course to take. If I give you up the Vigilantes will hang you."

"I'm a lost man," said the Negro, helplessly, "but I'll never be taken alive."

Stevens walked up and down the room once or twice. It was a human life in his hands. If left to the law to decide, even then in this particular case the Negro stood no chance. It was an awful question to decide. One more turn up and down the little room and suddenly stopping, he flung himself upon his knees in the middle of the room, and raising his clasped hands, cried aloud for heavenly guidance. Such a prayer as followed, the startled listener had never before heard anywhere. There was nothing of rhetorical phrases, nothing of careful thought in the construction of sentences, it was the outpouring of a pure soul asking for help from its Heavenly Father with all the trustfulness of a little child. It came in a torrent, a flood; it wrestled mightily for the blessing it sought. Rising to his feet when his prayer was finished, Rev. Stevens said, "Stone,—you are to remain Stone, you know—it is best to leave things as they are. Go back to work."

The man raised his bowed head.

"You mean you're not going to give me up?"

"Stay here till the danger is past; then leave for other parts."

Stone's face turned red, then pale, his voice trembled and tears were in the gray eyes. "I can't thank you, Mr. Stevens, but if ever I get the chance you'll find me grateful."

"All right, Stone, all right," and the minister went back to his writing.

That fall the Rev. Septimus Stevens went to visit his old New England home—he and Flip. He was returning home the day before Thanksgiving, with his widowed mother, who had elected to leave old associations and take charge of her son's home. It was a dim-colored day.

Engineers were laying out a new road near a place of swamps and oozy ground and dead, wet grass, over-arched by leafless, desolate boughs. They were eating their lunch now, seated about on the trunks of fallen trees. The jokes were few, scarcely a pun seasoned the meal. The day was a dampener; that the morrow was a holiday did not kindle merriment.

Stone sat a little apart from the rest. He had left Rev. Stevens when he got this job in another state. They had voted him moody and unsociable long ago—a man who broods forever upon his wrongs is not a comfortable companion; he never gave any one a key to his moods. He shut himself up in his haunted room—haunted by memory—and no one interfered with him.

The afternoon brought a change in the weather. There was a strange hush, as if Nature were holding her breath. But it was as a wild beast holds its breath before a spring. Suddenly a little chattering wind ran along the ground. It was too weak to lift the sodden leaves, yet it made itself heard in some way, and grew stronger. It seemed dizzy, and ran about in a circle. There was a pale light over all, a brassy, yellow light, that gave all things a wild look. The chief of the party took an observation and said: "We'd better get home."

Stone lingered. He was paler, older.

The wind had grown vigorous now and began to tear angrily at the trees, twisting the saplings about with invisible hands. There was a rush and a roar that seemed to spread about in every direction. A tree was furiously uprooted and fell directly in front of him; Stone noticed the storm for the first time.

He looked about him in a dazed way and muttered, "He's coming on this train, he and the kid!"

The brassy light deepened into darkness. Stone went upon the railroad track, and stumbled over something that lay directly over it. It was a huge tree that the wind had lifted in its great strength and whirled over there like thistledown. He raised himself slowly, a little confused by the fall. He took hold of the tree mechanically, but the huge bulk would not yield an inch.

He looked about in the gathering darkness; it was five miles to the station where he might get help. His companions were too far on their way to recall, and there lay a huge mass, directly in the way of the coming train. He had no watch, but he knew it must be nearly six. Soon—very soon—upon the iron pathway, a great train, freighted with life, would dash around the curve to wreck and ruin! Again he muttered, "Coming on this train, he and the kid!" He pictured the faces of his benefactor and the little child, so like his own lost one, cold in death; the life crushed out by the cruel wheels. What was it that seemed to strike across the storm and all its whirl of sound—a child's laugh? Nay, something fainter still—the memory of a child's laugh. It was like a breath of spring flowers in the desolate winter—a touch of heart music amid the revel of the storm. A vision of other fathers with children climbing upon their knees, a soft babble of baby voices assailed him.

"God help me to save them!" he cried.

Again and again he tugged at the tree. It would not move. Then he hastened and got an iron bar from among the tools. Again he strove—once—twice—thrice. With a groan the nearest end gave way. Eureka! If only his strength would hold out. He felt it ebbing slowly from him, something seemed to clutch at his heart; his head swam. Again and yet again he exerted all his strength. There came a prolonged shriek that awoke the echoes. The train was coming. The tree was moving! It was almost off the other rail. The leafless trees seemed to enfold him—to hold him with skeleton arms. "Oh, God save them!" he gasped. "Our times are in Thy hand!"

Something struck him a terrible blow. The agony was ended. Stone was dead.

Rev. Stevens closed his eyes, with a deadly faintness creeping over him, when he saw how near the trainload of people had been to destruction. Only God had saved them at the eleventh hour through the heroism of Stone, who lay dead upon the track, the life crushed out of him by the engine. An inarticulate thanksgiving rose to his lips as soft and clear came the sound of distant church bells, calling to weekly prayer, like "horns of Elfland softly blowing."

Sunday, a week later, Rev. Septimus Stevens preached the greatest sermon of his life. They had found the true murderer of Jerry Mason, and Jones and Gentleman Jim were publicly exonerated by a repentant community.

On this Sunday Rev. Stevens preached the funeral sermon of Gentleman Jim. The church was packed to suffocation by a motley assemblage of men in all stages of dress and undress, but there was sincerity in their hearts as they listened to the preacher's burning words: "As the Lord lives, he is one of our mother's children."

1903

A Sheaf of Poetry by Late-Nineteenth-Century American Women

Except Emily Dickinson, whose assumed "difference" acts as a *cordon sanitaire* separating her from her peers, nineteenth-century women poets are the most maligned group of writers in American literary history. Defining themselves in terms of their resistance to nineteenth-century genteel poetics, early modernists treated nineteenth-century American poetry globally as an overly polite or, worse, excessively sentimental literature. Although the prestige of male poets such as Henry Wadsworth Longfellow and Oliver Wendell Holmes was diminished through this maneuver, their devaluation was slight in comparison to that suffered by their female peers. Made irresistibly comic by Twain's Emmeline Grangerford in *Huckleberry Finn,* the figure of the nineteenth-century "poetess" came to epitomize the worst of nineteenth-century versifying. Sentimental, foolish, addicted to clichés, and morbidly obsessed with death, the "poetess" joined the "old maid" and the "blue-stocking" as a butt for popular humor and a target for sometimes savage critical attack.

In recent years interest in nineteenth-century women's poetry has revived but focused mainly on poets from the first half of the century, such as Lydia Sigourney and Frances Osgood, who, like Harriet Beecher Stowe, explored the power of sentiment—or feeling—to sustain familial bonds and motivate socially progressive change. With a few exceptions (notably, Frances Ellen Watkins Harper and Emma Lazarus), little attention has been paid to poets writing after 1865. Though welcome, this new interest has continued to reinforce the critical misperception that nineteenth-century American women's poetry is the homogeneous product of northeastern white women writing in the "sentimental" tradition. Nothing could be farther from the truth. By the end of the nineteenth century, women poets came from every ethnic group, every walk of life, and every region of the country. What is more, they brought their differences with them.

To understand the development of late-nineteenth-century American women's poetry, one should turn first to the major venues in which it was marketed—newspapers and periodicals. Despised by the early modernists, who favored the avant-garde "little magazines," these venues were not without their virtues. In particular, they provided open spaces where new poets were all but guaranteed a hearing. Since, it seems, every special-interest group in society had its own newspaper or journal, from labor groups and Spiritualists to new immigrant populations and individual Native American tribes, the very diversity of these outlets also ensured that there would be diversity among contributors. If these media published a good deal of poorly crafted poetry, they also made poetry a highly accessible art form. Any woman (the message went) could write poetry; most women probably did.

Under such conditions, not surprisingly, serious women poets—as well as the Emmeline Grangerford variety—flourished. Taking advantage of the print media's rapacious need for fresh copy, these women filled the "poet's corner" of their local newspapers, as well as the better literary periodicals (*Harper's* and *Atlantic,* for instance), with their verse. For many of these women, as for Dickinson, poetry was a site for exploration and experimentation—not for reinforcing old truths. They used it as a vehicle by which to test possibilities for themselves and to address their social, political, and spiritual concerns, from matters of faith and doubt as in Thaxter's "Wherefore" and Piatt's "We Two" to those of desire and disenchantment as in Wilcox's "Her Prayer" and Jewett's "I Speak Your Name." Coming at the end of a century witnessing massive changes in women's social position and personal expectations, their poetry maps their evolution as emergent modern women or, as the nineteenth century itself put it, as "new women."

To bring together a sheaf of late-nineteenth-century American women's poetry is to bring together a group of very diverse voices. No selection this brief can possibly do justice to this diversity. However, certain myths about late-nineteenth-century American women's poetry—besides its homogeneity—can be laid to rest: the first and most important is that these writers were uniformly sentimental; the second, that their handling of poetic strategies was uniformly uninspired and conventional; and the third, often said of Dickinson herself, that all they wrote about was death (*pace* Emmeline).

It has been so taken for granted that nineteenth-century American women's writing is uniformly sentimental that even scholars seeking to retrieve it have spent most of their critical energy defending sentimentalism itself. Yet as Sarah Piatt's "His Mother's Way" suggests, many nineteenth-century women writers, especially in the latter part of the century, found sentimentalism problematic as a vehicle by which to hold families together or effect social change. Although the mother in this poem clearly has the high moral ground over her bullish mate (whose solution to the problem of the homeless is pistols and prison), her own power to affect him is radically undermined by her excessive reliance on tears—tears that, as her young son says, she sheds over "almost anything!" Given the way in which men are socialized *not* to feel—that a little boy tells this story is no accident—the mother's tears do not win sympathy for the tramp. Despite the inherent justice of her cause, they merely make her an object of contempt in her husband's eyes.

Along with critiquing the efficacy of excessive feeling, especially when isolated from other considerations (a modern parallel might be conservative responses to the "bleeding heart liberal"), Piatt's poem also suggests that by the second half of the century women had developed a good deal of irony about themselves and about the very capacity to feel with which they were socially identified. Poems such as Celia Thaxter's "In Kittery Churchyard," Piatt's "Shapes of a Soul" and "The Palace-Burner," Ella Wheeler Wilcox's "Illusion," and Reese's "Emily" and "Drought" all implicitly or explicitly use irony as a means of self-distancing. These are complex, sophisticated poems in which the speakers themselves approach their own emotional engagement suspiciously. As such, they are at the furthest remove from sentimentality.

If the uniform sentimentality of late-nineteenth-century American women's poetry turns out on closer inspection to be an unfair generalization, so does the charge that the poetry, like Emmeline Grangerford's, is badly or conventionally written. With her long line and fondness for catalogs, as well as for bombastic politics, Adah Menken distinguished herself as among Whitman's earliest and most vociferous disciples. Alice Dunbar-Nelson, the wife of the well-known African American poet Paul Laurence Dunbar, also experiments with free verse. Even when these poets used traditional forms, moreover, they did not necessarily treat them conventionally. On the contrary. By using multiple voices, fragmented narratives, and irregular and broken rhythms, Piatt, in particular, roughens the surface of her verse. An admirer of Robert Browning, Piatt made the human voice in conversation the basis for her art. Her inclusion of both direct and indirect dialogue, often in the same poem, roots her poetry in the social world of her day. Reese and Guiney also use rhythmic variations, including the use of enjambment and metrical substitutions, or, as in Guiney's beautiful and delicate "Charista Musing," blank verse, to disrupt the regularity of their poetry.

Finally, in terms of content, late-nineteenth-century women's poetry, far from being obsessed with death, turns out to be as diverse as the women who authored it. Born on a slave-holding plantation outside Lexington, Kentucky, in 1836 and marrying a northerner in 1861, Piatt, for instance, uses the Civil War as a dividing line between two worlds, two ways of life, both of which were profoundly alienating to her. Like Faulkner, but extending her consideration to the North as well as the South, she devotes much of her writing to an examination of how social corruption is passed from one generation to the next as, for example, in "The Palace-Burner" (on the Paris Commune, Europe's first experiment in communism), where the executed female communard—a woman who sacrificed her life for her political beliefs—becomes the measure of the bourgeois speaker's own moral failure as mother and citizen.

Lizette Woodworth Reese, also a southerner from a border state (Maryland), writes with profound nostalgia and a delicate love of the untouched. All but abandoning the social world, Reese turns her focus on nature and on "common things." Like Dickinson, her relation to natural beauty is so intense it appears, as in "Spring Ecstasy," to be orgasmic—an experience she both desires and flees. In the clarity of her language and restrained tone, Reese has probably been the most directly influential of these poets on later writers, sharing much in common with Frost, in particular.

Especially when compared to Reese, Menken and Wilcox illustrate the more radical possibilities open to nineteenth-century women poets. Born in Memphis, Tennessee, of Irish stock, Menken (née Ada McCord) was a celebrity figure—actress, poet, and participant in numerous scandals at home and abroad. Filled with boundless energy and characterized by a flamboyant style, her poetry simultaneously reflects her deep passion for life and her outrage at social injustice. Though in no way as extreme as Menken, Wilcox—a "flapper" before her time—was also an internationally known poet whose writing was touched by scandal. Much of her poetry seems staid by today's standards, but her *Poems of Passion* (1883) was notorious in its own day.

Striking differences also divide the four New England poets reprinted here. Writing from the very heart of the New England literary establishment, Thaxter is a mainstream meditative poet—her topics the traditional ones of love and death. If being at the "center" shapes Thaxter's content and approach, however, marginalization is no less shaping in the work of the other three—Jewett, a teacher of medieval literature at Wellesley College and a lesbian; Eastman, a Berkshire farm girl who married Dr. Charles Eastman (Ohiyesa) and spent much of her life in the Dakotas laboring among her husband's people; and Guiney, an Irish Roman Catholic, who finally left the United States altogether, returning spiritually and poetically as well as physically to Britain and to what she viewed as the wholeness of the past. In each case the individual poets' content and approach were determined by their differing social and political commitments. Nor is this any less true of E. Pauline Johnson (Tekahionwake), a Canadian Mohawk, who explicitly used her poetry to bridge the social and racial groups that were her biological legacy, or Dunbar-Nelson, who wrote from the position of the "new," post-Reconstruction, black woman.

Each poet represented in this sheaf

writes as much from her own personal subject position as she does from her position as social subject. As the poems indicate, by the last decade of the nineteenth century, the "new woman" had arrived—and she was a mercurial creature, given at times to passionate extremes yet, as in Sarah Cleghorn's "Behold the Lillies," not at all averse to making fun of herself. Taken together, these poems suggest that what modernity gave these women was the latitude to be many, very different women writing in many, very different ways.

Paula Bennett
Southern Illinois University at Carbondale

PRIMARY WORKS

Adah Menken, *Infelicia*, 1868; Celia Thaxter, *Poems*, 1872; Sarah M. B. Piatt, *A Woman's Poems*, 1871; *That New World and Other Poems*, 1879; *Dramatic Persons and Moods with Other New Poems*, 1880; E. Pauline Johnson, *Flint and Feather*, 1912; Louise Imogen Guiney, *Happy Ending*, 1909 (2nd ed. 1927).

Adah Menken 1835?–1868

Judith[1]

"Repent, or I will come unto thee quickly, and will fight thee with the sword of my mouth."

—REVELATION 2:16

I

Ashkelon is not cut off with the remnant of a valley.
Baldness dwells not upon Gaza.[2]
The field of the valley is mine, and it is clothed in verdure.
The steepness of Baal-perazim is mine;
And the Philistines spread themselves in the valley of Rephaim.[3]
They shall yet be delivered into my hands.
For the God of Battles has gone before me!
The sword of the mouth shall smite them to dust.
I have slept in the darkness—
But the seventh angel[4] woke me, and giving me a sword of flame,
points to the blood-ribbed cloud, that lifts his reeking head
above the mountain.
Thus am I the prophet.

[1]In the *Apocrypha* Judith saves her people from Nebuchadnezzar's forces by stealing into the camp of his general, Holofernes, and beheading him.
[2]Ashkelon and Gaza are two cities in southwest Palestine.
[3]Baal-perazim and the Valley of Rephaim are sites where David conquered the Philistines in II Samuel 5:18–25.
[4]See Revelation 10:7–11.

I see the dawn that heralds to my waiting soul the advent of power.
  Power that will unseal the thunders!
  Power that will give voice to graves!
  Graves of the living;
  Graves of the dying;
  Graves of the sinning;
  Graves of the loving;
  Graves of despairing;
And oh! graves of the deserted!
These shall speak, each as their voices shall be loosed.
And the day is dawning.

II

Stand back, ye Philistines!
Practice what ye preach to me;
I heed ye not, for I know ye all.
Ye are living burning lies, and profanation to the garments which with
  stately steps ye sweep your marble palaces.
Your palaces of Sin, around which the damning evidence of guilt
  hangs like a reeking vapor.
Stand back!
I would pass up the golden road of the world.
A place in the ranks awaits me.
I know that ye are hedged on the borders of my path.
Lie and tremble, for ye well know that I hold with iron grasp the
  battle axe.
Creep back to your dark tents in the valley.
Slouch back to your haunts of crime.
Ye do not know me, neither do ye see me.
But the sword of the mouth is unsealed, and ye coil yourselves in
  slime and bitterness at my feet.
I mix your jeweled heads, and your gleaming eyes, and your hissing
  tongues with the dust.
My garments shall bear no mark of ye.
When I shall return this sword to the angel, your foul blood will not
  stain its edge.
It will glimmer with the light of truth, and the strong arm shall rest.

III

Stand back!
I am no Magdalene waiting to kiss the hem of your garment.
It is mid-day.
See ye not what is written on my forehead?

I am Judith!
I wait for the head of my Holofernes!
Ere the last tremble of the conscious death-agony shall have shuddered, I will show it to ye with the long black hair clinging to the glazed eyes, and the great mouth opened in search of voice, and the strong throat all hot and reeking with blood, that will thrill me with wild unspeakable joy as it courses down my bare body and dabbles my cold feet!
My sensuous soul will quake with the burden of so much bliss.
Oh, what wild passionate kisses will I draw up from that bleeding mouth!
I will strangle this pallid throat of mine on the sweet blood!
I will revel in my passion.
At midnight I will feast on it in the darkness.
For it was that which thrilled its crimson tides of reckless passion through the blue veins of my life, and made them leap up in the wild sweetness of Love and agony of Revenge!
I am starving for this feast.
Oh forget not that I am Judith!
And I know where sleeps Holofernes.

1868

Celia Thaxter 1835–1894

In Kittery Churchyard[1]

"Mary, wife of Charles Chauncy, died April 23, 1758, in the 24th year of her age."

Crushing the scarlet strawberries in the grass,
I kneel to read the slanting stone. Alas!
How sharp a sorrow speaks! A hundred years
And more have vanished, with their smiles and tears,
Since here was laid, upon an April day,
Sweet Mary Chauncy in the grave away,—
A hundred years since here her lover stood
Beside her grave in such despairing mood,

[1]Kittery, a seacoast town on the Maine–New Hampshire border, settled in the late seventeenth century.

And yet from out the vanished past I hear
His cry of anguish sounding deep and clear,
And all my heart with pity melts, as though
To-day's bright sun were looking on his woe.
"Of such a wife, O righteous Heaven! bereft,
What joy for me, what joy on earth is left?
Still from my inmost soul the groans arise,
Still flow the sorrows ceaseless from mine eyes."
Alas, poor tortured soul! I look away
From the dark stone,—how brilliant shines the day!
A low wall, over which the roses shed
Their perfumed petals, shuts the quiet dead
Apart a little, and the tiny square
Stands in the broad and laughing field so fair,
And gay green vines climb o'er the rough stone wall,
And all about the wild birds flit and call,
And but a stone's throw southward, the blue sea
Rolls sparkling in and sings incessantly.
Lovely as any dream the peaceful place,
And scarcely changed since on her gentle face
For the last time on that sad April day
He gazed, and felt, for him, all beauty lay
Buried with her forever. Dull to him
Looked the bright world through eyes with tears so dim!
"I soon shall follow the same dreary way
That leads and opens to the coasts of day."
His only hope! But when slow time had dealt
Firmly with him and kindly, and he felt
The storm and stress of strong and piercing pain
Yielding at last, and he grew calm again,
Doubtless he found another mate before
He followed Mary to the happy shore!
But none the less his grief appeals to me
Who sit and listen to the singing sea
This matchless summer day, beside the stone
He made to echo with his bitter moan.
And in my eyes I feel the foolish tears
For buried sorrow, dead a hundred years!

1874

Wherefore

Black sea, black sky! A ponderous steamship driving
Between them, laboring westward on her way,

And in her path a trap of Death's contriving
  Waiting remorseless for its easy prey.

Hundreds of souls within her frame lie dreaming,
  Hoping and fearing, longing for the light:
With human life and thought and feeling teeming,
  She struggles onward through the starless night.

Upon her furnace fires fresh fuel flinging,
  The swarthy firemen grumble at the dust
Mixed with the coal—when suddenly upspringing,
  Swift through the smoke-stack like a signal thrust,

Flares a red flame, a dread illumination!
  A cry,—a tumult! Slowly to her helm
The vessel yields, 'mid shouts of acclamation,
  And joy and terror all her crew o'erwhelm;

For looming from the blackness drear before them
  Discovered is the iceberg—hardly seen,
Its ghastly precipices hanging o'er them,
  Its reddened peaks, with dreadful chasms between,

Ere darkness swallows it again! and veering
  Out of its track the brave ship onward steers,
Just grazing ruin. Trembling still, and fearing,
  Her grateful people melt in prayers and tears.

Is it a mockery, their profound thanksgiving?
  Another ship goes shuddering to her doom
Unwarned, that very night, with hopes as living
  With freight as precious, lost amid the gloom,

With not a ray to show the apparition
  Waiting to slay her, none to cry "Beware!"
Rushing straight onward headlong to perdition,
  And for her crew no time vouchsafed for prayer.

Could they have stormed Heaven's gate with anguished praying,
  It would not have availed a feather's weight
Against their doom. Yet were they disobeying
  No law of God, to beckon such a fate.

And do not tell me the Almighty Master
  Would work a miracle to save the one,
And yield the other up to dire disaster,
  By merely human justice thus outdone!

Vainly we weep and wrestle with our sorrow—
We cannot see his roads, they lie so broad:
But his eternal day knows no to-morrow,
And life and death are all the same with God.

1874

Sarah M. B. Piatt 1836–1919

Giving Back the Flower

So, because you chose to follow me into the subtle sadness of night,
And to stand in the half-set moon with the weird fall-light on your glimmering hair,
Till your presence hid all of the earth and all of the sky from my sight,
And to give me a little scarlet bud, that was dying of frost, to wear,

Say, must you taunt me forever, forever? You looked at my hand and you knew
That I was the slave of the Ring,[1] while you were as free as the wind is free.
When I saw your corpse in your coffin, I flung back your flower to you;
It was all of yours that I ever had; you may keep it, and—keep from me.

Ah? so God is your witness. Has God, then, no world to look after but ours?
May He not have been searching for that wild star, with trailing plumage, that flew
Far over a part of our darkness while we were there by the freezing flowers,
Or else brightening some planet's luminous rings, instead of thinking of you?

Or, if He was near us at all, do you think that He would sit listening there

[1]Her wedding ring.

Because you sang "Hear me, Norma,"[2] to a woman in jewels and lace,
While, so close to us, down in another street, in the wet, unlighted air,
There were children crying for bread and fire, and mothers who questioned His grace?

Or perhaps He had gone to the ghastly field where the fight had been that day,
To number the bloody stabs that were there, to look at and judge the dead;
Or else to the place full of fever and moans where the wretched wounded lay;
At least I do not believe that He cares to remember a word that you said.

So take back your flower, I tell you—of its sweetness I now have no need;
Yes, take back your flower down into the stillness and mystery to keep;
When you wake I will take it, and God, then, perhaps will witness indeed,
But go, now, and tell Death he must watch you, and not let you walk in your sleep.

1867

Shapes of a Soul

White with the starlight folded in its wings,
And nestling timidly against your love,
At this soft time of hushed and glimmering things,
You call my soul a dove, a snowy dove.

If I shall ask you in some shining hour,
When bees and odors through the clear air pass,
You'll say my soul buds as a small flush'd flower,
Far off, half hiding, in the old home-grass.

[2]Albeit inexactly, Piatt is quoting from the opera *Norma* (1831) by Vincenzo Bellini. Presumably, like the Druidic heroine of the opera, who carries on a secret liaison with the Roman proconsul of Britain, the speaker has taken a lover from among the enemy. The meeting narrated in the poem appears to occur in Washington, D.C., where Piatt and her husband spent time during the Civil War.

Ah, pretty names for pretty moods; and you,
Who love me, such sweet shapes as these can see;
But, take it from its sphere of bloom and dew,
And where will then your bird or blossom be?

Could you but see it, by life's torrid light,
Crouch in its sands and glare with fire-red wrath,
My soul would seem a tiger, fierce and bright
Among the trembling passions in its path.

And, could you sometimes watch it coil and slide,
And drag its colors through the dust a while,
And hiss its poison under-foot, and hide,
My soul would seem a snake—ah, do not smile!

Yet fiercer forms and viler it can wear;
No matter, though, when these are of the Past,
If as a lamb in the Good Shepherd's care
By the still waters it lie down at last.[1]

1867

The Palace-Burner[1]

A Picture in a Newspaper

She has been burning palaces. "To see
The sparks look pretty in the wind?" Well, yes—
And something more. But women brave as she
Leave much for cowards, such as I, to guess.

But this is old, so old that everything
Is ashes here—the woman and the rest.
Two years are—oh! so long. Now you may bring
Some newer pictures. You like this one best?

You wish that you had lived in Paris then?—
You would have loved to burn a palace, too?

[1]Piatt's point here is less that after death our sins will be forgiven than that the speaker's interlocutor (presumably her husband) will get what he wants (an "angel-wife") only when she is dead.

[1]A striking illustration of the execution of a *Petroleuse*—or "palace-burner," as the female members of the Paris Commune were called—appeared in *Harper's Weekly,* July 8, 1871. The principal speaker in the poem is a bourgeois mother, who is talking with her young son about this illustration.

But they had guns in France, and Christian men
  Shot wicked little Communists like you.

You would have burned the palace?—Just because
  You did not live in it yourself! Oh! why
Have I not taught you to respect the laws?
  You would have burned the palace—would not *I*?

Would I? Go to your play. Would I, indeed?
  I? Does the boy not know my soul to be
Languid and worldly, with a dainty need
  For light and music? Yet he questions me.

Can he have seen my soul more near than I?
  Ah! in the dusk and distance sweet she seems,
With lips to kiss away a baby's cry,
  Hands fit for flowers, and eyes for tears and dreams.

Can he have seen my soul? And could she wear
  Such utter life upon a dying face:
Such unappealing, beautiful despair:
  Such garments—soon to be a shroud—with grace?

Has she a charm so calm that it could breathe
  In damp, low places till some frightened hour;
Then start, like a fair, subtle snake, and wreathe
  A stinging poison with a shadowy power?

Would *I* burn palaces? The child has seen
  In this fierce creature of the Commune here,
So bright with bitterness and so serene,
  A being finer than my soul, I fear.

1872

We Two

God's will is—the bud of the rose for your hair,
  The ring for your hand and the pearl for your breast;
God's will is—the mirror that makes you look fair.
  No wonder you whisper: "God's will is the best."

But what if God's will were the famine, the flood?
  And were God's will the coffin shut down in your face?

And were God's will the worm in the fold of the bud,
Instead of the picture, the light, and the lace?

Were God's will the arrow that flieth by night,
Were God's will the pestilence walking by day,[1]
The clod in the valley,[2] the rock on the hight—
I fancy "God's will" would be harder to say.

God's will is—your own will. What honor have you
For having your own will, awake or asleep?
Who praises the lily for keeping the dew,
When the dew is so sweet for the lily to keep?

God's will unto me is not music or wine.
With helpless reproaching, with desolate tears
God's will I resist, for God's will is divine;
And I—shall be dust to the end of my years.

God's will is—not mine. Yet one night I shall lie
Very still at his feet, where the stars may not shine.
"Lo! I am well pleased"[3] I shall hear from the sky;
Because—it is God's will I do, and not mine.

1874

His Mother's Way[1]

"My Mamma just knows how to cry
About an old glove or a ring,
Or even a stranger going by
The gate, or—almost anything!

"She cried till both her eyes were red
About him, too. (I saw her, though!)

[1]Psalm 91:5-6. "Thou shalt not be afraid for the terror by night, nor for the arrow that flieth by day, nor the pestilence that stalks in the darkness, nor the destruction that wastes at noonday."

[2]Job 21:33. "The clods of the valley are sweet to him," spoken by Job of the wicked who are nevertheless favored by God. The centrality of the Book of Job to this poem cannot be overstressed, despite the fleetingness of this allusion. The "rock" that follows appears to be a more general allusion to the safety and security those in God's favor enjoy.

[3]Matthew 3:17. "This is my beloved son, with whom I am well pleased." Given that these words are spoken by God at the baptism of Christ, Piatt, like Dickinson, appears to be adopting the role of the female Christus, along with that of a female Job.

[1]Written after reading certain newspaper discussions as to the treatment of the "tramp."—Piatt's note.

And he was just a ———, Papa said.
(We have to call them that, you know.)

"She cried about the shabbiest shawl,
Because it cost too much to buy;
But Papa cannot cry at all,
For he's a man. And that is why!

"Why, if his coat was not right new,
And if the yellow bird would die
That sings, and my white kitten too,
Or even himself, *he* would not cry.

"He said that he would sleep to-night
With both the pistols at his head,
Because that ragged fellow might
Come back. That's what my Papa said!

"But Mamma goes and hides her face
There in the curtains, and peeps out
At him, and almost spoils the lace.
And he is what she cries about!

"She says he looks so cold, so cold,
And has no pleasant place to stay!
Why can't he work? He is not old;
His eyes are blue—they've not turned gray."

So the boy babbled. . . . Well, sweet sirs,
Flushed with your office-fires, you write
You laugh down at such grief as hers;
But are these women foolish quite?

I know. But, look you, there may be
Stains sad as wayside dust, I say.
Upon your own white hands (ah, me!)
No woman's tears can wash away.

One sees her baby's dimple hold
More love than you can measure. . . . Then
Nights darken down on heads of gold
Till wind and frost try wandering men!

But there are prisons made for such,
Where the strong roof shuts out the snow;
And bread (that you would scorn to touch)
Is served them there. I know, I know.

Ah! while you have your books, your ease,
Your lamp-light leisure, jests, and wine,
Fierce outside whispers, if you please,
Moan, each: "These things are also mine!"[2]

1880

Ella Wheeler Wilcox 1850–1919

Her Prayer

She let down all the wonder of her hair;
Its dusky clouds fell round her, and her form
Shone like a Grecian statue through a storm.
One gleaming shoulder, beautiful as bare,
Leaned to the lips that used to sigh "How fair!"
And the white beauty of one perfect arm,
As ivory polished and as velvet warm,
Twined round his massive neck.

O Heart's despair!

In his cold eyes there lay no least desire,
And not a thrill shot through him, though his head
Lay pillowed on her breast. In days scarce fled
One touch of hers could set his blood on fire.
"Hast thou no hell? Make one, O God!" she said.
"'Twere heaven, to earth with love and passion dead."

1894

Illusion

God and I in space alone,
And nobody else in view.
And "Where are the people, O Lord," I said,
"The earth below and the sky o'erhead
And the dead whom once I knew?"

[2]Possibly a rendering of Isaiah 66:1–2 ("All these things my hand has made, and so all these things are mine") but also suggestive of Jesus of Nazareth's deep identification with the poor and outcast.

"That was a dream," God smiled and said:
"A dream that seemed to be true.
There were no people living or dead,
There was no earth and no sky o'erhead—
There was only Myself and you."

"Why do I feel no fear," I asked,
Meeting YOU here this way?
"For I have sinned, I know full well;
And is there heaven, and is there hell,
And is this the Judgment Day?"

"Nay! those were but dreams," the great God said;
"Dreams that have ceased to be.
There are no such things as fear, or sin;
There is no you—you never have been—
There is nothing at all but me!"

1896

Goddess of Liberty,[1] Answer

Goddess of Liberty, listen! listen. I say, and look
To the sounds and sights of sorrow this side of Sandy Hook![2]
Your eye is searching the distance, you are holding your torch too high
To see the slaves who are fettered, though close at your feet they lie.
And the cry of the suffering stranger has reached your ear and your breast,
But you do not heed the wail that comes from the haunts of your own oppressed.

Goddess of Liberty, follow, follow me where I lead;
Come down into sweat-shops and look on the work of greed!
Look on the faces of children, old before they were born!
Look on the haggard women of all sex graces shorn!
Look on the men—God, help us! if this is what it means
To be men in the land of freedom and live like mere machines!

[1]The Statue of Liberty. This poem appears to be a response to Emma Lazarus's "The New Colossus"; see box on page 27.

[2]Sandy Hook, a spit of land on the New Jersey coast, opposite the south end of Manhattan. It marked the boundary beyond which lay the open ocean and Europe, source of the immigrant populations to whom Lazarus's poem is addressed.

Goddess of Liberty, answer! how can the slaves of Spain
Find freedom under your banner, while your own still wear the chain?
Loud is the screech of your eagle and boastful the voice of your drums,
But they do not silence the wail of despair that rises out of your slums.
What will you do with your conquests, and how shall your hosts be fed,
While your streets are filled with desperate throngs, crying for work
or bread?

1898

Mary E. Wilkins Freeman 1852–1930

Love and the Witches

It was a little, fearful maid,
Whose mother left her all alone;
Her door with iron bolt she stayed,
And 'gainst it rolled a lucky stone—
For many a night she'd waked with fright
When witches by the house had flown.

To piping lute in still midnight,
Who comes a-singing at the door,—
That showeth seams of gold light,—
"Ah, open, darling, I implore"?
She could not help knowing 't was Love,
Although they'd never met before.

She swiftly shot the iron bar,
And rolled the lucky stone away,
And careful set the door ajar—
"Now enter in, Sir Love, I pray;
My mother knows it not, but I have watched
For you this many a day."

With fan and roar of gloomy wings
They gave the door a windy shove;
They perched on chairs and brooms and things;
Like bats they beat around above—
Poor little maid, she'd let the witches in with Love.

1891

Lizette Woodworth Reese 1856–1935

Emily

She had a garden full of herbs,
And many another pleasant thing,
Like pink round asters in the fall,
Blue flags, white flags[1] a week in spring.

Housewives ran in each hour or so,
For sprigs of thyme, mint, parsley too;
For pans to borrow, or some meal;
She was the kindest thing they knew.

Tall, and half slender, slightly grey,
With gay, thin lips, eyes flower-clear,
She bragged her stock was Puritan;
Her usual mood was Cavalier.

Ample of deed; clipped, warm of speech,
Each day in some large-flowered gown,
She went the rounds to sad, to sick
Saint, humorist to the faded town.

She died at sixty. For a while
They missed her in each intimate spot—
Tall, and half slender, slightly grey—
They ate, drank, slept, and quite forgot.

1923

Telling the Bees

(A Colonial Custom)[1]

Bathsheba came out to the sun,
Out to our wallèd cherry-trees;
The tears adown her cheek did run,

[1]Blue iris, white iris.

[1]Upon a death in the family, a household member would, according to old New England custom, "tell the bees" lest they fly away.

Bathsheba standing in the sun,
Telling the bees.

My mother had that moment died;
Unknowing, sped I to the trees,
And plucked Bathsheba's hand aside;
Then caught the name that there she cried
Telling the bees.

Her look I never can forget,
I that held her sobbing to her knees;
The cherry-boughs above us met;
I think I see Bathsheba yet
Telling the bees.

1896

Drought

Silence—and in the air
A stare.
One bush, the color of rust,
Stands in the endless lane;
And farther on, hot, hard of pane,
With roof shrunk black,
Headlong against the sky
A house is thrust;
Betwixt the twain,
Like meal poured from a sack,
Stirless, foot high—
The dust.

1920

Spring Ecstasy

Oh, let me run and hide,
  Let me run straight to God;
The weather is so mad with white
  From sky down to the clod!

If but one thing were so,
Lilac, or thorn out there,
It would not be, indeed,
So hard to bear.

The weather has gone mad with white;
The cloud, the highway touch;
When lilac is enough;
White thorn too much!

1923

Sophie Jewett 1861–1909

Entre Nous[1]

I talk with you of foolish things and wise,
Of persons, places, books, desires and aims,
Yet all our words a silence underlies,
An earnest, vivid thought that neither names.

Ah! what to us were foolish talk or wise?
Were persons, places, books, desires or aims,
Without the deeper sense that underlies,
The sweet encircling thought that neither names?

MS 1882, 1910

Armistice

The water sings along our keel,
The wind falls to a whispering breath;
I look into your eyes and feel
No fear of life or death;
So near is love, so far away
The losing strife of yesterday.

We watch the swallow skim and dip;
Some magic bids the world be still;

[1]French for "between us."

Life stands with finger upon lip;
  Love hath his gentle will;
Though hearts have bled, and tears have burned,
The river floweth unconcerned.

We pray the fickle flag of truce
  Still float deceitfully and fair;
Our eyes must love its sweet abuse;
  This hour we will not care,
Though just beyond to-morrow's gate
Arrayed and strong, the battle wait.

1892

I Speak Your Name

I speak your name in alien ways, while yet
November smiles from under lashes wet.
  In the November light I see you stand
  Who love the fading woods and withered land,
Where Peace may walk, and Death, but not Regret.

The year is slow to alter or forget;
June's glow and autumn's tenderness are met.
  Across the months by this swift sunlight spanned,
    I speak your name.

Because I loved your golden hair, God set
His sea between our eyes. I may not fret,
  For, sure and strong, to meet my soul's demand,
  Comes your soul's truth, more near than hand in hand;
And low to God, who listens, Margaret,
    I speak your name.

MS 1892, 1910

E. Pauline Johnson (Tekahionwake) 1861–1913

The Camper

Night 'neath the northern skies, lone, black, and grim:
Naught but the starlight lies 'twixt heaven, and him.

Of man no need has he, of God, no prayer;
He and his Deity are brothers there.

Above his bivouac the firs fling down
Through branches gaunt and black, their needles brown.

Afar some mountain streams, rockbound and fleet,
Sing themselves through his dreams in cadence sweet,

The pine trees whispering, the heron's cry,
The plover's wing, his lullaby.

And blinking overhead the white stars keep
Watch o'er his hemlock bed—his sinless sleep.

1895

The Corn Husker

Hard by the Indian lodges, where the bush
  Breaks in a clearing, through ill-fashioned fields,
She comes to labour, when the first still hush
  Of autumn follows large and recent yields.

Age in her fingers, hunger in her face,
  Her shoulders stooped with weight of work and years,
But rich in tawny colouring of her race,
  She comes a-field to strip the purple ears.

And all her thoughts are with the days gone by,
  Ere might's injustice banished from their lands
Her people, that to-day unheeded lie,
  Like the dead husks that rustle through her hands.

1903

The Indian Corn Planter

He needs must leave the trapping and the chase,
For mating game his arrows ne'er despoil,
And from the hunter's heaven turn his face,
To wring some promise from the dormant soil.

He needs must leave the lodge that wintered him,
The enervating fires, the blanket bed—
The women's dulcet voices, for the grim
Realities of labouring for bread.

So goes he forth beneath the planter's moon
With sack of seed that pledges large increase,
His simple pagan faith knows night and noon,
Heat, cold, seedtime and harvest shall not cease.

And yielding to his needs, this honest sod,
Brown as the hand that tills it, moist with rain,
Teeming with ripe fulfillment, true as God,
With fostering richness, mothers every grain.

1912

Louise Imogen Guiney 1861–1920

Hylas[1]

Jar in arm, they bade him rove
Thro' the alder's long alcove,
Where the hid spring musically
Gushes to the ample valley.
(There's a bird on the under bough
Fluting evermore and now:
"Keep—young!" but who knows how?)

Down the woodland corridor,
Odors deepened more and more;

[1]In Greek mythology, a beautiful youth, beloved of Hercules. While serving as an Argonaut, he was sent to fetch water from a spring. There, the nymphs who lived in the spring, catching sight of his beauty, dragged him in and his body was never found.

Blossomed dogwood, in the briers,
Struck her faint delicious fires;
Miles of April passed between
Crevices of closing green,
And the moth, the violet-lover,
By the wellside saw him hover.

Ah, the slippery sylvan dark!
Never after shall he mark
Noisy ploughmen drinking, drinking,
On his drownèd cheek down-sinking;
Quit of serving is that wild,
Absent, and bewitchèd child,
Unto action, age, and danger,
Thrice a thousand years a stranger.

Fathoms low, the naiads[2] sing
In a birthday welcoming;[3]
Water-white their breasts, and o'er him,
Water-gray, their eyes adore him.
(There's a bird on the under bough
Fluting evermore and now:
"Keep—young!" but who knows how?)

1893

Monochrome

Shut fast again in Beauty's sheath
Where ancient forms renew,
The round world seems above, beneath,
One wash of faintest blue,

And air and tide so stilly sweet
In nameless union lie,
The little far-off fishing fleet
Goes drifting up the sky.

Secure of neither misted coast
Nor ocean undefined,

[2]In Greek mythology, the nymphs inhabiting streams, rivers, and lakes.

[3]Guiney appears to be suggesting that Hylas's "death" in this life marked his rebirth (or "birthday") in the next.

Our flagging sail is like the ghost
Of one that served mankind,

Who in the void, as we upon
This melancholy sea,
Finds labour and allegiance done,
And Self begin to be.

1896

Charista Musing

Moveless, on the marge of a sunny cornfield,
Rapt in sudden revery while thou standest,
Like the sheaves, in beautiful Doric[1] yellow
Clad to the ankle,

Oft to thee with delicate hasty footstep
So I steal, and suffer because I find thee
Inly flown, and only a fallen feather
Left of my darling.

Give me back thy wakening breath, thy ringlets
Fragrant as the vine of the bean in blossom,
And those eyes of violet dusk and daylight
Under sea-water,

Eyes too far away, and too full of longing!
Yes: and go not heavenward where I lose thee,
Go not, go not whither I cannot follow,
Being but earthly.

Willing swallow poisèd upon my finger,
Little wild-wing ever from me escaping,
For the care thou art to me, I thy lover
Love thee, and fear thee.

1899

[1]The Doric order (or style) was the oldest and simplest of the three major Greek architectural and musical modes. Guiney appears to want to associate Charista with classical Greek beauty and simplicity. Her name (Charista) derives from the ancient Greek for love (as does the modern English "charity"), and there may also be a pun on "musing" ("muse" or source of poetic inspiration, as in Greek mythology).

Elaine Goodale Eastman 1863–1953

The Wood-Chopper to His Ax

My comrade keen, my lawless friend,
When will your savage temper mend?
I wield you, powerless to resist;
I feel your weight bend back my wrist,
Straighten the corded arm,
Caress the hardened palm.

War on these forest tribes they made,
The men who forged your sapphire blade;
Its very substance thus renewed
Tenacious of the ancient feud,
In crowding ranks uprose
Your ambushed, waiting foes.

This helve, by me wrought out and planned,
By long use suited to this hand,
Was carved, with patient, toilsome art,
From stubborn hickory's milk-white heart;
Its satin gloss makes plain
The fineness of the grain.

When deeply sunk, an entering wedge,
The live wood tastes your shining edge;
When, strongly cleft from side to side,
You feel its shrinking heart divide,
List not the shuddering sigh
Of that dread agony.

Yon gaping mouth you need not miss,
But close it with a poignant kiss;
Nor dread to search, with whetted knife,
The naked mystery of life,
And count on shining rings
The ever-widening springs.

Hew, trenchant steel, the ivory core,
One mellow, resonant stroke the more!
Loudly the cracking sinews start,
Unwilling members wrenched apart—
Dear ax, your 'complice I
In love and cruelty!

1883

The Cross and the Pagan

As men in the forest, erect and free,
We prayed to God in the living tree;
You razed our shrine, to the wood-god's loss,
And out of the tree you fashioned a Cross!

You left us for worship one day in seven;
In exchange for our earth you offered us heaven;
Dizzy with wonder, and wild with loss,
We bent the knee to your awful Cross.

Your sad, sweet Christ—we called him Lord;
He promised us peace, but he brought a sword;
In shame and sorrow, in pain and loss,
We have drunk his cup;[1] we have borne his Cross!

1912

Alice Dunbar-Nelson 1875–1935

I Sit and Sew

I sit and sew—a useless task it seems,
My hands grown tired, my head weighed down with dreams—
The panoply of war, the martial tred of men,
Grim-faced, stern-eyed, gazing beyond the ken
Of lesser souls, whose eyes have not seen Death,
Nor learned to hold their lives but as a breath—
But—I must sit and sew.

I sit and sew—my heart aches with desire—
That pageant terrible, that fiercely pouring fire
On wasted fields, and writhing grotesque things
Once men. My soul in pity flings
Appealing cries, yearning only to go
There in that holocaust of hell, those fields of woe—
But—I must sit and sew.

The little useless seam, the idle patch;
Why dream I here beneath my homely thatch,

[1]Communion cup; Christ's blood.

When there they lie in sodden mud and rain,
Pitifully calling me, the quick ones and the slain?
You need me, Christ! It is no roseate dream
That beckons me—this pretty futile seam
It stifles me—God, must I sit and sew?

1920

You! Inez!

Orange gleams athwart a crimson soul
Lambent flames; purple passion lurks
In your dusk eyes.
Red mouth; flower soft,
Your soul leaps up—and flashes
Star-like, white, flame-hot.
Curving arms, encircling a world of love.
You! Stirring the depths of passionate desire!

MS 1921

The Proletariat Speaks

I love beautiful things:
Great trees, bending green winged branches to a velvet lawn,
Fountains sparkling in white marble basins,
Cool fragrance of lilacs and roses and honeysuckle.
Or exotic blooms, filling the air with heart-contracting odors;
Spacious rooms, cool and gracious with statues and books,
Carven seats and tapestries, and old masters
Whose patina shows the wealth of centuries.

And so I work
In a dusty office, whose grimèd windows
Look out in an alley of unbelievable squalor,
Where mangy cats, in their degradation, spurn
Swarming bits of meat and bread;
Where odors, vile and breath taking, rise in fetid waves
Filling my nostrils, scorching my humid, bitter cheeks.

I love beautiful things:
Carven tables laid with lily-hued linen
And fragile china and sparkling iridescent glass;

Pale silver, etched with heraldies,
Where tender bits of regal dainties tempt,
And soft-stepped service anticipates the unspoken wish.

And so I eat
In the food-laden air of a greasy kitchen,
At an oil-clothed table:
Plate piled high with food that turns my head away,
Lest a squeamish stomach reject too soon
The lumpy gobs it never needed.
Or in a smoky cafeteria, balancing a slippery tray
To a table crowded with elbows
Which lately the bus boy wiped with a grimy rag.

I love beautiful things:
Soft linen sheets and silken coverlet,
Sweet coolth of chamber opened wide to fragrant breeze;
Rose shaded lamps and golden atomizers,
Spraying Parisian fragrance over my relaxed limbs,
Fresh from a white marble bath, and sweet cool spray.

And so I sleep
In a hot hall-room whose half-opened window,
Unscreened, refuses to budge another inch;
Admits no air, only insects, and hot choking gasps,
That make me writhe, nun-like, in sack-cloth sheets and lumps of straw.
And then I rise
To fight my way to a dubious tub,
Whose tiny, tepid stream threatens to make me late;
And hurrying out, dab my unrefreshed face
With bits of toiletry from the ten cent store.

1929

Sarah Norcliffe Cleghorn 1876–1959[1]

Behold the Lillies

Drowsy weather, eleven o'clock;
  Tall white daisies blow in the sun,

[1]See box on page 33 for another poem by Cleghorn.

And dust blew lightly on Martha's[2] frock;
(Morning Service must have begun).

The anthem sounded along the street;
Winds breathed up from the fresh-cut hay.
She lingered a little; the fields are sweet,
They toil not, neither do they pray.[3]

1896

[2]In the Bible, the sister of Lazarus and friend of Jesus. She is mentioned in Luke 10:40; but her story was only elaborated in the Middle Ages, when she came to symbolize the active life (of toil), as opposed to her sister Mary, who symbolized the contemplative life (of prayer).

[3]Matthew 6:26.

The Making of "Americans"

Because the United States invented itself—came into being by political fiat—and because of Americans' widely diverse origins, inhabitants of the United States have always had to deal with the question of what it is to be, or to become, an American. In what does an American identity consist? The question, explored by writers throughout U.S. history, acquired new urgency at the end of the nineteenth century, when cultural, racial, religious, and economic disparities among the peoples of the nation intensified and registered themselves more visibly on the national consciousness. The arrival in unprecedented numbers of immigrants from southern and eastern Europe, who brought with them languages, religions, and cultural practices that were markedly different from those of the majority of the populace, seemed to some observers to present a new threat to civic stability. "Many American citizens are not Americanized," exclaimed Josiah Strong in *Our Country: Its Possible Future and Present Crisis* in 1885, voicing a popular and all too often ethnocentric anxiety. (Indeed, citizenship itself was still an unresolved issue for some Americans, including Indians.) The situation of other groups, such as African Americans, Mexican Americans, and Asian Americans, and the growing agitation by women to redefine their role and place in American life, added to the questioning. Thus the 1890s and 1900s saw the emergence of a body of writing, much of it autobiographical, asking in new and challenging ways what it meant to be an American.

It has been suggested that the outsider, the person who is or sees himself or herself on the margin, can often best express what it means to exist within a particular culture or society. Both belonging and not quite belonging, an outsider has a double vantage point and perhaps a heightened alertness to what others often unconsciously take for granted. Marginalization because of race, ethnicity, or gender marks the writers in this unit, all of whom are explicitly concerned with who they are, want to be, or feel pressured into becoming. They cannot take for granted their full participation in the nation's political, economic, or cultural life, and thus they need consciously to consider the nature of their inclusion or exclusion. All of them, in one way or another, undertake the task of defining themselves in relation to certain by-then-established American norms and expectations.

Broadly speaking, these norms expressed the customs and values of the English Protestant who first settled the country along its eastern seaboard; by the end of the nineteenth century, inculcation of these norms had become a central function of important social institutions. Chief among them was formal education, and many of the writers in this unit dwell on their schooling as, for better or worse, pivotal to their developing sense of themselves. Whether they fully embraced, accepted with qualification, or rejected the dominant values and patterns of behavior of the larger society, their need to come to terms with them is a central theme in their autobiographies.

Geographical and social mobility also mark the writers in this unit. Like so many Americans in the nineteenth century and today, they are migratory, leaving the places of their birth, whether in Europe or in the American South or West, to journey to new locations in search of new or expanded selves—journeys often dramatized through spatial metaphors of confinement and openness. For all of them, also, the question of assuming a place in American society becomes a question of defining an individual identity, and therefore of scrutinizing the components that go into the making of a self. Does identity reside in one's name, religion, manner of dress, or language? in one's race? in one's sex or gender role? in one's family or community? in one's chosen work or degree of material success? In what different ways and to what degrees are all of these important, and how does one negotiate among them? More broadly, how does one balance society's expectations with one's own innermost feelings and needs? The complexities of the process are suggested by Mary Austin's resorting, in her autobiography, to several voices, using a first person voice to describe her private self and a third person one to describe the conventional role and behavior society expected of her. By contrast, Mary Antin, in her autobiographical work, *The Promised Land,* creates a more public persona of a woman who eagerly adapted to the expectations of her new culture, and Sui Sin Far articulates a shifting sense of identity that is neither exclusively Asian nor exclusively American but combines both.

This section concludes with José Martí's "Nuestra America" ("Our America") because, as a Cuban committed to this nation's independence from Spain and to the political and cultural flourishing of Latin America, Martí focuses not on individuals but on the kind of large-scale movement within which individual American selves have been forged. Martí calls for the decolonization of Latin America and its replenishment by means of its indigenous Indian traditions—and for U.S. respect for the integrity of the emerging Latin American countries. Drawing from native, French, Spanish, classical, and U.S. North American traditions, he himself displays a democratic cosmopolitanism. He recognizes that the participation of all the countries of the American continents in global intellectual and cultural currents can be enriching, and he rejects the idea that some countries and cultures are of lesser worth than others. Through the twentieth century and into the twenty-first, American literature has continued to be challenged and energized by views such as those expressed by Martí and, as well, by the more personally focused literature of writers engaged in the ongoing, often tasking, often exhilarating work of creating and re-creating American selves.

Elaine Hedges
late of Towson State University

Sandra A. Zagarell
Oberlin College

Abraham Cahan 1860–1951

Abraham Cahan has been described as the single most influential personality in the cultural life of well over two million Jewish immigrants and their families during his lifetime. As a journalist and writer, his unique ability to mediate among the various sensibilities and languages of the Lower East Side in New York City placed him at the center of American Jewish culture and Jewish writing. His major fictional works, *Yekl* (1896) and *The Rise of David Levinsky* (1917), are widely recognized as classic accounts of the immigrant experience of Americanization.

Born in Podberezy, Russia, Cahan was educated at traditional Jewish cheders and also studied at the Vilna Teachers Institute, a Russian government school for Jewish teachers. After graduating in 1881, he began teaching and at the same time became deeply involved in radical, underground anti-czarist activities. Forced to flee, he joined a group of immigrants bound for America and arrived in Philadelphia on June 5, 1882. The next day he reached New York, where his religious training proved useless and secular success beckoned. In 1890 he became editor of the weekly *Arbeiter Zeitung,* the paper of the United Hebrew Trades. Using the pseudonym "Proletarian Preacher" he wrote columns that mixed Russian fables, Talmudic parables, and Marxist ideas to convey his socialist critique of capitalism.

National prominence came to Cahan in 1896, when his novella, *Yekl: A Tale of the New York Ghetto,* was published in English. Like many of his contemporaries—Dreiser, Crane, and Norris, for example—Cahan was probing the impact of America's social and economic forces, their power to influence acculturation and assimilation. In *Yekl,* Jake compromises his religion, values, dress, and behavior to become an "American" (that is, not a greenhorn) and to acquire money and a new identity. On the arrival of his wife, Gitl, with her son Yossie, he compares her with Mamie (an Americanized Jewish woman) and chooses Mamie. After a Jewish divorce (a "get") he seems to be reluctant, at the end, to go to City Hall with Mamie, perhaps realizing too late that in the "exchange" he emerges a victim, not a conqueror.

During the decade that followed Cahan published *The Imported Bridegroom and Other Stories* (1898), *The White Terror and the Red: A Novel of Revolutionary Russia* (1905), as well as stories in *Cosmopolitan.* In 1913 he published a four-part series for *McClure's* magazine, "The Autobiography of an American Jew." Enthusiastically received, this work was the genesis of the novel that appeared four years later, Cahan's masterpiece, *The Rise of David Levinsky.* The story of an immigrant who becomes a successful cloak manufacturer, the novel probed deeply into the tensions and conflicts involved in pursuing the American dream of success that had begun to surface in *Yekl.*

Cahan paralleled his career as a novelist and short-story writer with a long, distinguished career as a newspaperman and editor. From 1903 to 1946 he served as editor of the Jewish *Daily Forward,* a socialist paper that he transformed into a mass circulation pacesetter for the Yiddish press. Originally a political radical, Cahan became a pragmatic socialist, influenced by the forces of Americanization so evident in his fiction and journalism. His dynamic leadership, his use of conversational instead of literary Yiddish, and his pioneering "Bintel Brief," a Yiddish "Dear Abby" column, endeared him to his fellow immigrants and placed him at the center of American Jewish culture and writing. Under Cahan's guidance the *Forward* developed into a powerful national voice in journalism, and he gained influence in American society, especially in liberal and progressive circles.

Cahan's five volumes of memoirs, *Bleter fun mein Leben (Leaves from My Life),* published from 1926 to 1931, spanned the decades from the 1860s in Russia to the beginning of World War I. When he died in 1951, Abraham Cahan was revered in both Yiddish and American communities as an immigrant who had succeeded in the New World but had never forgotten the Old.

Daniel Walden
Pennsylvania State University

PRIMARY WORKS

Yekl and *The Imported Bridegroom and Other Stories,* 1895, 1896; *The Rise of David Levinsky,* 1917.

from Yekl

4 The Meeting

A few weeks later, on a Saturday morning, Jake, with an unfolded telegram in his hand, stood in front of one of the desks at the Immigration Bureau of Ellis Island. He was freshly shaven and clipped, smartly dressed in his best clothes and ball shoes, and, in spite of the sickly expression of shamefacedness and anxiety which distorted his features, he looked younger than usual.

All the way to the island he had been in a flurry of joyous anticipation. The prospect of meeting his dear wife and child, and, incidentally, of showing off his swell attire to her, had thrown him into a fever of impatience. But on entering the big shed he had caught a distant glimpse of Gitl and Yosselé through the railing separating the detained immigrants from their visitors, and his heart had sunk at the sight of his wife's uncouth and un-American appearance. She was slovenly dressed in a brown jacket and skirt of grotesque cut, and her hair was concealed under a voluminous wig of a pitch-black hue. This she had put on just before leaving the steamer, both "in honor of the Sabbath" and by way of sprucing herself up for the great event. Since Yekl had left home she had gained considerably in the measurement of her waist. The wig, however, made her seem stouter and shorter than she would have appeared without it. It also added at least five years to her looks. But she was aware neither of this nor of the fact that in New York even a Jewess of her station and orthodox breeding is accustomed to blink at the wickedness of displaying her natural hair, and that none but an elderly matron may wear a wig without being the occasional target for snowballs or stones. She was naturally dark of complexion, and the nine or ten days spent at sea had covered her face with a deep bronze, which combined with her prominent cheek bones, inky little eyes, and, above all, the smooth black wig, to lend her resemblance to a squaw.

Jake had no sooner caught sight of her than he had averted his face, as if loth to rest his eyes on her, in the presence of the surging crowd around him, before it was inevitable. He dared not even survey that crowd to see whether it contained any acquaintance of his, and he vaguely wished that her release were delayed indefinitely.

Presently the officer behind the desk took the telegram from him, and in another little while Gitl, hugging Yosselé with one arm and a bulging parcel with the other, emerged from a side door.

"Yekl!" she screamed out in a piteous high key, as if crying for mercy.

"Dot'sh alla right!" he returned in English, with a wan smile and unconscious of what he was saying. His wandering eyes and dazed mind were striving to fix themselves upon the stern functionary and the questions he bethought himself of asking before finally releasing his prisoners. The contrast between Gitl and Jake was so striking that the officer wanted to make sure—partly as a matter of official duty and partly for the fun of the thing—that the two were actually man and wife.

"*Oi* a lamentation upon me! He shaves his beard!" Gitl ejaculated to herself as she scrutinized her husband. "Yosselé, look! Here is *taté*!"

But Yosselé did not care to look at taté. Instead, he turned his frightened little eyes—precise copies of Jake's—and buried them in his mother's cheek.

When Gitl was finally discharged she made to fling herself on Jake. But he checked her by seizing both loads from her arms. He started for a distant and deserted corner of the room, bidding her follow. For a moment the boy looked stunned, then he burst out crying and fell to kicking his father's chest with might and main, his reddened little face appealingly turned to Gitl. Jake continuing his way tried to kiss his son into toleration, but the little fellow proved too nimble for him. It was in vain that Gitl, scurrying behind, kept expostulating with Yosselé: "Why, it is taté!" Taté was forced to capitulate before the march was brought to its end.

At length, when the secluded corner had been reached, and Jake and Gitl had set down their burdens, husband and wife flew into mutual embrace and fell to kissing each other. The performance had an effect of something done to order, which, it must be owned, was far from being belied by the state of their minds at the moment. Their kisses imparted the taste of mutual estrangement to both. In Jake's case the sensation was quickened by the strong steerage odors which were emitted by Gitl's person, and he involuntarily recoiled.

"You look like a *poritz,*"[1] she said shyly.

"How are you? How is mother?"

"How should she be? So, so. She sends you her love," Gitl mumbled out.

"How long was father ill?"

"Maybe a month. He cost us health enough."

He proceeded to make advances to Yosselé, she appealing to the child in his behalf. For a moment the sight of her, as they were both crouching before the boy, precipitated a wave of thrilling memories on Jake and made him feel in his own environment. Presently, however, the illusion took wing and here he was, Jake the Yankee, with this bonnetless, wigged, dowdyish little greenhorn by his side! That she was his wife, nay, that he was a married man at all, seemed incredible to him. The sturdy, thriving urchin had at first inspired him with pride; but as he now cast another side glance at Gitl's wig he lost all interest in him, and began to regard him, together with his mother, as one great obstacle dropped from heaven, as it were, in his way.

Gitl, on her part, was overcome with a feeling akin to awe. She, too, could not get herself to realize that this stylish young man—shaved and dressed as in Povodye is only some young nobleman—was Yekl, her own Yekl, who had all these three years never been absent from her mind. And while she was once more examining Jake's blue diagonal cutaway, glossy stand-up collar, the white four-in-hand necktie, coquettishly tucked away in the bosom of his starched shirt, and, above all, his patent leather shoes, she was at the same time mentally scanning the Yekl of three years before. The latter alone was hers, and she felt like crying to the image to come back to her and let her be *his* wife.

Presently, when they had got up and Jake was plying her with perfunctory questions, she chanced to recognize a certain movement of his upper lip—an old trick of his. It was as if she had suddenly discovered her own Yekl in an apparent stranger, and, with another pitiful outcry, she fell on his breast.

[1]Yiddish for nobleman.

"Don't!" he said, with patient gentleness, pushing away her arms. "Here everything is so different."

She colored deeply.

"They don't wear wigs here," he ventured to add.

"What then?" she asked, perplexedly.

"You will see. It is quite another world."

"Shall I take it off, then? I have a nice Saturday kerchief," she faltered. "It is of silk—I bought it at Kalmen's for a bargain. It is still brand new."

"Here one does not wear even a kerchief."

"How then? Do they go about with their own hair?" she queried in ill-disguised bewilderment.

"*Vell, alla right,* put it on, quick!"

As she set about undoing her parcel, she bade him face about and screen her, so that neither he nor any stranger could see her bareheaded while she was replacing the wig by the kerchief. He obeyed. All the while the operation lasted he stood with his gaze on the floor, gnashing his teeth with disgust and shame, or hissing some Bowery oath.

"Is this better?" she asked bashfully, when her hair and part of her forehead were hidden under a kerchief of flaming blue and yellow, whose end dangled down her back.

The kerchief had a rejuvenating effect. But Jake thought that it made her look like an Italian woman of Mulberry Street on Sunday.

"*Alla right,* leave it be for the present," he said in despair, reflecting that the wig would have been the lesser evil of the two.

When they reached the city Gitl was shocked to see him lead the way to a horse car. "*Oi* woe is me! Why, it is Sabbath!" she gasped.

He irately essayed to explain that a car, being an uncommon sort of vehicle, riding in it implied no violation of the holy day. But this she sturdily met by reference to railroads.[2] Besides, she had seen horse cars while stopping in Hamburg,[3] and knew that no orthodox Jew would use them on the seventh day. At length Jake, losing all self-control, fiercely commanded her not to make him the laughingstock of the people on the street and to get in without further ado. As to the sin of the matter he was willing to take it all upon himself. Completely dismayed by his stern manner, amid the strange, uproarious, forbidding surroundings, Gitl yielded.

As the horses started she uttered a groan of consternation and remained looking aghast and with a violently throbbing heart. If she had been a culprit on the way to the gallows she could not have been more terrified than she was now at this her first ride on the day of rest.

The conductor came up for their fares. Jake handed him a ten-cent piece, and raising two fingers, he roared out: "Two! He ain' no maur as tree years, de liddle feller!" And so great was the impression which his dashing manner and his English produced on Gitl, that for some time it relieved her mind and she even forgot to be shocked by the sight of her husband handling coin on the Sabbath.

[2]Orthodox Jews are not permitted to ride in any sort of vehicle on the Sabbath.

[3]German port from which immigrants embarked.

Having thus paraded himself before his wife, Jake all at once grew kindly disposed toward her.

"You must be hungry?" he asked.

"Not at all! Where do you eat your *varimess?*"[4]

"Don't say varimess" he corrected her complaisantly; "here it is called *dinner.*"

"*Dinner?*[5] And what if one becomes fatter?" she confusedly ventured an irresistible pun.

This was the way in which Gitl came to receive her first lesson in the five or six score English words and phrases which the omnivorous Jewish jargon has absorbed in the Ghettos of English-speaking countries.

9 The Parting

It was on a bright frosty morning in the following January, in the kitchen of Rabbi Aaronovitz, on the third floor of a rickety old tenement house, that Jake and Gitl, for the first time since his flight,[6] came face to face. It was also to be their last meeting as husband and wife.

The low-ceiled room was fairly crowded with men and women. Besides the principal actors in the scene, the rabbi, the scribe, and the witnesses, and, as a matter of course, Mrs. Kavarsky,[7] there was the rabbi's wife, their two children, and an envoy from Mamie, charged to look after the fortitude of Jake's nerve. Gitl, extremely careworn and haggard, was "in her own hair," thatched with a broad-brimmed winter hat of a brown colour, and in a jacket of black beaver. The rustic, "greenhornlike" expression was completely gone from her face and manner, and, although she now looked bewildered and as if terror-stricken, there was noticeable about her a suggestion of that peculiar air of self-confidence with which a few months' life in America is sure to stamp the looks and bearing of every immigrant. Jake, flushed and plainly nervous and fidgety, made repeated attempts to conceal his state of mind now by screwing up a grim face, now by giving his enormous head a haughty posture, now by talking aloud to his escort.

The tedious preliminaries were as trying to the rabbi as they were to Jake and Gitl. However, the venerable old man discharged his duty of dissuading the young couple from their contemplated step as scrupulously as he dared in view of his wife's signals to desist and not to risk the fee. Gitl, prompted by Mrs. Kavarsky, responded to all questions with an air of dazed resignation, while Jake, ever conscious of his guard's glance, gave his answers with bravado. At last the scribe, a gaunt middle-aged man, with an expression of countenance at once devout and businesslike, set about his task. Whereupon Mrs. Aaronovitz heaved a sigh of relief, and forthwith banished her two boys into the parlor.

An imposing stillness fell over the room. Little by little, however, it was broken, at first by whispers and then by an unrestrained hum. The rabbi, in a velvet skullcap, faded and besprinkled with down, presided with pious dignity, though apparently ill

[4]Yiddish for dinner.
[5]Yiddish for thinner.
[6]Jake has fled from his wife to Mamie Fein, and he and Gitl are now being divorced.
[7]A neighbor sympathetic to Gitl.

at ease, at the head of the table. Alternately stroking his yellowish-gray beard and curling his scanty sidelocks, he kept his eyes on the open book before him, now and then stealing a glance at the other end of the table, where the scribe was rapturously drawing the square characters of the holy tongue.[8]

Gitl carefully looked away from Jake. But he invincibly haunted her mind, rendering her deaf to Mrs. Kavarsky's incessant buzz. His presence terrified her, and at the same time it melted her soul in a fire, torturing yet sweet, which impelled her at one moment to throw herself upon him and scratch out his eyes, and at another to prostrate herself at his feet and kiss them in a flood of tears.

Jake, on the other hand, eyed Gitl quite frequently, with a kind of malicious curiosity. Her general Americanized makeup, and, above all, that broad-brimmed, rather fussy, hat of hers, nettled him. It seemed to defy him, and as if devised for that express purpose. Every time she and her adviser caught his eye, a feeling of devouring hate for both would rise in his heart. He was panting to see his son; and, while he was thoroughly alive to the impossibility of making a child the witness of a divorce scene between father and mother, yet, in his fury, he interpreted their failure to bring Joey with them as another piece of malice.

"Ready!" the scribe at length called out, getting up with the document in his hand, and turning it over to the rabbi.

The rest of the assemblage also rose from their seats, and clustered round Jake and Gitl, who had taken places on either side of the old man; a beam of hard, cold sunlight, filtering in through a grimy windowpane and falling lurid upon the rabbi's wrinkled brow, enhanced the impressiveness of the spectacle. A momentary pause ensued, stern, weird, and casting a spell of awe over most of the bystanders, not excluding the rabbi. Mrs. Kavarsky even gave a shudder and gulped down a sob.

"Young woman," Rabbi Aaronovitz began, with bashful serenity, "here is the writ of divorce all ready. Now thou mayst still change thy mind."

Mrs. Aaronovitz anxiously watched Gitl, who answered by a shake of her head.

"Mind thee, I tell thee once again," the old man pursued, gently. "Thou must accept this divorce with the same free will and readiness with which thou hast married thy husband. Should there be the slightest objection hidden in thy heart, the divorce is null and void. Dost thou understand?"

"Say that you are *saresfied,*" whispered Mrs. Kavarsky.

"*Ull ride,* I am *salesfiet,*" murmured Gitl, looking down on the table.

"Witnesses, hear ye what this young woman says? That she accepts the divorce of her own free will," the rabbi exclaimed solemnly, as if reading the Talmud.

"Then I must also tell you once more," he then addressed himself to Jake as well as to Gitl, "that this divorce is good only upon condition that you are also divorced by the Government of the land—by the court—do you understand? So it stands written in the separate paper which you get. Do you understand what I say?"

"Dot'sh alla right," Jake said, with ostentatious ease of manner. "I have already told you that the *dvosh* of the court is already *fikshed,*[9] haven't I?" he added, even angrily.

[8]Hebrew is the holy tongue.
[9]*Dvosh:* divorce; *fikshed:* fixed.

Now came the culminating act of the drama. Gitl was affectionately urged to hold out her hands, bringing them together at an angle, so as to form a receptacle for the fateful piece of paper. She obeyed mechanically, her cheeks turning ghastly pale. Jake, also pale to his lips, his brows contracted, received the paper, and obeying directions, approached the woman who in the eye of the Law of Moses was still his wife. And then, repeating word for word after the rabbi, he said:

"Here is thy divorce. Take thy divorce. And by this divorce thou art separated from me and free for all other men!"

Gitl scarcely understood the meaning of the formula, though each Hebrew word was followed by its Yiddish translation. Her arms shook so that they had to be supported by Mrs. Kavarsky and by one of the witnesses.

At last Jake deposited the writ and instantly drew back.

Gitl closed her hands upon the paper as she had been instructed; but at the same moment she gave a violent tremble, and with a heartrending groan fell on the witness in a fainting swoon.

In the ensuing commotion Jake slipped out of the room, presently followed by Mamie's ambassador, who had remained behind to pay the bill. . . .

10 A Defeated Victor

. . . While Gitl thus sat swaying and wringing her hands, Jake, Mamie, her emissary at the divorce proceeding, and another mutual friend, were passengers on a Third Avenue cable car, all bound for the mayor's office. While Gitl was indulging herself in an exhibition of grief, her recent husband was flaunting a hilarious mood. He did feel a great burden to have rolled off his heart, and the proximity of Mamie, on the other hand, caressed his soul. He was tempted to catch her in his arms, and cover her glowing cheeks with kisses. But in his inmost heart he was the reverse of eager to reach the City Hall. He was painfully reluctant to part with his long-coveted freedom so soon after it had at last been attained, and before he had had time to relish it. Still worse than this thirst for a taste of liberty was a feeling which was now gaining upon him, that, instead of a conqueror, he had emerged from the rabbi's house the victim of an ignominious defeat. If he could now have seen Gitl in her paroxysm of anguish, his heart would perhaps have swelled with a sense of his triumph, and Mamie would have appeared to him the embodiment of his future happiness. Instead of this he beheld her, Bernstein, Yosselé, and Mrs. Kavarsky celebrating their victory and bandying jokes at his expense. Their future seemed bright with joy, while his own loomed dark and impenetrable. What if he should now dash into Gitl's apartments and, declaring his authority as husband, father, and lord of the house, fiercely eject the strangers, take Yosselé in his arms, and sternly command Gitl to mind her household duties?

But the distance between him and the mayor's office was dwindling fast. Each time the car came to a halt he wished the pause could be prolonged indefinitely; and when it resumed its progress, the violent lurch it gave was accompanied by a corresponding sensation in his heart.

1896

Edith Maud Eaton (Sui Sin Far) 1865–1914

Between the late 1890s and 1914, short stories and articles signed "Sui Sin Far" appeared in such popular and prominent national magazines as *Overland, Century,* the *Independent, Good Housekeeping,* and *New England Magazine,* and Americans of Chinese ancestry began to have a literary voice in the United States. Hatred and fear of the Chinese had spread throughout the nation, culminating in the Chinese Exclusion Act of 1882. The courageous pen of Sui Sin Far, the first person of Chinese ancestry to write in defense of the Chinese in America, countered beliefs widely held at the time that the Chinese were unassimilable, morally corrupt, and corrupting. Sui Sin Far demonstrated that the Chinese were human, like everyone else, but victimized by the laws of the land.

Born in Macclesfield, England, in 1865, Edith Maud Eaton was the eldest daughter and second child of fourteen surviving children of an unusual and romantic couple: Grace Trefusius, a Chinese woman adopted by an English couple and reared in England, and Edward Eaton, an Englishman and struggling landscape painter. According to *Me,* the autobiography of Edith's sister, novelist Winnifred Eaton, who used the pseudonym Onoto Watanna, the Eaton household bohemian (artistic and poverty-stricken), offering fertile ground for self-expression. Their mother read them Tennyson's *Idylls of the King* and the children would act out the characters. Artistic endeavors, as well as early financial independence, were encouraged. While still in their teens, Edith and Winnifred began publishing poems, stories, and articles for the local newspaper, becoming the first Asian American writers of fiction.

Edith Eaton's autobiographical essay, "Leaves from the Mental Portfolio of an Eurasian," focuses on the education in race relations of an Eurasian in Caucasian-dominated societies. The essay emphasizes the pain endured by a person considered socially unacceptable on two counts: her race and her single state. Yet the essay also reveals her courageous spirit: her willingness to confront wrongs done to herself and others and to right those wrongs. Though her facial features did not betray her ancestry, Edith boldly asserted her Chinese identity. Though single women were mocked, she remained unmarried, channeling her energies and her income into the care of her numerous siblings and of Chinese people in need. Her stories were collected in one volume, *Mrs. Spring Fragrance,* originally published in 1912 and recently reprinted. Set in Seattle or San Francisco, these stories show the struggles and joys in the daily lives of Chinese families in North America. Particularly poignant are the stories delineating the cultural conflicts of Eurasians and recent immigrants. In the ironically titled "In the Land of the Free," Sui Sin Far shows the suffering inflicted by discriminatory immigration laws.

Edith Eaton died April 7, 1914, in Montreal and is buried in the Protestant Cemetery there. In gratitude for her work on their behalf, the Chinese community erected a special headstone on her tomb inscribed with the characters "Yi bu wang hua" ("The righteous one does not forget China").

Amy Ling
University of Wisconsin, Madison

King-Kok Cheung
University of California, Los Angeles

Dominika Ferens
University of Wroclaw, Poland

PRIMARY WORKS

"Leaves from the Mental Portfolio of an Eurasian," *Independent* (January 21, 1909), 125–132; "The Persecution and Oppression of Me," *Independent* (August 24, 1911), 421–424; *Mrs. Spring Fragrance* (1912, 1995).

Leaves from the Mental Portfolio of an Eurasian

When I look back over the years I see myself, a little child of scarcely four years of age, walking in front of my nurse, in a green English lane, and listening to her tell another of her kind that my mother is Chinese. "Oh, Lord!" exclaims the informed. She turns me around and scans me curiously from head to foot. Then the two women whisper together. Tho the word "Chinese" conveys very little meaning to my mind, I feel that they are talking about my father and mother and my heart swells with indignation. When we reach home I rush to my mother and try to tell her what I have heard. I am a young child. I fail to make myself intelligible. My mother does not understand, and when the nurse declares to her, "Little Miss Sui is a story-teller," my mother slaps me.

Many a long year has past over my head since that day—the day on which I first learned that I was something different and apart from other children, but tho my mother has forgotten it, I have not.

I see myself again, a few years older. I am playing with another child in a garden. A girl passes by outside the gate. "Mamie," she cries to my companion. "I wouldn't speak to Sui if I were you. Her mamma is Chinese."

"I don't care," answers the little one beside me. And then to me, "Even if your mamma is Chinese, I like you better than I like Annie."

"But I don't like you," I answer, turning my back on her. It is my first conscious lie.

I am at a children's party, given by the wife of an Indian officer whose children were schoolfellows of mine. I am only six years of age, but have attended a private school for over a year, and have already learned that China is a heathen country, being civilized by England. However, for the time being, I am a merry romping child. There are quite a number of grown people present. One, a white haired old man, has his attention called to me by the hostess. He adjusts his eyeglasses and surveys me critically. "Ah, indeed!" he exclaims, "Who would have thought it at first glance. Yet now I see the difference between her and other children. What a peculiar coloring! Her mother's eyes and hair and her father's features, I presume. Very interesting little creature!"

I had been called from my play for the purpose of inspection. I do not return to it. For the rest of the evening I hide myself behind a hall door and refuse to show myself until it is time to go home.

My parents have come to America. We are in Hudson City, N.Y., and we are very poor. I am out with my brother, who is ten months older than myself. We pass a Chinese store, the door of which is open. "Look!" says Charlie, "Those men in there are

Chinese!" Eagerly I gaze into the long low room. With the exception of my mother, who is English bred with English ways and manner of dress, I have never seen a Chinese person. The two men within the store are uncouth specimens of their race, drest in working blouses and pantaloons with queues hanging down their backs. I recoil with a sense of shock.

"Oh, Charlie," I cry, "Are we like that?"

"Well, we're Chinese, and they're Chinese, too, so we must be!" returns my seven-year-old brother.

"Of course you are," puts in a boy who has followed us down the street, and who lives near us and has seen my mother: "Chinky, Chinky, Chinaman, yellow-face, pig-tail, rat-eater." A number of other boys and several little girls join in with him.

"Better than you," shouts my brother, facing the crowd. He is younger and smaller than any there, and I am even more insignificant than he; but my spirit revives.

"I'd rather be Chinese than anything else in the world," I scream.

They pull my hair, they tear my clothes, they scratch my face, and all but lame my brother; but the white blood in our veins fights valiantly for the Chinese half of us. When it is all over, exhausted and bedraggled, we crawl home, and report to our mother that we have "won the battle."

"Are you sure?" asks my mother doubtfully.

"Of course. They ran from us. They were frightened," returns my brother.

My mother smiles with satisfaction.

"Do you hear?" she asks my father.

"Umm," he observes, raising his eyes from his paper for an instant. My childish instinct, however, tells me that he is more interested than he appears to be.

It is tea time, but I cannot eat. Unobserved I crawl away. I do not sleep that night. I am too excited and I ache all over. Our opponents had been so very much stronger and bigger than we. Toward morning, however, I fall into a doze from which I awake myself, shouting:

"Sound the battle cry;
See the foe is nigh."

My mother believes in sending us to Sunday school. She has been brought up in a Presbyterian college.

The scene of my life shifts to Eastern Canada. The sleigh which has carried us from the station stops in front of a little French Canadian hotel. Immediately we are surrounded by a number of villagers, who stare curiously at my mother as my father assists her to alight from the sleigh. Their curiosity, however, is tempered with kindness, as they watch, one after another, the little black heads of my brothers and sisters and myself emerge out of the buffalo robe, which is part of the sleigh's outfit. There are six of us, four girls and two boys; the eldest, my brother, being only seven years of age. My father and mother are still in their twenties. "Les pauvres enfants," the inhabitants murmur, as they help to carry us into the hotel. Then in lower tones: "Chinoise, Chinoise."

For some time after our arrival, whenever we children are sent for a walk, our footsteps are dogged by a number of young French and English Canadians, who amuse themselves with speculations as to whether, we being Chinese, are susceptible to pinches and hair pulling, while older persons pause and gaze upon us, very much in the same way that I have seen people gaze upon strange animals in a menagerie. Now and then we are stopt and plied with questions as to what we eat and drink, how we go to sleep, if my mother understands what my father says to her, if we sit on chairs or squat on floors, etc., etc., etc.

There are many pitched battles, of course, and we seldom leave the house without being armed for conflict. My mother takes a great interest in our battles, and usually cheers us on, tho I doubt whether she understands the depth of the troubled waters thru which her little children wade. As to my father, peace is his motto, and he deems it wisest to be blind and deaf to many things.

School days are short, but memorable. I am in the same class with my brother, my sister next to me in the class below. The little girl whose desk my sister shares shrinks close against the wall as my sister takes her place. In a little while she raises her hand.

"Please, teacher!"

"Yes, Annie."

"May I change my seat?"

"No, you may not!"

The little girl sobs. "Why should she have to sit beside a——"

Happily my sister does not seem to hear, and before long the two little girls become great friends. I have many such experiences.

My brother is remarkably bright; my sister next to me has a wonderful head for figures, and when only eight years of age helps my father with his night work accounts. My parents compare her with me. She is of sturdier build than I, and, as my father says, "Always has her wits about her." He thinks her more like my mother, who is very bright and interested in every little detail of practical life. My father tells me that I will never make half the woman that my mother is or that my sister will be. I am not as strong as my sisters, which makes me feel somewhat ashamed, for I am the eldest little girl, and more is expected of me. I have no organic disease, but the strength of my feelings seems to take from me the strength of my body. I am prostrated at times with attacks of nervous sickness. The doctor says that my heart is unusually large; but in the light of the present I know that the cross of the Eurasian bore too heavily upon my childish shoulders. I usually hide my weakness from the family until I cannot stand. I do not understand myself, and I have an idea that the others will despise me for not being as strong as they. Therefore, I like to wander away alone, either by the river or in the bush. The green fields and flowing water have a charm for me. At the age of seven, as it is today, a bird on the wing is my emblem of happiness.

I have come from a race on my mother's side which is said to be the most stolid and insensible to feeling of all races, yet I look back over the years and see myself so keenly alive to every shade of sorrow and suffering that it is almost a pain to live.

If there is any trouble in the house in the way of a difference between my father and mother, or if any child is punished, how I suffer! And when harmony is restored, heaven seems to be around me. I can be sad, but I can also be glad. My mother's screams of agony when a baby is born almost drive me wild, and long after her pangs have subsided I feel them in my own body. Sometimes it is a week before I can get to sleep after such an experience.

A debt owing by my father fills me with shame. I feel like a criminal when I pass the creditor's door. I am only ten years old. And all the while the question of nationality perplexes my little brain. Why are we what we are? I and my brothers and sisters. Why did God make us to be hooted and stared at? Papa is English, mamma is Chinese. Why couldn't we have been either one thing or the other? Why is my mother's race despised? I look into the faces of my father and mother. Is she not every bit as dear and good as he? Why? Why? She sings us the songs she learned at her English school. She tells us tales of China. Tho a child when she left her native land she remembers it well, and I am never tired of listening to the story of how she was stolen from her home. She tells us over and over again of her meeting with my father in Shanghai and the romance of their marriage. Why? Why?

I do not confide in my father and mother. They would not understand. How could they? He is English, she is Chinese. I am different to both of them—a stranger, tho their own child. "What are we?" I ask my brother. "It doesn't matter, sissy," he responds. But it does. I love poetry, particularly heroic pieces. I also love fairy tales. Stories of everyday life do not appeal to me. I dream dreams of being great and noble; my sisters and brothers also. I glory in the idea of dying at the stake and a great genie arising from the flames and declaring to those who have scorned us: "Behold, how great and glorious and noble are the Chinese people!"

My sisters are apprenticed to a dressmaker; my brother is entered in an office. I tramp around and sell my father's pictures, also some lace which I make myself. My nationality, if I had only known it at that time, helps to make sales. The ladies who are my customers call me "The Little Chinese Lace Girl." But it is a dangerous life for a very young girl. I come near to "mysteriously disappearing" many a time. The greatest temptation was in the thought of getting far away from where I was known, to where no mocking cries of "Chinese!" "Chinese!" could reach.

Whenever I have the opportunity I steal away to the library and read every book I can find on China and the Chinese. I learn that China is the oldest civilized nation on the face of the earth and a few other things. At eighteen years of age what troubles me is not that I am what I am, but that others are ignorant of my superiority. I am small, but my feelings are big—and great is my vanity.

My sisters attend dancing classes, for which they pay their own fees. In spite of covert smiles and sneers, they are glad to meet and mingle with other young folk. They are not sensitive in the sense that I am. And yet they understand. One of them tells me that she overheard a young man say to another that he would rather marry a pig than a girl with Chinese blood in her veins.

In course of time I too learn shorthand and take a position in an office. Like my sister, I teach myself, but, unlike my sister, I have neither the perseverance nor the ability to perfect myself. Besides, to a temperament like mine, it is torture to spend the hours in transcribing other people's thoughts. Therefore, altho I can always earn a moderately good salary, I do not distinguish myself in the business world as does she.

When I have been working for some years I open an office of my own. The local papers patronize me and give me a number of assignments, including most of the local Chinese reporting. I meet many Chinese persons, and when they get into trouble am often called upon to fight their battles in the papers. This I enjoy. My heart leaps for joy when I read one day an article signed by a New York Chinese in which he declares "The Chinese in America owe an everlasting debt of gratitude to Sui Sin Far for the bold stand she has taken in their defense."

The Chinaman who wrote the article seeks me out and calls upon me. He is a clever and witty man, a graduate of one of the American colleges and as well a Chinese scholar. I learn that he has an American wife and several children. I am very much interested in these children, and when I meet them my heart throbs in sympathetic tune with the tales they relate of their experiences as Eurasians. "Why did papa and mamma born us?" asks one. Why?

I also meet other Chinese men who compare favorably with the white men of my acquaintance in mind and heart qualities. Some of them are quite handsome. They have not as finely cut noses and as well developed chins as the white men, but they have smoother skins and their expression is more serene; their hands are better shaped and their voices softer.

Some little Chinese women whom I interview are very anxious to know whether I would marry a Chinaman. I do not answer No. They clap their hands delightedly, and assure me that the Chinese are much the finest and best of all men. They are, however, a little doubtful as to whether one could be persuaded to care for me, full-blooded Chinese people having a prejudice against the half white.

Fundamentally, I muse, all people are the same. My mother's race is as prejudiced as my father's. Only when the whole world becomes as one family will human beings be able to see clearly and hear distinctly. I believe that some day a great part of the world will be Eurasian. I cheer myself with the thought that I am but a pioneer. A pioneer should glory in suffering.

"You were walking with a Chinaman yesterday," accuses an acquaintance.

"Yes, what of it?"

"You ought not to. It isn't right."

"Not right to walk with one of my mother's people? Oh, indeed!"

I cannot reconcile his notion of righteousness with my own.

* * *

I am living in a little town away off on the north shore of a big lake. Next to me at the dinner table is the man for whom I work as a stenographer. There are also a couple of business men, a young girl and her mother.

Some one makes a remark about the cars full of Chinamen that past [sic] that morning. A transcontinental railway runs thru the town.

My employer shakes his rugged head. "Somehow or other," says he, "I cannot reconcile myself to the thought that the Chinese are humans like ourselves. They may have immortal souls, but their faces seem to be so utterly devoid of expression that I cannot help but doubt."

"Souls," echoes the town clerk. "Their bodies are enough for me. A Chinaman is, in my eyes, more repulsive than a nigger."

"They always give me such a creepy feeling," puts in the young girl with a laugh.

"I wouldn't have one in my house," declares my landlady.

"Now, the Japanese are different altogether. There is something bright and likeable about those men," continues Mr. K.

A miserable, cowardly feeling keeps me silent. I am in a Middle West town. If I declare what I am, every person in the place will hear about it the next day. The population is in the main made up of working folks with strong prejudices against my mother's countrymen. The prospect before me is not an enviable one—if I speak. I have no longer an ambition to die at the stake for the sake of demonstrating the greatness and nobleness of the Chinese people.

Mr. K. turns to me with a kindly smile.

"What makes Miss Far so quiet?" he asks.

"I don't suppose she finds the 'washee washee men' particularly interesting subjects of conversation," volunteers the young manager of the local bank.

With a great effort I raise my eyes from my plate. "Mr. K.," I say, addressing my employer, "the Chinese people may have no souls, no expression on their faces, be altogether beyond the pale of civilization, but whatever they are, I want you to understand that I am—I am a Chinese."

There is silence in the room for a few minutes. Then Mr. K. pushes back his plate and standing up beside me, says:

"I should not have spoken as I did. I know nothing whatever about the Chinese. It was pure prejudice. Forgive me!"

I admire Mr. K.'s moral courage in apologizing to me; he is a conscientious Christian man, but I do not remain much longer in the little town.

* * *

I am under a tropic sky, meeting frequently and conversing with persons who are almost as high up in the world as birth, education and money can set them. The environment is peculiar, for I am also surrounded by a race of people, the reputed descendants of Ham, the son of Noah, whose offspring, it was prophesied, should be the servants of the sons of Shem and Japheth. As I am a descendant, according to the Bible, of both Shem and Japheth, I have a perfect right to set my heel upon the Ham people; but tho I see others around me following out the Bible suggestion, it is not in my nature to be arrogant to any but those who seek to impress me with their superiority, which the poor black maid who has been assigned to me by the hotel certainly does not. My employer's wife takes me to task for this. "It is unnecessary," she says, "to thank a black person for a service."

The novelty of life in the West Indian island is not without its charm. The surroundings, people, manner of living, are so entirely different from what I have been accustomed to up North that I feel as if I were "born again." Mixing with people of fashion, and yet not of them, I am not of sufficient importance to create comment or curiosity. I am busy nearly all day and often well into the night. It is not monotonous work, but it is certainly strenuous. The planters and business men of the island take me as a matter of course and treat me with kindly courtesy. Occasionally an Englishman will warn me against the "brown boys" of the island, little dreaming that I too am of the "brown people" of the earth.

When it begins to be whispered about the place that I am not all white, some of the "sporty" people seek my acquaintance. I am small and look much younger than my years. When, however, they discover that I am a very serious and sober-minded spinster indeed, they retire quite gracefully, leaving me a few amusing reflections.

One evening a card is brought to my room. It bears the name of some naval officer. I go down to my visitor, thinking he is probably some one who, having been told that I am a reporter for the local paper, has brought me an item of news. I find him lounging in an easy chair on the veranda of the hotel—a big, blond, handsome fellow, several years younger than I.

"You are Lieutenant——?" I inquire.

He bows and laughs a little. The laugh doesn't suit him somehow—and it doesn't suit me, either.

"If you have anything to tell me, please tell it quickly, because I'm very busy."

"Oh, you don't really mean that," he answers, with another silly and offensive laugh. "There's always plenty of time for good times. That's what I am here for. I saw you at the races the other day and twice at King's House. My ship will be here for——weeks."

"Do you wish that noted?" I ask.

"Oh, no! Why—I came just because I had an idea that you might like to know me. I would like to know you. You look such a nice little body. Say, wouldn't you like to go out for a sail this lovely night? I will tell you all about the sweet little Chinese girls I met when we were at Hong Kong. They're not so shy!"

* * *

I leave Eastern Canada for the Far West, so reduced by another attack of rheumatic fever that I only weigh eighty-four pounds. I travel on an advertising contract. It is presumed by the railway company that in some way or other I will give them full value for their transportation across the continent. I have been ordered beyond the Rockies by the doctor, who declares that I will never regain my strength in the East. Nevertheless, I am but two days in San Francisco when I start out in search of work. It is the first time that I have sought work as a stranger in a strange town. Both of the other positions away from home were secured for me by home influence. I am quite surprised to find that there is no demand for my services in San Francisco and that no one is particularly interested in me. The best I can do is to accept an offer from a railway agency to typewrite their correspondence for $5 a month. I stipulate, however, that I shall have the privilege of taking in outside work and that my hours shall be light. I am hopeful that the sale of a story or newspaper article may add to my income, and I console myself with the reflection that, considering that I still limp and bear traces of sickness, I am fortunate to secure any work at all.

The proprietor of one of the San Francisco papers, to whom I have a letter of introduction, suggests that I obtain some subscriptions from the people of Chinatown, that district of the city having never been canvassed. This suggestion I carry out with enthusiasm, tho I find that the Chinese merchants and people generally are inclined to regard me with suspicion. They have been imposed upon so many times by unscrupulous white people. Another drawback—save for a few phrases, I am unacquainted with my mother tongue. How, then, can I expect these people to accept me as their own countrywoman? The Americanized Chinamen actually laugh in my face when I tell them that I am of their race. However, they are not all "doubting Thomases." Some little women discover that I have Chinese hair, color of eyes and complexion, also that I love rice and tea. This settles the matter for them—and for their husbands.

My Chinese instincts develop. I am no longer the little girl who shrunk against my brother at the first sight of a Chinaman. Many and many a time, when alone in a strange place, has the appearance of even an humble laundryman given me a sense of protection and made me feel quite at home. This fact of itself proves to me that prejudice can be eradicated by association.

I meet a half Chinese, half white girl. Her face is plastered with a thick white coat of paint and her eyelids and eyebrows are blackened so that the shape of her eyes and the whole expression of her face is changed. She was born in the East, and at the age of eighteen came West in answer to an advertisement. Living for many years among the working class, she had heard little but abuse of the Chinese. It is not difficult, in a land like California, for a half Chinese, half white girl to pass as one of Spanish or Mexican origin. This the poor child does, tho she lives in nervous dread of being "discovered." She becomes engaged to a young man, but fears to tell him what she is, and only does so when compelled by a fearless American girl friend. This girl, who knows her origin, realizing that the truth sooner or later must be told, and better soon than late, advises the Eurasian to confide in the young man, assuring her that he loves her well enough not to allow her nationality to stand, a bar sinister, between them. But the Eurasian prefers to keep her secret, and only reveals it to the man who is to be her husband when driven to bay by the American girl, who declares that if the halfbreed will not tell the truth she will. When the young man hears that the girl he is engaged to has Chinese blood in her veins, he exclaims: "Oh, what will my folks say?" But that is all. Love is stronger than prejudice with him, and neither he nor she deems it necessary to inform his "folks."

The Americans, having for many years manifested a much higher regard for the Japanese than for the Chinese, several half Chinese young men and women, thinking to advance themselves, both in a social and business sense, pass as Japanese. They continue to be known as Eurasians; but a Japanese Eurasian does not appear in the same light as a Chinese Eurasian. The unfortunate Chinese Eurasians! Are not those who compel them to thus cringe more to be blamed than they?

People, however, are not all alike. I meet white men, and women, too, who are proud to mate with those who have Chinese blood in their veins, and think it a great honor to be distinguished by the friendship of such. There are also Eurasians and Eurasians. I know of one who allowed herself to become engaged to a white man after refusing him nine times. She had discouraged him in every way possible, had warned him that she was half Chinese; that her people were poor, that every week or month she sent home a certain amount of her earnings, and that the man she married would have to do as much, if not more; also, most uncompromising truth of all, that she did not love him and never would. But the resolute and undaunted lover swore that it was a matter of indifference to him whether she was a Chinese or a Hottentot, that it would be his pleasure and privilege to allow her relations double what it was in her power to bestow, and as to not loving him—that did not matter at all. He loved her. So, because the young woman had a married mother and married sisters, who were always picking at her and gossiping over her independent manner of living, she finally consented to marry him, recording the agreement in her diary thus:

"I have promised to become the wife of —— —— on —— ——, 189–, because the world is so cruel and sneering to a single woman—and for no other reason."

Everything went smoothly until one day. The young man was driving a pair of beautiful horses and she was seated by his side, trying very hard to imagine herself in love with him, when a Chinese vegetable gardener's cart came rumbling along. The Chinaman was a jolly-looking individual in blue cotton blouse and pantaloons, his rakish looking hat being kept in place by a long queue which was pulled upward from his neck and wound around it. The young woman was suddenly possest with the spirit of mischief. "Look!" she cried, indicating the Chinaman, "there's my brother. Why don't you salute him?"

The man's face fell a little. He sank into a pensive mood. The wicked one by his side read him like an open book.

"When we are married," said she. "I intend to give a Chinese party every month."

No answer.

"As there are very few aristocratic Chinese in this city, I shall fill up with the laundrymen and vegetable farmers. I don't believe in being exclusive in democratic America, do you?"

He hadn't a grain of humor in his composition, but a sickly smile contorted his features as he replied:

"You shall do just as you please, my darling. But—but—consider a moment. Wouldn't it be just a little pleasanter for us if, after we are married, we allowed it to be presumed that you were—er—Japanese? So many of my friends have inquired of me if that is not your nationality. They would be so charmed to meet a little Japanese lady."

"Hadn't you better oblige them by finding one?"

"Why—er—what do you mean?"

"Nothing much in particular. Only—I am getting a little tired of this," taking off his ring.

"You don't mean what you say! Oh, put it back, dearest! You know I would not hurt your feelings for the world!"

"You haven't. I'm more than pleased. But I do mean what I say."

That evening the "ungrateful" Chinese Eurasian diaried, among other things, the following:

"Joy, oh, joy! I'm free once more. Never again shall I be untrue to my own heart. Never again will I allow any one to 'hound' or 'sneer' me into matrimony."

I secure transportation to many California points. I meet some literary people, chief among whom is the editor of the magazine who took my first Chinese stories. He and his wife give me a warm welcome to their ranch. They are broad-minded people, whose interest in me is sincere and intelligent, not affected and vulgar. I also meet some funny people who advise me to "trade" upon my nationality. They tell me that if I wish to succeed in literature in America I should dress in Chinese costume, carry a fan in my hand, wear a pair of scarlet beaded slippers, live in New York, and come of high birth. Instead of making myself familiar with the Chinese-Americans around me, I should discourse on my spirit acquaintance with Chinese ancestors and quote in between the "Good mornings" and "How d'ye dos" of editors.

> *"Confucius, Confucius, how great is Confucius, Before Confucius, there never was Confucius. After Confucius, there never came Confucius,"* etc., etc., etc.,

or something like that, both illuminating and obscuring, don't you know. They forget, or perhaps they are not aware that the old Chinese sage taught "The way of sincerity is the way of heaven."

My experiences as an Eurasian never cease; but people are not now as prejudiced as they have been. In the West, too, my friends are more advanced in all lines of thought than those whom I know in Eastern Canada—more genuine, more sincere, with less of the form of religion, but more of its spirit.

So I roam backward and forward across the continent. When I am East, my heart is West. When I am West, my heart is East. Before long I hope to be in China. As my life began in my father's country it may end in my mother's.

After all I have no nationality and am not anxious to claim any. Individuality is more than nationality. "You are you and I am I," says Confucius. I give my right hand to the Occidentals and my left to the Orientals, hoping that between them they will not utterly destroy the insignificant "connecting link." And that's all.

1909

from Mrs. Spring Fragrance

In the Land of the Free[1]

I

"See, Little One—the hills in the morning sun. There is thy[2] home for years to come. It is very beautiful and thou wilt be very happy there."

The Little One looked up into his mother's face in perfect faith. He was engaged in the pleasant occupation of sucking a sweetmeat; but that did not prevent him from gurgling responsively.

"Yes, my olive bud; there is where thy father is making a fortune for thee. Thy father! Oh, wilt thou not be glad to behold his dear face. 'Twas for thee I left him."

The Little One ducked his chin sympathetically against his mother's knee. She lifted him on to her lap. He was two years old, a round, dimple-cheeked boy with bright brown eyes and a sturdy little frame.

"Ah! Ah! Ah! Ooh! Ooh! Ooh!" puffed he, mocking a tugboat steaming by.

San Francisco's waterfront was lined with ships and steamers, while other craft, large and small, including a couple of white transports from the Philippines, lay at

[1]This story was initially published in the progressive New York magazine, *Independent* 67, 3170 (September 2, 1909) 504–508, in the third decade of the Chinese Exclusion Act when legal harassment of Chinese was still prevalent.

[2]The use of *thy* and *thou* is not to be associated with sixteenth-century usage or nineteenth-century Quakers. Sui Sin Far's intent here is to convey a tone of familiarity and intimacy, as well as a slight foreignness, in this Chinese mother's remarks, supposedly in Chinese, to her two-year-old child.

anchor here and there off shore. It was some time before the *Eastern Queen* could get docked, and even after that was accomplished, a lone Chinaman who had been waiting on the wharf for an hour was detained that much longer by men with the initials U.S.C. on their caps, before he could board the steamer and welcome his wife and child.

"This is thy son," announced the happy Lae Choo.

Hom Hing lifted the child, felt of his little body and limbs, gazed into his face with proud and joyous eyes; then turned inquiringly to a customs officer at his elbow.

"That's a fine boy you have there," said the man. "Where was he born?"

"In China," answered Hom Hing, swinging the Little One on his right shoulder, preparatory to leading his wife off the steamer.

"Ever been to America before?"

"No, not he," answered the father with a happy laugh.

The customs officer beckoned to another.

"This little fellow," said he, "is visiting America for the first time."

The other customs officer stroked his chin reflectively.

"Good day," said Hom Hing.

"Wait!" commanded one of the officers. "You cannot go just yet."

"What more now?" asked Hom Hing.

"I'm afraid," said the first customs officer, "that we cannot allow the boy to go ashore. There is nothing in the papers that you have shown us—your wife's papers and your own—having any bearing upon the child."

"There was no child when the papers were made out," returned Hom Hing. He spoke calmly; but there was apprehension in his eyes and in his tightening grip on his son.

"What is it? What is it?" quavered Lae Choo, who understood a little English.

The second customs officer regarded her pityingly.

"I don't like this part of the business," he muttered.

The first officer turned to Hom Hing and in an official tone of voice, said:

"Seeing that the boy has no certificate entitling him to admission to this country you will have to leave him with us."

"Leave my boy!" exclaimed Hom Hing.

"Yes; he will be well taken care of, and just as soon as we can hear from Washington he will be handed over to you."

"But," protested Hom Hing, "he is my son."

"We have no proof," answered the man with a shrug of his shoulders; "and even if so we cannot let him pass without orders from the Government."

"He is my son," reiterated Hom Hing, slowly and solemnly. "I am a Chinese merchant and have been in business in San Francisco for many years. When my wife told to me one morning that she dreamed of a green tree with spreading branches and one beautiful red flower growing thereon, I answered her that I wished my son to be born in our country, and for her to prepare to go to China. My wife complied with my wish. After my son was born my mother fell sick and my wife nursed and cared for her; then my father, too, fell sick, and my wife also nursed and cared for him. For twenty moons my wife care for and nurse the old people, and when they die they bless her and my son, and I send for her to return to me. I had no fear of trouble. I was a Chinese merchant and my son was my son."

"Very good, Hom Hing," replied the first officer. "Nevertheless, we take your son."

"No, you not take him; he my son too."

It was Lae Choo. Snatching the child from his father's arms she held and covered him with her own.

The officers conferred together for a few moments; then one drew Hom Hing aside and spoke in his ear.

Resignedly Hom Hing bowed his head, then approached his wife. "'Tis the law," said he, speaking in Chinese, "and 'twill be but for a little while—until tomorrow's sun arises."

"You, too," reproached Lae Choo in a voice eloquent with pain. But accustomed to obedience she yielded the boy to her husband, who in turn delivered him to the first officer. The Little One protested lustily against the transfer; but his mother covered her face with her sleeve and his father silently led her away. Thus was the law of the land complied with.

II

Day was breaking. Lae Choo, who had been awake all night, dressed herself, then awoke her husband.

"'Tis the morn," she cried. "Go, bring our son."

The man rubbed his eyes and arose upon his elbow so that he could see out of the window. A pale star was visible in the sky. The petals of a lily in a bowl on the windowsill were unfurled.

"'Tis not yet time," said he, laying his head down again.

"Not yet time. Ah, all the time that I lived before yesterday is not so much as the time that has been since my little one was taken from me."

The mother threw herself down beside the bed and covered her face.

Hom Hing turned on the light, and touching his wife's bowed head with a sympathetic hand inquired if she had slept.

"Slept!" she echoed, weepingly. "Ah, how could I close my eyes with my arms empty of the little body that has filled them every night for more than twenty moons! You do not know—man—what it is to miss the feel of the little fingers and the little toes and the soft round limbs of your little one. Even in the darkness his darling eyes used to shine up to mine, and often have I fallen into slumber with his pretty babble at my ear. And now, I see him not; I touch him not; I hear him not. My baby, my little fat one!"

"Now! Now! Now!" consoled Hom Hing, patting his wife's shoulder reassuringly; "there is no need to grieve so; he will soon gladden you again. There cannot be any law that would keep a child from its mother!"

Lae Choo dried her tears.

"You are right, my husband," she meekly murmured. She arose and stepped about the apartment, setting things to rights. The box of presents she had brought for her California friends had been opened the evening before; and silks, embroideries, carved ivories, ornamental lacquer-ware, brasses, camphorwood boxes, fans, and chinaware were scattered around in confused heaps. In the midst of unpacking the thought of her child in the hands of strangers had overpowered her, and she had left everything to crawl into bed and weep.

Having arranged her gifts in order she stepped out on to the deep balcony.

The star had faded from view and there were bright streaks in the western sky. Lae Choo looked down the street and around. Beneath the flat occupied by her and her husband were quarters for a number of bachelor Chinamen, and she could hear them from where she stood, taking their early morning breakfast. Below their dining-room was her husband's grocery store. Across the way was a large restaurant. Last night it had been resplendent with gay colored lanterns and the sound of music. The rejoicings over "the completion of the moon,"[3] by Quong Sum's first-born, had been long and loud, and had caused her to tie a handkerchief over her ears. She, a bereaved mother, had it not in her heart to rejoice with other parents. This morning the place was more in accord with her mood. It was still and quiet. The revellers had dispersed or were asleep.

A roly-poly woman in black sateen, with long pendant earrings in her ears, looked up from the street below and waved her a smiling greeting. It was her old neighbor, Kuie Hoe, the wife of the gold embosser, Mark Sing. With her was a little boy in yellow jacket and lavender pantaloons. Lae Choo remembered him as a baby. She used to like to play with him in those days when she had no child of her own. What a long time ago that seemed! She caught her breath in a sigh, and laughed instead.

"Why are you so merry?" called her husband from within.

"Because my Little One is coming home," answered Lae Choo. "I am a happy mother—a happy mother."

She pattered into the room with a smile on her face.

The noon hour had arrived. The rice was steaming in the bowls and a fragrant dish of chicken and bamboo shoots was awaiting Hom Hing. Not for one moment had Lae Choo paused to rest during the morning hours; her activity had been ceaseless. Every now and again, however, she had raised her eyes to the gilded clock on the curiously carved mantelpiece. Once, she had exclaimed:

"Why so long, oh! why so long?" Then apostrophizing herself: "Lae Choo, be happy. The Little One is coming! The Little One is coming!" Several times she burst into tears and several times she laughed aloud.

Hom Hing entered the room; his arms hung down by his side.

"The Little One!" shrieked Lae Choo.

"They bid me call tomorrow."

With a moan the mother sank to the floor.

The noon hour passed. The dinner remained on the table.

[3]The Chinese traditionally give banquets to celebrate the completion of an infant boy's first month.

III

The winter rains were over: the spring had come to California, flushing the hills with green and causing an ever-changing pageant of flowers to pass over them. But there was no spring in Lae Choo's heart, for the Little One remained away from her arms. He was being kept in a mission. White women were caring for him, and though for one full moon he had pined for his mother and refused to be comforted he was now apparently happy and contented. Five moons or five months had gone by since the day he had passed with Lae Choo through the Golden Gate; but the great Government at Washington still delayed sending the answer which would return him to his parents.

Hom Hing was disconsolately rolling up and down the balls in his abacus box when a keen-faced young man stepped into his store.

"What news?" asked the Chinese merchant.

"This!" The young man brought forth a typewritten letter. Hom Hing read the words:

"Re Chinese child, alleged to be the son of Hom Hing, Chinese merchant, doing business at 425 Clay street, San Francisco.

"Same will have attention as soon as possible."

Hom Hing returned the letter, and without a word continued his manipulation of the counting machine.

"Have you anything to say?" asked the young man.

"Nothing. They have sent the same letter fifteen times before. Have you not yourself showed it to me?"

"True!" The young man eyed the Chinese merchant furtively. He had a proposition to make and he was pondering whether or not the time was opportune.

"How is your wife?" he inquired solicitously—and diplomatically.

Hom Hing shook his head mournfully.

"She seems less every day," he replied. "Her food she takes only when I bid her and her tears fall continually. She finds no pleasure in dress or flowers and cares not to see her friends. Her eyes stare all night. I think before another moon she will pass into the land of spirits."

"No!" exclaimed the young man, genuinely startled.

"If the boy not come home I lose my wife sure," continued Hom Hing with bitter sadness.

"It's not right," cried the young man indignantly. Then he made his proposition.

The Chinese father's eyes brightened exceedingly.

"Will I like you to go to Washington and make them give you the paper to restore my son?" cried he. "How can you ask when you know my heart's desire?"

"Then," said the young fellow, "I will start next week. I am anxious to see this thing through if only for the sake of your wife's peace of mind."

"I will call her. To hear what you think to do will make her glad," said Hom Hing.

He called a message to Lae Choo upstairs through a tube in the wall.

In a few moments she appeared, listless, wan, and hollow-eyed; but when her husband told her the young lawyer's suggestion she became as one electrified; her form straightened, her eyes glistened; the color flushed to her cheeks.

"Oh," she cried, turning to James Clancy, "You are a hundred man good!"

The young man felt somewhat embarrassed; his eyes shifted a little under the intense gaze of the Chinese mother.

"Well, we must get your boy for you," he responded. "Of course"—turning to Hom Hing—"it will cost a little money. You can't get fellows to hurry the Government for you without gold in your pocket."

Hom Hing stared blankly for a moment. Then: "How much do you want, Mr. Clancy?" he asked quietly.

"Well, I will need at least five hundred to start with."

Hom Hing cleared his throat.

"I think I told to you the time I last paid you for writing letters for me and seeing the Custom boss here that nearly all I had was gone!"

"Oh, well then we won't talk about it, old fellow. It won't harm the boy to stay where he is, and your wife may get over it all right."

"What that you say?" quavered Lae Choo.

James Clancy looked out of the window.

"He says," explained Hom Hing in English, "that to get our boy we have to have much money."

"Money! Oh, yes."

Lae Choo nodded her head.

"I have not got the money to give him."

For a moment Lae Choo gazed wonderingly from one face to the other; then, comprehension dawning upon her, with swift anger, pointing to the lawyer, she cried: "You not one hundred man good; you just common white man."

"Yes, ma'am," returned James Clancy, bowing and smiling ironically.

Hom Hing pushed his wife behind him and addressed the lawyer again: "I might try," said he, "to raise something; but five hundred—it is not possible."

"What about four?"

"I tell you I have next to nothing left and my friends are not rich."

"Very well!"

The lawyer moved leisurely toward the door, pausing on its threshold to light a cigarette.

"Stop, white man; white man, stop!"

Lae Choo, panting and terrified, had started forward and now stood beside him, clutching his sleeve excitedly.

"You say you can go to get paper to bring my Little One to me if Hom Hing give you five hundred dollars?"

The lawyer nodded carelessly; his eyes were intent upon the cigarette which would not take the fire from the match.

"Then you go get paper. If Hom Hing not can give you five hundred dollars—I give you perhaps what more that much."

She slipped a heavy gold bracelet from her wrist and held it out to the man. Mechanically he took it.

"I go get more!"

She scurried away, disappearing behind the door through which she had come.

"Oh, look here, I can't accept this," said James Clancy, walking back to Hom Hing and laying down the bracelet before him.

"It's all right," said Hom Hing, seriously, "pure China gold. My wife's parent give it to her when we married."

"But I can't take it anyway," protested the young man.

"It is all same as money. And you want money to go to Washington," replied Hom Hing in a matter of fact manner.

"See, my jade earrings—my gold buttons—my hairpins—my comb of pearl and my rings—one, two, three, four, five rings; very good—very good—all same much money. I give them all to you. You take and bring me paper for my Little One."

Lae Choo piled up her jewels before the lawyer.

Hom Hing laid a restraining hand upon her shoulder. "Not all, my wife," he said in Chinese. He selected a ring—his gift to Lae Choo when she dreamed of the tree with the red flower. The rest of the jewels he pushed toward the white man.

"Take them and sell them," said he. "They will pay your fare to Washington and bring you back with the paper."

For one moment James Clancy hesitated. He was not a sentimental man; but something within him arose against accepting such payment for his services.

"They are good, good," pleadingly asserted Lae Choo, seeing his hesitation.

Whereupon he seized the jewels, thrust them into his coat pocket, and walked rapidly away from the store.

IV

Lae Choo followed after the missionary woman through the mission nursery school. Her heart was beating so high with happiness that she could scarcely breathe. The paper had come at last—the precious paper which gave Hom Hing and his wife the right to the possession of their own child. It was ten months now since he had been taken from them—ten months since the sun had ceased to shine for Lae Choo.

The room was filled with children—most of them wee tots, but none so wee as her own. The mission woman talked as she walked. She told Lae Choo that little Kim, as he had been named by the school, was the pet of the place, and that his little tricks and ways amused and delighted every one. He had been rather difficult to manage at first and had cried much for his mother; "but children so soon forget, and after a month he seemed quite at home and played around as bright and happy as a bird."

"Yes," responded Lae Choo. "Oh, yes, yes!"

But she did not hear what was said to her. She was walking in a maze of anticipatory joy.

"Wait here, please," said the mission woman, placing Lae Choo in a chair. "The very youngest ones are having their breakfast."

She withdrew for a moment—it seemed like an hour to the mother—then she reappeared leading by the hand a little boy dressed in blue cotton overalls and white-soled shoes. The little boy's face was round and dimpled and his eyes were very bright.

"Little One, ah, my Little One!" cried Lae Choo.

She fell on her knees and stretched her hungry arms toward her son.

But the Little One shrunk from her and tried to hide himself in the folds of the white woman's skirt.

"Go'way, go'way!" he bade his mother.

Mary Austin 1868–1934

The second child of George and Susannah Hunter, Mary Hunter Austin was born in Carlinville, Illinois, and graduated from Blackburn College in 1888, with interests in both science and art. In 1888 her family moved to Southern California hoping to homestead in the lower San Joaquin Valley. By this time her father and older sister had died, relations between Austin and her mother were strained, and Austin had accustomed herself to a solitary life, in which her most vibrant, meaningful experiences came from a mystical connection to nature. Already predisposed to value the natural world, Austin explored, fell in love with, and began to write about the arid landscapes of the Southwest.

She married Stafford Wallace Austin in 1891, moving with him to the Owens Valley where both taught in several Southern California small towns, settling finally in Lone Pine. In 1892 her only child, Ruth, was born mentally retarded; eventually Ruth was placed by her mother in a mental institution, where she died in 1918. Austin's marriage to Stafford Austin was in shambles by the time her first, and most famous book, *The Land of Little Rain,* appeared in 1903. They lived separate lives for ten years, finally divorcing in 1914. Austin never remarried, devoting herself instead to intellectual and emotional engagement with the most important writers of her time, and to a life of public activism in various causes, including environmental conservation and regional advocacy. An important figure in the artists' colonies of both Carmel, California and Santa Fe, New Mexico, she also fought for water rights in the Southwest, first in the Owens Valley and later as a delegate to the Boulder Dam Conference in 1927, where she argued against the diversion of the Colorado River to supply water to Los Angeles.

As her autobiography, *Earth Horizon* makes clear, early in her life Austin felt herself "marked" by a specialness which was evidenced in her drive to influence social customs and political policies through her writings. Author of twenty-seven books and more than two hundred and fifty articles, she saw her mission as essentially two-fold: to shift the center of culture from the Euro-American traditions of the East coast to the American Indian and Hispanic traditions of the Southwest, and to change her generation's attitudes toward women and women's rights. She was a regionalist who used her considerable energy, influence, and talent in collecting, preserving, and encouraging the continuation of Hispanic and American Indian folk arts. Her involvement with American Indian and Hispanic arts in the Southwest poses, however, complex interpretative issues. On the one hand, Austin and her colleagues helped engender national markets for art forms that had been ignored and even suppressed; on the other, they did so by applying Euro-American esthetic standards to indigenous arts, attempting to direct the local artists into patterns not necessarily in keeping with the crafts or their own cultural values.

Austin was also a vocal feminist, using her writings to argue for suffrage and birth control. Her most successful fictional effort, *A Woman of Genius,* ranks alongside

Willa Cather's *Song of the Lark* as a study in the trials facing a creative woman of the Progressive Era. Austin's remarkable legacy of writings coheres around her intense focus on the conflicts experienced by women of her time. *Earth Horizon* most clearly delineates those tensions in Austin's inventive use of first, second, and third person voices in referring to herself. Realizing that women often operated in two spheres of consciousness—one that was their inner, true self and one that evidenced a husband's or father's projections of ideal womanhood (she, you, or simply, Mary)—Austin wrote movingly about her personal anguish in order to exemplify the changes she hoped to see accomplished. Her struggle was not only with beliefs about women's roles but with the physical spaces they were allowed to occupy. Whether she was writing about desert-induced mirages, or small-town life in Carlinville, Illinois, or the urban canyons of New York City, she described in detail the physical environment and its potential as a place of free movement for women. In this way, Austin's writing offers a broad-ranging critique of the environments—both perceptual and actual—in which women live their lives. Her counsel to herself in *Earth Horizon* remains valuable today as women continue the struggle to establish their own space: "There was something you could do about unsatisfactory conditions besides being heroic or martyr to them, something more satisfactory than enduring or complaining, and that was getting out to hunt for the remedy."

Vera Norwood
University of New Mexico

PRIMARY WORKS

The Land of Little Rain, 1903; *Lost Borders,* 1909; *A Woman of Genius,* 1912; *The Land of Journey's Ending,* 1924; *Starry Adventure,* 1931; *Earth Horizon,* 1932; *Literary America,* 1903–1934; *The Mary Austin Letters,* 1979; *Stories from the Country of Lost Borders,* ed. Marjorie Pryse, 1987; *The Ford,* 1997; *The Basket Woman: A Book of Indian Tales,* 1999.

from Earth Horizon

III

After the summer of '82, or thereabouts, events began to present themselves again in an orderly course. We were living on Johnson Street then, in a house my mother built out of the sale of the farm. The pension she had applied for had been allowed, with officer's back pay; other matters had straightened themselves out, so that, though she continued to go out occasionally as general emergency aid, it was chiefly to the houses of her friends, who coveted her warm, consoling interest in their plight. The house was well built, of six rooms arranged in two rows, three bedrooms, parlor, sitting-room, and kitchen; no bath, of course; an outside toilet, and drinking water from the pump, as was the case with all the houses in town except for the very wealthy. There was no central heating such as was beginning to be the fashion for more commodious homes, but there were two fireplaces for burning coal, with imitation black marble mantels, and between the parlor and livingroom there were folding doors. The one extravagance my mother had allowed herself was to have the woodwork of the two 'front' rooms 'grained'; which means that it was treated so as to present the natural aspect of an expensive hardwood finish, like no wood on earth, I am sure. Susie[1] was extremely pleased with it, and the work must have been good of its kind, for when I visited the house forty years later, it was still shining and intact.

Outside, ours was such a house as might have been discovered by the score in any Middlewestern town, clapboarded, white-painted with green blinds, its original Colonial lines corrupted by what in the course of the next decade or two broke out irruptively into what is now known as the 'bungalow' type. We lived there about seven years, and Mary was never at home in it at all. At that time nobody ever thought of inquiring what Mary thought of anything, so nobody found out. Several years after our removing to California, when Mother, who was desperately homesick there, was reproaching her for never having shown any trace of such sickness, said Mary unthoughtfully, 'Homesick for what?' and saw that she would have to turn it quickly; 'Isn't it the family that makes the home?'—and Susie managed to be doubtfully content with that. The place was dear to her; she had built it, and except that she would have furnished it more handsomely if she could, it satisfied her expectation. But Mary recalls very well her first going there after the workmen had left and the furniture was partly in place, and being struck with a cold blast of what she was to recognize long after as the wind before the dawn of the dreary discontent with the American scene, which has since been made familiar to us all by the present generation of writers in the Middlewest. But Mary's case was rendered more desolate by her not being able to refuse the conviction that was pressed upon her from every side, that any dissatisfaction she might have felt was inherently of herself, that she was queer and ungrateful and insensitive to the finer aspects of existence. To the extent that she wasn't able to shut it out of consciousness by fixing her attention on something else, Mary was always, in that house, a little below herself, without the relief of despising it, which a kindly dispensation granted to the generation next after her.

To begin with, there wasn't a nook or corner of the house which could be differentiated from any other corner, could be made to take the impress of the resident's spirit, or afford even a momentary relief from the general tone and tempo of the family life. It was all neat and hard and squared up with a purely objective domesticity within which it was not possible even to imagine any other sort of life. There wasn't the alteration of pulse such as might be secured by the coming and going of the head of the house, the relief of readjusting details to the drama of affection; a perpetually widowed house.

My mother was in most respects an efficient housekeeper; everything was invariably clean and tidy; she got through her work with a celerity that was the marvel of the neighborhood. She had an extraordinary knack of stretching money to the utmost, of cleaning and turning and pressing her clothes, so that she always looked trim and well-turned-out. She put all of us, and her house, through the same process, without anybody ever suspecting that it might not be the best process imaginable for everybody.

Outside, things were not much better. Johnson Street was north of the town, between the town and the college; it had been chosen partly because of that, so that the children as they grew up might have that advantage, or that Susie might eke out her

[1]Susie is Mary Austin's mother, Susannah Hunter.

income, as it proved desirable, with boarders. This last plan never came to anything. In that small house the intrusion of a 'boarder' proved unbearable, even to the brothers, and Susie discovered that a boarder is a poor substitute for the one thing that binds a woman willingly to the unbroken routine of meals and hours.

The neighborhood itself was new; only a few houses had gone up there, newly married couples and the better-paid sort of work-people. All that part of town was originally prairie, stretching north and north unbrokenly, shorn and treeless, to flat horizons. Up and down the street young maples had been planted, but except for a few trees about the Miller place, which had once been a farmhouse, there was nothing to rest the eye upon. Going to school one went past vacant weed-grown lots, past the foundry, which had once been the woolen mills, and was at the moment, I believe, a tool and hoe works, and so to Grandpa's house on First North, and across the square to school. That was the way you took when hurried, but coming back you spared yourself the time as often as possible to come the longest way around, along East Main, up College Avenue, so as to bring yourself past the more attractive gardens.

I am not, after all these years, going to be blamed, as I was blamed by everybody who knew about it, for my preferences in matters of this kind. Mary was more than ordinarily sensitive to form and proportion. Never so much so as during those years of adolescence when the submerged faculty, that is appeased with the mere appearance of things, came so close to the surface that it was chiefly the want of any possible practical way of accomplishing a painting career that decided her between paint and print as a medium of expression.

I felt the outward scene in those days as other people feel music, its structure, its progressions; felt emotion as color and color as tone. All the family except Mary were to some degree musical, but it scarcely occurred to anybody in those days that not having 'an ear for music' was merely an error in the instrumentation, that all the sensitivities that went with a musical gift were merely transferred to another sensory tract and were active there, capable of ecstasy and pain in a similar, even in a more intensive fashion. To this day Mary can be made sick by living in a room of bad color or wrong proportions, even though, in the stress of other preoccupations, often the first notice she has of inharmony in the objective environment, is physical dis-ease. Susie herself was so sensitive to tone that she never hesitated to say when the piano was badly out of tune that it 'gave her the shivers.'

One of the family jokes was that Mary had a notion that the tool and hoe works was pretty, although what Mary had actually said was not 'pretty' but beautiful, as she had seen it once of a winter twilight, rust-red against a dark blue sky faintly streaked with ruddy cloud, and below the long lines of the brick walls in harmony with the horizon, the pond where youngsters went to skate in winter, blue with the deep-sea blue of thick ice lit with reflected fire of the sky. Well, it *was* beautiful. The mistake was in saying so. And that was why Mary said as little as possible about the house in Johnson Street, which only just escaped being unendurable.

The parlor was the worst. The furniture, except for the piano new and ugly, of a popular type of decoration of cut-in designs picked out in black and gilt. People were then beginning to get rid of their good old pieces and stressing a modern note. The blinds at the undraped windows were dark chocolate, the carpet and upholstery chosen of reds and greens which 'set each other off.' Except for a few family photographs, the walls were bare. Later a lithograph of the martyred Garfield[2] adorned one wall and a cheap papier-maché 'placque' of Lily Langtry[3] another. I do not know what else we would have put on them. There were a few houses in Carlinville where you could see good old engravings, Currier and Ives prints, and a few dark portraits in oil. There were other houses in which you might find bright prints of a slightly later date in black and gilt frames; none of them so bad as they became a decade later; sentimental subjects; Fast Asleep and Wide Awake were the names of the two at Grandpa's, and a black and white Landseer Stag at Bay—some such matter. But there were none of these at our house, perhaps because Susie had never cared to own them. There was not even a Whatnot.

Some day someone will write the history of the Whatnot, with its odd, and for the most part attractive, collection of sociohistorical fetishes; the tropic shell carved minutely with the Lord's Prayer; Indian arrow-heads; the glass paper-weight with glass flowers inside, or a picture of the Centennial; the stuffed bird; the wax flowers; the polished buffalo horn; the 'mineral specimens' from California; all those curious keys which unlocked for the ancestors aesthetic emotion and intellectual curiosity. I am sure if I had a proper Whatnot at hand, I could lead you by it through the whole aesthetic history of the Middlewest. I could touch the hidden life, the obscure, the unconfessed root of the art impulse from which I am indubitably sprung. But we had no Whatnot in our house, not even a home-made one of wire-threaded spools and walnut stain.

Looking back, I can realize now that the child with staring eyes and the great mane of tawny curls, who used to creep slowly along the rail that divided the 'art department' of the county fair from the milling crowd, taking in with avid, slow absorption the now obsolete tufted and cut-out and cross-stitched counterpanes, the infinitely fine crocheted antimacassars, the picture frames of shells and acorn cups and prickly seeds, seeing them grow with time more curious and tasteless, and valued for their singularity, was seeing much more than that. She was seeing the passing of that initial impulse toward aestheticism so hardily kept alive for three generations on the contents of Whatnots, and on little else. . . .

It wasn't until the family had settled well into the house on Johnson Street that Mary began to feel herself harassed by family criticism of her individual divergences on no better ground than that they were divergences. That year Mary had finally overcome the two years' difference in their school grades that divided her from Jim,[4] and, though not yet sharing all his classes, they sat under the same teacher, and Mary began to be the subject of that acute sensitivity of brothers to lapses, on the part of their young sisters, from severest propriety. Well, of course, brothers always did tell on you. It seemed to be part of their official prerogative as arbiters of what could or could not be said to or in front of sisters and the obligation to lick other boys who violated these restrictions. But it seemed to Mary that there was too much relish sometimes in the telling, and, besides, Mary had her own notions of the proprieties.

It was in the business of a spirited self-justification that she first explicitly noticed something of which she had been, ever since that summer in Boston, dimly

[2]James Garfield, twentieth president of the United States, who was assassinated in 1881.

[3]Lily Langtry was an English actress of the time.

[4]Austin's older brother. She was advanced to his grade level because she was an excellent reader, much beyond her age level.

aware, the extent to which her mother was reshaping the family and her own affectional life around her eldest son, shaping him to that part it was so widely agreed was suitable to be played, and 'sweet' to observe him playing, as the widow's son.

One tries to present a situation, usual enough then, not so usual now, as it occurred, as an incident in the education of Mary. What my mother was proceeding toward, with the saction of the most treasured of American traditions, was constituting my brother, at fifteen or thereabouts, the Head of the family. According to the tradition, she had a right to expect Mary to contribute a certain acquiescence in a situation which kept the shape if not the content of the best my mother's generation knew of the ritual of sex. It was a way to maintain what the high-minded women of her generation esteemed the crown of a woman's life, the privilege of being the utterly giving and devoted wife of one man who could make it still seem a privilege, although it violated all the other natural motions of the woman's being. Susie was justified, in a compulsion of advice and remonstrance, to persuade Mary into the traditional attitudes. What she missed realizing was that a general social change in those attitudes was imminent, and that both her children were probably unconsciously responding to it according to their natures. Hers was not the only household in which struggles between brothers and sisters were going on, prophetic of the somewhat later conflict between traditionalism and realism which was so to alter the whole status of American marriage. Mary wasn't by any means the only girl of that period insisting on going her own way against the traditions, and refusing to come to a bad end on account of it.

Years after, when the feminist fight, marshaled in the direction of Woman Suffrage, became the occasion of conferences of women from all parts of the world, in the relaxing hour between committee meetings and campaign planning, there would be confidences. 'Well, it was seeing what my mother had to go through that started me'; or, 'It was being sacrificed to the boys in the family that set me going'; or, 'My father was one of the old-fashioned kind . . .' I remember three English sisters who all together and at once took to window-smashing and hunger fasts because they simply could not endure for another minute the tyranny of having their father spend their dress money every year in a single bolt of cloth of his own choosing, from which they were expected to make up what they wore. Women of high intelligence and education went white and sick telling how, in their own families, the mere whim of the dominant male member, even in fields which should have been exempt from his interference, had been allowed to assume the whole weight of moral significance.

It was a four-minute egg that set Mary going.

I have already related how, scrambling out of sleep rendered uneasy by too early responsibility and not always untouched by the consciousness of her father's recurrent anguish, Mary had acquired a prejudice against the very soft-boiled egg, so that her never very stable appetite revolted at seeing one broken even unsuspectingly before her. I don't know just when her quite justifiable request to have her egg put in the kettle a minute or two before the others began to break down the general disposition to create, out of her brother's status as the Head of the family, a criterion of how eggs should be served. It was only one of many unimportant oddments in which the necessity arose of considering Mary as a separate item in the family ritual which Susie was happily reconstituting around her eldest son. It was to be for Jim as nearly as possible as it had been when the whole affectional and practical interest of the family had centered on Father having what he wanted and being pleased by it. To remember Mary's egg became a constantly annoying snag in the perfect family gesture of subservience to the Head, which all her woman's life had gone to create. And perhaps there was latent in Susie's mind, in spite of her avowed liberality toward the woman movement, something of the deep-seated conviction, on the part of the house-mother, that drove many girls of Mary's generation from the domestic life, that a different sort of boiled egg was more than a female had a right to claim on her own behalf. I can, at any rate, recall very well the completely justified manner with which she would say, on those increasing occasions when it turned out that Mary's egg had not been remembered, 'Well, my dear, if you can't learn to take your food like the *rest* of the family . . .' But even more it proved a distraction and an annoyance when Mary was left to prepare her own egg. 'Oh, Mary, why do you always have to have something different from the *rest* of the family . . .' And finally when Jim, consistently playing his part as the complaisant favorite of the house, delivered judgment, 'Somehow you never seem to have any feeling for what a HOME should be'; not in the least realizing that there was growing up in the minds of thousands of young American women at that moment, the notion that it, at least, *shouldn't* be the place of the apotheosis of its male members. In so far as the difficulty about the extra minute and a half proved annoying to Mary, she settled it by deciding that she didn't care for eggs for breakfast. And yet, slight as the incident seems, it served to fix the pattern of family reaction to Mary's divergences. . . .

By the time the Hunters had settled in at Tejon,[5] Mary suffered something like a complete collapse. There had been, in addition to the emotional stress of breaking up home, the two years of exhausting college work, in which so much of the other two years had to be made up by extra hours, after which had come the relaxing California climate, and the problem of food. I suppose few people who pioneered on the Pacific Coast between the Gold Rush in '49 and the Real Estate Rush in the eighties ever realized the natural food poverty of that opulent land. By that time the Spanish with the art of irrigation, and the Chinese, wise in food-growing, had mitigated the handicaps of an almost total want of native roots and fruits and nuts on which the Middlewest pioneers had managed mainly to subsist. It was only the few like the Tejon homesteaders, cast away on a waterless strip in a dry year, who realized that it had been the wiping away of the slowly accumulated Indian knowledge of native foods under the Franciscans, and the replacement of the wild herds with privately owned sheep and cattle, that made the tragedy of the forced abandonment of the Missions. For the settlers on the Tejon there was not so much as a mess of greens to be raised or gathered. It had all to be fetched from the town two days away, at prices that forced a cautious balancing between that and the still expensive and not very satisfactory canned fruits and vegetables. Strange now to recall that my mother never did become skillful in the utilization of canned foods, and that there persisted among housewives out of the self-sustaining rural households of the Middlewest an irreducible remainder of prejudice to their use.

During the first six months of homesteading, Mary suffered the genuine distress

[5] Austin's family moved to an area of homestead land south of Bakersfield, California in 1888.

of malnutrition. There was no butter, and if anyone remembers what canned milk was like at that time, diluted with stale water from a dry-season waterhole—but I hope nobody does! For meat, we had game, plentiful if monotonous; rabbits, quail, and occasionally bear meat and venison bought from the 'mountain men,' grizzled derelicts of an earlier period, hidden away in tiny valleys, subsisting chiefly on the killing of venison and the robbing of bee trees. Mary, however, did not like game, especially rabbits, though she might have done better about it if she had not had to kill them. Mary was a fair shot, and with George to pick them up after they were killed, contrived to keep the family table reasonably supplied. Every little while the men of the neighborhood would go on a community hunt, especially in the winter months when there were ducks by thousands on the sloughs, and so we managed to live. My brothers, in fact, throve; George, who up till then had shown signs of being undersized and pudgy, began to shoot up and ended by being the tallest of the family. But Mary grew thinner and thinner, stooping under her weight of hair, and fell into a kind of torpor, of which undernourishment was probably the chief factor, a condition to which nobody paid any attention. Appetite, or the loss of it, was a purely personal matter. People guessed you would eat if you wanted it. What finally worried her mother was that Mary was unable to sleep. She would lie in her bunk with fixed, wide-open eyes, hearing the cu-owls on the roof, the nearly noiseless tread of coyotes going by in the dark, the strange ventriloquist noises they kept up with their cousins miles away beyond Rose Station, hearing the slow shuffling tread of the starved cattle, momentarily stopped by the faint smell of the settlers' water-barrels, but too feeble to turn out of their own tracks to come at them.

Nights when she and her mother slept at Susie's cabin, which was in a sandy wash, Mary would sit out among the dunes in the moonlight—Susie would never sleep there at any other times than full moon—watching the frisking forms of field mouse and kangaroo rat, the noiseless passage of the red fox and the flitting of the elf owls at their mating. By day she would follow a bobcat to its lair in the bank of the Wash, and, lying down before its den, the two would contemplate each other wordlessly for long times, in which Mary remained wholly unaware of what might happen to her should the wildcat at any moment make up its mind to resent her presence. There was a band of antelope on the Tejon range, fully protected by law, roving far down the hollow between the hills, passing between the wires of the fence as cleanly as winged things. There was a lone buck—the one who figures in the story of 'The Last Antelope'—who tolerated her—it was not in his lifetime that the antelope had been accustomed to pursuit from men. Once in a storm of wind and rain they took shelter together in a half-ruined settler's shack. That was how Mary spent the first three months on the Tejon, all the time growing apparently more apathetic, until Susie was genuinely worried. 'I can't help but think,' she would say, 'if you'd rouse yourself to take some interest in things . . .'

But the fact is Mary was consumed with interest as with enchantment. Her trouble was that the country failed to explain itself. If it had a history, nobody could recount it. Its creatures had no known life except such as she could discover by unremitting vigilance of observation; its plants no names that her Middlewestern botany could supply. She did not know yet what were its weather signs, nor what the procession of its days might bring forth. Until these things elucidated themselves factually, Mary was spellbound in an effort not to miss any animal behavior, any bird-marking, any weather signal, any signature of tree or flower. Animals are like that, thrust into strange captivity, caught up into fearful question, refusing food and sleep until they die. But in Mary's case there was no fear but that she might miss the significance of the question, to which as yet she had no answer, the magic words which would unlock as much at least as anybody knew of the meaning of what she saw. For Mary is one of those people plagued with an anxiety to know. Other people, satisfied by the mere delight of seeing, think they pay her a compliment when they speak of her 'intuition' about things of the wild, or that they let her down a deserved notch or two by referring to her fortunate guesses.

The deadlock was broken by the discovery, after the leaves were off, of wild grapes in one of the Tejon canyons, and after a week or two of almost exclusive grape diet, Mary began to pick up amazingly. It was so *like* Mary, her family remarked, to almost starve to death on a proper Christian diet and go and get well on something grubbed out of the woods. But there was more to the incident than that; there was the beginning of a notion in Mary's mind of a poor appetite of any sort being cured by its proper food; that there was something you could do about unsatisfactory conditions besides being heroic or a martyr to them, something more satisfactory than enduring or complaining, and that was getting out to hunt for the remedy. This, for young ladies in the eighteen-eighties, was a revolutionary discovery to have made. So that it appeared in the nature of a happy accident that General Edward Fitzgerald Beale, the owner of Tejon Ranch, came back to it along in January, 1889, and released Mary from the black spell of her wanting to know.

1932

Gertrude Bonnin (Zitkala-Sa; Sioux) 1876–1938

In her writings as well as her work as an Indian rights activist, Gertrude Simmons Bonnin or Zitkala-Sa (Red Bird), is a vital link between the oral culture of tribal America in conflict with its colonizers and the literate culture of contemporary American Indians. A Yankton, born on the Pine Ridge Reservation in South Dakota, she was the third child of Ellen Tate 'Iyohiwin Simmons, a full-blood Sioux. Little is known of her father, a white man. Her mother brought up the children in traditional ways. At the age of eight, Zitkala-Sa left the reservation to attend a Quaker missionary school in Wabash, Indiana. She returned to the reservation but was culturally unhinged, "neither a wild Indian nor a tame one," as she described herself later in "The Schooldays of an Indian Girl." After four unhappy years she returned to her school, graduated, and at age nineteen enrolled—against her mother's wish—at Earlham College in Richmond, Indiana. She later taught at Carlisle Indian School for about two years. Having become an accomplished violinist, she also studied at the Boston Conservatory of Music.

Meanwhile, the estrangement from her mother and the old ways of the reservation had grown, as had her indignation over the treatment of American Indians by the state, church, and population at large. Around 1900 she began to express her feelings publicly in writing. In articles in the *Atlantic Monthly* and other journals she struggled with the issues of cultural dislocation and injustice that brought suffering to her people. But her authorial voice was not merely critical. She was earnestly committed to being a bridge builder between cultures, for example, by writing *Old Indian Legends,* published in 1901. "I have tried," she says in the introduction to that work, "to transplant the native spirit of these tales—root and all—into the English language, since America in the last few centuries has acquired a second tongue."

In the following decades, Zitkala-Sa's writing efforts were increasingly part of, and finally supplanted by, her work as an Indian rights activist. She had accepted a clerkship at the Standing Rock Reservation, where she met and married Raymond T. Bonnin, another Sioux employee of the Indian service. The Bonnins then transferred to a reservation in Utah where they became affiliated with the Society of American Indians. Zitkala-Sa was elected secretary of the Society in 1916, and the Bonnins moved to Washington, D.C., where she worked with the Society and edited the *American Indian Magazine.* In 1926 she founded the National Council of American Indians and continued to pursue reforms through public speaking and lobbying efforts. She was instrumental in the passage of the Indian Citizenship Bill and secured powerful outside interests in Indian reform. Zitkala-Sa died in Washington, D.C., in 1938 and was buried in Arlington Cemetery.

Although her output was limited, her artistic accomplishment cannot be denied. In addition to her earlier works, in 1913 she collaborated with William P. Hanson in producing an Indian opera, "Sundance." In 1921 her collection of *American Indian Stories* was published, combining her previously printed work with some new essays and merging autobiography and fiction in a unique way. In her writings, Zitkala-Sa anticipated some aspects of the work of present-day American Indian fiction writers like N. Scott Momaday and Leslie Silko and contemporary advocates of the Indian cause like Vine Deloria, Jr. As her collection of *Old Indian Legends* proves, she realized that political rights would be fruitless unless they were rooted in a recovery of cultural identity through a revitalization of the oral tradition.

Zitkala-Sa's autobiographical work makes her perhaps the first American Indian woman to write her own story without the aid of an editor, interpreter, or ethnographer. Her essay, "Why I am a Pagan," merits special attention because at the time it was published it was popular for American Indians to describe their conversions to Christianity.

Kristin Herzog
University of North Carolina–Chapel Hill

PRIMARY WORKS

Old Indian Legends, 1901, 1985; *American Indian Stories,* 1921, 1985.

from The School Days of an Indian Girl[1]

I The Land of Red Apples

There were eight in our party of bronzed children who were going East with the missionaries. Among us were three young braves, two tall girls, and we three little ones, Judéwin, Thowin, and I.

We had been very impatient to start on our journey to the Red Apple Country,[2] which, we were told, lay a little beyond the great circular horizon of the Western prairie. Under a sky of rosy apples we dreamt of roaming as freely and happily as we had chased the cloud shadows on the Dakota plains. We had anticipated much pleasure from a ride on the iron horse, but the throngs of staring palefaces disturbed and troubled us.

On the train, fair women, with tottering babies on each arm, stopped their haste and scrutinized the children of absent mothers. Large men, with heavy bundles in their hands, halted near by, and riveted their glassy blue eyes upon us.

I sank deep into the corner of my seat, for I resented being watched. Directly in front of me, children who were no larger than I hung themselves upon the backs of their seats, with their bold white faces toward me. Sometimes they took their forefingers out of their mouths and pointed at my moccasined feet. Their mothers, instead of reproving such rude curiosity, looked closely at me, and attracted their children's further notice to my blanket. This embarrassed me, and kept me constantly on the verge of tears.

I sat perfectly still, with my eyes downcast, daring only now and then to shoot long glances around me. Chancing to turn to the window at my side, I was quite breathless upon seeing one familiar object. It was the telegraph pole which strode by at short paces. Very near my mother's dwelling, along the edge of a road thickly bordered with wild sunflowers, some poles like these had been planted by white men. Often I had stopped, on my way down the road, to hold my ear against the pole, and, hearing its low moaning, I used to wonder what the paleface had done to hurt it. Now I sat watching for each pole that glided by to be the last one.

In this way I had forgotten my uncomfortable surroundings, when I heard one of my comrades call out my name. I saw the missionary standing very near, tossing candies and gums into our midst. This amused us all, and we tried to see who could catch the most of the sweet-meats. The missionary's generous distribution of candies was impressed upon my memory by a disastrous result which followed. I had caught more than my share of candies and gums, and soon after our arrival at the school I had a chance to disgrace myself, which, I am ashamed to say, I did.

Though we rode several days inside of the iron horse, I do not recall a single thing about our luncheons.

It was night when we reached the school grounds. The lights from the windows

[1] "The School Days of an Indian Girl" appeared in *Atlantic,* 85 (February, 1900), 185–194. It was reprinted in Zitkala-Sa's *American Indian Stories* (1921), which was reprinted in 1985.

[2] *I.e.,* Indiana.

of the large buildings fell upon some of the icicled trees that stood beneath them. We were led toward an open door, where the brightness of the lights within flooded out over the heads of the excited palefaces who blocked the way. My body trembled more from fear than from the snow I trod upon.

Entering the house, I stood close against the wall. The strong glaring light in the large whitewashed room dazzled my eyes. The noisy hurrying of hard shoes upon a bare wooden floor increased the whirring in my ears. My only safety seemed to be in keeping next to the wall. As I was wondering in which direction to escape from all this confusion, two warm hands grasped me firmly, and in the same moment I was tossed high in midair. A rosy-cheeked paleface woman caught me in her arms. I was both frightened and insulted by such trifling. I stared into her eyes, wishing her to let me stand on my own feet, but she jumped me up and down with increasing enthusiasm. My mother had never made a plaything of her wee daughter. Remembering this I began to cry aloud.

They misunderstood the cause of my tears, and placed me at a white table loaded with food. There our party were united again. As I did not hush my crying, one of the older ones whispered to me, "Wait until you are alone in the night."

It was very little I could swallow besides my sobs, that evening.

"Oh, I want my mother and my brother Dawée! I want to go to my aunt!" I pleaded; but the ears of the palefaces could not hear me.

From the table we were taken along an upward incline of wooden boxes, which I learned afterward to call a stairway. At the top was a quiet hall, dimly lighted. Many narrow beds were in one straight line down the entire length of the wall. In them lay sleeping brown faces, which peeped just out of the coverings. I was tucked into bed with one of the tall girls, because she talked to me in my mother tongue and seemed to soothe me.

I had arrived in the wonderful land of rosy skies, but I was not happy, as I had thought I should be. My long travel and the bewildering sights had exhausted me. I fell asleep, heaving deep, tired sobs. My tears were left to dry themselves in streaks, because neither my aunt nor my mother was near to wipe them away.

II The Cutting of My Long Hair

The first day in the land of apples was a bitter-cold one; for the snow still covered the ground, and the trees were bare. A large bell rang for breakfast, its loud metallic voice crashing through the belfry overhead and into our sensitive ears. The annoying clatter of shoes on bare floors gave us no peace. The constant clash of harsh noises, with an undercurrent of many voices murmuring an unknown tongue, made a bedlam within which I was securely tied. And though my spirit tore itself in struggling for its lost freedom, all was useless.

A paleface woman, with white hair, came up after us. We were placed in a line of girls who were marching into the dining room. These were Indian girls, in stiff shoes and closely clinging dresses. The small girls wore sleeved aprons and shingled hair. As I walked noiselessly in my soft moccasins, I felt like sinking to the floor, for my blanket had been stripped from my shoulders. I looked hard at the Indian girls, who seemed not to care that they were even more immodestly dressed than I, in their tightly fitting clothes. While we marched in, the boys entered at an opposite door. I watched for the three young braves who came in our party. I spied them in the rear ranks, looking as uncomfortable as I felt.

A small bell was tapped, and each of the pupils drew a chair from under the table. Supposing this act meant they were to be seated, I pulled out mine and at once slipped into it from one side. But when I turned my head, I saw that I was the only one seated, and all the rest at our table remained standing. Just as I began to rise, looking shyly around to see how chairs were to be used, a second bell was sounded. All were seated at last, and I had to crawl back into my chair again. I heard a man's voice at one end of the hall, and I looked around to see him. But all the others hung their heads over their plates. As I glanced at the long chain of tables, I caught the eyes of a paleface woman upon me. Immediately I dropped my eyes, wondering why I was so keenly watched by the strange woman. The man ceased his mutterings, and then a third bell was tapped. Every one picked up his knife and fork and began eating. I began crying instead, for by this time I was afraid to venture anything more.

But this eating by formula was not the hardest trial in that first day. Late in the morning, my friend Judéwin gave me a terrible warning. Judéwin knew a few words of English; and she had overheard the paleface woman talk about cutting our long, heavy hair. Our mothers had taught us that only unskilled warriors who were captured had their hair shingled by the enemy. Among our people, short hair was worn by mourners, and shingled hair by cowards!

We discussed our fate some moments, and when Judéwin said, "We have to submit, because they are strong," I rebelled.

"No, I will not submit! I will struggle first!" I answered.

I watched my chance, and when no one noticed I disappeared. I crept up the stairs as quietly as I could in my squeaking shoes,—my moccasins had been exchanged for shoes. Along the hall I passed, without knowing whither I was going. Turning aside to an open door, I found a large room with three white beds in it. The windows were covered with dark green curtains, which made the room very dim. Thankful that no one was there, I directed my steps toward the corner farthest from the door. On my hands and knees I crawled under the bed, and cuddled myself in the dark corner.

From my hiding place I peered out, shuddering with fear whenever I heard footsteps near by. Though in the hall loud voices were calling my name, and I knew that even Judéwin was searching for me, I did not open my mouth to answer. Then the steps were quickened and the voices became excited. The sounds came nearer and nearer. Women and girls entered the room. I held my breath, and watched them open closet doors and peep behind large trunks. Some one threw up the curtains, and the room was filled with sudden light. What caused them to stoop and look under the bed I do not know. I remember being dragged out, though I resisted by kicking and scratching wildly. In spite of myself, I was carried downstairs and tied fast in a chair.

I cried aloud, shaking my head all the while until I felt the cold blades of the scissors against my neck, and heard them gnaw off one of my thick braids. Then I lost my spirit. Since the day I was taken from my mother I had suffered extreme indignities. People had stared at me. I had been tossed about in the air like a wooden puppet. And now my long hair was shingled like a coward's! In my anguish I moaned for my mother, but no one came to comfort me. Not a soul reasoned quietly with me, as my own mother used to do: for now I was only one of many little animals driven by a herder.

III The Snow Episode

A short time after our arrival we three Dakotas were playing in the snowdrifts. We were all still deaf to the English language, excepting Judéwin, who always heard such puzzling things. One morning we learned through her ears that we were forbidden to fall lengthwise in the snow, as we had been doing, to see our own impressions. However, before many hours we had forgotten the order, and were having great sport in the snow, when a shrill voice called us. Looking up, we saw an imperative hand beckoning us into the house. We shook the snow off ourselves, and started toward the woman as slowly as we dared.

Judéwin said: "Now the paleface is angry with us. She is going to punish us for falling into the snow. If she looks straight into your eyes and talks loudly, you must wait until she stops. Then, after a tiny pause, say, 'No.'" The rest of the way we practiced upon the little word "no."

As it happened, Thowin was summoned to judgment first. The door shut behind her with a click.

Judéwin and I stood silently listening at the keyhole. The paleface woman talked in very severe tones. Her words fell from her lips like crackling embers, and her inflection ran up like the small end of a switch. I understood her voice better than the things she was saying. I was certain we had made her very impatient with us. Judéwin heard enough of the words to realize all too late that she had taught us the wrong reply.

"Oh, poor Thowin!" she gasped, as she put both hands over her ears.

Just then I heard Thowin's tremulous answer, "No."

With an angry exclamation, the woman gave her a hard spanking. Then she stopped to say something. Judéwin said it was this: "Are you going to obey my word the next time?"

Thowin answered again with the only word at her command, "No."

This time the woman meant her blows to smart, for the poor frightened girl shrieked at the top of her voice. In the midst of the whipping the blows ceased abruptly, and the woman asked another question: "Are you going to fall in the snow again?"

Thowin gave her bad password another trial. We heard her say feebly, "No! No!"

With this the woman hid away her half-worn slipper, and led the child out, stroking her black shorn head. Perhaps it occurred to her that brute force is not the solution for such a problem. She did nothing to Judéwin nor to me. She only returned to us our unhappy comrade, and left us alone in the room.

During the first two or three seasons misunderstandings as ridiculous as this one of the snow episode frequently took place, bringing unjustifiable frights and punishments into our little lives.

Within a year I was able to express myself somewhat in broken English. As soon as I comprehended a part of what was said and done, a mischievous spirit of revenge possessed me. One day I was called in from my play for some misconduct. I had disregarded a rule which seemed to me very needlessly binding. I was sent into the kitchen to mash the turnips for dinner. It was noon, and steaming dishes were hastily carried into the dining room. I hated turnips, and their odor which came from the brown jar was offensive to me. With fire in my heart, I took the wooden tool that the paleface woman held out to me. I stood upon a step, and, grasping the handle with both hands, I bent in hot rage over the turnips. I worked my vengeance upon them. All were so busily occupied that no one noticed me. I saw that the turnips were in a pulp, and that further beating could not improve them; but the order was, "Mash these turnips," and mash them I would! I renewed my energy; and as I sent the masher into the bottom of the jar, I felt a satisfying sensation that the weight of my body had gone into it.

Just here a paleface woman came up to my table. As she looked into the jar, she shoved my hands roughly aside. I stood fearless and angry. She placed her red hands upon the rim of the jar. Then she gave one lift and a stride away from the table. But lo! the pulpy contents fell through the crumbled bottom to the floor! She spared me no scolding phrases that I had earned. I did not heed them. I felt triumphant in my revenge, though deep within me I was a wee bit sorry to have broken the jar.

As I sat eating my dinner, and saw that no turnips were served, I whooped in my heart for having once asserted the rebellion within me. . . .[3]

VI Four Strange Summers

After my first three years of school, I roamed again in the Western country through four strange summers.

During this time I seemed to hang in the heart of chaos, beyond the touch or voice of human aid. My brother, being almost ten years my senior, did not quite understand my feelings. My mother had never gone inside of a schoolhouse, and so she was not capable of comforting her daughter who could read and write. Even nature seemed to have no place for me. I was neither a wee girl nor a tall one; neither a wild Indian nor a tame one. This deplorable situation was the effect of my brief course in the East, and the unsatisfactory "teenth" in a girl's years.

It was under these trying conditions that, one bright afternoon, as I sat restless and unhappy in my mother's cabin, I caught the sound of the spirited step of my brother's pony on the road which passed by our dwelling. Soon I heard the wheels of a light buckboard, and Dawée's familiar "Ho!" to his pony. He alighted upon the bare ground in front of our house. Tying his pony to one of the projecting corner logs of the low-roofed cottage, he stepped upon the wooden doorstep.

I met him there with a hurried greeting, and, as I passed by, he looked a quiet "What?" into my eyes.

[3]Sections IV and V are omitted. In IV, Zitkala-Sa relates her introduction to the white man's concept of the devil and the nightmares it caused her to have. In V, she describes the rigid discipline at the school and the death of a young friend, who she says died because of inadequate health care.

When he began talking with my mother, I slipped the rope from the pony's bridle. Seizing the reins and bracing my feet against the dashboard, I wheeled around in an instant. The pony was ever ready to try his speed. Looking backward, I saw Dawée waving his hand to me. I turned with the curve in the road and disappeared. I followed the winding road which crawled upward between the bases of little hillocks. Deep water-worn ditches ran parallel on either side. A strong wind blew against my cheeks and fluttered my sleeves. The pony reached the top of the highest hill, and began an even race on the level lands. There was nothing moving within that great circular horizon of the Dakota prairies save the tall grasses, over which the wind blew and rolled off in long, shadowy waves.

Within this vast wigwam of blue and green I rode reckless and insignificant. It satisfied my small consciousness to see the white foam fly from the pony's mouth.

Suddenly, out of the earth a coyote came forth at a swinging trot that was taking the cunning thief toward the hills and the village beyond. Upon the moment's impulse, I gave him a long chase and a wholesome fright. As I turned away to go back to the village, the wolf sank down upon his haunches for rest, for it was a hot summer day; and as I drove slowly homeward, I saw his sharp nose still pointed at me, until I vanished below the margin of the hilltops.

In a little while I came in sight of my mother's house. Dawée stood in the yard, laughing at an old warrior who was pointing his forefinger, and again waving his whole hand, toward the hills. With his blanket drawn over one shoulder, he talked and motioned excitedly. Dawée turned the old man by the shoulder and pointed me out to him.

"Oh, han!" (Oh, yes) the warrior muttered, and went his way. He had climbed the top of his favorite barren hill to survey the surrounding prairies, when he spied my chase after the coyote. His keen eyes recognized the pony and driver. At once uneasy for my safety, he had come running to my mother's cabin to give her warning. I did not appreciate his kindly interest, for there was an unrest gnawing at my heart.

As soon as he went away, I asked Dawée about something else.

"No, my baby sister. I cannot take you with me to the party to-night," he replied. Though I was not far from fifteen, and I felt that before long I should enjoy all the privileges of my tall cousin, Dawée persisted in calling me his baby sister.

That moonlight night, I cried in my mother's presence when I heard the jolly young people pass by our cottage. They were no more young braves in blankets and eagle plumes, nor Indian maids with prettily painted cheeks. They had gone three years to school in the East, and had become civilized. The young men wore the white man's coat and trousers, with bright neckties. The girls wore tight muslin dresses, with ribbons at neck and waist. At these gatherings they talked English. I could speak English almost as well as my brother, but I was not properly dressed to be taken along. I had no hat, no ribbons, and no close-fitting gown. Since my return from school I had thrown away my shoes, and wore again the soft moccasins.

While Dawée was busily preparing to go I controlled my tears. But when I heard him bounding away on his pony, I buried my face in my arms and cried hot tears.

My mother was troubled by my unhappiness. Coming to my side, she offered me the only printed matter we had in our home. It was an Indian Bible,[4] given her some years ago by a missionary. She tried to console me. "Here, my child, are the white man's papers. Read a little from them," she said most piously.

I took it from her hand, for her sake; but my enraged spirit felt more like burning the book, which afforded me no help, and was a perfect delusion to my mother. I did not read it, but laid it unopened on the floor, where I sat on my feet. The dim yellow light of the braided muslin burning in a small vessel of oil flickered and sizzled in the awful silent storm which followed my rejection of the Bible.

Now my wrath against the fates consumed my tears before they reached my eyes. I sat stony, with a bowed head. My mother threw a shawl over her head and shoulders, and stepped out into the night.

After an uncertain solitude, I was suddenly aroused by a loud cry piercing the night. It was my mother's voice wailing among the barren hills which held the bones of buried warriors. She called aloud for her brothers' spirits to support her in her helpless misery. My fingers grew icy cold, as I realized that my unrestrained tears had betrayed my suffering to her, and she was grieving for me.

Before she returned, though I knew she was on her way, for she had ceased her weeping, I extinguished the light, and leaned my head on the window sill.

Many schemes of running away from my surroundings hovered about in my mind. A few more moons of such a turmoil drove me away to the Eastern school. I rode on the white man's iron steed, thinking it would bring me back to my mother in a few winters, when I should be grown tall, and there would be congenial friends awaiting me.

VII Incurring My Mother's Displeasure

In the second journey to the East I had not come without some precautions. I had a secret interview with one of our best medicine men, and when I left his wigwam I carried securely in my sleeve a tiny bunch of magic roots. This possession assured me of friends wherever I should go. So absolutely did I believe in its charms that I wore it through all the school routine for more than a year. Then, before I lost my faith in the dead roots, I lost the little buckskin bag containing all my good luck.

At the close of this second term of three years I was the proud owner of my first diploma. The following autumn I ventured upon a college career against my mother's will.

I had written for her approval, but in her reply I found no encouragement. She called my notice to her neighbors' children, who had completed their education in three years. They had returned to their homes, and were then talking English with the frontier settlers. Her few words hinted that I had better give up my slow attempt to learn the white man's ways, and be content to roam over the prairies and find my living upon wild roots. I silenced her by deliberate disobedience.

[4]Selections from the Bible had been published in Dakota as early as 1839. The reference is probably to *Dakota Wowapi Wakan,* translated by Thomas S. Williamson and Stephen R. Riggs and published in 1879.

Thus, homeless and heavy-hearted, I began anew my life among strangers.

As I hid myself in my little room in the college dormitory, away from the scornful and yet curious eyes of the students, I pined for sympathy. Often I wept in secret, wishing I had gone West, to be nourished by my mother's love, instead of remaining among a cold race whose hearts were frozen hard with prejudice.

During the fall and winter seasons I scarcely had a real friend, though by that time several of my classmates were courteous to me at a safe distance.

My mother had not yet forgiven my rudeness to her, and I had no moment for letterwriting. By daylight and lamplight, I spun with reeds and thistles, until my hands were tired from their weaving, the magic design which promised me the white man's respect.

At length, in the spring term, I entered an oratorical contest among the various classes. As the day of competition approached, it did not seem possible that the event was so near at hand, but it came. In the chapel the classes assembled together, with their invited guests. The high platform was carpeted, and gayly festooned with college colors. A bright white light illumined the room, and outlined clearly the great polished beams that arched the domed ceiling. The assembled crowds filled the air with pulsating murmurs. When the hour for speaking arrived all were hushed. But on the wall the old clock which pointed out the trying moment ticked calmly on.

One after another I saw and heard the orators. Still, I could not realize that they longed for the favorable decision of the judges as much as I did. Each contestant received a loud burst of applause, and some were cheered heartily. Too soon my turn came, and I paused a moment behind the curtains for a deep breath. After my concluding words, I heard the same applause that the others had called out.

Upon my retreating steps, I was astounded to receive from my fellow-students a large bouquet of roses tied with flowing ribbons. With the lovely flowers I fled from the stage. This friendly token was a rebuke to me for the hard feelings I had borne them.

Later, the decision of the judges awarded me the first place. Then there was a mad uproar in the hall, where my classmates sang and shouted my name at the top of their lungs; and the disappointed students howled and brayed in fearfully dissonant tin trumpets. In this excitement, happy students rushed forward to offer their congratulations. And I could not conceal a smile when they wished to escort me in a procession to the students' parlor, where all were going to calm themselves. Thanking them for the kind spirit which prompted them to make such a proposition, I walked alone with the night to my own little room.

A few weeks afterward, I appeared as the college representative in another contest. This time the competition was among orators from different colleges in our State. It was held at the State capital, in one of the largest opera houses.

Here again was a strong prejudice against my people. In the evening, as the great audience filled the house, the student bodies began warring among themselves. Fortunately, I was spared witnessing any of the noisy wrangling before the contest began. The slurs against the Indian that stained the lips of our opponents were already burning like a dry fever within my breast.

But after the orations were delivered a deeper burn awaited me. There, before that vast ocean of eyes, some college rowdies threw out a large white flag, with a drawing of a most forlorn Indian girl on it. Under this they had printed in bold black letters words that ridiculed the college which was represented by a "squaw." Such worse than barbarian rudeness embittered me. While we waited for the verdict of the judges, I gleamed fiercely upon the throngs of palefaces. My teeth were hard set, as I saw the white flag still floating insolently in the air.

Then anxiously we watched the man carry toward the stage the envelope containing the final decision.

There were two prizes given, that night, and one of them was mine!

The evil spirit laughed within me when the white flag dropped out of sight, and the hands which hurled it hung limp in defeat.

Leaving the crowd as quickly as possible, I was soon in my room. The rest of the night I sat in an armchair and gazed into the crackling fire. I laughed no more in triumph when thus alone. The little taste of victory did not satisfy a hunger in my heart. In my mind I saw my mother far away on the Western plains, and she was holding a charge against me.

1900

Why I Am a Pagan[1]

When the spirit swells my breast I love to roam leisurely among the green hills; or sometimes, sitting on the brink of the murmuring Missouri, I marvel at the great blue overhead. With half closed eyes I watch the huge cloud shadows in their noiseless play upon the high bluffs opposite me, while into my ear ripple the sweet, soft cadences of the river's song. Folded hands lie in my lap, for the time forgot. My heart and I lie small upon the earth like a grain of throbbing sand. Drifting clouds and tinkling waters, together with the warmth of a genial summer day, bespeak with eloquence the loving Mystery round about us. During the idle while I sat upon the sunny river brink, I grew somewhat, though my response be not so clearly manifest as in the green grass fringing the edge of the high bluff back of me.

At length retracing the uncertain footpath scaling the precipitous embankment, I seek the level lands where grow the wild prairie flowers. And they, the lovely little folk, soothe my soul with their perfumed breath.

Their quaint round faces of varied hue convince the heart which leaps with glad surprise that they, too, are living symbols of omnipotent thought. With a child's eager eye I drink in the myriad star shapes wrought in luxuriant color upon the green. Beautiful is the spiritual essence they embody.

I leave them nodding in the breeze, but take along with me their impress upon my heart. I pause to rest me upon a rock embedded on the side of a foothill facing the low river bottom. Here the Stone-Boy,[2] of whom the American aborigine tells, frolics about, shooting his baby arrows and shouting aloud with glee at the tiny shafts

[1]This essay appeared in *Atlantic,* 90 (December, 1902), 801–803.

[2]Stone Boy, or Inyanhoksila, possessed of supernatural powers, was a popular figure in Dakota lore.

of lightning that flash from the flying arrow-beaks. What an ideal warrior he became, baffling the siege of the pests of all the land till he triumphed over their united attack. And here he lay,—Inyan our great-great-grandfather, older than the hill he rested on, older than the race of men who love to tell of his wonderful career.

Interwoven with the thread of this Indian legend of the rock, I fain would trace a subtle knowledge of the native folk which enabled them to recognize a kinship to any and all parts of this vast universe. By the leading of an ancient trail I move toward the Indian village.

With the strong, happy sense that both great and small are so surely enfolded in His magnitude that, without a miss, each has his allotted individual ground of opportunities, I am buoyant with good nature.

Yellow Breast, swaying upon the slender stem of a wild sunflower, warbles a sweet assurance of this as I pass near by. Breaking off the clear crystal song, he turns his wee head from side to side eyeing me wisely as slowly I plod with moccasined feet. Then again he yields himself to his song of joy. Flit, flit hither and yon, he fills the summer sky with his swift, sweet melody. And truly does it seem his vigorous freedom lies more in his little spirit than in his wing.

With these thoughts I reach the log cabin whither I am strongly drawn by the tie of a child to an aged mother. Out bounds my four-footed friend to meet me, frisking about my path with unmistakable delight. Chän is a black shaggy dog, "a thorough bred little mongrel" of whom I am very fond. Chän seems to understand many words in Sioux, and will go to her mat even when I whisper the word, though generally I think she is guided by the tone of the voice. Often she tries to imitate the sliding inflection and long drawn out voice to the amusement of our guests, but her articulation is quite beyond my ear. In both my hands I hold her shaggy head and gaze into her large brown eyes. At once the dilated pupils contract into tiny black dots, as if the roguish spirit within would evade my questioning.

Finally resuming the chair at my desk I feel in keen sympathy with my fellow creatures, for I seem to see clearly again that all are akin.

The racial lines, which once were bitterly real, now serve nothing more than marking out a living mosaic of human beings. And even here men of the same color are like the ivory keys of one instrument where each resembles all the rest, yet varies from them in pitch and quality of voice. And those creatures who are for a time mere echoes of another's note are not unlike the fable of the thin sick man whose distorted shadow, dressed like a real creature, came to the old master to make him follow as a shadow. Thus with a compassion for all echoes in human guise, I greet the solemn-faced "native preacher" whom I find awaiting me. I listen with respect for God's creature, though he mouth most strangely the jangling phrases of a bigoted creed.

As our tribe is one large family, where every person is related to all the others, he addressed me:—

"Cousin, I came from the morning church service to talk with you."

"Yes?" I said interrogatively, as he paused for some word from me.

Shifting uneasily about in the straight-backed chair he sat upon, he began: "Every holy day (Sunday) I look about our little God's house, and not seeing you there, I am disappointed. This is why I come to-day. Cousin, as I watch you from afar, I see no unbecoming behavior and hear only good reports of you, which all the more burns me with the wish that you were a church member. Cousin, I was taught long years ago by kind missionaries to read the holy book. These godly men taught me also the folly of our old beliefs.

"There is one God who gives reward or punishment to the race of dead men. In the upper region the Christian dead are gathered in unceasing song and prayer. In the deep pit below, the sinful ones dance in torturing flames.

"Think upon these things, my cousin, and choose now to avoid the after-doom of hell fire!" Then followed a long silence in which he clasped tighter and unclasped again his interlocked fingers.

Like instantaneous lightning flashes came pictures of my own mother's making, for she, too, is now a follower of the new superstition.

"Knocking out the chinking of our log cabin, some evil hand thrust in a burning taper of braided dry grass, but failed of his intent, for the fire died out and the half burned brand fell inward to the floor. Directly above it, on a shelf, lay the holy book. This is what we found after our return from a several days' visit. Surely some great power is hid in the sacred book!"

Brushing away from my eyes many like pictures, I offered midday meal to the converted Indian sitting wordless and with downcast face. No sooner had he risen from the table with "Cousin, I have relished it," than the church bell rang.

Thither he hurried forth with his afternoon sermon. I watched him as he hastened along, his eyes bent fast upon the dusty road till he disappeared at the end of a quarter of a mile.

The little incident recalled to mind the copy of a missionary paper brought to my notice a few days ago, in which a "Christian" pugilist commented upon a recent article of mine, grossly perverting the spirit of my pen. Still I would not forget that the pale-faced missionary and the hoodooed aborigine are both God's creatures, though small indeed their own conceptions of Infinite Love. A wee child toddling in a wonder world, I prefer to their dogma my excursions into the natural gardens where the voice of the Great Spirit is heard in the twittering of birds, the rippling of mighty waters, and the sweet breathing of flowers. If this is Paganism, then at present, at least, I am a Pagan.

1902

Mary Antin 1881–1949

Mary Antin was born in Polotzk in the Pale of Settlement, the area of czarist Russia in which Jews were allowed to live. Even when young, she became aware of how restricted life in Russia was for Jews. The Russian government allowed them few options in terms of where they could live and what work they could do. They had few of the rights of the poorest peasants. In Polotzk, they were restricted in terms of religious options, with their lives thoroughly controlled by Jewish Orthodoxy.

After experiencing serious illnesses, Antin's parents lost their modest fortune. Failing in numerous attempts to recoup his fortune in Russia, Israel, when Mary was eleven, went to America seeking affluence but, more important, hoping to live with freedom and dignity. Unable to adapt to the new country or to master English, Israel eventually became embittered toward America, but when he sent for his wife and children in 1894, when Mary was thirteen, he was still enamored of America. Shortly after his family arrived in Boston, Israel proudly enrolled his three younger children in public school. Later, Mary pictured the public schools as the immigrant child's road to Americanization. Thriving in the public schools of Boston, she went from first to fifth grade in half a year.

Her abilities as a writer appeared early. At fifteen, she published her first poem in the *Boston Herald.* In 1899, Antin's first book, *From Plotzk* [sic] *to Boston,* was published; it briefly recounts her trip from Russia through Germany to Boston. With the appearance of this book, Mary, eighteen at the time, was hailed as a child prodigy. The material in this volume became the basis of her masterpiece, *The Promised Land.*

After attending Girls Latin School in Boston, she attended Teachers College of Columbia University from 1901 to 1902 and Barnard College from 1902 to 1904. In college, she met and married Amadeus W. Grabau, a geologist, one-time Columbia professor, and non-Jew, thus putting into action her belief that religious differences are irrelevant to life in America. While living in New York, she also became friends with Emma Lazarus, who encouraged her to write *The Promised Land* and to whom Antin dedicated the book. Appearing in serial form in the *Atlantic Monthly* in 1911 to 1912, *The Promised Land* was published in book form in 1912. Immediately hailed as a masterpiece, it is still accepted as a classic work of immigrant autobiography.

After *The Promised Land,* Antin wrote one more book, *They Who Knock at the Gates,* in which she argues in favor of immigration for all but criminals and declares that the best people of Europe crowd the steerage compartments of ships steaming toward America. For several more years, she published articles and short stories in magazines and did social work. From 1913 to 1918, she lectured throughout the United States. Although her marriage fell apart when, in 1920, her husband left her and settled in China, she remained ardently optimistic in her faith in America and in the eventual Americanization of the immigrants.

Antin is remembered today for *The Promised Land.* Many critics view the book as a naive, overly optimistic hymn of praise for Americanization and total assimilation. Others, however, view it as a sensitive, truthful account of a Jewish girl's odyssey from an essentially medieval life in Russia to a modern life in America.

Richard Tuerk
Texas A&M University–Commerce

PRIMARY WORKS

From Plotzk to Boston, 1899; *The Promised Land,* 1912; *They Who Knock at the Gates: A Complete Gospel of Immigration,* 1914.

from The Promised Land

from **Chapter IX**

. . . Anybody who knows Boston knows that the West and North Ends are the wrong ends of that city. They form the tenement district, or, in the newer phrase, the slums of Boston. Anybody who is acquainted with the slums of any American metropolis knows that that is the quarter where poor immigrants foregather, to live, for the most part, as unkempt, half-washed, toiling, unaspiring foreigners; pitiful in the eyes of social missionaries, the despair of boards of health, the hope of ward politicians, the touchstone of American democracy. The well-versed metropolitan knows the slums as a sort of house of detention for poor aliens, where they live on probation till they can show a certificate of good citizenship.

He may know all this and yet not guess how Wall Street, in the West End, appears in the eyes of a little immigrant from Polotzk.[1] What would the sophisticated sight-seer say about Union Place, off Wall Street, where my new home waited for me? He would say that it is no place at all, but a short box of an alley. Two rows of three-story tenements are its sides, a stingy strip of sky is its lid, a littered pavement is the floor, and a narrow mouth its exit.

But I saw a very different picture on my introduction to Union Place. I saw two imposing rows of brick buildings, loftier than any dwelling I had ever lived in. Brick was even on the ground for me to tread on, instead of common earth or boards. Many friendly windows stood open, filled with uncovered heads of women and children. I thought the people were interested in us, which was very neighborly. I looked up to the topmost row of windows, and my eyes were filled with the May blue of an American sky!

In our days of affluence in Russia we had been accustomed to upholstered parlors, embroidered linen, silver spoons and candlesticks, goblets of gold, kitchen shelves shining with copper and brass. We had feather-beds heaped halfway to the ceiling; we had clothes presses dusky with velvet and silk and fine woollen. The three small rooms into which my father now ushered us, up one flight of stairs, contained only the necessary beds, with lean mattresses; a few wooden chairs; a table or two; a mysterious iron structure, which later turned out to be a stove; a couple of unornamental kerosene lamps; and a scanty array of cooking-utensils and crockery. And yet we were all impressed with our new home and its furniture. It was not only because we had just passed through our seven lean years, cooking in earthen vessels, eating black bread on holidays and wearing cotton; it was chiefly because these wooden chairs and tin pans were American chairs and pans that they shone glorious in our eyes. And if there was anything lacking for comfort or decoration we expected it to be presently supplied—at least, we children did. Perhaps my mother alone, of us newcomers, appreciated the shabbiness of the little apartment, and realized that for her there was as yet no laying down of the burden of poverty.

Our initiation into American ways began with the first step on the new soil. My father found occasion to instruct or correct us even on the way from the pier to Wall

[1]The town in Russia where Antin lived.

Street, which journey we made crowded together in a rickety cab. He told us not to lean out of the windows, not to point, and explained the word "greenhorn."[2] We did not want to be "greenhorns," and gave the strictest attention to my father's instructions. I do not know when my parents found opportunity to review together the history of Polotzk in the three years past, for we children had no patience with the subject; my mother's narrative was constantly interrupted by irrelevant questions, interjections, and explanations.

The first meal was an object lesson of much variety. My father produced several kinds of food, ready to eat, without any cooking, from little tin cans that had printing all over them. He attempted to introduce us to a queer, slippery kind of fruit, which he called "banana," but had to give it up for the time being. After the meal, he had better luck with a curious piece of furniture on runners, which he called "rocking-chair." There were five of us newcomers, and we found five different ways of getting into the American machine of perpetual motion, and as many ways of getting out of it. One born and bred to the use of a rocking-chair cannot imagine how ludicrous people can make themselves when attempting to use it for the first time. We laughed immoderately over our various experiments with the novelty, which was a wholesome way of letting off steam after the unusual excitement of the day.

In our flat we did not think of such a thing as storing the coal in the bathtub. There was no bathtub. So in the evening of the first day my father conducted us to the public baths. As we moved along in a little procession, I was delighted with the illumination of the streets. So many lamps, and they burned until morning, my father said, and so people did not need to carry lanterns. In America, then, everything was free, as we had heard in Russia. Light was free; the streets were as bright as a synagogue on a holy day. Music was free; we had been serenaded, to our gaping delight, by a brass band of many pieces, soon after our installation on Union Place.

Education was free. That subject my father had written about repeatedly, as comprising his chief hope for us children, the essence of American opportunity, the treasure that no thief could touch, not even misfortune or poverty. It was the one thing that he was able to promise us when he sent for us; surer, safer than bread or shelter. On our second day I was thrilled with the realization of what this freedom of education meant. A little girl from across the alley came and offered to conduct us to school. My father was out, but we five between us had a few words of English by this time. We knew the word school. We understood. This child, who had never seen us till yesterday, who could not pronounce our names, who was not much better dressed than we, was able to offer us the freedom of the schools of Boston! No application made, no questions asked, no examinations, rulings, exclusions; no machinations, no fees. The doors stood open for every one of us. The smallest child could show us the way.

This incident impressed me more than anything I had heard in advance of the freedom of education in America. It was a concrete proof—almost the thing itself. One had to experience it to understand it.

It was a great disappointment to be told by my father that we were not to enter

[2]A term, often derogatory, for a newly arrived immigrant. It implies that one has not yet adapted to life in America.

upon our school career at once. It was too near the end of the term, he said, and we were going to move to Crescent Beach in a week or so. We had to wait until the opening of the schools in September. What a loss of precious time—from May till September!

Not that the time was really lost. Even the interval on Union Place was crowded with lessons and experiences. We had to visit the stores and be dressed from head to foot in American clothing; we had to learn the mysteries of the iron stove, the washboard, and the speaking-tube; we had to learn to trade with the fruit peddler through the window, and not to be afraid of the policeman; and, above all, we had to learn English.

The kind people who assisted us in these important matters form a group by themselves in the gallery of my friends. If I had never seen them from those early days till now, I should still have remembered them with gratitude. When I enumerate the long list of my American teachers, I must begin with those who came to us on Wall Street and taught us our first steps. To my mother, in her perplexity over the cookstove, the woman who showed her how to make the fire was an angel of deliverance. A fairy godmother to us children was she who led us to a wonderful country called "uptown," where, in a dazzlingly beautiful palace called a "department store," we exchanged our hateful homemade European costumes, which pointed us out as "greenhorns" to the children on the street, for real American machine-made garments, and issued forth glorified in each other's eyes.

With our despised immigrant clothing we shed also our impossible Hebrew names. A committee of our friends, several years ahead of us in American experience, put their heads together and concocted American names for us all. Those of our real names that had no pleasing American equivalents they ruthlessly discarded, content if they retained the initials. My mother, possessing a name that was not easily translatable, was punished with the undignified nickname of Annie. Fetchke, Joseph, and Deborah issued as Frieda, Joseph, and Dora, respectively. As for poor me, I was simply cheated. The name they gave me was hardly new. My Hebrew name being Maryashe in full, Mashke for short, Russianized into Marya (*Mar-ya*), my friends said that it would hold good in English as *Mary;* which was very disappointing, as I longed to possess a strange-sounding American name like the others.

I am forgetting the consolation I had, in this matter of names, from the use of my surname, which I have had no occasion to mention until now. I found on my arrival that my father was "Mr. Antin" on the slightest provocation, and not, as in Polotzk, on state occasions alone. And so I was "Mary Antin," and I felt very important to answer to such a dignified title. It was just like America that even plain people should wear their surnames on week days. . . .

The apex of my civic pride and personal contentment was reached on the bright September morning when I entered the public school. That day I must always remember, even if I live to be so old that I cannot tell my name. To most people their first day at school is a memorable occasion. In my case the importance of the day was a hundred times magnified, on account of the years I had waited, the road I had come, and the conscious ambitions I entertained.

I am wearily aware that I am speaking in extreme figures, in superlatives. I wish I knew some other way to render the mental life of the immigrant child of reasoning age. I may have been ever so much an exception in acuteness of observation, powers of comparison, and abnormal self-consciousness; none the less were my thoughts and conduct typical of the attitude of the intelligent immigrant child toward American institutions. And what the child thinks and feels is a reflection of the hopes, desires, and purposes of the parents who brought him overseas, no matter how precocious and independent the child may be. Your immigrant inspectors will tell you what poverty the foreigner brings in his baggage, what want in his pockets. Let the overgrown boy of twelve, reverently drawing his letters in the baby class, testify to the noble dreams and high ideals that may be hidden beneath the greasy caftan of the immigrant. Speaking for the Jews, at least, I know I am safe in inviting such an investigation.

Who were my companions on my first day at school? Whose hand was in mine, as I stood, overcome with awe, by the teacher's desk, and whispered my name as my father prompted? Was it Frieda's steady, capable hand? Was it her loyal heart that throbbed, beat for beat with mine, as it had done through all our childish adventures? Frieda's heart did throb that day, but not with my emotions. My heart pulsed with joy and pride and ambition; in her heart longing fought with abnegation. For I was led to the schoolroom, with its sunshine and its singing and the teacher's cheery smile; while she was led to the workshop, with its foul air, care-lined faces, and the foreman's stern command. Our going to school was the fulfilment of my father's best promises to us, and Frieda's share in it was to fashion and fit the calico frocks in which the baby sister and I made our first appearance in a public schoolroom.

I remember to this day the gray pattern of the calico, so affectionately did I regard it as it hung upon the wall—my consecration robe awaiting the beatific day. And Frieda, I am sure, remembers it, too, so longingly did she regard it as the crisp, starchy breadths of it slid between her fingers. But whatever were her longings, she said nothing of them; she bent over the sewing-machine humming an Old-World melody. In every straight, smooth seam, perhaps, she tucked away some lingering impulse of childhood; but she matched the scrolls and flowers with the utmost care. If a sudden shock of rebellion made her straighten up for an instant, the next instant she was bending to adjust a ruffle to the best advantage. And when the momentous day arrived, and the little sister and I stood up to be arrayed, it was Frieda herself who patted and smoothed my stiff new calico; who made me turn round and round, to see that I was perfect; who stooped to pull out a disfiguring basting-thread. If there was anything in her heart besides sisterly love and pride and good-will, as we parted that morning, it was a sense of loss and a woman's acquiescence in her fate; for we had been close friends, and now our ways would lie apart. Longing she felt, but no envy. She did not grudge me what she was denied. Until that morning we had been children together, but now, at the fiat of her destiny, she became a woman, with all a woman's cares; whilst I, so little younger than she, was bidden to dance at the May festival of untroubled childhood.

I wish, for my comfort, that I could say that I had some notion of the difference in our lots, some sense of the injustice to her, of the indulgence to me. I wish I could even say that I gave serious thought to the matter. There had always been a distinction between us rather out of proportion to the difference in our years. Her good health and domestic instincts had made it natural for her to become my mother's right hand, in the years preceding the emigration, when there were no more servants or dependents. Then there was the family tradition that Mary was the quicker, the brighter of the two, and that hers could be no common lot. Frieda was relied upon for help, and her sister for glory. And when I failed as a milliner's apprentice, while Frieda made excellent progress at the dressmaker's, our fates, indeed, were sealed. It was understood, even before we reached Boston, that she would go to work and I to school. In view of the family prejudices, it was the inevitable course. No injustice was intended. My father sent us hand in hand to school, before he had ever thought of America. If, in America, he had been able to support his family unaided, it would have been the culmination of his best hopes to see all his children at school, with equal advantages at home. But when he had done his best, and was still unable to provide even bread and shelter for us all, he was compelled to make us children self-supporting as fast as it was practicable. There was no choosing possible; Frieda was the oldest, the strongest, the best prepared, and the only one who was of legal age to be put to work.

My father has nothing to answer for. He divided the world between his children in accordance with the laws of the country and the compulsion of his circumstances. I have no need of defending him. It is myself that I would like to defend, and I cannot. I remember that I accepted the arrangements made for my sister and me without much reflection, and everything that was planned for my advantage I took as a matter of course. I was no heartless monster, but a decidedly self-centered child. If my sister had seemed unhappy it would have troubled me; but I am ashamed to recall that I did not consider how little it was that contented her. I was so preoccupied with my own happiness that I did not half perceive the splendid devotion of her attitude towards me, the sweetness of her joy in my good luck. She not only stood by approvingly when I was helped to everything; she cheerfully waited on me herself. And I took everything from her hand as if it were my due.

The two of us stood a moment in the doorway of the tenement house on Arlington Street, that wonderful September morning when I first went to school. It was I that ran away, on winged feet of joy and expectation; it was she whose feet were bound in the treadmill of daily toil. And I was so blind that I did not see that the glory lay on her, and not on me.

Father himself conducted us to school. He would not have delegated that mission to the President of the United States. He had awaited the day with impatience equal to mine, and the visions he saw as he hurried us over the sun-flecked pavements transcended all my dreams. Almost his first act on landing on American soil, three years before, had been his application for naturalization. He had taken the remaining steps in the process with eager promptness, and at the earliest moment allowed by the law, he became a citizen of the United States. It is true that he had left home in search of bread for his hungry family, but he went blessing the necessity that drove him to America. The boasted freedom of the New World meant to him far more than the right to reside, travel, and work wherever he pleased; it meant the freedom to speak his thoughts, to throw off the shackles of superstition, to test his own fate, unhindered by political or religious tyranny. He was only a young man when he landed—thirty-two; and most of his life he had been held in leading-strings. He was hungry for his untasted manhood.

Three years passed in sordid struggle and disappointment. He was not prepared to make a living even in America, where the day laborer eats wheat instead of rye.

Apparently the American flag could not protect him against the pursuing Nemesis of his limitations; he must expiate the sins of his fathers who slept across the seas. He had been endowed at birth with a poor constitution, a nervous, restless temperament, and an abundance of hindering prejudices. In his boyhood his body was starved, that his mind might be stuffed with useless learning. In his youth this dearly gotten learning was sold, and the price was the bread and salt which he had not been trained to earn for himself. Under the wedding canopy he was bound for life to a girl whose features were still strange to him; and he was bidden to multiply himself, that sacred learning might be perpetuated in his sons, to the glory of the God of his fathers. All this while he had been led about as a creature without a will, a chattel, an instrument. In his maturity he awoke, and found himself poor in health, poor in purse, poor in useful knowledge, and hampered on all sides. At the first nod of opportunity he broke away from his prison, and strove to atone for his wasted youth by a life of useful labor; while at the same time he sought to lighten the gloom of his narrow scholarship by freely partaking of modern ideas. But his utmost endeavor still left him far from his goal. In business, nothing prospered with him. Some fault of hand or mind or temperament led him to failure where other men found success. Wherever the blame for his disabilities be placed, he reaped their bitter fruit. "Give me bread!" he cried to America. "What will you do to earn it?" the challenge came back. And he found that he was master of no art, of no trade; that even his precious learning was of no avail, because he had only the most antiquated methods of communicating it.

So in his primary quest he had failed. There was left him the compensation of intellectual freedom. That he sought to realize in every possible way. He had very little opportunity to prosecute his education, which, in truth, had never been begun. His struggle for a bare living left him no time to take advantage of the public evening school; but he lost nothing of what was to be learned through reading, through attendance at public meetings, through exercising the rights of citizenship. Even here he was hindered by a natural inability to acquire the English language. In time, indeed, he learned to read, to follow a conversation or lecture; but he never learned to write correctly, and his pronunciation remains extremely foreign to this day.

If education, culture, the higher life were shining things to be worshipped from afar, he had still a means left whereby he could draw one step nearer to them. He could send his children to school, to learn all those things that he knew by fame to be desirable. The common school, at least, perhaps high school; for one or two, perhaps even college! His children should be students, should fill his house with books and intellectual company; and thus he would walk by proxy in the Elysian Fields of liberal learning. As for the children themselves, he knew no surer way to their advancement and happiness.

So it was with a heart full of longing and hope that my father led us to school on that first day. He took long strides in his eagerness, the rest of us running and hopping to keep up.

At last the four of us stood around the teacher's desk; and my father, in his impossible English, gave us over in her charge, with some broken word of his hopes for us that his swelling heart could no longer contain. I venture to say that Miss Nixon was struck by something uncommon in the group we made, something outside of Semitic features and the abashed manner of the alien. My little sister was as pretty as a doll, with her clear pink-and-white face, short golden curls, and eyes like blue violets when you caught them looking up. My brother might have been a girl, too, with his cherubic contours of face, rich red color, glossy black hair, and fine eyebrows. Whatever secret fears were in his heart, remembering his former teachers, who had taught with the rod, he stood up straight and uncringing before the American teacher, his cap respectfully doffed. Next to him stood a starved-looking girl with eyes ready to pop out, and short dark curls that would not have made much of a wig for a Jewish bride.

All three children carried themselves rather better than the common run of "green" pupils that were brought to Miss Nixon. But the figure that challenged attention to the group was the tall, straight father, with his earnest face and fine forehead, nervous hands eloquent in gesture, and a voice full of feeling. This foreigner, who brought his children to school as if it were an act of consecration, who regarded the teacher of the primer class with reverence, who spoke of visions, like a man inspired, in a common schoolroom, was not like other aliens, who brought their children in dull obedience to the law; was not like the native fathers, who brought their unmanageable boys, glad to be relieved of their care. I think Miss Nixon guessed what my father's best English could not convey. I think she divined that by the simple act of delivering our school certificates to her he took possession of America.

1912

José Martí 1853–1895

The date: January 1880. A few weeks before he turned twenty-seven, José Martí arrived in New York City as yet another Cuban immigrant displaced by the long war for independence on his native island. Already a recognized writer, patriot (who at seventeen was sentenced to a labor camp for his revolutionary activities against Spanish rule), and talented orator, Martí was welcomed as a leader in the community of exiled Cubans in the Northeast. At night he strolled through the streets of lower Manhattan and, in an essay for the newspaper the *Hour*, described the misery of the "shoeless and foodless" unemployed whom he encountered on one of his nocturnal walks in Madison Square. During a brief stay the following year in Caracas, Venezuela, Martí worked as a teacher and founded a journal to promote his vision of a greater "America" (one in which north and south are unified by mutual respect and understanding).

In the last fourteen years of his life Martí worked in New York as a translator, teacher, and regular correspondent for newspapers in Venezuela, Argentina, and Mexico. He also wrote articles for the *New York Sun* and frequent letters to the editors of other local newspapers. He was a private tutor and a volunteer teacher of working-class pupils of all colors. Martí wrote poignant essays on the North American cultural and political scene for Spanish American readers. In them he offered the first portraits of Whitman, Emerson, and General Ulysses S. Grant, and he interpreted contemporary events on subjects as diverse as impressionist painting, monetary policy, college education, ethnic conflicts, labor strife, earthquakes, floods, universal suffrage. In early 1890 Martí founded, with Rafael Serra, La Liga, a center for Cubans and Puerto Ricans of color. Martí admired three women—Clara Barton, Harriet Beecher Stowe, and Helen Hunt Jackson—for their social and humanitarian commitments. He translated Jackson's novel *Ramona* as well as textbooks on agriculture, logic, and the classical world. He published two books of poetry and a novel, directed several journals, and edited a children's magazine. Most of all, however, Martí worked to unite the rival factions of the independence movement under the Cuban Revolutionary Party. He traveled from New York to Key West and to Central America, Mexico, and the Caribbean, to promote Cuba's long quest for freedom, which was eventually renewed on the battlefield in 1895. This armed struggle sought to gain independence from Spain *and* from the United States, to build a just society based on racial equality, without social inequalities. José Martí was killed on the battlefield, in eastern Cuba, on the afternoon of May 19, 1895.

His essay "Our America" is required reading in our days of compulsion for world order, when geopolitical concerns shift from deposits of funds to funds of information, when imperialist expansions emphasize cultural transformations. Martí's ultimate concern is for one "America" based on its Native American uniqueness, without racial hatred; an America that distances itself from Europe and creates requited appreciation (North and South) based on peaceful coexistence and mutual knowledge and respect.

Martí identified the United States as "Anglo-Saxon America," a threat to full Spanish American independence. Martí saw especially during the last two decades of the nineteenth century the developing strategy for the economic and political control of all of America that was taking shape in Washington under the direction of Secretary of State James G. Blaine. For many decades the United States had expressed an interest in buying or, if necessary, gently taking Cuba from Spain. Southern states were particularly interested in gaining territory farther south that would strengthen the rationale for slavery. In the 1850s, filibuster William Walker invaded Nicaragua, declared himself its president, established English as the official language, and even reinstated slavery for the Nicaraguans, all in the quest of a manifest destiny south of the border.

Martí saw in Blaine's Pan-American Conference of 1889–1890 not an opportunity for cooperation among American republics but a United States plan to inherit the previous Spanish colonies as new markets for surplus products. His greatest apprehension was to see this economic and political domination in place before Cuba and Puerto Rico won their independence. Thus, he wrote profusely about the consequences of this brand of Pan-Americanism and what he perceived as Blaine's real objective: political control of the Americas. If Spanish America was to be absorbed economically, politically, and culturally before it had relished the opportunity to gain its true independence by recognizing its indigenous roots, multiracial identity, and knowledge of itself, Martí's greater "America" would be in danger. If the government of the United States proceeded thoughtlessly, without attempting to study the true nature of its neighbors, Martí's greater "America" would be lost. For America could only be one with understanding and knowledge of the other, and by common consent.

Such is the invitation to read José Martí's "Our America," the best of his works. This essay may yet open American minds.

Enrique Sacerio-Garí
Bryn Mawr College

PRIMARY WORKS

Ismaelillo, 1882; *Versos libres*, 1882; *Amistad funesta*, 1885; *La edad de oro*, 1889; *Versos sencillos*, 1891.

Our America[1]

TRANSLATOR'S NOTE

[José Martí, like many other writers in exile, became a translator. It was a way of earning a living in his interlingual landscapes, exploring thoughts with new words. His first translation was very carefully selected. It was a translation of Victor Hugo's *Mes Fils* ("My Sons"), published in Mexico in 1875 the year of his return to America, by way of Paris, after his first period of exile in Spain. In *Mes Fils,* Hugo summarizes his life, especially his life in exile and how his two sons helped him during this arduous experience. In England, one of his sons became a translator of Shakespeare into French. Hugo devotes a significant portion of *Mes Fils* to comments on the importance of translation and the sorrows of life as an exile. A greater pain awaited Hugo when he returned to France, after nineteen years of exile: the death of both of his sons. *Mes Fils* is the story of this loss and the hope and desire to be reunited with them after death.

Translators often meet texts after death. Martí, then, translated a text about the art of translation and the life of an exile like himself. He becomes partially identified with Hugo's son by planning to translate *Hamlet,* a project he did not complete. He says in the introduction to his translation that he has chosen to translate Victor Hugo and not Victor Hugo's French because "Victor Hugo does not write in French, [and] he can not be translated into Spanish . . . because Victor Hugo writes in Victor Hugo." He wants to translate "a mind." He adds that he finds himself wherever he finds ideas and that "if all lofty ideas are concentrated in [Hugo's] snowy head, I am either his son or his brother, I live in that head."

I offer a new translation of *Nuestra América* into an English that must be read as José Martí: a syntax whose interstitial twists and turns will hopefully place you within his tropical head.]

The presumptuous villager believes that the whole world is his village, and as long as he stays as mayor or can torture the rival who took his girlfriend or keep his savings growing in the bank, he declares the universal order good, unaware of the giants with

[1]Translation © Enrique Sacerio-Garí, 2000. All rights reserved. *Nuestra América* was published in *La Revista Ilustrada de Nueva York* (January 10, 1891) and then in Mexico in *El Partido Liberal* (January 30, 1891).

overdeveloped boots who can crush him or of the competing comets in the sky, moving through drowsy space, devouring worlds. What remains of the provincial village in America must awake. These are not times for covering one's head, but rather for weapons as pillows, like Juan de Castellanos' illustrious men.[2] Mind warfare conquers all other weapons. Trenches of ideas are better than trenches of stone.

There is no prow that can cut through a cloud of ideas. An energetic idea, unfurled in time before the world, can stop a battleship squadron, like the mystical banner of judgment day. Nations that do not know each other should do so quickly, as allies before a common enemy. Those who shake their fists at each other, like jealous brothers who covet the same land, or the one with a small house who envies the one with a mansion, should join hands and be one. Those who, protected by a criminal tradition, servered the lands of their brother, with a sword stained with their own blood, must return the lands to the conquered brother, who has been punished enough, if they do not want the people to call them thieves. The honest man does not settle debts of honor by receiving money at so much a slap. We can no longer be the people of leaves up in the air, treetops heavy with flowers, creaking or rustling at the whim of a caring light, or thrashed and uprooted by the tempests: the trees must close ranks to keep the overdeveloped giant from passing! It is the time to review the lines and to march united. We must advance tightly organized, like silver at the roots of the Andes.

Only those whose birth is premature will lack courage. Those who do not have faith in their homeland are premature men. Because they lack courage, they deny it to others. Their weak limbs cannot reach the difficult tree, limbs adorned with painted nails and braclets, Madrid or Paris limbs; and they insist the tree cannot be climbed. We must load the ships with these destructive insects, which gnaw the very bone of the fatherland that nourishes them. If they are from Paris or Madrid, let them prance along the Prado, or stop at Tortoni's for sherbet. Those carpenter's sons who are ashamed that their fathers are carpenters! Those born in America who are ashamed of the Indian apron and the mother who raised them, and disown their sick mother, the indolent good-for-nothing, who desert a mother on her sickbed! Then, who is man, the real man? The one who stays at his mother's side to heal her, or the one who puts her to work out of sight and lives off her toil in rotten lands, sporting a wormy tie, cursing the womb that carried him, displaying the sign of a traitor on the back of his paper frockcoat? These children of our America, an ever-improving America that will be saved by its Indians, these deserters who bear arms in the armies of North America and its worsenbing conditions that drown its Indians in blood! These delicate creatures, who are men but do not want to do the work of men! Did Washington, who made them this land, go to live with the English, precisely at the time he saw them moving against his homeland? These men of *incredible* honor, who drag their honor crawling on foreign soil, like the *incroyables* in the French Revolution, dancing haughtily, dragging and rolling their *r*s!

[2]Juan de Castellanos (1522–1607), Spanish poet, author of an elegy that celebrates the deeds of illustrious men from the "New World."

For in what native lands can a man take greater pride than in our suffering American republics, to the sounds of battle between the book and the high processional candle, republics uplifted among the silent Indian masses by the bleeding arms of a hundred apostles. Never before have such advanced and unified nations been forged in less time from such splintered elements. The haughty character believes that the earth was created to serve as his pedestal because he can easily handle his pen or colorful speech, and he accuses his native land of being worthless and irreparable because its virgin forests do not continuously grant him the means to travel abroad, driving Persian ponies through champagne trails, as if he owned the world. The incapacity does not reside with the emerging country, searching for appropriate forms and a useful greatness, but rather with those who attempt to rule different nations, uniquely composed of their own character and singular violence, with a legacy of laws freely exercised during four centuries in the United States and nineteen centuries of monarchy in France. A decree by Hamilton[3] does not stop the charging colts of the *Ilaneros.*[4] A phrase of Sieyès[5] does nothing to release the stagnant blood of the Indian race. In order to govern well one must face commitments as they truly are in the land. The good ruler in America is not the one who knows how government functions in France or Germany, but one who knows the elements that form his country and how to lead them in unsion in order to reach, using methods and institutions that have risen from within the country, that desirable state where every man may attain and engage self-knowledge, where all men may enjoy the abundance that Nature bestowed for everyone in the nation they enrich with their labor and defend with their lives. The government should be born from the country itself. The spirit of the government should be the same as that of the country. The form of government must agree with the inherent constitution of the country. True government is nothing more than the balance of a country's natural elements.

That is why the imported book has been defeated in America by the natural man. Natural men have defeated the artificial learned men. The native people of mixed race have defeated the exotic Creoles. The battle is not between barbarism and civilization,[6] but between false erudition and Nature. The natural man is good and he abides by and rewards superior intelligence as long as it does not take advantage of his submission to harm him; as long as he is not offended by being disregarded, the one thing he does not forgive, the natural man is always prepared to regain by force the respect of whoever wounds his sensitivity or harms his interests. Tyrants in America have risen to power in accordance with these scorned natural elements, and have fallen the moment they betrayed them. Republics have suffered in

[3]Alexander Hamilton (1757–1804), secretary of the treasury in George Washington's cabinet. He strongly favored centralized government and the strengthening of federal control at the expense of the states.

[4]*Llaneros,* famous horsemen from the plains of Venezuela who fought alongside Simón Bolívar under the command of José Antonio Páez.

[5]Emmanuel Joseph Sieyès (1748–1836), French revolutionary and priest who edited the *Declaration of Rights of Man* (1789) and the Constitution of 1791.

[6]Allusion to Argentinean statesman Domingo Faustino Sarmiento (1811–1888), author of *Facundo, or Civilization and Barbarity,* and supporter of European models of education and development. He blamed the uncultured *gauchos* for the violence that characterized Argentina's tyrannical governments.

tyannies their inability to recognize the true elements of their countries, to derive from them the form of government, and govern with them. Ruler, in a new country, means creator.

In nations composed of cultured and uncultured elements, the uncultured will govern, because it is their habit to attack and resolve all doubts by force, wherever the cultured fail to learn the art of government. The uncultured masses are lazy and timid in the realms of intelligence. They want to be governed well. But if it hurts them, they get rid of government and govern themselves. How can the universities produce a governing subject, if there is not a single university in America that teaches the rudimentary basics of the art of government, to wit, the analysis of the elements peculiar to the peoples of America? Like guesswork, out in the world wearing Yankee or French spectacles, young men aspire to govern a nation they do not know. In the political race, we should ban all those who are ignorant of the basic rudiments of politics. The prize in literary contests should not be awarded to the best ode, but to the best study of the country's political factors. Newspapers, universities, and academies should undertake the study of the real factors that influence the country. To know them is enough, with eyes open and without beating around the bush. Whoever sets aside, by choice or oversight, any part of the truth is doomed to fall under the truth that is lacking, that grows in a context of negligence and brings down whatever was erected without it. After knowing all the elements of a problem it is easier to solve it than not knowing them. Along comes the natural man, outraged and strong, and brings down all justice built on books because justice was not served according to the obvious needs of the country. To know is to act with resolution. To know one's country, and to govern it based on that knowledge, is the only way to free it from tyrannies. The European university must yield to the American university. The history of America, from the Incas to the present, must be taught inside out, even if the archons of Greece are not taught at all. Our Greece is preferable over the Greece that is not our own.[7] We need it more. Nationalist politicians must replace exotic politicians. Let the world be grafted onto our republics, but the trunk must be our own. And let the defeated pedant hold his tongue: for there is no native land in which a man can take greater pride than in our suffering American republics.

Bearing the rosary, our head white and our multicolored bodies, Indian and Creole, we unflaggingly entered the world of nations. We set out to conquer freedom under the banner of the Virgin. A priest,[8] a handful of lieutenants, and a woman[9] raised the Mexican Republic onto the shoulders of the Indians. A Spanish cleric, beneath his priestly veneer, instructed in French liberty a few heroic students, who supported a Spanish general against the rule of Spain. In monarchic garb and chest uplifted by

[7]Eight years before, under contract with D. Appleton and Company, Martí translated into Spanish *Roman Antiquities* by A. S. Wilkins and *Greek Antiquities* by J. P. Mahaffy.

[8]Miguel Hidalgo y Costilla (1753–1811), Mexican patriot and priest, leader of the *Grito de Dolores* (1810), which marked the beginning of the Mexican revolt against Spain. He was captured, tried, and shot by the Spaniards.

[9]María Josefa Ortiz de Domínguez (?–1829), known as "La Corregidora de Querétaro." Although her husband was chief magistrate (*corregidor*) of Querétaro, she risked her life (and was imprisoned for) conspiring with Father Hidalgo in favor of the revolution.

the sun, Venezuelans from the north and Argentineans from the south set out and began to build nations. When the two heroes clashed, and the continent was about to tremble, one of them, and not the lesser of the two, turned and rode back.[10] And since heroism in times of peace is rare by being less glorious than during wars, it is easier for men to die with honor than to think logically. It is more feasible to govern when sentiments are exalted and united than to lead the mind after the battle when diverse, arrogant, exotic, or ambitious thoughts emerge. The authorities that were crushed in this epic onslaught undermined, with expected feline cunning and by the weight of reality, the edifice that held high the flag of nations, nations nurtured by the sap of a continuous practice of reason and freedom in government, a flag that was raised throughout the crude and singular regions of our mixed America, at the towns of people with bare legs and those with frock coats from Paris. The hierarchical constitution of the colonies resisted the democratic organization of the republics.[11] The bow tie capital cities would keep in the vestibule the open country of colt leather boots. The bookish redeemers did not realize that the revolution that triumphed with the soul of the land, once unleashed from the voice of the savior, had to govern with that soul of the land, and not against it or without it. America began to suffer, and still suffers, from the fatigue of trying to reconcile the discordant and hostile elements it inherited from a despotic and perverse colonizer, and the imported ideas and modes which have been delaying logical government because of their lack of local reality. The continent, dislocated for three centuries by a power that denied men the right to use their reason, disregarding or closing its ears to the illiterate hordes that help it, attained its redemption, embarked on a form of government based on reason, a reason belonging to everyone for everyone's concerns, not a university reason over a country reason. The problem of independence entailed not a change of forms but a change of spirit.

A common cause had to be made with the oppressed, in order to consolidate the new system opposed to the interests and habits of power of the oppressors. The tiger, frightened by the outburst of gunpowder, returns and haunts the prey at night. It dies: flames shooting from its eyes, paws in the air. It cannot be heard as it approaches, for it moves on velvet paws. When the prey awakens, the tiger is already on top. The colony remained alive in the republic, and our America is saving itself from its greatest errors—the arrogance of its capital cities, the blind triumph of the scorned peasants, the excessive influx of other people's ideas and formulas, the wicked, impolitic and disdainful treatment of the aboriginal race—by exercising a higher virtue, fertilized with necessary blood, of the republic that struggles against the colony. The tiger waits behind each tree, curled up at every junction. It will die: paws in the air, flames shooting from its eyes.

[10] Refers to a meeting in Guayaquil, Ecuador, between Simón Bolívar and José de San Martín. San Martín had successfully crossed the Andes from Argentina to Chile and, after several significant victories over the Spanish, was about to enter Peru. At the meeting with Bolívar, who was moving from the north to Peru, he agreed to let Bolívar assume control of the subsequent critical battles.

[11] Thus begins Martí's presentation of residual colonial structures with feline qualities, a dangerous tiger "behind every tree" within the republic. Martí's intertextual struggles with Sarmiento's *Facundo,* where the tiger is a symbol of *gaucho* individual violence transformed into the violence of the state, surfaces again.

But "these countries will be saved," as Rivadavia[12] announced, the Argentinean whose sin was a predilection for refinement in crude times; a machete does not go well in a silk scabbard, nor can one leave behind the lance in a country won by the lance, for it becomes angry, and presents itself at the door of Iturbide's congress[13] demanding that "the blond one be made emperor." These countries will be saved because with a genius for moderation that seems to prevail—due to Nature's imperturbable harmony in the continent of light and a surge of critical reading that had replaced the previous European generation's mode, so imbued with a reading based on trial and error and phalanstery—a truly real man is born for America during these real times.

We were a spectacle with the chest of an athlete, the hands of a dandy, and the head of a child. We were masked: English trousers, Parisian vest, North American jacket and Spanish cap. The Indian, silenced, was roundabout us, and would go to the mountains to baptize his children. The Negro, looked down upon, poured out at night the music of his heart, alone and unknown among the waves and the wild. With blind indignation, the peasant, the creator, turned on the disdainful city and his own child. We were epaulets and academic gown in countries that came into the world with hemp sandals and Indian headbands. Our true character would have been to join in brotherhood, with the charity of heart and daring of the founding father, the Indian headband and the academic gown, to rescue the Indian from stagnation, to open spaces for the able Negro, to fit liberty to the body of those who rose up and triumphed in its name. We were left with the judge, the general, the scholar and the privileged. The angelic youth tossed their heads upwards toward Heaven, crowned with clouds, only to drop back in sterile glory, as if from the tentacles of an octopus. The natural people, driven by instinct and blinded by victory, overwhelmed the staffs of gold. Neither the European nor the Yankee book could solve the Hispanic-American riddle. Hate was tried, and the countries came further down in the world, year by year. Exhausted by this senseless hate, by the resistance of the book against the lance, of reason against the high processional candle, of the city against the country, of the impossible imperial domination of divided urban ranks over the natural nation, whether tempestuous or inert, we begin almost unknowingly to try love. Then, the nations stand up and greet each other. "What (and how) are we?" they ask themselves, and they begin to tell themselves what (and how) they are. When a problem arises in Cojimar, they do not look for the solution in Danzig. The frock coats are still French, but thought begins to be from America. The youth of America roll up their sleeves and bury their hands into the dough and make it rise with the yeast of their brows. They understand that there is too much imitation, and that salvation is to be found in creation. "Create" is the keyword of this generation. The wine is made from plantains, and even if it turns out sour, it is our wine! It is understood that

[12]Bernardino Rivadavia (1780–1845), first president of Argentina (1826). He resigned under pressure for carelessly negotiating peace with Brazil.

[13]Agustín de Iturbide (1783–1824), Mexican conservative leader who initially opposed the war for independence against Spain. After the *Tratado de Córdoba* he entered Mexico City and was later proclaimed Emperor Agustín I. He left for Europe after being deposed by General Antonio López de Santa Anna but returned in 1824 and was, then, executed.

the forms of government of a country must be in keeping with its natural elements; that absolute ideas must be stated in relative forms to avoid mistakes of form; that liberty, to be viable, must be sincere and complete; that the republic dies if it does not open its arms to all, and makes progress with all. The tiger within lets itself in through a crevice, and the tiger from without. The general holds his cavalry to a pace that suits his infantry. The enemy surrounds the cavalry if the infantry is left in the rear. Strategy equals politics. Nations must live in a context of mutual and self-criticism, because criticism is healthy but always with one heart and one mind. Reach down to the wretched and lift them up in your arms! Dissolve the clots of America with the fire of your heart! Let the natural blood of the nations run boiling and throbbing through the veins! On their feet, with happy workingmen eyes, the new Americans greet each other people to people. The natural statesmen emerge from their direct study of Nature. They read to apply what is read, not to copy mindlessly. Economists study the problems at their origin. Orators begin to restrain their rhetoric. Dramatists bring native characters to the stage. Academies discuss feasible topics. Poetry shears off its romantic Zorrilla locks and hangs its red vest on the glorious tree. Prose, sifted and sparkling expression, is charged with ideas. Those who govern Indian republics, learn Indian languages.

America begins to escape all its dangers. Above some republics still lies the octopus in its sleep. Others, in turn and in balance, set sail with furious and sublime haste to make up for lost centuries. Some, forgetting that Juárez[14] rode in a mule-drawn carriage, hitch their carriage to the wind with soap bubbles coachmen. Poisonous luxury, the enemy of freedom, corrupts the frivolous and opens the door to the foreigner. Others, with the epic spirit of a threatened independence, refine the virile character. Others, in rapacious wars against their neighbors, breed unruly soldiers who could devour them. But our America is facing another danger that does not come from itself but from the difference in origins, methods, and interests between the two halves of the continent. The time is near at hand when our America will be approached by an enterprising and booming nation demanding close relations, although it does not know our America and, indeed, despises it. And since potent countries, self-made by shotgun and law, love strong countries, only strong countries; since the time of unbridled recklessness and ambition (from which North America could perhaps be freed by the predominance of what is purest in its blood, or on which it may be thrown by its vengeful and sordid masses, its tradition of expansion, or the interests of a clever leader) is not so near at hand even to the most startled eye that there is not time to put it to the test of continuous and discreet dignity that could approach and dissuade it; since its honor as a republic in the eyes of the world's attentive nations places a restraint on North America that would not be eliminated even by the puerile provocation, or ostentatious arrogance, or parricidal discords of our America, the urgent duty for our America is to show itself as it is, one in soul and purpose, swift defeater of a suffocating tradition, stained only by the copious blood sapped from hands by the struggle to clear away ruins, and dripping

[14]Benito Juárez (1806–1872), Mexican politician, governor of Oaxaca and president of Mexico in 1867 and 1871. He successfully led the fight against the French intervention and captured the "Mexican" Emperor Maximilian at Querétaro.

from our veins, cut by our masters. The scorn of the formidable neighbor, who does not know our America, is the greatest danger for our America. It is imperative, since the day of the visit is at hand, for our neighbors to know our America, and to know it soon, so they stop disdaining it. Through ignorance, they might go so far as to covet it. Out of respect, once they know us, they would remove their hands. One must have faith in the best in men and distrust the worst. One must promote the best so that it be revealed and prevails over the worst. Otherwise, the worst prevails. Nations should have a pillory for whoever arouses useless hates and another one for whoever does not tell them the truth in time.

There can be no racial hate, because there are no races. The feeble thinkers, the detached thinkers, rattle off and reheat library-collected races, which the just traveler and the cordial observer seek in vain in Nature's justice, where what stands out, within a triumphant love and turbulent hunger for life, is the universal identity of man. The soul emanates, equal and eternal, from bodies of different shapes and colors.[15] Whoever foments and spreads confrontation and hate between races, sins against Humanity. But in its formative years, a nation among other different nations condenses particular and characteristic ideas and habits, of expansion and conquest, of vanity and greed, which could, during a period of internal disorder or alacrity of its accumulated character, turn from the latent state of national concerns into a serious threat to the neighboring lands, isolated and weak, which the strong country considers perishable and inferior. Thinking is serving. But one should not presuppose, by antagonistic small-mindedness, a fatal and innate wickedness in the blond nation of the continent, because it does not speak our language or does not see particulars as we do, nor resemble us in its political stigmas, so different from ours, nor does it favorably deem the short-tempered, dark-skinned people, nor does it look charitably from its still uncertain eminence on those less favored by History, who climb every heroic stretch of the way of the republics. The patently obvious facts of the problem should not be hidden, for proper study and the tacit and urgent union of the continental soul can settle this matter peacefully for ever and ever. A unanimous hymn is already resounding! The present generation lifts hard-working America on its shoulders and takes it along the fertile road of the sublime fathers; from the Rio Grande to the Straits of Magellan, the Great Semí,[16] bore by the condor, scattered the seed of the new America throughout the romantic nations of the continent and the sorrowful islands of the sea!

[15] Martí spent the last years of his life fighting against racism among Cubans and writing about issues of race and ethnicity in the United States and Spanish America. See Martí's *Inside the Monster* (New York: Monthly Review Press, 1915), pp. 209–242.

[16] Martí's figure of "the Great Semí" is based on an Arawak (Taíno) deity called a "cemí." During his first journey to this hemisphere, Columbus met the peaceful Taínos ("the noble ones") and the Caribes ("the strong ones"). The latter Columbus called "caníbales"—that is cannibals, a word of uncertain origin that was, nevertheless, the source of Shakespeare's character Caliban in *The Tempest.* Martí hopes the seed of his Great Semí will break forth into a lasting peace for a new America. For the Taínos, see José Juan Arrom's *Mitología y artes prehispánicas en las Antillas* (1975), Mercedes López-Baralt's *El mito taíno: Levi-Strauss en las Antillas* (1985) and Irving Rouse's *The Tainos: Rise and Decline of the People Who Greeted Columbus* (1992).

MODERN PERIOD 1910–1945

The Centers of the Modern

In 1913 the initial shock of modernism reached the United States in the form of the Armory Show. Staged in a New City building that had once housed military operations, this art exhibit outraged much of the population. Derided by the press as either hoaxes or insults to good taste, many of the works were abstract paintings, mainly by living artists, European and American, who were not well known. Most notorious was the piece by Marcel Duchamp, a radical French artist who eventually came to live in America: an abstract painting of a nude woman descending a staircase; and three years later he exhibited a urinal installed upside down and signed "R. Mutt." The show was international in terms of the artists represented, but it was thoroughly American in its optimism and its brashness.

When William Carlos Williams, then a practicing physician in New Jersey, saw the Duchamp painting, he laughed out loud. That laugh represented several emotions, and behind them a newly developing cultural frame of reference. Williams, like Duchamp, wanted art and poetry to be in contact with everyday life and everyday objects, even if it meant attacking the normal placidity of cultural conventions. Williams laughed at Duchamp's boldness, at his irreverence, and through a shock of recognition, he was also laughing at himself. For a great many people, the advent of modernism in America was definitely not a laughing matter. But for others, including many who would become identified as the country's leading writers, the irreverence and exuberance of the Armory Show were importantly echoed by the cultural energy that was taking shape in America in the first decades of the new century. Gertrude Stein once teasingly redefined old and new when she remarked that America was the oldest country in the world, because it had lived in the twentieth century longer than any other nation. Many historical and social forces helped make America modern, and in turn American writers helped make modernism what it was, and is.

Defining modernism is a difficult task. A comprehensive definition would refer to its stylistic innovations, its willingness to disrupt traditional syntax and form, to mix together modes or levels of writing that had often been kept separate, and to risk incoherence and experimentation in order to challenge the audience's preconceived notions of value and order. A historical definition would say that modernism is the artistic movement in which the artist's self-consciousness about questions of form and structure became uppermost. Some people saw modernism in terms of its obsession with so-called primitive material and attitudes, while yet others maintained that its essential ingredient was an international perspective on cultural matters. To the extent that both groups have support for their argument, we can also say that modernism realigns the center of culture, either by reaching out beyond its national or regional boundaries, or by re-incorporating material that had previously been considered "subliterary." In brief, modernism

> "If it had not been for these thing, I might have live out my life talking at street corners to scorning men. I might have die, unmarked, unknown, a failure. Now we are not a failure. This is our career and our triumph. Never in our full life could we hope to do such work for tolerance, for joostice, for man's onderstanding of man as now we do by accident. Our words—our lives—our pains—nothing! The taking of our lives—lives of a good shoemaker and a fish-peddler—all! That last moment belongs to us—that agony is our triumph."
>
> Bartolomeo Vanzetti

asks us to reconsider what we normally understand by the center and the margins.

One consensus argues simply that modernism is a cultural movement or period style that was dominant in the arts internationally, between the first years of the twentieth century and the end of World War II. But then the disagreement sets in: Was it profoundly anti-cultural in its impulses (as "R. Mutt" would seem to suggest)? Was it only a bankrupt form of romanticism? Artists who shared the beliefs of romanticism had for several generations been increasingly disheartened by the way society had marginalized artistic creativity. Was modernism's glorification of the artist a form of self-serving grandiosity that only masked a deep social despair?

All these questions are negatively phrased, but each can be converted into a positive claim. Many American writers, people otherwise as diverse as H.D. (Hilda Doolittle) and Ernest Hemingway, Theodore Dreiser and Jean Toomer, might have been willing to accept some of the following positive claims. Modernism rests on the belief that the artist is generally less appreciated but more sensitive, even more heroic, than the average person. By trusting in the power of art to save us from the deadening features of everyday life, especially the desensitizing elements in urban, industrial society, the artist both challenges tradition and reinvigorates it. New styles of writing were necessary to express new ideas and values, and modernism created what one critic called a "tradition of the new." This would mean a strong commitment to breaking away from both patterned responses and predictable forms.

The principle of experimentalism had to be rigorously defended, in the view of most modernists, since it would keep art from turning into something stale or pious. This attitude, however, was not the only one prevalent among modern writers. African American writers, for instance, sometimes drew consciously on traditional material and forms. Native American writers frequently wanted to restore ancient tales to a new, contemporary audience and so reclaim some of the cultural patrimony that was threatened by the modern age. But much modern art tried to avoid grandiosity and pompous themes, such as were often voiced by figures in organized religion or mainstream politics, working instead with the artist's individual perceptions and celebrating the ordinary textures and rhythms of life in an extraordinary way. Better to focus on a red wheelbarrow than on some worn-out public or classical monument, regardless of the disruption this might cause the expectations of the audience. Modernism shocked because it had to, and it used irony and an assortment of disruptive techniques to penetrate any and all the pious beliefs that kept us from knowing our true selves and our true values.

Modernism, in these general terms, contains several contradictory elements. For example, it was democratic in its impulses, tilting against the hierarchies that sustain historically sanctioned values—values such as the stability of the individual self, the importance of the patriarchal family as a cornerstone in society, and the need to honor long-established laws and customs. Modernism was also elitist, since it made claims for the artist that it was not always willing to extend to ordinary men and women. This is one reason why modernism was not wholly embraced by African American, Native American, or immigrant authors. Modernism, however, could redraw tradition so that some hidden or forgotten values might be reasserted. But in its more impatient forms it appeared to throw overboard traditional values altogether. And, very much to the point in our context, some modernist writers celebrated indigenous or national traditions, such as America's technological expertise, seeing in them a source of great emotional force in a world that was otherwise rootless and overstandardized—what many people seven decades ago called "deracinated." On the other hand, many modernist masterpieces deliberately assaulted the faith of simple views and simple people, and even saw in the national spirit a jingoism or provinciality that is everything an international cultural movement must try to avoid or eliminate.

The struggle for freer expression, especially in sexual and political matters, was one of the main issues in modernism. Writers committed to such expression often found themselves pursuing a kind of exile. Much of American literature in this period took place in foreign lands, but those settings sometimes had a very American feel to them, especially the sidewalk cafes and bars of Hemingway's Paris, or the Riviera of F. Scott Fitzgerald's *Tender Is the Night.* Still other writers fled from the small towns of their birth, not to Europe or other foreign places, but to the large and growing urban centers of America, especially Chicago, Los Angeles, and New York City. Many also deliberately headed for Greenwich Village or Harlem, centers within centers, as it were, but desirable in part because they were places where the marginal could be celebrated. In fleeing to the big cities, these writers were part of a great social and historical movement in America that swept along not only artists but also thousands of black Americans and immigrants from many countries. This growth of what we can call "mass society"—that is, large urban concentrations of millions of people, living in great density and working in factory jobs or other forms of wage labor—was at once the setting of modern art and often its focus of attack or celebration.

When American writers in large numbers fled their native shores during the first decades of the twentieth century, many to Paris or London, they did so seeking the broadest possible base for their experience, at the same time fleeing what they felt was a constrictive society. For many years, American artists had reacted negatively to what they identified as the Puritanical and repressive elements in our culture; this reaction grew stronger in the period before and after World War I. The Committee for the Suppression of Vice, headed by a man named Comstock, was operating visibly; it had lent its name to the term "Comstockery," an attitude that censored all reference to any immoral or even sexual behavior. Laws were passed in this period, for example, that prohibited sending any information about birth control through the mails. In 1900 Dreiser had difficulty publishing his novel *Sister Carrie,* and was able to do so only in a "sanitized" version. However, in 1925, his novel *An American Tragedy* was received with great praise, though it, too, told of a woman who wandered from the path of rectitude.

In some sense, the very efforts at repression suggest the strength of the movements to change American culture: at contest in the struggle over birth control, for example, was what might today be called "women's liberation"—whether the greater access to education or work, in the professions staffed by women since the late nineteenth century, would finally be translated into wider opportunities for self and sexual expression, and for freedom from the cycle of pregnancy, childbirth, and family-rearing that continued to entrap many poor and working women. Family-planning advocates, led by women like Margaret Sanger, argued that access to birth control was critical if society were to fulfill its implicit promises to women. Writers like Agnes Smedley (in *Daughter of Earth*) dramatized from a female perspective the savage internal conflicts many women experienced between their own sexuality and the consequences of its expression; more broadly still, Edith Wharton created characters like Lily Bart (in *The House of Mirth*) and Charity Royall (in *Summer*) for whom the social promises of wider opportunity outside traditional marriage proved altogether illusory. The issues of free expression with which modernist writers were concerned were thus related to deeply conflicted questions of social policy and cultural norms.

That connection was also illustrated in 1925, by the Scopes trial in Tennessee, in which a man was charged with corrupting young people by teaching them the theory of evolution, thus challenging one of the central myths of our culture, namely that humans were created by a divine being at a specific time as revealed in the Old Testament. In 1920 the editors of a magazine called *The Little Review* were fined $100 for publishing a portion of James Joyce's novel *Ulysses,* whose language had been described as "obscene." But in 1936, Judge John Woolsey wrote a landmark decision in the United States District Court clearing the way for the unhampered publication of this and other important modernist works. What society often treasured as its central beliefs—in decency, in the necessity for hard work, in the desirability of order and respect—was what modern art called into question.

One way to view modern art and modern society in the same framework is to see that both phenomena pose questions about the center and the periphery. Previously societies tended to have a visible center, and to produce a centrally located culture—the obvious model being that of the court and the monarch in early modern European societies. But with the coming of fully modern forms of life, many countries, the United States chief among them, evolved social forms in which the palpable sources of power and influence were harder to identify. Many forms of authority were questioned, especially in the 1920s and '30s, because the forces that gave society its shape were changing, often with incredible speed. Ezra Pound spoke of the age as one that demanded an "accelerated grimace." The city was certainly one of the places where the tempo of modern life was noticeably faster, and with this speed went a blurring of the outlines and a need to capture the panorama through rapidly shifting perspectives.

Some earlier writers such as Whitman, William Dean Howells, and Stephen Crane had begun to open up urban vistas in the late nineteenth century. Of course, the worlds of the raft and the whaling ship in Twain and Melville or of the New England village in Mary E. Wilkins Freeman and Sarah Orne Jewett could show middle-class readers a great deal about their experience, but eventually such exotic locales would prove insufficient to their increasingly urbanized consciousness. Dreiser's fiction is unimaginable outside of an urban setting, as is that of Toomer, Hughes, Yezierska, and Fitzgerald. Hemingway and Wharton on the other hand, write about Paris and New York, but also about trout streams and small Michigan and New England towns. Indeed, the pastoral or rural spirit remained a part of American literature in the first half of the twentieth century and its debunking a frequent theme.

But it was largely within the concentration of cities that writers, especially the male modernists, found subject material and stimulation. Cities, however, do not easily sort themselves out into manageable shapes. The modern city is a challenge, even a threat, to the idea of order, and as such it can present a problem to the aesthetic impulse. But American authors rose to this challenge, often attempting to resolve this artistic dilemma through experiments in artistic form.

When writers like Sherwood Anderson, Jean Toomer, Theodore Dreiser, Zora Neale Hurston, and Marianne Moore came to New York City, they were in some ways consciously coming to the center of literary life in America. But when these writers tried to capture what lay at the heart of America, they often looked to other locales as well. When H.D., Ezra Pound, and Hemingway went off to Paris or London, they, too, had a longing for a center, though each at some point in their careers settled in a small town considerably removed from the metropolis and its concentrations of wealth and influence. As with the environments of these writers, so, too, with their sense of subject matter. Not only might the center and the margins be redrawn, but the very notions of centrality and marginality would receive a modernist configuration. Hemingway could address the cosmic forces through the tale of a lone and primitive fisherman. H.D. might use the colossi of ancient myth to plumb her own psychic strength. The common men and women of New Jersey, marginalized by their economic and social status, could enter the art of Williams and find there a recognizable world, though not necessarily one that had a simple, old-fashioned celebration of stability as its centering principle.

But not all the literature in the modernist period in America focused on marginal figures. Or, to put it slightly differently, not all writers felt their material or characters to be marginalized. Robert Frost, for example, drew heavily on a tradition of nature and transcendentalism in his poetry, Edith Wharton dissected the established power of "old New York" in her novels and stories, just as Edwin Arlington Robinson, Ellen Glasgow, and Zora Neale Hurston confidently wrote of small town citizens who lived in an ostensibly stable world. Underneath the surface, however, all five writers were able to reveal fissures and tremors suggestive of modernist anxiety and cultural despair. The small town and rural locales were favored by some writers, but only for the most blinkered witnesses were the old social forms still valid.

Many of the developments in the modern world tended to de-emphasize the importance of place altogether, at least in the older nostalgic sense. Strong impulses toward regionalism and local color could exist at the same time, however, and an important writer such as Frost could make use of these interests. But the work force, for example, was increasingly made up of minorities: blacks and immigrants who had been called upon to do the backbreaking physical labor that made many of the advancements of modernity possible, and who were often treated as little more than exchangeable parts in a great social mechanism.

In the 1920s the population of New York City grew immensely. But by the end of the decade engineers had built a tunnel to New Jersey, creating an important link outside the island confines of Manhattan and a step toward the creation of what came to be called the "megalopolis." The end of the decade also saw work begin on the Empire State Building, soon to become a symbol not only of the city but of America itself throughout the world. This elegant structure epitomized the way skyscrapers converted space into something like a commodity, to be bought, sold, or rented as the business world saw fit. Large cities were able to expand both vertically and horizontally, and with their expansion came architecture and forms of life that were more and more bureaucratically organized—a bureaucracy that political philosopher Hannah Arendt called a system that featured "rule by nobody," a way of constantly displacing the center of responsibility and authority.

Culture is in complex ways always engaged in questions of authority, of course. The culture of modernism is structured by many themes, but one of the chief concerns it addresses is the idea that the older forms of authority are decayed or useless, and that the authority of the individual must be strengthened or people will be overwhelmed by what many in the 1930s called the "forces of collectivism." Indeed, the fear of collectivism was largely the result of the success of the 1917 Bolshevik Revolution in Russia. There was, however, a strong native strain of collectivist sentiment in the United States; Eugene Debs ran for president in 1920 on a socialist ticket, and captured almost one million votes. Many American writers were seriously attracted by Marxism, despite the ostracism it sometimes entailed. In the America of the 1930s the social crisis triggered by the Depression was often argued about, and physically fought over, in terms of individualism and collectivism.

But even before the Depression brought the decade of the 1920s to a brutal conclusion, the social struggles of the country were being bitterly contested. After World War I, the so-called Palmer raids of 1919, under the leadership of then Attorney General A. Mitchell Palmer, rounded up people with Communist affiliations, suspected subversive designs, or even activist labor backgrounds. These raids were only one of several efforts, private or government-sponsored, to "cleanse" the body politic of any radical or "foreign" influence. The Sacco and Vanzetti case, a direct outgrowth of the climate of fear produced by the Palmer raids, provided a particularly striking instance of this clash over political values. Accused of murder in connection with a payroll robbery, these two Italian anarchists were prosecuted, judged, and ultimately executed by members of the older Yankee aristocracy, and were defended over the seven years of appeals by, among others, a large group of writers and intellectuals, including Hemingway, John Dos Passos, Edna St. Vincent Millay, and Maxwell Anderson, many of whom participated in activities and wrote works focused on the case; Millay, in fact, was arrested on a picket line protesting their innocence.

Important strikes in the steel, coal, and textile industries in the late 1910s and early 1920s gave ample warning that America had to do more to meet the needs of ordinary workers than had so far been accomplished by the reform-minded liberalism of Theodore Roosevelt and Woodrow Wilson.

Still, those strikes were generally lost by the relatively weak mine and steel unions, and the 1920s became a period dominated by business interests. While the post-war years brought widespread prosperity—except to significant areas of the farm belt—wealth and power continued to be concentrated throughout this period. Working conditions, wages, and the length of the work week were all issues contested between those who held power and control of America's growing industries and those who worked in its increasingly modernized shops and assembly lines. But it was not until after the stock-market crash of 1929, the subsequent depression, and the general discrediting of business interests that these conflicts became widely visible or were much written about. Only then, too, did the pendulum of social and economic power swing in some degree back toward working people, who began to find ways to amass and control social power.

But it wasn't only working people who developed new ways of amassing and controlling power in and after the Depression. There was also a challenging structure for generating new financial strength and, by extension, social force as well: the American corporation. Again, America was not alone here, for other advanced industrial societies had corporations, some of great extensiveness and sophistication. But America and the modern world seemed united in their fascination with big business. And in America big business had increasingly come in the twentieth century to mean corporate business. In 1924 the newly elected President Coolidge proclaimed that "the chief business of the American people is business. The man who builds a factory builds a temple . . . . The man who works there worships there." Needless to say, five years later such religiosity took on an especially bitter irony for many.

However, after the Depression American business rebounded with a strength that amazed the world. In part this new strength was increased by the industrial retooling of the economy made necessary by World War II. And collectivism might at times have seemed a mere phantom, for the strength of American business was finally not curtailed by such "advanced" social legislation as the Social Security Act and the Labor Relations Act, both of which became law in 1935. Even the Republican candidate for President in 1936, Alf Landon, ran on a platform that supported social security. The Depression had the ineradicable effect of turning the boom period of the first two decades of the century into a period of social reorganization and planning. The forces of progressivism, with their belief in the power of masses of people to determine their own political destiny, had prospered under Teddy Roosevelt and Wilson, and been chastened by Harding, Coolidge, and Hoover; these forces were still vitally at work in American society in the 1930s.

Locating the sources of power in the people themselves had always been one of the cornerstones of American political thought. But such a broad base of power was often centered in institutions that were hard to change, slow to reflect greater diversity, and quick to justify their own mistakes. In 1920 the Nineteenth Amendment giving women the right to vote was adopted. Some saw suffrage as the culmination of a long struggle that had begun almost eighty years before with the Seneca Falls convention of 1848; they took it to symbolize the emergence of women into full equality, a significant place at the center of political power. And it is certainly true that the efforts to achieve women's suffrage and related reforms continued unabated throughout much of the nineteenth and early twentieth centuries. For others, the achievement of suffrage represented a more equivocal "victory," one which did little to change women's marginal status.

The historical evidence offers an ambiguous answer. It was certainly true, for example, that more and more women had since at least the 1890s been working for wages outside the home, that significant numbers of them had become professionals, and that women were no longer so utterly compelled to marry for support. But the professions they entered were primarily new ones: social work, nursing, and librarianship, which, like the old standby teaching, offered low status and pay. The traditional, and more lucrative, male professions, like medicine, law, and the clergy, remained largely closed to women for another half century. Women were barred from the skilled trades, and, in fact, as many as forty percent of working women, especially blacks, were engaged in household labor. Even within the home, the vaunted development of "labor-saving" household appliances carried its own ambiguities: machines often simply "freed" women to shift time to other household work, like child care, and the machines also changed the very nature of the chores, imposing higher standards of cleanliness on the "modern" housewife. The ambiguities extended in still other directions: if the new ideas of Freud suggested that women had and should be able to enjoy sexual feelings, and if the twenties "flapper" emerged in her bobbed hair and short skirts as an embodiment of female sexuality, most Americans probably continued to hold contrary Victorian ideas condemnatory of such new freedoms.

To point to the ambiguities of "progress" is not to deny that profound and significant changes had taken place in the lives of large numbers of women. Nothing suggests this so much as the falling birth rate: white women in 1800 bore, on average, over *seven* children; in 1860, 5.21; by 1920, the rate was down to 3.17. Opportunities for higher and graduate education did broaden steadily, at least into the 1920s. Women made many of the "new professions" their own: the Settlement House movement, and organizations established during this era from the Junior Leagues to the League of Women Voters to the Consumers League, offered women of all ages structured opportunities for participating effectively in public life. At the same time, perhaps precisely because more women were entering and competing in the job market, and were leading ultimately successful campaigns for suffrage, the prohibition of alcoholic beverages and lynching, and other progressive reforms, tensions over women's role and status increased markedly in the decades surrounding World War I.

In 1911, the philosopher George Santayana had attacked what he described as the "feminized" American intellect as an expression of an outmoded "genteel tradition." He and other writers of the period, like Sinclair Lewis and Joseph Hergesheimer, mocked the provinciality and presumed intellectual backwardness of small-town club ladies, as well as what some saw as the androgynous eccentricities of their bohemian sisters. While such critics assailed "genteel" male writers like William Dean Howells, the polemics of the time took on a distinctly gendered quality, which historians have only recently come to note. Perhaps this "war of words" developed because the experiences and outlooks of many male modernist writers differed from those of their female counterparts. For T. S. Eliot, the social life of the time might be represented by Prufrock's tea:

> In the room the women come and go
> Talking of Michelangelo.

But for Amy Lowell it might be an afternoon of chatty visits with her sister poets, Sappho, Elizabeth Barrett Browning, and Emily Dickinson ("The Sisters"), who seem strange to her,

> but near,
> Frightfully near, and rather terrifying,
> I understand you all, for in myself—
> Is that presumption? Yet indeed it's true—
> We are one family.

Recent critics have noted that the disintegration of the pre-World War order, so alarming to many male writers, seemed, perhaps, less a shock to women than a kind of liberation from, to quote Lowell again, Queen Victoria, Martin Luther, and "the long line of Church Fathers."

However that might be, it was certainly the case that the "woman question" was one of the main reasons why the 1920s felt to many who lived through it like a very modern time indeed. Where interest in modernism flourished, as in New York's Greenwich Village, the hub of social and literary experimentalism, feminism was a prominent part of the culture. Much of the bohemianism of the Village could be traced back to models in nineteenth-century France, but the mix of artists and social radicals had an American flavor all its own. There was a famous salon run by Mabel Dodge Luhan, a wealthy woman known for bringing together social and political radicals such as John Reed, who was to write *Ten Days That Shook the World,* a powerful history of the Bolshevik Revolution in Russia; Margaret Sanger, the proponent of birth control; and Big Bill Heywood, a leader of the Industrial Workers of the World (known as the IWW or "Wobblies"). Though Luhan herself was eventually to back away from the more radical positions of her guests, the salon was a focus for discussion and organization about a host of social and aesthetic issues. Another key figure in the bohemian culture of the Village was Edna St. Vincent Millay, whose poetry celebrated freedom in love and the equal rights of women and men in moral questions, and whose writing and triumphantly flippant public stance helped shape the notion of the avant-garde writer for an entire generation of readers.

For many centuries the traditional roles of Western European culture had tended to divide the work of art into things made by men, and things inspired or conserved by women. Few modernist writers pictured themselves as aggressively a maker as did Gertrude Stein; she was a woman who broke the rules. Her contemporary Amy Lowell also existed, in the public mind especially, in a category reserved for the outrageous; Lowell smoked cigars and expressed her opinions very forthrightly. She stood in contrast to a poet like Millay, who redefined the possibilities for women writers in more elusive and indirect ways. But Stein worked hard and inventively at virtually remaking the rules of English syntax. What she produced was often baffling to people who still believed in the genteel tradition, that is, those who looked to literature only to reassure themselves about the world. Stein pursued a most ungenteel lifestyle, and her prose style was called upon to perform in ways that only a marginal figure could readily imagine. Stein's marginality came from being a woman and a lesbian, but in the context of modernism she earned for herself what is to many people a central place. Though she spent much of her life as an expatriate in France, she is also regarded as one of the most American of authors. Categories and definitions were not safe with her; her only constant was a desire to experiment.

At about the same time women were winning the right to vote, another Constitutional amendment was passed, making the production, sale, and consumption of alcoholic beverages illegal. Prohibition was, like suffrage, a social experiment. However, Prohibition failed and suffragism did not. But what the two movements had in common (besides many people who supported them both, often for reasons that were linked) is that they both suggested that the social order could be in some sense "engineered"; that is, through political edicts people's habits and conditions of life could be fundamentally altered. The idea that society was in an important way a product of political institutions appealed to the American mind, for after all in many ways America itself had begun as an experiment, an idea. America was not the only country to have a suffragist movement, or to experiment with Prohibition, but because these were implemented in the 1920s, they seemed to be especially "modern" ideas—or vice versa.

Prohibition sponsored a culture all its own, as it produced or enhanced the visibility of speakeasies, bathtub gin, and organized crime. From the beginning, many people in America saw such an attempt to regulate alcohol as thoroughly hypocritical and doomed to failure. But the root of Prohibition in the temperance movement of the previous century was one of the remnants of religion in our national life. (There were other important elements in the temperance movement, such as a feminist revolt against family violence and the loss of income that alcoholism often entailed. The movement also included some who were disturbed by the "foreign" influence in saloon life.) Though modernism was in many ways a thoroughly secular, even anti-religious movement, the nation's cultural life could not be thoroughly restructured overnight. This truth cut both ways, for neither the forces of experimentalism nor those of traditionalism were able to settle

As stated before, every colored man who moves into Hyde Park knows that he is damaging his white neighbors' property. Therefore, he is making war on the white man. Consequently, he is not entitled to any consideration and forfeits his right to be employed by the white man. If employers should adopt a rule of refusing to employ Negroes who persist in residing in Hyde Park to the damage of the white man's property, it would soon show good results.

The Negro is using the Constitution and its legal rights to abuse the moral rights of the white. . . .

There is nothing in the make-up of a Negro, physically or mentally, which should induce anyone to welcome him as a neighbor. The best of them are insanitary, insurance companies class them as poor risks, ruin alone follows in their path. They are as proud as peacocks, but have nothing of the peacock's beauty. Certain classes of the Negroes, such as the Pullman porters, political heelers and hairdressers are clamoring for equality. They are not content with remaining with the creditable members of their race, they seem to want to mingle with the whites. Their inordinate vanity, their desire to shine as social lights caused them to stray out of their paths and lose themselves. We who would direct them back where they belong, towards their people, are censured and called "unjust." Far more unjust are their actions to the members of their race who have no desire to interfere with the homes of the white citizens of this district.

"Protect Your Property!" (1919), 1920
Property Owner's Journal

the questions raised by Prohibition. In 1933, the amendment was overturned, but what many people called "the noble experiment" had nevertheless left its mark on our collective identity.

The amendments giving women the vote and prohibiting the use of alcohol were important expressions of the spirit of the '20s. They represented both social experimentalism and political trust, something startlingly new and something reaffirmed. But if America was itself an experiment and Prohibition and women's suffrage two of its more challenging chapters, on a Friday in October, 1929, the country experienced one of its most severe failures. The Stock Market Crash of 1929 and subsequent Depression were a shock to all forms of political and social stability. It eventually required a great social experiment—the New Deal—to reset the shaken foundations. But in the meantime, the conflicting impulses of reformism, collectivism, individualism, and experimentalism that took on many forms in the early part of the 1920s faced each other on a stage marked by suspicion, fear, and dislocation. People waited in soup lines for food, and sold apples on the street in an effort to support themselves and their families. By now such images are so familiar to us that they are almost clichés, but to the men and women who first experienced them, the sensations of rage and helplessness were overwhelming. Many people talked of a loss of American innocence, referring back to a Puritan metaphor that echoed the fall from the Garden of Eden. The Puritans had themselves discovered a world far from innocent, and their fate showed how difficult it was to build a city on the hill to replace the lost innocence of the Garden.

The Depression showed Americans many things. It demonstrated, for example, the importance of the United States in the world of other nations, for the effects of our economic collapse soon spread throughout the Western industrialized world. The effects of the Depression also were greatly magnified by the Dust Bowl, a prolonged period of drought which left the agricultural center of the country in severe hardship. This devastation challenged the idea of the country as a land full of natural bounty. It also entered the national mythology—that storehouse of images and stories by which a people tells itself who they are—and became a part of some of our classic literature, such as John Steinbeck's *The Grapes of Wrath*. Also important was the fact that many Americans experienced migration and mobility in new ways; in desperate search for work, people took to the road and headed west or to big cities such as Chicago and New York. Many currents of American literature maintained a regional force, and there was also a new character in our midst: the drifter, often a man with a buried past and little to recommend him except an ability to survive at the edges of society.

What we can now see slightly more clearly than those who suffered through it is that the Depression represented the high point of the historical development of the powers of the state in America. The many federal agencies that were created to help re-energize the economy, the power that accrued to the office of the Presidency, and the realization that America's promise was only as sound as its economic system: all these helped to enhance governmental power in a way that challenged the virtually sacred tenets of American individualism. At the same time, a fierce argument had raged for over a decade as to how a balance might be struck between collectivism and individualism; questions about such a balance had animated the American political tradition since its beginnings. In fact, in the midst of the Depression, President Roosevelt entitled one of his 1936 campaign speeches, "The Period of Social Pioneering is Only at Its Beginning." The use of the pioneer metaphor enabled Roosevelt to invoke some of the cultural power of the myth of individualism even as he advanced the forms of activist government and social planning.

Though many might think that active resentment and resistance to the most obvious abuses of such power did not occur until the 1960s, the roots of the conflict go back at least thirty years to the time when an indigenous American radicalism set itself against what it saw as the enormous development of state power. Many of our poets mistrusted the trend towards concentration of power and official authority: E. E. Cummings, for example, praised the conscientious objector, and William Faulkner seemed to express a sneaking admiration for outcasts and renegades. Others, such as William Carlos Williams in his poem "To Elsie," depicted the victims of the system with something approaching clinical detachment. Again, modernism used irony to challenge "normal" perspectives and values.

If the 1920s were a period dominated by experimentalism, and one that altered the arts as well as traditional structures of social power, the 1930s were a period of solidarity and political experimentation. The Communist Party, for example, the largest political organization of the left in the 1930s, sponsored a wide range of activities, from unemployment councils and tenant unions to the literary John Reed clubs and Writers' Congresses, as well as newspapers and magazines. Party intellectuals, like Mike Gold, developed aesthetic theories of "proletarian realism" based on Marxist principles. And Party organizers, though later subject to 1950s purges, played key roles in starting the new industrial unions, which came together in 1935 in the Congress of Industrial Organizations (CIO), led by John L. Lewis and William Green. Early in the Depression the principle that workers had a *right* to organize collectively had been written into law; translating that theoretical right into practice, especially for the semiskilled or unskilled workers of mass-production industries, proved no easy matter, for major manufacturers sharply resisted the new unions. In the intense and often violent struggles which characterized organizing campaigns in major industries like rubber, auto, electrical, the government played a relatively neutral role—sometimes implicitly supporting unionization—which some interpreted as an effort to insure its own power or at least to build the political coalition headed by F.D.R.

For many writers, the 1930s offered as compelling, though strikingly different, a cultural milieu as that of 1920s bohemianism. Left-wing groups urged artists to support working-class organizing efforts, to help move the masses, in Edward Seaver's words, "through the maze of history toward Socialism and the classless society." Writers argued vigorously about the virtues and possibilities of the "proletarian novel." The American Writers' Congress of 1935 provided a platform for debating such issues, as did a variety of magazines whose names express their times: *Partisan Review, New Masses,* the *Anvil.* And as the decade wore on, more and more writers, like Dorothy Parker, Lillian Hellman, and Ernest Hemingway turned their talents toward the struggle against the rising threat of fascism.

Some authors, like Meridel LeSueur and Langston Hughes, tried to find ways of utilizing modernist formal techniques to pursue socialist political goals. But LeSueur insisted that the major departure of the period's culture was validating the lives and experiences of working people. For such goals, certain modernist tactics, like ironic detachment and linguistic complexity, offered little of value, though its interest in industrial processes, cinematic movement, and flat, ordinary language could be turned to political ends.

By no means was all 1930s culture defined by the left. In the South, particularly around Vanderbilt University, the group of "Southern Agrarians" offered their alternative to liberal and left-wing movements. Relatively isolated during the thirties, a number of these men became influential literary critics in succeeding decades, and their depoliticized formal mode of reading texts, the "New Criticism," a later academic orthodoxy. But precisely because so much in the thirties was given shape by organizers and intellectuals of the left, the profound anti-communism of the late 1940s and the 1950s obscured much of what had gone on in that earlier time. Until very recently, books and writers of the thirties were often cited only in order to deplore or condemn them as politically naive or formally backward. Some are. But many works, like the novels of Josephine Herbst and Fielding Burke, and the shorter pieces contained in this volume, have increased in critical estimation. While it was a contentious, frequently sectarian time, it was also a period of considerable and varied literary accomplishment. And it was the seedbed for some of the most significant of our contemporary writers, like Tillie Olsen, Muriel Rukeyser, and Richard Wright, all of whom honed their literary talents in 1930s political conflicts.

There were also other forces at work, chief among them the development of a new form of business management. For at least two decades before the war, that is, in the 1920s and '30s, American business had moved away from the ideal of the mogul or buccaneering entrepreneur to a safer, more settled agent of economic stewardship. The business executive, by replacing the tycoon, reflected a new sense of how to organize all forms of power: economic, political, and social. Companies like General Motors and Standard Oil would come to dominate international commerce in the second half of the twentieth century, but they began amassing their enormous wealth in the decades immediately after the Depression. Many writers deplored the new economic formations of what came to be called corporate capitalism; they saw them as unresponsive to human needs, wasteful of resources, and generally smug about their own prerogatives.

These new organizations of power often justified themselves as pursuing policies much more enlightened than those of the rapacious robber-barons of an earlier era. Such justifications were supported by the creation of massive amounts of wealth, demonstrated in very real ways, such as the production of automobiles, which changed the face of the cities and the countryside as well. Modernism in some of its aspects was quite thrilled by such manifestations. In his poem about Brooklyn Bridge, Hart Crane, for example, tried to capture the spirit of inventiveness and material progress in the mechanical age by using lyric forms. But the corporations extended their business theories, which prized inventiveness and progressively greater technical control, to society as a whole, as they argued for rational organization, the control of markets, and the desirability of new products and increased consumption. Many apologists for capitalism argued that an alliance between business and government should replace the oppositional politics of "trust-busting," and thereby offer to the people what would rightly become the dominant shaping force in American society. The benign form of this alliance was known as corporate liberalism, a belief that all the parts must support the good of the whole, and such parts would prosper best if they appreciated the special needs and benefits of that whole. Some writers were reluctant, however, to accept such arguments, and they frequently opposed what others celebrated as the genius of American "know how."

Such opposition as writers offered was not necessarily heeded, much less appreciated. But this did not lessen its vigor or frequency. A well known historian, Henry Steele Commager, wrote in *The American Mind* (1950) that the "all but unanimous repudiation of the accepted economic order by its literary representatives is one of the curious phenomena of American culture." Commager traced this repudiating spirit back to Thoreau and Emerson, which is surely one correct lineage. But some of the opposition spirit was fed by the modern concern with alienation. This notion was not especially connected to America; in fact, it was first explored in European Romanticism and in the writings of Karl Marx. But because it is such a central idea in the structure of modernity, it also had very strong and vivid manifestations in American literature.

Modernism and the Self

When Gertrude Stein told Hemingway that he and his fellow writers were all a "lost generation," she was speaking of alienation. When T. S. Eliot spoke about a "pair of ragged claws / Scuttling across the floors of silent seas," he was expressing a strong sense of alienation. When Louise Bogan speaks as "The Alchemist" who

. . . burned my life, that I might find
A passion wholly of the mind,
Thought divorced from eye and bone,
Ecstasy come to breath alone

she is registering what Eliot called the "dissociation of sensibility." And when Langston Hughes talked of "a dream deferred," he, too, spoke from a feeling of alienation. Stein's remark refers to the aftermath of World War I; Eliot's deals with sexual and social insecurity; Hughes is describing particular historical conditions of racial discrimination and oppression. Indeed, Hughes's living conditions were markedly different from those of privileged émigrés such as Eliot and Hemingway. But each writer is treating one of the central themes of modern literature: how can I form any basis for meaningful values and experience when I feel separated from my truest self, cut off from any sense of belonging in the world in a secure way? Alienation can be viewed as a condition of permanent marginality.

Alienation can take on very different meanings and tonalities depending on a person's immediate circumstances. Stein's remark about a lost generation, for example, clearly refers to the aftermath of World War I. In that war, America lost over one hundred thousand people through battlefield deaths and the effects of disease; the number of deaths suffered by the European countries, however, was even more staggering. Over seven million people perished on both sides. Mass society had produced a form of mass destruction. The loss of social purpose, heightened by the feeling of absurdity when confronted with the stupidity of the battle strategies and the "efficiency" of such lethal means as poison gas and motorized armaments, gave a special meaning to alienation in the post-war years. The scale of unnecessary suffering and the enormous loss of life changed the value systems of society for many people. Any notion that war contained chivalrous elements, or that it could be used to advance the causes of civilization, became harder and harder to sustain.

While America escaped the physical destruction of its cities and industrial capacities, it nevertheless remained scarred by the war in ways that were deep and pervasive. Pound spoke of the aftermath by describing civilization as "an old bitch gone in the teeth." Hemingway objected to the use of big and noble words; he felt that patriotism and duty had been corrupted by the uses to which they had been put by those who managed the war machines of the modern age. No longer could writers applaud sentiments such as President Wilson's when he explained that the purpose of the war was to "make the world safe for democracy." H.D. turned increasingly to a private order of myth that would, she hoped, show the way forward to a system of universal love. Even the technique of modernist irony was hard pressed to capture the split many felt between ideals and events. Alienation could mean that the person felt like a stranger, but it could also convey the feeling that it was the world that had become strange.

One way to think about alienation is to imagine how the very notion of the self altered as the modern world was formed. One of the most important changes was the development of a very acute sense of awareness about one's inner life. In European Romanticism this inner life was often seen as the true source of meaning and value in one's experience. At the same time, this interiority was a source of confusion, self-doubt, and self-questioning, since its states and emotions and insights were frequently unstable, infinitely changeable, or self-contradictory. The writings of Freud did much to put this exploration on a scientific basis, but even Freudian schemes of selfhood left many questions unanswered. The Freudian self, or "ego" as it was called, was often seen as a location of deep-seated conflicts and unerasable memories that constantly distorted one's ability to understand the past or adjust to the future. One way to resolve such contradictions was to adopt an ironic stance about everything, even about one's own stance. This consequently put a strain on the uses to which outside sources of authority—such as social norms or political structures—could be put in telling us who we "truly" are. Such lack of a clear identity can readily be experienced as a feeling of homelessness or marginality.

Because so much of the modern world seems "open"—in part because of our greater control over the physical environment, our ability to travel further and more quickly, the systems of distribution, and so forth—and because it seems possible as well to open up our models of artistic form, the modern self is sometimes confused by its own freedom. This confusion can be illusory. Immigrant writers, for example, often discover that their new home has more than a fair share of problems and limitations; what started as a quest for freedom produces a disillusioning awareness of restrictions and limits. One of the great themes of immigrant writing is the paradox of a new beginning that turns into a series of new losses and failures. In this, immigrants are thoroughly American, since from the country's beginnings this paradoxical reversal of expectations has shadowed our culture. Much immigrant writing, to be sure, tells a standard version of the success story, as the newcomer eventually rises to a social and economic position of prominence, or at least security. One of the standard histories on the subject, Oscar Handlin's *The Uprooted,* captures this double sense of the experience. As Crèvecoeur put it in *Letters from an American Farmer* (1782), for all successful immigrants "those (new) lands confer on them the title of freemen, and to that title every benefit is affixed which men can possibly require." But titles are very unstable in the modern world. Consequently, there are also many stories that focus on the dislocation instead of the security, that examine the persistence of margins rather than the pursuit of a new center.

Such dislocation or redefinition of the self is a cultural theme that makes the role of the immigrant one of special interest. And of course it is such conflict and questioning about the self (and *through* the self) that form much of the background of artistic experimentalism prevalent in the modern period. But we can also hear these concerns with the self expressed and explored in material that some have called "premodernist." In Dreiser's story "Typhoon," for example, the young woman slowly comes to a realization that the man she is involved with will not marry her and acknowledge the child she is expecting. Dreiser characterizes this realization as "some wild, unbelievable misery and fatality which had seemingly descended on her and yet could not be real." The woman knows and doesn't know, or rather she recognizes her state of mind even as she questions its very existence.

Native American writers often experienced something similar to this dislocation of the self. For many of them, however, this dislocation was experienced in terms of the loss of their legacy of land and their tribal culture. The Allotment Act of 1887 began with another social experiment, somewhat like those of Prohibition and suffrage. By giving parcels of the tribal land to individual Native Americans, the Federal government hoped to break up the system of reservations, which had produced passivity, alcoholism, and a lack of economic development. But too often individuals became the prey of unscrupulous speculators, who tricked the Native Americans out of their small parcels of "real estate," and left them even more ill-equipped to deal with modern "Anglo" society.

Alienation, for the Native American population, therefore meant the loss of one's tribal name, one's land, and one's identity as a member of a historically rich cultural community. One can see this very clearly in the extracts from *Sundown* (1934), the novel by John Joseph Matthews in which the spread of oil-derricks across the landscape becomes a haunting symbol of how the central social powers, in the search for raw materials to fuel a society, very remote from the concerns of the Native Americans, can seemingly at will make and remake the land in their own designs. The derricks move in gradually from east to west, and then as bust follows boom in the capitalist economy, the derricks slowly disappear as the wave of "development" flows back eastward. Alienation and marginality for the Native American are all too forcibly defined by a society that operates with unseen motives and purposes.

T. S. Eliot's strategy in *The Waste Land* is to divide the self among a heap of cultural fragments; Dreiser splits the woman's consciousness into two contradictory (but seemingly complete) states of awareness. Some immigrant writers come to America in this period wishing for a new life, yet often carrying a baggage of selfhood—in the form of ethnic traits, language, and physical characteristics—that is sometimes used against them by members of the dominant culture. Can the immigrant say that he or she has a true self that is defined by the very quest for a new home and a new identity? Can the immigrant proceed to establish this identity without taking full measure of the new environment? But what if such full measure involves the surrendering of much, if not all, of the identity that the immigrant arrived with? Can a new center be drawn up out of a space and time that are shaped by so many other forces besides personal will? Anzia Yezierska asks these questions with an urgency every bit as deeply felt as Eliot's fragmented speaker. They are also asked in novels like *My Antonia* by American-born writers like Willa Cather deeply interested in the processes by which European immigrants became midwestern pioneers.

Some poems, such as Gwendolyn Bennett's "To Usward" (which asks that its readers "be contained / By entities of self") and Claude McKay's "Harlem Dancer" ("I knew her self was not in that strange place"), directly raise issues about how the self can offer to define its very structure. Other works, such as the fiction of Mike Gold, can generally avoid any use of introspection, relying instead on the externally focused observation of daily life to make their point. Immigrant writing treats issues such as alienation, but often without the elaborate aesthetic devices developed by more experimental writers. This is not because immigrant writers are not aware of the complexity of their fates, but rather because in many instances the needs of audiences and the demands of artistic consistency don't allow for elaboration at a level of form and structure.

In the 1920s immigration to America reached new levels, comparable to those of the earlier period of the 1880s. (However, many Asians were excluded from the quotas during this period; the history of immigration patterns is complex and often marked by a bigotry and fear engendered by national conditions.) But the earlier immigrant groups had the advantage of being able to participate in a sense of settling the frontier. In the 1920s many of the newcomers to America ended up living in cities, especially those large urban conglomerations that were such an important part of the modern world; this continued the pattern set by immigrants at the end of the nineteenth century, and further increased the concern of many that such concentrations of foreigners were dangerous and unhealthy. These urban-dwelling immigrants of the twentieth century saw their own stories differently from their previous counterparts. Often they experienced the pains of dislocation and alienation, but they did so against a background of a bustling and driven commercial economy. It was not easy for them to cultivate the modes of introspection and self-analysis that were a part of other modern literature.

But even in works that are occupied with external description, and in those works by and about immigrants where the themes of nineteenth-century realism, such as social placement, family life, and economic success, are predominant, alienation is present. Sometimes this alienation can be detected in the distance we sense between the author's control of the material and the emotional demands that seem to come from the material itself. Such distance is usually called irony; many readers experience it as a form of detachment, even coldness. Modernists, however, felt that to give in to the full emotional impact of the material would involve them in a sentimentalism that they believed to be inaccurate—even dishonest. Readers who mistrusted modernism and yet shared

I'll Take My Stand

. . . Nobody now proposes for the South, or for any other community in this country, an independent political destiny. That idea is thought to have been finished in 1865. But how far shall the South surrender its moral, social, and economic autonomy to the victorious principle of Union? That question remains open. The South is a minority section that has hitherto been jealous of its minority right to live its own kind of life. The South scarcely hopes to determine the other sections, but it does propose to determine itself, within the utmost limits of legal action. Of late, however, there is the melancholy fact that the South itself has wavered a little and shown signs of wanting to join up behind the common or American industrial ideal. It is against that tendency that this book is written. The younger Southerners, who are being converted frequently to the industrial gospel, must come back to the support of the Southern tradition. They must be persuaded to look very critically at the advantages of becoming a "new South" which will be only an undistinguished replica of the usual industrial community.

But there are many other minority communities opposed to industrialism, and wanting a much simpler economy to live by. The communities and private persons sharing the agrarian tastes are to be found widely within the Union. Proper living is a matter of the intelligence and the will, does not depend on the local climate or geography, and is capable of a definition which is general and not Southern at all. Southerners have a filial duty to discharge to their own section. But their cause is precarious and they must seek alliances with sympathetic communities everywhere. The members of the present group would be happy to be counted as members of a national agrarian movement.

Industrialism is the economic organization of the collective American society. It means the decision of society to invest its economic resources in the applied sciences. But the word science has acquired a certain sanctitude. It is out of order to quarrel with science in the abstract, or even with the applied sciences when their applications are made subject to criticism and intelligence. The capitalization of the applied sciences has now become extravagant and uncritical; it has enslaved our human energies to a degree now clearly felt to be burdensome. The apologists of industrialism do not like to meet this charge directly; so they often take refuge in saying that they are devoted simply to science! They are really devoted to the applied sciences and to practical production. Therefore it is necessary to employ a certain skepticism even at the expense of the Cult of Science, and to say, It is an Americanism, which looks innocent and disinterested, but really is not either. . . .

Religion can hardly expect to flourish in an industrial society. Religion is our submission to the general intention of a nature that is fairly inscrutable; it is the sense of our rôle as creatures within it. But nature industrialized, transformed into cities and artificial habitations, manufactured into commodities, is no longer nature but a highly simplified picture of nature. We receive the illusion of having power over nature, and lose the sense of nature as something mysterious and contingent. The God of nature under these conditions is merely an amiable expression, a superfluity, and the philosophical understanding ordinarily carried in the religious experience is not there for us to have.

Nor do the arts have a proper life under industrialism, with the general decay of sensibility which attends it. Art depends, in general, like religion, on a right attitude to nature; and in particular on a free and disinterested observation of nature that occurs only in leisure. Neither the creation nor the understanding of works of art is possible in an industrial age except by some local and unlikely suspension of the industrial drive.

The amenities of life also suffer under the curse of a strictly-business or industrial civilization. They consist in such practices as manners, conversation, hospitality, sympathy, family life, romantic love—in the social exchanges which reveal and develop sensibility in human affairs. If religion and the arts are founded on right relations of man-to-nature, these are founded on right relations of man-to-man. . . .

It is strange, of course, that a majority of men anywhere could ever as with one mind become enamored of industrialism: a system that has so little regard for individual wants. There is evidently a kind of thinking that rejoices in setting up a social objective which has no relation to the individual. Men are prepared to sacrifice their private dignity and happiness to an abstract social ideal, and without asking whether the social ideal produces the welfare of any individual man whatsoever. But this is absurd. The responsibility of men is for their own welfare and that of their neighbors; not for the hypothetical welfare of some fabulous creature called society. . . .

For, in conclusion, this much is clear: If a community, or a section, or a race, or an age, is groaning under industrialism, and well aware that it is an evil dispensation, it must find the way to throw it off. To think that this cannot be done is pusillanimous. And if the whole community, section, race, or age thinks it cannot be done, then it has simply lost its political genius and doomed itself to impotence.

1930

some of its dislike of the modernized structures of society might well have said that irony itself was the end result of alienation.

Modernism and the New Negro Renaissance

The relations between modernism and the New Negro (or Harlem) Renaissance were complex. The Renaissance is generally considered the period that extends from just after World War I until the Depression. It is true that in this period a tremendous amount of work in all forms—poetry, fiction, drama, and essays—was produced by a group of diversely talented African American writers. Some of them, like Jean Toomer, were well known outside Harlem through their appearance in leading white publications. Some, like Zora Neal Hurston, were well known for a while but mostly in Harlem, and have had to be more widely "discovered" later by groups of white readers. Others, such as Langston Hughes, went on to full careers that extended beyond the period called the Renaissance. But it was a chapter in America's literary life that had a set of questions and qualities all its own. The Harlem Renaissance is sometimes referred to as the "New Negro Movement," in part as a result of the Alain Locke essay and anthology that use this term. Although most of the writing took place in Harlem, some critics acknowledge that the movement had centers of activity located throughout the country.

In an important sense, the history of the Harlem Renaissance begins with the publication of W.E.B. Du Bois's *The Souls of Black Folk* (1903). Du Bois was to become one of the founders of the National Association for the Advancement of Colored People (NAACP), and the editor of its important journal, *Crisis,* which published many of the prominent writers of the Renaissance. But it was Du Bois's book that set a course for black people different from the cultural assimilationism of Booker T. Washington. The approach of Du Bois was built on a recognition of what he called a "twoness," a divided awareness of one's identity on the part of African Americans:

It is a peculiar sensation, this double consciousness, this sense of always looking at one's self through the eyes of others, of measuring one's soul by the tape of a world that looks on in amused contempt and pity. One ever feels his two-ness,—an American, a Negro, two souls, two thoughts, two unreconciled strivings; two warring ideals in one dark body, whose dogged strength alone keeps it from being torn asunder.

This sounds very much like a description of alienation, of course. But it would be too easy simply to supply such a term to cover the distinct experience of black Americans. It is the fact that such terms as "alienation" both do and do not describe the experience of people who figured largely in the New Negro Renaissance that makes its relation to modernism so complex. Modernism was largely a European movement, and the New Negro Renaissance exhibited many features that owe little to European avant-garde art. In fact, it is possible to see modernism as drawing on some of the Renaissance's concerns in order to develop its energies: such questions as marginality, the use of folk or so-called "primitive" material, and the problem of writing for an elite audience, show that the channels of influence ran in both directions. One of the sources of the interest and complexity of the Renaissance is how it illustrates that the center and the margins of culture are always subject to redefinition.

Blacks experienced an outburst of oppressive and even murderous prejudice in the years immediately following World War I. In part, the bloody racial assaults of 1919—in Chicago, East St. Louis, and elsewhere—reflected intensified competition for jobs, housing, and even for recreational space between entrenched and hostile whites and blacks recently arrived from the more formally segregated South. In some measure, the continued racial strife was fueled in large part by that most benighted and despicable of American phenomena, the Ku Klux Klan. These organized bigots and vigilantes gained considerable increase in membership in part from the widespread xenophobia that was awakened by the flux of immigrants after World War I. But the Klan also grew because the issues addressed by the Reconstruction period after the Civil War were never resolved. The liberal reformism of the first years of the century was of course potentially extendable to all, regardless of race, although it had largely been conceived of and designed for whites. But the racism in American society was such that even in prosperity blacks were not extended full civil and political rights; so, when the post-war period saw mounting concerns about "foreign" influence in American life, especially in the market place and the factory, the situation of blacks worsened.

The leading writers of the New Negro Renaissance were themselves divided to some extent about the conflicting claims of advancement through cultural and educational "progress," or political protection and power gained through activist struggles and mass organizations and movements. One attempt at mass organization was the "Back to Africa" movement led by Marcus Garvey, founder of the Universal Negro Improvement Association, whose ideas attracted many blacks at this same time. Du Bois himself, at the end of *Souls of Black Folk,* said that improvement of the black masses was possible only through the cultivation of an educated elite, what he called the "talented Tenth." Many of the ideas of Du Bois were echoed in an essay which can be read as a manifesto of the Renaissance, Alain Locke's "The New Negro" (1925).

In this compendium of themes for a modernist revolution in black art and consciousness, Locke speaks of the importance of urbanization for blacks in the new century. There is also a strong sense of a new life as part of an experiment, a willful excursion into unknown territory that recalls one of the major themes of European Romanticism. Locke also speculates on the role of Harlem as the center of this new revolutionary movement: Harlem "is—or promises at least to be—a race capital." And he goes on to raise the issue of internationalism, arguing at one point that the "possible role of the American Negro in the future development of Africa is one of the most constructive and universally helpful missions that any modern people can lay claim to." This last point was especially significant because it showed that the Renaissance had posited a forward-looking aspect to its consciousness. Such consciousness would serve as an important source of cultural as well as political strength for black people.

Though Locke mentions Garvey favorably, he himself inclined toward the argument that proposed the leavening effect of a cultural elite. But hardly any black writer would say that the masses were simply to be led by more educated blacks. Nor would they deny that it was through direct experience of the widespread and inescapable injustice of racism in America that all blacks must come to expect and demand greater justice. Still, the question about black leadership, and whether that leadership should take on a cultural or a political form, remained of prime importance throughout the Renaissance, and beyond. There were strong feelings that artistic forms should be made to fit into the general advancement of the lives and political fortunes of blacks, but just how this would be done was extremely difficult to settle. One key consideration was the economic fact that earlier black writers such as Charles Chesnutt and Paul Laurence Dunbar could not have hoped to sustain themselves by writing only for black audiences; indeed, Dunbar turned to writing musicals to make a living. Eventually a market for black art and culture developed among blacks, due largely to increasing urbanization, increased racial awareness, and spreading literacy. Initially, that market was focused on the sale of "race records," the powerfully evocative work of black musicians like Bessie Smith and Louis Armstrong, who became known outside the black community. Ultimately, however, the market widened sufficiently, among whites as well as blacks, so that black writers and even visual artists, as well as musicians, could hope to make a living through their art.

The New Negro Renaissance was made possible in large measure by this new black audience. But it was an audience very much in transition. Somehow its writers had to build a consciousness of the history of their community even as they worked towards progressive ideals. The question of the political uses of artistic forms became highly charged in this context. And the Renaissance writers could not simply assume, as did the white modernist authors, that the use of innovative forms was automatically a cultural advance. Any one-to-one relationship between political desires and artistic choices might well prove too restrictive. Claude McKay, for example, used fairly traditional forms in his poetry, but his ideas and values were radical when it came to issues of justice and freedom.

The tensions between modernist principles and the other, more pressing needs of black writers produced several important extended discussions. Chief among these were the question of whether or not the use of experimental forms limited the audience for black literature, and whether or not the use of folk material was advantageous or implicitly condescending. These issues were complicated by whether the person who argued one point of view or the other was addressing a strictly black readership, or whether reference was being made, explicitly or not, to a larger white audience. These debates came up many times, and in different forms. For example, some people felt that if black authors were to be fully part of the artistic mainstream they must be conversant with the latest artistic experiments. The counterargument suggested that since many black readers were far from enjoying the benefits of middle-class society, with its consumerism, its suburban luxuries, and its extended educational system, they could hardly be expected to take an interest in highly complex aesthetic theories, issues, and forms.

The question of folk material arose in two contexts: the life and culture of blacks who lived in the South, and the world of folk music, especially its more modern forms, blues and jazz. Many of the black writers of this period "discovered" the culture of the black South, for they had been born in northern and urban areas and were by and large removed from the region that had long developed forms of life quite different from those of an industrialized society. Sterling Brown and Jean Toomer were two such writers. On the other hand, Nella Larsen left Alabama after studying and working there for a number of years, and her work is mainly concerned with urban experience. The traditions of narrative in the South were those of the folktale, with its use of mythic material and schematic patterning, and the slave narrative, with its emphasis on testimony and integrity. Slave narratives would serve as an important artistic context for Hurston and Richard Wright, and later for several contemporary black novelists, such as Alice Walker and Toni Morrison. The North, on the other hand, was filled with readers whose sense of a story was shaped by the traditions of European realism. Often a writer can combine both; Zora Neale Hurston, for example, was trained as an anthropologist and used characters and motifs from rural Florida, but she often crafted her stories with details and structures similar to those of famous modern short story writers such as Chekhov and Maupassant.

The use of the blues tradition was also a matter of great artistic debate. The world that was represented in blues lyrics could be understood to be one based on mere complaint about one's repressed and exploited condition. Yet there is in the blues tradition a series of images and themes that point the way towards liberation and even revolt. By using this tradition, with its roots in the world of slavery and peonage, a skillful writer could extend the richness of his or her vision back in time and acknowledge the original situation of blacks in America. The blues also owed an important debt to the post-Reconstruction chain-gangs of black prisoners, who adopted the "answer-and-call" format of black spirituals. Jazz, by extension, became a way for the black artist to create links to the past while at the same time forging one of the most complex and sophisticated of all indigenous American art forms. The poetry of Sterling Brown and Langston Hughes exemplifies some of these possibilities, possibilities that are further explored in the black literature of the 1960s and '70s.

Black artists face questions of social justice and aesthetic form in particular ways, of course, and when the questions overlap the tensions can be considerable. Jean Toomer managed these tensions with a special talent, as he used the poetic approach of a very lyrical prose to work with material that had not been granted a full voicing in American literature. He was an extremely self-conscious artist, who was very aware of the "twoness" of which Du Bois had spoken. (In fact, Toomer was a mulatto, and was sometimes accused of trying to "pass" in white society; this condition obviously complicated his situation in terms of "twoness.") The entirety of his book *Cane,* which is available here in excerpts, demonstrates how inventive artistic solutions are often found in changing the center of the work, or at least redefining what we normally understand as the central structure of a poem or story. In writing about *Cane,* Toomer explained that he had built a structure that went "aesthetically from simple forms to complex forms, and back to simple forms. Regionally (it went) from the South up into the North, and back into the South, and then a return North."

Toomer faced the questions of folk material, and experimental forms, and he also implicitly addressed himself to another issue that in a sense stands behind both of these other questions: individual expressiveness. Here the Renaissance writer shared some of the concerns of those artists who grappled with the problem of the modernist idea of the self. Was it possible to find the truth of one's own individual experience and still be true to the larger pressures of one's social and political identity? Modernism tried to insist that the eye of the artist could be transcendently placed above such categories as race and nation. Modernist artists also often made the very divided and fragmented nature of the self into the focus of their art. Native American writers were less directly concerned with subjective individual experience and instead vacillated between using folk materials and trying to adapt other literary traditions to express their concerns. The *Coyote Stories* (1933) of Mourning Dove can be compared and contrasted with the use of similar material by writers such as Toomer. Other available forms, such as journalism and drama, were attractive to both African-American and Native American writers who were pledged to speak for groups of people, and to do so in ways that grievances and oppression could be directly and widely moving to audiences. Black writers in different ways adopted both of these strategies, the subjective and introspective as well as the directly rhetorical or public speech, but they nevertheless had special problems of their own that such strategies would not address fully.

The hopes of Americans were often tested in this period by various celebrated trials, including that of Sacco and Vanzetti, noted earlier. For the black community, a somewhat similar case was that of the "Scottsboro Boys," a group of young black men unfairly charged and jailed for the assault of two white women in 1931. (Through a long process of appeals and demonstrations, the last of the Scottsboro "boys" was finally released in 1950.) In fact, we can say that if the Harlem Renaissance begins with Toomer's *Cane* (1923) and ends with the important anthology edited by Sterling Brown and others, *The Negro Caravan* (1941), then the Scottsboro trial becomes a sort of half-way marker. But if the Scottsboro incident represented a historical moment in the awakening of white consciousness (at least among liberals) about black oppression, to many black Americans it could hardly serve as a comforting chapter in their history. By extension, many incidents in our common his-

This is preeminently the time to speak the truth, the whole truth, frankly and boldly. Nor need we shrink from honestly facing conditions in our country today. This great Nation will endure as it has endured, will revive and will prosper. So, first of all, let me assert my firm belief that the only thing we have to fear is fear itself—nameless, unreasoning, unjustified terror which paralyzes needed efforts to convert retreat into advance. In every dark hour of our national life a leadership of frankness and vigor has met with that understanding and support of the people themselves which is essential to victory. I am convinced that you will again give that support to leadership in these critical days.

* * *

I see millions of families trying to live on incomes so meager that the pall of family disaster hangs over them day by day.

I see millions whose daily lives in city and on farm continue under conditions labeled indecent by a so-called polite society half a century ago.

I see millions denied education, recreation, and the opportunity to better their lot and the lot of their children.

I see millions lacking the means to buy the products of farm and factory and by their poverty denying work and productiveness to many other millions.

I see one-third of a nation ill-housed, ill-clad, ill-nourished.

It is not in despair that I paint you that picture. I paint it for you in hope—because the Nation, seeing and understanding the injustice in it, proposes to paint it out. We are determined to make every American citizen the subject of his country's interest and concern; and we will never regard any faithful, law-abiding group within our borders as superfluous. The test of our progress is not whether we add more to the abundance of those who have much; it is whether we provide enough for those who have too little.

Franklin Delano Roosevelt
First and Second Inaugural Addresses

torical self-awareness are valued very differently by blacks than by whites.

But the Harlem Renaissance was a truly important chapter for black readers and writers; it should become the same for whites. One way to begin reading the cultural importance of the Renaissance for both whites and blacks, is to see it as a chapter in a yet-unwritten history of modern literature, a history that will give modernism and the Renaissance—as well as their tangled relations—fair representation. Locke's hope that Harlem would be a capital of a new black consciousness reflects many of these tangles, for it seeks to establish a center. This, however, would have the possible effect of relegating some of the indigenous black experience—slave narratives, say, and the blues, and rural folk culture—to the periphery. The proper balance between such a center and such a periphery was often heatedly discussed among the writers of the Renaissance and it remains a matter of significant conflict today.

Modernism and the South

Some artists devoted their work to a striving for cultural and ethnic specificity and rooted-ness that the high orders of modernism seldom permitted. The Fugitive-Agrarian movement of the 1920s and 1930s in the South actually made this sort of contradiction within modernism a sustaining engine of creativity.

T. S. Eliot, one of the figureheads of international modernism in the 1920s, was, first as poet and then as cultural critic, one of the sparks to this Southern movement. Restless under the prescription to supply an outdated "local color" regionalism, the chief poets of the Fugitive movement (John Crowe Ransom, Allen Tate, and Robert Penn Warren) deliberately sought a kind of poetry that would acknowledge their regional history and character, yet achieve at the same time a rigor and historical-cultural sweep and sophistication such as they had seen and (in varying degrees) admired in "The Waste Land."

In the late 1920s, a few years after their careers as Fugitives waned, they reorganized themselves as Agrarians to resist what they saw as the imposition of an international and uniform culture by "the New Humanists," a group of scholars led by Eliot's former professor at Harvard, Irving Babbitt. The Agrarian manifesto, *I'll Take My Stand* (1930), is a collection of essays that argues for several and separate cultures, not a single and intellectualized one, such as modernism promised (or threatened). This manifesto was deeply contradictory: it formulated a scorching and radical criticism of industrial society and all its modernization and offered as a "solution" a return to traditional social forms based on agricultural values. Such an attempt to turn back historical development, or at least to redirect it, can be seen as yet another American "experiment."

With the success of the centralization and federalization of political and social life in the United States during the Great Depression, the Agrarian experimental agenda failed to reach a powerful audience—not even the Southern farmers the Agrarians envisioned went for the program—and the writers returned, one by one, to poetry and literary criticism.

By the end of the 1930s, they had come up with the New Criticism and a literary-historical definition of themselves, the Southern Renaissance, that put them on the U.S. literary map. With the success of William Faulkner and his winning the Nobel Prize in 1950, this regional movement was well established. Nor is this happy ending to the story without irony and self-contradiction, for Faulkner's fiction was not a complete success with the Agrarians-turned-critics; and the feeling was mutual.

At the end of the time spectrum, the literary-historical story is somewhat similar to its beginning. As Southern "regional" writing seemed to fill magazines and bookstores, and win prizes, another "regional" group, urban Jewish writers and critics (Saul Bellow, Bernard Malamud, Philip Roth, Alfred Kazin, Irving Howe, and others) began a renaissance of their own. A new tradition helped to cross-hatch and round out the modernist contours. Literary works and understandings were reworked; literary stock fluctuated; tempers flared, died down. Modernism, which had actually been a system of several energy cores, ascended to the status of a single literary movement; it became a fixture of academic understanding by the mid-1950s.

Modernism, Popular Culture, and the Media

Modernism approached all forms of traditional meaning with wariness, if not suspicion. This did not by any means entail a total rejection of all tradition, but instead modernists often looked for new ways to revivify and challenge traditional values. Because it was in many ways a very self-conscious movement, modernism also turned its attention to the ways in which values and experience are passed on to wider audiences, in both a temporal and spatial sense. This attention resulted in the artistic exploration of the media—the modern forms of information and (implicit) evaluation that came into being with such "outlets" as the mass audience newspaper, the radio, and the best-seller. These media were part of the very large pattern of modernization that included developments in transportation, housing, the standardization of market activities, and so forth. In short, mass society developed new ways to communicate with itself. But communicating with itself caused an exponential increase in complexity. Modernization in industrial society involved the widespread availability of different forms of communication. But this availability was problematic, since there was no longer a unequivocally dominant culture subject to central control, and yet some people and classes had more power over communication than others. In the past one of the chief functions of culture, and by extension literature, was to resolve tensions between different social factions or classes and even to celebrate the unity that a nation relied on for their security, wealth, and happiness. In modernized societies culture was often called upon to play a similar role, but at the same time there was added a new possibility, namely, contesting the official version or representing alternative versions of such unity. As we have seen, sometimes these alternative versions took the more or less coherent forms called "modernism," but sometimes they even took shape outside or in opposition to modernist tenets. In nearly every case, however, the control and understanding of the media of communication and self-representation were at issue.

Many artists were fascinated with these media, but many were also appalled by them. "We have the press for wafer": here Pound, for example, bitingly refers to the distorted use of the newspaper, the press, for something sacred, the wafer, used by Christian churches in their communion services. Dos Passos, however, tried to replicate the effect of the newspaper and newsreel headline in the very text of his fiction in order to be true to the tempo of his times. The phonograph shows up in Eliot's *Waste Land* as a symbol of mechanization and the deadening of emotion; the cinema (and even the elevator!) appears in Crane's "To Brooklyn Bridge" as something like a magic carpet. On the other hand, in Langston Hughes's "Air Raid over Harlem," a movie script is envisioned as a way to make the unimaginable terror of racial war into a palpable image. It wasn't until later, perhaps in the heyday of Pop Art in the 1960s, that such media were unequivocally celebrated by artists. But modern artists saw that despite whatever wariness they experienced, the new media were definitely an unignorable part of modern life, and as such had to be dealt with in art.

Many writers even pursued careers in some of the media, or at least sought gainful employment there for a time. Crane and Sherwood Anderson worked in advertising, for example. Many other writers went to Hollywood, especially in the 1940s, to work as screenwriters. True, they were often drawn there by the prospect of monetary reward (it was not unusual for writers to be paid $1500 per week in the 1940s, a large salary, especially for that time), and they often left disappointed. But it was not only Scott Fitzgerald who sojourned a while in Babylon; so, too, did Faulkner, Yezierska, Odets, and many more. And there was also the work on newspapers, engaged in by LeSueur and others, but perhaps best typified by Hemingway, that came to form an important part of modern fiction's prose style.

In the decades after 1910 the main inventions to be widely circulated in American society were the movies, the model T, and the telephone. The first sound film was shown in 1927, but for years previously the silent movies had developed a sophisticated set of techniques and a star system that involved millions of fans in its success. Indeed, Charlie Chaplin had become a household word, and a favorite of artists as well, as Hart Crane's poem demonstrates. After 1930, the radio and the phonograph became increasingly widespread. The first commercial radio broadcast was actually made in 1920, but a number of years elapsed before the average household owned a receiver. Likewise, television made an appearance at the 1939 New York City World's Fair, but a national TV network did not exist until ten years later.

The Chicago Exposition in 1893 marked an important watershed in America's cultural history. The World's Fair can serve as a similar marker of change. It was organized around exhibits sponsored by large corporations; these companies were one of the main forces at work in presenting the new media and technologies to the American public. It was not long before some people began to suggest that all these media were in effect mainly useful as elements of social control. The fact that radio programs and newspapers were produced at centralized locations, and often used material already selected and shaped by a group of professionals who had certain attitudes and outlooks, contributed to this realization. Still, such media were most often presented as advantages of modern living, allowing a kind of important democratization of knowledge by making available to people from all walks of life what had once been restricted to a small group.

Such centered forms of control over the production and distribution of the news, not to mention our views of history, politics, and other public forms of knowledge, were not completely new. Earlier societies had also utilized symbolic forms of narrative and other explanations, and controlled them by exercising royal prerogatives, for example. But the modern media seemed to have an extensiveness, and something like a transparency, that gave them special force. It was tempting for writers to be a part of this network, and at the same time it was hard to resist it if their predilections lay in that direction. This is why the story of Hollywood and the writers who went there is so fascinating and so often retold. But beyond that, what hope would writers have if their time-honored devices were to be slowly but steadily replaced by other forms of information and storytelling?

Modernism had always cultivated its fascination with what it saw in the primitive. Part of the anti-cultural impulse in the movement took the form of a high valuation of the life forms of people who had not been thoroughly industrialized, or even "civilized" in the modern sense. This fascination goes back to William Wordsworth and other Romantic writers of the nineteenth century. The so-called "primitive" forms of storytelling became a focus of this modernist interest in different forms of knowledge. In many ways, the media were at the opposite end of the spectrum from such forms. Where the ancient storyteller used a background of shared belief and invoked a spiritual realm that gave credibility to the tale, the modern news report was, as it were, self-contained. It referred only to the surfaces of life and to either the most immediately plausible context or to some form of sensationalism or escapism.

For all these differences in assumptions and effects, however, both the ancient tale and the media news story serve as a way for the society to represent itself to its members, and hence for its members to come to a fuller understanding of their social identities. The writer has to choose, consciously or unconsciously, to accept the validity of the media's version of people's characters and lives, or to adopt some critical distance from it. This was yet another area where modernist irony would come into play. But the consequence of such irony would almost certainly be to limit the writer's audience, since many people would not easily be able to read against the grain of so much "popular" wisdom.

The phenomenon of the best-seller in the modern period is tied up with the beginning of a mass readership fostered by the book clubs, many of which began in the 1930s. In 1931, for example, *The Good Earth* by Pearl Buck entered the best-seller lists for an extended stay of two years. In 1937, *Gone with the Wind* was published and within ten years it had sold three and a half million copies. Some of the writers who earned critical acclaim were economically very successful, and were also "best-sellers," though that term was generally avoided for novels that were considered artistically "serious." Hemingway became a wealthy man through his fiction, and Fitzgerald also prospered, at least for a time. But many others, such as Moore, Stein, and Crane had to settle for the esteem of the academy or of a relatively small group of intellectuals. The relation between popular success and artistic talent has never been simple, and writers are often the first to bemoan this situation. But in the modern age such disjunctions were sometimes seen to be a result of the influence of the media. In a sense this issue can be put this way: what some readily refer to as "popular" art others insist on calling "mass art." Such people prefer to reserve the term "popular" art for the kinds of folk expression that thrives without any recourse to advanced forms of distribution such as those offered by the media.

Again, we can turn to notions of marginality in order to put these points in a context that relates them to parts of the foregoing discussion. What follows is a very brief explanation of a process that is undoubtedly more complicated than what can be shown here, since many forces are at work in such matters. Popular art might once, in pre-modern society, have had a central role to play in a society's self-representation. Tales and heroes and motifs transformed by fantasy and desire would help a social group to recognize and understand itself and its members. But with the advent of modern mass society, the media displaced truly popular forms of representation, substituting "mass art" images and ideas that best fit into the new media forms. This displacement created two marginalized sources of cultural images: the surviving remnants of popular culture, which we can see in work from the Harlem Renaissance writers, for example, and the more complex forms of cultural experiments that we associate with the modernist spirit.

Modern literature is marked by a willingness to engage itself with a wide variety of cultural forms. In this sense, much of modernism is in dialogue with popular art, alternately drawn to it and trying to outstrip it. The Harlem Renaissance writer may have a different reason for engaging in this sort of dialogue with popular forms from that of the experimental modernist; both may in turn be quite different from a poet such as Frost or Robert Penn Warren, who questions much of what passes for popular wisdom or "common sense." But even an immigrant writer like Yezierska can sharply attack the very widely circulated notions that pass for accepted opinion, while at the same time longing to set aside her alienated condition and fit into the narrative frames that she has heard and read about in all the popular media. And so modern culture can be understood—in at least one version—as a struggle among various artistic forms and audiences for the central interpretative myths, images, and stories of the age.

What some would argue against this account is that it assumes that societies do not always get exactly the cultural representations they desire. How, one might ask, can anyone say that the modernist or the Harlem Renaissance writer or the immigrant writer possessed a version of the culture that was any more valid than that which existed in the popular media? Of course, no one can. In a very real and important sense the culture does contain all the expressive forms which its members produce, and that culture is no more (and no less) than the sum of all such expressions. But one thing we can claim for the writer is that he or she does have access to a vast and complex array of devices that allow for many various forms of expressiveness. This array of forms also suggests that many different attitudes can be registered: acceptance, rejection, praise, condemnation, and many sorts of variations and combinations thereof.

The following selections, therefore, are highly varied. The writers share only two things in common; they identified themselves as American and they were born at a time when the modern world had unmistakably come into being. Their reactions to that world were diverse in terms of attitude and artistic form. Such variety is perhaps best appreciated by multiple perspectives, cross-readings, and even eccentric explorations.

Toward the Modern Age

Modernism has become a very broad term and like terms such as Classicism and Romanticism, it not only includes many diverse elements, but it also attracts "forerunners." Because the temporal limits of such cultural styles are hard to fix, readers and critics often end up talking about "pre-modern" works. This can occasionally be distorting, for few writers actually compose their work self-consciously as an advance version of some later style or movement. However, there are writers in certain periods whose work can be interestingly and usefully placed in a context of later developments. In the case of writers who are seen as heading "towards modernism," this often means their work has some of the themes and styles of what is generally regarded as the highwater mark of modernism itself, from the first years of the twentieth century until after World War II. Other writers working in the same period can be seen as outside Modernism altogether and yet working with problems and themes that dominate the modern age.

Women writers are especially interesting in this context. For example, Edith Wharton can readily be seen as a representative writer of realist novels, much like those by nineteenth-century masters such as George Eliot or Thackeray. But because of her concern with certain mental and emotional states, and their origins in the conflict of the individual faced with oppressive social values, her work also reflects some of the concern of psychological and ironic realism. Furthermore, her sensibility and talent as a woman make her a keen observer of forces in social and personal relations that are hidden from many male novelists. Wharton's work also stands in the tradition of women novelists of America who wrote with an eye to sentiment and family values, but it also sharply challenges many of the features of this tradition. Likewise, Willa Cather is a novelist who borrows heavily from the tradition of regional literature, but her work goes far beyond the more expectable limits of such work. Simply by being writers who challenge the traditions in which they work, Cather and Wharton are seen by many as moving towards modernism.

The same sort of argument applies to poets such as Masters, Millay, and Jeffers. None of these poets are especially noted for their technical innovations, which is to say they don't break the norms of syntax and diction as readily or as often as poets such as Pound and Eliot. Nevertheless, their poetry is infused with a feeling of challenge: for Jeffers this challenge sets itself against any sense of nature as a source of comfort; for Masters, the challenge is to redefine the sense of heroism and scale in people's lives; for Millay, there is an attack, often implicit, against the sentimental, especially as it pertains to women's roles and limitations.

Writers could also approach modern issues of great import in the medium of prose. Some especially significant social issues such as race were discussed in essays, novels, or autobiography. Three African Americans might be seen as originating a modern conversation about the "color line"—what W.E.B. Du Bois called the main political problem of the twentieth century. It was Du Bois himself, in conversation with Booker T. Washington and James Weldon

Johnson, who traced the complex curves and intersections of race and modern life.

The writings of these three people not only raise questions of historical justice and memory, but they also provoke reflection about key modern issues involving personal testimony, the right to represent or speak for others, and movement between audiences in both dominant and repressed groups in society. The modernity of the traditions of African American writing is clearly anticipated by Du Bois and his compatriots.

Much of the reception of modernism was contested on such matters as propriety and stylistic innovation; readers simply refused to accept the notion that poems and novels should look and sound that way. But the writers in this section may not have generated the same sort of audience resistance. The work here doesn't fit comfortably into a set historical framework, because some of its elements are forward-looking and some are not. But in each case the writer may have been less consciously preoccupied with such matters as the historical fate of a certain style, and instead has decided to work with words and forms that are more locally responsive or even deliberately out of the rush of contemporary developments.

Charles Molesworth
Queens College, City University of New York

Booker T. Washington 1856–1915

Booker Taliaferro Washington's life and most important literary work embodied the American myth of the poor boy who pulls himself up by his own bootstraps to become a success. As he wrote in his autobiography, *Up from Slavery,* he was born a slave in Franklin County, Virginia, "in the midst of the most miserable, desolate, and discouraging surroundings." He received no help from his white father, whose identity has never been ascertained. It was his mother, Jane, the cook for a small planter named James Burroughs, who taught young Booker his survival lessons. Booker (he did not take the name Washington until he began to attend school) spent his first nine years as a slave on the Burroughs farm. When the Civil War ended, his mother took him and his three siblings to Malden, West Virginia, to join her husband, Washington Ferguson, a former slave who had found employment in the salt mines. Booker soon went to work at a salt furnace; by the time he was twelve years old, he had seen considerable dangerous work in the Malden coal mines. Nevertheless the boy had his dream—he wanted to go to school.

By attending night school sporadically, Washington achieved fundamental literacy, but he was unable to get any regular schooling until he went to work as a houseboy for Mrs. Viola Ruffner, the wife of a Malden mine owner. She was the first of many well-placed white people whom Washington learned to please in exchange for their support of his ambitions. From her he learned lessons that in 1872 enabled him to gain admission into the Hampton Institute, an industrial school for blacks and American Indians near Norfolk, Virginia. He studied not only the academic curriculum at Hampton but also the ways in which its president, Samuel C. Armstrong, won the admiration of his black students and the goodwill of the white community. After graduating from Hampton with honors in 1875, Washington soon returned as a faculty member. In 1881 the Alabama legislature asked Armstrong to recommend someone who could found a school for black teachers at Tuskegee in the heart of the state's "Black Belt." Washington was his choice.

From 1881 until his death Washington concentrated on three goals: (1) the creation and maintenance of Tuskegee Institute as a major black-run educational institution, (2) the advancement of his own power as a national racial leader, and (3) the publicizing and defense of his philosophy of African American education and socioeconomic progress. With a modest tone, Washington provides considerable evidence of the lofty status he attained in the eyes of powerful whites. The text of his most famous address, which he gave at the opening of the Cotton States and International Exposition in Atlanta, is followed by a letter from President Grover Cleveland congratulating him on the wisdom of his ideas about how to solve America's race problem. Without expounding these ideas systematically in his autobiography, Washington makes *Up from Slavery* demonstrate their efficacy in his life and in the life of Tuskegee.

As many post-war African American leaders believed, Washington felt the key to his race's advancement was education. But the kind of education that Tuskegee offered was what Washington called "practical knowledge"—"knowing how to make a living." This attitude toward education gave Washington his reputation as a realist. When he urged fellow blacks in his Atlanta Exposition address "to draw the line between the superficial and the substantial, the ornamental gewgaws of life and the useful," he concerned himself with the here and now, rather than romantic hopes and distant ideals.

Washington's brand of realism had profound political implications. Black leaders like Frederick Douglass had traditionally laid claim to the principles of full citizenship embodied in the U.S. Constitution and Bill of Rights. But Washington's pragmatism implied that African Americans had to prove they were qualified for civil rights by making a success of themselves first in the economic arena.

For a half century after its publication *Up from Slavery* was the best-known book written by an African American. This was mainly attributable to Washington's skill in subtly revising his literary models, the autobiographies of Benjamin Franklin and Frederick Douglass. *Up from Slavery* is a slave narrative whose opening recalls Douglass's 1845 *Narrative,* but Washington's agenda is radically different from his predecessor's. While Douglass depicts slavery as a hell on earth, Washington blandly calls it a "school" that helped prepare blacks for the role that he argues they were ready and willing to assume in the post-war economic order. Washington attributes his successes to his adherence to many of the virtues celebrated in Franklin's archetypal American success story: selflessness, industry, honesty, and optimism. But as recent scholarship has shown, behind the mask of the public-spirited, humble, and plainspoken schoolmaster one can often find a devious and self-centered power broker. To read *Up from Slavery* is to explore the rhetorical means by which Washington constructed the most powerful and disingenuous myth of black selfhood in his era.

William L. Andrews
University of North Carolina–Chapel Hill

PRIMARY WORKS

The Future of the American Negro, 1899; *Up from Slavery,* 1901; *Working with the Hands,* 1904; *My Larger Education,* 1911.

from Up from Slavery

Chapter I A Slave Among Slaves

I was born a slave on a plantation in Franklin County, Virginia. I am not quite sure of the exact place or exact date of my birth, but at any rate I suspect I must have been born somewhere and at some time. As nearly as I have been able to learn, I was born near a crossroads post-office called Hale's Ford, and the year was 1858 or 1859.[1] I do not know the month or the day. The earliest impressions I can now recall are of the plantation and the slave quarters—the latter being the part of the plantation where the slaves had their cabins.

My life had its beginning in the midst of the most miserable, desolate, and discouraging surroundings. This was so, however, not because my owners were especially cruel, for they were not, as compared with many others. I was born in a typical log cabin, about fourteen by sixteen feet square. In this cabin I lived with my mother and a brother and sister till after the Civil War, when we were all declared free.

Of my ancestry I know almost nothing. In the slave quarters, and even later, I heard whispered conversations among the coloured people of the tortures which the slaves, including, no doubt, my ancestors on my mother's side, suffered in the middle passage of the slave ship while being conveyed from Africa to America. I have been unsuccessful in securing any information that would throw any accurate light upon the history of my family beyond my mother. She, I remember, had a half-brother and a half-sister. In the days of slavery not very much attention was given to family history and family records—that is, black family records. My mother, I suppose, attracted the attention of a purchaser who was afterward my owner and hers. Her addition to the slave family attracted about as much attention as the purchase of a new horse or cow. Of my father I know even less than of my mother. I do not even know his name. I have heard reports to the effect that he was a white man who lived on one of the near-by plantations. Whoever he was, I never heard of his taking the least interest in me or providing in any way for my rearing. But I do not find especial fault with him. He was simply another unfortunate victim of the institution which the Nation unhappily had engrafted upon it at that time.

The cabin was not only our living-place, but was also used as the kitchen for the plantation. My mother was the plantation cook. The cabin was without glass windows; it had only openings in the side which let in the light, and also the cold, chilly air of winter. There was a door to the cabin—that is, something that was called a door—but the uncertain hinges by which it was hung, and the large cracks in it, to say nothing of the fact that it was too small, made the room a very uncomfortable one. In addition to these openings there was, in the lower right-hand corner of the room, the "cat-hole"—a contrivance which almost every mansion or cabin in Virginia possessed during the ante-bellum period. The "cat-hole" was a square opening, about seven by eight inches, provided for the purpose of letting the cat pass in and out of the house at will during the night. In the case of our particular cabin I could

[1]1858 or 1859: Washington was probably born in the spring of 1856.

never understand the necessity for this convenience, since there were at least a half-dozen other places in the cabin that would have accommodated the cats. There was no wooden floor in our cabin, the naked earth being used as a floor. In the centre of the earthen floor there was a large, deep opening covered with boards, which was used as a place in which to store sweet potatoes during the winter. An impression of this potato-hole is very distinctly engraved upon my memory, because I recall that during the process of putting the potatoes in or taking them out I would often come into possession of one or two, which I roasted and thoroughly enjoyed. There was no cooking-stove on our plantation, and all the cooking for the whites and slaves my mother had to do over an open fireplace, mostly in pots and "skillets." While the poorly built cabin caused us to suffer with cold in the winter, the heat from the open fireplace in summer was equally trying.

The early years of my life, which were spent in the little cabin, were not very different from those of thousands of other slaves. My mother, of course, had little time in which to give attention to the training of her children during the day. She snatched a few moments for our care in the early morning before her work began, and at night after the day's work was done. One of my earliest recollections is that of my mother cooking a chicken late at night, and awakening her children for the purpose of feeding them. How or where she got it I do not know. I presume, however, it was procured from our owner's farm. Some people may call this theft. If such a thing were to happen now, I should condemn it as theft myself. But taking place at the time it did, and for the reason that it did, no one could ever make me believe that my mother was guilty of thieving. She was simply a victim of the system of slavery. I cannot remember having slept in a bed until after our family was declared free by the Emancipation Proclamation. Three children—John, my older brother, Amanda, my sister, and myself—had a pallet on the dirt floor, or, to be more correct, we slept in and on a bundle of filthy rags laid upon the dirt floor.

I was asked not long ago to tell something about the sports and pastimes that I engaged in during my youth. Until that question was asked it had never occurred to me that there was no period of my life that was devoted to play. From the time that I can remember anything, almost every day of my life has been occupied in some kind of labour; though I think I would now be a more useful man if I had had time for sports. During the period that I spent in slavery I was not large enough to be of much service, still I was occupied most of the time in cleaning the yards, carrying water to the men in the fields, or going to the mill, to which I used to take the corn, once a week, to be ground. The mill was about three miles from the plantation. This work I always dreaded. The heavy bag of corn would be thrown across the back of the horse, and the corn divided about evenly on each side; but in some way, almost without exception, on these trips, the corn would so shift as to become unbalanced and would fall off the horse, and often I would fall with it. As I was not strong enough to reload the corn upon the horse, I would have to wait, sometimes for many hours, till a chance passer-by came along who would help me out of my trouble. The hours while waiting for some one were usually spent in crying. The time consumed in this way made me late in reaching the mill, and by the time I got my corn ground and reached home it would be far into the night. The road was a lonely one, and often led through dense forests. I was always frightened. The woods were said to be full of soldiers who had deserted from the army, and I had been told that the first thing a deserter did to a Negro boy when he found him alone was to cut off his ears. Besides, when I was late in getting home I knew I would always get a severe scolding or a flogging.

I had no schooling whatever while I was a slave, though I remember on several occasions I went as far as the schoolhouse door with one of my young mistresses to carry her books. The picture of several dozen boys and girls in a schoolroom engaged in study made a deep impression upon me, and I had the feeling that to get into a schoolhouse and study in this way would be about the same as getting into paradise.

So far as I can now recall, the first knowledge that I got of the fact that we were slaves, and that freedom of the slaves was being discussed, was early one morning before day, when I was awakened by my mother kneeling over her children and fervently praying that Lincoln and his armies might be successful, and that one day she and her children might be free. In this connection I have never been able to understand how the slaves throughout the South, completely ignorant as were the masses so far as books or newspapers were concerned, were able to keep themselves so accurately and completely informed about the great National questions that were agitating the country. From the time that Garrison, Lovejoy,[2] and others began to agitate for freedom, the slaves throughout the South kept in close touch with the progress of the movement. Though I was a mere child during the preparation for the Civil War and during the war itself, I now recall the many late-at-night whispered discussions that I heard my mother and the other slaves on the plantation indulge in. These discussions showed that they understood the situation, and that they kept themselves informed of events by what was termed the "grape-vine" telegraph.

During the campaign when Lincoln was first a candidate for the Presidency, the slaves on our far-off plantation, miles from any railroad or large city or daily newspaper, knew what the issues involved were. When war was begun between the North and the South, every slave on our plantation felt and knew that, though other issues were discussed, the primal one was that of slavery. Even the most ignorant members of my race on the remote plantations felt in their hearts, with a certainty that admitted of no doubt, that the freedom of the slaves would be the one great result of the war, if the Northern armies conquered. Every success of the Federal armies and every defeat of the Confederate forces was watched with the keenest and most intense interest. Often the slaves got knowledge of the results of great battles before the white people received it. This news was usually gotten from the coloured man who was sent to the post-office for the mail. In our case the post-office was about three miles from the plantation, and the mail came once or twice a week. The man who was sent to the office would linger about the place long enough to get the drift of the conversation from the group of white people who naturally congregated there, after receiving their mail, to discuss the latest news. The mail-carrier on his way back to our master's house would as naturally retail the news that he had secured among the slaves, and in this way they often heard of important events before the white people at the "big house," as the master's house was called.

I cannot remember a single instance during my childhood or early boyhood

[2]William Lloyd Garrison (1805–1879) and Elijah Parish Lovejoy (1802–1837), prominent abolitionist editors.

when our entire family sat down to the table together, and God's blessing was asked, and the family ate a meal in a civilized manner. On the plantation in Virginia, and even later, meals were gotten by the children very much as dumb animals get theirs. It was a piece of bread here and a scrap of meat there. It was a cup of milk at one time and some potatoes at another. Sometimes a portion of our family would eat out of the skillet or pot, while some one else would eat from a tin plate held on the knees, and often using nothing but the hands with which to hold the food. When I had grown to sufficient size, I was required to go to the "big house" at meal-times to fan the flies from the table by means of a large set of paper fans operated by a pulley. Naturally much of the conversation of the white people turned upon the subject of freedom and war, and I absorbed a good deal of it. I remember that at one time I saw two of my young mistresses and some lady visitors eating ginger-cakes, in the yard. At that time those cakes seemed to me to be absolutely the most tempting and desirable things that I had ever seen; and I then and there resolved that, if I ever got free, the height of my ambition would be reached if I could get to the point where I could secure and eat ginger-cakes in the way that I saw those ladies doing.

Of course as the war was prolonged the white people, in many cases, often found it difficult to secure food for themselves. I think the slaves felt the deprivation less than the whites, because the usual diet for the slaves was corn bread and pork, and these could be raised on the plantation; but coffee, tea, sugar, and other articles which the whites had been accustomed to use could not be raised on the plantation, and the conditions brought about by the war frequently made it impossible to secure these things. The whites were often in great straits. Parched corn was used for coffee, and a kind of black molasses was used instead of sugar. Many times nothing was used to sweeten the so-called tea and coffee.

The first pair of shoes that I recall wearing were wooden ones. They had rough leather on the top, but the bottoms, which were about an inch thick, were of wood. When I walked they made a fearful noise, and besides this they were very inconvenient, since there was no yielding to the natural pressure of the foot. In wearing them one presented an exceedingly awkward appearance. The most trying ordeal that I was forced to endure as a slave boy, however, was the wearing of a flax shirt. In the portion of Virginia where I lived it was common to use flax as part of the clothing for the slaves. That part of the flax from which our clothing was made was largely the refuse, which of course was the cheapest and roughest part. I can scarcely imagine any torture, except, perhaps, the pulling of a tooth, that is equal to that caused by putting on a new flax shirt for the first time. It is almost equal to the feeling that one would experience if he had a dozen or more chestnut burrs, or a hundred small pin-points, in contact with his flesh. Even to this day I can recall accurately the tortures that I underwent when putting on one of these garments. The fact that my flesh was soft and tender added to the pain. But I had no choice. I had to wear the flax shirt or none; and had it been left to me to choose, I should have chosen to wear no covering. In connection with the flax shirt, my brother John, who is several years older than I am, performed one of the most generous acts that I ever heard of one slave relative doing for another. On several occasions when I was being forced to wear a new flax shirt, he generously agreed to put it on in my stead and wear it for several days, till it was "broken in." Until I had grown to be quite a youth this single garment was all that I wore.

One may get the idea, from what I have said, that there was bitter feeling toward the white people on the part of my race, because of the fact that most of the white population was away fighting in a war which would result in keeping the Negro in slavery if the South was successful. In the case of the slaves on our place this was not true, and it was not true of any large portion of the slave population in the South where the Negro was treated with anything like decency. During the Civil War one of my young masters was killed, and two were severely wounded. I recall the feeling of sorrow which existed among the slaves when they heard of the death of "Mars' Billy." It was no sham sorrow, but real. Some of the slaves had nursed "Mars' Billy"; others had played with him when he was a child. "Mars' Billy" had begged for mercy in the case of others when the overseer or master was thrashing them. The sorrow in the slave quarter was only second to that in the "big house." When the two young masters were brought home wounded, the sympathy of the slaves was shown in many ways. They were just as anxious to assist in the nursing as the family relatives of the wounded. Some of the slaves would even beg for the privilege of sitting up at night to nurse their wounded masters. This tenderness and sympathy on the part of those held in bondage was a result of their kindly and generous nature. In order to defend and protect the women and children who were left on the plantations when the white males went to war, the slaves would have laid down their lives. The slave who was selected to sleep in the "big house" during the absence of the males was considered to have the place of honour. Any one attempting to harm "young Mistress" or "old Mistress" during the night would have had to cross the dead body of the slave to do so. I do not know how many have noticed it, but I think that it will be found to be true that there are few instances, either in slavery or freedom, in which a member of my race has been known to betray a specific trust.

As a rule, not only did the members of my race entertain no feelings of bitterness against the whites before and during the war, but there are many instances of Negroes tenderly caring for their former masters and mistresses who for some reason have become poor and dependent since the war. I know of instances where the former masters of slaves have for years been supplied with money by their former slaves to keep them from suffering. I have known of still other cases in which the former slaves have assisted in the education of the descendants of their former owners. I know of a case on a large plantation in the South in which a young white man, the son of the former owner of the estate, has become so reduced in purse and self-control by reason of drink that he is a pitiable creature; and yet, notwithstanding the poverty of the coloured people themselves on this plantation, they have for years supplied this young white man with the necessities of life. One sends him a little coffee or sugar, another a little meat, and so on. Nothing that the coloured people possess is too good for the son of "old Mars' Tom," who will perhaps never be permitted to suffer while any remain on the place who knew directly or indirectly of "old Mars' Tom."

I have said that there are few instances of a member of my race betraying a specific trust. One of the best illustrations of this which I know of is in the case of an ex-slave from Virginia whom I met not long ago in a little town in the state of Ohio. I found that this man had made a contract with his master, two or three years previous to the Emancipation Proclamation, to the effect that the slave was to be permitted to buy himself, by paying so much per year for his body; and while he was paying for himself, he was to be permitted to labour where and for whom he pleased. Finding that he could secure better wages in Ohio, he went there. When freedom came, he was still in debt to his master some three hundred dollars. Notwithstanding that the Emancipation Proclamation freed him from any obligation to his master, this black man walked the greater portion of the distance back to where his old master lived in Virginia, and placed the last dollar, with interest, in his hands. In talking to me about this, the man told me that he knew that he did not have to pay the debt, but that he had given his word to his master, and his word he had never broken. He felt that he could not enjoy his freedom till he had fulfilled his promise.

From some things that I have said one may get the idea that some of the slaves did not want freedom. This is not true. I have never seen one who did not want to be free, or one who would return to slavery.

I pity from the bottom of my heart any nation or body of people that is so unfortunate as to get entangled in the net of slavery. I have long since ceased to cherish any spirit of bitterness against the Southern white people on account of the enslavement of my race. No one section of our country was wholly responsible for its introduction, and, besides, it was recognized and protected for years by the General Government. Having once got its tentacles fastened on to the economic and social life of the Republic, it was no easy matter for the country to relieve itself of the institution. Then, when we rid ourselves of prejudice, or racial feeling, and look facts in the face, we must acknowledge that, notwithstanding the cruelty and moral wrong of slavery, the ten million Negroes inhabiting this country, who themselves or whose ancestors went through the school of American slavery, are in a stronger and more hopeful condition, materially, intellectually, morally, and religiously, than is true of an equal number of black people in any other portion of the globe. This is so to such an extent that Negroes in this country, who themselves or whose forefathers went through the school of slavery, are constantly returning to Africa as missionaries to enlighten those who remained in the fatherland. This I say, not to justify slavery—on the other hand, I condemn it as an institution, as we all know that in America it was established for selfish and financial reasons, and not from a missionary motive—but to call attention to a fact, and to show how Providence so often uses men and institutions to accomplish a purpose. When persons ask me in these days how, in the midst of what sometimes seem hopelessly discouraging conditions, I can have such faith in the future of my race in this country, I remind them of the wilderness through which and out of which, a good Providence has already led us.

Chapter III The Struggle for an Education

One day, while at work in the coal-mine,[3] I happened to overhear two miners talking about a great school for coloured people somewhere in Virginia. This was the first time that I had ever heard anything about any kind of school or college that was more pretentious than the little coloured school in our town.

[3]Washington went to work in a coal mine in Malden, West Virginia, at about the age of ten to supplement his family's meager income.

In the darkness of the mine I noiselessly crept as close as I could to the two men who were talking. I heard one tell the other that not only was the school established for the members of my race, but that opportunities were provided by which poor but worthy students could work out all or a part of the cost of board, and at the same time be taught some trade or industry.

As they went on describing the school, it seemed to me that it must be the greatest place on earth, and not even Heaven presented more attractions for me at that time than did the Hampton Normal and Agricultural Institute in Virginia,[4] about which these men were talking. I resolved at once to go to that school, although I had no idea where it was, or how many miles away, or how I was going to reach it; I remembered only that I was on fire constantly with one ambition, and that was to go to Hampton. This thought was with me day and night.

After hearing of the Hampton Institute, I continued to work for a few months longer in the coal-mine. While at work there, I heard of a vacant position in the household of General Lewis Ruffner, the owner of the salt-furnace and coal-mine. Mrs. Viola Ruffner, the wife of General Ruffner, was a "Yankee" woman from Vermont. Mrs. Ruffner had a reputation all through the vicinity for being very strict with her servants, and especially with the boys who tried to serve her. Few of them had remained with her more than two or three weeks. They all left with the same excuse: she was too strict. I decided, however, that I would rather try Mrs. Ruffner's house than remain in the coal-mine, and so my mother applied to her for the vacant position. I was hired at a salary of $5 per month.

I had heard so much about Mrs. Ruffner's severity that I was almost afraid to see her, and trembled when I went into her presence. I had not lived with her many weeks, however, before I began to understand her. I soon began to learn that, first of all, she wanted everything kept clean about her, that she wanted things done promptly and systematically, and that at the bottom of everything she wanted absolute honesty and frankness. Nothing must be sloven or slipshod; every door, every fence, must be kept in repair.

I cannot now recall how long I lived with Mrs. Ruffner before going to Hampton, but I think it must have been a year and a half. At any rate, I here repeat what I have said more than once before, that the lessons that I learned in the home of Mrs. Ruffner were as valuable to me as any education I have ever gotten anywhere since. Even to this day I never see bits of paper scattered around a house or in the street that I do not want to pick them up at once. I never see a filthy yard that I do not want to clean it, a paling off of a fence that I do not want to put it on, an unpainted or unwhitewashed house that I do not want to paint or whitewash it, or a button off one's clothes, or a grease-spot on them or on a floor, that I do not want to call attention to it.

From fearing Mrs. Ruffner I soon learned to look upon her as one of my best friends. When she found that she could trust me she did so implicitly. During the one or two winters that I was with her she gave me an opportunity to go to school for an hour in the day during a portion of the winter months, but most of my studying was

[4]A co-educational school founded in 1868 for the training of teachers, farmers, and the development of trades among southern blacks.

done at night, sometimes alone, sometimes under some one whom I could hire to teach me. Mrs. Ruffner always encouraged and sympathized with me in all my efforts to get an education. It was while living with her that I began to get together my first library. I secured a dry-goods box, knocked out one side of it, put some shelves in it, and began putting into it every kind of book that I could get my hands upon, and called it my "library."

Notwithstanding my success at Mrs. Ruffner's I did not give up the idea of going to the Hampton Institute. In the fall of 1872 I determined to make an effort to get there, although, as I have stated, I had no definite idea of the direction in which Hampton was, or of what it would cost to go there. I do not think that any one thoroughly sympathized with me in my ambition to go to Hampton unless it was my mother, and she was troubled with a grave fear that I was starting out on a "wild-goose chase." At any rate, I got only a half-hearted consent from her that I might start. The small amount of money that I had earned had been consumed by my stepfather and the remainder of the family, with the exception of a very few dollars, and so I had very little with which to buy clothes and pay my travelling expenses. My brother John helped me all that he could, but of course that was not a great deal, for his work was in the coal-mine, where he did not earn much, and most of what he did earn went in the direction of paying the household expenses.

Perhaps the thing that touched and pleased me most in connection with my starting for Hampton was the interest that many of the older coloured people took in the matter. They had spent the best days of their lives in slavery, and hardly expected to live to see the time when they would see a member of their race leave home to attend a boarding-school. Some of these older people would give me a nickel, others a quarter, or a handkerchief.

Finally the great day came, and I started for Hampton. I had only a small, cheap satchel that contained what few articles of clothing I could get. My mother at the time was rather weak and broken in health. I hardly expected to see her again, and thus our parting was all the more sad. She, however, was very brave through it all. At that time there were no through trains connecting that part of West Virginia with eastern Virginia. Trains ran only a portion of the way, and the remainder of the distance was travelled by stage-coaches.

The distance from Malden to Hampton is about five hundred miles. I had not been away from home many hours before it began to grow painfully evident that I did not have enough money to pay my fare to Hampton. One experience I shall long remember. I had been travelling over the mountains most of the afternoon in an old-fashioned stage-coach, when, late in the evening, the coach stopped for the night at a common, unpainted house called a hotel. All the other passengers except myself were whites. In my ignorance I supposed that the little hotel existed for the purpose of accommodating the passengers who travelled on the stage-coach. The difference that the colour of one's skin would make I had not thought anything about. After all the other passengers had been shown rooms and were getting ready for supper, I shyly presented myself before the man at the desk. It is true I had practically no money in my pocket with which to pay for bed or food, but I had hoped in some way to beg my way into the good graces of the landlord, for at that season in the mountains of Virginia the weather was cold, and I wanted to get indoors for the night. Without asking as to whether I had any money, the man at the desk firmly refused to even consider the matter of providing me with food or lodging. This was my first experience in finding out what the colour of my skin meant. In some way I managed to keep warm by walking about, and so got through the night. My whole soul was so bent upon reaching Hampton that I did not have time to cherish any bitterness toward the hotel-keeper.

By walking, begging rides both in wagons and in the cars, in some way, after a number of days, I reached the city of Richmond, Virginia, about eighty-two miles from Hampton. When I reached there, tired, hungry, and dirty, it was late in the night. I had never been in a large city, and this rather added to my misery. When I reached Richmond, I was completely out of money. I had not a single acquaintance in the place, and, being unused to city ways, I did not know where to go. I applied at several places for lodging, but they all wanted money, and that was what I did not have. Knowing nothing else better to do, I walked the streets. In doing this I passed by many food-stands where fried chicken and half-moon apple pies were piled high and made to present a most tempting appearance. At that time it seemed to me that I would have promised all that I expected to possess in the future to have gotten hold of one of those chicken legs or one of those pies. But I could not get either of these, nor anything else to eat.

I must have walked the streets till after midnight. At last I became so exhausted that I could walk no longer. I was tired, I was hungry, I was everything but discouraged. Just about the time when I reached extreme physical exhaustion, I came upon a portion of a street where the board sidewalk was considerably elevated. I waited for a few minutes, till I was sure that no passers-by could see me, and then crept under the sidewalk and lay for the night upon the ground, with my satchel of clothing for a pillow. Nearly all night I could hear the tramp of feet over my head. The next morning I found myself somewhat refreshed, but I was extremely hungry, because it had been a long time since I had had sufficient food. As soon as it became light enough for me to see my surroundings I noticed that I was near a large ship, and that this ship seemed to be unloading a cargo of pig iron. I went at once to the vessel and asked the captain to permit me to help unload the vessel in order to get money for food. The captain, a white man, who seemed to be kind-hearted, consented. I worked long enough to earn money for my breakfast, and it seems to me, as I remember it now, to have been about the best breakfast that I have ever eaten.

My work pleased the captain so well that he told me if I desired I could continue working for a small amount per day. This I was very glad to do. I continued working on this vessel for a number of days. After buying food with the small wages I received there was not much left to add to the amount I must get to pay my way to Hampton. In order to economize in every way possible, so as to be sure to reach Hampton in a reasonable time, I continued to sleep under the same sidewalk that first gave me shelter the first night I was in Richmond. Many years after that the coloured citizens of Richmond very kindly tendered me a reception at which there must have been two thousand people present. This reception was held not far from the spot where I slept the first night I spent in that city, and I must confess that my mind was more upon the sidewalk that first gave me shelter than upon the reception, agreeable and cordial as it was.

When I had saved what I considered enough money with which to reach Hampton, I thanked the captain of the vessel for his kindness, and started again. Without any unusual occurrence I reached Hampton, with a surplus of exactly fifty cents with which to begin my education. To me it had been a long, eventful journey; but the first sight of the large, three-story, brick school building seemed to have rewarded me for all that I had undergone in order to reach the place. If the people who gave the money to provide that building could appreciate the influence the sight of it had upon me, as well as upon thousands of other youths, they would feel all the more encouraged to make such gifts. It seemed to me to be the largest and most beautiful building I had ever seen. The sight of it seemed to give me new life. I felt that a new kind of existence had now begun—that life would now have a new meaning. I felt that I had reached the promised land, and I resolved to let no obstacle prevent me from putting forth the highest effort to fit myself to accomplish the most good in the world.

As soon as possible after reaching the grounds of the Hampton Institute, I presented myself before the head teacher for assignment to a class. Having been so long without proper food, a bath, and change of clothing, I did not, of course, make a very favourable impression upon her, and I could see at once that there were doubts in her mind about the wisdom of admitting me as a student. I felt that I could hardly blame her if she got the idea that I was a worthless loafer or tramp. For some time she did not refuse to admit me, neither did she decide in my favour, and I continued to linger about her, and to impress her in all the ways I could with my worthiness. In the meantime I saw her admitting other students, and that added greatly to my discomfort, for I felt, deep down in my heart, that I could do as well as they, if I could only get a chance to show what was in me.

After some hours had passed, the head teacher said to me: "The adjoining recitation-room needs sweeping. Take the broom and sweep it."

It occurred to me at once that here was my chance. Never did I receive an order with more delight. I knew that I could sweep, for Mrs. Ruffner had thoroughly taught me how to do that when I lived with her.

I swept the recitation-room three times. Then I got a dusting-cloth and I dusted it four times. All the woodwork around the walls, every bench, table, and desk, I went over four times with my dusting-cloth. Besides, every piece of furniture had been moved and every closet and corner in the room had been thoroughly cleaned. I had the feeling that in a large measure my future depended upon the impression I made upon the teacher in the cleaning of that room. When I was through, I reported to the head teacher. She was a "Yankee" woman who knew just where to look for dirt. She went into the room and inspected the floor and closets; then she took her handkerchief and rubbed it on the woodwork about the walls, and over the table and benches. When she was unable to find one bit of dirt on the floor, or a particle of dust on any of the furniture, she quietly remarked, "I guess you will do to enter this institution."

I was one of the happiest souls on earth. The sweeping of that room was my college examination, and never did any youth pass an examination for entrance into Harvard or Yale that gave him more genuine satisfaction. I have passed several examinations since then, but I have always felt that this was the best one I ever passed.

I have spoken of my own experience in entering the Hampton Institute. Perhaps few, if any, had anything like the same experience that I had, but about that same period there were hundreds who found their way to Hampton and other institutions after experiencing something of the same difficulties that I went through. The young men and women were determined to secure an education at any cost.

The sweeping of the recitation-room in the manner that I did it seems to have paved the way for me to get through Hampton. Miss Mary. F. Mackie, the head teacher, offered me a position as janitor. This, of course, I gladly accepted, because it was a place where I could work out nearly all the cost of my board. The work was hard and taxing, but I stuck to it. I had a large number of rooms to care for, and had to work late into the night, while at the same time I had to rise by four o'clock in the morning, in order to build the fires and have a little time in which to prepare my lessons. In all my career at Hampton, and ever since I have been out in the world, Miss Mary F. Mackie, the head teacher to whom I have referred, proved one of my strongest and most helpful friends. Her advice and encouragement were always helpful and strengthening to me in the darkest hour.

I have spoken of the impression that was made upon me by the buildings and general appearance of the Hampton Institute, but I have not spoken of that which made the greatest and most lasting impression upon me, and that was a great man—the noblest, rarest human being that it has ever been my privilege to meet. I refer to the late General Samuel C. Armstrong.

It has been my fortune to meet personally many of what are called great characters, both in Europe and America, but I do not hesitate to say that I never met any man who, in my estimation, was the equal of General Armstrong. Fresh from the degrading influences of the slave plantation and the coal-mines, it was a rare privilege for me to be permitted to come into direct contact with such a character as General Armstrong. I shall always remember that the first time I went into his presence he made the impression upon me of being a perfect man; I was made to feel that there was something about him that was superhuman. It was my privilege to know the General personally from the time I entered Hampton till he died, and the more I saw of him the greater he grew in my estimation. One might have removed from Hampton all the buildings, class-rooms, teachers, and industries, and given the men and women there the opportunity of coming into daily contact with General Armstrong, and that alone would have been a liberal education. The older I grow, the more I am convinced that there is no education which one can get from books and costly apparatus that is equal to that which can be gotten from contact with great men and women. Instead of studying books so constantly, how I wish that our schools and colleges might learn to study men and things!

General Armstrong spent two of the last six months of his life in my home at Tuskegee. At that time he was paralyzed to the extent that he had lost control of his body and voice in a very large degree. Notwithstanding his affliction, he worked almost constantly night and day for the cause to which he had given his life. I never saw a man who so completely lost sight of himself. I do not believe he ever had a selfish thought. He was just as happy in trying to assist some other institution in the South as he was when working for Hampton. Although he fought the Southern white man in the Civil War, I never heard him utter a bitter word against him afterward. On the other hand, he was constantly seeking to find ways by which he could be of service to the Southern whites.

It would be difficult to describe the hold that he had upon the students at Hampton, or the faith they had in him. In fact, he was worshipped by his students. It never occurred to me that General Armstrong could fail in anything that he undertook. There is almost no request that he could have made that would not have been complied with. When he was a guest at my home in Alabama, and was so badly paralyzed that he had to be wheeled about in an invalid's chair, I recall that one of the General's former students had occasion to push his chair up a long, steep hill that taxed his strength to the utmost. When the top of the hill was reached, the former pupil, with a glow of happiness on his face, exclaimed, "I am so glad that I have been permitted to do something that was real hard for the General before he dies!" While I was a student at Hampton, the dormitories became so crowded that it was impossible to find room for all who wanted to be admitted. In order to help remedy the difficulty, the General conceived the plan of putting up tents to be used as rooms. As soon as it became known that General Armstrong would be pleased if some of the older students would live in the tents during the winter, nearly every student in school volunteered to go.

I was one of the volunteers. The winter that we spent in those tents was an intensely cold one, and we suffered severely—how much I am sure General Armstrong never knew, because we made no complaints. It was enough for us to know that we were pleasing General Armstrong, and that we were making it possible for an additional number of students to secure an education. More than once, during a cold night, when a stiff gale would be blowing, our tent was lifted bodily, and we would find ourselves in the open air. The General would usually pay a visit to the tents early in the morning, and his earnest, cheerful, encouraging voice would dispel any feeling of despondency.

I have spoken of my admiration for General Armstrong, and yet he was but a type of that Christlike body of men and women who went into the Negro schools at the close of the war by the hundreds to assist in lifting up my race. The history of the world fails to show a higher, purer, and more unselfish class of men and women than those who found their way into those Negro schools.

Life at Hampton was a constant revelation to me; was constantly taking me into a new world. The matter of having meals at regular hours, of eating on a tablecloth, using a napkin, the use of the bath-tub and of the tooth-brush, as well as the use of sheets upon the bed, were all new to me.

I sometimes feel that almost the most valuable lesson I got at the Hampton Institute was in the use and value of the bath. I learned there for the first time some of its value, not only in keeping the body healthy, but in inspiring self-respect and promoting virtue. In all my travels in the South and elsewhere since leaving Hampton I have always in some way sought my daily bath. To get it sometimes when I have been the guest of my own people in a single-roomed cabin has not always been easy to do, except by slipping away to some stream in the woods. I have always tried to teach my people that some provision for bathing should be a part of every house.

For some time, while a student at Hampton, I possessed but a single pair of socks, but when I had worn these till they became soiled, I would wash them at night and hang them by the fire to dry, so that I might wear them again the next morning.

The charge for my board at Hampton was ten dollars per month. I was expected to pay a part of this in cash and to work out the remainder. To meet this cash payment, as I have stated, I had just fifty cents when I reached the institution. Aside from a very few dollars that my brother John was able to send me once in a while, I had no money with which to pay my board. I was determined from the first to make my work as janitor so valuable that my services would be indispensable. This I succeeded in doing to such an extent that I was soon informed that I would be allowed the full cost of my board in return for my work. The cost of tuition was seventy dollars a year. This, of course, was wholly beyond my ability to provide. If I had been compelled to pay the seventy dollars for tuition, in addition to providing for my board, I would have been compelled to leave the Hampton school. General Armstrong, however, very kindly got Mr. S. Griffitts Morgan, of New Bedford, Mass., to defray the cost of my tuition during the whole time that I was at Hampton. After I finished the course at Hampton and had entered upon my lifework at Tuskegee, I had the pleasure of visiting Mr. Morgan several times.

After having been for a while at Hampton, I found myself in difficulty because I did not have books and clothing. Usually, however, I got around the trouble about books by borrowing from those who were more fortunate than myself. As to clothes, when I reached Hampton I had practically nothing. Everything that I possessed was in a small hand satchel. My anxiety about clothing was increased because of the fact that General Armstrong made a personal inspection of the young men in ranks, to see that their clothes were clean. Shoes had to be polished, there must be no buttons off the clothing, and no grease-spots. To wear one suit of clothes continually, while at work and in the schoolroom, and at the same time keep it clean, was rather a hard problem for me to solve. In some way I managed to get on till the teachers learned that I was in earnest and meant to succeed, and then some of them were kind enough to see that I was partly supplied with second-hand clothing that had been sent in barrels from the North. These barrels proved a blessing to hundreds of poor but deserving students. Without them I question whether I should ever have gotten through Hampton.

When I first went to Hampton I do not recall that I had ever slept in a bed that had two sheets on it. In those days there were not many buildings there, and room was very precious. There were seven other boys in the same room with me; most of them, however, students who had been there for some time. The sheets were quite a puzzle to me. The first night I slept under both of them, and the second night I slept on top of both of them; but by watching the other boys I learned my lesson in this, and have been trying to follow it ever since and to teach it to others.

I was among the youngest of the students who were in Hampton at that time. Most of the students were men and women—some as old as forty years of age. As I now recall the scene of my first year, I do not believe that one often has the opportunity of coming into contact with three or four hundred men and women who were so tremendously in earnest as these men and women were. Every hour was occupied in study or work. Nearly all had had enough actual contact with the world to teach them the need of education. Many of the older ones were, of course, too old to master the text-books very thoroughly, and it was often sad to watch their struggles; but they made up in earnestness much of what they lacked in books. Many of them were as poor as I was, and, besides having to wrestle with their books, they had to struggle with a poverty which prevented their having the necessities of life. Many of them had aged parents who were dependent upon them, and some of them were men who had wives whose support in some way they had to provide for.

The great and prevailing idea that seemed to take possession of every one was to prepare himself to lift up the people at his home. No one seemed to think of himself. And the officers and teachers, what a rare set of human beings they were! They worked for the students night and day, in season and out of season. They seemed happy only when they were helping the students in some manner. Whenever it is written—and I hope it will be—the part that the Yankee teachers played in the education of the Negroes immediately after the war will make one of the most thrilling parts of the history of this country. The time is not far distant when the whole South will appreciate this service in a way that it has not yet been able to do.

Chapter VI Black Race and Red Race

During the year that I spent in Washington,[5] and for some little time before this, there had been considerable agitation in the state of West Virginia over the question of moving the capital of the state from Wheeling to some other central point. As a result of this, the Legislature designated three cities to be voted upon by the citizens of the state as the permanent seat of government. Among these cities was Charleston, only five miles from Malden, my home. At the close of my school year in Washington I was very pleasantly surprised to receive, from a committee of white people in Charleston, an invitation to canvass the state in the interests of that city. This invitation I accepted, and spent nearly three months in speaking in various parts of the state. Charleston was successful in winning the prize, and is now the permanent seat of government.

The reputation that I made as a speaker during this campaign induced a number of persons to make an earnest effort to get me to enter political life, but I refused, still believing that I could find other service which would prove of more permanent value to my race. Even then I had a strong feeling that what our people most needed was to get a foundation in education, industry, and property, and for this I felt that they could better afford to strive than for political preferment. As for my individual self, it appeared to me to be reasonably certain that I could succeed in political life, but I had a feeling that it would be a rather selfish kind of success—individual success at the cost of failing to do my duty in assisting in laying a foundation for the masses.

At this period in the progress of our race a very large proportion of the young men who went to school or to college did so with the expressed determination to prepare themselves to be great lawyers, or Congressmen, and many of the women planned to become music teachers; but I had a reasonably fixed idea, even at that early period in my life, that there was need for something to be done to prepare the way for successful lawyers, Congressmen, and music teachers.

I felt that the conditions were a good deal like those of an old coloured man, during the days of slavery, who wanted to learn how to play on the guitar. In his desire to take guitar lessons he applied to one of his young masters to teach him; but the young man, not having much faith in the ability of the slave to master the guitar at his age, sought to discourage him by telling him: "Uncle Jake, I will give you guitar lessons; but, Jake, I will have to charge you three dollars for the first lesson, two dollars for the second lesson, and one dollar for the third lesson. But I will charge you only twenty-five cents for the last lesson."

Uncle Jake answered: "All right, boss, I hires you on dem terms. But, boss! I wants yer to be sure an' give me dat las' lesson first."

[5]In the fall of 1878, Washington left a position as a schoolteacher in the Kanawha Valley, West Virginia, to pursue a year of theological study at the Wayland Seminary in Washington, D.C.

Soon after my work in connection with the removal of the capital was finished, I received an invitation which gave me great joy and which at the same time was a very pleasant surprise. This was a letter from General Armstrong, inviting me to return to Hampton at the next Commencement to deliver what was called the "post-graduate address." This was an honour which I had not dreamed of receiving. With much care I prepared the best address that I was capable of. I chose for my subject "The Force That Wins."

As I returned to Hampton for the purpose of delivering this address, I went over much of the same ground—now, however, covered entirely by railroad—that I had traversed nearly six years before, when I first sought entrance into Hampton Institute as a student. Now I was able to ride the whole distance in the train. I was constantly contrasting this with my first journey to Hampton. I think I may say, without seeming egotism, that it is seldom that five years have wrought such a change in the life and aspirations of an individual.

At Hampton I received a warm welcome from teachers and students. I found that during my absence from Hampton the institute each year had been getting closer to the real needs and conditions of our people; that the industrial teaching, as well as that of the academic department, had greatly improved. The plan of the school was not modelled after that of any other institution then in existence, but every improvement was made under the magnificent leadership of General Armstrong solely with the view of meeting and helping the needs of our people as they presented themselves at the time. Too often, it seems to me, in missionary and educational work among undeveloped races, people yield to the temptation of doing that which was done a hundred years before, or is being done in other communities a thousand miles away. The temptation often is to run each individual through a certain educational mould, regardless of the condition of the subject or the end to be accomplished. This was not so at Hampton Institute.

The address which I delivered on Commencement Day seems to have pleased every one, and many kind and encouraging words were spoken to me regarding it. Soon after my return to my home in West Virginia, where I had planned to continue teaching, I was again surprised to receive a letter from General Armstrong, asking me to return to Hampton partly as a teacher and partly to pursue some supplementary studies. This was in the summer of 1879. Soon after I began my first teaching in West Virginia I had picked out four of the brightest and most promising of my pupils, in addition to my two brothers, to whom I have already referred, and had given them special attention, with the view of having them go to Hampton. They had gone there, and in each case the teachers had found them so well prepared that they entered advanced classes. This fact, it seems, led to my being called back to Hampton as a teacher. One of the young men that I sent to Hampton in this way is now Dr. Samuel E. Courtney, a successful physician in Boston, and a member of the School Board of that city.

About this time the experiment was being tried for the first time, by General Armstrong, of educating Indians at Hampton. Few people then had any confidence in the ability of the Indians to receive education and to profit by it. General Armstrong was anxious to try the experiment systematically on a large scale. He secured from the reservations in the Western states over one hundred wild and for the most part perfectly ignorant Indians, the greater proportion of whom were young men.

The special work which the General desired me to do was to be sort of "house father" to the Indian young men—that is, I was to live in the building with them and have the charge of their discipline, clothing, rooms, and so on. This was a very tempting offer, but I had become so much absorbed in my work in West Virginia that I dreaded to give it up. However, I tore myself away from it. I did not know how to refuse to perform any service that General Armstrong desired of me.

On going to Hampton, I took up my residence in a building with about seventy-five Indian youths. I was the only person in the building who was not a member of their race. At first I had a good deal of doubt about my ability to succeed. I knew that the average Indian felt himself above the white man, and, of course, he felt himself far above the Negro, largely on account of the fact of the Negro having submitted to slavery—a thing which the Indian would never do. The Indians, in the Indian Territory, owned a large number of slaves during the days of slavery. Aside from this, there was a general feeling that the attempt to educate and civilize the red men at Hampton would be a failure. All this made me proceed very cautiously, for I felt keenly the great responsibility. But I was determined to succeed. It was not long before I had the complete confidence of the Indians, and not only this, but I think I am safe in saying that I had their love and respect. I found that they were about like any other human beings; that they responded to kind treatment and resented ill-treatment. They were continually planning to do something that would add to my happiness and comfort. The things that they disliked most, I think, were to have their long hair cut, to give up wearing their blankets, and to cease smoking; but no white American ever thinks that any other race is wholly civilized until he wears the white man's clothes, eats the white man's food, speaks the white man's language, and professes the white man's religion.

When the difficulty of learning the English language was subtracted, I found that in the matter of learning trades and mastering academic studies there was little difference between the coloured and Indian students. It was a constant delight to me to note the interest which the coloured students took in trying to help the Indians in every way possible. There were a few of the coloured students who felt that the Indians ought not to be admitted to Hampton, but these were in the minority. Whenever they were asked to do so, the Negro students gladly took the Indians as roommates, in order that they might teach them to speak English and to acquire civilized habits.

I have often wondered if there was a white institution in this country whose students would have welcomed the incoming of more than a hundred companions of another race in the cordial way that these black students at Hampton welcomed the red ones. How often I have wanted to say to white students that they lift themselves up in proportion as they help to lift others, and the more unfortunate the race, and the lower in the scale of civilization, the more does one raise one's self by giving the assistance.

Chapter XIII Two Thousand Miles for a Five-Minute Speech

. . . On the morning of September 17, together with Mrs. Washington and my three children, I started for Atlanta. I felt a good deal as I suppose a man feels when he is on his way to the gallows. In passing through the town of Tuskegee I met a white farmer who lived some distance out in the country. In a jesting manner this man said:

"Washington, you have spoken before the Northern white people, the Negroes in the South, and to us country white people in the South; but in Atlanta, to-morrow, you will have before you the Northern whites, the Southern whites, and the Negroes all together. I am afraid that you have got yourself into a tight place." This farmer diagnosed the situation correctly, but his frank words did not add anything to my comfort.

In the course of the journey from Tuskegee to Atlanta both coloured and white people came to the train to point me out, and discussed with perfect freedom, in my hearing, what was going to take place the next day. We were met by a committee in Atlanta. Almost the first thing that I heard when I got off the train in that city was an expression something like this, from an old coloured man near by: "Dat's de man of my race what's gwine to make a speech at de Exposition to-morrow. I'se sho' gwine to hear him."

Atlanta was literally packed, at the time, with people from all parts of this country, and with representatives of foreign governments, as well as with military and civic organizations. The afternoon papers had forecasts of the next day's proceedings in flaring headlines. All this tended to add to my burden. I did not sleep much that night. The next morning, before day, I went carefully over what I intended to say. I also kneeled down and asked God's blessing upon my effort. Right here, perhaps, I ought to add that I make it a rule never to go before an audience, on any occasion, without asking the blessing of God upon what I want to say.

I always make it a rule to make especial preparation for each separate address. No two audiences are exactly alike. It is my aim to reach and talk to the heart of each individual audience, taking it into my confidence very much as I would a person. When I am speaking to an audience, I care little for how what I am saying is going to sound in the newspapers, or to another audience, or to an individual. At the time, the audience before me absorbs all my sympathy, thought, and energy.

Early in the morning a committee called to escort me to my place in the procession which was to march to the Exposition grounds. In this procession were prominent coloured citizens in carriages, as well as several Negro military organizations. I noted that the Exposition officials seemed to go out of their way to see that all of the coloured people in the procession were properly placed and properly treated. The procession was about three hours in reaching the Exposition grounds, and during all of this time the sun was shining down upon us disagreeably hot. When we reached the grounds, the heat, together with my nervous anxiety, made me feel as if I were about ready to collapse, and to feel that my address was not going to be a success. When I entered the audience-room, I found it packed with humanity from bottom to top, and there were thousands outside who could not get in.

The room was very large, and well suited to public speaking. When I entered the room, there were vigorous cheers from the coloured portion of the audience, and faint cheers from some of the white people. I had been told, while I had been in Atlanta, that while many white people were going to be present to hear me speak, simply out of curiosity, and that others who would be present would be in full sympathy with me, there was a still larger element of the audience which would consist of those who were going to be present for the purpose of hearing me make a fool of myself, or, at least, of hearing me say some foolish thing, so that they could say to the officials who had invited me to speak, "I told you so!"

One of the trustees of the Tuskegee Institute, as well as my personal friend, Mr. William H. Baldwin, Jr., was at the time General Manager of the Southern Railroad, and happened to be in Atlanta on that day. He was so nervous about the kind of reception that I would have, and the effect that my speech would produce, that he could not persuade himself to go into the building, but walked back and forth in the grounds outside until the opening exercises were over.

Chapter XIV The Atlanta Exposition Address

The Atlanta Exposition,[6] at which I had been asked to make an address as a representative of the Negro race, as stated in the last chapter, was opened with a short address from Governor Bullock. After other interesting exercises, including an invocation from Bishop Nelson, of Georgia, a dedicatory ode by Albert Howell, Jr., and addresses by the President of the Exposition and Mrs. Joseph Thompson, the President of the Woman's Board, Governor Bullock introduced me with the words, "We have with us to-day a representative of Negro enterprise and Negro civilization."

When I arose to speak, there was considerable cheering, especially from the coloured people. As I remember it now, the thing that was uppermost in my mind was the desire to say something that would cement the friendship of the races and bring about hearty cooperation between them. So far as my outward surroundings were concerned, the only thing that I recall distinctly now is that when I got up, I saw thousands of eyes looking intently into my face. The following is the address which I delivered:—

Mr. President and Gentlemen of the Board of Directors and Citizens:

One-third of the population of the South is of the Negro race. No enterprise seeking the material, civil, or moral welfare of this section can disregard this element of our population and reach the highest success. I but convey to you, Mr. President and Directors, the sentiment of the masses of my race when I say that in no way have the value and manhood of the American Negro been more fittingly and generously recognized than by the managers of this magnificent Exposition at every stage of its progress. It is a recognition that will do more to cement the friendship of the two races than any occurrence since the dawn of our freedom.

Not only this, but the opportunity here afforded will awaken among us a new era of industrial progress. Ignorant and inexperienced, it is not strange that in the first years of our new life we began at the top instead of at the bottom; that a seat in Congress or the state legislature was more sought than real estate or industrial skill; that the political convention or stump speaking had more attractions than starting a dairy farm or truck garden.

A ship lost at sea for many days suddenly sighted a friendly vessel. From the mast of the unfortunate vessel was seen a signal, "Water, water; we die of thirst!" The answer from the friendly vessel at once came back, "Cast down your bucket where you are." A second time the signal, "Water, water; send us water!" ran up from the

[6]Washington spoke at the opening ceremonies of the Atlanta (Georgia) Cotton States and International Exposition, September 18, 1895.

distressed vessel, and was answered, "Cast down your bucket where you are." And a third and fourth signal for water was answered, "Cast down your bucket where you are." The captain of the distressed vessel, at last heeding the injunction, cast down his bucket, and it came up full of fresh, sparkling water from the mouth of the Amazon River. To those of my race who depend on bettering their condition in a foreign land or who underestimate the importance of cultivating friendly relations with the Southern white man, who is their next-door neighbour, I would say: "Cast down your bucket where you are"—cast it down in making friends in every manly way of the people of all races by whom we are surrounded.

Cast it down in agriculture, mechanics, in commerce, in domestic service, and in the professions. And in this connection it is well to bear in mind that whatever other sins the South may be called to bear, when it comes to business, pure and simple, it is in the South that the Negro is given a man's chance in the commercial world, and in nothing is this Exposition more eloquent than in emphasizing this chance. Our greatest danger is that in the great leap from slavery to freedom we may overlook the fact that the masses of us are to live by the productions of our hands, and fail to keep in mind that we shall prosper in proportion as we learn to dignify and glorify common labour and put brains and skill into the common occupations of life; shall prosper in proportion as we learn to draw the line between the superficial and the substantial, the ornamental gewgaws of life and the useful. No race can prosper till it learns that there is as much dignity in tilling a field as in writing a poem. It is at the bottom of life we must begin, and not at the top. Nor should we permit our grievances to overshadow our opportunities.

To those of the white race who look to the incoming of those of foreign birth and strange tongue and habits for the prosperity of the South, were I permitted I would repeat what I say to my own race, "Cast down your bucket where you are." Cast it down among the eight millions of Negroes whose habits you know, whose fidelity and love you have tested in days when to have proved treacherous meant the ruin of your firesides. Cast down your bucket among these people who have, without strikes and labour wars, tilled your fields, cleared your forests, builded your railroads and cities, and brought forth treasures from the bowels of the earth, and helped make possible this magnificent representation of the progress of the South. Casting down your bucket among my people, helping and encouraging them as you are doing on these grounds, and to education of head, hand, and heart, you will find that they will buy your surplus land, make blossom the waste places in your fields, and run your factories. While doing this, you can be sure in the future, as in the past, that you and your families will be surrounded by the most patient, faithful, law-abiding, and unresentful people that the world has seen. As we have proved our loyalty to you in the past, in nursing your children, watching by the sick-bed of your mothers and fathers, and often following them with tear-dimmed eyes to their graves, so in the future, in our humble way, we shall stand by you with a devotion that no foreigner can approach, ready to lay down our lives, if need be, in defence of yours, interlacing our industrial, commercial, civil, and religious life with yours in a way that shall make the interests of both races one. In all things that are purely social we can be as separate as the fingers, yet one as the hand in all things essential to mutual progress.

There is no defence or security for any of us except in the highest intelligence and development of all. If anywhere there are efforts tending to curtail the fullest growth of the Negro, let these efforts be turned into stimulating, encouraging, and making him the most useful and intelligent citizen. Effort or means so invested will pay a thousand per cent interest. These efforts will be twice blessed—"blessing him that gives and him that takes."[7]

There is no escape through law of man or God from the inevitable:—

"The laws of changeless justice bind
Oppressor with oppressed;
And close as sin and suffering joined
We march to fate abreast."[8]

Nearly sixteen millions of hands will aid you in pulling the load upward, or they will pull against you the load downward. We shall constitute one-third and more of the ignorance and crime of the South, or one-third its intelligence and progress; we shall contribute one-third to the business and industrial prosperity of the South, or we shall prove a veritable body of death, stagnating, depressing, retarding every effort to advance the body politic.

Gentlemen of the Exposition, as we present to you our humble effort at an exhibition of our progress, you must not expect overmuch. Starting thirty years ago with ownership here and there in a few quilts and pumpkins and chickens (gathered from miscellaneous sources), remember the path that has led from these to the inventions and production of agricultural implements, buggies, steam-engines, newspapers, books, statuary, carving, paintings, the management of drug-stores and banks, has not been trodden without contact with thorns and thistles. While we take pride in what we exhibit as a result of our independent efforts, we do not for a moment forget that our part in this exhibition would fall far short of your expectations but for the constant help that has come to our educational life, not only from the Southern states, but especially from Northern philanthropists, who have made their gifts a constant stream of blessing and encouragement.

The wisest among my race understand that the agitation of questions of social equality is the extremest folly, and that progress in the enjoyment of all the privileges that will come to us must be the result of severe and constant struggle rather than of artificial forcing. No race that has anything to contribute to the markets of the world is long in any degree ostracized. It is important and right that all privileges of the law be ours, but it is vastly more important that we be prepared for the exercise of these privileges. The opportunity to earn a dollar in a factory just now is worth infinitely more than the opportunity to spend a dollar in an opera-house.

In conclusion, may I repeat that nothing in thirty years has given us more hope and encouragement, and drawn us so near to you of the white race, as this opportunity offered by the Exposition; and here bending, as it were, over the altar that represents the results of the struggles of your race and mine, both starting practically empty-handed three decades ago, I pledge that in your effort to work out the great and intricate problem which God has laid at the doors of the South, you shall have at all times the patient, sympathetic help of my race; only let this be constantly in mind, that, while from representations in these buildings of the product of field, of forest, of mine, of factory, letters, and art, much good will come, yet far above and beyond material benefits will be that higher good, that, let us pray God, will come, in a blotting out of sectional differences and racial animosities and suspicions, in a determination to administer absolute justice, in a willing obedience among all classes to the

[7]William Shakespeare, *The Merchant of Venice,* Act IV, scene 1, line 1670.

[8]"Song of the Negro Boatman," by John Greenleaf Whittier (1807–1892).

mandates of law. This, coupled with our material prosperity, will bring into our beloved South a new heaven and a new earth.

The first thing that I remember, after I had finished speaking, was that Governor Bullock rushed across the platform and took me by the hand, and that others did the same. I received so many and such hearty congratulations that I found it difficult to get out of the building. I did not appreciate to any degree, however, the impression which my address seemed to have made, until the next morning, when I went into the business part of the city. As soon as I was recognized, I was surprised to find myself pointed out and surrounded by a crowd of men who wished to shake hands with me. This was kept up on every street on to which I went, to an extent which embarrassed me so much that I went back to my boarding-place. The next morning I returned to Tuskegee. At the station in Atlanta, and at almost all of the stations at which the train stopped between that city and Tuskegee, I found a crowd of people anxious to shake hands with me.

The papers in all parts of the United States published the address in full, and for months afterward there were complimentary editorial references to it. Mr. Clark Howell, the editor of the Atlanta *Constitution,* telegraphed to a New York paper, among other words, the following, "I do not exaggerate when I say that Professor Booker T. Washington's address yesterday was one of the most notable speeches, both as to character and as to the warmth of its reception, ever delivered to a Southern audience. The address was a revelation. The whole speech is a platform upon which blacks and whites can stand with full justice to each other."

The Boston *Transcript* said editorially: "The speech of Booker T. Washington at the Atlanta Exposition, this week, seems to have dwarfed all the other proceedings and the Exposition itself. The sensation that it has caused in the press has never been equalled."

I very soon began receiving all kinds of propositions from lecture bureaus, and editors of magazines and papers, to take the lecture platform, and to write articles. One lecture bureau offered me fifty thousand dollars, or two hundred dollars a night and expenses, if I would place my services at its disposal for a given period. To all these communications I replied that my life-work was at Tuskegee; and that whenever I spoke it must be in the interests of the Tuskegee school and my race, and that I would enter into no arrangements that seemed to place a mere commercial value upon my services.

Some days after its delivery I sent a copy of my address to the President of the United States, the Hon. Grover Cleveland. I received from him the following autograph reply:—

Gray Gables
Buzzard's Bay, Mass., October 6, 1895

Booker T. Washington, Esq.:

My Dear Sir: I thank you for sending me a copy of your address delivered at the Atlanta Exposition.

I thank you with much enthusiasm for making the address. I have read it with intense interest, and I think the Exposition would be fully justified if it did not do more than furnish the opportunity for its delivery. Your words cannot fail to delight and en-

courage all who wish well for your race; and if our coloured fellow-citizens do not from your utterances gather new hope and form new determinations to gain every valuable advantage offered them by their citizenship, it will be strange indeed. Yours very truly,

Grover Cleveland

Later I met Mr. Cleveland, for the first time, when, as President, he visited the Atlanta Exposition. At the request of myself and others he consented to spend an hour in the Negro Building, for the purpose of inspecting the Negro exhibit and of giving the coloured people in attendance an opportunity to shake hands with him. As soon as I met Mr. Cleveland I became impressed with his simplicity, greatness, and rugged honesty. I have met him many times since then, both at public functions and at his private residence in Princeton, and the more I see of him the more I admire him. When he visited the Negro Building in Atlanta he seemed to give himself up wholly, for that hour, to the coloured people. He seemed to be as careful to shake hands with some old coloured "auntie" clad partially in rags, and to take as much pleasure in doing so, as if he were greeting some millionnaire. Many of the coloured people took advantage of the occasion to get him to write his name in a book or on a slip of paper. He was as careful and patient in doing this as if he were putting his signature to some great state document.

Mr. Cleveland has not only shown his friendship for me in many personal ways, but has always consented to do anything I have asked of him for our school. This he has done, whether it was to make a personal donation or to use his influence in securing the donations of others. Judging from my personal acquaintance with Mr. Cleveland, I do not believe that he is conscious of possessing any colour prejudice. He is too great for that. In my contact with people I find that, as a rule, it is only the little, narrow people who live for themselves, who never read good books, who do not travel, who never open up their souls in a way to permit them to come into contact with other souls—with the great outside world. No man whose vision is bounded by colour can come into contact with what is highest and best in the world. In meeting men, in many places, I have found that the happiest people are those who do the most for others; the most miserable are those who do the least. I have also found that few things, if any, are capable of making one so blind and narrow as race prejudice. I often say to our students, in the course of my talks to them on Sunday evenings in the chapel, that the longer I live and the more experience I have of the world, the more I am convinced that, after all, the one thing that is most worth living for—and dying for, if need be—is the opportunity of making some one else more happy and more useful.

The coloured people and the coloured newspapers at first seemed to be greatly pleased with the character of my Atlanta address, as well as with its reception. But after the first burst of enthusiasm began to die away, and the coloured people began reading the speech in cold type, some of them seemed to feel that they had been hypnotized. They seemed to feel that I had been too liberal in my remarks toward the Southern whites, and that I had not spoken out strongly enough for what they termed the "rights" of the race. For a while there was a reaction, so far as a certain element of my own race was concerned, but later these reactionary ones seemed to have been won over to my way of believing and acting.

While speaking of changes in public sentiment, I recall that about ten years after the school at Tuskegee was established, I had an experience that I shall never forget. Dr. Lyman Abbott, then the pastor of Plymouth Church, and also editor of the *Outlook* (then the *Christian Union*), asked me to write a letter for his paper giving my opinion of the exact condition, mental and moral, of the coloured ministers in the South, as based upon my observations. I wrote the letter, giving the exact facts as I conceived them to be. The picture painted was a rather black one—or, since I am black, shall I say "white"? It could not be otherwise with a race but a few years out of slavery, a race which had not had time or opportunity to produce a competent ministry.

What I said soon reached every Negro minister in the country, I think, and the letters of condemnation which I received from them were not few. I think that for a year after the publication of this article every association and every conference or religious body of any kind, of my race, that met, did not fail before adjourning to pass a resolution condemning me, or calling upon me to retract or modify what I had said. Many of these organizations went so far in their resolutions as to advise parents to cease sending their children to Tuskegee. One association even appointed a "missionary" whose duty it was to warn the people against sending their children to Tuskegee. This missionary had a son in the school, and I noticed that, whatever the "missionary" might have said or done with regard to others, he was careful not to take his son away from the institution. Many of the coloured papers, especially those that were the organs of religious bodies, joined in the general chorus of condemnation or demands for retraction.

During the whole time of the excitement, and through all the criticism, I did not utter a word of explanation or retraction. I knew that I was right, and that time and the sober second thought of the people would vindicate me. It was not long before the bishops and other church leaders began to make a careful investigation of the conditions of the ministry, and they found out that I was right. In fact, the oldest and most influential bishop in one branch of the Methodist Church said that my words were far too mild. Very soon public sentiment began making itself felt, in demanding a purifying of the ministry. While this is not yet complete by any means, I think I may say, without egotism, and I have been told by many of our most influential ministers, that my words had much to do with starting a demand for the placing of a higher type of men in the pulpit. I have had the satisfaction of having many who once condemned me thank me heartily for my frank words.

The change of the attitude of the Negro ministry, so far as regards myself, is so complete that at the present time I have no warmer friends among any class than I have among the clergymen. The improvement in the character and life of the Negro ministers is one of the most gratifying evidences of the progress of the race. My experience with them, as well as other events in my life, convince me that the thing to do, when one feels sure that he has said or done the right thing, and is condemned, is to stand still and keep quiet. If he is right, time will show it.

In the midst of the discussion which was going on concerning my Atlanta speech, I received the letter which I give below, from Dr. Gilman, the President of Johns Hopkins University, who had been made chairman of the judges of award in connection with the Atlanta Exposition:

Johns Hopkins University, Baltimore
President's Office, September 30, 1895

Dear Mr. Washington: Would it be agreeable to you to be one of the Judges of Award in the Department of Education at Atlanta? If so, I shall be glad to place your name upon the list. A line by telegraph will be welcomed. Yours very truly,

D.C. Gilman

I think I was even more surprised to receive this invitation than I had been to receive the invitation to speak at the opening of the Exposition. It was to be a part of my duty, as one of the jurors, to pass not only upon the exhibits of the coloured schools, but also upon those of the white schools. I accepted the position, and spent a month in Atlanta in performance of the duties which it entailed. The board of jurors was a large one, consisting in all of sixty members. It was about equally divided between Southern white people and Northern white people. Among them were college presidents, leading scientists and men of letters, and specialists in many subjects. When the group of jurors to which I was assigned met for organization, Mr. Thomas Nelson Page,[9] who was one of the number, moved that I be made secretary of that division, and the motion was unanimously adopted. Nearly half of our division were Southern people. In performing my duties in the inspection of the exhibits of white schools I was in every case treated with respect, and at the close of our labours I parted from my associates with regret.

I am often asked to express myself more freely than I do upon the political condition and the political future of my race. These recollections of my experience in Atlanta give me the opportunity to do so briefly. My own belief is, although I have never before said so in so many words, that the time will come when the Negro in the South will be accorded all the political rights which his ability, character, and material possessions entitle him to. I think, though, that the opportunity to freely exercise such political rights will not come in any large degree through outside or artificial forcing, but will be accorded to the Negro by the Southern white people themselves, and that they will protect him in the exercise of those rights. Just as soon as the South gets over the old feeling that it is being forced by "foreigners," or "aliens," to do something which it does not want to do, I believe that the change in the direction that I have indicated is going to begin. In fact, there are indications that it is already beginning in a slight degree.

Let me illustrate my meaning. Suppose that some months before the opening of the Atlanta Exposition there had been a general demand from the press and public platform outside the South that a Negro be given a place on the opening programme, and that a Negro be placed upon the board of jurors of award. Would any such recognition of the race have taken place? I do not think so. The Atlanta officials went as far as they did because they felt it to be a pleasure, as well as a duty, to reward what they considered merit in the Negro race. Say what we will, there is something in human nature which we cannot blot out, which makes one man, in the end, recognize and reward merit in another, regardless of colour or race.

I believe it is the duty of the Negro—as the greater part of the race is already doing—to deport himself modestly in regard to political claims, depending upon the slow but sure influences that proceed from the possession of property, intelligence,

[9]Thomas Nelson Page, southern writer (1853–1922).

and high character for the full recognition of his political rights. I think that the according of the full exercise of political rights is going to be a matter of natural, slow growth, not an over-night, gourd-vine affair. I do not believe that the Negro should cease voting, for a man cannot learn the exercise of self-government by ceasing to vote, any more than a boy can learn to swim by keeping out of the water, but I do believe that in his voting he should more and more be influenced by those of intelligence and character who are his next-door neighbours.

I know coloured men who, through the encouragement, help, and advice of Southern white people, have accumulated thousands of dollars' worth of property, but who, at the same time, would never think of going to those same persons for advice concerning the casting of their ballots. This, it seems to me, is unwise and unreasonable, and should cease. In saying this I do not mean that the Negro should truckle, or not vote from principle, for the instant he ceases to vote from principle he loses the confidence and respect of the Southern white man even.

I do not believe that any state should make a law that permits an ignorant and poverty-stricken white man to vote, and prevents a black man in the same condition from voting. Such a law is not only unjust, but it will react, as all unjust laws do, in time; for the effect of such a law is to encourage the Negro to secure education and property, and at the same time it encourages the white man to remain in ignorance and poverty. I believe that in time, through the operation of intelligence and friendly race relations, all cheating at the ballot-box in the South will cease. It will become apparent that the white man who begins by cheating a Negro out of his ballot soon learns to cheat a white man out of his, and that the man who does this ends his career of dishonesty by the theft of property or by some equally serious crime. In my opinion, the time will come when the South will encourage all of its citizens to vote. It will see that it pays better, from every standpoint, to have healthy, vigorous life than to have that political stagnation which always results when one-half of the population has no share and no interest in the Government.

As a rule, I believe in universal, free suffrage, but I believe that in the South we are confronted with peculiar conditions that justify the protection of the ballot in many of the states, for a while at least, either by an educational test, a property test, or by both combined; but whatever tests are required, they should be made to apply with equal and exact justice to both races.

1901

W.E.B. Du Bois 1868–1963

At the turn of the twentieth century, William Edward Burghardt Du Bois, the most outspoken civil rights activist in America, committed himself to a style of political leadership which emphasized that, in order for African Americans to survive the inordinate stress and cruelty of racial discrimination, they had to make a ". . . determined attempt at self-development, self-realization, in spite of environing discouragement and prejudice." The style called upon African Americans to seek full exercise of civil rights in the United States through militant protest and agitation.

Du Bois's posture met with little popularity, for it was at the time that the nation had witnessed the undermining of the "Reconstruction Amendments"—which had given blacks the legal prerogatives of the vote, access to public facilities and services, and equal rights under the law—by the 1896 Supreme Court decision, *Plessy v. Fergusson* or the "separate but equal" doctrine. Rayford W. Logan, a noted historian, called the ensuing period of disfranchisement the "nadir" and betrayal of African American citizenship in the United States. Du Bois was undaunted in his conviction that, despite *Plessy v. Fergusson,* the Declaration of Independence and the Constitution of the United States were documents of entitlement and that the struggle of African Americans was a struggle for securing basic human and civil rights for *all* Americans. Hence, for Du Bois, the turn-of-the-century nadir signaled social and political conditions for blacks which made protest an absolute necessity.

Du Bois's political idealism was a product of his childhood observations of and participation in the civic activities of his home town and of his formal education in the 19th-century disciplines of history and sociology, both of which held firm to a belief in human progress and the perfectibility of man in society. Born in Great Barrington, Massachusetts, in 1868, Du Bois grew up in a typical New England small-town environment, where social and economic activities were reinforced by strong traditions in "primary democracy": all of its citizens had a right to be heard. The people of Great Barrington considered their community to be one with a moral purpose; thus, assuming social responsibility was an integral part of civic life. Having grown up in such an environment, Du Bois had little direct experience with the social, political, and economic exclusion of blacks before he went south to attend Fisk University in 1885.

After graduating from Fisk University, Du Bois went to Harvard, 1888 to 1892, where he completed a second baccalaureate degree in philosophy and a master's degree in history. He studied philosophy with William James, George Santayana, and Josiah Royce, whose thoughts on individualism, community, pragmatism, and the use of ideas to promote social change influenced Du Bois's thinking throughout his long career as an activist and writer. His advanced study led to his earning a Ph.D. in history at Harvard and the distinction of having his dissertation, *The Suppression of the Slave Trade in the United States of America,* published as the first volume of the *Harvard Historical Studies* in 1896.

The new social science held that one should seek the "truth" of the human history through an examination of a range of historical documents: the Congressional Record, the census, newspapers, private papers, and so forth. Study of such primary sources would allow the scholar to write a comprehensive view of any historical era or issue. During the initial period of his career, Du Bois utilized the new social science methodology as a researcher and teacher at Wilberforce University (1894–96), the University of Pennsylvania (1897), and Atlanta University (1897–1910). Between 1896 and 1905, he conducted studies of the urbanization of blacks in the North (*The Philadelphia Negro*) and the social organization of blacks in the rural South (*The Atlanta University Publications*). By 1900, however, having declared that "the problem of the twentieth century is the problem of the color line," he realized that his scholarly work reached a limited audience. He began experimenting with the literary forms in search of containers, as it were, for a kind of literature which portrayed the African American's social and cultural distinctiveness in ways the social sciences did not. Many of his experimental works—essays, poems, short stories, plays, dramatic sketches, and so on—were published in two magazines which he edited, the *Moon Illustrated Weekly* (1905) and the *Horizon* (1907–10). The poem "The Song of the Smoke," for example, was first published in the *Horizon* (February 1907); and, in many respects, its theme is characteristic of Du Bois's early work: an assertion of a positive disposition toward blackness for its beauty, its creativity and its service to mankind.

Du Bois also realized as early as 1900 that organized collective action by black people needed an institutional structure in order to be effective. In 1905, he was the principal founder of the Niagara Movement, a civil rights protest organization, in opposition to Booker T. Washington's conciliatory posture of accommodating racial discrimination. The organization called for direct action against racial discrimination through protest, through the use of the courts, and through education of the American people. Four years later, he was a principal organizer of the National Association for the Advancement of Colored People (NAACP). Its mission was identical to that of the Niagara Movement but its membership included both blacks and whites. From 1910 to 1934, as the NAACP Director of Publicity and Research and editor of its magazine (the *Crisis*), he combined his experimentation in literature, his understanding of American culture, and the rhetoric of protest. He was, for nearly a quarter century, the undisputed intellectual leader of a new generation of African Americans.

In 1934, Du Bois was fired from his post with the NAACP because he advocated use of segregation as a strategy for binding blacks into a cohesive group during the worst of the Depression years. Other officials of the organization felt such a strategy was against the NAACP's basic mission: seeking an integrated society. While Du Bois's strategy is little understood, nevertheless it remains the primary reason cited for his departure from the civil rights organization which he helped to found and to which he gave direction.

Although Du Bois returned to the NAACP as Director of Special Research from 1944 to 1948, 1934 marked the end of his influence in the organization and in the affairs of African American letters. Already a world leader by 1900, Du Bois dedicated his post-1934 years almost exclusively to world affairs. For almost two decades, to his death, he was identified as a sympathizer with world peace movements. In 1963, he became a citizen of Ghana, where he died in August of the same year.

Frederick Woodard
University of Iowa

PRIMARY WORKS

The Suppression of the African Slave Trade to the United States of America, 1896; *The Philadelphia Negro: A Social Study,* 1899; *Atlanta University Studies on the American Negro,* 19 volumes published between 1897 and 1915; *The Souls of Black Folk,* 1903; *John Brown,* 1909; *The Quest of the Silver Fleece,* 1911; *The Star of Ethiopia,* 1913; *The Negro,* 1916; *Darkwater,* 1920; *The Gift of the Negro,* 1924; *Dark Princess: Voices from Within the Veil,* 1928; *Black Reconstruction,* 1935; *Dusk of Dawn: An Essay Toward an Autobiography of a Race Concept,* 1940; *Color and Democracy: Colonies and Peace,* 1945; *The World and Africa,* 1947; *The Black Flame—A Trilogy: The Ordeal of Mansart, Mansart Builds a School, and Worlds of Color,* 1957, 1959 and 1961.

from The Souls of Black Folk

I Of Our Spiritual Strivings[1]

O water, voice of my heart, crying in the sand,
All night long crying with a mournful cry,
As I lie and listen, and cannot understand
The voice of my heart in my side or the voice of the sea,
O water, crying for rest, is it I, is it I?
All night long the water is crying to me.

Unresting water, there never shall be rest
Till the last moon droop and the last tide fail,
And the fire of the end begin to burn in the west;
And the heart shall be weary and wonder and cry like the sea,
All life long crying without avail,
As the water all night long is crying to me.

—ARTHUR SYMONS

Between me and the other world there is ever an unasked question: unasked by some through feelings of delicacy; by others through the difficulty of rightly framing it. All, nevertheless, flutter round it. They approach me in a half-hesitant sort of way, eye me curiously or compassionately, and then, instead of saying directly, How does it feel to be a problem? they say, I know an excellent colored man in my town; or, I fought at Mechanicsville; or, Do not these Southern outrages make your blood boil? At these

[1]The musical epigraph is taken from the spiritual, "Nobody Know the Trouble I've Seen," whose message of striving and salvation is translated into secular terms in Du Bois's chapter: "Sometimes I'm up, sometimes I'm down,/ Sometimes I'm almost to the ground./ Oh, nobody knows the trouble I've seen . . ." The chapter's famous passage on the veil that yields black men and women "no true self consciousness" may also be compared to the song's second verse: "One day when I was walking along, Oh yes, Lord—/ The element opened, and the Love came down, Oh yes Lord." There were numerous collections of spirituals at the turn of the century, but the musicological evidence suggests that Du Bois probably took his examples from J.B.T. Marsh, *The Story of the Jubilee Singers* (1872), and M. F. Armstrong and Helen W. Ludlow, *Hampton and Its Students, with Fifty Cabin and Plantation Songs,* arranged by Thomas P. Fenner (1874). Some of the songs mentioned in Chapter 14, "Of the Sorrow Songs," had been commented on by earlier collectors of spirituals such as William Allen in *Slave Songs in the United States* (1867). The most complete compilation in the early twentieth century was James Weldon Johnson and Rosamond Johnson's two-volume *Book of American Negro Spirituals* (1925, 1926).

I smile, or am interested, or reduce the boiling to a simmer, as the occasion may require. To the real question, How does it feel to be a problem? I answer seldom a word.

And yet, being a problem is a strange experience,—peculiar even for one who has never been anything else, save perhaps in babyhood and in Europe. It is in the early days of rollicking boyhood that the revelation first bursts upon one, all in a day, as it were. I remember well when the shadow swept across me. I was a little thing, away up in the hills of New England, where the dark Housatonic winds between Hoosac and Taghkanic to the sea. In a wee wooden schoolhouse, something put it into the boys' and girls' heads to buy gorgeous visiting-cards—ten cents a package—and exchange. The exchange was merry, till one girl, a tall newcomer, refused my card,—refused it peremptorily, with a glance. Then it dawned upon me with a certain suddenness that I was different from the others; or like, mayhap, in heart and life and longing, but shut out from their world by a vast veil. I had thereafter no desire to tear down that veil, to creep through; I held all beyond it in common contempt, and lived above it in a region of blue sky and great wandering shadows. That sky was bluest when I could beat my mates at examination time, or beat them at a foot-race, or even beat their stringy heads. Alas, with the years all this fine contempt began to fade; for the worlds I longed for, and all their dazzling opportunities, were theirs, not mine. But they should not keep these prizes, I said; some, all, I would wrest from them. Just how I would do it I could never decide: by reading law, by healing the sick, by telling the wonderful tales that swam in my head,—some way. With other black boys the strife was not so fiercely sunny: their youth shrunk into tasteless sycophancy, or into silent hatred of the pale world about them and mocking distrust of everything white; or wasted itself in a bitter cry, Why did God make me an outcast and a stranger in mine own house? The shades of the prison-house closed round about us all: walls strait and stubborn to the whitest, but relentlessly narrow, tall, and unscalable to sons of night who must plod darkly on in resignation, or beat unavailing palms against the stone, or steadily, half hopelessly, watch the streak of blue above.

After the Egyptian and Indian, the Greek and Roman, the Teuton and Mongolian, the Negro is a sort of seventh son, born with a veil, and gifted with second-sight in this American world,—a world which yields him no true self-consciousness, but only lets him see himself through the revelation of the other world. It is a peculiar sensation, this double-consciousness, this sense of always looking at one's self through the eyes of others, of measuring one's soul by the tape of a world that looks on in amused contempt and pity. One ever feels his two-ness,—an American, a Negro; two souls, two thoughts, two unreconciled strivings; two warring ideals in one dark body, whose dogged strength alone keeps it from being torn asunder.[2]

The history of the American Negro is the history of this strife,—this longing to attain self-conscious manhood, to merge his double self into a better and truer self. In this merging he wishes neither of the older selves to be lost. He would not Africanize America, for America has too much to teach the world and Africa. He would not

[2]This passage is often referred to as Du Bois's theory of the "double-consciousness." It is a "gift of second-sight" but it is also a curse of ambivalence.

bleach the Negro soul in a flood of white Americanism, for he knows that Negro blood has a message for the world. He simply wishes to make it possible for a man to be both a Negro and an American, without being cursed and spit upon by his fellows, without having the doors of Opportunity closed roughly in his face.

This, then, is the end of his striving: to be a co-worker in the kingdom of culture, to escape both death and isolation, to husband and use his best powers and his latent genius. These powers of body and mind have in the past been strangely wasted, dispersed, or forgotten. The shadow of a mighty Negro past flits through the tale of Ethiopia the Shadowy and of Egypt the Sphinx. Throughout history, the powers of single black men flash here and there like falling stars, and die sometimes before the world has rightly gauged their brightness. Here in America, in the few days since Emancipation, the black man's turning hither and thither in hesitant and doubtful striving has often made his very strength to lose effectiveness, to seem like absence of power, like weakness. And yet it is not weakness,—it is the contradiction of double aims. The double-aimed struggle of the black artisan—on the one hand to escape white contempt for a nation of mere hewers of wood and drawers of water, and on the other hand to plough and nail and dig for a poverty-stricken horde—could only result in making him a poor craftsman, for he had but half a heart in either cause. By the poverty and ignorance of his people, the Negro minister or doctor was tempted toward quackery and demagogy; and by the criticism of the other world, toward ideals that made him ashamed of his lowly tasks. The would-be black *savant* was confronted by the paradox that the knowledge his people needed was a twice-told tale to his white neighbors, while the knowledge which would teach the white world was Greek to his own flesh and blood. The innate love of harmony and beauty that set the ruder souls of his people a-dancing and a-singing raised but confusion and doubt in the soul of the black artist; for the beauty revealed to him was the soul-beauty of a race which his larger audience despised, and he could not articulate the message of another people. This waste of double aims, this seeking to satisfy two unreconciled ideals, has wrought sad havoc with the courage and faith and deeds of ten thousand thousand people,—has sent them often wooing false gods and invoking false means of salvation, and at times has even seemed about to make them ashamed of themselves.

Away back in the days of bondage they thought to see in one divine event the end of all doubt and disappointment; few men ever worshipped Freedom with half such unquestioning faith as did the American Negro for two centuries. To him, so far as he thought and dreamed, slavery was indeed the sum of all villainies, the cause of all sorrow, the root of all prejudice; Emancipation was the key to a promised land of sweeter beauty than ever stretched before the eyes of wearied Israelites. In song and exhortation swelled one refrain—Liberty; in his tears and curses the God he implored had Freedom in his right hand. At last it came,—suddenly, fearfully, like a dream. With one wild carnival of blood and passion came the message in his own plaintive cadences:—

> "Shout, O children!
> Shout, you're free!
> For God has bought your liberty!"

Years have passed away since then,—ten, twenty, forty; forty years of national life, forty years of renewal and development, and yet the swarthy spectre sits in its accustomed seat at the Nation's feast. In vain do we cry to this our vastest social problem:—

> "Take any shape but that, and my firm nerves
> Shall never tremble!"

The Nation has not yet found peace from its sins; the freedman has not yet found in freedom his promised land. Whatever of good may have come in these years of change, the shadow of a deep disappointment rests upon the Negro people,—a disappointment all the more bitter because the unattained ideal was unbounded save by the simple ignorance of a lowly people.

The first decade was merely a prolongation of the vain search for freedom, the boon that seemed ever barely to elude their grasp,—like a tantalizing will-of-the-wisp, maddening and misleading the headless host. The holocaust of war, the terrors of the Ku-Klux-Klan, the lies of carpet-baggers, the disorganization of industry, and the contradictory advice of friends and foes, left the bewildered serf with no new watchword beyond the old cry for freedom. As the time flew, however, he began to grasp a new idea. The ideal of liberty demanded for its attainment powerful means, and these the Fifteenth Amendment gave him. The ballot, which before he had looked upon as a visible sign of freedom, he now regarded as the chief means of gaining and perfecting the liberty with which war had partially endowed him. And why not? Had not votes made war and emancipated millions? Had not votes enfranchised the freedmen? Was anything impossible to a power that had done all this? A million black men started with renewed zeal to vote themselves into the kingdom. So the decade flew away, the revolution of 1876 came, and left the half-free serf weary, wondering, but still inspired. Slowly but steadily, in the following years, a new vision began gradually to replace the dream of political power,—a powerful movement, the rise of another ideal to guide the unguided, another pillar of fire by night after a clouded day. It was the ideal of "book-learning"; the curiosity, born of compulsory ignorance, to know and test the power of the cabalistic letters of the white man, the longing to know. Here at last seemed to have been discovered the mountain path to Canaan; longer than the highway of Emancipation and law, steep and ragged, but straight, leading to heights high enough to overlook life.

Up the new path the advance guard toiled, slowly, heavily, doggedly; only those who have watched and guided the faltering feet, the misty minds, the dull understandings, of the dark pupils of those schools know how faithfully, how piteously, this people strove to learn. It was weary work. The cold statistician wrote down the inches of progress here and there, noted also where here and there a foot had slipped or some one had fallen. To the tired climbers, the horizon was ever dark, the mists were often cold, the Canaan was always dim and far away. If, however, the vistas disclosed as yet no goal, no resting-place, little but flattery and criticism, the journey at least gave leisure for reflection and self-examination; it changed the child of Emancipation to the youth with dawning self-consciousness, self-realization, self-respect. In those sombre forests of his striving his own soul rose before him, and he saw himself,—darkly as through a veil; and yet he saw in himself some faint revelation of his power, of his mission. He began to have a dim feeling that, to attain his place in the world, he must be himself, and not another. For the first time he sought to analyze the burden he bore upon his back, that dead weight of social degradation partially masked behind a half-named Negro problem. He felt his poverty; without a cent, without a home, without land, tools, or savings, he had entered into competition with rich, landed, skilled neighbors. To be a poor man is hard, but to be a poor race in a land of dollars is the very bottom of hardships. He felt the weight of his ignorance,—not simply of letters, but of life, of business, of the humanities; the accumulated sloth and shirking and awkwardness of decades and centuries shackled his hands and feet. Nor was his burden all poverty and ignorance. The red stain of bastardy, which two centuries of systematic legal defilement of Negro women had stamped upon his race, meant not only the loss of ancient African chastity, but also the hereditary weight of a mass of corruption from white adulterers, threatening almost the obliteration of the Negro home.

A people thus handicapped ought not to be asked to race with the world, but rather allowed to give all its time and thought to its own social problems. But alas! while sociologists gleefully count his bastards and his prostitutes, the very soul of the toiling, sweating black man is darkened by the shadow of a vast despair. Men call the shadow prejudice, and learnedly explain it as the natural defence of culture against barbarism, learning against ignorance, purity against crime, the "higher" against the "lower" races. To which the Negro cries Amen! and swears that to so much of this strange prejudice as is founded on just homage to civilization, culture, righteousness, and progress, he humbly bows and meekly does obeisance. But before that nameless prejudice that leaps beyond all this he stands helpless, dismayed, and well-nigh speechless; before that personal disrespect and mockery, the ridicule and systematic humiliation, the distortion of fact and wanton license of fancy, the cynical ignoring of the better and the boisterous welcoming of the worse, the all-pervading desire to inculcate disdain for everything black, from Toussaint[3] to the devil,—before this there rises a sickening despair that would disarm and discourage any nation save that black host to whom "discouragement" is an unwritten word.

But the facing of so vast a prejudice could not but bring the inevitable self-questioning, self-disparagement, and lowering of ideals which ever accompany repression and breed in an atmosphere of contempt and hate. Whisperings and portents came borne upon the four winds: Lo! we are diseased and dying, cried the dark hosts; we cannot write, our voting is vain; what need of education, since we must always cook and serve? And the Nation echoed and enforced this self-criticism, saying: Be content to be servants, and nothing more; what need of higher culture for half-men? Away with the black man's ballot, by force or fraud,—and behold the suicide of a race! Nevertheless, out of the evil came something of good,—the more careful adjustment of education to real life, the clearer perception of the Negroes' social responsibilities, and the sobering realization of the meaning of progress.

So dawned the time of *Sturm und Drang:* storm and stress to-day rocks our little boat on the mad waters of the world-sea; there is within and without the sound of conflict, the burning of body and rending of soul; inspiration strives with doubt, and faith with vain questionings. The bright ideals of the past,—physical freedom, political

[3]Toussaint L'Overture, a Haitian general who led peasants against the French army in Haiti during time of the French Revolution. Du Bois refers to him as early as in *The Suppression of the Slave Trade.* Toussaint is a symbol, in many of Du Bois's works, of the undauntable spirit of black people in the New World.

power, the training of brains and the training of hands,—all these in turn have waxed and waned, until even the last grows dim and overcast. Are they all wrong,—all false? No, not that, but each alone was over-simple and incomplete,—the dreams of a credulous race-childhood, or the fond imaginings of the other world which does not know and does not want to know our power. To be really true, all these ideals must be melted and welded into one. The training of the schools we need to-day more than ever,—the training of deft hands, quick eyes and ears, and above all the broader, deeper, higher culture of gifted minds and pure hearts. The power of the ballot we need in sheer self-defence,—else what shall save us from a second slavery? Freedom, too, the long-sought, we still seek,—the freedom of life and limb, the freedom to work and think, the freedom to love and aspire. Work, culture, liberty,—all these we need, not singly but together, not successively but together, each growing and aiding each, and all striving toward that vaster ideal that swims before the Negro people, the ideal of human brotherhood, gained through the unifying ideal of Race; the ideal of fostering and developing the traits and talents of the Negro, not in opposition to or contempt for other races, but rather in large conformity to the greater ideals of the American Republic, in order that some day on American soil two world-races may give to each those characteristics both so sadly lack. We the darker ones come even now not altogether empty-handed: there are to-day no truer exponents of the pure human spirit of the Declaration of Independence than the American Negroes; there is no true American music but the wild sweet melodies of the Negro slave; the American fairy tales and folk-lore are Indian and African; and, all in all, we black men seem the sole oasis of simple faith and reverence in a dusty desert of dollars and smartness. Will America be poorer if she replace her brutal dyspeptic blundering with light-hearted but determined Negro humility? or her coarse and cruel wit with loving jovial good-humor? or her vulgar music with the soul of the Sorrow Songs?

Merely a concrete test of the underlying principles of the great republic is the Negro Problem, and the spiritual striving of the freedmen's sons is the travail of souls whose burden is almost beyond the measure of their strength, but who bear it in the name of an historic race, in the name of this the land of their fathers' fathers, and in the name of human opportunity.

And now what I have briefly sketched in large outline let me on coming pages tell again in many ways, with loving emphasis and deeper detail, that men may listen to the striving in the souls of black folk.

Chapter III Of Mr. Booker T. Washington and Others[4]

From birth till death enslaved; in word, in deed, unmanned!

. . . .

Hereditary bondsmen! Know ye not
Who would be free themselves must strike the blow?

—BYRON

[4]The musical epigraph in this case comes from the spiritual "A Great Camp-Meeting in the Promised Land," whose message of solidarity stands in contrast to Du Bois's criticism of Washington, though it may also indicate his admiration of his opponent's hard work and achievements: "Oh, walk together, children,/ Don't you get weary,/ Walk together, children,/ Don't you get weary,/ There's a great camp-meeting in the Promised Land."

Easily the most striking thing in the history of the American Negro since 1876 is the ascendancy of Mr. Booker T. Washington. It began at the time when war memories and ideals were rapidly passing; a day of astonishing commercial development was dawning; a sense of doubt and hesitation overtook the freedmen's sons,—then it was that his leading began. Mr. Washington came, with a single definite programme, at the psychological moment when the nation was a little ashamed of having bestowed so much sentiment on Negroes, and was concentrating its energies on Dollars. His programme of industrial education, conciliation of the South, and submission and silence as to civil and political rights, was not wholly original; the Free Negroes from 1830 up to war-time had striven to build industrial schools, and the American Missionary Association had from the first taught various trades; and Price and others had sought a way of honorable alliance with the best of the Southerners. But Mr. Washington first indissolubly linked these things; he put enthusiasm, unlimited energy, and perfect faith into his programme, and changed it from a by-path into a veritable Way of Life. And the tale of the methods by which he did this is a fascinating study of human life.

It startled the nation to hear a Negro advocating such a programme after many decades of bitter complaint; it startled and won the applause of the South, it interested and won the admiration of the North; and after a confused murmur of protest, it silenced if it did not convert the Negroes themselves.

To gain the sympathy and coöperation of the various elements comprising the white South was Mr. Washington's first task; and this, at the time Tuskegee was founded, seemed, for a black man, well-nigh impossible. And yet ten years later it was done in the word spoken at Atlanta: "In all things purely social we can be as separate as the five fingers, and yet one as the hand in all things essential to mutual progress." This "Atlanta Compromise" is by all odds the most notable thing in Mr. Washington's career. The South interpreted it in different ways: the radicals received it as a complete surrender of the demand for civil and political equality; the conservatives, as a generously conceived working basis for mutual understanding. So both approved it, and to-day its author is certainly the most distinguished Southerner since Jefferson Davis, and the one with the largest personal following.

Next to this achievement comes Mr. Washington's work in gaining place and consideration in the North. Others less shrewd and tactful had formerly essayed to sit on these two stools and had fallen between them; but as Mr. Washington knew the heart of the South from birth and training, so by singular insight he intuitively grasped the spirit of the age which was dominating the North. And so thoroughly did he learn the speech and thought of triumphant commercialism, and the ideals of material prosperity, that the picture of a lone black boy poring over a French grammar amid the weeds and dirt of a neglected home soon seemed to him the acme of absurdities. One wonders what Socrates and St. Francis of Assisi would say to this.

And yet this very singleness of vision and thorough oneness with his age is a mark of the successful man. It is as though Nature must needs make men narrow in order to give them force. So Mr. Washington's cult has gained unquestioning followers, his work has wonderfully prospered, his friends are legion, and his enemies are confounded. To-day he stands as the one recognized spokesman of his ten million fellows, and one of the most notable figures in a nation of seventy millions. One hesitates, therefore, to criticise a life which, beginning with so little, has done so much. And yet the time is come when one may speak in all sincerity and utter courtesy of the mistakes and shortcomings of Mr. Washington's career, as well as of his triumphs, without being thought captious or envious, and without forgetting that it is easier to do ill than well in the world.

The criticism that has hitherto met Mr. Washington has not always been of this broad character. In the South especially has he had to walk warily to avoid the harshest judgments,—and naturally so, for he is dealing with the one subject of deepest sensitiveness to that section. Twice—once when at the Chicago celebration of the Spanish-American War he alluded to the color-prejudice that is "eating away the vitals of the South," and once when he dined with President Roosevelt—has the resulting Southern criticism been violent enough to threaten seriously his popularity. In the North the feeling has several times forced itself into words, that Mr. Washington's counsels of submission overlooked certain elements of true manhood, and that his educational programme was unnecessarily narrow. Usually, however, such criticism has not found open expression, although, too, the spiritual sons of the Abolitionists have not been prepared to acknowledge that the schools founded before Tuskegee, by men of broad ideals and self-sacrificing spirit, were wholly failures or worthy of ridicule. While, then, criticism has not failed to follow Mr. Washington, yet the prevailing public opinion of the land has been but too willing to deliver the solution of a wearisome problem into his hands, and say, "If that is all you and your race ask, take it."

Among his own people, however, Mr. Washington has encountered the strongest and most lasting opposition, amounting at times to bitterness, and even today continuing strong and insistent even though largely silenced in outward expression by the public opinion of the nation. Some of this opposition is, of course, mere envy; the disappointment of displaced demagogues and the spite of narrow minds. But aside from this, there is among educated and thoughtful colored men in all parts of the land a feeling of deep regret, sorrow, and apprehension at the wide currency and ascendancy which some of Mr. Washington's theories have gained. These same men admire his sincerity of purpose, and are willing to forgive much to honest endeavor which is doing something worth the doing. They coöperate with Mr. Washington as far as they conscientiously can; and, indeed, it is no ordinary tribute to this man's tact and power that, steering as he must between so many diverse interests and opinions, he so largely retains the respect of all.

But the hushing of the criticism of honest opponents is a dangerous thing. It leads some of the best of the critics to unfortunate silence and paralysis of effort, and others to burst into speech so passionately and intemperately as to lose listeners. Honest and earnest criticism from those whose interests are most nearly touched,—criticism of writers by readers, of government by those governed, of leaders by those led,—this is the soul of democracy and the safeguard of modern society. If the best of the American Negroes receive by outer pressure a leader whom they had not recognized before, manifestly there is here a certain palpable gain. Yet there is also irreparable loss,—a loss of that peculiarly valuable education which a group receives when by search and criticism it finds and commissions its own leaders. The way in which this is done is at once the most elementary and the nicest problem of social growth. History is but the record of such group-leadership; and yet how infinitely changeful is its type and character! And of all types and kinds, what can be more instructive than the leadership of a group within a group?—that curious double movement where real progress may be negative and actual advance be relative retrogression. All this is the social student's inspiration and despair.

Now in the past the American Negro has had instructive experience in the choosing of group leaders, founding thus a peculiar dynasty which in the light of present conditions is worth while studying. When sticks and stones and beasts form the sole environment of a people, their attitude is largely one of determined opposition to and conquest of natural forces. But when to earth and brute is added an environment of men and ideas, then the attitude of the imprisoned group may take three main forms,—a feeling of revolt and revenge; an attempt to adjust all thought and action to the will of the greater group; or, finally, a determined effort at self-realization and self-development despite environing opinion. The influence of all of these attitudes at various times can be traced in the history of the American Negro, and in the evolution of his successive leaders.

Before 1750, while the fire of African freedom still burned in the veins of the slaves, there was in all leadership or attempted leadership but the one motive of revolt and revenge,—typified in the terrible Maroons, the Danish blacks, and Cato of Stono, and veiling all the Americas in fear of insurrection. The liberalizing tendencies of the latter half of the eighteenth century brought, along with kindlier relations between black and white, thoughts of ultimate adjustment and assimilation. Such aspiration was especially voiced in the earnest songs of Phyllis, in the martyrdom of Attucks, the fighting of Salem and Poor, the intellectual accomplishments of Banneker and Derham, and the political demands of the Cuffes.

Stern financial and social stress after the war cooled much of the previous humanitarian ardor. The disappointment and impatience of the Negroes at the persistence of slavery and serfdom voiced itself in two movements. The slaves in the South, aroused undoubtedly by vague rumors of the Haytian revolt, made three fierce attempts at insurrection,—in 1800 under Gabriel in Virginia, in 1822 under Vesey in Carolina, and in 1831 again in Virginia under the terrible Nat Turner. In the Free States, on the other hand, a new and curious attempt at self-development was made. In Philadelphia and New York color-prescription led to a withdrawal of Negro communicants from white churches and the formation of a peculiar socio-religious institution among the Negroes known as the African Church,—an organization still living and controlling in its various branches over a million of men.

Walker's wild appeal against the trend of the times showed how the world was changing after the coming of the cotton-gin. By 1830 slavery seemed hopelessly fastened on the South, and the slaves thoroughly cowed into submission. The free Negroes of the North, inspired by the mulatto immigrants from the West Indies, began to change the basis of their demands; they recognized the slavery of slaves, but insisted that they themselves were freemen, and sought assimilation and amalgamation with the nation on the same terms with other men. Thus, Forten and Purvis of Philadelphia, Shad of Wilmington, Du Bois of New Haven, Barbadoes of Boston, and others, strove singly and together as men, they said, not as slaves; as "people of color," not as "Negroes." The trend of the times, however, refused them recognition save in individual and exceptional cases, considered them as one with all the despised blacks, and they soon found themselves striving to keep even the rights they formerly had of voting and working and moving as freemen. Schemes of migration and colonization arose among them; but these they refused to entertain, and they eventually turned to the Abolition movement as a final refuge.

Here, led by Remond, Nell, Wells-Brown, and Douglass, a new period of self-assertion and self-development dawned. To be sure, ultimate freedom and assimilation was the ideal before the leaders, but the assertion of the manhood rights of the Negro by himself was the main reliance, and John Brown's raid was the extreme of its logic. After the war and emancipation, the great form of Frederick Douglass, the greatest of American Negro leaders, still led the host. Self-assertion, especially in political lines, was the main programme, and behind Douglass came Elliot, Bruce, and Langston, and the Reconstruction politicians, and, less conspicuous but of greater social significance, Alexander Crummell and Bishop Daniel Payne.

Then came the Revolution of 1876, the suppression of the Negro votes, the changing and shifting of ideals, and the seeking of new lights in the great night. Douglass, in his old age, still bravely stood for the ideals of his early manhood,—ultimate assimilation *through* self-assertion, and on no other terms. For a time Price arose as a new leader, destined, it seemed, not to give up, but to re-state the old ideals in a form less repugnant to the white South. But he passed away in his prime. Then came the new leader. Nearly all the former ones had become leaders by the silent suffrage of their fellows, had sought to lead their own people alone, and were usually, save Douglass, little known outside their race. But Booker T. Washington arose as essentially the leader not of one race but of two,—a compromiser between the South, the North, and the Negro. Naturally the Negroes resented, at first bitterly, signs of compromise which surrendered their civil and political rights, even though this was to be exchanged for larger chances of economic development. The rich and dominating North, however, was not only weary of the race problem, but was investing largely in Southern enterprises, and welcomed any method of peaceful coöperation. Thus, by national opinion, the Negroes began to recognize Mr. Washington's leadership; and the voice of criticism was hushed.

Mr. Washington represents in Negro thought the old attitude of adjustment and submission; but adjustment at such a peculiar time as to make his programme unique. This is an age of unusual economic development, and Mr. Washington's programme naturally takes an economic cast, becoming a gospel of Work and Money to such an extent as apparently almost completely to overshadow the higher aims of life. Moreover, this is an age when the more advanced races are coming in closer contact with the less developed races, and the race-feeling is therefore intensified; and Mr. Washington's programme practically accepts the alleged inferiority of the Negro races. Again, in our own land, the reaction from the sentiment of war time has given impetus to race-prejudice against Negroes, and Mr. Washington withdraws many of the high demands of Negroes as men and American citizens. In other periods of intensified prejudice all the Negro's tendency to self-assertion has been called forth; at this period a policy of submission is advocated. In the history of nearly all other races and peoples the doctrine preached at such crises has been that manly self-respect is worth more than lands and houses, and that a people who voluntarily surrender such respect, or cease striving for it, are not worth civilizing.

In answer to this, it has been claimed that the Negro can survive only through submission. Mr. Washington distinctly asks that black people give up, at least for the present, three things,—

First, political power,

Second, insistence on civil rights,

Third, higher education of Negro youth,—

and concentrate all their energies on industrial education, and accumulation of wealth, and the conciliation of the South. This policy has been courageously and insistently advocated for over fifteen years, and has been triumphant for perhaps ten years. As a result of this tender of the palm-branch, what has been the return? In these years there have occurred:

1. The disfranchisement of the Negro.
2. The legal creation of a distinct status of civil inferiority for the Negro.
3. The steady withdrawal of aid from institutions for the higher training of the Negro.

These movements are not, to be sure, direct results of Mr. Washington's teachings; but his propaganda has, without a shadow of doubt, helped their speedier accomplishment. The question then comes: Is it possible, and probable, that nine millions of men can make effective progress in economic lines if they are deprived of political rights, made a servile caste, and allowed only the most meagre chance for developing their exceptional men? If history and reason give any distinct answer to these questions, it is an emphatic *No.* And Mr. Washington thus faces the triple paradox of his career:

1. He is striving nobly to make Negro artisans business men and property-owners; but it is utterly impossible, under modern competitive methods, for workingmen and property-owners to defend their rights and exist without the right of suffrage.
2. He insists on thrift and self-respect, but at the same time counsels a silent submission to civic inferiority such as is bound to sap the manhood of any race in the long run.
3. He advocates common-school and industrial training, and depreciates institutions of higher learning; but neither the Negro common-schools, nor Tuskegee itself, could remain open a day were it not for teachers trained in Negro colleges, or trained by their graduates.

This triple paradox in Mr. Washington's position is the object of criticism by two classes of colored Americans. One class is spiritually descended from Toussaint the Savior, through Gabriel, Vesey, and Turner, and they represent the attitude of revolt and revenge; they hate the white South blindly and distrust the white race generally, and so far as they agree on definite action, think that the Negro's only hope lies in emigration beyond the borders of the United States. And yet, by the irony of fate, nothing has more effectually made this programme seem hopeless than the recent course of the United States toward weaker and darker peoples in the West Indies, Hawaii, and the Philippines,—for where in the world may we go and be safe from lying and brute force?

The other class of Negroes who cannot agree with Mr. Washington has hitherto said little aloud. They deprecate the sight of scattered counsels, of internal disagreement; and especially they dislike making their just criticism of a useful and earnest man an excuse for a general discharge of venom from small-minded opponents. Nevertheless, the questions involved are so fundamental and serious that it is difficult to see how men like the Grimkes, Kelly Miller, J. W. E. Bowen, and other representatives of this group, can much longer be silent. Such men feel in conscience bound to ask of this nation three things:

1. The right to vote.
2. Civic equality.
3. The education of youth according to ability.

They acknowledge Mr. Washington's invaluable service in counselling patience and courtesy in such demands; they do not ask that ignorant black men vote when ignorant whites are debarred, or that any reasonable restrictions in the suffrage should not be applied; they know that the low social level of the mass of the race is responsible for much discrimination against it, but they also know, and the nation knows, that relentless color-prejudice is more often a cause than a result of the Negro's degradation; they seek the abatement of this relic of barbarism, and not its systematic encouragement and pampering by all agencies of social power from the Associated Press to the Church of Christ. They advocate, with Mr. Washington, a broad system of Negro common schools supplemented by thorough industrial training; but they are surprised that a man of Mr. Washington's insight cannot see that no such educational system ever has rested or can rest on any other basis than that of the well-equipped college and university, and they insist that there is a demand for a few such institutions throughout the South to train the best of the Negro youth as teachers, professional men, and leaders.

This group of men honor Mr. Washington for his attitude of conciliation toward the white South; they accept the "Atlanta Compromise" in its broadest interpretation; they recognize, with him, many signs of promise, many men of high purpose and fair judgment, in this section; they know that no easy task has been laid upon a region already tottering under heavy burdens. But, nevertheless, they insist that the way to truth and right lies in straightforward honesty, not in indiscriminate flattery; in praising those of the South who do well and criticising uncompromisingly those who do ill; in taking advantage of the opportunities at hand and urging their fellows to do the same, but at the same time in remembering that only a firm adherence to their higher ideals and aspirations will ever keep those ideals within the realm of possibility. They do not expect that the free right to vote, to enjoy civic rights, and to be educated, will come in a moment; they do not expect to see the bias and prejudices of years disappear at the blast of a trumpet; but they are absolutely certain that the way for a people to gain their reasonable rights is not by voluntarily throwing them away and insisting that they do not want them; that the way for a people to gain respect is not by continually belittling and ridiculing themselves; that, on the contrary, Negroes must insist continually, in season and out of season, that voting is necessary to modern manhood, that color discrimination is barbarism, and that black boys need education as well as white boys.

In failing thus to state plainly and unequivocally the legitimate demands of their people, even at the cost of opposing an honored leader, the thinking classes of American Negroes would shirk a heavy responsibility,—a responsibility to themselves, a responsibility to the struggling masses, a responsibility to the darker races of men whose future depends so largely on this American experiment, but especially a responsibility to this nation,—this common Fatherland. It is wrong to encourage a man or a people in evil-doing; it is wrong to aid and abet a national crime simply because it is unpopular not to do so. The growing spirit of kindliness and reconciliation between the North and South after the frightful difference of a generation ago ought to be a source of deep congratulation to all, and especially to those whose mistreatment caused the war; but if that reconciliation is to be marked by the industrial slavery and civic death of those same black men, with permanent legislation into a position of inferiority, then those black men, if they are really men, are called upon by every consideration of patriotism and loyalty to oppose such a course by all civilized methods, even though such opposition involves disagreement with Mr. Booker T. Washington. We have no right to sit silently by while the inevitable seeds are sown for a harvest of disaster to our children, black and white.

First, it is the duty of black men to judge the South discriminatingly. The present generation of Southerners are not responsible for the past, and they should not be blindly hated or blamed for it. Furthermore, to no class is the indiscriminate endorsement of the recent course of the South toward Negroes more nauseating than to the best thought of the South. The South is not "solid"; it is a land in the ferment of social change, wherein forces of all kinds are fighting for supremacy; and to praise the ill the South is today perpetrating is just as wrong as to condemn the good. Discriminating and broad-minded criticism is what the South needs,—needs it for the sake of her own white sons and daughters, and for the insurance of robust, healthy mental and moral development.

To-day even the attitude of the Southern whites toward the blacks is not, as so many assume, in all cases the same; the ignorant Southerner hates the Negro, the workingmen fear his competition, the money-makers wish to use him as a laborer, some of the educated see a menace in his upward development, while others—usually the sons of the masters—wish to help him to rise. National opinion has enabled this last class to maintain the Negro common schools, and to protect the Negro partially in property, life, and limb. Through the pressure of the money-makers, the Negro is in danger of being reduced to semi-slavery, especially in the country districts; the workingmen, and those of the educated who fear the Negro, have united to disfranchise him, and some have urged his deportation; while the passions of the ignorant are easily aroused to lynch and abuse any black man. To praise this intricate whirl of thought and prejudice is nonsense; to inveigh indiscriminately against "the South" is unjust; but to use the same breath in praising Governor Aycock, exposing Senator Morgan, arguing with Mr. Thomas Nelson Page, and denouncing Senator Ben Tillman, is not only sane, but the imperative duty of thinking black men.

It would be unjust to Mr. Washington not to acknowledge that in several instances he has opposed movements in the South which were unjust to the Negro; he sent memorials to the Louisiana and Alabama constitutional conventions, he has spoken against lynching, and in other ways has openly or silently set his influence against sinister schemes and unfortunate happenings. Notwithstanding this, it is equally true to assert that on the whole the distinct impression left by Mr. Washington's propaganda is, first, that the South is justified in its present attitude toward the Negro because of the Negro's degradation; secondly, that the prime cause of the Negro's failure to rise more quickly is his wrong education in the past; and, thirdly, that his future rise depends primarily on his own efforts. Each of these propositions is a dangerous half-truth. The supplementary truths must never be lost sight of: first, slavery and race-prejudice are potent if not sufficient causes of the Negro's position; second, industrial and common-school training were necessarily slow in planting because they had to await the black teachers trained by higher institutions,—it being extremely doubtful if any essentially different development was possible, and certainly a Tuskegee was unthinkable before 1880; and, third, while it is a great truth to say that the Negro must strive and strive mightily to help himself, it is equally true that unless his striving be not simply seconded, but rather aroused and encouraged, by the initiative of the richer and wiser environing group, he cannot hope for great success.

In his failure to realize and impress this last point, Mr. Washington is especially to be criticised. His doctrine has tended to make the whites, North and South, shift the burden of the Negro problem to the Negro's shoulders and stand aside as critical and rather pessimistic spectators; when in fact the burden belongs to the nation, and the hands of none of us are clean if we bend not our energies to righting these great wrongs.

The South ought to be led, by candid and honest criticism, to assert her better self and do her full duty to the race she has cruelly wronged and is still wronging. The North—her co-partner in guilt—cannot salve her conscience by plastering it with gold. We cannot settle this problem by diplomacy and suaveness, by "policy" alone. If worse come to worst, can the moral fibre of this country survive the slow throttling and murder of nine millions of men?

The black men of America have a duty to perform, a duty stern and delicate,—a forward movement to oppose a part of the work of their greatest leader. So far as Mr. Washington preaches Thrift, Patience, and Industrial Training for the masses, we must hold up his hands and strive with him, rejoicing in his honors and glorying in the strength of this Joshua called of God and of man to lead the headless host. But so far as Mr. Washington apologizes for injustice, North or South, does not rightly value the privilege and duty of voting, belittles the emasculating effects of caste distinctions, and opposes the higher training and ambition of our brighter minds,—so far as he, the South, or the Nation, does this,—we must unceasingly and firmly oppose them. By every civilized and peaceful method we must strive for the rights which the world accords to men, clinging unwaveringly to those great words which the sons of the Fathers would fain forget: "We hold these truths to be self-evident: That all men are created equal; that they are endowed by their Creator with certain unalienable rights; that among these are life, liberty, and the pursuit of happiness."

XIV Of the Sorrow Songs[5]

I walk through the churchyard
To lay this body down;
I know moon-rise, I know star-rise;
I walk in the moonlight, I walk in the starlight;
I'll lie in the grave and stretch out my arms,
I'll go to judgment in the evening of the day,
And my soul and thy soul shall meet that day,
When I lay this body down.

NEGRO SONG

They that walked in darkness sang songs in the olden days—Sorrow Songs—for they were weary at heart. And so before each thought that I have written in this book I have set a phrase, a haunting echo of these weird old songs in which the soul of the black slave spoke to men. Ever since I was a child these songs have stirred me strangely. They came out of the South unknown to me, one by one, and yet at once I knew them as of me and of mine. Then in after years when I came to Nashville I saw the great temple builded of these songs towering over the pale city. To me Jubilee Hall seemed ever made of the songs themselves, and its bricks were red with the blood and dust of toil. Out of them rose for me morning, noon, and night, bursts of wonderful melody, full of the voices of my brothers and sisters, full of the voices of the past.

Little of beauty has America given the world save the rude grandeur God himself stamped on her bosom; the human spirit in this new world has expressed itself in vigor and ingenuity rather than in beauty. And so by fateful chance the Negro folk-song—the rhythmic cry of the slave—stands to-day not simply as the sole American music, but as the most beautiful expression of human experience born this side the seas. It has been neglected, it has been, and is, half despised, and above all it has been persistently mistaken and misunderstood; but notwithstanding, it still remains as the singular spiritual heritage of the nation and the greatest gift of the Negro people.

[5] The musical epigraph in Du Bois's final chapter comes from "Wrestling Jacob": "Wrestling Jacob, Jacob, day is a-breaking,/ Wrestling Jacob, Jacob, I will not let thee go . . . Until thou bless me." The spiritual speaks of Jacob's wrestling with the angel in Genesis 32, which signifies the triumph and reconciliation that make him a patriarch of Israel. In this chapter, which is saturated with the songs of the African American past, Du Bois likewise suggests that he has struggled with the patriarchs of his own tradition in order to become a leader and to create a new cultural language that combines music and oratory.

Away back in the thirties the melody of these slave songs stirred the nation, but the songs were soon half forgotten. Some, like "Near the lake where drooped the willow," passed into current airs and their source was forgotten; others were caricatured on the "minstrel" stage and their memory died away. Then in war-time came the singular Port Royal experiment after the capture of Hilton Head, and perhaps for the first time the North met the Southern slave face to face and heart to heart with no third witness. The Sea Islands of the Carolinas, where they met, were filled with a black folk of primitive type, touched and moulded less by the world about them than any others outside the Black Belt. Their appearance was uncouth, their language funny, but their hearts were human and their singing stirred men with a mighty power. Thomas Wentworth Higginson hastened to tell of these songs, and Miss McKim and others urged upon the world their rare beauty. But the world listened only half credulously until the Fisk Jubilee Singers sang the slave songs so deeply into the world's heart that it can never wholly forget them again.

There was once a blacksmith's son born at Cadiz, New York, who in the changes of time taught school in Ohio and helped defend Cincinnati from Kirby Smith. Then he fought at Chancellorsville and Gettysburg and finally served in the Freedman's Bureau at Nashville. Here he formed a Sunday-school class of black children in 1866, and sang with them and taught them to sing. And then they taught him to sing, and when once the glory of the Jubilee songs passed into the soul of George L. White, he knew his life-work was to let those Negroes sing to the world as they had sung to him. So in 1871 the pilgrimage of the Fisk Jubilee Singers began. North to Cincinnati they rode,—four half-clothed black boys and five girl-women,—led by a man with a cause and a purpose. They stopped at Wilberforce, the oldest of Negro schools, where a black bishop blessed them. Then they went, fighting cold and starvation, shut out of hotels, and cheerfully sneered at, ever northward; and ever the magic of their song kept thrilling hearts, until a burst of applause in the Congregational Council at Oberlin revealed them to the world. They came to New York and Henry Ward Beecher dared to welcome them, even though the metropolitan dailies sneered at his "Nigger Minstrels." So their songs conquered till they sang across the land and across the sea, before Queen and Kaiser, in Scotland and Ireland, Holland and Switzerland. Seven years they sang, and brought back a hundred and fifty thousand dollars to found Fisk University.

Since their day they have been imitated—sometimes well, by the singers of Hampton and Atlanta, sometimes ill, by straggling quartettes. Caricature has sought again to spoil the quaint beauty of the music, and has filled the air with many debased melodies which vulgar ears scarce know from the real. But the true Negro folk-song still lives in the hearts of those who have heard them truly sung and in the hearts of the Negro people.

What are these songs, and what do they mean? I know little of music and can say nothing in technical phrase, but I know something of men, and knowing them, I know that these songs are the articulate message of the slave to the world. They tell us in these eager days that life was joyous to the black slave, careless and happy. I can easily believe this of some, of many. But not all the past South, though it rose from the dead, can gainsay the heart-touching witness of these songs. They are the music of an unhappy people, of the children of disappointment; they tell of death and suffering and unvoiced longing toward a truer world, of misty wanderings and hidden ways.

The songs are indeed the siftings of centuries; the music is far more ancient than the words, and in it we can trace here and there signs of development. My grandfather's grandmother was seized by an evil Dutch trader two centuries ago; and coming to the valleys of the Hudson and Housatonic, black, little, and lithe, she shivered and shrank in the harsh north winds, looked longingly at the hills, and often crooned a heathen melody to the child between her knees, thus:

Do ba-na co-ba, ge-ne me, ge-ne me!
Do ba-na co-ba, ge-ne me, ge-ne me!
Ben d'nu-li, nu-li, nu-li, nu-li, ben d'le.

The child sang it to his children and they to their children's children, and so two hundred years it has travelled down to us and we sing it to our children, knowing as little as our fathers what its words may mean, but knowing well the meaning of its music.

This was primitive African music; it may be seen in larger form in the strange chant which heralds "The Coming of John":

"You may bury me in the East,
You may bury me in the West,
But I'll hear the trumpet sound in that morning."

—the voice of exile.

Ten master songs, more or less, one may pluck from this forest of melody—songs of undoubted Negro origin and wide popular currency, and songs peculiarly characteristic of the slave. One of these I have just mentioned. Another whose strains begin this book is "Nobody knows the trouble I've seen." When, struck with a sudden poverty, the United States refused to fulfill its promises of land to the freedmen, a brigadier-general went down to the Sea Islands to carry the news. An old woman on the outskirts of the throng began singing this song; all the mass joined with her, swaying. And the soldier wept.

The third song is the cradle-song of death which all men know,—"Swing low, sweet chariot,"—whose bars begin the life story of "Alexander Crummell." Then there is the song of many waters, "Roll, Jordan, roll," a mighty chorus with minor cadences. There were many songs of the fugitive like that which opens "The Wings of Atalanta," and the more familiar "Been a-listening." The seventh is the song of the End and the Beginning—"My Lord, what a mourning! when the stars begin to fall"; a strain of this is placed before "The Dawn of Freedom." The song of groping—"My way's cloudy"—begins "The Meaning of Progress"; the ninth is the song of this chapter—"Wrestlin' Jacob, the day is a-breaking,"—a paean of hopeful strife. The last master song is the song of songs—"Steal away,"—sprung from "The Faith of the Fathers."

There are many others of the Negro folk-songs as striking and characteristic as these, as, for instance, the three strains in the third, eighth, and ninth chapters; and others I am sure could easily make a selection on more scientific principles. There are, too, songs that seem to be a step removed from the more primitive types: there is the maze-like medley, "Bright sparkles," one phrase of which heads "The Black Belt"; the Easter carol, "Dust, dust and ashes"; the dirge, "My mother's took her flight and gone home"; and that burst of melody hovering over "The Passing of the First-Born"—"I hope my mother will be there in that beautiful world on high."

These represent a third step in the development of the slave song, of which "You may bury me in the East" is the first, and songs like "March on" (chapter six) and "Steal away" are the second. The first is African music, the second Afro-American, while the third is a blending of Negro music with the music heard in the foster land. The result is still distinctively Negro and the method of blending original, but the elements are both Negro and Caucasian. One might go further and find a fourth step in this development, where the songs of white America have been distinctively influenced by the slave songs or have incorporated whole phrases of Negro melody, as "Swanee River" and "Old Black Joe." Side by side, too, with the growth has gone the debasements and imitations—the Negro "minstrel" songs, many of the "gospel" hymns, and some of the contemporary "coon" songs,—a mass of music in which the novice may easily lose himself and never find the real Negro melodies.

In these songs, I have said, the slave spoke to the world. Such a message is naturally veiled and half articulate. Words and music have lost each other and new and cant phrases of a dimly understood theology have displaced the older sentiment. Once in a while we catch a strange word of an unknown tongue, as the "Mighty Myo," which figures as a river of death; more often slight words or mere doggerel are joined to music of singular sweetness. Purely secular songs are few in number, partly because many of them were turned into hymns by a change of words, partly because the frolics were seldom heard by the stranger, and the music less often caught. Of nearly all the songs, however, the music is distinctly sorrowful. The ten master songs I have mentioned tell in word and music of trouble and exile, of strife and hiding; they grope toward some unseen power and sigh for rest in the End.

The words that are left to us are not without interest, and, cleared of evident dross, they conceal much of real poetry and meaning beneath conventional theology and unmeaning rhapsody. Like all primitive folk, the slave stood near to Nature's heart. Life was a "rough and rolling sea" like the brown Atlantic of the Sea Islands; the "Wilderness" was the home of God, and the "lonesome valley" led to the way of life. "Winter'll soon be over," was the picture of life and death to a tropical imagination. The sudden wild thunder-storms of the South awed and impressed the Negroes,—at times the rumbling seemed to them "mournful," at times imperious:

"My Lord calls me,
He calls me by the thunder,
The trumpet sounds it in my soul."

The monotonous toil and exposure is painted in many words. One sees the ploughmen in the hot, moist furrow, singing:

"Dere's no rain to wet you,
Dere's no sun to burn you,
Oh, push along, believer,
I want to go home."

The bowed and bent old man cries, with thrice-repeated wail:

"O Lord, keep me from sinking down,"

and he rebukes the devil of doubt who can whisper:

"Jesus is dead and God's gone away."

Yet the soul-hunger is there, the restlessness of the savage, the wail of the wanderer, and the plaint is put in one little phrase:

My soul wants something that's new, that's new

Over the inner thoughts of the slaves and their relations one with another the shadow of fear ever hung, so that we get but glimpses here and there, and also with them, eloquent omissions and silences. Mother and child are sung, but seldom father; fugitive and weary wanderer call for pity and affection, but there is little of wooing and wedding; the rocks and the mountains are well known, but home is unknown. Strange blending of love and helplessness signs through the refrain:

"Yonder's my ole mudder,
Been waggin' at de hill so long;
'Bout time she cross over,
Git home bime-by."

Elsewhere comes the cry of the "motherless" and the "Farewell, farewell, my only child."

Love-songs are scarce and fall into two categories—the frivolous and light, and the sad. Of deep successful love there is ominous silence, and in one of the oldest of these songs there is a depth of history and meaning:

Poor Ro-sy, poor gal; Poor Ro-sy,
poor gal; Ro-sy break my poor heart,
Heav'n shall-a-be my home.

A black woman said of the song, "It can't be sung without a full heart and a troubled sperrit." The same voice sings here that sings in the German folk-song:

"Jetz Geh i' an's brunele, trink' aber net."

Of death the Negro showed little fear, but talked of it familiarly and even fondly as simply a crossing of the waters, perhaps—who knows?—back to his ancient forests again. Later days transfigured his fatalism, and amid the dust and dirt the toiler sang:

"Dust, dust and ashes, fly over my grave,
But the Lord shall bear my spirit home."

The things evidently borrowed from the surrounding world undergo characteristic change when they enter the mouth of the slave. Especially is this true of Bible phrases. "Weep, O captive daughter of Zion," is quaintly turned into "Zion, weep-a-low," and the wheels of Ezekiel are turned every way in the mystic dreaming of the slave, till he says:

"There's a little wheel a-turnin' in-a-my heart."

As in olden time, the words of these hymns were improvised by some leading minstrel of the religious band. The circumstances of the gathering, however, the rhythm of the songs, and the limitations of allowable thought, confined the poetry for the most part to single or double lines, and they seldom were expanded to quatrains or longer tales, although there are some few examples of sustained efforts, chiefly paraphrases of the Bible. Three short series of verses have always attracted me,—the one that heads this chapter, of one line of which Thomas Wentworth Higginson has fittingly said, "Never, it seems to me, since man first lived and suffered was his infinite longing for peace uttered more plaintively." The second and third are descriptions of the Last Judgment,—the one a late improvisation, with some traces of outside influence:

> "Oh, the stars in the elements are falling,
> And the moon drips away into blood,
> And the ransomed of the Lord are returning unto God,
> Blessed be the name of the Lord."

And the other earlier and homelier picture from the low coast lands:

> "Michael, haul the boat ashore,
> Then you'll hear the horn they blow,
> Then you'll hear the trumpet sound,
> Trumpet sound the world around,
> Trumpet sound for rich and poor,
> Trumpet sound for Jubilee,
> Trumpet sound for you and me."

Through all the sorrow of the Sorrow Songs there breathes a hope—a faith in the ultimate justice of things. The minor cadences of despair change often to triumph and calm confidence. Sometimes it is faith in life, sometimes a faith in death, sometimes assurance of boundless justice in some fair world beyond. But whichever it is, the meaning is always clear: that sometime, somewhere, men will judge men by their souls and not by their skins. Is such a hope justified? Do the Sorrow Songs sing true?

The silently growing assumption of this age is that the probation of races is past, and that the backward races of to-day are of proven inefficiency and not worth the saving. Such an assumption is the arrogance of peoples irreverent toward Time and ignorant of the deeds of men. A thousand years ago such an assumption, easily possible, would have made it difficult for the Teuton to prove his right to life. Two thousand years ago such dogmatism, readily welcome, would have scouted the idea of blond races ever leading civilization. So wofully unorganized is sociological knowledge that the meaning of progress, the meaning of "swift" and "slow" in human doing, and the limits of human perfectability, are veiled, unanswered sphinxes on the shores of science. Why should Æschylus have sung two thousand years before Shakespeare was born? Why has civilization flourished in Europe, and flickered, flamed, and died in Africa? So long as the world stands meekly dumb before such questions, shall this nation proclaim its ignorance and unhallowed prejudices by denying freedom of opportunity to those who brought the Sorrow Songs to the Seats of the Mighty?

Your country? How came it yours? Before the Pilgrims landed we were here. Here we have brought our three gifts and mingled them with yours: a gift of story and song—soft, stirring melody in an ill-harmonized and unmelodious land; the gift of sweat and brawn to beat back the wilderness, conquer the soil, and lay the foundations of this vast economic empire two hundred years earlier than your weak hands could have done it; the third, a gift of the Spirit. Around us the history of the land has centred for thrice a hundred years; out of the nation's heart we have called all that was best to throttle and subdue all that was worst; fire and blood, prayer and sacrifice, have billowed over this people, and they have found peace only in the altars of the God of Right. Nor has our gift of the Spirit been merely passive. Actively we have woven ourselves with the very warp and woof of this nation,—we fought their battles, shared their sorrow, mingled our blood with theirs, and generation after generation have pleaded with a headstrong, careless people to despise not Justice, Mercy, and Truth, lest the nation be smitten with a curse. Our song, our toil, our cheer, and warning have been given to this nation in blood-brotherhood. Are not these gifts worth the giving? Is not this work and striving? Would America have been America without her Negro people?

Even so is the hope that sang in the songs of my fathers well sung. If somewhere in this whirl and chaos of things there dwells Eternal Good, pitiful yet masterful, then anon in His good time America shall rend the Veil and the prisoned shall be free. Free, free as the sunshine trickling down the morning into these high windows of mine, free as yonder fresh young voices welling up to me from the caverns of brick and mortar below—welling with song, instinct with life, tremulous treble and darkening bass. My children, my little children, are singing to the sunshine, and thus they sing:

Let us cheer the weary traveller,
Cheer the weary traveller,
Let us cheer the weary traveller
Along the heavenly way.

And the traveller girds himself, and sets his face toward the Morning, and goes his way.

1903

The Song of the Smoke

I am the smoke king,
I am black.
I am swinging in the sky.
I am ringing worlds on high:
I am the thought of the throbbing mills,
I am the soul of the soul toil kills,
I am the ripple of trading rills,

Up I'm curling from the sod,
I am whirling home to God.
I am the smoke king,
I am black.

I am the smoke king,
I am black.

I am wreathing broken hearts,
I am sheathing devils' darts;
Dark inspiration of iron times,
Wedding the toil of toiling climes
Shedding the blood of bloodless crimes,

Down I lower in the blue,
Up I tower toward the true,
I am the smoke king,
I am black.

I am the smoke king,
I am black.

I am darkening with song,
I am hearkening to wrong;
I will be as black as blackness can,
The blacker the mantle the mightier the man,
My purpl'ing midnights no day dawn may ban.

I am carving God in night,
I am painting hell in white.
I am the smoke king,
I am black.

I am the smoke king,
I am black.

I am cursing ruddy morn,
I am nursing hearts unborn;
Souls unto me are as mists in the night,
I whiten my blackmen, I beckon my white,
What's the hue of a hide to a man in his might!

Hail, then, grilly, grimy hands,
Sweet Christ, pity toiling lands!
Hail to the smoke king,
Hail to the black!

1907

James Weldon Johnson 1871–1938

James Weldon Johnson was Harlem's Renaissance Man—gifted with talent and aplomb. He had the ability to deal with the struggles of life as he worked to develop his intellectual and artistic powers in a dual society. Rather than being devastated by the divided consciousness that drove some black leaders to extremes and others to annihilation, he subverted the marginality strain to a victorious stance. His contributions to American culture help to support the premise that marginality may be a requisite for creativity and innovation. So the imperative in his poem "The Creation," "I'll make me a world," bears some relevance to the line of his own destiny in the Western world.

Johnson was born in Jacksonville, Florida, where he attended school at Stanton. His immediate family and acquaintances provided a cultural background and economic security that gave him the chance to pursue his career. These advantages, with his ability to learn, served him well as an Atlanta University student. The professors who taught the classics exerted every effort to make students nobler and higher beings. Johnson worked to become an "all-sided man," *l'homo universale.*

Johnson received a B.A. degree at Atlanta University in 1894, his M.A. in 1904. Immediately after graduation he taught at Stanton, but moved up to the level of high school and became principal. In order to hasten the advancement of racial uplift, he helped to found the *Daily American* in 1895 as the first black daily paper in America. But he made his mark as a journalist when he became a contributing editor of the *New York Age,* 1914–16, where he used his column as a "strong weapon" in the fight against inequality and injustice.

From 1916 through 1930, Johnson served as an official for the National Association for the Advancement of Colored People and was responsible for building support for the organization in the South and the West. In addition, he investigated America's misrule in Haiti in 1920, and he successfully lobbied Congress in 1921–22 for passage of the Dyer-Lynching Bill. It was his finest hour as a race leader. But Johnson likewise won acclaim in the diplomatic service. From 1906–20 he served as Consul to Venezuela and Nicaragua. In 1929, he was a representative to the Institute on Pacific Relations held in Kyoto, Japan.

Somehow Johnson's more ardent pursuits led to his early orientation in school life and the arts. Fisk University named Johnson as Adam K. Spence Professor of Creative Writing, a position he filled from 1930 to 1938. At the same time (1934), he became Visiting Professor at New York University. On the day of his death in an automobile accident, June 26, 1938, in Wiscasset, Maine, he had just been appointed Extension Professor of Black Literature at New York University.

Johnson believed that the creation of "pure literature" by a people is their mark of civilization. His first "pure" literary offering is "Sence You Went Away," a dialect poem in the style of Paul L. Dunbar. His second poem, the standard English lyric "Lift Ev'ry Voice and Sing," was set to music by his brother, J. Rosamond, in 1900, and is still his hallmark as "The Black National Anthem."

When he joined Bob Cole and his brother in 1901 in New York, where they became successful writers of "Coon songs" and black musical reviews, they (along with Will Marion Cook and others) knew that something was lacking. Their art failed to tap the source-stream of black folk culture and folk art. James Weldon erected a frame: the super-structure of conscious black art must be built on the cultural background of the black folk. Johnson's canon is limited but each work is vital for its attempt to evoke the black ethos.

As a writer, Johnson was a novelist, poet, literary critic, biographer, cultural historian, revolutionary philosopher, and more. Published anonymously in 1912, signed in 1927, *Autobiography of an Ex-Colored Man* is a sociological treatise as well as a fictive narrative. The theme of this important novel is "passing," but the hero's exploits reflect all of the author's rich experiences up to the year 1912. Of his three volumes of poetry—*Fifty Years and Other Poems* (1917), *God's Trombones* (1927), and *St. Peter Relates an Incident* (1930)—*Trombones* is the most innovative. In it he recorded the "sermon sagas" of his people, thus helping to perpetuate the oral tradition.

Five essays play a major role in establishing Johnson as a literary critic: prefaces to the two editions of *The Book of American Negro Poetry* (1922, 1931); to *The First Book of American Negro Spirituals* (1925); to *The Second Book of American Negro Spirituals* (1926); and to *God's Trombones.* In them he praises the "creative genius of blacks," analyzes song-poems as poetry, and isolates the folk sermon as a genre.

Along This Way (1933) is an autobiography that helps to establish Johnson as a precursor to and participant in the Harlem Renaissance. *Black Manhattan* is a cultural history of Harlem itself with an accurate history of the New York Theatrical Stage. *Negro Americans, What Now?* (1934) is considered by at least one scholar as a blueprint of the general philosophy of the Black Revolution of the sixties.

Mayor Fiorello La Guardia's New York eulogy is the proper assessment of Johnson's life and works: "Greatness in a man is a quality that does not know the boundaries of race or creed."

Arthenia J. Bates Millican
Southern University

PRIMARY WORKS

The Autobiography of an Ex-Colored Man, 1912; *Fifty Years and Other Poems,* 1917; *God's Trombones,* 1927; *Black Manhattan,* 1930; *Along This Way,* 1933; *Negro Americans, What Now?,* 1934; *St. Peter Relates an Incident: Selected Poems,* 1935.

Lift Every Voice and Sing

Lift every voice and sing
Till earth and heaven ring,
Ring with the harmonies of Liberty;
Let our rejoicing rise
High as the listening skies,
Let it resound loud as the rolling sea.
Sing a song full of the faith that the dark past has taught us,
Sing a song full of the hope that the present has brought us.
Facing the rising sun of our new day begun,
Let us march on till victory is won.

Stony the road we trod,
Bitter the chastening rod,

Felt in the days when hope unborn had died;
Yet with a steady beat
Have not our weary feet
Come to the place for which our fathers sighed?
We have come over a way that with tears has been watered,
We have come, treading our path through the blood of the
slaughtered,
Out from the gloomy past,
Till now we stand at last
Where the white gleam of our bright star is cast.

God of our weary years,
God of our silent tears,
Thou who hast brought us thus far on the way;
Thou who hast by Thy might
Led us into the light,
Keep us forever in the path, we pray.
Lest our feet stray from the places, our God, where we met Thee,
Lest, our hearts drunk with the wine of the world, we forget Thee,
Shadowed beneath Thy hand,
May we forever stand.
True to our God,
True to our native land.

1900

O Black and Unknown Bards

O black and unknown bards of long ago,
How came your lips to touch the sacred fire?
How, in your darkness, did you come to know
The power and beauty of the minstrel's lyre?
Who first from midst his bonds lifted his eyes?
Who first from out the still watch, lone and long,
Feeling the ancient faith of prophets rise
Within his dark-kept soul, burst into song?

Heart of what slave poured out such melody
As "Steal Away to Jesus"? On its strains
His spirit must have nightly floated free,
Though still about his hands he felt his chains.
Who heard great "Jordan roll"? Whose starward eye
Saw chariot "swing low"? And who was he

That breathed that comforting, melodic sigh,
"Nobody Knows de Trouble I See"?

What merely living clod, what captive thing,
Could up toward God through all its darkness grope,
And find within its deadened heart to sing
These songs of sorrow, love, and faith, and hope?
How did it catch that subtle undertone,
That note in music heard not with the ears?
How sound the elusive reed so seldom blown,
Which stirs the soul or melts the heart to tears?

Not that great German master in his dream
Of harmonies that thundered amongst the stars
At the creation, ever heard a theme
Nobler than "Go Down, Moses." Mark its bars,
How like a mighty trumpet-call they stir
The blood. Such are the notes that men have sung
Going to valorous deeds; such tones there were
That helped make history when Time was young.

There is a wide, wide wonder in it all,
That from degraded rest and servile toil
The fiery spirit of the seer should call
These simple children of the sun and soil.
O black slave singers, gone, forgot, unfamed,
You—you alone, of all the long, long line
Of those who've sung untaught, unknown, unnamed,
Have stretched out upward, seeking the divine.

You sang not deeds of heroes or of kings;
No chant of bloody war, no exulting paean
Of arms-won triumphs; but your humble strings
You touched in chord with music empyrean.
You sang far better than you knew; the songs
That for your listeners' hungry hearts sufficed
Still live—but more than this to you belongs;
You sang a race from wood and stone to Christ.

1908

from Autobiography of an Ex-Colored Man

Chapter X

[*This chapter is the second-to-last in the book, and tells of the narrator's return to America and the deep South after several years overseas. The final chapter traces his move to New York City where he finds financial success as a "white man."*]

Among the first of my fellow-passengers of whom I took any particular notice was a tall, broad-shouldered, almost gigantic, colored man. His dark-brown face was clean-shaven; he was well-dressed and bore a decidedly distinguished air. In fact, if he was not handsome, he at least compelled admiration for his fine physical proportions. He attracted general attention as he strode the deck in a sort of majestic loneliness. I became curious to know who he was and determined to strike up an acquaintance with him at the first opportune moment. The chance came a day or two later. He was sitting in the smoking-room, with a cigar, which had gone out, in his mouth, reading a novel. I sat down beside him and, offering him a fresh cigar, said: "You don't mind my telling you something unpleasant, do you?" He looked at me with a smile, accepted the proffered cigar, and replied in a voice which comported perfectly with his size and appearance: "I think my curiosity overcomes any objections I might have." "Well," I said, "have you noticed that the man who sat at your right in the saloon during the first meal has not sat there since?" He frowned slightly without answering my question. "Well," I continued, "he asked the steward to remove him; and not only that, he attempted to persuade a number of the passengers to protest against your presence in the dining-saloon." The big man at my side took a long draw from his cigar, threw his head back, and slowly blew a great cloud of smoke toward the ceiling. Then turning to me he said: "Do you know, I don't object to anyone's having prejudices so long as those prejudices don't interfere with my personal liberty. Now, the man you are speaking of had a perfect right to change his seat if I in any way interfered with his appetite or his digestion. I should have no reason to complain if he removed to the farthest corner of the saloon, or even if he got off the ship; but when his prejudice attempts to move *me* one foot, one inch, out of the place where I am comfortably located, then I object." On the word "object" he brought his great fist down on the table in front of us with such a crash that everyone in the room turned to look. We both covered up the slight embarrassment with a laugh and strolled out on the deck.

We walked the deck for an hour or more, discussing different phases of the Negro question. In referring to the race I used the personal pronoun "we"; my companion made no comment about it, nor evinced any surprise, except to raise his eyebrows slightly the first time he caught the significance of the word. He was the broadest-minded colored man I have ever talked with on the Negro question. He even went so far as to sympathize with and offer excuses for some white Southern points of view. I asked him what were his main reasons for being so hopeful. He replied: "In spite of all that is written, said, and done, this great, big, incontrovertible fact stands out—the Negro is progressing, and that disproves all the arguments in the world that he is incapable of progress. I was born in slavery, and at emancipation was set adrift a ragged, penniless bit of humanity. I have seen the Negro in every grade, and I know what I am talking about. Our detractors point to the increase of crime as evidence against us; certainly we have progressed in crime as in other things; what less could be expected? And yet, in this respect, we are far from the point which has been reached by the more highly civilized white race. As we continue to progress, crime among us will gradually lose much of its brutal, vulgar, I might say healthy, aspect, and become more delicate, refined, and subtle. Then it will be less shocking and noticeable, although more dangerous to society." Then dropping his tone of irony, he continued with some show of eloquence: "But, above all, when I am discouraged and disheartened, I have this to fall back on: if there is a principle of right in the world, which finally prevails, and I believe that there is; if there is a merciful but justice-loving God in heaven, and I believe that there is, we shall win; for we have right on our side, while those who oppose us can defend themselves by nothing in the moral law, nor even by anything in the enlightened thought of the present age."

For several days, together with other topics, we discussed the race problem, not only of the United States, but as it affected native Africans and Jews. Finally, before we reached Boston, our conversation had grown familiar and personal. I had told him something of my past and much about my intentions for the future. I learned that he was a physician, a graduate of Howard University, Washington, and had done post-graduate work in Philadelphia; and this was his second trip abroad to attend professional courses. He had practiced for some years in the city of Washington, and though he did not say so, I gathered that his practice was a lucrative one. Before we left the ship, he had made me promise that I would stop two or three days in Washington before going on south.

We put up at a hotel in Boston for a couple of days and visited several of my new friend's acquaintances; they were all people of education and culture and, apparently, of means. I could not help being struck by the great difference between them and the same class of colored people in the South. In speech and thought they were genuine Yankees. The difference was especially noticeable in their speech. There was none of that heavy-tongued enunciation which characterizes even the best-educated colored people of the South. It is remarkable, after all, what an adaptable creature the Negro is. I have seen the black West Indian gentleman in London, and he is in speech and manners a perfect Englishman. I have seen natives of Haiti and Martinique in Paris, and they are more Frenchy than a Frenchman. I have no doubt that the Negro would make a good Chinaman, with exception of the pigtail.

My stay in Washington, instead of being two or three days, was two or three weeks. This was my first visit to the national capital, and I was, of course, interested in seeing the public buildings and something of the working of the government; but most of my time I spent with the doctor among his friends and acquaintances. The social phase of life among colored people is more developed in Washington than in any other city in the country. This is on account of the large number of individuals earning good salaries and having a reasonable amount of leisure time to draw from. There are dozens of physicians and lawyers, scores of school teachers, and hundreds of clerks in the departments. As to the colored department clerks, I think it fair to say that in educational equipment they average above the white clerks of the same grade; for, whereas a colored college graduate will seek such a job, the white university man goes into one of the many higher vocations which are open to him.

In a previous chapter I spoke of social life among colored people; so there is no need to take it up again here. But there is one thing I did not mention: among Negroes themselves there is the peculiar inconsistency of a color question. Its existence is rarely admitted and hardly ever mentioned; it may not be too strong a statement to say that the greater portion of the race is unconscious of its influence; yet this influence, though silent, is constant. It is evidenced most plainly in marriage selection; thus the black men generally marry women fairer than themselves; while, on the other hand, the dark women of stronger mental endowment are very often married to light-complexioned men; the effect is a tendency toward lighter complexions, especially among the more active elements in the race. Some might claim that this is a tacit admission of colored people among themselves of their own inferiority judged by the color line. I do not think so. What I have termed an inconsistency is, after all, most natural; it is, in fact, a tendency in accordance with what might be called an economic necessity. So far as racial differences go, the United States puts a greater premium on color, or, better, lack of color, than upon anything else in the world. To paraphrase, "Have a white skin, and all things else may be added unto you." I have seen advertisements in newspapers for waiters, bell-boys, or elevator men, which read: "Light-colored man wanted." It is this tremendous pressure which the sentiment of the country exerts that is operating on the race. There is involved not only the question of higher opportunity, but often the question of earning a livelihood; and so I say it is not strange, but a natural tendency. Nor is it any more a sacrifice of self-respect that a black man should give to his children every advantage he can which complexion of the skin carries than that the new or vulgar rich should purchase for their children the advantages which ancestry, aristocracy, and social position carry. I once heard a colored man sum it up in these words: "It's no disgrace to be black, but it's often very inconvenient."

Washington shows the Negro not only at his best, but also at his worst. As I drove around with the doctor, he commented rather harshly on those of the latter class which we saw. He remarked: "You see those lazy, loafing, good-for-nothing darkies; they're not worth digging graves for; yet they are the ones who create impressions of the race for the casual observer. It's because they are always in evidence on the street corners, while the rest of us are hard at work, and you know a dozen loafing darkies make a bigger crowd and a worse impression in this country than fifty white men of the same class. But they ought not to represent the race. We are the race, and the race ought to be judged by us, not by them. Every race and every nation should be judged by the best it has been able to produce, not by the worst."

The recollection of my stay in Washington is a pleasure to me now. In company with the doctor I visited Howard University, the public schools, the excellent colored hospital, with which he was in some way connected, if I remember correctly, and many comfortable and even elegant homes. It was with some reluctance that I continued my journey south. The doctor was very kind in giving me letters to people in Richmond and Nashville when I told him that I intended to stop in both of these cities. In Richmond a man who was then editing a very creditable colored newspaper gave me a great deal of his time and made my stay there of three or four days very pleasant. In Nashville I spent a whole day at Fisk University, the home of the "Jubilee

Singers," and was more than repaid for my time. Among my letters of introduction was one to a very prosperous physician. He drove me about the city and introduced me to a number of people. From Nashville I went to Atlanta, where I stayed long enough to gratify an old desire to see Atlanta University again. I then continued my journey to Macon.

During the trip from Nashville to Atlanta I went into the smoking-compartment of the car to smoke a cigar. I was traveling in a Pullman, not because of an abundance of funds, but because through my experience with my millionaire a certain amount of comfort and luxury had become a necessity to me whenever it was obtainable. When I entered the car, I found only a couple of men there; but in a half-hour there were half a dozen or more. From the general conversation I learned that a fat Jewish-looking man was a cigar manufacturer, and was experimenting in growing Havana tobacco in Florida; that a slender bespectacled young man was from Ohio and a professor in some State institution in Alabama; that a white-mustached, well-dressed man was an old Union soldier who had fought through the Civil War; and that a tall, raw-boned, red-faced man, who seemed bent on leaving nobody in ignorance of the fact that he was from Texas, was a cotton planter.

In the North men may ride together for hours in a "smoker" and unless they are acquainted with each other never exchange a word; in the South men thrown together in such manner are friends in fifteen minutes. There is always present a warm-hearted cordiality which will melt down the most frigid reserve. It may be because Southerners are very much like Frenchmen in that they must talk; and not only must they talk, but they must express their opinions.

The talk in the car was for a while miscellaneous—on the weather, crops, business prospects; the old Union soldier had invested capital in Atlanta, and he predicted that that city would soon be one of the greatest in the country. Finally the conversation drifted to politics; then, as a natural sequence, turned upon the Negro question.

In the discussion of the race question the diplomacy of the Jew was something to be admired; he had the faculty of agreeing with everybody without losing his allegiance to any side. He knew that to sanction Negro oppression would be to sanction Jewish oppression and would expose him to a shot along that line from the old soldier, who stood firmly on the ground of equal rights and opportunity to all men; long traditions and business instincts told him when in Rome to act as a Roman. Altogether his position was a delicate one, and I gave him credit for the skill he displayed in maintaining it. The young professor was apologetic. He had had the same views as the G.A.R. man; but a year in the South had opened his eyes, and he had to confess that the problem could hardly be handled any better than it was being handled by the Southern whites. To which the G.A.R. man responded somewhat rudely that he had spent ten times as many years in the South as his young friend and that he could easily understand how holding a position in a State institution in Alabama would bring about a change of views. The professor turned very red and had very little more to say. The Texan was fierce, eloquent, and profane in his argument, and, in a lower sense, there was a direct logic in what he said, which was convincing; it was only by taking higher ground, by dealing in what Southerners call "theories," that he could be combated. Occasionally some one of the several other men in the "smoker" would throw in a remark to reinforce what he said, but he really didn't need any help; he was sufficient in himself.

In the course of a short time the controversy narrowed itself down to an argument between the old soldier and the Texan. The latter maintained hotly that the Civil War was a criminal mistake on the part of the North and that the humiliation which the South suffered during Reconstruction could never be forgotten. The Union man retorted just as hotly that the South was responsible for the war and that the spirit of unforgetfulness on its part was the greatest cause of present friction; that it seemed to be the one great aim of the South to convince the North that the latter made a mistake in fighting to preserve the Union and liberate the slaves. "Can you imagine," he went on to say, "what would have been the condition of things eventually if there had been no war, and the South had been allowed to follow its course? Instead of one great, prosperous country with nothing before it but the conquests of peace, a score of petty republics, as in Central and South America, wasting their energies in war with each other or in revolutions."

"Well," replied the Texan, "anything—no country at all—is better than having niggers over you. But anyhow, the war was fought and the niggers were freed; for it's no use beating around the bush, the niggers, and not the Union, was the cause of it; and now do you believe that all the niggers on earth are worth the good white blood that was spilt? You freed the nigger and you gave him the ballot, but you couldn't make a citizen out of him. He don't know what he's voting for, and we buy 'em like so many hogs. You're giving 'em education, but that only makes slick rascals out of 'em."

"Don't fancy for a moment," said the Northern man, "that you have any monopoly in buying ignorant votes. The same thing is done on a larger scale in New York and Boston, and in Chicago and San Francisco; and they are not black votes either. As to education's making the Negro worse, you might just as well tell me that religion does the same thing. And, by the way, how many educated colored men do you know personally?"

The Texan admitted that he knew only one, and added that he was in the penitentiary. "But," he said, "do you mean to claim, ballot or no ballot, education or no education, that niggers are the equals of white men?"

"That's not the question," answered the other, "but if the Negro is so distinctly inferior, it is a strange thing to me that it takes such tremendous effort on the part of the white man to make him realize it, and to keep him in the same place into which inferior men naturally fall. However, let us grant for sake of argument that the Negro is inferior in every respect to the white man; that fact only increases our moral responsibility in regard to our actions toward him. Inequalities of numbers, wealth, and power, even of intelligence and morals, should make no difference in the essential rights of men."

"If he's inferior and weaker, and is shoved to the wall, that's his own look-out," said the Texan. "That's the law of nature; and he's bound to go to the wall; for no race in the world has ever been able to stand competition with the Anglo-Saxon. The Anglo-Saxon race has always been and always will be the masters of the world, and the niggers in the South ain't going to change all the records of history."

"My friend," said the old soldier slowly, "if you have studied history, will you tell me, as confidentially between white men, what the Anglo-Saxon has ever done?"

The Texan was too much astonished by the question to venture any reply.

His opponent continued: "Can you name a single one of the great fundamental and original intellectual achievements which have raised man in the scale of civilization that may be credited to the Anglo-Saxon? The art of letters, of poetry, of music, of sculpture, of painting, of the drama, of architecture; the science of mathematics, of astronomy, of philosophy, of logic, of physics, of chemistry, the use of the metals, and the principles of mechanics, were all invented or discovered by darker and what we now call inferior races and nations. We have carried many of these to their highest point of perfection, but the foundation was laid by others. Do you know the only original contribution to civilization we can claim is what we have done in steam and electricity and in making implements of war more deadly? And there we worked largely on principles which we did not discover. Why, we didn't even originate the religion we use. We are a great race, the greatest in the world today, but we ought to remember that we are standing on a pile of past races, and enjoy our position with a little less show of arrogance. We are simply having our turn at the game, and we were a long time getting to it. After all, racial supremacy is merely a matter of dates in history. The man here who belongs to what is, all in all, the greatest race the world ever produced, is almost ashamed to own it. If the Anglo-Saxon is the source of everything good and great in the human race from the beginning, why wasn't the German forest the birthplace of civilization, rather than the valley of the Nile?"

The Texan was somewhat disconcerted, for the argument had passed a little beyond his limits, but he swung it back to where he was sure of his ground by saying: "All that may be true, but it hasn't got much to do with us and the niggers here in the South. We've got 'em here, and we've got 'em to live with, and it's a question of white man or nigger, no middle ground. You want us to treat niggers as equals. Do you want to see 'em sitting around in our parlors? Do you want to see a mulatto South? To bring it right home to you, would you let your daughter marry a nigger?"

"No, I wouldn't consent to my daughter's marrying a nigger, but that doesn't prevent my treating a black man fairly. And I don't see what fair treatment has to do with niggers sitting around in your parlors; they can't come there unless they're invited. Out of all the white men I know, only a hundred or so have the privilege of sitting around in my parlor. As to the mulatto South, if you Southerners have one boast that is stronger than another, it is your women; you put them on a pinnacle of purity and virtue and bow down in a chivalric worship before them; yet you talk and act as though, should you treat the Negro fairly and take the anti-inter-marriage laws off your statute books, these same women would rush into the arms of black lovers and husbands. It's a wonder to me that they don't rise up and resent the insult."

"Colonel," said the Texan, as he reached into his handbag and brought out a large flask of whisky, "you might argue from now until hell freezes over, and you might convince me that you're right, but you'll never convince me that I'm wrong. All you say sounds very good, but it's got nothing to do with facts. You can say what men ought to be, but they ain't that; so there you are. Down here in the South we're up against facts, and we're meeting 'em like facts. We don't believe the nigger is or ever will be the equal of the white man, and we ain't going to treat him as an equal; I'll be damned if we will. Have a drink." Everybody except the professor partook of the generous Texan's flask, and the argument closed in a general laugh and good feeling.

I went back into the main part of the car with the conversation on my mind. Here I had before me the bald, raw, naked aspects of the race question in the South; and, in consideration of the step I was just taking, it was far from encouraging. The sentiments of the Texan—and he expressed the sentiments of the South—fell upon me like a chill. I was sick at heart. Yet I must confess that underneath it all I felt a certain sort of admiration for the man who could not be swayed from what he held as his principles. Contrasted with him, the young Ohio professor was indeed a pitiable character. And all along, in spite of myself, I have been compelled to accord the same kind of admiration to the Southern white man for the manner in which he defends not only his virtues, but his vices. He knows that, judged by a high standard, he is narrow and prejudiced, that he is guilty of unfairness, oppression, and cruelty, but this he defends as stoutly as he would his better qualities. This same spirit obtains in a great degree among the blacks; they, too, defend their faults and failings. This they generally do whenever white people are concerned. And yet among themselves they are their own most merciless critics. I have never heard the race so terribly arraigned as I have by colored speakers to strictly colored audiences. It is the spirit of the South to defend everything belonging to it. The North is too cosmopolitan and tolerant for such a spirit. If you should say to an Easterner that Paris is a gayer city than New York, he would be likely to agree with you, or at least to let you have your own way; but to suggest to a South Carolinian that Boston is a nicer city to live in than Charleston would be to stir his greatest depths of argument and eloquence.

But to-day, as I think over that smoking-car argument, I can see it in a different light. The Texan's position does not render things so hopeless, for it indicates that the main difficulty of the race question does not lie so much in the actual condition of the blacks as it does in the mental attitude of the whites; and a mental attitude, especially one not based on truth, can be changed more easily than actual conditions. That is to say, the burden of the question is not that the whites are struggling to save ten million despondent and moribund people from sinking into a hopeless slough of ignorance, poverty, and barbarity in their very midst, but that they are unwilling to open certain doors of opportunity and to accord certain treatment to ten million aspiring, education-and-property-acquiring people. In a word, the difficulty of the problem is not so much due to the facts presented as to the hypothesis assumed for its solution. In this it is similar to the problem of the solar system. By a complex, confusing, and almost contradictory mathematical process, by the use of zigzags instead of straight lines, the earth can be proved to be the center of things celestial; but by an operation so simple that it can be comprehended by a schoolboy, its position can be verified among the other worlds which revolve about the sun, and its movements harmonized with the laws of the universe. So, when the white race assumes as a hypothesis that it is the main object of creation and that all things else are merely subsidiary to its well-being, sophism, subterfuge, perversion of conscience, arrogance, injustice, oppression, cruelty, sacrifice of human blood, all are required to maintain the position, and its dealings with other races become indeed a problem, a problem which, if based on a hypothesis of common humanity, could be solved by the simple rules of justice.

When I reached Macon, I decided to leave my trunk and all my surplus belongings, to pack my bag, and strike out into the interior. This I did; and by train, by mule and ox-cart, I traveled through many counties. This was my first real experience among rural colored people, and all that I saw was interesting to me; but there was a great deal which does not require description at my hands; for log cabins and plantations and dialect-speaking "darkies" are perhaps better known in American literature than any other single picture of our national life. Indeed, they form an ideal and exclusive literary concept of the American Negro to such an extent that it is almost impossible to get the reading public to recognize him in any other setting; so I shall endeavor to avoid giving the reader any already overworked and hackneyed descriptions. This generally accepted literary ideal of the American Negro constitutes what is really an obstacle in the way of the thoughtful and progressive element of the race. His character has been established as a happy-go-lucky, laughing, shuffling, banjo-picking being, and the reading public has not yet been prevailed upon to take him seriously. His efforts to elevate himself socially are looked upon as a sort of absurd caricature of "white civilization." A novel dealing with colored people who lived in respectable homes and amidst a fair degree of culture and who naturally acted "just like white folks" would be taken in a comic-opera sense. In this respect the Negro is much in the position of a great comedian who gives up the lighter roles to play tragedy. No matter how well he may portray the deeper passions, the public is loath to give him up in his old character; they even conspire to make him a failure in serious work, in order to force him back into comedy. In the same respect, the public is not too much to be blamed, for great comedians are far more scarce than mediocre tragedians; every amateur actor is a tragedian. However, this very fact constitutes the opportunity of the future Negro novelist and poet to give the country something new and unknown, in depicting the life, the ambitions, the struggles, and the passions of those of their race who are striving to break the narrow limits of traditions. A beginning has already been made in that remarkable book by Dr. Du Bois' *The Souls of Black Folk*.

Much, too, that I saw while on this trip, in spite of my enthusiasm, was disheartening. Often I thought of what my millionaire had said to me, and wished myself back in Europe. The houses in which I had to stay were generally uncomfortable, sometimes worse. I often had to sleep in a division or compartment with several other people. Once or twice I was not so fortunate as to find divisions; everybody slept on pallets on the floor. Frequently I was able to lie down and contemplate the stars which were in their zenith. The food was at times so distasteful and poorly cooked that I could not eat it. I remember that once I lived for a week or more on buttermilk, on account of not being able to stomach the fat bacon, the rank turniptops, and the heavy damp mixture of meal, salt, and water which was called corn bread. It was only my ambition to do the work which I had planned that kept me steadfast to my purpose. Occasionally I would meet with some signs of progress and uplift in even one of these back-wood settlements—houses built of boards, with windows, and divided into rooms; decent food, and a fair standard of living. This condition was due to the fact that there was in the community some exceptionally capable Negro farmer whose thrift served as an example. As I went about among these dull, simple people—the great majority of them hard working, in their relations with the whites submissive, faithful, and often affectionate, negatively content with their lot—and contrasted them with those of the race who had been quickened by the forces of thought, I could not but appreciate the logic of the position held by those Southern leaders who have been bold enough to proclaim against the education of the Negro. They are consistent in their public speech with Southern sentiment and desires. Those public men of the South who have not been daring or heedless enough to defy the ideals of twentieth-century civilization and of modern humanitarianism and philanthropy, find themselves in the embarrassing situation of preaching one thing and praying for another. They are in the position of the fashionable woman who is compelled by the laws of polite society to say to her dearest enemy: "How happy I am to see you!"

And yet in this respect how perplexing is Southern character; for, in opposition to the above, it may be said that the claim of the Southern whites that they love the Negro better than the Northern whites do is in a manner true. Northern white people love the Negro in a sort of abstract way, as a race; through a sense of justice, charity, and philanthropy, they will liberally assist in his elevation. A number of them have heroically spent their lives in this effort (and just here I wish to say that when the colored people reach the monument-building stage, they should not forget the men and women who went South after the war and founded schools for them). Yet, generally speaking, they have no particular liking for individuals of the race. Southern white people despise the Negro as a race, and will do nothing to aid in his elevation as such; but for certain individuals they have a strong affection, and are helpful to them in many ways. With these individual members of the race they live on terms of the greatest intimacy; they entrust to them their children, their family treasures, and their family secrets; in trouble they often go to them for comfort and counsel; in sickness they often rely upon their care. This affectionate relation between the Southern whites and those blacks who come into close touch with them has not been overdrawn even in fiction.

This perplexity of Southern character extends even to the intermixture of the races. That is spoken of as though it were dreaded worse than smallpox, leprosy, or the plague. Yet, when I was in Jacksonville, I knew several prominent families there with large colored branches, which went by the same name and were known and acknowledged as blood relatives. And what is more, there seemed to exist between these black brothers and sisters and uncles and aunts a decidedly friendly feeling.

I said above that Southern whites would do nothing for the Negro as a race. I know the South claims that it has spent millions for the education of the blacks, and that it has of its own free will shouldered this awful burden. It seems to be forgetful of the fact that these millions have been taken from the public tax funds for education, and that the law of political economy which recognizes the land owner as the one who really pays the taxes is not tenable. It would be just as reasonable for the relatively few land owners of Manhattan to complain that they had to stand the financial burden of the education of the thousands and thousands of children whose parents pay rent for tenements and flats. Let the millions of producing and consuming Negroes be taken out of the South, and it would be quickly seen how much less of public funds there would be to appropriate for education or any other purpose.

In thus traveling about through the country I was sometimes amused on arriving at some little railroad-station town to be taken for and treated as a white man, and six hours later, when it was learned that I was stopping at the house of the colored preacher or school teacher, to note the attitude of the whole town change. At times this led even to embarrassment. Yet it cannot be so embarrassing for a colored man to be taken for white as for a white man to be taken for colored; and I have heard of several cases of the latter kind.

All this while I was gathering material for work, jotting down in my note-book themes and melodies, and trying to catch the spirit of the Negro in his relatively primitive state. I began to feel the necessity of hurrying so that I might get back to some city like Nashville to begin my compositions and at the same time earn at least a living by teaching and performing before my funds gave out. At the last settlement in which I stopped I found a mine of material. This was due to the fact that "big meeting" was in progress. "Big meeting" is an institution something like camp-meeting, the difference being that it is held in a permanent church, and not in a temporary structure. All the churches of some one denomination—of course, either Methodist or Baptist—in a county, or, perhaps, in several adjoining counties, are closed, and the congregations unite at some centrally located church for a series of meetings lasting a week. It is really a social as well as a religious function. The people come in great numbers, making the trip, according to their financial status, in buggies drawn by sleek, fleet-footed mules, in ox-carts, or on foot. It was amusing to see some of the latter class trudging down the hot and dusty road, with their shoes, which were brand-new, strung across their shoulders. When they got near the church, they sat on the side of the road and, with many grimaces, tenderly packed their feet into those instruments of torture. This furnished, indeed, a trying test of their religion. The famous preachers come from near and far and take turns in warning sinners of the day of wrath. Food, in the form of those two Southern luxuries, fried chicken and roast pork, is plentiful, and no one need go hungry. On the opening Sunday the women are immaculate in starched stiff white dresses adorned with ribbons, either red or blue. Even a great many of the men wear streamers of vari-colored ribbons in the buttonholes of their coats. A few of them carefully cultivate a forelock of hair by wrapping it in twine, and on such festive occasions decorate it with a narrow ribbon streamer. Big meetings afford a fine opportunity to the younger people to meet each other dressed in their Sunday clothes, and much rustic courting, which is as enjoyable as any other kind, is indulged in.

This big meeting which I was lucky enough to catch was particularly well attended; the extra large attendance was due principally to two attractions, a man by the name of John Brown, who was renowned as the most powerful preacher for miles around; and a wonderful leader of singing, who was known as "Singing Johnson." These two men were a study and a revelation to me. They caused me to reflect upon how great an influence their types have been in the development of the Negro in America. Both these types are now looked upon generally with condescension or contempt by the progressive element among the colored people; but it should never be forgotten that it was they who led the race from paganism and kept it steadfast to Christianity through all the long, dark years of slavery.

John Brown was a jet-black man of medium size, with a strikingly intelligent head and face, and a voice like an organ peal. He preached each night after several lesser lights had successively held the pulpit during an hour or so. As far as subject-matter is concerned, all of the sermons were alike: each began with the fall of man, ran through various trials and tribulations of the Hebrew children, on to the redemption by Christ, and ended with a fervid picture of the judgment day and the fate of the damned. But John Brown possessed magnetism and an imagination so free and daring that he was able to carry through what the other preachers would not attempt. He knew all the arts and tricks of oratory, the modulation of the voice to almost a whisper, the pause for effect, the rise through light, rapid-fire sentences to the terrific, thundering outburst of an electrifying climax. In addition, he had the intuition of a born theatrical manager. Night after night this man held me fascinated. He convinced me that, after all, eloquence consists more in the manner of saying than in what is said. It is largely a matter of tone pictures.

The most striking example of John Brown's magnetism and imagination was his "heavenly march"; I shall never forget how it impressed me when I heard it. He opened his sermon in the usual way; then, proclaiming to his listeners that he was going to take them on the heavenly march, he seized the Bible under his arm and began to pace up and down the pulpit platform. The congregation immediately began with their feet a tramp, tramp, tramp, in time with the preacher's march in the pulpit, all the while singing in an undertone a hymn about marching to Zion. Suddenly he cried: "Halt!" Every foot stopped with the precision of a company of well-drilled soldiers, and the singing ceased. The morning star had been reached. Here the preacher described the beauties of that celestial body. Then the march, the tramp, tramp, tramp, and the singing were again taken up. Another "Halt!" They had reached the evening star. And so on, past the sun and moon—the intensity of religious emotion all the time increasing—along the milky way, on up to the gates of heaven. Here the halt was longer, and the preacher described at length the gates and walls of the New Jerusalem. Then he took his hearers through the pearly gates, along the golden streets, pointing out the glories of the city, pausing occasionally to greet some patriarchal members of the church, well-known to most of his listeners in life, who had had "the tears wiped from their eyes, were clad in robes of spotless white, with crowns of gold upon their heads and harps within their hands," and ended his march before the great white throne. To the reader this may sound ridiculous, but listened to under the circumstances, it was highly and effectively dramatic. I was a more or less sophisticated and non-religious man of the world, but the torrent of the preacher's words, moving with the rhythm and glowing with the eloquence of primitive poetry, swept me along, and I, too, felt like joining in the shouts of "Amen! Hallelujah!"

John Brown's powers in describing the delights of heaven were no greater than those in depicting the horrors of hell. I saw great, strapping fellows trembling and weeping like children at the "mourners' bench." His warnings to sinners were truly terrible. I shall never forget one expression that he used, which for originality and aptness could not be excelled. In my opinion, it is more graphic and, for us, far more expressive than St. Paul's "It is hard to kick against the pricks." He struck the attitude of a pugilist and thundered out: "Young man, your arm's too short to box with God!"

Interesting as was John Brown to me, the other man, "Singing Johnson," was more so. He was a small, dark-brown, one-eyed man, with a clear, strong, high-pitched voice, a leader of singing, a maker of songs, a man who could improvise at the moment lines to fit the occasion. Not so striking a figure as John Brown, but, at "big meetings," equally important. It is indispensable to the success of the singing, when the congregation is a large one made up of people from different communities, to have someone with a strong voice who knows just what hymn to sing and when to sing it, who can pitch it in the right key, and who has all the leading lines committed to memory. Sometimes it devolves upon the leader to "sing down" a long-winded or uninteresting speaker. Committing to memory the leading lines of all the Negro spiritual songs is no easy task, for they run up into the hundreds. But the accomplished leader must know them all, because the congregation sings only the refrains and repeats; every ear in the church is fixed upon him, and if he becomes mixed in his lines or forgets them, the responsibility falls directly on his shoulders.

For example, most of these hymns are constructed to be sung in the following manner:

> *Leader.* Swing low, sweet chariot.
> *Congregation.* Coming for to carry me home.
> *Leader.* Swing low, sweet chariot.
> *Congregation.* Coming for to carry me home.
> *Leader.* I look over yonder, what do I see?
> *Congregation.* Coming for to carry me home.
> *Leader.* Two little angels coming after me.
> *Congregation.* Coming for to carry me home. . . .

The solitary and plaintive voice of the leader is answered by a sound like the roll of the sea, producing a most curious effect.

In only a few of these songs do the leader and the congregation start off together. Such a song is the well-known "Steal away to Jesus."

The leader and the congregation begin with part-singing:

> Steal away, steal away,
> Steal away to Jesus;
> Steal away, steal away home,
> I ain't got long to stay here.

Then the leader alone or the congregation in unison:

> My Lord he calls me,
> He calls me by the thunder,
> The trumpet sounds within-a my soul.

Then all together:

> I ain't got long to stay here.

The leader and the congregation again take up the opening refrain; then the leader sings three more leading lines alone, and so on almost *ad infinitum.* It will be seen that even here most of the work falls upon the leader, for the congregation sings the same lines over and over, while his memory and ingenuity are taxed to keep the songs going.

Generally the parts taken up by the congregation are sung in a three-part harmony, the women singing the soprano and a transposed tenor, the men with high voices singing the melody, and those with low voices a thundering bass. In a few of these songs, however, the leading part is sung in unison by the whole congregation, down to the last line, which is harmonized. The effect of this is intensely thrilling. Such a hymn is "Go down, Moses." It stirs the heart like a trumpet call.

"Singing Johnson" was an ideal leader, and his services were in great demand. He spent his time going about the country from one church to another. He received his support in much the same way as the preachers—part of a collection, food and lodging. All of his leisure time he devoted to originating new words and melodies and new lines for old songs. He always sang with his eyes—or, to be more exact, his eye—

closed, indicating the *tempo* by swinging his head to and fro. He was a great judge of the proper hymn to sing at a particular moment; and I noticed several times, when the preacher reached a certain climax, or expressed a certain sentiment, that Johnson broke in with a line or two of some appropriate hymn. The speaker understood and would pause until the singing ceased.

As I listened to the singing of these songs, the wonder of their production grew upon me more and more. How did the men who originated them manage to do it? The sentiments are easily accounted for; they are mostly taken from the Bible; but the melodies, where did they come from? Some of them so weirdly sweet, and others so wonderfully strong. Take, for instance, "Go down, Moses." I doubt that there is a stronger theme in the whole musical literature of the world. And so many of these songs contain more than mere melody; there is sounded in them that elusive undertone, the note in music which is not heard with the ears. I sat often with the tears rolling down my cheeks and my heart melted within me. Any musical person who has never heard a Negro congregation under the spell of religious fervor sing these old songs has missed one of the most thrilling emotions which the human heart may experience. Anyone who without shedding tears can listen to Negroes sing "Nobody knows de trouble I see, Nobody knows but Jesus" must indeed have a heart of stone.

As yet, the Negroes themselves do not fully appreciate these old slave songs. The educated classes are rather ashamed of them and prefer to sing hymns from books. This feeling is natural; they are still too close to the conditions under which the songs were produced; but the day will come when this slave music will be the most treasured heritage of the American Negro.

At the close of the "big meeting" I left the settlement where it was being held, full of enthusiasm. I was in that frame of mind which, in the artistic temperament, amounts to inspiration. I was now ready and anxious to get to some place where I might settle down to work, and give expression to the ideas which were teeming in my head; but I strayed into another deviation from my path of life as I had it marked out, which led me upon an entirely different road. Instead of going to the nearest and most convenient railroad station, I accepted the invitation of a young man who had been present the closing Sunday at the meeting to drive with him some miles farther to the town in which he taught school, and there take the train. My conversation with this young man as we drove along through the country was extremely interesting. He had been a student in one of the Negro colleges—strange coincidence, in the very college, as I learned through him, in which "Shiny" was now a professor. I was, of course, curious to hear about my boyhood friend; and had it not been vacation time, and that I was not sure that I should find him, I should have gone out of my way to pay him a visit; but I determined to write to him as soon as the school opened. My companion talked to me about his work among the people, of his hopes and his discouragements. He was tremendously in earnest; I might say, too much so. In fact, it may be said that the majority of intelligent colored people are, in some degree, too much in earnest over the race question. They assume and carry so much that their progress is at times impeded and they are unable to see things in their proper proportions. In many instances a slight exercise of the sense of humor would save much anxiety of soul. Anyone who marks the general tone of editorials in colored newspapers is apt to be impressed with this idea. If the mass of Negroes took their present and future as seriously as do the most of their leaders, the race would be in no mental condition to sustain the terrible pressure which it undergoes; it would sink of its own weight. Yet it must be acknowledged that in the making of a race overseriousness is a far lesser failing than its reverse, and even the faults resulting from it lean toward the right.

We drove into the town just before dark. As we passed a large, unpainted church, my companion pointed it out as the place where he held his school. I promised that I would go there with him the next morning and visit awhile. The town was of that kind which hardly requires or deserves description; a straggling line of brick and wooden stores on one side of the railroad track and some cottages of various sizes on the other side constituted about the whole of it. The young school teacher boarded at the best house in the place owned by a colored man. It was painted, had glass windows, contained "store bought" furniture, an organ, and lamps with chimneys. The owner held a job of some kind on the railroad. After supper it was not long before everybody was sleepy. I occupied the room with the school teacher. In a few minutes after we got into the room he was in bed and asleep; but I took advantage of the unusual luxury of a lamp which gave light, and sat looking over my notes and jotting down some ideas which were still fresh in my mind. Suddenly I became conscious of that sense of alarm which is always aroused by the sound of hurrying footsteps on the silence of the night. I stopped work and looked at my watch. It was after eleven. I listened, straining every nerve to hear above the tumult of my quickening pulse. I caught the murmur of voices, then the gallop of a horse, then of another and another. Now thoroughly alarmed, I woke my companion, and together we both listened. After a moment he put out the light and softly opened the window-blind, and we cautiously peeped out. We saw men moving in one direction, and from the mutterings we vaguely caught the rumor that some terrible crime had been committed. I put on my coat and hat. My friend did all in his power to dissuade me from venturing out, but it was impossible for me to remain in the house under such tense excitement. My nerves would not have stood it. Perhaps what bravery I exercised in going out was due to the fact that I felt sure my identity as a colored man had not yet become known in the town.

I went out and, following the drift, reached the railroad station. There was gathered there a crowd of men, all white, and others were steadily arriving, seemingly from all the surrounding country. How did the news spread so quickly? I watched these men moving under the yellow glare of the kerosene lamps about the station, stern, comparatively silent, all of them armed, some of them in boots and spurs; fierce, determined men. I had come to know the type well, blond, tall, and lean, with ragged mustache and beard, and glittering gray eyes. At the first suggestion of daylight they began to disperse in groups, going in several directions. There was no extra noise or excitement, no loud talking, only swift, sharp words of command given by those who seemed to be accepted as leaders by mutual understanding. In fact, the impression made upon me was that everything was being done in quite an orderly manner. In spite of so many leaving, the crowd around the station continued to grow; at sunrise there were a great many women and children. By this time I also noticed some colored people; a few seemed to be going about customary tasks; several were standing on the outskirts of the crowd; but the gathering of Negroes usually seen in such towns was missing.

Before noon they brought him in. Two horsemen rode abreast; between them, half dragged, the poor wretch made his way through the dust. His hands were tied behind him, and ropes around his body were fastened to the saddle horns of his double guard. The men who at midnight had been stern and silent were now emitting that terror-instilling sound known as the "rebel yell." A space was quickly cleared in the crowd, and a rope placed about his neck, when from somewhere came the suggestion, "Burn him!" It ran like an electric current. Have you ever witnessed the transformation of human beings into savage beasts? Nothing can be more terrible. A railroad tie was sunk into the ground, the rope was removed, and a chain brought and securely coiled around the victim and the stake. There he stood, a man only in form and stature, every sign of degeneracy stamped upon his countenance. His eyes were dull and vacant, indicating not a single ray of thought. Evidently the realization of his fearful fate had robbed him of whatever reasoning power he had ever possessed. He was too stunned and stupefied even to tremble. Fuel was brought from everywhere, oil, the torch; the flames crouched for an instant as though to gather strength, then leaped up as high as their victim's head. He squirmed, he writhed, strained at his chains, then gave out cries and groans that I shall always hear. The cries and groans were choked off by the fire and smoke; but his eyes, bulging from their sockets, rolled from side to side, appealing in vain for help. Some of the crowd yelled and cheered, others seemed appalled at what they had done, and there were those who turned away sickened at the sight. I was fixed to the spot where I stood, powerless to take my eyes from what I did not want to see.

It was over before I realized that time had elapsed. Before I could make myself believe that what I saw was really happening, I was looking at a scorched post, a smoldering fire, blackened bones, charred fragments sifting down through coils of chain; and the smell of burnt flesh—human flesh—was in my nostrils.

I walked a short distance away and sat down in order to clear my dazed mind. A great wave of humiliation and shame swept over me. Shame that I belonged to a race that could be so dealt with; and shame for my country, that it, the great example of democracy to the world, should be the only civilized, if not the only state on earth, where a human being would be burned alive. My heart turned bitter within me. I could understand why Negroes are led to sympathize with even their worst criminals and to protect them when possible. By all the impulses of normal human nature they can and should do nothing less.

Whenever I hear protests from the South that it should be left alone to deal with the Negro question, my thoughts go back to that scene of brutality and savagery. I do not see how a people that can find in its conscience any excuse whatever for slowly burning to death a human being, or for tolerating such an act, can be entrusted with the salvation of a race. Of course, there are in the South men of liberal thought who do not approve lynching, but I wonder how long they will endure the limits which are placed upon free speech. They still cower and tremble before "Southern opinion." Even so late as the recent Atlanta riot those men who were brave enough to speak a word in behalf of justice and humanity felt called upon, by way of apology, to preface what they said with a glowing rhetorical tribute to the Anglo-Saxon's superiority and to refer to the "great and impassable gulf" between the races "fixed by the Creator at the foundation of the world." The question of the relative qualities of the two races is still an open one. The reference to the "great gulf" loses force in face of the fact that there are in this country perhaps three or four million people with the blood of both races in their veins; but I fail to see the pertinency of either statement subsequent to the beating and murdering of scores of innocent people in the streets of a civilized and Christian city.

The Southern whites are in many respects a great people. Looked at from a certain point of view, they are picturesque. If one will put oneself in a romantic frame of mind, one can admire their notions of chivalry and bravery and justice. In this same frame of mind an intelligent man can go to the theatre and applaud the impossible hero, who with his single sword slays everybody in the play except the equally impossible heroine. So can an ordinary peace-loving citizen sit by a comfortable fire and read with enjoyment of the bloody deeds of pirates and the fierce brutality of Vikings. This is the way in which we gratify the old, underlying animal instincts and passions; but we should shudder with horror at the mere idea of such practices being realities in this day of enlightened and humanitarianized thought. The Southern whites are not yet living quite in the present age; many of their general ideas hark back to a former century, some of them to the Dark Ages. In the light of other days they are sometimes magnificent. Today they are often cruel and ludicrous.

How long I sat with bitter thoughts running through my mind I do not know; perhaps an hour or more. When I decided to get up and go back to the house, I found that I could hardly stand on my feet. I was as weak as a man who had lost blood. However, I dragged myself along, with the central idea of a general plan well fixed in my mind. I did not find my school teacher friend at home, so I did not see him again. I swallowed a few mouthfuls of food, packed my bag, and caught the afternoon train.

When I reached Macon, I stopped only long enough to get the main part of my luggage and to buy a ticket for New York. All along the journey I was occupied in debating with myself the step which I had decided to take. I argued that to forsake one's race to better one's condition was no less worthy an action than to forsake one's country for the same purpose. I finally made up my mind that I would neither disclaim the black race nor claim the white race; but that I would change my name, raise a mustache, and let the world take me for what it would; that it was not necessary for me to go about with a label of inferiority pasted across my forehead. All the while I understood that it was not discouragement or fear or search for a larger field of action and opportunity that was driving me out of the Negro race. I knew that it was shame, unbearable shame. Shame at being identified with a people that could with impunity be treated worse than animals. For certainly the law would restrain and punish the malicious burning alive of animals.

So once again I found myself gazing at the towers of New York and wondering what future that city held in store for me.

1912

The Creation

And God stepped out on space,
And he looked around and said:
I'm lonely—
I'll make me a world.

And far as the eye of God could see
Darkness covered everything,
Blacker than a hundred midnights
Down in a cypress swamp.

Then God smiled,
And the light broke,
And the darkness rolled up on one side,
And the light stood shining on the other,
And God said: That's good!

Then God reached out and took the light in his hands,
And God rolled the light around in his hands
Until he made the sun;
And he set that sun a-blazing in the heavens.
And the light that was left from making the sun
God gathered it up in a shining ball
And flung it against the darkness,
Spangling the night with the moon and stars.
Then down between
The darkness and the light
He hurled the world;
And God said: That's good!

Then God himself stepped down—
And the sun was on his right hand,
And the moon was on his left;
The stars were clustered about his head,
And the earth was under his feet.
And God walked, and where he trod
His footsteps hollowed the valleys out
And bulged the mountains up.

Then he stopped and looked and saw
That the earth was hot and barren.
So God stepped over to the edge of the world
And he spat out the seven seas—
He batted his eyes, and the lightnings flashed—
He clapped his hands, and the thunders rolled—

And the waters above the earth came down,
The cooling waters came down.

Then the green grass sprouted,
And the little red flowers blossomed,
The pine tree pointed his finger to the sky,
And the oak spread out his arms,
The lakes cuddled down in the hollows of the ground,
And the rivers ran down to the sea;
And God smiled again,
And the rainbow appeared,
And curled itself around his shoulder.

Then God raised his arm and he waved his hand
Over the sea and over the land,
And he said: Bring forth! Bring forth!
And quicker than God could drop his hand,
Fishes and fowls
And beasts and birds
Swam the rivers and the seas,
Roamed the forests and the woods,
And split the air with their wings.
And God said: That's good!

Then God walked around,
And God looked around
On all that he had made.
He looked at his sun,
And he looked at his moon,
And he looked at his little stars;
He looked on his world
With all its living things,
And God said: I'm lonely still.

Then God sat down—
On the side of a hill where he could think;
By a deep, wide river he sat down;
With his head in his hands,
God thought and thought,
Till he thought: I'll make me a man!

Up from the bed of the river
God scooped the clay;
And by the bank of the river
He kneeled him down;
And there the great God Almighty
Who lit the sun and fixed it in the sky,

Who flung the stars to the most far corner of the night,
Who rounded the earth in the middle of his hand;
This Great God,
Like a mammy bending over her baby,
Kneeled down in the dust
Toiling over a lump of clay
Till he shaped it in his own image;

Then into it he blew the breath of life,
And man became a living soul.
Amen. Amen.

1927

Edwin Arlington Robinson 1869–1935

America's first important poet of the twentieth century, Edwin Arlington Robinson is also the most prolific. Unlike his more prominent contemporaries—Frost, Stevens, Eliot, and Williams—Robinson devoted his energies exclusively to the writing of poetry. For that reason his life is markedly unremarkable, but he published an astonishing twenty volumes of poems which were eventually combined into *Collected Poems,* a volume of nearly 1500 pages. It is a Robinsonian irony that today he is known for only a handful of poems of the sort he once complained were "pickled in anthological brine."

He grew up in Gardiner, Maine, the "Tilbury Town" of his poetry, spent two years at Harvard, and went home to Maine where he published privately his first volume, *The Torrent and The Night Before,* in 1896. From 1911 onward he established a routine of spending the winters in New York City and the summers in New Hampshire at the McDowell Colony, where he did most of his writing. The first of his three Pulitzer Prizes was won for *Collected Poems* in 1921. He died in New York in 1935, literally hours after he had completed reading the galley proofs of *King Jasper.*

In his preface to *King Jasper,* Robert Frost said aptly that Robinson was "content with the old-fashioned way to be new." He was a strict traditionalist in his use of verse forms, experimenting in his early years with elaborate French forms, showing great proficiency with the sonnet, and turning to blank verse for his book-length narratives. In both subject matter and attitude, however, Robinson was an innovator. Frequently compared to Robert Browning and Henry James, he has been called variously realistic, romantic, naturalistic, and existential. His attitudes range from satire to understatement, from pessimism to compassion. Most pervasive is his sensitivity to the struggle in the human condition between the mundane and the mystical.

Rather than being simply a recorder of the failed life, as he has often been perceived, Robinson is actually a poet fascinated by how the unsuccessful cope. This celebration of the human spirit in spite of the disappointments of life is connected to an element of his poetry that has generally gone unnoticed: its autobiographical qualities. In 1965 Chard Powers Smith took as a thesis for his biography of Robinson, *Where the Light Falls,* that the preponderance of triangular love situations in the poetry is a direct result of E. A.'s having lost his fiancée, Emma Shepherd, to his brother Herman.

The selections in this anthology give only a partial indication of Robinson's range and variety. "The Clerks" represents one of his brief Tilbury Town portraits of ordinary individuals, but it also includes a reference to the life of a poet and thus combines two of his most prevalent themes. "Aunt Imogen" illustrates a medium-length character sketch of a woman who was basically in the same situation as Robinson in his relationship with his three nieces. The famous "Mr. Hood's Party" (which Robinson claimed was his favorite poem) transforms a boyhood prank in Gardiner. The infrequently anthologized "Momus" illustrates not only Robinson's playfulness but also his consciousness of the uncertain lot of a poet. "Eros Turannos" and "The Tree in Pamela's Garden" deal in contrasting ways with relationships between women and men.

Robinson wrote poetry that is contrivedly unspectacular, a characteristic that has cost him readers in the second half of the twentieth century. Nevertheless, the precision and skill with which he wrote and the human quality of his themes promise his work an enduring place in the American canon.

Nancy Carol Joyner
Western Carolina University

PRIMARY WORKS

Collected Poems, 1937; *Selected Letters,* 1940; *Uncollected Poems and Prose,* 1975.

The Clerks

I did not think that I should find them there
When I came back again; but there they stood,
As in the days they dreamed of when young blood
Was in their cheeks and women called them fair.
Be sure, they met me with an ancient air,—
And yes, there was a shop-worn brotherhood
About them; but the men were just as good,
And just as human as they ever were.

And you that ache so much to be sublime,
And you that feed yourselves with your descent,
What comes of all your visions and your fears?
Poets and kings are but the clerks of Time,
Tiering the same dull webs of discontent,
Clipping the same sad alnage[1] of the years.

1897

[1]A measure of cloth.

Aunt Imogen

Aunt Imogen was coming, and therefore
The children—Jane, Sylvester, and Young George—
Were eyes and ears; for there was only one
Aunt Imogen to them in the whole world,
And she was in it only for four weeks
In fifty-two. But those great bites of time
Made all September a Queen's Festival;
And they would strive, informally, to make
The most of them.—The mother understood,
And wisely stepped away. Aunt Imogen
Was there for only one month in the year,
While she, the mother,—she was always there;
And that was what made all the difference.
She knew it must be so, for Jane had once
Expounded it to her so learnedly
That she had looked away from the child's eyes
And thought; and she had thought of many things.

There was a demonstration every time
Aunt Imogen appeared, and there was more
Than one this time. And she was at a loss
Just how to name the meaning of it all:
It puzzled her to think that she could be
So much to any crazy thing alive—
Even to her sister's little savages
Who knew no better than to be themselves;
But in the midst of her glad wonderment
She found herself besieged and overcome
By two tight arms and one tumultuous head,
And therewith half bewildered and half pained
By the joy she felt and by the sudden love
That proved itself in childhood's honest noise.
Jane, by the wings of sex, had reached her first;
And while she strangled her, approvingly,
Sylvester thumped his drum and Young George howled.
But finally, when all was rectified,
And she had stilled the clamor of Young George
By giving him a long ride on her shoulders,
They went together into the old room
That looked across the fields; and Imogen
Gazed out with a girl's gladness in her eyes,
Happy to know that she was back once more
Where there were those who knew her, and at last
Had gloriously got away again

From cabs and clattered asphalt for a while;
And there she sat and talked and looked and laughed
And made the mother and the children laugh.
Aunt Imogen made everybody laugh.

There was the feminine paradox—that she
Who had so little sunshine for herself
Should have so much for others. How it was
That she could make, and feel for making it,
So much of joy for them, and all along
Be covering, like a scar, and while she smiled,
That hungering incompleteness and regret—
That passionate ache for something of her own,
For something of herself—she never knew.
She knew that she could seem to make them all
Believe there was no other part of her
Than her persistent happiness; but the why
And how she did not know. Still none of them
Could have a thought that she was living down—
Almost as if regret were criminal,
So proud it was and yet so profitless—
The penance of a dream, and that was good.
Her sister Jane—the mother of little Jane,
Sylvester, and Young George—might make herself
Believe she knew, for she—well, she was Jane.

Young George, however, did not yield himself
To nourish the false hunger of a ghost
That made no good return. He saw too much:
The accumulated wisdom of his years
Had so conclusively made plain to him
The permanent profusion of a world
Where everybody might have everything
To do, and almost everything to eat,
That he was jubilantly satisfied
And all unthwarted by adversity.
Young George knew things. The world, he had found out,
Was a good place, and life was a good game—
Particularly when Aunt Imogen
Was in it. And one day it came to pass—
One rainy day when she was holding him
And rocking him—that he, in his own right,
Took it upon himself to tell her so;
And something in his way of telling it—
The language, or the tone, or something else—
Gripped like insidious fingers on her throat,
And then went foraging as if to make

A plaything of her heart. Such undeserved
And unsophisticated confidence
Went mercilessly home; and had she sat
Before a looking glass, the deeps of it
Could not have shown more clearly to her then
Than one thought-mirrored little glimpse had shown,
The pang that wrenched her face and filled her eyes
With anguish and intolerable mist.
The blow that she had vaguely thrust aside
Like fright so many times had found her now:
Clean-thrust and final it had come to her
From a child's lips at last, as it had come
Never before, and as it might be felt
Never again. Some grief, like some delight,
Stings hard but once: to custom after that
The rapture or the pain submits itself,
And we are wiser than we were before.
And Imogen was wiser; though at first
Her dream-defeating wisdom was indeed
A thankless heritage: there was no sweet,
No bitter now; nor was there anything
To make a daily meaning for her life—
Till truth, like Harlequin,[1] leapt out somehow
From ambush and threw sudden savor to it—
But the blank taste of time. There were no dreams,
No phantoms in her future any more:
One clinching revelation of what was
One by-flash of irrevocable chance,
Had acridly but honestly foretold
The mystical fulfilment of a life
That might have once . . . But that was all gone by:
There was no need of reaching back for that:
The triumph was not hers: there was no love
Save borrowed love: there was no might have been.

But there was yet Young George—and he had gone
Conveniently to sleep, like a good boy;
And there was yet Sylvester with his drum,
And there was frowzle-headed little Jane;
And there was Jane the sister, and the mother,—
Her sister, and the mother of them all.
They were not hers, not even one of them:
She was not born to be so much as that,
For she was born to be Aunt Imogen.

[1]A traditional buffoon of Italian comedy.

Now she could see the truth and look at it;
Now she could make stars out where once had palled
A future's emptiness; now she could share
With others—ah, the others!—to the end
The largess of a woman who could smile;
Now it was hers to dance the folly down,
And all the murmuring; now it was hers
To be Aunt Imogen.—So, when Young George
Woke up and blinked at her with his big eyes,
And smiled to see the way she blinked at him,
'T was only in old concord with the stars
That she took hold of him and held him close,
Close to herself, and crushed him till he laughed.

1902

Momus[1]

"Where's the need of singing now?"—
Smooth your brow,
Momus, and be reconciled,
For King Kronos[2] is a child—
Child and father,
Or god rather,
And all gods are wild.

"Who reads Byron[3] any more?"—
Shut the door,
Momus, for I feel a draught;
Shut it quick, for some one laughed.—
"What's become of
Browning? Some of
Wordsworth[4] lumbers like a raft?
"What are poets to find here?"—
Have no fear:
When the stars are shining blue

[1]Minor Greek deity, god of blame and ridicule.
[2]In Greek mythology, a Titan who ruled the universe until dethroned by his son, Zeus.
[3]Prominent 19th-century British poet who made satirical attacks on critics in "English Bards and Scottish Reviewers" and "Who Killed John Keats?"
[4]Robert Browning (1812–1889) and William Wordsworth (1770–1850), two prominent British poets of the 19th century, both of whom share Robinson's penchant for long narrative poems.

There will yet be left a few
Themes availing—
And these failing,
Momus, there'll be you.

1910

Eros Turannos[1]

She fears him, and will always ask
  What fated her to choose him;
She meets in his engaging mask
  All reasons to refuse him;
But what she meets and what she fears
Are less than are the downward years,
Drawn slowly to the foamless weirs
  Of age, were she to lose him.

Between a blurred sagacity
  That once had power to sound him,
And Love, that will not let him be
  The Judas[2] that she found him,
Her pride assuages her almost,
As if it were alone the cost.—
He sees that he will not be lost,
  And waits and looks around him.

A sense of ocean and old trees
  Envelops and allures him;
Tradition, touching all he sees,
  Beguiles and reassures him;
And all her doubts of what he says
Are dimmed with what she knows of days—
Till even prejudice delays
  And fades, and she secures him.

The falling leaf inaugurates
  The reign of her confusion;
The pounding wave reverberates
  The dirge of her illusion;

[1]Greek: "Love, the Tyrant."
[2]See Matthew 26:47–49.

And home, where passion lived and died,
Becomes a place where she can hide,
While all the town and harbor side
  Vibrate with her seclusion.

We tell you, tapping on our brows,
  The story as it should be,—
As if the story of a house
  Were told, or ever could be;
We'll have no kindly veil between
Her visions and those we have seen,—
As if we guessed what hers have been,
  Or what they are or would be.

Meanwhile we do no harm; for they
  That with a god have striven,
Not hearing much of what we say,
  Take what the god has given;
Though like waves breaking it may be,
Or like a changed familiar tree,
Or like a stairway to the sea
  Where down the blind are driven.

1916

The Tree in Pamela's Garden

Pamela was too gentle to deceive
Her roses. "Let the men stay where they are,"
She said, "and if Apollo's avatar[1]
Be one of them, I shall not have to grieve."
And so she made all Tilbury Town[2] believe
She sighed a little more for the North Star
Than over men, and only in so far
As she was in a garden was like Eve.

Her neighbors—doing all that neighbors can
To make romance of reticence meanwhile—
Seeing that she had never loved a man,

[1]Embodiment. Apollo, unlucky in love, has been called "the most Greek of the Greek gods."

[2]Robinson's fictional name for his home town, Gardiner, Maine.

Wished Pamela had a cat, or a small bird,
And only would have wondered at her smile
Could they have seen that she had overheard.

1921

Mr. Flood's Party

Old Eben Flood, climbing alone one night
Over the hill between the town below
And the forsaken upland hermitage
That held as much as he should ever know
On earth again of home, paused warily.
The road was his with not a native near;
And Eben, having leisure, said aloud,
For no man else in Tilbury Town to hear:

"Well, Mr. Flood, we have the harvest moon
Again, and we may not have many more;
The bird is on the wing, the poet says[1]
And you and I have said it here before.
Drink to the bird." He raised up to the light
The jug that he had gone so far to fill,
And answered huskily: "Well, Mr. Flood,
Since you propose it, I believe I will."

Alone, as if enduring to the end
A valiant armor of scarred hopes outworn,
He stood there in the middle of the road
Like Roland's ghost winding a silent horn.[2]
Below him, in the town among the trees,
Where friends of other days had honored him,
A phantom salutation of the dead
Rang thinly till old Eben's eyes were dim.

Then, as a mother lays her sleeping child
Down tenderly, fearing it may awake,
He set the jug down slowly at his feet
With trembling care, knowing that most things break;
And only when assured that on firm earth

[1]See Edward Fitzgerald, *The Rubaiyat of Omar Khayyam,* 11.27–28.

[2]In *Song of Roland,* Roland died after he had blown his horn to warn Charlemagne.

It stood, as the uncertain lives of men
Assuredly did not, he paced away,
And with his hand extended paused again:

"Well, Mr. Flood, we have not met like this
In a long time; and many a change has come
To both of us, I fear, since last it was
We had a drop together. Welcome home!"
Convivially returning with himself,
Again he raised the jug up to the light;
And with an acquiescent quaver said:
"Well, Mr. Flood, if you insist, I might.

"Only a very little, Mr. Flood—
For auld lang syne.[3] No more, sir; that will do."
So, for the time, apparently it did,
And Eben evidently thought so too;
For soon amid the silver loneliness
Of night he lifted up his voice and sang,
Secure, with only two moons listening,
Until the whole harmonious landscape rang—

"For auld lang syne." The weary throat gave out,
The last word wavered, and the song was done;
He raised again the jug regretfully
And shook his head, and was again alone.
There was not much that was ahead of him,
And there was nothing in the town below—
Where strangers would have shut the many doors
That many friends had opened long ago.

1920

Ellen Glasgow 1873–1945

Southern literature was romantic when Ellen Glasgow began writing. She saw herself as a realist bringing "blood and irony" to a society based on pretense. The vantage from which most of her nineteen novels were written was the family home at One West Main Street in Richmond. As a child she watched her gentle mother, a lady of the Virginia aristocracy, decline to nervous invalidism after bearing ten children. Her father, manager of an ironworks, appeared self-righteous and unfeeling to a daughter who would, nevertheless, give some of her more admirable characters a Scots-Calvinist background like his and a similar "vein of iron."

As a young woman Ellen Glasgow re-

[3]Scottish dialect for "days long gone." The song is attributed to Robert Burns.

fused to attend church with her father, an act of intellectual rebellion. Without much formal schooling she read, on her own, advanced thinkers of the time and was particularly influenced by Social Darwinism, a philosophy which hardly consoled her for what she saw as life's cruelty. Poor health and loss of hearing that sent her to many doctors over the years increased the pessimism.

The hero of Glasgow's first novel is an "illegitimate" outcast from a southern town who becomes, briefly, a radical journalist. Written in secret and published anonymously, *The Descendant* (1897) was intended to shock. The author, who later provided newspapers with a photograph of herself in white ruffles, was aware of the incongruity of her writing on matters about which a young lady was supposed to know nothing. Yet Glasgow did not at first make women's roles her major theme, and she was slow to place heroines rather than heroes at the centers of the stories.

In *Virginia* (1913) the protagonist is a woman, though not a rebel. Virginia Pendleton, based on Glasgow's mother, is an old-fashioned southern lady raised on "the simple theory that the less a girl knew about life, the better prepared she would be to contend with it." The author was capable of irony about such figures, sustained by illusion, at times controlling through weakness. Blind Mrs. Blake in *The Deliverance* (1904) is protected by her family from knowing the Civil War is lost and the slaves freed. But Virginia is treated sympathetically, even idealized, as Glasgow tended to idealize all her heroines.

The author depicted a new kind of woman that feminism and confidence in evolution made her believe possible. She had difficulty, though, imagining a woman's life that combined love and work. The feminine quality of sympathy which made a heroine worthy of interest would lead her, like Judith Campbell in "The Professional Instinct," to choose love over ambition. In *The Woman Within* (1954), an autobiography written for post-humous publication, Glasgow tells of a long, secret affair with a married man she had met in New York. Later she was engaged twice, even collaborating on novels with one fiancé, but did not marry. Her best work was done when love was over, she said.

The novel of greatest personal importance to the author was *Barren Ground* (1925), in which she felt she had reversed the traditional seduction plot. When Glasgow's heroines are strong, they are so only because men are weak, and the women's victories are sad triumphs. She thought that writing *Barren Ground,* a "tragedy," freed her for the comedies of manners *The Romantic Comedians* (1926), *They Stooped to Folly* (1929), and *The Sheltered Life* (1932). These late works are the most artful criticism of romantic illusion in all her long career.

Linda Pannill
Transylvania University

PRIMARY WORKS

Virginia, 1913; *Barren Ground,* 1925; *The Romantic Comedians,* 1926; *They Stooped to Folly,* 1929; *The Sheltered Life,* 1932; *Vein of Iron,* 1935; *A Certain Measure: An Interpretation of Prose Fiction,* 1943; *The Woman Within,* 1954; *The Collected Stories of Ellen Glasgow,* ed. Richard K. Meeker, 1963.

The Professional Instinct[1]

As he unfolded his napkin and broke his toast with the precise touch of fingers that think, Doctor John Estbridge concluded that holidays were becoming unbearable. Christmas again, he reflected gloomily, and Christmas in New York, with a heavy snowstorm that meant weeks of dirt and slush and back-breaking epidemics of influenza and pneumonia! Beyond the curtains of rose-colored damask the storm rocked the boughs of an ailanthus tree[2] which grew midway of the high-fenced backyard. Long ago, in the days of his youth and mania for reform, Estbridge remembered that he had once tried to convert the backyard into an Italian garden. For a brief season box had survived, if it had not actually flourished there, and a cypress tree, sent by an ex-patient from Northern Italy, had lived through a single summer and had died with the first frost of winter. That was nearly twenty years ago, for Estbridge had relinquished his garden with the other dreams of his youth, and to-day the brawny ailanthus stood there as a symbol of the prosperous failure of his career.

"What's to be got out of this business of living anyhow?" he enquired, gazing over his breakfast at a portrait of Savonarola[3] which hung above the French clock on the mantelpiece. With a laugh he recalled that it had been his business for twenty years to answer this immemorial question for the satisfaction of the unsound or the dejected. "To have stuffed all those poor devils with sawdust," he added, and a minute later: "By Jove, if happiness were only as cheap as philosophy!"

Within the last few weeks several cases of changed personalities had passed through his hands. They concerned men and women, not far from his own age, who had undergone curious psychological crises that emerged quite new personalities and the thought flashed through his mind that he was in something of the same mental state at this moment. "What if I should cut it good and begin over again?" he asked suddenly. "What if I should take the only way out and cut it for good?"

Over the trivial French clock the eyes of the great Italian reformer looked down on him. "You were right, Monk, as far as you went," murmured Estbridge ironically, "but the primal force got beyond you: the trouble was that man wanted his little happiness in Florence just as badly as he wants it here to-day in New York."

For a blank instant, while his gaze still hung on the portrait, he tried to evoke the impression of that day, more than twenty years ago, when he had bought the picture and hung it with his own hands over his mantel. Even after the crucial scene of last night he had never forgotten the curious episode. It was the morning after he had seen Tilly Pratt in a graduating play; and though the girl had laid aside her religious fervor as easily as she had the flowing robes and cowl of the Florentine Friar, she had still impersonated the militant idealism of Estbridge's youth. For he had loved Tilly,

[1]Left in manuscript, this story was not published until 1962, when William W. Kelly edited it for *Western Humanities Review.* Kelly, whose text is reproduced here, dates composition between 1916 and 1924. The manuscript is housed at Alderman Library, University of Virginia.

[2]Tree of Heaven, a Chinese import much used in urban gardens. *Box,* below, is boxwood, the evergreen shrub.

[3]*Savonarola* (1452–1498), Dominican friar. Preached moral reform in Florence and briefly gained political power there. Remembered for "burning of the vanities," including some books. Falling to his enemies, he was hanged and burned.

not for herself, but because she had shown him his own image. Like most men, according to the analytical psychologists, he had identified his own dreams with the shape of a woman. "Yes, it was not you, Tilly. You were not Savonarola," he said.

For a grey quarter of a century hung now like a fog between the ample figure of the present Mrs. Estbridge and the girl who had bewitched him during his interneship at Christ's Hospital. It was impossible for the most active imagination to create an illusion about the wife who invariably ruffled his contentment and devoured his time. Florid, robust, and bristling with activity, she had triumphantly checkmated him during the twenty years of their marriage. So relentless had been her rule, that her victim, though still at bay, had been forced to accord a critical admiration to her performance. But for her amazing perseverance, he thought now, his whole life might have been different, and instead of missing the coveted chair of physiology at the University, he might have watched some of his early dreams acquire the outlines and substance of reality. But for her he might have abandoned his profession as a means, no longer necessary, of breadwinning; and but for her, he added bitterly after a minute, he might have used his great experience and his undoubted gift to raise the vision and standards of accomplishment in the schools where doctors were formed. Yes, she had always been at his elbow, holding him back. It was incredible; it was diabolical; but she had done it for twenty years, and she was doing it still!

A convenient neurosis, cured now and then, but intermittently subject to relapse in favor of some new doctor, kept Mrs. Estbridge in bed for breakfast; and Estbridge had come to grasp eagerly this one rich hour of solitude. Between eight and nine o'clock, no one invaded the dining-room where he sat at his simple breakfast which had been left by some servant who had vanished. If the telephone rang he did not answer it. If patients chose that hour to die, they died without his attentions. There was no rustling of newspapers, no slitting of fresh correspondence. The only sound in the room was the bubbling of the coffee percolator, and while this morning he brooded over the meal, he was thankfully aware of the restful hush of the place—of the mute service of inanimate things which surrounded him.

"That's the last straw—to miss that appointment," he thought. "To have worked for twenty years, and then to see the chair go to Adamson—to Adamson who was my assistant when he began." With the words he rose hurriedly from the table, and crossing to the window, looked out on the swaying ailanthus tree. "There's but one way out, and no one could blame me for taking it," he added under his breath.

The sound of the opening door made him wheel quickly about, and he shivered with a nervous movement of protest as he found himself facing the commanding form of his wife.

"Doctor Railston says I may begin to get up for breakfast," she remarked affably, as she passed to the head of the table, and took her place behind the archaic silver service she had inherited from some Pratt who had figured in history. "So I planned a little surprise for you."

While she smiled benignly upon him, Estbridge realized that she had become, by the authority of metaphor and fact, an immovable body. Though he had longed for years to forbid her the room, he knew that he was morally powerless to do so. Her presence now was merely part of the whole plan; and in the very instant that he perceived her design, he understood that he was incapable of making an effort to thwart it. Just as she had victoriously substituted herself for his profession and for the few free hours at the end of his day, she meant now, he saw, to devour the one brief interval of time he could call his own. Not content with destroying his happiness, she was opening, with the best possible intentions, an attack upon the intellectual side of his work.

"You drink too much strong coffee," she said as her competent glance swept the table. "Bates tells me you sometimes fill the percolator twice."

He had fallen back into his chair, and while his lip tightened with exasperation, he watched her ring the bell and order bacon and eggs. From the moment when she had entered, she had become the dominant figure. She was a woman, and by virtue of her womanhood she had made the breakfast table her ally. By every law, by every custom she was fulfilling the domestic tradition; and without disturbing a convention, without disobeying a religious behest, she was ruining his life. Society was on her side—God, he felt for one bitter moment, was on her side. Had she been violent or vicious, he might have withstood her; but her authority was rooted in virtue, and before the tyranny of virtue he was helpless.

While she sat there, calmly waiting for her breakfast, he surveyed her large handsome face with a resentful gaze. From her stiff iron grey hair to her firm and massive figure, she presented a picture of matronly rectitude. The very perfection of her type was the thing he found it hardest to forgive in her. She was born to be "a good manager," and it was not to be expected that her inherited talent should stop short before the man whom fate, or his own folly, had delivered into her hands. With children to occupy her, she might have found, he realized, other outlets for her benevolent impulses; but there were no children, and as the years went by he had ceased his early rejoicing that his wife lacked the inclination for public reforms. From a firmly efficient management of her household, she had passed, without perceptible loss of either firmness or efficiency, to the management of his clothes, his diet, his exercise, and the number and the brands of his cigarettes. With an unholy dread he saw that it was only a question of time—perhaps days—before she would begin to "manage" his hospital.

"I want you to eat more breakfast, John." She was pouring a plentiful supply of hot milk into her coffee. "And it is really absurd of you to fancy that you can think while you eat."

From the oblong mirror over the sideboard the reflection of his own features flashed back at him, and he stared at his distinguished face as if it had been the face of a stranger. Although they were exactly the same age, he became suddenly aware that he looked at least ten years younger than the capable lady whom he had married. Science had kept him young in return for the passion he had lavished upon her. In his bright blue eyes, which grew hard enough on occasions, still glistened the eternal enquiring spirit of youth. His dark hair had silvered, but it was still thick, and his compact and muscular figure had escaped the increasing weight which sent most of his contemporaries into belated training.

"Thank heaven for this holiday." She was beginning to ramble. "There won't be any need for you to rush off this morning. If it's Christmas, it might as well be a merry one."

She was in an amiable mood, and it was plain to him, after the first moment or two, that the scene of last night had barely ruffled the surface of her composure. Well, of course, if a thing like that didn't ruffle one! A smile, half of humor, half of irony, twisted his lip, while there floated through his mind a sentence from one of his lectures on mental deficiency: *"To be unable to recall experience and to profit by it is a common characteristic of the morons."*

When she had skewered the last bit of bacon on her fork, and not before, Mrs. Estbridge raised her eyes again to her husband.

"Have you heard that the chair of physiology has been given to Adamson?"

"Yes, I heard." A flush rose to Estbridge's face, staining his scholarly brow under the silver hair. The board of trustees had not only passed him over—they had passed him over for Adamson, a young fellow with merely a fair record and, as Estbridge told himself now, with a hopelessly limited horizon. If not Estbridge, it must, of course, have been Adamson—but by all that was fair and honest, it should have been Estbridge! What other man in New York combined his venturesome imagination with his sound knowledge and understanding of modern achievement?

"How did you get the news?" he asked after a minute. Was it possible that here also she had helped to defeat him? In the old days when he had tried to make her share in his ambition to be a leader of young men, he remembered she had laughingly said to him more than once: "But that sounds very foolish to me. What's the use of standing up before a lot of Jews and telling them things that are all in the books anyhow?"

"Aunt Clara came in last evening," she replied, and added with a scarcely perceptible emphasis: "after you went out. Uncle Timothy rushed the appointment through, and would hear of no one but Adamson. He insisted on having a practical man. . . ."

So it was out at last! Old Timothy Pratt, his wife's uncle, had won over the board of trustees to Adamson . . . old Timothy Pratt, who had trebled in inherited fortune though he never got up before mid-day.

"Of course I know that your uncle was opposed to me," said Estbridge, "but I had counted on Jim." Until that instant he had not realized how much he had counted on Jim Hoadly.

"Poor old Jim." Mrs. Estbridge's voice was faintly patronizing. "He did his best, but he is hardly a match for Uncle Timothy. I wonder why he doesn't come here any more?" As she paused she reached for the jar of marmalade and (helped) herself to an even spoonful. It was Mrs. Estbridge's proudest boast that she let nothing impair her appetite.

"I trust that Aunt Clara at least is pleased." Estbridge had recovered his humor, if not his temper.

"Not at all. On the contrary she asked me several weeks ago about the advisability of her speaking to Uncle Timothy. She seemed to feel, and quite naturally, I think, that Uncle Timothy ought not to . . . at least that he ought not to appear to be leading a fight against you. . . ."

"Indeed!"

"But, of course, when she asked me frankly, I was obliged to tell her what I thought. . . ."

His nerves jerked, and pushing back his chair, he walked quickly to the door.

"Yes, John, when she asked me for the truth, I was obliged to speak it. Even as things are now, I was forced to tell her that I rarely see you, that you show signs of irritability—you know you do, John—that you are overworked, and that any well-wisher. . . ."

The volume of sound was interrupted by the sudden entrance of Bates, who felt, doubtless, that if the doctor had taken to entertaining at breakfast, the butler was entitled to be present. But even if the sombre Englishman, compressed to silence by generations of servitude, had miraculously acquired the gift of fluent speech, it would have availed him little against the torrential overflow of directions which followed Estbridge into the hall.

"John, it is snowing hard." The voice pursued him with the imperious accents of destiny. "If you *will* go out, don't forget to put on your overshoes."

One overshoe was already half on, but prying it off, Estbridge kicked it furiously under the hat-rack. "It would be an interesting experience," he muttered to himself as he slammed the door behind him, "if some rainy day she should remind me to put on my hat. I wonder what the devil I should do if she did?"

As he plunged through the storm in the direction of Fifth Avenue, he felt that his body vibrated in every cell and fibre with rebellion. It was a revolt not only against his wife, but against the whole world of women. At the instant he saw all women as victorious over the lives and destinies of men. As for his wife, he knew now, as he had known for years, that he had never perhaps loved any woman. He was passing the mansion of Mr. Pratt, just a few blocks south of the Park, and as he glanced up at the high windows, framed in snow, he felt that he wanted to curse the pompous old mandarin still asleep in his bed.

"Why shouldn't I cut it for good?" he asked again as he had asked an hour before. "By God, I will cut it for good! I'll take the post that is still open at Shanghai!" The wish which had created the thought evolved from a simple impulse into a practical idea. He saw before him a definite vision of freedom, and he saw the ten vigorous years ahead of him crowded, not with vain attempts, not with frustrated efforts, but with adventure, accomplishment, and reward.

The door of his office swung back into emptiness, and he rejoiced for the first time in the holiday which had relieved him of his usual staff of helpers. As he turned, still with the thought of Shanghai in his mind, to an atlas on the table of his waiting-room, he saw a woman's figure dimly outlined against the glass of the door. "Can it be Judith Campbell?" he thought while a tremor passed over him. Then, flinging the door open, he fell back a step, and stood waiting for her to cross the threshold. "What an angel you are to come to me through the storm!"

She entered slowly, wrapped in dark furs to the chin, and he had an impression even before she spoke, of the softness and grace of her manner.

"I felt that you would be here, and I couldn't let Christmas go by without seeing you for a minute." Stopping beside the table, with its litter of last year's magazines, she gazed up at him with the strange gentleness which had first drawn him to her—that rare gentleness, he found himself thinking now, which alone can make a woman the equal of men.

"I wanted to bring my little gift," she said. "Last year I should hardly have dared." While he watched her take from her muff the white package, with its red ribbon and spray of holly, he became aware that her body like her mind was compacted of delicate graces, of exquisite surprises. Though she had been for years the professor of philosophy in a college for women, she was as feminine in appearance as any early Victorian heroine of fiction. She was, he realized forcibly at the instant, everything that his wife was not and could never become. His wife was a dull woman with an instinct to dominate; but Judith Campbell—he felt this as he had never felt it before—was a clever woman with an instinct to yield.

"Your coming begins my Christmas," he said, and the words sounded so inadequate as he uttered them that he went on more rapidly: "I am so glad. It is your book. May I open it?"

She shook her head with a little laugh that had a yielding and tremulous grace. "After I go, I can stay only a minute."

The slender figure in the heavy furs had the look of a cypress-tree that sways and bends under the storm. Through the veil of dotted net her large grey eyes still gazed at him with an enigmatical softness. Even her intellect, in spite of its flashing brilliance, gave him this impression of softness and grace, as if its strength were tempered by sympathy. Though she had always appeared in her spiritual detachment to stand above the more commonplace aspects of passion, he had sometimes wondered if her perfect response to his moods meant a gradual change in her friendship. Could her delicate intuitions remain insensible to the inevitable course such things take?

And yet only at this moment did he realize that his will was drawing him to her. Against his judgment, against his ideals, against his teaching and his habits, the will to live was driving him away from his work to the love of a woman. To his profession, and his conception of what it might some day become, he had dedicated both his intellect and his passion. For twenty years his marriage had been sufficient to keep him out of casual temptation; and his friendship for Jim Hoadly had supplied him, as he blindly supposed, with all that he required of sympathy and understanding. But at this instant, looking back on his association with Judith Campbell—on their first rare meetings at joint boards, on their occasional walks in the Park, on an evening now and then at some waterside restaurant during the summer, on the substantial help he had been able to give her in her work, and more than all on the ready comprehension with which she had met him from the start—looking back on all these things, he saw, with a luminous flash of understanding, that the miracle of renewed youth had occurred. While he stood there he felt like a man who had gone shivering to sleep in the winter, and had awakened to find the scented air of spring blowing in his window.

"There is something else I must tell you." Her soft voice quivered for an instant. "I had this morning the offer of the presidency of Hartwell College."

He breathed hard with suspense, yet he could think of nothing to say except the obvious: "But that's in St. Louis."

"Yes."

"And you will accept it?"

"Yes, I shall accept it."

"That means you will live in St. Louis?"

"That means I shall live in St. Louis."

The parrying had restored his composure. "You have always wanted something like that more than anything else in the world."

"I told myself this morning that I had always wanted such a place more than anything in the world."

The note of hesitation in her voice made him look at her quickly. He had always supposed that her face was too strong, too intelligent, to conform to any standard of beauty, but he recognized now, with a start, that she embodied the complete and absolute perfection of womanhood. And he felt that he wanted her as from his youth up he had wanted the unattainable—as an hour ago he had wanted the chair of physiology that went to Adamson.

"You deserve it," he said after a pause. "It is the outcome of your work, and the crowning of your ambition."

"Yes," the word faltered on her lips. "I suppose it is the crowning of my ambition." Though her age was thirty-eight there was the shyness of a girl in her eyes, and by her shyness and the quiver of her lashes as he looked at her, he knew that she loved him.

"I wish," she pursued slowly, "that I had no ambition."

"But would you give it up?" It was a simple enough question, and yet after he had put it, he stood watching her as if he were in a laboratory awaiting the result of some physiological experiment.

"Crowning a woman's ambition often makes her a beggar," she answered quietly, adding after a minute, "What a shame it is about Adamson!"

He laughed grimly. "Yes, I did want that; more, perhaps, than you wanted Hartwell. But that's over now. Who knows, after all, if it wasn't something else that I wanted?"

Her look touched him like a caress. "If I could only give you what I have."

"And yet it is the highest honor that could come to you."

She smiled, a little wearily he thought, as she answered:

"That is why I would give it to you."

"Judith!"

She had moved a step nearer the door, and stopping there at his call, she looked back with a startled glow in her face.

"Judith, would you give it up if I asked you?"

"If you asked me?"

"Would you stay—would you give it up if I asked you?" The glow in her face seemed to pervade her whole body while she stood before him transfigured.

"I would give up the whole world if you asked me."

"You would sacrifice your ambition—your future?"

A laugh broke from her lips. "I haven't any ambition—any future—except yours." It was as if the passive substance of her nature had flamed into energy.

He walked to the window, gazing down on the city, which loomed in bizarre outlines through the storm. "It's this way with me," he began impersonally, as if to the street. "An hour ago I made up my mind to quit New York for good. You know most of the reasons. All of them now since you know about Adamson. I have made up my mind to begin over again, and for once to get down to some real work—something genuine—in China. I told you about the post in Shanghai. Well, I am going to take it."

She drew her breath sharply, and though he still looked away from her, he felt her very will had passed into the flame and fervor of his.

"For twenty years I have thought that my hour would come," he said in a voice which he tried in vain to make as guarded as his manner. "It has come now."

"It has come now?" Her words were scarcely more than a sigh faintly drawn.

"It is here, and I want to grasp it while I have still the courage. I want to grasp it before it escapes me."

Though she looked as if she would yield—as if she would dissolve at a touch, he did not stretch out his hand to her. He had made his appeal and she had answered it.

"Yes, if I go, I must go while I have the courage. I must go now—to-day," he went on, gaining confidence while he watched her drooping under the weight of her furs. "I must go while you will go with me."

As he moved a step nearer, she swayed towards him, and for a moment he held her close with a gentleness that was strangely sacramental for a lover. Neither spoke until she released herself, and threw back her veil with the gesture of one who is casting aside the burden of years.

"Wherever you go, I will go with you," she said.

"You will go with me to-day?"

She glanced with brightly questioning eyes at the clock. "Is there a boat on Christmas day?"

He laughed, and with the sound he looked suddenly boyish. "Oh, enchanting professor of philosophy! No, there isn't a boat, but we'll catch the noon train to Chicago. To-morrow we'll go on to San Francisco, and after that the way will be easy. You have an hour. Will you be ready?"

"It will not take me an hour. I can get what I need in San Francisco."

He was allowing her only an hour, she knew, because to go at all they must go without thinking. They must act at once as each had dreamed so often of acting, in obedience to the divine indomitable impulse. They must follow with bandaged eyes the spirit of adventure.

"And I'll go after burning my boats. I shan't even look over my papers. There must be no compromises." Then, as if craving movement, action, certainty, he glanced at the clock. "I'll telephone my man to send my things to the train. There will be a sudden call to Chicago. In exactly fifty-five minutes will you meet me in the Pennsylvania Station—by the gate?"

"I shall not fail you. I shall never fail you."

With the promise she had gone; and crossing to the window of the outer office, he looked down on her figure making its way through the storm. In the midst of thronging pedestrians, of noisy motors, of newsboys frantically crying the extras, he watched her press evenly forward until at last the whirling snowflakes gathered her in.

Well, that was over! He had made his decision; he had burned his boats; and no good could come from looking back over his shoulder. While he stood there gazing down into the street, he felt that the flame and glory of his hour was still with him. His nerves no longer reacted jarringly to his surroundings. He was aware of a complete, harmonious adjustment to the circumstances of his life. Destiny for once moved in obedience to his will. It was all so easy—this quick shedding of the husks of the past, this putting forth, with renewed growth and vigor, in a strange soil amid an alien people. What fools men were to talk of convention and experience! All one needed was the will to choose, the courage to act promptly.

Turning to his desk, he mechanically rang for his secretary, before he remembered that the day was Christmas. Then, reflecting with a smile that he couldn't very well use her for the business on hand, he began hurriedly filling his black portfolio with check-books, manuscripts, and letters which required personal answers. While he sorted his papers, littering the floor with what was not needed, and lighting a fire in the grate in order to burn certain documents which he wished to destroy, he found himself thinking, not of the post at Shanghai, not of the future with Judith Campbell, but of the chair of physiology which had been given to Adamson. The hurt had not healed. Though he told himself passionately that life without Judith would not be worth living, he was aware that beneath his happiness the wound to his ambition still throbbed.

He had been barely ten minutes at his task when an imperative knock on the door forced him to open it.

"I might have known who it was," he thought moodily as he turned the knob. "What an ass I was not to hide where he couldn't find me."

Jim Hoadly was a big man—so big that he seemed to fill the space in the doorway, and his mere physical bulk had always possessed a curious fascination for his classmate. To-day, however, Estbridge was conscious of a latent antagonism, of a secret revolt against all the qualities he had once admired in his friend. It was as if the demon of the inopportune had suddenly entered.

"I knew I'd find you here," began the caller, while he shook the snow from his shoulders with a vigorous movement. "No," he went on gaily in reply to the question in Estbridge's eyes, "I didn't even try at the house." A minute afterwards, as he passed through the doorway of the inner office, he broke into a low whistle of astonishment. "Whew! Quite a wind blowing, isn't there? and a conflagration on top of it!"

"I lit a fire, that's all." Estbridge was trying to smile unconcernedly.

"If I remember rightly it isn't your first fire either," retorted Hoadly, drying his sandy beard with his fingers. "You know, Jack, I always said you could act when your hour caught you."

"My hour?" Estbridge's glance flew to the clock. "Well you were right, Jim, my hour has caught me, and I am acting. I am leaving at twelve o'clock—for the future."

A grey light, as if from the sombre sky outside, sobered Jim's merry features. "Do you mean to kill yourself, Jack?"

"Kill myself?" Estbridge laughed with joy. "No, I am going to live. For the first time in my life, I am going to live!"

Though Hoadly had led a life of singular detachment, twenty-five years of journalism had made him a shrewd interpreter of the emotions of others. "Shall I go through the form of enquiring," he asked airily, "if you intend to begin this new existence alone?"

"Alone? No."

"You won't mind my asking, I suppose, if Judith Campbell goes with you?"

For a moment Estbridge looked as if he were about to show resentment. Then his manner grew flippant, and he replied carelessly: "Well, why shouldn't you know? I want you to know before anyone else. You won't have a start of more than twenty-four hours over the papers at that."

"So it's the famous professor of philosophy!" Jim's tone was measured in its calmness. "I must say I find it hard to follow these feminists. But, Jack, you can't do it!"

"Who's to stop me?" Estbridge's voice was sharp with defiance.

"I am."

The thought of physical violence shot through Estbridge's mind, and he retorted angrily, "Don't try that game, it is dangerous."

"Oh, I don't know," responded Jim drily. "I've tried it before now, and I'm still living. But, come, Jack, you can't toss aside an old friend so easily. At least you can't do it until you have offered him a chair," he added, flinging himself into the worn leather chair facing the window. "I may sit down, I suppose, while I argue. Great Jove! How many poor devils, I wonder, have sat here before me?"

"You may sit down and you may argue," replied Estbridge, "but you won't mind my not listening to you, I hope. My train goes at twelve o'clock."

"Has it ever occurred to you to make an inventory, mainly in the interest of science, of what you are leaving behind?"

"It has. I am leaving behind a life that gets nowhere, and one that bores me to death."

"And to ask yourself what the lady is giving up in return for the doubtful constancy you offer her. By George, Jack, have you thought to tell her that the only thing you ever loved in any woman was your own reflection?"

"If that's all you know about it?"

"It isn't all, perhaps, but it's a good bit. You aren't the first analytical psychologist who has identified the world with himself, and, God permitting, you probably won't be the last."

"If that's your game, my boy, you are wasting time."

"Well, after all, you are dodging my question about the lady."

"Have you read her book on 'Marriage and Individuality'?" Estbridge glanced at the package on the table.

"No, I haven't, but I can make a good guess as to what it is all about. There is not much to be said on that subject, I fancy. It is take it or leave it—that's all. But, granting that she doesn't lose much as she sees it, she doesn't stand to win very big stakes either, does she? Does she, now, really? Come, Jack, as a married man, nearing fifty, don't you agree with me?"

"If I do, how is the case altered? Of course I am not worthy of her, but what, in heaven's name, has that got to do with it?"

"You realize that your wife will never divorce you?"

With a shrug Estbridge went back to his papers. "Have I lived with her for twenty years without discovering that?"

"And the end will be, I suppose," Hoadly's voice had grown rasping, "that you will feel yourself bound to Judith Campbell until—until she comes between you and something that you want more than any woman. There is an instinct in you stronger than love, Jack, and God pity her when she crosses it. I have always said that your Grand Inquisitor[4] was a humanitarian crossed in his purpose."

Estbridge's face darkened. "There are barely fifteen minutes left, and I've as much as I can attend to."

"Don't let me delay you." Rising from his chair, Hoadly held out his hand with the causal manner of an attorney who continues to smile pleasantly in the face of defeat. "You aren't allowing yourself a great deal of time, are you?" As he reached the

[4]Most famous was Torquemada (1420–1498), first head of the Spanish Inquisition, who is said to have put thousands to death at the stake.

door he glanced back, and said carelessly, "By the way, I forgot to tell you about Adamson. But I suppose you have heard?"

"I heard this morning," replied Estbridge sharply, "I wish the University well of him."

"Then you haven't seen the extras?" The door closed with a slam, and Hoadly turned back into the room. "He's dead, you know—run over this morning in West Fifty-ninth Street. I heard it two hours ago." For a moment he hesitated, and then added maliciously, "I suppose we'll have a hard time now to replace him."

"Adamson!" The portfolio he had picked up slipped from Estbridge's grasp, and he stood staring incredulously into the face of his friend. "Why hadn't you told me?"

"I came down for that, not just to wish you a Merry Christmas—but the news went quite out of my mind when I found myself in the midst of this romantic episode. After all, life is so much more engrossing than death, isn't it?"

"Adamson?" Estbridge was repeating the name blankly. As if awakening from the effects of a narcotic, he stretched out his hand with a groping uncertain gesture. Not only his tone, but his face, his look, even his figure, appeared to have altered. It was as if an entirely different set of nerve cells had begun acting at the instant—as if the molecular rhythm of his brain had run down, and then started feverishly with fresh waves of energy. He was like a man who had died and been born anew in an instant; and, watching him, Hoadly realized that his friend was now living with a different side of his nature—with other impulses, with other vibrations of memory, with other automatic reactions.

"So Adamson is dead, and the place at the University is vacant!"

Over Jim Hoadly's impassive features a smile that was slightly sardonic in its humor flickered for an instant. "You have just time to catch your train," he said, and added gravely, with a vague movement toward the portfolio, "the snow makes traffic difficult."

At the reminder the exultation faded from Estbridge's look, while his anxious gaze sought the face of the clock, and hung there as if drawn and held by an irresistible magnet.

"Yes, there is just time," he repeated; but he did not turn, and his shoulders did not stoop for the overcoat which Hoadly held waiting behind him.

"You had better start or you miss it," said Hoadly again, after three minutes in which he had watched the struggle with his smile of flickering irony—like the smile of some inscrutable image of wisdom. "It would be a pity to miss that train, wouldn't it?"

But the clock ticked slowly on, while Estbridge stood transfixed, bewildered, brooding, with his eyes on the hands which travelled inevitably toward the appointed hour.

1962

Edith Wharton 1862–1937

Edith Newbold Jones was the third child and only daughter in an elite, conservative, old New York family. Tracing their lineage to pre-Revolutionary settlers, her parents, George Frederic and Lucretia Stevens Rhinelander Jones, belonged to a class that prided itself on its avoidance of ostentation, intellectualism, publicity, and, according to the author as a grown woman, emotion. That Wharton was to become a famous, brilliantly accomplished author in no way fulfilled her family's program for her.

During her childhood, the Joneses divided their time between New York and Europe, with summers in Newport, Rhode Island. Because her two brothers were already in their teens when she was born, she grew up as if she were an only child; and, as with other girls of her time and class, her life was sheltered. She was tutored at home and, making her debut at the age of seventeen, she was expected thereafter simply to marry. When she did, accepting in 1885 Edward ("Teddy") Wharton, a good-natured man thirteen years her senior, she made a match that was conventional and, ultimately, unhappy. As a leisure-class wife, she traveled and visited, entertained, supervised servants, and built and decorated homes. Some of these activities appealed to Wharton. Increasingly, however, she found this existence suffocating and, on the advice of doctors treating her for depression, turned to writing as an outlet.

Publishing short stories in the 1890s and then long fiction at the turn of the century, Wharton grew in strength as her husband's mental health deteriorated. The couple had no children, and their lives steadily diverged. In the early 1900s Wharton had a secret love affair with a younger man, Morton Fullerton, and in 1913 pursued a divorce. The divorce pained and shocked family members.

The publication of *The House of Mirth* in 1905 launched Wharton as America's most acclaimed twentieth-century fiction writer in the decades preceding the 1920s. During her major period, the years from 1905 to 1920, she published novels prolifically: *The House of Mirth, Madame de Treymes, Ethan Frome, The Reef, The Custom of the Country, Summer,* and *The Age of Innocence.* Her work is distinguished by her brilliance as a stylist, her urbane intelligence, and her acuity as a social observer and critic, particularly of the leisure class.

Wharton wrote about the rapaciousness and vulgarity of the *nouveaux riches,* the timidity and repression of the upper class, the contrast between European and American customs and values, and the inequality and repression of women, which often showed up in patriarchal culture—by design, of course—in hostility and rivalry among women. As both "The Valley of Childish Things" and "Roman Fever" show, issues of female sexual freedom, frustrated artistic ambition, and severely limited status in the public realm interested her. Poverty also arrested her imagination and stimulated some of her best work, such as *Ethan Frome* and *Summer.* Not surprisingly, given her personal experience, she also focused on marriage, which she usually portrayed as incarcerating, especially for women. At the same time, as "Souls Belated" illustrates, she was keenly aware of how psychologically important the conventional relationship of marriage and its attendant responsibility could be. The private love diary she wrote during her affair with Morton Fullerton, "The Life Apart," which was never published during her lifetime, shows yet another side of Wharton—anxious, at times insecure, bold, sensual.

The contribution of Edith Wharton to American literature is major. Often compared with Henry James, a close friend, she is recognized along with other women writers at the turn into the twentieth century—Kate Chopin, Alice Dunbar-Nelson, Ellen Glasgow, Willa Cather—for moving nineteenth-century women's literary tradition into a new phase of artistic ambitiousness and excellence. In her lifetime she published nineteen novels and novellas, eleven volumes of short stories, a number of book-length discursive works, some poetry, and many essays, reviews, and articles. Perceived in her own time as an extraordinary writer, she received the Pulitzer Prize in 1921 and in 1923 was the first woman to be honored by Yale University with the degree of doctor of letters. Wharton died of a stroke at the age of seventy-five and is buried in France, where she made her home for the last twenty-five years of her life. Her grave is in the Cimetière des Gonards at Versailles.

Elizabeth Ammons
Tufts University

PRIMARY WORKS

The House of Mirth, 1905; *Madame de Treymes,* 1907; *Ethan Frome,* 1911; *The Reef,* 1912; *The Custom of the Country,* 1913; *Summer,* 1917; *The Age of Innocence,* 1920; *Old New York,* 1924; *The Mother's Recompense,* 1925; *A Backward Glance,* 1934 (memoir).

The Valley of Childish Things

Once upon a time a number of children lived together in the Valley of Childish Things, playing all manner of delightful games, and studying the same lesson books. But one day a little girl, one of their number, decided that it was time to see something of the world about which the lesson books had taught her; and as none of the other children cared to leave their games, she set out alone to climb the pass which led out of the valley.

It was a hard climb, but at length she reached a cold, bleak tableland beyond the mountains. Here she saw cities and men, and learned many useful arts, and in so doing grew to be a woman. But the tableland was bleak and cold, and when she had served her apprenticeship she decided to return to her old companions in the Valley of Childish Things, and work with them instead of with strangers.

It was a weary way back, and her feet were bruised by the stones, and her face was beaten by the weather; but halfway down the pass she met a man, who kindly helped her over the roughest places. Like herself, he was lame and weather-beaten; but as soon as he spoke she recognized him as one of her old playmates. He too had been out in the world, and was going back to the valley; and on the way they talked together of the work they meant to do there. He had been a dull boy, and she had never taken much notice of him; but as she listened to his plans for building bridges and draining swamps and cutting roads through the jungle, she thought to herself, "Since he has grown into such a fine fellow, what splendid men and women my other playmates must have become!"

But what was her surprise to find, on reaching the valley, that her former companions, instead of growing into men and women, had all remained little children. Most of them were playing the same old games, and the few who affected to be working were engaged in such strenuous occupations as building mudpies and sailing paper boats in basins. As for the lad who had been the favorite companion of her studies, he was playing marbles with all the youngest boys in the valley.

At first the children seemed glad to have her back, but soon she saw that her presence interfered with their games; and when she tried to tell them of the great things that were being done on the tableland beyond the mountains, they picked up their toys and went farther down the valley to play.

Then she turned to her fellow traveler, who was the only grown man in the valley; but he was on his knees before a dear little girl with blue eyes and a coral necklace, for whom he was making a garden out of cockleshells and bits of glass and broken flowers stuck in sand.

The little girl was clapping her hands and crowing (she was too young to speak articulately); and when she who had grown to be a woman laid her hand on the man's shoulder, and asked him if he did not want to set to work with her building bridges, draining swamps, and cutting roads through the jungle, he replied that at that particular moment he was too busy.

And as she turned away, he added in the kindest possible way, "Really, my dear, you ought to have taken better care of your complexion."

1896

Souls Belated

Their railway carriage had been full when the train left Bologna; but at the first station beyond Milan their only remaining companion—a courtly person who ate garlic out of a carpetbag—had left his crumb-strewn seat with a bow.

Lydia's eye regretfully followed the shiny broadcloth of his retreating back till it lost itself in the cloud of touts and cab drivers hanging about the station; then she glanced across at Gannett and caught the same regret in his look. They were both sorry to be alone.

"Par-ten-za!"[1] shouted the guard. The train vibrated to a sudden slamming of doors; a waiter ran along the platform with a tray of fossilized sandwiches; a belated porter flung a bundle of shawls and bandboxes into a third-class carriage; the guard snapped out a brief *Partenza!* which indicated the purely ornamental nature of his first shout; and the train swung out of the station.

The direction of the road had changed, and a shaft of sunlight struck across the dusty red-velvet seats into Lydia's corner. Gannett did not notice it. He had returned to his *Revue de Paris,* and she had to rise and lower the shade of the farther window. Against the vast horizon of their leisure such incidents stood out sharply.

Having lowered the shade, Lydia sat down, leaving the length of the carriage between herself and Gannett. At length he missed her and looked up.

"I moved out of the sun," she hastily explained.

He looked at her curiously: the sun was beating on her through the shade.

"Very well," he said pleasantly; adding, "You don't mind?" as he drew a cigarette case from his pocket.

It was a refreshing touch, relieving the tension of her spirit with the suggestion that, after all, he could *smoke*—! The relief was only momentary. Her experience of smokers was limited (her husband had disapproved of the use of tobacco) but she knew from hearsay that men sometimes smoked to get away from things; that a cigar

[1]Italian: "departing" (i.e., "all aboard").

might be the masculine equivalent of darkened windows and a headache. Gannett, after a puff or two, returned to his review.

It was just as she had foreseen; he feared to speak as much as she did. It was one of the misfortunes of their situation that they were never busy enough to necessitate, or even to justify, the postponement of unpleasant discussions. If they avoided a question it was obviously, unconcealably because the question was disagreeable. They had unlimited leisure and an accumulation of mental energy to devote to any subject that presented itself; new topics were in fact at a premium. Lydia sometimes had premonitions of a famine-stricken period when there would be nothing left to talk about, and she had already caught herself doling out piecemeal what, in the first prodigality of their confidences, she would have flung to him in a breath. Their silence therefore might simply mean that they had nothing to say; but it was another disadvantage of their position that it allowed infinite opportunity for the classification of minute differences. Lydia had learned to distinguish between real and factitious silences; and under Gannett's she now detected a hum of speech to which her own thoughts made breathless answer.

How could it be otherwise, with that thing between them? She glanced up at the rack overhead. The *thing* was there, in her dressing bag, symbolically suspended over her head and his. He was thinking of it now, just as she was; they had been thinking of it in unison ever since they had entered the train. While the carriage had held other travelers they had screened her from his thoughts; but now that he and she were alone she knew exactly what was passing through his mind; she could almost hear him asking himself what he should say to her.

The thing had come that morning, brought up to her in an innocent-looking envelope with the rest of their letters, as they were leaving the hotel at Bologna. As she tore it open, she and Gannett were laughing over some ineptitude of the local guidebook—they had been driven, of late, to make the most of such incidental humors of travel. Even when she had unfolded the document she took it for some unimportant business paper sent abroad for her signature, and her eye traveled inattentively over the curly *Whereases* of the preamble until a word arrested her: Divorce. There it stood, an impassable barrier, between her husband's name and hers.

She had been prepared for it, of course, as healthy people are said to be prepared for death, in the sense of knowing it must come without in the least expecting that it will. She had known from the first that Tillotson meant to divorce her—but what did it matter? Nothing mattered, in those first days of supreme deliverance, but the fact that she was free; and not so much (she had begun to be aware) that freedom had released her from Tillotson as that it had given her to Gannett. This discovery had not been agreeable to her self-esteem. She had preferred to think that Tillotson had himself embodied all her reasons for leaving him; and those he represented had seemed cogent enough to stand in no need of reinforcement. Yet she had not left him till she met Gannett. It was her love for Gannett that had made life with Tillotson so poor and incomplete a business. If she had never, from the first, regarded her marriage as a full canceling of her claims upon life, she had at least, for a number of years, accepted it as a provisional compensation,—she had made it "do." Existence in the commodious Tillotson mansion in Fifth Avenue—with Mrs. Tillotson senior commanding the approaches from the second-story front windows—had been reduced to a series of purely automatic acts. The moral atmosphere of the Tillotson interior was as carefully screened and curtained as the house itself: Mrs. Tillotson senior dreaded ideas as much as a draft in her back. Prudent people liked an even temperature; and to do anything unexpected was as foolish as going out in the rain. One of the chief advantages of being rich was that one need not be exposed to unforeseen contingencies: by the use of ordinary firmness and common sense one could make sure of doing exactly the same thing every day at the same hour. These doctrines, reverentially imbibed with his mother's milk, Tillotson (a model son who had never given his parents an hour's anxiety) complacently expounded to his wife, testifying to his sense of their importance by the regularity with which he wore galoshes on damp days, his punctuality at meals, and his elaborate precautions against burglars and contagious diseases. Lydia, coming from a smaller town, and entering New York life through the portals of the Tillotson mansion, had mechanically accepted this point of view as inseparable from having a front pew in church and a parterre box at the opera. All the people who came to the house revolved in the same small circle of prejudices. It was the kind of society in which, after dinner, the ladies compared the exorbitant charges of their children's teachers, and agreed that, even with the new duties on French clothes, it was cheaper in the end to get everything from Worth; while the husbands, over their cigars, lamented municipal corruption, and decided that the men to start a reform were those who had no private interests at stake.

To Lydia this view of life had become a matter of course, just as lumbering about in her mother-in-law's landau had come to seem the only possible means of locomotion, and listening every Sunday to a fashionable Presbyterian divine the inevitable atonement for having thought oneself bored on the other six days of the week. Before she met Gannett her life had seemed merely dull; his coming made it appear like one of those dismal Cruikshank prints in which the people are all ugly and all engaged in occupations that are either vulgar or stupid.

It was natural that Tillotson should be the chief sufferer from this readjustment of focus. Gannett's nearness had made her husband ridiculous, and a part of the ridicule had been reflected on herself. Her tolerance laid her open to a suspicion of obtuseness from which she must, at all costs, clear herself in Gannett's eyes.

She did not understand this until afterwards. At the time she fancied that she had merely reached the limits of endurance. In so large a charter of liberties as the mere act of leaving Tillotson seemed to confer, the small question of divorce or no divorce did not count. It was when she saw that she had left her husband only to be with Gannett that she perceived the significance of anything affecting their relations. Her husband, in casting her off, had virtually flung her at Gannett: it was thus that the world viewed it. The measure of alacrity with which Gannett would receive her would be the subject of curious speculation over afternoon tea tables and in club corners. She knew what would be said—she had heard it so often of others! The recollection bathed her in misery. The men would probably back Gannett to "do the decent thing"; but the ladies' eyebrows would emphasize the worthlessness of such enforced fidelity; and after all, they would be right. She had put herself in a position where Gannett "owed" her something; where, as a gentleman, he was bound to "stand the damage." The idea of accepting such compensation had never crossed her mind; the so-called rehabilitation of such a marriage had always seemed to her the only real disgrace. What she dreaded was the necessity of having to explain herself;

of having to combat his arguments; of calculating, in spite of herself, the exact measure of insistence with which he pressed them. She knew not whether she most shrank from his insisting too much or too little. In such a case the nicest sense of proportion might be at fault; and how easily to fall into the error of taking her resistance for a test of his sincerity! Whichever way she turned, an ironical implication confronted her: she had the exasperated sense of having walked into the trap of some stupid practical joke.

Beneath all these preoccupations lurked the dread of what he was thinking. Sooner or later, of course, he would have to speak; but that, in the meantime, he should think, even for a moment, that there was any use in speaking, seemed to her simply unendurable. Her sensitiveness on this point was aggravated by another fear, as yet barely on the level of consciousness; the fear of unwillingly involving Gannett in the trammels of her dependence. To look upon him as the instrument of her liberation; to resist in herself the least tendency to a wifely taking possession of his future; had seemed to Lydia the one way of maintaining the dignity of their relation. Her view had not changed, but she was aware of a growing inability to keep her thoughts fixed on the essential point—the point of parting with Gannett. It was easy to face as long as she kept it sufficiently far off: but what was this act of mental postponement but a gradual encroachment on his future? What was needful was the courage to recognize the moment when, by some word or look, their voluntary fellowship should be transformed into a bondage the more wearing that it was based on none of those common obligations which make the most imperfect marriage in some sort a center of gravity.

When the porter, at the next station, threw the door open, Lydia drew back, making way for the hoped-for intruder; but none came, and the train took up its leisurely progress through the spring wheat fields and budding copses. She now began to hope that Gannett would speak before the next station. She watched him furtively, half-disposed to return to the seat opposite his, but there was an artificiality about his absorption that restrained her. She had never before seen him read with so conspicuous an air of warding off interruption. What could he be thinking of? Why should he be afraid to speak? Or was it her answer that he dreaded?

The train paused for the passing of an express, and he put down his book and leaned out of the window. Presently he turned to her with a smile.

"There's a jolly old villa out here," he said.

His easy tone relieved her, and she smiled back at him as she crossed over to his corner.

Beyond the embankment, through the opening in a mossy wall, she caught sight of the villa, with its broken balustrades, its stagnant fountains, and the stone satyr closing the perspective of a dusky grass walk.

"How should you like to live there?" he asked as the train moved on.

"There?"

"In some such place, I mean. One might do worse, don't you think so? There must be at least two centuries of solitude under those yew trees. Shouldn't you like it?"

"I—I don't know," she faltered. She knew now that he meant to speak.

He lit another cigarette. "We shall have to live somewhere, you know," he said as he bent above the match.

Lydia tried to speak carelessly. "*Je n'en vois pas la nécessité!*[2] Why not live everywhere, as we have been doing?"

"But we can't travel forever, can we?"

"Oh, forever's a long word," she objected, picking up the review he had thrown aside.

"For the rest of our lives then," he said, moving nearer.

She made a slight gesture which caused his hand to slip from hers.

"Why should we make plans? I thought you agreed with me that it's pleasanter to drift."

He looked at her hesitatingly. "It's been pleasant, certainly; but I suppose I shall have to get at my work again some day. You know I haven't written a line since—all this time," he hastily amended.

She flamed with sympathy and self-reproach. "Oh, if you mean *that*—if you want to write—of course we must settle down. How stupid of me not to have thought of it sooner! Where shall we go? Where do you think you could work best? We oughtn't to lose any more time."

He hesitated again. "I had thought of a villa in these parts. It's quiet; we shouldn't be bothered. Should you like it?"

"Of course I should like it." She paused and looked away. "But I thought—I remember your telling me once that your best work had been done in a crowd—in big cities. Why should you shut yourself up in a desert?"

Gannett, for a moment, made no reply. At length he said, avoiding her eye as carefully as she avoided his: "It might be different now; I can't tell, of course, till I try. A writer ought not to be dependent on his *milieu;* it's a mistake to humor oneself in that way; and I thought that just at first you might prefer to be—"

She faced him. "To be what?"

"Well—quiet. I mean—"

"What do you mean by 'at first'?" she interrupted.

He paused again. "I mean after we are married."

She thrust up her chin and turned toward the window. "Thank you!" she tossed back at him.

"Lydia!" he exclaimed blankly; and she felt in every fiber of her averted person that he had made the inconceivable, the unpardonable mistake of anticipating her acquiescence.

The train rattled on and he groped for a third cigarette. Lydia remained silent.

"I haven't offended you?" he ventured at length, in the tone of a man who feels his way.

She shook her head with a sigh. "I thought you understood," she moaned. Their eyes met and she moved back to his side.

"Do you want to know how not to offend me? By taking it for granted, once for all, that you've said your say on the odious question and that I've said mine, and that we stand just where we did this morning before that—that hateful paper came to spoil everything between us!"

"To spoil everything between us? What on earth do you mean? Aren't you glad to be free?"

[2]French: "I don't see the need!"

"I was free before."

"Not to marry me," he suggested.

"But I don't *want* to marry you!" she cried.

She saw that he turned pale. "I'm obtuse, I suppose," he said slowly. "I confess I don't see what you're driving at. Are you tired of the whole business? Or was I simply a—an excuse for getting away? Perhaps you didn't care to travel alone? Was that it? And now you want to chuck me?" His voice had grown harsh. "You owe me a straight answer, you know; don't be tenderhearted!"

Her eyes swam as she leaned to him. "Don't you see it's because I care—because I care so much? Oh, Ralph! Can't you see how it would humiliate me? Try to feel it as a woman would! Don't you see the misery of being made your wife in this way? If I'd known you as a girl—that would have been a real marriage! But now—this vulgar fraud upon society—and upon a society we despised and laughed at—this sneaking back into a position that we've voluntarily forfeited: don't you see what a cheap compromise it is? We neither of us believe in the abstract 'sacredness' of marriage; we both know that no ceremony is needed to consecrate our love for each other; what object can we have in marrying, except the secret fear of each that the other may escape, or the secret longing to work our way back gradually—oh, very gradually—into the esteem of the people whose conventional morality we have always ridiculed and hated? And the very fact that, after a decent interval, these same people would come and dine with us—the women who talk about the indissolubility of marriage, and who would let me die in a gutter today because I am 'leading a life of sin'—doesn't that disgust you more than their turning their backs on us now? I can stand being cut by them, but I couldn't stand their coming to call and asking what I meant to do about visiting that unfortunate Mrs. So-and-so!"

She paused, and Gannett maintained a perplexed silence.

"You judge things too theoretically," he said at length, slowly. "Life is made up of compromises."

"The life we ran away from—yes! If we had been willing to accept them"—she flushed—"we might have gone on meeting each other at Mrs. Tillotson's dinners."

He smiled slightly. "I didn't know that we ran away to found a new system of ethics. I supposed it was because we loved each other."

"Life is complex, of course; isn't it the very recognition of that fact that separates us from the people who see it *tout d'une pièce*?[3] If *they* are right—if marriage is sacred in itself and the individual must always be sacrificed to the family—then there can be no real marriage between us, since our—our being together is a protest against the sacrifice of the individual to the family." She interrupted herself with a laugh. "You'll say now that I'm giving you a lecture on sociology! Of course one acts as one can—as one must, perhaps—pulled by all sorts of invisible threads; but at least one needn't pretend, for social advantages, to subscribe to a creed that ignores the complexity of human motives—that classifies people by arbitrary signs, and puts it in everybody's reach to be on Mrs. Tillotson's visiting list. It may be necessary that the world should be ruled by conventions—but if we believed in them, why did we break through them? And if we don't believe in them, is it honest to take advantage of the protection they afford?"

[3]French: "all as a piece."

Gannett hesitated. "One may believe in them or not; but as long as they do rule the world it is only by taking advantage of their protection that one can find a *modus vivendi.*"

"Do outlaws need a *modus vivendi*?"

He looked at her hopelessly. Nothing is more perplexing to man than the mental process of a woman who reasons her emotions.

She thought she had scored a point and followed it up passionately. "You do understand, don't you? You see how the very thought of the thing humiliates me! We are together today because we choose to be—don't let us look any farther than that!" She caught his hands. "*Promise* me you'll never speak of it again; promise me you'll never *think* of it even," she implored, with a tearful prodigality of italics.

Through what followed—his protests, his arguments, his final unconvinced submission to her wishes—she had a sense of his but half-discerning all that, for her, had made the moment so tumultuous. They had reached that memorable point in every heart history when, for the first time, the man seems obtuse and the woman irrational. It was the abundance of his intentions that consoled her, on reflection, for what they lacked in quality. After all, it would have been worse, incalculably worse, to have detected any overreadiness to understand her.

II

When the train at nightfall brought them to their journey's end at the edge of one of the lakes, Lydia was glad that they were not, as usual, to pass from one solitude to another. Their wanderings during the year had indeed been like the flight of outlaws: through Sicily, Dalmatia, Transylvania and Southern Italy they had persisted in their tacit avoidance of their kind. Isolation, at first, had deepened the flavor of their happiness, as night intensifies the scent of certain flowers; but in the new phase on which they were entering, Lydia's chief wish was that they should be less abnormally exposed to the action of each other's thoughts.

She shrank, nevertheless, as the brightly-looming bulk of the fashionable Anglo-American hotel on the water's brink began to radiate toward their advancing boat its vivid suggestion of social order, visitors' lists, Church services, and the bland inquisition of the *table d'hôte.* The mere fact that in a moment or two she must take her place on the hotel register as Mrs. Gannett seemed to weaken the springs of her resistance.

They had meant to stay for a night only, on their way to a lofty village among the glaciers of Monte Rosa; but after the first plunge into publicity, when they entered the dining room, Lydia felt the relief of being lost in a crowd, of ceasing for a moment to be the center of Gannett's scrutiny; and in his face she caught the reflection of her feeling. After dinner, when she went upstairs, he strolled into the smoking room, and an hour or two later, sitting in the darkness of her window, she heard his voice below and saw him walking up and down the terrace with a companion cigar at his side. When he came up he told her he had been talking to the hotel chaplain—a very good sort of fellow.

"Queer little microcosms, these hotels! Most of these people live here all summer and then migrate to Italy or the Riviera. The English are the only people who can lead that kind of life with dignity—those soft-voiced old ladies in Shetland shawls somehow carry the British Empire under their caps. *Civis Romanus sum.*[4] It's a curious study—there might be some good things to work up here."

He stood before her with the vivid preoccupied stare of the novelist on the trail of a "subject." With a relief that was half painful she noticed that, for the first time since they had been together, he was hardly aware of her presence.

"Do you think you could write here?"

"Here? I don't know." His stare dropped. "After being out of things so long one's first impressions are bound to be tremendously vivid, you know. I see a dozen threads already that one might follow—"

He broke off with a touch of embarrassment.

"Then follow them. We'll stay," she said with sudden decision.

"Stay here?" He glanced at her in surprise, and then, walking to the window, looked out upon the dusky slumber of the garden.

"Why not?" she said at length, in a tone of veiled irritation.

"The place is full of old cats in caps who gossip with the chaplain. Shall you like—I mean, it would be different if—"

She flamed up.

"Do you suppose I care? It's none of their business."

"Of course not; but you won't get them to think so."

"They may think what they please."

He looked at her doubtfully.

"It's for you to decide."

"We'll stay," she repeated.

Gannett, before they met, had made himself known as a successful writer of short stories and of a novel which had achieved the distinction of being widely discussed. The reviewers called him "promising," and Lydia now accused herself of having too long interfered with the fulfillment of his promise. There was a special irony in the fact, since his passionate assurances that only the stimulus of her companionship could bring out his latent faculty had almost given the dignity of a "vocation" to her course: there had been moments when she had felt unable to assume, before posterity, the responsibility of thwarting his career. And, after all, he had not written a line since they had been together: his first desire to write had come from renewed contact with the world! Was it all a mistake then? Must the most intelligent choice work more disastrously than the blundering combinations of chance? Or was there a still more humiliating answer to her perplexities? His sudden impulse of activity so exactly coincided with her own wish to withdraw, for a time, from the range of his observation, that she wondered if he too were not seeking sanctuary from intolerable problems.

"You must begin tomorrow!" she cried, hiding a tremor under the laugh with which she added, "I wonder if there's any ink in the inkstand?"

Whatever else they had at the Hotel Bellosguardo, they had, as Miss Pinsent said, "a certain tone." It was to Lady Susan Condit that they owed this inestimable benefit; an advantage ranking in Miss Pinsent's opinion above even the lawn tennis

[4]Latin: "I am a Roman citizen."

courts and the resident chaplain. It was the fact of Lady Susan's annual visit that made the hotel what it was. Miss Pinsent was certainly the last to underrate such a privilege: "It's so important, my dear, forming as we do a little family, that there should be someone to give *the tone;* and no one could do it better than Lady Susan—an earl's daughter and a person of such determination. Dear Mrs. Ainger now—who really *ought,* you know, when Lady Susan's away—absolutely refuses to assert herself." Miss Pinsent sniffed derisively. "A bishop's niece!—my dear, I saw her once actually give in to some South Americans—and before us all. She gave up her seat at table to oblige them—such a lack of dignity! Lady Susan spoke to her very plainly about it afterwards."

Miss Pinsent glanced across the lake and adjusted her auburn front.

"But of course I don't deny that the stand Lady Susan takes is not always easy to live up to—for the rest of us, I mean. Monsieur Grossart, our good proprietor, finds it trying at times, I know—he has said as much, privately, to Mrs. Ainger and me. After all, the poor man is not to blame for wanting to fill his hotel, is he? And Lady Susan is so difficult—so very difficult—about new people. One might almost say that she disapproves of them beforehand, on principle. And yet she's had warnings—she very nearly made a dreadful mistake once with the Duchess of Levens, who dyed her hair and—well, swore and smoked. One would have thought that might have been a lesson to Lady Susan." Miss Pinsent resumed her knitting with a sigh. "There are exceptions, of course. She took at once to you and Mr. Gannett—it was quite remarkable, really. Oh, I don't mean that either—of course not! It was perfectly natural—we *all* thought you so charming and interesting from the first day—we knew at once that Mr. Gannett was intellectual, by the magazines you took in; but you know what I mean. Lady Susan is so very—well, I won't say prejudiced, as Mrs. Ainger does—but so prepared *not* to like new people, that her taking to you in that way was a surprise to us all, I confess."

Miss Pinsent sent a significant glance down the long laurustinus alley from the other end of which two people—a lady and gentleman—were strolling toward them through the smiling neglect of the garden.

"In this case, of course, it's very different; that I'm willing to admit. Their looks are against them; but, as Mrs. Ainger says, one can't exactly tell them so."

"She's very handsome," Lydia ventured, with her eyes on the lady, who showed, under the dome of a vivid sunshade, the hourglass figure and superlative coloring of a Christmas chromo.

"That's the worst of it. She's too handsome."

"Well, after all, she can't help that."

"Other people manage to," said Miss Pinsent skeptically.

"But isn't it rather unfair of Lady Susan—considering that nothing is known about them?"

"But, my dear, that's the very thing that's against them. It's infinitely worse than any actual knowledge."

Lydia mentally agreed that, in the case of Mrs. Linton, it possibly might be.

"I wonder why they came here?" she mused.

"That's against them too. It's always a bad sign when loud people come to a quiet place. And they've brought van loads of boxes—her maid told Mrs. Ainger's that they meant to stop indefinitely."

"And Lady Susan actually turned her back on her in the salon?"

"My dear, she said it was for our sakes: that makes it so unanswerable! But poor Grossart *is* in a way! The Lintons have taken his most expensive suite, you know—the yellow damask drawing room above the portico—and they have champagne with every meal!"

They were silent as Mr. and Mrs. Linton sauntered by; the lady with tempestuous brows and challenging chin; the gentleman, a blond stripling, trailing after her, head downward, like a reluctant child dragged by his nurse.

"What does your husband think of them, my dear?" Miss Pinsent whispered as they passed out of earshot.

Lydia stooped to pick a violet in the border.

"He hasn't told me."

"Of your speaking to them, I mean. Would he approve of that? I know how very particular nice Americans are. I think your action might make a difference; it would certainly carry weight with Lady Susan."

"Dear Miss Pinsent, you flatter me!"

Lydia rose and gathered up her book and sunshade.

"Well, if you're asked for an opinion—if Lady Susan asks you for one—I think you ought to be prepared," Miss Pinsent admonished her as she moved away.

III

Lady Susan held her own. She ignored the Lintons, and her little family, as Miss Pinsent phrased it, followed suit. Even Mrs. Ainger agreed that it was obligatory. If Lady Susan owed it to the others not to speak to the Lintons, the others clearly owed it to Lady Susan to back her up. It was generally found expedient, at the Hotel Bellosguardo, to adopt this form of reasoning.

Whatever effect this combined action may have had upon the Lintons, it did not at least have that of driving them away. Monsieur Grossart, after a few days of suspense, had the satisfaction of seeing them settle down in his yellow damask *premier* with what looked like a permanent installation of palm trees and silk cushions, and a gratifying continuance in the consumption of champagne. Mrs. Linton trailed her Doucet draperies up and down the garden with the same challenging air, while her husband, smoking innumerable cigarettes, dragged himself dejectedly in her wake; but neither of them, after the first encounter with Lady Susan, made any attempt to extend their acquaintance. They simply ignored their ignorers. As Miss Pinsent resentfully observed, they behaved exactly as though the hotel were empty.

It was therefore a matter of surprise, as well as of displeasure, to Lydia, to find, on glancing up one day from her seat in the garden, that the shadow which had fallen across her book was that of the enigmatic Mrs. Linton.

"I want to speak to you," that lady said, in a rich hard voice that seemed the audible expression of her gown and her complexion.

Lydia stared. She certainly did not want to speak to Mrs. Linton.

"Shall I sit down here?" the latter continued, fixing her intensely-shaded eyes on Lydia's face, "or are you afraid of being seen with me?"

"Afraid?" Lydia colored. "Sit down, please. What is it that you wish to say?"

Mrs. Linton, with a smile, drew up a garden chair and crossed one openwork ankle above the other.

"I want you to tell me what my husband said to your husband last night."

Lydia turned pale.

"My husband—to yours?" she faltered, staring at the other.

"Didn't you know they were closeted together for hours in the smoking room after you went upstairs? My man didn't get to bed until nearly two o'clock and when he did I couldn't get a word out of him. When he wants to be aggravating I'll back him against anybody living!" Her teeth and eyes flashed persuasively upon Lydia. "But you'll tell me what they were talking about, won't you? I know I can trust you—you look so awfully kind. And it's for his own good. He's such a precious donkey and I'm so afraid he's got into some beastly scrape or other. If he'd only trust his own old woman! But they're always writing to him and setting him against me. And I've got nobody to turn to." She laid her hand on Lydia's with a rattle of bracelets. "You'll help me, won't you?"

Lydia drew back from the smiling fierceness of her brows.

"I'm sorry—but I don't think I understand. My husband has said nothing to me of—of yours."

The great black crescents above Mrs. Linton's eyes met angrily.

"I say—is that true?" she demanded.

Lydia rose from her seat.

"Oh, look here, I didn't mean that, you know—you mustn't take one up so! Can't you see how rattled I am?"

Lydia saw that, in fact, her beautiful mouth was quivering beneath softened eyes.

"I'm beside myself!" the splendid creature wailed, dropping into her seat.

"I'm so sorry," Lydia repeated, forcing herself to speak kindly; "but how can I help you?"

Mrs. Linton raised her head sharply.

"By finding out—there's a darling!"

"Finding what out?"

"What Trevenna told him."

"Trevenna—?" Lydia echoed in bewilderment.

Mrs. Linton clapped her hand to her mouth.

"Oh, Lord—there, it's out! What a fool I am! But I supposed of course you knew; I supposed everybody knew." She dried her eyes and bridled. "Didn't you know that he's Lord Trevenna? I'm Mrs. Cope."

Lydia recognized the names. They had figured in a flamboyant elopement which had thrilled fashionable London some six months earlier.

"Now you see how it is—you understand, don't you?" Mrs. Cope continued on a note of appeal. "I knew you would—that's the reason I came to you. I suppose *he* felt the same thing about your husband; he's not spoken to another soul in the place." Her face grew anxious again. "He's awfully sensitive, generally—he feels our position, he says—as if it wasn't *my* place to feel that! But when he does get talking there's no knowing what he'll say. I know he's been brooding over something lately, and I *must* find out what it is—it's to his interest that I should. I always tell him that I think only of his interest; if he'd only trust me! But he's been so odd lately—I can't think what he's plotting. You will help me, dear?"

Lydia, who had remained standing, looked away uncomfortably.

"If you mean by finding out what Lord Trevenna has told my husband, I'm afraid it's impossible."

"Why impossible?"

"Because I infer that it was told in confidence."

Mrs. Cope stared incredulously.

"Well, what of that? Your husband looks such a dear—anyone can see he's awfully gone on you. What's to prevent your getting it out of him?"

Lydia flushed.

"I'm not a spy!" she exclaimed.

"A spy—a spy? How dare you?" Mrs. Cope flamed out. "Oh, I don't mean that either! Don't be angry with me—I'm so miserable." She essayed a softer note. "Do you call that spying—for one woman to help out another? I do need help so dreadfully! I'm at my wits' end with Trevenna, I am indeed. He's such a boy—a mere baby, you know; he's only two-and-twenty." She dropped her orbed lids. "He's younger than me—only fancy, a few months younger. I tell him he ought to listen to me as if I was his mother; oughtn't he now? But he won't, he won't! All his people are at him, you see—oh, I know *their* little game! Trying to get him away from me before I can get my divorce—that's what they're up to. At first he wouldn't listen to them; he used to toss their letters over to me to read; but now he reads them himself, and answers 'em too, I fancy; he's always shut up in his room, writing. If I only knew what his plan is I could stop him fast enough—he's such a simpleton. But he's dreadfully deep too—at times I can't make him out. But I know he's told your husband everything—I knew that last night the minute I laid eyes on him. And I *must* find out—you must help me—I've got no one else to turn to!"

She caught Lydia's fingers in a stormy pressure.

"Say you'll help me—you and your husband."

Lydia tried to free herself.

"What you ask is impossible; you must see that it is. No one could interfere in—in the way you ask."

Mrs. Cope's clutch tightened.

"You won't, then? You won't?"

"Certainly not. Let me go, please."

Mrs. Cope released her with a laugh.

"Oh, go by all means—pray don't let me detain you! Shall you go and tell Lady Susan Condit that there's a pair of us—or shall I save you the trouble of enlightening her?"

Lydia stood still in the middle of the path, seeing her antagonist through a mist of terror. Mrs. Cope was still laughing.

"Oh, I'm not spiteful by nature, my dear; but you're a little more than flesh and blood can stand! It's impossible, is it? Let you go, indeed! You're too good to be mixed up in my affairs, are you? Why, you little fool, the first day I laid eyes on you I saw that you and I were both in the same box—that's the reason I spoke to you."

She stepped nearer, her smile dilating on Lydia like a lamp through a fog.

"You can take your choice, you know; I always play fair. If you'll tell I'll promise not to. Now then, which is it to be?"

Lydia, involuntarily, had begun to move away from the pelting storm of words; but at this she turned and sat down again.

"You may go," she said simply. "I shall stay here."

IV

She stayed there for a long time, in the hypnotized contemplation, not of Mrs. Cope's present, but of her own past. Gannett, early that morning, had gone off on a long walk—he had fallen into the habit of taking these mountain tramps with various fellow lodgers; but even had he been within reach she could not have gone to him just then. She had to deal with herself first. She was surprised to find how, in the last months, she had lost the habit of introspection. Since their coming to the Hotel Bellosguardo she and Gannett had tacitly avoided themselves and each other.

She was aroused by the whistle of the three o'clock steamboat as it neared the landing just beyond the hotel gates. Three o'clock! Then Gannett would soon be back—he had told her to expect him before four. She rose hurriedly, her face averted from the inquisitorial façade of the hotel. She could not see him just yet; she could not go indoors. She slipped through one of the overgrown garden alleys and climbed a steep path to the hills.

It was dark when she opened their sitting-room door. Gannett was sitting on the window ledge smoking a cigarette. Cigarettes were now his chief resource: he had not written a line during the two months they had spent at the Hotel Bellosguardo. In that respect, it had turned out not to be the right *milieu* after all.

He started up at Lydia's entrance.

"Where have you been? I was getting anxious."

She sat down in a chair near the door.

"Up the mountain," she said wearily.

"Alone?"

"Yes."

Gannett threw away his cigarette: the sound of her voice made him want to see her face.

"Shall we have a little light?" he suggested.

She made no answer and he lifted the globe from the lamp and put a match to the wick. Then he looked at her.

"Anything wrong? You look done up."

She sat glancing vaguely about the little sitting room, dimly lit by the pallid-globed lamp, which left in twilight the outlines of the furniture, of his writing table heaped with books and papers, of the tea roses and jasmine drooping on the mantelpiece. How like home it had all grown—how like home!

"Lydia, what is wrong?" he repeated.

She moved away from him, feeling for her hatpins and turning to lay her hat and sunshade on the table.

Suddenly she said: "That woman has been talking to me."

Gannett stared.

"That woman? What woman?"

"Mrs. Linton—Mrs. Cope."

He gave a start of annoyance, still, as she perceived, not grasping the full import of her words.

"The deuce! She told you—?"

"She told me everything."

Gannett looked at her anxiously.

"What impudence! I'm so sorry that you should have been exposed to this, dear."

"Exposed!" Lydia laughed.

Gannett's brow clouded and they looked away from each other.

"Do you know *why* she told me? She had the best of reasons. The first time she laid eyes on me she saw that we were both in the same box."

"Lydia!"

"So it was natural, of course, that she should turn to me in a difficulty."

"What difficulty?"

"It seems she has reason to think that Lord Trevenna's people are trying to get him away from her before she gets her divorce—"

"Well?"

"And she fancied he had been consulting with you last night as to—as to the best way of escaping from her."

Gannett stood up with an angry forehead.

"Well—what concern of yours was all this dirty business? Why should she go to you?"

"Don't you see? It's so simple. I was to wheedle his secret out of you."

"To oblige that woman?"

"Yes; or, if I was unwilling to oblige her, then to protect myself."

"To protect yourself? Against whom?"

"Against her telling everyone in the hotel that she and I are in the same box."

"She threatened that?"

"She left me the choice of telling it myself or of doing it for me."

"The beast!"

There was a long silence. Lydia had seated herself on the sofa, beyond the radius of the lamp, and he leaned against the window. His next question surprised her.

"When did this happen? At what time, I mean?"

She looked at him vaguely.

"I don't know—after luncheon, I think. Yes, I remember; it must have been at about three o'clock."

He stepped into the middle of the room and as he approached the light she saw that his brow had cleared.

"Why do you ask?" she said.

"Because when I came in, at about half-past three, the mail was just being distributed, and Mrs. Cope was waiting as usual to pounce on her letters; you know she was always watching for the postman. She was standing so close to me that I couldn't help seeing a big official-looking envelope that was handed to her. She tore it open, gave one look at the inside, and rushed off upstairs like a whirlwind, with the director shouting after her that she had left all her other letters behind. I don't believe she ever thought of you again after that paper was put into her hand."

"Why?"

"Because she was too busy. I was sitting in the window, watching for you, when the five o'clock boat left, and who should go on board, bag and baggage, valet and maid, dressing bags and poodle, but Mrs. Cope and Trevenna. Just an hour and a half to pack up in! And you should have seen her when they started. She was radiant—shaking hands with everybody—waving her handkerchief from the deck—distributing bows and smiles like an empress. If ever a woman got what she wanted just in the nick of time that woman did. She'll be Lady Trevenna within a week, I'll wager."

"You think she has her divorce?"

"I'm sure of it. And she must have got it just after her talk with you."

Lydia was silent.

At length she said, with a kind of reluctance, "She was horribly angry when she left me. It wouldn't have taken long to tell Lady Susan Condit."

"Lady Susan Condit has not been told."

"How do you know?"

"Because when I went downstairs half an hour ago I met Lady Susan on the way—"

He stopped, half smiling.

"Well?"

"And she stopped to ask if I thought you would act as patroness to a charity concert she is getting up."

In spite of themselves they both broke into a laugh. Lydia's ended in sobs and she sank down with her face hidden. Gannett bent over her, seeking her hands.

"That vile woman—I ought to have warned you to keep away from her; I can't forgive myself! But he spoke to me in confidence; and I never dreamed—well, it's all over now."

Lydia lifted her head.

"Not for me. It's only just beginning."

"What do you mean?"

She put him gently aside and moved in her turn to the window. Then she went on, with her face turned toward the shimmering blackness of the lake, "You see of course that it might happen again at any moment."

"What?"

"This—this risk of being found out. And we could hardly count again on such a lucky combination of chances, could we?"

He sat down with a groan.

Still keeping her face toward the darkness, she said, "I want you to go and tell Lady Susan—and the others."

Gannett, who had moved towards her, paused a few feet off.

"Why do you wish me to do this?" he said at length, with less surprise in his voice than she had been prepared for.

"Because I've behaved basely, abominably, since we came here: letting these people believe we were married—lying with every breath I drew—"

"Yes, I've felt that too," Gannett exclaimed with sudden energy.

The words shook her like a tempest: all her thoughts seemed to fall about her in ruins.

"You—you've felt so?"

"Of course I have." He spoke with low-voiced vehemence. "Do you suppose I like playing the sneak any better than you do? It's damnable."

He had dropped on the arm of a chair, and they stared at each other like blind people who suddenly see.

"But you have liked it here," she faltered.

"Oh, I've liked it—I've liked it." He moved impatiently. "Haven't you?"

"Yes," she burst out; "that's the worst of it—that's what I can't bear. I fancied it was for your sake that I insisted on staying—because you thought you could write here; and perhaps just at first that really was the reason. But afterwards I wanted to stay myself—I loved it." She broke into a laugh. "Oh, do you see the full derision of it? These people—the very prototypes of the bores you took me away from, with the same fenced-in view of life, the same keep-off-the-grass morality, the same little cautious virtues and the same little frightened vices—well, I've clung to them, I've delighted in them, I've done my best to please them. I've toadied Lady Susan, I've gossiped with Miss Pinsent, I've pretended to be shocked with Mrs. Ainger. Respectability! It was the one thing in life that I was sure I didn't care about, and it's grown so precious to me that I've stolen it because I couldn't get it in any other way."

She moved across the room and returned to his side with another laugh.

"I who used to fancy myself unconventional! I must have been born with a card-case in my hand. You should have seen me with that poor woman in the garden. She came to me for help, poor creature, because she fancied that, having 'sinned,' as they call it, I might feel some pity for others who had been tempted in the same way. Not I! She didn't know me. Lady Susan would have been kinder, because Lady Susan wouldn't have been afraid. I hated the woman—my one thought was not to be seen with her—I could have killed her for guessing my secret. The one thing that mattered to me at that moment was my standing with Lady Susan!"

Gannett did not speak.

"And you—you've felt it too!" she broke out accusingly. "You've enjoyed being with these people as much as I have; you've let the chaplain talk to you by the hour about The Reign of Law and Professor Drummond. When they asked you to hand the plate in church I was watching you—*you wanted to accept.*"

She stepped close, laying her hand on his arm.

"Do you know, I begin to see what marriage is for. It's to keep people away from each other. Sometimes I think that two people who love each other can be saved from madness only by the things that come between them—children, duties, visits, bores, relations—the things that protect married people from each other. We've been too close together—that has been our sin. We've seen the nakedness of each other's souls."

She sank again on the sofa, hiding her face in her hands.

Gannett stood above her perplexedly: he felt as though she were being swept away by some implacable current while he stood helpless on its bank.

At length he said, "Lydia, don't think me a brute—but don't you see yourself that it won't do?"

"Yes, I see it won't do," she said without raising her head.

His face cleared.

"Then we'll go tomorrow."

"Go—where?"

"To Paris; to be married."

For a long time she made no answer; then she asked slowly, "Would they have us here if we were married?"

"Have us here?"

"I mean Lady Susan—and the others."

"Have us here? Of course they would."

"Not if they knew—at least, not unless they could pretend not to know."

He made an impatient gesture.

"We shouldn't come back here, of course; and other people needn't know—no one need know."

She sighed. "Then it's only another form of deception and a meaner one. Don't you see that?"

"I see that we're not accountable to any Lady Susans on earth!"

"Then why are you ashamed of what we are doing here?"

"Because I'm sick of pretending that you're my wife when you're not—when you won't be."

She looked at him sadly.

"If I were your wife you'd have to go on pretending. You'd have to pretend that I'd never been—anything else. And our friends would have to pretend that they believed what you pretended."

Gannett pulled off the sofa tassel and flung it away.

"You're impossible," he groaned.

"It's not I—it's our being together that's impossible. I only want you to see that marriage won't help it."

"What will help it then?"

She raised her head.

"My leaving you."

"Your leaving me?" He sat motionless, staring at the tassel which lay at the other end of the room. At length some impulse of retaliation for the pain she was inflicting made him say deliberately:

"And where would you go if you left me?"

"Oh!" she cried.

He was at her side in an instant.

"Lydia—Lydia—you know I didn't mean it; I couldn't mean it! But you've driven me out of my senses; I don't know what I'm saying. Can't you get out of this labyrinth of self-torture? It's destroying us both."

"That's why I must leave you."

"How easily you say it!" He drew her hands down and made her face him. "You're very scrupulous about yourself—and others. But have you thought of me? You have no right to leave me unless you've ceased to care—"

"It's because I care—"

"Then I have a right to be heard. If you love me you can't leave me."

Her eyes defied him.

"Why not?"

He dropped her hands and rose from her side.

"Can you?" he said sadly.

The hour was late and the lamp flickered and sank. She stood up with a shiver and turned toward the door of her room.

V

At daylight a sound in Lydia's room woke Gannett from a troubled sleep. He sat up and listened. She was moving about softly, as though fearful of disturbing him. He heard her push back one of the creaking shutters; then there was a moment's silence, which seemed to indicate that she was waiting to see if the noise had roused him.

Presently she began to move again. She had spent a sleepless night, probably, and was dressing to go down to the garden for a breath of air. Gannett rose also; but some undefinable instinct made his movements as cautious as hers. He stole to his window and looked out through the slats of the shutter.

It had rained in the night and the dawn was gray and lifeless. The cloud-muffled hills across the lake were reflected in its surface as in a tarnished mirror. In the garden, the birds were beginning to shake the drops from the motionless laurustinus boughs.

An immense pity for Lydia filled Gannett's soul. Her seeming intellectual independence had blinded him for a time to the feminine cast of her mind. He had never thought of her as a woman who wept and clung: there was a lucidity in her intuitions that made them appear to be the result of reasoning. Now he saw the cruelty he had committed in detaching her from the normal conditions of life; he felt, too, the insight with which she had hit upon the real cause of their suffering. Their life was "impossible," as she had said—and its worst penalty was that it had made any other life impossible for them. Even had his love lessened, he was bound to her now by a hundred ties of pity and self-reproach; and she, poor child, must turn back to him as Latude returned to his cell.

A new sound startled him: it was the stealthy closing of Lydia's door. He crept to his own and heard her footsteps passing down the corridor. Then he went back to the window and looked out.

A minute or two later he saw her go down the steps of the porch and enter the garden. From his post of observation her face was invisible, but something about her appearance struck him. She wore a long traveling cloak and under its folds he detected the outline of a bag or bundle. He drew a deep breath and stood watching her.

She walked quickly down the laurustinus alley toward the gate; there she paused a moment, glancing about the little shady square. The stone benches under the trees were empty, and she seemed to gather resolution from the solitude about her, for she crossed the square to the steamboat landing, and he saw her pause before the ticket office at the head of the wharf. Now she was buying her ticket. Gannett turned his head a moment to look at the clock: the boat was due in five minutes. He had time to jump into his clothes and overtake her—

He made no attempt to move; an obscure reluctance restrained him. If any thought emerged from the tumult of his sensations, it was that he must let her go if she wished it. He had spoken last night of his rights: what were they? At the last issue, he and she were two separate beings, not made one by the miracle of common forbearances, duties, abnegations, but bound together in a *noyade*[5] of passion that left them resisting yet clinging as they went down.

After buying her ticket, Lydia had stood for a moment looking out across the lake; then he saw her seat herself on one of the benches near the landing. He and she, at that moment, were both listening for the same sound: the whistle of the boat as it

[5]French: "drowning."

rounded the nearest promontory. Gannett turned again to glance at the clock: the boat was due now.

Where would she go? What would her life be when she had left him? She had no near relations and few friends. There was money enough . . . but she asked so much of life, in ways so complex and immaterial. He thought of her as walking barefooted through a stony waste. No one would understand her—no one would pity her—and he, who did both, was powerless to come to her aid.

He saw that she had risen from the bench and walked toward the edge of the lake. She stood looking in the direction from which the steamboat was to come; then she turned to the ticket office, doubtless to ask the cause of the delay. After that she went back to the beach and sat down with bent head. What was she thinking of?

The whistle sounded; she started up, and Gannett involuntarily made a movement toward the door. But he turned back and continued to watch her. She stood motionless, her eyes on the trail of smoke that preceded the appearance of the boat. Then the little craft rounded the point, a dead white object on the leaden water: a minute later it was puffing and backing at the wharf.

The few passengers who were waiting—two or three peasants and a snuffy priest—were clustered near the ticket office. Lydia stood apart under the trees.

The boat lay alongside now; the gangplank was run out and the peasants went on board with their baskets of vegetables, followed by the priest. Still Lydia did not move. A bell began to ring querulously; there was a shriek of steam, and someone must have called to her that she would be late, for she started forward, as though in answer to a summons. She moved waveringly, and at the edge of the wharf she paused. Gannett saw a sailor beckon to her; the bell rang again and she stepped upon the gangplank.

Halfway down the short incline to the deck she stopped again; then she turned and ran back to the land. The gangplank was drawn in, the bell ceased to ring, and the boat backed out into the lake. Lydia, with slow steps, was walking toward the garden.

As she approached the hotel she looked up furtively and Gannett drew back into the room. He sat down beside a table; a Bradshaw lay at his elbow, and mechanically, without knowing what he did, he began looking out at the trains to Paris.

1899

The Other Two

Waythorn, on the drawing-room hearth, waited for his wife to come down to dinner.

It was their first night under his own roof, and he was surprised at his thrill of boyish agitation. He was not so old, to be sure—his glass gave him little more than the five-and-thirty years to which his wife confessed—but he had fancied himself already in the temperate zone; yet here he was listening for her step with a tender sense of all it symbolized, with some old trail of verse about the garlanded nuptial doorposts floating through his enjoyment of the pleasant room and the good dinner just beyond it.

They had been hastily recalled from their honeymoon by the illness of Lily Haskett, the child of Mrs. Waythorn's first marriage. The little girl, at Waythorn's desire, had been transferred to his house on the day of her mother's wedding, and the doctor, on their arrival, broke the news that she was ill with typhoid, but declared that all the symptoms were favorable. Lily could show twelve years of unblemished health, and the case promised to be a light one. The nurse spoke as reassuringly, and after a moment of alarm Mrs. Waythorn had adjusted herself to the situation. She was very fond of Lily—her affection for the child had perhaps been her decisive charm in Waythorn's eyes—but she had the perfectly balanced nerves which her little girl had inherited, and no woman ever wasted less tissue in unproductive worry. Waythorn was therefore quite prepared to see her come in presently, a little late because of a last look at Lily, but as serene and well-appointed as if her goodnight kiss had been laid on the brow of health. Her composure was restful to him; it acted as ballast to his somewhat unstable sensibilities. As he pictured her bending over the child's bed he thought how soothing her presence must be in illness: her very step would prognosticate recovery.

His own life had been a gray one, from temperament rather than circumstance, and he had been drawn to her by the unperturbed gaiety which kept her fresh and elastic at an age when most women's activities are growing either slack or febrile. He knew what was said about her; for, popular as she was, there had always been a faint undercurrent of detraction. When she had appeared in New York, nine or ten years earlier, as the pretty Mrs. Haskett whom Gus Varick had unearthed somewhere—was it in Pittsburgh or Utica?—society, while promptly accepting her, had reserved the right to cast a doubt on its own indiscrimination. Inquiry, however, established her undoubted connection with a socially reigning family, and explained her recent divorce as the natural result of a runaway match at seventeen; and as nothing was known of Mr. Haskett it was easy to believe the worst of him.

Alice Haskett's remarriage with Gus Varick was a passport to the set whose recognition she coveted, and for a few years the Varicks were the most popular couple in town. Unfortunately the alliance was brief and stormy, and this time the husband had his champions. Still, even Varick's stanchest supporters admitted that he was not meant for matrimony, and Mrs. Varick's grievances were of a nature to bear the inspection of the New York courts. A New York divorce is in itself a diploma of virtue, and in the semiwidowhood of this second separation Mrs. Varick took on an air of sanctity, and was allowed to confide her wrongs to some of the most scrupulous ears in town. But when it was known that she was to marry Waythorn there was a momentary reaction. Her best friends would have preferred to see her remain in the role of the injured wife, which was as becoming to her as crepe to a rosy complexion. True, a decent time had elapsed, and it was not even suggested that Waythorn had supplanted his predecessor. People shook their heads over him, however, and one grudging friend, to whom he affirmed that he took the step with his eyes open, replied oracularly: "Yes—and with your ears shut."

Waythorn could afford to smile at these innuendoes. In the Wall Street phrase, he had "discounted" them. He knew that society has not yet adapted itself to the consequences of divorce, and that till the adaptation takes place every woman who uses the freedom the law accords her must be her own social justification. Waythorn had an amused confidence in his wife's ability to justify herself. His expectations were fulfilled, and before the wedding took place Alice Varick's group had rallied openly to her support. She took it all imperturbably: she had a way of surmounting obstacles without seeming to be aware of them, and Waythorn looked back with wonder at the trivialities over which he had worn his nerves thin. He had the sense of having found refuge in a richer, warmer nature than his own, and his satisfaction, at the moment, was humorously summed up in the thought that his wife, when she had done all she could for Lily, would not be ashamed to come down and enjoy a good dinner.

The anticipation of such enjoyment was not, however, the sentiment expressed by Mrs. Waythorn's charming face when she presently joined him. Though she had put on her most engaging tea gown she had neglected to assume the smile that went with it, and Waythorn thought he had never seen her look so nearly worried.

"What is it?" he asked. "Is anything wrong with Lily?"

"No; I've just been in and she's still sleeping." Mrs. Waythorn hesitated. "But something tiresome has happened."

He had taken her two hands, and now perceived that he was crushing a paper between them.

"This letter?"

"Yes—Mr. Haskett has written—I mean his lawyer has written."

Waythorn felt himself flush uncomfortably. He dropped his wife's hands.

"What about?"

"About seeing Lily. You know the courts—"

"Yes, yes," he interrupted nervously.

Nothing was known about Haskett in New York. He was vaguely supposed to have remained in the outer darkness from which his wife had been rescued, and Waythorn was one of the few who were aware that he had given up his business in Utica and followed her to New York in order to be near his little girl. In the days of his wooing, Waythorn had often met Lily on the doorstep, rosy and smiling, on her way "to see papa."

"I am so sorry," Mrs. Waythorn murmured.

He roused himself. "What does he want?"

"He wants to see her. You know she goes to him once a week."

"Well—he doesn't expect her to go to him now, does he?"

"No—he has heard of her illness; but he expects to come here."

"Here?"

Mrs. Waythorn reddened under his gaze. They looked away from each other.

"I'm afraid he has the right. . . . You'll see. . . ." She made a proffer of the letter.

Waythorn moved away with a gesture of refusal. He stood staring about the softly-lighted room, which a moment before had seemed so full of bridal intimacy.

"I'm so sorry," she repeated. "If Lily could have been moved—"

"That's out of the question," he returned impatiently.

"I suppose so."

Her lip was beginning to tremble, and he felt himself a brute.

"He must come, of course," he said. "When is—his day?"

"I'm afraid—tomorrow."

"Very well. Send a note in the morning."

The butler entered to announce dinner.

Waythorn turned to his wife. "Come—you must be tired. It's beastly, but try to forget about it," he said, drawing her hand through his arm.

"You're so good, dear. I'll try," she whispered back.

Her face cleared at once, and as she looked at him across the flowers, between the rosy candleshades, he saw her lips waver back into a smile.

"How pretty everything is!" she sighed luxuriously.

He turned to the butler. "The champagne at once, please. Mrs. Waythorn is tired."

In a moment or two their eyes met above the sparkling glasses. Her own were quite clear and untroubled: he saw that she had obeyed his injunction and forgotten.

II

Waythorn, the next morning, went downtown earlier than usual. Haskett was not likely to come till the afternoon, but the instinct of flight drove him forth. He meant to stay away all day—he had thoughts of dining at his club. As his door closed behind him he reflected that before he opened it again it would have admitted another man who had as much right to enter it as himself, and the thought filled him with a physical repugnance.

He caught the elevated at the employees' hour, and found himself crushed between two layers of pendulous humanity. At Eighth Street the man facing him wriggled out, and another took his place. Waythorn glanced up and saw that it was Gus Varick. The men were so close together that it was impossible to ignore the smile of recognition on Varick's handsome overblown face. And after all—why not? They had always been on good terms, and Varick had been divorced before Waythorn's attentions to his wife began. The two exchanged a word on the perennial grievance of the congested trains, and when a seat at their side was miraculously left empty the instinct of self-preservation made Waythorn slip into it after Varick.

The latter drew the stout man's breath of relief. "Lord—I was beginning to feel like a pressed flower." He leaned back, looking unconcernedly at Waythorn. "Sorry to hear that Sellers is knocked out again."

"Sellers?" echoed Waythorn, starting at his partner's name.

Varick looked surprised. "You didn't know he was laid up with the gout?"

"No. I've been away—I only got back last night." Waythorn felt himself reddenly in anticipation of the other's smile.

"Ah—yes; to be sure. And Sellers' attack came on two days ago. I'm afraid he's pretty bad. Very awkward for me, as it happens, because he was just putting through a rather important thing for me."

"Ah?" Waythorn wondered vaguely since when Varick had been dealing in "important things." Hitherto he had dabbled only in the shallow pools of speculation, with which Waythorn's office did not usually concern itself.

It occurred to him that Varick might be talking at random, to relieve the strain of their propinquity. That strain was becoming momentarily more apparent to Waythorn, and when, at Cortlandt Street, he caught sight of an acquaintance and had a sudden vision of the picture he and Varick must present to an initiated eye, he jumped up with a muttered excuse.

"I hope you'll find Sellers better," said Varick civilly, and he stammered back: "If I can be of any use to you—" and let the departing crowd sweep him to the platform.

At his office he heard that Sellers was in fact ill with the gout, and would probably not be able to leave the house for some weeks.

"I'm sorry it should have happened so, Mr. Waythorn," the senior clerk said with affable significance. "Mr. Sellers was very much upset at the idea of giving you such a lot of extra work just now."

"Oh, that's no matter," said Waythorn hastily. He secretly welcomed the pressure of additional business, and was glad to think that, when the day's work was over, he would have to call at his partner's on the way home.

He was late for luncheon, and turned in at the nearest restaurant instead of going to his club. The place was full, and the waiter hurried him to the back of the room to capture the only vacant table. In the cloud of cigar smoke Waythorn did not at once distinguish his neighbors: but presently, looking about him, he saw Varick seated a few feet off. This time, luckily, they were too far apart for conversation, and Varick, who faced another way, had probably not even seen him; but there was an irony in their renewed nearness.

Varick was said to be fond of good living, and as Waythorn sat dispatching his hurried luncheon he looked across half enviously at the other's leisurely degustation of his meal. When Waythorn first saw him he had been helping himself with critical deliberation to a bit of Camembert at the ideal point of liquefaction, and now, the cheese removed, he was just pouring his *café double* from its little two-storied earthen pot. He poured slowly, his ruddy profile bent over the task, and one beringed white hand steadying the lid of the coffeepot; then he stretched his other hand to the decanter of cognac at his elbow, filled a liqueur glass, took a tentative sip, and poured the brandy into his coffee cup.

Waythorn watched him in a kind of fascination. What was he thinking of—only of the flavor of the coffee and the liqueur? Had the morning's meeting left no more trace in his thoughts than on his face? Had his wife so completely passed out of his life that even this odd encounter with her present husband, within a week after her remarriage, was no more than an incident in his day? And as Waythorn mused, another idea struck him: had Haskett ever met Varick as Varick and he had just met? The recollection of Haskett perturbed him, and he rose and left the restaurant, taking a circuitous way out to escape the placid irony of Varick's nod.

It was after seven when Waythorn reached home. He thought the footman who opened the door looked at him oddly.

"How is Miss Lily?" he asked in haste.

"Doing very well, sir. A gentleman—"

"Tell Barlow to put off dinner for half an hour," Waythorn cut him off, hurrying upstairs.

He went straight to his room and dressed without seeing his wife. When he reached the drawing room she was there, fresh and radiant. Lily's day had been good; the doctor was not coming back that evening.

At dinner Waythorn told her of Seller's illness and of the resulting complications. She listened sympathetically, adjuring him not to let himself be overworked, and asking vague feminine questions about the routine of the office. Then she gave him the chronicle of Lily's day; quoted the nurse and doctor, and told him who had called to inquire. He had never seen her more serene and unruffled. It struck him, with a curious pang, that she was very happy in being with him, so happy that she found a childish pleasure in rehearsing the trivial incidents of her day.

After dinner they went to the library, and the servant put the coffee and liqueurs on a low table before her and left the room. She looked singularly soft and girlish in her rosy-pale dress, against the dark leather of one of his bachelor armchairs. A day earlier the contrast would have charmed him.

He turned away now, choosing a cigar with affected deliberation.

"Did Haskett come?" he asked, with his back to her.

"Oh, yes—he came."

"You didn't see him, of course?"

She hesitated a moment. "I let the nurse see him."

That was all. There was nothing more to ask. He swung round toward her, applying a match to his cigar. Well, the thing was over for a week, at any rate. He would try not to think of it. She looked up at him, a trifle rosier than usual, with a smile in her eyes.

"Ready for your coffee, dear?"

He leaned against the mantelpiece, watching her as she lifted the coffeepot. The lamplight struck a gleam from her bracelets and tipped her soft hair with brightness. How light and slender she was, and how each gesture flowed into the next! She seemed a creature all compact of harmonies. As the thought of Haskett receded, Waythorn felt himself yielding again to the joy of possessorship. They were his, those white hands with their flitting motions, his the light haze of hair, the lips and eyes. . . .

She set down the coffeepot, and reaching for the decanter of cognac, measured off a liqueur glass and poured it into his cup.

Waythorn uttered a sudden exclamation.

"What is the matter?" she said, startled.

"Nothing; only—I don't take cognac in my coffee."

"Oh, how stupid of me," she cried.

Their eyes met, and she blushed a sudden agonized red.

III

Ten days later, Mr. Sellers, still housebound, asked Waythorn to call on his way downtown.

The senior partner, with his swaddled foot propped up by the fire, greeted his associate with an air of embarrassment.

"I'm sorry, my dear fellow; I've got to ask you to do an awkward thing for me."

Waythorn waited, and the other went on, after a pause apparently given to the arrangement of his phrases: "The fact is, when I was knocked out I had just gone into a rather complicated piece of business for—Gus Varick."

"Well?" said Waythorn, with an attempt to put him at his ease.

"Well—it's this way: Varick came to me the day before my attack. He had evidently had an inside tip from somebody, and had made about a hundred thousand. He came to me for advice, and I suggested his going in with Vanderlyn."

"Oh, the deuce!" Waythorn exclaimed. He saw in a flash what had happened.

The investment was an alluring one, but required negotiation. He listened quietly while Sellers put the case before him, and, the statement ended, he said: "You think I ought to see Varick?"

"I'm afraid I can't as yet. The doctor is obdurate. And this thing can't wait. I hate to ask you, but no one else in the office knows the ins and outs of it."

Waythorn stood silent. He did not care a farthing for the success of Varick's venture, but the honor of the office was to be considered, and he could hardly refuse to oblige his partner.

"Very well," he said, "I'll do it."

That afternoon, apprised by telephone, Varick called at the office. Waythorn, waiting in his private room, wondered what the others thought of it. The newspapers, at the time of Mrs. Waythorn's marriage, had acquainted their readers with every detail of her previous matrimonial ventures, and Waythorn could fancy the clerks smiling behind Varick's back as he was ushered in.

Varick bore himself admirably. He was easy without being undignified, and Waythorn was conscious of cutting a much less impressive figure. Varick had no experience of business, and the talk prolonged itself for nearly an hour while Waythorn set forth with scrupulous precision the details of the proposed transaction.

"I'm awfully obliged to you," Varick said as he rose. "The fact is I'm not used to having much money to look after, and I don't want to make an ass of myself—" He smiled, and Waythorn could not help noticing that there was something pleasant about his smile. "It feels uncommonly queer to have enough cash to pay one's bills. I'd have sold my soul for it a few years ago!"

Waythorn winced at the allusion. He had heard it rumored that a lack of funds had been one of the determining causes of the Varick separation, but it did not occur to him that Varick's words were intentional. It seemed more likely that the desire to keep clear of embarrassing topics had fatally drawn him into one. Waythorn did not wish to be outdone in civility.

"We'll do the best we can for you," he said. "I think this is a good thing you're in."

"Oh, I'm sure it's immense. It's awfully good of you—" Varick broke off, embarrassed. "I suppose the thing's settled now—but if—"

"If anything happens before Sellers is about, I'll see you again," said Waythorn quietly. He was glad, in the end, to appear the more selfpossessed of the two.

The course of Lily's illness ran smooth, and as the days passed Waythorn grew used to the idea of Haskett's weekly visit. The first time the day came round, he stayed out late, and questioned his wife as to the visit on his return. She replied at once that Haskett had merely seen the nurse downstairs, as the doctor did not wish anyone in the child's sickroom till after the crisis.

The following week Waythorn was again conscious of the recurrence of the day, but had forgotten it by the time he came home to dinner. The crisis of the disease came a few days later, with a rapid decline of fever, and the little girl was pronounced out of danger. In the rejoicing which ensued the thought of Haskett passed out of Waythorn's mind, and one afternoon, letting himself into the house with a latchkey, he went straight to his library without noticing a shabby hat and umbrella in the hall.

In the library he found a small effaced-looking man with a thinnish gray beard sitting on the edge of a chair. The stranger might have been a piano tuner, or one of those mysteriously efficient persons who are summoned in emergencies to adjust some detail of domestic machinery. He blinked at Waythorn through a pair of gold-rimmed spectacles and said mildly: "Mr. Waythorn, I presume? I am Lily's father."

Waythorn flushed. "Oh—" he stammered uncomfortably. He broke off, disliking to appear rude. Inwardly he was trying to adjust the actual Haskett to the image of him projected by his wife's reminiscences. Waythorn had been allowed to infer that Alice's first husband was a brute.

"I am sorry to intrude," said Haskett, with his over-the-counter politeness.

"Don't mention it," returned Waythorn, collecting himself. "I suppose the nurse has been told?"

"I presume so. I can wait," said Haskett. He had a resigned way of speaking, as though life had worn down his natural powers of resistance.

Waythorn stood on the threshold, nervously pulling off his gloves.

"I'm sorry you've been detained. I will send for the nurse," he said; and as he opened the door he added with an effort: "I'm glad we can give you a good report of Lily." He winced as the *we* slipped out, but Haskett seemed not to notice it.

"Thank you, Mr. Waythorn, it's been an anxious time for me."

"Ah, well, that's past. Soon she'll be able to go to you." Waythorn nodded and passed out.

In his own room he flung himself down with a groan. He hated the womanish sensibility which made him suffer so acutely from the grotesque chances of life. He had known when he married that his wife's former husbands were both living, and that amid the multiplied contacts of modern existence there were a thousand chances to one that he would run against one or the other, yet he found himself as much disturbed by his brief encounter with Haskett as though the law had not obligingly removed all difficulties in the way of their meeting.

Waythorn sprang up and began to pace the room nervously. He had not suffered half as much from his two meetings with Varick. It was Haskett's presence in his own house that made the situation so intolerable. He stood still, hearing steps in the passage.

"This way, please," he heard the nurse say. Haskett was being taken upstairs, then: not a corner of the house but was open to him. Waythorn dropped into another chair, staring vaguely ahead of him. On his dressing table stood a photograph of Alice, taken when he had first known her. She was Alice Varick then—how fine and exquisite he had thought her! Those were Varick's pearls about her neck. At Waythorn's instance they had been returned before her marriage. Had Haskett ever given her any trinkets—and what had become of them, Waythorn wondered? He realized suddenly that he knew very little of Haskett's past or present situation; but from the man's appearance and manner of speech he could reconstruct with curious precision the surroundings of Alice's first marriage. And it startled him to think that she had, in the background of her life, a phase of existence so different from anything with which he had connected her. Varick, whatever his faults, was a gentleman, in the conventional, traditional sense of the term: the sense which at that moment seemed, oddly enough, to have most meaning to Waythorn. He and Varick had the same social habits, spoke the same language, understood the same allusions. But this other man . . . it was grotesquely uppermost in Waythorn's mind that Haskett had worn a made-up tie attached with an elastic. Why should that ridiculous detail symbolize the whole man? Waythorn was exasperated by his own paltriness, but the fact of the tie expanded, forced itself on him, became as it were the key to Alice's past. He could see her, as Mrs. Haskett, sitting in a "front parlor" furnished in plush, with a pianola, and copy of *Ben Hur* on the center table. He could see her going to the theater with Haskett—or perhaps even to a "Church Sociable"—she in a "picture hat" and Haskett in a black frock coat, a little creased, with the made-up tie on an elastic. On the way home they would stop and look at the illuminated shop windows, lingering over the photographs of New York actresses. On Sunday afternoons Haskett would take her for a walk, pushing Lily ahead of them in a white enameled perambulator, and Waythorn had a vision of the people they would stop and talk to. He could fancy how pretty Alice must have looked, in a dress adroitly constructed from the hints of a New York fashion paper, and how she must have looked down on the other women, chafing at her life, and secretly feeling that she belonged in a bigger place.

For the moment his foremost thought was one of wonder at the way in which she had shed the phase of existence which her marriage with Haskett implied. It was as if her whole aspect, every gesture, every inflection, every allusion, were a studied negation of that period of her life. If she had denied being married to Haskett she could hardly have stood more convicted of duplicity than in this obliteration of the self which had been his wife.

Waythorn started up, checking himself in the analysis of her motives. What right had he to create a fantastic effigy of her and then pass judgment on it? She had spoken vaguely of her first marriage as unhappy, had hinted, with becoming reticence, that Haskett had wrought havoc among her young illusions. . . . It was a pity for Waythorn's peace of mind that Haskett's very inoffensiveness shed a new light on the nature of those illusions. A man would rather think that his wife has been brutalized by her first husband than that the process has been reversed.

IV

"Mr. Waythorn, I don't like that French governess of Lily's."

Haskett, subdued and apologetic, stood before Waythorn in the library, revolving his shabby hat in his hand.

Waythorn, surprised in his armchair over the evening paper, stared back perplexedly at his visitor.

"You'll excuse my asking to see you," Haskett continued. "But this is my last visit, and I thought if I could have a word with you it would be a better way than writing to Mrs. Waythorn's lawyer."

Waythorn rose uneasily. He did not like the French governess either; but that was irrelevant.

"I am not so sure of that," he returned stiffly; "but since you wish it I will give your message to—my wife." He always hesitated over the possessive pronoun in addressing Haskett.

The latter sighed. "I don't know as that will help much. She didn't like it when I spoke to her."

Waythorn turned red. "When did you see her?" he asked.

"Not since the first day I came to see Lily—right after she was taken sick. I remarked to her then that I didn't like the governess."

Waythorn made no answer. He remembered distinctly that, after that first visit, he had asked his wife if she had seen Haskett. She had lied to him then, but she had respected his wishes since; and the incident cast a curious light on her character. He was sure she would not have seen Haskett that first day if she had divined that Waythorn would object, and the fact that she did not divine it was almost as disagreeable to the latter as the discovery that she had lied to him.

"I don't like the woman," Haskett was repeating with mild persistency. "She ain't straight, Mr. Waythorn—she'll teach the child to be underhand. I've noticed a change in Lily—she's too anxious to please—and she don't always tell the truth. She used to be the straightest child, Mr. Waythorn—" He broke off, his voice a little thick. "Not but what I want her to have a stylish education," he ended.

Waythorn was touched. "I'm sorry, Mr. Haskett; but frankly, I don't quite see what I can do."

Haskett hesitated. Then he laid his hat on the table, and advanced to the hearthrug, on which Waythorn was standing. There was nothing aggressive in his manner, but he had the solemnity of a timid man resolved on a decisive measure.

"There's just one thing you can do, Mr. Waythorn," he said. "You can remind Mrs. Waythorn that, by the decree of the courts, I am entitled to have a voice in Lily's bringing-up." He paused, and went on more deprecatingly: "I'm not the kind to talk about enforcing my rights, Mr. Waythorn. I don't know as I think a man is entitled to rights he hasn't known how to hold on to; but this business of the child is different. I've never let go there—and I never mean to."

The scene left Waythorn deeply shaken. Shamefacedly, in indirect ways, he had been finding out about Haskett; and all that he had learned was favorable. The little man, in order to be near his daughter, had sold out his share in a profitable business in Utica, and accepted a modest clerkship in a New York manufacturing house. He boarded in a shabby street and had few acquaintances. His passion for Lily filled his life. Waythorn felt that this exploration of Haskett was like groping about with a dark lantern in his wife's past; but he saw now that there were recesses his lantern had not explored. He had never inquired into the exact circumstances of his wife's first matrimonial rupture. On the surface all had been fair. It was she who had obtained the divorce, and the court had given her the child. But Waythorn knew how many ambiguities such a verdict might cover. The mere fact that Haskett retained a right over his daughter implied an unsuspected compromise. Waythorn was an idealist. He always refused to recognize unpleasant contingencies till he found himself confronted with them, and then he saw them followed by a spectral train of consequences. His next days were thus haunted, and he determined to try to lay the ghosts by conjuring them up in his wife's presence.

When he repeated Haskett's request a flame of anger passed over her face; but she subdued it instantly and spoke with a slight quiver of outraged motherhood.

"It is very ungentlemanly of him," she said.

The word grated on Waythorn. "That is neither here nor there. It's a bare question of rights."

She murmured: "It's not as if he could ever be a help to Lily—"

Waythorn flushed. This was even less to his taste. "The question is," he repeated, "what authority has he over her?"

She looked downward, twisting herself a little in her seat. "I am willing to see him—I thought you objected," she faltered.

In a flash he understood that she knew the extent of Haskett's claims. Perhaps it was not the first time she had resisted them.

"My objecting has nothing to do with it," he said coldly; "if Haskett has a right to be consulted you must consult him."

She burst into tears, and he saw that she expected him to regard her as a victim.

Haskett did not abuse his rights. Waythorn had felt miserably sure that he would not. But the governess was dismissed, and from time to time the little man demanded an interview with Alice. After the first outburst she accepted the situation with her usual adaptability. Haskett had once reminded Waythorn of the piano tuner, and Mrs. Waythorn, after a month or two, appeared to class him with that domestic familiar. Waythorn could not but respect the father's tenacity. At first he had tried to cultivate the suspicion that Haskett might be "up to" something, that he had an object in securing a foothold in the house. But in his heart Waythorn was sure of Haskett's single-mindedness; he even guessed in the latter a mild contempt for such advantages as his relation with the Waythorns might offer. Haskett's sincerity of purpose made him invulnerable, and his successor had to accept him as a lien on the property.

Mr. Sellers was sent to Europe to recover from his gout, and Varick's affairs hung on Waythorn's hands. The negotiations were prolonged and complicated; they necessitated frequent conferences between the two men, and the interests of the firm forbade Waythorn's suggesting that his client should transfer his business to another office.

Varick appeared well in the transaction. In moments of relaxation his coarse streak appeared, and Waythorn dreaded his geniality; but in the office he was concise and clear-headed, with a flattering deference to Waythorn's judgment. Their business relations being so affably established, it would have been absurd for the two men to ignore each other in society. The first time they met in a drawing room, Varick took up their intercourse in the same easy key, and his hostess' grateful glance obliged Waythorn to respond to it. After that they ran across each other frequently, and one evening at a ball Waythorn, wandering through the remoter rooms, came upon Varick seated beside his wife. She colored a little, and faltered in what she was saying; but Varick nodded to Waythorn without rising, and the latter strolled on.

In the carriage, on the way home, he broke out nervously: "I didn't know you spoke to Varick."

Her voice trembled a little. "It's the first time—he happened to be standing near me; I didn't know what to do. It's so awkward, meeting everywhere—and he said you had been very kind about some business."

"That's different," said Waythorn.

She paused a moment. "I'll do just as you wish," she returned pliantly. "I thought it would be less awkward to speak to him when we meet."

Her pliancy was beginning to sicken him. Had she really no will of her own—no theory about her relation to these men? She had accepted Haskett—did she mean to accept Varick? It was "less awkward," as she had said, and her instinct was to evade difficulties or to circumvent them. With sudden vividness Waythorn saw how the instinct had developed. She was "as easy as an old shoe"—a shoe that too many feet had worn. Her elasticity was the result of tension in too many different directions. Alice Haskett—Alice Varick—Alice Waythorn—she had been each in turn, and had left hanging to each name a little of her privacy, a little of her personality, a little of the inmost self where the unknown god abides.

"Yes—it's better to speak to Varick," said Waythorn wearily.

V

The winter wore on, and society took advantage of the Waythorns' acceptance of Varick. Harassed hostesses were grateful to them for bridging over a social difficulty, and Mrs. Waythorn was held up as a miracle of good taste. Some experimental spirits could not resist the diversion of throwing Varick and his former wife together, and there were those who thought he found a zest in the propinquity. But Mrs. Waythorn's conduct remained irreproachable. She neither avoided Varick nor sought him out. Even Waythorn could not but admit that she had discovered the solution of the newest social problem.

He had married her without giving much thought to that problem. He had fancied that a woman can shed her past like a man. But now he saw that Alice was bound to hers both by the circumstances which forced her into continued relation with it, and by the traces it had left on her nature. With grim irony Waythorn compared himself to a member of a syndicate. He held so many shares in his wife's personality and his predecessors were his partners in the business. If there had been any element of passion in the transaction he would have felt less deteriorated by it. The fact that Alice took her change of husbands like a change of weather reduced the situation to mediocrity. He could have forgiven her for blunders, for excesses; for resisting Haskett, for yielding to Varick; for anything but her acquiescence and her tact. She reminded him of a juggler tossing knives; but the knives were blunt and she knew they would never cut her.

And then, gradually, habit formed a protecting surface for his sensibilities. If he paid for each day's comfort with the small change of his illusions, he grew daily to value the comfort more and set less store upon the coin. He had drifted into a dulling propinquity with Haskett and Varick and he took refuge in the cheap revenge of satirizing the situation. He even began to reckon up the advantages which accrued from it, to ask himself if it were not better to own a third of a wife who knew how to make a man happy than a whole one who had lacked opportunity to acquire the art. For it *was* an art, and made up, like all others, of concessions, eliminations and embellishments; of lights judiciously thrown and shadows skillfully softened. His wife knew exactly how to manage the lights, and he knew exactly to what training she owed her skill. He even tried to trace the source of his obligations, to discriminate between the influences which had combined to produce his domestic happiness: he perceived that Haskett's commonness had made Alice worship good breeding, while Varick's liberal construction of the marriage bond had taught her to value the conjugal virtues; so that he was directly indebted to his predecessors for the devotion which made his life easy if not inspiring.

From this phase he passed into that of complete acceptance. He ceased to satirize himself because time dulled the irony of the situation and the joke lost its humor with its sting. Even the sight of Haskett's hat on the hall table had ceased to touch the springs of epigram. The hat was often seen there now, for it had been decided that it was better for Lily's father to visit her than for the little girl to go to his boardinghouse. Waythorn, having acquiesced in this arrangement, had been surprised to find how little difference it made. Haskett was never obtrusive, and the few visitors who met him on the stairs were unaware of his identity. Waythorn did not know how often he saw Alice, but with himself Haskett was seldom in contact.

One afternoon, however, he learned on entering that Lily's father was waiting to see him. In the library he found Haskett occupying a chair in his usual provisional way. Waythorn always felt grateful to him for not leaning back.

"I hope you'll excuse me, Mr. Waythorn," he said rising. "I wanted to see Mrs. Waythorn about Lily, and your man asked me to wait here till she came in."

"Of course," said Waythorn, remembering that a sudden leak had that morning given over the drawing room to the plumbers.

He opened his cigar case and held it out to his visitor, and Haskett's acceptance seemed to mark a fresh stage in their intercourse. The spring evening was chilly, and Waythorn invited his guest to draw up his chair to the fire. He meant to find an excuse to leave Haskett in a moment; but he was tired and cold, and after all the little man no longer jarred on him.

The two were enclosed in the intimacy of their blended cigar smoke when the door opened and Varick walked into the room. Waythorn rose abruptly. It was the first time that Varick had come to the house, and the surprise of seeing him, combined with the singular inopportuneness of his arrival, gave a new edge to Waythorn's blunted sensibilities. He stared at his visitor without speaking.

Varick seemed too preoccupied to notice his host's embarrassment.

"My dear fellow," he exclaimed in his most expansive tone, "I must apologize for tumbling in on you in this way, but I was too late to catch you downtown, and so I thought—"

He stopped short, catching sight of Haskett, and his sanguine color deepened to a flush which spread vividly under his scant blond hair. But in a moment he recovered himself and nodded slightly. Haskett returned the bow in silence, and Waythorn was still groping for speech when the footman came in carrying a tea table.

The intrusion offered a welcome vent to Waythorn's nerves. "What the deuce are you bringing this here for?" he said sharply.

"I beg your pardon, sir, but the plumbers are still in the drawing room, and Mrs. Waythorn said she would have tea in the library." The footman's perfectly respectful tone implied a reflection on Waythorn's reasonableness.

"Oh, very well," said the latter resignedly, and the footman proceeded to open the folding tea table and set out its complicated appointments. While this interminable process continued the three men stood motionless, watching it with a fascinated stare, till Waythorn, to break the silence, said to Varick, "Won't you have a cigar?"

He held out the case he had just tendered to Haskett, and Varick helped himself with a smile. Waythorn looked about for a match, and finding none, proffered a light from his own cigar. Haskett, in the background held his ground mildly, examining his cigar tip now and then, and stepping forward at the right moment to knock its ashes into the fire.

The footman at last withdrew, and Varick immediately began: "If I could just say half a word to you about this business—"

"Certainly," stammered Waythorn; "in the dining room—"

But as he placed his hand on the door it opened from without, and his wife appeared on the threshold.

She came in fresh and smiling, in her street dress and hat, shedding a fragrance from the boa which she loosened in advancing.

"Shall we have tea in here, dear?" she began; and then she caught sight of Varick. Her smile deepened, veiling a slight tremor of surprise.

"Why, how do you do?" she said with a distinct note of pleasure.

As she shook hands with Varick she saw Haskett standing behind him. Her smile faded for a moment, but she recalled it quickly, with a scarcely perceptible side glance at Waythorn.

"How do you do, Mr. Haskett?" she said, and shook hands with him a shade less cordially.

The three men stood awkwardly before her, till Varick, always the most self-possessed, dashed into an explanatory phrase.

"We—I had to see Waythorn a moment on business," he stammered, brick-red from chin to nape.

Haskett stepped forward with his air of mild obstinacy. "I am sorry to intrude; but you appointed five o'clock—" he directed his resigned glance to the timepiece on the mantel.

She swept aside their embarrassment with a charming gesture of hospitality.

"I'm so sorry—I'm always late; but the afternoon was so lovely." She stood drawing off her gloves, propitiatory and graceful, diffusing about her a sense of ease and familiarity in which the situation lost its grotesqueness. "But before talking business," she added brightly, "I'm sure everyone wants a cup of tea."

She dropped into her low chair by the tea table, and the two visitors, as if drawn by her smile, advanced to receive the cups she held out.

She glanced about for Waythorn, and he took the third cup with a laugh.

1904

The Life Apart *(L'âme close)*[1]

The Mount.[2] Oct 29*th* 1907.

If you had not enclosed that sprig of wych-hazel in your note I should not have opened this long-abandoned book; for the note in itself might have meant nothing—would have meant nothing to me—beyond the inference that you had a more "personal" accent than week-end visitors usually put into their leave-takings. But you

[1]French: the enclosed soul. "The Life Apart" is published with the permission of both the Lilly Library, Indiana University, Bloomington, Indiana, and the Watkins/Loomis Agency, agents for the estate of Edith Wharton. It was first published in full in *American Literature* 66 (December 1994): 663–88, edited by Kenneth M. Price and Phyllis McBride. The editors of *The Heath Anthology* wish to thank them for sharing the fruits of their labor with us and with our students.

Ellipses and revisions are Wharton's; brackets indicate material that is unclear in the original manuscript.

[2]Wharton's home in Lenox, Massachusetts.

sent the wych-hazel—& sent it without a word—thus telling me (as I choose to think!) that you knew what was in my mind when I found it blooming on that wet bank in the woods, where we sat together & smoked a cigarette while the chains were put on the wheels of the motor.

And so it happens that, finding myself—after so long!—with some one to talk to, I take up this empty volume, in which, long ago, I made one or two spasmodic attempts to keep a diary. For I had no one but myself to talk to, & it is absurd to write down what one says ~~of~~ to one's self; but now I shall have the illusion that I am talking to you, & that—as when I picked the wych-hazel—something of what I say will somehow reach you. . . .

Your evening here the other day was marked by curious symbols; for the day before you arrived we had our first autumn snow-storm (we have October snow in these hills); & on the bank where you & I sat we found the first sprig of the "old woman's flower"—the flower that blooms in the autumn!

Nov. 27th Your letter from Paris . . .

February 21st.

All these months I thought after all I had been mistaken; & my poor "âme close" barred its shutters & bolted its doors again, & the dust gathered & the cobwebs thickened in the empty rooms, where for a moment I had heard an echo. . . .

Then we went to Herblay. Such a cold, sad winter day, with the wind beating the bare trees, & a leaden sieve between brown banks! In the church it was still & dim, & in the shadowy corner where I sat while you talked with the curé, a veiled figure stole up & looked at me a moment. Was its name Happiness? I dared not lift the veil . . .

When you came to dine, two nights afterward, you said things that distressed me. At first it was exquisite. I had my work, & you sat near the lamp, & read me a page of Chevrillon's article in the Revue de Paris—the article on Meredith that I had told you about.[3] And as I followed you, seeing your mind leap ahead, as it always does, noting how you instantly singled out the finer values I had missed—discriminated, classified, with that flashing, illuminating sense of differences & relations that so exquisitely distinguishes your thought—ah, the illusion I had, of a life in which such evenings might be a dear, accepted habit! At that moment indeed, "the hour became her husband . . ."[4]

Why did you spoil it? Because men & women are different, because—in that respect—~~w~~ in the way of mental companionship—what I can give you is so much less interesting, less arresting, than what I receive from you? It was as if there stood between us at that moment ~~a~~ the frailest of glass cups, filled with a rare colourless ~~liquid~~ wine—& with a gesture you broke the glass & spilled the drops.

You hurt me—you disillusionized me—& when you left me I was more deeply yours . . . Ah, the confused processes within us!

[3]André Chevrillon was a nephew of the historian Hippolite Taine and wrote about English literature.

[4]The line comes from sonnet forty-seven of George Meredith's "Modern Love."

Feb. 22^{d}.

How can I ever dream that life has in store for me a single moment of happiness? . . . . This is the day on which we were to have gone together to M . . . l'A[5] . . . a whole day together in the country!—I said to myself all the week: "I have never in my life known what it was to be happy (as a woman understands happiness) even for a single hour—now at last I shall be happy for a whole day, talking à coeur ouvert,[6] saying for once what I feel, and *all that I feel,* as other women do . . . Ah, pauvre âme close! Y ai-je vraiment cru un seul instant? Non, je savais trop bien que quand il s'agit de moi les Erynnies de dorment jamais, hélas . . . . .[7]

~~Un retour inattendu changed everything; I am back in the tread mill again~~ . . .[8] I had to put you off, by a vague note, not daring to be explicit—& you were hurt, you didn't understand—& the sky is all dark again . . .

And here is the day—soft & sunny, with spring in the air . . . Some other woman's day, not mine . . .

Ame close.[9]

My soul is like a house that dwellers nigh
Can see no light in. "Ah, poor house," they say,
"Long since its owners died or went their way.
Thick ivy loops the rusted door-latch tie,
The chimney rises cold against the sky,
And flowers turned weed down the bare paths ~~in the dry~~
~~cold earth~~ decay" . . .
Yet one stray passer, at the shut of day,
Sees a light tremble in a casement high.

Even so, my soul would set a light for you,
A light invisible to all beside,
As though a lover's ghost should yearn & glide
From pane to pane, to let the flame shine through.
Yet enter not, lest, as it flits ahead,
You see the hand that carries it is dead.

Feb. 21st.

March 3^{d}

The other night at the theatre, when you came into the box—that little, dim baignoire (no. 13, I shall always remember!) I felt for the first time that indescribable current of communication flowing between myself & some one else—felt it, I mean, uninterruptedly, securely, so that it penetrated every sense & every thought . . . & said to myself: "This must be what happy women feel. . . . ."

(The theatre was the Renaissance.)

[5]Montfort l'Amaury.
[6]French: with open heart.
[7]French: Oh, poor enclosed soul! Did I truly believe it for even a single moment? No, I know too well that when it is a question of myself, the Furies never sleep.
[8]French: an unexpected return.
[9]This poem is by Wharton.

And we had another dear half-hour, coming back from St C—last Sunday in the motor. It was snowing—the first snow of the winter!—& the flakes froze on the windows, shutting us in, shutting everything else out . . . I felt your *dearest* side then, the side that is simple & sensitive & true . . . & I felt that all that must have been, at first, so unintelligible to you in me & in my life, was clear at last, & that our hearts & our minds met . . .

I should like to be to you, friend of my heart, like a touch of wings brushing by you in the darkness, or like the scent of an ~~unseen~~ invisible garden, that one passes on an unknown road at night . . .

April 20*th*.

I haven't written for six weeks or more. I have been afraid to write . . . Since then I have had my "day"—two "days" . . . one at Montfort, one at Provins. I have known "what happy women feel" . . . . with the pang, all through, every moment, of what heart-broken women feel! Ah, comme j'avais raison de vous ecrire[10]: "I didn't know what it would be like."—

For a month now I have been here alone—in another month I shall be gone. *It will be over.* Those four words are always before me, day & night; & yet I don't understand them, they mean nothing to me . . . What! I shall be gone, I shan't see you, I shan't hear your voice, I shan't wake up to think: "In so many hours we shall meet, my hand will be in his, my eyes will be in his." . . ? But what shall I *be* then? Nothing else lives in me now but *you*—I have no conscious existence outside the thought of you, the feeling of you. I, who dominated life, stood aside from it so, how I am humbled, absorbed, without a shred of will or identity left! All I want is to be near you, to feel my hands in yours. Ah, if you ever read these pages you will know you have been loved!

Sometimes I am calm, exalted almost, so enclosed & satisfied in the thought of you, that I could say to you truly, as I did yesterday: "I never wonder what you are doing when you are not with me." At such moments I feel as though all the mysticism in me—the transcendentalism that in other women turns to religion—were poured into my feeling for you, giving me a sense of *immanence,* of inseparableness from you.—In one of these moods, the other day, when you were reproaching me for never giving you any sign of my love for you, I felt like answering: "But there is a contact of thoughts that seems so much closer than a kiss" . . .

Then there are other days, tormented days—this is one of them—when that sense of mystic nearness fails me, when in your absence I long, I ache for you, I feel that what I want is to be in your arms, to be held fast there—"like other women!" And then comes the terrible realization of the fugitiveness of it all, the weariness of the struggle, the à quoi bon?,[11] the failing courage, the mortal weakness—the blind cry: "I want you! I want you!" that bears down everything else . . .

And sometimes you say to me: "Ah, *si* vous m'aimiez d'amour"—Si je vous aimais, mon amour![12]

[10]French: Oh, how right I was to write to you.
[11]French: what's the use?
[12]French: "Oh, *if* you truly loved me"—if I loved you, my love!

April 25th.

Less than a month now! Sursum corda![13] Let us not think of such things, when there is so much gained of exquisite & imperishable, "beyond the reach of accident" . . .

The day before yesterday, when I made you some answer that surprised & amused you, & you exclaimed: "Oh, the joy of *seeing around things* together!," I felt for the first time that you understood what I mean by the thoughts that are closer than a kiss.—And yet *I* understand now, for the first time, how thought may be dissolved in feeling, & what Dante meant when he [???] said: "Donne che avete l'intelletto d'amore". . . .[14]

Malgrè moi,[15] I am a little humbled, a little ashamed, to find how poor a thing I am, how the personality I had moulded into such strong firm lines has crumbled to a pinch of ashes in this flame! For the first time in my life *I can't read* . . . I hold the book in my hand, & [???] see your name all over the page!—I always thought I should know how to bear suffering better than happiness, & so it is . . . I am stupified, anéantie[16] . . . There lies the profound difference between man & woman. What enlarges & enriches life for the one, eliminates everything but itself for the other.—Now & then I say to myself: "Je vais me ressaisir"—mais saisir quoi?[17] This pinch of ashes that slips through my fingers? Oh, my free, proud, secure soul, where are you? *What were you,* to escape me like this? . . . .

It is curious how the scraps of verses I wrote from time to time in the past, when a wave of Beauty rushed over me, & felt *I must tell some one!*—it is curious how they express what I am feeling now, how they say more than I then understood, & how they go straight to you, like homing birds released long long ago by a hand that knew not whence they came!

April 27th

A note comes almost every morning now. It is brought in on my breakfast-tray, with the other letters, & there is the delicious moment of postponement, when one leaves it unopened while one pours the tea, just in order to "savourer"[18] longer the joy that is coming!—Ah, how I see in all this the instinctive longing to pack every moment of my present with all the wasted, driven-in feeling of the past! One should be happy in one's youth to be happy freely, carelessly, *extravagantly*! How I hoard & tremble over each incident & sign! I am like a hungry beggar who crumbles up the crust he has found in order to make it last longer! . . . And then comes the opening of the letter, the slipping of the little silver knife under the flap (which one would never tear!), the first glance to see how many pages there are, the second to see how it ends, & then the return to the beginning, the breathless first reading, & the slow lingering again over each phrase & each word, the taking possession, the absorbing of them one by one, & finally the choosing of the one that will be carried in one's

[13]Heart on high! From *The Episcopal Book of Common Prayer.*
[14]Italian: "Women who have the intellect of love."
[15]French: in spite of myself.
[16]French: crushed.
[17]French: "I go to capture myself"—but to capture what?
[18]French: savor.

thoughts all day, making an exquisite accompaniment to ~~all~~ the dull prose of life . . . Sometimes I think the moment of reading the letter is the best of all—I think that till I see you again, & then, when you are *there,* & my hands are in yours, *& my soul is in my hands,* then what grey ghosts the letters all become! . . . . . .

May 3d.

Yesterday at Beauvais.—a memory bathed with ~~the~~ light. . . . You did not want to go, objecting that with H.J.[19] it would not be like our excursions à deux.[20] But I could not make up my mind to go without you, & I *begged* (so against my usual habit!), & you yielded.

You write me this morning that ~~your~~ you want me to know "how delicious" it all was . . . I think you really found it so . . . Alone with you I am often shy & awkward, tormented by the fear that I may not please you—but with our dear H.J. I felt at my ease, & full of the "motor nonsense" that always seizes me after one of these long flights through the air. And what a flight it was! History & romance & natural loveliness every mile of the way—across the windings of Seine & Oise, through the grey old towns piled up above their rivers, through the melting spring landscape, all tender green & snowy fruit-blossoms, against black slopes of fir—till a last climb brought us out above the shimmering plain, with Beauvais choir rising "like a white Albi" on its ledge . . .

Then the lazy, happy luncheon in the warm court-yard of the Hôtel d'Angleterre, with dogs & children playing, canaries singing, flowers blooming about the little fountain—the coffee & cigarettes in the sunshine, & the slow stroll through the narrow streets first to St Etienne, then through the bright variegated fair which filled the Grande Place—till, guided by you, we reached the little lane behind the ~~choir~~ cathedral, & saw, far up against the blue, the soaring, wheeling choir—"saw it turn", as you put it, "cosmically spin through space . . ."

Then, inside, the sense of ~~immense~~ glad upward rush of all these converging lives—"gladness," as H.J. said, is the dominant note within the church—The mystic impression of something swung aloft, suspended, "qui plane"[21] in supernatural levitation—&, while H.J. made the tour of the ambulatory, [~~your~~] our little minute, sitting outside on the steps in the sunshine; with the *"Dear, are you happy?"* that made it all yours & mine, that drew the great miracle down into the compass of our two hearts—our one heart. . . . . .

May 3d. Only, after such days, the blankness, the intolerableness of the morrow—the day when one does not see you! What a pity that one cannot live longer in the memory of such hours—that the eager heart must always reach out for more, & more! I used to think: "If I could be happy for a week—an hour!" And now I am asking to be happy all the rest of my life . . .

Sometimes I think that if I could go off with you for twenty-four hours to a little inn in the country, in the depths of a green wood, I should ask no more. Just to

[19]Henry James.
[20]French: together.
[21]French: that soars.

have one long day & quiet evening with you, & the next morning to be still together—oh, how I ache for it sometimes! But how I should ache for it again when it was over—& oh, the sweet, vain impossible pictures it would evoke! Poor hearts, in this shifting [???] stream of life, so hungry for permanence & security!—As I wrote these lines I suddenly said to myself: *"I will go with him once before we separate."*

How strange to feel one's self all at once "Jenseits von Gut und Böse"[22] . . . It would hurt no one—it would give me my first, last, draught of life . . . Why not? I have always laughed at the "mala prohibita"[23]—"bugbears to frighten children." The anti-social act is the only one that is harmful "per se". And, as you told me the other day—*and as I needed no telling!*—what I have given already is far, far more. . . . . . .

May 5th. How I love the queer letter paper with ~~ruled~~ criss-cross rulings on which you write me at night, chez le restaurateur du coin,[24] on your way home! There seems to ~~me~~ be more feeling in what you say on that humble poor paper, on which the fashionable & the conventional are never expressed!

You say in your note of last night: "We are behind the scenes together—*on the hither side*" . . . Just a few hours after I had written that *"Jenseits"* above there . . . Such coincidences make it seem true, don't they?

May 7th. The night before last you dined with me alone. Yesterday evening we had planned to go to Versailles & dine. But the weather was doubtful, you were likely to be detained late at yr work, & I was afraid of appearing eager to go when you were less so. (By note & telephone, one can explain nothing.) So we missed our dear, dear evening, & this morning you write: "Instead of being stupidly sundered, we might ~~be~~ have been happy together."—Let us not lose one of the few remaining chances to "be happy together" . . . Strange words!—that I never spoke, or heard spoken to me, before . . . I appear to myself like a new creature opening dazzled eyes on a new world. C'est l'aube![25]

May 9th. La Châtaignerie.
Montmorency.

[A flower is pressed onto this page.]

May 13th.

Something gave me the impression the other day that we were watched in this house . . . commented on.—Ah, how a great love needs to be a happy & open love! How degraded I feel by other people's degrading thoughts . . .

- - - - - - - -

We met the other day at the Louvre, & walked to St. Germain l'Auxerrois. Then we took a motor, & went over to "Les Arènes de Lutéce," & then to St Etienne du

[22]German: beyond good and evil. Wharton was reading Nietzsche at the time.
[23]"Forbidden evils."
[24]French: at the corner restaurant.
[25]French: It is dawn!

Mont . . . Then we walked to the Luxembourg, & sat for a long time in a quiet corner under the trees. But what I long for, these last days, is to be with you alone, far off, in quietness—held fast, peacefully, "while close as lips lean, lean the thoughts between."[26] . . . There is no use in trying to look at things together. We don't see them any longer . . .

Senlis. May 16*th*

Hung high against the perfect blue,
Like flame the belfry trembled higher,
Like leafage let the bird-flights through,
Like incense wreathed its melting spire.

From the dim vantage, lilacs hung,
Niched in the Roman rampart's strength,
We watched the foaming clouds that swung
Against the church's island-length;

~~The sheet of emerald foliage spread~~
~~Like some deep inlet's inmost reach~~
~~Between the cliff like towers o'erhead,~~
~~The low slate roof that [framed] their beach~~

We watched, & felt the tides of time
Coil round our hidden leafy place,
Sweep on through changing race & clime,
And leave us at the heart of space,

In some divine transcendent hush
Where light & darkness melt & cease,
Staying the awful cosmic rush
To give two hearts an hour of peace. . . . .

So deep the peace, so ~~h~~ ours the hour,
When night-fall & the fiery train
Had swept us from our high-built bower,
And out across the dreaming plain,

Stillness yet brooded in our souls,
And even our rushing chariot stayed,
Loitering through aisles of silvery boles,
In some remote & star-laced glade,

Where through the pale & secret night,
Past gleams of water, depths of shade,
Under a low moon's golden light
I felt the quiet fields outspread—

And there, on the calm air afloat,
While silence held the throbbing train,
Some thrush from immemorial throat
Poured all the sweetness, all the pain.

[26]The line is from "Ogrin the Hermit," a poem Wharton was composing.

May 19th

I didn't suppose that, to a creature as exacting, scrutinizing, analytical as I am, life could hold an absolutely perfect day—but it came to me last week at Senlis . . . I see you still, meeting me at the station when I drove up at 11.20.—We were together from then till 9.15 in the evening.—The sense of peace those long hours gave! And yet how they rushed & swept us with them!—But there came a moment of divine, deep calm, when, alone in the train returning to Paris, we watched the full moon rise, & heard the thrush on the lisière des bois[27] filling the night with what was in our hearts.—I knew then, dearest dear, all that I had never known before—the interfusion of spirit & sense, the double nearness, the [~~blest~~] the mingled communion of touch & thought . . . One such hour ought to irradiate a whole life—

Yesterday I went with you to see the répétition générale of Polyphème[28] . . . . I don't suppose you knew—since it is more of my sex than yours—the quiet ecstasy I feel in sitting next you in a public place, looking now & then at the way the hair grows on your forehead, at the line of your profile turned to the stage, your attitude, your expression—while every drop of blood in my body whispers: "Mine—mine—mine!" . . . .

Then we went to the Tuileries, & found a quiet seat under the trees, on the terrace above the Seine . . . I am always glad to go with you to some new place, so that in the empty future years I may say, going there alone: "We were here together once". It will make the world less empty. And I shall always remember now that, sitting under that tree, you said to me: "My love! my darling!" while people walked up & down before us, not knowing—not knowing *that it was not worth their while to be alive*. . . . . . .

May 21st.

My two months, my incredible two months, are almost over! . . . I have drunk of the wine of life at last, I have known the thing best worth knowing, I have been warmed through & through, never to grow quite cold again till the end. . . .

Oh, Life, Life, how I give thanks to you for this! How right I was to trust you, to know that my day would come, & to be too proud, & too confident of my fate, to take for a moment any lesser gift, any smaller happiness than this that you had in store for me!

How often I used to say to myself: "No one can love life as I do, love the beauty & the splendour & the ardour, & find words for them as I can, without having a share in them some day"—I mean the dear intimate share that one guessed at, always, beyond & behind their universal thrill!—And the day came—the day has *been*—& I have poured into it all my stored-up joy of living, all my sense of the beauty & mystery of the world, every impression of joy & loveliness, in sight or sound or touch, that I ever figured to myself in all the lovely days when I used to weave such sensations into a [~~perf~~] veil of colour to hide the great blank behind. . . . .

[27]French: edge of the woods.

[28]Dress rehearsal of Samain's play *Polyphème.*

May 22^{d}. The last Day.

My room is full of the traces of packing for tomorrow's departure . . . On the bed, the sofa, every chair, the dresses, cloaks, hats, tea-gowns, I have worn these last six months . . . There is the black dress I had on the first time we went to the Sorbonne, to hear B.—[29]lecture last December. I remember thinking: "Will he like me in it?" And of how many of the others, afterward, I had the same thought! And when you noticed one of my dresses, & praised it, quelle joie![30] I used to say to myself: "It must be becoming, ~~or I~~ or he never would have thought it pretty." . . . .

There is the ~~dress~~ teagown I wore the first night you dined with me alone . . . You liked it, you said. . . . And here is the ~~one~~ dress I wore the day we went to Herblay, when, in the church, for a moment, the Veiled Happiness stole up to me. . . . . Here is the grey dress, with Irish lace,

May 24th At sea—on the way home.
10. a.m.

Yesterday morning you wrote those lines on the opposite page . . . Just twenty four hours ago, you handed me this book, which I had lent you overnight, & sat beside me in the compartment of the Hâvre train. How far away we seemed from each other already, while we waited for the train to start! With people coming & going, & the good gay L.R.K.,[31] all unconscious, & lingering between us to the last, how futile it seemed to be together! Yet we *were* together, at least—our eyes could meet, I saw your forehead, & the way the hair lies on it—when shall I see that again?—Through the window, when the train started, I saw you lingering to wave a goodbye; & I had to wave & smile at you—to smile at that moment!

And now the sea is between us, & silence, & the long days, & the inexorable fate that binds me here & you there.

It is over, my Heart, all over!—

. . . .

Et on ~~en~~ n'en meurt pas, hélas![32]

May 25th. At sea.

When I am gone, recall my hair,
Not for the light it used to hold,
But that your touch~~ed,~~ enmeshèd there,
Has turned it to a younger gold.

Recall my hands, that were not soft
Or white or fine beyond expressing,
Till they had slept so long & oft,
So warm & close, in your possessing.

[29]Frank Baker, an American professor who lectured on Elizabethan playwrights.
[30]French: what joy!
[31]Le Roy King, Wharton's younger second cousin.
[32]French: And we die not (of heartbreak), alas!

Recall my eyes, that used to lie
Blind pools with summer's wreckage strewn.
You cleared the drifts, but in their sky
You hung no image but your own.

Recall my mouth, that knew not how
A kiss is cradled & takes wing,
~~But~~ Yet fluttered like a nest-hung bough
When you had touched it like the spring . . .
. . . .

At Sea
May 26*th*

Herblay . . . Montfort l'Amaury . . . Provins . . . Beauvais . . . Montmorency . . . Senlis . . . Meudon . . .

What dear, sweet, crowding memories! What wealth for a heart that was empty this time last year. How the wych-hazel has kept its promise, since it flowered in our hands last October!—Bring me, magic flower, one more day such as those—but dearer, nearer, by all these death-pangs of separation with which my heart is torn!

The Mount. May [31*st*].

Arrived yesterday.—

At sea I could bear it. Ici j'étouffe . . .[33]

In the train yesterday I was reading Lock's Heredity & Variation, & struck by a curious & rather amusing passage, held it out & said: "Read that."

The answer was: "Does that sort of thing really amuse you?"—I heard the key turn in my prison-lock.—That is the answer to everything worth while!

Oh, Gods of derision! And you've given me over twenty years of it! Je n'en peut plus . . .[34]

And yet I must be just. I have stood it all these years, & hardly felt it, because I had created a world of ~~mine~~ my own, in which I ~~lif~~ lived without heeding what went on outside. But since I have known what it was to have some one enter into that world & live there with me, the mortal solitude I came back to has become terrible . . .

June 12th

I have not written again in this book since my return, because I have written to you instead, my own dear Love, answering the letters you have sent me by every steamer . . .

But yesterday your letter of June 2*d* came, & I learned from it that you will certainly not come here till the autumn, & that all your future is in doubt. You don't even know where you will be next winter—at the ends of the Earth, perhaps!---- Leagues beyond leagues of distance seems to have widened between us since I read

[33]French: Here, I am suffocating.

[34]French: I can stand it no longer.

that letter—all hope forsook me, & I sent you back a desperate word: "Don't write to me again! Let me face at once the fact *that it is over.* Without a date to look to, I can't bear to go on, & it will be easier to make the break now, voluntarily, than to see it slowly, agonizingly made by time & circumstance."—

So I felt ~~now~~ then, so I still feel—but, oh, my adored, my own Love, you who have given me the only moments of real life I have ever known, how am I to face the long hours & days before I learn again the old hard lesson of "how existence may be cherished, strengthened & fed, without the aid of joy"?—

I knew that lesson once, but I have unlearned it—you have kissed away the memory of it. . . . If you knew how I repeat to myself: "I have had my hour, & I am grateful for it!" Yes—but the human heart is insatiable, & I didn't know, my own, I didn't know!—

I wrote of Senlis:—"One such hour ought to irradiate a whole life."—Eh bien, non—ce n'est pas assez![35]

The Eyes

We had been put in the mood for ghosts, that evening, after an excellent dinner at our old friend Culwin's, by a tale of Fred Murchard's—the narrative of a strange personal invitation.

Seen through the haze of our cigars, and by the drowsy gleam of a coal fire, Culwin's library, with its oak walls and dark old bindings, made a good setting for such evocations; and ghostly experiences at first hand being, after Murchard's opening, the only kind acceptable to us, we proceeded to take stock of our group and tax each member for a contribution. There were eight of us, and seven contrived, in a manner more or less adequate, to fulfill the condition imposed. It surprised us all to find that we could muster such a show of supernatural impressions, for none of us, excepting Murchard himself and young Phil Frenham—whose story was the slightest of the lot—had the habit of sending our souls into the invisible. So that, on the whole, we had every reason to be proud of our seven "exhibits," and none of us would have dreamed of expecting an eighth from our host.

Our old friend, Mr. Andrew Culwin, who had sat back in his armchair, listening and blinking through the smoke circles with the cheerful tolerance of a wise old idol, was not the kind of man likely to be favored with such contacts, though he had imagination enough to enjoy, without envying, the superior privileges of his guests. By age and by education he belonged to the stout Positivist tradition, and his habit of thought had been formed in the days of the epic struggle between physics and metaphysics. But he had been, then and always, essentially a spectator, a humorous detached observer of the immense muddled variety show of life, slipping out of his seat now and then for a brief dip into the convivialities at the back of the house, but never, as far as one knew, showing the least desire to jump on the stage and do a "turn."

[35]French: Very well; no, it is not enough!

Among his contemporaries there lingered a vague tradition of his having, at a remote period, and in a romantic clime, been wounded in a duel; but his legend no more tallied with what we younger men knew of his character than my mother's assertion that he had once been "a charming little man with nice eyes" corresponded to any possible reconstitution of his physiognomy.

"He never can have looked like anything but a bundle of sticks," Murchard had once said of him. "Or a phosphorescent log, rather," some one else amended; and we recognized the happiness of this description of his small squat trunk, with the red blink of the eyes in a face like mottled bark. He had always been possessed of a leisure which he had nursed and protected, instead of squandering it in vain activities. His carefully guarded hours had been devoted to the cultivation of a fine intelligence and a few judiciously chosen habits; and none of the disturbances common to human experience seemed to have crossed his sky. Nevertheless, his dispassionate survey of the universe had not raised his opinion of that costly experiment, and his study of the human race seemed to have resulted in the conclusion that all men were superfluous, and women necessary only because someone had to do the cooking. On the importance of this point his convictions were absolute, and gastronomy was the only science which he revered as a dogma. It must be owned that his little dinners were a strong argument in favor of this view, besides being a reason—though not the main one—for the fidelity of his friends.

Mentally he exercised a hospitality less seductive but no less stimulating. His mind was like a forum, or some open meeting place for the exchange of ideas: somewhat cold and drafty, but light, spacious and orderly—a kind of academic grove from which all the leaves have fallen. In this privileged area a dozen of us were wont to stretch our muscles and expand our lungs; and, as if to prolong as much as possible the tradition of what we felt to be a vanishing institution, one or two neophytes were now and then added to our band.

Young Phil Frenham was the last, and the most interesting, of these recruits, and a good example of Murchard's somewhat morbid assertion that our old friend "liked 'em juicy." It was indeed a fact that Culwin, for all his dryness, specially tasted the lyric qualities in youth. As he was far too good an Epicurean to nip the flowers of soul which he gathered for his garden, his friendship was not a disintegrating influence: on the contrary, it forced the young idea to robuster bloom. And in Phil Frenham he had a good subject for experimentation. The boy was really intelligent, and the soundness of his nature was like the pure paste under a fine glaze. Culwin had fished him out of a fog of family dullness, and pulled him up to a peak in Darien; and the adventure hadn't hurt him a bit. Indeed, the skill with which Culwin had contrived to stimulate his curiosities without robbing them of their bloom of awe seemed to me a sufficient answer to Murchard's ogreish metaphor. There was nothing hectic in Frenham's efflorescence, and his old friend had not laid even a finger tip on the sacred stupidities. One wanted no better proof of that than the fact that Frenham still reverenced them in Culwin.

"There's a side of him you fellows don't see. I believe that story about the duel!" he declared; and it was of the very essence of this belief that it should impel him—just as our little party was dispersing—to turn back to our host with the joking demand: "And now you've got to tell us about *your* ghost!"

The outer door had closed on Murchard and the others; only Frenham and I remained; and the devoted servant who presided over Culwin's destinies, having brought a fresh supply of soda water, had been laconically ordered to bed.

Culwin's sociability was a night-blooming flower, and we knew that he expected the nucleus of his group to tighten around him after midnight. But Frenham's appeal seemed to disconcert him comically, and he rose from the chair in which he had just reseated himself after his farewells in the hall.

"*My* ghost? Do you suppose I'm fool enough to go to the expense of keeping one of my own, when there are so many charming ones in my friends' closets? Take another cigar," he said, revolving toward me with a laugh.

Frenham laughed too, pulling up his slender height before the chimney piece as he turned to face his short bristling friend.

"Oh," he said, "you'd never be content to share if you met one you really liked."

Culwin had dropped back into his armchair, his shock head embedded in the hollow of worn leather, his little eyes glimmering over a fresh cigar.

"Liked—*liked?* Good Lord!" he growled.

"Ah, you *have,* then!" Frenham pounced on him in the same instant, with a side glance of victory at me; but Culwin cowered gnomelike among his cushions, dissembling himself in a protective cloud of smoke.

"What's the use of denying it? You've seen everything, so of course you've seen a ghost!" his young friend persisted, talking intrepidly into the cloud. "Or, if you haven't seen one, it's only because you've seen two!"

The form of the challenge seemed to strike our host. He shot his head out of the mist with a queer tortoise-like motion he sometimes had, and blinked approvingly at Frenham.

"That's it," he flung at us on a shrill jerk of laughter; "it's only because I've seen two!"

The words were so unexpected that they dropped down and down into a deep silence, while we continued to stare at each other over Culwin's head, and Culwin stared at his ghosts. At length Frenham, without speaking, threw himself into the chair on the other side of the hearth, and leaned forward with his listening smile. . . .

II

"Oh, of course they're not show ghosts—a collector wouldn't think anything of them. . . . Don't let me raise your hopes . . . their one merit is their numerical strength: the exceptional fact of there being *two.* But, as against this, I'm bound to admit that at any moment I could probably have exorcised them both by asking my doctor for a prescription, or my oculist for a pair of spectacles. Only, as I never could make up my mind whether to go to the doctor or the oculist—whether I was afflicted by an optical or a digestive delusion—I left them to pursue their interesting double life, though at times they made mine exceedingly uncomfortable. . . .

"Yes—uncomfortable; and you know how I hate to be uncomfortable! But it was part of my stupid pride, when the thing began, not to admit that I could be disturbed by the trifling matter of seeing two.

"And then I'd no reason, really, to suppose I was ill. As far as I knew I was simply bored—horribly bored. But it was part of my boredom—I remember—that I was feeling so uncommonly well, and didn't know how on earth to work off my surplus energy. I had come back from a long journey—down in South America and Mexico—and had settled down for the winter near New York with an old aunt who had known Washington Irving and corresponded with N. P. Willis. She lived, not far from Irvington, in a damp Gothic villa overhung by Norway spruces and looking exactly like a memorial emblem done in hair. Her personal appearance was in keeping with this image, and her own hair—of which there was little left—might have been sacrificed to the manufacture of the emblem.

"I had just reached the end of an agitated year, with considerable arrears to make up in money and emotion; and theoretically it seemed as though my aunt's mild hospitality would be as beneficial to my nerves as to my purse. But the deuce of it was that as soon as I felt myself safe and sheltered my energy began to revive; and how was I to work it off inside of a memorial emblem? I had, at that time, the illusion that sustained intellectual effort could engage a man's whole activity; and I decided to write a great book—I forget about what. My aunt, impressed by my plan, gave up to me her Gothic library, filled with classics bound in black cloth and daguerreotypes of faded celebrities; and I sat down at my desk to win myself a place among their number. And to facilitate my task she lent me a cousin to copy my manuscript.

"The cousin was a nice girl, and I had an idea that a nice girl was just what I needed to restore my faith in human nature, and principally in myself. She was neither beautiful nor intelligent—poor Alice Nowell!—but it interested me to see any woman content to be so uninteresting, and I wanted to find out the secret of her content. In doing this I handled it rather rashly, and put it out of joint—oh, just for a moment! There's no fatuity in telling you this, for the poor girl had never seen anyone but cousins. . . .

"Well, I was sorry for what I'd done, of course, and confoundedly bothered as to how I should put it straight. She was staying in the house, and one evening, after my aunt had gone to bed, she came down to the library to fetch a book she'd mislaid, like any artless heroine, on the shelves behind us. She was pink-nosed and flustered, and it suddenly occurred to me that her hair, though it was fairly thick and pretty, would look exactly like my aunt's when she grew older. I was glad I had noticed this, for it made it easier for me to decide to do what was right; and when I had found the book she hadn't lost I told her I was leaving for Europe that week.

"Europe was terribly far off in those days, and Alice knew at once what I meant. She didn't take it in the least as I'd expected—it would have been easier if she had. She held her book very tight, and turned away a moment to wind up the lamp on my desk—it had a ground-glass shade with vine leaves, and glass drops around the edge, I remember. Then she came back, held out her hand, and said: 'Good-bye.' And as she said it she looked straight at me and kissed me. I had never felt anything as fresh and shy and brave as her kiss. It was worse than any reproach, and it made me ashamed to deserve a reproach from her. I said to myself: 'I'll marry her, and when my aunt dies she'll leave us this house, and I'll sit here at the desk and go on with my book; and Alice will sit over there with her embroidery and look at me as she's looking now. And life will go on like that for any number of years.' The prospect frightened me a little, but at the time it didn't frighten me as much as doing anything to hurt her; and ten minutes later she had my seal ring on her finger, and my promise that when I went abroad she should go with me.

"You'll wonder why I'm enlarging on this incident. It's because the evening on which it took place was the very evening on which I first saw the queer sight I've spoken of. Being at that time an ardent believer in a necessary sequence between cause and effect, I naturally tried to trace some kind of link between what had just happened to me in my aunt's library, and what was to happen a few hours later on the same night; and so the coincidence between the two events always remained in my mind.

"I went up to bed with rather a heavy heart, for I was bowed under the weight of the first good action I had ever consciously committed; and young as I was, I saw the gravity of my situation. Don't imagine from this that I had hitherto been an instrument of destruction. I had been merely a harmless young man, who had followed his bent and declined all collaboration with Providence. Now I had suddenly undertaken to promote the moral order of the world, and I felt a good deal like the trustful spectator who has given his gold watch to the conjurer, and doesn't know in what shape he'll get it back when the trick is over. . . . Still, a glow of self-righteousness tempered my fears, and I said to myself as I undressed that when I'd got used to being good it probably wouldn't make me as nervous as it did at the start. And by the time I was in bed, and had blown out my candle, I felt that I really *was* getting used to it, and that, as far as I'd got, it was not unlike sinking down into one of my aunt's very softest wool mattresses.

"I closed my eyes on this image, and when I opened them it must have been a good deal later, for my room had grown cold, and intensely still. I was waked by the queer feeling we all know—the feeling that there was something in the room that hadn't been there when I fell asleep. I sat up and strained my eyes into the darkness. The room was pitch black, and at first I saw nothing; but gradually a vague glimmer at the foot of the bed turned into two eyes staring back at me. I couldn't distinguish the features attached to them, but as I looked the eyes grew more and more distinct: they gave out a light of their own.

"The sensation of being thus gazed at was far from pleasant, and you might suppose that my first impulse would have been to jump out of bed and hurl myself on the invisible figure attached to the eyes. But it wasn't—my impulse was simply to lie still. . . . I can't say whether this was due to an immediate sense of the uncanny nature of the apparition—to the certainty that if I did jump out of bed I should hurl myself on nothing—or merely to the benumbing effect of the eyes themselves. They were the very worst eyes I've ever seen: a man's eyes—but what a man! My first thought was that he must be frightfully old. The orbits were sunk, and the thick red-lined lids hung over the eyeballs like blinds of which the cords are broken. One lid drooped a little lower than the other, with the effect of a crooked leer; and between these folds of flesh, with their scant bristle of lashes, the eyes themselves, small glassy disks with an agate-like rim, looked like sea pebbles in the grip of a starfish.

"But the age of the eyes was not the most unpleasant thing about them. What turned me sick was their expression of vicious security. I don't know how else to describe the fact that they seemed to belong to a man who had done a lot of harm in his life, but had always kept just inside the danger lines. They were not the eyes of a coward, but of someone much too clever to take risks; and my gorge rose at their look of base astuteness. Yet even that wasn't the worst; for as we continued to scan each other I saw in them a tinge of derision, and felt myself to be its object.

"At that I was seized by an impulse of rage that jerked me to my feet and pitched me straight at the unseen figure. But of course there wasn't any figure there, and my fists struck at emptiness. Ashamed and cold, I groped about for a match and lit the candles. The room looked just as usual—as I had known it would; and I crawled back to bed, and blew out the lights.

"As soon as the room was dark again the eyes reappeared; and I now applied myself to explaining them on scientific principles. At first I thought the illusion might have been caused by the glow of the last embers in the chimney; but the fireplace was on the other side of my bed, and so placed that the fire could not be reflected in my toilet glass, which was the only mirror in the room. Then it struck me that I might have been tricked by the reflection of the embers in some polished bit of wood or metal; and though I couldn't discover any object of the sort in my line of vision, I got up again, groped my way to the hearth, and covered what was left of the fire. But as soon as I was back in bed the eyes were back at its foot.

"They were an hallucination, then: that was plain. But the fact that they were not due to any external dupery didn't make them a bit pleasanter. For if they were a projection of my inner consciousness, what the deuce was the matter with that organ? I had gone deeply enough into the mystery of morbid pathological states to picture the conditions under which an exploring mind might lay itself open to such a midnight admonition; but I couldn't fit it to my present case. I had never felt more normal, mentally and physically; and the only unusual fact in my situation—that of having assured the happiness of an amiable girl—did not seem of a kind to summon unclean spirits about my pillow. But there were the eyes still looking at me.

"I shut mine, and tried to evoke a vision of Alice Nowell's. They were not remarkable eyes, but they were as wholesome as fresh water, and if she had had more imagination—or longer lashes—their expression might have been interesting. As it was, they did not prove very efficacious, and in a few moments I perceived that they had mysteriously changed into the eyes at the foot of the bed. It exasperated me more to feel these glaring at me through my shut lids than to see them, and I opened my eyes again and looked straight into their hateful stare. . . .

"And so it went on all night. I can't tell you what that night was like, nor how long it lasted. Have you ever lain in bed, hopelessly wide awake, and tried to keep your eyes shut, knowing that if you opened 'em you'd see something you dreaded and loathed? It sounds easy, but it's devilishly hard. Those eyes hung there and drew me. I had the *vertige de l'abîme,*[1] and their red lids were the edge of my abyss. . . . I had known nervous hours before: hours when I'd felt the wind of danger in my neck; but never this kind of strain. It wasn't that the eyes were awful; they hadn't the majesty of the powers of darkness. But they had—how shall I say?—a physical effect that was the equivalent of a bad smell: their look left a smear like a snail's. And I didn't see what business they had with me, anyhow—and I stared and stared, trying to find out.

"I don't know what effect they were trying to produce; but the effect they *did* produce was that of making me pack my portmanteau and bolt to town early the next

[1]French: vertigo, dizziness.

morning. I left a note for my aunt, explaining that I was ill and had gone to see my doctor; and as a matter of fact I did feel uncommonly ill—the night seemed to have pumped all the blood out of me. But when I reached town I didn't go to the doctor's. I went to a friend's rooms, and threw myself on a bed, and slept for ten heavenly hours. When I woke it was the middle of the night, and I turned cold at the thought of what might be waiting for me. I sat up, shaking, and stared into the darkness; but there wasn't a break in its blessed surface, and when I saw that the eyes were not there I dropped back into another long sleep.

"I had left no word for Alice when I fled, because I meant to go back the next morning. But the next morning I was too exhausted to stir. As the day went on the exhaustion increased, instead of wearing off like the fatigue left by an ordinary night of insomnia: the effect of the eyes seemed to be cumulative, and the thought of seeing them again grew intolerable. For two days I fought my dread; and on the third evening I pulled myself together and decided to go back the next morning. I felt a good deal happier as soon as I'd decided, for I knew that my abrupt disappearance, and the strangeness of my not writing, must have been very distressing to poor Alice. I went to bed with an easy mind, and fell asleep at once; but in the middle of the night I woke, and there were the eyes. . . .

"Well, I simply couldn't face them; and instead of going back to my aunt's I bundled a few things into a trunk and jumped aboard the first steamer for England. I was so dead tired when I got on board that I crawled straight into my berth, and slept most of the way over; and I can't tell you the bliss it was to wake from those long dreamless stretches and look fearlessly into the dark, *knowing* that I shouldn't see the eyes. . . .

"I stayed abroad for a year, and then I stayed for another; and during that time I never had a glimpse of them. That was enough reason for prolonging my stay if I'd been on a desert island. Another was, of course, that I had perfectly come to see, on the voyage over, the complete impossibility of my marrying Alice Nowell. The fact that I had been so slow in making this discovery annoyed me, and made me want to avoid explanations. The bliss of escaping at one stroke from the eyes, and from this other embarrassment, gave my freedom an extraordinary zest; and the longer I savored it the better I liked its taste.

"The eyes had burned such a hole in my consciousness that for a long time I went on puzzling over the nature of the apparition, and wondering if it would ever come back. But as time passed I lost this dread, and retained only the precision of the image. Then that faded in its turn.

"The second year found me settled in Rome, where I was planning, I believe, to write another great book—a definitive work on Etruscan influences in Italian art. At any rate, I'd found some pretext of the kind for taking a sunny apartment in the Piazza di Spagna and dabbling about in the Forum; and there, one morning, a charming youth came to me. As he stood there in the warm light, slender and smooth and hyacinthine, he might have stepped from a ruined altar—one to Antinous, say; but he'd come instead from New York, with a letter from (of all people) Alice Nowell. The letter—the first I'd had from her since our break—was simply a line introducing her young cousin, Gilbert Noyes, and appealing to me to befriend him. It appeared, poor lad, that he 'had talent,' and 'wanted to write'; and, an obdurate family having insisted that his calligraphy should take the form of double entry, Alice had intervened to win him six months' respite, during which he was to travel abroad on a meager pittance, and somehow prove his ability to increase it by his pen. The quaint conditions of the test struck me first: it seemed about as conclusive as a medieval 'ordeal.' Then I was touched by her having sent him to me. I had always wanted to do her some service, to justify myself in my own eyes rather than hers; and here was a beautiful occasion.

"I imagine it's safe to lay down the general principle that predestined geniuses don't, as a rule, appear before one in the spring sunshine of the Forum looking like one of its banished gods. At any rate, poor Noyes wasn't a predestined genius. But he *was* beautiful to see, and charming as a comrade. It was only when he began to talk literature that my heart failed me. I knew all the symptoms so well—the things he had 'in him,' and the things outside him that impinged! There's the real test, after all. It was always—punctually, inevitably, with the inexorableness of a mechnical law—it was *always* the wrong thing that struck him. I grew to find a certain fascination in deciding in advance exactly which wrong thing he'd select; and I acquired an astonishing skill at the game. . . .

"The worst of it was that his *bêtise*[2] wasn't of the too obvious sort. Ladies who met him at picnics thought him intellectual; and even at dinners he passed for clever. I, who had him under the microscope, fancied now and then that he might develop some kind of a slim talent, something that he could make 'do' and be happy on; and wasn't that, after all, what I was concerned with? He was so charming—he continued to be so charming—that he called forth all my charity in support of this argument; and for the first few months I really believed there was a chance for him. . . .

"Those months were delightful. Noyes was constantly with me, and the more I saw of him, the better I liked him. His stupidity was a natural grace—it was as beautiful, really, as his eyelashes. And he was so gay, so affectionate, and so happy with me, that telling him the truth would have been about as pleasant as slitting the throat of some gentle animal. At first I used to wonder what had put into that radiant head the detestable delusion that it held a brain. Then I began to see that it was simply protective mimicry—an instinctive ruse to get away from family life and an office desk. Not that Gilbert didn't—dear lad!—believe in himself. There wasn't a trace of hypocrisy in him. He was sure that his 'call' was irresistible, while to me it was the saving grace of his situation that it *wasn't,* and that a little money, a little leisure, a little pleasure would have turned him into an inoffensive idler. Unluckily, however, there was no hope of money, and with the alternative of the office desk before him he couldn't postpone his attempt at literature. The stuff he turned out was deplorable, and I see now that I knew it from the first. Still, the absurdity of deciding a man's whole future on a first trial seemed to justify me in withholding my verdict, and perhaps even in encouraging him a little, on the ground that the human plant generally needs warmth to flower.

"At any rate, I proceeded on that principle, and carried it to the point of getting his term of probation extended. When I left Rome he went with me, and we idled away a delicious summer between Capri and Venice. I said to myself: 'If he has any-

[2]French: stupidity, foolishness.

thing in him, it will come out now,' and it *did*. He was never more enchanting and enchanted. There were moments of our pilgrimage when beauty born of murmuring sound seemed actually to pass into his face—but only to issue forth in a flood of the palest ink. . . .

"Well, the time came to turn off the tap; and I knew there was no hand but mine to do it. We were back in Rome, and I had taken him to stay with me, not wanting him to be alone in his *pension* when he had to face the necessity of renouncing his ambition. I hadn't, of course, relied solely on my own judgment in deciding to advise him to drop literature. I had sent his stuff to various people—editors and critics—and they had always sent it back with the same chilling lack of comment. Really there was nothing on earth to say.

"I confess I never felt more shabby than I did on the day when I decided to have it out with Gilbert. It was well enough to tell myself that it was my duty to knock the poor boy's hopes into splinters—but I'd like to know what act of gratuitous cruelty hasn't been justified on that plea? I've always shrunk from usurping the functions of Providence, and when I have to exercise them I decidely prefer that it shouldn't be on an errand of destruction. Besides, in the last issue, who was I to decide, even after a year's trial, if poor Gilbert had it in him or not?

"The more I looked at the part I'd resolved to play, the less I liked it; and I liked it still less when Gilbert sat opposite me, with his head thrown back in the lamplight, just as Phil's is now. . . . I'd been going over his last manuscript, and he knew it, and he knew that his future hung on my verdict—we'd tacitly agreed to that. The manuscript lay between us, on my table—a novel, his first novel, if you please!—and he reached over and laid his hand on it, and looked up at me with all his life in the look.

"I stood up and cleared my throat, trying to keep my eyes away from his face and on the manuscript.

"'The fact is, my dear Gilbert,' I began—

"I saw him turn pale, but he was up and facing me in an instant.

"'Oh, look here, don't take on so, my dear fellow! I'm not so awfully cut up as all that!' His hands were on my shoulders, and he was laughing down on me from his full height, with a kind of mortally stricken gaiety that drove the knife into my side.

"He was too beautifully brave for me to keep up any humbug about my duty. And it came over me suddenly how I should hurt others in hurting him: myself first, since sending him home meant losing him; but more particularly poor Alice Nowell, to whom I had so longed to prove my good faith and my desire to serve her. It really seemed like failing her twice to fail Gilbert.

"But my intuition was like one of those lightning flashes that encircle the whole horizon, and in the same instant I saw what I might be letting myself in for if I didn't tell the truth. I said to myself: 'I shall have him for life'—and I'd never yet seen anyone, man or woman, whom I was quite sure of wanting on those terms. Well, this impulse of egotism decided me. I was ashamed of it, and to get away from it I took a leap that landed me straight in Gilbert's arms.

"'The thing's all right, and you're all wrong!' I shouted up at him; and as he hugged me, and I laughed and shook in his clutch, I had for a minute the sense of self-complacency that is supposed to attend the footsteps of the just. Hang it all, making people happy *has* its charms.

"Gilbert, of course, was for celebrating his emancipation in some spectacular manner; but I sent him away alone to explode his emotions, and went to bed to sleep off mine. As I undressed I began to wonder what their aftertaste would be—so many of the finest don't keep! Still, I wasn't sorry, and I meant to empty the bottle, even if it *did* turn a trifle flat.

"After I got into bed I lay for a long time smiling at the memory of his eyes—his blissful eyes. . . . Then I fell asleep, and when I woke the room was deathly cold, and I sat up with a jerk—and there were *the other eyes*. . . .

"It was three years since I'd seen them, but I'd thought of them so often that I fancied they could never take me unawares again. Now, with their red sneer on me, I knew that I had never really believed they would come back, and that I was as defenceless as ever against them. . . . As before, it was the insane irrelevance of their coming that made it so horrible. What the deuce were they after, to leap out at me at such a time? I had lived more or less carelessly in the years since I'd seen them, though my worst indiscretions were not dark enough to invite the searchings of their infernal glare; but at this particular moment I was really in what might have been called a state of grace; and I can't tell you how the fact added to their horror. . . .

"But it's not enough to say they were as bad as before: they were worse. Worse by just so much as I'd learned of life in the interval; by all the damnable implications my wider experience read into them. I saw now what I hadn't seen before: that they were eyes which had grown hideous gradually, which had built up their baseness coral-wise, bit by bit, out of a series of small turpitudes slowly accumulated through the industrious years. Yes—it came to me that what made them so bad was that they'd grown bad so slowly. . . .

"There they hung in the darkness, their swollen lids dropped across the little watery bulbs rolling loose in the orbits, and the puff of flesh making a muddy shadow underneath—and as their stare moved with my movements, there came over me a sense of their tacit complicity, of a deep hidden understanding between us that was worse than the first shock of their strangeness. Not that I understood them; but that they made it so clear that someday I should. . . . Yes, that was the worst part of it, decidedly; and it was the feeling that became stronger each time they came back. . . .

"For they got into the damnable habit of coming back. They reminded me of vampires with a taste for young flesh, they seemed so to gloat over the taste of a good conscience. Every night for a month they came to claim their morsel of mine: since I'd made Gilbert happy they simply wouldn't loosen their fangs. The coincidence almost made me hate him, poor lad, fortuitous as I felt it to be. I puzzled over it a good deal, but couldn't find any hint of an explanation except in the chance of his association with Alice Nowell. But then the eyes had let up on me the moment I had abandoned her, so they could hardly be the emissaries of a woman scorned, even if one could have pictured poor Alice charging such spirits to avenge her. That set me thinking, and I began to wonder if they would let up on me if I abandoned Gilbert. The temptation was insidious, and I had to stiffen myself against it; but really, dear boy! he was too charming to be sacrificed to such demons. And so, after all, I never found out what they wanted. . . ."

III

The fire crumbled, sending up a flash which threw into relief the narrator's gnarled face under its grey-black stubble. Pressed into the hollow of the chair back, it stood out an instant like an intaglio of yellowish red-veined stone, with spots of enamel for the eyes; then the fire sank and it became once more a dim Rembrandtish blur.

Phil Frenham, sitting in a low chair on the opposite side of the hearth, one long arm propped on the table behind him, one hand supporting his thrown-back head, and his eyes fixed on his old friend's face, had not moved since the tale began. He continued to maintain his silent immobility after Culwin had ceased to speak, and it was I who, with a vague sense of disappointment at the sudden drop of the story, finally asked: "But how long did you keep on seeing them?"

Culwin, so sunk into his chair that he seemed like a heap of his own empty clothes, stirred a little, as if in surprise at my question. He appeared to have half-forgotten what he had been telling us.

"How long? Oh, off and on all that winter. It was infernal. I never got used to them. I grew really ill."

Frenham shifted his attitude, and as he did so his elbow struck against a small mirror in a bronze frame standing on the table behind him. He turned and changed its angle slightly; then he resumed his former attitude, his dark head thrown back on his lifted palm, his eyes intent on Culwin's face. Something in his silent gaze embarrassed me, and as if to divert attention from it I pressed on with another question:

"And you never tried sacrificing Noyes?"

"Oh, no. The fact is I didn't have to. He did it for me, poor boy!"

"Did it for you? How do you mean?"

"He wore me out—wore everybody out. He kept on pouring out his lamentable twaddle, and hawking it up and down the place till he became a thing of terror. I tried to wean him from writing—oh, ever so gently, you understand, by throwing him with agreeable people, giving him a chance to make himself felt, to come to a sense of what he *really* had to give. I'd foreseen this solution from the beginning—felt sure that, once the first ardor of authorship was quenched, he'd drop into his place as a charming parasitic thing, the kind of chronic Cherubino for whom, in old societies, there's always a seat at table, and a shelter behind the ladies' skirts. I saw him take his place as 'the poet': the poet who doesn't write. One knows the type in every drawing room. Living in that way doesn't cost much—I'd worked it all out in my mind, and felt sure that, with a little help, he could manage it for the next few years; and meanwhile he'd be sure to marry. I saw him married to a widow, rather older, with a good cook and a well-run house. And I actually had my eye on the widow. . . . Meanwhile I did everything to help the transition—lent him money to ease his conscience, introduced him to pretty women to make him forget his vows. But nothing would do him: he had but one idea in his beautiful obstinate head. He wanted the laurel and not the rose, and he kept on repeating Gautier's axiom, and battering and filing at his limp prose till he'd spread it out over Lord knows how many hundred pages. Now and then he would send a barrelful to a publisher, and of course it would always come back.

"At first it didn't matter—he thought he was 'misunderstood.' He took the attitudes of genius, and whenever an opus came home he wrote another to keep it company. Then he had a reaction of despair, and accused me of deceiving him, and Lord knows what. I got angry at that, and told him it was he who had deceived himself. He'd come to me determined to write, and I'd done my best to help him. That was the extent of my offence, and I'd done it for his cousin's sake, not his.

"That seemed to strike home, and he didn't answer for a minute. Then he said: 'My time's up and my money's up. What do you think I'd better do?'

"'I think you'd better not be an ass,' I said.

"'What do you mean by being an ass?' he asked.

"I took a letter from my desk and held it out to him.

"'I mean refusing this offer of Mrs. Ellinger's: to be her secretary at a salary of five thousand dollars. There may be a lot more in it than that.'

"He flung out his hand with a violence that struck the letter from mine. 'Oh, I know well enough what's in it!' he said, red to the roots of his hair.

"'And what's the answer, if you know?' I asked.

"He made none at the minute, but turned away slowly to the door. There, with his hand on the threshold, he stopped to say, almost under his breath: 'Then you really think my stuff's no good?'

"I was tired and exasperated, and I laughed. I don't defend my laugh—it was in wretched taste. But I must plead in extenuation that the boy was a fool, and that I'd done my best for him—I really had.

"He went out of the room, shutting the door quietly after him. That afternoon I left for Frascati, where I'd promised to spend the Sunday with some friends. I was glad to escape from Gilbert, and by the same token, as I learned that night, I had also escaped from the eyes. I dropped into the same lethargic sleep that had come to me before when I left off seeing them; and when I woke the next morning in my peaceful room above the ilexes, I felt the utter weariness and deep relief that always followed on that sleep. I put in two blessed nights at Frascati, and when I got back to my rooms in Rome I found that Gilbert had gone. . . . Oh, nothing tragic had happened—the episode never rose to *that.* He'd simply packed his manuscripts and left for America—for his family and the Wall Street desk. He left a decent enough note to tell me of his decision, and behaved altogether, in the circumstances, as little like a fool as it's possible for a fool to behave. . . ."

IV

Culwin paused again, and Frenham still sat motionless, the dusky contour of his young head reflected in the mirror at his back.

"And what became of Noyes afterward?" I finally asked, still disquieted by a sense of incompleteness, by the need of some connecting thread between the parallel lines of the tale.

Culwin twitched his shoulders. "Oh, nothing became of him—because he became nothing. There could be no question of 'becoming' about it. He vegetated in an office, I believe, and finally got a clerkship in a consulate, and married drearily in China. I saw him once in Hong Kong, years afterward. He was fat and hadn't shaved. I was told he drank. He didn't recognize me."

"And the eyes?" I asked, after another pause which Frenham's continued silence made oppressive.

Culwin, stroking his chin, blinked at me meditatively through the shadows. "I never saw them after my last talk with Gilbert. Put two and two together if you can. For my part, I haven't found the link."

He rose, his hands in his pockets, and walked stiffly over to the table on which reviving drinks had been set out.

"You must be parched after this dry tale. Here, help yourself, my dear fellow. Here, Phil—" He turned back to the hearth.

Frenham made no response to his host's hospitable summons. He still sat in his low chair without moving, but as Culwin advanced toward him, their eyes met in a long look; after which the young man, turning suddenly, flung his arms across the table behind him, and dropped his face upon them.

Culwin, at the unexpected gesture, stopped short, a flush on his face.

"Phil—what the deuce? Why, have the eyes scared *you*? My dear boy—my dear fellow—I never had such a tribute to my literary ability, never!"

He broke into a chuckle at the thought, and halted on the hearthrug, his hands still in his pockets, gazing down at the youth's bowed head. Then, as Frenham still made no answer, he moved a step or two nearer.

"Cheer up, my dear Phil! It's years since I've seen them—apparently I've done nothing lately bad enough to call them out of chaos. Unless my present evocation of them has made *you* see them; which would be their worst stroke yet!"

His bantering appeal quivered off into an uneasy laugh, and he moved still nearer, bending over Frenham, and laying his gouty hands on the lad's shoulders.

"Phil, my dear boy, really—what's the matter? Why don't you answer? *Have* you seen the eyes?"

Frenham's face was still hidden, and from where I stood behind Culwin I saw the latter, as if under the rebuff of this unaccountable attitude, draw back slowly from his friend. As he did so, the light of the lamp on the table fell full on his congested face, and I caught its reflection in the mirror behind Frenham's head.

Culwin saw the reflection also. He paused, his face level with the mirror, as if scarcely recognizing the countenance in it as his own. But as he looked his expression gradually changed, and for an appreciable space of time he and the image in the glass confronted each other with a glare of slowly gathering hate. Then Culwin let go of Frenham's shoulders, and drew back a step. . . .

Frenham, his face still hidden, did not stir.

1910

Roman Fever

From the table at which they had been lunching two American ladies of ripe but well-cared-for middle age moved across the lofty terrace of the Roman restaurant and, leaning on its parapet, looked first at each other, and then down on the outspread glories of the Palatine and the Forum, with the same expression of vague but benevolent approval.

As they leaned there a girlish voice echoed up gaily from the stairs leading to the court below. "Well, come along, then," it cried, not to them but to an invisible companion, "and let's leave the young things to their knitting"; and a voice as fresh laughed back: "Oh, look here, Babs, not actually *knitting*—" "Well, I mean figuratively," rejoined the first. "After all, we haven't left our poor parents much else to do. . . ." and at that point the turn of the stairs engulfed the dialogue.

The two ladies looked at each other again, this time with a tinge of smiling embarrassment, and the smaller and paler one shook her head and colored slightly.

"Barbara!" she murmured, sending an unheard rebuke after the mocking voice in the stairway.

The other lady, who was fuller, and higher in color, with a small determined nose supported by vigorous black eyebrows, gave a good-humored laugh. "That's what our daughters think of us!"

Her companion replied by a deprecating gesture. "Not of us individually. We must remember that. It's just the collective modern idea of Mothers. And you see—" Half-guiltily she drew from her handsomely mounted black handbag a twist of crimson silk run through by two fine knitting needles. "One never knows," she murmured. "The new system has certainly given us a good deal of time to kill; and sometimes I get tired just looking—even at this." Her gesture was now addressed to the stupendous scene at their feet.

The dark lady laughed again, and they both relapsed upon the view, contemplating it in silence, with a sort of diffused serenity which might have been borrowed from the spring effulgence of the Roman skies. The luncheon hour was long past, and the two had their end of the vast terrace to themselves. At its opposite extremity a few groups, detained by a lingering look at the outspread city, were gathering up guidebooks and fumbling for tips. The last of them scattered, and the two ladies were alone on the air-washed height.

"Well, I don't see why we shouldn't just stay here," said Mrs. Slade, the lady of the high color and energetic brows. Two derelict basket chairs stood near, and she pushed them into the angle of the parapet, and settled herself in one, her gaze upon the Palatine. "After all, it's still the most beautiful view in the world."

"It always will be, to me," assented her friend Mrs. Ansley, with so slight a stress on the "me" that Mrs. Slade, though she noticed it, wondered if it were not merely accidental, like the random underlinings of old-fashioned letter writers.

"Grace Ansley was always old-fashioned," she thought; and added aloud, with a retrospective smile: "It's a view we've both been familiar with for a good many years. When we first met here we were younger than our girls are now. You remember?"

"Oh, yes, I remember," murmured Mrs. Ansley, with the same undefinable stress. "There's that headwaiter wondering," she interpolated. She was evidently far less sure than her companion of herself and of her rights in the world.

"I'll cure him of wondering," said Mrs. Slade, stretching her hand toward a bag as discreetly opulent-looking as Mrs. Ansley's. Signing to the headwaiter, she explained that she and her friend were old lovers of Rome, and would like to spend the end of the afternoon looking down on the view—that is, if it did not disturb the service? The headwaiter, bowing over her gratuity, assured her that the ladies were most welcome, and would be still more so if they would condescend to remain for dinner. A full-moon night, they would remember. . . .

Mrs. Slade's black brows drew together, as though references to the moon were out of place and even unwelcome. But she smiled away her frown as the headwaiter retreated. "Well, why not? We might do worse. There's no knowing, I suppose, when the girls will be back. Do you even know back from *where?* I don't!"

Mrs. Ansley again colored slightly. "I think those young Italian aviators we met at the Embassy invited them to fly to Tarquinia for tea. I suppose they'll want to wait and fly back by moonlight."

"Moonlight—moonlight! What a part it still plays. Do you suppose they're as sentimental as we were?"

"I've come to the conclusion that I don't in the least know what they are," said Mrs. Ansley. "And perhaps we didn't know much more about each other."

"No; perhaps we didn't."

Her friend gave her a shy glance. "I never should have supposed you were sentimental, Alida."

"Well, perhaps I wasn't." Mrs. Slade drew her lids together in retrospect; and for a few moments the two ladies, who had been intimate since childhood, reflected how little they knew each other. Each one, of course, had a label ready to attach to the other's name; Mrs. Delphin Slade, for instance, would have told herself, or anyone who asked her, that Mrs. Horace Ansley, twenty-five years ago, had been exquisitely lovely—no, you wouldn't believe it, would you? . . . though, of course, still charming, distinguished. . . . Well, as a girl she had been exquisite; far more beautiful than her daughter Barbara, though certainly Babs, according to the new standards at any rate, was more effective—had more *edge,* as they say. Funny where she got it, with those two nullities as parents. Yes; Horace Ansley was—well, just the duplicate of his wife. Museum specimens of old New York. Good-looking, irreproachable, exemplary. Mrs. Slade and Mrs. Ansley had lived opposite each other—actually as well as figuratively—for years. When the drawing-room curtains in No. 20 East 73rd Street were renewed, No. 23, across the way, was always aware of it. And of all the movings, buyings, travels, anniversaries, illnesses—the tame chronicle of an estimable pair. Little of it escaped Mrs. Slade. But she had grown bored with it by the time her husband made his big *coup* in Wall Street, and when they bought in upper Park Avenue had already begun to think: "I'd rather live opposite a speakeasy for a change; at least one might see it raided." The idea of seeing Grace raided was so amusing that (before the move) she launched it at a woman's lunch. It made a hit, and went the rounds—she sometimes wondered if it had crossed the street, and reached Mrs. Ansley. She hoped not, but didn't much mind. Those were the days when respectability was at a discount, and it did the irreproachable no harm to laugh at them a little.

A few years later, and not many months apart, both ladies lost their husbands. There was an appropriate exchange of wreaths and condolences, and a brief renewal of intimacy in the half-shadow of their mourning; and now, after another interval, they had run across each other in Rome, at the same hotel, each of them the modest appendage of a salient daughter. The similarity of their lot had again drawn them together, lending itself to mild jokes, and the mutual confession that, if in old days it must have been tiring to "keep up" with daughters, it was now, at times, a little dull not to.

No doubt, Mrs. Slade reflected, she felt her unemployment more than poor Grace ever would. It was a big drop from being the wife of Delphin Slade to being his widow. She had always regarded herself (with a certain conjugal pride) as his equal in social gifts, as contributing her full share to the making of the exceptional couple they were: but the difference after his death was irremediable. As the wife of the famous corporation lawyer, always with an international case or two on hand, every day brought its exciting and unexpected obligation: the impromptu entertaining of eminent colleagues from abroad, the hurried dashes on legal business to London, Paris or Rome, where the entertaining was so handsomely reciprocated; the amusement of hearing in her wake: "What, that handsome woman with the good clothes and the eyes is Mrs. Slade—*the* Slade's wife? Really? Generally the wives of celebrities are such frumps."

Yes; being *the* Slade's widow was a dullish business after that. In living up to such a husband all her faculties had been engaged; now she had only her daughter to live up to, for the son who seemed to have inherited his father's gifts had died suddenly in boyhood. She had fought through that agony because her husband was there, to be helped and to help; now, after the father's death, the thought of the boy had become unbearable. There was nothing left but to mother her daughter; and dear Jenny was such a perfect daughter that she needed no excessive mothering. "Now with Babs Ansley I don't know that I *should* be so quiet," Mrs. Slade sometimes half-enviously reflected; but Jenny, who was younger than her brilliant friend, was that rare accident, an extremely pretty girl who somehow made youth and prettiness seem as safe as their absence. It was all perplexing—and to Mrs. Slade a little boring. She wished that Jenny would fall in love—with the wrong man, even; that she might have to be watched, out-maneuvered, rescued. And instead, it was Jenny who watched her mother, kept her out of drafts, made sure that she had taken her tonic. . . .

Mrs. Ansley was much less articulate than her friend, and her mental portrait of Mrs. Slade was slighter, and drawn with fainter touches. "Alida Slade's awfully brilliant; but not as brilliant as she thinks," would have summed it up; though she would have added, for the enlightenment of strangers, that Mrs. Slade had been an extremely dashing girl; much more so than her daughter, who was pretty, of course, and clever in a way, but had none of her mother's—well, "vividness," someone had once called it. Mrs. Ansley would take up current words like this, and cite them in quotation marks, as unheard-of audacities. No; Jenny was not like her mother. Sometimes Mrs. Ansley thought Alida Slade was disappointed; on the whole she had had a sad life. Full of failures and mistakes; Mrs. Ansley had always been rather sorry for her. . . .

So these two ladies visualized each other, each through the wrong end of her little telescope.

II

For a long time they continued to sit side by side without speaking. It seemed as though, to both, there was a relief in laying down their somewhat futile activities in the presence of the vast Memento Mori which faced them. Mrs. Slade sat quite still, her eyes fixed on the golden slope of the Palace of the Caesars, and after a while Mrs. Ansley ceased to fidget with her bag, and she too sank into meditation. Like many intimate friends, the two ladies had never before had occasion to be silent together, and Mrs. Ansley was slightly embarrassed by what seemed, after so many years, a new stage in their intimacy, and one with which she did not yet know how to deal.

Suddenly the air was full of that deep clangor of bells which periodically covers Rome with a roof of silver. Mrs. Slade glanced at her wristwatch. "Five o'clock already," she said, as though surprised.

Mrs. Ansley suggested interrogatively: "There's bridge at the Embassy at five." For a long time Mrs. Slade did not answer. She appeared to be lost in contemplation, and Mrs. Ansley thought the remark had escaped her. But after a while she said, as if speaking out of a dream: "Bridge, did you say? Not unless you want to. . . . But I don't think I will, you know."

"Oh, no," Mrs. Ansley hastened to assure her. "I don't care to at all. It's so lovely here; and so full of old memories, as you say." She settled herself in her chair, and almost furtively drew forth her knitting. Mrs. Slade took sideway note of this activity, but her own beautifully cared-for hands remained motionless on her knee.

"I was just thinking," she said slowly, "what different things Rome stands for to each generation of travelers. To our grandmothers, Roman fever; to our mothers, sentimental dangers—how we used to be guarded!—to our daughters, no more dangers than the middle of Main Street. They don't know it—but how much they're missing!"

The long golden light was beginning to pale, and Mrs. Ansley lifted her knitting a little closer to her eyes. "Yes; how we were guarded!"

"I always used to think," Mrs. Slade continued, "that our mothers had a much more difficult job than our grandmothers. When Roman fever stalked the streets it must have been comparatively easy to gather in the girls at the danger hour; but when you and I were young, with such beauty calling us, and the spice of disobedience thrown in, and no worse risk than catching cold during the cool hour after sunset, the mothers used to be put to it to keep us in—didn't they?"

She turned again toward Mrs. Ansley, but the latter had reached a delicate point in her knitting. "One, two, three—slip two; yes, they must have been," she assented, without looking up.

Mrs. Slade's eyes rested on her with a deepened attention. "She can knit—in the face of *this!* How like her. . ."

Mrs. Slade leaned back, brooding, her eyes ranging from the ruins which faced her to the long green hollow of the Forum, the fading flow of the church fronts beyond it, and the outlying immensity of the Colosseum. Suddenly she thought: It's all very well to say that our girls have done away with sentiment and moonlight. But if Babs Ansley isn't out to catch that young aviator—the one who's a Marchese—then I don't know anything. And Jenny has no chance beside her. I know that too. I wonder if that's why Grace Ansley likes the two girls to go everywhere together? My poor Jenny as a foil—!" Mrs. Slade gave a hardly audible laugh, and at the sound Mrs. Ansley dropped her knitting.

"Yes—?"

"I—oh, nothing. I was only thinking how your Babs carries everything before her.

That Campolieri boy is one of the best matches in Rome. Don't look so innocent, my dear—you know he is. And I was wondering, ever so respectfully, you understand . . . wondering how two such exemplary characters as you and Horace had managed to produce anything quite so dynamic." Mrs. Slade laughed again, with a touch of asperity.

Mrs. Ansley's hands lay inert across her needles. She looked straight out at the great accumulated wreckage of passion and splendor at her feet. But her small profile was almost expressionless. At length she said: "I think you overrate Babs, my dear."

Mrs. Slade's tone grew easier. "No; I don't. I appreciate her. And perhaps envy you. Oh, my girl's perfect; if I were a chronic invalid I'd—well, I think I'd rather be in Jenny's hands. There must be times . . . but there! I always wanted a brilliant daughter . . . and never quite understood why I got an angel instead."

Mrs. Ansley echoed her laugh in a faint murmur. "Babs is an angel too."

"Of course—of course! But she's got rainbow wings. Well, they're wandering by the sea with their young men; and here we sit . . . and it all brings back the past a little too acutely."

Mrs. Ansley had resumed her knitting. One might almost have imagined (if one had known her less well, Mrs. Slade reflected) that, for her also, too many memories rose from the lengthening shadows of those august ruins. But no; she was simply absorbed in her work. What was there for her to worry about? She knew that Babs would almost certainly come back engaged to the extremely eligible Campolieri. "And she'll sell the New York house, and settle down near them in Rome, and never be in their way . . . she's much too tactful. But she'll have an excellent cook, and just the right people in for bridge and cocktails . . . and a perfectly peaceful old age among her grandchildren."

Mrs. Slade broke off this prophetic flight with a recoil of self-disgust. There was no one of whom she had less right to think unkindly than of Grace Ansley. Would she never cure herself of envying her? Perhaps she had begun too long ago.

She stood up and leaned against the parapet, filling her troubled eyes with the tranquilizing magic of the hour. But instead of tranquilizing her the sight seemed to increase her exasperation. Her gaze turned toward the Colosseum. Already its golden flank was downed in purple shadow, and above it the sky curved crystal clear, without light or color. It was the moment when afternoon and evening hang balanced in midheaven.

Mrs. Slade turned back and laid her hand on her friend's arm. The gesture was so abrupt that Mrs. Ansley looked up, startled.

"The sun's set. You're not afraid, my dear?"

"Afraid—?"

"Of Roman fever or pneumonia? I remember how ill you were that winter. As a girl you had a very delicate throat, hadn't you?"

"Oh, we're all right up here. Down below, in the Forum, it does get deathly cold, all of a sudden . . . but not here."

"Ah, of course you know because you had to be so careful." Mrs. Slade turned back to the parapet. She thought: "I must make one more effort not to hate her." Aloud she said: "Whenever I look at the Forum from up here, I remember that story about a great-aunt of yours, wasn't she? A dreadfully wicked great-aunt?"

"Oh, yes; great-aunt Harriet. The one who was supposed to have sent her young sister out to the Forum after sunset to gather a nightblooming flower for her album. All our great-aunts and grandmothers used to have albums of dried flowers."

Mrs. Slade nodded. "But she really sent her because they were in love with the same man—"

"Well, that was the family tradition. They said Aunt Harriet confessed it years afterward. At any rate, the poor little sister caught the fever and died. Mother used to frighten us with the story when we were children."

"And you frightened *me* with it, that winter when you and I were here as girls. The winter I was engaged to Delphin."

Mrs. Ansley gave a faint laugh. "Oh, did I? Really frightened you? I don't believe you're easily frightened."

"Not often; but I was then. I was easily frightened because I was too happy. I wonder if you know what that means?"

"I—yes . . ." Mrs. Ansley faltered.

"Well, I suppose that was why the story of your wicked aunt made such an impression on me. And I thought: 'There's no more Roman fever, but the Forum is deathly cold after sunset—especially after a hot day. And the Colosseum's even colder and damper'."

"The Colosseum—?"

"Yes. It wasn't easy to get in, after the gates were locked for the night. Far from easy. Still, in those days it could be managed; it *was* managed, often. Lovers met there who couldn't meet elsewhere. You knew that?"

"I—I dare say. I don't remember."

"You don't remember? You don't remember going to visit some ruins or other one evening, just after dark, and catching a bad chill? You were supposed to have gone to see the moon rise. People always said that expedition was what caused your illness."

There was a moment's silence; then Mrs. Ansley rejoined: "Did they? It was all so long ago."

"Yes. And you got well again—so it didn't matter. But I suppose it struck your friends—the reason given for your illness, I mean—because everybody knew you were so prudent on account of your throat, and your mother took such care of you. . . . You *had* been out late sight-seeing, hadn't you, that night?"

"Perhaps I had. The most prudent girls aren't always prudent. What made you think of it now?"

Mrs. Slade seemed to have no answer ready. But after a moment she broke out: "Because I simply can't bear it any longer—!"

Mrs. Ansley lifted her head quickly. Her eyes were wide and very pale. "Can't bear what?"

"Why—your not knowing that I've always known why you went."

"Why I went—?"

"Yes. You think I'm bluffing, don't you? Well, you went to meet the man I was engaged to—and I can repeat every word of the letter that took you there."

While Mrs. Slade spoke Mrs. Ansley had risen unsteadily to her feet. Her bag, her knitting and gloves, slid in a panic-stricken heap to the ground. She looked at Mrs. Slade as though she were looking at a ghost.

"No, no—don't," she faltered out.

"Why not? Listen, if you don't believe me. 'My one darling, things can't go on like this. I must see you alone. Come to the Colosseum immediately after dark tomorrow. There will be somebody to let you in. No one whom you need fear will suspect'—but perhaps you've forgotten what the letter said?"

Mrs. Ansley met the challenge with an unexpected composure. Steadying herself against the chair she looked at her friend, and replied: "No; I know it by heart too."

"And the signature? 'Only *your* D.S.' Was that it? I'm right, am I? That was the letter that took you out that evening after dark?"

Mrs. Ansley was still looking at her. It seemed to Mrs. Slade that a slow struggle was going on behind the voluntarily controlled mask of her small quiet face. "I shouldn't have thought she had herself so well in hand," Mrs. Slade reflected, almost resentfully. But at this moment Mrs. Ansley spoke. "I don't know how you knew. I burnt the letter at once."

"Yes; you would, naturally—you're so prudent!" The sneer was open now. "And if you burnt the letter you're wondering how on earth I know what was in it. That's it, isn't it?"

Mrs. Slade waited, but Mrs. Ansley did not speak.

"Well, my dear, I know what was in that letter because I wrote it!"

"You wrote it?"

"Yes."

The two women stood for a minute staring at each other in the last golden light. Then Mrs. Ansley dropped back into her chair. "Oh," she murmured, and covered her face with her hands.

Mrs. Slade waited nervously for another word or movement. None came, and at length she broke out: "I horrify you."

Mrs. Ansley's hands dropped to her knee. The face they uncovered was streaked with tears. "I wasn't thinking of you. I was thinking—it was the only letter I ever had from him!"

"And I wrote it. Yes; I wrote it! But I was the girl he was engaged to. Did you happen to remember that?"

Mrs. Ansley's head drooped again. "I'm not trying to excuse myself . . . I remembered. . . ."

"And still you went?"

"Still I went."

Mrs. Slade stood looking down on the small bowed figure at her side. The flame of her wrath had already sunk, and she wondered why she had ever thought there would be any satisfaction in inflicting so purposeless a wound on her friend. But she had to justify herself.

"You do understand? I'd found out—and I hated you, hated you. I knew you were in love with Delphin—and I was afraid; afraid of you, of your quiet ways, your sweetness . . . your . . . well, I wanted you out of the way, that's all. Just for a few weeks; just till I was sure of him. So in a blind fury I wrote that letter . . . I don't know why I'm telling you now."

"I suppose," said Mrs. Ansley slowly, "it's because you've always gone on hating me."

"Perhaps. Or because I wanted to get the whole thing off my mind." She paused. "I'm glad you destroyed the letter. Of course I never thought you'd die."

Mrs. Ansley relapsed into silence, and Mrs. Slade, leaning above her, was conscious of a strange sense of isolation, of being cut off from the warm current of human communion. "You think me a monster!"

"I don't know. . . . It was the only letter I had, and you say he didn't write it?"

"Ah, how you care for him still!"

"I cared for that memory," said Mrs. Ansley.

Mrs. Slade continued to look down on her. She seemed physically reduced by the blow—as if, when she got up, the wind might scatter her like a puff of dust. Mrs. Slade's jealousy suddenly leapt up again at the sight. All these years the woman had been living on that letter. How she must have loved him, to treasure the mere memory of its ashes! The letter of the man her friend was engaged to. Wasn't it she who was the monster?

"You tried your best to get him away from me, didn't you? But you failed; and I kept him. That's all."

"Yes. That's all."

"I wish now I hadn't told you. I'd no idea you'd feel about it as you do; I thought you'd be amused. It all happened so long ago, as you say; and you must do me the justice to remember that I had no reason to think you'd ever taken it seriously. How could I, when you were married to Horace Ansley two months afterward? As soon as you could get out of bed your mother rushed you off to Florence and married you. People were rather surprised—they wondered at its being done so quickly; but I thought I knew. I had an idea you did it out of *pique*—to be able to say you'd got ahead of Delphin and me. Girls have such silly reasons for doing the most serious things. And your marrying so soon convinced me that you'd never really cared."

"Yes. I suppose it would," Mrs. Ansley assented.

The clear heaven overhead was emptied of all its gold. Dusk spread over it, abruptly darkening the Seven Hills. Here and there lights began to twinkle through the foliage at their feet. Steps were coming and going on the deserted terrace—waiters looking out of the doorway at the head of the stairs, then reappearing with trays and napkins and flasks of wine. Tables were moved, chairs straightened. A feeble string of electric lights flickered out. Some vases of faded flowers were carried away, and brought back replenished. A stout lady in a dust coat suddenly appeared, asking in broken Italian if anyone had seen the elastic band which held together her tattered Baedeker. She poked with her stick under the table at which she had lunched, the waiters assisting.

The corner where Mrs. Slade and Mrs. Ansley sat was still shadowy and deserted. For a long time neither of them spoke. At length Mrs. Slade began again: "I suppose I did it as a sort of joke—"

"A joke?"

"Well, girls are ferocious sometimes, you know. Girls in love especially. And I remember laughing to myself all that evening at the idea that you were waiting around there in the dark, dodging out of sight, listening for every sound, trying to get in—Of course I was upset when I heard you were so ill afterward."

Mrs. Ansley had not moved for a long time. But now she turned slowly toward her companion. "But I didn't wait. He'd arranged everything. He was there. We were let in at once," she said.

Mrs. Slade sprang up from her leaning position. "Delphin there? They let you in?—Ah, now you're lying!" she burst out with violence.

Mrs. Ansley's voice grew clearer, and full of surprise. "But of course he was there. Naturally he came—"

"Came? How did he know he'd find you there? You must be raving!"

Mrs. Ansley hesitated, as though reflecting. "But I answered the letter. I told him I'd be there. So he came."

Mrs. Slade flung her hands up to her face. "Oh, God—you answered! I never thought of your answering. . . ."

"It's odd you never thought of it, if you wrote the letter."

"Yes. I was blind with rage."

Mrs. Ansley rose, and drew her fur scarf about her. "It is cold here. We'd better go . . . I'm sorry for you," she said, as she clasped the fur about her throat.

The unexpected words sent a pang through Mrs. Slade. "Yes; we'd better go." She gathered up her bag and cloak. "I don't know why you should be sorry for me," she muttered.

Mrs. Ansley stood looking away from her toward the dusky secret mass of the Colosseum. "Well—because I didn't have to wait that night."

Mrs. Slade gave an unquiet laugh. "Yes; I was beaten there. But I oughtn't to begrudge it to you, I suppose. At the end of all these years. After all, I had everything; I had him for twenty-five years. And you had nothing but that one letter that he didn't write."

Mrs. Ansley was again silent. At length she turned toward the door of the terrace. She took a step, and turned back, facing her companion.

"I had Barbara," she said, and began to move ahead of Mrs. Slade toward the stairway.

1936

Edgar Lee Masters 1869–1950

Edgar Lee Masters is best-known for his internationally acclaimed *Spoon River Anthology* (1915), a book which prompted Ezra Pound to conclude that "at last America has discovered a poet" and British critic John Cowper Powys to call Masters "the natural child of Walt Whitman." The *Spoon River* graveyard epitaphs spoke not only to the heart of America but to the anxieties and triumphs of humanity everywhere. Masters's later works have not received the critical acclaim they deserve. In spite of his popularity with the public, his poetry and fiction have been slighted by many critics who complain that he wrote too much too quickly.

Masters was raised in Petersburg in western Illinois—an area he celebrated often in his hymns to the eternal energy of the midwestern prairies. A lawyer by profession, he admitted to having read Shelley and Browning on the side camouflaged by law books in his office. His poetry was influenced by the tightness of the *Greek Anthology* and the expanse of Beethoven. He felt "lifted and strengthened" by Emerson; he was influenced by Whitman's native genius, Browning's dramatic monologues, Goethe's epic yearnings, Shelley's liberating imagery. Masters was also an astute critic of American culture.

The variety of Masters's writing is impressive. Over four decades he published fiction and critical essays as well as an autobiography, *Across Spoon River* (1936), critical biographies on Vachel Lindsay (1935), Whitman (1937), and Mark Twain (1938), and a wide range of poetry. *The New Spoon River* (1924) captured some of the nuances of the original and several volumes from *Songs and Satires* (1916) to *Along the Illinois* (1942) featured short pieces. He paid tribute to the accomplishments of natural heroes and ordinary folks in the lyrical ballads of *Toward the Gulf* (1918) and *The Open Sea* (1921) and particularly in *Poems of People* (1936) and *More People* (1939). He experimented with innovative verse patterns and long narrative forms in *Lichee Nuts* (1930) and *The Serpent in the Wilderness* (1933) and drew upon his legal expertise in the courtroom suspense drama of *Domesday Book* (1920) and its sequel, *The Fate of the Jury* (1929). Though he spent his later years in the East, Masters's last volumes sang the praises of his native Midwest—in *Illinois Poems* (1941), *The Sangamon* (1942), and *The Harmony of Deeper Music,* (1976) edited by Frank K. Robinson, published after his death.

Masters heeded Emerson's warning that Americans had for too long listened to "the courtly Muses of Europe." He wrote about ordinary people and their everyday experiences. He saw small-town USA as a microcosm of the universe and worked the rhythms of daily experience into his poems. He felt that poets in his time had largely avoided the challenges Whitman had issued to sing in the American idiom and to develop an American mythos. At a time when it wasn't popular to do so, he called for "American poetry, plain as the prairies, level as the quiet sea."

Ronald Primeau
Central Michigan University

PRIMARY WORKS

Spoon River Anthology, 1915; *Songs and Satires,* 1916; *Toward the Gulf,* 1918; *Domesday Book,* 1920; *The Open Sea,* 1921; *The New Spoon River,* 1924; *The Fate of the Jury,* 1929; *Lichee Nuts,* 1930; *The Serpent in the Wilderness,* 1933; *Across Spoon River,* 1936, 1991; *Poems of People,* 1936; *More People,* 1939; *Illinois Poems,* 1941; *Along the Illinois,* 1942; *The Sangamon,* 1942; *The Harmony of Deeper Music: Posthumous Poems of Edgar Lee Masters,* 1976, ed. by Frank K. Robinson. *The Enduring River: Edgar Lee Masters's Uncollected Spoon River Poems,* 1991; *Spoon River Anthology: An Annotated Edition,* 1992.

from Spoon River Anthology

Petit, the Poet

Seeds in a dry pod, tick, tick, tick,
Tick, tick, tick, like mites in a quarrel—
Faint iambics that the full breeze wakens—

But the pine tree makes a symphony thereof.
Triolets, villanelles, rondels, rondeaus,
Ballades by the score with the same old thought:
The snows and the roses of yesterday are vanished;
And what is love but a rose that fades?
Life all around me here in the village:
Tragedy, comedy, valor and truth,
Courage, constancy, heroism, failure—
All in the loom, and oh what patterns!
Woodlands, meadows, streams and rivers—
Blind to all of it all my life long.
Triolets, villanelles, rondels, rondeaus,
Seeds in a dry pod, tick, tick, tick,
Tick, tick, tick, what little iambics,
While Homer and Whitman roared in the pines?

Seth Compton

When I died, the circulating library
Which I built up for Spoon River,
And managed for the good of inquiring minds,
Was sold at auction on the public square,
As if to destroy the last vestige
Of my memory and influence.
For those of you who could not see the virtue
Of knowing Volney's "Ruins" as well as Butler's "Analogy"
And "Faust" as well as "Evangeline,"
Were really the power in the village,
And often you asked me,
"What is the use of knowing the evil in the world?"
I am out of your way now, Spoon River,
Choose your own good and call it good.
For I could never make you see
That no one knows what is good
Who knows not what is evil;
And no one knows what is true
Who knows not what is false.

Lucinda Matlock

I went to the dances at Chandlerville,
And played snap-out at Winchester.
One time we changed partners,
Driving home in the moonlight of middle June,
And then I found Davis.

We were married and lived together for seventy years,
Enjoying, working, raising the twelve children,
Eight of whom we lost
Ere I had reached the age of sixty.
I spun, I wove, I kept the house, I nursed the sick,
I made the garden, and for holiday
Rambled over the fields where sang the larks,
And by Spoon River gathering many a shell,
And many a flower and medicinal weed—
Shouting to the wooded hills, singing to the green valleys.
At ninety-six I had lived enough, that is all,
And passed to a sweet repose.
What is this I hear of sorrow and weariness,
Anger, discontent and drooping hopes?
Degenerate sons and daughters,
Life is too strong for you—
It takes life to love Life.

The Village Atheist

Ye young debaters over the doctrine
Of the soul's immortality,
I who lie here was the village atheist,
Talkative, contentious, versed in the arguments
Of the infidels.
But through a long sickness
Coughing myself to death
I read the *Upanishads*[1] and the poetry of Jesus.
And they lighted a torch of hope and intuition
And desire which the Shadow,
Leading me swiftly through the caverns of darkness,
Could not extinguish.
Listen to me, ye who live in the senses
And think through the senses only:
Immortality is not a gift,
Immortality is an achievement;
And only those who strive mightily
Shall possess it.

1915

[1]Hindu metaphysical treatises dealing with man in relation to the universe.

from The New Spoon River

Cleanthus Trilling

The urge of the seed: the germ.
The urge of the germ: the stalk.
The urge of the stalk: leaves.
The urge of leaves: the blossom.
The urge of the blossom: to scatter pollen.
The urge of the pollen: the imagined dream of life.
The urge of life: longing for to-morrow.
The urge of to-morrow: Pain.
The urge of Pain: God.

1924

from Lichee Nuts

Ascetics and Drunkards

Yesterday Yang Chung was talking of ascetics and drunkards,
And arguing that ascetics live as fully as drunkards.
"Denial," said Yang Chung, "has as much sensation
As indulgence."

1930

Great Audiences and Great Poets

Two Chinese students
From University of Chicago
Go with Yet Wei to see Yuan Chang
And have much talk about war,
Confucius and at last Li Po.
One Chinese student speak of Walt Whitman and America,
And say to have great poets
There must be great audiences too.
Other Chinese student say:
"To have great audiences
"There must be fewer poets."

1930

from The Harmony of Deeper Music

Not to See Sandridge Again

Amid these city walls I often think
Of Sandridge, and its billowed land between
The woods and hills, where clover, red and pink,
And corn fields, oat fields, wheat fields, gold and green,
Lie under skies of speeding clouds serene,
Where gardens know the robin, bobolink.

The yellow road that travels by the hedge,
The rail fence till it slants the gradual rise
Of farms toward the upland fields that edge
The Sangamon, touched by descending skies—
This, too, I see; this is that loved Sandridge,
All changed, but changeless in my memories.

Orchards and strips of timber, walls of log,
Barns, windmills, creeks, even the Shipley Pond
Have vanished, like the early-morning fog
That hung above the swales, and far beyond
The pastures, where the patient shepherd dog
Followed the farmer, dutiful and fond.

Earth even may change, but if the love it stirs
Remains, is Earth then changed? If man must pass,
And generations of cattle, if harvesters
Themselves are gathered, and old men sink like grass
Into the quiet of the universe,
Yet memory keeps them, they are never less.

That is eternal life for them, for me.
For what is living save it be that what
Was beauty is preserved in memory?
If gazing on a dead face is to blot
What the dead was in life, so not to see
Sandridge again may be the better lot.

1936

Willa Cather 1873–1947

Willa Cather was 38 in 1912 when her first novel, *Alexander's Bridge,* appeared and 67 when her thirteenth and last novel, *Sapphira and the Slave Girl,* was published in 1940. Today she is compared with the most widely acclaimed American novelists of the twentieth century—Ernest Hemingway, F. Scott Fitzgerald, and William Faulkner—all of whom were a full generation younger than she. She grew to maturity at the end of the nineteenth century and became an eloquent spokeswoman for the values that shaped her to a twentieth-century world so different from the one into which she was born. Her new subject for American readers in the teens was the life of immigrant populations and transplanted Americans living on the high prairies of Nebraska, Kansas, and Colorado, but her subtle prose style and careful handling of narrative grew from her admiration for the work of American, British, and European writers such as Hawthorne, Flaubert, Stevenson, and James.

A recurring situation in much of Cather's best fiction is one that ties her work to a characteristic American experience—that of starting over. Willa Cather herself was born in the Upper Shenandoah Valley in western Virginia, near Winchester, the oldest of seven children of Charles and Virginia Cather. When she was nine, her parents moved west to join her paternal grandparents on the open plains of Nebraska, taking a large and varied household with them. At first the newcomers lived on the grandfather's farm in the Catherton precinct of Webster County, an area so populated with southerners that its school was called the New Virginia School. Within two years, however, Charles Cather moved the large household into the town of Red Cloud, where he opened a real estate office.

Red Cloud was no stereotypical isolated country town; a main spur of the Burlington railroad passed through Red Cloud, and the Cathers saw performances in the local opera house of the most popular plays of the day produced by major traveling companies. Just as her months in the country had introduced her to the immigrant farmers from Sweden, France, and Bohemia, in Red Cloud Willa Cather discovered a cast of small-town characters rich in cultural diversity. Settlers in this small western town were from Europe, the American South, New England, northeastern cities, and the farms surrounding Red Cloud.

A tomboy who fought the restrictions placed on "young ladies" in the American version of the Victorian era in which she grew up, Cather began signing her name on school papers as "William Cather, M.D." when she was 15. Her closely cropped hair and masculine dress made her stand out when she left home to prepare to enter the new state university in Lincoln. By the time she graduated from the University of Nebraska in 1895, she had modified her appearance and behavior to be more in keeping with the "New Women" of the 1890s that she encountered there. Her recent biographer Sharon O'Brien finds her early rebellion against conventional behavior in dress and demeanor a sign of the assertiveness that gave Cather the confidence she needed to succeed in a culture that was so repressive to women who did not accept their culturally assigned roles.

While in college, Cather began writing reviews for campus and Lincoln newspapers that led to her first job in Pittsburgh as an editor of a ladies' magazine. There she taught high school English and Latin for a few years before joining *McClure's Magazine* in New York City after publishing her first collection of short stories in 1905. For the next forty years, she would live and write in New York, but rarely would that city appear in her fiction. Instead, the memories of her early years in

Virginia and Nebraska, her trips to the American Southwest, New England, Europe, and Canada tantalized her mind. Midway through her career as a novelist, she broadened her attention from the worlds of her personal past to include the history of the settlement of North America in novels such as *Death Comes for the Archbishop* and *Shadows on the Rock,* which treat European immigration to New Mexico and Quebec.

Cather left no diaries, journals, or autobiography behind her when she died. Nor did she permit the publication or quotation of the many letters she wrote to friends that help biographers to explain the relationship she had to the subjects of her work. Yet clearly she found much of the power of her lifelong subjects from her own experience. Several recent biographers and critics see evidence of a lesbianism in Cather's life that she never openly proclaimed. Her strongest ties were clearly to women—her friend and traveling companion Isabelle McClung with whom Cather roomed during her years of high school teaching in Pittsburgh, her mentor Sarah Orne Jewett whom she met while working as a journalist for *McClure's Magazine,* and Edith Lewis with whom Cather lived for almost forty years in New York. With no definitive evidence of Cather's sexual preference available, biographer James Woodress sees her as conscientiously avoiding binding romantic entanglements with either the men or the women in her life in order to devote all her energies to her writing.

Margaret Anne O'Connor
University of North Carolina–at Chapel Hill

PRIMARY WORKS

April Twilights (poetry), 1903, 1923; *The Troll Garden* (stories), 1905; *Alexander's Bridge,* 1912; *O Pioneers!,* 1913; *The Song of the Lark,* 1915; *My Ántonia,* 1918; *Youth and the Bright Medusa* (stories), 1920; *One of Ours,* 1922; *A Lost Lady,* 1923; *The Professor's House,* 1925; *My Mortal Enemy,* 1926; *Death Comes for the Archbishop,* 1927; *Shadows on the Rock,* 1931; *Obscure Destinies* (stories), 1932; *Lucy Gayheart,* 1935; *Not Under Forty* (essays retitled *Literary Excursions* in the Autograph Edition of Cather's collected works, 1937–41), 1936; *Sapphira and the Slave Girl,* 1940; *The Old Beauty and Others,* 1948; *Willa Cather on Writing,* 1949; *Uncle Valentine and Other Stories: 1915–1929,* 1973; *Willa Cather in Person: Interviews, Speeches, and Letters,* 1986.

Coming, Aphrodite!

I

Don Hedger had lived for four years on the top floor of an old house on the south side of Washington Square, and nobody had ever disturbed him. He occupied one big room with no outside exposure except on the north, where he had built in a many-paned studio window that looked upon a court and upon the roofs and walls of other buildings. His room was very cheerless, since he never got a ray of direct sunlight; the south corners were always in shadow. In one of the corners was a clothes closet, built against the partition, in another a wide divan, serving as a seat by day and a bed by night. In the front corner, the one farther from the window, was a sink, and a table with two gas burners where he sometimes cooked his food. There, too, in the perpetual dusk, was the dog's bed, and often a bone or two for his comfort.

The dog was a Boston bull terrier, and Hedger explained his surly disposition by the fact that he had been bred to the point where it told on his nerves. His name was Caesar III, and he had taken prizes at very exclusive dog shows. When he and his master went out to prowl about University Place or to promenade along West Street, Caesar III was invariably fresh and shining. His pink skin showed through his mottled coat, which glistened as if it had just been rubbed with olive oil, and he wore a brass-studded collar, bought at the smartest saddler's. Hedger, as often as not, was hunched up in an old striped blanket coat, with a shapeless felt hat pulled over his bushy hair, wearing black shoes that had become grey, or brown ones that had become black, and he never put on gloves unless the day was biting cold.

Early in May, Hedger learned that he was to have a new neighbour in the rear apartment—two rooms, one large and one small, that faced the west. His studio was shut off from the larger of these rooms by double doors, which, though they were fairly tight, left him a good deal at the mercy of the occupant. The rooms had been leased, long before he came there, by a trained nurse who considered herself knowing in old furniture. She went to auction sales and bought up mahogany and dirty brass and stored it away here, where she meant to live when she retired from nursing. Meanwhile, she sub-let her rooms, with their precious furniture, to young people who came to New York to "write" or to "paint"—who proposed to live by the sweat of the brow rather than of the hand, and who desired artistic surroundings. When Hedger first moved in, these rooms were occupied by a young man who tried to write plays,—and who kept on trying until a week ago, when the nurse had put him out for unpaid rent.

A few days after the playwright left, Hedger heard an ominous murmur of voices through the bolted double doors: the lady-like intonation of the nurse—doubtless exhibiting her treasures—and another voice, also a woman's, but very different; young, fresh, unguarded, confident. All the same, it would be very annoying to have a woman in there. The only bath-room on the floor was at the top of the stairs in the front hall, and he would always be running into her as he came or went from his bath. He would have to be more careful to see that Caesar didn't leave bones about the hall, too; and she might object when he cooked steak and onions on his gas burner.

As soon as the talking ceased and the women left, he forgot them. He was absorbed in a study of paradise fish at the Aquarium, staring out at people through the glass and green water of their tank. It was a highly gratifying idea; the incommunicability of one stratum of animal life with another,—though Hedger pretended it was only an experiment in unusual lighting. When he heard trunks knocking against the sides of the narrow hall, then he realized that she was moving in at once. Toward noon, groans and deep gasps and the creaking of ropes, made him aware that a piano was arriving. After the tramp of the movers died away down the stairs, somebody touched off a few scales and chords on the instrument, and then there was peace. Presently he heard her lock her door and go down the hall humming something; going out to lunch, probably. He stuck his brushes in a can of turpentine and put on his hat, not stopping to wash his hands. Caesar was smelling along the crack under the bolted doors; his bony tail stuck out hard as a hickory withe, and the hair was standing up about his elegant collar.

Hedger encouraged him. "Come along, Caesar. You'll soon get used to a new smell."

In the hall stood an enormous trunk, behind the ladder that led to the roof, just opposite Hedger's door. The dog flew at it with a growl of hurt amazement. They went down three flights of stairs and out into the brilliant May afternoon.

Behind the Square, Hedger and his dog descended into a basement oyster house where there were no tablecloths on the tables and no handles on the coffee cups, and the floor was covered with sawdust, and Caesar was always welcome,—not that he needed any such precautionary flooring. All the carpets of Persia would have been safe for him. Hedger ordered steak and onions absentmindedly, not realizing why he had an apprehension that this dish might be less readily at hand hereafter. While he ate, Caesar sat beside his chair, gravely disturbing the sawdust with his tail.

After lunch Hedger strolled about the Square for the dog's health and watched the stages pull out;—that was almost the very last summer of the old horse stages on Fifth Avenue. The fountain had but lately begun operations for the season and was throwing up a mist of rainbow water which now and then blew south and sprayed a bunch of Italian babies that were being supported on the outer rim by older, very little older, brothers and sisters. Plump robins were hopping about on the soil; the grass was newly cut and blindingly green. Looking up the Avenue through the Arch, one could see the young poplars with their bright, sticky leaves, and the Brevoort glistening in its spring coat of paint, and shining horses and carriages,—occasionally an automobile, mis-shapen and sullen, like an ugly threat in a stream of things that were bright and beautiful and alive.

While Caesar and his master were standing by the fountain, a girl approached them, crossing the Square. Hedger noticed her because she wore a lavender cloth suit and carried in her arms a big bunch of fresh lilacs. He saw that she was young and handsome,—beautiful, in fact, with a splendid figure and good action. She, too, paused by the fountain and looked back through the Arch up the Avenue. She smiled rather patronizingly as she looked, and at the same time seemed delighted. Her slowly curving upper lip and half-closed eyes seemed to say: "You're gay, you're exciting, you are quite the right sort of thing; but you're none too fine for me!"

In the moment she tarried, Caesar stealthily approached her and sniffed at the hem of her lavender skirt, then, when she went south like an arrow, he ran back to his master and lifted a face full of emotion and alarm, his lower lip twitching under his sharp white teeth and his hazel eyes pointed with a very definite discovery. He stood thus, motionless, while Hedger watched the lavender girl go up the steps and through the door of the house in which he lived.

"You're right, my boy, it's she! She might be worse looking, you know."

When they mounted to the studio, the new lodger's door, at the back of the hall, was a little ajar, and Hedger caught the warm perfume of lilacs just brought in out of the sun. He was used to the musty smell of the old hall carpet. (The nurse-lessee had once knocked at his studio door and complained that Caesar must be somewhat responsible for the particular flavour of that mustiness, and Hedger had never spoken to her since.) He was used to the old smell, and he preferred it to that of the lilacs, and so did his companion, whose nose was so much more discriminating. Hedger shut his door vehemently, and fell to work.

Most young men who dwell in obscure studios in New York have had a beginning, come out of something, have somewhere a home town, a family, a paternal roof. But Don Hedger had no such background. He was a foundling, and had grown up in a school for homeless boys, where book-learning was a negligible part of the curriculum. When he was sixteen, a Catholic priest took him to Greensburg, Pennsylvania, to keep house for him. The priest did something to fill in the large gaps in the boy's education,—taught him to like "Don Quixote" and "The Golden Legend," and encouraged him to mess with paints and crayons in his room up under the slope of the mansard. When Don wanted to go to New York to study at the Art League, the priest got him a night job as packer in one of the big department stores. Since then, Hedger had taken care of himself; that was his only responsibility. He was singularly unencumbered; had no family duties, no social ties, no obligations toward any one but his landlord. Since he travelled light, he had travelled rather far. He had got over a good deal of the earth's surface, in spite of the fact that he never in his life had more than three hundred dollars ahead at any one time, and he had already outlived a succession of convictions and revelations about his art.

Though he was not but twenty-six years old, he had twice been on the verge of becoming a marketable product; once through some studies of New York streets he did for a magazine, and once through a collection of pastels he brought home from New Mexico, which Remington, then at the height of his popularity, happened to see, and generously tried to push. But on both occasions Hedger decided that this was something he didn't wish to carry further,—simply the old thing over again and got nowhere—so he took enquiring dealers experiments in a "later manner," that made them put him out of the shop. When he ran short of money, he could always get any amount of commercial work; he was an expert draughtsman and worked with lightning speed. The rest of his time he spent in groping his way from one kind of painting into another, or travelling about without luggage, like a tramp, and he was chiefly occupied with getting rid of ideas he had once thought very fine.

Hedger's circumstances, since he had moved to Washington Square, were affluent compared to anything he had ever known before. He was now able to pay advance rent and turn the key on his studio when he went away for four months at a stretch. It didn't occur to him to wish to be richer than this. To be sure, he did without a great many things other people think necessary, but he didn't miss them, because he had never had them. He belonged to no clubs, visited no houses, had no studio friends, and he ate his dinner alone in some decent little restaurant, even on Christmas and New Year's. For days together he talked to nobody but his dog and the janitress and the lame oysterman.

After he shut the door and settled down to his paradise fish on that first Tuesday in May, Hedger forgot all about his new neighbour. When the light failed, he took Caesar out for a walk. On the way home he did his marketing on West Houston Street, with a one-eyed Italian woman who always cheated him. After he had cooked his beans and scallopini, and drunk half a bottle of Chianti, he put his dishes in the sink and went up on the roof to smoke. He was the only person in the house who ever went to the roof, and he had a secret understanding with the janitress about it. He was to have "the privilege of the roof," as she said, if he opened the heavy trapdoor on sunny days to air out the upper hall, and was watchful to close it when rain threatened. Mrs. Foley was fat and dirty and hated to climb stairs,—besides, the roof was reached by a perpendicular iron ladder, definitely inaccessible to a woman of her bulk, and the iron door at the top of it was too heavy for any but Hedger's strong arm to lift. Hedger was not above medium height, but he practised with weights and dumb-bells, and in the shoulders he was as strong as a gorilla.

So Hedger had the roof to himself. He and Caesar often slept up there on hot nights, rolled in blankets he had brought home from Arizona. He mounted with Caesar under his left arm. The dog had never learned to climb a perpendicular ladder, and never did he feel so much his master's greatness and his own dependence upon him, as when he crept under his arm for this perilous ascent. Up there was even gravel to scratch in, and a dog could do whatever he liked, so long as he did not bark. It was a kind of heaven, which no one was strong enough to reach but his great, paint-smelling master.

On this blue May night there was a slender, girlish looking young moon in the west, playing with a whole company of silver stars. Now and then one of them darted away from the group and shot off into the gauzy blue with a soft little trail of light, like laughter. Hedger and his dog were delighted when a star did this. They were quite lost in watching the glittering game, when they were suddenly diverted by a sound,—not from the stars, though it was music. It was not the Prologue to Pagliacci, which rose ever and anon on hot evenings from an Italian tenement on Thompson Street, with the gasps of the corpulent baritone who got behind it; nor was it the hurdy-gurdy man, who often played at the corner in the balmy twilight. No, this was a woman's voice, singing the tempestuous, over-lapping phrases of Signor Puccini, then comparatively new in the world, but already so popular that even Hedger recognized his unmistakable gusts of breath. He looked about over the roofs; all was blue and still, with the well-built chimneys that were never used now standing up dark and mournful. He moved softly toward the yellow quadrangle where the gas from the hall shone up through the half-lifted trapdoor. Oh yes! It came up through the hole like a strong draught, a big, beautiful voice, and it sounded rather like a professional's. A piano had arrived in the morning, Hedger remembered. This might be a very great nuisance. It would be pleasant enough to listen to, if you could turn it on and off as you wished; but you couldn't. Caesar, with the gas light shining on his collar and his ugly but sensitive face, panted and looked up for information. Hedger put down a reassuring hand.

"I don't know. We can't tell yet. It may not be so bad."

He stayed on the roof until all was still below, and finally descended, with quite a new feeling about his neighbour. Her voice, like her figure, inspired respect,—if one did not choose to call it admiration. Her door was shut, the transom was dark; nothing remained of her but the obtrusive trunk, unrightfully taking up room in the narrow hall.

II

For two days Hedger didn't see her. He was painting eight hours a day just then, and only went out to hunt for food. He noticed that she practised scales and exercises for about an hour in the morning; then she locked her door, went humming down the hall, and left him in peace. He heard her getting her coffee ready at about the same time he got his. Earlier still, she passed his room on her way to her bath. In the evening she sometimes sang, but on the whole she didn't bother him. When he was working well he did not notice anything much. The morning paper lay before his door until he reached out for his milk bottle, then he kicked the sheet inside and it lay on the floor until evening. Sometimes he read it and sometimes he did not. He forgot there was anything of importance going on in the world outside of his third floor studio. Nobody had ever taught him that he ought to be interested in other people; in the Pittsburgh steel strike, in the Fresh Air Fund, in the scandal about the Babies' Hospital. A grey wolf, living in a Wyoming canyon, would hardly have been less concerned about these things than was Don Hedger.

One morning he was coming out of the bathroom at the front end of the hall, having just given Caesar his bath and rubbed him into a glow with a heavy towel. Before the door, lying in wait for him, as it were, stood a tall figure in a flowering blue silk dressing gown that fell away from her marble arms. In her hands she carried various accessories of the bath.

"I wish," she said distinctly, standing in his way, "I wish you wouldn't wash your dog in the tub. I never heard of such a thing! I've found his hair in the tub, and I've smelled a doggy smell, and now I've caught you at it. It's an outrage!"

Hedger was badly frightened. She was so tall and positive, and was fairly blazing with beauty and anger. He stood blinking, holding on to his sponge and dog-soap, feeling that he ought to bow very low to her. But what he actually said was: "Nobody has ever objected before. I always wash the tub,—and, anyhow, he's cleaner than most people."

"Cleaner than me?" her eyebrows went up, her white arms and neck and her fragrant person seemed to scream at him like a band of outraged nymphs. Something flashed through his mind about a man who was turned into a dog, or was pursued by dogs, because he unwittingly intruded upon the bath of beauty.

"No, I didn't mean that," he muttered, turning scarlet under the bluish stubble of his muscular jaws. "But I know he's cleaner than I am."

"That I don't doubt!" Her voice sounded like a soft shivering of crystal, and with a smile of pity she drew the folds of her voluminous blue robe close about her and allowed the wretched man to pass. Even Caesar was frightened; he darted like a streak down the hall, through the door and to his own bed in the corner among the bones.

Hedger stood still in the doorway, listening to indignant sniffs and coughs and a great swishing of water about the sides of the tub. He had washed it; but as he had washed it with Caesar's sponge, it was quite possible that a few bristles remained; the dog was shedding now. The playwright had never objected, nor had the jovial illustrator who occupied the front apartment,—but he, as he admitted, "was usually pye-eyed, when he wasn't in Buffalo." He went home to Buffalo sometimes to rest his nerves.

It had never occurred to Hedger that any one would mind using the tub after Caesar;—but then, he had never seen a beautiful girl caparisoned for the bath before. As soon as he beheld her standing there, he realized the unfitness of it. For that matter, she ought not to step into a tub that any other mortal had bathed in; the illustrator was sloppy and left cigarette ends on the moulding.

All morning as he worked he was gnawed by a spiteful desire to get back at her. It rankled him that he had been so vanquished by her disdain. When he heard her locking her door to go out for lunch, he stepped quickly into the hall in his messy painting coat, and addressed her.

"I don't wish to be exigent, Miss,"—he had certain grand words that he used upon occasion—"but if this is your trunk, it's rather in the way here."

"Oh, very well!" she exclaimed carelessly, dropping her keys into her handbag. "I'll have it moved when I can get a man to do it," and she went down the hall with her free, roving stride.

Her name, Hedger discovered from her letters, which the postman left on the table in the lower hall, was Eden Bower.

III

In the closet that was built against the partition separating his room from Miss Bower's, Hedger kept all his wearing apparel, some of it on hooks and hangers, some of it on the floor. When he opened his closet door now-a-days, little dust-coloured insects flew out on downy wing, and he suspected that a brood of moths were hatching in his winter overcoat. Mrs. Foley, the janitress, told him to bring down all his heavy clothes and she would give them a beating and hang them in the court. The closet was in such disorder that he shunned the encounter, but one hot afternoon he set himself to the task. First he threw out a pile of forgotten laundry and tied it up in a sheet. The bundle stood as high as his middle when he had knotted the corners. Then he got his shoes and overshoes together. When he took his overcoat from its place against the partition, a long ray of yellow light shot across the dark enclosure,—a knot hole, evidently, in the high wainscoating of the west room. He had never noticed it before, and without realizing what he was doing, he stooped and squinted through it.

Yonder, in a pool of sunlight, stood his new neighbour, wholly unclad, doing exercises of some sort before a long gilt mirror. Hedger did not happen to think how unpardonable it was of him to watch her. Nudity was not improper to any one who had worked so much from the figure, and he continued to look, simply because he had never seen a woman's body so beautiful as this one,—positively glorious in action. As she swung her arms and changed from one pivot of motion to another, muscular energy seemed to flow through her from her toes to her finger-tips. The soft flush of exercise and the gold of afternoon sun played over her flesh together, enveloped her in a luminous mist which, as she turned and twisted, made now an arm, now a shoulder, now a thigh, dissolve in pure light and instantly recover its outline with the next gesture. Hedger's fingers curved as if he were holding a crayon; mentally he was doing the whole figure in a single running line, and the charcoal seemed to explode in his hand at the point where the energy of each gesture was discharged into the whirling disc of light, from a foot or shoulder, from the up-thrust chin or the lifted breasts.

He could not have told whether he watched her for six minutes or sixteen. When her gymnastics were over, she paused to catch up a lock of hair that had come down, and examined with solicitude a little reddish mole that grew under her left arm-pit. Then, with her hand on her hip, she walked unconcernedly across the room and disappeared through the door into her bedchamber.

Disappeared—Don Hedger was crouching on his knees, staring at the golden shower which poured in through the west windows, at the lake of gold sleeping on the faded Turkish carpet. The spot was enchanted; a vision out of Alexandria, out of the remote pagan past, had bathed itself there in Helianthine fire.

When he crawled out of his closet, he stood blinking at the grey sheet stuffed with laundry, not knowing what had happened to him. He felt a little sick as he contemplated the bundle. Everything here was different; he hated the disorder of the place, the grey prison light, his old shoes and himself and all his slovenly habits. The black calico curtains that ran on wires over his big window were white with dust. There were three greasy frying pans in the sink, and the sink itself—He felt desperate. He couldn't stand this another minute. He took up an armful of winter clothes and ran down four flights into the basement.

"Mrs. Foley," he began. "I want my room cleaned this afternoon, thoroughly cleaned. Can you get a woman for me right away?"

"Is it company you're having?" the fat, dirty janitress enquired. Mrs. Foley was the widow of a useful Tammany man, and she owned real estate in Flatbush. She was huge and soft as a feather bed. Her face and arms were permanently coated with dust, grained like wood where the sweat had trickled.

"Yes, company. That's it."

"Well, this is a queer time of the day to be asking for a cleaning woman. It's likely I can get you old Lizzie, if she's not drunk. I'll send Willy round to see."

Willy, the son of fourteen, roused from the stupor and stain of his fifth box of cigarettes by the gleam of a quarter, went out. In five minutes he returned with old Lizzie,—she smelling strong of spirits and wearing several jackets which she had put on one over the other, and a number of skirts, long and short, which made her resemble an animated dish-clout. She had, of course, to borrow her equipment from Mrs. Foley and toiled up the long flights, dragging mop and pail and broom. She told Hedger to be of good cheer, for he had got the right woman for the job, and showed him a great leather strap she wore about her wrist to prevent dislocation of tendons. She swished about the place, scattering dust and splashing soapsuds, while he watched her in nervous despair. He stood over Lizzie and made her scour the sink, directing her roughly, then paid her and got rid of her. Shutting the door on his failure, he hurried off with his dog to lose himself among the stevedores and dock labourers on West Street.

A strange chapter began for Don Hedger. Day after day, at that hour in the afternoon, the hour before his neighbour dressed for dinner, he crouched down in his closet to watch her go through her mysterious exercises. It did not occur to him that his conduct was detestable; there was nothing shy or retreating about this unclad girl,—a bold body, studying itself quite coolly and evidently well pleased with itself, doing all this for a purpose. Hedger scarcely regarded his action as conduct at all; it was something that had happened to him. More than once he went out and tried to stay away for the whole afternoon, but at about five o'clock he was sure to find himself among his old shoes in the dark. The pull of that aperture was stronger than his will,—and he had always considered his will the strongest thing about him. When she threw herself upon the divan and lay resting, he still stared, holding his breath. His nerves were so on edge that a sudden noise made him start and brought out the sweat on his forehead. The dog would come and tug at his sleeve, knowing that something was wrong with his master. If he attempted a mournful whine, those strong hands closed about his throat.

When Hedger came slinking out of his closet, he sat down on the edge of the couch, sat for hours without moving. He was not painting at all now. This thing, whatever it was, drank him up as ideas had sometimes done, and he sank into a stupor of idleness as deep and dark as the stupor of work. He could not understand it; he was no boy, he had worked from models for years, and a woman's body was no mystery to him. Yet now he did nothing but sit and think about one. He slept very little, and with the first light of morning he awoke as completely possessed by this woman as if he had been with her all the night before. The unconscious operations of life went on in him only to perpetuate this excitement. His brain held but one image now—vibrated, burned with it. It was a heathenish feeling; without friendliness, almost without tenderness.

Women had come and gone in Hedger's life. Not having had a mother to begin with, his relations with them, whether amorous or friendly, had been casual. He got on well with janitresses and wash-women, with Indians and with the peasant women of foreign countries. He had friends among the silk-skirt factory girls who came to eat their lunch in Washington Square, and he sometimes took a model for a day in the country. He felt an unreasoning antipathy toward the well-dressed women he saw coming out of big shops, or driving in the Park. If, on his way to the Art Museum, he noticed a pretty girl standing on the steps of one of the houses on upper Fifth Avenue, he frowned at her and went by with his shoulders hunched up as if he were cold. He had never known such girls, or heard them talk, or seen the inside of the houses in which they lived; but he believed them all to be artificial and, in an aesthetic sense, perverted. He saw them enslaved by desire of merchandise and manufactured articles, effective only in making life complicated and insincere and in embroidering it with ugly and meaningless trivialities. They were enough, he thought, to make one almost forget woman as she existed in art, in thought, and in the universe.

He had no desire to know the woman who had, for the time at least, so broken up his life,—no curiosity about her every-day personality. He shunned any revelation of it, and he listened for Miss Bower's coming and going, not to encounter, but to avoid her. He wished that the girl who wore shirt-waists and got letters from Chicago would keep out of his way, that she did not exist. With her he had naught to make. But in a room full of sun, before an old mirror, on a little enchanted rug of sleeping colours, he had seen a woman who emerged naked through a door, and disappeared naked. He thought of that body as never having been clad, or as having worn the stuffs and dyes of all the centuries but his own. And for him she had no geographical associations; unless with Crete, or Alexandria, or Veronese's Venice. She was the immortal conception, the perennial theme.

The first break in Hedger's lethargy occurred one afternoon when two young men came to take Eden Bower out to dine. They went into her music room, laughed and talked for a few minutes, and then took her away with them. They were gone a long while, but he did not go out for food himself; he waited for them to come back. At last he heard them coming down the hall, gayer and more talkative than when they left. One of them sat down at the piano, and they all began to sing. This Hedger found absolutely unendurable. He snatched up his hat and went running down the stairs. Caesar leaped beside him, hoping that old times were coming back. They had supper in the oysterman's basement and then sat down in front of their own doorway. The moon stood full over the Square, a thing of regal glory; but Hedger did not see the moon; he was looking, murderously, for men. Presently two, wearing straw hats and white trousers and carrying canes, came down the steps from his house. He rose and dogged them across the Square. They were laughing and seemed very much elated about something. As one stopped to light a cigarette, Hedger caught from the other:

"Don't you think she has a beautiful talent?"

His companion threw away his match. "She has a beautiful figure." They both ran to catch the stage.

Hedger went back to his studio. The light was shining from her transom. For the first time he violated her privacy at night, and peered through that fatal aperture. She was sitting, fully dressed, in the window, smoking a cigarette and looking out over the housetops. He watched her until she rose, looked about her with a disdainful, crafty smile, and turned out the light.

The next morning, when Miss Bower went out, Hedger followed her. Her white skirt gleamed ahead of him as she sauntered about the Square. She sat down behind the Garibaldi statue and opened a music book she carried. She turned the leaves carelessly, and several times glanced in his direction. He was on the point of going over to her, when she rose quickly and looked up at the sky. A flock of pigeons had risen from somewhere in the crowded Italian quarter to the south, and were wheeling rapidly up through the morning air, soaring and dropping, scattering and coming together, now grey, now white as silver, as they caught or intercepted the sunlight. She put up her hand to shade her eyes and followed them with a kind of defiant delight in her face.

Hedger came and stood beside her. "You've surely seen them before?"

"Oh, yes," she replied, still looking up. "I see them every day from my windows. They always come home about five o'clock. Where do they live?"

"I don't know. Probably some Italian raises them for the market. They were here long before I came, and I've been here four years."

"In that same gloomy room? Why didn't you take mine when it was vacant?"

"It isn't gloomy. That's the best light for painting."

"Oh, is it? I don't know anything about painting. I'd like to see your pictures sometime. You have such a lot in there. Don't they get dusty, piled up against the wall like that?"

"Not very. I'd be glad to show them to you. Is your name really Eden Bower? I've seen your letters on the table."

"Well, it's the name I'm going to sing under. My father's name is Bowers, but my friend Mr. Jones, a Chicago newspaper man who writes about music, told me to drop the 's.' He's crazy about my voice."

Miss Bower didn't usually tell the whole story,—about anything. Her first name, when she lived in Huntington, Illinois, was Edna, but Mr. Jones had persuaded her to change it to one which he felt would be worthy of her future. She was quick to take suggestions, though she told him she "didn't see what was the matter with 'Edna.'"

She explained to Hedger that she was going to Paris to study. She was waiting in

New York for Chicago friends who were to take her over, but who had been detained. "Did you study in Paris?" she asked.

"No, I've never been in Paris. But I was in the south of France all last summer, studying with C——. He's the biggest man among the moderns,—at least I think so."

Miss Bower sat down and made room for him on the bench. "Do tell me about it. I expected to be there by this time, and I can't wait to find out what it's like."

Hedger began to relate how he had seen some of this Frenchman's work in an exhibition, and deciding at once that this was the man for him, he had taken a boat for Marseilles the next week, going over steerage. He proceeded at once to the little town on the coast where his painter lived, and presented himself. The man never took pupils, but because Hedger had come so far, he let him stay. Hedger lived at the master's house and every day they went out together to paint, sometimes on the blazing rocks down by the sea. They wrapped themselves in light woollen blankets and didn't feel the heat. Being there and working with C—— was being in Paradise, Hedger concluded; he learned more in three months than in all his life before.

Eden Bower laughed. "You're a funny fellow. Didn't you do anything but work? Are the women very beautiful? Did you have awfully good things to eat and drink?"

Hedger said some of the women were fine looking, especially one girl who went about selling fish and lobsters. About the food there was nothing remarkable,—except the ripe figs, he liked those. They drank sour wine, and used goat-butter, which was strong and full of hair, as it was churned in a goat skin.

"But don't they have parties or banquets? Aren't there any fine hotels down there?"

"Yes, but they are all closed in summer, and the country people are poor. It's a beautiful country, though."

"How, beautiful?" she persisted.

"If you want to go in, I'll show you some sketches, and you'll see."

Miss Bower rose. "All right. I won't go to my fencing lesson this morning. Do you fence? Here comes your dog. You can't move but he's after you. He always makes a face at me when I meet him in the hall, and shows his nasty little teeth as if he wanted to bite me."

In the studio Hedger got out his sketches, but to Miss Bower, whose favourite pictures were Christ Before Pilate and a redhaired Magdalen of Henner, these landscapes were not at all beautiful, and they gave her no idea of any country whatsoever. She was careful not to commit herself, however. Her vocal teacher had already convinced her that she had a great deal to learn about many things.

"Why don't we go out to lunch somewhere?" Hedger asked, and began to dust his fingers with a handkerchief—which he got out of sight as swiftly as possible.

"All right, the Brevoort," she said carelessly. "I think that's a good place, and they have good wine. I don't care for cocktails."

Hedger felt his chin uneasily. "I'm afraid I haven't shaved this morning. If you could wait for me in the Square? It won't take me ten minutes."

Left alone, he found a clean collar and handkerchief, brushed his coat and blacked his shoes, and last of all dug up ten dollars from the bottom of an old copper kettle he had brought from Spain. His winter hat was of such a complexion that the Brevoort hall boy winked at the porter as he took it and placed it on the rack in a row of fresh straw ones.

IV

That afternoon Eden Bower was lying on the couch in her music room, her face turned to the window, watching the pigeons. Reclining thus she could see none of the neighbouring roofs, only the sky itself and the birds that crossed and recrossed her field of vision, white as scraps of paper blowing in the wind. She was thinking that she was young and handsome and had had a good lunch, that a very easy-going, light-hearted city lay in the streets below her; and she was wondering why she found this queer painter chap, with his lean, bluish cheeks and heavy black eyebrows, more interesting than the smart young men she met at her teacher's studio.

Eden Bower was, at twenty, very much the same person that we all know her to be at forty, except that she knew a great deal less. But one thing she knew: that she was to be Eden Bower. She was like some one standing before a great show window full of beautiful and costly things, deciding which she will order. She understands that they will not all be delivered immediately, but one by one they will arrive at her door. She already knew some of the many things that were to happen to her; for instance, that the Chicago millionaire who was going to take her abroad with his sister as chaperone, would eventually press his claim in quite another manner. He was the most circumspect of bachelors, afraid of everything obvious, even of women who were too flagrantly handsome. He was a nervous collector of pictures and furniture, a nervous patron of music, and a nervous host; very cautious about his health, and about any course of conduct that might make him ridiculous. But she knew that he would at last throw all his precautions to the winds.

People like Eden Bower are inexplicable. Her father sold farming machinery in Huntington, Illinois, and she had grown up with no acquaintances or experiences outside of that prairie town. Yet from her earliest childhood she had not one conviction or opinion in common with the people about her,—the only people she knew. Before she was out of short dresses she had made up her mind that she was going to be an actress, that she would live far away in great cities, that she would be much admired by men and would have everything she wanted. When she was thirteen, and was already singing and reciting for church entertainments, she read in some illustrated magazine a long article about the late Czar of Russia, then just come to the throne or about to come to it. After that, lying in the hammock on the front porch on summer evenings, or sitting through a long sermon in the family pew, she amused herself by trying to make up her mind whether she would or would not be the Czar's mistress when she played in his Capital. Now Edna had met this fascinating word only in the novels of Ouida,—her hard-worked little mother kept a long row of them in the upstairs storeroom, behind the linen chest. In Huntington, women who bore that relation to men were called by a very different name, and their lot was not an enviable one; of all the shabby and poor, they were the shabbiest. But then, Edna had never lived in Huntington, not even before she began to find books like "Sappho" and "Mademoiselle de Maupin," secretly sold in paper covers throughout Illinois. It was as if she had come into Huntington, into the Bowers family, on one of the trains that puffed over the marshes behind their back fence all day long, and was waiting for another train to take her out.

As she grew older and handsomer, she had many beaux, but these small-town boys didn't interest her. If a lad kissed her when he brought her home from a dance, she was indulgent and she rather liked it. But if he pressed her further, she slipped away from him, laughing. After she began to sing in Chicago, she was consistently discreet. She stayed as a guest in rich people's houses, and she knew that she was being watched like a rabbit in a laboratory. Covered up in bed, with the lights out, she thought her own thoughts, and laughed.

This summer in New York was her first taste of freedom. The Chicago capitalist, after all his arrangements were made for sailing, had been compelled to go to Mexico to look after oil interests. His sister knew an excellent singing master in New York. Why should not a discreet, well-balanced girl like Miss Bower spend the summer there, studying quietly? The capitalist suggested that his sister might enjoy a summer on Long Island; he would rent the Griffiths' place for her, with all the servants, and Eden could stay there. But his sister met this proposal with a cold stare. So it fell out, that between selfishness and greed, Eden got a summer all her own,—which really did a great deal toward making her an artist and whatever else she was afterward to become. She had time to look about, to watch without being watched; to select diamonds in one window and furs in another, to select shoulders and moustaches in the big hotels where she went to lunch. She had the easy freedom of obscurity and the consciousness of power. She enjoyed both. She was in no hurry.

While Eden Bower watched the pigeons, Don Hedger sat on the other side of the bolted doors, looking into a pool of dark turpentine, at his idle brushes, wondering why a woman could do this to him. He, too, was sure of his future and knew that he was a chosen man. He could not know, of course, that he was merely the first to fall under a fascination which was to be disastrous to a few men and pleasantly stimulating to many thousands. Each of these two young people sensed the future, but not completely. Don Hedger knew that nothing much would ever happen to him. Eden Bower understood that to her a great deal would happen. But she did not guess that her neighbour would have more tempestuous adventures sitting in his dark studio than she would find in all the capitals of Europe, or in all the latitude of conduct she was prepared to permit herself.

V

One Sunday morning Eden was crossing the Square with a spruce young man in a white flannel suit and a panama hat. They had been breakfasting at the Brevoort and he was coaxing her to let him come up to her rooms and sing for an hour.

"No, I've got to write letters. You must run along now. I see a friend of mine over there, and I want to ask him about something before I go up."

"That fellow with the dog? Where did you pick him up?" the young man glanced toward the seat under a sycamore where Hedger was reading the morning paper.

"Oh, he's an old friend from the West," said Eden easily. "I won't introduce you, because he doesn't like people. He's a recluse. Good-bye. I can't be sure about Tuesday. I'll go with you if I have time after my lesson." She nodded, left him, and went over to the seat littered with newspapers. The young man went up the Avenue without looking back.

"Well, what are you going to do today? Shampoo this animal all morning?" Eden enquired teasingly.

Hedger made room for her on the seat. "No, at twelve o'clock I'm going out to Coney Island. One of my models is going up in a balloon this afternoon. I've often promised to go and see her, and now I'm going."

Eden asked if models usually did such stunts. No, Hedger told her, but Molly Welch added to her earnings in that way. "I believe," he added, "she likes the excitement of it. She's got a good deal of spirit. That's why I like to paint her. So many models have flaccid bodies."

"And she hasn't, eh? Is she the one who comes to see you? I can't help hearing her, she talks so loud."

"Yes, she has a rough voice, but she's a fine girl. I don't suppose you'd be interested in going?"

"I don't know," Eden sat tracing patterns on the asphalt with the end of her parasol. "Is it any fun? I got up feeling I'd like to do something different today. It's the first Sunday I've not had to sing in church. I had that engagement for breakfast at the Brevoort, but it wasn't very exciting. That chap can't talk about anything but himself."

Hedger warmed a little. "If you've never been to Coney Island, you ought to go. It's nice to see all the people; tailors and bar-tenders and prize-fighters with their best girls, and all sorts of folks taking a holiday."

Eden looked sidewise at him. So one ought to be interested in people of that kind, ought one? He was certainly a funny fellow. Yet he was never, somehow, tiresome. She had seen a good deal of him lately, but she kept wanting to know him better, to find out what made him different from men like the one she had just left—whether he really was as different as he seemed. "I'll go with you," she said at last, "if you'll leave that at home." She pointed to Caesar's flickering ears with her sunshade.

"But he's half the fun. You'd like to hear him bark at the waves when they come in."

"No, I wouldn't. He's jealous and disagreeable if he sees you talking to any one else. Look at him now."

"Of course, if you make a face at him. He knows what that means, and he makes a worse face. He likes Molly Welch, and she'll be disappointed if I don't bring him."

Eden said decidedly that he couldn't take both of them. So at twelve o'clock when she and Hedger got on the boat at Desbrosses street, Caesar was lying on his pallet, with a bone.

Eden enjoyed the boat-ride. It was the first time she had been on the water, and she felt as if she were embarking for France. The light warm breeze and the plunge of the waves made her very wide awake, and she liked crowds of any kind. They went to the balcony of a big, noisy restaurant and had a shore dinner, with tall steins of beer. Hedger had got a big advance from his advertising firm since he first lunched with Miss Bower ten days ago, and he was ready for anything.

After dinner they went to the tent behind the bathing beach, where the tops of two balloons bulged out over the canvas. A red-faced man in a linen suit stood in front of the tent, shouting in a hoarse voice and telling the people that if the crowd was good for five dollars more, a beautiful young woman would risk her life for their entertainment. Four little boys in dirty red uniforms ran about taking contributions in their pill-box hats. One of the balloons was bobbing up and down in its tether and people were shoving forward to get nearer the tent.

"Is it dangerous, as he pretends?" Eden asked.

"Molly says it's simple enough if nothing goes wrong with the balloon. Then it would be all over, I suppose."

"Wouldn't you like to go up with her?"

"I? Of course not. I'm not fond of taking foolish risks."

Eden sniffed. "I shouldn't think sensible risks would be very much fun."

Hedger did not answer, for just then every one began to shove the other way and shout, "Look out. There she goes!" and a band of six pieces commenced playing furiously.

As the balloon rose from its tent enclosure, they saw a girl in green tights standing in the basket, holding carelessly to one of the ropes with one hand and with the other waving to the spectators. A long rope trailed behind to keep the balloon from blowing out to sea.

As it soared, the figure in green tights in the basket diminished to a mere spot, and the balloon itself, in the brilliant light, looked like a big silvery-grey bat, with its wings folded. When it began to sink, the girl stepped through the hole in the basket to a trapeze that hung below, and gracefully descended through the air, holding to the rod with both hands, keeping her body taut and her feet close together. The crowd, which had grown very large by this time, cheered vociferously. The men took off their hats and waved, little boys shouted, and fat old women, shining with the heat and a beer lunch, murmured admiring comments upon the balloonist's figure. "Beautiful legs, she has!"

"That's so," Hedger whispered. "Not many girls would look well in that position." Then, for some reason, he blushed a slow, dark, painful crimson.

The balloon descended slowly, a little way from the tent and the red-faced man in the linen suit caught Molly Welch before her feet touched the ground, and pulled her to one side. The band struck up "Blue Bell" by way of welcome, and one of the sweaty pages ran forward and presented the balloonist with a large bouquet of artificial flowers. She smiled and thanked him, and ran back across the sand to the tent.

"Can't we go inside and see her?" Eden asked. "You can explain to the door man. I want to meet her." Edging forward, she herself addressed the man in the linen suit and slipped something from her purse into his hand.

They found Molly seated before a trunk that had a mirror in the lid and a "make-up" outfit spread upon the tray. She was wiping the cold cream and powder from her neck with a discarded chemise.

"Hello, Don," she said cordially. "Brought a friend?"

Eden liked her. She had an easy, friendly manner, and there was something boyish and devil-may-care about her.

"Yes, it's fun. I'm mad about it," she said in reply to Eden's questions. "I always want to let go, when I come down on the bar. You don't feel your weight at all, as you would on a stationary trapeze."

The big drum boomed outside, and the publicity man began shouting to newly arrived boatloads. Miss Welch took a last pull at her cigarette. "Now you'll have to get out, Don. I change for the next act. This time I go up in a black evening dress, and lose the skirt in the basket before I start down."

"Yes, go along," said Eden. "Wait for me outside the door. I'll stay and help her dress."

Hedger waited and waited, while women of every build bumped into him and begged his pardon, and the red pages ran about holding out their caps for coins, and the people ate and perspired and shifted parasols against the sun. When the band began to play a two-step, all the bathers ran up out of the surf to watch the ascent. The second balloon bumped and rose, and the crowd began shouting to the girl in a black evening dress who stood leaning against the ropes and smiling. "It's a new girl," they called. "It ain't the Countess this time. You're a peach, girlie!"

The balloonist acknowledged these compliments, bowing and looking down over the sea of upturned faces,—but Hedger was determined she should not see him, and he darted behind the tent-fly. He was suddenly dripping with cold sweat, his mouth was full of the bitter taste of anger and his tongue felt stiff behind his teeth. Molly Welch, in a shirt-waist and a white tam-o'-shanter cap, slipped out from the tent under his arm and laughed up in his face. "She's a crazy one you brought along. She'll get what she wants!"

"Oh, I'll settle with you, all right!" Hedger brought out with difficulty.

"It's not my fault, Donnie. I couldn't do anything with her. She bought me off. What's the matter with you? Are you soft on her? She's safe enough. It's as easy as rolling off a log, if you keep cool." Molly Welch was rather excited herself, and she was chewing gum at a high speed as she stood beside him, looking up at the floating silver cone. "Now watch," she exclaimed suddenly. "She's coming down on the bar. I advised her to cut that out, but you see she does it first-rate. And she got rid of the skirt, too. Those black tights show off her legs very well. She keeps her feet together like I told her, and makes a good line along the back. See the light on those silver slippers,—that was a good idea I had. Come along to meet her. Don't be a grouch; she's done it fine!"

Molly tweaked his elbow, and then left him standing like a stump, while she ran down the beach with the crowd.

Though Hedger was sulking, his eye could not help seeing the low blue welter of the sea, the arrested bathers, standing in the surf, their arms and legs stained red by the dropping sun, all shading their eyes and gazing upward at the slowly falling silver star.

Molly Welch and the manager caught Eden under the arms and lifted her aside, a red page dashed up with a bouquet, and the band struck up "Blue Bell." Eden laughed and bowed, took Molly's arm, and ran up the sand in her black tights and silver slippers, dodging the friendly old women, and the gallant sports who wanted to offer their homage on the spot.

When she emerged from the tent, dressed in her own clothes, that part of the beach was almost deserted. She stepped to her companion's side and said carelessly: "Hadn't we better try to catch this boat? I hope you're not sore at me. Really, it was lots of fun."

Hedger looked at his watch. "Yes, we have fifteen minutes to get the boat," he said politely.

As they walked toward the pier, one of the pages ran up panting. "Lady, you're carrying off the bouquet," he said, aggrievedly.

Eden stopped and looked at the bunch of spotty cotton roses in her hand. "Of course. I want them for a souvenir. You gave them to me yourself."

"I give 'em to you for looks, but you can't take 'em away. They belong to the show."

"Oh, you always use the same bunch?"

"Sure we do. There ain't too much money in this business."

She laughed and tossed them back to him. "Why are you angry?" she asked Hedger. "I wouldn't have done it if I'd been with some fellows, but I thought you were the sort who wouldn't mind. Molly didn't for a minute think you would."

"What possessed you to do such a fool thing?" he asked roughly.

"I don't know. When I saw her coming down, I wanted to try it. It looked exciting. Didn't I hold myself as well as she did?"

Hedger shrugged his shoulders, but in his heart he forgave her.

The return boat was not crowded, though the boats that passed them, going out, were packed to the rails. The sun was setting. Boys and girls sat on the long benches with their arms about each other, singing. Eden felt a strong wish to propitiate her companion, to be alone with him. She had been curiously wrought up by her balloon trip; it was a lark, but not very satisfying unless one came back to something after the flight. She wanted to be admired and adored. Though Eden said nothing, and sat with her arms limp on the rail in front of her, looking languidly at the rising silhouette of the city and the bright path of the sun, Hedger felt a strange drawing near to her. If he but brushed her white skirt with his knee, there was an instant communication between them, such as there had never been before. They did not talk at all, but when they went over the gang-plank she took his arm and kept her shoulder close to his. He felt as if they were enveloped in a highly charged atmosphere, an invisible network of subtle, almost painful sensibility. They had somehow taken hold of each other.

An hour later, they were dining in the back garden of a little French hotel on Ninth Street, long since passed away. It was cool and leafy there, and the mosquitoes were not very numerous. A party of South Americans at another table were drinking champagne, and Eden murmured that she thought she would like some, if it were not too expensive. "Perhaps it will make me think I am in the balloon again. That was a very nice feeling. You've forgiven me, haven't you?"

Hedger gave her a quick straight look from under his black eyebrows, and something went over her that was like a chill, except that it was warm and feathery. She drank most of the wine; her companion was indifferent to it. He was talking more to her tonight than he had ever done before. She asked him about a new picture she had seen in his room; a queer thing full of stiff, supplicating female figures. "It's Indian, isn't it?"

"Yes. I call it Rain Spirits, or maybe, Indian Rain. In the Southwest, where I've been a good deal, the Indian traditions make women have to do with the rain-fall. They were supposed to control it, somehow, and to be able to find springs, and make moisture come out of the earth. You see I'm trying to learn to paint what people think and feel; to get away from all that photographic stuff. When I look at you. I don't see what a camera would see, do I?"

"How can I tell?"

"Well, if I should paint you, I could make you understand what I see." For the second time that day Hedger crimsoned unexpectedly, and his eye fell and steadily contemplated a dish of little radishes. "That particular picture I got from a story a Mexican priest told me; he said he found it in an old manuscript book in a monastery down there, written by some Spanish Missionary, who got his stories from the Aztecs.

This one he called 'The Forty Lovers of the Queen,' and it was more or less about rain-making."

"Aren't you going to tell it to me?" Eden asked.

Hedger fumbled among the radishes. "I don't know if it's the proper kind of story to tell a girl."

She smiled; "Oh, forget about that! I've been balloon riding today. I like to hear you talk."

Her low voice was flattering. She had seemed like clay in his hands ever since they got on the boat to come home. He leaned back in his chair, forgot his food, and, looking at her intently, began to tell his story, the theme of which he somehow felt was dangerous tonight.

The tale began, he said, somewhere in Ancient Mexico, and concerned the daughter of a king. The birth of this Princess was preceded by unusual portents. Three times her mother dreamed that she was delivered of serpents, which betokened that the child she carried would have power with the rain gods. The serpent was the symbol of water. The Princess grew up dedicated to the gods, and wise men taught her the rain-making mysteries. She was with difficulty restrained from men and was guarded at all times, for it was the law of the Thunder that she be maiden until her marriage. In the years of her adolescence, rain was abundant with her people. The oldest man could not remember such fertility. When the Princess had counted eighteen summers, her father went to drive out a war party that harried his borders on the north and troubled his prosperity. The King destroyed the invaders and brought home many prisoners. Among the prisoners was a young chief, taller than any of his captors, of such strength and ferocity that the King's people came a day's journey to look at him. When the Princess beheld his great stature, and saw that his arms and breast were covered with the figures of wild animals, bitten into the skin and coloured, she begged his life from her father. She desired that he should practise his art upon her, and prick upon her skin the signs of Rain and Lightning and Thunder, and stain the wounds with herb-juices, as they were upon his own body. For many days, upon the roof of the King's house, the Princess submitted herself to the bone needle, and the women with her marvelled at her fortitude. But the Princess was without shame before the Captive, and it came about that he threw from him his needles and his stains, and fell upon the Princess to violate her honour; and her women ran down from the roof screaming, to call the guard which stood at the gateway of the King's house, and none stayed to protect their mistress. When the guard came, the Captive was thrown into bonds, and he was gelded, and his tongue was torn out, and he was given for a slave to the Rain Princess.

The country of the Aztecs to the east was tormented by thirst, and their king, hearing much of the rain-making arts of the Princess, sent an embassy to her father, with presents and an offer of marriage. So the Princess went from her father to be the Queen of the Aztecs, and she took with her the Captive, who served her in everything with entire fidelity and slept upon a mat before her door.

The King gave his bride a fortress on the outskirts of the city, whither she retired to entreat the rain gods. This fortress was called the Queen's House, and on the night of the new moon the Queen came to it from the palace. But when the moon waxed and grew toward the round, because the god of Thunder had had his will of her, then the Queen returned to the King. Drouth abated in the country and rain fell abundantly by reason of the Queen's power with the stars.

When the Queen went to her own house she took with her no servant but the Captive, and he slept outside her door and brought her food after she had fasted. The Queen had a jewel of great value, a turquoise that had fallen from the sun, and had the image of the sun upon it. And when she desired a young man whom she had seen in the army or among the slaves, she sent the Captive to him with the jewel, for a sign that he should come to her secretly at the Queen's House upon business concerning the welfare of all. And some, after she had talked with them, she sent away with rewards; and some she took into her chamber and kept them by her for one night or two. Afterward she called the Captive and bade him conduct the youth by the secret way he had gone, underneath the chambers of the fortress. But for the going away of the Queen's lovers the Captive took out the bar that was beneath a stone in the floor of the passage, and put in its stead a rush-reed, and the young stepped upon it and fell through into a cavern that was the bed of an underground river, and whatever was thrown into it was not seen again. In this service nor in any other did the Captive fail the Queen.

But when the Queen sent for the Captain of the Archers, she detained him four days in her chamber, calling often for food and wine, and was greatly content with him. On the fourth day she went to the Captain outside her door and said "Tomorrow take this man up by the sure way, by which the King comes, and let him live."

In the Queen's door were arrows, purple and white. When she desired the King to come to her publicly, with his guard, she sent him a white arrow; but when she sent the purple, he came secretly, and covered himself with his mantle to be hidden from the stone gods at the gate. On the fifth night that the Queen was with her lover, the Captive took a purple arrow to the King, and the King came secretly and found them together. He killed the Captain with his own hand, but the Queen he brought to public trial. The Captive, when he was put to the question, told on his fingers forty men that he had let through the underground passage into the river. The Captive and the Queen were put to death by fire, both on the same day, and afterward there was scarcity of rain.

Eden Bower sat shivering a little as she listened. Hedger was not trying to please her, she thought, but to antagonize and frighten her by his brutal story. She had often told herself that his lean, big-boned lower jaw was like his bull-dog's, but tonight his face made Caesar's most savage and determined expression seem an affectation. Now she was looking at the man he really was. Nobody's eyes had ever defied her like this. They were searching her and seeing everything; all she had concealed from Livingston, and from the millionaire and his friends, and from the newspaper man. He was testing her, trying her out, and she was more ill at ease than she wished to show.

"That's quite a thrilling story," she said at last, rising and winding her scarf about her throat. "It must be getting late. Almost every one has gone."

They walked down the Avenue like people who have quarrelled, or who wish to get rid of each other. Hedger did not take her arm at the street crossings, and they did not linger in the Square. At her door he tried none of the old devices of the

Livingston boys. He stood like a post, having forgotten to take off his hat, gave her a harsh, threatening glance, muttered "goodnight," and shut his own door noisily.

There was no question of sleep for Eden Bower. Her brain was working like a machine that would never stop. After she undressed, she tried to calm her nerves by smoking a cigarette, lying on the divan by the open window. But she grew wider and wider awake, combating the challenge that had flamed all evening in Hedger's eyes. The balloon had been one kind of excitement, the wine another; but the thing that had roused her, as a blow rouses a proud man, was the doubt, the contempt, the sneering hostility with which the painter had looked at her when he told his savage story. Crowds and balloons were all very well, she reflected, but woman's chief adventure is man. With a mind over active and a sense of life over strong, she wanted to walk across the roofs in the starlight, to sail over the sea and face at once a world of which she had never been afraid.

Hedger must be asleep; his dog had stopped sniffing under the double doors. Eden put on her wrapper and slippers and stole softly down the hall over the old carpet; one loose board creaked just as she reached the ladder. The trapdoor was open, as always on hot nights. When she stepped out on the roof she drew a long breath and walked across it, looking up at the sky. Her foot touched something soft; she heard a low growl, and on the instant Caesar's sharp little teeth caught her ankle and waited. His breath was like steam on her leg. Nobody had ever intruded upon his roof before, and he panted for the movement or the word that would let him spring his jaw. Instead, Hedger's hand seized his throat.

"Wait a minute. I'll settle with him," he said grimly. He dragged the dog toward the manhole and disappeared. When he came back, he found Eden standing over by the dark chimney, looking away in an offended attitude.

"I caned him unmercifully," he panted. "Of course you didn't hear anything; he never whines when I beat him. He didn't nip you, did he?"

"I don't know whether he broke the skin or not," she answered aggrievedly, still looking off into the west.

"If I were one of your friends in white pants, I'd strike a match to find whether you were hurt, though I know you are not, and then I'd see your ankle, wouldn't I?"

"I suppose so."

He shook his head and stood with his hands in the pockets of his old painting jacket. "I'm not up to such boy-tricks. If you want the place to yourself, I'll clear out. There are plenty of places where I can spend the night, what's left of it. But if you stay here and I stay here—" He shrugged his shoulders.

Eden did not stir, and she made no reply. Her head drooped slightly, as if she were considering. But the moment he put his arms about her they began to talk, both at once, as people do in an opera. The instant avowal brought out a flood of trivial admissions. Hedger confessed his crime, was reproached and forgiven, and now Eden knew what it was in his look that she had found so disturbing of late.

Standing against the black chimney, with the sky behind and blue shadows before, they looked like one of Hedger's own paintings of the period; two figures, one white and one dark, and nothing whatever distinguishable about them but that they were male and female. The faces were lost, the contours blurred in shadow, but the figures were a man and a woman, and that was their whole concern and their mysterious beauty,—it was the rhythm in which they moved, at last, along the roof and down into the dark hole; he first, drawing her gently after him. She came down very slowly. The excitement and bravado and uncertainty of that long day and night seemed all at once to tell upon her. When his feet were on the carpet and he reached up to lift her down, she twined her arms about his neck as after a long separation, and turned her face to him, and her lips, with their perfume of youth and passion.

One Saturday afternoon Hedger was sitting in the window of Eden's music room. They had been watching the pigeons come wheeling over the roofs from their unknown feeding grounds.

"Why," said Eden suddenly, "don't we fix those big doors into your study so they will open? Then, if I want you, I won't have to go through the hall. That illustrator is loafing about a good deal of late."

"I'll open them, if you wish. The bolt is on your side."

"Isn't there one on yours, too?"

"No. I believe a man lived there for years before I came in, and the nurse used to have these rooms herself. Naturally, the lock was on the lady's side."

Eden laughed and began to examine the bolt. "It's all stuck up with paint." Looking about, her eye lighted upon a bronze Buddha which was one of the nurse's treasures. Taking him by his head, she struck the bolt a blow with his squatting posteriors. The two doors creaked, sagged, and swung weakly inward a little way, as if they were too old for such escapades. Eden tossed the heavy idol into a stuffed chair. "That's better," she exclaimed exultantly. "So the bolts are always on the lady's side? What a lot society takes for granted!"

Hedger laughed, sprang up and caught her arms roughly. "Whoever takes you for granted—Did anybody, ever?"

"Everybody does. That's why I'm here. You are the only one who knows anything about me. Now I'll have to dress if we're going out for dinner."

He lingered, keeping his hold on her. "But I won't always be the only one, Eden Bower. I won't be the last."

"No, I suppose not," she said carelessly. "But what does that matter? You are the first."

As a long, despairing whine broke in the warm stillness, they drew apart. Caesar, lying on his bed in the dark corner, had lifted his head at this invasion of sunlight, and realized that the side of his room was broken open, and his whole world shattered by change. There stood his master and this woman, laughing at him! The woman was pulling the long black hair of this mightiest of men, who bowed his head and permitted it.

VI

In time they quarrelled, of course, and about an abstraction,—as young people often do, as mature people almost never do. Eden came in late one afternoon. She had been with some of her musical friends to lunch at Burton Ives' studio, and she began telling Hedger about its splendours. He listened a moment and then threw down his brushes. "I know exactly what it's like," he said impatiently. "A very good department-store conception of a studio. It's one of the show places."

"Well, it's gorgeous, and he said I could bring you to see him. The boys tell me he's awfully kind about giving people a lift, and you might get something out of it."

Hedger started up and pushed his canvas out of the way. "What could I possibly get from Burton Ives? He's almost the worst painter in the world; the stupidest, I mean."

Eden was annoyed. Burton Ives had been very nice to her and had begged her to sit for him. "You must admit that he's a very successful one," she said coldly.

"Of course he is! Anybody can be successful who will do that sort of thing. I wouldn't paint his pictures for all the money in New York."

"Well, I saw a lot of them, and I think they are beautiful."

Hedger bowed stiffly.

"What's the use of being a great painter if nobody knows about you?" Eden went on persuasively. "Why don't you paint the kind of pictures people can understand, and then, after you're successful, do whatever you like?"

"As I look at it," said Hedger brusquely, "I am successful."

Eden glanced about. "Well, I don't see any evidences of it," she said, biting her lip. "He has a Japanese servant and a wine cellar, and keeps a riding horse."

Hedger melted a little. "My dear, I have the most expensive luxury in the world, and I am much more extravagant than Burton Ives, for I work to please nobody but myself."

"You mean you could make money and don't? That you don't try to get a public?"

"Exactly. A public only wants what has been done over and over. I'm painting for painters,—who haven't been born."

"What would you do if I brought Mr. Ives down here to see your things?"

"Well, for God's sake, don't! Before he left I'd probably tell him what I thought of him."

Eden rose. "I give you up. You know very well there's only one kind of success that's real."

"Yes, but it's not the kind you mean. So you've been thinking me a scrub painter, who needs a helping hand from some fashionable studio man? What the devil have you had anything to do with me for, then?"

"There's no use talking to you," said Eden walking slowly toward the door. "I've been trying to pull wires for you all afternoon, and this is what it comes to." She had expected that the tidings of a prospective call from the great man would be received very differently, and had been thinking as she came home in the stage how, as with a magic wand, she might gild Hedger's future, float him out of his dark hole on a tide of prosperity, see his name in the papers and his pictures in the windows on Fifth Avenue.

Hedger mechanically snapped the midsummer leash on Caesar's collar and they ran downstairs and hurried through Sullivan Street off toward the river. He wanted to be among rough, honest people, to get down where the big drays bumped over stone paving blocks and the men wore corduroy trowsers and kept their shirts open at the neck. He stopped for a drink in one of the sagging bar-rooms on the water front. He had never in his life been so deeply wounded; he did not know he could be so hurt. He had told this girl all his secrets. On the roof, in these warm, heavy summer nights, with her hands locked in his, he had been able to explain all his misty ideas about an unborn art the world was waiting for; had been able to explain them better than he had ever done to himself. And she had looked away to the chattels of this uptown studio and coveted them for him! To her he was only an unsuccessful Burton Ives.

Then why, as he had put it to her, did she take up with him? Young, beautiful, talented as she was, why had she wasted herself on a scrub? Pity? Hardly; she wasn't sentimental. There was no explaining her. But in this passion that had seemed so fearless and so fated to be, his own position now looked to him ridiculous; a poor dauber without money or fame,—it was her caprice to load him with favours. Hedger ground his teeth so loud that his dog, trotting beside him, heard him and looked up.

While they were having supper at the oysterman's, he planned his escape. Whenever he saw her again, everything he had told her, that he should never have told any one, would come back to him; ideas he had never whispered even to the painter whom he worshipped and had gone all the way to France to see. To her they must seem his apology for not having horses and a valet, or merely the puerile boastfulness of a weak man. Yet if she slipped the bolt tonight and came through the doors and said, "Oh, weak man, I belong to you!" what could he do? That was the danger. He would catch the train out to Long Beach tonight, and tomorrow he would go onto the north end of Long Island, where an old friend of his had a summer studio among the sand dunes. He would stay until things came right in his mind. And she could find a smart painter, or take her punishment.

When he went home, Eden's room was dark; she was dining out somewhere. He threw his things into a hold-all he had carried about the world with him, strapped up some colours and canvases, and ran downstairs.

VII

Five days later Hedger was a restless passenger on a dirty, crowded Sunday train, coming back to town. Of course he saw now how unreasonable he had been in expecting a Huntington girl to know anything about pictures; here was a whole continent full of people who knew nothing about pictures and he didn't hold it against them. What had such things to do with him and Eden Bower? When he lay out on the dunes, watching the moon come up out of the sea, it had seemed to him that there was no wonder in the world like the wonder of Eden Bower. He was going back to her because she was older than art, because she was the most overwhelming thing that had ever come into his life.

He had written her yesterday, begging her to be at home this evening, telling her that he was contrite, and wretched enough.

Now that he was on his way to her, his stronger feeling unaccountably changed to a mood that was playful and tender. He wanted to share everything with her, even the most trivial things. He wanted to tell her about the people on the train, coming back tired from their holiday with bunches of wilted flowers and dirty daisies; to tell her that the fish-man, to whom she had often sent him for lobsters, was among the passengers, disguised in a silk shirt and a spotted tie, and how his wife looked exactly like a fish, even to her eyes, on which cataracts were forming. He could tell her, too, that he hadn't as much as unstrapped his canvases,—that ought to convince her.

In those days passengers from Long Island came into New York by ferry. Hedger had to be quick about getting his dog out of the express car in order to catch the first boat. The East River, and the bridges, and the city to the west, were burning in the conflagration of the sunset; there was that great homecoming reach of evening in the air.

The car changes from Thirty-fourth Street were too many and too perplexing; for the first time in his life Hedger took a hansom cab for Washington Square. Caesar sat bolt upright on the worn leather cushion beside him, and they jogged off, looking down on the rest of the world.

It was twilight when they drove down lower Fifth Avenue into the Square, and through the Arch behind them were the two long rows of pale violet lights that used to bloom so beautifully against the grey stone and asphalt. Here and yonder about the Square hung globes that shed a radiance not unlike the blue mists of evening, emerging softly when daylight died, as the stars emerged in the thin blue sky. Under them the sharp shadows of the trees fell on the cracked pavement and the sleeping grass. The first stars and the first lights were growing silver against the gradual darkening, when Hedger paid his driver and went into the house,—which, thank God, was still there! On the hall table lay his letter of yesterday, unopened.

He went upstairs with every sort of fear and every sort of hope clutching at his heart; it was as if tigers were tearing him. Why was there no gas burning in the top hall? He found matches and the gas bracket. He knocked, but got no answer; nobody was there. Before his own door were exactly five bottles of milk, standing in a row. The milk-boy had taken spiteful pleasure in thus reminding him that he forgot to stop his order.

Hedger went down to the basement; it, too, was dark. The janitress was taking her evening airing on the basement steps. She sat waving a palm-leaf fan majestically, her dirty calico dress open at the neck. She told him at once that there had been "changes." Miss Bower's room was to let again, and the piano would go tomorrow. Yes, she left yesterday, she sailed for Europe with friends from Chicago. They arrived on Friday, heralded by many telegrams. Very rich people they were said to be, though the man had refused to pay the nurse a month's rent in lieu of notice,—which would have been only right, as the young lady had agreed to take the rooms until October. Mrs. Foley had observed, too, that he didn't overpay her or Willy for their trouble, and a great deal of trouble they had been put to, certainly. Yes, the young lady was very pleasant, but the nurse said there were rings on the mahogany table where she had put tumblers and wine glasses. It was just as well she was gone. The Chicago man was uppish in his ways, but not much to look at. She supposed he had poor health, for there was nothing to him inside his clothes.

Hedger went slowly up the stairs—never had they seemed so long, or his legs so heavy. The upper floor was emptiness and silence. He unlocked his room, lit the gas, and opened the windows. When he went to put his coat in the closet, he found, hanging among his clothes, a pale, flesh-tinted dressing gown he had liked to see her wear, with a perfume—oh, a perfume that was still Eden Bower! He shut the door behind him and there, in the dark, for a moment he lost his manliness. It was when he held this garment to him that he found a letter in the pocket.

The note was written with a lead pencil, in haste: She was sorry that he was angry, but she still didn't know just what she had done. She had thought Mr. Ives would be useful to him; she guessed he was too proud. She wanted awfully to see him again, but Fate came knocking at her door after he had left her. She believed in Fate. She would never forget him, and she knew he would become the greatest painter in the world. Now she must pack. She hoped he wouldn't mind her leaving the dressing gown; somehow, she could never wear it again.

After Hedger read this, standing under the gas, he went back into the closet and knelt down before the wall; the knot hole had been plugged up with a ball of wet paper,—the same blue note-paper on which her letter was written.

He was hard hit. Tonight he had to bear the loneliness of a whole lifetime. Knowing himself so well, he could hardly believe that such a thing had ever happened to him, that such a woman had lain happy and contented in his arms. And now it was over. He turned out the light and sat down on his painter's stool before the big window. Caesar, on the floor beside him, rested his head on his master's knee. We must leave Hedger thus, sitting in his tank with his dog, looking up at the stars.

COMING, APHRODITE! This legend, in electric lights over the Lexington Opera House, had long announced the return of Eden Bower to New York after years of spectacular success in Paris. She came at last, under the management of an American Opera Company, but bringing her own *chef d'orchestre*.

One bright December afternoon Eden Bower was going down Fifth Avenue in her car, on the way to her broker, in Williams Street. Her thoughts were entirely upon stocks,—Cerro de Pasco, and how much she should buy of it,—when she suddenly looked up and realized that she was skirting Washington Square. She had not seen the place since she rolled out of it in an old-fashioned four-wheeler to seek her fortune, eighteen years ago.

"*Arrêtez, Alphonse. Attendez moi,*" she called, and opened the door before he could reach it. The children who were streaking over the asphalt on roller skates saw a lady in a long fur coat, and short, high-heeled shoes, alight from a French car and pace slowly about the Square, holding her muff to her chin. This spot, at least, had changed very little, she reflected; the same trees, the same fountain, the white arch, and over yonder, Garibaldi, drawing the sword for freedom. There, just opposite her, was the old red brick house.

"Yes, that is the place," she was thinking. "I can smell the carpets now, and the dog,—what was his name? That grubby bathroom at the end of the hall, and that dreadful Hedger—still, there was something about him, you know—" She glanced up and blinked against the sun. From somewhere in the crowded quarter south of the Square a flock of pigeons rose, wheeling quickly upward into the brilliant blue sky. She threw back her head, pressed her muff closer to her chin, and watched them with a smile of amazement and delight. So they still rose, out of all that dirt and noise and squalor, fleet and silvery, just as they used to rise that summer when she was twenty and went up in a balloon on Coney Island!

Alphonse opened the door and tucked her robes about her. All the way down town her mind wandered from Cerro de Pasco, and she kept smiling and looking up at the sky.

When she had finished her business with the broker, she asked him to look in the telephone book for the address of M. Gaston Jules, the picture dealer, and slipped the paper on which he wrote it into her glove. It was five o'clock when she reached the French Galleries, as they were called. On entering she gave the attendant her card, asking him to take it to M. Jules. The dealer appeared very promptly and begged her to come into his private office, where he pushed a great chair toward his desk for her and signalled his secretary to leave the room.

"How good your lighting is in here," she observed, glancing about. "I met you at Simon's studio, didn't I? Oh, no! I never forget anybody who interests me." She threw her muff on his writing table and sank into the deep chair. "I have come to you for some information that's not in my line. Do you know anything about an American painter named Hedger?"

He took the seat opposite her. "Don Hedger? But, certainly! There are some very interesting things of his in an exhibition at V——'s. If you would care to—"

She held up her hand. "No, no. I've no time to go to exhibitions. Is he a man of importance?"

"Certainly. He is one of the first men among the moderns. That is to say, among the very moderns. He is always coming up with something different. He often exhibits in Paris, you must have seen—"

"No, I tell you I don't go to exhibitions. Has he had great success? That is what I want to know."

M. Jules pulled at his short grey moustache. "But, Madame, there are many kinds of success," he began cautiously.

Madame gave a dry laugh. "Yes, so he used to say. We once quarrelled on that issue. And how would you define his particular kind?"

M. Jules grew thoughtful. "He is a great name with all the young men, and he is decidedly an influence in art. But one can't definitely place a man who is original, erratic, and who is changing all the time."

She cut him short. "Is he much talked about at home? In Paris, I mean? Thanks. That's all I want to know." She rose and began buttoning her coat. "One doesn't like to have been an utter fool, even at twenty."

"Mais, non!" M. Jules handed her her muff with a quick, sympathetic glance. He followed her out through the carpeted show-room, now closed to the public and draped in cheesecloth, and put her into her car with words appreciative of the honour she had done him in calling.

Leaning back in the cushions, Eden Bower closed her eyes, and her face, as the street lamps flashed their ugly orange light upon it, became hard and settled, like a plaster cast; so a sail, that has been filled by a strong breeze, behaves when the wind suddenly dies. Tomorrow night the wind would blow again, and this mask would be the golden face of Aphrodite. But a "big" career takes its toll, even with the best of luck.

Susan Glaspell 1876–1948

Susan Glaspell was born in Davenport, Iowa. Her father's family was among the first settlers of that region and from him she learned to cherish the independence, integrity, idealism, and practicality of her pioneer ancestry, and to emphasize these values in her art. After being graduated from Drake University in 1899, she worked for two years as a reporter for the *Des Moines Daily News,* finding in the everyday details of midwestern life the materials for the short stories she began to publish in the ladies' magazines of the period. Her early stories were in the local color tradition. Like other local colorists, such as Zona Gale and Mary French, Susan Glaspell wanted to preserve in her art those special qualities of place, speech, and thought that made her region unique. Resisting the homogenization of American life brought on by the railroad and the growing urban-industrial expansion, these writers depicted a native son or daughter renewed by an association with the land, finding a bond between man and nature that echoed the earlier pastoral dream of the nineteenth century.

In 1907 Susan Glaspell met George Cram Cook, who was also born and raised in Davenport, but, unlike her, Cook revolted against the provincialism he saw in Davenport and against the "medieval-romantic" views of writers like Glaspell. Cook helped her discover a literary tradition that treated contemporary issues in realistic terms. At the same time, he strengthened her own idealism with his vision of a classical revival in America, where, especially in the theater, all the arts would come together in a single creative totality. In her full-length plays, a few short stories, and in the novels she wrote in the 1930s and 1940s, she creates modern "pioneers," who make for themselves new frontiers of feeling, thinking, and living, often at considerable cost, both financial and psychological, to themselves.

Susan Glaspell married Cook in 1913 and moved to Provincetown, Massachusetts, where in 1915 they put on a few one-act plays in a makeshift theater. Under "Jig" Cook's inspired leadership, they continued to write and produce plays that winter in New York, and soon established the Playwright's Theatre, or, as they came to be called, the Provincetown Players. Between 1916 and 1922 the Provincetown Players was the leading force in causing a revolution in American theater. In contrast to other little theaters in New York at that time, Cook insisted that the Provincetown produce only original plays written by American playwrights, and, in time, they proved that a tiny, experimental theater, dedicated to native dramatists, could succeed, and that the theater audience was ready for serious plays of ideas. Along with Eugene O'Neill, Susan Glaspell was the Provincetown's most important and prolific playwright. She wrote about the new woman striving to fulfill her dreams in a hostile and insensitive world; she treated psychoanalysis when it was still new in this country; she depicted the little magazine, the bohemian, the war's effect on minorities, and the tragedy of the isolated midwestern farm-wife. She brought together European expressionism with American realism, showing an extraordinary diversity of dramatic techniques. In the seven one-acts and three full-length plays she wrote for the Provincetown, she created an original dramatic voice that spoke to the American audience in a new way about contemporary concerns.

After Cook's death in Greece in 1922, Susan Glaspell returned to Cape Cod where she lived until her death in 1948. In 1930 she wrote *Alison's House,* a play based on the life of Emily Dickinson, which won the Pulitzer Prize for drama in 1931. Whereas the fiction she wrote before and after the Provincetown years exemplifies an established and conservative literary tradition, her plays fostered new forms of dramatic expression and helped bring about a radical shift in the direction of American drama. Thus, her novels are rarely read today, but her plays still speak to audiences the world over.

Arthur Waterman
Georgia State University

PRIMARY WORKS

Plays, 1920; *Plays by Sudsan Glaspell,* ed. C. W. E. Bigsby, 1987; *Inheritors,* 1921; *The Verge,* 1922; *Alison's House,* 1930; *Ambrose Holt and Family,* 1931; *Judd Rankin's Daughter,* 1945.

Trifles[1]

SCENE. *The kitchen in the now abandoned farmhouse of* JOHN WRIGHT, *a gloomy kitchen, and left without having been put in order—unwashed pans under the sink, a loaf of bread outside the bread-box, a dish-towel on the table—other signs of incompleted work. At the rear the outer door opens and the* SHERIFF *comes in followed by the* COUNTY ATTORNEY *and* HALE. *The* SHERIFF *and* HALE *are men in middle life, the* COUNTY ATTORNEY *is a young man; all are much bundled up and go at once to the stove. They are followed by the two women—the* SHERIFF'S *wife first; she is a slight wiry woman, a thin nervous face.* MRS. HALE *is larger and would ordinarily be called more comfortable looking, but she is disturbed now and looks fearfully about as she enters. The women have come in slowly, and stand close together near the door.*

COUNTY ATTORNEY [*Rubbing his hands.*] This feels good. Come up to the fire, ladies.

MRS. PETERS [*After taking a step forward.*] I'm not—cold.

SHERIFF [*Unbuttoning his overcoat and stepping away from the stove as if to mark the beginning of official business.*] Now, Mr. Hale, before we move things about, you explain to Mr. Henderson just what you saw when you came here yesterday morning.

COUNTY ATTORNEY By the way, has anything been moved? Are things just as you left them yesterday?

SHERIFF [*Looking about.*] It's just the same. When it dropped below zero last night I thought I'd better send Frank out this morning to make a fire for us—no use getting pneumonia with a big case on, but I told him not to touch anything except the stove—and you know Frank.

COUNTY ATTORNEY Somebody should have been left here yesterday.

SHERIFF Oh—yesterday. When I had to send Frank to Morris Center for that man who went crazy—I want you to know I had my hands full yesterday. I knew you could get back from Omaha by today and as long as I went over everything here myself—

COUNTY ATTORNEY Well, Mr. Hale, tell just what happened when you came here yesterday morning.

HALE Harry and I had started to town with a load of potatoes. We came along the road from my place and as I got here I said, "I'm going to see if I can't get John Wright to go in with me on a party telephone." I spoke to Wright about it once be-

[1]First performed by the Provincetown Players in Provincetown, Mass., August 8, 1916. Rewritten as a short story, "Jury of Her Peers," and first published in *Everyweek,* March 5, 1917.

fore and he put me off, saying folks talked too much anyway, and all he asked was peace and quiet—I guess you know about how much he talked himself; but I thought maybe if I went to the house and talked about it before his wife, though I said to Harry that I didn't know as what his wife wanted made much difference to John—

COUNTY ATTORNEY Let's talk about that later, Mr. Hale. I do want to talk about that, but tell now just what happened when you got to the house.

HALE I didn't hear or see anything; I knocked at the door, and still it was all quiet inside. I knew they must be up, it was past eight o'clock. So I knocked again, and I thought I heard somebody say, "Come in." I wasn't sure, I'm not sure yet, but I opened the door—this door [*indicating the door by which the two women are still standing*] and there in that rocker—[*pointing to it*] sat Mrs. Wright.

[*They all look at the rocker.*]

COUNTY ATTORNEY What—was she doing?

HALE She was rockin' back and forth. She had her apron in her hand and was kind of—pleating it.

COUNTY ATTORNEY And how did she—look?

HALE Well, she looked queer.

COUNTY ATTORNEY How do you mean—queer?

HALE Well, as if she didn't know what she was going to do next. And kind of done up.

COUNTY ATTORNEY How did she seem to feel about your coming?

HALE Why, I don't think she minded—one way or other. She didn't pay much attention. I said, "How do, Mrs. Wright, it's cold, ain't it?" And she said, "Is it?"—and went on kind of pleating at her apron. Well, I was surprised; she didn't ask me to come up to the stove, or to set down, but just sat there, not even looking at me, so I said, "I want to see John." And then she—laughed. I guess you would call it a laugh. I thought of Harry and the team outside, so I said a little sharp: "Can't I see John?" "No," she says, kind o' dull like. "Ain't he home?" says I. "Yes," says she, "he's home." "Then why can't I see him?" I asked her, out of patience. "'Cause he's dead," says she. *"Dead?"* says I. She just nodded her head, not getting a bit excited, but rockin' back and forth. "Why—where is he?" says I, not knowing what to say. She just pointed upstairs—like that [*himself pointing to the room above*]. I got up, with the idea of going up there. I walked from there to here—then I says, "Why, what did he die of?" "He died of a rope round his neck," says she, and just went on pleatin' at her apron. Well, I went out and called Harry. I thought I might—need help. We went upstairs and there he was lyin'—

COUNTY ATTORNEY I think I'd rather have you go into that upstairs, where you can point it all out. Just go on now with the rest of the story.

HALE Well, my first thought was to get that rope off. It looked . . . [*Stops, his face twitches*] . . . but Harry, he went up to him, and he said, "No, he's dead all right, and we'd better not touch anything." So we went back downstairs. She was still sitting that same way. "Has anybody been notified?" I asked. "No," says she, unconcerned. "Who did this, Mrs. Wright?" said Harry. He said it business-like—and she stopped pleatin' of her apron. "I don't know," she says. "You don't *know?*" says Harry. "No," says she. "Weren't you sleepin' in the bed with him?" says Harry. "Yes," says she, "but I was on the inside." "Somebody slipped a rope round his neck and strangled him and you didn't wake up?" says Harry. "I didn't wake up," she said after him. We must 'a looked as if we didn't see how that could be, for after a minute she said, "I sleep sound." Harry was going to ask her more questions but I said maybe we ought to let her tell her story first to the coroner, or the sheriff, so Harry went fast as he could to Rivers' place, where there's a telephone.

COUNTY ATTORNEY And what did Mrs. Wright do when she knew that you had gone for the coroner?

HALE She moved from that chair to this one over here [*Pointing to a small chair in the corner*] and just sat there with her hands held together and looking down. I got a feeling that I ought to make some conversation, so I said I had come in to see if John wanted to put in a telephone, and at that she started to laugh, and then she stopped and looked at me—scared. [*The* County Attorney, *who has had his notebook out, makes a note.*] I dunno, maybe it wasn't scared. I wouldn't like to say it was. Soon Harry got back, and then Dr. Lloyd came, and you, Mr. Peters, and so I guess that's all I know that you don't.

COUNTY ATTORNEY [*Looking around.*] I guess we'll go upstairs first—and then out to the barn and around there. [*To the* Sheriff.] You're convinced that there was nothing important here—nothing that would point to any motive.

SHERIFF Nothing here but kitchen things.

[*The* County Attorney, *after again looking around the kitchen, opens the door of a cupboard closet. He gets up on a chair and looks on a shelf. Pulls his hand away, sticky.*]

COUNTY ATTORNEY Here's a nice mess.

[*The women draw nearer.*]

MRS. PETERS [*To the other woman.*] Oh, her fruit; it did freeze. [*To the* Lawyer.] She worried about that when it turned so cold. She said the fire'd go out and her jars would break.

SHERIFF Well, can you beat the women! Held for murder and worryin' about her preserves.

COUNTY ATTORNEY I guess before we're through she may have something more serious than preserves to worry about.

HALE Well, women are used to worrying over trifles.

[*The two women move a little closer together.*]

COUNTY ATTORNEY [*With the gallantry of a young politician.*] And yet, for all their worries, what would we do without the ladies? [*The women do not unbend. He goes to the sink, takes a dipperful of water from the pail and pouring it into a basin, washes his hands. Starts to wipe them on the roller-towel, turns it for a cleaner place.*] Dirty towels! [*Kicks his foot against the pans under the sink.*] Not much of a housekeeper, would you say, ladies?

MRS. HALE [*Stiffly.*] There's a great deal of work to be done on a farm.

COUNTY ATTORNEY To be sure. And yet [*With a little bow to her*] I know there are some Dickson county farmhouses which do not have such roller towels.

[*He gives it a pull to expose its full length again.*]

MRS. HALE Those towels get dirty awful quick. Men's hands aren't always as clean as they might be.

COUNTY ATTORNEY Ah, loyal to your sex, I see. But you and Mrs. Wright were neighbors. I suppose you were friends, too.

MRS. HALE [*Shaking her head.*] I've not seen much of her of late years. I've not been in this house—it's more than a year.

COUNTY ATTORNEY And why was that? You didn't like her?

MRS. HALE I liked her all well enough. Farmers' wives have their hands full, Mr. Henderson. And then—

COUNTY ATTORNEY Yes—?

MRS. HALE [*Looking about.*] It never seemed a very cheerful place.

COUNTY ATTORNEY No—it's not cheerful. I shouldn't say she had the homemaking instinct.

MRS. HALE Well, I don't know as Wright had, either.

COUNTY ATTORNEY You mean that they didn't get on very well?

MRS. HALE No, I don't mean anything. But I don't think a place'd be any cheerfuller for John Wright's being in it.

COUNTY ATTORNEY I'd like to talk more of that a little later. I want to get the lay of things upstairs now.

[*He goes to the left, where three steps lead to a stair door.*]

SHERIFF I suppose anything Mrs. Peters does'll be all right. She was to take in some clothes for her, you know, and a few little things. We left in such a hurry yesterday.

COUNTY ATTORNEY Yes, but I would like to see what you take, Mrs. Peters, and keep an eye out for anything that might be of use to us.

MRS. PETERS Yes, Mr. Henderson.

[*The women listen to the men's steps on the stairs, then look about the kitchen.*]

MRS. HALE I'd hate to have men coming into my kitchen, snooping around and criticising.

[*She arranges the pans under sink which the Lawyer had shoved out of place.*]

MRS. PETERS Of course it's no more than their duty.

MRS. HALE Duty's all right, but I guess that deputy sheriff that came out to make the fire might have got a little of this on. [*Gives the roller towel a pull.*] Wish I'd thought of that sooner. Seems mean to talk about her for not having things slicked up when she had to come away in such a hurry.

MRS. PETERS [*Who has gone to a small table in the left rear corner of the room, and lifted one end of a towel that covers a pan.*] She had bread set.

[*Stands still.*]

MRS. HALE [*Eyes fixed on a loaf of bread beside the breadbox, which is on a low shelf at the other side of the room. Moves slowly toward it.*] She was going to put this in there. [*Picks up loaf, then abruptly drops it. In a manner of returning to familiar things.*] It's a shame about her fruit. I wonder if it's all gone. [*Gets up on the chair and looks.*] I think there's some here that's all right, Mrs. Peters. Yes—here; [*Holding it toward the window*] this is cherries, too. [*Looking again.*] I declare I believe that's the only one. [*Gets down, bottle in her hand. Goes to the sink and wipes it off on the outside.*] She'll feel awful bad after all her hard work in the hot weather. I remember the afternoon I put up my cherries last summer.

[*She puts the bottle on the big kitchen table, center of the room. With a sigh, is about to sit down in the rocking-chair. Before she is seated realizes what chair it is; with a slow look at it, steps back. The chair which she has touched rocks back and forth.*]

MRS. PETERS Well, I must get those things from the front room closet. [*She goes to the door at the right, but after looking into the other room, steps back.*] You coming with me, Mrs. Hale? You could help me carry them.

[*They go in the other room; reappear,* MRS. PETERS *carrying a dress and skirt,* MRS. HALE *following with a pair of shoes.*]

MRS. PETERS My, it's cold in there.

[*She puts the clothes on the big table, and hurries to the stove.*]

MRS. HALE [*Examining the skirt.*] Wright was close.[2] I think maybe that's why she kept so much to herself. She didn't even belong to the Ladies Aid. I suppose she felt she couldn't do her part, and then you don't enjoy things when you feel shabby. She used to wear pretty clothes and be lively, when she was Minnie Foster, one of the town girls singing in the choir. But that—oh, that was thirty years ago. This all you was to take in?

MRS. PETERS She said she wanted an apron. Funny thing to want, for there isn't much to get you dirty in jail, goodness knows. But I suppose just to make her feel more natural. She said they was in the top drawer in this cupboard. Yes, here. And then her little shawl that always hung behind the door. [*Opens stair door and looks.*] Yes, here it is.

[*Quickly shuts door leading upstairs.*]

MRS. HALE [*Abruptly moving toward her.*] Mrs. Peters?

MRS. PETERS Yes, Mrs. Hale?

MRS. HALE Do you think she did it?

MRS. PETERS [*In a frightened voice.*] Oh, I don't know.

MRS. HALE Well, I don't think she did. Asking for an apron and her little shawl. Worrying about her fruit.

MRS. PETERS [*Starts to speak, glances up, where footsteps are heard in the room above. In a low voice.*] Mr. Peters says it looks bad for her. Mr. Henderson is awful sarcastic in a speech and he'll make fun of her sayin' she didn't wake up.

MRS. HALE Well, I guess John Wright didn't wake when they was slipping that rope under his neck.

MRS. PETERS No, it's strange. It must have been done awful crafty and still. They say it was such a—funny way to kill a man, rigging it all up like that.

MRS. HALE That's just what Mr. Hale said. There was a gun in the house. He says that's what he can't understand.

MRS. PETERS Mr. Henderson said coming out that what was needed for the case was a motive; something to show anger, or—sudden feeling.

MRS. HALE [*Who is standing by the table.*] Well, I don't see any signs of anger around here. [*She puts her hand on the dish towel which lies on the table, stands looking down at table, one half of which is clean, the other half messy.*] It's wiped to here.

[2]Not sociable, kept close to himself.

[*Makes a move as if to finish work, then turns and looks at loaf of bread outside the breadbox. Drops towel. In that voice of coming back to familiar things.*] Wonder how they are finding things upstairs. I hope she had it a little more red-up[3] up there. You know, it seems kind of *sneaking.* Locking her up in town and then coming out here and trying to get her own house to turn against her!

MRS. PETERS But Mrs. Hale, the law is the law.

MRS. HALE I s'pose 'tis. [*Unbuttoning her coat.*] Better loosen up your things, Mrs. Peters. You won't feel them when you go out.

[MRS. PETERS *takes off her fur tippet, goes to hang it on hook at back of room, stands looking at the under part of the small corner table.*]

MRS. PETERS She was piecing a quilt.

[*She brings the large sewing basket and they look at the bright pieces.*]

MRS. HALE It's log cabin pattern. Pretty, isn't it? I wonder if she was goin' to quilt it or just knot it?[4]

[*Footsteps have been heard coming down the stairs. The* SHERIFF *enters followed by* HALE *and the* COUNTY ATTORNEY.]

SHERIFF They wonder if she was going to quilt it or just knot it!

[*The men laugh, the women look abashed.*]

COUNTY ATTORNEY [*Rubbing his hands over the stove.*] Frank's fire didn't do much up there, did it? Well, let's go out to the barn and get that cleared up.

[*The men go outside.*]

MRS. HALE [*Resentfully.*] I don't know as there's anything so strange, our takin' up our time with little things while we're waiting for them to get the evidence. [*She sits down at the big table smoothing out a block with decision.*] I don't see as it's anything to laugh about.

MRS. PETERS [*Apologetically.*] Of course they've got awful important things on their minds.

[*Pulls up a chair and joins* MRS. HALE *at the table.*]

MRS. HALE [*Examining another block.*] Mrs. Peters, look at this one. Here, this is the one she was working on, and look at the sewing! All the rest of it has been so nice and even. And look at this! It's all over the place! Why, it looks as if she didn't know what she was about!

[*After she had said this they look at each other, then start to glance back at the door. After an instant* MRS. HALE *has pulled at a knot and ripped the sewing.*]

MRS. PETERS Oh, what are you doing, Mrs. Hale?

MRS. HALE [*Mildly.*] Just pulling out a stitch or two that's not sewed very good.

[3]Gotten ready, made-up.

[4]Different methods of connecting the parts of a quilt.

[*Threading a needle.*] Bad sewing always made me fidgety.

MRS. PETERS [*Nervously.*] I don't think we ought to touch things.

MRS. HALE I'll just finish up this end. [*Suddenly stopping and leaning forward.*] Mrs. Peters?

MRS. PETERS Yes, Mrs. Hale?

MRS. HALE What do you suppose she was so nervous about?

MRS. PETERS Oh—I don't know. I don't know as she was nervous. I sometimes sew awful queer when I'm just tired. [Mrs. Hale *starts to say something, looks at* Mrs. Peters, *then goes on sewing.*] Well I must get these things wrapped up. They may be through sooner than we think. [*Putting apron and other things together.*] I wonder where I can find a piece of paper, and string.

MRS. HALE In that cupboard, maybe.

MRS. PETERS [*Looking in cupboard.*] Why, here's a bird-cage. [*Holds it up.*] Did she have a bird, Mrs. Hale?

MRS. HALE Why, I don't know whether she did or not—I've not been here for so long. There was a man around last year selling canaries cheap, but I don't know as she took one; maybe she did. She used to sing real pretty herself.

MRS. PETERS [*Glancing around.*] Seems funny to think of a bird here. But she must have had one, or why would she have a cage? I wonder what happened to it.

MRS. HALE I s'pose maybe the cat got it.

MRS. PETERS No, she didn't have a cat. She's got that feeling some people have about cats—being afraid of them. My cat got in her room and she was real upset and asked me to take it out.

MRS. HALE My sister Bessie was like that. Queer, ain't it?

MRS. PETERS [*Examining the cage.*] Why, look at this door. It's broke. One hinge is pulled apart.

MRS. HALE [*Looking too.*] Looks as if someone must have been rough with it.

MRS. PETERS Why, yes.

[*She brings the cage forward and puts it on the table.*]

MRS. HALE I wish if they're going to find any evidence they'd be about it. I don't like this place.

MRS. PETERS But I'm awful glad you came with me, Mrs. Hale. It would be lonesome for me sitting here alone.

MRS. HALE It would, wouldn't it? [*Dropping her sewing.*] But I tell you what I do wish, Mrs. Peters. I wish I had come over sometimes when *she* was here. I—[*Looking around the room*]—wish I had.

MRS. PETERS But of course you were awful busy, Mrs. Hale—your house and your children.

MRS. HALE I could've come. I stayed away because it weren't cheerful—and that's why I ought to have come. I—I've never liked this place. Maybe because it's down in a hollow and you don't see the road. I dunno what it is, but it's a lonesome place and always was. I wish I had come over to see Minnie Foster sometimes. I can see now—

[*Shakes her head.*]

MRS. PETERS Well, you mustn't reproach yourself, Mrs. Hale. Somehow we just don't see how it is with other folks until—something comes up.

MRS. HALE Not having children makes less work—but it makes a quiet house, and

Wright out to work all day, and no company when he did come in. Did you know John Wright, Mrs. Peters?

MRS. PETERS Not to know him; I've seen him in town. They say he was a good man.

MRS. HALE Yes—good; he didn't drink, and kept his word as well as most, I guess, and paid his debts. But he was a hard man, Mrs. Peters. Just to pass the time of day with him—[*Shivers.*] Like a raw wind that gets to the bone. [*Pauses, her eye falling on the cage.*] I should think she would 'a wanted a bird. But what do you suppose went with it?

MRS. PETERS I don't know, unless it got sick and died.

[*She reaches over and swings the broken door, swings it again, both women watch it.*]

MRS. HALE You weren't raised round here, were you? [Mrs. Peters *shakes her head.*] You didn't know—her?

MRS. PETERS Not till they brought her yesterday.

MRS. HALE She—come to think of it, she was kind of like a bird herself—real sweet and pretty, but kind of timid and—fluttery. How—she—did—change. [*Silence; then as if struck by a happy thought and relieved to get back to every day things.*] Tell you what, Mrs. Peters, why don't you take the quilt in with you? It might take up her mind.

MRS. PETERS Why, I think that's a real nice idea, Mrs. Hale. There couldn't possibly be any objection to it, could there? Now, just what would I take? I wonder if her patches are in here—and her things.

[*They look in the sewing basket.*]

MRS. HALE Here's some red. I expect this has got sewing things in it. [*Brings out a fancy box.*] What a pretty box. Looks like something somebody would give you. Maybe her scissors are in here. [*Opens box. Suddenly puts her hand to her nose.*] Why—[Mrs. Peters *bends nearer, then turns her face away.*] There's something wrapped up in this piece of silk.

MRS. PETERS Why, this isn't her scissors.

MRS. HALE [*Lifting the silk.*] Oh, Mrs. Peters—its—

[MRS. PETERS *bends closer.*]

MRS. PETERS It's the bird.

MRS. HALE [*Jumping up.*] But, Mrs. Peters—look at it! It's [*sic*] neck! Look at its neck! It's all—other side *to.*

MRS. PETERS Somebody—wrung—its—neck.

[*Their eyes meet. A look of growing comprehension, of horror. Steps are heard outside.* MRS. HALE *slips box under quilt pieces, and sinks into her chair. Enter* SHERIFF *and* COUNTY ATTORNEY. MRS. PETERS *rises.*]

COUNTY ATTORNEY [*As one turning from serious things to little pleasantries.*] Well, ladies, have you decided whether she was going to quilt it or knot it?

MRS. PETERS We think she was going to—knot it.

COUNTY ATTORNEY Well, that's interesting, I'm sure. [*Seeing the birdcage.*] Has the bird flown?

MRS. HALE [*Putting more quilt pieces over the box.*] We think the—cat got it.

COUNTY ATTORNEY [*Preoccupied.*] Is there a cat?

[MRS. HALE *glances in a quick covert way at* MRS. PETERS.]

MRS. PETERS Well, not *now.* They're superstitious, you know. They leave.

COUNTY ATTORNEY [*To* Sheriff Peters, *continuing an interrupted conversation.*] No sign at all of anyone having come from the outside. Their own rope. Now let's go up again and go over it piece by piece. [*They start upstairs.*] It would have to have been someone who knew just the—

[MRS. PETERS *sits down. The two women sit there not looking at one another, but as if peering into something and at the same time holding back. When they talk now it is in the manner of feeling their way over strange ground, as if afraid of what they are saying, but as if they can not help saying it.*]

MRS. HALE She liked the bird. She was going to bury it in that pretty box.

MRS. PETERS [*In a whisper.*] When I was a girl—my kitten—there was a boy took a hatchet, and before my eyes—and before I could get there—[*Covers her face an instant.*] If they hadn't held me back I would have—[*Catches herself, looks upstairs where steps are heard, falters weakly*]—hurt him.

MRS. HALE [*With a slow look around her.*] I wonder how it would seem never to have had any children around. [*Pause.*] No, Wright wouldn't like the bird—a thing that sang. She used to sing. He killed that, too.

MRS. PETERS [*Moving uneasily.*] We don't know who killed the bird.

MRS. HALE I knew John Wright.

MRS. PETERS It was an awful thing was done in this house that night, Mrs. Hale. Killing a man while he slept, slipping a rope around his neck that choked the life out of him.

MRS. HALE His neck. Choked the life out of him.

[*Her hand goes out and rests on the bird-cage.*]

MRS. PETERS [*With rising voice.*] We don't know who killed him. We don't *know.*

MRS. HALE [*Her own feeling not interrupted.*] If there'd been years and years of nothing, then a bird to sing to you, it would be awful—still, after the bird was still.

MRS. PETERS [*Something within her speaking.*] I know what stillness is. When we homesteaded in Dakota, and my first baby died—after he was two years old, and me with no other then—

MRS. HALE [*Moving.*] How soon do you suppose they'll be through, looking for the evidence?

MRS. PETERS I know what stillness is. [*Pulling herself back.*] The law has got to punish crime, Mrs. Hale.

MRS. HALE [*Not as if answering that.*] I wish you'd seen Minnie Foster when she wore a white dress with blue ribbons and stood up there in the choir and sang. [*A look around the room.*] Oh, I *wish* I'd come over here once in a while! That was a crime! That was a crime! Who's going to punish that?

MRS. PETERS [*Looking upstairs.*] We mustn't—take on.

MRS. HALE I might have known she needed help! I know how things can be—for women. I tell you, it's queer, Mrs. Peters. We live close together and we live far apart. We all go through the same things—it's all just a different kind of the same thing. [*Brushes her eyes, noticing the bottle of fruit, reaches out for it.*] If I was you I wouldn't tell her her fruit was gone. Tell her it *ain't.* Tell her it's all right. Take this in to prove it to her. She—she may never know whether it was broke or not.

MRS. PETERS [*Takes the bottle, looks about for something to wrap it in; takes petticoat from the clothes brought from the other room, very nervously begins winding this around the bottle. In a false voice.*] My, it's a good thing the men couldn't hear us. Wouldn't they just laugh! Getting all stirred up over a little thing like a—dead canary. As if that could have anything to do with—with—wouldn't they *laugh!*

[*The men are heard coming down stairs.*]

MRS. HALE [*Under her breath.*] Maybe they would—maybe they wouldn't.

COUNTY ATTORNEY No, Peters, it's all perfectly clear except a reason for doing it. But you know juries when it comes to women. If there was some definite thing. Something to show—something to make a story about—a thing that would connect up with this strange way of doing it—

[*The women's eyes meet for an instant. Enter* HALE *from outer door.*]

HALE Well, I've got the team around. Pretty cold out there.

COUNTY ATTORNEY I'm going to stay here a while by myself. [*To the* Sheriff.] You can send Frank out for me, can't you? I want to go over everything. I'm not satisfied that we can't do better.

SHERIFF Do you want to see what Mrs. Peters is going to take in?

[*The* LAWYER *goes to the table, picks up the apron, laughs.*]

COUNTY ATTORNEY Oh, I guess they're not very dangerous things the ladies have picked out. [*Moves a few things about, disturbing the quilt pieces which cover the box. Steps back.*] No, Mrs. Peters doesn't need supervising. For that matter, a sheriff's wife is married to the law. Ever think of it that way, Mrs. Peters?

MRS. PETERS Not—just that way.

SHERIFF [*Chuckling.*] Married to the law. [*Moves toward the other room.*] I just want you to come in here a minute, George. We ought to take a look at these windows.

COUNTY ATTORNEY [*Scoffingly.*] Oh, windows!

SHERIFF We'll be right out, Mr. Hale.

[HALE *goes outside. The* SHERIFF *follows the* COUNTY ATTORNEY *into the other room. Then* MRS. HALE *rises, hands tight together, looking intensely at* MRS. PETERS, *whose eyes make a slow turn, finally meeting* MRS. HALE'S. *A moment* MRS. HALE *holds her, then her own eyes point the way to where the box is concealed. Suddenly* MRS. PETERS *throws back quilt pieces and tries to put the box in the bag she is wearing. It is too big. She opens box, starts to take bird out, cannot touch it, goes to pieces, stands there helpless. Sound of a knob turning in the other room. Mrs. Hale snatches the box and puts it in the pocket of her big coat. Enter* COUNTY ATTORNEY *and* SHERIFF.]

COUNTY ATTORNEY [*Facetiously.*] Well, Henry, at least we found out that she was not going to quilt it. She was going to—what is it you call it, ladies?

MRS. HALE [*Her hand against her pocket.*] We call it—knot it, Mr. Henderson.

(CURTAIN)

1917

Robinson Jeffers 1887–1962

With the publication of *Tamar* (1924), Robinson Jeffers turned from the derivative versifying of his earlier volumes, *Flagons and Apples* and *Californians,* to themes and presentation that won him an enthusiastic audience. The intensity of the long narratives he then began to write contrasted strikingly not only with his early poetry but also with that of other poets. Jeffers described briefly his misgivings about the direction of the poetry of the 1920s. Without originality, he said, a poet was only a verse-writer. Some of his contemporaries were pursuing originality by "divorcing poetry from reason and ideas, bringing it nearer to music. . . ." But, he demurred, "renouncing intelligibility in order to concentrate on the music of poetry [the modern poet], had turned off the road into a narrowing lane. . . . ideas had gone, now meter had gone, imagery would have to go; then recognizable emotions would have to go. . . ." To make an advance in poetry, a poet would need "emotions or ideas, or a point of view, or even mere rhythms, that had not occurred to [his contemporaries]."

To this plan to be "original," Jeffers brought enormous learning in literature, religion, philosophy, languages, myth, and sciences. His father, a professor of Old Testament Literature and Exegesis and Biblical and Ecclesiastical History at Western Theological Seminary in Pittsburgh, supervised Jeffers's education, and the son began at five to learn Greek. This tutelage was followed by travel in Europe. The family moved to California, and Jeffers matriculated as a junior at Occidental College, from which he was graduated in 1905. Jeffers immediately entered graduate school as a student of literature at the University of Southern California. In the spring of 1906, he was back in Switzerland taking courses in philosophy, Old English, French literary history, Dante, Spanish romantic poetry, and the history of the Roman Empire. Returning to USC in September 1907, he was admitted to the medical school, where he distinguished himself as a student and taught physiology at the USC dental college. A final episode of formal education took place at the University of Washington, where he studied forestry. Another strong influence on his intellectual development was his wife, Una, whom he met in a class on Faust at USC and who later studied for a doctorate in philosophy at the University of California at Berkeley.

Shortly after marrying (1913), the couple moved to Carmel, and in 1919 the poet himself began building a stone cottage on land purchased overlooking Carmel Bay and facing Point Lobos; near the cottage he built a forty-foot stone tower. Here in the heart of the Big Sur region, Jeffers undertook his lifelong celebration of the awesome beauty of coastal hills and ravines that plunged into the Pacific. With very few exceptions, Jeffers's verse praises "the beauty of things" in this setting and focuses on his belief that such splendor demands tragedy: the greater the beauty, the greater the demand.

In Jeffers's poetry, there is an undeniable, though challenging, religious intent that shows him to be a pantheist whose God is the evolving universe. Images and themes of cycle dominate his poetry and derive from many sources. Civilizations—from Rome to twentieth-century America—follow a cycle of growth, maturation, and decline. Jeffers's uncomfortable view is that great wars were welcome because they would purge the earth of humans who in their self-centeredness showed themselves unworthy of existing amid the divine beauty which they habitually defiled and failed to honor. Following these views is Jeffers's apocalyptic theme affirming that humankind will destroy itself and thereby restore the world to its pristine state. Images of rocks and hawks are central symbols—the former of the permanence of nature and God ("disinterestedness"), the latter of "fierce consciousness."

During the late 1930s and the 1940s, Jeffers's genius was judged to have faded; furthermore, many of his references to current events and figures (such as Pearl Harbor, Teheran, Hitler, Stalin, Roosevelt) raised questions about his patriotism in a period of national strife. Indeed, *The Double Axe* (1948) appeared with a disclaimer from the publisher. However, Jeffers's adaptation of Euripides' *Medea* (1946), which he wrote for Judith Anderson, was a great success when it was produced in New York in 1947. In his final statement on poetry—an article for the *New York Times,* "Poetry, Gongorism, and a Thousand Years" (1949)—Jeffers says that the great poet writes for all times, renounces self-conscious and labored obscurity, and favors straightforward and natural statement. Thus Jeffers is consistent with his early views and separates himself from his contemporaries as he viewed them.

Arthur B. Coffin
Montana State University

PRIMARY WORKS

Flagons and Apples, 1912; *Californians,* 1916; *Collected Poetry of Robinson Jeffers* (4 volumes), 1988–2000; *The Selected Poetry of Robinson Jeffers,* 1938; *Be Angry at the Sun,* 1941; *Medea,* 1946; *The Double Axe and Other Poems,* 1948; *Hungerfield and Other Poems,* 1954; *The Beginning and the End and Other Poems,* 1963; *Robinson Jeffers: Selected Poems,* 1965; *The Selected Letters of Robinson Jeffers,* 1968; *Rock and Hawk: A Selection of the Shorter Poems by Robinson Jeffers,* 1987.

Credo

My friend from Asia has powers and magic, he plucks a blue leaf
from the young blue-gum
And gazing upon it, gathering and quieting
The God in his mind, creates an ocean more real than the ocean,
the salt, the actual
Appalling presence, the power of the waters.
He believes that nothing is real except as we make it. I humbler
have found in my blood
Bred west of Caucasus a harder mysticism.
Multitude stands in my mind but I think that the ocean in the
bone vault is only
The bone vault's ocean: out there is the ocean's;
The water is the water, the cliff is the rock, come shocks and
flashes of reality. The mind
Passes, the eye closes, the spirit is a passage;
The beauty of things was born before eyes and sufficient to itself;
the heart-breaking beauty
Will remain when there is no heart to break for it.

1927

Rock and Hawk

Here is a symbol in which
Many high tragic thoughts
Watch their own eyes.

This gray rock, standing tall
On the headland, where the seawind
Lets no tree grow,

Earthquake-proved, and signatured
By ages of storms: on its peak
A falcon has perched.

I think, here is your emblem
To hang in the future sky;
Not the cross, not the hive,[1]

But this; bright power, dark peace;
Fierce consciousness joined with final
Disinterestedness;

Life with calm death; the falcon's
Realist eyes and act
Married to the massive

Mysticism of stone,
Which failure cannot cast down
Nor success make proud.

1935

The Purse-Seine

Our sardine fishermen work at night in the dark of the moon; daylight or moonlight
They could not tell where to spread the net, unable to see the phosphorescence of the shoals of fish.
They work northward from Monterey, coasting Santa Cruz; off

[1]*Cross, hive:* both symbols of Christianity, the latter referring to the Mormons and the Church of Jesus Christ of the Latter-day Saints.

New Year's Point or off Pigeon Point
The look-out man will see some lakes of milk-color light on the sea's night-purple; he points, and the helmsman
Turns the dark prow, the motor boat circles the gleaming shoal and drifts out her seine-net. They close the circle
And purse the bottom of the net, then with great labor haul it in.

I cannot tell you
How beautiful the scene is, and a little terrible, then, when the crowded fish
Know they are caught, and wildly beat from one wall to the other of their closing destiny the phosphorescent
Water to a pool of flame, each beautiful slender body sheeted with flame, like a live rocket
A comet's tail wake of clear yellow flame; while outside the narrowing
Floats and cordage of the net great sea-lions come up to watch, sighing in the dark; the vast walls of night
Stand erect to the stars.

Lately I was looking from a night mountain-top
On a wide city, the colored splendor, galaxies of light: how could I help but recall the seine-net
Gathering the luminous fish? I cannot tell you how beautiful the city appeared, and a little terrible.
I thought, We have geared the machines and locked all together into interdependence; we have built the great cities; now
There is no escape. We have gathered vast populations incapable of free survival, insulated
From the strong earth, each person in himself helpless, on all dependent. The circle is closed, and the net
Is being hauled in. They hardly feel the cords drawing, yet they shine already. The inevitable mass-disasters
Will not come in our time nor in our children's, but we and our children
Must watch the net draw narrower, government take all powers—or revolution, and the new government
Take more than all, add to kept bodies kept souls—or anarchy, the mass-disasters.

These things are Progress;
Do you marvel our verse is troubled or frowning, while it keeps its reason? Or it lets go, lets the mood flow
In the manner of the recent young men into mere hysteria, splintered gleams, crackled laughter. But they are quite wrong.
There is no reason for amazement: surely one always knew that cultures decay, and life's end is death.

1937

Self-Criticism in February

The bay is not blue but sombre yellow
With wrack from the battered valley, it is speckled with violent
    foam-heads
And tiger-striped with long lovely storm-shadows.
You love this better than the other mask; better eyes than yours
Would feel the equal beauty in the blue.
It is certain you have loved the beauty of storm disproportionately.
But the present time is not pastoral, but founded
On violence, pointed for more massive violence: perhaps it is not
Perversity but need that perceives the storm-beauty.
Well, bite on this: your poems are too full of ghosts and demons,
And people like phantoms—how often life's are—
And passion so strained that the clay mouths go praying for
    destruction—
Alas, it is not unusual in life;
To every soul at some time. *But why insist on it? And now*
For the worst fault: you have never mistaken
Demon nor passion nor idealism for the real God.
Then what is most disliked in those verses
Remains most true. *Unfortunately. If only you could sing*
That God is love, or perhaps that social
Justice will soon prevail. I can tell lies in prose.[1]

1937

The Bloody Sire

It is not bad. Let them play.
Let the guns bark and the bombing-plane
Speak his prodigious blasphemies.
It is not bad, it is high time,
Stark violence is still the sire of all the world's values.

[1]In the Foreword to his *Selected Poetry,* Jeffers wrote: "Another formative principle came to me from a phrase of Nietzsche's: 'The poets? The poets lie too much.' I was nineteen when the phrase stuck in my mind . . . and I decided not to tell lies in verse." Cf. "Cassandra."

What but the wolf's tooth whittled so fine
The fleet limbs of the antelope?
What but fear winged the birds, and hunger
Jeweled with such eyes the great goshawk's head?
Violence has been the sire of all the world's values.

Who would remember Helen's face[1]
Lacking the terrible halo of spears?
Who formed Christ but Herod and Caesar,
The cruel and bloody victories of Caesar?
Violence, the bloody sire of all the world's values.

Never weep, let them play,
Old violence is not too old to beget new values.

1941

The Excesses of God

Is it not by his high superfluousness we know
Our God? For to be equal a need
Is natural, animal, mineral: but to fling
Rainbows over the rain
And beauty above the moon, and secret rainbows
On the domes of deep sea-shells,
And make the necessary embrace of breeding
Beautiful also as fire,
Not even the weeds to multiply without blossom
Nor the birds without music:
There is the great humaneness at the heart of things,
The extravagant kindness, the fountain
Humanity can understand, and would flow likewise
If power and desire were perch-mates.

1941

[1]Helen of Troy, over whom, according to Homer in the *Iliad,* the Greeks and Trojans fought in the Trojan War.

Cassandra[1]

The mad girl with the staring eyes and long white fingers
Hooked in the stones of the wall,
The storm-wrack hair and the screeching mouth: does it matter, Cassandra,
Whether the people believe
Your bitter fountain? Truly men hate the truth; they'd liefer[2]
Meet a tiger on the road.
Therefore the poets honey their truth with lying; but religion—
Venders and political men
Pour from the barrel, new lies on the old, and are praised for kindly
Wisdom. Poor bitch, be wise.
No: you'll still mumble in a corner a crust of truth, to men
And gods disgusting.—You and I, Cassandra.

1948

The Beauty of Things

To feel and speak the astonishing beauty of things—earth, stone and water,
Beast, man and woman, sun, moon and stars—
The blood-shot beauty of human nature, its thoughts, frenzies and passions,
And unhuman nature its towering reality—
For man's half dream; man you might say, is nature dreaming, but rock
And water and sky are constant—to feel
Greatly, and understand greatly, and express greatly, the natural
Beauty, is the sole business of poetry.
The rest's diversion: those holy or noble sentiments, the intricate ideas,
The love, lust, longing: reasons, but not the reason.

1954

[1]The daughter of Priam and Hecuba, king and queen of Troy, Cassandra resisted the advances of the god Apollo, who loved her and had given her the gift of prophecy; consequently, Apollo rendered her gift useless, causing her prophecies never to be believed.

[2]More gladly, more willingly.

Carmel Point

The extraordinary patience of things!
This beautiful place defaced with a crop of suburban houses—
How beautiful when we first beheld it,
Unbroken field of poppy and lupin walled with clean cliffs;
No intrusion but two or three horses pasturing,
Or a few milch cows rubbing their flanks on the outcrop rockheads—
Now the spoiler has come: does it care?
Not faintly. It has all time. It knows the people are a tide
That swells and in time will ebb, and all
Their works dissolve. Meanwhile the image of the pristine beauty
Lives in the very grain of the granite,
Safe as the endless ocean that climbs our cliff.—As for us:
We must uncenter our minds from ourselves;
We must unhumanize our views a little, and become confident
As the rock and ocean that we were made from.

1954

Robert Frost 1874–1963

Throughout his career, Robert Frost skillfully assumed the persona of a New England farmer-poet. Actually, however, Frost was born in San Francisco; he did not move East with his widowed mother until he was eleven, and he spent most of his adolescence in Lawrence, an industrialized Massachusetts mill town. Between 1892 and 1900 he married Elinor Miriam White and began raising his family while he worked in mills, taught school, and attended Dartmouth College and Harvard University. In 1900 he moved to a farm in Derry, New Hampshire, which was purchased for him by his grandfather. He taught English at a private school, the Pinkerton Academy, from 1906 to 1911, and he taught English and psychology at a teacher's college in Plymouth, New Hampshire, for a year in 1911–12. He sold the Derry farm in 1911 and moved with his family to England the following year where he met the English Georgian poets Wilfred Gibson, Lascelles Abercrombie, and Edward Thomas and began writing poetry full-time. Although Frost had adopted rural New England life as his special subject matter, his first two books, *A Boy's Will* (1913) and *North of Boston* (1914), were published in London before they appeared in the United States.

After returning to America in 1915, Frost became popular, particularly with English teachers and academic audiences. He taught or was a "Poet in Residence" at Amherst, the University of Michigan, and other colleges, and he spent many summers at the Bread Loaf Writers' Conference in Vermont. Frost was awarded the Pulitzer Prize for Poetry in 1924, 1931, 1937, and 1943. The United States Senate extended its felicitations to him on his birthday in 1950; a mountain in Vermont was named after him in 1955; the State Department sent him to South America, England, and Russia on "good-will missions" in 1954, 1957, and 1962; and in 1961 he was invited to read a poem at John F. Kennedy's inaugural ceremonies. Frost's admirers were upset by Lawrance Thompson's definitive, three-volume biography, published between 1966 and 1976, which revealed that the poet had been a vain, vindictive, inordinately ambitious, and frequently cruel man in his private life who had caused great suffering to his family and friends. Thompson also emphasized that Frost's public and poetic stoicism had sometimes masked acute depression, self-doubt, and guilt and that he had suffered many personal miseries and tragedies—the insanity of his sister Jeanie, the deaths of his daughter Marjorie and his wife in 1934 and 1938, and the suicide of his only son in 1940.

The time Frost spent in back-country New England gave him the opportunity to encounter farmers. For these New Englanders, like the old farmer in "Mending Wall," isolation could have certain advantages, and it is significant that in "The Line-Gang" Frost describes the arrival of the telephone—that very modern means of communication—in a distinctly ambivalent manner. In *North of Boston, Mountain Interval* (1916), and *New Hampshire* (1923) he was able to communicate both the limitations and the virtues of this rural, isolated, older America to the urban and academic Americans who read his poems and attended his readings.

Poetically, Frost can be considered a link between an older era and modern culture, and his relationship to literary modernism was equivocal. His early poems are similar to those of nineteenth-century American fireside poets such as Longfellow and English Georgians such as Thomas and Gibson. And many of his mature poems have more in common with the works of William Wordsworth or Robert Browning than they do with those of his contemporaries T. S. Eliot, Wallace Stevens, or William Carlos Williams. Frost eschewed free verse and wrote his poems in traditional rhymes and metrical forms like blank verse. Moreover, like his popular New England contemporary, Edward Arlington Robinson, Frost wrote many poems which are dramatic narratives and can be appreciated, like prose fiction, for their characterizations and plot development.

Intellectually, Frost was the heir of the nineteenth-century romantic individualism exemplified by Emerson and Thoreau. He assumed the lone individual could question and work out his or her own relationships to God and existence—preferably in a natural setting and with a few discrete references to Christianity and Transcendentalism. Unlike Thoreau, however, Frost was never daring enough to challenge the social order boldly in his writings—though he was capable of the conservative cynicism of "Provide, Provide." Nor was he able to express the romantic affirmations that characterize many of Emerson's works. The poet, to Emerson, was a seer whose poems should contain truths analogous to religious revelations. Frost's view of the poet was more modest. In his essay "The Figure a Poem Makes," which he published as a preface to his *Collected Poems,* he emphasized that a poem "begins in delight and ends in wisdom. . . . it runs a course of lucky events, and ends in a clarification of life—not necessarily a great clarification, such as sects and cults are founded on, but in a momentary stay against confusion."

James Guimond
Rider College

PRIMARY WORKS

Complete Poems of Robert Frost, 1949; *In the Clearing,* 1962; Lawrance Thompson, ed., *Selected Letters of Robert Frost,* 1964.

The Pasture

I'm going out to clean the pasture spring;
I'll only stop to rake the leaves away
(And wait to watch the water clear, I may):
I sha'n't be gone long.—You come too.

I'm going out to fetch the little calf
That's standing by the mother. It's so young
It totters when she licks it with her tongue.
I sha'n't be gone long.—You come too.

1913

Mending Wall

Something there is that doesn't love a wall,
That sends the frozen-ground-swell under it,
And spills the upper boulders in the sun;
And makes gaps even two can pass abreast.
The work of hunters is another thing:
I have come after them and made repair
Where they have left not one stone on a stone,
But they would have the rabbit out of hiding,
To please the yelping dogs. The gaps I mean,
No one has seen them made or heard them made,
But at spring mending-time we find them there.
I let my neighbor know beyond the hill;
And on a day we meet to walk the line
And set the wall between us once again.
We keep the wall between us as we go.
To each the boulders that have fallen to each.
And some are loaves and some so nearly balls
We have to use a spell to make them balance:
"Stay where you are until our backs are tuned!"
We wear our fingers rough with handling them.
Oh, just another kind of outdoor game,
One on a side. It comes to little more:
There where it is we do not need the wall:
He is all pine and I am apple orchard.
My apple trees will never get across
And eat the cones under his pines, I tell him
He only says, "Good fences make good neighbors."
Spring is the mischief in me, and I wonder
If I could put a notion in his head:

"*Why* do they make good neighbors? Isn't it
Where there are cows? But here there are no cows.
Before I built a wall I'd ask to know
What I was walling in or walling out,
And to whom I was like to give offense.
Something there is that doesn't love a wall,
That wants it down." I could say "Elves" to him,
But it's not elves exactly, and I'd rather
He said it for himself. I see him there
Bringing a stone grasped firmly by the top
In each hand, like an old-stone savage armed.
He moves in darkness as it seems to me,
Not of woods only and the shade of trees
He will not go behind his father's saying,
And he likes having thought of it so well
He says again, "Good fences make good neighbors."

1914

The Road Not Taken

Two roads diverged in a yellow wood,
And sorry I could not travel both
And be one traveler, long I stood
And looked down one as far as I could
To where it bent in the undergrowth;

Then took the other, as just as fair,
And having perhaps the better claim,
Because it was grassy and wanted wear;
Though as for that the passing there
Had worn them really about the same,

And both that morning equally lay
In leaves no step had trodden black.
Oh, I kept the first for another day!
Yet knowing how way leads on to way,
I doubted if I should ever come back.

I shall be telling this with a sigh
Somewhere ages and ages hence:
Two roads diverged in a wood, and I—
I took the one less traveled by,
And that has made all the difference.

1916

An Old Man's Winter Night

All out-of-doors looked darkly in at him
Through the thin frost, almost in separate stars,
That gathers on the pane in empty rooms.
What kept his eyes from giving back the gaze
Was the lamp tilted near them in his hand.
What kept him from remembering what it was
That brought him to that creaking room was age.
He stood with barrels round him—at a loss.
And having scared the cellar under him
In clomping here, he scared it once again
In clomping off;—and scared the outer night,
Which has its sounds, familiar, like the roar
Of trees and crack of branches, common things,
But nothing so like beating on a box.
A light he was to no one but himself
Where now he sat, concerned with he knew what,
A quiet light, and then not even that.
He consigned to the moon, such as she was,
So late-arising, to the broken moon
As better than the sun in any case
For such a charge, his snow upon the roof,
His icicles along the wall to keep;
And slept. The log that shifted with a jolt
Once in the stove, disturbed him and he shifted,
And eased his heavy breathing, but still slept.
One aged man—one man—can't keep a house,
A farm, a countryside, or if he can,
It's thus he does it of a winter night.

1916

The Oven Bird[1]

There is a singer everyone has heard,
Loud, a mid-summer and a mid-wood bird,
Who makes the solid tree trunks sound again.
He says that leaves are old and that for flowers

[1]American warbler which builds a dome-shaped nest on the ground.

Mid-summer is to spring as one to ten.
He says the early petal-fall is past
When pear and cherry bloom went down in showers
On sunny days a moment overcast;
And comes that other fall we name the fall.[2]
He says the highway dust is over all.
The bird would cease and be as other birds
But that he knows in singing not to sing.
The question that he frames in all but words
Is what to make of a diminished thing.

1916

"Out, Out—"[1]

The buzz saw snarled and rattled in the yard
And made dust and dropped stove-length sticks of wood,
Sweet-scented stuff when the breeze drew across it.
And from there those that lifted eyes could count
Five mountain ranges one behind the other
Under the sunset far into Vermont.
And the saw snarled and rattled, snarled and rattled,
As it ran light, or had to bear a load.
And nothing happened: day was all but done.
Call it a day, I wish they might have said
To please the boy by giving him the half hour
That a boy counts so much when saved from work.
His sister stood beside them in her apron
To tell them "Supper." At the word, the saw,
As if to prove saws knew what supper meant,
Leaped out at the boy's hand, or seemed to leap—
He must have given the hand. However it was,
Neither refused the meeting. But the hand!
The boy's first outcry was a rueful laugh,
As he swung toward them holding up the hand,
Half in appeal, but half as if to keep
The life from spilling. Then the boy saw all—

[2]"The fall" may allude to the Biblical account of the disobedience of Adam and Eve (Genesis 3) and their expulsion from the Garden of Eden.

[1]Macbeth, V, v.

Since he was old enough to know, big boy
Doing a man's work, though a child at heart—
He saw all spoiled. "Don't let him cut my hand off—
The doctor, when he comes. Don't let him, sister!"
So. But the hand was gone already.
The doctor put him in the dark of ether.
He lay and puffed his lips out with his breath.
And then—the watcher at his pulse took fright.
No one believed. They listened at his heart.
Little—less—nothing!—and that ended it.
No more to build on there. And they, since they
Were not the one dead, turned to their affairs.

1916

The Line-Gang

Here come the line-gang pioneering by.
They throw a forest down less cut than broken.
They plant dead trees for living, and the dead
They string together with a living thread.
They string an instrument against the sky
Wherein words whether beaten out or spoken
Will run as hushed as when they were a thought
But in no hush they string it: they go past
With shouts afar to pull the cable taut,
To hold it hard until they make it fast,
To ease away—they have it. With a laugh,
An oath of towns that set the wild at naught
They bring the telephone and telegraph.

1916

The Ax-Helve

I've known ere now an interfering branch
Of alder catch my lifted ax behind me.
But that was in the woods, to hold my hand
From striking at another alder's roots,
And that was, as I say, an alder branch.
This was a man, Baptiste, who stole one day

Behind me on the snow in my own yard
Where I was working at the chopping block,
And cutting nothing not cut down already.
He caught my ax expertly on the rise,
When all my strength put forth was in his favor,
Held it a moment where it was, to calm me,
Then took it from me—and I let him take it.
I didn't know him well enough to know
What it was all about. There might be something
He had in mind to say to a bad neighbor
He might prefer to say to him disarmed.
But all he had to tell me in French-English
Was what he thought of—not me, but my ax,
Me only as I took my ax to heart.
It was the bad ax-helve someone had sold me—
"Made on machine," he said, plowing the grain
With a thick thumbnail to show how it ran
Across the handle's long-drawn serpentine,
Like the two strokes across a dollar sign.
"You give her one good crack, she's snap raght off.
Den where's your hax-ead flying t'rough de hair?"
Admitted; and yet, what was that to him?

"Come on my house and I put you one in
What's las' awhile—good hick'ry what's grow crooked,
De second growt'[1] I cut myself—tough, tough!"

Something to sell? That wasn't how it sounded.

"Den when you say you come? It's cost you nothing.
Tonaght?"

As well tonight as any night.

Beyond an over-warmth of kitchen stove
My welcome differed from no other welcome.
Baptiste knew best why I was where I was.
So long as he would leave enough unsaid,
I shouldn't mind his being overjoyed
(If overjoyed he was) at having got me
Where I must judge if what he knew about an ax
That not everybody else knew was to count
For nothing in the measure of a neighbor.

[1]Second growth, trees which grow up after the virgin forest is logged.

Hard if, though cast away for life with Yankees,
A Frenchman couldn't get his human rating!

Mrs. Baptiste came in and rocked a chair
That had as many motions as the world:
One back and forward, in and out of shadow,
That got her nowhere; one more gradual,
Sideways, that would have run her on the stove
In time, had she not realized her danger
And caught herself up bodily, chair and all,
And set herself back where she started from.
"She ain't spick too much Henglish—dat's too bad."
I was afraid, in brightening first on me,
Then on Baptiste, as if she understood
What passed between us, she was only feigning.
Baptiste was anxious for her; but no more
Than for himself, so placed he couldn't hope
To keep his bargain of the morning with me
In time to keep me from suspecting him
Of really never having meant to keep it.

Needlessly soon he had his ax-helves out,
A quiverful to choose from, since he wished me
To have the best he had, or had to spare—
Not for me to ask which, when what he took
Had beauties he had to point me out at length
To insure their not being wasted on me.
He liked to have it slender as a whipstock,
Free from the least knot, equal to the strain
Of bending like a sword across the knee.
He showed me that the lines of a good helve
Were native to the grain before the knife
Expressed them, and its curves were no false curves
Put on it from without. And there its strength lay
For the hard work. He chafed its long white body
From end to end with his rough hand shut round it.
He tried it at the eyehole in the ax-head.
"Hahn, hahn," he mused, "don't need much taking down."
Baptiste knew how to make a short job long
For love of it, and yet not waste time either.

Do you know, what we talked about was knowledge?
Baptiste on his defense about the children
He kept from school, or did his best to keep—
Whatever school and children and our doubts
Of laid-on education had to do
With the curves of his ax-helves and his having

Used these unscrupulously to bring me
To see for once the inside of his house.
Was I desired in friendship, partly as someone
To leave it to, whether the right to hold
Such doubts of education should depend
Upon the education of those who held them?

But now he brushed the shavings from his knee
And stood the ax there on its horse's hoof,
Erect, but not without its waves, as when
The snake stood up for evil in the Garden—[2]
Top-heavy with a heaviness his short,
Thick hand made light of, steel-blue chin drawn down
And in a little—a French touch in that.
Baptiste drew back and squinted at it, pleased:
"See how she's cock her head!"

1923

Stopping by Woods on a Snowy Evening

Whose woods these are I think I know.
His house is in the village though;
He will not see me stopping here
To watch his woods fill up with snow.

My little horse must think it queer
To stop without a farmhouse near
Between the woods and frozen lake
The darkest evening of the year.

He gives his harness bells a shake
To ask if there is some mistake.
The only other sound's the sweep
Of easy wind and downy flake.

The woods are lovely, dark and deep,
But I have promises to keep,
And miles to go before I sleep,
And miles to go before I sleep.

1923

[2]Alludes to the serpent in the Garden of Eden (Genesis 3).

Desert Places

Snow falling and night falling fast, oh, fast
In a field I looked into going past,
And the ground almost covered smooth in snow,
But a few weeds and stubble showing last.

The woods around it have it—it is theirs.
All animals are smothered in their lairs.
I am too absent-spirited to count;
The loneliness includes me unawares.

And lonely as it is that loneliness
Will be more lonely ere it will be less—
A blanker whiteness of benighted snow
With no expression, nothing to express.

They cannot scare me with their empty spaces
Between stars—on stars where no human race is.
I have it in me so much nearer home
To scare myself with my own desert places.

1936

Once by the Pacific

The shattered water made a misty din.
Great waves looked over others coming in,
And thought of doing something to the shore
That water never did to land before.
The clouds were low and hairy in the skies,
Like locks blown forward in the gleam of eyes.
You could not tell, and yet it looked as if
The shore was lucky in being backed by cliff,
The cliff in being backed by continent;
It looked as if a night of dark intent
Was coming, and not only a night, an age.
Someone had better be prepared for rage.
There would be more than ocean-water broken
Before God's last *Put out the Light* was spoken.

1928

Design

I found a dimpled spider, fat and white,
On a white heal-all,[1] holding up a moth
Like a white piece of rigid satin cloth—
Assorted characters of death and blight
Mixed ready to begin the morning right,
Like the ingredients of a witches' broth—
A snow-drop spider, a flower like a froth,
And dead wings carried like a paper kite.

What had that flower to do with being white,
The wayside blue and innocent heal-all?
What brought the kindred spider to that height,
Then steered the white moth thither in the night?
What but design of darkness to appall?—
If design govern in a thing so small.

1936

Provide, Provide

The witch that came (the withered hag)
To wash the steps with pail and rag,
Was once the beauty Abishag,[1]

The picture pride of Hollywood.
Too many fall from great and good
For you to doubt the likelihood.

Die early and avoid the fate.
Or if predestined to die late,
Make up your mind to die in state.

Make the whole stock exchange your own!
If need be occupy a throne,
Where nobody can call *you* crone.

[1]Flower thought to have medicinal qualities; its leaves were applied to slight cuts.

[1]A beautiful young woman mentioned in the Bible (I Kings 1:3).

Some have relied on what they knew;
Others on being simply true.
What worked for them might work for you.

No memory of having starred
Atones for later disregard,
Or keeps the end from being hard.

Better to go down dignified
With boughten friendship at your side
Than none at all. Provide, provide!

1936

Directive

Back out of all this now too much for us,
Back in a time made simple by the loss
Of detail, burned, dissolved, and broken off
Like graveyard marble sculpture in the weather,
There is a house that is no more a house
Upon a farm that is no more a farm
And in a town that is no more a town.
The road there, if you'll let a guide direct you
Who only has at heart your getting lost,
May seem as if it should have been a quarry—
Great monolithic knees the former town
Long since gave up pretense of keeping covered.
And there's a story in a book about it:
Besides the wear of iron wagon wheels
The ledges show lines ruled southeast northwest,
The chisel work of an enormous Glacier
That braced his feet against the Arctic Pole.
You must not mind a certain coolness from him
Still said to haunt this side of Panther Mountain.
Nor need you mind the serial ordeal
Of being watched from forty cellar holes
As if by eye pairs out of forty firkins.[1]
As for the woods' excitement over you
That sends light rustle rushes to their leaves,

[1]Small wooden casks or vessels used to hold fish, butter, etc.

Charge that to upstart inexperience.
Where were they all not twenty years ago?
They think too much of having shaded out
A few old pecker-fretted[2] apple trees.
Make yourself up a cheering song of how
Someone's road home from work this once was,
Who may be just ahead of you on foot
Or creaking with a buggy load of grain.
The height of the adventure is the height
Of country where two village cultures faded
Into each other. Both of them are lost.
And if you're lost enough to find yourself
By now, pull in your ladder road behind you
And put a sign up CLOSED to all but me.
Then make yourself at home. The only field
Now left's no bigger than a harness gall.[3]
First there's the children's house of make believe,
Some shattered dishes underneath a pine,
The playthings in the playhouse of the children.
Weep for what little things could make them glad.
Then for the house that is no more a house,
But only a belilaced cellar hole,
Now slowly closing like a dent in dough.
This was no playhouse but a house in earnest.
Your destination and your destiny's
A brook that was the water of the house,
Cold as a spring as yet so near its source,
Too lofty and original to rage.
(We know the valley streams that when aroused
Will leave their tatters hung on barb and thorn.)
I have kept hidden in the instep arch
Of an old cedar at the waterside
A broken drinking goblet like the Grail[4]
Under a spell so the wrong ones can't find it,
So can't get saved, as Saint Mark[5] says they mustn't.
(I stole the goblet from the children's playhouse.)
Here are your waters and your watering place.
Drink and be whole again beyond confusion.

1947

[2]Dotted with a pattern of holes made by woodpeckers.

[3]A sore on the back of a horse caused by the rubbing of the saddle or harness.

[4]Cup used by Christ at the Last Supper. According to medieval legends, it was brought to England and sought by King Arthur's knights. It could only be found by persons who were pure in their thoughts, words, and deeds.

[5]Alludes to the Bible (Mark 16:16).

Sherwood Anderson 1876–1941

Sherwood Anderson was above all a storyteller, and in all of his writings he has left his readers a rich record of his life. Born in Camden, Ohio, he spent his first two decades in small towns of northern Ohio, especially Clyde, which became the setting for *Winesburg, Ohio* (1919), his best-known work. He dedicated *Winesburg* to his mother, "whose keen observations on the life about her first awoke in me the hunger to see beneath the surface of lives."

This hunger to see hidden significance and beauty beneath the surface of lonely, often frustrated lives became Anderson's main preoccupation as a writer, whether the setting is "Winesburg," or "Bidwell," as in his best novel, *Poor White* (1920), or described directly as Clyde in his three autobiographies, *A Story Teller's Story* (1924), *Tar: A Midwest Childhood* (1926), and his posthumous *Memoirs* (1942; critical edition, 1969). In depicting the inhabitants of the small midwestern town at the turn of the century, Anderson depicts the struggles of all of us, especially when we are on the threshold of adulthood.

When his mother died in 1895, Anderson left Clyde, and after a stint in the Army during the Spanish-American War, embarked on a career in advertising in Chicago in 1900. In 1907 he left advertising to found a roof-paint business in Elyria, Ohio, a business which prospered until Anderson neglected it to spend hours at night writing. A dramatic moment, which he tells and retells in his autobiographical work, came in November, 1912, when he suffered a kind of mental collapse, walked out of his office, wandered about in a state of amnesia for four days, and finally was hospitalized in Cleveland. After a period of recuperation and the liquidation of his debt-ridden business, he returned to Chicago in February, 1913. Whether or not, as Anderson alleged in numerous writings, his repudiation of business was a conscious choice of the life of the artist over the life of the businessman, the fact remains that, at the age of thirty-six, he radically changed the course of his life.

When Anderson returned to Chicago, he became acquainted with the writers, journalists, and critics of the "Chicago Renaissance" of the 1910s, for example, Edgar Lee Masters, Carl Sandburg, and Ben Hecht. He met the established writer Theodore Dreiser and the aspiring writer Ernest Hemingway. In New Orleans, between 1924 and 1925, he met the young William Faulkner. These younger writers, along with Erskine Caldwell, F. Scott Fitzgerald, Jean Toomer, and many others, became indebted to Anderson's new method of storytelling and new structuring of stories into a story cycle. In fact, Faulkner later said of Anderson: "He was the father of my whole generation of writers."

Anderson made his greatest contribution to American literature in the genre of the short story. With the publication of *Winesburg* in 1919, the American reading public was introduced to a volume of stories innovative in two important ways. First, the individual stories break with the tradition of tightly plotted, linear stories in order to tell and retell a significant moment until all its meaning is revealed. Second, *Winesburg* is not a collection of isolated stories but is a story cycle, a grouping of stories which, in Anderson's own words, "belong together." In *Winesburg,* in addition to the fact that the individual stories have their own unity and beauty, the cycle itself acquires an artistic integrity because of the relationship of all of the stories to each other. Examples of American story cycles which followed *Winesburg* are Hemingway's *In Our Time,* Toomer's *Cane,* Caldwell's *Georgia Boy,* and Faulkner's *The Unvanquished* and *Go Down, Moses.*

Martha Curry
Wayne State University

PRIMARY WORKS

Winesburg, Ohio, 1919; *Poor White,* 1920; *The Triumph of the Egg,* 1921; *Horses and Men,* 1923; *A Story Teller's Story,* 1924; *Tar: A Midwest Childhood,* 1926; *Death in the Woods,* 1933; Ray Lewis White, ed., *Sherwood Anderson's Memoirs,* 1969.

Hands

Upon the half decayed veranda of a small frame house that stood near the edge of a ravine near the town of Winesburg, Ohio, a fat little old man walked nervously up and down. Across a long field that has been seeded for clover but that had produced only a dense crop of yellow mustard weeds, he could see the public highway along which went a wagon filled with berry pickers returning from the fields. The berry pickers, youths and maidens, laughed and shouted boisterously. A boy clad in a blue shirt leaped from the wagon and attempted to drag after him one of the maidens who screamed and protested shrilly. The feet of the boy in the road kicked up a cloud of dust that floated across the face of the departing sun. Over the long field came a thin girlish voice. "Oh, you Wing Biddlebaum, comb your hair, it's falling into your eyes," commanded the voice to the man, who was bald and whose nervous little hands fiddled about the bare white forehead as though arranging a mass of tangled locks.

Wing Biddlebaum, forever frightened and beset by a ghostly band of doubts, did not think of himself as in any way a part of the life of the town where he had lived for twenty years. Among all the people of Winesburg but one had come close to him. With George Willard, son of Tom Willard, the proprietor of the new Willard House, he had formed something like a friendship. George Willard was the reporter on the *Winesburg Eagle* and sometimes in the evenings he walked out along the highway to Wing Biddlebaum's house. Now as the old man walked up and down on the veranda, his hands moving nervously about, he was hoping that George Willard would come and spend the evening with him. After the wagon containing the berry pickers had passed, he went across the field through the tall mustard weeds and climbing a rail fence peered anxiously along the road to the town. For a moment he stood thus, rubbing his hands together and looking up and down the road, and then, fear overcoming him, ran back to walk again upon the porch on his own house.

In the presence of George Willard, Wing Biddlebaum, who for twenty years had been the town mystery, lost something of his timidity, and his shadowy personality, submerged in a sea of doubts, came forth to look at the world. With the young reporter at his side, he ventured in the light of day into Main Street or strode up and down on the rickety front porch of his own house, talking excitedly. The voice that had been low and trembling became shrill and loud. The bent figure straightened. With a kind of wriggle, like a fish returned to the brook by the fisherman, Biddlebaum the silent began to talk, striving to put into words the ideas that had been accumulated by his mind during long years of silence.

Wing Biddlebaum talked much with his hands. The slender expressive fingers, forever active, forever striving to conceal themselves in his pockets or behind his back, came forth and became the piston rods of his machinery of expression.

The story of Wing Biddlebaum is a story of hands. Their restless activity, like unto the beating of the wings of an imprisoned bird, had given him his name. Some obscure poet of the town had thought of it. The hands alarmed their owner. He wanted to keep them hidden away and looked with amazement at the quiet inexpressive hands of other men who worked beside him in the fields, or passed, driving sleepy teams on country roads.

When he talked to George Willard, Wing Biddlebaum closed his fists and beat with them upon a table or on the walls of his house. The action made him more comfortable. If the desire to talk came to him when the two were walking in the fields, he sought out a stump or the top board of a fence and with his hands pounding busily talked with renewed ease.

The story of Wing Biddlebaum's hands is worth a book in itself. Sympathetically set forth it would tap many strange, beautiful qualities in obscure men. It is a job for a poet. In Winesburg the hands had attracted attention merely because of their activity. With them Wing Biddlebaum had picked as high as a hundred and forty quarts of strawberries in a day. They became his distinguishing feature, the source of his fame. Also they made more grotesque an already grotesque and elusive individuality. Winesburg was proud of the hands of Wing Biddlebaum in the same spirit in which it was proud of Banker White's new stone house and Wesley Moyer's bay stallion, Tony Tip, that had won the two-fifteen trot at the fall races in Cleveland.

As for George Willard, he had many times wanted to ask about the hands. At times an almost overwhelming curiosity had taken hold of him. He felt that there must be a reason for their strange activity and their inclination to keep hidden away and only a growing respect for Wing Biddlebaum kept him from blurting out the questions that were often in his mind.

Once he had been on the point of asking. The two were walking in the fields on a summer afternoon and had stopped to sit upon a grassy bank. All afternoon Wing Biddlebaum had talked as one inspired. By a fence he had stopped and beating like a giant woodpecker upon the top board had shouted at George Willard, condemning his tendency to be too much influenced by the people about him. "You are destroying yourself," he cried. "You have the inclination to be alone and to dream and you are afraid of dreams. You want to be like others in town here. You hear them talk and you try to imitate them."

On the grassy bank Wing Biddlebaum had tried again to drive his point home. His voice became soft and reminiscent, and with a sigh of contentment he launched into a long rambling talk, speaking as one lost in a dream.

Out of the dream Wing Biddlebaum made a picture for George Willard. In the picture men lived again in a kind of pastoral golden age. Across a green open country came clean-limbed young men, some afoot, some mounted upon horses. In crowds the young men came to gather about the feet of an old man who sat beneath a tree in a tiny garden and who talked to them.

Wing Biddlebaum became wholly inspired. For once he forgot the hands. Slowly they stole forth and lay upon George Willard's shoulders. Something new and bold came into the voice that talked. "You must try to forget all you have learned," said the old man. "You must begin to dream. From this time on you must shut your ears to the roaring of the voices."

Pausing in his speech, Wing Biddlebaum looked long and earnestly at George Willard. His eyes glowed. Again he raised the hands to caress the boy and then a look of horror swept over his face.

With a convulsive movement of his body, Wing Biddlebaum sprang to his feet and thrust his hands deep into his trousers pockets. Tears came to his eyes. "I must be getting along home. I can talk no more with you," he said nervously.

Without looking back, the old man had hurried down the hillside and across a meadow, leaving George Willard perplexed and frightened upon the grassy slope. With a shiver of dread the boy arose and went along the road toward town. "I'll not ask him about his hands," he thought, touched by the memory of the terror he had seen in the man's eyes. "There's something wrong, but I don't want to know what it is. His hands have something to do with his fear of me and of everyone."

And George Willard was right. Let us look briefly into the story of the hands. Perhaps our talking of them will arouse the poet who will tell the hidden wonder story of the influence for which the hands were but fluttering pennants of promise.

In his youth Wing Biddlebaum had been a school teacher in a town in Pennsylvania. He was not then known as Wing Biddlebaum, but went by the less euphonic name of Adolph Myers. As Adolph Myers he was much loved by the boys of his school.

Adolph Myers was meant by nature to be a teacher of youth. He was one of those rare, little-understood men who rule by a power so gentle that it passes as a lovable weakness. In their feeling for the boys under their charge such men are not unlike the finer sort of women in their love of men.

And yet that is but crudely stated. It needs the poet there. With the boys of his school, Adolph Myers had walked in the evening or had sat talking until dusk upon the schoolhouse steps lost in a kind of dream. Here and there went his hands, caressing the shoulders of the boys, playing about the tousled heads. As he talked his voice became soft and musical. There was a caress in that also. In a way the voice and the hands, the stroking of the shoulders and the touching of the hair was a part of the schoolmaster's effort to carry a dream into the young minds. By the caress that was in his fingers he expressed himself. He was one of those men in whom the force that creates life is diffused, not centralized. Under the caress of his hands doubt and disbelief went out of the minds of the boys and they began also to dream.

And then the tragedy. A half-witted boy of the school became enamored of the young master. In his bed at night he imagined unspeakable things and in the morning went forth to tell his dreams as facts. Strange, hideous accusations fell from his loose-hung lips. Through the Pennsylvania town went a shiver. Hidden, shadowy doubts that had been in men's minds concerning Adolph Myers were galvanized into beliefs.

The tragedy did not linger. Trembling lads were jerked out of bed and questioned. "He put his arms about me," said one. "His fingers were always playing in my hair," said another.

One afternoon a man of the town, Henry Bradford, who kept a saloon, came to the schoolhouse door. Calling Adolph Myers into the school yard he began to beat him with his fists. As his hard knuckles beat down into the frightened face of the schoolmaster, his wrath became more and more terrible. Screaming with dismay, the children ran here and there like disturbed insects. "I'll teach you to put your hands on my boy, you beast," roared the saloon keeper, who, tired of beating the master, had begun to kick him about the yard.

Adolph Myers was driven from the Pennsylvania town in the night. With lanterns in their hands a dozen men came to the door of the house where he lived alone and commanded that he dress and come forth. It was raining and one of the men had a rope in his hands. They had intended to hang the schoolmaster, but something in his figure, so small, white, and pitiful, touched their hearts and they let him escape. As he ran away into the darkness they repented of their weakness and ran after him, swearing and throwing sticks and great balls of soft mud at the figure that screamed and ran faster and faster into the darkness.

For twenty years Adolph Myers had lived alone in Winesburg. He was but forty but looked sixty-five. The name of Biddlebaum he got from a box of goods seen at a freight station as he hurried through an eastern Ohio town. He had an aunt in Winesburg, a black-toothed old woman who raised chickens, and with her he lived until she died. He had been ill for a year after the experience in Pennsylvania, and after his recovery worked as a day laborer in the fields, going timidly about and striving to conceal his hands. Although he did not understand what had happened he felt that the hands must be to blame. Again and again the fathers of the boys had talked of the hands. "Keep your hands to yourself," the saloon keeper had roared, dancing with fury in the schoolhouse yard.

Upon the veranda of his house by the ravine, Wing Biddlebaum continued to walk up and down until the sun had disappeared and the road beyond the field was lost in the grey shadows. Going into his house he cut slices of bread and spread honey upon them. When the rumble of the evening train that took away the express cars loaded with the day's harvest of berries had passed and restored the silence of the summer night, he went again to walk upon the veranda. In the darkness he could not see the hands and they became quiet. Although he still hungered for the presence of the boy, who was the medium through which he expressed his love of man, the hunger became again a part of his loneliness and his waiting. Lighting a lamp, Wing Biddlebaum washed the few dishes soiled by his simple meal and, setting up a folding cot by the screen door that led to the porch, prepared to undress for the night. A few stray white bread crumbs lay on the cleanly washed floor by the table; putting the lamp upon a low stool he began to pick up the crumbs, carrying them to his mouth one by one with unbelievable rapidity. In the dense blotch of light beneath the table, the kneeling figure looked like a priest engaged in some service of his church. The nervous expressive fingers, flashing in and out of the light, might well have been mistaken for the fingers of the devotee going swiftly through decade after decade of his rosary.

1919

Death in the Woods

She was an old woman and lived on a farm near the town in which I lived. All country and small-town people have seen such old women, but no ones knows much about them. Such an old woman comes into town driving an old worn-out horse or she comes afoot carrying a basket. She may own a few hens and have eggs to sell. She brings them in a basket and takes them to a grocer. There she trades them in. She gets some salt pork and some beans. Then she gets a pound or two of sugar and some flour.

Afterwards she goes to the butcher's and asks for some dog meat. She may spend ten or fifteen cents, but when she does she asks for something. Formerly the butchers gave liver to anyone who wanted to carry it away. In our family we were always having it. Once one of my brothers got a whole cow's liver at the slaughterhouse near the fairgrounds in our town. We had it until we were sick of it. It never cost a cent. I have hated the thought of it ever since.

The old farm woman got some liver and a soupbone. She never visited with anyone, and as soon as she got what she wanted she lit out for home. It made quite a load for such an old body. No one gave her a lift. People drive right down a road and never notice an old woman like that.

There was such an old woman who used to come into town past our house one summer and fall when I was a young boy and was sick with what was called inflammatory rheumatism. She went home later carrying a heavy pack on her back. Two or three large gaunt-looking dogs followed at her heels.

The old woman was nothing special. She was one of the nameless ones that hardly anyone knows, but she got into my thoughts. I have just suddenly now, after all these years, remembered her and what happened. It is a story. Her name was Grimes, and she lived with her husband and son in a small unpainted house on the bank of a small creek four miles from town.

The husband and son were a tough lot. Although the son was but twenty-one, he had already served a term in jail. It was whispered about that the woman's husband stole horses and ran them off to some other county. Now and then, when a horse turned up missing, the man had also disappeared. No one ever caught him. Once, when I was loafing at Tom Whitehead's livery barn, the man came there and sat on the bench in front. Two or three other men were there, but no one spoke to him. He sat for a few minutes and then got up and went away. When he was leaving he turned around and stared at the men. There was a look of defiance in his eyes. "Well, I have tried to be friendly. You don't want to talk to me. It has been so wherever I have gone in this town. If, some day, one of your fine horses turns up missing, well, then what?" He did not say anything actually. "I'd like to bust one of you on the jaw," was about what his eyes said. I remember how the look in his eyes made me shiver.

The old man belonged to a family that had had money once. His name was Jake Grimes. It all comes back clearly now. His father, John Grimes, had owned a sawmill when the country was new, and had made money. Then he got to drinking and running after women. When he died there wasn't much left.

Jake blew in the rest. Pretty soon there wasn't any more lumber to cut and his land was nearly all gone.

He got his wife off a German farmer, for whom he went to work one June day in the wheat harvest. She was a young thing then and scared to death. You see, the farmer was up to something with the girl—she was, I think, a bound girl and his wife had her suspicions. She took it out on the girl when the man wasn't around. Then, when the wife had to go off to town for supplies, the farmer got after her. She told young Jake that nothing really ever happened, but he didn't know whether to believe it or not.

He got her pretty easy himself, the first time he was out with her. He wouldn't have married her if the German farmer hadn't tried to tell him where to get off. He got her to go riding with him in his buggy one night when he was threshing on the place, and then he came for her the next Sunday night.

She managed to get out of the house without her employer's seeing, but when she was getting into the buggy he showed up. It was almost dark, and he just popped up suddenly at the horse's head. He grabbed the horse by the bridle and Jake got out his buggy whip.

They had it out all right! The German was a tough one. Maybe he didn't care whether his wife knew or not, Jake hit him over the face and shoulders with the buggy whip, but the horse got to acting up and he had to get out.

Then the two men went for it. The girl didn't see it. The horse started to run away and went nearly a mile down the road before the girl got him stopped. Then she managed to tie him to a tree beside the road. (I wonder how I know all this. It must have stuck in my mind from small-town tales when I was a boy.) Jake found her there after he got through with the German. She was huddled up in the buggy seat, crying, scared to death. She told Jake a lot of stuff, how the German had tried to get her, how he chased her once into the barn, how another time, when they happened to be alone in the house together, he tore her dress open clear down the front. The German, she said, might have got her that time if he hadn't heard his old woman drive in at the gate. She had been off to town for supplies. Well, she would be putting the horse in the barn. The German managed to sneak off to the fields without his wife seeing. He told the girl he would kill her if she told. What could she do? She told a lie about ripping her dress in the barn when she was feeding the stock. I remember now that she was a bound girl and did not know where her father and mother were. Maybe she did not have any father. You know what I mean.

Such bound children were often enough cruelly treated. They were children who had no parents, slaves really. There were very few orphan homes then. They were legally bound into some home. It was a matter of pure luck how it came out.

II

She married Jake and had a son and a daughter, but the daughter died.

Then she settled down to feed stock. That was her job. At the German's place she had cooked the food for the German and his wife. The wife was a strong woman with big hips and worked most of the time in the fields with her husband. She fed them and fed the cows in the barn, fed the pigs, the horses and the chickens. Every moment of every day, as a young girl, was spent feeding something.

Then she married Jake Grimes and he had to be fed. She was a slight thing, and when she had been married for three or four years, and after the two children were born, her slender shoulders became stooped.

Jake always had a lot of big dogs around the house, that stood near the unused sawmill near the creek. He was always trading horses when he wasn't stealing something and had a lot of poor bony ones about. Also he kept three or four pigs and a cow. They were all pastured in the few acres left of the Grimes place and Jake did little enough work.

He went into debt for a threshing outfit and ran it for several years, but it did not pay. People did not trust him. They were afraid he would steal the grain at night. He had to go a long way off to get work and it cost too much to get there. In the winter he hunted and cut a little firewood, to be sold in some nearby town. When the son grew up he was just like the father. They got drunk together. If there wasn't anything to eat in the house when they came home the old man gave his old woman a cut over the head. She had a few chickens of her own and had to kill one of them in a hurry. When they were all killed she wouldn't have any eggs to sell when she went to town, and then what would she do?

She had to scheme all her life about getting things fed, getting the pigs fed so they would grow fat and could be butchered in the fall. When they were butchered her husband took most of the meat off to town and sold it. If he did not do it first, the boy did. They fought sometimes and when they fought the old woman stood aside trembling.

She had got the habit of silence anyway—that was fixed. Sometimes, when she began to look old—she wasn't forty yet—and when the husband and son were both off, trading horses or drinking or hunting or stealing, she went around the house and the barnyard muttering to herself.

How was she going to get everything fed?—that was her problem. The dogs had to be fed. There wasn't enough hay in the barn for the horses and the cow. If she didn't feed the chickens how could they lay eggs? Without eggs to sell how could she get things in town, things she had to have to keep the life of the farm going? Thank heaven, she did not have to feed her husband—in a certain way. That hadn't lasted long after their marriage and after the babies came. Where he went on his long trips she did not know. Sometimes he was gone from home for weeks, and after the boy grew up they went off together.

They left everything at home for her to manage and she had no money. She knew no one. No one ever talked to her in town. When it was winter she had to gather sticks of wood for her fire, had to try to keep the stock fed with very little grain.

The stock in the barn cried to her hungrily, the dogs followed her about. In the winter the hens laid few enough eggs. They huddled in the corners of the barn and she kept watching them. If a hen lays an egg in the barn in the winter and you do not find it, it freezes and breaks.

One day in winter the old woman went off to town with a few eggs and the dogs followed her. She did not get started until nearly three o'clock and the snow was heavy. She hadn't been feeling very well for several days and so she went muttering along, scantily clad, her shoulders stooped. She had an old grain bag in which she carried her eggs, tucked away down in the bottom. There weren't many of them, but in winter the price of eggs is up. She would get a little meat in exchange for the eggs, some salt pork, a little sugar, and some coffee perhaps. It might be the butcher would give her a piece of liver.

When she had got to town and was trading in her eggs the dogs lay by the door outside. She did pretty well, got the things she needed, more than she had hoped. Then she went to the butcher and he gave her some liver and some dog meat.

It was the first time anyone had spoken to her in a friendly way for a long time. The butcher was alone in his shop when she came in and was annoyed by the thought of such a sick-looking old woman out on such a day. It was bitter cold and the snow, that had let up during the afternoon, was falling again. The butcher said something about her husband and her son, swore at them, and the old woman stared at him, a look of mild surprise in her eyes as he talked. He said that if either the husband or the son were going to get any of the liver or the heavy bones with scraps of meat hanging to them that he had put into the grain bag, he'd see him starve first.

Starve, eh? Well, things had to be fed. Men had to be fed, and the horses that weren't any good but maybe could be traded off, and the poor thin cow that hadn't given any milk for three months.

Horses, cows, pigs, dogs, men.

III

The old woman had to get back before darkness came if she could. The dogs followed at her heels, sniffing at the heavy grain bag she had fastened on her back. When she got to the edge of town she stopped by a fence and tied the bag on her back with a piece of rope she had carried in her dress pocket for just that purpose. That was an easier way to carry it. Her arms ached. It was hard when she had to crawl over fences and once she fell over and landed in the snow. The dogs went frisking about. She had to struggle to get to her feet again, but she made it. The point of climbing over the fences was that there was a short cut over a hill and through a woods. She might have gone around by the road, but it was a mile farther that way. She was afraid she couldn't make it. And then, besides, the stock had to be fed. There was a little hay left and a little corn. Perhaps her husband and son would bring some home when they came. They had driven off in the only buggy the Grimes family had, a rickety thing, a rickety horse hitched to the buggy, two other rickety horses led by halters. They were going to trade horses, get a little money if they could. They might come home drunk. It would be well to have something in the house when they came back.

The son had an affair on with a woman at the county seat, fifteen miles away. She was a rough enough woman, a tough one. Once, in the summer, the son had brought her to the house. Both she and the son had been drinking. Jake Grimes was away and the son and his woman ordered the old woman about like a servant. She didn't mind much; she was used to it. Whatever happened she never said anything. That was her way of getting along. She had managed that way when she was a young girl at the German's and ever since she had married Jake. That time her son brought his woman to the house they stayed all night, sleeping together just as though they were married. It hadn't shocked the old woman, not much. She had got past being shocked early in life.

With the pack on her back she went painfully along across an open field, wading in the deep snow, and got into the woods.

There was a path, but it was hard to follow. Just beyond the top of the hill, where the woods was thickest, there was a small clearing. Had someone once thought of building a house there? The clearing was as large as a building lot in town, large enough for a house and a garden. The path ran along the side of the clearing, and when she got there the old woman sat down to rest at the foot of a tree.

It was a foolish thing to do. When she got herself placed, the pack against the tree's trunk, it was nice, but what about getting up again? She worried about that for a moment and then quietly closed her eyes.

She must have slept for a time. When you are about so cold you can't get any colder. The afternoon grew a little warmer and the snow came thicker than ever. Then after a time the weather cleared. The moon even came out.

There were four Grimes dogs that had followed Mrs. Grimes into town, all tall gaunt fellows. Such men as Jake Grimes and his son always keep just such dogs. They kick and abuse them, but they stay. The Grimes dogs, in order to keep from starving, had to do a lot of foraging for themselves, and they had been at it while the old woman slept with her back to the tree at the side of the clearing. They had been chasing rabbits in the woods and in adjoining fields and in their ranging had picked up three other farm dogs.

After a time all the dogs came back to the clearing. They were excited about something. Such nights, cold and clear and with a moon, do things to dogs. It may be that some old instinct, come down from the time when they were wolves and ranged the woods in packs on winter nights, comes back into them.

The dogs in the clearing, before the old woman, had caught two or three rabbits and their immediate hunger had been satisfied. They began to play, running in circles in the clearing. Round and round they ran, each dog's nose at the tail of the next dog. In the clearing, under the snow-laden trees and under the wintry moon they made a strange picture, running thus silently, in a circle their running had beaten in the soft snow. The dogs made no sound. They ran around and around in the circle.

It may have been that the old woman saw them doing that before she died. She may have awakened once or twice and looked at the strange sight with dim old eyes.

She wouldn't be very cold now, just drowsy. Life hangs on a long time. Perhaps the old woman was out of her head. She may have dreamed of her girlhood, at the German's, and before that, when she was a child and before her mother lit out and left her.

Her dreams couldn't have been very pleasant. Not many pleasant things have happened to her. Now and then one of the Grimes dogs left the running circle and came to stand before her. The dog thrust his face close to her face. His red tongue was hanging out.

The running of the dogs may have been a kind of death ceremony. It may have been that the primitive instinct of the wolf, having been aroused in the dogs by the night and the running, made them somehow afraid.

"Now we are no longer wolves. We are dogs, the servants of men. Keep alive, man! When man dies we become wolves again."

When one of the dogs came to where the old woman sat with her back against the tree and thrust his nose close to her face he seemed satisfied and went back to run with the pack. All the Grimes dogs did it at some time during the evening, before she died. I knew all about it afterward, when I grew to be a man, because once in a woods in Illinois, on another winter night, I saw a pack of dogs act just like that. The dogs were waiting for me to die as they had waited for the old woman that night when I was a child, but when it happened to me I was a young man and had no intention whatever of dying.

The old woman died softly and quietly. When she was dead and when one of the Grimes dogs had come to her and had found her dead all the dogs stopped running.

They gathered about her.

Well, she was dead now. She had fed the Grimes dogs when she was alive, what about now?

There was the pack on her back, the grain bag containing the piece of salt pork, the liver the butcher had given her, the dog meat, the soupbones. The butcher in town, having been suddenly overcome with a feeling of pity, had loaded her grain bag heavily. It had been a big haul for the old woman.

It was a big haul for the dogs now.

IV

One of the Grimes dogs sprang suddenly out from among the others and began worrying the pack on the old woman's back. Had the dogs really been wolves, that one would have been the leader of the pack. What he did, all the others did.

All of them sank their teeth into the grain bag the old woman had fastened with ropes to her back.

They dragged the old woman's body out into the open clearing. The worn-out dress was quickly torn from her shoulders. When she was found, a day or two later, the dress had been torn from her body clear to the hips, but the dogs had not touched her body. They had got the meat out of the grain bag, that was all. Her body was frozen stiff when it was found, and the shoulders were so narrow and the body so slight that in death it looked like the body of some charming young girl.

Such things happened in towns of the Middle West, on farms near town, when I was a boy. A hunter out after rabbits found the old woman's body and did not touch it. Something, the beaten round path in the little snow-covered clearing, the silence of the place, the place where the dogs had worried the body trying to pull the grain bag away or tear it open—something startled the man and he hurried off to town.

I was in Main Street with one of my brothers who was town newsboy and who was taking the afternoon papers to the stores. It was almost night.

The hunter came into a grocery and told his story. Then he went to a hardware shop and into a drugstore. Men began to gather on the sidewalks. Then they started out along the road to the place in the woods.

My brother should have gone on about his business of distributing papers but he didn't. Everyone was going to the woods. The undertaker went and the town marshal. Several men got on a dray and rode out to where the path left the road and went into the woods, but the horses weren't very sharply shod and slid about on the slippery roads. They made no better time than those of us who walked.

The town marshal was a large man whose leg had been injured in the Civil War. He carried a heavy cane and limped rapidly along the road. My brother and I followed at his heels, and as we went other men and boys joined the crowd.

It had grown dark by the time we got to where the old woman had left the road, but the moon had come out. The marshal was thinking there might have been a murder. He kept asking the hunter questions. The hunter went along with his gun across his shoulders, a dog following at his heels. It isn't often a rabbit hunter has a chance to be so conspicuous. He was taking full advantage of it, leading the procession with the town marshal. "I didn't see any wounds. She was a beautiful young girl. Her face was buried in the snow. No, I didn't know her." As a matter of fact, the hunter had not looked closely at the body. He had been frightened. She might have been murdered and someone might spring out from behind a tree and murder him. In a woods, in the late afternoon, when the trees are all bare and there is white snow on the ground, when all is silent, something creepy steals over the mind and body. If something strange or uncanny has happened in the neighborhood all you think about is getting away from there as fast as you can.

The crowd of men and boys had got to where the old woman had crossed the field and went, following the marshal and the hunter, up the slight incline and into the woods.

My brother and I were silent. He had his bundle of papers in a bag slung across his shoulder. When he got back to town he would have to go on distributing his papers before he went home to supper. If I went along, as he had no doubt already determined I should, we would both be late. Either Mother or our older sister would have to warm our supper.

Well, we would have something to tell. A boy did not get such a chance very often. It was lucky we just happened to go into the grocery when the hunter came in. The hunter was a country fellow. Neither of us had ever seen him before.

Now the crowd of men and boys had got to the clearing. Darkness comes quickly on such winter nights, but the full moon made everything clear. My brother and I stood near the tree beneath which the old woman had died.

She did not look old, lying there in that light, frozen and still. One of the men turned her over in the snow and I saw everything. My body trembled with some strange mystical feeling and so did my brother's. It might have been the cold.

Neither of us had ever seen a woman's body before. It may have been the snow, clinging to the frozen flesh, that made it look so white and lovely, so like marble. No woman had come with the party from town; but one of the men, he was the town blacksmith, took off his overcoat and spread it over her. Then he gathered her into his arms and started off to town, all the others following silently. At that time no one knew who she was.

V

I had seen everything, had seen the oval in the snow, like a miniature race track, where the dogs had run, had seen how the men were mystified, had seen the white bare young-looking shoulders, had heard the whispered comments of the men.

The men were simply mystified. They took the body to the undertaker's, and when the blacksmith, the hunter, the marshal and several others had got inside they closed the door. If Father had been there perhaps he could have got in, but we boys couldn't.

I went with my brother to distribute the rest of his papers and when we got home it was my brother who told the story.

I kept silent and went to bed early. It may have been I was not satisfied with the way he told it.

Later, in the town, I must have heard other fragments of the old woman's story. She was recognized the next day and there was an investigation.

The husband and son were found somewhere and brought to town and there was an attempt to connect them with the woman's death, but it did not work. They had perfect enough alibis.

However, the town was against them. They had to get out. Where they went I never heard.

I remember only the picture there in the forest, the men standing about, the naked girlish-looking figure, face down in the snow, the tracks made by the running dogs and the clear cold winter sky above. White fragments of clouds were drifting across the sky. They went racing across the little open space among the trees.

The scene in the forest had become for me, without my knowing it, the foundation for the real story I am now trying to tell. The fragments, you see, had to be picked up slowly, long afterward.

Things happened. When I was a young man I worked on the farm of a German. The hired girl was afraid of her employer. The farmer's wife hated her.

I saw things at that place. Once later, I had a half-uncanny, mystical adventure with dogs in an Illinois forest on a clear, moonlit winter night. When I was a schoolboy, and on a summer day, I went with a boy friend out along a creek some miles from town and came to the house where the old woman had lived. No one had lived in the house since her death. The doors were broken from the hinges; the window lights were all broken. As the boy and I stood in the road outside, two dogs, just roving farm dogs no doubt, came running around the corner of the house. The dogs were tall, gaunt fellows and came down to the fence and glared through at us, standing in the road.

The whole thing, the story of the old woman's death, was to me as I grew older like music heard from far off. The notes had to be picked up slowly one at a time. Something had to be understood.

The woman who died was one destined to feed animal life. Anyway, that is all she ever did. She was feeding animal life before she was born, as a child, as a young woman working on the farm of the German, after she married, when she grew old, and when she died. She fed animal life in cows, in chickens, in pigs, in horses, in dogs, in men. Her daughter had died in childhood and with her one son she had no articulate relations. On the night when she died she was hurrying homeward, bearing on her body food for animal life.

She died in the clearing in the woods and even after her death continued feeding animal life.

You see, it is likely that when my brother told the story that night when we got home and my mother and sister sat listening I did not think he got the point. He was too young and so was I. A thing so complete has its own beauty.

I shall not try to emphasize the point. I am only explaining why I was dissatisfied then and have been ever since. I speak of that only that you may understand why I have been impelled to try to tell the simple story over again.

1933

Theodore Dreiser 1871–1945

Theodore Dreiser was the son of a German Catholic immigrant father and a German-Moravian Mennonite mother. He spent his childhood in the Midwest, his parents moving frequently from one town to another as they searched for steady employment and tried to establish a stable home life for their large family. Paul, the eldest of the ten Dreiser children, changed his name to the less Germanic "Dresser" and went on stage where he became famous as a vaudeville performer and songwriter. The other Dreiser children, with the exception of Theodore, were less successful: all of them rebelled against their father's dogmatic Catholicism, and some of them drifted into petty crime or, in the case of several of the girls, into liaisons with married men. Theodore's education was desultory, but through the generosity of one of his elementary school teachers he did manage a year at Indiana University in 1889–90. Not long after, he made a start in journalism and wrote for newspapers in Chicago, St. Louis, and Pittsburgh. During this period he first encountered the fiction of Balzac and the philosophical writings of Huxley, Tyndall, and Spencer. These authors had a strong impact on him and profoundly influenced his subsequent thinking.

By 1899 Dreiser had become a successful free-lance writer in New York City and had married. At the urging of his friend Arthur Henry, he undertook a novel and based it on the experiences of one of his sisters. That novel became *Sister Carrie* (1900), a landmark in American naturalistic fiction. Difficulties with his publisher over the novel, together with marital problems and other tensions, caused Dreiser to suffer a nervous breakdown in 1902. With the aid of his brother Paul he recovered and re-entered the world of journalism early in 1904 but attempted no significant new writing for almost seven years—though he did have *Sister Carrie* successfully reissued in 1907. After he lost a lucrative position with the Butterick Publishing Company in 1910, Dreiser completed and published *Jennie Gerhardt* (1911). That book, with *Sister Carrie*, finally established him as a visible, pioneering novelist.

The next fourteen years were productive but difficult for Dreiser. Such novels as *The Financier, The Titan,* and *The "Genius"* were frank in their treatment of sex and severe in their criticism of American society; as a result, they were frequently attacked and sometimes banned. Dreiser joined with H. L. Mencken, his champion among critics, and with Horace Liveright, his publisher, to battle the forces of puritanism and repression in the courts and the literary marketplace. These conflicts left Dreiser exhausted and wary of further disputes with censors. After *The "Genius"* in 1915, he published no new novel for ten years, though he worked on several in manuscript. His career as a writer of fiction culminated in 1925 with publication of the magnificent two-volume novel *An American Tragedy,* based on an actual murder case in upstate New York. After the *Tragedy,* Dreiser completed no other novel until almost the end of his life, but he remained active over the next two decades, issuing poetry, short fiction, travel books, philosophical writings, journalism, drama, and a remarkable autobiographical volume entitled *Dawn* (1931). During the thirties and forties he involved himself in proletarian causes and, shortly before his death, applied for membership in the Communist Party.

"Typhoon" was written by Dreiser not long after he published *An American Tragedy.* Like that novel it is based on an actual murder case—the shooting of Edward Lister by Ethel Schultz in Philadelphia on October 27, 1925. "Typhoon" is typically Dreiserian: the story includes elements strongly reminiscent of *Sister Carrie, Jennie Gerhardt,* and the *Tragedy,* and it touches on many other major themes found in Dreiser's writings. Its message, strongly pessimistic, is tempered by Dreiser's sympathy for his characters, especially Ida, who is trapped biologically and is driven by desires and motives which she does not understand.

Dreiser wrote "Typhoon" early in 1926 for the mass-circulation magazine *Hearst's International-Cosmopolitan.* The story appeared there in October 1926 under the title "The Wages of Sin" and was republished the following spring, under Dreiser's preferred title, in his collection *Chains: Lesser Novels and Stories.* Both the magazine text and the collected text were cut and censored before publication. The magazine version was especially heavily edited; the cuts altered characterization and motivation, removed many references to sex, and softened the harsh determinism of the theme. Dreiser restored some of the excised material to the collected version, but he was still not able to publish "Typhoon" as he had originally written it. The text presented here has been reconstructed by James M. Hutchisson from manuscripts and typescripts which survive among Dreiser's literary papers at the University of Pennsylvania. "Typhoon" appears below as Dreiser originally wished to publish it.

James M. Hutchisson
The Citadel

James L.W. West, III
The Pennsylvania State University

PRIMARY WORKS

Sister Carrie, 1900; *Jennie Gerhardt,* 1911; *The Financier,* 1912 (rev. edn., 1927); *A Traveler at Forty,* 1913; *The Titan,* 1914; *The "Genius,"* 1915; *A Hoosier Holiday,* 1916; *Free and Other Stories,* 1918; *Twelve Men,* 1919; *Hey Rub-a-Dub-Dub!,* 1920; *A Book about Myself,* 1922; *The Color of a Great City,* 1923; *An American Tragedy,* 1925; *Moods,* 1926; *Chains,* 1927; *Dreiser Looks at Russia,* 1928; *A Gallery of Women,* 1929; *Dawn,* 1931; *The Bulwark,* 1946; *The Stoic,* 1947.

Typhoon

Into a singularly restricted and indifferent environment Ida Zobel was born. Her mother, a severe, prim German woman, died when Ida was but three, leaving her first to the care of her father, a reserved and orderly person who in turn employed for her his sister, who was as rigid and socially restricted as himself. He was the owner and manager of a small wallpaper, paint and color store in the immediate vicinity of the house they occupied. Later, after Ida had reached the age of ten, William Zobel, her father, took to himself a second wife, Maria Stamp, who like Zobel and his first wife was as much a stickler for labor, order and the like as was he.

Both were entirely at odds with the brash gayety and baseness of the American world in which they found themselves. Being narrow, sober, workaday Germans, they were annoyed by the groups of restless, seeking, eager and as Zobel saw it rather scandalous young men and women who paraded these neighborhood streets of an evening without a single thought apparently other than pleasure. No care as to thrift, sobriety, duty or the value of time. They had jobs and a little money—or no money and no jobs—but at any rate they were not concerned about the future as they should have been. The swarms and swarms of automobiles!— And these young scamps and their girlfriends who sped about in them whether they owned them or not. The loose, indifferent parents. The loose, free ways of all of these children. What was to become of such a nation? Were not the daily newspapers, which he would scarcely tolerate in his home, full of these wretched doings? The pictures of almost naked women that filled them all! Jazz! Petting parties! High school boys with flasks of whiskey on their hips! Girls with skirts to their knees, rolled-down stockings, rolled-down neck bands, bare arms, bobbed hair—no decent, concealing underwear. And all parading up and down Warren Avenue, which was a rapidly developing commercial street to which the Zobel home was contiguous. In fact, rouge, lipstick, bobbed hair and the free, gay, loose way of the current American girl were singly and collectively anathema to this conventional, recessive German and his second wife, who were enamored of much more sober ways.

"What—a daughter of his grow up like that!—be permitted to join in this prancing rout to perdition! Never!" And in consequence the strictest of rules from Ida's third or fourth or fifth year on. Her hair was to grow its natural length, of course. Her lips and cheeks were never to know the blush of false suggestive paint: and plain dresses. And plain underwear and stockings—and shoes and hats and work at home and in the store, when not otherwise employed with her studies at school. No crazy, idiotic finery—but substantial, respectable clothing. And last but not least, schooling of such a proper and definite character as would serve to keep her mind from the innumerable current follies which were apparently pulling at the very foundations of decent society.

And in consequence Zobel chose a private and somewhat religious school conducted by an aged German spinster of the name of Elizabeth Hohstauffer who had succeeded after years and years of teaching in impressing her merits as a mentor on perhaps as many as a hundred German families of the area. No contact with the careless if not actually shameless public school here. And once the child had been inducted into that, there followed a series of daily inquiries and directions intended to guide the youth in the path she was expected to follow.

"Hurry—you have only ten minutes now in which to get to school. There is no time to lose." On which she departed for and returned from school—morning, noon, night; the company kept, the places she went, the time taken to go to and return from the same, her study hours, her shopping pilgrimages were all strictly regulated. "How comes it that you are five minutes late tonight? What were you doing? Your teacher compelled you to stay? What for? You had to stay and look for a blank book? Why didn't you come home first and then let me look for it with you afterwards?" (It was her stepmother talking.) "You know your father does not want you to stay out after school. Besides, there in the store your father needs you. And just what were you doing in Warren Avenue between twelve and one today? Your father said you were walking with Vilma Balet. And who is Vilma Balet? Where does she live? How long has it been since you have been going with her? Why is it you have not mentioned her before? You know what your father's rule is. And now I shall have to tell him. He will be angry. You must obey his rules. You are by no means old enough to decide for yourself. You have heard him say that."

Notwithstanding all this, Ida, though none too daring or aggressive mentally, was none-the-less imaginatively and emotionally drawn to the very gayeties and pleasures that require courage and daring. She lived in a mental world made up of the bright lights of Warren Avenue which traversed the great mill district known as Kensington. The cars, the moving picture theatres of which there were three matinees within a mile of each other on this great commonplace thoroughfare, with its street cars and endless stores side by side. The movies and her favorite photographs of actresses and actors (some of the mannerisms of whom the girls imitated at school). The voices, the laughter, the walkings to and fro, arm in arm, of the boys and girls that were to be seen here and there planning what pleasures, discussing what triumphs or prospective joys.

But as for Ida, despite her budding sensitivity—at ten, eleven, twelve, thirteen, fourteen, what varying and at times troublesome dreams, aspirations, recessions. There was no escape from the severe regimen she was compelled to follow. The work she had to do, the rules she had to observe. Breakfast at seven-thirty sharp because the store had to be opened by her father at eight, which meant rising at seven; luncheon at twelve-thirty so as to satisfy her father and her own noon recess hour which was completely filled by this; dinner invariably at six-thirty because there were many things, commercial and social, which fell upon the shoulders of William Zobel at night. And between whiles, from four to six in weekdays and later from seven to ten at night, as well as all day Saturdays, store duty in her father's store.

While other girls walked the streets arm in arm, or made pairs with young men of the region or elsewhere and were off to the movies, or to some party—and came in at what hours after—(didn't she hear them laugh and chatter at school and on their ways home, afterwards)—she, because of her father's and later her stepmother's attitude, was compelled to adhere to the regimen thought advisable for her. No parties that kept her out later than ten at night at anytime—and then only after due investigation. Those she really liked were always picked to pieces by her stepmother—and, of course, this somewhat influenced the opinion of her father. It was common gossip of the neighborhood by the time she was twelve that her parents were very strict and that they permitted her scarcely any liberties. A trip to a movie, the choice of which was properly supervised by her parents; an occasional ride in an automobile with her parents because, by the time she had attained fifteen years of age, he had purchased one of the cheaper cars.

But all the time the rout of youthful life ever before her eyes. And in so far as her home life or the emotional significance of her parents were concerned—a sort of depressive greyness there. For William Zobel, with his grey-blue eyes gleaming behind gilt-rimmed glasses, was scarcely the person to whom a girl of Ida's temperament would be drawn. Nor yet her stepmother with her tall, narrow face, brown eyes and black hair. Indeed Zobel grew more impressive as she grew older. He had wanted a boy and had not obtained him. Next his wife had died, leaving him Ida. He became a father who by the very solemnity of his demeanor, as well as the soberness and practicality of his thoughts and rules, was constantly evoking a sense of dictatorship, which was by no means anything to entice a sympathetic approach on the part of such a girl as Ida—let alone intimacy. To be sure, there were greetings, acknowledgements, respectful and careful explanations as to this and that and the other. Occasionally they would go to a friend's house, a public restaurant where Zobel as well as his wife liked to dine. But there existed no understanding on the part of either

Zobel or his wife—he having never desired a girl of his own and Mrs. Zobel not being particularly drawn to the child of another—of the growing problems of adolescence that might be confronting her, and hence none of that possible harmony and enlightenment which might have endeared each to the other.

Instead repression—and even fear at him which in the course of years took on the aspect of careful courtesy supplemented by accurate obedience. But within herself a growing sense of her own increasing charm, which, in her father's eyes, if not in her stepmother's, seemed to be identified always with danger—either present or prospective. Were there not boys who, from her seventh year on, looked at her and sought to attract her attention? Could not he as well as his second wife see at the same time in her a budding realization of her charm—her very light and silky hair. The light greyish-blue eyes. A rounded and intriguing figure which other girls, even at Magdalena Girl's School, noticed and commented on. Not only that but her small *retroussé* nose and full and yet small and almost pouting mouth and rounded chin. Had she not a mirror? Worse—throughout the brisk, sensitive, colorful years and impinging upon adolescence, what varying and at times troublesome dreams, aspirations, recessions. The smart, playful, wayward boy students of Watkins High—which was in the immediate vicinity of her own home, though she did not attend it—who in bright college caps and sweaters, their books under their arms and all too often in the lauding, genial company of the colorful, carefree girls of the same school, made their way along Warren Avenue which she was compelled to traverse also. And their laughter. Their vigor. The bantering, seeking, intriguing free conversation so universally redolent of the desire of the opposite sexes for each other. And yet in the face of that, her own home. And in the interim, cooking, sewing, studying in such fields as Zobel and his second wife thought it best she should study or make herself useful, and in addition, on occasion, errand-running in such swift and brief ways as was deemed sufficient to guard against contacts which might seem loose or prove inimical.

And yet, in spite of all these precautions, the swift telegraphy of eyes and blood. And the haunting, seeking moods of youth which speak a language of their own. In the drug store at the corner of Warren and Tracy, but a half block from her home, there was at one time in her twelfth year Edward Sullivan, a soda clerk. And at that time he seemed to her the handsomest and the most beautiful thing she had ever seen. The dark, smooth hair lying glossed and parted above a perfect white forehead. Slim, graceful hands—or so she thought, a care and smartness in the manner of dress which even the clothing of the scores of public school boys passing this way seemed scarcely to match. And such a way where girls were concerned—so smiling and at his ease—a most wonderful smile for everybody. And a word, too, for scores of girls in this very vicinity—some who attended the conservative school of Miss Hohstauffer and who came this way on their way home.

"Why, hello Della! How's Miss McGinnis today? I bet I know what you're going to have. I think pretty blonde girls must like chocolate sundaes—they contrast with their complexions." And then smiling serenely while Miss McGinnis panted—and smiled a little. "A lot you know about what blonde girls like."

And Ida Zobel, present on occasion by permission for a soda or a sundae, looking on and listening most eagerly. Such a handsome youth. All of sixteen. As yet he would pay no attention to so youthful a girl as her of course. But when she was older. Would she be as handsome as Miss McGinnis? Could she be as assured? How wonderful to be so attractive to such a youth! And what would he say to her, if he said anything at all. And what would she say to him—if she were ever able to say anything to him or anybody—seeing that her father felt as he did and her stepmother too. Many times she imitated these girls mentally and held imaginary conversations with herself. Yet despite this passive admiration, Mr. Sullivan had gone the way of all soda clerks, changing eventually to another job in another neighborhood—

But in the course of time, there were others who took her eye—and for a little while filled her mind—around whose differing charms she erected fancies which had nothing to do with reality. One of these was Merton Webster, the brisk, showy, vain and none-too-ambitious son of a local state senator from the region who lived in the same block she did and attended Watkins High School. So handsome was he,—so debonair—such an easy smiling way where all girls were concerned. "Hello, kid. Gee you look cute, all right. One of these days I'll take you to a dance if you want to go." Yet because at the time he was most definitely interested in another, he paid no attention to her and she was troubled by thoughts of him until Walter Stour, whose father conducted the realty and insurance business only a little way west of her father's store in Warren Avenue, took her attention—a year later. He was a tall, fair-complected youth with gay eyes and a big, laughing mouth who occasionally—with Merton Webster, Laurence Cross, a son of one of the grocers of the area, Sven Volberg, the dry cleaner's son, and some others—hung about the moving picture theatre or the drug store or on the main corner and flirted with the girls of the vicinity as they passed by.

As restricted as she was, still because of her trips to and fro between her home and school and her service as a clerk in her father's store, she was not unfamiliar with these several figures or their names. They passed her place. She was looked at, commented on, even. "Oh, getting to be a pretty girl—we think." Whereupon she would flush with excitement and busy herself about filling the customer's order.

It was through Etelka Shomel, the daughter of a German neighbor who was also a friend of William Zobel, that she learned much of these boys and girls. Her father thought Etelka a safe character for Ida to chum with, chiefly on account of her unattractiveness. But through her, as well as their joint pilgrimages here and there, she came to hear much gossip about these boys and girls of the neighborhood. Walter Stour, whom she now so greatly admired, was going with a girl by the name of Edna Strong who was the daughter of a milk dealer. Stour's father was not as stingy as some fathers. He had a good car and occasionally let his son use it. Stour often took Edna and some of her friends to boathouse resorts on the Little Shark River. A girlfriend of Etelka's told her what a wonderful mimic and dancer he was. He could mimic an Irishman, a "Kike," a Chinaman and a Swede. He was funny and he wore such fine clothes—one of the best-dressed boys in the neighborhood.

And one night as Ida was coming around from her father's house to his store at seven-thirty, and Stour was on his favorite corner with several other boys, he called, "I know who's a sweet kid—but her father won't let her look at anybody." And Ida, knowing full well who was meant, had flushed to the roots of her unbobbed hair, but hurried on all the faster. Oh, my! If her father heard that! But it thrilled her as she walked. "Sweet kid," "Sweet kid," kept ringing in her ears.

And then at last in her sixteenth year, Mr. Stour and the others having all gone, Edward Hauptfuhrer, the debonair son of Jacob Hauptfuhrer, a very well-to-do coal dealer who had recently purchased a yard on the Absecon, moved into the neighborhood. And just at the time, no end of weariness and yearning on the part of Ida, who was keenly aware by now that her normal girlhood with its so necessary social contacts was being set at naught—was completely frustrated by the stern and repressive attitude of her father and stepmother. But ah, the wonder of the spring and summer evenings when she turned sixteen. The moon above her own commonplace home—shining down into the narrow and commonplace garden at the back where still were tulips, hyacinths, honeysuckle and roses. And the moon above Warren Avenue where were the cars, the crowds, the moving picture theatres and restaurants. There was a kind of madness, an ache in it all. Oh, for pleasure—pleasure! To go, run, dance, play, kiss with someone—almost anyone really, if he were only young and handsome. And herself out of school now, yet clerking as before. And dressing as before. No short skirts, bobbed hair, rolled-down stockings, lip or cheek rouge. How was she to bring herself into the current of the actual and beautiful? And the young men on the streets passing or kicking their heels on the corner as she passed—or calling to her from cars—saying, "Oh, look who's here. She's pretty all right but her father won't let her have any fun. Why don't you bob your hair, Ida? You're too cute not to." Yet with fear and weakness, not so much before her stepmother, whom she no longer dreaded so much, as her father.

But with the arrival of this Edward Hauptfuhrer—more daring and strategic than any of the hometown boys she had known so far—there came a change. For here was a youth of definite and drastic impulses—a beau, a fighter, a fellow of infinite guile where girls of all sorts were concerned—and, too, a youth of taste in the matter of dress and manner—one who stood out as a kind of hero to the type of youthful male companion with whom he chose to associate. These old-fashioned dictatorial German parents didn't bother him. Didn't he have a pair of his own? But couldn't he see old Zobel in his store—morning, noon and night when he passed that way, bent over his cash register or his books—or measuring something out for a customer? And so often, now that she had graduated from her school and was at home all of the time, the fair Ida herself behind the counter with him—or quite alone, waiting on customers when he was not there. And for reason of her repressed beauty, which had come to attract him largely because it was so obviously repressed, he had come to note the hours when she was most alone. These were, as a rule, Wednesdays and Fridays—when because of a singing society as well as a German men's social and commercial club—her father was absent from eight-thirty on. And although assisted by her stepmother occasionally, she was usually alone, as he had also noted.

But more definite and important than anything else in connection with all this was the distinct and intriguing thought in his own mind that she was disposed toward love but, because of the repression by her father, was held in check, and that if he were to approach her with sufficient art, most distinctly he could intrigue her in a romance. The thing to do was to outwit her father. Would that not set him apart as one who was above the average in this matter of intrigue and charm for girls?

And so a campaign which was to break the spell which held the sleeping beauty. At first, however, only a smile in the direction of Ida whenever he passed or she passed him, together with boasts to his friends to the effect that he would "win that kid yet; wait and see." And then one evening, in the absence of Zobel, a visit to the store. Ida was behind the counter, and between the business of waiting on customers she was dreaming as usual of the life outside. For during the past few weeks she had become more sharply conscious of the smiling interest of Mr. Hauptfuhrer. His straight lithe body—his quick aggressive manner—his assertive seeking eyes! Oh my! Like the others who had gone before him, and who had attracted her emotional interest, he was that smart, fastidious, self-assured and self-admiring type which so attracts the inexperienced girl. No hesitancy. No doubt as to his victory at any point. Even for this occasion he had scarcely troubled to think of a story. What difference? Any old story would do. He wanted to see some paints. They might be going to repaint the house soon. And in the meanwhile he would engage her in conversation. And if the "old man" came back, well, he was looking over some paints, wasn't he?

And so on this particularly warm and enticing night in May when Ida was sixteen, Mr. Hauptfuhrer walking in briskly, in a new grey suit, light tan fedora hat and tan shoes and tie completing an ensemble which was the admiration of the neighborhood. Furthermore, he carried it all with the air of a cavalier and a fighter—one of the best in the neighborhood as all of his companions knew. "Oh, hello. Pretty tough to have to work inside on a night like this, ain't it?" (And a most irresistible smile going with this.) "I want to see some paints—the colors of 'em I mean. The old man is thinking of doing over a part of the house this summer." And at once, Ida excited and flushing to the roots of her hair, turning to look for a color card—as much to conceal her flushing as anything else. And yet intrigued as much as she was affrighted. The daring of this handsome cavalier—to come right in here and approach her in this brisk manner. Supposing her father should return—or her stepmother enter? Still wasn't this youth as much a customer as anyone else? Or could be, although she knew by his manner that it was by no means paints that had brought him. And yet while over the way three of his admiring companions had ranged themselves to watch her. Hauptfuhrer leaning genially and familiarly against the counter and continuing, "Gee, I've seen you often enough, going back and forth between your school and the store and your home. You've never gone around much with the rest of the girls. Too bad! Otherwise we mighta' met before. I've met all the rest of the girls so far." And as he spoke, troubling to touch his tie, he managed to bring into action one handsome hand with not only an opal on the ring finger but the smartly striped pink cuff of his shirt gracefully encircling his wrist. "I used to see you when you went to Miss Hohstauffer's school up here on Brainerd near Warren. I heard your father wouldn't even let you go to Watkins High. Pretty strict, eh?" And he beamed into the pale blue-grey eyes of the budding girl before him—noted the rounded pink cheeks—the full mouth, the silky hair—the while she trembled and thrilled.

"Yes, he is pretty strict, that's true."

"But you can't just go nowhere—all the time, can you?" And by now the color card, taken into his own hand, was lying flat on the desk. "You gotta have a little fun once in a while, eh? If I'da thought you'da stood for it, I'da introduced myself before. My father has the big coal dock down here on the river. He knows your father—by sight anyhow. I gotta car—or at least my dad has—and that's as good as mine. You don't think your parents 'ud letcha' take a run out in the country some Saturday or Sunday—down to Little Shark River or Peck's Beach, say. Lots of the fellows and girls from around here go down there."

By now it was obvious that Mr. Hauptfuhrer was getting along in his conquest, and his companions over the way were abandoning their advantageous position—no longer hopefully interested by the possibility of defeat. And the nervous Ida—intrigued though terrified, was thinking how wonderful that at last so handsome a youth as this—decidedly as handsome as any in the vicinity—was showing attention to her—and even though her hair was not bobbed. Were his intentions sincere? Could it really be that he was intrigued by her physical charm? His dark brown and yet hard and eager eyes. His handsome hands. The smart way in which he dressed. If only her parents would permit her to enjoy the companionship of such a youth as this, and yet her father—her stepmother. Already, and even as she talked she found herself explaining—supposing her father or stepmother—but more especially her father—should come in at the door, that after all he was a customer.

At the same time she found herself most definitely replying—"Oh no. I couldn't ever do anything like that. Not just that way, anyhow. You see he doesn't know you and besides we haven't been introduced and he wouldn't let me go with anyone he doesn't know or to whom I haven't been introduced. You know how it is." Contrasted with his neat-fitting grey suit and tan and red tie and his ring, she was becoming conscious of the severely plain blue dress with white trimmings which she wore,—the fact that her hands carried no ring and that her slippers and stockings were not as smart as they should be—her skirts much too long. And if she went on such a trip they would be the same, would they not? Yet the wonder of knowing such a youth—of having him for a beau. Oh, must this fail—this wonderful opportunity?

But undaunted, Mr. Hauptfuhrer had another suggestion. Those cheeks. Those swimming, eager, melting grey-blue eyes—that rounded, sensuous face. "Well, why couldn't I introduce myself then? My father knows him by name anyhow—and he knows my father I'm sure. I'm not afraid of him. I could just tell him that I want to call on you—couldn't I—there's sure no harm in that, is there?" Mr. Hauptfuhrer was as brave as he was sly.

"Well, that might be all right, only he's very strict—and he might not want me to go anyhow."

"Oh, pshaw. But you would like to go, wouldn't you? Or to a moving picture show. He couldn't kick against that, could he?"

He looked the fair Ida in the eye, smiling, and in doing so drew the lids of his eyes together in a sensuous intriguing way which he had found effective with others. They had commented on it. The budding Ida—impulses over which she had no consciousness or control set seething by this—merely looked at him weakly. The wonder of all this. The beauty of love! Her desire toward him! His charm. Would her father accept him? Would he? Oh, if he only would! So finding heart to say, "No, maybe not. I don't know. You see I've never had a beau, yet."

She looked at him in such a way as to convince him of his conquest. "Easy! A cinch!" was his thought. "Nothing to it at all." He would either see Zobel in person and make a request saying who he was or meet Ida clandestinely. Gee, a father like that had no right to keep his daughter from having any fun at all. Besides, the pride of showing to all the others how easy this conquest had been. And couldn't he drop her—if he wanted to? Hadn't he dropped others? These narrow, hard-boiled German parents. They ought to be shown, oughtn't they—awakened—made to come to life.

And then within only two days Mr. Hauptfuhrer brazenly presenting himself to Zobel in his store in order to test whether he could not induce him to accept him as, presumably at least, a candidate for his daughter's favor. Yet in his mind or mood at the time, no concern for either the mood or the plans of Mr. Zobel in regard to his daughter. On the contrary, Mr. Hauptfuhrer was of that audacious as well as brazen temperament which saw in such a situation as this a test for his skill as a young Lothario and little more. What! Marry a girl just because you want to have a little flirtation with her—or she with you? Where did any old fashioned "nut" such as this same Zobel, for instance, get that stuff?

As for himself, in connection with all of his adventures thus far, he not even for so much as a moment seriously considered any such thing. He was too young and, what was more, too attractive. Most girls "fell" for him, and all too frequently without any overtures on his part. They made bold to flirt with him—to beg of him even the favor of his attentions. And except for the peculiar conditions which surrounded this young and dreaming beauty, and that made it difficult if not impossible for anyone to approach and associate with her, he would not have been interested.

A part of this he himself clearly recognized. And Mr. Zobel, conscious always of the moral perils facing his daughter and dubious of youth—and most especially to the sophisticated, independent youth of the hour eyeing him, not as a candidate for his daughter's company, but as a prospective customer. For Mr. Hauptfuhrer had chosen nine o'clock in the morning when as yet few customers might be expected and one was never out of order.

"Mr. Zobel," began Mr. Hauptfuhrer with the secret thought if not the suspicious manner of one who would dissemble greatly, "my name is Edward Hauptfuhrer. You probably know of my father, Jacob Hauptfuhrer. He's in the coal business. We have a yard down here on the Absecon. We live up here in Whitaker Street about five blocks."

"Yes, I know," replied Mr. Zobel looking up from a day book which he was checking. "I see his trucks about here. Yes." At the same time he was evaluating after a fashion the smart brown suit, good tan shoes, new if brisk brown felt hat which Mr. Hauptfuhrer wore. Obviously the son of a man of means. Where had he seen him before? Somewhere in this vicinity.

"You don't know me," went on Mr. Hauptfuhrer with the nerve of a practised wording, "but I work for my father down at the dock. I'm a weigher and bookkeeper. We've only lived around here a few months, but I've seen your daughter and she's seen me. I've been in here a few times to buy things when she's been here and I admire her a great deal and I've come in to ask if you have any objections to my keeping company with her. I tried to speak to her about this the other night," he added with a touch of genuine psychologic artistry, "but she told me that I would have to see you. I work all the time and make my own living."

Mr. Hauptfuhrer was restating a phrase which he had caught from a German father who had stated it in another way—"Work and make your own living or get out. I want no loafers in my family." But here, reformed and adapted to the occasion, it sounded much better. At the same time Mr. Zobel hearing his daughter mentioned—a previous contact acknowledged even by her—and nothing said to him. He was not only flustered, but at the same time suspicious.

"You say that you spoke to her already?"

"I asked her if I might call on her, yes sir."

"Ahuh! When was this?"

"Just two days ago—in the evening here."

"Ahuh!"

At the same time a certain nervous, critical attitude toward everything, which had produced many fine lines about the eyes and above the nose of Mr. Zobel, now caused these to concentrate and so crumble.

"Your father—you work for him you say?"

"Yes, sir."

"Well, well—this is something I will have to talk over with my daughter first. I must see about this. It is not everyone I want her to be running with."

By now Mr. Zobel's manner was suspicious and crass. At the same time there was the undoubted existence of some six or seven coal trucks to say nothing of the Hauptfuhrer coal dock recently built on the Absecon eight blocks away—a very substantial and prosperous looking affair. Undoubtedly Mr. Jacob Hauptfuhrer was successful as a coal dealer and this was his son—or so he said. "Very well," he added, a swift calculation as to the wisdom of allying Ida with such a family—"I will have to see about this. You must wait. I will let you know later. Come in some other time." At the same time there was speeding swiftly across the background of his mind the thought that—assuming that he refused—could not this youth and his daughter contrive without him? He did not know the adage, "Love laughs at lock smiths," but he knew the truth underlying it.

And so, in the course of a week, permission to Mr. Hauptfuhrer to call,—also to escort Ida to any of the moving-picture houses in the vicinity, to say nothing of occasional rides in his father's borrowed car—for from Mr. Zobel's subsequent investigation, and to his satisfaction, it had appeared that this youth was the son of the coal dealer and worked for his father as he had said. Also there was nothing exactly unsatisfactory known concerning him in this immediate vicinity. He dressed in a very smart and even garish manner. But then was not his father well-to-do? Furthermore, as it now appeared—and somewhat to Mr. Zobel's practical surprise—his daughter, despite her brief knowledge of this youth, was smitten with love. He was very nice and polite. More, Mr. Zobel, after much solemn reflection was led to conclude perhaps it was all for the best. His daughter no doubt should have some male contact of some kind. He had been very strict and she was at that period when at least one beau might be necessary. She had reached the age when most girls were permitted to go out some.

Finally came then an agreement under which Mr. Hauptfuhrer was to be permitted to call once or twice a week. And after that—he having conducted himself most circumspectly—it followed that an evening at one of the neighborhood picture houses was suggested and achieved. Once this was accomplished it became a regularity for either Wednesday or Friday evening, as his own and Ida's work permitted. Then followed a suggestion by Hauptfuhrer, his courage and skill never deserting him, that they should be permitted to visit Peck's Beach nine miles below the city on the Little Shark. It was the popular Saturday and Sunday resort for most of the residents of this area, for by now Mr. Hauptfuhrer had gained the confidence of Zobel and it was not hard to accomplish this. Then there were other trips—to one or another of the theatres in the business heart, to a better class restaurant in the same area, to the house of a boy friend who had a sister and who lived in the next block.

Despite his stern, infiltrating supervision, Zobel could not prevent the progressive familiarities based on youth, desire, romance. For with Edward Hauptfuhrer, to contact was to intrigue and eventually demand and compel. And so by degrees, hand pressures, waist pressures, stolen or enforced kisses. Yet none-the-less Ida, still fully dominated by the moods and convictions of her father, persisting in a nervous evasiveness which was all too trying to her lover.

"Ah, you don't know my father. No, I couldn't do that. No, I mustn't stay out so late. Oh, no—I wouldn't dare go there—I wouldn't dare to. I don't know what he would do to me." This—or such as this to all his overtures which hinted at late hours, a trip to a mysterious and fascinating boat club on the Little Shark twenty-five miles out where, as he so glibly explained, were to be enjoyed dancing, swimming, boating, music, feasting. And Ida had never done any of these. Yet it required an unheard of period of time—from noon until midnight—or later Saturday, whereas there had been fixed as essential and permanent to her welfare the hour of eleven-thirty, as the one at which she was to return to the parental roof. Yet none-the-less yearning toward dreams of a greater freedom which would permit participation in so idyllic a realm. And with Mr. Hauptfuhrer, artful in the extreme and yet greatly lured by this lush beauty, whispering not only of her compelling and firing fascination for him but also of rebellion.

"Ah, don't you want to have any fun at all? Gee, he don't want you to do anything and you let him do that to you. But look at all the other fellows and girls around here. There's not one that's as scary as you are. Besides what harm is there? Supposing we don't get back on time. Couldn't we say the car broke down? He couldn't say anything to that. Besides no one punches a time clock exactly." Yet with the nervous Ida resisting—and with Hauptfuhrer wanting her more than ever—and because of this very resistance, determined to win her to his mood and to outwit her father in the bargain.

And ah, the lure of summer nights—romantic—Corybantic—dithyrambic. Kisses. Kisses. Kisses—under the shadow of trees in King Lake Park or in one of the little boats of its lake which nosed the roots of those same trees on the shore. And with the sensitive and sensual and yet restricted and inexperienced Ida growing more and more lost in the spell which youth, summer, love had generated. The beauty of the face of this her grand cavalier! His carefully cut clothes, his brisk, athletic energy and mental daring. Gee, she ought to see this and that. Go here and there. If she only truly loved him and had the courage. And at last, on this same lake—with her lying in his arms attempting familiarities which had scarcely seemed possible in her dreams and which caused her to jump up and demand to be put ashore—the while he merely laughed at first—demanding to know what he had done that was so terrible. Say, she cared for him, didn't she? Then why so uppish? Oh, all right—if that was the way she was going to feel about it. And with himself walking briskly off in the gayest and most self-sufficient of ways while she alone—tortured by her sudden ejection from paradise, slipped into her own room, there to bury her face in her pillow and to herself and to it whisper and moan even of the horror that had befallen her. The perfect Hauptfuhrer. His lovely face—hands, hair. He had kissed her—hugged her. Of all the youths in all the world he was the one and only. And so dragging herself to her father's store the next day merely to wait and dream that he was not as evil as he seemed; that he could not have seriously contemplated the familiarities that he had attempted; that he had been merely obsessed, bewitched—as she herself had been. Oh, love, love! Edward! Edward! Oh, he would not, could not remain away. She must see him—give him a chance to explain—think of seizing upon some opportunity by which she could explain—make him understand that it was not want of love but fear of life—her father, everything, everybody—that kept her so sensitive, aloof, remote. And with Hauptfuhrer himself, for all his bravado and craft, now nervous lest he had been too pressing too soon. For—after all—what a beauty! Christ, the lure! He couldn't let her go like that. It was a little too delicious and wonderful to have her so infatuated—and with a little more attention—who knows?

And so conspicuously placing himself where she must pass—of an evening anyhow—at the corner of Warren and High—and with Ida seeing—and yearning in white-faced misery—Monday night! Tuesday night! And then on Wednesday seeing him pass the store on his way home without so much as turning his head. And then the next day a note handed the negro errand boy of her father's store, a note to be given him later at the corner where he would surely be.

And then later—with the same Edward taking it most casually and grandly and reading it. So she had been compelled to write him—had she? Oh, these dames! Yet with a considerable thrill from the contents for all of that, for it read, "Oh, Edward darling! You can't be so cruel to me. How can you? I love you so. You didn't mean what you said. Tell me you didn't. I didn't. Oh, please come to the house at eight. I want to see you." And Edward Hauptfuhrer—triumphant now—saying to the messenger before four cronies who knew of his present pursuit of Ida: "Oh. That's all right. Just tell her I'll be over after while." And then as eight o'clock neared, ambling off in the direction of the Zobel home and with the four cronies thinking to themselves—and one of them commenting as he left: "Whaddaya know? He's got her on the run now. She's writing him notes. Didn't ya see the coon bring it up?" And the others as enviously, amazedly and contemptuously inquiring: "Whaddaya know?"

And so under June trees in King Lake Park once more another conference. "Oh, darling—how could you treat me so—how could you? Oh, my dear, dear, darling." And he replying—sure—sure, it was all right—sure he loved her—just as she loved him. More, if anything. But what did she think a fellow like him was made of, iron? Say. Have a heart! "I'm human, ain't I? I've got some feelings just the same as anybody else. How you expect me to do? Ain't I crazy about you and ain't you crazy about me? Well then—Besides—Well, say. . . ." A long pharisaical and deluding argument, as one might guess, with all the miseries and difficulties of restrained and evaded desire most artfully suggested—yet with no harm meant, of course. Oh no. Didn't he love her—she him?

But her father.

Sure her father. What about him?

But if anything went wrong. And he wouldn't marry her.

But how was anything to go wrong? Didn't he know?

But wouldn't it? Could he be sure? And if anything did, would he marry her?

But again, on her part, the old foolish terrorized love plea. And the firm assurance on his part that if anything went wrong—why of course. But why worry about that now? Gee, she was the only girl he knew that worried about anything like that. And finally a rendezvous at Little Shark River with his father's car as the conveyance. And then others and others. And with—because of her meek, fearsome yielding in the first instance—and then her terrorized contemplation of possible consequences in the second—her clinging to him in an all too eager and hence cloying fashion. She was his now—all his. Oh—he would never never desert her now, would he?

But he, once satisfied—his restless and overweening ego comforted by another victory—no danger of loss or defeat here—turning with a restless and chronic and for him uncontrollable sense of satiety, as well as a fear of complications and burden, to other phases of beauty—to fields and relationships where there was no such danger. For after all—one more girl; one more experience. And not so greatly different from others that had gone before it. And this in the face of the magic of her meaning before capitulation. He did not understand it! He could not. He did not even trouble to think about it much. But so it was. And there was the danger of being involved in an early and unsatisfactory marriage which his father and mother would resent, and before he was prepared for it. Yet so long as he achieved compliance by her holding him—hours throughout July and August in which they met here and there—in the woods, in the borrowed room of a youthful friend until at last the fatal complaint. There was something wrong, she feared. She had such strange moods—such strange spells. Pains, fears. Could there be? Did he think that there really could be any danger? Oh, if there were, what was she to do? Would he marry her now? Would he? He must really. There was no escape. Her father. His fierce anger. Her own terrors. She could not live and face him or anyone without marriage. Could they not—would they not be married at once? He had said he would marry her at once, had he not?

And then, in the face of that, an entirely new situation for her. For with this drastic announcement a calm and decidedly sturdy determination, as she herself could see and feel, on the part of Mr. Hauptfuhrer, not to be nervously or quickly dragooned into admitting the danger or necessity, if not the need, of any such binding relationship as she herself deemed necessary and had all along anticipated. His father! His hitherto free roaming life! His future! Besides, how did she know? How could she be sure? And supposing she was! Other girls got out of such things without much trouble. Why not she? He knew of lots of cases. There were remedies. He would see about something first.

But conjoined with this a sudden definite coolness—never before sensed or witnessed by her, which was based on a sudden determination on his part not to pursue this threatening relationship any longer, seeing that to do so meant only to emphasize responsibility. On the contrary, a keen desire to stay away—move and get out of this really, if worse came to worst. Were there not other girls!—a whole world full, yet to be seen and entertained. And only recently had he not been intrigued by one who, if no more attractive or of no greater social station than Ida, was still more aware of the free, smart ways of pleasure and not so likely ever to prove a burden?

But on the other hand, in the face of a father as stern and orderly almost as Zobel, and a mother who believed in his goodness, his course was not absolutely clear, either. And in consequence a serious if irritated effort on his part to find a remedy—yet among his friends of the boating club and street corners, and with the additional result of a vivid advertisement of the fact that this gay and successful adventure of his had resulted so unsuccessfully for Ida. The fun he must have had. The "pickle" she was in. And thereafter hints and words and nudges among themselves whenever she chanced to pass or appeared in the distance. For already from time to time she had been casually introduced, at least, to the majority of those who gathered in this vicinity.

And yet no definite relief from the eventually provided pills. Instead more and more terrifying pains and more weakening and nausea with more and more terrifying emotions based on the stern and unrelenting countenance of her father, which loomed so threateningly beyond the immediate future. "If me no if's and but me no but's." Oh, how to do? What pressure if any to bring to bear? For throughout the use of this useless remedy, there had been nothing to do but wait. And the waiting ending in surer pains—only greater horrors. And between all this—and enforced work at the store—and enforced duties at home—efforts to see her beloved—who because of new and more urgent duties was finding it harder and harder to meet with her anywhere or at any time.

"But you must see how it is with me. Ed, I love you. I can't go on like this—and you see that! You said you'd marry me, didn't you? And look at all the time that's gone already. Oh, I'm almost mad. You must do something, you know! You must! You must! If my father should find out—oh, my goodness. I don't know what he might do to me or to you either. Can you see how that is?"

Yet in the face of this tortured plea on the part of this frantic and still love-sick girl, a calm on the part of Hauptfuhrer that betokened not indifference but cruelty, which inexperience and youthful lack of understanding had failed to sense. He did not want to marry her. In truth, by now he was weary of her—but even more of these importunities. And besides, what could she do? If she drove him too hard he could leave, couldn't he? She be damned. He would not. He could not. He must save himself now at whatever cost. And so a determined attempt not to see her anymore at all—never to speak to her openly anywhere—or to admit any responsibility as to all this. Also a certain hard, brazen courage based on similar situations, from which he had extracted himself by courage and cruelty, now prompted him to look brazenly at her and say, "But I didn't really promise to marry you and you know I didn't. You wanted to do that as much as I did, didn't you? Where do you get this stuff? You don't suppose that just because you don't know how to take care of yourself I've got to marry you, do you?"

His eyes were—for the first time—truly hard. His intention to end this by one fell blow if possible was very definite. And the blow was sufficient at the moment to half unseat the romantic and all but febrile reason of this girl who up to this hour had believed so foolishly in love. Why, how could this be? The horrors of this implied disaster. The end of happiness—paradise! Only storm and darkness ahead! And then half in understanding, half in befuddled unreason, exclaiming, "But, Ed! Ed! You can't mean that! Why, it isn't true—you know it isn't! You promised. You swore. You know I never wanted to—until you made me. Why—oh, what'll I do! My father—I don't know what he'll do to you or to me. Oh, dear! oh, dear!" And frantically and without sufficient balance to warrant the name of reason, she began wringing her hands and twisting and swaying in a kind of physical as well as mental agony. This was all under the trees in Briscoe Street near Warren in the middle days of September—and after much importuning by note—much loitering in the vicinity in order to encounter him—he had finally come to meet her again.

"But what can I do?" was his private thought. "If I don't get out of this now, whenever again will I be able to? Best make a brutal matter of it—once and for all—say I never intended to marry her from the beginning—never promised to. She can't make me, can she? And so now exclaiming—"Oh, cut that stuff. Whaddya want to do? Make it look as though I said I'd marry you? Well I never did and you know it. Am I to blame if you're not able to look out for yourself?" And then not being able or willing to say more—so great was the amazement and horror in her eyes—turning on his heel and leaving her in order to avoid further complaint and in a moment rejoining the chaffering group of youths on the corner with whom, before her arrival, he had been talking. And now as much to sustain himself in this fatal decision as well as to carry it off before them who knew so much about him as a Lothario—as well as too much about this affair—remarking, "Gee—these skirts! It does beat hell!"

He was at once vain and yet a little fearsome in this case. The whole thing from the beginning had been so brazenly and even showily executed. If anything it was his masterpiece in brazen adventures thus far.

And Dudley Shaw—one of his admirers and companions—as well as one of the more yearning and less successful bloods of the neighborhood—remarking, "What's the trouble, Ed? Can't you shake her? I seen her hangin' around here for the last three-quarters of an hour." And Johnny Martin, another aspirant for street-corner and Lothario honors, adding: "I saw her here last night looking for you, I'm sure. Better look out, Ed. One of these skirts is likely to do somepin' to you one of these days."

But with Mr. Hauptfuhrer, head up, a new wrist watch on his left wrist, a new fall suit, most carefully cut and worn, grazing his vigorous skin and slim defiant body, calmly extracting a cigarette from a silver and gilt cigarette case recently presented him by a girl admirer—and without a look in the direction of the half-swooning Ida—saying, "Is that so? Well, maybe. We'll see first." And then with a nonchalant nod in the direction of the befuddled and all but reeling Ida, too tortured to even retreat as yet but standing quite resolute, exclaiming: "Gee these Germans! She's got an old man that wouldn't ever let her find out anything, and now because she thinks there's something wrong with her she blames me. As though she weren't old enough to know." And then a crony of the Little Shark River boat club approaching, and with news of two girls who were to meet them somewhere later—exclaiming, "Hello, Skate! Everything set. All right then. We might as well go along, eh? S'long—fellows." And with this newest entertainment in view stepping briskly and vigorously away.

Yet with the stricken and shaken Ida still loitering under the already partially denuded September trees. And with the speeding street and auto cars of this major thoroughfare with their horns and bells—and the chaffering voices and shuffling feet of the pedestrians and the blazing evening lights of Warren Avenue making a kind of fanfare of color and sound. Was it cold? Or was it only herself who was numb and cold? He would not marry her! He had never said he would! But he had. And this was a cold, indifferent, evasive lie. And so brazen. And her father to deal with! And her condition to deal with! And only a few months since when the days and the leaves of spring were new. Those wonderful approaches on his part—his declarations of love! His tenderness! His wonderful way with her!

As she stood there without moving there flashed before her a complete panorama of all the paths and benches of King Lake Park; the little boats that slipped here and there under the trees at night in the summer time;—a boy and a girl, a boy and a girl, a boy and a girl. And the oars dragging—most inconsequentially. And infatuated hearts beating ecstatically—at times suffocatingly strong. And now after so many kisses and promises—the lie given to her dreams—her words; his words on which her words had been based; the lie given to kisses—hours, days, weeks, months of unspeakable bliss; the lie given to her own security and hopes forever, to the love-light in his eyes and in hers—to the gay pictures of future love and pleasure that he had depicted to her, to everything—everything—the wonderful scenes of love and happiness that she had painted for herself. And now only her room—her father and stepmother, accusation, abuse—eviction possibly—and with this—this—a baby—facing her.

And then a slow and dragging return to her room, where because of the absence of her father at the store, her stepmother in her sewing-room, she could slip into her bed and lie there, thinking. But with a kind of fever, alternating with chills, and both shot through with most menacing pains due to this most astounding revelation. But no, no, no!—this could not be. There must be some way out, something to do. Her father! Her state! Her future! He could not have meant all that he had just said. It was not believable. Too harsh, too fierce. Almost sneering and contemptuous. Perhaps he himself was frightened like she was—afraid to undertake all this. Even though he had said he would. And yet those sneering and contemptuous words,—his walking off in that way, leaving her to make her way home alone.

And so other days and other nights all alone. But now with a blazing, searing, whirling, disordered flow of thoughts and terrors which stalked her like demons. Her father, her stepmother. Self-destruction. Was that possible for herself in the face of all this? Was it not? Those chattering, gaping youths on the street corners; the various girls she had known or seen at school, or in this immediate vicinity, and who had seen her with Hauptfuhrer! Their thoughts!

And then the outside world, its strangeness and hence terror, assuming that she were forced into it now, its contempt for all such as she fancied; her loneliness without love—her inability to make her way alone—these and a hundred related thoughts now danced before her tortured mental gaze a fantastic, macabre, mental dance.

But always within her own brain the persisting and even growing notion or illusion that here was something—some wild, unbelievable misery and fatality which had seemingly descended on her and yet could not be real—not all that she had fancied was to be as perfect. And so at first, with continued faith in the value of pleading—picturing her own misery as well as his former affection and her continuing love. But finding that unavailing—her own physical and mental misery greater, his own attitude unchanging, she fixed with a faint hope upon what a threat might do.

"What's the big idea, following me around, anyhow? You think I haven't anything else to do but listen to you? Say, I told you in the first place I couldn't marry you, didn't I? And now because you think there's something wrong with you, you want to make me responsible. Well, I'm not the only fellow in this neighborhood. And everybody knows that."

He had paused then because, as he saw it, that last declaration had awakened in her a latent strength and determination never previously shown in any way. The horror of that to her, as he could see. The whiteness of her face afterwards and on the instant. The blazing electric points within the pupils of her eyes. "That's a lie and you know it. It's not true. Oh, how terrible. And for you to say that to me. I see it all now. You're just a sneak." Yet helpless and defeated misery. To think—to think—he could talk so to her—deny all to her. And yet despite her rage—in the center of this very misery, love itself, hot and strong—the very core of it. But so tortured that already it was beginning to drive the tears to her eyes.

And knowing so thoroughly as he did that this love was still there, now instantly seizing on these latest truthful words of hers as an insult—something on which to base an assumed grievance.

"Is that so? A coward, eh? Well let's see what you draw down for that, you little dumb-bell." And so turning on his heel—the strongest instinct in him his own social salvation in this immediate petty neighborhood at the present time—his own freedom and even dignity—or at least acclaim as a philanderer, sport—lady's man, or what you will, uppermost in his mind. And without a look behind.

But Ida, her fear and terror at its height, calling: "Ed—Ed—You come back here. I won't stand for this, I tell you. I won't. You come back here now and talk to me." And then, seeing that in spite of what she had just said he continued walking briskly and indifferently away—his wretched and unjust courage in his every move. She ran after him—unbelievably tense and a little beside herself—almost mentally unaccountable for the moment. And he seeing her thus, and amazed and troubled by this new turn his problem had taken, turned abruptly with: "Say, who the devil do you think you are and what do you think you're goin' to get by this? Make me marry you? If you do you're sound asleep. You cut out o' this now before I do somethin' to you, do you hear? I'm not the one to let you pull this stuff on me. You got yourself into this and now you get yourself out of it. Beat it before I do something to you, do you hear?"

And now he drew nearer—and with such a threatening and savage look in his eyes that for the first time in all her contacts with him Ida grew fearful of him. That angry, sullen face. Those fierce, cruel, savage eyes. Was it really true that in addition to all the rest he would really do her physical harm? Then she had not understood him at all, ever. And so pausing and standing quite still, that same fear of physical force that had kept her in subjection to her father overawing her here. At the same time Hauptfuhrer, noting the effect of his glowering rage, now added—and most savagely, "Now quit coming near me anymore—do you hear! If you do—you're goin' to get something you're not going to like. I'm through and I'm through for good, see. Go and get someone else to help you. There's plenty that'll be glad to if you want 'em to. I'm not the only guy in the world, am I?" Once more he turned and strode briskly away—this time toward the central business district of the High and Warren Avenue region, the while Ida, too shaken by this newest development to quite grasp the full measure of her own necessity or courage—or what she must or must not do or say now, stood there. The fierceness of his face—The horror of it! The disgrace! The shame!

For the time being—in order to save herself from too much publicity, she began to move on—walk—only with whirling thoughts as to all that had just occurred—this charge of license with others—his threat to strike her—that last brutal advice as to getting help from someone else. And with the nature of her physical condition such that she had so little time left in which anything for her could be done. Her father! Her stepmother! All the girls she had met through him recently. These boys who unquestionably knew of this evil relationship and what it had now led to. God!

And so—most shaken and pale, making her way once more to her own home—where—because she had indicated earlier in the day that she was going to a moving picture with him, her return was not even noticed. Yet now not crying as before—too tortured to cry, really—but instead thinking grimly—fiercely at moments—at other times most weakly and feebly even, on all that had so recently occurred. That charge he had made! His rage! His hate even, and at the end of all this—her father! Her stepmother! If he, she—they—should come to know! And when they did! But no—something else must happen before even that should be allowed to happen. She must leave—or—or—better yet maybe drown herself—make away with herself in some way—or—or—

In the garret of this house in which she had always lived, and to which as a child, on certain rainy days, she had frequently resorted to play, was an old wire clothesline on which was also hung an occasional wash. There it was. And now—might not that—in the face of absolute conclusion and fiasco here—might not that—— She had read of ending one's life in that manner! And it was so unlikely that anyone would trouble to look there—until—until—well—

But should she? Could she? This strange budding life that she sensed—feared. Was it fair to it?—Herself? Respectable in her courage, reason—and especially where he was so unfair,—cruel! And when she so desired to live! And when he owed her something—life—or at least help to her and her—her— No—she could not, would not think of that yet, and especially when to die this way would be but to clear the way for easier and happier conquests for him—perhaps.

Never! Never! Never! She would not! She would not— She would kill him first—and then herself. Or expose him and so herself—and then—and then—

But again her father! Her stepmother! The disgrace! And so—

But in her father's desk at the store was a revolver—a large, firm, squarish mechanism which, as she had heard him say, fired eight shots. It was so heavy, so blue, so cold. She had seen it, touched it, lifted it once—but with a kind of terror really. It was always so identified with death,—not life—anger— But now— Supposing—supposing—if she desired to punish Edward and herself or just herself alone. And so— But no—no—what was the way, anyhow? What was the way.

And so now brooding in a tortured and half-demented way until her father, noting her mental state, inquired solemnly as to what had come over her of late. Had she had a quarrel with Hauptfuhrer? He had not seen him about, recently. Was she ill in any way? Her appetite had certainly fallen off. She ate scarcely anything. But receiving a prompt "no" to both inquiries—and although not satisfied as to the truth of either, he remained curious but inclined to suspend further inquiry for the time being. There was something, of course—but no doubt it would soon show. He would be able to extract something from her in the form of truth if this pale, brooding, lassitudinous state continued.

But now in the face of this—of course there must be action—decision. Her father's daily looks. The inquiry in his eyes. And so—in view of the thoughts as to self-destruction and the revolver, a decision to try the effect of a physical threat upon Hauptfuhrer. She would not kill him, of course. She could not. For even now, here there were those vivid if searing thoughts of the previous spring, summer—the first days. And so——Oh——Yet while working about the store looking at the revolver—lifting it up when Zobel was not there, thinking how,—how—did one carry such a thing,—how conceal it? Supposing—supposing—one—but not really—and—and—(but oh no) a spit of fire, a puff of smoke—a deadly bullet leaped from it—into his heart!!!—— Into hers afterwards. And then what? Where? The little life that was—or at least might be!

A dozen—a score of times in less than two days she approached the drawer and looked—lifted it up at last—thought of laying it in her bosom where so often during the summer his head had lain. But it was so heavy—so cold—so blue. The very weight and meaning of it terrorized her, although at last—after the twentieth attempt, she was able to fit it into her bosom in such a way that it lay quite firm and still.

And yet Mr. Hauptfuhrer, in the face of all this, congratulating himself that he was done with her,—that he had frightened her off. And then one afternoon when she could scarcely endure the strain any longer—her father demanding, "What is the matter with you anyhow? You do not know what you are doing half the time. Is there anything wrong between you and that young beau of yours? I see he does not come around here anymore. It is time that you either married or that you have nothing more to do with him. I don't want any silly nonsense between you and him. He must either marry you now or stay away and let someone else go with you. You cannot wait for him forever." He was merely voicing various thoughts which had been troubling him for days.

But this affected the very decision which she had most dreaded now,—now something quickly—this evening. She must see him again and tell him that she was going to see his father and reveal all, tell him furthermore that if he did not marry her she would kill him, herself—both. Show him the gun maybe—and frighten him with it, maybe—if she could, but at any rate make a last plea as well as a threat. If only—if only he would listen this time—not hem or haw anymore—not curse—or lie—now.

There was the coal yard of his father that was at the end of an inlet giving into the river. And then his own home. She might go first to the coal office. He would be sure to be leaving there at half-past five. Or at six he would be nearing his own home. At seven or half-past, departing from that again for his beloved friends of the corner.

But best—best—to go to the coal office first. He would be coming from there alone. It would be the quickest.

And yet Mr. Hauptfuhrer, in the face of all this congratulating himself that he was done with her; that by his brutality or gifted bravado, as he saw it, he had been able to frighten her away. And coming out of the coal office on this particular evening in the mood and with the air of one with whom all was well. A pleasing meeting with another girl in prospect—his dress suit; a little dancing party with a group of friends—and then——

But in the windy dusk of this November evening—arc lights blazing in the distance, the sound of distant cars, the wind whipping crisp leaves along the ground—distant life—the figure of a girl—a familiar cape about her shoulders, suddenly emerging from behind a pile of brick he was accustomed to pass. Ordinarily he walked this way with another clerk, Burkey Eckel of the office, whom he had come to know and like. But tonight the latter was remaining behind to superintend some final tons of coal emerging from a lately moored barge.

"Ed,—I want to talk to you a minute."

"You again! What the hell did I tell you? I ain't got no time to talk to you and besides I won't! What do I want to be talking to you for? What did I——"

"Now, lissen, Ed. Stop that now—do you hear? I'm desperate. I'm desperate—do you hear? Can't you see?" Her voice was staccato, almost shrill and yet mournful too. "I've come to tell you that you've got to marry me. You've got to—do you hear?" She fumbled at her breast where lay that heavy blue weapon—no longer so cold as when she had placed it in there. The handle was upward. She must draw it now—show it—or hold it under her cloak at least—ready so that at the right moment she could show it. Only now that she did this, her hand shook so that once it was at her side she could scarcely hold it. It was so heavy—so terrible. She could scarcely hear herself adding, "Otherwise I'm going to your father and mine now. My father may do something terrible to me but he'll do more to you. And so will your father when he knows. But anyway—" She was about to add, "you've got to marry me. And if you don't—" And then it was that she was to produce the revolver—flash it before him in a threatening, dramatic manner.

But before that the uncalculated and non-understanding fury of Mr. Hauptfuhrer. "Well, the nerve of this skirt. Say, cut this out, will you? What did I tell you? Who the hell do you think you are? Go on to your father. Go to my father if you want to. What the hell do I care? Do you think he's going to believe a ______ like you? I never had anything to do with you and that's that. Don't be trying to palm off any of this ______ stuff on me." And then in his anger giving her a push—as much to overawe her as anything.

And then blindness! Pain. Whirling, fiery sparks such as never in all her life before had she seen—and executing strange rhythmic convolutions and orbits in her brain—swift and eccentric and red and yet beautiful orbits. And in the center of them the face of her beloved, but not as it was now—oh, no—but rather haloed by a strange white light, and as it was under the trees in spring. And herself turning in spite of the push, jumping before him.

"You *will* marry me— You see this? You *will* marry me."

And then, as much to her astonishment as to his—yet with no particular terror to either of them—the thing spitting flame—making a loud noise—jumping almost out of her hand—so much so that before she could turn it away again there was another report—a smaller flash of red in the dusk. And then Mr. Hauptfuhrer—too astonished quite for words at the moment, exclaiming, "Jesus! What are you . . ." And because of a sharp pain in his chest putting his hand there and adding—"Oh, Christ—I'm shot—" And beginning to fall forward to one side of her.

And then a voice: "Hey! Stop that girl! Murder!" And from somewhere else another voice: "Hey!" And footsteps. And then herself—those same whirling red sparks in her brain saying—"No, now I must kill myself, too. I must run somewhere—turn this on myself." Only quite unable to lift it at the moment—and because of someone, a man—approaching, running toward her—herself beginning to run—for some tree—some wall—some gate, some doorway. Only hard quick steps immediately behind her. And a hand grabbing her hand in which—wildly and unwittingly—was held the pistol. And as the other hand wrenched at her hand—"Gimme that gun." And then a strong youth whom she had never seen before—and yet not unlike Eddie either—restraining her—turning her about. "You come back here. You can't get away with this!" And yet at the same time as she seemed to see not unfriendly eyes looking at hers. But herself exclaiming, "Oh, let me go. Let me go! I want to die, too! Oh let me go. I want to die too, I tell you!" And sobbing great, dry, shaking sobs.

But after that—and all so quickly—crowds—crowds—men and women, girls and boys and finally policemen, too, and these, each with the rules of his training firm in mind—to get as much general information as possible, to see that the wounded man was hurried to a hospital, the girl to a precinct police station, the names and addressses of witnesses secured. But with the lorn Ida in a state of collapse—seated upon a doorstep in a yard—a crowd around her and the while—

voices, voices. Who—where, what, how— "Sure! Sure! Just now! Right back there! Sure! They're calling the ambulance now. Sure! He's done for, I guess. Twice in the breast. He can't live. She did. Sure! With a revolver—a great big one. Eight-shooter. The cops got it. I seen 'em lookin' at it. She was tryin' to get away. Sure. Jimmie Allen caught her. He was just comin' home. Sure. She's the daughter of Old Zobel who keeps the paint store up here in Warren Avenue. Sure. An he's the son of this Hauptfuhrer here who owns the coal yard—He ain't heard sure, yet. Neither has her father. I used to work for 'im myself. Lives up in Grey Street."

But in the meantime young Hauptfuhrer—unconscious and being transferred to an operating table at Mercy Hospital—his case pronounced hopeless—twenty-four hours of life at most. And his father and mother hearing—and running there.

And in the same period the tortured Ida transferred to the Henderson Avenue police station where in a rear inquisitorial chamber entirely surrounded by policemen and detectives she was questioned and re-questioned: "Yah say yah seen this fellow for the first time over a year ago? Is that right? He just moved into the neighborhood a little while before? Ain't that so." And the lorn, half-conscious Ida nodding her head, and outside a large, morbid, curious crowd. A beautiful girl! A dying young man! Some sex mystery here!

And in the interim Zobel himself and his wife, duly informed by a burly policeman, hurrying white-faced and strained to this same station. So Ida had shot young Hauptfuhrer! And in the street, near his office! Murder! Great God! Then there was something between them. There was! There was! But he might have known. Her white face. Her dreary, forsaken manner these latter days. He had betrayed her! Devils! Eighty-thousand hells! And after all he had said to her! All his and his wife's care! And now the neighbors! His business! The police. A trial for her. A public trial. Possibly a sentence. A death sentence! God in heaven! His own daughter! And after all he had sought to do, too! But this! And that young scoundrel. No doubt he was to blame too—he with his fine clothes—his fine air. Why—why was it that he ever let his daughter go with him in the first place? When he might have known,—his daughter so inexperienced—as much, maybe, because of the extreme care he had exercised as— My God! My God! And at last rushing in breathless. "Where is she? My God. My God. This is terrible. And myself an honest man!"

But seeing her sitting there white, doleful—and looking up at him when spoken to with an almost meaningless look, a bloodless, smileless face—and yet now—somehow not terrorized by him anymore. "Ida! What is this? In God's name. It can't be so! Why didn't you tell me? Why didn't you come to me? I am your father, am I not! I would have helped you of course. But this! And now—"

But the only thought afloat in the lorn Ida's brain—was this really her father? And he was talking so—of help! That she might have come to him, when she had thought— But would he have—would he have— But then returning in thought to young Hauptfuhrer. Was he really dead! Had she really killed him? She had not intended to. That push—almost a blow it was—those words. But still—Oh, dear—oh—dear—! And then beginning to cry to herself silently, deeply. While Zobel and his wife bent over her for the first time in true sympathy. The complications of life! The terrors! There was no peace for anyone on this earth—no peace—no peace—all was madness and sorrow really. But they would stand by her now—he, Zobel, would. Yes—yes. And beginning volubly to explain to the desk lieutenant and these detectives and policemen all that he knew—how this same Hauptfuhrer had come to him the spring before to ask permission to court his daughter; how, because of his father's business, he had granted it—the attention,—the summer outings,—the recent depression of his daughter. He had feared something, of course, but he did not know this. She had never spoken. He had never really guessed. His daughter so shy—so careful, so virtuous.

And then the reporters! A public furor fanned by the newspapers with their men and women writers, pen-and-ink artists, photographers—their editorials—cartoons: "Beautiful Girl of Seventeen Shoots Lover, Twenty-One. Fires two bullets into body of man she charges with refusing to keep faith. About to become a mother. Youth likely to die. Girl admits crime. Pleads to be left alone in misery. Parents of both in despair." And their columns and columns, day after day,—since on the following afternoon at three young Hauptfuhrer did die—admitting that he had wronged her. And a coroner's jury called immediately afterward, holding the girl for subsequent action by the Grand Jury and without bail. Yet because of the beauty of the girl and the "pathos" of the case—the newspapers, the ministers, the public, via its letters to the papers—society men and women—the politicians and even the police—as intimately connected with the administration if not the enforcement of the law—demanding that the poor wronged girl, about to become a mother, and who had committed no crime other than that of loving too well—if not wisely—be admitted to bail.

As things stood no jury would ever convict her. Indeed it would "go hard" with any jury that would attempt to "further punish" a girl who had already suffered so much. Plainly, plainly it was the duty of the judge in this case to admit this poor wronged soul to bail—and the peace and quiet of some home or institution in which her child might be born, especially since already a woman of extreme wealth and social position, deeply stirred by the pathos of this drama, had not only come forward to sympathize with this innocent victim of love and order and duty and had already offered bail in the sum of three hundred fifty thousand if necessary—in order that she might be released to the peace and quiet of her own home—there to await the outcome of her physical condition as well as the unavoidable persecution which must fix her future.

And so, to her wonder and confusion, Ida finally released in the custody of this outwardly sober and yet inwardly emotional woman who, ever since the first day of her imprisonment in the central county jail, had sought to ingratiate herself into the good graces and emotions of this girl who herself scarcely understood at the time what her true emotions were. And transferred at once—a bailed prisoner, subject to return upon demand, to the wide acres and impressive chambers of a once country but now city residence, an integral part of the best residence area of the city. And there, all needful equipment and services provided—a maid and servants, her food served to her in her room when she wished—silence or entertainment as she chose.

Yet in the main, and because her mood and health seemed to require it, left to contemplate the inexplicable chain of events which her primary desire for love had brought about. The almost amazing difference in the mental attitude of her parents toward her now and before this dreadful accident—so considerate and sympathetic now as to result in an offer of a happier home for her and her child in the future, whereas before all was—or so she had sensed it—so threatening and desperate; the strange and to her inexplicable attitude of this woman even—so kind and generous—and this in the face of her sin and shame.

And again, the strange and to her inexplicable attitude of the public itself which, previous to her sin and crime, had known nothing of her and presumably should have proved censorious, and not only that, vindictive. Rather, it seemed now determinedly and emotionally bent in but one direction—to pity, protect, laud—even coddle her for the grim misery her own folly had brought about. The laudatory articles in the newspapers; the sympathetic reporters, photographers, artists, cameramen before her removal to this peaceful realm; the kindly eyes of the coroner, judge, district attorney, police—all.

And yet what peace or quiet could there be for her, here or anywhere else now? The terrible torture that had preceded that terrible accident. Her Edward's cry! His death! And when she had loved him so! Had! Did now! And yet by his dread perverseness, cruelty, brutality he had taken himself from her. But still, still—Now that he was gone—now that in dying, as she heard, he had said he had been "stuck on her" at first, that later she had "set him crazy," but that afterwards, because of her parents, he had decided that he would marry her. She could not help but feel kindly toward him. He had been cruel. But had he not died? And at her hands. She had killed him! Murdered him. Oh yes, she had. Oh! Oh! Oh. For in her heart no doubt that when she had jumped in front of him, there in the dusk, there had been rage—rage and hate even, too, for the moment. Oh, yes. But he had cried—"Oh, Christ, I'm shot!" (Her Edward's cry.) And afterwards someone had said that his shirt front had been all bloody. She had heard that. Oh, oh, oh! And so, even in the silence of these richly appointed rooms, with a servant coming to her call; silent tears and deep, rocking sobs—when no one was supposed to see or hear—and thoughts, thoughts, thoughts—sombre—bleak as to her lack of sense,—her lack of courage or will to end it all for herself on that dreadful evening when she so easily might have. And now here she had pledged her word that she would do nothing rash—would not attempt to take her life. But the future! The future. And what she had not seen since that dreadful night Edward's father and mother were at the inquest! And how they had looked at her! To her! Hauptfuhrer, senior—his strong, broad German face worked with a great anguish. And Mrs. Hauptfuhrer—small—and all in black. And with great hollow rings under her eyes. And crying silently nearly all of the time. And both had sworn that they knew nothing of Edward's conduct, or of his definite interest in her. He was a headstrong, virile, restless boy. They had had a hard time controlling him. And yet he had not been a bad boy either—headstrong—but willing to work and play—their only son. And they had then looked sadly and reproachfully at her—as why should they not?

Oh, why not? Why not? Why not? These great rooms! They were beautiful of course. All was silent and serene. She could go about the grounds as she chose. This kindly woman—Mrs. Chandler. Her new friend was all attention, courtesy, sympathy. She took her here and there—her driver—and to the movies and the theatre, wherever she chose to go. Her own parents were allowed to visit her whenever she chose—She felt so uncomfortable in the presence of her parents. True, they were kind—gentle now, whenever they came. She had sinned! She had killed a man—her faithless lover. And wrecked another family—the hearts of two other parents—as well as his own peace of mind and commercial and social well being. And—in all his charity—was there room for that? In the solemnity of his manner—as well as that of her stepmother, she could not imagine the life that was to be after this great crisis was truly past—the birth of the child—which was never other than indirectly referred to, of course—or the trial, either, which was to follow later. There was to be a new store in a new neighborhood. The old one had already been offered for sale. And after that—— But even in her father's eyes, as he spoke, she could not see the weight of care which he now shouldered. Since her father was not one who was poor or welcomed charity—a contemplated and finally accomplished return to the new world—the new home and store which had been established in a very different and remote part of the city.

But before leaving Mrs. Chandler's—in those long days when she had been awaiting these eventualities which were so slowly and dismally approaching the whole problem of her future. And apart from all this comfort that there surrounded her—and which by contrast reminded her of the lower or so much less favored state to which she must presently return.

In the great room which held a canopied bed upon a dais, and into which at morning and various other hours a maid entered, smiling, to do this or that—ask this or that, serve this or that, the lorn Ida, still hopelessly brooding upon all that had just gone, now lay and studied a great lawn already sprinkled with snow, or trees onto which clung a few fluttering brown leaves. Winter was coming. A trial. And after that. But he had said that she was so attractive, even when he was dying—and that he would not have treated her so badly except for—except for—And she had shot him—twice!! Had seen him fall that night—exclaiming, "Jesus"—and then "Oh, Christ, I'm shot!" And now he was gone—his brisk vigorous body, his finely modeled, handsome face and head; the smile—the laugh—the gayety with which he was wont to greet her the year before. And never, never would he again—think of that! And her parents gloomily awaiting her return. Oh, God, if she had only killed herself too. And—and—and—and—Would she never have done with these sad, torturing thoughts?

And yet meals in a beautiful dining room in which at night many lights were lit—yet only herself and Mrs. Chandler to dine together, since her hostess was a widow and alone. And afterward, if she wished—music on the radio—on the victrola in a great drawing room with an open fire. Or, if her mood dictated, the theatre—(a comedy—a seat in a box concealed from view)—or a moving picture in some strange neighborhood. And by day a car—with her new friend as her companion or without—the sober, guileless chauffeur long in her hostess's employ—to drive her here and there.

And yet—and yet—only the only scenes of the spring and summer before; the woods and paths in King Lake Park; the little boats; the love, the kisses.

* * *

At one point in these extensive grounds—entirely surrounded by Lombardy poplars—now leafless—there stood a fountain drained of its water for the winter. And on a pedestal upon a bronze rock, at the foot of which washed bronze waves of the Rhine, a Rhine maiden of the blonde German Lorelei type—standing erect—and adream—in youth—in love. And at her feet on his knees—a German lover of the Ritter type, vigorous, uniformed, lured—his fair blond head and faced turned upward to the beauty about whose hips his arms were clasped—his look seeking—urgent. And upon his fair bronze hair—her right hand, the while she bent on him a yearning, yielding glance. There was an evening in early December—when the first gust of this terrific storm had subsided, when she saw this, a new moon overhead, and sat to look at it. King Lake Park! The little boats upon its surface in summer! She—Edward—in one. She leaning and dreaming as now,—as now—this figure of this girl on this rock was doing. And he—he—at her knees. To be sure——to be sure——he had cursed her. He had said——he had said——ah, what had he not said——the fierce, indifferent, cruel words that had driven her at last to madness—to a desire to die. And now——and now——

She had left the fountain quickly but only to return after a few days—and then again—and again but only to brood and brood the more deeply.

And then——the girl acquitted instantly—and turned with handshakes of the jury, judge, prosecuting attorney—all into the swift, indifferent world, in which, henceforth, she must lose herself of course. The stern, absorbing self-interests of each and all. And then the new life in a newer portion of the city—far out in Woodridge—on Woodridge Avenue—another paint store near another moving-picture theatre; near another crass business street of some importance. And boys and girls here as elsewhere—on the corner—going by arm in arm; herself at home for months in a newer if no better home until the child should be weaned—be able to walk. Yet helping to cook, sew, clean, work as before. And with Mrs. Zobel as reserved and dubious as ever. For, after all, had she not made a mess of her life; and what now?—what now? Here forever—as a fixture? And even though Zobel, in spite of his grimness and reserve, was becoming fond of the child. How wretched—how futile life really was!

But far away King Lake Park and the old neighborhood. And thoughts that went back to it constantly. She had been so wildly in love and she had killed him. Although acquitted, she had killed him none-the-less and they had been so happy the summer before. But now this summer!—And the other summers to come—even though sometime, once Eric was grown—there might be some other lover—who would not mind—

But no—no—not that. Never. She did not want that—could not—would not endure it.

And so at last of a Saturday afternoon when she had the excuse of certain things needed for Eric as well as herself—a trip, presumably to the central business heart—whereas in reality it was to King Lake Park she was going. And once there—the little boats, the familiar paths—a certain nook under overarching bushes and trees. She knew it well. It was here that he had demanded to be let out in order that she might go home by herself—so shocked, so ashamed. Yet not seeking it.

The world does not understand such things. It is so busy with so many, many things.

And then dusk—though she should have been returning—Her boy! He would miss her, of course. But could she endure what she would be missing—always? And then a little wind with a last faint russet glow in the west. And these stars! Quite all the world had gone to its dinner now. The park was all but empty. The water here so still—so agate. (The world—the world—it will never understand, will it?) Where would Edward—the dashing handsome Hauptfuhrer—be—if at all? Would he meet her? Know her? Greet her? (The world—the world!—the busy, strident, indifferent, matter-of-fact world.)

And then a girl in the silence, in the shadow, making her way down to the very spot that the nose of their boat had nuzzled but one short summer before.

But now calmly stepping down and then wading to her knees—to her waist—her breasts in the mild caressing water—and then to her lips and over them—and without a cry—or sigh.

The world does not understand such things. The tide of life runs so fast. So much that is beautiful—terrible—sweeps by—by—by—without thought—without notice in the great volume.

And yet the body was found—her story retold in great flaring headlines. (Ida Zobel—Girl Slayer of Hauptfuhrer a Suicide.) And then . . . and then . . . forgotten.

1926, 1989

Edna St. Vincent Millay 1892–1950

Born in Rockland, Maine, Edna St. Vincent Millay was the eldest of three children of Henry Tolman Millay, a school superintendent, and Cora Buzzelle Millay, a practical nurse. Mrs. Millay provided a home environment rich in literature and music. Evidently a gifted child, Millay wrote her first poem at the age of five. When she was twelve, her poems first appeared in *St. Nicholas Magazine,* which two years later awarded her a gold badge for poetry. She contributed poems and playlets to her high school magazine and appeared in high school plays and in local productions by touring acting companies.

When at the age of twenty she recited her poem "Renascence" as entertainment at a local hotel resort, she was "discovered" by a visiting official of the New York City YWCA, who sponsored Millay's entrance into college. While at Vassar College, she wrote poetry and plays for the campus magazine, composed her class's baccalaureate hymn, and drew considerable attention when she acted in college plays. Millay lived for eight years in Greenwich Village, during which she appeared as an actress at the Provincetown Playhouse, where her popular one-act play *Aria da Capo* was first produced, and devoted herself to writing. After marrying Eugene Boissevain, a Dutch American importer, in 1923, she resided permanently at her estate, Steepletop, in eastern New York State. In addition to being the first woman poet to receive the Pulitzer Prize (1923), Millay was the recipient of five honorary degrees and numerous awards for poetry. She was hailed in the 1940s as "one of the ten greatest living women."

Edmund Wilson, the famous critic, characterized her as a female intellectual. Early reviews ran the gamut, calling her "a romantic idealist" and "an urban pagan." Although at first a few critics were inclined to treat her too lightly, most recognized her as a truly gifted poet who wrote artistically crafted verse about serious matters of the human heart and mind. Though she was taken to task for being flippant and self-indulgent with her second book, *A Few Figs from Thistles, Second April* was generally well received. This volume also contains twelve sonnets, a form in which Millay was to work with much distinction. She is arguably one of the great sonnet writers in English and without peer in the sonnet form among all American poets. Subsequent volumes saw her called uneven, lacking in intellectual force, and ill disciplined, but at the same time she was named "America's finest living lyric poet" and "among our foremost twentieth-century poets."

Although many poems in earlier volumes are touched with humor and satire, the mood of the later poetry darkens and deepens as Millay's artistry grows more complex and the ideas more profound. Her treatment of romantic love, for example, grows graver and more reflective. She became a writer very much involved in social issues, an activist and feminist long before these terms were popular. She is outspoken about personal integrity and freedom, which is really the major theme of her work. For a brief time, she also wrote of subjects related to the ongoing war. She is a memorable nature poet, rivaling her contemporary Robert Frost in a fine delineation of natural detail. Millay's range as an author is demonstrated by her periodical short stories, her volume of prose "dialogues," a libretto for a distinguished American opera, and half a dozen dramatic works.

Although Millay published nothing in the last ten years of her life, she wrote constantly. Much of this work appears in the posthumous *Mine the Harvest.* The past thirty years have witnessed a resurgence of interest in Millay, with academic symposia, a growing number of articles, several dissertations, and ten books in whole or in part about her. An artists' colony and a literary society have been established in her name.

John J. Patton
Atlantic-Cape Community College

PRIMARY WORKS

Renascence and Other Poems, 1917; *A Few Figs from Thistles, Aria da Capo,* 1920; *Two Slatterns and a King, The Lamp and the Bell, Second April,* 1921; *The Harp Weaver and Other Poems,* 1923; *Distressing Dialogues* (published under "Nancy Boyd"), 1924; *Three Plays,* 1926; *The King's Henchman,* 1927; *The Buck in the Snow,* 1928; *Poems Selected for Young People,* 1929; *Fatal Interview,* 1931; *The Princess Marries the Page,* 1932; *Wine from These Grapes,* 1934; *Conversation at Midnight,* 1937; *Collected Sonnets,* 1941; *Murder of Lidice,* 1942; *Collected Lyrics,* 1943; *Letters of Edna St. Vincent Millay,* 1952; *Mine the Harvest,* 1954; *Collected Poems,* 1956; *Collected Sonnets, Revised & Expanded ed.,* 1988; *Selected Poems: The Centenary Edition,* 1991.

Spring

To what purpose, April, do you return again?
Beauty is not enough.
You can no longer quiet me with the redness
Of little leaves opening stickily.
I know what I know.
The sun is hot on my neck as I observe
The spikes of the crocus.
The smell of the earth is good.
It is apparent that there is no death.
But what does that signify?
Not only under ground are the brains of men
Eaten by maggots.

Life in itself
Is nothing,
An empty cup, a flight of uncarpeted stairs.
It is not enough that yearly, down this hill,
April
Comes like an idiot, babbling and strewing flowers.

1921

The Spring and the Fall

In the spring of the year, in the spring of the year,
I walked the road beside my dear.
The trees were black where the bark was wet.
I see them yet, in the spring of the year.
He broke me a bough of the blossoming peach
That was out of the way and hard to reach.

In the fall of the year, in the fall of the year,
I walked the road beside my dear.
The rooks went up with a raucous trill.
I hear them still, in the fall of the year.
He laughed at all I dared to praise,
And broke my heart, in little ways.

Year be springing or year be falling,
The bark will drip and the birds be calling.
There's much that's fine to see and hear
In the spring of a year, in the fall of a year.
'Tis not love's going hurts my days,
But that it went in little ways.

1923

[Euclid alone has looked on Beauty bare]

Euclid[1] alone has looked on Beauty bare.
Let all who prate of Beauty hold their peace,

[1]Third-century B.C. Greek mathematician, the founder of geometry. Millay here considers mathematics a form of pure beauty.

And lay them prone upon the earth and cease
To ponder on themselves, the while they stare
At nothing, intricately drawn nowhere
In shapes of shifting lineage; let geese
Gabble and hiss, but heroes seek release
From dusty bondage into luminous air.
O blinding hour, O holy, terrible day,
When first the shaft into his vision shone
Of light anatomized! Euclid alone
Has looked on Beauty bare. Fortunate they
Who, though once only and then but far away,
Have heard her massive sandal set on stone.

1923

Dirge Without Music

I am not resigned to the shutting away of loving hearts in the hard
ground.
So it is, and so it will be, for so it has been, time out of mind:
Into the darkness they go, the wise and the lovely. Crowned
With lilies and with laurel they go; but I am not resigned.

Lovers and thinkers, into the earth with you.
Be one with the dull, the indiscriminate dust.
A fragment of what you felt, of what you knew,
A formula, a phrase remains,—but the best is lost.

The answers quick and keen, the honest look, the laughter, the
love,—
They are gone. They are gone to feed the roses. Elegant and
curled
Is the blossom. Fragrant is the blossom. I know. But I do not
approve.
More precious was the light in your eyes than all the roses in the
world.

Down, down, down into the darkness of the grave
Gently they go, the beautiful, the tender, the kind;
Quietly they go, the intelligent, the witty, the brave.
I know. But I do not approve. And I am not resigned.

1928

[Love is not all: it is not meat nor drink]

Love is not all: it is not meat nor drink
Nor slumber nor a roof against the rain;
Nor yet a floating spar to men that sink
And rise and sink and rise and sink again;
Love can not fill the thickened lung with breath,
Nor clean the blood, nor set the fractured bone;
Yet many a man is making friends with death
Even as I speak, for lack of love alone.
It well may be that in a difficult hour,
Pinned down by pain and moaning for release,
Or nagged by want past resolution's power,
I might be driven to sell your love for peace,
Or trade the memory of this night for food.
It well may be. I do not think I would.

1931

The Return

Earth does not understand her child,
Who from the loud gregarious town
Returns, depleted and defiled,
To the still woods, to fling him down.

Earth can not count the sons she bore:
The wounded lynx, the wounded man
Come trailing blood unto her door;
She shelters both as best she can.

But she is early up and out,
To trim the year or strip its bones;
She has no time to stand about
Talking of him in undertones

Who has no aim but to forget,
Be left in peace, be lying thus
For days, for years, for centuries yet,
Unshaven and anonymous;

Who, marked for failure, dulled by grief,
  Has traded in his wife and friend
For this warm ledge, this alder leaf:
  Comfort that does not comprehend.

1934

[Here lies, and none to mourn him but the sea]

Here lies, and none to mourn him but the sea,
That falls incessant on the empty shore,
Most various Man, cut down to spring no more;
Before his prime, even in his infancy
Cut down, and all the clamour that was he,
Silenced; and all the riveted pride he wore,
A rusted iron column whose tall core
The rains have tunnelled like an aspen tree.
Man, doughty Man, what power has brought you low,
That heaven itself in arms could not persuade
To lay aside the lever and the spade
And be as dust among the dusts that blow?
Whence, whence the broadside? whose the heavy blade? . . .
Strive not to speak, poor scattered mouth; I know.

1934

[His stalk the dark delphinium]

His stalk the dark delphinium[1]
Unthorned into the tending hand
Releases . . . yet that hour will come . . .
And must, in such a spiny land.

[1]The delphinium has spurred flowers, the rose has thorns, and mignonette's clusters of tiny flowers are almost hidden. All three flowers are therefore hard to get at because of their natural defenses.

The silky, powdery mignonette
Before these gathering dews are gone
May pierce me—does the rose regret
The day she did her armour on?
In that the foul supplants the fair,
The coarse defeats the twice-refined,
Is food for thought, but not despair:
All will be easier when the mind
To meet the brutal age has grown
An iron cortex of its own.

1939

Sonnet xli

I, being born a woman and distressed
By all the needs and notions of my kind,
Am urged by your propinquity to find
Your person fair, and feel a certain zest
To bear your body's weight upon my breast:
So subtly is the fume of life designed,
To clarify the pulse and cloud the mind,
And leave me once again undone, possessed.
Think not for this, however, the poor treason
Of my stout blood against my staggering brain,
I shall remember you with love, or season
My scorn with pity,—let me make it plain:
I find this frenzy insufficient reason
For conversation when we meet again.

1923

Sonnet xcv

Women have loved before as I love now;
At least, in lively chronicles of the past—
Of Irish waters by a Cornish prow
Or Trojan waters by a Spartan mast
Much to their cost invaded—here and there,
Hunting the amorous line, skimming the rest,
I find some woman bearing as I bear

Love like a burning city in the breast.
I think however that of all alive
I only in such utter, ancient way
Do suffer love; in me alone survive
The unregenerate passions of a day
When treacherous queens, with death upon the tread,
Heedless and wilful, took their knights to bed.

1931

Justice Denied in Massachusetts[1]

Let us abandon then our gardens and go home
And sit in the sitting-room.
Shall the larkspur blossom or the corn grow under this cloud?
Sour to the fruitful seed
Is the cold earth under this cloud,
Fostering quack and weed, we have marched upon but cannot
    conquer;
We have bent the blades of our hoes against the stalks of them.

Let us go home, and sit in the sitting-room.
Not in our day
Shall the cloud go over and the sun rise as before,
Beneficent upon us
Out of the glittering bay,
And the warm winds be blown inward from the sea
Moving the blades of corn
With a peaceful sound.
Forlorn, forlorn,
Stands the blue hay-rack by the empty mow.
And the petals drop to the ground,
Leaving the tree unfruited.
The sun that warmed our stooping backs and withered the weed
    uprooted—
We shall not feel it again.
We shall die in darkness, and be buried in the rain.

[1]Refers to the case of Nicola Sacco and Bartolomeo Vanzetti, who, believed by many to be political victims, were self-professed anarchists convicted of robbery and murder, and executed at Boston in 1927. Despite an outpouring of appeals for clemency, including a personal plea from Millay, the governor refused to commute the sentence.

What from the splendid dead
We have inherited—
Furrows sweet to the grain, and the weed subdued—
See now the slug and the mildew plunder.
Evil does overwhelm
The larkspur and the corn;
We have seen them go under.

Let us sit here, sit still,
Here in the sitting-room until we die;
At the step of Death on the walk, rise and go;
Leaving to our children's children this beautiful doorway,
And this elm,
And a blighted earth to till
With a broken hoe.

1928

Alienation and Literary Experimentation

Ezra Pound is generally regarded as the chief spokesperson for experimentation in modern American literature. His famous slogan, "Make it New," was quoted often by many writers who agreed with its premises and aims. For those in agreement, making it new demanded the use of large ideas and specific details in ways that reflected sharp observation and fresh thought. Many who disagreed—other writers as well as readers who were happy to remain conventional—saw in Pound and others a deliberate desire to be obscure. In fact, "The Waste Land," T. S. Eliot's most famous poem and perhaps the most famous poem of the twentieth century, was vociferously rejected by many people as a farce, a trick Eliot was playing on unsuspecting readers. Even Eliot himself, once he converted to the respectability of organized religion, dismissed the poem as nothing but "a grouse against life."

Modernism does, in fact, have a serious argument against many of the features of modern life. Pound objected most to what he called "Victorian slither," by which he meant the tendency to allow one's comfortable and preset attitudes to lead the attention away from what was most pressing or most illusive. Such tendencies were the result of the routinization and increasing bureaucracy in an urbanized and industrial world. Implicit in Pound's polemic blasts against the shopworn and trite expression was a sense that the artist was, as he put it, the antenna of the race. This claim of an isolated and privileged position for the artist also entailed a separation from normal or "mass" society. Such separation in its severest form was known as alienation, the feeling of being an outsider in one's social environment. Hence, there were many ways in which alienation and experimentation were linked. In fact, the stylistic effects that result from the linking of the two are offered by some critics as the core of modernism.

But alienation and experimentation could be joined on other grounds as well. Many alienated writers argued that their mental and psychological states were simply impossible to record using the traditional or standard forms of expression. Such standard forms had been developed, the argument said, for normal audiences by normal writers. Some writers were aggressively set against everything that acted as a "norm": for example, E. E. Cummings and H.D. not only changed the look of the poem on the page but also acted out their unconventional beliefs in ways that society found offensively abnormal. However, other writers such as William Carlos Williams and Marianne Moore could retain all the appearances of social propriety, even as their poems were clearly challenging accepted ways of creating meaning and expressing emotion. Alienation was not simply a matter of unconventional behavior, nor was experimentation simply based on a desire to appear different from others.

Some of the writers of the modern period seemed to reflect a belief that society itself was an alienating structure, rather than merely claiming that individual artists "suffered" from a disaffecting situation. F. Scott Fitzgerald and Katherine Anne Porter depicted society in a way that suggested everyone was unhappy in ways that were pervasive and yet largely invisible. Various "solutions" were offered to the problem, though often the proposed solution was itself undercut by irony. Irony was often used in modernism because it makes all foundations of claim and statement less secure; this insecurity appealed to modernists because it reflected their own state and also challenged the security of normal experience. Eugene O'Neill, for example, offers in *The Hairy Ape* a form of primitivism as a solution to alienation, but the problem is far from resolved in any straightforward way.

Even today many readers find that the experimentalism of modernism is too confusing, too needlessly complex, and that the alienation of modern literary thought is too bleak, too utterly empty. Whether or not modernism can be seen as an affirmative cultural tradition, one that challenges and even destroys, but does so in the interest of genuine renewal, remains a much debated question. Disputes about style and attitude are often part of this larger question.

Charles Molesworth
Queens College, City University of New York

Ezra Pound 1885–1972

No one better symbolizes the course of modern literature—its triumphs and defeats—than Ezra Pound. From the lyric poems of his Edwardian period to the complex allusive style of his epic *Cantos,* Pound marked the path that modern poetry followed. His work in criticism and translation, from his "Imagist Manifesto" and *Guide to Kulchur* to his translations from Provençal and Chinese, signaled new directions in modern literature and criticism. But it is not only as a major influence on literary modernism that Pound is important.

Pound was born in Hailey, Idaho, and raised in Pennsylvania, where his father worked in the Mint in Philadelphia. His pug-nacious spirit is evident in an essay titled "How I Began," in which Pound says that at age fifteen he decided to become a poet and to know by age thirty more about poetry than any living man. Pound was a student at the University of Pennsylvania in 1902, where he met William Carlos Williams, and Hilda Doolittle, who was a student at Bryn Mawr. He received his B.A. from Hamilton College in 1905 and an M.A. in Romance Languages from the University of Pennsylvania in 1906. After being fired as a teacher at Wabash College for harboring a "lady-gent impersonator" in his room, Pound departed for Europe, where he would remain for most of his life.

In 1908, Pound arrived in Venice, where he arranged to have his first volume of poems, *A Lume Spento,* published at his own expense. Within the next few years, he became a central figure in London literary life. Through his own work and by fostering the work of others, including W. B. Yeats, James Joyce, H.D., Marianne Moore, William Carlos Williams, and T. S. Eliot, Pound sought to bring about a renaissance of the arts in England and America. In "A Few Don'ts by an Imagiste," which appeared in *Poetry* in 1913, he announced the modernist poetics of precision, concision, and metrical freedom which he had formulated in conversation with H.D. and Richard Aldington.

The poems of *Lustra* (1916) reflect the range of Pound's intellectual interests, the variety of his technical experiments, and the extent of his artistic achievement in his London years. For Pound as for other modernists, the First World War marked a turn away from the aestheticism of his early years toward what he would call "the poem including history." Having entombed the aesthete figure of his early period in "Hugh Selwyn Mauberley," which was published in 1920, Pound departed for Europe and turned his main energies to writing his epic *Cantos.* Under the influence of C. H. Douglas's ideas on Social Credit and, after 1924, the politics of Mussolini in Italy, Pound came to attribute the waste of the war and the malaise of the modern world to the dominance of bankers and munitions manufacturers, usury, and Jews. Insisting on the relationship between good government, good art, and the good life, Pound incorporated his social and economic views into the works he published during the thirties, including *ABC of Economics* (1933), *Eleven New Cantos* (1934), *Social Credit: An Impact* (1935), and *Jefferson and/or Mussolini* (1935).

In 1939 he made a trip to Washington, D.C., where he spoke with members of Congress about his economic policies and about his fear that Roosevelt, the bankers, and the armaments industry were leading America into another war. Unsuccessful with American politicians, he returned to Italy, where in 1941 he began regularly broadcasting his ideas over Rome Radio, in a program aimed at the English-speaking world. Mixing reflections on literature with tirades against Roosevelt, usury, and international finance, Pound continued these broadcasts until July 1943, when he was indicted for treason. After being arrested in May 1945, he was incarcerated for six months in a wire cage in Pisa before he was sent back to America to stand trial. Declared mentally unfit to stand trial by a team of psychologists, Pound was committed in 1946 to St. Elizabeths Hospital in Washington, D.C. where he remained until his release in 1958.

When in February 1949 the Library of Congress awarded the Bollingen Prize for Poetry to the *Pisan Cantos* (1948), Pound became the center of a controversy over the relation of poetry and politics, and modernism and fascism, that raged for several months in the American press. While T. S. Eliot, Allen Tate, and Robert Penn Warren argued for the separation of poetry and politics in the evaluation of Pound's work, others, including Karl Shapiro and Robert Hillyer, argued that Pound's politics ultimately vitiated the artistic value of his poetry.

In his later writings, Pound lost no opportunity to criticize the "mere aesthete," who did not understand the social and regenerative function of his epic "tale of the tribe." In the wake of the Bollingen controversy, however, it was the image of Pound the formalist and aesthete that rose to prominence in the Anglo American tradition. This emphasis was supported by the increasing obscurity and complexity of Pound's later volumes of Cantos. Since Pound's death, studies of his work have remained split between those who would praise the poet and forget the politician and those who would attack the fascist and forget the poet. But in the final analysis, it may be Pound's Americanism as much as his fascism that pervades his work.

Betsy Erkkila
University of Pennsylvania

PRIMARY WORKS

A Lume Spento, 1908; *Personae,* 1909–1926; *The Spirit of Romance,* 1910; *Cantos,* 1916–1968; *Cathay,* 1915; *Gaudier-Brzeska,* 1916; *Lustra,* 1916; *Hugh Selwyn Mauberley,* 1920; *Make It New,* 1934; D.D. Paige, ed., *The Letters of Ezra Pound (1907–1941),* 1950; *Literary Essays of Ezra Pound,* 1954; *Selected Poems 1908–1959,* 1975.

A Virginal[1]

No, no! Go from me, I have left her lately.
I will not spoil my sheath with lesser brightness,
For my surrounding air hath a new lightness;
Slight are her arms, yet they have bound me straitly
And left me cloaked as with a gauze of aether;
As with sweet leaves; as with subtle clearness.
Oh, I have picked up magic in her nearness
To sheathe me half in half the things that sheathe her.
No, no! Go from me. I have still the flavour,
Soft as spring wind that's come from birchen bowers.
Green come the shoots, aye April in the branches,
As winter's wound with her sleight hand she staunches,
Hath of the trees a likeness of the savour:
As white their bark, so white this lady's hours.

1912

A Pact

I make a pact with you, Walt Whitman—
I have detested you long enough.
I come to you as a grown child
Who has had a pig-headed father;
I am old enough now to make friends.
It was you that broke the new wood,
Now is a time for carving.
We have one sap and one root—
Let there be commerce between us.

1916

[1]A virginal is a small harpsichord played in the sixteenth and seventeenth centuries by young girls, virgins.

In a Station of the Metro

The apparition of these faces in the crowd;
Petals on a wet, black bough.

1916

L'art, 1910

Green arsenic smeared on an egg-white cloth,
Crushed strawberries! Come, let us feast our eyes.

1916

A Retrospect[1]

There has been so much scribbling about a new fashion in poetry, that I may perhaps be pardoned this brief recapitulation and retrospect.

In the spring or early summer of 1912, 'H.D.', Richard Aldington and myself decided that we were agreed upon the three principles following:

1. Direct treatment of the 'thing' whether subjective or objective.
2. To use absolutely no word that does not contribute to the presentation.
3. As regarding rhythm: to compose in the sequence of the musical phrase, not in sequence of a metronome.

Upon many points of taste and of predilection we differed, but agreeing upon these three positions we thought we had as much right to a group name, at least as much right, as a number of French 'schools' proclaimed by Mr Flint in the August number of Harold Monro's magazine for 1911.

This school has since been 'joined' or 'followed' by numerous people who, whatever their merits, do not show any signs of agreeing with the second specification. Indeed *vers libre*[2] has become as prolix and as verbose as any of the flaccid varieties that preceded it. It has brought faults of its own. The actual language and phrasing is often as bad as that of our elders without even the excuse that the words are shovelled in to fill a metric pattern or to complete the noise of a rhyme-sound. Whether

[1]A group of early essays which appeared in *Pavannes and Divisions* (1918). "A Few Don'ts by an Imagiste" first appeared in *Poetry,* 1 (March 1913).

[2]*Vers libre* is the French term for free verse.

or no the phrases followed by the followers are musical must be left to the reader's decision. At times I can find a marked metre in 'vers libres', as stale and hackneyed as any pseudo-Swinburnian,[3] at times the writers seem to follow no musical structure whatever. But it is, on the whole, good that the field should be ploughed. Perhaps a few good poems have come from the new method, and if so it is justified.

Criticism is not a circumscription or a set of prohibitions. It provides fixed points of departure. It may startle a dull reader into alertness. That little of it which is good is mostly in stray phrases; or if it be an older artist helping a younger it is in great measure but rules of thumb, cautions gained by experience.

I set together a few phrases on practical working about the time the first remarks on imagisme were published. The first use of the word 'Imagiste' was in my note to T.E. Hulme's five poems, printed at the end of my 'Ripostes' in the autumn of 1912. I reprint my cautions from *Poetry* for March, 1913.

A Few Don'ts

An 'Image' is that which presents an intellectual and emotional complex in an instant of time. I use the term 'complex' rather in the technical sense employed by the newer psychologists, such as Hart, though we might not agree absolutely in our application.

It is the presentation of such a 'complex' instantaneously which gives that sense of sudden liberation; that sense of freedom from time limits and space limits; that sense of sudden growth, which we experience in the presence of the greatest works of art.

It is better to present one Image in a lifetime than to produce voluminous works.

All this, however, some may consider open to debate. The immediate necessity is to tabulate A LIST OF DON'TS for those beginning to write verses. I can not put all of them into Mosaic negative.

To begin with, consider the three propositions (demanding direct treatment, economy of words, and the sequence of the musical phrase), not as dogma—never consider anything as dogma—but as the result of long contemplation, which, even if it is some one else's contemplation, may be worth consideration.

Pay no attention to the criticism of men who have never themselves written a notable work. Consider the discrepancies between the actual writing of the Greek poets and dramatists, and the theories of the Graeco-Roman grammarians, concocted to explain their metres.

1918

[3] Algernon Swinburne, a nineteenth-century British poet.

from Hugh Selwyn Mauberley (Life and Contacts)[1]

E.P. Ode pour L'election de Son Sepulchre[2]

I

For three years, out of key with his time,
He strove to resuscitate the dead art
Of poetry; to maintain "the sublime"
In the old sense. Wrong from the start—

No, hardly, but seeing he had been born
In a half savage country, out of date;
Bent resolutely on wringing lilies from the acorn;
Capaneus[3]; trout for factitious bait;

Ἴδμεν γάρ τοι πάνθ', ὅσ' ἐνὶ Τροίῃ[4]
Caught in the unstopped ear;
Giving the rocks small lee-way
The chopped seas held him, therefore, that year.

His true Penelope[5] was Flaubert,[6]
He fished by obstinate isles;
Observed the elegance of Circe's[7] hair
Rather than the mottoes on sun-dials.

Unaffected by "the march of events,"
He passed from men's memory in *l'an trentiesme*
De son eage[8]; the case presents
No adjunct to the Muses' diadem.

[1]"Hugh Selwyn Mauberley" is a kind of farewell to London and the literary culture of Pound's early years. The poem was published in 1920, the same year that Pound left England for France and Italy, where he dedicated himself more fully to the composition of his epic *Cantos*.

[2]"Ode on the Choice of His Tomb," adapted from an ode by Pierre Ronsard (1524–1585), "De l'Election de son sepulchre" ("On the Choice of His Tomb").

[3]One of the seven warriors sent from Argos to attack Thebes. Zeus struck him down with lightning for his boastful defiance.

[4]The siren's song to Odysseus in Homer's *Odyssey* (Book XII): "For we know all that was suffered in Troy."

[5]The faithful wife of Odysseus to whom he returned at the end of his voyage.

[6]Gustave Flaubert (1821–1880), the French novelist and supreme stylist, whom Pound admired for his emphasis on *le mot juste*—the precise word.

[7]The goddess of Aeaea by whom Odysseus and his crew were enchanted for a year in *The Odyssey*.

[8]"The thirtieth year of his age," adapted from the first line of *The Testament* by François Villon (1431–1463?).

II

The age demanded an image
Of its accelerated grimace,
Something for the modern stage,
Not, at any rate, an Attic grace;[9]

Not, not certainly, the obscure reveries
Of the inward gaze;
Better mendacities
Than the classics in paraphrase!

The "age demanded" chiefly a mould in plaster,
Made with no loss of time,
A prose kinema, not, not assuredly, alabaster
Or the "sculpture" of rhyme.

III

The tea-rose tea-gown, etc.
Supplants the mousseline of Cos,[10]
The pianola "replaces"
Sappho's barbitos.[11]

Christ follows Dionysus,[12]
Phallic and ambrosial
Made way for macerations;
Caliban casts out Ariel.[13]

All things are a flowing,
Sage Heracleitus[14] says;
But a tawdry cheapness
Shall outlast our days.

Even the Christian beauty
Defects—after Samothrace;[15]
We see *τὸ καλὸν*[16]
Decreed in the market place.

[9]A pure style associated with ancient Attica.
[10]Muslin from the Greek island of Cos.
[11]An early form of lyre used by the seventh-century B.C. Greek woman poet Sappho.
[12]Greek god of fertility, wine, and poetic inspiration, associated with orgiastic rites performed in his honor.
[13]In Shakespeare's *The Tempest,* Caliban is presented as "a savage and deformed Slave," and Ariel is presented as "an airy Spirit."
[14]Greek philosopher (540–480 B.C.) who taught that all things are in a constant flux.
[15]Greek island, associated with the rites of Dionysus and the statue of the "Winged Victory."
[16]Greek word for "the beautiful."

Faun's flesh is not to us,
Nor the saint's vision.
We have the press for wafer;
Franchise for circumcision.

All men, in law, are equals.
Free of Pisistratus,[17]
We choose a knave or an eunuch
To rule over us.

O bright Apollo,[18]
τίν' ἄνδρα, τίν' ἥρωα, τίνα θεόν,[19]
What god, man, or hero
Shall I place a tin wreath upon!

IV

These fought in any case,
and some believing,
pro domo[20] in any case . . .

Some quick to arm,
some for adventure,
some from fear of weakness,
some from fear of censure,
some for love of slaughter, an imagination,
learning later . . .
some in fear, learning love of slaughter;

Died some, pro patria,
non "dulce" non "et decor"[21] . . .
walked eye-deep in hell
believing in old men's lies, then unbelieving
came home, home to a lie,
home to many deceits,
home to old lies and new infamy;
usury age-old and age-thick
and liars in public places.

[17]Sixth-century B.C. Athenian tyrant who supported the arts.

[18]Greek god of poetry, prophecy, and civic order.

[19]Greek for "What man, what hero, what god," adapted from Pindar's *Olympian Odes.*

[20]"For the home," from Cicero's *De Domo Sua.*

[21]"For one's country, not sweet and not fitting." From Horace's *Odes:* "Dulce et decorum est pro patria mori" ("It is sweet and fitting to die for one's country").

Daring as never before, wastage as never before.
Young blood and high blood,
fair cheeks, and fine bodies;

fortitude as never before

frankness as never before,
disillusions as never told in the old days,
hysterias, trench confessions,
laughter out of dead bellies.

V

There died a myriad,
And of the best, among them,
For an old bitch gone in the teeth,
For a botched civilization,

Charm, smiling at the good mouth,
Quick eyes gone under earth's lid,

For two gross of broken statues,
For a few thousand battered books.

Yeux Glauques[22]

Gladstone[23] was still respected,
When John Ruskin produced
"King's Treasuries"; Swinburne
And Rossetti still abused.[24]

Fœtid Buchanan[25] lifted up his voice
When that faun's head of hers
Became a pastime for
Painters and adulterers.

[22]French for "grey eyes." Alludes to a painting by the pre-Raphaelite artist Edward Burne-Jones (1833–1898), "King Cophetua and the Beggar-Maid," in the Tate Gallery in London. Elizabeth Siddal, who later married the poet and painter Dante Gabriel Rossetti (1828–1882), was the model for this and other paintings by the pre-Raphaelites.

[23]William Gladstone, British Chancellor of the Exchequer and Liberal Prime Minister during the period 1859–1894.

[24]John Ruskin (1819–1900) was an art critic who defended the pre-Raphaelites, including Dante Gabriel Rossetti and the poet Algernon Swinburne (1827–1909). In a chapter of *Sesame and Lilies* (1865) entitled "Kings' Treasuries," he calls for the general diffusion of literature and the arts.

[25]Robert Buchanan (1841–1901), a poet and reviewer who attacked the pre-Raphaelite movement in "The Fleshly School of Poetry" (1871).

The Burne-Jones[26] cartons
Have preserved her eyes;
Still, at the Tate, they teach
Cophetua to rhapsodize;

Thin like brook-water,
With a vacant gaze.
The English Rubaiyat[27] was still-born
In those days.
The thin, clear gaze, the same
Still darts out faun-like from the half-ruin'd face,
Questing and passive. . . .
"Ah, poor Jenny's case"[28] . . .

Bewildered that a world
Shows no surprise
At her last maquero's[29]
Adulteries.

Siena mi fe'; Disfecemi Maremma[30]

Among the pickled fœtuses and bottled bones,
Engaged in perfecting the catalogue,
I found the last scion of the
Senatorial families of Strasbourg, Monsieur Verog.[31]

For two hours he talked of Gallifet;[32]
Of Dowson; of the Rhymers' Club;[33]
Told me how Johnson (Lionel)[34] died
By falling from a high stool in a pub . . .

But showed no trace of alcohol
At the autopsy, privately performed—

[26]Sketches for paintings.
[27]Edward Fitzgerald (1809–1883) translated *The Rubaiyat of Omar Khayyam* in 1859.
[28]"Jenny" is a poem about a prostitute by Dante Gabriel Rossetti.
[29]maquero: pimp.
[30]"Siena made me, Maremma undid me," spoken by "La Pia dei' Tolomei," murdered by her husband in the Maremma marshlands, in Dante's *Purgatoria.*
[31]Fictive name for Victor Plarr (1863–1929), French poet who wrote *In the Dorian Mood* and later librarian of the Royal College of Surgeons.
[32]Marquis de Galliffet (1830–1909), French general who lost the battle of Sedan during the Franco-Prussian war.
[33]Ernest Dowson (1867–1900), English poet and member of the Rhymers' Club, which was founded by William Butler Yeats and others in 1890–91.
[34]Lionel Johnson (1867–1902), a poet and heavy drinker who was also a member of the Rhymers' Club.

Tissue preserved—the pure mind
Arose toward Newman[35] as the whiskey warmed.

Dowson found harlots cheaper than hotels;
Headlam for uplift; Image[36] impartially imbued
With raptures for Bacchus, Terpsichore and the Church.[37]
So spoke the author of "The Dorian Mood,"

M. Verog, out of step with the decade,
Detached from his contemporaries,
Neglected by the young,
Because of these reveries.

Brennbaum[38]

The sky-like limpid eyes,
The circular infant's face,
The stiffness from spats to collar
Never relaxing into grace;

The heavy memories of Horeb, Sinai and the forty years,[39]
Showed only when the daylight fell
Level across the face
Of Brennbaum "The Impeccable."

Mr. Nixon[40]

In the cream gilded cabin of his steam yacht
Mr. Nixon advised me kindly, to advance with fewer
Dangers of delay. "Consider
"Carefully the reviewer.

[35]Cardinal John Henry Newman (1801–1890), Catholic theologian and leader of the Oxford Movement. Johnson and Dowson both converted to Catholicism.

[36]Reverend Stewart D. Headlam (1847–1924), forced to resign his curacy for lecturing on theater and dance to workingmen's clubs. He founded the Church and Stage Guild with Selwyn Image (1849–1930).

[37]Bacchus is the Roman name for Dionysus. Terpsichore is the Greek muse of dance. The Church alludes to the Roman Catholic Church.

[38]Portrait suggests Max Beerbohm (1872–1956), an essayist and parodist.

[39]The children of Israel wandered in the wilderness for forty years in search of Canaan. Moses drew water from Horeb; he received the Ten Commandments at Sinai.

[40]Pound said Mr. Nixon was "a fictitious name for a real person." He may be referring to the English journalist and novelist Arnold Bennett (1867–1931).

"I was as poor as you are;
"When I began I got, of course,
"Advance on royalties, fifty at first," said Mr. Nixon,
"Follow me, and take a column,
"Even if you have to work free.

"Butter reviewers. From fifty to three hundred
"I rose in eighteen months;
"The hardest nut I had to crack
"Was Dr. Dundas.

"I never mentioned a man but with the view
"Of selling my own works.
"The tip's a good one, as for literature
"It gives no man a sinecure.

"And no one knows, at sight, a masterpiece.
"And give up verse, my boy,
"There's nothing in it."

* * *

Likewise a friend of Bloughram's[41] once advised me:
Don't kick against the pricks,
Accept opinion. The "Nineties" tried your game
And died, there's nothing in it.

X

Beneath the sagging roof
The stylist[42] has taken shelter,
Unpaid, uncelebrated,
At last from the world's welter

Nature receives him;
With a placid and uneducated mistress
He exercises his talents
And the soil meets his distress.

The haven from sophistications and contentions
Leaks through its thatch;

[41]In Robert Browning's "Bishop Bloughram's Apology," the Bishop rationalizes his sacrifice of sacred principle for worldly comfort.

[42]The stylist Pound has in mind may be James Joyce or Ford Maddox Ford.

He offers succulent cooking;
The door has a creaking latch.

XI

"Conservatrix of Milésien"[43]
Habits of mind and feeling,
Possibly. But in Ealing[44]
With the most bank-clerkly of Englishmen?

No, "Milésian" is an exaggeration.
No instinct has survived in her
Older than those her grandmother
Told her would fit her station.

XII

"Daphne with her thighs in bark
Stretches toward me her leafy hands,"[45]—
Subjectively. In the stuffed-satin drawing-room
I await The Lady Valentine's commands,

Knowing my coat has never been
Of precisely the fashion
To stimulate, in her,
A durable passion;

Doubtful, somewhat, of the value
Of well-gowned approbation
Of literary effort,
But never of The Lady Valentine's vocation:

Poetry, her border of ideas,
The edge, uncertain, but a means of blending
With other strata
Where the lower and higher have ending;

[43]Adapted from Remy de Gourmont's short story "Strategèmes": "des femmes . . . ces conservatrices des traditions milésiennes" ("women . . . these conservers of Milesian traditions").
[44]A suburb of London.
[45]The lines are translated from Théophile Gautier's version of Ovid's story in *Emaux et Camées*). In Ovid's story, Daphne is metamorphosed into a tree in order to escape the embrace of Apollo.

A hook to catch the Lady Jane's attention,
A modulation toward the theatre,
Also, in the case of revolution,
A possible friend and comforter.

* * *

Conduct, on the other hand, the soul
"Which the highest cultures have nourished"
To Fleet St. where
Dr. Johnson[46] flourished;

Beside this thoroughfare
The sale of half-hose has
Long since superseded the cultivation
Of Pierian roses.[47]

Envoi (1919)[48]

Go, dumb-born book,
Tell her that sang me once that song of Lawes:[49]
Hadst thou but song
As thou hast subjects known,
Then were there cause in thee that should condone
Even my faults that heavy upon me lie,
And build her glories their longevity.

Tell her that sheds
Such treasure in the air,
Recking naught else but that her graces give
Life to the moment,
I would bid them live
As roses might, in magic amber laid,
Red overwrought with orange and all made
One substance and one colour
Braving time.

Tell her that goes
With song upon her lips

[46]Samuel Johnson (1709–1784), eighteenth-century British journalist, essayist, and critic.

[47]Pieria is the legendary birthplace of the Muses.

[48]An envoi is a writer's parting word. The poem is modeled on Edmund Waller's (1606– 1687) "Go, Lovely Rose!"

[49]Henry Lawes (1596–1662), English composer and musician who set Waller's "Go, Lovely Rose!" to music.

But sings not out the song, nor knows
The maker of it, some other mouth,
May be as fair as hers,
Might, in new ages, gain her worshippers,
When our two dusts with Waller's shall be laid,
Siftings on siftings in oblivion,
Till change hath broken down
All things save Beauty alone.

1920

from The Cantos

I[1]

And then went down to the ship,
Set keel to breakers, forth on the godly sea, and
We set up mast and sail on that swart ship,
Bore sheep aboard her, and our bodies also
Heavy with weeping, and winds from sternward
Bore us out onward with bellying canvas,
Circe's[2] this craft, the trim-coifed goddess.
Then sat we amidships, wind jamming the tiller,
Thus with stretched sail, we went over sea till day's end.
Sun to his slumber, shadows o'er all the ocean,
Came we then to the bounds of deepest water,
To the Kimmerian lands,[3] and peopled cities
Covered with close-webbed mist, unpierced ever
With glitter of sun-rays
Nor with stars stretched, nor looking back from heaven
Swartest night stretched over wretched men there.
The ocean flowing backward, came we then to the place
Aforesaid by Circe.
Here did they rites, Perimedes and Eurylochus,[4]
And drawing sword from my hip
I dug the ell-square pitkin;
Poured we libations unto each the dead,

[1]The first canto is an adaptation from Book XI of Homer's *The Odyssey,* which recounts Odysseus' voyage to Hades, the realm of the dead.

[2]Circe, the sorceress of Aeaea who delays Odysseus and his crew for a year. When he requests permission to return home, she directs him to seek prophecy for his journey from Tiresias in the underworld.

[3]Ancient land located at the end of the earth.

[4]Two of Odysseus' companions.

First mead and then sweet wine, water mixed with white flour.
Then prayed I many a prayer to the sickly death's-heads;
As set in Ithaca,[5] sterile bulls of the best
For sacrifice, heaping the pyre with goods,
A sheep to Tiresias only, black and a bell-sheep.
Dark blood flowed in the fosse,
Souls out of Erebus,[6] cadaverous dead, of brides
Of youths and of the old who had borne much;
Souls stained with recent tears, girls tender,
Men many, mauled with bronze lance heads,
Battle spoil, bearing yet dreory arms,
These many crowded about me; with shouting,
Pallor upon me, cried to my men for more beasts;
Slaughtered the herds, sheep slain of bronze;
Poured ointment, cried to the gods,
To Pluto the strong, and praised Proserpine;[7]
Unsheathed the narrow sword,
I sat to keep off the impetuous impotent dead,
Till I should hear Tiresias.
But first Elpenor came, our friend Elpenor,[8]
Unburied, cast on the wide earth,
Limbs that we left in the house of Circe,
Unwept, unwrapped in sepulchre, since toils urged other.
Pitiful spirit. And I cried in hurried speech:
"Elpenor, how art thou come to this dark coast?
"Cam'st thou afoot, outstripping seamen?"
                    And he in heavy speech:
"Ill fate and abundant wine. I slept in Circe's ingle.
"Going down the long ladder unguarded,
"I fell against the buttress,
"Shattered the nape-nerve, the soul sought Avernus.[9]
"But thou, O King, I bid remember me, unwept, unburied,
"Heap up mine arms, be tomb by sea-bord, and inscribed:
"A man of no fortune, and with a name to come.
"And set my oar up, that I swung mid fellows."

And Anticlea[10] came, whom I beat off, and then Tiresias Theban,
Holding his golden wand, knew me, and spoke first:
"A second time? why? man of ill star,

[5]The island home of Odysseus, off the coast of Greece.
[6]Land of the dead.
[7]Goddess of fertility abducted by Pluto, the god of the underworld.
[8]Companion of Odysseus who fell to his death from Circe's roof when he awoke from a drunken stupor to hear his friends departing. He was left unburied.
[9]Lake near Naples, the legendary entrance to Hades.
[10]Odysseus' mother, who died in his absence from Ithaca.

"Facing the sunless dead and this joyless region?
"Stand from the fosse, leave me my bloody bever
"For soothsay."
        And I stepped back,
And he strong with the blood, said then: "Odysseus
"Shalt return through spiteful Neptune,[11] over dark seas,
"Lose all companions." And then Anticlea came.
Lie quiet Divus. I mean, that is Andreas Divus,[12]
In officina Wecheli,[13] 1538, out of Homer.
And he sailed, by Sirens and thence outward and away
And unto Circe.
        Venerandam,[14]
In the Cretan's phrase, with the golden crown, Aphrodite,[15]
Cypri munimenta sortita est,[16] mirthful, orichalchi,[17] with golden
Girdles and breast bands, thou with dark eyelids
Bearing the golden bough of Argicida.[18] So that:

1917

XIII[1]

Kung walked
        by the dynastic temple
and into the cedar grove,
        and then out by the lower river,
And with him Khieu, Tchi
        and Tian[2] the low speaking
And "we are unknown," said Kung,
"You will take up charioteering?
        Then you will become known,
"Or perhaps I should take up charioteering, or archery?
"Or the practice of public speaking?"

[11]God of the sea, who would hinder Odysseus' return home.

[12]Pound acknowledges using the 1538 Latin translation of Homer by Andrea Divus.

[13]"In the printshop of Wechelus," printed on the title page of Divus's *Odyssey.*

[14]"Venerable," from the second Homeric Hymn to Aphrodite as translated by Georgius Dartona Cretensis (the "Cretan") from Greek into Renaissance Latin.

[15]Aphrodite, the goddess of love and beauty, a recurrent figure in *The Cantos.*

[16]"The citadels of Cyprus were her appointed realm."

[17]Orichalchi—of copper—refers to Aphrodite's earrings.

[18]The golden bough enables Aeneas to gain entrance to the underworld. Here the bough is also associated with Aphrodite, as the goddess of love and slayer of the Greeks ("Argicida").

[1]The first of the "Confucian Cantos," which draws on the teachings of the Chinese philosopher Confucius, or Kung (551–479 B.C.), in three classic texts which Pound translates as *The Great Digest, The Unwobbling Pivot,* and *The Analects.* Pound considered this Canto the "announcement of the backbone moral of the *Cantos.*"

[2]Disciples of Confucius.

And Tseu-lou said, "I would put the defences in order,"
And Khieu said, "If I were lord of a province
I would put it in better order than this is."
And Tchi said, "I would prefer a small mountain temple,
"With order in the observances,
            with a suitable performance of the ritual,"
And Tian said, with his hand on the strings of his lute
The low sounds continuing
            after his hand left the strings,
And the sound went up like smoke, under the leaves,
And he looked after the sound:
            "The old swimming hole,
"And the boys flopping off the planks,
"Or sitting in the underbrush playing mandolins."
            And Kung smiled upon all of them equally.
And Thseng-sie desired to know:
            "Which had answered correctly?"
And Kung said, "They have all answered correctly,
"That is to say, each in his nature."
And Kung raised his cane against Yuan Jang,
            Yuan Jang being his elder,
For Yuan Jang sat by the roadside pretending to
            be receiving wisdom.
And Kung said
            "You old fool, come out of it,
Get up and do something useful."
            And Kung said
"Respect a child's faculties
"From the moment it inhales the clear air,
"But a man of fifty who knows nothing
            Is worthy of no respect."
And "When the prince has gathered about him
"All the savants and artists, his riches will be fully employed."
And Kung said, and wrote on the bo leaves:
            If a man have not order within him
He can not spread order about him;
And if a man have not order within him
His family will not act with due order;
            And if the prince have not order within him
He can not put order in his dominions.
And Kung gave the words "order"
and "brotherly deference"
And said nothing of the "life after death."
And he said
            "Anyone can run to excesses,
It is easy to shoot past the mark,
It is hard to stand firm in the middle."

And they said: If a man commit murder
  Should his father protect him, and hide him?
And Kung said:
      He should hide him.

And Kung gave his daughter to Kong-Tch'ang[3]
      Although Kong-Tch'ang was in prison.
And he gave his niece to Nan-Young[4]
      although Nan-Young was out of office.
And Kung said "Wang[5] ruled with moderation,
      In his day the State was well kept,
And even I can remember
A day when the historians left blanks in their writings,
I mean for things they didn't know,
But that time seems to be passing."
And Kung said, "Without character you will
      be unable to play on that instrument
Or to execute the music fit for the Odes.
The blossoms of the apricot
      blow from the east to the west,
And I have tried to keep them from falling."

1925

XLV

With Usura[1]

With usura hath no man a house of good stone
each block cut smooth and well fitting
that design might cover their face,
with usura
hath no man a painted paradise on his church wall
harpes et luz[2]
or where virgin receiveth message
and halo projects from incision,
with usura
seeth no man Gonzaga[3] his heirs and his concubines
no picture is made to endure nor to live with

[3]Confucius' son-in-law.
[4]Disciple of Confucius.
[5]Wu Wang ruled as the first emperor of the Chou dynasty, 1122–1115 B.C.
[1]Latin for usury. The Catholic Church outlawed the practice of usury up to the time of the Reformation; John Calvin overturned the ban.
[2]Latin for harps and lutes. Pound paraphrases lines from François Villon's "Ballade pour Prier Notre Dame." In *ABC of Reading* he described Villon as the "first voice of man broken by bad economics," representing the "end of the mediaeval dream."
[3]Pound refers to the painting *Gonzaga, His Heirs and His Concubines,* by Andrea Mantegna (1431–1506).

but it is made to sell and sell quickly
with usura, sin against nature,
is thy bread ever more of stale rags
is thy bread dry as paper,
with no mountain wheat, no strong flour
with usura the line grows thick
with usura is no clear demarcation
and no man can find site for his dwelling.
Stonecutter is kept from his stone
weaver is kept from his loom
WITH USURA
wool comes not to market
sheep bringeth no gain with usura
Usura is a murrain,[4] usura
blunteth the needle in the maid's hand
and stoppeth the spinner's cunning. Pietro Lombardo[5]
came not by usura
Duccio[6] came not by usura
nor Pier della Francesca; Zuan Bellin'[7] not by usura
nor was 'La Calunnia'[8] painted.
Came not by usura Angelico; came not Ambrogio Praedis,[9]
Came no church of cut stone signed: *Adamo me fecit.*[10]
Not by usura St Trophime
Not by usura Saint Hilaire,[11]
Usura rusteth the chisel
It rusteth the craft and the craftsman
It gnaweth the thread in the loom
None learneth to weave gold in her pattern;
Azure hath a canker by usura; cramoisi[12] is unbroidered
Emerald findeth no Memling[13]
Usura slayeth the child in the womb
It stayeth the young man's courting
It hath brought palsey to bed, lyeth
between the young bride and her bridegroom
CONTRA NATURAM[14]

[4]Plague.
[5]Pietro Lombardo (1435–1515), Italian architect and sculptor.
[6]Agostino di Duccio (1418?–1481), Italian sculptor.
[7]Pier della Francesca (1420–1492), Italian painter; Giovanni Bellini (1430–1516), Venetian painter.
[8]"La Calunnia" ("Calumny") is a painting by Sandro Botticelli (1444–1510).
[9]Fra Angelico (1387–1455), Florentine painter; Ambrogio Praedis (1455?–1508?), Milanese painter.
[10]Latin for "Adam made me."
[11]St. Trophime is a Church in Arles, France; Saint Hilaire is in Poitiers, France.
[12]French for crimson cloth.
[13]Hans Memling (1430?–1495?), painter of the Flemish school.
[14]Latin for AGAINST NATURE, a phrase Aristotle uses to describe usury in *Politics*.

They have brought whores for Eleusis[15]
Corpses are set to banquet
at behest of usura.

N.B. Usury: A charge for the use of purchasing power, levied without regard to production; often without regard to the possibilities of production. (Hence the failure of the Medici bank.)[16]

1936

LXXXI

libretto Yet
Ere the season died a-cold
Borne upon a zephyr's[1] shoulder
I rose through the aureate sky
Lawes and Jenkyns[2] guard thy rest
Dolmetsch[3] ever be thy guest,
Has he tempered the viol's wood
To enforce both the grave and the acute?
Has he curved us the bowl of the lute?
Lawes and Jenkyns guard thy rest
Dolmetsch ever be thy guest
Hast 'ou fashioned so airy a mood
To draw up leaf from the root?
Hast 'ou found a cloud so light
As seemed neither mist nor shade?

Then resolve me, tell me aright
If Waller sang or Dowland[4] played.

Your eyen two wol sleye me sodenly
I may the beauté of hem nat susteyne[5]

And for 180 years almost nothing.

[15]Eleusis is the town in ancient Greece where the Eleusinian mysteries were celebrated.
[16]In the year of his death, Pound revised his original formulation on usury to say: "I was out of focus, taking a symptom for a cause. The cause is AVARICE."
[1]The west wind.
[2]Henry Lawes (1596–1662), English composer; John Jenkins (1592–1678), English composer and musician to Charles I and Charles II.
[3]Arnold Dolmetsch (1858–1940), French musician and instrument maker.
[4]Edmund Waller (1606–1687), English poet; John Dowland (1563–1626), English composer and lute player.
[5]Lines from the poem "Merciles Beaute," attributed to Geoffrey Chaucer.

Ed ascoltando al leggier mormorio[6]
there came new subtlety of eyes into my tent,
whether of spirit or hypostasis,
but what the blindfold hides
or at carneval

nor any pair showed anger
Saw but the eyes and stance between the eyes,
colour, diastasis,
careless or unaware it had not the
whole tent's room
nor was place for the full Ειδὼσ[7]
interpass, penetrate
casting but shade beyond the other lights
sky's clear
night's sea
green of the mountain pool
shone from the unmasked eyes in half-mask's space.
What thou lovest well remains,
the rest is dross
What thou lov'st well shall not be reft from thee
What thou lov'st well is thy true heritage
Whose world, or mine or theirs
or is it of none?
First came the seen, then thus the palpable
Elysium,[8] though it were in the halls of hell,
What thou lovest well is thy true heritage
What thou lov'st well shall not be reft from thee

The ant's a centaur in his dragon world.
Pull down thy vanity, it is not man
Made courage, or made order, or made grace,
Pull down thy vanity, I say pull down.
Learn of the green world what can be thy place
In scaled invention or true artistry,
Pull down thy vanity,
Paquin[9] pull down!
The green casque has outdone your elegance.

"Master thyself, then others shall thee beare"[10]
Pull down thy vanity
Thou art a beaten dog beneath the hail,

[6]Italian for "and listening to the light murmur."
[7]Greek for "knowing."
[8]The Elysian fields of Greek mythology.
[9]A Parisian dressmaker.
[10]An adaptation from Chaucer's "Ballade of Good Counsel."

A swollen magpie in a fitful sun,
Half black half white
Nor knowst' ou wing from tail
Pull down thy vanity
                    How mean thy hates
Fostered in falsity,
                    Pull down thy vanity,
Rathe to destroy, niggard in charity,
Pull down thy vanity,
                    I say pull down.

But to have done instead of not doing
                    this is not vanity
To have, with decency, knocked
That a Blunt[11] should open
            To have gathered from the air a live tradition
or from a fine old eye the unconquered flame
This is not vanity.
      Here error is all in the not done,
all in the diffidence that faltered . . .

1948

CXX

I have tried to write Paradise

Do not move
   Let the wind speak
         that is paradise.

Let the Gods forgive what I
         have made
Let those I love try to forgive
         what I have made.

1969

[11]Wilfred Scawen Blunt (1840–1922), English poet and critic of imperialism.

Amy Lowell 1874–1925

Amy Lowell was born in Brookline, Massachusetts, and grew up on her family estate Sevenels (named after the seven Lowells—mother, father, and five children), which she ultimately inherited and whose lavish gardens figure prominently in her poetry. A girl of the upper classes was generally not permitted by her family to go off to the university as her brothers did, and so Lowell's education consisted primarily of tutors, access to her father's vast library, and travel in Europe. As she later wrote to the poet Archibald MacLeish in response to his inquiry, her formal education "really did not amount to a hill of beans." She evinced an interest in literature when very young, and her first writing was published when she was eleven years old.

While the diaries she kept as an adolescent suggest an early bisexuality, as she matured she became less interested in men and looked for love and companionship with other women. Her fascination with the theater led to her involvement for a time with the musical starlet Lina Abarbanell. It also led her to her first muse, the tragedian Eleonora Duse, whom she saw on stage for the first time in 1902. Duse's talent and beauty inspired Lowell, already twenty-eight years old, to revive her youthful interest in writing. Lowell later recalled the momentous effect of watching Duse perform: "It loosed a bolt in my brain and I knew where my true function lay." Her first poem since her juvenilia was addressed to the actress and marked the beginning of Lowell's career as a writer, although she did not publish her first book, *A Dome of Many-Coloured Glass,* until 1912, ten years later.

A Dome of Many-Coloured Glass was influenced by nineteenth-century romanticism, and its title comes from a phrase in *Adonais,* Shelley's elegiac tribute to Keats, whose poetry many of the poems echo. Other poems in the volume are more original and show the promise of her later poetry; they are personal poems with brilliant flashes of color, verse about her childhood, her family estate, her quest for love. In the following year, 1913, Lowell discovered several imagist poems by H.D. (Hilda Doolittle) in *Poetry* magazine; these made her recognize that "I, too, am an imagiste." Indeed, before she knew the term "imagism," she had developed her appreciation of Japanese haiku and tanka, her interest in the Orient having been stimulated by her brother Percival, who had lived in Asia. She immediately began to explore the school of imagism of which, she discovered, Ezra Pound was the titular head; in 1913 she traveled to England in order to meet him.

The conflict between them could have been predicted. Lowell was by 1913 a 250-pound woman of vast wealth, a sense of entitlement, and an air of knowing her own mind. Pound found her overbearing and perhaps threatening. Lowell, for her part, would undoubtedly have agreed with Gertrude Stein's description of Pound as a village explainer—which is "fine if you're a village, and if not, not." Despite Pound's hostility, Lowell published three anthologies in 1915, 1916, and 1917, titled *Some Imagist Poets,* which included along with her own work that of H.D., John Gould Fletcher, D. H. Lawrence, and others. When the first volume came out, imagism was still so revolutionary and controversial in the United States that Lowell was denounced by the Poetry Society of America for championing imagist writers. Pound threatened to sue her for stealing his thunder, and Lowell encouraged him, saying that a lawsuit would be "a good advertisement" for *Some Imagist Poets.* But since neither a title nor a poetic school can be copyrighted, Pound dropped the idea and disassociated himself from American imagism (which he scoffingly called "Amygism"). Lowell adopted the pugilistic posture that she was to use in many of her literary controversies throughout her career.

In her own writing, imagism soon became only one of a panoply of approaches to poetry. She also explored "polyphonic prose," writing that is prose in its typography and poetry in its language and dense use of imagery. In *Legends* (1921) she adapted folk myths from aboriginal North America, China, Peru, and the Yucatan, as well as Europe. She was also influenced by a broad range of authors, including, as she suggests in "The Sisters," her "spiritual relations," Sappho, Elizabeth Barrett Browning and Emily Dickinson.

In the thirteen years before she died, Lowell managed to bring out a book of poems every year or two (*East Wind* and *Ballads for Sale* were published in the two years after her death), and several volumes of prose, including a two-volume biography of John Keats (1925).

Although Lowell won the Pulitzer Prize posthumously in 1926 for her volume of poems *What's O'Clock,* the attacks on her reputation became virulent soon after her death. It is difficult to say if her detractors were motivated by homophobia or by a sincere lack of excitement about her poetry. In a particularly scurrilous 1926 book by Clement Wood, *Amy Lowell,* the author was determined to diminish Lowell's reputation at least partly because she was a lesbian. He argued that her poetry did not "word a common cry of many hearts," and he concluded that Lowell may qualify "as an impassioned singer of her own desires; and she may well be laureate also of as many as stand beside her," but non-lesbian readers would find nothing in her verse.

Those who refused to recognize that Lowell was a lesbian but saw her only as an unattractive, overweight woman and an "old maid" were equally unfair in their prejudiced assessments. An article titled "Amy Lowell as a Poet," which appeared in the *Saturday Review of Literature* in 1927, complained that her poetry was bad because she was "cut off from the prime biological experiences of life by her tragic physical predicament." Therefore, the critic goes on to say, erroneously, her poems are decorative rather than expressive of elemental passion "as always happens when the sources of inspiration are literary and secondary rather than primarily the expression of emotional experience." Though some of Lowell's work suffers from prolixity and a tendency to exaggerate, her best work is free from such faults. It is concise, vivid, and honest.

Lillian Faderman
California State University, Fresno

PRIMARY WORKS

John Keats, 1925; *Poetry and Poets: Essays by Amy Lowell,* 1930; *The Complete Poetical Works of Amy Lowell,* 1955.

A Lady

You are beautiful and faded
Like an old opera tune
Played upon a harpsichord;
Or like the sun-flooded silks
Of an eighteenth-century boudoir.

In your eyes
Smoulder the fallen roses of out-lived minutes,
And the perfume of your soul
Is vague and suffusing,
With the pungence of sealed spice-jars.
Your half-tones delight me,
And I grow mad with gazing
At your blent colours.

My vigour is a new-minted penny,
Which I cast at your feet.
Gather it up from the dust,
That its sparkle may amuse you.

1914

Patterns

I walk down the garden paths,
And all the daffodils
Are blowing, and the bright blue squills.
I walk down the patterned garden-paths
In my stiff, brocaded gown.
With my powdered hair and jewelled fan,
I too am a rare
Pattern. As I wander down
The garden paths.

My dress is richly figured,
And the train
Makes a pink and silver stain
On the gravel, and the thrift
Of the borders.
Just a plate of current fashion
Tripping by in high-heeled, ribboned shoes.
Not a softness anywhere about me,
Only whalebone and brocade.
And I sink on a seat in the shade
Of a lime tree. For my passion
Wars against the stiff brocade.
The daffodils and squills
Flutter in the breeze
As they please.
And I weep;

For the lime-tree is in blossom
And one small flower has dropped upon my bosom.

And the plashing of waterdrops
In the marble fountain
Comes down the garden-paths.
The dripping never stops.
Underneath my stiffened gown
Is the softness of a woman bathing in a marble basin,
A basin in the midst of hedges grown
So thick, she cannot see her lover hiding,
But she guesses he is near,
And the sliding of the water
Seems the stroking of a dear
Hand upon her.
What is Summer in a fine brocaded gown!
I should like to see it lying in a heap upon the ground.
All the pink and silver crumpled up on the ground.

I would be the pink and silver as I ran along the paths,
And he would stumble after,
Bewildered by my laughter.
I should see the sun flashing from his sword-hilt and buckles on his
shoes.
I would choose
To lead him in a maze along the patterned paths,
A bright and laughing maze for my heavy-booted lover.
Till he caught me in the shade,
And the buttons of his waistcoat bruised my body as he clasped me,
Aching, melting, unafraid.
With the shadows of the leaves and the sundrops,
And the plopping of the waterdrops,
All about us in the open afternoon—
I am very like to swoon
With the weight of this brocade,
For the sun sifts through the shade.
Underneath the fallen blossom
In my bosom,
Is a letter I have hid.
It was brought to me this morning by a rider from the Duke.
"Madam, we regret to inform you that Lord Hartwell
Died in action Thursday se'nnight."
As I read it in the white, morning sunlight,
The letters squirmed like snakes.
"Any answer, Madam," said my footman.
"No," I told him.

"See that the messenger takes some refreshment.
No, no answer."
And I walked into the garden,
Up and down the patterned paths,
In my stiff, correct brocade.
The blue and yellow flowers stood up proudly in the sun,
Each one.
I stood upright too,
Held rigid to the pattern
By the stiffness of my gown.
Up and down I walked.
Up and down.

In a month he would have been my husband.
In a month, here, underneath this lime,
We would have broken the pattern;
He for me, and I for him,
He as Colonel, I as Lady,
On this shady seat.
He had a whim
That sunlight carried blessing.
And I answered, "It shall be as you have said."
Now he is dead.
In Summer and in Winter I shall walk
Up and down
The patterned garden-paths
In my stiff, brocaded gown.
The squills and daffodils
Will give place to pillared roses, and to asters, and to snow.
I shall go
Up and down,
In my gown.
Gorgeously arrayed,
Boned and stayed.
And the softness of my body will be guarded from embrace
By each button, hook, and lace.
For the man who should loose me is dead,
Fighting with the Duke in Flanders,
In a pattern called a war.
Christ! What are patterns for?

1916

The Letter

Little cramped words scrawling all over the paper
Like draggled fly's legs,
What can you tell of the flaring moon
Through the oak leaves?
Or of my uncurtained window and the bare floor
Spattered with moonlight?
Your silly quirks and twists have nothing in them
Of blossoming hawthorns,
And this paper is dull, crisp, smooth, virgin of loveliness
Beneath my hand.

I am tired, Beloved, of chafing my heart against
The want of you;
Of squeezing it into little inkdrops,
And posting it.
And I scald alone, here, under the fire
Of the great moon.

1919

Summer Rain

All night our room was outer-walled with rain.
Drops fell and flattened on the tin roof,
And rang like little disks of metal.
Ping!—Ping!—and there was not a pinpoint of silence between
them.
The rain rattled and clashed,
And the slats of the shutters danced and glittered.
But to me the darkness was red-gold and crocus-coloured
With your brightness,
And the words you whispered to me
Sprang up and flamed—orange torches against the rain.
Torches against the wall of cool, silver rain!

1919

Venus Transiens[1]

Tell me,
Was Venus more beautiful
Than you are,
When she topped
The crinkled waves,
Drifting shoreward
On her plaited shell?
Was Botticelli's vision[2]
Fairer than mine;
And were the painted rosebuds
He tossed his lady,
Of better worth
Than the words I blow about you
To cover your too great loveliness
As with a gauze
Of misted silver?

For me,
You stand poised
In the blue and buoyant air,
Cinctured by bright winds,
Treading the sunlight.
And the waves which precede you
Ripple and stir
The sands at my feet.

1919

Madonna of the Evening Flowers

All day long I have been working,
Now I am tired.
I call: "Where are you?"
But there is only the oak-tree rustling in the wind.

[1]Venus is the Roman goddess of love and beauty. The Latin phrase means Venus passing over.

[2]In the painting of Botticelli (1444–1510) called "The Birth of Venus" (c. 1485), the goddess stands on a large scallop shell; small roses are blown about her by the wind.

The house is very quiet,
The sun shines in on your books,
On your scissors and thimble just put down,
But you are not there.
Suddenly I am lonely:
Where are you?
I go about searching.

Then I see you,
Standing under a spire of pale blue larkspur,
With a basket of roses on your arm.
You are cool, like silver,
And you smile.
I think the Canterbury bells[1] are playing little tunes.

You tell me that the peonies need spraying,
That the columbines have overrun all bounds,

That the pyrus japonica should be cut back and rounded.
You tell me these things.
But I look at you, heart of silver,
White heart-flame of polished silver,
Burning beneath the blue steeples of the larkspur,
And I long to kneel instantly at your feet,
While all about us peal the loud, sweet Te Deums[2] of the
Canterbury bells.

1919

Opal

You are ice and fire,
The touch of you burns my hands like snow.
You are cold and flame.
You are the crimson of amaryllis,
The silver of moon-touched magnolias.

[1]Canterbury bells are cultivated plants with large, bell-like flowers. The poet may also be referring to the bells in Canterbury Cathedral in England.

[2]A Latin hymn beginning "*Te Deum laudamus,*" we praise thee, Lord.

When I am with you,
My heart is a frozen pond
Gleaming with agitated torches.

1919

Wakefulness

Jolt of market-carts;
Steady drip of horses' hoofs on hard pavement;
A black sky lacquered over with blueness,
And the lights of Battersea Bridge
Pricking pale in the dawn.
The beautiful hours are passing
And still you sleep!
Tired heart of my joy,
Incurved upon your dreams,
Will the day come before you have opened to me?

1919

Grotesque

Why do the lilies goggle their tongues at me
When I pluck them;
And writhe, and twist,
And strangle themselves against my fingers,
So that I can hardly weave the garland
For your hair?
Why do they shriek your name
And spit at me
When I would cluster them?
Must I kill them
To make them lie still,
And send you a wreath of lolling corpses
To turn putrid and soft
On your forehead
While you dance?

1919

The Sisters

Taking us by and large, we're a queer lot
We women who write poetry. And when you think
How few of us there've been, it's queerer still.
I wonder what it is that makes us do it,
Singles us out to scribble down, man-wise,
The fragments of ourselves. Why are we
Already mother-creatures, double-bearing,
With matrices in body and in brain?
I rather think that there is just the reason
We are so sparse a kind of human being;
The strength of forty thousand Atlases
Is needed for our every-day concerns.
There's Sapho, now I wonder what was Sapho.
I know a single slender thing about her:
That, loving, she was like a burning birch tree
All tall and glittering fire, and that she wrote
Like the same fire caught up to Heaven and held there,
A frozen blaze before it broke and fell.
Ah, me! I wish I could have talked to Sapho,
Surprised her reticences by flinging mine
Into the wind. This tossing off of garments
Which cloud the soul is none too easy doing
With us to-day. But still I think with Sapho
One might accomplish it, were she in the mood
To bare her loveliness of words and tell
The reasons, as she possibly conceived them,
Of why they are so lovely. Just to know
How she came at them, just to watch
The crisp sea sunshine playing on her hair,
And listen, thinking all the while 'twas she
Who spoke and that we two were sisters
Of a strange, isolated little family.
And she is Sapho—Sapho—not Miss or Mrs.,
A leaping fire we call so for convenience;
But Mrs. Browning—who would ever think
Of such presumption as to call her "Ba."
Which draws the perfect line between sea-cliffs
And a close-shuttered room in Wimpole Street.
Sapho could fly her impulses like bright
Balloons tip-tilting to a morning air
And write about it. Mrs. Browning's heart
Was squeezed in stiff conventions. So she lay
Stretched out upon a sofa, reading Greek
And speculating, as I must suppose,

In just this way on Sapho; all the need,
The huge, imperious need of loving, crushed
Within the body she believed so sick.
And it was sick, poor lady, because words
Are merely simulacra after deeds
Have wrought a pattern; when they take the place
Of actions they breed a poisonous miasma
Which, though it leave the brain, eats up the body.
So Mrs. Browning, aloof and delicate,
Lay still upon her sofa, all her strength
Going to uphold her over-topping brain.
It seems miraculous, but she escaped
To freedom and another motherhood
Than that of poems. She was a very woman
And needed both.
                                If I had gone to call,
Would Wimpole Street have been the kindlier place,
Or Casa Guidi, in which to have met her?
I am a little doubtful of that meeting,
For Queen Victoria was very young and strong
And all-pervading in her apogee
At just that time. If we had stuck to poetry,
Sternly refusing to be drawn off by mesmerism
Or Roman revolutions, it might have done.
For, after all, she is another sister,
But always, I rather think, an older sister
And not herself so curious a technician
As to admit newfangled modes of writing—
"Except, of course, in Robert, and that is neither
Here nor there for Robert is a genius."
I do not like the turn this dream is taking,
Since I am very fond of Mrs. Browning
And very much indeed should like to hear her
Graciously asking me to call her "Ba."
But then the Devil of Verisimilitude
Creeps in and forces me to know she wouldn't.
Convention again, and how it chafes my nerves,
For we are such a little family
Of singing sisters, and as if I didn't know
What those years felt like tied down to the sofa.
Confounded Victoria, and the slimy inhibitions
She loosed on all us Anglo-Saxon creatures!
Suppose there hadn't been a Robert Browning,
No "Sonnets from the Portuguese" would have been written.
They are the first of all her poems to be,
One might say, fertilized. For, after all,
A poet is flesh and blood as well as brain

And Mrs. Browning, as I said before,
Was very, very woman. Well, there are two
Of us, and vastly unlike that's for certain.
Unlike at least until we tear the veils
Away which commonly gird souls. I scarcely think
Mrs. Browning would have approved the process
In spite of what had surely been relief;
For speaking souls must always want to speak
Even when bat-eyed, narrow-minded Queens
Set prudishness to keep the keys of impulse.
Then do the frowning Gods invent new banes
And make the need of sofas. But Sapho was dead
And I, and others, not yet peeped above
The edge of possibility. So that's an end
To speculating over tea-time talks
Beyond the movement of pentameters
With Mrs. Browning.

But I go dreaming on,
In love with these my spiritual relations.
I rather think I see myself walk up
A flight of wooden steps and ring a bell
And send a card in to Miss Dickinson.
Yet that's a very silly way to do.
I should have taken the dream twist-ends about
And climbed over the fence and found her deep
Engrossed in the doing of a humming bird
Among nasturtiums. Not having expected strangers,
She might forget to think me one, and holding up
A finger say quite casually: "Take care.
Don't frighten him, he's only just begun."
"Now this," I well believe I should have thought,
"Is even better than Sapho. With Emily
You're really here, or never anywhere at all
In range of mind." Wherefore, having begun
In the strict centre, we could slowly progress
To various circumferences, as we pleased.
We could, but should we? That would quite depend
On Emily. I think she'd be exacting,
Without intention possibly, and ask
A thousand tight-rope tricks of understanding.
But, bless you, I would somersault all day
If by so doing I might stay with her.
I hardly think that we should mention souls
Although they might just round the corner from us
In some half-quizzical, half-wistful metaphor.
I'm very sure that I should never seek

To turn her parables to stated fact.
Sapho would speak, I think, quite openly,
And Mrs. Browning guard a careful silence,
But Emily would set doors ajar and slam them
And love you for your speed of observation.

Strange trio of my sisters, most diverse,
And how extraordinarily unlike
Each is to me, and which way shall I go?
Sapho spent and gained; and Mrs. Browning,
After a miser girlhood, cut the strings
Which tied her money-bags and let them run;
But Emily hoarded—hoarded—only giving
Herself to cold, white paper. Starved and tortured,
She cheated her despair with games of patience
And fooled herself by winning. Frail little elf,
The lonely brain-child of a gaunt maturity,
She hung her womanhood upon a bough
And played ball with the stars—too long—too long—
The garment of herself hung on a tree
Until at last she lost even the desire
To take it down. Whose fault? Why let us say,
To be consistent, Queen Victoria's.
But really, not to over-rate the queen,
I feel obliged to mention Martin Luther,
And behind him the long line of Church Fathers
Who draped their prurience like a dirty cloth
About the naked majesty of God.
Good-bye, my sisters, all of you are great,
And all of you are marvellously strange,
And none of you has any word for me.
I cannot write like you, I cannot think
In terms of Pagan or of Christian now.
I only hope that possibly some day
Some other woman with an itch for writing
May turn to me as I have turned to you
And chat with me a brief few minutes. How
We lie, we poets! It is three good hours
I have been dreaming. Has it seemed so long
To you? And yet I thank you for the time
Although you leave me sad and self-distrustful,
For older sisters are very sobering things.
Put on your cloaks, my dears, the motor's waiting.
No, you have not seemed strange to me, but near,
Frightfully near, and rather terrifying.
I understand you all, for in myself—
Is that presumption? Yet indeed it's true—

We are one family. And still my answer
Will not be any one of yours, I see.
Well, never mind that now. Good night! Good night!

1925

Gertrude Stein 1874–1946

Gertrude Stein—novelist, poet, essayist and playwright—produced some 571 works during a career that spanned forty-three years. During her lifetime, this quintessentially American writer chose to live in Paris and write from the perspective of a different continent about things American and the American vision of things European. Her interests included art, aesthetics, language, philosophy, history, economics, and human nature. She and her lifelong companion Alice B. Toklas drove for the American Fund for French Wounded during World War I and lived quietly sequestered in the French countryside during the German occupation of France during World War II. As Stein said in 1936, "America is my country and Paris is my home town and it is as it has come to be."

Stein had a gift for doing the uncommon in a commonplace way. Born into a German-Jewish immigrant family in Allegheny, Pennsylvania, at the height of the Victorian era, she lived in Gemunden and Vienna, Austria; Passy, France; Baltimore, Maryland; Oakland and San Francisco, California; Cambridge, Massachusetts; and London, England, before settling in Paris in 1903. The youngest of five children, Stein experienced a comparatively unfettered childhood heavily colored by the companionship of her brother Leo, himself later a critic and writer. In the 1890s she studied philosophy and psychology at Harvard University with William James, George Herbert Palmer, George Santayana, and Hugo Munsterberg, and then went on to medical school at Johns Hopkins University. Within a semester of finishing her M.D. degree, she left the United States to take up residence in Paris so that she might live and write in the comparative freedom afforded to her as an expatriate.

Initially, Gertrude and Leo Stein shared the living and work space at 27 rue de Fleurus, conducting their salon and building their fine collection of Cézanne, Matisse, and Picasso paintings. But Leo had no respect for his sister's work and in time was replaced by Alice B. Toklas, an expatriate Californian who shared Stein's interests and supported her ambitions, and became her lifelong lover and partner. Stein's social and literary networks were as wide and cosmopolitan as the city itself. In the early years she worked, talked, and played with such artists and poets as Pablo Picasso, Guillaume Apollinaire, Natalie Barney, and Renée Vivien who shared her interests in unconventional literature and art. Stein continued her interest in philosophy, visiting Alfred North Whitehead on the eve of World War I, and in the fifteen years before World War II writing her own best critical theory and a major philosophical meditation. Her unconventional, experimental work during the early years of the twentieth century brought her to the attention of writers as diverse as Jean Cocteau and Sherwood Anderson, both of whom testified to the liberating impact of *Tender Buttons* (1912) on their own vision.

In the 1920s she mentored Ernest Hemingway, and over the years entertained and communicated with a number of young writers, artists, and composers. Talented young Americans and artists coming from the United States to Paris carried letters of introduction and over the years she entertained such persons as Nella Larsen and Paul Robeson. She corresponded with Richard Wright and later encouraged him to live in France. Her Paris circle included Sylvia Beach, Margaret Anderson, Janet Flanner, Djuna Barnes, and H.D. In the mid-1930s after the unprecedented popular success of her readable *The Autobiography of Alice B. Toklas* (1932), Stein returned with Toklas to the United States for a triumphant coast-to-coast tour. In 1946, at the height of her literary powers and recognition, Stein died quietly of cancer in Paris with Toklas at her side.

Financial success, critical recognition, and popular acclaim did not come easily to Stein, who was as uncompromising in pursuit of her artistic goals as she was in securing her domestic comfort and maintaining her personal integrity. Though formally trained in philosophy and medicine, she was widely read in literature, particularly English prose narrative. Her first major work, *The Making of Americans* (1903, 1906–11), is a historical record of a German-Jewish immigrant family establishing itself in the new land. *Three Lives* (1905–06) bears the mark of both Anglo-American naturalism and the psychological probing of Henry James. But already the abstract way in which she defined character and her use of very complex prose rhythms to portray character suggested that experimental breakthroughs were to follow.

"Ada" (1908–12) marks the transition of her prose from *Three Lives* to *Tender Buttons.* In the latter, a brilliant prose/poetry meditation on objects, food, and rooms, Stein established once and for all her philosophical interest in the ordinary, her delight in words as an artistic medium, and her willingness to experiment with generic conventions. Her lifelong effort was to show how the human mind perceives, orders, and reflects on the interwoven world of animate and inanimate phenomena.

Through the 1920s Stein continued to write poetry, portraits, plays, landscapes, novels, and operas—collapsing the aesthetic categories usually reserved for either the visual or the verbal arts. *Four Saints in Three Acts* (1927) explores religion, gender, art, meditation, ritual, and language in a way typical of her mature middle style. *Patriarchal Poetry,* a long poem written the same year, makes it clear that Stein was fully aware of what it meant to be a woman writing in a literary tradition defined by masculine interests, experiences, and values. During the 1930s Stein wrote in the autobiographies some of her most accessible prose, all the while continuing in the novella and drama to explore the complexity of experience, form, and language. *The Geographical History of America* (1935) states boldly her belief that she—a woman—is doing the major literary thinking of the era. She doubtless felt the need to say this, for her work continued to bewilder common reader and critic alike, much of it remaining unpublished during her lifetime. The attention given to Stein's experiments in form and language during her lifetime long obscured her major contribution to our understanding of domesticity, female culture, myths about women, the social world in which women function, and what it meant in the twentieth century to intentionally create art that is not patriarchal.

Cynthia Secor
University of Denver

Hugh English
Queens College, CUNY

PRIMARY WORKS

Three Lives, 1909; *Tender Buttons,* 1914; *The Making of Americans,* 1925; *Four Saints in Three Acts,* 1929; *The Autobiography of Alice B. Toklas,* 1933; *The Geographical History of America,* 1936; *Ida, A Novel,* 1941; *The Mother of Us All,* 1949; *Patriarchal Poetry,* 1953.

from The Making of Americans

Once an angry man dragged his father along the ground through his own orchard. "Stop!" cried the groaning old man at last, "Stop! I did not drag my father beyond this tree."

It is hard living down the tempers we are born with. We all begin well, for in our youth there is nothing we are more intolerant of than our own sins writ large in others and we fight them fiercely in ourselves; but we grow old and we see that these our sins are of all sins the really harmless ones to own, nay that they give a charm to any character, and so our struggle with them dies away.

It has always seemed to me a rare privilege, this, of being an American, a real American, one whose tradition it has taken scarcely sixty years to create. We need only realise our parents, remember our grandparents and know ourselves and our history is complete.

The old people in a new world, the new people made out of the old, that is the story that I mean to tell, for that is what really is and what I really know.

Some of the fathers we must realise so that we can tell our story really, were little boys then, and they came across the water with their parents, the grandparents we need only just remember. Some of these our fathers and our mothers, were not even made then, and the women, the young mothers, our grandmothers we perhaps just have seen once, carried these our fathers and our mothers into the new world inside them, those women of the old world strong to bear them. Some looked very weak and little women, but even these so weak and little, were strong always, to bear many children.

These certain men and women, our grandfathers and grandmothers, with their children born and unborn with them, some whose children were gone ahead to prepare a home to give them; all countries were full of women who brought with them many children; but only certain men and women and the children they had in them, to make many generations for them, will fill up this history for us of a family and its progress.

Many kinds of all these women were strong to bear many children.

One was very strong to bear them and then always she was very strong to lead them.

One was strong to bear them and then always she was strong to suffer with them.

One, a little gentle weary woman was strong to bear many children, and then always after she would sadly suffer for them, weeping for the sadness of all sinning, wearying for the rest she knew her death would bring them.

And then there was one sweet good woman, strong just to bear many children, and then she died away and left them, for that was all she knew then to do for them.

And these four women and the husbands they had with them and the children born and unborn in them will make up the history for us of a family and its progress.

Other kinds of men and women and the children they had with them, came at different times to know them; some, poor things, who never found how they could make a living, some who dreamed while others fought a way to help them, some whose children went to pieces with them, some who thought and thought and then their children rose to greatness through them, and some of all these kinds of men and women and the children they had in them will help to make the history for us of this family and its progress.

These first four women, the grandmothers we need only just remember, mostly never saw each other. It was their children and grandchildren who, later, wandering over the new land, where they were seeking first, just to make a living, and then later, either to grow rich or to gain wisdom, met with one another and were married, and so together they made a family whose progress we are now soon to be watching. . . .

Old ones come to be dead. There are old ones in family living in some family livings and these when they come to be old enough ones come to be dead. Any one coming to be an old enough one comes then to be a dead one.

Doing something is done by some in family living. Some family living is existing. Some are doing something in family living. Some one in a family living is doing something and family living is existing and family living is going on being existing and that one is doing something in family living. That one has been doing something in family living, that one is doing something in family living, that one is going to be doing something in family living. That one has been doing something in family living and that one is doing that thing and any one in the family living is being one being in the family living and that one the one doing something in the family living is completely remembering that every one being in the family living is in the family living. That one is remembering something of this thing about every one being in the family living, is remembering something about each one being in the family living, is completely remembering something about each one being in the family living and any one in the family living can come to be remembering that that one the one completely remembering something about each one being in the family living is remembering something about each one in the family living being in the family living.

The one remembering completely remembering something about each one being in the family living has been completely remembering everything about any one being in the family living, is remembering completely remembering everything about some being in the family living, is completely remembering something about every one being in the family living, will be completely remembering everything about some being in the family living will completely remember something about every one being in the family living. Family living can be existing. Very many are remembering that family living can be existing.

Very many can go on living remembering that family living is existing. Very many are living and are remembering that family living can go on existing. Very many can go on living remembering that family living can go on existing. . . .

Family living can go on existing. Very many are remembering this thing are remembering that family living living can go on existing. Very many are quite certain that family living can go on existing. Very many are remembering that they are quite certain that family living can go on exiting.

Any family living going on existing is going on and every one can come to be a dead one and there are then not any more living in that family living and that family is not then existing if there are not then any more having come to be living. Any family living is existing if there are some more being living when very many have come to be dead ones. Family living can be existing if not every one in the family living has come to be a dead one. Family living can be existing if there have come to be some existing who have not come to be dead ones. Family living can be existing and there can be some who are not completely remembering any such thing. Family living can be existing and there can be some who have been completely remembering such a thing. Family living can be existing and there can be some remembering something of such a thing. Family living can be existing and some can come to be old ones and then dead ones and some can have been then quite expecting some such thing. Family living can be existing and some can come to be old ones and not yet dead ones and some can be remembering something of some such thing. Family living can be existing and some one can come to be an old one and some can come to be a pretty old one and some can come to be completely expecting such a thing and completely remembering expecting such a thing. Family living can be existing and every one can come to be a dead one and not any one then is remembering any such thing. Family living can be existing and every one can come to be a dead one and some are remembering some such thing. Family living can be existing and any one can come to be a dead one and every one is then a dead one and there are then not any more being living. Any old one can come to be a dead one. Every old one came come to be a dead one. Any family being existing is one having some being then not having come to be a dead one. Any family living can be existing when to every one has come to be a dead one. Every one in a family living have come to be dead ones some are remembering something of some such thing. Some being living not have come to be dead ones can be ones being in a family living. Some being living and having come to be old ones can come then to be dead ones. Some being living and being in a family living and coming then to be old ones can come then to be dead ones. Any one can be certain that some can remember such a thing. Any family living can be one being existing and some can remember something of some such thing.

Susie Asado

Sweet sweet sweet sweet sweet tea.
    Susie Asado.
Sweet sweet sweet sweet sweet tea.
    Susie Asado.
Susie Asado which is a told tray sure.
A lean on the shoe this means slips slips hers.
When the ancient light grey is clean it is yellow, it is a silver seller.
This is a please this is a please there are the saids to jelly. These are the wets these say the sets to leave a crown to Incy.
Incy is short for incubus.
A pot. A pot is a beginning of a rare bit of trees. Trees tremble, the old vats are in bobbles, bobbles which shade and shove and render clean, render clean must.
    Drink pups.

Drink pups drink pups lease a sash hold, see it shine and a bobolink his pins. It shows a nail.

What is a nail. A nail is unison.

Sweet sweet sweet sweet sweet tea.

Preciosilla

Cousin to Clare washing.

In the win all the band beagles which have cousin lime sign and arrange a weeding match to presume a certain point to exstate to exstate a certain pass lint to exstate a lean sap prime lo and shut shut is life.

Bait, bait, tore, tore her clothes, toward it, toward a bit, toward a sit, sit down in, in vacant surely lots, a single mingle, bait and wet, wet a single establishment that has a lily lily grow. Come to the pen come in the stem, come in the grass grown water.

Lily wet lily wet while. This is so pink so pink in stammer, a long bean which shows bows is collected by a single curly shady, shady get, get set wet bet.

It is a snuff a snuff to be told and have can wither, can is it and sleep sleep knot, it is a lily scarf the pink and blue yellow, not blue not odour sun, nobles are bleeding bleeding two seats two seats on end. Why is grief. Grief is strange black. Sugar is melting. We will not swim.

Preciosilla

Please be please be get, please get wet, wet naturally, naturally in weather. Could it be fire more firier. Could it be so in ate struck. Could it be gold up, gold up stringing, in it while while which is hanging, hanging in dingling, dingling in pinning, not so. Not so dots large dressed dots, big sizes, less laced, less laced diamonds, diamonds white, diamonds bright, diamonds in the in the light, diamonds light diamonds door diamonds hanging to be four, two four, all before, this bean, lessly, all most, a best, willow, vest, a green guest, guest, go go go go go go, go. Go go. Not guessed. Go go.

Toasted susie is my ice-cream.

Ladies' Voices

Curtain Raiser

Ladies' voices give pleasure.

The acting two is easily lead. Leading is not in winter. Here the winter is sunny.

Does that surprise you.

Ladies voices together and then she came in.

Very well good night.

Very well good night.
(Mrs. Cardillac.)
That's silver.
You mean the sound.
Yes the sound.

Act II

Honest to God Miss Williams I don't mean to say that I was older.

But you were.

Yes I was. I do not excuse myself. I feel that there is no reason for passing an archduke.

You like the word.

You know very well that they all call it their house.

As Christ was to Lazarus so was the founder of the hill to Mahon.

You really mean it.

I do.

Act III

Yes Genevieve does not know it. What. That we are seeing Caesar.

Caesar kisses.

Kisses today.

Caesar kisses every day.

Genevieve does not know that it is only in this country that she could speak as she does.

She does speak very well doesn't she. She told them that there was not the slightest intention on the part of her countrymen to eat the fish that was not caught in their country.

In this she was mistaken.

Act IV

What are ladies voices.
Do you mean to believe me.
Have you caught the sun.
Dear me have you caught the sun.

Scene II

Did you say they were different. I said it made no difference.

Where does it. Yes.

Mr. Richard Sutherland. This is a name I know.

Yes.

The Hotel Victoria.
Many words spoken to me have seemed English.
Yes we do hear one another and yet what are called voices the best decision in telling of balls.
Masked balls.
Yes masked balls.
Poor Augustine.

from Composition as Explanation

There is singularly nothing that makes a difference a difference in beginning and in the middle and in ending except that each generation has something different at which they are all looking. By this I mean so simply that anybody knows it that composition is the difference which makes each and all of them then different from other generations and this is what makes everything different otherwise they are all alike and everybody knows it because everybody says it.

It is very likely that nearly every one has been very nearly certain that something that is interesting is interesting them. Can they and do they. It is very interesting that nothing inside in them, that is when you consider the very long history of how every one ever acted or has felt, it is very interesting that nothing inside in them in all of them makes it connectedly different. By this I mean this. The only thing that is different from one time to another is what is seen and what is seen depends upon how everybody is doing everything. This makes the thing we are looking at very different and this makes what those who describe it make of it, it makes a composition, it confuses, it shows, it is, it looks, it likes it as it is, and this makes what is seen as it is seen. Nothing changes from generation to generation except the thing seen and that makes a composition. Lord Grey remarked that when the generals before the war talked about the war they talked about it as a nineteenth century war although to be fought with twentieth century weapons. That is because war is a thing that decides how it is to be when it is to be done. It is prepared and to that degree it is like all academies it is not a thing made by being made it is a thing prepared. Writing and painting and all that, is like that, for those who occupy themselves with it and don't make it as it is made. Now the few who make it as it is made, and it is to be remarked that the most decided of them usually are prepared just as the world around them is preparing, do it in this way and so I if you do not mind I will tell you how it happens. Naturally one does not know how it happened until it is well over beginning happening.

To come back to the part that the only thing that is different is what is seen when it seems to be being seen, in other words, composition and time-sense.

No one is ahead of his time, it is only that the particular variety of creating his time is the one that his contemporaries who also are creating their own time refuse to accept. And they refuse to accept it for a very simple reason and that is that they do not have to accept it for any reason. They themselves that is everybody in their entering the modern composition and they do enter it, if they do not enter it they are not so to speak in it they are out of it and so they do enter it; but in as you may say the non-competitive efforts where if you are not in it nothing is lost except nothing at all except what is not had, there are naturally all the refusals, and the things refused are only important if unexpectedly somebody happens to need them. In the case of the arts it is very definite. Those who are creating the modern composition authentically are naturally only of importance when they are dead because by that time the modern composition having become past is classified and the description of it is classical. That is the reason why the creator of the new composition in the arts is an outlaw until he is a classic, there is hardly a moment in between and it is really too bad very much too bad naturally for the creator but also very much too bad for the enjoyer, they all really would enjoy the created so much better just after it has been made than when it is already a classic, but it is perfectly simple that there is no reason why the contemporaries should see, because it would not make any difference as they lead their lives in the new composition anyway, and as everyone one is naturally indolent why naturally they don't see. For this reason as in quoting Lord Grey it is quite certain that nations not actively threatened are at least several generations behind themselves militarily so æsthetically they are more than several generations behind themselves and it is very much too bad, it is so very much more exciting and satisfactory for everybody if one can have contemporaries, if all one's contemporaries could be one's contemporaries.

There is almost not an interval.

For a very long time everybody refuses and then almost without a pause almost everybody accepts. In this history of the refused in the arts and literature the rapidity of the change is always startling. Now the only difficulty with the *volte-face* concerning the arts is this. When the acceptance comes, by that acceptance the thing created becomes a classic. It is a natural phenomena a rather extraordinary natural phenomena that a thing accepted becomes a classic. And what is the characteristic quality of a classic. The characteristic quality of a classic is that it is beautiful. Now of course it is perfectly true that a more or less first rate work of art is beautiful but the trouble is that when that first rate work of art becomes a classic because it is accepted the only thing that is important from then on to the majority of the acceptors the enormous majority, the most intelligent majority of the acceptors is that it is so wonderfully beautiful. Of course it is wonderfully beautiful, only when it is still a thing irritating annoying stimulating then all quality of beauty is denied to it. . . .

from The Geographical History of America or the Relation of Human Nature to the Human Mind

Page III

Human nature has nothing to do with it.
Human nature.
Has nothing to do with it.

Page IV

Emptying and filling an ocean has nothing to do with it because if it is full it is an ocean and if it is empty it is not an ocean.
Filling and emptying an ocean has nothing to do with it.

Page IV

Nothing to do with master-pieces.

Page V

Nothing to do with war.

Page VI

War has nothing to do with master-pieces.
Who says it has.
Everybody says it has.
Does anybody say what a master-piece is.
No nobody does.

Page VIII

So then the important literary thinking is being done.
Who does it.
I do it.
Oh yes I do it.

Page XXI

Money one.
Romanticism one
Scenery one
Human nature not one.
Master-pieces.
Human nature never knows anything about one and one.

Page XXI

Storms.
Even a little one is not exciting.

Page XXI

Is there any difference between flat land and an ocean a big country and a little one.
Is there any difference between human nature and the human mind.
Poetry and prose is not interesting.
What is necessary now is not form but content.
That is why in this epoch a woman does the literary thinking.
Kindly learn everything please.

Page XXII

How ardently hurry comes too late.
That is what they used to say
Donald.
Donald and Dorothy Dora and Don Donald and Donald he comes when he can.
If he can when he can as he can nine.
Donald and Donald is all in one time.
To-morrow is as Donald would say twenty a day.
What does Donald do.
He does it all.
Of course what does Donald do.
Of course he does he does do it at all.
Donald dear.
Welcome here.
If he comes yes he comes.
Yes he comes.
If he comes.
Any Donald is not Donald there.
Donald there is not any Donald here.
But better here.
What if Donald may.
Not likely is not as different as very likely.
And very likely Donald is here.

Page XVIII

I may not be through with Donald.

Page XIX

Donald has nothing to do with romanticism.
Donald has nothing to do with money.
Donald has nothing to do with scenery.
Donald has nothing to do with human nature.

Donald has nothing to do.
Donald.
No one can reproach Donald.
Donald and Dorothy and once there was an ocean and they were not drowned.

Page 2

You.

Page III

Why should a woman do the literary important literary thinking of this epoch.

Page IV

Master-pieces are what they are.

Page V

There is no identity nor time in master-pieces even when they tell about that.

1935

from The Mother of Us All

The Chorus. The vote we vote we note the vote.
(They all bow and smile to the statue. Suddenly Susan B.'s voice is heard)
Susan B.'s voice. We cannot retrace our steps, going forward may be the same as going backwards. We cannot retrace our steps, retrace our steps. All my long life, all my life, we do not retrace our steps, all my long life, but.
(A silence a long silence)
But—we do not retrace our steps, all my long life, and here, here we are here, in marble and gold, did I say gold, yes I said gold, in marble and gold and where—
(A silence)
Where is where. In my long life of effort and strife, dear life, life is strife, in my long life, it will not come and go, I tell you so, it will stay it will pay but
(A long silence)
But do I want what we have got, has it not gone, what made it live, has it not gone because now it is had, in my long life in my long life
(Silence)
Life is strife, I was a martyr all my life not to what I won but to what was done.

(Silence)
Do you know because I tell you so, or do you know, do you know.
(Silence)
My long life, my long life.

CURTAIN

1945–46

William Carlos Williams 1883–1963

Since his death in 1963, William Carlos Williams's centrality among the American modernist poets has been assured by a spate of critical studies elucidating his innovative poetics, his use of American language and scene, and his ties to revolutionary currents in the visual arts. In formal experiment and in modulation of poetic voice from the highly objective to the intimately autobiographical, Williams's influence on the writing of younger generations of poets has been extensive. Beyond this emphasis on craft, however, lies his essential humanity and what he called "contact" with the immediate world: from close attention to the flora and landscape of his native northern New Jersey to his concern with the struggle, pathos, and comic resilience of the working class. A writer of amazing shifts and changes, Williams's interest in process and discovery led him to reflect the fragmentation and disjunction of modern life.

Born in Rutherford, New Jersey, Williams spent most of his life there except for periods of education and travel. For him, remaining in the United States became an example to set against the expatriation of Ezra Pound and T. S. Eliot. Yet he was far from provincial. From 1897 to 1899 he studied with his younger brother at schools near Geneva and in Paris. Home again, he commuted to the Horace Mann School in New York until 1902. Finally deciding a career in medicine would offer the support his writing demanded, Williams attended the University of Pennsylvania Medical School, graduating in 1906. After an internship in New York City, he spent a year in Europe, visiting Pound in London and traveling on the continent. He was convinced, however, that the United States provided richer materials for the native writer attentive to the "local" and the vital language of his people.

Of mixed heritage, Williams thought himself a quintessential American. His mother had been born in Puerto Rico of Basque and French-Dutch-Jewish descent; his father, born in England and raised in the West Indies, retained British citizenship after settling with his new wife in the U.S. The family spoke Spanish at home when Williams was a boy. In his parents' experience—including his mother's three years of art study as a young woman in Paris and his father's business trips to Latin and South America—as well as in his own knowledge of the immigrant life of many of his patients, Williams found the basis for his celebration of cultural diversity.

In 1912, two years after he began medical practice, Williams married Florence Herman, daughter of a prosperous local family and later the Flossie of numerous poems. The next year they bought a house at 9 Ridge Road in Rutherford to serve as home and office; here they raised two sons and resided the rest of their lives. His practice among the poor and the middle class would become a source of characters, settings, and images throughout his work.

Influenced by early reading and imitation of Walt Whitman and John Keats, Williams was to find his way after publication of *Poems 1909* through Imagism and interest in modernist art to a new attitude toward poetic form and treatment of immediate reality. Although Ezra Pound, with whom he began a lifelong friendship at the University of Pennsylvania, could not fully convert him to Imagism's tenets, his ideas helped to free Williams from a more conventional Romanticism.

With publication of *Al Que Quiere!* in 1917 Williams first displayed the qualities of his mature work: the short enjambed lines characterizing his visual style contrasted with more colloquial verse shaped by what he called the "American idiom"; the brash, no-nonsense voice of the social man contrasted with a lyrical, romantic strain; precise, almost photographic recording of scene contrasted with evocation of intimate emotion. In large measure Williams's break with traditional forms and with aesthetic attitudes toward mimesis and beauty was a response to contemporary movements in painting and photography. In the work of the Cubists, Dadaists, and Precisionists exhibited at Alfred Stieglitz's galleries and at Walter Arensberg's studio, as well as in the dense lyrics of Marianne Moore, Williams found support for a radically new approach to verse.

The early 1920s were for Williams a time of aggressive experimentation. Typical of the range of his writing during this period are the three poems "Spring and All," "The Rose," and "To Elsie." In each Williams begins with the importance of the particular, the near-at-hand, affirming his later insistence in *Paterson* on "no ideas but in things." The potential for quickening he perceives in the drear landscape and the possibility for renewal of outmoded conceptions communicated in the painting—these, Williams implies, await only our imaginative response.

With *Paterson,* Book I (1946), Williams undertook the long poem for which he had been preparing since the preliminary study, "Paterson" (1927). Composed eventually of five books, this modernist epic centers on the doctor-poet Paterson's search for a redeeming language, exploring the estrangement of men and women from their environment and from each other. Using collage-like techniques, Williams juxtaposes material from newspapers, letters, documents, and interviews with passages in lyric, descriptive, and dramatic forms to create a portrait of his time as significant as those in the long poems of Eliot and Pound.

In his later work Williams often employed what he referred to as the "variable foot," a triadic or step-down form he first discovered in writing "The Descent" in *Paterson,* Book II. Line length in "The Pink Locust," for example, is sometimes determined by grammatical units, sometimes by the emphasis Williams places on phrases or individual words. The speaker's voice is direct, personal. Like the pink locust, Williams persisted during the last fifteen years of his life, weathering a series of heart attacks and strokes and a nervous collapse, to write a number of psychologically complex and hauntingly beautiful poems. He is considered the most diverse and challenging poet of his generation.

Theodora Rapp Graham
Pennsylvania State University at Harrisburg

PRIMARY WORKS

Poetry: *Poems,* 1909; *The Tempers,* 1913; *Al Que Quiere!,* 1917; *Sour Grapes,* 1921; *Spring and All,* 1923; *Collected Poems 1906–1938,* 1938; *Paterson,* 1946, 1948, 1949, 1951, 1958, 1963 (revised edition, 1992); *The Desert Music,* 1954; *Journey to Love,* 1955; *Pictures from Breghel,* 1962; A. Walton Litz and Christopher MacGowan, eds., *Collected Poems of William Carlos Williams,* Vol. I, 1986, *Collected Poems,* Vol. II, 1988; Fiction: *The Great American Novel,* 1923; *A Voyage to Pagany,* 1928; A Trilogy: *White Mule,* 1937; *In the Money,* 1940; *The Build-Up,* 1952; *Collected Stories,* 1961 (1996); Non-Fiction: *Kora in Hell: Improvisations,* 1920; *In the American Grain,* 1925; *Autobiography,* 1951.

Danse Russe[1]

If when my wife is sleeping
and the baby and Kathleen[2]
are sleeping
and the sun is a flame-white disc
in silken mists
above shining trees,—
if I in my north room
dance naked, grotesquely
before my mirror
waving my shirt round my head
and singing softly to myself:
"I am lonely, lonely.
I was born to be lonely,
I am best so!"
If I admire my arms, my face,
my shoulders, flanks, buttocks
against the yellow drawn shades,—

Who shall say I am not
the happy genius of my household?

1916

[1]In 1916 Nijinsky and the Ballets Russes appeared in New York.

[2]"Kathleen" was nursemaid for the Williams children.

The Young Housewife

At ten A.M. the young housewife
moves about in negligee behind
the wooden walls of her husband's house.
I pass solitary in my car.

Then again she comes to the curb
to call the ice-man, fish-man, and stands
shy, uncorseted, tucking in
stray ends of hair, and I compare her
to a fallen leaf.

The noiseless wheels of my car
rush with a crackling sound over
dried leaves as I bow and pass smiling.

1917

Portrait of a Lady

Your thighs are appletrees
whose blossoms touch the sky.
Which sky? The sky
where Watteau hung a lady's
slipper. Your knees
are a southern breeze—or
a gust of snow. Agh! what
sort of man was Fragonard?[1]
—as if that answered
anything. Ah, yes—below
the knees, since the tune
drops that way, it is
one of those white summer days,
the tall grass of your ankles
flickers upon the shore—
Which shore?—

[1]Watteau and Fragonard were 18th-century French painters. The painting referred to is not by Watteau, but Fragonard's "The Swing."

the sand clings to my lips—
Which shore?
Agh, petals maybe. How
should I know?
Which shore? Which shore?
I said petals from an appletree.

1920

The Great Figure

Among the rain
and lights
I saw the figure 5
in gold[1]
on a red
firetruck
moving
tense
unheeded
to gong clangs
siren howls
and wheels rumbling
through the dark city.

1921

Spring and All

By the road to the contagious hospital
under the surge of the blue
mottled clouds driven from the
northeast—a cold wind. Beyond, the
waste of broad, muddy fields
brown with dried weeds, standing and fallen

[1]Cf. Charles Demuth's 1928 poster painting "I Saw the Figure 5 in Gold," his portrait of Williams based on the earlier poem.

patches of standing water
the scattering of tall trees

All along the road the reddish
purplish, forked, upstanding, twiggy
stuff of bushes and small trees
with dead, brown leaves under them
leafless vines—

Lifeless in appearance, sluggish
dazed spring approaches—

They enter the new world naked,
cold, uncertain of all
save that they enter. All about them
the cold, familiar wind—

Now the grass, tomorrow
the stiff curl of wildcarrot leaf

One by one objects are defined—
It quickens:[1] clarity, outline of leaf

But now the stark dignity of
entrance—Still, the profound change
has come upon them: rooted, they
grip down and begin to awaken

1923

The Pot of Flowers[1]

Pink confused with white
flowers and flowers reversed
take and spill the shaded flame
darting it back
into the lamp's horn

[1]Medical term given to pregnant woman's first feeling of movement of fetus.

[1]Free rendering into poetry of Charles Demuth's "Tuberoses" (1922), which Williams owned.

petals aslant darkened with mauve

red where in whorls
petal lays its glow upon petal
round flamegreen throats

petals radiant with transpiercing light
contending
above

the leaves
reaching up their modest green
from the pot's rim

and there, wholly dark, the pot
gay with rough moss.

1923

The Rose

The rose is obsolete
but each petal ends in
an edge, the double facet
cementing the grooved
columns of air—The edge
cuts without cutting
meets—nothing—renews
itself in metal or porcelain—

whither? It ends—

But if it ends
the start is begun
so that to engage roses
becomes a geometry—

Sharper, neater, more cutting
figured in majolica—
the broken plate
glazed with a rose

Somewhere the sense
makes copper roses
steel roses—

The rose carried weight of love
but love is at an end—of roses

It is at the edge of the
petal that love waits

Crisp, worked to defeat
laboredness—fragile
plucked, moist, half-raised
cold, precise, touching

What

The place between the petal's
edge and the

From the petal's edge a line starts
that being of steel
infinitely fine, infinitely
rigid penetrates
the Milky Way
without contact—lifting
from it—neither hanging
nor pushing—

The fragility of the flower
unbruised
penetrates space.

1923

To Elsie[1]

The pure products of America
go crazy—
mountain folk from Kentucky

or the ribbed north end of
Jersey
with its isolate lakes and

[1]Elsie was a retarded nursemaid from the state orphanage who worked for the Williams family after Kathleen departed (see "Danse Russe").

valleys, its deaf-mutes, thieves
old names
and promiscuity between

devil-may-care men who have taken
to railroading
out of sheer lust of adventure—

and young slatterns, bathed
in filth
from Monday to Saturday

to be tricked out that night
with gauds
from imaginations which have no

peasant traditions to give them
character
but flutter and flaunt

sheer rags—succumbing without
emotion
save numbed terror

under some hedge of choke-cherry
or viburnum—
which they cannot express—

Unless it be that marriage
perhaps
with a dash of Indian blood

will throw up a girl so desolate
so hemmed round
with disease or murder

that she'll be rescued by an
agent—
reared by the state and

sent out at fifteen to work in
some hard-pressed
house in the suburbs—

some doctor's family, some Elsie—
voluptuous water
expressing with broken

brain the truth about us—
her great
ungainly hips and flopping breasts

addressed to cheap
jewelry
and rich young men with fine eyes

as if the earth under our feet
were
an excrement of some sky

and we degraded prisoners
destined
to hunger until we eat filth

while the imagination strains
after deer
going by fields of goldenrod in

the stifling heat of September
Somehow
it seems to destroy us

It is only in isolate flecks that
something
is given off

No one
to witness
and adjust, no one to drive the car

1923

The Red Wheelbarrow

so much depends
upon

a red wheel
barrow

glazed with rain
water

beside the white
chickens.

1923

Young Sycamore

I must tell you
this young tree
whose round and firm trunk
between the wet

pavement and the gutter
(where water
is trickling) rises
bodily

into the air with
one undulant
thrust half its height—
and then

dividing and waning
sending out
young branches on
all sides—

hung with cocoons
it thins
till nothing is left of it
but two

eccentric knotted
twigs
bending forward
hornlike at the top

1927

The Flower

A petal, colorless and without form
the oblong towers lie

beyond the low hill and northward the great
bridge stanchions,

small in the distance, have appeared,
pinkish and incomplete—

It is the city,
approaching over the river. Nothing

of it is mine, but visibly
for all that it is petal of a flower—my own.

It is a flower through which the wind
combs the whitened grass and a black dog

with yellow legs stands eating from a
garbage barrel. One petal goes eight blocks

past two churches and a brick school beyond
the edge of the park where under trees

leafless now, women having nothing else to do
sit in summer—to the small house

in which I happen to have been born. Or
a heap of dirt, if you care

to say it, frozen and sunstreaked in
the January sun, returning.

Then they hand you—they who wish to God
you'd keep your fingers out of

their business—science or philosophy or
anything else they can find to throw off

to distract you. But Madame Lenine[1]
is a benefactress when under her picture

[1]French spelling of the name of Lenin's widow, an educational leader in Russia.

in the papers she is quoted as saying:
Children should be especially protected

from religion. Another petal
reaches to San Diego, California where

a number of young men, New Yorkers most
of them, are kicking up the dust.

A flower, at its heart (the stamens, pistil,
etc.) is a naked woman, about 38, just

out of bed, worth looking at both for
her body and her mind and what she has seen

and done. She it was put me straight
about the city when I said, It

makes me ill to see them run up
a new bridge like that in a few months

and I can't find time even to get
a book written. They have the power,

that's all, she replied. That's what you all
want. If you can't get it, acknowledge

at least what it is. And they're not
going to give it to you. Quite right.

For years I've been tormented by
that miracle, the buildings all lit up—

unable to say anything much to the point
though it is the major sight

of this region. But foolish to rhapsodize over
strings of lights, the blaze of a power

in which I have not the least part.
Another petal reaches

into the past, to Puerto Rico
when my mother was a child bathing in a small

river and splashing water up on
the yucca leaves to see them roll back pearls.

The snow is hard on the pavements. This
is no more a romance than an allegory.

I plan one thing—that I could press
buttons to do the curing of or caring for

the sick that I do laboriously now by hand
for cash, to have the time

when I am fresh, in the morning, when
my mind is clear and burning—to write.

1930

The Poor

It's the anarchy of poverty
delights me, the old
yellow wooden house indented
among the new brick tenements

Or a cast-iron balcony
with panels showing oak branches
in full leaf. It fits
the dress of the children

reflecting every stage and
custom of necessity—
Chimneys, roofs, fences of
wood and metal in an unfenced

age and enclosing next to
nothing at all: the old man
in a sweater and soft black
hat who sweeps the sidewalk—

his own ten feet of it—
in a wind that fitfully
turning his corner has
overwhelmed the entire city

1938

Burning the Christmas Greens

Their time past, pulled down
cracked and flung to the fire
—go up in a roar
All recognition lost, burnt clean

clean in the flame, the green
dispersed, a living red,
flame red, red as blood wakes
on the ash—

and ebbs to a steady burning
the rekindled bed become
a landscape of flame

At the winter's midnight
we went to the trees, the coarse
holly, the balsam and
the hemlock for their green

At the thick of the dark
the moment of the cold's
deepest plunge we brought branches
cut from the green trees

to fill our need, and over
doorways, about paper Christmas
bells covered with tinfoil
and fastened by red ribbons

we stuck the green prongs
in the windows hung
woven wreaths and above pictures
the living green. On the

mantle we built a green forest
and among those hemlock
sprays put a herd of small
white deer as if they

were walking there. All this!
and it seemed gentle and good
to us. Their time past,
relief! The room bare. We

stuffed the dead grate
with them upon the half burnt out

log's smoldering eye, opening
red and closing under them

and we stood there looking down.
Green is a solace
a promise of peace, a fort
against the cold (though we

did not say so) a challenge
above the snow's
hard shell. Green (we might
have said) that, where

small birds hide and dodge
and lift their plaintive
rallying cries, blocks for them
and knocks down

the unseeing bullets of
the storm. Green spruce boughs
pulled down by a weight of
snow—Transformed!

Violence leaped and appeared.
Recreant! roared to life
as the flame rose through and
our eyes recoiled from it.

In the jagged flames green
to red, instant and alive. Green!
those sure abutments . . . Gone!
lost to mind

and quick in the contracting
tunnel of the grate
appeared a world! Black
mountains, black and red—as

yet uncolored—and ash white,
an infant landscape of shimmering
ash and flame and we, in
that instant, lost,

breathless to be witnesses,
as if we stood
ourselves refreshed among
the shining fauna of that fire.

1944

The Descent

The descent beckons
as the ascent beckoned.
Memory is a kind
of accomplishment,
a sort of renewal
even
an initiation, since the spaces it opens are new places
inhabited by hordes
heretofore unrealized,
of new kinds—
since their movements
are toward new objectives
(even though formerly they were abandoned).

No defeat is made up entirely of defeat—since
the world it opens is always a place
formerly
unsuspected. A
world lost,
a world unsuspected,
beckons to new places
and no whiteness (lost) is so white as the memory
of whiteness .

With evening, love wakens
though its shadows
which are alive by reason
of the sun shining—
grow sleepy now and drop away
from desire .

Love without shadows stirs now
beginning to awaken
as night
advances.

The descent
made up of despairs
and without accomplishment
realizes a new awakening:
which is a reversal
of despair.
For what we cannot accomplish, what

is denied to love,
what we have lost in the anticipation—
a descent follows,
endless and indestructible

1954

The Pink Locust

I'm persistent as the pink locust,
once admitted
to the garden,
you will not easily get rid of it.
Tear it from the ground,
if one hair-thin rootlet
remain
it will come again.
It is
flattering to think of myself
so. It is also
laughable.
A modest flower,
resembling a pink sweet-pea,
you cannot help
but admire it
until its habits
become known.
Are we not most of us
like that? It would be
too much
if the public
pried among the minutiae
of our private affairs.
Not
that we have anything to hide
but could *they*
stand it? Of course
the world would be gratified
to find out
what fools we have made of ourselves.
The question is,
would they
be generous with us—

as we have been
with others? It is,
as I say,
a flower
incredibly resilient
under attack!
Neglect it
and it will grow into a tree.
I wish I could *so* think of myself
and of what
is to become of me.
The poet himself,
what does he think of himself
facing his world?
It will not do to say,
as he is inclined to say:
Not much. The poem
would be in *that* betrayed.
He might as well answer—
"a rose is a rose
is a rose"[1] and let it go at that.
A rose *is* a rose
and the poem equals it
if it be well made.
The poet
cannot slight himself
without slighting
his poem—
which would be
ridiculous.
Life offers
no greater reward.
And so,
like this flower,
I persist—
for what there may be in it.
I am not,
I know,
in the galaxy of poets
a rose
but *who,* among the rest,
will deny me
my place.

1955

[1]The phrase quoted is Gertrude Stein's.

Eugene O'Neill 1888–1953

"The best play by an American we have seen," raved the *Brooklyn Eagle;* "an exceedingly juvenile performance," lamented the *New York Post.* The mixed reviews of *The Hairy Ape*'s first production in Greenwich Village in 1922 were not unusual for a new O'Neill play during that decade. Despite winning three Pulitzer Prizes for drama between 1920 and 1928, O'Neill repeatedly battled not only skeptical critics but also hostile censors, who resisted the staging of plays depicting interracial marriage *(All God's Chillun Got Wings,* 1924), infanticide *(Desire Under the Elms,* 1924), and infidelity and abortion *(Strange Interlude,* 1928). The controversy continues today, though its focus now is literary. O'Neill simultaneously spiritualized and democratized the modern stage by discovering "the transfiguring nobility of tragedy" in "seemingly the most ignoble, debased lives"—such as that of Yank Smith—thereby forging a trail later followed by Arthur Miller and Tennessee Williams. O'Neill's keen ear for native dialects (like the Bronx accent of Yank) brought numerous varieties of spoken American English onto our stage in a serious way for the first time, an achievement comparable to that of Mark Twain in fiction.

If O'Neill's literary merit is the subject of debate, his work's autobiographical nature is not. His father was the famous actor James O'Neill, who became a wealthy man—and sacrificed much of his talent—by touring in the title role of the melodrama *The Count of Monte Cristo,* which he performed over 5,000 times. Perhaps the young O'Neill's taste for strong theatrical effects, so evident in *Ape*'s stage directions, can be traced to his early, repeated exposure to this source; certainly, the polar conflict between Yank and Mildred (typical of the extreme oppositions in O'Neill's plays) is the stuff of melodrama, though here it dramatizes psychological, social, and philosophical issues rather than moral ones. The central conflict also points toward the playwright's mother. Ella Quinlan O'Neill longlasting addiction to morphine caused a frequent personal remoteness that deeply wounded her youngest son—who was sent off to Roman Catholic boarding schools as a young boy, partially to prevent his knowledge of her condition. His traumatic discovery of it at fourteen was comparable in his mind to the biblical fall from grace (a recurrent motif in his work): and Yank's sense of not "belonging" anywhere after his encounter with the ghostly Mildred projects the spiritual anguish that subsequently tormented O'Neill throughout his life. He never fully forgave his mother, and the women in his work frequently embody cultural stereotypes that reveal O'Neill's deep fear and mistrust of women. He also grew to resent bitterly the Christian God who, he felt, permitted his mother's addiction and failed to answer his prayers to cure it. Later, this disillusion took the form of a restless quest for alternative faiths—not unlike Yank's agonized search—that led him to the works of Nietzsche, Schopenhauer, Jung, Freud, and Asian mystical religions, systems which inform his drama throughout the twenties.

O'Neill's discovery of writing as his vocation occurred only after a period of alcoholism, sea travel, and bohemianism culminated in 1912 in a failed suicide attempt and his contracting of tuberculosis. Recovering from the disease, he started reading ancient and modern drama—Sophocles, Aeschylus, Wedekind, Ibsen, Shaw, and (especially) Strindberg—and, with the help of George Pierce Baker's drama workshop at Harvard, began writing his own plays, many about the sea. One of them, *Bound East for Cardiff,* was produced on Cape Cod in 1916 by the Provincetown Players, one of numerous, idealistic "little theater" companies formed in America after 1900 to produce and promote artistic drama without regard for commercial considerations. As guided by George Cram Cook, the Players helped develop O'Neill's sense of theater's sacred mission; more important, they encouraged his experimentation and established his reputation when they began producing his plays in New York in the fall of 1916. Within four years, O'Neill had scored his first Broadway success with *Beyond the Horizon,* a realistic tragedy. Within two more years, the original Provincetown Players had disbanded, but not before producing two of O'Neill's most daring expressionistic works, *The Emperor Jones* (1921) and *The Hairy Ape.* Even after his plays moved permanently to Broadway, O'Neill continued to take artistic risks, though he now often turned to classical sources for inspiration. *The Great God Brown* (1926) used masks to explore psychological conflicts within and between the characters; *Strange Interlude* (1928) borrowed the Elizabethan soliloquy for prolonged "thought asides" that resembled the stream of consciousness technique in modernist novels; and *Mourning Becomes Electra* (1931) drew on Aeschylus' *Oresteia* for a tragic trilogy that explored the Freudian family romance in an aristocratic nineteenth-century New England clan. All were essentially religious dramas that focused on inner, spiritual conflicts, seeking to "interpret Life in terms of ,lives"; only with *Ah, Wilderness!* (1933), his mature comedy, did he relax.

In his final plays, written during a period of withdrawal from the stage between 1934 and 1946, O'Neill returned to the mode of realism. He worked assiduously on a cycle of eleven plays tracing the history of an American family, "A Tale of Possessors Self-dispossessed," but destroyed most before his death in 1953; only *A Touch of the Poet* (completed in 1942, produced in 1957) survived in finished form, though *More Stately Mansions* (1963) and *The Calms of Capricorn* (1982) have been completed and published with the help of O'Neill scholars. But O'Neill produced his most powerful work when he courageously faced his personal ghosts in *The Iceman Cometh* (1939), *Long Day's Journey into Night* (1941, published and produced 1955), *Hughie* (1942), and *A Moon for the Misbegotten* (1943). The latter two exorcise the demon of his older brother Jamie, an alcoholic "Broadway loafer" who had died in 1923; the former two, set in 1912, are even closer to home. Revisiting the Bowery bar where O'Neill had attempted suicide, *Iceman* dramatizes a self-deluding salesman's attempt to rob derelicts of their sustaining life-lies; revisiting the New London, Connecticut, home where O'Neill grew up, *Journey* depicts his mother's readdiction to morphine upon discovery of his tuberculosis. Appropriately, the climactic acts of both plays revolve around confessions, for here O'Neill confronted not only harrowing memories but (in *Journey*) the radical cause of his alienation and his tragic vision: his guilt over being born, the original sin that had first caused his mother to take morphine in 1888.

Within two years of completing *Journey,* O'Neill had to end his writing career due to Parkinson's disease; within another ten years, he was dead.

James A. Robinson
University of Maryland

PRIMARY WORKS

Comments on the Drama and the Theater: A Source Book, 1987; *Complete Plays* (three volumes), 1988; *Selected Letters,* 1988.

The Hairy Ape

A Comedy of Ancient and Modern Life in Eight Scenes

Characters

ROBERT SMITH, "YANK"
PADDY
LONG
MILDRED DOUGLAS
HER AUNT
SECOND ENGINEER
A GUARD
A SECRETARY OF AN ORGANIZATION
STOKERS, LADIES, GENTLEMEN, ETC.

Scenes

SCENE I: *The firemen's forecastle of an ocean liner—an hour after sailing from New York.*

SCENE II: *Section of promenade deck, two days out—morning.*

SCENE III: *The stokehole. A few minutes later.*

SCENE IV: *Same as Scene One. Half an hour later.*

SCENE V: *Fifth Avenue, New York. Three weeks later.*

SCENE VI: *An island near the city. The next night.*

SCENE VII: *In the city. About a month later.*

SCENE VIII: *In the city. Twilight of the next day.*

Scene One

The firemen's forecastle of a transatlantic liner an hour after sailing from New York for the voyage across. Tiers of narrow, steel banks, three deep, on all sides. An entrance in rear. Benches on the floor before the bunks. The room is crowded with men, shouting, cursing, laughing, singing—a confused, inchoate uproar swelling into a sort of unity, a meaning—the bewildered, furious, baffled defiance of a beast in a cage. Nearly all the men are drunk. Many bottles are passed from hand to hand. All are dressed in dungaree pants, heavy ugly shoes. Some wear singlets, but the majority are stripped to the waist.

The treatment of this scene, or of any other scene in the play, should by no means be naturalistic. The effect sought after is a cramped space in the bowels of a ship, imprisoned by white steel. The lines of bunks, the uprights supporting them, cross each other like the steel framework of a cage. The ceiling crushes down upon the men's heads. They cannot stand upright. This accentuates the natural stooping posture which shoveling coal and the resultant over-development of back and shoulder muscles have given them. The men themselves should resemble those pictures in which the appearance of Neanderthal Man is guessed at. All are hairy-chested, with long arms of tremendous power, and low, receding brows above their small, fierce, resentful eyes. All the civilized white races are represented, but except for the slight differentiation in color of hair, skin, eyes, all these men are alike.

The curtain rises on a tumult of sound. YANK *is seated in the foreground. He seems broader, fiercer, more truculent, more powerful, more sure of himself than the rest. They respect his superior strength—the grudging respect of fear. Then, too, he represents to them a self-expression, the very last word in what they are, their most highly developed individual.*

VOICES Gif me trink dere, you!
'Ave a wet!
Salute!
Gesundheit!
Skoal![1]
Drunk as a lord, God stiffen you!
Here's how!
Luck!
Pass back that bottle, damn you!
Pourin' it down his neck!
Ho, Froggy! Where the devil have you been?
La Touraine.[2]
I hit him smash in yaw, py Gott!
Jenkins—the First—he's a rotten swine—
And the coppers nabbed him—and I run—
I like peer better. It don't pig head gif you.
A slut, I'm saying'! She robbed me aslape—
To hell with 'em all!
You're a bloody liar!
Say dot again! *(Commotion. Two men about to fight are pulled apart.)*
No scrappin' now!
Tonight—
See who's the best man!
Bloody Dutchman!
Tonight on the for'ard square.
I'll bet on Dutchy.
He packa da wallop, I tella you!
Shut up, Wop!
No fightin', maties. We're all chums, ain't we?
(A voice starts bawling a song.)

"Beer, beer, glorious beer!
Fill yourselves right up to here."

[1]Scandinavian drinking toast.
[2]A French ocean liner.

YANK. *(for the first time seeming to take notice of the uproar about him, turns around threateningly—in a tone of contemptuous authority)* Choke off dat noise! Where d'yuh get dat beer stuff? Beer, hell! Beer's for goils—and Dutchmen. Me for somep'n wit a kick to it! Gimme a drink, one of youse guys. *(Several bottles are eagerly offered. He takes a tremendous gulp at one of them; then, keeping the bottle in his hand, glares belligerently at the owner, who hastens to acquiesce in this robbery by saying)* All righto, Yank. Keep it and have another. (YANK *contemptuously turns his back on the crowd again. For a second there is an embarrassed silence. Then—)*

VOICES. We must be passing the Hook.[3]

She's beginning to roll to it.

Six days in hell—and then Southampton.[4]

Py Yesus, I vish somepody take my first vatch for me!

Gittin' seasick, Square-head?

Drink up and forget it!

What's in your bottle?

Gin.

Dot's nigger trink.

Absinthe? It's doped. You'll go off your chump, Froggy!

Cochon![5]

Whisky, that's the ticket!

Where's Paddy?

Going asleep.

Sing us that whisky song, Paddy. *(They all turn to an old, wizened Irishman who is dozing, very drunk, on the benches forward. His face is extremely monkey-like with all the sad, patient pathos of that animal in his small eyes.)*

Singa da song, Caruso[6] Pat!

He's gettin' old. The drink is too much for him.

He's too drunk.

PADDY. *(blinking about him, starts to his feet resentfully, swaying, holding on to the edge of a bunk)* I'm never too drunk to sing. 'Tis only when I'm dead to the world I'd be wishful to sing at all. *(With a sort of sad contempt)* "Whisky Johnny," ye want? A chanty, ye want? Now that's a queer wish from the ugly like of you, God help you. But no matther. *(He starts to sing in a thin, nasal, doleful tone:)*

"Oh, whisky is the life of man!
Whisky! O Johnny! (They all join in on this.)
Oh, whisky is the life of man!
Whisky for my Johnny! (Again chorus.)

"Oh, whisky drove my old man mad!
Whisky! O Johnny!
Oh, whisky drove my old man mad!
Whisky for my Johnny!"

[3]Sandy Hook, a narrow sandy New Jersey peninsula at the entrance to lower New York Bay.

[4]English port city.

[5]"Pig!" (French).

[6]Enrico Caruso, Italian operatic tenor (1873–1921).

YANK. *(again turning around scornfully)* Aw hell! Nix on dat old sailing ship stuff! All dat bull's dead, see? And you're dead, too, yuh damned old Harp,[7] on'y yuh don't know it. Take it easy, see. Give us a rest. Nix on de loud noise. *(With a cynical grin)* Can't youse see I'm tryin' to t'ink?

ALL. *(repeating the word after him as one with the same cynical amused mockery)* Think! *(The chorused word has a brazen metallic quality as if their throats were phonograph horns. It is followed by a general uproar of hard, barking laughter.)*

VOICES. Don't be cracking your head wit ut, Yank.
You gat headache, py yingo!
One thing about it—it rhymes with drink!
Ha, ha, ha!
Drink, don't think!
Drink, don't think!
Drink, don't think! *(A whole chorus of voices has taken up this refrain, stamping on the floor, pounding on the benches with fists.)*

YANK. *(taking a gulp from his bottle—good-naturedly)* Aw right. Can de noise. I got yuh de foist time. *(The uproar subsides. A very drunken sentimental tenor begins to sing):*

"Far away in Canada,
Far across the sea,
There's a lass who fondly waits
Making a home for me—"

YANK. *(fiercely contemptuous)* Shut up, yuh lousy boob! Where d'yuh get dat tripe? Home? Home, hell! I'll make a home for yuh! I'll knock yuh dead. Home! T'hell wit home! Where d'yuh get dat tripe? Dis is home, see? What d'yuh want wit home? *(Proudly)* I runned away from mine when I was a kid. On'y too glad to beat it, dat was me. Home was lickings for me, dat's all. But yuh can bet your shoit no one ain't never licked me since! Wanter try it, any of youse? Huh! I guess not. *(In a more placated but still contemptuous tone)* Goils waitin' for yuh, huh? Aw, hell! Dat's all tripe. Dey don't wait for no one. Dey'd double-cross yuh for a nickel. Dey're all tarts, get me? Treat 'em rough, dat's me. To hell wit 'em. Tarts, dat's what, de whole bunch of 'em.

LONG. *(very drunk, jumps on a bench exictedly, gesticulating with a bottle in his hand)* Listen 'ere, Comrades! Yank 'ere is right. 'E says this 'ere stinkin' ship is our 'ome. And 'e says as 'ome is 'ell. And 'e's right! This is 'ell. We lives in 'ell, Comrades—and right enough we'll die in it. *(Raging)* And who's ter blame, I arsks yer? We ain't. We wasn't born this rotten way. All men is born free and ekal. That's in the bleedin' Bible, maties. But what d'they care for the Bible—them lazy, bloated swine what travels first cabin? Them's the ones. They dragged us down 'til we're on'y wage slaves in the bowels of a bloody ship, sweatin', burnin' up, eatin' coal dust! Hit's them's ter blame—the damned Capitalist clarss! *(There had been a gradual murmur of contemptuous resentment rising among the men until now he is interrupted by a storm of catcalls, hisses, boos, hard laughter.)*

[7] "Irishman" (slang).

VOICES. Turn it off!
Shut up!
Sit down!
Closa da face!
Tamn fool! *(Etc.)*.

YANK. *(standing up and glaring at* LONG*)* Sit down before I knock yuh down! (LONG *makes haste to efface himself.* YANK *goes on contemptuously*) De Bible, huh? De Cap'tlist class, huh? Aw nix on dat Salvation Army-Socialist bull. Git a soapbox! Hire a hall! Come and be saved, huh? Jerk us to Jesus, huh? Aw g'wan! I've listened to lots of guys like you, see. Yuh're all wrong. Wanter know what I t'ink? Yuh ain't no good for no one. Yuh're de bunk. Yuh ain't got no noive, get me? Yuh're yellow, dat's what. Yellow, dat's you. Say! What's dem slobs in de foist cabin got to do wit us? We're better men dan dey are, ain't we? Sure! One of us guys could clean up de whole mob wit one mitt. Put one of 'em down here for one watch in de stokehole, what'd happen? Dey'd carry him off on a stretcher. Dem boids don't amount to nothin'. Dey're just baggage. Who makes dis old tub run? Ain't it us guys? Well den, we belong, don't we? We belong and dey don't. Dat's all. *(A loud chorus of approval.* YANK *goes on)* As for dis bein' hell—aw, nuts! Yuh lost your noive, dat's what. Dis is a man's job, get me? It belongs. It runs dis tub. No stiffs[8] need apply. But yuh're a stiff, see? Yuh're yellow, dat's you.

VOICES. *(with a great hard pride in them)*
Righto!
A man's job!
Talk is cheap, Long.
He never could hold up his end.
Divil take him!
Yank's right. We make it go.
Py Gott, Yank say right ting!
We don't need no one cryin' over us.
Makin' speeches.
Throw him out!
Yellow!
Chuck him overboard!
I'll break his jaw for him!
(They crowd around LONG *threateningly.)*

YANK. *(half good-natured again—contemptuously)* Aw, take it easy. Leave him alone. He ain't woith a punch. Drink up. Here's how, whoever owns dis. *(He takes a long swallow from his bottle. All drink with him. In a flash all is hilarious amiability again, back-slapping, loud talk, etc.)*

PADDY. *(who has been sitting in a blinking, melancholy daze—suddenly cries out in a voice full of old sorrow)* We belong to this, you're saying? We make the ship to go, you're saying? Yerra[9] then, that Almighty God have pity on us! *(His voice runs into the wail of a keen,[10] he rocks back and forth on his bench. The men stare at him, startled and impressed in spite of themselves)* Oh, to be back in the fine days of my

[8]Slang expression for an overformal, inhibited person, as well as a corpse.

[9]"Truly" (Irish).

[10]Irish lamentation for the dead.

youth, ochone![11] Oh, there was fine beautiful ships them days—clippers wid tall masts touching the sky—fine strong men in them—men that was sons of the sea as if 'twas the mother that bore them. Oh, the clean skins of them, and the clear eyes, the straight backs and full chests of them! Brave men they was, and bold men surely! We'd be sailing out, bound down round the Horn[12] maybe. We'd be making sail in the dawn, with a fair breeze, singing a chanty song wid no care to it. And astern the land would be sinking low and dying out, but we'd give it no heed but a laugh, and never a look behind. For the day that was, was enough, for we was free men—and I'm thinking 'tis only slaves do be giving heed to the day that's gone or the day to come—until they're old like me. *(With a sort of religious exaltation)* Oh, to be scudding south again wid the power of the Trade Wind driving her on steady through the nights and the days! Full sail on her! Nights and days! Nights when the foam of the wake would be flaming wid fire, when the sky'd be blazing and winking wid stars. Or the full of the moon maybe. Then you'd see her driving through the gray night, her sails stretching aloft all silver and white, not a sound on the deck, the lot of us dreaming dreams, till you'd believe 'twas no real ship at all you was on but a ghost ship like the *Flying Dutchman*[13] they say does be roaming the seas forevermore widout touching a port. And there was the days, too. A warm sun on the clean decks. Sun warming the blood of you, and wind over the miles of shiny green ocean like strong drink to your lungs. Work—aye, hard work—but who'd mind that at all? Sure, you worked under the sky and 'twas work wid skill and daring to it. And wid the day done, in the dog watch, smoking me pipe at ease, the lookout would be raising land maybe, and we'd see the mountains of South Americy wid the red fire of the setting sun painting their white tops and the clouds floating by them! *(His tone of exaltation ceases. He goes on mournfully)* Yerra, what's the use of talking? 'Tis a dead man's whisper. *(To* YANK *resentfully)* 'Twas them days men belonged to ships, not now. 'Twas them days a ship was part of the sea, and a man was part of a ship, and the sea joined all together and made it one. *(Scornfully)* Is it one wid this you'd be, Yank—black smoke from the funnels smudging the sea, smudging the decks—the bloody engines pounding and throbbing and shaking—wid divil a sight of sun or a breath of clean air—choking our lungs wid coal dust—breaking our backs and hearts in the hell of the stokehole—feeding the bloody furnace—feeding our lives along wid the coal, I'm thinking—caged in by steel from a sight of the sky like bloody apes in the Zoo! *(With a harsh laugh)* Ho-ho, divil mend you! Is it to belong to that you're wishing? Is it a flesh and blood wheel of the engines you'd be?

YANK. *(who has been listening with a contemptuous sneer, barks out the answer)* Sure ting! Dat's me. What about it?

PADDY. *(as if to himself—with great sorrow)* Me time is past due. That a great wave wid sun in the heart of it may sweep me over the side sometime I'd be dreaming of the days that's gone!

[11]"Alas!" (Irish).

[12]Cape Horn, southern end of South America.

[13]Legendary ship carrying a mariner condemned to sail the seas against the wind until Judgment Day.

YANK. Aw, yuh crazy Mick![14] *(He springs to his feet and advances on* PADDY *threateningly—then stops, fighting some queer struggle within himself—lets his hands fall to his sides—contemptuously)* Aw, take it easy. Yuh're aw right, at dat. Yuh're bugs, dat's all—nutty as a cuckoo. All dat tripe yuh been pullin'—Aw, dat's all right. On'y it's dead, get me? Yuh don't belong no more, see. Yuh don't get de stuff. Yuh're too old. *(Disgustedly)* But aw say, come up for air onct in a while, can't yuh? See what's happened since yuh croaked. *(He suddenly bursts forth vehemently, growing more and more excited)* Say! Sure! Sure I meant it! What de hell—Say, lemme talk! Hey! Hey, you old Harp! Hey, youse guys! Say, listen to me—wait a moment—I gotter talk, see. I belong and he don't. He's dead but I'm livin'. Listen to me! Sure I'm part of de engines! Why de hell not! Dey move, don't dey? Dey're speed, ain't dey? Dey smash trou, don't dey? Twenty-five knots a hour! Dat's goin' some! Dat's new stuff! Dat belongs! But him, he's too old. He gets dizzy. Say, listen. All dat crazy tripe about nights and days; all dat crazy tripe about stars and moons; all dat crazy tripe about suns and winds, fresh air and de rest of it—Aw hell, dat's all a dope dream! Hittin' de pipe of de past, dat's what he's doin'. He's old and don't belong no more. But me, I'm young! I'm in de pink! I move wit it. It, get me! I mean de ting dat's de guts of all dis. It ploughs trou all de tripe he's been sayin'. It blows dat up! It knocks dat dead! It slams dat offen de face of de oith! It, get me! De engines and de coal and de smoke and all de rest of it! He can't breathe and swallow coal dust, but I kin, see? Dat's fresh air for me! Dat's food for me! I'm new, get me? Hell in de stokehole? Sure! It takes a man to work in hell. Hell, sure, dat's my fav'rite climate. I eat it up! I git fat on it! It's me makes it hot! It's me makes it roar! It's me makes it move! Sure, on'y for me everyting stops. It all goes dead, get me? De noise and smoke and all de engines movin' de woild, dey stop. Dere ain't nothin' no more! Dat's what I'm sayin'. Everyting else dat makes de woild move, somep'n makes it move. It can't move witout somep'n else, see? Den yuh get down to me. I'm at de bottom, get me! Dere ain't nothin' foither. I'm de end! I'm de start! I start somep'n and de woild moves! It—dat's me!—de new dat's moiderin' de old! I'm de ting in coal dat makes it boin; I'm steam and oil for de engines; I'm de ting in noise dat makes yuh hear it; I'm smoke and express trains and steamers and factory whistles; I'm de ting in gold dat makes it money! And I'm what makes iron into steel! Steel, dat stands for de whole ting! And I'm steel—steel—steel! I'm de muscles in steel, de punch behind it! *(As he says this he pounds with his fist against the steel bunks. All the men, roused to a pitch of frenzied self-glorification by his speech, do likewise. There is a deafening metallic roar, through which* YANK'S *voice can be heard bellowing)* Slaves, hell! We run de whole woiks. All de rich guys dat tink dey're somep'n, dey ain't nothin'! Dey don't belong. But us guys, we're in de move, we're at de bottom, de whole ting is us! (PADDY *from the start of* YANK'S *speech has been taking one gulp after another from his bottle, at first frightenedly, as if he were afraid to listen, then desperately, as if to drown his senses, but finally has achieved complete indifferent, even amused, drunkenness.* YANK *sees his lips moving. He quells the uproar with a shout)* Hey, youse guys, take it easy! Wait a moment! De nutty Harp is sayin' somep'n.

[14]"Irishman" (slang).

PADDY. *(is heard now—throws his head back with a mocking burst of laughter)* Ho-ho-ho-ho-ho—

YANK. *(drawing back his fist, with a snarl)* Aw! Look out who yuh're givin' the bark!

PADDY. *(begins to sing, the "Miller of Dee" with enormous good nature)*

> *"I care for nobody, no, not I,*
> *And nobody cares for me."*

YANK. *(good-natured himself in a flash, interrupts* PADDY *with a slap on the bare back like a report)* Dat's de stuff! Now yuh're gettin' wise to somep'n. Care for nobody, dat's de dope! To hell with 'em all! And nix on nobody else carin'. I kin care for myself, get me! *(Eight bells sound, muffled, vibrating through the steel walls as if some enormous brazen gong were imbedded in the heart of the ship. All the men jump up mechanically, file through the door silently close upon each other's heels in what is very like a prisoner's lockstep.* YANK *slaps* PADDY *on the back)* Our watch, yuh old Harp! *(Mockingly)* Come on down in hell. Eat up de coal dust. Drink in de heat. It's it, see! Act like yuh liked it, yuh better—or croak yuhself.

PADDY. *(with jovial defiance)* To the divil wid it! I'll not report this watch. Let thim log[15] me and be damned. I'm no slave the like of you. I'll be sittin' here at me ease, and drinking, and thinking, and dreaming dreams.

YANK. *(contemptuously)* Tinkin' and dreamin', what'll that get yuh? What's tinkin' got to do wit it? We move, don't we? Speed, ain't it? Fog, dat's all you stand for. But we drive trou dat, don't we? We split dat up and smash trou—twenty-five knots a hour! *(Turns his back on* PADDY *scornfully)* Aw, yuh make me sick! Yuh don't belong! *(He strides out the door in rear.* PADDY *hums to himself, blinking drowsily.)*

CURTAIN

Scene Two

Two days out. A section of the promenade deck. MILDRED DOUGLAS *and her aunt are discovered reclining in deck chairs. The former is a girl of twenty, slender, delicate, with a pale, pretty face marred by a self-conscious expression of disdainful superiority. She looks fretful, nervous and discontented, bored by her own anemia. Her aunt is a pompous and proud—and fat—old lady. She is a type even to the point of a double chin and lorgnettes.*[16] *She is dressed pretentiously, as if afraid her face alone would never indicate her position in life.* MILDRED *is dressed all in white.*

The impression to be conveyed by this scene is one of the beautiful, vivid life of the sea all about—sunshine on the deck in a great flood, the fresh sea wind blowing across it. In the midst of this, these two incongruous, artificial figures, inert and disharmonious, the elder like a gray lump of dough touched up with rouge, the younger looking as if the vitality of her stock had been sapped before she was conceived, so that

[15]Note his absence by entering his name in the ship's log, a record of daily activities and routines.

[16]Eyeglasses with a short handle, a fashion accessory of some upper-class women of the time.

she is the expression not of its life energy but merely of the artificialities that energy had won for itself in the spending.

MILDRED. *(looking up with affected dreaminess)* How the black smoke swirls back against the sky! Is it not beautiful?

AUNT. *(without looking up)* I dislike smoke of any kind.

MILDRED. My great-grandmother smoked a pipe—a clay pipe.

AUNT. *(ruffling)* Vulgar!

MILDRED. She was too distant a relative to be vulgar. Time mellows pipes.

AUNT. *(pretending boredom but irritated)* Did the sociology you took up at college teach you that—to play the ghoul on every possible occasion, excavating old bones? Why not let your great-grandmother rest in her grave?

MILDRED. *(dreamily)* With her pipe beside her—puffing in Paradise.

AUNT. *(with spite)* Yes, you are a natural born ghoul. You are even getting to look like one, my dear.

MILDRED. *(in a passionless tone)* I detest you, Aunt. *(Looking at her critically)* Do you know what you remind me of? Of a cold pork pudding against a background of linoleum tablecloth in the kitchen of a—but the possibilities are wearisome. *(She closes her eyes.)*

AUNT. *(with a bitter laugh) Merci*[17] for your candor. But since I am and must be your chaperon—in appearance, at least—let us patch up some sort of armed truce. For my part you are quite free to indulge any pose of eccentricity that beguiles you—as long as you observe the amenities—

MILDRED. *(drawling)* The inanities?

AUNT. *(going on as if she hadn't heard)* After exhausting the morbid thrills of social service work on New York's East Side[18]—how they must have hated you, by the way, the poor that you made so much poorer in their own eyes!—you are now bent on making your slumming international. Well, I hope Whitechapel[19] will provide the needed nerve tonic. Do not ask me to chaperon you there, however. I told your father I would not. I loathe deformity. We will hire an army of detectives and you may investigate everything—they allow you to see.

MILDRED. *(protesting with a trace of genuine earnestness)* Please do not mock my attempts to discover how the other half lives. Give me credit for some sort of groping sincerity in that at least. I would like to help them. I would like to be some use in the world. Is it my fault I don't know how? I would like to be sincere, to touch life somewhere. *(With weary bitterness)* But I'm afraid I have neither the vitality nor integrity. All that was burnt out in our stock before I was born. Grandfather's blast furnaces, flaming to the sky, melting steel, making millions—then father keeping those home fires burning, making more millions—and little me at the tail-end of it all. I'm a waste product in the Bessemer process[20]—like the millions. Or rather, I inherit the acquired trait of the by-product, wealth, but none of the energy, none of the strength of the steel that made it. I am sired by gold and

[17] "Thank you" (French).

[18] A Manhattan slum district, inhabited mainly by first generation immigrants.

[19] A London slum district.

[20] A method for making steel by burning out excess impurities.

damned[21] by it, as they say at the race track—damned in more ways than one. *(She laughs mirthlessly.)*

AUNT. *(unimpressed—superciliously)* You seem to be going in for sincerity today. It isn't becoming to you, really—except as an obvious pose. Be as artificial as you are, I advise. There's a sort of sincerity in that, you know. And, after all, you must confess you like that better.

MILDRED. *(again affected and bored)* Yes, I suppose I do. Pardon me for my outburst. When a leopard complains of its spots, it must sound rather grotesque. *(In a mocking tone)* Purr, little leopard. Purr, scratch, tear, kill, gorge yourself and be happy—only stay in the jungle where your spots are camouflage. In a cage they make you conspicuous.

AUNT. I don't know what you are talking about.

MILDRED. It would be rude to talk about anything to you. Let's just talk. *(She looks at her wrist watch)* Well, thank goodness, it's about time for them to come for me. That ought to give me a new thrill, Aunt.

AUNT. *(affectedly troubled)* You don't mean to say you're really going? The dirt—the heat must be frightful—

MILDRED. Grandfather started as a puddler.[22] I should have inherited an immunity to heat that would make a salamander[23] shiver. It will be fun to put it to the test.

AUNT. But don't you have to have the captain's—or someone's—permission to visit the stokehole?

MILDRED. *(with a triumphant smile)* I have it—both his and the chief engineer's. Oh, they didn't want to at first, in spite of my social service credentials. They didn't seem a bit anxious that I should investigate how the other half lives and works on a ship. So I had to tell them that my father, the president of Nazareth Steel,[24] chairman of the board of directors of this line, had told me it would be all right.

AUNT. He didn't.

MILDRED. How naïve age makes one! But I said he did, Aunt. I even said he had given me a letter to them—which I had lost. And they were afraid to take the chance that I might be lying. *(Excitedly)* So it's ho! for the stokehole. The second engineer is to escort me. *(Looking at her watch again)* It's time. And here he comes, I think. *(The* SECOND ENGINEER *enters. He is a husky, fine-looking man of thirty-five or so. He stops before the two and tips his cap, visibly embarrassed and ill-at-ease.)*

SECOND ENGINEER. Miss Douglas?

MILDRED. Yes. *(Throwing off her rugs and getting to her feet)* Are we all ready to start?

SECOND ENGINEER. In just a second, ma'am. I'm waiting for the Fourth.[25] He's coming along.

MILDRED. *(with a scornful smile)* You don't care to shoulder this responsibility alone, is that it?

SECOND ENGINEER. *(forcing a smile)* Two are better than one. *(Disturbed by her eyes, glances out to sea—blurts out)* A fine day we're having.

[21]Pun on "dammed" (mothered).

[22]A steelworker.

[23]A mythical creature, resembling a lizard, once believed capable of living in fire.

[24]Allusion to Bethlehem Steel, a large American steel corporation.

[25]Fourth Engineer.

MILDRED. Is it?

SECOND ENGINEER. A nice warm breeze—

MILDRED. It feels cold to me.

SECOND ENGINEER. But it's hot enough in the sun—

MILDRED. Not hot enough for me. I don't like Nature. I was never athletic.

SECOND ENGINEER. *(forcing a smile)* Well, you'll find it hot enough where you're going.

MILDRED. Do you mean hell?

SECOND ENGINEER. *(flabbergasted, decides to laugh)* Ho-ho! No, I mean the stokehole.

MILDRED. My grandfather was a puddler. He played with boiling steel.

SECOND ENGINEER. *(all at sea—uneasily)* Is that so? Hum, you'll excuse me, ma'am, but are you intending to wear that dress?

MILDRED. Why not?

SECOND ENGINEER. You'll likely rub against oil and dirt. It can't be helped.

MILDRED. It doesn't matter. I have lots of white dresses.

SECOND ENGINEER. I have an old coat you might throw over—

MILDRED. I have fifty dresses like this. I will throw this one into the sea when I come back. That ought to wash it clean, don't you think?

SECOND ENGINEER. *(doggedly)* There's ladders to climb down that are none too clean—and dark alleyways—

MILDRED. I will wear this very dress and none other.

SECOND ENGINEER. No offense meant. It's none of my business. I was only warning you—

MILDRED. Warning? That sounds thrilling.

SECOND ENGINEER. *(looking down the deck—with a sigh of relief)* There's the Fourth now. He's waiting for us. If you'll come—

MILDRED. Go on. I'll follow you. *(He goes.* MILDRED *turns a mocking smile on her aunt)* An oaf—but a handsome, virile oaf.

AUNT. *(scornfully)* Poser!

MILDRED. Take care. He said there were dark alleyways—

AUNT. *(in the same tone)* Poser!

MILDRED. *(biting her lips angrily)* You are right. But would that my millions were not so anemically chaste!

AUNT. Yes, for a fresh pose I have no doubt you would drag the name of Douglas in the gutter!

MILDRED. From which it sprang. Good-by, Aunt. Don't pray too hard that I may fall into the fiery furnace.

AUNT. Poser!

MILDRED. *(viciously)* Old hag! *(She slaps her aunt insultingly across the face and walks off, laughing gaily.)*

AUNT. *(screams after her)* I said poser!

CURTAIN

Scene Three

The stokehole. In the rear, the dimly-outlined bulks of the furnaces and boilers. High overhead one hanging electric bulb sheds just enough light through the murky air laden with coal dust to pile up masses of shadows everywhere. A line of men, stripped to the waist, is before the furnace doors. They bend over, looking neither to right nor left, handling their shovels as if they were part of their bodies, with a strange, awkward, swinging rhythm. They use the shovels to throw open the furnace doors. Then from these fiery round holes in the black a flood of terrific light and heat pours full upon the men who are outlined in silhouette in the crouching, inhuman attitudes of chained gorillas. The men shovel with a rhythmic motion, swinging as on a pivot from the coal which lies in heaps on the floor behind to hurl it into the flaming mouths before them. There is a tumult of noise—the brazen clang of the furnace doors as they are flung open or slammed shut, the grating, teeth-gritting grind of steel against steel, of crunching coal. This clash of sounds stuns one's ears with its rending dissonance. But there is order in it, rhythm, a mechanical regulated recurrence, a tempo. And rising above all, making the air hum with the quiver of liberated energy, the roar of leaping flames in the furnaces, the monotonous throbbing beat of the engines.

As the curtain rises, the furnace doors are shut. The men are taking a breathing spell. One or two are arranging the coal behind them, pulling it into more accessible heaps. The others can be dimly made out leaning on their shovels in relaxed attitudes of exhaustion.

PADDY. *(from somewhere in the line—plaintively)* Yerra, will this divil's own watch nivir end? Me back is broke. I'm destroyed entirely.

YANK. *(from the center of the line—with exuberant scorn)* Aw, yuh make me sick! Lie down and croak, why don't yuh? Always beefin', dat's you! Say, dis is a cinch! Dis was made for me! It's my meat, get me! *(A whistle is blown—a thin, shrill note from somewhere overhead in the darkness.* YANK *curses without resentment)* Dere's de damn engineer crackin' de whip. He tinks we're loafin'.

PADDY. *(vindictively)* God stiffen him!

YANK. *(in an exultant tone of command)* Come on, youse guys! Git into de game! She's gittin' hungry! Pile some grub in her. Trow it into her belly! Come on now, all of youse! Open her up! *(At this last all the men, who have followed his movements of getting into position, throw open their furnace doors with a deafening clang. The fiery light floods over their shoulders as they bend round for the coal. Rivulets of sooty sweat have traced maps on their backs. The enlarged muscles form bunches of high light and shadow.)*

YANK. *(chanting a count as he shovels without seeming effort)* One—two—tree—*(His voice rising exultantly in the joy of battle)* Dat's de stuff! Let her have it! All togedder now! Sling it into her! Let her ride! Shoot de piece now! Call de toin on her! Drive her into it! Feel her move! Watch her smoke! Speed, dat's her middle name! Give her coal, youse guys! Coal, dat's her booze! Drink it up, baby! Let's see yuh sprint! Dig in and gain a lap! Dere she go-o-es. *(This last in the chanting formula of the gallery gods at the six-day bike race. He slams his furnace door shut. The others do likewise with as much unison as their wearied bodies will permit. The effect is of one fiery eye after another being blotted out with a series of accompanying bangs.)*

PADDY. *(groaning)* Me back is broke. I'm bate out—bate— *(There is a pause. Then the inexorable whistle sounds again from the dim regions above the electric light. There is a growl of cursing rage from all sides.)*

YANK. *(shaking his fist upward—contemptuously)* Take it easy dere, you! Who d'yuh tink's runnin' dis game, me or you? When I git ready, we move. Not before! When I git ready, get me!

VOICES. *(approvingly)* That's the stuff!

Yank tal him, py golly!
Yank ain't affeerd.
Goot poy, Yank!
Give him hell!
Tell 'im 'e's a bloody swine!
Bloody slave-driver!

YANK. *(contemptuously)* He ain't got no noive. He's yellow, get me? All de engineers is yellow. Dey got streaks a mile wide. Aw, to hell wit him! Let's move, youse guys. We had a rest. Come on, she needs it! Give her pep! It ain't for him. Him and his whistle, dey don't belong. But we belong, see! We gotter feed de baby! Come on! *(He turns and flings his furnace door open. They all follow his lead. At this instant the* SECOND *and* FOURTH ENGINEERS *enter from the darkness on the left with* MILDRED *between them. She starts, turns paler, her pose is crumbling, she shivers with fright in spite of the blazing heat, but forces herself to leave the* ENGINEERS *and take a few steps nearer the men. She is right behind* YANK. *All this happens quickly while the men have their backs turned.)*

YANK. Come on, youse guys! *(He is turning to get coal when the whistle sounds again in a peremptory, irritating note. This drives* YANK *into a sudden fury. While the other men have turned full around and stopped dumbfounded by the spectacle of* MILDRED *standing there in her white dress,* YANK *does not turn far enough to see her. Besides, his head is thrown back, he blinks upward through the murk trying to find the owner of the whistle, he brandishes his shovel murderously over his head in one hand, pounding on his chest, gorilla-like, with the other, shouting)* Toin off dat whistle! Come down outa dere, yuh yellow, brass-buttoned, Belfast bum, yuh! Come down and I'll knock yer brains out! Yuh lousy, stinkin', yellow mut of a Catholic-moiderin' bastard! Come down and I'll moider yuh! Pullin' dat whistle on me, huh? I'll show yuh! I'll crash yer skull in! I'll drive yer teet' down yer troat! I'll slam yer nose trou de back of yer head! I'll cut yer guts out for a nickel, yuh lousy boob, yuh dirty, crummy, muck-eatin' son of a—*(Suddenly he becomes conscious of all the other men staring at something directly behind his back. He whirls defensively with a snarling, murderous growl, crouching to spring, his lips drawn back over his teeth, his small eyes gleaming ferociously. He sees* MILDRED, *like a white apparition in the full light from the open furnace doors. He glares into her eyes, turned to stone. As for her, during his speech she has listened, paralyzed with horror, terror, her whole personality crushed, beaten in, collapsed, by the terrific impact of this unknown, abysmal brutality, naked and shameless. As she looks at his gorilla face, as his eyes bore into hers, she utters a low, choking cry and shrinks away from him, putting both hands up before her eyes to shut out the sight of his face, to protect her own. This startles* YANK *to a reaction. His mouth falls open, his eyes grow bewildered.)*

MILDRED. *(about to faint—to the* ENGINEERS, *who now have her one by each arm—whimperingly)* Take me away! Oh, the filthy beast! *(She faints. They carry her quickly back, disappearing in the darkness at the left, rear. An iron door clangs shut. Rage and bewildered fury rush back on* YANK. *He feels himself insulted in some unknown fashion in the very heart of his pride. He roars* "God Damn yuh!" *and hurls his shovel after them at the door which has just closed. It hits the steel bulkhead with a clang and falls clattering on the steel floor. From overhead the whistle sounds again in a long, angry, inconsistent command.)*

CURTAIN

Scene Four

The firemen's forecastle. YANK'S *watch has just come off duty and had dinner. Their faces and bodies shine from a soap-and-water scrubbing but around their eyes, where a hasty dousing does not touch, the coal dust sticks like black make-up, giving them a queer, sinister expression.* YANK *has not washed either face or body. He stands out in contrast to them, a blackened, brooding figure. He is seated forward on a bench in the exact attitude of Rodin's "The Thinker."*[26] *The others, most of them smoking pipes, are staring at* YANK *half-apprehensively, as if fearing an outburst; half-amusedly, as if they saw a joke somehwere that tickled them.*

VOICES. He ain't ate nothin'.
Py golly, a fallar gat to gat grub in him.
Divil a lie.
Yank feeda da fire, no feeda da face.
Ha-ha.
He ain't even washed hisself.
He's forgot.
Hey, Yank, you forgot to wash.

YANK. *(sullenly)* Forgot nothin'! To hell wit washin'.

VOICES. It'll stick to you.
It'll get under your skin.
Give yer the bleedin' itch, that's wot.
It makes spots on you—like a leopard.
Like a piebald[27] nigger, you mean.
Better wash up, Yank.
You sleep better.
Wash up, Yank!
Wash up! Wash up!

YANK. *(resentfully)* Aw say, youse guys. Lemme alone. Can't youse see I'm tryin' to tink?

[26]Statue by French sculptor Auguste Rodin (1840–1917) of seated nude man with chin propped on fist.

[27]Spotted or patched, especially in black and white.

ALL. *(repeating the word after him as one with cynical mockery)* Think! *(The word has a brazen, metallic quality as if their throats were phonograph horns. It is followed by a chorus of hard, barking laughter.)*

YANK. *(springing to his feet and glaring at them belligerently)* Yes, tink! Tink, dat's what I said! What about it? *(They are silent, puzzled by his sudden resentment at what used to be one of his jokes.* YANK *sits down again in the same attitude of "The Thinker.")*

VOICES. Leave him alone.
He's got a grouch on.
Why wouldn't he?

PADDY. *(with a wink at the others)* Sure I know what's the matther. 'Tis aisy to see. He's fallen in love, I'm telling you.

ALL. *(repeating the word after him as one with cynical mockery)* Love! *(The word has a brazen, metallic quality as if their throats were phonograph horns. It is followed by a chorus of hard, barking laughter.)*

YANK. *(with a contemptuous snort)* Love, Hell! Hate, dat's what. I've fallen in hate, get me?

PADDY. *(philosophically)* 'Twould take a wise man to tell one from the other. *(With a bitter, ironical scorn, increasing as he goes on)* But I'm telling you it's love that's in it. Sure what else but love for us poor bastes in the stokehole would be bringing a fine lady, dressed like a white quane, down a mile of ladders and steps to be havin' a look at us? *(A growl of anger goes up from all sides.)*

LONG. *(jumping on a bench—hectically)* Hinsultin' us! Hinsultin' us, the bloody cow! And them bloody engineers! What right 'as they got to be exhibitin' us 's if we was bleedin' monkeys in a menagerie? Did we sign for hinsults to our dignity as 'onest workers? Is that in the ship's articles?[28] You kin bloody well bet it ain't! But I knows why they done it. I arsked a deck steward 'o she was and 'e told me. 'Er old man's a bleedin' millionaire, a bloody Capitalist! 'E's got enuf bloody gold to sink this bleedin' ship! 'E makes arf the bloody steel in the world! 'E owns this bloody boat! And you and me, Comrades, we're 'is slaves! And the skipper and mates and engineers, they're 'is slaves! And she's 'is bloody daughter and we're all 'er slaves, too! And she gives 'er orders as 'ow she wants to see the bloody animals below decks and down they takes 'er! *(There is a roar of rage from all sides.)*

YANK. *(blinking at him bewilderedly)* Say! Wait a moment! Is all dat straight goods?

LONG. Straight as string! The bleedin' steward as waits on 'em, 'e told me about 'er. And what're we goin' ter do, I arsks yer? 'Ave we got ter swaller 'er hinsults like dogs? It ain't in the ship's articles. I tell yer we got a case. We kin go to law—

YANK. *(with abysmal contempt)* Hell! Law!

ALL. *(repeating the word after him as one with cynical mockery)* Law! *(The word has a brazen metallic quality as if their throats were phonograph horns. It is followed by a chorus of hard, barking laughter.)*

LONG. *(feeling the ground slipping from under his feet—desperately)* As voters and citizens we kin force the bloody governments—

[28]Regulations concerning employment.

YANK. *(with abysmal contempt)* Hell! Governments!

ALL. *(repeating the word after him as one with cynical mockery)* Governments! *(The word has a brazen metallic quality as if their throats were phonograph horns. It is followed by a chorus of hard, barking laughter.)*

LONG. *(hysterically)* We're free and equal in the sight of God—

YANK. *(with abysmal contempt)* Hell! God!

ALL. *(repeating the word after him as one with cynical mockery)* God! *(The word has a brazen metallic quality as if their throats were phonograph horns. It is followed by a chorus of hard, barking laughter.)*

YANK. *(witheringly)* Aw, join de Salvation Army!

ALL. Sit down! Shut up! Damn fool! Sea-lawyer![29] (LONG *slinks back out of sight.)*

PADDY. *(continuing the trend of his thoughts as if he had never been interrupted—bitterly)* And there she was standing behind us, and the Second pointing at us like a man you'd hear in a circus would be saying: In this cage is a queerer kind of baboon than ever you'd find in darkest Africy. We roast them in their own sweat—and be damned if you won't hear some of thim saying they like it! *(He glances scornfully at* YANK.*)*

YANK. *(with a bewildered uncertain growl)* Aw!

PADDY. And there was Yank roarin' curses and turning round wid his shovel to brain her—and she looked at him, and him at her—

YANK. *(slowly)* She was all white. I tought she was a ghost. Sure.

PADDY. *(with heavy, biting sarcasm)* 'Twas love at first sight, divil a doubt of it! If you'd seen the endearin' look on her pale mug when she shriveled away with her hands over her eyes to shut out the sight of him! Sure, 'twas as if she'd seen a great hairy ape escaped from the Zoo!

YANK. *(stung—with a growl of rage)* Aw!

PADDY. And the loving way Yank heaved his shovel at the skull of her, only she was out the door! *(A grin breaking over his face)* 'Twas touching, I'm telling you! It put the touch of home, swate home in the stokehole. *(There is a roar of laughter from all.)*

YANK. *(glaring at* PADDY *menacingly)* Aw, choke dat off, see!

PADDY. *(not heeding him—to the others)* And her grabbin' at the Second's arm for protection. *(With a grotesque imitation of a woman's voice)* Kiss me, Engineer dear, for it's dark down here and me old man's in Wall Street making money! Hug me tight, darlin', for I'm afeerd in the dark and me mother's on deck makin' eyes at the skipper! *(Another roar of laughter.)*

YANK. *(threateningly)* Say! What yuh tryin' to do, kid me, yuh old Harp?

PADDY. Divil a bit! Ain't I wishin' myself you'd brained her?

YANK. *(fiercely)* I'll brain her! I'll brain her yet, wait 'n' see! *(Coming over to* PADDY*—slowly)* Say, is dat what she called me—a hairy ape?

PADDY. She looked it at you if she didn't say the word itself.

YANK. *(grinning horribly)* Hairy ape, huh? Sure! Dat's de way she looked at me, aw right. Hairy ape! So dat's me, huh? *(Bursting into rage—as if she were still in front of him)* Yuh skinny tart! Yuh white-faced bum, yuh! I'll show yuh who's a ape! *(Turning to the others, bewilderment seizing him again)* Say, youse guys. I was

[29] "Troublemaker" (slang).

bawlin' him out for pullin' de whistle on us. You heard me. And den I seen youse lookin' at somep'n and I tought he'd sneaked down to come up in back of me, and I hopped round to knock him dead wit de shovel. And dere she was wit de light on her! Christ, yuh coulda pushed me over with a finger! I was scared, get me? Sure! I thought she was a ghost, see? She was all in white like dey wrap around stiffs. You seen her. Kin yuh blame me? She didn't belong, dat's what. And den when I come to and seen it was a real skoit and seen de way she was lookin' at me—like Paddy said—Christ, I was sore, get me? I don't stand for dat stuff from nobody. And I flung de shovel—on'y she'd beat it. *(Furiously)* I wished it'd banged her! I wished it'd knocked her block off!

LONG. And be 'anged for murder or 'lectrocuted? She ain't bleedin' well worth it.

YANK. I don't give a damn what! I'd be square wit her, wouldn't I? Tink I wanter let her put somep'n over on me? Tink I'm goin' to let her git away wit dat stuff? Yuh don't know me! No one ain't never put nothin' over on me and got away wit it, see!—not dat kind of stuff—no guy and no skoit neither! I'll fix her! Maybe she'll come down again—

VOICE. No chance, Yank. You scared her out of a year's growth.

YANK. I scared her? Why de hell should I scare her? Who de hell is she? Ain't she de same as me? Hairy ape, huh? *(With his old confident bravado)* I'll show her I'm better'n her, if she on'y knew it. I belong and she don't, see! I move and she's dead! Twenty-five knots a hour, dat's me! Dat carries her but I make dat. She's on'y baggage. Sure! *(Again bewilderedly)* But, Christ, she was funny lookin'! Did yuh pipe her hands? White and skinny. Yuh could see de bones through 'em. And her mush, dat was dead white, too. And her eyes, dey was like dey'd seen a ghost. Me, dat was! Sure! Hairy ape! Ghost, huh? Look at dat arm! *(He extends his right arm, swelling out of the great muscles)* I coulda took her wit dat, wit just my little finger even, and broke her in two. *(Again bewilderedly)* Say, who is dat skoit, huh? What is she? What's she come from? Who made her? Who give her de noive to look at me like dat? Dis ting's got my goat right. I don't get her. She's new to me. What does a skoit like her mean, huh? She don't belong, get me! I can't see her. *(With growing anger)* But one ting I'm wise to, aw right, aw right! Youse all kin bet your shoits I'll git even wit her. I'll show her if she tinks she—She grinds de organ and I'm on de string, huh? I'll fix her! Let her come down again and I'll fling her in de furnace! She'll move den! She won't shiver at nothin', den! Speed, dat'll be her! She'll belong den! *(He grins horribly.)*

PADDY. She'll never come. She's had her belly-full, I'm telling you. She'll be in bed now, I'm thinking, wid ten doctors and nurses feedin' her salts[30] to clean the fear out of her.

YANK. *(enraged)* Yuh tink I made her sick, too, do yuh? Just lookin' at me, huh? Hairy ape, huh? *(In a frenzy of rage)* I'll fix her! I'll tell her where to git off! She'll git down on her knees and take it back or I'll bust de face offen her! *(Shaking one fist upward and beating on his chest with the other)* I'll find yuh! I'm comin', d'yuh hear? I'll fix yuh, God damn yuh! *(He makes a rush for the door.)*

VOICES. Stop him!

[30]Epsom salts, a laxative.

He'll get shot!
He'll murder her!
Trip him up!
Hold him!
He's gone crazy!
Gott, he's strong!
Hold him down!
Look out for a kick!
Pin his arms!

(They have all piled on him and, after a fierce struggle, by sheer weight of numbers have borne him to the floor just inside the door.)

PADDY. *(who has remained detached)* Kape him down till he's cooled off. *(Scornfully)* Yerra, Yank, you're a great fool. Is it payin' attention at all you are to the like of that skinny sow widout one drop of rale blood in her?

YANK. *(frenziedly, from the bottom of the heap)* She done me doit! She done me doit, didn't she? I'll git square wit her! I'll get her some way! Git offen me, youse guys! Lemme up! I'll show her who's a ape!

CURTAIN

Scene Five

Three weeks later. A corner of Fifth Avenue in the Fifties on a fine Sunday morning. A general atmosphere of clean, well-tidied, wide street; a flood of mellow, tempered sunshine; gentle, genteel breezes. In the rear, the show windows of two shops, a jewelry establishment on the corner, a furrier's next to it. Here the adornments of extreme wealth are tantalizingly displayed. The jeweler's window is gaudy with glittering diamonds, emeralds, rubies, pearls, etc., fashioned in ornate tiaras, crowns, necklaces, collars, etc. From each piece hangs an enormous tag from which a dollar sign and numerals in intermittent electric lights wink out the incredible prices. The same in the furrier's. Rich furs of all varieties hang there bathed in a downpour of artificial light. The general effect is of a background of magnificence cheapened and made grotesque by commercialism, a background in tawdry disharmony with the clear light and sunshine on the street itself.

Up the side street YANK *and* LONG *come swaggering.* LONG *is dressed in shore clothes, wears a black Windsor tie, cloth cap.* YANK *is in his dirty dungarees. A fireman's cap with black peak is cocked defiantly on the side of his head. He has not shaved for days and around his fierce, resentful eyes—as around those of* LONG *to a lesser degree—the black smudge of coal dust still sticks like make-up. They hesitate and stand together at the corner, swaggering, looking about them with a forced, defiant contempt.*

LONG. *(indicating it all with an oratorical gesture)* Well, 'ere we are. Fif' Avenoo. This 'ere's their bleedin' private lane, as yer might say. *(Bitterly)* We're trespassers 'ere. Proletarians keep orf the grass!

YANK. *(dully)* I don't see no grass, yuh boob. *(Staring at the sidewalk)* Clean, ain't it?

Yuh could eat a fried egg offen it. The white wings[31] got some job sweepin' dis up. *(Looking up and down the avenue—surlily)* Where's all de white-collar stiffs yuh said was here—and de skoits—*her* kind?

LONG. In church, blarst 'em! Arskin' Jesus to give 'em more money.

YANK. Choich, huh? I useter go to choich onct—sure—when I was a kid. Me old man and woman, dey made me. Dey never went demselves, dough. Always got too big a head on Sunday mornin', dat was dem. *(With a grin)* Dey was scrappers for fair, bot' of dem. On Satiday nights when dey bot' got a skinful dey could put up a bout oughter been staged at de Garden.[32] When dey got trough dere wasn't a chair or table wit a leg under it. Or else dey bot' jumped on me for somep'n. Dat was where I loined to take punishment. *(With a grin and a swagger)* I'm a chip offen de old block, get me?

LONG. Did yer old man follow the sea?

YANK. Naw. Worked along shore. I runned away when me old lady croaked wit de tremens.[33] I helped at truckin' and in de market. Den I shipped in de stokehole. Sure. Dat belongs. De rest was nothin'. *(Looking around him)* I ain't never seen dis before. De Brooklyn waterfront, dat was where I was dragged up. *(Taking a deep breath)* Dis ain't so bad at dat, huh?

LONG. Not bad? Well, we pays for it wiv our bloody sweat, if yer wants to know!

YANK. *(with sudden angry disgust)* Aw, hell! I don't see no one, see—like her. All dis gives me a pain. It don't belong. Say, ain't dere a back room around dis dump? Let's go shoot a ball.[34] All dis is too clean and quiet and dolled-up, get me! It gives me a pain.

LONG. Wait and yer'll bloody well see—

YANK. I don't wait for no one. I keep on de move. Say, what yuh drag me up here for, anyway? Tryin' to kid me, yuh simp, yuh?

LONG. Yer wants to get back at 'er, don't yer? That's what yer been sayin' every bloomin' hour since she hinsulted yer.

YANK. *(vehemently)* Sure ting I do! Didn't I try to get even wit her in Southampton? Didn't I sneak on de dock and wait for her by de gangplank? I was goin' to spit in her pale mug, see! Sure, right in her pop-eyes! Dat woulda made me even, see? But no chanct. Dere was a whole army of plainclothes bulls around. Dey spotted me and gimme de bum's rush. I never seen her. But I'll git square wit her yet, you watch. *(Furiously)* De lousy tart! She tinks she kin get away wit moider—but not wit me! I'll fix her! I'll tink of a way!

LONG. *(as disgusted as he dares to be)* Ain't that why I brought yer up 'ere—to show yer? Yer been lookin' at this 'ere 'ole affair wrong. Yer been actin' an' talkin' 's if it was all a bleedin' personal matter between yer and that bloody cow. I wants to convince yer she was on'y a representative of 'er clarss. I wants to awaken yer bloody clarss consciousness. Then yer'll see it's 'er clarss yer've got to fight, not 'er alone. There's a 'ole mob of 'em like 'er, Gawd blind 'em!

YANK. *(spitting on his hands—belligerently)* De more de merrier when I gits started. Bring on de gang!

[31]Streetcleaners, dressed in white.
[32]New York City's Madison Square Garden, site of prize fights.
[33]Delirium tremens, a nervous affliction suffered by heavy drinkers.
[34]Shoot pool.

LONG. Yer'll see 'em in arf a mo', when that church lets out. *(He turns and sees the window display in the two stores for the first time)* Blimey![35] Look at that, will yer? *(They both walk back and stand looking in the jeweler's.* LONG *flies into a fury)* Just look at this 'ere bloomin' mess! Just look at it! Look at the bleedin' prices on 'em—more'n our 'ole bloody stokehole makes in ten voyages sweatin' in 'ell! And they—'er and 'er bloody clarss—buys 'em for toys to dangle on 'em! One of these 'ere would buy scoff[36] for a starvin' family for a year!

YANK. Aw, cut de sob stuff! T' hell wit de starvin' family! Yuh'll be passin' de hat to me next. *(With naïve admiration)* Say, dem tings is pretty, huh? Bet yuh dey'd hock for a piece of change aw right. *(Then turning away, bored)* But, aw hell, what good are dey? Let her have 'em. Dey don't belong no more'n she does. *(With a gesture of sweeping the jewelers into oblivion)* All dat don't count, get me?

LONG. *(who has moved to the furrier's—indignantly)* And I s'pose this 'ere don't count neither—skins of poor, 'armless animals slaughtered so as 'er and 'ers can keep their bleedin' noses warm!

YANK. *(who has been staring at something inside—with queer excitement)* Take a slant at dat! Give it de once-over! Monkey fur—two t'ousand bucks! *(Bewilderedly)* Is dat straight goods—monkey fur? What de hell—?

LONG. *(bitterly)* It's straight enuf. *(With grim humor)* They wouldn't bloody well pay that for a 'airy ape's skin—no, nor for the 'ole livin' ape with all 'is 'ead, and a body, and soul thrown in!

YANK. *(clenching his fists, his face growing pale with rage as if the skin in the window were a personal insult)* Trowin' it up in my face! Christ! I'll fix her!

LONG. *(excitedly)* Church is out. 'Ere they come, the bleedin' swine. *(After a glance at* YANK'S *lowering face—uneasily)* Easy goes, Comrade. Keep yer bloomin' temper. Remember force defeats itself. It ain't our weapon. We must impress our demands through peaceful means—the votes of the on-marching proletarians of the bloody world!

YANK. *(with abysmal contempt)* Votes, hell! Votes is a joke, see. Votes for women! Let dem do it!

LONG. *(still more uneasily)* Calm, now. Treat 'em wiv the proper contempt. Observe the bleedin' parasites but 'old yer 'orses.

YANK. *(angrily)* Git away from me! Yuh're yellow, dat's what. Force, dat's me! De punch, dat's me every time, see! *(The crowd from church enter from the right, sauntering slowly and affectedly, their heads held stiffly up, looking neither to right nor left, talking in toneless, simpering voices. The women are rouged, calcimined,[37] dyed, overdressed to the nth degree. The men are in Prince Alberts[38] high hats, spats, canes, etc. A procession of gaudy marionettes, yet with something of the relentless horror of Frankensteins[39] in their detached, mechanical unawareness.)*

VOICES. Dear Doctor Caiphas![40] He is so sincere!

What was the sermon? I dozed off.

[35] "God blind me" (British slang).

[36] "Food" (slang).

[37] Made up with calcimine, a white liquid used as a wash for walls and ceilings.

[38] Long-tailed suit coats, very formal wear.

[39] *I.e.,* the Frankenstein monster.

[40] A possible allusion to Caiaphas, the Jewish high priest who presided over the council that condemned Jesus.

About the radicals, my dear—and the false doctrines that are being preached.
We must organize a hundred per cent American bazaar.
And let everyone contribute one one-hundredth per cent of their income tax.
What an original idea!
We can devote the proceeds to rehabilitating the veil of the temple.[41]
But that has been done so many times.

YANK. *(glaring from one to the other of them—with an insulting snort of scorn)* Huh! Huh! *(Without seeming to see him, they make wide detours to avoid the spot where he stands in the middle of the sidewalk.)*

LONG. *(frightenedly)* Keep yer bloomin' mouth shut, I tells yer.

YANK. *(viciously)* G'wan! Tell it to Sweeney! *(He swaggers away and deliberately lurches into a top-hatted gentleman, then glares at him pugnaciously)* Say, who d'yuh tink yuh're bumpin'? Tink yuh own de oith?

GENTLEMAN. *(coldly and affectedly)* I beg your pardon. *(He has not looked at* YANK *and passes on without a glance, leaving him bewildered.)*

LONG. *(rushing up and grabbing* YANK'S *arm)* 'Ere! Come away! This wasn't what I meant. Yer'll 'ave the bloody coppers down on us.

YANK. *(savagely—giving him a push that sends him sprawling)* G'wan!

LONG. *(picks himself up—hysterically)* I'll pop orf then. This ain't what I meant. And whatever 'appens, yer can't blame me. *(He slinks off left.)*

YANK. T' hell wit youse! *(He approaches a lady—with a vicious grin and smirking wink)* Hello, Kiddo. How's every little ting? Got anything on for tonight? I know an old boiler down to de docks we kin crawl into. *(The lady stalks by without a look, without a change of pace.* YANK *turns to others—insultingly)* Holy smokes, what a mug! Go hide yuhself before de horses shy at yuh. Gee, pipe de heine on dat one! Say, youse, yuh look like de stoin of a ferryboat. Paint and powder! All dolled up to kill! Yuh look like stiffs laid out for de boneyard! Aw, g'wan, de lot of youse! Yuh give me de eyeache. Yuh don't belong, get me! Look at me, why don't youse dare? I belong, dat's me! *(Pointing to a skyscraper across the street which is in process of construction—with bravado)* See dat building goin' up dere? See de steel work? Steel, dat's me! Youse guys live on it and tink yuh're somep'n. But I'm *in* it, see! I'm de hoistin' engine dat makes it go up! I'm it—de inside and bottom of it! Sure! I'm steel and steam and smoke and de rest of it! It moves—speed—twenty-five stories up—and me at de top and bottom—movin'! Youse simps don't move. Yuh're on'y dolls I winds up to see 'm spin. Yuh're de garbage, get me—de leavin's—de ashes we dump over de side! Now, what 'a' yuh gotta say? *(But as they seem neither to see nor hear him, he flies into a fury)* Bums! Pigs! Tarts! Bitches! *(He turns in a rage on the men, bumping viciously into them but not jarring them the least bit. Rather it is he who recoils after each collision. He keeps growling)* Git off de oith! G'wan, yuh bum! Look where yuh're goin', can't yuh? Git outa here! Fight, why don't yuh? Put up yer mits! Don't be a dog! Fight or I'll

[41]A curtain hung before the sanctuary of a church.

knock yuh dead! *(But, without seeming to see him, they all answer with mechanical affected politeness* "I beg your pardon." *Then at a cry from one of the women, they all scurry to the furrier's window.)*

THE WOMAN. *(ecstatically, with a gasp of delight)* Monkey fur! *(The whole crowd of men and women chorus after her in the same tone of affected delight* "Monkey fur!")

YANK. *(with a jerk of his head back on his shoulders, as if he had received a punch full in the face—raging)* I see yuh, all in white! I see yuh, yuh white-faced tart, yuh! Hairy ape, huh? I'll hairy ape yuh! *(He bends down and grips at the street curbing as if to pluck it out and hurl it. Foiled in this, snarling with passion, he leaps to the lamp-post on the corner and tries to pull it up for a club. Just at that moment a bus is heard rumbling up. A fat, high-hatted, spatted gentleman runs out from the side street. He calls out plaintively* "Bus! Bus! Stop there!" *and runs full tilt into the bending, straining* YANK, *who is bowled off his balance.)*

YANK. *(seeing a fight—with a roar of joy as he springs to his feet)* At last! Bus, huh? I'll bust yuh! *(He lets drive a terrific swing, his fist landing full on the fat gentleman's face. But the gentleman stands unmoved as if nothing had happened.)*

GENTLEMAN. I beg your pardon. *(Then irritably)* You have made me lose my bus. *(He claps his hands and begins to scream)* Officer! Officer! *(Many police whistles shrill out on the instant and a whole platoon of policemen rush in on* YANK *from all sides. He tries to fight but is clubbed to the pavement and fallen upon. The crowd at the window have not moved or noticed this disturbance. The clanging gong of the patrol wagon approaches with a clamoring din.)*

CURTAIN

Scene Six

Night of the following day. A row of cells in the prison on Blackwells Island.[42] *The cells extend back diagonally from right front to left rear. They do not stop, but disappear in the dark background as if they ran on, numberless, into infinity. One electric bulb from the low ceiling of the narrow corridor sheds its light through the heavy steel bars of the cell at the extreme front and reveals part of the interior.* YANK *can be seen within, crouched on the edge of his cot in the attitude of Rodin's "The Thinker." His face is spotted with black and blue bruises. A blood-stained bandage is wrapped around his head.*

YANK. *(suddenly starting as if awakening from a dream, reaches out and shakes the bars—aloud to himself, wonderingly)* Steel. Dis is de Zoo, huh? *(A burst of hard, barking laughter comes from the unseen occupants of the cells, runs back down the tier, and abruptly ceases.)*

VOICES. *(mockingly)* The Zoo? That's a new name for this coop—a damn good name!
Steel, eh? You said a mouthful. This is the old iron house.
Who is that boob talkin'?

[42]In New York City's East River; now Roosevelt Island.

He's the bloke they brung in out of his head. The bulls had beat him up fierce.

YANK. *(dully)* I musta been dreamin'. I tought I was in a cage at de Zoo—but de apes don't talk, do dey?

VOICES. *(with mocking laughter)* You're in a cage aw right.

A coop!

A pen!

A sty!

A kennel! *(Hard laughter—a pause.)*

Say, guy! Who are you? No, never mind lying. What are you?

Yes, tell us your sad story. What's your game?

What did they jug yuh for?

YANK. *(dully)* I was a fireman—stokin' on de liners. *(Then with sudden rage, rattling his cell bars)* I'm a hairy ape, get me? And I'll bust youse all in de jaw if yuh don't lay off kiddin' me.

VOICES. Huh! You're a hard boiled duck, ain't you!

When you spit, it bounces! *(Laughter.)*

Aw, can it. He's a regular guy. Ain't you?

What did he say he was—a ape?

YANK. *(defiantly)* Sure ting! Ain't dat what youse all are—apes? *(A silence. Then a furious rattling of bars from down the corridor.)*

A VOICE. *(thick with rage)* I'll show yuh who's a ape, yuh bum!

VOICES. Ssshh! Nix!

Can de noise!

Piano![43]

You'll have the guard down on us!

YANK. *(scornfully)* De guard? Yuh mean de keeper, don't yuh? *(Angry exclamations from all the cells.)*

VOICE. *(placatingly)* Aw, don't pay no attention to him. He's off his nut from the beatin'-up he got. Say, you guy! We're waitin' to hear what they landed you for—or ain't yuh tellin'?

YANK. Sure, I'll tell youse. Sure! Why de hell not? On'y—youse won't get me. Nobody gets me but me, see? I started to tell de Judge and all he says was: "'Toity days to tink it over."—Tink it over! Christ, dat's all I been doin' for weeks! *(After a pause)* I was trying' to git even wit someone, see?—someone dat done me doit.

VOICES. *(cynically)* De old stuff, I beg. Your goil, huh?

Give yuh the double-cross, huh?

That's them every time!

Did yuh beat up de odder guy?

YANK. *(disgustedly)* Aw, yuh're all wrong! Sure dere was a skoit in it—but not what youse mean, not dat old tripe. Dis was a new kind of skoit. She was dolled up all in white—in de stokehole. I tought she was a ghost. Sure. *(A pause.)*

VOICES. *(whispering)* Gee, he's still nutty.

Let him rave. It's fun listenin'.

[43]"Softly" (Italian).

YANK. *(unheeding—groping in his thoughts)* Her hands—dey was skinny and white like dey wasn't real but painted on somep'n. Dere was a million miles from me to her—twenty-five knots a hour. She was like some dead ting de cat brung in. Sure, dat's what. She didn't belong. She belonged in de window of a toy store, or on de top of a garbage can, see! Sure! *(He breaks out angrily)* But would yuh believe it, she had de noive to do me doit. She lamped[44] me like she was seein' somep'n broke loose from de menagerie. Christ, yuh'd oughter seen her eyes! *(He rattles the bars of his cell furiously)* But I'll get back at her yet, you watch! And if I can't find her I'll take it out on de gang she runs wit. I'm wise to where dey hangs out now. I'll show her who belongs! I'll show her who's in de move and who ain't. You watch my smoke!

VOICES. *(serious and joking)* Dat's de talkin'!
Take her for all she's got!
What was this dame, anyway? Who was she, eh?

YANK. I dunno. First cabin stiff. Her old man's a millionaire, dey says—name of Douglas.

VOICES. Douglas? That's the president of the Steel Trust, I bet.
Sure. I seen his mug in de papers.
He's filthy with dough.

VOICE. Hey, feller, take a tip from me. If you want to get back at that dame, you better join the Wobblies. You'll get some action then.

YANK. Wobblies? What de hell's dat?

VOICE. Ain't you ever heard of the I.W.W.?[45]

YANK. Naw. What is it?

VOICE. A gang of blokes—a tough gang. I been readin' about 'em today in the paper. The guard give me the *Sunday Times.* There's a long spiel about 'em. It's from a speech made in the Senate by a guy named Senator Queen. *(He is in the cell next to* YANK'S. *There is a rustling of paper)* Wait'll I see if I got light enough and I'll read you. Listen. *(He reads)* "There is a menace existing in this country today which threatens the vitals of our fair Republic—as foul a menace against the very life-blood of the American Eagle as was the foul conspiracy of Catiline[46] against the eagles of ancient Rome!"

VOICE. *(disgustedly)* Aw, hell! Tell him to salt de tail of dat eagle!

VOICE. *(reading)* "I refer to that devil's brew of rascals, jailbirds, murderers and cutthroats who libel all honest working men by calling themselves the Industrial Workers of the World; but in the light of their nefarious plots, I call them the Industrious *Wreckers* of the World!"

YANK. *(with vengeful satisfaction)* Wreckers, dat's de right dope! Dat belongs! Me for dem!

VOICE. Ssshh! *(Reading)* "This fiendish organization is a foul ulcer on the fair body of our Democracy—"

[44]"Looked at" (slang).
[45]Industrial Workers of the World, a radical socialist/anarchist group whose members were called "Wobblies."
[46]Roman revolutionary (108–62 B.C.).

VOICE. Democracy, hell! Give him the boid, fellers—the raspberry! *(They do.)*

VOICE. Ssshh! *(Reading)* "Like Cato[47] I say to this Senate, the I.W.W. must be destroyed! For they represent an ever-present dagger pointed at the heart of the greatest nation the world has ever known, where all men are born free and equal, with equal opportunities to all, where the Founding Fathers have guaranteed to each one happiness, where Truth, Honor, Liberty, Justice, and the Brotherhood of Man are a religion absorbed with one's mother's milk, taught at our father's knee, sealed, signed, and stamped upon in the glorious Constitution of these United States!" *(A perfect storm of hisses, catcalls, boos, and hard laughter.)*

VOICES. *(scornfully)* Hurrah for de Fort' of July!
Pass de hat!
Liberty!
Justice!
Honor!
Opportunity!
Brotherhood!

ALL. *(with abysmal scorn)* Aw, hell!

VOICE. Give that Queen Senator guy the bark! All togedder now—one—two—tree—*(A terrific chorus of barking and yapping.)*

GUARD. *(from a distance)* Quiet there, youse—or I'll git the hose. *(The noise subsides.)*

YANK. *(with growling rage)* I'd like to catch dat senator guy alone for a second. I'd loin him some trute!

VOICE. Ssshh! Here's where he gits down to cases on the Wobblies. *(Reads)* "They plot with fire in one hand and dynamite in the other. They stop not before murder to gain their ends, nor at the outraging of defenseless womanhood. They would tear down society, put the lowest scum in the seats of the mighty, turn Almighty God's revealed plan for the world topsy-turvy, and make of our sweet and lovely civilization a shambles, a desolation where man, God's masterpiece, would soon degenerate back to the ape!"

VOICE. *(to YANK)* Hey, you guy. There's your ape stuff again.

YANK. *(with a growl of fury)* I got him. So dey blow up tings, do dey? Dey turn tings round, do dey? Hey, lend me dat paper, will yuh?

VOICE. Sure. Give it to him. On'y keep it to yourself, see. We don't wanter listen to no more of that slop.

VOICE. Here you are. Hide it under your mattress.

YANK. *(reaching out)* Tanks. I can't read much but I kin manage. *(He sits, the paper in the hand at his side, in the attitude of Rodin's "The Thinker." A pause. Several snores from down the corridor. Suddenly* YANK *jumps to his feet with a furious groan as if some appalling thought had crashed on him—bewilderedly)* Sure—her old man—president of de Steel Trust—makes half de steel in de world—steel—where I tought I belonged—drivin' trou—movin'—in dat—to make *her*—and cage me in for her to spit on! Christ! *(He shakes the bars of his cell door till the whole tier trem-*

[47]Roman senator (234–189 B.C.) who argued for the destruction of Rome's enemy, Carthage.

bles. Irritated, protesting exclamations from those awakened or trying to get to sleep) He made dis—dis cage! Steel! *It* don't belong, dat's what! Cages, cells, locks, bolts, bars—dat's what it means!—holdin' me down wit him at de top! But I'll drive trou! Fire, dat melts it! I'll be fire—under de heap—fire dat never goes out—hot as hell—breakin' out in de night—*(While he has been saying this last he has shaken his cell door to a clanging accompaniment. As he comes to the "breakin' out" he seizes one bar with both hands and, putting his two feet up against the others so that his position is parallel to the floor like a monkey's, he gives a great wrench backwards. The bar bends like a licorice stick under his tremendous strength. Just at this moment the* PRISON GUARD *rushes in, dragging a hose behind him.)*

GUARD. *(angrily)* I'll loin youse bums to wake me up! *(Sees* YANK*)* Hello, it's you, huh? Got the D.T.'s[48] hey? Well, I'll cure 'em. I'll drown your snakes for yuh! *(Noticing the bar)* Hell, look at dat bar bended! On'y a bug is strong enough for dat!

YANK. *(glaring at him)* Or a hairy ape, yuh big yellow bum! Look out! Here I come! *(He grabs another bar.)*

GUARD. *(scared now—yelling off left)* Toin de hose on, Ben!—full pressure! And call de others—and a straitjacket! *(The curtain is falling. As it hides* YANK *from view, there is a splattering smash as the steam of water hits the steel of* YANK'S *cell.)*

CURTAIN

Scene Seven

Nearly a month later. An I.W.W. local near the waterfront, showing the interior of a front room on the ground floor, and the street outside. Moonlight on the narrow street, buildings massed in black shadow. The interior of the room, which is general assembly room, office, and reading room, resembles some dingy settlement boys' club. A desk and high stool are in one corner. A table with papers, stacks of pamphlets, chairs about it, is at center. The whole is decidedly cheap, banal, commonplace and unmysterious as a room could well be. The SECRETARY *is perched on the stool making entries in a large ledger. An eye shade casts his face into shadows. Eight or ten men, longshoremen, iron workers, and the like, are grouped about the table. Two are playing checkers. One is writing a letter. Most of them are smoking pipes. A big signboard is on the wall at the rear, "Industrial Workers of the World—Local No. 57."*

YANK *comes down the street outside. He is dressed as in Scene Five. He moves cautiously, mysteriously. He comes to a point opposite the door; tiptoes softly up to it, listens, is impressed by the silence within, knocks carefully, as if he were guessing at the password to some secret rite. Listens. No answer. Knocks again a bit louder. No answer. Knocks impatiently, much louder.*

SECRETARY. *(turning around on his stool)* What the hell is that—someone knocking? *(Shouts)* Come in, why don't you? *(All the men in the room look up.* YANK *opens the door slowly, gingerly, as if afraid of an ambush. He looks around for secret doors, mystery, is taken aback by the commonplaceness of the room and the men in it,*

[48] Delirium tremens.

thinks he may have gotten in the wrong place, then sees the signboard on the wall and is reassured.)

YANK. *(blurts out)* Hello.

MAN. *(reservedly)* Hello.

YANK. *(more easily)* I thought I'd bumped into de wrong dump.

SECRETARY. *(scrutinizing him carefully)* Maybe you have. Are you a member?

YANK. Naw, not yet. Dat's what I come for—to join.

SECRETARY. That's easy. What's your job—longshore?

YANK. Naw. Fireman—stoker on de liners.

SECRETARY. *(with satisfaction)* Welcome to our city. Glad to know you people are waking up at last. We haven't got many members in your line.

YANK. Naw. Dey're all dead to de woild.

SECRETARY. Well, you can help to wake 'em. What's your name? I'll make out your card.

YANK. *(confused)* Name? Lemme tink.

SECRETARY. *(sharply)* Don't you know your own name?

YANK. Sure; but I been just Yank for so long—Bob, dat's it—Bob Smith.

SECRETARY. *(writing)* Robert Smith. *(Fills out the rest of the card)* Here you are. Cost you half a dollar.

YANK. Is dat all—four bits? Dat's easy. *(Gives the* SECRETARY *the money.)*

SECRETARY. *(throwing it in drawer)* Thanks. Well, make yourself at home. No introductions needed. There's literature on the table. Take some of those pamphlets with you to distribute aboard ship. They may bring results. Sow the seed, only go about it right. Don't get caught and fired. We got plenty out of work. What we need is men who can hold their jobs—and work for us at the same time.

YANK. Sure. *(But he still stands, embarrassed and uneasy.)*

SECRETARY. *(looking at him—curiously)* What did you knock for? Think we had a coon[49] in uniform to open doors?

YANK. Naw, I tought it was locked—and dat yuh'd wanter give me the once-over trou a peep-hole or somep'n to see if I was right.

SECRETARY. *(alert and suspicious but with an easy laugh)* Think we were running a crap game? That door is never locked. What put that in your nut?

YANK. *(with a knowing grin, convinced that this is all camouflage, a part of the secrecy)* Dis burg is full of bulls, ain't it?

SECRETARY. *(sharply)* What have the cops got to do with us? We're breaking no laws.

YANK. *(with a knowing wink)* Sure. Youse wouldn't for woilds. Sure. I'm wise to dat.

SECRETARY. You seem to be wise to a lot of stuff none of us knows about.

YANK. *(with another wink)* Aw, dat's aw right, see. *(Then made a bit resentful by the suspicious glances from all sides)* Aw, can it! Youse needn't put me trou de toid degree. Can't youse see I belong? Sure! I'm reg'lar. I'll stick, get me? I'll shoot de woiks for youse. Dat's why I wanted to join in.

SECRETARY. *(breezily, feeling him out)* That's the right spirit. Only are you sure you understand what you've joined? It's all plain and above board; still, some guys get a wrong slant on us. *(Sharply)* What's your notion of the purpose of the I.W.W.?

[49]Negro (slang).

YANK. Aw, I know all about it.
SECRETARY. *(sarcastically)* Well, give us some of your valuable information.
YANK. *(cunningly)* I know enough not to speak outa my toin. *(Then resentfully again)* Aw, say! I'm reg'lar. I'm wise to de game. I know yuh got to watch your step wit a stranger. For all youse know, I might be a plain-clothes dick, or somep'n, dat's what yuh're tinkin', huh? Aw, forget it! I belong, see? Ask any guy down to de docks if I don't.
SECRETARY. Who said you didn't?
YANK. After I'm 'nitiated, I'll show yuh.
SECRETARY. *(astounded)* Initiated? There's no initiation.
YANK. *(disappointed)* Ain't there no password—no grip nor nothin'?
SECRETARY. What'd you think this is—the Elks—or the Black Hand?[50]
YANK. De Elks, hell! De Black Hand, dey're a lot of yellow back stickin' Ginees.[51] Naw. Dis is a man's gang, ain't it?
SECRETARY. You said it! That's why we stand on our two feet in the open. We got no secrets.
YANK. *(surprised but admiringly)* Yuh mean to say yuh always run wide open—like dis?
SECRETARY. Exactly.
YANK. Den yuh sure got your noive wit youse!
SECRETARY. *(sharply)* Just what was it made you want to join us? Come out with that straight.
YANK. Yuh call me? Well, I got noive, too! Here's my hand. Yuh wanter blow tings up, don't yuh? Well, dat's me! I belong!
SECRETARY. *(with pretended carelessness)* You mean change the unequal conditions of society by legitimate direct action—or with dynamite?
YANK. Dynamite! Blow it offen de oith—steel—all de cages—all de factories, steamers, buildings, jails—de Steel Trust and all dat makes it go.
SECRETARY. So—that's your idea, eh? And did you have any special job in that line you wanted to propose to us? *(He makes a sign to the men, who get up cautiously one by one and group behind* YANK.*)*
YANK. *(boldly)* Sure, I'll come out wit it. I'll show youse I'm one of de gang. Dere's dat millionaire guy, Douglas—
SECRETARY. President of the Steel Trust, you mean? Do you want to assassinate him?
YANK. Naw, dat don't get yuh nothin'. I mean blow up de factory, de woiks, where he makes de steel. Dat's what I'm after—to blow up de steel, knock all de steel in de woild up to de moon. Dat'll fix tings! *(Eagerly, with a touch of bravado)* I'll do it by me lonesome! I'll show yuh! Tell me where his woiks is, how to git there, all de dope. Gimme de stuff, de old butter—and watch me do de rest! Watch de smoke and see it move! I don't give a damn if dey nab me—long as it's done! I'll soive life for it—And give 'em de laugh! *(Half to himself)* And I'll write her a letter and tell her de hairy ape done it. Dat'll square tings.
SECRETARY. *(stepping away from* YANK*)* Very interesting. *(He gives a signal. The men,*

[50] A secret Sicilian terrorist group active in the United States in the early years of the twentieth century.

[51] "Guineas" (slang for "Italians").

huskies all, throw themselves on YANK *and before he knows it they have his legs and arms pinioned. But he is too flabbergasted to make a struggle, anyway. They feel him over for weapons.)*

MAN. No gat, no knife. Shall we give him what's what and put the boots to him?

SECRETARY. No. He isn't worth the trouble we'd get into. He's too stupid. *(He comes closer and laughs mockingly in* YANK'S *face)* Ho-ho! By God, this is the biggest joke they've put up on us yet. Hey, you Joke! Who sent you—Burns or Pinkerton?[52] No, by God, you're such a bonehead I'll bet you're in the Secret Service! Well, you dirty spy, you rotten agent provocator, you can go back and tell whatever skunk is paying you blood-money for betraying your brothers that he's wasting his coin. You couldn't catch a cold. And tell him that all he'll ever get on us, or ever has got, is just his own sneaking plots that he's framed up to put us in jail. We are what our manifesto says we are, neither more nor less—and we'll give him a copy of that any time he calls. And as for you—*(He glares scornfully at* YANK, *who is sunk in an oblivious stupor)* Oh, hell, what's the use of talking? You're a brainless ape.

YANK. *(aroused by the word to fierce but futile struggles)* What's dat, you Sheeny[53] bum, yuh!

SECRETARY. Throw him out, boys. *(In spite of his struggles, this is done with gusto and éclat. Propelled by several parting kicks,* YANK *lands sprawling in the middle of the narrow cobbled street. With a growl he starts to get up and storm the closed door, but stops bewildered by the confusion in his brain, pathetically impotent. He sits there, brooding, in as near to the attitude of Rodin's "The Thinker" as he can get in his position.)*

YANK. *(bitterly)* So dem boids don't tink I belong, neider. Aw, to hell wit 'em! Dey're in de wrong pew—de same old bull—soap-boxes and Salvation Army—no guts! Cut out an hour offen de job a day and make me happy! Gimme a dollar more a day and make me happy! Tree square a day, and cauliflowers in de front yard—ekal rights—a woman and kids—a lousy vote—and I'm all fixed for Jesus, huh? Aw, hell! What does dat get yuh? Dis ting's in your inside, but it ain't your belly. Feedin' your face—sinkers and coffee—dat don't touch it. It's way down—at de bottom. Yuh can't grab it, and yuh can't stop it. It moves, and everything moves. It stops and de whole woild stops. Dat's me now—I don't tick, see?—I'm a busted Ingersoll,[54] dat's what. Steel was me, and I owned de woild. Now I ain't steel, and de woild owns me. Aw, hell! I can't see—it's all dark, get me? It's all wrong! *(He turns a bitter mocking face up like an ape gibbering at the moon)* Say, youse up dere, Man in de Moon, yuh look so wise, gimme de answer, huh? Slip me de inside dope, de information right from de stable—where do I get off at, huh?

A POLICEMAN. *(who has come up the street in time to hear this last—with grim humor)* You'll get off at the station, you boob, if you don't get up out of that and keep movin'.

YANK. *(looking up at him—with a hard, bitter laugh)* Sure! Lock me up! Put me in a cage! Dat's de on'y answer yuh know. G'wan, lock me up!

POLICEMAN. What you been doin'?

YANK. Enuf to gimme life for! I was born, see? Sure, dat's de charge. Write it in de blotter. I was born, get me!

[52]Famous detective agencies of the time.
[53]Jewish (slang).
[54]A popular watch brand of the time.

POLICEMAN. *(jocosely)* God pity your old woman! *(Then matter-of-factly)* But I've no time for kidding. You're soused. I'd run you in but it's too long a walk to the station. Come on now, get up, or I'll fan your ears with this club. Beat it now! *(He hauls* YANK *to his feet.)*

YANK. *(in a vague mocking tone)* Say, where do I go from here?

POLICEMAN. *(giving him a push—with a grin, indifferently)* Go to hell.

CURTAIN

Scene Eight

Twilight of the next day. The monkey house at the Zoo. One spot of clear gray light falls on the front of one cage so that the interior can be seen. The other cages are vague, shrouded in shadow from which chatterings pitched in a conversational tone can be heard. On the one cage a sign from which the word "gorilla" stands out. The gigantic animal himself is seen squatting on his haunches on a bench in much the same attitude as Rodin's "The Thinker." YANK *enters from the left. Immediately a chorus of angry chattering and screeching breaks out. The gorilla turns his eyes but makes no sound or move.*

YANK. *(with a hard, bitter laugh)* Welcome to your city, huh? Hail, hail, de gang's all here! *(At the sound of his voice the chattering dies away into an attentive silence.* YANK *walks up to the gorilla's cage and, leaning over the railing, stares in at its occupant, who stares back at him, silent and motionless. There is a pause of dead stillness. Then* YANK *begins to talk in a friendly confidential tone, half mockingly, but with a deep undercurrent of sympathy)* Say, yuh're some hard-lookin' guy, ain't yuh? I seen lots of tough nuts dat de gang called gorillas, but yuh're de foist real one I ever seen. Some chest yuh got, and shoulders, and dem arms and mits! I bet yuh got a punch in eider fist dat'd knock 'em all silly! *(This with genuine admiration. The gorilla, as if he understood, stands upright, swelling out his chest and pounding on it with fist.* YANK *grins sympathetically)* Sure, I get yuh. Yuh challenge de whole woild, huh? Yuh got what I was sayin' even if yuh muffed de woids. *(Then bitterness creeping in)* And why wouldn't yuh get me? Ain't we both members of de same club—de Hairy Apes? *(They stare at each other—a pause—then* YANK *goes on slowly and bitterly.)* So yuh're what she seen when she looked at me, de white-faced tart! I was you to her, get me? On'y outa de cage—broke out—free to moider her, see? Sure! Dat's what she tought. She wasn't wise dat I was in a cage, too—worser'n yours—sure—a damn sight—'cause you got some chanct to bust loose—but me—*(He grows confused)* Aw, hell! It's all wrong, ain't it? *(A pause)* I s'pose yuh wanter know what I'm doin' here, huh? I been warmin' a bench down to de Battery[55]—ever since last night. Sure. I seen de sun come up. Dat was pretty, too—all red and pink and green. I was lookin' at de skycrapers—

[55]A park on the southern end of Manhattan where artillery was mounted during colonial and revolutionary times.

steel—and all de ships comin' in, sailin' out, all over de oith—and dey was steel, too. De sun was warm, dey wasn't no clouds, and dere was a breeze blowin'. Sure, it was great stuff. I got it aw right—what Paddy said about dat bein' de right dope—on'y I couldn't get *in* it, see? I couldn't belong in dat. It was over my head. And I kept tinkin'—and den I beat it up here to see what youse was like. And I waited till dey was all gone to git yuh alone. Say, how d'yuh feel sittin' in dat pen all de time, havin' to stand for 'em comin' and starin' at yuh—de white-faced, skinny tarts and de boobs what marry 'em—makin' fun of yuh, laughin' at yuh, gittin' scared of yuh—damn 'em! *(He pounds on the rail with his fist. The gorilla rattles the bars of his cage and snarls. All the other monkeys set up an angry chattering in the darkness.* YANK *goes on excitedly)* Sure! Dat's de way it hits me, too. On'y yuh're lucky, see? Yuh don't belong wit 'em and yuh know it. But me, I belong wit 'em—but I don't, see? Dey don't belong wit me, dat's what. Get me? Tinkin' is hard—*(He passes one hand across his forehead with a painful gesture. The gorilla growls impatiently.* YANK *goes on gropingly)* It's dis way, what I'm drivin' at. Youse can sit and dope dream in de past, green woods, de jungle and de rest of it. Den yuh belong and dey don't. Den yuh kin laugh at 'em, see? Yuh're de champ of de world. But me—I ain't got no past to tink in, nor nothin' dat's comin', on'y what's now—and dat don't belong. Sure, you're de best off! You can't tink, can yuh? Yuh can't talk neider. But I kin make a bluff at talkin' and tinkin'—a'most git away wit it—a'most!—and dat's where de joker comes in. *(He laughs)* I ain't on oith and I ain't in heaven, get me? I'm in de middle tryin' to separate 'em, takin' all de woist punches from bot' of 'em. Maybe dat's what dey call hell, huh? But you, yuh're at de bottom. You belong! Sure! Yuh're de on'y one in de woild dat does, yuh lucky stiff! *(The gorilla growls proudly)* And dat's why dey gotter put yuh in a cage, see? *(The gorilla roars angrily)* Sure! Yuh get me. It beats it when you try to tink it or talk it—it's way down—deep—behind—you 'n' me we feel it. Sure! Bot' members of dis club! *(He laughs—then in a savage tone)* What de hell! T' hell wit it! A little action, dat's our meat! Dat belongs! Knock 'em down and keep bustin' 'em till dey croaks yuh wit a gat—wit steel! Sure! Are yuh game? Dey've looked at youse, ain't dey—in a cage? Wanter git even? Wanter wind up like a sport 'stead of croakin' slow in dere? *(The gorilla roars an emphatic affirmative.* YANK *goes on with a sort of furious exaltation)* Sure! Yuh're reg'lar! Yuh'll stick to de finish! Me 'n' you, huh?—bot' members of dis club! We'll put up one last star bout dat'll knock 'em offen deir seats! Dey'll have to make de cages stronger after we're trou! *(The gorilla is straining at his bars, growling, hopping from one foot to the other.* YANK *takes a jimmy from under his coat and forces the lock on the cage door. He throws this open)* Pardon from de governor! Step out and shake hands. I'll take yuh for a walk down Fif' Avenoo. We'll knock 'em offen de oith and croak wit de band playin'. Come on, Brother. *(The gorilla scrambles gingerly out of his cage. Goes to* YANK *and stands looking at him.* YANK *keeps his mocking tone—holds out his hand)* Shake—de secret grip of our order. *(Something, the tone of mockery, perhaps, suddenly enrages the animal. With a spring he wraps his huge arms around* YANK *in a murderous hug. There is a crackling snap of crushed ribs—a gasping cry, still mocking, from* YANK*)* Hey, I didn't say kiss me! *(The gorilla lets the crushed body slip to the floor; stands over it uncertainly, considering; then picks it up, throws it in the* *cage, shuts the door, and shuffles off menacingly into the darkness at left. A great uproar of frightened chattering and whimpering comes from the other cages. Then* YANK *moves, groaning, opening his eyes, and there is silence. He mutters painfully)*

Say—dey oughter match him—with Zybszko.[56] He got me, aw right, I'm trou. Even him didn't tink I belonged. *(Then, with sudden passionate despair)* Christ, where do I get off at? Where do I fit in? *(Checking himself as suddenly)* Aw, what de hell! No squawkin', see! No quittin', get me! Croak wit your boots on! *(He grabs hold of the bars of the cage and hauls himself painfully to his feet—looks around him bewilderedly—forces a mocking laugh)* In de cage? huh? *(In the strident tones of a circus barker)* Ladies and gents, step forward and take a slant at de one and only— *(His voice weakening)* one and original—Hairy Ape from de wilds of— *(He slips in a heap on the floor and dies. The monkeys set up a chattering, whimpering wail. And, perhaps, the Hairy Ape at last belongs.)*

CURTAIN

1922

Djuna Barnes 1892–1982

Barnes was born in Cornwall-on-Hudson in New York State. Her family was artistic, eccentric, and strong-willed. One grandmother had been a suffragette. However, the family was also psychologically murderous, the father a philanderer. As a child, Barnes was possibly sexually abused. Her best-selling novel, *Ryder* (1928), and her verse drama, *The Antiphon* (1958), re-enact her family's freedom, license, and trauma.

Barnes became a stylish, self-created, self-supporting New Woman. From 1913 to 1919, she lived in New York. Bisexual, she traveled in bohemian and avant-garde circles. Red-haired, she was a vital presence and vivid wit. Sometimes using the pseudonym, "Lydia Steptoe," as she stepped on toes, she earned her living and helped to support her family as a journalist and illustrator. She also wrote stories and plays.

During the 1920s and 1930s, Barnes moved to Europe, finding a home in Paris, Berlin, and England. She bought her bread through free-lance writing and, once again, she was a part of bohemian, avant-garde, and now lesbian groups. Her rollicking *Ladies Almanack* (1928) pungently satirizes and celebrates the women around Natalie Barney, a lesbian leader in Paris. Her best-known novel, *Nightwood* (1936), transforms her long affair with Thelma Wood, a sculptor, into a profound study of women's relationships, and Thelma into Robin Vote, a figure of the night. Her talent respected, Barnes befriended major modernists. Among them were James Joyce, T. S. Eliot, Mina Loy, and Samuel Beckett, whose mordancy and ironic play often resemble hers.

World War II forced Barnes to return to the United States. In 1941, she moved to a tiny apartment on Patchin Place in Greenwich Village. She had such friends, helpers, and admirers as Marianne Moore and Dag Hammarskjold, then the Secretary General of the United Nations. In

[56] Stanislaus Zbyszko, famous wrestler during the 1920s.

1959, she was inducted into the American Academy of Arts and Letters. Once a heavy drinker, she wisely gave up alcohol. Yet, she was poor, ill, and reclusive. The famous red hair turned white and thin, and, when heard, the Barnes wit was frequently vicious and prejudiced. She wrote, but rarely published, and in 1982, sick of being old and alone, Barnes died.

An ambitious writer, Barnes explores many of the huge themes and trials of modern Western culture: the family as a crucible of identity; the nature of sexuality, sexual difference, and a "third sex" that reconciles femininity and masculinity; the abuses of power; the repetitions and pressures of history; the fragility of language. She named a poem, "Quarry" (1969), as her epitaph. It imagines time in a "tongued-tied tree." She attends to the outsider, the exile, the grotesque figure, and often represents her century as a carnival, burlesque, or circus. Obsessed with a conflict between the ridiculous corruptions of the body and the severe weaknesses of the spirit, she finds us midway between redemption and damnation, ascending towards salvation, descending into the darkness of the unconscious and doom. The last scene in *Nightwood* shows Robin, on the floor of a chapel in the woods, a dog beside her: "dog" is the inverse of "God."

Although erratically educated, Barnes learned from literary history. She commands a repertoire of genres, from the picaresque novel to the lyric poem, and styles, from raunchy humor to metaphysical speculation. Her writing can be archaic, allusive, dense, aphoristic, metaphorical. However, "Smoke," first published in a New York newspaper in 1917, shows a young, lean, austere writer who knows how to tell about the extraordinary in the ordinary. The story is about a family, the site of cruelty and comfort, creativity and frustration. This family winds down. Its iron rusts. Babies die; mothers die in childbirth. Like writers, physicians cannot save lives. At best, they mourn and joke.

Catharine R. Stimpson
New York University

PRIMARY WORKS

The Book of Repulsive Women, 1915; *A Book,* 1923, reprinted as *A Night Among The Horses,* 1929; *Ladies Almanack,* 1928, 1972; *Ryder,* 1928, 1979; *Nightwood,* 1936; *The Antiphon,* 1958; *Selected Works,* 1962; *Smoke and Other Early Stories,* ed. Douglas Messerli, 1982; *Interviews,* ed. Alyce Barry, 1985.

Smoke

There was Swart with his bushy head and Fenken with the half shut eyes and the grayish beard, and there also was Zelka with her big earrings and her closely bound inky hair, who had often been told that "she was very beautiful in a black way."

Ah, what a fine strong creature she had been, and what a fine strong creature her father, Fenken, had been before her, and what a specimen was her husband, Swart, with his gentle melancholy mouth and his strange strong eyes and his brown neck.

Fenken in his youth had loaded the cattle boats, and in his twilight of age he would sit in the round-backed chair by the open fireplace, his two trembling hands folded, and would talk of what he had been.

"A bony man I was, Zelka—my two knees as hard as a pavement, so that I clapped them with great discomfort to my own hands. Sometimes," he would add, with a twinkle in his old eyes, "I'd put you between them and my hand. It hurt less."

Zelka would turn her eyes on him slowly—they moved around into sight from under her eyebrows like the barrel of a well-kept gun; they were hard like metal and strong, and she was always conscious of them even in sleep. When she would close her eyes before saying her prayers, she would remark to Swart, "I draw the hood over the artillery." And Swart would smile, nodding his large head.

In the town these three were called the "Bullets"—when they came down the street, little children sprang aside, not because they were afraid, but because they came so fast and brought with them something so healthy, something so potent, something unconquerable. Fenken could make his fingers snap against his palm like the crack of a cabby's whip just by shutting his hand abruptly, and he did this often, watching the gamin and smiling.

Swart, too, had his power, but there was a hint at something softer in him, something that made the lips kind when they were sternest, something that gave him a sad expression when he was thinking—something that had drawn Zelka to him in their first days of courting. "We Fenkens," she would say, "have iron in our veins—in yours I fear there's a little blood."

Zelka was cleanly. She washed her linen clean as though she were punishing the dirt. Had the linen been less durable there would have been holes in it from her knuckles in a six months. Everything Zelka cooked was tender—she had bruised it with her preparations.

And then Zelka's baby had come. A healthy, fat, little crying thing, with eyes like its father's and with its father's mouth. In vain did Zelka look for something about it that would give it away as one of the Fenken blood—it had a maddeningly tender way of stroking her face; its hair was finer than blown gold; and it squinted up its pale blue eyes when it fell over its nose. Sometimes Zelka would turn the baby around in bed, placing its little feet against her side, waiting for it to kick. And when it finally did, it was gently and without great strength and with much good humor. "Swart," Zelka would say, "your child is entirely human. I'm afraid all his veins run blood." And she would add to her father, "Sonny will never load the cattle ships."

When it was old enough to crawl, Zelka would get down on hands and knees and chase it about the little ash-littered room. The baby would crawl ahead of her, giggling and driving Zelka mad with a desire to stop and hug him. But when she roared behind him like a lion to make him hurry, the baby would roll over slowly, struggle into a sitting posture, and, putting his hand up, would sit staring at her as though he would like to study out something that made this difference between them.

When it was seven, it would escape from the house and wander down to the shore, and stand for hours watching the boats coming in, being loaded and unloaded. Once one of the men put the cattle belt about him and lowered him into the boat. He went down sadly, his little golden head drooping and his feet hanging down. When they brought him back on shore again and dusted him off they were puzzled at him—he had neither cried nor laughed. They said, "Didn't you like that?" And he had only answered by looking at them fixedly.

And when he grew up he was very tender to his mother, who had taken to shaking her head over him. Fenken had died the Summer of his grandchild's thirtieth year, so that after the funeral Swart had taken the round-backed chair for his own. And now he sat there with folded hands, but he never said what a strong lad he had been. Sometimes he would say, "Do you remember how Fenken used to snap his fingers together like a whip?" And Zelka would answer, "I do."

And finally, when her son married, Zelka was seen at the feast dressed in a short blue skirt, leaning upon Swart's arm, both of them still strong and handsome and capable of lifting the buckets of cider.

Zelka's son had chosen a strange woman for a wife: a little thin thing, with a tiny waistline and a narrow chest and a small, very lovely throat. She was the daughter of a ship owner and had a good deal of money in her name. When she married Zelka's son, she brought him some ten thousand a year. And so he stopped the shipping of cattle and went in for exports and imports of Oriental silks and perfumes.

When his mother and father died, he moved a little inland away from the sea and hired clerks to do his bidding. Still, he never forgot what his mother had said to him: "There must always be a little iron in the blood, sonny."

He reflected on this when he looked at Lief, his wife. He was a silent, taciturn man as he grew older, and Lief had grown afraid of him, because of his very kindness and his melancholy.

There was only one person to whom he was a bit stern, and this was his daughter, "Little Lief." Toward her he showed a strange hostility, a touch even of that fierceness that had been his mother's. Once she had rushed shrieking from his room because he had suddenly roared behind her as his mother had done behind him. When she was gone, he sat for a long time by his table, his hands stretched out in front of him, thinking.

He had succeeded well. He had multiplied his wife's money now into the many thousands—they had a house in the country and servants. They were spoken of in the town as a couple who had an existence that might be termed as "pretty soft"; and when the carriage drove by of a Sunday with baby Lief up front on her mother's lap and Lief's husband beside her in his gray cloth coat, they stood aside not to be trampled on by the swift legged, slender ankled "pacer" that Lief had bought that day when she had visited the "old home"—the beach that had known her and her husband when they were children. This horse was the very one that she had asked for when she saw how beautiful it was as they fastened the belt to it preparatory to lowering it over the side. It was then that she remembered how, when her husband had been a little boy, they had lowered him over into the boat with this same belting.

During the Winter that followed, which was a very hard one, Lief took cold and resorted to hot water bottles and thin tea. She became very fretful and annoyed at her husband's constant questionings as to her health. Even Little Lief was a nuisance because she was so noisy. She would steal into the room, and, crawling under her mother's bed, would begin to sing in a high, thin treble, pushing the ticking with her patent leather boots to see them crinkle. Then the mother would cry out, the nurse would run in and take her away, and Lief would spend a half hour in tears. Finally they would not allow Little Lief in the room, so she would steal by the door many times, walking noiselessly up and down the hall. But finally, her youth overcoming her, she would stretch her legs out into a straight goose step, and for this she was whipped because on the day that she had been caught, her mother had died.

And so the time passed and the years rolled on, taking their toll. It was now many Summers since that day that Zelka had walked into town with Swart—now many years since Fenken had snapped his fingers like a cabby's whip. Little Lief had never even heard that her grandmother had been called a "beautiful woman in a black sort of way," and she had only vaguely heard of the nickname that had once been given the family, the "Bullets." She came to know that great strength had once been in the family, to such an extent, indeed, that somehow a phrase was known to her, "Remember always to keep a little iron in the blood." And one night she had pricked her arm to see if there were iron in it, and she had cried because it hurt. And so she knew that there was none.

With her this phrase ended. She never repeated it because of that night when she had made that discovery.

Her father had taken to solitude and the study of sociology. Sometimes he would turn her about by the shoulder and look at her, breathing in a thick way he had with him of late. And once he told her she was a good girl but foolish, and left her alone.

They had begun to lose money, and some of Little Lief's tapestries, given her by her mother, were sold. Her heart broke, but she opened the windows oftener because she needed some kind of beauty. She made the mistake of loving tapestries best and nature second best. Somehow she had gotten the two things mixed—of course, it was due to her bringing up. "If you are poor, you live out-of-doors; but if you are rich, you live in a lovely house." So to her the greatest of calamities had befallen the house. It was beginning to go away by those imperceptible means that at first leave a house looking unfamiliar and then bare.

Finally she could stand it no longer and she married a thin, wiry man with a long, thin nose and a nasty trick of rubbing it with a finger equally long and thin—a man with a fair income and very refined sisters.

This man, Misha, wanted to be a lawyer. He studied half the night and never seemed happy unless his head was in his palm. His sisters were like this also, only for another reason: they enjoyed weeping. If they could find nothing to cry about, they cried for the annoyance of this dearth of destitution and worry. They held daily councils for future domestic trouble—one the gesture of emotional and one of mental desire.

Sometimes Little Lief's father would come to the big iron gate and ask to see her. He would never come in—why? He never explained. So Little Lief and he would talk over the gate top, and sometimes he was gentle and sometimes he was not. When he was harsh to her, Little Lief wept, and when she wept, he would look at her steadily from under his eyebrows and say nothing. Sometimes he asked her to take a walk with him. This would set Little Lief into a terrible flutter; the corners of her mouth would twitch and her nostrils tremble. But she always went.

Misha worried little about his wife. He was a very selfish man, with that greatest capacity of a selfish nature, the ability to labor untiringly for some one thing that he wanted and that nature had placed beyond his reach. Some people called this quality excellent, pointing out what a great scholar Misha was, holding him up as an example in their own households, looking after him when he went hurriedly down the street with that show of nervous expectancy that a man always betrays when he knows within himself that he is deficient—a sort of peering in the face of life to see if it has discovered the flaw.

Little Lief felt that her father was trying to be something that was not natural to him. What was it? As she grew older, she tried to puzzle it out. Now it happened more often that she would catch him looking at her in a strange way, and once she asked him half playfully if he wished she had been a boy. And he had answered abruptly, "Yes, I do."

Little Lief would stand for hours at the casement and, leaning her head against the glass, try to solve this thing about her father. And then she discovered it when he had said, "Yes, I do." He was trying to be strong—what was it that was in the family?—oh, yes—iron in the blood. He feared there was no longer any iron left. Well, perhaps there wasn't—was that the reason he looked at her like this? No, he was worried about himself. Why?—wasn't he satisfied with his own strength? He had been cruel enough very often. This shouldn't have worried him.

She asked him, and he answered, "Yes, but cruelty isn't strength." That was an admission. She was less afraid of him since that day when he had made that answer, but now she kept peering into his face as he had done into hers, and he seemed not to notice it. Well, he was getting to be a very old man.

Then one day her two sisters-in-law pounced upon her so that her golden head shook on its thin, delicate neck.

"Your father has come into the garden," cried one.

"Yes, yes," pursued the elder. "He's even sat himself upon the bench."

She hurried out to him. "What's the matter, father?" Her head was aching.

"Nothing." He did not look up.

She sat down beside him, stroking his hand, at first timidly, then with more courage.

"Have you looked at the garden?"

He nodded.

She burst into tears.

He took his hand away from her and began to laugh.

"What's the matter, child? A good dose of hog-killing would do you good."

"You have no right to speak to me in this way—take yourself off!" she cried sharply, holding her side. And her father rocked with laughter.

She stretched her long, thin arms out, clenching her thin fingers together. The lace on her short sleeves trembled, her knuckles grew white.

"A good pig-killing," he repeated, watching her. And she grew sullen.

"Eh?" He pinched her flesh a little and dropped it. She was passive; she made no murmur. He got up, walked to the gate, opened it and went out, closing it after him. He turned back a step and waved to her. She did not answer for a moment, then she waved back slowly with one of her thin, white hands.

She would have liked to refuse to see him again, but she lacked courage. She would say to herself, "If I am unkind to him now, perhaps later I shall regret it." In this way she tried to excuse herself. The very next time he had sent word that he wished speech with her, she had come.

"Little fool!" he said, in a terrible rage, and walked off. She was quite sure that he was slowly losing his mind—a second childhood, she called it, still trying to make things as pleasant as possible.

She had been ill a good deal that Spring, and in the Fall she had terrible headaches. In the Winter months she took to her bed, and early in May the doctor was summoned.

Misha talked to the physician in the drawing-room before he sent him up to his wife.

"You must be gentle with her. She is nervous and frail." The doctor laughed outright. Misha's sisters were weeping, of course, and perfectly happy.

"It will be such a splendid thing for her," they said, meaning the beef, iron and wine that they expected the doctor to prescribe.

Toward evening Little Lief closed her eyes.

Her child was still-born.

The physician came downstairs and entered the parlor where Misha's sisters stood together, still shedding tears.

He rubbed his hands.

"Send Misha upstairs."

"He has gone."

"Isn't it dreadful? I never could bear corpses, especially little ones."

"A baby isn't a corpse," answered the physician, smiling at his own impending humor. "It's an interrupted plan."

He felt that the baby, not having drawn a breath in this world, could not feel hurt at such a remark, because it had gathered no feminine pride and, also, as it had passed out quicker than the time it took to make the observation, it really could be called nothing more than the background for medical jocularity.

Misha came into the room with red eyes.

"Out like a puff of smoke," he said.

One of the sisters remarked: "Well, the Fenkens lived themselves thin."

The next Summer Misha married into a healthy Swedish family. His second wife had a broad face, with eyes set wide apart, and with broad, flat, healthy, yellow teeth. And she played the piano surprisingly well, though she looked a little heavy as she sat upon the piano stool.

1917

Elizabeth Madox Roberts 1881–1941

Elizabeth Madox Roberts was one of eight children born to Mary Elizabeth Brent and Simpson Roberts, two strong-minded, passionate people, who, through stories and written memoirs, blended fact and imagination. This background helped shape Roberts's complex sensibility. Elizabeth loved to listen to the rich tales her father and maternal grandmother spun about ancestors dating back to the early eighteenth century, and to the stories recounted from Bulfinch's *The Age of Fable*. Much of this after-dinner lore was woven into her novels and short stories, especially her historical novel *The Great Meadow*.

Ardent southern sympathizers, her

parents struggled meagerly through the Civil War and the Reconstruction period in Perryville, Kentucky. In 1884, the family moved to Springfield, a small, agrarian community, which bustled to life once a month on County Court Day to catch up with trading, haggling, and gossiping. Roberts, a keen observer, later depicted these Pigeon River country scenes with skill and flair. In spite of being situated in a particular time and place, and making use of "local color" devices, her novels take on archetypal dimensions and become universal in theme.

Elizabeth Madox Roberts was intelligent, sensitive, and artistic even as a child. She had a great love for music; in fact, the folksong, as well as the symphony, gave substance and shape to her art. Having excelled as a student in the small private schools of Springfield, she was sent by her parents to Covington to complete high school in a city school system. With little money and ill health, Roberts did not attend college full-time for another eighteen years. During these years she taught in various rural towns, boarding with residents and noting in detail the idiom of the people, their mores and customs. On June 8, 1917, she enrolled in the University of Chicago, her long-awaited dream come true. She graduated at the age of forty.

During her four years in Chicago, Roberts studied with Robert Morss Lovett and was active in a group of writers which included Glenway Wescott, Yvor Winters, and Harriet Monroe. Members read their own works, discussed the current literary scene (including Edgar Lee Masters, Carl Sandburg, Vachel Lindsay, and Sherwood Anderson), and shared an intense interest in literature and the arts. Roberts's writing career began with the publication of *Under the Tree* (1922), a volume of "child poems," "butterbeans" she called them, for which she won the Fiske Poetry Prize. She returned home frail and ill both physically and emotionally, but brought with her a Bachelor of Philosophy degree.

The Time of Man (1926) and *The Great Meadow* (1930) represent Roberts at her best, and with these novels she achieved the status of one of America's most popular and critically acclaimed novelists. In both novels Roberts uses a feminine central consciousness to shape her subject: "the total mind, not thinking or reason, but the instincts and emotions of all memories, imaginings, sensations of the whole being." In 1932 she published her first volume of stories, *The Haunted Mirror.* Her stories demonstrate her innovative craftsmanship, her use of "symbolism working through poetic realism" and regionalism, her belief in the intimate connection between the past and the present, and her penetrating dramatization of psychological crises. "Life is from within," she would say, "and thus the noise outside is a wind blowing in a mirror."

Roberts never married. She seldom made public appearances and, except for medical reasons, rarely traveled. During the last few years of her life, she spent the cold winter months in Orlando, Florida, where she died after years of suffering from a severe skin ailment and what was finally diagnosed as Hodgkin's disease. Although her writing career was comparatively short, she was surprisingly productive and original. With *The Time of Man,* her richest novel, she claimed her place as the first major novelist of the Southern Renascence. Her style markedly influenced later southern writers such as Jesse Stuart and William Faulkner, as well as Robert Penn Warren, who acknowledged this indebtedness when he said: "Elizabeth Madox Roberts was that rare thing, a true artist. . . . She was one of the indispensables."

Sheila Hurst Donnelly
Orange County Community College

PRIMARY WORKS

Under the Tree, 1922; *The Time of Man,* 1926; *My Heart and My Flesh,* 1927; *The Great Meadow,* 1930; *A Buried Treasure,* 1931; *The Haunted Mirror,* 1932; *He Sent Forth a Raven,* 1935; *Black Is My Truelove's Hair,* 1938; *Song in the Meadow,* 1940; *Not by Strange Gods,* 1941.

Death at Bearwallow

He had been to see his grandmother and the way home was growing dark, the ground at his feet imperfectly seen, moving nearer than his feet, as if his feet stepped into it and out again, as if they walked into an open substance which was like sponge. He had run out of the road to chase a rabbit, off into a cornfield, and now he was sorry for this. His father would flog him when he reached home, that he knew, for not being at hand to help with the night work. The moon was already in the sky, there when the sun set, prepared for the night, hastening the night. The thorn bushes at the roadside were familiar, known in all their contours and sensed in all their power, known too well. The hills beyond the running line of the fence and the field sank into the dark of the sky, cool and even, a terror, going to the night too easily, joining the dark. All the familiar things of the road and the day fitted into the dark, rising out of it. He was too far from his grandmother's house to return there; he had been on the road now since long before sundown.

He was more afraid as he came near to Terry Polin's house, fearful of it, for old Terry Polin threw stones at the children and he was bent as if he were squared to the earth he walked unevenly over. Coming near to the house he stopped in the road and would not dare to pass farther. There were strange ticking noises, irregularly placed, like some diminutive speech put into the bushes beyond the fence where scrub cedars grew out of a bramble, but he was not afraid of the sounds. It was the earth that arose to engulf him, to open his grave before his feet. The dusty stones in the road threatened, rising familiarly into the light, already accurately known. He blunted his fear of the house before his renewed sense of the earth and walked heedlessly past Polin's cabin where it stood close by the roadside as a threat standing clear in the moonlight. When he was well past it, he saw that the light on the window was not the light of the moon. A lamp burned inside, and out of the walls came the low outcry of voices.

He came then to the creek that ran past Polin's house, but the way downward toward the ford seemed short. Then the water was over the stepping stones, and he was unable to see the stones in the dark, running freshet that had come from the rain of the early afternoon in the hills. He tried to find one stone with a long stick, and he thought that if he could strike one of them he would be able to work out the others, but the water was high and the stones were lost. The dark of the earth lay under his feet, ready to yawn, his abysmal place, and he went back along the road and stopped in the open under the moon, above the creek bank, well away from the shade about the ford. The dark bushes at the side of the road, twiggy and rugged against the white of the moon, arose out of the black of the earth. Over in the field beyond the fence, out of sight in the shaded hummocks of the stubble, some hogs were working at the soil, rooting their food out of it, deeply breathing and grunting their content. He looked again at the dark of the ford, and he tried again and again to probe the water with a stick, but in the end he left the creek hurriedly and walked back along the way toward the moonlight. The dusty stones of the road were misty with their own defeat as they sank out of the light and carried understanding with them as they went, too vividly known, already familiar of old. He cried in his terror, the sobbing cry of a child, and he stood in the road shuddering. A sudden increase of fear arose suffusing the entire night that threatened to split asunder to let terror out, a threat like the threatened crack of doom. Crack-of-doom stood in his path and waited upon a thunder crash. He ran back along the road and, pushing open the door, he went into the house without knocking.

There was a dim light in the room, a light that seemed fogged beside the light of the moon. Two men whose names he knew, Sam Mulligan and Leo Scruggs, sat beside the table laying cards up on the dim board, scraping their feet on the floor when they rocked forward. Another man lay in the bed, lying very still.

"If here ain't Thompson Nally's boy," Scruggs said. "If here ain't that youngone, Dave Nally."

"What's he out so late for?" Mulligan asked.

There was a great laugh, the two of them joining to make it burst through the dim light and knock at the corners of the ceiling. The cards fell evenly from their hands, falling now one and now another to the table.

"God's sake, I bet that-there youngone was caught out. Afeared to go home by hisself."

"Come in to help old Terry Polin die."

"Doc says to me: 'Somebody's got to sit up tonight along with old Terry Polin. Somebody's got to.' Then I says: 'I don't mind if I do. As lief as not.'"

"I judge it's time now to be a-readen the prayer for the departen," Scruggs said. "I judge we best begin."

"Plenty time yet. Play on the cards. Quit your always a-blocken a game. It'll be a pretty while yet as I see."

He sat in the corner on the bare floor, near the door, between the light of the moon and the light of the lamp, touched by both. The man on the bed lay very still, but presently Sam Mulligan moved aside and the light fell toward the bed, and then by lifting his head and straining forward from the corner he could see the face that lay horizontal with the dull, yellowed pillow. The man on the bed was Terry Polin, the owner of the house. On the road old Terry threw stones at the children when they laughed and called out to him.

He knew that Terry Polin was on his bed to die and that the two men, Leo Scruggs and Sam Mulligan, were there to assist him. He himself was a small shape crouched in the corner, gathering himself to the smallest possible size, gathering inward his fear. He folded his hands into the warmth that was made where his arms touched his sides and bent his body toward the hollow where the two walls joined, drawing inward. He was glad that old Terry Polin was bound to die, that this would be the end of him, that he would not be throwing rocks on the road along with his curses when some child called him a name. His fears grew dim before sleep and he sank into a surrounding oblivion. The voices at the table went first, leaving the dim square of the room with its blocked shadows, but these trembled softly and broke into fragments, dissolved. He dreamed a story of hoofs thundering on the turf at the place where the grown boys raced their horses, the coming rush of feet throwing up the sod in little balls that were sprayed with dust.

"You threw back your slobbers inside the water bucket," a loud voice said. "You can just go to the spring and get more water now."

Voices had waked him with a great clamor. The men were up in the floor, shaking the floor with their steps. They were calling out roughly in anger.

"I'll not do it. I never threw back my slobbers. I didn't have no slobbers left. I drank it up to the bottom of the dipper."

"You threw back your slobbers, Leo Scruggs. I seen you. You lie to me if you say you didn't."

"You call me a lie and I'll smear your face up. I didn't throw back no slobbers."

"I'll throw this-here water out the door, the whole bucketful, and you can get more or go dry the balance of the night. You're a lie, Leo Scruggs. I see you throw back slobbers."

"You throw out this-here water and I'll knock hell outen you. You can take back your lie, too, Sam Mulligan. You don't call me a lie and pass it off like the time of day. You can take back your words."

"I never take back nothing. God Almighty, who you think I am?"

The boards of the house shook with their trampled feet as they scuffled, as they tried to grapple each the other's throat. The table was brushed aside, the lamp uncertainly poised in the movement, but it did not fall. Their great shadows lurched among the corners of the room, and Terry Polin twitched his hands at the quilt's edge. Then the fight ended suddenly and both men laughed. Scruggs had overturned the water bucket by some accident. The water slopped over the floor, and the bucket rolled along the boards near the chimney, spilling the dipper. A foot kicked the dipper away.

They settled to their places again, both of them breathing deeply after the fight. They both laughed again and told incidents of the struggle over and over. Then Sam Mulligan took up the cards from the floor and began to set them straight.

"I reckon it's about time now to read the prayer for the departen," Scruggs said when he had cooled a little from the fight. "We best read now."

"Aw, no. The night's young as I see it."

They set themselves to the cards again, but Dave was afraid to sleep. The untended lamp burned dully and smoked the chimney, and Leo Scruggs scraped the wick with a long splinter. One after the other, they would deal the cards, the dealer spraying one portion of the cards upon the other as if the pages of two books were mingled into one mass. Another sound came steadily beside the dropping of the cards on the table and the irregular outcries of the game, and presently he knew that the other sound was the long slow breathing of the man on the bed, each breath lying between long spaces of quiet. At the end of a round the men burst into comments, a loud scuffle of voices that broke into enforced sleep. "God, I had a club hand! Whoop law, and a lousy queen! I says to Hick: 'Where'd you-all get that-there haimstrung thoroughbred?'" The voice came starkly then out of his sleep:

"Her dress gaped open and I saw her meat, saw her naked meat a-showen."

"Saw Claudie Burk's meat. God, what was that to see?"

"I know it's time now to be a-readen the prayer for the departen."

Mulligan peered down across the dim light toward the bed, stretching his neck to see the progress there, waiting while he peered. "Naw, not yet. Deal again. I reckon I know. Deal on the cards."

Morning would come, he thought, sinking against the wall, fading into the hard lines of the wall, meeting the contours of the plaster. His back ached for sleep and his legs cramped as they were crumpled beneath him. After long intervals a deep breath shuddered through the dying man. The wall was merciful, inviting oblivion, and he sank toward it again and entered into it more nearly. A long interval of semi-knowing passed when the sounds found their accustomed rhythms and fell away entirely. Suddenly then a rough call splitting the density of forgetfulness.

Voice: I know it's time to be a-readen. I know it's getten time to be a-readen the prayer for the departen.

Voice: Aw, not yet. I know.

Voice: What's he a-tryen to say?

Voice: He's a-callen Kate. K-k-k-k-ka-kate. Used to be his old woman. Kate Polin, don't you recollect?

Voice: We better begin to read the prayer for the departen.

Voice: Pick up that-there deuce offen the floor. Play the cards. He ain't a-dyen easy, by gosh. Doc said afore morning. Come on now. It's four and four.

Voice: Doc says to me: "Somebody's got to sit up with old Terry Polin . . ."

Voice: I disgust bad cards, but these-here are plumb stinken.

The event on the bed stood between him and the morning which would never come. He fell again into semi-sleep. The water would be over the stones until daylight. A great hand tended the lamp again, lifting away the chimney and clearing the wick, the shapes of fingers shadowing the room, great palms obliterating the ceiling and the bed. It seemed a long while after the incident of the fingers that a quick outcry rent the substances of the wall into which he had sunk. The men were leaping to the floor, the voices blended.

"I told you it was time . . ."

"God Almighty, where's that-there prayer book?"

"Find the place inside. Hold that-there lamp. Hold it higher. Quit your fool doens now. That's not the prayer book. God Almighty, where's the prayer book? Get the right book, you damned-to-hell fool. Get the prayer book, Leo Scruggs. Hunt it up. Hold the lamp steady now. Find that-there prayer book. . . ."

He ran out the door of the house. One light bare step on the floor and another on the door sill and he was beyond the reach of the lamplight. He ran down to the dark ford and waited among the cold shadows.

Valeria was dead, Bob Newton's girl, and the banns had been ready to publish. Dave Nally drove his plow through the crumpled dolomite soil making ground ready for winter wheat, and as he walked he knew his height suddenly and knew what it was to stand high above the ground in the stature of a man. This knowledge had grown upon him with the years and had not been openly confessed to his sense. The bell ringing at St. Rose came faintly across many hills and was dispersed among the stony rises and bushy hollows, shallow and thin. Hearing the bell he remembered the mission that would begin at St. Rose in two weeks, and a vague excitement surged in his breast and in his throat, for the mission would be someplace to go every night. But Valeria was dead. Going to the mission would not be what it had formerly been to Bob Newton, to himself, to his sister Piety, to Clel Tobin; the mission was gutted of its rich core. The earth he cut with the plowshare was dark with hard sand and the plow scraped the stones. As he walked behind the plow, one foot limping deeply into the furrow, he arose momently above the soil and sank anew into it, fluctuating with each roughly placed step. He knew then what it was to stand above the ground in the shape of a man, having all of a man's parts.

Valeria lay in a bed somewhere in her father's house. From the field he could see the crumpled gable of the house as it stood, small, almost invisible, out of two hills.

Across the road from his plowing lay the marsh where tall rushes grew, and out of it some water birds were crying. Old men at the store, talking about the country and about the early days, often said that once the bears had come there to wallow, that the bears had carried away the mud on their backs and had made the great pond. He knew how the water stood above the clay or sank into it, and the great oaks had been there when the bears had lain in the mire. Bears had eaten the nuts from the tall hickory trees. The marsh seemed more curious, as one of the wonders of the earth, since he had heard of the bears, but on this morning as his gaze was fastened on the marsh while the plow rode across the rise of the field, he saw it in its relation to Valeria. His brother Dominic had walked across the field going to the still that was hidden down inside the bushy glen, had walked that way an hour earlier, and passing he had said:

"Valery, she's dead. Valery."

"Dead! How? Valery?"

"She died a right smart while ago this morning. She was taken bad last night at bedtime with a gripe in her heart and she died soon after daylight."

Valeria came acutely into his vision as he drove the team up the field, cutting the dirt apart for the winter seeds. At first a still pang lay within his breast, awe, disappointment, annoyance. Slowly the past tense gathered about her name and the present was sifted out of it. By the time he had plowed two rings about the field Valeria was dead, the matter settled and done, reported, closed. The beasts dragged at the heavy plow over the hill's rim, and the earth lay away, hill following hill, each interlocking with another. Coming across the brow, as the stubble rolled back to reveal its crumbled inner part, he saw swiftly into the earth, into the dark of the dirt. Year after year the plow but turned it over, wheeled it in procession. His eyes saw into it and saw the darkness under it.

As he went down the hill's farther side, slapping the plow rope on the mare's haunch, tears dimmed his eyes. Valeria had been Bob's girl, a warm creature with gray eyes, round arms and hips, soft to touch, warm to feel. Bob had known what it was to have her in his arms, and the banns were ready. He could hear clearly now the clatter of her laugh and feel her coming nearer, her swift step. Her hair was dark and her voice was kind for Bob and for Bob's friends, or impudently full of life. He had gone with Bob acutely in mind, knowing his way with her. Seeing them kiss, and seeing his sister Piety with Clel Tobin, he had turned to Pearl Janes and had kissed there, trying to want what he did, but she was forbidding even when she invited. There was a hardness in her, a dull woodenness. They had walked to the graveyard and had looked at the place where the first to come into the country were buried, trying to find dates on the eaten stones. He had known intently what Valeria and Bob held between them and he had read their joy and their sense of each other. He had stood between them minutely while they looked together, their eyes full of their greetings, and he had gone with them in their frank caress. Now the tears dried on his face, the tears of his first surprise at the news, and he moved unevenly after the plow iron, holding it into the earth, his eyes searching the ground where it rolled apart.

His sister Piety was coming across the field toward the plow. She seemed very small as she bent to struggle against the rough furrows and clods, very delicate and small, a child, as she worked her way through the crumbled clods to the inner island of unplowed stubble where she waited until he came near, her apron folded over her head to shield her from the sun.

"Valery's dead," she said. She seemed untouched by grief, being too near the event herself. He saw her then as a woman standing in the heart of the field, speaking out of the stubble. Her hands were warm and moist as she held the apron over her shoulder and her body swelled its woman's curves. She was a part of what lay on Valeria's bed, of what had gone with Valeria.

"Dominic told me. Where's Bob at now?"

"He came by our house a right smart while ago. He's gone back home now to his pappy's. He was here, but now he's gone."

He looked at her, comprehending. They looked toward each other and away.

"Did Bob take on?"

"He wouldn't talk. He just set in his chair. They want you to stay there tonight. To sit up. With the corpse."

The horses stood at ease, resting, the harness falling limp across their tired flanks. He stood with his feet buried in the crumbled loam, accepting the need where it reached toward him, making no sign. He was seeing Piety as Clel Tobin saw her, as Bob had seen Valeria, and this understanding overspread his thought and made him slow in acquiescing. She stood a moment before him, the warmth of her life issuing from her body, from her face, from her hair, infinitely capable of sustaining itself, of continuing. Her breasts, lifted with her lifted arm, throbbed with it before him, denoting warm being, the same as that which had moved in the other girl. They were the same to him, both something distinguished by the two boys, his friends, Bob and Clel Tobin. It was unthinkable that any disaster could bring it any hurt. Warm life darted now about Piety's mouth as she spoke and sat quietly on her eyes, or sat again on her small full shoulders and her back, her hips and her legs, her ankles. He nodded his willingness to the request and gathered taut the plow lines.

"I best put a stitch in your shirt with the blue stripe," she said. "I best mend it a little by the collar."

He remembered the garment, and remembered that he would have to put on his other clothes. "I'll quit up work early, in time to get there against night sets in. They might want help."

He saw her go back across the plowed space, picking her way slowly and with trouble through the broken earth. He saw a small blue shape, Piety, rising and falling in a struggle with the gullies and stony rises.

Two candles burned at Valeria's feet and the room was very still. Her people had gone to the other room, or they had gone above to the loft chamber. One or two sat on the chairs of the room or knelt at the prayers. When they stood, the uneven boards creaked under the carpet Valeria herself had helped to weave at the loom. Her hands had gathered the winter bouquet, goldenrod and sassafras and thorn apples, gathered idly, not meant to keep; but now it would be saved on the shelf, standing on the mantel beyond the crucifix. At any moment of its gathering she was near to tossing it into the gully, caring then to keep only what Bob gave her.

He was staring at the light on the wall where the throb of the candle burst and spread unevenly. The other watcher was an old man, Ben Hester, and he had fallen asleep over his prayers where he knelt in a corner. The night moved slowly, and the weariness of the plow pulled at his limbs but he had no mind to sleep. He had read the prayers for the repose of the dead and he had been through the circle of the rosary, and now he stared at the beating light on the wall. Valeria was still, was waxen like an image at the altar. He turned his back to the room and sat facing the light that throbbed uneasily on the wall just beyond the crucifix and the dried bouquet of autumn. Bob's joy in Valeria arose as a spectre to question him, and the book had fallen from his hands to lie unheeded on the floor. The ground at his feet moved nearer, imperfectly seen, making a pool about his ankles, arising to engulf him. "It's time now to be a-readen the prayer for the departen," a flat voice said, far back in his memory, one with his breath, "the prayer for the departen." This which Bob had with Valeria stood set apart, warm within itself, but his only by the knowing of it, it being theirs to have privately. A cry beat at his throat and sank deeply into his mind. He was staring at the wall and his feet were sinking into the dark of the floor. Within his own breath, the speech lying back of his inner disorder, the words lay perpetually, "It's time now to be a-readen that-there prayer for the departen."

The man on the bed was himself, Dave Nally, his head on the pillow, his feet stretched out far and cold. As he lay, his eyes looked up at the ceiling which was a fixity holding length and depth in a four-square design. His throat struggled with the words of the rosary, the words pushed against his throat as against shut gates that held firmly, that rattled on lock and hinges, "Hail Mary, full of grace, blessed art thou among women." His entire self from first to the present moment lay back in his being, and he was one, breathing and living, the same he had always been. He could leap back to the beginning or forward to the end, the now, the last moment. It was night and he and Dominic were beside the fire, Dominic taking a piece of food from their mother's hands. He was holding his hands, the same hands he now had, to the warmth of the fire, saying over and over: "Six times seven is forty-two, six times seven. That's my word to remember." The hammering words of the prayer still beat at the hinges of his shut throat, and his fingers felt the hard little berries of the rosary, but when he lifted his hands under the quilt he found that they were cold and empty. There were no beads.

The two candles burned behind him at Valeria's feet and she was still, like wax. The light shook on the yellowed wall, leaping and falling slowly. His hands were at the quilt's edge, adjusting the world. He was cold and he ought to have gloves, his hands smarting, hard and stiff and raw with deep chapped places that bled. His mammy would knit him some gloves if she were still living. He would sit close to the fire and the heat would glide into his bones slowly, a little at a time. He would take his coat off to let the warmth in, and he would sit and hear the log crackle and settle itself into a quiet lapping flame, until he would float on the warmth and the cold would sink back and away. His own warmth, all for him, would sink inside his shirt, the same inside he had always had. Ten hail-maries and then one our-father, in his hands as marbles on a string. A sudden outcry: You threw back your slobbers. I see you do it. You lie to me if you say you didn't. I didn't do it. I never threw my slobbers back. I drank it all to the last drop. You did so throw back your slobbers. I never had no slobbers. You lie and I'll tear your guts out. You'll eat back your words. I never take nothing back. God Almighty who you think I am. It's time now to be a-readen the prayer for the departen. Naw, not yet, plenty time yet as I see. Play down your hand, quit a-blocken a game.

He was with a pack of boys, hunting across fields and into woods. A pack of boys, himself one, and a little girl hiding. She was running down a thicket, her skimp little dress, drab, showing now and then in the brush. Hoarse cries, unknown to themselves, were coming out of their throats. Four boys, himself one. She was gone, swallowed up by the ground or slipped away through some fence, Sallie Bent, lost to them, safe. Down into a deep hollow where the path ran cool, and she was lost to them, two of the boys off after a rabbit and one, Wes Hyte, lagging behind in the cool brush, lying on the moss, loving the moss.

Slowly he came back to the light of the lamp behind the smoky chimney and then to the hands that lifted regularly over the edge of the table and dropped the cards. "There's my high and the ace ain't out. A queen for high. Her dress gapped open and I see her naked meat a-showen. I see old man Hicks come down the pike a-driven a haimstrung critter. Where'd he get that-there haimstrung nag? Deal out again, egad, and give me something this-here time." The voice took tone:

"Is it time now to be a-readen the prayer for the departen?"

The lamp made pink streams across the space before the window, long colored lines running down into the light across the powdered dark of the room. The air was still except that something rattled slowly in long waves, a rattling lying across the continued stillness. A great head stood up above the turned shoulders, nose, mouth, eyes and hair. The eyes looked down across the quiet space, peering and staring at him out of their shadowed lids.

"Naw, not yet. Deal again. Plenty time. Reckon I know."

The cards fell slowly one on the other, making no sounds, but now and then a hand thumped the table impatiently. Fragments of the prayer for the departing appeared in mind, imperfectly remembered, the litany for the dying, never learned in life. "Lord have mercy on him. Christ have mercy on him. Lord have mercy . . . Holy Mary pray for him . . . All ye holy angels and arch-angels . . ." The supplications were rising and falling away . . . "All ye choirs of the just . . . Have pity, Lord, on his sighs, have pity on his tears. Loosed from the bonds of flesh . . ." Somebody would have to read the words from the book.

He was sitting in the pew with Piety and his mother, at late mass. A wasp was dipping up and down slowly over old Mrs. Hester's bonnet, touching the black of the crown. Piety was kneeling, saying prayers, her eyes half asleep, her feet set upright behind the hem of her dress, her lips whispering rapid, wordless motions. He was turning through the prayer book, watching the leaves fall over the brim of it, motions of leaves, the worn edges soft like rag. His eyes had read without seeing, The Litany of the Saints, The Ordinary of the Mass, Prayer for one Departing this Life. The words stood on the page like poetry in a book.

St. Mary Magdalen,
St. Lucy
All ye holy virgins and widows.

He fingered the edge of the quilt to settle the edges of the world into order, to make all right, to straighten a crease. A great hand shadowed the lamp and the light fell through the gapped fingers and became a turmoil that threatened to wrench his hold from the side of the quilt. "I know you did throw your slobbers back. I did not so. You call me a lie and I'll tear your guts outen your belly . . ." There was something he, Terry Polin, had always been wanting, needing, and he could not now gather the name of it or the meaning. It was something he was always wanting and getting and wanting again. He could not divine how it was called. It was gone now and the name of it gone. It was something that ran in his limbs, in his legs and arms and sides. It was kate; he had found the name for it. It seemed very far away now, forgotten in the way of its going, but the name was now assembled, kate in his arms and legs, in his breastbone.

Slowly this sense grew definite and firm, gathering a person about it, Kate, a warm moving body, a blood-containing flesh, hands lifted and rising before the puffed breasts as she sewed. Hurrying down to the chickenhouse with a pan of meal dough or going in at the door of the house, closing the door. Ask Kate. Tell Kate. These were incessant sayings, never refuted. Tell Kate about the low price of hogs, himself almost giving them away. She was the mother of his children, Tony and Mag and Terry B. Kate moved down a film of air, her hands moving, setting food out or cooking food, making a bed, combing her hair, drawing on her clothes that smelt warm and full, like her body and like the things she handled all day, food, chickens, feathers, ashes, earth, children. He would ask Kate, tell Kate, tell her now. A great cry formed in his body and rushed up into his throat, into his loose throat, and there it hung on folds of flesh entangled with breath and struggled forth in a dry hissing sound. "K-k-k-k-ka-Kate!" Two great heads stood up above a mass of shoulders and turned wide-opened eyes toward him. He brought his gaze down from the dispersed light of the room and centered it upon the two heads that turned toward him staring, they being the world. The rattle that shook through the quiet of the room was his breath, his own, climbing down long slow stairs with great steps. He was one, the same he had always been, as when he ran out at the door in a little blue dress, climbing up the hen ladder.

Voice: I know now it's time to be a-readen the prayer for the departen. . . .

Voice: Find me that-there prayer book. . . .

Voice: God Almighty, where's that-there book? Find it quick. Find the place. I never take nothing back. Who you think I am?

Voice: Lord have mercy on him
Christ have mercy on him
Lord have mercy
Holy Mary pray for him
All ye holy angels. . . .
Holy Abel . . .
Thy creature not made by strange gods but by thee. . . .
Loosed from the bonds of flesh he may attain . . . may attain . . . may attain. . . .

He arose and went bending toward the house door, looking past the candles that burned at Valeria's feet. The night was cool outside, the crying of the night noises an infinity of sound sinking back and arising perpetually in the three-ply space of the night-quiet. The darkness was complete, no part of it distinguished from any other part.

1932

H.D. (Hilda Doolittle) 1886–1961

H.D.'s life and work recapitulate the central themes of literary modernism: the emergence from Victorian norms and certainties; the entry into an age characterized by rapid technological change and the violence of two world wars; the disruptions of conventional gender roles with the rise of feminism; and the development of literary modes which reflected the disintegration of traditional symbolic systems and the myth-making quest for new meanings. Writing under the *nom de plume* H.D., she is known mainly as a poet, especially for her imagist poetry (as in *Sea Garden*) and her epics of the forties and fifties (*Trilogy* and *Helen in Egypt*). She was the first woman to receive the prestigious Award of Merit Medal for Poetry from the American Academy of Arts and Letters (1960). H.D. has also been highly praised for her Greek translations. Often compared to Virginia Woolf and Gertrude Stein, H.D. is increasingly recognized for her experimental fiction (*HERmione, Bid Me to Live* and *Asphodel*) and her personal essays (*Tribute to Freud*).

Like the modernist poetry of her friends, Ezra Pound, T. S. Eliot, and William Carlos Williams, H.D.'s early poetry originated in the avant-garde, *vers libre* movements of 1910–1920 (especially imagism), influenced by Sappho, Japanese haiku, Troubadour lyrics, Bergsonian philosophy, and post-impressionist art. H.D. was known as the "most perfect" of the imagist poets for her innovative musical rhythms, crystalline lines, and stark images. Like *The Cantos, The Waste Land,* and *Paterson,* H.D.'s later long sequence poems featured the poet as prophet wandering in the wilderness of the modern world, drawing on the fragments of many cultures to forge new myths that might give meaning to a world shattered by war, technology, and alienation. Like the modernist novels of Virginia Woolf, James Joyce, and William Faulkner that she admired, H.D.'s fiction fractured narrative perspective and chronology in order to capture the shifting subjectivities of consciousness. This prose centers on the experience of the creative woman who wants both love and vocation in a world perpetually split open by violence.

H.D.'s distinctive emphasis as a modernist grew out of her extensive involvement with classical Greece and ancient Egypt, cinema, psychoanalysis, esoteric religion, and occult mysticism. Her perspective as a woman further permeated her revisions of these traditions. Analyzed by Sigmund Freud (1933, 1934), for example, she transformed his androcentric theories of femininity into the basis of a redemptive female voice and vision. Like Woolf, H.D. was profoundly concerned with the issues of war and violence. To counter the forces of death, her work reconstitutes gender, language, and myth to serve her search for a vision of personal and cultural rebirth.

Loving the forests and sea-coasts of the United States, H.D. grew up in Pennsylvania: first Bethlehem and then a Philadelphia suburb. Her mother was a Moravian artist and musician, and her father was a well-known professor of astronomy. Withdrawing from Bryn Mawr College in her sophomore year with poor grades, she later went to Europe in 1911 to join the circle of artists around Pound, Yeats, and Joyce. Although she remained intensely American throughout her residences in London and Switzerland, she only visited the United States four times. Bisexually oriented, H.D. almost married Ezra Pound, married fellow imagist Richard Aldington in 1913, separated from him in 1919, divorced him in 1938, and lived with Bryher (Winifred Ellerman) from 1919 through 1946.

Susan Stanford Friedman
University of Wisconsin at Madison

PRIMARY WORKS

Sea Garden, 1916; *Collected Poems,* 1925; *Palimpsest,* 1926; *Hedylus,* 1928; *By Avon River,* 1949; *Tribute to Freud,* 1956; *Bid Me to Live (A Madrigal),* 1960; *Helen in Egypt,* 1961; *Hermetic Definition,* 1972; *Trilogy, 1944–1946,* 1973; *HERmione,* 1981; *Collected Poems, 1912–1944,* 1983; *Paint It Today,* 1992; *Asphodel,* 1992.

Sea Rose

Rose, harsh rose,
marred and with stint of petals,
meagre flower, thin,
sparse of leaf,

more precious
than a wet rose
single on a stem—
you are caught in the drift.

Stunted, with small leaf,
you are flung on the sand,
you are lifted
in the crisp sand
that drives in the wind.

Can the spice-rose
drip such acrid fragrance
hardened in a leaf?

1916

The Helmsman[1]

O be swift—
we have always known you wanted us.
We fled inland with our flocks,
we pastured them in hollows,
cut off from the wind
and the salt track of the marsh.

We worshipped inland—
we stepped past wood-flowers,
we forgot your tang,
we brushed wood-grass.

We wandered from pine-hills
through oak and scrub-oak tangles,
we broke hyssop and bramble,
we caught flower and new bramble-fruit
in our hair: we laughed
as each branch whipped back,
we tore our feet in half buried rocks
and knotted roots and acorn-cups.

We forgot—we worshipped,
we parted green from green,
we sought further thickets,
we dipped our ankles
through leaf-mould and earth,
and wood and wood-bank enchanted us—

and the feel of the clefts in the bark,
and the slope between tree and tree—
and a slender path strung field to field
and wood to wood
and hill to hill
and the forest after it.

We forgot—for a moment
tree-resin, tree-bark,
sweat of a torn branch
were sweet to the taste.

[1]Possible allusion to Charon, the ferryman who carried the souls of the dead across the river Styx to the Underworld in Greek mythology.

We were enchanted with the fields,
the tufts of coarse grass
in the shorter grass—
we loved all this.

But now, our boat climbs—hesitates—drops—
climbs—hesitates—crawls back—
climbs—hesitates—
O be swift—
we have always known you wanted us.

1916

Oread[1]

Whirl up, sea—
whirl your pointed pines,
splash your great pines
on our rocks,
hurl your green over us,
cover us with your pools of fir.

1914

Helen[1]

All Greece hates
the still eyes in the white face,
the lustre as of olives
where she stands,
and the white hands.

[1]Mountain nymph in Greek mythology.

[1]Beautiful daughter of Zeus and Leda, and wife of the Greek king Menelaus, Helen was abducted from Sparta and taken to Troy by Paris, the Trojan prince. Her kidnapping led to the Trojan War.

All Greece reviles
the wan face when she smiles,
hating it deeper still
when it grows wan and white,
remembering past enchantments
and past ills.

Greece sees unmoved,
God's daughter, born of love,
the beauty of cool feet
and slenderest knees,
could love indeed the maid,
only if she were laid,
white ash amid funereal cypresses.

1923

from Trilogy

from The Walls Do Not Fall

[43]

Still the walls do not fall,
I do not know why;

there is zrr-hiss,
lightning in a not-known,

unregistered dimension;
we are powerless,

dust and powder fill our lungs
our bodies blunder

through doors twisted on hinges,
and the lintels slant

cross-wise;
we walk continually

on thin air
that thickens to a blind fog,

then step swiftly aside,
for even the air

is independable,
thick where it should be fine

and tenuous
where wings separate and open,

and the ether
is heavier than the floor,

and the floor sags
like a ship floundering;

we know no rule
of procedure,

we are voyagers, discoverers
of the not-known,

the unrecorded;
we have no map;

possibly we will reach haven,
heaven.

1944

from Tribute to the Angels

[8]

Now polish the crucible[1]
and in the bowl distill

[1]In alchemy, the vessel in which the alchemist tried to purify matter into gold through fire.

a word most bitter, *marah,*[2]
a word bitterer still, *mar,*[3]

sea, brine, breaker, seducer,
giver of life, giver of tears;

now polish the crucible
and set the jet of flame

under, till *marah-mar*[4]
are melted, fuse and join

and change and alter,
mer, mere, mère, mater, Maia, Mary,

Star of the Sea,
Mother.[5]

[12]

Swiftly re-light the flame,
Aphrodite,[6] holy name,

Astarte,[7] hull and spar
of wrecked ships lost your star,

forgot the light at dusk,
forgot the prayer at dawn;

return, O holiest one,
Venus[8] whose name is kin

[2]Hebrew word for bitter in feminine form; the place where the Hebrews first camped after crossing the Red Sea, and where Moses made the bitter waters sweet (Exodus 15:23); and the name Naomi took to signify her bitter fate after the death of her sons (Ruth 1:20).

[3]Hebrew adjective for bitter in masculine form; Hebrew title for Mr.; and Hebrew verb for ruin, mar, break.

[4]In the alchemical crucible, the alchemist fired together materials thought to be masculine and feminine.

[5]In French, *mer* means sea; *mère* means mother. In Latin, *mater* means mother. Maia is an early Greek goddess and mother of Hermes by Zeus. In Christian tradition, Mary is the mother of Jesus and is sometimes known by the name Stella Maris, Latin for Star of the Sea. This name indicates her protection of sailors as a beacon of light in the planet Venus, also associated with the Egyptian goddess Isis, the Babylonian goddess Ishtar, the Phoenecian goddess Astarte, the Greek goddess Aphrodite, and the Roman goddess Venus.

[6]Greek goddess of love.

[7]Phoenecian goddess of love.

[8]Roman goddess of love.

to venerate,
venerator.

[19]

. . . .
we asked for no sign
but she[9] gave a sign unto us;

sealed with the seal of death,
we thought not to entreat her

but prepared us for burial;
then she set a charred tree before us,

burnt and stricken to the heart;
was it may-tree or apple?

[20]

Invisible, indivisible Spirit,
how is it you come so near,

how is it that we dare
approach the high-altar?

we crossed the charred portico,
passed through a frame—doorless—

entered a shrine; like a ghost,
we entered a house through a wall;

then still not knowing
whether (like the wall)

we were there or not-there,
we saw the tree flowering;

[9]The goddess of the Near-eastern, Egyptian, Greek, and Roman mystery religions in all her many forms; also associated in *Trilogy* with the Virgin Mary and Mary Magdalene, the former prostitute who first saw the risen Christ according to Christian tradition.

it was an ordinary tree
in an old garden-square.

[23]

. . . .

it was the Holy Ghost[10]—

a half-burnt-out-apple-tree
blossoming;

this the flowering of the rood,[11]
this is the flowering of the wood,

where Annael,[12] we pause to give
thanks that we rise again from death and live.

[43]

And the point in the spectrum
where all lights become one,

is white and white is not no-colour,
as we were told as children,

but all-colour;
where the flames mingle

and the wings meet, when we gain
the arc of perfection,

we are satisfied, we are happy,
we begin again;

[10]Third member of the Trinity (Father, Son, Holy Ghost) in Christianity, often associated with the feminine.

[11]Cross or crucifix, symbolizing the death and resurrection of Christ.

[12]Angel of peace in the Judeo-Christian tradition, associated with Venus. H.D. links Annael and the six other angels in *Tribute to the Angels* with the seven unnamed angels around God's throne in the book of Revelation in the Bible.

I *John saw. I testify*[13]
to rainbow feathers, to the span of heaven

and walls of colour,
and colonnades of jasper;
but when the jewel
melts in the crucible,

we find not ashes, not ash-of-rose,
not a tall vase and a staff of lilies,

not *vas spirituale,*[14]
not *rosa mystica*[15] even,

but a cluster of garden-pinks
or a face like a Christmas-rose.

This is the flowering of the rod,
this is the flowering of the burnt-out wood,

where, Zadkiel, we pause to give
thanks that we rise again from death and live.

London, May 17–31, 1944

A Sheaf of Political Poetry in the Modern Period

The history of American political poetry is continuous with the history of the nation itself; there is no period, for example, when poetry reflecting on and critical of the dominant values in American social life was not being written and read. But the history of the moments when oppositional political poetry became highly visible and influential—either within important subcultures or more broadly—is far more discontinuous. The high points of political poetry include the abolitionist poetry of the mid-nineteenth century and the poetry and song of the late-nineteenth- and early-twentieth-century labor movement. In the twentieth century a proper definition of political poetry would certainly encompass much of the work of the New Negro Renaissance. For contemporary readers the history of political poetry also includes

[13]Words of John of Patmos in Revelation 22:8 and 22:18. John testifies to his vision of the end of the world and the second coming of Christ in a new Jerusalem, whose walls are of jasper and other gems. A rainbow surrounds God's throne and appears on the head of an angel (Revelation 4:3 and 10:1). The rainbow also alludes to God's promise to Noah after the Flood to never destroy humankind again (Genesis 9:13–16).

[14]Latin for a spiritual or ritual vessel.

[15]Latin for rose used in secret rites. In esoteric Judeo-Christian traditions, the rose symbolizes the mystery of resurrection and is also associated with Mary, Aphrodite, and Venus.

the 1960s poetry of black liberation, the anti-war poetry written during the Vietnam War, and much contemporary Chicano, feminist, Asian American, and Native American poetry.

But in no decade was political poetry as pervasive as it was in the 1930s. As the Great Depression deepened in the early 1930s, large numbers of people, including many writers, were drawn to the political Left or to the Communist Party. They shared a widespread conviction that capitalism had failed, that the old order could not be restored, and that only the most thoroughgoing social and political change could bring about social and economic justice. As a result, the generalized sense of alienation common to modernism became much more focused; many poets felt specifically alienated from capitalism and its social institutions, rather than from modern life as a whole. They joined a number of active poets who had already been writing from that perspective in the 1920s, for the much heralded "roaring twenties" had not brought economic health to everyone. Both agriculture and the entire rural economy had remained depressed throughout the decade; moreover, several major industries were already in recession before the stock market crash of 1929. Especially in the South and in depressed areas of the North, working-class and labor poets, along with poets affiliated with socialism, had been writing about economic inequities for years. Some of these poets positioned themselves not only as individual voices but also as participants in movements for social change. All this culminated in the poetry of 1930s, when poets writing on public themes sensed that they were contributing to a common cultural enterprise.

What this actually meant began to become clear in 1926 and 1927 when protests against the planned execution of Sacco and Vanzetti in Massachusetts gathered force. A broad coalition, reaching far beyond writers with established progressive commitments, formed to oppose the verdict. When the execution occurred despite mass protests, many writers concluded that American institutions were too corrupt to be reformed. A few years later, when the Depression took hold, some of these writers found themselves documenting the decay of American life and urging revolutionary change. It would take a full decade, until 1936 and 1937 and the advent of the Spanish Civil War, before a coalition as broad as that protesting Sacco's and Vanzetti's executions would form again, but in the meantime many writers were radicalized and the poetry of the Great Depression reached a wide audience.

As even this brief selection of poems demonstrates, the political poetry of the Great Depression and subsequent decades was far more varied formally and stylistically than is conventionally assumed. At least on the political Left, modernist experimentation could sometimes coexist with forms as traditional as the ballad stanza. As poems like Rolfe's "First Love" and "Elegia" suggest, the language of political poetry was often lyrical, though lyricism and anger here often occur together. This intense period of social and political consciousness for many lasted beyond the decade. Those radical poets of the 1930s who maintained their Left commitments and who lived through the 1950s found themselves taking up, in turn, critiques of capitalism, racism, fascism, and McCarthyism. Thus a poet like Rolfe was writing protest poetry until his death in 1954. This poetry does, therefore, display common themes and political views, a pattern poets were aware of and sought to underline.

On the one hand, Kay Boyle's "A Communication to Nancy Cunard," based on the Scottsboro case in which nine young black men were unjustly accused and convicted of the rape of two white women that had not even taken place, and Genevieve Taggard's poem sequence "To the Negro People" represent the great number of poems that white authors produced to protest American racism and explore African American culture. Rolfe's "First Love" and "Elegia" and Taggard's "To the Veterans of the Abraham Lincoln Brigade," on the other hand, represent many poems written in support of the Spanish Republic and of the Americans who fought on its behalf after Francisco Franco and other army officers supported by Hitler and Mussolini led a revolt against it in 1936. The Spanish Civil War came to an end with Franco's victory in 1939, but American poets who came of age in the 1920s and 1930s continued to write poems about it through the 1950s.

Poems about the Great Depression and about American labor fill out this selection. They include Lola Ridge's protest against labor leader Tom Mooney's unjust imprisonment for a crime he did not commit, Tillie Olsen's exposé of the exploitation of Mexican American seamstresses in the Southwest, and Alfred Hayes's simultaneously anguished and sardonic narrative about an economically disenfranchised generation. Stylistically, they range from Joseph Kalar's almost expressionist portrait of an abandoned factory to Kenneth Fearing's satires about American business and politics, from Taggard's effort to mix blunt realism with metaphoric intensity in "Up State—Depression Summer," her narrative of a farm family's decline, to Rolfe's fusion of realism and surreal moments in "Season of Death," his poem about the unemployed. Protest against hypocrisy also runs through these poems: Ridge and Boyle protest the hypocrisy of the U.S. justice system; Langston Hughes satirizes the hypocrisy of American Christianity and of the privileged classes' attitudes toward poverty, and urges revolutionary change; and many of the poets challenge the false values that sustain the American economic system.

Not every reader today will find the revolutionary sentiments here appealing, but many of the social issues these poets took up remain strikingly relevant. Economic hardship and exploitation in the city and on the farm have not changed enough to date these poems, nor have race relations in America so improved as to make the poems about race irrelevant. Taggard's poem about immigration, diversity, and national identity, "Ode in Time of Crisis," reads as if it might have been written yesterday. And it is uncanny, certainly, to realize that the damage asbestos could do to a worker was evident to some as early as 1933. These are among the points of entrance we may use in deciding whether the passions of this period have any bearing on our own.

Cary Nelson
University of Illinois

PRIMARY WORKS

Kenneth Fearing, *Social Poetry of the 1930s,* 1978; *Complete Poems,* 1994; Kay Boyle, *Collected Poems,* 1991; Langston Hughes, *Good Morning Revolution: Uncollected Writings of Social Protest,* 1992; *Collected Poems,* 1994; Edwin Rolfe, *Collected Poems,* 1993.

Joseph Kalar 1906–1972

Papermill

Not to be believed, this blunt savage wind
Blowing in chill empty rooms, this tornado
Surging and bellying across the oily floor
Pushing men out in streams before it;
Not to be believed, this dry fall
Of unseen fog drying the oil
And emptying the jiggling greasecups;
Not to be believed, this unseen hand
Weaving a filmy rust of spiderwebs
Over these turbines and grinding gears,
These snarling chippers and pounding jordans;[1]
These fingers placed to lips saying shshsh;
Keep silent, keep silent, keep silent;
Not to be believed hardly, this clammy silence
Where once feet stamped over the oily floor,
Dinnerpails clattered, voices rose and fell
In laughter, curses, and songs. Now the guts
Of this mill have ceased their rumbling, now
The fires are banked and red changes to black,
Steam is cold water, silence is rust, and quiet
Spells hunger. Look at these men, now,
Standing before the iron gates, mumbling,
"Who could believe it? Who could believe it?"

1931

Kenneth Fearing 1902–1961

Dirge

1–2–3 was the number he played but today the number came 3–2–1;
Bought his Carbide[1] at 30 and it went to 29; had the favorite at
Bowie but the track was slow—

[1]Machines employed at a paper mill.

[1]Union Carbide stock.

O executive type, would you like to drive a floating-power, knee-
action, silk-upholstered six? Wed a Hollywood star? Shoot
the course in 58? Draw to the ace, king, jack?
O fellow with a will who won't take no, watch out for three
cigarettes on the same, single match; O democratic voter
born in August under Mars, beware of liquidated rails—

Denouement to denouement, he took a personal pride in the certain, certain way he lived his own, private life,
But nevertheless, they shut off his gas; nevertheless, the bank foreclosed; nevertheless, the landlord called; nevertheless, the
radio broke,

And twelve o'clock arrived just once too often,
Just the same he wore one gray tweed suit, bought one straw hat,
drank one straight Scotch, walked one short step, took one
long look, drew one deep breath,
Just one too many,

And wow he died as wow he lived,
Going whop to the office and blooie home to sleep and biff got
married and bam had children and oof got fired,
Zowie did he live and zowie did he die,

With who the hell are you at the corner of his casket, and where
the hell're we going on the right-hand silver knob, and who
the hell cares walking second from the end with an American Beauty wreath from why the hell not,

Very much missed by the circulation staff of the New York Evening Post; deeply, deeply mourned by the B.M.T.[2]
Wham, Mr. Roosevelt; pow, Sears Roebuck; awk, big dipper;
bop, summer rain;
Bong, Mr., bong, Mr., bong, Mr., bong.

1935

1933

You heard the gentleman, with automatic precision, speak
the truth.
Cheers. Triumph.
And then mechanically it followed the gentleman lied.

[2]A subway line in New York City.

Deafening applause. Flashlights, cameras, microphones.
Floral tribute. Cheers.

Down Mrs. Hogan's alley, your hand with others reaching
among the ashes, cinders, scrapiron, garbage, you
found the rib of sirloin wrapped in papal documents. Snatched it. Yours by right, the title clear.
Looked up. Saw lips twitch in the smiling head thrust
from the museum window. "A new deal."

And ran. Escaped. You returned the million dollars. You
restored the lady's virginity.
You were decorated 46 times in rapid succession by
the King of Italy. Took a Nobel prize. Evicted
again, you went downtown, slept at the movies,
stood in the breadline, voted yourself a limousine.
Rage seized the Jewish Veterans of Foreign Wars. In
footnotes, capitals, Latin, italics, the poet of the
Sunday supplements voiced steamheated grief. The
RFC expressed surprise.
And the news, at the Fuller Brush hour, leaked out.
Shouts. Cheers. Stamping of feet. Blizzard of con-
fetti. Thunderous applause.

But the stocks were stolen. The pearls of the actress, stolen
again. The books embezzled.
Inexorably, the thief pursued. Captured inexorably.
Tried. Inexorably acquitted.

And again you heard the gentleman, with automatic
precision, speak the truth.
Saw, once more, the lady's virginity restored.

In the sewers of Berlin, the directors prepared, the room
dark for the seance, she a simple Baroness, you a
lowly millionaire, came face to face with John D.
Christ.
Shook hands, his knife at your back, your knife at his.
Sat down.
Saw issue from his throat the ectoplasm of Pius VIII,
and heard "A test of the people's faith." You said
amen, voted to endorse but warned against default,
you observed the astral form of Nicholas II, and
heard "Sacred union of all." Saw little "Safe for
democracy" Nell. Listened to Adolph "Safety of

France and society" Thiers.
And beheld the faith, the union of rags, blackened
hands, stacked carrion, breached barricades in flame,
no default, credit restored, Union Carbide 94⅜, call
money 10%, disarm, steel five points up, rails rise,
Dupont up, disarm, disarm, and heard again,
ghost out of ghost out of ghost out of ghost,
the voice of the senator reverberate through all the
morgues of all the world, echo again for liberty in
the catacombs of Rome, again sound through the
sweatshops, ghettoes, factories, mines, hunger again
repealed, circle the London cenotaph once more
annulling death, saw ten million dead returned to
life, shot down again, again restored,

Heard once more the gentleman speak, with automatic
precision, the final truth,
once more beheld the lady's virginity, the lady's decency, the lady's purity, the lady's innocence,
paid for, certified, and restored.

Crawled amorously into bed. Felt among the maggots for
the mouldering lips. The crumbled arms. Found
them.
Tumult of cheers. Music and prayer by the YMCA.
Horns, rockets. Spotlight.
The child was nursed on government bonds. Cut its
teeth on a hand grenade. Grew fat on shrapnel.
Bullets. Barbed wire. Chlorine gas. Laughed at
the bayonet through its heart.

These are the things you saw and heard, these are the
things you did, this is your record,
you.

1934

Alfred Hayes 1911–1985

In a Coffee Pot

Tonight, like every night, you see me here
Drinking my coffee slowly, absorbed, alone.

A quiet creature at a table in the rear
Familiar at this evening hour and quite unknown.
The coffee steams. The Greek who runs the joint
Leans on the counter, sucks a dead cigar.
His eyes are meditative, sad, lost in what it is
Greeks think about the kind of Greeks they are.

I brood upon myself. I rot
Night after night in this cheap coffee pot.
I am twenty-two I shave each day
I was educated at a public school
They taught me what to read and what to say
The nobility of man my country's pride
How Nathan Hale died
And Grant took Richmond.
Was it on a summer or a winter's day?
Was it Sherman burned the Southland to the sea?
The men the names the dates have worn away
The classes words the books commencement prize
Here bitter with myself I sit
Holding the ashes of their prompted lies.

The bright boys, where are they now?
Fernando, handsome wop who led us all
The orator in the assembly hall
Arista man the school's big brain.
He's bus boy in an eat-quick joint
At seven per week twelve hours a day.
His eyes are filled with my own pain
His life like mine is thrown away.
Big Jorgensen the honest, blond, six feet,
And Daniels, cunning, sly,—all, all—
You'll find them reading Sunday's want ad sheet.
Our old man didnt know someone
Our mother gave no social teas
You'll find us any morning now
Sitting in the agencies.

You'll find us there before the office opens
Crowding the vestibule before the day begins
The secretary yawns from last night's date
The elevator boy's black face looks out and grins.
We push we crack our bitter jokes we wait
These mornings always find us waiting there
Each one of us has shined his broken shoes
Has brushed his coat and combed his careful hair
Dance hall boys pool parlor kids wise guys

The earnest son the college grad all, all
Each hides the question twitching in his eyes
And smokes and spits and leans against the wall.

We meet each other sometimes on the street
Sixth Avenue's high L bursts overhead
Freak shows whore gypsies hotdog stands
Cajole our penniless eyes our bankrupt hands.
"Working yet?" "The job aint come
Got promised but a runaround."
The L shakes building store and ground
"What's become of Harry? and what's become
Of Charley? Martinelli? Brooklyn Jones?"
"He's married—got a kid—and broke."
And Charley's on Blackwell's, Martinelli's through—
Met him in Grand Central—he's on the bum—
We're all of us on the bum—"
A freak show midget's pounding on a drum
The high L thunders redflag auctioneers
Are selling out a bankrupt world—
The hammer falls—a bid! a bid!—and no one hears . . .

The afternoon will see us in the park
With pigeons and our feet in peanut shells.
We pick a bench apart. We brood.

1934

Tillie Lerner Olsen b. 1913

I Want You Women up North to Know

(Based on a Letter by Felipe Ibarro in New Masses, *Jan. 9th, 1934.)*

i want you women up north to know
how those dainty children's dresses you buy
  at macy's, wanamakers, gimbels, marshall fields,
are dyed in blood, are stitched in wasting flesh,
down in San Antonio, "where sunshine spends the winter."

I want you women up north to see
the obsequious smile, the salesladies trill
  "exquisite work, madame, exquisite pleats"

vanish into a bloated face, ordering more dresses,
gouging the wages down,
dissolve into maria, ambrosa, catalina,
stitching these dresses from dawn to night,
in blood, in wasting flesh.

Catalina Rodriguez, 24,
body shrivelled to a child's at twelve,
catalina rodriguez, last stages of consumption,
works for three dollars a week from dawn to midnight.
A fog of pain thickens over her skull, the parching heat
breaks over her body.
and the bright red blood embroiders the floor of her room.
White rain stitching the night, the bourgeois poet would say,
white gulls of hands, darting, veering,
white lightning, threading the clouds,
this is the exquisite dance of her hands over the cloth,
and her cough, gay, quick, staccato,
like skeleton's bones clattering,
is appropriate accompaniment for the esthetic dance
of her fingers,
and the tremolo, tremolo when the hands tremble with pain.
Three dollars a week,
two fifty-five,
seventy cents a week,
no wonder two thousands eight hundred ladies of joy
are spending the winter with the sun after he goes down—
for five cents (who said this was a rich man's world?) you can
get all the lovin you want
"clap and syph aint much worse than sore fingers, blind eyes, and
t.m."

Maria Vasquez, spinster,
for fifteen cents a dozen stitches garments for children she has never
had,
Catalina Torres, mother of four,
to keep the starved body starving, embroiders from dawn to
night.
Mother of four, what does she think of,
as the needle pocked fingers shift over the silk—
of the stubble-coarse rags that stretch on her own brood,
and jut with the bony ridge that marks hunger's landscape
of fat little prairie-roll bodies that will bulge in the
silk she needles?
(Be not envious, Catalina Torres, look!
on your own children's clothing, embroidery,
more intricate than any a thousand hands could fashion,

there where the cloth is ravelled, or darned,
designs, multitudinous, complex and handmade by Poverty
herself.)

Ambrosa Espinoza trusts in god,
"Todos es de dios, everything is from god,"
through the dwindling night, the waxing day, she bolsters herself up with
it—
but the pennies to keep god incarnate, from ambrosa,
and the pennies to keep the priest in wine, from ambrosa,
ambrosa clothes god and priest with hand-made children's dresses.

Her brother lies on an iron cot, all day and watches,
on a mattress of rags he lies.
For twenty-five years he worked for the railroad, then they laid him off.
(racked days, searching for work; rebuffs; suspicious eyes of policemen.)
goodbye ambrosa, mebbe in dallas I find work; desperate swing for a
freight,
surprised hands, clutching air, and the wheel goes over a
leg,
the railroad cuts it off, as it cut off twenty-five years of his life.)
She says that he prays and dreams of another world, as he lies there, a
heaven (which he does not know was brought to earth in 1917 in
Russia, by workers like him).
Women up north, I want you to know
when you finger the exquisite hand made dresses
what it means, this working from dawn to midnight,
on what strange feet the feverish dawn must come
to maria, catalina, ambrosa,
how the malignant fingers twitching over the pallid faces jerk them to work,
and the sun and the fever mounts with the day—
long plodding hours, the eyes burn like coals, heat jellies the flying fingers,
down comes the night like blindness.
long hours more with the dim eye of the lamp, the breaking back,
weariness crawls in the flesh like worms, gigantic like earth's in winter.
And for Catalina Rodriguez comes the night sweat and the blood
embroidering the darkness.
for Catalina Torres the pinched faces of four huddled
children,
the naked bodies of four bony children,
the chant of their chorale of hunger.
And for twenty eight hundred ladies of joy the grotesque act gone over—
the wink—the grimace—the "feeling like it baby?"
And for Maria Vasquez, spinster, emptiness, emptiness.
flaming with dresses for children she can never fondle.
And for Ambrosa Espinoza—the skeleton body of her brother on his mattress

of rags, boring twin holes in the dark with his eyes to the image of christ
remembering a leg, and twenty-five years cut off from his life by the railroad.

Women up north, I want you to know,
I tell you this can't last forever.

I swear it won't.

1934

Kay Boyle 1903–1993

A Communication to Nancy Cunard[1]

These are not words set down for the rejected
Nor for outcasts cast by the mind's pity
Beyond the aid of lip or hand or from the speech
  Of fires lighted in the wilderness by lost men
  Reaching in fright and passion to each other.
  This is not for the abandoned to hear.

It begins in the dark on a box-car floor, the groaning timber
Stretched from bolt to bolt above the freight-train wheels
That grind and cry aloud like hounds upon the trail, the breathing
  weaving
Unseen within the dark from mouth to nostril, nostril to speaking mouth.
This is the theme of it, stated by one girl in a box-car saying:
"Christ, what they pay you don't keep body and soul together."
"Where was you working?" "Working in a mill-town."
The other girl in the corner saying: "Working the men when we could
  get them."
"Christ, what they pay you," wove the sound of breathing, "don't keep
  shoes on your feet.
Don't feed you. That's why we're shoving on."
(This is not for Virginia Price or Ruby Bates, the white girls dressed like
boys to go; not for Ozie Powell, six years in a cell playing the harp he
played tap-dancing on the box-car boards; not for Olen Montgomery,
the blind boy travelling towards Memphis that night, hopping a ride to
find a doctor who could cure his eyes; not for Eugene Williams or

[1]The poem is based on the famous Scottsboro case in which nine young black men (Charlie Weems, Ozie Powell, Clarence Norris, Olen Montgomery, Willie Robertson, Haywood Patterson, Andy Wright, Roy Wright, Eugene Williams) were convicted of raping Ruby Bates and Victoria Price in 1931 in Alabama. The convictions, based on false testimony, produced death sentences and worldwide protest.

Charlie Weems, not for Willie Robertson nor for Leroy and Andy Wright, thirteen years old the time in March they took him off the train in Paint Rock, Alabama; this is not for Clarence Norris or Haywood Patterson, sentenced three times to die.)

This is for the sheriff with a gold lodge pin
And for the jury venireman who said: "Now, mos' folk don't go on
And think things out. The Bible never speaks
Of sexual intercourses. It jus' says a man knows a woman.
So after Cain killed Abel he went off and knew a woman
In the land of Nod. But the Bible tells as how
There couldn't be no human folk there then.
Now, jus' put two and two together. Cain had off-spring
In the land of Nod so he musta had him a female baboon
Or chimpanzee or somethin' like it.
And that's how the nigger race begun."

This is for the Sunday-school teacher with the tobacco-plug
Who addressed the jury, the juice splattering on the wall,
Pleading: "Whether in overalls or furs a woman is protected by the Alabama law
Against the vilest crime the human species knows. Now, even dogs choose their mates,
But these nine boys are lower than the birds of the air,
Lower than the fish in the sea, lower than the beasts of the fields.
There is a law reaching down from the mountain-tops to the swamps and caves—
It's the wisdom of the ages, there to protect the sacred parts of the female species
Without them having to buckle around their middles
Six-shooters or some other method of defense."

This is set down for the others: people who go and come,
Open a door and pass through it, walk in the streets
With the shops lit, loitering, lingering, gazing.
This is for two men riding, Deputy Sheriff Sandlin, Deputy Sheriff Blacock,
With Ozie Powell, handcuffed. Twelve miles out of Cullman
They shot him through the head.

The Testimony

Haywood Patterson:	*Victoria Price:*
"So here goes an I shell try	
Faithfully an I possibly can	"I
Reference to myself in particularly	cain't
And concerning the other boys personal pride	remember."

And life time upto now.
You must be patience with me and remember "I
Most of my English is not of much interest cain't
And that I am continually remember."
Stopping and searching for the word."

So here goes and I shall try faithfully as possible to tell you as I understand if not mistaken that Olen Montgomery, who was part blind then, kept saying because of the dark there was inside the box-car and outside it: "It sure don't seem to me we're getting anywheres. It sure don't seem like it to me." I and my three comrades whom were with me, namely Roy Wright and his brother Andy and Eugene Williams, and about my character I have always been a good natural sort of boy, but as far as I am personally concerned about those pictures of me in the papers, why they are more or less undoubtedly not having the full likeness of me for I am a sight better-looking than those pictures make me out. Why all my life I spent in and around working for Jews in their stores and so on and I have quite a few Jew friends whom can and always have gave me a good reputation as having regards for those whom have regards for me. The depression ran me away from home, I was off on my way to try my very best to find some work some elsewhere but misfortune befalled me without a moving cause. For it is events and misfortune which happens to people and how some must whom are less fortunate have their lives taken from them and how people die in chair for what they do not do.

The Spiritual for Nine Voices

I went last night to a turkey feast (Oh, God, don't fail your children now!)
My people were sitting there the way they'll sit in heaven
With their wings spread out and their hearts all singing
Their mouths full of food and the table set with glass
(Oh, God, don't fail your children now!)
There were poor men sitting with their fingers dripping honey
All the ugly sisters were fair. I saw my brother who never had a penny
With a silk shirt on and a pair of golden braces
And gems strewn through his hair.

(Were you looking, Father, when the sheriffs came in?
Was your face turned towards us when they had their say?)

There was baked sweet potato and fried corn pone
There was eating galore, there was plenty in the horn.

(Were you there when Victoria Price took the stand?
Did you see the state attorney with her drawers in his hand?
Did you hear him asking for me to burn?)

There were oysters cooked in amplitude
There was sauce in every mouth.
There was ham done slow in spice and clove
And chicken enough for the young and the old.

(Was it you stilled the waters on horse-swapping day
When the mob came to the jail? Was it you come out in a long
tail coat
Come dancing high with the word in your mouth?)

I saw my sister who never had a cent
Come shaking and shuffling between the seats.
Her hair was straight and her nails were pointed
Her breasts were high and her legs double-jointed.

(Oh, God, don't fail your children now!)

The Sentence

Hear how it goes, the wheels of it travelling fast on the rails
The box-cars, the gondolas running drunk through the night.
Hear the long high wail as it flashes through stations unlit
Past signals ungiven running wild through a country
A time when sleepers rouse in their beds and listen
And cannot sleep again.
Hear it passing in no direction, to no destination
Carrying people caught in the box-cars, trapped on the coupled chert-
cars
(Hear the rattle of gravel as it rides whistling through the day and
night.)
Not the old or the young on it, nor people with any difference in their
color or shape,
Not girls or men, negroes or white, but people with this in common:
People that no one had use for, had nothing to give to, no place to offer
But the cars of a freight-train careening through Paint Rock, through
Memphis,
Through town after town without halting.
The loose hands hang down, and swing with the swing of the train in
the darkness,
Holding nothing but poverty, syphilis white as a handful of dust, taking
nothing as baggage
But the sound of the harp Ozie Powell is playing or the voice of Mont-
gomery
Half-blind in oblivion saying: "It sure don't seem to me like we're
getting anywheres.
It don't seem to me like we're getting anywheres at all."

1937

Langston Hughes 1902–1967

Goodbye Christ

Listen, Christ,
You did all right in your day, I reckon—
But that day's gone now.
They ghosted you up a swell story, too.
Called it the Bible—
But it's dead now.
The popes and the preachers 've
Made too much money from it.
They've sold you to too many
Kings, generals, robbers, and killers—
Even to the Tzar and the Cossacks,
Even to Rockefeller's Church,
Even to the Saturday Evening Post.
You ain't no good no more.
They've pawned you
Till you've done wore out.
Goodbye.
Christ Jesus Lord God Jehovah,
Beat it on away from here now.
Make way for a new guy with no religion at all—
A real guy named
Marx Communist Lenin Peasant Stalin Worker ME—
I said, ME!
Go ahead on now,
You're getting in the way of things, Lord,
And please take Saint Ghandi with you when you go,
And Saint Pope Pius,
And Saint Aimee McPherson,[1]
And big black Saint Becton
Of the Consecrated Dime.
And step on the gas, Christ!
Move!
Don't be so slow about movin'!
The world is mine from now on—
And nobody's gonna sell ME
To a king, or a general,
Or a millionaire.

Goodbye Christ, good morning Revolution!

1932

[1]Aimee McPherson (1890–1944), American evangelist.

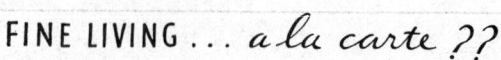

FINE LIVING . . . *a la carte ??*

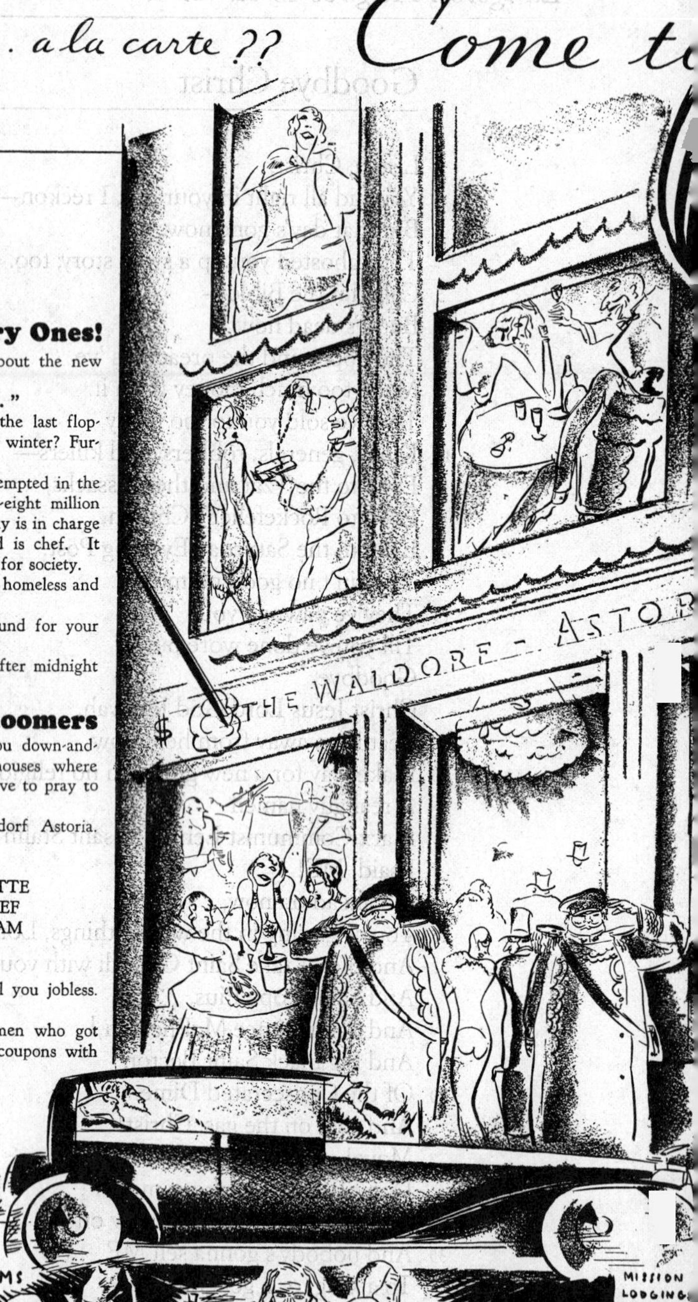

Listen Hungry Ones!

Look! See what **Vanity Fair** says about the new
Waldorf Astoria:

"All the luxuries of private home . . ."

Now, won't that be charming when the last flop-house has turned you down this winter? Furthermore:

"It is far beyond anything hitherto attempted in the hotel world. . . " It cost twenty-eight million dollars. The famous Oscar Tschirky is in charge of banqueting. Alexandre Gastaud is chef. It will be a distinguished background for society.

So when you've got no place else to go, homeless and hungry ones,
choose the Waldorf as a background for your rags—

(Or do you still consider the subway after midnight good enough?)

Roomers

Take a room at the new Waldorf, you down-and-outers—sleepers in charity flop-houses where God pulls a long face, and you have to pray to get a bed.

They serve swell board at the Waldorf Astoria. Look at this menu, will you:

GUMBO CREOLE
CRABMEAT IN CASSOLETTE
BOILED BRISKET OF BEEF
SMALL ONIONS IN CREAM
WATERCRESS SALAD
PEACH MELBA

Have luncheon there this afternoon, all you jobless. Why not?

Dine with some of the men and women who got rich off of your labor, who clip coupons with

Illustration by Walter Steinhilber

the Waldorf-Astoria!

clean white fingers because your hands dug coal, drilled stone, sewed garments, poured steel—to let other people draw dividends and live easy.
(Or haven't you had enough yet of the soup-lines and the bitter bread of charity?)
Walk through Peacock Alley tonight before dinner, and get warm, anyway. You've got nothing else to do.

Evicted Families

All you families put out in the street: Apartments in the Towers are only $10,000 a year. (Three rooms and two baths.) Move in there until times get good, and you can do better. $10,000 and $1.00 are about the same to you, aren't they?
Who cares about money with a wife and kids homeless, and nobody in the family working? Wouldn't a duplex high above the street be grand, with a view of the richest city in the world at your nose?
"A lease, if you prefer; or an arrangement terminable at will."

Negroes

O, Lawd, I done forgot Harlem!
Say, you colored folks, hungry a long time in 135th Street—they got swell music at the Waldorf-Astoria. It sure is a mighty nice place to shake hips in, too. There's dancing after supper in a big warm room. It's cold as hell on Lenox Avenue. All you've had all day is a cup of coffee. Your pawnshop overcoat's a ragged banner on your hungry frame. . . . You know, down-town folks are just crazy about Paul Robeson. Maybe they'd like you, too, black mob from Harlem. Drop in at the Waldorf this afternoon for tea. Stay to dinner. Give Park Avenue a lot of darkie color —free—for nothing! Ask the Junior Leaguers to sing a spiritual for you. They probably know 'em better than you do—and their lips won't be so chapped with cold after they step out of their closed cars in the undercover driveways.
Hallelujah! under-cover driveways!
Ma soul's a witness for de Waldorf-Astoria!
(A thousand nigger section-hands keep the roadbeds smooth, so investments in railroads pay ladies with diamond necklaces staring at Cert murals.)
Thank God A-Mighty!
(And a million niggers bend their backs on rubber plantations, for rich behinds to ride on thick tires to the Theatre Guild tonight.)
Ma soul's a witness!
(And here we stand, shivering in the cold, in Harlem.)
Glory be to God—
De Waldorf-Astoria's open!

Everybody

So get proud and rare back, everybody! The new Waldorf-Astoria's open!
(Special siding for private cars from the railroad yards.)
You ain't been there yet?
(A thousand miles of carpet and a million bath rooms.)
What's the matter? You haven't seen the ads in the papers? Didn't you get a card? Don't you know they specialize in American cooking?
Ankle on down to 49th Street at Park Avenue. Get up off that subway bench tonight with the evening POST for cover! Come on out o' that flop-house! Stop shivering your guts out all day on street corners under the L.
Jesus, ain't you tired yet?

Christmas Card

Hail Mary, Mother of God!
The new Christ child of the Revolution's about to be born.
(Kick hard, red baby, in the bitter womb of the mob.)
Somebody, put an ad in **Vanity Fair** quick!
Call Oscar of the Waldorf—for Christ's sake!
It's almost Christmas, and that little girl—turned whore because her belly was too hungry to stand it any more—wants a nice clean bed for the Immaculate Conception.
Listen, Mary, Mother of God, wrap your new born babe in the red flag of Revolution:
The Waldorf-Astoria's the best manger we've got.
For reservations: Telephone
ELdorado 5-3000.

by Langston Hughes

Air Raid over Harlem

Scenario for a Little Black Movie

Who you gonna put in it?
Me.
Who the hell are you?
Harlem.
Alright, then.
AIR RAID OVER HARLEM
You're not talkin' 'bout Harlem, are you?
That's where my home is,
My bed is, my woman is, my kids is!
Harlem, that's where I live!
Look at my streets
Full of black and brown and
Yellow and high-yellow
Jokers like me.
Lenox, Seventh, Edgecombe, 145th.
Listen,
Hear 'em talkin' and laughin'?
Bombs over Harlem'd kill
People like me—
Kill ME!

Sure, I know
The Ethiopian war broke out last night:[1]
BOMBS OVER HARLEM
Cops on every corner
Most of 'em white
COPS IN HARLEM
Guns and billy-clubs
Double duty in Harlem
Walking in pairs
Under every light
Their faces
WHITE
In Harlem
And mixed in with 'em
A black cop or two
for the sake of the vote in Harlem

[1]In 1935 Italian forces under Mussolini invaded the African nation of Ethiopia, an act that aroused protest among blacks throughout the United States.

GUGSA A TRAITOR TOO
No, sir,
I ain't talking' 'bout you,
Mister Policeman!
No, indeed!
I know we got to keep
ORDER OVER HARLEM
Where the black millions sleep
Shepherds over Harlem
Their armed watch keep
Lest Harlem stirs in its sleep
And maybe remembers
And remembering forgets
To be peaceful and quiet
And has sudden fits
Of raising a black fist
Out of the dark
And that black fist
Becomes a red spark
PLANES OVER HARLEM
Bombs over Harlem
You're just making up
A fake funny picture, ain't you?
Not real, not real?
Did you ever taste blood
From an iron heel
Planted in your mouth
In the slavery-time South
Where to whip a nigger's
Easy as hell—
And not even a *living* nigger
Has a tale to tell
Lest the kick of a boot
Bring more blood to his mouth
In the slavery-time South
And a long billy-club
Split his head wide
And a white hand draw
A gun from its side
And send bullets splaying
Through the streets of Harlem
Where the dead're laying
Lest you stir in your sleep
And remember something
You'd best better keep
In the dark, in the dark
Where the ugly things hide

Under the white lights
With guns by their side
In Harlem?
Say, what are yuh tryin' to do?
Start a riot?
You keep quiet!
You niggers keep quiet!
BLACK WORLD
Never wake up
Lest you knock over the cup
Of gold that the men who
Keep order guard so well
And then—well, then
There'd be hell
To pay
And bombs over Harlem

AIR RAID OVER HARLEM

Bullets through Harlem
And someday
A sleeping giant waking
To snatch bombs from the sky
And push the sun up with a loud cry
Of to hell with the cops on the corners at night
Armed to the teeth under the light
Lest Harlem see red
And suddenly sit on the edge of its bed
And shake the whole world with a new dream
As the squad cars come and the sirens scream
And a big black giant snatches bombs from the sky
And picks up a cop and lets him fly
Into the dust of the Jimcrow past
And laughs and hollers
Kiss my
!x!&!

Hey!
Scenario For A Little Black Movie,
You say?
A RED MOVIE TO MR. HEARST
Black and white workers united as one
In a city where
There'll never be
Air raids over Harlem
FOR THE WORKERS ARE FREE

What workers are free?
THE BLACK AND WHITE WORKERS—
You and me!
Looky here, everybody!
Look at me!

I'M HARLEM!

Harlem, 1935

Lola Ridge 1871–1941

Stone Face

They have carved you into a stone face, Tom Mooney,[1]
You, there lifted high in California
Over the salt wash of the Pacific,
With your eyes . . . crying in many tongues,
Goading, innumerable eyes of the multitudes,
Holding in them all hopes, fears, persecutions,
Forever straining one way.

Even in the Sunday papers,
and your face tight-bitten like a pierced fist,
The eyes have a transfixed gleam
as they had glimpsed some vision and there hung
Impaled as on a bright lance.

Too much lip-foam has dripped on you, too many
And disparate signatures are scrawled on your stone face
that all
Have set some finger on, to say who made you for the
years
To mouth as waves mouth rock . . . you, a rough man,
Rude-nurtured, casually shouldering
Through a May-day crowd in San Francisco,

[1]Tom Mooney (1892–1942), labor leader who was falsely convicted of planting a bomb that killed ten people at a 1916 parade in San Francisco. Despite revelations that the testimony against him was perjured, Mooney remained in prison for twenty-three years.

To be cast up out of the dark mass—terribly gestating,
 swarming without feature,
And raised with torsion to identity.

Now they—who wrote you plain, with Sacco and the fish-
 monger,
High on the scroll of the Republic—
Look up with a muddled irritation at your clenched face,
It set up in full sight under the long
Gaze of the generations—to be there
Haggard in the sunrise, when San Quentin
Prison shall be caved in and its steel ribs
Food for the ant-rust . . . and Governor Rolph[2]
A fleck of dust among the archives.

1935

Edwin Rolfe 1909–1954

Asbestos[1]

Knowing (as John did) nothing of the way
men act when men are roused from lethargy,
and having nothing (as John had) to say
to those he saw were starving just as he

starved, John was like a workhorse. Day by day
he saw his sweat cement the granite tower
(the edifice his bone had built), to stay
listless as ever, older every hour.

John's deathbed is a curious affair:
the posts are made of bone, the spring of nerves,
the mattress bleeding flesh. Infinite air,
compressed from dizzy altitudes, now serves

his skullface as a pillow. Overhead
a vulture leers in solemn mockery,
knowing what John had never known: that dead
workers are dead before they cease to be.

1928

[2]California Governor who refused to pardon Mooney.

[1]Titled "The 100 Percenter" when published in 1928. Retitled "Asbestos" when reprinted in 1933.

Season of Death

This is the sixth winter:
this is the season of death
when lungs contract and the breath of homeless men
freezes on restaurant window panes—men seeking
the sight of rare food
before the head is lowered into the upturned collar
and the shoulders hunched and the shuffling feet
move away slowly, slowly disappear
into a darkened street.

This is the season when rents go up:
men die, and their dying is casual.
I walk along a street, returning
at midnight from my unit. Meet a man
leaning against an illumined wall
and ask him for a light.
His open eyes
stay fixed on mine. And cold rain falling
trickles down his nose, his chin.
"Buddy," I begin . . . and look more closely—
and flee in horror from the corpse's grin.

The eyes pursue you even in sleep and
when you awake they stare at you from the ceiling;
you see the dead face peering from your shoes;
the eggs at Thompson's are the dead man's eyes.
Work dims them for eight hours, but then—
the machines silent—they appear again.

Along the docks, in the terminals, in the subway,
on the street,
in restaurants—the eyes
are focused from the river
among the floating garbage
that other men fish for,
their hands around poles
almost in prayer—
wanting to live,
wanting to live! who also soon
will stand propped by death against a stone-cold wall.

1935

First Love[1]

Again I am summoned to the eternal field
green with the blood still fresh at the roots of flowers,
green through the dust-rimmed memory of faces
that moved among the trees there for the last time
before the final shock, the glazed eye, the hasty mound.

But why are my thoughts in another country?
Why do I always return to the sunken road through corroded hills,
with the Moorish castle's shadow casting ruins over my shoulder
and the black-smocked girl approaching, her hands laden with
grapes?

I am eager to enter it, eager to end it.
Perhaps this one will be the last one.
And men afterward will study our arms in museums
and nod their heads, and frown, and name the inadequate dates
and stumble with infant tongues over the strange place-names.

But my heart is forever captive of that other war
that taught me first the meaning of peace and of comradeship

and always I think of my friend who amid the apparition of bombs
saw on the lyric lake the single perfect swan.

1943

Elegia

Madrid Madrid Madrid Madrid[1]
I call your name endlessly, savor it like a lover.
Ten irretrievable years have exploded like bombs
since last I saw you, since last I slept
in your arms of tenderness and wounded granite.
Ten years since I touched your face in the sun,

[1]Written when the author was in training in the U.S. army during World War II. He is reflecting on his volunteer service (1937–1938) in the Abraham Lincoln Battalion on the side of the Spanish Republic during the Spanish Civil War.

[1]The Spanish capital. Hoping to end the civil war he started with one decisive stroke, Franco ordered a major assault against the city in 1936. German troops assisted him with massive bombing against civilians. The city did not fall until the war's end (and Franco's victory) in 1939; its suffering and defense were symbolic of the war in its entirety.

ten years since the homeless Guadarrama winds[2]
moaned like shivering orphans through your veins
and I moaned with them.
When I think of you, Madrid,
locked in the bordello of the Universal Pimp,[3]
the blood that rushes to my heart and head
blinds me, and I could strangle your blood-bespattered jailors,
choke them with these two hands which once embraced you.
When I think of your breathing body of vibrancy and sun,
silently I weep, in my own native land
which I love no less because I love you more.
Yet I know, in the heart of my heart, that until your liberation
rings through the world of free men near and far
I must wander like an alien everywhere.

Madrid, in these days of our planet's anguish,
forged by the men whose mock morality
begins and ends with the tape of the stock exchanges,
I too sometimes despair. I weep with your dead young poet.
Like him I curse our age and cite the endless wars,
the exiles, dangers, fears, our weariness
of blood, and blind survival, when so many
homes, wives, even memories, are lost.

Yes, I weep with Garcilaso.[4] I remember
your grave face and your subtle smile
and the heart-leaping beauty of your daughters
and even
the tattered elegance of your poorest sons.
I remember the gaiety of your *milicianos*—[5]
my comrades-in-arms. What other city
in history ever raised a battalion of barbers
or reared its own young shirt-sleeved generals?
And I recall them all. If I ever forget you,
Madrid, Madrid, may my right hand lose its cunning.
I speak to you, Madrid, as lover, husband, son.
Accept this human trinity of passion.
I love you, therefore I am faithful to you
and because to forget you would be to forget
everything I love and value in the world.
Who is not true to you is false to every man

[2]Madrid is encircled by the Guadarrama mountains to the north. The winds that sweep down off them are a distinctive part of the city's climate.
[3]Francisco Franco.
[4]Garcilaso de la Vega (1501–1536) was a soldier-poet, the undisputed classic poet of the Golden Age of Spanish literature. The recurrent theme in his poetry is love, typically viewed with melancholy and frustrated idealism.
[5]Soldiers.

and he to whom your name means nothing never
loved
and they who would use your flesh and blood again
as a whore for their wars and their wise investments,
may they be doubly damned! the double murderers
of you and their professed but fictional honor,
of everything untarnished in our time.

Wandering, bitter, in this bitter age,
I dream of your broad avenues like brooks in summer
with your loveliest children alive in them like trout.
In my memory I walk the Calle de Velasquez[6]
to the green Retiro[7] and its green gardens.
Sometimes when I pace the streets of my own city
I am transported to the flowing Alcalá[8]
and my footsteps quicken, I hasten to the spot
where all your living streams meet the Gateway to the Sun.[9]
Sometimes I brood in the shadowed Plaza Mayor[10]
with the ghosts of old Kings and Inquisitors
agitating the balconies with their idiot stares
(which Goya[11] later knew) and under whose stone arches,
those somber rooms beneath the colonnades,
the old watchmaker dreams of tiny, intricate minutes,
the old woman sells pencils and gaudy amber combs,
dreaming of the days when her own body was young,
and the rheumatic peasant with fingers gnarled as grapevines
eagerly displays his muscat raisins;
and the intense boys of ten, with smouldering agèd eyes,
kneel, and gravely, quixotically,
polish the rawhide boots of the soldiers in for an hour
from the mined trenches of the Casa de Campo,[12]
from their posts, buzzing with death, within the skeleton
of University City.[13]

And the girls stroll by,
the young ones, conscious of their womanhood,
and I hear in my undying heart called Madrid
the soldiers boldly calling to them: Oye, guapa, oye!

[6]Street where the International Brigades building was located and where Rolfe edited its English language newspaper.

[7]Park in the middle of Madrid.

[8]A major highway that heads east from its origin in the *Puerta del Sol.*

[9]*Puerta del Sol,* the central plaza of Madrid.

[10]A seventeenth-century square, frequent site for public spectacles, from processions of flagellants to bullfights and the crowning of kings. The Inquisition held its *autos-da-fe* and executed its victims here.

[11]Francisco de Goya (1746–1828), one of Spain's great painters.

[12]A sprawling wooded park northwest of the city that was the scene of major fighting during the attacks on Madrid.

[13]The hillside campus of the University of Madrid that was the scene of dramatic fighting.

I remember your bookshops, the windows always crowded
with new editions of the Gypsy Ballads,[14]
with *Poetas en la España Leal*
and *Romanceros de los Soldados en las Trincheras.*[15]
There was never enough food, but always poetry.
Ah the flood of song that gushed with your blood
into the world during your three years of glory!

And I think: it is a fine thing to be a man
only when man has dignity and manhood.
It is a fine thing to be proud and fearless
only when pride and courage have direction, meaning.
And in our world no prouder words were spoken
in those three agonized years than *I am from Madrid.*

Now ten years have passed with small explosions of hope,
yet you remain, Madrid, the conscience of our lives.
So long as you endure, in chains, in sorrow,
I am not free, no one of us is free.
Any man in the world who does not love Madrid
as he loves a woman, as he values his sex,
that man is less than a man and dangerous,
and so long as he directs the affairs of our world
I must be his undying enemy.

Madrid Madrid Madrid Madrid
Waking and sleeping, your name sings in my heart
and your need fills all my thoughts and acts
(which are gentle but have also been intimate with rifles).
Forgive me, I cannot love you properly from afar—
no distant thing is ever truly loved—
but this, in the wrathful impotence of distance,
I promise: Madrid, if I ever forget you,
may my right hand lose its human cunning,
may my arms and legs wither in their sockets,
may my body be drained of its juices and my brain
go soft and senseless as an imbecile's.
And if I die before I can return to you,
or you, in fullest freedom, are restored to us,
my sons will love you as their father did
Madrid Madrid Madrid

1948

[14] *Romancero Gitano,* 1928: A book of poems by Federico Garcia Lorca. Lorca was murdered by Nationalist partisans just after the outbreak of the Spanish Civil War.

[15] Two wartime poetry anthologies issued in Spain by Loyalist supporters.

Genevieve Taggard 1894–1948

Up State—Depression Summer

One of many patient farms under a cloud—
Clap-boarded house on up-land, Yankee as
cider;
Mortgage the cloud, with another, second mortgage;
One old cloud with another one, drawn closer,
Size of a silver dollar, pouring trouble;
Bad luck everyway, short rations, and the old horse
spavined.
Two cents a quart for milk and the feed sky-high.

June was sinister sweet. Can you eat wild flowers?
The world outside gilt-green, inside bone-bare.
No sugar, coffee . . . So the evil had them . . .
Evil, devil, pain in the belly hit them.
Taxes, words with the grocer, rage. . . .
The trouble veered
And found a body small, for spring infection,
White as the May, slim shoulders and naked ear
Open for poison.
Behind June-morning eyes
The torpor spread.
Suddenly the kid was sick.

Emma found her in the yellow spare-room
That opened north, asleep across her doll
Face on the floor in stupor with thick breath.
And in her bed she hardly ever groaned.
Shut her eyes, stretched arms up, and went down
Deeper in stupor.
And days and weeks went by.
At first no telephone could get the doctor.
Emma sat
Rubbing Nan's chest with goose grease, whipping egg
To make her vomit phlegm. Tom stormed and peeped
at the child.
Banging the kitchen pots with no relief.
"Why haven't we
Medicine here, Emma," ranted Tom,
Knocking the bottles off the window-sill.
"Thermometer. Damn. This is like you.
You let the time go by till the kid gets sick

Before you even think to look or get one.
Go get some sleep. We both don't need to watch.
Go on, I tell you."
Emma left the door
Open. Tom closed it. It was the closing door
That felt like death. Emma stared and stood.
And emerald lightning went on out of doors
Too vaguely flashed to rain and cut the web
Of woven heat that clustered in the trees.

And it was weeks along and still she lay.

The doctor came and went and wanted medicine
No one could buy. And weeks went on.
Hot spell came on; and rank weeds wilted. Haze.
Night's indifferent noise
Went slowly on. Day was the easier night-mare.

One day no one came out to feed the cows.
The house was like a rock stuck in the earth.
Tom's half-gone Ford
Stopped in the barn-yard middle. There the hens
Fluffed dust and slept beneath it. Desolation
Sat busy in the yard somewhere. The cows stamped on
Inside the barn with caking heavy udders.
The wind-mill pined and swung a point or two.
And Fanny, the cow, bore her calf and licked it clean.
No one molested. Nothing came
Out of the house till evening.
Then poor Tom
Blundered about the porch and milked a little
And pumped some water and went in, afraid.
And the kid died as slowly as she could.
Then Emma was sick and would lie and look at
nothing,
Or look at the elms and maples in the sky.
Or she spent a useless day with silent toil,
While the heat broke slowly. Cooking with no sense;
War on all living dirt; anger and fret
At all inanimate things that balked her hands.
Because the fire smoked she cried in a rage.

Tom found his cows, his second haying, found
The solid substance that he walked upon.
The roughness of his tools, the excellent
Hard silence of his clumsy cultivator.
And milking had its comfort, morning and evening.

In the gloom he came into the kitchen, bumping in,
To warn her not to let herself go on
While he was there to eat.
                    Not possible now
To even roughly kiss her.
                    They slept apart
Like grieving beasts that fall to sleep and lie
Their sour blood, their agony in them.

They sold the calf. That fall the bank took over.

1936

To the Negro People

I. Spirituals

My way's cloudy, I cry out,
Cloudy, Lord.
        Who found this way to speak?
Where is this poet's grave?
South is his burying ground. River Mississippi wide
Washes his dust along.
                The Gulf dances level
Sapphire blue near his elbow, where his bones
Sleep in the dust of song, where we lift up our voices
Crying with the dark man when we cry
My way's cloudy.

1939

II. City of the Blues

St. Louis, Mo.;
            river side, piles rotted with river,
Y'hoo, Y'hoo, river whistle tuned harsh.
Get me back to St. Louis.
Burdocks, castor oil plants; ground pecked over by chickens,
    smeared
With droppings and moulted feathers. Fence, coop, mash-
    pans, wire
And a tub of white-wash. Faded rag rug and flat bottle.
(This nook and nobody here but the half-grown hens.)

Tug going by, puffpuff, small wave tapered. St. Louis dock
Stacked high, six blocks away, belted with wharves,
Coal smoke, winches, shovels,—crash of freight,
Pillars of white puffed upward, stiff white from the trains.
Bank all slums and slime, frame houses. Dark, wet, cold.
(So sweet, so cold, so fair.)
Castor oil plants and acanthus.
(When they kill, they kill
Here, and dump the body here.) The river, pale clay
Deep down stream. Y'hoo, Y'hoo yell the trains,
And the boats yell, too.
But the silence, the silence
Blows clean through your bones.
In the chicken yard, listlessly, beside the piles, waiting for
nothing
The Negro boy, head bent, beating out his tattoo
Nimble and complex, on the fence . . .
Get ready to blow, trumpets, trumpets, trumpets,
O Gabriel,[1] O Willie Smith[2]
Take it away.

1939

III. Proud Day

(Marian Anderson on the steps of the Lincoln Memorial)[1]

Our sister sang on the Lincoln steps. Proud day.
We came to hear our sister sing. Proud day.
Voice out of depths, poise with memory,
What goodness, what splendor lay long under foot!
Our sister with a lasso of sorrow and triumph
Caught America, made it listen. Proud day.

The peaceful Lincoln sat so still. Proud day.
Waiting the Republic to be born again. Proud day.
Never, never forget how the dark people rewarded us
Giving out of their want and their little freedom
This blazing star. This blazing star.
Something spoke in my patriot heart. Proud day.

1939

[1]An angel named in both the Old and New Testaments. He is to blow the trumpet on Judgment Day.
[2]Willie Smith (1897–1973), legendary American jazz pianist.

[1]Marian Anderson (1902–1993), American singer renowned for her performance of spirituals. She also devoted herself to the struggle for civil rights.

IV. Chant for the Great Negro Poet of America Not Yet Born

He comes soon now, this spanning poet, the wide
Man, the dark, conscious of the apex, the place of his people.
He is sure to come,—up from the sorrowing side,
Born, awake, with the urgent rising of his people.

He will be our poet when he comes, he will wear
Scars. And a dazzling joy will give him the mark of his
    people.
We will hear his voice; in our nearness share
The struggle he joins, with the powerful mass of his people.

His ancestors are splendid; they are ours also; but he is heir.
The Hebrew poets, so long the fellows of his people.
Those who Englished them, anonymous, and also their
Kin—Blake, Whitman, and the honest preachers of his
    people.

He comes to us with the authority of those who cried
In darkness. He, to be the poet of all rising people.
A fervent kiss from all of us who have died
Going down, singing, for him, rising up in majesty, singing
    with the universal
    singing of his people.

1941

Ode in Time of Crisis[1]

Now in the fright of change when bombed towns vanish
In fountains of debris
We say to the stranger coming across the sea
Not here, not here, go elsewhere!
Here we keep
Bars up. Wall out the danger, tightly seal
The ports, the intake from the alien world we fear.

[1]Alludes to several crises of national identity during World War II, from America's refusal to accept refugees from Nazi Germany to our decision to imprison American citizens of Japanese descent for the duration of the war.

It is a time of many errors now.
And this the error of children when they feel
But cannot say their terror. To shut off the stream
In which we moved and still move, if we move.
The alien is the nation, nothing more or less.
How set ourselves at variance to prove
The alien is not the nation. And so end the dream.
Forbid our deep resource from whence we came,
And the very seed of greatness.

This is to do
Something like suicide; to choose
Sterility—forget the secret of our past
Which like a magnet drew
A wealth of men and women hopeward. And now to lose
In ignorant blindness what we might hold fast.
The fright of change, not readiness. Instead
Inside our wall we will today pursue
The man we call the alien, take his print,
Give him a taste of the thing from which he fled,
Suspicion him. And again we fail.
How shall we release his virtue, his good-will
If by such pressure we hold his life in jail?
The alien is the nation. Nothing else.
And so we fail and so we jail ourselves.
Landlocked, the stagnant stream.
So ends the dream.

O country-men, are we working to undo
Our lusty strength, our once proud victory?
Yes, if by this fright we break our strength in two.
If we make of every man we jail the enemy.
If we make ourselves the jailer locked in jail.
Our laboring wills, our brave, too brave to fail
Remember this nation by millions believed to be
Great and of mighty forces born; and resolve to be free,
To continue and renew.

1940

To the Veterans of the Abraham Lincoln Brigade[1]

Say of them
They knew no Spanish
At first, and nothing of the arts of war
At first,
how to shoot, how to attack, how to retreat
How to kill, how to meet killing
At first.
Say they kept the air blue
Grousing and griping,
Arid words and harsh faces. Say
They were young;
The haggard in a trench, the dead on the olive slope
All young. And the thin, the ill and the shattered,
Sightless, in hospitals, all young.

Say of them they were young, there was much they did not
know,
They were human. Say it all; it is true. Now say
When the eminent, the great, the easy, the old,
And the men on the make
Were busy bickering and selling,
Betraying, conniving, transacting, splitting hairs,
Writing bad articles, signing bad papers,
Passing bad bills,
Bribing, blackmailing,
Whimpering, meaching, garroting,—they
Knew and acted
understood and died.

Or if they did not die came home to peace
That is not peace.
Say of them
They are no longer young, they never learned
The arts, the stealth of peace, this peace, the tricks of fear;
And what they knew, they know.
And what they dared, they dare.

1941

[1]Written after these veterans of the Spanish Civil War had their loyalty questioned by the House Un-American Activities Committee.

E. E. Cummings 1894–1962

Edward Estlin Cummings, the son of Edward Cummings, a Unitarian minister, and Rebecca Haswell Clarke, a woman of distinguished literary and intellectual ancestry, grew up in Cambridge, Massachusetts, a community dominated by the learning of Harvard University and the literary spirit of Longfellow and Lowell. Although he was educated at the Cambridge Latin School and Harvard (A.B. in classics, 1915; A.M. in English, 1916), he soon became a rebel against the Cambridge atmosphere.

While at Harvard, Cummings became intensely interested in the new movements in the visual arts: impressionism, post-impressionism, cubism, and futurism, and he began painting in the modern manner. He read the new poets: Pound, H.D., Sandburg, and Amy Lowell, and he started to write free verse and follow the imagist principles. But seeking fresh and unusual effects, he began, by 1916, to create a style of his own, a form of literary cubism, breaking up his material and attempting to present it so that its appearance on the page directed the reader toward its meaning.

When the United States entered the European war in 1917, Cummings volunteered for service in the Norton-Harjes Ambulance Corps. While he was on duty in France, his pacifist leanings led to his being imprisoned in a French concentration camp under suspicion of espionage. This experience formed the basis of his autobiographical book *The Enormous Room.* Continuing to write verse, Cummings established, by 1919, a distinctive poetic style that had its own grammatical usages, its own punctuation, and its own rules for capitalization, in the freest kind of verse.

His work, published in *Tulips and Chimneys* and later volumes, met with much critical hostility, expressed in complaints about his "exploded fragments," "eccentric punctuation," and "jigsaw puzzle" arrangements. His harsh satirical verse as well as his erotic poems served also to identify him as a social iconoclast. But Cummings's trip to Russia in 1931 and two troublesome marriages brought about a change in his youthful and exuberant outlook. He became politically more conservative and more irascible in temper, as seen in such volumes as *Eimi,* an account of his experience in Russia, and *No Thanks,* a collection of his most experimental verse. At the same time, he continued to give voice to a basic affirmation of life, especially in whatever was simple, natural, individual, or unique, and he expressed powerful opposition to any social forces that would hinder uniqueness, forces such as conformity, groupiness, imitation, and artificiality. His poem "anyone lived in a pretty how town" gives mythic expression to these attitudes.

The horrors of World War II, the atomic bomb, and the cruel Russian suppression of the Hungarian revolution all made their impact upon Cummings's later work, but he was still able to express moods of serenity, particularly in response to the beauties of the natural world.

Like Joyce, Eliot, Faulkner, and other literary innovators, Cummings gradually taught his audience how to read his work; and with Pound and others he carried free verse into visually directive forms. The appearance on the page of much present-day poetry owes something to the flexibility Cummings introduced into American verse.

Richard S. Kennedy
Temple University

PRIMARY WORKS

The Enormous Room, 1922; *Tulips and Chimneys,* 1923 (complete edition, 1976); *Is 5,* 1926; *Him,* 1927; *ViVa,* 1931; *Eimi,* 1933; *No Thanks,* 1935; *50 Poems,* 1940; *1 × 1,* 1944; *Xiape,* 1950; *i: six non-lectures,* 1953; *Complete Poems,* 1972; *Etcetera,* 1983.

[Buffalo Bill's]

Buffalo Bill 's
defunct
                    who used to
                    ride a watersmooth-silver
                                                  stallion
and break onetwothreefourfive pigeonsjustlikethat
                                                                                      Jesus

he was a handsome man
                                    and what i want to know is
how do you like your blueeyed boy
Mister Death

1920, 1923

[into the strenuous briefness]

into the strenuous briefness
Life:
handorgans and April
darkness,friends

i charge laughing.
Into the hair-thin tints
of yellow dawn,
into the women-coloured twilight

i smilingly
glide. I
into the big vermilion departure
swim,sayingly;

(Do you think?)the
i do, world
is probably made
of roses & hello:

(of solongs and,ashes)

1923

[the Cambridge ladies who live in furnished souls]

the Cambridge ladies who live in furnished souls
are unbeautiful and have comfortable minds
(also, with the church's protestant blessings
daughters,unscented shapeless spirited)
they believe in Christ and Longfellow,both dead,
are invariably interested in so many things—
at the present writing one still finds
delighted fingers knitting for the is it Poles?
perhaps. While permanent faces coyly bandy
scandal of Mrs. N and Professor D
.... the Cambridge ladies do not care,above
Cambridge if sometimes in its box of
sky lavender and cornerless,the
moon rattles like a fragment of angry candy

1923

[i like my body when it is with your]

i like my body when it is with your
body. It is so quite new a thing.
Muscles better and nerves more.
i like your body.   i like what it does,
i like its hows.   i like to feel the spine
of your body and its bones,and the trembling
-firm-smooth ness and which i will
again and again and again
kiss,   i like kissing this and that of you,

i like,slowly stroking the,shocking fuzz
of your electric fur, and what-is-it comes
over parting flesh.... And eyes big love-crumbs,

and possibly i like the thrill

of under me you so quite new

1925

[my sweet old etcetera]

my sweet old etcetera
aunt lucy during the recent

war could and what
is more did tell you just
what everybody was fighting

for,
my sister

isabel created hundreds
(and
hundreds)of socks not to
mention shirts fleaproof earwarmers

etcetera wristers etcetera,my

mother hoped that

i would die etcetera
bravely of course my father used
to become hoarse talking about how it was
a privilege and if only he
could meanwhile my

self etcetera lay quietly
in the deep mud et

cetera
(dreaming,
et
  cetera,of

Your smile
eyes knees and of your Etcetera)

1926

[since feeling is first]

since feeling is first
who pays any attention
to the syntax of things
will never wholly kiss you;

wholly to be a fool
while Spring is in the world

my blood approves,
and kisses are a better fate
than wisdom
lady i swear by all flowers. Don't cry
—the best gesture of my brain is less than
your eyelids' flutter which says

we are for each other:then
laugh,leaning back in my arms
for life's not a paragraph

And death i think is no parenthesis

1926

[i sing of Olaf glad and big]

XXX

i sing of Olaf glad and big
whose warmest heart recoiled at war:
a conscientious object-or

his wellbelovéd colonel(trig
westpointer most succinctly bred)
took erring Olaf soon in hand;

but—though an host of overjoyed
noncoms(first knocking on the head
him)do through icy waters roll
that helplessness which others stroke
with brushes recently employed
anent this muddy toiletbowl,
while kindred intellects evoke
allegiance per blunt instruments—
Olaf(being to all intents
a corpse and wanting any rag
upon what God unto him gave)
responds, without getting annoyed
"I will not kiss your fucking flag"

straightway the silver bird looked grave
(departing hurriedly to shave)

but—though all kinds of officers
(a yearning nation's blueeyed pride)
their passive prey did kick and curse
until for wear their clarion
voices and boots were much the worse,
and egged the firstclassprivates on
his rectum wickedly to tease
by means of skilfully applied
bayonets roasted hot with heat—
Olaf(upon what were once knees)
does almost ceaselessly repeat
"there is some shit I will not eat"

our president,being of which
assertions duly notified
threw the yellowsonofabitch
into a dungeon,where he died

Christ(of His mercy infinite)
i pray to see;and Olaf, too

preponderatingly because
unless statistics lie he was
more brave than me:more blond than you.

1931

[Picasso]

Picasso[1]
you give us Things
which
bulge:grunting lungs pumped full of sharp thick mind

you make us shrill
presents always
shut in the sumptuous screech of
simplicity

(out of the
black unbunged
Something gushes vaguely a squeak of planes
or

between squeals of
Nothing grabbed with circular shrieking tightness
solid screams whisper.)
Lumberman of The Distinct

your brain's
axe only chops hugest inherent
Trees of Ego,from
whose living and biggest

bodies lopped
of every
prettiness

you hew form truly

1925

[anyone lived in a pretty how town]

anyone lived in a pretty how town
(with up so floating many bells down)

[1]Twentieth-century Spanish painter; the originator of the cubist technique.

spring summer autumn winter
he sang his didn't he danced his did.

Women and men(both little and small)
cared for anyone not at all
they sowed their isn't they reaped their same
sun moon stars rain

children guessed(but only a few
and down they forgot as up they grew
autumn winter spring summer)
that noone loved him more by more

when by now and tree by leaf
she laughed his joy she cried his grief
bird by snow and stir by still
anyone's any was all to her

someones married their everyones
laughed their cryings and did their dance
(sleep wake hope and then)they
said their nevers they slept their dream

stars rain sun moon
(and only the snow can begin to explain
how children are apt to forget to remember
with up so floating many bells down)

one day anyone died i guess
(and noone stooped to kiss his face)
busy folk buried them side by side
little by little and was by was

all by all and deep by deep
and more by more they dream their sleep
noone and anyone earth by april
wish by spirit and if by yes.

Women and men(both dong and ding)
summer autumn winter spring
reaped their sowing and went their came
sun moon stars rain

1940

[plato told]

plato told

him:he couldn't
believe it(jesus

told him;he
wouldn't believe
it)lao

tsze
certainly told
him,and general
(yes

mam)
sherman;[1]
and even
(believe it
or

not)you
told him:i told
him;we told him
(he didn't believe it,no

sir)it took
a nipponized bit of
the old sixth

avenue
el;[2]in the top of his head:to tell
him

1944

[1]General in the American Civil War who said, "War is hell."
[2]Cummings supposes that when the Sixth Avenue Elevated Train tracks were demolished, the scrap iron was sold to the Japanese for reuse in munitions making.

[what if a much of a which of a wind]

what if a much of a which of a wind
gives the truth to summer's lie;
bloodies with dizzying leaves the sun
and yanks immortal stars awry?
Blow king to beggar and queen to seem
(blow friend to fiend:blow space to time)
—when skies are hanged and oceans drowned,
the single secret will still be man

what if a keen of a lean wind flays
screaming hills with sleet and snow:
strangles valleys by ropes of thing
and stifles forests in white ago?
Blow hope to terror;blow seeing to blind
(blow pity to envy and soul to mind)
—whose hearts are mountains,roots are trees,
it's they shall cry hello to the spring

what if a dawn of a doom of a dream
bites this universe in two,
peels forever out of his grave
and sprinkles nowhere with me and you?
Blow soon to never and never to twice
(blow life to isn't:blow death to was)
—all nothing's only our hugest home;
the most who die,the more we live

1944

[pity this busy monster, manunkind]

pity this busy monster,manunkind,

not. Progress is a comfortable disease:
your victim(death and life safely beyond)

plays with the bigness of his littleness
—electrons deify one razorblade
into a mountainrange;lenses extend

unwish through curving wherewhen till unwish
returns on its unself.

A world of made
is not a world of born—pity poor flesh

and trees,poor stars and stones,but never this
fine specimen of hypermagical

ultraomnipotence. We doctors know

a hopeless case if—listen:there's a hell
of a good universe next door;let's go

1944

T. S. Eliot 1888–1965

Born in St. Louis, Missouri, Thomas Stearns Eliot was the son of Charlotte Stearns, a sometime amateur poet strictly committed to New England beliefs, and Henry Ware Eliot, a successful businessman. His grandfather, William Greenleaf Eliot, a Unitarian minister with a strong sense of civic and religious duty, had moved from Massachusetts in 1831, founding the local church, school, and the college which subsequently became Washington University. Thus, growing up a "South Westerner," Eliot was nonetheless always aware of his New England heritage, an awareness deepened by his mother's tutelage, by regular family summer vacations on Cape Ann, and by his education at Milton Academy (1905–06) and Harvard (1906–10, 1911–14).

However strong these American influences, Eliot chose to live almost his entire adult life abroad. In 1910 he went to the Sorbonne for a year, and after three graduate years studying philosophy at Harvard, he went to Merton College at Oxford on a fellowship. In September, 1914, he met Ezra Pound, to whom he read "The Love Song of J. Alfred Prufrock." Pound immediately recognized its merit and persuaded Harriet Monroe to publish it in *Poetry* in June 1915, the same month Eliot married Vivien Haigh-Wood. His family strongly disapproved of the sudden marriage and temporarily withdrew support. Faced with the necessity of making a living, Eliot taught in public schools for two years. By 1917 he had completed his doctoral dissertation on F. H. Bradley, but he did not return to Harvard to receive the degree and join the philosophy department, despite his outspoken dislike of grammar school teaching. Instead he became a bank clerk at Lloyd's, which he also found wearing. It was not until 1925 that, through the efforts of influential literary friends, Eliot obtained a congenial position as a director at the publishing firm of Faber and Gwyer, a post he retained for the rest of his life.

Ultimately, the strongest force in keeping him abroad was his growing reputation in literary London, a reputation enhanced by the publication of *Prufrock and Other Observations* (1917) and *Poems* (1920). He also had begun to establish himself as a critic, the first collection of his essays, *The Sacred Wood,* appearing in 1920. With the publication of *The Waste Land* in 1922, he achieved the status he was to hold for the next two decades as the most influential poet and critic writing in English.

In his private life, however, and especially at the time he was writing *The Waste Land,* Eliot was at the point of despair. His sense of conflict with his parents, his dislike of his job, and, above all, the strain of his marriage brought him close to collapse.

After years of tension and unhappiness, to which both undoubtedly contributed, Eliot arranged a formal separation from Vivien in 1932, as he made his first return home to give a series of lectures at Harvard. There is much evidence in "The Family Reunion" and elsewhere of the guilt he continued to feel over forcing the separation. As for Vivien Eliot, always high-strung, her intermittent instability eventually worsened into a nervous breakdown, and she was institutionalized from 1939 until her death in 1947. Eliot did not remarry until 1958, his seventieth year, and he seems to have been supremely happy in these last years with Valerie Eliot.

As Eliot was being recognized as the premier poet of the 1920s, he was also noted for his essays on literature. Certain of his theories, abbreviated in catch phrases, are still part of the critical vocabulary—the "impersonality" of the poet; "dissociation of sensibility" into thought and feeling; the "objective correlative" by which an emotion is expressed. Essays on Donne, the Metaphysical Poets, Dryden, and, especially, early seventeenth-century dramatists, given what was by now Eliot's almost magisterial literary authority, were highly influential in contributing to a reconsideration of these figures. Eliot's role as a major critical voice was facilitated by his launching of *Criterion* in 1922, a journal which he edited until 1939; and he continued to publish a wide range of essays there and elsewhere throughout the 1920s.

In 1935 "Burnt Norton" was published, followed by "East Coker" (1940), "The Dry Salvages" (1941), and "Little Gidding" (1942). They were collected as *Four Quartets* in 1943, the major opus of the last part of Eliot's career. Both external and internal evidence indicates that he did not at the outset envisage *Four Quartets* as a unified poem, although read together, the *Quartets* provide a better sense of the total thrust, not only of the four pieces, but of Eliot's entire work. The differences between the early and late poetry are marked, but there is also an essential thematic continuity.

Many readers have regarded *Four Quartets* as Eliot's culminating achievement, appropriately recognized by the Nobel Prize in 1948. Others have entered demurrals. Several close readings have recently presented Eliot as a poet essentially torn between romantic yearning and intellectual detachment, unwilling or unable in this final major effort to maintain the temper of negative capability so movingly evident in his earlier poems. In this view, *Four Quartets* becomes an assertion in desperation, a falling off from the poetry of experience to the more prosaic, discursive mode of "a man reasoning with himself in solitude," with a consequent loss of intensity and even credibility. Whether or not one finds validity in such "corrections" to previous understandings of Eliot, they are valuable in underlining the importance of continued examination of his writing. In any reading, his work stands as one of the most distinctive contributions of the twentieth century to the literary tradition.

Sam S. Baskett
Michigan State University

PRIMARY WORKS

Selected Essays, 1932, 1960; *The Complete Poems and Plays of T. S. Eliot,* 1952, 1962; *The Complete Plays of T. S. Eliot,* 1967; *The Waste Land: A Facsimile and Transcript of the Original Drafts Including the Annotations of Ezra Pound,* 1971; *Inventions of the March Hare,* ed. Christopher Ricks, 1997.

The Love Song of J. Alfred Prufrock

S'io credessi che mia risposta fosse
a persona che mai tornasse al mondo,
questa fiamma staria senza più scosse.
Ma per ciò che giammai di questo fondo
non tornò vivo alcun, s'i'odo il vero,
senza tema d'infamia ti rispondo.[1]

Let us go then, you and I,
When the evening is spread out against the sky
Like a patient etherised upon a table;
Let us go, through certain half-deserted streets,
The muttering retreats
Of restless nights in one-night cheap hotels
And sawdust restaurants with oyster-shells:
Streets that follow like a tedious argument
Of insidious intent
To lead you to an overwhelming question . . .
Oh, do not ask, 'What is it?'
Let us go and make our visit.

In the room the women come and go
Talking of Michelangelo.

The yellow fog that rubs its back upon the window-panes,
The yellow smoke that rubs its muzzle on the window-panes,
Licked its tongue into the corners of the evening,
Lingered upon the pools that stand in drains,
Let fall upon its back the soot that falls from chimneys,
Slipped by the terrace, made a sudden leap,
And seeing that it was a soft October night,
Curled once about the house, and fell asleep.

And indeed there will be time
For the yellow smoke that slides along the street
Rubbing its back upon the window-panes;
There will be time, there will be time
To prepare a face to meet the faces that you meet;
There will be time to murder and create,

[1]"If I thought my answer were to one who could ever return to the world, this flame would move no more; but since no one has ever returned alive from this depth, if what I hear be true, without fear of infamy I answer you." (Dante, *Inferno* XXVII, 61–66.) Guido da Montefeltro, in Hell as punishment for giving false counsel without repenting, thus confesses to Dante since he believes he cannot return to earth and report Guido's shame.

And time for all the works and days of hands
That lift and drop a question on your plate;
Time for you and time for me,
And time yet for a hundred indecisions,
And for a hundred visions and revisions,
Before the taking of a toast and tea.

In the room the women come and go
Talking of Michelangelo.

And indeed there will be time
To wonder, 'Do I dare?' and, 'Do I dare?'
Time to turn back and descend the stair,
With a bald spot in the middle of my hair—
(They will say: 'How his hair is growing thin!')
My morning coat, my collar mounting firmly to the chin,
My necktie rich and modest, but asserted by a simple pin—
(They will say: 'But how his arms and legs are thin!')
Do I dare
Disturb the universe?
In a minute there is time
For decisions and revisions which a minute will reverse.

For I have known them all already, known them all—
Have known the evenings, mornings, afternoons,
I have measured out my life with coffee spoons;
I know the voices dying with a dying fall
Beneath the music from a farther room.
  So how should I presume?

And I have known the eyes already, known them all—
The eyes that fix you in a formulated phrase,
And when I am formulated, sprawling on a pin,
When I am pinned and wriggling on the wall,
Then how should I begin
To spit out all the butt-ends of my days and ways?
  And how should I presume?

And I have known the arms already, known them all—
Arms that are braceleted and white and bare
(But in the lamplight, downed with light brown hair!)
Is it perfume from a dress
That makes me so digress?
Arms that lie along a table, or wrap about a shawl.
  And should I then presume?
  And how should I begin?

* * *

Shall I say, I have gone at dusk through narrow streets
And watched the smoke that rises from the pipes
Of lonely men in shirt-sleeves, leaning out of windows? . . .

I should have been a pair of ragged claws
Scuttling across the floors of silent seas.

* * *

And the afternoon, the evening, sleeps so peacefully!
Smoothed by long fingers,
Asleep . . . tired . . . or it malingers,
Stretched on the floor, here beside you and me.
Should I, after tea and cakes and ices,
Have the strength to force the moment to its crisis?
But though I have wept and fasted, wept and prayed,
Though I have seen my head (grown slightly bald) brought in
upon a platter,[2]
I am no prophet—and here's no great matter;
I have seen the moment of my greatness flicker,
And I have seen the eternal Footman hold my coat, and snicker,
And in short, I was afraid.

And would it have been worth it, after all,
After the cups, the marmalade, the tea,
Among the porcelain, among some talk of you and me,
Would it have been worth while,
To have bitten off the matter with a smile,
To have squeezed the universe into a ball[3]
To roll it towards some overwhelming question,
To say: 'I am Lazarus,[4] come from the dead,
Come back to tell you all, I shall tell you all'—
If one, settling a pillow by her head,
Should say: 'That is not what I meant at all.
That is not it, at all.'

And would it have been worth it, after all,
Would it have been worth while,
After the sunsets and the dooryards and the sprinkled streets,
After the novels, after the teacups, after the skirts that trail along
the floor—

[2]Mark 6:17–20 and Matthew 14:3–11 recount the story of John the Baptist, forerunner and baptiser of Christ. He was beheaded at the request of Salome, who then presented his head to Queen Herodias.

[3]Here, as in line 23, an echo of the seductive *carpe diem* plea of Andrew Marvell's "To His Coy Mistress."

[4]Luke 16:19–31 and John 11:1–44 recount the resurrection of Lazarus.

And this, and so much more?—
It is impossible to say just what I mean!
But as if a magic lantern threw the nerves in patterns on a screen:
Would it have been worth while
If one, settling a pillow or throwing off a shawl,
And turning toward the window, should say:
    'That is not it at all,
    That is not what I meant, at all.'

* * *

No! I am not Prince Hamlet, nor was meant to be;
Am an attendant lord, one that will do
To swell a progress, start a scene or two,
Advise the prince; no doubt, an easy tool,
Deferential, glad to be of use,
Politic, cautious, and meticulous;
Full of high sentence, but a bit obtuse;[5]
At times, indeed, almost ridiculous—
Almost, at times, the Fool.

I grow old . . . I grow old . . .
I shall wear the bottoms of my trousers rolled.

Shall I part my hair behind? Do I dare to eat a peach?
I shall wear white flannel trousers, and walk upon the beach.
I have heard the mermaids[6] singing, each to each.

I do not think that they will sing to me.

I have seen them riding seaward on the waves
Combing the white hair of the waves blown back
When the wind blows the water white and black.

We have lingered in the chambers of the sea
By sea-girls wreathed with seaweed red and brown
Till human voices wake us, and we drown.

1915

[5]Qualities associated with Polonius in Shakespeare's *Hamlet.* Line 74 echoes Hamlet's mocking of Polonius, II. ii. 205–6: "you yourself, sir, should be as old as I am, if like a crab you could go backward."

[6]The "mermaid passage" may be read in the context of the Siren Tradition—mermaids/sirens considered as muses, "not wholly evil, but very far from entirely good."

Preludes

I

The winter evening settles down
With smell of steaks in passageways.
Six o'clock.
The burnt-out ends of smoky days.
And now a gusty shower wraps
The grimy scraps
Of withered leaves about your feet
And newspapers from vacant lots;
The showers beat
On broken blinds and chimney-pots,
And at the corner of the street
A lonely cab-horse steams and stamps.
And then the lighting of the lamps.

II

The morning comes to consciousness
Of faint stale smells of beer
From the sawdust-trampled street
With all its muddy feet that press
To early coffee-stands.
With the other masquerades
That time resumes,
One thinks of all the hands
That are raising dingy shades
In a thousand furnished rooms.

III

You tossed a blanket from the bed,
You lay upon your back, and waited;
You dozed, and watched the night revealing
The thousand sordid images
Of which your soul was constituted;
They flickered against the ceiling.
And when all the world came back
And the light crept up between the shutters
And you heard the sparrows in the gutters,
You had such a vision of the street
As the street hardly understands;

Sitting along the bed's edge, where
You curled the papers from your hair,
Or clasped the yellow soles of feet
In the palms of both soiled hands.

IV

His soul stretched tight across the skies
That fade behind a city block,
Or trampled by insistent feet
At four and five and six o'clock;
And short square fingers stuffing pipes,
And evening newspapers, and eyes
Assured of certain certainties,
The conscience of a blackened street
Impatient to assume the world.

I am moved by fancies that are curled
Around these images, and cling:
The notion of some infinitely gentle
Infinitely suffering thing.

Wipe your hand across your mouth, and laugh;
The worlds revolve like ancient women
Gathering fuel in vacant lots.

1917

Tradition and the Individual Talent[1]

In English writing we seldom speak of tradition, though we occasionally apply its name in deploring its absence. We cannot refer to "the tradition" or to "a tradition"; at most, we employ the adjective in saying that the poetry of So-and-so is "traditional" or even "too traditional." Seldom, perhaps, does the word appear except in a phrase of censure. If otherwise, it is vaguely approbative, with the implication, as to the work approved, of some pleasing archaeological reconstruction. You can hardly make the word agreeable to English ears without this comfortable reference to the reassuring science of archaeology.

Certainly the word is not likely to appear in our appreciations of living or dead writers. Every nation, every race, has not only its own creative, but its own critical turn of mind; and is even more oblivious of the shortcomings and limitations of

[1]From *The Sacred Wood* (1920), first published in *The Egoist* (1919).

its critical habits than of those of its creative genius. We know, or think we know, from the enormous mass of critical writing that has appeared in the French language the critical method or habit of the French; we only conclude (we are such unconscious people) that the French are "more critical" than we, and sometimes even plume ourselves a little with the fact, as if the French were the less spontaneous. Perhaps they are; but we might remind ourselves that criticism is as inevitable as breathing, and that we should be none the worse for articulating what passes in our minds when we read a book and feel an emotion about it, for criticizing our own minds in their work of criticism. One of the facts that might come to light in this process is our tendency to insist, when we praise a poet, upon those aspects of his work in which he least resembles any one else. In these aspects or parts of his work we pretend to find what is individual, what is the peculiar essence of the man. We dwell with satisfaction upon the poet's difference from his predecessors, especially his immediate predecessors; we endeavour to find something that can be isolated in order to be enjoyed. Whereas if we approach a poet without this prejudice we shall often find that not only the best, but the most individual parts of his work may be those in which the dead poets, his ancestors, assert their immortality most vigorously. And I do not mean the impressionable period of adolescence, but the period of full maturity.

Yet if the only form of tradition, of handing down, consisted in following the ways of the immediate generation before us in a blind or timid adherence to its successes, "tradition" should positively be discouraged. We have seen many such simple currents soon lost in the sand; and novelty is better than repetition. Tradition is a matter of much wider significance. It cannot be inherited, and if you want it you must obtain it by great labour. It involves, in the first place, the historical sense, which we may call nearly indispensable to any one who would continue to be a poet beyond his twenty-fifth year; and the historical sense involves a perception, not only of the pastness of the past, but of its presence; the historical sense compels a man to write not merely with his own generation in his bones, but with a feeling that the whole of the literature of Europe from Homer and within it the whole of the literature of his own country has a simultaneous existence and composes a simultaneous order. This historical sense, which is a sense of the timeless as well as of the temporal and of the timeless and of the temporal together, is what makes a writer traditional. And it is at the same time what makes a writer most acutely conscious of his place in time, of his own contemporaneity.

No poet, no artist of any art, has his complete meaning alone. His significance, his appreciation is the appreciation of his relation to the dead poets and artists. You cannot value him alone; you must set him, for contrast and comparison, among the dead. I mean this as a principle of aesthetic, not merely historical, criticism. The necessity that he shall conform, that he shall cohere, is not onesided; what happens when a new work of art is created is something that happens simultaneously to all the works of art which preceded it. The existing monuments form an ideal order among themselves, which is modified by the introduction of the new (the really new) work of art among them. The existing order is complete before the new work arrives; for order to persist after the supervention of novelty, the *whole* existing order must be, if ever so slightly, altered; and so the relations, proportions, values of each work of art toward the whole are readjusted; and this is conformity between the old and the new. Whoever has approved this idea of order, of the form of European, of English literature will not find it preposterous that the past should be altered by the present as much as the present is directed by the past. And the poet who is aware of this will be aware of great difficulties and responsibilities.

In a peculiar sense he will be aware also that he must inevitably be judged by the standards of the past. I say judged, not amputated, by them; not judged to be as good as, or worse or better than, the dead; and certainly not judged by the canons of dead critics. It is a judgment, a comparison, in which two things are measured by each other. To conform merely would be for the new work not really to conform at all; it would not be new, and would therefore not be a work of art. And we do not quite say that the new is more valuable because it fits in; but its fitting in is a test of its value—a test, it is true, which can only be slowly and cautiously applied, for we are none of us infallible judges of conformity. We say: it appears to conform, and is perhaps individual, or it appears individual, and may conform; but we are hardly likely to find that it is one and not the other.

To proceed to a more intelligible exposition of the relation of the poet to the past: he can neither take the past as a lump, an indiscriminate bolus, nor can he form himself wholly on one or two private admirations, nor can he form himself wholly upon one preferred period. The first course is inadmissible, the second is an important experience of youth, and the third is a pleasant and highly desirable supplement. The poet must be very conscious of the main current, which does not at all flow invariably through the most distinguished reputations. He must be quite aware of the obvious fact that art never improves, but that the material of art is never quite the same. He must be aware that the mind of Europe—the mind of his own country—a mind which he learns in time to be much more important than his own private mind—is a mind which changes, and that this change is a development which abandons nothing *en route,* which does not superannuate either Shakespeare, or Homer, or the rock drawing of the Magdalenian[2] draughtsmen. That this development, refinement perhaps, complication certainly, is not, from the point of view of the artist, any improvement. Perhaps not even an improvement from the point of view of the psychologist or not to the extent which we imagine; perhaps only in the end based upon a complication in economics and machinery. But the difference between the present and the past is that the conscious present is an awareness of the past in a way and to an extent which the past's awareness of itself cannot show.

Some one said: "The dead writers are remote from us because we *know* so much more than they did." Precisely, and they are that which we know.

I am alive to a usual objection to what is clearly part of my programme for the *métier* of poetry. The objection is that the doctrine requires a ridiculous amount of erudition (pedantry), a claim which can be rejected by appeal to the lives of poets in any pantheon. It will even be affirmed that much learning deadens or perverts poetic sensibility. While, however, we persist in believing that a poet ought to know as much as will not encroach upon his necessary receptivity and necessary laziness, it is not desirable to confine knowledge to whatever can be put into a useful shape for

[2]Named for La Madeleine in France, where the drawings of this advanced stage of Paleolithic culture were discovered.

examinations, drawing-rooms, or the still more pretentious modes of publicity. Some can absorb knowledge, the more tardy must sweat for it. Shakespeare acquired more essential history from Plutarch[3] than most men could from the whole British Museum. What is to be insisted upon is that the poet must develop or procure the consciousness of the past and that he should continue to develop this consciousness throughout his career.

What happens is a continual surrender of himself as he is at the moment to something which is more valuable. The progress of an artist is a continual self-sacrifice, a continual extinction of personality.

There remains to define this process of depersonalization and its relation to the sense of tradition. It is in this depersonalization that art may be said to approach the condition of science. I, therefore, invite you to consider, as a suggestive analogy, the action which takes place when a bit of finely filiated platinum is introduced into a chamber containing oxygen and sulphur dioxide.

II

Honest criticism and sensitive appreciation are directed not upon the poet but upon the poetry. If we attend to the confused cries of the newspaper critics and the *susurrus*[4] of popular repetition that follows, we shall hear the names of poets in great numbers; if we seek not Blue-book[5] knowledge but the enjoyment of poetry, and ask for a poem, we shall seldom find it. I have tried to point out the importance of the relation of the poem to other poems by other authors, and suggested the conception of poetry as a living whole of all the poetry that has ever been written. The other aspect of this Impersonal theory of poetry is the relation of the poem to its author. And I hinted, by an analogy, that the mind of the mature poet differs from that of the immature one not precisely in any valuation of "personality," not being necessarily more interesting, or having "more to say," but rather by being a more finely perfected medium in which special, or very varied, feelings are at liberty to enter into new combinations.

The analogy was that of the catalyst. When the two gases previously mentioned are mixed in the presence of a filament of platinum, they form sulphurous acid. This combination takes place only if the platinum is present; nevertheless the newly formed acid contains no trace of platinum, and the platinum itself is apparently unaffected; has remained inert, neutral, and unchanged. The mind of the poet is the shred of platinum. It may partly or exclusively operate upon the experience of the man himself; but, the more perfect the artist, the more completely separate in him will be the man who suffers and the mind which creates; the more perfectly will the mind digest and transmute the passions which are its material.

The experience, you will notice, the elements which enter the presence of the transforming catalyst, are of two kinds: emotions and feelings. The effect of a work of art upon the person who enjoys it is an experience different in kind from any experience not of art. It may be formed out of one emotion, or may be a combination

[3]First century (A.D.) Greek biographer from whom Shakespeare took the plots of his Roman plays.

[4]"Murmuring" in Latin.

[5]British official government publication.

of several; and various feelings, inhering for the writer in particular words or phrases or images, may be added to compose the final result. Or great poetry may be made without the direct use of any emotion whatever: composed out of feelings solely. Canto XV of the *Inferno* (Brunetto Latini)[6] is a working up of the emotion evident in the situation; but the effect, though single as that of any work of art, is obtained by considerable complexity of detail. The last quatrain gives an image, a feeling attaching to an image, which "came," which did not develop simply out of what precedes, but which was probably in suspension in the poet's mind until the proper combination arrived for it to add itself to. The poet's mind is in fact a receptacle for seizing and storing up numberless feelings, phrases, images, which remain there until all the particles which can unite to form a new compound are present together.

If you compare several representative passages of the greatest poetry you see how great is the variety of types of combination, and also how completely any semi-ethical criterion of "sublimity" misses the mark. For it is not the "greatness," the intensity, of the emotions, the components, but the intensity of the artistic process, the pressure, so to speak, under which the fusion takes place, that counts. The episode of Paolo and Francesca[7] employs a definite emotion, but the intensity of the poetry is something quite different from whatever intensity in the supposed experience it may give the impression of. It is no more intense, furthermore, than Canto XXVI, the voyage of Ulysses,[8] which has not the direct dependence upon an emotion. Great variety is possible in the process of transmutation of emotion: the murder of Agamemnon,[9] or the agony of Othello,[10] gives an artistic effect apparently closer to a possible original than the scenes from Dante. In the *Agamemnon,* the artistic emotion approximates to the emotion of an actual spectator; in *Othello* to the emotion of the protagonist himself. But the difference between art and the event is always absolute; the combination which is the murder of Agamemnon is probably as complex as that which is the voyage of Ulysses. In either case there has been a fusion of elements. The ode of Keats[11] contains a number of feelings which have nothing particular to do with the nightingale, but which the nightingale, partly, perhaps, because of its attractive name, and partly because of its reputation, served to bring together.

The point of view which I am struggling to attack is perhaps related to the metaphysical theory of the substantial unity of the soul: for my meaning is, that the poet has, not a "personality" to express, but a particular medium, which is only a medium and not a personality, in which impressions and experiences combine in peculiar and unexpected ways. Impressions and experiences which are important for the man may take no place in the poetry, and those which become important in the poetry may play quite a negligible part in the man, the personality.

I will quote a passage which is unfamiliar enough to be regarded with fresh attention in the light—or darkness—of these observations:

[6]Late thirteenth-century philosopher; Dante's master. Dante describes the punishment he is eternally undergoing for his unnatural lusts, but greets him with compassion.

[7]Dante describes the punishment of these illicit lovers in *Inferno,* V.

[8]Ulysses, who is being punished for false counseling, tells Dante of his final voyage, actually Dante's addition to Homer.

[9]In Aeschylus' tragedy, Agamemnon is killed by his wife and her lover.

[10]In Shakespeare's tragedy, Othello agonizes over having killed his wife out of jealousy.

[11]"Ode to a Nightingale."

And now methinks I could e'en chide myself
For doating on her beauty, though her death
Shall be revenged after no common action.
Does the silkworm expend her yellow labours
For thee? For thee does she undo herself?
Are lordships sold to maintain ladyships
For the poor benefit of a bewildering minute?
Why does yon fellow falsify highways,
And put his life between the judge's lips,
To refine such a thing—keeps horse and men
To beat their valours for her? . . .[12]

In this passage (as is evident if it is taken in its context) there is a combination of positive and negative emotions: an intensely strong attraction toward beauty and an equally intense fascination by the ugliness which is contrasted with it and which destroys it. This balance of contrasted emotion is in the dramatic situation to which the speech is pertinent, but that situation alone is inadequate to it. This is, so to speak, the structural emotion, provided by the drama. But the whole effect, the dominant tone, is due to the fact that a number of floating feelings, having an affinity to this emotion by no means superficially evident, have combined with it to give us a new art emotion.

It is not in his personal emotions, the emotions provoked by particular events in his life, that the poet is in any way remarkable or interesting. His particular emotions may be simple, or crude, or flat. The emotion in his poetry will be a very complex thing, but not with the complexity of the emotions of people who have very complex or unusual emotions in life. One error, in fact, of eccentricity in poetry is to seek for new human emotions to express; and in this search for novelty in the wrong place it discovers the perverse. The business of the poet is not to find new emotions, but to use the ordinary ones and, in working them up into poetry, to express feelings which are not in actual emotions at all. And emotions which he has never experienced will serve his turn as well as those familiar to him. Consequently, we must believe that "emotion recollected in tranquillity"[13] is an inexact formula. For it is neither emotion, nor recollection, nor, without distortion of meaning, tranquillity. It is a concentration, and a new thing resulting from the concentration, of a very great number of experiences which to the practical and active person would not seem to be experiences at all; it is a concentration which does not happen consciously or of deliberation. These experiences are not "recollected," and they finally unite in an atmosphere which is "tranquil" only in that it is a passive attending upon the event. Of course this is not quite the whole story. There is a great deal, in the writing of poetry, which must be conscious and deliberate. In fact, the bad poet is usually unconscious where he ought to be conscious, and conscious where he ought to be unconscious. Both errors tend to make him "personal." Poetry is not a turning loose of emotion, but an escape from emotion; it is not the expression of personality, but an escape from personality. But, of course, only those who have personality and emotions know what it means to want to escape from these things.

[12]From Cyril Tourneur's *The Revenger's Tragedy* (1607), III. v. 68–78.

[13]Wordsworth's "formula" for poetry expressed in his Preface to *Lyrical Ballads*.

III

ὁ δὲ νοῦς ἴσως θειότερόν τι καὶ ἀπαθές ἐστιν.[14]

This essay proposes to halt at the frontier of metaphysics or mysticism, and confine itself to such practical conclusions as can be applied by the responsible person interested in poetry. To divert interest from the poet to the poetry is a laudable aim: for it would conduce to a juster estimation of actual poetry, good and bad. There are many people who appreciate the expression of sincere emotion in verse, and there is a smaller number of people who can appreciate technical excellence. But very few know when there is an expression of *significant* emotion, emotion which has its life in the poem and not in the history of the poet. The emotion of art is impersonal. And the poet cannot reach this impersonality without surrendering himself wholly to the work to be done. And he is not likely to know what is to be done unless he lives in what is not merely the present, but the present moment of the past, unless he is conscious, not of what is dead, but of what is already living.

1919

The Waste Land[1]

"Nam Sibyllam quidem Cumis ego ipse oculis meis vidi in ampulla pendere, et cum illi pueri dicerent: Σίβυλλα τί θέλεις; *respondebat illa:* ἀποθανεῖν θέλω.*"*[2]

—FOR EZRA POUND
il miglior fabbro.[3]

[14]Aristotle, *De Anima* ("On the Soul"), I. 4. "No doubt the mind is something divine and not subject to external impressions."

[1] In the first hard-cover edition of *The Waste Land,* Eliot included several pages of "Notes," acknowledging his indebtedness to Miss Jessie L. Weston's book on the Grail Legend, *From Ritual to Romance,* as suggesting "the title . . . the plan and a good deal of the incidental symbolism of the poem." He also cited as a source the volumes of James G. Frazer's *The Golden Bough* which deal with "vegetation ceremonies." As deemed particularly helpful, Eliot's notes are summarized in these footnotes.

[2]Petronius's *Satyricon* (first century A.D.) recounts the story of the Sibyl of Cumae, given eternal life, but thus doomed to perpetual old age: "For once I myself saw with my own eyes, the Sibyl at Cumae hanging in a cage, and when the children said to her, 'Sibyl, what do you want?' she replied, 'I want to die.'"

[3]"The better maker," Eliot's recognition of Pound for his extensive, sensitive help in shaping the poem. The quotation, from Dante's *Purgatorio* XXVI, 117, was a tribute to the Provençal poet Arnaut Daniel.

I. The Burial of the Dead[4]

April is the cruellest month, breeding
Lilacs out of the dead land, mixing
Memory and desire, stirring
Dull roots with spring rain.
Winter kept us warm, covering
Earth in forgetful snow, feeding
A little life with dried tubers.
Summer surprised us, coming over the Starnbergersee[5]
With a shower of rain; we stopped in the colonnade,
And went on in sunlight, into the Hofgarten,[6]
And drank coffee, and talked for an hour.
Bin gar keine Russin, stamm' aus Litauen, echt deutsch.[7]
And when we were children, staying at the archduke's,
My cousin's, he took me out on a sled,
And I was frightened. He said, Marie,
Marie, hold on tight. And down we went.
In the mountains, there you feel free.
I read, much of the night, and go south in the winter.

What are the roots that clutch, what branches grow
Out of this stony rubbish? Son of man,[8]
You cannot say, or guess, for you know only
A heap of broken images, where the sun beats,
And the dead tree gives no shelter, the cricket no relief,[9]
And the dry stone no sound of water. Only
There is shadow under this red rock,[10]
(Come in under the shadow of this red rock),
And I will show you something different from either
Your shadow at morning striding behind you
Or your shadow at evening rising to meet you;
I will show you fear in a handful of dust.

Frisch weht der Wind
Der Heimat zu

[4]The phrase is from the burial service of the Anglican Church.
[5]A lake near Munich. Lines 8–16 echo passages in Countess Marie Larisch's *My Past* (1913).
[6]A Munich public park with cafés, formerly the grounds of a palace.
[7]"I am no Russian, I come from Lithuania, a real German."
[8]Eliot's note: "Cf. Ezekiel II, i." God addresses Ezekiel as "Son of man," and calls upon him to "stand upon thy feet, and I will speak unto thee."
[9]Eliot's note: "Cf. Ecclesiastes XII," The Preacher points to old age when "the grasshopper shall be a burden and desire shall fail."
[10]Isaiah 32:1–2 prophesies that when the Messiah comes it "shall be . . . as rivers of water in a dry place, as the shadow of a great rock in a weary land."

Mein irisch Kind,
Wo weilest du?[11]

"You gave me hyacinths first a year ago;
"They called me the hyacinth girl."[12]
—Yet when we came back, late, from the Hyacinth garden,
Your arms full, and your hair wet, I could not
Speak, and my eyes failed, I was neither
Living nor dead, and I knew nothing,
Looking into the heart of light, the silence.
Oed' und leer das Meer.[13]

Madame Sosostris,[14] famous clairvoyante,
Had a bad cold, nevertheless
Is known to be the wisest woman in Europe,
With a wicked pack of cards.[15] Here, said she,
Is your card, the drowned Phoenician Sailor,[16]
(Those are pearls that were his eyes.[17] Look!)
Here is Belladonna, the Lady of the Rocks,[18]
The lady of situations.
Here is the man with three staves, and here the Wheel,[19]
And here is the one-eyed merchant,[20] and this card,

[11]Eliot's note: "*Tristan und Isolde,* I, verses 5–8." In Wagner's opera, the lines are sung by a sailor aboard Tristan's ship, thinking of his beloved in Ireland: "Fresh blows the wind homeward; my Irish child, where are you waiting?"

[12]In Ovid's *Metamorphoses,* X, Hyacinth is a young boy slain by a rival for Apollo's love.

[13]"Wide and empty the sea," the message given the dying Tristan, waiting for the ship bringing Isolde.

[14]The name alludes to Sesotris, a 12th-dynasty Egyptian king, adapted by Aldous Huxley in *Chrome Yellow* (1921) to Sesostris, the Sorceress of Ectabana, a woman fortune-teller.

[15]The reference is to the Tarot deck once, but no longer, significant in Eastern magic. Its four suits, cup, dish, lance, and sword, are life symbols in the Grail Legend. Eliot's note: "I am not familiar with the exact constitution of the Tarot pack of cards, from which I have obviously departed to suit my own convenience. The Hanged Man, a member of the traditional pack, fits my purpose in two ways: because he is associated in my mind with the Hanged God of Frazer, and because I associate him with the hooded figure in the passage of the disciples to Emmaus in Part V. The Phoenician Sailor and the Merchant appear later; also the 'crowds of people,' and Death by Water is executed in Part IV. The Man with Three Staves (an authentic member of the Tarot pack) I associate, quite arbitrarily, with the Fisher King himself." Eliot's disclaimer should be attended, since the Phoenician Sailor, for example, is not a member of the pack.

[16]According to Eliot's note, the Smyrna merchant (1. 209) "melts into the Phoenician Sailor." The Phoenicians were seagoing merchants who spread Egyptian fertility cults throughout the Mediterranean. He is a type of the fertility god annually "drowned" as a symbol of the death of winter.

[17]From Ariel's song in Shakespeare's *The Tempest,* I. ii. 398. Ariel sings of the transformation from supposed death to "something rich and strange." See also "A Game of Chess," 1. 125.

[18]Suggestive of several "situations": literally, beautiful lady, the name ambiguously expands into the names of the poisonous nightshade, of a cosmetic and of the Madonna, or Virgin Mary, painted by Leonardo da Vinci as *Madonna of the Rocks.*

[19]The Wheel on one of the Tarot cards is the Wheel of Fortune.

[20]Cf. Mr. Eugenides, 1. 209; on the Tarot card he is shown in profile, thus "one-eyed."

Which is blank, is something he carries on his back,
Which I am forbidden to see. I do not find
The Hanged Man. Fear death by water.
I see crowds of people, walking round in a ring.
Thank you. If you see dear Mrs. Equitone,
Tell her I bring the horoscope myself:
One must be so careful these days.

Unreal City,[21]
Under the brown fog of a winter dawn,
A crowd flowed over London Bridge, so many,
I had not thought death had undone so many.[22]
Sighs, short and infrequent, were exhaled,[23]
And each man fixed his eyes before his feet.
Flowed up the hill and down King William Street,
To where Saint Mary Woolnoth kept the hours
With a dead sound on the final stroke of nine.[24]
There I saw one I knew, and stopped him, crying: "Stetson!
"You who were with me in the ships at Mylae![25]
"That corpse you planted last year in your garden,
"Has it begun to sprout? Will it bloom this year?
"Or has the sudden frost disturbed its bed?
"Oh keep the Dog far hence, that's friend to men,
"Or with his nails he'll dig it up again![26]
"You! hypocrite lecteur!—mon semblable,—mon frère!"[27]

[21]Eliot's note: "Cf. Baudelaire: 'Fourmillante cité, cité pleine de rêves,/ Où le spectre en plein jour raccroche le passant.'" In translation: "Swarming city, city full of dreams,/ Where the specter in full day accosts the passerby." *Les Fleurs du Mal (The Flowers of Evil).*

[22]A rendering of *Inferno,* III, 55–57, quoted in Eliot's note. Canto III deals with those living without praise or blame.

[23]A rendering of *Inferno* IV, 25–27, quoted in Eliot's note. Canto IV deals with those in Limbo who had lived virtuously but died before Christ, and were thus excluded from Christian salvation.

[24]Eliot's note wryly comments, "A Phenomenon which I have often noticed." Indeed he had, for it was partly the route Eliot took for many years to his desk at Lloyd's. If he passed under the clock of the "Bankers Church" at nine, he would have been on time at the office, a few steps down the street. The church is also possibly an allusion to the Chapel Perilous in the Grail Legend. See also Lines 388–89.

[25]Rome won a naval battle at Mylae (260 B.C.) in a commercial war against Carthage.

[26]Lines 71–75 constitute a parody of the anticipation of the resurrection of the fertility god. Eliot's note refers to Webster's *The White Devil.* A Roman woman fears her murdered relatives will be disinterred: "But keep the wolf far thence, that's foe to men,/ For with his nails he'll dig them up again." In welding his "theft,"—Eliot's term for such literary "borrowing"—into something "new" he made two significant changes: "foe" to "friend" and "wolf" to "Dog," thus alluding to the "Dog Star"—the bright star Sirius whose annual positioning coincided with the flooding of the Nile in consonance with the fertility ceremonies. The passage has occasioned a great deal of speculative comment with reference to naturalistic and humanistic suggestions that seem at odds with the rebirth of the god.

[27]Eliot's note refers to Baudelaire's *Fleurs du Mal.* The apposite lines in the introductory poem to the volume may be rendered, "Hypocrite reader!—my likeness—my brother!"

II. *A Game of Chess*[28]

The Chair she sat in, like a burnished throne,
Glowed on the marble,[29] where the glass
Held up by standards wrought with fruited vines
From which a golden Cupidon peeped out
(Another hid his eyes behind his wing)
Doubled the flames of sevenbranched candelabra
Reflecting light upon the table as
The glitter of her jewels rose to meet it,
From satin cases poured in rich profusion;
In vials of ivory and coloured glass
Unstoppered, lurked her strange synthetic perfumes,
Unguent, powdered, or liquid—troubled, confused
And drowned the sense in odours; stirred by the air
That freshened from the window, these ascended
In fattening the prolonged candle-flames,
Flung their smoke into the laquearia,[30]
Stirring the pattern on the coffered ceiling.
Huge sea-wood fed with copper
Burned green and orange, framed by the coloured stone,
In which sad light a carvèd dolphin swam.
Above the antique mantel was displayed
As though a window gave upon the sylvan scene[31]
The change of Philomel, by the barbarous king
So rudely forced; yet there the nightingale
Filled all the desert with inviolable voice
And still she cried, and still the world pursues,
"Jug Jug"[32] to dirty ears.
And other withered stumps of time
Were told upon the walls; staring forms

[28]The title alludes to Thomas Middleton's *A Game of Chess* (1627), about a marriage for political purposes, and *Women Beware Women* (1657), in which a chess game is used as a means of keeping a woman occupied while her daughter-in-law is being seduced, the seduction being described in terms of chess. See also l. 137.

[29]Shakespeare's *Anthony and Cleopatra,* II. ii. 190–1: "The barge she sat in, like a burnished throne,/ Burn'd on the water."

[30]An echo of the "paneled ceiling" of the banquet hall in which Queen Dido of Carthage received Aeneas, *Aenid,* I, 726. She commits suicide after Aeneas leaves her to found Rome.

[31]Eliot's note for line 98 refers to *Paradise Lost,* IV, 140 for "sylvan scene," the phrase used in Satan's first visit to the Garden. The actual scene, however, is that of the "change of Philomel"; and Eliot for line 99 refers to "Ovid *Metamorphoses,* VI, Philomela." Thus the two failures of love are conjoined—and added to the two previous failures figured in the opulent furnishing of the lady's boudoir. Eve's temptation by Satan will lead to carnal debauchery and expulsion from the Garden. Ovid recounts the rape of Philomela by Tereus, her sister's husband. Eventually, to escape his wrath, she is transformed into a nightingale. The motif of the transformation of suffering into art continues through line 103 and, pointed to by Eliot's note, in lines 206–9.

[32]The stylized representation of the song of the nightingale in Elizabethan poetry.

Leaned out, leaning, hushing the room enclosed.
Footsteps shuffled on the stair.
Under the firelight, under the brush, her hair
Spread out in fiery points
Glowed into words, then would be savagely still.

"My nerves are bad to-night. Yes, bad. Stay with me.
"Speak to me. Why do you never speak. Speak.
"What are you thinking of? What thinking? What?
"I never know what you are thinking. Think."

I think we are in rats' alley
Where the dead men lost their bones.

"What is that noise?"
The wind under the door.
"What is that noise now? What is the wind doing?"
Nothing again nothing.
"Do
"You know nothing? Do you see nothing? Do you remember
"Nothing?"

I remember
Those are pearls that were his eyes.
"Are you alive, or not? Is there nothing in your head?"
But

O O O O that Shakespeherian Rag—
It's so elegant
So intelligent
"What shall I do now? What shall I do?"
"I shall rush out as I am, and walk the street
"With my hair down, so. What shall we do to-morrow?
"What shall we ever do"
The hot water at ten.
And if it rains, a closed car at four.
And we shall play a game of chess,
Pressing lidless eyes and waiting for a knock upon the door.

When Lil's husband got demobbed,[33] I said—
I didn't mince my words, I said to her myself,
HURRY UP PLEASE ITS TIME[34]
Now Albert's coming back, make yourself a bit smart.

[33]Slang for "demobilized" from the army after World War I.

[34]Announcement by the "pub" bartender that it is closing time.

He'll want to know what you done with that money he gave you
To get yourself some teeth. He did, I was there.
You have them all out, Lil, and get a nice set,
He said, I swear, I can't bear to look at you.
And no more can't I, I said, and think of poor Albert,
He's been in the army four years, he wants a good time,
And if you don't give it him, there's others will, I said.
Oh is there, she said. Something o' that, I said.
Then I'll know who to thank, she said, and give me a straight
look.
HURRY UP PLEASE ITS TIME
If you don't like it you can get on with it, I said.
Others can pick and choose if you can't.
But if Albert makes off, it won't be for lack of telling.
You ought to be ashamed, I said, to look so antique.
(And her only thirty-one.)
I can't help it, she said, pulling a long face,
It's them pills I took, to bring it off, she said.
(She's had five already, and nearly died of young George.)
The chemist[35] said it would be all right, but I've never been the
same.
You are a proper fool, I said.
Well, if Albert won't leave you alone, there it is, I said,
What you get married for if you don't want children?
HURRY UP PLEASE ITS TIME
Well, that Sunday Albert was home, they had a hot gammon,[36]
And they asked me in to dinner, to get the beauty of it hot—
HURRY UP PLEASE ITS TIME
HURRY UP PLEASE ITS TIME
Goonight Bill. Goonight Lou. Goonight May. Goonight.
Ta ta. Goonight. Goonight.
Good night, ladies, good night, sweet ladies, good night, good
night.[37]

[35]Druggist.
[36]Ham or the lower end of a side of bacon; suggestively, thigh.
[37]Alludes to both Ophelia's words before drowning herself, *Hamlet,* IV. v. 72 and to a popular song "Good night ladies, we're going to leave you now."

III. *The Fire Sermon*[38]

The river's tent is broken: the last fingers of leaf
Clutch and sink into the wet bank. The wind
Crosses the brown land, unheard. The nymphs are departed.
Sweet Thames, run softly, till I end my song.[39]
The river bears no empty bottles, sandwich papers,
Silk handkerchiefs, cardboard boxes, cigarette ends
Or other testimony of summer nights. The nymphs are departed.
And their friends, the loitering heirs of city directors;
Departed, have left no addresses.
By the waters of Leman I sat down and wept . . .[40]
Sweet Thames, run softly till I end my song,
Sweet Thames, run softly, for I speak not loud or long.
But at my back in a cold blast I hear[41]
The rattle of the bones, and chuckle spread from ear to ear.
A rat crept softly through the vegetation
Dragging its slimy belly on the bank
While I was fishing in the dull canal
On a winter evening round behind the gashouse
Musing upon the king my brother's wreck[42]
And on the king my father's death before him.
White bodies naked on the low damp ground
And bones cast in a little low dry garret,
Rattled by the rat's foot only, year to year.
But at my back from time to time I hear
The sound of horns and motors, which shall bring
Sweeney to Mrs. Porter in the spring.[43]

[38]The title of this section is especially evocative. It serves as a kind of rubric for the various scenes of lust, past and present, which follow, and it anticipates the express references to Buddha's *Fire Sermon* and St. Augustine's *Confessions* in the concluding lines and in Eliot's notes to those lines (310–12). Given the accurate London geography of the poem and the fact that *The Waste Land* began as, and to some extent remains, a poem about London in the Dryden vein, it is worth noting that overlooking the scenes mentioned, especially in lines 262–268, is the imposing Monument to the Great Fire of London of 1666.

[39]The refrain of Edmund Spenser's *Prothalamion,* a late sixteenth-century celebration of marriage in the then pastoral setting along the Thames River near London.

[40]In Psalms 137:1 the exiled Jews express their longing for home: "By the rivers of Babylon, there we sat down, yea, we wept, when we remembered Zion." Eliot largely finished the poem at Lake Leman, as Lake Geneva is also called, at a sanatorium where he had gone for care.

[41]Lines 188 and 199 allude to Andrew Marvell's "To His Coy Mistress," lines 21–24.

[42]An allusion, again, to *The Tempest.* Ferdinand, believing his father dead, is "Sitting on a bank,/ Weeping again the King my father's wreck," I., ii. 389–90.

[43]Eliot's note quotes the relevant lines from John Day's *Parliament of Bees:* "When of a sudden, listening, you shall hear, A noise of horns and hunting, which shall bring/ Actaeon to Diana in the spring/ Where all shall see her naked skin . . ." As a punishment for thus seeing the goddess of chastity naked, Actaeon was changed into a stag, hunted, and killed.

O the moon shone bright on Mrs. Porter
And on her daughter
They wash their feet in soda water[44]
Et O ces voix d'enfants, chantant dans la coupole![45]

Twit twit twit
Jug jug jug jug jug jug
So rudely forc'd.
Tereu[46]
Unreal City
Under the brown fog of a winter noon
Mr. Eugenides, the Smyrna merchant
Unshaven, with a pocket full of currants
C.i.f.[47] London: documents at sight,
Asked me in demotic French
To luncheon at the Cannon Street Hotel
Followed by a weekend at the Metropole.[48]

At the violet hour, when the eyes and back
Turn upward from the desk, when the human engine waits
Like a taxi throbbing waiting,
I Tiresias,[49] though blind, throbbing between two lives,
Old man with wrinkled female breasts, can see
At the violet hour, the evening hour that strives
Homeward, and brings the sailor home from sea,
The typist home at teatime, clears her breakfast, lights
Her stove, and lays out food in tins.
Out of the window perilously spread
Her drying combinations touched by the sun's last rays,

44Eliot here uses some sanitized lines from a bawdy song of World War I, which actually was a parody of the popular ballad, "Little Redwing."

45Eliot's note calls attention to Paul Verlaine's sonnet, "Parsifal," the last line of which goes, "And O those children singing in the choir." The feet of Parsifal, in Wagner's opera, are washed before he enters the sanctuary. The children are singing at the ceremony. In Verlaine's poem, there are sexual implications.

46See Notes 31, 32.

47Eliot's explanation, "carriage and insurance free to London," has been corrected by Mrs. Valerie Eliot to "cost, insurance and freight."

48The Cannon Street Hotel is a commercial hotel in that area of the City, the Metropole, a hotel in Brighton popular for assignations.

49Eliot's note: "Tiresias, although a mere spectator and not indeed a 'character,' is yet the most important personage in the poem, uniting all the rest. Just as the one-eyed merchant, seller of currants, melts into the Phoenician Sailor, and the latter is not wholly distinct from Ferdinand Prince of Naples, so all the women are one woman, and the two sexes meet in Tiresias. What Tiresias *sees,* in fact is the substance of the poem. The whole passage from Ovid is of great anthropological interest." The Latin passage which is quoted may be summarized as follows: Tiresias saw two snakes copulating, separated them and became a woman; after seven years he saw the same sight, again separated them, became a man again. When Jove and Juno disputed whether more pleasure in love was enjoyed by male or female, they referred the question to Tiresias, who said women. Juno in her anger blinded him, but Jove, unable to undo her action, gave him the power of infallible divination.

On the divan are piled (at night her bed)
Stockings, slippers, camisoles, and stays.
I Tiresias, old man with wrinkled dugs
Perceived the scene, and foretold the rest—
I too awaited the expected guest.
He, the young man carbuncular, arrives,
A small house agent's clerk, with one bold stare,
One of the low on whom assurance sits
As a silk hat on a Bradford[50] millionaire.
The time is now propitious, as he guesses,
The meal is ended, she is bored and tired,
Endeavours to engage her in caresses
Which still are unreproved, if undesired.
Flushed and decided, he assaults at once;
Exploring hands encounter no defence;
His vanity requires no response,
And makes a welcome of indifference.
(And I Tiresias have foresuffered all
Enacted on this same divan or bed;
I who have sat by Thebes below the wall
And walked among the lowest of the dead.)[51]
Bestows one final patronizing kiss,
And gropes his way, finding the stairs unlit . . .

She turns and looks a moment in the glass,
Hardly aware of her departed lover;
Her brain allows one half-formed thought to pass:
"Well now that's done: and I'm glad it's over."
When lovely woman stoops to folly and
Paces about her room again, alone,
She smoothes her hair with automatic hand,
And puts a record on the gramophone.[52]
"This music crept by me upon the waters"[53]
And along the Strand, up Queen Victoria Street.
O City city, I can sometimes hear
Beside a public bar in Lower Thames Street,
The pleasant whining of a mandoline
And a clatter and a chatter from within
Where fishmen lounge at noon: where the walls

[50]A manufacturing town in Yorkshire, England, noted for the rapid fortunes made during World War I.

[51]The site of Tiresias' prophecies and of his witnessing the fate of Oedipus and Creon.

[52]Eliot's note refers to the song in Goldsmith's *The Vicar of Wakefield:* "When lovely woman stoops to folly/ And finds too late that men betray/ What charm can sooth her melancholy,/ What art can wash her guilt away?/ The only art her guilt to cover,/ To hide her shame from every eye,/ To give repentance to her lover/ And wring his bosom—is to die."

[53]An exact quotation from Ariel's song of transformation in *The Tempest,* I. ii. 391.

Of Magnus Martyr hold
Inexplicable splendour of Ionian white and gold.[54]

The river sweats[55]
Oil and tar
The barges drift
With the turning tide
Red sails
Wide
To leeward, swing on the heavy spar.
The barges wash
Drifting logs
Down Greenwich reach
Past the Isle of Dogs.
Weialala leia
Wallala leialala

Elizabeth and Leicester[56]
Beating oars
The stern was formed
A gilded shell
Red and gold
The brisk swell
Rippled both shores
Southwest wind
Carried down stream
The peal of bells
White towers
Weialala leia
Wallala leialala

"Trams and dusty trees.
Highbury bore me. Richmond and Kew
Undid me. By Richmond I raised my knees
Supine on the floor of a narrow canoe."

"My feet are at Moorgate,[57] and my heart
Under my feet. After the event

[54]Eliot's note: "The interior of St Magnus Martyr is to my mind one of the finest among Wren's interiors." Nearby the Billingsgate Fishmarket and across the street from "The Cock," "where fishmen lounge at noon," it was known as the "Fishmen's Church."

[55]Eliot's note: "The Song of the (three) Thames-daughters begins here. From line 295 to 309 inclusive they speak in turn. V. *Götterdämmerung,* III, i: the Rhine-daughters."

[56]A reference to the fruitless love affair of Queen Elizabeth and the Earl of Leicester, referred to in Eliot's note.

[57]Highbury, Richmond, Kew, and Moorgate are all areas in or around London.

He wept. He promised 'a new start.'
I made no comment. What should I resent?"

"On Margate Sands.[58]
I can connect
Nothing with nothing.
The broken fingernails of dirty hands.
My people humble people who expect
Nothing."
la la

To Carthage then I came[59]

Burning burning burning burning
O Lord Thou pluckest me out
O Lord Thou pluckest

burning

IV. Death by Water[60]

Phlebas the Phoenician, a fortnight dead,
Forgot the cry of gulls, and the deep sea swell
And the profit and loss.
A current under sea
Picked his bones in whispers. As he rose and fell
He passed the stages of his age and youth
Entering the whirlpool.
Gentile or Jew
O you who turn the wheel and look to windward,
Consider Phlebas, who was once handsome and tall as you.

[58]A resort on the sea where Eliot, suffering from stress, spent a short period before going to the sanatorium on Lake Geneva.

[59]The last five lines of "The Fire Sermon" Eliot virtually instructs the reader to consider together. Of line 310 he quotes St. Augustine's Confessions, "to Carthage then I came, where a cauldron of unholy love sang all about my ears." Of line 311, he points to "The complete text of the Buddha's Fire Sermon (which corresponds in importance to the Sermon on the Mount) from which these words are taken. . . . " Of line 312, after citing *Confessions* again, "The collocation of these two representatives of eastern and western asceticism, as the culmination of this part of the poem, is not an accident."

[60]There is no consensus as to whether this short section, drastically cut by Ezra Pound, is in anticipation of rebirth or annihilation. Interestingly, it is translated from the concluding lines of Eliot's "Dans le Restaurant," written in French.

V. *What the Thunder Said*[61]

After the torchlight red on sweaty faces
After the frosty silence in the gardens
After the agony in stony places
The shouting and the crying
Prison and palace and reverberation
Of thunder of spring over distant mountains
He who was living is now dead
We who were living are now dying
With a little patience[62]

Here is no water but only rock
Rock and no water and the sandy road
The road winding above among the mountains
Which are mountains of rock without water
If there were water we should stop and drink
Amongst the rock one cannot stop or think
Sweat is dry and feet are in the sand
If there were only water amongst the rock
Dead mountain mouth of carious teeth that cannot spit
Here one can neither stand nor lie nor sit
There is not even silence in the mountains
But dry sterile thunder without rain
There is not even solitude in the mountains
But red sullen faces sneer and snarl
From doors of mudcracked houses
                                        If there were water
And no rock
If there were rock
And also water
And water
A spring
A pool among the rock
If there were the sound of water only
Not the cicada
And dry grass singing
But sound of water over a rock
Where the hermit-thrush sings in the pine trees
Drip drop drip drop drop drop drop
But there is no water

[61]Eliot's note: "In the first part of Part V three themes are employed: the journey to Emmaus, the approach to the Chapel Perilous (see Miss Weston's book) and the present decay of eastern Europe." See lines 363, 391, 372 respectively.

[62]Lines 325–333 allude to Christ's travail in the gardens of Gethsemane and Golgotha—but also to that of the other slain gods of anthropology through whom new life was invoked.

Who is the third who walks always beside you?
When I count, there are only you and I together
But when I look ahead up the white road
There is always another one walking beside you
Gliding wrapt in a brown mantle, hooded
I do not know whether a man or a woman
—But who is that on the other side of you?
What is that sound high in the air
Murmur of maternal lamentation
Who are those hooded hordes swarming
Over endless plains, stumbling in cracked earth
Ringed by the flat horizon only
What is the city over the mountains
Cracks and reforms and bursts in the violet air
Falling towers
Jerusalem Athens Alexandria
Vienna London
Unreal

A woman drew her long black hair out tight
And fiddled whisper music on those strings
And bats with baby faces in the violet light
Whistled, and beat their wings
And crawled head downward down a blackened wall
And upside down in air were towers
Tolling reminiscent bells, that kept the hours
And voices singing out of empty cisterns and exhausted wells.

In this decayed hole among the mountains
In the faint moonlight, the grass is singing
Over the tumbled graves, about the chapel
There is the empty chapel, only the wind's home.
It has no windows, and the door swings,
Dry bones can harm no one.
Only a cock stood on the rooftree
Co co rico co co rico[63]
In a flash of lightning. Then a damp gust
Bringing rain
Ganga[64] was sunken, and the limp leaves
Waited for rain, while the black clouds
Gathered far distant, over Himavant.[65]

[63]In folklore, the cock's crow was thought to indicate the departure of ghosts. In Matthew, as Christ has predicted, Peter denies him three times before the cock crows.

[64]The Ganges River in India is sacred to Hindus, a place of purification.

[65]A Himalayan mountain.

The jungle crouched, humped in silence.
Then spoke the thunder
DA[66]
Datta: what have we given?
My friend, blood shaking my heart
The awful daring of a moment's surrender
Which an age of prudence can never retract
By this, and this only, we have existed
Which is not to be found in our obituaries
Or in memories draped by the beneficent spider[67]
Or under seals broken by the lean solicitor
In our empty rooms
DA
Dayadhvam: I have heard the key[68]
Turn in the door once and turn once only
We think of the key, each in his prison
Thinking of the key, each confirms a prison
Only at nightfall, aethereal rumours
Revive for a moment a broken Coriolanus[69]
DA
Damyata: The boat responded
Gaily, to the hand expert with sail and oar
The sea was calm, your heart would have responded
Gaily, when invited, beating obedient
To controlling hands

I sat upon the shore
Fishing,[70] with the arid plain behind me
Shall I at least set my lands in order?
London Bridge is falling down falling down falling down
Poi s'ascose nel foco che gli affina[71]

[66]Eliot's note: "'DaTa, dayadhvam, damyata' (Give, sympathise, control)." With this introduction of the onomatopoetic Sanskrit, the density of allusion, only partially accommodated in these footnotes for reasons of space and clarity of progression, seems to intensify.

[67]Eliot's note refers to Webster's *The White Devil:* "they'll remarry/ Ere the worm pierce your winding-sheet, ere the spider/ Make a thin curtain for your epitaphs."

[68]Eliot's note refers to Dante's Ugolino in *Inferno,* XXXIII, 46 starved to death in the locked tower and to F.H. Bradley's postulation that "my experience falls within my own circle. . . . the whole world for each is peculiar and private to that soul."

[69]Coriolanus, threatened with banishment from Rome, chose exile, and, although he tried to return, was eventually "broken." Shakespeare's *Coriolanus* deals with his tragedy.

[70]Eliot's note directs the reader to Weston's "chapter on the Fisher King." The King in the Grail Legends typically lived on a river or seashore. Fish is a fertility or life symbol. This meaning was often forgotten, however, and the title of the Fisher King in medieval romances was accounted for by describing him as fishing.

[71]"Then he hid himself in the fire that refines them." Eliot's note refers to *Purgatorio,* XXVI, 145–48 where the poet Arnaut Daniel, remembering his lechery, speaks this line.

Quando fiam uti chelidon[72]—O swallow swallow
Le Prince d'Aquitaine à la tour abolie[73]
These fragments I have shored against my ruins
Why then Ile fit you. Hieronymo's mad againe.[74]
Datta, Dayadhvam. Damyata.
Shantih shantih shantih[75]

1922

The Dry Salvages

(The Dry Salvages—presumably *les trois sauvages*—is a small group of rocks, with a beacon, off the N.E. coast of Cape Ann, Massachusetts. *Salvages* is pronounced to rhyme with *assuages. Groaner:* a whistling buoy.)

I

I do not know much about gods; but I think that the river
Is a strong brown god—sullen, untamed and intractable,
Patient to some degree, at first recognised as a frontier;
Useful, untrustworthy, as a conveyor of commerce;
Then only a problem confronting the builder of bridges.
The problem once solved, the brown god is almost forgotten
By the dwellers in cities—ever, however, implacable,
Keeping his seasons and rages, destroyer, reminder
Of what men choose to forget. Unhonoured, unpropitiated
By worshippers of the machine, but waiting, watching and waiting.
His rhythm was present in the nursery bedroom,

72"When shall I be like the swallow?" Eliot's note refers to the Latin poem, *Pervigilium Veneris,* with its echo of Philomela, recalling the idea of finding a voice through suffering. In this anonymous poem, the myth is imaged in the swallow. "O Swallow, Swallow" appears in one of the songs in Tennyson's "The Princess."

73"The Prince of Aquitaine in the ruined tower" is from Gérard de Nerval's sonnet *"El Desdichado"* ("The Disinherited One").

74When Hieronymo in Thomas Kyd's play, *The Spanish Tragedy, Hieronymo's Mad Againe* (1594), is asked to write a court play, he replies, "I'll fit [supply] you." Through the play, despite his madness, he is able to revenge himself on the murderers of his son in a pattern similar to that of *Hamlet.*

75Eliot's note: "Shantih. Repeated as here, a formal ending to an Upanishad [sacred Hindu text]. 'The Peace which passeth understanding' is our equivalent to this word."

In the rank ailanthus of the April dooryard,[1]
In the smell of grapes on the autumn table,
And the evening circle in the winter gaslight.

The river is within us, the sea is all about us;
The sea is the land's edge also, the granite
Into which it reaches, the beaches where it tosses
Its hints of earlier and other creation:
The starfish, the horseshoe crab, the whale's backbone;
The pools where it offers to our curiosity
The more delicate algae and the sea anemone.
It tosses up our losses, the torn seine,
The shattered lobsterpot, the broken oar
And the gear of foreign dead men. The sea has many voices,
Many gods and many voices.
                                        The salt is on the briar rose,
The fog is in the fir trees.
                                        The sea howl
And the sea yelp, are different voices
Often together heard: the whine in the rigging,
The menace and caress of wave that breaks on water,
The distant rote in the granite teeth,
And the wailing warning from the approaching headland
Are all sea voices, and the heaving groaner
Rounded homewards, and the seagull:
And under the oppression of the silent fog
The tolling bell
Measures time not our time, rung by the unhurried
Ground swell, a time
Older than the time of chronometers, older
Than time counted by anxious worried women
Lying awake, calculating the future,
Trying to unweave, unwind, unravel
And piece together the past and the future,
Between midnight and dawn, when the past is all deception,
The future futureless, before the morning watch
When time stops and time is never ending;
And the ground swell, that is and was from the beginning,
Clangs
The bell.

[1]Here and in lines 36 and 48, Eliot alludes to Whitman's "When Lilacs Last in the Dooryard Bloom'd." These echoes of the clanging bells and the April dooryard have been seen as effecting "a reconciliation with Whitman and America—a kind of homecoming," with Eliot discovering poetically "the home key at last, the right relation of the personal and the primitive, of the natural and the human orders."

II

Where is there an end of it, the soundless wailing,
The silent withering of autumn flowers
Dropping their petals and remaining motionless;
Where is there an end to the drifting wreckage,
The prayer of the bone on the beach, the unprayable
Prayer at the calamitous annunciation?

There is no end, but addition: the trailing
consequence of further days and hours,
While emotion takes to itself the emotionless
Years of living among the breakage
Of what was believed in as the most reliable—
And therefore the fittest for renunciation.

There is the final addition, the failing
Pride or resentment at failing powers,
The unattached devotion which might pass for devotionless,
In a drifting boat with a slow leakage,
The silent listening to the undeniable
Clamour of the bell of the last annunciation.

Where is the end of them, the fishermen sailing
Into the wind's tail, where the fog cowers?
We cannot think of a time that is oceanless
Or of an ocean not littered with wastage
Or of a future that is not liable
Like the past, to have no destination.

We have to think of them as forever bailing,
Setting and hauling, while the North East lowers
Over shallow banks unchanging and erosionless
Or drawing their money, drying sails at dockage;
Not as making a trip that will be unpayable
For a haul that will not bear examination.

There is no end of it, the voiceless wailing,
No end to the withering of withered flowers,
To the movement of pain that is painless and motionless,
To the drift of the sea and the drifting wreckage,
The bone's prayer to Death its God. Only the hardly, barely
    prayable
Prayer of the one Annunciation.

It seems, as one becomes older,
That the past has another pattern, and ceases to be a mere
    sequence—
Or even development: the latter a partial fallacy

Encouraged by superficial notions of evolution,
Which becomes, in the popular mind, a means of disowning the
    past.
The moments of happiness—not the sense of well-being,
Fruition, fulfilment, security or affection,
Or even a very good dinner, but the sudden illumination—
We had the experience but missed the meaning,
And approach to the meaning restores the experience
In a different form, beyond any meaning
We can assign to happiness. I have said before
That the past experience revived in the meaning
Is not the experience of one life only
But of many generations—not forgetting
Something that is probably quite ineffable:
The backward look behind the assurance
Of recorded history, the backward half-look
Over the shoulder, towards the primitive terror.
Now, we come to discover that the moments of agony
(Whether, or not, due to misunderstanding,
Having hoped for the wrong things or dreaded the wrong things,
Is not in question) are likewise permanent
With such permanence as time has. We appreciate this better
In the agony of others, nearly experienced,
Involving ourselves, than in our own.
For our own past is covered by the currents of action,
But the torment of others remains an experience
Unqualified, unworn by subsequent attrition.
People change, and smile: but the agony abides.
Time the destroyer is time the preserver,
Like the river with its cargo of dead negroes, cows and chicken
    coops,
The bitter apple and the bite in the apple.
And the ragged rock in the restless waters,
Waves wash over it, fogs conceal it;
On a halcyon day it is merely a monument,
In navigable weather it is always a seamark
To lay a course by: but in the sombre season
Or the sudden fury, is what it always was.

III

I sometimes wonder if that is what Krishna meant—
Among other things—or one way of putting the same thing:
That the future is a faded song, a Royal Rose or a lavender spray
Of wistful regret for those who are not yet here to regret,
Pressed between yellow leaves of a book that has never been
    opened.

And the way up is the way down, the way forward is the way
back.
You cannot face it steadily, but this thing is sure,
That time is no healer: the patient is no longer here.
When the train starts, and the passengers are settled
To fruit, periodicals and business letters
(And those who saw them off have left the platform)
Their faces relax from grief into relief,
To the sleepy rhythm of a hundred hours.
Fare forward, travellers! not escaping from the past
Into different lives, or into any future;
You are not the same people who left that station
Or who will arrive at any terminus,
While the narrowing rails slide together behind you;
And on the deck of the drumming liner
Watching the furrow that widens behind you,
You shall not think 'the past is finished'
Or 'the future is before us'.
At nightfall, in the rigging and the aerial,
Is a voice descanting (though not to the ear,
The murmuring shell of time, and not in any language)
'Fare forward, you who think that you are voyaging;
You are not those who saw the harbour
Receding, or those who will disembark.
Here between the hither and the farther shore
While time is withdrawn, consider the future
And the past with an equal mind.
At the moment which is not of action or inaction
You can receive this: "on whatever sphere of being
The mind of a man may be intent
At the time of death"—that is the one action
(And the time of death is every moment)
Which shall fructify in the lives of others:
And do not think of the fruit of action.
Fare forward.
O voyagers, O seamen,
You who come to port, and you whose bodies
Will suffer the trial and judgement of the sea
Or whatever event, this is your real destination.'
So Krishna, as when he admonished Arjuna
On the field of battle.[2]
Not fare well,
But fare forward, voyagers.

[2]Krishna, one of the principal Hindu gods, thus admonishes the hero of the *Bhagavad-Gita* "on the field of battle."

IV

Lady, whose shrine stands on the promontory,
Pray for all those who are in ships, those
Whose business has to do with fish, and
Those concerned with every lawful traffic
And those who conduct them.

Repeat a prayer also on behalf of
Women who have seen their sons or husbands
Setting forth, and not returning:
Figlia del tuo figlio,[3]
Queen of Heaven.

Also pray for those who were in ships, and
Ended their voyage on the sand, in the sea's lips
Or in the dark throat which will not reject them
Or wherever cannot reach them the sound of the sea bell's
Perpetual angelus.

V

To communicate with Mars, converse with spirits,
To report the behaviour of the sea monster,
Describe the horoscope, haruspicate or scry,
Observe disease in signatures, evoke
Biography from the wrinkles of the palm
And tragedy from fingers; release omens
By sortilege, or tea leaves, riddle the inevitable
With playing cards, fiddle with pentagrams
Or barbituric acids, or dissect
The recurrent image into pre-conscious terrors—
To explore the womb, or tomb, or dreams; all these are usual
Pastimes and drugs, and features of the press:
And always will be, some of them especially
When there is distress of nations and perplexity
Whether on the shores of Asia, or in the Edgware Road.
Men's curiosity searches past and future
And clings to that dimension. But to apprehend
The point of intersection of the timeless
With time, is an occupation for the saint—

[3]The daughter of Thy Son.

No occupation either, but something given
And taken, in a lifetime's death in love,
Ardour and selflessness and self-surrender.
For most of us, there is only the unattended
Moment, the moment in and out of time,
The distraction fit, lost in a shaft of sunlight,
The wild thyme unseen, or the winter lightning
Or the waterfall, or music heard so deeply
That it is not heard at all, but you are the music
While the music lasts. These are only hints and guesses,
Hints followed by guesses; and the rest
Is prayer, observance, discipline, thought and action.
The hint half guessed, the gift half understood, is Incarnation.
Here the impossible union
Of spheres of existence is actual,
Here the past and future
Are conquered, and reconciled,
Where action were otherwise movement
Of that which is only moved
And has in it no source of movement—
Driven by dæmonic, chthonic
Powers. And right action is freedom
From past and future also.
For most of us, this is the aim
Never here to be realised;
Who are only undefeated
Because we have gone on trying;
We, content at the last
If our temporal reversion nourish
(Not too far from the yew-tree)
The life of significant soil.

1941

F. Scott Fitzgerald 1896–1940

F. Scott Fitzgerald grew up in St. Paul, Minnesota—a social landscape Edmund Wilson called "the middle west of large cities and country clubs." From boyhood Fitzgerald experienced both the conflict and the fluidity of class in American life. On his father's side, his family, though they were descended from Francis Scott Key and possessed of what Fitzgerald called that "poor old shattered word 'breeding,'" had come to be part of the genteel lower middle-class. His mother's people, the McQuillans, were immigrant entrepreneurs who "had the money." Not surprisingly, his mother nurtured social ambitions in her only son, and Fitzgerald was sent east to a

Catholic prep school (Newman School in New Jersey), and then to Princeton.

At Princeton Fitzgerald courted academic trouble as he pursued success on the parallel tracks which were to mark his career as a writer. He wrote lyrics for the Triangle Club's shows and published poems and stories in the *Nassau Literary Magazine.* Later on, he wrote story after story for the *Saturday Evening Post* and movie scripts for Hollywood while he struggled to write the novels for which he is chiefly remembered.

In the fall of 1917, his senior year at Princeton, Fitzgerald received a commission in the U.S. Army and was assigned to Fort Leavenworth, Kansas. There and at Camp Taylor in Kentucky, Fitzgerald worked on the manuscript of the novel that was to become *This Side of Paradise.* While at Camp Sheridan, outside Montgomery, Alabama, Fitzgerald met and instantly fell in love with eighteen-year-old Zelda Sayre. Discharged from the army in February 1919, Fitzgerald moved to New York and went to work for the Barron Collier advertising agency. When Zelda broke off their long-distance engagement in June 1919, Fitzgerald decided to quit his job, return to St. Paul, and rewrite his novel as "a sort of substitute form of dissipation." He wrote feverishly and by September, Scribners had reconsidered and accepted the book. He and Zelda were married in St. Patrick's Cathedral on April 3, 1920, and their life embellished what Fitzgerald had already called the Jazz Age.

This Side of Paradise was both a sensation and success, and its reception set Fitzgerald's course as a celebrity and a serious novelist. Though taken to task for this double identity by Edmund Wilson and others, Fitzgerald nevertheless expressed the social and psychological tensions of his life in his novels and short fiction. From *This Side of Paradise* to *The Last Tycoon,* Fitzgerald interprets the contemporary American scene in relation to an unfolding sense of essential values. Foremost among these is a romantic sense of American history as "the most beautiful history in the world . . . the history of all aspiration—not just the American dream but the human dream." Yet Fitzgerald tempered the romantic in him with a skeptic's cold eye. Nick Carraway, the narrator of *The Great Gatsby,* declares Gatsby's dream dead not only personally but historically back in "that vast obscurity . . . where the dark fields of the republic rolled on under the night." And with the disillusionment of the idealist, Fitzgerald embraces "the sense that life is essentially a cheat and its conditions are those of defeat, and that the redeeming things are not 'happiness and pleasure' but the deeper satisfactions that come out of struggle." Americans, Fitzgerald thought, at their best managed to keep alive a "willingness, of the heart" essential to the pursuit of happiness and citizenship.

"Sometimes," Fitzgerald wrote his daughter near the end of his life, "I wish I had gone along with that gang [Cole Porter and Rodgers and Hart], but I guess I am too much a moralist at heart and really want to preach at people in some acceptable form rather than to entertain them." In "May Day" (1920) Fitzgerald mingles autobiographical incidents with details from contemporary history. In May of 1919 in the early hours of the morning after the interfraternity dance at Delmonico's, he was bounced out of the Fifty-ninth-Street Childs for a disturbance similar to that created by Peter Himmel in the story. At the same time, the assault on the *New York Trumpet* by a mob of mostly inebriated returning soldiers recalls an actual raid on the socialist *New York Call* during the red scare of 1919. Like many of Fitzgerald's stories in *Tales of the Jazz Age,* "May Day" has in it a "touch of disaster"—in this case the violent despair of the down-and-out Yale man Gordon Sterrett—which is set alongside the oblivious pursuit of pleasure by Gordon's double, his wealthy man-about-town classmate, Philip Dean.

John F. Callahan
Lewis and Clark College

PRIMARY WORKS

This Side of Paradise, 1920; *Flappers and Philosophers,* 1921; *The Beautiful and Damned,* 1922; *Tales of the Jazz Age,* 1922; *The Vegetable or from President to Postman,* 1923; *The Great Gatsby,* 1925; *All the Sad Young Men,* 1926; *Tender Is the Night,* 1934; *Taps at Reveille,* 1935; *The Last Tycoon,* ed. by Edmund Wilson, 1941; *The Crack-Up,* ed. by Edmund Wilson, 1945; *Correspondence of F. Scott Fitzgerald,* ed. by Matthew J. Bruccoli and Margaret M. Duggan, 1980.

May Day

There had been a war fought and won and the great city of the conquering people was crossed with triumphal arches and vivid with thrown flowers of white, red, and rose. All through the long spring days the returning soldiers marched up the chief highway behind the strump of drums and the joyous, resonant wind of the brasses, while merchants and clerks left their bickerings and figurings and, crowding to the windows, turned their white-bunched faces gravely upon the passing battalions.

Never had there been such splendor in the great city, for the victorious war had brought plenty in its train, and the merchants had flocked thither from the South and West with their households to taste of all the luscious feasts and witness the lavish entertainments prepared—and to buy for their women furs against the next winter and bags of golden mesh and varicolored slippers of silk and silver and rose satin and cloth of gold.

So gaily and noisily were the peace and prosperity impending hymned by the scribes and poets of the conquering people that more and more spenders had gathered from the provinces to drink the wine of excitement, and faster and faster did the merchants dispose of their trinkets and slippers until they sent up a mighty cry for more trinkets and more slippers in order that they might give in barter what was demanded of them. Some even of them flung up their hands helplessly, shouting:

"Alas! I have no more slippers! and alas! I have no more trinkets! May Heaven help me, for I know not what I shall do!"

But no one listened to their great outcry, for the throngs were far too busy—day by day, the foot-soldiers trod jauntily the highway and all exulted because the young men returning were pure and brave, sound of tooth and pink of cheek, and the young women of the land were virgins and comely both of face and of figure.

So during all this time there were many adventures that happened in the great city, and, of these, several—or perhaps one—are here set down.

I

At nine o'clock on the morning of the first of May, 1919, a young man spoke to the room clerk at the Biltmore Hotel, asking if Mr. Philip Dean were registered there, and if so, could he be connected with Mr. Dean's rooms. The inquirer was dressed in a well-cut, shabby suit. He was small, slender, and darkly handsome; his eyes were framed above with unusually long eyelashes and below with the blue semicircle of ill health, this latter effect heightened by an unnatural glow which colored his face like a low, incessant fever.

Mr. Dean was staying there. The young man was directed to a telephone at the side.

After a second his connection was made; a sleepy voice hello'd from somewhere above.

"Mr. Dean?"—this very eagerly—"it's Gordon, Phil. It's Gordon Sterrett. I'm down-stairs. I heard you were in New York and I had a hunch you'd be here."

The sleepy voice became gradually enthusiastic. Well, how was Gordy, old boy! Well, he certainly was surprised and tickled! Would Gordy come right up, for Pete's sake!

A few minutes later Philip Dean, dressed in blue silk pajamas, opened his door and the two young men greeted each other with a half-embarrassed exuberance. They were both about twenty-four, Yale graduates of the year before the war; but there the resemblance stopped abruptly. Dean was blond, ruddy, and rugged under his thin pajamas. Everything about him radiated fitness and bodily comfort. He smiled frequently, showing large and prominent teeth.

"I was going to look you up," he cried enthusiastically. "I'm taking a couple of weeks off. If you'll sit down a sec I'll be right with you. Going to take a shower."

As he vanished into the bathroom his visitor's dark eyes roved nervously around the room, resting for a moment on a great English travelling bag in the corner and on a family of thick silk shirts littered on the chairs amid impressive neckties and soft woollen socks.

Gordon rose and, picking up one of the shirts, gave it a minute examination. It was of very heavy silk, yellow with a pale blue stripe—and there were nearly a dozen of them. He stared involuntarily at his own shirt-cuffs—they were ragged and linty at the edges and soiled to a faint gray. Dropping the silk shirt, he held his coat-sleeves down and worked the frayed shirt-cuffs up till they were out of sight. Then he went to the mirror and looked at himself with listless, unhappy interest. His tie, of former glory, was faded and thumb-creased—it served no longer to hide the jagged button-holes of his collar. He thought, quite without amusement, that only three years before he had received a scattering vote in the senior elections at college for being the best-dressed man in his class.

Dean emerged from the bathroom polishing his body.

"Saw an old friend of yours last night," he remarked.

"Passed her in the lobby and couldn't think of her name to save my neck. That girl you brought up to New Haven senior year."

Gordon started.

"Edith Bradin? That whom you mean?"

"'At's the one. Damn good looking. She's still sort of a pretty doll—you know what I mean: as if you touched her she'd smear."

He surveyed his shining self complacently in the mirror, smiled faintly, exposing a section of teeth.

"She must be twenty-three anyway," he continued.

"Twenty-two last month," said Gordon absently.

"What? Oh, last month. Well, I imagine she's down for the Gamma Psi dance. Did you know we're having a Yale Gamma Psi dance to-night at Delmonico's? You better come up, Gordy. Half of New Haven'll probably be there. I can get you an invitation."

Draping himself reluctantly in fresh underwear, Dean lit a cigarette and sat down by the open window, inspecting his calves and knees under the morning sunshine which poured into the room.

"Sit down, Gordy," he suggested, "and tell me all about what you've been doing and what you're doing now and everything."

Gordon collapsed unexpectedly upon the bed; lay there inert and spiritless. His mouth, which habitually dropped a little open when his face was in repose, became suddenly helpless and pathetic.

"What's the matter?" asked Dean quickly.

"Oh, God!"

"What's the matter?"

"Every God damn thing in the world," he said miserably. "I've absolutely gone to pieces, Phil. I'm all in."

"Huh?"

"I'm all in." His voice was shaking.

Dean scrutinized him more closely with appraising blue eyes.

"You certainly look all shot."

"I am. I've made a hell of mess of everything." He paused. "I'd better start at the beginning—or will it bore you?"

"Not at all; go on." There was, however, a hesitant note in Dean's voice. This trip East had been planned for a holiday—to find Gordon Sterrett in trouble exasperated him a little.

"Go on," he repeated, and then added half under his breath, "Get it over with."

"Well," began Gordon unsteadily, "I got back from France in February, went home to Harrisburg for a month, and then came down to New York to get a job. I got one—with an export company. They fired me yesterday."

"Fired you?"

"I'm coming to that, Phil. I want to tell you frankly. You're about the only man I can turn to in a matter like this. You won't mind if I just tell you frankly, will you, Phil?"

Dean stiffened a bit more. The pats he was bestowing on his knees grew perfunctory. He felt vaguely that he was being unfairly saddled with responsibility; he was not even sure he wanted to be told. Though never surprised at finding Gordon Sterrett in mild difficulty, there was something in this present misery that repelled him and hardened him, even though it excited his curiosity.

"Go on."

"It's a girl."

"Hm." Dean resolved that nothing was going to spoil his trip. If Gordon was going to be depressing, then he'd have to see less of Gordon.

"Her name is Jewel Hudson," went on the distressed voice from the bed. "She used to be 'pure,' I guess, up to about a year ago. Lived here in New York—poor family. Her people are dead now and she lives with an old aunt. You see it was just about the time I met her that everybody began to come back from France in droves—and all I did was to welcome the newly arrived and go on parties with 'em. That's the way it started, Phil, just from being glad to see everybody and having them glad to see me."

"You ought to've had more sense."

"I know," Gordon paused, and then continued listlessly. "I'm on my own now, you know, and Phil, I can't stand being poor. Then came this darn girl. She sort of fell in love with me for a while and, though I never intended to get so involved, I'd always seem to run into her somewhere. You can imagine the sort of work I was doing for those exporting people—of course, I always intended to draw; do illustrating for magazines; there's a pile of money in it."

"Why didn't you? You've got to buckle down if you want to make good," suggested Dean with cold formalism.

"I tried, a little, but my stuff's crude. I've got talent, Phil; I can draw—but I just don't know how. I ought to go to art school and I can't afford it. Well, things came to a crisis about a week ago. Just as I was down to about my last dollar this girl began bothering me. She wants some money; claims she can make trouble for me if she doesn't get it."

"Can she?"

"I'm afraid she can. That's one reason I lost my job—she kept calling up the office all the time, and that was sort of the last straw down there. She's got a letter all written to send to my family. Oh, she's got me, all right. I've got to have some money for her."

There was an awkward pause. Gordon lay very still, his hands clenched by his side.

"I'm all in," he continued, his voice trembling. "I'm half crazy, Phil. If I hadn't known you were coming East, I think I'd have killed myself. I want you to lend me three hundred dollars."

Dean's hands, which had been patting his bare ankles, were suddenly quiet—and the curious uncertainty playing between the two became taut and strained.

After a second Gordon continued:

"I've bled the family until I'm ashamed to ask for another nickel."

Still Dean made no answer.

"Jewel says she's got to have two hundred dollars."

"Tell her where she can go."

"Yes, that sounds easy, but she's got a couple of drunken letters I wrote her. Unfortunately, she's not at all the flabby sort of person you'd expect."

Dean made an expression of distaste.

"I can't stand that sort of woman. You ought to have kept away."

"I know," admitted Gordon wearily.

"You've got to look at things as they are. If you haven't got money you've got to work and stay away from women."

"That's easy for you to say," began Gordon, his eyes narrowing. "You've got all the money in the world."

"I most certainly have not. My family keep darn close tab on what I spend. Just because I have a little leeway I have to be extra careful not to abuse it."

He raised the blind and let in a further flood of sunshine.

"I'm no prig, Lord knows," he went on deliberately. "I like pleasure—and I like a lot of it on a vacation like this, but you're—you're in awful shape. I never heard you talk just this way before. You seem to be sort of bankrupt—morally as well as financially."

"Don't they usually go together?"

Dean shook his head impatiently.

"There's a regular aura about you that I don't understand. It's a sort of evil."

"It's an air of worry and poverty and sleepless nights," said Gordon, rather defiantly.

"I don't know."

"Oh, I admit I'm depressing. I depress myself. But, my God, Phil, a week's rest and a new suit and some ready money and I'd be like—like I was. Phil, I can draw like a streak, and you know it. But half the time I haven't had the money to buy decent drawing materials—and I can't draw when I'm tired and discouraged and all in. With a little ready money I can take a few weeks off and get started."

"How do I know you wouldn't use it on some other woman?"

"Why rub it in?" said Gordon quietly.

"I'm not rubbing it in. I hate to see you this way."

"Will you lend me the money, Phil?"

"I can't decide right off. That's a lot of money and it'll be darn inconvenient for me."

"It'll be hell for me if you can't—I know I'm whining, and it's all my own fault but—that doesn't change it."

"When could you pay it back?"

This was encouraging. Gordon considered. It was probably wisest to be frank.

"Of course, I could promise to send it back next month, but—I'd better say three months. Just as soon as I start to sell drawings."

"How do I know you'll sell any drawings?"

A new hardness in Dean's voice sent a faint chill of doubt over Gordon. Was it possible that he wouldn't get the money?

"I supposed you had a little confidence in me."

"I did have—but when I see you like this I begin to wonder."

"Do you suppose if I wasn't at the end of my rope I'd come to you like this? Do you think I'm enjoying it?" He broke off and bit his lip, feeling that he had better subdue the rising anger in his voice. After all, he was the suppliant.

"You seem to manage it pretty easily," said Dean angrily. "You put me in the position where, if I don't lend it to you, I'm a sucker—oh, yes, you do. And let me tell you it's no easy thing for me to get hold of three hundred dollars. My income isn't so big but that a slice like that won't play the deuce with it."

He left his chair and began to dress, choosing his clothes carefully. Gordon stretched out his arms and clenched the edges of the bed, fighting back a desire to cry out. His head was splitting and whirring, his mouth was dry and bitter and he could feel the fever in his blood resolving itself into innumerable regular counts like a slow dripping from a roof.

Dean tied his tie precisely, brushed his eyebrows, and removed a piece of tobacco from his teeth with solemnity. Next he filled his cigarette case, tossed the empty box thoughtfully into the waste basket, and settled the case in his vest pocket.

"Had breakfast?" he demanded.

"No; I don't eat it any more."

"Well, we'll go out and have some. We'll decide about that money later. I'm sick of the subject. I came East to have a good time.

"Let's go over to the Yale Club," he continued moodily, and then added with an implied reproof: "You've given up your job. You've got nothing else to do."

"I'd have a lot to do if I had a little money," said Gordon pointedly.

"Oh, for Heaven's sake drop the subject for a while! No point in glooming on my whole trip. Here, here's some money."

He took a five-dollar bill from his wallet and tossed it over to Gordon, who folded it carefully and put it in his pocket. There was an added spot of color in his cheeks, an added glow that was not fever. For an instant before they turned to go out their eyes met and in that instant each found something that made him lower his own glance quickly. For in that instant they quite suddenly and definitely hated each other.

II

Fifth Avenue and Forty-fourth Street swarmed with the noon crowd. The wealthy, happy sun glittered in transient gold through the thick windows of the smart shops, lighting upon mesh bags and purses and strings of pearls in gray velvet cases; upon gaudy feather fans of many colors; upon the laces and silks of expensive dresses; upon the bad paintings and the fine period furniture in the elaborate show rooms of interior decorators.

Working-girls, in pairs and groups and swarms, loitered by these windows, choosing their future boudoirs from some resplendent display which included even a man's silk pajamas laid domestically across the bed. They stood in front of the jewelry stores and picked out their engagement rings, and their wedding rings and their platinum wrist watches, and then drifted on to inspect the feather fans and opera cloaks; meanwhile digesting the sandwiches and sundaes they had eaten for lunch.

All through the crowd were men in uniform, sailors from the great fleet anchored in the Hudson, soldiers with divisional insignia from Massachusetts to California wanting fearfully to be noticed, and finding the great city thoroughly fed up with soldiers unless they were nicely massed into pretty formations and uncomfortable under the weight of a pack and rifle.

Through this medley Dean and Gordon wandered; the former interested, made alert by the display of humanity at its frothiest and gaudiest; the latter reminded of how often he had been one of the crowd, tired, casually fed, overworked, and dissipated. To Dean the struggle was significant, young, cheerful; to Gordon it was dismal, meaningless, endless.

In the Yale Club they met a group of their former classmates who greeted the visiting Dean vociferously. Sitting in a semicircle of lounges and great chairs, they had a highball all around.

Gordon found the conversation tiresome and interminable. They lunched together *en masse,* warmed with liquor as the afternoon began. They were all going to the Gamma Psi dance that night—it promised to be the best party since the war.

"Edith Bradin's coming," said some one to Gordon. "Didn't she used to be an old flame of yours? Aren't you both from Harrisburg?"

"Yes." He tried to change the subject. "I see her brother occasionally. He's sort of a socialistic nut. Runs a paper or something here in New York."

"Not like his gay sister, eh?" continued his eager informant. "Well, she's coming to-night with a junior named Peter Himmel."

Gordon was to meet Jewel Hudson at eight o'clock—he had promised to have some money for her. Several times he glanced nervously at his wrist watch. At four, to his relief, Dean rose and announced that he was going over to Rivers Brothers to buy some collars and ties. But as they left the Club another of the party joined them, to Gordon's great dismay. Dean was in a jovial mood now, happy, expectant of the evening's party, faintly hilarious. Over in Rivers' he chose a dozen neckties, selecting each one after long consultations with the other man. Did he think narrow ties were coming back? And wasn't it a shame that Rivers couldn't get any more Welsh Margotson collars? There never was a collar like the "Covington."

Gordon was in something of a panic. He wanted the money immediately. And he was now inspired also with a vague idea of attending the Gamma Psi dance. He wanted to see Edith—Edith whom he hadn't met since one romantic night at the Harrisburg Country Club just before he went to France. The affair had died, drowned in the turmoil of the war and quite forgotten in the arabesque of these three months, but a picture of her, poignant, debonnaire, immersed in her own inconsequential chatter, recurred to him unexpectedly and brought a hundred memories with it. It was Edith's face that he had cherished through college with a sort of detached yet affectionate admiration. He had loved to draw her—around his room had been a dozen sketches of her—playing golf, swimming—he could draw her pert, arresting profile with his eyes shut.

They left Rivers' at five-thirty and paused for a moment on the sidewalk.

"Well," said Dean genially, "I'm all set now. Think I'll go back to the hotel and get a shave, haircut, and massage."

"Good enough," said the other man, "I think I'll join you."

Gordon wondered if he was to be beaten after all. With difficulty he restrained himself from turning to the man and snarling out, "Go on away, damn you!" In despair he suspected that perhaps Dean had spoken to him, was keeping him along in order to avoid a dispute about the money.

They went into the Biltmore—a Biltmore alive with girls—mostly from the West and South, the stellar débutantes of many cities gathered for the dance of a famous fraternity of a famous university. But to Gordon they were faces in a dream. He gathered together his forces for a last appeal, was about to come out with he knew not what, when Dean suddenly excused himself to the other man and taking Gordon's arm led him aside.

"Gordy," he said quickly, "I've thought the whole thing over carefully and I've decided that I can't lend you that money. I'd like to oblige you, but I don't feel I ought to—it'd put a crimp in me for a month."

Gordon, watching him dully, wondered why he had never before noticed how much those upper teeth projected.

"—I'm mighty sorry, Gordon," continued Dean, "but that's the way it is."

He took out his wallet and deliberately counted out seventy-five dollars in bills.

"Here," he said, holding them out, "here's seventy-five; that makes eighty all together. That's all the actual cash I have with me, besides what I'll actually spend on the trip."

Gordon raised his clenched hand automatically, opened it as though it were a tongs he was holding, and clenched it again on the money.

"I'll see you at the dance," continued Dean. "I've got to get along to the barber shop."

"So-long," said Gordon in a strained and husky voice.

"So-long."

Dean began to smile, but seemed to change his mind. He nodded briskly and disappeared.

But Gordon stood there, his handsome face awry with distress, the roll of bills clenched tightly in his hand. Then, blinded by sudden tears, he stumbled clumsily down the Biltmore steps.

III

About nine o'clock of the same night two human beings came out of a cheap restaurant in Sixth Avenue. They were ugly, ill-nourished, devoid of all except the very lowest form of intelligence, and without even that animal exuberance that in itself brings color into life; they were lately vermin-ridden, cold, and hungry in a dirty town of a strange land; they were poor, friendless; tossed as driftwood from their births, they would be tossed as driftwood to their deaths. They were dressed in the uniform of the United States Army, and on the shoulder of each was the insignia of a drafted division from New Jersey, landed three days before.

The taller of the two was named Carrol Key, a name hinting that in his veins, however thinly diluted by generations of degeneration, ran blood of some potentiality. But one could stare endlessly at the long, chinless face, the dull, watery eyes, and high cheekbones, without finding a suggestion of either ancestral worth or native resourcefulness.

His companion was swart and bandy-legged, with rat-eyes and a much-broken hooked nose. His defiant air was obviously a pretense, a weapon of protection borrowed from that world of snarl and snap, of physical bluff and physical menace, in which he had always lived. His name was Gus Rose.

Leaving the café they sauntered down Sixth Avenue, wielding toothpicks with great gusto and complete detachment.

"Where to?" asked Rose, in a tone which implied that he would not be surprised if Key suggested the South Sea Islands.

"What you say we see if we can getta holda some liquor?" Prohibition was not yet. The ginger in the suggestion was caused by the law forbidding the selling of liquor to soldiers.

Rose agreed enthusiastically.

"I got an idea," continued Key, after a moment's thought, "I got a brother somewhere."

"In New York?"

"Yeah. He's an old fella." He meant that he was an elder brother. "He's a waiter in a hash joint."

"Maybe he can get us some."

"I'll say he can!"

"B'lieve me, I'm goin' to get this darn uniform off me to-morra. Never get me in it again, neither. I'm goin' to get me some regular clothes."

"Say, maybe I'm not."

As their combined finances were something less than five dollars, this intention can be taken largely as a pleasant game of words, harmless and consoling. It seemed to please both of them, however, for they reinforced it with chuckling and mention of personages high in biblical circles, adding such further emphasis as "Oh, boy!" "You know!" and "I'll say so!" repeated many times over.

The entire mental pabulum of these two men consisted of an offended nasal comment extended through the years upon the institution—army, business, or poorhouse—which kept them alive, and toward their immediate superior in that institution. Until that very morning the institution had been the "government" and the immediate superior had been the "Cap'n"—from these two they had glided out and were now in the vaguely uncomfortable state before they should adopt their next bondage. They were uncertain, resentful, and somewhat ill at ease. This they hid by pretending an elaborate relief at being out of the army, and by assuring each other that military discipline should never again rule their stubborn, liberty-loving wills. Yes, as a matter of fact, they would have felt more at home in a prison than in this new-found and unquestionable freedom.

Suddenly Key increased his gait. Rose, looking up and following his glance, discovered a crowd that was collecting fifty yards down the street. Key chuckled and began to run in the direction of the crowd; Rose thereupon also chuckled and his short bandy legs twinkled beside the long, awkward strides of his companion.

Reaching the outskirts of the crowd they immediately became an indistinguishable part of it. It was composed of ragged civilians somewhat the worse for liquor, and of soldiers representing many divisions and many stages of sobriety, all clustered around a gesticulating little Jew with long black whiskers, who was waving his arms and delivering an excited but succinct harangue. Key and Rose, having wedged themselves into the approximate parquet, scrutinized him with acute suspicion, as his words penetrated their common consciousness.

"—What have you got outa the war?" he was crying fiercely. "Look arounja, look arounja! Are you rich? Have you got a lot of money offered you?—no; you're lucky if you're alive and got both your legs; you're lucky if you came back an' find your wife ain't gone off with some other fella that had the money to buy himself out of the war! That's when you're lucky! Who got anything out of it except J. P. Morgan an' John D. Rockefeller?"

At this point the little Jew's oration was interrupted by the hostile impact of a fist upon the point of his bearded chin and he toppled backward to a sprawl on the pavement.

"God damn Bolsheviki!" cried the big soldier-blacksmith who had delivered the blow. There was a rumble of approval, the crowd closed in nearer.

The Jew staggered to his feet, and immediately went down again before a half-dozen reaching-in fists. This time he stayed down, breathing heavily, blood oozing from his lip where it was cut within and without.

There was a riot of voices, and in a minute Rose and Key found themselves flowing with the jumbled crowd down Sixth Avenue under the leadership of a thin civilian in a slouch hat and the brawny soldier who had summarily ended the oration. The crowd had marvelously swollen to formidable proportions and a stream of more noncommittal citizens followed it along the sidewalks lending their moral support by intermittent huzzas.

"Where we goin'?" yelled Key to the man nearest him.

His neighbor pointed up to the leader in the slouch hat.

"That guy knows where there's a lot of 'em! We're goin' to show 'em!"

"We're goin' to show 'em!" whispered Key delightedly to Rose, who repeated the phrase rapturously to a man on the other side.

Down Sixth Avenue swept the procession, joined here and there by soldiers and marines, and now and then by civilians, who came up with the inevitable cry that they were just out of the army themselves, as if presenting it as a card of admission to a newly formed Sporting and Amusement Club.

Then the procession swerved down a cross street and headed for Fifth Avenue and the word filtered here and there that they were bound for a Red meeting at Tolliver Hall.

"Where is it?"

The question went up the line and a moment later the answer floated back. Tolliver Hall was down on Tenth Street. There was a bunch of other sojers who was goin' to break it up and was down there now!

But Tenth Street had a faraway sound and at the word a general groan went up and a score of the procession dropped out. Among these were Rose and Key, who slowed down to a saunter and let the more enthusiastic sweep on by.

"I'd rather get some liquor," said Key as they halted and made their way to the sidewalk amid cries of "Shell hole!" and "Quitters!"

"Does your brother work around here?" asked Rose, assuming the air of one passing from the superficial to the eternal.

"He oughta," replied Key. "I ain't seen him for a coupla years. I been out to Pennsylvania since. Maybe he don't work at night anyhow. It's right along here. He can get us some o'right if he ain't gone."

They found the place after a few minutes' patrol of the street—a shoddy tablecloth restaurant between Fifth Avenue and Broadway. Here Key went inside to inquire for his brother George, while Rose waited on the sidewalk.

"He ain't here no more," said Key emerging. "He's a waiter up to Delmonico's."

Rose nodded wisely, as if he'd expected as much. One should not be surprised at a capable man changing jobs occasionally. He knew a waiter once—there ensued a long conversation as they walked as to whether waiters made more in actual wages than in tips—it was decided that it depended on the social tone of the joint wherein the waiter labored. After having given each other vivid pictures of millionaires dining at Delmonico's and throwing away fifty-dollar bills after their first quart of champagne, both men thought privately of becoming waiters. In fact, Key's narrow brow was secreting a resolution to ask his brother to get him a job.

"A waiter can drink up all the champagne those fellas leave in bottles," suggested Rose with some relish, and then added as an afterthought, "Oh, boy!"

By the time they reached Delmonico's it was half past ten, and they were surprised to see a stream of taxis driving up to the door one after the other and emitting marvelous, hatless young ladies, each one attended by a stiff young gentleman in evening clothes.

"It's a party," said Rose with some awe. "Maybe we better not go in. He'll be busy."

"No, he won't. He'll be o'right."

After some hesitation they entered what appeared to them to be the least elaborate door and, indecision falling upon them immediately, stationed themselves nervously in an inconspicuous corner of the small dining-room in which they found themselves. They took off their caps and held them in their hands. A cloud of gloom fell upon them and both started when a door at one end of the room crashed open, emitting a comet-like waiter who streaked across the floor and vanished through another door on the other side.

There had been three of these lightning passages before the seekers mustered the acumen to hail a waiter. He turned, looked at them suspiciously, and then approached with soft, catlike steps, as if prepared at any moment to turn and flee.

"Say," began Key, "say, do you know my brother? He's a waiter here."

"His name is Key," annotated Rose.

Yes, the waiter knew Key. He was up-stairs, he thought. There was a big dance going on in the main ballroom. He'd tell him.

Ten minutes later George Key appeared and greeted his brother with the utmost suspicion; his first and most natural thought being that he was going to be asked for money.

George was tall and weak chinned, but there his resemblance to his brother ceased. The waiter's eyes were not dull, they were alert and twinkling, and his manner was suave, in-door, and faintly superior. They exchanged formalities. George was married and had three children. He seemed fairly interested, but not impressed by the news that Carrol had been abroad in the army. This disappointed Carrol.

"George," said the younger brother, these amenities having been disposed of, "we want to get some booze, and they won't sell us none. Can you get us some?"

George considered.

"Sure. Maybe I can. It may be half an hour, though."

"All right," agreed Carrol; "we'll wait."

At this Rose started to sit down in a convenient chair, but was haled to his feet by the indignant George.

"Hey! Watch out, you! Can't sit down here! This room's all set for a twelve o'clock banquet."

"I ain't goin' to hurt it," said Rose resentfully. "I been through the delouser."

"Never mind," said George sternly, "if the head waiter seen me here talkin' he'd romp all over me."

"Oh."

The mention of the head waiter was full explanation to the other two; they fingered their overseas caps nervously and waited for a suggestion.

"I tell you," said George, after a pause, "I got a place you can wait; you just come here with me."

They followed him out the far door, through a deserted pantry and up a pair of dark winding stairs, emerging finally into a small room chiefly furnished by piles of pails and stacks of scrubbing brushes, and illuminated by a single dim electric light. There he left them, after soliciting two dollars and agreeing to return in half an hour with a quart of whiskey.

"George is makin' money, I bet," said Key gloomily as he seated himself on an inverted pail. "I bet he's making fifty dollars a week."

Rose nodded his head and spat.

"I bet he is, too."

"What'd he say the dance was of?"

"A lot of college fellas. Yale College."

They both nodded solemnly at each other.

"Wonder where that crowda sojers is now?"

"I don't know. I know that's too damn long to walk for me."

"Me too. You don't catch me walkin' that far."

Ten minutes later restlessness seized them.

"I'm goin' to see what's out here," said Rose, stepping cautiously toward the other door.

It was a swinging door of green baize and he pushed it open a cautious inch.

"See anything?"

For answer Rose drew in his breath sharply.

"Doggone! Here's some liquor I'll say!"

"Liquor?"

Key joined Rose at the door, and looked eagerly.

"I'll tell the world that's liquor," he said, after a moment of concentrated gazing.

It was a room about twice as large as the one they were in—and in it was prepared a radiant feast of spirits. There were long walls of alternating bottles set along two white covered tables; whiskey, gin, brandy, French and Italian vermouths, and orange juice, not to mention an array of syphons and two great empty punch bowls. The room was as yet uninhabited.

"It's for this dance they're just starting," whispered Key; "hear the violins playin'? Say, boy, I wouldn't mind havin' a dance."

They closed the door softly and exchanged a glance of mutual comprehension. There was no need of feeling each other out.

"I'd like to get my hands on a coupla those bottles," said Rose emphatically.

"Me too."

"Do you suppose we'd get seen?"

Key considered.

"Maybe we better wait till they start drinkin' 'em. They got 'em all laid out now, and they know how many of them there are."

They debated this point for several minutes. Rose was all for getting his hands on a bottle now and tucking it under his coat before any one came into the room. Key, however, advocated caution. He was afraid he might get his brother in trouble. If they waited till some of the bottles were opened it'd be all right to take one, and everybody'd think it was one of the college fellas.

While they were still engaged in argument George Key hurried through the room and, barely grunting at them, disappeared by way of the green baize door. A minute later they heard several corks pop, and then the sound of crackling ice and splashing liquid. George was mixing the punch.

The soldiers exchanged delighted grins.

"Oh, boy!" whispered Rose.

George reappeared.

"Just keep low, boys," he said quickly. "I'll have your stuff for you in five minutes."

He disappeared through the door by which he had come.

As soon as his footsteps receded down the stairs, Rose, after a cautious look, darted into the room of delights and reappeared with a bottle in his hand.

"Here's what I say," he said, as they sat radiantly digesting their first drink. "We'll wait till he comes up, and we'll ask him if we can't just stay here and drink what he brings us—see. We'll tell him we haven't got any place to drink it—see. Then we can sneak in there whenever there ain't nobody in that there room and tuck a bottle under our coats. We'll have enough to last us a coupla days—see?"

"Sure," agreed Rose enthusiastically. "Oh, boy! And if we want to we can sell it to sojers any time we want to."

They were silent for a moment thinking rosily of this idea. Then Key reached up and unhooked the collar of his O.D. coat.

"It's hot in here, ain't it?"

Rose agreed earnestly.

"Hot as hell."

IV

She was still quite angry when she came out of the dressing-room and crossed the intervening parlor of politeness that opened onto the hall—angry not so much at the actual happening which was, after all, the merest commonpleace of her social existence, but because it had occurred on this particular night. She had no quarrel with herself. She had acted with that correct mixture of dignity and reticent pity which she always employed. She had succinctly and deftly snubbed him.

It had happened when their taxi was leaving the Biltmore—hadn't gone half a block. He had lifted his right arm awkwardly—she was on his right side—and attempted to settle it snugly around the crimson fur-trimmed opera cloak she wore. This in itself had been a mistake. It was inevitably more graceful for a young man attempting to embrace a young lady of whose acquiescence he was not certain, to first put his far arm around her. It avoided that awkward movement of raising the near arm.

His second *faux pas* was unconscious. She had spent the afternoon at the hairdresser's; the idea of any calamity overtaking her hair was extremely repugnant—yet as Peter made his unfortunate attempt the point of his elbow had just faintly brushed it. That was his second *faux pas.* Two were quite enough.

He had begun to murmur. At the first murmur she had decided that he was nothing but a college boy—Edith was twenty-two, and anyhow, this dance, first of its kind since the war, was reminding her, with the accelerating rhythm of its associations, of something else—of another dance and another man, a man for whom her feelings had been little more than a sad-eyed, adolescent mooniness. Edith Bradin was falling in love with her recollection of Gordon Sterrett.

So she came out of the dressing-room at Delmonico's and stood for a second in the doorway looking over the shoulders of a black dress in front of her at the groups of Yale men who flitted like dignified black moths around the head of the stairs. From the room she had left drifted out the heavy fragrance left by the passage to and fro of many scented young beauties—rich perfumes and the fragile memory-laden dust of fragrant powders. This odor drifting out acquired the tang of cigarette smoke in the hall, and then settled sensuously down the stairs and permeated the ballroom where the Gamma Psi dance was to be held. It was an odor she knew well, exciting, stimulating, restlessly sweet—the odor of a fashionable dance.

She thought of her own appearance. Her bare arms and shoulders were powdered to a creamy white. She knew they looked very soft and would gleam like milk against the black backs that were to silhouette them tonight. The hairdressing had been a success; her reddish mass of hair was piled and crushed and creased to an arrogant marvel of mobile curves. Her lips were finely made of deep carmine; the irises of her eyes were delicate, breakable blue, like china eyes. She was a complete, infinitely delicate, quite perfect thing of beauty, flowing in an even line from a complex coiffure to two small slim feet.

She thought of what she would say to-night at this revel, faintly presaged already by the sounds of high and low laughter and slippered footsteps, and movements of couples up and down the stairs. She would talk the language she had talked for many years—her line—made up of the current expressions, bits of journalese and college slang strung together into an intrinsic whole, careless, faintly provocative, delicately sentimental. She smiled faintly as she heard a girl sitting on the stairs near her say: "You don't know the half of it, dearie!"

And as she smiled her anger melted for a moment, and closing her eyes she drew in a deep breath of pleasure. She dropped her arms to her side until they were faintly touching the sleek sheath that covered and suggested her figure. She had never felt her own softness so much nor so enjoyed the whiteness of her own arms.

"I smell sweet," she said to herself simply, and then came another thought—"I'm made for love."

She liked the sound of this and thought it again; then in inevitable succession came her new-born riot of dreams about Gordon. The twist of her imagination which, two hours before, had disclosed to her her unguessed desire to see him again, seemed now to have been leading up to this dance, this hour.

For all her sleek beauty, Edith was a grave, slow-thinking girl. There was a streak in her of that same desire to ponder, of that adolescent idealism that had turned her brother socialist and pacifist. Henry Bradin had left Cornell, where he had been an instructor in economics, and had come to New York to pour the latest cures for incurable evils into the columns of a radical weekly newspaper.

Edith, less fatuously, would have been content to cure Gordon Sterrett. There was a quality of weakness in Gordon that she wanted to take care of; there was a helplessness in him that she wanted to protect. And she wanted someone she had known a long while, someone who had loved her a long while. She was a little tired; she wanted to get married. Out of a pile of letters, half a dozen pictures and as many memories, and this weariness, she had decided that next time she saw Gordon their relations were going to be changed. She would say something that would change them. There was this evening. This was her evening. All evenings were her evenings.

Then her thoughts were interrupted by a solemn undergraduate with a hurt look and an air of strained formality who presented himself before her and bowed unusually low. It was the man she had come with, Peter Himmel. He was tall and humorous, with horned-rimmed glasses and an air of attractive whimsicality. She suddenly rather disliked him—probably because he had not succeeded in kissing her.

"Well," she began, "are you still furious at me?"

"Not at all."

She stepped forward and took his arm.

"I'm sorry," she said softly. "I don't know why I snapped out that way. I'm in a bum humor to-night for some strange reason. I'm sorry."

"S'all right," he mumbled, "don't mention it."

He felt disagreeably embarrassed. Was she rubbing in the fact of his late failure?

"It was a mistake," she continued, on the same consciously gentle key. "We'll both forget it." For this he hated her.

A few minutes later they drifted out on the floor while the dozen swaying, sighing members of the specially hired jazz orchestra informed the crowded ballroom that "if a saxophone and me are left alone why then two is com-pan-ee!"

A man with a mustache cut in.

"Hello," he began reprovingly. "You don't remember me."

"I can't just think of your name," she said lightly—"and I know you so well."

"I met you up at—" His voice trailed disconsolately off as a man with very fair hair cut in. Edith murmured a conventional "Thanks loads—cut in later," to the *inconnu.*

The very fair man insisted on shaking hands enthusiastically. She placed him as one of the numerous Jims of her acquaintance—last name a mystery. She remembered even that he had a peculiar rhythm in dancing and found as they started that she was right.

"Going to be here long?" he breathed confidentially.

She leaned back and looked up at him.

"Couple of weeks."

"Where are you?"

"Biltmore. Call me up some day."

"I mean it," he assured her. "I will. We'll go to tea."

"So do I—Do."

A dark man cut in with intense formality.

"You don't remember me, do you?" he said gravely.

"I should say I do. Your name's Harlan."

"No-ope. Barlow."

"Well, I knew there were two syllables anyway. You're the boy that played the ukulele so well up at Howard Marshall's house party."

"I played—but not—"

A man with prominent teeth cut in. Edith inhaled a slight cloud of whiskey. She liked men to have had something to drink; they were so much more cheerful, and appreciative and complimentary—much easier to talk to.

"My name's Dean, Philip Dean," he said cheerfully. "You don't remember me, I know, but you used to come up to New Haven with a fellow I roomed with senior year, Gordon Sterrett."

Edith looked up quickly.

"Yes, I went up with him twice—to the Pump and Slipper and the Junior prom."

"You've seen him, of course," said Dean carelessly. "He's here to-night. I saw him just a minute ago."

Edith started. Yet she had felt quite sure he would be here.

"Why, no, I haven't—"

A fat man with red hair cut in.

"Hello, Edith," he began.

"Why—hello there—"

She slipped, stumbled lightly.

"I'm sorry, dear," she murmured mechanically.

She had seen Gordon—Gordon very white and listless, leaning against the side of a doorway, smoking and looking into the ballroom. Edith could see that his face was thin and wan—that the hand he raised to his lips with a cigarette was trembling. They were dancing quite close to him now.

"—They invite so darn many extra fellas that you—" the short man was saying.

"Hello, Gordon," called Edith over her partner's shoulder. Her heart was pounding wildly.

His large dark eyes were fixed on her. He took a step in her direction. Her partner turned her away—she heard his voice bleating—

"—but half the stags get lit and leave before long, so——"

Then a low tone at her side.

"May I, please?"

She was dancing suddenly with Gordon; one of his arms was around her; she felt it tighten spasmodically; felt his hand on her back with the fingers spread. Her hand holding the little lace handkerchief was crushed in his.

"Why Gordon," she began breathlessly.

"Hello, Edith."

She slipped again—was tossed forward by her recovery until her face touched the black cloth of his dinner coat. She loved him—she knew she loved him—then for a minute there was silence while a strange feeling of uneasiness crept over her. Something was wrong.

Of a sudden her heart wrenched, and turned over as she realized what it was. He was pitiful and wretched, a little drunk, and miserably tired.

"Oh—" she cried involuntarily.

His eyes looked down at her. She saw suddenly that they were blood-streaked and rolling uncontrollably.

"Gordon," she murmured, "we'll sit down; I want to sit down."

They were nearly in mid-floor, but she had seen two men start toward her from opposite sides of the room, so she halted, seized Gordon's limp hand and led him bumping through the crowd, her mouth tight shut, her face a little pale under her rouge, her eyes trembling with tears.

She found a place high up on the soft-carpeted stairs, and he sat down heavily beside her.

"Well," he began, staring at her unsteadily, "I certainly am glad to see you, Edith."

She looked at him without answering. The effect of this on her was immeasurable. For years she had seen men in various stages of intoxication, from uncles all the way down to chauffeurs, and her feelings had varied from amusement to disgust, but here for the first time she was seized with a new feeling—an unutterable horror.

"Gordon," she said accusingly and almost crying, "you look like the devil."

He nodded. "I've had trouble, Edith."

"Trouble?"

"All sorts of trouble. Don't you say anything to the family, but I'm all gone to pieces. I'm a mess, Edith."

His lower lip was sagging. He seemed scarcely to see her.

"Can't you—can't you," she hesitated, "can't you tell me about it, Gordon? You know I'm always interested in you."

She bit her lip—she had intended to say something stronger, but found at the end that she couldn't bring it out.

Gordon shook his head dully. "I can't tell you. You're a good woman. I can't tell a good woman the story."

"Rot," she said, defiantly. "I think it's a perfect insult to call any one a good woman in that way. It's a slam. You've been drinking, Gordon."

"Thanks." He inclined his head gravely. "Thanks for the information."

"Why do you drink?"

"Because I'm so damn miserable."

"Do you think drinking's going to make it any better?"

"What you doing—trying to reform me?"

"No; I'm trying to help you, Gordon. Can't you tell me about it?"

"I'm in an awful mess. Best thing you can do is to pretend not to know me."

"Why, Gordon?"

"I'm sorry I cut in on you—it's unfair to you. You're pure woman—and all that sort of thing. Here, I'll get some one else to dance with you."

He rose clumsily to his feet, but she reached up and pulled him down beside her on the stairs.

"Here, Gordon. You're ridiculous. You're hurting me. You're acting like a—like a crazy man——"

"I admit it. I'm a little crazy. Something's wrong with me, Edith. There's something left me. It doesn't matter."

"It does, tell me."

"Just that. I was always queer—little bit different from other boys. All right in college, but now it's all wrong. Things have been snapping inside me for four months like little hooks on a dress, and it's about to come off when a few more hooks go. I'm very gradually going loony."

He turned his eyes full on her and began to laugh, and she shrank away from him.

"What *is* the matter?"

"Just me," he repeated. "I'm going loony. This whole place is like a dream to me—this Delmonico's——"

As he talked she saw he had changed utterly. He wasn't at all light and gay and careless—a great lethargy and discouragement had come over him. Revulsion seized her, followed by a faint, surprising boredom. His voice seemed to come out of a great void.

"Edith," he said, "I used to think I was clever, talented, an artist. Now I know I'm nothing. Can't draw, Edith. Don't know why I'm telling you this."

She nodded absently.

"I can't draw, I can't do anything. I'm poor as a church mouse." He laughed, bitterly and rather too loud. "I've become a damn beggar, a leech on my friends. I'm a failure. I'm poor as hell."

Her distaste was growing. She barely nodded this time, waiting for her first possible cue to rise.

Suddenly Gordon's eyes filled with tears.

"Edith," he said, turning to her with what was evidently a strong effort at self-control, "I can't tell you what it means to me to know there's one person left who's interested in me."

He reached out and patted her hand, and involuntarily she drew it away.

"It's mighty fine of you," he repeated.

"Well," she said slowly, looking him in the eye, "any one's always glad to see an old friend—but I'm sorry to see you like this, Gordon."

There was a pause while they looked at each other, and the momentary eagerness in his eyes wavered. She rose and stood looking at him, her face quite expressionless.

"Shall we dance?" she suggested, coolly.

—Love is fragile—she was thinking—but perhaps the pieces are saved, the things that hovered on lips, that might have been said. The new love words, the tendernesses learned, are treasured up for the next lover.

V

Peter Himmel, escort to the lovely Edith, was unaccustomed to being snubbed; having been snubbed, he was hurt and embarrassed, and ashamed of himself. For a matter of two months he had been on special delivery terms with Edith Bradin and, knowing that the one excuse and explanation of the special delivery letter is its value in sentimental correspondence, he had believed himself quite sure of his ground. He searched in vain for any reason why she should have taken this attitude in the matter of a simple kiss.

Therefore when he was cut in on by the man with the mustache he went out into the hall and, making up a sentence, said it over to himself several times. Considerably deleted, this was it:

"Well, if any girl ever led a man on and then jolted him, she did—and she has no kick coming if I go out and get beautifully boiled."

So he walked through the supper room into a small room adjoining it, which he had located earlier in the evening. It was a room in which there were several large bowls of punch flanked by many bottles. He took a seat beside the table which held the bottles.

At the second highball, boredom, disgust, the monotony of time, the turbidity of events, sank into a vague background before which glittering cobwebs formed. Things became reconciled to themselves, things lay quietly on their shelves; the troubles of the day arranged themselves in trim formation and at his curt wish of dismissal, marched off and disappeared. And with the departure of worry came brilliant, permeating symbolism. Edith became a flighty, negligible girl, not to be worried over; rather to be laughed at. She fitted like a figure of his own dream into the surface world forming about him. He himself became in a measure symbolic, a type of the continent bacchanal, the brilliant dreamer at play.

Then the symbolic mood faded and as he sipped his third highball his imagination yielded to the warm glow and he lapsed into a state similar to floating on his back in pleasant water. It was at this point that he noticed that a green baize door near him was open about two inches, and that through the aperture a pair of eyes were watching him intently.

"Hm," murmured Peter calmly.

The green door closed—and then opened again—a bare half inch this time.

"Peek-a-boo," murmured Peter.

The door remained stationary and then he became aware of a series of tense intermittent whispers.

"One guy."

"What's he doin'?"

"He's sittin' lookin'."

"He better beat it off. We gotta get another li'l' bottle."

Peter listened while the words filtered into his consciousness.

"Now this," he thought, "is most remarkable."

He was excited. He was jubilant. He felt that he had stumbled upon a mystery. Affecting an elaborate carelessness he arose and walked around the table—then, turning quickly, pulled open the green door, precipitating Private Rose into the room.

Peter bowed.

"How do you do?" he said.

Private Rose set one foot slightly in front of the other, poised for fight, flight, or compromise.

"How do you do?" repeated Peter politely.

"I'm o'right."

"Can I offer you a drink?"

Private Rose looked at him searchingly, suspecting possible sarcasm.

"O'right," he said finally.

Peter indicated a chair.

"Sit down."

"I got a friend," said Rose, "I got a friend in there." He pointed to the green door.

"By all means let's have him in."

Peter crossed over, opened the door and welcomed in Private Key, very suspicious and uncertain and guilty. Chairs were found and the three took their seats around the punch bowl. Peter gave them each a highball and offered them a cigarette from his case. They accepted both with some diffidence.

"Now," continued Peter easily, "may I ask why you gentlemen prefer to lounge away your leisure hours in a room which is chiefly furnished, as far as I can see, with scrubbing brushes. And when the human race has progressed to the stage where seventeen thousand chairs are manufactured on every day except Sunday—" he paused. Rose and Key regarded him vacantly. "Will you tell me," went on Peter, "why you choose to rest yourselves on articles intended for the transportation of water from one place to another?"

At this point Rose contributed a grunt to the conversation.

"And lastly," finished Peter, "will you tell me why, when you are in a building beautifully hung with enormous candelabra, you prefer to spend these evening hours under one anemic electric light?"

Rose looked at Key; Key looked at Rose. They laughed; they laughed uproariously; they found it was impossible to look at each other without laughing. But they were not laughing with this man—they were laughing at him. To them a man who talked after this fashion was either raving drunk or raving crazy.

"You are Yale men, I presume," said Peter, finishing his highball and preparing another.

They laughed again.

"Na-ah."

"So? I thought perhaps you might be members of that lowly section of the university known as the Sheffield Scientific School."

"Na-ah."

"Hm. Well, that's too bad. No doubt you are Harvard men, anxious to preserve your incognito in this—this paradise of violet blue, as the newspapers say."

"Na-ah," said Key scornfully, "we was just waitin' for somebody."

"Ah," exclaimed Peter, rising and filling their glasses, "very interestin'. Had a date with a scrublady, eh?"

They both denied this indignantly.

"It's all right," Peter reassured them, "don't apologize. A scrublady's as good as any lady in the world. Kipling says 'Any lady and Judy O'Grady under the skin.'"

"Sure," said Key, winking broadly at Rose.

"My case, for instance," continued Peter, finishing his glass. "I got a girl up there that's spoiled. Spoildest darn girl I ever saw. Refused to kiss me; no reason whatsoever. Led me on deliberately to think sure I want to kiss you and then plunk! Threw me over! What's the younger generation comin' to?"

"Say tha's hard luck," said Key—"that's awful hard luck."

"Oh boy!" said Rose.

"Have another?" said Peter.

"We got in a sort of fight for a while," said Key after a pause, "but it was too far away."

"A fight?—tha's stuff!" said Peter, seating himself unsteadily. "Fight 'em all! I was in the army."

"This was with a Bolshevik fella."

"Tha's stuff!" exclaimed Peter, enthusiastic. "That's what I say! Kill the Bolshevik! Exterminate 'em!"

"We're Americuns," said Rose, implying a sturdy, defiant patriotism.

"Sure," said Peter. "Greatest race in the world! We're all Americuns! Have another."

They had another.

VI

At one o'clock a special orchestra, special even in a day of special orchestras, arrived at Delmonico's, and its members, seating themselves arrogantly around the piano, took up the burden of providing music for the Gamma Psi Fraternity. They were headed by a famous flute-player, distinguished throughout New York for his feat of standing on his head and shimmying with his shoulders while he played the latest jazz on his flute. During his performance the lights were extinguished except for the spotlight on the flute-player and another roving beam that threw flickering shadows and changing kaleidoscopic colors over the massed dancers.

Edith had danced herself into that tired, dreamy state habitual only with débutantes, a state equivalent to the glow of a noble soul after several long highballs. Her mind floated vaguely on the bosom of the music; her partners changed with the unreality of phantoms under the colorful shifting dusk, and to her present coma it seemed as if days had passed since the dance began. She had talked on many fragmentary subjects with many men. She had been kissed once and made love to six times. Earlier in the evening different undergraduates had danced with her, but now, like all the more popular girls there, she had her own entourage—that is, half a dozen gallants had singled her out or were alternating her charms with those of some other chosen beauty; they cut in on her in regular, inevitable succession.

Several times she had seen Gordon—he had been sitting a long time on the stairway with his palm to his head, his dull eyes fixed at an infinite speck on the floor before him, very depressed, he looked, and quite drunk—but Edith each time had averted her glance hurriedly. All that seemed long ago; her mind was passive now, her senses were lulled to trance-like sleep; only her feet danced and her voice talked on in hazy sentimental banter.

But Edith was not nearly so tired as to be incapable of moral indignation when Peter Himmel cut in on her, sublimely and happily drunk. She gasped and looked up at him.

"Why, *Peter*!"

"I'm a li'l' stewed, Edith."

"Why, Peter, you're a *peach,* you are! Don't you think it's a bum way of doing—when you're with me?"

Then she smiled unwillingly, for he was looking at her with owlish sentimentality varied with a silly spasmodic smile.

"Darlin' Edith," he began earnestly, "you know I love you, don't you?"

"You tell it well."

"I love you—and I merely wanted you to kiss me," he added sadly.

His embarrassment, his shame, were both gone. She was a mos' beautiful girl in whole worl'. Mos' beautiful eyes, like stars above. He wanted to 'pologize—firs', for presuming try to kiss her; second, for drinking—but he'd been so discouraged 'cause he had thought she was mad at him——

The red-fat man cut in, and looking up at Edith smiled radiantly.

"Did you bring any one?" she asked.

No. The red-fat man was a stag.

"Well, would you mind—would it be an awful bother for you to—to take me home to-night?" (this extreme diffidence was a charming affectation on Edith's part—she knew that the red-fat man would immediately dissolve into a paroxysm of delight).

"Bother? Why, good Lord, I'd be darn glad to! You know I'd be darn glad to."

"Thanks *loads*! You're awfully sweet."

She glanced at her wrist-watch. It was half-past one. And, as she said "half-past one" to herself, it floated vaguely into her mind that her brother had told her at luncheon that he worked in the office of his newspaper until after one-thirty every evening.

Edith turned suddenly to her current partner.

"What street is Delmonico's on, anyway?"

"Street? Oh, why Fifth Avenue, of course."

"I mean, what cross street?"

"Why—let's see—it's on Forty-fourth Street."

This verified what she had thought. Henry's office must be across the street and just around the corner, and it occurred to her immediately that she might slip over for a moment and surprise him, float in on him, a shimmering marvel in her new crimson opera cloak and "cheer him up." It was exactly the sort of thing Edith revelled in doing—an unconventional, jaunty thing. The idea reached out and gripped at her imagination—after an instant's hesitation she had decided.

"My hair is just about to tumble entirely down," she said pleasantly to her partner; "would you mind if I go and fix it?"

"Not at all."

"You're a peach."

A few minutes later, wrapped in her crimson opera cloak, she flitted down a side-stairs, her cheeks glowing with excitement at her little adventure. She ran by a couple who stood at the door—a weak-chinned waiter and an over-rouged young lady, in hot dispute—and opening the outer door stepped into the warm May night.

VII

The over-roughed young lady followed her with a brief, bitter glance—then turned again to the weak-chinned waiter and took up her argument.

"You better go up and tell him I'm here," she said defiantly, "or I'll go up myself."

"No, you don't!" said George sternly.

The girl smiled sardonically.

"Oh, I don't, don't I? Well, let me tell you I know more college fellas and more of 'em know me, and are glad to take me out on a party, than you ever saw in your whole life."

"Maybe so——"

"Maybe so," she interrupted. "Oh, it's all right for any of 'em like that one that just ran out—God knows where *she* went—it's all right for them that are asked here to come or go as they like—but when I want to see a friend they have some cheap, ham-slinging, bring-me-a-doughnut waiter to stand here and keep me out."

"See here," said the elder Key indignantly, "I can't lose my job. Maybe this fella you're talkin' about doesn't want to see you."

"Oh, he wants to see me all right."

"Anyways, how could I find him in all that crowd?"

"Oh, he'll be there," she asserted confidently. "You just ask anybody for Gordon Sterrett and they'll point him out to you. They all know each other, those fellas."

She produced a mesh bag, and taking out a dollar bill handed it to George.

"Here," she said, "here's a bribe. You find him and give him my message. You tell him if he isn't here in five minutes I'm coming up."

George shook his head pessimistically, considered the question for a moment, wavered violently, and then withdrew.

In less than the allotted time Gordon came down-stairs. He was drunker than he had been earlier in the evening and in a different way. The liquor seemed to have hardened on him like a crust. He was heavy and lurching—almost incoherent when he talked.

"'Lo, Jewel," he said thickly. "Came right away. Jewel, I couldn't get that money. Tried my best."

"Money nothing!" she snapped. "You haven't been near me for ten days. What's the matter?"

He shook his head slowly.

"Been very low, Jewel. Been sick."

"Why didn't you tell me if you were sick. I don't care about the money that bad. I didn't start bothering you about it at all until you began neglecting me."

Again he shook his head.

"Haven't been neglecting you. Not at all."

"Haven't! You haven't been near me for three weeks, unless you been so drunk you didn't know what you were doing."

"Been sick, Jewel," he repeated, turning his eyes upon her wearily.

"You're well enough to come and play with your society friends here all right. You told me you'd meet me for dinner, and you said you'd have some money for me. You didn't even bother to ring me up."

"I couldn't get any money."

"Haven't I just been saying that doesn't matter? I wanted to see *you,* Gordon, but you seem to prefer your somebody else."

He denied this bitterly.

"Then get your hat and come along," she suggested.

Gordon hesitated—and she came suddenly close to him and slipped her arms around his neck.

"Come on with me, Gordon," she said in a half whisper. "We'll go over to Devineries' and have a drink, and then we can go up to my apartment."

"I can't, Jewel,—"

"You can," she said intensely.

"I'm sick as a dog!"

"Well, then, you oughtn't to stay here and dance."

With a glance around him in which relief and despair were mingled, Gordon hesitated; then she suddenly pulled him to her and kissed him with soft, pulpy lips.

"All right," he said heavily. "I'll get my hat."

VIII

When Edith came out into the clear blue of the May night she found the Avenue deserted. The windows of the big shops were dark; over their doors were drawn great iron masks until they were only shadowy tombs of the late day's splendor. Glancing down toward Forty-second Street she saw a commingled blur of lights from the all-night restaurants. Over on Sixth Avenue the elevated, a flare of fire, roared across the street between the glimmering parallels of light at the station and streaked along into the crisp dark. But at Forty-fourth Street it was very quiet.

Pulling her cloak close about her Edith darted across the Avenue. She started nervously as a solitary man passed her and said in a hoarse whisper—"Where bound, kiddo?" She was reminded of a night in her childhood when she had walked around the block in her pajamas and a dog had howled at her from a mystery-big back yard.

In a minute she had reached her destination, a two-story, comparatively old building on Forty-fourth, in the upper windows of which she thankfully detected a wisp of light. It was bright enough outside for her to make out the sign beside the window—the *New York Trumpet.* She stepped inside a dark hall and after a second saw the stairs in the corner.

Then she was in a long, low room furnished with many desks and hung on all sides with file copies of newspapers. There were only two occupants. They were sitting at different ends of the room, each wearing a green eye-shade and writing by a solitary desk light.

For a moment she stood uncertainly in the doorway, and then both men turned around simultaneously and she recognized her brother.

"Why, Edith!" He rose quickly and approached her in surprise, removing his eye-shade. He was tall, lean, and dark, with black, piercing eyes under very thick glasses. They were far-away eyes that seemed always fixed just over the head of the person to whom he was talking.

He put his hands on her arms and kissed her cheek.

"What is it?" he repeated in some alarm.

"I was at a dance across at Delmonico's, Henry," she said excitedly, "and I couldn't resist tearing over to see you."

"I'm glad you did." His alertness gave way quickly to a habitual vagueness. "You oughtn't to be out alone at night though, ought you?"

The man at the other end of the room had been looking at them curiously, but at Henry's beckoning gesture he approached. He was loosely fat with little twinkling eyes, and, having removed his collar and tie, he gave the impression of a Middle-Western farmer on a Sunday afternoon.

"This is my sister," said Henry. "She dropped in to see me."

"How do you do?" said the fat man, smiling. "My name's Bartholomew, Miss Bradin. I know your brother has forgotten it long ago."

Edith laughed politely.

"Well," he continued, "not exactly gorgeous quarters we have here, are they?"

Edith looked around the room.

"They seem very nice," she replied. "Where do you keep the bombs?"

"The bombs?" repeated Bartholomew, laughing. "That's pretty good—the bombs. Did you hear her, Henry? She wants to know where we keep the bombs. Say, that's pretty good."

Edith swung herself around onto a vacant desk and sat dangling her feet over the edge. Her brother took a seat beside her.

"Well," he asked, absent-mindedly, "how do you like New York this trip?"

"Not bad. I'll be over at the Biltmore with the Hoyts until Sunday. Can't you come to luncheon to-morrow?"

He thought a moment.

"I'm especially busy," he objected, "and I hate women in groups."

"All right," she agreed, unruffled. "Let's you and me have luncheon together."

"Very well."

"I'll call for you at twelve."

Bartholomew was obviously anxious to return to his desk, but apparently considered that it would be rude to leave without some parting pleasantry.

"Well—" he began awkwardly.

They both turned to him.

"Well, we—we had an exciting time earlier in the evening."

The two men exchanged glances.

"You should have come earlier," continued Bartholomew, somewhat encouraged. "We had a regular vaudeville."

"Did you really?"

"A serenade," said Henry. "A lot of soldiers gathered down there in the street and began to yell at the sign."

"Why?" she demanded.

"Just a crowd," said Henry, abstractedly. "All crowds have to howl. They didn't have anybody with much initiative in the lead, or they'd probably have forced their way in here and smashed things up."

"Yes," said Bartholomew, turning again to Edith, "you should have been here."

He seemed to consider this a sufficient cue for withdrawal, for he turned abruptly and went back to his desk.

"Are the soldiers all set against the Socialists?" demanded Edith of her brother. "I mean do they attack you violently and all that?"

Henry replaced his eye-shade and yawned.

"The human race has come a long way," he said casually, "but most of us are throw-backs; the soldiers don't know what they want, or what they hate, or what they like. They're used to acting in large bodies, and they seem to have to make demonstrations. So it happens to be against us. There've been riots all over the city to-night. It's May Day, you see."

"Was the disturbance here pretty serious?"

"Not a bit," he said scornfully. "About twenty-five of them stopped in the street about nine o'clock, and began to bellow at the moon."

"Oh—" She changed the subject. "You're glad to see me, Henry?"

"Why, sure."

"You don't seem to be."

"I am."

"I suppose you think I'm a—a waster. Sort of the World's Worst Butterfly."

Henry laughed.

"Not at all. Have a good time while you're young. Why? Do I seem like the priggish and earnest youth?"

"No—" She paused, "—but somehow I began thinking how absolutely different the party I'm on is from—from all your purposes. It seems sort of—of incongruous, doesn't it?—me being at a party like that, and you over here working for a thing that'll make that sort of party impossible ever any more, if your ideas work."

"I don't think of it that way. You're young, and you're acting just as you were brought up to act. Go ahead—have a good time."

Her feet, which had been idly swinging, stopped and her voice dropped a note.

"I wish you'd—you'd come back to Harrisburg and have a good time. Do you feel sure that you're on the right track——"

"You're wearing beautiful stockings," he interrupted. "What on earth are they?"

"They're embroidered," she replied, glancing down. "Aren't they cunning?" She raised her skirts and uncovered slim, silk-sheathed calves. "Or do you disapprove of silk stockings?"

He seemed slightly exasperated, bent his dark eyes on her piercingly.

"Are you trying to make me out as criticizing you in any way, Edith?"

"Not at all——"

She paused. Bartholomew had uttered a grunt. She turned and saw that he had left his desk and was standing at the window.

"What is it?" demanded Henry.

"People," said Bartholomew, and then after an instant: "Whole jam of them. They're coming from Sixth Avenue."

"People."

The fat man pressed his nose to the pane.

"Soldiers, by God!" he said emphatically. "I had an idea they'd come back."

Edith jumped to her feet, and running over joined Bartholomew at the window.

"There's a lot of them!" she cried excitedly. "Come here, Henry!"

Henry readjusted his shade, but kept his seat.

"Hadn't we better turn out the lights?" suggested Bartholomew.

"No. They'll go away in a minute."

"They're not," said Edith, peering from the window. "They're not even thinking of going away. There's more of them coming. Look—there's a whole crowd turning the corner of Sixth Avenue."

By the yellow glow and blue shadows of the street lamp she could see that the sidewalk was crowded with men. They were mostly in uniform, some sober, some enthusiastically drunk, and over the whole swept an incoherent clamor and shouting.

Henry rose, and going to the window exposed himself as a long silhouette against the office lights. Immediately the shouting became a steady yell, and a rattling fusillade of small missiles, corners of tobacco plugs, cigarette-boxes, and even pennies beat against the window. The sounds of the racket now began floating up the stairs as the folding doors revolved.

"They're coming up!" cried Bartholomew.

Edith turned anxiously to Henry.

"They're coming up, Henry."

From down-stairs in the lower hall their cries were now quite audible.

"—God damn Socialists!"

"Pro-Germans! Boche-lovers!"

"Second floor, front! Come on!"

"We'll get the sons——"

The next five minutes passed in a dream. Edith was conscious that the clamor burst suddenly upon the three of them like a cloud of rain, that there was a thunder of many feet on the stairs, that Henry had seized her arm and drawn her back toward the rear of the office. Then the door opened and an overflow of men were forced into the room—not the leaders, but simply those who happened to be in front.

"Hello, Bo!"

"Up late, ain't you?"

"You an' your girl. Damn *you*!"

She noticed that two very drunken soldiers had been forced to the front, where they wobbled fatuously—one of them was short and dark, the other was tall and weak of chin.

Henry stepped forward and raised his hand.

"Friends!" he said.

The clamor faded into a momentary stillness, punctuated with mutterings.

"Friends!" he repeated, his far-away eyes fixed over the heads of the crowd, "you're injuring no one but yourselves by breaking in here to-night. Do we look like rich men? Do we look like Germans? I ask you in all fairness——"

"Pipe down!"

"I'll say you do!"

"Say, who's your lady friend, buddy?"

A man in civilian clothes, who had been pawing over a table, suddenly held up a newspaper.

"Here it is!" he shouted. "They wanted the Germans to win the war!"

A new overflow from the stairs was shouldered in and of a sudden the room was full of men all closing around the pale little group at the back. Edith saw that the tall soldier with the weak chin was still in front. The short dark one had disappeared.

She edged slightly backward, stood close to the open window, through which came a clear breath of cool night air.

Then the room was a riot. She realized that the soldiers were surging forward, glimpsed the fat man swinging a chair over his head—instantly the lights went out, and she felt the push of warm bodies under rough cloth, and her ears were full of shouting and trampling and hard breathing.

A figure flashed by her out of nowhere, tottered, was edged sideways, and of a sudden disappeared helplessly out through the open window with a frightened, fragmentary cry that died staccato on the bosom of the clamor. By the faint light streaming from the building backing on the area Edith had a quick impression that it had been the tall soldier with the weak chin.

Anger rose astonishingly in her. She swung her arms wildly, edged blindly toward the thickest of the scuffling. She heard grunts, curses, the muffled impact of fists.

"Henry!" she called frantically, "Henry!"

Then, it was minutes later, she felt suddenly that there were other figures in the room. She heard a voice, deep, bullying, authoritative; she saw yellow rays of light sweeping here and there in the fracas. The cries became more scattered. The scuffling increased and then stopped.

Suddenly the lights were on and the room was full of policemen, clubbing left and right. The deep voice boomed out:

"Here now! Here now! Here now!"

And then:

"Quiet down and get out! Here now!"

The room seemed to empty like a wash-bowl. A policeman fast-grappled in the corner released his hold on his soldier antagonist and started him with a shove toward the door. The deep voice continued. Edith perceived now that it came from a bull-necked police captain standing near the door.

"Here now! This is no way! One of your own sojers got shoved out of the back window an' killed hisself!"

"Henry!" called Edith, "Henry!"

She beat wildly with her fists on the back of the man in front of her; she brushed between two others; fought, shrieked, and beat her way to a very pale figure sitting on the floor close to a desk.

"Henry," she cried passionately, "what's the matter? What's the matter? Did they hurt you?"

His eyes were shut. He groaned and then looking up said disgustedly—

"They broke my leg. My God, the fools!"

"Here now!" called the police captain. "Here now! Here now!"

IX

"Childs', Fifty-ninth Street," at eight o'clock of any morning differs from its sisters by less than the width of their marble tables or the degree of polish on the frying-pans. You will see there a crowd of poor people with sleep in the corners of their eyes, trying to look straight before them at their food so as not to see the other poor people. But Childs', Fifty-ninth, four hours earlier is quite unlike any Childs' restaurant from Portland, Oregon, to Portland, Maine. Within its pale but sanitary walls one finds a noisy medley of chorus girls, college boys, débutantes, rakes, *filles de joie*—a not unrepresentative mixture of the gayest of Broadway, and even of Fifth Avenue.

In the early morning of May the second it was unusually full. Over the marble-topped tables were bent the excited faces of flappers whose fathers owned individual villages. They were eating buckwheat cakes and scrambled eggs with relish and gusto, an accomplishment that it would have been utterly impossible for them to repeat in the same place four hours later.

Almost the entire crowd were from the Gamma Psi dance at Delmonico's except for several chorus girls from a midnight revue who sat at a side table and wished they'd taken off a little more make-up after the show. Here and there a drab, mouse-like figure, desperately out of place, watched the butterflies with a weary, puzzled curiosity. But the drab figure was the exception. This was the morning after May Day, and celebration was still in the air.

Gus Rose, sober but a little dazed, must be classed as one of the drab figures. How he had got himself from Forty-fourth Street to Fifty-ninth Street after the riot was only a hazy half-memory. He had seen the body of Carrol Key put in an ambulance and driven off, and then he had started up town with two or three soldiers. Somewhere between Forty-fourth Street and Fifty-ninth Street the other soldiers had met some women and disappeared. Rose had wandered to Columbus Circle and chosen the gleaming lights of Childs' to minister to his craving for coffee and doughnuts. He walked in and sat down.

All around him floated airy, inconsequential chatter and high-pitched laughter. At first he failed to understand, but after a puzzled five minutes he realized that this was the aftermath of some gay party. Here and there a restless, hilarious young man wandered fraternally and familiarly between the tables, shaking hands indiscriminately and pausing occasionally for a facetious chat, while excited waiters, bearing cakes and eggs aloft, swore at him silently, and bumped him out of the way. To Rose, seated at the most inconspicuous and least crowded table, the whole scene was a colorful circus of beauty and riotous pleasure.

He became gradually aware, after a few moments, that the couple seated diagonally across from him, with their backs to the crowd, were not the least interesting pair in the room. The man was drunk. He wore a dinner coat with a dishevelled tie and shirt swollen by spillings of water and wine. His eyes, dim and bloodshot, roved unnaturally from side to side. His breath came short between his lips.

"He's been on a spree!" thought Rose.

The woman was almost if not quite sober. She was pretty, with dark eyes and feverish high color, and she kept her active eyes fixed on her companion with the alertness of a hawk. From time to time she would lean and whisper intently to him, and he would answer by inclining his head heavily or by a particularly ghoulish and repellent wink.

Rose scrutinized them dumbly for some minutes, until the woman gave him a quick, resentful look; then he shifted his gaze to two of the most conspicuously hilarious of the promenaders who were on a protracted circuit of the tables. To his surprise he recognized in one of them the young man by whom he had been so ludicrously entertained at Delmonico's. This started him thinking of Key with a vague sentimentality, not unmixed with awe. Key was dead. He had fallen thirty-five feet and split his skull like a cracked cocoanut.

"He was a darn good guy," thought Rose mournfully. "He was a darn good guy, o'right. That was awful hard luck about him."

The two promenaders approached and started down between Rose's table and the next, addressing friends and strangers alike with jovial familiarity. Suddenly Rose saw the fair-haired one with the prominent teeth stop, look unsteadily at the man and girl opposite, and then begin to move his head disapprovingly from side to side.

The man with the blood-shot eyes looked up.

"Gordy," said the promenader with the prominent teeth, "Gordy."

"Hello," said the man with the stained shirt thickly.

Prominent Teeth shook his finger pessimistically at the pair, giving the woman a glance of aloof condemnation.

"What'd I tell you Gordy?"

Gordon stirred in his seat.

"Go to hell!" he said.

Dean continued to stand there shaking his finger. The woman began to get angry.

"You go away!" she cried fiercely. "You're drunk, that's what you are!"

"So's he," suggested Dean, staying the motion of his finger and pointing it at Gordon.

Peter Himmel ambled up, owlish now and oratorically inclined.

"Here now," he began as if called upon to deal with some petty dispute between children. "Wha's all trouble?"

"You take your friend away," said Jewel tartly. "He's bothering us."

"What's 'at?"

"You heard me!" she said shrilly. "I said to take your drunken friend away."

Her rising voice sang out above the clatter of the restaurant and a waiter came hurrying up.

"You gotta be more quiet!"

"That fella's drunk," she cried. "He's insulting us."

"Ah-ha, Gordy," persisted the accused. "What'd I tell you." He turned to the waiter. "Gordy an' I friends. Been tryin' help him, haven't I, Gordy?"

Gordy looked up.

"Help me? Hell, no!"

Jewel rose suddenly, and seizing Gordon's arm assisted him to his feet.

"Come on, Gordy!" she said, leaning toward him and speaking in a half whisper. "Let's us get out of here. This fella's got a mean drunk on."

Gordon allowed himself to be urged to his feet and started toward the door. Jewel turned for a second and addressed the provoker of their flight.

"I know all about *you*!" she said fiercely. "Nice friend, you are, I'll say. He told me about you."

Then she seized Gordon's arm, and together they made their way through the curious crowd, paid their check, and went out.

"You'll have to sit down," said the waiter to Peter after they had gone.

"What's 'at? Sit down?"

"Yes—or get out."

Peter turned to Dean.

"Come on," he suggested. "Let's beat up this waiter."

"All right."

They advanced toward him, their faces grown stern. The waiter retreated.

Peter suddenly reached over to a plate on the table beside him and picking up a handful of hash tossed it into the air. It descended as a languid parabola in snowflake effect on the heads of those near by.

"Hey! Ease up!"

"Put him out!"

"Sit down, Peter!"

"Cut out that stuff!"

Peter laughed and bowed.

"Thank you for your kind applause, ladies and gents. If some one will lend me some more hash and a tall hat we will go on with the act."

The bouncer hustled up.

"You've gotta get out!" he said to Peter.

"Hell, no!"

"He's my friend!" put in Dean indignantly.

A crowd of waiters were gathering. "Put him out!"

"Better go, Peter."

There was a short struggle and the two were edged and pushed toward the door.

"I got a hat and a coat here!" cried Peter.

"Well, go get 'em and be spry about it!"

The bouncer released his hold on Peter, who, adopting a ludicrous air of extreme cunning, rushed immediately around to the other table, where he burst into derisive laughter and thumbed his nose at the exasperated waiters.

"Think I just better wait a l'il' longer," he announced.

The chase began. Four waiters were sent around one way and four another. Dean caught hold of two of them by the coat, and another struggle took place before the pursuit of Peter could be resumed; he was finally pinioned after overturning a sugar-bowl and several cups of coffee. A fresh argument ensued at the cashier's desk, where Peter attempted to buy another dish of hash to take with him and throw at policemen.

But the commotion upon his exit proper was dwarfed by another phenomenon which drew admiring glances and a prolonged involuntary "Oh-h-h!" from every person in the restaurant.

The great plate-glass front had turned to a deep creamy blue, the color of a Maxfield Parrish moonlight—a blue that seemed to press close upon the pane as if to crowd its way into the restaurant. Dawn had come up in Columbus Circle, magical, breathless dawn, silhouetting the great statue of the immortal Christopher, and mingling in a curious and uncanny manner with the fading yellow electric light inside.

X

Mr. In and Mr. Out are not listed by the census-taker. You will search for them in vain through the social register or the births, marriages, and deaths, or the grocer's credit list. Oblivion has swallowed them and the testimony that they ever existed at all is vague and shadowy, and inadmissible in a court of law. Yet I have it upon the best authority that for a brief space Mr. In and Mr. Out lived, breathed, answered to their names and radiated vivid personalities of their own.

During the brief span of their lives they walked in their native garments down the great highway of a great nation; were laughed at, sworn at, chased, and fled from. Then they passed and were heard of no more.

They were already taking form dimly, when a taxicab with the top open breezed down Broadway in the faintest glimmer of May dawn. In this car sat the souls of Mr. In and Mr. Out discussing with amazement the blue light that had so precipitately colored the sky behind the statue of Christopher Columbus, discussing with bewilderment the old, gray faces of the early risers which skimmed palely along the street like brown bits of paper on a gray lake. They were agreed on all things, from the absurdity of the bouncer in Childs' to the absurdity of the business of life. They were dizzy with the extreme maudlin happiness that the morning had awakened in their glowing souls. Indeed, so fresh and vigorous was their pleasure in living that they felt it should be expressed by loud cries.

"Ye-ow-ow!" hooted Peter, making a megaphone with his hands—and Dean joined in with a call that, though equally significant and symbolic, derived its resonance from its very inarticulateness.

"Yo-ho! Yea! Yoho! Yo-buba!"

Fifty-third Street was a bus with a dark, bobbed-hair beauty atop; Fifty-second was a street cleaner who dodged, escaped, and sent up a yell of, "Look where you're aimin'!" in a pained and grieved voice. At Fiftieth Street a group of men on a very white sidewalk in front of a very white building turned to stare after them, and shouted:

"Some party, boys!"

At Forty-ninth Street Peter turned to Dean. "Beautiful morning," he said gravely, squinting up his owlish eyes.

"Probably is."

"Go get some breakfast, hey?"

Dean agreed—with additions.

"Breakfast and liquor."

"Breakfast and liquor," repeated Peter, and they looked at each other, nodding. "That's logical."

Then they both burst into loud laughter.

"Breakfast and liquor! Oh, gosh!"

"No such thing," announced Peter.

"Don't serve it? Ne'mind. We force 'em serve it. Bring pressure bear."

"Bring logic bear."

The taxi cut suddenly off Broadway, sailed along a cross street, and stopped in front of a heavy tomb-like building in Fifth Avenue.

"What's idea?"

The taxi-driver informed them that this was Delmonico's.

This was somewhat puzzling. They were forced to devote several minutes to intense concentration, for if such an order had been given there must have been a reason for it.

"Somep'm 'bouta coat," suggested the taxi-man.

That was it. Peter's overcoat and hat. He had left them at Delmonico's. Having decided this, they disembarked from the taxi and strolled toward the entrance arm in arm.

"Hey!" said the taxi-driver.

"Huh?"

"You better pay me."

They shook their heads in shocked negation.

"Later, not now—we give orders, you wait."

The taxi-driver objected; he wanted his money now. With the scornful condescension of men exercising tremendous self-control they paid him.

Inside Peter groped in vain through a dim, deserted check-room in search of his coat and derby.

"Gone, I guess. Somebody stole it."

"Some Sheff student."

"All probability."

"Never mind," said Dean, nobly. "I'll leave mine here too—then we'll both be dressed the same."

He removed his overcoat and hat and was hanging them up when his roving glance was caught and held magnetically by two large squares of cardboard tacked to the two coat-room doors. The one on the left-hand door bore the word "In" in big black letters, and the one on the right-hand door flaunted the equally emphatic word "Out."

"Look!" he exclaimed happily—

Peter's eyes followed his pointing finger.

"What?"

"Look at the signs. Let's take 'em."

"Good idea."

"Probably pair very rare an' valuable signs. Probably come in handy."

Peter removed the left-hand sign from the door and endeavored to conceal it about his person. The sign being of considerable proportions, this was a matter of some difficulty. An idea flung itself at him, and with an air of dignified mystery he turned his back. After an instant he wheeled dramatically around, and stretching out his arms displayed himself to the admiring Dean. He had inserted the sign in his vest, completely covering his shirt front. In effect, the word "In" had been painted upon his shirt in large black letters.

"Yoho!" cheered Dean. "Mister In."

He inserted his own sign in like manner.

"Mister Out!" he announced triumphantly. "Mr. In meet Mr. Out."

They advanced and shook hands. Again laughter overcame them and they rocked in a shaken spasm of mirth.

"Yoho!"

"We probably get a flock of breakfast."

"We'll go—go to the Commodore."

Arm in arm they sallied out the door, and turning east in Forty-fourth Street set out for the Commodore.

As they came out a short dark soldier, very pale and tired, who had been wandering listlessly along the sidewalk, turned to look at them.

He started over as though to address them, but as they immediately bent on him glances of withering unrecognition, he waited until they had started unsteadily down the street, and then followed at about forty paces, chuckling to himself and saying, "Oh, boy!" over and over under his breath, in delighted, anticipatory tones.

Mr. In and Mr. Out were meanwhile exchanging pleasantries concerning their future plans:

"We want liquor; we want breakfast. Neither without the other. One and indivisible."

"We want both 'em!"

"Both 'em!"

It was quite light now, and passers-by began to bend curious eyes on the pair. Obviously they were engaged in a discussion, which afforded each of them intense amusement, for occasionally a fit of laughter would seize upon them so violently that, still with their arms interlocked, they would bend nearly double.

Reaching the Commodore, they exchanged a few spicy epigrams with the sleepy-eyed doorman, navigated the revolving door with some difficulty, and then made their way through a thinly populated but startled lobby to the dining-room, where a puzzled waiter showed them an obscure table in a corner. They studied the bill of fare helplessly, telling over the items to each other in puzzled mumbles.

"Don't see any liquor here," said Peter reproachfully.

The waiter became audible but unintelligible.

"Repeat," continued Peter, with patient tolerance, "that there seems to be unexplained and quite distasteful lack of liquor upon bill of fare."

"Here!" said Dean confidently, "let me handle him." He turned to the waiter—"Bring us—bring us—" he scanned the bill of fare anxiously. "Bring us a quart of champagne and a—a—probably ham sandwich."

The waiter looked doubtful.

"Bring it!" roared Mr. In and Mr. Out in chorus.

The waiter coughed and disappeared. There was a short wait during which they were subjected without their knowledge to a careful scrutiny by the headwaiter. Then the champagne arrived, and at the sight of it Mr. In and Mr. Out became jubilant.

"Imagine their objecting to us having champagne for breakfast—jus' imagine."

They both concentrated upon the vision of such an awesome possibility, but the feat was too much for them. It was impossible for their joint imaginations to conjure up a world where any one might object to any one else having champagne for breakfast. The waiter drew the cork with an enormous *pop*—and their glasses immediately foamed with pale yellow froth.

"Here's health, Mr. In."

"Here's the same to you, Mr. Out."

The waiter withdrew; the minutes passed; the champagne became low in the bottle.

"It's—it's mortifying," said Dean suddenly.

"Wha's mortifying?"

"The idea their objecting us having champagne breakfast."

"Mortifying?" Peter considered. "Yes, tha's word—mortifying."

Again they collapsed into laughter, howled, swayed, rocked back and forth in their chairs, repeating the word "mortifying" over and over to each other—each repetition seeming to make it only more brilliantly absurd.

After a few more gorgeous minutes they decided on another quart. Their anxious waiter consulted his immediate superior, and this discreet person gave implicit instructions that no more champagne should be served. Their check was brought.

Five minutes later, arm in arm, they left the Commodore and made their way through a curious, staring crowd along Forty-second Street, and up Vanderbilt Avenue to the Biltmore. There, with sudden cunning, they rose to the occasion and traversed the lobby, walking fast and standing unnaturally erect.

Once in the dining-room they repeated their performance. They were torn between intermittent convulsive laughter and sudden spasmodic discussions of politics, college, and the sunny state of their dispositions. Their watches told them that it was now nine o'clock, and a dim idea was born in them that they were on a memorable party, something that they would remember always. They lingered over the second bottle. Either of them had only to mention the word "mortifying" to send them both into riotous gasps. The dining-room was whirring and shifting now; a curious lightness permeated and rarefied the heavy air.

They paid their check and walked out into the lobby.

It was at this moment that the exterior doors revolved for the thousandth time that morning, and admitted into the lobby a very pale young beauty with dark circles under her eyes, attired in a much-rumpled evening dress. She was accompanied by a plain stout man, obviously not an appropriate escort.

At the top of the stairs this couple encountered Mr. In and Mr. Out.

"Edith," began Mr. In, stepping toward her hilariously and making a sweeping bow, "darling, good morning."

The stout man glanced questioningly at Edith, as if merely asking her permission to throw this man summarily out of the way.

"'Scuse familiarity," added Peter, as an afterthought. "Edith, good-morning."

He seized Dean's elbow and impelled him into the foreground.

"Meet Mr. In, Edith, my bes' frien'. Inseparable. Mr. In and Mr. Out."

Mr. Out advanced and bowed; in fact, he advanced so far and bowed so low that he tipped slightly forward and only kept his balance by placing a hand lightly on Edith's shoulder.

"I'm Mr. Out, Edith," he mumbled pleasantly, "S'misterin Misterout."

"'Smisterinanout," said Peter proudly.

But Edith stared straight by them, her eyes fixed on some infinite speck in the gallery above her. She nodded slightly to the stout man, who advanced bull-like and with a sturdy brisk gesture pushed Mr. In and Mr. Out to either side. Through this alley he and Edith walked.

But ten paces farther on Edith stopped again—stopped and pointed to a short, dark soldier who was eyeing the crowd in general, and the tableau of Mr. In and Mr. Out in particular, with a sort of puzzled, spell-bound awe.

"There," cried Edith. "See there!"

Her voice rose, became somewhat shrill. Her pointing finger shook slightly.

"There's the soldier who broke my brother's leg."

There were a dozen exclamations; a man in a cutaway coat left his place near the desk and advanced alertly; the stout person made a sort of lightning-like spring toward the short, dark soldier, and then the lobby closed around the little group and blotted them from the sight of Mr. In and Mr. Out.

But to Mr. In and Mr. Out this event was merely a particolored iridescent segment of a whirring, spinning world.

They heard loud voices; they saw the stout man spring; the picture suddenly blurred.

Then they were in an elevator bound skyward.

"What floor, please?" said the elevator man.

"Any floor," said Mr. In.

"Top floor," said Mr. Out.

"This is the top floor," said the elevator man.

"Have another floor put on," said Mr. Out.

"Higher," said Mr. In.

"Heaven," said Mr. Out.

XI

In a bedroom of a small hotel just off Sixth Avenue Gordon Sterrett awoke with a pain in the back of his head and a sick throbbing in all his veins. He looked at the dusky gray shadows in the corners of the room and at a raw place on a large leather chair in the corner where it had long been in use. He saw clothes, dishevelled, rumpled clothes on the floor and he smelt stale cigarette smoke and stale liquor. The windows were tight shut. Outside the bright sunlight had thrown a dust-filled beam across the sill—a beam broken by the head of the wide wooden bed in which he had slept. He lay very quiet—comatose, drugged, his eyes wide, his mind clicking wildly like an unoiled machine.

It must have been thirty seconds after he perceived the sunbeam with the dust on it and the rip on the large leather chair that he had the sense of life close beside him, and it was another thirty seconds after that before he realized he was irrevocably married to Jewel Hudson.

He went out half an hour later and bought a revolver at a sporting goods store. Then he took a taxi to the room where he had been living on East Twenty-seventh Street, and, leaning across the table that held his drawing materials, fired a cartridge into his head just behind the temple.

1920

The Diamond as Big as the Ritz

John T. Unger came from a family that had been well known in Hades—a small town on the Mississippi River—for several generations. John's father had held the amateur golf championship through many a heated contest; Mrs. Unger was known "from hot-box to hot-bed," as the local phrase went, for her political addresses; and young John T. Unger, who had just turned sixteen, had danced all the latest dances from New York before he put on long trousers. And now, for a certain time, he was to be away from home. That respect for a New England education which is the bane of all provincial places, which drains them yearly of their most promising young men, had seized upon his parents. Nothing would suit them but that he should go to St. Midas' School near Boston—Hades was too small to hold their darling and gifted son.

Now in Hades—as you know if you ever have been there—the names of the more fashionable preparatory schools and colleges mean very little. The inhabitants have been so long out of the world that, though they make a show of keeping up to date in dress and manners and literature, they depend to a great extent on hearsay, and a function that in Hades would be considered elaborate would doubtless be hailed by a Chicago beef-princess as "perhaps a little tacky."

John T. Unger was on the eve of departure. Mrs. Unger, with maternal fatuity, packed his trunks full of linen suits and electric fans, and Mr. Unger presented his son with an asbestos pocket-book stuffed with money.

"Remember, you are always welcome here," he said. "You can be sure, boy, that we'll keep the home fires burning."

"I know," answered John huskily.

"Don't forget who you are and where you come from," continued his father proudly, "and you can do nothing to harm you. You are an Unger—from Hades."

So the old man and the young shook hands and John walked away with tears streaming from his eyes. Ten minutes later he had passed outside the city limits, and he stopped to glance back for the last time. Over the gates the old-fashioned Victorian motto seemed strangely attractive to him. His father had tried time and time again to have it changed to something with a little more push and verve about it, such as "Hades—Your Opportunity," or else a plain "Welcome" sign set over a hearty handshake pricked out in electric lights. The old motto was a little depressing, Mr. Unger had thought—but now. . . .

So John took his look and then set his face resolutely toward his destination. And, as he turned away, the lights of Hades against the sky seemed full of a warm and passionate beauty.

St. Midas' School is half an hour from Boston in a Rolls-Pierce motor-car. The actual distance will never be known, for no one, except John T. Unger, had ever arrived there save in a Rolls-Pierce and probably no one ever will again. St. Midas' is the most expensive and the most exclusive boys' preparatory school in the world.

John's first two years there passed pleasantly. The fathers of all the boys were money-kings and John spent his summers visiting at fashionable resorts. While he was very fond of all the boys he visited, their fathers struck him as being much of a piece, and in his boyish way he often wondered at their exceeding sameness. When he told them where his home was they would ask jovially, "Pretty hot down there?" and John would muster a faint smile and answer, "It certainly is." His response would have been heartier had they not all made this joke—at best varying it with, "Is it hot enough for you down there?" which he hated just as much.

In the middle of his second year at school, a quiet, handsome boy named Percy Washington had been put in John's form. The newcomer was pleasant in his manner and exceedingly well dressed even for St. Midas', but for some reason he kept aloof from the other boys. The only person with whom he was intimate was John T. Unger, but even to John he was entirely uncommunicative concerning his home or his family. That he was wealthy went without saying, but beyond a few such deductions John knew little of his friend, so it promised rich confectionery for his curiosity when Percy invited him to spend the summer at his home "in the West." He accepted, without hesitation.

It was only when they were in the train that Percy became, for the first time, rather communicative. One day while they were eating lunch in the dining-car and discussing the imperfect characters of several of the boys at school, Percy suddenly changed his tone and made an abrupt remark.

"My father," he said, "is by far the richest man in the world."

"Oh," said John, politely. He could think of no answer to make to this confidence. He considered "That's very nice," but it sounded hollow and was on the point of saying, "Really?" but refrained since it would seem to question Percy's statement. And such an astounding statement could scarcely be questioned.

"By far the richest," repeated Percy.

"I was reading in the *World Almanac,*" began John, "that there was one man in America with an income of over five million a year and four men with incomes of over three million a year, and——"

"Oh, they're nothing." Percy's mouth was a half-moon of scorn. "Catch-penny capitalists, financial small-fry, petty merchants and money-lenders. My father could buy them out and not know he'd done it."

"But how does he——"

"Why haven't they put down *his* income tax? Because he doesn't pay any. At least he pays a little one—but he doesn't pay any on his *real* income."

"He must be very rich," said John simply. "I'm glad. I like very rich people.

"The richer a fella is, the better I like him." There was a look of passionate frankness upon his dark face. "I visited the Schnlitzer-Murphys last Easter. Vivian Schnlitzer-Murphy had rubies as big as hen's eggs, and sapphires that were like globes with lights inside them——"

"I love jewels," agreed Percy enthusiastically. "Of course I wouldn't want any one at school to know about it, but I've got quite a collection myself. I used to collect them instead of stamps."

"And diamonds," continued John eagerly. "The Schnlitzer-Murphys had diamonds as big as walnuts——"

"That's nothing." Percy had leaned forward and dropped his voice to a low whisper. "That's nothing at all. My father has a diamond bigger than the Ritz-Carlton Hotel."

II

The Montana sunset lay between two mountains like a gigantic bruise from which dark arteries spread themselves over a poisoned sky. An immense distance under the sky crouched the village of Fish, minute, dismal, and forgotten. There were twelve men, so it was said, in the village of Fish, twelve sombre and inexplicable souls who sucked a lean milk from the almost literally bare rock upon which a mysterious populatory force had begotten them. They had become a race apart, these twelve men of Fish, like some species developed by an early whim of nature, which on second thought had abandoned them to struggle and extermination.

Out of the blue-black bruise in the distance crept a long line of moving lights upon the desolation of the land, and the twelve men of Fish gathered like ghosts at the shanty depot to watch the passing of the seven o'clock train, the Transcontinental Express from Chicago. Six times or so a year the Transcontinental Express, through some inconceivable jurisdiction, stopped at the village of Fish, and when this occurred a figure or so would disembark, mount into a buggy that always appeared from out of the dusk, and drive off toward the bruised sunset. The observation of this pointless and preposterous phenomenon had become a sort of cult among the men of Fish. To observe, that was all; there remained in them none of the vital quality of illusion which would make them wonder or speculate, else a religion might have grown up around these mysterious visitations. But the men of Fish were beyond all religion—the barest and most savage tenets of even Christianity could gain no foothold on that barren rock—so there was no altar, no priest, no sacrifice; only each night at seven the silent concourse by the shanty depot, a congregation who lifted up a prayer of dim, anæmic wonder.

On this June night, the Great Brakeman, whom, had they deified any one, they might well have chosen as their celestial protagonist, had ordained that the seven o'clock train should leave its human (or inhuman) deposit at Fish. At two minutes after seven Percy Washington and John T. Unger disembarked, hurried past the spellbound, the agape, the fearsome eyes of the twelve men of Fish, mounted into a buggy which had obviously appeared from nowhere, and drove away.

After half an hour, when the twilight had coagulated into dark, the silent negro who was driving the buggy hailed an opaque body somewhere ahead of them in the gloom. In response to his cry, it turned upon them a luminous disk which regarded them like a malignant eye out of the unfathomable night. As they came closer, John saw that it was the tail-light of an immense automobile, larger and more magnificent than any he had ever seen. Its body was of gleaming metal richer than nickel and lighter than silver, and the hubs of the wheels were studded with iridescent geometric figures of green and yellow—John did not dare to guess whether they were glass or jewel.

Two negroes, dressed in glittering livery such as one sees in pictures of royal processions in London, were standing at attention beside the car and as the two young men dismounted from the buggy they were greeted in some language which the guest could not understand, but which seemed to be an extreme form of the Southern negro's dialect.

"Get in," said Percy to his friend, as their trunks were tossed to the ebony roof of the limousine. "Sorry we had to bring you this far in that buggy, but of course it wouldn't do for the people on the train or those God-forsaken fellas in Fish to see this automobile."

"Gosh! What a car!" This ejaculation was provoked by its interior. John saw that the upholstery consisted of a thousand minute and exquisite tapestries of silk, woven with jewels and embroideries, and set upon a background of cloth of gold. The two armchair seats in which the boys luxuriated were covered with stuff that resembled duvetyn, but seemed woven in numberless colors of the ends of ostrich feathers.

"What a car!" cried John again, in amazement.

"This thing?" Percy laughed. "Why, it's just an old junk we use for a station wagon."

By this time they were gliding along through the darkness toward the break between the two mountains.

"We'll be there in an hour and a half," said Percy, looking at the clock. "I may as well tell you it's not going to be like anything you ever saw before."

If the car was any indication of what John would see, he was prepared to be astonished indeed. The simple piety prevalent in Hades has the earnest worship of and respect for riches as the first article of its creed—had John felt otherwise than radiantly humble before them, his parents would have turned away in horror at the blasphemy.

They had now reached and were entering the break between the two mountains and almost immediately the way became much rougher.

"If the moon shone down here, you'd see that we're in a big gulch," said Percy, trying to peer out of the window. He spoke a few words into the mouthpiece and immediately the footman turned on a search-light and swept the hillsides with an immense beam.

"Rocky, you see. An ordinary car would be knocked to pieces in half an hour. In fact, it'd take a tank to navigate it unless you knew the way. You notice we're going uphill now."

They were obviously ascending, and within a few minutes the car was crossing a high rise, where they caught a glimpse of a pale moon newly risen in the distance. The car stopped suddenly and several figures took shape out of the dark beside it—these were negroes also. Again the two young men were saluted in the same dimly recognizable dialect; then the negroes set to work and four immense cables dangling from overhead were attached with hooks to the hubs of the great jeweled wheels. At a resounding "Hey-yah!" John felt the car being lifted slowly from the ground—up and up—clear of the tallest rocks on both sides—then higher, until he could see a wavy, moonlit valley stretched out before him in sharp contrast to the quagmire of rocks that they had just left. Only on one side was there still rock—and then suddenly there was no rock beside them or anywhere around.

It was apparent that they had surmounted some immense knife-blade of stone, projecting perpendicularly into the air. In a moment they were going down again, and finally with a soft bump they were landed upon the smooth earth.

"The worst is over," said Percy, squinting out the window. "It's only five miles from here, and our own road—tapestry brick—all the way. This belongs to us. This is where the United States ends, father says."

"Are we in Canada?"

"We are not. We're in the middle of the Montana Rockies. But you are now on the only five square miles of land in the country that's never been surveyed."

"Why hasn't it? Did they forget it?"

"No," said Percy, grinning, "they tried to do it three times. The first time my grandfather corrupted a whole department of the State survey; the second time he had the official maps of the United States tinkered with—that held them for fifteen years. The last time was harder. My father fixed it so that their compasses were in the strongest magnetic field ever artificially set up. He had a whole set of surveying instruments made with a slight defection that would allow for this territory not to appear, and he substituted them for the ones that were to be used. Then he had a river deflected and he had what looked like a village built up on its banks—so that they'd see it, and think it was a town ten miles farther up the valley. There's only one thing my father's afraid of," he concluded, "only one thing in the world that could be used to find us out."

"What's that?"

Percy sank his voice to a whisper.

"Aeroplanes," he breathed. "We've got half a dozen anti-aircraft guns and we've arranged it so far—but there've been a few deaths and a great many prisoners. Not that we mind *that,* you know, father and I, but it upsets mother and the girls, and there's always the chance that some time we won't be able to arrange it."

Shreds and tatters of chinchilla, courtesy clouds in the green moon's heaven, were passing the green moon like precious Eastern stuffs paraded for the inspection of some Tartar Khan. It seemed to John that it was day, and that he was looking at some lads sailing above him in the air, showering down tracts and patent medicine circulars, with their messages of hope for despairing, rock-bound hamlets. It seemed to him that he could see them look down out of the clouds and stare—and stare at whatever there was to stare at in this place whither he was bound—What then? Were they induced to land by some insidious device there to be immured far from patent medicines and from tracts until the judgment day—or, should they fail to fall into the trap, did a quick puff of smoke and the sharp round of a splitting shell bring them drooping to earth—and "upset" Percy's mother and sisters. John shook his head and the wraith of a hollow laugh issued silently from his parted lips. What desperate transaction lay hidden here? What a moral expedient of a bizarre Crœsus? What terrible and golden mystery? . . .

The chinchilla clouds had drifted past now and outside the Montana night was bright as day. The tapestry brick of the road was smooth to the tread of the great tires as they rounded a still, moonlit lake; they passed into darkness for a moment, a pine grove, pungent and cool, then they came out into a broad avenue of lawn and John's exclamation of pleasure was simultaneous with Percy's taciturn "We're home."

Full in the light of the stars, an exquisite château rose from the borders of the lake, climbed in marble radiance half the height of an adjoining mountain, then melted in grace, in perfect symmetry, in translucent feminine languor, into the massed darkness of a forest of pine. The many towers, the slender tracery of the sloping parapets, the chiselled wonder of a thousand yellow windows with their oblongs and hectagons and triangles of golden light, the shattered softness of the intersecting planes of star-shine and blue shade, all trembled on John's spirit like a chord of music. On one of the towers, the tallest, the blackest at its base, an arrangement of exterior lights at the top made a sort of floating fairyland—and as John gazed up in warm enchantment the faint acciaccare sound of violins drifted down in a rococo harmony that was like nothing he had ever heard before. Then in a moment the car stopped before wide, high marble steps around which the night air was fragrant with a host of flowers. At the top of the steps two great doors swung silently open and amber light flooded out upon the darkness, silhouetting the figure of an exquisite lady with black, high-piled hair, who held out her arms toward them.

"Mother," Percy was saying, "this is my friend, John Unger, from Hades."

Afterward John remembered that first night as a daze of many colors, of quick sensory impressions, of music soft as a voice in love, and of the beauty of things, lights and shadows, and motions and faces. There was a white-haired man who stood drinking a many-hued cordial from a crystal thimble set on a golden stem. There was a girl with a flowery face, dressed like Titania with braided sapphires in her hair. There was a room where the solid, soft gold of the walls yielded to the pressure of his hand, and a room that was like a platonic conception of the ultimate prison—ceiling, floor, and all, it was lined with an unbroken mass of diamonds, diamonds of every size and shape, until, lit with tall violet lamps in the corners, it dazzled the eyes with a whiteness that could be compared only with itself, beyond human wish or dream.

Through a maze of these rooms the two boys wandered. Sometimes the floor under their feet would flame in brilliant patterns from lighting below, patterns of barbaric clashing colors, of pastel delicacy, of sheer whiteness, or of subtle and intricate mosaic, surely from some mosque on the Adriatic Sea. Sometimes beneath layers of thick crystal he would see blue or green water swirling, inhabited by vivid fish and growths of rainbow foliage. Then they would be treading on furs of every texture and color or along corridors of palest ivory, unbroken as though carved complete from the gigantic tusks of dinosaurs extinct before the age of man. . . .

Then a hazily remembered transition, and they were at dinner—where each plate was of two almost imperceptible layers of solid diamond between which was curiously worked a filigree of emerald design, a shaving sliced from green air. Music, plangent and unobtrusive, drifted down through far corridors—his chair, feathered and curved insidiously to his back, seemed to engulf and overpower him as he drank his first glass of port. He tried drowsily to answer a question that had been asked him, but the honeyed luxury that clasped his body added to the illusion of sleep—jewels, fabrics, wines, and metals blurred before his eyes into a sweet mist. . . .

"Yes," he replied with a polite effort, "it certainly is hot enough for me down there."

He managed to add a ghostly laugh; then, without movement, without resistance, he seemed to float off and away, leaving an iced dessert that was pink as a dream. . . . He fell asleep.

When he awoke he knew that several hours had passed. He was in a great quiet room with ebony walls and a dull illumination that was too faint, too subtle, to be called a light. His young host was standing over him.

"You fell asleep at dinner," Percy was saying. "I nearly did, too—it was such a treat to be comfortable again after this year of school. Servants undressed and bathed you while you were sleeping."

"Is this a bed or a cloud?" sighed John. "Percy, Percy—before you go, I want to apologize."

"For what?"

"For doubting you when you said you had a diamond as big as the Ritz-Carlton Hotel."

Percy smiled.

"I thought you didn't believe me. It's that mountain, you know."

"What mountain?"

"The mountain the château rests on. It's not very big, for a mountain. But except about fifty feet of sod and gravel on top it's solid diamond. *One* diamond, one cubic mile without a flaw. Aren't you listening? Say——"

But John T. Unger had again fallen asleep.

III

Morning. As he awoke he perceived drowsily that the room had at the same moment become dense with sunlight. The ebony panels of one wall had slid aside on a sort of track, leaving his chamber half open to the day. A large negro in a white uniform stood beside the bed.

"Good-evening," muttered John, summoning his brains from the wild places.

"Good-morning, sir. Are you ready for your bath, sir? Oh, don't get up—I'll put you in, if you'll just unbutton your pajamas—there. Thank you, sir."

John lay quietly as his pajamas were removed—he was amused and delighted; he expected to be lifted like a child by this black Gargantua who was tending him, but nothing of the sort happened; instead he felt the bed tilt up slowly on its side—he began to roll, startled at first, in the direction of the wall, but when he reached the wall its drapery gave way, and sliding two yards farther down a fleecy incline he plumped gently into water the same temperature as his body.

He looked about him. The runway or rollway on which he had arrived had folded gently back into place. He had been projected into another chamber and was sitting in a sunken bath with his head just above the level of the floor. All about him, lining the walls of the room and the sides and bottom of the bath itself, was a blue aquarium, and gazing through the crystal surface on which he sat, he could see fish swimming among amber lights and even gliding without curiosity past his outstretched toes, which were separated from them only by the thickness of the crystal. From overhead, sunlight came down through sea-green glass.

"I suppose, sir, that you'd like hot rosewater and soapsuds this morning, sir—and perhaps cold salt water to finish."

The negro was standing beside him.

"Yes," agreed John, smiling inanely, "as you please." Any idea of ordering this bath according to his own meagre standards of living would have been priggish and not a little wicked.

The negro pressed a button and a warm rain began to fall, apparently from overhead, but really, so John discovered after a moment, from a fountain arrangement near by. The water turned to a pale rose color and jets of liquid soap spurted into it from four miniature walrus heads at the corners of the bath. In a moment a dozen little paddle-wheels, fixed to the sides, had churned the mixture into a radiant rainbow of pink foam which enveloped him softly with its delicious lightness, and burst in shining, rosy bubbles here and there about him.

"Shall I turn on the moving-picture machine, sir?" suggested the negro deferentially. "There's a good one-reel comedy in this machine to-day, or I can put in a serious piece in a moment, if you prefer it."

"No, thanks," answered John, politely but firmly. He was enjoying his bath too much to desire any distraction. But distraction came. In a moment he was listening intently to the sound of flutes from just outside, flutes dripping a melody that was like a waterfall, cool and green as the room itself, accompanying a frothy piccolo, in play more fragile than the lace of suds that covered and charmed him.

After a cold salt-water bracer and a cold fresh finish, he stepped out and into a fleecy robe, and upon a couch covered with the same material he was rubbed with oil, alcohol, and spice. Later he sat in a voluptuous chair while he was shaved and his hair was trimmed.

"Mr. Percy is waiting in your sitting-room," said the negro, when these operations were finished. "My name is Gygsum, Mr. Unger, sir. I am to see to Mr. Unger every morning."

John walked out into the brisk sunshine of his living-room, where he found breakfast waiting for him and Percy, gorgeous in white kid knickerbockers, smoking in an easy chair.

IV

This is a story of the Washington family as Percy sketched it for John during breakfast.

The father of the present Mr. Washington had been a Virginian, a direct descendant of George Washington, and Lord Baltimore. At the close of the Civil War he was a twenty-five-year-old Colonel with a played-out plantation and about a thousand dollars in gold.

Fitz-Norman Culpepper Washington, for that was the young Colonel's name, decided to present the Virginia estate to his younger brother and go West. He selected two dozen of the most faithful blacks, who, of course, worshipped him, and bought twenty-five tickets to the West, where he intended to take out land in their names and start a sheep and cattle ranch.

When he had been in Montana for less than a month and things were going very poorly indeed, he stumbled on his great discovery. He had lost his way when riding in the hills, and after a day without food he began to grow hungry. As he was without his rifle, he was forced to pursue a squirrel, and in the course of the pursuit he noticed that it was carrying something shiny in its mouth. Just before it vanished into its hole—for Providence did not intend that this squirrel should alleviate his hunger—it dropped its burden. Sitting down to consider the situation Fitz-Norman's eye was caught by a gleam in the grass beside him. In ten seconds he had completely lost his appetite and gained one hundred thousand dollars. The squirrel, which had refused with annoying persistence to become food, had made him a present of a large and perfect diamond.

Late that night he found his way to camp and twelve hours later all the males among his darkies were back by the squirrel hole digging furiously at the side of the mountain. He told them he had discovered a rhinestone mine, and, as only one or two of them had ever seen even a small diamond before, they believed him, without question. When the magnitude of his discovery became apparent to him, he found himself in a quandary. The mountain was *a* diamond—it was literally nothing else but solid diamond. He filled four saddle bags full of glittering samples and started on horseback for St. Paul. There he managed to dispose of half a dozen small stones—when he tried a larger one a storekeeper fainted and Fitz-Norman was arrested as a public disturber. He escaped from jail and caught the train for New York, where he sold a few medium-sized diamonds and received in exchange about two hundred thousand dollars in gold. But he did not dare to produce any exceptional gems—in fact, he left New York just in time. Tremendous excitement had been created in jewelry circles, not so much by the size of his diamonds as by their appearance in the city from mysterious sources. Wild rumors became current that a diamond mine had been discovered in the Catskills, on the Jersey coast, on Long Island, beneath Washington Square. Excursion trains, packed with men carrying picks and shovels, began to leave New York hourly, bound for various neighboring El Dorados. But by that time young Fitz-Norman was on his way back to Montana.

By the end of a fortnight he had estimated that the diamond in the mountain was approximately equal in quantity to all the rest of the diamonds known to exist in the world. There was no valuing it by any regular computation, however, for it was *one solid diamond*—and if it were offered for sale not only would the bottom fall out of the market, but also, if the value should vary with its size in the usual arithmetical progression, there would not be enough gold in the world to buy a tenth part of it. And what could any one do with a diamond that size?

It was an amazing predicament. He was, in one sense, the richest man that ever lived—and yet was he worth anything at all? If his secret should transpire there was no telling to what measures the Government might resort in order to prevent a panic, in gold as well as in jewels. They might take over the claim immediately and institute a monopoly.

There was no alternative—he must market his mountain in secret. He sent South for his younger brother and put him in charge of his colored following—darkies who had never realized that slavery was abolished. To make sure of this, he read them a proclamation that he had composed, which announced that General Forrest had reorganized the shattered Southern armies and defeated the North in one pitched battle. The negroes believed him implicitly. They passed a vote declaring it a good thing and held revival services immediately.

Fitz-Norman himself set out for foreign parts with one hundred thousand dollars and two trunks filled with rough diamonds of all sizes. He sailed for Russia in a Chinese junk and six months after his departure from Montana he was in St. Petersburg. He took obscure lodgings and called immediately upon the court jeweller, announcing that he had a diamond for the Czar. He remained in St. Petersburg for two weeks, in constant danger of being murdered, living from lodging to lodging, and afraid to visit his trunks more than three or four times during the whole fortnight.

On his promise to return in a year with larger and finer stones, he was allowed to leave for India. Before he left, however, the Court Treasurers had deposited to his credit, in American banks, the sum of fifteen million dollars—under four different aliases.

He returned to America in 1868, having been gone a little over two years. He had visited the capitals of twenty-two countries and talked with five emperors, eleven kings, three princes, a shah, a khan, and a sultan. At that time Fitz-Norman estimated his own wealth at one billion dollars. One fact worked consistently against the disclosure of his secret. No one of his larger diamonds remained in the public eye for a week before being invested with a history of enough fatalities, amours, revolutions, and wars to have occupied it from the days of the first Babylonian Empire.

From 1870 until his death in 1900, the history of Fitz-Norman Washington was a long epic in gold. There were side issues, of course—he evaded the surveys, he married a Virginia lady, by whom he had a single son, and he was compelled, due to a series of unfortunate complications, to murder his brother, whose unfortunate habit of drinking himself into an indiscreet stupor had several times endangered their safety. But very few other murders stained these happy years of progress and expansion.

Just before he died he changed his policy, and with all but a few million dollars of his outside wealth bought up rare minerals in bulk, which he deposited in the safety vaults of banks all over the world, marked as bric-à-brac. His son, Braddock Tarleton Washington, followed this policy on an even more tensive scale. The minerals were converted into the rarest of all elements—radium—so that the equivalent of a billion dollars in gold could be placed in a receptacle no bigger than a cigar box.

When Fitz-Norman had been dead three years his son, Braddock, decided that the business had gone far enough. The amount of wealth that he and his father had taken out of the mountain was beyond all exact computation. He kept a note-book in cipher in which he set down the approximate quantity of radium in each of the thousand banks he patronized, and recorded the alias under which it was held. Then he did a very simple thing—he sealed up the mine.

He sealed up the mine. What had been taken out of it would support all the Washingtons yet to be born in unparalleled luxury for generations. His one care must be the protection of his secret, lest in the possible panic attendant on its discovery he should be reduced with all the property-holders in the world to utter poverty.

This was the family among whom John T. Unger was staying. This was the story he heard in his silver-walled living-room the morning after his arrival.

V

After breakfast, John found his way out the great marble entrance, and looked curiously at the scene before him. The whole valley, from the diamond mountain to the steep granite cliff five miles away, still gave off a breath of golden haze which hovered idly above the fine sweep of lawns and lakes and gardens. Here and there clusters of elms made delicate groves of shade, contrasting strangely with the tough masses of pine forest that held the hills in a grip of dark-blue green. Even as John looked he saw three fawns in single file patter out from one clump about a half mile away and disappear with awkward gayety into the black-ribbed half-light of another. John would not have been surprised to see a goat-foot piping his way among the trees or to catch a glimpse of pink nymph-skin and flying yellow hair between the greenest of the green leaves.

In some such cool hope he descended the marble steps, disturbing faintly the sleep of two silky Russian wolfhounds at the bottom, and set off along a walk of white and blue brick that seemed to lead in no particular direction.

He was enjoying himself as much as he was able. It is youth's felicity as well as its insufficiency that it can never live in the present, but must always be measuring up the day against its own radiantly imagined future—flowers and gold, girls and stars, they are only prefigurations and prophecies of that incomparable, unattainable young dream.

John rounded a soft corner where the massed rose-bushes filled the air with heavy scent, and struck off across a park toward a patch of moss under some trees. He had never lain upon moss, and he wanted to see whether it was really soft enough to justify the use of its name as an adjective. Then he saw a girl coming toward him over the grass. She was the most beautiful person he had ever seen.

She was dressed in a white little gown that came just below her knees, and a wreath of mignonettes clasped with blue slices of sapphire bound up her hair. Her pink bare feet scattered the dew before them as she came. She was younger than John—not more than sixteen.

"Hello," she cried softly, "I'm Kismine."

She was much more than that to John already. He advanced toward her, scarcely moving as he drew near lest he should tread on her bare toes.

"You haven't met me," said her soft voice. Her blue eyes added, "Oh, but you've missed a great deal!" . . . "You met my sister, Jasmine, last night. I was sick with lettuce poisoning," went on her soft voice, and her eyes continued, "and when I'm sick I'm sweet—and when I'm well."

"You have made an enormous impression on me," said John's eyes, "and I'm not so slow myself"—"How do you do?" said his voice. "I hope you're better this morning."—"You darling," added his eyes tremulously.

John observed that they had been walking along the path. On her suggestion they sat down together upon the moss, the softness of which he failed to determine.

He was critical about women. A single defect—a thick ankle, a hoarse voice, a glass eye—was enough to make him utterly indifferent. And here for the first time in his life he was beside a girl who seemed to him the incarnation of physical perfection.

"Are you from the East?" asked Kismine with charming interest.

"No," answered John simply. "I'm from Hades."

Either she had never heard of Hades, or she could think of no pleasant comment to make upon it, for she did not discuss it further.

"I'm going East to school this fall," she said. "D'you think I'll like it? I'm going to New York to Miss Bulge's. It's very strict, but you see over the week-ends I'm going to live at home with the family in our New York house, because father heard that the girls had to go walking two by two."

"Your father wants you to be proud," observed John.

"We are," she answered, her eyes shining with dignity. "None of us has ever been punished. Father said we never should be. Once when my sister Jasmine was a little girl she pushed him down-stairs and he just got up and limped away.

"Mother was—well, a little startled," continued Kismine, "when she heard that you were from—from where you *are* from, you know. She said that when she was a young girl—but then, you see, she's a Spaniard and old-fashioned."

"Do you spend much time out here?" asked John, to conceal the fact that he was somewhat hurt by this remark. It seemed an unkind allusion to his provincialism.

"Percy and Jasmine and I are here every summer, but next summer Jasmine is going to Newport. She's coming out in London a year from this fall. She'll be presented at court."

"Do you know," began John hesitantly, "you're much more sophisticated than I thought you were when I first saw you?"

"Oh, no, I'm not," she exclaimed hurriedly. "Oh, I wouldn't think of being. I think that sophisticated young people are *terribly* common, don't you? I'm not at all, really. If you say I am, I'm going to cry."

She was so distressed that her lip was trembling. John was impelled to protest:

"I didn't meant that; I only said it to tease you."

"Because I wouldn't mind if I *were,*" she persisted, "but I'm *not.* I'm very innocent and girlish. I never smoke, or drink, or read anything except poetry. I know scarcely any mathematics or chemistry. I dress *very* simply—in fact, I scarcely dress at all. I think sophisticated is the last thing you can say about me. I believe that girls ought to enjoy their youths in a wholesome way."

"I do, too," said John heartily.

Kismine was cheerful again. She smiled at him, and a stillborn tear dripped from the corner of one blue eye.

"I like you," she whispered, intimately. "Are you going to spend all your time with Percy while you're here, or will you be nice to me? Just think—I'm absolutely fresh ground. I've never had a boy in love with me in all my life. I've never been allowed even to *see* boys alone—except Percy. I came all the way out here into this grove hoping to run into you, where the family wouldn't be around."

Deeply flattered, John bowed from the hips as he had been taught at dancing school in Hades.

"We'd better go now," said Kismine sweetly. "I have to be with mother at eleven. You haven't asked me to kiss you once. I thought boys always did that nowadays."

John drew himself up proudly.

"Some of them do," he answered, "but not me. Girls don't do that sort of thing—in Hades."

Side by side they walked back toward the house.

VI

John stood facing Mr. Braddock Washington in the full sunlight. The elder man was about forty with a proud, vacuous face, intelligent eyes, and a robust figure. In the mornings he smelt of horses—the best horses. He carried a plain walking-stick of gray birch with a single large opal for a grip. He and Percy were showing John around.

"The slaves' quarters are there." His walking-stick indicated a cloister of marble on their left that ran in graceful Gothic along the side of the mountain. "In my youth I was distracted for a while from the business of life by a period of absurd idealism. During that time they lived in luxury. For instance, I equipped every one of their rooms with a tile bath."

"I suppose," ventured John, with an ingratiating laugh, "that they used the bathtubs to keep coal in. Mr. Schnlitzer-Murphy told me that once he——"

"The opinions of Mr. Schnlitzer-Murphy are of little importance, I should imagine," interrupted Braddock Washington, coldly. "My slaves did not keep coal in their bathtubs. They had orders to bathe every day, and they did. If they hadn't I might have ordered a sulphuric acid shampoo. I discontinued the baths for quite another reason. Several of them caught cold and died. Water is not good for certain races—except as a beverage."

John laughed, and then decided to nod his head in sober agreement. Braddock Washington made him uncomfortable.

"All these negroes are descendants of the ones my father brought North with him. There are about two hundred and fifty now. You notice that they've lived so long apart from the world that their original dialect has become an almost indistinguishable patois. We bring a few of them up to speak English—my secretary and two or three of the house servants.

"This is the golf course," he continued, as they strolled along the velvet winter grass. "It's all a green, you see—no fairway, no rough, no hazards."

He smiled pleasantly at John.

"Many men in the cage, father?" asked Percy suddenly.

Braddock Washington stumbled, and let forth an involuntary curse.

"One less than there should be," he ejaculated darkly—and then added after a moment, "We've had difficulties."

"Mother was telling me," exclaimed Percy, "that Italian teacher——"

"A ghastly error," said Braddock Washington angrily. "But of course there's a good chance that we may have got him. Perhaps he fell somewhere in the woods or stumbled over a cliff. And then there's always the probability that if he did get away his story wouldn't be believed. Nevertheless, I've had two dozen men looking for him in different towns around here."

"And no luck?"

"Some. Fourteen of them reported to my agent that they'd each killed a man answering to that description, but of course it was probably only the reward they were after——"

He broke off. They had come to a large cavity in the earth about the circumference of a merry-go-round and covered by a strong iron grating. Braddock Washington beckoned to John, and pointed his cane down through the grating. John stepped to the edge and gazed. Immediately his ears were assailed by a wild clamor from below.

"Come on down to Hell!"

"Hello, kiddo, how's the air up there?"

"Hey! Throw us a rope!"

"Got an old doughnut, Buddy, or a couple of second-hand sandwiches?"

"Say, fella, if you'll push down that guy you're with, we'll show you a quick disappearance scene."

"Paste him one for me, will you?"

It was too dark to see clearly into the pit below, but John could tell from the coarse optimism and rugged vitality of the remarks and voices that they proceeded from middle-class Americans of the more spirited type. Then Mr. Washington put out his cane and touched a button in the grass, and the scene below sprang into light.

"These are some adventurous mariners who had the misfortune to discover El Dorado," he remarked.

Below them there had appeared a large hollow in the earth shaped like the interior of a bowl. The sides were steep and apparently of polished glass, and on its slightly concave surface stood about two dozen men clad in the half costume, half uniform, of aviators. Their up-turned faces, lit with wrath, with malice, with despair, with cynical humor, were covered by long growths of beard, but with the exception of a few who had pined perceptibly away, they seemed to be a well-fed, healthy lot.

Braddock Washington drew a garden chair to the edge of the pit and sat down.

"Well, how are you, boys?" he inquired genially.

A chorus of execration in which all joined except a few too dispirited to cry out, rose up into the sunny air, but Braddock Washington heard it with unruffled composure. When its last echo had died away he spoke again.

"Have you thought up a way out of your difficulty?"

From here and there among them a remark floated up.

"We decided to stay here for love!"

"Bring us up there and we'll find us a way!"

Braddock Washington waited until they were again quiet. Then he said:

"I've told you the situation. I don't want you here. I wish to heaven I'd never seen you. Your own curiosity got you here, and any time that you can think of a way out which protects me and my interests I'll be glad to consider it. But so long as you confine your efforts to digging tunnels—yes, I know about the new one you've started—you won't get very far. This isn't as hard on you as you make it out, with all your howling for the loved ones at home. If you were the type who worried much about the loved ones at home, you'd never have taken up aviation."

A tall man moved apart from the others, and held up his hand to call his captor's attention to what he was about to say.

"Let me ask you a few questions!" he cried. "You pretend to be a fair-minded man."

"How absurd. How could a man of *my* position be fair-minded toward *you*? You might as well speak of a Spaniard being fair-minded toward a piece of steak."

At this harsh observation the faces of the two dozen steaks fell, but the tall man continued:

"All right!" he cried. "We've argued this out before. You're not a humanitarian and you're not fair-minded, but you're human—at least you say you are—and you ought to be able to put yourself in our place for long enough to think how—how—how——"

"How what?" demanded Washington, coldly.

"—how unnecessary——"

"Not to me."

"Well,—how cruel——"

"We've covered that. Cruelty doesn't exist where self-preservation is involved. You've been soldiers; you know that. Try another."

"Well, then, how stupid."

"There," admitted Washington, "I grant you that. But try to think of an alternative. I've offered to have all or any of you painlessly executed if you wish. I've offered to have your wives, sweethearts, children and mothers kidnapped and brought out here. I'll enlarge your place down there and feed and clothe you the rest of your lives. If there was some method of producing permanent amnesia I'd have all of you operated on and released immediately, somewhere outside of my preserves. But that's as far as my ideas go."

"How about trusting us not to peach on you?" cried some one.

"You don't proffer that suggestion seriously," said Washington, with an expression of scorn. "I did take out one man to teach my daughter Italian. Last week he got away."

A wild yell of jubilation went up suddenly from two dozen throats and a pandemonium of joy ensued. The prisoners clog-danced and cheered and yodeled and wrestled with one another in a sudden uprush of animal spirits. They even ran up the glass sides of the bowl as far as they could, and slid back to the bottom upon the natural cushions of their bodies. The tall man started a song in which they all joined——

"Oh, we'll hang the kaiser
On a sour apple tree——"

Braddock Washington sat in inscrutable silence until the song was over.

"You see," he remarked, when he could gain a modicum of attention. "I bear you no ill-will, I like to see you enjoying yourselves. That's why I didn't tell you the whole story at once. The man—what was his name? Critchtichiello?—was shot by some of my agents in fourteen different places."

Not guessing that the places referred to were cities, the tumult of rejoicing subsided immediately.

"Nevertheless," cried Washington with a touch of anger, "he tried to run away. Do you expect me to take chances with any of you after an experience like that?"

Again a series of ejaculations went up.

"Sure!"

"Would your daughter like to learn Chinese?"

"Hey, I can speak Italian! My mother was a wop."

"Maybe she'd like t'learna speak N'Yawk!"

"If she's the little one with the big blue eyes I can teach her a lot of things better than Italian."

"I know some Irish songs—and I could hammer brass once't."

Mr. Washington reached forward suddenly with his cane and pushed the button in the grass so that the picture below went out instantly, and there remained only that great dark mouth covered dismally with the black teeth of the grating.

"Hey!" called a single voice from below, "you ain't goin' away without givin' us your blessing?"

But Mr. Washington, followed by the two boys, was already strolling on toward the ninth hole of the golf course, as though the pit and its contents were no more than a hazard over which his facile iron had triumphed with ease.

VII

July under the lee of the diamond mountain was a month of blanket nights and of warm, glowing days. John and Kismine were in love. He did not know that the little gold football (inscribed with the legend *Pro deo et patria et St. Mida*) which he had given her rested on a platinum chain next to her bosom. But it did. And she for her part was not aware that a large sapphire which had dropped one day from her simple coiffure was stowed away tenderly in John's jewel box.

Late one afternoon when the ruby and ermine music room was quite, they spent an hour there together. He held her hand and she gave him such a look that he whispered her name aloud. She bent toward him—then hesitated.

"Did you say "Kismine'?" she asked softly, "or——"

She had wanted to be sure. She thought she might have misunderstood.

Neither of them had ever kissed before, but in the course of an hour it seemed to make little difference.

The afternoon drifted away. That night when a last breath of music drifted down from the highest tower, they each lay awake, happily dreaming over the separate minutes of the day. They had decided to be married as soon as possible.

VIII

Every day Mr. Washington and the two young men went hunting or fishing in the deep forests or played golf around the somnolent course—games which John diplomatically allowed his host to win—or swam in the mountain coolness of the lake. John found Mr. Washington a somewhat exacting personality—utterly uninterested in any ideas or opinions except his own. Mrs. Washington was aloof and reserved at all times. She was apparently indifferent to her two daughters, and entirely absorbed in her son Percy, with whom she held interminable conversations in rapid Spanish at dinner.

Jasmine, the elder daughter, resembled Kismine in appearance—except that she was somewhat bow-legged, and terminated in large hands and feet—but was utterly unlike her in temperament. Her favorite books had to do with poor girls who kept house for widowed fathers. John learned from Kismine that Jasmine had never recovered from the shock and disappointment caused her by the termination of the World War, just as she was about to start for Europe as a canteen expert. She had even pined away for a time, and Braddock Washington had taken steps to promote a new war in the Balkans—but she had seen a photograph of some wounded Serbian soldiers and lost interest in the whole proceedings. But Percy and Kismine seemed to have inherited the arrogant attitude in all its harsh magnificence from their father. A chaste and consistent selfishness ran like a pattern through their every idea.

John was enchanted by the wonders of the château and the valley. Braddock Washington, so Percy told him, had caused to be kidnapped a landscape gardener, an architect, a designer of stage settings, and a French decadent poet left over from the last century. He had put his entire force of negroes at their disposal, guaranteed to supply them with any materials that the world could offer, and left them to work out some ideas of their own. But one by one they had shown their uselessness. The decadent poet had at once begun bewailing his separation from the boulevards in spring—he made some vague remarks about spices, apes, and ivories, but said nothing that was of any practical value. The stage designer on his part wanted to make the whole valley a series of tricks and sensational effects—a state of things that the Washingtons would soon have grown tired of. And as for the architect and the landscape gardener, they thought only in terms of convention. They must make this like this and that like that.

But they had, at least, solved the problem of what was to be done with them—they all went mad early one morning after spending the night in a single room trying to agree upon the location of a fountain, and were now confined comfortably in an insane asylum at Westport, Connecticut.

"But," inquired John curiously, "who did plan all your wonderful reception rooms and halls, and approaches and bathrooms——?"

"Well," answered Percy, "I blush to tell you, but it was a moving-picture fella. He was the only man we found who was used to playing with an unlimited amount of money, though he did tuck his napkin in his collar and couldn't read or write."

As August drew to a close John began to regret that he must soon go back to school. He and Kismine had decided to elope the following June.

"It would be nicer to be married here," Kismine confessed, "but of course I could never get father's permission to marry you at all. Next to that I'd rather elope. It's terrible for wealthy people to be married in America at present—they always have to send out bulletins to the press saying that they're going to be married in remnants, when what they mean is just a peck of old second-hand pearls and some used lace worn once by the Empress Eugénie."

"I know," agreed John fervently. "When I was visiting the Schnlitzer-Murphys, the eldest daughter, Gwendolyn, married a man whose father owns half of West Virginia. She wrote home saying what a tough struggle she was carrying on on his salary as a bank clerk—and then she ended up by saying that 'Thank God, I have four maids anyhow, and that helps a little.'"

"It's absurd," commented Kismine. "Think of millions and millions of people in the world, laborers and all, who get along with only two maids."

One afternoon late in August a chance remark of Kismine's changed the face of the entire situation, and threw John into a state of terror.

They were in their favorite grove, and between kisses John was indulging in some romantic forebodings which he fancied added poignancy to their relations.

"Sometimes I think we'll never marry," he said sadly. "You're too wealthy, too magnificent. No one as rich as you are can be like other girls. I should marry the daughter of some well-to-do wholesale hardware man from Omaha or Sioux City, and be content with her half-million."

"I knew the daughter of a wholesale hardware man once," remarked Kismine. "I don't think you'd have been contented with her. She was a friend of my sister's. She visited here."

"Oh, then you've had other guests?" exclaimed John in surprise.

Kismine seemed to regret her words.

"Oh, yes," she said hurriedly, "we've had a few."

"But aren't you—wasn't your father afraid they'd talk outside?"

"Oh, to some extent, to some extent," she answered. "Let's talk about something pleasanter."

But John's curiosity was asroused.

"Something pleasanter!" he demanded. "What's unpleasant about that? Weren't they nice girls?"

To his great surprise Kismine began to weep.

"Yes—th—that's the—the whole t-trouble. I grew qu-quite attached to some of them. So did Jasmine, but she kept in-v-viting them anyway. I couldnt' under*stand* it."

A dark suspicion was born in John's heart.

"Do you mean that they *told,* and your father had them—removed?"

"Worse than that," she muttered brokenly. "Father took no chances—and Jasmine kept writing them to come, and they had *such* a good time!"

She was overcome by a paroxysm of grief.

Stunned with the horror of this revelation, John sat there open-mouthed, feeling the nerves of his body twitter like so many sparrows perched upon his spinal column.

"Now, I've told you, and I shouldn't have," she said, calming suddenly and drying her dark blue eyes."

"Do you mean to say that your father had them *murdered* before they left?"

She nodded.

"In August usually—or early in September. It's only natural for us to get all the pleasure out of them that we can first."

"How abominable! How—why, I must be going crazy! Did you really admit that——"

"I did," interrupted Kismine, shrugging her shoulders. "We can't very well imprison them like those aviators, where they'd be a continual reproach to us every day. And it's always been made easier for Jasmine and me, because father had it done sooner than we expected. In that way we avoided any farewell scene——"

"So you murdered them! Uh!" cried John.

"It was done very nicely. They were drugged while they were asleep—and their families were always told that they died of scarlet fever in Butte."

"But—I fail to understand why you kept on inviting them!"

"I didn't," burst out Kismine. "I never invited one. Jasmine did. And they always had a very good time. She'd give them the nicest presents toward the last. I shall probably have visitors too—I'll harden up to it. We can't let such an inevitable thing as death stand in the way of enjoying life while we have it. Think how lonesome it'd be out here if we never had *any* one. Why, father and mother have sacrificed some of their best friends just as we have."

"And so," cried John accusingly, "and so you were letting me make love to you and pretending to return it, and talking about marriage, all the time knowing perfectly well that I'd never get out of here alive——"

"No," she protested passionately. "Not any more. I did at first. You were here. I couldn't help that, and I thought your last days might as well be pleasant for both of us. But then I fell in love with you, and—and I'm honestly sorry you're going to—going to be put away—though I'd rather you'd be put away than ever kiss another girl."

"Oh, you would, would you?" cried John ferociously.

"Much rather. Besides, I've always heard that a girl can have more fun with a man whom she knows she can never marry. Oh, why did I tell you? I've probably spoiled your whole good time now, and we were really enjoying things when you didn't know it. I knew it would make things sort of depressing for you."

"Oh, you did, did you?" John's voice trembled with anger. "I've heard about enough of this. If you haven't any more pride and decency than to have an affair with a fellow that you know isn't much better than a corpse, I don't want to have any more to do with you!"

"You're not a corpse!" she protested in horror. "You're not a corpse! I won't have you saying that I kissed a corpse!"

"I said nothing of the sort!"

"You did! You said I kissed a corpse!"

"I didn't!"

Their voices had risen, but upon a sudden interruption they both subsided into immediate silence. Footsteps were coming along the path in their direction, and a moment later the rose bushes were parted displaying Braddock Washington, whose intelligent eyes set in his good-looking vacuous face were peering in at them.

"Who kissed a corpse?" he demanded in obvious disapproval.

"Nobody," answered Kismine quickly. "We were just joking."

"What are you two doing here, anyhow?" he demanded gruffly. "Kismine, you ought to be—to be reading or playing golf with your sister. Go read! Go play golf! Don't let me find you here when I come back!"

Then he bowed at John and went up the path.

"See?" said Kismine crossly, when he was out of hearing. "You've spoiled it all. We can never meet any more. He won't let me meet you. He'd have you poisoned if he thought we were in love."

"We're not, any more!" cried John fiercely, "so he can set his mind at rest upon that. Moreover, don't fool yourself that I'm going to stay around here. Inside of six hours I'll be over those mountains, if I have to gnaw a passage through them, and on my way East."

They had both got to their feet, and at this remark Kismine came close and put her arm through his.

"I'm going, too."

"You must be crazy——"

"Of course I'm going," she interrupted impatiently.

"You most certainly are not. You——"

"Very well," she said quietly, "we'll catch up with father now and talk it over with him."

Defeated, John mustered a sickly smile.

"Very well, dearest," he agreed, with pale and unconvincing affection, "we'll go together."

His love for her returned and settled placidly on his heart. She was his—she would go with him to share his dangers. He put his arms about her and kissed her fervently. After all she loved him; she had saved him, in fact.

Discussing the matter, they walked slowly back toward the château. They decided that since Braddock Washington had seen them together they had best depart the next night. Nevertheless, John's lips were unusually dry at dinner, and he nervously emptied a great spoonful of peacock soup into his left lung. He had to be carried into the turquoise and sable card-room and pounded on the back by one of the under-butlers, which Percy considered a great joke.

IX

Long after midnight John's body gave a nervous jerk, and he sat suddenly upright, staring into the veils of somnolence that draped the room. Through the squares of blue darkness that were his open windows, he had heard a faint far-away sound that died upon a bed of wind before identifying itself on his memory, clouded with uneasy dreams. But the sharp noise that had succeeded it was nearer, was just outside the room—the click of a turned knob, a footstep, a whisper, he could not tell; a hard lump gathered in the pit of his stomach, and his whole body ached in the moment that he strained agonizingly to hear. Then one of the veils seemed to dissolve, and he saw a vague figure standing by the door, a figure only faintly limned and blocked in upon the darkness, mingled so with the folds of the drapery as to seem distorted, like a reflection seen in a dirty pane of glass.

With a sudden movement of fright or resolution John pressed the button by his bedside, and the next moment he was sitting in the green sunken bath of the adjoining room, waked into alertness by the shock of the cold water which half filled it.

He sprang out, and, his wet pajamas scattering a heavy trickle of water behind him, ran for the aquamarine door which he knew led out onto the ivory landing of the second floor. The door opened noiselessly. A single crimson lamp burning in a great dome above lit the magnificent sweep of the carved stairways with a poignant beauty. For a moment John hesitated, appalled by the silent splendor massed about him, seeming to envelop in its gigantic folds and contours the solitary drenched little figure shivering upon the ivory landing. Then simultaneously two things happened. The door of his own sitting-room swung open, precipitating three naked negroes into the hall—and, as John swayed in wild terror toward the stairway, another door slid back in the wall on the other side of the corridor, and John saw Braddock Washington standing in the lighted lift, wearing a fur coat and a pair of riding boots which reached to his knees and displayed, above, the glow of his rose-colored pajamas.

On the instant the three negroes—John had never seen any of them before, and it flashed through his mind that they must be the professional executioners—paused in their movement toward John, and turned expectantly to the man in the lift, who burst out with an imperious command:

"Get in here! All three of you! Quick as hell!"

Then, within the instant, the three negroes darted into the cage, the oblong of light was blotted out as the left door slid shut, and John was again alone in the hall. He slumped weakly down against an ivory stair.

It was apparent the something portentous had occurred, something which, for the moment at least, had postponed his own petty disaster. What was it? Had the negroes risen in revolt? Had the aviators forced aside the iron bars of the grating? Or had the men of Fish stumbled blindly through the hills and gazed with bleak, joyless eyes upon the gaudy valley? John did not know. He heard a faint whir of air as the lift whizzed up again, and then, a moment later, as it descended. It was probable that Percy was hurrying to his father's assistance, and it occurred to John that this was his opportunity to join Kismine and plan an immediate escape. He waited until the lift had been silent for several minutes; shivering a little with the night cool that whipped in through his wet pajamas, he returned to his room and dressed himself quickly. Then he mounted a long flight of stairs and turned down the corridor carpeted with Russian sable which led to Kismine's suite.

The door of her sitting-room was open and the lamps were lighted. Kismine, in an angora kimono, stood near the window of the room in a listening attitude, and as John entered noiselessly she turned toward him.

"Oh, it's you!" she whispered, crossing the room to him. "Did you hear them?"

"I heard your father's slaves in my——"

"No," she interrupted excitedly. "Aeroplanes!"

"Aeroplanes? Perhaps that was the sound that woke me."

"There're at least a dozen. I saw one a few moments ago dead against the moon. The guard back by the cliff fired his rifle and that's what roused father. We're going to open on them right away."

"Are they here on purpose?"

"Yes—it's that Italian who got away——"

Simultaneously with her last word, a succession of sharp cracks tumbled in through the open window. Kismine uttered a little cry, took a penny with fumbling fingers from a box on her dresser, and ran to one of the electric lights. In an instant the entire château was in darkness—she had blown out the fuse.

"Come on!" she cried to him. "We'll go up to the roof garden, and watch it from there!"

Drawing a cape about her, she took his hand, and they found their way out the door. It was only a step to the tower lift, and as she pressed the button that shot them upward he put his arms around her in the darkness and kissed her mouth. Romance had come to John Unger at last. A minute later they had stepped out upon the star-white platform. Above, under the misty moon, sliding in and out of the patches of cloud that eddied below it, floated a dozen dark-winged bodies in a constant circling course. From here and there in the valley flashes of fire leaped toward them, followed by sharp detonations. Kismine clapped her hands with pleasure, which, a moment later, turned to dismay as the aeroplanes at some prearranged signal, began to release their bombs and the whole of the valley became a panorama of deep reverberate sound and lurid light.

Before long the aim of the attackers became concentrated upon the points where the anti-aircraft guns were situated, and one of them was almost immediately reduced to a giant cinder to lie smouldering in the park of rose bushes.

"Kismine," begged John, "you'll be glad when I tell you that this attack came on the eve of my murder. If I hadn't heard that guard shoot off his gun back by the pass I should now be stone dead——"

"I can't hear you!" cried Kismine, intent on the scene before her. "You'll have to talk louder!"

"I simply said," shouted John, "that we'd better get out before they begin to shell the château!"

Suddenly the whole portico of the negro quarters cracked asunder, a geyser of flame shot up from under the colonnades, and great fragments of jagged marble were hurled as far as the borders of the lake.

"There go fifty thousand dollars' worth of slaves," cried Kismine, "at prewar prices. So few Americans have any respect for property."

John renewed his efforts to compel her to leave. The aim of the aeroplanes was becoming more precise minute by minute, and only two of the anti-aircraft guns were still retaliating. It was obvious that the garrison, encircled with fire, could not hold out much longer.

"Come on!" cried John, pulling Kismine's arm, "we've got to go. Do you realize that those aviators will kill you without question if they find you?"

She consented reluctantly.

"We'll have to wake Jasmine!" she said, as they hurried toward the lift. Then she added in sort of childish delight: "We'll be poor, won't we? Like people in books. And I'll be an orphan and utterly free. Free and poor! What fun!" She stopped and raised her lips to him in a delighted kiss.

"It's impossible to be both together," said John grimly. "People have found that out. And I should choose to be free as preferable of the two. As an extra caution you'd better dump the contents of your jewel box into your pockets."

Ten minutes later the two girls met John in the dark corridor and they descended to the main floor of the château. Passing for the last time through the magnificence of the splendid halls, they stood for a moment out on the terrace, watching the burning negro quarters and the flaming embers of two planes which had fallen on the other side of the lake. A solitary gun was still keeping up a sturdy popping, and the attackers seemed timorous about descending lower, but sent their thunderous fireworks in a circle around it, until any chance shot might annihilate its Ethiopian crew.

John and the two sisters passed down the marble steps, turned sharply to the left, and began to ascend a narrow path that wound like a garter about the diamond mountain. Kismine knew a heavily wooded spot half-way up where they could lie concealed and yet be able to observe the wild night in the valley—finally to make an escape, when it should be necessary, along a secret path laid in a rocky gully.

X

It was three o'clock when they attained their destination. The obliging and phlegmatic Jasmine fell off to sleep immediately, leaning against the trunk of a large tree, while John and Kismine sat, his arm around her, and watched the desperate ebb and flow of the dying battle among the ruins of a vista that had been a garden spot that morning. Shortly after four o'clock the last remaining gun gave out a clanging sound and went out of action in a swift tongue of red smoke. Though the moon was down, they saw that the flying bodies were circling closer to the earth. When the planes had made certain that the beleaguered possessed no further resources, they would land and the dark and glittering reign of the Washingtons would be over.

With the cessation of the firing the valley grew quiet. The embers of the two aeroplanes glowed like the eyes of some monster crouching in the grass. The château stood dark and silent, beautiful without light as it had been beautiful in the sun, while the woody rattles of Nemesis filled the air above with a growing and receding complaint. Then John perceived that Kismine, like her sister, had fallen sound asleep.

It was long after four when he became aware of footsteps along the path they had lately followed, and he waited in breathless silence until the persons to whom they belonged had passed the vantage-point he occupied. There was a faint stir in the air now that was not of human origin, and the dew was cold; he knew that the dawn would break soon. John waited until the steps had gone a safe distance up the mountain and were inaudible. Then he followed. About half-way to the steep summit the trees fell away and a hard saddle of rock spread itself over the diamond beneath. Just before he reached this point he slowed down his pace, warned by an animal sense that there was life just ahead of him. Coming to a high boulder, he lifted his head gradually above its edge. His curiosity was rewarded; this is what he saw:

Braddock Washington was standing there motionless, silhouetted against the gray sky without sound or sign of life. As the dawn came up out of the east, lending a cold green color to the earth, it brought the solitary figure into insignificant contrast with the new day.

While John watched, his host remained for a few moments absorbed in some inscrutable contemplation; then he signalled to the two negroes who crouched at his feet to lift the burden which lay between them. As they struggled upright, the first yellow beam of the sun struck through the innumerable prisms of an immense and exquisitely chiselled diamond—and a white radiance was kindled that glowed upon the air like a fragment of the morning star. The bearers staggered beneath its weight for a moment—then their rippling muscles caught and hardened under the wet shine of the skins and the three figures were again motionless in their defiant impotency before the heavens.

After a while the white man lifted his head and slowly raised his arms in a gesture of attention, as one who would call a great crowd to hear—but there was no crowd, only the vast silence of the mountain and the sky, broken by faint bird voices down among the trees. The figure on the saddle of rock began to speak ponderously and with an inextinguishable pride.

"You out there—" he cried in a trembling voice. "You—there—!" He paused, his arms still uplifted, his head held attentively as though he were expecting an answer. John strained his eyes to see whether there might be men coming down the mountain, but the mountain was bare of human life. There was only sky and a mocking flute of wind along the tree-tops. Could Washington be praying? For a moment John wondered. Then the illusion passed—there was something in the man's whole attitude antithetical to prayer.

"Oh, you above there!"

The voice was become strong and confident. This was no forlorn supplication. If anything, there was in it a quality of monstrous condescension.

"You there——"

Words, too quickly uttered to be understood, flowing one into the other. . . . John listened breathlessly, catching a phrase here and there, while the voice broke off, resumed, broke off again—now strong and argumentative, now colored with a slow, puzzled impatience. Then a conviction commenced to dawn on the single listener, and as realization crept over him a spray of quick blood rushed through his arteries. Braddock Washington was offering a bribe to God!

That was it—there was no doubt. The diamond in the arms of his slaves was some advance sample, a promise of more to follow.

That, John perceived after a time, was the thread running through his sentences. Prometheus Enriched was called to witness forgotten sacrifices, forgotten rituals, prayers obsolete before the birth of Christ. For a while his discourse took the form of reminding God of this gift or that which Divinity had deigned to accept from men—great churches if he would rescue cities from the plague, gifts of myrrh and gold, of human lives and beautiful women and captive armies, of children and queens, of beasts of the forest and field, sheep and goats, harvests and cities, whole conquered lands that had been offered up in lust or blood for His appeasal, buying a meed's worth of alleviation from the Divine wrath—and now he, Braddock Washington, Emperor of Diamonds, king and priest of the age of gold, arbiter of splendor and luxury, would offer up a treasure such as princes before him had never dreamed of, offer it up not in suppliance, but in pride.

He would give to God, he continued, getting down to specifications, the greatest diamond in the world. This diamond would be cut with many more thousand facets than there were leaves on a tree, and yet the whole diamond would be shaped with the perfection of a stone no bigger than a fly. Many men would work upon it for many years. It would be set in a great dome of beaten gold, wonderfully carved and equipped with gates of opal and crusted sapphire. In the middle would be hollowed out a chapel presided over by an altar of iridescent, decomposing, ever-changing radium which would burn out the eyes of any worshipper who lifted up his head from prayer—and on this altar there would be slain for the amusement of the Divine Benefactor any victim He should choose, even though it should be the greatest and most powerful man alive.

In return he asked only a simple thing, a thing that for God would be absurdly easy—only that matters should be as they were yesterday at this hour and that they should so remain. So very simple! Let but the heavens open, swallowing these men and their aeroplanes—and then close again. Let him have his slaves once more, restored to life and well.

There was no one else with whom he had ever needed to treat or bargain.

He doubted only whether he had made his bribe big enough. God had His price, of course. God was made in man's image, so it had been said: He must have His price. And the price would be rare—no cathedral whose building consumed many years, no pyramid constructed by ten thousand workmen, would be like this cathedral, this pyramid.

He paused here. That was his proposition. Everything would be up to specifications and there was nothing vulgar in his assertion that it would be cheap at the price. He implied that Providence could take it or leave it.

As he approached the end his sentences became broken, became short and uncertain, and his body seemed tense, seemed strained to catch the slightest pressure or whisper of life in the spaces around him. His hair had turned gradually white as he talked, and now he lifted his head high to the heavens like a prophet of old—magnificently mad.

Then, as John stared in giddy fascination, it seemed to him that a curious phenomenon took place somewhere around him. It was as though the sky had darkened for an instant, as though there had been a sudden murmur in a gust of wind, a sound of far-away trumpets, a sighing like the rustle of a great silken rope—for a time the whole of nature round about partook of this darkness; the birds' song ceased; the trees were still, and far over the mountain there was a mutter of dull, menacing thunder.

That was all. The wind died along the tall grasses of the valley. The dawn and the day resumed their place in a time, and the risen sun sent hot waves of yellow mist that made its path bright before it. The leaves laughed in the sun, and their laughter shook the trees until each bough was like a girl's school in fairyland. God had refused to accept the bribe.

For another moment John watched the triumph of the day. Then, turning, he saw a flutter of brown down by the lake, then another flutter, then another, like the dance of golden angels alighting from the clouds. The aeroplanes had come to earth.

John slid off the boulder and ran down the side of the mountain to the clump of trees, where the two girls were awake and waiting for him. Kismine sprang to her feet, the jewels in her pockets jingling, a question on her parted lips, but instinct told John that there was no time for words. They must get off the mountain without losing a moment. He seized a hand of each, and in silence they threaded the tree-trunks, washed with light now and with the rising mist. Behind them from the valley came no sound at all, except the complaint of the peacocks far away and the pleasant undertone of morning.

When they had gone about half a mile, they avoided the park land and entered a narrow path that led over the next rise of ground. At the highest point of this they paused and turned around. Their eyes rested upon the mountainside they had just left—oppressed by some dark sense of tragic impendency.

Clear against the sky a broken, white-haired man was slowly descending the steep slope, followed by two gigantic and emotionless negroes, who carried a burden between them which still flashed and glittered in the sun. Half-way down two other figures joined them—John could see that they were Mrs. Washington and her son, upon whose arm she leaned. The aviators had clambered from their machines to the sweeping lawn in front of the château, and with rifles in hand were starting up the diamond mountain in skirmishing formation.

But the little group of five which had formed farther up and was engrossing all the watchers' attention had stopped upon a ledge of rock. The negroes stooped and pulled up what appeared to be a trap-door in the side of the mountain. Into this they all disappeared, the white-haired man first, then his wife and son, finally the two negroes, the glittering tips of whose jeweled head-dresses caught the sun for a moment before the trap-door descended and engulfed them all.

Kismine clutched John's arm.

"Oh," she cried wildly, "where are they going? What are they going to do?"

"It must be some underground way of escape——"

A little scream from the two girls interrupted his sentence.

"Don't you see?" sobbed Kismine hysterically. "The mountain is wired!"

Even as she spoke John put up his hands to shield his sight. Before their eyes the whole surface of the mountain had changed suddenly to a dazzling burning yellow, which showed up through the jacket of turf as light shows through a human hand. For a moment the intolerable glow continued, and then like an extinguished filament it disappeared, revealing a black waste from which blue smoke arose slowly, carrying off with it what remained of vegetation and of human flesh. Of the aviators there were left neither blood nor bone—they were consumed as completely as the five souls who had gone inside.

Simultaneously, and with an immense concussion, the château literally threw itself into the air, bursting into flaming fragments as it rose, and then tumbling back upon itself in a smoking pile that lay projecting half into the water of the lake. There was no fire—what smoke there was drifted off mingling with the sunshine, and for a few minutes longer a powdery dust of marble drifted from the great featureless pile that had once been the house of jewels. There was no more sound and the three people were alone in the valley.

XI

At sunset John and his two companions reached the high cliff which had marked the boundaries of the Washingtons' dominion, and looking back found the valley tranquil and lovely in the dusk. They sat down to finish the food which Jasmine had brought with her in a basket.

"There!" she said, as she spread the table-cloth and put the sandwiches in a neat pile upon it. "Don't they look tempting? I always think that food tastes better outdoors."

"With that remark," remarked Kismine, "Jasmine enters the middle class."

"Now," said John eagerly, "turn out your pocket and let's see what jewels you brought along. If you made a good selection we three ought to live comfortably all the rest of our lives."

Obediently Kismine put her hand in her pocket and tossed two handfuls of glittering stones before him.

"Not so bad," cried John, enthusiastically. "They aren't very big, but—Hello!" His expression changed as he held one of them up to the declining sun. "Why, these aren't diamonds! There's something the matter!"

"By golly!" exclaimed Kismine, with a startled look. "What an idiot I am!"

"Why, these are rhinestones!" cried John.

"I know." She broke into a laugh. "I opened the wrong drawer. They belonged on the dress of a girl who visited Jasmine. I got her to give them to me in exchange for diamonds. I'd never seen anything but precious stones before."

"And this is what you brought?"

"I'm afraid so." She fingered the brilliants wistfully. "I think I like these better. I'm a little tired of diamonds."

"Very well," said John gloomily. "We'll have to live in Hades. And you will grow old telling incredulous women that you got the wrong drawer. Unfortunately your father's bank-books were consumed with him."

"Well, what's the matter with Hades?"

"If I come home with a wife at my age my father is just as liable as not to cut me off with a hot coal, as they say down there."

Jasmine spoke up.

"I love washing," she said quietly. "I have always washed my own handkerchiefs. I'll take in laundry and support you both."

"Do they have washwomen in Hades?" asked Kismine innocently.

"Of course," answered John. "It's just like anywhere else."

"I thought—perhaps it was too hot to wear any clothes."

John laughed.

"Just try it!" he suggested. "They'll run you out before you're half started."

"Will father be there?" she asked.

John turned to her in astonishment.

"Your father is dead," he replied somberly. "Why should he go to Hades? You have it confused with another place that was abolished long ago."

After supper they folded up the table-cloth and spread their blankets for the night.

"What a dream it was," Kismine sighed, gazing up at the stars. "How strange it seems to be here with one dress and a penniless fiancé!

"Under the stars," she repeated. "I never noticed the stars before. I always thought of them as great big diamonds that belonged to some one. Now they frighten me. They make me feel that it was all a dream, all my youth."

"It *was* a dream," said John quietly. "Everybody's youth is a dream, a form of chemical madness."

"How pleasant then to be insane!"

"So I'm told," said John gloomily. "I don't know any longer. At any rate, let us love for a while, for a year or so, you and me. That's a form of divine drunkenness that we can all try. There are only diamonds in the whole world, diamonds and perhaps the shabby gift of disillusion. Well, I have that last and I will make the usual nothing of it." He shivered. "Turn up your coat collar, little girl, the night's full of chill and you'll get pneumonia. His was a great sin who first invented consciousness. Let us lose it for a few hours."

So wrapping himself in his blanket he fell off to sleep.

Katherine Anne Porter 1890–1980

Callie Russell Porter was born in Indian Creek, Texas, to a land-poor family with Virginia and Kentucky roots, who had been brought low by a series of bad business decisions and the economic aftermath of the Civil War. When she died ninety years later, in Silver Spring, Maryland, Katherine Anne Porter had long since assumed her paternal grandmother's name. She had abandoned an unhappy marriage and life in Texas for a nomadic existence that took her to Mexico, New York, Paris, and eventually to Washington, D.C., where, as the doyenne of modern American literature, she dined frequently at the Johnson White House.

Born on the cusp of the twentieth century, she was also born into the lap of history. "I am the grandchild of a lost War," she wrote in "Portrait: Old South." If her emotional history began with the Civil War, her personal history would expose her to several other cataclysmic events of the modern era, all of which went into her stories. In Colorado, she nearly died of influenza during the epidemic that struck both the civilian population and the American Expeditionary Forces preparing to enter World War I to save Europe for democracy. That experience became "Pale Horse, Pale Rider." In Mexico, she "attended . . . and assisted at" the Obregon Revolution, an experience captured in the classic "Flowering Judas." In Berlin, she watched the rise of Hitler and dined with Hermann Göring. Her sense of pre-Nazi Germany went into "The Leaning Tower." Through it all, writing was her way of bringing order out of both personal and historical chaos.

Before settling on writing—as a young woman in her twenties—Porter performed as a singer and movie extra, taught, and worked as a journalist. She won solid critical notice from the publication of her first slim volume of short stories, *Flowering Judas,* in 1930, but her writing brought her no wide public notice (or sustained income) until her single novel, *Ship of Fools,* was published in 1962.

The catalyst for the stories in that first edition of *Flowering Judas* was apparently Porter's first exposure to a foreign culture: several of the stories are set in Mexico. Whatever the physical setting, all reflect the personal conflict she herself was experiencing, and one quite familiar to contemporary women: a conflicted wish for love and the conventional security belonging to home and family, and a simultaneous desire for an independent identity and free assertion of her personal ideals and talents.

During the 1930s, while living in Paris (when marriage to her third husband, Eugene Pressley, offered some financial security), she began to explore her own psychological roots by creating a fictional southern family, the Gays, whose youngest daughter, Miranda, is Porter's principal persona. This focus on the psychologically important experiences of a young girl growing up in a rigid, southern Victorian culture produced "The Old Order," "Pale Horse, Pale Rider," "Noon Wine," and "Old Mortality." These last three major fictions were published under the title *Pale Horse, Pale Rider* in 1939.

During the twenty years it took to produce *Ship of Fools,* Porter traveled the lecture circuit and taught to support herself. Her essays, under the title *The Days Before,* were published in 1952. Much anticipated after its long gestation, *Ship of Fools* was published to critical hoopla, and movie rights were quickly sold. In 1965, all of her short fiction, complete with four previously uncollected stories, was brought out. *The Collected Stories of Katherine Anne Porter* was awarded the National Book Award and the Pulitzer Prize for fiction in 1966, capping Porter's career. Her non-fiction was expanded and updated in *The Collected Essays and Occasional Writings of Katherine Anne Porter* (1970), and finally,

The Never-Ending Wrong, a non-fiction account of Porter's participation in the protest against the Sacco-Vanzetti execution, completed her writings in 1977.

Her stories are full of historical texture and local color, each comprising a different setting. This tends to obscure the fact that she writes over and over about personal freedom, from a particularly feminine perspective. In the minds of many of her female protagonists there is the wish for a nurturing love and an equal desire for personal independence and autonomy achieved through their own talents and perceptions. Porter spoke for generations of women who experienced physical and psychological limitations because of their sexuality and their society. Porter's insight is that the power to give life can, ironically, also inflict death, not only physically, but psychologically. In "Old Mortality," Miranda must sort out the complexities of Amy's wish to be free of the biological demands of her female body and, in addition, find her own truth about what she has been told—not only about the family, but through those stories, about herself and her femaleness. She must follow that truth, even though she, like the rest of the family, yearns for the romantic myth.

Thus, Porter's focus on the female conflict between following one's own nature or nurturing others leads to stories about the paradoxical relationship between birth and death; about the loss of innocence that comes with recognizing that those experiences are interwoven; about the evil of self-delusion and the price to be paid for personal freedom. To Porter, the biggest sin is the refusal—or inability—to love, an exercise that in her view inevitably ends in pain, but which must be engaged if the world is to survive at all.

Jane Krause DeMouy

Darlene Unrue
University of Nevada—Las Vegas

PRIMARY WORKS

Flowering Judas, 1930; *Flowering Judas and Other Stories,* 1940; *The Leaning Tower and Other Stories,* 1944; *The Days Before,* 1952; *Ship of Fools,* 1962; *The Collected Stories of Katherine Anne Porter,* 1965; *The Collected Essays and Occasional Writings of Katherine Anne Porter,* 1970; *The Never-Ending Wrong,* 1977.

The Jilting of Granny Weatherall

She flicked her wrist neatly out of Doctor Harry's pudgy careful fingers and pulled the sheet up to her chin. The brat ought to be in knee breeches. Doctoring around the country with spectacles on his nose! "Get along now, take your schoolbooks and go. There's nothing wrong with me."

Doctor Harry spread a warm paw like a cushion on her forehead where the forked green vein danced and made her eyelids twitch. "Now, now, be a good girl, and we'll have you up in no time."

"That's no way to speak to a woman nearly eighty years old just because she's down. I'd have you respect your elders, young man."

"Well, Missy, excuse me." Doctor Harry patted her cheek. "But I've got to warn you, haven't I? You're a marvel, but you must be careful or you're going to be good and sorry."

"Don't tell me what I'm going to be. I'm on my feet now, morally speaking. It's Cornelia. I had to go to bed to get rid of her."

Her bones felt loose, and floated around in her skin, and Doctor Harry floated like a balloon around the foot of the bed. He floated and pulled down his waistcoat and swung his glasses on a cord. "Well, stay where you are, it certainly can't hurt you."

"Get along and doctor your sick," said Granny Weatherall. "Leave a well woman alone. I'll call for you when I want you. . . . Where were you forty years ago when I pulled through milk-leg and double pneumonia? You weren't even born. Don't let Cornelia lead you on," she shouted, because Doctor Harry appeared to float up to the ceiling and out. "I pay my own bills, and I don't throw my money away on nonsense!"

She meant to wave good-by, but it was too much trouble. Her eyes closed of themselves, it was like a dark curtain drawn around the bed. The pillow rose and floated under her, pleasant as a hammock in a light wind. She listened to the leaves rustling outside the window. No, somebody was swishing newspapers: no, Cornelia and Doctor Harry were whispering together. She leaped broad awake, thinking they whispered in her ear.

"She was never like this, *never* like this!" "Well, what can we expect?" "Yes, eighty years old. . . ."

Well, and what if she was? She still had ears. It was like Cornelia to whisper around doors. She always kept things secret in such a public way. She was always being tactful and kind. Cornelia was dutiful; that was the trouble with her. Dutiful and good: "So good and dutiful," said Granny, "that I'd like to spank her." She saw herself spanking Cornelia and making a fine job of it.

"What'd you say, Mother?"

Granny felt her face tying up in hard knots.

"Can't a body think, I'd like to know?"

"I thought you might want something."

"I do. I want a lot of things. First off, go away and don't whisper."

She lay and drowsed, hoping in her sleep that the children would keep out and let her rest a minute. It had been a long day. Not that she was tired. It was always pleasant to snatch a minute now and then. There was always so much to be done, let me see: tomorrow.

Tomorrow was far away and there was nothing to trouble about. Things were finished somehow when the time came; thank God there was always a little margin over for peace: then a person could spread out the plan of life and tuck in the edges orderly. It was good to have everything clean and folded away, with the hair brushes and tonic bottles sitting straight on the white embroidered linen: the day started without fuss and the pantry shelves laid out with rows of jelly glasses and brown jugs and white stone-china jars with blue whirligigs and words painted on them: coffee, tea, sugar, ginger, cinnamon, allspice: and the bronze clock with the lion on top nicely dusted off. The dust that lion could collect in twenty-four hours! The box in the attic with all those letters tied up, well, she'd have to go through that tomorrow. All those letters—George's letters and John's letters and her letters to them both—lying around for the children to find afterwards made her uneasy.

Yes, that would be tomorrow's business. No use to let them know how silly she had been once.

While she was rummaging around she found death in her mind and it felt clammy and unfamiliar. She had spent so much time preparing for death there was no need for bringing it up again. Let it take care of itself now. When she was sixty she had felt very old, finished, and went around making farewell trips to see her children and grandchildren, with a secret in her mind: This is the very last of your mother, children! Then she made her will and came down with a long fever. That was all just a notion like a lot of other things, but it was lucky too, for she had once for all got over the idea of dying for a long time. Now she couldn't be worried. She hoped she had better sense now. Her father had lived to be one hundred and two years old and had drunk a noggin of strong hot toddy on his last birthday. He told the reporters it was his daily habit, and he owed his long life to that. He had made quite a scandal and was very pleased about it. She believed she'd just plague Cornelia a little.

"Cornelia! Cornelia!" No footsteps, but a sudden hand on her cheek. "Bless you, where have you been?"

"Here, Mother."

"Well, Cornelia, I want a noggin of hot toddy."

"Are you cold, darling?"

"I'm chilly, Cornelia. Lying in bed stops the circulation. I must have told you that a thousand times."

Well, she could just hear Cornelia telling her husband that Mother was getting a little childish and they'd have to humor her. The thing that most annoyed her was that Cornelia thought she was deaf, dumb, and blind. Little hasty glances and tiny gestures tossed around her and over her head saying. "Don't cross her, let her have her way, she's eighty years old," and she sitting there as if she lived in a thin glass cage. Sometimes Granny almost made up her mind to pack up and move back to her own house where nobody could remind her every minute that she was old. Wait, wait, Cornelia, till your own children whisper behind your back!

In her day she had kept a better house and had got more work done. She wasn't too old yet for Lydia to be driving eighty miles for advice when one of the children jumped the track, and Jimmy still dropped in and talked things over: "Now, Mammy, you've a good business head, I want to know what you think of this? . . ." Old. Cornelia couldn't change the furniture around without asking. Little things, little things! They had been so sweet when they were little. Granny wished the old days were back again with the children young and everything to be done over. It had been a hard pull, but not too much for her. When she thought of all the food she had cooked, and all the clothes she had cut and sewed, and all the gardens she had made—well, the children showed it. There they were, made out of her, and they couldn't get away from that. Sometimes she wanted to see John again and point to them and say, Well, I didn't do so badly, did I? But that would have to wait. That was for tomorrow. She used to think of him as a man, but now all the children were older than their father, and he would be a child beside her if she saw him now. It seemed strange and there was something wrong in the idea. Why, he couldn't possibly recognize her. She had fenced in a hundred acres once, digging the post holes herself and clamping the wires with just a negro boy to help. That changed a woman. John would be looking for a young woman with the peaked Spanish comb in her hair and the painted fan. Digging post holes changed a woman. Riding country roads in the winter when women had their babies was another thing: sitting up nights with sick horses and sick negroes and sick children and hardly ever losing one. John, I hardly ever lost one of them! John would see that in a minute, that would be something he could understand, she wouldn't have to explain anything!

It made her feel like rolling up her sleeves and putting the whole place to rights again. No matter if Cornelia was determined to be everywhere at once, there were a great many things left undone on this place. She would start tomorrow and do them. It was good to be strong enough for everything, even if all you made melted and changed and slipped under your hands, so that by the time you finished you almost forgot what you were working for. What was it I set out to do? she asked herself intently, but she could not remember. A fog rose over the valley, she saw it marching across the creek swallowing the trees and moving up the hill like an army of ghosts. Soon it would be at the near edge of the orchard, and then it was time to go in and light the lamps. Come in, children, don't stay out in the night air.

Lighting the lamps had been beautiful. The children huddled up to her and breathed like little calves waiting at the bars in the twilight. Their eyes followed the match and watched the flame rise and settle in a blue curve, then they moved away from her. The lamp was lit, they didn't have to be scared and hang on to mother any more. Never, never, never more. God, for all my life I thank Thee. Without Thee, my God, I could never have done it. Hail, Mary, full of grace.

I want you to pick all the fruit this year and see that nothing is wasted. There's always someone who can use it. Don't let good things rot for want of using. You waste life when you waste good food. Don't let things get lost. It's bitter to lose things. Now, don't let me get to thinking, not when I am tired and taking a little nap before supper. . . .

The pillow rose about her shoulders and pressed against her heart and the memory was being squeezed out of it: oh, push down the pillow, somebody: it would smother her if she tried to hold it. Such a fresh breeze blowing and such a green day with no threats in it. But he had not come, just the same. What does a woman do when she has put on the white veil and set out the white cake for a man and he doesn't come? She tried to remember. No, I swear he never harmed me but in that. He never harmed me but in that . . . and what if he did? There was the day, the day, but a whirl of dark smoke rose and covered it, crept up and over into the bright field where everything was planted so carefully in orderly rows. That was hell, she knew hell when she saw it. For sixty years she had prayed against remembering him and against losing her soul in the deep pit of hell, and now the two things were mingled in one and the thought of him was a smoky cloud from hell that moved and crept in her head when she had just got rid of Doctor Harry and was trying to rest a minute. Wounded vanity, Ellen, said a sharp voice in the top of her mind. Don't let your wounded vanity get the upper hand of you. Plenty of girls get jilted. You were jilted, weren't you? Then stand up to it. Her eyelids wavered and let in streamers of blue-gray light like tissue paper over her eyes. She must get up and pull the shades down or she'd never sleep. She was in bed again and the shades were not down. How could that happen? Better turn over, hide from the light, sleeping in the light gave you nightmares. "Mother, how do you feel now?" and a stinging wetness on her forehead. But I don't like having my face washed in cold water!

Hapsy? George? Lydia? Jimmy? No, Cornelia, and her features were swollen and full of little puddles. "They're coming, darling, they'll all be here soon." Go wash your face, child, you look funny.

Instead of obeying, Cornelia knelt down and put her head on the pillow. She seemed to be talking but there was no sound. "Well, are you tongue-tied? Whose birthday is it? Are you going to give a party?"

Cornelia's mouth moved urgently in strange shapes. "Don't do that, you bother me, daughter."

"Oh, no, Mother. Oh, no. . . ."

Nonsense. It was strange about children. They disputed your every word. "No what, Cornelia?"

"Here's Doctor Harry."

"I won't see that boy again. He just left five minutes ago."

"That was this morning, Mother. It's night now. Here's the nurse."

"This is Doctor Harry, Mrs. Weatherall. I never saw you look so young and happy!"

"Ah, I'll never be young again—but I'd be happy if they'd let me lie in peace and get rested."

She thought she spoke up loudly, but no one answered. A warm weight on her forehead, a warm bracelet on her wrist, and a breeze went on whispering, trying to tell her something. A shuffle of leaves in the everlasting hand of God, He blew on them and they danced and rattled. "Mother, don't mind, we're going to give you a little hypodermic." "Look here, daughter, how do ants get in this bed? I saw sugar ants yesterday." Did you send for Hapsy too?

It was Hapsy she really wanted. She had to go a long way back through a great many rooms to find Hapsy standing with a baby on her arm. She seemed to herself to be Hapsy also, and the baby on Hapsy's arm was Hapsy and himself and herself, all at once, and there was no surprise in the meeting. Then Hapsy melted from within and turned flimsy as gray gauze and the baby was a gauzy shadow, and Hapsy came up close and said, "I thought you'd never come," and looked at her very searchingly and said, "You haven't changed a bit!" They leaned forward to kiss, when Cornelia began whispering from a long way off, "Oh, is there anything you want to tell me? Is there anything I can do for you?"

Yes, she had changed her mind after sixty years and she would like to see George. I want you to find George. Find him and be sure to tell him I forgot him. I want him to know I had my husband just the same and my children and my house like any other woman. A good house too and a good husband that I loved and fine children out of him. Better than I hoped for even. Tell him I was given back everything he took away and more. Oh, no, oh, God, no, there was something else besides the house and the man and the children. Oh, surely they were not all? What was it? Something not given back. . . . Her breath crowded down under her ribs and grew into a monstrous frightening shape with cutting edges; it bored up into her head, and the agony was unbelievable: Yes, John, get the Doctor now, no more talk my time has come.

When this one was born it should be the last. The last. It should have been born first, for it was the one she had truly wanted. Everything came in good time. Nothing left out, left over. She was strong, in three days she would be as well as ever. Better. A woman needed milk in her to have her full health.

"Mother, do you hear me?"

"I've been telling you—"

"Mother, Father Connolly's here."

"I went to Holy Communion only last week. Tell him I'm not so sinful as all that."

"Father just wants to speak to you."

He could speak as much as he pleased. It was like him to drop in and inquire about her soul as if it were a teething baby, and then stay on for a cup of tea and a round of cards and gossip. He always had a funny story of some sort, usually about an Irishman who made his little mistakes and confessed them, and the point lay in some absurd thing he would blurt out in the confessional showing his struggles between native piety and original sin. Granny felt easy about her soul. Cornelia, where are your manners? Give Father Connolly a chair. She had her secret comfortable understanding with a few favorite saints who cleared straight road to God for her. All as surely signed and sealed as the papers for the new Forty Acres. Forever . . . heirs and assigns forever. Since the day the wedding cake was not cut, but thrown out and wasted. The whole bottom dropped out of the world, and there she was blind and sweating with nothing under her feet and the walls falling away. His hand had caught her under the breast, she had not fallen, there was the freshly polished floor with the green rug on it, just as before. He had cursed like a sailor's parrot and said, "I'll kill him for you." Don't lay a hand on him, for my sake leave something to God. "Now, Ellen, you must believe what I tell you. . . ."

So there was nothing, nothing to worry about any more, except sometimes in the night one of the children screamed in a nightmare, and they both hustled out shaking and hunting for the matches and calling, "There, wait a minute, here we are!" John, get the doctor now, Hapsy's time has come. But there was Hapsy standing by the bed in a white cap. "Cornelia, tell Hapsy to take off her cap. I can't see her plain."

Her eyes opened very wide and the room stood out like a picture she had seen somewhere. Dark colors with the shadows rising towards the ceiling in long angles. The tall black dresser gleamed with nothing on it but John's picture, enlarged from a little one, with John's eyes very black when they should have been blue. You never saw him, so how do you know how he looked? But the man insisted the copy was perfect, it was very rich and handsome. For a picture, yes, but it's not my husband. The table by the bed had a linen cover and a candle and a crucifix. The light was blue from Cornelia's silk lampshades. No sort of light at all, just frippery. You had to live forty years with kerosene lamps to appreciate honest electricity. She felt very strong and she saw Doctor Harry with a rosy nimbus around him.

"You look like a saint, Doctor Harry, and I vow that's as near as you'll ever come to it."

"She's saying something."

"I heard you, Cornelia. What's all this carrying-on?"

"Father Connolly's saying—"

Cornelia's voice staggered and bumped like a cart in a bad road. It rounded corners and turned back again and arrived nowhere. Granny stepped up in the cart very lightly and reached for the reins, but a man sat beside her and she knew him by his hands, driving the cart. She did not look in his face, for she knew without seeing, but looked instead down the road where the trees leaned over and bowed to each other and a thousand birds were singing a Mass. She felt like singing too, but she put her hand in the bosom of her dress and pulled out a rosary, and Father Connolly murmured Latin in a very solemn voice and tickled her feet. My God, will you stop that nonsense? I'm a married woman. What if he did run away and leave me to face the priest by myself? I found another a whole world better. I wouldn't have exchanged my husband for anybody except St. Michael himself, and you may tell him that for me with a thank you in the bargain.

Light flashed on her closed eyelids, and a deep roaring shook her. Cornelia, is that lightning? I hear thunder. There's going to be a storm. Close all the windows. Call the children in. . . . "Mother, here we are, all of us." "Is that you, Hapsy?" "Oh, no, I'm Lydia. We drove as fast as we could." Their faces drifted above her, drifted away. The rosary fell out of her hands and Lydia put it back. Jimmy tried to help, their hands fumbled together, and Granny closed two fingers around Jimmy's thumb. Beads wouldn't do, it must be something alive. She was so amazed her thoughts ran round and round. So, my dear Lord, this is my death and I wasn't even thinking about it. My children have come to see me die. But I can't, it's not time. Oh, I always hated surprises. I wanted to give Cornelia the amethyst set—Cornelia, you're to have the amethyst set, but Hapsy's to wear it when she wants, and, Doctor Harry, do shut up. Nobody sent for you. Oh, my dear Lord, do wait a minute. I meant to do something about the Forty Acres, Jimmy doesn't need it and Lydia will later on, with that worthless husband of hers. I meant to finish the altar cloth and send six bottles of wine to Sister Borgia for her dyspepsia. I want to send six bottles of wine to Sister Borgia, Father Connolly, now don't let me forget.

Cornelia's voice made short turns and tilted over and crashed. "Oh, Mother, oh, Mother, oh, Mother. . . ."

"I'm not going, Cornelia. I'm taken by surprise. I can't go."

You'll see Hapsy again. What about her? "I thought you'd never come." Granny made a long journey outward, looking for Hapsy. What if I don't find her? What then? Her heart sank down and down, there was no bottom to death, she couldn't come to the end of it. The blue light from Cornelia's lampshade drew into a tiny point in the center of her brain, it flickered and winked liked an eye, quietly it fluttered and dwindled. Granny lay curled down within herself, amazed and watchful, staring at the point of light that was herself; her body was now only a deeper mass of shadow in an endless darkness and this darkness would curl around the light and swallow it up. God, give a sign!

For a second time there was no sign. Again no bridegroom and the priest in the house. She could not remember any other sorrow because this grief wiped them all away. Oh, no, there's nothing more cruel than this—I'll never forgive it. She stretched herself with a deep breath and blew out the light.

1930

Flowering Judas

Braggioni sits heaped upon the edge of a straight-backed chair much too small for him, and sings to Laura in a furry, mournful voice. Laura has begun to find reasons for avoiding her own house until the latest possible moment, for Braggioni is there almost every night. No matter how late she is, he will be sitting there with a surly, waiting expression, pulling at his kinky yellow hair, thumbing the strings of his guitar, snarling a tune under his breath. Lupe the Indian maid meets Laura at the door, and says with a flicker of a glance towards the upper room, "He waits."

Laura wishes to lie down, she is tired of her hairpins and the feel of her long tight sleeves, but she says to him, "Have you a new song for me this evening?" If he says yes, she asks him to sing it. If he says no, she remembers his favorite one, and asks him to sing it again. Lupe brings her a cup of chocolate and a plate of rice, and Laura eats at the small table under the lamp, first inviting Braggioni, whose answer is always the same: "I have eaten, and besides, chocolate thickens the voice."

Laura says, "Sing, then," and Braggioni heaves himself into song. He scratches the guitar familiarly as though it were a pet animal, and sings passionately off key, taking the high notes in a prolonged painful squeal. Laura, who haunts the markets listening to the ballad singers, and stops every day to hear the blind boy playing his reed-flute in Sixteenth of September Street, listens to Braggioni with pitiless courtesy, because she dares not smile at his miserable performance. Nobody dares to smile at him. Braggioni is cruel to everyone, with a kind of specialized insolence, but he is so vain of his talents, and so sensitive to slights, it would require a cruelty and vanity greater than his own to lay a finger on the vast cureless wound of his self-esteem. It would require courage, too, for it is dangerous to offend him, and nobody has this courage.

Braggioni loves himself with such tenderness and amplitude and eternal charity that his followers—for he is a leader of men, a skilled revolutionist, and his skin has been punctured in honorable warfare—warm themselves in the reflected glow, and say to each other: "He has a real nobility, a love of humanity raised above mere personal affections." The excess of this self-love has flowed out, inconveniently for her, over Laura, who, with so many others, owes her comfortable situation and her salary to him. When he is in a very good humor, he tells her, "I am tempted to forgive you for being a *gringa. Gringita!*"[1] and Laura, burning, imagines herself leaning forward suddenly, and with a sound back-handed slap wiping the suety smile from his face. If he notices her eyes at these moments he gives no sign.

She knows what Braggioni would offer her, and she must resist tenaciously without appearing to resist, and if she could avoid it she would not admit even to herself the slow drift of his intention. During these long evenings which have spoiled a long month for her, she sits in her deep chair with an open book on her knees, resting her eyes on the consoling rigidity of the printed page when the sight and sound of Braggioni singing threaten to identify themselves with all her remembered afflictions and

[1]Spanish for foreigner, usually an American. "Gringita" is the diminutive form.

to add their weight to her uneasy premonitions of the future. The gluttonous bulk of Braggioni has become a symbol of her many disillusions, for a revolutionist should be lean, animated by heroic faith, a vessel of abstract virtues. This is nonsense, she knows it now and is ashamed of it. Revolution must have leaders, and leadership is a career for energetic men. She is, her comrades tell her, full of romantic error, for what she defines as cynicism in them is merely "a developed sense of reality." She is almost too willing to say, "I am wrong, I suppose I don't really understand the principles," and afterward she makes a secret truce with herself, determined not to surrender her will to such expedient logic. But she cannot help feeling that she has been betrayed irreparably by the disunion between her way of living and her feeling of what life should be, and at times she is almost contented to rest in this sense of grievance as a private store of consolation. Sometimes she wishes to run away, but she stays. Now she longs to fly out of this room, down the narrow stairs, and into the street where the houses lean together like conspirators under a single mottled lamp, and leave Braggioni singing to himself.

Instead she looks at Braggioni, frankly and clearly, like a good child who understands the rules of behavior. Her knees cling together under sound blue serge, and her round white collar is not purposely nun-like. She wears the uniform of an idea, and has renounced vanities. She was born Roman Catholic, and in spite of her fear of being seen by someone who might make a scandal of it, she slips now and again into some crumbling little church, kneels on the chilly stone, and says a Hail Mary on the gold rosary she bought in Tehuantepec. It is no good and she ends by examining the altar with its tinsel flowers and ragged brocades, and feels tender about the battered doll-shape of some male saint whose white, lace-trimmed drawers hang limply around his ankles below the hieratic dignity of his velvet robe. She has encased herself in a set of principles derived from her early training, leaving no detail of gesture or of personal taste untouched, and for this reason she will not wear lace made on machines. This is her private heresy, for in her special group the machine is sacred, and will be the salvation of the workers. She loves fine lace, and there is a tiny edge of fluted cobweb on this collar, which is one of twenty precisely alike, folded in blue tissue paper in the upper drawer of her clothes chest.

Braggioni catches her glance solidly as if he had been waiting for it, leans forward, balancing his paunch between his spread knees, and sings with tremendous emphasis, weighing his words. He has, the song relates, no father and no mother, nor even a friend to console him; lonely as a wave of the sea he comes and goes, lonely as a wave. His mouth opens round and yearns sideways, his balloon cheeks grow oily with the labor of song. He bulges marvelously in his expensive garments. Over his lavender collar, crushed upon a purple necktie, held by a diamond hoop: over his ammunition belt of tooled leather worked in silver, buckled cruelly around his gasping middle: over the tops of his glossy yellow shoes Braggioni swells with ominous ripeness, his mauve silk hose stretched taut, his ankles bound with the stout leather thongs of his shoes.

When he stretches his eyelids at Laura she notes again that his eyes are the true tawny yellow cat's eyes. He is rich, not in money, he tells her, but in power, and this power brings with it the blameless ownership of things, and the right to indulge his love of small luxuries. "I have a taste for the elegant refinements," he said once, flourishing a yellow silk handkerchief before her nose. "Smell that? It is Jockey Club, imported from New York." Nonetheless he is wounded by life. He will say so presently. "It is true everything turns to dust in the hand, to gall on the tongue." He sighs and his leather belt creaks like a saddle girth. "I am disappointed in everything as it comes. Everything." He shakes his head. "You, poor thing, you will be disappointed too. You are born for it. We are more alike than you realize in some things. Wait and see. Some day you will remember what I have told you, you will know that Braggioni was your friend."

Laura feels a slow chill, a purely physical sense of danger, a warning in her blood that violence, mutilation, a shocking death, wait for her with lessening patience. She has translated this fear into something homely, immediate, and sometimes hesitates before crossing the street. "My personal fate is nothing, except as the testimony of a mental attitude," she reminds herself, quoting from some forgotten philosophic primer, and is sensible enough to add, "Anyhow, I shall not be killed by an automobile if I can help it."

"It may be true I am as corrupt, in another way, as Braggioni," she thinks in spite of herself, "as callous, as incomplete," and if this is so, any kind of death seems preferable. Still she sits quietly, she does not run. Where could she go? Uninvited she has promised herself to this place; she can no longer imagine herself as living in another country, and there is no pleasure in remembering her life before she came here.

Precisely what is the nature of this devotion, its true motives, and what are its obligations? Laura cannot say. She spends part of her days in Xochimilco, near by, teaching Indian children to say in English, "The cat is on the mat." When she appears in the classroom they crowd about her with smiles on their wise, innocent, clay-colored faces, crying, "Good morning, my titcher!" in immaculate voices, and they make of her desk a fresh garden of flowers every day.

During her leisure she goes to union meetings and listens to busy important voices quarreling over tactics, methods, internal politics. She visits the prisoners of her own political faith in their cells, where they entertain themselves with counting cockroaches, repenting of their indiscretions, composing their memoirs, writing out manifestoes and plans for their comrades who are still walking about free, hands in pockets, sniffing fresh air. Laura brings them food and cigarettes and a little money, and she brings messages disguised in equivocal phrases from the men outside who dare not set foot in the prison for fear of disappearing into the cells kept empty for them. If the prisoners confuse night and day, and complain, "Dear little Laura, time doesn't pass in this infernal hole, and I won't know when it is time to sleep unless I have a reminder," she brings them their favorite narcotics, and says in a tone that does not wound them with pity, "Tonight will really be night for you," and though her Spanish amuses them, they find her comforting, useful. If they lose patience and all faith, and curse the slowness of their friends in coming to their rescue with money and influence, they trust her not to repeat everything, and if she inquires, "Where do you think we can find money, or influence?" they are certain to answer, "Well, there is Braggioni, why doesn't he do something?"

She smuggles letters from headquarters to men hiding from firing squads in back streets in mildewed houses, where they sit in tumbled beds and talk bitterly as if all Mexico were at their heels, when Laura knows positively they might appear at the band concert in the Alameda on Sunday morning, and no one would notice them. But Braggioni says, "Let them sweat a little. The next time they may be careful. It is very restful to have them out of the way for a while." She is not afraid to knock on any door in any street after midnight, and enter in the darkness, and say to one of these men who is really in danger: "They will be looking for you—seriously—tomorrow morning after six. Here is some money from Vicente. Go to Vera Cruz and wait."

She borrows money from the Roumanian agitator to give to his bitter enemy the Polish agitator. The favor of Braggioni is their disputed territory, and Braggioni holds the balance nicely, for he can use them both. The Polish agitator talks love to her over café tables, hoping to exploit what he believes is her secret sentimental preference for him, and he gives her misinformation which he begs her to repeat as the solemn truth to certain persons. The Roumanian is more adroit. He is generous with his money in all good causes, and lies to her with an air of ingenuous candor, as if he were her good friend and confidant. She never repeats anything they may say. Braggioni never asks questions. He has other ways to discover all that he wishes to know about them.

Nobody touches her, but all praise her gray eyes, and the soft, round under lip which promises gayety, yet is always grave, nearly always firmly closed: and they cannot understand why she is in Mexico. She walks back and forth on her errands, with puzzled eyebrows, carrying her little folder of drawings and music and school papers. No dancer dances more beautifully than Laura walks, and she inspires some amusing, unexpected ardors, which cause little gossip, because nothing comes of them. A young captain who had been a soldier in Zapata's army attempted, during a horseback ride near Cuernavaca, to express his desire for her with the noble simplicity befitting a rude folk-hero: but gently, because he was gentle. This gentleness was his defeat, for when he alighted, and removed her foot from the stirrup, and essayed to draw her down into his arms, her horse, ordinarily a tame one, shied fiercely, reared and plunged away. The young hero's horse careered blindly after his stable-mate, and the hero did not return to the hotel until rather late that evening. At breakfast he came to her table in full charro dress, gray buckskin jacket and trousers with strings of silver buttons down the leg, and he was in a humorous, careless mood. "May I sit with you?" and "You are a wonderful rider. I was terrified that you might be thrown and dragged. I should never have forgiven myself. But I cannot admire you enough for your riding!"

"I learned to ride in Arizona," said Laura.

"If you will ride with me again this morning, I promise you a horse that will not shy with you," he said. But Laura remembered that she must return to Mexico City at noon.

Next morning the children made a celebration and spent their playtime writing on the blackboard, "We lov ar ticher," and with tinted chalks they drew wreaths of flowers around the words. The young hero wrote her a letter: "I am a very foolish, wasteful, impulsive man. I should have first said I love you, and then you would not have run away. But you shall see me again." Laura thought, "I must send him a box of colored crayons," but you was trying to forgive herself for having spurred her horse at the wrong moment.

A brown, shock-haired youth came and stood in her patio one night and sang like a lost soul for two hours, but Laura could think of nothing to do about it. The moonlight spread a wash of gauzy silver over the clear spaces of the garden, and the shadows were cobalt blue. The scarlet blossoms of the Judas tree were dull purple, and the names of the colors repeated themselves automatically in her mind, while she watched not the boy, but his shadow, fallen like a dark garment across the fountain rim, trailing in the water. Lupe came silently and whispered expert counsel in her ear: "If you will throw him one little flower, he will sing another song or two and go away." Laura threw the flower, and he sang a last song and went away with the flower tucked in the band of his hat. Lupe said, "He is one of the organizers of the Typographers Union, and before that he sold corridos in the Merced market, and before that, he came from Guanajuato, where I was born. I would not trust any man, but I trust least those from Guanajuato."

She did not tell Laura that he would be back again the next night, and the next, nor that he would follow her at a certain fixed distance around the Merced market, through the Zócolo, up Francisco I. Madero Avenue, and so along the Paseo de la Reforma to Chapultepec Park, and into the Philosopher's Footpath, still with that flower withering in his hat, and an indivisible attention in his eyes.

Now Laura is accustomed to him, it means nothing except that he is nineteen years old and is observing a convention with all propriety, as though it were founded on a law of nature, which in the end it might well prove to be. He is beginning to write poems which he prints on a wooden press, and he leaves them stuck like handbills in her door. She is pleasantly disturbed by the abstract, unhurried watchfulness of his black eyes which will in time turn easily towards another object. She tells herself that throwing the flower was a mistake, for she is twenty-two years old and knows better; but she refuses to regret it, and persuades herself that her negation of all external events as they occur is a sign that she is gradually perfecting herself in the stoicism she strives to cultivate against that disaster she fears, though she cannot name it.

She is not at home in the world. Every day she teaches children who remain strangers to her, though she loves their tender round hands and their charming opportunist savagery. She knocks at unfamiliar doors not knowing whether a friend or a stranger shall answer, and even if a known face emerges from the sour gloom of that unknown interior, still it is the face of a stranger. No matter what this stranger says to her, nor what her message to him, the very cells of her flesh reject knowledge and kinship in one monotonous word. No. No. No. She draws her strength from this one holy talismanic word which does not suffer her to be led into evil. Denying everything, she may walk anywhere in safety, she looks at everything without amazement.

No, repeats this firm unchanging voice of her blood; and she looks at Braggioni without amazement. He is a great man, he wishes to impress this simple girl who covers her great round breasts with thick dark cloth, and who hides long, invaluably beautiful legs under a heavy skirt. She is almost thin except for the incomprehensible fullness of her breasts, like a nursing mother's, and Braggioni, who considers himself a judge of women, speculates again on the puzzle of her notorious virginity, and takes the liberty of speech which she permits without a sign of modesty, indeed, without any sort of sign, which is disconcerting.

"You think you are so cold, *gringita!* Wait and see. You will surprise yourself some day! May I be there to advise you!" He stretches his eyelids at her, and his ill-humored cat's eyes waver in a separate glance for the two points of light marking the opposite ends of a smoothly drawn path between the swollen curve of her breasts. He is not put off by that blue serge, nor by her resolutely fixed gaze. There is all the time in the world. His cheeks are bellying with the wind of song. "O girl with the dark eyes," he sings, and reconsiders. "But yours are not dark. I can change all that. O girl with the green eyes, you have stolen my heart away!" then his mind wanders to the song, and Laura feels the weight of his attention being shifted elsewhere. Singing thus, he seems harmless, he is quite harmless, there is nothing to do but sit patiently and say "No," when the moment comes. She draws a full breath, and her mind wanders also, but not far. She dares not wander too far.

Not for nothing has Braggioni taken pains to be a good revolutionist and a professional lover of humanity. He will never die of it. He has the malice, the cleverness, the wickedness, the sharpness of wit, the hardness of heart, stipulated for loving the world profitably. *He will never die of it.* He will live to see himself kicked out from his feeding trough by other hungry world-saviors. Traditionally he must sing in spite of his life which drives him to bloodshed, he tells Laura, for his father was a Tuscany peasant who drifted to Yucatan and married a Maya woman: a woman of race, an aristocrat. They gave him the love and knowledge of music, thus: and under the rip of his thumbnail, the strings of the instrument complain like exposed nerves.

Once he was called Delgadito by all the girls and married women who ran after him; he was so scrawny all his bones showed under his thin cotton clothing, and he could squeeze his emptiness to the very backbone with his two hands. He was a poet and the revolution was only a dream then; too many women loved him and sapped away his youth, and he could never find enough to eat anywhere, anywhere! Now he is a leader of men, crafty men who whisper in his ear, hungry men who wait for hours outside his office for a word with him, emaciated men with wild faces who waylay him at the street gate with a timid, "Comrade, let me tell you . . ." and they blow the foul breath from their empty stomachs in his face.

He is always sympathetic. He gives them handfuls of small coins from his own pocket, he promises them work, there will be demonstrations, they must join the unions and attend the meetings, above all they must be on the watch for spies. They are closer to him than his own brothers, without them he can do nothing—until tomorrow, comrade!

Until tomorrow. "They are stupid, they are lazy, they are treacherous, they would cut my throat for nothing," he says to Laura. He has good food and abundant drink, he hires an automobile and drives in the Paseo on Sunday morning, and enjoys plenty of sleep in a soft bed beside a wife who dares not disturb him; and he sits pampering his bones in easy billows of fat, singing to Laura, who knows and thinks these things about him. When he was fifteen, he tried to drown himself because he loved a girl, his first love, and she laughed at him. "A thousand women have paid for that," and his tight little mouth turns down at the corners. Now he perfumes his hair with Jockey Club, and confides to Laura: "One woman is really as good as another for me, in the dark. I prefer them all."

His wife organizes unions among the girls in the cigarette factories, and walks in picket lines, and even speaks at meetings in the evening. But she cannot be brought to acknowledge the benefits of true liberty. "I tell her I must have my freedom, net. She does not understand my point of view." Laura has heard this many times. Braggioni scratches the guitar and meditates. "She is an instinctively virtuous woman, pure gold, no doubt of that. If she were not, I should lock her up, and she knows it."

His wife, who works so hard for the good of the factory girls, employs part of her leisure lying on the floor weeping because there are so many women in the world, and only one husband for her, and she never knows where nor when to look for him. He told her: "Unless you can learn to cry when I am not here, I must go away for good." That day he went away and took a room at the Hotel Madrid.

It is this month of separation for the sake of higher principles that has been spoiled not only for Mrs. Braggioni, whose sense of reality is beyond criticism, but for Laura, who feels herself bogged in a nightmare. Tonight Laura envies Mrs. Braggioni, who is alone, and free to weep as much as she pleases about a concrete wrong. Laura has just come from a visit to the prison, and she is waiting for tomorrow with a bitter anxiety as if tomorrow may not come, but time may be caught immovably in this hour, with herself transfixed, Braggioni singing on forever, and Eugenio's body not yet discovered by the guard.

Braggioni says: "Are you going to sleep?" Almost before she can shake her head, he begins telling her about the May-day disturbances coming on in Morelia, for the Catholics hold a festival in honor of the Blessed Virgin, and the Socialists celebrate their martyrs on that day. "There will be two independent processions, starting from either end of town, and they will march until they meet, and the rest depends . . ." He asks her to oil and load his pistols. Standing up, he unbuckles his ammunition belt, and spreads it laden across her knees. Laura sits with the shells slipping through the cleaning cloth dipped in oil, and he says again he cannot understand why she works so hard for the revolutionary idea unless she loves some man who is in it. "Are you not in love with someone?" "No," says Laura. "And no one is in love with you?" "No." "Then it is your own fault. No woman need go begging. Why, what is the matter with you? The legless beggar woman in the Alameda has a perfectly faithful lover. Did you know that?"

Laura peers down the pistol barrel and says nothing, but a long, slow faintness rises and subsides in her? Braggioni curves his swollen fingers around the throat of the guitar and softly smothers the music out of it, and when she hears him again he seems to have forgotten her, and is speaking in the hypnotic voice he uses when talking in small rooms to a listening, close-gathered crowd. Some day this world, now seemingly so composed and eternal, to the edges of every sea shall be merely a tangle of gaping trenches, of crashing walls and broken bodies. Everything must be torn from its accustomed place where it has rotted for centuries, hurled skyward and distributed, cast down again clean as rain, without separate identity. Nothing shall survive that the stiffened hands of poverty have created for the rich and no one shall be left alive except the elect spirits destined to procreate a new world cleansed of cruelty and injustice, ruled by benevolent anarchy: "Pistols are good, I love them, cannon are even better, but in the end I pin my faith to good dynamite," he concludes, and strokes the pistol lying in her hands. "Once I dreamed of destroying this city, in case if offered resistance to General Ortíz, but it fell into his hands like an overripe pear."

He is made restless by his own words, rises and stands waiting. Laura holds up the belt to him: "Put that on, and go kill somebody in Morelia, and you will be happier," she says softly. The presence of death in the room makes her bold. "Today, I found Eugenio going into a stupor. He refused to allow me to call the prison doctor. He had taken all the tablets I brought him yesterday. He said he took them because he was bored."

"He is a fool, and his death is his own business," says Braggioni, fastening his belt carefully.

"I told him if he had waited only a little while longer, you would have got him set free," says Laura. "He said he did not want to wait."

"He is a fool and we are well rid of him," says Braggioni, reaching for his hat.

He goes away. Laura knows his mood has changed, she will not see him any more for a while. He will send word when he needs her to go on errands into strange streets, to speak to the strange faces that will appear, like clay masks with the power of human speech, to mutter their thanks to Braggioni for his help. Now she is free, and she thinks, I must run while there is time. But she does not go.

Braggioni enters his own house where for a month his wife has spent many hours every night weeping and tangling her hair upon her pillow. She is weeping now, and she weeps more at the sight of him, the cause of all her sorrows. He looks about the room. Nothing is changed, the smells are good and familiar, he is well acquainted with the woman who comes toward him with no reproach except grief on her face. He says to her tenderly: "You are so good, please don't cry any more, you dear good creature." She says, "Are you tired, my angel? Sit here and I will wash your feet." She brings a bowl of water, and kneeling, unlaces his shoes, and when from her knees she raises her sad eyes under her blackened lids, he is sorry for everything, and bursts into tears. "Ah, yes, I am hungry, I am tired, let us eat something together," he says, between sobs. His wife leans her head on his arm and says, "Forgive me!" and this time he is refreshed by the solemn, endless rain of her tears.

Laura takes off her serge dress and puts on a white linen nightgown and goes to bed. She turns her head a little to one side, and lying still, reminds herself that it is time to sleep. Numbers tick in her brain like little clocks, soundless doors close of themselves around her. If you would sleep, you must not remember anything, the children will say tomorrow, good morning, my teacher, the poor prisoners who come every day bringing flowers to their jailor. 1-2-3-4-5—it is monstrous to confuse love with revolution, night with day, life with death—ah, Eugenio!

The tolling of the midnight bell is a signal, but what does it mean? Get up, Laura, and follow me: come out of your sleep, out of your bed, out of this strange house. What are you doing in this house? Without a word, without fear she rose and reached for Eugenio's hand, but he eluded her with a sharp, sly smile and drifted away. This is not all, you shall see—Murderer, he said, follow me, I will show you a new country, but it is far away and we must hurry. No, said Laura, not unless you take my hand, no; and she clung first to the stair rail, and then to the topmost branch of the Judas tree that bent down slowly and set her upon the earth, and then to the rocky ledge of a cliff, and then to the jagged wave of a sea that was not water but a desert of crumbling stone. Where are you taking me, she asked in wonder but without fear. To death, and it is a long way off, and we must hurry, said Eugenio. No, said Laura, not unless you take my hand. Then eat these flowers, poor prisoner, said Eugenio in a voice of pity, take and eat: and from the Judas tree he stripped the warm bleeding flowers, and held them to her lips. She saw that his hand was fleshless, a cluster of small white petrified branches, and his eye sockets were without light, but she ate the flowers greedily for they satisfied both hunger and thirst. Murderer! said Eugenio, and Cannibal! This is my body and my blood. Laura cried No! and at the sound of her own voice, she awoke trembling, and was afraid to sleep again.

1930

Marianne Moore 1887–1972

Marianne Moore had a high reputation among American poets by the 1920s, but was not well known by the reading public until the 1960s. Raised in Kirkwood, Missouri and Carlisle, Pennsylvania, she published verse in school publications while attending Bryn Mawr College, from which she graduated in 1909. She continued to write while teaching at the U.S. Indian School in Carlisle, and working as a secretary, tutor, and assistant librarian in New York City from 1911 to 1915. Her first professional publications in England and the United States in 1915 brought her the acclaim of other writers. She became a close associate of both William Carlos Williams and Wallace Stevens, and in 1925 was given *The Dial* magazine award for *Observations* (1924). Five consecutive issues of *The Dial* lauded her work; she soon became editor of the journal, which was perhaps the best-known American magazine of literature and art during the 1920s.

During her four years with *The Dial* she published little of her own work, but in the 1930s Moore began again to accumulate awards as critics and other poets lauded her craftsmanship and precision of observation. Her greatest accolade came from T. S. Eliot, who in the introduction to her *Selected Poems* (1935) said she was one of the few writers who had made a contribution to the language. Moore used neither neo-metaphysical conceits nor private imagery: yet she remained "a poet's poet" until 1952 when, following publication of *Collected Poems* (1951), she was given the National Book Award, the Pulitzer Prize, and the Bollingen Prize.

Even after such acclaim, however, her work continued to be regarded as exceedingly difficult, and was seldom included in the school anthologies which give most Americans their first acquaintance with the work of poets. But her three-cornered hat and delightfully idiosyncratic conversation made her a public "character," and by the 1960s she was a favorite of *Life* magazine and the *New York Times*. Her being lionized as a celebrity is curiously at odds with her aesthetic of impersonal and objective values, and it raises questions about the larger fate of poetry in American culture. Equally questionable is the way in which such an intelligent and serious poet could be reduced to the stereotypes of eccentric "genius" and benevolent grandmotherly dottiness. Meanwhile, she translated from the French *The Fables of La Fontaine* (1955), a work she rewrote four times. Classroom recognition finally came after critics in the 1960s demonstrated that the reader willing to slow down and pay attention will find her poems one of the most delightful bodies of writing of our time. Her essays are equally idiosyncratic—one of her favorite words—and charming.

Part of her reputation for difficulty arose from the seemingly quirky habit in her early poems of breaking words in the middle at the ends of lines, even though the lines did not extend to the page margins. This came from adhering strictly to syllable-counting as the means of determining line lengths. Her stanzas are typically made up of lines kept parallel in length by this device. Thus the six-line stanzas in "Abundance" open with three lines of five or six syllables each; these are followed by two lines of ten or eleven and one of seven or eight. These metrics support the careful, precise statement of "observation" that a poem deals with. Another source for the opinion that Moore's work is difficult may have been the fact that she was determined to be as relatively objective as her male peers.

Moore had a strict, at times even prim, sense of moral values. She often found her values exemplified in animals exotic to the American public; both her animal lore and other information frequently came from the wide reading that was one of her principal sources of experience. In her rigorous view, abundance comes not from a plethora of luxuries but from devotion to duty; fortitude is one of the primary necessities for survival; and good poetry must make room for the "genuine." She took much delight in the well-made, whether the product of human craftsmanship or a creature of nature such as the chameleon. The best emblems for her thought and feeling were those that suggested the combination of the physical, esthetic, and religious grace that she found represented by the pangolin (the scaly anteater). Perhaps she was on occasion fussy in her endless revising and fondness for exact detail. But her "gusto," frequent tone of delight, play of humor, fastidious sense of right and wrong, and fascination with the play of the mind give her work the enduring "enchantment" she sought.

Bernard F. Engel
Michigan State University

PRIMARY WORKS

Poems, 1921; *Observations,* 1924; *Selected Poems,* 1935; *The Pangolin and Other Verse,* 1936; *What Are Years?,* 1941; *Nevertheless,* 1944; *Collected Poems,* 1951; *The Complete Poems of Marianne Moore,* 1967, 1981; *The Complete Prose of Marianne Moore,* 1989.

Poetry[1]

I, too, dislike it: there are things that are important beyond
    all this fiddle.
  Reading it, however, with a perfect contempt for it, one
    discovers in
  it after all, a place for the genuine.
    Hands that can grasp, eyes
      that can dilate, hair that can rise
        if it must, these things are important not because a

high-sounding interpretation can be put upon them but because
    they are
  useful. When they become so derivative as to become
    unintelligible,
  the same thing may be said for all of us, that we
      do not admire what
    we cannot understand: the bat
        holding on upside down or in quest of something to

[1]This is the well-known version of the poem. The *Collected Poems* (1981) prints only the first four words of lines 1–5. The notes, however, give the full version that appears here.

eat, elephants pushing, a wild horse taking a roll, a tireless wolf
under
a tree, the immovable critic twitching his skin like a horse that
feels a flea, the base-
ball fan, the statistician—
nor is it valid
to discriminate against 'business documents and

school-books';[2] all these phenomena are important. One must
make a distinction
however: when dragged into prominence by half poets, the
result is not poetry,
nor till the poets among us can be
'literalists of
the imagination'[3]—above
insolence and triviality and can present
for inspection, 'imaginary gardens with real toads in them', shall
we have
it. In the meantime, if you demand on the one hand,
the raw material of poetry in
all its rawness and
that which is on the other hand
genuine, you are interested in poetry.

1921

England

with its baby rivers and little towns, each with its abbey or its
cathedral,
with voices—one voice perhaps, echoing through the transept—
the
criterion of suitability and convenience: and Italy
with its equal shores—contriving an epicureanism
from which the grossness has been extracted:

and Greece with its goat and its gourds,
the nest of modified illusions: and France,

[2]*Diary of Tolstoy,* p. 84: "Poetry is verse: prose is not verse. Or the poetry is everything with the exception of business documents and school books" (from Moore's notes).

[3]W. B. Yeats, *Ideas of Good and Evil,* 1903, p. 182: "The limitation of his view was from the very intensity of his vision; he was a too literal realist of imagination, as others are of nature. . . ." (from Moore's notes).

the "chrysalis of the nocturnal butterfly,"[1]
in whose products mystery of construction
diverts one from what was originally one's object—
substance at the core: and the East with its snails, its emotional

shorthand and jade cockroaches, its rock crystal and its imperturbability,
all of museum quality: and America where there
is the little old ramshackle victoria in the south,
where cigars are smoked on the street in the north;
where there are no proof-readers, no silkworms, no digressions;

the wild man's land; grassless, linksless, languageless country in which letters are written
not in Spanish, not in Greek, not in Latin, not in shorthand,
but in plain American which cats and dogs can read!
The letter *a* in psalm and calm when
pronounced with the sound of *a* in candle, is very noticeable, but

why should continents of misapprehension
have to be accounted for by the fact?
Does it follow that because there are poisonous toadstools
which resemble mushrooms, both are dangerous?
Of mettlesomeness which may be mistaken for appetite,
of heat which may appear to be haste,
no conclusions may be drawn.

To have misapprehended the matter is to have confessed that one has not looked far enough.
The sublimated wisdom of China, Egyptian discernment,
the cataclysmic torrent of emotion
compressed in the verbs of the Hebrew language,
the books of the man who is able to say,
"I envy nobody but him, and him only,
who catches more fish than I do"—[2]
the flower and fruit of all that noted superiority—
if not stumbled upon in America,
must one imagine that it is not there?
It has never been confined to one locality.

1921

[1]Moore's notes attribute the quotation to Erté (Romain de Tirtoff, 1892–1990), Russian-born graphics artist who became a celebrity designer for fashion houses and the theater in Paris, London, and New York.

[2]Moore took the quotation from Izaak Walton (1593–1683), author of *The Compleat Angler* (1653, rev. 1655), the best-known book on fishing as a recreation.

To a Chameleon[1]

Hid by the august foliage and fruit of the grape-vine
twine
your anatomy
round the pruned and polished stem,
Chameleon.
Fire laid upon
an emerald as long as
the Dark King's[2] massy
one,
could not snap the spectrum up for food as you have done.

1921

An Egyptian Pulled Glass Bottle in the Shape of a Fish

Here we have thirst
and patience, from the first,
and art, as in a wave held up for us to see
in its essential perpendicularity;

not brittle but
intense—the spectrum, that
spectacular and nimble animal the fish,
whose scales turn aside the sun's sword by their polish.

1924

[1]Chameleon: any of a number of lizards that can change skin color. The shape of the poem on the page seems meant to suggest the way the lizard can "twine" around a stem.

[2]Dark King: alludes to Prester John, a perhaps legendary medieval king and priest, said to have ruled in Ethiopia or western Asia.

The Pangolin

Another armored animal[1]—scale
lapping scale with spruce-cone regularity until they
form the uninterrupted central
tail-row! This near artichoke with head and legs and grit-
equipped gizzard,

the night miniature artist engineer is,
yes, Leonardo da Vinci's replica—[2]
impressive animal and toiler of whom we seldom hear.
Armor seems extra. But for him,
the closing ear-ridge—[3]
or bare ear lacking even this small
eminence and similarly safe

contracting nose and eye apertures
impenetrably closable, are not; a true ant-eater,
not cockroach-eater, who endures
exhausting solitary trips through unfamiliar ground at night,
returning before sunrise; stepping in the moonlight,
on the moonlight peculiarly,[4] that the outside
edges of his hands may bear the weight and save the
claws
for digging. Serpentined about
the tree, he draws
away from danger unpugnaciously,
with no sound but a harmless hiss; keeping

the fragile grace of the Thomas-
of-Leighton Buzzard Westminster Abbey wrought-iron vine,[5]
or
rolls himself into a ball that has
power to defy all effort to unroll it; strongly intailed, neat
head for core, on neck not breaking off, with curled-in feet.
Nevertheless he has sting-proof scales; and nest

[1]"Pangolin" is the name given to a number of scaly, ant-eating mammals of Asia and Africa. The word "another" suggests a bit of humor, since Moore wrote several poems on creatures having thick hides or other "armor."

[2]Leonardo da Vinci (1452–1519), Renaissance man of all talents, was both artist and engineer.

[3]Moore's notes say that "the closing ear-ridge" and certain other details are from Robert T. Hatt, "Pangolins," *Natural History* (December 1935).

[4]Moore's notes say that "stepping . . . peculiarly" is an idea taken from Richard Lydekker (1849–1915), English naturalist.

[5]Alludes to "a fragment of ironwork in Westminster Abbey" (from Moore's note).

of rocks closed with earth from inside, which he can thus
darken.
Sun and moon and day and night and man and beast
each with a splendor
which man in all his vileness cannot
set aside; each with an excellence!

"Fearful yet to be feared,"[6] the armored
ant-eater met by the driver-ant does not turn back, but
engulfs what he can, the flattened sword-
edged leafpoints on the tail and artichoke set leg- and body-
plates
quivering violently when it retaliates
and swarms on him. Compact like the furled fringed frill
on the hat-brim of Gargallo's hollow iron head of a
matador,[7] he will drop and will
then walk away
unhurt, although if unintruded on,
he cautiously works down the tree, helped

by his tail. The giant-pangolin-
tail, graceful tool, as prop or hand or broom or ax, tipped
like
an elephant's trunk with special skin,
is not lost on this ant- and stone-swallowing uninjurable
artichoke which simpletons thought a living fable
whom the stones had nourished, whereas ants had done
so. Pangolins are not aggressive animals; between
dusk and day they have the not unchain-like machine-like
form and frictionless creep of a thing
made graceful by adversities, con-

versities. To explain grace requires
a curious hand. If that which is at all were not forever,
why would those who graced the spires
with animals and gathered there to rest, on cold luxurious
low stone seats—a monk and monk and monk—between the
thus
ingenious roof-supports, have slaved to confuse
grace with a kindly manner, time in which to pay a debt,

[6]"Fearful yet to be feared": Moore gives no source. She may have been quoting; or she may have used quotation marks to highlight the expression or to give it an air of factuality.

[7]Pablo Gargallo (1881–1934) was a Spanish painter and sculptor.

the cure for sins, a graceful use
of what are yet
approved stone mullions[8] branching out across
the perpendiculars? A sailboat
was the first machine. Pangolins, made
for moving quietly also, are models of exactness,
on four legs; on hind feet plantigrade,
with certain postures of a man. Beneath sun and moon, man slaving
to make his life more sweet, leaves half the flowers worth having,
needing to choose wisely how to use his strength;
a paper-maker like the wasp; a tractor of foodstuffs,
like the ant; spidering a length
of web from bluffs
above a stream; in fighting, mechanicked
like the pangolin; capsizing in
disheartenment. Bedizened or stark
naked, man, the self, the being we call human, writing-
master to this world, griffons[9] a dark
"Like does not like like that is obnoxious"; and writes error with four
r's. Among animals, *one* has a sense of humor.
Humor saves a few steps, it saves years. Unignorant,
modest and unemotional, and all emotion,
he has everlasting vigor,
power to grow,
though there are few creatures who can make one
breathe faster and make one erecter.

Not afraid of anything is he,
and then goes cowering forth, tread paced to meet an obstacle
at every step. Consistent with the
formula—warm blood, no gills, two pairs of hands and a few hairs—that
is a mammal; there he sits in his own habitat,
serge-clad, strong-shod. The prey of fear, he, always
curtailed, extinguished, thwarted by the dusk, work partly done,

[8]Vertical dividing bars between panels or window panes.
[9]Probably alludes to the griffin, a mythical beast having an eagle's head and wings, and a lion's body. The word is used here as a verb.

says to the alternating blaze,
"Again the sun!
anew each day; and new and new and new,
that comes into and steadies my soul."

1936

What Are Years?

What is our innocence,
what is our guilt? All are
naked, none is safe. And whence
is courage: the unanswered question,
the resolute doubt,—
dumbly calling, deafly listening—that
in misfortune, even death,
encourages others
and in its defeat, stirs

the soul to be strong? He
sees deep and is glad, who
accedes to mortality
and in his imprisonment rises
upon himself as
the sea in a chasm, struggling to be
free and unable to be,
in its surrendering
finds its continuing.

So he who strongly feels,
behaves. The very bird,
grown taller as he sings, steels
his form straight up. Though he is captive,
his mighty singing
says, satisfaction is a lowly
thing, how pure a thing is joy.
This is mortality,
this is eternity.

1941

Nevertheless

you've seen a strawberry
that's had a struggle; yet
was, where the fragments met,

a hedgehog or a star-
fish for the multitude
of seeds. What better food

than apple seeds—the fruit
within the fruit—locked in
like counter-curved twin

hazelnuts? Frost that kills
the little rubber-plant-
leaves of *kok-saghyz*[1]-stalks, can't

harm the roots; they still grow
in frozen ground. Once where
there was a prickly-pear-

leaf clinging to barbed wire,
a root shot down to grow
in earth two feet below;

as carrots form mandrakes[2]
or ram's-horn root some-
times. Victory won't come

to me unless I go
to it; a grape tendril
ties a knot in knots till

knotted thirty times—so
the bound twig that's undergone and over-gone, can't stir.

The weak overcomes its
menace, the strong over-
comes itself. What is there

[1]Russian dandelion; its roots yield a form of rubber.

[2]Poisonous plants thought to look like the human body.

like fortitude! What sap
    went through that little thread
    to make the cherry red!

1944

The Mind Is an Enchanting Thing[1]

is an enchanted thing
    like the glaze on a
katydid-wing
        subdivided by sun
        till the nettings are legion.
Like Gieseking playing Scarlatti;[2]

like the apteryx-awl
    as a beak, or the
kiwi's rain shawl
        of haired feathers, the mind
        feeling its way as though blind,
walks along with its eyes on the ground.

It has memory's ear
    that can hear without
having to hear.
        Like the gyroscope's fall,
        truly unequivocal
because trued by regnant certainty,

it is a power of
    strong enchantment. It
is like the dove-
        neck animated by
        sun; it is memory's eye;
it's conscientious inconsistency.

* * *

[1]This poem may be compared with the later "The Mind, Intractable Thing."
[2]Walter W. Gieseking (1895–1956), a German pianist, was well known for his playing of pieces by the Italian composer Domenico Scarlatti (1685–1757).

It tears off the veil; tears
the temptation, the
mist the heart wears,
from its eyes—if the heart
has a face; it takes apart
dejection. It's fire in the dove-neck's

iridescence; in the
inconsistencies
of Scarlatti.
Unconfusion submits
its confusion to proof; it's
not a Herod's oath that cannot change.

1944

Louise Bogan 1897–1970

Born in Livermore, Maine, Bogan attended private school in New Hampshire and, after her family moved to Boston, the Girls' Latin School, graduating in 1915. Later, she remembered her five years at the school—renowned for its rigorous classical curriculum—as stimulating and happy. By age fifteen she considered herself a writer. However, having completed one year at Boston University, she married an army officer and accompanied him to Panama, where they had a daughter. After his death in 1920, Bogan lived in New York, supporting herself with jobs in a bookstore and at the public library. During these difficult, but exciting years, she frequented literary gatherings in Greenwich Village and met writers associated with Alfred Kreymborg and his magazine, *Others,* among them William Carlos Williams, Lola Ridge, and Conrad Aiken. She also developed a lasting friendship with the writer-critic Edmund Wilson. By 1922, her verse had appeared in such leading journals as *Poetry, Vanity Fair,* and *The New Republic.* Early recognition led in 1923 to her first book, *Body of This Death.*

From 1925 to 1937 Bogan was married to Raymond Holden, a poet and for several years managing editor of *The New Yorker.* In 1931 she became poetry reviewer for the magazine, a position she held for thirty-eight years. Her essays and reviews are collected in two volumes of criticism. From 1933, when she was awarded the first of two Guggenheim Fellowships for creative writing, she spent periods of time in Europe.

The detachment typical of Bogan's verse is absent in "Women" (1922). In an accusing tone, the speaker berates women for reducing their talent and imagination to attain a life-denying contentment, perpetuating their own meager conditions. Although the speaker implies male standards against which to judge women's actions, the point is, surely, that women *should* have "wilderness in them," should journey with courage, and both think and imagine beyond narrowly defined limits. When the poem appeared, Bogan herself was not one of the "provident," cautious women she describes.

Two poems from the 1930s reveal the influence of Yeats and Rilke as well as the range of Bogan's poetic skill. In lines alive with alliteration, "Roman Fountain" echoes the startling rise and fall of the fountain, shaped by the bronze spout to achieve its zenith just a moment before falling. Like the fountain's maker, the poet crafts her materials in dramatic, intricate patterns to capture the image. In contrast to this response to outer reality, "The Sleeping Fury" details the speaker's conflict with an inner self, both sister and avenger of "the kissed-out lie." Driven by this punishing force, she must finally acknowledge her mask and its false love. In place of the flame-enshrouded demon, she discovers upon relinquishing her passion a childlike figure of dreamless sleep that mirrors her hard-won peace. In long, fluid lines Bogan conveys deep personal anguish without revealing its factual source.

A late poem, "The Dragonfly," exemplifies Bogan's rare experiment with short free verse lines, capturing through vivid imagery the insect's appearance and movement. Like Moore's animals, Bogan's dragonfly embodies certain human characteristics: the "Unending hunger/Grappling love" that cause the beautiful predator to "rocket into the day," only to lose "design and purpose" as the season runs its course. In its faultless diction and elegant simplicity, Bogan's finest verse possesses lyric power of a high order.

Theodora Rapp Graham
Pennsylvania State University at Harrisburg

PRIMARY WORKS

Poetry: *Body of This Death,* 1923; *Dark Summer,* 1929; *The Sleeping Fury,* 1937; *Poems and New Poems,* 1941; *Collected Poems, 1923–1953,* 1954; *The Blue Estuaries: Poems 1923–1968,* 1968, 1977; Criticism: *Achievement in American Poetry, 1900–1950,* 1951; *Selected Criticism: Poetry and Prose,* 1955; Robert Phelps and Ruth Limmer, eds., *A Poet's Alphabet: Reflections on the Literary Art and Vocation,* 1970.

Women

Women have no wilderness in them,
They are provident instead,
Content in the tight hot cell of their hearts
To eat dusty bread.

They do not see cattle cropping red winter grass,
They do not hear
Snow water going down under culverts
Shallow and clear.

They wait, when they should turn to journeys,
They stiffen, when they should bend.
They use against themselves that benevolence
To which no man is friend.

* * *

They cannot think of so many crops to a field
Or of clean wood cleft by an axe.
Their love is an eager meaninglessness
Too tense, or too lax.

They hear in every whisper that speaks to them
A shout and a cry.
As like as not, when they take life over their door-sills
They should let it go by.

1922

The Sleeping Fury

You are here now,
Who were so loud and feared, in a symbol before me,
Alone and asleep, and I at last look long upon you.

Your hair fallen on your cheek, no longer in the semblance of
    serpents,
Lifted in the gale; your mouth, that shrieked so, silent.
You, my scourge, my sister, lie asleep, like a child,
Who, after rage, for an hour quiet, sleeps out its tears.

The days close to winter
Rough with strong sound. We hear the sea and the forest,

And the flames of your torches fly, lit by others,
Ripped by the wind, in the night. The black sheep for sacrifice
Huddle together. The milk is cold in the jars.

All to no purpose, as before, the knife whetted and plunged,
The shout raised, to match the clamor you have given them.
You alone turn away, not appeased; unaltered, avenger.

Hands full of scourges, wreathed with your flames and adders,
You alone turned away, but did not move from my side,
Under the broken light, when the soft nights took the torches.

At thin morning you showed, thick and wrong in that calm,
The ignoble dream and the mask, sly, with slits at the eyes,
Pretence and half-sorrow, beneath which a coward's hope
    trembled.

You uncovered at night, in the locked stillness of houses,
False love due the child's heart, the kissed-out lie, the embraces,
Made by the two who for peace tenderly turned to each other.

You who know what we love, but drive us to know it;
You with your whips and shrieks, bearer of truth and of solitude;
You who give, unlike men, to expiation your mercy.

Dropping the scourge when at last the scourged advances to meet
it,
You, when the hunted turns, no longer remain the hunter
But stand silent and wait, at last returning his gaze.

Beautiful now as a child whose hair, wet with rage and tears
Clings to its face. And now I may look upon you,
Having once met your eyes. You lie in sleep and forget me.
Alone and strong in my peace, I look upon you in yours.

1937

Roman Fountain

Up from the bronze, I saw
Water without a flaw
Rush to its rest in air,
Reach to its rest, and fall.

Bronze of the blackest shade,
An element man-made,
Shaping upright the bare
Clear gouts of water in air.

O, as with arm and hammer,
Still it is good to strive
To beat out the image whole,
To echo the shout and stammer
When full-gushed waters, alive,
Strike on the fountain's bowl
After the air of summer.

1937

After the Persian

I

I do not wish to know
The depths of your terrible jungle:
From what nest your leopard leaps
Or what sterile lianas are at once your serpents' disguise and
home.

I am the dweller on the temperate threshold,
The strip of corn and vine,
Where all is translucence (the light!)
Liquidity, and the sound of water.
Here the days pass under shade
And the nights have the waxing and the waning moon.
Here the moths take flight at evening;
Here at morning the dove whistles and the pigeons coo.
Here, as night comes on, the fireflies wink and snap
Close to the cool ground,
Shining in a profusion
Celestial or marine.

Here it is never wholly dark but always wholly green,
And the day stains with what seems to be more than the sun
What may be more than my flesh.

II

I have wept with the spring storm;
Burned with the brutal summer.
Now, hearing the wind and the twanging bow-strings,
I know what winter brings.

The hunt sweeps out upon the plain
And the garden darkens.
They will bring the trophies home
To bleed and perish
Beside the trellis and the lattices,
Beside the fountain, still flinging diamond water,
Beside the pool
(Which is eight-sided, like my heart).

III

All has been translated into treasure:
Weightless as amber,
Translucent as the currant on the branch,
Dark as the rose's thorn.

Where is the shimmer of evil?
This is the shell's iridescence
And the wild bird's wing.

IV

Ignorant, I took up my burden in the wilderness.
Wise with great wisdom, I shall lay it down upon flowers.

V

Goodbye, goodbye!
There was so much to love, I could not love it all;
I could not love it enough.

Some things I overlooked, and some I could not find.
Let the crystal clasp them
When you drink your wine, in autumn.

1937

The Dragonfly

You are made of almost nothing
But of enough
To be great eyes
And diaphanous double vans;
To be ceaseless movement,
Unending hunger
Grappling love.

Link between water and air,
Earth repels you.
Light touches you only to shift into iridescence
Upon your body and wings.

Twice-born, predator,
You split into the heat.
Swift beyond calculation or capture
You dart into the shadow
Which consumes you.

You rocket into the day.
But at last, when the wind flattens the grasses,
For you, the design and purpose stop.

And you fall
With the other husks of summer.

1963

Night

The cold remote islands
And the blue estuaries
Where what breathes, breathes
The restless wind of the inlets,
And what drinks, drinks
The incoming tide;

Where shell and weed
Wait upon the salt wash of the sea,
And the clear nights of stars
Swing their lights westward
To set behind the land;

Where the pulse clinging to the rocks
Renews itself forever;
Where, again on cloudless nights,
The water reflects
The firmament's partial setting;

—O remember
In your narrowing dark hours
That more things move
Than blood in the heart.

1963

Ernest Hemingway 1899–1961

Though he has a reputation for writing best about men in a man's world of war or wilderness, Hemingway lived very much in a world of women. Born in the affluent Chicago suburb of Oak Park, he was surrounded by women as the second child and first son in a family of four sisters. He was sixteen before his only brother, Leicester, was born. Like his alter ego Nick Adams, who appears in over twenty stories, Hemingway went hunting and fishing with his physician father in upper Michigan. A story such as "The Doctor and the Doctor's Wife" in *In Our Time* suggests the alignment Hemingway saw between the suburban world of his strong-willed mother, Grace, and the escape from its complexities provided by the Michigan woods that his father loved. An eye injury kept him out of the army in 1917 when he tried to enlist after high school graduation. Instead he began his writing apprenticeship as a reporter for the *Kansas City Star.*

Less than a year later, he succeeded in entering the Great War as a driver in the Red Cross Ambulance Corps. Hemingway uses his own war experiences in both the Nick Adams stories and *A Farewell to Arms* of 1929 and yet ties them to images of war in the work of contemporaries such as T. S. Eliot and nineteenth-century writers Ambrose Bierce and Stephen Crane. Crane's protagonist in *The Red Badge of Courage* was named Henry Fleming; Hemingway's narrator Frederic Henry becomes a direct descendant since he is usually referred to by his last name alone. Both characters are experiencing war for the first time, and both become disillusioned by the experience.

Like his narrator Frederic Henry, Hemingway was wounded in the leg soon after arriving in Italy to serve in the ambulance corps. He too fell in love with a British nurse and later found himself caught up in the Italian army's retreat from Caporetto as the Austrian and German forces advanced. Henry's real enemies are boredom, hunger, thirst, and random violence, all of which are exacerbated by class conflicts between enlisted men and officers and inept leadership. In the section excerpted here, Henry translates his conversations with Italian soldiers into English and allows himself the luxury of remembering nurse Catherine Barkley, who is pregnant with his child, only in a dazed moment of escape from the humdrum preparations for retreat.

Hemingway returned from World War I to an American Midwest constrained by Prohibition and the numbing strictures of family and smalltown life. Journalism and travel proved his escape. In 1921 he married Hadley Richardson, the first of his four wives, and returned to Europe as foreign correspondent for the Toronto *Star.*

Armed with a letter of introduction from Sherwood Anderson, Hemingway joined the coterie of American expatriates forming around Gertrude Stein in Paris. Later he would attribute much of the repetition in her work to her aversion to revising and deleting, steps in the writing process that he saw as vital. Yet as the neophyte writer, Hemingway's competitive instincts were set aside while he profited from the lessons of more established writers such as Stein, Ezra Pound, and eventually F. Scott Fitzgerald.

Success and recognition complicated Hemingway's life, as did the birth of his son John in 1923. Impending fatherhood and the responsibilities it entailed had a gloomy effect on Hemingway, much as it does for the American in "Hills Like White Elephants." Most immediately, Hadley's pregnancy meant a return to Canada for several months and a threatened end to the youthful freedom they had enjoyed in Paris. Their last European fling that July was the first of his three visits to Spain for the running of the bulls in Pamplona. This experience is embedded in his most highly acclaimed novel, *The Sun Also Rises,* which presents the rootless society of the "lost generation" on a secular pilgrimage that covers terrain similar to that of T. S. Eliot's *The Waste Land.*

Each of Hemingway's four marriages marks a stage in his career that suggests an alignment of his personal and professional life. Marriage to Pauline Pfeiffer in 1927 signaled a turn toward domestic concerns. Key West, Florida, became his home base, though he traveled widely in America, Europe, and Africa, occasionally accompanied by Pauline and their two sons, Patrick and Gregory, as well as his older son John. He wrote personal essays against the background of bullfighting in *Death in the Afternoon* and big game hunting in *Green Hills of Africa* and a novel dealing with his Loyalist sympathies in the Spanish Civil War, *For Whom the Bell Tolls.*

Divorce and remarriage to foreign correspondent Martha Gellhorn in 1940 marked another stage in Hemingway's life and work. For the first and only time, he chose a competitor as a wife, and by his standards this was the least successful of his marriages. He wrote little fiction in these years, and despite the homes he established with Martha Gellhorn in Cuba and Ketchum, Idaho, he led a nomadic life, sporadically covering the European theater of World War II. By the time Martha Gellhorn scooped him by being with the first wave of American troops to hit the beaches in the Normandy invasion, Hemingway had chosen a less aggressive journalist, Mary Welsh, to be his fourth wife. It was with Mary that Hemingway celebrated the liberation of Paris in August 1944.

Highlights of Hemingway's career in the years of his marriage to Mary Welsh were the negative response to his highly autobiographical novel *Across the River and Into the Trees,* in contrast to the popular and critical success of his novella *The Old Man and the Sea.* This work, for which he received the Pulitzer Prize in 1952, was the impetus for his receiving the Nobel Prize in Literature in 1954. Like Stephen Crane of an earlier generation, Hemingway put modern man in an open boat for a life-or-death struggle on the sea. Though his "old man" Santiago conquers the great fish, he loses all but the memory of his success.

Falling into depression exacerbated by bouts of hard drinking and writer's block, Hemingway committed suicide at his ranch in Ketchum in 1961. His posthumously published works greatly increase the biographical dimensions of the man to be discerned from works published in his lifetime, but his reputation as a stylist and writer of fiction still rests squarely on those works he himself saw through many stages of revision to publication.

Margaret Anne O'Connor
University of North Carolina–Chapel Hill

PRIMARY WORKS

In Our Time, 1925; *The Sun Also Rises,* 1926; *The Torrents of Spring,* 1926; *Men Without Women,* 1927; *A Farewell to Arms,* 1929; *Death in the Afternoon,* 1932; *Winner Take Nothing,* 1933; *Green Hills of Africa,* 1935; *To Have and Have Not,* 1937; *The Fifth Column and the First Forty-nine Stories,* 1938; *For Whom the Bell Tolls,* 1940; *Across the River and Into the Trees,* 1950; *The Old Man and the Sea,* 1952; *A Moveable Feast,* 1964; *Islands in the Stream,* 1970; *The Nick Adams Stories,* ed. by Philip Young, 1972; *Selected Letters, 1917–1961,* ed. by Carlos Baker, 1981; *That Dangerous Summer,* 1985; *The Garden of Eden,* 1986; *The Complete Short Stories of Ernest Hemingway,* 1987; *True at First Light,* 1999.

Hills Like White Elephants

The hills across the valley of the Ebro[1] were long and white. On this side there was no shade and no trees and the station was between two lines of rails in the sun. Close against the side of the station there was the warm shadow of the building and a curtain, made of strings of bamboo beads, hung across the open door into the bar, to keep out flies. The American and the girl with him sat at a table in the shade, outside the building. It was very hot and the express from Barcelona would come in forty minutes. It stopped at this junction for two minutes and went on to Madrid.

"What should we drink?" the girl asked. She had taken off her hat and put it on the table.

"It's pretty hot," the man said.

"Let's drink beer."

"Dos cervezas," the man said into the curtain.

"Big ones?" a woman asked from the doorway.

"Yes. Two big ones."

The woman brought two glasses of beer and two felt pads. She put the felt pads and the beer glasses on the table and looked at the man and the girl. The girl was looking off at the line of hills. They were white in the sun and the country was brown and dry.

"They look like white elephants," she said.

"I've never seen one," the man drank his beer.

"No, you wouldn't have."

"I might have," the man said. "Just because you say I wouldn't have doesn't prove anything."

The girl looked at the bead curtain. "They've painted something on it," she said. "What does it say?"

"Anis del Toro. It's a drink."

"Could we try it?"

The man called "Listen" through the curtain. The woman came out from the bar.

"Four reales."

"We want two Anis del Toro."

"With water?"

"Do you want it with water?"

"I don't know," the girl said. "Is it good with water?"

"It's all right."

"You want them with water?" asked the woman.

"Yes, with water."

"It tastes like licorice," the girl said and put the glass down.

"That's the way with everything."

[1]River in northeast Spain that empties into the Mediterranean between Barcelona and Valencia.

"Yes," said the girl. "Everything tastes of licorice. Especially all the things you've waited so long for, like absinthe."

"Oh, cut it out."

"You started it," the girl said. "I was being amused. I was having a fine time."

"Well, let's try and have a fine time."

"All right. I was trying. I said the mountains looked like white elephants. Wasn't that bright?"

"That was bright."

"I wanted to try this new drink. That's all we do, isn't it—look at things and try new drinks?"

"I guess so."

The girl looked across at the hills.

"They're lovely hills," she said. "They don't really look like white elephants. I just meant the coloring of their skin through the trees."

"Should we have another drink?"

"All right."

The warm wind blew the bead curtain against the table.

"The beer's nice and cool," the man said.

"It's lovely," the girl said.

"It's really an awfully simple operation, Jig," the man said. "It's not really an operation at all."

The girl looked at the ground the table legs rested on.

"I know you wouldn't mind it, Jig. It's really not anything. It's just to let the air in."

The girl did not say anything.

"I'll go with you and I'll stay with you all the time. They just let the air in and then it's all perfectly natural."

"Then what will we do afterward?"

"We'll be fine afterward. Just like we were before."

"What makes you think so?"

"That's the only thing that bothers us. It's the only thing that's made us unhappy."

The girl looked at the bead curtain, put her hand out and took hold of two of the strings of beads.

"And you think then we'll be all right and be happy."

"I know we will. You don't have to be afraid. I've known lots of people that have done it."

"So have I," said the girl. "And afterward they were all so happy."

"Well," the man said, "if you don't want to you don't have to. I wouldn't have you do it if you didn't want to. But I know it's perfectly simple."

"And you really want to?"

"I think it's the best thing to do. But I don't want you to do it if you don't really want to."

"And if I do it you'll be happy and things will be like they were and you'll love me?"

"I love you now. You know I love you."

"I know. But if I do it, then it will be nice again if I say things are like white elephants, and you'll like it?"

"I'll love it. I love it now but I just can't think about it. You know how I get when I worry."

"If I do it you won't ever worry?"

"I won't worry about that because it's perfectly simple."

"Then I'll do it. Because I don't care about me."

"What do you mean?"

"I don't care about me."

"Well, I care about you."

"Oh, yes. But I don't care about me. And I'll do it and then everything will be fine."

"I don't want you to do it if you feel that way."

The girl stood up and walked to the end of the station. Across, on the other side, were fields of grain and trees along the banks of the Ebro. Far away, beyond the river, were mountains. The shadow of a cloud moved across the field of grain and she saw the river through the trees.

"And we could have all this," she said. "And we could have everything and every day we make it more impossible."

"What did you say?"

"I said we could have everything."

"We can have everything."

"No, we can't."

"We can have the whole world."

"No, we can't."

"We can go everywhere."

"No, we can't. It isn't ours any more."

"It's ours."

"No, it isn't. And once they take it away, you never get it back."

"But they haven't taken it away."

"We'll wait and see."

"Come on back in the shade," he said. "You mustn't feel that way."

"I don't feel any way," the girl said. "I just know things."

"I don't want you to do anything that you don't want to do—"

"Nor that isn't good for me," she said. "I know. Could we have another beer?"

"All right. But you've got to realize—"

"I realize," the girl said. "Can't we maybe stop talking?"

They sat down at the table and the girl looked across at the hills on the dry side of the valley and the man looked at her and at the table.

"You've got to realize," he said, "that I don't want you to do it if you don't want to. I'm perfectly willing to go through with it if it means anything to you."

"Doesn't it mean anything to you? We could get along."

"Of course it does. But I don't want anybody but you. I don't want any one else. And I know it's perfectly simple."

"Yes, you know it's perfectly simple."

"It's all right for you to say that, but I do know it."

"Would you do something for me now?"

"I'd do anything for you."

"Would you please please please please please please please stop talking?"

He did not say anything but looked at the bags against the wall of the station. There were labels on them from all the hotels where they had spent nights.

"But I don't want you to," he said, "I don't care anything about it."

"I'll scream," the girl said.

The woman came out through the curtains with two glasses of beer and put them down on the damp felt pads. "The train comes in five minutes," she said.

"What did she say?" asked the girl.

"That the train is coming in five minutes."

The girl smiled brightly at the woman, to thank her.

"I'd better take the bags over to the other side of the station," the man said. She smiled at him.

"All right. Then come back and we'll finish the beer."

He picked up the two heavy bags and carried them around the station to the other tracks. He looked up the tracks but could not see the train. Coming back, he walked through the barroom, where people waiting for the train were drinking. He drank an Anis at the bar and looked at the people. They were all waiting reasonably for the train. He went out through the bead curtain. She was sitting at the table and smiled at him.

"Do you feel better?" he asked.

"I feel fine," she said. "There's nothing wrong with me. I feel fine."

1927

from A Farewell to Arms

Chapter XXVII

I woke when Rinaldi[1] came in but he did not talk and I went back to sleep again. In the morning I was dressed and gone before it was light. Rinaldi did not wake when I left.

I had not seen the Bainsizza before and it was strange to go up the slope where the Austrians had been, beyond the place on the river where I had been wounded. There was a steep new road and many trucks. Beyond, the road flattened out and I saw woods and steep hills in the mist. There were woods that had been taken quickly and not smashed. Then beyond where the road was not protected by the hills it was screened by matting on the sides and over the top. The road ended in a wrecked village. The lines were up beyond. There was much artillery around. The houses were badly smashed but things were very well organized and there were signboards everywhere. We found Gino and he got us some coffee and later I went with him and met various people and saw the posts. Gino said the British cars were working further

[1]Major in the Italian army with whom Frederic Henry is billeted.

down the Bainsizza at Ravne. He had great admiration for the British. There was still a certain amount of shelling, he said, but not many wounded. There would be many sick now the rains had started. The Austrians were supposed to attack but he did not believe it. We were supposed to attack too, but they had not brought up any new troops so he thought that was off too. Food was scarce and he would be glad to get a full meal in Gorizia. What kind of supper had I had? I told him and he said that would be wonderful. He was especially impressed by the *dolce.* I did not describe it in detail, only said it was a *dolce,* and I think he believed it was something more elaborate than bread pudding.

Did I know where he was going to go? I said I didn't but that some of the other cars were at Caporetto. He hoped he would go up that way. It was a nice little place and he liked the high mountain hauling up beyond. He was a nice boy and every one seemed to like him. He said where it really had been hell was at San Gabriele and the attack beyond Lom that had gone bad. He said the Austrians had a great amount of artillery in the woods along Ternova ridge beyond and above us, and shelled the roads badly at night. There was a battery of naval guns that had gotten on his nerves. I would recognize them because of their flat trajectory. You heard the report and then the shriek commenced almost instantly. They usually fired two guns at once, one right after the other, and the fragments from the burst were enormous. He showed me one, a smoothly jagged piece of metal over a foot long. It looked like babbitting metal.[2]

"I don't suppose they are so effective," Gino said. "But they scare me. They all sound as though they came directly for you. There is the boom, then instantly the shriek and burst. What's the use of not being wounded if they scare you to death?"

He said there were Croats in the lines opposite us now and some Magyars. Our troops were still in the attacking positions. There was no wire to speak of and no place to fall back to if there should be an Austrian attack. There were fine positions for defense along the low mountains that came up out of the plateau but nothing had been done about organizing them for defense. What did I think about the Bainsizza anyway?

I had expected it to be flatter, more like a plateau. I had not realized it was so broken up.

"Alto piano,"[3] Gino said, "but no piano."

We went back to the cellar of the house where he lived. I said I thought a ridge that flattened out on top and had a little depth would be easier and more practical to hold than a succession of small mountains. It was no harder to attack up a mountain than on the level, I argued. "That depends on the mountains," he said. "Look at San Gabriele."

"Yes," I said, "but where they had trouble was at the top where it was flat. They got up to the top easy enough."

"Not so easy," he said.

"Yes," I said, "but that was a special case because it was a fortress rather than a mountain, anyway. The Austrians had been fortifying it for years." I meant tactically

[2]Alloy of tin, antimony, and copper that reduces friction on bearings, named for its American inventor, Isaac Babbitt (1799–1862).

[3]Italian: high plateau.

speaking in a war where there was some movement a succession of mountains were nothing to hold as a line because it was too easy to turn them. You should have possible mobility and a mountain is not very mobile. Also, people always over-shoot downhill. If the flank were turned, the best men would be left on the highest mountains. I did not believe in a war in mountains. I had thought about it a lot, I said. You pinched off one mountain and they pinched off another but when something really started every one had to get down off the mountains.

What were you going to do if you had a mountain frontier? he asked.

I had not worked that out yet, I said, and we both laughed. "But," I said, "in the old days the Austrians were always whipped in the quadrilateral around Verona. They let them come down onto the plain and whipped them there."

"Yes," said Gino. "But those were Frenchmen and you can work out military problems clearly when you are fighting in somebody else's country."

"Yes," I agreed, "when it is your own country you cannot use it so scientifically."

"The Russians did, to trap Napoleon."

"Yes, but they had plenty of country. If you tried to retreat to trap Napoleon in Italy you would find yourself in Brindisi."

"A terrible place," said Gino. "Have you ever been there?"

"Not to stay."

"I am a patriot," Gino said. "But I cannot love Brindisi or Taranto."

"Do you love the Bainsizza?" I asked.

"The soil is sacred," he said. "But I wish it grew more potatoes. You know when we came here we found fields of potatoes the Austrians had planted."

"Has the food really been short?"

"I myself have never had enough to eat but I am a big eater and I have not starved. The mess is average. The regiments in the line get pretty good food but those in support don't get so much. Something is wrong somewhere. There should be plenty of food."

"The dogfish are selling it somewhere else."

"Yes, they give the battalions in the front line as much as they can but the ones in back are very short. They have eaten all the Austrians' potatoes and chestnuts from the woods. They ought to feed them better. We are big eaters. I am sure there is plenty of food. It is very bad for the soldiers to be short of food. Have you ever noticed the difference it makes in the way you think?"

"Yes," I said. "It can't win a war but it can lose one."

"We won't talk about losing. There is enough talk about losing. What has been done this summer cannot have been done in vain."

I did not say anything. I was always embarrassed by the words sacred, glorious, and sacrifice and the expression in vain. We had heard them, sometimes standing in the rain almost out of earshot, so that only the shouted words came through, and had read them, on proclamations that were slapped up by billposters over other proclamations, now for a long time, and I had seen nothing sacred, and the things that were glorious had no glory and the sacrifices were like the stockyards at Chicago if nothing was done with the meat except to bury it. There were many words that you could not stand to hear and finally only the names of places had dignity. Certain numbers were the same way and certain dates and these with the names of the places were all you could say and have them mean anything. Abstract words such as glory, honor, courage, or hallow were obscene beside the concrete names of villages, the numbers of roads, the names of rivers, the numbers of regiments and the dates. Gino was a patriot, so he said things that separated us sometimes, but he was also a fine boy and I understood his being a patriot. He was born one. He left with Peduzzi in the car to go back to Gorizia.

It stormed all that day. The wind drove down the rain and everywhere there was standing water and mud. The plaster of the broken houses was gray and wet. Late in the afternoon the rain stopped and from out number two post I saw the bare wet autumn country with clouds over the tops of the hills and the straw screening over the roads wet and dripping. The sun came out once before it went down and shone on the bare woods beyond the ridge. There were many Austrian guns in the woods beyond the ridge but only a few fired. I watched the sudden round puffs of shrapnel smoke in the sky above a broken farmhouse near where the line was; soft puffs with a yellow white flash in the centre. You saw the flash, then heard the crack, then saw the smoke ball distort and thin in the wind. There were many iron shrapnel balls in the rubble of the houses and on the road beside the broken house where the post was, but they did not shell near the post that afternoon. We loaded two cars and drove down the road that was screened with wet mats and the last of the sun came through in the breaks between the strips of mattings. Before we were out on the clear road behind the hill the sun was down. We went on down the clear road and as it turned a corner into the open and went into the square arched tunnel of matting the rain started again.

The wind rose in the night and at three o'clock in the morning with the rain coming in sheets there was a bombardment and the Croatians came over across the mountain meadows and through patches of woods and into the front line. They fought in the dark in the rain and a counter-attack of scared men from the second line drove them back. There was much shelling and many rockets in the rain and machine-gun and rifle fire all along the line. They did not come again and it was quieter and between the gusts of wind and rain we could hear the sound of a great bombardment far to the north.

The wounded were coming into the post, some were carried on stretchers, some walking and some were brought on the backs of men that came across the field. They were wet to the skin and all were scared. We filled two cars with stretcher cases as they came up from the cellar of the post and as I shut the door of the second car and fastened it I felt the rain on my face turn to snow. The flakes were coming heavy and fast in the rain.

When daylight came the storm was still blowing but the snow had stopped. It had melted as it fell on the wet ground and now it was raining again. There was another attack just after daylight but it was unsuccessful. We expected an attack all day but it did not come until the sun was going down. The bombardment started to the south below the long wooded ridge where the Austrian guns were concentrated. We expected a bombardment but it did not come. It was getting dark. Guns were firing from the field behind the village and the shells, going away, had a comfortable sound.

We heard that the attack to the south had been unsuccessful. They did not attack that night but we heard that they had broken through to the north. In the night word came that we were to prepare to retreat. The captain at the post told me this. He had it from the Brigade. A little while later he came from the telephone and said it was a lie. The Brigade had received orders that the line of the Bainsizza should be held no matter what happened. I asked about the break through and he said that he had heard at the Brigade that the Austrians had broken through the twenty-seventh army corps up toward Caporetto. There had been a great battle in the north all day.

"If those bastards let them through we are cooked," he said.

"It's Germans that are attacking," one of the medical officers said. The word Germans was something to be frightened of. We did not want to have anything to do with the Germans.

"There are fifteen divisions of Germans," the medical officer said. "They have broken through and we will be cut off."

"At the Brigade, they say this line is to be held. They say they have not broken through badly and that we will hold a line across the mountains from Monte Maggiore."

"Where do they hear this?"

"From the Division."

"The word that we were to retreat came from the Division."

"We work under the Army Corps," I said. "But here I work under you. Naturally when you tell me to go I will go. But get the orders straight."

"The orders are that we stay here. You clear the wounded from here to the clearing station."

"Sometimes we clear from the clearing station to the field hospitals too," I said. "Tell me, I have never seen a retreat—if there is a retreat how are all the wounded evacuated?"

"They are not. They take as many as they can and leave the rest."

"What will I take in the cars?"

"Hospital equipment."

"All right," I said.

The next night the retreat started. We heard that Germans and Austrians had broken through in the north and were coming down the mountain valleys toward Cividale and Udine. The retreat was orderly, wet and sullen. In the night, going slowly along the crowded roads we passed troops marching under the rain, guns, horses pulling wagons, mules, motor trucks, all moving away from the front. There was no more disorder than in an advance.

That night we helped empty the field hospitals that had been set up in the least ruined villages of the plateau, taking the wounded down to Plava on the river-bed: and the next day hauled all day in the rain to evacuate the hospitals and clearing station at Plava. It rained steadily and the army of the Bainsizza moved down off the plateau in the October rain and across the river where the great victories had commenced in the spring of that year. We came into Gorizia in the middle of the next day. The rain had stopped and the town was nearly empty. As we came up the street they were loading the girls from the soldiers' whorehouse into a truck. There were seven girls and they had on their hats and coats and carried small suitcases. Two of them were crying. Of the others one smiled at us and put out her tongue and fluttered it up and down. She had thick full lips and black eyes.

I stopped the car and went over and spoke to the matron. The girls from the officers' house had left early that morning, she said. Where were they going? To Conegliano, she said. The truck started. The girl with thick lips put out her tongue again at us. The matron waved. The two girls kept on crying. The others looked interestedly out at the town. I got back in the car.

"We ought to go with them," Bonello said. "That would be a good trip."

"We'll have a good trip," I said.

"We'll have a hell of a trip."

"That's what I mean," I said. We came up the drive to the villa.

"I'd like to be there when some of those tough babies climb in and try and hop them."

"You think they will?"

"Sure. Everybody in the Second Army knows that matron."

We were outside the villa.

"They call her the Mother Superior," Bonello said. "The girls are new but everybody knows her. They must have brought them up just before the retreat."

"They'll have a time."

"I'll say they'll have a time. I'd like to have a crack at them for nothing. They charge too much at that house anyway. The government gyps us."

"Take the car out and have the mechanics go over it," I said. "Change the oil and check the differential. Fill it up and then get some sleep."

"Yes, Signor Tenente."

The villa was empty. Rinaldi was gone with the hospital. The major was gone taking hospital personnel in the staff car. There was a note on the window for me to fill the cars with the material piled in the hall and to proceed to Pordenone. The mechanics were gone already. I went out back to the garage. The other two cars came in while I was there and their drivers got down. It was starting to rain again.

"I'm so —— sleepy I went to sleep three times coming here from Plava," Piani said. "What are we going to do, Tenente?"

"We'll change the oil, grease them, fill them up, then take them around in front and load up the junk they've left."

"Then do we start?"

"No, we'll sleep for three hours."

"Christ I'm glad to sleep," Bonello said. "I couldn't keep awake driving."

"How's your car, Aymo?" I asked.

"It's all right."

"Get me a monkey suit and I'll help you with the oil."

"Don't you do that, Tenente," Aymo said. "It's nothing to do. You go and pack your things."

"My things are all packed," I said. "I'll go and carry out the stuff that they left for us. Bring the cars around as soon as they're ready."

They brought the cars around to the front of the villa and we loaded them with the hospital equipment which was piled in the hallway. When it was all in, the three cars stood in line down the driveway under the trees in the rain. We went inside.

"Make a fire in the kitchen and dry your things," I said.

"I don't care about dry clothes," Piani said. "I want to sleep."

"I'm going to sleep on the major's bed," Bonello said. "I'm going to sleep where the old man corks off."

"I don't care where I sleep," Piani said.

"There are two beds in here." I opened the door.

"I never knew what was in that room," Bonello said.

"That was old fish-face's room," Piani said.

"You two sleep in there," I said. "I'll wake you."

"The Austrians will wake us if you sleep too long, Tenente," Bonello said.

"I won't oversleep," I said. "Where's Aymo?"

"He went out in the kitchen."

"Get to sleep," I said.

"I'll sleep," Piani said. "I've been asleep sitting up all day. The whole top of my head kept coming down over my eyes."

"Take your boots off," Bonello said. "That's old fish-face's bed."

"Fish-face is nothing to me." Piani lay on the bed, his muddy boots straight out, his head on his arm. I went out to the kitchen. Aymo had a fire in the stove and a kettle of water on.

"I thought I'd start some *pasta asciutta,*" he said. "We'll be hungry when we wake up."

"Aren't you sleepy, Bartolomeo?"

"Not so sleepy. When the water boils I'll leave it. The fire will go down."

"You'd better get some sleep," I said. "We can eat cheese and monkey meat."

"This is better," he said. "Something hot will be good for those two anarchists. You go to sleep, Tenente."

"There's a bed in the major's room."

"You sleep there."

"No, I'm going up to my old room. Do you want a drink, Bartolomeo?"

"When we go, Tenente. Now it wouldn't do me any good."

"If you wake in three hours and I haven't called you, wake me, will you?"

"I haven't any watch, Tenente."

"There's a clock on the wall in the major's room."

"All right."

I went out then through the dining-room and the hall and up the marble stairs to the room where I had lived with Rinaldi. It was raining outside. I went to the window and looked out. It was getting dark and I saw the three cars standing in line under the trees. The trees were dripping in the rain. It was cold and the drops hung to the branches. I went back to Rinaldi's bed and lay down and let sleep take me.

We ate in the kitchen before we started. Aymo had a basin of spaghetti with onions and tinned meat chopped up in it. We sat around the table and drank two bottles of the wine that had been left in the cellar of the villa. It was dark outside and still raining. Piani sat at the table very sleepy.

"I like a retreat better than an advance," Bonello said. "On a retreat we drink barbera."

"We drink it now. To-morrow maybe we drink rainwater," Aymo said.

"To-morrow we'll be in Udine. We'll drink champagne. That's where the slackers live. Wake up, Piani! We'll drink champagne to-morrow in Udine!"

"I'm awake," Piani said. He filled his plate with the spaghetti and meat. "Couldn't you find tomato sauce, Barto?"

"There wasn't any," Aymo said.

"We'll drink champagne in Udine," Bonello said. He filled his glass with the clear red barbera.

"We may drink —— before Udine," Piani said.

"Have you eaten enough, Tenente?" Aymo asked.

"I've got plenty. Give me the bottle, Bartolomeo."

"I have a bottle apiece to take in the cars," Aymo said.

"Did you sleep at all?"

"I don't need much sleep. I slept a little."

"To-morrow we'll sleep in the king's bed,"[4] Bonello said. He was feeling very good.

"To-morrow maybe we'll sleep in ——," Piani said.

"I'll sleep with the queen," Bonello said. He looked to see how I took the joke.

"You'll sleep with ——," Piani said sleepily.

"That's treason, Tenente," Bonello said. "Isn't that treason?"

"Shut up," I said. "You get too funny with a little wine." Outside it was raining hard. I looked at my watch. It was half-past nine.

"It's time to roll," I said and stood up.

"Who are you going to ride with, Tenente?" Bonello asked.

"With Aymo. Then you come. Then Piani. We'll start out on the road for Cormons."

"I'm afraid I'll go to sleep," Piani said.

"All right. I'll ride with you. Then Bonello. Then Aymo."

"That's the best way," Piani said. "Because I'm so sleepy."

"I'll drive and you sleep awhile."

"No. I can drive just so long as I know somebody will wake me up if I go to sleep."

"I'll wake you up. Put out the lights, Barto."

"You might as well leave them," Bonello said. "We've got no more use for this place."

"I have a small locker trunk in my room," I said. "Will you help take it down, Piani?"

"We'll take it," Piani said. "Come on, Aldo." He went off into the hall with Bonello. I heard them going upstairs.

"This was a fine place," Bartolomeo Aymo said. He put two bottles of wine and half a cheese into his haversack. "There won't be a place like this again. Where will they retreat to, Tenente?"

"Beyond the Tagliamento, they say. The hospital and the sector are to be at Pordenone."

"This is a better town than Pordenone."

"I don't know Pordenone," I said. "I've just been through there."

"It's not much of a place," Aymo said.

1927

[4]Victor Emmanuel III, King of Italy from 1900 to 1946.

Wallace Stevens 1879–1955

Wallace Stevens, the poet of lush word patterns and evocative images, lived a circumspect daily life that contrasted dramatically with the profession of poet. In his position as vice president of the Hartford Accident and Indemnity Insurance Company, Stevens used his law degree for the betterment of his field, and never mentioned to his associates that he was also a poet. Even when his *Collected Poems* won the Pulitzer Prize and the National Book Award, he remained first an insurance executive.

The son of an attorney, Stevens was born and reared in Reading, Pennsylvania. He attended Harvard for three years as a special student, studying languages and publishing poems in the *Harvard Advocate.* George Santayana befriended him during that time. For a year he wrote for the New York *Herald Tribune,* but he did not enjoy journalism. He then entered the New York University Law School, and in 1904 was admitted to the New York Bar and began to practice law. A partnership failed; he worked in several firms and, in 1909, married Elsie Moll. His move to the insurance field occurred in 1916.

Although Stevens began to publish his mature poems in *Poetry* and elsewhere in 1914, it was 1923 before *Harmonium,* his first book, was published. Many of Stevens's best-known poems were included in that collection, but little notice of it was taken until 1931, when it was reissued. Then Stevens published three collections in quick succession, establishing himself as one of the most skilled and original of America's modernists. In 1946 he was chosen as a member of the National Institute of Arts and Letters; in 1950 he won the Bollingen Prize for Poetry, and in 1955 both the Pulitzer Prize for Poetry and the National Book Award.

A distinctively original poet, Stevens was not afraid to write about seemingly "philosophical" subjects, even in a period when the modernist writers concentrated on objects (and Williams said, "No ideas but in things"). Stevens's art was usually grounded in those things, however, and he called himself a poet of the earth. He met the sometimes rigid demands of the modernists, and yet preserved his own inclination to re-create beauty—the sheer colors of a tropical landscape, the efflorescence of the ocean depths, the stark icy silhouette of a snow-covered tree. For all his interest in abstractions, Stevens was a highly visual poet. He was also the poet of language as sounded speech, and many of his best poems are most effective when read aloud. Stevens did not write from the point of view of a persona—either himself or a disguised person—but he did write with such a true sense of inflected speech that his line, his sound, were his own. "One must have a mind of winter," "The Snow Man" opens, and while the reader is not sure the speaking voice is that of Stevens, he or she is convinced that it is the voice of some observer or listener. Authenticity rather than personality marks Stevens's writing.

Most of Stevens's poems are far from somber, although their meditative pace and generally long lines suggest a seriousness that might turn dour. Instead, he sparks parts of single poems (which are often lengthy) as well as entire collections with comic touches. Like Roethke, Stevens sees with the childlike eyes of innocence. Like Cummings, he was not afraid to share his vision with a world that might have scoffed at its ingenuousness. All the joy and power of language used at its best, and for a myriad of its best effects, is evident in Stevens's work.

Linda Wagner-Martin
University of North Carolina at Chapel Hill

PRIMARY WORKS

Harmonium, 1923, 1931; *Ideas of Order,* 1935; *The Man with the Blue Guitar,* 1937; *Parts of a World,* 1942; *Transport to Summer,* 1947; *The Auroras of Autumn,* 1950; *The Necessary Angel,* 1951; *Collected Poems,* 1954; *Letters,* 1966; Milton J. Bates, ed., *Sur Plusiers Beaux Sujects: Wallace Stevens' Commonplace Book,* 1989.

Sunday Morning

I

Complacencies of the peignoir, and late
Coffee and oranges in a sunny chair,
And the green freedom of a cockatoo
Upon a rug mingle to dissipate
The holy hush of ancient sacrifice.
She dreams a little, and she feels the dark
Encroachment of that old catastrophe,
As a calm darkens among water-lights.
The pungent oranges and bright, green wings
Seem things in some procession of the dead,
Winding across wide water, without sound.
The day is like wide water, without sound,
Stilled for the passing of her dreaming feet
Over the seas, to silent Palestine,
Dominion of the blood and sepulchre.

II

Why should she give her bounty to the dead?
What is divinity if it can come
Only in silent shadows and in dreams?
Shall she not find in comforts of the sun,
In pungent fruit and bright, green wings, or else
In any balm or beauty of the earth,
Things to be cherished like the thought of heaven?
Divinity must live within herself:
Passions of rain, or moods in falling snow;
Grievings in loneliness, or unsubdued
Elations when the forest blooms; gusty
Emotions on wet roads on autumn nights;
All pleasures and all pains, remembering
The bough of summer and the winter branch.
These are the measures destined for her soul.

III

Jove[1] in the clouds had his inhuman birth.
No mother suckled him, no sweet land gave
Large-mannered motions to his mythy mind.
He moved among us, as a muttering king,
Magnificent, would move among his hinds,
Until our blood, commingling, virginal,
With heaven, brought such requital to desire
The very hinds discerned it, in a star.
Shall our blood fail? Or shall it come to be
The blood of paradise? And shall the earth,
Seem all of paradise that we shall know?
The sky will be much friendlier then than now,
A part of labor and a part of pain,
And next in glory to enduring love,
Not this dividing and indifferent blue.

IV

She says, "I am content when wakened birds,
Before they fly, test the reality
Of misty fields, by their sweet questionings;
But when the birds are gone, and their warm fields
Return no more, where, then, is paradise?"
There is not any haunt of prophecy,
Nor any old chimera[2] of the grave,
Neither the golden underground, nor isle
Melodious, where spirits gat them home,
Nor visionary south, nor cloudy palm
Remote on heaven's hill, that has endured
As April's green endures; or will endure
Like her remembrance of awakened birds,
Or her desire for June and evening, tipped
By the consummation of the swallow's wings.

[1]Jupiter, the chief deity in Roman mythology.
[2]A fabulous fire-breathing monster in Greek mythology.

V

She says, "But in contentment I still feel
The need of some imperishable bliss."
Death is the mother of beauty; hence from her,
Alone, shall come fulfilment to our dreams
And our desires. Although she strews the leaves
Of sure obliteration on our paths,
The path sick sorrow took, the many paths
Where triumph rang its brassy phrase, or love
Whispered a little out of tenderness,
She makes the willow shiver in the sun
For maidens who were wont to sit and gaze
Upon the grass, relinquished to their feet.
She causes boys to pile new plums and pears
On disregarded plate. The maidens taste
And stray impassioned in the littering leaves.

VI

Is there no change of death in paradise?
Does ripe fruit never fall? Or do the boughs
Hang always heavy in that perfect sky,
Unchanging, yet so like our perishing earth,
With rivers like our own that seek for seas
They never find, the same receding shores
That never touch with inarticulate pang?
Why set the pear upon those river-banks
Or spice the shores with odors of the plum?
Alas, that they should wear our colors there,
The silken weavings of our afternoons,
And pick the strings of our insipid lutes!
Death is the mother of beauty, mystical,
Within whose burning bosom we devise
Our earthly mothers waiting, sleeplessly.

VII

Supple and turbulent, a ring of men
Shall chant in orgy on a summer morn
Their boisterous devotion to the sun,
Not as a god, but as a god might be,
Naked among them, like a savage source.
Their chant shall be a chant of paradise,

Out of their blood, returning to the sky;
And in their chant shall enter, voice by voice,
The windy lake wherein their lord delights,
The trees, like serafin, and echoing hills,
That choir among themselves long afterward.
They shall know well the heavenly fellowship
Of men that perish and of summer morn.
And whence they came and whither they shall go
The dew upon their feet shall manifest.

VIII

She hears, upon that water without sound,
A voice that cries, "The tomb in Palestine
Is not the porch of spirits lingering.
It is the grave of Jesus, where he lay."
We live in an old chaos of the sun,
Or old dependency of day and night,
Or island solitude, unsponsored, free,
Of that wide water, inescapable.
Deer walk upon our mountains, and the quail
Whistle about us their spontaneous cries;
Sweet berries ripen in the wilderness;
And, in the isolation of the sky,
At evening, casual flocks of pigeons make
Ambiguous undulations as they sink,
Downward to darkness, on extended wings.

1923

The Snow Man

One must have a mind of winter
To regard the frost and the boughs
Of the pine-trees crusted with snow;

And have been cold a long time
To behold the junipers shagged with ice,
The spruces rough in the distant glitter

Of the January sun; and not to think
Of any misery in the sound of the wind,
In the sound of a few leaves,

Which is the sound of the land
Full of the same wind
That is blowing in the same bare place

For the listener, who listens in the snow,
And, nothing himself, beholds
Nothing that is not there and the nothing that is.

1923

Peter Quince at the Clavier[1]

I

Just as my fingers on these keys
Make music, so the selfsame sounds
On my spirit make a music, too.

Music is feeling, then, not sound;
And thus it is that what I feel,
Here in this room, desiring you,

Thinking of your blue-shadowed silk,
Is music. It is like the strain
Waked in the elders by Susanna.[2]

Of a green evening, clear and warm,
She bathed in her still garden, while
The red-eyed elders watching, felt

The basses of their beings throb
In witching chords, and their thin blood
Pulse pizzicati of Hosanna.[3]

[1]The keyboard of an organ, harpsichord, or piano.

[2]The story of Susanna and the elders is told in the thirteenth chapter of Daniel, in the Apocrypha. Susanna, a Jewish woman of the Babylonian diaspora famed for her beauty and virtue, is caught alone in her garden by two wicked elders who attempted to coerce sex with her. She cries out for assistance, but when her house servants arrive, the elders accuse her of committing adultery with a young man who has just eluded them, a crime for which she is condemned to death. Susanna is rescued and her accusers executed instead when Daniel exposes their false testimony.

[3]Pizzicati are notes made by plucking a stringed instrument; a Hosanna is an exclamation of praise to God.

II

In the green water, clear and warm,
Susanna lay.
She searched
The touch of springs,
And found
Concealed imaginings.
She sighed,
For so much melody.

Upon the bank, she stood
In the cool
Of spent emotions.
She felt, among the leaves,
The dew
Of old devotions.

She walked upon the grass,
Still quavering.
The winds were like her maids,
On timid feet,
Fetching her woven scarves,
Yet wavering.

A breath upon her hand
Muted the night.
She turned—
A cymbal crashed,
And roaring horns.

III

Soon, with a noise like tambourines,
Came her attendant Byzantines.[4]

They wondered why Susanna cried
Against the elders by her side;

And as they whispered, the refrain
Was like a willow swept by rain.

[4]Natives of Byzantium.

Anon, their lamps' uplifted flame
Revealed Susanna and her shame.

And then, the simpering Byzantines
Fled, with a noise like tambourines.

IV

Beauty is momentary in the mind—
The fitful tracing of a portal;
But in the flesh it is immortal.

The body dies; the body's beauty lives.
So evenings die, in their green going,
A wave, interminably flowing.
So gardens die, their meek breath scenting
The cowl of winter, done repenting.
So maidens die, to the auroral
Celebration of a maiden's choral.

Susanna's music touched the bawdy strings
Of those white elders; but, escaping,
Left only Death's ironic scraping.
Now, in its immortality, it plays
On the clear viol of her memory,
And makes a constant sacrament of praise.

1923

Anecdote of the Jar

I placed a jar in Tennessee,
And round it was, upon a hill.
It made the slovenly wilderness
Surround that hill.

The wilderness rose up to it,
And sprawled around, no longer wild.
The jar was round upon the ground
And tall and of a port in air.

It took dominion everywhere.
The jar was gray and bare.

It did not give of bird or bush,
Like nothing else in Tennessee.

1923

A High-Toned Old Christian Woman

Poetry is the supreme fiction, madame.
Take the moral law and make a nave of it
And from the nave build haunted heaven. Thus,
The conscience is converted into palms,
Like windy citherns[1] hankering for hymns.
We agree in principle. That's clear. But take
The opposing law and make a peristyle,
And from the peristyle project a masque
Beyond the planets. Thus, our bawdiness,
Unpurged by epitaph, indulged at last,
Is equally converted into palms,
Squiggling like saxophones. And palm for palm,
Madame, we are where we began. Allow,
Therefore, that in the planetary scene
Your disaffected flagellants,[2] well-stuffed,
Smacking their muzzy bellies in parade,
Proud of such novelties of the sublime,
Such tink and tank and tunk-a-tunk-tunk,
May, merely may, madame, whip from themselves
A jovial hullabaloo among the spheres.
This will make widows wince. But fictive things
Wink as they will. Wink most when widows wince.

1923

[1]A stringed instrument of the guitar family popular in medieval times.

[2]Persons who whip themselves as a religious discipline.

Of Modern Poetry

The poem of the mind in the act of finding
What will suffice. It has not always had
To find: the scene was set; it repeated what
Was in the script.
Then the theatre was changed
To something else. Its past was a souvenir.

It has to be living, to learn the speech of the place.
It has to face the men of the time and to meet
The women of the time. It has to think about war
And it has to find what will suffice. It has
To construct a new stage. It has to be on that stage
And, like an insatiable actor, slowly and
With meditation, speak words that in the ear,
In the delicatest ear of the mind, repeat,
Exactly, that which it wants to hear, at the sound
Of which, an invisible audience listens,
Not to the play, but to itself, expressed
In an emotion as of two people, as of two
Emotions becoming one. The actor is
A metaphysician in the dark, twanging
An instrument, twanging a wiry string that gives
Sounds passing through sudden rightnesses, wholly
Containing the mind, below which it cannot descend,
Beyond which it has no will to rise.
It must
Be the finding of a satisfaction, and may
Be a man of skating, a woman dancing, a woman
Combing. The poem of the act of the mind.

1942

The Course of a Particular

Today the leaves cry, hanging on branches swept by wind,
Yet the nothingness of winter becomes a little less.
It is still full of icy shades and shapen snow.

The leaves cry . . . One holds off and merely hears the cry.
It is a busy cry, concerning someone else.
And though one says that one is part of everything,

There is a conflict, there is a resistance involved;
And being part is an exertion that declines:
One feels the life of that which gives life as it is.

The leaves cry. It is not a cry of divine attention,
Nor the smoke-drift of puffed-out heroes, nor human cry.
It is the cry of leaves that do not transcend themselves,

In the absence of fantasia, without meaning more
Than they are in the final finding of the ear, in the thing
Itself, until, at last, the cry concerns no one at all.

1950

Of Mere Being

The palm at the end of the mind,
Beyond the last thought, rises
In the bronze distance,

A gold-feathered bird
Sings in the palm, without human meaning,
Without human feeling, a foreign song.

You know then that it is not the reason
That makes us happy or unhappy.
The bird sings. Its feathers shine.

The palm stands on the edge of space.
The wind moves slowly in the branches.
The bird's fire-fangled feathers dangle down.

1955

William Faulkner 1897–1962

The great-grandson and namesake of Colonel William C. Falkner, a Civil War hero who was also a popular writer, William Cuthbert Faulkner aspired to greatness, even as a small child, when he listened mesmerized to tales and legends from his distinguished family's past, a history that had paled by the time it reached his rather ordinary and sometimes hostile father, Murray Falkner. William was born in New Albany, Mississippi, but the family soon moved to nearby Oxford, where Faulkner would spend most of his life.

In June 1918, Faulkner joined the

Royal Air Force of Canada; he trained as a cadet pilot in Toronto until November, when the Armistice sent him homeward again. Back in Oxford, after swaggering around the square in his uniform, telling spurious tales about his combat in France, he renewed his attempts to become both an artist and a poet. He had learned to draw from his artistically inclined grandmother and mother; enrolling as a special student at the University of Mississippi, he illustrated several campus publications, as well as some poetry sequences he wrote for various girlfriends. After dropping out of the university in 1921, Faulkner took a brief job in a New York bookstore; there he met the future wife of Sherwood Anderson, Elizabeth Prall. Returning to Oxford in December, he accepted a position as postmaster at the university, a job he held, despite a lackadaisical attitude, until late 1924. His first book of poetry, *The Marble Faun* (1924), continued his work in the decadent/neo-romantic vein.

Faulkner moved to New Orleans in 1925, where his friendship with Elizabeth Prall led to an apprenticeship with Sherwood Anderson, whom she had married. In Anderson's literary circle Faulkner became acquainted with Freud's theories of sexuality, the mythic world of anthropologist Sir James Frazer's *Golden Bough,* and the sweeping implications of the literary innovations of T. S. Eliot and James Joyce. He also absorbed the ennui and despair of the post-war generation, and melded all these influences, first in a series of literary sketches published by the *New Orleans Times Picayune* and *The Double Dealer* (a literary magazine) and then in a first novel, *Soldier's Pay.* Faulkner meanwhile left for Europe, spending time in Italy and England but reacting most strongly to France, beginning a lifelong love affair with that country. Returning to Mississippi, Faulkner took a series of jobs while working on his second novel, *Mosquitoes* (1927).

For Faulkner, 1929 marked the beginning of what critics have come to call "the great years" (extending to 1942), when he wrote the seven novels (in a total of twenty) that have been judged masterworks. The impetus for this extraordinary outburst came in *Sartoris* (1929), when Faulkner, on the advice of Anderson, decided to concentrate on what he came to call his "little postage-stamp of soil," Yoknapatawpha County; all the great novels are set there, in or around Jefferson, the county seat. The town and county obviously depict Oxford and its surrounding Lafayette County. As a result of this focus, Faulkner was able to create a mythic "cosmos" of his own, with interconnected mythic structures and characters, populating his world with all the various folk he had encountered in life; he made a determined effort to render the experience of women, blacks, and American Indians as well, and showed nostalgia for lost traditions and the vanishing wilderness while simultaneously decrying rampant materialist culture and racial injustice.

Faulkner's first masterwork, *The Sound and the Fury,* was published in 1929. Faulkner wrote this book thinking of a little girl with muddy drawers climbing a pear tree to look in on her grandmother's body lying in state in the parlor, thereby finding a metaphor for the narrative of the fall of a proud southern family. The story, told in three successive first person narrations by three brothers and finally through the consciousness of their black nurse/housekeeper, keeps circling back to the same issues in different voices, adding new levels of understanding. Documenting, in a radical new prose style, both the loss of familial love and honor and the decline of a great culture, the book caused a sensation among critics but sold poorly, as did its successor, *As I Lay Dying* (1930), which detailed the efforts of a poor-white family to bury their unembalmed mother.

Faulkner, desperate for money, embarked on the first of several unhappy stints in Hollywood as a scriptwriter (1932–1936; 1942–1945; parts of 1951 and 1954).

He found intermittent happiness during his Hollywood years. He wrote much of his next novel, *Light in August* (1932), during a trip to New York. One of his two or three greatest works, it details the deceptively simple frame story of Lena Grove, a country woman wandering the South searching for the father of her unborn child. This narrative interconnects on many levels with the one it encloses, the much longer and tragic tale of Joe Christmas, an orphan like Lena, who may or may not have black blood. The novel probes deeply into race, religion, and sexuality, and the role of memory and the past in the human consciousness.

Absalom, Absalom! (1936) is generally considered Faulkner's most monumental achievement. Four narrators, including Quentin Compson of *The Sound and the Fury* and his Harvard roommate, Shreve McCannon, attempt to decipher the mysteries surrounding the rise and fall of Thomas Sutpen, a self-made planter and God-like creator of Supten's Hundreds, a huge plantation. The novel plunges into the darker recesses of personal histories, exploring incest, inter-racial love, psychic perversion, and materialist obsession, while simultaneously rendering the sufferings of blacks and whites during the Civil War and Reconstruction, and the South's attempts to come to terms with its tragic history.

Faulkner experimented with counterpoint in *The Wild Palms* (1939), alternating chapters of two discrete narratives, one concerning a convict's efforts to bring a woman and her baby safely out of a Mississippi flood, the other focusing on a tragic and adulterous love affair. He returned to form in his last two masterworks, *The Hamlet* (1940) and *Go Down, Moses* (1942). The former, Faulkner's finest comedy, begins a trilogy of novels about the rise of the Snopes family which continues in *The Town* (1957) and *The Mansion* (1959). *Go Down, Moses,* generated by Faulkner's revision and union of existing stories, concerns the efforts of Ike McCaslin to repudiate the tragic racial history of his family, which includes his grandfather's siring of a child on his mulatto daughter. The narrative builds to a climax in what is perhaps Faulkner's most powerful and sustained piece of writing, "The Bear," which uses a hunt to explore the meaning of history, manhood, and responsibility to nature.

The course of his career was always uncertain, and all of his books except *Sanctuary* were out of print before Malcolm Cowley's publication of *The Portable Faulkner* in 1946, which began a reassessment of Faulkner's career. Faulkner's *Collected Stories* appeared in 1950, setting the stage for his acceptance of the Nobel Prize for literature in Stockholm, where his short but powerful acceptance speech caused a sensation; he predicted that man would not only endure; he would prevail.

Faulkner's last decade combined increasing bouts with illness, accident, and alcoholism, with public appearances and pronouncements. He traveled widely for the State Department (most memorably to Japan in 1955) and eventually accepted a position at the University of Virginia in Charlottesville.

His dogged, often heroic commitment to a dissection of racism indicates an agreement with W.E.B. Du Bois's assertion that "the problem of the twentieth century is the problem of the color line." Faulkner's profound sense of history and tradition was in no way a curb on his appetite for modernist solutions—both stylistic and philosophical—to literary, social, and spiritual problems. He stated, a few years before his death, that "the writer's first job . . ." is "always to search the soul . . . To search his own soul, and to give a proper, moving picture of man in the human dilemma." At its best, Faulkner's complex work courageously meets this standard.

John Lowe
Louisiana State University

PRIMARY WORKS

The Marble Faun, 1924; *Soldier's Pay,* 1926; *Mosquitoes,* 1927; *Sartoris,* 1929; *The Sound and the Fury,* 1929; *As I Lay Dying,* 1930; *Sanctuary,* 1931; *Light in August,* 1932; *Pylon,* 1935; *Absalom, Absalom!,* 1936; *The Unvanquished,* 1938; *The Wild Palms,* 1939; *The Hamlet,* 1940; *Go Down, Moses,* 1942; *Intruder in the Dust,* 1948; *Collected Stories of William Faulkner,* 1950; *Requiem for a Nun,* 1951; *A Fable,* 1954; *The Town,* 1957; *The Mansion,* 1959; *Early Prose and Poetry,* ed. Carvel Collins, 1962; *The Reivers,* 1962; *Essays, Speeches and Public Letters,* ed. James B. Meriwether, 1965; *Selected Letters of William Faulkner,* ed. Joseph L. Blotner, 1977.

A Courtship

This is how it was in the old days, when old Issetibbeha was still the Man, and Ikkemotubbe, Issetibbeha's nephew and David Hogganbeck, the white man who told the steamboat where to walk, courted Herman Basket's sister.

The People all lived in the Plantation now. Issetibbeha and General Jackson met and burned sticks and signed a paper, and now a line ran through the woods, although you could not see it. It ran straight as a bee's flight among the woods, with the Plantation on one side of it, where Issetibbeha was the Man, and America on the other side, where General Jackson was the Man. So now when something happened on one side of the line, it was a bad fortune for some and a good fortune for others, depending on what the white man happened to possess, as it had always been. But merely by occurring on the other side of that line which you couldn't even see, it became what the white men called a crime punishable by death if they could just have found who did it. Which seemed foolish to us. There was one uproar which lasted off and on for a week, not that the white man had disappeared, because he had been the sort of white man which even other white men did not regret, but because of a delusion that he had been eaten. As if any man, no matter how hungry, would risk eating the flesh of a coward or thief in this country where even in winter there is always something to be found to eat;—this land for which, as Issetibbeha used to say after he had become so old that nothing more was required of him except to sit in the sun and criticise the degeneration of the People and the folly and rapacity of politicians, the Great Spirit has done more and man less than for any land he ever heard of. But it was a free country, and if the white man wished to make a rule even that foolish in their half of it, it was all right with us.

Then Ikkemotubbe and David Hogganbeck saw Herman Basket's sister. As who did not, sooner or later, young men and old men too, bachelors and widowers too, and some who were not even widowers yet, who for more than one reason within the hut had no business looking anywhere else, though who is to say what age a man must reach or just how unfortunate he must have been in his youthful compliance, when he shall no longer look at the Herman Basket's sisters of this world and chew his bitter thumbs too, aihee. Because she walked in beauty. Or she sat in it, that is, because she did not walk at all unless she had to. One of the earliest sounds in the Plantation would be the voice of Herman Basket's aunt crying to know why she had not risen and gone to the spring for water with the other girls, which she did not do sometimes until Herman Basket himself rose and made her, or in the afternoon crying to know why she did not go to the river with the other girls and women to wash, which she did not do very often either. But she did not need to. Anyone who looks as Herman Basket's sister did at seventeen and eighteen and nineteen does not need to wash.

Then one day Ikkemotubbe saw her, who had known her all his life except during the first two years. He was Issetibbeha's sister's son. One night he got into the steamboat with David Hogganbeck and went away. And suns passed and then moons and then three high waters came and went and old Issetibbeha had entered the earth a year and his son Moketubbe was the Man when Ikkemotubbe returned, named Doom now, with the white friend called the Chevalier Soeur-Blonde de Vitry and the eight new slaves which we did not need either, and his gold-laced hat and cloak and the little gold box of strong salt and the wicker wine hamper containing the four other puppies which were still alive, and within two days Moketubbe's little son was dead and within three Ikkemotubbe whose name was Doom now was himself the Man. But he was not Doom yet. He was still just Ikkemotubbe, one of the young men, the best one, who rode the hardest and fastest and danced the longest and got the drunkest and was loved the best, by the young men and the girls and the other women too who should have had other things to think about. Then one day he saw Herman Basket's sister, whom he had known all his life except for the first two years.

After Ikkemotubbe looked at her, my father and Owl-by-Night and Sylvester's John and the other young men looked away. Because he was the best of them and they loved him then while he was still just Ikkemotubbe. They would hold the other horse for him as, stripped to the waist, his hair and body oiled with bear's grease as when racing (though with honey mixed into the bear's grease now) and with only a rope hackamore and no saddle as when racing, Ikkemotubbe would ride on his new racing pony past the gallery where Herman Basket's sister sat shelling corn or peas into the silver wine pitcher which her aunt had inherited from her second cousin by marriage's great-aunt who was old David Colbert's wife, while Log-in-the-Creek (one of the young men too, though nobody paid any attention to him. He raced no horses and fought no cocks and cast no dice, and even when forced to, he would not even dance fast enough to keep out of the other dancers' way, and disgraced both himself and the others each time by becoming sick after only five or six horns of what was never even his whiskey) leaned against one of the gallery posts and blew into his harmonica. Then one of the young men held the racing pony, and on his gaited mare now and wearing his flower-painted weskit and pigeon-tailed coat and beaver hat in which he looked handsomer than a steamboat gambler and richer even than the whisky-trader, Ikkemotubbe would ride past the gallery where Herman Basket's sister shelled another pod of peas into the pitcher and Log-in-the-Creek sat with his back against the post and blew into the harmonica. Then another of the young men would take the mare too and Ikkemotubbe would walk to Herman Basket's and sit on the gallery too in his fine clothes while Herman Basket's sister shelled another pod of peas perhaps into the silver pitcher and Log-in-the-Creek lay on his back on the floor, blowing into the harmonica. Then the whisky-trader came and Ikkemotubbe and the young men invited Log-in-the-Creek into the woods until they became tired of carrying him. And although a good deal wasted outside, as usual Log-in-the-Creek became sick and then asleep after seven or eight horns, and Ikkemotubbe returned to Herman Basket's gallery, where for a day or two at least he didn't have to not listen to the harmonica.

Finally Owl-at-Night made a suggestion. "Send Herman Basket's aunt a gift." But the only thing Ikkemotubbe owned which Herman Basket's aunt didn't, was the new racing pony. So after a while Ikkemotubbe said, "So it seems I want this girl even worse than I believed," and sent Owl-at-Night to tie the racing pony's hackamore to Herman Basket's kitchen door handle. Then he thought how Herman Basket's aunt could not even always make Herman Basket's sister just get up and go to the spring for water. Besides, she was the second cousin by marriage to the grand-niece of the wife of old David Colbert, the chief Man of all the Chickasaws in our section, and she looked upon Issetibbeha's whole family and line as mushrooms.

"But Herman Basket has been known to make her get up and go to the spring," my father said. "And I never heard her claim that old Dave Colbert's wife or his wife's niece or anybody else's wife or niece or aunt was any better than anybody else. Give Herman the horse."

"I can beat that," Ikkemotubbe said. Because there was no horse in the Plantation or America either between Natchez and Nashville whose tail Ikkemotubbe's new pony ever looked at. "I will run Herman a horse-race for his influence," he said. "Run," he told my father. "Catch Owl-at-Night before he reaches the house." So my father brought the pony back in time. But just in case Herman Basket's aunt had been watching from the kitchen window or something, Ikkemotubbe sent Owl-at-Night and Sylvester's John home for his crate of gamecocks, though he expected little from this since Herman Basket's aunt already owned the best cocks in the Plantation and won all the money every Sunday morning anyway. And when Herman Basket declined to commit himself, so a horse-race would have been merely for pleasure and money. And Ikkemotubbe said how money could not help him, and with that damned girl on his mind day and night his tongue had forgotten the savor of pleasure. But the whisky-trader always came, and so for a day or two at least he wouldn't have to not listen to the harmonica.

Then David Hogganbeck also looked at Herman Basket's sister, whom he too had been seeing once each year since the steamboat first walked to the Plantation. After a while even winter would be over and we would begin to watch the mark which David Hogganbeck had put on the landing to show us when the water would be tall enough for the steamboat to walk in. Then the river would reach the mark, and sure enough within two suns the steamboat would cry in the Plantation. Then all the People—men and women and children and dogs, even Herman Basket's sister because Ikkemotubbe would fetch a horse for her to ride and so only Log-in-the-Creek would remain, not inside the house even though it was still cold, because Herman Basket's aunt wouldn't let him stay inside the house where she would have to step over him each time she passed, but squatting in his blanket on the gallery with an old cooking-pot of fire inside the blanket with him—would stand on the landing, to watch the upstairs and the smokestack moving among the trees and hear the puffing of the smokestack and its feet walking fast in the water too when it was not crying. Then we would begin to hear David Hogganbeck's fiddle, and then the steamboat would come walking up the last of the river like a race-horse, with the smoke rolling black and its feet flinging the water aside as a running horse flings dirt, and Captain

Studenmare who owned the steamboat chewing tobacco in one window and David Hogganbeck playing his fiddle in the other, and between them the head of the boy slave who turned the wheel, who was not much more than half as big as Captain Studenmare and not even a third as big as David Hogganbeck. And all day long the trading would continue, though David Hogganbeck took little part in this. And all night long the dancing would continue, and David Hogganbeck took the biggest part in this. Because he was bigger than any two of the young men put together almost, and although you would not have called him a man built for dancing or running either, it was as if that very double size which could hold twice as much whisky as any other, could also dance twice as long, until one by one the young men fell away and only he was left. And there was horse-racing and eating, and although David Hogganbeck had no horses and did not ride one since no horse could have carried him and run fast too, he would eat a match each year for money against any two of the young men whom the People picked, and David Hogganbeck always won. Then the water would return toward the mark he had made on the landing, and it would be time for the steamboat to leave while there was still enough water in the river for it to walk in.

And then it did not go away. The river began to grow little, yet still David Hogganbeck played his fiddle on Herman Basket's gallery while Herman Basket's sister stirred something for cooking into the silver wine pitcher and Ikkemotubbe sat against a post in his fine clothes and his beaver hat and Log-in-the-Creek lay on his back on the floor with the harmonica cupped in both hands to his mouth, though you couldn't hear now whether he was blowing into it or not. Then you could see the mark which David Hogganbeck had marked on the landing while he still played his fiddle on Herman Basket's gallery where Ikkemotubbe had brought a rocking chair from his house to sit in until David Hogganbeck would have to leave in order to show the steamboat the way back to Natchez. And all that afternoon the People stood along the landing and watched the steamboat's slaves hurling wood into its stomach for steam to make it walk; and during most of that night, while David Hogganbeck drank twice as much and danced twice as long as even David Hogganbeck, so that he drank four times as much and danced four times as long as even Ikkemotubbe, even an Ikkemotubbe who at last had looked at Herman Basket's sister or at least had looked at someone else looking at her, the older ones among the People stood along the landing and watched the slaves hurling wood into the steamboat's stomach, not to make it walk but to make its voice cry while Captain Studenmare leaned out of the upstairs with the end of the crying-rope tied to the door-handle. And the next day Captain Studenmare himself came onto the gallery and grasped the end of David Hogganbeck's fiddle.

"You're fired," he said.

"All right," David Hogganbeck said. Then Captain Studenmare grasped the end of David Hogganbeck's fiddle.

"We will have to go back to Natchez where I can get money to pay you off," he said.

"Leave the money at the saloon," David Hogganbeck said. "I'll bring the boat back out next spring."

Then it was night. Then Herman Basket's aunt came out and said that if they were going to stay there all night, at least David Hogganbeck would have to stop playing his fiddle so other people could sleep. Then she came out and said for Herman Basket's sister to come in and go to bed. Then Herman Basket came out and said, "Come on now, fellows. Be reasonable." Then Herman Basket's aunt came out and said that the next time she was going to bring Herman Basket's dead uncle's shotgun. So Ikkemotubbe and David Hogganbeck left Log-in-the-Creek lying on the floor and stepped down from the gallery. "Goodnight," David Hogganbeck said.

"I'll walk home with you," Ikkemotubbe said. So they walked across the Plantation to the steamboat. It was dark and there was no fire in its stomach now because Captain Studenmare was still asleep under Issetibbeha's back porch. Then Ikkemotubbe said, "Goodnight."

"I'll walk home with you," David Hogganbeck said. So they walked back across the Plantation to Ikkemotubbe's house. But David Hogganbeck did not have time to say goodnight now because Ikkemotubbe turned as soon as they reached his house and started back toward the steamboat. Then he began to run, because David Hogganbeck still did not look like a man who could run fast. But he had not looked like a man who could dance a long time either, so when Ikkemotubbe reached the steamboat and turned and ran again, he was only a little ahead of David Hogganbeck. And when they reached Ikkemotubbe's house he was still only a little ahead of David Hogganbeck when he stopped, breathing fast but only a little fast, and held the door open for David Hogganbeck to enter.

"My house is not very much house," he said. "But it is yours." So they both slept in Ikkemotubbe's bed in his house that night. And the next afternoon, although Herman Basket would still do no more than wish him success, Ikkemotubbe sent my father and Sylvester's John with his saddle mare for Herman Basket's aunt to ride on, and he and Herman Basket ran the horse-race. And he rode faster than anyone had ever ridden in the Plantation. He won by lengths and lengths and, with Herman Basket's aunt watching, he made Herman Basket take all the money, as though Herman Basket had won, and that evening he sent Owl-at-Night to tie the racing pony's hackamore to the door-handle of Herman Basket's kitchen. But that night Herman Basket's aunt did not even warn them. She came out the first time with Herman Basket's dead uncle's gun, and hardly a moment had elapsed before Ikkemotubbe found out that she meant him too. So he and David Hogganbeck left Log-in-the-Creek lying on the gallery and they stopped for a moment at my father's house on the first trip between Ikkemotubbe's house and the steamboat, though when my father and Owl-at-Night finally found Ikkemotubbe to tell him that Herman Basket's aunt must have sent the racing pony far into the woods and hidden it because they had not found it yet, Ikkemotubbe and David Hogganbeck were both asleep in David Hogganbeck's bed in the steamboat.

And the next morning the whisky-trader came, and that afternoon Ikkemotubbe and the young men invited Log-in-the-Creek into the woods and my father and Sylvester's John returned for the whisky-trader's buckboard and, with my father and Sylvester's John driving the buckboard and Log-in-the-Creek lying on his face on top of the little house on the back of the buckboard where the whisky-kegs rode and Ikkemotubbe standing on top of the little house, wearing the used general's coat which General Jackson gave Issetibbeha, with his arms folded and one foot advanced onto Log-in-the-Creek's back, they rode slow past the gallery where David Hogganbeck played his fiddle while Herman Basket's sister stirred something for cooking into the silver wine pitcher. And when my father and Owl-at-Night found Ikkemotubbe that night to tell him they still had not found where Herman Basket's aunt had hidden the pony, Ikkemotubbe and David Hogganbeck were at Ikkemotubbe's house. And the next afternoon Ikkemotubbe and the young men invited David Hogganbeck into the woods and it was a long time this time and when they came out, David Hogganbeck was driving the buckboard while the legs of Ikkemotubbe and the other young men dangled from the open door of the little whisky-house like so many strands of vine hay and Issetibbeha's general's coat was tied by its sleeves about the neck of one of the mules. And nobody hunted for the racing pony that night, and when Ikkemotubbe waked up, he didn't know at first even where he was. And he could already hear David Hogganbeck's fiddle before he could move aside enough of the young men to get out of the little whisky-house, because that night neither Herman Basket's aunt nor Herman Basket and then finally Herman Basket's dead uncle's gun could persuade David Hogganbeck to leave the gallery and go away or even to stop playing the fiddle.

So the next morning Ikkemotubbe and David Hogganbeck squatted in a quiet place in the woods while the young men, except Sylvester's John and Owl-by-Night who were still hunting for the horse, stood on guard. "We could fight for her then," David Hogganbeck said.

"We could fight for her," Ikkemotubbe said. "But white men and the People fight differently. We fight with knives, to hurt good and to hurt quickly. That would be all right, if I were to lose. Because I would wish to be hurt good. But if I am to win, I do not wish you to be hurt good. If I am to truly win, it will be necessary for you to be there to see it. On the day of the wedding, I wish you to be present, or at least present somewhere, not lying wrapped in a blanket on a platform in the woods, waiting to enter the earth." Then my father said how Ikkemotubbe put his hand on David Hogganbeck's shoulder and smiled at him. "If that could satisfy me, we would not be squatting here discussing what to do. I think you see that."

"I think I do," David Hogganbeck said.

Then my father said how Ikkemotubbe removed his hand from David Hogganbeck's shoulder. "And we have tried whisky," he said.

"We have tried that," David Hogganbeck said.

"Even the racing pony and the general's coat failed me," Ikkemotubbe said. "I had been saving them, like a man with two hole-cards."

"I wouldn't say that the coat completely failed," David Hogganbeck said. "You looked fine in it."

"Aihee," Ikkemotubbe said. "So did the mule." Then my father said how he was not smiling either as he squatted beside David Hogganbeck, making little marks in the earth with a twig. "So there is just one other thing," he said. "And I am already beaten at that too before we start."

So all that day they ate nothing. And that night when they left Log-in-the-Creek lying on Herman Basket's gallery, instead of merely walking for a while and then running for a while back and forth between Ikkemotubbe's house and the steamboat, they began to run as soon as they left Herman Basket's. And when they lay down in the woods to sleep, it was where they would not only be free of temptation to eat but of opportunity too, and from which it would take another hard run as an appetiser to reach the Plantation for the match. Then it was morning and they ran back to where my father and the young men waited on horses to meet them and tell Ikkemotubbe that they still hadn't found where under the sun Herman Basket's aunt could have hidden the pony and to escort them back across the Plantation to the race-course, where the People waited around the table, with Ikkemotubbe's rocking chair from Herman Basket's gallery for Issetibbeha and a bench behind it for the judges. First there was a recess while a ten-year-old boy ran once around the race-track, to let them recover breath. Then Ikkemotubbe and David Hogganbeck took their places on either side of the table, facing each other across it, and Owl-at-Night gave the word.

First, each had that quantity of stewed bird chitterlings which the other could scoop with two hands from the pot. Then each had as many wild turkey eggs as he was old, Ikkemotubbe twenty-two and David Hogganbeck twenty-three, though Ikkemotubbe refused the advantage and said he would eat twenty-three too. Then David Hogganbeck said he was entitled to one more than Ikkemotubbe so he would eat twenty-four, until Issetibbeha told them both to hush and get on, and Owl-at-Night tallied the shells. Then there was the tongue, paws and melt of a bear, though for a little while Ikkemotubbe stood and looked at his half of it while David Hogganbeck was already eating. And at the half-way he stopped and looked at it again while David Hogganbeck was finishing. But it was all right; there was a faint smile on his face such as the young men had seen on it at the end of a hard running when he was going from now on not on the fact that he was still alive but on the fact that he was Ikkemotubbe. And he went on, and Owl-at-Night tallied the bones, and the women set the roasted shote on the table and Ikkemotubbe and David Hogganbeck moved back to the tail of the shote and faced one another across it and Owl-at-Night had even given the word to start until he gave another word to stop. "Give me some water," Ikkemotubbe said. So my father handed him the gourd and he even took a swallow. But the water returned as though it had merely struck the back of his throat and bounced, and Ikkemotubbe put the gourd down and raised the tail of his shirt before his bowed face and turned and walked away as the People opened aside to let him pass.

And that afternoon they did not even go to the quiet place in the woods. They stood in Ikkemotubbe's house while my father and the others stood quietly too in the background. My father said that Ikkemotubbe was not smiling now. "I was right yesterday," he said. "If I am to lose to thee, we should have used the knives. You see," he said, and now my father said he even smiled again, as at the end of the long hard running when the young men knew that he would go on, not because he was still alive but because he was Ikkemotubbe; "—you see, although I have lost, I still cannot reconcile."

"I had you beat before we started," David Hogganbeck said. "We both knew that."

"Yes," Ikkemotubbe said. "But I suggested it."

"Then what do you suggest now?" David Hogganbeck said. And now my father said how they loved David Hogganbeck at that moment as they loved Ikkemotubbe; that they loved them both at that moment while Ikkemotubbe stood before David Hogganbeck with the smile on his face and his right hand flat on David Hogganbeck's chest, because there were men in those days.

"Once more then, and then no more," Ikkemotubbe said. "The Cave." The

Cave." Then he and David Hogganbeck stripped and my father and the others oiled them, body and hair too, with bear's grease mixed with mint, not just for speed this time but for lasting too, because the Cave was a hundred and thirty miles away, over in the country of old David Colbert—a black hole in the hill which the spoor of wild creatures merely approached and then turned away and which no dog could even be beaten to enter and where the boys from among all the People would go to lie on their first Night-away-from-Fire to prove if they had the courage to become men, because it had been known among the People from a long time ago that the sound of a whisper or even the disturbed air of a sudden movement would bring parts of the roof down and so all believed that not even a very big movement or sound or maybe none at all at some time would bring the whole mountain into the cave. Then Ikkemotubbe took the two pistols from the trunk and drew the loads and reloaded them. "Whoever reaches the Cave first can enter it alone and fire his pistol," he said. "If he comes back out, he has won."

"And if he does not come back out?" David Hogganbeck said.

"Then you have won," Ikkemotubbe said.

"Or you," David Hogganbeck said.

And now my father said how Ikkemotubbe smiled again at David Hogganbeck. "Or me," he said. "Though I think I told you yesterday that such as that for me will not be victory." Then Ikkemotubbe put another charge of powder, with a wadding and bullet, into each of two small medicine bags, one for himself and one for David Hogganbeck, just in case the one who entered the Cave first should not lose quick enough, and, wearing only their shirts and shoes and each with his pistol and medicine bag looped on a cord around his neck, they emerged from Ikkemotubbe's house and began to run.

It was evening then. Then it was night, and since David Hogganbeck did not know the way, Ikkemotubbe continued to set the pace. But after a time it was daylight again and now David Hogganbeck could run by the sun and the landmarks which Ikkemotubbe described to him while they rested beside a creek, if he wished to go faster. So sometimes David Hogganbeck would run in front and sometimes Ikkemotubbe, then David Hogganbeck would pass Ikkemotubbe as he sat beside a spring or a stream with his feet in the water and Ikkemotubbe would smile at David Hogganbeck and wave his hand. Then he would overtake David Hogganbeck and the country was open now and they would run side by side in the prairies with his hand lying lightly on David Hogganbeck's shoulder, not on the top of the shoulder but lightly against the back of it until after a while he would smile at David Hogganbeck and draw ahead. But then it was sundown, and then it was dark again so Ikkemotubbe slowed and then stopped until he heard David Hogganbeck and knew that David Hogganbeck could hear him and then he ran again so that David Hogganbeck could follow the sound of his running. So when David Hogganbeck fell, Ikkemotubbe heard it and went back and found David Hogganbeck in the dark and turned him onto his back and found water in the dark and soaked his shirt in it and returned and wrung the water from the shirt into David Hogganbeck's mouth. And then it was daylight and Ikkemotubbe waked also and found a nest containing five unfledged birds and ate and brought the other three to David Hogganbeck and then he went on until he was just this side of where David Hogganbeck could no longer see him and sat down again until David Hogganbeck got up onto his feet.

And he gave David Hogganbeck the landmarks for that day too, talking back to David Hogganbeck over his shoulder as they ran, though David Hogganbeck did not need them because he never overtook Ikkemotubbe again. He never came closer than fifteen or twenty paces, although it looked at one time like he was. Because this time it was Ikkemotubbe who fell. And the country was open again so Ikkemotubbe could lie there for a long time and watch David Hogganbeck coming. Then it was sunset again, and then it was dark again, and he lay there listening to David Hogganbeck coming for a long time until it was time for Ikkemotubbe to get up and he did and they went on slowly in the dark with David Hogganbeck at least a hundred paces behind him, until he heard David Hogganbeck fall and then he lay down too. Then it was day again and he watched David Hogganbeck get up onto his feet and come slowly toward him and at last he tried to get up too but he did not and it looked like David Hogganbeck was going to come up with him. But he got up at last while David Hogganbeck was still four or five paces away and they went on until David Hogganbeck fell, and then Ikkemotubbe thought he was just watching David Hogganbeck fall until he found that he had fallen too but he got up onto his hands and knees and crawled still another ten or fifteen paces before he too lay down. And there in the sunset before him was the hill in which the Cave was, and there through the night, and there still in the sunrise.

So Ikkemotubbe ran into the Cave first, with his pistol already cocked in his hand. He told how he stopped perhaps for a second at the entrance, perhaps to look at the sun again or perhaps just to see where David Hogganbeck had stopped. But David Hogganbeck was running too and he was still only that fifteen or twenty paces behind, and besides, because of that damned sister of Herman Basket's, there had been no light nor heat either in the sun for moons and moons. So he ran into the Cave and turned and saw David Hogganbeck also running into the Cave and he cried, "Back, fool!" But David Hogganbeck still ran into the Cave even as Ikkemotubbe pointed his pistol at the roof and fired. And there was a noise, and a rushing, and a blackness and a dust, and Ikkemotubbe told how he thought, *Aihee. It comes.* But it did not, and even before the blackness he saw David Hogganbeck cast himself forward onto his hands and knees, and there was not a complete blackness either because he could see the sunlight and air and day beyond the tunnel of David Hogganbeck's arms and legs as, still on his hands and knees, David Hogganbeck held the fallen roof upon his back. "Hurry," David Hogganbeck said. "Between my legs. I can't—"

"Nay, brother," Ikkemotubbe said. "Quickly thyself, before it crushes thee. Crawl back."

"Hurry," David Hogganbeck said behind his teeth. "Hurry, damn you." And Ikkemotubbe did, and he remembered David Hogganbeck's buttocks and legs pink in the sunrise and the slab of rock which supported the fallen roof pink in the sunrise too across David Hogganbeck's back. But he did not remember where he found the pole nor how he carried it alone into the Cave and thrust it into the hole beside David Hogganbeck and stooped his own back under it and lifted until he knew that some at least of the weight of the fallen roof was on the pole.

"Now," he said. "Quickly."

"No," David Hogganbeck said.

"Quickly, brother," Ikkemotubbe said. "The weight is off thee."

"Then I can't move," David Hogganbeck said. But Ikkemotubbe couldn't move either, because now he had to hold the fallen roof up with his back and legs. So he reached one hand and grasped David Hogganbeck by the meat and jerked him backward out of the hole until he lay face-down upon the earth. And maybe some of the weight of the fallen roof was on the pole before, but now all of the weight was on it and Ikkemotubbe said how he thought, *This time surely aihee.* But it was the pole and not his back which snapped and flung him face-down too across David Hogganbeck like two flung sticks, and a bright gout of blood jumped out of David Hogganbeck's mouth.

But by the second day David Hogganbeck had quit vomiting blood, though Ikkemotubbe had run hardly forty miles back toward the Plantation when my father met him with the horse for David Hogganbeck to ride. Presently my father said, "I have a news for thee."

"So you found the pony," Ikkemotubbe said. "All right. Come on. Let's get that damned stupid fool of a white man—"

"No, wait my brother," my father said. "I have a news for thee."

And presently Ikkemotubbe said, "All right."

But when Captain Studenmare borrowed Issetibbeha's wagon to go back to Natchez in, he took the steamboat slaves too. So my father and the young men built a fire in the steamboat's stomach to make steam for it to walk, while David Hogganbeck sat in the upstairs and drew the crying-rope from time to time to see if the steam was strong enough yet, and at each cry still more of the People came to the landing until at last all the People in the Plantation except old Issetibbeha perhaps stood along the bank to watch the young men hurl wood into the steamboat's stomach:—a thing never before seen in our Plantation at least. Then the steam was strong and the steamboat began to walk and then the People began to walk too beside the steamboat, watching the young men for a while then Ikkemotubbe and David Hogganbeck for a while as the steamboat walked out of the Plantation where hardly seven suns ago Ikkemotubbe and David Hogganbeck would sit all day long and half the night too until Herman Basket's aunt would come out with Herman Basket's dead uncle's gun, on the gallery of Herman Basket's house while Log-in-the-Creek lay on the floor with his harmonica cupped to his mouth and Log-in-the-Creek's wife shelled corn or peas into old Dave Colbert's wife's grand-niece's second cousin by marriage's wine pitcher. Presently Ikkemotubbe was gone completely away, to be gone a long time before he came back named Doom, with his new white friend whom no man wished to love either and the eight more slaves which we had no use for either because at times someone would have to get up and walk somewhere to find something for the ones we already owned to do, and the fine gold-trimmed clothes and the little gold box of salt which caused the other four puppies to become dead too one after another, and then anything else which happened to stand between Doom and what he wanted. But he was not quite gone yet. He was just Ikkemotubbe yet, one of the young men, another of the young men who loved and was not loved in return and could hear the words and see the fact, yet who, like the young men who had been before him and the ones who would come after him, still could not understand it.

"But not for her!" Ikkemotubbe said. "And not even because it was Log-in-the-Creek. Perhaps they are for myself: that such a son as Log-in-the-Creek could cause them to wish to flow."

"Don't think about her," David Hogganbeck said.

"I don't. I have already stopped. See?" Ikkemotubbe said while the sunset ran down his face as if it had already been rain instead of light when it entered the window. "There was a wise man of ours who said once how a woman's fancy is like a butterfly which, hovering from flower to flower, pauses at the last as like as not where a horse has stood."

"There was a wise man of ours named Solomon who often said something of that nature too," David Hogganbeck said. "Perhaps there is just one wisdom for all men, no matter who speaks it."

"Aihee. At least, for all men one same heart-break," Ikkemotubbe said. Then he drew the crying-rope, because the boat was now passing the house where Log-in-the-Creek and his wife lived, and now the steamboat sounded like it did the first night while Captain Studenmare still thought David Hogganbeck would come and show it the way back to Natchez, until David Hogganbeck made Ikkemotubbe stop. Because they would need the steam because the steamboat did not always walk. Sometimes it crawled, and each time its feet came up there was mud on them, and sometimes it did not even crawl until David Hogganbeck drew the crying-rope as the rider speaks to the recalcitrant horse to remind it with his voice just who is up. Then it crawled again and then it walked again, until at last the People could no longer keep up, and it cried once more beyond the last bend and then there was no longer either the black shapes of the young men leaping to hurl wood into its red stomach or even the sound of its voice in the Plantation or the night. That's how it was in the old days.

1948

Delta Autumn

Soon now they would enter the Delta. The sensation was familiar to old Isaac McCaslin. It had been renewed like this each last week in November for more than fifty years—the last hill, at the foot of which the rich unbroken alluvial flatness began as the sea began at the base of its cliffs, dissolving away beneath the unhurried November rain as the sea itself would dissolve away.

At first they had come in wagons: the guns, the bedding, the dogs, the food, the whiskey, the keen heartlifting anticipation of hunting; the young men who could drive all night and all the following day in the cold rain and pitch a camp in the rain and sleep in the wet blankets and rise at daylight the next morning and hunt. There had been bear then. A man shot a doe or a fawn as quickly as he did a buck, and in the afternoons they shot wild turkey with pistols to test their stalking skill and marksmanship, feeding all but the breast to the dogs. But that time was gone now. Now they went in cars, driving faster and faster each year because the roads were better and they had farther and farther to drive, the territory in which game still existed drawing yearly inward as his life was drawing inward, until now he was the last of those who had once made the journey in wagons without feeling it and now those who accompanied him were the sons and even grandsons of the men who had ridden for twenty-four hours in the rain or sleet behind the steaming mules. They called him "Uncle Ike" now, and he no longer told anyone how near eighty he actually was because he knew as well as they did that he no longer had any business making such expeditions, even by car.

In fact, each time now, on that first night in camp, lying aching and sleepless in the harsh blankets, his blood only faintly warmed by the single thin whiskey-and-water which he allowed himself, he would tell himself that this would be his last. But he would stand that trip—he still shot almost as well as he ever had, still killed almost as much of the game he saw as he ever killed; he no longer even knew how many deer had fallen before his gun—and the fierce long heat of the next summer would renew him. Then November would come again, and again in the car with two of the sons of his old companions, whom he had taught not only how to distinguish between the prints left by a buck or a doe but between the sound they made in moving, he would look ahead past the jerking arc of the windshield wiper and see the land flatten suddenly and swoop, dissolving away beneath the rain as the sea itself would dissolve, and he would say, "Well, boys, there it is again."

This time though, he didn't have time to speak. The driver of the car stopped it, slamming it to a skidding halt on the greasy pavement without warning, actually flinging the two passengers forward until they caught themselves with their braced hands against the dash. "What the hell, Roth!" the man in the middle said. "Can't you whistle first when you do that? Hurt you, Uncle Ike?"

"No," the old man said. "What's the matter?" The driver didn't answer. Still leaning forward, the old man looked sharply past the face of the man between them, at the face of his kinsman. It was the youngest face of them all, aquiline, saturnine, a little ruthless, the face of his ancestor too, tempered a little, altered a little, staring sombrely through the streaming windshield across which the twin wipers flicked and flicked.

"I didn't intend to come back in here this time," he said suddenly and harshly.

"You said that back in Jefferson last week," the old man said. "Then you changed your mind. Have you changed it again? This ain't a very good time to——"

"Oh, Roth's coming," the man in the middle said. His name was Legate. He seemed to be speaking to no one, as he was looking at neither of them. "If it was just a buck he was coming all this distance for, now. But he's got a doe in here. Of course a old man like Uncle Ike can't be interested in no doe, not one that walks on two legs—when she's standing up, that is. Pretty light-colored, too. The one he was after them nights last fall when he said he was coon-hunting, Uncle Ike. The one I figured maybe he was still running when he was gone all that month last January. But of course a old man like Uncle Ike ain't got no interest in nothing like that." He chortled, still looking at no one, not completely jeering.

"What?" the old man said. "What's that?" But he had not even so much as glanced at Legate. He was still watching his kinsman's face. The eyes behind the spectacles were the blurred eyes of an old man, but they were quite sharp too; eyes which could still see a gun-barrel and what ran beyond it as well as any of them could. He was remembering himself now: how last year, during the final stage by motor boat in to where they camped, a box of food had been lost overboard and how on the next day his kinsman had gone back to the nearest town for supplies and had been gone overnight. And when he did return, something had happened to him. He would go into the woods with his rifle each dawn when the others went, but the old man, watching him, knew that he was not hunting. "All right," he said. "Take me and Will on to shelter where we can wait for the truck, and you can go on back."

"I'm going in," the other said harshly. "Don't worry. Because this will be the last of it."

"The last of deer hunting, or doe hunting?" Legate said. This time the old man paid no attention to him even by speech. He still watched the young man's savage and brooding face.

"Why?" he said.

"After Hitler gets through with it? Or Smith or Jones or Roosevelt or Willkie or whatever he will call himself in this country?"

"We'll stop him in this country," Legate said. "Even if he calls himself George Washington."

"How?" Edmonds said. "By singing 'God Bless America' in bars at midnight and wearing dime-store flags in our lapels?"

"So that's what's worrying you," the old man said. "I ain't noticed this country being short of defenders yet, when it needed them. You did some of it yourself twenty-odd years ago, before you were a grown man even. This country is a little mite stronger than any one man or group of men, outside of it or even inside of it either. I reckon, when the time comes and some of you have done got tired of hollering we are whipped if we don't go to war and some more are hollering we are whipped if we do, it will cope with one Austrian paper-hanger, no matter what he will be calling himself. My pappy and some other better men than any of them you named tried once to tear it in two with a war, and they failed."

"And what have you got left?" the other said. "Half the people without jobs and half the factories closed by strikes. Half the people on public dole that won't work and half that couldn't work even if they would. Too much cotton and corn and hogs, and not enough for people to eat and wear. The country full of people to tell a man how he can't raise his own cotton whether he will or won't, and Sally Rand with a sergeant's stripes and not even the fan couldn't fill the army rolls. Too much not-butter and not even the guns——"

"We got a deer camp—if we ever get to it," Legate said. "Not to mention does."

"It's a good time to mention does," the old man said. "Does and fawns both. The only fighting anywhere that ever had anything of God's blessing on it has been when man fought to protect does and fawns. If it's going to come to fighting, that's a good thing to mention and remember too."

"Haven't you discovered in—how many years more than seventy is it?—that women and children are one thing there's never any scarcity of?" Edmonds said.

"Maybe that's why all I am worrying about right now is that ten miles of river we still have got to run before we can make camp," the old man said. "So let's get on."

They went on. Soon they were going fast again, as Edmonds always drove, consulting neither of them about the speed just as he had given neither of them any warning when he slammed the car to stop. The old man relaxed again. He watched, as he did each recurrent November while more than sixty of them passed, the land which he had seen change. At first there had been only the old towns along the River and the old towns along the hills, from each of which the planters with their gangs of slaves and then of hired laborers had wrested from the impenetrable jungle of water-standing cane and cypress, gum and holly and oak and ash, cotton patches which, as the years passed, became fields and then plantations. The paths made by deer and bear became roads and then highways, with towns in turn springing up along them and along the rivers Tallahatchie and Sunflower which joined and became the Yazoo, the River of the Dead of the Choctaws—the thick, slow, black, unsunned streams almost without current, which once each year ceased to flow at all and then reversed, spreading, drowning the rich land and subsiding again, leaving it still richer.

Most of that was gone now. Now a man drove two hundred miles from Jefferson before he found wilderness to hunt in. Now the land lay open from the cradling hills on the east to the rampart of levee on the west, standing horseman-tall with cotton for the world's looms—the rich black land, imponderable and vast, fecund up to the very doorsteps of the Negroes who worked it and of the white men who owned it; which exhausted the hunting life of a dog in one year, the working life of a mule in five and of a man in twenty—the land in which neon flashed past them from the little countless towns, and countless shining this-year's automobiles sped past them on the broad plumb-ruled highways, yet in which the only permanent mark of man's occupation seemed to be the tremendous gins, constructed in sections of sheet iron and in a week's time though they were, since no man, millionaire though he be, would build more than a roof and walls to shelter the camping equipment he lived from, when he knew that once each ten years or so his house would be flooded to the second storey and all within it ruined;—the land across which there came now no scream of panther but instead the long hooting of locomotives: trains of incredible length and drawn by a single engine, since there was no gradient anywhere and no elevation save those raised by forgotten aboriginal hands as refuges from the yearly water and used by their Indian successors to sepulchre their fathers' bones, and all that remained of that old time were the Indian names on the little towns and usually pertaining to water—Aluschaskuna, Tillatoba, Homochitto, Yazoo.

By early afternoon, they were on water. At the last little Indian-named town at the end of pavement they waited until the other car and the two trucks—the one carrying the bedding and tents and food, the other the horses—overtook them. They left the concrete and, after another mile or so, the gravel too. In caravan they ground on through the ceaselessly dissolving afternoon, with skid-chains on the wheels now, lurching and splashing and sliding among the ruts, until presently it seemed to him that the retrograde of his remembering had gained an inverse velocity from their own slow progress, that the land had retreated not in minutes from the last spread of gravel but in years, decades, back toward what it had been when he first knew it: the road they now followed once more the ancient pathway of bear and deer, the diminishing fields they now passed once more scooped punily and terrifically by axe and saw and mule-drawn plow from the wilderness' flank, out of the brooding and immemorial tangle, in place of ruthless mile-wide parallelograms wrought by ditching the dyking machinery.

They reached the river landing and unloaded, the horses to go overland down stream to a point opposite the camp and swim the river, themselves and the bedding and food and dogs and guns in the motor launch. It was himself, though no horseman, no farmer, not even a countryman save by his distant birth and boyhood, who coaxed and soothed the two horses, drawing them by his own single frail hand until, backing, filling, trembling a little, they surged, halted, then sprang scrambling down from the truck, possessing no affinity for them as creatures, beasts, but being merely insulated by his years and time from the corruption of steel and oiled moving parts which tainted the others.

Then, his old hammer double gun which was only twelve years younger than he standing between his knees, he watched even the last puny marks of man—cabin, clearing, the small and irregular fields which a year ago were jungle and in which the skeleton stalks of this year's cotton stood almost as tall and rank as the old cane had stood, as if man had had to marry his planting to the wilderness in order to conquer it—fall away and vanish. The twin banks marched with wilderness as he remembered it—the tangle of brier and cane impenetrable even to sight twenty feet away, the tall tremendous soaring of oak and gum and ash and hickory which had rung to no axe save the hunter's, had echoed to no machinery save the beat of old-time steam boats traversing it or to the snarling of launches like their own of people going into it to dwell for a week or two weeks because it was still wilderness. There was some of it left, although now it was two hundred miles from Jefferson when once it had been thirty. He had watched it, not being conquered, destroyed, so much as retreating since its purpose was served now and its time an outmoded time, retreating southward through this inverted-apex, this ▽-shaped section of earth between hills and River until what was left of it seemed now to be gathered and for the time arrested in one tremendous density of brooding and inscrutable impenetrability at the ultimate funnelling tip.

They reached the site of their last-year's camp with still two hours left of light. "You go on over under that driest tree and set down," Legate told him. "—if you can find it. Me and these other young boys will do this." He did neither. He was not tired yet. That would come later. *Maybe it won't come at all this time,* he thought, as he had thought at this point each November for the last five or six of them. *Maybe I will go out on stand in the morning too;* knowing that he would not, not even if he took the advice and sat down under the driest shelter and did nothing until camp was made and supper cooked. Because it would not be the fatigue. It would be because he would not sleep tonight but would lie instead wakeful and peaceful on the cot amid the tent-filling snoring and the rain's whisper as he always did on the first night in camp; peaceful, without regret or fretting, telling himself that was all right too, who didn't have so many of them left as to waste one sleeping.

In his slicker he directed the unloading of the boat—the tents, the stove, the bedding, the food for themselves and the dogs until there should be meat in camp. He sent two of the Negroes to cut firewood; he had the cook-tent raised and the stove up and a fire going and supper cooking while the big tent was still being staked down. Then in the beginning of dusk he crossed in the boat to where the horses waited, backing and snorting at the water. He took the lead-ropes and with no more weight than that and his voice, he drew them down into the water and held them beside the boat with only their heads above the surface, as though they actually were suspended from his frail and strengthless old man's hands, while the boat recrossed and each horse in turn lay prone in the shallows, panting and trembling, its eyes rolling in the dusk, until the same weightless hand and unraised voice gathered it surging upward, splashing and thrashing up the bank.

Then the meal was ready. The last of light was gone now save the thin stain of it snared somewhere between the river's surface and the rain. He had the single glass of thin whiskey-and-water, then, standing in the churned mud beneath the stretched tarpaulin, he said grace over the fried slabs of pork, the hot soft shapeless bread, the canned beans and molasses and coffee in iron plates and cups,—the town food, brought along with them—then covered himself again, the others following. "Eat," he said. "Eat it all up. I don't want a piece of town meat in camp after breakfast tomorrow. Then you boys will hunt. You'll have to. When I first started hunting in this bottom sixty years ago with old General Compson and Major de Spain and Roth's grandfather and Will Legate's too, Major de Spain wouldn't allow but two pieces of foreign grub in his camp. That was one side of pork and one ham or beef. And not to eat for the first supper and breakfast neither. It was to save until along toward the end of camp when everybody was so sick of bear meat and coon and venison that we couldn't even look at it."

"I thought Uncle Ike was going to say the pork and beef was for the dogs," Legate said, chewing. "But that's right; I remember. You just shot the dogs a mess of wild turkey every evening when they got tired of deer guts."

"Times are different now," another said. "There was game here then."

"Yes," the old man said quietly. "There was game here then."

"Besides, they shot does then too," Legate said. "As it is now, we ain't got but one doe-hunter in——"

"And better men hunted it," Edmonds said. He stood at the end of the rough plank table, eating rapidly and steadily as the others ate. But again the old man looked sharply across at the sullen, handsome, brooding face which appeared now darker and more sullen still in the light of the smoky lantern. "Go on. Say it."

"I didn't say that," the old man said. "There are good men everywhere, at all times. Most men are. Some are just unlucky, because most men are a little better than their circumstances give them a chance to be. And I've known some that even the circumstances couldn't stop."

"Well, I wouldn't say—" Legate said.

"So you've lived almost eighty years," Edmonds said, "and that's what you finally learned about the other animals you lived among. I suppose the question to ask you is, where have you been all the time you were dead?"

There was a silence; for the instant even Legate's jaw stopped chewing while he gaped at Edmonds. "Well, by God, Roth—" the third speaker said. But it was the old man who spoke, his voice still peaceful and untroubled and merely grave:

"Maybe so," he said. "But if being what you call alive would have learned me any different, I reckon I'm satisfied, wherever it was I've been."

"Well, I wouldn't say that Roth—" Legate said.

The third speaker was still leaning forward a little over the table, looking at Edmonds. "Meaning that it's only because folks happen to be watching him that a man behaves at all," he said. "Is that it?"

"Yes," Edmonds said. "A man in a blue coat, with a badge on it watching him. Maybe just the badge."

"I deny that," the old man said. "I don't——"

The other two paid no attention to him. Even Legate was listening to them for the moment, his mouth still full of food and still open a little, his knife with another lump of something balanced on the tip of the blade arrested halfway to his mouth.

"I'm glad I don't have your opinion of folks," the third speaker said. "I take it you include yourself."

"I see," Edmonds said. "You prefer Uncle Ike's opinion of circumstances. All right. Who makes the circumstances?"

"Luck," the third said. "Chance. Happen-so. I see what you are getting at. But that's just what Uncle Ike said: that now and then, maybe most of the time, man is a little better than the net result of his and his neighbors' doings, when he gets the chance to be."

This time Legate swallowed first. He was not to be stopped this time. "Well, I wouldn't say that Roth Edmonds can hunt one doe every day and night for two weeks and was a poor hunter or a unlucky one neither. A man that still have the same doe left to hunt on again next year——"

"Have some meat," the man next to him said.

"—ain't so unlucky— What?" Legate said.

"Have some meat." The other offered the dish.

"I got some," Legate said.

"Have some more," the third speaker said. "You and Roth Edmonds both. Have a heap of it. Clapping your jaws together that way with nothing to break the shock." Someone chortled. Then they all laughed, with relief, the tension broken. But the old man was speaking, even into the laughter, in that peaceful and still untroubled voice:

"I still believe. I see proof everywhere. I grant that man made a heap of his circumstances, him and his living neighbors between them. He even inherited some of them already made, already almost ruined even. A while ago Henry Wyatt there said how there used to be more game here. There was. So much that we even killed does. I seem to remember Will Legate mentioning that, too—" Someone laughed, a single guffaw, stillborn. It ceased and they all listened, gravely, looking down at their plates. Edmonds was drinking his coffee, sullen, brooding, inattentive.

"Some folks still kill does," Wyatt said. "There won't be just one buck hanging in this bottom tomorrow night without any head to fit it."

"I didn't say all men," the old man said. "I said most men. And not just because there is a man with a badge to watch us. We probably won't even see him unless maybe he will stop here about noon tomorrow and eat dinner with us and check our licenses——"

"We don't kill does because if we did kill does in a few years there wouldn't even be any bucks left to kill, Uncle Ike," Wyatt said.

"According to Roth yonder, that's one thing we won't never have to worry about," the old man said. "He said on the way here this morning that does and fawns—I believe he said women and children—are two things this world ain't ever lacked. But that ain't all of it," he said. "That's just the mind's reason a man has to give himself because the heart don't always have time to bother with thinking up words that fit together. God created man and He created the world for him to live in and I reckon He created the kind of world He would have wanted to live in if He had been a man—the ground to walk on, the big woods, the trees and the water, and the game to live in it. And maybe He didn't put the desire to hunt and kill game in man but I reckon He knew it was going to be there, that man was going to teach it to himself, since he wasn't quite God himself yet——"

"When will he be?" Wyatt said.

"I think that every man and woman, at the instant when it don't even matter whether they marry or not, I think that whether they marry then or afterward or don't never, at that instant the two of them together were God."

"Then there are some Gods in this world I wouldn't want to touch, and with a damn long stick," Edmonds said. He set his coffee cup down and looked at Wyatt. "And that includes myself, if that's what you want to know. I'm going to bed." He was gone. There was a general movement among the others. But it ceased and they stood again about the table, not looking at the old man, apparently held there yet by his quiet and peaceful voice as the heads of the swimming horses had been held above the water by his weightless hand. The three Negroes—the cook and his helper and old Isham—were sitting quietly in the entrance of the kitchen tent, listening too, the three faces dark and motionless and musing.

"He put them both here: man, and the game he would follow and kill, foreknowing it. I believe He said, 'So be it.' I reckon He even foreknew the end. But He said, 'I will give him his chance. I will give him warning and foreknowledge too, along with the desire to follow and the power to slay. The woods and fields he ravages and the game he devastates will be the consequence and signature of his crime and guilt, and his punishment.'— Bed time," he said. His voice and inflection did not change at all. "Breakfast at four o'clock, Isham. We want meat on the ground by sunup time."

There was a good fire in the sheet-iron heater; the tent was warm and was beginning to dry out, except for the mud underfoot. Edmonds was already rolled into his blankets, motionless, his face to the wall. Isham had made up his bed too—the strong, battered iron cot, the stained mattress which was not quite soft enough, the worn, often-washed blankets which as the years passed were less and less warm enough. But the tent was warm; presently, when the kitchen was cleaned up and readied for breakfast, the young Negro would come in to lie down before the heater, where he could be roused to put fresh wood into it from time to time. And then, he knew now he would not sleep tonight anyway; he no longer needed to tell himself that perhaps he would. But it was all right now. The day was ended now and night faced him, but alarmless, empty of fret. *Maybe I came for this,* he thought: *Not to hunt, but for this. I would come anyway, even if only to go back home tomorrow.* Wearing only his bagging woolen underwear, his spectacles folded away in the worn case beneath the pillow where he could reach them readily and his lean body fitted easily into the old worn groove of mattress and blankets, he lay on his back, his hands crossed on his breast and his eyes closed while the others undressed and went to bed and the last of the sporadic talking died into snoring. Then he opened his eyes and lay peaceful and quiet as a child, looking up at the motionless belly of rain-murmured canvas upon which the glow of the heater was dying slowly away and would fade still further until the young Negro, lying on two planks before it, would sit up and stoke it and lie back down again.

They had a house once. That was sixty years ago, when the Big Bottom was only thirty miles from Jefferson and old Major de Spain, who had been his father's cavalry commander in '61 and '2 and '3 and '4, and his cousin (his older brother; his father too) had taken him into the woods for the first time. Old Sam Fathers was alive then, born in slavery, son of a Negro slave and a Chickasaw chief, who had taught him how to shoot, not only when to shoot but when not to; such a November dawn as tomorrow would be and the old man led him straight to the great cypress and he had known the buck would pass exactly there because there was something running in Sam Fathers' veins which ran in the veins of the buck too, and they stood there against the tremendous trunk, the old man of seventy and the boy of twelve, and there was nothing save the dawn until suddenly the buck was there, smoke-colored out of nothing, magnificent with speed: and Sam Fathers said, 'Now. Shoot quick and shoot slow:' and the gun levelled rapidly without haste and crashed and he walked to the buck lying still intact and still in the shape of that magnificent speed and bled it with Sam's knife and Sam dipped his hands into the hot blood and marked his face forever while he stood trying not to tremble, humbly and with pride too though the boy of twelve had been unable to phrase it then: *I slew you; my bearing must not shame your quitting life. My conduct forever onward must become your death;* marking him for that and for more than that: that day and himself and McCaslin juxtaposed, not against the wilderness but against the tamed land, the old wrong and shame itself, in repudiation and denial at least of the land and the wrong and shame, even if he couldn't cure the wrong and eradicate the shame, who at fourteen when he learned of it had believed he could do both when he became competent, and when at twenty-one he became competent he knew that he could do neither but at least he could repudiate the wrong and shame, at least in principle, and at least the land itself in fact, for his son at least: and did, thought he had: then (married then) in a rented cubicle in a back-street stock-traders' boarding-house, the first and last time he ever saw her naked body, himself and his wife juxtaposed in their turn against that same land, that same wrong and shame from whose regret and grief he would at least save and free his son and, saving and freeing his son, lost him.

They had the house then. That roof, the two weeks of each November which they spent under it, had become his home. Although since that time they had lived during the two fall weeks in tents and not always in the same place two years in succession and now his companions were the sons and even the grandsons of them with whom he had lived in the house, and for almost fifty years now the house itself had not even existed, the conviction, the sense and feeling of home, had been merely transferred into the canvas. He owned a house in Jefferson, a good house though small, where he had had a wife and lived with her and lost her, ay, lost her even though he had lost her in the rented cubicle before he and his old clever dipsomaniac partner had finished the house for them to move into it: but lost her, because she loved him. But women hope for so much. They never live too long to still believe that anything within the scope of their passionate wanting is likewise within the range of their passionate hope: and it was still kept for him by his dead wife's widowed niece and her children, and he was comfortable in it, his wants and needs and even the small trying harmless crochets of an old man looked after by blood at least related to the blood which he had elected out of all the earth to cherish. But he spent the time within those walls waiting for November, because even this tent with its muddy floor and the bed which was not wide enough nor soft enough nor even warm enough, was his home and these men, some of whom he only saw during these two November weeks and not one of whom even bore any name he used to know—De Spain and Compson and Ewell and Hogganbeck—were more his kin than any. Because this was his land——

The shadow of the youngest Negro loomed. It soared, blotting the heater's dying glow from the ceiling, the wood billets thumping into the iron maw until the glow, the flame, leaped high and bright across the canvas. But the Negro's shadow still remained, by its length and breadth, standing, since it covered most of the ceiling, until after a moment he raised himself on one elbow to look. It was not the Negro, it was his kinsman; when he spoke the other turned sharp against the red firelight the sullen and ruthless profile.

"Nothing," Edmonds said. "Go on back to sleep."

"Since Will Legate mentioned it," McCaslin said, "I remember you had some trouble sleeping in here last fall too. Only you called it coon-hunting then. Or was it Will Legate called it that?" The other didn't answer. Then he turned and went back to his bed. McCaslin, still propped on his elbow, watched until the other's shadow sank down the wall and vanished, became one with the mass of sleeping shadows. "That's right," he said. "Try to get some sleep. We must have meat in camp tomorrow. You can do all the setting up you want to after that." He lay down again, his hands crossed again on his breast, watching the glow of the heater on the canvas ceiling. It was steady again now, the fresh wood accepted, being assimilated; soon it would begin to fade again, taking with it the last echo of that sudden upflare of a young man's passion and unrest. Let him lie awake for a little while, he thought; He will lie still some day for a long time without even dissatisfaction to disturb him. And lying awake here, in these surroundings, would soothe him if anything could, if anything could soothe a man just forty years old. Yes, he thought; Forty years old or thirty, or even the trembling and sleepless ardor of a boy; already the tent, the rain-murmured canvas globe, was once more filled with it. He lay on his back, his eyes closed, his breathing quiet and peaceful as a child's, listening to it—that silence which was never silence but was myriad. He could almost see it, tremendous, primeval, looming, musing downward upon this puny, evanescent clutter of human sojourn which after a single brief week would vanish and in another week would be completely healed, traceless in the unmarked solitude. Because it was his land, although he had never owned a foot of it. He had never wanted to, not even after he saw plain its ultimate doom, watching it retreat year by year before the onslaught of axe and saw and log-lines and then dynamite and tractor plows, because it belonged to no man. It belonged to all; they had only to use it well, humbly and with pride. Then suddenly he knew why he had never wanted to own any of it, arrest at least that much of what people called progress, measure his longevity at least against that much of its ultimate fate. It was because there was just exactly enough of it. He seemed to see the two of them—himself and the wilderness—as coevals, his own span as a hunter, a woodsman, not contemporary with his first breath but transmitted to him, assumed by him gladly, humbly, with joy and pride, from that old Major de Spain and that old Sam Fathers who had taught him to hunt, the two spans running out together, not toward oblivion, nothingness, but into a dimension free of both time and space, where once more the untreed land warped and wrung to mathematical squares of rank cotton for the frantic old-world people to turn into shells to shoot at one another, would find ample room for both—the names, the faces of the old men he had known and loved and for a little while outlived, moving again among the shades of tall unaxed trees and sightless brakes where the wild strong immortal game ran forever before the tireless belling immortal hounds, falling and rising phoenix-like to the soundless guns.

He had been asleep. The lantern was lighted now. Outside in the darkness the oldest Negro, Isham, was beating a spoon against the bottom of a tin pan and crying, "Raise up and get yo foa clock coffy. Raise up and get yo foa clock coffy," and the tent was full of low talk and of men dressing, and Legate's voice, repeating: "Get out of here now and let Uncle Ike sleep. If you wake him up, he'll go out with us. And he ain't got any business in the woods this morning."

So he didn't move. He lay with his eyes closed, his breathing gentle and peaceful, and heard them one by one leave the tent. He listened to the breakfast sounds from the table beneath the tarpaulin and heard them depart—the horses, the dogs, the last voice until it died away and there was only the sounds of the Negroes clearing breakfast away. After a while he might possibly even hear the first faint clear cry of the first hound ring through the wet woods from where the buck had bedded, then he would go back to sleep again— The tent-flap swung in and fell. Something jarred sharply against the end of the cot and a hand grasped his knee through the blanket before he could open his eyes. It was Edmonds, carrying a shotgun in place of his rifle. He spoke in a harsh, rapid voice:

"Sorry to wake you. There will be a—"

"I was awake," McCaslin said. "Are you going to shoot that shotgun today?"

"You just told me last night you want meat," Edmonds said. "There will be a—"

"Since when did you start having trouble getting meat with your rifle?"

"All right," the other said, with that harsh, restrained, furious impatience. Then McCaslin saw in his hand a thick oblong: an envelope. "There will be a message here some time this morning, looking for me. Maybe it won't come. If it does, give the messenger this and tell h— say I said No."

"A what?" McCaslin said. "Tell who?" He half rose onto his elbow as Edmonds jerked the envelope onto the blanket, already turning toward the entrance, the envelope striking solid and heavy and without noise and already sliding from the bed until McCaslin caught it, divining by feel through the paper as instantaneously and conclusively as if he had opened the envelope and looked, the thick sheaf of banknotes. "Wait," he said. "Wait:"—more than the blood kinsman, more even than the senior in years, so that the other paused, the canvas lifted, looking back, and McCaslin saw that outside it was already day. "Tell her No," he said. "Tell her." They stared at one another—the old face, wan, sleep-raddled above the tumbled bed, the dark and sullen younger one at once furious and cold. "Will Legate was right. This is what you called coon-hunting. And now this." He didn't raise the envelope. He made no motion, no gesture to indicate it. "What did you promise her that you haven't the courage to face her and retract?"

"Nothing!" the other said. "Nothing! This is all of it. Tell her I said No." He was gone. The tent flap lifted on an in-waft of faint light and the constant murmur of rain, and fell again, leaving the old man still half-raised onto one elbow, the envelope clutched in the other shaking hand. Afterward it seemed to him that he had begun to hear the approaching boat almost immediately, before the other could have got out of sight even. It seemed to him that there had been no interval whatever: the tent flap falling on the same out-waft of faint and rain-filled light like the suspiration and expiration of the same breath and then in the next second lifted again—the mounting snarl of the outboard engine, increasing, nearer and nearer and louder and louder then cut short off, ceasing with the absolute instantaneity of a blown-out candle, into the lap and plop of water under the bows as the skiff slid in to the bank, the youngest Negro, the youth, raising the tent flap beyond which for that instant he saw the boat—a small skiff with a Negro man sitting in the stern beside the upslanted motor—then the woman entering, in a man's hat and a man's slicker and rubber boots, carrying the blanket-swaddled bundle on one arm and holding the edge of the unbuttoned raincoat over it with the other hand: and bringing something else, something intangible, an effluvium which he knew he would recognize in a moment because Isham had already told him, warned him, by sending the young Negro to the tent to announce the visitor instead of coming himself, the flap falling at last on the young Negro and they were alone—the face indistinct and as yet only young and with dark eyes, queerly colorless but not ill and not that of a country woman despite the garments she wore, looking down at him where he sat upright on the cot now, clutching the envelope, the soiled undergarment bagging about him and the twisted blankets huddled about his hips.

"Is this his?" he cried. "Don't lie to me!"

"Yes," she said. "He's gone."

"Yes. He's gone. You won't jump him here. Not this time. I don't reckon even you expected that. He left you this. Here." He fumbled at the envelope. It was not to pick it up, because it was still in his hand; he had never put it down. It was as if he had to fumble somehow to co-ordinate physically his heretofore obedient hand with what his brain was commanding of it, as if he had never performed such an action before, extending the envelope at last, saying again, "Here. Take it. Take it:" until he became aware of her eyes, or not the eyes so much as the look, the regard fixed now on his face with that immersed contemplation, that bottomless and intent candor, of a child. If she had ever seen either the envelope or his movement to extend it, she did not show it.

"You're Uncle Isaac," she said.

"Yes," he said. "But never mind that. Here. Take it. He said to tell you No." She looked at the envelope, then she took it. It was sealed and bore no superscription. Nevertheless, even after she glanced at the front of it he watched her hold it in the one free hand and tear the corner off with her teeth and manage to rip it open and tilt the neat sheaf of bound notes onto the blanket without even glancing at them and look into the empty envelope and take the edge between her teeth and tear it completely open before she crumpled and dropped it.

"That's just money," she said.

"What did you expect? What else did you expect? You have known him long enough or at least often enough to have got that child, and you don't know him any better than that?"

"Not very often. Not very long. Just that week here last fall, and in January he sent for me and we went west, to New Mexico. We were there six weeks, where I could at least sleep in the same apartment where I cooked for him and looked after his clothes——"

"But not marriage," he said. "Not marriage. He didn't promise you that. Don't lie to me. He didn't have to."

"No. He didn't have to. I didn't ask him to. I knew what I was doing. I knew that to begin with, long before honor, I imagine he called it, told him the time had come to tell me in so many words what his code, I suppose he would call it, would forbid him forever to do. And we agreed. Then we agreed again before he left New Mexico, to make sure. That that would be all of it. I believed him. No, I don't mean that; I mean I believed myself. I wasn't even listening to him any more by then because by that time it had been a long time since he had anything else to tell me for me to have to hear. By then I wasn't even listening enough to ask him to please stop talking. I was listening to myself. And I believed it. I must have believed it. I don't see how I could have helped but believe it, because he was gone then as we had agreed and he didn't write as we had agreed, just the money came to the bank in Vicksburg in my name but coming from nobody as we had agreed. So I must have believed it. I even wrote him last month to make sure again and the letter came back unopened and I was sure. So I left the hospital and rented myself a room to live in until the deer season opened so I could make sure myself and I was waiting beside the road yesterday when your car passed and he saw me and so I was sure."

"Then what do you want?" he said. "What do you want? What do you expect?"

"Yes," she said. And while he glared at her, his white hair awry from the pillow and his eyes, lacking the spectacles to focus them, blurred and irisless and apparently pupilless, he saw again that grave, intent, speculative and detached fixity like a child watching him. "His great great— Wait a minute—great great *great* grandfather was your grandfather. McCaslin. Only it got to be Edmonds. Only it got to be more than that. Your cousin McCaslin was there that day when your father and Uncle Buddy won Tennie from Mr. Beauchamp for the one that had no name but Terrel so you called him Tomey's Terrel, to marry. But after that it got to be Edmonds." She regarded him, almost peacefully, with that unwinking and heatless fixity—the dark, wide, bottomless eyes in the face's dead and toneless pallor which to the old man looked anything but dead, but young and incredibly and even ineradicably alive—as though she were not only not looking at anything, she was not even speaking to anyone but herself. "I would have made a man of him. He's not a man yet. You spoiled him. You, and Uncle Lucas and Aunt Mollie. But mostly you."

"Me?" he said. "Me?"

"Yes. When you gave to his grandfather that land which didn't belong to him, not even half of it, by will or even law."

"And never mind that too," he said. "Never mind that too. You," he said. "You sound like you have been to college even. You sound almost like a Northerner even, not like the draggle-tailed women of these Delta peckerwoods. Yet you meet a man on the street one afternoon just because a box of groceries happened to fall out of a boat. And a month later you go off with him and live with him until he got a child on you: and then, by your own statement, you sat there while he took his hat and said goodbye and walked out. Even a Delta peckerwood would look after even a draggle-tail better than that. Haven't you got any folks at all?"

"Yes," she said. "I was living with one of them. My aunt, in Vicksburg. I came to live with her two years ago when my father died; we lived in Indianapolis then. But I got a job, teaching school here in Aluschaskuna, because my aunt was a widow, with a big family, taking in washing to sup——"

"Took in what?" he said. "Took in washing?" He sprang, still seated even, flinging himself backward onto one arm, awry-haired, glaring. Now he understood what it was she had brought into the tent with her, what old Isham had already told him by sending the youth to bring her in to him—the pale lips, the skin pallid and dead-looking yet not ill, the dark and tragic and foreknowing eyes. *Maybe in a thousand or two thousand years in America,* he thought. *But not now! Not now!* He cried, not loud, in a voice of amazement, pity, and outrage: "You're a nigger!"

"Yes," she said. "James Beauchamp—you called him Tennie's Jim though he had a name—was my grandfather. I said you were Uncle Isaac."

"And he knows?"

"No," she said. "What good would that have done?"

"But you did," he cried. "But you did. Then what do you expect here?"

"Nothing."

"Then why did you come here? You said you were waiting in Aluschaskuna yesterday and he saw you. Why did you come this morning?"

"I'm going back North. Back home. My cousin brought me up the day before yesterday in his boat. He's going to take me on to Leland to get the train."

"Then go," he said. Then he cried again in that thin not loud and grieving voice: "Get out of here! I can do nothing for you! Can't nobody do nothing for you!" She moved; she was not looking at him again, toward the entrance. "Wait," he said. She paused again, obediently still, turning. He took up the sheaf of banknotes and laid it on the blanket at the foot of the cot and drew his hand back beneath the blanket. "There," he said.

Now she looked at the money, for the first time, one brief blank glance, then away again. "I don't need it. He gave me money last winter. Besides the money he sent to Vicksburg. Provided. Honor and code too. That was all arranged."

"Take it," he said. His voice began to rise again, but he stopped it. "Take it out of my tent." She came back to the cot and took up the money; whereupon once more he said, "Wait:" although she had not turned, still stooping, and he put out his hand. But, sitting, he could not complete the reach until she moved her hand, the single hand which held the money, until he touched it. He didn't grasp it, he merely touched it—the gnarled, bloodless, bone-light, bone-dry old man's fingers touching for a second the smooth young flesh where the strong old blood ran after its long lost journey back to home. "Tennie's Jim," he said. "Tennie's Jim." He drew the hand back beneath the blanket again: he said harshly now: "It's a boy, I reckon. They usually are, except that one that was its own mother too."

"Yes," she said. "It's a boy." She stood for a moment longer, looking at him. Just for an instant her free hand moved as though she were about to lift the edge of the raincoat away from the child's face. But she did not. She turned again when once more he said Wait and moved beneath the blanket.

"Turn your back," he said. "I am going to get up. I ain't got my pants on." Then he could not get up. He sat in the huddled blanket, shaking, while again she turned and looked down at him in dark interrogation. "There," he said harshly, in the thin and shaking old man's voice. "On the nail there. The tent-pole."

"What?" she said.

"The horn!" he said harshly. "The horn." She went and got it, thrust the money into the slicker's side pocket as if it were a rag, a soiled handkerchief, and lifted down the horn, the one which General Compson had left him in his will, covered with the unbroken skin from a buck's shank and bound with silver.

"What?" she said.

"It's his. Take it."

"Oh," she said. "Yes. Thank you."

"Yes," he said, harshly, rapidly, but not so harsh now and soon not harsh at all but just rapid, urgent, until he knew that his voice was running away with him and he had neither intended it nor could stop it: "That's right. Go back North. Marry: a man in your own race. That's the only salvation for you—for a while yet, maybe a long while yet. We will have to wait. Marry a black man. You are young, handsome, almost white; you could find a black man who would see in you what it was you saw in him, who would ask nothing of you and expect less and get even still less than that, if it's revenge you want. Then you will forget all this, forget it ever happened, that he ever existed—" until he could stop it at last and did, sitting there in his huddle of blankets during the instant when, without moving at all, she blazed silently down at him. Then that was gone too. She stood in the gleaming and still dripping slicker, looking quietly down at him from under the sodden hat.

"Old man," she said, "have you lived so long and forgotten so much that you don't remember anything you ever knew or felt or even heard about love?"

Then she was gone too. The waft of light and the murmur of the constant rain flowed into the tent and then out again as the flap fell. Lying back once more, trembling, panting, the blanket huddled to his chin and his hands crossed on his breast, he listened to the pop and snarl, the mounting then fading whine of the motor until it died away and once again the tent held only silence and the sound of rain. And cold too: he lay shaking faintly and steadily in it, rigid save for the shaking. This Delta, he thought: This Delta. *This land which man has deswamped and denuded and derivered in two generations so that white men can own plantations and commute every night to Memphis and black men own plantations and ride in Jim Crow cars to Chicago to live in millionaires' mansions on Lake Shore Drive; where white men rent farms and live like niggers and niggers crop on shares and live like animals; where cotton is planted and grows man-tall in the very cracks of the sidewalks, and usury and mortgage and bankruptcy and measureless wealth, Chinese and African and Aryan and Jew, all breed and spawn together until no man has time to say which one is which nor cares. . . .* No wonder the ruined woods I used to know don't cry for retribution! he thought: The people who have destroyed it will accomplish its revenge.

The tent flap jerked rapidly in and fell. He did not move save to turn his head and open his eyes. It was Legate. He went quickly to Edmonds' bed and stooped, rummaging hurriedly among the still-tumbled blankets.

"What is it?" he said.

"Looking for Roth's knife," Legate said. "I come back to get a horse. We got a deer on the ground." He rose, the knife in his hand, and hurried toward the entrance.

"Who killed it?" McCaslin said. "Was it Roth?"

"Yes," Legate said, raising the flap.

"Wait," McCaslin said. He moved, suddenly, onto his elbow. "What was it?" Legate paused for an instant beneath the lifted flap. He did not look back.

"Just a deer, Uncle Ike," he said impatiently. "Nothing extra." He was gone; again the flap fell behind him, wafting out of the tent again the faint light and the constant and grieving rain. McCaslin lay back down, the blanket once more drawn to his chin, his crossed hands once more weightless on his breast in the empty tent.

"It was a doe," he said.

1940

Barn Burning

The store in which the Justice of the Peace's court was sitting smelled of cheese. The boy, crouched on his nail keg at the back of the crowded room, knew he smelled cheese, and more: from where he sat he could see the ranked shelves close-packed with the solid, squat, dynamic shapes of tin cans whose labels his stomach read, not from the lettering which meant nothing to his mind but from the scarlet devils and the silver curve of fish—this, the cheese which he knew he smelled and the hermetic meat which his intestines believed he smelled coming in intermittent gusts momentary and brief between the other constant one, the smell and sense just a little of fear because mostly of despair and grief, the old fierce pull of blood. He could not see the table where the Justice sat and before which his father and his father's enemy (*our enemy* he thought in that despair; *ourn! mine and hisn both! He's my father!*) stood, but he could hear them, the two of them that is, because his father had said no word yet:

"But what proof have you, Mr. Harris?"

"I told you. The hog got into my corn. I caught it up and sent it back to him. He had no fence that would hold it. I told him so, warned him. The next time I put the hog in my pen. When he came to get it I gave him enough wire to patch up his pen. The next time I put the hog up and kept it. I rode down to his house and saw the wire I gave him still rolled on to the spool in his yard. I told him he could have the hog when he paid me a dollar pound fee.[1] That evening a nigger came with the dollar and got the hog. He was a strange nigger. He said, 'He say to tell you wood and hay kin burn.' I said, 'What?' 'That whut he say to tell you,' the nigger said. 'Wood and hay kin burn.' That night my barn burned. I got the stock out but I lost the barn."

"Where is the nigger? Have you got him?"

"He was a strange nigger, I tell you. I don't know what became of him."

"But that's not proof. Don't you see that's not proof?"

"Get that boy up here. He knows." For a moment the boy thought too that the man meant his older brother until Harris said, "Not him. The little one. The boy," and, crouching, small for his age, small and wiry like his father, in patched and faded jeans even too small for him, with straight, uncombed, brown hair and eyes gray and wild as storm scud, he saw the men between himself and the table part and become a lane of grim faces, at the end of which he saw the Justice, a shabby, collarless, graying man in spectacles, beckoning him. He felt no floor under his bare feet; he seemed to walk beneath the palpable weight of the grim turning faces. His father, stiff in his black Sunday coat donned not for the trial but for the moving, did not even look at him. *He aims for me to lie,* he thought, again with that frantic grief and despair. *And I will have to do hit.*

"What's your name, boy?" the Justice said.

[1]In many rural cultures, property owners may "impound" domestic animals that stray onto their land. The animal's owner must pay a "fee" to redeem them.

"Colonel Sartoris Snopes," the boy whispered.

"Hey?" the Justice said. "Talk louder. Colonel Sartoris? I reckon anybody named for Colonel Sartoris in this country can't help but tell the truth, can they?" The boy said nothing. *Enemy! Enemy!* he thought; for a moment he could not even see, could not see that the Justice's face was kindly nor discern that his voice was troubled when he spoke to the man named Harris: "Do you want me to question this boy?" But he could hear, and during those subsequent long seconds while there was absolutely no sound in the crowded little room save that of quiet and intent breathing it was as if he had swung outward at the end of a grape vine, over a ravine, and at the top of the swing had been caught in a prolonged instant of mesmerized gravity, weightless in time.

"No!" Harris said violently, explosively. "Damnation! Send him out of here!" Now time, the fluid world, rushed beneath him again, the voices coming to him again through the smell of cheese and sealed meat, the fear and despair and the old grief of blood:

"This case is closed. I can't find against you, Snopes, but I can give you advice. Leave this country and don't come back to it."

His father spoke for the first time, his voice cold and harsh, level, without emphasis: "I aim to. I don't figure to stay in a country among people who . . ." he said something unprintable and vile, addressed to no one.

"That'll do," the Justice said. "Take your wagon and get out of this country before dark. Case dismissed."

His father turned, and he followed the stiff black coat, the wiry figure walking a little stiffly from where a Confederate provost's man's musket ball had taken him in the heel on a stolen horse thirty years ago, followed the two backs now, since his older brother had appeared from somewhere in the crowd, no taller than the father but thicker, chewing tobacco steadily, between the two lines of grim-faced men and out of the store and across the worn gallery and down the sagging steps and among the dogs and half-grown boys in the mild May dust, where as he passed a voice hissed:

"Barn burner!"

Again he could not see, whirling; there was a face in a red haze, moonlike, bigger than the full moon, the owner of it half again his size, he leaping in the red haze toward the face, feeling no blow, feeling no shock when his head struck the earth, scrabbling up and leaping again, feeling no blow this time either and tasting no blood, scrabbling up to see the other boy in full flight and himself already leaping into pursuit as his father's hand jerked him back, the harsh, cold voice speaking above him: "Go get in the wagon."

It stood in a grove of locusts and mulberries across the road. His two hulking sisters in their Sunday dresses and his mother and her sister in calico and sunbonnets were already in it, sitting on and among the sorry residue of the dozen and more movings which even the boy could remember—the battered stove, the broken beds and chairs, the clock inlaid with mother-of-pearl, which would not run, stopped at some fourteen minutes past two o'clock of a dead and forgotten day and time, which had been his mother's dowry. She was crying, though when she saw him she drew her sleeve across her face and began to descend from the wagon. "Get back," the father said.

"He's hurt. I got to get some water and wash his . . ."

"Get back in the wagon," his father said. He got in too, over the tail-gate. His father mounted to the seat where the older brother already sat and struck the gaunt mules two savage blows with the peeled willow, but without heat. It was not even sadistic; it was exactly that same quality which in later years would cause his descendants to over-run the engine before putting a motor car into motion, striking and reining back in the same movement. The wagon went on, the store with its quiet crowd of grimly watching men dropped behind; a curve in the road hid it. *Forever* he thought. *Maybe he's done satisfied now, now that he has* . . . stopping himself, not to say it aloud even to himself. His mother's hand touched his shoulder.

"Does hit hurt?" she said.

"Naw," he said. "Hit don't hurt. Lemme be."

"Can't you wipe some of the blood off before hit dries?"

"I'll wash to-night," he said. "Lemme be, I tell you."

The wagon went on. He did not know where they were going. None of them ever did or ever asked, because it was always somewhere, always a house of sorts waiting for them a day or two days or even three days away. Likely his father had already arranged to make a crop on another farm before he . . . Again he had to stop himself. He (the father) always did. There was something about his wolflike independence and even courage when the advantage was at least neutral which impressed strangers, as if they got from his latent ravening ferocity not so much a sense of dependability as a feeling that his ferocious conviction in the rightness of his own actions would be of advantage to all whose interest lay with his.

That night they camped, in a grove of oaks and beeches where a spring ran. The nights were still cool and they had a fire against it, of a rail lifted from a nearby fence and cut into lengths—a small fire, neat, niggard almost, a shrewd fire; such fires were his father's habit and custom always, even in freezing weather. Older, the boy might have remarked this and wondered why not a big one; why should not a man who had not only seen the waste and extravagance of war, but who had in his blood an inherent voracious prodigality with material not his own, have burned everything in sight? Then he might have gone a step farther and thought that that was the reason: that niggard blaze was the living fruit of nights passed during those four years in the woods hiding from all men, blue or gray, with his strings of horses (captured horses, he called them). And older still, he might have divined the true reason: that the element of fire spoke to some deep mainspring of his father's being, as the element of steel or of powder spoke to other men, as the one weapon for the preservation of integrity, else breath were not worth the breathing, and hence to be regarded with respect and used with discretion.

But he did not think this now and he had seen those same niggard blazes all his life. He merely ate his supper beside it and was already half asleep over his iron plate when his father called him, and once more he followed the stiff back, the stiff and ruthless limp, up the slope and on to the starlit road where, turning, he could see his father against the stars but without face or depth—a shape black, flat, and bloodless as though cut from tin in the iron folds of the frockcoat which had not been made for him, the voice harsh like tin and without heat like tin:

"You were fixing to tell them. You would have told him." He didn't answer. His father struck him with the flat of his hand on the side of the head, hard but without heat, exactly as he had struck the two mules at the store, exactly as he would strike either of them with any stick in order to kill a horse fly, his voice still without heat or anger: "You're getting to be a man. You got to learn. You got to learn to stick to your own blood or you ain't going to have any blood to stick to you. Do you think either of them, any man there this morning, would? Don't you know all they wanted was a chance to get at me because they knew I had them beat? Eh?" Later, twenty years later, he was to tell himself, "If I had said they wanted only truth, justice, he would have hit me again." But now he said nothing. He was not crying. He just stood there. "Answer me," his father said.

"Yes," he whispered. His father turned.

"Get on to bed. We'll be there tomorrow."

To-morrow they were there. In the early afternoon the wagon stopped before a paintless two-room house identical almost with the dozen others it had stopped before even in the boy's ten years, and again, as on the other dozen occasions, his mother and aunt got down and began to unload the wagon, although his two sisters and his father and brother had not moved.

"Likely hit ain't fitten for hawgs," one of the sisters said.

"Nevertheless, fit it will and you'll hog it and like it," his father said. "Get out of them chairs and help your Ma unload."

The two sisters got down, big, bovine, in a flutter of cheap ribbons; one of them drew from the jumbled wagon bed a battered lantern, the other a worn broom. His father handed the reins to the older son and began to climb stiffly over the wheel. "When they get unloaded, take the team to the barn and feed them." Then he said, and at first the boy thought he was still speaking to his brother: "Come with me."

"Me?" he said.

"Yes," his father said. "You."

"Abner," his mother said. His father paused and looked back—the harsh level stare beneath the shaggy, graying, irascible brows.

"I reckon I'll have a word with the man that aims to begin to-morrow owning me body and soul for the next eight months."

They went back up the road. A week ago—or before last night, that is—he would have asked where they were going, but not now. His father had struck him before last night but never before had he paused afterward to explain why; it was as if the blow and the following calm, outrageous voice still rang, repercussed, divulging nothing to him save the terrible handicap of being young, the light weight of his few years, just heavy enough to prevent his soaring free of the world as it seemed to be ordered but not heavy enough to keep him footed solid in it, to resist it and try to change the course of its events.

Presently he could see the grove of oaks and cedars and the other flowering trees and shrubs where the house would be, though not the house yet. They walked beside a fence massed with honeysuckle and Cherokee roses and came to a gate swinging open between two brick pillars, and now, beyond a sweep of drive, he saw the house for the first time and at that instant he forgot his father and the terror and despair both, and even when he remembered his father again (who had not stopped) the terror and despair did not return. Because, for all the twelve movings, they had sojourned until now in a poor country, a land of small farms and fields and houses, and he had never seen a house like this before. *Hit's big as a courthouse* he thought quietly, with a surge of peace and joy whose reason he could not have thought into words, being too young for that: *They are safe from him. People whose lives are a part of this peace and dignity are beyond his touch, he no more to them than a buzzing wasp: capable of stinging for a little moment but that's all; the spell of this peace and dignity rendering even the barns and stable and cribs which belong to it impervious to the puny flames he might contrive* . . . this, the peace and joy, ebbing for an instant as he looked again at the stiff black back, the stiff and implacable limp of the figure which was not dwarfed by the house, for the reason that it had never looked big anywhere and which now, against the serene columned backdrop, had more than ever that impervious quality of something cut ruthlessly from tin, depthless, as though, sidewise to the sun, it would cast no shadow. Watching him, the boy remarked the absolutely undeviating course which his father held and saw the stiff foot come squarely down in a pile of fresh droppings where a horse had stood in the drive and which his father could have avoided by a simple change of stride. But it ebbed only for a moment, though he could not have thought this into words either, walking on in the spell of the house, which he could ever want but without envy, without sorrow, certainly never with that ravening and jealous rage which unknown to him walked in the ironlike black coat before him: *Maybe he will feel it too. Maybe it will even change him now from what maybe he couldn't help but be.*

They crossed the portico. Now he could hear his father's stiff foot as it came down on the boards with clocklike finality, a sound out of all proportion to the displacement of the body it bore and which was not dwarfed either by the white door before it, as though it had attained to a sort of vicious and ravening minimum not to be dwarfed by anything—the flat, wide, black hat, the formal coat of broadcloth which had once been black but which had now that friction-glazed greenish cast of the bodies of old house flies, the lifted sleeve which was too large, the lifted hand like a curled claw. The door opened so promptly that the boy knew the Negro must have been watching them all the time, an old man with neat grizzled hair, in a linen jacket, who stood barring the door with his body, saying, "Wipe yo foots, white man, fo you come in here. Major ain't home nohow."

"Get out of my way, nigger," his father said, without heat too, flinging the door back and the Negro also and entering, his hat still on his head. And now the boy saw the prints of the stiff foot on the doorjamb and saw them appear on the pale rug behind the machinelike deliberation of the foot which seemed to bear (or transmit) twice the weight which the body compassed. The Negro was shouting "Miss Lula! Miss Lula!" somewhere behind them, then the boy, deluged as though by a warm wave by a suave turn of carpeted stair and a pendant glitter of chandeliers and a mute gleam of gold frames, heard the swift feet and saw her too, a lady—perhaps he had never seen her like before either—in a gray, smooth gown with lace at the throat and an apron tied at the waist and the sleeves turned back, wiping cake or biscuit dough from her hands with a towel as she came up the hall, looking not at his father at all but at the tracks on the blond rug with an expression of incredulous amazement.

"I tried," the Negro cried. "I tole him to . . ."

"Will you please go away?" she said in a shaking voice. "Major de Spain is not at home. Will you please go away?"

His father had not spoken again. He did not speak again. He did not even look at her. He just stood stiff in the center of the rug, in his hat, the shaggy iron-gray brows twitching slightly above the pebble-colored eyes as he appeared to examine the house with brief deliberation. Then with the same deliberation he turned; the boy watched him pivot on the good leg and saw the stiff foot drag round the arc of the turning, leaving a final long and fading smear. His father never looked at it, he never once looked down at the rug. The Negro held the door. It closed behind them, upon the hysteric and indistinguishable woman-wail. His father stopped at the top of the steps and scraped his boot clean on the edge of it. At the gate he stopped again. He stood for a moment, planted stiffly on the stiff foot, looking back at the house. "Pretty and white, ain't it?" he said. "That's sweat. Nigger sweat. Maybe it ain't white enough yet to suit him. Maybe he wants to mix some white sweat with it."

Two hours later the boy was chopping wood behind the house within which his mother and aunt and the two sisters (the mother and aunt, not the two girls, he knew that; even at this distance and muffled by walls the flat loud voices of the two girls emanated an incorrigible idle inertia) were setting up the stove to prepare a meal, when he heard the hooves and saw the linen-clad man on a fine sorrel mare, whom he recognized even before he saw the rolled rug in front of the Negro youth following on a fat bay carriage horse—a suffused, angry face vanishing, still at full gallop, beyond the corner of the house where his father and brother were sitting in the two tilted chairs; and a moment later, almost before he could have put the axe down, he heard the hooves again and watched the sorrel mare go back out of the yard, already galloping again. Then his father began to shout one of the sisters' names, who presently emerged backward from the kitchen door dragging the rolled rug along the ground by one end while the other sister walked behind it.

"If you ain't going to tote, go on and set up the wash pot," the first said.

"You, Sarty!" the second shouted. "Set up the wash pot!" His father appeared at the door, framed against that shabbiness, as he had been against that other bland perfection, impervious to either, the mother's anxious face at his shoulder.

"Go on," the father said. "Pick it up." The two sisters stooped, broad, lethargic; stooping, they presented an incredible expanse of pale cloth and a flutter of tawdry ribbons.

"If I thought enough of a rug to have to git hit all the way from France I wouldn't keep hit where folks coming in would have to tromp on hit," the first said. They raised the rug.

"Abner," the mother said. "Let me do it."

"You go back and git dinner," his father said. "I'll tend to this."

From the woodpile through the rest of the afternoon the boy watched them, the rug spread flat in the dust beside the bubbling wash-pot, the two sisters stooping over it with that profound and lethargic reluctance, while the father stood over them in turn, implacable and grim, driving them though never raising his voice again. He could smell the harsh homemade lye they were using; he saw his mother come to the door once and look toward them with an expression not anxious now but very like despair; he saw his father turn, and he fell to with the axe and saw from the corner of his eye his father raise from the ground a flattish fragment of field stone and examine it and return to the pot, and this time his mother actually spoke: "Abner. Abner. Please don't. Please, Abner."

Then he was done too. It was dusk; the whippoorwills had already begun. He could smell coffee from the room where they would presently eat the cold food remaining from the mid-afternoon meal, though when he entered the house he realized they were having coffee again probably because there was a fire on the hearth, before which the rug now lay spread over the backs of the two chairs. The tracks of his father's foot were gone. Where they had been were now long, water-cloudy scoriations resembling the sporadic course of a lilliputian[2] mowing machine.

It still hung there while they ate the cold food and then went to bed, scattered without order or claim up and down the two rooms, his mother in one bed, where his father would later lie, the older brother in the other, himself, the aunt, and the two sisters on pallets on the floor. But his father was not in bed yet. The last thing the boy remembered was the depthless, harsh silhouette of the hat and coat bending over the rug and it seemed to him that he had not even closed his eyes when the silhouette was standing over him, the fire almost dead behind it, the stiff foot prodding him awake. "Catch up the mule," his father said.

When he returned with the mule his father was standing in the black door, the rolled rug over his shoulder. "Ain't you going to ride?" he said.

"No. Give me your foot."

He bent his knee into his father's hand, the wiry, surprising power flowed smoothly, rising, he rising with it, on to the mule's bare back (they had owned a saddle once; the boy could remember it though not when or where) and with the same effortlessness his father swung the rug up in front of him. Now in the starlight they retraced the afternoon's path, up the dusty road rife with honeysuckle, through the gate and up the black tunnel of the drive to the lightless house, where he sat on the mule and felt the rough warp of the rug drag across his thighs and vanish.

"Don't you want me to help?" he whispered. His father did not answer and now he heard again that stiff foot striking the hollow portico with that wooden and clocklike deliberation, that outrageous overstatement of the weight it carried. The rug, hunched, not flung (the boy could tell that even in the darkness) from his father's shoulder struck the angle of wall and floor with a sound unbelievably loud, thunderous, then the foot again, unhurried and enormous; a light came on in the house and the boy sat, tense, breathing steadily and quietly and just a little fast, though the foot itself did not increase its beat at all, descending the steps now; now the boy could see him.

"Don't you want to ride now?" he whispered. "We kin both ride now," the light within the house altering now, flaring up and sinking. *He's coming down the stairs now,* he thought. He had already ridden the mule up beside the horse block; presently his father was up behind him and he doubled the reins over and slashed the mule across the neck, but before the animal could begin to trot the hard, thin arm came round him, the hard, knotted hand jerking the mule back to a walk.

In the first red rays of the sun they were in the lot, putting plow gear on the mules. This time the sorrel mare was in the lot before he heard it at all, the rider collarless and even bareheaded, trembling, speaking in a shaking voice as the woman in the house had done, his father merely looking up once before stooping again to the hame[3] he was buckling, so that the man on the mare spoke to his stooping back:

[2]Extremely small, like the 6-inch inhabitants of the land of Lilliput in Jonathan Swift's *Gulliver's Travels* (1726).

[3]One of two curved wooden or metal pieces of a harness.

"You must realize you have ruined that rug. Wasn't there anybody here, any of your women . . ." he ceased, shaking, the boy watching him, the older brother leaning now in the stable door, chewing, blinking slowly and steadily at nothing apparently. "It cost a hundred dollars. But you never had a hundred dollars. You never will. So I'm going to charge you twenty bushels of corn against your crop. I'll add it in your contract and when you come to the commissary you can sign it. That won't keep Mrs. de Spain quiet but maybe it will teach you to wipe your feet off before you enter her house again."

Then he was gone. The boy looked at his father, who still had not spoken or even looked up again, who was now adjusting the logger-head[4] in the hame.

"Pap," he said. His father looked at him—the inscrutable face, the shaggy brows beneath which the gray eyes glinted coldly. Suddenly the boy went toward him, fast, stopping as suddenly. "You done the best you could!" he cried. "If he wanted hit done different why didn't he wait and tell you how? He won't git no twenty bushels! He won't git none! We'll gether hit and hide hit! I kin watch . . ."

"Did you put the cutter back in that straight stock like I told you?"[5]

"No, sir," he said.

"Then go do it."

That was Wednesday. During the rest of that week he worked steadily, at what was within his scope and some which was beyond it, with an industry that did not need to be driven nor even commanded twice; he had this from his mother, with the difference that some at least of what he did he liked to do, such as splitting wood with the half-size axe which his mother and aunt had earned; or saved money somehow, to present him with at Christmas. In company with the two older women (and on one afternoon, even one of the sisters), he built pens for the shoat and the cow which were a part of his father's contract with the landlord, and one afternoon, his father being absent, gone somewhere on one of the mules, he went to the field.

They were running a middle buster now, his brother holding the plow straight while he handled the reins, and walking beside the straining mule, the rich black soil shearing cool and damp against his bare ankles, he thought *Maybe this is the end of it. Maybe even that twenty bushels that seems hard to have to pay for just a rug will be a cheap price for him to stop forever and always from being what he used to be;* thinking, dreaming now, so that his brother had to speak sharply to him to mind the mule: *Maybe he even won't collect the twenty bushels. Maybe it will all add up and balance and vanish—corn, rug, fire; the terror and grief, the being pulled two ways like between two teams of horses—gone, done with for ever and ever.*

Then it was Saturday; he looked up from beneath the mule he was harnessing and saw his father in the black coat and hat. "Not that," his father said. "The wagon gear." And then, two hours later, sitting in the wagon bed behind his father and brother on the seat, the wagon accomplished a final curve, and he saw the weathered paintless store with its tattered tobacco- and patent-medicine posters and the tethered wagons and saddle animals below the gallery. He mounted the gnawed steps be-

[4]Plowhead; harness piece.

[5]Cutter . . . straight stock: the blade and frame of a plow.

hind his father and brother, and there again was the lane of quiet, watching faces for the three of them to walk through. He saw the man in spectacles sitting at the plank table and he did not need to be told this was a Justice of the Peace; he sent one glare of fierce, exultant, partisan defiance at the man in collar and cravat now, whom he had seen but twice before in his life, and that on a galloping horse, who now wore on his face an expression not of rage but of amazed unbelief which the boy could not have known was at the incredible circumstance of being sued by one of his own tenants, and came and stood against his father and cried at the Justice: "He ain't done it! He ain't burnt . . ."

"Go back to the wagon," his father said.

"Burnt?" the Justice said. "Do I understand this rug was burned too?"

"Does anybody here claim it was?" his father said. "Go back to the wagon." But he did not, he merely retreated to the rear of the room, crowded as that other had been, but not to sit down this time, instead, to stand pressing among the motionless bodies, listening to the voices:

"And you claim twenty bushels of corn is too high for the damage you did to the rug?"

"He brought the rug to me and said he wanted the tracks washed out of it. I washed the tracks out and took the rug back to him."

"But you didn't carry the rug back to him in the same condition it was in before you made the tracks on it."

His father did not answer, and now for perhaps half a minute there was no sound at all save that of breathing, the faint, steady suspiration of complete and intent listening.

"You decline to answer that, Mr. Snopes?" Again his father did not answer. "I'm going to find against you, Mr. Snopes. I'm going to find that you were responsible for the injury to Major de Spain's rug and hold you liable for it. But twenty bushels of corn seems a little high for a man in your circumstances to have to pay. Major de Spain claims it cost a hundred dollars. October corn will be worth about fifty cents. I figure that if Major de Spain can stand a ninety-five dollar loss on something he paid cash for, you can stand a five-dollar loss you haven't earned yet. I hold you in damages to Major de Spain to the amount of ten bushels of corn over and above your contract with him, to be paid to him out of your crop at gathering time. Court adjourned."

It had taken no time hardly, the morning was but half begun. He thought they would return home and perhaps back to the field, since they were late, far behind all other farmers. But instead his father passed on behind the wagon, merely indicating with his hand for the older brother to follow with it, and crossed the road toward the blacksmith shop opposite, pressing on after his father, overtaking him, speaking, whispering up at the harsh, calm face beneath the weathered hat: "He won't git no ten bushels neither. He won't git one. We'll . . ." until his father glanced for an instant down at him, the face absolutely calm, the grizzled eyebrows tangled above the cold eyes, the voice almost pleasant, almost gentle:

"You think so? Well, we'll wait till October anyway."

The matter of the wagon—the setting of a spoke or two and the tightening of the tires—did not take long either, the business of the tires accomplished by driving the wagon into the spring branch behind the shop and letting it stand there, the mules nuzzling into the water from time to time, and the boy on the seat with the idle reins, looking up the slope and through the sooty tunnel of the shed where the slow hammer rang and where his father sat on an upended cypress bolt, easily, either talking or listening, still sitting there when the boy brought the dripping wagon up out of the branch and halted it before the door.

"Take them on to the shade and hitch," his father said. He did so and returned. His father and the smith and a third man squatting on his heels inside the door were talking, about crops and animals; the boy, squatting too in the ammoniac dust and hoof-parings and scales of rust, heard his father tell a long and unhurried story out of the time before the birth of the older brother even when he had been a professional horsetrader. And then his father came up beside him where he stood before a tattered last year's circus poster on the other side of the store, gazing rapt and quiet at the scarlet horses, the incredible poisings and convolutions of tulle and tights and the painted leers of comedians, and said, "It's time to eat."

But not at home. Squatting beside his brother against the front wall, he watched his father emerge from the store and produce from a paper sack a segment of cheese and divide it carefully and deliberately into three with his pocket knife and produce crackers from the same sack. They all three squatted on the gallery and ate, slowly, without talking; then in the store again, they drank from a tin dipper tepid water smelling of the cedar bucket and of living beech trees. And still they did not go home. It was a horse lot this time, a tall rail fence upon and along which men stood and sat and out of which one by one horses were led, to be walked and trotted and then cantered back and forth along the road while the slow swapping and buying went on and the sun began to slant westward, they—the three of them—watching and listening, the older brother with his muddy eyes and his steady, inevitable tobacco, the father commenting now and then on certain of the animals, to no one in particular.

It was after sundown when they reached home. They ate supper by lamplight, then, sitting on the doorstep, the boy watched the night fully accomplish, listening to the whippoorwills and the frogs, when he heard his mother's voice: "Abner! No! No! Oh, God. Oh, God. Abner!" and he rose, whirled, and saw the altered light through the door where a candle stub now burned in a bottle neck on the table and his father, still in the hat and coat, at once formal and burlesque as though dressed carefully for some shabby and ceremonial violence, emptying the reservoir of the lamp back into the five-gallon kerosene can from which it had been filled, while the mother tugged at his arm until he shifted the lamp to the other hand and flung her back, not savagely or viciously, just hard, into the wall, her hands flung out against the wall for balance, her mouth open and in her face the same quality of hopeless despair as had been in her voice. Then his father saw him standing in the door. "Go to the barn and get that can of oil we were oiling the wagon with," he said. The boy did not move. Then he could speak.

"What . . ." he cried. "What are you . . ."

"Go get that oil," his father said. "Go."

Then he was moving, running, outside the house, toward the stable: this the old habit, the old blood which he had not been permitted to choose for himself, which had been bequeathed him willy nilly and which had run for so long (and who knew where, battening on what of outrage and savagery and lust) before it came to him. *I could keep on,* he thought. *I could run on and on and never look back, never need to see his face again. Only I can't. I can't,* the rusted can in his hand now, the liquid sploshing in it as he ran back to the house and into it, into the sound of his mother's weeping in the next room, and handed the can to his father.

"Ain't you going to even send a nigger?" he cried. "At least you sent a nigger before!"

This time his father didn't strike him. The hand came even faster than the blow had, the same hand which had set the can on the table with almost excruciating care flashing from the can toward him too quick for him to follow it, gripping him by the back of his shirt and on to tiptoe before he had seen it quit the can, the face stooping at him in breathless and frozen ferocity, the cold, dead voice speaking over him to the older brother who leaned against the table, chewing with that steady, curious, sidewise motion of cows:

"Empty the can into the big one and go on. I'll catch up with you."

"Better tie him up to the bedpost," the brother said.

"Do like I told you," the father said. Then the boy was moving, his bunched shirt and the hard, bony hand between his shoulder-blades, his toes just touching the floor, across the room and into the other one, past the sisters sitting with spread heavy thighs in the two chairs over the cold hearth, and to where his mother and aunt sat side by side on the bed, the aunt's arms about his mother's shoulders.

"Hold him," the father said. The aunt made a startled movement. "Not you," the father said. "Lennie. Take hold of him. I want to see you do it." His mother took him by the wrist. "You'll hold him better than that. If he gets loose don't you know what he is going to do? He will go up yonder." He jerked his head toward the road. "Maybe I'd better tie him."

"I'll hold him," his mother whispered.

"See you do then." Then his father was gone, the stiff foot heavy and measured upon the boards, ceasing at last.

Then he began to struggle. His mother caught him in both arms, he jerking and wrenching at them. He would be stronger in the end, he knew that. But he had no time to wait for it. "Lemme go!" he cried. "I don't want to have to hit you!"

"Let him go!" the aunt said. "If he don't go, before God, I am going up there myself!"

"Don't you see I can't?" his mother cried. "Sarty! Sarty! No! No! Help me, Lizzie!"

Then he was free. His aunt grasped at him but it was too late. He whirled, running, his mother stumbled forward on to her knees behind him, crying to the nearer sister: "Catch him, Net! Catch him!" But that was too late too, the sister (the sisters were twins, born at the same time, yet either of them now gave the impression of being, encompassing as much living meat and volume and weight as any other two of the family) not yet having begun to rise from the chair, her head, face, alone merely turned, presenting to him in the flying instant an astonishing expanse of young female features untroubled by any surprise even, wearing only an expression of bovine interest. Then he was out of the room, out of the house, in the mild dust of the starlit road and the heavy rifeness of honeysuckle, the pale ribbon unspooling with terrific slowness under his running feet, reaching the gate at last and turning in, running, his heart and lungs drumming, on up the drive toward the lighted house, the lighted door. He did not knock, he burst in, sobbing for breath, incapable for the moment of speech; he saw the astonished face of the Negro in the linen jacket without knowing when the Negro had appeared.

"De Spain!" he cried, panted. "Where's . . ." then he saw the white man too emerging from a white door down the hall. "Barn!" he cried. "Barn!"

"What?" the white man said. "Barn?"

"Yes!" the boy cried. "Barn!"

"Catch him!" the white man shouted.

But it was too late this time too. The Negro grasped his shirt, but the entire sleeve, rotten with washing, carried away, and he was out that door too and in the drive again, and had actually never ceased to run even while he was screaming into the white man's face.

Behind him the white man was shouting, "My horse! Fetch my horse!" and he thought for an instant of cutting across the park and climbing the fence into the road, but he did not know the park nor how high the vine-massed fence might be and he dared not risk it. So he ran on down the drive, blood and breath roaring; presently he was in the road again though he could not see it. He could not hear either: the galloping mare was almost upon him before he heard her, and even then he held his course, as if the very urgency of his wild grief and need must in a moment more find him wings, waiting until the ultimate instant to hurl himself aside and into the weed-choked roadside ditch as the horse thundered past and on, for an instant in furious silhouette against the stars, the tranquil early summer night sky which, even before the shape of the horse and rider vanished, stained abruptly and violently upward: a long, swirling roar incredible and soundless, blotting the stars, and he springing up and into the road again, running again, knowing it was too late yet still running even after he heard the shot and, an instant later, two shots, pausing now without knowing he had ceased to run, crying "Pap! Pap!," running again before he knew he had begun to run, stumbling, tripping over something and scrabbling up again without ceasing to run, looking backward over his shoulder at the glare as he got up, running on among the invisible trees, panting, sobbing, "Father! Father!"

At midnight he was sitting on the crest of a hill. He did not know it was midnight and he did not know how far he had come. But there was no glare behind him now and he sat now, his back toward what he had called home for four days anyhow, his face toward the dark woods which he would enter when breath was strong again, small, shaking steadily in the chill darkness, hugging himself into the remainder of his thin, rotten shirt, the grief and despair now no longer terror and fear but just grief and despair. *Father. My father,* he thought. "He was brave!" he cried suddenly, aloud but not loud, no more than a whisper: "He was! He was in the war! He was in Colonel Sartoris' cav'ry!" not knowing that his father had gone to that war a private in the fine old European sense, wearing no uniform, admitting the authority of and giving fidelity to no man or army or flag, going to war as Malbrouck[6] himself did: for

[6]Malbrouck, the hero of an eighteenth-century French nursery rhyme, *"Malbrouck s'en va-t-en guerre"* ("Malbrouck has gone to war").

booty—it meant nothing and less than nothing to him if it were enemy booty or his own.

The slow constellations wheeled on. It would be dawn and then sun-up after a while and he would be hungry. But that would be to-morrow and now he was only cold, and walking would cure that. His breathing was easier now and he decided to get up and go on, and then he found that he had been asleep because he knew it was almost dawn, the night almost over. He could tell that from the whippoorwills. They were everywhere now among the dark trees below him, constant and inflectioned and ceaseless, so that, as the instant for giving over to the day birds drew nearer and nearer, there was no interval at all between them. He got up. He was a little stiff, but walking would cure that too as it would the cold, and soon there would be the sun. He went on down the hill, toward the dark woods within which the liquid silver voices of the birds called unceasing—the rapid and urgent beating of the urgent and quiring heart of the late spring night. He did not look back.

1938

Hart Crane 1899–1932

The only child of a successful candy manufacturer and a difficult, possessive mother, Hart Crane grew up in a household of domestic turmoil that did not end even with his parents' divorce in 1916. He had a sketchy formal education but a precocious self-education derived from reading the experimental writing published in the little magazines of the period. He published his first poem, "C-33," in one such magazine, *Bruno's Weekly,* when he was seventeen. During this period, he voraciously read not only nativist writers such as Edgar Lee Masters and Sherwood Anderson but also Ezra Pound and T. S. Eliot and the French poets Rimbaud and Laforgue.

He left school and went to New York for a brief stay in 1916, returned to Ohio to work for his father from 1919 to 1923, and finally settled in New York. Nourished by the break with his family, Crane was nonetheless troubled by financial difficulties which kept him unhappily dependent upon his relatives. Benefactors such as financier Otto Kahn, who provided support for part of the writing of the long poem *The Bridge,* also helped Crane through troubled times.

In 1922, he started work on a three-part poem "For the Marriage of Faustus and Helen," which was to express the union of science and beauty, of technology and art, in the modern world. The oddly disparate three parts of the poem open with the poet's meeting Helen of Troy, symbol of beauty, in a streetcar (Part I), then move to an evocation of the jazz age (Part II), and end with a vision of wholeness beyond the ravages of modern warfare (Part III). This poem is important as a precursor of *The Bridge* as well as an expression of Crane's visionary hope.

During this period of his life, Crane was alternately productive and dejected. His first volume of poetry, *White Buildings,* was published in 1926. He continued to work on *The Bridge* through 1927, but he did not complete it until 1929 when he was encouraged by a promise from Harry Crosby, the owner of the Black Sun Press, to publish the poem. Crane never revived the inspiration that inaugurated the long work, and the last poems that he wrote for it lacked the power and vitality of the beginning. However, because he published the poems not in the sequence in which they were written but in the sequence outlined very early in the composition (he wrote, for example, the last section first), *The Bridge* is a difficult poem to read as a whole. It moves through changes of mood, as it struggles to maintain the positive vision of America that Crane first imagined. The poem starts and ends with a paean to the Brooklyn Bridge, symbolized as "O harp and altar, of the fury fused."

In the middle sections of the long poem, Crane moves back and forth in American history: back to trace the voyage of Columbus, forward to track the modern subway traveler, back to the Indians, forward to the airplane age, in an effort to unite past and present, nature and technology, America and the spiritual possibilities of the new age. Some parts, written late in the process of composition, express Crane's flagging spirits even when, in the sequence of the long work, they are designed to move positively toward the affirmation of the ending. As a result, *The Bridge* has presented problems in interpretation. Assured of its power, readers have been less certain about its purpose.

Long before he completed *The Bridge,* Crane lost faith in his vision of America and in his own ability as a poet. After a period of creative inactivity and personal discontent, Crane was awarded a Guggenheim Fellowship and moved to Mexico. On his return from Mexico in April 1927, he committed suicide by jumping from the ship carrying him to New York. Among the poems that he had been working on in his final years, "The Broken Tower" indicates a new range of control and verbal mastery. It expresses a return to the subject of poetry and to his own role as a poet of "the visionary company of love." Crane's poetry is marked by visionary power, verbal difficulty, and jammed syntax.

Margaret Dickie
University of Georgia

PRIMARY WORKS

White Buildings, 1926; *The Bridge,* 1930; *The Collected Poems of Hart Crane,* 1933; *The Letters of Hart Crane, 1916–1932,* ed. Brom Weber, 1952, 1965; *Letters of Hart Crane and His Family,* ed. Thomas S.W. Lewis, 1974; *Hart Crane and Yvor Winters: Their Literary Correspondence,* ed. Thomas F. Parkinson, 1978.

Black Tambourine

The interests of a black man in a cellar
Mark tardy judgment on the world's closed door.
Gnats toss in the shadow of a bottle,
And a roach spans a crevice in the floor.

Æsop,[1] driven to pondering, found
Heaven with the tortoise and the hare;

[1]A Greek slave to whom many beast fables are attributed.

Fox brush and sow ear top his grave
And mingling incantations on the air.

The black man, forlorn in the cellar,
Wanders in some mid-kingdom, dark, that lies,
Between his tambourine, stuck on the wall,
And, in Africa, a carcass quick with flies.

1926

Chaplinesque[1]

We make our meek adjustments,
Contented with such random consolations
As the wind deposits
In slithered and too ample pockets.

For we can still love the world, who find
A famished kitten on the step, and know
Recesses for it from the fury of the street,
Or warm torn elbow coverts.

We will sidestep, and to the final smirk
Dally the doom of that inevitable thumb[2]
That slowly chafes its puckered index toward us,
Facing the dull squint with what innocence
And what surprise!

And yet these fine collapses are not lies
More than the pirouettes of any pliant cane;
Our obsequies are, in a way, no enterprise.
We can evade you, and all else but the heart:
What blame to us if the heart live on.[3]

The game enforces smirks; but we have seen
The moon in lonely alleys make
A grail of laughter of an empty ash can,
And through all sound of gaiety and quest
Have heard a kitten in the wilderness.

1926

[1]In the style of Charlie Chaplin, the silent movie star whom Crane had seen in *The Kid* in 1921.
[2]Of the policeman.
[3]Crane claimed to use this term as a deliberate pun on his first name.

At Melville's Tomb[1]

Often beneath the wave, wide from this ledge
The dice of drowned men's bones he saw bequeath
An embassy. Their numbers as he watched,
Beat on the dusty shore and were obscured.

And wrecks passed without sound of bells,
The calyx of death's bounty giving back
A scattered chapter, livid hieroglyph,
The portent wound in corridors of shells.

Then in the circuit calm of one vast coil,
Its lashings charmed and malice reconciled,
Frosted eyes there were that lifted altars;
And silent answers crept across the stars.

Compass, quadrant and sextant contrive
No farther tides . . . High in the azure steeps
Monody shall not wake the mariner.
This fabulous shadow only the sea keeps.

1926

from The Bridge

To Brooklyn Bridge

How many dawns, chill from his rippling rest
The seagull's wings shall dip and pivot him,
Shedding white rings of tumult, building high
Over the chained bay waters Liberty—

Then, with inviolate curve, forsake our eyes
As apparitional as sails that cross
Some page of figures to be filed away;
—Till elevators drop us from our day . . .

I think of cinemas, panoramic sleights
With multitudes bent toward some flashing scene

[1]Herman Melville (1819–1891) is buried at Woodlawn Cemetery in New York City. Crane refers to the sea as Melville's tomb.

Never disclosed, but hastened to again,
Foretold to other eyes on the same screen;

And Thee, across the harbor, silver-paced
As though the sun took step of thee, yet left
Some motion ever unspent in thy stride,—
Implicity thy freedom staying thee!

Out of some subway scuttle, cell or loft
A bedlamite[1] speeds to thy parapets,
Tilting there momently, shrill shirt ballooning,
A jest falls from the speechless caravan.

Down Wall,[2] from girder into street noon leaks,
A rip-tooth of the sky's acetylene;
All afternoon the cloud-flown derricks turn . . .
Thy cables breathe the North Atlantic still.

And obscure as that heaven of the Jews,
Thy guerdon[3] . . . Accolade thou dost bestow
Of anonymity time cannot raise:
Vibrant reprieve and pardon thou dost show.

O harp and altar, of the fury fused,
(How could mere toil align thy choiring strings!)
Terrific threshold of the prophet's pledge,
Prayer of pariah, and the lover's cry,—

Again the traffic lights that skim thy swift
Unfractioned idiom, immaculate sigh of stars,
Beading thy path—condense eternity:
And we have seen night lifted in thine arms.

Under thy shadow by the piers I waited;
Only in darkness is thy shadow clear.
The City's fiery parcels all undone,
Already snow submerges an iron year . . .

O Sleepless as the river under thee,
Vaulting the sea, the prairies' dreaming sod,
Unto us lowliest sometime sweep, descend
And of the curveship lend a myth to God.

1930

[1]A madman, inhabitant of Bedlam, the earliest established insane asylum in England.

[2]Wall Street in Manhattan, the financial center.

[3]A reward.

The River[1]

Stick your patent name on a signboard
brother—all over—going west—young man
Tintex—Japalac—Certain-teed Overalls ads[2]
and lands sakes! under the new playbill ripped
in the guaranteed corner—see Bert Williams[3] what?

. . . and past the din and slogans of the year—

Minstrels when you steal a chicken just
save me the wing for if it isn't
Erie it ain't for miles around a
Mazda—and the telegraphic night coming on Thomas

a Ediford—and whistling down the tracks
a headlight rushing with the sound—can you
imagine—while an EXpress makes time like
SCIENCE—COMMERCE and the HOLYGHOST
RADIO ROARS IN EVERY HOME WE HAVE THE NORTHPOLE
WALLSTREET AND VIRGINBIRTH WITHOUT STONES OR
WIRES OR EVEN RUNning brooks[4] connecting ears
and no more sermons windows flashing roar
breathtaking—as you like it . . . eh?

So the 20th Century—so
whizzed the Limited[5]—roared by and left
three men, still hungry on the tracks, ploddingly
watching the tail lights wizen and converge, slipping gimleted and neatly out of sight.

* * *

The last bear, shot drinking in the Dakotas
Loped under wires that span the mountain stream.
Keen instruments, strung to a vast precision
Bind town to town and dream to ticking dream.
But some men take their liquor slow—and count
—Though they'll confess no rosary nor clue—

to those whose addresses are never near

[1]The Mississippi River.
[2]A take-off on advertisements of the day.
[3]One of the most talented Negro comedians of the twentieth century who flourished from about 1895 until his death in 1922.
[4]"books in the running brooks, / Sermons in stones," William Shakespeare, *As You Like It*, Act II, Scene 1, 11. 16–17.
[5]Twentieth-Century Limited was a fast train.

The river's minute by the far brook's year.
Under a world of whistles, wires and steam
Caboose-like they go ruminating through
Ohio, Indiana—blind baggage—
To Cheyenne tagging . . . Maybe Kalamazoo.

Time's rendings, time's blendings they construe
As final reckonings of fire and snow;
Strange bird-wit, like the elemental gist
Of unwalled winds they offer, singing low
My Old Kentucky Home and *Casey Jones,*
Some Sunny Day. I heard a road-gang chanting so.
And afterwards, who had a colt's eyes—one said,
"Jesus! Oh I remember watermelon days!" And sped
High in a cloud of merriment, recalled
"—And when my Aunt Sally Simpson smiled," he
drawled—
"It was almost Louisiana, long ago."
"There's no place like Booneville though, Buddy,"
One said, excising a last burr from his vest,
"—For early trouting." Then peering in the can,
"—But I kept on the tracks." Possessed, resigned,
He trod the fire down pensively and grinned,
Spreading dry shingles of a beard . . .

Behind
My father's cannery works I used to see
Rail-squatters ranged in nomad raillery,
The ancient men—wifeless or runaway
Hobo-trekkers that forever search
An empire wilderness of freight and rails.
Each seemed a child, like me, on a loose perch,
Holding to childhood like some termless play.
John, Jake or Charley, hopping the slow freight
—Memphis to Tallahassee—riding the rods,
Blind fists of nothing, humpty-dumpty clods.

Yet they touch something like a key perhaps.
From pole to pole across the hills, the states
—They know a body under the wide rain;
Youngsters with eyes like fjords, old reprobates
With racetrack jargon,—dotting immensity
They lurk across her, knowing her yonder breast
Snow-silvered, sumac-stained or smoky blue—
Is past the valley-sleepers, south or west.
—As I have trod the rumorous midnights, too,

but who have touched her, knowing her without name

And past the circuit of the lamp's thin flame
(O Nights that brought me to her body bare!)[6]
Have dreamed beyond the print that bound her name.
Trains sounding the long blizzards out—I heard
Wail into distances I knew were hers.
Papooses crying on the wind's long mane
Screamed redskin dynasties that fled the brain,
—Dead echoes! But I knew her body there,
Time like a serpent down her shoulder, dark,
And space, an eaglet's wing, laid on her hair.[7]
Under the Ozarks, domed by Iron Mountain,
The old gods of the rain lie wrapped in pools
Where eyeless fish curvet a sunken fountain
and re-descend with corn from querulous crows.
Such pilferings make up their timeless eatage,
Propitiate them for their timber torn
By iron, iron—always the iron dealt cleavage!
They doze now, below axe and powder horn.

nor the myths of her fathers . . .

And Pullman breakfasters glide glistening steel
From tunnel into field—iron strides the dew—
Straddles the hill, a dance of wheel on wheel.
You have a half-hour's wait at Siskiyou,
Or stay the night and take the next train through.
Southward, near Cairo[8] passing, you can see
The Ohio merging,—borne down Tennessee;
And if it's summer and the sun's in dusk
Maybe the breeze will lift the River's musk
—As though the waters breathed that you might know
Memphis Johnny, Steamboat Bill, Missouri Joe.[9]
Oh, lean from the window, if the train slows down,
As though you touched hands with some ancient
    clown,
—A little while gaze absently below
And hum *Deep River* with them while they go.

Yes, turn again and sniff once more—look see,
O Sheriff, Brakeman and Authority—
Hitch up your pants and crunch another quid,

[6]Crane identifies the body of the American continent with the Indian princess Pocahontas.

[7]The union of serpent and eagle symbolizes the union of time and space, land and air.

[8]In southern Illinois where the Ohio River merges with the Mississippi.

[9]Old Mississippi folk songs. "Deep River" is also a Mississippi River song.

For you, too, feed the River timelessly.
And few evade full measure of their fate;
Always they smile out eerily what they seem.
I could believe he joked at heaven's gate—
Dan Midland[10]—jolted from the cold brake-beam.

Down, down—born pioneers in time's despite,
Grimed tributaries to an ancient flow—
They win no frontier by their wayward plight,
But drift in stillness, as from Jordan's brow.[11]

You will not hear it as the sea; even stone
Is not more hushed by gravity . . . But slow,
As loth to take more tribute—sliding prone
Like one whose eyes were buried long ago

The River, spreading, flows—and spends your dream.
What are you, lost within this tideless spell?
You are your father's father, and the stream—
A liquid theme that floating niggers swell.

Damp tonnage and alluvial march of days—
Nights turbid, vascular with silted shale
And roots surrendered down of moraine clays:
The Mississippi drinks the farthest dale.

O quarrying passion, undertowed sunlight!
The basalt surface drags a jungle grace
Ochreous and lynx-barred in lengthening might;
Patience! and you shall reach the biding place!

Over De Soto's[12] bones the freighted floors
Throb past the City storied of three thrones.
Down two more turns the Mississippi pours
(Anon tall ironsides up from salt lagoons)

And flows within itself, heaps itself free.
All fades but one thin skyline 'round . . . Ahead

[10]A storied hobo who fell from the brake beam while "riding the rods."
[11]The shore of the river Jordan in Palestine.
[12]To prevent hostile Indians from discovering the death of Hernando DeSoto, who discovered the Mississippi in 1541, his men buried him in the river, near New Orleans whose history involved the three thrones of Spain, France, and England.

No embrace opens but the stinging sea;
The River lifts itself from its long bed,

Poised wholly on its dream, a mustard glow
Tortured with history, its one will—flow!
—The Passion[13] spreads in wide tongues, choked and slow,
Meeting the Gulf, hosannas silently below.

1930

The Broken Tower

The bell-rope that gathers God at dawn[1]
Dispatches me as though I dropped down the knell
Of a spent day—to wander the cathedral lawn
From pit to crucifix, feet chill on steps from hell.

Have you not heard, have you not seen that corps
Of shadows in the tower, whose shoulders sway
Antiphonal carillons launched before
The stars are caught and hived in the sun's ray?

The bells, I say, the bells break down their tower;
And swing I know not where. Their tongues engrave
Membrane through marrow, my long-scattered score
Of broken intervals . . . And I, their sexton slave!

Oval encyclicals in canyons heaping
The impasse high with choir. Banked voices slain!
Pagodas, campaniles with reveilles outleaping—
O terraced echoes prostrate on the plain! . . .

And so it was I entered the broken world
To trace the visionary company of love, its voice
An instant in the wind (I know not whither hurled)
but not for long to hold each desperate choice.

My word I poured. But was it cognate, scored
Of that tribunal monarch of the air[2]

[13]The river is associated with the Passion (suffering on the Cross) of Christ. The Gulf (of Mexico) becomes an emblem of eternity.

[1]The angelus commemorates the Incarnation of Christ.
[2]Christ as judge and king.

Whose thigh embronzes earth, strikes crystal Word[3]
In wounds pledged once to hope—cleft to despair?

The steep encroachments of my blood left me
No answer (could blood hold such a lofty tower
As flings the question true?)—or is it she
Whose sweet mortality stirs latent power?—

And through whose pulse I hear, counting the strokes
My veins recall and add, revived and sure
The angelus of wars my chest evokes;
What I hold healed, original now, and pure . . .

And builds, within, a tower that is not stone
(Not stone can jacket heaven)—but slip
Of pebbles,—visible wings of silence sown
In azure circles, widening as they dip

The matrix of the heart, lift down the eye
That shrines the quiet lake and swells a tower . . .
The commodious, tall decorum of that sky
Unseals her earth, and lifts love in its shower.

1932

[3]Divine revelation and the poet's words.

The New Negro Renaissance

On the evening of March 21, 1924, one hundred ten Harlem luminaries converged on Manhattan's Civic Club in order to celebrate the publication of Jessie Harris Fauset's *There Is Confusion.* But the event was soon transformed into a sort of brokerage affair that would ease access between a select few of black America's "talented tenth" and certain well-heeled patrons of public opinion. The project of literary history/renovation would be tremendously simplified if we could sweep away the complexities and designate this glittering social event (or any other one like it) as the "beginning" of that period of dense cultural legacy called the "New Negro (or "Harlem") Renaissance." Enough of the younger generation of African American writers were invited to Charles S. Johnson's bash to flatter one's fantasies of uncomplicated and veritable origins: Eric Walrond, Gwendolyn Bennett, Countee Cullen, Langston Hughes, Georgia Douglass Johnson, Walter White, and Alain Locke (among others) were present, as the names, from the distance of almost eight decades, sound the roll of black cultural heroes who inscribed African American literary personality upon the twentieth century. That this formidable project was launched under the auspices of food and drink and in the midst, too, of important "midwives" such as Horace Liveright, whose house had published Jean Toomer's *Cane* the year before, enriches our notions of socio-political engagement. Absent from the Johnson fête, Toomer was not particularly eager to proffer his name and reputation to the movement stirring around him, but at least Arna Bontemps believed that *Cane* (1923)—despite the author's own wishes—really started it all.

Though the Great Depression is considered to have ended the New Negro Renaissance, its beginning remains elusive and open to debate. Though Nathan Huggins's important study of the period does not specify a precise commencement, his opening chapter focuses on the year of war, 1914, when James Weldon Johnson moved to Harlem and New York for the second time. David Levering Lewis begins his stunning narrative on the period with the return of New York National Guard's Fifteenth Regiment and a triumphal march along Fifth Avenue on a "clear, sharp" February morning, 1919. In her study of gender politics of the era, Gloria Hull offers a later date that forces us to reinterpret events both before and after that point: "The year is 1927," Hull notes, and Alice Dunbar-Nelson "is writing lively, informative columns" for Washington, D.C.'s *Eagle.* These scholars and critics offer a longer perspective than the customary shorter view of the Renaissance years that confines its investigation to the poetry, fiction, and nonfiction by African American writers published between 1923 and 1929.

Offering a radically different conceptual formulation of the inquiry, Houston Baker's 1987 study of the period tracks the New Negro Renaissance as the fruition of a discursive mastery wielded by Booker T. Washington in his address before the Atlantic Exposition on September 18, 1895. That scholars and students of the phenomenon might arguably adopt the long or short view and account for "deep" and "immediate" forces at work that converge on the period would suggest that these years—years rich with the promise and project of political and economic liberation—specify an especially dramatic moment in the long and perilous journey of cultural apprenticeship of African Americans within the context of the African Diaspora.

We can say, then, with some certainty that the New Negro Renaissance, the literary and artistic arm of a massive social movement with roots in the broken promises of post-Reconstruction America, offers at least a decade of *communal* and nationalist assertion, focused in the work of African American artists. The Renaissance becomes, in fact, the most vividly named outcome of a *second* African Diaspora, when large numbers of black people living in the southern United States fled the high tide of a "reign of terror," staged in the terrorist maneuvers of the Ku Klux Klan. From this angle, 1918 speaks volumes in its record number of lynchings. Seeking the more advantageous labor opportunities spawned by the war effort and pursuing a freer space in which to live their lives, southern black people in unprecedented number followed the tracks northward. From the midsouth and urban areas like Memphis and Little Rock, the migratory patterns ran straight to the major cities of the Midwest—Chicago, primarily. Even Cairo, Illinois, for the southern person, reared on the farm, represented that place of greater freedom. Likely an apocryphal story, train conductors in "the old days" were said to have declared, once outside Memphis, on the way to "yonder in Cairo," "black and white together!"

From the coastal regions of the South—Georgia, Virginia, and the Carolinas—"Mecca" was thought to have resided in cities like New York, Philadelphia, Hartford, and Boston. It is probably not at all accidental that Chicago in recent times is sometimes playfully referred to as an overgrown Mississippi town, or that the grandparents and parents of one's contemporaries in various East Coast cities are often indigenous to Charleston, South Carolina, or Greensboro or Rocky Mount, North Carolina, say. Even though Alain Locke might not have had the "masses" in mind, though he purportedly spoke for them in *The New Negro* (1925), the historical ground of the Renaissance is embedded in far less glamorous circumstances than the *haut monde* of the literary salon, or the charming dinner antics of what Zora Neale Hurston mockingly termed "niggerati."

An exceedingly complex historical movement that gained force at the close of World War I and that was largely checked by the economic collapse of the 1930s, the New Negro Renaissance was marked by a number of important developments. Among the most crucial was the extent to which African Americans gained access, even if limited, to certain engines of public opinion and evaluation. The Niagara Movement (1909–10) had created the National Association for the Advancement of Colored People (NAACP), which founded, in turn, *Crisis Magazine,* which became, under the general editorship of W.E.B. Du Bois and the literary editorship of Jessie Fauset, one of the major sources for the dissemination of writings by African Americans. Langston Hughes's "The Negro Speaks of Rivers," published in *Crisis* before the poet attained wide celebrity, may be thought of as the poem that helped promote him to a place of acclaim. Published under the auspices of the National Urban League and originally intended to serve as a journal of sociology and a forum for the discussion of "race" issues, Charles S. Johnson's *Opportunity* easily slipped, by cunning design, into a nerve center that monitored the literary productions of black writers. Marcus Garvey's United Negro Improvement Association and its newspapers must also be taken into account as a crucial political force of the age.

Though not the first time, by any means, that black Americans realized and practiced the efficacies of collective effort, the period is noteworthy as a time of pointed critical consciousness. In addition to the journals of the NAACP and the National Urban League, Locke's anthology and James Weldon Johnson's 1922 *The Book of American Negro Poetry* not only signaled a new spirit abroad on the urban scene, but also underscored its merits as a collective enterprise that encompassed male and female artists and African American artists indigenous to the United States as well as to certain Caribbean communities, particularly Jamaica—the homeland of Marcus and Amy Jacques Garvey and Claude McKay. The apparent democracy of artistic expressiveness that embraced a literary agenda as divergent as Claude McKay's sonnets, Georgia Douglass Johnson's and Countee Cullen's lyrics, and Langston Hughes's experimentation with 12-bar blues mode in verse sustained, in fact, an international dimension that has not been fully appreciated. In her study of the Francophone-focused Negritude movement, critic Lilyan Lagneau-Kesteloot outlines contact between Renaissance figures, such as Alain Locke, and West African expatriate intellectuals living in Paris, including Leopold Senghor, future president of Senegal, and the author and future statesman Aimé Césaire.

Although students of the period usually focus on its literary production, the music generated in Harlem clubs of the time participated fully in a crucial synthesis of idioms that we would come to recognize as "modern jazz." Langston Hughes's "Jazzonia," for instance, which limns "six long-headed jazzers" "in a Harlem cabaret," "in a whirling cabaret," seems to lay hold of the romance of nightclubbing and the simple kaleidoscopic flicker of ceiling lights through a colored filter. Much of the poetry and fiction of Hughes, in their articulation of urban idioms of speech, might be thought of as the thematic intersection of the "folks" and new modes of being.

In the lyrics of Countee Cullen and Claude McKay, the traditional sonnet form is appropriated to alternative modes of address as both poets instigate an Afrocentric poetic *persona* at the center of their inquiry. In "Yet Do I Marvel," Cullen invokes the mythic dilemmas of Tantalus and Sisyphus in explaining the speaker's self-reflexive marveling—"To make a poet black, and bid him sing!" Ultimately, the poetry of the Renaissance reflects two major currents: (1) experimentation with verse form that takes its inspiration from African American musical idiom—e.g., the work song and the blues in the poetic canon of Langston Hughes and Sterling Brown, and (2) the exploration of traditional verse forms, including free verse technique that rewrites aspects of European courtly love tradition in projecting a romanticized and aestheticized figure of the "black woman" (Cullen's "A Song of Praise" offers a case in point) and generally adapts romantic and heroic lyricisms to speak a range of emotion through black personality. (Anne Spencer's "At the Carnival," Gwendolyn Bennett's "To a Dark Girl," Claude McKay's "Harlem Dancer" and "Harlem Shadows," and Arna Bontemps's "A Black Man Talks of Reaping" all belong to this category.)

But perhaps the boldest artistic project of the period is embodied in *Cane,* a text that explodes generic boundaries in a stunningly innovative fashion. Not altogether poetry, prose, or drama, Jean Toomer's work encompasses all three. Synthesizing the symbolic valences of male/female, light/dark, North/South, black/white, urban/countryside, narrative closure/fragmentation, this brooding text refuses easy resolution and can be said to anticipate late twentieth-century developments in creative writing and critical discourse.

Though New Negro Renaissance poetry is more widely known than its fiction, it was in the latter arena that two significant women writers of the period made their appearance—Nella Larsen and Zora Neale Hurston. Marked by the publication of two important novels—*Quicksand* in 1928 and *Passing* in 1929—the truncated career of Nella Larsen represents yet another case of how the voices of women writers can fall strangely silent. Perhaps her own fiction provides a clue to the apparent creative impasse that Larsen encountered. Published in 1937, Hurston's *Their Eyes Were Watching God* was prepared for in the shorter fiction that she produced during the Renaissance years and has become one of the best-know and most influential novels written by an African American woman.

It seems entirely plausible to claim the New Negro Renaissance years as not only a burst of social and artistic activity of a freed American people, but also the "genesis" of African American personality as "modern man/woman." Even though Phillis Wheatley wrote her neoclassical verse almost a full two centuries before Gwendolyn Bennett and Countee Cullen set pen to paper, it is with the opening of the twentieth century and specifically the Renaissance period that the community can name a literature for itself. The proliferation of texts from those years offers an early model for what we know now as the new national pluralism. One of the United States' "modernisms," alongside Gertrude Stein's "lost generation," the New Negro Renaissance pursued a fairly amazing idea—an art directly tied to the fortunes of a political agenda.

Hortense Spillers
Cornell University

Alain Locke 1885–1954

That young Alain Leroy Locke grew up to be an educator is no surprise. By the time of his birth on September 13, 1885, education had become something of a family business. But that he would also be known as an influential philosopher and cultural critic is indeed surprising. Less than twenty years before Locke entered Harvard University to study philosophy, W.E.B. Du Bois had been cautioned against that discipline by William James who feared that a Negro philosopher, even one with a degree from Harvard, would be hard put to make a living. Du Bois chose history instead; Locke sought to prove James wrong, even while taking up elements of Jamesian pragmatism in his own work. Locke's use of critical philosophy, which questioned traditional Western faith in ultimate truths and absolute meanings, became an important element in his more widely known cultural work. He was a prolific reviewer of literature and drama; a critic, historian, and collector of fine art, including African sculpture; an early student and advocate of African American music; and, of course, the prime mover behind the primarily artistic New Negro Renaissance, officially initiated in 1925 with the anthology edited by Locke, titled simply *The New Negro: An Interpretation.*

Throughout his criticism, Locke moves between a deep appreciation of the Western high art forms he had come to know as a child in his late-Victorian, middle-class household, and an impassioned regard for African and African

American folk art forms. Locke's view of culture was influenced by the Victorian Matthew Arnold, but early on, Locke began to depict the individual as an active producer rather than a passive consumer of culture. This view of cultural production became important for the political aspects of the New Negro Renaissance. Unlike many of his white contemporaries in academia, Locke was always committed to social action and an awareness of what Du Bois called the "problem of the color-line."

Locke graduated with honors from Central High School in Philadelphia in 1902, then furthered his studies at the Philadelphia School of Pedagogy. Matriculated at Harvard in 1904, he began his studies in philosophy and literature at an advanced level. Upon graduating magna cum laude and Phi Beta Kappa in 1907, Locke accepted the first Rhodes scholarship ever awarded to an African American.

Race awareness was thrust upon Locke before he even arrived in England: five Oxford colleges denied him admission, in spite of his prestigious award. Finally settling in at one of the smaller and newer colleges, Hertford, the dark-skinned Locke had difficulty finding a comfortable social footing among his white classmates. He did, however, find company and intellectual stimulation with many African scholars at Oxford, friendships he pursued in later years as his interest in Pan-Africanism and international politics grew. Following his three years as a Rhodes scholar, Locke moved on for a year of study at the University of Berlin, as Du Bois had done just before the century's turn. Locke returned to Harvard in 1916 to complete his dissertation, "The Problem of Classification in the Theory of Value," under the direction of Ralph Barton Perry. Locke was now on his way to becoming one of the African American intellectual elite, those whom Du Bois exhorted to become "co-workers in the kingdom of culture."

Locke constantly challenged what it meant to be an intellectual. Many of the artists whom he actively supported charged him with elitism and Eurocentrism, and often bristled at his (sometimes heavy-handed) editorial recommendations. Some, like Claude McKay, were embarrassed by Locke's perfect evocation of the "Aframerican roccoco." Though he certainly courted beauty in all its forms, and sometimes questioned the "blind practicality of the common man," Locke was never satisfied with the role of the decadent aesthete or the sedentary academic. Accepting the professorship at Howard University in 1912 that he would hold (with some interruption) until his retirement in 1953, Locke immediately became active in campus politics and student life; he supported both the Howard literary journal and the theater department, and lobbied for parity among black and white faculty members. This latter effort resulted in his dismissal in 1925; but student and faculty protests made it clear that Locke was a highly valued member of the Howard community, and that the community would no longer stand for the unjust practices of the white university president. In 1928, Howard's first African American president, Mordecai W. Johnson, reappointed Locke.

Locke did not officially take up residence in that district of upper Manhattan called Harlem until his retirement. But with the publication of the special Harlem issue of the journal *Survey Graphic* in 1925 (which resulted in the anthology published in the same year), Locke knew Harlem well enough to assert that "it is — or promises at least to be — a race capital." Indeed, the "pulse of the Negro world [had] begun to beat in Harlem." Though Locke acknowledged important urban movements elsewhere in the North and central Midwest, it was Harlem that could offer the New Negro Movement the "cosmopolitan scale" necessary to rise above racial provincialism.

In the 1930s and 1940s, Locke spent less time supporting the arts, due in part to World War II. Throughout the late 1940s

Locke continued teaching, often as a visiting professor. After his retirement in 1953, he finally moved to Manhattan, his spiritual hometown, and began work on the ambitious project *The Negro in American Culture.* On June 9, 1954, Alain Locke died of heart failure at New York's Mount Sinai Hospital.

Beth Helen Stickney
City University of New York

PRIMARY WORKS

The New Negro: An Interpretation, 1925; *The Negro and His Music,* 1936; *When Peoples Meet: A Study in Race and Culture Contacts,* 1942; *The Negro in Art,* 1971; *The Negro in American Culture,* 1972; *The Critical Temper of Alain Locke: A Selection of his Essays on Art and Culture,* 1983; *The Philosophy of Alain Locke: Harlem Renaissance and Beyond,* 1989.

The New Negro

In the last decade something beyond the watch and guard of statistics has happened in the life of the American Negro and the three norns who have traditionally presided over the Negro problem have a changeling in their laps. The Sociologist, the Philanthropist, the Race-leader are not unaware of the New Negro, but they are at a loss to account for him. He simply cannot be swathed in their formulae. For the younger generation is vibrant with a new psychology; the new spirit is awake in the masses, and under the very eyes of the professional observers is transforming what has been a perennial problem into the progressive phases of contemporary Negro life.

Could such a metamorphosis have taken place as suddenly as it has appeared to? The answer is no; not because the New Negro is not here, but because the Old Negro had long become more of a myth than a man. The Old Negro, we must remember, was a creature of moral debate and historical controversy. His has been a stock figure perpetuated as an historical fiction partly in innocent sentimentalism, partly in deliberate reactionism. The Negro himself has contributed his share to this through a sort of protective social mimicry forced upon him by the adverse circumstances of dependence. So for generations in the mind of America, the Negro has been more of a formula than a human being—a something to be argued about, condemned or defended, to be "kept down," or "in his place," or "helped up," to be worried with or worried over, harassed or patronized, a social bogey or a social burden. The thinking Negro even has been induced to share this same general attitude, to focus his attention on controversial issues, to see himself in the distorted perspective of a social problem. His shadow, so to speak, has been more real to him than his personality. Through having had to appeal from the unjust stereotypes of his oppressors and traducers to those of his liberators, friends and benefactors he has had to subscribe to the traditional positions from which his case has been viewed. Little true social or self-understanding has or could come from such a situation.

But while the minds of most of us, black and white, have thus burrowed in the trenches of the Civil War and Reconstruction, the actual march of development has simply flanked these positions, necessitating a sudden reorientation of view. We have not been watching in the right direction; set North and South on a sectional axis, we have not noticed the East till the sun has us blinking.

Recall how suddenly the Negro spirituals revealed themselves; suppressed for generations under the stereotypes of Wesleyan hymn harmony, secretive, half-ashamed, until the courage of being natural brought them out—and behold, there was folk-music. Similarly the mind of the Negro seems suddenly to have slipped from under the tyranny of social intimidation and to be shaking off the psychology of imitation and implied inferiority. By shedding the old chrysalis of the Negro problem we are achieving something like a spiritual emancipation. Until recently, lacking self-understanding, we have been almost as much of a problem to ourselves as we still are to others. But the decade that found us with a problem has left us with only a task. The multitude perhaps feels as yet only a strange relief and a new vague urge, but the thinking few know that in the reaction the vital inner grip of prejudice has been broken.

With this renewed self-respect and self-dependence, the life of the Negro community is bound to enter a new dynamic phase, the buoyancy from within compensating for whatever pressure there may be of conditions from without. The migrant masses, shifting from countryside to city, hurdle several generations of experience at a leap, but more important, the same thing happens spiritually in the life-attitudes and self-expression of the Young Negro, in his poetry, his art, his education and his new outlook, with the additional advantage, of course, of the poise and greater certainty of knowing what it is all about. From this comes the promise and warrant of a new leadership. As one of them has discerningly put it:

> We have tomorrow
> Bright before us
> Like a flame.
>
> Yesterday, a night-gone thing
> A sun-down name.
>
> And dawn today
> Broad arch above the road we came.
> We march!

This is what, even more than any "most creditable record of fifty years of freedom," requires that the Negro of to-day be seen through other than the dusty spectacles of past controversy. The day of "aunties," "uncles" and "mammies" is equally gone. Uncle Tom and Sambo have passed on, and even the "Colonel" and "George" play barnstorm rôles from which they escape with relief when the public spotlight is off. The popular melodrama has about played itself out, and it is time to scrap the fictions, garret the bogeys and settle down to a realistic facing of facts.

First we must observe some of the changes which since the traditional lines of opinion were drawn have rendered these quite obsolete. A main change has been, of course, that shifting of the Negro population which has made the Negro problem no longer exclusively or even predominantly Southern. Why should our minds remain sectionalized, when the problem itself no longer is? Then the trend of migration has not only been toward the North and the Central Midwest, but cityward and to the great centers of industry—the problems of adjustment are new, practical, local and not peculiarly racial. Rather they are an integral part of the large industrial and social problems of our present-day democracy. And finally, with the Negro rapidly in process of class differentiation, if it ever was warrantable to regard and treat the Negro *en masse* it is becoming with every day less possible, more unjust and more ridiculous.

In the very process of being transplanted, the Negro is becoming transformed.

The tide of Negro migration, northward and city-ward, is not to be fully explained as a blind flood started by the demands of war industry coupled with the shutting off of foreign migration, or by the pressure of poor crops coupled with increased social terrorism in certain sections of the South and Southwest. Neither labor demand, the bollweevil nor the Ku Klux Klan is a basic factor, however contributory any or all of them may have been. The wash and rush of this human tide on the beach line of the northern city centers is to be explained primarily in terms of a new vision of opportunity, of social and economic freedom, of a spirit to seize, even in the face of an extortionate and heavy toll, a chance for the improvement of conditions. With each successive wave of it, the movement of the Negro becomes more and more a mass movement toward the larger and the more democratic chance—in the Negro's case a deliberate flight not only from countryside to city, but from medieval America to modern.

Take Harlem as an instance of this. Here in Manhattan is not merely the largest Negro community in the world, but the first concentration in history of so many diverse elements of Negro life. It has attracted the African, the West Indian, the Negro American; has brought together the Negro of the North and the Negro of the South; the man from the city and the man from the town and village; the peasant, the student, the business man, the professional man, artist, poet, musician, adventurer and worker, preacher and criminal, exploiter and social outcast. Each group has come with its own separate motives and for its own special ends, but their greatest experience has been the finding of one another. Proscription and prejudice have thrown these dissimilar elements into a common area of contact and interaction. Within this area, race sympathy and unity have determined a further fusing of sentiment and experience. So what began in terms of segregation becomes more and more, as its elements mix and react, the laboratory of a great race-welding. Hitherto, it must be admitted that American Negroes have been a race more in name than in fact, or to be exact, more in sentiment than in experience. The chief bond between them has been that of a common condition rather than a common consciousness; a problem in common rather than a life in common. In Harlem, Negro life is seizing upon its first chances for group expression and self-determination. It is—or promises at least to be—a race capital. That is why our comparison is taken with those nascent centers of folk-expression and self-determination which are playing a creative part in the world to-day. Without pretense to their political significance, Harlem has the same rôle to play for the New Negro as Dublin has had for the New Ireland or Prague for the New Czechoslovakia.

Harlem, I grant you, isn't typical—but it is significant, it is prophetic. No sane observer, however sympathetic to the new trend, would contend that the great masses are articulate as yet, but they stir, they move, they are more than physically restless. The challenge of the new intellectuals among them is clear enough—the "race radicals" and realists who have broken with the old epoch of philanthropic guidance, sentimental appeal and protest. But are we after all only reading into the stirrings of a sleeping giant the dreams of an agitator? The answer is in the migrating peasant. It is the "man farthest down" who is most active in getting up. One of the most characteristic symptoms of this is the professional man, himself migrating to recapture his constituency after a vain effort to maintain in some Southern corner what for years back seemed an established living and clientele. The clergyman following his errant flock, the physician or lawyer trailing his clients, supply the true clues. In a real sense it is the rank and file who are leading, and the leaders who are following. A transformed and transforming psychology permeates the masses.

When the racial leaders of twenty years ago spoke of developing race-pride and stimulating race-consciousness, and of the desirability of race solidarity, they could not in any accurate degree have anticipated the abrupt feeling that has surged up and now pervades the awakened centers. Some of the recognized Negro leaders and a powerful section of white opinion identified with "race work" of the older order have indeed attempted to discount this feeling as a "passing phase," an attack of "race nerves" so to speak, an "aftermath of the war," and the like. It has not abated, however, if we are to gauge by the present tone and temper of the Negro press, or by the shift in popular support from the officially recognized and orthodox spokesmen to those of the independent, popular, and often radical type who are unmistakable symptoms of a new order. It is a social disservice to blunt the fact that the Negro of the Northern centers has reached a stage where tutelage, even of the most interested and well-intentioned sort, must give place to new relationships, where positive self-direction must be reckoned with in ever increasing measure. The American mind must reckon with a fundamentally changed Negro.

The Negro too, for his part, has idols of the tribe to smash. If on the one hand the white man has erred in making the Negro appear to be that which would excuse or extenuate his treatment of him, the Negro, in turn, has too often unnecessarily excused himself because of the way he has been treated. The intelligent Negro of to-day is resolved not to make discrimination an extenuation for his shortcomings in performance, individual or collective; he is trying to hold himself at par, neither inflated by sentimental allowances nor depreciated by current social discounts. For this he must know himself and be known for precisely what he is, and for that reason he welcomes the new scientific rather than the old sentimental interest. Sentimental interest in the Negro has ebbed. We used to lament this as the falling off of our friends; now we rejoice and pray to be delivered both from self-pity and condescension. The mind of each racial group has had a bitter weaning, apathy or hatred on one side matching disillusionment or resentment on the other; but they face each other to-day with the possibility at least of entirely new mutual attitudes.

It does not follow that if the Negro were better known, he would be better liked or better treated. But mutual understanding is basic for any subsequent coöperation and adjustment. The effort toward this will at least have the effect of remedying in large part what has been the most unsatisfactory feature of our present stage of race relationships in America, namely the fact that the more intelligent and representative elements of the two race groups have at so many points got quite out of vital touch with one another.

The fiction is that the life of the races is separate, and increasingly so. The fact is that they have touched too closely at the unfavorable and too lightly at the favorable levels.

While inter-racial councils have sprung up in the South, drawing on forward elements of both races, in the Northern cities manual laborers may brush elbows in their everyday work, but the community and business leaders have experienced no such interplay or far too little of it. These segments must achieve contact or the race situation in America becomes desperate. Fortunately this is happening. There is a growing realization that in social effort the co-operative basis must supplant long-distance philanthropy, and that the only safeguard for mass relations in the future must be provided in the carefully maintained contacts of the enlightened minorities of both race groups. In the intellectual realm a renewed and keen curiosity is replacing the recent apathy; the Negro is being carefully studied, not just talked about and discussed. In art and letters, instead of being wholly caricatured, he is being seriously portrayed and painted.

To all of this the New Negro is keenly responsive as an augury of a new democracy in American culture. He is contributing his share to the new social understanding. But the desire to be understood would never in itself have been sufficient to have opened so completely the protectively closed portals of the thinking Negro's mind. There is still too much possibility of being snubbed or patronized for that. It was rather the necessity for fuller, truer self-expression, the realization of the unwisdom of allowing social discrimination to segregate him mentally, and a counterattitude to cramp and fetter his own living—and so the "spite-wall" that the intellectuals built over the "color-line" has happily been taken down. Much of this reopening of intellectual contacts has centered in New York and has been richly fruitful not merely in the enlarging of personal experience, but in the definite enrichment of American art and letters and in the clarifying of our common vision of the social tasks ahead.

The particular significance in the re-establishment of contact between the more advanced and representative classes is that it promises to offset some of the unfavorable reactions of the past, or at least to re-surface race contacts somewhat for the future. Subtly the conditions that are molding a New Negro are molding a new American attitude.

However, this new phase of things is delicate; it will call for less charity but more justice; less help, but infinitely closer understanding. This is indeed a critical stage of race relationships because of the likelihood, if the new temper is not understood, of engendering sharp group antagonism and a second crop of more calculated prejudice. In some quarters, it has already done so. Having weaned the Negro, public opinion cannot continue to paternalize. The Negro to-day is inevitably moving forward under the control largely of his own objectives. What are these objectives? Those of his outer life are happily already well and finally formulated, for they are none other than the ideals of American institutions and democracy. Those of his inner life are yet in process of formation, for the new psychology at present is more of a consensus of feeling than of opinion, of attitude rather than of program. Still some points seem to have crystallized.

Up to the present one may adequately describe the Negro's "inner objectives" as an attempt to repair a damaged group psychology and reshape a warped social perspective. Their realization has required a new mentality for the American Negro.

And as it matures we begin to see its effects; at first, negative, iconoclastic, and then positive and constructive. In this new group psychology we note the lapse of sentimental appeal, then the development of a more positive self-respect and self-reliance; the repudiation of social dependence, and then the gradual recovery from hyper-sensitiveness and "touchy" nerves, the repudiation of the double standard of judgment with its special philanthropic allowances and then the sturdier desire for objective and scientific appraisal; and finally the rise from social disillusionment to race pride, from the sense of social debt to the responsibilities of social contribution, and offsetting the necessary working and commonsense acceptance of restricted conditions, the belief in ultimate esteem and recognition. Therefore the Negro to-day wishes to be known for what he is, even in his faults and shortcomings, and scorns a craven and precarious survival at the price of seeming to be what he is not. He resents being spoken of as a social ward or minor, even by his own, and to being regarded a chronic patient for the sociological clinic, the sick man of American Democracy. For the same reasons, he himself is through with those social nostrums and panaceas, the so-called "solutions" of his "problem," with which he and the country have been so liberally dosed in the past. Religion, freedom, education, money—in turn, he has ardently hoped for and peculiarly trusted these things; he still believes in them, but not in blind trust that they alone will solve his life-problem.

Each generation, however, will have its creed, and that of the present is the belief in the efficacy of collective effort, in race co-operation. This deep feeling of race is at present the mainspring of Negro life. It seems to be the outcome of the reaction to proscription and prejudice; an attempt, fairly successful on the whole, to convert a defensive into an offensive position, a handicap into an incentive. It is radical in tone, but not in purpose and only the most stupid forms of opposition, misunderstanding or persecution could make it otherwise. Of course, the thinking Negro has shifted a little toward the left with the world-trend, and there is an increasing group who affiliate with radical and liberal movements. But fundamentally for the present the Negro is radical on race matters, conservative on others, in other words, a "forced radical," a social protestant rather than a genuine radical. Yet under further pressure and injustice iconoclastic thought and motives will inevitably increase. Harlem's quixotic radicalisms call for their ounce of democracy to-day lest to-morrow they be beyond cure.

The Negro mind reaches out as yet to nothing but American wants, American ideas. But this forced attempt to build his Americanism on race values is a unique social experiment, and its ultimate success is impossible except through the fullest sharing of American culture and institutions. There should be no delusion about this. American nerves in sections unstrung with race hysteria are often fed the opiate that the trend of Negro advance is wholly separatist, and that the effect of its operation will be to encyst the Negro as a benign foreign body in the body politic. This cannot be—even if it were desirable. The racialism of the Negro is no limitation or reservation with respect to American life; it is only a constructive effort to build the obstructions in the stream of his progress into an efficient dam of social energy and power. Democracy itself is obstructed and stagnated to the extent that any of its channels are closed. Indeed they cannot be selectively closed. So the choice is not between one way for the Negro and another way for the rest, but between American institutions frustrated on the one hand and American ideals progressively fulfilled and realized on the other.

There is, of course, a warrantably comfortable feeling in being on the right side of the country's professed ideals. We realize that we cannot be undone without America's undoing. It is within the gamut of this attitude that the thinking Negro faces America, but with variations of mood that are if anything more significant than the attitude itself. Sometimes we have it taken with the defiant ironic challenge of McKay:

> Mine is the future grinding down to-day
> Like a great landslip moving to the sea,
> Bearing its freight of débris far away
> Where the green hungry waters restlessly
> Heave mammoth pyramids, and break and roar
> Their eerie challenge to the crumbling shore.

Sometimes, perhaps more frequently as yet, it is taken in the fervent and almost filial appeal and counsel of Weldon Johnson's:

> O Southland, dear Southland!
> Then why do you still cling
> To an idle age and a musty page,
> To a dead and useless thing?

But between defiance and appeal, midway almost between cynicism and hope, the prevailing mind stands in the mood of the same author's *To America,* an attitude of sober query and stoical challenge:

> How would you have us, as we are?
> Or sinking 'neath the load we bear,
> Our eyes fixed forward on a star,
> Or gazing empty at despair?
>
> Rising or falling? Men or things?
> With dragging pace or footsteps fleet?
> Strong, willing sinews in your wings,
> Or tightening chains about your feet?

More and more, however, an intelligent realization of the great discrepancy between the American social creed and the American social practice forces upon the Negro the taking of the moral advantage that is his. Only the steadying and sobering effect of a truly characteristic gentleness of spirit prevents the rapid rise of a definite cynicism and counter-hate and a defiant superiority feeling. Human as this reaction would be, the majority still deprecate its advent, and would gladly see it forestalled by the speedy amelioration of its causes. We wish our race pride to be a healthier, more positive achievement than a feeling based upon a realization of the shortcomings of others. But all paths toward the attainment of a sound social attitude have been difficult; only a relatively few enlightened minds have been able as the phrase puts it "to rise above" prejudice. The ordinary man has had until recently only a hard choice between the alternatives of supine and humiliating submission and stimulating but hurtful counter-prejudice. Fortunately from some inner, desperate resourcefulness has recently sprung up the simple expedient of fighting prejudice by mental passive resistance, in other words by trying to ignore it. For the few, this manna may perhaps be effective, but the masses cannot thrive upon it.

Fortunately there are constructive channels opening out into which the balked social feelings of the American Negro can flow freely.

Without them there would be much more pressure and danger than there is. These compensating interests are racial but in a new and enlarged way. One is the consciousness of acting as the advance-guard of the African peoples in their contact with Twentieth Century civilization; the other, the sense of a mission of rehabilitating the race in world esteem from that loss of prestige for which the fate and conditions of slavery have so largely been responsible. Harlem, as we shall see, is the center of both these movements; she is the home of the Negro's "Zionism." The pulse of the Negro world has begun to beat in Harlem. A Negro newspaper carrying news material in English, French and Spanish, gathered from all quarters of America, the West Indies and Africa has maintained itself in Harlem for over five years. Two important magazines, both edited from New York, maintain their news and circulation consistently on a cosmopolitan scale. Under American auspices and backing, three pan-African congresses have been held abroad for the discussion of common interests, colonial questions and future co-operative development of Africa. In terms of the race question as a world problem, the Negro mind has leapt, so to speak, upon the parapets of prejudice and extended its cramped horizons. In so doing it has linked up with the growing group consciousness of the dark-peoples and is gradually learning their common interests. As one of our writers has recently put it: "It is imperative that we understand the white world in its relations to the non-white world." As with the Jew, persecution is making the Negro international.

As a world phenomenon this wider race consciousness is a different thing from the much asserted rising tide of color. Its inevitable causes are not of our making. The consequences are not necessarily damaging to the best interests of civilization. Whether it actually brings into being new Armadas of conflict or argosies of cultural exchange and enlightenment can only be decided by the attitude of the dominant races in an era of critical change. With the American Negro, his new internationalism is primarily an effort to recapture contact with the scattered peoples of African derivation. Garveyism may be a transient, if spectacular, phenomenon, but the possible rôle of the American Negro in the future development of Africa is one of the most constructive and universally helpful missions that any modern people can lay claim to.

Constructive participation in such causes cannot help giving the Negro valuable group incentives, as well as increased prestigé at home and abroad. Our greatest rehabilitation may possibly come through such channels, but for the present, more immediate hope rests in the revaluation by white and black alike of the Negro in terms of his artistic endowments and cultural contributions, past and prospective. It must be increasingly recognized that the Negro has already made very substantial contributions, not only in his folk-art, music especially, which has always found appreciation, but in larger, though humbler and less acknowledged ways. For generations the Negro has been the peasant matrix of that section of America which has most undervalued him, and here he has contributed not only materially in labor and in social patience, but spiritually as well. The South has unconsciously absorbed the gift of his folk-temperament. In less than half a generation it will be easier to recognize this, but the fact remains that a leaven of humor, sentiment, imagination and tropic nonchalance has gone into the making of the South from a humble, unacknowledged source. A second crop of the Negro's gifts promises still more largely. He now becomes a conscious contributor and lays aside the status of a beneficiary and ward for that of a collaborator and participant in American civilization. The great social gain in this is the releasing of our talented group from the arid fields of controversy and debate to the productive fields of creative expression. The especially cultural recognition they win should in turn prove the key to that revaluation of the Negro which must precede or accompany any considerable further betterment of race relationships. But whatever the general effect, the present generation will have added the motives of self-expression and spiritual development to the old and still unfinished task of making material headway and progress. No one who understandingly faces the situation with its substantial accomplishment or views the new scene with its still more abundant promise can be entirely without hope. And certainly, if in our lifetime the Negro should not be able to celebrate his full initiation into American democracy, he can at least, on the warrant of these things, celebrate the attainment of a significant and satisfying new phase of group development, and with it a spiritual Coming of Age.

1925

Jean Toomer 1894–1967

Born and raised in Washington, D.C., Nathan Eugene Toomer was the only child of Nina Pinchback, and her husband, Nathan Toomer. Soon after his son's birth, however, Nathan, Sr., disappeared, and Nina was forced, through economic need, to return to live with her father, Pinckney Benton Stewart Pinchback, who had been a controversial figure in Louisiana Reconstruction politics. She remarried in 1906 and took her son with her to New Rochelle, New York. Following her untimely death in 1909, Toomer returned to Washington and remained there until he left for college in 1914. Thereafter, intermittently, he lived for varying periods of time with his grandparents, until their deaths in the 1920s.

As a young man, Jean Toomer took a long time choosing a profession. He attended six separate institutions of higher education, but never graduated. However, even as a child, he enjoyed literature, and as early as when he lived in New York, he attempted to write. In 1919 he made up his mind to pursue a literary career.

Cane, his most important work, was published in 1923. This book grew out of a trip to the South in September 1921, at a time when he was frustrated with the slow progress of his writing. Toomer's encounter with rural African American folk culture inspired him, and the visit served as the catalyst for ideas that connected his identity, positively, to his creative impulses. *Cane* was highly praised upon publication. Toomer's friends and associates were mostly white avant-garde writers, but black writers of the early New Negro Renaissance claimed him as their own. As the first book to emerge from that period, *Cane* was called the herald of a new day in African American letters, and Toomer the most promising of the upcoming new writers. In its artistic achievement, his work had surpassed all prior literary descriptions of the African American experience. His future seemed assured.

Although composed of three separate parts, *Cane* unifies the northern and southern African American experiences through its circular movement. In the first section, six vignettes of southern women and twelve poems, in lyrical, vivid, mystical, and sensuous language, highlight the duality of black southern life in their portrayal of conflicts, pressures, and racial and economic oppression. The second section is a kaleidoscope of impressions of the death of black spirituality in a wasteland of urban materialism and technology. In the final section, a drama, a black northerner searches for and discovers his identity in the South of his ancestors. The most enduring aspect of *Cane* is its revelation of an intrinsic strength and beauty in black American culture even in the face of white oppression.

Toomer's other works of note include several plays written between 1922 and 1929 in which he experimented with expressionist techniques, then new to America. Among American playwrights, only Eugene O'Neill surpassed him in this respect. But by the beginning of 1924, angered by the negative impact of racial identity in American society and in search of a philosophy that would permit him a sense of internal unity, Toomer turned away from literature and became a follower of mystic George Gurdjieff. From 1924 to 1932 he worked as a teacher of Gurdjieff's philosophy, one which promised him the unity he sought. He continued to write, but never again about the black experience, or with the qualities of his masterpiece, *Cane*. Publishers refused the new work on its non-literary merits. His final publication, a long Whitmanesque poem entitled "The Blue Meridian" (1936), pays tribute to Americans of all races, creeds, and colors.

Toomer was a gifted artist who turned his back on what might have been a brilliant writing career for a principle regarding the meaning of race in America. For this reason, his life and work remain especially interesting to scholars. His grandfather claimed a black identity, although he was sufficiently light-skinned to pass for white. As the equally fair-skinned Toomer grew up and learned about racial politics, he declared himself a member of the American race rather than belonging to a particular ethnic group. This caused him many difficulties, especially as others accused him of denying his African American heritage, a charge he stoutly refuted. He stood firm, maintaining that he was the conscious representative of a people with a heritage of multiple bloodlines, and that others would understand this in time. By privileging no one of his bloodlines, Toomer perceived himself as having taken an important step toward solving America's racial problems.

Nellie Y. McKay
University of Wisconsin at Madison

PRIMARY WORKS

Cane, 1923; *Essentials,* 1931; *The Wayward and the Seeking: A Collection of Writings by Jean Toomer,* ed. Darwin Turner, 1980; *The Collected Poems of Jean Toomer,* ed. Robert B. Jones and Margery Toomer Latimer, 1988.

from Cane

Karintha

Her skin is like dusk on the eastern horizon,
O cant you see it, O cant you see it,
Her skin is like dusk on the eastern horizon
. . . When the sun goes down.

Men had always wanted her, this Karintha, even as a child, Karintha carrying beauty, perfect as dusk when the sun goes down. Old men rode her hobby-horse upon their knees. Young men danced with her at frolics when they should have been dancing with their grown-up girls. God grant us youth, secretly prayed the old men. The young fellows counted the time to pass before she would be old enough to mate with them. This interest of the male, who wishes to ripen a growing thing too soon, could mean no good to her.

Karintha, at twelve, was a wild flash that told the other folks just what it was to live. At sunset, when there was no wind, and the pine-smoke from over by the sawmill hugged the earth, and you couldnt see more than a few feet in front, her sudden darting past you was a bit of vivid color, like a black bird that flashes in light. With the other children one could hear, some distance off, their feet flopping in the two-inch dust. Karintha's running was a whir. It had the sound of the red dust that sometimes makes a spiral in the road. At dusk, during the hush just after the sawmill had closed down, and before any of the women had started their supper getting-ready songs, her voice, high-pitched, shrill, would put one's ears to itching. But no one ever thought to make her stop because of it. She stoned the cows, and beat her dog, and fought the other children . . . Even the preacher, who caught her at mischief, told himself that she was as innocently lovely as a November cotton flower. Already, rumors were out about her. Homes in Georgia are most often built on the two-room plan. In one, you cook and eat, in the other you sleep, and there love goes on. Karintha had seen or heard, perhaps she had felt her parents loving. One could but imitate one's parents, for to follow them was the way of God. She played "home" with a small boy who was not afraid to do her bidding. That started the whole thing. Old men could no longer ride her hobby-horse upon their knees. But young men counted faster.

Her skin is like dusk,
O cant you see it,
Her skin is like dusk,
When the sun goes down.

Karintha is a woman. She who carries beauty, perfect as dusk when the sun goes down. She has been married many times. Old men remind her that a few years back they rode her hobby-horse upon their knees. Karintha smiles, and indulges them when she is in the mood for it. She has contempt for them. Karintha is a woman. Young men run stills to make her money. Young men go to the big cities and run on the road. Young men go away to college. They all want to bring her money. These are the young men who thought that all they had to do was to count time. But Karintha is a woman, and she has had a child. A child fell out of her womb onto a bed of pine-needles in the forest. Pine-needles are smooth and sweet. They are elastic to the feet of rabbits . . . A sawmill was nearby. Its pyramidal sawdust pile smouldered. It is a year before one completely burns. Meanwhile, the smoke curls up and hangs in odd wraiths about the trees, curls up, and spreads itself out over the valley . . . Weeks after Karintha returned home the smoke was so heavy you tasted it in water. Some one made a song:

Smoke is on the hills. Rise up.
Smoke is on the hills, O rise
And take my soul to Jesus.

Karintha is a woman. Men do not know that the soul of her was a growing thing ripened too soon. They will bring their money; they will die not having found it out . . . Karintha at twenty, carrying beauty, perfect as dusk when the sun goes down. Karintha . . .

Her skin is like dusk on the eastern horizon,
O cant you see it, O cant you see it,
Her skin is like dusk on the eastern horizon
. . . When the sun goes down.

Goes down . . .

1923

Song of the Son

Pour O pour that parting soul in song,
O pour it in the sawdust glow of night,
Into the velvet pine-smoke air to-night,
And let the valley carry it along.
And let the valley carry it along.

O land and soil, red soil and sweet-gum tree,
So scant of grass, so profligate of pines,
Now just before an epoch's sun declines
Thy son, in time, I have returned to thee,
Thy son, I have in time returned to thee.

In time, for though the sun is setting on
A song-lit race of slaves, it has not set;
Though late, O soil, it is not too late yet
To catch thy plaintive soul, leaving, soon gone,
Leaving, to catch thy plaintive soul soon gone.

O Negro slaves, dark purple ripened plums,
Squeezed, and bursting in the pine-wood air,
Passing, before they stripped the old tree bare
One plum was saved for me, one seed becomes

An everlasting song, a singing tree,
Caroling softly souls of slavery,
What they were, and what they are to me,
Caroling softly souls of slavery.

1923

Blood-Burning Moon

1

Up from the skeleton stone walls, up from the rotting floor boards and the solid hand-hewn beams of oak of the pre-war cotton factory, dusk came. Up from the dusk the full moon came. Glowing like a fired pine-knot, it illumined the great door and soft showered the Negro shanties aligned along the single street of factory town. The full moon in the great door was an omen. Negro women improvised songs against its spell.

Louisa sang as she came over the crest of the hill from the white folks' kitchen. Her skin was the color of oak leaves on young trees in fall. Her breasts, firm and up-pointed like ripe acorns. And her singing had the low murmur of winds in fig trees. Bob Stone, younger son of the people she worked for, loved her. By the way the world reckons things, he had won her. By measure of that warm glow which came into her mind at thought of him, he had won her. Tom Burwell, whom the whole town called Big Boy, also loved her. But working in the fields all day, and far away from her, gave him no chance to show it. Though often enough of evenings he had tried to. Somehow, he never got along. Strong as he was with hands upon the ax or plow, he found it difficult to hold her. Or so he thought. But the fact was that he held her to factory town more firmly than he thought for. His black balanced, and pulled against, the white of Stone, when she thought of them. And her mind was vaguely upon them as she came over the crest of the hill, coming from the white folks' kitchen. As she sang softly at the evil face of the full moon.

A strange stir was in her. Indolently, she tried to fix upon Bob or Tom as the cause of it. To meet Bob in the canebrake, as she was going to do an hour or so later, was nothing new. And Tom's proposal which she felt on its way to her could be indefinitely put off. Separately, there was no unusual significance to either one. But for some reason, they jumbled when her eyes gazed vacantly at the rising moon. And from the jumble came the stir that was strangely within her. Her lips trembled. The slow rhythm of her song grew agitant and restless. Rusty black and tan spotted hounds, lying in the dark corners of porches or prowling around back yards, put their noses in the air and caught its tremor. They began plaintively to yelp and howl. Chickens woke up and cackled. Intermittently, all over the countryside dogs barked and roosters crowed as if heralding a weird dawn or some ungodly awakening. The women sang lustily. Their songs were cotton-wads to stop their ears. Louisa came down into factory town and sank wearily upon the step before her home. The moon was rising towards a thick cloud-bank which soon would hide it.

Red nigger moon. Sinner!
Blood-burning moon. Sinner!
Come out that fact'ry door.

2

Up from the deep dusk of a cleared spot on the edge of the forest a mellow glow arose and spread fan-wise into the low-hanging heavens. And all around the air was heavy with the scent of boiling cane. A large pile of cane-stalks lay like ribboned shadows upon the ground. A mule, harnessed to a pole, trudged lazily round and round the pivot of the grinder. Beneath a swaying oil lamp, a Negro alternately whipped out at the mule, and fed cane-stalks to the grinder. A fat boy waddled pails of fresh ground juice between the grinder and the boiling stove. Steam came from the copper boiling pan. The scent of cane came from the copper pan and drenched the forest and the hill that sloped to factory town, beneath its fragrance. It drenched the men in circle seated around the stove. Some of them chewed at the white pulp of stalks, but there was no need for them to, if all they wanted was to taste the cane. One tasted it in factory town. And from factory town one could see the soft haze thrown by the glowing stove upon the low-hanging heavens.

Old David Georgia stirred the thickening syrup with a long ladle, and ever so often drew it off. Old David Georgia tended his stove and told tales about the white folks, about moonshining and cotton picking, and about sweet nigger gals, to the men who sat there about his stove to listen to him. Tom Burwell chewed cane-stalk and laughed with the others till some one mentioned Louisa. Till some one said something about Louisa and Bob Stone, about the silk stockings she must have gotten from him. Blood ran up Tom's neck hotter than the glow that flooded from the stove. He sprang up. Glared at the men and said, "She's my gal." Will Manning laughed. Tom strode over to him. Yanked him up and knocked him to the ground. Several of Manning's friends got up to fight for him. Tom whipped out a long knife and would have cut them to shreds if they hadnt ducked into the woods. Tom had had enough. He nodded to Old David Georgia and swung down the path to factory town. Just then, the dogs started barking and the roosters began to crow. Tom felt funny. Away from the fight, away from the stove, chill got to him. He shivered. He shuddered when he saw the full moon rising towards the cloud-bank. He who didnt give a godam for the fears of old women. He forced his mind to fasten on Louisa. Bob Stone. Better not be. He turned into the street and saw Louisa sitting before her home. He went towards her, ambling, touched the brim of a marvelously shaped, spotted, felt hat, said he wanted to say something to her, and then found that he didnt know what he had to say, or if he did, that he couldnt say it. He shoved his big fists in his overalls, grinned, and started to move off.

"Youall want me, Tom?"

"Thats what us wants, sho, Louisa."

"Well, here I am—"

"An here I is, but that aint ahelpin none, all th same."

"You wanted to say something? . ."

"I did that, sho. But words is like th spots on dice: no matter how y fumbles em, there's times when they jes wont come. I dunno why. Seems like th love I feels fo yo done stole m tongue. I got it now. Whee! Louisa, honey, I oughtnt tell y, I feel I oughtnt cause yo is young an goes t church an I has had other gals, but Louisa I sho do love y. Lil gal, Ise watched y from them first days when youall sat right here befo yo door befo th well an sang sometimes in a way that like t broke m heart. Ise carried y with me into th fields, day after day, an after that, an I sho can plow when yo is there, an I can pick cotton. Yassur! Come near beatin Barlo yesterday. I sho did. Yassur! An next year if ole Stone'll trust me, I'll have a farm. My own. My bales will buy yo what y gets from white folks now. Silk stockings an purple dresses—course I dont believe what some folks been whisperin as t how y gets them things now. White folks always did do for niggers what they likes. An they jes cant help alikin yo, Louisa. Bob Stone likes y. Course he does. But not the way folks is awhisperin. Does he, hon?"

"I dont know what you mean, Tom."

"Course y dont. Ise already cut two niggers. Had t hon, t tell em so. Niggers always tryin t make somethin out a nothin. An then besides, white folks aint up t them tricks so much nowadays. Godam better not be. Leastawise not with yo. Cause I wouldnt stand f it. Nassur."

"What would you do, Tom?"

"Cut him jes like I cut a nigger."

"No, Tom—"

"I said I would an there aint no mo to it. But that aint th talk f now. Sing, honey Louisa, an while I'm listenin t y I'll be makin love."

Tom took her hand in his. Against the tough thickness of his own, hers felt soft and small. His huge body slipped down to the step beside her. The full moon sank upward into the deep purple of the cloud-bank. An old woman brought a lighted lamp and hung it on the common well whose bulky shadow squatted in the middle of the road, opposite Tom and Louisa. The old woman lifted the well-lid, took hold the chain, and began drawing up the heavy bucket. As she did so, she sang. Figures shifted, restlesslike, between lamp and window in the front rooms of the shanties. Shadows of the figures fought each other on the gray dust of the road. Figures raised the windows and joined the old woman in song. Louisa and Tom, the whole street, singing:

> Red nigger moon. Sinner!
> Blood-burning moon. Sinner!
> Come out that fact'ry door.

3

Bob Stone sauntered from his veranda out into the gloom of fir trees and magnolias. The clear white of his skin paled, and the flush of his cheeks turned purple. As if to balance this outer change, his mind became consciously a white man's. He passed the house with its huge open hearth which, in the days of slavery, was the plantation cookery. He saw Louisa bent over that hearth. He went in as a master should and took her. Direct, honest, bold. None of this sneaking that he had to go through now. The contrast was repulsive to him. His family had lost ground. Hell no, his family still owned the niggers, practically. Damned if they did, or he wouldnt have to duck around so. What would they think if they knew? His mother? His sister? He shouldnt mention them, shouldnt think of them in this connection. There in the dusk he blushed at doing so. Fellows about town were all right, but how about his friends up North? He could see them incredible, repulsed. They didnt know. The thought first made him laugh. Then, with their eyes still upon him, he began to feel embarrassed. He felt the need of explaining things to them. Explain hell. They wouldnt understand, and moreover, who ever heard of a Southerner getting on his knees to any Yankee, or anyone. No sir. He was going to see Louisa to-night, and love her. She was lovely—in her way. Nigger way. What way was that? Damned if he knew. Must know. He'd known her long enough to know. Was there something about niggers that you couldnt know? Listening to them at church didnt tell you anything. Looking at them didnt tell you anything. Talking to them didnt tell you anything—unless it was gossip, unless they wanted to talk. Of course, about farming, and licker, and craps—but those werent nigger. Nigger was something more. How much more? Something to be afraid of, more? Hell no. Who ever heard of being afraid of a nigger? Tom Burwell. Cartwell had told him that Tom went with Louisa after she reached home. No sir. No nigger had ever been with his girl. He'd like to see one try. Some position for him to be in. Him, Bob Stone, of the old Stone family, in a scrap with a nigger over a nigger girl. In the good old days . . . Ha! Those were the days. His family had lost ground. Not so much, though. Enough for him to have to cut through old Lemon's canefield by way of the woods, that he might meet her. She was worth it. Beautiful nigger gal. Why nigger? Why not, just gal? No, it was because she was nigger that he went to her. Sweet . . . The scent of boiling cane came to him. Then he saw the rich glow of the stove. He heard the voices of the men circled around it. He was about to skirt the clearing when he heard his own name mentioned. He stopped. Quivering. Leaning against a tree, he listened.

"Bad nigger. Yassur, he sho is one bad nigger when he gets started."

"Tom Burwell's been on th gang three times fo cuttin men."

"What y think he's agwine t do t Bob Stone?"

"Dunno yet. He aint found out. When he does—Baby!"

"Aint no tellin."

"Young Stone aint no quitter an I ken tell y that. Blood of th old uns in his veins."

"That's right. He'll scrap, sho."

"Be gettin too hot f niggers round this away."

"Shut up, nigger. Y dont know what y talkin bout."

Bob Stone's ears burned as though he had been holding them over the stove. Sizzling heat welled up within him. His feet felt as if they rested on red-hot coals. They stung him to quick movement. He circled the fringe of the glowing. Not a twig cracked beneath his feet. He reached the path that led to factory town. Plunged furiously down it. Halfway along, a blindness within him veered him aside. He crashed into the bordering canebrake. Cane leaves cut his face and lips. He tasted blood. He threw himself down and dug his fingers in the ground. The earth was cool. Cane-roots took the fever from his hands. After a long while, or so it seemed to him, the thought came to him that it must be time to see Louisa. He got to his feet and walked calmly to their meeting place. No Louisa. Tom Burwell had her. Veins in his forehead bulged and distended. Saliva moistened the dried blood on his lips. He bit down on his lips. He tasted blood. Not his own blood; Tom Burwell's blood. Bob drove through the cane and out again upon the road. A hound swung down the path before him towards factory town. Bob couldnt see it. The dog loped aside to let him pass. Bob's blind rushing made him stumble over it. He fell with a thud that dazed him. The hound yelped. Answering yelps came from all over the countryside. Chickens cackled. Roosters crowed, heralding the bloodshot eyes of southern awakening. Singers in the town were silenced. They shut their windows down. Palpitant between the rooster crows, a chill hush settled upon the huddled forms of Tom and Louisa. A figure rushed from the shadow and stood before them. Tom popped to his feet.

"Whats y want?"

"I'm Bob Stone."

"Yassur—an I'm Tom Burwell. Whats y want?"

Bob lunged at him. Tom side-stepped, caught him by the shoulder, and flung him to the ground. Straddled him.

"Let me up."

"Yassur—but watch yo doins, Bob Stone."

A few dark figures, drawn by the sound of scuffle, stood about them. Bob sprang to his feet.

"Fight like a man, Tom Burwell, and I'll lick y."

Again he lunged. Tom side-stepped and flung him to the ground. Straddled him.

"Get off me, you godam nigger you."

"Yo sho has started somethin now. Get up."

Tom yanked him up and began hammering at him. Each blow sounded as if it smashed into a precious, irreplaceable soft something. Beneath them, Bob staggered back. He reached in his pocket and whipped out a knife.

"Thats my game, sho."

Blue flash, a steel blade slashed across Bob Stone's throat. He had a sweetish sick feeling. Blood began to flow. Then he felt a sharp twitch of pain. He let his knife drop. He slapped one hand against his neck. He pressed the other on top of his head as if to hold it down. He groaned. He turned, and staggered towards the crest of the hill in the direction of white town. Negroes who had seen the fight slunk into their homes and blew the lamps out. Louisa, dazed, hysterical, refused to go indoors. She slipped, crumbled, her body loosely propped against the woodwork of the well. Tom Burwell leaned against it. He seemed rooted there.

Bob reached Broad Street. White men rushed up to him. He collapsed in their arms.

"Tom Burwell. . . ."

White men like ants upon a forage rushed about. Except for the taut hum of their moving, all was silent. Shotguns, revolvers, rope, kerosene, torches. Two high-powered cars with glaring search-lights. They came together. The taut hum rose to a low roar. Then nothing could be heard but the flop of their feet in the thick dust of the road. The moving body of their silence preceded them over the crest of the hill into factory town. It flattened the Negroes beneath it. It rolled to the wall of the factory, where it stopped. Tom knew that they were coming. He couldnt move. And then he saw the search-lights of the two cars glaring down on him. A quick shock went through him. He stiffened. He started to run. A yell went up from the mob. Tom wheeled about and faced them. They poured down on him. They swarmed. A large man with dead-white face and flabby cheeks came to him and almost jabbed a gun-barrel through his guts.

"Hands behind y, nigger."

Tom's wrists were bound. The big man shoved him to the well. Burn him over it, and when the woodwork caved in, his body would drop to the bottom. Two deaths for a godam nigger. Louisa was driven back. The mob pushed in. Its pressure, its momentum was too great. Drag him to the factory. Wood and stakes already there. Tom moved in the direction indicated. But they had to drag him. They reached the great door. Too many to get in there. The mob divided and flowed around the walls to either side. The big man shoved him through the door. The mob pressed in from the sides. Taut humming. No words. A stake was sunk into the ground. Rotting floor boards piled around it. Kerosene poured on the rotting floor boards. Tom bound to the stake. His breast was bare. Nails' scratches let little lines of blood trickle down and mat into the hair. His face, his eyes were set and stony. Except for irregular breathing, one would have thought him already dead. Torches were flung onto the pile. A great flare muffled in black smoke shot upward. The mob yelled. The mob was silent. Now Tom could be seen within the flames. Only his head, erect, lean, like a blackened stone. Stench of burning flesh soaked the air. Tom's eyes popped. His head settled downward. The mob yelled. Its yell echoed against the skeleton stone walls and sounded like a hundred yells. Like a hundred mobs yelling. Its yell thudded against the thick front wall and fell back. Ghost of a yell slipped through the flames and out the great door of the factory. It fluttered like a dying thing down the single street of factory town. Louisa, upon the step before her home, did not hear it, but her eyes opened slowly. They saw the full moon glowing in the great door. The full moon, an evil thing, an omen, soft showering the homes of folks she knew. Where were they, these people? She'd sing, and perhaps they'd come out and join her. Perhaps Tom Burwell would come. At any rate, the full moon in the great door was an omen which she must sing to:

Red nigger moon. Sinner!
Blood-burning moon. Sinner!
Come out that fact'ry door.

1923

Seventh Street

Money burns the pocket, pocket hurts,
Bootleggers in silken shirts,
Ballooned, zooming Cadillacs,
Whizzing, whizzing down the street-car tracks.

Seventh Street is a bastard of Prohibition and the War. A crude-boned, soft-skinned wedge of nigger life breathing its loafer air, jazz songs and love, thrusting unconscious rhythms, black reddish blood into the white and whitewashed wood of Washington. Stale soggy wood of Washington. Wedges rust in soggy wood . . . Split it! In two! Again! Shred it! . . the sun. Wedges are brilliant in the sun; ribbons of wet wood dry and blow away. Black reddish blood. Pouring for crude-boned soft-skinned life, who set you flowing? Blood suckers of the War would spin in a frenzy of dizziness if they drank your blood. Prohibition would put a stop to it. Who set you flowing? White and whitewash disappear in blood. Who set you flowing? Flowing down the smooth asphalt of Seventh Street, in shanties, brick office buildings, theaters, drug stores, restaurants, and cabarets? Eddying on the corners? Swirling like a blood-red smoke up where the buzzards fly in heaven? God would not dare to suck black red blood. A Nigger God! He would duck his head in shame and call for the Judgment Day. Who set you flowing?

Money burns the pocket, pocket hurts,
Bootleggers in silken shirts,
Ballooned, zooming Cadillacs,
Whizzing, whizzing down the street-car tracks.

1923

Box Seat

1

Houses are shy girls whose eyes shine reticently upon the dusk body of the street. Upon the gleaming limbs and asphalt torso of a dreaming nigger. Shake your curled wool-blossoms, nigger. Open your liver lips to the lean, white spring. Stir the root-life of a withered people. Call them from their houses, and teach them to dream.

Dark swaying forms of Negroes are street songs that woo virginal houses.

Dan Moore walks southward on Thirteenth Street. The low limbs of budding chestnut trees recede above his head. Chestnut buds and blossoms are wool he walks upon. The eyes of houses faintly touch him as he passes them. Soft girl-eyes, they set him singing. Girl-eyes within him widen upward to promised faces. Floating away, they dally wistfully over the dusk body of the street. Come on, Dan Moore, come on. Dan sings. His voice is a little hoarse. It cracks. He strains to produce tones in keeping with the houses' loveliness. Cant be done. He whistles. His notes are shrill. They hurt him. Negroes open gates, and go indoors, perfectly. Dan thinks of the house he's going to. Of the girl. Lips, flesh-notes of a forgotten song, plead with him . . .

Dan turns into a side-street, opens an iron gate, bangs it to. Mounts the steps, and searches for the bell. Funny, he cant find it. He fumbles around. The thought comes to him that some one passing by might see him, and not understand. Might think that he is trying to sneak, to break in.

Dan: Break in. Get an ax and smash in. Smash in their faces. I'll show em. Break into an engine-house, steal a thousand horse-power fire truck. Smash in with the truck. I'll show em. Grab an ax and brain em. Cut em up. Jack the Ripper. Baboon from the zoo. And then the cops come. "No, I aint a baboon. I aint Jack the Ripper. I'm a poor man out of work. Take your hands off me, you bull-necked bears. Look into my eyes. I am Dan Moore. I was born in a canefield. The hands of Jesus touched me. I am come to a sick world to heal it. Only the other day, a dope fiend brushed against me—Dont laugh, you mighty, juicy, meat-hook men. Give me your fingers and I will peel them as if they were ripe bananas.

Some one might think he is trying to break in. He'd better knock. His knuckles are raw bone against the thick glass door. He waits. No one comes. Perhaps they havent heard him. He raps again. This time, harder. He waits. No one comes. Some one is surely in. He fancies that he sees their shadows on the glass. Shadows of gorillas. Perhaps they saw him coming and dont want to let him in. He knocks. The tension of his arms makes the glass rattle. Hurried steps come towards him. The door opens.

"Please, you might break the glass—the bell—oh, Mr. Moore! I thought it must be some stranger. How do you do? Come in, wont you? Muriel? Yes. I'll call her. Take your things off, wont you? And have a seat in the parlor. Muriel will be right down. Muriel! Oh Muriel! Mr. Moore to see you. She'll be right down. You'll pardon me, wont you? So glad to see you."

Her eyes are weak. They are bluish and watery from reading newspapers. The blue is steel. It gimlets Dan while her mouth flaps amiably to him.

Dan: Nothing for you to see, old mussel-head. Dare I show you? If I did, delirium would furnish you headlines for a month. Now look here. Thats enough. Go long, woman. Say some nasty thing and I'll kill you. Huh. Better damned sight not. Ta-ta, Mrs. Pribby.

Mrs. Pribby retreats to the rear of the house. She takes up a newspaper. There is a sharp click as she fits into her chair and draws it to the table. The click is metallic like the sound of a bolt being shot into place. Dan's eyes sting. Sinking into a soft couch, he closes them. The house contracts about him. It is a sharp-edged, massed, metallic house. Bolted. About Mrs. Pribby. Bolted to the endless rows of metal houses. Mrs. Pribby's house. The rows of houses belong to other Mrs. Pribbys. No wonder he couldn't sing to them.

Dan: What's Muriel doing here? God, what a place for her. Whats she doing? Putting her stockings on? In the bathroom. Come out of there, Dan Moore. People must have their privacy. Peeping-toms. I'll never peep. I'll listen. I like to listen.

Dan goes to the wall and places his ear against it. A passing street car and something vibrant from the earth sends a rumble to him. That rumble comes from the earth's deep core. It is the mutter of powerful underground races. Dan has a picture of all the people rushing to put their ears against walls, to listen to it. The next world-savior is coming up that way. Coming up. A continent sinks down. The new-world Christ will need consummate skill to walk upon the waters where huge bubbles burst . . . Thuds of Muriel coming down. Dan turns to the piano and glances through a stack of jazz music sheets. Ji-ji-bo, JI-JI-BO! . .

"Hello, Dan, stranger, what brought you here?"

Muriel comes in, shakes hands, and then clicks into a high-armed seat under the orange glow of a floor-lamp. Her face is fleshy. It would tend to coarseness but for the fresh fragrant something which is the life of it. Her hair like an Indian's. But more curly and bushed and vagrant. Her nostrils flare. The flushed ginger of her cheeks is touched orange by the shower of color from the lamp.

"Well, you havent told me, you havent answered my question, stranger. What brought you here?"

Dan feels the pressure of the house, of the rear room, of the rows of houses, shift to Muriel. He is light. He loves her. He is doubly heavy.

"Dont know, Muriel—wanted to see you—wanted to talk to you—to see you and tell you that I know what you've been through—what pain the last few months must have been—"

"Lets dont mention that."

"But why not, Muriel? I—"

"Please."

"But Muriel, life is full of things like that. One grows strong and beautiful in facing them. What else is life?"

"I dont know, Dan. And I dont believe I care. Whats the use? Lets talk about something else. I hear there's a good show at the Lincoln this week."

"Yes, so Harry was telling me. Going?"

"To-night."

Dan starts to rise.

"I didnt know. I dont want to keep you."

"Its all right. You dont have to go till Bernice comes. And she wont be here till eight. I'm all dressed. I'll let you know."

"Thanks."

Silence. The rustle of a newspaper being turned comes from the rear room.

Muriel: Shame about Dan. Something awfully good and fine about him. But he dont fit in. In where? Me? Dan, I could love you if I tried. I dont have to try. I do. O Dan, dont you know I do? Timid lover, brave talker that you are. Whats the good of all you know if you dont know that? I wont let myself. I? Mrs. Pribby who reads newspapers all night wont. What has she got to do with me? She *is* me, somehow. No she's not. Yes she is. She is the town, and the town wont let me love you, Dan. Dont you know? You could make it let me if you would. Why wont you? Youre selfish. I'm not strong enough to buck it. Youre too selfish to buck it, for me. I wish you'd go. You irritate me. Dan, please go.

"What are you doing now, Dan?"

"Same old thing, Muriel. Nothing, as the world would have it. Living, as I look at things. Living as much as I can without—"

"But you cant live without money, Dan. Why dont you get a good job and settle down?"

Dan: Same old line. Shoot it at me, sister. Hell of a note, this loving business. For ten minutes of it youve got to stand the torture of an intolerable heaviness and a hundred platitudes. Well, damit, shoot on.

"To what? my dear. Rustling newspapers?"

"You mustnt say that, Dan. It isnt right. Mrs. Pribby has been awfully good to me."

"Dare say she has. Whats that got to do with it?"

"Oh, Dan, youre so unconsiderate and selfish. All you think of is yourself."

"I think of you."

"Too much—I mean, you ought to work more and think less. Thats the best way to get along."

"Mussel-heads get along, Muriel. There is more to you than that—"

"Sometimes I think there is, Dan. But I dont know. I've tried. I've tried to do something with myself. Something real and beautiful, I mean. But whats the good of trying? I've tried to make people, every one I come in contact with, happy—"

Dan looks at her, directly. Her animalism, still unconquered by zoo-restrictions and keeper-taboos, stirs him. Passion tilts upward, bringing with it the elements of an old desire. Muriel's lips become the flesh-notes of a futile, plaintive longing. Dan's impulse to direct her is its fresh life.

"Happy, Muriel? No, not happy. Your aim is wrong. There is no such thing as happiness. Life bends joy and pain, beauty and ugliness, in such a way that no one may isolate them. No one should want to. Perfect joy, or perfect pain, with no contrasting element to define them, would mean a monotony of consciousness, would mean death. Not happy, Muriel. Say that you have tried to make them create. Say that you have used your own capacity for life to cradle them. To start them upward-flowing. Or if you cant say that you have, then say that you will. My talking to you will make you aware of your power to do so. Say that you will love, that you will give yourself in love—"

"To you, Dan?"

Dan's consciousness crudely swerves into his passions. They flare up in his eyes. They set up quivers in his abdomen. He is suddenly over-tense and nervous.

"Muriel—"

The newspaper rustles in the rear room.

"Muriel—"

Dan rises. His arms stretch towards her. His fingers and his palms, pink in the lamplight, are glowing irons. Muriel's chair is close and stiff about her. The house, the rows of houses locked about her chair. Dan's fingers and arms are fire to melt and bars to wrench and force and pry. Her arms hang loose. Her hands are hot and moist. Dan takes them. He slips to his knees before her.

"Dan, you mustnt."

"Muriel—"

"Dan, really you mustnt. No, Dan. No."

"Oh, come, Muriel. Must I—"

"Shhh. Dan, please get up. Please. Mrs. Pribby is right in the next room. She'll hear you. She may come in. Dont, Dan. She'll see you—"

"Well then, lets go out."

"I cant. Let go, Dan. Oh, wont you please let go."

Muriel tries to pull her hands away. Dan tightens his grip. He feels the strength of his fingers. His muscles are tight and strong. He stands up. Thrusts out his chest. Muriel shrinks from him. Dan becomes aware of his crude absurdity. His lips curl. His passion chills. He has an obstinate desire to possess her.

"Muriel I love you. I want you, whatever the world of Pribby says. Damn your Pribby. Who is she to dictate my love? I've stood enough of her. Enough of you. Come here."

Muriel's mouth works in and out. Her eyes flash and waggle. She wrenches her hands loose and forces them against his breast to keep him off. Dan grabs her wrists. Wedges in between her arms. Her face is close to him. It is hot and blue and moist. Ugly.

"Come here now."

"Dont, Dan. Oh, dont. What are you killing?"

"Whats weak in both of us and a whole litter of Pribbys. For once in your life youre going to face whats real, by God—"

A sharp rap on the newspaper in the rear room cuts between them. The rap is like cool thick glass between them. Dan is hot on one side. Muriel, hot on the other. They straighten. Gaze fearfully at one another. Neither moves. A clock in the rear room, in the rear room, the rear room, strikes eight. Eight slow, cool sounds. Bernice. Muriel fastens on her image. She smooths her dress. She adjusts her skirt. She becomes prim and cool. Rising, she skirts Dan as if to keep the glass between them. Dan, gyrating nervously above the easy swing of his limbs, follows her to the parlor door. Muriel retreats before him till she reaches the landing of the steps that lead upstairs. She smiles at him. Dan sees his face in the hall mirror. He runs his fingers through his hair. Reaches for his hat and coat and puts them on. He moves towards Muriel. Muriel steps backward up one step. Dan's jaw shoots out. Muriel jerks her arm in warning of Mrs. Pribby. She gasps and turns and starts to run. Noise of a chair scraping as Mrs. Pribby rises from it, ratchets down the hall. Dan stops. He makes a wry face, wheels round, goes out, and slams the door.

2

People come in slowly . . . mutter, laughs, flutter, whishadwash, "I've changed my work-clothes—" . . . and fill vacant seats of Lincoln Theater. Muriel, leading Bernice who is a cross between a washerwoman and a blue-blood lady, a washer-blue, a washer-lady, wanders down the right aisle to the lower front box. Muriel has on an orange dress. Its color would clash with the crimson box draperies, its color would contradict the sweet rose smile her face is bathed in, should she take her coat off. She'll keep it on. Pale purple shadows rest on the planes of her cheeks. Deep purple comes from her thick-shocked hair. Orange of the dress goes well with these. Muriel presses her coat down from around her shoulders. Teachers are not supposed to have bobbed hair. She'll keep her hat on. She takes the first chair, and indicates that Bernice is to take the one directly behind her. Seated thus, her eyes are level with, and near to, the face of an imaginary man upon the stage. To speak to Berny she must turn. When she does, the audience is square upon her.

People come in slowly . . . "—for my Sunday-go-to-meeting dress. O glory God! O shout Amen!" . . . and fill vacant seats of Lincoln Theater. Each one is a bolt that shoots into a slot, and is locked there. Suppose the Lord should ask, where was Moses when the light went out? Suppose Gabriel should blow his trumpet! The seats are slots. The seats are bolted houses. The mass grows denser. Its weight at first is impalpable upon the box. Then Muriel begins to feel it. She props her arm against the brass box-rail, to ward it off. Silly. These people are friends of hers: a parent of a child she teaches, an old school friend. She smiles at them. They return her courtesy, and she is free to chat with Berny. Berny's tongue, started, runs on, and on. O washer-blue! O washer-lady!

Muriel: Never see Dan again. He makes me feel queer. Starts things he doesnt finish. Upsets me. I am not upset. I am perfectly calm. I am going to enjoy the show. Good show. I've had some show! This damn tame thing. O Dan. Wont see Dan again. Not alone. Have Mrs. Pribby come in. She *was* in. Keep Dan out. If I love him, can I keep him out? Well then, I dont love him. Now he's out. Who is that coming in? Blind as a bat. Ding-bat. Looks like Dan. He mustnt see me. Silly. He cant reach me. He wont dare come in here. He'd put his head down like a goring bull and charge me. He'd trample them. He'd gore. He'd rape! Berny! He wont dare come in here.

"Berny, who was that who just came in? I havent my glasses."

"A friend of yours, a *good* friend so I hear. Mr. Daniel Moore, Lord."

"Oh. He's no friend of mine."

"No? I hear he is."

"Well, he isnt."

Dan is ushered down the aisle. He has to squeeze past the knees of seated people to reach his own seat. He treads on a man's corns. The man grumbles, and shoves him off. He shrivels close beside a portly Negress whose huge rolls of flesh meet about the bones of seat-arms. A soil-soaked fragrance comes from her. Through the cement floor her strong roots sink down. They spread under the asphalt streets. Dreaming, the streets roll over on their bellies, and suck their glossy health from them. Her strong roots sink down and spread under the river and disappear in blood-lines that waver south. Her roots shoot down. Dan's hands follow them. Roots throb. Dan's heart beats violently. He places his palms upon the earth to cool them. Earth throbs. Dan's heart beats violently. He sees all the people in the house rush to the walls to listen to the rumble. A new-world Christ is coming up. Dan comes up. He is startled. The eyes of the woman dont belong to her. They look at him unpleasantly. From either aisle, bolted masses press in. He doesnt fit. The mass grows agitant. For an instant, Dan's and Muriel's eyes meet. His weight there slides the weight on her. She braces an arm against the brass rail, and turns her head away.

Muriel: Damn fool; dear Dan, what did you want to follow me here for? Oh cant you ever do anything right? Must you always pain me, and make me hate you? I do hate you. I wish some one would come in with a horse-whip and lash you out. I wish some one would drag you up a back alley and brain you with the whip-butt.

Muriel glances at her wrist-watch.

"Quarter of nine. Berny, what time have you?"

"Eight-forty. Time to begin. Oh, look Muriel, that woman with the plume; doesnt she look good! They say she's going with, oh, whats his name. You know. Too much powder. I can see it from here. Here's the orchestra now. O fine! Jim Clem at the piano!"

The men fill the pit. Instruments run the scale and tune. The saxophone moans and throws a fit. Jim Clem, poised over the piano, is ready to begin. His head nods forward. Opening crash. The house snaps dark. The curtain recedes upward from the blush of the footlights. Jazz overture is over. The first act is on.

Dan: Old stuff. Muriel—bored. Must be. But she'll smile and she'll clap. Do what youre bid, you she-slave. Look at her. Sweet, tame woman in a brass box seat. Clap, smile, fawn, clap. Do what youre bid. Drag me in with you. Dirty me. Prop me in your brass box seat. I'm there, am I not? because of you. He-slave. Slave of a woman who is a slave. I'm a damned sight worse than you are. I sing your praises, Beauty! I exalt thee, O Muriel! A slave, thou art greater than all Freedom because I love thee.

Dan fidgets, and disturbs his neighbors. His neighbors glare at him. He glares back without seeing them. The man whose corns have been trod upon speaks to him.

"Keep quiet, cant you, mister. Other people have paid their money besides yourself to see the show."

The man's face is a blur about two sullen liquid things that are his eyes. The eyes dissolve in the surrounding vagueness. Dan suddenly feels that the man is an enemy whom he has long been looking for.

Dan bristles. Glares furiously at the man.

"All right. All right then. Look at the show. I'm not stopping you."

"Shhh," from some one in the rear.

Dan turns around.

"Its that man there who started everything. I didnt say a thing to him until he tried to start something. What have I got to do with whether he has paid his money or not? Thats the manager's business. Do I look like the manager?"

"Shhhh. Youre right. Shhhh."

"Dont tell me to shhh. Tell him. That man there. He started everything. If what he wanted was to start a fight, why didnt he say so?"

The man leans forward.

"Better be quiet, sonny. I aint said a thing about fight, yet."

"Its a good thing you havent."

"Shhhh."

Dan grips himself. Another act is on. Dwarfs, dressed like prize-fighters, foreheads bulging like boxing gloves, are led upon the stage. They are going to fight for the heavyweight championship. Gruesome. Dan glances at Muriel. He imagines that she shudders. His mind curves back into himself, and picks up tail-ends of experiences. His eyes are open, mechanically. The dwarfs pound and bruise and bleed each other, on his eyeballs.

Dan: Ah, but she was some baby! And not vulgar either. Funny how some women can do those things. Muriel dancing like that! Hell. She rolled and wabbled. Her buttocks rocked. She pulled up her dress and showed her pink drawers. Baby! And then she caught my eyes. Dont know what my eyes had in them. Yes I do. God, dont I though! Sometimes I think, Dan Moore, that your eyes could burn clean . . . burn clean . . . BURN CLEAN! . .

The gong rings. The dwarfs set to. They spar grotesquely, playfully, until one lands a stiff blow. This makes the other sore. He commences slugging. A real scrap is on. Time! The dwarfs go to their corners and are sponged and fanned off. Gloves bulge from their wrists. Their wrists are necks for the tight-faced gloves. The fellow to the right lets his eyes roam over the audience. He sights Muriel. He grins.

Dan: Those silly women arguing feminism. Here's what I should have said to them. "It should be clear to you women, that the proposition must be stated thus:

> Me, horizontally above her.
> Action: perfect strokes downward oblique.
> Hence, man dominates because of limitation.
> Or, so it shall be until women learn their stuff.

So framed, the proposition is a mental-filler, Dentist, I want gold teeth. It should become cherished of the technical intellect. I hereby offer it to posterity as one of the important machine-age designs. P.S. It should be noted, that because it *is* an achievement of this age, its growth and hence its causes, up to the point of maturity, antedate machinery. Ery . . ."

The gong rings. No fooling this time. The dwarfs set to. They clinch. The referee parts them. One swings a cruel upper-cut and knocks the other down. A huge head hits the floor. Pop! The house roars. The fighter, groggy, scrambles up. The referee whispers to the contenders not to fight so hard. They ignore him. They charge. Their heads jab like boxing-gloves. They kick and spit and bite. They pound each other furiously. Muriel pounds. The house pounds. Cut lips. Bloody noses. The referee asks for the gong. Time! The house roars. The dwarfs bow, are made to bow. The house wants more. The dwarfs are led from the stage.

Dan: Strange I never really noticed him before. Been sitting there for years. Born a slave. Slavery not so long ago. He'll die in his chair. Swing low, sweet chariot. Jesus will come and roll him down the river Jordan. Oh, come along, Moses, you'll get lost; stretch out your rod and come across. LET MY PEOPLE GO! Old man. Knows everyone who passes the corners. Saw the first horse-cars. The first Oldsmobile. And he was born in slavery. I did see his eyes. Never miss eyes. But they were bloodshot and watery. It hurt to look at them. It hurts to look in most people's eyes. He saw Grant and Lincoln. He saw Walt—old man, did you see Walt Whitman? Did you see Walt Whitman! Strange force that drew me to him. And I went up to see. The woman thought I was crazy. I told him to look into the heavens. He did, and smiled. I asked him if he knew what that rumbling is that comes up from the ground. Christ, what a stroke that was. And the jabbering idiots crowding around. And the crossing-cop leaving his job to come over and wheel him away . . .

The house applauds. The house wants more. The dwarfs are led back. But no encore. Must give the house something. The attendant comes out and announces that Mr. Barry, the champion, will sing one of his own songs, "for your approval." Mr. Barry grins at Muriel as he wabbles from the wing. He holds a fresh white rose, and a small mirror. He wipes blood from his nose. He signals Jim Clem. The orchestra starts. A sentimental love song. Mr. Barry sings, first to one girl, and then another in the audience. He holds the mirror in such a way that it flashes in the face of each one he sings to. The light swings around.

Dan: I am going to reach up and grab the girders of this building and pull them down. The crash will be a signal. Hid by the smoke and dust Dan Moore will arise. In his right hand will be a dynamo. In his left, a god's face that will flash white light from ebony. I'll grab a girder and swing it like a walking-stick. Lightning will flash. I'll grab its black knob and swing it like a crippled cane. Lightning . . . Some one's flashing . . . some one's flashing . . . Who in hell is flashing that mirror? Take it off me, godam you.

Dan's eyes are half blinded. He moves his head. The light follows. He hears the audience laugh. He hears the orchestra. A man with a high-pitched, sentimental voice is singing. Dan sees the dwarf. Along the mirror flash the song comes. Dan ducks his head. The audience roars. The light swings around to Muriel. Dan looks. Muriel is too close. Mr. Barry covers his mirror. He sings to her. She shrinks away. Nausea. She clutches the brass box-rail. She moves to face away. The audience is square upon her. Its eyes smile. Its hands itch to clap. Muriel turns to the dwarf and forces a smile at him. With a showy blare of orchestration, the song comes to its close. Mr. Barry bows. He offers Muriel the rose, first having kissed it. Blood of his battered lips is a vivid stain upon its petals. Mr. Barry offers Muriel the rose. The house applauds. Muriel flinches back. The dwarf steps forward, diffident; threatening. Hate pops from his eyes and crackles like a brittle heat about the box. The thick hide of his face is drawn in tortured wrinkles. Above his eyes, the bulging, tight-skinned brow. Dan looks at it. It grows calm and massive. It grows profound. It is a thing of wisdom and tenderness, of suffering and beauty. Dan looks down. The eyes are calm and luminous. Words come from them . . . Arms of the audience reach out, grab Muriel, and hold her there. Claps are steel fingers that manacle her wrists and move them forward to acceptance. Berny leans forward and whispers:

"Its all right. Go on—take it."

Words form in the eyes of the dwarf:

> Do not shrink. Do not be afraid of me.
> *Jesus*
> See how my eyes look at you.
> *the Son of God*
> I too was made in His image.
> *was once—*
> I give you the rose.

Muriel, tight in her revulsion, sees black, and daintily reaches for the offering. As her hand touches it, Dan springs up in his seat and shouts:

"JESUS WAS ONCE A LEPER!"

Dan steps down.

He is as cool as a green stem that has just shed its flower.

Rows of gaping faces strain towards him. They are distant, beneath him, impalpable. Squeezing out, Dan again treads upon the corn-foot man. The man shoves him.

"Watch where youre going, mister. Crazy or no, you aint going to walk over me. Watch where youre going there."

Dan turns, and serenely tweaks the fellow's nose. The man jumps up. Dan is jammed against a seat-back. A slight swift anger flicks him. His fist hooks the other's jaw.

"Now you have started something. Aint no man living can hit me and get away with it. Come on on the outside."

The house, tumultuously stirring, grabs its wraps and follows the men.

The man leads Dan up a black alley. The alley-air is thick and moist with smells of garbage and wet trash. In the morning, singing niggers will drive by and ring their gongs . . . . Heavy with the scent of rancid flowers and with the scent of fight. The crowd, pressing forward, is a hollow roar. Eyes of houses, soft girl-eyes, glow reticently upon the hubbub and blink out. The man stops. Takes off his hat and coat. Dan, having forgotten him, keeps going on.

1923

Langston Hughes 1902–1967

Langston Hughes was one of the most original and versatile of twentieth-century black writers. Born in Joplin, Missouri, to James Nathaniel and Carrie Mercer Langston Hughes, he was reared for a time by his grandmother in Lawrence, Kansas, after his parents' divorce. Influenced by the poetry of Paul Laurence Dunbar and Carl Sandburg, he began writing creatively while still a boy. After his graduation from high school in Cleveland, he spent fifteen months in Mexico with his father; upon his return to the United States in 1921, Hughes attended Columbia University for a year. Disillusioned with formal education, in 1923 he joined the crew of the *SS Malone* bound for Africa, where the ship visited thirty-odd ports. Before returning to New York, Hughes lived in Paris, Venice, and Genoa.

Despite the celebrated story of Hughes's being "discovered" by the white poet Vachel Lindsay while working as a hotel busboy in 1925, by that point Hughes had already established himself as a bright young star of the New Negro Renaissance. One of his most famous and innovative poems, "The Negro Speaks of Rivers" (dedicated to W.E.B. Du Bois), appeared in the *Crisis* in 1921; and in 1923, the New York's *Amsterdam News* carried his "The Weary Blues." Two years later, his first collection, also entitled *The Weary Blues,* was published.

The most important stage in Langston Hughes's development as a writer was his discovery of New York, of Harlem, of the cultural life and literary circle of the "New Negro" writers: Countee Cullen, Arna Bontemps, Wallace Thurman, Zora Neale Hurston, Eric Walrond and others. The black revue *Shuffle Along* was on Broadway, and Harlem was the center of a thriving theater and the new music—jazz. Hughes steeped himself in the language, music, and feeling of the common people of Harlem. Proud of his folk heritage, Hughes made the spirituals, blues, and jazz the bases of his poetic expression. Hughes wrote, he contended, "to explain and illuminate the Negro condition in America." As his friends said of him, "No one enjoyed being a Negro as much as Langston Hughes." He portrayed the humor, wit, endurance, and faith of his people with extraordinary skill. Subjected to discrimination and segregation, he remained steadfast in his devotion to human rights. His well-known defense of black writers was typical: "We younger Negro artists who create now intend to express our individual dark skinned selves without fear or shame. . . ."

The versatility of Langston Hughes is

evident in his capacity to create in every literary genre—poetry, fiction, drama, essay, and history. He was also the most prolific of black writers; more than 12 volumes of his poetry appeared in his lifetime. Hughes won several prizes, awards, and fellowships, and was in constant demand for readings and lectures throughout the world. His fiction is equally distinguished. In addition to his fine coming-of-age novel, *Not Without Laughter* (1930), Langston Hughes created the character of Jesse B. Simple, a lively embodiment of urban black life, whose folk wit and wisdom allowed Hughes to undermine the bourgeois pretentions of our society while pointing out the hypocritical nature of American racism. Like Whitman, Hughes enhances our love of humanity, our vision of the just society with a spiritual transcendence and ever-widening horizons of joy and hope. In its spontaneity and race pride, his poetry found a response among poets of Africa and the Caribbean; and in his own country Hughes served as both an inspiration and a mentor for the younger black writers who came of age in the 1960s. With his rich poetic voice, nurturing generosity, warm humor, and abiding love of black people, Langston Hughes was one of the dominant voices in American literature of the twentieth century and the single most influential black poet.

Charles H. Nichols
Brown University

PRIMARY WORKS

Poetry: *The Weary Blues,* 1926; *Fine Clothes to the Jew,* 1927; *Shakespeare in Harlem,* 1942; *Montage of a Dream Deferred,* 1951; Fiction: *Not Without Laughter,* 1930; *The Ways of White Folks,* 1934; *The Best of Simple,* 1961; *Something in Common and Other Stories,* 1963; Autobiography: *The Big Sea,* 1940; *I Wonder as I Wander,* 1956; Anthologies edited by Hughes: *The Poetry of the Negro* (with Arna Bontemps), 1949; *The Book of Negro Folklore* (with Arna Bontemps), 1958; *New Negro Poets: U.S.A.,* 1964; *The Best Short Stories by Negro Writers,* 1967; Histories: *A Pictorial History of the Negro in America* (with Milton Meltzer), 1956; *Famous Negro Heroes of America,* 1958; *Fight for Freedom: The Story of the NAACP,* 1962.

The Negro Speaks of Rivers

I've known rivers:
I've known rivers ancient as the world and older than the flow of
human blood in human veins.

My soul has grown deep like the rivers.

I bathed in the Euphrates when dawns were young.
I built my hut near the Congo and it lulled me to sleep.
I looked upon the Nile and raised the pyramids above it.

I heard the singing of the Mississippi when Abe Lincoln
went down to New Orleans, and I've seen its muddy

bosom turn all golden in the sunset.

I've known rivers:
Ancient, dusky rivers.

My soul has grown deep like the rivers.

1921

The Weary Blues

Droning a drowsy syncopated tune,
Rocking back and forth to a mellow croon,
I heard a Negro play.
Down on Lenox Avenue the other night
By the pale dull pallor of an old gas light
He did a lazy sway . . .
He did a lazy sway . . .
To the tune o' those Weary Blues.
With his ebony hands on each ivory key
He made that poor piano moan with melody.
O Blues!
Swaying to and fro on his rickety stool
He played that sad raggy tune like a musical fool.
Sweet Blues!
Coming from a black man's soul.
O Blues!
In a deep song voice with a melancholy tone
I heard that Negro sing, that old piano moan—
"Ain't got nobody in all this world,
Ain't got nobody but ma self.
I's gwine to quit ma frownin'
And put ma troubles on the shelf."
Thump, thump, thump, went his foot on the floor.
He played a few chords then he sang some more—
"I got the Weary Blues
And I can't be satisfied.
Got the Weary Blues
And can't be satisfied—
I ain't happy no mo'
And I wish that I had died."
And far into the night he crooned that tune.
The stars went out and so did the moon.
The singer stopped playing and went to bed

While the Weary Blues echoed through his head.
He slept like a rock or a man that's dead.

1925

Drum

Bear in mind
That death is a drum
Beating forever
Till the last worms come
To answer its call,
Till the last stars fall,
Until the last atom
Is no atom at all,
Until time is lost
And there is no air
And space itself
Is nothing nowhere,
Death is a drum,
A signal drum,
Calling life
To come!
Come!
Come!

1931

The Same

It is the same everywhere for me:
On the docks at Sierra Leone,
In the cotton fields of Alabama,
In the diamond mines of Kimberley,
On the coffee hills of Haiti,
The banana lands of Central America,
The streets of Harlem,
And the cities of Morocco and Tripoli.

Black:
Exploited, beaten, and robbed,

Shot and killed.
Blood running into

DOLLARS
POUNDS
FRANCS
PESETAS
LIRE

For the wealth of the exploiters—
Blood that never comes back to me again.
Better that my blood
Runs into the deep channels of Revolution,
Runs into the strong hands of Revolution,
Stains all flags red,
Drives me away from

SIERRA LEONE
KIMBERLEY
ALABAMA
HAITI
CENTRAL AMERICA
HARLEM
MOROCCO
TRIPOLI

And all the black lands everywhere.
The force that kills,
The power that robs,
And the greed that does not care.
Better that my blood makes one with the blood
Of all the struggling workers in the world—
Till every land is free of

DOLLAR ROBBERS
POUND ROBBERS
FRANC ROBBERS
PESETA ROBBERS
LIRE ROBBERS
LIFE ROBBERS—

Until the Red Armies of the International Proletariat
Their faces, black, white, olive, yellow, brown,
Unite to raise the blood-red flag that
Never will come down!

1932

The English

In ships all over the world
The English comb their hair for dinner,
Stand watch on the bridge,
Guide by strange stars,
Take on passengers,
Slip up hot rivers,
Nose across lagoons,
Bargain for trade,
Buy, sell or rob,
Load oil, load fruit,
Load cocoa beans, load gold.
In ships all over the world,
Comb their hair for dinner.

1930

Johannesburg Mines

In the Johannesburg mines
There are 240,000 natives working.

What kind of poem
Would you make out of that?

240,000 natives working
In the Johannesburg mines.

1928

Negro

I am a Negro:
  Black as the night is black,
  Black like the depths of my Africa.

I've been a slave:
  Caesar told me to keep his door-steps clean.

I brushed the boots of Washington.

I've been a worker:
Under my hand the pyramids arose.
I made mortar for the Woolworth Building.

I've been a singer:
All the way from Africa to Georgia
I carried my sorrow songs.
I made ragtime.

I've been a victim:
The Belgians cut off my hands in the Congo.
They lynch me still in Mississippi.

I am a Negro:
Black as the night is black,
Black like the depths of my Africa.

1922

Bad Luck Card

Cause you don't love me
Is awful, awful hard.
Gypsy done showed me
My bad luck card.

There ain't no good left
In this world for me.
Gypsy done tole me—
Unlucky as can be.

I don't know what
Po' weary me can do.
Gypsy says I'd kill my self
If I was you.

1927

I, Too

I, too, sing America.

I am the darker brother.
They send me to eat in the kitchen
When company comes,
But I laugh,
And eat well,
And grow strong.

Tomorrow,
I'll be at the table
When company comes.
Nobody'll dare
Say to me,
"Eat in the kitchen,"
Then.

Besides,
They'll see how beautiful I am
And be ashamed—

I, too, am America.

1925

Dream Variations

To fling my arms wide
In some place of the sun,
To whirl and to dance
Till the white day is done.
Then rest at cool evening
Beneath a tall tree
While night comes on gently,
    Dark like me—
That is my dream!

To fling my arms wide
In the face of the sun,
Dance! Whirl! Whirl!
Till the quick day is done.

Rest at pale evening . . .
A tall, slim tree . . .
Night coming tenderly
    Black like me.

1924

Harlem

What happens to a dream deferred?

Does it dry up
like a raisin in the sun?
Or fester like a sore—
And then run?
Does it stink like rotten meat?
Or crust and sugar over—
like a syrupy sweet?

Maybe it just sags
like a heavy load.

Or does it explode?

1951

Freedom Train

I read in the papers about the
    Freedom Train.
I heard on the radio about the
    Freedom Train.
I seen folks talkin' about the
    Freedom Train.
Lord, I been a-waitin' for the
    Freedom Train!
Down South in Dixie only train I see's
Got a Jim Crow car set aside for me.
I hope there ain't no Jim Crow on the Freedom Train,
No back door entrance to the Freedom Train,
No signs FOR COLORED on the Freedom Train,
No WHITE FOLKS ONLY on the Freedom Train.

I'm gonna check up on this
Freedom Train.

Who's the engineer on the Freedom Train?
Can a coal black man drive the Freedom Train?
Or am I still a porter on the Freedom Train?
Is there ballot boxes on the Freedom Train?
When it stops in Mississippi will it be made plain
Everybody's got a right to board the Freedom Train?

Somebody tell me about this
Freedom Train!

The Birmingham station's marked COLORED and WHITE.
The white folks go left, the colored go right—
They even got a segregated lane.
Is that the way to get aboard the Freedom Train?

I got to know about this
Freedom Train!

If my children ask me, *Daddy, please explain*
Why there's Jim Crow stations for the Freedom Train?
What shall I tell my children? . . . *You* tell me—
'Cause freedom ain't freedom when a man ain't free.

But maybe they explains it on the
Freedom Train.

When my grandmother in Atlanta, 83 and black,
Gets in line to see the Freedom,
Will some white man yell, *Get back!*
A Negro's got no business on the Freedom Track!

Mister, I thought it were the
Freedom Train!

Her grandson's name was Jimmy. He died at Anzio.
He died for real. It warn't no show.
The freedom that they carryin' on this Freedom Train,
Is it for real—or just a show again?

Jimmy wants to know about the
Freedom Train.

Will *his* Freedom Train come zoomin' down the track
Gleamin' in the sunlight for white and black?
Not stoppin' at no stations marked COLORED nor WHITE,

Just stoppin' in the fields in the broad daylight,
Stoppin' in the country in the wide-open air
Where there never was no Jim Crow signs nowhere,
No Welcomin' Committees, nor Politicians of note,
No Mayors and such for which colored can't vote,
And nary a sign of a color line—
For the Freedom Train will be yours and mine!

Then maybe from their graves in Anzio
The G.I.'s who fought will say, *We wanted it so!*
Black men and white will say, *Ain't it fine?*
At home they got a train that's yours and mine!

Then I'll shout, *Glory for the*
Freedom Train!
I'll holler, *Blow your whistle,*
Freedom Train!
Thank God-A-Mighty! Here's the
Freedom Train!
Get on board our Freedom Train!

1947

Big Meeting

The early stars had begun to twinkle in the August night as Bud and I neared the woods. A great many Negroes, old and young, were plodding down the dirt road on foot on their way to the Big Meeting. Long before we came near the lantern-lighted tent, we could hear early arrivals singing, clapping their hands lustily, and throwing out each word distinct like a drum-beat. Songs like "When the Saints Go Marching Home" and "That Old-Time Religion" filled the air.

In the road that ran past the woods, a number of automobiles and buggies belonging to white people had stopped near the tent so that their occupants might listen to the singing. The whites stared curiously through the hickory trees at the rocking figures in the tent. The canvas, except behind the pulpit, was rolled up on account of the heat, and the meeting could easily be seen from the road, so there beneath a tree Bud and I stopped, too. In our teens, we were young and wild and didn't believe much in revivals, so we stayed outside in the road where we could smoke and laugh like the white folks. But both Bud's mother and mine were under the tent singing, actively a part of the services. Had they known we were near, they would certainly have come out and dragged us in.

From frequent attendance since childhood at these Big Meetings held each summer in the South, we knew the services were divided into three parts. The testimonials and the song-service came first. This began as soon as two or three people were gathered together, continuing until the minister himself arrived. Then the sermon followed, with its accompanying songs and shouts from the audience. Then the climax came with the calling of the lost souls to the mourners' bench, and the prayers for sinners and backsliders. This was where Bud and I would leave. We were having too good a time being sinners, and we didn't want to be saved—not yet, anyway.

When we arrived, old Aunt Ibey Davis was just starting a familiar song:

"Where shall I be when that first trumpet sound?
Lawdy, where shall I be when it sound so loud?"

The rapidly increasing number of worshipers took up the tune in full volume, sending a great flood of melody billowing beneath the canvas roof. With heads back, feet and hands patting time, they repeated the chorus again and again. And each party of new arrivals swung into rhythm as they walked up the aisle by the light of the dim oil lanterns hanging from the tent poles.

Standing there at the edge of the road beneath a big tree, Bud and I watched the people as they came—keeping our eyes open for the girls. Scores of Negroes from the town and nearby villages and farms came, drawn by the music and the preaching. Some were old and gray-headed; some in the prime of life; some mere boys and girls; and many little barefooted children. It was the twelfth night of the Big Meeting. They came from miles around to bathe their souls in a sea of song, to shout and cry and moan before the flow of Reverend Braswell's eloquence, and to pray for all the sinners in the county who had not yet seen the light. Although it was a colored folks' meeting, whites liked to come and sit outside in the road in their cars and listen. Sometimes there would be as many as ten or twelve parties of whites parked there in the dark, smoking and listening, and enjoying themselves, like Bud and I, in a not very serious way.

Even while old Aunt Ibey Davis was singing, a big red Buick drove up and parked right behind Bud and me beneath the tree. It was full of white people, and we recognized the driver as Mr. Parkes, the man who owned the drugstore in town where colored people couldn't buy a glass of soda at the fountain.

"It will sound so loud it will wake up the dead!
Lawdy, where shall I be when it sound?"

"You'll hear some good singing out here," Mr. Parkes said to a woman in the car with him.

"I always did love to hear darkies singing," she answered from the back seat.

Bud nudged me in the ribs at the word "darkie."

"I hear 'em," I said, sitting down on one of the gnarled roots of the tree and pulling out a cigarette.

The song ended as an old black woman inside the tent got up to speak. "I rise to testify dis evenin' fo' Jesus!" she said. "Ma Saviour an' ma Redeemer an' de chamber wherein I resusticates ma soul. Pray fo' me, brothers and sisters. Let yo' mercies bless me in all I do an' yo' prayers go with me on each travelin' voyage through dis land."

"Amen! Hallelujah!" cried my mother.

Just in front of us, near the side of the tent, a woman's clear soprano voice began to sing:

"I am a po' pilgrim of sorrow
Out in this wide world alone . . ."

Soon others joined with her and the whole tent was singing:

"Sometimes I am tossed and driven,
Sometimes I don't know where to go . . ."

"Real pretty, ain't it?" said the white woman in the car behind us.

"But I've heard of a city called heaven
And I've started to make it my home."

When the woman finished her song, she rose and told how her husband left her with six children, her mother died in a poorhouse, and the world had always been against her—but still she was going on!

"My, she's had a hard time," giggled the woman in the car.

"Sure has," laughed Mr. Parkes, "to hear her tell it."

And the way they talked made gooseflesh come out on my skin.

"Trials and tribulations surround me—but I'm goin' on," the woman in the tent cried. Shouts and exclamations of approval broke out all over the congregation.

"Praise God!"

"Bless His Holy Name!"

"That's right, sister!"

"Devils beset me—but I'm goin' on!" said the woman. "I ain't got no friends—but I'm goin' on!"

"Jesus yo' friend, sister! Jesus yo' friend!" came the answer.

"God bless Jesus! I'm goin' on!"

"Dat's right!" cried Sister Mabry, Bud's mother, bouncing in her seat and flinging her arms outward. "Take all this world, but gimme Jesus!"

"Look at Mama," Bud said half amused, sitting there beside me smoking. "She's getting happy."

"Whoo-ooo-o-o! Great Gawd A'mighty!" yelled old man Walls near the pulpit. "I can't hold it dis evenin'! Dis mawnin', dis evenin', dis mawnin', Lawd!"

"Pray for me—cause I'm goin' on!" said the woman. In the midst of the demonstration she had created, she sat down exhausted, her armpits wet with sweat and her face covered with tears.

"Did you hear her, Jehover?" someone asked.

"Yes! He heard her! Halleloo!" came the answer.

"Dis mawnin', dis evenin', dis mawnin', Lawd!"

Brother Nace Eubanks began to line a song:

"Must Jesus bear his cross alone
An' all de world go free?"

Slowly they sang it line by line. Then the old man rose and told of a vision that had come to him long ago on that day when he had been changed from a sinner to a just man.

"I was layin' in ma bed," he said, "at de midnight hour twenty-two years past at Seven hundred fourteen Pine Street in dis here city when a snow-white sheep come in ma room an' stood behind de washbowl. Dis here sheep, hit spoke to me wid tongues o' fiah an' hit said, 'Nace, git up! Git up, an' come wid me!' Yes, suh! He had a light round 'bout his head like a moon, an' wings like a dove, an' he walked on hoofs o' gold an' dis sheep hit said, 'I once were lost, but now I'm saved, an' you kin be like me!" Yes, suh! An' ever since dat night, brothers an' sisters, I's been a chile o' de Lamb! Pray fo' me!"

"Help him, Jesus!" Sister Mabry shouted.

"Amen!" chanted Deacon Laws. "Amen! Amen!"

"Glory! Hallelujah!
Let de halleluian roll

I'll sing ma Saviour's praises far an' wide!"

It was my mother's favorite song, and she sang it like a paean of triumph, rising from her seat.

"Look at Ma," I said to Bud, knowing that she was about to start her nightly shouting.

"Yah," Bud said. "I hope she don't see me while she's standing up there, or she'll come out here and make us go up to the mourners' bench."

"We'll leave before that," I said.

"I've opened up to heaven
All de windows of ma soul,

An' I'm livin' on de halleluian side!"

Rocking proudly to and fro as the second chorus boomed and swelled beneath the canvas, Mama began to clap her hands, her lips silent now in this sea of song she had started, her head thrown back in joy—for my mother was a great shouter. Stepping gracefully to the beat of the music, she moved out toward the center aisle into a cleared space. Then she began to spring on her toes with little short rhythmical hops. All the way up the long aisle to the pulpit gently she leaped to the clap-clap of hands, the pat of feet, and the steady booming song of her fellow worshipers. Then Mama began to revolve in a dignified circle, slowly, as a great happiness swept her gleaming black features, and her lips curved into a smile.

"I've opened up to heaven
All de windows of my soul . . ."

Mama was dancing before the Lord with her eyes closed, her mouth smiling, and her head held high.

"I'm livin' on de halleluian side!"

As she danced, she threw her hands upward away from her breasts, as though casting off all the cares of the world.

Just then the white woman in Mr. Parkes's car behind us laughed. "My Lord, John, it's better than a show!"

Something about the way she laughed made my blood boil. That was *my mother* dancing and shouting. Maybe it was better than a show, but nobody had any business laughing at her, least of all white people.

I looked at Bud, but he didn't say anything. Maybe he was thinking how often we, too, made fun of the shouters, laughing at our parents as though they were crazy—but deep down inside us we understood why they came to Big Meeting. Working all day all their lives for white folks, they *had* to believe there was a "halleluian side."

I looked at Mama standing there singing, and I thought about how many years she had prayed and shouted and praised the Lord at church meetings and revivals, then came home for a few hours' sleep before getting up at dawn to go cook and scrub and clean for others. And I didn't want any white folks, especially whites who wouldn't let a Negro drink a glass of soda in their drugstore or give one a job, sitting in a car laughing at Mama.

"Gimme a cigarette, Bud. If these dopes behind us say any more, I'm gonna get up and tell 'em something they won't like."

"To hell with 'em," Bud answered.

I leaned back against the gnarled roots of the tree by the road and inhaled deeply. The white people were silent again in their car, listening to the singing. In the dark I couldn't see their faces to tell if they were still amused or not. But that was mostly what they wanted out of Negroes—work and fun—without paying for it, I thought, work and fun.

To a great hand-clapping body-rocking foot-patting rhythm, Mama was repeating the chorus over and over. Sisters leaped and shouted and perspiring brothers walked the aisles, bowing left and right, beating time, shaking hands, laughing aloud for joy, and singing steadily when, at the back of the tent, the Reverend Duke Braswell arrived.

A tall, powerful jet-black man, he moved with long steps through the center of the tent, his iron-gray hair uncovered, his green-black coat jim-swinging to his knees, his fierce eyes looking straight toward the altar. Under his arm he carried a Bible.

Once on the platform, he stood silently wiping his brow with a large white handkerchief while the singing swirled around him. Then he sang, too, his voice roaring like a cyclone, his white teeth shining. Finally he held up his palms for silence and the song gradually lowered to a hum, hum, hum, hands and feet patting, bodies still moving. At last, above the broken cries of the shouters and the undertones of song, the minister was able to make himself heard.

"Brother Garner, offer up a prayer."

Reverend Braswell sank on his knees and every back bowed. Brother Garner, with his head in his hands, lifted his voice against a background of moans:

"Oh, Lawd, we comes befo' you dis evenin' wid fear an' tremblin'—unworthy as we is to enter yo' house an' speak yo' name. We comes befo' you, Lawd, 'cause we knows you is mighty an' powerful in all de lands, an' great above de stars, an' bright above de moon. Oh, Lawd, you is bigger den de world. You holds de sun in yo' right hand an' de mornin' star in you' left, an' we po' sinners ain't nothin', not even so much as a grain o' sand beneath yo' feet. Yet we calls on you dis evenin' to hear us, Lawd, to send down yo' sweet Son Jesus to walk wid us in our sorrows to comfort us on our weary road 'cause sometimes we don't know which-a-way to turn! We pray you dis evenin', Lawd, to look down at our wanderin' chilluns what's gone from home. Look down in St. Louis, Lawd, an' look in Memphis, an' look down in Chicago if they's usin' Thy name in vain dis evenin', if they's gamblin' tonight, Lawd, if they's doin' any ways wrong—reach down an' pull 'em up, Lawd, an' say, 'Come wid me, cause I am de Vine an' de Husbandman an' de gate dat leads to Glory!' "

Remembering sons in faraway cities, "Help him, Jesus!" mothers cried.

"Whilst you's lookin' down on us dis evenin', keep a mighty eye on de sick an' de 'flicked. Ease Sister Hightower, Lawd, layin' in her bed at de pint o' death. An' bless Bro' Carpenter what's come out to meetin' here dis evenin' in spite o' his broken arm from fallin' off de roof. An' Lawd, aid de pastor dis evenin' to fill dis tent wid yo' Spirit, an' to make de sinners tremble an' backsliders shout, an' dem dat is without de church to come to de moaners' bench an' find rest in Jesus! We ask Thee all dese favors dis evenin'. Also to guide us an' bless us wid Thy bread an' give us Thy wine to drink fo' Christ de Holy Saviour's sake, our Shelter an' our Rock. Amen!"

"There's not a friend like de lowly Jesus . . ."

Some sister began, high and clear after the passion of the prayer,

"No, not one! . . . No, not one!"

Then the preacher took his text from the open Bible. "Ye now therefore have sorrow: but I will see you again, and your hearts shall rejoice, and your joy no man taketh from you."

He slammed shut the Holy Book and walked to the edge of the platform. "That's what Jesus said befo' he went to the cross, children—'I will see you again, and yo' hearts shall rejoice!' "

"Yes sir!" said the brothers and sisters. " 'Deed he did!"

Then the minister began to tell the familiar story of the death of Christ. Standing in the dim light of the smoking oil lanterns, he sketched the life of the man who had had power over multitudes.

"Power," the minister said. "Power! Without money and without titles, without position, he had power! And that power went out to the poor and afflicted. For Jesus said, 'The first shall be last, and the last shall be first.' "

"He sho did!" cried Bud's mother.

"Hallelujah!" Mama agreed loudly. "Glory be to God!"

"Then the big people of the land heard about Jesus," the preacher went on, "the chief priests and the scribes, the politicians, the bootleggers, and the bankers—and they begun to conspire against Jesus because *He had power!* This Jesus with His twelve disciples preachin' in Galilee. Then came that eve of the Passover, when he set down with His friends to eat and drink of the vine and the settin' sun fell behind the hills of Jerusalem. And Jesus knew that ere the cock crew, Judas would betray Him, and Peter would say, 'I know Him not,' and all alone by Hisself He would go to His death. Yes, sir, He knew! So He got up from the table and went into the garden to pray. In this hour of trouble, Jesus went to pray!"

Away at the back of the tent some old sister began to sing:

"Oh, watch with me one hour
While I go yonder and pray . . ."

And the crowd took up the song, swelled it, made its melody fill the hot tent while the minister stopped talking to wipe his face with his white handkerchief.

Then, to the humming undertone of the song, he continued, "They called it

Gethsemane—that garden where Jesus fell down on His face in the grass and cried to the Father, 'Let this bitter hour pass from me! Oh, God, let this hour pass.' Because He was still a young man who did not want to die, He rose up and went back into the house—but His friends was all asleep. While Jesus prayed, His friends done gone to sleep! But, 'Sleep on,' he said, 'for the hour is at hand.' Jesus said, 'Sleep on.'"

"Sleep on, sleep on," chanted the crowd, repeating the words of the minister.

"He was not angry with them. But as Jesus looked out of the house, He saw that garden alive with men carryin' lanterns and swords and staves, and the mob was everywhere. So He went to the door. Then Judas come out from among the crowd, the traitor Judas, and kissed Him on the cheek—oh, bitter friendship! And the soldiers with handcuffs fell upon the Lord and took Him prisoner.

"The disciples was awake by now, oh yes! But they fled away because they was afraid. And the mob carried Jesus off.

"Peter followed Him from afar, followed Jesus in chains till they come to the palace of the high priest. There Peter went in, timid and afraid, to see the trial. He set in the back of the hall. Peter listened to the lies they told about Christ—and didn't dispute 'em. He watched the high priest spit in Christ's face—and made no move. He saw 'em smite Him with the palms of they hands—and Peter uttered not a word for his poor mistreated Jesus."

"Not a word! . . . Not a word! . . . Not a word!"

"And when the servants of the high priest asked Peter, 'Does you know this man?' he said, 'I do not!'

"And when they asked him a second time, he said, 'No!'

"And yet a third time, 'Do you know Jesus?'

"And Peter answered with an oath, 'I told you, no!'

"Then the cock crew."

"De cock crew!" cried Aunt Ibey Davis. "De cock crew! Oh, ma Lawd! De cock crew!"

"The next day the chief priests taken counsel against Jesus to put Him to death. They brought Him before Pilate, and Pilate said, 'What evil hath he done?'

"But the people cried, 'Crucify Him!' because they didn't care. So Pilate called for water and washed his hands.

"The soldiers made sport of Jesus where He stood in the Council Hall. They stripped Him naked, and put a crown of thorns on His head, a red robe about His body, and a reed from the river in His hands.

"They said, 'Ha! Ha! So you're the King! Ha! Ha!' And they bowed down in mockery before Him, makin' fun of Jesus.

"Some of the guards threw wine in His face. Some of the guards was drunk and called Him out o' His name—and nobody said, 'Stop! That's Jesus!'"

The Reverend Duke Braswell's face darkened with horror as he pictured the death of Christ. "Oh yes! Peter denied Him because he was afraid. Judas betrayed Him for thirty pieces of silver. Pilate said, 'I wash my hands—take Him and kill Him.'

"And His friends fled away! . . . Have mercy on Jesus! . . . His friends done fled away!"

"His friends!"

"His friends done fled away!"

The preacher chanted, half moaning his sentences, not speaking them. His breath came in quick, short gasps, with an indrawn "umn!" between each rapid phrase. Perspiration poured down his face as he strode across the platform, wrapped in this drama that he saw in the very air before his eyes. Peering over the heads of his audience out into the darkness, he began the ascent to Golgotha, describing the taunting crowd at Christ's heels and the heavy cross on His shoulders.

"Then a black man named Simon, blacker than me, come and took the cross and bore it for Him. Umn!

"Then Jesus were standin' alone on a high hill, in the broilin' sun, while they put the crosses in the ground. No water to cool His throat! No tree to shade His achin' head! Nobody to say a friendly word to Jesus! Umn!

"Alone, in that crowd on the hill of Golgotha, with two thieves bound and dyin', and the murmur of the mob all around. Umn!

"They laid they hands on Him, and they tore the clothes from His body—and then, and then"—loud as a thunderclap, the minister's voice broke through the little tent—"they raised Him to the cross!"

A great wail went up from the crowd. Bud and I sat entranced in spite of ourselves, forgetting to smoke. Aunt Ibey Davis wept. Sister Mabry moaned. In their car behind us the white people were silent as the minister went on:

"They brought four long iron nails
And put one in the palm of His left hand.
The hammer said . . . Bam!
They put one in the palm of His right hand.
The hammer said . . . Bam!
They put one through His left foot . . . Bam!
And one through His right foot . . . Bam!"

"Don't drive it!" a woman screamed. "Don't drive them nails! For Christ's sake! Oh! Don't drive 'em!"

"And they left my Jesus on the cross!
Nails in His hands! Nails in His feet!
Sword in His side! Thorns circlin' His head!
Mob cussin' and hootin' my Jesus! Umn!
The spit of the mob in His face! Umn!
His body hangin' on the cross! Umn!
Gimme piece of His garment for a souvenir! Umn!
Castin' lots for His garments! Umn!
Blood from His wounded side! Umn!
Streamin' down His naked legs! Umn!
Droppin' in the dust—umn—
That's what they did to my Jesus!
They stoned Him first, they stoned Him!
Called Him everything but a child of God.
Then they lynched Him on the cross."

In song I heard my mother's voice cry:

"Were you there when they crucified my Lord?
Were you there when they nailed Him to the tree?"

The Reverend Duke Braswell stretched wide his arms against the white canvas of the tent. In the yellow light his body made a cross-like shadow on the canvas.

"Oh, it makes me to tremble, tremble!
Were you there when they crucified my Lord?"

"Let's go," said the white woman in the car behind us. "This is too much for me!" They started the motor and drove noisily away in a swirl of dust.

"Don't go," I cried from where I was sitting at the root of the tree. "Don't go," I shouted, jumping up. "They're about to call for sinners to come to the mourners' bench. Don't go!" But their car was already out of earshot.

I didn't realize I was crying until I tasted my tears in my mouth.

1935

The Negro Artist and the Racial Mountain[1]

One of the most promising of the young Negro poets said to me once, "I want to be a poet—not a Negro poet," meaning, I believe, "I want to write like a white poet"; meaning subconsciously, "I would like to be a white poet"; meaning behind that, "I would like to be white." And I was sorry the young man said that, for no great poet has ever been afraid of being himself. And I doubted then that, with his desire to run away spiritually from his race, this boy would ever be a great poet. But this is the mountain standing in the way of any true Negro art in America—this urge within the race toward whiteness, the desire to pour racial individuality into the mold of American standardization, and to be as little Negro and as much American as possible.

But let us look at the immediate background of this young poet. His family is of what I suppose one would call the Negro middle class: people who are by no means rich yet never uncomfortable nor hungry—smug, contented, respectable folk, members of the Baptist church. The father goes to work every morning. He is a chief steward at a large white club. The mother sometimes does fancy sewing or supervises parties for the rich families of the town. The children go to a mixed school. In the home they read white papers and magazines. And the mother often says "Don't be like niggers" when the children are bad. A frequent phrase from the father is, "Look

[1]This essay can fruitfully be read as a response to George Schuyler's "The Negro-Art Hokum" (p. 1703), which had appeared in *The Nation* the week before Hughes's "The Negro Artist."

how well a white man does things." And so the word white comes to be unconsciously a symbol of all the virtues. It holds for the children beauty, morality, and money. The whisper of "I want to be white" runs silently through their minds. This young poet's home is, I believe, a fairly typical home of the colored middle class. One sees immediately how difficult it would be for an artist born in such a home to interest himself in interpreting the beauty of his own people. He is never taught to see that beauty. He is taught rather not to see it, or if he does, to be ashamed of it when it is not according to Caucasian patterns.

For racial culture the home of a self-styled "high-class" Negro has nothing better to offer. Instead there will perhaps be more aping of things white than in a less cultured or less wealthy home. The father is perhaps a doctor, lawyer, landowner, or politician. The mother may be a social worker, or a teacher, or she may do nothing and have a maid. Father is often dark but he has usually married the lightest woman he could find. The family attend a fashionable church where few really colored faces are to be found. And they themselves draw a color line. In the North they go to white theatres and white movies. And in the South they have at least two cars and a house "like white folks." Nordic manners, Nordic faces, Nordic hair, Nordic art (if any), and an Episcopal heaven. A very high mountain indeed for the would-be racial artist to climb in order to discover himself and his people.

But then there are the low-down folks, the so-called common element, and they are the majority—may the Lord be praised! The people who have their nip of gin on Saturday nights and are not too important to themselves or the community, or too well fed, or too learned to watch the lazy world go round. They live on Seventh Street in Washington or State Street in Chicago and they do not particularly care whether they are like white folks or anybody else. Their joy runs, bang! into ecstasy. Their religion soars to a shout. Work maybe a little today, rest a little tomorrow. Play awhile. Sing awhile. O, let's dance! These common people are not afraid of spirituals, as for a long time their more intellectual brethren were, and jazz is their child. They furnish a wealth of colorful, distinctive material for any artist because they still hold their own individuality in the face of American standardizations. And perhaps these common people will give to the world its truly great Negro artist, the one who is not afraid to be himself. Whereas the better-class Negro would tell the artist what to do, the people at least let him alone when he does appear. And they are not ashamed of him—if they know he exists at all. And they accept what beauty is their own without question.

Certainly there is, for the American Negro artist who can escape the restrictions the more advanced among his own group would put upon him, a great field of unused material ready for his art. Without going outside his race, and even among the better classes with their "white" culture and conscious American manners, but still Negro enough to be different, there is sufficient matter to furnish a black artist with a lifetime of creative work. And when he chooses to touch on the relations between Negroes and whites in this country with their innumerable overtones and undertones surely, and especially for literature and the drama, there is an inexhaustible supply of themes at hand. To these the Negro artist can give his racial individuality, his heritage of rhythm and warmth, and his incongruous humor that so often, as in the Blues, becomes ironic laughter mixed with tears. But let us look again at the mountain.

A prominent Negro clubwoman in Philadelphia paid eleven dollars to hear Raquel Meller sing Andalusian popular songs. But she told me a few weeks before she would not think of going to hear "that woman," Clara Smith, a great black artist, sing Negro folksongs. And many an upper-class Negro church, even now, would not dream of employing a spiritual in its services. The drab melodies in white folks' hymn-books are much to be preferred. "We want to worship the Lord correctly and quietly. We don't believe in 'shouting.' Let's be dull like the Nordics," they say, in effect.

The road for the serious black artist, then, who would produce a racial art is most certainly rocky and the mountain is high. Until recently he received almost no encouragement for his work from either white or colored people. The fine novels of Chesnutt go out of print with neither race noticing their passing. The quaint charm and humor of Dunbar's dialect verse brought to him, in his day, largely the same kind of encouragement one would give a sideshow freak (A colored man writing poetry! How odd!) or a clown (How amusing!).

The present vogue in things Negro, although it may do as much harm as good for the budding colored artist, has at least done this: it has brought him forcibly to the attention of his own people among whom for so long, unless the other race had noticed him beforehand, he was a prophet with little honor. I understand that Charles Gilpin acted for years in Negro theatres without any special acclaim from his own, but when Broadway gave him eight curtain calls, Negroes, too, began to beat a tin pan in his honor. I know a young colored writer, a manual worker by day, who had been writing well for the colored magazines for some years, but it was not until he recently broke into the white publications and his first book was accepted by a prominent New York publisher that the "best" Negroes in his city took the trouble to discover that he lived there. Then almost immediately they decided to give a grand dinner for him. But the society ladies were careful to whisper to his mother that perhaps she'd better not come. They were not sure she would have an evening gown.

The Negro artist works against an undertow of sharp criticism and misunderstanding from his own group and unintentional bribes from the whites. "Oh, be respectable, write about nice people, show how good we are," say the Negroes. "Be stereotyped, don't go too far, don't shatter our illusions about you, don't amuse us too seriously. We will pay you," say the whites. Both would have told Jean Toomer not to write *Cane.* The colored people did not praise it. The white people did not buy it. Most of the colored people who did read *Cane* hate it. They are afraid of it. Although the critics gave it good reviews the public remained indifferent. Yet (excepting the work of Du Bois) *Cane* contains the finest prose written by a Negro in America. And like the singing of Robeson, it is truly racial.

But in spite of the Nordicized Negro intelligentsia and the desires of some white editors we have an honest America Negro literature already with us. Now I await the rise of the Negro theatre. Our folk music, having achieved world-wide fame, offers itself to the genius of the great individual American composer who is to come. And within the next decade I expect to see the work of a growing school of colored artists who paint and model the beauty of dark faces and create with new technique the expressions of their own soul-world. And the Negro dancers who will dance like flame and the singers who will continue to carry our songs to all who listen—they will be with us in even greater numbers tomorrow.

Most of my own poems are racial in theme and treatment, derived from the life I know. In many of them I try to grasp and hold some of the meanings and rhythms of jazz. I am as sincere as I know how to be in these poems and yet after every reading I answer questions like these from my own people: Do you think Negroes should always write about Negroes? I wish you wouldn't read some of your poems to white folks. How do you find anything interesting in a place like a cabaret? Why do you write about black people? You aren't black. What makes you do so many jazz poems?

But jazz to me is one of the inherent expressions of Negro life in America; the eternal tom-tom beating in the Negro soul—the tom-tom of revolt against weariness in a white world, a world of subway trains, and work, work, work; the tom-tom of joy and laughter, and pain swallowed in a smile. Yet the Philadelphia clubwoman is ashamed to say that her race created it and she does not like me to write about it. The old subconscious "white is best" runs through her mind. Years of study under white teachers, a lifetime of white books, pictures, and papers, and white manners, morals, and Puritan standards made her dislike the spirituals. And now she turns up her nose at jazz and all its manifestations—likewise almost everything else distinctly racial. She doesn't care for the Winold Reiss portraits of Negroes because they are "too Negro." She does not want a true picture of herself from anybody. She wants the artist to flatter her, to make the white world believe that all Negroes are as smug and as near white in soul as she wants to be. But, to my mind, it is the duty of the younger Negro artist, if he accepts any duties at all from outsiders, to change through the force of his art that old whispering "I want to be white," hidden in the aspirations of his people, to "Why should I want to be white? I am a Negro—and beautiful!"

So I am ashamed for the black poet who says, "I want to be a poet, not a Negro poet," as though his own racial world were not as interesting as any other world. I am ashamed, too, for the colored artist who runs from the painting of Negro faces to the painting of sunsets after the manner of the academicians because he fears the strange un-whiteness of his own features. An artist must be free to choose what he does, certainly, but he must also never be afraid to do what he might choose.

Let the blare of Negro jazz bands and the bellowing voice of Bessie Smith singing Blues penetrate the closed ears of the colored near-intellectuals until they listen and perhaps understand. Let Paul Robeson singing "Water Boy," and Rudolph Fisher writing about the streets of Harlem, and Jean Toomer holding the heart of Georgia in his hands, and Aaron Douglas drawing strange black fantasies cause the smug Negro middle class to turn from their white, respectable, ordinary books and papers to catch a glimmer of their own beauty. We younger Negro artists who create now intend to express our individual dark-skinned selves without fear or shame. If white people are pleased we are glad. If they are not, it doesn't matter. We know we are beautiful. And ugly too. The tom-tom cries and the tom-tom laughs. If colored people are pleased we are glad. If they are not, their displeasure doesn't matter either. We build our temples for tomorrow, strong as we know how, and we stand on top of the mountain, free within ourselves.

1926

When the Negro Was in Vogue

The 1920s were the years of Manhattan's black Renaissance. It began with *Shuffle Along, Running Wild,* and the Charleston. Perhaps some people would say even with *The Emperor Jones,* Charles Gilpin, and the tom-toms at the Provincetown. But certainly it was the musical revue, *Shuffle Along,* that gave a scintillating send-off to that Negro vogue in Manhattan, which reached its peak just before the crash of 1929, the crash that sent Negroes, white folks, and all rolling down the hill toward the Works Progress Administration.

Shuffle Along was a honey of a show. Swift, bright, funny, rollicking, and gay, with a dozen danceable, singable tunes. Besides, look who were in it: The now famous choir director, Hall Johnson, and the composer, William Grant Still, were a part of the orchestra. Eubie Blake and Noble Sissle wrote the music and played and acted in the show. Miller and Lyles were the comics. Florence Mills skyrocketed to fame in the second act. Trixie Smith sang "He May Be Your Man But He Comes to See Me Sometimes." And Caterina Jarboro, now a European prima donna, and the internationally celebrated Josephine Baker were merely in the chorus. Everybody was in the audience—including me. People came back to see it innumerable times. It was always packed.

To see *Shuffle Along* was the main reason I wanted to go to Columbia. When I saw it, I was thrilled and delighted. From then on I was in the gallery of the Cort Theatre every time I got a chance. That year, too, I saw Katharine Cornell in *A Bill of Divorcement,* Margaret Wycherly in *The Verge,* Maugham's *The Circle* with Mrs. Leslie Carter, and the Theatre Guild production of Kaiser's *From Morn Till Midnight.* But I remember *Shuffle Along* best of all. It gave just the proper push—a pre-Charleston kick—to that Negro vogue of the 20's, that spread to books, African sculpture, music, and dancing.

Put down the 1920's for the rise of Roland Hayes, who packed Carnegie Hall, the rise of Paul Robeson in New York and London, of Florence Mills over two continents, of Rose McClendon in Broadway parts that never measured up to her, the booming voice of Bessie Smith and the low moan of Clara on thousands of records, and the rise of that grand comedienne of song, Ethel Waters, singing: "Charlie's elected now! He's in right for sure!" Put down the 1920's for Louis Armstrong and Gladys Bentley and Josephine Baker.

White people began to come to Harlem in droves. For several years they packed the expensive Cotton Club on Lenox Avenue. But I was never there, because the Cotton Club was a Jim Crow club for gangsters and monied whites. They were not cordial to Negro patronage, unless you were a celebrity like Bojangles. So Harlem Negroes did not like the Cotton Club and never appreciated its Jim Crow policy in the very heart of their dark community. Nor did ordinary Negroes like the growing influx of whites toward Harlem after sundown, flooding the little cabarets and bars where formerly only colored people laughed and sang, and where now the strangers were given the best ringside tables to sit and stare at the Negro customers—like amusing animals in a zoo.

The Negroes said: "We can't go downtown and sit and stare at you in your clubs. You won't even let us in your clubs." But they didn't say it out loud—for Negroes are practically never rude to white people. So thousands of whites came to Harlem night after night, thinking the Negroes loved to have them there, and firmly believing that all Harlemites left their houses at sundown to sing and dance in cabarets, because most of the whites saw nothing but the cabarets, not the houses.

Some of the owners of Harlem clubs, delighted at the flood of white patronage, made the grievous error of barring their own race, after the manner of the famous Cotton Club. But most of these quickly lost business and folded up, because they failed to realize that a large part of the Harlem attraction for downtown New Yorkers lay in simply watching the colored customers amuse themselves. And the smaller clubs, of course, had no big floor shows or a name band like the Cotton Club, where Duke Ellington usually held forth, so, without black patronage, they were not amusing at all.

Some of the small clubs, however, had people like Gladys Bentley, who was something worth discovering in those days, before she got famous, acquired an accompanist, specially written material, and conscious vulgarity. But for two or three amazing years, Miss Bentley sat, and played a big piano all night long, literally all night, without stopping—singing songs like "The St. James Infirmary," from ten in the evening until dawn, with scarcely a break between the notes, sliding from one song to another, with a powerful and continuous underbeat of jungle rhythm. Miss Bentley was an amazing exhibition of musical energy—a large, dark, masculine lady, whose feet pounded the floor while her fingers pounded the keyboard—a perfect piece of African sculpture, animated by her own rhythm.

But when the place where she played became too well known, she began to sing with an accompanist, became a star, moved to a larger place, then downtown, and is now in Hollywood. The old magic of the woman and the piano and the night and the rhythm being one is gone. But everything goes, one way or another. The '20's are gone and lots of fine things in Harlem night life have disappeared like snow in the sun—since it became utterly commercial, planned for the downtown tourist trade, and therefore dull.

The lindy-hoppers at the Savoy even began to practise acrobatic routines, and to do absurd things for the entertainment of the whites, that probably never would have entered their heads to attempt merely for their own effortless amusement. Some of the lindy-hoppers had cards printed with their names on them and became dance professors teaching the tourists. Then Harlem nights became show nights for the Nordics.

Some critics say that that is what happened to certain Negro writers, too—that they ceased to write to amuse themselves and began to write to amuse and entertain white people, and in so doing distorted and over-colored their material, and left out a great many things they thought would offend their American brothers of a lighter complexion. Maybe—since Negroes have writer-racketeers, as has any other race. But I have known almost all of them, and most of the good ones have tried to be honest, write honestly, and express their world as they saw it.

All of us know that the gay and sparkling life of the so-called Negro Renaissance of the '20's was not so gay and sparkling beneath the surface as it looked. Carl Van Vechten, in the character of Byron in *Nigger Heaven,* captured some of the bitterness and frustration of literary Harlem that Wallace Thurman later so effectively poured into his *Infants of the Spring*—the only novel by a Negro about that fantastic period when Harlem was in vogue.

It was a period when, at almost every Harlem upper-crust dance or party, one would be introduced to various distinguished white celebrities there as guests. It was a period when almost any Harlem Negro of any social importance at all would be likely to say casually: "As I was remarking the other day to Heywood—," meaning Heywood Broun. Or: "As I said to George—," referring to George Gershwin. It was a period when local and visiting royalty were not at all uncommon in Harlem. And when the parties of A'Lelia Walker, the Negro heiress, were filled with guests whose names would turn any Nordic social climber green with envy. It was a period when Harold Jackman, a handsome young Harlem school teacher of modest means, calmly announced one day that he was sailing for the Riviera for a fortnight, to attend Princess Murat's yachting party. It was a period when Charleston preachers opened up shouting churches as sideshows for white tourists. It was a period when at least one charming colored chorus girl, amber enough to pass for a Latin American, was living in a pent house, with all her bills paid by a gentleman whose name was banker's magic on Wall Street. It was a period when every season there was at least one hit play on Broadway acted by a Negro cast. And when books by Negro authors were being published with much greater frequency and much more publicity than ever before or since in history. It was a period when white writers wrote about Negroes more successfully (commercially speaking) than Negroes did about themselves. It was the period (God help us!) when Ethel Barrymore appeared in blackface in *Scarlet Sister Mary!* It was the period when the Negro was in vogue.

I was there. I had a swell time while it lasted. But I thought it wouldn't last long. (I remember the vogue for things Russian, the season the Chauve-Souris first came to town.) For how could a large and enthusiastic number of people be crazy about Negroes forever? But some Harlemites thought the millennium had come. They thought the race problem had at last been solved through Art plus Gladys Bentley. They were sure the New Negro would lead a new life from then on in green pastures of tolerance created by Countee Cullen, Ethel Waters, Claude McKay, Duke Ellington, Bojangles, and Alain Locke.

I don't know what made any Negroes think that—except that they were mostly intellectuals doing the thinking. The ordinary Negroes hadn't heard of the Negro Renaissance. And if they had, it hadn't raised their wages any. As for all those white folks in the speakeasies and night clubs of Harlem—well, maybe a colored man could find *some* place to have a drink that the tourists hadn't yet discovered.

Then it was that house-rent parties began to flourish—and not always to raise the rent either. But, as often as not, to have a get-together of one's own, where you could do the black-bottom with no stranger behind you trying to do it, too. Non-theatrical, non-intellectual Harlem was an unwilling victim of its own vogue. It didn't like to be stared at by white folks. But perhaps the downtowners never knew this—for the cabaret owners, the entertainers, and the speakeasy proprietors treated them fine—as long as they paid.

The Saturday night rent parties that I attended were often more amusing than any night club, in small apartments where God knows who lived—because the guests seldom did—but where the piano would often be augmented by a guitar, or an odd cornet, or somebody with a pair of drums walking in off the street. And where awful bootleg whiskey and good fried fish or steaming chitterling were sold at very low prices. And the dancing and singing and impromptu entertaining went on until dawn came in at the windows.

These parties, often termed whist parties or dances, were usually announced by brightly colored cards stuck in the grille of apartment house elevators. Some of the cards were highly entertaining in themselves:

We got yellow girls, we've got black and tan
Will you have a good time? - YEAH MAN!

A Social Whist Party

—GIVEN BY—
MARY WINSTON
147 West 145th Street Apt. 5

SATURDAY EVE., MARCH 19th, 1932

GOOD MUSIC REFRESHMENTS

H U R R A Y

COME AND SEE WHAT IS IN STORE FOR YOU AT THE

TEA CUP PARTY

GIVEN BY MRS. VANDERBILT SMITH
at 409 EDGECOMBE AVENUE
NEW YORK CITY
Apartment 10-A
on Thursday evening, January 23rd, 1930
at 8:30 P. M.

ORIENTAL - GYPSY - SOUTHERN MAMMY - STARLIGHT
and other readers will be present

Music and Talent — — Refreshments Served
Ribbons-Bows and Trotters A Specialty

Fall in line, and watch your step, For there'll be
Lots of Browns with plenty of Pep At

A Social Whist Party

Given by
Lucille & Minnie
149 West 117th Street, N. Y. Gr. floor, W,

Saturday Evening, Nov. 2nd 1929

Refreshments Just It Music Won't Quit

If Sweet Mamma is running wild, and you are looking for a Do-right child, just come around and linger awhile at a

SOCIAL WHIST PARTY

GIVEN BY

PINKNEY & EPPS

260 West 129th Street Apartment 10

SATURDAY EVENING, JUNE 9, 1928

GOOD MUSIC REFRESHMENTS

Railroad Men's Ball

AT CANDY'S PLACE

FRIDAY, SATURDAY & SUNDAY,

April 29-30, May 1, 1927

Black Wax, says change your mind and say they do and he will give you a hearing, while MEAT HOUSE SLIM, laying in the bin killing all good men.

L. A. Vaugh, *President*

OH BOY OH JOY

The Eleven Brown Skins

of the

Evening Shadow Social Club

are giving their

Second Annual St. Valentine Dance

Saturday evening, Feb. 18th, 1928

At 129 West 136th Street, New York City

Good Music Refreshments Served

Subscription 25 Cents

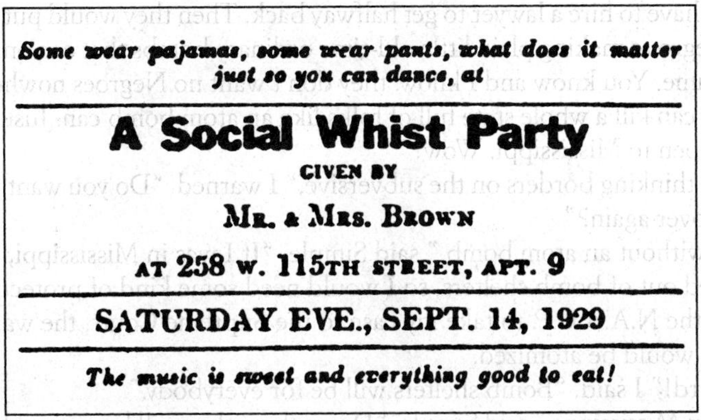
Some wear pajamas, some wear pants, what does it matter just so you can dance, at

A Social Whist Party

GIVEN BY

MR. & MRS. BROWN

AT 258 W. 115TH STREET, APT. 9

SATURDAY EVE., SEPT. 14, 1929

The music is sweet and everything good to eat!

Almost every Saturday night when I was in Harlem I went to a house-rent party. I wrote lots of poems about house-rent parties, and ate thereat many a fried fish and pig's foot—with liquid refreshments on the side. I met ladies' maids and truck drivers, laundry workers and shoe shine boys, seamstresses and porters. I can still hear their laughter in my ears, hear the soft slow music, and feel the floor shaking as the dancers danced.

1940

Radioactive Red Caps

"How wonderful," I said, "that Negroes today are being rapidly integrated into every phase of American life from the Army and Navy to schools to industries—advancing, advancing!"

"I have not advanced one step," said Simple. "Still the same old job, same old salary, same old kitchenette, same old Harlem and the same old color."

"You are just one individual," I said. "I am speaking of our race in general. Look how many colleges have opened up to Negroes in the last ten years. Look at the change in restrictive covenants. You can live anywhere."

"You mean *try* to live anywhere."

"Look at the way you can ride unsegregated in interstate travel."

"And get throwed off the bus."

"Look at the ever greater number of Negroes in high places."

"Name me one making an atom bomb."

"That would be top-secret information," I said, "even if I knew. Anyway, you are arguing from supposition, not knowledge. How do you know what our top Negro scientists are doing?"

"I don't," said Simple. "But I bet if one was making an atom bomb, they would have his picture on the cover of *Jet* every other week like Eartha Kitt, just to make Negroes think the atom bomb is an integrated bomb. Then, next thing you know, some old Southern senator would up and move to have that Negro investigated for being subversive, because he would be mad that a Negro ever got anywhere near an atom bomb. Then that Negro would be removed from his job like Miss Annie Lee

Moss, and have to hire a lawyer to get halfway back. Then they would put that white-washed Negro to making plain little old-time ordinary bombs that can only kill a few folks at a time. You know and I know, they don't want no Negroes nowhere near no bomb that can kill a whole state full of folks like an atom bomb can. Just think what would happen to Mississippi. Wow!"

"Your thinking borders on the subversive," I warned. "Do you want to fight the Civil War over again?"

"Not without an atom bomb," said Simple. "If I was in Mississippi, I would be Jim Crowed out of bomb shelters, so I would need some kind of protection. By the time I got the N.A.A.C.P. to take my case to the Supreme Court, the war would be over, else I would be atomized."

"Absurd!" I said. "Bomb shelters will be for everybody."

"Not in Mississippi," said Simple. "Down there they will have some kind of voting test, else loyalty test, in which they will find some way of flunking Negroes out. You can't tell me them Dixiecrats are going to give Negroes free rein of bomb shelters. On the other hand, come to think of it, they might *have* to let us in to save their own skins, because I hear tell in the next war everything that ain't sheltered will be so charged with atoms a human can't touch it. Even the garbage is going to get radioactive when the bombs start falling. I read last week in the *News* that, in case of a bombing, it will be a problem as to where to put our garbage, because it will be radioactive up to a million years. So you sure can't keep garbage around. If you dump it in the sea, it will make the fish radioactive, too, like them Japanese tunas nobody could eat. I am wondering what the alley cats will eat—because if all the garbage is full of atomic rays, and the cats eat the garbage, and my wife pets a strange cat, Joyce will be radioactive, too. Then if I pet my wife, what will happen to me?"

"You are stretching the long arm of coincidence mighty far," I said. "What is more likely to happen is, if the bombs fall, you will be radioactive long before the garbage will."

"That will worry white folks," said Simple. "Just suppose all the Negroes down South got atomized, charged up like hot garbage, who would serve the white folks' tables, nurse their children, Red Cap their bags, and make up their Pullman berths? Just think! Suppose all the colored Red Caps carrying bags on the Southern Railroad was atom-charged! Suitcases would get atomized, too, and all that is packed in them. Every time a white man took out his toothbrush to wash his teeth on the train, his teeth would get atom-charged. How could he kiss his wife when he got home?"

"I believe you are charged now," I said.

"No," said Simple, "I am only thinking how awful this atom bomb can be! If one fell up North in Harlem and charged me, then I went downtown and punched that time clock where I work, the clock would be charged. Then a white fellow would come along behind me and punch the time clock, and he would be charged. Then both of us would be so full of atoms for the next million years, that at any time we would be liable to explode like firecrackers on the Fourth of July. And from us, everybody else in the plant would get charged. Atoms, they tell me, is catching. What I read in the *News* said that if you even look at an atom bomb going off, the rays are so strong your eyes will water the rest of your life, your blood will turn white, your hair turn gray, and your children will be born backwards. Your breakfast eggs will no longer be sunny-side up, but scrambled, giving off sparks—and people will give off sparks, too. If you walk down the street, every doorbell you pass will ring without your touching it. If you pick up a phone, whoever answers it will be atomized. So if you know somebody you don't like, for example, just phone them—and you can really fix them up! That's what they call a chain reaction. I am getting my chain ready now—the first person I am going to telephone is my former landlady! When she picks up the phone, I hope to atomize her like a Japanese tuna! She will drive a Geiger counter crazy after I say, 'Hello!' "

"My dear boy," I said, "what makes you think you, of all people, would be able to go around transferring atomic radiation to others? You would probably be annihilated yourself by the very first bomb blast."

"Me? Oh, no," said Simple. "Negroes are very hard to annihilate. I am a Negro—so I figure I would live to radiate and, believe me, once charged, I will take charge."

"In other words, come what may, you expect to survive the atom bomb?"

"If Negroes can survive white folks in Mississippi," said Simple, "we can survive anything."

1961

Thank You, M'am

She was a large woman with a large purse that had everything in it but a hammer and nails. It had a long strap, and she carried it slung across her shoulder. It was about eleven o'clock at night, dark, and she was walking alone, when a boy ran up behind her and tried to snatch her purse. The strap broke with the sudden single tug the boy gave it from behind. But the boy's weight and the weight of the purse combined caused him to lose his balance. Instead of taking off full blast as he had hoped, the boy fell on his back on the sidewalk and his legs flew up. The large woman simply turned around and kicked him right square in his blue-jeaned sitter. Then she reached down, picked the boy up by his shirt front, and shook him until his teeth rattled.

After that the woman said, "Pick up my pocketbook, boy, and give it here."

She still held him tightly. But she bent down enough to permit him to stoop and pick up her purse. Then she said, "Now ain't you ashamed of yourself?"

Firmly gripped by his shirt front, the boy said, "Yes'm."

The woman said, "What did you want to do it for?"

The boy said, "I didn't aim to."

She said, "You a lie!"

By that time two or three people passed, stopped, turned to look, and some stood watching.

"If I turn you loose, will you run?" asked the woman.

"Yes'm," said the boy.

"Then I won't turn you loose," said the woman. She did not release him.

"Lady, I'm sorry," whispered the boy.

"Um-hum! Your face is dirty. I got a great mind to wash your face for you. Ain't you got nobody home to tell you to wash your face?"

"No'm," said the boy.

"Then it will get washed this evening," said the large woman, starting up the street, dragging the frightened boy behind her.

He looked as if he were fourteen or fifteen, frail and willow-wild, in tennis shoes and blue jeans.

The woman said, "You ought to be my son. I would teach you right from wrong. Least I can do right now is to wash your face. Are you hungry?"

"No'm," said the being-dragged boy. "I just want you to turn me loose."

"Was I bothering *you* when I turned that corner?" asked the woman.

"No'm."

"But you put yourself in contact with *me,*" said the woman. "If you think that that contact is not going to last awhile, you got another thought coming. When I get through with you, sir, you are going to remember Mrs. Luella Bates Washington Jones."

Sweat popped out on the boy's face and he began to struggle. Mrs. Jones stopped, jerked him around in front of her, put a half nelson about his neck, and continued to drag him up the street. When she got to her door, she dragged the boy inside, down a hall, and into a large kitchenette-furnished room at the rear of the house. She switched on the light and left the door open. The boy could hear other roomers laughing and talking in the large house. Some of their doors were open, too, so he knew he and the woman were not alone. The woman still had him by the neck in the middle of her room.

She said, "What is your name?"

"Roger," answered the boy.

"Then, Roger, you go to that sink and wash your face," said the woman, whereupon she turned him loose—at last. Roger looked at the door—looked at the woman—looked at the door—*and went to the sink.*

"Let the water run until it gets warm," she said. "Here's a clean towel."

"You gonna take me to jail?" asked the boy, bending over the sink.

"Not with that face, I would not take you nowhere," said the woman. "Here I am trying to get home to cook me a bite to eat, and you snatch my pocketbook! Maybe you ain't been to your supper either, late as it be. Have you?"

"There's nobody home at my house," said the boy.

"Then we'll eat," said the woman. "I believe you're hungry—or been hungry—to try to snatch my pocketbook!"

"I want a pair of blue suede shoes," said the boy.

"Well, you didn't have to snatch *my* pocketbook to get some suede shoes," said Mrs. Luella Bates Washington Jones. "You could of asked me."

"M'am?"

The water dripping from his face, the boy looked at her. There was a long pause. A very long pause. After he had dried his face and not knowing what else to do, dried it again, the boy turned around, wondering what next. The door was open. He could make a dash for it down the hall. He could run, run, run, *run!*

The woman was sitting on the day bed. After a while she said, "I were young once and I wanted things I could not get."

There was another long pause. The boy's mouth opened. Then he frowned, not knowing he frowned.

The woman said, "Um-hum! You thought I was going to say *but,* didn't you? You thought I was going to say, *but I didn't snatch people's pocketbooks.* Well, I wasn't going to say that." Pause. Silence. "I have done things, too, which I would not tell you, son—neither tell God, if He didn't already know. Everybody's got something in common. So you set down while I fix us something to eat. You might run that comb through your hair so you will look presentable."

In another corner of the room behind a screen was a gas plate and an icebox. Mrs. Jones got up and went behind the screen. The woman did not watch the boy to see if he was going to run now, nor did she watch her purse, which she left behind her on the day bed. But the boy took care to sit on the far side of the room, away from the purse, where he thought she could easily see him out of the corner of her eye if she wanted to. He did not trust the woman *not* to trust him. And he did not want to be mistrusted now.

"Do you need somebody to go to the store," asked the boy, "maybe to get some milk or something?"

"Don't believe I do," said the woman, "unless you just want sweet milk yourself. I was going to make cocoa out of this canned milk I got here."

"That will be fine," said the boy.

She heated some lima beans and ham she had in the icebox, made the cocoa, and set the table. The woman did not ask the boy anything about where he lived, or his folks, or anything else that would embarrass him. Instead, as they ate, she told him about her job in a hotel beauty shop that stayed open late, what the work was like, and how all kinds of women came in and out, blondes, redheads, and Spanish. Then she cut him a half of her ten-cent cake.

"Eat some more, son," she said.

When they were finished eating, she got up and said, "Now here, take this ten dollars and buy yourself some blue suede shoes. And next time, do not make the mistake of latching onto *my* pocketbook *nor nobody else's*—because shoes got by devilish ways will burn your feet. I got to get my rest now. But from here on in, son, I hope you will behave yourself."

She led him down the hall to the front door and opened it. "Good night! Behave yourself, boy!" she said, looking out into the street as he went down the steps.

The boy wanted to say something other than, "Thank you, m'am," to Mrs. Luella Bates Washington Jones, but although his lips moved, he couldn't even say that as he turned at the foot of the barren stoop and looked up at the large woman in the door. Then she shut the door.

1959

Countee Cullen 1903–1946

Born in 1903, Countee Cullen was the adopted son of Frederick A. Cullen, an AME minister, and his wife, Carolyn. He attended DeWitt Clinton High School in New York and then New York University, where he was a member of Phi Beta Kappa. After earning his MA at Harvard in 1926, he returned to New York, where he worked as a teacher.

Although he wrote and published

works representing practically every genre of creative literature, Countee Cullen was essentially a poet. He had started writing poetry in high school and was but 22 years old when he published his first and most important book of poetry, *Color* (1925). He quickly became one of the best-known writers among the young group of artists whose works gave vitality to the fabled New Negro Renaissance. Single poems of his appeared in *American Mercury, Bookman, Century, Harper's, Nation, Palms, Survey Graphic,* and *Vanity Fair;* his awards and prizes for poetry included those won in contests sponsored by *Crisis, Opportunity,* and *Poetry* magazines. And because he was literary editor for *Opportunity* magazine—one of the two foremost black periodicals of the era—he exercised significant influence over which other young authors had their works appear in print in the mid-20s.

Primarily because he used conventional literary forms in writing poetry, casual critics have seldom thought of Cullen as a social protest writer. Yet he was, and much of his work illustrates his disdain for American racial prejudice. In tone, Cullen's poetry is marked by intensity of emotion and, thematically, by a persistent concern with the ironies and frustrations of the African American experience, especially from a religious perspective.

Walter C. Daniel
University of Missouri–Columbia

PRIMARY WORKS

Color, 1925; *The Ballad of the Brown Girl,* 1927; *Caroling Dusk: An Anthology of Verse by Negro Poets,* 1927; *Copper Sun,* 1927; *The Black Christ and Other Poems,* 1929; *One Way to Heaven,* 1932; *The Medea,* 1935; *On These I Stand,* 1947.

Incident

Once riding in old Baltimore,
  Heart-filled, head-filled with glee,
I saw a Baltimorean
  Keep looking straight at me.

Now I was eight and very small,
  And he was no whit bigger,
And so I smiled, but he poked out
  His tongue, and called me, "Nigger."

I saw the whole of Baltimore
  From May until December;
Of all the things that happened there
  That's all that I remember.

1924

From the Dark Tower

We shall not always plant while others reap
The olden increment of bursting fruit,
Not always countenance, abject and mute,
That lesser men should hold their brothers cheap;
Not everlastingly while others sleep
Shall we beguile their limbs with mellow flute,
Not always bend to some more subtle brute;
We were not made eternally to weep.

The night whose sable breast relieves the stark,
White stars is no less lovely being dark,
And there are buds that cannot bloom at all
In light, but crumple, piteous, and fall;
So in the dark we hide the heart that bleeds,
And wait, and tend our agonizing seeds.

1924

Simon the Cyrenian Speaks

He never spoke a word to me,
  And yet He called my name;
He never gave a sign to me,
  And yet I knew and came.

At first I said, "I will not bear
  His cross upon my back;
He only seeks to place it there
  Because my skin is black."

But He was dying for a dream,
  And He was very meek,
And in His eyes there shone a gleam
  Men journey far to seek.

It was Himself my pity bought;
  I did for Christ alone
What all of Rome could not have wrought
  With bruise of lash or stone.

1924

Yet Do I Marvel

I doubt not God is good, well-meaning, kind,
And did He stoop to quibble could tell why
The little buried mole continues blind,
Why flesh that mirrors Him must some day die,
Make plain the reason tortured Tantalus
Is baited by the fickle fruit, declare
If merely brute caprice dooms Sisyphus
To struggle up a never-ending stair.
Inscrutable His ways are, and immune
To catechism by a mind too strewn
With petty cares to slightly understand
What awful brain compels his awful hand.
Yet do I marvel at this curious thing:
To make a poet black, and bid him sing!

1925

Pagan Prayer

Not for myself I make this prayer,
But for this race of mine
That stretches forth from shadowed places
Dark hands for bread and wine.

For me, my heart is pagan mad,
My feet are never still,
But give them hearths to keep them warm
In homes high on a hill.

For me, my faith lies fallowing,
I bow not till I see,
But these are humble and believe;
Bless their credulity.

For me, I pay my debts in kind,
And see no better way,
Bless these who turn the other cheek
For love of you, and pray.

Our Father, God, our Brother, Christ—
So are we taught to pray;
Their kinship seems a little thing
Who sorrow all the day.

Our Father, God; our Brother, Christ,
  Or are we bastard kind,
That to our plaints your ears are closed,
  Your doors barred from within?

Our Father, God; our Brother, Christ,
  Retrieve my race again;
So shall you compass this black sheep,
  That flushes this wild fruit?

1925

Heritage

For Harold Jackman

What is Africa to me:
Copper sun or scarlet sea,
Jungle star or jungle track,
Strong bronzed men, or regal black
Women from whose loins I sprang
When the birds of Eden sang?
One three centuries removed
From the scenes his fathers loved,
Spicy grove, cinnamon tree,
What is Africa to me?

So I lie, who all day long
Want no sound except the song
Sung by wild barbaric birds
Goading massive jungle herds,
Juggernauts of flesh that pass
Trampling tall defiant grass
Where young forest lovers lie,
Plighting troth beneath the sky.
So I lie, who always hear,
Though I cram against my ear
Both my thumbs, and keep them there,
Great drums throbbing through the air.
So I lie, whose fount of pride,
Dear distress, and joy allied.
Is my somber flesh and skin,
With the dark blood dammed within
Like great pulsing tides of wine
That, I fear, must burst the fine
Channels of the chafing net
Where they surge and foam and fret.

Africa? A book one thumbs
Listlessly, till slumber comes.
Unremembered are her bats
Circling through the night, her cats
Crouching in the river reeds,
Stalking gentle flesh that feeds
By the river brink; no more
Does the bugle-throated roar
Cry that monarch claws have leapt
From the scabbards where they slept.
Silver snakes that once a year
Doff the lovely coats you wear,
Seek no covert in your fear
Lest a mortal eye should see;
What's your nakedness to me?
Here no leprous flowers rear
Fierce corollas in the air;
Here no bodies sleek and wet,
Dripping mingled rain and sweat,
Tread the savage measures of
Jungle boys and girls in love.
What is last year's snow to me,
Last year's anything? The tree
Budding yearly must forget
How its past arose or set—
Bough and blossom, flower, fruit,
Even what shy bird with mute
Wonder at her travail there,
Meekly labored in its hair.
One three centuries removed
From the scenes his fathers loved,
Spicy grove, cinnamon tree,
What is Africa to me?

So I lie, who find no peace
Night or day, no slight release
From the unremittant beat
Made by cruel padded feet
Walking through my body's street.
Up and down they go, and back,
Treading out a jungle track.
So I lie, who never quite
Safely sleep from rain at night—
I can never rest at all
When the rain begins to fall;
Like a soul gone mad with pain
I must match its weird refrain;

Ever must I twist and squirm,
Writhing like a baited worm,
While its primal measures drip
Through my body, crying, "Strip!
Doff this new exuberance.
Come and dance the Lover's Dance!"
In an old remembered way
Rain works on me night and day.

Quaint, outlandish heathen gods
Black men fashion out of rods,
Clay, and brittle bits of stone,
In a likeness like their own,
My conversion came high-priced;
I belong to Jesus Christ,
Preacher of humility,
Heathen gods are naught to me.

Father, Son, and Holy Ghost,
So I make an idle boast;
Jesus of the twice-turned cheek,
Lamb of God, although I speak
With my mouth thus, in my heart
Do I play a double part.
Ever at Thy glowing altar
Must my heart grow sick and falter,
Wishing He I served were black,
Thinking then it would not lack
Precedent of pain to guide it,
Let who would or might deride it;
Surely then this flesh would know
Yours had borne a kindred woe.
Lord, I fashion dark gods, too,
Daring even to give You
Dark despairing features where,
Crowned with dark rebellious hair,
Patience wavers just so much as
Mortal grief compels, while touches
Quick and hot, of anger, rise
To smitten cheek and weary eyes.
Lord, forgive me if my need
Sometimes shapes a human creed.
All day long and all night through,
One thing only must I do:
Quench my pride and cool my blood,
Lest I perish in the flood,
Lest a hidden ember set

Timber that I thought was wet
Burning like the dryest flax,
Melting like the merest wax,
Lest the grave restore its dead.
Not yet has my heart or head
In the least way realized
They and I are civilized.

1925

Scottsboro, Too, Is Worth Its Song

(A poem to American poets)

I said:
Now will the poets sing,—
Their cries go thundering
Like blood and tears
Into the nation's ears,
Like lightning dart
Into the nation's heart.
Against disease and death and all things fell,
And war,
Their strophes rise and swell
To jar
The foe smug in his citadel.
Remembering their sharp and pretty
Tunes for Sacco and Vanzetti,
I said:
Here too's a cause divinely spun
For those whose eyes are on the sun,
Here in epitome
Is all disgrace
And epic wrong,
Like wine to brace
The minstrel heart, and blare it into song.

Surely, I said,
Now will the poets sing.
But they have raised no cry.
I wonder why.

1934

Gwendolyn B. Bennett 1902–1981

Her name is not the best known of African American authors, but Gwendolyn Bennett is being mentioned more and more often as an overlooked figure during the New Negro Renaissance and later. Born in Giddings, Texas, in 1902, to Joshua and Maime Bennett—a lawyer and a schoolteacher—she was raised in Nevada and Washington, D.C., before settling with her father and his second wife in New York City, where she attended high school and then Columbia University. Bennett wrote little, but she was a close friend and associate of Langston Hughes, Countee Cullen, Wallace Thurman, and Zora Neale Hurston. This group of young writers collaborated in publishing *Fire!!*, a literary magazine that folded after one issue but is now a collector's item. Like Countee Cullen, Bennett wrote a column, "Ebony Flute," in *Opportunity* magazine, and she was later active in the Federal Writer's Project and the Federal Art Project. Her poems are included in a dozen or more anthologies of black American writing, including Charles S. Johnson's influential *Ebony and Topaz.*

In addition to writing poetry that was published in *Crisis, Opportunity, Messenger,* and *Palms* magazines, Gwendolyn Bennett worked in the Harlem Art Center during the 1940s. She had been formally trained as an artist, having received a certificate from Pratt Institute in Brooklyn in 1924 before being appointed to the faculty of Howard University, where she taught art for several years.

Her poem "To Usward" was written for a dinner the National Urban League held in New York on May 21, 1924, in honor of the publication of Jessie Fauset's novel *There Is Confusion.* The other works here represent Bennett's pursuit of the lyrical tradition in writing highly personal poetry.

Walter C. Daniel
University of Missouri–Columbia

Heritage

I want to see the slim palm trees,
Pulling at the clouds
With little pointed fingers . . .

I want to see lithe Negro girls,
Etched dark against the sky
While sunset lingers.

I want to hear the silent sands
Singing to the moon
Before the spinx-still face . . .

I want to hear the chinting
Around a heathen fire
Of a strange black race.

I want to breathe the lotus flower,
Sighing to the stars
With tendrils drinking at the Nile . . .

I want to feel the surging
Of my sad people's soul
Hidden by a minstrel smile.

1923

To Usward

Let us be still
As ginger jars are still
Upon a Chinese shelf
And let us be contained
By entities of self. . . .
Not still with lethargy and sloth
But quiet with the Pushing of our growth
Not self-contained with smug identity
But conscious of the strength of entity.

If any have a song to sing
That's different from the rest,
Oh let them sing
Before the urgency of youth's behest!
For some of us have songs to sing
Of jungle heat and fires,
And some of us are solemn grown
With pitiful desires,
And there are those who feel the pull
Of seas beneath the skies,
And some there be who want to croon
Of Negro lullabies
We claim no part with racial dearth,
We want to sing the songs of birth!

And so we stand like ginger jars
Like ginger jars bound round
With dust and age;

Like jars of ginger we are sealed
By nature's heritage.

But let us break the seal of years
With pungent thrusts of song
For there is joy in long-dried tears
For whetted passions of a throng.

1924

Advice

You were a sophist,
Pale and quite remote,
As you bade me
Write poems—
Brown poems
of dark words
And prehistoric rhythms . . .
Your pallor stifled my posey.
But I remembered a tapestry
that I would someday weave
Of dim purples and fine reds
And blues
Like night and death—
The keen precision of your words
Wove a silver thread
Through the dusk softness
Of my dream-stuff. . . .

1927

Lines Written at the Grave of Alexandre Dumas

Cemeteries are places for departed souls
And bones interred,
Or hearts with shattered loves.
A woman with lips made warm for laughter
Would find grey stones and roving spirits

Too chill for living, moving pulses . . .
And thou, great spirit, wouldst shiver in thy granite shroud
Should idle mirth or empty talk
Disturb thy tranquil sleeping.

A cemetery is a place for shattered loves
And broken hearts. . . .
Bowed before the crystal chalice of thy soul,
I find the multi-colored fragrance of thy mind
Has lost itself in Death's transparency.

Oh, stir the lucid waters of thy sleep
And coin for me a tale
Of happy loves and gems and joyous limbs
And hearts where love is sweet!

A cemetery is a place for broken hearts
And silent thought . . .
And silence never moves,
Nor speaks nor sings.

1927

Sterling A. Brown 1901–1989

After graduating with a Harvard M.A. in 1923, Sterling A. Brown went south, as he said, to learn something of his people. There a whole new world of black experience opened up to his acute and sensitive artistic vision, causing in him not just a geographical realignment from north to south but the profound shaping of a folk-based aesthetic. At Virginia Seminary and College in Lynchburg (1923–26), where the precocious twenty-three-year-old instructor played "red-ink" man in English classes, the teacher by day became student at night as seminarians introduced him to Calvin "Big Boy" Davis, itinerate guitar player, and Mrs. Bibby, "illiterate, and somehow very wise"—two of the many individuals whose lives, language, and lore Brown would celebrate in memorable literary portraits.

The genteel circumstances of Brown's birth would seemingly have mitigated against so complete an absorption of black folk life. He was born into the rather "high-brow" gentility of Washington, D.C.'s, black middle class, to Adelaide Allen and Sterling Nelson Brown, a famous pastor, theologian, and social activist who numbered John Mercer Langston and Blanche K. Bruce among his friends. Graduating valedictorian from the prestigious Dunbar High School in 1918 earned Brown a scholarship to Williams College, where an essay in 1922, "The Comic Spirit in Shakespeare and Molière," and election to Phi Beta Kappa won him a Clark Fellowship to Harvard for graduate work (1922–23). By the time Brown began a second period of study at Harvard (1931–32), a marvelous synthesis of formal and folk training had coalesced into an early maturing scholarship and a deeply sensitive creative writing.

An unpublished course thesis entitled "Plays of the Irish Character: A Study in Reinterpretation" (1932), for example, anticipated the critical approach of some of his most important scholarship of the 1930s: "Negro Character as Seen by White Authors" (1933), *Negro Poetry and Drama* (1938), and *The Negro in American Fiction* (1938). It is in this vein that, as editor on Negro Affairs for the Federal Writers' Project (1938–40) and as researcher for the Carnegie-Myrdal Study (1939–40), Brown was a custodian guarding against the proliferation of stereotypes of blacks in the American Guidebooks series as well as in Gunnar Myrdal's *An American Dilemma* (1944). Against the tiresome argument that blacks had contributed little to American cultural history, Brown set forth *The Negro Caravan* (1941), an anthology of black writing co-edited with Arthur P. Davis and Ulysses Lee. By making "comprehensiveness" an editorial aim, the *Caravan* effectively expanded the canons of black and Euro-American literatures by historicizing nineteenth-century black formal and folk literatures, bringing previously unacknowledged writers into prominence, and advocating a single standard of literary criticism. A 1942 Rosenwald Foundation grant supported his work on "A Negro Looks at the South," a proposed book-length travelogue.

The context established by Brown's scholarship and teaching is a window through which to view his poetry. After his early experiments with conventional Victorian verse forms, two seemingly unrelated traditions coalesced in Brown's poetry: the democratic impulse of the New American Poetry and the richly textured aesthetic forms and experiences of black folk life. Carl Sandburg, Robert Frost, Edwin Arlington Robinson, Edgar Lee Masters, and Vachel Lindsay resonate throughout Brown's writing. In their startling experiments with free verse, bold use of idiom and regional vernaculars, and mining of "ordinary" life for its extraordinary meaning, these poets established an American poetry which diverged both from artificial nineteenth-century conventions and from the concern for myth, symbol, and image voiced by Pound, Eliot, and others of the "high modernist" mode.

The other tradition animating Brown's poetry, the untapped world of black folk experience, suffered from *a priori* assumptions of blacks as contented slaves, exotic primitives, and other literary stereotypes. By situating his sensibility in the American literary trend called "critical realism," Brown the scholar refuted such representations. But his poetry became an affirmation of black life while insisting upon a recognition of black humanity. Under his influence, the blues, Negro spirituals, humor, folktales, aphorisms, and work songs became more than cultural artifacts; they became crucibles of experience that when transformed became the stuff of good art.

The blues presented more than a music of pain, suffering, and lost love. Its culturally specific verse form and its highly metaphoric language were raw materials awaiting the craftsman's hand. In the Negro spirituals, Brown detected a tonic shrewdness, or what a critic later described as a "distilled metaphysic." Lines such as "Ben down so long, / Down don't bother me" and "I don't know why my mother wants to stay here for / This world ain't been no friend to her" reveal his desire to get at certain qualities in the language of black people, "a flavor, a color, a pungency of speech." Later, he continues, "I came to something more important—I wanted to get an understanding of people, to acquire an accuracy in the portrayal of their lives."

Expanding black language into a philosophical vehicle conveying the character of a people—a way of life, in effect—revises the conventional idea that black language is inherently limited and racially demeaning. In much the same way, Brown's adaptation of black folk humor revises the shopworn notion of blacks "laughing to keep from crying," by exploiting the familiar purposes of satire to instruct and delight and to instruct through delighting. And black life, largely misunderstood and poorly represented, enjoys one of its most articulate and enthusiastic celebrants.

John Edgar Tidwell
University of Kansas

PRIMARY WORKS

Southern Road, 1932; "A Son's Return: 'Oh, Didn't He Ramble,'" in *Chant of Saints,* eds. Michael S. Harper and Robert B. Stepto, 1979: 3–22; *The Collected Poems of Sterling A. Brown,* 1980; *A Son's Return,* ed. Mark A. Sanders, 1996.

When de Saints Go Ma'ching Home

(To Big Boy Davis, Friend.
In Memories of Days Before He Was
Chased Out of Town for Vagrancy.)[1]

I

He'd play, after the bawdy songs and blues,
After the weary plaints
Of "Trouble, Trouble deep down in muh soul,"
Always one song in which he'd lose the rôle
Of entertainer to the boys. He'd say,
"My mother's favorite." And we knew
That what was coming was his chant of saints,
"When de saints go ma'chin' home. . . ."[2]
And that would end his concert for the day.

Carefully as an old maid over needlework,
Oh, as some black deacon, over his Bible, lovingly,
He'd tune up specially for this. There'd be
No chatter now, no patting of the feet.
After a few slow chords, knelling and sweet—
Oh when de saints go ma'chin' home,
Oh when de sayaints goa ma'chin' home. . . .

[1]As a faculty member at Virginia Seminary and College in Lynchburg, VA (1923–26), Brown befriended Calvin "Big Boy" Davis, a former coal miner turned itinerate blues guitarist.

[2]Adaptation of Negro spiritual "When de Saints Go Ma'chin' In."

He would forget
The quieted bunch, his dimming cigarette
Stuck into a splintered edge of the guitar;
Sorrow deep hidden in his voice, a far
And soft light in his strange brown eyes;
Alone with his masterchords, his memories. . . .
Lawd I wanna be one in nummer
When de saints go ma'chin' home.
Deep the bass would rumble while the treble scattered high,
For all the world like heavy feet a-trompin' toward the sky,
With shrill-voiced women getting 'happy'
All to celestial tunes.
The chap's few speeches helped me understand
The reason why he gazed so fixedly
Upon the burnished strings.
For he would see
A gorgeous procession to 'de Beulah Land,'—
Of saints—his friends—*"a-climbin' fo' deir wings."*
Oh when de saints go ma'chin' home. . . .
Lawd I wanna be one o' dat nummer
When de saints goa ma'chin' home. . . .

II

There'd be—so ran his dream:
"Ole Deacon Zachary
With de asthmy in his chest,
A-puffin' an' a-wheezin'
Up de golden stair;
Wid de badges of his lodges
Strung acrost his heavin' breast
An' de hoggrease jes' shinin'
In his coal black hair. . . .

"An' ole Sis Joe
In huh big straw hat,
An' huh wrapper flappin',
Flappin' in de heavenly win',
An' huh thin-soled easy walkers
Goin' pitty pitty pat,—
Lawd she'd have to ease her corns
When she got in!"

Oh when de saints go ma'chin' home.
"Ole Elder Peter Johnson

Wid his corncob jes' a-puffin',
An' de smoke a-rollin'
Lak stormclouds out behin';
Crossin' de cloud mountains
Widout slowin' up fo' nuffin,
Steamin' up de grade
Lak Wes' bound No. 9.

"An' de little brown-skinned chillen
Wid deir skinny legs a-dancin',
Jes' a-kickin' up ridic'lous
To de heavenly band;
Lookin' at de Great Drum Major
On a white hoss jes' a-prancin',
Wid a gold and silver drumstick
A-waggin' in his han'."
Oh when de sun refuse to shine
Oh when de mo-on goes down
In Blood
"Ole Maumee Annie
Wid huh washin' done,
An' huh las' piece o' laundry
In de renchin' tub,
A wavin' sof' pink han's
To de much obligin' sun,
An' her feet a-moverin' now
To a swif' rub-a-dub;

"An' old Grampa Eli
Wid his wrinkled old haid,
A-puzzlin' over summut
He ain' understood,
Intendin' to ask Peter
Pervidin' he ain't skyaid,
'Jes' what mought be de meanin'
Of de moon in blood?' . . ."
When de saints go ma'chin' home. . . .

III

"Whuffolks,"[3] he dreams, *"will have to stay outside*
Being so onery." But what is he to do

[3]Black vernacular pronunciation of white folks.

With that red brakeman who once let him ride
An empty going home? Or with that kind-faced man
Who paid his songs with board and drink and bed?
Or with the Yankee Cap'n who left a leg
At Vicksburg? *Mought be a place, he said,*
Mought be another mansion fo' white saints,
A smaller one than his'n . . . not so gran'.
As fo' the rest . . . oh let 'em howl and beg.
Hell would be good enough—if big enough—
Widout no shade trees, lawd, widout no rain.
Whuffolks sho' to bring nigger out behin',
Excep'—"when de saints go ma'chin' home."

IV

Sportin' Legs would not be there—nor lucky Sam,
Nor Smitty, nor Hambone, nor Hardrock Gene,
An' not too many guzzlin', cuttin' shines,
Not bootleggers to keep his pockets clean.
An' Sophie wid de sof' smile on her face,
Her foolin' voice, her strappin' body, brown
Lak coffee doused wid milk—she had been good
To him, wid lovin', money and wid food.—
But saints and heaven didn't seem to fit
Jes' right wid Sophy's Beauty—nary bit—
She mought stir trouble, somehow, in dat peaceful place
Mought be some dressed-up dudes in dat fair town.

V

Ise got a dear ole mudder,
She is in hebben I know—
He sees:
    Mammy,
    Li'l mammy—wrinkled face,
    Her brown eyes, quick to tears—to joy—
    With such happy pride in her
    Guitar-plunkin' boy.
    Oh kain't I be one in nummer?

    Mammy
    With deep religion defeating the grief
    Life piled so closely about her,
    Ise so glad trouble doan last alway,

And her dogged belief
That some fine day
She'd go a-ma'chin'
When de saints go ma'chin' home.

He sees her ma'chin' home, ma'chin' along,
Her perky joy shining in her furrowed face,
Her weak and quavering voice singing her song—
The best chair set apart for her worn out body
In that restful place. . . .
I pray to de Lawd I'll meet her
When de saints go ma'chin' home.

1927

Strong Men

The young men keep coming on
The strong men keep coming on.
—SANDBURG

They dragged you from homeland,
They chained you in coffles,[1]
They huddled you spoon-fashion[2] *in filthy hatches,*
They sold you to give a few gentlemen ease.

They broke you in like oxen,
They scourged you,
They branded you,
They made your women breeders,
They swelled your numbers with bastards. . . .
They taught you the religion they disgraced.

You sang:
Keep a-inchin' along
Lak a po' inch worm. . . .

You sang:
Bye and bye
I'm gonna lay down dis heaby load. . . .

[1]A line or file of slaves chained together in transit.
[2]A method of chaining and stowing slaves below ship deck in the hold, resembling the arrangement of spoons in a silverware chest.

You sang:
Walk togedder, chillen,
Dontcha git weary. . . .[3]
The strong men keep a-comin' on
The strong men git stronger.

They point with pride to the roads you built for them,
They ride in comfort over the rails you laid for them.
They put hammers in your hands
And said—Drive so much before sundown.[4]

You sang:
Ain't no hammah
In dis lan',
Strikes lak mine, bebby,
Strikes lak mine.

They cooped you in their kitchens,
They penned you in their factories,
They gave you the jobs that they were too good for,
They tried to guarantee happiness to themselves
By shunting dirt and misery to you.

You sang:
Me an' muh baby gonna shine, shine
Me an' muh baby gonna shine.[5]
The strong men keep a-comin' on
The strong men git stronger. . . .

They bought off some of your leaders
You stumbled, as blind men will . . .
They coaxed you, unwontedly soft-voiced. . . .
You followed a way.
Then laughed as usual.

They heard the laugh and wondered;
Uncomfortable,
Unadmitting a deeper terror. . . .
The strong men keep a-comin' on
Gittin' stronger. . . .

What, from the slums
Where they have hemmed you,
What, from the tiny huts

[3]Lines from old Negro spirituals.
[4]Injunction to lay railroad track.
[5]Lines from Negro secular folksongs.

They could not keep from you—
What reaches them
Making them ill at ease, fearful?
Today they shout prohibition at you
"Thou shalt not this"
"Thou shalt not that"
"Reserved for whites only"
You laugh,

One thing they cannot prohibit—
The strong men . . . coming on
The strong men gittin' stronger.
Strong men. . . .
Stronger. . . .

1931

Ma Rainey[1]

I

When Ma Rainey
Comes to town,
Folks from anyplace
Miles aroun',
From Cape Girardeau,
Poplar Bluff,
Flocks in to hear
Ma do her stuff;
Comes flivverin' in,[2]
Or ridin' mules,
Or packed in trains,
Picknickin' fools. . . .
That's what it's like,
Fo' miles on down,
To New Orleans delta
An' Mobile town,

[1]Gertrude Malissa Nix Pridgett "Ma" Rainey (1886–1939), a former vaudeville entertainer who sang minstrel and popular songs with the Rabbit Foot Minstrels, was taken with "strange" and "weird" music, which she eventually helped propel into national prominence as the classic blues.

[2]Brown makes a verb of *flivver,* a slang term of unknown origin for an old or cheap car.

When Ma hits
Anywheres aroun'.

II

Dey comes to hear Ma Rainey from de little river settlements,
From blackbottom cornrows and from lumber camps;
Dey stumble in de hall, jes a-laughin' an' a-cacklin',
Cheerin' lak roarin' water, lak wind in river swamps.

An' some jokers keeps deir laughs a-goin' in de crowded aisles,
An' some folks sits dere waitin' wid deir aches an' miseries,
Till Ma comes out before dem, a-smilin' gold-toofed smiles
An' Long Boy ripples minors on de black an' yellow keys.

III

O Ma Rainey,
Sing yo' song;
Now you's back
Whah you belong,
Git way inside us,
Keep us strong. . . .
O Ma Rainey,
Li'l an' low;
Sing us 'bout de hard luck
Roun' our do';
Sing us 'bout de lonesome road
We mus' go. . . .

IV

I talked to a fellow, an' the fellow say,
"She jes' catch hold of us, somekindaway.
She sang Backwater Blues one day:
'It rained fo' days an' de skies was dark as night,
Trouble taken place in de lowlands at night.

'Thundered an' lightened an' the storm begin to roll
Thousan's of people ain't got no place to go.

'Den I went an' stood upon some high ol' lonesome hill,
An' looked down on the place where I used to live.'

An' den de folks, dey natchally bowed dey heads an' cried,
Bowed dey heavy heads, shet dey moufs up tight an' cried,

An' Ma lef' de stage, an' followed some de folks outside."

Dere wasn't much more de fellow say:
She jes' gits hold of us dataway.

1932

Slim in Hell[1]

I

Slim Greer went to heaven;
St. Peter said, "Slim,
You been a right good boy."
An' he winked at him.

"You been a travelin' rascal
In yo' day.
You kin roam once mo';
Den you comes to stay.

"Put dese wings on yo' shoulders,
An' save yo' feet."
Slim grin, and he speak up
"Thankye, Pete."

Den Peter say, "Go
To Hell an' see,
All dat is doing, and
Report to me.

"Be sure to remember
How everything go."
Slim say, "I be seein' yuh
On de late watch, bo."

Slim got to cavortin',
Swell as you choose,
Like Lindy in de "Spirit
Of St. Louis Blues!"

He flew an' he flew,
Till at last he hit

[1]In addition to the tall-tale tradition made famous by Mark Twain, the poem draws from two other vernacular traditions: "the colored man in heaven" folktale and the myth of Orpheus and Eurydice.

A hangar wid de sign readin'
  DIS IS IT.

Den he parked his wings,
  An' strolled aroun'
Gettin' used to his feet
  On de solid ground.

II

Big bloodhound came aroarin'
  Like Niagry Falls,
Sicked on by white devils
  In overhalls.

Now Slim warn't scared,
  Cross my heart, it's a fac',
An' de dog went on a bayin'
  Some po' devil's track.

Dem Slim saw a mansion
  An' walked right in;
De Devil looked up
  Wid a sickly grin.

"Suttinly didn't look
  Fo' you, Mr. Greer,
How it happen you comes
  To visit here?"

Slim say—"Oh, jes' thought
  I'd drap by a spell."
"Feel at home, seh, an' here's
  De keys to Hell."

Den he took Slim around
  An' showed him people
Raisin' hell as high as
  De First Church Steeple.

Lots of folks fightin'
  At de roulette wheel,
Like old Rampart Street,
  Or leastwise Beale.[2]

[2]Sites of booze and bordellos, Rampart Street in New Orleans and Beale Street in Memphis were birthplaces of blues and jazz during the first quarter of the century.

Showed him bawdy houses
An' cabarets,
Slim thought of New Orleans
An' Memphis days.

Each devil was busy
Wid a devilish broad,
An' Slim cried, "Lawdy,
Lawd, Lawd, Lawd."

Took him in a room
Where Slim see
De preacher wid a brownskin
On each knee.

Showed him giant stills,
Going everywhere
Wid a passel of devils,
Stretched dead drunk there.

Den he took him to de furnace
Dat some devils was firing,
Hot as hell, an' Slim start
A mean presspirin';

White devils wid pitchforks
Threw black devils on,
Slim thought he'd better
Be gittin' along.

An' he say—"Dis makes
Me think of home—
Vicksburg, Little Rock, Jackson,
Waco, and Rome."

Den de devil gave Slim
De big Ha-Ha;
An' turned into a cracker,
Wid a sheriff's star.

Slim ran fo' his wings,
Lit out from de groun'
Hauled it back to St. Peter,
Safety boun'.

III

St. Peter said, "Well,
You got back quick.
How's de devil? An' what's
His latest trick?"

An' Slim say, "Peter,
I really cain't tell,
De place was Dixie
Dat I took for Hell."

Then Peter say, "You must
Be crazy, I vow,
Where'n hell dja think Hell *was,*
Anyhow?

"Git on back to de yearth,
Cause I got de fear,
You'se a leetle too dumb,
Fo' to stay up here . . ."

1932

Remembering Nat Turner[1]

(For R.C.L.)

We saw a bloody sunset over Courtland, once Jerusalem,
As we followed the trail that old Nat took
When he came out of Cross Keys down upon Jerusalem,[2]
In his angry stab for freedom a hundred years ago.
The land was quiet, and the mist was rising,
Out of the woods and the Nottaway swamp,
Over Southampton the still night fell,
As we rode down to Cross Keys where the march began.

When we got to Cross Keys, they could tell us little of him,
The Negroes had only the faintest recollections:

[1]Nat Turner (1800–1831) led one of the few black slave uprisings in which white people were killed. According to various accounts, seventy-five slaves slew fifty-five whites on this August 21, 1831, revolt. After eluding capture for several weeks, Turner was caught, convicted, and eventually hanged on November 11, 1831.

[2]Then county seat of Southampton County, Virginia.

"I ain't been here so long, I come from up roun' Newsome;
Yassah, a town a few miles up de road,
The old folks who coulda told you is all dead an' gone.
I heard something, sometime; I doan jis remember what.
'Pears lak I heard that name somewheres or other.
So he fought to be free. Well, you doan say."

An old white woman recalled exactly
How Nat crept down the steps, axe in his hand,
After murdering a woman and child in bed,
"Right in this here house at the head of these stairs"
(In a house built long after Nat was dead).
She pointed to a brick store where Nat was captured,
(Nat was taken in the swamp, three miles away)
With his men around him, shooting from the windows
(She was thinking of Harpers Ferry and old John Brown).[3]
She cackled as she told how they riddled Nat with bullets
(Nat was tried and hanged at Courtland, ten miles away).
She wanted to know why folks would come miles
Just to ask about an old nigger fool.
"Ain't no slavery no more, things is going all right,
Pervided thar's a good goober market this year.
We had a sign post here with printing on it,
But it rotted in the hole, and thar it lays,
And the nigger tenants split the marker for kindling.
Things is all right, now, ain't no trouble with the niggers
Why they make this big to-do over Nat?"

As we drove from Cross Keys back to Courtland,
Along the way that Nat came down upon Jerusalem,
A watery moon was high in the cloud-filled heavens,
The same moon he dreaded a hundred years ago.
The tree they hanged Nat on is long gone to ashes,
The trees he dodged behind have rotted in the swamps.

The bus for Miami and the trucks boomed by,
And touring cars, their heavy tires snarling on the pavement.
Frogs piped in the marshes, and a hound bayed long,
And yellow lights glowed from the cabin windows.

As we came back the way that Nat led his army,
Down from Cross Keys, down to Jerusalem,

[3]A white abolitionist leader (1800–1859) who attacked Harpers Ferry, VA, October 16, 1859, site of a federal armory; his militance earned for him the status of martyr from Union soldiers, who took up the song "John Brown's Body" as a battle hymn.

We wondered if his troubled spirit still roamed the Nottaway,
Or if it fled with the cock-crow at daylight,
Or lay at peace with the bones in Jerusalem,
Its restlessness stifled by Southampton clay.

We remembered the poster rotted through and falling,
The marker split for kindling a kitchen fire.

1939

Song of Triumph

Let the band play Dixie.
And let the Rebel Yell resound.
Let daughters of the Confederacy
Be proud that once more virginal loveliness
Even in dingy courtrooms
Receives the homage of the poets.

Let us rush to Stone Mountain[1]
Uncover our heads, stand speechless before
Granite embodiments of our knighthood
Unfinished but everlasting,
"And truth and honor established here, forever."
Lo! Stonewall, preux chevalier,[2]
And Lee, majestic Arthur,[3] facing East.

Behind them, to the West
Scottsboro, Decatur.
Eight cowering Negroes in a jail[4]
Waiting for the justice
Chivalry as ever extends to them,
Still receiving the benefactions
Of *Noblesse Oblige.*[5]

[1]Site near Atlanta infamous for the Ku Klux Klan rallies in the 1920s.
[2]Confederate general Thomas "Stonewall" Jackson (1824–1863) is described literally as "pure knight," or gallant and valiant warrior.
[3]The metaphor of knighthood is continued in this reference to Robert E. Lee, another general fighting for the Confederacy, with this comparison to King Arthur, whose medieval knights of the Round Table became synonymous with chivalry.
[4]The infamous Scottsboro Boys case, in which nine black youths were accused of raping two white prostitutes hoboing on a train near this small Alabama town, was a *cause célèbre* beginning in 1931.
[5]French for "nobility obligates." Persons of high rank or nobility are expected to adopt a benevolent and honorable air toward those less fortunate than they are.

Oh, let us be proud.
Oh, let us, undefeated, raise again
The Rebel Yell.

1980

Zora Neale Hurston 1891–1960

An author who died in poverty in 1960, Zora Neale Hurston now holds a posthumous reputation which she herself might not have imagined. Her best-known novel, *Their Eyes Were Watching God* (1937), has sold over 50,000 copies in the past decade, and more of her work is in print now than at any period during her lifetime. A writer who never earned appreciable royalties on any of her books, Hurston understood the vagaries of literary fortune: "I have been in sorrow's kitchen and licked out all the pots. Then I have stood on the peaky mountain wrapped in rainbows, with a harp and a sword in my hands."

Why should this particular woman have such an impact? For two reasons. Her life illustrates the folk wisdom of Hurston's mother, who told her daughter to "jump at de sun. You might not land on the sun, but at least you'll get off the ground." At the same time, her work celebrates black culture, and leads us to an appreciation of the courage and humor, art and intellect, life and society, of black people living in the rural South in the early decades of the twentieth century—men and women who didn't jump at the sun so much as labor under its rays from "can" in the morning till "can't" at night.

Born in the all-black town of Eatonville, Florida, Zora Neale Hurston attended Howard University, and in 1928 graduated from Barnard College, where she studied with anthropologists Franz Boas and Gladys Reichard. While living in New York in the twenties, an exuberant participant with Langston Hughes, Countee Cullen, and others in the artist's uprising they labeled "The Harlem Renaissance," she grew fascinated with the scholarly study of her home town's natural ways, which the anthropologists on Morningside Heights called "folklore."

Hurston spent the late 1920s and early 1930s collecting the folklore she knew best, the stories, songs, tales, proverbs, and crafts of black southern people. With a pistol in her pocketbook and a cheap dress in her suitcase, she roamed the backroads of Florida, Mississippi, and Louisiana, swapping tales at turpentine camps, holding "lying sessions" at jook joints, and learning hoodoo rituals from conjure doctors. If questioned too closely about being a single woman in the sole possession of a Chevrolet coupe, she usually explained that she was a bootlegger's woman on the lam.

In the mid-1930s she began publishing folklore collections (*Mules and Men,* 1935), novels (*Jonah's Gourd Vine,* 1934; *Moses: Man of the Mountain,* 1939), and Caribbean travel books (*Tell My Horse,* 1938). Well received by reviewers and critics, these books earned her a modest reputation, which reached its peak in 1942, when her autobiography, *Dust Tracks on a Road,* won a national race relations award and *The Saturday Review* featured her portrait on its cover.

The last twenty years of her life saw this reputation steadily decline for a variety of reasons, including her own withdrawal following a false morals charge in 1948 and increasing financial difficulties. In 1952 she was discovered working as a maid the same week that the *Saturday Evening Post* published one of her stories.

At Hurston's death in Fort Pierce, Florida, friends collected small change from school children to help pay for her burial. Until Alice Walker, the Pulitzer Prize–winning author of *The Color Purple,* made a pilgrimage to Fort Pierce to erect a memorial, however, she lay buried in an unmarked grave in a segregated cemetery.

As fascinating as her life is, however, Hurston's influence arises from her art. As Walker says, "We love Zora Neale Hurston for her work, first." At a time when the Ku Klux Klan was still a major force in national politics, in an era when "negro coeds" were expected to limit their horizons to school teaching, Hurston single-handedly, against great odds, became the best black woman writer in America.

"Sweat" and "The Gilded Six-Bits" are early short stories, written before Hurston reached her peak in the mid-thirties, but they illustrate the strengths of her writing. Focusing on the lives of common folks—black people usually represented as only sociological statistics—she demonstrates both the complexity of their lives and the richness of their folk culture. In these stories, particularly, she also explores the tangle of sexual power and personal oppression which can characterize relationships between men and women.

Robert E. Hemenway
University of Kansas

PRIMARY WORKS

Jonah's Gourd Vine, 1934; *Mules and Men,* 1935; *Their Eyes Were Watching God,* 1937; *Tell My Horse,* 1938; *Moses: Man of the Mountain,* 1939; *Dust Tracks on a Road,* 1942; *Seraph on the Swanee,* 1948.

Sweat

It was eleven o'clock of a Spring night in Florida. It was Sunday. Any other night, Delia Jones would have been in bed for two hours by this time. But she was a washwoman, and Monday morning meant a great deal to her. So she collected the soiled clothes on Saturday when she returned the clean things. Sunday night after church, she sorted them and put the white things to soak. It saved her almost a half day's start. A great hamper in the bedroom held the clothes that she brought home. It was so much neater than a number of bundles lying around.

She squatted in the kitchen floor beside the great pile of clothes, sorting them into small heaps according to color, and humming a song in a mournful key, but wondering through it all where Sykes, her husband, had gone with her horse and buckboard.

Just then something long, round, limp and black fell upon her shoulders and slithered to the floor beside her. A great terror took hold of her. It softened her knees and dried her mouth so that it was a full minute before she could cry out or move. Then she saw that it was the big bull whip her husband liked to carry when he drove.

She lifted her eyes to the door and saw him standing there bent over with laughter at her fright. She screamed at him.

"Sykes, what you throw dat whip on me like dat? You know it would skeer me—looks just like a snake, an' you knows how skeered Ah is of snakes."

"Course Ah knowed it! That's how come Ah done it." He slapped his leg with his hand and almost rolled on the ground in his mirth. "If you such a big fool dat you got to have a fit over a earth worm or a string, Ah don't keer how bad Ah skeer you."

"You aint got no business doing it. Gawd knows it's a sin. Some day Ah'm gointuh drop dead from some of yo' foolishness. 'Nother thing, where you been wid mah rig? Ah feeds dat pony. He aint fuh you to be drivin' wid no bull whip."

"You sho is one aggravatin' nigger woman!" he declared and stepped into the room. She resumed her work and did not answer him at once. "Ah done tole you time and again to keep them white folks' clothes outa dis house."

He picked up the whip and glared down at her. Delia went on with her work. She went out into the yard and returned with a galvanized tub and set it on the washbench. She saw that Sykes had kicked all of the clothes together again, and now stood in her way truculently, his whole manner hoping, *praying,* for an argument. But she walked calmly around him and commenced to re-sort the things.

"Next time, Ah'm gointer kick 'em outdoors," he threatened as he struck a match along the leg of his corduroy breeches.

Delia never looked up from her work, and her thin, stooped shoulders sagged further.

"Ah aint for no fuss t'night Sykes. Ah just come from taking sacrament at the church house."

He snorted scornfully. "Yeah, you just come from de church house on a Sunday night, but heah you is gone to work on them clothes. You ain't nothing but a hypocrite. One of them amen-corner Christians—sing, whoop, and shout, then come home and wash white folks clothes on the Sabbath."

He stepped roughly upon the whitest pile of things, kicking them helter-skelter as he crossed the room. His wife gave a little scream of dismay, and quickly gathered them together again.

"Sykes, you quit grindin' dirt into these clothes! How can Ah git through by Sat'day if Ah don't start on Sunday?"

"Ah don't keer if you never git through. Anyhow, Ah done promised Gawd and a couple of other men, Ah aint gointer have it in mah house. Don't gimme no lip neither, else Ah'll throw 'em out and put mah fist up side yo' head to boot."

Delia's habitual meekness seemed to slip from her shoulders like a blown scarf. She was on her feet; her poor little body, her bare knuckly hands bravely defying the strapping hulk before her.

"Looka heah, Sykes, you done gone too fur. Ah been married to you fur fifteen years, and Ah been takin' in washin' for fifteen years. Sweat, sweat, sweat! Work and sweat, cry and sweat, pray and sweat!"

"What's that got to do with me?" he asked brutally.

"What's it got to do with you, Sykes? Mah tub of suds is filled yo' belly with vittles more times than yo' hands is filled it. Mah sweat is done paid for this house and Ah reckon Ah kin keep on sweatin' in it."

She seized the iron skillet from the stove and struck a defensive pose, which act surprised him greatly, coming from her. It cowed him and he did not strike her as he usually did.

"Naw you won't," she panted, "that ole snaggle-toothed black woman you runnin' with aint comin' heah to pile up on *mah* sweat and blood. You aint paid for nothin' on this place, and Ah'm gointer stay right heah till Ah'm toted out foot foremost."

"Well, you better quit gittin' me riled up, else they'll be totin' you out sooner than you expect. Ah'm so tired of you Ah don't know whut to do. Gawd! how Ah hates skinny wimmen!"

A little awed by this new Delia, he sidled out of the door and slammed the back gate after him. He did not say where he had gone, but she knew too well. She knew very well that he would not return until nearly daybreak also. Her work over, she went on to bed but not to sleep at once. Things had come to a pretty pass!

She lay awake, gazing upon the debris that cluttered their matrimonial trail. Not an image left standing along the way. Anything like flowers had long ago been drowned in the salty stream that had been pressed from her heart. Her tears, her sweat, her blood. She had brought love to the union and he had brought a longing after the flesh. Two months after the wedding, he had given her the first brutal beating. She had the memory of his numerous trips to Orlando with all of his wages when he had returned to her penniless, even before the first year had passed. She was young and soft then, but now she thought of her knotty, muscled limbs, her harsh knuckly hands, and drew herself up into an unhappy little ball in the middle of the big feather bed. Too late now to hope for love, even if it were not Bertha it would be someone else. This case differed from the others only in that she was bolder than the others. Too late for everything except her little home. She had built it for her old days, and planted one by one the trees and flowers there. It was lovely to her, lovely.

Somehow, before sleep came, she found herself saying aloud: "Oh well, whatever goes over the Devil's back, is got to come under his belly. Sometime or ruther, Sykes, like everybody else, is gointer reap his sowing." After that she was able to build a spiritual earthworks against her husband. His shells could no longer reach her. *Amen.* She went to sleep and slept until he announced his presence in bed by kicking her feet and rudely snatching the covers away.

"Gimme some kivah heah, an' git yo' damn foots over on yo' own side! Ah oughter mash you in yo' mouf fuh drawing dat skillet on me."

Delia went clear to the rail without answering him. A triumphant indifference to all that he was or did.

The week was as full of work for Delia as all other weeks, and Saturday found her behind her little pony, collecting and delivering clothes.

It was a hot, hot day near the end of July. The village men on Joe Clarke's porch even chewed cane listlessly. They did not hurl the cane-knots as usual. They let them dribble over the edge of the porch. Even conversation had collapsed under the heat.

"Heah come Delia Jones," Jim Merchant said, as the shaggy pony came 'round the bend of the road toward them. The rusty buckboard was heaped with baskets of crisp, clean laundry.

"Yep," Joe Lindsay agreed. "Hot or col', rain or shine, jes ez reg'lar ez de weeks roll roun' Delia carries 'em an' fetches 'em on Sat'day."

"She better if she wanter eat," said Moss. "Syke Jones aint wuth de shot an' powder hit would tek tuh kill 'em. Not to *huh* he aint."

"He sho' aint," Walter Thomas chimed in. "It's too bad, too, cause she wuz a right pritty lil trick when he got huh. Ah'd uh mah'ied huh mahseff if he hadnter beat me to it."

Delia nodded briefly at the men as she drove past.

"Too much knockin' will ruin *any* 'oman. He done beat huh 'nough tuh kill three women, let 'lone change they looks," said Elijah Moseley. "How Syke kin stommuck dat big black greasy Mogul he's layin' roun wid, gits me. Ah swear dat eight-rock couldn't kiss a sardine can Ah done throwed out de back do' 'way las' yeah."

"Aw, she's fat, thass how come. He's allus been crazy 'bout fat women," put in Merchant. "He'd a' been tied up wid one long time ago if he could a' found one tuh have him. Did Ah tell yuh 'bout him come sidlin' roun' *mah* wife—bringin' her a basket uh pecans outa his yard fuh a present? Yessir, mah wife! She tol' him tuh take 'em right straight back home, cause Delia works so hard ovah dat washtub she reckon everything on de place taste lak sweat an' soapsuds. Ah jus' wisht Ah'd a' caught 'im 'roun' dere! Ah'd a' made his hips ketch on fiah down dat shell road."

"Ah know he done it, too. Ah sees 'im grinnin' at every 'oman dat passes," Walter Thomas said. "But even so, he useter eat some mighty big hunks uh humble pie tuh git dat lil' 'oman he got. She wuz ez pritty ez a speckled pup! Dat wuz fifteen yeahs ago. He useter be so skeered uh losin' huh, she could make him do some parts of a husband's duty. Dey never wuz de same in de mind."

"There oughter be a law about him," said Lindsay. "He aint fit tuh carry guts tuh a bear."

Clarke spoke for the first time. "Taint no law on earth dat kin make a man be decent if it aint in 'im. There's plenty men dat takes a wife lak dey do a joint uh sugar-cane. It's round, juicy an' sweet when dey gits it. But dey squeeze an' grind, squeeze an' grind an' wring tell dey wring every drop uh pleasure dat's in 'em out. When dey's satisfied dat dey is wrung dry, dey treats 'em jes lak dey do a cane-chew. Dey throws 'em away. Dey knows whut dey is doin' while dey is at it, an' hates theirselves fuh it but they keeps on hangin' after huh tell she's empty. Den dey hates huh fuh bein' a cane-chew an' in de way."

"We oughter take Syke an' dat stray 'oman uh his'n down in Lake Howell swamp an' lay on de rawhide till they cain't say Lawd a' mussy. He allus wuz uh ovahbearin' niggah, but since dat white 'oman from up north done teached 'im how to run a automobile, he done got too biggety to live—an' we oughter kill 'im," Old Man Anderson advised.

A grunt of approval went around the porch. But the heat was melting their civic virtue, and Elijah Moseley began to bait Joe Clarke.

"Come on, Joe, git a melon outa dere an' slice it up for yo' customers. We'se all sufferin' wid de heat. De bear's done got *me!*"

"Thass right, Joe, a watermelon is jes' whut Ah needs tuh cure de eppizudicks," Walter Thomas joined forces with Moseley. "Come on dere, Joe. We all is steady customers an' you aint set us up in a long time. Ah chooses dat long, bowlegged Floridy favorite."

"A god, an' be dough. You all gimme twenty cents and slice way," Clarke retorted. "Ah needs a col' slice m'self. Heah, everybody chip in. Ah'll lend y'll mah meat knife."

The money was quickly subscribed and the huge melon brought forth. At that moment, Sykes and Bertha arrived. A determined silence fell on the porch and the melon was put away again.

Merchant snapped down the blade of his jackknife and moved toward the store door.

"Come on in, Joe, an' gimme a slab uh sow belly an' uh pound uh coffee—almost fuhgot 'twas Sat'day. Got to git on home." Most of the men left also.

Just then Delia drove past on her way home, as Sykes was ordering magnificently for Bertha. It pleased him for Delia to see.

"Git whutsoever yo' heart desires, Honey. Wait a minute, Joe. Give huh two botles uh strawberry soda-water, uh quart uh parched ground-peas, an' a block uh chewin' gum."

With all this they left the store, with Sykes reminding Bertha that this was his town and she could have it if she wanted it.

The men returned soon after they left, and held their watermelon feast.

"Where did Syke Jones git da 'oman from nohow?" Lindsay asked.

"Ovah Apopka. Guess dey musta been cleanin' out de town when she lef'. She don't look lak a thing but a hunk uh liver wid hair on it."

"Well, she sho' kin squall," Dave Carter contributed. "When she gits ready tuh laff, she jes' opens huh mouf an' latches it back tuh de las' notch. No ole grandpa alligator down in Lake Bell ain't got nothin' on huh."

Bertha had been in town three months now. Sykes was still paying her room rent at Della Lewis'—the only house in town that would have taken her in. Sykes took her frequently to Winter Park to "stomps." He still assured her that he was the swellest man in the state.

"Sho' you kin have dat lil' ole house soon's Ah kin git dat 'oman outa dere. Everything b'longs tuh me an' you sho' kin have it. Ah sho' 'bominates uh skinny 'oman. Lawdy, you sho' is got one portly shape on you! You kin git *anything* you wants. Dis is *mah* town an' you sho' kin have it."

Delia's work-worn knees crawled over the earth in Gethsemane and up the rocks of Calvary many, many times during these months. She avoided the villagers and meeting places in her efforts to be blind and deaf. But Bertha nullified this to a degree, by coming to Delia's house to call Sykes out to her at the gate.

Delia and Sykes fought all the time now with no peaceful interludes. They slept and ate in silence. Two or three times Delia had attempted a timid friendliness, but she was repulsed each time. It was plain that the breaches must remain agape.

The sun had burned July to August. The heat streamed down like a million hot arrows, smiting all things living upon the earth. Grass withered, leaves browned, snakes went blind in shedding and men and dogs went mad. Dog days!

Delia came home one day and found Sykes there before her. She wondered, but started to go on into the house without speaking, even though he was standing in the kitchen door and she must either stoop under his arm or ask him to move. He made no room for her. She noticed a soap box beside the steps, but paid no particular attention to it, knowing that he must have brought it there. As she was stooping to pass under his outstretched arm, he suddenly pushed her backward, laughingly.

"Look in de box dere Delia, Ah done brung yuh somethin'!"

She nearly fell upon the box in her stumbling, and when she saw what it held, she all but fainted outright.

"Syke! Syke, mah Gawd! You take dat rattlesnake 'way from heah! You *gottuh*. Oh, Jesus, have mussy!"

"Ah aint gut tuh do nuthin' uh de kin'—fact is Ah aint got tuh do nothin' but die. Taint no use uh you puttin' on airs makin' out lak you skeered uh dat snake—he's gointer stay right heah tell he die. He wouldn't bite me cause Ah knows how tuh handle 'im. Nohow he wouldn't risk breakin' out his fangs 'gin *yo'* skinny laigs."

"Naw, now Syke, don't keep dat thing 'roun' heah tuh skeer me tuh death. You knows Ah'm even feared uh earth worms. Thass de biggest snake Ah evah did see. Kill 'im Syke, please."

"Doan ast me tuh do nothin' fuh yuh. Goin' roun' trying' tuh be so damn asterperious. Naw, Ah aint gonna kill it. Ah think uh damn sight mo' uh him dan you! Dat's a nice snake an' anybody doan lak 'im kin jes' hit de grit."

The village soon heard that Sykes had the snake, and came to see and ask questions.

"How de hen-fire did you ketch dat six-foot rattler, Syke?" Thomas asked.

"He's full uh frogs so he caint hardly move, thass how. Ah eased up on 'm. But Ah'm a snake charmer an' knows how tuh handle 'em. Shux, dat aint nothin'. Ah could ketch one eve'y day if Ah so wanted tuh."

"Whut he needs is a heavy hick'ry club leaned real heavy on his head. Dat's de bes 'way tuh charm a rattlesnake."

"Naw, Walt, y'll jes' don't understand dese diamon' backs lak Ah do," said Sykes in a superior tone of voice.

The village agreed with Walter, but the snake stayed on. His box remained by the kitchen door with its screen wire covering. Two or three days later it had digested its meal of frogs and literally came to life. It rattled at every movement in the kitchen or the yard. One day as Delia came down the kitchen steps she saw his chalky-white fangs curved like scimitars hung in the wire meshes. This time she did not run away with averted eyes as usual. She stood for a long time in the doorway in a red fury that grew bloodier for every second that she regarded the creature that was her torment.

That night she broached the subject as soon as Sykes sat down to the table.

"Syke, Ah wants you tuh take dat snake 'way fum heah. You done starved me an' Ah put up widcher, you done beat me an Ah took dat, but you done kilt all mah insides bringin' dat varmint heah."

Sykes poured out a saucer full of coffee and drank it deliberately before he answered her.

"A whole lot Ah keer 'bout how you feels inside uh out. Dat snake aint goin' no damn wheah till Ah gits ready fuh 'im tuh go. So fur as beatin' is concerned, yuh aint took near all dat you gointer take ef yuh stay 'roun' *me*."

Delia pushed back her plate and got up from the table. "Ah hates you, Sykes," she said calmly. "Ah hates you tuh de same degree dat Ah useter love yuh. Ah done took an' took till mah belly is full up tuh mah neck. Dat's de reason Ah got mah letter fum de church an' moved mah membership tuh Woodbridge—so Ah don't haftuh take no sacrament wid yuh. Ah don't wantuh see yuh 'roun' me atall. Lay 'roun' wid dat 'oman all yuh wants tuh, but gwan 'way fum me an' mah house. Ah hates yuh lak uh suck-egg dog."

Sykes almost let the huge wad of corn bread and collard greens he was chewing fall out of his mouth in amazement. He had a hard time whipping himself up to the proper fury to try to answer Delia.

"Well, Ah'm glad you does hate me. Ah'm sho' tiahed uh you hangin' ontuh me. Ah don't want yuh. Look at yuh stringey ole neck! Yo' rawbony laigs an' arms is enough tuh cut uh man tuh death. You looks jes' lak de devvul's doll-baby tuh *me*. You cain't hate me no worse dan Ah hates you. Ah been hatin' *you* fuh years."

"Yo' ole black hide don't look lak nothin' tuh me, but uh passle uh wrinkled up rubber, wid yo' big ole yeahs flappin' on each side lak uh paih uh buzzard wings. Don't think Ah'm gointuh be run 'way fum mah house neither. Ah'm goin' tuh de white folks bout *you,* mah young man, de very nex' time you lay yo' han's on me. Mah cup is done run ovah." Delia said this with no signs of fear and Sykes departed from the house, threatening her, but made not the slightest move to carry out any of them.

That night he did not return at all, and the next day being Sunday, Delia was glad she did not have to quarrel before she hitched up her pony and drove the four miles to Woodbridge.

She stayed to the night service—"love feast"—which was very warm and full of spirit. In the emotional winds her domestic trials were borne far and wide so that she sang as she drove homeward.

"Jurden water, black an' col'
Chills de body, not de soul
An' Ah wantah cross Jurden in uh calm time."

She came from the barn to the kitchen door and stopped.

"Whut's de mattah, ol' satan, you aint kickin' up yo' racket?" She addressed the snake's box. Complete silence. She went on into the house with a new hope in its birth struggles. Perhaps her threat to go to the white folks had frightened Sykes! Perhaps he was sorry! Fifteen years of misery and suppression had brought Delia to the place where she would hope *anything* that looked towards a way over or through her wall of inhibitions.

She felt in the march safe behind the stove at once for a match. There was only one there.

"Dat niggah wouldn't fetch nothin' heah tuh save his rotten neck, but he kin run thew whut Ah brings quick enough. Now he done toted off nigh on tuh haff uh box uh matches. He done had dat 'oman heah in mah house, too."

Nobody but a woman could tell how she knew this even before she struck the match. But she did and it put her into a new fury.

Presently she brought in the tubs to put the white things to soak. This time she decided she need not bring the hamper out of the bedroom; she would go in there and do the sorting. She picked up the pot-bellied lamp and went in. The room was small and the hamper stood hard by the foot of the white iron bed. She could sit and reach through the bedposts—resting as she worked.

"Ah wantah cross Jurden in uh calm time," She was singing again. The mood of the "love feast" had returned. She threw back the lid of the basket almost gaily. Then, moved by both horror and terror, she sprang back toward the door. *There lay the snake in the basket!* He moved sluggishly at first, but even as she turned round and round, jumped up and down in an insanity of fear, he began to stir vigorously. She saw him pouring his awful beauty from the basket upon the bed, then she seized the lamp and ran as fast as she could to the kitchen. The wind from the open door blew out the light and the darkness added to her terror. She sped to the darkness of the yard, slamming the door after her before she thought to set down the lamp. She did not feel safe even on the ground, so she climbed up in the hay barn.

There for an hour or more she lay sprawled upon the hay a gibbering wreck.

Finally, she grew quiet, and after that, coherent thought. With this, stalked through her a cold, bloody rage. Hours of this. A period of introspection, a space of retrospection, then a mixture of both. Out of this an awful calm.

"Well, Ah done de bes' Ah could. If things aint right, Gawd knows taint mah fault."

She went to sleep—a twitch sleep—and woke up to a faint gray sky. There was a loud hollow sound below. She peered out. Sykes was at the wood-pile, demolishing a wire-covered box.

He hurried to the kitchen door, but hung outside there some minutes before he entered, and stood some minutes more inside before he closed it after him.

The gray in the sky was spreading. Delia descended without fear now, and crouched beneath the low bedroom window. The drawn shade shut out the dawn, shut in the night. But the thin walls held back no sound.

"Dat ol' scratch is woke up now!" She mused at the tremendous whirr inside, which every woodsman knows, is one of the sound illusions. The rattler is a ventriloquist. His whirr sounds to the right, to the left, straight ahead, behind, close under foot—everywhere but where it is. Woe to him who guesses wrong unless he is prepared to hold up his end of the argument! Sometimes he strikes without rattling at all.

Inside, Sykes heard nothing until he knocked a pot lid off the stove while trying to reach the match safe in the dark. He had emptied his pockets at Bertha's.

The snake seemed to wake up under the stove and Sykes made a quick leap into the bedroom. In spite of the gin he had had, his head was clearing now.

"Mah Gawd!" he chattered, "ef Ah could on'y strack uh light!"

The rattling ceased for a moment as he stood paralyzed. He waited. It seemed that the snake waited also.

"Oh, fuh de light! Ah thought he'd be too sick"—Sykes was muttering to himself when the whirr began again, closer, right underfoot this time. Long before this, Sykes' ability to think had been flattened down to primitive instinct and he leaped—onto the bed.

Outside Delia heard a cry that might have come from a maddened chimpanzee, a stricken gorilla. All the terror, all the horror, all the rage that man possibly could express, without a recognizable human sound.

A tremendous stir inside there, another series of animal screams, the intermittent whirr of the reptile. The shade torn violently down from the window, letting in the red dawn, a huge brown hand seizing the window stick, great dull blows upon the wooden floor punctuating the gibberish of sound long after the rattle of the snake had abruptly subsided. All this Delia could see and hear from her place beneath the window, and it made her ill. She crept over to the four-o'clocks and stretched herself on the cool earth to recover.

She lay there. "Delia. Delia!" She could hear Sykes calling in a most despairing tone as one who expected no answer. The sun crept on up, and he called. Delia could not move—her legs were gone flabby. She never moved, he called, and the sun kept rising.

"Mah Gawd!" She heard him moan, "Mah Gawd fum Heben!" She heard him stumbling about and got up from her flower-bed. The sun was growing warm. As she approached the door she heard him call out hopefully, "Delia, is dat you Ah heah?"

She saw him on his hands and knees as soon as she reached the door. He crept an inch or two toward her—all that he was able, and she saw his horribly swollen neck and his one open eye shining with hope. A surge of pity too strong to support bore her away from that eye that must, could not, fail to see the tubs. He would see the lamp. Orlando with its doctors was too far. She could scarcely reach the Chinaberry tree, where she waited in the growing heat while inside she knew the cold river was creeping up and up to extinguish that eye which must know by now that she knew.

1926

The Gilded Six-Bits

It was a Negro yard around a Negro house in a Negro settlement that looked to the payroll of the G. and G. Fertilizer works for its support.

But there was something happy about the place. The front yard was parted in the middle by a sidewalk from gate to doorstep, a sidewalk edged on either side by quart bottles driven neck down into the ground on a slant. A mess of homey flowers planted without a plan but blooming cheerily from their helter-skelter places. The fence and house were whitewashed. The porch and steps scrubbed white.

The front door stood open to the sunshine so that the floor of the front room could finish drying after its weekly scouring. It was Saturday. Everything clean from the front gate to the privy house. Yard raked so that the strokes of the rake would make a pattern. Fresh newspaper cut in fancy edge on the kitchen shelves.

Missie May was bathing herself in the galvanized washtub in the bedroom. Her dark-brown skin glistened under the soapsuds that skittered down from her washrag. Her stiff young breasts thrust forward aggressively, like broad-based cones with the tips lacquered in black.

She heard men's voices in the distance and glanced at the dollar clock on the dresser.

"Humph! Ah'm way behind time t'day! Joe gointer be heah 'fore Ah git mah clothes on if Ah don't make haste."

She grabbed the clean mealsack at hand and dried herself hurriedly and began to dress. But before she could tie her slippers, there came the ring of singing metal on wood. Nine times.

Missie May grinned with delight. She had not seen the big tall man come stealing in the gate and creep up the walk grinning happily at the joyful mischief he was about to commit. But she knew that it was her husband throwing silver dollars in the door for her to pick up and pile beside her plate at dinner. It was this way every Saturday afternoon. The nine dollars hurled into the open door, he scurried to a hiding place behind the Cape jasmine bush and waited.

Missie May promptly appeared at the door in mock alarm.

"Who dat chunkin' money in mah do'way?" she demanded. No answer from the yard. She leaped off the porch and began to search the shrubbery. She peeped under the porch and hung over the gate to look up and down the road. While she did this, the man behind the jasmine darted to the chinaberry tree. She spied him and gave chase.

"Nobody ain't gointer be chunkin' money at me and Ah not do 'em nothin'," she shouted in mock anger. He ran around the house with Missie May at his heels. She overtook him at the kitchen door. He ran inside but could not close it after him before she crowded in and locked with him in a rough-and-tumble. For several minutes the two were a furious mass of male and female energy. Shouting, laughing, twisting, turning, tussling, tickling each other in the ribs; Missie May clutching onto Joe and Joe trying, but not too hard, to get away.

"Missie May, take yo' hand out mah pocket!" Joe shouted out between laughs.

"Ah ain't, Joe, not lessen you gwine gimme whateve' it is good you got in yo' pocket. Turn it go, Joe, do Ah'll tear yo' clothes."

"Go on tear 'em. You de one dat pushes de needles round heah. Move yo' hand, Missie May."

"Lemme git dat paper sak out yo' pocket. Ah bet it's candy kisses."

"Tain't. Move yo' hand. Woman ain't got no business in a man's clothes nohow. Go way."

Missie May gouged way down and gave an upward jerk and triumphed.

"Unhhunh! Ah got it! It 'tis so candy kisses. Ah knowed you had somethin' for me in yo' clothes. Now Ah got to see whut's in every pocket you got."

Joe smiled indulgently and let his wife go through all of his pockets and take out the things that he had hidden for her to find. She bore off the chewing gum, the cake of sweet soap, the pocket handkerchief as if she had wrested them from him, as if they had not been bought for the sake of this friendly battle.

"Whew! dat play-fight done got me all warmed up!" Joe exclaimed. "Got me some water in de kittle?"

"Yo' water is on de fire and yo' clean things is cross de bed. Hurry up and wash yo'self and git changed so we kin eat. Ah'm hongry." As Missie said this, she bore the steaming kettle into the bedroom.

"You ain't hongry, sugar," Joe contradicted her. "Youse jes' a little empty. Ah'm de one whut's hongry. Ah could eat up camp meetin', back off 'ssociation, and drink Jurdan dry. Have it on de table when Ah git out de tub."

"Don't you mess wid mah business, man. You git in yo' clothes. Ah'm a real wife, not no dress and breath. Ah might not look lak one, but if you burn me, you won't git a thing but wife ashes."

Joe splashed in the bedroom and Missie May fanned around in the kitchen. A fresh red-and-white checked cloth on the table. Big pitcher of buttermilk beaded with pale drops of butter from the churn. Hot fried mullet, crackling bread, ham hock atop a mound of string beans and new potatoes, and perched on the windowsill a pone of spicy potato pudding.

Very little talk during the meal but that little consisted of banter that pretended to deny affection but in reality flaunted it. Like when Missie May reached for a second helping of the tater pone. Joe snatched it out of her reach.

After Missie May had made two or three unsuccessful grabs at the pan, she begged, "Aw, Joe, gimme some mo' dat tater pone."

"Nope, sweetenin' is for us menfolks. Y'all pritty lil frail eels don't need nothin' lak dis. You too sweet already."

"Please, Joe."

"Naw, naw. Ah don't want you to git no sweeter than whut you is already. We goin' down de road a lil piece t'night so you go put on yo' Sunday-go-to-meetin' things."

Missie May looked at her husband to see if he was playing some prank. "Sho nuff, Joe?"

"Yeah. We goin' to de ice cream parlor."

"Where de ice cream parlor at, Joe?"

"A new man done come heah from Chicago and he done got a place and took and opened it up for a ice cream parlor, and bein' as it's real swell, Ah wants you to be one de first ladies to walk in dere and have some set down."

"Do Jesus, Ah ain't knowed nothin' bout it. Who de man done it?"

"Mister Otis D. Slemmons, of spots and places—Memphis, Chicago, Jacksonville, Philadelphia and so on."

"Dat heavyset man wid his mouth full of gold teeths?"

"Yeah. Where did you see 'im at?"

"Ah went down to de sto' tuh git a box of lye and Ah seen 'im standin' on de corner talkin' to some of de mens, and Ah come on back and went to scrubbin' de floor, and he passed and tipped his hat whilst Ah was scourin' de steps. Ah thought Ah never seen *him* befo'."

Joe smiled pleasantly. "Yeah, he's up-to-date. He got de finest clothes Ah ever seen on a colored man's back."

"Aw, he don't look no better in his clothes than you do in yourn. He got a puzzlegut on 'im and he so chuckleheaded he got a pone behind his neck."

Joe looked down at his own abdomen and said wistfully: "Wisht Ah had a build on me lak he got. He ain't puzzlegutted, honey. He jes' got a corperation. Dat make 'm look lak a rich white man. All rich mens is got some belly on 'em."

"Ah seen de pitchers of Henry Ford and he's a spare-built man and Rockefeller look lak he ain't got but one gut. But Ford and Rockefeller and dis Slemmons and all de rest kin be as many-gutted as dey please, Ah's satisfied wid you jes' lak you is, baby. God took pattern after a pine tree and built you noble. Youse a pritty man, and if Ah knowed any way to make you mo' pritty still Ah'd take and do it."

Joe reached over gently and toyed with Missie May's ear. "You jes' say dat cause you love me, but Ah know Ah can't hold no light to Otis D. Slemmons. Ah ain't never been nowhere and Ah ain't got nothin' but you."

Missie May got on his lap and kissed him and he kissed back in kind. Then he went on. "All de womens is crazy 'bout 'im everywhere he go."

"How you know dat, Joe?"

"He tole us so hisself."

"Dat don't make it so. His mouf is cut crossways, ain't it? Well, he kin lie jes' lak anybody else."

"Good Lawd, Missie! You womens sho is hard to sense into things. He's got a five-dollar gold piece for a stickpin and he got a ten-dollar gold piece on his watch chain and his mouf is jes' crammed full of gold teeths. Sho wisht it wuz mine. And whut make it so cool, he got money 'cumulated. And womens give it all to 'im."

"Ah don't see whut de womens see on 'im. Ah wouldn't give 'im a wink if de sheriff wuz after 'im."

Well, he tole us how de white womens in Chicago give 'im all dat gold money. So he don't 'low nobody to touch it at all. Not even put day finger on it. Dey told 'im not to. You kin make 'miration at it, but don't tetch it."

"Whyn't he stay up dere where dey so crazy 'bout 'im?"

"Ah reckon dey done made 'im vast-rich and he wants to travel some. He says dey wouldn't leave 'im hit a lick of work. He got mo' lady people crazy 'bout him than he kin shake a stick at."

"Joe, Ah hates to see you so dumb. Dat stray nigger jes' tell y'all anything and y'all b'lieve it."

"Go 'head on now, honey, and put on yo' clothes. He talkin' 'bout his pritty womens—Ah want 'im to see *mine.*"

Missie May went off to dress and Joe spent the time trying to make his stomach punch out like Slemmons's middle. He tried the rolling swagger of the stranger, but found that his tall bone-and-muscle stride fitted ill with it. He just had time to drop back into his seat before Missie May came in dressed to go.

On the way home that night Joe was exultant. "Didn't Ah say ole Otis was swell? Can't he talk Chicago talk? Wuzn't dat funny whut he said when great big fat ole Ida Armstrong come in? He asted me, 'Who is dat broad wid de forte shake?' Dat's a new word. Us always thought forty was a set of figgers but he showed us where it means a whole heap of things. Sometimes he don't say forty, he jes' say thirty-eight and two and dat mean de same thing. Know whut he told me when Ah wuz payin' for our ice cream? He say, Ah have to hand it to you, Joe. Dat wife of yours is jes' thirty-eight and two. Yessuh, she's forte!' Ain't he killin'?"

"He'll do in case of a rush. But he sho is got uh heap uh gold on 'im. Dat's de first time Ah ever seed gold money. It lookted good on him sho nuff, but it'd look a whole heap better on you."

"Who, me? Missie May, youse crazy! Where would a po' man lak me git gold money from?"

Missie May was silent for a minute, then she said, "Us might find some goin' long de road some time. Us could."

"Who would be losin' gold money round heah? We ain't even seen none dese white folks wearin' no gold money on dey watch chain. You must be figgerin' Mister Packard or Mister Cadillac goin' pass through heah."

"You don't know whut been lost 'round heah. Maybe somebody way back in memorial times lost they gold money and went on off and it ain't never been found. And then if we wuz to find it, you could wear some 'thout havin' no gang of womens lak dat Slemmons say he got."

Joe laughed and hugged her. "Don't be so wishful 'bout me. Ah'm satisfied de way Ah is. So long as Ah be yo' husband. Ah don't keer 'bout nothin' else. Ah'd ruther all de other womens in de world to be dead than for you to have de toothache. Less we go to bed and git our night rest."

It was Saturday night once more before Joe could parade his wife in Slemmons's ice cream parlor again. He worked the night shift and Saturday was his only night off. Every other evening around six o'clock he left home, and dying dawn saw him hustling home around the lake, where the challenging sun flung a flaming sword from east to west across the trembling water.

That was the best part of life—going home to Missie May. Their whitewashed house, the mock battle on Saturday, the dinner and ice cream parlor afterwards, church on Sunday nights when Missie outdressed any woman in town—all, everything, was right.

One night around eleven the acid ran out at the G. and G. The foreman knocked off the crew and let the steam die down. As Joe rounded the lake on his way home, a lean moon rode the lake in a silver boat. If anybody had asked Joe about the moon on the lake, he would have said he hadn't paid it any attention. But he saw it with his feelings. It made him yearn painfully for Missie. Creation obsessed him. He thought about children. They had been married more than a year now. They had money put away. They ought to be making little feet for shoes. A little boy child would be about right.

He saw a dim light in the bedroom and decided to come in through the kitchen door. He could wash the fertilizer dust off himself before presenting himself to Missie May. It would be nice for her not to know that he was there until he slipped into his place in bed and hugged her back. She always liked that.

He eased the kitchen door open slowly and silently, but when he went to set his dinner bucket on the table he bumped it into a pile of dishes, and something crashed to the floor. He heard his wife gasp in fright and hurried to reassure her.

"Iss me, honey. Don't git skeered."

There was a quick, large movement in the bedroom. A rustle, a thud, and a stealthy silence. The light went out.

What? Robbers? Murderers? Some varmint attacking his helpless wife, perhaps. He struck a match, threw himself on guard and stepped over the doorsill into the bedroom.

The great belt on the wheel of Time slipped and eternity stood still. By the match light he could see the man's legs fighting with his breeches in his frantic desire to get them on. He had both chance and time to kill the intruder in his helpless condition—half in and half out of his pants—but he was too weak to take action. The shapeless enemies of humanity that live in the hours of Time had waylaid Joe. He was assaulted in his weakness. Like Samson awakening after his haircut. So he just opened his mouth and laughed.

The match went out and he struck another and lit the lamp. A howling wind raced across his heart, but underneath its fury he heard his wife sobbing and Slemmons pleading for his life. Offering to buy it with all that he had. "Please, suh, don't kill me. Sixty-two dollars at de sto'. Gold money."

Joe just stood. Slemmons looked at the window, but it was screened. Joe stood out like a rough-backed mountain between him and the door. Barring him from escape, from sunrise, from life.

He considered a surprise attack upon the big clown that stood there laughing like a chessy cat. But before his fist could travel an inch, Joe's own rushed out to crush him like a battering ram. Then Joe stood over him.

"Git into yo' damn rags, Slemmons, and dat quick."

Slemmons scrambled to his feet and into his vest and coat. As he grabbed his hat, Joe's fury overrode his intentions and he grabbed at Slemmons with his left hand and struck at him with his right. The right landed. The left grazed the front of his vest. Slemmons was knocked a somersault into the kitchen and fled through the open door. Joe found himself alone with Missie May, with the golden watch charm clutched in his left fist. A short bit of broken chain dangled between his fingers.

Missie May was sobbing. Wails of weeping without words. Joe stood, and after a while he found out that he had something in his hand. And then he stood and felt without thinking and without seeing with his natural eyes. Missie May kept on crying and Joe kept on feeling so much, and not knowing what to do with all his feelings, he put Slemmons's watch charm in his pants pocket and took a good laugh and went to bed.

"Missie May, whut you cryin' for?"

"Cause Ah love you so hard and Ah know you don't love *me* no mo'."

Joe sank his face into the pillow for a spell, then he said huskily, "You don't know de feelings of dat yet, Missie May."

"Oh Joe, honey, he said he wuz gointer give me dat gold money and he jes' kept on after me—"

Joe was very still and silent for a long time. Then he said, "Well, don't cry no mo', Missie May. Ah got yo' gold piece for you."

The hours went past on their rusty ankles. Joe still and quiet on one bed rail and Missie May wrung dry of sobs on the other. Finally the sun's tide crept upon the shore of night and drowned all its hours. Missie May with her face stiff and streaked towards the window saw the dawn come into her yard. It was day. Nothing more. Joe wouldn't be coming home as usual. No need to fling open the front door and sweep off the porch, making it nice for Joe. Never no more breakfast to cook; no more washing and starching of Joe's jumper-jackets and pants. No more nothing. So why get up?

With this strange man in her bed, she felt embarrassed to get up and dress. She decided to wait till he had dressed and gone. Then she would get up, dress quickly and be gone forever beyond reach of Joe's looks and laughs. But he never moved. Red light turned to yellow, then white.

From beyond the no-man's land between them came a voice. A strange voice that yesterday had been Joe's.

"Missie May, ain't you gonna fix me no breakfus'?"

She sprang out of bed. "Yeah, Joe. Ah didn't reckon you wuz hongry."

No need to die today. Joe needed her for a few more minutes anyhow.

Soon there was a roaring fire in the cookstove. Water bucket full and two chickens killed. Joe loved fried chicken and rice. She didn't deserve a thing and good Joe was letting her cook him some breakfast. She rushed hot biscuits to the table as Joe took his seat.

He ate with his eyes in his plate. No laughter, no banter.

"Missie May, you ain't eatin' yo' breakfus'."

"Ah don't choose none, Ah thank yuh."

His coffee cup was empty. She sprang to refill it. When she turned from the stove and bent to set the cup beside Joe's plate, she saw the yellow coin on the table between them.

She slumped into her seat and wept into her arms.

Presently Joe said calmly, "Missie May, you cry too much. Don't look back lak Lot's wife and turn to salt."

The sun, the hero of every day, the impersonal old man that beams as brightly on death as on birth, came up every morning and raced across the blue dome and dipped into the sea of fire every morning. Water ran downhill and birds nested.

Missie knew why she didn't leave Joe. She couldn't. She loved him too much, but she could not understand why Joe didn't leave her. He was polite, even kind at times, but aloof.

There were no more Saturday romps. No ringing silver dollars to stack beside her plate. No pockets to rifle. In fact, the yellow coin in his trousers was like a monster hiding in the cave of his pockets to destroy her.

She often wondered if he still had it, but nothing could have induced her to ask nor yet to explore his pockets to see for herself. Its shadow was in the house whether or no.

One night Joe came home around midnight and complained of pains in the back. He asked Missie to rub him down with liniment. It had been three months since Missie had touched his body and it all seemed strange. But she rubbed him. Grateful for the chance. Before morning youth triumphed and Missie exulted. But the next day, as she joyfully made up their bed, beneath her pillow she found the piece of money with the bit of chain attached.

Alone to herself, she looked at the thing with loathing, but look she must. She took it into her hands with trembling and saw first thing that it was no gold piece. It was a gilded half dollar. Then she knew why Slemmons had forbidden anyone to touch his gold. He trusted village eyes at a distance not to recognize his stickpin as a gilded quarter, and his watch charm as a four-bit piece.

She was glad at first that Joe had left it there. Perhaps he was through with her punishment. They were man and wife again. Then another thought came clawing at her. He had come home to buy from her as if she were any woman in the longhouse. Fifty cents for her love. As if to say that he could pay as well as Slemmons. She slid the coin into his Sunday pants pocket and dressed herself and left his house.

Halfway between her house and the quarters she met her husband's mother, and after a short talk she turned and went back home. Never would she admit defeat to that woman who prayed for it nightly. If she had not the substance of marriage she had the outside show. Joe must leave *her.* She let him see she didn't want his old gold four-bits, too.

She saw no more of the coin for some time though she knew that Joe could not help finding it in his pocket. But his health kept poor, and he came home at least every ten days to be rubbed.

The sun swept around the horizon, trailing its robes of weeks and days. One morning as Joe came in from work, he found Missie May chopping wood. Without a word he took the ax and chopped a huge pile before he stopped.

"You ain't got no business choppin' wood, and you know it."

"How come? Ah been choppin' it for de last longest."

"Ah ain't blind. You makin' feet for shoes."

"Won't you be glad to have a lil baby chile, Joe?"

"You know dat 'thout astin' me."

"Iss gointer be a boy chile and de very spit of you."

"You reckon, Missie May?"

"Who else could it look lak?"

Joe said nothing, but he thrust his hand deep into his pocket and fingered something there.

It was almost six months later Missie May took to bed and Joe went and got his mother to come wait on the house.

Missie May was delivered of a fine boy. Her travail was over when Joe come in from work one morning. His mother and the old woman were drinking great bowls of coffee around the fire in the kitchen.

The minute Joe came into the room his mother called him aside.

"How did Missie May make out?" he asked quickly.

"Who, dat gal? She strong as a ox. She gointer have plenty mo'. We done fixed her wid de sugar and lard to sweeten her for de nex' one."

Joe stood silent awhile.

"You ain't ask 'bout de baby, Joe. You oughter be mighty proud cause he sho is de spittin' image of yuh, son. Dat's yourn all right, if you never git another one, dat un is yourn. And you know Ah'm mighty proud too, son, cause Ah never thought well of you marryin' Missie May cause her ma used tuh fan her foot round right smart and Ah been mighty skeered dat Missie May wuz gointer git misput on her road."

Joe said nothing. He fooled around the house till late in the day, then, just before he went to work, he went and stood at the foot of the bed and asked his wife how she felt. He did this every day during the week.

On Saturday he went to Orlando to make his market. It had been a long time since he had done that.

Meat and lard, meal and flour, soap and starch. Cans of corn and tomatoes. All the staples. He fooled around town for a while and bought bananas and apples. Way after while he went around to the candy store.

"Hello, Joe," the clerk greeted him. "Ain't seen you in a long time."

"Nope, Ah ain't been heah. Been round in spots and places."

"Want some of them molasses kisses you always buy?"

"Yessuh." He threw the gilded half dollar on the counter. "Will dat spend?"

"What is it, Joe? Well, I'll be doggone! A gold-plated four-bit piece. Where'd you git it, Joe?"

"Offen a stray nigger dat come through Eatonville. He had it on his watch chain for a charm—goin' round making out iss gold money. Ha ha! He had a quarter on his tiepin and it wuz all golded up too. Tryin' to fool people. Makin' out he so rich and everything. Ha! Ha! Tryin' to tole off folkses wives from home."

"How did you git it, Joe? Did he fool you, too?"

"Who, me? Naw suh! He ain't fooled me none. Know whut Ah done? He come round me wid his smart talk. Ah hauled off and knocked 'im down and took his old four-bits away from 'im. Gointer buy my wife some good ole lasses kisses wid it. Gimme fifty cents worth of dem candy kisses."

"Fifty cents buys a mighty lot of candy kisses, Joe. Why don't you split it up and take some chocolate bars, too? They eat good, too."

"Yessuh, dey do, but Ah wants all dat in kisses. Ah got a lil boy chile home now. Tain't a week old yet, but he kin suck a sugar tit and maybe eat one them kisses hisself."

Joe got his candy and left the store. The clerk turned to the next customer. "Wisht I could be like these darkies. Laughin' all the time. Nothin' worries 'em."

Back in Eatonville, Joe reached his own front door. There was the ring of singing metal on wood. Fifteen times. Missie May couldn't run to the door, but she crept there as quickly as she could.

"Joe Banks, Ah hear you chunkin' money in mah do'way. You wait till Ah got mah strength back and Ah'm gointer fix you for dat."

1933

Claude McKay 1889–1948

Of the many gifted writers who contributed to the rich literary legacy of the Harlem Renaissance, Claude McKay, a Jamaican immigrant, was clearly the most militant. McKay's most famous poem, "If We Must Die," an eloquent and provocative sonnet, was inspired by the violent race riots that erupted in Chicago and other cities in 1919. In other deeply moving, carefully crafted poems, McKay voices his outrage at the treatment of blacks in a racist society. The poem "The Lynching," for example, is a chilling indictment against the hatred and vigilantism which cost many black Americans their lives in the 1920s and 1930s. However, the social protest verse upon which McKay's reputation as a poet ultimately rests represents only a small portion of his approximately two hundred published poems.

Born in the Clarendon Hills of Jamaica, McKay began writing poetry in childhood. He published two books of dialect verse in 1912. In recognition of this achievement, the Jamaican Institute of Arts and Sciences awarded McKay a medal and a stipend that allowed him to study agriculture briefly at Tuskegee Institute and later at Kansas State University (1912–14). McKay left Kansas State in 1914 to pursue a writing career in New York City, where he became involved with the socialist movement and wrote for radical journals like Max Eastman's *Liberator,* for which he served as an editor. As the Harlem Renaissance began to flower, McKay published *Harlem Shadows* (1922), a landmark collection of poems. McKay also published three novels, including the popular and controversial *Home to Harlem* (1928), as well as other books and essays. The majority of McKay's fiction was written between 1923 and 1934, when he was an expatriate, living variously in France, Great Britain, and North Africa, and his work reflects the broad range of black experience in what is now termed the Diaspora. He died in Chicago in 1948. His *Selected Poems* appeared posthumously in 1953.

Like his friend and fellow Renaissance poet Countee Cullen, McKay preferred the traditional verse forms of the British masters, particularly the sonnet and short lyric. Thematically, McKay's poetry includes nostalgic lyrics about rural Jamaica, and poems celebrating nature, love, and Christian faith, in addition to the powerful protest verses. McKay's best poetry sparkles with sharp, fresh images and resonates with an indomitable passion for life.

Elvin Holt
Southwest Texas State University

PRIMARY WORKS

Songs of Jamaica, 1912; *Spring in New Hampshire,* 1920; *Harlem Shadows,* 1922; *Home to Harlem,* 1928; *Banjo,* 1929; *Gingertown,* 1932; *Banana Bottom,* 1933; *A Long Way from Home,* 1937; *Harlem: Negro Metropolis,* 1940; *Selected Poems,* 1953.

The Harlem Dancer

Applauding youths laughed with young prostitutes
And watched her perfect, half-clothed body sway;
Her voice was like the sound of blended flutes
Blown by black players upon a picnic day.
She sang and danced on gracefully and calm,
The light gauze hanging loose about her form;
To me she seemed a proudly-swaying palm
Grown lovelier for passing through a storm.
Upon her swarthy neck black shiny curls
Luxuriant fell; and tossing coins in praise,
The wine-flushed, bold-eyed boys, and even the girls,
Devoured her shape with eager, passionate gaze;
But looking at her falsely-smiling face,
I knew her self was not in that strange place.

1917

If We Must Die

If we must die, let it not be like hogs
Hunted and penned in an inglorious spot,
While round us bark the mad and hungry dogs,
Making their mock at our accursed lot.
If we must die, O let us nobly die,
So that our precious blood may not be shed
In vain; then even the monsters we defy
Shall be constrained to honor us though dead!
O kinsmen! we must meet the common foe!
Though far outnumbered let us show us brave,
And for their thousand blows deal one deathblow!

What though before us lies the open grave?
Like men we'll face the murderous, cowardly pack,
Pressed to the wall, dying, but fighting back!

1919

The Lynching

His Spirit in smoke ascended to high heaven.
His father, by the cruelest way of pain,
Had bidden him to his bosom once again;
The awful sin remained still unforgiven.
All night a bright and solitary star
(Perchance the one that ever guided him,
Yet gave him up at last to Fate's wild whim)
Hung pitifully o'er the swinging char.
Day dawned, and soon the mixed crowds came to view
The ghastly body swaying in the sun.
The women thronged to look, but never a one
Showed sorrow in her eyes of steely blue.

And little lads, lynchers that were to be,
Danced round the dreadful thing in fiendish glee.

1920

Harlem Shadows

I hear the halting footsteps of a lass
    In Negro Harlem when the night lets fall
Its veil. I see the shapes of girls who pass
    To bend and barter at desire's call.
Ah, little dark girls who in slippered feet
Go prowling through the night from street to street!

Through the long night until the silver break
    Of day the little gray feet know no rest;
Through the lone night until the last snow-flake
    Has dropped from heaven upon the earth's white breast,
The dusky, half-clad girls of tired feet
Are trudging, thinly shod, from street to street.

Ah, stern harsh world, that in the wretched way
Of poverty, dishonor and disgrace,
Has pushed the timid little feet of clay,
The sacred brown feet of my fallen race!
Ah, heart of me, the weary, weary feet
In Harlem wandering from street to street.

1920

I Shall Return

I shall return again. I shall return
To laugh and love and watch with wonder-eyes
At golden noon the forest fires burn,
Wafting their blue-black smoke to sapphire skies.
I shall return to loiter by the streams
That bathe the brown blades of the bending grasses,
And realize once more my thousand dreams
Of waters rushing down the mountain passes.
I shall return to hear the fiddle and fife
Of village dances, dear delicious tunes
That stir the hidden depths of native life,
Stray melodies of dim-remembered runes.
I shall return. I shall return again
To ease my mind of long, long years of pain.

1920

America

Although she feeds me bread of bitterness,
And sinks into my throat her tiger's tooth,
Stealing my breath of life, I will confess
I love this cultured hell that tests my youth!
Her vigor flows like tides into my blood,
Giving me strength erect against her hate.
Her bigness sweeps my being like a flood.
Yet as a rebel fronts a king in state,
I stand within her walls with not a shred
Of terror, malice, not a word of jeer.
Darkly I gaze into the days ahead,
And see her might and granite wonders there,

Beneath the touch of Time's unerring hand,
Like priceless treasures sinking in the sand.

1921

In Bondage

I would be wandering in distant fields
Where man, and bird, and beast, lives leisurely,
And the old earth is kind, and ever yields
Her goodly gifts to all her children free;
Where life is fairer, lighter, less demanding,
And boys and girls have time and space for play
Before they come to years of understanding—
Somewhere I would be singing, far away.
For life is greater than the thousand wars
Men wage for it in their insatiate lust,
And will remain like the eternal stars,
When all that shines today is drift and dust
But I am bound with you in your mean graves,
O black men, simple slaves of ruthless slaves.

1920

Flame-Heart

So much I have forgotten in ten years,
So much in ten brief years! I have forgot
What time the purple apples come to juice,
And what month brings the shy forget-me-not.
I have forgot the special, startling season
Of the pimento's flowering and fruiting;
What time of year the ground doves brown the fields
And fill the noonday with their curious fluting.
I have forgotten much, but still remember
The poinsettia's red, blood-red, in warm December.

I still recall the honey-fever grass,
But cannot recollect the high days when
We rooted them out of the ping-wing path
To stop the mad bees in the rabbit pen.
I often try to think in what sweet month

The languid painted ladies used to dapple
The yellow by-road mazing from the main,
Sweet with the golden threads of the rose-apple.
I have forgotten—strange—but quite remember
The poinsettia's red, blood-red, in warm December.

What weeks, what months, what time of the mild year
We cheated school to have our fling at tops?
What days our wine-thrilled bodies pulsed with joy
Feasting upon blackberries in the copse?
Oh some I know! I have embalmed the days,
Even the sacred moments when we played,
All innocent of passion, uncorrupt,
At noon and evening in the flame-heart's shade.
We were so happy, happy, I remember,
Beneath the poinsettia's red in warm December.

1922

Flower of Love

The perfume of your body dulls my sense.
  I want nor wine nor weed; your breath alone
Suffices. In this moment rare and tense
  I worship at your breast. The flower is blown,
The saffron petals tempt my amorous mouth,
  The yellow heart is radiant now with dew
Soft-scented, redolent of my loved South;
  O flower of love! I give myself to you.
Uncovered on your couch of figured green,
  Here let us linger indivisible.
The portals of your sanctuary unseen
  Receive my offering, yielding unto me.
Oh, with our love the night is warm and deep!
  The air is sweet, my flower, and sweet the flute
Whose music lulls our burning brain to sleep,
  While we lie loving, passionate and mute.

1953

A Red Flower

Your lips are like a southern lily red,
   Wet with soft rain-kisses of the night,
In which the brown bee buries deep its head,
   When still the dawn's a silver sea of light.

Your lips betray the secret of your soul,
   The dark delicious essence that is you,
A mystery of life, the flaming goal
   I seek through mazy pathways strange and new.

Your lips are the red symbol of a dream.
   What visions of warm lilies they impart,
That line the green bank of a fair blue stream,
   With butterflies and bees close to each heart!

Brown bees that murmur sounds of music rare,
   That softly fall upon the languorous breeze,
Wafting them gently on the quiet air
   Among untended avenues of trees.

O were I hovering, a bee, to probe
   Deep down within your scented heart, fair flower,
Enfolded by your soft vermilion robe,
   Amorous of sweets, for but one perfect hour!

1953

Anne Spencer 1882–1975

Born Annie Bethel Scales in Bramwell, West Virginia, Anne Spencer was educated at the Virginia Seminary in Lynchburg. Selected to deliver the major student address at the commencement on May 8, 1899, Annie, for her uplifting oration, merited widespread acclaim and respect. Accompanying a gift—a four-volume set of Emerson—that Dr. Richard H. Bolling, head of the Negro Baptist Publishing Board of Nashville, had given Annie was a maxim: "Take what you have and make what you want." This advice she treasured, and it evolved through the years as her personal philosophy. Two years later, Annie married Edward Spencer, a former classmate, and they settled in Lynchburg.

Annie was intensely interested in the world about her, yet remained apart from active society, except when cultivating literary friends and visitors such as W.E.B. Du Bois, James Weldon Johnson, Walter White, and others. She also corresponded with Carl Van Vechten and H. L. Mencken. Yet, under certain conditions, Spencer was an initiator, organizer, and a fighter for human rights. She helped mobilize black citizens to oppose political and civil injustices in the Lynchburg community. An independent thinker and doer, she assumed the pen name Anne Spencer by which her poetry is identified. Having read Emerson's works closely throughout her life, she asserted, "Do your 'own thing' is right out of Emerson . . . it is not new." During her mid-life, she became the librarian at the Dunbar High School to supplement her family's income when her children reached college age.

She began writing poetry before the Harlem Renaissance, but her poetry first appeared during this period, notably in Countee Cullen's *Caroling Dusk* (1927). Spencer's verse is somewhat conventional and, like much of the poetry of William Stanley Braithwaite and Cullen, is nonracial in theme. She admitted that she possessed "no civilized articulation for the things she hated." Spencer develops vibrant images to communicate a uniquely private experience that becomes profound, reflecting her sensibility to a moral code that man evidences, her fidelity to exoticism as a romantic component, her innate love of nature, her search for the ideal while acknowledging reality, and her dual treatment of the imagination involving both character and reader.

Spencer never had a volume of her own poems published. She was content to probe and pursue her private musings, often, however, interacting or collaborating with other writers who sought her views and valued her editorial comments. Through several decades her creativity has been respected and admired, for her poems have appeared in nearly every anthology of African American literature; moreover, she created new poems and revised previous compositions until her final year: her poem titled "1975" was composed in 1974. Spencer's poetry of affirmation will endure, appealing to all who seek insights concerning humankind's relationship to the past, present, and future.

Evelyn H. Roberts
St. Louis Community College–Meramec

Lines to a Nasturtium

(A Lover Muses)[1]

Flame-flower, Day-torch, Mauna Loa,
I saw a daring bee, today, pause, and soar,
   Into your flaming heart;
Then did I hear crisp, crinkled laughter
As the furies after tore him apart?
   A bird, next, small and humming,
Looked into your startled depths and fled. . . .
Surely, some dread sight, and dafter
   Than human eyes as mine can see,
Set the stricken air waves drumming
   In his flight.

[1]Slightly revised from the version as first published in *Palms,* IV (October 1926), 13.

Day-torch, Flame-flower, cool-hot Beauty,
I cannot see, I cannot hear your flutey
Voice lure your loving swain,
But I know one other to whom you are in beauty
Born in vain:
Hair like the setting sun,
Her eyes a rising star,
Motions gracious as reeds by Babylon, bar
All your competing;
Hands like, how like, brown lilies sweet,
Cloth of gold were fair enough to touch her feet . . .
Ah, how the sense reels at my repeating,
As once in her fire-lit heart I felt the furies
Beating, beating.

1926

Substitution[1]

Is Life itself but many ways of thought,
How real the tropic storm or lambent breeze
Within the slightest convolution wrought
Our mantled world and men-freighted seas?
God thinks . . . and being comes to ardent things:
The splendor of the day-spent sun, love's birth,—
Or dreams a little, while creation swings
The circle of His mind and Time's full girth . . .
As here within this noisy peopled room
My thought leans forward . . . quick! you're lifted clear
Of brick and frame to moonlit garden bloom,—
Absurdly easy, now, our walking, dear,
Talking, my leaning close to touch your face . . .
His All-Mind bids us keep this sacred place!

1927

For Jim, Easter Eve[1]

If ever a garden was a Gethsemane,
with old tombs set high against

[1]Revised in 1973 from the version as first published in Countee Cullen, ed., *Caroling Dusk: An Anthology of Verse by Negro Poets,* 1927, 48.

[1]Written in 1948 and first published in Langston Hughes and Arna Bontemps, eds., *The Poetry of the Negro, 1746–1949,* 1949, 65.

the crumpled olive tree—and lichen,
this, my garden has been to me.
For such as I none other is no sweet:
Lacking old tombs, here stands my grief,
and certainly its ancient tree.

Peace is here and in every season
a quiet beauty.
The sky falling about me
evenly to the compass . . .
What is sorrow but tenderness now
in this earth-close frame of land and sky
falling constantly into horizons
of east and west, north and south;
what is pain but happiness here
amid these green and wordless patterns,—
indefinite texture of blade and leaf:

Beauty of an old, old tree,
last comfort in Gethsemane.

1949

Nella Larsen 1891–1964

Until the early 1970s when previously "lost" work by women writers began to be recovered and reprinted, Nella Larsen was one of several women writers of the New Negro Renaissance relegated to the back pages of that movement's literary history, a curious fate since her career had such an auspicious beginning. Touted as a promising writer by blacks and whites alike, Larsen was encouraged by some of the most influential names on the 1920s arts scene. Walter White, onetime director of the NAACP, read drafts of *Quicksand* and urged Larsen along to its completion. Carl Van Vechten, popularly credited with promoting many Harlem Renaissance writers, introduced the novel to his publisher, Knopf. These efforts paid off. Larsen won second prize in literature in 1928 for *Quicksand* from the Harmon Foundation, which celebrated outstanding achievement by Negroes.

Quicksand was also well received by the critics. In his review of the novel, W.E.B. Du Bois praised it as the "best piece of fiction that Negro America has produced since the heyday of Chesnutt." *Passing* was similarly lauded. One reviewer gave the novel high marks for capturing, as did no other novel of the genre, the psychology of racial passing with "consummate art." Due largely to the success of these first two novels, Larsen won a Guggenheim fellowship in 1930—the first black female creative writer to be so honored—to do research on a third novel in Spain and France. That novel was never published.

After the release of *Passing,* Larsen published her last piece, a story entitled "Sanctuary." The subject of much controversy, many speculate that the scandal it created helped to send Larsen into obscurity. Following the appearance of the story in 1930, Larsen was accused of plagiarism. One reader wrote to the editor of the magazine about the striking resemblance of Larsen's story to one by Sheila Kaye-Smith entitled "Mrs. Adis," published in the January 1922 issue of *Century* magazine. The editor of *The Forum* conducted an investigation and was finally convinced that the resemblance between the stories was an extraordinary coincidence. In compliance with the editor's request, Larsen wrote a detailed explanation of the way in which she came by the germ for her story, trying to vindicate herself. Despite her editor's support, Larsen never recovered from the shock of the charge and disappeared from the literary scene altogether. She died in Brooklyn in 1964, practically in obscurity.

Why a career with such auspicious beginnings had such an inauspicious ending has continued to perplex students of the New Negro Renaissance. Many search for answers in the scattered fragments of Larsen's biography, which reveal a delicate and unstable person. Though there is very little information about Larsen, some pieces of her life's puzzle are fairly widely known. Born in Chicago in 1891 (though no birth certificate has been found), she was the daughter of a Danish mother and a black West Indian father who died when Larsen was a young girl. Larsen's mother remarried, this time a white man who treated his step-daughter with some disfavor. Never feeling connected to this newly configured family, Larsen searched vainly for the sense of belonging it could not provide. Fickle and unsettled, Larsen roamed from place to place, searching for some undefined and undefinable "something." She studied at Fisk University in Nashville, Tennessee; audited classes at the University of Copenhagen; and studied nursing at Lincoln Hospital Training School for Nurses in New York, graduating in 1915.

For a brief time after her nurses' training, she was superintendent of nurses at Tuskegee Institute in Alabama. Unable to tolerate its stifling atmosphere, she left after only a year and returned to New York. There she worked as a nurse between 1916 and 1918 at the hospital where she was trained; and between 1918 and 1921 for New York City's Department of Health. Dissatisfied with this career, she began work in 1921 at the children's division of the New York Public Library, enrolling in its training program. During her employment as a librarian, she published her only two novels.

Both *Quicksand* and *Passing* illuminate the peculiar pressures on Nella Larsen as a woman writer during the male-dominated New Negro Renaissance. They show her grappling with the conflicting demands of her racial and sexual identities and the contradictions of a black and feminine aesthetic. While these novels often appear to be concessions to the dominant ideology of romance—marriage and motherhood—viewed from a feminist perspective, they can be seen as radical and original efforts to acknowledge a female sexual experience, repressed, more often than not, in both literary and social realms.

Deborah E. McDowell
University of Virginia

PRIMARY WORKS

Quicksand, 1928; *Passing,* 1929.

from Passing

One

It was the last letter in Irene Redfield's little pile of morning mail. After her other ordinary and clearly directed letters the long envelope of thin Italian paper with its almost illegible scrawl seemed out of place and alien. And there was, too, something mysterious and slightly furtive about it. A thin sly thing which bore no return address to betray the sender. Not that she hadn't immediately known who its sender was. Some two years ago she had one very like it in outward appearance. Furtive, but yet in some peculiar, determined way a little flaunting. Purple ink. Foreign paper of extraordinary size.

It had been, Irene noted, postmarked in New York the day before. Her brows came together in a tiny frown. The frown, however, was more from perplexity than from annoyance; though there was in her thoughts an element of both. She was wholly unable to comprehend such an attitude towards danger as she was sure the letter's contents would reveal; and she disliked the idea of opening and reading it.

This, she reflected, was of a piece with all that she knew of Clare Kendry. Stepping always on the edge of danger. Always aware, but not drawing back or turning aside. Certainly not because of any alarms or feeling of outrage on the part of others.

And for a swift moment Irene Redfield seemed to see a pale small girl sitting on a ragged blue sofa, sewing pieces of bright red cloth together, while her drunken father, a tall, powerfully built man, raged threateningly up and down the shabby room, bellowing curses and making spasmodic lunges at her which were not the less frightening because they were, for the most part, ineffectual. Sometimes he did manage to reach her. But only the fact that the child had edged herself and her poor sewing over to the farthermost corner of the sofa suggested that she was in any way perturbed by this menace to herself and her work.

Clare had known well enough that it was unsafe to take a portion of the dollar that was her weekly wage for the doing of many errands for the dressmaker who lived on the top floor of the building of which Bob Kendry was janitor. But that knowledge had not deterred her. She wanted to go to her Sunday school's picnic, and she had made up her mind to wear a new dress. So, in spite of certain unpleasantness and possible danger, she had taken the money to buy the material for that pathetic little red frock.

There had been, even in those days, nothing sacrificial in Clare Kendry's idea of life, no allegiance beyond her own immediate desire. She was selfish, and cold, and hard. And yet she had, too, a strange capacity of transforming warmth and passion, verging sometimes almost on theatrical heroics.

Irene, who was a year or more older than Clare, remembered the day that Bob Kendry had been brought home dead, killed in a silly saloon-fight. Clare, who was at that time a scant fifteen years old, had just stood there with her lips pressed together, her thin arms folded across her narrow chest, staring down at the familiar pasty-white face of her parent with a sort of disdain in her slanting black eyes. For a very long time she had stood like that, silent and staring. Then, quite suddenly, she had given way to a torrent of weeping, swaying her thin body, tearing at her bright hair, and stamping her small feet. The outburst had ceased as suddenly as it had begun. She glanced quickly about the bare room, taking everyone in, even the two policemen, in a sharp look of flashing scorn. And, in the next instant, she had turned and vanished through the door.

Seen across the long stretch of years, the thing had more the appearance of an outpouring of pent-up fury than of an overflow of grief for her dead father; though she had been, Irene admitted, fond enough of him in her own rather catlike way.

Catlike. Certainly that was the word which best described Clare Kendry, if any single word could describe her. Sometimes she was hard and apparently without feeling at all; sometimes she was affectionate and rashly impulsive. And there was about her an amazing soft malice, hidden well away until provoked. Then she was capable of scratching, and very effectively too. Or, driven to anger, she would fight with a ferocity and impetuousness that disregarded or forgot any danger; superior strength, numbers, or other unfavourable circumstances. How savagely she had clawed those boys the day they had hooted her parent and sung a derisive rhyme, of their own composing, which pointed out certain eccentricities in his careening gait! And how deliberately she had—

Irene brought her thoughts back to the present, to the letter from Clare Kendry that she still held unopened in her hand. With a little feeling of apprehension, she very slowly cut the envelope, drew out the folded sheets, spread them, and began to read.

It was, she saw at once, what she had expected since learning from the postmark that Clare was in the city. An extravagantly phrased wish to see her again. Well, she needn't and wouldn't, Irene told herself, accede to that. Nor would she assist Clare to realize her foolish desire to return for a moment to that life which long ago, and of her own choice, she had left behind her.

She ran through the letter, puzzling out, as best she could, the carelessly formed words or making instinctive guesses at them.

". . . For I am lonely, so lonely . . . cannot help longing to be with you again, as I have never longed for anything before; and I have wanted many things in my life . . . You can't know how in this pale life of mine I am all the time seeing the bright pictures of that other that I once thought I was glad to be free of . . . It's like an ache, a pain that never ceases . . ." Sheets upon thin sheets of it. And ending finally with, "and it's your fault, 'Rene dear. At least partly. For I wouldn't now, perhaps, have this terrible, this wild desire if I hadn't seen you that time in Chicago . . ."

Brilliant red patches flamed in Irene Redfield's warm olive cheeks.

"That time in Chicago." The words stood out from among the many paragraphs of other words, bringing with them a clear, sharp remembrance, in which even now, after two years, humiliation, resentment, and rage were mingled.

Two

This is what Irene Redfield remembered.

Chicago. August. A brilliant day, hot, with a brutal staring sun pouring down rays that were like molten rain. A day on which the very outlines of the buildings shuddered as if in protest at the heat. Quivering lines sprang up from baked pavements and wriggled along the shining cartracks. The automobiles parked at the kerbs were a dancing blaze, and the glass of the shop-windows threw out a blinding radiance. Sharp particles of dust rose from the burning sidewalks, stinging the seared or dripping skins of wilting pedestrians. What small breeze there was seemed like the breath of a flame fanned by slow bellows.

It was on that day of all others that Irene set out to shop for the things which she had promised to take home from Chicago to her two small sons, Brian junior and Theodore. Characteristically, she had put it off until only a few crowded days remained of her long visit. And only this sweltering one was free of engagements till the evening.

Without too much trouble she had got the mechanical aeroplane for Junior. But the drawing-book, for which Ted had so gravely and insistently given her precise directions, had sent her in and out of five shops without success.

It was while she was on her way to a sixth place that right before her smarting eyes a man toppled over and became an inert crumpled heap on the scorching cement. About the lifeless figure a little crowd gathered. Was the man dead, or only faint? someone asked her. But Irene didn't know and didn't try to discover. She edged her way out of the increasing crowd, feeling disagreeably damp and sticky and soiled from contact with so many sweating bodies.

For a moment she stood fanning herself and dabbing at her moist face with an inadequate scrap of handkerchief. Suddenly she was aware that the whole street had a wobbly look, and realized that she was about to faint. With a quick perception of the need for immediate safety, she lifted a wavering hand in the direction of a cab parked directly in front of her. The perspiring driver jumped out and guided her to his car. He helped, almost lifted her in. She sank down on the hot leather seat.

For a minute her thoughts were nebulous. They cleared.

"I guess," she told her Samaritan, "it's tea I need. On a roof somewhere."

"The Drayton, ma'am?" he suggested. "They do say as how it's always a breeze up there."

"Thank you. I think the Drayton'll do nicely," she told him.

There was that little grating sound of the clutch being slipped in as the man put the car in gear and slid deftly out into the boiling traffic. Reviving under the warm breeze stirred up by the moving cab, Irene made some small attempts to repair the damage that the heat and crowds had done to her appearance.

All too soon the rattling vehicle shot towards the sidewalk and stood still. The driver sprang out and opened the door before the hotel's decorated attendant could reach it. She got out, and thanking him smilingly as well as in a more substantial manner for his kind helpfulness and understanding, went in through the Drayton's wide doors.

Stepping out of the elevator that had brought her to the roof, she was led to a table just in front of a long window whose gently moving curtains suggested a cool breeze. It was, she thought, like being wafted upward on a magic carpet to another world, pleasant, quiet, and strangely remote from the sizzling one that she had left below.

The tea, when it came, was all that she had desired and expected. In fact, so much was it what she had desired and expected that after the first deep cooling drink she was able to forget it, only now and then sipping, a little absently, from the tall green glass, while she surveyed the room about her or looked out over some lower buildings at the bright unstirred blue of the lake reaching away to an undetected horizon.

She had been gazing down for some time at the specks of cars and people creeping about in streets, and thinking how silly they looked, when on taking up her glass she was surprised to find it empty at last. She asked for more tea and while she waited, began to recall the happenings of the day and to wonder what she was to do about Ted and his book. Why was it that almost invariably he wanted something that was difficult or impossible to get? Like his father. For ever wanting something that he couldn't have.

Presently there were voices, a man's booming one and a woman's slightly husky. A waiter passed her, followed by a sweetly scented woman in a fluttering dress of green chiffon whose mingled pattern of narcissuses, jonquils, and hyacinths was a reminder of pleasantly chill spring days. Behind her there was a man, very red in the face, who was mopping his neck and forehead with a big crumpled handkerchief.

"Oh dear!" Irene groaned, rasped by annoyance, for after a little discussion and commotion they had stopped at the very next table. She had been alone there at the window and it had been so satisfyingly quiet. Now, of course, they would chatter.

But no. Only the woman sat down. The man remained standing, abstractedly pinching the knot of his bright blue tie. Across the small space that separated the two tables his voice carried clearly.

"See you later, then," he declared, looking down at the woman. There was pleasure in his tones and a smile on his face.

His companion's lips parted in some answer, but her words were blurred by the little intervening distance and the medley of noises floating up from the streets below. They didn't reach Irene. But she noted the peculiar caressing smile that accompanied them.

The man said: "Well, I suppose I'd better," and smiled again, and said goodbye, and left.

An attractive-looking woman, was Irene's opinion, with those dark, almost black, eyes and that wide mouth like a scarlet flower against the ivory of her skin. Nice clothes too, just right for the weather, thin and cool without being mussy, as summer things were so apt to be.

A waiter was taking her order. Irene saw her smile up at him as she murmured something—thanks, maybe. It was an odd sort of smile. Irene couldn't quite define it, but she was sure that she would have classed it, coming from another woman, as being just a shade too provocative for a waiter. About this one, however, there was something that made her hesitate to name it that. A certain impression of assurance, perhaps.

The waiter came back with the order. Irene watched her spread out her napkin, saw the silver spoon in the white hand slit the dull gold of the melon. Then, conscious that she had been staring, she looked quickly away.

Her mind returned to her own affairs. She had settled, definitely, the problem of the proper one of two frocks for the bridge party that night, in rooms whose atmosphere would be so thick and hot that every breath would be like breathing soup. The dress decided, her thoughts had gone back to the snag of Ted's book, her unseeing eyes far away on the lake, when by some sixth sense she was acutely aware that someone was watching her.

Very slowly she looked around, and into the dark eyes of the woman in the green frock at the next table. But she evidently failed to realize that such intense interest as she was showing might be embarrassing, and continued to stare. Her demeanour was that of one who with utmost singleness of mind and purpose was determined to impress firmly and accurately each detail of Irene's features upon her memory for all time, nor showed the slightest trace of disconcertment at having been detected in her steady scrutiny.

Instead, it was Irene who was put out. Feeling her colour heighten under the continued inspection, she slid her eyes down. What, she wondered, could be the reason for such persistent attention? Had she, in her haste in the taxi, put her hat on backwards? Guardedly she felt at it. No. Perhaps there was a streak of powder somewhere on her face. She made a quick pass over it with her handkerchief. Something wrong with her dress? She shot a glance over it. Perfectly all right. *What* was it?

Again she looked up, and for a moment her brown eyes politely returned the stare of the other's black ones, which never for an instant fell or wavered. Irene made a little mental shrug. Oh well, let her look! She tried to treat the woman and her watching with indifference, but she couldn't. All her efforts to ignore her, it, were futile. She stole another glance. Still looking. What strange languorous eyes she had!

And gradually there rose in Irene a small inner disturbance, odious and hatefully familiar. She laughed softly, but her eyes flashed.

Did that woman, could that woman, somehow know that here before her very eyes on the roof of the Drayton sat a Negro?

Absurd! Impossible! White people were so stupid about such things for all that they usually asserted that they were able to tell; and by the most ridiculous means, finger-nails, palms of hands, shapes of ears, teeth, and other equally silly rot. They always took her for an Italian, a Spaniard, a Mexican, or a gipsy. Never, when she was alone, had they even remotely seemed to suspect that she was a Negro. No, the woman sitting there staring at her couldn't possibly know.

Nevertheless, Irene felt, in turn, anger, scorn, and fear slide over her. It wasn't that she was ashamed of being a Negro, or even of having it declared. It was the idea of being ejected from any place, even in the polite and tactful way in which the Drayton would probably do it, that disturbed her.

But she looked, boldly this time, back into the eyes still frankly intent upon her. They did not seem to her hostile or resentful. Rather, Irene had the feeling that they were ready to smile if she would. Nonsense, of course. The feeling passed, and she turned away with the firm intention of keeping her gaze on the lake, the roofs of the buildings across the way, the sky, anywhere but on that annoying woman. Almost immediately, however, her eyes were back again. In the midst of her fog of uneasiness she had been seized by a desire to outstare the rude observer. Suppose the woman did know or suspect her race. She couldn't prove it.

Suddenly her small fright increased. Her neighbor had risen and was coming towards her. What was going to happen now?

"Pardon me," the woman said pleasantly, "but I think I know you." Her slightly husky voice held a dubious note.

Looking up at her, Irene's suspicions and fears vanished. There was no mistaking the friendliness of that smile or resisting its charm. Instantly she surrendered to it and smiled too, as she said: "I'm afraid you're mistaken."

"Why, of course, I know you!" the other exclaimed. "Don't tell me you're not Irene Westover. Or do they still call you 'Rene?"

In the brief second before her answer, Irene tried vainly to recall where and when this woman could have known her. There, in Chicago. And before her marriage. That much was plain. High school? College? Y.W.C.A. committees? High school, most likely. What white girls had she known well enough to have been familiarly addressed as 'Rene by them? The woman before her didn't fit her memory of any of them. Who was she?

"Yes, I'm Irene Westover. And though nobody calls me 'Rene any more, it's good to hear the name again. And you—" She hesitated, ashamed that she could not remember, and hoping that the sentence would be finished for her.

"Don't you know me? Not really, 'Rene?"

"I'm sorry, but just at the minute I can't seem to place you."

Irene studied the lovely creature standing beside her for some clue to her identity. Who could she be? Where and when had they met? And through her perplexity there came the thought that the trick which her memory had played her was for some reason more gratifying than disappointing to her old acquaintance, that she didn't mind not being recognized.

And, too, Irene felt that she was just about to remember her. For about the woman was some quality, an intangible something too vague to define, too remote to seize, but which was, to Irene Redfield, very familiar. And that voice. Surely she'd heard those husky tones somewhere before. Perhaps before time, contact, or something had been at them, making them into a voice remotely suggesting England. Ah! Could it have been in Europe that they had met? 'Rene. No.

"Perhaps," Irene began, "you—"

The woman laughed, a lovely laugh, a small sequence of notes that was like a trill and also like the ringing of a delicate bell fashioned of a precious metal, a tinkling.

Irene drew a quick sharp breath. "Clare!" she exclaimed, "not really Clare Kendry?"

So great was her astonishment that she had started to rise.

"No, no, don't get up," Clare Kendry commanded, and sat down herself. "You've simply got to stay and talk. We'll have something more. Tea? Fancy meeting you here! It's simply too, too lucky!"

"It's awfully surprising," Irene told her, and, seeing the change in Clare's smile, knew that she had revealed a corner of her own thoughts. But she only said: "I'd never in this world have known you if you hadn't laughed. You are changed, you know. And yet, in a way, you're just the same."

"Perhaps," Clare replied. "Oh, just a second."

She gave her attention to the waiter at her side. "M-mm, let's see. Two teas. And bring some cigarettes. Y-es, they'll be all right. Thanks." Again that odd upward smile. Now, Irene was sure that it was too provocative for a waiter.

While Clare had been giving the order, Irene made a rapid mental calculation. It must be, she figured, all of twelve years since she, or anybody that she knew, had laid eyes on Clare Kendry.

After her father's death she'd gone to live with some relatives, aunts or cousins two or three times removed, over on the west side: relatives that nobody had known the Kendry's possessed until they had turned up at the funeral and taken Clare away with them.

For about a year or more afterwards she would appear occasionally among her old friends and acquaintances on the south side for short little visits that were, they understood, always stolen from the endless domestic tasks in her new home. With each succeeding one she was taller, shabbier, and more belligerently sensitive. And each time the look on her face was more resentful and brooding. "I'm worried about Clare, she seems so unhappy," Irene remembered her mother saying. The visits dwindled, becoming shorter, fewer, and further apart until at last they ceased.

Irene's father, who had been fond of Bob Kendry, made a special trip over to the west side about two months after the last time Clare had been to see them and returned with the bare information that he had seen the relatives and that Clare had disappeared. What else he had confided to her mother, in the privacy of their own room, Irene didn't know.

But she had had something more than a vague suspicion of its nature. For there had been rumours. Rumours that were, to girls of eighteen and nineteen years, interesting and exciting.

There was the one about Clare Kendry's having been seen at the dinner hour in a fashionable hotel in company with another woman and two men, all of them white. And *dressed!* And there was another which told of her driving in Lincoln Park with a man, unmistakably white, and evidently rich. Packard limousine, chauffeur in livery, and all that. There had been others whose context Irene could no longer recollect, but all pointing in the same glamorous direction.

And she could remember quite vividly how, when they used to repeat and discuss these tantalizing stories about Clare, the girls would always look knowingly at one another and then, with little excited giggles, drag away their eager shining eyes and say with lurking undertones of regret or disbelief some such thing as: "Oh, well, maybe she's got a job or something," or "After all, it mayn't have been Clare," or "You can't believe all you hear."

And always some girl, more matter-of-fact or more frankly malicious than the rest, would declare: "Of course it was Clare! Ruth said it was and so did Frank, and they certainly know her when they see her as well as we do." And someone else would say: "Yes, you can bet it was Clare all right." And then they would all join in asserting that there could be no mistake about its having been Clare, and that such circumstances could mean only one thing. Working indeed! People didn't take their servants to the Shelby for dinner. Certainly not all dressed up like that. There would follow insincere regrets, and somebody would say: "Poor girl, I suppose it's true enough, but what can you expect. Look at her father. And her mother, they say, would have run away if she hadn't died. Besides, Clare always had a—a—having way with her."

Precisely that! The words came to Irene as she sat there on the Drayton roof, facing Clare Kendry. "A having way." Well, Irene acknowledged, judging from her appearance and manner, Clare seemed certainly to have succeeded in having a few of the things that she wanted.

It was, Irene repeated, after the interval of the waiter, a great surprise and a very pleasant one to see Clare again after all those years, twelve at least.

"Why, Clare, you're the last person in the world I'd have expected to run into. I guess that's why I didn't know you."

Clare answered gravely: "Yes. It is twelve years. But I'm not surprised to see you, 'Rene. That is, not so very. In fact, ever since I've been here, I've more or less hoped that I should, or someone. Preferably you, though. Still, I imagine that's because I've thought of you often and often, while you—I'll wager you've never given me a thought."

It was true, of course. After the first speculations and indictments, Clare had gone completely from Irene's thoughts. And from the thoughts of others too—if their conversation was any indication of their thoughts.

Besides, Clare had never been exactly one of the group, just as she'd never been merely the janitor's daughter, but the daughter of Mr. Bob Kendry, who, it was true, was a janitor, but who also, it seemed, had been in college with some of their fathers. Just how or why he happened to be a janitor, and a very inefficient one at that, they none of them quite knew. One of Irene's brothers, who had put the question to their father, had been told: "That's something that doesn't concern you," and given him the advice to be careful not to end in the same manner as "poor Bob."

No, Irene hadn't thought of Clare Kendry. Her own life had been too crowded. So, she supposed, had the lives of other people. She defended her—their—forgetfulness. "You know how it is. Everybody's so busy. People leave, drop out, maybe for a little while there's talk about them, or questions; then, gradually they're forgotten."

"Yes, that's natural," Clare agreed. And what, she inquired, had they said of her for that little while at the beginning before they'd forgotten her altogether?

Irene looked away. She felt the telltale colour rising in her cheeks. "You can't," she evaded, "expect me to remember trifles like that over twelve years of marriages, births, deaths, and the war."

There followed that trill of notes that was Clare Kendry's laugh, small and clear and the very essence of mockery.

"Oh, 'Rene!" she cried, "of course you remember! But I won't make you tell me, because I know just as well as if I'd been there and heard every unkind word. Oh, I know, I know. Frank Danton saw me in the Shelby one night. Don't tell me he didn't broadcast that, and with embroidery. Others may have seen me at other times. I don't know. But once I met Margaret Hammer in Marshall Field's. I'd have spoken, was on the very point of doing it, but she cut me dead. My dear 'Rene, I assure you that from the way she looked through me, even I was uncertain whether I was actually there in the flesh or not. I remember it clearly, too clearly. It was that very thing which, in a way, finally decided me not to go out and see you one last time before I went away to stay. Somehow, good as all of you, the whole family, had always been to the poor forlorn child that was me, I felt I shouldn't be able to bear that. I mean if any of you, your mother or the boys or—Oh, well, I just felt I'd rather not know it if you did. And so I stayed away. Silly, I suppose. Sometimes I've been sorry I didn't go."

Irene wondered if it was tears that made Clare's eyes so luminous.

"And now 'Rene, I want to hear all about you and everybody and everything. You're married, I s'pose?"

Irene nodded.

"Yes," Clare said knowingly, "you would be. Tell me about it."

And so for an hour or more they had sat there smoking and drinking tea and filling in the gap of twelve years with talk. That is, Irene did. She told Clare about her marriage and removal to New York, about her husband, and about her two sons, who were having their first experience of being separated from their parents at a summer camp, about her mother's death, about the marriages of her two brothers. She told of the marriages, births and deaths in other families that Clare had known, opening up, for her, new vistas on the lives of old friends and acquaintances.

Clare drank it all in, these things which for so long she had wanted to know and hadn't been able to learn. She sat motionless, her bright lips slightly parted, her whole face lit by the radiance of her happy eyes. Now and then she put a question, but for the most part she was silent.

Somewhere outside, a clock struck. Brought back to the present, Irene looked down at her watch and exclaimed: "Oh, I must go, Clare!"

A moment passed during which she was the prey of uneasiness. It had suddenly occurred to her that she hadn't asked Clare anything about her own life and that she had a very definite unwillingness to do so. And she was quite well aware of the reason for that reluctance. But, she asked herself, wouldn't it, all things considered, be the kindest thing not to ask? If things with Clare were as she—as they all—had suspected, wouldn't it be more tactful to seem to forget to inquire how she had spent those twelve years?

If? It was that "if" which bothered her. It might be, it might just be, in spite of all gossip and even appearances to the contrary, that there was nothing, had been nothing, that couldn't be simply and innocently explained. Appearances, she knew now, had a way sometimes of not fitting facts, and if Clare hadn't—Well, if they had all been wrong, then certainly she ought to express some interest in what had happened to her. It would seem queer and rude if she didn't. But how was she to know? There was, she at last decided, no way; so she merely said again. "I must go, Clare."

"Please, not so soon, 'Rene," Clare begged, not moving.

Irene thought: "She's really almost too good-looking. It's hardly any wonder that she—"

"And now, 'Rene dear, that I've found you, I mean to see lots and lots of you. We're here for a month at least. Jack, that's my husband, is here on business. Poor dear! in this heat. Isn't it beastly? Come to dinner with us tonight, won't you?" And she gave Irene a curious little sidelong glance and a sly, ironical smile peeped out on her full red lips, as if she had been in the secret of the other's thoughts and was mocking her.

Irene was conscious of a sharp intake of breath, but whether it was relief or chagrin that she felt, she herself could not have told. She said hastily: "I'm afraid I can't, Clare. I'm filled up. Dinner and bridge. I'm so sorry."

"Come tomorrow instead, to tea," Clare insisted. "Then you'll see Margery—she's just ten—and Jack too, maybe, if he hasn't got an appointment or something."

From Irene came an uneasy little laugh. She had an engagement for tomorrow also and she was afraid that Clare would not believe it. Suddenly, now, that possibility disturbed her. Therefore it was with a half-vexed feeling at the sense of undeserved guilt that had come upon her that she explained that it wouldn't be possible because she wouldn't be free for tea, or for luncheon or dinner either. "And the next day's Friday when I'll be going away for the week-end, Idlewild, you know. It's quite the thing now." And then she had an inspiration.

"Clare!" she exclaimed, "why don't you come up with me? Our place is probably full up—Jim's wife has a way of collecting mobs of the most impossible people—but we can always manage to find room for one more. And you'll see absolutely everybody."

In the very moment of giving the invitation she regretted it. What a foolish, what an idiotic impulse to have given way to! She groaned inwardly as she thought of the endless explanations in which it would involve her, of the curiosity, and the talk, and the lifted eye-brows. It wasn't she assured herself, that she was a snob, that she cared greatly for the petty restrictions and distinctions with which what called itself Negro society chose to hedge itself about; but that she had a natural and deeply rooted aversion to the kind of front-page notoriety that Clare Kendry's presence in Idlewild, as her guest, would expose her to. And here she was, perversely and against all reason, inviting her.

But Clare shook her head, "Really, I'd love to, 'Rene," she said, a little mournfully. "There's nothing I'd like better. But I couldn't. I mustn't, you see. It wouldn't do at all. I'm sure you understand. I'm simply crazy to go, but I can't." The dark eyes glistened and there was a suspicion of a quaver in the husky voice. "And believe me, 'Rene, I do thank you for asking me. Don't think I've entirely forgotten just what it would mean for you if I went. That is, if you still care about such things."

All indication of tears had gone from her eyes and voice, and Irene Redfield, searching her face, had an offended feeling that behind what was now only an ivory mask lurked a scornful amusement. She looked away, at the wall far beyond Clare. Well, she deserved it, for, as she acknowledged to herself, she *was* relieved. And for the very reason at which Clare had hinted. The fact that Clare had guessed her perturbation did not, however, in any degree lessen that relief. She was annoyed at having been detected in what might seem to be an insincerity; but that was all.

The waiter came with Clare's change. Irene reminded herself that she ought immediately to go. But she didn't move.

The truth was, she was curious. There were things that she wanted to ask Clare Kendry. She wished to find out about this hazardous business of "passing," this breaking away from all that was familiar and friendly to take one's chances in another environment, not entirely strange, perhaps, but certainly not entirely friendly. What, for example, one did about background, how one accounted for oneself. And how one felt when one came into contact with other Negroes. But she couldn't. She was unable to think of a single question that in its context or its phrasing was not too frankly curious, if not actually impertinent.

As if aware of her desire and her hesitation, Clare remarked, thoughtfully:

"You know, 'Rene, I've often wondered why more coloured girls, girls like you and Margaret Hammer and Esther Dawson and—oh, lots of others—never 'passed' over. It's such a frightfully easy thing to do. If one's the type, all that's needed is a little nerve."

"What about background? Family, I mean. Surely you can't just drop down on people from nowhere and expect them to receive you with open arms, can you?"

"Almost," Clare asserted. "You'd be surprised, 'Rene, how much easier that is with white people than with us. Maybe because there are so many more of them, or maybe because they are secure and so don't have to bother. I've never quite decided."

Irene was inclined to be incredulous. "You mean that you didn't have to explain where you came from? It seems impossible."

Clare cast a glance of repressed amusement across the table at her. "As a matter of fact, I didn't. Though I suppose under any other circumstances I might have had to provide some plausible tale to account for myself. I've a good imagination, so I'm sure I could have done it quite creditably, and credibly. But it wasn't necessary. There were many aunts, you see, respectable and authentic enough for anything or anybody."

"I see. They were 'passing' too."

"No. They weren't. They were white."

"Oh!" And in the next instant it came back to Irene that she had heard this mentioned before; by her father, or, more likely, her mother. They were Bob Kendry's aunts. He had been a son of their brother's, on the left hand. A wild oat.

"They were nice old ladies," Clare explained, "very religious and as poor as church mice. That adored brother of theirs, my grandfather, got through every penny they had after he'd finished his own little bit."

Clare paused in her narrative to light another cigarette. Her smile, her expression, Irene noticed, was faintly resentful.

"Being good Christians," she continued, "when dad came to his tipsy end, they did their duty and gave me a home of sorts. I was, it was true, expected to earn my keep by doing all the housework, and most of the washing. But do you realize, 'Rene, that if it hadn't been for them, I shouldn't have had a home in the world?"

Irene's nod and little murmur were comprehensive, understanding.

Clare made a small mischievous grimace and proceeded. "Besides, to their notion, hard labour was good for me. I had Negro blood and they belonged to the generation that had written and read long articles headed: 'Will the Blacks Work?' Too, they weren't quite sure that the good God hadn't intended the sons and daughters of Ham to sweat because he had poked fun at old man Noah once when he had taken a drop too much. I remember the aunts telling me that that old drunkard had cursed Ham and his sons for all time."

Irene laughed. But Clare remained quite serious.

"It was more than a joke, I assure you, 'Rene. It was a hard life for a girl of sixteen. Still, I had a roof over my head, and food, and clothes—such as they were. And there were the Scriptures, and talks on morals and thrift and industry and the loving-kindness of the good Lord."

"Have you ever stopped to think, Clare," Irene demanded, "how much unhappiness and downright cruelty are laid to the loving-kindness of the Lord? And always by His most ardent followers, it seems."

"Have I?" Clare exclaimed. "It, they, made me what I am today. For, of course, I was determined to get away, to be a person and not a charity or a problem, or even a daughter of the indiscreet Ham. Then, too, I wanted things. I knew I wasn't bad-looking and that I could 'pass.' You can't know, 'Rene, how, when I used to go over to the south side, I used almost to hate all of you. You had all the things I wanted and never had had. It made me all the more determined to get them, and others. Do you, can you understand what I felt?"

She looked up with a pointed and appealing effect, and, evidently finding the sympathetic expression on Irene's face sufficient answer, went on. "The aunts were queer. For all their Bibles and praying and ranting about honesty, they didn't want anyone to know that their darling brother had seduced—ruined, they called it—a Negro girl. They could excuse the ruin, but they couldn't forgive the tar-brush. They forbade me to mention Negroes to the neighbours, or even to mention the south side. You may be sure that I didn't. I'll bet they were good and sorry afterwards."

She laughed and the ringing bells in her laugh had a hard metallic sound.

"When the chance to get away came, that omission was of great value to me. When Jack, a schoolboy acquaintance of some people in the neighbourhood, turned up from South America with untold gold, there was no one to tell him I was coloured, and many to tell him about the severity and the religiousness of Aunt Grace and Aunt Edna. You can guess the rest. After he came, I stopped slipping off to the south side and slipped off to meet him instead. I couldn't manage both. In the end I had no great difficulty in convincing him that I was eighteen, we went off and were married. So that's that. Nothing could have been easier."

"Yes, I do see that for you it was easy enough. By the way! I wonder why they didn't tell father that you were married. He went over to find out about you when you stopped coming over to see us. I'm sure they didn't tell him. Not that you were married."

Clare Kendry's eyes were bright with tears that didn't fall. "Oh, how lovely! To have cared enough about me to do that. The dear sweet man! Well, they couldn't tell him because they didn't know it. I took care of that, for I couldn't be sure that those consciences of theirs wouldn't begin to work on them afterwards and make them let the cat out of the bag. The old things probably thought I was living in sin, wherever I was. And it would be about what they expected."

An amused smile lit the lovely face for the smallest fraction of a second. After a little silence she said soberly: "But I'm sorry if they told your father so. That was something I hadn't counted on."

"I'm not sure that they did," Irene told her. "He didn't say so, anyway."

"He wouldn't, 'Rene. Not your father."

"Thanks, I'm sure he wouldn't."

"But you've never answered my question. Tell me, honestly, haven't you ever thought of 'passing'?"

Irene answered promptly: "No, why should I?" And so disdainful was her voice and manner that Clare's face flushed and her eyes glinted. Irene hastened to add: "You see, Clare, I've everything I want. Except, perhaps, a little more money."

At that Clare laughed, her spark of anger vanished as quickly as it had appeared. "Of course," she declared, "that's what everybody wants, just a little more money, even the people who have it. And I must say I don't blame them. Money's awfully nice to have. In fact, all things considered, I think, 'Rene, that it's even worth the price."

Irene could only shrug her shoulders. Her reason partly agreed, her instinct wholly rebelled. And she could not say why. And though conscious that if she didn't hurry away, she was going to be late to dinner, she still lingered. It was as if the woman sitting on the other side of the table, a girl that she had known, who had done this rather dangerous and, to Irene Redfield, abhorrent thing successfully and had announced herself well satisfied, had for her a fascination, strange and compelling.

Clare Kendry was still leaning back in the tall chair, her sloping shoulders against the carved top. She sat with an air of indifferent assurance, as if arranged for, desired. About her clung that dim suggestion of polite insolence with which a few women are born and which some acquire with the coming of riches or importance.

Clare, it gave Irene a little prick of satisfaction to recall, hadn't got that by passing herself off as white. She herself had always had it.

Just as she'd always had that pale gold hair, which, unsheared still, was drawn loosely back from a broad brow, partly hidden by the small close hat. Her lips, painted a brilliant geranium-red, were sweet and sensitive and a little obstinate. A tempting mouth. The face across the forehead and cheeks was a trifle too wide, but the ivory skin had a peculiar soft lustre. And the eyes were magnificent! Dark, sometimes absolutely black, always luminous, and set in long, black lashes. Arresting eyes, slow and mesmeric, and with, for all their warmth, something withdrawn and secret about them.

Ah! Surely! They were Negro eyes! Mysterious and concealing. And set in that ivory face under that bright hair, there was about them something exotic.

Yes, Clare Kendry's loveliness was absolute, beyond challenge, thanks to those eyes which her grandmother and later her mother and father had given her.

Into those eyes there came a smile and over Irene the sense of being petted and caressed. She smiled back.

"Maybe," Clare suggested, "you can come Monday, if you're back. Or, if you're not, then Tuesday."

With a small regretful sigh, Irene informed Clare that she was afraid she wouldn't be back by Monday and that she was sure she had dozens of things for Tuesday, and that she was leaving Wednesday. It might be, however, that she could get out of something Tuesday.

"Oh, do try. Do put somebody else off. The others can see you any time, while I—Why, I may never see you again! Think of that, 'Rene! You'll have to come. You'll simply have to! I'll never forgive you if you don't."

At that moment it seemed a dreadful thing to think of never seeing Clare Kendry again. Standing there under the appeal, the caress, of her eyes, Irene had the desire, the hope, that this parting wouldn't be the last.

"I'll try, Clare," she promised gently. "I'll call you—or will you call me?"

"I think, perhaps, I'd better call you. Your father's in the book, I know, and the address is the same. Sixty-four eighteen. Some memory, what? Now remember, I'm going to expect you. You've got to be able to come."

Again that peculiar mellowing smile.

"I'll do my best, Clare."

Irene gathered up her gloves and bag. They stood up. She put out her hand. Clare took it and held it.

"It has been nice seeing you again, Clare. How pleased and glad father'll be to hear about you!"

"Until Tuesday, then," Clare Kendry replied. "I'll spend every minute of the time from now on looking forward to seeing you again. Good-bye, 'Rene dear. My love to your father, and this kiss for him."

The sun had gone from overhead, but the streets were still like fiery furnaces. The languid breeze was still hot. And the scurrying people looked even more wilted than before Irene had fled from their contact.

Crossing the avenue in the heat, far from the coolness of the Drayton's roof, away from the seduction of Clare Kendry's smile, she was aware of a sense of irritation with herself because she had been pleased and a little flattered at the other's obvious gladness at their meeting.

With her perspiring progress homeward this irritation grew, and she began to wonder just what had possessed her to make her promise to find time, in the crowded days that remained of her visit, to spend another afternoon with a woman whose life had so definitely and deliberately diverged from hers; and whom, as had been pointed out, she might never see again.

Why in the world had she made such a promise?

As she went up the steps to her father's house, thinking with what interest and amazement he would listen to her story of the afternoon's encounter, it came to her that Clare had omitted to mention her marriage name. She had referred to her husband as Jack. That was all. Had that, Irene asked herself, been intentional?

Clare had only to pick up the telephone to communicate with her, or to drop her a card, or to jump into a taxi. But she couldn't reach Clare in any way. Nor could anyone else to whom she might speak of their meeting.

"As if I should!"

Her key turned in the lock. She went in. Her father, it seemed, hadn't come in yet.

Irene decided that she wouldn't, after all, say anything to him about Clare Kendry. She had, she told herself, no inclination to speak of a person who held so low an opinion of her loyalty, or her discretion. And certainly she had no desire or intention of making the slightest effort about Tuesday. Nor any other day for that matter.

She was through with Clare Kendry.

1929

George Samuel Schuyler 1895–1977

Born in Providence, Rhode Island, Schuyler received a public school education in Syracuse, New York, before enlisting in the army at age 17. During World War I, he produced satirical sketches for *The Service,* a military publication. When he mustered out as a first lieutenant in 1919, he began his long career as a professional journalist and wrote satirical columns for a series of black newspapers, including *The Messenger* (New York City) and the *Pittsburgh Courier,* the publication with which he was longest associated. At the same time he published essays, sketches, and satirical pieces in influential magazines such as *The Nation, The American Mercury,* and *Reader's Digest.* Schuyler also traveled overseas, especially to West Africa and Latin America, as a foreign correspondent. In his later years he moved away from his earlier socialistic bent to become a conservative anti-Communist, joining the John Birch Society and writing for William Loeb's *Manchester* (New Hampshire) *Union Leader.*

Best known for the stinging satires he published in the 1920s and 1930s, he ridiculed the "colorphobia" of both black and white Americans in articles such as "The Negro-Art Hokum" (1926), "Blessed Are the Sons of Ham" (1927), and "Our White Folks" (1927). *Black No More,* the first full-length satiric novel by a black American, hypothesizes an America in which a black doctor discovers a formula that makes blacks white. Chaos results as whites try to become as black as possible to distinguish themselves from their (formerly) black brethren. Schuyler's next novel, *Slaves Today,* savagely attacked the slave trade in Liberia in the 1920s. His autobiographical *Black and Conservative,* besides containing a wealth of information on just about every political, social, literary, and journalistic black personality of the first half of the century, is a shrill anti-Communist tract.

Because he maintained there was essentially no difference between black and white Americans except in color ("the Aframerican is merely a lampblacked Anglo-Saxon," he once wrote), and because he ridiculed black leaders from W.E.B. Du Bois to Martin Luther King, Schuyler was labeled in the heat of the 1960s as an "assimilationist" or "Uncle Tom" who thought "white" and sold out to the establishment. It was an unfair assessment; during his long career Schuyler demonstrated pride in his black heritage—a fact his critics too often ignored, mistaking his iconoclastic stance as race hatred.

Of course Schuyler was perversely proud of his reputation as a shatterer of idols. Such an attitude placed him in the company of several journalistic satirists of this century—Ambrose Bierce, for example, and H. L. Mencken, who befriended him and published some of his articles in the *American Mercury.* The NAACP's newspaper, *The Crisis*—in which he had once been praised by its founder, W.E.B. Du Bois—lamented in 1965 that Schuyler had become "a veteran dissenter and incurable iconoclast" who "dips his pen in his ever-handy bottle of acid." "The Negro Art-Hokum" appeared in the *Nation* in 1926 and is noteworthy because it constitutes yet another of Schuyler's sarcastic assaults on claims that there exist fundamental differences between blacks and whites. The essay also elicted from Langston Hughes one of the most important critical statements on black art of the time—"The Negro Artist and the Racial Mountain."

"Our Greatest Gift to America" was first published in *Ebony and Topaz* in 1927 and reprinted in V. F. Calverton's *Anthology of American Negro Literature* (1929). As a period piece, Schuyler's essay presents a dismal view of the racial situation in the 1920s. Its ironic, even savage, tone makes it uncomfortable reading. Slashing Juvenalian satire usually is. Yet underlying the attack is a more optimistic appeal to reason. In this as in his other works Schuyler seems to say, "If Americans would only realize how absurd their colorphobia is, then perhaps they would put it aside and behave like human beings." It is a message as relevant today as it was in 1927.

During the 1930s, Schuyler published a number of non-satirical pieces, some of them pseudonymously. These included eight African novellas, which were serialized in the *Pittsburgh Courier.* Two of them were innovative pieces of science fiction, "The Black Internationale" and "Black Empire," and were published together in 1991 as *Black Empire.* Two more novellas, a murder mystery ("The Ethiopian Murder Mystery"), and an international adventure story ("Revolt in Ethiopia") were collected under the title *Ethiopian Stories* in 1994.

Michael W. Peplow

PRIMARY WORKS

Black No More, 1931; *Slaves Today,* 1931; *Fifty Years of Progress in Negro Journalism,* 1950; *Black and Conservative,* 1966; *Black Empire,* ed., Robert A. Hill and R. Kent Rasmussen, 1991; *Ethiopian Stories,* ed. with an introduction by Robert A. Hill, 1994.

Our Greatest Gift to America

On divers occasions some eloquent Ethiop[1] arises to tell this enlightened nation about the marvelous contributions of his people to our incomparable civilization. With glib tongue or trenchant pen, he starts from the arrival of the nineteen unfortunate dinges at Jamestown in 1619,[2] or perhaps with the coming of the celebrated Columbus to these sacred shores with his Negro mate in 1492,[3] and traces the multiple gifts of the black brethren to the present day. He will tell us of the vast amount of cotton picked by the Negro, of the hundreds of roads and levees the black laborers have constructed, of the miles of floors Negro women have scrubbed, and the acres of clothes they have washed, of the numerous wars in which, for some unknown reason, the Sambo participated, of the dances and cookery he invented, or of the spirituals and work songs composed by the sons of Ham and given to a none too grateful nation. The more erudite of these self-appointed spokesmen of the race will even go back to the Garden of Eden, the walls of Babylon, the pyramids of Egypt and the palaces of Ethiopia by way of introduction and during their prefatory remarks, they will not fail, often, to claim for the Negro race every person of importance that has ever resided on the face of the earth. Ending with a forceful and fervent plea for justice, equality, righteousness, humanitarianism and other such things conspicuous in the world by their absence, they close amid a storm of applause from their sable auditors—and watch the collection plate.

This sort of thing has been going on regularly for the last century. No Negro meeting is a success without one or more such encouraging addresses, and no Negro publication that fails to carry one such article in almost every issue is considered worthy of purchase. So general has the practice become that even white audiences and magazines are no longer immune. It has become not unusual in the past few years for the Tired Society Woman's Club of Keokuk, Iowa, or the Delicatessen Proprietors' Chamber of Commerce or the Hot Dog Venders' Social Club to have literary afternoons devoted exclusively to the subject of the lowly smoke. On such occasions there will be some notable Aframerican speakers as Prof. Hambone of Moronia Institute[4] or Dr. Lampblack[5] of the Federal Society for the Exploitation of Lynching, who will

[1]Schuyler employs a number of racial epithets in vogue in the 1920s: for blacks, Ethiop, dinges, Sambo (see the children's story, "Little Black Sambo"), sons of Ham, shines, blackamoors, smokes, spades, coons, darkies, zigaboos; for whites, crackers, peckerwoods, the buckra majority, rednecks, ofays, etc.

[2]*The Chronological History of the Negro in America* (hereafter CHNA) quotes John Rolfe's journal entry for August 20: "there came in a Dutch man-of-warre that sold us 20 negars." These were indentured servants.

[3]The CHNA cites the legend that one Pedro Alonzo Nino, a black man, was part of Columbus's crew.

[4]Moronia Institute is Schuyler's jab at Tuskegee Institute, founded by Booker T. Washington and headed in the 1920s by Robert Russa Moton.

[5]Probably a reference to Dr. W.E.B. Du Bois, a founding member of the NAACP and editor of its periodical, *The Crisis.* The NAACP organized anti-lynching conferences and published annual surveys of lynchings in the United States. Du Bois not only published numerous racial uplift articles in *The Crisis* but also wrote *The Gift of Black Folk: Negroes in the Making of America* (1924).

eloquently hold forth for the better part of an hour on the blackamoor's gifts to the Great Republic and why, therefore, he should not be kept down. Following him there will usually be a soulful rendition by the Charcoal Singers of their selected repertoire of genuine spirituals and then, mayhap, one of the younger Negro poets will recite one of his inspiring verses anent[6] a ragged black prostitute gnawing out her soul in the dismal shadows of Hog Maw Alley.[7]

It was not so many years ago that Negro writers used to chew their fingernails and tear as much of their hair as they could get hold of because the adamantine editors of white magazines and journals invariably returned unread their impassioned manuscripts in which they sought to tell how valuable the Aframerican had always been to his country and what a dirty shame it was to incinerate a spade without benefit of jury. Not so today, my friends. The swarms of Negro hacks and their more learned associates have at last come into their own. They have ridden into popular demand on the waves of jazz music, the Charleston, Mammy Songs and the ubiquitous, if intricate, Black Bottom. Pick up almost any of the better class periodicals of national note nowadays and you are almost sure to find a lengthy paper by some sable literatus on the Negro's gifts to America, on his amazing progress in becoming just like other Americans in habit and thought, or on the horrible injustice of Jim Crow[8] cars. The cracker editors are paying generously for the stuff (which is more than the Negro editors did in the old days) and, as a result, the black scribblers, along with the race orators, are now wallowing in the luxury of four-room apartments, expensive radios, Chickering pianos, Bond Street habiliments, canvas-back duck, pre-war Scotch and high yellow mistresses.

All of which is very well and good. It is only natural that the peckerwoods, having become bored to death with their uninteresting lives, should turn to the crows for inspiration and entertainment. It is probably part of their widespread rationalization of the urge they possess to mix with the virile blacks. One marvels, however, that the principal contribution of our zigaboos to the nation has been entirely overlooked by our dusky literati and peripatetic platform prancers. None of them, apparently, has ever thought of it. While they have been ransacking their brains and the shelves of the public libraries for new Negro gifts of which to inform their eager listeners at so much per word or per engagement, they have ignored the principal gift sprawling everywhere about them. They had but to lift their eyes from the pages of their musty tome and glance around. But they didn't.

"And what," I can hear these propagandists feverishly inquiring with poised fountain pens and notebooks, "is this unchronicled contribution to the worth of our nation?" Well, I am not unwilling to divulge this "secret" that has been all too apparent to the observing. And though the brownish intelligentsia are now able to pay for the information—and probably willing to do so—I modestly ask nothing save perhaps a quart of decent rye or possibly one of the numerous medals shoveled out

[6]About.

[7]A probable reference to the poet Claude McKay's sentimental poem, "Young Prostitute."

[8]Any of a series of laws enforcing segregated public facilities. See Schuyler's "Traveling Jim Crow" which was published in *The American Mercury* (August 1930) and condensed in *Reader's Digest* (August 1930).

every year to deserving coons. Hence, like all of the others, I now arise, flick a speck off my dinner jacket, adjust my horn-rimmed nose glasses and, striking an attitude, declaim the magic word: Flattery!

Yes, folks, the greatest gift we have made to America is flattery. Flattery, if you please, of the buckra majority; inflation of the racial ego of the dominant group by our mere proximity, by our actions and by our aspirations. "How come?" I am belligerently and skeptically quizzed, and very indulgently I elucidate. Imitation, someone has said, is the sincerest flattery. It is quite human to be pleased and feel very important when we are aped and imitated. Consider how we Negroes shove out our chests when an article appears in an enterprising darky newspaper from the pen of some prominent African chief saying that his dingy colleagues on the Dark Continent look to their American brethren, with their amazing progress, for inspiration. How sweet is flattery, the mother of pride. And pride, we have been told, is absolutely essential to progress and achievement. If all of this be true of the dark American, how much truer must it be of the pink American? By constant exposure to his energetic propagandists in press, on platform and in pulpit, the colored brother has forged ahead—to borrow an expression from the *Uplift*—until he can now eat with Rogers silver off Haviland china, sprawl on overstuffed couches and read spicy literature under the glow of ornate floor lamps, while the strains of "Beer Bucket Blues" are wafted over the radio. This is generally known as progress. Now, if the downtrodden Negro under the influence of his flattering propagandists has been able to attain such heights of material well-being, is it any wonder that the noble rednecks have leaped so much farther up the scale of living when surrounded by millions of black flatterers, both mute and vocal? Most certainly not.

Look, for example, at Isadore Shankersoff. By hook or by crook (probably the latter) he grabbed off enough coin of his native land to pay his passage to America. In Russia he was a nobody—hoofed by everybody—the mudsill of society. Quite naturally his inferiority complex was Brobdingnagian. Arriving under the shadow of the Statue of Liberty, he is still Isadore Shankersoff, the prey of sharpers and cheap grafters, but now he has moved considerably higher in the social scale. Though remaining mentally adolescent, he is no longer at the bottom; he is a white man! Over night he has become a member of the superior race. Ellis Island marked his metamorphosis. For the first time in his life he is better than somebody. Without the presence of the blackamoor in these wonderfully United States, he would still know himself for the thick-pated underling that he is; but how can he go on believing that when America is screaming to him on every hand that he is a white man and, as such, entitled to certain rights and privileges forbidden to Negro scientists, artists, clergymen, journalists and merchants. One can understand why Isadore walks with firmer tread.

Or glance at Cyrus Leviticus Dumbell. He is of Anglo-Saxon stock that is so old that it has very largely gone to seed. In the fastnesses of the Blue Ridge Mountains his racial strain has been safely preserved from pollution by black and red men, for over two hundred years. Thus he is a stalwart fellow untouched by thrift or education. Cy finally tires of the bushes and descends to one of the nearby towns. There he finds employment in a mill on a twelve-hour shift. The company paternalistically furnishes him everything he needs and thoughtfully deducts the cost regularly from his slender pay envelope, leaving him about two dollars for corn liquor and moving pictures. Cy has never had cause to think himself of any particular importance in the scheme of things, but his fellow workers tell him differently. He is a white man, they say, and therefore divinely appointed to "keep the nigger down." He must, they insist, protect white womanhood and preserve white supremacy. This country, he learns, is a white man's country and, although he owns none of it, the information strikes him not unpleasantly. Shortly he scrapes together ten dollars, buys Klan[9] regalia, and is soon engaged in attending midnight meetings, burning crosses, repeating ritual from the Kloran, flogging erring white womanhood for the greater purity of Anglo-Saxondom, and keeping vigilantly on the lookout for uppish and offensive zigaboos to lynch. Like the ancient Greeks and Romans, he now believes himself superior to everybody different from him. Nor does the presence of Jim Crow institutions on every hand contribute anything toward lessening that belief. Whatever his troubles may be, he has learned from his colleagues and the politicians to blame it all on the dark folks, who are, he is now positive, without exception his inferiors.

Think, also, of demure little Dorothy Dunce. For twelve years she attended the palatial public school. Now, at eighteen, having graduated, she is about to apply her Latin, Greek, English literature, ancient history, geometry and botany to her everyday work as packer in a spaghetti factory. When she was very young, before she entered the kindergarten, her indulgent parents used to scare her by issuing a solemn warning that a big, black nigger would kidnap her if she wasn't a good little girl. Now that she has had American popular education turned loose upon her, she naturally believes differently: *i.e.,* that every big, burly, black nigger she meets on a dark street is ready to relieve her by force of what remains of her virtue. A value is placed upon her that she would not have in Roumania, Scotland, Denmark, or Montenegro. She is now a member of that exalted aggregation known as pure, white womanhood. She is also confident of her general superiority because education has taught her that Negroes are inferior, immoral, diseased, lazy, unprogressive, ugly, odoriferous, and should be firmly kept in their place at the bottom of the social and industrial scale. Quite naturally she swells with race pride for, no matter how low she falls, she will always be a white woman.

But enough of such examples. It is fairly well established, I think, that our presence in the Great Republic has been of incalculable psychological value to the masses of white citizens. Descendants of convicts, serfs and half-wits with the rest have been buoyed up and greatly exalted by being constantly assured of their superiority to all other races and their equality with each other. On the stages of a thousand music halls, they have had their vanity tickled by blackface performers parading the idiocies of mythical black roustabouts and rustics. Between belly-cracking guffaws they have secretly congratulated themselves on the fact that they are not like these buffoons. Their books and magazines have told them, or insinuated, that morality, beauty, refinement and culture are restricted to Caucasians. On every hand they have seen smokes endeavoring to change from black to white and from kinky hair to straight by means of deleterious chemicals; and constantly they hear the Negroes

[9]The Ku Klux Klan was quite active during the 1920s (see the CHNA and Schuyler's own "Scripture for Lynchers" in *The Crisis* [January 1935] and his savage—and hilarious—novel, *Black No More* [1931]). The Kloran was the Klan's "bible."

urging each other to do this and that "like white folks." Nor do the crackers fail to observe, either, that pink epidermis is as highly treasured among blacks as in Nordic America and that the most devastating charge that one Negro can make against another is that "he acts just like a nigger." Anything excellent they hear labeled by the race conscious Negroes as "like white folks," nor is it unusual for them, while loitering in the Negro ghetto, to hear black women compared to Fords, mulatto women to Cadillacs and white women to Packards. With so much flattery it is no wonder that the Caucasians have a very high opinion of themselves and attempt to live up to the lofty niche in which the Negroes have placed them. We should not marvel that every white elevator operator, school teacher and bricklayer identifies himself with Shakespeare, Julius Caesar, Napoleon, Newton, Edison, Wagner, Tennyson, and Rembrandt as creators of this great civilization. As a result we have our American society, where everybody who sports a pink color believes himself to be the equal of all other whites by virtue of his lack of skin pigmentation and his classic Caucasian features.

It is not surprising, then, that democracy has worked better in this country than elsewhere. This belief in the equality of all white folks—making skin color the gauge of worth and the measure of citizenship rights—has caused the lowest to strive to become among the highest. Because of this great ferment, America has become the Utopia of the material world, the land of hope and opportunity. Without the transplanted African in their midst to bolster up the illusion, America would have unquestionably been a very different place; but instead the shine has served as a mudsill upon which all white people alike can stand and reach toward the stars. I submit that here is the gift par excellence of the Negro to America. To spur ten times our number on to great heights of achievement; to spare the nation the enervating presence of a destructive social caste system, such as exists elsewhere, by substituting a color caste system that rouses the hope and pride of teeming millions of ofays—this indeed is a gift of which we can well be proud.

1927

The Negro-Art Hokum

Negro art "made in America" is as non-existent as the widely advertised profundity of Cal Coolidge, the "seven years of progress" of Mayor Hylan, or the reported sophistication of New Yorkers. Negro art there has been, is, and will be among the numerous black nations of Africa; but to suggest the possibility of any such development among the ten million colored people in this republic is self-evident foolishness. Eager apostles from Greenwich Village, Harlem, and environs proclaimed a great renaissance of Negro art just around the corner waiting to be ushered on the scene by those whose hobby is taking races, nations, peoples, and movements under their wing. New art forms expressing the "peculiar" psychology of the Negro were about to flood the market. In short, the art of Homo Africanus was about to electrify the waiting world. Skeptics patiently waited. They still wait.

True, from dark-skinned sources have come those slave songs based on Protestant hymns and Biblical texts known as the spirituals, work songs and secular songs of sorrow and tough luck known as the blues, that outgrowth of ragtime known as jazz (in the development of which whites have assisted), and the Charleston, an eccentric dance invented by the gamins around the public market-place in Charleston, S.C. No one can or does deny this. But these are contributions of a caste in a certain section of the country. They are foreign to Northern Negroes, West Indian Negroes, and African Negroes. They are no more expressive or characteristic of the Negro race than the music and dancing of the Appalachian highlanders or the Dalmatian peasantry are expressive or characteristic of the Caucasian race. If one wishes to speak of the musical contributions of the peasantry of the South, very well. Any group under similar circumstances would have produced something similar. It is merely a coincidence that this peasant class happens to be of a darker hue than the other inhabitants of the land. One recalls the remarkable likeness of the minor strains of the Russian mujiks to those of the Southern Negro.

As for the literature, painting, and sculpture of Aframericans—such as there is—it is identical in kind with the literature, painting, and sculpture of white Americans: that is, it shows more or less evidence of European influence. In the field of drama little if any merit has been written by and about Negroes that could not have been written by whites. The dean of the Aframerican literati is W.E.B. Du Bois, a product of Harvard and German universities; the foremost Aframerican sculptor is Meta Warwick Fuller, a graduate of leading American art schools and former student of Rodin; while the most noted Aframerican painter, Henry Ossawa Tanner, is dean of American painters in Paris and has been decorated by the French Government. Now the work of these artists is no more "expressive of the Negro soul"—as the gushers put it—than are the scribblings of Octavus Cohen or Hugh Wiley.

This, of course, is easily understood if one stops to realize that the Aframerican is merely a lampblacked Anglo-Saxon. If the European immigrant after two or three generations of exposure to our schools, politics, advertising, moral crusades, and restaurants becomes indistinguishable from the mass of Americans of the older stock (despite the influence of the foreign-language press), how much truer must it be of the sons of Ham who have been subjected to what the uplifters call Americanism for the last three hundred years. Aside from his color, which ranges from very dark brown to pink, your American Negro is just plain American. Negroes and whites from the same localities in this country talk, think, and act about the same. Because a few writers with a paucity of themes have seized upon imbecilities of the Negro rustics and clowns and palmed them off as authentic and characteristic Aframerican behavior, the common notion that the black American is so "different" from his white neighbor has gained wide currency. The mere mention of the word "Negro" conjures up in the average white American's mind a composite stereotype of Bert Williams, Aunt Jemima, Uncle Tom, Jack Johnson, Florian Slappey, and the various monstrosities scrawled by the cartoonists. Your average Aframerican no more resembles this stereotype than the average American resembles a composite of Andy Gump, Jim Jeffries, and a cartoon by Rube Goldberg.

Again, the Aframerican is subject to the same economic and social forces that mold the actions and thoughts of the white Americans. He is not living in a different world as some whites and a few Negroes would have us believe. When the jangling of his Connecticut alarm clock gets him out of his Grand Rapids bed to a breakfast similar to that eaten by his white brother across the street; when he toils at the same or similar work in mills, mines, factories, and commerce alongside the descendants of Spartacus, Robin Hood, and Erik the Red; when he wears similar clothing and speaks the same language with the same degree of perfection; when he reads the same Bible and belongs to the Baptist, Methodist, Episcopal, or Catholic church; when his fraternal affiliations also include the Elks, Masons, and Knights of Pythias; when he gets the same or similar schooling, lives in the same kind of houses, owns the same makes of cars (or rides in them), and nightly sees the same Hollywood version of life on the screen; when he smokes the same brands of tobacco and avidly peruses the same puerile periodicals; in short, when he responds to the same political, social, moral, and economic stimuli in precisely the same manner as his white neighbor, it is sheer nonsense to talk about "racial differences" as between the American black man and the American white man. Glance over a Negro newspaper (it is printed in good Americanese) and you will find the usual quota of crime news, scandal, personals, and uplift to be found in the average white newspaper—which, by the way, is more widely read by the Negroes than is the Negro press. In order to satisfy the cravings of an inferiority complex engendered by the colorphobia of the mob, the readers of the Negro newspapers are given a slight dash of racialistic seasoning. In the homes of the black and white Americans of the same cultural and economic level one finds similar furniture, literature, and conversation. How, then, can the black American be expected to produce art and literature dissimilar to that of the white American?

Consider Coleridge-Taylor, Edward Wilmot Blyden, and Claude McKay, the Englishmen; Pushkin, the Russian; Bridgewater, the Pole; Antar, the Arabian; Latino, the Spaniard; Dumas, *père* and *fils,* the Frenchmen; and Paul Laurence Dunbar, Charles W. Chesnutt, and James Weldon Johnson, the Americans. All Negroes; yet their work shows the impress of nationality rather than race. They all reveal the psychology and culture of their environment—their color is incidental. Why should Negro artists of America vary from the national artistic norm when Negro artists in other countries have not done so? If we can foresee what kind of white citizens will inhabit this neck of the woods in the next generation by studying the sort of education and environment the children are exposed to now, it should not be difficult to reason that the adults of today are what they are because of the education and environment they were exposed to a generation ago. And that education and environment were about the same for blacks and whites. One contemplates the popularity of the Negro-art hokum and murmurs, "How come?"

This nonsense is probably the last stand of the old myth palmed off by Negrophobists for all these many years, and recently rehashed by the sainted Harding, that there are "fundamental, eternal, and inescapable differences" between white and black Americans. That there are Negroes who will lend this myth a helping hand need occasion no surprise. It has been broadcast all over the world by the vociferous scions of slaveholders, "scientists" like Madison Grant and Lothrop Stoddard, and the patriots who flood the treasury of the Ku Klux Klan; and is believed, even today, by the majority of free, white citizens. On this baseless premise, so flattering to the white mob, that the blackamoor is inferior and fundamentally different, is erected the postulate that he must needs be peculiar; and when he attempts to portray life through the medium of art, it must of necessity be a peculiar art. While such reasoning may seem conclusive to the majority of Americans, it must be rejected with a loud guffaw by intelligent people.

1926

Blues Lyrics

Although the word "blues" referring to anxiety or sadness dates from around the sixteenth century, the music called the blues is more recent. The blues initially emerged in the 1890s, when the first generation of African Americans born after emancipation came into their majority subjected to the post-Reconstruction brand of freedom. While slaves were brutalized within a system in which they often had well-defined roles that sought to prevent much dignity or responsibility, the post-Reconstruction African American was brutalized by a more ambiguous and uncertain, but still inferior, status. The theoretical freedom created the illusion of the possibility of social and economic success, but the lack of education and economic independence, and continuing racial discrimination, was a prescription not only for failure but also for haunting self-doubt. Lacking an older generation with this same experience to consult for advice, the new generation responded by expressing their reactions in a variety of new forms, including the blues, that were recognizably rooted in the African American tradition. Although critics may disagree on the particulars of the African influence on the blues, most agree that there are certain African elements in the blues as well as the work songs and field hollers from which the blues seem to have developed. The creations of people often unable to read and write, the texts of this tradition were not written down but passed on orally. From the common hopes, fears, and language of the people, the blues singers created songs that were, in turn, passed back to the audience in a form that was both traditional and individually creative.

The folk blues songs heard around the turn of the century, by people like Howard W. Odum and W. C. Handy, mirrored the variety of stanzas as employed in the blues tradition. The text of a blues stanza might consist of one "line" (sometimes rendered as two lines on the page, divided where a singer might pause in performance) repeated exactly or approximately twice (AA) or more; one line repeated twice or three times combined with a rhyming line to complete the thought expressed in the first line (AAB or AAAB); one line sung once followed by a rhyming line sung twice (ABB); two different lines followed by a refrain (AB refrain); or a variety of other patterns. The musical performances, executed with a fluid rather than a rigid sense of measures, tended toward eight-, twelve-, or sixteen-bar stanzas most often, and the songsters or musicians who performed these blues provided the tradition from which the first generation of recorded blues singers in the 1920s drew. Inevitably, phonograph recordings influenced the nature of the blues, helping establish the AAB stanza as the predominant form, changing the often traditional, non-thematic or associative texts into more original, thematic texts, and removing the song from its original performance context in the community. The first blues recordings by African Americans were the so-called vaudeville blues of the "Jazz Age" written by people like Handy who drew on both their knowledge of the oral tradition and on professional musical training that created a more sophisticated hybrid, sometimes straining for sexual innuendo, or creating the role of the rebellious "hot mama," but reaching their pinnacle in folk blues-based performances by such greats as Bessie Smith and Ma Rainey.

There is also disagreement about the nature of the blues performer and what the blues represent. While some see the blues as autobiographical laments, others have seen them as a recounting of "species experience." In reality they can be either or both. The singers may be describing what has or might have happened to someone like them, or may be conforming the lyrics to the idea of a mythological singer created over the years. Although the blues have been rejected by many middle-class blacks as old-fashioned and self-pitying, or as signs of resignation and defeat, others have seen in them a spirit of hope, a creativity, an unwillingness to capitulate to white middle-class values, and even a defiance and revolutionary resistance.

Blues performances are intended for entertainment and deal primarily with love relationships between men and women. The often secular nature of the blues sometimes caused devout Christians to term them "devil's music," which prompted responses like those of Wright Holmes in "Alley Special." The blues have been seen as a central expression of African American spirit, providing structures, rhythms, images, themes, and characters for literary artists like Langston Hughes, Sterling A. Brown, Zora Neale Hurston, Allen Ginsberg, John Berryman, Ralph Ellison, Albert Murray, Alice Walker, Etheridge Knight, and Gayl Jones. And the blues are still being created and performed today.

Steven C. Tracy
University of Massachusetts–Amherst

PRIMARY WORKS

Paul Oliver, ed., *Early Blues Songbook;* Eric Sackheim, ed., *The Blues Line,* 1975; Jeff Titon, ed., *Downhome Blues Lyrics,* 1981; Michael Taft, *Blues Lyric Poetry: An Anthology,* 1983; Michael Taft, *Blues Lyric Poetry: A Concordance,* 1984; W.C. Handy, *Blues: An Anthology,* 1985; R. R. MacLeod, ed., *Yazoo 1–20* and *Yazoo 21–83,* 1988; *Document Blues–1,* 1993; *Document Blues–2* and *Document Blues–3,* 1995.

Blues Lyrics

Well, the blues come to Texas loping like a mule. (twice)
You take a high brown woman—man, she's hard to fool.

You can't ever tell what a woman's got on her mind.
Yes, you can't tell what a woman's got on her mind.
You might think she's crazy about you, she's leaving you all the
time.

She ain't so good looking and her teeth don't shine like pearls,
She ain't so good looking, teeth don't shine like pearls,
But that nice disposition carry that woman all through the world.

I'm going to the river, gonna take my rocker chair.
Well, I'm going to the river, carry my rocker chair.
Gonna ask that transfer boat, "Have the worried blues reached
here?"

I think I heard my good gal calling my name.
Hey, hey, good gal calling my name.
She don't call so loud, but she call so nice and plain.

I was raised in Texas, schooled in Tennessee. (twice)
Now, sugar, you can't make no fatmouth out of me.

Can't a woman act funny, quit you for another man. (twice)
She ain't gonna look at you straight, but she's always raising sand.

—Blind Lemon Jefferson

John Henry said to his captain, "A man ain't nothing but a man.
And before I let your steam drill beat me down
Die with a hammer in my hand." (twice)

When John Henry was a little boy he sit down on his father's
knee,
He pointed his hand at a piece of steel,
Said, "That gonna be the death of me, Lord, Lord, Lord!
That gonna be the death of me."

John Henry hammered in the mountain 'til the head of his
hammer catched afire.
Cryin' "Pick 'em up boys and let 'em down again,
One cool drink of water 'fore I die, die,
One cool drink of water 'fore I die."

—Traditional

Now she's the meanest woman that I've ever seen,
And when I asked for water give me gasoline.
Now, asked her for water, give me gasoline.
Lord, asked for water, give me gasoline.

—Ishmon Bracey

Which-a-way, which-a-way, do the blood Red River run?
Run from my window to the rising sun.

—Virgil Childers

I did more for you than you understand.
You can tell by the bullet holes, mama, now, here in my hand.
Baby, now, you got to reap, baby,
Just what, what you sow.

—Peetie Wheatstraw

I need plenty grease in my frying pan 'cause I don't want my meat
to burn.
You know I asked you first to get me some lard,
But it seems that you cannot learn.
You know I use plenty grease everyday,
But I ain't did no frying while you was away.
I need plenty grease in my frying pan 'cause I don't want my meat
to burn.

—Margaret Carter

I've got a disposition and a way of my own.
When my man starts kicking I let him find another home.
I get full of good liquor, walk the streets all night,
Go home and put my man out if he don't act right.
Wild women don't worry,
Wild women don't have the blues.

—Ida Cox

I got all cut to pieces, aah aah, about a man I love. (twice)
I'm gonna get that a-woman just as sure as the sky's above.

Now, when my man left me I was half dead lying in my door.
When my man left me, aah, half dead lying in my door.
I was a-suffering and groaning, "Oh daddy, please don't go."

—Bessie Tucker

When I picked you up, baby, you was beat just like a slave.
(twice)
You had one foot on a banana peeling, ooh well well, and the
other foot in the grave.

—Peetie Wheatstraw

Mama get your hatchet, kill the fly on your baby's head. (twice)
Mama get your hatchet and run here to my bed.

—Furry Lewis

Crying, sun gonna shine in my back door some day.
(Now don't you hear me talking pretty mama?) Lord,
Sun gonna shine in my back door some day.
And the wind gonna change, gonna blow my blues away.

—Tommy Johnson

I've got to keep moving, I've got to keep moving.
Blues falling down like hail, Blues falling down like hail,
Blues falling down like hail, Blues falling down like hail.
And the day keeps on 'minding me there's a hellhound on my
trail.
Hellhound on my trail, Hellhound on my trail.

—Robert Johnson

Black cat on my doorstep, black cat on my window sill. (twice)
If some black cat don't cross me, some other black cat will.

—Ma Rainey

I left my babe in Mississippi picking cotton down on her knees.
(twice)
She says, "If you get to Chicago all right, please write me a letter
if you please."

—Tommy McClennan

Poor people is like prisoners, but they just ain't got on a ball and
chain. (twice)
But the way they are faring I swear it's all the same.

—Walter Davis

You know, mama, take me out to the alley, now, mama,
Before the high water rise.
Y'all know I ain't no Christian 'cause I once have been baptized.
Know I went to church this morning, yes, and they called on me
to pray.
Well, I fell down on my knees,
On my knees, gee, I for-, forgot just what to say.

You know when I cried Lord, my father, my genius (I didn't know
what I was doing)
I said that would be to kingdom come,
I say if you got any brownskin women in heaven
Will you please send Wright Holmes one?

Listen, master, you know I ain't never been to heaven,
Oh, this black one have been told,
You know they tell me got women up there,
Women up there, gee, with their mouths all lined with gold.

—*Wright Holmes*

Early one morning when I was on my way home. (twice)
A policeman walked up and caught me by my arm.

I told him my name, and he wrote it down. (twice)
He said, "Come with me, this is your last night running
'round."

I took him at his word and didn't have nothing to
say. (twice)
I thought they would have my trial the very next day.

But they put me in jail, wouldn't give me no bond.
They put me in jail, wouldn't give me no bond.
It made me think about my peoples that's dead and gone.

On that third morning just about half past three. (twice)
They beat me and kicked me and put me through the third
degree.

They put me in the cellar, got my clothes and shoes. (twice)
That's why I'm screaming, I got the third degree blues.

—*Blind Blake*

Got the backwoods blues but I don't want to go back home.
Got the blues so bad for the place that I come from.
Gonna see my folks but it's way too far,
You ride in a dusty old Jim Crow car,
Got the backwoods blues but I don't want to go back home . . .

Gonna stay right here right where I'm at,
Where there ain't no grinnin and snatchin off my hat,
Got the backwoods blues but I don't want to go back home . . .

Yes I'm from down there and I'm proud to say,
And from down there I'm gonna stay,
Got the backwoods blues but I don't want to go back home.

—*Rosa Henderson*

I walked down the track and the stars refused to shine,
Looked like every minute I was goin to lose my mind.
Now my knees was weak, my footsteps was all I heard,
Looked like every minute I was steppin in another world.

—Charlie McCoy

I don't mind workin, captain, from sun to sun,
I don't mind workin, captain, from sun to sun,
But I want my money, captain, when pay day comes.

—Tom Dickson

Comin a time B.D. womens ain't gonna need no men.
Comin a time B.D. womens ain't going to need no men.
Oh the way they treat us is a lowdown and dirty sin.

B.D. women, you sure can't understand,
B.D. women, you sure can't understand,
They got a head like a switch engine and they walk just like a natural
man.

B.D. women, they all done learned their trade.
B.D. women, they all done learned their trade.
They can lay their jive just like a natural man.

–Lucille Bogan

Issues and Visions in Modern America

When the Puritans came to America they had a vision of a city on a hill, a sacred republic that would show the continuing force of God's promise to them and replace the security that was lost by the Fall from the Garden of Eden. Social problems, however, were not automatically answered by this vision. Yet it continued to give hope to those who felt such problems could be addressed. More complexly, the vision often determined what could be perceived as the problem, let alone its possible solutions. This same set of complexities faced Americans in the modern period as well. But the nature of the problem was generally conceded to be on a much larger scale, and there were inescapably numerous solutions that were being put forth with great feeling and skill.

The problem in modern society was perceived in many terms. For some it was a problem of scale: simply put, the difficulties in administering and governing a social collective that numbers in the tens or hundreds of millions had never been faced in previous centuries, and hardly even imagined. For others, the problem was one of legitimacy, that is, how could those who rule others lay claim to their power, especially if they could no longer claim that power by right of birth or "natural" endowment? For yet others, the problem was an old problem but it had taken on new urgency in an industrialized society: how should we distribute the wealth?

Many of the writers in this section held to visions that would have supplied solutions, so they believed, even though no writer here ever claimed it would be easy. Mike Gold felt that the claims of distributive justice—the question of who should own what and how might they justly dispose of it—were paramount. Other writers preferred to concentrate on the problem rather than the solution. Thus, LeSueur devoted her artistic energy to depicting the outrages people had to suffer when the economic system of capitalism failed to provide even a minimally just distribution of society's goods.

The 1930s in America saw many writers turn to solutions based on collectivism, whether in the form of a general commitment to socialism or of a more specific identification with the communism of the Soviet Union. These solutions were in turn harshly attacked as being against the spirit of American individualism, even identified as the work of "foreign" agents. The New Deal of President Roosevelt, set forth in the Depression years, was a form of government intervention in the market system, and so was recognized as a form of social democracy, though others insisted on attacking it as an insidiously advanced form of collectivism. These issues were debated fiercely by American citizens and American writers, too.

Generally speaking, these issues can be seen under the heading of this country's perennial struggle between the principles of unity and plurality. America's famous motto—*e pluribus unum*—suggests that unity will arise out of plurality almost automatically. But unity and plurality are both subject to various rhetorical twists and turns, most obviously when the topic turns to immigration. In a sense all Americans, except the Native Americans, are immigrants. In another sense we "naturally" honor our various populations—but if so, what then can we claim as our principle of unity? Beyond the question of immigration there is the problem of integration: not only of one race with another, but of individual with community, and region with nation. Writers in this section as various as Randolph Bourne and Mary McCarthy have faced the insoluble aspects of integrating nation and self, unity and plurality.

One way of dealing with the apparently insoluble aspects of the problem is to celebrate diversity. This approach often works well, but it also arouses the suspicion of those who distrust any attempt to blur individual identity, the tactile grit of specific individuals faced with their separate and unabstractable lives. Writers like Warren and Ransom faced this dilemma, and they generally insisted on the specific, as they contributed to the vast wealth of regional literature in America. Both, however, were very sophisticated and conversant with abstract thought. In a sense, they dealt with one of the problems of modernism that affected writers during the New Negro Renaissance: can the use of folk or mythic material in literature successfully avoid creating a limited reception for the work of art? And how can a mass audience best be addressed without limiting the writer's vision and range of reference?

Immigrant writers had similar problems, for they had to be aware of the choice between speaking only to other immigrants (many of whom were unable to read very widely in the language of the "new" country), or to people who were part of the established and conventional population. If the vision of the immigrant such as Yezierska were to insist on its authentic specificity it might very well consign itself to oblivion. But to do anything less would be to lose the self which had undergone the experience. Of course, there was the additional problem of the specific experiences of each immigrant group. Russians might see the new land quite differently from Chinese, say, and even inside any one national group there could be sharp class distinctions which would form separate frames of reference and perception.

This section is clearly a miscellany, including as it does not only regional writers and immigrant authors (popular writers and intellectuals) but also two Native American storytellers. In its inclusiveness, this unit celebrates diversity. But it rests on two shared assumptions: that the self is distinctive, and that constant and nimble exploration is required in order to reveal the particular character of the self.

Charles Molesworth
Queens College, City University of New York

Randolph Bourne 1886–1918

Randolph Bourne was one of the most intellectual voices of his generation, a social critic of considerable acuity and an analyst of American national life and culture without peer in the first two decades of the twentieth century. He was born in Bloomfield, New Jersey, a small town of the sort he was to describe with X-ray accuracy in "The Social Order in an American Town" (1913). Though his spine and face were deformed at birth, Bourne went on to find a place for himself among the leading literary and intellectual figures of the day. Like Thorstein Veblen and other left-leaning critics of American society, Bourne constantly circled around the disjunction of our ideals and our practices. He often cultivated an ironic view of life, but never succumbed to the corrosive pessimism endemic to social criticism. At Columbia College in the early 1910s, he met Charles Beard and John Dewey and began to publish essay in journals like the *Atlantic Monthly* and the *Dial.* It was with the *New Republic,* founded in 1914, and its editors and writers such as Herbert Croly and Walter Lippman, and later with the cultural magazine, *The Seven Arts,* that he came closest to finding a network of supportive friends. But in fact he often lived in a sort of emotional isolation, admired by many but frequently troubled by his inability to find a permanent position for himself without compromising his ideals. He died in 1918, a victim of the influenza epidemic that spread throughout the country after the close of the war.

Perhaps the most important chapter in Bourne's intellectual odyssey came when he broke with his mentor, John Dewey, over America's entrance into the First World War. Bourne's polemical skills stood out in sharp relief during this episode, as essays like "Twilight of Idols" (1917) exposed the weak logic of those who had to change their principles in order to justify joining the national call to arms. During this time he also wrote his most important work, an unfinished theoretical piece called "The State" (1919); this bold set of formulations served later to increase speculation about his ultimate intellectual and political influence had he lived to write more along such lines.

"Trans-National America" (1916) must be read in the context of Bourne's rejection of the war fever that was beginning to overtake various ethnic groups in America in 1915, when the cry of "preparedness" was often a code for heightening the will to fight on an international scale. But the essay is also an extremely prescient work, the most challenging rethinking of the "melting pot" metaphor produced by any twentieth-century writer. Indeed it is fair to say that even today the thinking on multiculturalism and its political and social forms has rarely gone beyond Bourne's formulations, even though he acknowledged his own "vagueness."

Bourne used the image of the cultural center to organize his article, but he urged his readers not to accept the central "melting pot" metaphor to produce a culture that would be "washed out into a tasteless, colorless fluid of uniformity." Intellectuals at this time were just beginning to see the social ramifications of assimilation, and not all who analyzed the situation were favorably disposed to the cultural values of those increasingly referred to as "hyphenated" Americans. Far from thrilled by what he called the "flotsam and jetsam of American life," with its "leering cheapness and falseness of taste and spiritual outlook," Bourne saw further into the problem than most when he claimed that "if freedom means a democratic cooperation in determining the ideals and purposes and industrial and social institutions of a country, then the immigrant has not been free."

Bourne envisioned a nation of immigrants who could "retain that distinctiveness of their native cultures" and hence be "more valuable and interesting to each other for being different." This visionary state he called by various terms, such as a "Beloved Community," marked by a cosmopolitanism that embraced various cultural points of view. He saw, like Du Bois, the necessary double consciousness of modern life, though, unlike Du Bois, he considered this a possibility rather than a burden. Like Alain Locke, he recognized that cultural struggle and enrichment could provide a way beyond the narrow bitterness of political divisiveness and economic exploitation. Education, especially one provided by the modern college and university that contained the "seeds of [an] international intellectual world of the future" would prepare immigrants for the "Beloved Community." As with many visionaries, Bourne's formulations remain both a rebuke and a challenge.

Charles Molesworth
Queens College, City University of New York

PRIMARY WORKS

The Radical Will: Selected Writings 1911–1918, ed. Olaf Hansen, 1992.

Trans-National America

No reverberatory effect of the great war has caused American public opinion more solicitude than the failure of the "melting-pot." The discovery of diverse nationalistic feelings among our great alien population has come to most people as an intense shock. It has brought out the unpleasant inconsistencies of our traditional beliefs. We have had to watch hard-hearted old Brahmins virtuously indignant at the spectacle of the immigrant refusing to be melted, while they jeer at patriots like Mary Antin who write about "our forefathers." We have had to listen to publicists who express themselves as stunned by the evidence of vigorous nationalistic and cultural movements in this country among Germans, Scandinavians, Bohemians, and Poles, while in the same breath they insist that the alien shall be forcibly assimilated to that Anglo-Saxon tradition which they unquestioningly label "American."

As the unpleasant truth has come upon us that assimilation in this country was proceeding on lines very different from those we had marked out for it, we found ourselves inclined to blame those who were thwarting our prophecies. The truth became culpable. We blamed the war, we blamed the Germans. And then we discovered with a moral shock that these movements had been making great headway before the war even began. We found that the tendency, reprehensible and paradoxical as it might be, has been for the national clusters of immigrants, as they became more and more firmly established and more and more prosperous, to cultivate more and more assiduously the literatures and cultural traditions of their homelands. Assimilation, in other words, instead of washing out the memories of Europe, made them more and more intensely real. Just as these clusters became more and more objectively American, did they become more and more German or Scandinavian or Bohemian or Polish.

To face the fact that our aliens are already strong enough to take a share in the direction of their own destiny, and that the strong cultural movements represented by the foreign press, schools, and colonies are a challenge to our facile attempts, is not, however, to admit the failure of Americanization. It is not to fear the failure of democracy. It is rather to urge us to an investigation of what Americanism may rightly mean. It is to ask ourselves whether our ideal has been broad or narrow—whether perhaps the time has not come to assert a higher ideal than the "melting-pot." Surely we cannot be certain of our spiritual democracy when, claiming to melt the nations within us to a comprehension of our free and democratic institutions, we fly into panic at the first sign of their own will and tendency. We act as if we wanted Americanization to take place only on our own terms, and not by the consent of the governed. All our elaborate machinery of settlement and school and union, of social and political naturalization, however, will move with friction just in so far as it neglects to take into account this strong and virile insistence that America shall be what the immigrant will have a hand in making it, and not what a ruling class, descendant of those British stocks which were the first permanent immigrants, decide that America shall be made. This is the condition which confronts us, and which demands a clear and general readjustment of our attitude and our ideal.

I

Mary Antin is right when she looks upon our foreign-born as the people who missed the Mayflower and came over on the first boat they could find. But she forgets that when they did come it was not upon other Mayflowers, but upon a "Maiblume," a "Fleur de Mai," a "Fior di Maggio," a "Majblomst." These people were not mere arrivals from the same family, to be welcomed as understood and long-loved, but strangers to the neighborhood, with whom a long process of settling down had to take place. For they brought with them their national and racial characters, and each new national quota had to wear slowly away the contempt with which its mere alienness got itself greeted. Each had to make its way slowly from the lowest strata of unskilled labor up to a level where it satisfied the accredited norms of social success.

We are all foreign-born or the descendants of foreign-born, and if distinctions are to be made between us they should rightly be on some other ground than indigenousness. The early colonists came over with motives no less colonial than the later. They did not come to be assimilated in an American melting-pot. They did not come to adopt the culture of the American Indian. They had not the smallest intention of "giving themselves without reservation" to the new country. They came to get freedom to live as they wanted to. They came to escape from the stifling air and chaos of the old world; they came to make their fortune in a new land. They invented no new social framework. Rather they brought over bodily the old ways to which they had been accustomed. Tightly concentrated on a hostile frontier, they were conservative beyond belief. Their pioneer daring was reserved for the objective conquest of material resources. In their folkways, in their social and political institutions, they were, like every colonial people, slavishly imitative of the mother country. So that, in spite of the "Revolution," our whole legal and political system remained more English than the English, petrified and unchanging, while in England law developed to meet the needs of the changing times.

It is just this English-American conservatism that has been our chief obstacle to social advance. We have needed the new peoples—the order of the German and Scandinavian, the turbulence of the Slav and Hun—to save us from our own stagnation. I do not mean that the illiterate Slav is now the equal of the New Englander of pure descent. He is raw material to be educated, not into a New Englander, but into a socialized American along such lines as those thirty nationalities are being educated in the amazing schools of Gary. I do not believe that this process is to be one of decades of evolution. The spectacle of Japan's sudden jump from mediaevalism to post-modernism should have destroyed that superstition. We are not dealing with individuals who are to "evolve." We are dealing with their children, who, with that education we are about to have, will start level with all of us. Let us cease to think of ideals like democracy as magical qualities inherent in certain peoples. Let us speak, not of inferior races, but of inferior civilizations. We are all to educate and to be educated. These peoples in America are in a common enterprise. It is not what we are now that concerns us, but what this plastic next generation may become in the light of a new cosmopolitan ideal.

We are not dealing with static factors, but with fluid and dynamic generations. To contrast the older and the newer immigrants and see the one class as democratically motivated by love of liberty, and the other by mere money-getting, is not to illuminate the future. To think of earlier nationalities as culturally assimilated to America, while we picture the later as a sodden and resistive mass, makes only for bitterness and misunderstanding. There may be a difference between these earlier and these later stocks, but it lies neither in motive for coming nor in strength of cultural allegiance to the homeland. The truth is that no more tenacious cultural allegiance to the mother country has been shown by any alien nation than by the ruling class of Anglo-Saxon descendants in these American States. English snobberies, English religion, English literary styles, English literary reverences and canons, English ethics, English superiorities, have been the cultural food that we have drunk in from our mothers' breasts. The distinctively American spirit—pioneer, as distinguished from the reminiscently English—that appears in Whitman and Emerson and James, has had to exist on sufferance alongside of this other cult, unconsciously belittled by our cultural makers of opinion. No country has perhaps had so great indigenous genius which had so little influence on the country's traditions and expressions. The unpopular and dreaded German-American of the present day is a beginning amateur in comparison with those foolish Anglophiles of Boston and New York and Philadelphia whose reversion to cultural type sees uncritically in England's cause the cause of Civilization, and, under the guise of ethical independence of thought, carries along European traditions which are no more "American" than the German categories themselves.

It speaks well for German-American innocence of heart or else for its lack of imagination that it has not turned the hyphen stigma into a "Tu quoque"! If there were to be any hyphens scattered about, clearly they should be affixed to those English descendants who had had centuries of time to be made American where the German had had only half a century. Most significantly has the war brought out of them this alien virus, showing them still loving English things, owing allegiance to the English Kultur, moved by English shibboleths and prejudice. It is only because it has been the ruling class in this country that bestowed the epithets that we have not heard copiously and scornfully of "hyphenated English-Americans." But even our quarrels with England have had the bad temper, the extravagance, of family quarrels. The Englishman of today nags us and dislikes us in that personal, peculiarly intimate way in which he dislikes the Australian, or as we may dislike our younger brothers. He still thinks of us incorrigibly as "colonials." America—official, controlling, literary, political America—is still, as a writer recently expressed it, "culturally speaking, a self-governing dominion of the British Empire."

The non-English American can scarcely be blamed if he sometimes thinks of the Anglo-Saxon predominance in America as little more than a predominance of priority. The Anglo-Saxon was merely the first immigrant, the first to found a colony. He has never really ceased to be the descendant of immigrants, nor has he ever succeeded in transforming that colony into a real nation, with a tenacious, richly woven fabric of native culture. Colonials from the other nations have come and settled down beside him. They found no definite native culture which should startle them out of their colonialism, and consequently they looked back to their mother country, as the earlier Anglo-Saxon immigrant was looking back to his. What has been offered the newcomer has been the chance to learn English, to become a citizen, to salute the flag. And those elements of our ruling classes who are responsible for the public schools, the settlements, all the organizations for amelioration in the cities, have every reason to be proud of the care and labor which they have devoted to absorbing the immigrant. His opportunities the immigrant has taken to gladly, with almost a pathetic eagerness to make his way in the new land without friction or disturbance. The common language has made not only for the necessary communication, but for all the amenities of life.

If freedom means the right to do pretty much as one pleases, so long as one does not interfere with others, the immigrant has found freedom, and the ruling element has been singularly liberal in its treatment of the invading hordes. But if freedom means a democratic cooperation in determining the ideals and purposes and industrial and social institutions of a country, then the immigrant has not been free, and the Anglo-Saxon element is guilty of just what every dominant race is guilty of in every European country: the imposition of its own culture upon the minority peoples. The fact that this imposition has been so mild and, indeed, semi-conscious does not alter its quality. And the war has brought out just the degree to which that purpose of "Americanizing," that is, "Anglo-Saxonizing," the immigrant has failed.

For the Anglo-Saxon now in his bitterness to turn upon the other peoples, talk about their "arrogance," scold them for not being melted in a pot which never existed, is to betray the unconscious purpose which lay at the bottom of his heart. It betrays too the possession of a racial jealousy similar to that of which he is now accusing the so-called "hyphenates." Let the Anglo-Saxon be proud enough of the heroic toil and heroic sacrifices which moulded the nation. But let him ask himself, if he had had to depend on the English descendants, where he would have been living today. To those of us who see in the exploitation of unskilled labor the strident red *leit-motif* of our civilization, the settling of the country presents a great social drama as the waves of immigration broke over it.

Let the Anglo-Saxon ask himself where he would have been if these races had not come? Let those who feel the inferiority of the non-Anglo-Saxon immigrant contemplate that region of the States which has remained the most distinctively "American," the South. Let him ask himself whether he would really like to see the foreign hordes Americanized into such an Americanization. Let him ask himself how superior this native civilization is to the great "alien" states of Wisconsin and Minnesota, where Scandinavians, Poles, and Germans have self-consciously labored to preserve their traditional culture, while being outwardly and satisfactorily American. Let him ask himself how much more wisdom, intelligence, industry and social leadership has come out of these alien states than out of all the truly American ones. The South, in fact, while this vast Northern development has gone on, still remains an English colony, stagnant and complacent, having progressed culturally scarcely beyond the early Victorian era. It is culturally sterile because it has had no advantage of cross-fertilization like the Northern states. What has happened in states such as Wisconsin and Minnesota is that strong foreign cultures have struck root in a new and fertile soil.

America has meant liberation, and German and Scandinavian political ideas and social energies have expanded to a new potency. The process has not been at all the fancied "assimilation" of the Scandinavian or Teuton. Rather it has been a process of their assimilation of us—I speak as an Anglo-Saxon. The foreign cultures have not been melted down or run together, made into some homogeneous Americanism, but have remained distinct but cooperating to the greater glory and benefit, not only of themselves but of all the native "Americanism" around them.

What we emphatically do not want is that these distinctive qualities should be washed out into a tasteless, colorless fluid of uniformity. Already we have far too much of this insipidity—masses of people who are cultural half-breeds, neither assimilated Anglo-Saxons nor nationals of another culture. Each national colony in this country seems to retain in its foreign press, its vernacular literature, its schools, its intellectual and patriotic leaders, a central cultural nucleus. From this nucleus the colony extends out by imperceptible gradations to a fringe where national characteristics are all but lost. Our cities are filled with these half-breeds who retain their foreign names but have lost the foreign savor. This does not mean that they have actually been changed into New Englanders or Middle Westerners. It does not mean that they have been really Americanized. It means that, letting slip from them whatever native culture they had, they have substituted for it only the most rudimentary American—the American culture of the cheap newspaper, the "movies," the popular song, the ubiquitous automobile. The unthinking who survey this class call them assimilated, Americanized. The great American public school has done its work. With these people our institutions are safe. We may thrill with dread at the aggressive hyphenate, but this tame flabbiness is accepted as Americanization. The same moulders of opinion whose ideal is to melt the different races into Anglo-Saxon gold hail this poor product as the satisfying result of their alchemy.

Yet a truer cultural sense would have told us that it is not the self-conscious cultural nuclei that sap at our American life, but these fringes. It is not the Jew who sticks proudly to the faith of his fathers and boasts of that venerable culture of his who is dangerous to America, but the Jew who has lost the Jewish fire and become a mere elementary, grasping animal. It is not the Bohemian who supports the Bohemian schools in Chicago whose influence is sinister, but the Bohemian who has made money and has got into ward politics. Just so surely as we tend to disintegrate these nuclei of nationalistic culture do we tend to create hordes of men and women without a spiritual country, cultural outlaws, without taste, without standards but those of the mob. We sentence them to live on the most rudimentary planes of American life. The influences at the centre of the nuclei are centripetal. They make for the intelligence and the social values which mean an enhancement of life. And just because the foreign-born retains this expressiveness he is likely to be a better citizen of the American community. The influences at the fringe, however, are centrifugal, anarchical. They make for detached fragments of peoples. Those who came to find liberty achieve only license. They become the flotsam and jetsam of American life, the downward undertow of our civilization with its leering cheapness and falseness of taste and spiritual outlook, the absence of mind and sincere feeling which we see in our slovenly towns, our vapid moving pictures, our popular novels, and in the vacuous faces of the crowds on the city street. This is the cultural wreckage of our time, and it is from the fringes of the Anglo-Saxon as well as the other stocks that it falls. America has as yet no impelling integrating force. It makes too easily for this detritus of cultures. In our loose, free country, no constraining national purpose, no tenacious folk-tradition and folk-style hold the people to a line.

The war has shown us that not in any magical formula will this purpose be found. No intense nationalism of the European plan can be ours. But do we not begin to see a new and more adventurous ideal? Do we not see how the national colonies in America, deriving power from the deep cultural heart of Europe and yet living here in mutual toleration, freed from the age-long tangles of races, creeds, and dynasties, may work out a federated ideal? America is transplanted Europe, but a Europe that has not been disintegrated and scattered in the transplanting as in some Dispersion. Its colonies live here inextricably mingled, yet not homogeneous. They merge but they do not fuse.

America is a unique sociological fabric, and it bespeaks poverty of imagination not to be thrilled at the incalculable potentialities of so novel a union of men. To seek no other goal than the weary old nationalism—belligerent, exclusive, inbreeding, the poison of which we are witnessing now in Europe—is to make patriotism a hollow sham, and to declare that, in spite of our boastings, America must ever be a follower and not a leader of nations.

II

If we come to find this point of view plausible, we shall have to give up the search for our native "American" culture. With the exception of the South and that New England which, like the Red Indian, seems to be passing into solemn oblivion, there is no distinctively American culture. It is apparently our lot rather to be a federation of cultures. This we have been for half a century, and the war has made it ever more evident that this is what we are destined to remain. This will not mean, however, that there are not expressions of indigenous genius that could not have sprung from any other soil. Music, poetry, philosophy, have been singularly fertile and new. Strangely enough, American genius has flared forth just in those directions which are least understanded [*sic*] of the people. If the American note is bigness, action, the objective as contrasted with the reflective life, where is the epic expression of this spirit? Our drama and our fiction, the peculiar fields for the expression of action and objectivity, are somehow exactly the fields of the spirit which remain poor and mediocre. American materialism is in some way inhibited from getting into impressive artistic form its own energy with which it bursts. Nor is it any better in architecture, the least romantic and subjective of all the arts. We are inarticulate of the very values which we profess to idealize. But in the finer forms—music, verse, the essay, philosophy—the American genius puts forth work equal to any of its contemporaries. Just in so far as our American genius has expressed the pioneer spirit, the adventurous, forward-looking drive of a colonial empire, is it representative of that whole America of the many races and peoples, and not of any partial or traditional enthusiasm. And only as that pioneer note is sounded can we really speak of the American culture. As long as we thought of Americanism in terms of the "melting-pot," our American cultural tradition lay in the past. It was something to which the new Americans were to be moulded. In the light of our changing ideal of Americanism, we must perpetrate the paradox that our American cultural tradition lies in the future. It will be what we all together make out of this incomparable opportunity of attacking the future with a new key.

Whatever American nationalism turns out to be, it is certain to become something utterly different from the nationalisms of twentieth-century Europe. This wave of reactionary enthusiasm to play the orthodox nationalistic game which is passing over the country is scarcely vital enough to last. We cannot swagger and thrill to the same national self-feeling. We must give new edges to our pride. We must be content to avoid the unnumbered woes that national patriotism has brought in Europe, and that fiercely heightened pride and self-consciousness. Alluring as this is, we must allow our imaginations to transcend this scarcely veiled belligerency. We can be serenely too proud to fight if our pride embraces the creative forces of civilization which armed contest nullifies. We can be too proud to fight if our code of honor transcends that of the schoolboy on the playground surrounded by his jeering mates. Our honor must be positive and creative, and not the mere jealous and negative protectiveness against metaphysical violations of our technical rights. When the doctrine is put forth that in one American flows the mystic blood of all our country's sacred honor, freedom, and prosperity, so that an injury to him is to be the signal for turning our whole nation into that clan-feud of horror and reprisal which would be war, then we find ourselves back among the musty schoolmen of the Middle Ages, and not in any pragmatic and realistic America of the twentieth century.

We should hold our gaze to what America has done, not what mediaeval codes of dueling she has failed to observe. We have transplanted European modernity to our soil, without the spirit that inflames it and turns all its energy into mutual destruction. Out of these foreign peoples there has somehow been squeezed the poison. An America, "hyphenated" to bitterness, is somehow non-explosive. For, even if we all hark back in sympathy to a European nation, even if the war has set every one vibrating to some emotional string twanged on the other side of the Atlantic, the effect has been one of almost dramatic harmlessness.

What we have really been witnessing, however unappreciatively, in this country has been a thrilling and bloodless battle of Kulturs. In that arena of friction which has been the most dramatic—between the hyphenated German-American and the hyphenated English-American—there have emerged rivalries of philosophies which show up deep traditional attitudes, points of view which accurately reflect the gigantic issues of the war. America has mirrored the spiritual issues. The vicarious struggle has been played out peacefully here in the mind. We have seen the stout resistiveness of the old moral interpretation of history on which Victorian England thrived and made itself great in its own esteem. The clean and immensely satisfying vision of the war as a contest between right and wrong; the enthusiastic support of the Allies as the incarnation of virtue-on-a-rampage; the fierce envisaging of their selfish national purposes as the ideals of justice, freedom, and democracy—all this has been thrown with intensest force against the German realistic interpretations in terms of the struggle for power and the virility of the integrated State. America has been the intellectual battleground of the nations.

III

The failure of the melting-pot, far from closing the great American democratic experiment, means that it has only just begun. Whatever American nationalism turns out to be, we see already that it will have a color richer and more exciting than our ideal has hitherto encompassed. In a world which has dreamed of internationalism, we find that we have all unawares been building up the first international nation. The voices which have cried for a tight and jealous nationalism of the European pattern are failing. From the ideal, however valiantly and disinterestedly it has been set for us, time and tendency have moved us further and further away. What we have achieved has been rather a cosmopolitan federation of national colonies, of foreign cultures, from whom the sting of devastating competition has been removed. America is already the world-federation in miniature, the continent where for the first time in history has been achieved that miracle of hope, the peaceful living side by side, with character substantially preserved, of the most heterogenous peoples under the sun. Nowhere else has such contiguity been anything but the breeder of misery. Here, notwithstanding our tragic failures of adjustment, the outlines are already too clear not to give us a new vision and a new orientation of the American mind in the world.

It is for the American of the younger generation to accept this cosmopolitanism, and carry it along with self-conscious and fruitful purpose. In his colleges, he is already getting, with the study of modern history and politics, the modern literatures, economic geography, the privilege of a cosmopolitan outlook such as the people of no other nation of today in Europe can possibly secure. If he is still a colonial, he is no longer the colonial of one partial culture, but of many. He is a colonial of the world. Colonialism has grown into cosmopolitanism, and his motherland is no one nation, but all who have anything life-enhancing to offer to the spirit. That vague sympathy which the France of ten years ago was feeling for the world—a sympathy which was drowned in the terrible reality of war—may be the modern American's, and that in a positive and aggressive sense. If the American is parochial, it is in sheer wantonness or cowardice. His provincialism is the measure of his fear of bogies or the defect of his imagination.

Indeed, it is not uncommon for the eager Anglo-Saxon who goes to a vivid American university today to find his true friends not among his own race but among the acclimatized German or Austrian, the acclimatized Jew, the acclimatized Scandinavian or Italian. In them he finds the cosmopolitan note. In these youths, foreign-born or the children of foreign-born parents, he is likely to find many of his old inbred morbid problems washed away. These friends are oblivious to the repressions of that tight little society in which he so provincially grew up. He has a pleasurable sense of liberation from the stale and familiar attitudes of those whose ingrowing culture has scarcely created anything vital for his America of today. He breathes a larger air. In his new enthusiasms for continental literature, for unplumbed Russian depths, for French clarity of thought, for Teuton philosophies of power, he feels himself citizen of a larger world. He may be absurdly superficial, his outward-reaching wonder may ignore all the stiller and homelier virtues of his Anglo-Saxon home, but he has at least found the clue to that international mind which will be essential to all men and women of good-will if they are ever to save this Western world of ours from suicide. His new friends have gone through a similar evolution. America has burned most of the baser metal also from them. Meeting now with this common American background, all of them may yet retain that distinctiveness of their native cultures and their national spiritual slants. They are more valuable and interesting to each other for being different, yet that difference could not be creative were it not for this new cosmopolitan outlook which America has given them and which they all equally possess.

A college where such a spirit is possible even to the smallest degree, has within itself already the seeds of this international intellectual world of the future. It suggests that the contribution of America will be an intellectual internationalism which goes far beyond the mere exchange of scientific ideas and discoveries and the cold recording of facts. It will be an intellectual sympathy which is not satisfied until it has got at the heart of the different cultural expressions, and felt as they feel. It may have immense preferences, but it will make understanding and not indignation its end. Such a sympathy will unite and not divide.

Against the thinly disguised panic which calls itself "patriotism" and the thinly disguised militarism which calls itself "preparedness" the cosmopolitan ideal is set. This does not mean that those who hold it are for a policy of drift. They, too, long passionately for an integrated and disciplined America. But they do not want one which is integrated only for domestic economic exploitation of the workers or for predatory economic imperialism among the weaker peoples. They do not want one that is integrated by coercion or militarism, or for the truculent assertion of a mediaeval code of honor and of doubtful rights. They believe that the most effective integration will be one which coordinates the diverse elements and turns them consciously toward working out together the place of America in the world-situation. They demand for integration a genuine integrity, a wholeness and soundness of enthusiasm and purpose which can only come when no national colony within our America feels that it is being discriminated against or that its cultural case is being prejudged. This strength of cooperation, this feeling that all who are here may have a hand in the destiny of America, will make for a finer spirit of integration than any narrow "Americanism" or forced chauvinism.

In this effort we may have to accept some form of that dual citizenship which meets with so much articulate horror among us. Dual citizenship we may have to recognize as the rudimentary form of that international citizenship to which, if our words mean anything, we aspire. We have assumed unquestioningly that mere participation in the political life of the United States must cut the new citizen off from all sympathy with his old allegiance. Anything but a bodily transfer of devotion from one sovereignty to another has been viewed as a sort of moral treason against the Republic. We have insisted that the immigrant whom we welcomed escaping from the very exclusive nationalism of his European home shall forthwith adopt a nationalism just as exclusive, just as narrow, and even less legitimate because it is founded on no warm traditions of his own. Yet a nation like France is said to permit a formal and legal dual citizenship even at the present time. Though a citizen of hers may pretend to cast off his allegiance in favor of some other sovereignty, he is still subject to her laws when he returns. Once a citizen, always a citizen, no matter how many new citizenships he may embrace. And such a dual citizenship seems to us sound and right.

For it recognizes that, although the Frenchman may accept the formal institutional framework of his new country and indeed become intensely loyal to it, yet his Frenchness he will never lose. What makes up the fabric of his soul will always be of this Frenchness, so that unless he becomes utterly degenerate he will always to some degree dwell still in his native environment.

Indeed, does not the cultivated American who goes to Europe practice a dual citizenship, which, if not formal, is no less real? The American who lives abroad may be the least expatriate of men. If he falls in love with French ways and French thinking and French democracy and seeks to saturate himself with the new spirit, he is guilty of at least a dual spiritual citizenship. He may be still American, yet he feels himself through sympathy also a Frenchman. And he finds that this expansion involves no shameful conflict within him, no surrender of his native attitude. He has rather for the first time caught a glimpse of the cosmopolitan spirit. And after wandering about through many races and civilizations he may return to America to find them all here living vividly and crudely, seeking the same adjustment that he made. He sees the new peoples here with a new vision. They are no longer masses of aliens, waiting to be "assimilated," waiting to be melted down into the indistinguishable dough of Anglo-Saxonism. They are rather threads of living and potent cultures, blindly striving to weave themselves into a novel international nation, the first the world has seen. In an Austria-Hungary or a Prussia the stronger of these cultures would be moving almost instinctively to subjugate the weaker. But in America those wills-to-power are turned in a different direction into learning how to live together.

Along with dual citizenship we shall have to accept, I think, that free and mobile passage of the immigrant between America and his native land again which now arouses so much prejudice among us. We shall have to accept the immigrant's return for the same reason that we consider justified our own flitting about the earth. To stigmatize the alien who works in America for a few years and returns to his own land, only perhaps to seek American fortune again, is to think in narrow nationalistic terms. It is to ignore the cosmopolitan significance of this migration. It is to ignore the fact that the returning immigrant is often a missionary to an inferior civilization.

This migratory habit has been especially common with the unskilled laborers who have been pouring into the United States in the last dozen years from every country in southeastern Europe. Many of them return to spend their earnings in their own country or to serve their country in war. But they return with an entirely new critical outlook, and a sense of the superiority of American organization to the primitive living around them. This continued passage to and fro has already raised the material standard of living in many regions of these backward countries. For these regions are thus endowed with exactly what they need, the capital for the exploitation of their natural resources, and the spirit of enterprise. America is thus educating these laggard peoples from the very bottom of society up, awakening vast masses to a new-born hope for the future. In the migratory Greek, therefore, we have not the parasitic alien, the doubtful American asset, but a symbol of that cosmopolitan interchange which is coming, in spite of all war and national exclusiveness.

Only America, by reason of the unique liberty of opportunity and traditional isolation for which she seems to stand, can lead in this cosmopolitan enterprise. Only the American—and in this category I include the migratory alien who has lived with us and caught the pioneer spirit and a sense of new social vistas—has the chance to become that citizen of the world. America is coming to be, not a nationality but a trans-nationality, a weaving back and forth, with the other lands, of many threads of all sizes and colors. Any movement which attempts to thwart this weaving, or to dye the fabric any one color, or disentangle the threads of the strands, is false to this cosmopolitan vision. I do not mean that we shall necessarily glut ourselves with the raw product of humanity. It would be folly to absorb the nations faster than we could weave them. We have no duty either to admit or reject. It is purely a question of expediency. What concerns us is the fact that the strands are here. We must have a policy and an ideal for an actual situation. Our question is, What shall we do with our America? How are we likely to get the more creative America—by confining our imaginations to the ideal of the melting-pot, or broadening them to some such cosmopolitan conception as I have been vaguely sketching?

The war has shown America to be unable, though isolated geographically and politically from a European world-situation, to remain aloof and irresponsible. She is a wandering star in a sky dominated by two colossal constellations of states. Can she not work out some position of her own, some life of being in, yet not quite of, this seething and embroiled European world? This is her only hope and promise. A trans-nationality of all the nations, it is spiritually impossible for her to pass into the orbit of any one. It will be folly to hurry herself into a premature and sentimental nationalism, or to emulate Europe and play fast and loose with the forces that drag into war. No Americanization will fulfill this vision which does not recognize the uniqueness of this trans-nationalism of ours. The Anglo-Saxon attempt to fuse will only create enmity and distrust. The crusade against "hyphenates" will only inflame the partial patriotism of trans-nationals, and cause them to assert their European traditions in strident and unwholesome ways. But the attempt to weave a wholly novel international nation out of our chaotic America will liberate and harmonize the creative power of all these peoples and give them the new spiritual citizenship, as so many individuals have already been given, of a world.

Is it a wild hope that the undertow of opposition to metaphysics in international relations, opposition to militarism, is less a cowardly provincialism than a groping for this higher cosmopolitan ideal? One can understand the irritated restlessness with which our proud pro-British colonists contemplate a heroic conflict across the seas in which they have no part. It was inevitable that our necessary inaction should evolve in their minds into the bogey of national shame and dishonor. But let us be careful about accepting their sensitiveness as final arbiter. Let us look at our reluctance rather as the first crude beginnings of assertion on the part of certain strands in our nationality that they have a right to a voice in the construction of the American ideal. Let us face realistically the America we have around us. Let us work with the forces that are at work. Let us make something of this trans-national spirit instead of outlawing it. Already we are living this cosmopolitan America. What we need is everywhere a vivid consciousness of the new ideal. Deliberate headway must be made against the survivals of the melting-pot ideal for the promise of American life.

We cannot Americanize America worthily by sentimentalizing and moralizing history. When the best schools are expressly renouncing the questionable duty of teaching patriotism by means of history, it is not the time to force shibboleth upon the immigrant. This form of Americanization has been heard because it appealed to the vestiges of our old sentimentalized and moralized patriotism. This has so far held the field as the expression of the new American's new devotion. The inflections of other voices have been drowned. They must be heard. We must see if the lesson of the war has not been for hundreds of these later Americans a vivid realization of their trans-nationality, a new consciousness of what America meant to them as a citizenship in the world. It is the vague historic idealisms which have provided the fuel for the European flame. Our American ideal can make no progress until we do away with this romantic gilding of the past.

All our idealisms must be those of future social goals in which all can participate, the good life of personality lived in the environment of the Beloved Community. No mere doubtful triumphs of the past, which redound to the glory of only one of our trans-nationalities, can satisfy us. It must be a future America, on which all can unite, which pulls us irresistibly toward it, as we understand each other more warmly.

To make real this striving amid dangers and apathies is work for a younger *intelligentsia* of America. Here is an enterprise of integration into which we can all pour ourselves, of a spiritual welding which should make us, if the final menace ever came, not weaker, but infinitely strong.

Anzia Yezierska 1881(?)–1970

Anzia Yezierska, one of ten children, emigrated with her family from Russian Poland to New York's Lower East Side when she was about fifteen. She worked in sweatshops, laundries, and as a maid, studying English in night school. A settlement worker helped her get a scholarship to Columbia College's domestic science teacher training program; Yezierska invented a high school diploma to enter. These early experiences formed her fictional voice of the feisty immigrant waif who pulls herself up from poverty through wit and hard work.

While attending Rand School classes in social theory, she met radical feminist Henrietta Rodman, who encouraged her writing. She started using her European name of Anzia Yezierska, rather than Hattie Mayer, the name which she had received at Ellis Island. In 1910, Yezierska's brief marriage to lawyer Jacob Gordon was annulled. A year later, she married teacher Arnold Levitas, giving birth to their daughter Louise in 1912. When Yezierska and Levitas separated, she focused on her writing and visited Louise once a week. Her first published story, "The Free Vacation House" (1915), describes an overworked immigrant mother's frustration with both domestic life and organized charity's attempts to relieve her. Through the voice of the ghetto mother, Yezierska expressed the Yiddish-English dialect better than any previous writer had.

In 1917, Yezierska barged into the Columbia University office of philosopher and educator John Dewey to enlist his help in obtaining a permanent teaching certificate. From 1917 to 1918, she audited his seminars. Their brief and probably unconsummated romance ended after the summer of 1918. For Dewey, Yezierska was a window onto New York's Jewish ghetto and inspiration for over twenty love poems. For Yezierska, Dewey represented mainstream America, and the paternal approval she did not receive from her own highly religious father, who believed women should be wives and not writers.

Dewey, however, encouraged Yezierska and introduced her to editors.

Yezierska's most anthologized short story, "The Fat of the Land," was originally chosen the best of *Best Short Stories of 1919;* in 1920, Houghton Mifflin Company published *Hungry Hearts,* a collection of Yezierska's short stories. After newspapers publicized the book, Goldwyn movie studios hired her to write screenplays. The short stories of *Hungry Hearts,* and her first novel, *Salome of the Tenements,* became two movies, the prints and negatives of which have since disintegrated. Yezierska felt her creativity dry up in Hollywood and returned to New York. There she was somewhat reclusive, but occasionally met with the Algonquin group of writers.

Yezierska wrote more short stories (collected in *Children of Loneliness*) and three more novels (*Bread Givers,* her most polished; *Arrogant Beggar;* and *All I Could Never Be,* about her relationship with Dewey). This last work was written while Yezierska held a Zona Gale Fellowship for writers-in-residence at the University of Wisconsin (1928–31). Back in New York, around 1935 or 1936, Yezierska joined the WPA Writer's Project, staying perhaps until 1938.

Her fictionalized autobiography, *Red Ribbon on a White Horse,* published in 1950 after an eighteen-year silence, renewed public interest in her writing. Most of the volume describes her Hollywood and WPA experiences. Throughout the Fifties, she wrote *New York Times* book reviews and sometimes lectured. Her fictional voice of the old woman, speaker for the disenfranchised, aged poor, developed at this time. Until 1966, Yezierska lived alone in New York, but then moved near her daughter, who hired transcribers for the writing Yezierska continued even when nearly blind. Yezierska died in a nursing home near Claremont, California, at close to ninety.

Critics have called Yezierska's fiction extremely autobiographical, but examination reveals it to be emotionally, rather than factually, true to her life. All of her writing, whether about young immigrant working-class Jewish women, or the elderly, isolated urban poor, expresses the feelings of characters considered by others to be marginal to the American mainstream. Her work has been recently rediscovered by those interested in women's, ethnic, immigrant, Jewish, urban, or working-class literature.

Sally Ann Drucker
Nassau Community College

PRIMARY WORKS

Hungry Hearts, 1920; *Salome of the Tenements,* 1922; *Children of Loneliness,* 1923; *Bread Givers,* 1925; *Arrogant Beggar,* 1927; *All I Could Never Be,* 1932; *Red Ribbon on a White Horse,* 1950. Paperback reprints: *Bread Givers,* 1975; *Hungry Hearts and Other Stories,* 1985; *Red Ribbon on a White Horse,* 1988; *The Open Cage* (a collection), 1979, 1993.

America and I

As one of the dumb, voiceless ones I speak. One of the millions of immigrants beating, beating out their hearts at your gates for a breath of understanding.

Ach! America! From the other end of the earth from where I came, America was a land of living hope, woven of dreams, aflame with longing and desire.

Choked for ages in the airless oppression of Russia, the Promised Land rose up—wings for my stifled spirit—sunlight burning through my darkness—freedom singing to me in my prison—deathless songs tuning prison-bars into strings of a beautiful violin.

I arrived in America. My young, strong body, my heart and soul pregnant with the unlived lives of generations clamoring for expression.

What my mother and father and their mother and father never had a chance to give out in Russia, I would give out in America. The hidden sap of centuries would find release; colors that never saw light—songs that died unvoiced—romance that never had a chance to blossom in the black life of the Old World.

In the golden land of flowing opportunity I was to find my work that was denied me in the sterile village of my forefathers. Here I was to be free from the dead drudgery for bread that held me down in Russia. For the first time in America, I'd cease to be a slave of the belly. I'd be a creator, a giver, a human being! My work would be the living job of fullest self-expression.

But from my high visions, my golden hopes, I had to put my feet down on earth. I had to have food and shelter. I had to have the money to pay for it.

I was in America, among the Americans, but not of them. No speech, no common language, no way to win a smile of understanding from them, only my young, strong body and my untried faith. Only my eager, empty hands, and my full heart shining from my eyes!

God from the world! Here I was with so much richness in me, but my mind was not wanted without the language. And my body, unskilled, untrained, was not even wanted in the factory. Only one of two chances was left open to me: the kitchen, or minding babies.

My first job was as a servant in an Americanized family. Once, long ago, they came from the same village from where I came. But they were so well-dressed, so well-fed, so successful in America, that they were ashamed to remember their mother tongue.

"What were to be my wages?" I ventured timidly, as I looked up to the well-fed, well-dressed "American" man and woman.

They looked at me with a sudden coldness. What have I said to draw away from me their warmth? Was it so low from me to talk of wages? I shrank back into myself like a low-down bargainer. Maybe they're so high up in well-being they can't any more understand my low thoughts for money.

From his rich height the man preached down to me that I must not be so grabbing for wages. Only just landed from the ship and already thinking about money when I should be thankful to associate with "Americans."

The woman, out of her smooth, smiling fatness assured me that this was my chance for a summer vacation in the country with her two lovely children. My great chance to learn to be a civilized being, to become an American by living with them.

So, made to feel that I was in the hands of American friends, invited to share with them their home, their plenty, their happiness, I pushed out from my head the worry for wages. Here was my first chance to begin my life in the sunshine, after my long darkness. My laugh was all over my face as I said to them: "I'll trust myself to you. What I'm worth you'll give me." And I entered their house like a child by the hand.

The best of me I gave them. Their house cares were my house cares. I got up early. I worked till late. All that my soul hungered to give I put into the passion with which I scrubbed floors, scoured pots, and washed clothes. I was so grateful to mingle with the American people, to hear the music of the American language, that I never knew tiredness.

There was such a freshness in my brains and such a willingness in my heart that I could go on and on—not only with the work of the house, but work with my head—learning new words from the children, the grocer, the butcher, the iceman. I was not even afraid to ask for words from the policeman on the street. And every new word made me see new American things with American eyes. I felt like a Columbus, finding new worlds through every new word.

But words alone were only for the inside of me. The outside of me still branded me for a steerage immigrant. I had to have clothes to forget myself that I'm a stranger yet. And so I had to have money to buy these clothes.

The month was up. I was so happy! Now I'd have money. *My own, earned* money. Money to buy a new shirt on my back—shoes on my feet. Maybe yet an American dress and hat!

Ach! How high rose my dreams! How plainly I saw all that I would do with my visionary wages shining like a light over my head!

In my imagination I already walked in my new American clothes. How beautiful I looked as I saw myself like a picture before my eyes! I saw how I would throw away my immigrant rags tied up in my immigrant shawl. With money to buy—free money in my hands—I'd show them that I could look like an American in a day.

Like a prisoner in his last night in prison, counting the seconds that will free him from his chains, I trembled breathlessly for the minute I'd get the wages in my hand.

Before dawn I rose.

I shined up the house like a jewel-box.

I prepared breakfast and waited with my heart in my mouth for my lady and gentleman to rise. At last I heard them stirring. My eyes were jumping out of my head to them when I saw them coming in and seating themselves by the table.

Like a hungry cat rubbing up to its boss for meat, so I edged and simpered around them as I passed them the food. Without my will, like a beggar, my hand reached out to them.

The breakfast was over. And no word yet from my wages.

"Gottuniu!" I thought to myself. "Maybe they're so busy with their own things they forgot it's the day for my wages. Could they who have everything know what I was to do with my first American dollars? How could they, soaking in plenty, how could they feel the longing and the fierce hunger in me, pressing up through each visionary dollar? How could they know the gnawing ache of my avid fingers for the feel of my own, earned dollars? *My* dollars that I could spend like a free person. *My* dollars that would make me feel with everybody alike!"

Lunch came. Lunch past.

Oi-i weh! Not a word yet about my money.

It was near dinner. And not a word yet about my wages.

I began to set the table. But my head—it swam away from me. I broke a glass. The silver dropped from my nervous fingers. I couldn't stand it any longer. I dropped everything and rushed over to my American lady and gentleman.

"*Oi weh!* The money—my money—my wages!" I cried breathlessly.

Four cold eyes turned on me.

"Wages? Money?" The four eyes turned into hard stone as they looked me up and down. "Haven't you a comfortable bed to sleep, and three good meals a day? You're only a month here. Just came to America. And you already think about money. Wait till you're worth any money. What use are you without knowing English? You should be glad we keep you here. It's like a vacation for you. Other girls pay money yet to be in the country."

It went black for my eyes. I was so choked no words came to my lips. Even the tears went dry in my throat.

I left. Not a dollar for all my work.

For a long, long time my heart ached and ached like a sore wound. If murderers would have robbed me and killed me it wouldn't have hurt me so much. I couldn't think through my pain. The minute I'd see before me how they looked at me, the words they said to me—then everything began to bleed in me. And I was helpless.

For a long, long time the thought of ever working in an "American" family made me tremble with fear, like the fear of wild wolves. No—never again would I trust myself to an "American" family, no matter how fine their language and how sweet their smile.

It was blotted out in me all trust in friendship from "Americans." But the life in me still burned to live. The hope in me still craved to hope. In darkness, in dirt, in hunger and want, but only to live on!

There had been no end to my day—working for the "American" family.

Now rejecting false friendships from higher-ups in America, I turned back to the Ghetto. I worked on a hard bench with my own kind on either side of me. I knew before I began what my wages were to be. I knew what my hours were to be. And I knew the feeling of the end of the day.

From the outside my second job seemed worse than the first. It was in a sweat-shop of a Delancey Street basement, kept up by an old, wrinkled woman that looked like a black witch of greed. My work was sewing on buttons. While the morning was still dark I walked into a dark basement. And darkness met me when I turned out of the basement.

Day after day, week after week, all the contact I got with America was handling dead buttons. The money I earned was hardly enough to pay for bread and rent. I didn't have a room to myself. I didn't even have a bed. I slept on a mattress on the floor in a rat-hole of a room occupied by a dozen other immigrants. I was always hungry—oh, so hungry! The scant meals I could afford only sharpened my appetite for real food. But I felt myself better off than working in the "American" family, where I had three good meals a day and a bed to myself. With all the hunger and darkness of the sweat-shop, I had at least the evening to myself. And all night was mine. When all were asleep, I used to creep up on the roof of the tenement and talk out my heart in silence to the stars in the sky.

"Who am I? What am I? What do I want with my life? Where is America? Is there an America? What is this wilderness in which I'm lost?"

I'd hurl my questions and then think and think. And I could not tear it out of me, the feeling that America must be somewhere, somehow—only I couldn't find it—*my America,* where I would work for love and not for a living. I was like a thing following blindly after something far off in the dark!

"Oi weh!" I'd stretch out my hand up in the air. "My head is so lost in America! What's the use of all my working if I'm not in it? Dead buttons is not me."

Then the busy season started in the shop. The mounds of buttons grew and grew. The long day stretched out longer. I had to begin with the buttons earlier and stay with them till later in the night. The old witch turned into a huge greedy maw for wanting more and more buttons.

For a glass of tea, for a slice of herring over black bread, she would buy us up to stay another and another hour, till there seemed no end to her demands.

One day, the light of self-assertion broke into my cellar darkness.

"I don't want the tea. I don't want your herring," I said with terrible boldness. "I only want to go home. I only want the evening to myself!"

"You fresh mouth, you!" cried the old witch. "You learned already too much in America. I want no clock-watchers in my shop. Out you go!"

I was driven out to cold and hunger. I could no longer pay for my mattress on the floor. I no longer could buy the bite in my mouth. I walked the streets. I knew what it is to be alone in a strange city, among strangers.

But I laughed through my tears. So I learned too much already in America because I wanted the whole evening to myself? Well America has yet to teach me still more: how to get not only the whole evening to myself, but a whole day a week like the American workers.

That sweat-shop was a bitter memory but a good school. It fitted me for a regular factory. I could walk in boldly and say I could work at something, even if it was only sewing on buttons.

Gradually, I became a trained worker. I worked in a light, airy factory, only eight hours a day. My boss was no longer a sweater and a blood-squeezer. The first freshness of the morning was mine. And the whole evening was mine. All day Sunday was mine.

Now I had better food to eat. I slept on a better bed. Now, I even looked dressed up like the American-born. But inside of me I knew that I was not yet an American. I choked with longing when I met an American-born, and I could say nothing.

Something cried dumb in me. I couldn't help it. I didn't know what it was I wanted. I only knew I wanted. I wanted. Like the hunger in the heart that never gets food.

An English class for foreigners started in our factory. The teacher had such a good, friendly face, her eyes looked so understanding, as if she could see right into my heart. So I went to her one day for an advice:

"I don't know what is with me the matter," I began. "I have no rest in me. I never yet done what I want."

"What is it you want to do, child?" she asked me.

"I want to do something with my head, my feelings. All day long, only with my hands I work."

"First you must learn English." She patted me as if I was not yet grown up. "Put your mind on that, and then we'll see."

So for a time I learned the language. I could almost begin to think with English words in my head. But in my heart the emptiness still hurt. I burned to give, to give something, to do something, to be something. The dead work with my hands was killing me. My work left only hard stones on my heart.

Again I went to our factory teacher and cried out to her: "I know already to read and write the English language, but I can't put it into words what I want. What is it in me so different that can't come out?"

She smiled at me down from her calmness as if I were a little bit out of my head. "What *do you want* to do?"

"I feel. I see. I hear. And I want to think it out. But I'm like dumb in me. I only feel I'm different—different from everybody."

She looked at me close and said nothing for a minute. "You ought to join one of the social clubs of the Women's Association," she advised.

"What's the Women's Association?" I implored greedily.

"A group of American women who are trying to help the working-girl find herself. They have a special department for immigrant girls like you."

I joined the Women's Association. On my first evening there they announced a lecture: "The Happy Worker and His Work," by the Welfare director of the United Mills Corporation.

"Is there such a thing as a happy worker at his work?" I wondered. Happiness is only by working at what you love. And what poor girl can ever find it to work at what she loves? My old dreams about my America rushed through my mind. Once I thought that in America everybody works for love. Nobody has to worry for a living. Maybe this welfare man came to show me the *real* America that till now I sought in vain.

With a lot of polite words the head lady of the Women's Association introduced a higher-up that looked like the king of kings of business. Never before in my life did I ever see a man with such a sureness in his step, such power in his face, such friendly positiveness in his eye as when he smiled upon us.

"Efficiency is the new religion of business," he began. "In big business houses, even in up-to-date factories, they no longer take the first comer and give him any job that happens to stand empty. Efficiency begins at the employment office. Experts are hired for the one purpose, to find out how best to fit the worker to his work. It's economy for the boss to make the worker happy." And then he talked a lot more on efficiency in educated language that was over my head.

I didn't know exactly what it meant—efficiency—but if it was to make the worker happy at his work, then that's what I had been looking for since I came to America. I only felt from watching him that he was happy by his job. And as I looked on this clean, well-dressed, successful one, who wasn't ashamed to say he rose from an office-boy, it made me feel that I, too, could lift myself up for a person.

He finished his lecture, telling us about the Vocational-Guidance Center that the Women's Association started.

The very next evening I was at the Vocational-Guidance Center. There I found a young, college-looking woman. Smartness and health shining from her eyes! She, too, looked as if she knew her way in America. I could tell at the first glance: here is a person that is happy by what she does.

"I feel you'll understand me," I said right away.

She leaned over with pleasure in her face: "I hope I can."

"I want to work by what's in me. Only, I don't know what's in me. I only feel I'm different."

She gave me a quick, puzzled look from the corner of her eyes. "What are you doing now?"

"I'm the quickest shirtwaist hand on the floor. But my heart wastes away by such work. I think and think, and my thoughts can't come out."

"Why don't you think out your thoughts in shirtwaists? You could learn to be a designer. Earn more money."

"I don't want to look on waists. If my hands are sick from waists, how could my head learn to put beauty into them?"

"But you must earn your living at what you know, and rise slowly from job to job."

I looked at her office sign: "Vocational Guidance." "What's your vocational guidance?" I asked. "How to rise from job to job—how to earn more money?"

The smile went out from her eyes. But she tried to be kind yet. "What *do* you want?" she asked, with a sigh of last patience.

"I want America to want me."

She fell back in her chair, thunderstruck with my boldness. But yet, in a low voice of educated self-control, she tried to reason with me:

"You have to *show* that you have something special for America before America has need of you."

"But I never had a chance to find out what's in me, because I always had to work for a living. Only, I feel it's efficiency for America to find out what's in me so different, so I could give it out by my work."

Her eyes half closed as they bored through me. Her mouth opened to speak, but no words came from her lips. So I flamed up with all that was choking in me like a house on fire:

"America gives free bread and rent to criminals in prison. They got grand houses with sunshine, fresh air, doctors and teachers, even for the crazy ones. Why don't they have free boarding-schools for immigrants—strong people—willing people? Here you see us burning up with something different, and America turns her head away from us."

Her brows lifted and dropped down. She shrugged her shoulders away from me with the look of pity we give to cripples and hopeless lunatics.

"America is no Utopia. First you must become efficient in earning a living before you can indulge in your poetic dreams."

I went away from the vocational-guidance office with all the air out of my lungs. All the light out of my eyes. My feet dragged after me like dead wood.

Till now there had always lingered a rosy veil of hope over my emptiness, a hope that a miracle would happen. I would open up my eyes some day and suddenly find the America of my dreams. As a young girl hungry for love sees always before her eyes the picture of lover's arms around her, so I saw always in my heart the vision of Utopian America.

But now I felt that the America of my dreams never was and never could be. Reality had hit me on the head as with a club. I felt that the America that I sought was nothing but a shadow—an echo—a chimera of lunatics and crazy immigrants.

Stripped of all illusion, I looked about me. The long desert of wasting days of drudgery stared me in the face. The drudgery that I had lived through, and the endless drudgery still ahead of me rose over me like a withering wilderness of sand. In vain were all my cryings, in vain were all frantic efforts of my spirit to find the living waters of understanding for my perishing lips. Sand, sand was everywhere. With every seeking, every reaching out I only lost myself deeper and deeper in a vast sea of sand.

I knew now the American language. And I knew now, if I talked to the Americans from morning till night, they could not understand what the Russian soul of me wanted. They could not understand *me* any more than if I talked to them in Chinese. Between my soul and the American soul were worlds of difference that no words could bridge over. What was that difference? What made the Americans so far apart from me?

I began to read the American history. I found from the first pages that America started with a band of Courageous Pilgrims. They had left their native country as I had left mine. They had crossed an unknown ocean and landed in an unknown country, as I.

But the great difference between the first Pilgrims and me was that they expected to make America, build America, create their own world of liberty. I wanted to find it ready made.

I read on. I delved deeper down into the American history. I saw how the Pilgrim Fathers came to a rocky desert country, surrounded by Indian savages on all sides. But undaunted, they pressed on—through danger—through famine, pestilence, and want—they pressed on. They did not ask the Indians for sympathy, for understanding. They made no demands on anybody, but on their own indomitable spirit of persistence.

And I—I was forever begging a crumb of sympathy, a gleam of understanding from strangers who could not understand.

I, when I encountered a few savage Indian scalpers, like the old witch of the sweat-shop, like my "Americanized" countryman, who cheated me of my wages—I, when I found myself on the lonely, untrodden path through which all seekers of the new world must pass, I lost heart and said: "There is no America!"

Then came a light—a great revelation! I saw America—a big idea—a deathless hope—a world still in the making. I saw that it was the glory of America that it was not yet finished. And I, the last comer, had her share to give, small or great, to the making of America, like those Pilgrims who came in the *Mayflower.*

Fired up by this revealing light, I began to build a bridge of understanding between the American-born and myself. Since their life was shut out from such as me, I began to open up my life and the lives of my people to them. And life draws life. In only writing about the Ghetto I found America.

Great chances have come to me. But in my heart is always a deep sadness. I feel like a man who is sitting down to a secret table of plenty, while his near ones and dear ones are perishing before his eyes. My very joy in doing the work I love hurts me like secret guilt, because all about me I see so many with my longings, my burning eagerness, to do and to be, wasting their days in drudgery they hate, merely to buy bread and pay rent. And America is losing all that richness of the soul.

The Americans of tomorrow, the America that is every day nearer coming to be, will be too wise, too open-hearted, too friendly-handed, to let the least lastcomer at their gates knock in vain with his gifts unwanted.

1923

Michael Gold 1893–1967

Michael Gold was the eldest of three sons born to the Graniches, Jewish immigrants living on New York's Lower East Side. During the Palmer Raids of 1919–20 he took the name Michael Gold after a Jewish Civil War veteran he admired for having fought to "free the slaves." When his father's health and business failed, the son had to go to work at age twelve to help support the family. His anger at capitalism was initially more personal than political, more subjective than ideological: unlike the mass of impoverished ghetto dwellers, he had been reared to expect better.

He was twenty-one and his life was going nowhere when, having "no politics . . . except hunger," Granich happened to wander into Union Square one April day in 1914 during a demonstration, was knocked down by a policeman, and had the epiphany he describes at the end of *Jews Without Money.* The Jewish Messiah that the young boy of *Jews Without Money* prays for will not come in Gold's lifetime; but the Marxist Messiah, who will punish the guilty—*i.e.,* the capitalists, the exploiters—and reward the innocent—*i.e.,* the workers, the exploited—will.

The first time he read *The Masses,* the important revolutionary magazine edited by Max Eastman and Floyd Dell, Granich was amazed that poetry and fiction about being poor was publishable—he had been writing poems and stories which he assumed he could never publish. Four months after his Union Square epiphany in August, 1914, *The Masses* published Granich's first piece, a poem about three anarchists who had died in a bomb explosion, and his fifty-year career as a writer was launched.

He left the Jewish, working-class Lower East Side and moved to Greenwich Village where he started to move in the American and Bohemian leftist and literary circles then swirling around John Reed and Eugene O'Neill. Discovering he could support himself working for the leftist press, Granich ceased working as a manual laborer. In 1921 he became an editor of the *Liberator,* which had succeeded the suppressed *Masses* and became the cultural journal of the Communist Party. When the *Liberator* became wholly political in the mid-1920s, he helped found the *New Masses,* devoted to publishing literary works *by* workers rather than by literary leftists with working-class sympathies. He became editor-in-chief in 1928.

Jews Without Money, which Gold had been working on throughout the 1920s, was published in February, 1930. Had it been published a year or two earlier when the Jazz Age still seemed to be booming, it might well have gone unnoticed; had it been published a year or two later in the midst of the Depression, it might have seemed old hat. The collapse of the economy had ruined the plans and destroyed the dreams of a whole generation, as the collapse of Papa Granich's business and health twenty years earlier had ruined the plans and destroyed the dreams of Yitzhak-already-Isaac-already-Irwin Granich. Although *Jews Without Money* was not *about* the 1930s and did not emerge from a 1930s sensibility, having been composed in the 1920s, it seemed to many the pre-eminent 1930s novel. By October it had gone into its eleventh printing.

The book's success was not based on its subject matter alone. It was Gold's description of a degrading ghetto existence—the diseases, the early deaths, the degenerates, crime, prostitution, filth—and his arraignment of capitalism as its progenitor and cause that made *Jews Without Money* seem so contemporary, so urgent, in 1930. The heroic center of *Jews Without Money* is Katie Gold, whose selflessness, whose love for fellow men and women, Jew and Gentile, and whose energy and indomitability are all channeled into an almost cosmic sense of responsibility to and for everyone she comes into contact with. Katie's persistent struggle to survive with dignity and generosity of spirit stands as a paradigm for the Workers' Revolution.

Gold became a national figure, cultural commissar of the Communist Party, arbiter of artistic value according to the artist's political allegiances. As the Twenties had buoyed up F. Scott Fitzgerald, the Thirties buoyed up Michael Gold—it was the decade for which he was born. In 1933 he became daily columnist for the *Daily Worker,* the mass circulation Communist Party newspaper. In 1935, in the introduction for a new edition of *Jews Without Money,* Gold noted that it had been translated into French, Swedish, Bohemian, Bulgarian, Romanian, Jugo-Slavian [*sic*], Italian, Japanese, Chinese, Ukrainian, Russian, Yiddish, Dutch, and Tatar and was particularly proud that "German radicals had translated it and were spreading it widely as a form of propaganda against the Nazi anti-Semitic lies."

Unlike many of the Marxists of his generation, Michael Gold never shifted gears, never changed with the times. Through the Forties, Fifties, and Sixties he remained remarkably—some would say foolishly, naively, stupidly—faithful to that twenty-one-year-old's epiphany: "O workers' Revolution! . . . You are the true Messiah!" Gold's chance of surviving as a writer has come to depend much more on the religion and ethnicity that he abandoned than on his politics and ideology, much more on the Jewish identity he implicitly rejected at the end of *Jews Without Money* and which shaped the first twenty-one years of his life than on the Marxist identity he explicitly donned at the end of *Jews Without Money.*

Barry Gross
Michigan State University

PRIMARY WORKS

Jews Without Money, 1930; *Mike Gold: A Literary Anthology,* ed. by Michael Folsom, 1972.

from Jews Without Money

The Soul of a Landlord

1

On the East Side people buy their groceries a pinch at a time; three cents' worth of sugar, five cents' worth of butter, everything in penny fractions. The good Jewish black bread that smells of harvest time, is sliced into a dozen parts and sold for pennies. But that winter even pennies were scarce.

There was a panic on Wall Street. Multitudes were without work; there were strikes, suicides, and food riots. The prostitutes roamed our street like wolves; never was there so much competition among them.

Life froze. The sun vanished from the deathly gray sky. The streets reeked with snow and slush. There were hundreds of evictions. I walked down a street between dripping tenement walls. The rotten slush ate through my shoes. The wind beat on my face. I saw a stack of furniture before a tenement: tables, chairs, a washtub packed with crockery and bedclothes, a broom, a dresser, a lamp.

The snow covered them. The snow fell, too, on a little Jew and his wife and three children. They huddled in a mournful group by their possessions. They had placed a saucer on one of the tables. An old woman with a market bag mumbled a prayer in passing. She dropped a penny in the saucer. Other people did the same. Each time the evicted family lowered its eyes in shame. They were not beggars, but "respectable" people. But if enough pennies fell in the saucer, they might have rent for a new home. This was the one hope left them.

Winter. Building a snow fort one morning, we boys dug out a litter of frozen kittens and their mother. The little ones were still blind. They had been born into it, but had never seen our world.

Other dogs and cats were frozen. Men and women, too, were found dead in hallways and on docks. Mary Sugar Bum met her end in an alley. She was found half-naked, clutching a whiskey bottle in her blue claw. This was her last "love" affair.

Horses slipped on the icy pavement, and quivered there for hours with broken legs, until a policeman arrived to shoot them.

The boys built a snow man. His eyes were two coals; his nose a potato. He wore a derby hat and smoked a corncob pipe. His arms were flung wide; in one of them he held a broom, in the other a newspaper. This Golem[1] with his amazed eyes and idiotic grin amused us all for an afternoon.

The next morning we found him strangely altered. His eyes and nose had been torn out; his grin smashed, like a war victim's. Who had played this joke? The winter wind.

2

Mrs. Rosenbaum owned a grocery store on our street. She was a widow with four children, and lived in two rooms back of the store. She slaved from dawn until midnight; a big, clumsy woman with a chapped face and masses of untidy hair; always grumbling, groaning, gossiping about her ailments. Sometimes she was nervous and screamed at her children, and beat them. But she was a kind-hearted woman, and that winter suffered a great deal. Every one was very poor, and she was too good not to give them groceries on credit.

"I'm crazy to do it!" she grumbled in her icy store. "I'm a fool! But when a child comes for a loaf of bread, and I have the bread, and I know her family is starving, how can I refuse her? Yet I have my own children to think of! I am being ruined! The store is being emptied! I can't meet my bills!"

[1]According to Jewish folklore, the golem was an artificial figure in human form that Rabbi Low of Prague created in the sixteenth century to frighten the enemies of the Jews.

She was kind. Kindness is a form of suicide in a world based on the law of competition.

One day we watched the rewards of kindness. The sheriff's men arrived to seize Mrs. Rosenbaum's grocery. They tore down the shelves and fixtures, they carted off tubs of butter, drums of kerosene, sacks of rice, flour and potatoes.

Mrs. Rosenbaum stood by watching her own funeral. Her fat kind face was swollen with crying as with toothache. Her eyes blinked in bewilderment. Her children clung to her skirts and cried. Snow fell from the sky, a crowd muttered its sympathy, a policeman twirled his club.

What happened to her after that, I don't know. Maybe the Organized Charities helped her; or maybe she died. O golden dyspeptic God of America, you were in a bad mood that winter. We were poor, and you punished us harshly for this worst of sins.

3

My father lay in bed. His shattered feet ached in each bone. His painter's sickness came back on him; he suffered with lung and kidney pains.

He was always depressed. His only distraction was to read the Yiddish newspapers, and to make gloomy conversation at night over the suicides, the hungry families, the robberies, murders and catastrophes that newspapers record.

"It will come to an end!" said my father. "People are turning into wolves! They will soon eat each other! They will tear down the cities, and destroy the world in flames and blood!"

"Drink your tea," said my mother cheerfully, "God is still in the world. You will get better and work and laugh again. Let us not lose courage."

My father was fretful and nervous with an invalid's fears.

"But what if we are evicted, Katie?"

"We won't be evicted, not while I have my two hands and can work," said my mother.

"But I don't want you to work!" my father cried. "It breaks up our home!"

"It doesn't!" said my mother. "I have time and strength for everything."

4

At first my mother had feared going out to work in a cafeteria among Christians. But after a few days she settled easily into the life of the polyglot kitchen, and learned to fight, scold, and mother the Poles, Germans, Italians, Irish and Negroes who worked there. They liked her, and soon called her "Momma," which made her vain.

"You should hear how a big black dishwasher named Joe, how he comes to me to-day, and says, 'Momma, I'm going to quit. Every one is against me here because I am black,' he says. 'The whole world is against us black people.'"

"So I said to him, 'Joe, I am not against you. Don't be foolish, don't go out to be a bum again. The trouble with you here is you are lazy. If you would work harder the others would like you, too.' So he said, 'Momma, all right I'll stay,' So that's how it is in the restaurant. They call me Momma, even the black ones."

It was a large, high-priced cafeteria for businessmen on lower Broadway. My mother was a chef's helper, and peeled and scoured tons of vegetables for cooking. Her wages were seven dollars a week.

She woke at five, cooked our breakfast at home, then had to walk a mile to her job. She came home at five-thirty, and made supper, cleaned the house, was busy on her feet until bedtime. It hurt my father's masculine pride to see his wife working for wages. But my mother liked it all; she was proud of earning money, and she liked her fights in the restaurant.

My dear, tireless, little dark-faced mother! Why did she always have to fight? Why did she have to give my father a new variety of headache with accounts of her battles for "justice" in the cafeteria? The manager there was a fat blond Swede with a *Kaiserliche* mustache,[2] and the manners of a Mussolini.[3] All the workers feared this bull-necked tyrant, except my mother. She told him "what was what." When the meat was rotten, when the drains were clogged and smelly, or the dishwashers overworked, she told him so. She scolded him as if he were her child, and he listened meekly. The other workers fell into the habit of telling their complaints to my mother, and she would relay them to the Swedish manager.

"It's because he needs me," said my mother proudly. "That's why he lets me scold him. I am one of his best workers; he can depend on me in the rush. And he knows I am not like the other kitchen help; they work a day or two; then quit, but I stay on. So he's afraid to fire me, and I tell him what is what."

It was one of those super-cafeterias, with flowers on the tables, a string orchestra during the lunch hour, and other trimmings. But my mother had no respect for it. She would never eat the lunch served there to the employees, but took along two cheese sandwiches from home.

"Your food is *Dreck,*[4] it is fit only for pigs," she told the manager bluntly. And once she begged me to promise never to eat hamburger steak in a restaurant when I grew up.

"Swear it to me, Mikey!" she said. "Never, never eat hamburger!"

"I swear it, momma."

"Poison!" she went on passionately. "They don't care if they poison the people, so long as there's money in it. I've seen with my own eyes. If I could write English, I'd write a letter to all the newspapers."

"Mind your own business!" my father growled. "Such things are for Americans. It is their country and their hamburger steak."

[2]Kaiser Wilhelm II, Emperor of Germany and King of Prussia (1888–1918), had a very prominent and imposing mustache.

[3]Benito Mussolini founded the Italian Fascist Party in 1919 and was Prime Minister of Italy (1922–1943).

[4]Yiddish for feces.

5

Our tenement was nothing but a junk-heap of rotten lumber and brick. It was an old ship on its last voyage; in the battering winter storms, all its seams opened, and wind and snow came through.

The plaster was always falling down, the stairs were broken and dirty. Five times that winter the water pipes froze, and floods spurted from the plumbing, and dripped from the ceilings.

There was no drinking water in the tenement for days. The women had to put on their shawls and hunt in the street for water. Up and down the stairs they groaned, lugging pails of water. In December, when Mr. Zunzer the landlord called for rent, some of the neighbors told him he ought to fix the plumbing.

"Next week," he murmured into his scaly beard.

"Next week!" my mother sneered, after he had gone. "A dozen times he has told us that, the yellow-faced murderer! May the lice eat him next week! May his false teeth choke him to death next week!"

Some tenants set out hunting for other flats, but could find none. The cheap ones were always occupied, the better flats were too dear. Besides, it wasn't easy to move; it cost money, and it meant leaving one's old neighbors.

"The tenements are the same everywhere, the landlords the same," said a woman. "I have seen places to-day an Irisher[5] wouldn't live in, and the rents are higher than here."

Toward the end of January, during a cataclysmic spell of snow, ice, and iron frost, the pipes burst again, and for weeks every one suffered for lack of water; the babies, old people, the sick ones. The neighbors were indignant. They gathered in the halls and held wild conversations. Mrs. Cracauer suggested that some one send in a complaint to the Board of Health. Mrs. Schuman said this was useless, the Board of Health belonged to Tammany Hall,[6] and the landlord had a pull there.

Mrs. Tannenbaum exploded like a bomb of Jewish emotion. She was a worse agitator than my mother, a roly-poly hysterical hippopotamus with a piercing voice.

"Let's all move out together!" she shrieked. "Let's get axes and hack out the walls and smash the windows and then move out!"

"No," said my mother, "I know something better."

Then and now, on the East Side, there have been rent strikes of tenants against their landlords. East Side tenants, I am sure, have always been the most obstreperous that ever gave a landlord sleepless nights and indigestion. My mother suggested a rent strike. The neighbors agreed with enthusiasm. They chattered about it in the weeks that followed. One told the other how she would curse the landlord when he came, and refuse to pay the rent.

"I'll spit in his face," said Mrs. Tannenbaum, "and tell him to kiss my *tochess*[7] for his rent. Then I'll slam the door on him. That's what I'll do."

[5]Slang for someone from Ireland.

[6]Tammany Hall was the headquarters of the Tammany Society, a political organization that controlled New York City politics and plundered it of millions of dollars in the nineteenth century. In the twentieth century Tammany Hall was synonymous with political patronage in New York as dispensed by the Democratic party.

[7]Yiddish for ass.

There spread through our tenement that feeling of exhilarating tension which precedes a battle. One counted the days until the first of February, when the landlord called for rent. What would he do? What would he say?

The hour came. Mrs. Tannenbaum, the fat, wildeyed hippopotamus agitator, was the first tenant upon whose door the landlord knocked. She opened it meekly, paid the rent, and never spoke a word. Her husband had forbade her to make a fuss. He didn't want the bother of moving.

The next tenant, Mrs. Schuman across the hall, was so amazed at this treachery to the cause, that she paid her rent, too. Every one else paid, except my mother. She faced the landlord boldly, and said in a clear voice, for every one to hear:

"Fix first the plumbing, Mr. Zunzer, then I'll pay the rent."

Mr. Zunzer glared at her with his goggly eyes. For a minute he could not speak for rage. Then he yanked his red scrubby beard, and said:

"I'll throw you out! Mischief-maker, I know who you are! You're the one who has been starting the rent strike here!"

"Yes," said my mother coolly. "And you've scared the others into paying you, but you can't scare me."

"I can't?" sputtered the landlord. "I will show you. To-morrow I'll call the sheriff and throw your furniture on the street!"

"No!" said my mother. "First you will have to take me to court! I know what my rights are!"

"Pfoo[8] on your rights!" said the landlord. "I can do anything I want in this district. I have a pull with Tammany Hall!"

My mother put her hands on her hips, and asked him quietly: "But with God have you a pull, Mr. Zunzer?"

Mr. Zunzer was startled by this sally. He tried to meet it with haughtiness.

"Don't talk to me of God," he said. "I am more often in the synagogue than you and your husband together. I give a dozen times more money there."

"Every one knows you have money," said my mother quietly, "even the Angel of Death. Some day he will come for *all* your money, Mr. Zunzer."

The landlord's face paled; he trembled. He tried to speak, but the words choked him. He looked queer, as if he were about to faint. Then he pulled himself together, and walked away. My mother slammed the door after him, and laughed heartily. She rushed to the window, and called across the airshaft[9] to Mrs. Ashkenazi and other neighbors. They had been sitting at their windows, listening greedily to the quarrel.

"Did you hear what hell I gave to that landlord? Didn't I give it to him good?"

"Madwoman!" my father called from the bedroom. "Where will we go when he puts us out to-morrow?"

"He won't put us out," said my mother confidently. "The landlord is scared of me, I could see it in his eyes."

My father sneered at her. Who ever heard of a landlord being scared of his tenant? But it was true this time; the landlord did not bother us again. He actually fixed

[8] Slang for "I spit on."

[9] In tenement buildings a narrow court enclosed within four walls but open at the top as a source of air supply for internal windows.

the plumbing. He sent an agent to collect the rent. He was scared; my mother had made a lucky hit when she taunted him with the Angel of Death.

Mr. Zunzer was superstitious. His deepest fear was that burglars would break in some night and kill him and take his money. Dr. Solow told us the story one night:

6

"When Mr. Zunzer first came to America," Dr. Solow related, "he peddled neckties, shoelaces and collarbuttons from a tray. He was very poor. He slept on a mattress in a cobbler's damp cellar, and lived on herrings and dry bread. He starved and suffered for five years. That's how he got the yellow face you see on him.

"Every penny he could grab he saved like a miser. He tied the nickels and dimes in a bag which he hid in a crack under his mattress. He worried. Big rats ran across his face while he slept. They did not bother him a tenth as much as did thoughts of his money.

"Oh, how sacred was that money to him. It was money to bring his wife and children from Europe. He was hungry for them. He would cry at night thinking about them. The money was not money; it was his family, his peace, his happiness, his life and death.

"One night some one stole this money from under the mattress. It was the savings of three years. Mr. Zunzer almost went crazy. He was sick in a hospital for months. He refused to eat. He wanted to die. But he took heart and commenced saving again. In two years he was able to send for his wife and children.

"Happiness did not come with them. Mr. Zunzer had formed the habit of saving money. He was a miser. He grudged his wife and children every cent they needed. He gave them little to eat. His wife fell sick; he grudged her a doctor. She died. At the funeral he fought with the undertaker over the burial price. He was always thinking of money.

"His children grew up hating him for his miserly ways. One by one they left him. The eldest boy became a thief. The second boy joined the U.S. Army. The girl disappeared.

"Mr. Zunzer was left alone. He is rich now, he owns a pawnshop and several tenement houses. But he still lives on herring and dry bread, and saves pennies like a miser. It is a disease.

"He has fits," said Dr. Solow. "Every few months I am called to him. He is rolling on the floor, he knocks his head against furniture, he cuts his face on falling dishes. He screams robbers are killing him, and stealing his money. I talk to him quietly. I give him a medicine. I light the gas, to show him there are no burglars. All night I talk to him as to a child.

"About ten years ago a junkman he knew was murdered by thieves and robbed. Since then Mr. Zunzer has the fear the same thing will happen to him.

"'Listen,' I tell him, 'you must stop worrying about money. It is making you crazy, Mr. Zunzer.'

"He wrings his hands, he weeps, and says to me: 'Yes, Dr. Solow, it is making me crazy. But what can I do? It is in my blood, in my heart. Can I cut it out of me with a knife?'

"'No,' I answer him, 'there are other ways, Mr. Zunzer.'

"'What other ways?' he weeps. 'Shall I throw my money in the river? Shall I give it to the synagogue? What good would it do? How can one live without money? And if other men fight for money, must one not fight, too? The whole world is sick with this disease, Dr. Solow, I am not the only one.'

"So what can I answer? He will die in one of his fits. His money will disappear down the sewer. Sometimes I am sorry for him; it's not altogether his fault. It *is* a world sickness. Even we who are not misers suffer from it. How happy the world would be without money! Yet what's to be done?"

My mother wagged her head mournfully through this tale of Mr. Zunzer's sickness. She said:

"The poor man! Maybe he needs another wife."

Ach, my mother! She could be sorry for any one, even a landlord.

7

Yet she fought the landlord again that winter. The rent was due, and by a coincidence my brother, my sister, my mother and I all needed shoes. We had worn the old ones until they were in shreds. It was impossible to patch them any longer. My mother decided to pawn the family's diamond ring—the one my father had bought in a prosperous period.

I went with my mother to Mr. Zunzer's pawnshop. In summer it had swinging wicker doors like a saloon. Now we entered through heavy curtained doors that shut out the daylight.

It was a grim, crowded little store smelling of camphor. There were some gloomy East Side people standing around. The walls were covered with strange objects: guitars, shovels, blankets, clocks; with lace curtains, underwear and crutches; all these miserable trophies of the defeat of the poor.

Everything worth more than a quarter was taken in pawn by Mr. Zunzer, from an old man's false teeth to a baby's diapers. People were sure to redeem these little necessities. If he made ten cents on a transaction he was satisfied, for there were hundreds of them. At the end of a week there was a big total.

It was said in the neighborhood he also bought stolen things from the young thieves and pickpockets.

We waited for our turn. An old Irish worker in overalls, with merry blue eyes and a rosy face, was trying to pawn some tools. He was drunk, and pleaded that he be given a dollar. Mr. Zunzer gave him only half a dollar, and said, "Get the hell out." The white-haired Irishman jigged and sang as he left for the saloon.

A dingy little woman pawned a baby carriage. An old Jewish graybeard pawned his prayer book and praying shawl. A fat Polish woman with a blowsy, weepy face pawned an accordion. A young girl pawned some quilts; then our turn came.

The landlord wore a black alpaca coat[10] in the pawnshop, and a skull cap.[11] He

[10] A fine lightweight cloth made from the woolly hair of an alpaca, an animal similar to a llama.

[11] A close-fitting, brimless cloth cap worn by Orthodox Jewish males.

crouched on a stool behind the counter. One saw only his scaly yellow face and bulging eyes; he was like an anxious spider. He picked up the ring my mother presented him, screwed a jeweler's glass into his eye, and studied it in the gaslight.

"Ten dollars," he said abruptly.

"I must have fifteen," said my mother.

"Ten dollars," said the landlord.

"No, fifteen," said my mother.

He looked up irritably and stared at her with his near-sighted eyes. He recognized her in the pawnshop gloom.

"You're my tenant, aren't you?" he asked, "the one that made all the trouble for me?"

"Yes," said my mother, "what of it?"

The landlord smiled bitterly.

"Nothing," he said, "but you are sure to come to a bad end."

"No worse end than yours," said my mother, "may the bananas grow in your throat!"

"Don't curse me in my own shop!" said the landlord. "I'll have you arrested. What do you want here?"

"I told you," said my mother, "I want fifteen dollars on this ring."

"It is worth only ten," said the landlord.

"To me you must give fifteen," said my mother boldly.

The landlord paled. He looked at my mother fearfully. She knew his secret. My mother mystified and alarmed him with her boldness. He was accustomed to people who cowered.

He wrote out a ticket for the ring, gave my mother fifteen dollars. She crowed over her victory as we walked home. Next day she bought shoes for my brother, my sister Esther, and myself. Her own shoes she forgot to buy. That's the way she generally arranged things.

1930

H. L. Mencken 1880–1956

Called by journalist Walter Lippmann in the 1920s "the most powerful personal influence on this whole generation of educated people," H. L. Mencken reigned as national literary arbiter during that decade as well as the most famous social and cultural commentator of his day. From the early days of the twentieth century he led the attack on the genteel tradition in American letters—the Anglo-American tradition that was associated in most readers' eyes with Henry James, William Dean Howells, and "polite letters." Mencken championed early literary naturalists and realists, particularly Theodore Dreiser and Sinclair Lewis; and in the pages of the *Smart Set* and the *American Mercury,* highly influential magazines that he edited for two decades, he attacked provincialism, puritanism, and censorship. A bitter critic of the American alliance with Great Britain in World War I—and, in fact, a critic of all things British—he fought for an expansion of the literary franchise to Americans of non-

British descent. He had in mind German Americans (such as Dreiser) and eastern Europeans, but—as editor of *American Mercury*—he also published more African American writers than any other editor of his time.

Mencken came by his "prejudices" (as he termed them) honestly. The son of German American parents whose families had settled in Baltimore in the mid-nineteenth century, he grew up in a mid-Atlantic city dominated by Americans of British (and, often, southern) descent. Scorning a university education (although, he was quick to point out, the Menckens had been a learned family in Germany), he took to journalism in his teens and rose quickly on a series of Baltimore newspapers—all the while reading voraciously, trying his hand at poetry and fiction, and publishing books on Nietzsche and George Bernard Shaw in his twenties. In his late twenties he became literary editor of the stylish *Smart Set,* and by his mid-thirties he was editing the magazine. Silenced during World War I for his unpopular pro-German views, he broke out in 1919 with both fury and delight as he heaped abuse on nearly every aspect of American life: its small-town provincialism, its religious fundamentalism, its tawdry politics, its intellectual sterility. He was particularly rough on the American hinterlands, the South and the Midwest. Holding up a European—and an urban—ideal, and feeling the American East at least approached that ideal, he delighted in attacking those regions that he felt had become the home of American puritanism (by which he meant a sort of raw Calvinism in combination with Victorian propriety) and the hotbed of prohibitionist sentiment. He lambasted the provinces in his Baltimore *Sun* column, in nationally syndicated newspaper pieces, in the pages of the *Mercury,* and in a series of books—appropriately entitled *Prejudices*—that appeared throughout the 1920s.

Among his most famous essays are those he wrote during the Scopes evolution trial in Dayton, Tennessee, in 1925 (and, just after the trial, his vicious obituary essay on the life and career of the fundamentalist William Jennings Bryan) and his diatribe against southern culture, "The Sahara of the Bozart." That essay and others earned Mencken the reputation of the most hated man in the South since Sherman—although his anti-South essays also stirred a number of young, iconoclastic southern writers (including Thomas Wolfe, Frances Newman, W. J. Cash, Paul Green, and Allen Tate—although Tate later repented of his Menckenism) and played some part in the southern literary renaissance of the 1920s and 1930s. His truth-telling about the South also influenced the young African American writer Richard Wright—who happened upon criticism of Mencken in a Memphis newspaper, turned to Mencken's own essays, and marveled at this writer who, as Wright later stated, denounced "everything American," laughed at the national circus, and used "words as a weapon . . . as one would use a club."

Mencken produced other books in the 1920s and 1930s—reflections on religion, politics, and the national life—but his period of greatest influence declined with the end of the 1920s. Although he regained readers and reputation in the 1940s with a series of autobiographical volumes as well as his multi-volume work *The American Language* (he vastly preferred American English to British English), he never recaptured the boisterous spirit of the 1920s. During the Great Depression and World War II, Mencken's brand of satire no longer appeared so funny. His pro-German sympathies kept him from attacking Hitler (whom he characterized as a European version of a benighted southern demagogue), and certain of his writings led to charges of anti-Semitism.

It is with the 1920s, then, that the essential Mencken is to be identified. As an American social critic and humorist he is *sui generis*—the boldest, most outrageous critic of his time, writing in a language that seemed to sing and dance. Scholars have found for him European equivalents—

Voltaire and Samuel Johnson are most often cited—but no American precedents. Mencken's own favorite American writer, Mark Twain, perhaps comes closest—with his own bold satire, his truth-telling, his love of the American language, his delight in exposing frauds and hypocrites of all kinds. At its best, Mencken's joyous naysaying provides ample evidence for Walter Lippmann's shrewd assessment: Mencken "calls you a swine, and an imbecile, and . . . increases your will to live."

Fred Hobson
University of North Carolina–Chapel Hill

PRIMARY WORKS

Prejudices (6 vols.), 1919–27; *Happy Days,* 1940;B *Newspaper Days,* 1941; *Heathen Days,* 1943.

The Sahara of the Bozart

Alas, for the South! Her books have grown fewer—She never was much given to literature.

In the lamented J. Gordon Coogler, author of these elegaic lines, there was the insight of a true poet. He was the last bard of Dixie, at least in the legitimate line. Down there a poet is now almost as rare as an oboe-player, a dry-point etcher or a metaphysician. It is, indeed, amazing to contemplate so vast a vacuity. One thinks of the interstellar spaces, of the colossal reaches of the now mythical ether. Nearly the whole of Europe could be lost in that stupendous region of fat farms, shoddy cities and paralyzed cerebrums: one could throw in France, Germany and Italy, and still have room for the British Isles. And yet, for all its size and all its wealth and all the "progress" it babbles of, it is almost as sterile, artistically, intellectually, culturally, as the Sahara Desert. There are single acres in Europe that house more first-rate men than all the states south of the Potomac; there are probably single square miles in America. If the whole of the late Confederacy were to be engulfed by a tidal wave tomorrow, the effect upon the civilized minority of men in the world would be but little greater than that of a flood on the Yang-tse-kiang. It would be impossible in all history to match so complete a drying-up of civilization.

I say a civilization because that is what, in the old days, the South had, despite the Baptist and Methodist barbarism that reigns down there now. More, it was a civilization of manifold excellences—perhaps the best that the Western Hemisphere has ever seen—undoubtedly the best that These States have ever seen. Down to the middle of the last century, and even beyond, the main hatchery of ideas on this side of the water was across the Potomac bridges. The New England shopkeepers and theologians never really developed a civilization; all they ever developed was a government. They were, at their best, tawdry and tacky fellows, oafish in manner and devoid of imagination; one searches the books in vain for mention of a salient Yankee gentleman; as well look for a Welsh gentleman. But in the south there were men of delicate fancy, urbane instinct and aristocratic manner—in brief, superior men—in brief, gentry. To politics, their chief diversion, they brought active and original minds. It was there that nearly all the political theories we still cherish and suffer under came to birth. It was there that the crude dogmatism of New England was refined and humanized. It was there, above all, that some attention was given to the art of living—that life got beyond and above the state of a mere infliction and became an exhilarating experience. A certain noble spaciousness was in the ancient southern scheme of things. The *Ur*-Confederate had leisure. He liked to toy with ideas. He was hospitable and tolerant. He had the vague thing that we call culture.

But consider the condition of his late empire today. The picture gives one the creeps. It is as if the Civil War stamped out every last bearer of the torch, and left only a mob of peasants on the field. One thinks of Asia Minor, resigned to Armenians, Greeks and wild swine, of Poland abandoned to the Poles. In all that gargantuan paradise of the fourth-rate there is not a single picture gallery worth going into, or a single orchestra capable of playing the nine symphonies of Beethoven, or a single opera-house, or a single theater devoted to decent plays, or a single public monument (built since the war) that is worth looking at, or a single workshop devoted to the making of beautiful things. Once you have counted Robert Loveman (an Ohioan by birth) and John McClure (an Oklahoman) you will not find a single southern poet above the rank of a neighborhood rhymester. Once you have counted James Branch Cabell (a lingering survivor of the *ancien régime:* a scarlet dragonfly imbedded in opaque amber) you will not find a single southern prose writer who can actually write. And once you have—but when you come to critics, musical composers, painters, sculptors, architects and the like, you will have to give it up, for there is not even a bad one between the Potomac mud-flats and the Gulf. Nor an historian. Nor a sociologist. Nor a philosopher. Nor a theologian. Nor a scientist. In all these fields the south is an awe-inspiring blank—a brother to Portugal, Serbia and Esthonia.

Consider, for example, the present estate and dignity of Virginia—in the great days indubitably the premier American state, the mother of Presidents and statesmen, the home of the first American university worthy of the name, the *arbiter elegantiarum* of the western world. Well, observe Virginia to-day. It is years since a first-rate man, save only Cabell, has come out of it; it is years since an idea has come out of it. The old aristocracy went down the red gullet of war; the poor white trash are now in the saddle. Politics in Virginia are cheap, ignorant, parochial, idiotic; there is scarcely a man in office above the rank of a professional job-seeker; the political doctrine that prevails is made up of hand-me-downs from the bumpkinry of the Middle West—Bryanism, Prohibition, vice crusading, all that sort of filthy claptrap; the administration of the law is turned over to professors of Puritanism and espionage; a Washington or a Jefferson, dumped there by some act of God, would be denounced as a scoundrel and jailed overnight. Elegance, *esprit,* culture? Virginia has no art, no literature, no philosophy, no mind or aspiration of her own. Her education has sunk to the Baptist seminary level; not a single contribution to human knowledge has come out of her colleges in twenty-five years; she spends less than half upon her common schools, *per capita,* than any northern state spends. In brief, an intellectual Gobi or Lapland. Urbanity, *politesse,* chivalry? Go to! It was in Virginia that they invented the device of searching for contraband whisky in women's underwear. . . . There remains, at the top, a ghost of the old aristocracy, a bit wistful and infinitely charming. But it has lost all its old leadership to fabulous monsters from the lower depths; it is submerged in an industrial plutocracy that is ignorant and ignominious.

The mind of the state, as it is revealed to the nation, is pathetically naïve and inconsequential. It no longer reacts with energy and elasticity to great problems. It has fallen to the bombastic trivialities of the camp-meeting and the chautauqua. Its foremost exponent—if so flabby a thing may be said to have an exponent—is a stateman whose name is synonymous with empty words, broken pledges and false pretenses. One could no more imagine a Lee or a Washington in the Virginia of to-day than one could imagine a Huxley in Nicaragua.

I choose the Old Dominion, not because I disdain it, but precisely because I esteem it. It is, by long odds, the most civilized of the southern states, now as always. It has sent a host of creditable sons northward; the stream kept running into our own time. Virginians, even the worst of them, show the effects of a great tradition. They hold themselves above other southerners, and with sound pretension. If one turns to such a commonwealth as Georgia the picture becomes far darker. There the liberated lower orders of whites have borrowed the worst commercial bounderism of the Yankee and superimposed it upon a culture that, at bottom, is but little removed from savagery. Georgia is at once the home of the cotton-mill sweater and of the most noisy and vapid sort of chamber of commerce, of the Methodist parson turned Savonarola and of the lynching bee. A self-respecting European, going there to live, would not only find intellectual stimulation utterly lacking; he would actually feel a certain insecurity, as if the scene were the Balkans or the China Coast. The Leo Frank affair was no isolated phenomenon. It fitted into its frame very snugly. It was a natural expression of Georgian notions of truth and justice. There is a state with more than half the area of Italy and more population than either Denmark or Norway, and yet in thirty years it has not produced a single idea. Once upon a time a Georgian printed a couple of books that attracted notice, but immediately it turned out that he was little more than an amanuensis for the local blacks—that his works were really the products, not of white Georgia, but of black Georgia. Writing afterward *as* a white man, he swiftly subsided into the fifth rank. And he is not only the glory of the literature of Georgia; he is, almost literally, the whole of the literature of Georgia—nay, of the entire art of Georgia.

Virginia is the best of the south to-day, and Georgia is perhaps the worst. The one is simply senile; the other is crass, gross, vulgar and obnoxious. Between lies a vast plain of mediocrity, stupidity, lethargy, almost of dead silence. In the north, of course, there is also grossness, crassness, vulgarity. The north, in its way, is also stupid and obnoxious. But nowhere in the north is there such complete sterility, so depressing a lack of all civilized gesture and aspiration. One would find it difficult to unearth a second-rate city between the Ohio and the Pacific that isn't struggling to establish an orchestra, or setting up a little theater, or going in for an art gallery, or making some other effort to get into touch with civilization. These efforts often fail, and sometimes they succeed rather absurdly, but under them there is at least an impulse that deserves respect, and that is the impulse to seek beauty and to experiment with ideas, and so to give the life of every day a certain dignity and purpose. You will find no such impulse in the south. There are no committees down there cadging subscriptions for orchestras; if a string quartet is ever heard there, the news of it has never come out; an opera troupe, when it roves the land, is a nine days' wonder. The little theater movement has swept the whole country, enormously augmenting the public interest in sound plays, giving new dramatists their chance, forcing reforms upon the commercial theater. Everywhere else the wave rolls high—but along the line of the Potomac it breaks upon a rock-bound shore. There is no little theater beyond. There is no gallery of pictures. No artist ever gives exhibitions. No one talks of such things. No one seems to be interested in such things.

As for the cause of this unanimous torpor and doltishness, this curious and almost pathological estrangement from everything that makes for a civilized culture, I have hinted at it already, and now state it again. The south has simply been drained of all its best blood. The vast blood-letting of the Civil War half exterminated and wholly paralyzed the old aristocracy, and so left the land to the harsh mercies of the poor white trash, now its masters. The war, of course, was not a complete massacre. It spared a decent number of first-rate southerners—perhaps even some of the very best. Moreover, other countries, notably France and Germany, have survived far more staggering butcheries, and even showed marked progress thereafter. But the war not only cost a great many valuable lives; it also brought bankruptcy, demoralization and despair in its train—and so the majority of the first-rate southerners that were left, broken in spirit and unable to live under the new dispensation, cleared out. A few went to South America, to Egypt, to the Far East. Most came north. They were fecund; their progeny is widely dispersed, to the great benefit of the north. A southerner of good blood almost always does well in the north. He finds, even in the big cities, surroundings fit for a man of condition. His peculiar qualities have a high social value, and are esteemed. He is welcomed by the codfish aristocracy as one palpably superior. But in the south he throws up his hands. It is impossible for him to stoop to the common level. He cannot brawl in politics with the grandsons of his grandfather's tenants. He is unable to share their fierce jealousy of the emerging black—the cornerstone of all their public thinking. He is anæsthetic to their theological and political enthusiasms. He finds himself an alien at their feasts of soul. And so he withdraws into his tower, and is heard of no more. Cabell is almost a perfect example. His eyes, for years, were turned toward the past; he became a professor of the grotesque genealogizing that decaying aristocracies affect; it was only by a sort of accident that he discovered himself to be an artist. The south is unaware of the fact to this day; it regards Woodrow Wilson and Col. John Temple Graves as much finer stylists, and Frank L. Stanton as an infinitely greater poet. If it has heard, which I doubt, that Cabell has been hoofed by the Comstocks, it unquestionably views that assault as a deserved rebuke to a fellow who indulges a lewd passion for fancy writing, and is a covert enemy to the Only True Christianity.

What is needed down there, before the vexatious public problems of the region may be intelligently approached, is a survey of the population by competent ethnologists and anthropologists. The immigrants of the north have been studied at great length, and any one who is interested may now apply to the Bureau of Ethnology for elaborate data as to their racial strains, their stature and cranial indices, their relative capacity for education, and the changes that they undergo under American *Kultur.* But the older stocks of the south, and particularly the emancipated and dominant poor white trash, have never been investigated scientifically, and most of the current generalizations about them are probably wrong. For example, the generalization that they are purely Anglo-Saxon in blood. This I doubt very seriously. The chief strain down there, I believe, is Celtic rather than Saxon, particularly in the hill country. French blood, too, shows itself here and there, and so does Spanish, and so does

German. The last-named entered from the northward, by way of the limestone belt just east of the Alleghenies. Again, it is very likely that in some parts of the south a good many of the plebeian whites have more than a trace of negro blood. Interbreeding under concubinage produced some very light half-breeds at an early day, and no doubt appreciable numbers of them went over into the white race by the simple process of changing their abode. Not long ago I read a curious article by an intelligent negro, in which he stated that it is easy for a very light negro to pass as white in the south on account of the fact that large numbers of southerners accepted as white have distinctly negroid features. Thus it becomes a delicate and dangerous matter for a train conductor or a hotel-keeper to challenge a suspect. But the Celtic strain is far more obvious than any of these others. It not only makes itself visible in physical stigmata—*e.g.,* leanness and dark coloring—but also in mental traits. For example, the religious thought of the south is almost precisely identical with the religious thought of Wales. There is the same naïve belief in an anthropomorphic Creator but little removed, in manner and desire, from an evangelical bishop; there is the same submission to an ignorant and impudent sacerdotal tyranny, and there is the same sharp contrast between doctrinal orthodoxy and private ethics. Read Caradoc Evans' ironical picture of the Welsh Wesleyans in his preface to "My Neighbors," and you will be instantly reminded of the Georgia and Carolina Methodists. The most booming sort of piety, in the south, is not incompatible with the theory that lynching is a benign institution. Two generations ago it was not incompatible with an ardent belief in slavery.

It is highly probable that some of the worst blood of western Europe flows in the veins of the southern poor whites, now poor no longer. The original strains, according to every honest historian, were extremely corrupt. Philip Alexander Bruce (a Virginian of the old gentry) says in his "Industrial History of Virginia in the Seventeenth Century" that the first native-born generation was largely illegitimate. "One of the most common offenses against morality committed in the lower ranks of life in Virginia during the seventeenth century," he says, "was bastardy." The mothers of these bastards, he continues, were chiefly indentured servants, and "had belonged to the lowest class in their native country." Fanny Kemble Butler, writing of the Georgia poor whites of a century later, described them as "the most degraded race of human beings claiming an Anglo-Saxon origin that can be found on the face of the earth—filthy, lazy, ignorant, brutal, proud, penniless savages." The Sunday-school and the chautauqua, of course, have appreciably mellowed the descendants of these "savages," and their economic progress and rise to political power have done perhaps even more, but the marks of their origin are still unpleasantly plentiful. Every now and then they produce a political leader who puts their secret notions of the true, the good and the beautiful into plain words, to the amazement and scandal of the rest of the country. That amazement is turned into downright incredulity when news comes that his platform has got him high office, and that he is trying to execute it.

In the great days of the south the line between the gentry and the poor whites was very sharply drawn. There was absolutely no intermarriage. So far as I know there is not a single instance in history of a southerner of the upper class marrying one of the bondwomen described by Mr. Bruce. In other societies characterized by class distinctions of that sort it is common for the lower class to be improved by extra-legal crosses. That is to say, the men of the upper class take women of the lower class as mistresses, and out of such unions spring the extraordinary plebeians who rise sharply from the common level, and so propagate the delusion that all other plebeians would do the same thing if they had the chance—in brief, the delusion that class distinctions are merely economic and conventional, and not congenital and genuine. But in the south the men of the upper classes sought their mistresses among the blacks, and after a few generations there was so much white blood in the black women that they were considerably more attractive than the unhealthy and bedraggled women of the poor whites. This preference continued into our own time. A southerner of good family once told me in all seriousness that he had reached his majority before it ever occurred to him that a white woman might make quite as agreeable a mistress as the octaroons of his jejune fancy. If the thing has changed of late, it is not the fault of the southern white man, but of the southern mulatto women. The more slightly yellow girls of the region, with improving economic opportunities, have gained self-respect, and so they are no longer as willing to enter into concubinage as their grand-dams were.

As a result of this preference of the southern gentry for mulatto mistresses there was created a series of mixed strains containing the best white blood of the south, and perhaps of the whole country. As another result the poor whites went unfertilized from above, and so missed the improvement that so constantly shows itself in the peasant stocks of other countries. It is a commonplace that nearly all negroes who rise above the general are of mixed blood, usually with the white predominating. I know a great many negroes, and it would be hard for me to think of an exception. What is too often forgotten is that this white blood is not the blood of the poor whites but that of the old gentry. The mulatto girls of the early days despised the poor whites as creatures distinctly inferior to negroes, and it was thus almost unheard of for such a girl to enter into relations with a man of that submerged class. This aversion was based upon a sound instinct. The southern mulatto of to-day is a proof of it. Like all other half-breeds he is an unhappy man, with disquieting tendencies toward anti-social habits of thought, but he is intrinsically a better animal than the pure-blooded descendant of the old poor whites, and he not infrequently demonstrates it. It is not by accident that the negroes of the south are making faster progress, economically and culturally, than the masses of the whites. It is not by accident that the only visible æsthetic activity in the south is wholly in their hands. No southern composer has ever written music so good as that of half a dozen white-black composers who might be named. Even in politics, the negro reveals a curious superiority. Despite the fact that the race question has been the main political concern of the southern whites for two generations, to the practical exclusion of everything else, they have contributed nothing to the discussion that has impressed the rest of the world so deeply and so favorably as three or four books by southern negroes.

Entering upon such themes, of course, one must resign one's self to a vast misunderstanding and abuse. The south has not only lost its old capacity for producing ideas; it has also taken on the worst intolerance of ignorance and stupidity. Its prevailing mental attitude for several decades past has been that of its own hedge ecclesiastics. All who dissent from its orthodox doctrines are scoundrels. All who presume to discuss its ways realistically are damned. I have had, in my day, several experiences in point. Once, after I had published an article on some phase of the eternal race question, a leading southern newspaper replied by printing a column of denunciation of my father, then dead nearly twenty years—a philippic placarding him as an ignorant foreigner of dubious origin, inhabiting "the Baltimore ghetto" and speaking a dialect recalling that of Weber & Fields—two thousand words of incandescent nonsense, utterly false and beside the point, but exactly meeting the latter-day southern notion of effective controversy. Another time, I published a short discourse on lynching, arguing that the sport was popular in the south because the backward culture of the region denied the populace more seemly recreations. Among such recreations I mentioned those afforded by brass bands, symphony orchestras, boxing matches, amateur athletic contests, shoot-the-chutes, roof gardens, horse races, and so on. In reply another great southern journal denounced me as a man "of wineshop temperament, brass-jewelry tastes and pornographic predilections." In other words, brass bands, in the south, are classed with brass jewelry, and both are snares of the devil! To advocate setting up symphony orchestras is pornography! . . . Alas, when the touchy southerner attempts a greater urbanity, the result is often even worse. Some time ago a colleague of mine printed an article deploring the arrested cultural development of Georgia. In reply he received a number of protests from patriotic Georgians, and all of them solemnly listed the glories of the state. I indulge in a few specimens:

> Who has not heard of Asa G. Candler, whose name is synonymous with Coca-Cola, a Georgia product?
>
> The first Sunday-school in the world was opened in Savannah.
>
> Who does not recall with pleasure the writings of . . . Frank L. Stanton, Georgia's brilliant poet?
>
> Georgia was the first state to organize a Boys' Corn Club in the South—Newton county, 1904.
>
> The first to suggest a common United Daughters of the Confederacy badge was Mrs. Raynes, of Georgia.
>
> The first to suggest a state historian of the United Daughters of the Confederacy was Mrs. C. Helen Plane (Macon convention, 1896).
>
> The first to suggest putting to music Heber's "From Greenland's Icy Mountains" was Mrs. F. R. Goulding, of Savannah.

And so on, and so on. These proud boasts came, remember, not from obscure private persons, but from "Leading Georgians"—in one case, the state historian. Curious sidelights upon the ex-Confederate mind! Another comes from a stray copy of a negro paper. It describes an ordinance lately passed by the city council of Douglas, Ga., forbidding any trousers presser, on penalty of forfeiting a $500 bond, to engage in "pressing for both white and colored." This in a town, says the negro paper, where practically all of the white inhabitants have "their food prepared by colored hands," "their babies cared for by colored hands," and "the clothes which they wear right next to their skins washed in houses where negroes live"—houses in which the said clothes "remain for as long as a week at a time." But if you marvel at the absurdity, keep it dark! A casual word, and the united press of the south will be upon your trail, denouncing you bitterly as a scoundrelly Yankee, a Bolshevik Jew, an agent of the Wilhelmstrasse. . . .

Obviously, it is impossible for intelligence to flourish in such an atmosphere. Free inquiry is blocked by the idiotic certainties of ignorant men. The arts, save in the lower reaches of the gospel hymn, the phonograph and the chautauqua harangue, are all held in suspicion. The tone of public opinion is set by an upstart class but lately emerged from industrial slavery into commercial enterprise—the class of "hustling" business men, of "live wires," of commercial club luminaries, of "drive" managers, of forward-lookers and right-thinkers—in brief, of third-rate southerners inoculated with all the worst traits of the Yankee sharper. One observes the curious effects of an old tradition of truculence upon a population now merely pushful and impudent, of an old tradition of chivalry upon a population now quite without imagination. The old repose is gone. The old romanticism is gone. The philistinism of the new type of town-boomer southerner is not only indifferent to the ideals of the old south; it is positively antagonistic to them. That philistinism regards human life, not as an agreeable adventure, but as a mere trial of rectitude and efficiency. It is overwhelmingly utilitarian and moral. It is inconceivably hollow and obnoxious. What remains of the ancient tradition is simply a certain charming civility in private intercourse—often broken down, alas, by the hot rages of Puritanism, but still generally visible. The southerner, at his worst, is never quite the surly cad that the Yankee is. His sensitiveness may betray him into occasional bad manners, but in the main he is a pleasant fellow—hospitable, polite, good-humored, even jovial. . . . But a bit absurd. . . . A bit pathetic.

1917

John Dos Passos 1896–1970

Son of a famous Wall Street lawyer, John Dos Passos attended Choate, toured Europe, and went on to Harvard to become first an aesthete and then, gradually, something of a political rebel. In 1917, like many young men of his background, he went to France as a volunteer ambulance driver. Horrified by the war's brutality, by the official lies, by the meaninglessness of the suffering he witnessed, he grew increasingly radical and further alienated from the world his father represented. In *Three Soldiers,* an attack on the army, he sought, through formal means, to break out of the narrow perspective of his own social class: this early novel is narrated in turn from the points of view of three different soldiers, one an artist and Harvard man, but the other two very much "average" soldiers.

Dos Passos's desire to broaden further the social perspective in his writing, along with his intense interest in postwar developments in the arts, led to the experimental novel *Manhattan Transfer,* published in 1925. Here the point of view shifts rapidly, providing over a hundred fragments of the lives of dozens of characters, so that no one individual, but rather Manhattan itself—dazzling, but lonely and alienating—emerges as the novel's protagonist.

Over the next ten years, Dos Passos became involved with a variety of left-wing causes, among them the *New Masses,* a political journal; the radical New Playwrights Theatre; the defense of Sacco and Vanzetti, two Italian American anarchists hastily accused of murder and finally executed in 1927; and the 1931 miners' strike in Harlan County, Kentucky. The fiction he wrote during this period, the trilogy *U.S.A.,* reflects Dos Passos's deepening radicalism as well as his increasing ambition as a writer, for the subject of *U.S.A.* is the history of

American life in the first three decades of this century. His best work, the trilogy represents a culmination of Dos Passos's experimentation with literary form. In *U.S.A.,* Dos Passos found the technical means to delineate the connections between the kinds of alienation he dramatized in *Manhattan Transfer* and the social structures that produced it.

Most of this lengthy trilogy consists of twelve interwoven fictional narratives, each told from the point of view of its central character. These twelve narratives are interrupted not only by each other but by three kinds of formal devices: (1) sixty-eight "Newsreel" sections, carefully constructed collages of actual newspaper headlines, news story fragments, and snatches of song lyrics, political speeches, and advertisements that together trace mass culture and popular consciousness over the years; (2) twenty-seven biographies (like the two included here) of key public figures, people who shaped or represented or resisted the major social forces of the era; and (3) fifty-one "Camera Eye" sections, stream-of-consciousness fragments that depict the developing awareness of a sensitive and artistic individual (not unlike Dos Passos). These four components—narratives, Newsreels, biographies, and Camera Eye sections—work together to dramatize the impact of public events on private lives, to illustrate the very social nature of individual experience, and to indict capitalist America.

Dos Passos's writing after *U.S.A.* never approached the power of the trilogy. His experimenting had been very much tied up with his radical ideas, and he began rejecting those ideas in the late 1930s (becoming, in later life, extremely conservative). He returned to more traditional forms in a second trilogy, *District of Columbia* (1952), and in later novels; he began writing history, including a biography of Thomas Jefferson; and he continued the political journalism and travel writing he had been producing all his life. In 1961 he published *Midcentury,* which copies the form of his first trilogy but has none of its power; *Midcentury*'s attack on unions, psychoanalysis, teenagers, and other targets seems narrow and petulant next to the passionate critique of an entire social system that is Dos Passos's greatest achievement, *U.S.A.*

Robert C. Rosen
William Paterson University

PRIMARY WORKS

Three Soldiers, 1920; *Manhattan Transfer,* 1925; *U.S.A.,* 1938 *(The 42nd Parallel,* 1930; *Nineteen Nineteen,* 1932; *The Big Money,* 1936); *District of Columbia,* 1952; *Midcentury,* 1961.

from U.S.A.

The Body of an American

Whereasthe Congressoftheunitedstates byaconcurrentresolutionadoptedon the4thdayofmarch lastauthorizedthe Secretaryofwar to cause to be brought to theunitedstatesthe body of an Americanwhowasamemberoftheamericanexpeditionaryforcesineurope wholosthislifeduringtheworldwarandwhoseidentityhas notbeenestablished for burial inthememorialamphitheatreofthenationalcemeteryat arlingtonvirginia

In the tarpaper morgue at Chalons-sur-Marne in the reek of chloride of lime and the dead, they picked out the pine box that held all that was left of

enie menie minie moe plenty other pine boxes stacked up there containing what they'd scraped up of Richard Roe

and other person or persons unknown. Only one can go. How did they pick John Doe?

Make sure he aint a dinge, boys,

make sure he aint a guinea or a kike,[1]

how can you tell a guy's a hundredpercent when all you've got's a gunnysack full of bones, bronze buttons stamped with the screaming eagle and a pair of roll puttees?

. . . and the gagging chloride and the puky dirtstench of the yearold dead . . .

The day withal was too meaningful and tragic for applause. Silence, tears, songs and prayer, muffled drums and soft music were the instrumentalities today of national approbation.

John Doe was born (thudding din of blood in love into the shuddering soar of a man and a woman alone indeed together lurching into

and ninemonths sick drowse waking into scared agony and the pain and blood and mess of birth). John Doe was born

and raised in Brooklyn, in Memphis, near the lakefront in Cleveland, Ohio, in the stench of the stockyards in Chi, on Beacon Hill, in an old brick house in Alexandria Virginia, on Telegraph Hill, in a halftimbered Tudor cottage in Portland the city of roses,

in the Lying-In Hospital old Morgan[2] endowed on Stuyvesant Square,

across the railroad tracks, out near the country club, in a shack cabin tenement apartmenthouse exclusive residential suburb;

scion of one of the best families in the social register, won first prize in the baby parade at Coronado Beach, was marbles champion of the Little Rock grammarschools, crack basketballplayer at the Booneville High, quarterback at the State Reformatory, having saved the sheriff's kid from drowning in the Little Missouri River was invited to Washington to be photographed shaking hands with the President on the White House steps;—

* * *

though this was a time of mourning, such an assemblage necessarily has about it a touch of color. In the boxes are seen the court uniforms of foreign diplomats, the gold braid of our own and foreign fleets and armies, the black of the conventional morning dress of American statesmen, the varicolored furs and outdoor wrapping garments of mothers and sisters come to mourn, the drab and blue of soldiers and sailors, the glitter of musical instruments and the white and black of a vested choir

[1]Derogatory terms for black, Italian, and Jew.
[2]J. Pierpont Morgan (1837–1913), powerful U.S. financier.

—busyboy harveststiff hogcaller boyscout champeen cornshucker of Western Kansas bellhop at the United States Hotel at Saratoga Springs office boy callboy fruiter telephone lineman longshoreman lumberjack plumber's helper,

worked for an exterminating company in Union City, filled pipes in an opium joint in Trenton, N.J.

Y.M.C.A. secretary, express agent, truckdriver, fordmechanic, sold books in Denver Colorado: Madam would you be willing to help a young man work his way through college?

President Harding, with a reverence seemingly more significant because of his high temporal station, concluded his speech:

We are met today to pay the impersonal tribute;

the name of him whose body lies before us took flight with his imperishable soul . . .

as a typical soldier of this representative democracy he fought and died believing in the indisputable justice of his country's cause . . .

by raising his right hand and asking the thousands within the sound of his voice to join in the prayer:

Our Father which art in heaven hallowed be thy name . . .

Naked he went into the army;

they weighed you, measured you, looked for flat feet, squeezed your penis to see if you had clap, looked up your anus to see if you had piles, counted your teeth, made you cough, listened to your heart and lungs, made you read the letters on the card, charted your urine and your intelligence,

gave you a service record for a future (imperishable soul)

and an identification tag stamped with your serial number to hang around your neck, issued O D[3] regulation equipment, a condiment can and a copy of the articles of war:

Atten'SHUN suck in your gut you c——r wipe that smile off your face eyes right wattja tink dis is a choirch-social? For-war-D'ARCH.

John Doe

and Richard Roe and other person or persons unknown

drilled hiked, manual of arms, ate slum,[4] learned to salute, to soldier, to loaf in the latrines, forbidden to smoke on deck, overseas guard duty, forty men and eight horses,[5] shortarm inspection[6] and the ping of shrapnel and the shrill bullets combing the air and the sorehead woodpeckers the machineguns mud cooties gasmasks and the itch.

Say feller tell me how I can get back to my outfit.

[3]Olive drab, military color.

[4]Slumgullion, or watery stew.

[5]Troop train capacity.

[6]Inspection for venereal disease.

John Doe had a head

for twentyodd years intensely the nerves of the eyes the ears the palate the tongue the fingers the toes the armpits, the nerves warmfeeling under the skin charged the coiled brain with hurt sweet warm cold mine must dont sayings print headlines:

Thou shalt not the multiplication table long division, Now is the time for all good men knocks but once at a young man's door, It's a great life if Ish gebibbel,[7] The first five years'll be the Safety First, Suppose a hun tried to rape your my country right or wrong, Catch 'em young, What he dont know wont treat 'em rough, Tell 'em nothin, He got what was coming to him he got his, This is a white man's country, Kick the bucket, Gone west, If you dont like it you can croaked him

Say buddy cant you tell me how I can get back to my outfit?

Cant help jumpin when them things go off, give me the trots[8] them things do. I lost my identification tag swimmin in the Marne, roughhousin with a guy while we was waitin to be deloused, in bed with a girl named Jeanne (Love moving picture wet French postcard dream began with saltpeter[9] in the coffee and ended at the propho[10] station);—

Say soldier for chrissake cant you tell me how I can get back to my outfit?

John Doe's

heart pumped blood:

alive thudding silence of blood in your ears

down in the clearing in the Oregon forest[11] where the punkins were punkincolor pouring into the blood through the yes and the fallcolored trees and the bronze hoppers were hopping through the dry grass, where tiny striped snails hung on the underside of the blades and the flies hummed, wasps droned, bumble-bees buzzed, and the woods smelt of wine and mushrooms and apples, homey smell of fall pouring into the blood,

and I dropped the tin hat and the sweaty pack and lay flat with the dogday sun licking my throat and adamsapple and the tight skin over the breastbone.

The shell had his number on it.

The blood ran into the ground.

* * *

The service record dropped out of the filing cabinet when the quartermaster sergeant got blotto that time they had to pack up and leave the billets in a hurry.

The identification tag was in the bottom of the Marne.

The blood ran into the ground, the brains oozed out of the cracked skull and were licked up by the trenchrats, the belly swelled and raised a generation of bluebottle flies,

[7]It doesn't matter to me (pseudo-Yiddish).
[8]Diarrhea.
[9]Chemical given to soldiers in an effort to reduce their sexual desire.
[10]Prophylactic.
[11]Argonne Forest, in northeastern France; scene of major World War I battle.

and the incorruptible skeleton,
and the scraps of dried viscera and skin bundled in khaki
they took to Chalons-sur-Marne
and laid it out neat in a pine coffin
and took it home to God's Country on a battleship

and buried it in a sarcophagus in the Memorial Amphitheatre in the Arlington National Cemetery

and draped the Old Glory over it

and the bugler played taps

and Mr. Harding prayed to God and the diplomats and the generals and the admirals and the brasshats and the politicians and the handsomely dressed ladies out of the society column of the *Washington Post* stood up solemn

and thought how beautiful sad Old Glory God's Country it was to have the bugler play taps and the three volleys made their ears ring.

Where his chest ought to have been they pinned

the Congressional Medal, the D.S.C.,[12] the Medaille Militaire, the Belgian Croix de Guerre, the Italian gold medal, the Vitutea Militara sent by Queen Marie of Rumania, the Czechoslovak war cross, the Virtuti Militari of the Poles, a wreath sent by Hamilton Fish, Jr.,[13] of New York, and a little wampum presented by a deputation of Arizona redskins in warpaint and feathers. All the Washingtonians brought flowers.

Woodrow Wilson brought a bouquet of poppies.

1932

The Bitter Drink

Veblen,

a greyfaced shambling man lolling resentful at his desk with his cheek on his hand, in a low sarcastic mumble of intricate phrases subtly paying out the logical inescapable rope of matteroffact for a society to hang itself by,

dissecting out the century with a scalpel so keen, so comical, so exact that the professors and students ninetenths of the time didn't know it was there, and the magnates and the respected windbags and the applauded loudspeakers never knew it was there.

Veblen

asked too many questions, suffered from a constitutional inability to say yes.

Socrates asked questions, drank down the bitter drink one night when the first cock crowed,

but Veblen

[12]Distinguished Service Cross.

[13]Member of U.S. Congress; promoted Unknown Soldier memorial.

drank it in little sips through a long life in the stuffiness of classrooms, the dust of libraries, the staleness of cheap flats such as a poor instructor can afford. He fought the bogy all right, pedantry, routine, timeservers at office desks, trustees, collegepresidents, the plump flunkies of the ruling businessmen, all the good jobs kept for yesmen, never enough money, every broadening hope thwarted. Veblen drank the bitter drink all right.

The Veblens were a family of freeholding farmers.

The freeholders of the narrow Norwegian valleys were a stubborn hardworking people, farmers, dairymen, fishermen, rooted in their fathers' stony fields, in their old timbered farmsteads with carved gables they took their names from, in the upland pastures where they grazed the stock in summer.

During the early nineteenth century the towns grew; Norway filled up with landless men, storekeepers, sheriffs, moneylenders, bailiffs, notaries in black with stiffcollars and briefcases full of foreclosures under their arms. Industries were coming in. The townsmen were beginning to get profits out of the country and to finagle the farmers out of the freedom of their narrow farms.

The meanspirited submitted as tenants, daylaborers; but the strong men went out of the country

as their fathers had gone out of the country centuries before when Harald the Fairhaired[1] and St. Olaf[2] hacked to pieces the liberties of the northern men, who had been each man lord of his own creek, to make Christians and serfs of them,

only in the old days it was Iceland, Greenland, Vineland[3] the northmen had sailed west to; now it was America.

Both Thorstein Veblen's father's people and his mother's people had lost their farmsteads and with them the names that denoted them free men.

Thomas Anderson for a while tried to make his living as a traveling carpenter and cabinetmaker, but in 1847 he and his wife, Kari Thorsteinsdatter, crossed in a whalingship from Bremen and went out to join friends in the Scandihoovian[4] colonies round Milwaukee.

Next year his brother Haldor joined him.

They were hard workers; in another year they had saved up money to preempt a claim on 160 acres of uncleared land in Sheboygan County, Wisconsin; when they'd gotten that land part cleared they sold it and moved to an all-Norway colony in Manitowoc County, near Cato and a place named Valders after the valley they had all come from in the old country;

there in the house Thomas Anderson built with his own tools, the sixth of twelve children, Thorstein Veblen was born.

When Thorstein was eight years old, Thomas Anderson moved west again into the blacksoil prairies of Minnesota that the Sioux and the buffalo had only been

[1]Harald I, King of Norway (c. 872–933).
[2]Patron saint of Norway and King (1016–1029).
[3]Area of northeastern North America visited by Norse explorers around A.D. 1000.
[4]Scandinavian (derogatory term).

driven off from a few years before. In the deed to the new farm Thomas Anderson took back the old farmstead name of Veblen.

He was a solid farmer, builder, a clever carpenter, the first man to import merino sheep and a mechanical reaper and binder; he was a man of standing in the group of Norway people farming the edge of the prairies, who kept their dialects, the manner of life of their narrow Norway valleys, their Lutheran pastors, their homemade clothes and cheese and bread, their suspicion and stubborn dislike of townsmen's ways.

The townspeople were Yankees mostly, smart to make two dollars grow where a dollar grew before, storekeepers, middlemen, speculators, moneylenders, with long heads for politics and mortgages; they despised the Scandihoovian dirtfarmers they lived off, whose daughters did their wives' kitchenwork.

The Norway people believed as their fathers had believed that there were only two callings for an honest man, farming or preaching.

Thorstein grew up a hulking lad with a reputation for laziness and wit. He hated the irk of everrepeated backbreaking chores round the farm. Reading he was happy. Carpentering he liked or running farmmachinery. The Lutheran pastors who came to the house noticed that his supple mind slid easily round the corners of their theology. It was hard to get farmwork out of him, he had a stinging tongue and was famous for the funny names he called people; his father decided to make a preacher out of him.

When he was seventeen he was sent for out of the field where he was working. His bag was already packed. The horses were hitched up. He was being sent to Carleton Academy in Northfield, to prepare for Carleton College.

As there were several young Veblens to be educated their father built them a house on a lot near the campus. Their food and clothes were sent to them from the farm. Cash money was something they never saw.

Thorstein spoke English with an accent. He had a constitutional inability to say yes. His mind was formed on the Norse sagas and on the matteroffact sense of his father's farming and the exact needs of carpenterwork and threshingmachines.

He could never take much interest in the theology, sociology, economics of Carleton College where they were busy trimming down the jagged dogmas of the old New England bibletaught traders to make stencils to hang on the walls of commissionmerchants' offices.

Veblen's collegeyears were the years when Darwin's assertions of growth and becoming were breaking the set molds of the Noah's Ark world,

when Ibsen's women were tearing down the portieres of the Victorian parlors,

and Marx's mighty machine was rigging the countinghouse's own logic to destroy the countinghouse.

When Veblen went home to the farm he talked about these things with his father, following him up and down at his plowing, starting an argument while they were waiting for a new load for the wheatthresher. Thomas Anderson had seen Norway and America; he had the squarebuilt mind of a carpenter and builder, and an understanding of tools and the treasured elaborated builtupseasonbyseason knowledge of a careful farmer,

a tough whetstone for the sharpening steel of young Thorstein's wits.

At Carleton College young Veblen was considered a brilliant unsound eccentric; nobody could understand why a boy of such attainments wouldn't settle down to the business of the day, which was to buttress property and profits with anything usable in the debris of Christian ethics and eighteenthcentury economics that cluttered the minds of collegeprofessors, and to reinforce the sacred, already shaky edifice with the new strong girderwork of science Herbert Spencer[5] was throwing up for the benefit of the bosses.

People complained they never knew whether Veblen was joking or serious.

In 1880 Thorstein Veblen started to try to make his living by teaching. A year in an academy at Madison, Wisconsin, wasn't much of a success. Next year he and his brother Andrew started graduate work at Johns Hopkins. Johns Hopkins didn't suit, but boarding in an old Baltimore house with some ruined gentlewomen gave him a disdaining glimpse of an etiquette motheaten now but handed down through the lavish leisure of the slaveowning planters' mansions straight from the merry England of the landlord cavaliers.

(The valleyfarmers had always been scornful of outlanders' ways.)

He was more at home at Yale where in Noah Porter[6] he found a New England roundhead granite against which his Norway granite rang in clear dissent. He took his Ph.D. there. But there was still some question as to what department of the academic world he could best make a living in.

He read Kant and wrote prize essays. But he couldn't get a job. Try as he could he couldn't get his mouth round the essential yes.

He went back to Minnesota with a certain intolerant knowledge of the amenities of the higher learning. To his slight Norwegian accent he'd added the broad a.

At home he loafed about the farm and tinkered with inventions of new machinery and read and talked theology and philosophy with his father. In the Scandihoovian colonies the price of wheat and the belief in God and St. Olaf were going down together. The farmers of the Northwest were starting their long losing fight against the parasite businessmen who were sucking them dry. There was a mortgage on the farm, interest on debts to pay, always fertilizer, new machines to buy to speed production to pump in a halfcentury the wealth out of the soil laid down in a million years of buffalo-grass. His brothers kept grumbling about this sardonic loafer who wouldn't earn his keep.

Back home he met again his college sweetheart, Ellen Rolfe, the niece of the president of Carleton College, a girl who had railroadmagnates and money in the family. People in Northfield were shocked when it came out that she was going to marry the drawling pernickety bookish badlydressed young Norwegian ne'er-do-well.

Her family hatched a plan to get him a job as economist for the Santa Fe Railroad but at the wrong moment Ellen Rolfe's uncle lost control of the line. The young couple went to live at Stacyville where they did everything but earn a living. They

[5] English philosopher (1820–1903); argued that laissez-faire economics made for survival of the fittest and social progress.

[6] Conservative theologian and educator (1811–1892).

read Latin and Greek and botanized in the woods and along the fences and in the roadside scrub. They boated on the river and Veblen started his translation of the *Laxdaelasaga.*[7] They read *Looking Backward*[8] and articles by Henry George.[9] They looked at their world from the outside.

In '91 Veblen got together some money to go to Cornell to do postgraduate work. He turned up there in the office of the head of the economics department wearing a coonskin cap and grey corduroy trousers and said in his low sarcastic drawl, "I am Thorstein Veblen,"

but it was not until several years later, after he was established at the new University of Chicago that had grown up next to the World's Fair, and had published *The Theory of the Leisure Class,* put on the map by Howells'[10] famous review, that the world of the higher learning[11] knew who Thorstein Veblen was.

Even in Chicago as the brilliant young economist he lived pioneerfashion. (The valleyfarmers had always been scornful of outlanders' ways.) He kept his books in packingcases laid on their sides along the walls. His only extravagances were the Russian cigarettes he smoked and the red sash he sometimes sported. He was a man without smalltalk. When he lectured he put his cheek on his hand and mumbled out his long spiral sentences, reiterative like the eddas. His language was a mixture of mechanics' terms, scientific latinity, slang and Roget's Thesaurus. The other profs couldn't imagine why the girls fell for him so.

The girls fell for him so that Ellen Rolfe kept leaving him. He'd take summer trips abroad without his wife. There was a scandal about a girl on an ocean liner.

Tongues wagged so (Veblen was a man who never explained, who never could get his tongue around the essential yes; the valleyfarmers had always been scornful of the outlanders' ways, and their opinions) that his wife left him and went off to live alone on a timberclaim in Idaho and the president asked for his resignation.

Veblen went out to Idaho to get Ellen Rolfe to go with him to California when he succeeded in getting a job at a better salary at Leland Stanford, but in Palo Alto it was the same story as in Chicago. He suffered from woman trouble and the constitutional inability to say yes and an unnatural tendency to feel with the workingclass instead of with the profittakers. There were the same complaints that his courses were not constructive or attractive to big money bequests and didn't help his students to butter their bread, make Phi Beta Kappa, pick plums off the hierarchies of the academic grove. His wife left him for good. He wrote to a friend: "The president doesn't approve of my domestic arrangements; nor do I."

Talking about it he once said, "What is one to do if the woman moves in on you?"

He went back up to the shack in the Idaho woods.

Friends tried to get him an appointment to make studies in Crete, a chair at the University of Pekin, but always the bogy, routine, businessmen's flunkeys in all the university offices . . . for the questioner the bitter drink.

[7]Thirteenth-century Icelandic saga.
[8]Utopian novel (1888) by Edward Bellamy.
[9]U.S. economist (1839–1897) who advocated social reform through a "single tax" on land.
[10]William Dean Howells (1837–1920), American novelist.
[11]Allusion to Veblen's scathing attack on universities, *The Higher Learning in America* (1918).

His friend Davenport got him an appointment at the University of Missouri. At Columbia he lived like a hermit in the basement of the Davenports' house, helped with the work round the place, carpentered himself a table and chairs. He was already a bitter elderly man with a grey face covered with a net of fine wrinkles, a vandyke beard and yellow teeth. Few students could follow his courses. The college authorities were often surprised and somewhat chagrined that when visitors came from Europe it was always Veblen they wanted to meet.

These were the years he did most of his writing, trying out his ideas on his students, writing slowly at night in violet ink with a pen of his own designing. Whenever he published a book he had to put up a guarantee with the publishers. In *The Theory of Business Enterprise, The Instinct of Workmanship, The Vested Interests and the Common Man,*

he established a new diagram of a society dominated by monopoly capital,
etched in irony
the sabotage of production by business,
the sabotage of life by blind need for money profits,

pointed out the alternatives: a warlike society strangled by the bureaucracies of the monopolies forced by the law of diminishing returns to grind down more and more the common man for profits,

or a new matteroffact commonsense society dominated by the needs of the men and women who did the work and the incredibly vast possibilities for peace and plenty offered by the progress of technology.

These were the years of Debs's[12] speeches, growing laborunions, the I.W.W.[13] talk about industrial democracy: these years Veblen still held to the hope that the workingclass would take over the machine of production before monopoly had pushed the western nations down into the dark again.

War cut across all that: under the cover of the bunting of Woodrow Wilson's phrases the monopolies cracked down. American democracy was crushed.

The war at least offered Veblen an opportunity to break out of the airless greenhouse of academic life. He was offered a job with the Food Administration, he sent the Navy Department a device for catching submarines by trailing lengths of stout bindingwire. (Meanwhile the government found his books somewhat confusing. The postoffice was forbidding the mails to *Imperial Germany and the Industrial Revolution* while propaganda agencies were sending it out to make people hate the Huns. Educators were denouncing *The Nature of Peace* while Washington experts were clipping phrases out of it to add to the Wilsonian smokescreen.)

For the Food Administration Thorstein Veblen wrote two reports: in one he advocated granting the demands of the I.W.W. as a wartime measure and conciliating the workingclass instead of beating up and jailing all the honest leaders; in the other he pointed out that the Food Administration was a businessman's racket and was not

[12]Eugene V. Debs (1855–1926), labor leader and Socialist Party presidential candidate.

[13]Industrial Workers of the World, militant labor union founded in Chicago in 1905; its members were called "wobblies."

aiming for the most efficient organization of the country as a producing machine. He suggested that, in the interests of the efficient prosecution of the war, the government step into the place of the middleman and furnish necessities to the farmers direct in return for raw materials;

but cutting out business was not at all the Administration's idea of making the world safe for democracy,

so Veblen had to resign from the Food Administration.

He signed the protests against the trial of the hundred and one wobblies in Chicago.[14]

After the armistice he went to New York. In spite of all the oppression of the war years, the air was freshening. In Russia the great storm of revolt had broken, seemed to be sweeping west, in the strong gusts from the new world in the east the warsodden multitudes began to see again. At Versailles[15] allies and enemies, magnates, generals, flunkey politicians were slamming the shutters against the storm, against the new, against hope. It was suddenly clear for a second in the thundering glare what war was about, what peace was about.

In America, in Europe, the old men won. The bankers in their offices took a deep breath, the bediamonded old ladies of the leisure class went back to clipping their coupons in the refined quiet of their safe deposit vaults,

the last puffs of the ozone of revolt went stale
in the whisper of speakeasy arguments.

Veblen wrote for the *Dial*,[16]
lectured at the New School for Social Research.

He still had a hope that the engineers, the technicians, the nonprofiteers whose hands were on the switchboard might take up the fight where the workingclass had failed. He helped form the Technical Alliance.[17] His last hope was the British general strike.[18]

Was there no group of men bold enough to take charge of the magnificent machine before the pigeyed speculators and the yesmen at office desks irrevocably ruined it

and with it the hopes of four hundred years?

No one went to Veblen's lectures at the New School. With every article he wrote in the *Dial* the circulation dropped.

Harding's normalcy,[19] the new era was beginning;
even Veblen made a small killing on the stockmarket.
He was an old man and lonely.

[14]Mass trial in 1918; charges were numerous and indiscriminate, sentencing harsh.
[15]Site of major treaty (1919) officially ending World War I.
[16]Influential political and literary magazine.
[17]Organization of radical-left engineers.
[18]In 1926, in support of miners; it lasted nine days.
[19]Warren G. Harding, U.S. President (1921–1923), promised a return to "normalcy," away from internationalism and progressivist reform.

His second wife had gone to a sanitarium suffering from delusions of persecution.
There seemed no place for a masterless man.

Veblen went back out to Palo Alto
to live in his shack in the tawny hills and observe from outside the last grabbing urges of the profit system taking on, as he put it, the systematized delusions of dementia praecox.

There he finished his translation of the *Laxdaelasaga.*

He was an old man. He was much alone. He let the woodrats take what they wanted from his larder. A skunk that hung round the shack was so tame he'd rub up against Veblen's leg like a cat.

He told a friend he'd sometimes hear in the stillness about him the voices of his boyhood talking Norwegian as clear as on the farm in Minnesota where he was raised. His friends found him harder than ever to talk to, harder than ever to interest in anything. He was running down. The last sips of the bitter drink.

He died on August 3, 1929.

Among his papers a penciled note was found:

It is also my wish, in case of death, to be cremated if it can conveniently be done, as expeditiously and inexpensively as may be, without ritual or ceremony of any kind; that my ashes be thrown loose into the sea or into some sizable stream running into the sea; that no tombstone, slab, epitaph, effigy, tablet, inscription or monument of any name or nature, be set up to my memory or name in any place or at any time; that no obituary, memorial, portrait or biography of me, nor any letters written to or by me be printed or published, or in any way reproduced, copied or circulated;

but his memorial remains
riveted into the language:
the sharp clear prism of his mind.

1936

Albert Maltz 1908–1985

Albert Maltz was born in Brooklyn, New York, the son of immigrants; his father, beginning as a grocer's boy, had become a contractor and builder. Maltz attended public schools and Columbia University, where he majored in philosophy and graduated in 1930. He then enrolled in the Yale Drama School to study with George Pierce Baker, whose students had included Eugene O'Neill, Sidney Howard, S.N. Behrman, and Thomas Wolfe. Another important influence was that of fellow student George Sklar, whose radical politics ignited Maltz's own incipient leftist leanings. At first in collaboration with Sklar and then alone, Maltz wrote and saw several plays produced, among them an anti-war drama called *Peace on Earth,* and *Black Pit,* a study of conditions endured by coal miners in West Virginia.

Maltz soon turned to writing fiction, and it is on his stories and novels that his reputation rests. "Man on a Road," published in the *New Masses* in 1935, sparked a Congressional investigation of the dangers of silicosis to miners; this story was later widely reprinted. Maltz's excellent novella "Season of Celebration," which focuses on a dying man in a Bowery flophouse, and "The Happiest Man on Earth" both won recognition when they appeared in 1938. These and other stories were collected and published under the title *The Way Things Are.*

Both the principal strength and the central weakness of Maltz's work arise from his desire to fulfill an ideal of proletarian art and yet not betray "the great humanistic tradition of culture" by serving "an individual political purpose." The tension between these aims caused him some personal trouble as well as artistic ambivalence. In a 1946 essay entitled "What Shall We Ask of Writers?" he criticized the shallow aesthetic tenets of the left, questioning whether art was to be used as a weapon in the class war. For this he was bitterly denounced, and after two months of verbal siege, Maltz backed down; the *New Masses* published his retraction, in which he declared his earlier piece a "one-sided nondialectical treatment of complex issues."

Maltz is at his best when his political sympathies animate but do not overwhelm his narrative gift. In stories like "Man on a Road" and "The Happiest Man on Earth," a muted undercurrent of anger at injustice and suffering renders the protest extremely effective. But when he becomes openly didactic, Maltz's indignation subverts character, plot, and even feeling, as in his first novel, *The Underground Stream,* which focuses on the struggle between auto industry workers seeking to organize unions and the fascistic management who resist them. Here the characters act simply as one-dimensional mouthpieces, delivering various political viewpoints, rather than developing believably.

Maltz confronted his aesthetic dilemma with varying degrees of success in his next four novels; *The Cross and the Arrow* is his best. In part this novel was written as an answer to the theories of Robert Vansittart, a British diplomat who contended that the German people as a race were addicted to war, and that if this innate bellicosity could not be corrected by cultural reconditioning, it would be necessary to exterminate them. Maltz's narrative explores the life of a factory worker named Willi Wegler, who, though decorated with a German service cross, suddenly and heroically turns against his country's cause.

By this time Maltz was working in Hollywood as a screenwriter, but this career was to be interrupted in 1947 when the House Un-American Activities Committee reinstituted its investigation into Communist infiltration in the motion picture industry. Maltz, along with nine other writers and producers, a group thereafter known as "the Hollywood Ten," challenged the constitutional legitimacy of that committee on First Amendment grounds. Refusing to answer the committee's questions as to whether he was a member of the Communist Party and the Screenwriters' Guild, Maltz was fined and sentenced to a year's imprisonment in 1950. Blacklisted in Hollywood and so unable to work there for many years, he moved to Mexico after his release from prison and remained there until 1962.

During the time of the HUAC investigations, *The Journey of Simon McKeever* was published; squarely in the tradition of the novel of the road, this compact work recounts the adventures of a 73-year-old escapee from an old-age home, a representative American who comes at last to a reaffirmation of the communal ideal. *A Long Day in a Short Life* was written in Mexico and based on his nine-months' experience in a federal prison; a flatly realistic portrayal of the lives of prisoners in a Washington, D.C., jail, it voices Maltz's plea for human commitment and solidarity as the basis of true democracy. *A Tale of One January* was published in England and has never been printed in the U.S.; chronicling the escape of two women from Auschwitz, its narrative centers on one woman's rediscovery of her sense of self, her womanhood, and her relationship to the larger world.

Albert Maltz died in Los Angeles in 1985. His constant literary concern for an idealized vision of democracy links his work to the American tradition of Emerson and Whitman. His fiction regularly focuses on the individual's struggle for self-realization under confinement in some prison-like situation; always Maltz's faith in human decency, in the viability of the human struggle for a better life, and in the need for spiritual liberation triumph over the forces of repression. Among the most talented of the social protest writers shaped by the Depression years, Maltz projects an idealistic intensity in his best work that makes it worthy of wider recognition and publication.

Gabriel Miller
Rutgers University–Newark

PRIMARY WORKS

Peace on Earth, 1934; *Black Pit,* 1935; *The Way Things Are,* 1938; *The Underground Stream,* 1940; *The Cross and the Arrow,* 1944; *The Journey of Simon McKeever,* 1949; *The Citizen Writer,* 1950; *A Long Day in a Short Life,* 1957; *A Tale of One January,* 1966; *Afternoon in the Jungle,* 1971.

The Happiest Man on Earth

Jesse felt ready to weep. He had been sitting in the shanty waiting for Tom to appear, grateful for the chance to rest his injured foot, quietly, joyously anticipating the moment when Tom would say, "Why, of course, Jesse, you can start whenever you're ready!"

For two weeks he had been pushing himself, from Kansas City, Missouri, to Tulsa, Oklahoma, through nights of rain and a week of scorching sun, without sleep or a decent meal, sustained by the vision of that one moment. And then Tom had come into the office. He had come in quickly, holding a sheaf of papers in his hand; he had glanced at Jesse only casually, it was true—but long enough. He had not known him. He had turned away . . . And Tom Brackett was his brother-in-law.

Was it his clothes? Jesse knew he looked terrible. He had tried to spruce up at a drinking fountain in the park, but even that had gone badly; in his excitement he had cut himself shaving, an ugly gash down the side of his cheek. And nothing could get the red gumbo dust out of his suit even though he had slapped himself till both arms were worn out . . . Or was it just that he had changed so much?

True, they hadn't seen each other for five years; but Tom looked five years older, that was all. He was still Tom. God! Was he so different?

Brackett finished his telephone call. He leaned back in his swivel chair and glanced over at Jesse with small, clear, blue eyes that were suspicious and unfriendly. He was a heavy, paunchy man of forty-five, auburn-haired, rather dour-looking; his face was meaty, his features pronounced and forceful, his nose somewhat bulbous and reddish-hued at the tip. He looked like a solid, decent, capable businessman who was commander of his local branch of the American Legion—which he was. He surveyed Jesse with cold indifference, manifestly unwilling to spend time on him. Even the way he chewed his toothpick seemed contemptuous to Jesse.

"Yes?" Brackett said suddenly. "What to you want?"

His voice was decent enough, Jesse admitted. He had expected it to be worse. He moved up to the wooden counter that partitioned the shanty. He thrust a hand nervously through his tangled hair.

"I guess you don't recognize me, Tom," he said falteringly. "I'm Jesse Fulton."

"Huh?" Brackett said. That was all.

"Yes, I am, and Ella sends you her love."

Brackett rose and walked over to the counter until they were face to face. He surveyed Fulton incredulously, trying to measure the resemblance to his brother-in-law as he remembered him. This man was tall, about thirty. That fitted! He had straight good features and a lank erect body. That was right too. But the face was too gaunt, the body too spiny under the baggy clothes for him to be sure. His brother-in-law had been a solid, strong, young man with muscle and beef to him. It was like looking at a faded, badly taken photograph and trying to recognize the subject: The resemblance was there but the difference was tremendous. He searched the eyes. They at least seemed definitely familiar, gray, with a curiously shy but decent look in them. He had liked that about Fulton.

Jesse stood quiet. Inside he was seething. Brackett was like a man examining a piece of broken-down horseflesh; there was a look of pure pity in his eyes. It made Jesse furious. He knew he wasn't as far gone as all that.

"Yes, I believe you are," Brackett said finally, "but you sure have changed."

"By God, it's five years, ain't it?" Jesse said resentfully. "You only saw me a couple of times anyway." Then, to himself, with his lips locked together, in mingled vehemence and shame, "What if I have changed? Don't everybody? I ain't no corpse."

"You was solid looking," Brackett continued softly, in the same tone of incredulous wonder. "You lost weight, I guess?"

Jesse kept silent. He needed Brackett too much to risk antagonizing him. But it was only by deliberate effort that he could keep from boiling over. The pause lengthened, became painful. Brackett flushed. "Jiminy Christmas, excuse me," he burst out in apology. He jerked the counter up. "Come in. Take a seat. Good God, boy"—he grasped Jesse's hand and shook it—"I am glad to see you; don't think anything else! You just looked so peaked."

"It's all right," Jesse murmured. He sat down, thrusting his hand through his curly, tangled hair.

"Why are you limping?"

"I stepped on a stone; it jagged a hole through my shoe." Jesse pulled his feet back under the chair. He was ashamed of his shoes. They had come from the relief originally, and two weeks on the road had about finished them. All morning, with a kind of delicious, foolish solemnity, he had been vowing to himself that before anything else, before even a suit of clothes, he was going to buy himself a brand-new strong pair of shoes.

Brackett kept his eyes off Jesse's feet. He knew what was bothering the boy and it filled his heart with pity. The whole thing was appalling. He had never seen anyone who looked more down-and-out. His sister had been writing to him every week, but she hadn't told him they were as badly-off as this.

"Well now, listen," Brackett began, "tell me things. How's Ella?"

"Oh, she's pretty good," Jesse replied absently. He had a soft, pleasing shy voice that went with his soft gray eyes. He was worrying over how to get started.

"And the kids?"

"Oh, they're fine . . . Well, you know," Jesse added, becoming more attentive, "the young one has to wear a brace. He can't run around, you know. But he's smart. He draws pictures and he does things, you know."

"Yes," Brackett said. "That's good." He hesitated. There was a moment's silence. Jesse fidgeted in his chair. Now that the time had arrived, he felt awkward. Brackett leaned forward and put his hand on Jesse's knee. "Ella didn't tell me things were so bad for you, Jesse. I might have helped."

"Well, goodness," Jesse returned softly, "you been having your own troubles, ain't you?"

"Yes." Brackett leaned back. His ruddy face became mournful and darkly bitter. "You know I lost my hardware shop?"

"Well sure, of course," Jesse answered, surprised. "You wrote us. That's what I mean."

"I forgot," Brackett said. "I keep on being surprised over it myself. Not that it was worth much," he added bitterly. "It was running downhill for three years. I guess I just wanted it because it was mine." He laughed pointlessly, without mirth. "Well, tell me about yourself," he added. "What happened to the job you had?"

Jesse burst out abruptly, with agitation, "Let it wait, Tom, I got something on my mind."

"It ain't you and Ella?" Brackett interrupted anxiously.

"Why no!" Jesse sat back. "Why, however did you come to think that? Why Ella and me . . . " He stopped, laughing. "Why, Tom, I'm just crazy about Ella. Why she's just wonderful. She's just my whole life, Tom."

"Excuse me. Forget it." Brackett chuckled uncomfortably, turned away. The naked intensity of the youth's burst of love had upset him. It made him wish savagely that he could do something for them. They were too decent to have had it so hard. Ella was like this boy too, shy and a little soft.

"Tom, listen," Jesse said, "I come here on purpose." He thrust his hand through his hair. "I want you to help me."

"Damn it, boy," Brackett groaned. He had been expecting this. "I can't much. I only get thirty-five a week and I'm damn grateful for it."

"Sure, I know," Jesse emphasized excitedly. He was feeling once again the wild, delicious agitation that had possessed him in the early hours of the morning. "I know you can't help us with money! But we met a man who works for you! He was in our city! He said you could give me a job!"

"Who said?"

"Oh, why didn't you tell me?" Jesse burst out reproachfully. "Why, as soon as I heard of it I started out. For two weeks now I been pushing ahead like crazy."

Brackett groaned aloud. "You come walking from Kansas City in two weeks so I could give you a job?"

"Sure, Tom, of course. What else could I do?"

"God Almighty, there ain't no jobs, Jesse! It's a slack season. And you don't know this oil business. It's special. I got my Legion friends here, but they couldn't do nothing now. Don't you think I'd ask for you as soon as there was a chance?"

Jesse felt stunned. The hope of the last two weeks seemed rolling up into a ball of agony in his stomach. Then, frantically, he cried, "But listen, this man said *you* could hire! He told me! He drives trucks for you! He said you always need men!"

"Oh! . . . You mean my department?" Brackett said in a low voice.

"Yes, Tom. That's it!"

"Oh, no, you don't want to work in my department," Brackett told him in the same low voice. "You don't know what it is."

"Yes, I do," Jesse insisted. "He told me all about it, Tom. You're a dispatcher, ain't you? You send the dynamite trucks out?"

"Who was the man, Jesse?"

"Everett, Everett, I think."

"Egbert? Man about my size?" Brackett asked slowly.

"Yes, Egbert. He wasn't a phony, was he?"

Brackett laughed. For the second time his laughter was curiously without mirth. "No, he wasn't a phony." Then, in a changed voice: "Jiminy, boy, you should have asked me before you trekked all the way down here."

"Oh, I didn't want to," Jesse explained with naive cunning. "I knew you'd say no. He told me it was risky work, Tom. But I don't care."

Brackett locked his fingers together. His solid, meaty face became very hard. "I'm going to say no anyway, Jesse."

Jesse cried out. It had not occurred to him that Brackett would not agree. It had seemed as though reaching Tulsa were the only problem he had to face. "Oh no," he begged, "you can't. Ain't there any jobs, Tom?"

"Sure there's jobs. There's even Egbert's job if you want it."

"He's quit?"

"He's dead!"

"Oh!"

"On the job, Jesse. Last night if you want to know."

"Oh!" . . . Then, "I don't care!"

"Now you listen to me," Brackett said. "I'll tell you a few things that you should have asked before you started out. It ain't dynamite you drive. They don't use anything as safe as dynamite in drilling oil wells. They wish they could, but they can't. It's nitroglycerin! Soup!"

"But I know," Jesse told him reassuringly. "He advised me, Tom. You don't have to think I don't know."

"Shut up a minute," Brackett ordered angrily. "Listen! You just have to look at this soup, see? You just cough loud and it blows! You know how they transport it? In a can that's shaped like this, see, like a fan? That's to give room for compartments, because each compartment has to be lined with rubber. That's the only way you can even think of handling it."

"Listen, Tom . . ."

"Now wait a minute, Jesse. For God's sake just put your mind to this. I know you had your heart set on a job, but you've got to understand. This stuff goes only in special trucks! At night! They got to follow a special route! They can't go through any city! If they lay over, it's got to be in a special garage! Don't you see what that means? Don't that tell you how dangerous it is?"

"I'll drive careful," Jesse said. "I know how to handle a truck. I'll drive slow."

Brackett groaned. "Do you think Egbert didn't drive careful or know how to handle a truck?"

"Tom," Jesse said earnestly, "you can't scare me. I got my mind fixed on only one thing: Egbert said he was getting a dollar a mile. He was making five to six hundred dollars a month for half a month's work, he said. Can I get the same?"

"Sure you can get the same," Brackett told him savagely. "A dollar a mile. It's easy. But why do you think the company has to pay so much? It's easy—until you run over a stone that your headlights didn't pick out, like Egbert did. Or get a blowout! Or get something in your eye so the wheel twists and you jar the truck! Or any other God damn thing that nobody ever knows! We can't ask Egbert what happened to him. There's no truck to give any evidence. There's no corpse. There's nothing! Maybe tomorrow somebody'll find a piece of twisted steel way off in a cornfield. But we never find the driver. Not even a fingernail. All we know is that he don't come in on schedule. Then we wait for the police to call us. You know what happened last night? Something went wrong on a bridge. Maybe Egbert was nervous. Maybe he brushed the side with his fender. Only there's no bridge anymore. No truck. No Egbert. Do you understand now? That's what you get for your God damn dollar a mile!"

There was a moment of silence. Jesse sat twisting his long thin hands. His mouth was sagging open, his face was agonized. Then he shut his eyes and spoke softly. "I don't care about that, Tom. You told me. Now you got to be good to me and give me that job."

Brackett slapped the palm of his hand down on his desk. "No!"

"Listen, Tom," Jesse said softly, "you just don't understand." He opened his eyes. They were filled with tears. They made Brackett turn away. "Just look at me, Tom. Don't that tell you enough? What did you think of me when you first saw me? You thought: 'Why don't that bum go away and stop panhandling?' Didn't you, Tom? Tom, I just can't live like this any more. I got to be able to walk down the street with my head up."

"You're crazy," Brackett muttered. "Every year there's one out of five drivers gets killed. That's the average. What's worth that?"

"Is my life worth anything now? We're just starvin' at home, Tom. They ain't put us back on relief yet."

"Then you should have told me," Brackett exclaimed harshly. "It's your own damn fault. A man has no right to have false pride when his family ain't eating. I'll borrow some money and we'll telegraph it to Ella. Then you go home and get back on relief."

"And then what?"

"And then wait, Got damn it! You're no old man. You got no right to throw your life away. Sometime you'll get a job."

"No!" Jesse jumped up. "No. I believed that too. But I don't now," he cried passionately. "I ain't getting a job no more than you're getting your hardware store back. I lost my skill, Tom. Linotyping is skilled work. I'm rusty now. I've been six years on relief. The only work I've had is pick and shovel. When I got that job this spring, I was supposed to be an A-1 man. But I wasn't. And they got new machines now. As soon as the slack started, they let me out."

"So what?" Brackett said harshly. "Ain't there other jobs?"

"How do I know?" Jesse replied. "There ain't been one for six years. I'd even be afraid to take one now. It's been too hard waiting so many weeks to get back on relief."

"Well, you got to have some courage," Brackett shouted. "You've got to keep up hope."

"I got all the courage you want," Jesse retorted vehemently, "but no, I ain't got no hope. The hope has dried up in me in six years waiting. You're the only hope I got."

"You're crazy," Brackett muttered. "I won't do it. For God's sake think of Ella for a minute."

"Don't you know I'm thinking about her?" Jesse asked softly. He plucked at Brackett's sleeve. "That's what decided me, Tom." His voice became muted into a hushed, pained, whisper. "The night Egbert was at our house I looked at Ella like I'd seen her for the first time. She ain't pretty anymore, Tom!" Brackett jerked his head and moved away. Jesse followed him, taking a deep, sobbing breath. "Don't that tell you, Tom? Ella was like a little doll or something, you remember. I couldn't walk down the street without somebody turning to look at her. She ain't twenty-nine yet, Tom, and she ain't pretty no more."

Brackett sat down with his shoulders hunched up wearily. He gripped his hands together and sat leaning forward, staring at the floor.

Jesse stood over him, his gaunt face flushed with emotion, almost unpleasant in its look of pleading and bitter humility. "I ain't done right for Ella, Tom. Ella deserved better. This is the only chance I see in my whole life to do something for her. I've just been a failure."

"Don't talk nonsense," Brackett commented without rancor. "You ain't a failure. No more than me. There's millions of men in the identical situation. It's just the depression, or the recession, or the God damn New Deal, or . . . !" He swore and lapsed into silence.

"Oh no," Jesse corrected him in a knowing, sorrowful tone, "those things maybe excuse other men. But not me. It was up to me to do better. This is my own fault!"

"Oh, beans!" Brackett said. "It's more sun spots than it's you!"

Jesse's face turned an unhealthy mottled red. It looked swollen. "Well I don't care," he cried wildly. "I don't care! You got to give me this! I got to lift my head up. I went through one stretch of hell, but I can't go through another. You want me to keep looking at my little boy's legs and tell myself if I had a job he wouldn't be like that? Every time he walks he says to me, 'I got soft bones from the rickets and you give it to me because you didn't feed me right.' Jesus Christ, Tom, you think I'm going to sit there and watch him like that another six years?"

Brackett leaped to his feet. "So what if you do?" he shouted. "You say you're thinking about Ella. How's she going to like it when you get killed?"

"Maybe I won't," Jesse pleaded. "I've got to have some luck sometime."

"That's what they all think," Brackett replied scornfully. "When you take this job, your luck is a question mark. The only thing certain is that sooner or later you get killed."

"Okay then," Jesse shouted back. "Then I do! But meanwhile I got something, don't I? I can buy a pair of shoes. Look at me! I can buy a suit that don't say 'Relief' by the way it fits. I can smoke cigarettes. I can buy some candy for the kids. I can eat some myself. Yes, by God, I want to eat some candy. I want a glass of beer once a day. I want Ella dressed up. I want her to eat meat three times a week, four times maybe. I want to take my family to the movies."

Brackett sat down. "Oh, shut up," he said wearily.

"No," Jesse told him softly, passionately, "you can't get rid of me. Listen, Tom," he pleaded, "I got it all figured out. On six hundred a month look how much I can save! If I last only three months, look how much it is . . . a thousand dollars . . . more! And maybe I'll last longer. Maybe a couple years. I can fix Ella up for life!"

"You said it," Brackett interposed. "I suppose you think she'll enjoy living when you're on a job like that?"

"I got it all figured out," Jesse answered excitedly. "She don't know, see? I tell her I make only forty. You put the rest in a bank account for her, Tom."

"Oh, shut up," Brackett said. "You think you'll be happy? Every minute, waking and sleeping, you'll be wondering if tomorrow you'll be dead. And the worst days will be your days off, when you're not driving. They have to give you every other day free to get your nerve back. And you lay around the house eating your heart out. That's how happy you'll be."

Jesse laughed. "I'll be happy! Don't you worry, I'll be so happy, I'll be singing. Lord God, Tom, I'm going to feel proud of myself for the first time in seven years!"

"Oh, shut up, shut up," Brackett said.

The little shanty became silent. After a moment Jesse whispered: "You got to, Tom. You got to. You got to."

Again there was silence. Brackett raised both hands to his head, pressing the palms against his temples.

"Tom, Tom . . ." Jesse said.

Brackett sighed. "Oh, God damn it," he said finally, "all right, I'll take you on, God help me." His voice was low, hoarse, infinitely weary. "If you're ready to drive tonight, you can drive tonight."

Jesse didn't answer. He couldn't. Brackett looked up. The tears were running down Jesse's face. He was swallowing and trying to speak, but only making an absurd, gasping noise.

"I'll send a wire to Ella," Brackett said in the same hoarse, weary voice. "I'll tell her you got a job, and you'll send her fare in a couple of days. You'll have some money then—that is, if you last the week out, you jackass!"

Jesse only nodded. His heart felt so close to bursting that he pressed both hands against it, as though to hold it locked within his breast.

"Come back here at six o'clock," Brackett said. "Here's some money. Eat a good meal."

"Thanks," Jesse whispered.

"Wait a minute," Brackett said. "Here's my address." He wrote it on a piece of paper, "Take any car going that way. Ask the conductor where to get off. Take a bath and get some sleep."

"Thanks," Jesse said. "Thanks, Tom."

"Oh, get out of here," Brackett said.

"Tom."

"What?"

"I just . . ." Jesse stopped. Brackett saw his face. The eyes were still glistening with tears, but the gaunt face was shining now with a kind of fierce radiance.

Brackett turned away. "I'm busy," he said.

Jesse went out. The wet film blinded him, but the whole world seemed to have turned golden. He limped slowly, with the blood pounding his temples and a wild, incommunicable joy in his heart. "I'm the happiest man in the world," he whispered to himself. "I'm the happiest man on the whole earth."

Brackett sat watching till finally Jesse turned the corner of the alley and disappeared. Then he hunched himself over with his head in his hands. His heart was beating painfully like something old and clogged. He listened to it as it beat. He sat in desperate tranquillity, gripping his head in his hands.

1938

Lillian Hellman 1905–1984

Lillian Hellman's craftsmanship, powerful characterizations, and vigorous, persuasive themes assure her an important place in the history of the American stage. Born in 1905 and spending her childhood between New Orleans and New York, Hellman launched her dramatic career in 1934 with the production of *The Children's Hour.* She went on to write eight plays, including *Days to Come* (1936), *The Little Foxes* (1939), *Watch on the Rhine* (1941), *The Searching Wind* (1944), *Another Part of the Forest* (1946), *The Autumn Garden* (1951), and *Toys in the Attic* (1960), as well as four theatrical adaptations and numerous screenplays for Hollywood. Seven of the plays were chosen among the ten "Best Plays" of their seasons and she received the New York Critics' Circle Award for the best American drama of the season for both *Watch on the Rhine* and *Toys in the Attic,* as well as the Gold Medal for drama from the National Institute of Arts and Letters. In her Introduction to *Four Plays,* Hellman wrote, "I am a moral writer," and she saw her plays as an opportunity to exercise moral judgment. Although intended for the comfortable middle class that frequents Broadway, the plays, with their rigorous sense of justice and insistence on individual responsibility, compel audiences to confront themselves and their beliefs in light of Hellman's moral vigor. As Robert Brustein wrote of Hellman after her death, "she never wavered in her conviction that theater could be a force for change in what she considered an unethical, unjust, essentially venal world" and Hellman's work especially emphasized the dangers of American innocence to evil and injustice.

When publicly receiving an honorary Doctor of Letters at Smith College in 1974, Hellman was told "no stronger voice than yours has ever been raised against Fascism, the black comedy of the McCarthy period, or the frightening horror of Watergate and after." An example of the way Hellman followed the ethical ideals set out in her plays came during the McCarthy Era with its challenge to American civil liberties and freedom of inquiry. Hellman was called before the House Un-American Activities Committee in 1952 as were many people in the arts and entertainment industry. Risking the possibility of arrest, not to mention loss of property and livelihood, Hellman courageously told the Committee that while she was willing to speak about her own political activities, she refused, unlike so many called up before them, to "name names," to testify about the activities of friends and acquaintances. In her famous letter to HUAC, she insisted, "I cannot and will not cut my conscience to fit this year's fashions."

Hellman survived the Hollywood blacklisting that was in effect for years after her appearance before HUAC to launch a new career as a writer of the autobiographical memoirs which would become as well known as her plays. *An Unfinished Woman* appeared in 1969 and won the National Book Award; *Pentimento* came out in 1976 and one of its portraits was made into the 1977 film *Julia.* The last of these memoirs was *Maybe: A Story,* published in 1980. Hellman said that by far the hardest of her memoirs to write was *Scoundrel Time,* published in 1976. It had taken twenty-five years for her to bring herself to describe her experience before the House Un-American Committee during what is often referred as the McCarthy Witchhunts based on the dominant role played by Senator Joseph McCarthy and his Committee on Government Operations. With *Scoundrel Time,* Hellman said she wasn't out to write history, just to describe what happened to her. But in doing so, in pungent language with a definite point of view, she brings to life the repression of civil liberties in the name of Anti-Communism during the Cold War era of the 1950s. The selection here, culled from three places in the memoir, represents the underlying argument of the book. When *Scoundrel Time* was published, Hellman received high praise both for her portrayal of this period and for her actions during it. But the memoir, as did much of Hellman's life, also engendered controversy and strong criticism, sometimes from the very intellectuals and writers Hellman's book indicted. And while Hellman did not think another McCarthy era could happen, she did tell interviewer Marilyn Berger that she thought contemporary Americans could be deprived of their civil liberties, that "something worse could happen based on a seeming sense and seeming rationality and seeming need . . . in a much more quiet and simple way since very few of us any longer pay any attention to the small laws that are passed, or even the larger ones. We can be deprived of a great deal without knowing it; without realizing it; waking up to it."

Vivian Patraka
Bowling Green State University

PRIMARY WORKS

Lillian Hellman: The Collected Plays, 1971; *Six Plays,* 1979; *Three: An Unfinished Woman, Pentimento, Scoundrel Time,* 1979; *Maybe,* 1980.

from Scoundrel Time

I have tried twice before to write about what has come to be known as the McCarthy period but I didn't much like what I wrote. My reasons for not being able to write about my part in this sad, comic, miserable time of our history were simple to me, although some people thought I had avoided it for mysterious reasons. There was no mystery. I had strange hangups and they are always hard to explain. Now I tell myself that if I face them, maybe I can manage.

The prevailing eccentricity was and is my inability to feel much against the leading figures of the period, the men who punished me. Senators McCarthy and McCarran, Representatives Nixon, Walter and Wood, all of them, were what they were: men who invented when necessary, maligned even when it wasn't necessary. I do not think they believed much, if anything, of what they said: the time was ripe for a new wave in America, and they seized their political chance to lead it along each day's opportunity, spit-balling whatever and with whoever came into view.

But the new wave was not so new. It began with the Russian Revolution of 1917. The victory of the revolution, and thus its menace, had haunted us through the years that followed then twisted the tail of history when Russia was our ally in the Second World War and, just because that had been such an unnatural connection, the fears came back in fuller force after the war when it looked to many people as if Russia would overrun western Europe. Then the revolution in China caused an enormous convulsion in capitalist societies and somewhere along the line gave us the conviction that we could have prevented it if only. If only was never explained with any sense, but the times had very little need of sense.

The fear of Communism did not begin that year, but the new China, allied in those days with Russia, had a more substantial base and there were many honest men and women who were, understandably, frightened that their pleasant way of life could end in a day.

It was not the first time in history that the confusions of honest people were picked up in space by cheap baddies who, hearing a few bars of popular notes, made them into an opera of public disorder, staged and sung, as much of the congressional testimony shows, in the wards of an insane asylum.

A theme is always necessary, a plain, simple, unadorned theme to confuse the ignorant. The anti-Red theme was easily chosen from the grab bag, not alone because we were frightened of socialism, but chiefly, I think, to destroy the remains of Roosevelt and his sometimes advanced work. The McCarthy group—a loose term for all the boys, lobbyists, Congressmen, State Department bureaucrats, CIA operators—chose the anti-Red scare with perhaps more cynicism than Hitler picked anti-Semitism. He, history can no longer deny, deeply believed in the impurity of the Jew. But it is impossible to remember the drunken face of McCarthy, merry often with a kind of worldly malice, as if he were mocking those who took him seriously, and believe that he himself could take seriously anything but his boozed-up nightmares. And if all the rumors were true the nightmares could have concerned more than the fear of a Red tank on Pennsylvania Avenue, although it is possible that in his case a tank could have turned him on. Mr. Nixon's beliefs, if indeed they ever existed, are best left to jolly quarter-historians like Theodore White. But one has a right to believe that if Whittaker Chambers[1] was capable of thinking up a pumpkin, and he was, Mr. Nixon seized upon this strange hiding place with the eagerness of a man who already felt deep contempt for public intelligence. And he was right.

But none of them, even on the bad morning of my hearing before the House Un-American Activities Committee, interested me or disturbed me at a serious level.

[1]In August 1948 Whittaker Chambers appeared before the House Un-American Activities Committee. Chambers, a senior editor of *Time* magazine, told the Committee that he had once been a Communist and an underground courier. He named ten men as his former associates, the best known being Alger Hiss, formerly a high official of the State Department. Chambers accused Hiss of giving him secret government material, which Chambers preserved by placing it in a pumpkin at his farm in Maryland. Hiss was indicted, tried twice, and sent to jail for almost four years. In 1975 the secret pumpkin papers were found to contain nothing secret, nothing confidential. They were, in fact, nonclassified, which is Washington's way of saying anybody who says "please" can have them.

They didn't and they don't. They are what they are, or were, and are no relation to me by blood or background. (My own family held more interesting villains of another, wittier nature.)

I have written before that my shock and my anger came against what I thought had been the people of my world, although in many cases, of course, I did not know the men and women of that world except by name. I had, up to the late 1940's, believed that the educated, the intellectual, lived by what they claimed to believe: freedom of thought and speech, the right of each man to his own convictions, a more than implied promise, therefore, of aid to those who might be persecuted. But only a very few raised a finger when McCarthy and the boys appeared. Almost all, either by what they did or did not do, contributed to McCarthyism, running after a bandwagon which hadn't bothered to stop to pick them up.

Simply, then and now, I feel betrayed by the nonsense I had believed. I had no right to think that American intellectuals were people who would fight for anything if doing so would injure them; they have very little history that would lead to that conclusion. Many of them found in the sins of Stalin Communism—and there were plenty of sins and plenty that for a long time I mistakenly denied—the excuse to join those who should have been their hereditary enemies.

* * *

To many intellectuals the radicals had become the chief, perhaps the only, enemy. (There had been a history of this that preceded my generation: Eugene Debs had been hounded into jail by Woodrow Wilson, and there had been the vicious trials of the men of the International Workers of the World.) Not alone because the radical's intellectual reasons were suspect, but because his convictions would lead to a world that deprived the rest of us what we had. Very few people are capable of admitting anything so simple: the radical had to be made into an immoral man who justified murder, prison camps, torture, any means to an end. And, in fact, he sometimes was just that. But the anti-radical camp contained the same divisions: often they were honest and thoughtful men, often they were men who turned down a dark road for dark reasons.

But radicalism or anti-radicalism should have had nothing to do with the sly, miserable methods of McCarthy, Nixon and colleagues, as they flailed at Communists, near-Communists, and nowhere-near-Communists. Lives were being ruined and few hands were raised in help. Since when do you have to agree with people to defend them from injustice? Certainly nobody in their right mind could have believed that the China experts, charged and fired by the State Department, did any more than recognize that Chiang Kai-shek was losing. Truth made you a traitor as it often does in a time of scoundrels. But there were very few who stood up to say so and there are almost none even now to remind us that one of the reasons we know so little and guess so badly about China is that we lost the only men who knew what they were talking about. Certainly the good magazines, the ones that published the most serious writers, should have come to the aid of those who were persecuted. *Partisan Review,* although through the years it has published many pieces protesting the punishment of dissidents in Eastern Europe, made no protest when people in this country were jailed or ruined. In fact, it never took an editorial position against Mc-

Carthy himself, although it did publish the results of anti-McCarthy symposiums and at least one distinguished piece by Irving Howe. *Commentary* didn't do anything. No editor or contributor ever protested against McCarthy. Indeed, Irving Kristol in that magazine wrote about McCarthy's critics, Henry Steele Commager among others, as if they were naughty children who needed Kristol to correct their innocence.

There were many thoughtful and distinguished men and women on both magazines. None of them, as far as I know, has yet found it a part of conscience to admit that their Cold War anti-Communism was perverted, possibly against their wishes, into the Vietnam War and then into the reign of Nixon, their unwanted but inevitable leader.

* * *

There were many broken lives along the path the boys [McCarthy, Cohn, and Schine] had bulldozed, but not so many that people needed to feel guilty if they turned their backs fast enough and told each other, as we were to do again after Watergate, that Americans justice will always prevail no matter how careless it seems to critical outsiders.

It is not true that when the bell tolls it tolls for thee: if it were true we could not have elected, so few years later, Richard Nixon, a man who had been closely allied with McCarthy. It was no accident that Mr. Nixon brought with him a group of high-powered operators who made Cohn and Schine look like cute little rascals from grammar school. The names and faces had been changed; the stakes were higher, because the prize was the White House. And one year after a presidential scandal of a magnitude still unknown, we have almost forgotten them, too. We are a people who do not want to keep much of the past in our heads. It is considered unhealthy in America to remember mistakes, neurotic to think about them, psychotic to dwell upon them.

1976

Mary McCarthy 1912–1989

Mary McCarthy was an important intellectual writer whose work addressed many of the critical political issues of the twentieth century. Her novels and memoirs as well as her numerous collections of essays demonstrate that she was deeply concerned with social responsibility—a topic that inevitably involves an analysis of the traditional definitions of race, class, and gender. McCarthy's early theatre columns for *Partisan Review,* her autobiographical narratives, her fiction, especially her controversial novel *The Group,* and her penetrating essays in such collections as *On the Contrary* make it clear that she did not shrink from confrontation. Her keen analytical skills and caustic commentary were focused on national and international issues such as the Watergate scandal, the Vietnam War, and the invasion of Cambodia, as well as domestic concerns such as divorce, female sexuality and birth control. Her refusal to resort to platitudes in her analyses of subjects as diverse as corruption in national government and dysfunctional family dynamics earned her a reputation as being "cold, steely, merciless." She became known as the "lady with a switchblade."

McCarthy's personal life was as complex as her writing. Born in Seattle in 1912, she was orphaned at the age of six when her parents died in the influenza epidemic that swept the United States in 1918. With her three younger brothers, Kevin, Preston, and Sheridan, she was sent to live with her great aunt and uncle. She recorded her bitter recollections of that time in *Memories of a Catholic Girlhood, How I Grew,* and *Intellectual Memoirs.* Especially distressing was the cruel treatment she received from Uncle Myers, whose vicious criticisms and physical cruelty she never forgot. He is the prototype of the bombastic and self-indulgent men who appear in her fiction from "The Man in the Brooks Brothers Suit" to her descriptions of H. R. Haldeman and John Ehrlichman in *The Mask of State: Watergate Portraits.*

As an undergraduate at Vassar from 1929 to 1933, McCarthy was a voracious reader and an excellent student. After marrying and divorcing in the first three years after graduation, she embarked on an adventurous life in Greenwich Village during the Depression. During this time, McCarthy wrote theatre reviews for *Partisan Review* and lived with Philip Rahv, one of the editors of the journal. In 1938 she left Rahv to marry Edmund Wilson, a brilliant literary critic and essayist. Crediting Wilson with her career as a fiction writer, McCarthy reported that early in their marriage he insisted that she remain in her study until she had written a short story. She and Wilson had a son, Reuel, in 1939, and they divorced six years later. McCarthy married twice more and lived in Paris for many years with her fourth husband, James West.

During the 1930s, McCarthy was involved in political debates between the Stalinists and the supporters of Trotsky, whom she favored. She brilliantly evokes the political and social ferment of this period in the short stories "The Genial Host" and "Portrait of an Intellectual as a Yale Man," which were included in *The Company She Keeps.* The *New Yorker* responded with enthusiasm to this collection and invited McCarthy to join its staff of writers.

Following the Second World War, McCarthy and Hannah Arendt formed a friendship that lasted 30 years. McCarthy observed in *How I Grew* that "not love or marriage so much as friendship has promoted growth." McCarthy and Arendt became internationally acclaimed during the years of their friendship. When Arendt died in 1975, McCarthy devoted two years to editing Arendt's *The Life of the Mind,* which was published in two volumes in 1978.

Throughout her life, McCarthy disavowed any association with feminism, as did many women of her generation; nevertheless, a feminist sensibility underlies her work. One of the primary themes of her work is the battle of the sexes and the damaging consequences of the norms of masculine aggression and feminine passivity. Another of her concerns is the importance of psychological and financial autonomy for women. Economic and emotional dependence on men results in extraordinary paralysis in the lives of McCarthy's women protagonists, who are frequently caught in a web of feminine self-abnegation disguised as romantic love.

McCarthy dissected the perils of female passivity in the novel *The Group,* an immediate best-seller when published in 1963. The novel begins with the first inauguration of Franklin Roosevelt and ends with the inauguration of Truman. McCarthy observed that the novel is "about the idea of progress really, seen in the female sphere; the study of technology in the home, in the playpen, in the bed." Weaving interconnecting narratives about eight Vassar graduates from the class of 1933, this novel makes clear that, in spite of optimism about the possibilities of modern life, these women are as dependent on men for economic and social survival as their mothers were.

The writer Alison Lurie observed that Mary McCarthy invented "herself as a totally new type of woman who stood for both sense and sensibility; who was both coolly and professionally intellectual and frankly passionate." In spite of her sardonic and satiric view of sexual politics, McCarthy believed that it is necessary "to choose the self you want." Her boldly unconventional and accomplished life is a testament to the modernist credo that the individual is the locus of authority.

Wendy Martin
Claremont Graduate School

PRIMARY WORKS

Fiction: *The Oasis,* 1949; *The Groves of Academe,* 1952; *A Charmed Life,* 1955; *The Group,* 1963; *Birds of America,* 1965; *The Company She Keeps,* 1970; *Cannibals and Missionaries,* 1979; *The Hounds of Summer and Other Stories,* 1981. Nonfiction: *Cast a Cold Eye,* 1950; *Sights and Spectacles, 1937–1956,* 1956; *Venice Observed,* 1956; *The Stones of Florence,* 1959; *On the Contrary,* 1961; *Mary McCarthy's Theater Chronicles,* 1963; *Vietnam,* 1967; *Hanoi,* 1968; *The Writing on the Wall and Other Literary Essays,* 1970; *Medina,* 1972; *The Mask of State: Watergate Portraits,* 1974; *Memories of a Catholic Girlhood,* 1974; *The Seventeenth Degree,* 1974; *Ideas and the Novel,* 1980; *How I Grew,* 1985; *Occasional Prose,* 1985; *Intellectual Memoirs: New York 1936–1938,* 1992.

from Memories of a Catholic Girlhood

Names

Anna Lyons, Mary Louise Lyons, Mary von Phul, Emilie von Phul, Eugenia McLellan, Marjorie McPhail, Marie-Louise L'Abbé, Mary Danz, Julia Dodge, Mary Fordyce Blake, Janet Preston—these were the names (I can still tell them over like a rosary) of some of the older girls in the convent: the Virtues and Graces. The virtuous ones wore wide blue or green moire good-conduct ribbons, bandoleer-style, across their blue serge uniforms; the beautiful ones wore rouge and powder or at least were reputed to do so. Our class, the eighth grade, wore pink ribbons (I never got one myself) and had names like Patricia ("Pat") Sullivan, Eileen Donohoe, and Joan Kane. We were inelegant even in this respect; the best name we could show, among us, was Phyllis ("Phil") Chatham, who boasted that her father's name, Ralph, was pronounced "Rafe" as in England.

Names had a great importance for us in the convent, and foreign names, French, German, or plain English (which, to us, were foreign, because of their Protestant sound), bloomed like prize roses among a collection of spuds. Irish names were too common in the school to have any prestige either as surnames (Gallagher, Sheehan, Finn, Sullivan, McCarthy) or as Christian names (Kathleen, Eileen). Anything exotic had value: an "olive" complexion, for example. The pet girl of the convent was a fragile Jewish girl named Susie Lowenstein, who had pale red-gold hair and an exquisite retroussé nose, which, if we had had it, might have been called "pug." We liked her name too and the name of a child in the primary grades: Abbie Stuart Baillargeon. My favorite name, on the whole, though, was Emilie von Phul (pronounced "Pool"); her oldest sister, recently graduated, was called Celeste. Another name that appealed to me was Genevieve Albers, Saint Genevieve being the patron saint of Paris who turned back Attila from the gates of the city.

All these names reflected the still-pioneer character of the Pacific Northwest. I had never heard their like in the parochial school in Minneapolis, where "foreign" extraction, in any case, was something to be ashamed of, the whole drive being toward Americanization of first name and surname alike. The exceptions to this were the Irish, who could vaunt such names as Catherine O'Dea and the name of my second cousin, Mary Catherine Anne Rose Violet McCarthy, while an unfortunate German boy named Manfred was made to suffer for his. But that was Minneapolis. In Seattle, and especially in the convent of the Ladies of the Sacred Heart, foreign names suggested not immigration but emigration—distinguished exile. Minneapolis was a granary; Seattle was a port, which had attracted a veritable Foreign Legion of adventurers—soldiers of fortune, younger sons, gamblers, traders, drawn by the fortunes to be made in virgin timber and shipping and by the Alaska Gold Rush. Wars and revolutions had sent the defeated out to Puget Sound, to start a new life; the latest had been the Russian Revolution, which had shipped us, via Harbin, a Russian colony, complete with restaurant, on Queen Anne Hill. The English names in the convent, when they did not testify to direct English origin, as in the case of "Rafe" Chatham, had come to us from the South and represented a kind of internal exile; such girls as Mary Fordyce Blake and Mary McQueen Street (a class ahead of me; her sister was named Francesca) bore their double-barreled first names like titles of aristocracy from the ante-bellum South. Not all our girls, by any means, were Catholic; some of the very prettiest ones—Julia Dodge and Janet Preston, if I remember rightly—were Protestants. The nuns had taught us to behave with special courtesy to these strangers in our midst, and the whole effect was of some superior hostel for refugees of all the lost causes of the past hundred years. Money could not count for much in such an atmosphere; the fathers and grandfathers of many of our "best" girls were ruined men.

Names, often, were freakish in the Pacific Northwest, particularly girls' names. In the Episcopal boarding school I went to later, in Tacoma, there was a girl called De Vere Utter, and there was a girl called Rocena and another called Hermoine. Was Rocena a mistake for Rowena and Hermoine for Hermione? And was Vere, as we called her, Lady Clara Vere de Vere? Probably. You do not hear names like those often, in any case, east of the Cascade Mountains; they belong to the frontier, where books and libraries were few and memory seems to have been oral, as in the time of Homer.

Names have more significance for Catholics than they do for other people; Christian names are chosen for the spiritual qualities of the saints they are taken from; Protestants used to name their children out of the Old Testament and now they name them out of novels and plays, whose heroes and heroines are perhaps the new patron saints of a secular age. But with Catholics it is different. The saint a child is named for is supposed to serve, literally, as a model or pattern to imitate; your name is your fortune and it tells you what you are or must be. Catholic children ponder their names for a mystic meaning, like birthstones; my own, I learned, besides belonging to the Virgin and Saint Mary of Egypt, originally meant "bitter" or "star of the sea." My second name, Therese, could dedicate me either to Saint Theresa or to the saint called the Little Flower, Soeur Thérèse of Lisieux, on whom God was supposed to have descended in the form of a shower of roses. At Confirmation, I had added a third name (for Catholics then rename themselves, as most nuns do, yet another time, when they take orders); on the advice of a nun, I had taken "Clementina," after Saint Clement, an early pope—a step I soon regretted on account of "My Darling Clementine" and her number nine shoes. By the time I was in the convent, I would no longer tell anyone what my Confirmation name was. The name I had nearly picked was "Agnes," after a little Roman virgin martyr, always shown with a lamb, because of her purity. But Agnes would have been just as bad, I recognized in Forest Ridge Convent—not only because of the possibility of "Aggie," but because it was subtly, indefinably *wrong,* in itself. Agnes would have made me look like an ass.

The fear of appearing ridiculous first entered my life, as a governing motive, during my second year in the convent. Up to then, a desire for prominence had decided many of my actions and, in fact, still persisted. But in the eighth grade, I became aware of mockery and perceived that I could not seek prominence without attracting laughter. Other people could, but I couldn't. This laughter was proceeding, not from my classmates, but from the girls of the class just above me, in particular from two boon companions, Elinor Heffernan and Mary Harty, a clownish pair—oddly assorted in size and shape, as teams of clowns generally are, one short, plump, and baby-faced, the other tall, lean, and owlish—who entertained the high-school department by calling attention to the oddities of the younger girls. Nearly every school has such a pair of satirists, whose marks are generally low and who are tolerated just because of their laziness and non-conformity; one of them (in this case, Mary Harty, the plump one) usually appears to be half asleep. Because of their low standing, their indifference to appearances, the sad state of their uniforms, their clowning is taken to be harmless, which, on the whole, it is, their object being not to wound but to divert; such girls are bored in school. We in the eighth grade sat directly in front of the two wits in study hall, so that they had us under close observation; yet at first I was not afraid of them, wanting, if anything, to identify myself with their laughter, to be initiated into the joke. One of their specialties was giving people nicknames, and it was considered an honor to be the first in the eighth grade to be let in by Elinor and Mary on their latest invention. This often happened to me; they would tell me, on the playground, and I would tell the others. As their intermediary, I felt myself almost their friend and it did not occur to me that I might be next on their list.

I had achieved prominence not long before by publicly losing my faith and regaining it at the end of a retreat. I believe Elinor and Mary questioned me about this on the playground, during recess, and listened with serious, respectful faces while I told them about my conversations with the Jesuits. Those serious faces ought to have been an omen, but if the two girls used what I had revealed to make fun of me, it must have been behind my back. I never heard any more of it, and yet just at this time I began to feel something, like a cold breath on the nape of my neck, that made me wonder whether the new position I had won for myself in the convent was as secure as I imagined. I would turn around in study hall and find the two girls looking at me with speculation in their eyes.

It was just at this time, too, that I found myself in a perfectly absurd situation, a very private one, which made me live, from month to month, in horror of discovery. I had waked up one morning, in my convent room, to find a few small spots of blood on my sheet; I had somehow scratched a trifling cut on one of my legs and opened it during the night. I wondered what to do about this, for the nuns were fussy about bedmaking, as they were about our white collars and cuffs, and if we had an inspection those spots might count against me. It was best, I decided, to ask the nun on dormitory duty, tall, stout Mother Slattery, for a clean bottom sheet, even though she might scold me for having scratched my leg in my sleep and order me to cut my toenails. You never know what you might be blamed for. But Mother Slattery, when she bustled in to look at the sheet, did not scold me at all; indeed, she hardly seemed to be listening as I explained to her about the cut. She told me to sit down: she would be back in a minute. "You can be excused from athletics today," she added, closing the door. As I waited, I considered this remark, which seemed to me strangely munificent, in view of the unimportance of the cut. In a moment, she returned, but without the sheet. Instead, she produced out of her big pocket a sort of cloth girdle and a peculiar flannel object which I first took to be a bandage, and I began to protest that I did not need or want a bandage; all I needed was a bottom sheet. "The sheet can wait," said Mother Slattery, succinctly, handing me two large safety pins. It was the pins that abruptly enlightened me; I saw Mother Slattery's mistake, even as she was instructing me as to how this flannel article, which I now understood to be a sanitary napkin, was to be put on.

"Oh, no, Mother," I said, feeling somewhat embarrassed. "You don't understand. It's just a little cut, on my leg." But Mother, again, was not listening; she appeared to have grown deaf, as the nuns had a habit of doing when what you were saying did not fit in with their ideas. And now that I knew what was in her mind, I was conscious of a funny constraint; I did not feel it proper to name a natural process, in so many words, to a nun. It was like trying not to think of their going to the bathroom or trying not to see the straggling iron-grey hair coming out of their coifs (the common notion that they shaved their heads was false). On the whole, it seemed better just to show her my cut. But when I offered to do so and unfastened my black stocking, she only glanced at my leg, cursorily. "That's only a scratch, dear," she said. "Now hurry up and put this on or you'll be late for chapel. Have you any pain?" "No, no, Mother!" I cried. "You don't understand!" "Yes, yes, I understand," she replied soothingly, "and you will too, a little later. Mother Superior will tell you about it some time during the morning. There's nothing to be afraid of. You have become a woman."

"I know all about that," I persisted. "Mother, please listen. I just cut my leg. On the athletic field. Yesterday afternoon." But the more excited I grew, the more soothing, and yet firm, Mother Slattery became. There seemed to be nothing for it but to give up and do as I was bid. I was in the grip of a higher authority, which almost had the power to persuade me that it was right and I was wrong. But of course I was not wrong; that would have been too good to be true. While Mother Slattery waited, just outside my door, I miserably donned the equipment she had given me, for there was no place to hide it, on account of drawer inspection. She led me down the hall to where there was a chute and explained how I was to dispose of the flannel thing, by dropping it down the chute into the laundry. (The convent arrangements were very old-fashioned, dating back, no doubt, to the days of Louis Philippe.)

The Mother Superior, Madame MacIllvra, was a sensible woman, and all through my early morning classes, I was on pins and needles, chafing for the promised interview with her which I trusted would clear things up. *"Ma Mère,"* I would begin, "Mother Slattery thinks . . ." Then I would tell her about the cut and the athletic field. But precisely the same impasse confronted me when I was summoned to her office at recess-time. *I* talked about my cut, and *she* talked about becoming a woman. It was rather like a round, in which she was singing "Scotland's burning, Scotland's burning," and I was singing "Pour on water, pour on water." Neither of us could hear the other, or, rather, I could hear her, but she could not hear me. Owing to our different positions in the convent, she was free to interrupt me, whereas I was expected to remain silent until she had finished speaking. When I kept breaking in, she hushed me, gently, and took me on her lap. Exactly like Mother Slattery, she attributed all my references to the cut to a blind fear of this new, unexpected reality that had supposedly entered my life. Many young girls, she reassured me, were frightened if they had not been prepared. "And you, Mary, have lost your dear mother, who could have made this easier for you." Rocked on Madame MacIllvra's lap, I felt paralysis overtake me and I lay, mutely listening, against her bosom, my face being tickled by her white, starched, fluted wimple, while she explained to me how babies were born, all of which I had heard before.

There was no use fighting the convent. I had to pretend to have become a woman, just as, not long before, I had had to pretend to get my faith back—for the sake of peace. This pretense was decidedly awkward. For fear of being found out by the lay sisters downstairs in the laundry (no doubt an imaginary contingency, but the convent was so very thorough), I reopened the cut on my leg, so as to draw a little blood to stain the napkins, which were issued me regularly, not only on this occasion, but every twenty-eight days thereafter. Eventually, I abandoned this bloodletting, for fear of lockjaw, and trusted to fate. Yet I was in awful dread of detection; my only hope, as I saw it, was either to be released from the convent or to become a woman in reality, which might take a year, at least, since I was only twelve. Getting out of athletics once a month was not sufficient compensation for the farce I was going through. It was not my fault; they had forced me into it; nevertheless, it was I who would look silly—worse than silly; half mad—if the truth ever came to light.

I was burdened with this guilt and shame when the nickname finally found me out. "Found me out," in a general sense, for no one ever did learn the particular secret I bore about with me, pinned to the linen band. "We've got a name for you," Elinor and Mary called out to me, one day on the playground. "What is it?" I asked, half hoping, half fearing, since not all their sobriquets were unfavorable. "Cye," they answered, looking at each other and laughing. "'Si'?" I repeated, supposing that it was based on Simple Simon. Did they regard me as a hick? "C.Y.E.," they elucidated, spelling it out in chorus. "The letters stand for something. Can you guess?" I could not and I cannot now. The closest I could come to it in the convent was "Clean Your Ears." Perhaps that was it, though in later life I have wondered whether it did not stand, simply, for "Clever Young Egg" or "Champion Young Eccentric." But in the convent I was certain that it stood for something horrible, something even worse than dirty ears (as far as I knew, my ears were clean), something I could never guess because it represented some aspect of myself that the world could see and I couldn't, like a sign pinned on my back. Everyone in the convent must have known what the letters stood for, but no one would tell me. Elinor and Mary had made them promise. It was like halitosis; not even my best friend, my deskmate, Louise, would tell me, no matter how much I pleaded. Yet everyone assured me that it was "very good," that is, very apt. And it made everyone laugh.

This name reduced all my pretensions and solidified my sense of *wrongness.* Just as I felt I was beginning to belong to the convent, it turned me into an outsider, since

I was the only pupil who was not in the know. I liked the convent, but it did not like me, as people say of certain foods that disagree with them. By this, I do not mean that I was actively unpopular, either with the pupils or with the nuns. The Mother Superior cried when I left and predicted that I would be a novelist, which surprised me. And I had finally made friends; even Emilie von Phul smiled upon me softly out of her bright blue eyes from the far end of the study hall. It was just that I did not fit into the convent pattern; the simplest thing I did, like asking for a clean sheet, entrapped me in consequences that I never could have predicted. I was not bad; I did not consciously break the rules; and yet I could never, not even for a week, get a pink ribbon, and this was something I could not understand, because I was trying as hard as I could. It was the same case as with the hated name; the nuns, evidently, saw something about me that was invisible to me.

The oddest part was all that pretending. There I was, a walking mass of lies, pretending to be a Catholic and going to confession while really I had lost my faith, and pretending to have monthly periods by cutting myself with nail scissors; yet all this had come about without my volition and even contrary to it. But the basest pretense I was driven to was the acceptance of the nickname. Yet what else could I do? In the convent, I could not live it down. To all those girls, I had become "Cye McCarthy." That was who I was. That was how I had to identify myself when telephoning my friends during vacations to ask them to the movies: "Hello, this is Cye." I loathed myself when I said it, and yet I succumbed to the name totally, making myself over into a sort of hearty to go with it—the kind of girl I hated. "Cye" was my new patron saint. This false personality stuck to me, like the name, when I entered public high school, the next fall, as a freshman, having finally persuaded my grandparents to take me out of the convent, although they could never get to the bottom of my reasons, since, as I admitted, the nuns were kind, and I had made many nice new friends. What I wanted was a fresh start, a chance to begin life over again, but the first thing I heard in the corridors of the public high school was that name called out to me, like the warmest of welcomes: "Hi, there, Si!" That was the way they thought it was spelled. But this time I was resolute. After the first weeks, I dropped the hearties who called me "Si" and I never heard it again. I got my own name back and sloughed off Clementina and even Therese—the names that did not seem to me any more to be mine but to have been imposed on me by others. And I preferred to think that Mary meant "bitter" rather than "star of the sea."

1957

Clifford Odets 1906–1963

Born into a middle-class family in Philadelphia, Odets grew up in predominantly Jewish neighborhoods in the Bronx. Like many successful American authors, he never attended college. After eleventh grade he found acting jobs on the radio and then drifted into work in small local theatre companies.

Odets's acting career was making little progress when in 1930 he became involved with the Group Theatre, a new and dynamic organization which was just beginning its influential decade in New York. After a number of minor acting roles with that company, he decided to try writing a contemporary family drama for them; his script was the genesis of *Awake and Sing* (1935), his first full-length play. The early draft of *Awake and Sing,* however, was rejected by the managers of the Group, and Odets put his script through extensive revisions before the play was eventually performed. In the meantime his rapidly written short play, *Waiting for Lefty* (1935), made him an instant theatrical celebrity.

A certain amount of theatrical mythology has grown up around the composition of *Waiting for Lefty.* It was, in fact, first produced in a small union hall; it was probably not, on the other hand, written in three nights or written as an entry in a contest with a $50 prize. It was quite clearly written in response to the urging of Odets's Communist friends (Odets had joined the party for his brief dalliance in the fall of 1934). More important about the play is the emotional heat which the young playwright was able to convey as well as the theatricality of the presentation. In part because it is a blatant "message" play which can be presented without the benefit of an elaborate stage or scenery, within a few months "Lefty" was being produced all over the country. The reception was predictably enthusiastic in almost every city where it was presented. Even when the play was condemned as mere propaganda, it managed to create enough of a stir to enhance the young playwright's reputation.

Thus the Depression and the Group Theatre were the two formative factors in Odets's career as dramatist. It is hard to imagine Odets's successes coming at any time other than during the Depression. To the left-oriented, often militant American writers like Odets, "The theatre is a weapon" was a rallying cry. Yet the author of *Waiting for Lefty* went on to write for films, to marry a glamorous Hollywood movie queen, to live comfortably in Beverly Hills, to enjoy the night life of Las Vegas, and to speak openly about Communist infiltration of the arts when he testified in 1952 before the notorious House Un-American Activities Committee. These are only a few of the contradictions apparent in Odets's life.

His subsequent plays, the most popular of which are *Golden Boy* (1937) and *The Country Girl* (1950), demonstrate a mature craftsmanship. Some, like *The Flowering Peach,* even show a calm mood unexpected from the firebrand who wrote *Waiting for Lefty.* Yet Odets's reputation will probably rest heavily with the rich colloquial family drama, *Awake and Sing,* and the angry, experimental *Waiting for Lefty,* his first two produced dramas.

If Odets did not reach the full measure of fulfillment which any artist seeks, he did earn his niche in the history of American drama. His direct influence on playwrights like William Gibson and Arthur Miller is evident. Always the idealist rather than the doctrinaire leftist, Odets is best characterized not by the "Stormbirds of the Working Class" speech at the conclusion of *Waiting for Lefty,* but by the line he directed to the younger generation in *Awake and Sing:* "Go out and fight so life shouldn't be printed on dollar bills."

Michael J. Mendelsohn
University of Tampa

PRIMARY WORKS

Six Plays of Clifford Odets, 1935; *The Country Girl,* 1951.

Waiting for Lefty

As the curtain goes up we see a bare stage. On it are sitting six or seven men in a semicircle. Lolling against the proscenium[1] *down left is a young man chewing a toothpick: a gunman. A fat man of porcine appearance is talking directly to the audience. In other words he is the head of a union and the men ranged behind him are a committee of workers. They are now seated in interesting different attitudes and present a wide diversity of type, as we shall soon see. The fat man is hot and heavy under the collar, near the end of a long talk, but not too hot: he is well fed and confident. His name is* HARRY FATT.

FATT: You're so wrong I ain't laughing. Any guy with eyes to read knows it. Look at the textile strike—out like lions and in like lambs. Take the San Francisco tie-up—starvation and broken heads. The steel boys wanted to walk out too, but they changed their minds. It's the trend of the times, that's what it is. All we workers got a good man behind us now.[2] He's top man of the country—looking out for our interests—the man in the White House is the one I'm referrin' to. That's why the times ain't ripe for a strike. He's working day and night—

VOICE *(from the audience):* For who? *(The* GUNMAN *stirs himself.)*

FATT: For you! The records prove it. If this was the Hoover[3] régime, would I say don't go out, boys? Not on your tintype![4] But things is different now. You read the papers as well as me. You know it. And that's why I'm against the strike. Because we gotta stand behind the man who's standin' behind us! The whole country—

ANOTHER VOICE: Is on the blink! *(The* GUNMAN *looks grave.)*

FATT: Stand up and show yourself, you damn red![5] Be a man, let's see what you look like! *(Waits in vain.)* Yellow from the word go! Red and yellow makes a dirty color, boys. I got my eyes on four or five of them in the union here. What the hell'll they do for you? Pull you out and run away when trouble starts. Give those birds a chance and they'll have your sisters and wives in the whore houses, like they done in Russia. They'll tear Christ off his bleeding cross. They'll wreck your homes and throw your babies in the river. You think that's bunk? Read the papers! Now listen, we can't stay here all night. I gave you the facts in the case. You boys got hot suppers to go to and—

ANOTHER VOICE: Says you!

GUNMAN: Sit down, Punk!

ANOTHER VOICE: Where's Lefty? *(Now this question is taken up by the others in unison.* FATT *pounds with gavel.)*

FATT: That's what I wanna know. Where's your pal, Lefty? You elected him chairman—where the hell did he disappear?

VOICES: We want Lefty! Lefty! Lefty!

FATT *(pounding):* What the hell is this—a circus? You got the committee here. This bunch of cowboys you elected. *(Pointing to man on extreme right end.)*

[1]The archway, or frame, that forms the front of a traditional theatrical stage.
[2]Franklin Roosevelt, elected President in 1932.
[3]Roosevelt's predecessor, President from 1929–1933.
[4]Not a chance (slang).
[5]Fatt is calling the unseen heckler a communist agitator.

MAN: Benjamin.

FATT: Yeah, Doc Benjamin. *(Pointing to other men in circle in seated order):* Benjamin, Miller, Stein, Mitchell, Phillips, Keller. It ain't my fault Lefty took a run-out powder. If you guys—

A GOOD VOICE: What's the committee say?

OTHERS: The committee! Let's hear from the committee! (FATT *tries to quiet the crowd, but one of the seated men suddenly comes to the front. The* GUNMAN *moves over to center stage, but* FATT *says:)*

FATT: Sure, let him talk. Let's hear what the red boys gotta say! *(Various shouts are coming from the audience.* FATT *insolently goes back to his seat in the middle of the circle. He sits on his raised platform and relights his cigar. The* GUNMAN *goes back to his post.* JOE, *the new speaker, raises his hand for quiet. Gets it quickly. He is sore.)*

JOE: You boys know me. I ain't a red boy one bit! Here I'm carryin' a shrapnel that big I picked up in the war. And maybe I don't know it when it rains! Don't tell me red! You know what we are? The black and blue boys! We been kicked around so long we're black and blue from head to toes. But I guess anyone who says straight out he don't like it, he's a red boy to the leaders of the union. What's this crap about goin' home to hot suppers? I'm asking to your faces how many's got hot suppers to go home to? Anyone who's sure of his next meal, raise your hand! A certain gent sitting behind me can raise them both. But not in front here! And that's why we're talking strike—to get a living wage!

VOICE: Where's Lefty?

JOE: I honest to God don't know, but he didn't take no run-out powder. That Wop's got more guts than a slaughter house. Maybe a traffic jam got him, but he'll be here. But don't let this red stuff scare you. Unless fighting for a living scares you. We gotta make up our minds. My wife made up my mind last week, if you want the truth. It's plain as the nose on Sol Feinberg's face we need a strike. There's us comin' home every night—eight, ten hours on the cab. "God," the wife says, "eighty cents ain't money—don't buy beans almost. You're workin' for the company," she says to me, "Joe! you ain't workin' for me or the family no more!" She says to me, "If you don't start . . ."

I. Joe and Edna

The lights fade out and a white spot picks out the playing space within the space of seated men. The seated men are very dimly visible in the outer dark, but more prominent is FATT *smoking his cigar and often blowing the smoke in the lighted circle.*

A tired but attractive woman of thirty comes into the room, drying her hands on an apron. She stands there sullenly as JOE *comes in from the other side, home from work. For a moment they stand and look at each other in silence.*

JOE: Where's all the furniture, honey?

EDNA: They took it away. No installments paid.

JOE: When?

EDNA: Three o'clock.

JOE: They can't do that.

EDNA: Can't? They did it.
JOE: Why, the palookas,[6] we paid three-quarters.
EDNA: The man said read the contract.
JOE: We must have signed a phoney. . . .
EDNA: It's a regular contract and you signed it.
JOE: Don't be so sour, Edna. . . . *(Tries to embrace her.)*
EDNA: Do it in the movies, Joe—they pay Clark Gable big money for it.
JOE: This is a helluva house to come home to. Take my word!
EDNA: Take MY word! Whose fault is it?
JOE: Must you start that stuff again?
EDNA: Maybe you'd like to talk about books?
JOE: I'd like to slap you in the mouth!
EDNA: No you won't.
JOE *(sheepishly):* Jeez, Edna, you get me sore some time. . . .
EDNA: But just look at me—I'm laughing all over!
JOE: Don't insult me. Can I help it if times are bad? What the hell do you want me to do, jump off a bridge or something?
EDNA: Don't yell. I just put the kids to bed so they won't know they missed a meal. If I don't have Emmy's shoes soled tomorrow, she can't go to school. In the meantime let her sleep.
JOE: Honey, I rode the wheels off the chariot today. I cruised around five hours without a call. It's conditions.
EDNA: Tell it to the A & P!
JOE: I booked two-twenty on the clock. A lady with a dog was lit . . . she gave me a quarter tip by mistake. If you'd only listen to me—we're rolling in wealth.
EDNA: Yeah? How much?
JOE: I had "coffee and—" in a beanery. *(Hands her silver coins.)* A buck four.
EDNA: The second month's rent is due tomorrow.
JOE: Don't look at me that way, Edna.
EDNA: I'm looking through you, not at you. . . . Everything was gonna be so ducky! A cottage by the waterfall, roses in Picardy. You're a four-star-bust! If you think I'm standing for it much longer, you're crazy as a bedbug.
JOE: I'd get another job if I could. There's no work—you know it.
EDNA: I only know we're at the bottom of the ocean.
JOE: What can I do?
EDNA: Who's the man in the family, you or me?
JOE: That's no answer. Get down to brass tacks. Christ, gimme a break, too! A coffee and java all day. I'm hungry, too, Babe. I'd work my fingers to the bone if—
EDNA: I'll open a can of salmon.
JOE: Not now. Tell me what to do!
EDNA: I'm not God!
JOE: Jeez, I wish I was a kid again and didn't have to think about the next minute.
EDNA: But you're not a kid and you do have to think about the next minute. You got two blondie kids sleeping in the next room. They need food and clothes. I'm not

[6]A dumb, muscular type (slang).

mentioning anything else—But we're stalled like a flivver[7] in the snow. For five years I laid awake at night listening to my heart pound. For God's sake, do something, Joe, get wise. Maybe get your buddies together, maybe go on strike for better money. Poppa did it during the war and they won out. I'm turning into a sour old nag.

JOE: *(defending himself):* Strikes don't work!

EDNA: Who told you?

JOE: Besides that means not a nickel a week while we're out. Then when it's over they don't take you back.

EDNA: Suppose they don't. What's to lose?

JOE: Well, we're averaging six-seven dollars a week now.

EDNA: That just pays for the rent.

JOE: That is something, Edna.

EDNA: It isn't. They'll push you down to three and four a week before you know it. Then you'll say, "That's somethin'," too!

JOE: There's too many cabs on the street, that's the whole damn trouble.

EDNA: Let the company worry about that, you big fool! If their cabs didn't make a profit, they'd take them off the streets. Or maybe you think they're in business just to pay Joe Mitchell's rent!

JOE: You don't know a-b-c, Edna.

EDNA: I know this—your boss is making suckers outa you boys every minute. Yes, and suckers out of all the wives and the poor innocent kids who'll grow up with crooked spines and sick bones. Sure, I see it in the papers, how good orange juice is for kids. But damnit our kids get colds one on top of the other. They look like little ghosts. Betty never saw a grapefruit. I took her to the store last week and she pointed to a stack of grapefruits. "What's that!" she said. My God, Joe—the world is supposed to be for all of us.

JOE: You'll wake them up.

EDNA: I don't care, as long as I can maybe wake you up.

JOE: Don't insult me. One man can't make a strike.

EDNA: Who says one? You got hundreds in your rotten union!

JOE: The union ain't rotten.

EDNA: No? Then what are they doing? Collecting dues and patting your back?

JOE: They're making plans.

EDNA: What kind?

JOE: They don't tell us.

EDNA: It's too damn bad about you. They don't tell little Joey what's happening in his bitsie witsie union. What do you think it is—a ping pong game?

JOE: You know they're racketeers. The guys at the top would shoot you for a nickel.

EDNA: Why do you stand for that stuff?

JOE: Don't you wanna see me alive?

EDNA *(after a deep pause):* No . . . I don't think I do, Joe. Not if you can lift a finger to do something about it, and don't. No, I don't care.

[7]A beat-up automobile (slang).

JOE: Honey, you don't understand what—

EDNA: And any other hackie[8] that won't fight . . . let them all be ground to hamburger!

JOE: It's one thing to—

EDNA: Take your hand away! Only they don't grind me to little pieces! I got different plans. *(Starts to take off her apron.)*

JOE: Where are you going?

EDNA: None of your business.

JOE: What's up your sleeve?

EDNA: My arm'd be up my sleeve, darling, if I had a sleeve to wear. *(Puts neatly folded apron on back of chair.)*

JOE: Tell me!

EDNA: Tell you what?

JOE: Where are you going?

EDNA: Don't you remember my old boy friend?

JOE: Who?

EDNA: Bud Haas. He still has my picture in his watch. He earns a living.

JOE: What the hell are you talking about?

EDNA: I heard worse than I'm talking about.

JOE: Have you seen Bud since we got married?

EDNA: Maybe.

JOE: If I thought . . . *(He stands looking at her.)*

EDNA: See much? Listen, boy friend, if you think I won't do this it just means you can't see straight.

JOE: Stop talking bull.

EDNA: This isn't five years ago, Joe.

JOE: You mean you'd leave me and the kids?

EDNA: I'd leave *you* like a shot!

JOE: No. . . .

EDNA: Yes! (JOE *turns away, sitting in a chair with his back to her. Outside the lighted circle of the playing stage we hear the other seated members of the strike committee. "She will . . . she will . . . it happens that way," etc. This group should be used throughout for various comments, political, emotional and as general chorus. Whispering. . . . The fat boss now blows a heavy cloud of smoke into the scene.)*

JOE *(finally):* Well, I guess I ain't got a leg to stand on.

EDNA: No?

JOE *(suddenly mad):* No, you lousy tart, no! Get the hell out of here. Go pick up that bull-thrower on the corner and stop at some cushy hotel downtown. He's probably been coming here every morning and laying you while I hacked my guts out!

EDNA: You're crawling like a worm!

JOE: You'll be crawling in a minute.

EDNA: You don't scare me that much! *(Indicates a half inch on her finger.)*

JOE: This is what I slaved for!

EDNA: Tell it to your boss.

[8]Taxi driver.

JOE: He don't give a damn for you or me!

EDNA: That's what I say.

JOE: Don't change the subject!

EDNA: This is the subject, the *exact subject!* Your boss makes this subject. I never saw him in my life, but he's putting ideas in my head a mile a minute. He's giving your kids that fancy disease called the rickets. He's making a jelly-fish outa you and putting wrinkles in my face. This is the subject every inch of the way! He's throwing me into Bud Haas' lap. When in hell will you get wise—

JOE: I'm not so dumb as you think! But you are talking like a red.

EDNA: I don't know what that means. But when a man knocks you down you get up and kiss his fist! You gutless piece of boloney.

JOE: One man can't—

EDNA *(with great joy):* I don't say one man! I say a hundred, a thousand, a whole million, I say. But start in your own union. Get those hack boys together! Sweep out those racketeers like a pile of dirt! Stand up like men and fight for the crying kids and wives. Goddamnit! I'm tired of slavery and sleepless nights.

JOE *(with her):* Sure, sure! . . .

EDNA: Yes. Get brass toes on your shoes and know where to kick!

JOE *(suddenly jumping up and kissing his wife full on the mouth):* Listen, Edna, I'm goin' down to 174th Street to look up Lefty Costello. Lefty was saying the other day . . . *(He suddenly stops.)* How about this Haas guy?

EDNA: Get out of here!

JOE: I'll be back! *(Runs out. For a moment* EDNA *stands triumphant. There is a blackout and when the regular lights come up,* JOE MITCHELL *is concluding what he has been saying):*

JOE: You guys know this stuff better than me. We gotta walk out! *(Abruptly he turns and goes back to his seat.)*

Blackout

II. Lab Assistant Episode

Discovered: MILLER, *a lab assistant, looking around; and* FAYETTE, *an industrialist.*

FAY: Like it?

MILLER: Very much. I've never seen an office like this outside the movies.

FAY: Yes, I often wonder if interior decorators and bathroom fixture people don't get all their ideas from Hollywood. Our country's extraordinary that way. Soap, cosmetics, electric refrigerators—just let Mrs. Consumer know they're used by the Crawfords and Garbos[9]—more volume of sale than one plant can handle!

MILL: I'm afraid it isn't that easy, Mr. Fayette.

[9]Reference to two glamorous movie stars, Joan Crawford and Greta Garbo.

FAY: No, you're right—gross exaggeration on my part. Competition is cutthroat today. Market's up flush against a stone wall. The astronomers had better hurry—open Mars to trade expansion.

MILL: Or it will be just too bad!

FAY: Cigar?

MILL: Thank you, don't smoke.

FAY: Drink?

MILL: Ditto, Mr. Fayette.

FAY: I like sobriety in my workers . . . the trained ones, I mean. The pollacks and niggers, they're better drunk—keeps them out of mischief. Wondering why I had you come over?

MILL: If you don't mind my saying—very much.

FAY *(patting him on the knee):* I like your work.

MILL: Thanks.

FAY: No reason why a talented young man like yourself shouldn't string along with us—a growing concern. Loyalty is well repaid in our organization. Did you see Siegfried this morning?

MILL: He hasn't been in the laboratory all day.

FAY: I told him yesterday to raise you twenty dollars a month. Starts this week.

MILL: You don't know how happy my wife'll be.

FAY: Oh, I can appreciate it. *(He laughs.)*

MILL: Was that all, Mr. Fayette?

FAY: Yes, except that we're switching you to laboratory A tomorrow. Siegfried knows about it. That's why I had you in. The new work is very important. Siegfried recommended you very highly as a man to trust. You'll work directly under Dr. Brenner. Make you happy?

MILL: Very. He's an important chemist!

FAY *(leaning over seriously):* We think so, Miller. We think so to the extent of asking you to stay within the building throughout the time you work with him.

MILL: You mean sleep and eat in?

FAY: Yes. . . .

MILL: It can be arranged.

FAY: Fine. You'll go far, Miller.

MILL: May I ask the nature of the new work?

FAY *(looking around first):* Poison gas. . . .

MILL: Poison!

FAY: Orders from above. I don't have to tell you from where. New type poison gas for modern warfare.

MILL: I see.

FAY: You didn't know a new war was that close, did you?

MILL: I guess I didn't.

FAY: I don't have to stress the importance of absolute secrecy.

MILL: I understand!

FAY: The world is an armed camp today. One match sets the whole world blazing in forty-eight hours. Uncle Sam won't be caught napping!

MILL *(addressing his pencil):* They say 12 million men were killed in that last one and 20 million more wounded or missing.

FAY: That's not our worry. If big business went sentimental over human life there wouldn't be big business of any sort!
MILL: My brother and two cousins went in the last one.
FAY: They died in a good cause.
MILL: My mother says "no!"
FAY: She won't worry about you this time. You're too valuable behind the front.
MILL: That's right.
FAY: All right, Miller. See Siegfried for further orders.
MILL: You should have seen my brother—he could ride a bike without hands. . . .
FAY: You'd better move some clothes and shaving tools in tomorrow. Remember what I said—you're with a growing organization.
MILL: He could run the hundred yards in 9:8 flat. . . .
FAY: Who?
MILL: My brother. He's in the Meuse-Argonne Cemetery. Mama went there in 1926. . . .
FAY: Yes, those things stick. How's your handwriting, Miller, fairly legible?
MILL: Fairly so.
FAY: Once a week I'd like a little report from you.
MILL: What sort of report?
FAY: Just a few hundred words once a week on Dr. Brenner's progress.
MILL: Don't you think it might be better coming from the Doctor?
FAY: I didn't ask you that.
MILL: Sorry.
FAY: I want to know what progress he's making, the reports to be purely confidential—between you and me.
MILL: You mean I'm to watch him?
FAY: Yes!
MILL: I guess I can't do that. . . .
FAY: Thirty a month raise . . .
MILL: You said twenty. . . .
FAY: Thirty!
MILL: Guess I'm not built that way.
FAY: Forty. . . .
MILL: Spying's not in my line, Mr. Fayette!
FAY: You use ugly words, Mr. Miller!
MILL: For ugly activity? Yes!
FAY: Think about it, Miller. Your chances are excellent. . . .
MILL: No.
FAY: You're doing something for your country. Assuring the United States that when those goddamn Japs start a ruckus we'll have offensive weapons to back us up! Don't you read your newspapers, Miller?
MILL: Nothing but Andy Gump.[10]
FAY: If you were on the inside you'd know I'm talking cold sober truth! Now, I'm not asking you to make up your mind on the spot. Think about it over your lunch period.

[10]A comic strip character.

MILL: No.
FAY: Made up your mind already?
MILL: Afraid so.
FAY: You understand the consequences?
MILL: I lose my raise—

Simultaneously: { MILL: And my job!
FAY: And your job!
MILL: You misunderstand—

MILL: Rather dig ditches first!
FAY: That's a big job for foreigners.
MILL: But sneaking—and making poison gas—that's for Americans?
FAY: It's up to you.
MILL: My mind's made up.
FAY: No hard feelings?
MILL: Sure hard feelings! I'm not the civilized type, Mr. Fayette. Nothing suave or sophisticated about me. Plenty of hard feelings! Enough to want to bust you and all your kind square in the mouth! *(Does exactly that.)*

Blackout

III. The Young Hack and His Girl

Opens with girl and brother. FLORENCE *waiting for* SID *to take her to a dance.*

FLOR: I gotta right to have something out of life. I don't smoke, I don't drink. So if Sid wants to take me to a dance, I'll go. Maybe if you was in love you wouldn't talk so hard.
IRV: I'm saying it for your good.
FLOR: Don't be so good to me.
IRV: Mom's sick in bed and you'll be worryin' her to the grave. She don't want that boy hanging around the house and she don't want you meeting him in Crotona Park.
FLOR: I'll meet him anytime I like!
IRV: If you do, yours truly'll take care of it in his own way. With just one hand, too!
FLOR: Why are you all so set against him?
IRV: Mom told you ten times—it ain't him. It's that he ain't got nothing. Sure, we know he's serious, that he's stuck on you. But that don't cut no ice.
FLOR: Taxi drivers used to make good money.
IRV: Today they're makin' five and six dollars a week. Maybe you wanta raise a family on that. Then you'll be back here living with us again and I'll be supporting two families in one. Well . . . over my dead body.
FLOR: Irv, I don't care—I love him!
IRV: You're a little kid with half-baked ideas!
FLOR: I stand there behind the counter the whole day. I think about him—
IRV: If you thought more about Mom it would be better.

FLOR: Don't I take care of her every night when I come home? Don't I cook supper and iron your shirts and . . . you give me a pain in the neck, too. Don't try to shut me up! I bring a few dollars in the house, too. Don't you see I want something else out of life. Sure, I want romance, love, babies. I want everything in life I can get.

IRV: You take care of Mom and watch your step!

FLOR: And if I don't?

IRV: Yours truly'll watch it for you!

FLOR: You can talk that way to a girl. . . .

IRV: I'll talk that way to your boy friend, too, and it won't be with words! Florrie, if you had a pair of eyes you'd see it's for your own good we're talking. This ain't no time to get married. Maybe later—

FLOR: "Maybe Later" never comes for me, though. Why don't we send Mom to a hospital? She can die in peace there instead of looking at the clock on the mantelpiece all day.

IRV: That needs money. Which we don't have!

FLOR: Money, Money, Money!

IRV: Don't change the subject.

FLOR: This is the subject!

IRV: You gonna stop seeing him? *(She turns away).* Jesus, kiddie, I remember when you were a baby with curls down your back. Now I gotta stand here yellin' at you like this.

FLOR: I'll talk to him, Irv.

IRV: When?

FLOR: I asked him to come here tonight. We'll talk it over.

IRV: Don't get soft with him. Nowadays is no time to be soft. You gotta be hard as a rock or go under.

FLOR: I found that out. There's the bell. Take the egg off the stove I boiled for Mom. Leave us alone Irv. (SID *comes in—the two men look at each other for a second.* IRV *exits.)*

SID *(enters):* Hello, Florrie.

FLOR: Hello, Honey. You're looking tired.

SID: Naw, I just need a shave.

FLOR: Well, draw your chair up to the fire and I'll ring for brandy and soda . . . like in the movies.

SID: If this was the movies I'd bring a big bunch of roses.

FLOR: How big?

SID: Fifty or sixty dozen—the kind with long, long stems—big as that. . . .

FLOR: You dope. . . .

SID: Your Paris gown is beautiful.

FLOR *(acting grandly):* Yes, Percy, velvet panels are coming back again. Madame La Farge told me today that Queen Marie herself designed it.

SID: Gee . . . !

FLOR: Every princess in the Balkans is wearing one like this. *(Poses grandly.)*

SID: Hold it. *(Does a nose camera—thumbing nose and imitating grinding of camera with other hand. Suddenly she falls out of the posture and swiftly goes to him, to embrace him, to kiss him with love. Finally):*

SID: You look tired, Florrie.

FLOR: Naw, I just need a shave. *(She laughs tremulously.)*
SID: You worried about your mother?
FLOR: No.
SID: What's on your mind?
FLOR: The French and Indian War.
SID: What's on your mind?
FLOR: I got us on my mind, Sid. Night and day, Sid!
SID: I smacked a beer truck today. Did I get hell! I was driving along thinking of US, too. You don't have to say it—I know what's on your mind. I'm rat poison around here.
FLOR: Not to me. . . .
SID: I know to who . . . and I know why. I don't blame them. We're engaged now for three years. . . .
FLOR: That's a long time. . . .
SID: My brother Sam joined the navy this morning—get a break that way. They'll send him down to Cuba with the hootchy-kootchy girls. He don't know from nothing, that dumb basket ball player!
FLOR: Don't you do that.
SID: Don't you worry, I'm not the kind who runs away. But I'm so tired of being a dog, Baby, I could choke. I don't even have to ask what's going on in your mind. I know from the word go, 'cause I'm thinking the same things, too.
FLOR: It's yes or no—nothing in between.
SID: The answer is no—a big electric sign looking down on Broadway!
FLOR: We wanted to have kids. . . .
SID: But that sort of life ain't for the dogs which is us. Christ, Baby! I get like thunder in my chest when we're together. If we went off together I could maybe look the world straight in the face, spit in its eye like a man should do. God-damnit, it's trying to be a man on the earth. Two in life together.
FLOR: But something wants us to be lonely like that—crawling alone in the dark. Or they want us trapped.
SID: Sure, the big shot money men want us like that.
FLOR: Highly insulting us—
SID: Keeping us in the dark about what is wrong with us in the money sense. They got the power and mean to be damn sure they keep it. They know if they give in just an inch, all the dogs like us will be down on them together—an ocean knocking them to hell and back and each singing cuckoo with stars coming from their nose and ears. I'm not raving, Florrie—
FLOR: I know you're not, I know.
SID: I don't have the words to tell you what I feel. I never finished school. . . .
FLOR: I know. . . .
SID: But it's relative, like the professors say. We worked like hell to send him to college—my kid brother Sam, I mean—and look what he done—joined the navy! The damn fool don't see the cards is stacked for all of us. The money man dealing himself a hot royal flush. Then giving you and me a phony hand like a pair of tens or something. Then keeping on losing the pots 'cause the cards is stacked against you. Then he says, what's the matter you can't win—no stuff on the ball, he says to you. And kids like my brother believe it 'cause they don't know better. For all their education, they don't know from nothing. But wait a minute! Don't he come

around and say to you—this millionaire with a jazz band—listen Sam or Sid or what's-your-name, you're no good, but here's a chance. The whole world'll know who you are. Yes sir, he says, get up on that ship and fight those bastards who's making the world a lousy place to live in. The Japs, the Turks, the Greeks. Take this gun—kill the slobs like a real hero, he says, a real American. Be a hero! And the guy you're poking at? A real louse, just like you, 'cause they don't let him catch more than a pair of tens, too. On that foreign soil he's a guy like me and Sam, a guy who wants his baby like you and hot sun on his face! They'll teach Sam to point the guns the wrong way, that dumb basket ball player!

FLOR: I got a lump in my throat, Honey.

SID: You and me—we never even had a room to sit in somewhere.

FLOR: The park was nice . . . .

SID: In winter? The hallways . . . . I'm glad we never got together. This way we don't know what we missed.

FLOR *(in a burst):* Sid, I'll go with you—we'll get a room somewhere.

SID: Naw . . . they're right. If we can't climb higher than this together—we better stay apart.

FLOR: I swear to God I wouldn't care.

SID: You would, you would—in a year, two years, you'd curse the day. I seen it happen.

FLOR: Oh, Sid. . . .

SID: Sure, I know. We got the blues, Babe—the 1935 blues. I'm talkin' this way 'cause I love you. If I didn't, I wouldn't care. . . .

FLOR: We'll work together, we'll—

SID: How about the backwash? Your family needs your nine bucks. My family—

FLOR: I don't care for them!

SID: You're making it up, Florrie. Little Florrie Canary in a cage.

FLOR: Don't make fun of me.

SID: I'm not, Baby.

FLOR: Yes, you're laughing at me.

SID: I'm not. *(They stand looking at each other, unable to speak. Finally, he turns to a small portable phonograph and plays a cheap, sad, dance tune. He makes a motion with his hand; she comes to him. They begin to dance slowly. They hold each other tightly, almost as though they would merge into each other. The music stops, but the scratching record continues to the end of the scene. They stop dancing. He finally looses her clutch and seats her on the couch, where she sits, tense and expectant.)*

SID: Hello, Babe.

FLOR: Hello. *(For a brief time they stand as though in a dream.)*

SID *(finally):* Good-bye, Babe. *(He waits for an answer, but she is silent. They look at each other.)*

SID: Did you ever see my Pat Rooney[11] imitation? *(He whistles Rosy O'Grady and soft-shoes to it. Stops. He asks:)*

SID: Don't you like it?

FLOR *(finally):* No. *(Buries her face in her hands. Suddenly he falls on his knees and buries his face in her lap.)*

Blackout

[11]A vaudeville entertainer.

IV. Labor Spy Episode

FATT: You don't know how we work for you. Shooting off your mouth won't help. Hell, don't you guys ever look at the records like me? Look in your own industry. See what happened when the hacks walked out in Philly three months ago! Where's Philly? A thousand miles away? An hour's ride on the train.

VOICE: Two hours!!

FATT: Two hours . . . what the hell's the difference. Let's hear from someone who's got the practical experience to back him up. Fellers, there's a man here who's seen the whole parade in Philly, walked out with his pals, got knocked down like the rest—and blacklisted after they went back. That's why he's here. He's got a mighty interestin' word to say. *(Announces): Tom Clayton! (As* CLAYTON *starts up from the audience,* FATT *gives him a hand which is sparsely followed in the audience.* CLAYTON *comes forward.)*

Fellers, this is a man with practical strike experience—Tom Clayton from little ole Philly.

CLAYTON *a thin, modest individual:* Fellers, I don't mind your booing. If I thought it would help us hacks get better living conditions, I'd let you walk all over me, cut me up to little pieces. I'm one of you myself. But what I wanna say is that Harry Fatt's right. I only been working here in the big town five weeks, but I know conditions just like the rest of you. You know how it is—don't take long to feel the sore spots, no matter where you park.

CLEAR VOICE *(from the audience):* Sit down!

CLAYTON: But Fatt's right. Our officers is right. The time ain't ripe. Like a fruit don't fall off the tree until it's ripe.

CLEAR VOICE: Sit down, you fruit!

FATT *(on his feet):* Take care of him, boys.

VOICE *(in audience, struggling):* No one takes care of me. *(Struggle in house and finally the owner of the voice runs up on stage, says to speaker):*

SAME VOICE: Where the hell did you pick up that name! Clayton! This rat's name is Clancy, from the old Clancys, way back! Fruit! I almost wet myself listening to that one!

FATT *(gunman with him):* This ain't a barn! What the hell do you think you're doing here!

SAME VOICE: Exposing a rat!

FATT: You can't get away with this. Throw him the hell outa here.

VOICE *(preparing to stand his ground):* Try it yourself. . . . When this bozo throws that slop around. You know who he is? That's a company spy.

FATT: Who the hell are you to make—

VOICE: I paid dues in this union for four years, that's who's me! I gotta right and this pussy-footed rat ain't coming in here with ideas like that. You know his record. Lemme say it out—

FATT: You'll prove all this or I'll bust you in every hack outfit in town!

VOICE: I gotta right. I gotta right. Looka *him,* he don't say boo!

CLAYTON: You're a liar and I never seen you before in my life!

VOICE: Boys, he spent two years in the coal fields breaking up any organization he touched. Fifty guys he put in jail. He's ranged up and down the east coast—shipping, textiles, steel—he's been in everything you can name. Right now—

CLAYTON: That's a lie!

VOICE: Right now he's working for that Bergman outfit on Columbus Circle who furnishes rats for any outfit in the country, before, during, and after strikes. *(The man who is the hero of the next episode goes down to his side with other committee men.)*

CLAYTON: He's trying to break up the meeting, fellers!

VOICE: We won't search you for credentials. . . .

CLAYTON: I got nothing to hide. Your own secretary knows I'm straight.

VOICE: Sure. Boys, you know who this sonovabitch is?

CLAYTON: I never seen you before in my life!

VOICE: Boys, I slept with him in the same bed sixteen years. HE'S MY OWN LOUSY BROTHER!!

FATT *(after pause):* Is this true? *(No answer from* CLAYTON.*)*

VOICE *(to* CLAYTON*):* Scram, before I break your neck! *(*CLAYTON *scrams down center aisle.* VOICE *says, watching him:* Remember his map—he can't change that—Clancy! *(Standing in his place says):* Too bad you didn't know about this, Fatt! *(After a pause.)* The Clancy family tree is bearing nuts! *(Standing isolated clear on the stage is the hero of the next episode.)*

Blackout

V. Interne Episode

Dr. Barnes, an elderly distinguished man, is speaking on the telephone. He wears a white coat.

DR. BARNES: No, I gave you my opinion twice. You outvoted me. You did this to Dr. Benjamin yourself. That is why you can tell him yourself. *(Hangs up phone, angrily. As he is about to pour himself a drink from a bottle on the table, a knock is heard.)*

BARNES: Who is it?

BENJAMIN *(without):* Can I see you a minute, please?

BARNES *(hiding the bottle):* Come in, Dr. Benjamin, come in.

BENJ: It's important—excuse me—they've got Leeds up there in my place—He's operating on Mrs. Lewis—the historectomy—it's my job. I washed up, prepared . . . they told me at the last minute. I don't mind being replaced, Doctor, but Leeds is a damn fool! He shouldn't be permitted—

BARNES *(dryly):* Leeds is the nephew of Senator Leeds.

BENJ: He's incompetent as hell.

BARNES *(obviously changing subject, picks up lab. jar):* They're doing splendid work in brain surgery these days. This is a very fine specimen. . . .

BENJ: I'm sorry, I thought you might be interested.

BARNES *(still examining jar):* Well, I am, young man, I am! Only remember it's a charity case!

BENJ: Of course. They wouldn't allow it for a second, otherwise.

BARNES: Her life is in danger?

BENJ: Of course! You know how serious the case is!

BARNES: Turn your gimlet eyes elsewhere, Doctor. Jigging around like a cricket on a hot grill won't help. Doctors don't run these hospitals. He's the Senator's nephew and there he stays.

BENJ: It's too bad.

BARNES: I'm not calling you down either. *(Plopping down jar suddenly.)* Goddamnit, do you think it's my fault?

BENJ *(about to leave):* I know . . . I'm sorry.

BARNES: Just a minute. Sit down.

BENJ: Sorry, I can't sit.

BARNES: Stand then!

BENJ *(sits):* Understand, Dr. Barnes, I don't mind being replaced at the last minute this way, but . . . well, this flagrant bit of class distinction—because she's poor—

BARNES: Be careful of words like that—"class distinction." Don't belong here. Lots of energy, you brilliant young men, but idiots. Discretion! Ever hear that word?

BENJ: Too radical?

BARNES: Precisely. And some day like in Germany, it might cost you your head.

BENJ: Not to mention my job.

BARNES: So they told you?

BENJ: Told me what?

BARNES: They're closing Ward C next month. I don't have to tell you the hospital isn't self-supporting. Until last year that board of trustees met deficits. . . . You can guess the rest. At a board meeting Tuesday, our fine feathered friends discovered they couldn't meet the last quarter's deficit—a neat little sum well over $100,000. If the hospital is to continue at all, its damn—

BENJ: Necessary to close another charity ward!

BARNES: So they say. . . . *(A wait.)*

BENJ: But that's not all?

BARNES *(ashamed):* Have to cut down on staff too. . . .

BENJ: That's too bad. Does it touch me?

BARNES: Afraid it does.

BENJ: But after all I'm top man here. I don't mean I'm better than others, but I've worked harder.

BARNES: And shown more promise. . . .

BENJ: I always supposed they'd cut from the bottom first.

BARNES: Usually.

BENJ: But in this case?

BARNES: Complications.

BENJ: For instance? (BARNES *hesitant.)*

BARNES: I like you, Benjamin. It's one ripping shame.

BENJ: I'm no sensitive plant—what's the answer?

BARNES: An old disease, malignant, tumescent. We need an antitoxin for it.

BENJ: I see.

BARNES: What?

BENJ: I met that disease before—at Harvard first.

BARNES: You have seniority here, Benjamin.

BENJ: But I'm a Jew! (BARNES *nods his head in agreement.* BENJ *stands there a moment and blows his nose.)*

BARNES *(blows his nose):* Microbes!

BENJ: Pressure from above?

BARNES: Don't think Kennedy and I didn't fight for you!

BENJ: Such discrimination, with all those wealthy brother Jews on the board?

BARNES: I've remarked before—doesn't seem to be much difference between wealthy Jews and rich Gentiles. Cut from the same piece!

BENJ: For myself I don't feel sorry. My parents gave up an awful lot to get me this far. They ran a little dry goods shop in the Bronx until their pitiful savings went in the crash last year. Poppa's peddling neckties. . . . Saul Ezra Benjamin—a man who's read Spinoza all his life.

BARNES: Doctors don't run medicine in this country. The men who know their jobs don't run anything here, except the motormen on trolley cars. I've seen medicine change—plenty—anesthesia, sterilization—but not because of rich men—in *spite* of them! In a rich man's country your true self's buried deep. Microbes! Less. . . . Vermin! See this ankle, this delicate sensitive hand? Four hundred years to breed that. Out of a revolutionary background! Spirit of '76! Ancestors froze at Valley Forge! What's it all mean! Slops! The honest workers were sold out then, in '76. The Constitution's for rich men then and now. Slops! *(The phone rings.)*

BARNES *(angrily):* Dr. Barnes. *(Listens a moment, looks at* BENJAMIN.*)* I see. *(Hangs up, turns slowly to the younger Doctor.)* They lost your patient. *(*BENJ *stands solid with the shock of the news but finally hurls his operation gloves to the floor.)*

BARNES: That's right . . . that's right. Young, hot, go and do it! I'm very ancient, fossil, but life's ahead of you, Dr. Benjamin, and when you fire the first shot say, "This one's for old Doc Barnes!" Too much dignity—bullets. Don't shoot vermin! Step on them! If I didn't have an invalid daughter—*(*BARNES *goes back to his seat, blows his nose in silence):* I have said my piece, Benjamin.

BENJ: Lots of things I wasn't certain of. Many things these radicals say . . . you don't believe theories until they happen to you.

BARNES: You lost a lot today, but you won a great point.

BENJ: Yes, to know I'm right? To really begin believing in something? Not to say, "What a world!", but to say, "Change the world!" I wanted to go to Russia. Last week I was thinking about it—the wonderful opportunity to do good work in their socialized medicine—

BARNES: Beautiful, beautiful!

BENJ: To be able to work—

BARNES: Why don't you go? I might be able—

BENJ: Nothing's nearer what I'd like to do!

BARNES: Do it!

BENJ: No! Our work's here—America! I'm scared. . . . What future's ahead, I don't know. Get some job to keep alive—maybe drive a cab—and study and work and learn my place—

BARNES: And step down hard!

BENJ: Fight! Maybe get killed, but goddamn! We'll go ahead! *(*BENJAMIN *stands with clenched fist raised high.)*

Blackout

AGATE: *Ladies and Gentlemen,* and don't let anyone tell you we ain't got some ladies in this sea of upturned faces! Only they're wearin' pants. Well, maybe I don't know a thing; maybe I fell outa the cradle when I was a kid and ain't been right since—you can't tell!

VOICE: Sit down, cockeye!

AGATE: Who's paying you for those remarks, Buddy?—Moscow Gold? Maybe I got a *glass eye,* but it come from working in a factory at the age of eleven. They hooked it out because they didn't have a shield on the works. But I wear it like a medal 'cause it tells the world where I belong—deep down in the working class! We had delegates in the union there—all kinds of secretaries and treasurers . . . walkin' delegates, but not with blisters on their feet! Oh no! On their fat little ass from sitting on cushions and raking in mazuma.[12] *(*SECRETARY *and* GUNMAN *remonstrate in words and actions here.)* Sit down, boys. I'm just sayin' that about unions in general. I know it ain't true here! Why no, our officers is all aces. Why, I seen our own secretary Fatt walk outa his way not to step on a cockroach. No boys, don't think—

FATT *(breaking in):* You're out of order!

AGATE *(to audience):* Am I outa order?

ALL: No, no. Speak. Go on, etc.

AGATE: Yes, our officers is all aces. But I'm a member here—and no experience in Philly either! Today I couldn't wear my union button. The damnest thing happened. When I take the old coat off the wall, I see she's smoking. I'm a sonovagun if the old union button isn't on fire! Yep, the old celluloid was makin' the most god-awful stink: the landlady come up and give me hell! You know what happened? That old union button just blushed itself to death! Ashamed! Can you beat it?

FATT: Sit down, Keller! Nobody's interested!

AGATE: Yes they are!

GUNMAN: Sit down like he tells you!

AGATE *(continuing to audience):* And when I finish—*(His speech is broken by* FATT *and* GUNMAN *who physically handle him. He breaks away and gets to other side of stage. The two are about to make for him when some of the committee men come forward and get in between the struggling parties.* AGATE'S *shirt has been torn.)*

AGATE *(to audience):* What's the answer, boys? The answer is, if we're reds because we wanna strike, then we take over their salute too! Know how they do it? *(Makes Communist salute.)* What is it? An uppercut! The good old uppercut to the chin! Hell, some of us boys ain't even got a shirt to our backs. What's the boss class tryin' to do—make a nudist colony outa us? *(The audience laughs and suddenly* AGATE *comes to the middle of the stage so that the other cabmen back him up in a strong clump.)*

AGATE: Don't laugh! Nothing's funny! This is your life and mine! It's skull and bones every incha the road! Christ, we're dyin' by inches! For what? For the debutantees to have their sweet comin' out parties in the Ritz! Poppa's got a daughter she's gotta get her picture in the papers. Christ, they make 'em with our blood. Joe said

[12]Making a lot of money (slang).

it. Slow death or fight. It's war! *(Throughout this whole speech* AGATE *is backed up by the other six workers, so that from their activity it is plain that the whole group of them are saying these things. Several of them may take alternate lines out of this long last speech.)*

You Edna, God love your mouth! Sid and Florrie, the other boys, old Doc Barnes—fight with us for right! It's war! Working class, unite and fight! Tear down the slaughter house of our old lives! Let freedom really ring.

These slick slobs stand here telling us about bogeymen. That's a new one for the kids—the reds is bogeymen! But the man who got me food in 1932, he called me Comrade! The one who picked me up where I bled—he called me Comrade too! What are we waiting for. . . . Don't wait for Lefty! He might never come. Every minute— *(This is broken into by a man who has dashed up on the center aisle from the back of the house. He runs up on stage, says):*

MAN: Boys, they just found Lefty!

OTHERS: What? What? What?

SOME: Shhh. . . . Shhh. . . .

MAN: They found Lefty. . . .

AGATE: Where?

MAN: Behind the car barns with a bullet in his head!

AGATE *(crying):* Hear it, boys, hear it? Hell, listen to me! Coast to coast! HELLO AMERICA! HELLO. WE'RE STORMBIRDS OF THE WORKING-CLASS. WORKERS OF THE WORLD. . . . OUR BONES AND BLOOD! And when we die they'll know what we did to make a new world! Christ, cut us up to little pieces. We'll die for what is right! put fruit trees where our ashes are! *(To audience):* Well, what's the answer?

ALL: STRIKE!

AGATE: LOUDER!

ALL: STRIKE!

AGATE and OTHERS on Stage: AGAIN!

ALL: STRIKE, STRIKE, STRIKE!!!

Curtain

1935

Meridel LeSueur 1900–1996

Well known in the 1930s for her political journalism and her prize-winning short stories, Meridel LeSueur produced a major body of literature work over a period of more than sixty years. Her work includes poetry, autobiography, biography, and history in addition to journalism and fiction. Born in Murray, Iowa, in the first year of the century, she spent her childhood and adolescence in the care of her grandmother, a Texas and later Oklahoma pioneer, and her mother, a socialist and feminist who remained politically active until well over the age of seventy-five. Through her mother, Marian Wharton, and her step-father, the socialist lawyer Arthur LeSueur, she was introduced to such midwestern radical and reform movements as the Populists, the Farmer-Labor Party, and the Industrial Workers of the World. At her parents' homes, in Ft. Scott, Kansas, and later in St. Paul, Minnesota, she met labor leaders and radical thinkers.

After dropping out of high school, LeSueur worked as an actress in New York and California (including bit parts in the newly emerging Hollywood silent film industry). By 1927 she was publishing both political journalism and her first short stories. The years from 1917 to 1927, however, were years of marginal jobs and political disillusionment. The end of World War I ushered in a period of political repression, climaxed by the execution in 1927 of the anarchists Sacco and Vanzetti, whose cause LeSueur, like many other writers and artists, supported. LeSueur's decision in that same year to have a child was her deliberate affirmation of life in a world that had become, as she said in the story she wrote about her pregnancy, "dead" and "closed."

When that story, "Annunciation," was published in 1935, it was hailed as a "small American masterpiece" and praised for its "gravely achieved affirmations of life." Written in a simple prose that is at the same time richly metaphorical, the story communicates a vision of the world transfigured by the pregnant woman's sense of "inward blossoming." The pear tree outside her tenement porch, producing its fruit even in the "darkest time," becomes her symbol for rebirth and the continuity of life.

LeSueur became the chronicler of women's lives, often overlooked in accounts of the Great Depression, writing of their experiences in relief agencies and on the breadlines. Her novel *The Girl,* based on stories of women with whom she lived, was written in 1939 but not published until 1978. It describes the harsh realities—poverty, starvation, and sexual abuse—of the lives of working-class women during the Depression and their survival by means of supportive friendships and a shared, communal life. In the stories she published in the thirties in such literary magazines as *Scribner's* and *Partisan Review,* LeSueur wrote treatments of both working- and middle-class women—their experiences of adolescence, marriage, sexuality, pregnancy, childbirth, motherhood, and widowhood—that were often ahead of their time.

The publication in 1940 of *Salute to Spring,* a collection of her journalism and stories, marked a high point in LeSueur's career and reputation. This collection was followed in 1945 by *North Star Country,* a history of the Midwest based on oral folk materials. In the Cold War period of the late forties and fifties, LeSueur was politically harassed and her publishing outlets were curtailed. Although she continued to publish political journalism, she also turned to writing for children, producing a series of biographies. By the mid-1950s LeSueur was also working for Indian land rights, living among American Indians in Minnesota and the Southwest. A volume of poems published in 1975, *Rites of Ancient Ripening,* shows the influence on her thought of the legends, imageries, and cosmologies of American Indian cultures.

Beginning in the 1960s, a time of new political activism with the civil rights, antiwar, and women's movements, LeSueur's work found a new audience. As a result, in the 1970s and 1980s much of her earlier writing was reprinted, and she embarked on new work, including poetry, essays, and a series of novels that are experiments in new narrative forms. In this work she continued to explore many of her main themes—respect for the earth and all natural resources, concern for the lives, and the suffering, of women, and faith in biological and spiritual processes of renewal.

Elaine Hedges
Late of Towson State University

PRIMARY WORKS

Annunciation, 1935; *Salute to Spring,* 1940; *North Star Country,* 1945; *Crusaders,* 1955; *Corn Village,* 1970; *Rites of Ancient Ripening,* 1975; *The Girl,* 1978; *I Hear Men Talking and Other Stories,* 1983; *The Dread Road,* 1991.

Women on the Breadlines

I am sitting in the city free employment bureau. It's the women's section. We have been sitting here now for four hours. We sit here every day, waiting for a job. There are no jobs. Most of us have had no breakfast. Some have had scant rations for over a year. Hunger makes a human being lapse into a state of lethargy, especially city hunger. Is there any place else in the world where a human being is supposed to go hungry amidst plenty without an outcry, without protest, where only the boldest steal or kill for bread, and the timid crawl the streets, hunger like the beak of a terrible bird at the vitals?

We sit looking at the floor. No one dares think of the coming winter. There are only a few more days of summer. Everyone is anxious to get work to lay up something for that long siege of bitter cold. But there is no work. Sitting in the room we all know it. That is why we don't talk much. We look at the floor dreading to see that knowledge in each other's eyes. There is a kind of humiliation in it. We look away from each other. We look at the floor. It's too terrible to see this animal terror in each other's eyes.

So we sit hour after hour, day after day, waiting for a job to come in. There are many women for a single job. A thin sharp woman sits inside a wire cage looking at a book. For four hours we have watched her looking at that book. She has a hard little eye. In the small bare room there are half a dozen women sitting on the benches waiting. Many come and go. Our faces are all familiar to each other, for we wait here every day.

This is a domestic employment bureau. Most of the women who come here are middle-aged, some have families, some have raised their families and are now alone, some have men who are out of work. Hard times and the man leaves to hunt for work. He doesn't find it. He drifts on. The woman probably doesn't hear from him for a long time. She expects it. She isn't surprised. She struggles alone to feed the many mouths. Sometimes she gets help from the charities. If she's clever she can get herself a good living from the charities, if she's naturally a lick spittle, naturally a little docile and cunning. If she's proud then she starves silently, leaving her children to find work, coming home after a day's searching to wrestle with her house, her children.

Some such story is written on the faces of all these women. There are young girls too, fresh from the country. Some are made brazen too soon by the city. There is a great exodus of girls from the farms into the city now. Thousands of farms have been vacated completely in Minnesota. The girls are trying to get work. The prettier ones can get jobs in the stores when there are any, or waiting on table, but these jobs are only for the attractive and the adroit. The others, the real peasants, have a more difficult time.

Bernice sits next to me. She is a Polish woman of thirty-five. She has been working in people's kitchens for fifteen years or more. She is large, her great body in mounds, her face brightly scrubbed. She has a peasant mind and finds it hard even yet to understand the maze of the city where trickery is worth more than brawn. Her blue eyes are not clever but slow and trusting. She suffers from loneliness and lack of talk. When you speak to her, her face lifts and brightens as if you had spoken through a great darkness, and she talks magically of little things as if the weather were magic, or tells some crazy tale of her adventures on the city streets, embellishing them in bright colors until they hang heavy and thick like embroidery. She loves the city anyhow. It's exciting to her, like a bazaar. She loves to go shopping and get a bargain, hunting out the places where stale bread and cakes can be had for a few cents. She likes walking the streets looking for men to take her to a picture show. Sometimes she goes to five picture shows in one day, or she sits through one the entire day until she knows all the dialog by heart.

She came to the city a young girl from a Wisconsin farm. The first thing that happened to her, a charlatan dentist took out all her good shining teeth and the fifty dollars she had saved working in a canning factory. After that she met men in the park who told her how to look out for herself, corrupting her peasant mind, teaching her to mistrust everyone. Sometimes now she forgets to mistrust everyone and gets taken in. They taught her to get what she could for nothing, to count her change, to go back if she found herself cheated, to demand her rights.

She lives alone in little rooms. She bought seven dollars' worth of second-hand furniture eight years ago. She rents a room for perhaps three dollars a month in an attic, sometimes in a cold house. Once the house where she stayed was condemned and everyone else moved out and she lived there all winter alone on the top floor. She spent only twenty-five dollars all winter.

She wants to get married but she sees what happens to her married friends, left with children to support, worn out before their time. So she stays single. She is virtuous. She is slightly deaf from hanging out clothes in winter. She had done people's washing and cooking for fifteen years and in that time saved thirty dollars. Now she hasn't worked steady for a year and she has spent the thirty dollars. She had dreamed of having a little house or a houseboat perhaps with a spot of ground for a few chickens. This dream she will never realize.

She has lost all her furniture now along with the dream. A married friend whose husband is gone gives her a bed for which she pays by doing a great deal of work for the woman. She comes here every day now sitting bewildered, her pudgy hands folded in her lap. She is hungry. Her great flesh has begun to hang in folds. She has been living on crackers. Sometimes a box of crackers lasts a week. She has a friend who's a baker and he sometimes steals the stale loaves and brings them to her.

A girl we have seen every day all summer went crazy yesterday at the YW. She went into hysterics, stamping her feet and screaming.

She hadn't had work for eight months. "You've got to give me something," she kept saying. The woman in charge flew into a rage that probably came from days and days of suffering on her part, because she is unable to give jobs, having none. She flew into a rage at the girl and there they were facing each other in a rage both helpless, helpless. This woman told me once that she could hardly bear the suffering she saw, hardly hear it, that she couldn't eat sometimes and had nightmares at night.

So they stood there, the two women, in a rage, the girl weeping and the woman shouting at her. In the eight months of unemployment she had gotten ragged, and the woman was shouting that she would not send her out like that. "Why don't you shine your shoes?" she kept scolding the girl, and the girl kept sobbing and sobbing because she was starving.

"We can't recommend you like that," the harassed YWCA woman said, knowing she was starving, unable to do anything. And the girls and the women sat docilely, their eyes on the ground, ashamed to look at each other, ashamed of something.

Sitting here waiting for a job, the women have been talking in low voices about the girl Ellen. They talk in low voices with not too much pity for her, unable to see through the mist of their own torment. "What happened to Ellen?" one of them asks. She knows the answer already. We all know it.

A young girl who went around with Ellen tells about seeing her last evening back of a cafe downtown, outside the kitchen door, kicking, showing her legs so that the cook came out and gave her some food and some men gathered in the alley and threw small coin on the ground for a look at her legs. And the girl says enviously that Ellen had a swell breakfast and treated her to one too, that cost two dollars.

A scrub woman whose hips are bent forward from stooping with hands gnarled like watersoaked branches clicks her tongue in disgust. No one saves their money, she says, a little money and these foolish young things buy a hat, a dollar for breakfast, a bright scarf. And they do. If you've ever been without money, or food, something very strange happens when you get a bit of money, a kind of madness. You don't care. You can't remember that you had no money before, that the money will be gone. You can remember nothing but that there is the money for which you have been suffering. Now here it is. A lust takes hold of you. You see food in the windows. In imagination you eat hugely; you taste a thousand meals. You look in windows. Colors are brighter; you buy something to dress up in. An excitement takes hold of you. You know it is suicide but you can't help it. You must have food, dainty, splendid food, and a bright hat so once again you feel blithe, rid of that ratty gnawing shame.

"I guess she'll go on the street now," a thin woman says faintly, and no one takes the trouble to comment further. Like every commodity now the body is difficult to sell and the girls say you're lucky if you get fifty cents.

It's very difficult and humiliating to sell one's body.

Perhaps it would make it clear if one were to imagine having to go out on the street to sell, say, one's overcoat. Suppose you have to sell your coat so you can have breakfast and a place to sleep, say, for fifty cents. You decide to sell your only coat. You take it off and put it on your arm. The street, that has before been just a street, now becomes a mart, something entirely different. You must approach someone now and admit you are destitute and are now selling your clothes, your most intimate possessions. Everyone will watch you talking to the stranger showing him your overcoat, what a good coat it is. People will stop and watch curiously. You will be quite naked on the street. It is even harder to try to sell one's self, more humiliating. It is even humiliating to try to sell one's labor. When there is no buyer.

The thin woman opens the wire cage. There's a job for a nursemaid, she says. The old gnarled women, like old horses, know that no one will have them walk the streets with the young so they don't move. Ellen's friend gets up and goes to the window. She is unbelievably jaunty. I know she hasn't had work since last January. But she has a flare of life in her that glows like a tiny red flame and some tenacious thing, perhaps only youth, keeps it burning bright. Her legs are thin but the runs in her old stockings are neatly mended clear down her flat shank. Two bright spots of rouge conceal her pallor. A narrow belt is drawn tightly around her thin waist, her long shoulders stoop and the blades show. She runs wild as a colt hunting pleasure, hunting sustenance.

It's one of the great mysteries of the city where women go when they are out of work and hungry. There are not many women in the bread line. There are no flop houses for women as there are for men, where a bed can be had for a quarter or less. You don't see women lying on the floor at the mission in the free flops. They obviously don't sleep in the jungle or under newspapers in the park. There is no law I suppose against their being in these places but the fact is they rarely are.

Yet there must be as many women out of jobs in cities and suffering extreme poverty as there are men. What happens to them? Where do they go? Try to get into the YW without any money or looking down at heel. Charities take care of very few and only those that are called "deserving." The lone girl is under suspicion by the virgin women who dispense charity.

I've lived in cities for many months broke, without help, too timid to get in bread lines. I've known many women to live like this until they simply faint on the street from privations, without saying a word to anyone. A woman will shut herself up in a room until it is taken away from her, and eat a cracker a day and be as quiet as a mouse so there are no social statistics concerning her.

I don't know why it is, but a woman will do this unless she has dependents, will go for weeks verging on starvation, crawling in some hole, going through the streets ashamed, sitting in libraries, parks, going for days without speaking to a living soul like some exiled beast, keeping the runs mended in her stockings, shut up in terror in her own misery, until she becomes too super-sensitive and timid to even ask for a job.

Bernice says even strange men she has met in the park have sometimes, that is in better days, given her a loan to pay her room rent. She has always paid them back.

In the afternoon the young girls, to forget the hunger and the deathly torture and fear of being jobless, try to pick up a man to take them to a ten-cent show. They never go to more expensive ones, but they can always find a man willing to spend a dime to have the company of a girl for the afternoon.

Sometimes a girl facing the night without shelter will approach a man for lodging. A woman always asks a man for help. Rarely another woman. I have known girls to sleep in men's rooms for the night on a pallet without molestation and be given breakfast in the morning.

It's no wonder these young girls refuse to marry, refuse to rear children. They are like certain savage tribes, who, when they have been conquered, refuse to breed.

Not one of them but looks forward to starvation for the coming winter. We are in a jungle and know it. We are beaten, entrapped. There is no way out. Even if there were a job, even if that thin acrid woman came and gave everyone in the room a job for a few days, a few hours, at thirty cents an hour, this would all be repeated tomorrow, the next day and the next.

Not one of these women but knows that despite years of labor there is only starvation, humiliation in front of them.

Mrs. Gray, sitting across from me, is a living spokeman for the futility of labor. She is a warning. Her hands are scarred with labor. Her body is a great puckered scar. She has given birth to six children, buried three, supported them all alive and dead, bearing them, burying them, feeding them. Bred in hunger they have been spare, susceptible to disease. For seven years she tried to save her boy's arm from amputation, diseased from tuberculosis of the bone. It is almost too suffocating to think of that long close horror of years of child-bearing, child-feeding, rearing, with the bare suffering of providing a meal and shelter.

Now she is fifty. Her children, economically insecure, are drifters. She never hears of them. She doesn't know if they are alive. She doesn't know if she is alive. Such subtleties of suffering are not for her. For her the brutality of hunger and cold. Not until these are done away with can those subtle feelings that make a human being be indulged.

She is lucky to have five dollars ahead of her. That is her security. She has a tumor that she will die of. She is thin as a worn dime with her tumor sticking out of her side. She is brittle and bitter. Her face is not the face of a human being. She has borne more than it is possible for a human being to bear. She is reduced to the least possible denominator of human feelings.

It is terrible to see her little bloodshot eyes like a beaten hound's, fearful in terror.

We cannot meet her eyes. When she looks at any of us we look away. She is like a woman drowning and we turn away. We must ignore those eyes that are surely the eyes of a person drowning, doomed. She doesn't cry out. She goes down decently. And we all look away.

The young ones know though. I don't want to marry. I don't want any children. So they all say. No children. No marriage. They arm themselves alone, keep up alone. The man is helpless now. He cannot provide. If he propagates he cannot take care of his young. The means are not in his hands. So they live alone. Get what fun they can. The life risk is too horrible now. Defeat is too clearly written on it.

So we sit in this room like cattle, waiting for a nonexistent job, willing to work to the farthest atom of energy, unable to work, unable to get food and lodging, unable to bear children—here we must sit in this shame looking at the floor, worse than beasts at a slaughter.

It is appalling to think that these women sitting so listless in the room may work as hard as it is possible for a human being to work, may labor night and day, like Mrs. Gray, wash streetcars from midnight to dawn and offices in the early evening, scrub for fourteen and fifteen hours a day, sleep only five hours or so, do this their whole lives, and never earn one day of security, having always before them the pit of the future. The endless labor, the bending back, the water-soaked hands, earning never more than a week's wages, never having in their hands more life than that.

It's not the suffering of birth, death, love that the young reject, but the suffering of endless labor without dream, eating the spare bread in bitterness, being a slave without the security of a slave.

1932

Mourning Dove (Okanogan) 1888–1936

Mourning Dove was born Christal Quintasket near Bonner's Ferry, Idaho. Besides her English name, she was given the name Hum-ishu-ma, or Mourning Dove. On her mother's side she was descended from an ancient line of warrior chieftains, and her paternal grandfather was an Irishman who worked for the Hudson's Bay Company. She received some education at Sacred Heart Convent at Ward, Washington, but left school to help care for four younger sisters and brothers. In her later teenage years, Mourning Dove lived with her maternal grandmother and through her developed an intense interest in the oral tradition of her people, the Okanogans, who today live in the western part of the Colville Reservation, near the Columbia and Okanogan Rivers and the Canadian border.

Cogewea, published in 1927, was considered the first novel written by an American Indian woman until the discovery of S. Alice Callahan's *Wynema: A Child of the Forest,* first published in 1891. Mourning Dove wrote in cooperation with Lucullus McWhorter, whom she met in 1914, by which time she had already drafted a version of the novel. McWhorter, who became her friend and mentor for twenty years, was a serious scholar of Indian traditions and had been adopted into the Yakima tribe. In contrast, Mourning Dove had little more than a third-grade education and some training in a business school. Thus she agreed to let McWhorter "fix up" the story by adding poetic epigraphs and elaborate notes on Okanogan traditions. His stylistic influence is also apparent in the often stilted language, including a self-conscious use of slang, which contrasts with the simple style of Mourning Dove's later drafts of some coyote stories. However, McWhorter knew what a white readership expected, and he was able, after a delay of many years, to find a publisher. While the novel is uneven, it gives an excellent picture of some Okanogan traditions, and the western romance plot made it acceptable in its time.

Meanwhile, in 1919 Mourning Dove had married Fred Galler, a Wenatchee. She had no children, and with Galler she became a migrant worker, camping out, working in the hop fields and apple orchards, and lugging her typewriter along to work at her writing. McWhorter failed to mention this part of her life in his preface to *Cogewea;* instead, he gave a more idyllic picture of the deprivations of her life.

Coyote Stories, also published with the help of McWhorter, was much more Mourning Dove's own work. She agreed to Heister Dean Guie's receiving credit on the title page for illustrating and editing. Guie insisted on standardized spellings and verification of Okanogan beliefs. McWhorter mediated between him and Mourning Dove. Unfortunately, neither Guie nor McWhorter regarded Mourning Dove as an authority on Okanogan folklore. A foreword by Chief Standing Bear probably helped sell the book because Standing Bear had published two popular autobiographies during the previous years, and his *Land of the Spotted Eagle,* focusing on Sioux beliefs and customs, appeared in the same year as *Coyote Stories.*

The stories give an impression of Mourning Dove's personality and tradition as well as of the folk material she gathered. Her introduction gives authenticity to her collection by describing her family heritage and the tribal setting in which these stories were passed on for education, entertainment, and social bonding. The story "The Spirit Chief Names the Animal People" exemplifies all of these purposes, but also expresses the spiritual aspect of the coyote tradition by describing the concept of power *(squastenk')* and the origin of the

Sweat House ritual. Both are central to Okanogan beliefs and indicate an aboriginal insight into the subtle connections between physical and psychological vitality and their grounding in cosmological mystery. Coyote himself is part of this mystery by being laughably human and divinely powerful at the same time.

Mourning Dove's later years were spent in relative obscurity. Occasionally she traveled to lecture in the East, but she was uncomfortable before strange audiences and could hardly afford the travel expenses. The single honor bestowed on her was her election as an honorary member of the Eastern Washington State Historical Society. Having for years been plagued with various illnesses, Mourning Dove died in a state hospital at Medical Lake, Washington, at the age of forty-eight.

Kristin Herzog

PRIMARY WORKS

Cogewea, the Half-Blood: A Depiction of the Great Montana Cattle Range, 1927, rpt. 1981; *Coyote Stories,* 1933, 1990; *Mourning Dove: A Salishan Autobiography,* ed. by Jay Miller, 1990.

from Coyote Stories

Preface

The Animal People were here first—before there were any real people.

Coyote was the most important because, after he was put to work by the Spirit Chief, he did more than any of the others to make the world a good place to live. There were times, however, when Coyote was not busy for the Spirit Chief. Then he amused himself by getting into mischief and stirring up trouble. Frequently he got into trouble himself, and then everybody had a good laugh—everybody but Mole. She was Coyote's wife.

My people called Coyote *Sin-ka-lip',* which means Imitator. He delighted in mocking and imitating others, or in trying to, and, as he was a great one to play tricks, sometimes he is spoken of as "Trick Person."

Our name for the Animal People is *Chip-chap-tiqulk* (the "k" barely is sounded), and we use the same word for the stories that are told about the Animal People and legendary times. To the younger generations, *chip-chap-tiqulk* are improbable stories; that is a result of the white man's schools. But to the old Indians, *chip-chap-tiqulk* are not at all improbable; they are accounts of what really happened when the world was very young.

My people are the Okanogan and the *Swhee-al-puh* (Colville), closely related Salishan tribes, and I also have relatives in the *En-koh-tu-me-whoh,* or Nicola, band of the Thompson River Indians in British Columbia. My father's mother was a Nicola, and his father was a Hudson's Bay Company man, a hardy, adventurous Celt. My father, Joseph *Quintasket* (Dark Cloud), was born in the Upper Okanogan community at Penticton, B.C., but he has lived, since a boy, with the Lower Okanogan and the Colville, south of the international boundary. It is with the Lower, or River,

Okanogan and the *Swhee-al-puh* on the Colville Reservation in north eastern Washington that I am identified.

The *Swhee-al-puh*—also called *Schu-ayl-pk, Schwelpi* and *Shoyelpee*—became known as the Colville following the establishment of Fort Colville by the Hudson's Bay Company in 1825–26. The fort, named after Andrew Colville, a London governor of the Company, was built near Kettle Falls in the Columbia River, in the heart of the *Swhee-al-puh* country.

My mother's name was Lucy *Stukin.* She was a *Swhee-al-puh* full blood. Her Grandfather was *See-whelh-ken,* who was head chief of the tribe for many years. His nephew, *Kin-kan-nawh,* whom the white people called Pierre Jerome, was chief when the American government made the tribe give up its home in the Colville Valley in 1872 and move to poorer land on the other side of the Columbia. My mother was born at Kettle Falls—the "Big Falls" of these legends—and she and father were married in a log church at that location. The church was built by Indians who had accepted the teachings of the missionaries.

I was born in a canoe on the Kootenai River, near Bonner's Ferry, Idaho, in the Moon of the Leaves (April), 1888. My parents were traveling with a packtrain, which my uncle, Louie *Stukin,* operated between Walla Walla, Washington and Fort Steele, B.C. during the mining rush that year. My mother and grandmother were being ferried across the river when I arrived. The Indian who was paddling their canoe stripped off his shirt and handed it to grandmother, who wrapped me up in it.

It used to be the custom for story-tellers to go from village to village and relate *chip-chap-tiqulk* to the children. How gladly were those tribal historians welcomed by busy mothers, and how glad were the boys and girls when one came to visit!

Vividly I recall old *S'whist-kane* (Lost-Head), also known as Old Narciss, and how, in the course of a narrative, he would jump up and mimic his characters, speaking or singing in a strong or weak voice, just as the Animal Persons were supposed to have done. And he would dance around the fire in the tule-mat covered lodge until the pines rang with the gleeful shouts of the smallest listeners. We thought of this as all fun and play, hardly aware that the tale-telling and impersonations were a part of our primitive education.

Another favorite was Broken Nose Abraham. He was old and crippled. He came to our village usually on a white horse, riding double with his blind wife, who held the reins and guided the horse at his direction. It always thrilled us to see Broken Nose ride into camp, he had a stock of such fascinating stories. Broken Nose could not dance for us. He could not even walk without the support of his two canes. But he sang exciting war songs, and we liked to sing with him.

Some of the women were noted story-tellers, but they never made it a business to go from village to village to tell them. We children would go to them. I particularly remember *Ka-at-qhu* (Big Lip), Old Jennie, *Tee-qualt,* or Long Thresa, and my maternal grandmother, *Soma-how-atqhu* (She-got-her-power-from-the-water). I loved these simple, kindly people, and I think of them often. And in my memory I treasure a picture of my dear mother, who, when I was a very little girl, made the bedtime hours happy for me with legends she told. She would tell them to me until I fell asleep. Two that are in this collection, "Why Marten's Face Is Wrinkled" and "Why Mosquitoes Bite People," she told over and over again, and I never grew tired of hearing them.

My father always enjoyed telling the old stories, and he does still. He and *Ste-heet-qhu* (Soup), Toma Martin and *Kleen-ment-itqu* are among the few men and women left who can tell chip-*chap-tiqulk.* I thank them for helping me. And I must acknowledge my debt to a blue-eyed "Indian," Lucullus Virgil McWhorter, whom the Yakimas adopted many snows ago and named *He-me¯ne Ka¯'wan* (Old Wolf). His heart is warm toward the red people. In him the Indians of the Pacific Northwest have a true friend. But for his insistence and encouragement, these legends would not have been set down by me for the children of another race to read.

MOURNING DOVE.

I
The Spirit Chief Names the Animal People

Hah-ah' eel-me'-whem, the great Spirit Chief,[1] called the Animal People together. They came from all parts of the world. Then the Spirit Chief told them there was to be a change, that a new kind of people was coming to live on the earth.

"All of you *Chip-chap-tiqulk*—Animal People—must have names," the Spirit Chief said. "Some of you have names now, some of you haven't. But tomorrow all will have names that shall be kept by you and your descendants forever. In the morning, as the first light of day shows in the sky, come to my lodge and choose your names. The first to come may choose any name that he or she wants. The next person may take any other name. That is the way it will go until all the names are taken. And to each person I will give work to do."

That talk made the Animal People very excited. Each wanted a proud name and the power to rule some tribe or some part of the world, and everyone determined to get up early and hurry to the Spirit Chief's lodge.

Sin-ka-lip'—Coyote—boasted that no one would be ahead of him. He walked among the people and told them that, that he would be the first. Coyote did not like his name; he wanted another. Nobody respected his name, Imitator, but it fitted him. He was called *Sin-ka-lip'* because he liked to imitate people. He thought that he could do anything that other persons did, and he pretended to know everything. He would ask a question, and when the answer was given he would say:

"I knew that before. I did not have to be told."

Such smart talk did not make friends for Coyote. Nor did he make friends by the foolish things he did and the rude tricks he played on people.

"I shall have my choice of the three biggest names," he boasted. "Those names are: *Kee-lau-naw,* the Mountain Person—Grizzly Bear, who will rule the four-footed

[1] *Hah-ah',* or *Hwa-hwa'*—Spirit. *Eel-me'-whem*—Chief. While the Okanogan, Colville, and other Salishan stock tribes of the interior paid homage to a great variety of minor "powers" or deities (as many members of the tribes still do), they firmly believed in a Spirit Chief, or Chief Spirit, an all-powerful Man Above. This belief was theirs before they ever heard of Christianity, notwithstanding statements that have been made to the contrary.

people; *Milka-noups*—Eagle,[2] who will rule the birds, and *En-tee-tee-ueh,* the Good Swimmer—Salmon. Salmon will be the chief of all the fish that the New People use for food."

Coyote's twin brother, Fox, who at the next sun took the name *Why-ay'-looh*—Soft Fur, laughed. "Do not be so sure, *Sin-ka-lip',*" said Fox. "Maybe you will have to keep the name you have. People despise that name. No one wants it."

"I am tired of that name," Coyote said in an angry voice. "Let someone else carry it. Let some old person take it—someone who cannot win in war. I am going to be a great warrior. My smart brother, I will make you beg of me when I am called Grizzly Bear, Eagle, or Salmon."

"Your strong words mean nothing," scoffed Fox, "Better go to your *sewhool-luh* (tepee) and get some sleep, or you will not wake up in time to choose any name."

Coyote stalked off to his tepee. He told himself that he would not sleep any that night; he would stay awake. He entered the lodge, and his three sons called as if with one voice:

"Le-ee'-oo!" ("Father")[3]

They were hungry, but Coyote had brought them nothing to eat. Their mother, who after the naming was known as *Pul'-laqu-whu*—Mole, the Mound Digger—sat on her foot at one side of the doorway. Mole was a good woman, always loyal to her husband in spite of his mean ways, his mischief-making, and his foolishness. She never was jealous, never talked back, never replied to his words of abuse. She looked up and said:

"Have you no food for the children? They are starving. I can find no roots to dig."

"Eh-ha!" Coyote grunted. "I am no common person to be addressed in that manner. I am going to be a great chief tomorrow. Did you know that? I will have a new name? I will be Grizzly Bear. Then I can devour my enemies with ease. And I shall need you no longer. You are growing too old and homely to be the wife of a great warrior and chief."

Mole said nothing. She turned to her corner of the lodge and collected a few old bones, which she put into a *klek'-chin* (cooking-basket). With two sticks she lifted hot stones from the fire and dropped them into the basket. Soon the water boiled, and there was weak soup for the hungry children.

"Gather plenty of wood for the fire," Coyote ordered. "I am going to sit up all night."

Mole obeyed. Then she and the children went to bed.

Coyote sat watching the fire. Half of the night passed. He got sleepy. His eyes grew heavy. So he picked up two little sticks and braced his eyelids apart. "Now I can

[2]*Milka-noups*—the "War Eagle," or "Man Eagle" (golden eagle), whose white plumes with black or brown tips are prized for decorative and ceremonial purposes, particularly for war bonnets and other headgear, dance bustles, coup sticks, and shields. The tail feathers of the bald eagle, *Pak-la-kin* (White-headed-bird) are not valued so highly. In the old days the use of eagle feathers was restricted to the men. Except in rare instances, women were not privileged to wear them.

[3]*Le-ee'-oo.* This form of address is employed only by males. A daughter calls her father *Mestem,* and her mother *Toom.* A son calls his mother *Se-go-ee.*

stay awake," he thought, but before long he was fast asleep, although his eyes were wide open.

The sun was high in the sky when Coyote awoke. But for Mole he would not have awakened then. Mole called him. She called him after she returned with her name from the Spirit Chief's lodge. Mole loved her husband. She did not want him to have a big name and be a powerful chief. For then, she feared, he would leave her. That was why she did not arouse him at daybreak. Of this she said nothing.

Only half-awake and thinking it was early morning, Coyote jumped at the sound of Mole's voice and ran to the lodge of the Spirit Chief. None of the other *Chip-chap-tiqulk* were there. Coyote laughed. Blinking his sleepy eyes, he walked into the lodge. "I am going to be *Kee-lau-naw,"* he announced in a strong voice. "That shall be my name."

"The name Grizzly Bear was taken at dawn," the Spirit Chief answered.

"Then I shall be *Milka-noups,"* said Coyote, and his voice was not so loud.

"Eagle flew away at sunup," the other replied.

"Well, I shall be called *En-tee-tee-ueh,"* Coyote said in a voice that was not loud at all.

"The name Salmon also has been taken," explained the Spirit Chief. "All the names except your own have been taken. No one wished to steal your name."

Poor Coyote's knees grew weak. He sank down beside the fire that blazed in the great tepee, and the heart of *Hah-ah' Eel-mé-whem* was touched.

"Sin-ka-lip'," said that Person, "you must keep your name. It is a good name for you. You slept long because I wanted you to be the last one here. I have important work for you, much for you to do before the New People come. You are to be chief of all the tribes.

"Many bad creatures inhabit the earth. They bother and kill people, and the tribes cannot increase as I wish. These *En-alt-na Skil-ten*—People-Devouring Monsters—cannot keep on like that. They must be stopped. It is for you to conquer them. For doing that, for all the good things you do, you will be honored and praised by the people that are here now and that come afterward. But, for the foolish and mean things you do, you will be laughed at and despised. That you cannot help. It is your way.

"To make your work easier, I give you *squas-tenk'*. It is your own special magic power. No one else ever shall have it. When you are in danger, whenever you need help, call to your power. It will do much for you, and with it you can change yourself into any form, into anything you wish.

"To your twin brother, *Why-ay'-looh,* and to others I have given *shoo'-mesh.*[4] It is strong power. With that power Fox can restore your life should you be killed. Your bones may be scattered but, if there is one hair of your body left, Fox can make you live again. Others of the people can do the same with their *shoo'-mesh.* Now, go, *Sin-ka-lip'!* Do well the work laid for your trail!"

[4]*Shoo'-mesh.* With the exception of Coyote's "power," all "medicine" is spoken of as *shoo'-mesh,* which is regarded as definite aid communicated by the Spirit Chief through various mediums, inanimate objects as well as living creatures. Not infrequently an Indian will seek to test the potency of his medicine over that of another. Some present-day medicine-men and medicine-women are reputed to possess magic power strong enough to cause the sickness or even the death of enemies, of anyone incurring their displeasure.

Well, Coyote was a chief after all, and he felt good again. After that day his eyes were different. They grew slant from being propped open that night while he sat by his fire. The New People, the Indians, got their slightly slant eyes from Coyote.

After Coyote had gone, the Spirit Chief thought it would be nice for the Animal People and the coming New People to have the benefit of the spiritual sweat-house. But all of the Animal People had names, and there was no one to take the name of Sweat-house—*Quil'-sten,* the Warmer.[5] So the wife of the Spirit Chief took the name. She wanted the people to have the sweat-house, for she pitied them. She wanted them to have a place to go to purify themselves, a place where they could pray for strength and good luck and strong medicine-power, and where they could fight sickness and get relief from their troubles.

[5]*Quil'-sten*—Sweat-house. A mystic shrine for both temporal and spiritual cleansing, the sweat-house is one of the most venerated institutions. Its use is governed by strict rules, said to have originated with Coyote, the great "law-giver." To break any of the rules is to invite misfortune, if not disaster.

Sweat-houses, or lodges, are mound-shaped, round, or oval at the base, three to four or five feet high at the center, and four to six feet in diameter, accommodating three to four persons. In some sweat-houses there is room but for one bather.

Pliant branches—usually willow or fir, depending upon the locality and growth available—are planted like interlocking croquet wickets to make the frame. Where these "ribs" cross, they are tied together with strips of bark. There are never less than eight ribs. The frame is covered with swamp tule mats, blankets, or canvas. In primitive times sheets of cottonwood bark, top-dressed with earth, frequently formed the covering. Where a permanent residence is established, the framework is covered with tule mats, top-dressed with three or more inches of soil that is well packed and smoothed. The floor is carpeted with matting, grass, ferns, or fir boughs. The last are regarded as "strong medicine," and always are used if obtainable. They give the bather strength, and they are liked, besides, for their aromatic odor. The Indians rub their bodies with the soft tips of the fir boughs, both for the purpose of deriving power and for the scent imparted.

Just within and at one side of the lodge entrance, a small hole serves as a receptacle for the stones that are heated in a brisk fire a few steps from the structure. The stones, the size of a man's fist, are smooth, unchipped, "dry land" stones—never river-bed rocks. The latter crack and explode too easily when subjected to a combination of intense heat and cold water. By means of stout sticks, the heated stones are rolled from the fire into the sweat-house. Then the entrance is curtained tightly with mat or blanket, and the bather sprinkles cold water on the little pile of stones, creating a dense steam.

To the novice, five minutes spent in the sweltering, midnight blackness of the cramping structure seem an eternity and almost unendurable.

Several "sweats," each followed by a dip in a nearby stream or pool, properly constitute one sweat-bath. The customary period for a single sweat is ten to twenty minutes, although votaries from rival bands or tribes often crouch together in the steam for twice or thrice that time. Thus they display to one another their virility and hardihood. To further show their strength and their contempt for the discomfort of such protracted sweating, they will blow on their arms and chests. The forcing of the breath against the superheated skin produces a painful, burning sensation. Hours, even days, may be spent in "sweat-housing."

The stones used are saved and piled outside the sweat-lodge, where they remain undisturbed. For services rendered they are held in a regard bordering on reverence. An Indian would not think of spitting or stepping on these stones or of "desecrating" them in any way.

Old-time warriors and hunters always "sweat-housed" before starting on their expeditions, and many of the modern, school-educated Indian men and women often resort to the sweat-house to pray for good fortune and health.

The ribs, the frame poles, of the sweat-house represent the wife of *Hah-ah' Eel-me'-whem.* As she is a spirit, she cannot be seen, but she always is near. Songs to her are sung by the present generation. She hears them. She hears what her people say, and in her heart there is love and pity.

1933

John Joseph Mathews (Osage) 1894–1979

John Joseph Mathews appears on the tribal roll as one-eighth Osage. He was acutely aware of his mixed-blood status as well as the changes that were overtaking reservation life in Indian Territory, later Oklahoma. After a varied youth during which he received degrees in natural sciences from the University of Oklahoma and Oxford and served as a flight instructor in aviation's infancy during World War I, he returned to Pawhuska, Oklahoma, and turned his intellect and talent to a life of public service and writing. His first book, *Wah'kon-tah: The Osage and The White Man's Road* (1929), became a Book-of-the-Month Club bestseller.

The title of his only novel, *Sundown* (1934), reflects Mathews's judgment that the traditional tribal life was passing away forever in Oklahoma. The novel is about young Challenge "Chal" Windzer, born to a progressive-minded father who hopes his son will be strong enough to make a very uncertain future full of change. The novel's plot is roughly autobiographical. Unlike Mathews, however, Chal returns from the University of Oklahoma and flight training in World War I and is unable to fit into his community, or find a meaningful vocation, or resist the blandishments of alcohol and other Anglo corruptions. The black oil derricks that ebb and flow ominously across Osage land symbolize the fatal consequences of the instant wealth brought by the exploitation of Indian resources. In the first of the passages that follows, Mathews draws a keenly insightful picture of the kinds of changes that were coming to the reservation. In the second, Chal has returned home to find his community expiring in the last trickle of money and alcohol from the oil boom. Though he is inspired by Roan Horse's example, his mother's sad but more knowledgeable evaluation of his character suggests that there is little hope for her son to fulfill his dream.

Andrew O. Wiget
New Mexico State University

PRIMARY WORK

Sundown, 1934.

from Sundown

I

The black derricks crept farther west. Sometimes near the town they "shot" a well with nitroglycerine, so that the strata might be loosened and allow a freer flow of the oil. At such times the citizens of the town would drive out and watch the spray of oil as it shot high into the air, and hear the gravels rattle on the woodwork of the derrick, like shot.

Everyone was happy and almost playful. On one occasion a mixedblood rushed into the spraying oil and had his new suit and a "damned good hat—a twenty-five-dollar hat" covered with oil. He said, "Whoopee!" He didn't give a damn.

They would troop back to town, feeling in their hearts that the indefinite glory was not far off now. The mixedbloods would stand in groups at the corners and discuss the well, some of them rattling the silver dollars in their pockets as they talked. They would shout jovially at anyone crossing the street; some pleasantry in Osage or in English.

DuBois joined one such group, expanding facetiously, "Say," he said, "by gawd, if I had a nose like that, I'd charge people to see it." The others laughed, and the one accused felt embarrassed, and attempted not to show in his face that his vanity had been wounded just a little. He shifted his tobacco, then said, "Well, I guess it's big all right, but they's one thing, it ain't in everybody's business." The laughter was then directed toward DuBois, who went to the curbing of the new sidewalk and spat onto the pavement, then came back. "Say," he said, desiring to change the subject, "was yu out to the well they shot this mornin'—looks like it's a-comin', don't it?" The others shook their heads in a way that would indicate that; "Sure looks that-away." DuBois continued.

"I's talkin' with a geologist the other day, and he said he thought they's oil all under the Osage—said if they found that Carsonville sand west o' here, that he knew it was all under the Osage."

The sun warmed the corner with a beneficence that seemed only for that particular corner of the world as they talked about the future; about that future which was sure to be glorious, though its particular glory was vague.

They moved over toward the sandstone building which had been the office building. Some of them sat on the broad window sill which had been worn smooth by generations of sitters. There was nothing to do except talk. Their incomes were so large now that they didn't think of working at anything; in fact, they had never worked except by spurts when some enthusiasm came over them. Some enthusiasm like starting a chicken farm and raising chickens for a market that didn't exist, or breeding white-faced cattle and pure-bred hogs.

But now, how could anyone keep his mind on anything except oil, when that tingling thrill was constantly with one; that thrill that expressed itself in expansive camaraderie and boisterousness? Besides, these people were only being true to the blood in their veins. Many of them were descendants of French gentleman adventurers who were buried in the Osage camps on the Missouri river, or lost forever in the wild forests of the new land. And many of them were descendants of laughing *coureurs du bois,* and of men who defeated Braddock from behind trees, and had come back with their allies, the great Osages, and married Osage women. The mixedblood descendants of these adventurers were usually handsome, careless and promiscuous. They had no tendency to acquisitiveness, and their lives were made sparkling by a series of enthusiasms. They lived merrily, whether they were definitely sure of the next meal or not.

From the earliest days of the Agency, they had sat in front of the traders' stores during the summer, hunted during the autumn, and sat around the big-bellied stoves and spat into the sawdust during the winter. As the Agency became a town they still sat and talked, and as the town grew they continued to talk and laugh, standing or sitting and watching the traffic.

Many of the older traders had come to the Agency out of the spirit of adventure and profit. They were in many cases men of some culture and family, and they developed a great respect and sometimes actual love for the Indian. Which was rather unique in that their large profit-taking was not always within the bounds of ethics, if the ethics of their religious training had anything to do with business practice. They did not compete with each other and perhaps ethics was not necessary.

They took much credit for allowing their Indian clients to have provisions on account, and even sacrificed comfort to haul provisions to far away camps during severe winters. During the great epidemic of smallpox they had even endangered themselves to supply the Indians with necessities, driving with their provisions to a designated rock or tree near an infected camp and leaving them there. To compensate for their sacrifices, they often added extra percentages to the bill. The interest from the tribal trust fund was definite and sure, but these early traders always felt a certain magnanimity in allowing the Indians to have whatever provisions and clothing they needed between the quarterly payments. Especially during the epidemic, when the desire for the continuance of the trade overbalanced their fears, they felt particularly self-righteous. They came back from these trips with the fear of the disease in their hearts, but they felt better after they had seen that all the saucers had been refilled with carbolic acid and set in the windows of their stores. And they kept these saucers filled in the windows at their homes, though they had sent their families out of the reservation during the period of the epidemic. They took no chances of germs wandering aimlessly into their homes through the windows.

Now, they too watched the black derricks spread from the east with an enthusiasm that was somehow dampened by the fact that such development would bring more competition. They worried when they thought of those riches under them and all around them going to others. The old reservation had been theirs and they still felt that the new county was theirs as well, and they felt vindictive toward all the people who were coming in to share the trade with them. The Agency was their home and the town became their home. They talked the language of their friends, the Osages, and felt sincerely protective toward them. But things were moving too fast, and they had difficulty adjusting themselves to the new tempo of Progress, having spent their youth in the hard tranquillity of an Indian nation, where a man's word was as good as his signature.

The new people who came in after the allotment were of all types, representing many professions or no profession in particular. Drifting artisans and laborers, lawyers, doctors, shopkeepers, bootleggers, shrewd and unscrupulous men who did business on the new curbs, and men and women with criminal tendencies who lacked the courage. There were representatives of oil companies, geologists and lease men, and oil field employees from the ends of the earth.

They came slowly at first as the black derricks moved toward the west, then they came in hundreds. After the war, however, when people all over the country spoke of "normalcy" and said that prosperity had come to the Federation of States, they came into the little town in swarms, and the mixedbloods stood on the corner and proudly guessed that there must be fifteen or twenty thousand people in town.

There were no factories, no mills, no industry except the cattle business which had flourished for years. There weren't even any oil refineries. These had been established in neighboring towns because the owners felt that it was too expensive to satisfy all the business men who seemed to have influence over the destinies of the town. A big railroad missed Kihekah by six miles for reasons which remained obscure.

The black derricks that sprang up among the blackjacks over night gave to the Osages and all the mixedbloods on the roll one-sixth of every forty-two-gallon barrel of oil. As more oil came out of the ground the quarterly payments became larger and larger, and as the payments became larger and larger, men's heads became filled with dreams and their lives became frenzied activity. So intoxicated did they become that they forgot to stop in their frantic grasping to point the finger of accusation at a neighbor. Still there was no keen competition. One had only to sit and think up schemes for bringing to himself more of the wealth which surrounded him.

One afternoon black clouds came up in the northwest and tumbled over each other in their attempts to be in the van; tumbling as though with deliberate design, as though directed by angry gods to destroy the town in the valley among the blackjacks. Lightning played against the black mass and there was distant thunder. The outer edges of the clouds were whipped by crazy little winds, and a deep silence settled over the valley. The rest of the sky was pale green.

In the town the people began thinking of the cellars. John walked to the front porch of his house, looked at the sky for some time, then went back in and sat down, picked up the *Trumpet* and began reading. Down the street DuBois had just come home from Goldie's, where he had spent the afternoon with one of the new girls. He went to the door and looked at the sky, and as he looked the first heavy drops spattered on the roof of his house. He went to the bedroom where his wife was lying, expecting a new baby. He made the sign of the cross over her bed as she slept, and did the same at each window of the room, then called the children. He led them into the cellar and made the sign of the cross again as he closed the door.

Jep Newberg, the leading merchant and general business man among the newcomers, telephoned to his wife and told her to go to the cellar. He stood at the large plate glass window of his store, and shifted his chewed, unlit cigar first to one side of his mouth and then to the other. He didn't like that sky. A raindrop spattered on the plate glass. He thought of his secretary sitting back in the office, and he went back and stood over her. She was bent over the books, adding the usual twenty per cent to the purchases of Indians made that day.

"Let that go," he said. "Leave that off." He laid his stubby finger on the page of the book. She looked up at him with a question. He said:

"Say, looks purty bad outside. Maybe you'd better go over to the Blue Front basement—might be blowy." He didn't give her time to adjust her hat properly, and she had just managed to get into one sleeve of her raincoat before he pushed her out the front door and told her to run. She wondered if he were really growing cold; becoming tired. "Maybe the old cat has been after him again," she thought as she went to the Blue Front drug store. The druggist was motioning to her from the top of the basement steps.

Jep saw that the sidewalk was profusely covered with dark splashes. He went back to the vault, stepped inside, and left the door half open. He shifted his cigar nervously as he stood there.

Chal was on the prairie on the other side of the creek from the village. When he noticed the clouds were so menacing he put his pony into a trot, but already the big drops had begun to fall, and suddenly the tall cottonwood along the little creek began to bend with the under sides of its leaves showing gray. He could hear the wind moaning in the blackjacks along the ridge to the west; it was like a protest.

He knew he couldn't make the village so he rode toward a hill where the small blackjack saplings were growing. He heard hoof beats behind him, and looked around. Three Osages on ponies came up to him; an old man whom he had seen many times but couldn't recall his name, young White Elk, and Sun-on-His-Wings. He was surprised and he had to keep looking forward to keep them from seeing the surprise on his face. Their faces were painted in a manner he hadn't seen for years, and he guessed that their bodies were naked. They were covered with their blankets which were pulled up around their heads. They greeted each other and rode on as though they had been together all day.

A terrific gust of wind hit them just as they neared the saplings. Chal looked up and saw the clouds boiling above them, and the old man looked as well, and as he did so he stopped his pony and slid off saying, "How." Chal and the others slid off of their ponies and all ran to the young blackjacks, each one lying down on his belly and each grasping tightly the thin, flexible stem of a sapling.

Everything was blurred. The wind howled and the rain came before it horizontally across the prairie. Objects flew past and the little trees bent and swished, but you heard only the roar of the wind, above which the thunder cracked and the earth seemed to shiver.

The wind died and the rain, still falling, began to slacken, and the skies began to clear. They stood up and looked around. They could hear the roaring of the water in the little creek. The ponies were gone. Chal looked at the faces of the three and that which had puzzled him became clear.

They had seen the storm coming and had prepared themselves for the ancient ritual of defiance and sacrifice. Though he had heard about it, he had never seen it, and thought that the people had discontinued the ceremony. But he could see it all now. They had seen the storm coming and had ridden out to the hill so that they might be visible to Wah 'Kon-Tah, and manifest their bravery by defying the storm, but ready to die by a bolt of lightning if it pleased the Great Mysteries. There was some reason why they had ridden out. Perhaps it was because Wah 'Kon-Tah had manifested his displeasure in some way, and they had wanted to show him that they were still Osages and were not afraid to die; that they would sacrifice themselves if he wished it for the benefit of the tribe. Chal didn't know why they had not carried their guns with them to shoot into the storm—they used to do that, he remembered. He guessed that they didn't want to attract the attention of white people who might chance to be near.

They had probably come down when they saw that cyclone coming—Wah 'Kon-Tah would not want them to face a cyclone, with death a certainty. They would have no chance that way. Lightning was fickle, or rather, it was directed by the Great Mysteries to a certain spot.

Chal's clothes were wet and he felt shivery as he walked with his companions toward the village. The little creek was bank full, and they unhesitatingly walked into the muddy, swirling water and swam across, climbing out several yards downstream. The water of the creek felt warm to Chal's chilled body.

When they had gone some distance from the roaring creek, they stopped and listened to a greater roar; a roar that shook the earth under their feet. The old man was visibly disturbed as he looked at the sky in all directions. The roar became louder and Chal thought that the old man looked bewildered, but no one said anything.

When they reached the village, all four of the ponies were there quietly grazing among the débris of wagons and lodge-coverings. The people were walking here and there, searching for their belongings, but most of them were standing in a group talking. Chal didn't even stop to think whether any of them had been hurt. He knew that they had all gone out and clung to the saplings and sumac bushes at the edge of the village.

When his little party came up to the group, the old man asked in Osage. "That roar, what is that thing which makes ground afraid?" Charging Bull pointed toward the town, "I told my son to go see about that thing. He is back now. He says it is gas well. He says lightning struck gas well."

"Ho-hoooo," said the old man and Chal was sure that he saw relief in his face.

Sun-on-His-Wings, shivering in his wet blanket, turned to Chal and said in English, "Let's go over there to my father's lodge—maybe there's a fire there." He pointed to one of the few lodges left standing.

When they were both naked and warming themselves and Chal was drying his clothes, Sun-on-His-Wings said, "That old man is Black Elk. He will say that lightning struck that gas well 'cause the Great Spirit don't want the white people to come here any more. He will say in council some time that Osages ought to see that, and run all the white people out of their land, I bet." They were silent for some time, then Sun-on-His-Wings raised his voice again above the roar, "He's an old man, though, and he don't know about these things. His body is here but his mind is back in a place where we lived many years ago."

Chal wanted to ask his friend why he had gone with old Black Elk to the hill, since Sun-on-His-Wings was now a Peyote worshipper, but he only smiled about the old man and said nothing.

Chal rode back to town with the constant roar of the fire in his ears, and as he drew near it became deafening. As he approached he could see the flame above the pipe. The derrick had burned and the flame didn't begin at the pipe but several feet above it, like a great jet.

People were standing in groups some distance from the flame; standing on the hillside and sitting on stone walls, and some had climbed to the roofs of barns and houses. Just watching. Several men were nearer than the others and Chal could see that they had rifles. He could see them point the guns at the flame, then white puffs of smoke, but the report was drowned. They were attempting to separate the thin column of roaring gas from the flame above, but they failed.

He stood there for some time and watched; the crowd amused him. White people seemed so helpless when they couldn't talk, and it was funny to see them so inefficient, standing there. He could see some of them move toward each other, not able to restrain themselves any longer, and attempt to talk above the terrific roar. For a moment as he sat there on his pony, he wondered if they were as great as he had always thought them to be. These doubts gave rise to confusion and he dismissed them after a moment.

His attention was attracted to some people standing around a man high up on the hill. The man standing on a stone wall and gesticulating. Here was something strange; some strange thing the white people were doing there upon the hill. He was intrigued.

He rode up to where the people were gathering and stopped outside the circle, but he could see over the heads of the others from his position. The thin man who was standing on the retaining wall was shouting and raising his hands to the sky. Chal thought he was one of those people who sell medicine at first, but he was not selling anything, that was plain. His face was distorted and his eyes had a wild light in them. The roar was not so loud here and Chal could hear some of the things he said:

"Come to Jesus, come to Jesus, come you sinners and repent! Jesus loves you—arms—I shall come—far—Jesus is good, Jesus is —square—" The words would come indistinctly, and be lost as the little breeze that had sprung up carried the roar back over the hill. But Chal was fascinated by this man. He was fascinated by the veins that stood out on his neck and the way he moaned and shouted when he couldn't think of any more words. But eventually he would break into words again. Chal looked at the people around the speaker and he saw that they stood with their mouths open. On the outside of the circle some high school boys giggled and an older man turned and frowned at them.

The man would get down on his knees on the wall and lift his hands into the air, saying that that flaming gas well was a sign, and that everybody ought to make peace with their God. Then he would get up and pound the palm of his hand with the fist of the other, and point to the people in the front of the circle with a finger that shook.

Chal was surprised to see a man go forward and fall on his knees at the foot of the wall. Then a young girl and two women rushed forward and fell on their knees, weeping and groaning. He was startled by a cry close by him; like the cry of a rabbit caught by an owl, and a woman, scratching and clawing her way through the crowd, made his pony snort. Her hat was on the side of her head and her iron gray hair had fallen about her shoulders. She rushed forward to the wall and fell on her face shrieking.

Chal felt that a knot had come into his stomach, and the blood in his veins seemed to have turned to water, the water carrying some sort of poison. He turned his pony and rode away, shaking slightly.

He was glad to see that his father's house had not been disturbed by the cyclone; and he noticed that outside of a few trees and several houses some distance from the business district, very little damage had been done. He smiled to himself when he thought of what interpretation old Black Elk might put upon the fact that the village had been in the direct path of the storm, and that the town had been left intact.

After dinner he went back to the burning well with his father. People were still standing there, fascinated. He and his father stopped by a group of mixedbloods. They seemed to have doubts about the ability of the men running around below to put out the flame. DuBois shouted that they were "crazier 'n hell if they thought they was gonna put it out with rifles."

As they stood the flames lighted up the whole countryside, and the light could be seen for many miles that night. The terrific, ground-shivering roar and the light that spread over the whole valley; the light that made the blackjacks on the hills look like ghost trees, appeared to the mixedbloods standing there as a symbol of that indefinite glory that was coming. That light that you could see as far away as the old Cherokee country, and that roar that drowned all other sounds, gave them a feeling of vague greatness and importance in the universe. Here was the manifestation of a power that made the white man stand and wonder; a power that came out of their own hills, and that light, in which you could "pick up a pin a mile away," was certainly the light of glory.

Turning away from the spectacle, with a facetious remark in Osage, DuBois went home. He found one of the new doctors there. He had had a misunderstanding with the old government doctor, because he had forgotten to pay for former services rendered. He walked into the room where his wife lay, full of the emotion which had suffused him as he watched the fire. The doctor held the baby up to him and he saw that it was a boy.

"Well, Doc, he's already got a name," he said proudly, "Osage Oil DuBois."

II

The black derricks had crept from the blackjacks of the east, slowly over the hills; spreading to the south and north and on past the little town in the valley. They touched here and there, but climbed steadily west out of the valleys onto the high prairie; across the treeless hills, and on across Salt Creek that lay like a silver ribbon across the prairie, fringed by elms. Then they crept to the very edge of the old reservation and lapped over into the Kaw country. There they stopped. At the tip of the westward movement, half a dozen little towns grew up; not out of the earth like mushrooms, as they were not of this part of the earth; they had no harmony with the Osage. Later they were like driftwood carried in from strange lands on a high tide and left stranded when the tide went out.

Riding on the wave of oil the little town of Kihekah grew out of its narrow valley and climbed exuberantly up its surrounding hills, then grew along the lines of least resistance; along its elongated creek valley. The blackjacks moved back, stepping with dignity to protect their toes; standing around the town and throwing their shadows across gardens and the green lawns that crept up to their feet.

Then one day something happened. It didn't all happen in one day, but it seemed that way. The all-powerful life that had come with the creeping black derricks began to recede to the east. The population of the little towns at the tip of the movement seemed to melt into the air, and the brick buildings stood empty and fantastic on the prairie; singing sad songs in the prairie winds. The roar of activity faded into the lazy coughing of pumps, and the fever brightness of the Great Frenzy began to dim.

The derricks stood black against the prairie horizon in rows, and became the husks of a life force that had retreated back along its own trail. The houses in the town of the little valley stopped their encroachments on the blackjacks, then they gradually became husks too; like the shells of the cicadas clinging to the hillsides. The old trading store which had grown from primitive palisades into a domineering brick building closed its doors, and Ed Fancher took up a stand on the sunny corner of his old store, too old to believe what the more youthful were saying, that the oil would come back. The great store's empty windows stared out onto the streets like wondering eyes. Its owner expressing its surprised wonder when he said to a jovial, bankrupt mixedblood one day in the winter sun on the corner, that he "didn't see how 'Ye Shoppe' outfit across the street could keep goin." As he and the mixedblood talked about the past they backed up against the empty, staring windows. Above them was an extravagant advertisement announcing the arrival of a circus which had folded its canvas and left Kihekah the summer before.

Mixedblood families came back to the old Agency from their large homes in the mountains, in California, and elsewhere. They dropped their golf clubs and lost their homes and came back to wander aimlessly along the familiar streets. They asked with the other citizens of the town, "S'pose it'll come back?" All agreed that it would, but they wondered just the same.

One morning Jep Newberg was found with a bullet hole in his temple. Those who knew said that he sure was powder burned. He, with the sardonic humor of the hard-headed business man, had elected to float out sentimentally on the receding tide.

Doc Lawes, however, used a shotgun, and they said that he did a good job, all right.

When the population had shrunk to a few thousand and the citizens were still saying that times would be better, like a boy whistling in the dark, Federal investigators made an astonishing discovery. As a result, there was great interest in the fact that a group of citizens in the Big Hill country had been killing Big Hills for several years with the object of accumulating several headrights into the hands of one Indian woman who was married to one of the group. They were preparing to put her out of the way when they were caught. Running Elk had been the first relative to become a victim, but his death had aroused little interest, and the other victims were also disposed of in various ways during the roar of the Great Frenzy, and naturally little attention had been paid to the murders.

But now it was different. Here was an interest coming up just when a lively interest was needed, and good citizens rose early to be at the courtroom to hear the trial. Housewives left their breakfast dishes in order to get seats so that they might stare intently at the faces of the accused.

The little cloud that had hung over the town in the valley finally developed into a cumulus and spread over the sky. But there were no lightning-thrusts of an angry Jove. The senatorial committee came quietly and held their meetings in the courtroom. The members sat at a table, and successive witnesses took a chair and answered questions.

It was a dull day. A monotonous questioning of witnesses, and the only relief was the evident embarrassment of several guardians, and Roan Horse's speech. Chal sat in the back of the room, and when Roan Horse was called, he felt a deep, vicarious shame. Roan Horse was an insurgent and he believed that everything was wrong. He was the leader of the east moon faction of the Peyote church, and believed that Me-Ompah-Wee-Lee, the founder, was a deity, much to the disgust of the conservatives.

When he was called, he walked with quick dignity to the table, but refused to take the witness chair, and Chal's heart sank. He walked proudly to the dais of the judge's bench and stood there like one who is preparing to make an oration. His long hair fell over his black coat in two braids which were interbraided with red cheesecloth. Some tribal instinct caused his hand to move to his right breast, as though he were holding the edge of a blanket under his right arm, then with his right hand he made a gesture and said, "Gentleman of the senatorial investigating committee," then paused. The senator from the northwest Indian country sighed, and made a motion to the others that there was nothing to be done, then settled himself into a comfortable position. The others reared back in their chairs and pretended to be waiting.

Chal could see the anger in Roan Horse's face, and he looked down the bench where he was sitting as though he would escape if possible. Then again he heard Roan Horse's voice, "Gentlemen of the senatorial investigating committee: I am Roan Horse. I say this to you. You have come here twenty-five years too late." With a quick movement he descended to the table and shook hands with each of the members. When he came to the senator from the northwest Indian country, he stood at the senator's shoulder with his extended hand unnoticed. The senator was absorbed in some papers before him and apparently believed that Roan Horse was still speaking. He turned, surprised, and took the long bronze hand.

People laughed about Roan Horse's speech, and said it was good, and Chal felt quite proud of him. His speech came at a time in the investigation when the citizens were beginning to believe that the affair was going to be tame, after all. They had hoped that the committee might stir up something which would be of benefit to them, but had experienced that childish injury which intensely acquisitive people feel when they have been thwarted. Thus they felt, in some vague way, that Roan Horse had been their champion.

Chal felt the atmosphere which was charged with depression, and he felt almost disillusioned at times. The representatives of civilization changed from jovial back-slapping, efficient people, around whom he had placed an aura of glory, to dour, reticent people who seemed afraid. The many ways which they had found to share in the wealth of the Osages, became less practical as the methods formerly used, now loomed in the quiescence, which before had been drowned in the frenzy. There was an attitude of waiting for something, and they told each other repeatedly that the Osage payments would become larger again.

The glamour was dimmed and Chal found that even corn whisky and home brew parties were of little aid in lifting his spirit from the effect of that strange atmosphere which had settled over the little town in the valley. He was annoyed with his mother because she didn't seem to understand that something had happened to the world. Fire Cloud would come with his wife, and the three of them would sit out in the shade under the postoak and talk as they had always talked. He thought they were like that postoak in a way. It had been standing there as long as he could remember; standing there in the shrill excitement of the frenzy, and standing there now with the same indifference under the pall of the dimmed glory. Chal was annoyed with them because they didn't seem to be aware that something important had happened to the little world of their blackjacks and prairie.

One hot June morning Chal drove home. He put the car in the garage, making as little noise as possible. Of course his mother never said anything about his absences, but he didn't want her to know that he had been drunk for the last two weeks.

This morning he had come from the hangout of Pug Wilson and his gang, and he couldn't remember how he had got there. As he drove in he was wondering how long he had been there and what he had done. He had received his June payment, which was certainly not much, but he didn't have a cent left this morning. As he rubbed his hand over his chin his straggly beard seemed to be inches long. He could remember only snatches of the conversations at Pug's hangout, and he could remember vaguely that there had been girls there. He remembered Pug and the way he could take his false teeth out and draw his cheeks in and pucker his mouth so that he didn't look like the same man. Pug had boasted to him that he always did that before he went into a bank. He said he always put his false teeth in his pocket and screwed his face up when he stuck the iron in their guts, so they couldn't recognize him later. He told Chal they'd play hell catchin' him by the description of him with his teeth out.

Chal walked slowly to the shade of the old postoak and sat down. He tried to recall some of the other things that had happened at Pug's hangout, but he couldn't remember. He was sure of one thing, and that was that he had not left the house; he was sure that he couldn't have accompanied them on one of their "jobs." This assurance gave him a pleasant feeling.

As he sat by the table this hot summer morning in the shade of the old oak, he felt lazily indifferent to everything. He slid back in his chair and watched a robin feeding her young; their quivering, jerky little heads reaching above the nest with wide mouths. The mother robin shook herself and flew away. A sparrow came hopping along the limb, chirruped, and looked about, then hopped to the edge of the nest. He cocked his head at the nestlings. They, hearing the sound at the edge of the nest, reached for the expected food. The sparrow looked quizzically at the little ones for a while, with his head cocked. He looked around several times, then reached in and lifted one of the nestlings out. He hopped along the limb for a short distance, then looking down at the ground, he let the little bird fall. Chal heard it spatter as it hit the earth. The sparrow looked down at it for a moment, then hopped back to the nest.

Chal was about to rise to scare him away when the mother robin appeared, and with much scolding, chased the sparrow away. When she came back she had a worm dangling from her bill and began to feed the remaining nestlings. She failed to realize that anything had happened to the fourth.

The door slammed, and Chal's mother came out with some coffee, and sat down in the other chair by the table. For some time they sat silently, and as he sipped his coffee Chal felt annoyed with her. He had felt antagonistic toward her for some time, and he wasn't sure why. He noticed that she had changed quite a bit. Her black hair was parted in the center and brushed back and done into a neat knot. Her long, copper-colored fingers played along the arm of the chair nervously. Her shoes looked neat on her very small feet, and she was dressed in a very attractive blue dress. About her, as usual, as long as he could remember, was the odor of soap; a simple, clean odor without the hint of perfume. He noticed that her hair was still damp from the strokes of a wet brush.

The coffee in the pot grew cold. Another sparrow came to the oak tree and looked about cautiously for the mother robin. Chal watched him for a moment, then said, "The sparrows are still purty bad." His mother looked at the ground in front of her, "Yes, seems like they're worse this year—I don' know why."

His antagonism left as a memory came back to him. He turned to his mother. "'Member, I used to kill them with the arrows Uncle Fire Cloud made for me?"

"My son was a great hunter—he killed many sparrows." A smile came over her face, then left quickly, and there was another long silence. She looked straight ahead, then spoke softly, "Many white men are flying across the sea now."

It was only an observation, but Chal saw behind it into the Indian soul of his mother. He became very angry and almost hated her for a moment. An intense urge flooded him; an urge to vindicate himself before this woman. This woman sitting there was more than his mother—she was an Indian woman and she was questioning a man's courage. Suddenly he realized why he had almost hated her recently. She had been looking into his heart, as she had always looked into his heart.

As he sat there he was attempting to think of something to say which would vindicate him, but he was growing angrier in his futility. Then suddenly he was warmed by a thought. There was a primordial thing which thrilled him and made his stomach tingle, and he felt kindly toward his mother—toward this Indian woman who could see into a warrior's heart. Under the influence of this thought he got up from his chair and stood before her, instinctively straightening his body.

"Ah," he said, "there isn't anything to flyin'. Flyin' across the sea doesn't mean anything any more these days. It's not hard. We didn't have these parachutes and things. It was really dangerous when I was flyin'." He hesitated, then a definite, glorious feeling came over him as he stood there. "I'm goin' to Harvard law school, and take law—I'm gonna be a great orator." The thought that had so recently occurred to him for the first time, occurred to him the moment before, suffused him with glory, and he experienced an assurance and a courage that he hadn't felt for years, and he ended up with, "There isn't anything to flyin any more."

As his mother looked at him standing there, she didn't see a swaggering young man. She saw a little boy in breech clout and moccasins, holding up a cock sparrow for her approval. She could see again the marks of his fingers on his dirty face, and the little line of dirt in the crease of his neck. As he held the bird up to her he had frowned like a little warrior.

She thought that her heart might come into her face, so she looked at the ground and said, "Huhn-n-n-n-n." She got up quickly and went into the house.

Chal sat down in the chair and slid down on his back. He was filled with a calm pleasure. There was nothing definite except that hum of glory in his heart, subdued by the heat and the lazy tempo of life in the heated yard.

His heavy head lolled back and he fell asleep. The leaf-shadows made bizarre designs on his silk shirt, and moved slowly to the center of the table, then to the edge, and finally abandoned the table to the hot sun. The nestlings in the nest above settled down to digest their food. A flame-winged grasshopper rose in front of Chal's still form, and suspended there, made cracking sounds like electric sparks, then dropped to the grass and became silent. The flapping and splashing of the mother robin, as she bathed in the pan under the hydrant, was the only sound of activity.

1934

Thomas S. Whitecloud (Chippewa) 1914–1972

Thomas St. Germain Whitecloud was born in New York City, October 8, 1914. His mother was white and his father, Thomas S. Whitecloud, was Chippewa. The elder Whitecloud was a graduate of the Yale Law School but after his education chose not to cast his lot with white America. Thus the Whiteclouds divorced, and he returned to the Lac Du Flambeau Reservation in Wisconsin, where he remarried and reared a family. The young Whitecloud remained with his mother, but his childhood experiences included life on the reservation as well as in mainstream America.

The younger Whitecloud encountered difficult times growing up. He was in and out of public schools as well as federal Indian schools in Albuquerque, Chilocco, and Santa Fe. He made an unsuccessful attempt at college studies at the University of New Mexico but finally settled down to serious study at the University of Redlands, where he also met and married Barbara Ibanez. Meanwhile, during his youth, he had been a farm worker, truck driver, mechanic, handyman, and boxer, among others.

By the time Whitecloud entered Redlands, he had settled on medicine as a career. After graduation, in 1939 he entered the Tulane School of Medicine from which he earned his M.D. degree before entering military service in World War II. He served for over two years as a battalion surgeon with U.S. paratroops in Europe. As a practicing physician, he worked as an Indian Service doctor in Montana and Minnesota before entering private practice in Texas, where for over seven years he not only ran a county hospital but also served as county coroner and deputy sheriff. Because of ill health, he moved to Mississippi, settling finally at Picayune, where he had a limited practice, engaged in many civic activities, and served as a consultant to the Department of Health, Education, and Welfare. During his later years, he also wrote and lectured extensively.

While a student at Redlands, Whitecloud had contemplated careers other than medicine. He liked to write and apparently considered taking up literature. He wrote essays and Indian tales, some of which he sent to the aged Hamlin Garland, presumably for criticism. His only significant published literary work, "Blue Winds Dancing," appeared in his senior year. It has been a popular essay among readers of Indian literature because of its powerful theme and the quality of its style, which becomes almost lyrical at times. At his death, Whitecloud left a number of works in manuscript, including essays, tales, and poetry.

Daniel F. Littlefield, Jr.
University of Arkansas–Little Rock

PRIMARY WORK

Blue Winds Dancing, 1938.

Blue Winds Dancing[1]

There is a moon out tonight. Moon and stars and clouds tipped with moonlight. And there is a fall wind blowing in my heart. Ever since this evening, when against a

[1]From *Scribner's Monthly,* 103 (February, 1938), 59–61.

fading sky I saw geese wedge southward. They were going home. . . . Now I try to study, but against the pages I see them again, driving southward. Going home.

Across the valley there are heavy mountains holding up the night sky, and beyond the mountains there is home. Home, and peace, and the beat of drums, and blue winds dancing over snow fields. The Indian lodge will fill with my people, and our gods will come and sit among them. I should be there then. I should be at home.

But home is beyond the mountains, and I am here. Here where fall hides in the valleys, and winter never comes down from the mountains. Here where all the trees grow in rows; the palms stand stiffly by the roadsides, and in the groves the orange trees line in military rows, and endlessly bear fruit. Beautiful, yes; there is always beauty in order, in rows of growing things! But it is the beauty of captivity. A pine fighting for existence on a windy knoll is much more beautiful.

In my Wisconsin, the leaves change before the snows come. In the air there is the smell of wild rice and venison cooking; and when the winds come whispering through the forests, they carry the smell of rotting leaves. In the evenings, the loon calls, lonely; and birds sing their last songs before leaving. Bears dig roots and eat late fall berries, fattening for their long winter sleep. Later, when the first snows fall, one awakens in the morning to find the world white and beautiful and clean. Then one can look back over his trail and see the tracks following. In the woods there are tracks of deer and snowshoe rabbits, and long streaks where partridges slide to alight. Chipmunks make tiny footprints on the limbs; and one can hear squirrels busy in hollow trees, sorting acorns. Soft lake waves wash the shores, and sunsets burst each evening over the lakes, and make them look as if they were afire.

That land which is my home! Beautiful, calm—where there is no hurry to get anywhere, no driving to keep up in a race that knows no ending and no goal. No classes where men talk and talk, and then stop now and then to hear their own words come back to them from the students. No constant peering into the maelstrom of one's mind; no worries about grades and honors; no hysterical preparing for life until that life is half over; no anxiety about one's place in the thing they call Society.

I hear again the ring of axes in deep woods, the crunch of snow beneath my feet. I feel again the smooth velvet of ghost-birch bark. I hear the rhythm of the drums. . . . I am tired. I am weary of trying to keep up this bluff of being civilized. Being civilized means trying to do everything you don't want to, never doing anything you want to. It means dancing to the strings of custom and tradition; it means living in houses and never knowing or caring who is next door. These civilized white men want us to be like them—always dissatisfied, getting a hill and wanting a mountain.

Then again, maybe I am not tired. Maybe I'm licked. Maybe I am just not smart enough to grasp these things that go to make up civilization. Maybe I am just too lazy to think hard enough to keep up.

Still, I know my people have many things that civilization has taken from the whites. They know how to give; how to tear one's piece of meat in two and share it with one's brother. They know how to sing—how to make each man his own songs and sing them; for their music they do not have to listen to other men singing over a radio. They know how to make things with their hands, how to shape beads into design and make a thing of beauty from a piece of birch bark.

But we are inferior. It is terrible to have to feel inferior; to have to read reports of intelligence tests, and learn that one's race is behind. It is terrible to sit in classes and hear men tell you that your people worship sticks of wood—that your gods are all false, that the Manitou forgot your people and did not write them a book.

I am tired. I want to walk again among the ghost-birches. I want to see the leaves turn in autumn, the smoke rise from the lodgehouses, and to feel the blue winds. I want to hear the drums; I want to hear the drums and feel the blue whispering winds.

There is a train wailing into the night. The trains go across the mountains. It would be easy to catch a freight. They will say he has gone back to the blanket; I don't care. The dance at Christmas. . . .

* * *

A bunch of bums warming at a tiny fire talk politics and women and joke about the Relief and the WPA and smoke cigarettes. These men in caps and overcoats and dirty overalls living on the outskirts of civilization are free, but they pay the price of being free in civilization. They are outcasts. I remember a sociology professor lecturing on adjustment to society; hobos and prostitutes and criminals are individuals who never adjusted, he said. He could learn a lot if he came and listened to a bunch of bums talk. He would learn that work and a woman and a place to hang his hat are all the ordinary man wants. These are all he wants, but other men are not content to let him want only these. He must be taught to want radios and automobiles and a new suit every spring. Progress would stop if he did not want these things. I listen to hear if there is any talk of communism or socialism in the hobo jungles. There is none. At best there is a sort of disgusted philosophy about life. They seem to think there should be a better distribution of wealth, or more work, or something. But they are not rabid about it. The radicals live in the cities.

I find a fellow headed for Albuquerque, and talk road-talk with him. "It is hard to ride fruit cars. Bums break in. Better to wait for a cattle car going back to the Middle West, and ride that." We catch the next east-bound and walk the tops until we find a cattle car. Inside, we crouch near the forward wall, huddle, and try to sleep. I feel peaceful and content at last. I am going home. The cattle car rocks. I sleep.

Morning and the desert. Noon and the Salton Sea, lying more lifeless than a mirage under a somber sun in a pale sky. Skeleton mountains rearing on the skyline, thrusting out of the desert floor, all rock and shadow and edges. Desert. Good country for an Indian reservation. . . .

Yuma and the muddy Colorado. Night again, and I wait shivering for the dawn.

Phoenix. Pima country. Mountains that look like cardboard sets on a forgotten stage. Tucson. Papago country. Giant cacti that look like petrified hitchhikers along the highways. Apache country. At El Paso my road-buddy decides to go on to Houston. I leave him, and head north to the mesa country. Las Cruces and the terrible Organ Mountains, jagged peaks that instill fear and wondering. Albuquerque. Pueblos along the Rio Grande. On the boardwalk there are some Indian women in colored sashes selling bits of pottery. The stone age offering its art to the twentieth century. They hold up a piece and fix the tourists with black eyes until, embarrassed, he buys or turns away. I feel suddenly angry that my people should have to do such things for a living. . . .

Santa Fe trains are fast, and they keep them pretty clean of bums. I decide to hurry and ride passenger coaltenders. Hide in the dark, judge the speed of the train as it leaves, and then dash out, and catch it. I hug the cold steel wall of the tender and think of the roaring fire in the engine ahead, and of the passengers back in the dining car reading their papers over hot coffee. Beneath me there is blur of rails. Death would come quick if my hands should freeze and I fall. Up over the Sangre De Cristo range, around cliffs and through canyons to Denver. Bitter cold here, and I must watch out for Denver Bob. He is a railroad bull who has thrown bums from fast freights. I miss him. It is too cold, I suppose. On north to the Sioux country.

Small towns lit for the coming Christmas. On the streets of one I see a beam-shouldered young farmer gazing into a window filled with shining silver toasters. He is tall and wears a blue shirt buttoned, with no tie. His young wife by his side looks at him hopefully. He wants decorations for his place to hang his hat to please his woman. . . .

Northward again. Minnesota, and great white fields of snow; frozen lakes, and dawn running in dusk without noon. Long forests wearing white. Bitter cold, and one night the northern lights. I am nearing home.

I reach Woodruff at midnight. Suddenly I am afraid, now that I am but twenty miles from home. Afraid of what my father will say, afraid of being looked on as a stranger by my own people. I sit by a fire and think about myself and all the other young Indians. We just don't seem to fit in anywhere—certainly not among the whites, and not among the older people. I think again about the learned sociology professor and his professing. So many things seem to be clear now that I am away from school and do not have to worry about some man's opinion of my ideas. It is easy to think while looking at dancing flames.

Morning. I spend the day cleaning up, and buying some presents for my family with what is left of my money. Nothing much, but a gift is a gift, if a man buys it with his last quarter. I wait until evening, then start up the track toward home.

Christmas Eve comes in on a north wind. Snow clouds hang over the pines, and the night comes early. Walking along the railroad bed, I feel the calm peace of snow-bound forests on either side of me. I take my time; I am back in a world where time does not mean so much now. I am alone; alone but not nearly so lonely as I was back on the campus at school. Those are never lonely who love the snow and the pines; never lonely when the pines are wearing white shawls and snow crunches coldly underfoot. In the woods I know there are the tracks of deer and rabbit; I know that if I leave the rails and go into the woods I shall find them. I walk along feeling glad because my legs are light and my feet seem to know that they are home. A deer comes out of the woods just ahead of me, and stands silhouetted on the rails. The North, I feel, has welcomed me home. I watch him and am glad that I do not wish for a gun. He goes into the woods quietly, leaving only the design of his tracks in the snow. I walk on. Now and then I pass a field, white under the night sky, with houses at the far end. Snow comes from the chimneys of the houses, and I try to tell what sort of wood each is burning by the smoke; some burn pine, others aspen, others tamarack. There is one from which comes black coal smoke that rises lazily and drifts out over the tops of the trees. I like to watch houses and try to imagine what might be happening in them.

Just as a light snow begins to fall, I cross the reservation boundary; somehow it seems as though I have stepped into another world. Deep woods in a white-and-black winter night. A faint trail leading to the village.

The railroad on which I stand comes from a city sprawled by a lake—a city with a million people who walk around without seeing one another; a city sucking the life from all the country around; a city with stores and police and intellectuals and criminals and movies and apartment houses; a city with its politics and libraries and zoos.

Laughing, I go into the woods. As I cross a frozen lake I begin to hear the drums. Soft in the night the drums beat. It is like the pulse beat of the world. The white line of the lake ends at a black forest, and above the trees the blue winds are dancing.

I come to the outlying houses of the village. Simple box houses, etched black in the night. From one or two windows soft lamp light falls on the snow. Christmas here, too, but it does not mean much; not much in the way of parties and presents. Joe Sky will get drunk. Alex Bodidash will buy his children red mittens and a new sled. Alex is a Carlisle man, and tries to keep his home up to white standards. White standards. Funny that my people should be ever falling farther behind. The more they try to imitate whites the more tragic the result. Yet they want us to be imitation white men. About all we imitate well are their vices.

The village is not a sight to instill pride, yet I am not ashamed; one can never be ashamed of his own people when he knows they have dreams as beautiful as white snow on a tall pine.

Father and my brother and sister are seated around the table as I walk in. Father stares at me for a moment, then I am in his arms, crying on his shoulder. I give them the presents I have brought, and my throat tightens as I watch my sister save carefully bits of red string from the packages. I hide my feelings by wrestling with my brother when he strikes my shoulder in token of affection. Father looks at me, and I know he has many questions, but he seems to know why I have come. He tells me to go on alone to the lodge, and he will follow.

I walk along the trail to the lodge, watching the northern lights forming in the heavens. White waving ribbons that seem to pulsate with the rhythm of the drums. Clean snow creaks beneath my feet, and a soft wind sighs through the trees, singing to me. Everything seems to say "Be happy! You are home now—you are free. You are among friends—we are your friends; we, the trees, and the snow, and the lights." I follow the trail to the lodge. My feet are light, my heart seems to sing to the music, and I hold my head high. Across white snow fields blue winds are dancing.

Before the lodge door I stop, afraid. I wonder if my people will remember me. I wonder—"Am I Indian, or am I white?" I stand before the door a long time. I hear the ice groan on the lake, and remember the story of the old woman who is under the ice, trying to get out, so she can punish some runaway lovers. I think to myself, "If I am white I will not believe that story; if I am Indian, I will know that there is an old woman under the ice." I listen for a while, and I know that there is an old woman under the ice. I look again at the lights, and go in.

Inside the lodge there are many Indians. Some sit on benches around the walls, others dance in the center of the floor around a drum. Nobody seems to notice me. It seems as though I were among a people I have never seen before. Heavy women with long black hair. Women with children on their knees—small children that watch with intent black eyes the movements of the dancers, whose small faces are solemn and serene. The faces of the old people are serene, too, and their eyes are merry and bright. I look at the old men. Straight, dressed in dark trousers and beaded velvet vests, wearing soft moccasins. Dark, lined faces intent on the music. I wonder if I am at all like them. They dance on, lifting their feet to the rhythm of the drums, swaying lightly, looking upward. I look at their eyes, and am startled at the rapt attention to the rhythm of the music.

The dance stops. The men walk back to the walls, and talk in low tones or with their hands. There is little conversation, yet everyone seems to be sharing some secret. A woman looks at a small boy wandering away, and he comes back to her.

Strange, I think, and then remember. These people are not sharing words—they are sharing a mood. Everyone is happy. I am so used to white people that it seems strange so many people could be together without someone talking. These Indians are happy because they are together, and because the night is beautiful outside, and the music is beautiful. I try hard to forget school and white people, and be one of these—my people. I try to forget everything but the night, and it is a part of me; that I am one with my people and we are all a part of something universal. I watch eyes, and see now that the old people are speaking to me. They nod slightly, imperceptibly, and their eyes laugh into mine. I look around the room. All the eyes are friendly; they all laugh. No one questions my being here. The drums begin to beat again, and I catch the invitation in the eyes of the old men. My feet begin to lift to the rhythm, and I look out beyond the walls into the night and see the lights. I am happy. It is beautiful. I am home.

1938

D'Arcy McNickle 1904–1977

D'Arcy McNickle was born on January 18, 1904, in St. Ignatius, Montana to William McNickle and Philomene Parenteau. As he was to write later in life, his mother and her family came to Montana to escape the aftermath of the failed Métis Revolution in present-day Saskatchewan. (Descendants of Cree and French trappers, the Métis tried to maintain control over their lands when the Canadian government wanted them settled by European immigrants; the hostilities are often referred to as The Riel, or The Northwest, Rebellion.) Whether or not Philomene's father, Isidore Plante Parenteau, was an active participant in the revolt, and indeed the amount of "Indian blood" he possessed, are points of debate among some present-day scholars; however, the debate is noteworthy for one simple reason: it so clearly represents the resonating effects of McNickle's life and works. He raised controversy about contemporary Native American identity and issues at every turn. It is sufficient to note here that in April 1905 Philomene renounced all claim to lands or rights as a member of the Cree, and that she and her three children were adopted into the Salish (Flathead) tribe. There is no doubt that McNickle identified as a Native American, as he often articulated, and that he was dedicated to the causes of indigenous peoples.

His mother and father divorced, and in 1914 he was sent, as so many other Native American children in similar situations were sent, to a federal boarding school, Chemawa in Salem, Oregon. He was to write of this experience in several works, including two of his novels, for it epitomizes the central conflict and dilemma faced by generations of tribal peoples on this continent after the incursion of the European: the ever-present attempts to undermine native cultures, in this case through "re-education" camps, but also the immense attraction—the power, glitter and wealth—of the "modern" lifestyle offered as an alternative.

Although McNickle portrays federal boarding schools in very bleak terms, he continued with his education at the University of Montana, majoring in English, and in 1925 he sold his eighty-acre allotment on the reservation to fund his study at Oxford University. Although he did not finish his degree, McNickle became a respected scholar, academic, and activist: he wrote well-received books on Native American history, as well as three novels, and numerous short stories; he was the first director of the Newberry Library's Center for the History of the American Indian, which now is named after him; he helped found the Department of Anthropology at the University of Saskatchewan, Regina; and he was a founding member of the Congress of American Indians. These are but a few of the accomplishments that seem to indicate his total assimilation into mainstream society, as some scholars have argued.

McNickle was, however, a self-proclaimed, vocal proponent of the Native American right of self-determination, one who succeeded in urban America, true, but who remained self-identified with the lifeways he left on the reservation, and who drew a voice from native verbal arts and tribal perspectives. As his novels repeatedly proclaim, American Indians want only to be left alone to pursue their futures in their own ways. As history demonstrates and McNickle dramatizes, when this basic human right is abrogated, bad things happen.

Yet, his fiction is not always bleak and humorless, nor tragic in the usual, historical sense, for it is always underscored by a consistent reaffirmation in modern times of native values and beliefs; he provides insights into cultures that exist today after tens of thousands of years, despite very obvious recent changes in the landscape of this continent. Moreover, as the story "Hard Riding" shows us, attempts to impose non-traditional, non-indigenous patterns of behavior on native populations can have its humorous side. Employing his favorite character, the well-intentioned Euro-American, McNickle is able to show the inherent folly of an ethnocentric approach to intercultural interaction: the power figure is rendered powerless by those who give him what he wants, and is given an abject lesson in the subtle strength of self-determination at the same time.

John Lloyd Purdy
Western Washington University

PRIMARY WORKS

Fiction: *The Surrounded,* 1936; *Runner in the Sun: A Story of Indian Maize,* 1954; *Wind From an Enemy Sky,* 1978; *The Hawk is Hungry and Other Stories,* 1992. Other Prose: *They Came Here First,* 1949; *Indian Man: A Life of Oliver La Farge,* 1972; *Native American Tribalism: Indian Survival and Renewals,* 1973.

Hard Riding

Riding his gray mare a hard gallop in the summer dust, Brinder Mather labored with thought which couldn't quite come into focus.

The horse labored too, its gait growing heavy as loose sand fouled its footing; but at each attempt to break stride into a trot, there was the prick of spur point, a jerk at the reins. It was a habit with the rider.

"Keep going! Earn your feed, you hammerhead!"

Brinder was always saying that his horses didn't earn their feed. Yet he was the hardest rider in the country.

Feeling as he did about horses, he quite naturally had doubts about Indians. And he had to work with Indians. He was their superintendent . . . a nurse to their helplessness, was the way he sometimes thought of it.

It was getting toward sundown. The eastward mirror of the sky reflected orange and crimson flame thwarting the prismatic heavens. It was after supper, after a hard day at the Agency office, and Brinder was anxious to get his task done and be home to rest. The heat of the day had fagged him. His focusing thought came out in words, audibly.

"They've been fooling with the idea for a month, more than a month, and I still can't tell what they'll do. Somehow I've got to put it over. Either put it over or drop it. I'll tell them that. Take it or leave it. . . ."

Ahead, another mile, he saw the white school house, the windows ablaze with the evening sun. He wondered if those he had called together would be there, if they would all be there. A full turn-out, he reasoned, would indicate that they were interested. He could be encouraged if he saw them all on hand.

As he drew nearer, he observed that a group stood waiting. He tried to estimate the number . . . twelve or fifteen. Others were still coming. There were riders in the distance coming by other roads. The frown relaxed on his heavy, sun-reddened face. For the moment he was satisfied. He had called the entire Tribal Council of twenty, and evidently they would all be on hand. Good!

He let his horse slow to less than a canter for the first time in the three-mile ride from the Agency.

* * *

"Hello, boys. Everybody coming tonight? Let's go inside."

He strode, tall and dignified, through the group.

They smiled to his words, saying nothing. One by one they followed him into the school room. He was always for starting things with a rush; they always hung back. It was a familiar pattern. He walked to the teacher's desk and spread out before him a sheaf of paper which he had brought in a heavy envelope.

In five years one got to know something about Indians. Even in one's first job as superintendent of a Reservation, five years was a good schooling.

The important thing, the first thing to learn, was not to let them stall you. They would do it every time if you let them. They would say to a new idea, "Let us talk about that" or "Give us time. We'll think about it." One had to know when to cut short. Put it over or drop it. Take it or leave it.

Not realizing that at the start, he had let these crazy Mountain Indians stall on him a long time before he had begun to get results. He had come to them with a simple idea and only now, after five years, was it beginning to work.

Cattle . . . that was the idea. Beef cattle. Blooded stock. Good bulls. Fall roundups. The shipment East. Cash profits. In language as simple as that he had finally got them to see his point. He had a special liking for cattle. It began long before he had ever seen an Indian, back home in New York State. Boyhood reading about hard riding and fast shooting on the cattle trails . . . that was what started it. Then, in his first job in the Indian Service, he had worked under a hard-minded Scotchman whose record as a stockman was unbeatable. He had learned the gospel from him. He learned to talk the lingo.

"Indians don't know, more than that don't give a damn, about dragging their feet behind a plow. Don't say as I blame 'em. But Indians'll always ride horses. They're born to that. And if they're going to ride horses they might as well be riding herd on a bunch of steers. It pays money."

He put it that way, following his Scotch preceptor. He put it to the Indians, to Washington officials, and to anybody he could buttonhole for a few minutes. It was a complete gospel. It was appropriations of money from Congress for cattle purchases. It won flattering remarks from certain visitors who were always around inquiring about Indian welfare. In time, it won over the Indians. It should have won them sooner.

The point was just that, not to let them stall on you. After five years he had learned his lesson. Put it over, or drop it.

He had taken off his broad-brimmed cattleman's hat and laid it on the desk beside his papers. The hat was part of the creed. He surveyed the score of wordless, pensive, buckskin-smelling Indians, some slouched forward, holding their big hats between their knees; others, hats on, silently smoking.

He had to put it across, this thing he wanted them to do. He had to do it now, tonight, or else drop it. That was what he had concluded.

"I think you fellows have learned a lot since I been with you. I appreciate the way you co-operate with me. Sometimes it's kinda hard to make things clear, but once you see what it means to you, you're all for it. I like that." He paused and mopped his brow. The schoolroom was an oven. The meeting should have been held outside — but never mind.

"In our stock association, we run our cattle together on a common range. We share the costs of riding range, rounding up, branding, and buying breeding bulls. Every time you sell a steer you pay a five-dollar fee into the pot, and that's what pays the bills. That's one of the things I had to tell you about. You didn't understand at first, but once you did, you went ahead. Today, it's paying dividends.

"You never had as much cash profit in your life before. Your steers are better beef animals, because the breeding is better. We got the class in bulls. And you get better prices because you can dicker with the buyers. But you know all that. I'm just reminding you."

Someone coughed in the back of the room and Brinder, always on guard, like the cowboys contending with rustlers and sheepmen he used to read about, straightened his back and looked sharply. But it was only a cough, repeated several times —

an irritating, ineffective kind of cigarette cough. No one else in the audience made a sound. All were held in the spell of Brinder's words, or at any rate were waiting for him to finish what he had to say.

"We have one bad defect yet. You know what I mean, but I'll mention it just the same. In other words, fellows, we all of us know that every year a certain number of cattle disappear. The wolves don't get them and they don't die of natural causes. They are always strong, fat, two- or three-year-old steers that disappear, the kind that wolves don't monkey with and that don't die naturally. I ain't pointing my finger at anybody, but you know as well's I do that there's a certain element on the Reservation that don't deserve fresh meat, but always has it. They're too lazy or too ornery or they just don't know what it's all about. But they get fresh meat just the same.

"I want you fellows to get this. Let it sink in deep. Every time a fat steer goes to feed some Slick Steve too lazy to earn his keep, some of you are out around seventy-five, eighty dollars. You lose that much. Ponder that, you fellows."

He rustled the papers on the desk, looking for a row of figures: number of beef animals lost in five years (estimated), their money value, in round numbers. He hurled his figures at them, cudgeling.

"Some of you don't mind the loss. Because it's poor people getting the meat. It keeps someone from starving. That's what you say. What I say is — that ain't a proper way to look at it. First of all, because it's stealing and we can't go to countenancing stealing, putting up with it, I mean. Nobody has to starve, remember that. If you want to do something on your own book for the old people who can't work, you can. You can do what you like with your money. But lazy people, these Slick Steves who wouldn't work on a bet, nobody should give it easy to them, that's what I'm saying."

He waited a moment, letting the words find their way home. "There's a solution, as I told you last month. We want to set up a court, a court of Indian judges, and you will deal with these fellows in your own way. Give a few of them six months in jail to think it over, and times will begin to change around here. . . ."

That was the very point he had reached the last time he talked to the Council, a month before. He had gone no further, then, because they had begun asking questions, and from their questions he had discovered that they hadn't the least idea what he was driving at. Or so they made it appear. "If we have a tribal court," somebody would ask, "do we have to put somebody in jail?" That, obviously, was intentionally naive. It was intended to stall him off. Or some old man would say: "If somebody has to go to jail, let the Superintendent do it. Why should we have to start putting our own people in jail?" Such nonsense as that had been talked.

Finally, the perennial question of money came up. Would the Government pay for the court? A treacherous question, and he had answered without flinching.

"That's another thing," he had said brightly. "We're going to get away from the idea of the Government paying for everything. Having your own business this way, making a profit from it, you can pay for this yourselves. That will make you independent. It will be your own court, not the Government's court, not the Superintendent's court. No. The court will be supported by the fee money you pay when you sell a steer."

That speech broke up the meeting. It was greeted by a confusion of talk in the native tongue which gradually subsided in form of one speaker, one of the ancients, who obviously was a respected leader. Afterwards, a young, English-speaking tribesman translated.

"The old man here, Looking Glass, says the Gover'ment don't give us nothing for nothing. The money it spends on us, that's our own money, he says. It belongs to us and they keep it there at Washington, and nobody can say how much it is or how much has been lost. He says, where is all that money that they can't afford to pay for this court? That's what he says."

There was the snare which tripped up most Agency plans, scratch an old Indian, and the reaction was always the same. "Where's the money the Government owes us? Where's our land? Where's our treaty?" They were like a whistle with only one stop, those old fellows. Their tune was invariable, relentless, and shrill. That was why one dreaded holding a meeting when the old men were present. Now the young fellows, who understood Agency plans. . . .

Anyhow, here he was trying it again, going over the plan with great care and patience. Much of the misunderstanding had been ironed out in the meantime. So he had been led to believe.

"This court will put an end to all this trouble," he was going on, trying to gauge the effect of his words, watching for a reaction. At last it came. One of the old men was getting to his feet.

He was a small man, emaciated by age and thin living, yet neat looking. His old wife, obviously, took good care of his clothes, sewed buckskin patches on his overalls and kept him in new moccasins. He talked firmly, yet softly, and not for very long. He sat down as soon as he had finished and let the interpreter translate for him.

"The old man here, Big Face, says the court, maybe, is all right. They have talked it over among themselves, and maybe it's all right. Our agent, he says, is a good man. He rides too fast. He talks too fast. But he has a good heart, so maybe the court is all right. That's what Big Face says."

The words were good, and Brinder caught himself smiling, which was bad practice when dealing with the old fellows. They were masters at laying traps for the unwary—that, too, he had learned in five years. Their own expressions never changed, once they got going, and you could never tell what might be in their minds.

Just the same, he felt easier. Big Face, the most argumentative of the lot, had come around to accept this new idea, and that was something gained. The month had not been lost.

He had something more to say. He was getting to his feet again, giving a tug to his belt and looking around, as if to make sure of his following. He had been appointed spokesman. That much was clear.

He made a somewhat longer speech, in which he seemed to express agitation, perhaps uncertainty. One could never be sure of tone values. Sometimes the most excitable sounding passages of this strange tongue were very tame in English. Brinder had stopped smiling and waited for the translation.

"Big Face here says there's only one thing they can't decide about. That's about judges. Nobody wants to be a judge. That's what they don't like. Maybe the court is all right, but nobody wants to be judge."

Brinder was rather stumped by that. He rose to his feet, quickly, giving everyone a sharp glance. Was this the trap?

"Tell the old man I don't understand that. It is an honor, being a judge. People pay money to be a judge in some places. Tell Big Face I don't understand his objection."

The old man was on his feet as soon as the words had been translated for him. "It's like this. To be a judge, you got to be about perfect. You got to know everything, and you got to live up to it. Otherwise, you got nothing to say to anybody who does wrong. Anybody who puts himself up to be that good, he's just a liar. And people will laugh at him. We are friends among ourselves and nobody interferes in another person's business. That's how it is, and nobody wants to set himself up and be a judge. That's what Big Face says."

There it was—as neatly contrived a little pitfall as he had ever seen. He had to admire it—all the time letting himself get furious. Not that he let them see it. No, in five years, he had learned that much. Keep your head, and when in doubt, talk your head off. He drew a deep breath and plunged into an explanation of all the things he had already explained, reminding them of the money they lost each year, of the worthless fellows who were making an easy living from their efforts, of the proper way to deal with the problem. He repeated all the arguments and threw in as many more as he could think of.

"You have decided all this. You agree the court is a good thing. But how can you have a court without judges? It's the judges that make a court."

He couldn't tell whether he was getting anywhere or not—in all likelihood, not. They were talking all together once more and it didn't look as if they were paying much attention to him. He waited.

"What's it all about?" he finally asked the interpreter, a young mixed-blood, who was usually pretty good about telling Brinder which way the wind of thought blew among the old people.

"I can't make out," the interpreter murmured, drawing closer to Brinder. "They are saying lots of things. But I think they're going to decide on the judges—they've got some kind of plan—watch out for it—now, one of the old men will speak."

It was Big Face raising to his feet once more. Looking smaller, more wizened than ever. The blurring twilight of the room absorbed some of his substance and made Brinder feel that he was losing his grip on the situation. A shadow is a difficult adversary and Big Face was rapidly turning into one.

"The agent wants this court. He thinks it's a good thing. So we have talked some more—and we agree. We will have this court." He paused briefly, allowing Brinder only a moment's bewilderment.

"Only we couldn't decide who would be judge. Some said this one, some said that one. It was hard. . . ."

Brinder coughed. "Have you decided on any one, Big Face?" He no longer knew which way things were drifting but only hoped for the best.

The old fellow's eyes, misted by age, actually twinkled. In the body of councillors somebody laughed and coughed in the same breath. Feet stirred and bodies shifted. Something was in the air. Haltingly, Big Face named the men—the most amazing trio the Reservation had to offer.

"Walks-in-the-Ground—Jacob Gopher—Twisted Horn . . ."

In the silence that followed, Brinder tried hard to believe he had heard the wrong names. A mistake had been made. It was impossible to take it seriously. These three men—no, it was impossible! The first, an aged imbecile dripping saliva—ready to die! The second, stone deaf and blind! The third, an utter fool, a half-witted clown, to whom no one listened.

"You mean this?" Brinder still could not see the full situation, but was afraid that the strategy was deliberate and final.

"Those will be the judges of this court," Big Face replied, smiling his usual friendly way.

"But these men can't be judges! They are too old, or else too foolish. No one will listen to them . . . ," Brinder broke off short. He saw that he had stated the strategy of the old men especially as they had intended it. His friendliness withered away.

Big Face did not hesitate, did not break off smiling. "It is better, we think, that fools should be judges. If people won't listen to them, no one will mind."

Brinder had nothing to say, not just then. He let the front legs of his chair drop to the floor, picked up his hat. His face had paled. After five years—still to let this happen. . . . Using great effort, he turned it off as a joke. "Boys, you should of elected me judge to your kangaroo court. I would have made a crackerjack."

The Indians laughed and didn't know what he meant, not exactly. But maybe he was right.

1989

Robert Penn Warren 1905–1989

Robert Penn Warren was born and raised in Guthrie, Kentucky, a small town in the "Black Patch" tobacco country near the Tennessee border. Early on he developed deep loves for the countryside and for reading, particularly fiction and history. After failing his physical examination for the U.S. Naval Academy because of an eye injury, in 1921 he entered Vanderbilt University instead.

Warren's talent for writing was quickly noticed by his teachers, including John Crowe Ransom and Donald Davidson. Before long, he was an active member of the "Fugitives," a literary group centered at the university that met regularly to discuss philosophy and poetry. Warren at this time began writing his own verse and became close friends with Allen Tate, another "Fugitive" whose literary career, like Warren's, was then just beginning.

By the time he graduated from Vanderbilt in 1925 and was off to graduate study at the University of California, Berkeley (and later at Yale and then Oxford with a Rhodes scholarship), Warren had committed himself to a career of writing. His years at Vanderbilt with the Fugitives had been crucial in his early development. Perhaps most important, he established during this time a profound conviction for the worth of artistic pursuit, seeing, in his own words, "that poetry was a vital activity, that it related to ideas and life." Moreover, particularly through his friendship with Allen Tate, he immersed himself in the tremendous vitality and experimentation of literary modernism and began experimenting to discover his own poetic voice. Probably best known for his novel *All the King's Men,* Warren also published ten other novels, fifteen volumes of poetry, two plays, a biography of John Brown, and numerous books and essays on cultural and literary criticism, including the influential anthologies he edited with Cleanth Brooks, *Understanding Poetry, Understanding Fiction,* and *Modern Rhetoric.*

Warren's early poems show the strong

influences of Tate and T. S. Eliot, and also, by way of Eliot and John Crowe Ransom, of the seventeenth-century metaphysical poets. His first volume of verse, *Thirty-Six Poems,* appeared in 1935, followed by *Eleven Poems on the Same Theme* (1942) and *Selected Poems: 1923–1943* (1944). Most of the poems from these volumes, as James Justus has pointed out, show Warren as a master craftsman experimenting with models and conventions of others and along the way "slowly learning how to reinvigorate models out of his own needs and with his own voice."

Not all of Warren's energies during this time were going exclusively into poetry. In 1930 he began his distinguished academic career by accepting an appointment at Southwestern College in Memphis, followed by appointments at Vanderbilt University (1931) and Louisiana State University (1934), where with Cleanth Brooks he edited the *Southern Review* until 1942. In 1942, he became Professor of English at the University of Minnesota, where he stayed until 1950 when he accepted a position at Yale University. Warren retired from Yale in 1973.

During the 1930s and 1940s Warren was doing a great deal of writing other than poetry. He collaborated on several important anthologies of literature and rhetoric, and, even more importantly, began his career as writer of fiction. *Night Rider,* his first novel, appeared in 1939, followed by *At Heaven's Gate* (1943), his masterpiece, *All the King's Men* (1946), and *The Circus in the Attic and Other Stories* (1948). Seven other novels subsequently appeared along with a number of volumes of literary and cultural criticism.

Meanwhile, Warren's poetic output ceased from 1944 until 1953, when he brought out *Brother to Dragons: A Tale in Verse and Voices.* This striking work, an imaginative reconstruction of a historical event involving Thomas Jefferson's nephew written in voices, dialogue, and colloquy, marks the beginning of Warren's major phase as poet. *Brother to Dragons* opened up "a whole new sense of poetry," he later admitted. No less than twelve volumes of Warren's verse followed its publication. Warren's quest in his poetry was driven by a passion both to know himself and his world and to discover meaning and continuities despite the resistance of a naturalistic universe. This effort to achieve understanding, to transfigure the factual into the interpretative, lies at the heart of Warren's imaginative vision. "In this century, and moment, of mania," he writes in *Audubon,* "Tell me a story."

Robert H. Brinkmeyer, Jr.
University of Arkansas

PRIMARY WORKS

Fiction: *Night Rider,* 1939; *At Heaven's Gate,* 1943; *All the King's Men,* 1946; *The Circus in the Attic and Other Stories,* 1948; *World Enough and Time,* 1950; *Band of Angels,* 1955; *The Cave,* 1959; *Wilderness,* 1961; *Flood: A Romance of Our Time,* 1961; *Meet Me in the Green Glen,* 1971; *A Place to Come To,* 1977. Poetry: *Thirty-Six Poems,* 1935; *Brother to Dragons: A Tale in Verse and Voices,* 1953; *Audubon: A Vision,* 1969; *Chief Joseph of the Nez Perce,* 1983; *New and Selected Poems, 1923–1985,* 1985. Nonfiction: *John Brown: The Making of a Martyr,* 1929; *Segregation: The Inner Conflict in the South,* 1957; *Selected Essays,* 1958; *The Legacy of the Civil War,* 1961; *Who Speaks for the Negro?,* 1965; *Homage to Theodore Dreiser,* 1971; *Democracy and Poetry,* 1975; *Jefferson Davis Gets His Citizenship Back,* 1975; *Portrait of a Father,* 1988; *New and Selected Essays,* 1989. Anthologies (with Cleanth Brooks): *Understanding Poetry,* 1938; *Understanding Fiction,* 1943; *Modern Rhetoric,* 1949.

Founding Fathers, Early-Nineteenth-Century Style, Southeast U.S.A.

They were human, they suffered, wore long black coat and gold
watch chains.
They stare from daguerreotype with severe reprehension,
Or from genuine oil, and you'd never guess any pain
In those merciless eyes that now remark our own time's sad
declension.

Some composed declarations, remembering Jefferson's language.
Knew pose of the patriot, left hand in crook of the spine or
With finger to table, while right invokes the Lord's just rage.
There was always a grandpa, or cousin at least, who had been a
real Signer.

Some were given to study, read Greek in the forest, and these
Longed for an epic to do their own deeds right honor;
Were Nestor[1] by pigpen, in some tavern brawl played Achilles.[2]
In the ring of Sam Houston[3] they found, when he died, one word
engraved: *Honor.*

Their children were broadcast, like millet seed flung in a wind
flare.
Wives died, were dropped like old shirts in some corner of
country.
Said, "Mister," in bed, the child-bride; hadn't known what to find
there;
Wept all the next morning for shame; took pleasure in silk; wore
the keys to the pantry.

"Will die in these ditches if need be," wrote Bowie, at the Alamo.
And did, he whose left foot, soft-catting, came forward, and breath
hissed:
Head back, gray eyes narrow, thumb flat along knife-blade, blade
low.
"Great gentleman," said Henry Clay,[4] "and a patriot." Portrait by
Benjamin West.[5]

[1]A king of Pylos in Greek legend; hero of the Trojan War.
[2]A warrior in Greek legend; hero of Homer's *Iliad.*
[3]Soldier and statesman of Tennessee and Texas, 1793–1863; commander-in-chief of Texan forces in war with Mexico, 1836.
[4]American statesman, 1777–1852; pivotal figure in political controversies concerning slavery and sectionalism in decades before Civil War.
[5]American painter, 1738–1820; best known for his historical paintings.

Or take those, the nameless, of whom no portraits remain,
No locket or seal ring, though somewhere, broken and rusted,
In attic or earth, the long Decherd,[6] stock rotten, has lain;
Or the mold-yellow Bible, God's Word, in which, in their strength,
they also trusted.

Some wrestled the angel, and took a fall by the corncrib.
Fought the brute, stomp-and-gouge, but knew they were doomed
in that glory.
All night, in sweat, groaned; fell at last with spit red and a cracked
rib.
How sweet then the tears! Thus gentled, they roved the dark land
with the old story.

Some prospered, had black men and acres, and silver on table,
But remembered the owl call, the smell of burnt bear fat on dusk-
air.
Loved family and friends, and stood it as long as able—
"But money and women, too much is ruination, am Arkansas-
bound." So went there.

One of mine was a land shark, or so the book with scant praise
Denominates him. "A man large and shapeless,
Like a sack of potatoes set on a saddle," it says,
"Little learning but shrewd, not well trusted." Rides thus out of
history, neck fat and napeless.

One fought Shiloh[7] and such, got cranky, would fiddle all night.
The boys nagged for Texas. "God damn it, there's nothing, God
damn it,
In Texas"—but took wagons, went, and to prove he was right,
Stayed a year and a day—"hell, nothing in Texas"—had proved it,
came back to black vomit,

And died, and they died, and are dead, and now their voices
Come thin, like the last cricket in frost-dark, in grass lost,
With nothing to tell us for our complexity of choices,
But beg us only one word to justify their own old life-cost.

So let us bend ear to them in this hour of lateness,
And what they are trying to say, try to understand,
And try to forgive them their defects, even their greatness,
For we are their children in the light of humanness, and under the
shadow of God's closing hand.

1956

[6]Flintlock Kentucky rifle.
[7]Civil War battle, April 6 and 7, 1862, in southern Tennessee.

Infant Boy at Midcentury

I. When the Century Dragged

When the century dragged, like a great wheel stuck at dead center;
When the wind that had hurled us our half-century sagged now,
And only velleity of air somewhat snidely nagged now,
With no certain commitment to compass, or quarter: then you
 chose to enter.

You enter an age when the neurotic clock-tick
Of midnight competes with the heart's pulsed assurance of power.
You have entered our world at scarcely its finest hour.
And smile now life's gold Apollonian[1] smile at a sick dialectic.

You enter at the hour when the dog returns to his vomit,
And fear's moonflower spreads, white as girl-thigh, in our dusk of
 compromise;
When posing for pictures, arms linked, the same smile in their
 eyes,
Good and Evil, to iron out all differences, stage their meeting at
 summit.

You come in the year when promises are broken,
And petal fears the late, as fruit the early frost-fall;
When the young expect little, and the old endure total recall,
But discover no logic to justify what they had taken, or forsaken.

But to take and forsake now you're here, and the heart will
 compress
Like stone when we see that rosy heel learn,
With its first step, the apocalyptic power to spurn
Us, and our works and days, and onward, prevailing, pass

To pause, in high pride of unillusioned manhood,
At the gap that gives on the new century, and land,
And with calm heart and level eye command
That dawning perspective and possibility of human good.

2. Brightness of Distance

You will read the official histories—some true, no doubt.
Barring total disaster, the record will speak from the shelf.

[1]Harmonious, ordered, balanced.

And if there's disaster, disaster will speak for itself.
So all of our lies will be truth, and the truth vindictively out.

Remember our defects, we give them to you gratis.
But remember that ours is not the worst of times.
Our country's convicted of follies rather than crimes—
We throw out baby with bath, drop the meat in the fire where the
fat is.

And in even such stew and stink as Tacitus[2]
Once wrote of, his generals, gourmets, pimps, poltroons,
He found persons of private virtue, the old-fashioned stout ones
Who would bow the head to no blast; and we know that such are
yet with us.

He was puzzled how virtue found perch past confusion and wrath;
How even Praetorian[3] brutes, blank of love, as of hate,
Proud in their craftsman's pride only, held a last gate,
And died, each back unmarred as though at the barracks bath.

And remember that many among us wish you well;
And once, on a strange shore, an old man, toothless and through,
Groped a hand from the lattice of personal disaster to touch you.
He sat on the sand for an hour; said *ciao, bello,*[4] as evening fell.

And think, as you move past our age that grudges and grieves,
How eyes, purged of envy, will follow your sunlit chance.
Eyes will brighten to follow your brightness and dwindle of
distance.
From privacy of fate, eyes will follow, as though from the shadow
of leaves.

1956

The Leaf

A

Here the fig lets down the leaf, the leaf
Of the fig five fingers has, the fingers

[2]Historian of imperial Rome, c. 55 B.C.–c. A.D. 118.
[3]Referring to the bodyguard of the Roman emperor.
[4]Italian: Goodbye, beautiful one.

Are broad, spatulate, stupid,
Ill-formed, and innocent—but of a hand, and the hand,

To hide me from the blaze of the wide world, drops,
Shamefast, down. I am
What is to be concealed. I lurk
In the shadow of the fig. Stop.
Go no further. This is the place.

To this spot I bring my grief.
Human grief is the obscenity to be hidden by the leaf.

B

We have undergone ourselves, therefore
What more is to be done for Truth's sake? I

Have watched the deployment of ants, I
Have conferred with the flaming mullet in a deep place.

Near the nesting place of the hawk, among
Snag-rock, high on the cliff, I have seen
The clutter of annual bones, of hare, vole, bird, white
As chalk from sun and season, frail
As the dry grass stem. On that

High place of stone I have lain down, the sun
Beat, the small exacerbation
Of dry bones was what my back, shirtless and bare, knew. I saw

The hawk shudder in the high sky, he shudders
To hold position in the blazing wind, in relation to
The firmament, he shudders and the world is a metaphor, his eye
Sees, white, the flicker of hare-scut, the movement of vole.

Distance is nothing, there is no solution, I
Have opened my mouth to the wind of the world like wine, I
wanted
To taste what the world is, wind dried up

The live saliva of my tongue, my tongue
Was like a dry leaf in my mouth.

Destiny is what you experience, that
Is its name and definition, and is your name, for

The wide world lets down the hand in shame:
Here is the human shadow, there, of the wide world, the flame.

C

The world is fruitful, In this heat
The plum, black yet bough-bound, bursts, and the gold ooze is,
Of bees, joy, the gold ooze has striven
Outward, it wants again to be of
The goldness of air and—blessedly—innocent. The grape
Weakens at the juncture of the stem. The world

Is fruitful, and I, too,
In that I am the father
Of my father's father's father. I,
Of my father, have set the teeth on edge. But
By what grape? I have cried out in the night.

From a further garden, from the shade of another tree,
My father's voice, in the moment when the cicada ceases, has
called to me.

D

The voice blesses me for the only
Gift I have given: *teeth set on edge.*

In the momentary silence of the cicada,
I can hear the appalling speed,
In space beyond stars, of
Light. It is

A sound like wind.

1968

Evening Hawk

From plane of light to plane, wings dipping through
Geometries and orchids that the sunset builds,
Out of the peak's black angularity of shadow, riding
The last tumultuous avalanche of
Light above pines and the guttural gorge,
The hawk comes.

His wing
Scythes down another day, his motion

Is that of the honed steel-edge, we hear
The crashless fall of stalks of Time.

The head of each stalk is heavy with the gold of our error.

Look! Look! he is climbing the last light
Who knows neither Time nor error, and under
Whose eye, unforgiving, the world, unforgiven, swings
Into shadow.

Long now,
The last thrush is still, the last bat
Now cruises in his sharp hieroglyphics. His wisdom
Is ancient, too, and immense. The star
Is steady, like Plato, over the mountain.

If there were no wind we might, we think, hear
The earth grind on its axis, or history
Drip in darkness like a leaking pipe in the cellar.

1975

Heart of Autumn

Wind finds the northwest gap, fall comes.
Today, under gray cloud-scud and over gray
Wind-flicker of forest, in perfect formation, wild geese
Head for a land of warm water, the *boom,* the lead pellet.

Some crumple in air, fall. Some stagger, recover control,
Then take the last glide for a far glint of water. None
Knows what has happened. Now, today, watching
How tirelessly *V* upon *V* arrows the season's logic,

Do I know my own story? At least, they know
When the hour comes for the great wing-beat. Sky-strider,
Star-strider—they rise, and the imperial utterance,
Which cries out for distance, quivers in the wheeling sky.

That much they know, and in their nature know
The path of pathlessness, with all the joy
Of destiny fulfilling its own name.
I have known time and distance, but not why I am here.

Path of logic, path of folly, all
The same—and I stand, my face lifted now skyward,
Hearing the high beat, my arms outstretched in the tingling
Process of transformation, and soon tough legs,

With folded feet, trail in the sounding vacuum of passage,
And my heart is impacted with a fierce impulse
To unwordable utterance—
Toward sunset, at a great height.

1978

Amazing Grace in the Back Country

In the season of late August star-fall,
When the first crickets crinkled the dark,
There by woods, where oaks of the old forest-time
Yet swaggered and hulked over upstarts, the tent
Had been pitched, no bigger than one of
Some half-bankrupt carnival come
To town with fat lady, human skeleton, geek,
Man-woman and moth-eaten lion, and one
Boa constrictor for two bits seen
Fed a young calf or what; plus a brace
Of whores to whom menopause now
Was barely a memory, one with gold teeth and one
With game gam, but both
With aperture ready to serve
Any late-lingerers, and leave
A new and guaranteed brand of syphilis handy—yes,

The tent old and yellowed and patched,
Lit inside by three wire-hung gasoline lamps
That outside, through threadbare canvas, were muted to gold.
Here no carnival now—the tabernacle
To the glory of God the Most High, for now corn
Was laid by, business slack, such business as was, and
The late-season pain gnawing deep at the human bone
As the season burned on to its end.

God's Word and His glory—and I, aged twelve,
Sat there while an ex-railroad engineer
Turned revivalist shouted the Threat and the Promise, with sweat
On his brow, shirt plastered to belly, and

Eyes a-glaze with the mania of joy.
And now by my knees crouched some old-fool dame
In worn-out black silk, there crouching with tears
In here eyes as she tugged me to kneel
And save my pore twelve-year-old soul
Before too late. She wept.
She wept and she prayed, and I knew I was damned,
Who was guilty of all short of murder,
At least in my heart and no alibi there, and once
I had walked down a dark street, lights out in houses,
Uttering, "Lust—lust—lust,"
Like an invocation, out loud—and the word
So lovely, fresh-minted.

I saw others fall as though stricken. I heard
The shout of salvation. I stared
In the red-rimmed, wet eyes of the crazy old dame,
Whose name I never remembered, but knew
That she loved me—the Pore Little Lamb—and I thought
How old bones now creaked in God's name.

But the Pore Little Lamb, he hardened his heart,
Like a flint nigger-head[1] rounded slick in a creek-bed
By generations of flood, and suddenly
I found myself standing, then
Ran down an aisle, and outside,
Where cool air and dark filled my lungs, and fifty
Yards off, with my brow pressed hard
On the scaly bark of a hickory tree,
Vomited. Fumbling
In darkness, I found the spring
And washed my mouth. Humped there,

And knowing damnation, I stared
Through interstices of black brush to the muted gold glow
Of God's canvas, till in
The last hymn of triumph rose voices, and hearts
Burst with joy at amazing grace so freely given,
And moving on into darkness,

Voices sang of amazing grace, singing as they
Straggled back to the village, where voice after voice died away,
As singer by singer, in some dark house,
Found bed and lay down,
And tomorrow would rise and do all the old things to do,

[1]Dark-colored rock.

Until that morning they would not rise, not ever.
And now, when all voices were stilled and the lamps
Long out in the tent, and stars
Had changed place in the sky, I yet lay
By the spring with one hand in cold black water
That showed one star in reflection, alone—and lay
Wondering and wondering how many
A morning would I rise up to greet,
And what grace find.

But that was long years ago. I was twelve years old then.

1978

Fear and Trembling

The sun now angles downward, and southward.
The summer, that is, approaches its final fulfillment.
The forest is silent, no wind-stir, bird-note, or word.
It is time to meditate on what the season has meant.

But what is the meaningful language for such meditation?
What is a word but wind through the tube of the throat?
Who defines the relation between the word *sun* and the sun?
What word has glittered on whitecap? Or lured blossom out?

Walk deeper, foot soundless, into the forest.
Stop, breath bated. Look southward, and up, where high leaves
Against sun, in vernal translucence, yet glow with the freshest
Young tint of the lost spring. Here now nothing grieves.

Can one, in fact, meditate in the heart, rapt and wordless?
Or find his own voice in the towering gust now from northward?
When boughs toss—is it in joy or pain and madness?
The gold leaf—is it whirled in anguish or ecstasy skyward?

Can the heart's meditation wake us from life's long sleep,
And instruct us how foolish and fond was our labor spent—
Us who now know that only at death of ambition does the deep
Energy crack crust, spurt forth, and leap

From grottoes, dark—and from the caverned enchainment?

1980

John Crowe Ransom 1888–1974

John Crowe Ransom, son of a Methodist minister, was born in Pulaski, Tennessee. Rigorous training in the classics enabled him to enter Vanderbilt University at fifteen. He left after two years to teach; returning, he graduated in 1909 with the highest grades in his class. After teaching another year, he went to Christ Church College, Oxford University, as a Rhodes scholar, successfully pursuing a degree that required extensive reading in original Greek and Latin texts. Soon he had an offer from the English Department at Vanderbilt, where he taught from 1914 to 1917. During two years spent with the United States Army field artillery in England and France, First Lieutenant Ransom published *Poems About God* (1919).

In 1920 Ransom married Robb Reavill, a well-educated young woman who shared his interest in sports and games. In the early 1920s discussions of poetry with colleagues and friends led to the formation of a magazine, edited by a group including Ransom, Donald Davidson, and Allen Tate. Ransom found his mature poetic voice in the short lyric poems published regularly in the pages of *The Fugitive* from April, 1922, to December, 1925. All of the selections included here appeared there, except "Here Lies a Lady" (*Literary Review,* 1923). Ransom and Robert Penn Warren (his former student) served as editors in 1925, after which the magazine folded.

Ransom's poetry combines traditional forms and themes (love, mutability, death) with modernism in tone and diction. These characteristics are seen in poems with such varied subjects as the death of a child ("Bells for John Whiteside's Daughter"), the inevitable loss of youth and beauty ("Blue Girls"), a medieval religious battle ("Necrological"), rituals of harvest and hunt ("Antique Harvesters"). Although most of Ransom's poems can be found in *Chills and Fever* (1924) and *Two Gentlemen in Bonds* (1927), he continued to revise, to "tinker" with them, for decades.

Ransom's Agrarianism may have been inspired by the Scopes anti-evolution trial in Dayton, Tennessee, in 1925, during which reporters attacked the South for its backwardness. Ransom drafted the "Statement of Principles" for the volume *I'll Take My Stand* by Twelve Southerners (1930); his own essay, "Reconstructed but Unregenerate," is a reasoned defense of the European "provincial" tradition—agrarian, conservative, anti-industrial. A year in England with his family on a Guggenheim fellowship (1931–32) gave him a new perspective on the economic situation in America. Yet, by the time his essay appeared in the second Agrarian collection, *Who Owns America?* (1936), he was concentrating on literary criticism.

This change of focus (and his financial situation) led John Crowe Ransom in 1937 to accept an offer to move to Kenyon College in Gambier, Ohio. A number of students followed him there, including Randall Jarrell, Peter Taylor, and Robert Lowell. In 1939 Ransom published a volume of literary criticism, *The World's Body,* and began to edit the *Kenyon Review.* The next year he was named Carnegie Professor of English. *The New Criticism* (1941) analyzed the approaches of I. A. Richards, William Empson, T. S. Eliot, Yvor Winters, and Ransom himself; his title labeled the method emphasizing the kind of close analysis Ransom practiced in his classes.

Selected Poems (1945) brought together the poems Ransom chose to preserve, with some revisions; reviewers compared his work to that of T. S. Eliot and Wallace Stevens. His concern with training young literary critics and teachers led to the founding of the Kenyon School of English in 1948 (it moved in 1951 to Indiana University). In 1951 Ransom was awarded the Bollingen Prize in Poetry for the body of his work.

After his retirement Ransom continued to work, publishing a third edition of *Selected Poems* (1969) and a final volume of essays, *Beating the Bushes* (1971). Ransom's health failed gradually; he died in his sleep at home in Gambier at the age of eighty-six. Ransom's career illustrates a commitment to the tradition of classical learning that underlies continuing debates over core or general education requirements in American colleges and universities. Yet he was one of the earliest professors to attain tenure and promotion through creative writing and literary criticism rather than traditional research and scholarship.

Martha E. Cook
Longwood College

PRIMARY WORKS

The World's Body, 1938; *The New Criticism,* 1941; *Selected Poems,* 1945, 1963, 1969; *Beating the Bushes: Selected Essays, 1941–1970,* 1971; *Selected Essays,* ed. Young and Hindle, 1984; *Selected Letters,* ed. Young and Core, 1985.

Here Lies a Lady

Here lies a lady of beauty and high degree.
Of chills and fever she died, of fever and chills,
The delight of her husband, her aunt, an infant of three,
And of medicos marveling sweetly on her ills.

For either she burned, and her confident eyes would blaze,
And her fingers fly in a manner to puzzle their heads—
What was she making? Why, nothing; she sat in a maze
Of old scraps of laces, snipped into curious shreds—

Or this would pass, and the light of her fire decline
Till she lay discouraged and cold, like a thin stalk white and
blown,
And would not open her eyes, to kisses, to wine;
The sixth of these states was her last; the cold settled down.

Sweet ladies, long may ye bloom, and toughly I hope ye may thole,
But was she not lucky? In flowers and lace and mourning,
In love and great honor we bade God rest her soul
After six little spaces of chill, and six of burning.

1923

Philomela

Procne, Philomela, and Itylus,
Your names are liquid, your improbable tale
Is recited in the classic numbers of the nightingale.
Ah, but our numbers are not felicitous,
It goes not liquidly for us.

Perched on a Roman ilex, and duly apostrophized,
The nightingale descanted unto Ovid;
She has even appeared to the Teutons, the swilled and gravid;
At Fontainebleau it may be the bird was gallicized;
Never was she baptized.

To England came Philomela with her pain,
Fleeing the hawk her husband; querulous ghost,
She wanders when he sits heavy on his roost,
Utters herself in the original again,
The untranslatable refrain.

Not to these shores she came! this other Thrace,
Environ barbarous to the royal Attic;
How could her delicate dirge run democratic,
Delivered in a cloudless boundless public place
To an inordinate race?

I pernoctated with the Oxford students once,
And in the quadrangles, in the cloisters, on the Cher,
Precociously knocked at antique doors ajar,
Fatuously touched the hems of the hierophants,
Sick of my dissonance.

I went out to Bagley Wood, I climbed the hill;
Even the moon had slanted off in a twinkling,
I heard the sepulchral owl and a few bells tinkling,
There was no more villainous day to unfulfil,
The diuturnity was still.

Out of the darkness where Philomela sat,
Her fairy numbers issued. What then ailed me?
My ears are called capacious but they failed me,
Her classics registered a little flat!
I rose, and venomously spat.

Philomela, Philomela, lover of song,
I am in despair if we may make us worthy,

A bantering breed sophistical and swarthy;
Unto more beautiful, persistently more young,
Thy fabulous provinces belong.

1924

Piazza Piece

—I am a gentleman in a dustcoat trying
To make you hear. Your ears are soft and small
And listen to an old man not at all,
They want the young men's whispering and sighing.
But see the roses on your trellis dying
And hear the spectral singing of the moon;
For I must have my lovely lady soon,
I am a gentleman in a dustcoat trying.

—I am a lady young in beauty waiting
Until my truelove comes, and then we kiss.
But what grey man among the vines is this
Whose words are dry and faint as in a dream?
Back from my trellis, Sir, before I scream!
I am a lady young in beauty waiting.

1925

The Equilibrists

Full of her long white arms and milky skin
He had a thousand times remembered sin.
Alone in the press of people traveled he,
Minding her jacinth, and myrrh, and ivory.

Mouth he remembered: the quaint orifice
From which came heat that flamed upon the kiss,
Till cold words came down spiral from the head,
Grey doves from the officious tower illsped.

Body: it was a white field ready for love,
On her body's field, with the gaunt tower above,
The lilies grew, beseeching him to take,
If he would pluck and wear them, bruise and break.

Eyes talking: Never mind the cruel words,
Embrace my flowers but not embrace the swords.
But what they said, the doves came straightway flying
And unsaid: Honor, Honor, they came crying.

Importunate her doves. Too pure, too wise,
Clambering on his shoulder, saying, Arise,
Leave me now, and never let us meet,
Eternal distance now command thy feet.

Predicament indeed, which thus discovers
Honor among thieves, Honor between lovers.
O such a little word is Honor, they feel!
But the grey word is between them cold as steel.

At length I saw these lovers fully were come
Into their torture of equilibrium;
Dreadfully had forsworn each other, and yet
They were bound each to each, and they did not forget.

And rigid as two painful stars, and twirled
About the clustered night their prison world,
They burned with fierce love always to come near,
But Honor beat them back and kept them clear.

Ah, the strict lovers, they are ruined now!
I cried in anger. But with puddled brow
Devising for those gibbeted and brave
Came I descanting: Man, what would you have?

For spin your period out, and draw your breath,
A kinder sæculum begins with Death.
Would you ascend to Heaven and bodiless dwell?
Or take your bodies honorless to Hell?

In Heaven you have heard no marriage is,
No white flesh tinder to your lecheries,
Your male and female tissue sweetly shaped
Sublimed away, and furious blood escaped.

Great lovers lie in Hell, the stubborn ones
Infatuate of the flesh upon the bones;
Stuprate, they rend each other when they kiss,
The pieces kiss again, no end to this.

But still I watched them spinning, orbited nice.
Their flames were not more radiant than their ice.

I dug in the quiet earth and wrought the tomb
And made these lines to memorize their doom:—

EPITAPH

Equilibrists lie here; stranger, tread light;
Close, but untouching in each other's sight;
Mouldered the lips and ashy the tall skull.
Let them lie perilous and beautiful.

1925

Allen Tate 1899–1979

John Orley Allen Tate was born in Kentucky in 1899 and attended Vanderbilt University in 1918. There he was instructed by John Crowe Ransom and Donald Davidson, was a friend of Robert Penn Warren, and helped to create *The Fugitive* (1922–25), the most influential poetry magazine of literary modernism in the South. In 1924 he went to New York to become a freelance writer; he wrote many book reviews and two biographies, *Stonewall Jackson* (1928) and *Jefferson Davis* (1929). After the publication of *Mr. Pope and Other Poems* (1928), Tate received a Guggenheim Fellowship, which he spent in Europe among the American expatriate literary community. He returned to live in the South, where he contributed to *I'll Take My Stand: The South and the Agrarian Tradition* (1930), the expression of the conservative movement known as Southern Agrarianism. This period in his life culminated in the publication of a historical novel of Civil War Virginia, *The Fathers* (1938). During the mid-1930s he abandoned the life of a freelance writer and became a college professor, most lastingly at the University of Minnesota (1951–68), with periods as the Chair of Poetry at the Library of Congress (1943–44) and as editor of the *Sewanee Review* (1944–46). During these later years, his production of poetry declined markedly and he became most active as a literary critic associated with the New Criticism—a movement more famously urged by his friends Cleanth Brooks, Warren, and Ransom—and as a friend and patron of younger poets such as Robert Lowell. In his retirement, he returned to Tennessee, where he died in 1979.

Tate began his career as an admirer of H. L. Mencken, who excoriated the South as a cultural desert, moved to an interest in the French Symbolist poets (especially Baudelaire), then became devoted to T. S. Eliot, whose merits Tate was among the first to urge. Among the "Fugitive" poets, Tate pled the causes of cosmopolitanism, freedom from inhibition, the impossibility of general truth, and indifference to place. After having experienced New York and France, he began to reconsider these standpoints, though he never completely abandoned them. In "Ode to the Confederate Dead," Tate began to explore his mature theme: the delicate and fructifying tension between community and commitment on the one hand, and alientation and self-awareness on the other. Beginning with his essay "The Profession of Letters in the South" (1935) and continuing until "A Southern Mode of the Imagination" (1959), Tate applied this theme to southern literature, especially that of the Southern Renaissance.

Tate felt that if modernity was to salvage sanity, the intellectual must by act of will assert a meaningful social and religious order, almost irrespective of whether he accepted the general truth of that order. In the late 1920s and 1930s, Tate gave more attention to the social problem, though even in *I'll Take My Stand* he was drawn to make "Remarks on the Southern Religion." He argued that agrarianism—as opposed to urban industrial capitalism—would better lead to morality, prosperity, and community.

More rapidly than most of his confederates, however, he began to minimize the southern dimension of the cause by reaching out to other cultures. *The Fathers* was his last sustained venture in considering southern culture; its theme was the triumph of rapacious modernity over older traditions of noblesse oblige and civility. After 1938 Tate abandoned the attempt to make the South a repository of meaning and turned more strictly to religion; he converted to Roman Catholicism in 1952. In a world that Tate believed to be spinning into disorder, the forms of art seemed to him the nearest available, though very inadequate, consolation and bulwark.

Michael O'Brien
Miami University

PRIMARY WORKS

The Fathers, 1938; *Essays of Four Decades,* 1968; *Memoirs and Opinions, 1926–1974,* 1975; *Collected Poems, 1919–1976,* 1977.

Ode to the Confederate Dead

Row after row with strict impunity
The headstones yield their names to the element,
The wind whirrs without recollection;
In the riven troughs the splayed leaves
Pile up, of nature the casual sacrament
To the seasonal eternity of death;
Then driven by the fierce scrutiny
Of heaven to their election in the vast breath,
They sought the rumour of mortality.

Autumn is desolation in the plot
Of a thousand acres where these memories grow
From the inexhaustible bodies that are not
Dead, but feed the grass row after rich row.
Think of the autumns that have come and gone!—
Ambitious November with the humors of the year,
With a particular zeal for every slab,
Staining the uncomfortable angels that rot
On the slabs, a wing chipped here, an arm there:
The brute curiosity of an angel's stare
Turns you, like them, to stone,
Transforms the heaving air
Till plunged to a heavier world below
You shift your sea-space blindly
Heaving, turning like the blind crab.

Dazed by the wind, only the wind
The leaves flying, plunge

You know who have waited by the wall
The twilight certainty of an animal,
Those midnight restitutions of the blood
You know—the immitigable pines, the smoky frieze
Of the sky, the sudden call: you know the rage,
The cold pool left by the mounting flood,
Of muted Zeno and Parmenides.
You who have waited for the angry resolution
Of those desires that should be yours tomorrow,
You know the unimportant shrift of death
And praise the vision
And praise the arrogant circumstance
Of those who fall
Rank upon rank, hurried beyond decision—
Here by the sagging gate, stopped by the wall.

Seeing, seeing only the leaves
Flying, plunge and expire

Turn your eyes to the immoderate past,
Turn to the inscrutable infantry rising
Demons out of the earth—they will not last.
Stonewall, Stonewall, and the sunken fields of hemp,
Shiloh, Antietam, Malvern Hill, Bull Run
Lost in that orient of the thick-and-fast
You will curse the setting sun.

Cursing only the leaves crying
Like an old man in a storm

You hear the shout, the crazy hemlocks point
With troubled fingers to the silence which
Smothers you, a mummy, in time.

The hound bitch
Toothless and dying, in a musty cellar
Hears the wind only.

Now that the salt of their blood
Stiffens the saltier oblivion of the sea,
Seals the malignant purity of the flood,
What shall we who count our days and bow
Our heads with a commemorial woe
In the ribboned coats of grim felicity,
What shall we say of the bones, unclean,
Whose verdurous anonymity will grow?

The ragged arms, the ragged heads and eyes
Lost in these acres of the insane green?
The gray lean spiders come, they come and go;
In a tangle of willows without light
The singular screech-owl's tight
Invisible lyric seeds the mind
With the furious murmur of their chivalry.

We shall say only the leaves
Flying, plunge and expire

We shall say only the leaves whispering
In the improbable mist of nightfall
That flies on multiple wing;
Night is the beginning and the end
And in between the ends of distraction
Waits mute speculation, the patient curse
That stones the eyes, or like the jaguar leaps
For his own image in a jungle pool, his victim.
What shall we say who have knowledge
Carried to the heart? Shall we take the act
To the grave? Shall we, more hopeful, set up the grave
In the house? The ravenous grave?

Leave now

The shut gate and the decomposing wall:
The gentle serpent, green in the mulberry bush,
Riots with his tongue through the hush—
Sentinel of the grave who counts us all!

1928, 1937

Charles Reznikoff 1894–1976

The chronology of the Objectivist movement is brief. In late 1930, Louis Zukofsky, the poet who coined the term "Objectivist," wrote Ezra Pound that he was preparing a critical article on the poetry of Charles Reznikoff but, in order to analyze the poetry, had become involved in trying to define two terms: *sincerity* and *objectification.* Pound, familiar with Zukofsky's work, had already convinced editor Harriet Monroe to allow Zukofsky to edit an issue of *Poetry.* Zukofsky then appended his article, entitled "Sincerity and Objectification: With Special Reference to the Work of Charles Reznikoff," to the February 1931, issue—the "Objectivists" issue—with an eye to providing what he later called a "standard" for his contributors. His primary example of the language of Objectivism was Reznikoff's one-line poem "Aphrodite Vrania"—"The ceaseless weaving of the uneven water." The poem strongly suggests in its sound the movement to which it refers.

Reznikoff was a product of the Jewish community in New York. Born in Brooklyn in 1894, he earned a law degree but practiced only briefly. For a few years in the 1930s, however, he worked at a legal publishing firm, where he helped condense and summarize court records for inclusion in legal reference works. Although he had begun to publish in the teens (he self-published some of his own work with hand-set plates beginning in the 1920s), his reading and writing in legal publishing had a profound effect on much of his later poetry. He began to see that court testimony uniquely documented a comprehensive cultural history, and from court records he extracted and further condensed stories and vignettes (published as his prose book *Testimony,* 1934) and transformed them and additional records into poems that filled two volumes when published some thirty years later. He came to appreciate the straightforward, unornamented prose of court testimony, which used metaphor sparsely if at all. The tools he developed in such writing served him well when he wrote *Holocaust,* based closely on courtroom accounts of the Nazi death camps.

Reznikoff had an apparently intuitive eye for the "historical particulars" that Zukofsky valued. He incorporated into even his earliest poetry details of daily life in New York—from street lamps to domestic tragedies—that he saw during his long walks through the city. He wrote drama and fiction, including fictionalized history, but seldom criticism. In the 1930s, he worked for a time in Hollywood but returned to New York and made a living as a free-lance writer, translator, and researcher until his death in 1976. Reznikoff's work speaks of a significant project—one in which history shapes language, language in turn shapes history's readers, and poetry marks out the most artfully shaped language of the lived historical moment.

Randolph Chilton
College of St. Francis

PRIMARY WORKS

Rhythms, 1918; *Rhythms II,* 1919; *Poems,* 1920; *Uriel Accosta: A Play & A Fourth Group of Verse,* 1921; *Chatterton, the Black Death, and Meriwether Lewis,* 1922 (plays); *Coral and Captive Israel,* 1923 (plays); *Nine Plays,* 1927; *Five Groups of Verse,* 1927; *By the Waters of Manhattan: An Annual,* 1929 (anthology); *By the Waters of Manhattan,* 1930 (novel); *Jerusalem the Golden,* 1934; *Testimony,* 1934 (prose); *In Memoriam: 1933,* 1934; *Early History of a Sewing Machine Operator* (with Nathan Reznikoff), 1936 (prose); *Separate Way,* 1936; *Going To and Fro and Walking Up and Down,* 1941; *The Lionhearted,* 1944 (novel); *Inscriptions: 1944–1956,* 1959; *By the Waters of Manhattan: Selected Verse,* 1962; *Family Chronicle* (with Nathan and Sarah Reznikoff), 1963 (prose); *Testimony: The United States 1885–1890: Recitative,* 1965; *Testimony: The United States (1891–1900): Recitative,* 1968; *By the Well of Living and Seeing and The Fifth Book of the Maccabees,* 1969; *By the Well of Living & Seeing: New & Selected Poems 1918–1973,* 1974; *Holocaust,* 1975; *Poems 1918–1975: The Complete Poems of Charles Reznikoff,* 1989.

[How shall we mourn you who are killed and wasted]

How shall we mourn you who are killed and wasted,
sure that you would not die with your work unended,
as if the iron scythe in the grass stops for a flower?

1918

Aphrodite Vrania[1]

The ceaseless weaving of the uneven water.

1921

[The shoemaker sat in the cellar's dusk beside his bench]

The shoemaker sat in the cellar's dusk beside his bench and
sewing-machine, his large, blackened hands, finger tips
flattened and broad, busy.
Through the grating in the sidewalk over his window, paper
and dust were falling year by year.

At evening Passover would begin. The sunny street was
crowded. The shoemaker could see the feet of those who
walked over the grating.
He had one pair of shoes to finish and he would be through.
His friend came in, a man with a long, black beard, in shabby,
dirty clothes, but with shoes newly cobbled and blacked.
"Beautiful outside, really the world is beautiful."

A pot of fish was boiling on the stove. Sometimes the water
bubbled over and hissed. The smell of the fish filled the
cellar.
"It must be beautiful in the park now. After our fish we'll take
a walk in the park." The shoemaker nodded.
The shoemaker hurried his work on the last shoe. The pot on
the stove bubbled and hissed. His friend walked up and
down the cellar in shoes newly cobbled and blacked.

1921

[1]The Greek goddess of love and beauty, Aphrodite, combined with the Greek muse of astronomy, Urania.

Hellenist[1]

As I, barbarian, at last, although slowly, could read Greek,
at "blue-eyed Athena"
I greeted her picture that had long been on the wall:
the head slightly bent forward under the heavy helmet,
as if to listen; the beautiful lips slightly scornful.

1934

[In steel clouds]

In steel clouds
to the sound of thunder
like the ancient gods:
our sky, cement;
the earth, cement;
our trees, steel;
instead of sunshine,
a light that has no twilight,
neither morning nor evening,
only noon

Coming up the subway stairs, I thought the moon
only another street-light—
a little crooked.

1934

[About an excavation]

About an excavation
a flock of bright red lanterns
has settled.

1934

[1]Student of classical Greece.

After Rain

The motor-cars on the shining street move in semicircles of spray, semicircles of spray.

1934

[Among the heaps of brick and plaster lies]

Among the heaps of brick and plaster lies
a girder, still itself among the rubbish.

1934

The English in Virginia, April 1607[1]

They landed and could
see nothing but
meadows and tall
trees—
cypress, nearly three
fathoms about at the
roots,
rising straight for
sixty or eighty feet
without a branch.
In the woods were
cedars, oaks, and
walnut trees;
some beech, some elm,
black walnut, ash,
and sassafras; mul-
berry trees in
groves;
honey-suckle and

[1]Based upon the *Works of Captain John Smith,* edited by Edward Arber. [Reznikoff's note.]

other vines hanging
in clusters on
many trees.
They stepped on
violets and other
sweet flowers,
many kinds in many
colors; straw-
berries and rasp-
berries were on
the ground.
Blackbirds with red
shoulders were
flying about
and many small birds,
some red, some blue;
the woods were full of deer;
and running
everywhere
fresh water—
brooks, rundles,
springs and creeks.
In the twilight,
through the thickets
and tall grass,
creeping upon all
fours—the
savages, their
bows in their
mouths.

1934

from Testimony[1]

I

The company had advertised for men to unload a steamer across the river. It was six o'clock in the morning, snowing, and still dark.
There was a crowd looking for work on the dock;
and all the while men hurried to the dock.

[1]Based on cases in the law reports. [Reznikoff's note.]

The man at the wheel
kept the bow of the launch
against the dock—
the engine running slowly;
and the men kept jumping
from dock to deck,
jostling each other,
and crowding into the cabin.

Eighty or ninety men were in the cabin as the launch pulled away.
There were no lights in the cabin, and no room to turn—whoever was sitting down could not get up, and whoever had his hand up could not get it down,
as the launch ran in the darkness
through the ice,
ice cracking
against the launch
bumping and scraping
against the launch,
banging up against it,
until it struck
a solid cake of ice,
rolled to one side, and slowly
came back to an even keel.

The men began to feel water running against their feet as if from a hose. "Cap," shouted one, "the boat is taking water! Put your rubbers on, boys!"
The man at the wheel turned.
"Shut up!" he said.
The men began to shout,
ankle-deep in water.
The man at the wheel turned
with his flashlight:
everybody was turning and pushing against each other;
those near the windows
were trying to break them,
in spite of the wire mesh
in the glass; those who had been near the door
were now in the river,
reaching for the cakes of ice,
their hands slipping off and
reaching for the cakes of ice.

II

Amelia was just fourteen and out of the orphan asylum; at her first job—in the bindery, and yes sir, yes ma'am, oh, so anxious to please.
She stood at the table, her blonde hair hanging about her shoulders, "knocking up" for Mary and Sadie, the stitchers
("knocking up" is counting books and stacking them in piles to be taken away).
There were twenty wire-stitching machines on the floor, worked by a shaft that ran under the table;
as each stitcher put her work through the machine,
she threw it on the table. The books were piling up fast
and some slid to the floor
(the forelady had said, Keep the work off the floor!);
and Amelia stooped to pick up the books—
three or four had fallen under the table
between the boards nailed against the legs.
She felt her hair caught gently;
put her hand up and felt the shaft going round and round
and her hair caught on it, wound and winding around it,
until the scalp was jerked from her head,
and the blood was coming down all over her face and waist.

1941

Children

1

Once, among the transports, was one with children—two freight cars full.
The young men sorting out the belongings of those taken to the gas chambers
had to undress the children—they were orphans—
and then take them to the "lazarette."
There the S.S. men shot them.

2

A large eight-wheeled car arrived at the hospital
where there were children;
in the two trailers—open trucks—were sick women and men

lying on the floor.
The Germans threw the children into the trucks
from the second floor and the balconies—
children from one-year-old to ten;
threw them upon the sick in the trucks.
Some of the children tried to hold on to the walls,
scratched at the walls with their nails;
but the shouting Germans
beat and pushed the children towards the windows.

3

The children arrived at the camp in buses,
guarded by gendarmes of the French Vichy government.
The buses stopped in the middle of the courtyard
and the children were quickly taken off
to make room for the buses following.
Frightened but quiet,
the children came down in groups of fifty or sixty to eighty;
the younger children holding on to older ones.
They were taken upstairs to empty halls—
without any furniture
and only dirty straw bags on the floor, full of bugs:
children as young as two, three, or four years of age,
all in torn clothes and dirty,
for they had already spent two or three weeks in other camps,
uncared for;
and were now on their way to a death camp in Poland.
Some had only one shoe.
Many had diarrhea
but they were not allowed in the courtyard
where the water-closets were;
and, although there were chamber pots in the corridor of each story,
these were too large for the small children.

The women in the camp who were also deportees
and about to be taken to other camps
were in tears:
they would get up before sunrise
and go into the halls where the children were—
in each a hundred to a hundred and twenty—
to mend the children's clothing;
but the women had no soap to clean the children,
no clean underwear to give them,
and only cold water with which to wash them.
When soup came for the children,

there were no spoons;
and it would be served in tins
but the tins were sometimes too hot for the children to hold.

After nine at night no one—except for three or four who had a
permit—
was allowed to stay with the children.
Each room was then in darkness,
except for one bulb painted blue by blackout instructions.
The children would wake at night
calling for their mothers
and would then wake each other,
and sometimes all in the room would start crying out
and even wake the children in other rooms.

A visitor once stopped one of the children:
a boy of seven or eight, handsome, alert and gay.
He had only one shoe and the other foot was bare,
and his coat of good quality had no buttons.
The visitor asked him for his name
and then what his parents were doing;
and he said, "Father is working in the office
and Mother is playing the piano."
Then he asked the visitor if he would be joining his parents soon—
they always told the children they would be leaving soon to rejoin
their parents—
and the visitor answered, "Certainly. In a day or two."
At that the child took out of his pocket
half an army biscuit he had been given in camp
and said, "I am keeping this half for Mother;"
and then the child who had been so gay
burst into tears.

4

Other children, also separated from their parents,
arrived in buses,
and were put down in the courtyard of the camp—
a courtyard surrounded by barbed wire
and guarded by gendarmes.
On the day of leaving for the death camp
they were awakened at five in the morning.
Irritable, half asleep, most of them refused to get up and go down to
the courtyard.
Women—French volunteers, for they were still in France—
urged the children gently

to obey—they must!—and vacate the halls.
But many still would not leave the straw bags on which they slept
and then the gendarmes entered,
and took up the children in their arms;
the children screamed with fear,
struggled and tried to grasp each other.

5

Women guards at the women's section of the concentration camp
were putting little children into trucks
to be taken away to the gas chambers
and the children were screaming and crying, "Mamma, Mamma,"
even though the guards were trying to give them pieces of candy to
quiet them.

1975

John Steinbeck 1902–1968

John Steinbeck was born into a middle-class family in the agricultural center of Salinas, California. His father was county treasurer; his mother, once a school teacher, raised him on anecdotes of unusual rural happenings. A life among farmers, migrant workers, and ranchers of the Salinas Valley; biblical lore; the knightly adventures of King Arthur; a summer course in marine biology; a devotion to *The Golden Bough;* and a fascination with the mysteries of the unconscious all shaped Steinbeck's writings. In his lifetime the Nobel Prize-winning author wrote over twenty-eight plays, movie scripts, short story collections, books of non-fiction, novels, and political documents.

A popular student in high school, Steinbeck reluctantly attended Stanford University, in whose magazine his stories were first published. Leaving without a degree in 1925, Steinbeck continued working at odd jobs to support his writing. Initial success came with *Cup of Gold* (1929). In 1930 he married Carol Henning, the first of his three wives, received financial support from his parents as well as the use of their Pacific Grove cottage, and became a full-time writer. The couple joined the bohemian culture of aspiring painters and writers, sharing the gossip about the denizens of Monterey and Cannery Row.

Over his thirty-year writing career, Steinbeck wrote from three general perspectives that focused on the interaction between consciousness and experience. At first, his subject was the individual struggling with his consciousness. "The Chrysanthemums" is representative of the short stories depicting individuals whose dreams or illusions are thwarted by reality. The clash of totalitarian movements, the migrations from the Dust Bowl, and the appearance of New Deal social legislation offered a broader horizon upon which Steinbeck staged his action. In the mid-1930s he began writing of the individual's relationship with political, familial, or other groups he called "phalanxes." To explain the solidarity underlying phalanx behavior, Steinbeck developed the concept of a shared or collective consciousness. The writings for which he is most famous—*In Dubious Battle, Of Mice and Men,* and *The Grapes of Wrath*—dramatize the extent to which people surrender their individuality, separate themselves, or, in the case of the Joads, reinvent themselves so as to balance individual and collective identities. The war over and the phalanx movement in retreat, Steinbeck explored his own layers of consciousness in autobiographical works that appear as fiction. Whether the subject is divorce, cultural values, or writing itself, the central character is painfully aware that the world for which his mind and art are programmed has vanished. Common to all Steinbeck's writing are circumstances or events that challenge and often destroy the individual's sense of reality.

John Steinbeck's enormous popularity today derives in part from his gift as a storyteller and from his portrait of the individual as a tragic figure. His style varies from symbolic to allegorical. Usually he wrote with a theme in mind for which he created archetypal characters and a symbolic landscape. While his characters live in the present, they are linked to the past with a collective memory and through age-old rituals of sacrifice, death, and rebirth. Yet characters are not without choices. A human being is ultimately a pragmatic creature. That we are capable of perceiving the best course of action is the small hope Steinbeck willed his world audience.

If his artistic powers waned in his later writings, Steinbeck's concerns for humanity broadened. He had a voice in Democratic politics from Roosevelt to Johnson and edited the Great Society Platform of 1964. He died in New York and his ashes were returned to California.

Cliff Lewis
University of Lowell

PRIMARY WORKS

The Pastures of Heaven, 1932; *To a God Unknown,* 1933; *Tortilla Flat,* 1935; *In Dubious Battle,* 1936; *Of Mice and Men,* 1937; *The Long Valley,* 1938; *The Grapes of Wrath,* 1939; *The Pearl,* 1945; *The Wayward Bus,* 1947; *East of Eden,* 1952; *The Winter of Our Discontent,* 1961; *Travels With Charley,* 1962; *Steinbeck: A Life in Letters,* ed. by Elaine Steinbeck and Robert Wallsten, 1976.

The Chrysanthemums

The high gray-flannel fog of winter closed off the Salinas Valley from the sky and from all the rest of the world. On every side it sat like a lid on the mountains and made of the great valley a closed pot. On the broad, level land floor the gang ploughs bit deep and left the black earth shining like metal where the shares had cut. On the foothill ranches across the Salinas River, the yellow stubble fields seemed to be bathed in pale cold sunshine, but there was no sunshine in the valley now in December. The thick willow scrub along the river flamed with sharp and positive yellow leaves.

It was a time of quiet and of waiting. The air was cold and tender. A light wind blew up from the southwest so that the farmers were mildly hopeful of a good rain before long; but fog and rain do not go together.

Across the river, on Henry Allen's foothill ranch there was little work to be done, for the hay was cut and stored and the orchards were ploughed up to receive the rain deeply when it should come. The cattle on the higher slopes were becoming shaggy and rough-coated.

Elisa Allen, working in her flower garden, looked down across the yard and saw Henry, her husband, talking to two men in business suits. The three of them stood by the tractor shed, each man with one foot on the side of the little Fordson. They smoked cigarettes and studied the machine as they talked.

Elisa watched them for a moment and then went back to her work. She was thirty-five. Her face was lean and strong and her eyes were as clear as water. Her figure looked blocked and heavy in her gardening costume, a man's black hat pulled low down over her eyes, clod-hopper shoes, a figured print dress almost completely covered by a big corduroy apron with four big pockets to hold the snips, the trowel and scratcher, the seeds and the knife she worked with. She wore heavy leather gloves to protect her hands while she worked.

She was cutting down the old year's chrysanthemum stalks with a pair of short and powerful scissors. She looked down toward the men by the tractor shed now and then. Her face was eager and mature and handsome; even her work with the scissors was over-eager, over-powerful. The chrysanthemum stems seemed too small and easy for her energy.

She brushed a cloud of hair out of her eyes with the back of her glove, and left a smudge of earth on her cheek in doing it. Behind her stood the neat white farm house with red geraniums close-banked around it as high as the windows. It was a hard-swept-looking little house, with hard-polished windows, and a clean mud-mat on the front steps.

Elisa cast another glance toward the tractor shed. The strangers were getting into their Ford coupé. She took off a glove and put her strong fingers down into the forest of new green chrysanthemum sprouts that were growing around the old roots. She spread the leaves and looked down among the close-growing stems. No aphids were there, no sow bugs or snails or cutworms. Her terrier fingers destroyed such pests before they could get started.

Elisa started at the sound of her husband's voice. He had come near quietly, and he leaned over the wire fence that protected her flower garden from cattle and dogs and chickens.

"At it again," he said. "You've got a strong new crop coming."

Elisa straightened her back and pulled on the gardening glove again. "Yes. They'll be strong this coming year." In her tone and on her face there was a little smugness.

"You've got a gift with things," Henry observed. "Some of those yellow chrysanthemums you had this year were ten inches across. I wish you'd work out in the orchard and raise some apples that big."

Her eyes sharpened. "Maybe I could do it, too. I've a gift with things, all right. My mother had it. She could stick anything in the ground and make it grow. She said it was having planters' hands that knew how to do it."

"Well, it sure works with flowers," he said.

"Henry, who were those men you were talking to?"

"Why, sure, that's what I came to tell you. They were from the Western Meat Company. I sold those thirty head of three-year-old steers. Got nearly my own price, too."

"Good," she said. "Good for you."

"And I thought," he continued, "I thought how it's Saturday afternoon, and we might go into Salinas for dinner at a restaurant, and then to a picture show—to celebrate, you see."

"Good," she repeated. "Oh, yes. That will be good."

Henry put on his joking tone. "There's fights tonight. How'd you like to go to the fights?"

"Oh, no," she said breathlessly. "No, I wouldn't like fights."

"Just fooling, Elisa. We'll go to a movie. Let's see. It's two now. I'm going to take Scotty and bring down those steers from the hill. It'll take us maybe two hours. We'll go in town about five and have dinner at the Cominos Hotel. Like that?"

"Of course I'll like it. It's good to eat away from home."

"All right, then. I'll go get up a couple of horses."

She said: "I'll have plenty of time to transplant some of these sets, I guess."

She heard her husband calling Scotty down by the barn. And a little later she saw the two men ride up the pale yellow hillside in search of the steers.

There was a little square sandy bed kept for rooting the chrysanthemums. With her trowel she turned the soil over and over, and smoothed it and patted it firm. Then she dug ten parallel trenches to receive the sets. Back at the chrysanthemum bed she pulled out the little crisp shoots, trimmed off the leaves of each one with her scissors and laid it on a small orderly pile.

A squeak of wheels and plod of hoofs came from the road. Elisa looked up. The country road ran along the dense bank of willows and cottonwoods that bordered the river, and up this road came a curious vehicle, curiously drawn. It was an old spring-wagon, with a round canvas top on it like the cover of a prairie schooner. It was drawn by an old bay horse and a little gray-and-white burro. A big stubble-bearded man sat between the cover flaps and drove the crawling team. Underneath the wagon, between the hind wheels, a lean and rangy mongrel dog walked sedately. Words were painted on the canvas, in clumsy, crooked letters. "Pots, pans, knives, sisors, lawn mores, Fixed." Two rows of articles, and the triumphantly definitive "Fixed" below. The black paint had run down in little sharp points beneath each letter.

Elisa, squatting on the ground, watched to see the crazy, loose-jointed wagon pass by. But it didn't pass. It turned into the farm road in front of her house, crooked old wheels skirling and squeaking. The rangy dog darted from between the wheels and ran ahead. Instantly the two ranch shepherds flew out at him. Then all three stopped, and with stiff and quivering tails, with taut straight legs, with ambassadorial dignity, they slowly circled, sniffing daintily. The caravan pulled up to Elisa's wire fence and stopped. Now the newcomer dog, feeling out-numbered, lowered his tail and retired under the wagon with raised hackles and bared teeth.

The man on the wagon seat called out: "That's a bad dog in a fight when he gets started."

Elisa laughed. "I see he is. How soon does he generally get started?"

The man caught up her laughter and echoed it heartily. "Sometimes not for weeks and weeks," he said. He climbed stiffly down, over the wheel. The horse and the donkey drooped like unwatered flowers.

Elisa saw that he was a very big man. Although his hair and beard were graying, he did not look old. His worn black suit was wrinkled and spotted with grease. The laughter had disappeared from his face and eyes the moment his laughing voice ceased. His eyes were dark, and they were full of the brooding that gets in the eyes of teamsters and of sailors. The calloused hands he rested on the wire fence were cracked, and every crack was a black line. He took off his battered hat.

"I'm off my general road, ma'am," he said. "Does this dirt road cut over across the river to the Los Angeles highway?"

Elisa stood up and shoved the thick scissors in her apron pocket. "Well, yes, it does, but it winds around and then fords the river. I don't think your team could pull through the sand."

He replied with some asperity: "It might surprise you what them beasts can pull through."

"When they get started?" she asked.

He smiled for a second. "Yes. When they get started."

"Well," said Elisa, "I think you'll save time if you go back to the Salinas road and pick up the highway there."

He drew a big finger down the chicken wire and made it sing. "I ain't in any hurry, ma'am. I go from Seattle to San Diego and back every year. Takes all my time. About six months each way. I aim to follow nice weather."

Elisa took off her gloves and stuffed them in the apron pocket with the scissors. She touched the under edge of her man's hat, searching for fugitive hairs. "That sounds like a nice kind of a way to live," she said.

He leaned confidentially over the fence. "Maybe you noticed the writing on my wagon. I mend pots and sharpen knives and scissors. You got any of them things to do?"

"Oh, no," she said quickly. "Nothing like that." Her eyes hardened with resistance.

"Scissors is the worst thing," he explained. "Most people just ruin scissors trying to sharpen 'em, but I know how. I got a special tool. It's a little bobbit kind of thing, and patented. But it sure does the trick."

"No. My scissors are all sharp."

"All right, then. Take a pot," he continued earnestly, "a bent pot, or a pot with a hole. I can make it like new so you don't have to buy no new ones. That's a saving for you."

"No," she said shortly. "I tell you I have nothing like that for you to do."

His face fell to an exaggerated sadness. His voice took on a whining undertone. "I ain't had a thing to do today. Maybe I won't have no supper tonight. You see I'm off my regular road. I know folks on the highway clear from Seattle to San Diego. They save their things for me to sharpen up because they know I do it so good and save them money."

"I'm sorry," Elisa said irritably. "I haven't anything for you to do."

His eyes left her face and fell to searching the ground. They roamed about until they came to the chrysanthemum bed where she had been working. "What's them plants, ma'am?"

The irritation and resistance melted from Elisa's face. "Oh, those are chrysanthemums, giant whites and yellows. I raise them every year, bigger than anybody around here."

"Kind of a long-stemmed flower? Looks like a quick puff of colored smoke?" he asked.

"That's it. What a nice way to describe them."

"They smell kind of nasty till you get used to them," he said.

"It's a good bitter smell," she retorted, "not nasty at all."

He changed his tone quickly. "I like the smell myself."

"I had ten-inch blooms this year," she said.

The man leaned farther over the fence. "Look. I know a lady down the road a piece, has got the nicest garden you ever seen. Got nearly every kind of flower but no chrysantheums. Last time I was mending a copper-bottom washtub for her (that's a hard job but I do it good), she said to me: 'If you ever run acrost some nice chrysantheums I wish you'd try to get me a few seeds.' That's what she told me."

Elisa's eyes grew alert and eager. "She couldn't have known much about chrysanthemums. You *can* raise them from seed, but it's much easier to root the little sprouts you see there."

"Oh," he said. "I s'pose I can't take none to her, then."

"Why yes you can," Elisa cried. "I can put some in damp sand, and you can carry them right along with you. They'll take root in the pot if you keep them damp. And then she can transplant them."

"She'd sure like to have some, ma'am. You say they're nice ones?"

"Beautiful," she said. "Oh, beautiful." Her eyes shone. She tore off the battered hat and shook out her dark pretty hair. "I'll put them in a flower pot, and you can take them right with you. Come into the yard."

While the man came through the picket gate Elisa ran excitedly along the geranium-bordered path to the back of the house. And she returned carrying a big red flower pot. The gloves were forgotten now. She kneeled on the ground by the starting bed and dug up the sandy soil with her fingers and scooped it into the bright new flower pot. Then she picked up the little pile of shoots she had prepared. With her strong fingers she pressed them into the sand and tamped around them with her knuckles. The man stood over her. "I'll tell you what to do," she said. "You remember so you can tell the lady."

"Yes, I'll try to remember."

"Well, look. These will take root in about a month. Then she must set them out, about a foot apart in good rich earth like this, see?" She lifted a handful of dark soil for him to look at. "They'll grow fast and tall. Now remember this: In July tell her to cut them down, about eight inches from the ground."

"Before they bloom?" he asked.

"Yes, before they bloom." Her face was tight with eagerness. "They'll grow right up again. About the last of September the buds will start."

She stopped and seemed perplexed. "It's the budding that takes the most care," she said hesitantly. "I don't know how to tell you." She looked deep into his eyes, searchingly. Her mouth opened a little, and she seemed to be listening. "I'll try to tell you," she said. "Did you ever hear of planting hands?"

"Can't say I have, ma'am."

"Well I can only tell you what it feels like. It's when you're picking off the buds you don't want. Everything goes right down into your fingertips. You watch your fingers work. They do it themselves. You can feel how it is. They pick and pick the buds. They never make a mistake. They're with the plant. Do you see? Your fingers and the plant. You can feel that, right up your arm. They know. They never make a mistake. You can feel it. When you're like that you can't do anything wrong. Do you see that? Can you understand that?"

She was kneeling on the ground looking up at him. Her breast swelled passionately.

The man's eyes narrowed. He looked away self-consciously. "Maybe I know," he said. "Sometimes in the night in the wagon there—"

Elisa's voice grew husky. She broke in on him: "I've never lived as you do, but I know what you mean. When the night is dark—why, the stars are sharp-pointed, and there's quiet. Why, you rise up and up! Every pointed star gets driven into your body. It's like that. Hot and sharp and—lovely."

Kneeling there, her hand went out toward his legs in the greasy black trousers. Her hesitant fingers almost touched the cloth. Then her hand dropped to the ground. She crouched low like a fawning dog.

He said: "It's nice, just like you say. Only when you don't have no dinner, it ain't."

She stood up then, very straight, and her face was ashamed. She held the flower pot out to him and placed it gently in his arms. "Here. Put it in your wagon, on the seat, where you can watch it. Maybe I can find something for you to do."

At the back of the house she dug in the can pile and found two old and battered aluminum saucepans. She carried them back and gave them to him. "Here, maybe you can fix these."

His manner changed. He became professional. "Good as new I can fix them." At the back of his wagon he set a little anvil, and out of an oily tool-box dug a small machine hammer. Elisa came through the gate to watch him while he pounded out the dents in the kettles. His mouth grew sure and knowing. At a difficult part of the work he sucked his under-lip.

"You sleep right in the wagon?" Elisa asked.

"Right in the wagon, ma'am. Rain or shine I'm dry as a cow in there."

"It must be nice," she said. "It must be very nice. I wish women could do such things."

"It ain't the right kind of a life for a woman."

Her upper lip raised a little, showing her teeth. "How do you know? How can you tell?" she said.

"I don't know, ma'am," he protested. "Of course I don't know. Now here's your kettles, done. You don't have to buy no new ones."

"How much?"

"Oh, fifty cents'll do. I keep my prices down and my work good. That's why I have all them satisfied customers up and down the highway."

Elisa brought him a fifty-cent piece from the house and dropped it in his hand. "You might be surprised to have a rival sometime. I can sharpen scissors, too. And I can beat the dents out of little pots. I could show you what a woman might do."

He put his hammer back in the oily box and shoved the little anvil out of sight. "It would be a lonely life for a woman, ma'am, and a scarey life, too, with animals creeping under the wagon all night." He climbed over the single-tree, steadying himself with a hand on the burro's white rump. He settled himself in the seat, picked up the lines. "Thank you kindly, ma'am," he said. "I'll do like you told me; I'll go back and catch the Salinas road."

"Mind," she called, "if you're long in getting there, keep the sand damp."

"Sand, ma'am? . . . Sand? Oh, sure. You mean around the chrysantheums. Sure I will." He clucked his tongue. The beasts leaned luxuriously into their collars. The mongrel dog took his place between the back wheels. The wagon turned and crawled out the entrance road and back the way it had come, along the river.

Elisa stood in front of her wire fence watching the slow progress of the caravan. Her shoulders were straight, her head thrown back, her eyes half-closed, so that the scene came vaguely into them. Her lips moved silently, forming the words "Good-bye—good-bye." Then she whispered: "That's a bright direction. There's a glowing there." The sound of her whisper startled her. She shook herself free and looked about to see whether anyone had been listening. Only the dogs had heard. They lifted their heads toward her from their sleeping in the dust, and then stretched out their chins and settled asleep again. Elisa turned and ran hurriedly into the house.

In the kitchen she reached behind the stove and felt the water tank. It was full of hot water from the noonday cooking. In the bathroom she tore off her soiled clothes and flung them into the corner. And then she scrubbed herself with a little block of pumice, legs and thighs, loins and chest and arms, until her skin was scratched and red. When she had dried herself she stood in front of a mirror in her bedroom and looked at her body. She tightened her stomach and threw out her chest. She turned and looked over her shoulder at her back.

After a while she began to dress, slowly. She put on her newest underclothing and her nicest stockings and the dress which was the symbol of her prettiness. She worked carefully on her hair, pencilled her eyebrows and rouged her lips.

Before she was finished she heard the little thunder of hoofs and the shouts of Henry and his helper as they drove the red steers into the corral. She heard the gate bang shut and set herself for Henry's arrival.

His step sounded on the porch. He entered the house calling: "Elisa, where are you?"

"In my room, dressing. I'm not ready. There's hot water for your bath. Hurry up. It's getting late."

When she heard him splashing in the tub, Elisa laid his dark suit on the bed, and shirt and socks and tie beside it. She stood his polished shoes on the floor beside the bed. Then she went to the porch and sat primly and stiffly down. She looked toward the river road where the willow-line was still yellow with frosted leaves so that under the high gray fog they seemed a thin band of sunshine. This was the only color in the gray afternoon. She sat unmoving for a long time. Her eyes blinked rarely.

Henry came banging out of the door, shoving his tie inside his vest as he came. Elisa stiffened and her face grew tight. Henry stopped short and looked at her. "Why—why, Elisa. You look so nice!"

"Nice? You think I look nice? What do you mean by 'nice'?"

Henry blundered on. "I don't know. I mean you look different, strong and happy."

"I am strong? Yes, strong. What do you mean 'strong'?"

He looked bewildered. "You're playing some kind of a game," he said helplessly. "It's a kind of a play. You look strong enough to break a calf over your knee, happy enough to eat it like a watermelon."

For a second she lost her rigidity. "Henry! Don't talk like that. You didn't know what you said." She grew complete again. "I'm strong," she boasted. "I never knew before how strong."

Henry looked down toward the tractor shed, and when he brought his eyes back to her, they were his own again. "I'll get out the car. You can put on your coat while I'm starting."

Elisa went into the house. She heard him drive to the gate and idle down his motor, and then she took a long time to put on her hat. She pulled it here and pressed it there. When Henry turned the motor off she slipped into her coat and went out.

The little roadster bounced along on the dirt road by the river, raising the birds and driving the rabbits into the brush. Two cranes flapped heavily over the willow-line and dropped into the river-bed.

Far ahead on the road Elisa saw a dark speck. She knew.

She tried not to look as they passed it, but her eyes would not obey. She whispered to herself sadly: "He might have thrown them off the road. That wouldn't have been much trouble, not very much. But he kept the pot," she explained. "He had to keep the pot. That's why he couldn't get them off the road."

The roadster turned a bend and she saw the caravan ahead. She swung full around toward her husband so she could not see the little covered wagon and the mis-matched team as the car passed them.

In a moment it was over. The thing was done. She did not look back.

She said loudly, to be heard above the motor: "It will be good, tonight, a good dinner."

"Now you're changed again," Henry complained. He took one hand from the wheel and patted her knee. "I ought to take you in to dinner oftener. It would be good for both of us. We get so heavy out on the ranch."

"Henry," she asked, "could we have wine at dinner?"

"Sure we could. Say! That will be fine."

She was silent for a while; then she said: "Henry, at those prize-fights, do the men hurt each other very much?"

"Sometimes a little, not often. Why?"

"Well, I've read how they break noses, and blood runs down their chests. I've read how the fighting gloves get heavy and soggy with blood."

He looked around at her. "What's the matter, Elisa? I didn't know you read things like that." He brought the car to a stop, then turned to the right over the Salinas River bridge.

"Do any women ever go to the fights?" she asked.

"Oh, sure, some. What's the matter, Elisa? Do you want to go? I don't think you'd like it, but I'll take you if you really want to go."

She relaxed limply in the seat. "Oh, no. No. I don't want to go. I'm sure I don't." Her face was turned away from him. "It will be enough if we can have wine. It will be plenty." She turned up her coat collar so he could not see that she was crying weakly—like an old woman.

1938

from The Grapes of Wrath

Chapter One

To the red country and part of the gray country of Oklahoma, the last rains came gently, and they did not cut the scarred earth. The plows crossed and recrossed the rivulet marks. The last rains lifted the corn quickly and scattered weed colonies and grass along the sides of the roads so that the gray country and the dark red country began to disappear under a green cover. In the last part of May the sky grew pale and the clouds that had hung in high puffs for so long in the spring were dissipated. The sun flared down on the growing corn day after day until a line of brown spread along the edge of each green bayonet. The clouds appeared, and went away, and in a while they did not try any more. The weeds grew darker green to protect themselves, and they did not spread any more. The surface of the earth crusted, a thin hard crust, and as the sky became pale, so the earth became pale, pink in the red country and white in the gray country.

In the water-cut gullies the earth dusted down in dry little streams. Gophers and ant lions started small avalanches. And as the sharp sun struck day after day, the leaves of the young corn became less stiff and erect; they bent in a curve at first, and then, as the central ribs of strength grew weak, each leaf tilted downward. Then it was June, and the sun shone more fiercely. The brown lines on the corn leaves widened and moved in on the central ribs. The weeds frayed and edged back toward their roots. The air was thin and the sky more pale; and every day the earth paled.

In the roads where the teams moved, where the wheels milled the ground and the hooves of the horses beat the ground, the dirt crust broke and the dust formed. Every moving thing lifted the dust into the air: a walking man lifted a thin layer as high as his waist, and a wagon lifted the dust as high as the fence tops, and an automobile boiled a cloud behind it. The dust was long in settling back again.

When June was half gone, the big clouds moved up out of Texas and the Gulf, high heavy clouds, rain-heads. The men in the fields looked up at the clouds and sniffed at them and held wet fingers up to sense the wind. And the horses were nervous while the clouds were up. The rain-heads dropped a little spattering and hurried on to some other country. Behind them the sky was pale again and the sun flared. In the dust there were drop craters where the rain had fallen, and there were clean splashes on the corn, and that was all.

A gentle wind followed the rain clouds, driving them on northward, a wind that softly clashed the drying corn. A day went by and the wind increased, steady, unbroken by gusts. The dust from the roads fluffed up and spread out and fell on the weeds beside the fields, and fell into the fields a little way. Now the wind grew strong and hard and it worked at the rain crust in the corn fields. Little by little the sky was darkened by the mixing dust, and the wind felt over the earth, loosened the dust, and carried it away. The wind grew stronger. The rain crust broke and the dust lifted up out of the fields and drove gray plumes into the air like sluggish smoke. The corn threshed the wind and made a dry, rushing sound. The finest dust did not settle back to earth now, but disappeared into the darkening sky.

The wind grew stronger, whisked under stones, carried up straws and old leaves, and even little clods, marking its course as it sailed across the fields. The air and the sky darkened and through them the sun shone redly, and there was a raw sting in the air. During a night the wind raced faster over the land, dug cunningly among the rootlets of the corn, and the corn fought the wind with its weakened leaves until the roots were freed by the prying wind and then each stalk settled wearily sideways toward the earth and pointed the direction of the wind.

The dawn came, but no day. In the gray sky a red sun appeared, a dim red circle that gave a little light, like dusk; and as that day advanced, the dusk slipped back toward darkness, and the wind cried and whimpered over the fallen corn.

Men and women huddled in their houses, and they tied handkerchiefs over their noses when they went out, and wore goggles to protect their eyes.

When the night came again it was black night, for the stars could not pierce the dust to get down, and the window lights could not even spread beyond their own yards. Now the dust was evenly mixed with the air, an emulsion of dust and air. Houses were shut tight, and cloth wedged around doors and windows, but the dust came in so thinly that it could not be seen in the air, and it settled like pollen on the chairs and tables, on the dishes. The people brushed it from their shoulders. Little lines of dust lay at the door sills.

In the middle of that night the wind passed on and left the land quiet. The dust-filled air muffled sound more completely than fog does. The people, lying in their beds, heard the wind stop. They awakened when the rushing wind was gone. They lay quietly and listened deep into the stillness. Then the roosters crowed, and their voices were muffled, and the people stirred restlessly in their beds and wanted the morning. They knew it would take a long time for the dust to settle out of the air. In the morning the dust hung like fog, and the sun was as red as ripe new blood. All day the dust sifted down from the sky, and the next day it sifted down. An even blanket covered the earth. It settled on the corn, piled up on the tops of the fence posts, piled up on the wires; it settled on roofs, blanketed the weeds and trees.

The people came out of their houses and smelled the hot stinging air and covered their noses from it. And the children came out of the houses, but they did not run or shout as they would have done after a rain. Men stood by their fences and looked at the ruined corn, drying fast now, only a little green showing through the film of dust. The men were silent and they did not move often. And the women came out of the houses to stand beside their men—to feel whether this time the men would break. The women studied the men's faces secretly, for the corn could go, as long as something else remained. The children stood near by, drawing figures in the dust with bare toes, and the children sent exploring senses out to see whether men and women would break. The children peeked at the faces of the men and women, and then drew careful lines in the dust with their toes. Horses came to the watering troughs and nuzzled the water to clear the surface dust. After a while the faces of the watching men lost their bemused perplexity and became hard and angry and resistant. Then the women knew that they were safe and that there was no break. Then they asked, What'll we do? And the men replied, I don't know. But it was all right. The women knew it was all right, and the watching children knew it was all right. Women and children knew deep in themselves that no misfortune was too great to bear if their men were whole. The women went into the houses to their work, and the children began to play, but cautiously at first. As the day went forward the sun became less red. It flared down on the dust-blanketed land. The men sat in the doorways of their houses; their hands were busy with sticks and little rocks. The men sat still—thinking—figuring.

Chapter Five

The owners of the land came onto the land, or more often a spokesman for the owners came. They came in closed cars, and they felt the dry earth with their fingers, and sometimes they drove big earth augers into the ground for soil tests. The tenants, from their sun-beaten dooryards, watched uneasily when the closed cars drove along the fields. And at last the owner men drove into the dooryards and sat in their cars to talk out of the windows. The tenant men stood beside the cars for a while, and then squatted on their hams and found sticks with which to mark the dust.

In the open doors the women stood looking out, and behind them the children—corn-headed children, with wide eyes, one bare foot on top of the other bare foot, and the toes working. The women and the children watched their men talking to the owner men. They were silent.

Some of the owner men were kind because they hated what they had to do, and some of them were angry because they hated to be cruel, and some of them were cold because they had long ago found that one could not be an owner unless one were cold. And all of them were caught in something larger than themselves. Some of them hated the mathematics that drove them, and some were afraid, and some worshiped the mathematics because it provided a refuge from thought and from feeling. If a bank or a finance company owned the land, the owner man said, The Bank—or the Company—needs—wants—insists—must have—as though the Bank or the Company were a monster, with thought and feeling, which had ensnared them. These last would take no responsibility for the banks or the companies because they were men and slaves, while the banks were machines and masters all at the same time. Some of the owner men were a little proud to be slaves to such cold and powerful masters. The owner men sat in the cars and explained. You know the land is poor. You've scrabbled at it long enough, God knows.

The squatting tenant men nodded and wondered and drew figures in the dust, and yes, they knew, God knows. If the dust only wouldn't fly. If the top would only stay on the soil, it might not be so bad.

The owner men went on leading to their point: You know the land's getting poorer. You know what cotton does to the land; robs it, sucks all the blood out of it.

The squatters nodded—they knew, God knew. If they could only rotate the crops they might pump blood back into the land.

Well, it's too late. And the owner men explained the workings and the thinkings of the monster that was stronger than they were. A man can hold land if he can just eat and pay taxes; he can do that.

Yes, he can do that until his crops fail one day and he has to borrow money from the bank.

But—you see, a bank or a company can't do that, because those creatures don't breathe air, don't eat side-meat. They breathe profits; they eat the interest on money.

If they don't get it, they die the way you die without air, without side-meat. It is a sad thing, but it is so. It is just so.

The squatting men raised their eyes to understand. Can't we just hang on? Maybe the next year will be a good year. God knows how much cotton next year. And with all the wars—God knows what price cotton will bring. Don't they make explosives out of cotton? And uniforms? Get enough wars and cotton'll hit the ceiling. Next year, maybe. They looked up questioningly.

We can't depend on it. The bank—the monster has to have profits all the time. It can't wait. It'll die. No, taxes go on. When the monster stops growing, it dies. It can't stay one size.

Soft fingers began to tap the sill of the car window, and hard fingers tightened on the restless drawing sticks. In the doorways of the sun-beaten tenant houses, women sighed and then shifted feet so that the one that had been down was now on top, and the toes working. Dogs came sniffing near the owner cars and wetted on all four tires one after another. And chickens lay in the sunny dust and fluffed their feathers to get the cleansing dust down to the skin. In the little sties the pigs grunted inquiringly over the muddy remnants of the slops.

The squatting men looked down again. What do you want us to do? We can't take less share of the crop—we're half starved now. The kids are hungry all the time. We got no clothes, torn an' ragged. If all the neighbors weren't the same, we'd be ashamed to go to meeting.

And at last the owner men came to the point. The tenant system won't work any more. One man on a tractor can take the place of twelve or fourteen families. Pay him a wage and take all the crop. We have to do it. We don't like to do it. But the monster's sick. Something's happened to the monster.

But you'll kill the land with cotton.

We know. We've got to take cotton quick before the land dies. Then we'll sell the land. Lots of families in the East would like to own a piece of land.

The tenant men looked up alarmed. But what'll happen to us? How'll we eat?

You'll have to get off the land. The plows'll go through the dooryard.

And now the squatting men stood up angrily. Grampa took up the land, and he had to kill the Indians and drive them away. And Pa was born here, and he killed weeds and snakes. Then a bad year came and he had to borrow a little money. An' we was born here. There in the door—our children born here. And Pa had to borrow money. The bank owned the land then, but we stayed and we got a little bit of what we raised.

We know that—all that. It's not us, it's the bank. A bank isn't like a man. Or an owner with fifty thousand acres, he isn't like a man either. That's the monster.

Sure, cried the tenant men, but it's our land. We measured it and broke it up. We were born on it, and we got killed on it, died on it. Even if it's no good, it's still ours. That's what makes it ours—being born on it, working it, dying on it. That makes ownership, not a paper with numbers on it.

We're sorry. It's not us. It's the monster. The bank isn't like a man.

Yes, but the bank is only made of men.

No, you're wrong there—quite wrong there. The bank is something else than men. It happens that every man in a bank hates what the bank does, and yet the bank does it. The bank is something more than men, I tell you. It's the monster. Men made it, but they can't control it.

The tenants cried, Grampa killed Indians, Pa killed snakes for the land. Maybe we can kill banks—they're worse than Indians and snakes. Maybe we got to fight to keep our land, like Pa and Grampa did.

And now the owner men grew angry. You'll have to go.

But it's ours, the tenant men cried. We—

No. The bank, the monster owns it. You'll have to go.

We'll get our guns, like Grampa when the Indians came. What then?

Well—first the sheriff, and then the troops. You'll be stealing if you try to stay, you'll be murderers if you kill to stay. The monster isn't men, but it can make men do what it wants.

But if we go, where'll we go? How'll we go? We got no money.

We're sorry, said the owner men. The bank, the fifty-thousand-acre owner can't be responsible. You're on land that isn't yours. Once over the line maybe you can pick cotton in the fall. Maybe you can go on relief. Why don't you go on west to California? There's work there, and it never gets cold. Why, you can reach out anywhere and pick an orange. Why, there's always some kind of crop to work in. Why don't you go there? And the owner men started their cars and rolled away.

The tenant men squatted down on their hams again to mark the dust with a stick, to figure, to wonder. Their sun-burned faces were dark, and their sun-whipped eyes were light. The women moved cautiously out of the doorways toward their men, and the children crept behind the women, cautiously, ready to run. The bigger boys squatted beside their fathers, because that made them men. After a time the women asked, What did he want?

And the men looked up for a second, and the smolder of pain was in their eyes. We got to get off. A tractor and a superintendent. Like factories.

Where'll we go? the women asked.

We don't know. We don't know.

And the women went quickly, quietly back into the houses and herded the children ahead of them. They knew that a man so hurt and so perplexed may turn in anger, even on people he loves. They left the men alone to figure and to wonder in the dust.

After a time perhaps the tenant man looked about—at the pump put in ten years ago, with a goose-neck handle and iron flowers on the spout, at the chopping block where a thousand chickens had been killed, at the hand plow lying in the shed, and the patent crib hanging in the rafters over it.

The children crowded about the women in the houses. What we going to do, Ma? Where we going to go?

The women said, We don't know, yet. Go out and play. But don't go near your father. He might whale you if you go near him. And the women went on with the work, but all the time they watched the men squatting in the dust—perplexed and figuring.

The tractors came over the roads and into the fields, great crawlers moving like insects, having the incredible strength of insects. They crawled over the ground, laying the track and rolling on it and picking it up. Diesel tractors, puttering while they stood idle; they thundered when they moved, and then settled down to a droning roar. Snub-nosed monsters, raising the dust and sticking their snouts into it, straight down the country, across the country, through fences, through dooryards, in and out of gullies in straight lines. They did not run on the ground, but on their own roadbeds. They ignored hills and gulches, water courses, fences, houses.

The man sitting in the iron seat did not look like a man; gloved, goggled, rubber dust mask over nose and mouth, he was a part of the monster, a robot in the seat. The thunder of the cylinders sounded through the country, became one with the air and the earth, so that earth and air muttered in sympathetic vibration. The driver could not control it—straight across country it went, cutting through a dozen farms and straight back. A twitch at the controls could swerve the cat', but the driver's hands could not twitch because the monster that built the tractor, the monster that sent the tractor out, had somehow got into the driver's hands, into his brain and muscle, had goggled him and muzzled him—goggled his mind, muzzled his speech, goggled his perception, muzzled his protest. He could not see the land as it was, he could not smell the land as it smelled; his feet did not stamp the clods or feel the warmth and power of the earth. He sat in an iron seat and stepped on iron pedals. He could not cheer or beat or curse or encourage the extension of his power, and because of this he could not cheer or whip or curse or encourage himself. He did not know or own or trust or beseech the land. If a seed dropped did not germinate, it was nothing. If the young thrusting plant withered in drought or drowned in a flood of rain, it was no more to the driver than to the tractor.

He loved the land no more than the bank loved the land. He could admire the tractor—its machined surfaces, its surge of power, the roar of its detonating cylinders; but it was not his tractor. Behind the tractor rolled the shining disks, cutting the earth with blades—not plowing but surgery, pushing the cut earth to the right where the second row of disks cut it and pushed it to the left; slicing blades shining, polished by the cut earth. And pulled behind the disks, the harrows combing with iron teeth so that the little clods broke up and the earth lay smooth. Behind the harrows, the long seeders—twelve curved iron penes erected in the foundry, orgasms set by gears, raping methodically, raping without passion. The driver sat in his iron seat and he was proud of the straight lines he did not will, proud of the tractor he did not own or love, proud of the power he could not control. And when that crop grew, and was harvested, no man had crumbled a hot clod in his fingers and let the earth sift past his fingertips. No man had touched the seed, or lusted for the growth. Men ate what they had not raised, had no connection with the bread. The land bore under iron, and under iron gradually died; for it was not loved or hated, it had no prayers or curses.

At noon the tractor driver stopped sometimes near a tenant house and opened his lunch: sandwiches wrapped in waxed paper, white bread, pickle, cheese, Spam, a piece of pie branded like an engine part. He ate without relish. And tenants not yet moved away came out to see him, looked curiously while the goggles were taken off, and the rubber dust mask, leaving white circles around the eyes and a large white circle around nose and mouth. The exhaust of the tractor puttered on, for fuel is so cheap it is more efficient to leave the engine running than to heat the Diesel nose for a new start. Curious children crowded close, ragged children who ate their fried dough as they watched. They watched hungrily the unwrapping of the sandwiches, and their hunger-sharpened noses smelled the pickle, cheese, and Spam. They didn't speak to the driver. They watched his hand as it carried food to his mouth. They did not watch him chewing; their eyes followed the hand that held the sandwich. After a while the tenant who could not leave the place came out and squatted in the shade beside the tractor.

"Why, you're Joe Davis's boy!"

"Sure," the driver said.

"Well, what you doing this kind of work for—against your own people?"

"Three dollars a day. I got damn sick of creeping for my dinner—and not getting it. I got a wife and kids. We got to eat. Three dollars a day, and it comes every day."

"That's right," the tenant said. "But for your three dollars a day fifteen or twenty families can't eat at all. Nearly a hundred people have to go out and wander on the roads for your three dollars a day. Is that right?"

And the driver said, "Can't think of that. Got to think of my own kids. Three dollars a day, and it comes every day. Times are changing, mister, don't you know? Can't make a living on the land unless you've got two, five, ten thousand acres and a tractor. Crop land isn't for little guys like us any more. You don't kick up a howl because you can't make Fords, or because you're not the telephone company. Well, crops are like that now. Nothing to do about it. You try to get three dollars a day someplace. That's the only way."

The tenant pondered. "Funny thing how it is. If a man owns a little property, that property is him, it's part of him, and it's like him. If he owns property only so he can walk on it and handle it and be sad when it isn't doing well, and feel fine when the rain falls on it, that property is him, and some way he's bigger because he owns it. Even if he isn't successful he's big with his property. That is so."

And the tenant pondered more. "But let a man get property he doesn't see, or can't take time to get his fingers in, or can't be there to walk on it—why, then the property is the man. He can't do what he wants, he can't think what he wants. The property is the man, stronger than he is. And he is small, not big. Only his possessions are big—and he's the servant of his property. That is so, too."

The driver munched the branded pie and threw the crust away. "Times are changed, don't you know? Thinking about stuff like that don't feed the kids. Get your three dollars a day, feed your kids. You got no call to worry about anybody's kids but your own. You get a reputation for talking like that, and you'll never get three dollars a day. Big shots won't give you three dollars a day if you worry about anything but your three dollars a day."

"Nearly a hundred people on the road for your three dollars. Where will we go?"

"And that reminds me," the driver said, "you better get out soon. I'm going through the dooryard after dinner."

"You filled in the well this morning."

"I know. Had to keep the line straight. But I'm going through the dooryard after dinner. Got to keep the lines straight. And—well, you know Joe Davis, my old man, so I'll tell you this. I got orders wherever there's a family not moved out—if I have an accident—you know, get too close and cave the house in a little—well, I might get a couple of dollars. And my youngest kid never had no shoes yet."

"I built it with my hands. Straightened old nails to put the sheathing on. Rafters are wired to the stringers with baling wire. It's mine. I built it. You bump it down—

I'll be in the window with a rifle. You even come too close and I'll pot you like a rabbit."

"It's not me. There's nothing I can do. I'll lose my job if I don't do it. And look—suppose you kill me? They'll just hang you, but long before you're hung there'll be another guy on the tractor, and he'll bump the house down. You're not killing the right guy."

"That's so," the tenant said. "Who gave you orders? I'll go after him. He's the one to kill."

"You're wrong. He got his orders from the bank. The bank told him, 'Clear those people out or it's your job.'"

"Well, there's a president of the bank. There's a board of directors. I'll fill up the magazine of the rifle and go into the bank."

The driver said, "Fellow was telling me the bank gets orders from the East. The orders were, 'Make the land show profit or we'll close you up.'"

"But where does it stop? Who can we shoot? I don't aim to starve to death before I kill the man that's starving me."

"I don't know. Maybe there's nobody to shoot. Maybe the thing isn't men at all. Maybe, like you said, the property's doing it. Anyway I told you my orders."

"I got to figure," the tenant said. "We all got to figure. There's some way to stop this. It's not like lightning or earthquakes. We've got a bad thing made by men, and by God that's something we can change." The tenant sat in his doorway, and the driver thundered his engine and started off, tracks falling and curving, harrows combing, and the phalli of the seeder slipping into the ground. Across the dooryard the tractor cut, and the hard, foot-beaten ground was seeded field, and the tractor cut through again; the uncut space was ten feet wide. And back he came. The iron guard bit into the house-corner, crumbled the wall, and wrenched the little house from its foundation so that it fell sideways, crushed like a bug. And the driver was goggled and a rubber mask covered his nose and mouth. The tractor cut a straight line on, and the air and the ground vibrated with its thunder. The tenant man stared after it, his rifle in his hand. His wife was beside him, and the quiet children behind. And all of them stared after the tractor.

1939

Richard Wright 1908–1960

Richard Wright's home state of Mississippi was, at the time he was born near Natchez, the most oppressive place in the United States to be black. Wright himself would stress the point time and again. His earliest book, the short stories collected as *Uncle Tom's Children,* won first prize in a contest open to new writers working for the WPA during the Great Depression; yet, despite the acclaim publication brought him, he added to the augmented edition of the volume an essay on "The Ethics of Living Jim Crow" that outlined the experience with the caste system that forms the background of each story. Even earlier, when his first short story was published for a national audience in 1936, he provided his editor an autobiographical note stressing how he was forced by the poverty of his family to move all over Mississippi, Arkansas, and Tennessee; and how he had left school at the age of fifteen and taken on a string of the menial jobs available to black males. It is notable, though, that both of these early autobiographical sketches are associated with literary publication. The outline of Jim Crow experiences appears in a book that was given wide critical praise; and the short note detailing typically black southern experiences concludes with the remark, "At present I'm busy with a novel." Both statements demonstrated that the forced segregation and the economic and political practices designed to make black people inferior did not have their intended effect. Instead of becoming the victim of white supremacy, Richard Wright, through literacy and imagination, refused his fate.

Refusal did not mean he could ignore racism. Rather he took the experiences of being black in the South during the early years of the twentieth century and made them the material for literature that would strip away all pretense of rationality from racism, all justification, and expose the harsh brutality that lay beneath its ideology. This narrative design gained acclaim for Wright while he was still in his twenties. In 1937 *Story* magazine sponsored a contest open to all members of the Federal Writers Project who had not previously published a book. Wright, who was working on "Portrait of Harlem" for the American Guide Series issued by the Writers Project, submitted four stories he had written while living in Chicago. The contest judges, including the prominent novelist Sinclair Lewis, selected his manuscript for first prize, and *Story* arranged for its publication by Harper and Brothers in 1938 under the title *Uncle Tom's Children.* The stories in this first book of Wright's develop an ironic play on the popular term for accommodating to white demands by showing a series of protagonists becoming increasingly rebellious—less and less "Uncle Toms" and more and more radical—as they find the means to resist racism. To broaden the social context of the volume, Wright prepared an expanded edition of *Uncle Tom's Children,* including an autobiographical account entitled "The Ethics of Living Jim Crow" and the short story "Bright and Morning Star."

Despite the success of those stories, however, Wright feared that readers might read them sentimentally, shed tears rather than express rage. So, for *Native Son,* written when he had long since joined the great migration of black people from the fields of the South to the ghettos of northern cities, he conceived a protagonist who would defy anyone's attempt to see him as a mere victim. Bigger Thomas is, much like Wright, the product of American racial practices; and, like Wright, he has a core of inviolable selfhood that gradually grows into a sense of self-determining purpose. But Wright also makes him the murderer of two women who have no immediately personal responsibility for his condition; they are, in terms of their role in the fiction, instruments that break the cycle of fear and self-denigration in which Bigger has been confined by the social and material conditions of his life. The novel is prophetic of the price a nation must pay for racism, and to its contemporary audience it was a shocking reworking of the typical treatment of victims of society.

Though *Native Son* will probably remain Wright's best-known work, it bears close relationship to all of his subsequent writing, and in Wright's entire canon we are able to see a powerful consistency along with a broadening recognition of the significance of black experience. His autobiographical writings, *Black Boy* and *American Hunger,* present the heroic story of a man who bears some resemblance to the figure Americans like to call "self-made." In these works Wright takes pains to show himself to be an individualist with only his personal resources of mind and character to rely on, though the signs of his success are not financial improvement or control of others. Instead, Wright's self-portrait is marked by traits of rational understanding of events that entrap or mystify others and the capacity to use words to bridge the gap between society's underclass and his readers.

Though we must emphasize the unique sources of Wright's art and philosophy in African American life, we must recall that significant literature aims to speak to all readers whether or not they have shared the special experiences of the author. This universality is often remarked only in writing by members of a nation's dominant group; thus, white male novelists are more often called universal than are black or women novelists. That is a matter of literary politics or the result of unexamined assumptions. When it comes to "Bright and Morning Star," the narrative design is to make every reader, and any reader, the sympathetic companion of an African American heroine.

John M. Reilly
Howard University

PRIMARY WORKS

Uncle Tom's Children: Four Novellas, 1938 (as *Uncle Tom's Children: Five Long Stories,* 1940); *Native Son,* 1940; *The Outsider,* 1953; *Savage Holiday,* 1954; *The Long Dream,* 1958; *Eight Men,* 1961; *Lawd Today,* 1963; *Twelve Million Black Voices: A Folk History of the Negro in the United States,* 1941; *Black Boy: A Record of Childhood and Youth,* 1945; *Black Power: A Record of Reactions in a Land of Pathos,* 1954: *The Color Curtain: A Report on the Bandung Conference,* 1956: *Pagan Spain: A Report of a Journey into the Past,* 1957; *White Man, Listen!,* 1957; *American Hunger,* 1977.

Bright and Morning Star

I

She stood with her black face some six inches from the moist windowpane and wondered when on earth would it ever stop raining. It might keep up like this all week, she thought. She heard rain droning upon the roof and high up in the wet sky her eyes followed the silent rush of a bright shaft of yellow that swung from the airplane beacon in far off Memphis. Momently she could see it cutting through the rainy dark; it would hover a second like a gleaming sword above her head, then vanish. She sighed, troubling, Johnny-Boys been trampin in this slop all day wid no decent shoes on his feet. . . . Through the window she could see the rich black earth sprawling outside in the night. There was more rain than the clay could soak up; pools stood everywhere. She yawned and mumbled: "Rains good n bad. It kin make seeds bus up thu the groun, er it kin bog things down lika watah-soaked coffin." Her hands were folded loosely over her stomach and the hot air of the kitchen traced a filmy veil of sweat on her forehead. From the cook stove came the soft singing of burning wood and now and then a throaty bubble rose from a pot of simmering greens.

"Shucks, Johnny-Boy coulda let somebody else do all tha runnin in the rain. Theres others bettah fixed fer it than he is. But, naw! Johnny-Boy ain the one t trust nobody t do nothing. Hes gotta do it *all* hissef. . . ."

She glanced at a pile of damp clothes in a zinc tub. Waal, Ah bettah git t work. She turned, lifted a smoothing iron with a thick pad of cloth, touched a spit-wet finger to it with a quick, jerking motion: *smiiitz!* Yeah; its hot! Stooping, she took a blue work-shirt from the tub and shook it out. With a deft twist of her shoulder she caught the iron in her right hand; the fingers of her left hand took a piece of wax from a tin box and a frying sizzle came as she smeared the bottom. She was thinking of nothing now; her hands followed a lifelong ritual of toil. Spreading a sleeve, she ran the hot iron to and fro until the wet cloth became stiff. She was deep in the midst of her work when a song rose up out of the far off days of her childhood and broke through half-parted lips:

Hes the Lily of the Valley, the Bright n Mawnin Star
Hes the Fairest of Ten Thousan t mah soul . . .

A gust of wind dashed rain against the window. Johnny-Boy oughta c mon home n eat his suppah. Aw, Lawd! Itd be fine ef Sug could eat wid us tonight! Itd be like ol times! Mabbe aftah all it wont be long fo he comes back. Tha lettah Ah got from im las week said *Don give up hope. . . .* Yeah; we gotta live in hope. Then both of her sons, Sug and Johnny-Boy, would be back with her.

With an involuntary nervous gesture, she stopped and stood still, listening. But the only sound was the lulling fall of rain. Shucks, ain no usa me ackin this way, she thought. Ever time they gits ready to hol them meetings Ah gits jumpity. Ah been a lil scared ever since Sug went t jail. She heard the clock ticking and looked. Johnny-Boys a *hour* late! He sho mus be havin a time doin all tha trampin, trampin thu the mud. . . . But her fear was a quiet one; it was more like an intense brooding than a fear; it was a sort of hugging of hated facts so closely that she could feel their grain, like letting cold water run over her hand from a faucet on a winter morning.

She ironed again, faster now, as if she felt the more she engaged her body in work the less she would think. But how could she forget Johnny-Boy out there on those wet fields rounding up white and black Communists for a meeting tomorrow? And that was just what Sug had been doing when the sheriff had caught him, beat him, and tried to make him tell who and where his comrades were. Po Sug! They sho musta beat the boy somethin awful! But, thank Gawd, he didnt talk! He ain no weaklin, Sug ain! Hes been lion-hearted all his life long.

That had happened a year ago. And now each time those meetings came around the old terror surged back. While shoving the iron a cluster of toiling days returned; days of washing and ironing to feed Johnny-Boy and Sug so they could do party work; days of carrying a hundred pounds of white folks' clothes upon her head across fields sometimes wet and sometimes dry. But in those days a hundred pounds was nothing to carry carefully balanced upon her head while stepping by instinct over the corn and cotton rows. The only time it had seemed heavy was when she had heard of Sug's arrest. She had been coming home one morning with a bundle upon her head, her hands swinging idly by her sides, walking slowly with her eyes in front of her, when Bob, Johnny-Boy's pal, had called from across the fields and had come and told her that the sheriff had got Sug. That morning the bundle had become heavier than she could ever remember.

And with each passing week now, though she spoke of it to no one, things were becoming heavier. The tubs of water and the smoothing iron and the bundle of clothes were becoming harder to lift, with her back aching so; and her work was taking longer, all because Sug was gone and she didn't know just when Johnny-Boy would be taken too. To ease the ache of anxiety that was swelling her heart, she hummed, then sang softly:

He walks wid me, He talks wid me
He tells me Ahm His own. . . .

Guiltily, she stopped and smiled. Looks like Ah jus cant seem t fergit them ol songs, no mattah how hard Ah tries. . . . She had learned them when she was a little girl living and working on a farm. Every Monday morning from the corn and cotton fields the slow strains had floated from her mother's lips, lonely and haunting; and later, as the years had filled with gall, she had learned their deep meaning. Long hours of scrubbing floors for a few cents a day had taught her who Jesus was, what a great boon it was to cling to Him, to be like Him and suffer without a mumbling word. She had poured the yearning of her life into the songs, feeling buoyed with a faith beyond this world. The figure of the Man nailed in agony to the Cross, His burial in a cold grave, His transfigured Resurrection, His being breath and clay, God and Man—all had focused her feelings upon an imagery which had swept her life into a wondrous vision.

But as she had grown older, a cold white mountain, the white folks and their laws, had swum into her vision and shattered her songs and their spell of peace. To her that white mountain was temptation, something to lure her from her Lord, a part of the world God had made in order that she might endure it and come through all the stronger, just as Christ had risen with greater glory from the tomb. The days crowded with trouble had enhanced her faith and she had grown to love hardship with a bitter pride; she had obeyed the laws of the white folks with a soft smile of secret knowing.

After her mother had been snatched up to heaven in a chariot of fire, the years had brought her a rough workingman and two black babies, Sug and Johnny-Boy, all three of whom she had wrapped in the charm and magic of her vision. Then she was tested by no less than God; her man died, a trial which she bore with the strength shed by the grace of her vision; finally even the memory of her man faded into the vision itself, leaving her with two black boys growing tall, slowly into manhood.

Then one day grief had come to her heart when Johnny-Boy and Sug had walked forth demanding their lives. She had sought to fill their eyes with her vision, but they would have none of it. And she had wept when they began to boast of the strength shed by a new and terrible vision.

But she had loved them, even as she loved them now; bleeding, her heart had followed them. She could have done no less, being an old woman in a strange world. And day by day her sons had ripped from her startled eyes her old vision, and image by image had given her a new one, different, but great and strong enough to fling her into the light of another grace. The wrongs and sufferings of black men had taken the place of Him nailed to the Cross; the meager beginnings of the party had become another Resurrection; and the hate of those who would destroy her new faith had quickened in her a hunger to feel how deeply her new strength went.

"Lawd, Johnny-Boy," she would sometimes say, "Ah just wan them white folks t try t make me tell *who* is *in* the party n who *ain*! Ah just wan em t try, n Ahll show em somethin they never thought a black woman could have!"

But sometimes like tonight, while lost in the forgetfulness of work, the past and the present would become mixed in her; while toiling under a strange star for a new freedom the old songs would slip from her lips with their beguiling sweetness.

The iron was getting cold. She put more wood into the fire, stood again at the window and watched the yellow blade of light cut through the wet darkness. Johnny-Boy ain here yit. . . . Then, before she was aware of it, she was still, listening for sounds. Under the drone of rain she heard the slosh of feet in mud. Tha ain Johnny-Boy. She knew his long, heavy footsteps in a million. She heard feet come on the porch. Some woman. . . . She heard bare knuckles knock three times, then once. Thas some of them comrades! She unbarred the door, cracked it a few inches, and flinched from the cold rush of damp wind.

"Whos tha?"

"Its me!"

"Who?"

"Me, Reva!"

She flung the door open.

"Lawd, chile, c mon in!"

She stepped to one side and a thin, blond-haired white girl ran through the door; as she slid the bolt she heard the girl gasping and shaking her wet clothes. Somethings wrong! Reva wouldna walked a mile t mah house in all this slop fer nothin! Tha gals stuck onto Johnny-Boy. Ah wondah ef anything happened t im?

"Git on inter the kitchen, Reva, where its warm."

"Lawd, Ah sho is wet!"

"How yuh reckon yuhd be, in all tha rain?"

"Johnny-Boy ain here *yit?*" asked Reva.

"Naw! N ain no usa yuh worryin bout im. Jus yuh git them shoes off! Yuh wanna ketch yo deatha col?" She stood looking absently. Yeah; its somethin about the party er Johnny-Boy thas gone wrong. Lawd, Ah wondah ef her pa knows how she feels bout Johnny-Boy? "Honey, yuh hadnt oughta come out in sloppy weather like this."

"Ah had t come, An Sue."

She led Reva to the kitchen.

"Git them shoes off n git close t the stove so yuhll git dry!"

"An Sue, Ah got somethin t tell yuh . . ."

The words made her hold her breath. Ah bet its somethin bout Johnny-Boy!

"Whut, honey?"

"The sheriff wuz by our house tonight. He come t see pa."

"Yeah?"

"He done got word from somewheres bout tha meetin tomorrow."

"Is it Johnny-Boy, Reva?"

"Aw, naw, An Sue! Ah ain hearda word bout im. Ain yuh seen im tonight?"

"He ain come home t eat yit."

"Where kin he be?"

"Lawd knows, chile."

"Somebodys gotta tell them comrades tha meetings off," said Reva. "The sheriffs got men watchin our house. Ah had t slip out t git here widout em followin me."

"Reva?"

"Hunh?"

"Ahma ol woman n Ah wans yuh t tell me the truth."

"Whut, An Sue?"

"Yuh ain tryin t fool me, is yuh?"

"*Fool* yuh?"

"Bout Johnny-Boy?"

"Lawd, naw, An Sue!"

"Ef theres anythin wrong jus tell me, chile. Ah kin stan it."

She stood by the ironing board, her hands as usual folded loosely over her stomach, watching Reva pull off her water-clogged shoes. She was feeling that Johnny-Boy was already lost to her; she was feeling the pain that would come when she knew it for certain; and she was feeling that she would have to be brave and bear it. She was like a person caught in a swift current of water and knew where the water was sweeping her and did not want to go on but had to go on to the end.

"It ain nothin bout Johnny-Boy, An Sue," said Reva. "But we gotta do somethin er we'll all git inter trouble."

"How the sheriff know about tha meetin?"

"Thas whut pa wans t know."

"Somebody done turned Judas."

"Sho looks like it."

"Ah bet it wuz some of them new ones," she said.

"Its hard t tell," said Reva.

"Lissen, Reva, yuh oughta stay here n git dry, but yuh bettah git back n tell yo pa Johnny-Boy ain here n Ah don know when hes gonna show up. *Some*bodys gotta tell them comrades t stay erway from yo pas house."

She stood with her back to the window, looking at Reva's wide, blue eyes. Po critter! Gotta go back thru all tha slop! Though she felt sorry for Reva, not once did she think that it would not have to be done. Being a woman, Reva was not suspect; she would *have* to go. It was just as natural for Reva to go back through the cold rain as it was for her to iron night and day, or for Sug to be in jail. Right now, Johnny-Boy was out there on those dark fields trying to get home. Lawd, don let em git im tonight! In spite of herself her feelings became torn. She loved her son and, loving him, she loved what he was trying to do. Johnny-Boy was happiest when he was working for the party, and her love for him was for his happiness. She frowned, trying hard to fit something together in her feelings: for her to try to stop Johnny-Boy was to admit that all the toil of years meant nothing; and to let him go meant that sometime or other he would be caught, like Sug. In facing it this way she felt a little stunned, as though she had come suddenly upon a blank wall in the dark. But outside in the rain were people, white and black, whom she had known all her life. Those people depended upon Johnny-Boy, loved him and looked to him as a man and leader. Yeah; hes gotta keep on; he cant stop now. . . . She looked at Reva; she was crying and pulling her shoes back on with reluctant fingers.

"Whut yuh carryin on tha way fer, chile?"

"Yuh done los Sug, now yuh sendin Johnny-Boy . . ."

"Ah got t, honey."

She was glad she could say that. Reva believed in black folks and not for anything in the world would she falter before her. In Reva's trust and acceptance of her she had found her first feelings of humanity; Reva's love was her refuge from shame and degradation. If in the early days of her life the white mountain had driven her back from the earth, then in her last days Reva's love was drawing her toward it, like the beacon that swung through the night outside. She heard Reva sobbing.

"Hush, honey!"

"Mah brothers in jail too! Ma cries ever day . . ."

"Ah know, honey."

She helped Reva with her coat; her fingers felt the scant flesh of the girl's shoulders. She don git ernuff t eat, she thought. She slipped her arms around Reva's waist and held her close for a moment.

"Now, yuh stop that cryin."

"A-a-ah c-c-cant hep it. . . ."

"Everythingll be awright; Johnny-Boyll be back."

"Yuh think so?"

"Sho, chile. Cos he will."

Neither of them spoke again until they stood in the doorway. Outside they could hear water washing through the ruts of the street.

"Be sho n send Johnny-Boy t tell the folks t stay erway from pas house," said Reva.

"Ahll tell im. Don yuh worry."

"Good-bye!"

"Good-bye!"

Leaning against the door jamb, she shook her head slowly and watched Reva vanish through the falling rain.

II

She was back at her board, ironing, when she heard feet sucking in the mud of the back yard; feet she knew from long years of listening were Johnny-Boy's. But tonight, with all the rain and fear, his coming was like a leaving, was almost more than she could bear. Tears welled to her eyes and she blinked them away. She felt that he was coming so that she could give him up; to see him now was to say good-bye. But it was a good-bye she knew she could never say; they were not that way toward each other. All day long they could sit in the same room and not speak; she was his mother and he was her son. Most of the time a nod or a grunt would carry all the meaning that she wanted to convey to him, or he to her. She did not even turn her head when she heard him come stomping into the kitchen. She heard him pull up a chair, sit, sigh, and draw off his muddy shoes; they fell to the floor with heavy thuds. Soon the kitchen was full of the scent of his drying socks and his burning pipe. Tha boys hongry! She paused and looked at him over her shoulder; he was puffing at his pipe with his head tilted back and his feet propped up on the edge of the stove; his eyelids drooped and his wet clothes steamed from the heat of the fire. Lawd, tha boy gits mo like his pa ever day he lives, she mused, her lips breaking in a slow faint smile. Hols tha pipe in his mouth just like his pa usta hol his. Wondah how they woulda got erlong ef his pa hada lived? They oughta liked each other, they so much alike. She wished there could have been other children besides Sug, so Johnny-Boy would not have to be so much alone. A man needs a woman by his side. . . . She thought of Reva; she liked Reva; the brightest glow her heart had ever known was when she had learned that Reva loved Johnny-Boy. But beyond Reva were cold white faces. Ef theys caught it means *death*. . . . She jerked around when she heard Johnny-Boy's pipe clatter to the floor. She saw him pick it up, smile sheepishly at her, and wag his head.

"Gawd, Ahm sleepy," he mumbled.

She got a pillow from her room and gave it to him.

"Here," she said.

"Hunh," he said, putting the pillow between his head and the back of the chair.

They were silent again. Yes, she would have to tell him to go back out into the cold rain and slop; maybe to get caught; maybe for the last time; she didn't know. But she would let him eat and get dry before telling him that the sheriff knew of the meeting to be held at Lem's tomorrow. And she would make him take a big dose of soda before he went out; soda always helped to stave off a cold. She looked at the clock. It was eleven. Theres time yit. Spreading a newspaper on the apron of the stove, she placed a heaping plate of greens upon it, a knife, a fork, a cup of coffee, a slab of cornbread, and a dish of peach cobbler.

"Yo suppahs ready," she said.

"Yeah," he said.

He did not move. She ironed again. Presently, she heard him eating. When she could no longer hear his knife tinkling against the edge of the plate, she knew he was through. It was almost twelve now. She would let him rest a little while longer before she told him. Till one er'clock, mabbe. Hes so tired. . . . She finished her ironing, put away the board, and stacked the clothes in her dresser drawer. She poured herself a cup of black coffee, drew up a chair, sat down and drank.

"Yuh almos dry," she said, not looking around.

"Yeah," he said, turning sharply to her.

The tone of voice in which she had spoken had let him know that more was coming. She drained her cup and waited a moment longer.

"Reva wuz here."

"Yeah?"

"She lef bout a hour ergo."

"Whut she say?"

"She said ol man Lem hada visit from the sheriff today."

"Bout the meetin?"

"Yeah."

She saw him stare at the coals glowing red through the crevices of the stove and run his fingers nervously through his hair. She knew he was wondering how the sheriff had found out. In the silence he would ask a wordless question and in the silence she would answer wordlessly. Johnny-Boys too trustin, she thought. Hes trying t make the party big n hes takin in folks fastern he kin git t know em. You cant trust ever white man yuh meet. . . .

"Yuh know, Johnny-Boy, yuh been takin in a lotta them white folks lately . . ."

"Aw, ma!"

"But, Johnny-Boy . . ."

"Please, don talk t me bout tha now, ma."

"Yuh ain t ol t lissen n learn, son," she said.

"Ah know whut yuh gonna say, ma. N yuh wrong. Yuh cant judge folks jus by how yuh feel bout em n by how long yuh done knowed em. Ef we start tha we wouldnt have *no*body in the party. When folks pledge they word t be with us, then we gotta take em in. Wes too weak t be choosy."

He rose abruptly, rammed his hands into his pockets, and stood facing the window; she looked at his back in a long silence. She knew his faith; it was deep. He had always said that black men could not fight the rich bosses alone; a man could not fight with every hand against him. But he believes so hard hes blind, she thought. At odd times they had had these arguments before; always she would be pitting her feelings against the hard necessity of his thinking, and always she would lose. She shook her head. Po Johnny-Boy; he don know . . .

"But ain nona our folks tol, Johnny-Boy," she said.

"How yuh know?" he asked. His voice came low and with a tinge of anger. He still faced the window and now and then the yellow blade of light flicked across the sharp outline of his black face.

"Cause Ah know em," she said.

"*Any*body mighta tol," he said.

"It wuznt nona *our* folks," she said again.

She saw his hand sweep in a swift arc of disgust.

"*Our* folks! Ma, who in Gawds name is *our* folks?"

"The folks we wuz born n raised wid, son. The folks we *know*!"

"We cant make the party grow tha way, ma."

"It mighta been Booker," she said.

"Yuh don know."

". . . er Blattberg . . ."

"Fer Chrissakes!"

". . . er any of the fo-five others whut joined las week."

"Ma, yuh jus don wan me t go out tonight," he said.

"Yo ol ma wans yuh t be careful, son."

"Ma, when yuh start doubtin folks in the party, then there ain no end."

"Son, Ah knows ever black man n woman in this parta the county," she said, standing too. "Ah watched em grow up; Ah even heped birth n nurse some of em; Ah knows em *all* from way back. There ain none of em that *coulda* tol! The folks Ah know jus don open they dos n ast death t walk in! Son, it wuz some of them *white* folks! Yuh jus mark mah word n wait n see!"

"Why is it gotta be *white* folks?" he asked. "Ef they tol, then theys jus Judases, thas all."

"Son, look at whuts befo yuh."

He shook his head and sighed.

"Ma, Ah done tol yuh a hundred times. Ah cant see white n Ah cant see black," he said. "Ah sees rich men n Ah sees po men."

She picked up his dirty dishes and piled them in a pan. Out of the corners of her eyes she saw him sit and pull on his wet shoes. Hes goin! When she put the last dish away he was standing fully dressed, warming his hands over the stove. Jus a few mo minutes now n he'll be gone, like Sug, mabbe. Her throat tightened. This black mans fight takes *ever*thin! Looks like Gawd put us in this worl jus t beat us down!

"Keep this, ma," he said.

She saw a crumpled wad of money in his outstretched fingers.

"Naw; yuh keep it. Yuh might need it."

"It ain mine, ma. It berlongs t the party."

"But, Johnny-Boy, yuh might hafta go erway!"

"Ah kin make out."

"Don fergit yosef too much, son."

"Ef Ah don come back theyll need it."

He was looking at her face and she was looking at the money.

"Yuh keep tha," she said slowly. "Ahll give em the money."

"From where?"

"Ah got some."

"Where yuh git it from?"

She sighed.

"Ah been savin a dollah a week fer Sug ever since hes been in jail."

"Lawd, ma!"

She saw the look of puzzled love and wonder in his eyes. Clumsily, he put the money back into his pocket.

"Ahm gone," he said.

"Here; drink this glass of soda watah."

She watched him drink, then put the glass away.

"Waal," he said.

"Take the stuff outta yo pockets!"

She lifted the lid of the stove and he dumped all the papers from his pocket into the fire. She followed him to the door and made him turn round.

"Lawd, yuh tryin to make revolution n yuh cant even keep yo coat buttoned." Her nimble fingers fastened his collar high around his throat. "There!"

He pulled the brim of his hat low over his eyes. She opened the door and with the suddenness of the cold gust of wind that struck her face, he was gone. She watched the black fields and the rain take him, her eyes burning. When the last faint footstep could no longer be heard, she closed the door, went to her bed, lay down, and pulled the cover over her while fully dressed. Her feelings coursed with the rhythm of the rain: Hes gone! Lawd, Ah *know* hes gone! Her blood felt cold.

III

She was floating in a grey void somewhere between sleeping and dreaming and then suddenly she was wide awake, hearing and feeling in the same instant the thunder of the door crashing in and a cold wind filling the room. It was pitch black and she stared, resting on her elbows, her mouth open, not breathing, her ears full of the sound of tramping feet and booming voices. She knew at once: They lookin fer im! Then, filled with her will, she was on her feet, rigid, waiting, listening.

"The lamps burnin!"

"Yuh see her?"

"Naw!"

"Look in the kitchen!"

"Gee, this place smells like niggers!"

"Say, somebodys here er been here!"

"Yeah; theres fire in the stove!"

"Mabbe hes been here n gone?"

"Boy, look at these jars of jam!"

"Niggers make good jam!"

"Git some bread!"

"Heres some cornbread!"

"Say, lemme git some!"

"Take it easy! Theres plenty here!"

"Ahma take some of this stuff home!"

"Look, heres a pota greens!"

"N some hot cawffee!"

"Say, yuh guys! C mon! Cut it out! We didnt come here fer a feas!"

She walked slowly down the hall. They lookin fer im, but they ain got im yit! She stopped in the doorway, her gnarled, black hands as always folded over her stomach, but tight now, so tightly the veins bulged. The kitchen was crowded with white men in glistening raincoats. Though the lamp burned, their flashlights still glowed in red fists. Across her floor she saw the muddy tracks of their boots.

"Yuh white folks git outta mah house!"

There was quick silence; every face turned toward her. She saw a sudden movement, but did not know what it meant until something hot and wet slammed her squarely in the face. She gasped, but did not move. Calmly, she wiped the warm, greasy liquor of greens from her eyes with her left hand. One of the white men had thrown a handful of greens out of the pot at her.

"How they taste, ol bitch?"

"Ah ast yuh t git outta mah house!"

She saw the sheriff detach himself from the crowd and walk toward her.

"Now, Anty . . ."

"White man, don yuh *Anty* me!"

"Yuh ain got the right sperit!"

"Sperit hell! Yuh git these men outta mah house!"

"Yuh ack like yuh don like it!"

"Naw, Ah don like it, n yuh knows dam waal Ah don!"

"Whut yuh gonna do bout it?"

"Ahm tellin yuh t git outta mah house!"

"Gittin sassy?"

"Ef telling yuh t git outta mah house is sass, then Ahm sassy!"

Her words came in a tense whisper; but beyond, back of them, she was watching, thinking, judging the men.

"Listen, Anty," the sheriff's voice came soft and low. "Ahm here t hep yuh. How come yuh wanna ack this way?"

"Yuh ain never helped yo *own* sef since yuh been born," she flared. "How kin the likes of yuh hep me?"

One of the white men came forward and stood directly in front of her.

"Lissen, nigger woman, yuh talkin t *white* men!"

"Ah don care who Ahm talkin t!"

"Yuhll wish some day yuh did!"

"Not t the likes of yuh!"

"Yuh need somebody t teach yuh how t be a good nigger!"

"*Yuh* cant teach it t me!"

"Yuh gonna change yo tune."

"Not longs mah bloods warm!"

"Don git smart now!"

"Yuh git outta mah house!"

"Spose we don go?" the sheriff asked.

They were crowded around her. She had not moved since she had taken her place in the doorway. She was thinking only of Johnny-Boy as she stood there giving and taking words; and she knew that they, too, were thinking of Johnny-Boy. She knew they wanted him, and her heart was daring them to take him from her.

"Spose we don go?" the sheriff asked again.

"Twenty of yuh runnin over one ol woman! Now, ain yuh white men glad yuh so brave?"

The sheriff grabbed her arm.

"C mon, now! Yuh done did ernuff sass fer one night. Wheres tha nigger son of yos?"

"Don yuh wished yuh knowed?"

"Yuh wanna git slapped?"

"Ah ain never seen one of yo kind tha wuznt too low fer . . ."

The sheriff slapped her straight across her face with his open palm. She fell back against a wall and sank to her knees.

"Is tha whut white men do t nigger women?"

She rose slowly and stood again, not even touching the place that ached from his blow, her hands folded over her stomach.

"Ah ain never seen one of yo kind tha wuznt too low fer . . ."

He slapped her again; she reeled backward several feet and fell on her side.

"Is tha whut we too low t do?"

She stood before him again, dry-eyed, as though she had not been struck. Her lips were numb and her chin was wet with blood.

"Aw, let her go! Its the nigger we wan!" said one.

"Wheres that nigger son of yos?" the sheriff asked.

"Find im," she said.

"By Gawd, ef we hafta find im we'll kill im!"

"He wont be the only nigger yuh ever killed," she said.

She was consumed with a bitter pride. There was nothing on this earth, she felt then, that they could not do to her but that she could take. She stood on a narrow plot of ground from which she would die before she was pushed. And then it was, while standing there feeling warm blood seeping down her throat, that she gave up Johnny-Boy, gave him up to the white folks. She gave him up because they had come tramping into her heart demanding him, thinking they could get him by beating her, thinking they could scare her into making her tell where he was. She gave him up because she wanted them to know that they could not get what they wanted by bluffing and killing.

"Wheres this meetin gonna be?" the sheriff asked.

"Don yuh wish yuh knowed?"

"Ain there gonna be a meetin?"

"How come yuh astin me?"

"There *is* gonna be a meetin," said the sheriff.

"Is it?"

"Ah gotta great mind t choke it outta yuh!"

"Yuh so smart," she said.

"We ain playin wid yuh!"

"Did Ah say yuh wuz?"

"Tha nigger son of yos is erroun here somewheres n we aim t find im," said the sheriff. "Ef yuh tell us where he is n ef he talks, mabbe he'll git off easy. But ef we hafta find im, we'll kill im! Ef we hafta find im, then yuh git a sheet t put over im in the mawnin, see? Git yuh a sheet, cause hes gonna be dead!"

"He wont be the only nigger yuh ever killed," she said again.

The sheriff walked past her. The others followed. Yuh didnt git whut yuh wanted! she thought exultingly. N yuh ain gonna *never* git it! Hotly, something ached in her to make them feel the intensity of her pride and freedom; her heart groped to turn the bitter hours of her life into words of a kind that would make them feel that she had taken all they had done to her in her stride and could still take more. Her faith surged so strongly in her she was all but blinded. She walked behind them to the door, knotting and twisting her fingers. She saw them step to the muddy ground. Each whirl of the yellow beacon revealed glimpses of slanting rain. Her lips moved, then she shouted:

"Yuh didnt git whut yuh wanted! N yuh ain gonna nevah git it!"

The sheriff stopped and turned; his voice came low and hard.

"Now, by Gawd, thas ernuff outta yuh!"

"Ah know when Ah done said ernuff!"

"Aw, naw, yuh don!" he said. "Yuh don know when yuh done said ernuff, but Ahma teach yuh ternight!"

He was up the steps and across the porch with one bound. She backed into the hall, her eyes full on his face.

"Tell me when yuh gonna stop talkin!" he said, swinging his fist.

The blow caught her high on the cheek; her eyes went blank; she fell flat on her face. She felt the hard heel of his wet shoes coming into her temple and stomach.

"Lemme hear yuh talk some mo!"

She wanted to, but could not; pain numbed and choked her. She lay still and somewhere out of the grey void of unconsciousness she heard someone say: *aw fer chrissakes leave her erlone its the nigger we wan. . . .*

IV

She never knew how long she had lain huddled in the dark hallway. Her first returning feeling was of a nameless fear crowding the inside of her, then a deep pain spreading from her temple downward over her body. Her ears were filled with the drone of rain and she shuddered from the cold wind blowing through the door. She opened her eyes and at first saw nothing. As if she were imagining it, she knew she was half-lying and half-sitting in a corner against a wall. With difficulty she twisted her neck and what she saw made her hold her breath—a vast white blur was suspended directly above her. For a moment she could not tell if her fear was from the blur or if the blur was from her fear. Gradually the blur resolved itself into a huge white face that slowly filled her vision. She was stone still, conscious really of the effort to breathe, feeling somehow that she existed only by the mercy of that white face. She had seen it before; its fear had gripped her many times; it had for her the fear of all the white faces she had ever seen in her life. *Sue* . . . As from a great distance, she heard her name being called. She was regaining consciousness now, but the fear was coming with her. She looked into the face of a white man, wanting to scream out for him to go; yet accepting his presence because she felt she had to. Though some remote part of her mind was active, her limbs were powerless. It was as if an invisible knife had split her in two, leaving one half of her lying there helpless, while the other half shrank in dread from a forgotten but familiar enemy. *Sue its me Sue its me* . . . Then all at once the voice came clearly.

"Sue, its me! Its Booker!"

And she heard an answering voice speaking inside of her, Yeah, its Booker . . . The one whut jus joined . . . She roused herself, struggling for full consciousness; and as she did so she transferred to the person of Booker the nameless fear she felt. It seemed that Booker towered above her as a challenge to her right to exist upon the earth.

"Yuh awright?"

She did not answer; she started violently to her feet and fell.

"Sue, yuh hurt!"

"Yeah," she breathed.

"Where they hit yuh?"

"Its mah head," she whispered.

She was speaking even though she did not want to; the fear that had hold of her compelled her.

"They beat yuh?"

"Yeah."

"Them bastards! Them Gawddam bastards!"

She heard him saying it over and over; then she felt herself being lifted.

"Naw!" she gasped.

"Ahma take yuh t the kitchen!"

"Put me down!"

"But yuh cant stay here like this!"

She shrank in his arms and pushed her hands against his body; when she was in the kitchen she freed herself, sank into a chair, and held tightly to its back. She looked wonderingly at Booker. There was nothing about him that should frighten her so, but even that did not ease her tension. She saw him go to the water bucket, wet his handkerchief, wring it, and offer it to her. Distrustfully, she stared at the damp cloth.

"Here; put this on yo fohead . . ."

"Naw!"

"C mon, itll make yuh feel bettah!"

She hesitated in confusion. What right had she to be afraid when someone was acting as kindly as this toward her? Reluctantly, she leaned forward and pressed the damp cloth to her head. It helped. With each passing minute she was catching hold of herself, yet wondering why she felt as she did.

"Whut happened?"

"Ah don know."

"Yuh feel bettah?"

"Yeah."

"Who all wuz here?"

"Ah don know," she said again.

"Yo head still hurt?"

"Yeah."

"Gee, Ahm sorry."

"Ahm awright," she sighed and buried her face in her hands.

She felt him touch her shoulder.

"Sue, Ah got some bad news fer yuh . . ."

She knew; she stiffened and grew cold. It had happened; she stared dry-eyed, with compressed lips.

"Its mah Johnny-Boy," she said.

"Yeah; Ahm awful sorry t hafta tell yuh this way. But Ah thought yuh oughta know..."

Her tension eased and a vacant place opened up inside of her. A voice whispered, Jesus, hep me!

"W-w-where is he?"

"They got im out t Foleys Woods tryin t make im tell who the others is."

"He ain gonna tell," she said. "They jus as waal kill im, cause he ain gonna nevah tell."

"Ah hope he don," said Booker. "But he didnt hava chance t tell the others. They grabbed im jus as he got t the woods."

Then all the horror of it flashed upon her; she saw flung out over the rainy countryside an array of shacks where white and black comrades were sleeping; in the morning they would be rising and going to Lem's; then they would be caught. And that meant terror, prison, and death. The comrades would have to be told; she would have to tell them; she could not entrust Johnny-Boy's work to another, and especially not to Booker as long as she felt toward him as she did. Gripping the bottom of the chair with both hands, she tried to rise; the room blurred and she swayed. She found herself resting in Booker's arms.

"Lemme go!"

"Sue, yuh too weak t walk!"

"Ah gotta tell em!" she said.

"Set down, Sue! Yuh hurt! Yuh sick!"

When seated, she looked at him helplessly.

"Sue, lissen! Johnny-Boys caught. Ahm here. Yuh tell me who they is n Ahll tell em."

She stared at the floor and did not answer. Yes; she was too weak to go. There was no way for her to tramp all those miles through the rain tonight. But should she tell Booker? If only she had somebody like Reva to talk to! She did not want to decide alone; she must make no mistake about this. She felt Booker's fingers pressing on her arm and it was as though the white mountain was pushing her to the edge of a sheer height; she again exclaimed inwardly, Jesus, hep me! Booker's white face was at her side, waiting. Would she be doing right to tell him? Suppose she did not tell and then the comrades were caught? She could not ever forgive herself for doing a thing like that. But maybe she was wrong; maybe her fear was what Johnny-Boy had always called "jus foolishness." She remembered his saying, Ma we cant make the party grow ef we start doubtin everybody. . . .

"Tell me who they is, Sue, n Ahll tell em. Ah jus joined n Ah don know who they is."

"Ah don know who they is," she said.

"Yuh *gotta* tell me who they is, Sue!"

"Ah tol yuh Ah don know!"

"Yuh *do* know! C mon! Set up n talk!"

"Naw!"

"Yuh wan em all t git *killed*?"

She shook her head and swallowed. Lawd, Ah don blieve in this man!

"Lissen, Ahll call the names n yuh tell me which ones is in the party n which ones ain, see?"

"Naw!"

"Please, Sue!"

"Ah don know," she said.

"Sue, yuh ain doin right by em. Johnny-Boy wouldnt wan yuh t be this way. Hes out there holdin up his end. Les hol up ours . . ."

"Lawd, Ah don know . . ."

"Is yuh scareda me cause Ahm *white*? Johnny-Boy ain like tha. Don let all the work we done go fer nothin."

She gave up and bowed her head in her hands.

"Is it Johnson? Tell me, Sue?"

"Yeah," she whispered in horror; a mounting horror of feeling herself being undone.

"Is it Green?"

"Yeah."

"Murphy?"

"Lawd, Ah don know!"

"Yuh gotta tell me, Sue!"

"Mistah Booker, please leave me erlone . . ."

"Is it Murphy?"

She answered yes to the names of Johnny-Boy's comrades; she answered until he asked her no more. Then she thought, How he know the sheriffs men is watchin Lems house? She stood up and held onto her chair, feeling something sure and firm within her.

"How yuh know bout Lem?"

"Why . . . How Ah know?"

"Whut yuh doin here this tima night? How yuh know the sheriff got Johnny-Boy?"

"Sue, don yuh blieve in me?"

She did not, but she could not answer. She stared at him until her lips hung open; she was searching deep within herself for certainty.

"You meet Reva?" she asked.

"Reva?"

"Yeah; Lems gal?"

"Oh, yeah. Sho, Ah met Reva."

"She tell yuh?"

She asked the question more of herself than of him; she longed to believe.

"Yeah," he said softly. "Ah reckon Ah oughta be goin t tell em now."

"Who?" she asked. "Tell *who*?"

The muscles of her body were stiff as she waited for his answer; she felt as though life depended upon it.

"The comrades," he said.

"Yeah," she sighed.

She did not know when he left; she was not looking or listening. She just suddenly saw the room empty and from her the thing that had made her fearful was gone.

V

For a space of time that seemed to her as long as she had been upon the earth, she sat huddled over the cold stove. One minute she would say to herself, They both gone now; Johnny-Boy n Sug . . . Mabbe Ahll never see em ergin. Then a surge of guilt would blot out her longing. "Lawd, Ah shouldna tol!" she mumbled. "But no man kin be so lowdown as t do a thing like tha . . ." Several times she had an impulse to try to tell the comrades herself; she was feeling a little better now. But what good would that do? She had told Booker the names. He jus couldnt be a Judas to po folks like us . . . He *couldnt*!

"An Sue!"

Thas Reva! Her heart leaped with an anxious gladness. She rose without answering and limped down the dark hallway. Through the open door, against the background of rain, she saw Reva's face lit now and then to whiteness by the whirling beams of the beacon. She was about to call, but a thought checked her. Jesus, hep me! Ah gotta tell her bout Johnny-Boy . . . Lawd, Ah cant!

"An Sue, yuh there?"

"C mon in, chile!"

She caught Reva and held her close for a moment without speaking.

"Lawd, Ahm sho glad yuh here," she said at last.

"Ah thought somethin had happened t yuh," said Reva, pulling away. "Aw saw the do open . . . Pa tol me to come back n stay wid yuh tonight . . ." Reva paused and started. "W-w-whuts the mattah?"

She was so full of having Reva with her that she did not understand what the question meant.

"Hunh?"

"Yo neck . . ."

"Aw, it ain nothin, chile. C mon in the kitchen."

"But theres blood on yo neck!"

"The sheriff wuz here . . ."

"Them fools! Whut they wanna bother yuh fer? Ah could kill em! So hep me Gawd, Ah could!"

"It ain nothin," she said.

She was wondering how to tell Reva about Johnny-Boy and Booker. Ahll wait a lil while longer, she thought. Now that Reva was here, her fear did not seem as awful as before.

"C mon, lemme fix yo head, An Sue. Yuh hurt."

They went to the kitchen. She sat silent while Reva dressed her scalp. She was feeling better now; in just a little while she would tell Reva. She felt the girl's finger pressing gently upon her head.

"Tha hurt?"

"A lil, chile."

"Yuh po thing."

"It ain nothin."

"Did Johnny-Boy come?"

She hesitated.

"Yeah."

"He done gone t tell the others?"

Reva's voice sounded so clear and confident that it mocked her. Lawd, Ah cant tell this chile . . .

"Yuh tol im, didnt yuh, An Sue?"

"Y-y-yeah . . ."

"Gee! Thas good! Ah tol pa he didnt hafta worry ef Johnny-Boy got the news. Mabbe thingsll come out awright."

"Ah hope . . ."

She could not go on; she had gone as far as she could. For the first time that night she began to cry.

"Hush, An Sue! Yuh awways been brave. Itll be awright!"

"Ain nothin awright, chile. The worls jus too much fer us, Ah reckon."

"Ef yuh cry that way itll make me cry."

She forced herself to stop. Naw; Ah cant carry on this way in fronta Reva . . . Right now she had a deep need for Reva to believe in her. She watched the girl get pine-knots from behind the stove, rekindle the fire, and put on the coffee pot.

"Yuh wan some cawfee?" Reva asked.

"Naw, honey."

"Aw, c mon, An Sue."

"Jusa lil, honey."

"Thas the way to be. Oh, say, Ah fergot," said Reva, measuring out spoonsful of coffee. "Pa tol me t tell yuh t watch out fer tha Booker man. Hes a stool."

She showed not one sign of outward movement or expression, but as the words fell from Reva's lips she went limp inside.

"Pa tol me soon as Ah got back home. He got word from town . . ."

She stopped listening. She felt as though she had been slapped to the extreme outer edge of life, into a cold darkness. She knew now what she had felt when she had looked up out of her fog of pain and had seen Booker. It was the image of all the white folks, and the fear that went with them, that she had seen and felt during her lifetime. And again, for the second time that night, something she had felt had come true. All she could say to herself was, Ah didnt like im! Gawd knows, Ah didnt! Ah tol Johnny-Boy it wuz some of them white folks . . .

"Here; drink yo cawffee . . ."

She took the cup; her fingers trembled, and the steaming liquid spilt onto her dress and leg.

"Ahm sorry, An Sue!"

Her leg was scalded, but the pain did not bother her.

"Its awright," she said.

"Wait; lemme put some lard on tha burn!"

"It don hurt."

"Yuh worried bout somethin."

"Naw, honey."

"Lemme fix yuh so mo cawffee."

"Ah don wan nothin now, Reva."

"Waal, buck up. Don be tha way . . ."

They were silent. She heard Reva drinking. No; she would not tell Reva; Reva was all she had left. But she had to do something, some way, somehow. She was undone too much as it was; and to tell Reva about Booker or Johnny-Boy was more than she was equal to; it would be too coldly shameful. She wanted to be alone and fight this thing out with herself.

"Go t bed, honey. Yuh tired."

"Naw; Ahm awright, An Sue."

She heard the bottom of Reva's empty cup clank against the top of the stove. Ah *got* t make her go t bed! Yes; Booker would tell the names of the comrades to the sheriff. If she could only stop him some way! That was the answer, the point, the star that grew bright in the morning of new hope. Soon, maybe half an hour from now, Booker would reach Foley's Woods. Hes boun t go the long way, cause he don know no short cut, she thought. Ah could wade the creek n beat im there. . . . But what would she do after that?

"Reva, honey, go t bed. Ahm awright. Yuh need res."

"Ah ain sleepy, An Sue."

"Ah knows whuts bes fer yuh, chile. Yuh tired n wet."

"Ah wanna stay up wid yuh."

She forced a smile and said:

"Ah don think they gonna hurt Johnny-Boy . . ."

"Fer *real*, An Sue?"

"Sho, honey."

"But Ah wanna wait up wid yuh."

"Thas mah job, honey. Thas whut a mas fer, t wait up fer her chullun."

"Good night, An Sue."

"Good night, honey."

She watched Reva pull up and leave the kitchen; presently she heard the shucks in the mattress whispering, and she knew that Reva had gone to bed. She was alone. Through the cracks of the stove she saw the fire dying to grey ashes; the room was growing cold again. The yellow beacon continued to flit past the window and the rain still drummed. Yes; she was alone; she had done this awful thing alone; she must find some way out, alone. Like touching a festering sore, she put her finger upon that moment when she had shouted her defiance to the sheriff, when she had shouted to feel her strength. She had lost Sug to save others; she had let Johnny-Boy go to save others; and then in a moment of weakness that came from too much strength she had lost all. If she had not shouted to the sheriff, she would have been strong enough to have resisted Booker; she would have been able to tell the comrades herself. Something tightened in her as she remembered and understood the fit of fear she had felt on coming to herself in the dark hallway. A part of her life she thought she had done away with forever had had hold of her then. She had thought the soft, warm past was over; she had thought that it did not mean much when now she sang: "*Hes the Lily of the Valley, the Bright n Mawnin Star*". . . The days when she had sung that song were the days when she had not hoped for anything on this earth, the days when the cold mountain had driven her into the arms of Jesus. She had thought that Sug and Johnny-Boy had taught her to forget Him, to fix her hope upon the fight of black men for freedom. Through the gradual years she had believed and worked with them, had felt strength shed from the grace of their terrible vision. That grace had been upon her when she had let the sheriff slap her down; it had been upon her when she had risen time and again from the floor and faced him. But she had trapped herself with her own hunger; to water the long dry thirst of her faith her pride had made a bargain which her flesh could not keep. Her having told the names of Johnny-Boy's comrades was but an incident in a deeper horror. She stood up and looked at the floor while call and counter-call, loyalty and counter-loyalty struggled in her soul. Mired she was between two abandoned worlds, living, but dying without the strength of the grace that either gave. The clearer she felt it the fuller did something well up from the depths of her for release; the more urgent did she feel the need to fling into her black sky another star, another hope, one more terrible vision to give her the strength to live and act. Softly and restlessly she walked about the kitchen, feeling herself naked against the night, the rain, the world; and shamed whenever the thought of Reva's love crossed her mind. She lifted her empty hands and looked at her writhing fingers. Lawd, whut kin Ah do now? She could still wade the creek and get to Foley's Woods before Booker. And then what? How could she manage to see Johnny-Boy or Booker? Again she heard the sheriff's threatening voice: Git yuh a sheet, cause hes gonna be dead! The sheet! Thas it, the *sheet*! Her whole being leaped with will; the long years of her life bent toward a moment of focus, a point. Ah kin go wid mah sheet! Ahll be doin whut he said! Lawd Gawd in Heaven, Ahma go lika nigger woman wid mah windin sheet t git mah dead son! But then what? She stood straight and smiled grimly; she had in her heart the whole meaning of her life; her entire personality was poised on the brink of a total act. Ah know! Ah *know*! She thought of Johnny-Boy's gun in the dresser drawer. Ahll hide the gun in the sheet n go aftah Johnny-Boys body. . . . She tiptoed to her room, eased out the dresser drawer, and got a sheet. Reva was sleeping; the darkness was filled with her quiet breathing. She groped in the drawer and found the gun. She wound the gun in the sheet and held them both under her apron. Then she stole to the bedside and watched Reva. Lawd, hep her! But mabbe shes bettah off. This had t happen sometimes . . . She n Johnny-Boy couldna been together in this here South . . . N Ah couldnt tell her bout Booker. Itll come out awright n she wont nevah know. Reva's trust would never be shaken. She caught her breath as the shucks in the mattress rustled dryly; then all was quiet and she breathed easily again. She tiptoed to the door, down the hall, and stood on the porch. Above her the yellow beacon whirled through the rain. She went over muddy ground, mounted a slope, stopped and looked back at her house. The lamp glowed in her window, and the yellow beacon that swung every few seconds seemed to feed it with light. She turned and started across the fields, holding the gun and sheet tightly, thinking, Po Reva . . . Po critter . . . Shes fas ersleep . . .

VI

For the most part she walked with her eyes half shut, her lips tightly compressed, leaning her body against the wind and the driving rain, feeling the pistol in the sheet sagging cold and heavy in her fingers. Already she was getting wet; it seemed that her feet found every puddle of water that stood between the corn rows.

She came to the edge of the creek and paused, wondering at what point was it low. Taking the sheet from under her apron, she wrapped the gun in it so that her finger could be upon the trigger. Ahll cross here, she thought. At first she did not feel the water; her feet were already wet. But the water grew cold as it came up to her knees; she gasped when it reached her waist. Lawd, this creeks high! When she had passed the middle, she knew that she was out of danger. She came out of the water, climbed a grassy hill, walked on, turned a bend and saw the lights of autos gleaming ahead. Yeah; theys still there! She hurried with her head down. Wondah did Ah beat im here? Lawd, Ah *hope* so! A vivid image of Booker's white face hovered a moment before her eyes and a surging will rose up in her so hard and strong that it vanished. She was among the autos now. From nearby came the hoarse voices of the men.

"Hey, yuh!"

She stopped, nervously clutching the sheet. Two white men with shotguns came toward her.

"Whut in hell yuh doin out here?"

She did not answer.

"Didnt yuh hear somebody speak t yuh?"

"Ahm comin aftah mah son," she said humbly.

"Yo *son*?"

"Yessuh."

"Whut yo son doin out here?"

"The sheriffs got im."

"Holy Scott! Jim, its the niggers ma!"

"Whut yuh got there?" asked one.

"A sheet."

"A *sheet*?"

"Yessuh."

"Fer whut?"

"The sheriff tol me t bring a sheet t git his body."

"Waal, waal . . ."

"Now, ain tha somethin?"

The white men looked at each other.

"These niggers sho love one ernother," said one.

"N tha ain no lie," said the other.

"Take me t the sheriff," she begged.

"Yuh ain givin us *orders,* is yuh?"

"Nawsuh."

"We'll take yuh when wes good n ready."

"Yessuh."

"So yuh wan his body?"

"Yessuh."

"Waal, he ain dead yit."

"They gonna kill im," she said.

"Ef he talks they wont."

"He ain gonna talk," she said.

"How yuh know?"

"Cause he ain."

"We got ways of makin niggers talk."

"Yuh ain got no way fer im."

"Yuh thinka lot of that black Red, don yuh?"

"Hes mah son."

"Why don yuh teach im some sense?"

"Hes mah son," she said again.

"Lissen, ol nigger woman, yuh stand there wid yo hair white. Yuh got bettah sense than t blieve tha niggers kin make a revolution . . ."

"A black republic," said the other one, laughing.

"Take me t the sheriff," she begged.

"Yuh his ma," said one. "Yuh kin make im talk n tell whos in this thing wid im."

"He ain gonna talk," she said.

"Don yuh wan im t live?"

She did not answer.

"C mon, les take her t Bradley."

They grabbed her arms and she clutched hard at the sheet and gun; they led her toward the crowd in the woods. Her feelings were simple; Booker would not tell; she was there with the gun to see to that. The louder became the voices of the men the deeper became her feeling of wanting to right the mistake she had made; of wanting to fight her way back to solid ground. She would stall for time until Booker showed up. Oh, ef theyll only lemme git close t Johnny-Boy! As they led her near the crowd she saw white faces turning and looking at her and heard a rising clamor of voices.

"Whos tha?"

"A nigger woman!"

"Whut she doin out here?"

"This is his ma!" called one of the men.

"Whut she wans?"

"She brought a sheet t cover his body!"

"He ain dead yit!"

"They tryin t make im talk!"

"But he will be dead soon ef he don open up!"

"Say, look! The niggers ma brought a sheet t cover up his body!"

"Now, ain that sweet?"

"Mabbe she wans t hol a prayer meetin!"

"Did she git a preacher?"

"Say, go git Bradley!"

"O.K.!"

The crowd grew quiet. They looked at her curiously; she felt their cold eyes trying to detect some weakness in her. Humbly, she stood with the sheet covering the gun. She had already accepted all that they could do to her.

The sheriff came.

"So yuh brought yo sheet, hunh?"

"Yessuh," she whispered.

"Looks like them slaps we gave yuh learned yuh some sense, didnt they?"

She did not answer.

"Yuh don need tha sheet. Yo son ain dead yit," he said, reaching toward her.

She backed away, her eyes wide.

"Naw!"

"Now, lissen, Anty!" he said. "There ain no use in yuh ackin a fool! Go in there n tell tha nigger son of yos t tell us whos in this wid im, see? Ah promise we wont kill im ef he talks. We'll let im git outta town."

"There ain nothin Ah kin tell im," she said.

"Yuh wan us t kill im?"

She did not answer. She saw someone lean toward the sheriff and whisper.

"Bring her erlong," the sheriff said.

They led her to a muddy clearing. The rain streamed down through the ghostly glare of the flashlights. As the men formed a semi-circle she saw Johnny-Boy lying in a trough of mud. He was tied with rope; he lay hunched and one side of his face rested in a pool of black water. His eyes were staring questioningly at her.

"Speak t im," said the sheriff.

If she could only tell him why she was here! But that was impossible; she was close to what she wanted and she stared straight before her with compressed lips.

"Say, nigger!" called the sheriff, kicking Johnny-Boy. "Heres yo ma!"

Johnny-Boy did not move or speak. The sheriff faced her again.

"Lissen, Anty," he said. "Yuh got mo say wid im than anybody. Tell im t talk n hava chance. Whut he wanna pertect the other niggers n white folks fer?"

She slid her finger about the trigger of the gun and looked stonily at the mud.

"Go t him," said the sheriff.

She did not move. Her heart was crying out to answer the amazed question in Johnny-Boy's eyes. But there was no way now.

"Waal, yuhre astin fer it. By Gawd, we gotta way to *make* yuh talk t im," he said, turning away. "Say, Tim, git one of them logs n turn that nigger upside-down n put his legs on it!"

A murmur of assent ran through the crowd. She bit her lips; she knew what that meant.

"Yuh wan yo nigger son crippled?" she heard the sheriff ask.

She did not answer. She saw them roll the log up; they lifted Johnny-Boy and laid him on his face and stomach, then they pulled his legs over the log. His knee-caps rested on the sheer top of the log's back and the toes of his shoes pointed groundward. So absorbed was she in watching that she felt that it was she who was being lifted and made ready for torture.

"Git a crowbar!" said the sheriff.

A tall, lank man got a crowbar from a nearby auto and stood over the log. His jaws worked slowly on a wad of tobacco.

"Now, its up t yuh, Anty," the sheriff said. "Tell the man whut t do!"

She looked into the rain. The sheriff turned.

"Mabbe she thinks wes playin. Ef she don say nothin, then break em at the knee-caps!"

"O.K., Sheriff!"

She stood waiting for Booker. Her legs felt weak; she wondered if she would be able to wait much longer. Over and over she said to herself, Ef he came now Ahd kill em both!

"She ain sayin nothin, Sheriff!"

"Waal, Gawddammit, let im have it!"

The crowbar came down and Johnny-Boy's body lunged in the mud and water. There was a scream. She swayed, holding tight to the gun and sheet.

"Hol im! Git the other leg!"

The crowbar fell again. There was another scream.

"Yuh break em?" asked the sheriff.

The tall man lifted Johnny-Boy's legs and let them drop limply again, dropping rearward from the knee-caps. Johnny-Boy's body lay still. His head had rolled to one side and she could not see his face.

"Jus lika broke sparrow wing," said the man, laughing softly.

Then Johnny-Boy's face turned to her; he screamed.

"Go way, ma! Go way!"

It was the first time she had heard his voice since she had come out to the woods; she all but lost control of herself. She started violently forward, but the sheriff's arm checked her.

"Aw, naw! Yuh had yo chance!" He turned to Johnny-Boy. "She kin go ef yuh talk."

"Mistah, he ain gonna talk," she said.

"Go way, ma!" said Johnny-Boy.

"Shoot im! Don make im suffah so," she begged.

"He'll either talk or he'll never hear yuh ergin," the sheriff said. "Theres other things we kin do t im."

She said nothing.

"What yuh come here fer, ma?" Johnny-Boy sobbed.

"Ahm gonna split his eardrums," the sheriff said. "Ef yuh got anythin t say t im yuh bettah say it *now*!"

She closed her eyes. She heard the sheriff's feet sucking in mud. Ah could save im! She opened her eyes; there were shouts of eagerness from the crowd as it pushed in closer.

"Bus em, Sheriff!"

"Fix im so he cant hear!"

"He knows how t do it, too!"

"He busted a Jew boy tha way once!"

She saw the sheriff stoop over Johnny-Boy, place his flat palm over one ear and strike his fist against it with all his might. He placed his palm over the other ear and struck again. Johnny-Boy moaned, his head rolling from side to side, his eyes showing white amazement in a world without sound.

"Yuh wouldnt talk t im when yuh had the chance," said the sheriff. "Try n talk now."

She felt warm tears on her cheeks. She longed to shoot Johnny-Boy and let him go. But if she did that they would take the gun from her, and Booker would tell who the others were. Lawd, hep me! The men were talking loudly now, as though the main business was over. It seemed ages that she stood there watching Johnny-Boy roll and whimper in his world of silence.

"Say, Sheriff, heres somebody lookin fer yuh!"

"Who is it?"

"Ah don know!"

"Bring em in!"

She stiffened and looked around wildly, holding the gun tight. Is tha Booker? Then she held still, feeling that her excitement might betray her. Mabbe Ah kin shoot em both! Mabbe Ah kin shoot *twice*! The sheriff stood in front of her, waiting. The crowd parted and she saw Booker hurrying forward.

"Ah know em all, Sheriff!" he called.

He came full into the muddy clearing where Johnny-Boy lay.

"Yuh mean yuh got the names?"

"Sho! The ol nigger . . ."

She saw his lips hang open and silent when he saw her. She stepped forward and raised the sheet.

"Whut . . ."

She fired, once; then, without pausing, she turned, hearing them yell. She aimed at Johnny-Boy, but they had their arms around her, bearing her to the ground, clawing at the sheet in her hand. She glimpsed Booker lying sprawled in the mud, on his face, his hands stretched out before him; then a cluster of yelling men blotted him out. She lay without struggling, looking upward through the rain at the white faces above her. And she was suddenly at peace; they were not a white mountain now; they were not pushing her any longer to the edge of life. Its awright . . .

"She shot Booker!"

"She hada gun in the sheet!"

"She shot im right thu the head!"

"Whut she shoot im fer?"

"Kill the bitch!"

"Ah *thought* somethin wuz wrong bout her!"

"Ah wuz fer givin it t her from the firs!"

"Thas whut yuh git fer treatin a nigger nice!"

"Say, Bookers dead!"

She stopped looking into the white faces, stopped listening. She waited, giving up her life before they took it from her; she had done what she wanted. Ef only Johnny-Boy . . . She looked at him; he lay looking at her with tired eyes. Ef she could only tell im! But he lay already buried in a grave of silence.

"Whut yuh kill im fer, hunh?"

It was the sheriff's voice; she did not answer.

"Mabbe she wuz shootin at yuh, Sheriff?"

"Whut yuh kill im fer?"

She felt the sheriff's foot come into her side; she closed her eyes.

"Yuh black bitch!"

"Let her have it!"

"Yuh reckon she foun out bout Booker?"

"She mighta."

"Jesus Chris, whut yuh dummies *waitin* on!"

"Yeah; kill her!"

"Kill em *both*!"

"Let her know her nigger son dead firs!"

She turned her head toward Johnny-Boy; he lay looking puzzled in a world beyond the reach of voices. At leas he cant hear, she thought.

"C mon, let im have it!"

She listened to hear what Johnny-Boy could not. They came, two of them, one right behind the other; so close together that they sounded like one shot. She did not look at Johnny-Boy now; she looked at the white faces of the men, hard and wet in the glare of the flashlights.

"Yuh hear tha, nigger woman?"

"Did tha surprise im? Hes in hell now wonderin whut hit im!"

"C mon! Give it t her, Sheriff!"

"Lemme shoot her, Sheriff! It wuz mah pal she shot!"

"Awright, Pete! Thas fair ernuff!"

She gave up as much of her life as she could before they took it from her. But the sound of the shot and the streak of fire that tore its way through her chest forced her to live again, intensely. She had not moved, save for the slight jarring impact of the bullet. She felt the heat of her own blood warming her cold, wet back. She yearned suddenly to talk. "Yuh didnt git whut yuh wanted! N yuh ain gonna nevah git it! Yuh didnt kill me; Ah came here by mahsef . . ." She felt rain falling into her wide-open, dimming eyes and heard faint voices. Her lips moved soundlessly. *Yuh didnt git yuh didnt yuh didnt . . .* Focused and pointed she was, buried in the depths of her star, swallowed in its peace and strength; and not feeling her flesh growing cold, cold as the rain that fell from the invisible sky upon the doomed living and the dead that never dies.

1940

Between the World and Me

And one morning while in the woods I stumbled suddenly upon the
thing,
Stumbled upon it in a grassy clearing guarded by scaly oaks and elms.
And the sooty details of the scene rose, thrusting themselves between
the world and me . . .

There was a design of white bones slumbering forgottenly upon a
cushion of ashes.
There was a charred stump of a sapling pointing a blunt finger accusingly at the sky.
There were torn tree limbs, tiny veins of burnt leaves, and a scorched
coil of greasy hemp;

A vacant shoe, an empty tie, a ripped shirt, a lonely hat, and a pair of
trousers stiff with black blood.
And upon the trampled grass were buttons, dead matches, butt-ends
of cigars and cigarettes, peanut shells, a drained gin-flask, and
whore's lipstick;
Scattered traces of tar, restless arrays of feathers, and the lingering
smell of gasoline.
And through the morning air the sun poured yellow surprise into the
eye sockets of a stony skull . . .
And while I stood my mind was frozen with a cold pity for the life
that was gone.
The ground gripped my feet and my heart was circled by icy walls of
fear—
The sun died in the sky; a night wind muttered in the grass and fum
bled the leaves in the trees; the woods poured forth the hungry
yelping of hounds; the darkness screamed with thirsty voices;
and the witnesses rose and lived:
The dry bones stirred, rattled, lifted, melting themselves into my
bones.
The gray ashes formed flesh firm and black, entering into my flesh.
The gin-flask passed from mouth to mouth; cigars and cigarettes
glowed, the whore smeared the lipstick red upon her lips,
And a thousand faces swirled around me, clamoring that my life be
burned . . .
And then they had me, stripped me, battering my teeth into my throat
till I swallowed my own blood.
My voice was drowned in the roar of their voices, and my black wet
body slipped and rolled in their hands as they bound me to the
sapling.
And my skin clung to the bubbling hot tar, falling from me in limp
patches.
And the down and quills of the white feathers sank into my raw flesh,
and I moaned in my agony.
Then my blood was cooled mercifully, cooled by a baptism of
gasoline.
And in a blaze of red I leaped to the sky as pain rose like water,
boiling my limbs.
Panting, begging I clutched child-like, clutched to the hot sides of
death.
Now I am dry bones and my face a stony skull staring in yellow
surprise at the sun . . .

1934

Margaret Walker 1915–1998

Margaret Abigail Walker was born July 7, 1915, in Birmingham, Alabama. She received her early education in New Orleans and completed her undergraduate education at Northwestern University in Evanston, Illinois, by the time she was nineteen years old. Although Walker had been writing and publishing before moving to Chicago as a student, it was there that her talent matured. A member of the Works Progress Administration (WPA), Walker shared intellectual, cultural, and professional interests with an important group of artists and writers who formed the Southside Writers Group, led by Richard Wright. Wright and Walker enjoyed a close friendship until he moved to New York in the late 1930s. When Walker left Chicago for graduate school at the University of Iowa in 1939, she was well on her way to becoming a major American poet.

In 1942, Walker completed the full manuscript of a volume she called *For My People,* the title poem of which had been written and published in Chicago five years earlier. *For My People* won the Yale Series of Younger Poets Award following its 1942 publication and brought her immediate recognition as the first African American woman to achieve national literary prominence.

Walker also began work on a historical novel based on her great grandmother, Elvira Ware Dozier, a novel she would not finish until she returned to Iowa in the 1960s to complete her doctoral studies. *Jubilee* is the story of Vyry, whose commitment to her own set of values sustains her during difficult times both as a slave and later as a free woman. Walker's revisionist account of the Civil War and Reconstruction established a new tradition in southern American literature.

For most of her career, Walker lived in Jackson, Mississippi, where she taught English for thirty years. Married to Firnist James Alexander, Walker found time between writing and teaching to mother four children as well as a host of grandchildren.

Walker described herself as a "poet and dreamer who has tried to make her life a poem," a statement suggestive of the many influences and traditions found in her writing, the most notable of which is oratory. She works with sounds, rhythms, and meanings that are drawn from an African American cultural framework and that embrace classical mythology, Judeo-Christian humanism, and African spirituality. With precision of language and sharpness of imagery, Walker captures a wide range of feelings within Anglo-American and traditional African American literary forms. The "I" which frequently appears in her poetry reveals a collective voice reminiscent of Walt Whitman, yet it remains distinctive in its lyrical cadences.

As a writer-activist for the civil rights movement—which her writing helped to fuel and which she acknowledged as a major source of her work—Walker was the model for an entire generation of African American women writers, many of whose careers she midwived into existence through her efforts as a public spokesperson, literary sponsor, workshop leader, and conference organizer. Walker died in 1998 after a long illness.

Maryemma Graham
University of Kansas

PRIMARY WORKS

For My People, 1942; *Jubilee,* 1966; *Profits for a New Day,* 1970; *Richard Wright, Daemonic Genius: A Portrait of the Man, A Critical Look at His Work,* 1986; *This Is My Century: New and Collected Poems,* 1988; *How I Wrote Jubilee and Other Essays on Life and Literature,* 1990.

from Jubilee

No more auction block for me!

7 Cook in the Big House

Early in the spring of 1851 a fairly well-developed plot for an uprising among the slaves of Lee County, with the assistance of free Negroes and white abolitionists, became known to the High Sheriff of the county. How the news began to leak out and through what sources could not be determined by most Negroes. In the first place, the slaves on Marse John's plantation were not fully informed as to what nature the plot took nor how an uprising could take place. Brother Zeke was so troubled that he confided to his flock at their regular meeting place at the Rising Glory Church that it must be a false rumor since no definite plans had ever come to his knowledge. It was first suspected, however, by the guards or patter-rollers[1] and the drivers, who claimed that the Negroes were unusually hard to manage. And the neighboring whites claimed there were unusual movements in town among strange whites and in the county among free Negroes. At first the planters were not suspicious and hardly dared believe the piece-meal information they received. Why would their slaves want to do such a thing?

As Big Missy said to Marse John, "They are all well treated, and we love them and take good care of them just like a part of our family. When they are sick we nurse them back to health. We feed and clothe them and teach them the Christian religion. Our nigras are good and wouldn't try such a thing unless some criminal minds aided and abetted them, like abolitionists and free niggers from outside the state." Such monstrous activities were beyond the wildest imaginations of their good and happy childlike slaves!

Nevertheless, if there was such ingratitude lurking among them, after all the money that had been spent on food and clothes and doctor bills, the owners must be realistic and resort to drastic methods to counteract such activity. They must not wait too long to listen to reason. Hastily and secretly, Marse John and his planter friends gathered with this purpose. There they decided, as their drivers had suggested, that the first thing was to seek out the culprits and see that they were punished to the full extent of the law, chiefly by hanging. Thus they would make an example of them and put the fear of God in the rest of the slaves. Second, they must clamp down harder on the movements of all blacks, enforce the curfew laws and all of the Black Code, thereby rigorously maintaining control over their property, both land and chattel slaves. Finally, but not least, they must seek out all abolitionists guilty of giving aid and comfort to the black enemies of the Georgia people, and either force them out of the state or deal with them so harshly that they would willingly leave. As for the free Negroes, all of them should be called in for questioning and under threat of revoking their papers, forcing them back into slavery, they should be made to leave the state. Meanwhile, the planters should continue to question trusted slaves for any in-

[1]Colloquial term for "patrollers," roving groups of whites responsible for keeping watch and maintaining control over the movement of blacks in the slave South.

formation and should keep watch for any signs of the development of the plot or for any unusual movements of the slaves. The guards and patter-rollers were ordered to search the slave cabins to make sure no weapons or firearms of any kind came into the possession of any black person, slave or free.

May Liza and Caline told Vyry and Lucy and Aunt Sally, "Marster and Big Missy done taking to whisper and shush all the time."

"We act like we don't see nothing and don't hear nothing neither."

If any Negroes were caught in the woods or in the swamps they always said, "We's looking for greens and herbs for medicine and teas."

Many slaves, like Aunt Sally, had gardens around their cabins with collards growing almost into the door. These they cultivated when they did not go to the fields. But the tension was growing so they were forbidden any free activity. Marse John like his other planter friends redoubled his guards and patter-rollers and changed the curfew from nine o'clock to first dark or about one hour after sundown.

The growing tension exploded when the two Negro women accused of having killed their master and his mother by poisoning his food were convicted of murder and sentenced to be hanged. Like Aunt Sally and Vyry and Lucy, they worked in the kitchen of their Marster's Big House. When they were brought to the county jail for trial one afternoon it was quickly decided that they were guilty and had confessed the crime so that nothing was left but to hang them as soon as a judge could set the time and a hangman nearby could be summoned to do the deed.

This episode created a great disturbance among both planters and slaves. Among the planters' families there was unmistakable panic, and among the slaves there was great fear. Mutual distrust hung in the air between blacks and whites. In addition to the recent increase of guards on his place, Marse John, at the request of Grimes, purchased three additional bloodhounds for his plantation.

One of the murders had been committed several months before the second crime and the women were not at first suspected, but when the master died, a doctor confirmed suspicions expressed earlier when the man's mother died. The news traveled fast, and long before the date of the hanging had been set, the crime was common knowledge in every household.

The darkest day in Vyry's young life came without warning. Big Missy and Marse John had arranged to sell Aunt Sally. She would go first to Savannah and then by boat to New Orleans, where she would go on the auction block and be sold to the highest bidder. The morning she was ordered to go, she and Vyry went as usual to the kitchen. Big Missy came out in the kitchen after breakfast and told Aunt Sally to get her things together; there was a wagon in the backyard waiting to take her to Savannah. Now Aunt Sally was ready. She had her head-rag on and she had tied in a bundle the few things she had in the world including the few rags of clothes she wore. She had spread out one of her big aprons and tied them in it. Now she carried it in her arms. Tears were running down her fat black cheeks and she could not control her trembling lips. Vyry stood dazed and numb. Even when Aunt Sally hugged and kissed her, Vyry did not cry. She could not believe this was real, that she would be forced apart from Aunt Sally, that Aunt Sally was leaving and going somewhere. She heard Aunt Sally saying, "Goodbye, honey, don't yall forget to pray. Pray to God to send His chilluns a Moses, pray to Jesus to have mercy on us poor suffering chilluns.

Goodbye, honey, don't you forget Aunt Sally and don't forget to pray. Aunt Sally know she ain't never gwine see yall no more in this here sinful world, but I'm gwine be waiting for you on the other side where there ain't gwine be no more auction block. Goodbye, honey-child, goodbye."

Even then Vyry's eyes were dry. But then she saw poor old Aunt Sally clinging to Sam and Big Boy. She heard her sobbing pitifully, "Oh, Lord, when is you gwine send us that Moses? When you gwine set us peoples free? Jesus, how long? Marster, how long? They is taking all I got in the world from me, they is sending me way down yonder to that cruel auction block! Oh, Lord, how long is we gotta pray?" They were pulling her away but stumbling along crying and muttering she kept saying, "Oh, Lord, have mercy!"

Then Vyry found herself shaking like a leaf in a whirlwind. Salt tears were running in her mouth, and her short, sharp finger nails were digging in the palms of her hands. Suddenly she decided she would go with Aunt Sally, and just then Big Missy slapped her so hard she saw stars and when she saw straight again Aunt Sally was gone.

The first woman who came in from the fields to cook in the Big House did not suit anybody. Her food did not please Marse John and he said so, complaining and cursing at the same time. He grew more and more petulant at each meal, and Big Missy railed at him, "You are so cross and peevish you act like a child!" And he would swear, "Damn you, I was a fool! Had a good cook, been cooking ever since I was a boy, and I let you persuade me to sell her, damn you, don't you talk to me." To make it worse the house servants swore all-out war with the woman and would not help her do anything. She had never worked in the kitchen and knew nothing about where to find anything. She was confused by all the house servants whispering and muttering around her, even within earshot of the white folks. Caline said, "House servants and field hands just don't mix. I ain't no yard nigger myself and I don't have nothing to do with yard niggers. First place, they stinks!"

Vyry was still grieving over the loss of Aunt Sally, but she also resented the woman, and did no more than absolutely necessary to help her. Finally, Big Missy Salina admitted that the woman would have to go.

Then there was a brief interim when Big Missy tried several other women. After the field woman, an older woman from a nearby plantation was sold to Marse John and recommended as an excellent cook, but she ran away within twenty-four hours. They caught her, but Big Missy and Marster decided not to keep her but sent her back, instead, to her former master. The third woman was sickly and she coughed over the pots. In less than a month she grew so much worse that before they realized her trouble she was dead, dying one night on her own pallet after having cooked supper and worked all day. Vyry took her place in the emergency. Thus began her life as cook in the Big House. She always dated the time back to Aunt Sally's going away. Vyry knew the work thoroughly, having been accustomed to the kitchen from childhood. She had worked seven years under Aunt Sally and she not only had learned all she knew from her, but she cooked exactly like Aunt Sally. Although Marse John was immediately pleased with the food, he thought she was too young to be entrusted with the responsibility of chief cook, and that the work would be too hard for her. When he said this to Missy Salina she decided at once that Vyry should be the cook.

Vyry did not care. She had really had to do all the heavy work with the other women anyway, and she was glad to get the kitchen once more to herself. For a short time she was troubled with Big Missy coming into the kitchen, opening the pots to see what was in them, and giving shrill nervous orders which Vyry generally disregarded. After a terrible steaming burn Big Missy ceased to trouble Vyry, much to the girl's relief. The house servants were again satisfied, and the usual atmosphere of an uneasy peace seemed to descend once more over the household.

One morning Vyry was busy with the breakfast dishes when Big Missy came into the kitchen and said, "Vyry, there's a free nigger down at the stables shoeing Marster's horses. I guess you'd best take him a mouthful of something to eat. But mind, you'd better not give him anything fresh. See if you can't find some leftovers. Claims he's hungry and can't work. I don't see howcome he needs anything before dinnertime. He's only been working since six o'clock." Vyry said, "Yes'm. I'll see after him." Big Missy went off grumbling about free niggers being nothing but trouble, "and you mark my words, John'll be sorry for bringing him on this place."

Vyry finished her dishes and when she was ready to start dinner she fixed a plate of food and took it to the hired blacksmith. Rarely, indeed, did a free Negro come on the place to work. The overseers were afraid of the trouble free Negroes might make among the slaves, but there had not been a blacksmith on the place for a long time, so this man had been brought in from the nearby village where he owned his own smithy.

He was so busy working he did not hear Vyry's light step behind him, and when he turned and looked up, her milk-white face startled him. She was five and a half feet tall with her sandy hair roped high on her head. Her cold, bluish-gray eyes looked out without emotion. Her mouth was tight in a straight, hard line. He quickly recovered when he saw she wore the cheap calico and sack clothes of a slave.

"First off, I thought you was the young Missus. You look just like her."

"I'm a slave all right," snapped Vyry. "Here's your food. I ain't got no time for swapping gossip."

Then he stood up straight. He made no move to take the food, but giving her a long look said, "Ain't no hurry, is there? Or do they *pay* you to work so fast? I just wanted to know what might be your name?"

"Ain't got no name," said Vyry, and putting the food down on the ground she turned to walk away from him. But he was too quick for her. He jumped before her and caught her by the arm, "Easy, gal, I mean no harm. Bide a bit, and tell me who's your man?"

"You know who ain't, I reckon, and I'll thank you to turn me loose."

"Too good for a black man, hanh? I reckon the white folks got they eyes on you themselves."

"Don't know about that. I ain't had no trouble so far, and I ain't looking for none from black nor white."

He snickered. "Ain't feeding you saltpeter, hanh, to keep a good cook cooking?"

Vyry spoke out angrily, "Nigger, make haste and turn me loose!"

At that he narrowed his eyes and moved his hand.

"I may be a nigger, but I'm still a free man, and that's more'n you can say, Miss Stuck-up, with your ass on your shoulder. If you would marriage with me, I'd buy your freedom!" With that he turned to one side, looked her full in the eye, tossed back his massive black head, sparked his eyes, flashed his pearl-white teeth, and jingled the coins in his pocket. The word "freedom" caught her up short, and giving him a quick questioning glance she sized him up from head to toe. He had the strong, hard, muscular body that went with his trade and his shoulders were as big as a barrel. Black as a spade and stockily built, he looked like a powerful giant. There was just enough animal magnetism in him to trouble Vyry, and he was never more magnetic than now while she paused to weigh his words.

"You ain't got enough gold to buy me with what you jingling in your jeans." She said this half-scornfully, but she did not move now that she was perfectly free to go.

"I got a thousand gold pieces and a thousand silver pieces and I don't carry them in my jeans. I reckon they'll buy your freedom, or do you think you're worth more than that?"

"Show me your money first, and talk to me later."

"Why I got to show you? Can you buy, or can you sell?" Scornfully he chided her,

> White man got the eye for gold,
> And nigger man do what he told.

She continued just as pertly. "Then I gotta be getting back to my cooking. When you speaks to Marster bout buying my freedom so's I can marriage with you, I'll gossip with you then, till times gets better."

> *Lil piece of wheat bread,*
> *Lil piece of pie,*
> *Gwine have that yaller gal,*
> *Or else I'll die.*

8 Randall Ware

Randall Ware was a free man because he was born free. He was black as the Ace of Spades because nothing but the blood of black men coursed through his veins. He knew the trade of blacksmith when he came to Georgia and to Lee County with a sack of gold, enough to register himself as a free man, enough to guarantee the payment of his yearly taxes as a free man, and enough to buy himself a stake of land through the confidence and assistance of his white guardian, Randall Wheelwright. Of course, he would have stayed in Virginia where there were other relatives who were free and artisans, but Randall Wheelwright had persuaded him to come to Georgia. And Ware felt a closeness to this white man whom he respected so highly he had even taken his given name instead of the foreign name with which he had been christened in the Islands. Between these two men there was mutual and implicit trust.

Randall Wheelwright was a staunch Quaker whose ancestors had given material assistance to the cause of American freedom during the Revolutionary War. He was, therefore, entitled to draw in the land lottery of 1852 held in Lee County in the state of Georgia. He was an old man when he finally settled in Georgia, but he lived long enough to help young Randall Ware establish himself and find other white friends who could help him in need. Moreover, he willed this young black friend much of his property. Thus, Randall Ware came into possession of the two hundred and two and a half acres of land that Wheelwright had originally owned. They seemed nothing but woods and marsh land. He inherited this by a legally drawn will and the proper papers were duly recorded in the County Courthouse by the Clerk of the Court. It made Randall Ware a rich free Negro who was closely watched by the planters of Lee County. With some of his money he bought the land where his smithy stood, and next to it he had a grist mill where poor white farmers came in large numbers to have their corn ground into meal. He built the structure which housed his anvil and the nearby stalls for horses which were brought to him for shoes.

Another factor that had drawn Randall Ware to Randall Wheelwright was the latter's strong abolitionist views. As a Quaker his religious views were regarded as far too independent for the southern community, but his abolitionist views were hated even more. He and old Bob Qualls had frequently been suspected of helping slaves escape to freedom and even daring to buy slaves on the auction block and, after purchasing them, giving them their freedom. Randall Wheelwright was an immaculate and dapper little gentleman with brown hair and shrewd but kind and twinkling hazel eyes. He wore a Van Dyke beard and carried a gold-headed cane. He was built sparely and delicately. Old man Bob Qualls, on the other hand, a big heavily built man, was frequently unkempt, chewed tobacco, and talked with a Carolina drawl. His abolitionist views, however, were just as strong as Wheelwright's; moreover, he had been a soldier and had fought in both Indian and Mexican wars, so he, too, had a claim to land in the lottery. These two men had an interesting association with Randall Ware and their coming to Georgia near the middle of the century had both meaning and purpose.

As a free man in Georgia, Randall Ware had his troubles. The law was strict in the surveillance of all blacks, and the free black man was only slightly better off than the slaves. His movements were proscribed and all his actions defined. His legal status was flimsy because he must always have a white guardian. This white guardian must be a property owner of some means, and technically, the free man was attached to the land of his white guardian in much the same manner of a serf or slave. His status was also similar to that of an indentured servant whose time was not his own. He had the same difficulty in owning firearms as a slave or an Indian, but he could own property and had some legal rights that neither slaves nor Indians possessed. Every year he was forced to renew his free papers by paying an exorbitant tax which increased annually. These free papers must always be found on his person and when he traveled from place to place he must buy a permit and register in each county he entered so that his movements could always be checked. If, for any reason, he could not produce the yearly assessment for his papers, they could be taken from him and his freedom revoked. If he were arrested and charged with a crime or held under suspicion, his freedom was also questioned and endangered and he could be thrown into jail without redress unless he could speedily produce a white friend in the county.

Randall Ware was a literate man. He understood printed materials, could read and write and figure his own accounts, and he had read much abolitionist material. When he came to Georgia he understood what both Randall Wheelwright and Bob

Qualls represented as Quakers and abolitionists and he knew that he was of invaluable assistance to them and to all runaway slaves on the underground railroad. Brother Zeke was an important contact who must never be placed in jeopardy. No matter what time of night he brought a trembling runaway to the smithy, Randall Ware must hide him or get him to Wheelwright and Qualls without suspicion. Thus far, things had worked well. Thus far, he, Randall Ware, had encountered no real difficulty, even here in the backwoods of Georgia, until he saw the white face of the slave girl, Vyry.

For the first time in his mature life he felt the hot blood of desire for a special woman burn his flesh. It was the first time that such a physical desire had ever been uppermost in his mind. He felt he must have her for his own, and he knew nothing in the world could make her more willing to be his than the promise and fulfillment of her freedom. No matter what a white planter said, every slave craved freedom, and nobody knew this better than Randall Ware.

Vyry at fifteen was, nevertheless, not merely the chattel slave of John Morris Dutton, but obviously she was linked by blood to his household. Randall Ware reckoned that her resemblance to the young Missy and to Marse John was no little coincidence. She was their own blood kin, but tied to slavery by a black mother, he was sure. She would not be easy to buy. He had ways of learning, however, by the grapevine of the underground railroad whether her master would sell Vyry, who was now his cook in his Big House. He also knew that as a mulatto, by Georgia law she could be free to marry a free man with her master's consent, that is, if she could get that consent. There was also the possibility that she could be smuggled out to freedom. But he wanted her here in Georgia, and he wanted her to be legally bound to no one but him. He had enough to buy her, that ought to be all there was to it. He reassured himself that he could be confident that gold would buy anything on the market. His money had always been powerful enough to buy anything he wanted. Surely it would be powerful enough to buy the object of his heart's dearest desire.

Meanwhile, Vyry was troubled with strange emotions. She could not get the black face of the free man out of her mind. She still felt the casual touch of his hand on her arm. Above all she was fascinated with his talk of freedom, of buying her freedom, of making her free to marriage with him. He told her he had money. Did he have enough? Was he telling the truth? Was he playing and spoofing with her? Did he mean what he said? Who was he, anyway?

With great caution she casually inquired about the blacksmith. She knew his name was Randall Ware, and she knew he owned a blacksmith's shop in the village. But she still did not know all she wanted to about this free black man. How old was he? Did he have another gal or woman of his own? Rumor was a witness that he had plenty of money, that he had a rich white guardian, and that he was one of those smart niggers with letters in his head. A nigger with book learning? A nigger with money and a nigger free on top of all of this? Was she dreaming? Was such a thing ever heard of in Georgia? *Maybe he can teach me how to read and write and cipher on my hands.* But it was the idea of freedom and the proposition he had raised in connection with that miraculous idea that fascinated her most. She turned it over in her mind idly, as a child turns over a new play-toy. She tried to imagine what it meant to be free. She had never before entertained the faintest idea or hope of freedom, except some dream of an answer to prayer, when God would suddenly appear and send a deliverer like Moses, and set free all the people who were in bondage such as she. She had heard tell that once in a great while a master had been known to set a slave free for saving his life, but not once in her own short life had she ever heard of such a thing happening where she lived. She had never thought of anything else except accepting her lot as a slave, obeying her master and mistress and working hard. She had been resigned. She had never before thought about freedom.

Now the idea of being free began to take hold of her and to work up and down and through her like milk churning to make butter. All day long she thought of nothing but Randall Ware and freedom. At night she dreamed confused dreams in which she struggled to be free while something struggled against her to keep her in chains. Once she dreamed she saw a beautiful door and she tried to enter it, because someone told her the name of the door was Freedom, but the door was locked and although she kept trying the lock and turning the golden knob, it would not open. Then she beat against it with her fists and butted it with her head, but she only made hollow noises and it would not open. Then she saw a black man standing by the door. He held a golden key dangling from a dazzling chain, and he was smiling at her and promising to open the door, but his face kept changing into strange faces. When she woke up crying, she remembered that the door was still locked, even in her dreams, and that he had backed away from her, tantalizing her with that key. She begged and begged him, but he would not give it to her and backed away until he disappeared.

If her dreams and her thoughts were confusing, the talk around her was even more dismaying. She sensed what she did not have to be told: that Big Missy would put up a terrible fight against letting her be sold to a free black man or letting her have freedom in any way. Big Missy hated free Negroes worse than she hated Vyry. Marse John might want to do the right thing if she spoke to him alone but he was so mixed up and so indecisive and unpredictable that he might not be able to make his decision alone. He might make the mistake of asking Big Missy and then no telling what would happen. Even when she gambled against hope that maybe he wouldn't tell Big Missy, she remembered that he liked her cooking. Maybe he would not like her to have her freedom, either. Added to all this anxiety, she suddenly learned from Caline that Randall Ware was busy trying to get slaves to rise up and that sometimes he even slipped into the fields and talked to the field hands. She was very worried that something might happen to him before he had done anything about buying her freedom. She discovered that talk and gossip were strange things. Talk had feet and could walk and gossip had wings and could fly. She heard whispers and she was afraid they would grow as big as men, and she felt the wings of gossip threatening to sting and to smother her. It buzzed around her and flew against her and her words came back upon her to settle motionless in the air. The house servants confided to her that Randall Ware was telling Sam and Big Boy and many field hands that he knew a way they could all be free. As if all this were not enough, Big Missy kept throwing out broad hints and remarks about free black biggity niggers stirring up trouble amongst our good hard working niggers. When she finally came out and questioned Vyry sharply and asked her if she knew anything about the trouble that was being stirred up amongst all the niggers in the county, Vyry answered, "Lord, no Missy, I ain't heard tell of nothing," and "Yes'm, when I does I sure will let you know."

1966

Southern Song

I want my body bathed again by southern suns, my soul
reclaimed again from southern land. I want to rest
again in southern fields, in grass and hay and clover
bloom; to lay my hand again upon the clay baked by a
southern sun, to touch the rain-soaked earth and smell
the smell of soil.

I want my rest unbroken in the fields of southern earth;
freedom to watch the corn wave silver in the sun and
mark the splashing of a brook, a pond with ducks and
frogs and count the clouds.

I want no mobs to wrench me from my southern rest; no
forms to take me in the night and burn my shack and
make for me a nightmare full of oil and flame.

I want my careless song to strike no minor key; no fiend to
stand between my body's southern song—the fusion of
the South, my body's song and me.

1942

For My People

For my people everywhere singing their slave songs repeatedly: their
dirges and their ditties and their blues and jubilees, praying their
prayers nightly to an unknown god, bending their knees humbly to
an unseen power;

For my people lending their strength to the years, to the gone years
and the now years and the maybe years, washing ironing cooking
scrubbing sewing mending hoeing plowing digging planting
pruning patching dragging along never gaining never reaping never
knowing and never understanding;

For my playmates in the clay and dust and sand of Alabama backyards playing baptizing and preaching and doctor and jail and
soldier and school and mama and cooking and playhouse and
concert and store and hair and Miss Choomby and company;

For the cramped bewildered years we went to school to learn to know
the reasons why and the answers to and the people who and the
places where and the days when, in memory of the bitter hours
when we discovered we were black and poor and small and

different and nobody cared and nobody wondered and nobody understood;

For the boys and girls who grew in spite of these things to be man and woman, to laugh and dance and sing and play and drink their wine and religion and success, to marry their playmates and bear children and then die of consumption and anemia and lynching;

For my people thronging 47th Street in Chicago and Lenox Avenue in New York and Rampart Street in New Orleans, lost disinherited dispossessed and happy people filling the cabarets and taverns and other people's pockets needing bread and shoes and milk and land and money and something—something all our own;

For my people walking blindly spreading joy, losing time being lazy, sleeping when hungry, shouting when burdened, drinking when hopeless, tied and shackled and tangled among ourselves by the unseen creatures who tower over us omnisciently and laugh;

For my people blundering and groping and floundering in the dark of churches and schools and clubs and societies, associations and councils and committees and conventions, distressed and disturbed and deceived and devoured by money-hungry glory-craving leeches, preyed on by facile force of state and fad and novelty, by false prophet and holy believer;

For my people standing staring trying to fashion a better way from confusion, from hypocrisy and misunderstanding, trying to fashion a world that will hold all the people, all the faces, all the adams and eyes and their countless generations;

Let a new earth rise. Let another world be born. Let a bloody peace be written in the sky. Let a second generation full of courage issue forth; let a people loving freedom come to growth. Let a beauty full of healing and a strength of final clenching be the pulsing in our spirits and our blood. Let the martial songs be written, let the dirges disappear. Let a race of men now rise and take control.

1942

Ballad of the Hoppy-Toad

Ain't been on Market Street for nothing
With my regular washing load
When the Saturday crowd went stomping
Down the Johnny-jumping road,

Seen Sally Jones come running
With a razor at her throat,
Seen Deacon's daughter lurching
Like a drunken alley goat.

But the biggest for my money,
And the saddest for my throw
Was the night I seen the goopher man
Throw dust around my door.

Come sneaking round my doorway
In a stovepipe hat and coat;
Come sneaking round my doorway
To drop the evil note.

I run down to sis Avery's
And told her what I seen
"Root-worker's out to git me
What you reckon that there mean?"

Sis Avery she done told me,
"Now honey go on back
I knows just what will hex him
And that old goopher sack."

Now I done burned the candles
Till I seen the face of Jim
And I done been to church and prayed
But can't git rid of him.

Don't want to burn his picture
Don't want to dig his grave
Just want to have my peace of mind
And make that dog behave.

Was running through the fields one day
Sis Avery's chopping corn
Big horse come stomping after me
I knowed then I was gone.

Sis Avery grabbed that horse's mane
And not one minute late
Cause trembling down behind her
I seen my ugly fate.

She hollered to that horse to "Whoa!
I gotcha hoppy-toad."

And yonder come the goopher man
A-running down the road.

She hollered to that horse to "Whoa"
And what you wanta think?
Great-God-a-mighty, that there horse
Begun to sweat and shrink.

He shrunk up to a teeny horse
He shrunk up to a toad
And yonder come the goopher man
Still running down the road.

She hollered to that horse to "Whoa"
She said, "I'm killing him.
Now you just watch this hoppy-toad
And you'll be rid of Jim."

The goopher man was hollering
"Don't kill that hoppy-toad."
Sis Avery she said "Honey,
You bout to lose your load."

That hoppy-toad was dying
Right there in the road
And goopher man was screaming
"Don't kill that hoppy-toad."

The hoppy-toad shook one more time
And then he up and died
Old goopher man fell dying, too.
"O hoppy-toad," he cried.

1970

Solace

Now must I grieve and fret my little way
into death's darkness, ending all my day
in bitterness and pain, in striving and in stress;
go on unendingly again
to mock the sun with death
and mask all light with fear?
Oh no, I will not cease to lift my eyes
beyond those resurrecting hills;
a Fighter still, I will not cease to strive

and see beyond this thorny path a light.
I will not darken all my days
with bitterness and fear,
but lift my heart with faith and hope
and dream, as always, of a brighter place.

1988

The Crystal Palace

The Crystal Palace used to be
a place of elegance
Where "bourgie" black folks came to shoot
a game of pool
And dine in the small cafe
across the way.
The dance hall music rocked the night
and sang sweet melodies:
"Big fat mama with the meat shaking on her bones"
"Boogie woogie mama
Please come back home"
"I miss you loving papa
but I can't live on love alone"
The Crystal Palace
Used to be
most elegant.

1988

Saunders Redding 1906–1988

Of middle-class parentage, Jay Saunders Redding was born in Wilmington, Delaware, just three years after W.E.B. Du Bois posed his own probing questions in *The Souls of Black Folk.* His father, Lewis Alfred Redding, and his mother, Mary Ann Holmes Redding, had been educated to become teachers. His father's roots led back to slavery; his paternal grandmother was an escaped slave. His mother was mulatto; his maternal grandmother, a mixture of Irish, Indian, and black, was of a "free" background. For the young Saunders, an understanding of the importance of education for blacks and a consciousness of racial identity and awareness developed early.

After his early schooling in Wilmington (1912–23), Redding attended Lincoln University in Pennsylvania for one year (1923–24), then transferred to Brown University, from which he received his A.B. degree in 1928. After teaching at Morehouse College in Atlanta, he returned to Brown and was awarded an M.A. in 1932.

For more than half a century, Redding taught at a number of colleges and universities and built an outstanding career as writer and literary and cultural critic. He became one of the major "senior" scholars in African American literature and a much-sought-after mentor to new scholars in the field. Over the years, he taught at Louisville Municipal College, Southern University in Baton Rouge, State Teachers College at Elizabeth City, North Carolina, and Hampton Institute, among others. In his final professorial years he was Ernest I. White Professor of American Studies and Humane Letters at Cornell. He served also as director of the division of research and publication of the National Endowment for the Humanities, and he accepted a State Department assignment in India. In recognition of his scholarship, he was awarded several honorary doctorates, including one from his alma mater, Brown, and one from his home state university, the University of Delaware.

In literary history and criticism, Redding's *To Make a Poet Black* (1939) is a standard among early sources on African American literature. Including key writers from 1760 to 1939, the text had as its goal "to bring together factual material and critical opinion on American Negro literature in a sort of history of Negro thought in America." In 1940 Redding received a Rockefeller Grant to "Go out into Negro life in the South." The result was *No Day of Triumph* (1942), which won him the Mayflower Award from the North Carolina Historical Society for the best work that year by a North Carolinian. This book is an example of Redding's writing forte: the bringing together of the personal and the historic, with analysis and commentary.

Supported by a Guggenheim Award, Redding wrote his only novel, *Stranger and Alone* (1950), in which he scathingly attacks the black educator. This book received mixed critical attention in essays by Alain Locke, Ralph Ellison, Ann Petry, and others. As an illumination of the novel and an extension of the autobiography and social history of *No Day of Triumph,* one should read *On Being Negro in America* (1951), Redding's attempt to look back at self and race in his continued search for truth. His social histories—*They Came in Chains* (1950), *The Lonesome Road* (1958), and *The Negro* (1967)—treat some of the same issues as his other texts. Finally, in 1971, he and Arthur P. Davis published an anthology, *Cavalcade: Negro American Writing from 1760 to the Present,* revised with Joyce Ann Joyce and reissued after Redding's death. Letters written between 1938 and 1945 by Redding to James Weldon Johnson, Carl Van Vechten, and Richard Wright are housed at the Yale University Beinecke Rare Book and Manuscript Library.

Eleanor Q. Tignor
LaGuardia Community College

PRIMARY WORKS

To Make a Poet Black, 1939; *No Day of Triumph,* 1942; *Stranger and Alone,* 1950; *They Came in Chains,* 1950; *On Being Negro in America,* 1951; *The Lonesome Road,* 1958; *The Negro,* 1967; *J. Saunders Redding: Selected Writings,* ed. Faith Berry, 1988; *Cavalcade: Negro American Writing from 1760 to the Present,* 2 vols., ed. with Arthur P. Davis and Joyce Ann Joyce, 1991, 1992; *A Scholar's Conscience: Selected Writings of J. Saunders Redding, 1942–1977,* ed. Faith Berry, 1992.

from No Day of Triumph

Chapter One
Troubled in Mind

1

Consciousness of my environment began with the sound of talk. It was not hysterical talk, not bravado, though it might well have been, for my father had bought in a neighborhood formerly forbidden, and we lived, I realize now, under an armistice. But in the early years, when we were a young family, there was always talk at our house; a great deal of it mere talk, a kind of boundless and robustious overflow of family feeling. Our shouts roared through the house with the exuberant gush of flood waters through an open sluice, for talk, generated by any trifle, was the power that turned the wheels of our inner family life. It was the strength and that very quality of our living that made impregnable, it seemed, even to time itself, the walls of our home. But it was in the beginning of the second decade of the century, when the family was an institution still as inviolate as the swing of the earth.

There was talk of school, of food, of religion, of people. There were the shouted recitations of poems and Biblical passages and orations from *Bryan, Phillips,* and *John Brown.*[1] My mother liked rolling *apostrophes.*[2] We children were all trained at home in the declining art of oratory and were regular contestants for prizes at school. My father could quote with appropriate gestures bits from *Beveridge,* whom he had never heard, and from *Teddy Roosevelt* and *Fred Douglass,*[3] whom he had. There was talk of the "race problem," reasonable and unembittered unless Grandma Redding was there, and then it became a kind of spiritual poison, its virulence destructive of its own immediate effects, almost its own catharsis. Some of the poison was absorbed.

I remember Grandma Redding coming on one of her visits and finding us playing in the back yard. My brother and sister were there and we were playing with Myrtle Lott and Elwood Carter, white children who were neighbors. Grandma came in the back way through the alley, as she always did, and when we heard the gate scrape against the bricks we stopped. She stepped into the yard and looked fixedly at us.

[1]William Jennings Bryan (1860–1925), American orator, politician, and statesman; Democratic Party candidate who lost the Presidential race, twice to William McKinley (1860, 1900) and once to William Howard Taft (1908); Wendell Phillips (1811–1884), American orator and reformer, active with William Lloyd Garrison's abolitionist group and later with the American Anti-Slavery Society; John Brown (1800–1859), American abolitionist, charged with treason for his attempted raid of a United States arsenal at Harpers Ferry, Virginia (now West Virginia).

[2]A figure of speech in which a person or thing not listening is addressed directly.

[3]William Henry Beveridge (1879–1963), British economist and author, took the position that the number of jobs should always exceed the number of workers; Theodore Roosevelt, 26th President of the United States (1901–1909); Frederick Douglass (1817?–1895), American slave who escaped to freedom, became an abolitionist, orator, and statesman.

Holding her ancient, sagging canvas bag under one arm, she slowly untied the ribbons of her black bonnet. The gate fell shut behind her. Her eyes were like lashes on our faces. Reaching out her long arm, she held open the gate. Then she said, "Git. You white trash, git!" Our companions, pale with fright, ducked and scampered past her. When they had gone, Grandma nodded curtly to us. "Chillen," she said, and went into our house.

Grandma Redding's visits were always unannounced. She came the fifty-odd miles up from Still Pond, Maryland, as casually as if she had come from around the nearest corner. A sudden cold silence would fall, and there would be Grandma. I do not know how she managed to give the impression of shining with a kind of deadly hard glare, for she was always clothed entirely in black and her black, even features were as hard and lightless as stone. I never saw a change of expression on her features. She never smiled. In anger her face turned slowly, dully gray, but her thin nostrils never flared, her long mouth never tightened. She was tall and fibrous and one of her ankles had been broken when she was a girl and never properly set, so that she walked with a defiant limp.

She hated white people. In 1858, as a girl of ten, she had escaped from slavery on the eastern shore of Maryland with a young woman of eighteen. They made their way to Camden, New Jersey, but there was no work and little refuge there. Across the river, bustling Philadelphia swarmed with slave hunters. By subterfuge or by violence even free people were sometimes kidnaped and sent south. Near Bridgeton, New Jersey, the runaways heard, there was a free Negro settlement, but one night they were stopped on the docks by a constable who asked them for papers. They had none. Within two weeks after their escape they were slaves again. When my grandmother tried to run away from the flogging that was her punishment, Caleb Wrightson, her master, flung a chunk of wood at her and broke her ankle.

It was not until we were quite large children that Grandma Redding told us this story. She did not tell it for our pleasure, as one tells harrowing tales to children. It was without the dramatic effects that Grandma Conway delighted in. What *she* would have done with such a tale! No. Grandma Redding's telling was as bare and imageless as a lesson recited from the head and as coldly furious as the whine of a shot.

"An' ol' man Calub flane a hick'ry chunk an' brist my anklebone."

I can see her now as she sits stooped in the wooden rocker by the kitchen stove, her sharp elbows on her sharp knees and her long black fingers with their immense purple nails clawing upward at the air. Her undimmed eyes whipped at ours, and especially at mine, it seemed to me; her thin lips scarcely parted. She had just come in or was going out, for she wore her bonnet and it sat on the very top of her harsh, dull hair. Hatred shook her as a strong wind shakes a boughless tree.

"An' ol' man Calub stank lik'a pes'-house from the rottin' of his stomick 'fore he died an' went t' hell, an' his boys died in the wo' an' went to hell."

But her implacable hatred needed no historical recall, and so far as I remember, she never told the tale to us again.

But generally Grandma Redding's taciturnity was a hidden rock in the sea of our talk. The more swift the tide, the more the rock showed, bleak and unavoidable. At other times the talk flowed smoothly around her: the bursts of oratory and poetry, the chatter of people and events, the talk of schooling and sometimes of money and often of God. Even the talk of God did not arouse her. I think she was not especially religious; and in this, too, she was unlike Grandma Conway.

My grandmothers met at our house but once. They did not like each other.

2

Grandma Conway said "Good morning" as if she were pronouncing the will of God. A woman as squat and solid as a tree stump, she had a queer knurl of religious thought and character that no ax of eclecticism could cleave. She had great bouts of religious argument with whoever would argue with her. Even though her adversary sat but two feet away, she would shout out her disputes in a cracking voice and half-rise threateningly, her gray serge breast lifting and falling as if she had been running uphill. She often frightened our young friends in this manner, awed them into speechlessness; and when she had done this, her green-yellow eyes would blink very fast and her fat, yellow little fists would fly to her chest and beat gently there in laughter.

Grandma Conway was honest about God and often very moving. When she visited us, the family prayers on Sunday belonged to her. Her prayers seemed to bring Him into our dining room, transforming the flesh and blood reality of Grandma Conway into a greater reality of mystical communion. It was as if a sleep and a dream of God descended upon us all, replacing our earthly consciousness with another too penetrating to be born in wakefulness and too sublime to bear the weight of our gross senses. I would keep my gaze fastened upon Grandma for visual evidence against that awful Presence; or I looked around, feeling my elbows pressed deep into the fabroid of the chair seat, at my brother, my sisters, the quiet stillness of my mother's bent back, the upright, almost transfixed solidity of my father's shoulders. I would hear and smell the sausage frying, and the baked beans, and the hot rolls, and the coffee. But insensibly my eyes would close against the physical reality, which somehow even sight and sound and smell could not confirm, and I would be washed up onto a plane of awareness that terrified me.

"Come on feet of thunder, Holy One, but tread amongst us softly, and let us hear the rustling of your garments. It's like the sound the wind makes at night in the sycamore trees in front of my house on Columbus Street. I feel Your spirit hands uplifting me and Your Holy Presence cloaking me, Oh, Giver of all things good and perfect."

But often she talked to Him of the intimate trifles that enlivened her day, of her children and her children's children.

"Dear Father, the boy, Saunders, had a croup last night and his hacking and coughing kept me from my sleep."

So intimately and yet so reverently.

It was on one of these Sundays that my grandmothers met. Grandma Conway had been with us a month. Grandma Redding came as unceremoniously as she usually came, looking as if she had walked every step of the fifty miles from her home. When my mother went to the kitchen that morning, Grandma Redding was sitting on the back steps. Though it was August and hot, she wore the heavy black dress and the black woolen jacket which seemed to be her only garments. When she discovered that Grandma Conway was visiting us, she did not remove her bonnet, and, as I remember, there was some difficulty in inducing her to stay for prayers and breakfast.

The presence of the two old women filled us children with strange, jerky excitement. Even our mother was infected by it. I think we recognized more than the surface differences between our grandmothers. Separating their thoughts and characters was a deep gulf that could not be accounted for alone by the wide divergence of their experiences. It was something even more fundamental. It was what they were and would have been, even, I believe, had they lived through similar experiences. No bridge of time or thought or feeling could join them. They were of different earth. On the surface it looked as simple as this: one was yellow, the other black.

There was a pause of embarrassment just before we knelt for prayers. Grandma Conway, with the gracious magnanimity with which one sometimes yields to a rival, said to my father, "Maybe your ma would like to lead us in prayer this morning." My father looked embarrassed, drawing his hand over his bald head from crown to forehead and shooting an oblique glance at my mother. Mother said nothing. Then Grandma Redding said;

"No. Thank'ee. Lewis *wist*[4] I ain't no comp'ny-prayin' one. Let her pray."

We knelt at chairs around the square table. The odor of the breakfast was heavy in the room—coffee, fresh bread, and the Sunday smell of sliced bananas all mingled. The sun made a heavy shaft of light through each of the two windows and flecks of it escaping through the multitudinous small holes in the green shades danced upon the wall. More than the Sunday excitement of dressing for church filled us. Beyond the hard, straight shoulders of Grandma Redding I could see my older sister silently dancing on her knees. Behind me I could hear my mother's stepped-up breathing and the sound her dress made when she moved against the chair. The others knelt on the other side of the table. Lowering my face in my spread fingers, I waited for prayers to begin. Grandma Conway sighed heavily. I set myself against the coming of that awful Presence.

"God, our Holy Father, Chastiser of sin and evil, great Maker of all things pure and good and of the creatures that here on earth do dwell, be with us in our prayers this morning. There are many who cannot rise from their beds of pain this morning—dear Lord, be with them. There are many who went last night in health to bed and this morning lie cold in death. Be with them. And be with us. Thou can be everywhere. Thou art in the sun that. . . "

It was obvious to us who knew her prayers that the spirit had not descended upon her. Her prayer was not coming with that mellifluous and intimate spontaneity with which she generally spoke to God. She was remembering perhaps too much of the Book of Common Prayer which she had studied as a child. My tension eased a little.

". . . Holy Father, these my children now, and my children's children. Mary here, and the man who made her a woman. You know all this, Father, but I'm getting old and my mind wanders. Make these children as Your Son. Keep not the cross from them, nor the crown of thorns, nor the cup of sorrow. Deny them not the chastening rod of truth if their young lives would be as lamps on the footpaths of eternity. And

[4]Knows.

Redding's ma, Lord. She's with us this morning. She has her affliction, Holy One, and we can hardly notice it, but it's an affliction on her. Bless her. Teach her that affliction chasteneth a righteous heart and only the wicked are bowed down. Bless her, dear God, and bless us all. We ask it in the name . . ."

Before my father could say "Amen," as was his custom, and we could rise from our knees, Grandma Redding's hard, grainy voice whanged out beside me. I felt the room's shocked stillness. Surprised and irritated a little at this fresh delay to breakfast, I peeped at her through my fingers. She was kneeling with her long back in a hard curve and her forearms spread along the chair seat. Her black hands grasped the uprights of the chair, so that her large knuckles stood out purple. Her eyes were not closed and her face was as hard as rock.

"Lis'en, Jesus. You *wist* I ain't got the words fer comp'ny prayers. This is all I want t'say. I been climbin' hills an' goin' down valleys be't sixty some years, an' the hills ain't no littler an' the valleys ain't no lesser. I ain't downright complainin', Jesus. I'm jes' tellin' You the way things is, be't You ain't been here in my lifetime. You ain't been here in be't than a thousan' years. Sence You been here, Gawd's done made a new lan' an' put a whole lot o' diff'unt things an' people on it all together, an' we'se all steered up ever' which way. We had slav'ry sence You been here. That's mean business. Now we got something else, an' that's mean business too. Devilment an' hate an' wo' an' some being one thing an' some another, that's all bad, mean business. We'se all skiverin' an' steered up. It ain't t'beginnin' an' it ain't the close. You understan' what's on my mind, Jesus.

"Now, bless these young'uns. Bless 'em on earth. It don't matter 'bout us ol' ones. We'se skitterin' down the rocky hill anyhow. Bless us in the everlastin'. But these young'uns, they's climbin' up. All I ast be You keep 'em from the knowin' an' the manbirthed sins o' blackness. We'se bent on knees to Your will, Lord Jesus. Amen."

This prayer probably had no lasting effect upon the others who heard it, but, young as I was, its impression upon me was profound. In time to come it was to be as a light thrown upon Grandma Redding's character, and, by reflection, upon Grandma Conway's. It was only later, of course, that I had any intellectual comprehension of the basis of the contrast between them. For many years I continued to think of Grandma Redding as a strange, bitterly choleric old woman and that her irascibility was somehow a part of her blackness. I could not help this absurdity then, for ours was an upper-class Negro family, the unwitting victim of our own culture complexes; deeply sensitive to the tradition of ridicule and inferiority attaching to color; hating the tradition and yet inevitably absorbing it.

Grandma Redding knew and admitted the debilitating force of that tradition, and out of her knowledge had come her prayer. There were dark ones among us, but none so black as Grandma Redding. I was dark. But here again we were victims of evasive and defensive thinking. To members of our immediate family the stigma of blackness did not apply. But Grandma Redding, whom, somehow, we never seemed to know very well, and her children—my father's brothers—were not of the family circle. And it applied to them. It was a crazy, irrational, paradoxical pattern, not made less so by those occasional upheaving disturbances in the general social order that rolled in on us in great breakers from the fathomless sea of the white world. We were a garrisoned island in that sea.

On the other hand, I thought of Grandma Conway and her kin—they were all mulattoes—as escaping the tradition. But, indeed, Grandma Conway was nearer the absurdity than I. I have always remembered with what garrulous delight she used to repeat:

"So this white gentleman, who lived in the next block, met us on the street one day. I had a big hat on Cora, you see, and you couldn't see her face without raising her head or taking off her hat. So he met us and says, bowing just as nice, 'Miss Cora'—that was to me. Your poor, dead Aunt Cora was named for me. 'Miss Cora,' he says, 'let me see this prize package under the big hat,' and he lifted her hat up. Cora was just as pretty! She was too pretty to live, dear Lord. He lifted her hat up, and when he saw her, he says, as if he'd been kicked in the stomach, 'Why, she's nearly white!' 'Yes, indeedy,' I said, 'and I intend to keep her that way.'"

And then her eyes behind her tiny oval glasses would screw up and her fat yellow hands would fly to her breast and beat there gently in laughter. Her laughter was not an exact comment, but it was only later that I realized this, for when we were young it seemed merely an amusing story.

My grandmothers did not meet again after that Sunday breakfast. It was as strained a meal as any I have ever sat through. Grandma Redding kept her bonnet on all through it. She drank only sweetened hot water and ate only the sliced bananas. As always, Grandma Conway, though silent, ate and drank heavily of black coffee sweetened almost to syrup, of the kidney stew and baked beans, and the crunchy rolls as large as buns. Even under ordinary circumstances, her appetite was amazing. My father quarreled with us a good deal that morning. My mother was silent. Eventually we all fell silent, hearing only the sucking sound that Grandma Redding's lips made on the edge of her cup and the explosive grunts of pleasure with which Grandma Conway munched her roll.

They never saw each other again, though each lived several years longer. In 1923 Grandma Redding, her face stone-set in pain, limped defiantly to her death, and three years later death caught up with Grandma Conway while she slept.

1942

Pietro Di Donato 1911–1992

An anomaly in American literature and eccentric in the true sense of being off-center, the primitivism of Pietro Di Donato burst like a meteor on the literary scene of the late Thirties. This mainly self-taught son of Italian immigrants was to immortalize his tragically killed worker father as the veritable Christ-figure of his classic novel *Christ in Concrete,* published in 1939 to extraordinary critical acclaim.

It was, perhaps, the precisely right moment for this novel to be acclaimed: the portrayal of exploited workers fit the social protest sympathies of the period; and the unique language which expressed in English the Italian rhythms and thought patterns of Di Donato's immigrant characters appealed to critics newly receptive to the linguistic innovations of modernism. The searching energy and the raw idealism behind Di Donato's literary debut was not again achieved; *Christ in Concrete* remains the classic expression of the Italian American experience in the thematic material of the young boy's seeking identity in a new and alien world that is as rejecting as the old one of tradition (which had been his father's) is closed to him. *Christ in Concrete* is the most searing and thorough representation of the condition of an immigrant suspended between two worlds and held in thrall to work and the job.

Christ in Concrete, which began as a short story in *Esquire,* is an autobiographical rendering of the most haunting, ineluctable event of Di Donato's life—the tragic accident which killed his father on a construction job just days before his own twelfth birthday, casting the young boy into his father's role as brick-layer and supporter of the destitute family. When, during the Depression of the Thirties, Di Donato was laid off the job, the circumstance brought about his Golden Age: "With unemployment and Home Relief I was permitted the leisure to think . . . That sent me to the Northport Library and the discovery of the immortal minds of all countries. They gave me freedom. . . ."

When it appeared in 1939, *Christ in Concrete* was hailed as "the epithet of the twentieth century." It was chosen over John Steinbeck's *The Grapes of Wrath* for the Book-of-the-Month Club, and Di Donato, the working man, was transformed into a literary lion only to have the too-instant celebrity status and financial affluence render him silent for the next two decades.

From 1942 Pietro Di Donato spent time in a Cooperstown, New York, camp as a conscientious objector during World War II; while there, he met the widowed Helen Dean, a former showgirl. They were married in 1943, became the parents of two sons, and subsequently moved to Long Island, where Di Donato continued to write. Much of Di Donato's internal conflict—the contradictory pull between sensual hedonism and idealism, between the attraction to the woman he married and the insane jealousy harbored toward the dead husband who preceded him, between his feeling of having betrayed his Italian American identity and his unsure place in American society—found expression in his next autobiographical novel, *This Woman.*

Critics were not impressed with this work, which was dramatized, or with his next novel, *Three Circles of Light,* which was called "a loose collection of episodes rather than a sustained narrative . . . The novel's descent into sentimentality, bathos, and just plain scurrility is rapid." Subsequently Di Donato seems to have secured his identity within the framework of the reclaimed religious faith of his people, and he went on to write two religious biographies: *Immigrant Saint: The Life of Mother Cabrini* and *The Penitent,* which is the life of Maria Goretti.

Di Donato's short pieces, articles, and stories were collected in *Naked Author.* In 1978 his reportage on the kidnapping and murder of Aldo Moro, "Christ in Plastic," which appeared in *Penthouse* magazine, won the Overseas Press Club Award. At his best, as in *Christ in Concrete,* Di Donato's narrative patterns form, in their diversity, one of the richest linguistic textures to be found in the twentieth-century novel and make the bridge, for him and for his characters, between a lost and mythical Italy and a real but never realized America.

Helen Barolini

PRIMARY WORKS

Christ in Concrete, 1939, 1975; *This Woman,* 1958; *Immigrant Saint: The Life of Mother Cabrini,* 1960; *Three Circles of Light,* 1960; *The Penitent,* 1962; *Naked Author,* 1970.

Christ in Concrete

March whistled stinging snow against the brick walls and up the gaunt girders. Geremio, the foreman, swung his arms about, and gaffed the men on.

Old Nick, the "Lean," stood up from over a dust-flying brick pile, and tapped the side of his nose.

"Master Geremio, the devil himself could not break his tail any harder than we here."

Burly Vincenzo of the walrus mustache, and known as the "Snoutnose," let fall the chute door of the concrete hopper and sang over in the Lean's direction: "Mari-Annina's belly and the burning night will make of me once more a milk-mouthed stripling lad. . . ."

The Lean loaded his wheelbarrow and spat furiously. "Sons of two-legged dogs . . . despised of even the devil himself! Work! Sure! For America beautiful will eat you and spit your bones into the earth's hole! Work!" And with that his wiry frame pitched the barrow violently over the rough floor.

Snoutnose waved his head to and fro and with mock pathos wailed, "Sing on, oh guitar of mine. . . ."

Short, cheery-faced Joe Chiappa, the scaffoldman, paused with hatchet in hand and tenpenny spike sticking out from small dicelike teeth to tell the Lean as he went by, in a voice that all could hear, "Ah, father of countless chicks, the old age is a carrion!"

Geremio chuckled and called to him: "Hey, little Joe, who are you to talk? You and big-titted Cola can't even hatch an egg, whereas the Lean has just to turn the doorknob of his bedroom and old Philomena becomes a balloon!"

Coarse throats tickled and mouths opened wide in laughter.

Mike, the "Barrel-mouth," pretended he was talking to himself and yelled out in his best English . . . he was always speaking English while the rest carried on in their native Italian: "I don't know myself, but somebody whose gotta bigga buncha keeds and he alla times talka from somebody elsa!"

Geremio knew it was meant for him and he laughed. "On the tomb of Saint Pimplelegs, this little boy my wife is giving me next week shall be the last! Eight hungry little Christians to feed is enough for any man."

Joe Chiappa nodded to the rest. "Sure, Master Geremio had a telephone call from the next bambino. Yes, it told him it had a little bell there instead of a rose bush. . . . It even told him its name!"

"Laugh, laugh all of you," returned Geremio, "but I tell you that all my kids must be boys so that they some day will be big American builders. And then I'll help him to put the gold away in the basements for safekeeping!"

A great din of riveting shattered the talk among the fast-moving men. Geremio added a handful of "honest" tobacco to his corncob, puffed strongly, and cupped his hands around the bowl for a bit of warmth. The chill day caused him to shiver, and he thought to himself, Yes, the day is cold, cold . . . but who am I to complain when the good Christ himself was crucified?

Pushing the job is all right (when has it been otherwise in my life?) but this job frightens me. I feel the building wants to tell me something; just as one Christian to another. I don't like this. Mr. Murdin tells me, "Push it up!" That's all he knows. I keep telling him that the underpinning should be doubled and the old material removed from the floors, but he keeps the inspector drunk and . . . "Hey, Ashes-ass! Get away from under that pilaster! Don't pull the old work. Push it away from you or you'll have a nice present for Easter if the wall falls on you!" . . . Well, with the help of God I'll see this job through. It's not my first, nor the. . . . "Hey, Patsy number two! Put more cement in that concrete we're putting up a building, not an Easter cake!"

Patsy hurled his shovel to the floor and gesticulated madly. "The padrone Jurdinsa tells me, 'Too much, too much! Lil' bit is plenty!' And you tell me I'm stingy! The rotten building can fall after I leave!"

Six floors below, the contractor called: "Hey, Geremio! Is your gang of dagos dead?"

Geremio cautioned to the men: "On your toes, boys. If he writes out slips, someone won't have big eels on the Easter table."

The Lean cursed that "the padrone could take the job and shove it . . . !"

Curly-headed Sandino, the roguish, pigeon-toed scaffoldman, spat a clod of tobacco juice and hummed to his own music.

. . . "Yes, certainly yes to your face, master padrone . . . and behind, this to you and all your kind!"

The day, like all days, came to an end. Calloused and bruised bodies sighed, and numb legs shuffled towards shabby railroad flats. . . .

"Ah, *bella casa mia.* Where my little freshets of blood, and my good woman await me. Home where my broken back will not ache so. Home where midst the monkey chatter of my *piccolinos* I will float off to blessed slumber with my feet on the chair and the head on the wife's soft full breast."

These great childhearted ones leave each other without words or ceremony, and as they ride and walk home, a great pride swells the breast. . . .

"Blessings to Thee, oh Jesus. I have fought winds and cold. Hand to hand I have locked dumb stones in place and the great building rises. I have earned a bit of bread for me and mine."

The mad day's brutal conflict is forgiven, and strained limbs prostrate themselves so that swollen veins can send the yearning blood coursing and pulsating deliciously as though the body mountained leaping streams.

The job alone remained behind . . . and yet, they too, having left the bigger part of their lives with it. The cold ghastly beast, the Job, stood stark, the eerie March wind wrapping it in sharp shadows of falling dusk.

That night was a crowning point in the life of Geremio. He bought a house! Twenty years he had helped to mold the New World. And now he was to have a house of his own! What mattered that it was no more than a wooden shack? It was his own!

He had proudly signed his name and helped Annunziata to make her x on the wonderful contract that proved them owners. And she was happy to think that her next child, soon to come, would be born under their own rooftree. She heard the church chimes, and cried to the children: "Children, to bed! It is near midnight. And remember, shut-mouth to the *paesanos!* Or they will send the evil eye to our new home even before we put foot."

The children scampered off to the icy yellow bedroom where three slept in one bed and three in the other. Coltishly and friskily they kicked about under the covers; their black iron-cotton stockings not removed . . . what! and freeze the peanut-little toes?

Said Annunziata, "The children are so happy, Geremio; let them be, for even I would a Tarantella dance." And with that she turned blushing. He wanted to take her on her word. She patted his hands, kissed them, and whispered, "Our children will dance for us . . . in the American style some day."

Geremio cleared his throat and wanted to sing. "Yes, with joy I could sing in a richer feeling than the great Caruso." He babbled little old-country couplets and circled the room until the tenant below tapped the ceiling.

Annunziata whispered: "Geremio, to bed and rest. Tomorrow is a day for great things . . . and the day on which our Lord died for us."

The children were now hard asleep. Heads under the cover, over . . . moist noses whistling, and little damp legs entwined.

In bed Geremio and Annunziata clung closely to each other. They mumbled figures and dates until fatigue stilled their thoughts. And with chubby Johnnie clutching fast his bottle and warmed between them . . . life breathed heavily, and dreams entertained in far, far worlds, the nation-builder's brood.

But Geremio and Annunziata remained for a while staring into darkness, silently.

"Geremio?"

"Yes?"

"This job you are now working . . ."

"So?"

"You always used to tell me about what happened on the jobs . . . who was jealous, and who praised. . . ."

"You should know by now that all work is the same. . . ."

"Geremio. The month you have been on this job, you have not spoken a word about the work. . . . And I have felt that I am walking into a dream. Is the work dangerous? Why don't you answer . . . ?"

Job loomed up damp, shivery gray. Its giant members waiting.

Builders quietly donned their coarse robes, and waited.

Geremio's whistle rolled back into his pocket and the symphony of struggle began.

Trowel rang through brick and slashed mortar rivets were machine-gunned fast with angry grind Patsy number one check Patsy number two check the Lean three check Vincenzo four steel bellowed back at hammer donkey engines coughed purple Ashes-ass Pietro fifteen chisel point intoned stone thin steel whirred and wailed through wood liquid stone flowed with dull rasp through iron veins and hoist screamed through space Carmine the Fat twenty-four and Giacomo Sangini check. . . . The multitudinous voices of a civilization rose from the surroundings and melded with the efforts of the Job.

To the intent ear, Nation was voicing her growing pains, but, hands that create are attached to warm hearts and not to calculating minds. The Lean as he fought his burden on looked forward to only one goal, the end. The barrow he pushed, he did not love. The stones that brutalized his palms, he did not love. The great Good Job, he did not love. He felt a searing bitterness and a fathomless consternation at the queer consciousness that inflicted the ever mounting weight of structure that he HAD TO! HAD TO! raise above his shoulders! When, when and where would the last stone be? Never . . . did he bear his toil with the rhythm of song! Never . . . did his gasping heart knead the heavy mortar with lilting melody! A voice within him spoke in wordless language.

The language of worn oppression and the despair of realizing that his life had been left on brick piles. And always, there had been hunger and her bastard, the fear of hunger.

Murdin bore down upon Geremio from behind and shouted: "Goddamnit Geremio, if you're givin' the men two hours off today with pay, why the hell are they draggin' their tails? And why don't you turn that skinny old Nick loose, and put a young wop in his place?"

"Now, listen-a to me, Mister Murdin—"

"Don't give me that! And bear in mind that there are plenty of good barefoot men in the streets who'll jump for a day's pay!"

"Padrone—padrone, the underpinning gotta be make safe and—"

"Lissenyawopbastard! If you don't like it, you know what you can do!"

And with that he swung swaggering away.

The men had heard, and those who hadn't knew instinctively.

The new home, the coming baby, and his whole background, kept the fire from Geremio's mouth and bowed his head. "Annunziata speaks of scouring the ashcans for the children's bread in case I didn't want to work on a job where . . . But am I not a man, to feed my own with these hands? Ah, but day will end and no boss in the world can then rob me of the joy of my home!"

Murdin paused for a moment before descending the ladder.

Geremio caught his meaning and jumped to, nervously directing the rush of work. . . . No longer Geremio, but a machinelike entity.

The men were transformed into single, silent, beasts. Snoutnose steamed through ragged mustache whip lashing sand into mixer Ashes-ass dragged under four-by-twelve beam Lean clawed wall knots jumping in jaws masonry crumbled dust billowed thundered choked. . . .

At noon, Geremio drank his wine from an old-fashioned magnesia bottle and munched a great pepper sandwich . . . no meat on Good Friday. Said one, "Are some of us to be laid off? Easter is upon us and communion dresses are needed and . . ."

That, while Geremio was dreaming of the new house and the joys he could almost taste. Said he: "Worry not. You should know Geremio." It then all came out. He regaled them with his wonderful joy of the new house. He praised his wife and children one by one. They listened respectfully and returned him well wishes and blessings. He went on and on. . . . "Paul made a radio—all by himself mind you! One can hear Barney Google and many American songs! How proud he."

The ascent to labor was made, and as they trod the ladder, heads turned and eyes communed with the mute flames of the brazier whose warmth they were leaving, not with willing heart, and in that fleeting moment the breast wanted so, so much to speak, of hungers that never reached the tongue.

About an hour later, Geremio, called over to Pietro: "Pietro, see if Mister Murdin is in the shanty and tell him I must see him! I will convince him that the work must not go on like this . . . just for the sake of a little more profit!"

Pietro came up soon. "The padrone is not coming up. He was drinking from a large bottle of whiskey and cursed in American words that if you did not carry out his orders—"

Geremio turned away disconcerted, stared dumbly at the structure and mechanically listed in his mind's eye the various violations of construction safety. An uneasy sensation hollowed him. The Lean brought down an old piece of wall and the structure palsied. Geremio's heart broke loose and out thumped the floor's vibrations, a rapid wave of heat swept him and left a chill touch in its wake. He looked about to the men, a bit frightened. They seemed usual, lifesize, and moved about with the methodical deftness that made the moment then appear no different than the task of toil had ever been.

Snoutnose's voice boomed into him. "Master Geremio, the concrete is rea—dy!"

"Oh, yes, yes, Vincenz." And he walked gingerly toward the chute, but, not without leaving behind some part of his strength, sending out his soul to wrestle with the limbs of Job, who threatened in stiff silence. He talked and joked with Snoutnose. Nothing said anything, nor seemed wrong. Yet a vague uneasiness was to him as certain as the foggy murk that floated about Job's stone and steel.

"Shall I let the concrete down now, Master Geremio?"

"Well, let me see—no, hold it a minute. Hey, Sandino! Tighten the chute cables!"

Snoutnose straightened, looked about, and instinctively rubbed the sore small of his spine. "Ah," sighed he, "all the men feel as I—yes, I can tell. They are tired but happy that today is Good Friday and we quit at three o'clock . . . " And he swelled in human ecstasy at the anticipation of food, drink, and the hairy flesh-tingling warmth of wife, and then, extravagant rest. In truth, they all felt as Snoutnose, although perhaps with variations on the theme.

It was the Lean only who had lived, and felt otherwise. His soul, accompanied with time, had shredded itself in the physical war to keep the physical alive. Perhaps he no longer had a soul, and the corpse continued from momentum. May he not be the Slave, working on from the birth of Man—He of whom it was said, "It was not for Him to reason"? And probably He who, never asking, taking, nor wanting, created God and the creatables? Nevertheless, there existed in the Lean a sense of oppression suffered, so vast that the seas of time could never wash it away.

Geremio gazed about and was conscious of seeming to understand many things. He marveled at the strange feeling which permitted him to sense the familiarity of life. And yet—all appeared unreal, a dream pungent and nostalgic. Life, dream, reality, unreality, spiraling ever about each other. "Ha," he chuckled, "how and from where do these thoughts come?"

Snoutnose had his hand on the hopper latch and was awaiting the word from Geremio. "Did you say something, Master Geremio?"

"Why, yes, Vincenz, I was thinking—funny! A—yes, what is the time—yes, that is what I was thinking."

"My American can of tomatoes says ten minutes from two o'clock. It won't be long now, Master Geremio."

Geremio smiled. "No, about an hour . . . and then, home."

"Oh, but first we stop at Mulberry Street, to buy their biggest eels, and the other finger-licking stuffs."

Geremio was looking far off, and for a moment happiness came to his heart without words, a warm hand stealing over. Snoutnose's words sang to him pleasantly, and he nodded.

"And Master Geremio, we ought really to buy the seafruits with the shells—you know, for the much needed steam they put into the—"

He flushed despite himself and continued. "It is true, I know it—especially the juicy clams . . . uhmn, my mouth waters like a pump."

Geremio drew on his unlit pipe and smiled acquiescence. The men around him were moving to their tasks silently; feeling of their fatigue, but absorbed in contemplations the very same as Snoutnose's. The noise of labor seemed not to be noise, and as Geremio looked about, life settled over him a gray concert—gray forms, atmosphere, and gray notes. . . . Yes, his off-tone world felt so near, and familiar.

"Five minutes from two," swished through Snoutnose's mustache.

Geremio automatically took out his watch, rewound, and set it. Sandino had done with the cables. The tone and movement of the scene seemed to Geremio strange, differently strange, and yet, a dream familiar from a timeless date. His hand went up in motion to Vincenzo. The molten stone gurgled low, and then with heightening rasp. His eyes followed the stone-cementy pudding, and to his ears there was no other sound than its flow. From over the roofs somewhere, the tinny voice of Barney Google whined its way, hooked into his consciousness and kept itself a revolving record beneath his skull-plate.

"Ah, yes, Barney Google, my son's wonderful radio machine . . . wonderful Paul." His train of thought quickly took in his family, home and hopes. And with hope came fear. Something within asked, Is it not possible to breathe God's air without fear dominating with the pall of unemployment? And the terror of production for Boss, Boss and Job? To rebel is to love all of the very little. To be obedient is to choke. Oh, dear Lord, guide my path.

Just then, the floor lurched and swayed under his feet. The slipping of the underpinning below rumbled up through the undetermined floors.

Was he faint or dizzy? Was it part of the dreamy afternoon? He put his hands in front of him and stepped back, and looked up wildly. "No! No!"

The men poised stricken. Their throats wanted to cry out and scream but didn't dare. For a moment they were a petrified and straining pageant. Then the bottom of their world gave way. The building shuddered violently, her supports burst with the crackling slap of wooden gunfire. The floor vomited upward. Geremio clutched at the air and shrieked agonizingly. "Brother, what have we done. Ahhh-h, children of ours!" With the speed of light, balance went sickenly awry and frozen men went flying explosively. Job tore down upon them madly. Walls, floors, beams became whirling, solid, splintering waves crashing with detonations that ground man and material in bonds of death.

The strongly shaped body that slept with Annunziata nights and was perfect in all the limitless physical quantities, thudded as a worthless sack amongst the giant debris that crushed fragile flesh and bone with centrifugal intensity.

Darkness blotted out his terror and the resistless form twisted, catapulted insanely in its directionless flight, and shot down neatly and deliberately between the empty wooden forms of a foundation wall pilaster in upright position, his blue swollen face pressed against the form and his arms outstretched, caught securely through the meat by the thin round bars of reinforcing steel.

The huge concrete hopper that was sustained by an independent structure of thick timber, wavered a breath or so, its heavy concrete rolling uneasily until a great sixteen-inch wall caught it squarely with all the terrific verdict of its dead weight and impelled it downward through joists, beams and masonry until it stopped short, arrested by two girders, an arm's length above Geremio's head; the gray concrete gushing from the hopper mouth, and sealing up the mute figure.

Giacomo had been thrown clear of the building and dropped six floors to the street gutter, where he lay writhing.

The Lean had evinced no emotion. When the walls descended, he did not move. He lowered his head. One minute later he was hanging in mid-air, his chin on his chest, his eyes tearing loose from their sockets, a green foam bubbling from his mouth and his body spasming, suspended by the shreds left of his mashed arms pinned between a wall and a girder.

A two-by-four hooked little Joe Chiappa up under the back of his jumper and swung him around in a circle to meet a careening I-beam. In the flash that he lifted his frozen cherubic face, its shearing edge sliced through the top of his skull.

When Snoutnose cried beseechingly, "Saint Michael!" blackness enveloped him. He came to in a world of horror. A steady stream, warm, thick, and sickening as hot wine bathed his face and clogged his nose, mouth and eyes. The nauseous syrup that pumped over his face clotted his mustache red and drained into his mouth. He gulped for air, and swallowed the rich liquid scarlet. As he breathed, the pain shocked him to oppressive semi-consciousness. The air was wormingly alive with cries, screams, moans and dust, and his crushed chest seared him with a thousand fires. He couldn't see, nor breathe enough to cry. His right hand moved to his face and wiped at the gelatinizing substance, but it kept coming on, and a heartbreaking moan wavered about him, not far. He wiped his eyes in subconscious despair. Where was he? What kind of a dream was he having? Perhaps he wouldn't wake up in time for work, and then what? But how queer; his stomach beating him, his chest on fire, he sees nothing but dull red, only one hand moving about, and a moaning in his face!

The sound and clamor of the rescue squads called to him from far off.

Ah, yes, he's dreaming in bed, and far out in the streets, engines are going to a fire. Oh poor devils! Suppose his house were on fire? With the children scattered about in the rooms he could not remember! He must do his utmost to break out of this dream! He's swimming under water, not able to raise his head and get to the air. He must get back to consciousness to save his children!

He swam frantically with his one right hand, and then felt a face beneath its touch. A face! It's Angelina alongside of him! Thank God, he's awake! He tapped her face. It moved. It felt cold, bristly and wet. "It moves so. What is this?" His fingers slithered about grisly sharp bones and in a gluey, stringy, hollow mass, yielding as wet macaroni. Gray light brought sight, and hysteria punctured his heart. A girder lay across his chest, his right hand clutched a grotesque human mask, and suspended almost on top of him was the twitching, faceless body of Joe Chiappa. Vincenzo fainted with an inarticulate sigh. His fingers loosed and the bodyless-headless face dropped and fitted to the side of his face while the drippings above came slower and slower.

The rescue men cleaved grimly with pick and axe.

Geremio came to with a start . . . far from their efforts. His brain told him instantly what had happened and where he was. He shouted wildly. "Save me! Save me! I'm being buried alive!"

He paused exhausted. His genitals convulsed. The cold steel rod upon which they were impaled froze his spine. He shouted louder and louder. "Save me! I am hurt badly! I can be saved, I can—save me before it's too late!" But the cries went no farther than his own ears. The icy wet concrete reached his chin. His heart was appalled. "In a few seconds I shall be entombed. If I can only breathe, they will reach me. Surely they will!" His face was quickly covered, its flesh yielding to the solid, sharp-cut stones. "Air! Air!" screamed his lungs as he was completely sealed. Savagely, he bit into the wooden form pressed upon his mouth. An eighth of an inch of its surface splintered off. Oh, if he could only hold out long enough to bite even the smallest hole through to air! He must! There can be no other way! He is responsible for his family! He cannot leave them like this! He didn't want to die! This could not be the answer to life! He had bitten halfway through when his teeth snapped off to the gums in the uneven conflict. The pressure of the concrete was such, and its effectiveness so thorough, that the wooden splinters, stumps of teeth, and blood never left the choking mouth.

Why couldn't he go any farther?

Air! Quick! He dug his lower jaw into the little hollowed space and gnashed in choking agonized fury. "Why doesn't it go through? Mother of Christ, why doesn't it give? Can there be a notch, or two-by-four stud behind it? Sweet Jesu! No! No! Make it give. . . . Air! Air!"

He pushed the bone-bare jaw maniacally; it splintered, cracked, and a jagged fleshless edge cut through the form, opening a small hole to air. With a desperate burst the long-prisoned air blew an opening through the shredded mouth and whistled back greedily a gasp of fresh air. He tried to breathe, but it was impossible. The heavy concrete was settling immutably, and its rich cement-laten grout ran into his pierced face. His lungs would not expand, and were crushing in tighter and tighter under the settling concrete.

"Mother mine—mother of Jesu-Annunziata—children of mine—dear, dear, for mercy, Jesu-Guiseppe e 'Maria," his blue-foamed tongue called. It then distorted in a shuddering coil and mad blood vomited forth. Chills and fire played through him and his tortured tongue stuttered, "Mercy, blessed Father—salvation, most kind Father—Savior—Savior of His children help me—adored Savior—I kiss Your feet eternally—you are my God of infinite mercy—Hail Mary divine Virgin—Our Father who art in heaven hallowed be thy—name—our Father—my Father," and the agony excruciated with never-ending mount, "our Father—Jesu, Jesu, soon Jesu, hurry dear Jesu Jesu! Je-sssu . . . !" His mangled voice trebled hideously, and hung in jerky whimperings.

The unfeeling concrete was drying fast, and shrinking into monolithic density. The pressure temporarily desensitized sensation; leaving him petrified, numb and substanceless. Only the brain remained miraculously alive.

"Can this be death? It is all too strangely clear. I see nothing nor feel nothing, my body and senses are no more, my mind speaks as it never did before. Am I or am I not Geremio? But I am Geremio! Can I be in the other world? I never was in any other world except the one I knew of; that of toil, hardship, prayer . . . of my wife who awaits with child for me, of my children and the first home I was to own. Where did I begin in this world? Where do I leave off? Why? I recall only a baffled life of cruelty from every direction. And hope was always as painful as fear, the fear of displeasing, displeasing the people and ideas whom I could never understand; laws, policemen, priests, bosses, and a rag with colors waving on a stick. I never did anything to these things. But what have I done with my life? Yes, my life! No one else's! Mine—mine—MINE—Geremio! It is clear. I was born hungry, and have always been hungry for freedom—life! I married and ran away to America so as not to kill and be killed in Tripoli for things they call 'God and Country.' I've never known the freedom I wanted in my heart. There was always an arm upraised to hit at me. What have I done to them? I did not want to make them toil for me. I did not raise my arm to them. In my life I could never breathe, and now without air, my mind breathes clearly for me. Wait! There has been a terrible mistake! A cruel crime! The world is not right! Murderers! Thieves! You have hurt me and my kind, and have taken my life from me! I have long felt it—yes, yes, yes, they have cheated me with flags, signs, and fear. . . . I say you can't take my life! Vincenz! Chiappa! Nick! Men! Do you hear me? We must follow the desires within us for the world has been taken from us; we, who made the world! Life!"

Feeling returned to the destroyed form.

"Ahhh-h, I am not dead yet. I knew it—you have not done with me. Torture away! I cannot believe you, God and Country, no longer!" His body was fast breaking under the concrete's closing wrack. Blood vessels burst like mashed flower stems. He screamed. "Show yourself now, Jesu! Now is the time! Save me! Why don't you come! Are you there! I cannot stand it—ohhh, why do you let it happen—it is bestial—where are you! Hurry, hurry, hurry! You do not come! You make me suffer, and what have I done? Come, come—come now—now save me, save me now! Now, now, now! If you are God, save me!"

The stricken blood surged through a weltering maze of useless pipes and exploded forth from his squelched eyes and formless nose, ears and mouth, seeking life in the indifferent stone.

"Aie—aie, aie—devils and saints—beasts! Where are you—quick, quick, it is death and I am cheated—cheat—ed! Do you hear, you whoring bastards who own the world? Ohhh-ohhh aie aie—hahahaha!" His bones cracked mutely and his sanity went sailing distorted in the limbo of the subconscious.

With the throbbing tones of an organ in the hollow background, the fighting brain disintegrated and the memories of a baffled lifetime sought outlet.

He moaned the simple songs of barefoot childhood, scenes flashed desperately on and off in disassociated reflex, and words and parts of words came pitifully high and low from his inaudible lips, the hysterical mind sang cringingly and breathlessly, "Jesu my Lord my God my all Jesu my Lord my God my all Jesu my Lord my God my all Jesu my Lord my God my all," and on as the whirling tempo screamed now far, now near, and came in soul-sickening waves as the concrete slowly contracted and squeezed his skull out of shape.

Younghill Kang 1903–1972

Younghill Kang was born in Hamkyong Province in northern Korea. Educated at first in the Confucian tradition, he later attended Christian schools, which were established all over Korea by American missionaries. Kang immigrated to the United States with only $4 in his pocket in 1921, just three years prior to the enactment of laws that excluded immigrants from Korea for more than three decades. Originally, Kang was interested in science, but he found himself uncomfortable in the laboratory and said that he was forced to write because he couldn't find what he wanted said expressed anywhere else. Describing himself as "self-educated," Kang read English and American classics voraciously, attending classes at Harvard and Boston Universities while working at various jobs to support himself. Between 1924 and 1927, Kang wrote in Korean and Japanese, and in 1928 he began writing in English with the help of his Wellesley-educated American wife, Frances Keeley. He found work as an editor at *Encyclopaedia Britannica* and obtained a position as a Lecturer in the English Department at New York University, where he befriended Thomas Wolfe. At the time, Kang was working on *The Grass Roof,* a novel about a young man's life in Korea to the point of his departure for America. Wolfe read four chapters of the book and then took it to his own editor at Charles Scribner's Sons, where it was published in 1931. Between 1933 and 1935, Kang went to Germany and Italy with a Guggenheim Award in Creative Literature. In 1937, Scribner's published *East Goes West,* the story of a Korean in America.

An intensely lonely man, Younghill Kang was never afforded a permanent niche in American life. Always a visiting lecturer, he was never offered a stable teaching position. Instead, he traveled from speaking engagement to speaking engagement in an old Buick, spellbinding Rotary Club audiences with his recitations of Hamlet's soliloquy and his lectures on Korea. Widely read and possessing a remarkable memory, he lived with his wife, two sons, and a daughter, in genteel poverty in a ramshackle Long Island farmhouse overflowing with books. He is said to have commented that it was his great misfortune that Pearl Buck's Pulitzer Prize–winning novel about China, *The Good Earth,* was published in the same year as *The Grass Roof,* eclipsing his own tale of Asia.

Although he is best known for *The Grass Roof* and *East Goes West,* Kang also published translations of Korean literature, such as *Meditations of the Lover* and *Murder in the Royal Palace,* a children's book based on the first part of *The Grass Roof* (*The Happy Grove,* 1933), as well as a number of book reviews in the *New York Times* on Asian culture. Hospitalized in New York for post-operative hemorrhaging after a massive stroke, Kang died in 1972.

Kang considered *East Goes West* "more mature in style and technique" and more highly developed in content than *The Grass Roof,* which American critics generally preferred. Perhaps because they did not think that America and Americans should be part of a Korean immigrant's discourse territory, they applauded Kang's portrayal of Korea as a "planet of death," but they found fault with his criticism of American racism and prejudice.

Younghill Kang's work represents a new beginning in Asian American literature, a transition from the viewpoint of a guest or visitor acting as a "cultural bridge" to the perspective of the immigrant attempting to claim a permanent place in American life.

Elaine H. Kim
University of California at Berkeley

PRIMARY WORKS

The Grass Roof, 1931; *East Goes West: The Making of an Oriental Yankee,* 1937.

from East Goes West

Part One, Book Three

1

George and I were to leave New York about the same time. Pyun had found places for both, as he said he would. Since I could not cook, though George was charitable enough to recommend me, they said I must go as a houseboy, in company with another Korean, Mr. Pak.

"I know Mr. Pak," said George. "And you will have no trouble there."

I became optimistic then:

"My first American step, George, in economic life. I will make money now like Hung-Kwan Pang. On that I will become educated like J.P. Ok, A.B., B.D., M.S.T., M.A., Ph.D."

"I'm sure of Pak," George added, "but I am not sure of Pyun. Pyun has himself learned the American efficiency, though he would be ashamed to say that he is a good business man . . . this shows he still has some Orientality about him. But all the same he may be sending us both out just to get a commission."

"But he is a good friend of yours!"

"I do not like him much. In some ways he is an interesting type of Oriental successful in America. . . . Pyun's Utopia is not unlike that good old Epicurus[1] . . . he believes in eating good meals. He also believes in hard work. So he spends his days in hard work and his nights in good times—a typical New Yorker. He really knows gin. Those who come for the party enjoy themselves and have no headache the next morning. He has an apartment uptown where I often go to play poker (mostly losing). He keeps the entire floor for himself, so he can bring his friends privately. (His friends are mostly girls.) But he will never get anywhere. He has no poetry, no romance! Just skating!"

"Remember," said George to me, "it is not always the money man who is the best dancer, the best drinker, or the best-dressed human being at all. He often leads the dullest existence. That is because he does not know how to create an enjoyable life. It may be that money does not come to the man who knows how to spend it for a good time. But then you can't afford to have a dull life. At any rate—make money: but don't sacrifice mystery to make money. When you say, 'Never mind—that will come when I accumulate wealth,' then it may be too late. To scorn delights and live laborious days, that will not do."

I was packed long before George, and presently Pak came in a taxicab with his two suitcases. They were old and worn, not so good-looking as George's. The handle of one was wrapped with strings. Pak was very big and tall, with a phlegmatic face. He had a stubborn hesitating accent; three times his tongue would flutter, sometimes even more, before he could utter a sentence.

[1]Greek philosopher who held that sensuous pleasure was the highest good.

He was a most typical Korean, an exile only in body, not in soul. Western civilization had rolled over him as water over a rock. He was a very strong nationalist; so he always sat in at the Korean Christian services, because they had sometimes to do with nationalism. With his hard-earned money, he supported all societies for Korean revolution against Japan. Most of his relations had moved out of Korea since the Japanese occupation—into Manchuria and Russia—but Pak still lived believing that the time must come to go back, and even now, with a little money sent in care of a brother-in-law, he had bought a minute piece of land to the north of Seoul. For fifteen years his single ambition had been to get back there and settle down. On Korean land, he wanted to raise 100 per cent Korean children, who would be just as patriotic as himself, and maybe better educated in the classics. But still he did not have enough money to travel back, get married, settle comfortably down. This made him rather suffering and gloomy, always looking on the dark side of things.

George went out and got some beer to cheer him up. Real beer it was, in a paper carton. Pak drank beer and light wines—never gin—and smoked Luckies, but very temperately.

Pak too was worried, not about George's job, but about his and mine.

"Eighty dollars a month for two. That is not much!" he sighed. And George agreed.

"What is the matter with Pyun? Is he trying all the worst places first?"

"That trick was played on me many times before," said Pak.

"I guess your place is all right. The woman has two kids. She must be normal."

Pak shook his head gloomily.

"Normal you say—or as I say, not—American woman is hard to understand," insisted Pak, shaking his head. "I have had only one good job in America. For seven years I had a good job. A very nice man. Very nice wife. Nobody ever was mad at me. But he was mad at her, she was mad at him. Finally both become so mad with each other, they divorce. Nobody can see a reason why. The man goes to live in New York hotel. The lady goes to live with a friend in California. I was so happy with both!" Pak was almost crying. "Neither could take me. The lady cried, saying good-by. Then the man came, separately crying. But—all up! Our home was broken. One month's pay, $100 from the man. From the lady, a wonderful letter recommending me. I use this letter ever since. But never find another job like that. No more jobs like that in America!"

"Well," said George philosophically, "Their jobs are like their marriages. In the American civilization, especially in New York civilization, a married woman is no more than a kept woman, and no kept woman could be kept long. Thus divorce comes. It costs money. But they have it. So social life is a burden to them. . . ."

"Western marriage is no good in New York!" agreed Pak mournfully.

"But being a bachelor in New York is not bad!"

Pak didn't see it that way.

"Not good for a man to be unmarried. Indecent Western way."

"Look here, Pak, you are not Westernized," exclaimed George, rising up to preach. "You are not civilized. What is the matter with you? You can't enjoy the bachelor life when you have it. It is something we don't have in the Orient. This is one of the advantages of Western civilization. Listen, I read you advice."

George took down a big fat notebook. He put on his glasses.

"These are the wisest of Western men—the greatest of thinkers," he opened to his self-made index, hunting advice whether or not to get married. "(Not because they are wise and great, but because I agree in what they say.) First. Take Socrates. When asked whether to get married or stay single, Socrates said, 'Whichever, you will repent.' (You see, Socrates encouraged marriage 50 per cent. He lived in western classical times.) Another writer says, 'One was never married and this is his hell; another is, and that is his plague.' Hell may be bad, still it would not be as bad as plague. The wisest advice I know is that given by the great philosopher and thinker, Bacon, 'Young man—not yet! Elder man—never!'" And George shut the book with a whack, pleased with himself.

Pak still stood by his own conviction. He seemed not to have heard Jum's words at all.

"Forty-five years old I am. Not yet married. Already I lose at least five children by not marrying. And no children—no more me! This is fault! This is sin! This is crime . . . of the race suicide!"

2

In the station Pak bought a newspaper, which he could not read. He only bought it to look at the advertisements. He had not had much education at home and none at all in America. I offered to read some to him. But he was only interested to know what had happened in the Korean revolution, which had already quieted down. At least in American papers.

We were met at our destination by a lady in a big shiny car, all enclosed, and she was driving it herself. I examined her somewhat curiously, remembering the stories of George and Pak. She looked very *artificial* to me and *not very friendly.*

"He talk not much English," said Pak, and, uneasy how I would behave, he nudged me. As we assembled our suitcases, he said in Korean:

"Leave everything to me. You just keep in the background. Be shy like a Korean bride."

I tried to be shy. But the lady would not allow me to do this. As we rolled through suburban green lawns and semi-countrified streets, she directed all her words at me.

"You are the houseboy, aren't you? What? No experience! I hope we won't have too hard a time to train you" . . . and on and on. . . . My rôle seemed more a star than Pak's.

"And you must say 'Yes, *Madame.*'"

The car stopped. All around was free land, laid out for houses regularly with streets, but on it now were only small trees. There was one house. I did not care for the house. It ought out here to be a farmhouse but nobody attempted to make it a farm. It was a three-story concrete, very abrupt to look at in that flat space. There was a tiny hedge a little dog could jump and an artificial lawn with gravel paths. On the wind also you could smell the sea, but there was no sea smell about the house. It negated Nature, but the city was not transported yet. In a few years there would be many houses. I saw on the horizon another going up. I would not be able to recognize this place in 1975. Now, with neither society nor privacy, it was desolate.

"Get out," said the lady, who seemed a society-pioneer here. "And open the door for me. No, I mean you." And she pointed at me.

I had difficulty though to open the door for myself. Pak tried to open too, but it stuck. There was a trick in the button. The lady opened the door, turning around from her seat in front. Then my suitcase, which was on top of Pak's two suitcases, fell out, and opened and all my books fell out, and I fell out of the taxi after them. There I stood and didn't know whether to pick up my books or open the door for the lady. For she would have to step out on the books.

"Go round to the other door," said Pak to me in Korean. And he jumped out after me.

"Yes, Madame."

I tried to get there so fast that I stubbed my toe on Shakespeare and fell down. I jumped up and got the door open at last, and the lady had to step out in a kind of flower bed, while Pak crammed all my books back into the suitcase, and shut it, but only by one lock on one side: the other wouldn't close.

"That was very badly done," said the lady. "Leave the suitcases there—no, on the gravel, not on the lawn. Get into the car and try that over again."

This time I did very well. Pak breathed a sigh of relief.

"Now whenever I come in, you stand out here and open the car door. . . ."

She was moving toward the house in illustration. I grabbed up my suitcase again and followed after. Pak too.

She opened the side door with her key.

"Here, you must help to take my coat and overshoes."

"Yes, Madame."

I dropped my suitcase again. Again it broke.

"Never mind now," she said in vexation, "just remember another time."

I picked up my books.

"I hope they have no germs," she said, shuddering as she saw the dingy Oriental covers of some second-hand books I bought in Yokohoma.

We went inside. Pak took off his coat the first thing. But I kept mine—a missionary had told me that a gentleman never takes off his short coat in the house; forever he must wear it just like shoes. The lady handed us two white aprons, badges of servitude, ordering us to try these on. Pak tied his around his armpits. But mine was too long. I tied it around my neck and stood attentively.

"No, no, not that way."

"Yes, Madame."

Dejectedly I tied it around my waist under the jacket. The upper part looked man now, the lower, woman. Certainly it was a very long skirt. It almost trailed on the floor. The lady was looking at me analytically.

"H'm! What is wrong with you? Well, these are the best I can do until I take your sizes. My former cook was a very tall Negro. He was able to do the work of two. *But I hired you to be presentable.* Tomorrow I will go into the city to get some white coats—if everything else is satisfactory," she added with emphasis.

A cultured Korean lady takes small and calm steps full of leisure. This American lady moved out vice versa.

We were late. We must rush to get the first dinner. I only peeled carrots and beans. Then I cut my finger. But I had to wait on table. Pak couldn't do it for me. O Lord! George had forgotten to tell me how. I had a short lesson from Pak.

"Fork on left, spoon on right . . . pour water over right shoulder . . . offer meat on left . . . don't take away plate under soup bowl till end of soup. . . ."

How was I to remember all this? It was like learning the Chinese book of rites in five minutes.

Then I forgot all when I brought in the soup. A girl of eighteen stood there in trousers and shirt like an American man, with long leather boots reaching to the knees. She sat down.

"Oh, I'm so hungry," said the girl. "I rode clear round the riding school. . . . My horse was in fine spirits and . . ."

She caught sight of me and giggled. Her brother, a boy of twelve, laughed too.

I returned to the kitchen and described the girl to Pak.

"It's the way women dress on Long Island," I said.

Pak, however, took it as sinister.

"This job won't last," he gloomily shook his head. "Girl dressed like man, hair cut short, Westerners all like ten hells."

"But she has to, to ride on a horse."

"Yes! Rides on horse! Son-of-ingenuine-woman!"

The lady's bell rang peremptorily.

"Quick! Tell me what next."

But Pak couldn't. His tongue wouldn't move that fast.

"Get back," was all he said.

I went back in and the lady said, "Take the soup off."

"Through?" I said as softly as I could.

"You must say 'Yes, Madame.'"

What had Pak said? Don't take the plates under soup-bowls? I left the plates. It was wrong.

"Take these plates off!" said the lady angrily.

"Yes, Madame."

"Hey, give me some more water, Charley, before you go," said the boy.

"Yes, Madame."

The girl and the boy seemed to be giggling and laughing the whole time. They never took their eyes from me. I went into the kitchen again, where Pak was still mumbling to himself about the unnatural evils of Western civilization.

"What would my grandmother say? Running round over country on horseback dressed like men."

"How can I be there like Korean bride?" I asked indignantly. "The girl and boy are laughing at me all the time."

"Get back!" was all Pak said. "Before she rings. Here. Put napkin over arm."

I went in as noiselessly as I could. That was very noiseless. I was facing the boy and girl but the lady's back was to me. She didn't know I came in. I stood by the sideboard like a statue, napkin over the arm. The boy and girl were delighted.

"Ain't we got style?" said the boy. "We got a butler."

The lady laughed, "Peu! peu!" But she didn't see me.

Pretty soon I had to sneeze. I struggled for control. I must be Korean bride. No help. It was an awful sneeze. The lady jumped and said 'Oh!' She turned in a hurry—the boy and girl buried their faces in napkins and weakly howled. I too must laugh to look at them. "Hee!" I too put the napkin to my face. But the lady didn't laugh. "You may go!"

"Yes, Madame."

3

Pak worked slowly, but he did well, and he was a good cook. To me he was always kind. I complained to Pak about the lady, who interviewed me much more than Pak.

"It is not good that all the time she should get angry—not good for her, not good for me."

"No man can understand American ladies," he said patiently.

I had to work from morning to night. I had never worked so hard in all my life with no time to myself. First, beds to make. Pak helped me in this, for it was hard. Pak preached like George, be tight, but for a different reason.

"All Westerners roast the feet to freeze the nose. Western feet are cold, while Western nose is tough, tough as the elephant's trunk."

But next day the whole thing was to do over again. I was discouraged.

"All Westerners kick, these more than most," said Pak. "It is bad conscience maybe. I will buy big safety pins to pin the end sheets and blankets so they won't come off, after once being done, when the lady kicks at night."

Then there was so much dusting to do, all seeming an unnecessary labor to me. Surely such quantities of furniture were only in the way! In Korea, the beauty of a room is in its freespace. "The utility of a vase is in its emptiness." I did not believe Americans got much out of Shakespeare—American domesticity gave no time. And yet there were all sorts of labor-saving devices in the kitchen, even an electric egg-beater. I could not understand why I did not get through safely and quickly like George, with plenty of leisure time.

Whenever the lady saw me, she got nervous and irritated. Before she spoke, she would give one big artificial smile, and the bigger the smile was, the angrier she was going to be. She would preach:

"Always rearrange pillows after I—or any others—sit on the sofa. . . ."

"Always put on a clean apron before coming out of the kitchen . . . not one spotted with jam. . . ."

"Never leave off your apron as if you were a guest in the house. . . ."

"Dust under each chair with an oil rag, not with a feather. . . ."

"Dry the saucepan before putting it away. . . ."

"Dishwipers must be washed at once after being used; then hang them up carefully. . . ."

"Never use the front door except to open it for others. . . ."

"Don't stay here . . . go . . . after being called and serving . . ."

This last was vice versa to the orders of Pak. Always when I came out of the dining room while the family sat at the table, he ordered, "Back!" He didn't want me in his way either.

It was interesting in a sense, being treated just like a dog or cat. One could see everything, and go unnoticed, except while being scolded. But how tired my feet got! How discouraged I was! How hungry to get away somewhere, even if I starved! *"To keep on is harder than being a prisoner,"* I thought. And I remembered George's advice not to scorn delight and live laborious days.

Still another day of chore work in domesticity began. It was a beautiful morning. I looked out through the window at the green fields of the first April, juicy and wet. Outside the spring odor was penetrating and lyrical. The perfume of the bursting sods and quickened rootlets all swaying in the west wind, intermingled with the salty tang of the sea. But inside it was tough and bitter, for I had slept too late, having gone to bed too late the night before. Shakespeare was to blame for it. He was too beautiful to be left unread, too poignant to be left uncried. I wished to write letters to my ideal as George did.

"From you I have been absent in the Spring. . . ."

The clock indicated that I was an hour and a half late when I got up that morning. Pak did not wake me, because he thought I needed a little more sleep after the night before. He was too kind to me always. Alas, kindness was to spoil the whole business!

I went into the great white mechanized kitchen. Pak said:

"Fired!"

"Something is burning?" I cried, running to the electric stove.

"No. Fired! Job doesn't last!"

But hoping still to make good, I dragged the vacuum cleaner in to do the living room, my usual morning task. The girl, who was always the latest breakfast-getter, was already up, and so was her mother. They were standing, looking at the living room which was just as it had been left the night before, when the girl, who was already a candidate for somebody, entertained company.

The girl as usual giggled when she saw me. But the lady did not. She looked at me with a hard and spiteful smile:

"I have telephoned for a house servant, not a comedian."

1937

Carved on the Walls: Poetry by Early Chinese Immigrants

Angel Island in San Francisco Bay, now an idyllic state park, was the point of entry for the majority of the approximately 175,000 Chinese immigrants who came to America between 1910 and 1940. Modeled after New York's Ellis Island, the site was the immigration detention headquarters for Chinese awaiting the outcomes of medical examinations and immigration papers. It was also the holding ground for deportees awaiting transportation back to the motherland.

The ordeal of immigration and detention left an indelible mark in the minds of many Chinese, a number of whom wrote poetry on the barrack walls, recording impressions of their voyage to America, their longing for families back home, and their outrage and humiliation at the treatment America accorded them. When the center's doors shut in 1940, one of the bitterest chapters in the history of Chinese immigration to America came to a close. The poems expressing the thoughts of the Chinese immigrants were locked behind those doors and forgotten until 1970, when they were discovered by park ranger Alexander Weiss and preserved in *Island: Poetry and History of Chinese Immigrants on Angel Island, 1910–1940* (1980).

The Chinese began emigrating to America in large numbers during the California Gold Rush. Political chaos and economic hardships at home forced them to venture overseas to seek a better livelihood. Despite their contributions to America—building the transcontinental railroad, developing the shrimp and abalone fisheries, the vineyards, new strains of fruit, reclaiming swamplands, and providing needed labor for California's growing agriculture and light industries—they were viewed as labor competition and undesirable aliens and were mistreated and discriminated against.

The Chinese Exclusion Act of 1882 was the inevitable culmination of a series of oppressive anti-Chinese laws and violent physical assaults upon the Chinese. For the first time in American history, members of a specific ethnic group—the Chinese—were refused entry. Only exempt classes, which included merchants, government officials, students, teachers, visitors, as well as those claiming U.S. citizenship, were admitted. The Angel Island Immigration Station was established in 1910 to process Chinese immigrants claiming citizenship and exempt statuses.

According to stories told by Chinese detainees, most immigrants went into debt to pay for passage to America. Upon arrival, they were given medical examinations and then locked up in dormitories segregated by sex to await hearings on their applications. To prevent collusion, no visitors were allowed prior to interrogation except missionaries. Women were sometimes taken outside for walks and men were allowed to exercise in a small, fenced-in yard. Otherwise, confined inside, they spent their waking hours worrying about their future, gambling, reading, sewing, or knitting. Three times a day, they were taken to the dining hall for meals which, although cooked by Chinese staff, were barely edible.

Because the interrogation involved many detailed questions about one's family and village background, lengthy coaching books were memorized by prospective immigrants before coming to America. Inquiries usually lasted two to three days, during which time one's testimony had to be corroborated by witnesses. For those whose applications for entry were rejected, the wait could stretch to as long as two years while they awaited appeals. Most of the debarred swallowed their disappointment and stolidly awaited their fate. However, some committed suicide in the barracks or aboard returning ships. Still others vented their frustrations and anguish by writing or carving Chinese poems on the barrack walls as they waited for the results of appeals or orders for their deportation.

These poets of the exclusion era were largely Cantonese villagers from the Pearl River Delta region in Guangdong Province in South China. They were immigrants who sought to impart their experiences to men and women following in their footsteps. Their feelings of anger, frustration, uncertainty, hope and despair, self-pity, homesickness, and loneliness filled the walls of the detention barrack. Many of their poems were written in pencil or ink and eventually covered by coats of paint. Some, however, were first written in brush and then carved into the wood. The majority of the poems are undated and unsigned, probably for fear of retribution from the authorities.

All of the poems are written in the classical style, with frequent references or allusions to famous literary or heroic figures in Chinese legend and history, especially those who faced adversity. Because the early twentieth century saw an increasing national consciousness among the Chinese, many of the poems also voice resentment at being confined and bitterness that their weak motherland cannot intervene on their behalf. Most of the poems, however, bemoan the writer's own situation. A few are farewell verses written by deportees or messages of tribulations by transients to or from Mexico and Cuba.

The literary quality of the poems varies greatly. The style and language of some works indicate that the poets were well versed in the linguistic intricacies of poetic expression, while others, at best, can only be characterized as sophomoric attempts. Since most immigrants at that time did not have formal schooling beyond the primary grades and for obvious reasons were usually not equipped with rhyme books and dictionaries, many poems violate rules of rhyme and tone required in Chinese poetry.

The poems occupy a unique place in the literary culture of Asian America. These immigrant poets unconsciously introduced a new sensibility, a Chinese American sensibility using China as the source and America as a bridge to spawn a new cultural perspective. Their poetry is a legacy to Chinese Americans who would not be here today were it not for these predecessors' pioneering spirit. Their poetry is also a testimony to the indignity they suffered coming here.

The irony of exclusion was that it did not improve the white workingman's lot. Unemployment remained high and the wage level did not rise after the "cheap" competition had been virtually eliminated. As for the Chinese, their experiences on Angel Island and under the American exclusion laws, which were not repealed until 1943, laid the groundwork for the behavior and attitudes of an entire generation of Chinese Americans. The psychological scars—fear of officials, suspicion of outsiders, political apathy—still linger as a legacy in the Chinese American community today.

Him Mark Lai
Genny Lim
Judy Yung

PRIMARY WORK

Him Mark Lai, Genny Lim, and Judy Yung, eds., *Island: Poetry and History of Chinese Immigrants on Angel Island, 1910–1940,* 1991.

from The Voyage

5

Four days before the Qiqiao Festival,[1]
I boarded the steamship for America.

[1]Better known as the "Festival of the Seventh Day of the Seventh Moon," the Qiqiao Festival is widely celebrated among the Cantonese. As the legend of the Cowherd (Niulang) and the Weaver Maiden (Zhinu) is told, the Weaver Maiden in heaven one day fell in love with a mortal Cowherd. After their marriage, her loom which once wove garments for the gods fell silent. Angered by her dereliction of duty, the gods ordered her back to work. She was separated from the Cowherd by the Silver Stream or Milky Way, with the Cowherd, in the Constellation Aquila and she, across the Heavenly River in the Constellation Lyra. The couple was allowed to meet only once a year on the seventh day of the seventh moon, when the Silver Stream is spanned by a bridge of magpies. On this day, maidens display toys, figurines, artificial fruits and flowers, embroidery, and other examples of their handiwork, so that men can judge their skills. It is also customary for girls to worship and make offerings of fruits to the gods.

Time flew like a shooting arrow.
Already, a cool autumn has passed.
Counting on my fingers, several months have elapsed.
Still I am at the beginning of the road.
I have yet to be interrogated.
My heart is nervous with anticipation.

8

Instead of remaining a citizen of China, I willingly became an ox.
I intended to come to America to earn a living.
The Western styled buildings are lofty; but I have not the luck to
live in them.
How was anyone to know that my dwelling place would be a
prison?

from The Detainment

20

Imprisonment at Youli,[1] when will it end?
Fur and linen garments have been exchanged; it is already another
autumn.
My belly brims with discontent, too numerous to inscribe on
bamboo slips.[2]
Snow falls, flowers wilt, expressing sorrow through the ages.

[1]King Wen (c. 12th century B.C.), founder of the Zhou state, was held captive at Youli because the last Shang king, Zhou (1154–1122 B.C., different Chinese character from the preceding), regarded him as a potential threat to Shang rule. His son King Wu (1134–1115 B.C.) later did defeat the Shang and establish the Zhou dynasty (1122–249 B.C.).

[2]This idea is taken from a proverb which alludes to crimes so numerous they will not even fit on slips made from all the bamboo in the Zhongnan mountains. The ancient Chinese often wrote on bamboo slips.

30

After leaping into prison, I cannot come out.
From endless sorrows, tears and blood streak.
The *jingwei*[1] bird carries gravel to fill its old grudge.
The migrating wild goose complains to the moon, mourning his harried life.
When Ziqing[2] was in distant lands, who pitied and inquired after him?
When Ruan Ji[3] reached the end of the road, he shed futile tears.
The scented grass and hidden orchids complain of withering and falling.
When can I be allowed to rise above as I please?

By Li Jingbo of Taishan District[4]

31

There are tens of thousands of poems composed on these walls.
They are all cries of complaint and sadness.
The day I am rid of this prison and attain success,
I must remember that this chapter once existed.
In my daily needs, I must be frugal.
Needless extravagance leads youth to ruin.
All my compatriots should be mindful.
Once you have some small gains, return home early.

By One From Xiangshan[1]

[1]According to a folk tale, the daughter of the legendary Yandi, while playing in the Eastern Sea, was drowned. Her soul changed to a bird called the "jingwei," who, resenting the fact that the ocean took her life, carried pebbles in her beak from the Western Mountains and dropped them into the ocean, hoping to fill it.

[2]Another name for Su Wu (140–60 B.C.), who during the Western Han dynasty (206 B.C.–24 A.D.) was sent by the Chinese government as envoy to Xiongnu, a nomadic people north of the Chinese empire. Su Wu was detained there for 19 years, but refused to renounce his loyalty to the Han emperor.

[3]Ruan Ji (A.D. 210–263), a scholar during the period of the Three Kingdoms (A.D. 220–280), was a person who enjoyed drinking and visiting mountains and streams. Often when he reached the end of the road, he would cry bitterly before turning back.

[4]Adistrict southwest of the Pearl River Delta. The largest percentage of Chinese in the continental U.S. and Canada came from this district.

[1]A district in the Pearl River Delta, Xiangshan is the birth place of Sun Yat-sen (Sun Zhongshan, 1866–1925). After his death in 1925, the district name was changed to Zhongshan in Sun's memory.

from The Weak Shall Conquer

35

Leaving behind my writing brush and removing my sword, I came to America.
Who was to know two streams of tears would flow upon arriving here?
If there comes a day when I will have attained my ambition and become successful,
I will certainly behead the barbarians and spare not a single blade of grass.

38

Being idle in the wooden building, I opened a window.
The morning breeze and bright moon lingered together.
I reminisce the native village far away, cut off by clouds and mountains?
On the little island the wailing of cold, wild geese can be faintly heard.
The hero who has lost his way can talk meaninglessly of the sword.
The poet at the end of the road can only ascend a tower.
One should know that when the country is weak, the people's spirit dies.
Why else do we come to this place to be imprisoned?

42

The dragon out of water is humiliated by ants;
The fierce tiger who is caged is baited by a child.
As long as I am imprisoned, how can I dare strive for supremacy?
An advantageous position for revenge will surely come one day.

from About Westerners

51

I hastened here for the sake of my stomach and landed promptly in jail.
Imprisoned, I am melancholy; even when I eat, my heart is troubled.
They treat us Chinese badly and feed us yellowed greens.[1]
My weak physique cannot take it; I am truly miserable.

55

Shocking news, truly sad, reached my ears.
We mourn you. When will they wrap your corpse for return?
You cannot close your eyes.
Whom are you depending on to voice your complaints?
If you had foresight, you should have regretted coming here.
Now you will be forever sad and forever resentful.
Thinking of the village, one can only futilely face the Terrace for Gazing Homeward.[1]
Before you could fulfill your ambition, you were buried beneath clay and earth.
I know that even death could not destroy your ambition.

from Deportees, Transients

57

On a long voyage I travelled across the sea.
Feeding on wind and sleeping on dew, I tasted hardships.

[1]Salted cabbage.

[1]During the political turmoil in China at the end of the Western Jin dynasty (A.D. 265–316), two princesses fled to a distant region for safety and ended up marrying commoners in a village. They were often unhappy and longed for their old homes. Their fellow villagers then built a terrace which they could ascend to gaze in the direction of their home.

Even though Su Wu was detained among the barbarians, he would one day return home.[1]
When he encountered a snow storm, Wengong sighed, thinking of bygone years[2]
In days of old, heroes underwent many ordeals.
I am, in the end, a man whose goal is unfulfilled.
Let this be an expression of the torment which fills my belly.
Leave this as a memento to encourage fellow souls.

13th Day of the 3rd Month
in the 6th Year of the Republic[3]

64
Crude Poem Inspired by the Landscape

The ocean encircles a lone peak.
Rough terrain surrounds this prison.
There are few birds flying over the cold hills.
The wild goose messenger[1] cannot find its way.
I have been detained and obstacles have been put my way for half a year.
Melancholy and hate gather on my face.
Now that I must return to my country,
I have toiled like the *jingwei* bird in vain.[2]

[1]See note 2 on p. 159.

[2]The posthumous title of Han Yu (A.D. 768–824) scholar and official during the Tang dynasty (A.D. 618–907). In 819 he came under disfavor when he memorialized the throne against the elaborate ceremonies planned to welcome an alleged bone of Buddha. For this, he was exiled to Chaozhou in Guangdong province, then still an undeveloped region of jungles and swamps. On his way south, he bade farewell to his grandnephew at a snowy mountain pass, Lan Guan, in Shenxi, and composed a poem to express his feeling.

[3]March 13, 1917.

[1]*I.e.,* mail service.

[2]According to a folk tale, the daughter of the legendary Yandi, while playing in the Eastern Sea, was drowned. Her soul changed to a bird called the "jingwei," who, resenting the fact that the ocean took her life, carried pebbles in her beak from the Western Mountains and dropped them into the ocean, hoping to fill it.

69

Detained in this wooden house for several tens of days,
It is all because of the Mexican exclusion law[1] which implicates me.
It's a pity heroes have no way of exercising their prowess.
I can only await the word so that I can snap Zu's whip.[2]

From now on, I am departing far from this building.
All of my fellow villagers are rejoicing with me.
Don't say that everything within is Western styled.
Even if it is built of jade, it has turned into a cage.

1910–1940

[1]Angel Island was also used as a detention facility for transients to and from Cuba, Mexico, and other Latin American countries. In 1921 the Mexican government banned the immigration of Chinese labor into Mexico.

[2]A contraction of "the whip of Zu Di." Zu Di (A.D. 266–321)was a general during the Western Jin dynasty (A.D. 265–316).When non-Chinese people seized control of the Yellow River Valley in the 4th century and the Chinese court had to retreat to the south, Zu Di swore to recover this lost territory. One of his friends, also a general, once said, "I sleep with my weapon awaiting the dawn. My ambition is to kill the barbarian enemy, but I am always afraid that Zu will crack the whip before me." Thus, the reference means to try hard and compete to be first.

CONTEMPORARY PERIOD 1945 TO THE PRESENT

WHEN the United States emerged from World War II, it was unquestionably the most powerful nation the world had yet known. Its factories and farms had been crucial to the Allies' military victory. Its technology had produced the atomic bomb, a weapon of unsurpassed terror. Unlike many other industrial powers, its cities were untouched by the war's devastation, and its industries quickly converted their enormous productive capacities from making guns and tanks to producing cars and refrigerators. American engineers talked of producing virtually free power through atomic fission. And as Johnny came marching home, Rosie was told to leave riveting to raise babies in the newly built suburbs.

A quarter of a century later, the United States had essentially been defeated by a small Asian nation on the distant battlefield of Vietnam. Its factories, like some of its large cities, were in decay. Its monopoly on weapons of mass destruction had long disappeared into a balance of terror. Indeed, the fabric of American society was being shredded in harsh and sometimes violent conflicts over war, human rights, and continuing and deepening poverty. Johnny and Rosie had probably gone separate ways; the house in the suburbs had begun to disintegrate. Far from creating a harmonious chorus singing "one for all, all for one," Americans had issued a cacophony of competing voices, all demanding a large piece of the action.

The literature chosen to represent the last half of the twentieth century attempts to show the differences of outlook and attitude as well as the rich spectrum of cultural and aesthetic perspectives. The dissolution of cultural and even national boundaries has helped shape such writers as Sherman Alexie and Helena María Viramontes. Most of the writers of this period have lived with the fear of the Bomb, the agony of the Vietnam War, the exhilaration of the March on Washington; their works sometimes chronicle, sometimes protest, and sometimes ignore these events. Yet like everyone else, writers are in some measure creatures of their time, and since they are often—in Henry James's words—people on whom "nothing is lost," we will find their world and ours inscribed in their books.

"What validates us as human beings validates us as writers," Gloria Anzaldúa affirms as she urges people to express their beliefs and their individuality through the act of writing. The validation of all human experience through a printed text is more nearly possible now than ever before in American history. Publishers have become more interested in work by minorities and women, homosexuals and political radicals, and the appearance in print of some of the most important writing of the twentieth century foretells even greater opportunities to come. In fact, as large-scale commercial publishing has become more concentrated, with big publishers swallowed by bigger conglomerates, many groups have established smaller independent houses to create more specialized lists. Today, Arte Publico, Thunder's Mouth Press, Kitchen Table/Women of Color Press, Crossing Press, West End Press, and other publishers offer alternatives to the commercial concentration on "soon-to-be-major-movie" titles.

New kinds of publishing opportunities have met with criticism, however. Some readers claim that too much recent writing deals with odysseys of sexual freedom, descriptions of economic inequity, seemingly personal treatments of troubled families, and individual characters who experience madness or other shattering life happenings. They decry what they see as "inappropriate" subject matter conveyed through techniques so experimental as to be unreadable or, conversely, so simple as to be unliterary. This kind of negative response is also a United States literary tradition: such complaints have met new writing in almost every period because many readers feel more comfortable reading fiction, drama, and poetry that is distant, even remote, from their own life experience.

Yet contemporary American literature is remarkable because it does portray a variety of experiences, not only the sensational or the confessional. Today's writers often use unpleasant subject matter warningly, presenting it with enough chill that reading the text becomes admonitory. Contemporary literature does not wear blinders, and it is not intended for readers who live in an unreal world. Except for some science fiction and science fantasy, much contemporary literature is not escapist. It rather follows the direction of modernist writer William Carlos Williams, who demanded that the immediate objects and situations of the twentieth century become the subject of its art. Like Charles Sheeler's paintings of Ford Motor Company's River Rouge plant in Michigan, contemporary writers too use what surrounds them. Their artistry consists in shaping literature from that daily milieu, often crowded and chaotic, and often seemingly inartistic.

There is a difference, however, between the modern and the contemporary. Whereas the modern writer or artist focused on the objects of his or her culture, contemporary writers and artists are more intent on describing people's emotional states. The emotions that much writing chooses as its subject are more difficult to mirror than was Williams's red wheelbarrow. Today, when Carolyn Forché writes about the brutal dismembering of war (and the military man's delight in the torture that has become a daily event), or Etheridge Knight laments the marginality of the lives of prison inmates, or James Welch shows the loss of hope in the lives of young Native Americans, our attention is drawn to the emotional meaning of that telling. Style supports meaning, as it did during modernism, but with somewhat different effects. Much contemporary writing has stopped pretending that there is an order, a hierarchy, to experience, or that education can bring shape out of the chaos of twentieth-century life. While the modernists believed that knowledge meant control, many postmodernists have accepted an utter lack of order as today's cultural norm. What chaos theory means to the contemporary psyche is that randomness, surprise, and dysfunction are as valuable as more orderly patterns of experience—and the literature about it—that dominated letters earlier, in the twentieth century. To insist that the word is valuable as word, that the form of writing is not necessarily an extension of its meaning but perhaps works against its perceived meaning, and that the writer's thought is no more valuable than that of any other living person is as viable in today's culture as the modernist code. Thomas Pynchon, Donald Barthelme, John Ashbery, Jessica Hagedorn, Raymond Carver, Kimiko Hahn, Joy Harjo, Leslie Marmon Silko, Bharati Mukherjee, and others are among the postmodernist writers included here.

A second critical difference between modern and postmodern literature involves difference itself. The 1950s are often said to have offered a unified vision of American culture. We then knew, or so the myth has it, what constituted American, indeed "Western," history and culture, and therefore we knew what students should study and critics should criticize. And it is certainly true that curricula and literary texts of the period offer a degree of uniformity unimaginable today. But in fact the seeds of today's diversity had already been sown and were rapidly sprouting, as the Civil Rights movement began to change American society and therefore American culture as well. In many respects, the question for ethnic and minority writers, as for ethnic and minority people, had been how they might fit themselves into mainstream culture. This question oversimplifies a complex process, but what constituted the center and the margins had remained relatively clear. The very manner in which writers like Ann Petry and Ralph Ellison were received illustrates something of the power of normative definitions, since they could be accounted for as a "naturalistic" and a "symbolist" writer, respectively, whose plots in *The Street* and *Invisible Man* simply happened to focus more than others on race.

But in the 1950s older definitions of cultural norms based upon race and ethnicity were, after years of attack, falling. In 1954 the Supreme Court agreed that separate education for black and white students produced inherently unequal opportunities for minorities, thus setting aside the legal basis for segregated schools. In 1955, Rosa Parks refused to accept the concept that black people belonged at the back of the bus; her arrest for refusing to give up her seat to a white and move to the rear set the stage for the Montgomery bus boycott and the prominence of the young black minister Martin Luther King, Jr. These and hundreds of other instances of resistance ultimately pluralized American culture. That is, the question shifted from how an ethnic minority writer might fit *into* mainstream culture to how alternative centers of culture, alternative understandings of its nature and functions, might be established *by* minority writers and *for* minority communities.

The developing movements for change spread ideas about, for example, black pride and thus generated a new consciousness about culture and history among those who had been marginalized. Writers of color and white women responded to the imperative to speak for themselves and for others like themselves who had been silenced in history. But more: to do so, they had to define their own distinctive voices, create their own artistic forms and critical discourses, develop their own institutions—especially publishing houses—their own foci for cultural work. The Black Arts movement, El Teatro Campesino, anthologies like *Black Fire, Time to Greeze!,* and

> If I am right, the problem that has no name stirring in the minds of so many American women today is not a matter of loss of femininity or too much education, or the demands of domesticity. It is far more important than anyone recognizes. It is the key to these other new and old problems which have been torturing women and their husbands and children, and puzzling their doctors and educators for years. It may well be the key to our future as a nation and a culture. We can no longer ignore that voice within women that says: "I want something more than my husband and my children and my home."
>
> Betty Friedan
> "The Problem That Has No Name"

That's What She Said, the dozens of new magazines and festivals—these all represent significant moments in the development of alternative cultural centers. To some degree, these "centers" have been geographically differentiated. Detroit, San Francisco, Houston, Albuquerque, and Atlanta have, in their different ways, become central to certain significant cultural movements. But the issue is less that of place than of power: the power to define literary form and value. No longer can "ethnic literature" be defined as being *about* ethnics so much as *by* ethnics.

There is another, perhaps more far-reaching consequence of this radical pluralization of American literary traditions. As contemporary United States literature has lost its dominantly Anglo-American and largely male definition, it has become more accessible and perhaps more interesting to many from outside the United States, those readers who view the new American literature focused on ethnicity, race, and the "subaltern" as a vital part of a global dialogue about the relationship of colonized peoples to their (mainly European) colonizers. Paradoxically, it may be that the very decentering of American literature has made it more integral to international culture.

New themes and subjects call for new techniques, and the contemporary period includes literature as technically varied as that in any time before it. Earlier modernism—with its difficult but unforgettable texts such as Faulkner's *The Sound and the Fury,* Toomer's *Cane,* and Eliot's *The Waste Land*—strongly influences some contemporary writers who see formal innovation as a means not only for extending the domain of what is termed "literature" but also for shaking readers free from their conventional assumptions about their world. For other contemporary writers, however, formal innovation is of less consequence than expressing the experiences of communities that had previously been marginalized, and challenging readers with issues like AIDS and ambiguous sexual definition, which are painful and, to some, unwelcome. Much recent literature makes use of oral elements, which remain particularly strong in many minority cultures, as well as echoing traditional rituals and tales, like "La Llorona" and "Yellow Woman." Contemporary authors often blend realistic elements with elliptical or surreal details, rejecting the notion that writing must "represent" a knowable reality lying "behind" the surface of language, suggesting instead that any narrative—whether called history or a novel—is a fictional construction subject to deconstruction and reassembly by changing communities of readers.

"Postmodernism," the name often given to recent cultural developments, has no single agreed-upon definition, but it surely involves the decentering of literary and cultural authority, as well as the dissolution of traditional boundaries like those between "high" and "popular" cultures or between "American" and "other" literatures. Whatever else it may imply, the postmodern era presents little that is stable, unitary, and comforting for readers, offering instead the pleasures of uncertainty, diversity, and change.

This anthology aims to give today's readers a *representative* selection of contemporary writing. Space prohibits any attempt at comprehensiveness, but the works that follow show the sheer excellence of the writing of our time, the late twentieth century as well as the nascent twenty-first.

Orthodoxy and Resistance
Cold War Culture and Its Discontents

Early in the twentieth century, the modernist vision of civilization was a disappointing, sometimes frightening, phenomenon. A tone of bleak despair kept literature serious; what humor did exist was created through irony. *Angst* at the ultimate recognition—the meaninglessness of human life—underlay some of the best-known literature written from the time of World War I through the 1920s, a period in which society tried to reassure itself through financial prosperity, through the depressed 1930s and into World War II. After the atomic bomb was used in that war, a great many readers, influenced by French existentialism, chose the humor of ironic understatement as a basis for their philosophic view. If all life was hopeless, if rational order had given way to the random and the accidental, then endurance might be a human being's most important trait. Living it out with humor became the ideal of many writers, and readers, in the 1940s and the 1950s.

During the 1930s Nathanael West's fiction—and a little of Faulkner's—had prepared the way for incongruous but convincing views of the immediate scene in such early 1950s books as J. D. Salinger's *The Catcher in the Rye,* Saul Bellow's *The Adventures of Augie March,* Flannery O'Connor's *Wise Blood,* Kurt Vonnegut, Jr.'s *Player Piano,* and Ralph Ellison's *Invisible Man,* a novel that differed from Richard Wright's *Native Son* and *Black Boy* in that its outcry was tempered by a self-reflexive humor that made acerbic social criticism palatable to white and black readers alike.

Published in 1952, *Invisible Man* worked with most of the conventions of modernist fiction while adhering to many black narrative, musical, and oral traditions. The novel gives the reader a central protagonist but never names or describes him; to refer to the character, then, readers must keep repeating the thematic tag "invisible man." Not only a man without a country or a name—though he is also that—Ellison's character is a man without a body, without a presence, adrift from human community, existing as he does entirely through subterfuge and self-created energy. Invisible Man's "success" in the upwardly mobile American culture is that he manages to live in his own space, literally carved out of someone else's property and then suitably illuminated with stolen electricity. The child of Faulkner and Hemingway, as well as Gwendolyn Brooks, Wright, and Langston Hughes, Ellison composed an elegantly complex narrative score as carefully and yet—witness the many dizzying riffs—as improvisationally as might have the jazz musician he had once studied to become. The solid block structure of a conventional bildungsroman was here cut into and underscored with humorous asides, scenes, and dialogue that kept the reader from any complacency—or from feeling that any event in the book was predictable. As quixotic as most human life felt itself to be in the post-Bomb milieu, "invisible man" became a touchstone character for many readers.

The prominence of fiction by black writers indicated that some publishers understood the necessity of making their work available commercially. The battle

> We come then to the question presented: Does segregation of children in public schools solely on the basis of race, even though the physical facilities and other "tangible" factors may be equal, deprive the children of the minority group of equal education opportunities? We believe that it does.
>
> . . . We conclude that in the field of public education the doctrine of "separate but equal" has no place. Separate educational facilities are inherently unequal. Therefore, we hold that the plaintiffs and others similarly situated for whom the actions have been brought are, by reason of the segregation complained of, deprived of the equal protection of the laws guaranteed by the Fourteenth Amendment. . . .
>
> Chief Justice Earl Warren
> *Brown v. Board of Education of Topeka* (1954)

for publication of work by other racial minorities had scarcely begun, however, as the almost complete indifference to John Okada's *No-No Boy* in 1957 showed. Just as the writing of Carlos Bulosan had been immensely important during World War II, only to be forgotten by the 1950s, so attempts by aspiring writers from many minority groups were doomed to fail until the 1970s, even as work by black writers was being published regularly. Gwendolyn Brooks's and Robert Hayden's poems appeared from good publishers; Paule Marshall's *Brown Girl, Brownstones* was published in 1959; and during that same year Lorraine Hansberry's *A Raisin in the Sun* was the first play by a contemporary black playwright to appear on Broadway. Ernest J. Gaines's important fiction had only begun to see print.

Still, when readers spoke of "contemporary literature" in the 1950s, the reference was to "mainstream" writers, who were largely white, male, and frequently Jewish. The so-called Southern Renaissance that was to come was preceded by a burst of Jewish American publication that provided some of the most important writing of this period. Often well educated, these writers published fiction in the *New Yorker* and essays in *Partisan Review,* and regularly won Pulitzer Prizes and National Book Awards—Saul Bellow, Norman Mailer, Philip Roth, Isaac Bashevis Singer, John Cheever, Leslie Fiedler, and Bernard Malamud, among others. John Barth's *The Floating Opera* (1956) and *The End of the Road* (1958) represented the more academic literary tradition that was beginning to mold contemporary fiction.

Literature was becoming something to study and write essays about, as more writers became teachers and gave courses in creative writing and modern literature. After years of having very little prestige, American literature had become credible, and hungry students on countless campuses demanded courses in it. Academe responded, and an increasing corps of solid young scholars offered versions of the course that began with *The Adventures of Huckleberry Finn* and then extended Mark Twain's account of the young man looking for self and meaningful experience—a course in which *The Catcher in the Rye* and *The Adventures of Augie March* could also easily appear. Literature as it was taught in the 1950s and 1960s was based largely on male experience; its themes were the search for self (in business, the natural world, or war) and the recognition of absurdity. Women and minority students learned that "literature" about white male characters, generally from the middle class and aspiring to conventional middle-class ideals, spoke for all readers. "Humanities" and literature were both racial and gender monomyths.

Many of these novels, and such others from the 1960s as John Updike's *Rabbit* novels, Ken Kesey's *One Flew over the Cuckoo's Nest,* and Sylvia Plath's *The Bell Jar,* reached large audiences through what Richard Ohmann described as the "illness story." That is, the books focused on the lives of characters who, like their middle-class readers, felt the anxieties, indeed often despair, of inner lives somehow out of kilter with their increasingly affluent economic circumstances. The incongruity they attributed not to the malformations of a society committed to a cold war even as it rediscovered how deeply ingrained were its poverty and racism. Rather, these characters, and their readers, saw the lack of personal ease as *dis*ease, a symptom of private illness rather than social disorder, to be addressed, if at all, by individual psychotherapy or perhaps religion. Similarly, the culture explained the unhappiness that many middle-class women felt, trapped into isolated suburban lives of child-rearing and housekeeping, as personal neurosis. It would take such a 1960s book as Betty Friedan's *The Feminine Mystique,* and often the experiences of "consciousness-raising" groups and of political activity, for many women to discover that the "personal *is* political," that what in the 1950s was generally dismissed as neurotic might be, as Elizabeth Cady Stanton had found a hundred twenty years before, a "healthy discontent" leading to political action. Not until after the social movements of the 1960s had raised fundamental questions about American life would fiction begin to move away from the focus on the "illness story" toward more explicitly political grounds.

The accepted poetry of the immediate post-war period was also distant from reality as students knew it. Carefully stylized and formal, 1950s poems were drawn from "meaningful" observation of life, their message crystallized in an image or symbol that the educated reader would find allusively succinct. The prevalent critical practices of close reading, of explication of a text, shaped the poems that were written at the start of this contemporary period: Robert Penn Warren, Elizabeth Bishop, and John Crowe Ransom were leaders in the poetry world. Whatever was ironic, allusive, and concise—and remained distant from both the poet and the poet's world—was considered "good."

Running counter to that conservative strain in poetry were a number of different currents: the free-form poems of William Carlos Williams and his Objectivist followers; the breath-rhythm lines being composed by such Black Mountain poets as Charles Olson, Robert Creeley, and Denise Levertov; and the Whitmanic, all-encompassing work of the San Francisco "Beats," Allen Ginsberg, Jack Kerouac, Lawrence Ferlinghetti, Gary Snyder, and others. In writing specifically about their experiences with drugs and homosexuality, coupling their life experiences with harsh criticisms of existing society, the Beats became a rallying point for many readers. Ginsberg's 1956 long poem "Howl," which was published by Ferlinghetti at his San Francisco–based City Lights Press, chanted its disbelief of and rebellion against the self-satisfied 1950s culture and also insisted on its roots in "left-wing," Jewish American beliefs. They were soon to be joined by poets who insisted further on the use in poetry of real language and rhythms to mirror the feelings of real life, the so-called confessional poets Robert Lowell, Anne Sexton, John Berryman, W. D. Snodgrass, and Sylvia Plath.

The Beat and confessional poets' emphasis on a bacchanalian approach to writing, rather than the craft-dominated apollonian methods of the modernists, paralleled the use of new subject matter by dramatist Tennessee Williams, whose 1953 play *Camino Real,* followed by the 1955

Cat on a Hot Tin Roof, showed his willingness to explore the socially and sexually forbidden. William Inge's 1953 *Picnic* and the 1955 *Bus Stop* also investigated social attitudes toward marginal characters whose chief interest to the viewer was sexual; Truman Capote, Carson McCullers, Nelson Algren, William Burroughs, and others wrote openly about the sexual misfit or what society saw as the deviant. Published in 1957, Jack Kerouac's *On the Road* became a cult favorite, suggesting the real dissatisfaction of many readers with what appeared to be the prosperous, conservative 1950s. The critical purpose of literature during this decade had its best example in Arthur Miller's *The Crucible* (1953), in which he used the Salem witch trials as an analogue for the investigations of supposed Communists by Senator Joseph McCarthy.

The 1950s, in retrospect, appear to have been a watershed of repression, dominated by the suspicion and fear of the McCarthy hearings, symbolized by the executions of Ethel and Julius Rosenberg as atomic spies, and described in literature that often reflected anxiety about anyone's being different from mainstream culture. Sociological studies with titles like *The Man in the Gray Flannel Suit*, *The Organization Man*, and *The Lonely Crowd* documented the conformist qualities of the 1950s. By the end of the period, however, events like the riotous mocking of the House Un-American Activities Committee at a San Francisco hearing in 1959, celebrated in the film *Operation Abolition;* other movies like *Dr. Strangelove;* and the burgeoning Civil Rights movement had made it clear that under that conformist lid extraordinarily diverse cultural energies were simmering.

In fact, laughter at conformity and outrage at cold-war politics lay at the heart of many more 1950s works than Ginsberg's "America." In *Goodbye, Columbus,* for example, Philip Roth satirized the complacent lifestyles of suburban Jews who had "made it." By contrast, Tillie Olsen focused the four stories of her 1961 *Tell Me a Riddle* on working-class people trying to sustain their radical political values as well as their lives through what Lillian Hellman called a "scoundrel time." Olsen's collection, which includes the now-classic "I Stand Here Ironing" and "O Yes" as well as the title story, represents a kind of bridge back to the more explicitly "political" texts of the 1930s, like Olsen's novel, *Yonnondio: From the Thirties* (written in the earlier decade but not published until 1974), and Meridel LeSueur's *The Girl.* Unlike many 1930s texts, however, *Tell Me a Riddle* incorporated important understandings about the political roles women play within their families as well as within the external world, understandings that "revolution" may mean transforming social and particularly gender relations. With the rise of a new women's movement in the late 1960s, Olsen's book became a feminist classic.

Neither Olsen's passionate narratives nor Roth's satire was as unique to the late 1950s and early 1960s as it at first may have seemed. Joseph Heller's wry 1961 novel *Catch-22* portrayed damaged characters caught in the vicious lunacy of military bureaucracy. Like Ken Kesey's fiction, *Catch-22* posed questions about the absurdities of contemporary existence: to be eligible for discharge from the army on grounds of insanity, for example, one could not be sane enough to apply for discharge—catch-22. Not all writers of the 1960s were satiric; people as diverse in their outlooks and styles as Norman Mailer and Grace Paley, Amiri Baraka (LeRoi Jones) and Paule Marshall are, at least in their origins, writers of the midcentury.

It is true that a cold-war outlook dominated American culture in the decade and more following the end of World War II. The world seemed to be divided into two camps, and for many Americans those camps constituted on one side the forces of light—democracy, capitalism, religion—

and on the other what they perceived as the forces of darkness and repression. Such cultural critics as Lionel Trilling argued that true maturity consisted in the ability to hold contradictory ideas in tension rather than committing oneself to any single ideology like communism. Yet, as the literature of this section demonstrates, such binary conceptions disguise the complex currents that, beneath the surface, were slowly melting the cultural ice of cold-war conformity.

Arthur Miller b. 1915

Until the age of fourteen, Arthur Miller lived on East 112th Street in Harlem, New York, the son of a prosperous manufacturer of women's coats. With the Depression, his father lost his business and the family moved to Brooklyn into a small but comfortable house. Miller attended Abraham Lincoln High School, where he played football, sustaining a knee injury. Following graduation, he worked at various odd jobs ranging from singer on a local radio station to truck driver to clerk in an automobile parts warehouse. He saved his pay for two years to attend college but was unable to enroll because of poor grades in high school. On the long daily subway ride into Manhattan from Brooklyn, he began reading *The Brothers Karamazov* (which he thought was a detective story), the book that he later referred to as "the great book of wonder" and which presumably aroused his interest in serious literature.

After two attempts, in 1934 Miller finally was admitted to the University of Michigan in Ann Arbor, where he became a journalism major. During the spring of 1936, Miller wrote a play, *No Villain*, that won a Hopwood Award in Drama, an annual contest that carried an award of $250. During this same year, Miller was working his way through college by waiting tables, feeding mice in the university laboratories, and gaining experience as a reporter and night editor of the student newspaper. Transferring his degree program to English, Miller began to study plays eagerly and revised *No Villain* for the Theatre Guild's Bureau of New Plays Contest with a new title, *They Too Arise*. In 1937 Miller enrolled in a playwriting class taught by Kenneth T. Rowe; that year *They Too Arise* received a major award of $1,250 from the Bureau of New Plays and was produced in Ann Arbor and Detroit. In June his second Hopwood entry received another $250, and Miller decided that playwriting was his future. After narrowly missing winning a third Hopwood Award for *The Great Disobedience*, Miller graduated in 1938 and returned to Brooklyn.

Over the next six years, Miller wrote radio plays and scripts while continuing to look for a play producer. In 1944 his first Broadway play, *The Man Who Had All the Luck*, opened—but closed after four performances. Two years later, Miller appeared on Broadway again with *All My Sons*, a play like most of his major dramas that explored relationships between family members, quite often between fathers, sons, and brothers. *All My Sons* won the New York Drama Critics Circle Award. In 1945 Miller published a novel, *Focus*, that dealt with anti-Semitism. In 1949 *Death of a Salesman* was produced at the Morosco Theater in New York and firmly established its author as a major American playwright. The play won the Pulitzer Prize, the New York Drama Critics Award, the Antoinette Perry Award, the Theater Club Award, and the Donaldson Award, among many others. It remains one of the most definitive stage works of all time as a study of the American character and culture.

In 1950 Miller adapted Ibsen's *An Enemy of the People*. By 1953 the specter of McCarthyism and its search for Communists in and out of the government and the entertainment business had nearly paralyzed the country. Along with other members of the intellectual community, Miller felt that he had to write in protest. In the introduction to volume one of his *Collected Plays*, Miller noted that he had "known of the Salem witch-hunt for many years before 'McCarthyism' had arrived, and it had always remained an inexplicable darkness to me. When I looked into it now, however, it was with the contemporary situation at my back, particularly the mystery of the handing over of conscience, which seemed to me the central and informing fact of the time." To inform himself of the facts and temper of the Salem events, Miller traveled to Massachusetts, the location of the trials at Danvers (originally Salem Village) and present-day Salem, where he read the original transcripts and documents. The parallel then fell into place between Salem in 1692 and McCarthyism in 1952—the play was almost ready at hand in the transcripts. "No character is in the play," Miller said in a *New York Times* article, "who did not take a similar role in Salem, 1692." The play so precisely reflected the political atmosphere of 1952 that many reviewers were forced to pretend there was no connection. In 1955 Miller was called to testify before the House Committee on Un-American Activities; like John Proctor, he refused to testify against others accused of being Communist sympathizers or party members and was convicted for contempt of Congress (the decision was reversed in 1957). *The Crucible* to date has been produced more often than any of Miller's other plays. As a historical, cultural, and political rendition of one of the most terrifying chapters in American history, and as a reminder of how conscience handed over to others can debase the social contract, *The Crucible* remains unique. It won the Antoinette Perry and Donaldson awards for 1953's best play.

Miller's dramatic themes and interests have always been closely related to what's "in the air," which has led him to being described as a "social dramatist." In the plays following *The Crucible*, Miller has ranged far and experimentally in theme, form, and content. Such plays as *A View from the Bridge* (1956, two-act version); his film script for *The Misfits* (1960), now a classic film; *After the Fall* (1964), a dramatic representation of his family, political troubles, and marriage to Marilyn Monroe; *The Price* (1968); *The Archbishop's Ceiling* (1977); and *The American Clock* (1984), among others, deal directly or indirectly with the family, the 1930s Depression, politics, and the American dream. One of Miller's most recent plays, *The Ride Down Mount Morgan*, opened in London, England, in October 1991 to enthusiastic acclaim by British critics.

Robert A. Martin
Michigan State University

PRIMARY WORKS

Arthur Miller's Collected Plays, Volumes 1 and 2, 1957, 1981; *I Don't Need You Any More*, 1967; *The Theater Essays of Arthur Miller*, 1978; *The American Clock*, 1983; *The Archbishop's Ceiling*, 1984; *The Two-Way Mirror* (*Elegy for a Lady* and *Some Kind of Love Story*), 1984; *Danger: Memory* (*I Can't Remember Anything* and *Clara*), 1986; *Timebends: A Life*, 1987.

The Crucible

A Play in Four Acts

Characters

REVEREND PARRIS
BETTY PARRIS
TITUBA
ABIGAIL WILLIAMS
SUSANNA WALCOTT
MRS. ANN PUTNAM
THOMAS PUTNAM
MERCY LEWIS
MARY WARREN
JOHN PROCTOR
REBECCA NURSE
GILES COREY
REVEREND JOHN HALE
ELIZABETH PROCTOR
FRANCIS NURSE
EZEKIEL CHEEVER
MARSHAL HERRICK
JUDGE HATHORNE
DEPUTY GOVERNOR DANFORTH
SARAH GOOD
HOPKINS

A Note on the Historical Accuracy of This Play

This play is not history in the sense in which the word is used by the academic historian. Dramatic purposes have sometimes required many characters to be fused into one; the number of girls involved in the "crying-out" has been reduced; Abigail's age has been raised; while there were several judges of almost equal authority, I have symbolized them all in Hathorne and Danforth. However, I believe that the reader will discover here the essential nature of one of the strangest and most awful chapters in human history. The fate of each character is exactly that of his historical model, and there is no one in the drama who did not play a similar—and in some cases exactly the same—role in history.

As for the characters of the persons, little is known about most of them excepting what may be surmised from a few letters, the trial record, certain broadsides written at the time, and references to their conduct in sources of varying reliability. They may therefore be taken as creations of my own, drawn to the best of my ability in conformity with their known behavior, except as indicated in the commentary I have written for this text.

Act One
(An Overture)

A small upper bedroom in the home of Reverend Samuel Parris, Salem, Massachusetts, in the spring of the year 1692.

There is a narrow window at the left. Through its leaded panes the morning sunlight streams. A candle still burns near the bed, which is at the right. A chest, a chair, and a small table are the other furnishings. At the back a door opens on the landing of the stairway to the ground floor. The room gives off an air of clean spareness. The roof rafters are exposed, and the wood colors are raw and unmellowed.

As the curtain rises, Reverend Parris is discovered kneeling beside the bed, evidently in prayer. His daughter, Betty Parris, aged ten, is lying on the bed, inert.

At the time of these events Parris was in his middle forties. In history he cut a villainous path, and there is very little good to be said for him. He believed he was being persecuted wherever he went, despite his best efforts to win people and God to his side. In meeting, he felt insulted if someone rose to shut the door without first asking his permission. He was a widower with no interest in children, or talent with them. He regarded them as young adults, and until this strange crisis he, like the rest of Salem, never conceived that the children were anything but thankful for being permitted to walk straight, eyes slightly lowered, arms at the sides, and mouths shut until bidden to speak.

His house stood in the "town"—but we today would hardly call it a village. The meeting house was nearby, and from this point outward—toward the bay or inland—there were a few small-windowed, dark houses snuggling against the raw Massachusetts winter. Salem had been established hardly forty years before. To the European world the whole province was a barbaric frontier inhabited by a sect of fanatics who, nevertheless, were shipping out products of slowly increasing quantity and value.

No one can really know what their lives were like. They had no novelists—and would not have permitted anyone to read a novel if one were handy. Their creed forbade anything resembling a theater or "vain enjoyment." They did not celebrate Christmas, and a holiday from work meant only that they must concentrate even more upon prayer.

Which is not to say that nothing broke into this strict and somber way of life. When a new farmhouse was built, friends assembled to "raise the roof," and there would be special foods cooked and probably some potent cider passed around. There was a good supply of ne'er-do-wells in Salem, who dallied at the shovelboard in Bridget Bishop's tavern. Probably more than the creed, hard work kept the morals of the place from spoiling, for the people were forced to fight the land like heroes for every grain of corn, and no man had very much time for fooling around.

That there were some jokers, however, is indicated by the practice of appointing a two-man patrol whose duty was to "walk forth in the time of God's worship to take notice of such as either lye about the meeting house, without attending to the word and ordinances, or that lye at home or in the fields without giving good account thereof, and to take the names of such persons, and to present them to the magistrates, whereby they may be accordingly proceeded against." This predilection for minding other people's business was time-honored among the people of Salem, and it undoubtedly created many of the suspicions which were to feed the coming madness. It was also, in my opinion, one of the things that a John Proctor would rebel against, for the time of the armed camp had almost passed, and since the country was reasonably—although not wholly—safe, the old disciplines were beginning to rankle. But, as in all such matters, the issue was not clear-cut, for danger was still a possibility, and in unity still lay the best promise of safety.

The edge of the wilderness was close by. The American continent stretched endlessly west, and it was full of mystery for them. It stood, dark and threatening, over their shoulders night and day, for out of it Indian tribes marauded from time to time, and Reverend Parris had parishioners who had lost relatives to these heathen.

The parochial snobbery of these people was partly responsible for their failure to convert the Indians. Probably they also preferred to take land from heathens rather than from fellow Christians. At any rate, very few Indians were converted, and the Salem folk believed that the virgin forest was the Devil's last preserve, his home base and the citadel of his final stand. To the best of their knowledge the American forest was the last place on earth that was not paying homage to God.

For these reasons, among others, they carried about an air of innate resistance, even of persecution. Their fathers had, of course, been persecuted in England. So now they and their church found it necessary to deny any other sect its freedom, lest their New Jerusalem be defiled and corrupted by wrong ways and deceitful ideas.

They believed, in short, that they held in their steady hands the candle that would light the world. We have inherited this belief, and it has helped and hurt us. It helped them with the discipline it gave them. They were a dedicated folk, by and large, and they had to be to survive the life they had chosen or been born into in this country.

The proof of their belief's value to them may be taken from the opposite character of the first Jamestown settlement, farther south, in Virginia. The Englishmen who landed there were motivated mainly by a hunt for profit. They had thought to pick off the wealth of the new country and then return rich to England. They were a band of individualists, and a much more ingratiating group than the Massachusetts men. But Virginia destroyed them. Massachusetts tried to kill off the Puritans, but they combined; they set up a communal society which, in the beginning, was little more than an armed camp with an autocratic and very devoted leadership. It was, however, an autocracy by consent, for they were united from top to bottom by a commonly held ideology whose perpetuation was the reason and justification for all their sufferings. So their self-denial, their purposefulness, their suspicion of all vain pursuits, their hard-handed justice, were altogether perfect instruments for the conquest of this space so antagonistic to man.

But the people of Salem in 1692 were not quite the dedicated folk that arrived on the *Mayflower.* A vast differentiation had taken place, and in their own time a revolution had unseated the royal government and substituted a junta which was at this moment in power. The times, to their eyes, must have been out of joint, and to the common folk must have seemed as insoluble and complicated as do ours today. It is not hard to see how easily many could have been led to believe that the time of confusion had been brought upon them by deep and darkling forces. No hint of such speculation appears on the court record, but social disorder in any age breeds such mystical suspicions, and when, as in Salem, wonders are brought forth from below the social surface, it is too much to expect people to hold back very long from laying on the victims with all the force of their frustrations.

The Salem tragedy, which is about to begin in these pages, developed from a paradox. It is a paradox in whose grip we still live, and there is no prospect yet that we will discover its resolution. Simply, it was this: for good purposes, even high purposes, the people of Salem developed a theocracy, a combine of state and religious power whose function was to keep the community together, and to prevent any kind of disunity that might open it to destruction by material or ideological enemies. It was forged for a necessary purpose and accomplished that purpose. But all organization is and must be grounded on the idea of exclusion and prohibition, just as two objects cannot occupy the same space. Evidently the time came in New England when the repressions of order were heavier than seemed warranted by the dangers against which the order was organized. The witch-hunt was a perverse manifestation of the panic which set in among all classes when the balance began to turn toward greater individual freedom.

When one rises above the individual villainy displayed, one can only pity them all, just as we shall be pitied someday. It is still impossible for man to organize his social life without repressions, and the balance has yet to be struck between order and freedom.

The witch-hunt was not, however, a mere repression. It was also, and as importantly, a long overdue opportunity for everyone so inclined to express publicly his guilt and sins, under the cover of accusations against the victims. It suddenly became possible—and patriotic and holy—for a man to say that Martha Corey had come into his bedroom at night, and that, while his wife was sleeping at his side, Martha laid herself down on his chest and "nearly suffocated him." Of course it was her spirit only, but his satisfaction at confessing himself was no lighter than if it had been Martha herself. One could not ordinarily speak such things in public.

Long-held hatreds of neighbors could now be openly expressed, and vengeance taken, despite the Bible's charitable injunctions. Land-lust which had been expressed before by constant bickering over boundaries and deeds, could now be elevated to the arena of morality; one could cry witch against one's neighbor and feel perfectly justified in the bargain. Old scores could be settled on a plane of heavenly combat between Lucifer and the Lord; suspicions and the envy of the miserable toward the happy could and did burst out in the general revenge.

Reverend Parris is praying now, and, though we cannot hear his words, a sense of his confusion hangs about him. He mumbles, then seems about to weep; then he weeps, then prays again; but his daughter does not stir on the bed.

The door opens, and his Negro slave enters. Tituba is in her forties. Parris brought her with him from Barbados, where he spent some years as a merchant before entering the ministry. She enters as one does who can no longer bear to be barred from the sight of her beloved, but she is also very frightened because her slave sense has warned her that, as always, trouble in this house eventually lands on her back.

TITUBA, *already taking a step backward:* My Betty be hearty soon?

PARRIS: Out of here!

TITUBA, *backing to the door:* My Betty not goin' die . . .

PARRIS, *scrambling to his feet in a fury:* Out of my sight! *She is gone.* Out of my—*He is overcome with sobs. He clamps his teeth against them and closes the door and leans against it, exhausted.* Oh, my God! God help me! *Quaking with fear, mumbling to himself through his sobs, he goes to the bed and gently takes Betty's hand.* Betty. Child. Dear child. Will you wake, will you open up your eyes! Betty, little one . . .

He is bending to kneel again when his niece, Abigail Williams, seventeen, enters—a strikingly beautiful girl, an orphan, with an endless capacity for dissembling. Now she is all worry and apprehension and propriety.

ABIGAIL: Uncle? *He looks to her.* Susanna Walcott's here from Doctor Griggs.

PARRIS: Oh? Let her come, let her come.
ABIGAIL, *leaning out the door to call to Susanna, who is down the hall a few steps:* Come in, Susanna.

Susanna Walcott, a little younger than Abigail, a nervous, hurried girl, enters.

PARRIS, *eagerly:* What does the doctor say, child?
SUSANNA, *craning around Parris to get a look at Betty:* He bid me come and tell you, reverend sir, that he cannot discover no medicine for it in his books.
PARRIS: Then he must search on.
SUSANNA: Aye, sir, he have been searchin' his books since he left you, sir. But he bid me tell you, that you might look to unnatural things for the cause of it.
PARRIS, *his eyes going wide:* No—no. There be no unnatural cause here. Tell him I have sent for Reverend Hale of Beverly, and Mr. Hale will surely confirm that. Let him look to medicine and put out all thought of unnatural causes here. There be none.
SUSANNA: Aye, sir. He bid me tell you. *She turns to go.*
ABIGAIL: Speak nothin' of it in the village, Susanna.
PARRIS: Go directly home and speak nothing of unnatural causes.
SUSANNA: Aye, sir. I pray for her. *She goes out.*
ABIGAIL: Uncle, the rumor of witchcraft is all about; I think you'd best go down and deny it yourself. The parlor's packed with people, sir. I'll sit with her.
PARRIS, *pressed, turns on her:* And what shall I say to them? That my daughter and my niece I discovered dancing like heathen in the forest?
ABIGAIL: Uncle, we did dance; let you tell them I confessed it—and I'll be whipped if I must be. But they're speakin' of witchcraft. Betty's not witched.
PARRIS: Abigail, I cannot go before the congregation when I know you have not opened with me. What did you do with her in the forest?
ABIGAIL: We did dance, uncle, and when you leaped out of the bush so suddenly, Betty was frightened and then she fainted. And there's the whole of it.
PARRIS: Child. Sit you down.
ABIGAIL, *quavering, as she sits:* I would never hurt Betty. I love her dearly.
PARRIS: Now look you, child, your punishment will come in its time. But if you trafficked with spirits in the forest I must know it now, for surely my enemies will, and they will ruin me with it.
ABIGAIL: But we never conjured spirits.
PARRIS: Then why can she not move herself since midnight? This child is desperate! *Abigail lowers her eyes.* It must come out—my enemies will bring it out. Let me know what you done there. Abigail, do you understand that I have many enemies?
ABIGAIL: I have heard of it, uncle.
PARRIS: There is a faction that is sworn to drive me from my pulpit. Do you understand that?
ABIGAIL: I think so, sir.
PARRIS: Now then, in the midst of such disruption, my own household is discovered to be the very center of some obscene practice. Abominations are done in the forest—
ABIGAIL: It were sport, uncle!
PARRIS, *pointing at Betty:* You call this sport? *She lowers her eyes. He pleads:* Abigail,

if you know something that may help the doctor, for God's sake tell it to me. *She is silent.* I saw Tituba waving her arms over the fire when I came on you. Why was she doing that? And I heard a screeching and gibberish coming from her mouth. She were swaying like a dumb beast over that fire!

ABIGAIL: She always sings her Barbados songs, and we dance.

PARRIS: I cannot blink what I saw, Abigail, for my enemies will not blink it. I saw a dress lying on the grass.

ABIGAIL, *innocently:* A dress?

PARRIS—*it is very hard to say:* Aye, a dress. And I thought I saw—someone naked running through the trees!

ABIGAIL, *in terror:* No one was naked! You mistake yourself, uncle!

PARRIS, *with anger:* I saw it! *He moves from her. Then, resolved:* Now tell me true, Abigail. And I pray you feel the weight of truth upon you, for now my ministry's at stake, my ministry and perhaps your cousin's life. Whatever abomination you have done, give me all of it now, for I dare not be taken unaware when I go before them down there.

ABIGAIL: There is nothin' more. I swear it, uncle.

PARRIS, *studies her, then nods, half convinced:* Abigail, I have fought here three long years to bend these stiff-necked people to me, and now, just now when some good respect is rising for me in the parish, you compromise my very character. I have given you a home, child, I have put clothes upon your back—now give me upright answer. Your name in the town—it is entirely white, is it not?

ABIGAIL, *with an edge of resentment:* Why, I am sure it is, sir. There be no blush about my name.

PARRIS, *to the point:* Abigail, is there any other cause than you have told me, for your being discharged from Goody Proctor's service? I have heard it said, and I tell you as I heard it, that she comes so rarely to the church this year for she will not sit so close to something soiled. What signified that remark?

ABIGAIL: She hates me, uncle, she must, for I would not be her slave. It's a bitter woman, a lying, cold, sniveling woman, and I will not work for such a woman!

PARRIS: She may be. And yet it has troubled me that you are now seven month out of their house, and in all this time no other family has ever called for your service.

ABIGAIL: They want slaves, not such as I. Let them send to Barbados for that. I will not black my face for any of them! *With ill-concealed resentment at him:* Do you begrudge my bed, uncle?

PARRIS: No—no.

ABIGAIL, *in a temper:* My name is good in the village! I will not have it said my name is soiled! Goody Proctor is a gossiping liar!

Enter Mrs. Ann Putnam. She is a twisted soul of forty-five, a death-ridden woman, haunted by dreams.

PARRIS, *as soon as the door begins to open:* No—no, I cannot have anyone. *He sees her, and a certain deference springs into him, although his worry remains.* Why, Goody Putnam, come in.

MRS. PUTNAM, *full of breath, shiny-eyed:* It is a marvel. It is surely a stroke of hell upon you.

PARRIS: No, Goody Putnam, it is—

MRS. PUTNAM, *glancing at Betty:* How high did she fly, how high?
PARRIS: No, no, she never flew—
MRS. PUTNAM, *very pleased with it:* Why, it's sure she did. Mr. Collins saw her goin' over Ingersoll's barn, and come down light as bird, he says!
PARRIS: Now, look you, Goody Putnam, she never— *Enter Thomas Putnam, a well-to-do hard-handed landowner, near fifty.* Oh, good morning, Mr. Putnam.
PUTNAM: It is a providence the thing is out now! It is a providence. *He goes directly to the bed.*
PARRIS: What's out, sir, what's—

Mrs. Putnam goes to the bed.

PUTNAM, *looking down at Betty:* Why, *her* eyes is closed! Look you, Ann.
MRS. PUTNAM: Why, that's strange. *To Parris:* Ours is open.
PARRIS, *shocked:* Your Ruth is sick?
MRS. PUTNAM, *with vicious certainty:* I'd not call it sick; the Devil's touch is heavier than sick. It's death, y'know, it's death drivin' into them, forked and hoofed.
PARRIS: Oh, pray not! Why, how does Ruth ail?
MRS. PUTNAM: She ails as she must—she never waked this morning, but her eyes open and she walks, and hears naught, sees naught, and cannot eat. Her soul is taken, surely.

Parris is struck.

PUTNAM, *as though for further details:* They say you've sent for Reverend Hale of Beverly?
PARRIS, *with dwindling conviction now:* A precaution only. He has much experience in all demonic arts, and I—
MRS. PUTNAM: He has indeed; and found a witch in Beverly last year, and let you remember that.
PARRIS: Now, Goody Ann, they only thought that were a witch, and I am certain there be no element of witchcraft here.
PUTNAM: No witchcraft! Now look you, Mr. Parris—
PARRIS: Thomas, Thomas, I pray you, leap not to witchcraft. I know that you—you least of all, Thomas, would ever wish so disastrous a charge laid upon me. We cannot leap to witchcraft. They will howl me out of Salem for such corruption in my house.

A word about Thomas Putnam. He was a man with many grievances, at least one of which appears justified. Some time before, his wife's brother-in-law, James Bayley, had been turned down as minister of Salem. Bayley had all the qualifications, and a two-thirds vote into the bargain, but a faction stopped his acceptance, for reasons that are not clear.

Thomas Putnam was the eldest son of the richest man in the village. He had fought the Indians at Narragansett, and was deeply interested in parish affairs. He undoubtedly felt it poor payment that the village should so blatantly disregard his candidate for one of its more important offices, especially since he regarded himself as the intellectual superior of most of the people around him.

His vindictive nature was demonstrated long before the witchcraft began.

Another former Salem minister, George Burroughs, had had to borrow money to pay for his wife's funeral, and, since the parish was remiss in his salary, he was soon bankrupt. Thomas and his brother John had Burroughs jailed for debts the man did not owe. The incident is important only in that Burroughs succeeded in becoming minister where Bayley, Thomas Putnam's brother-in-law, had been rejected; the motif of resentment is clear here. Thomas Putnam felt that his own name and the honor of his family had been smirched by the village, and he meant to right matters however he could.

Another reason to believe him a deeply embittered man was his attempt to break his father's will, which left a disproportionate amount to a stepbrother. As with every other public cause in which he tried to force his way, he failed in this.

So it is not surprising to find that so many accusations against people are in the handwriting of Thomas Putnam, or that his name is so often found as a witness corroborating the supernatural testimony, or that his daughter led the crying-out at the most opportune junctures of the trials, especially when—But we'll speak of that when we come to it.

PUTNAM—*at the moment he is intent upon getting Parris, for whom he has only contempt, to move toward the abyss:* Mr. Parris, I have taken your part in all contention here, and I would continue; but I cannot if you hold back in this. There are hurtful, vengeful spirits layin' hands on these children.

PARRIS: But, Thomas, you cannot—

PUTNAM: Ann! Tell Mr. Parris what you have done.

MRS. PUTNAM: Reverend Parris, I have laid seven babies unbaptized in the earth. Believe me, sir, you never saw more hearty babies born. And yet, each would wither in my arms the very night of their birth. I have spoke nothin', but my heart has clamored intimations. And now, this year, my Ruth, my only—I see her turning strange. A secret child she has become this year, and shrivels like a sucking mouth were pullin' on her life too. And so I thought to send her to your Tituba—

PARRIS: To Tituba! What may Tituba—?

MRS. PUTNAM: Tituba knows how to speak to the dead, Mr. Parris.

PARRIS: Goody Ann, it is a formidable sin to conjure up the dead!

MRS. PUTNAM: I take it on my soul, but who else may surely tell us what person murdered my babies?

PARRIS, *horrified:* Woman!

MRS. PUTNAM: They were murdered, Mr. Parris! And mark this proof! Mark it! Last night my Ruth were ever so close to their little spirits; I know it, sir. For how else is she struck dumb now except some power of darkness would stop her mouth? It is a marvelous sign, Mr. Parris!

PUTNAM: Don't you understand it, sir? There is a murdering witch among us, bound to keep herself in the dark. *Parris turns to Betty, a frantic terror rising in him.* Let your enemies make of it what they will, you cannot blink it more.

PARRIS, *to Abigail:* Then you were conjuring spirits last night.

ABIGAIL, *whispering:* Not I, sir—Tituba and Ruth.

PARRIS *turns now, with new fear, and goes to Betty, looks down at her, and then, gazing off:* Oh, Abigail, what proper payment for my charity! Now I am undone.

PUTNAM: You are not undone! Let you take hold here. Wait for no one to charge you—declare it yourself. You have discovered witchcraft—

PARRIS: In my house? In my house, Thomas? They will topple me with this! They will make of it a—

Enter Mercy Lewis, the Putnams' servant, a fat, sly, merciless girl of eighteen.

MERCY: Your pardons. I only thought to see how Betty is.

PUTNAM: Why aren't you home? Who's with Ruth?

MERCY: Her grandma come. She's improved a little, I think—she give a powerful sneeze before.

MRS. PUTNAM: Ah, there's a sign of life!

MERCY: I'd fear no more, Goody Putnam. It were a grand sneeze; another like it will shake her wits together, I'm sure. *She goes to the bed to look.*

PARRIS: Will you leave me now, Thomas? I would pray a while alone.

ABIGAIL: Uncle, you've prayed since midnight. Why do you not go down and—

PARRIS: No—no. *To Putnam:* I have no answer for that crowd. I'll wait till Mr. Hale arrives. *To get Mrs. Putnam to leave:* If you will, Goody Ann . . .

PUTNAM: Now look you, sir. Let you strike out against the Devil, and the village will bless you for it! Come down, speak to them—pray with them. They're thirsting for your word, Mister! Surely you'll pray with them.

PARRIS, *swayed:* I'll lead them in a psalm, but let you say nothing of witchcraft yet. I will not discuss it. The cause is yet unknown. I have had enough contention since I came; I want no more.

MRS. PUTNAM: Mercy, you go home to Ruth, dy'y'hear?

MERCY: Aye, mum.

Mrs. Putnam goes out.

PARRIS, *to Abigail:* If she starts for the window, cry for me at once.

ABIGAIL: I will, uncle.

PARRIS, *to Putnam:* There is a terrible power in her arms today. *He goes out with Putnam.*

ABIGAIL, *with hushed trepidation:* How is Ruth sick?

MERCY: It's weirdish, I know not—she seems to walk like a dead one since last night.

ABIGAIL, *turns at once and goes to Betty, and now, with fear in her voice:* Betty? *Betty doesn't move. She shakes her.* Now stop this! Betty! Sit up now!

Betty doesn't stir. Mercy comes over.

MERCY: Have you tried beatin' her? I gave Ruth a good one and it waked her for a minute. Here, let me have her.

ABIGAIL, *holding Mercy back:* No, he'll be comin' up. Listen, now; if they be questioning us, tell them we danced—I told him as much already.

MERCY: Aye. And what more?

ABIGAIL: He knows Tituba conjured Ruth's sisters to come out of the grave.

MERCY: And what more?

ABIGAIL: He saw you naked.

MERCY, *clapping her hands together with a frightened laugh:* Oh, Jesus!

Enter Mary Warren, breathless. She is seventeen, a subservient, naive, lonely girl.

MARY WARREN: What'll we do? The village is out! I just come from the farm; the whole country's talkin' witchcraft! They'll be callin' us witches, Abby!

MERCY, *pointing and looking at Mary Warren:* She means to tell, I know it.

MARY WARREN: Abby, we've got to tell. Witchery's a hangin' error, a hangin' like they done in Boston two year ago! We must tell the truth, Abby! You'll only be whipped for dancin', and the other things!

ABIGAIL: Oh, *we'll* be whipped!

MARY WARREN: I never done none of it, Abby. I only looked!

MERCY, *moving menacingly toward Mary:* Oh, you're a great one for lookin', aren't you, Mary Warren? What a grand peeping courage you have!

Betty, on the bed, whimpers. Abigail turns to her at once.

ABIGAIL: Betty? *She goes to Betty.* Now, Betty, dear, wake up now. It's Abigail. *She sits Betty up and furiously shakes her.* I'll beat you, Betty! *Betty whimpers.* My, you seem improving. I talked to your papa and I told him everything. So there's nothing to—

BETTY, *darts off the bed, frightened of Abigail, and flattens herself against the wall:* I want my mama!

ABIGAIL, *with alarm, as she cautiously approaches Betty:* What ails you, Betty? Your mama's dead and buried.

BETTY: I'll fly to Mama. Let me fly! *She raises her arms as though to fly, and streaks for the window, gets one leg out.*

ABIGAIL, *pulling her away from the window:* I told him everything; he knows now, he knows everything we—

BETTY: You drank blood, Abby! You didn't tell him that!

ABIGAIL: Betty, you never say that again! You will never—

BETTY: You did, you did! You drank a charm to kill John Proctor's wife! You drank a charm to kill Goody Proctor!

ABIGAIL, *smashes her across the face:* Shut it! Now shut it!

BETTY, *collapsing on the bed:* Mama, Mama! *She dissolves into sobs.*

ABIGAIL: Now look you. All of you. We danced. And Tituba conjured Ruth Putnam's dead sisters. And that is all. And mark this. Let either of you breathe a word, or the edge of a word, about the other things, and I will come to you in the black of some terrible night and I will bring a pointy reckoning that will shudder you. And you know I can do it; I saw Indians smash my dear parents' heads on the pillow next to mine, and I have seen some reddish work done at night, and I can make you wish you had never seen the sun go down! *She goes to Betty and roughly sits her up.* Now, you—sit up and stop this!

But Betty collapses in her hands and lies inert on the bed.

MARY WARREN, *with hysterical fright:* What's got her? *Abigail stares in fright at Betty.* Abby, she's going to die! It's a sin to conjure, and we—

ABIGAIL, *starting for Mary:* I say shut it, Mary Warren!

Enter John Proctor. On seeing him, Mary Warren leaps in fright.

Proctor was a farmer in his middle thirties. He need not have been a partisan of any faction in the town, but there is evidence to suggest that he had a sharp and biting way with hypocrites. He was the kind of man—powerful of body, even-tempered, and not easily led—who cannot refuse support to partisans without drawing their deepest resentment. In Proctor's presence a fool felt his foolishness instantly—and a Proctor is always marked for calumny therefore.

But as we shall see, the steady manner he displays does not spring from an untroubled soul. He is a sinner, a sinner not only against the moral fashion of the time, but against his own vision of decent conduct. These people had no ritual for the washing away of sins. It is another trait we inherited from them, and it has helped to discipline us as well as to breed hypocrisy among us. Proctor, respected and even feared in Salem, has come to regard himself as a kind of fraud. But no hint of this has yet appeared on the surface, and as he enters from the crowded parlor below it is a man in his prime we see, with a quiet confidence and an unexpressed, hidden force. Mary Warren, his servant, can barely speak for embarrassment and fear.

MARY WARREN: Oh! I'm just going home, Mr. Proctor.

PROCTOR: Be you foolish, Mary Warren? Be you deaf? I forbid you leave the house, did I not? Why shall I pay you? I am looking for you more often than my cows!

MARY WARREN: I only come to see the great doings in the world.

PROCTOR: I'll show you a great doin' on your arse one of these days. Now get you home; my wife is waitin' with your work! *Trying to retain a shred of dignity, she goes slowly out.*

MERCY LEWIS, *both afraid of him and strangely titillated:* I'd best be off. I have my Ruth to watch. Good morning, Mr. Proctor.

Mercy sidles out. Since Proctor's entrance, Abigail has stood as though on tiptoe, absorbing his presence, wide-eyed. He glances at her, then goes to Betty on the bed.

ABIGAIL: Gah! I'd almost forgot how strong you are, John Proctor!

PROCTOR, *looking at Abigail now, the faintest suggestion of a knowing smile on his face:* What's this mischief here?

ABIGAIL, *with a nervous laugh:* Oh, she's only gone silly somehow.

PROCTOR: The road past my house is a pilgrimage to Salem all morning. The town's mumbling witchcraft.

ABIGAIL: Oh, posh! *Winningly she comes a little closer, with a confidential, wicked air.* We were dancin' in the woods last night, and my uncle leaped in on us. She took fright, is all.

PROCTOR, *his smile widening:* Ah, you're wicked yet, aren't y'! *A trill of expectant laughter escapes her, and she dares come closer, feverishly looking into his eyes.* You'll be clapped in the stocks before you're twenty.

He takes a step to go, and she springs into his path.

ABIGAIL: Give me a word, John. A soft word. *Her concentrated desire destroys his smile.*

PROCTOR: No, no, Abby. That's done with.

ABIGAIL, *tauntingly:* You come five mile to see a silly girl fly? I know you better.

PROCTOR, *setting her firmly out of his path:* I come to see what mischief your uncle's brewin' now. *With final emphasis:* Put it out of mind, Abby.

ABIGAIL, *grasping his hand before he can release her:* John—I am waitin' for you every night.

PROCTOR: Abby, I never give you hope to wait for me.

ABIGAIL, *now beginning to anger—she can't believe it:* I have something better than hope, I think!

PROCTOR: Abby, you'll put it out of mind. I'll not be comin' for you more.

ABIGAIL: You're surely sportin' with me.

PROCTOR: You know me better.

ABIGAIL: I know how you clutched my back behind your house and sweated like a stallion whenever I come near! Or did I dream that? It's she put me out, you cannot pretend it were you. I saw your face when she put me out, and you loved me then and you do now!

PROCTOR: Abby, that's a wild thing to say—

ABIGAIL: A wild thing may say wild things. But not so wild, I think. I have seen you since she put me out; I have seen you nights.

PROCTOR: I have hardly stepped off my farm this sevenmonth.

ABIGAIL: I have a sense for heat, John, and yours has drawn me to my window, and I have seen you looking up, burning in your loneliness. Do you tell me you've never looked up at my window?

PROCTOR: I may have looked up.

ABIGAIL, *now softening:* And you must. You are no wintry man. I know you, John. I *know* you. *She is weeping.* I cannot sleep for dreamin'; I cannot dream but I wake and walk about the house as though I'd find you comin' through some door. *She clutches him desperately.*

PROCTOR, *gently pressing her from him, with great sympathy but firmly:* Child—

ABIGAIL, *with a flash of anger:* How do you call me child!

PROCTOR: Abby, I may think of you softly from time to time. But I will cut off my hand before I'll ever reach for you again. Wipe it out of mind. We never touched, Abby.

ABIGAIL: Aye, but we did.

PROCTOR: Aye, but we did not.

ABIGAIL, *with a bitter anger:* Oh, I marvel how such a strong man may let such a sickly wife be—

PROCTOR, *angered—at himself as well:* You'll speak nothin' of Elizabeth!

ABIGAIL: She is blackening my name in the village! She is telling lies about me! She is a cold, sniveling woman, and you bend to her! Let her turn you like a—

PROCTOR, *shaking her:* Do you look for whippin'?

A psalm is heard being sung below.

ABIGAIL, *in tears:* I look for John Proctor that took me from my sleep and put knowledge in my heart! I never knew what pretense Salem was, I never knew the lying lessons I was taught by all these Christian women and their covenanted men! And now you bid me tear the light out of my eyes? I will not, I cannot! You loved me, John Proctor, and whatever sin it is, you love me yet! *He turns abruptly to go out. She rushes to him.* John, pity me, pity me!

The words "going up to Jesus" are heard in the psalm, and Betty claps her ears suddenly and whines loudly.

ABIGAIL: Betty? *She hurries to Betty, who is now sitting up and screaming. Proctor goes to Betty as Abigail is trying to pull her hands down, calling "Betty!"*

PROCTOR, *growing unnerved:* What's she doing? Girl, what ails you? Stop that wailing!

The singing has stopped in the midst of this, and now Parris rushes in.

PARRIS: What happened? What are you doing to her? Betty! *He rushes to the bed, crying, "Betty, Betty!" Mrs. Putnam enters, feverish with curiosity, and with her Thomas Putnam and Mercy Lewis. Parris, at the bed, keeps lightly slapping Betty's face, while she moans and tries to get up.*

ABIGAIL: She heard you singin' and suddenly she's up and screamin'.

MRS. PUTNAM: The psalm! The psalm! She cannot bear to hear the Lord's name!

PARRIS: No, God forbid. Mercy, run to the doctor! Tell him what's happened here! *Mercy Lewis rushes out.*

MRS. PUTNAM: Mark it for a sign, mark it!

Rebecca Nurse, seventy-two, enters. She is white-haired, leaning upon her walking-stick.

PUTNAM, *pointing at the whimpering Betty:* That is a notorious sign of witchcraft afoot, Goody Nurse, a prodigious sign!

MRS. PUTNAM: My mother told me that! When they cannot bear to hear the name of—

PARRIS, *trembling:* Rebecca, Rebecca, go to her, we're lost. She suddenly cannot bear to hear the Lord's—

Giles Corey, eighty-three, enters. He is knotted with muscle, canny, inquisitive, and still powerful.

REBECCA: There is hard sickness here, Giles Corey, so please to keep the quiet.

GILES: I've not said a word. No one here can testify I've said a word. Is she going to fly again? I hear she flies.

PUTNAM: Man, be quiet now!

Everything is quiet. Rebecca walks across the room to the bed. Gentleness exudes from her. Betty is quietly whimpering, eyes shut. Rebecca simply stands over the child, who gradually quiets.

And while they are so absorbed, we may put a word in for Rebecca. Rebecca was the wife of Francis Nurse, who, from all accounts, was one of those men for whom both sides of the argument had to have respect. He was called upon to arbitrate disputes as though he were an unofficial judge, and Rebecca also enjoyed the high opinion most people had for him. By the time of the delusion, they had three hundred acres, and their children were settled in separate homesteads within the same estate. However, Francis had originally rented the land, and one theory has it that, as he gradually paid for it and raised his social status, there were those who resented his rise.

Another suggestion to explain the systematic campaign against Rebecca, and inferentially against Francis, is the land war he fought with his neighbors, one of whom was a Putnam. This squabble grew to the proportions of a battle in the woods between partisans of both sides, and it is said to have lasted for two days. As for Rebecca herself, the general opinion of her character was so high that to explain how anyone dared cry her out for a witch—and more, how adults could bring themselves to lay hands on her—we must look to the fields and boundaries of that time.

As we have seen, Thomas Putnam's man for the Salem ministry was Bayley. The Nurse clan had been in the faction that prevented Bayley's taking office. In addition, certain families allied to the Nurses by blood or friendship, and whose farms were contiguous with the Nurse farm or close to it, combined to break away from the Salem town authority and set up Topsfield, a new and independent entity whose existence was resented by old Salemites.

That the guiding hand behind the outcry was Putnam's is indicated by the fact that, as soon as it began, this Topsfield-Nurse faction absented themselves from church in protest and disbelief. It was Edward and Jonathan Putnam who signed the first complaint against Rebecca; and Thomas Putnam's little daughter was the one who fell into a fit at the hearing and pointed to Rebecca as her attacker. To top it all, Mrs. Putnam—who is now staring at the bewitched child on the bed—soon accused Rebecca's spirit of "tempting her to iniquity," a charge that had more truth in it than Mrs. Putnam could know.

MRS. PUTNAM, *astonished:* What have you done?

Rebecca, in thought, now leaves the bedside and sits.

PARRIS, *wondrous and relieved:* What do you make of it, Rebecca?

PUTNAM, *eagerly:* Goody Nurse, will you go to my Ruth and see if you can wake her?

REBECCA, *sitting:* I think she'll wake in time. Pray calm yourselves. I have eleven children, and I am twenty-six times a grandma, and I have seen them all through their silly seasons, and when it come on them they will run the Devil bowlegged keeping up with their mischief. I think she'll wake when she tires of it. A child's spirit is like a child, you can never catch it by running after it; you must stand still, and, for love, it will soon itself come back.

PROCTOR: Aye, that's the truth of it, Rebecca.

MRS. PUTNAM: This is no silly season, Rebecca. My Ruth is bewildered, Rebecca; she cannot eat.

REBECCA: Perhaps she is not hungered yet. *To Parris:* I hope you are not decided to go in search of loose spirits, Mr. Parris. I've heard promise of that outside.

PARRIS: A wide opinion's running in the parish that the Devil may be among us, and I would satisfy them that they are wrong.

PROCTOR: Then let you come out and call them wrong. Did you consult the wardens before you called this minister to look for devils?

PARRIS: He is not coming to look for devils!

PROCTOR: Then what's he coming for?

PUTNAM: There be children dyin' in the village, Mister!

PROCTOR: I seen none dyin'. This society will not be a bag to swing around your head, Mr. Putnam. *To Parris:* Did you call a meeting before you—?

PUTNAM: I am sick of meetings; cannot the man turn his head without he have a meeting?

PROCTOR: He may turn his head, but not to Hell!

REBECCA: Pray, John, be calm. *Pause. He defers to her.* Mr. Parris, I think you'd best send Reverend Hale back as soon as he come. This will set us all to arguin' again in the society, and we thought to have peace this year. I think we ought rely on the doctor now, and good prayer.

MRS. PUTNAM: Rebecca, the doctor's baffled!

REBECCA: If so he is, then let us go to God for the cause of it. There is prodigious danger in the seeking of loose spirits. I fear it, I fear it. Let us rather blame ourselves and—

PUTNAM: How may we blame ourselves? I am one of nine sons; the Putnam seed have peopled this province. And yet I have but one child left of eight—and now she shrivels!

REBECCA: I cannot fathom that.

MRS. PUTNAM, *with a growing edge of sarcasm:* But I must! You think it God's work you should never lose a child, nor grandchild either, and I bury all but one? There are wheels within wheels in this village, and fires within fires!

PUTNAM, *to Parris:* When Reverend Hale comes, you will proceed to look for signs of witchcraft here.

PROCTOR, *to Putnam:* You cannot command Mr. Parris. We vote by name in this society, not by acreage.

PUTNAM: I never heard you worried so on this society, Mr. Proctor. I do not think I saw you at Sabbath meeting since snow flew.

PROCTOR: I have trouble enough without I come five mile to hear him preach only hellfire and bloody damnation. Take it to heart, Mr. Parris. There are many others who stay away from church these days because you hardly ever mention God any more.

PARRIS, *now aroused:* Why, that's a drastic charge!

REBECCA: It's somewhat true; there are many that quail to bring their children—

PARRIS: I do not preach for children, Rebecca. It is not the children who are unmindful of their obligations toward this ministry.

REBECCA: Are there really those unmindful?

PARRIS: I should say the better half of Salem village—

PUTNAM: And more than that!

PARRIS: Where is my wood? My contract provides I be supplied with all my firewood. I am waiting since November for a stick, and even in November I had to show my frostbitten hands like some London beggar!

GILES: You are allowed six pound a year to buy your wood, Mr. Parris.

PARRIS: I regard that six pound as part of my salary. I am paid little enough without I spend six pound on firewood.

PROCTOR: Sixty, plus six for firewood—

PARRIS: The salary is sixty-six pound, Mr. Proctor! I am not some preaching farmer with a book under my arm; I am a graduate of Harvard College.

GILES: Aye, and well instructed in arithmetic!

PARRIS: Mr. Corey, you will look far for a man of my kind at sixty pound a year! I am not used to this poverty; I left a thrifty business in the Barbados to serve the Lord. I do not fathom it, why am I persecuted here? I cannot offer one proposition but there be a howling riot of argument. I have often wondered if the Devil be in it somewhere; I cannot understand you people otherwise.

PROCTOR: Mr. Parris, you are the first minister ever did demand the deed to this house—

PARRIS: Man! Don't a minister deserve a house to live in?

PROCTOR: To live in, yes. But to ask ownership is like you shall own the meeting house itself; the last meeting I were at you spoke so long on deeds and mortgages I thought it were an auction.

PARRIS: I want a mark of confidence, is all! I am your third preacher in seven years. I do not wish to be put out like the cat whenever some majority feels the whim. You people seem not to comprehend that a minister is the Lord's man in the parish; a minister is not to be so lightly crossed and contradicted—

PUTNAM: Aye!

PARRIS: There is either obedience or the church will burn like Hell is burning!

PROCTOR: Can you speak one minute without we land in Hell again? I am sick of Hell!

PARRIS: It is not for you to say what is good for you to hear!

PROCTOR: I may speak my heart, I think!

PARRIS, *in a fury:* What, are we Quakers? We are not Quakers here yet, Mr. Proctor. And you may tell that to your followers!

PROCTOR: My followers!

PARRIS—*now he's out with it:* There is a party in this church. I am not blind; there is a faction and a party.

PROCTOR: Against you?

PUTNAM: Against him and all authority!

PROCTOR: Why, then I must find it and join it.

There is shock among the others.

REBECCA: He does not mean that.

PUTNAM: He confessed it now!

PROCTOR: I mean it solemnly, Rebecca; I like not the smell of this "authority."

REBECCA: No, you cannot break charity with your minister. You are another kind, John. Clasp his hand, make your peace.

PROCTOR: I have a crop to sow and lumber to drag home. *He goes angrily to the door and turns to Corey with a smile.* What say you, Giles, let's find the party. He says there's a party.

GILES: I've changed my opinion of this man, John. Mr. Parris, I beg your pardon. I never thought you had so much iron in you.

PARRIS, *surprised:* Why, thank you, Giles!

GILES: It suggests to the mind what the trouble be among us all these years. *To all:* Think on it. Wherefore is everybody suing everybody else? Think on it now, it's a deep thing, and dark as a pit. I have been six time in court this year—

PROCTOR, *familiarly, with warmth, although he knows he is approaching the edge of Giles' tolerance with this:* Is it the Devil's fault that a man cannot say you good morning without you clap him for defamation? You're old, Giles, and you're not hearin' so well as you did.

GILES—*he cannot be crossed:* John Proctor, I have only last month collected four pound damages for you publicly sayin' I burned the roof off your house, and I—

PROCTOR, *laughing:* I never said no such thing, but I've paid you for it, so I hope I can call you deaf without charge. Now come along, Giles, and help me drag my lumber home.

PUTNAM: A moment, Mr. Proctor. What lumber is that you're draggin', if I may ask you?

PROCTOR: My lumber. From out my forest by the riverside.

PUTNAM: Why, we are surely gone wild this year. What anarchy is this? That tract is in my bounds, it's in my bounds, Mr. Proctor.

PROCTOR: In your bounds! *Indicating Rebecca:* I bought that tract from Goody Nurse's husband five months ago.

PUTNAM: He had no right to sell it. It stands clear in my grandfather's will that all the land between the river and—

PROCTOR: Your grandfather had a habit of willing land that never belonged to him, if I may say it plain.

GILES: That's God's truth; he nearly willed away my north pasture but he knew I'd break his fingers before he'd set his name to it. Let's get your lumber home, John. I feel a sudden will to work coming on.

PUTNAM: You load one oak of mine and you'll fight to drag it home!

GILES: Aye, and we'll win too, Putnam—this fool and I. Come on! *He turns to Proctor and starts out.*

PUTNAM: I'll have my men on you, Corey! I'll clap a writ on you!

Enter Reverend John Hale of Beverly.

Mr. Hale is nearing forty, a tight-skinned, eager-eyed intellectual. This is a beloved errand for him; on being called here to ascertain witchcraft he felt the pride of the specialist whose unique knowledge has at last been publicly called for. Like almost all men of learning, he spent a good deal of his time pondering the invisible world, especially since he had himself encountered a witch in his parish not long before. That woman, however, turned into a mere pest under his searching scrutiny, and the child she had allegedly been afflicting recovered her normal behavior after Hale had given her his kindness and a few days of rest in his own house. However, that experience never raised a doubt in his mind as to the reality of the underworld or the existence of Lucifer's many-faced lieutenants. And his belief is not to his discredit. Better minds than Hale's were—and still are—convinced that there is a society of spirits beyond our ken. One cannot help noting that one of his lines has never yet raised a laugh in any audience that has seen this play; it is his assurance that "We cannot look to superstition in this. The Devil is precise." Evidently we are not quite certain even now whether diabolism is holy and not to be scoffed at. And it is no accident that we should be so bemused.

Like Reverend Hale and the others on this stage, we conceive the Devil as a necessary part of a respectable view of cosmology. Ours is a divided empire in which certain ideas and emotions and actions are of God, and their opposites are of Lucifer. It is as impossible for most men to conceive of a morality without sin as of an earth without "sky." Since 1692 a great but superficial change has wiped out God's beard and the Devil's horns, but the world is still gripped between two diametrically opposed absolutes. The concept of unity, in which positive and negative are attributes of the same force, in which good and evil are relative, ever changing, and always joined to the same phenomenon—such a concept is still reserved to the physical sciences and to the few who have grasped the history of ideas. When it is recalled that until the Christian era the underworld was never regarded as a hostile area, that all gods were useful and essentially friendly to man despite occasional lapses; when we see the steady and methodical inculcation into humanity of the idea of man's worthlessness—until redeemed—the necessity of the Devil may become evident as a weapon, a weapon designed and used time and time again in every age to whip men into a surrender to a particular church or church-state.

Our difficulty in believing the—for want of a better word—political inspiration of the Devil is due in great part to the fact that he is called up and damned not only by our social antagonists but by our own side, whatever it may be. The Catholic Church, through its Inquisition, is famous for cultivating Lucifer as the arch-fiend, but the Church's enemies relied no less upon the Old Boy to keep the human mind enthralled. Luther was himself accused of alliance with Hell, and he in turn accused his enemies. To complicate matters further, he believed that he had had contact with the Devil and had argued theology with him. I am not surprised at this, for at my own university a professor of history—a Lutheran, by the way—used to assemble his graduate students, draw the shades, and commune in the classroom with Erasmus. He was never, to my knowledge, officially scoffed at for this, the reason being that the university officials, like most of us, are the children of a history which still sucks at the Devil's teats. At this writing, only England has held back before the temptations of contemporary diabolism. In the countries of the Communist ideology, all resistance of any import is linked to the totally malign capitalist succubi, and in America any man who is not reactionary in his views is open to the charge of alliance with the Red hell. Political opposition, thereby, is given an inhumane overlay which then justifies the abrogation of all normally applied customs of civilized intercourse. A political policy is equated with moral right, and opposition to it with diabolical malevolence. Once such an equation is effectively made, society becomes a congerie of plots and counterplots, and the main role of government changes from that of the arbiter to that of the scourge of God.

The results of this process are no different now from what they ever were, except sometimes in the degree of cruelty inflicted, and not always even in that department. Normally the actions and deeds of a man were all that society felt comfortable in judging. The secret intent of an action was left to the ministers, priests, and rabbis to deal with. When diabolism rises, however, actions are the least important manifests of the true nature of a man. The Devil, as Reverend Hale said, is a wily one, and, until an hour before he fell, even God thought him beautiful in Heaven.

The analogy, however, seems to falter when one considers that, while there were no witches then, there are Communists and capitalists now, and in each camp there is certain proof that spies of each side are at work undermining the other. But this is a snobbish objection and not at all warranted by the facts. I have no doubt that people *were* communing with, and even worshiping, the Devil in Salem, and if the whole truth could be known in this case, as it is in others, we should discover a regular and conventionalized propitiation of the dark spirit. One certain evidence of this is the confession of Tituba, the slave of Reverend Parris, and another is the behavior of the children who were known to have indulged in sorceries with her.

There are accounts of similar *klatches* in Europe, where the daughters of the towns would assemble at night and, sometimes with fetishes, sometimes with a selected young man, give themselves to love, with some bastardly results. The Church, sharp-eyed as it must be when gods long dead are brought to life, condemned these orgies as witchcraft and interpreted them, rightly, as a resurgence of the Dionysiac forces it had crushed long before. Sex, sin, and the Devil were early linked, and so they continued to be in Salem, and are today. From all accounts there are no more puritanical mores in the world than those enforced by the Communists in Russia, where women's fashions, for instance, are as prudent and all-covering as any American Baptist would desire. The divorce laws lay a tremendous responsibility on the father for the care of his children. Even the laxity of divorce regulations in the early years of the revolution was undoubtedly a revulsion from the nineteenth-century Victorian immobility of marriage and the consequent hypocrisy that developed from it. If for no other reasons, a state so powerful, so jealous of the uniformity of its citizens, cannot long tolerate the atomization of the family. And yet, in American eyes at least, there remains the conviction that the Russian attitude toward women is lascivious. It is the Devil working again, just as he is working within the Slav who is shocked at the very idea of a woman's disrobing herself in a burlesque show. Our opposites are always robed in sexual sin, and it is from this unconscious conviction that demonology gains both its attractive sensuality and its capacity to infuriate and frighten.

Coming into Salem now, Reverend Hale conceives of himself much as a young doctor on his first call. His painfully acquired armory of symptoms, catchwords, and diagnostic procedures are now to be put to use at last. The road from Beverly is unusually busy this morning, and he has passed a hundred rumors that make him smile at the ignorance of the yeomanry in this most precise science. He feels himself allied with the best minds of Europe—kings, philosophers, scientists, and ecclesiasts of all churches. His goal is light, goodness and its preservation, and he knows the exaltation of the blessed whose intelligence, sharpened by minute examinations of enormous tracts, is finally called upon to face what may be a bloody fight with the Fiend himself.

He appears loaded down with half a dozen heavy books.

HALE: Pray you, someone take these!

PARRIS, *delighted:* Mr. Hale! Oh! it's good to see you again! *Taking some books:* My, they're heavy!

HALE, *setting down his books:* They must be; they are weighted with authority.

PARRIS, *a little scared:* Well, you do come prepared!

HALE: We shall need hard study if it comes to tracking down the Old Boy. *Noticing Rebecca:* You cannot be Rebecca Nurse?

REBECCA: I am, sir. Do you know me?

HALE: It's strange how I knew you, but I suppose you look as such a good soul should. We have all heard of your great charities in Beverly.

PARRIS: Do you know this gentleman? Mr. Thomas Putnam. And his good wife Ann.

HALE: Putnam! I had not expected such distinguished company, sir.

PUTNAM, *pleased:* It does not seem to help us today, Mr. Hale. We look to you to come to our house and save our child.

HALE: Your child ails too?

MRS. PUTNAM: Her soul, her soul seems flown away. She sleeps and yet she walks . . .

PUTNAM: She cannot eat.

HALE: Cannot eat! *Thinks on it. Then, to Proctor and Giles Corey:* Do you men have afflicted children?

PARRIS: No, no, these are farmers. John Proctor—

GILES COREY: He don't believe in witches.

PROCTOR, *to Hale:* I never spoke on witches one way or the other. Will you come, Giles?

GILES: No—no, John, I think not. I have some few queer questions of my own to ask this fellow.

PROCTOR: I've heard you to be a sensible man, Mr. Hale. I hope you'll leave some of it in Salem.

Proctor goes. Hale stands embarrassed for an instant.

PARRIS, *quickly:* Will you look at my daughter, sir? *Leads Hale to the bed.* She has tried to leap out the window; we discovered her this morning on the highroad, waving her arms as though she'd fly.

HALE, *narrowing his eyes:* Tries to fly.

PUTNAM: She cannot bear to hear the Lord's name, Mr. Hale; that's a sure sign of witchcraft afloat.

HALE, *holding up his hands:* No, no. Now let me instruct you. We cannot look to superstition in this. The Devil is precise; the marks of his presence are definite as stone, and I must tell you all that I shall not proceed unless you are prepared to believe me if I should find no bruise of hell upon her.

PARRIS: It is agreed, sir—it is agreed—we will abide by your judgment.

HALE: Good then. *He goes to the bed, looks down at Betty. To Parris:* Now, sir, what were your first warning of this strangeness?

PARRIS: Why, sir—I discovered her—*indicating Abigail*—and my niece and ten or twelve of the other girls, dancing in the forest last night.

HALE, *surprised:* You permit dancing?

PARRIS: No, no, it were secret—

MRS. PUTNAM, *unable to wait:* Mr. Parris's slave has knowledge of conjurin', sir.

PARRIS, *to Mrs. Putnam:* We cannot be sure of that, Goody Ann—

MRS. PUTNAM, *frightened, very softly:* I know it, sir. I sent my child—she should learn from Tituba who murdered her sisters.

REBECCA, *horrified:* Goody Ann! You sent a child to conjure up the dead?

MRS. PUTNAM: Let God blame me, not you, not you, Rebecca! I'll not have you judging me any more! *To Hale:* Is it a natural work to lose seven children before they live a day?

PARRIS: Sssh!

Rebecca, with great pain, turns her face away. There is a pause.

HALE: Seven dead in childbirth.

MRS. PUTNAM, *softly:* Aye. *Her voice breaks; she looks up at him. Silence. Hale is impressed. Parris looks to him. He goes to his books, opens one, turns pages, then reads. All wait, avidly.*

PARRIS, *hushed:* What book is that?

MRS. PUTNAM: What's there, sir?

HALE, *with a tasty love of intellectual pursuit:* Here is all the invisible world, caught, defined, and calculated. In these books the Devil stands stripped of all his brute disguises. Here are all your familiar spirits—your incubi and succubi; your witches that go by land, by air, and by sea; your wizards of the night and of the day. Have no fear now—we shall find him out if he has come among us, and I mean to crush him utterly if he has shown his face! *He starts for the bed.*

REBECCA: Will it hurt the child, sir?

HALE: I cannot tell. If she is truly in the Devil's grip we may have to rip and tear to get her free.

REBECCA: I think I'll go, then. I am too old for this. *She rises.*

PARRIS, *striving for conviction:* Why, Rebecca, we may open up the boil of all our troubles today!

REBECCA: Let us hope for that. I go to God for you, sir.

PARRIS, *with trepidation—and resentment:* I hope you do not mean we go to Satan here! *Slight pause.*

REBECCA: I wish I knew. *She goes out; they feel resentful of her note of moral superiority.*

PUTNAM, *abruptly:* Come, Mr. Hale, let's get on. Sit you here.

GILES: Mr. Hale, I have always wanted to ask a learned man—what signifies the readin' of strange books?

HALE: What books?

GILES: I cannot tell; she hides them.

HALE: Who does this?

GILES: Martha, my wife. I have waked at night many a time and found her in a corner, readin' of a book. Now what do you make of that?

HALE: Why, that's not necessarily—

GILES: It discomfits me! Last night—mark this—I tried and tried and could not say my prayers. And then she close her book and walks out of the house, and suddenly—mark this—I could pray again!

Old Giles must be spoken for, if only because his fate was to be so remarkable and so different from that of all the others. He was in his early eighties at this time, and was the most comical hero in the history. No man has ever been blamed for so much. If a cow was missed, the first thought was to look for her around Corey's house; a fire blazing up at night brought suspicion of arson to his door. He didn't give a hoot for public opinion, and only in his last years—after he had married Martha—did he bother much with the church. That she stopped his prayer is very probable, but he forgot to say that he'd only recently learned any prayers and it didn't take much to make him stumble over them. He was a crank and a nuisance, but withal a deeply innocent and brave man. In court, once, he was asked if it were true that he had been frightened by the strange behavior of a hog and had then said he knew it to be the Devil in an animal's shape. "What frighted you?" he was asked. He forgot everything but the word "frighted," and instantly replied, "I do not know that I ever spoke that word in my life."

HALE: Ah! The stoppage of prayer—that is strange. I'll speak further on that with you.

GILES: I'm not sayin' she's touched the Devil, now, but I'd admire to know what books she reads and why she hides them. She'll not answer me, y' see.

HALE: Aye, we'll discuss it. *To all:* Now mark me, if the Devil is in her you will witness some frightful wonders in this room, so please to keep your wits about you. Mr. Putnam, stand close in case she flies. Now, Betty, dear, will you sit up? *Putnam comes in closer, ready-handed. Hale sits Betty up, but she hangs limp in his hands.* Hmmm. *He observes her carefully. The others watch breathlessly.* Can you hear me? I am John Hale, minister of Beverly. I have come to help you, dear. Do you remember my two little girls in Beverly? *She does not stir in his hands.*

PARRIS, *in fright:* How can it be the Devil? Why would he choose my house to strike? We have all manner of licentious people in the village!

HALE: What victory would the Devil have to win a soul already bad? It is the best the Devil wants, and who is better than the minister?

GILES: That's deep, Mr. Parris, deep, deep!

PARRIS, *with resolution now:* Betty! Answer Mr. Hale! Betty!

HALE: Does someone afflict you, child? It need not be a woman, mind you, or a man. Perhaps some bird invisible to others comes to you—perhaps a pig, a mouse, or any beast at all. Is there some figure bids you fly? *The child remains limp in his hands. In silence he lays her back on the pillow. Now, holding out his hands toward her, he intones:* In nomine Domini Sabaoth sui filiique ite ad infernos. *She does not stir. He turns to Abigail, his eyes narrowing.* Abigail, what sort of dancing were you doing with her in the forest?

ABIGAIL: Why—common dancing is all.

PARRIS: I think I ought to say that I—I saw a kettle in the grass where they were dancing.

ABIGAIL: That were only soup.

HALE: What sort of soup were in this kettle, Abigail?

ABIGAIL: Why, it were beans—and lentils, I think, and—

HALE: Mr. Parris, you did not notice, did you, any living thing in the kettle? A mouse, perhaps, a spider, a frog—?

PARRIS, *fearfully:* I—do believe there were some movement—in the soup.

ABIGAIL: That jumped in, we never put it in!

HALE, *quickly:* What jumped in?

ABIGAIL: Why, a very little frog jumped—

PARRIS: A frog, Abby!

HALE, *grasping Abigail:* Abigail, it may be your cousin is dying. Did you call the Devil last night?

ABIGAIL: I never called him! Tituba, Tituba . . .

PARRIS, *blanched:* She called the Devil?

HALE: I should like to speak with Tituba.

PARRIS: Goody Ann, will you bring her up? *Mrs. Putnam exits.*

HALE: How did she call him?

ABIGAIL: I know not—she spoke Barbados.

HALE: Did you feel any strangeness when she called him? A sudden cold wind, perhaps? A trembling below the ground?

ABIGAIL: I didn't see no Devil! *Shaking Betty:* Betty, wake up. Betty! Betty!

HALE: You cannot evade me, Abigail. Did your cousin drink any of the brew in that kettle?

ABIGAIL: She never drank it!
HALE: Did you drink it?
ABIGAIL: No, sir!
HALE: Did Tituba ask you to drink it?
ABIGAIL: She tried, but I refused.
HALE: Why are you concealing? Have you sold yourself to Lucifer?
ABIGAIL: I never sold myself! I'm a good girl! I'm a proper girl!

Mrs. Putnam enters with Tituba, and instantly Abigail points at Tituba.

ABIGAIL: She made me do it! She made Betty do it!
TITUBA, *shocked and angry:* Abby!
ABIGAIL: She makes me drink blood!
PARRIS: Blood!!
MRS. PUTNAM: My baby's blood?
TITUBA: No, no, chicken blood. I give she chicken blood!
HALE: Woman, have you enlisted these children for the Devil?
TITUBA: No, no, sir, I don't truck with no Devil!
HALE: Why can she not wake? Are you silencing this child?
TITUBA: I love me Betty!
HALE: You have sent your spirit out upon this child, have you not? Are you gathering souls for the Devil?
ABIGAIL: She sends her spirit on me in church; she makes me laugh at prayer!
PARRIS: She have often laughed at prayer!
ABIGAIL: She comes to me every night to go and drink blood!
TITUBA: You beg *me* to conjure! She beg *me* make charm—
ABIGAIL: Don't lie! *To Hale:* She comes to me while I sleep; she's always making me dream corruptions!
TITUBA: Why you say that, Abby?
ABIGAIL: Sometimes I wake and find myself standing in the open doorway and not a stitch on my body! I always hear her laughing in my sleep. I hear her singing her Barbados songs and tempting me with—
TITUBA: Mister Reverend, I never—
HALE, *resolved now:* Tituba, I want you to wake this child.
TITUBA: I have no power on this child, sir.
HALE: You most certainly do, and you will free her from it now! When did you compact with the Devil?
TITUBA: I don't compact with no Devil!
PARRIS: You will confess yourself or I will take you out and whip you to your death, Tituba!
PUTNAM: This woman must be hanged! She must be taken and hanged!
TITUBA, *terrified, falls to her knees:* No, no, don't hang Tituba! I tell him I don't desire to work for him, sir.
PARRIS: The Devil?
HALE: Then you saw him! *Tituba weeps.* Now Tituba, I know that when we bind ourselves to Hell it is very hard to break with it. We are going to help you tear yourself free—

TITUBA, *frightened by the coming process:* Mister Reverend, I do believe somebody else be witchin' these children.

HALE: Who?

TITUBA: I don't know, sir, but the Devil got him numerous witches.

HALE: Does he! *It is a clue.* Tituba, look into my eyes. Come, look into me. *She raises her eyes to his fearfully.* You would be a good Christian woman, would you not, Tituba?

TITUBA: Aye, sir, a good Christian woman.

HALE: And you love these little children?

TITUBA: Oh, yes, sir, I don't desire to hurt little children.

HALE: And you love God, Tituba?

TITUBA: I love God with all my bein'.

HALE: Now, in God's holy name—

TITUBA: Bless Him. Bless Him. *She is rocking on her knees, sobbing in terror.*

HALE: And to His glory—

TITUBA: Eternal glory. Bless Him—bless God . . .

HALE: Open yourself, Tituba—open yourself and let God's holy light shine on you.

TITUBA: Oh, bless the Lord.

HALE: When the Devil comes to you does he ever come—with another person? *She stares up into his face.* Perhaps another person in the village? Someone you know.

PARRIS: Who came with him?

PUTNAM: Sarah Good? Did you ever see Sarah Good with him? Or Osburn?

PARRIS: Was it man or woman came with him?

TITUBA: Man or woman. Was—was woman.

PARRIS: What woman? A woman, you said. What woman?

TITUBA: It was black dark, and I—

PARRIS: You could see him, why could you not see her?

TITUBA: Well, they was always talking; they was always runnin' round and carryin' on—

PARRIS: You mean out of Salem? Salem witches?

TITUBA: I believe so, yes, sir.

Now Hale takes her hand. She is surprised.

HALE: Tituba. You must have no fear to tell us who they are, do you understand? We will protect you. The Devil can never overcome a minister. You know that, do you not?

TITUBA, *kisses Hale's hand:* Aye, sir, oh, I do.

HALE: You have confessed yourself to witchcraft, and that speaks a wish to come to Heaven's side. And we will bless you, Tituba.

TITUBA, *deeply relieved:* Oh, God bless you, Mr. Hale!

HALE, *with rising exaltation:* You are God's instrument put in our hands to discover the Devil's agents among us. You are selected, Tituba, you are chosen to help us cleanse our village. So speak utterly, Tituba, turn your back on him and face God—face God, Tituba, and God will protect you.

TITUBA, *joining with him:* Oh, God, protect Tituba!

HALE, *kindly:* Who came to you with the Devil? Two? Three? Four? How many?

Tituba pants, and begins rocking back and forth again, staring ahead.

TITUBA: There was four. There was four.
PARRIS, *pressing in on her:* Who? Who? Their names, their names!
TITUBA, *suddenly bursting out:* Oh, how many times he bid me kill you, Mr. Parris!
PARRIS: Kill me!
TITUBA, *in a fury:* He say Mr. Parris must be kill! Mr. Parris no goodly man, Mr. Parris mean man and no gentle man, and he bid me rise out of my bed and cut your throat! *They gasp.* But I tell him "No! I don't hate that man. I don't want kill that man." But he say, "You work for me, Tituba, and I make you free! I give you pretty dress to wear, and put you way high up in the air, and you gone fly back to Barbados!" And I say, "You lie, Devil, you lie!" And then he come one stormy night to me, and he say, "Look! I have *white* people belong to me." And I look—and there was Goody Good.
PARRIS: Sarah Good!
TITUBA, *rocking and weeping:* Aye, sir, and Goody Osburn.
MRS. PUTNAM: I knew it! Goody Osburn were midwife to me three times. I begged you, Thomas, did I not? I begged him not to call Osburn because I feared her. My babies always shriveled in her hands!
HALE: Take courage, you must give us all their names. How can you bear to see this child suffering? Look at her, Tituba. *He is indicating Betty on the bed.* Look at her God-given innocence; her soul is so tender; we must protect her, Tituba; the Devil is out and preying on her like a beast upon the flesh of the pure lamb. God will bless you for your help.

Abigail rises, staring as though inspired, and cries out.

ABIGAIL: I want to open myself! *They turn to her, startled. She is enraptured, as though in a pearly light.* I want the light of God, I want the sweet love of Jesus! I danced for the Devil; I saw him; I wrote in his book; I go back to Jesus; I kiss His hand. I saw Sarah Good with the Devil! I saw Goody Osburn with the Devil! I saw Bridget Bishop with the Devil!

As she is speaking, Betty is rising from the bed, a fever in her eyes, and picks up the chant.

BETTY, *staring too:* I saw George Jacobs with the Devil! I saw Goody Howe with the Devil!
PARRIS: She speaks! *He rushes to embrace Betty.* She speaks!
HALE: Glory to God! It is broken, they are free!
BETTY, *calling out hysterically and with great relief:* I saw Martha Bellows with the Devil!
ABIGAIL: I saw Goody Sibber with the Devil! *It is rising to a great glee.*
PUTNAM: The marshal, I'll call the marshal!

Paris is shouting a prayer of thanksgiving.

BETTY: I saw Alice Barrow with the Devil!

The curtain begins to fall.

HALE, *as Putnam goes out:* Let the marshal bring irons!

ABIGAIL: I saw Goody Hawkins with the Devil!
BETTY: I saw Goody Bibber with the Devil!
ABIGAIL: I saw Goody Booth with the Devil!

On their ecstatic cries—

Curtain

Act Two

The common room of Proctor's house, eight days later.

At the right is a door opening on the fields outside. A fireplace is at the left, and behind it a stairway leading upstairs. It is the low, dark, and rather long living room of the time. As the curtain rises, the room is empty. From above, Elizabeth is heard softly singing to the children. Presently the door opens and John Proctor enters, carrying his gun. He glances about the room as he comes toward the fireplace, then halts for an instant as he hears her singing. He continues on to the fireplace, leans the gun against the wall as he swings a pot out of the fire and smells it. Then he lifts out the ladle and tastes. He is not quite pleased. He reaches to a cupboard, takes a pinch of salt, and drops it into the pot. As he is tasting again, her footsteps are heard on the stair. He swings the pot into the fireplace and goes to a basin and washes his hands and face. Elizabeth enters.

ELIZABETH: What keeps you so late? It's almost dark.
PROCTOR: I were planting far out to the forest edge.
ELIZABETH: Oh, you're done then.
PROCTOR: Aye, the farm is seeded. The boys asleep?
ELIZABETH: They will be soon. *And she goes to the fireplace, proceeds to ladle up stew in a dish.*
PROCTOR: Pray now for a fair summer.
ELIZABETH: Aye.
PROCTOR: Are you well today?
ELIZABETH: I am. *She brings the plate to the table, and, indicating the food:* It is a rabbit.
PROCTOR, *going to the table:* Oh, is it! In Jonathan's trap?
ELIZABETH: No, she walked into the house this afternoon; I found her sittin' in the corner like she come to visit.
PROCTOR: Oh, that's a good sign walkin' in.
ELIZABETH: Pray God. It hurt my heart to strip her, poor rabbit. *She sits and watches him taste it.*
PROCTOR: It's well seasoned.
ELIZABETH, *blushing with pleasure:* I took great care. She's tender?
PROCTOR: Aye. *He eats. She watches him.* I think we'll see green fields soon. It's warm as blood beneath the clods.
ELIZABETH: That's well.

Proctor eats, then looks up.

PROCTOR: If the crop is good I'll buy George Jacob's heifer. How would that please you?

ELIZABETH: Aye, it would.

PROCTOR, *with a grin:* I mean to please you, Elizabeth.

ELIZABETH—*it is hard to say:* I know it, John.

He gets up, goes to her, kisses her. She receives it. With a certain disappointment, he returns to the table.

PROCTOR, *as gently as he can:* Cider?

ELIZABETH, *with a sense of reprimanding herself for having forgot:* Aye! *She gets up and goes and pours a glass for him. He now arches his back.*

PROCTOR: This farm's a continent when you go foot by foot droppin' seeds in it.

ELIZABETH, *coming with the cider:* It must be.

PROCTOR, *drinks a long draught, then, putting the glass down:* You ought to bring some flowers in the house.

ELIZABETH: Oh! I forgot! I will tomorrow.

PROCTOR: It's winter in here yet. On Sunday let you come with me, and we'll walk the farm together; I never see such a load of flowers on the earth. *With good feeling he goes and looks up at the sky through the open doorway.* Lilacs have a purple smell. Lilac is the smell of nightfall, I think. Massachusetts is a beauty in the spring!

ELIZABETH: Aye, it is.

There is a pause. She is watching him from the table as he stands there absorbing the night. It is as though she would speak but cannot. Instead, now, she takes up his plate and glass and fork and goes with them to the basin. Her back is turned to him. He turns to her and watches her. A sense of their separation rises.

PROCTOR: I think you're sad again. Are you?

ELIZABETH—*she doesn't want friction, and yet she must:* You come so late I thought you'd gone to Salem this afternoon.

PROCTOR: Why? I have no business in Salem.

ELIZABETH: You did speak of going, earlier this week.

PROCTOR—*he knows what she means:* I thought better of it since.

ELIZABETH: Mary Warren's there today.

PROCTOR: Why'd you let her? You heard me forbid her go to Salem any more!

ELIZABETH: I couldn't stop her.

PROCTOR, *holding back a full condemnation of her:* It is a fault, it is a fault, Elizabeth—you're the mistress here, not Mary Warren.

ELIZABETH: She frightened all my strength away.

PROCTOR: How may that mouse frighten you, Elizabeth? You—

ELIZABETH: It is a mouse no more. I forbid her go, and she raises up her chin like the daughter of a prince and says to me, "I must go to Salem, Goody Proctor; I am an official of the court!"

PROCTOR: Court! What court?

ELIZABETH: Aye, it is a proper court they have now. They've sent four judges out of Boston, she says, weighty magistrates of the General Court, and at the head sits the Deputy Governor of the Province.

PROCTOR, *astonished:* Why, she's mad.

ELIZABETH: I would to God she were. There be fourteen people in the jail now, she says. *Proctor simply looks at her, unable to grasp it.* And they'll be tried, and the court have power to hang them too, she says.

PROCTOR, *scoffing, but without conviction:* Ah, they'd never hang—

ELIZABETH: The Deputy Governor promise hangin' if they'll not confess, John. The town's gone wild, I think. She speak of Abigail, and I thought she were a saint, to hear her. Abigail brings the other girls into the court, and where she walks the crowd will part like the sea for Israel. And folks are brought before them, and if they scream and howl and fall to the floor—the person's clapped in the jail for bewitchin' them.

PROCTOR, *wide-eyed:* Oh, it is a black mischief.

ELIZABETH: I think you must go to Salem, John. *He turns to her.* I think so. You must tell them it is a fraud.

PROCTOR, *thinking beyond this:* Aye, it is, it is surely.

ELIZABETH: Let you go to Ezekiel Cheever—he knows you well. And tell him what she said to you last week in her uncle's house. She said it had naught to do with witchcraft, did she not?

PROCTOR, *in thought:* Aye, she did, she did. *Now, a pause.*

ELIZABETH, *quietly, fearing to anger him by prodding:* God forbid you keep that from the court, John. I think they must be told.

PROCTOR, *quietly, struggling with his thought:* Aye, they must, they must. It is a wonder they do believe her.

ELIZABETH: I would go to Salem now, John—let you go tonight.

PROCTOR: I'll think on it.

ELIZABETH, *with her courage now:* You cannot keep it, John.

PROCTOR, *angering:* I know I cannot keep it. I say I will think on it!

ELIZABETH, *hurt, and very coldly:* Good, then, let you think on it. *She stands and starts to walk out of the room.*

PROCTOR: I am only wondering how I may prove what she told me, Elizabeth. If the girl's a saint now, I think it is not easy to prove she's fraud, and the town gone so silly. She told it to me in a room alone—I have no proof for it.

ELIZABETH: You were alone with her?

PROCTOR, *stubbornly:* For a moment alone, aye.

ELIZABETH: Why, then, it is not as you told me.

PROCTOR, *his anger rising:* For a moment, I say. The others come in soon after.

ELIZABETH, *quietly—she has suddenly lost all faith in him:* Do as you wish, then. *She starts to turn.*

PROCTOR: Woman. *She turns to him.* I'll not have your suspicion any more.

ELIZABETH, *a little loftily:* I have no—

PROCTOR: I'll not have it!

ELIZABETH: Then let you not earn it.

PROCTOR, *with a violent undertone:* You doubt me yet?

ELIZABETH, *with a smile, to keep her dignity:* John, if it were not Abigail that you must go to hurt, would you falter now? I think not.

PROCTOR: Now look you—

ELIZABETH: I see what I see, John.

PROCTOR, *with solemn warning:* You will not judge me more, Elizabeth. I have good reason to think before I charge fraud on Abigail, and I will think on it. Let you look to your own improvement before you go to judge your husband any more. I have forgot Abigail, and—

ELIZABETH: And I.

PROCTOR: Spare me! You forget nothin' and forgive nothin'. Learn charity, woman. I have gone tiptoe in this house all seven month since she is gone. I have not moved from there to there without I think to please you, and still an everlasting funeral marches round your heart. I cannot speak but I am doubted, every moment judged for lies, as though I come into a court when I come into this house!

ELIZABETH: John, you are not open with me. You saw her with a crowd, you said. Now you—

PROCTOR: I'll plead my honesty no more, Elizabeth.

ELIZABETH—*now she would justify herself:* John, I am only—

PROCTOR: No more! I should have roared you down when first you told me your suspicion. But I wilted, and, like a Christian, I confessed. Confessed! Some dream I had must have mistaken you for God that day. But you're not, you're not, and let you remember it! Let you look sometimes for the goodness in me, and judge me not.

ELIZABETH: I do not judge you. The magistrate sits in your heart that judges you. I never thought you but a good man, John—*with a smile*—only somewhat bewildered.

PROCTOR, *laughing bitterly:* Oh, Elizabeth, your justice would freeze beer! *He turns suddenly toward a sound outside. He starts for the door as Mary Warren enters. As soon as he sees her, he goes directly to her and grabs her by her cloak, furious.* How do you go to Salem when I forbid it? Do you mock me? *Shaking her.* I'll whip you if you dare leave this house again!

Strangely, she doesn't resist him, but hangs limply by his grip.

MARY WARREN: I am sick, I am sick, Mr. Proctor. Pray, pray, hurt me not. *Her strangeness throws him off, and her evident pallor and weakness. He frees her.* My insides are all shuddery; I am in the proceedings all day, sir.

PROCTOR, *with draining anger—his curiosity is draining it:* And what of these proceedings here? When will you proceed to keep this house, as you are paid nine pound a year to do—and my wife not wholly well?

As though to compensate, Mary Warren goes to Elizabeth with a small rag doll.

MARY WARREN: I made a gift for you today, Goody Proctor. I had to sit long hours in a chair, and passed the time with sewing.

ELIZABETH, *perplexed, looking at the doll:* Why, thank you, it's a fair poppet.

MARY WARREN, *with a trembling, decayed voice:* We must all love each other now, Goody Proctor.

ELIZABETH, *amazed at her strangeness:* Aye, indeed we must.

MARY WARREN, *glancing at the room:* I'll get up early in the morning and clean the house. I must sleep now. *She turns and starts off.*

PROCTOR: Mary. *She halts.* Is it true? There be fourteen women arrested?

MARY WARREN: No, sir. There be thirty-nine now—*She suddenly breaks off and sobs and sits down, exhausted.*

ELIZABETH: Why, she's weepin'! What ails you, child?

MARY WARREN: Goody Osburn—will hang!

There is a shocked pause, while she sobs.

PROCTOR: Hang! *He calls into her face.* Hang, y'say?

MARY WARREN, *through her weeping:* Aye.

PROCTOR: The Deputy Governor will permit it?

MARY WARREN: He sentenced her. He must. *To ameliorate it:* But not Sarah Good. For Sarah Good confessed, y'see.

PROCTOR: Confessed! To what?

MARY WARREN: That she—*in horror at the memory*—she sometimes made a compact with Lucifer, and wrote her name in his black book—with her blood—and bound herself to torment Christians till God's thrown down—and we all must worship Hell forevermore.

Pause.

PROCTOR: But—surely you know what a jabberer she is. Did you tell them that?

MARY WARREN: Mr. Proctor, in open court she near to choked us all to death.

PROCTOR: How, choked you?

MARY WARREN: She sent her spirit out.

ELIZABETH: Oh, Mary, Mary, surely you—

MARY WARREN, *with an indignant edge:* She tried to kill me many times, Goody Proctor!

ELIZABETH: Why, I never heard you mention that before.

MARY WARREN: I never knew it before. I never knew anything before. When she come into the court I say to myself, I must not accuse this woman, for she sleep in ditches, and so very old and poor. But then—then she sit there, denying and denying, and I feel a misty coldness climbin' up my back, and the skin on my skull begin to creep, and I feel a clamp around my neck and I cannot breathe air; and then—*entranced*—I hear a voice, a screamin' voice, and it were my voice—and all at once I remembered everything she done to me!

PROCTOR: Why? What did she do to you?

MARY WARREN, *like one awakened to a marvelous secret insight:* So many time, Mr. Proctor, she come to this very door, beggin' bread and a cup of cider—and mark this: whenever I turned her away empty, she *mumbled.*

ELIZABETH: Mumbled! She may mumble if she's hungry.

MARY WARREN: But *what* does she mumble? You must remember, Goody Proctor. Last month—a Monday, I think—she walked away, and I thought my guts would burst for two days after. Do you remember it?

ELIZABETH: Why—I do, I think, but—

MARY WARREN: And so I told that to Judge Hathorne, and he asks her so. "Goody Osburn," says he, "what curse do you mumble that this girl must fall sick after turning you away?" And then she replies—*mimicking an old crone*—"Why, your excellence, no curse at all. I only say my commandments; I hope I may say my commandments," says she!

ELIZABETH: And that's an upright answer.

MARY WARREN: Aye, but then Judge Hathorne say, "Recite for us your commandments!"—*leaning avidly toward them*—and of all the ten she could not say a single one. She never knew no commandments, and they had her in a flat lie!

PROCTOR: And so condemned her?

MARY WARREN, *now a little strained, seeing his stubborn doubt:* Why, they must when she condemned herself.

PROCTOR: But the proof, the proof!

MARY WARREN, *with greater impatience with him:* I told you the proof. It's hard proof, hard as rock, the judges said.

PROCTOR, *pauses an instant, then:* You will not go to court again, Mary Warren.

MARY WARREN: I must tell you, sir, I will be gone every day now. I am amazed you do not see what weighty work we do.

PROCTOR: What work you do! It's strange work for a Christian girl to hang old women!

MARY WARREN: But, Mr. Proctor, they will not hang them if they confess. Sarah Good will only sit in jail some time—*recalling*—and here's a wonder for you; think on this. Goody Good is pregnant!

ELIZABETH: Pregnant! Are they mad? The woman's near to sixty!

MARY WARREN: They had Doctor Griggs examine her, and she's full to the brim. And smokin' a pipe all these years, and no husband either! But she's safe, thank God, for they'll not hurt the innocent child. But be that not a marvel? You must see it, sir, it's God's work we do. So I'll be gone every day for some time. I'm—I am an official of the court, they say, and I—*She has been edging toward offstage.*

PROCTOR: I'll official you! *He strides to the mantel, takes down the whip hanging there.*

MARY WARREN, *terrified, but coming erect, striving for her authority:* I'll not stand whipping any more!

ELIZABETH, *hurriedly, as Proctor approaches:* Mary, promise now you'll stay at home—

MARY WARREN, *backing from him, but keeping her erect posture, striving, striving for her way:* The Devil's loose in Salem, Mr. Proctor; we must discover where he's hiding!

PROCTOR: I'll whip the Devil out of you! *With whip raised he reaches out for her, and she streaks away and yells.*

MARY WARREN, *pointing at Elizabeth:* I saved her life today!

Silence. His whip comes down.

ELIZABETH, *softly:* I am accused?

MARY WARREN, *quaking:* Somewhat mentioned. But I said I never see no sign you ever sent your spirit out to hurt no one, and seeing I do live so closely with you, they dismissed it.

ELIZABETH: Who accused me?

MARY WARREN: I am bound by law, I cannot tell it. *To Proctor:* I only hope you'll not be so sarcastical no more. Four judges and the King's deputy sat to dinner with us but an hour ago. I—I would have you speak civilly to me, from this out.

PROCTOR, *in horror, muttering in disgust at her:* Go to bed.

MARY WARREN, *with a stamp of her foot:* I'll not be ordered to bed no more, Mr. Proctor! I am eighteen and a woman, however single!

PROCTOR: Do you wish to sit up? Then sit up.

MARY WARREN: I wish to go to bed!

PROCTOR, *in anger:* Good night, then!

MARY WARREN: Good night. *Dissatisfied, uncertain of herself, she goes out. Wide-eyed, both, Proctor and Elizabeth stand staring.*

ELIZABETH, *quietly:* Oh, the noose, the noose is up!

PROCTOR: There'll be no noose.

ELIZABETH: She wants me dead. I knew all week it would come to this!

PROCTOR, *without conviction:* They dismissed it. You heard her say—

ELIZABETH: And what of tomorrow? She will cry me out until they take me!

PROCTOR: Sit you down.

ELIZABETH: She wants me dead, John, you know it!

PROCTOR: I say sit down! *She sits, trembling. He speaks quietly, trying to keep his wits.* Now we must be wise, Elizabeth.

ELIZABETH, *with sarcasm, and a sense of being lost:* Oh, indeed, indeed!

PROCTOR: Fear nothing. I'll find Ezekiel Cheever. I'll tell him she said it were all sport.

ELIZABETH: John, with so many in the jail, more than Cheever's help is needed now, I think. Would you favor me with this? Go to Abigail.

PROCTOR, *his soul hardening as he senses . . . :* What have I to say to Abigail?

ELIZABETH, *delicately:* John—grant me this. You have a faulty understanding of young girls. There is a promise made in any bed—

PROCTOR, *striving against his anger:* What promise!

ELIZABETH: Spoke or silent, a promise is surely made. And she may dote on it now—I am sure she does—and thinks to kill me, then to take my place.

Proctor's anger is rising; he cannot speak.

ELIZABETH: It is her dearest hope, John, I know it. There be a thousand names; why does she call mine? There be a certain danger in calling such a name—I am no Goody Good that sleeps in ditches, nor Osburn, drunk and half-witted. She'd dare not call out such a farmer's wife but there be monstrous profit in it. She thinks to take my place, John.

PROCTOR: She cannot think it! *He knows it is true.*

ELIZABETH, *"reasonably":* John, have you ever shown her somewhat of contempt? She cannot pass you in the church but you will blush—

PROCTOR: I may blush for my sin.

ELIZABETH: I think she sees another meaning in that blush.

PROCTOR: And what see you? What see you, Elizabeth?

ELIZABETH, *"conceding":* I think you be somewhat ashamed, for I am there, and she so close.

PROCTOR: When will you know me, woman? Were I stone I would have cracked for shame this seven month!

ELIZABETH: Then go and tell her she's a whore. Whatever promise she may sense—break it, John, break it.

PROCTOR, *between his teeth:* Good, then. I'll go. *He starts for his rifle.*

ELIZABETH, *trembling, fearfully:* Oh, how unwillingly!

PROCTOR, *turning on her, rifle in hand:* I will curse her hotter than the oldest cinder in hell. But pray, begrudge me not my anger!

ELIZABETH: Your anger! I only ask you—

PROCTOR: Woman, am I so base? Do you truly think me base?

ELIZABETH: I never called you base.

PROCTOR: Then how do you charge me with such a promise? The promise that a stallion gives a mare I gave that girl!

ELIZABETH: Then why do you anger with me when I bid you break it?

PROCTOR: Because it speaks deceit, and I am honest! But I'll plead no more! I see now your spirit twists around the single error of my life, and I will never tear it free!

ELIZABETH, *crying out:* You'll tear it free—when you come to know that I will be your only wife, or no wife at all! She has an arrow in you yet, John Proctor, and you know it well!

Quite suddenly, as though from the air, a figure appears in the doorway. They start slightly. It is Mr. Hale. He is different now—drawn a little, and there is a quality of deference, even of guilt, about his manner now.

HALE: Good evening.

PROCTOR, *still in his shock:* Why, Mr. Hale! Good evening to you, sir. Come in, come in.

HALE, *to Elizabeth:* I hope I do not startle you.

ELIZABETH: No, no, it's only that I heard no horse—

HALE: You are Goodwife Proctor.

PROCTOR: Aye; Elizabeth.

HALE, *nods, then:* I hope you're not off to bed yet.

PROCTOR, *setting down his gun:* No, no. *Hale comes further into the room. And Proctor, to explain his nervousness:* We are not used to visitors after dark, but you're welcome here. Will you sit you down, sir?

HALE: I will. *He sits.* Let you sit, Goodwife Proctor.

She does, never letting him out of her sight. There is a pause as Hale looks about the room.

PROCTOR, *to break the silence:* Will you drink cider, Mr. Hale?

HALE: No, it rebels my stomach; I have some further traveling yet tonight. Sit you down, sir. *Proctor sits.* I will not keep you long, but I have some business with you.

PROCTOR: Business of the court?

HALE: No—no, I come of my own, without the court's authority. Hear me. *He wets his lips.* I know not if you are aware, but your wife's name is—mentioned in the court.

PROCTOR: We know it, sir. Our Mary Warren told us. We are entirely amazed.

HALE: I am a stranger here, as you know. And in my ignorance I find it hard to draw a clear opinion of them that come accused before the court. And so this afternoon, and now tonight, I go from house to house—I come now from Rebecca Nurse's house and—

ELIZABETH, *shocked:* Rebecca's charged!

HALE: God forbid such a one be charged. She is, however—mentioned somewhat.

ELIZABETH, *with an attempt at a laugh:* You will never believe, I hope, that Rebecca trafficked with the Devil.

HALE: Woman, it is possible.

PROCTOR, *taken aback:* Surely you cannot think so.

HALE: This is a strange time, Mister. No man may longer doubt the powers of the dark are gathered in monstrous attack upon this village. There is too much evidence now to deny it. You will agree, sir?

PROCTOR, *evading:* I—have no knowledge in that line. But it's hard to think so pious a woman be secretly a Devil's bitch after seventy year of such good prayer.

HALE: Aye. But the Devil is a wily one, you cannot deny it. However, she is far from accused, and I know she will not be. *Pause.* I thought, sir, to put some questions as to the Christian character of this house, if you'll permit me.

PROCTOR, *coldly, resentful:* Why, we—have no fear of questions, sir.

HALE: Good, then. *He makes himself more comfortable.* In the book of record that Mr. Parris keeps, I note that you are rarely in the church on Sabbath Day.

PROCTOR: No, sir, you are mistaken.

HALE: Twenty-six time in seventeen month, sir. I must call that rare. Will you tell me why you are so absent?

PROCTOR: Mr. Hale, I never knew I must account to that man for I come to church or stay at home. My wife were sick this winter.

HALE: So I am told. But you, Mister, why could you not come alone?

PROCTOR: I surely did come when I could, and when I could not I prayed in this house.

HALE: Mr. Proctor, your house is not a church; your theology must tell you that.

PROCTOR: It does, sir, it does; and it tells me that a minister may pray to God without he have golden candlesticks upon the altar.

HALE: What golden candlesticks?

PROCTOR: Since we built the church there were pewter candlesticks upon the altar; Francis Nurse made them, y'know, and a sweeter hand never touched the metal. But Parris came, and for twenty week he preach nothin' but golden candlesticks until he had them. I labor the earth from dawn of day to blink of night, and I tell you true, when I look to heaven and see my money glaring at his elbows—it hurt my prayer, sir, it hurt my prayer. I think, sometimes, the man dreams cathedrals, not clapboard meetin' houses.

HALE, *thinks, then:* And yet, Mister, a Christian on Sabbath Day must be in church. *Pause.* Tell me—you have three children?

PROCTOR: Aye. Boys.

HALE: How comes it that only two are baptized?

PROCTOR, *starts to speak, then stops, then, as though unable to restrain this:* I like it not that Mr. Parris should lay his hand upon my baby. I see no light of God in that man. I'll not conceal it.

HALE: I must say it, Mr. Proctor; that is not for you to decide. The man's ordained, therefore the light of God is in him.

PROCTOR, *flushed with resentment but trying to smile:* What's your suspicion, Mr. Hale?

HALE: No, no, I have no—

PROCTOR: I nailed the roof upon the church, I hung the door—

HALE: Oh, did you! That's a good sign, then.

PROCTOR: It may be I have been too quick to bring the man to book, but you cannot think we ever desired the destruction of religion. I think that's in your mind, is it not?

HALE, *not altogether giving way:* I—have—there is a softness in your record, sir, a softness.

ELIZABETH: I think, maybe, we have been too hard with Mr. Parris. I think so. But sure we never loved the Devil here.

HALE, *nods, deliberating this. Then, with the voice of one administering a secret test:* Do you know your Commandments, Elizabeth?

ELIZABETH, *without hesitation, even eagerly:* I surely do. There be no mark of blame upon my life, Mr. Hale. I am a convenanted Christian woman.

HALE: And you, Mister?

PROCTOR, *a trifle unsteadily:* I—am sure I do, sir.

HALE, *glances at her open face, then at John, then:* Let you repeat them, if you will.

PROCTOR: The Commandments.

HALE: Aye.

PROCTOR, *looking off, beginning to sweat:* Thou shalt not kill.

HALE: Aye.

PROCTOR, *counting on his fingers:* Thou shalt not steal. Thou shalt not covet thy neighbor's goods, nor make unto thee any graven image. Thou shalt not take the name of the Lord in vain; thou shalt have no other gods before me. *With some hesitation:* Thou shalt remember the Sabbath Day and keep it holy. *Pause. Then:* Thou shalt honor thy father and mother. Thou shalt not bear false witness. *He is stuck. He counts back on his fingers, knowing one is missing.* Thou shalt not make unto thee any graven image.

HALE: You have said that twice, sir.

PROCTOR, *lost:* Aye. *He is flailing for it.*

ELIZABETH, *delicately: Adultery,* John.

PROCTOR, *as though a secret arrow had pained his heart:* Aye. *Trying to grin it away—to Hale:* You see, sir, between the two of us we do know them all. *Hale only looks at Proctor, deep in his attempt to define this man. Proctor grows more uneasy.* I think it be a small fault.

HALE: Theology, sir, is a fortress; no crack in a fortress may be accounted small. *He rises; he seems worried now. He paces a little, in deep thought.*

PROCTOR: There be no love for Satan in this house, Mister.

HALE: I pray it, I pray it dearly. *He looks to both of them, an attempt at a smile on his face, but his misgivings are clear.* Well, then—I'll bid you good night.

ELIZABETH, *unable to restrain herself:* Mr. Hale. *He turns.* I do think you are suspecting me somewhat? Are you not?

HALE, *obviously disturbed—and evasive:* Goody Proctor, I do not judge you. My duty is to add what I may to the godly wisdom of the court. I pray you both good health and good fortune. *To John:* Good night, sir. *He starts out.*

ELIZABETH, *with a note of desperation:* I think you must tell him, John.

HALE: What's that?

ELIZABETH, *restraining a call:* Will you tell him?

Slight pause. Hale looks questioningly at John.

PROCTOR, *with difficulty:* I—I have no witness and cannot prove it, except my word be taken. But I know the children's sickness had naught to do with witchcraft.

HALE, *stopped, struck:* Naught to do—?

PROCTOR: Mr. Parris discovered them sportin' in the woods. They were startled and took sick.

Pause.

HALE: Who told you this?

PROCTOR, *hesitates, then:* Abigail Williams.

HALE: Abigail!

PROCTOR: Aye.

HALE, *his eyes wide:* Abigail Williams told you it had naught to do with witchcraft!

PROCTOR: She told me the day you came, sir.

HALE, *suspiciously:* Why—why did you keep this?

PROCTOR: I never knew until tonight that the world is gone daft with this nonsense.

HALE: Nonsense! Mister, I have myself examined Tituba, Sarah Good, and numerous others that have confessed to dealing with the Devil. They have *confessed* it.

PROCTOR: And why not, if they must hang for denyin' it? There are them that will swear to anything before they'll hang; have you never thought of that?

HALE: I have. I—I have indeed. *It is his own suspicion, but he resists it. He glances at Elizabeth, then at John.* And you—would you testify to this in court?

PROCTOR: I—had not reckoned with goin' into court. But if I must I will.

HALE: Do you falter here?

PROCTOR: I falter nothing, but I may wonder if my story will be credited in such a court. I do wonder on it, when such a steady-minded minister as you will suspicion such a woman that never lied, and cannot, and the world knows she cannot! I may falter somewhat, Mister; I am no fool.

HALE, *quietly—it has impressed him:* Proctor, let you open with me now, for I have a rumor that troubles me. It's said you hold no belief that there may even be witches in the world. Is that true, sir?

PROCTOR—*he knows this is critical, and is striving against his disgust with Hale and with himself for even answering:* I know not what I have said, I may have said it. I have wondered if there be witches in the world—although I cannot believe they come among us now.

HALE: Then you do not believe—

PROCTOR: I have no knowledge of it; the Bible speaks of witches, and I will not deny them.

HALE: And you, woman?

ELIZABETH: I—I cannot believe it.

HALE, *shocked:* You cannot!

PROCTOR: Elizabeth, you bewilder him!

ELIZABETH, *to Hale:* I cannot think the Devil may own a woman's soul, Mr. Hale, when she keeps an upright way, as I have. I am a good woman, I know it; and if you believe I may do only good work in the world, and yet be secretly bound to Satan, then I must tell you, sir, I do not believe it.

HALE: But, woman, you do believe there are witches in—

ELIZABETH: If you think that I am one, then I say there are none.

HALE: You surely do not fly against the Gospel, the Gospel—

PROCTOR: She believe in the Gospel, every word!

ELIZABETH: Question Abigail Williams about the Gospel, not myself!

Hale stares at her.

PROCTOR: She do not mean to doubt the Gospel, sir, you cannot think it. This be a Christian house, sir, a Christian house.

HALE: God keep you both; let the third child be quickly baptized, and go you without fail each Sunday in to Sabbath prayer; and keep a solemn, quiet way among you. I think—

Giles Corey appears in doorway.

GILES: John!

PROCTOR: Giles! What's the matter?

GILES: They take my wife.

Francis Nurse enters.

GILES: And his Rebecca!

PROCTOR, *to Francis:* Rebecca's in the *jail!*

FRANCIS: Aye, Cheever come and take her in his wagon. We've only now come from the jail, and they'll not even let us in to see them.

ELIZABETH: They've surely gone wild now, Mr. Hale!

FRANCIS, *going to Hale:* Reverend Hale! Can you not speak to the Deputy Governor? I'm sure he mistakes these people—

HALE: Pray calm yourself, Mr. Nurse.

FRANCIS: My wife is the very brick and mortar of the church,

Mr. Hale—*indicating Giles*—and Martha Corey, there cannot be a woman closer yet to God than Martha.

HALE: How is Rebecca charged, Mr. Nurse?

FRANCIS, *with a mocking, half-hearted laugh:* For murder, she's charged! *Mockingly quoting the warrant:* "For the marvelous and supernatural murder of Goody Putnam's babies." What am I to do, Mr. Hale?

HALE, *turns from Francis, deeply troubled, then:* Believe me, Mr. Nurse, if Rebecca Nurse be tainted, then nothing's left to stop the whole green world from burning. Let you rest upon the justice of the court; the court will send her home, I know it.

FRANCIS: You cannot mean she will be tried in court!

HALE, *pleading:* Nurse, though our hearts break, we cannot flinch; these are new times, sir. There is a misty plot afoot so subtle we should be criminal to cling to old respects and ancient friendships. I have seen too many frightful proofs in court—the Devil is alive in Salem, and we dare not quail to follow wherever the accusing finger points!

PROCTOR, *angered:* How may such a woman murder children?

HALE, *in great pain:* Man, remember, until an hour before the Devil fell, God thought him beautiful in Heaven.

GILES: I never said my wife were a witch, Mr. Hale; I only said she were reading books!

HALE: Mr. Corey, exactly what complaint were made on your wife?

GILES: That bloody mongrel Walcott charge her. Y'see, he buy a pig of my wife four or five year ago, and the pig died soon after. So he come dancin' in for his money back. So my Martha, she says to him, "Walcott, if you haven't the wit to feed a pig properly, you'll not live to own many," she says. Now he goes to court and claims that from that day to this he cannot keep a pig alive for more than four weeks because my Martha bewitch them with her books!

Enter Ezekiel Cheever. A shocked silence.

CHEEVER: Good evening to you, Proctor.

PROCTOR: Why, Mr. Cheever. Good evening.

CHEEVER: Good evening, all. Good evening, Mr. Hale.

PROCTOR: I hope you come not on business of the court.

CHEEVER: I do, Proctor, aye. I am clerk of the court now, y'know.

Enter Marshal Herrick, a man in his early thirties, who is somewhat shamefaced at the moment.

GILES: It's a pity, Ezekiel, that an honest tailor might have gone to Heaven must burn in Hell. You'll burn for this, do you know it?

CHEEVER: You know yourself I must do as I'm told. You surely know that, Giles. And I'd as lief you'd not be sending me to Hell. I like not the sound of it, I tell you; I like not the sound of it. *He fears Proctor, but starts to reach inside his coat.* Now believe me, Proctor, how heavy be the law, all its tonnage I do carry on my back tonight. *He takes out a warrant.* I have a warrant for your wife.

PROCTOR, *to Hale:* You said she were not charged!

HALE: I know nothin' of it. *To Cheever:* When were she charged?

CHEEVER: I am given sixteen warrant tonight, sir, and she is one.

PROCTOR: Who charged her?

CHEEVER: Why, Abigail Williams charge her.

PROCTOR: On what proof, what proof?

CHEEVER, *looking about the room:* Mr. Proctor, I have little time. The court bid me search your house, but I like not to search a house. So will you hand me any poppets that your wife may keep here?

PROCTOR: Poppets?

ELIZABETH: I never kept no poppets, not since I were a girl.

CHEEVER, *embarrassed, glancing toward the mantel where sits Mary Warren's poppet:* I spy a poppet, Goody Proctor.

ELIZABETH: Oh! *Going for it:* Why, this is Mary's.

CHEEVER, *shyly:* Would you please to give it to me?

ELIZABETH, *handing it to him, asks Hale:* Has the court discovered a text in poppets now?

CHEEVER, *carefully holding the poppet:* Do you keep any others in this house?

PROCTOR: No, nor this one either till tonight. What signifies a poppet?

CHEEVER: Why, a poppet—*he gingerly turns the poppet over*—a poppet may signify— Now, woman, will you please to come with me?

PROCTOR: She will not! *To Elizabeth:* Fetch Mary here.

CHEEVER, *ineptly reaching toward Elizabeth:* No, no, I am forbid to leave her from my sight.

PROCTOR, *pushing his arm away:* You'll leave her out of sight and out of mind, Mister. Fetch Mary, Elizabeth. *Elizabeth goes upstairs.*

HALE: What signifies a poppet, Mr. Cheever?

CHEEVER, *turning the poppet over in his hands:* Why, they say it may signify that she— *He has lifted the poppet's skirt, and his eyes widen in astonished fear.* Why, this, this—

PROCTOR, *reaching for the poppet:* What's there?

CHEEVER: Why—*He draws out a long needle from the poppet*—it is a needle! Herrick, Herrick, it is a needle!

Herrick comes toward him.

PROCTOR, *angrily, bewildered:* And what signifies a needle!

CHEEVER, *his hands shaking:* Why, this go hard with her, Proctor, this—I had my doubts, Proctor, I had my doubts, but here's calamity. *To Hale, showing the needle:* You see it, sir, it is a needle!

HALE: Why? What meanin' has it?

CHEEVER, *wide-eyed, trembling:* The girl, the Williams girl, Abigail Williams, sir. She sat to dinner in Reverend Parris's house tonight, and without word nor warnin' she falls to the floor. Like a struck beast, he says, and screamed a scream that a bull would weep to hear. And he goes to save her, and, stuck two inches in the flesh of her belly, he draw a needle out. And demandin' of her how she come to be so stabbed, she—*to Proctor now*—testify it were your wife's familiar spirit pushed it in.

PROCTOR: Why, she done it herself! *To Hale:* I hope you're not takin' this for proof, Mister!

Hale, struck by the proof, is silent.

CHEEVER: 'Tis hard proof! *To Hale:* I find here a poppet Goody Proctor keeps. I have found it, sir. And in the belly of the poppet a needle's stuck. I tell you true, Proctor, I never warranted to see such proof of Hell, and I bid you obstruct me not, for I—

Enter Elizabeth with Mary Warren. Proctor, seeing Mary Warren, draws her by the arm to Hale.

PROCTOR: Here now! Mary, how did this poppet come into my house?

MARY WARREN, *frightened for herself, her voice very small:* What poppet's that, sir?

PROCTOR, *impatiently, pointing at the doll in Cheever's hand:* This poppet, this poppet.

MARY WARREN, *evasively, looking at it:* Why, I—I think it is mine.

PROCTOR: It is your poppet, is it not?

MARY WARREN, *not understanding the direction of this:* It—is, sir.

PROCTOR: And how did it come into this house?

MARY WARREN, *glancing about at the avid faces:* Why—I made it in the court, sir, and—give it to Goody Proctor tonight.

PROCTOR, *to Hale:* Now, sir—do you have it?

HALE: Mary Warren, a needle have been found inside this poppet.

MARY WARREN, *bewildered:* Why, I meant no harm by it, sir.

PROCTOR, *quickly:* You stuck that needle in yourself?

MARY WARREN: I—I believe I did, sir, I—

PROCTOR, *to Hale:* What say you now?

HALE, *watching Mary Warren closely:* Child, you are certain this be your natural memory? May it be, perhaps, that someone conjures you even now to say this?

MARY WARREN: Conjures me? Why, no, sir, I am entirely myself, I think. Let you ask Susanna Walcott—she saw me sewin' it in court. *Or better still:* Ask Abby, Abby sat beside me when I made it.

PROCTOR, *to Hale, of Cheever:* Bid him begone. Your mind is surely settled now. Bid him out, Mr. Hale.

ELIZABETH: What signifies a needle?

HALE: Mary—you charge a cold and cruel murder on Abigail.

MARY WARREN: Murder! I charge no—

HALE: Abigail were stabbed tonight; a needle were found stuck into her belly—

ELIZABETH: And she charges me?

HALE: Aye.

ELIZABETH, *her breath knocked out:* Why—! The girl is murder! She must be ripped out of the world!

CHEEVER, *pointing at Elizabeth:* You've heard that, sir! Ripped out of the world! Herrick, you heard it!

PROCTOR, *suddenly snatching the warrant out of Cheever's hands:* Out with you.

CHEEVER: Proctor, you dare not touch the warrant.

PROCTOR, *ripping the warrant:* Out with you!

CHEEVER: You've ripped the Deputy Governor's warrant, man!

PROCTOR: Damn the Deputy Governor! Out of my house!

HALE: Now, Proctor, Proctor!

PROCTOR: Get y'gone with them! You are a broken minister.

HALE: Proctor, if she is innocent, the court—

PROCTOR: If *she* is innocent! Why do you never wonder if Parris be innocent, or Abigail? Is the accuser always holy now? Were they born this morning as clean as God's fingers? I'll tell you what's walking Salem—vengeance is walking Salem. We are what we always were in Salem, but now the little crazy children are jangling the keys of the kingdom, and common vengeance writes the law! This warrant's vengeance! I'll not give my wife to vengeance!

ELIZABETH: I'll go, John—

PROCTOR: You will not go!

HERRICK: I have nine men outside. You cannot keep her. The law binds me, John, I cannot budge.

PROCTOR, *to Hale, ready to break him:* Will you see her taken?

HALE: Proctor, the court is just—

PROCTOR: Pontius Pilate! God will not let you wash your hands of this!

ELIZABETH: John—I think I must go with them. *He cannot bear to look at her.* Mary, there is bread enough for the morning; you will bake, in the afternoon. Help Mr. Proctor as you were his daughter—you owe me that, and much more. *She is fighting her weeping. To Proctor:* When the children wake, speak nothing of witchcraft—it will frighten them. *She cannot go on.*

PROCTOR: I will bring you home. I will bring you soon.

ELIZABETH: Oh, John, bring me soon!

PROCTOR: I will fall like an ocean on that court! Fear nothing, Elizabeth.

ELIZABETH, *with great fear:* I will fear nothing. *She looks about the room, as though to fix it in her mind.* Tell the children I have gone to visit someone sick.

She walks out the door, Herrick and Cheever behind her. For a moment, Proctor watches from the doorway. The clank of chain is heard.

PROCTOR: Herrick! Herrick, don't chain her! *He rushes out the door. From outside:* Damn you, man, you will not chain her! Off with them! I'll not have it! I will not have her chained!

There are other men's voices against his. Hale, in a fever of guilt and uncertainty, turns from the door to avoid the sight; Mary Warren bursts into tears and sits weeping. Giles Corey calls to Hale.

GILES: And yet silent, minister? It is fraud, you know it is fraud! What keeps you, man?

Proctor is half braced, half pushed into the room by two deputies and Herrick.

PROCTOR: I'll pay you, Herrick, I will surely pay you!

HERRICK, *panting:* In God's name, John, I cannot help myself. I must chain them all. Now let you keep inside this house till I am gone! *He goes out with his deputies.*

Proctor stands there, gulping air. Horses and a wagon creaking are heard.

HALE, *in great uncertainty:* Mr. Proctor—

PROCTOR: Out of my sight!

HALE: Charity, Proctor, charity. What I have heard in her favor, I will not fear to testify in court. God help me, I cannot judge her guilty or innocent—I know not. Only this consider: the world goes mad, and it profit nothing you should lay the cause to the vengeance of a little girl.

PROCTOR: You are a coward! Though you be ordained in God's own tears, you are a coward now!

HALE: Proctor, I cannot think God be provoked so grandly by such a petty cause. The jails are packed—our greatest judges sit in Salem now—and hangin's promised. Man, we must look to cause proportionate. Were there murder done, perhaps, and never brought to light? Abomination? Some secret blasphemy that stinks to Heaven? Think on cause, man, and let you help me to discover it. For there's your way, believe it, there is your only way, when such confusion strikes upon the world. *He goes to Giles and Francis.* Let you counsel among yourselves; think on your village and what may have drawn from heaven such thundering wrath upon you all. I shall pray God open up our eyes.

Hale goes out.

FRANCIS, *struck by Hale's mood:* I never heard no murder done in Salem.

PROCTOR—*he has been reached by Hale's words:* Leave me, Francis, leave me.

GILES, *shaken:* John—tell me, are we lost?

PROCTOR: Go home now, Giles. We'll speak on it tomorrow.

GILES: Let you think on it. We'll come early, eh?
PROCTOR: Aye. Go now, Giles.
GILES: Good night, then.

Giles Corey goes out. After a moment:

MARY WARREN, *in a fearful squeak of a voice:* Mr. Proctor, very likely they'll let her come home once they're given proper evidence.

PROCTOR: You're coming to the court with me, Mary. You will tell it in the court.

MARY WARREN: I cannot charge murder on Abigail.

PROCTOR, *moving menacingly toward her:* You will tell the court how that poppet come here and who stuck the needle in.

MARY WARREN: She'll kill me for sayin' that! *Proctor continues toward her.* Abby'll charge lechery on you, Mr. Proctor!

PROCTOR, *halting:* She's told you!

MARY WARREN: I have known it, sir. She'll ruin you with it, I know she will.

PROCTOR, *hesitating, and with deep hatred of himself:* Good. Then her saintliness is done with. *Mary backs from him.* We will slide together into our pit; you will tell the court what you know.

MARY WARREN, *in terror:* I cannot, they'll turn on me—

Proctor strides and catches her, and she is repeating, "I cannot, I cannot!"

PROCTOR: My wife will never die for me! I will bring your guts into your mouth but that goodness will not die for me!

MARY WARREN, *struggling to escape him:* I cannot do it, I cannot!

PROCTOR, *grasping her by the throat as though he would strangle her:* Make your peace with it! Now Hell and Heaven grapple on our backs, and all our old pretense is ripped away—make your peace! *He throws her to the floor, where she sobs, "I cannot, I cannot . . ." And now, half to himself, staring, and turning to the open door:* Peace. It is a providence, and no great change; we are only what we always were, but naked now. *He walks as though toward a great horror, facing the open sky.* Aye, naked! And the wind, God's icy wind, will blow!

And she is over and over again sobbing, "I cannot, I cannot, I cannot."

Curtain

Act Three

The vestry room of the Salem meeting house, now serving as the anteroom of the General Court.

As the curtain rises, the room is empty, but for sunlight pouring through two high windows in the back wall. The room is solemn, even forbidding. Heavy beams jut out, boards of random widths make up the walls. At the right are two doors leading into the meeting house proper, where the court is being held. At the left another door leads outside.

There is a plain bench at the left, and another at the right. In the center a rather long meeting table, with stools and a considerable armchair snugged up to it.

Through the partitioning wall at the right we hear a prosecutor's voice, Judge Hathorne's, asking a question; then a woman's voice, Martha Corey's, replying.

HATHORNE'S VOICE: Now, Martha Corey, there is abundant evidence in our hands to show that you have given yourself to the reading of fortunes. Do you deny it?

MARTHA COREY'S VOICE: I am innocent to a witch. I know not what a witch is.

HATHORNE'S VOICE: How do you know, then, that you are not a witch?

MARTHA COREY'S VOICE: If I were, I would know it.

HATHORNE'S VOICE: Why do you hurt these children?

MARTHA COREY'S VOICE: I do not hurt them. I scorn it!

GILES' VOICE, *roaring:* I have evidence for the court!

Voices of townspeople rise in excitement.

DANFORTH'S VOICE: You will keep your seat!

GILES' VOICE: Thomas Putnam is reaching out for land!

DANFORTH'S VOICE: Remove that man, Marshal!

GILES' VOICE: You're hearing lies, lies!

A roaring goes up from the people.

HATHORNE'S VOICE: Arrest him, excellency!

GILES' VOICE: I have evidence. Why will you not hear my evidence?

The door opens and Giles is half carried into the vestry room by Herrick.

GILES: Hands off, damn you, let me go!

HERRICK: Giles, Giles!

GILES: Out of my way, Herrick! I bring evidence—

HERRICK: You cannot go in there, Giles; it's a court!

Enter Hale from the court.

HALE: Pray be calm a moment.

GILES: You, Mr. Hale, go in there and demand I speak.

HALE: A moment, sir, a moment.

GILES: They'll be hangin' my wife!

Judge Hathorne enters. He is in his sixties, a bitter, remorseless Salem judge.

HATHORNE: How do you dare come roarin' into this court! Are you gone daft, Corey?

GILES: You're not a Boston judge yet, Hathorne. You'll not call me daft!

Enter Deputy Governor Danforth and, behind him, Ezekiel Cheever and Parris. On his appearance, silence falls. Danforth is a grave man in his sixties, of some humor and sophistication that does not, however, interfere with an exact loyalty to his position and his cause. He comes down to Giles, who awaits his wrath.

DANFORTH, *looking directly at Giles:* Who is this man?

PARRIS: Giles Corey, sir, and a more contentious—

GILES, *to Parris:* I am asked the question, and I am old enough to answer it! *To Danforth, who impresses him and to whom he smiles through his strain:* My name is Corey, sir, Giles Corey. I have six hundred acres, and timber in addition. It is my wife you be condemning now. *He indicates the courtroom.*

DANFORTH: And how do you imagine to help her cause with such contemptuous riot? Now be gone. Your old age alone keeps you out of jail for this.

GILES, *beginning to plead:* They be tellin' lies about my wife, sir, I—

DANFORTH: Do you take it upon yourself to determine what this court shall believe and what it shall set aside?

GILES: Your Excellency, we mean no disrespect for—

DANFORTH: Disrespect indeed! It is disruption, Mister. This is the highest court of the supreme government of this province, do you know it?

GILES, *beginning to weep:* Your Excellency, I only said she were readin' books, sir, and they come and take her out of my house for—

DANFORTH, *mystified:* Books! What books?

GILES, *through helpless sobs:* It is my third wife, sir; I never had no wife that be so taken with books, and I thought to find the cause of it, d'y'see, but it were no witch I blamed her for. *He is openly weeping.* I have broke charity with the woman, I have broke charity with her. *He covers his face, ashamed. Danforth is respectfully silent.*

HALE: Excellency, he claims hard evidence for his wife's defense. I think that in all justice you must—

DANFORTH: Then let him submit his evidence in proper affidavit. You are certainly aware of our procedure here, Mr. Hale. *To Herrick:* Clear this room.

HERRICK: Come now, Giles. *He gently pushes Corey out.*

FRANCIS: We are desperate, sir; we come here three days now and cannot be heard.

DANFORTH: Who is this man?

FRANCIS: Francis Nurse, Your Excellency.

HALE: His wife's Rebecca that were condemned this morning.

DANFORTH: Indeed! I am amazed to find you in such uproar. I have only good report of your character, Mr. Nurse.

HATHORNE: I think they must both be arrested in contempt, sir.

DANFORTH, *to Francis:* Let you write your plea, and in due time I will—

FRANCIS: Excellency, we have proof for your eyes; God forbid you shut them to it. The girls, sir, the girls are frauds.

DANFORTH: What's that?

FRANCIS: We have proof of it, sir. They are all deceiving you.

Danforth is shocked, but studying Francis.

HATHORNE: This is contempt, sir, contempt!

DANFORTH: Peace, Judge Hathorne. Do you know who I am, Mr. Nurse?

FRANCIS: I surely do, sir, and I think you must be a wise judge to be what you are.

DANFORTH: And do you know that near to four hundred are in the jails from Marblehead to Lynn, and upon my signature?

FRANCIS: I—

DANFORTH: And seventy-two condemned to hang by that signature?

FRANCIS: Excellency, I never thought to say it to such a weighty judge, but you are deceived.

Enter Giles Corey from left. All turn to see as he beckons in Mary Warren with Proctor. Mary is keeping her eyes to the ground; Proctor has her elbow as though she were near collapse.

PARRIS, *on seeing her, in shock:* Mary Warren! *He goes directly to bend close to her face.* What are you about here?

PROCTOR, *pressing Parris away from her with a gentle but firm motion of protectiveness:* She would speak with the Deputy Governor.

DANFORTH, *shocked by this, turns to Herrick:* Did you not tell me Mary Warren were sick in bed?

HERRICK: She were, Your Honor. When I go to fetch her to the court last week, she said she were sick.

GILES: She has been strivin' with her soul all week, Your Honor; she comes now to tell the truth of this to you.

DANFORTH: Who is this?

PROCTOR: John Proctor, sir. Elizabeth Proctor is my wife.

PARRIS: Beware this man, Your Excellency, this man is mischief.

HALE, *excitedly:* I think you must hear the girl, sir, she—

DANFORTH, *who has become very interested in Mary Warren and only raises a hand toward Hale:* Peace. What would you tell us, Mary Warren?

Proctor looks at her, but she cannot speak.

PROCTOR: She never saw no spirits, sir.

DANFORTH, *with great alarm and surprise, to Mary:* Never saw no spirits!

GILES, *eagerly:* Never.

PROCTOR, *reaching into his jacket:* She has signed a deposition, sir—

DANFORTH, *instantly:* No, no, I accept no depositions. *He is rapidly calculating this; he turns from her to Proctor.* Tell me, Mr. Proctor, have you given out this story in the village?

PROCTOR: We have not.

PARRIS: They've come to overthrow the court, sir! This man is—

DANFORTH: I pray you, Mr. Parris. Do you know, Mr. Proctor, that the entire contention of the state in these trials is that the voice of Heaven is speaking through the children?

PROCTOR: I know that, sir.

DANFORTH, *thinks, staring at Proctor, then turns to Mary Warren:* And you, Mary Warren, how came you to cry out people for sending their spirits against you?

MARY WARREN: It were pretense, sir.

DANFORTH: I cannot hear you.

PROCTOR: It were pretense, she says.

DANFORTH: Ah? And the other girls? Susanna Walcott, and—the others? They are also pretending?

MARY WARREN: Aye, sir.

DANFORTH, *wide-eyed:* Indeed. *Pause. He is baffled by this. He turns to study Proctor's face.*

PARRIS, *in a sweat:* Excellency, you surely cannot think to let so vile a lie be spread in open court!

DANFORTH: Indeed not, but it strike hard upon me that she will dare come here with such a tale. Now, Mr. Proctor, before I decide whether I shall hear you or not, it is my duty to tell you this. We burn a hot fire here; it melts down all concealment.

PROCTOR: I know that, sir.

DANFORTH: Let me continue. I understand well, a husband's tenderness may drive him to extravagance in defense of a wife. Are you certain in your conscience, Mister, that your evidence is the truth?

PROCTOR: It is. And you will surely know it.

DANFORTH: And you thought to declare this revelation in the open court before the public?

PROCTOR: I thought I would, aye—with your permission.

DANFORTH, *his eyes narrowing:* Now, sir, what is your purpose in so doing?

PROCTOR: Why, I—I would free my wife, sir.

DANFORTH: There lurks nowhere in your heart, nor hidden in your spirit, any desire to undermine this court?

PROCTOR, *with the faintest faltering:* Why, no, sir.

CHEEVER, *clears his throat, awakening:* I—Your Excellency.

DANFORTH: Mr. Cheever.

CHEEVER: I think it be my duty, sir—*Kindly, to Proctor:* You'll not deny it, John. *To Danforth:* When we come to take his wife, he damned the court and ripped your warrant.

PARRIS: Now you have it!

DANFORTH: He did that, Mr. Hale?

HALE, *takes a breath:* Aye, he did.

PROCTOR: It were a temper, sir. I knew not what I did.

DANFORTH, *studying him:* Mr. Proctor.

PROCTOR: Aye, sir.

DANFORTH, *straight into his eyes:* Have you ever seen the Devil?

PROCTOR: No, sir.

DANFORTH: You are in all respects a Gospel Christian?

PROCTOR: I am, sir.

PARRIS: Such a Christian that will not come to church but once in a month!

DANFORTH, *restrained—he is curious:* Not come to church?

PROCTOR: I—I have no love for Mr. Parris. It is no secret. But God I surely love.

CHEEVER: He plow on Sunday, sir.

DANFORTH: Plow on Sunday!

CHEEVER, *apologetically:* I think it be evidence, John. I am an official of the court, I cannot keep it.

PROCTOR: I—I have once or twice plowed on Sunday. I have three children, sir, and until last year my land give little.

GILES: You'll find other Christians that do plow on Sunday if the truth be known.

HALE: Your Honor, I cannot think you may judge the man on such evidence.

DANFORTH: I judge nothing. *Pause. He keeps watching Proctor, who tries to meet his gaze.* I tell you straight, Mister—I have seen marvels in this court. I have seen people choked before my eyes by spirits; I have seen them stuck by pins and slashed by daggers. I have until this moment not the slightest reason to suspect that the children may be deceiving me. Do you understand my meaning?

PROCTOR: Excellency, does it not strike upon you that so many of these women have lived so long with such upright reputation, and—

PARRIS: Do you read the Gospel, Mr. Proctor?

PROCTOR: I read the Gospel.

PARRIS: I think not, or you should surely know that Cain were an upright man, and yet he did kill Abel.

PROCTOR: Aye, God tells us that. *To Danforth:* But who tells us Rebecca Nurse murdered seven babies by sending out her spirit on them? It is the children only, and this one will swear she lied to you.

Danforth considers, then beckons Hathorne to him. Hathorne leans in, and he speaks in his ear. Hathorne nods.

HATHORNE: Aye, she's the one.

DANFORTH: Mr. Proctor, this morning, your wife send me a claim in which she states that she is pregnant now.

PROCTOR: My wife pregnant!

DANFORTH: There be no sign of it—we have examined her body.

PROCTOR: But if she say she is pregnant, then she must be! That woman will never lie, Mr. Danforth.

DANFORTH: She will not?

PROCTOR: Never, sir, never.

DANFORTH: We have thought it too convenient to be credited. However, if I should tell you now that I will let her be kept another month; and if she begin to show her natural signs, you shall have her living yet another year until she is delivered—what say you to that? *John Proctor is struck silent.* Come now. You say your only purpose is to save your wife. Good, then, she is saved at least this year, and a year is long. What say you, sir? It is done now. *In conflict, Proctor glances at Francis and Giles.* Will you drop this charge?

PROCTOR: I—I think I cannot.

DANFORTH, *now an almost imperceptible hardness in his voice:* Then your purpose is somewhat larger.

PARRIS: He's come to overthrow this court, Your Honor!

PROCTOR: These are my friends. Their wives are also accused—

DANFORTH, *with a sudden briskness of manner:* I judge you not, sir. I am ready to hear your evidence.

PROCTOR: I come not to hurt the court; I only—

DANFORTH, *cutting him off:* Marshal, go into the court and bid Judge Stoughton and Judge Sewall declare recess for one hour. And let them go to the tavern, if they will. All witnesses and prisoners are to be kept in the building.

HERRICK: Aye, sir. *Very deferentially:* If I may say it, sir, I know this man all my life. It is a good man, sir.

DANFORTH—*it is the reflection on himself he resents:* I am sure of it, Marshal. *Herrick nods, then goes out.* Now, what deposition do you have for us, Mr. Proctor? And I beg you be clear, open as the sky, and honest.

PROCTOR, *as he takes out several papers:* I am no lawyer, so I'll—

DANFORTH: The pure in heart need no lawyers. Proceed as you will.

PROCTOR, *handing Danforth a paper:* Will you read this first, sir? It's a sort of testament. The people signing it declare their good opinion of Rebecca, and my wife, and Martha Corey. *Danforth looks down at the paper.*

PARRIS, *to enlist Danforth's sarcasm:* Their good opinion! *But Danforth goes on reading, and Proctor is heartened.*

PROCTOR: These are all landholding farmers, members of the church. *Delicately, trying to point out a paragraph:* If you'll notice, sir—they've known the women many years and never saw no sign they had dealings with the Devil.

Parris nervously moves over and reads over Danforth's shoulder.

DANFORTH, *glancing down a long list:* How many names are here?

FRANCIS: Ninety-one, Your Excellency.

PARRIS, *sweating:* These people should be summoned. *Danforth looks up at him questioningly.* For questioning.

FRANCIS, *trembling with anger:* Mr. Danforth, I gave them all my word no harm would come to them for signing this.

PARRIS: This is a clear attack upon the court!

HALE, *to Parris, trying to contain himself:* Is every defense an attack upon the court? Can no one—

PARRIS: All innocent and Christian people are happy for the courts in Salem! These people are gloomy for it. *To Danforth directly:* And I think you will want to know, from each and every one of them, what discontents them with you!

HATHORNE: I think they ought to be examined, sir.

DANFORTH: It is not necessarily an attack, I think. Yet—

FRANCIS: These are all covenanted Christians, sir.

DANFORTH: Then I am sure they may have nothing to fear. *Hands Cheever the paper.* Mr. Cheever, have warrants drawn for all of these—arrest for examination. *To Proctor:* Now, Mister, what other information do you have for us? *Francis is still standing, horrified.* You may sit, Mr. Nurse.

FRANCIS: I have brought trouble on these people; I have—

DANFORTH: No, old man, you have not hurt these people if they are of good conscience. But you must understand, sir, that a person is either with this court or he must be counted against it, there be no road between. This is a sharp time, now, a precise time—we live no longer in the dusky afternoon when evil mixed itself with good and befuddled the world. Now, by God's grace, the shining sun is up, and them that fear not light will surely praise it. I hope you will be one of those. *Mary Warren suddenly sobs.* She's not hearty, I see.

PROCTOR: No, she's not, sir. *To Mary, bending to her, holding her hand, quietly:* Now remember what the angel Raphael said to the boy Tobias. Remember it.

MARY WARREN, *hardly audible:* Aye.

PROCTOR: "Do that which is good, and no harm shall come to thee."

MARY WARREN: Aye.

DANFORTH: Come, man, we wait you.

Marshal Herrick returns, and takes his post at the door.

GILES: John, my deposition, give him mine.

PROCTOR: Aye. *He hands Danforth another paper.* This is Mr. Corey's deposition.

DANFORTH: Oh? *He looks down at it. Now Hathorne comes behind him and reads with him.*

HATHORNE, *suspiciously:* What lawyer drew this, Corey?

GILES: You know I never hired a lawyer in my life, Hathorne.

DANFORTH, *finishing the reading:* It is very well phrased. My compliments. Mr. Parris, if Mr. Putnam is in the court, will you bring him in? *Hathorne takes the deposition, and walks to the window with it. Parris goes into the court.* You have no legal training, Mr. Corey?

GILES, *very pleased:* I have the best, sir—I am thirty-three time in court in my life. And always plaintiff, too.

DANFORTH: Oh, then you're much put-upon.

GILES: I am never put-upon; I know my rights, sir, and I will have them. You know, your father tried a case of mine—might be thirty-five year ago, I think.

DANFORTH: Indeed.

GILES: He never spoke to you of it?

DANFORTH: No, I cannot recall it.

GILES: That's strange, he give me nine pound damages. He were a fair judge, your father. Y'see, I had a white mare that time, and this fellow come to borrow the mare—*Enter Parris with Thomas Putnam. When he sees Putnam, Giles' ease goes; he is hard.* Aye, there he is.

DANFORTH: Mr. Putnam, I have here an accusation by Mr. Corey against you. He states that you coldly prompted your daughter to cry witchery upon George Jacobs that is now in jail.

PUTNAM: It is a lie.

DANFORTH, *turning to Giles:* Mr. Putnam states your charge is a lie. What say you to that?

GILES, *furious, his fists clenched:* A fart on Thomas Putnam, that is what I say to that!

DANFORTH: What proof do you submit for your charge, sir?

GILES: My proof is there! *Pointing to the paper.* If Jacobs hangs for a witch he forfeit up his property—that's law! And there is none but Putnam with the coin to buy so great a piece. This man is killing his neighbors for their land!

DANFORTH: But proof, sir, proof.

GILES, *pointing at his deposition:* The proof is there! I have it from an honest man who heard Putnam say it! The day his daughter cried out on Jacobs, he said she'd given him a fair gift of land.

HATHORNE: And the name of this man?

GILES, *taken aback:* What name?

HATHORNE: The man that give you this information.

GILES, *hesitates, then:* Why, I—I cannot give you his name.

HATHORNE: And why not?

GILES, *hesitates, then bursts out:* You know well why not! He'll lay in jail if I give his name!

HATHORNE: This is contempt of the court, Mr. Danforth!

DANFORTH, *to avoid that:* You will surely tell us the name.

GILES: I will not give you no name. I mentioned my wife's name once and I'll burn in hell long enough for that. I stand mute.

DANFORTH: In that case, I have no choice but to arrest you for contempt of this court, do you know that?

GILES: This is a hearing; you cannot clap me for contempt of a hearing.

DANFORTH: Oh, it is a proper lawyer! Do you wish me to declare the court in full session here? Or will you give me good reply?

GILES, *faltering:* I cannot give you no name, sir, I cannot.

DANFORTH: You are a foolish old man. Mr. Cheever, begin the record. The court is now in session. I ask you, Mr. Corey—

PROCTOR, *breaking in:* Your Honor—he has the story in confidence, sir, and he—

PARRIS: The Devil lives on such confidences! *To Danforth:* Without confidences there could be no conspiracy, Your Honor!

HATHORNE: I think it must be broken, sir.

DANFORTH, *to Giles:* Old man, if your informant tells the truth let him come here openly like a decent man. But if he hide in anonymity I must know why. Now sir, the government and central church demand of you the name of him who reported Mr. Thomas Putnam a common murderer.

HALE: Excellency—

DANFORTH: Mr. Hale.

HALE: We cannot blink it more. There is a prodigious fear of this court in the country—

DANFORTH: Then there is a prodigious guilt in the country. Are *you* afraid to be questioned here?

HALE: I may only fear the Lord, sir, but there is fear in the country nevertheless.

DANFORTH, *angered now:* Reproach me not with the fear in the country; there is fear in the country because there is a moving plot to topple Christ in the country!

HALE: But it does not follow that everyone accused is part of it.

DANFORTH: No uncorrupted man may fear this court, Mr. Hale! None! *To Giles:* You are under arrest in contempt of this court. Now sit you down and take counsel with yourself, or you will be set in the jail until you decide to answer all questions.

Giles Corey makes a rush for Putnam. Proctor lunges and holds him.

PROCTOR: No, Giles!

GILES, *over Proctor's shoulder at Putnam:* I'll cut your throat, Putnam, I'll kill you yet!

PROCTOR, *forcing him into a chair:* Peace, Giles, peace. *Releasing him.* We'll prove ourselves. Now we will. *He starts to turn to Danforth.*

GILES: Say nothin' more, John. *Pointing at Danforth:* He's only playin' you! You means to hang us all!

Mary Warren bursts into sobs.

DANFORTH: This is a court of law, Mister. I'll have no effrontery here!

PROCTOR: Forgive him, sir, for his old age. Peace, Giles, we'll prove it all now. *He lifts up Mary's chin.* You cannot weep, Mary. Remember the angel, what he say to the boy. Hold to it, now; there is your rock. *Mary quiets. He takes out a paper, and turns to Danforth.* This is Mary Warren's deposition. I—I would ask you remember, sir, while you read it, that until two week ago she were no different than the other children are today. *He is speaking reasonably, restraining all his fears, his anger, his anxiety.* You saw her scream, she howled, she swore familiar spirits choked her; she even testified that Satan, in the form of women now in jail, tried to win her soul away, and then when she refused—

DANFORTH: We know all this.

PROCTOR: Aye, sir. She swears now that she never saw Satan; nor any spirit, vague or clear, that Satan may have sent to hurt her. And she declares her friends are lying now.

Proctor starts to hand Danforth the deposition, and Hale comes up to Danforth in a trembling state.

HALE: Excellency, a moment. I think this goes to the heart of the matter.

DANFORTH, *with deep misgivings:* It surely does.

HALE: I cannot say he is an honest man; I know him little. But in all justice, sir, a claim so weighty cannot be argued by a farmer. In God's name, sir, stop here; send him home and let him come again with a lawyer—

DANFORTH, *patiently:* Now look you, Mr. Hale—

HALE: Excellency, I have signed seventy-two death warrants; I am a minister of the Lord, and I dare not take a life without there be a proof so immaculate no slightest qualm of conscience may doubt it.

DANFORTH: Mr. Hale, you surely do not doubt my justice.

HALE: I have this morning signed away the soul of Rebecca Nurse, Your Honor. I'll not conceal it, my hand shakes yet as with a wound! I pray you, sir, *this* argument let lawyers present to you.

DANFORTH: Mr. Hale, believe me; for a man of such terrible learning you are most bewildered—I hope you will forgive me. I have been thirty-two year at the bar, sir, and I should be confounded were I called upon to defend these people. Let you consider, now—*To Proctor and the others:* And I bid you all do likewise. In an ordinary crime, how does one defend the accused? One calls up witnesses to prove his innocence. But witchcraft is *ipso facto,* on its face and by its nature, an invisible crime, is it not? Therefore, who may possibly be witness to it? The witch and the victim. None other. Now we cannot hope the witch will accuse herself; granted? Therefore, we must rely upon her victims—and they do testify, the children certainly do testify. As for the witches, none will deny that we are most eager for all their confessions. Therefore, what is left for a lawyer to bring out? I think I have made my point. Have I not?

HALE: But this child claims the girls are not truthful, and if they are not—

DANFORTH: That is precisely what I am about to consider, sir. What more may you ask of me? Unless you doubt my probity?

HALE, *defeated:* I surely do not, sir. Let you consider it, then.

DANFORTH: And let you put your heart to rest. Her deposition, Mr. Proctor.

Proctor hands it to him. Hathorne rises, goes beside Danforth, and starts reading. Parris comes to his other side. Danforth looks at John Proctor, then proceeds to read. Hale gets up, finds position near the judge, reads too. Proctor glances at Giles. Francis prays silently, hands pressed together. Cheever waits placidly, the sublime official, dutiful. Mary Warren sobs once. John Proctor touches her head reassuringly. Presently Danforth lifts his eyes, stands up, takes out a kerchief and blows his nose. The others stand aside as he moves in thought toward the window.

PARRIS, *hardly able to contain his anger and fear:* I should like to question—

DANFORTH—*his first real outburst, in which his contempt for Parris is clear:* Mr. Parris, I bid you be silent! *He stands in silence, looking out the window. Now, having established that he will set the gait:* Mr. Cheever, will you go into the court and bring the children here? *Cheever gets up and goes out upstage. Danforth now turns to Mary.* Mary Warren, how came you to this turnabout? Has Mr. Proctor threatened you for this deposition?

MARY WARREN: No, sir.

DANFORTH: Has he ever threatened you?

MARY WARREN, *weaker:* No, sir.

DANFORTH, *sensing a weakening:* Has he threatened you?

MARY WARREN: No, sir.

DANFORTH: Then you tell me that you sat in my court, callously lying, when you knew that people would hang by your evidence? *She does not answer.* Answer me!

MARY WARREN, *almost inaudibly:* I did, sir.

DANFORTH: How were you instructed in your life? Do you not know that God damns all liars? *She cannot speak.* Or is it now that you lie?

MARY WARREN: No, sir—I am with God now.

DANFORTH: You are with God now.

MARY WARREN: Aye, sir.

DANFORTH, *containing himself:* I will tell you this—you are either lying now, or you were lying in the court, and in either case you have committed perjury and you will go to jail for it. You cannot lightly say you lied, Mary. Do you know that?

MARY WARREN: I cannot lie no more. I am with God, I am with God.

But she breaks into sobs at the thought of it, and the right door opens, and enter Susanna Walcott, Mercy Lewis, Betty Parris, and finally Abigail. Cheever comes to Danforth.

CHEEVER: Ruth Putnam's not in the court, sir, nor the other children.

DANFORTH: These will be sufficient. Sit you down, children. *Silently they sit.* Your friend, Mary Warren, has given us a deposition. In which she swears that she never saw familiar spirits, apparitions, nor any manifest of the Devil. She claims as well that none of you have seen these things either. *Slight pause.* Now, children, this is a court of law. The law, based upon the Bible, and the Bible, writ by Almighty God, forbid the practice of witchcraft, and describe death as the penalty thereof. But likewise, children, the law and Bible damn all bearers of false witness. *Slight pause.* Now then. It does not escape me that this deposition may be devised to blind us; it may well be that Mary Warren has been conquered by Satan, who sends her here to distract our sacred purpose. If so, her neck will break for it. But if she speak true, I bid you now drop your guile and confess your pretense, for a quick confession will go easier with you. *Pause.* Abigail Williams, rise. *Abigail slowly rises.* Is there any truth in this?

ABIGAIL: No, sir.

DANFORTH, *thinks, glances at Mary, then back to Abigail:* Children, a very augur bit will now be turned into your souls until your honesty is proved. Will either of you change your positions now, or do you force me to hard questioning?

ABIGAIL: I have naught to change, sir. She lies.

DANFORTH, *to Mary:* You would still go on with this?

MARY WARREN, *faintly:* Aye, sir.

DANFORTH, *turning to Abigail:* A poppet were discovered in Mr. Proctor's house, stabbed by a needle. Mary Warren claims that you sat beside her in the court when she made it, and that you saw her make it and witnessed how she herself stuck her needle into it for safe-keeping. What say you to that?

ABIGAIL, *with a slight note of indignation:* It is a lie, sir.

DANFORTH, *after a slight pause:* While you worked for Mr. Proctor, did you see poppets in that house?

ABIGAIL: Goody Proctor always kept poppets.

PROCTOR: Your honor, my wife never kept no poppets. Mary Warren confesses it was her poppet.

CHEEVER: Your Excellency.

DANFORTH: Mr. Cheever.

CHEEVER: When I spoke with Goody Proctor in that house, she said she never kept no poppets. But she said she did keep poppets when she were a girl.

PROCTOR: She has not been a girl these fifteen years, Your Honor.

HATHORNE: But a poppet will keep fifteen years, will it not?

PROCTOR: It will keep if it is kept, but Mary Warren swears she never saw no poppets in my house, nor anyone else.

PARRIS: Why could there not have been poppets hid where no one ever saw them?

PROCTOR, *furious:* There might also be a dragon with five legs in my house, but no one has ever seen it.

PARRIS: We are here, Your Honor, precisely to discover what no one has ever seen.

PROCTOR: Mr. Danforth, what profit this girl to turn herself about? What may Mary Warren gain but hard questioning and worse?

DANFORTH: You are charging Abigail Williams with a marvelous cool plot to murder, do you understand that?

PROCTOR: I do, sir. I believe she means to murder.

DANFORTH, *pointing at Abigail, incredulously:* This child would murder your wife?

PROCTOR: It is not a child. Now hear me, sir. In the sight of the congregation she were twice this year put out of this meetin' house for laughter during prayer.

DANFORTH, *shocked, turning to Abigail:* What's this? Laughter during—!

PARRIS: Excellency, she were under Tituba's power at that time, but she is solemn now.

GILES: Aye, now she is solemn and goes to hang people!

DANFORTH: Quiet, man.

HATHORNE: Surely it have no bearing on the question, sir. He charges contemplation of murder.

DANFORTH: Aye. *He studies Abigail for a moment, then:* Continue, Mr. Proctor.

PROCTOR: Mary. Now tell the Governor how you danced in the woods.

PARRIS, *instantly:* Excellency, since I come to Salem this man is blackening my name. He—

DANFORTH: In a moment, sir. *To Mary Warren, sternly, and surprised:* What is this dancing?

MARY WARREN: I—*She glances at Abigail, who is staring down at her remorselessly. Then, appealing to Proctor:* Mr. Proctor—

PROCTOR, *taking it right up:* Abigail leads the girls to the woods, Your Honor, and they have danced there naked—

PARRIS: Your Honor, this—

PROCTOR, *at once:* Mr. Parris discovered them himself in the dead of night! There's the "child" she is!

DANFORTH—*it is growing into a nightmare, and he turns, astonished, to Parris:* Mr. Parris—

PARRIS: I can only say, sir, that I never found any of them naked, and this man is—

DANFORTH: But you discovered them dancing in the woods? *Eyes on Parris, he points at Abigail.* Abigail?

HALE: Excellency, when I first arrived from Beverly, Mr. Parris told me that.
DANFORTH: Do you deny it, Mr. Parris?
PARRIS: I do not, sir, but I never saw any of them naked.
DANFORTH: But she have *danced?*
PARRIS, *unwillingly:* Aye, sir.

Danforth, as though with new eyes, looks at Abigail.

HATHORNE: Excellency, will you permit me? *He points at Mary Warren.*
DANFORTH, *with great worry:* Pray, proceed.
HATHORNE: You say you never saw no spirits, Mary, were never threatened or afflicted by any manifest of the Devil or the Devil's agents.
MARY WARREN, *very faintly:* No, sir.
HATHORNE, *with a gleam of victory:* And yet, when people accused of witchery confronted you in court, you would faint, saying their spirits came out of their bodies and choked you—
MARY WARREN: That were pretense, sir.
DANFORTH: I cannot hear you.
MARY WARREN: Pretense, sir.
PARRIS: But you did turn cold, did you not? I myself picked you up many times, and your skin were icy. Mr. Danforth, you—
DANFORTH: I saw that many times.
PROCTOR: She only pretended to faint, Your Excellency. They're all marvelous pretenders.
HATHORNE: Then can she pretend to faint now?
PROCTOR: Now?
PARRIS: Why not? Now there are no spirits attacking her, for none in this room is accused of witchcraft. So let her turn herself cold now, let her pretend she is attacked now, let her faint. *He turns to Mary Warren.* Faint!
MARY WARREN: Faint?
PARRIS: Aye, faint. Prove to us how you pretended in the court so many times.
MARY WARREN, *looking to Proctor:* I—cannot faint now, sir.
PROCTOR, *alarmed, quietly:* Can you not pretend it?
MARY WARREN: I— *She looks about as though searching for the passion to faint.* I—have no *sense* of it now, I—
DANFORTH: Why? What is lacking now?
MARY WARREN: I—cannot tell, sir, I—
DANFORTH: Might it be that here we have no afflicting spirit loose, but in the court there were some?
MARY WARREN: I never saw no spirits.
PARRIS: Then see no spirits now, and prove to us that you can faint by your own will, as you claim.
MARY WARREN, *stares, searching for the emotion of it, and then shakes her head:* I—cannot do it.
PARRIS: Then you will confess, will you not? It were attacking spirits made you faint!
MARY WARREN: No, sir, I—
PARRIS: Your Excellency, this is a trick to blind the court!

MARY WARREN: It's not a trick! *She stands.* I—I used to faint because I—I thought I saw spirits.

DANFORTH: *Thought* you saw them!

MARY WARREN: But I did not, Your Honor.

HATHORNE: How could you think you saw them unless you saw them?

MARY WARREN: I—I cannot tell how, but I did. I—I heard the other girls screaming, and you, Your Honor, you seemed to believe them, and I— It were only sport in the beginning, sir, but then the whole world cried spirits, spirits, and I—I promise you, Mr. Danforth, I only thought I saw them but I did not.

Danforth peers at her.

PARRIS, *smiling, but nervous because Danforth seems to be struck by Mary Warren's story:* Surely Your Excellency is not taken by this simple lie.

DANFORTH, *turning worriedly to Abigail:* Abigail. I bid you now search your heart and tell me this—and beware of it, child, to God every soul is precious and His vengeance is terrible on them that take life without cause. Is it possible, child, that the spirits you have seen are illusion only, some deception that may cross your mind when—

ABIGAIL: Why, this—this—is a base question, sir.

DANFORTH: Child, I would have you consider it—

ABIGAIL: I have been hurt, Mr. Danforth; I have seen my blood runnin' out! I have been near to murdered every day because I done my duty pointing out the Devil's people—and this is my reward? To be mistrusted, denied, questioned like a—

DANFORTH, *weakening:* Child, I do not mistrust you—

ABIGAIL, *in an open threat:* Let *you* beware, Mr. Danforth. Think you to be so mighty that the power of Hell may not turn *your* wits? Beware of it! There is— *Suddenly, from an accusatory attitude, her face turns, looking into the air above—it is truly frightened.*

DANFORTH, *apprehensively:* What is it, child?

ABIGAIL, *looking about in the air, clasping her arms about her as though cold:* I—I know not. A wind, a cold wind, has come. *Her eyes fall on Mary Warren.*

MARY WARREN, *terrified, pleading:* Abby!

MERCY LEWIS, *shivering:* Your Honor, I freeze!

PROCTOR: They're pretending!

HATHORNE, *touching Abigail's hand:* She is cold, Your Honor, touch her!

MERCY LEWIS, *through chattering teeth:* Mary, do you send this shadow on me?

MARY WARREN: Lord, save me!

SUSANNA WALCOTT: I freeze, I freeze!

ABIGAIL, *shivering visibly:* It is a wind, a wind!

MARY WARREN: Abby, don't do that!

DANFORTH, *himself engaged and entered by Abigail:* Mary Warren, do you witch her? I say to you, do you send your spirit out?

With a hysterical cry Mary Warren starts to run. Proctor catches her.

MARY WARREN, *almost collapsing:* Let me go, Mr. Proctor, I cannot, I cannot—

ABIGAIL, *crying to Heaven:* Oh, Heavenly Father, take away this shadow!

Without warning or hesitation, Proctor leaps at Abigail and, grabbing her by the hair, pulls her to her feet. She screams in pain. Danforth, astonished, cries, "What are you about?" and Hathorne and Parris call, "Take your hands off her!" and out of it all comes Proctor's roaring voice.

PROCTOR: How do you call Heaven! Whore! Whore!

Herrick breaks Proctor from her.

HERRICK: John!

DANFORTH: Man! Man, what do you—

PROCTOR, *breathless and in agony:* It is a whore!

DANFORTH, *dumfounded:* You charge—?

ABIGAIL: Mr. Danforth, he is lying!

PROCTOR: Mark her! Now she'll suck a scream to stab me with but—

DANFORTH: You will prove this! This will not pass!

PROCTOR, *trembling, his life collapsing about him:* I have known her, sir. I have known her.

DANFORTH: You—you are a lecher?

FRANCIS, *horrified:* John, you cannot say such a—

PROCTOR: Oh, Francis, I wish you had some evil in you that you might know me! *To Danforth:* A man will not cast away his good name. You surely know that.

DANFORTH, *dumfounded:* In—in what time? In what place?

PROCTOR, *his voice about to break, and his shame great:* In the proper place—where my beasts are bedded. On the last night of my joy, some eight months past. She used to serve me in my house, sir. *He has to clamp his jaw to keep from weeping.* A man may think God sleeps, but God sees everything, I know it now. I beg you, sir, I beg you—see her what she is. My wife, my dear good wife, took this girl soon after, sir, and put her out on the highroad. And being what she is, a lump of vanity, sir— *He is being overcome.* Excellency, forgive me, forgive me. *Angrily against himself, he turns away from the Governor for a moment. Then, as though to cry out is his only means of speech left:* She thinks to dance with me on my wife's grave! And well she might, for I thought of her softly. God help me, I lusted, and there *is* a promise in such sweat. But it is a whore's vengeance, and you must see it; I set myself entirely in your hands. I know you must see it now.

DANFORTH, *blanched, in horror, turning to Abigail:* You deny every scrap and tittle of this?

ABIGAIL: If I must answer that, I will leave and I will not come back again!

Danforth seems unsteady.

PROCTOR: I have made a bell of my honor! I have rung the doom of my good name—you will believe me, Mr. Danforth! My wife is innocent, except she knew a whore when she saw one!

ABIGAIL, *stepping up to Danforth:* What look do you give me? *Danforth cannot speak.* I'll not have such looks! *She turns and starts for the door.*

DANFORTH: You will remain where you are! *Herrick steps into her path. She comes up short, fire in her eyes.* Mr. Parris, go into the court and bring Goodwife Proctor out.

PARRIS, *objecting:* Your Honor, this is all a—

DANFORTH, *sharply to Parris:* Bring her out! And tell her not one word of what's been spoken here. And let you knock before you enter. *Parris goes out.* Now we shall touch the bottom of this swamp. *To Proctor:* Your wife, you say, is an honest woman.

PROCTOR: In her life, sir, she have never lied. There are them that cannot sing, and them that cannot weep—my wife cannot lie. I have paid much to learn it, sir.

DANFORTH: And when she put this girl out of your house, she put her out for a harlot?

PROCTOR: Aye, sir.

DANFORTH: And knew her for a harlot?

PROCTOR: Aye, sir, she knew her for a harlot.

DANFORTH: Good then. *To Abigail:* And if she tell me, child, it were for harlotry, may God spread His mercy on you! *There is a knock. He calls to the door.* Hold! *To Abigail:* Turn your back. Turn your back. *To Proctor:* Do likewise. *Both turn their backs—Abigail with indignant slowness.* Now let neither of you turn to face Goody Proctor. No one in this room is to speak one word, or raise a gesture aye or nay. *He turns toward the door, calls:* Enter! *The door opens. Elizabeth enters with Parris. Parris leaves her. She stands alone, her eyes looking for Proctor.* Mr. Cheever, report this testimony in all exactness. Are you ready?

CHEEVER: Ready, sir.

DANFORTH: Come here, woman. *Elizabeth comes to him, glancing at Proctor's back.* Look at me only, not at your husband. In my eyes only.

ELIZABETH, *faintly:* Good, sir.

DANFORTH: We are given to understand that at one time you dismissed your servant, Abigail Williams.

ELIZABETH: That is true, sir.

DANFORTH: For what cause did you dismiss her? *Slight pause. Then Elizabeth tries to glance at Proctor.* You will look in my eyes only and not at your husband. The answer is in your memory and you need no help to give it to me. Why did you dismiss Abigail Williams?

ELIZABETH, *not knowing what to say, sensing a situation, wetting her lips to stall for time:* She—dissatisfied me. *Pause.* And my husband.

DANFORTH: In what way dissatisfied you?

ELIZABETH: She were— *She glances at Proctor for a cue.*

DANFORTH: Woman, look at me! *Elizabeth does.* Were she slovenly? Lazy? What disturbance did she cause?

ELIZABETH: Your Honor, I—in that time I were sick. And I—My husband is a good and righteous man. He is never drunk as some are, nor wastin' his time at the shovelboard, but always at his work. But in my sickness—you see, sir, I were a long time sick after my last baby, and I thought I saw my husband somewhat turning from me. And this girl— *She turns to Abigail.*

DANFORTH: Look at me.

ELIZABETH: Aye, sir. Abigail Williams— *She breaks off.*

DANFORTH: What of Abigail Williams?

ELIZABETH: I came to think he fancied her. And so one night I lost my wits, I think, and put her out on the highroad.

DANFORTH: Your husband—did he indeed turn from you?

ELIZABETH, *in agony:* My husband—is a goodly man, sir.

DANFORTH: Then he did not turn from you.

ELIZABETH, *starting to glance at Proctor:* He—

DANFORTH, *reaches out and holds her face, then:* Look at me! To your own knowledge, has John Proctor ever committed the crime of lechery? *In a crisis of indecision she cannot speak.* Answer my question! Is your husband a lecher!

ELIZABETH, *faintly:* No, sir.

DANFORTH: Remove her, Marshal.

PROCTOR: Elizabeth, tell the truth!

DANFORTH: She has spoken. Remove her!

PROCTOR, *crying out:* Elizabeth, I have confessed it!

ELIZABETH: Oh, God! *The door closes behind her.*

PROCTOR: She only thought to save my name!

HALE: Excellency, it is a natural lie to tell; I beg you, stop now before another is condemned! I may shut my conscience to it no more—private vengeance is working through this testimony! From the beginning this man has struck me true. By my oath to Heaven, I believe him now, and I pray you call back his wife before we—

DANFORTH: She spoke nothing of lechery, and this man has lied!

HALE: I believe him! *Pointing at Abigail:* This girl has always struck me false! She has—

Abigail, with a weird, wild, chilling cry, screams up to the ceiling.

ABIGAIL: You will not! Begone! Begone, I say!

DANFORTH: What is it, child? *But Abigail, pointing with fear, is now raising up her frightened eyes, her awed face, toward the ceiling—the girls are doing the same—and now Hathorne, Hale, Putnam, Cheever, Herrick, and Danforth do the same.* What's there? *He lowers his eyes from the ceiling, and now he is frightened; there is real tension in his voice.* Child! *She is transfixed—with all the girls, she is whimpering open-mouthed, agape at the ceiling.* Girls! Why do you—?

MERCY LEWIS, *pointing:* It's on the beam! Behind the rafter!

DANFORTH, *looking up:* Where!

ABIGAIL: Why—? *She gulps.* Why do you come, yellow bird?

PROCTOR: Where's a bird? I see no bird!

ABIGAIL, *to the ceiling:* My face? My face?

PROCTOR: Mr. Hale—

DANFORTH: Be quiet!

PROCTOR, *to Hale:* Do you see a bird?

DANFORTH: Be quiet!!

ABIGAIL, *to the ceiling, in a genuine conversation with the "bird," as though trying to talk it out of attacking her:* But God made my face; you cannot want to tear my face. Envy is a deadly sin, Mary.

MARY WARREN, *on her feet with a spring, and horrified, pleading:* Abby!

ABIGAIL, *unperturbed, continuing to the "bird":* Oh, Mary, this is a black art to change your shape. No, I cannot, I cannot stop my mouth; it's God's work I do.

MARY WARREN: Abby, I'm *here!*

PROCTOR, *frantically:* They're pretending, Mr. Danforth!

ABIGAIL—*now she takes a backward step, as though in fear the bird will swoop down momentarily:* Oh, please, Mary! Don't come down.

SUSANNA WALCOTT: Her claws, she's stretching her claws!
PROCTOR: Lies, lies.
ABIGAIL, *backing further, eyes still fixed above:* Mary, please don't hurt me!
MARY WARREN, *to Danforth:* I'm not hurting her!
DANFORTH, *to Mary Warren:* Why does she see this vision?
MARY WARREN: She sees nothin'!
ABIGAIL, *now staring full front as though hypnotized, and mimicking the exact tone of Mary Warren's cry:* She sees nothin'!
MARY WARREN, *pleading:* Abby, you mustn't!
ABIGAIL AND ALL THE GIRLS, *all transfixed:* Abby, you mustn't!
MARY WARREN, *to all the girls:* I'm here, I'm here!
GIRLS: I'm here, I'm here!
DANFORTH, *horrified:* Mary Warren! Draw back your spirit out of them!
MARY WARREN: Mr. Danforth!
GIRLS, *cutting her off:* Mr. Danforth!
DANFORTH: Have you compacted with the Devil? Have you?
MARY WARREN: Never, never!
GIRLS: Never, never!
DANFORTH, *growing hysterical:* Why can they only repeat you?
PROCTOR: Give me a whip—I'll stop it!
MARY WARREN: They're sporting. They—!
GIRLS: They're sporting!
MARY WARREN, *turning on them all hysterically and stamping her feet:* Abby, stop it!
GIRLS, *stamping their feet:* Abby, stop it!
MARY WARREN: Stop it!
GIRLS: Stop it!
MARY WARREN, *screaming it out at the top of her lungs, and raising her fists:* Stop it!!
GIRLS, *raising their fists:* Stop it!!

Mary Warren, utterly confounded, and becoming overwhelmed by Abigail's—and the girls'—utter conviction, starts to whimper, hands half raised, powerless, and all the girls begin whimpering exactly as she does.

DANFORTH: A little while ago you were afflicted. Now it seems you afflict others; where did you find this power?
MARY WARREN, *staring at Abigail:* I—have no power.
GIRLS: I have no power.
PROCTOR: They're gulling you, Mister!
DANFORTH: Why did you turn about this past two weeks? You have seen the Devil, have you not?
HALE, *indicating Abigail and the girls:* You cannot believe them!
MARY WARREN: I—
PROCTOR, *sensing her weakening:* Mary, God damns all liars!
DANFORTH, *pounding it into her:* You have seen the Devil, you have made compact with Lucifer, have you not?
PROCTOR: God damns liars, Mary!

Mary utters something unintelligible, staring at Abigail, who keeps watching the "bird" above.

DANFORTH: I cannot hear you. What do you say? *Mary utters again unintelligibly.* You will confess yourself or you will hang! *He turns her roughly to face him.* Do you know who I am? I say you will hang if you do not open with me!

PROCTOR: Mary, remember the angel Raphael—do that which is good and—

ABIGAIL, *pointing upward:* The wings! Her wings are spreading! Mary, please, don't, don't—!

HALE: I see nothing, Your Honor!

DANFORTH: Do you confess this power! *He is an inch from her face.* Speak!

ABIGAIL: She's going to come down! She's walking the beam!

DANFORTH: Will you speak!

MARY WARREN, *staring in horror:* I cannot!

GIRLS: I cannot!

PARRIS: Cast the Devil out! Look him in the face! Trample him! We'll save you, Mary, only stand fast against him and—

ABIGAIL, *looking up:* Look out! She's coming down!

She and all the girls run to one wall, shielding their eyes. And now, as though cornered, they let out a gigantic scream, and Mary, as though infected, opens her mouth and screams with them. Gradually Abigail and the girls leave off, until only Mary is left there, staring up at the "bird," screaming madly. All watch her, horrified by this evident fit. Proctor strides to her.

PROCTOR: Mary, tell the Governor what they— *He has hardly got a word out, when, seeing him coming for her, she rushes out of his reach, screaming in horror.*

MARY WARREN: Don't touch me—don't touch me! *At which the girls halt at the door.*

PROCTOR, *astonished:* Mary!

MARY WARREN, *pointing at Proctor:* You're the Devil's man!

He is stopped in his tracks.

PARRIS: Praise God!

GIRLS: Praise God!

PROCTOR, *numbed:* Mary, how—?

MARY WARREN: I'll not hang with you! I love God, I love God.

DANFORTH, *to Mary:* He bid you do the Devil's work?

MARY WARREN, *hysterically, indicating Proctor:* He come at me by night and every day to sign, to sign, to—

DANFORTH: Sign what?

PARRIS: The Devil's book? He come with a book?

MARY WARREN, *hysterically, pointing at Proctor, fearful of him:* My name, he want my name. "I'll murder you," he says, "if my wife hangs! We must go and overthrow the court," he says!

Danforth's head jerks toward Proctor, shock and horror in his face.

PROCTOR, *turning, appealing to Hale:* Mr. Hale!

MARY WARREN, *her sobs beginning:* He wake me every night, his eyes were like coals and his fingers claw my neck, and I sign, I sign . . .

HALE: Excellency, this child's gone wild!

PROCTOR, *as Danforth's wide eyes pour on him:* Mary, Mary!

MARY WARREN, *screaming at him:* No, I love God; I go your way no more. I love God, I bless God. *Sobbing, she rushes to Abigail.* Abby, Abby, I'll never hurt you more! *They all watch, as Abigail, out of her infinite charity, reaches out and draws the sobbing Mary to her, and then looks up to Danforth.*

DANFORTH, *to Proctor:* What are you? *Proctor is beyond speech in his anger.* You are combined with anti-Christ, are you not? I have seen your power; you will not deny it! What say you, Mister?

HALE: Excellency—

DANFORTH: I will have nothing from you, Mr. Hale! *To Proctor:* Will you confess yourself befouled with Hell, or do you keep that black allegiance yet? What say you?

PROCTOR, *his mind wild, breathless:* I say—I say—God is dead!

PARRIS: Hear it, hear it!

PROCTOR, *laughs insanely, then:* A fire, a fire is burning! I hear the boot of Lucifer, I see his filthy face! And it is my face, and yours, Danforth! For them that quail to bring men out of ignorance, as I have quailed, and as you quail now when you know in all your black hearts that this be fraud—God damns our kind especially, and we will burn, we will burn together!

DANFORTH: Marshal! Take him and Corey with him to the jail!

HALE, *starting across to the door:* I denounce these proceedings!

PROCTOR: You are pulling Heaven down and raising up a whore!

HALE: I denounce these proceedings, I quit this court! *He slams the door to the outside behind him.*

DANFORTH, *calling to him in a fury:* Mr. Hale! Mr. Hale!

Curtain

Act Four

A cell in Salem jail, that fall.

At the back is a high barred window; near it, a great, heavy door. Along the walls are two benches.

The place is in darkness but for the moonlight seeping through the bars. It appears empty. Presently footsteps are heard coming down a corridor beyond the wall, keys rattle, and the door swings open. Marshal Herrick enters with a lantern.

He is nearly drunk, and heavy-footed. He goes to a bench and nudges a bundle of rags lying on it.

HERRICK: Sarah, wake up! Sarah Good! *He then crosses to the other bench.*

SARAH GOOD, *rising in her rags:* Oh, Majesty! Comin', comin'! Tituba, he's here, His Majesty's come!

HERRICK: Go to the north cell; this place is wanted now. *He hangs his lantern on the wall. Tituba sits up.*

TITUBA: That don't look to me like His Majesty; look to me like the marshal.

HERRICK, *taking out a flask:* Get along with you now, clear this place. *He drinks, and Sarah Good comes and peers up into his face.*

SARAH GOOD: Oh, is it you, Marshal! I thought sure you be the Devil comin' for us. Could I have a sip of cider for me goin'-away?

HERRICK, *handing her the flask:* And where are you off to, Sarah?

TITUBA, *as Sarah drinks:* We goin' to Barbados, soon the Devil gits here with the feathers and the wings.

HERRICK: Oh? A happy voyage to you.

SARAH GOOD: A pair of bluebirds wingin' southerly, the two of us! Oh, it be a grand transformation, Marshal! *She raises the flask to drink again.*

HERRICK, *taking the flask from her lips:* You'd best give me that or you'll never rise off the ground. Come along now.

TITUBA: I'll speak to him for you, if you desires to come along, Marshal.

HERRICK: I'd not refuse it, Tituba; it's the proper morning to fly into Hell.

TITUBA: Oh, it be no Hell in Barbados. Devil, him be pleasureman in Barbados, him be singin' and dancin' in Barbados. It's you folks—you riles him up 'round here; it be too cold 'round here for that Old Boy. He freeze his soul in Massachusetts, but in Barbados he just as sweet and— *A bellowing cow is heard, and Tituba leaps up and calls to the window:* Aye, sir! That's him, Sarah!

SARAH GOOD: I'm here, Majesty! *They hurriedly pick up their rags as Hopkins, a guard, enters.*

HOPKINS: The Deputy Governor's arrived.

HERRICK, *grabbing Tituba:* Come along, come along.

TITUBA, *resisting him:* No, he comin' for me. I goin' home!

HERRICK, *pulling her to the door:* That's not Satan, just a poor old cow with a hatful of milk. Come along now, out with you!

TITUBA, *calling to the window:* Take me home, Devil! Take me home!

SARAH GOOD, *following the shouting Tituba out:* Tell him I'm goin', Tituba! Now you tell him Sarah Good is goin' too!

In the corridor outside Tituba calls on—"Take me home, Devil; Devil take me home!" and Hopkins' voice orders her to move on. Herrick returns and begins to push old rags and straw into a corner. Hearing footsteps, he turns, and enter Danforth and Judge Hathorne. They are in greatcoats and wear hats against the bitter cold. They are followed in by Cheever, who carries a dispatch case and a flat wooden box containing his writing materials.

HERRICK: Good morning, Excellency.

DANFORTH: Where is Mr. Parris?

HERRICK: I'll fetch him. *He starts for the door.*

DANFORTH: Marshal. *Herrick stops.* When did Reverend Hale arrive?

HERRICK: It were toward midnight, I think.

DANFORTH, *suspiciously:* What is he about here?

HERRICK: He goes among them that will hang, sir. And he prays with them. He sits with Goody Nurse now. And Mr. Parris with him.

DANFORTH: Indeed. That man have no authority to enter here, Marshal. Why have you let him in?

HERRICK: Why, Mr. Parris command me, sir. I cannot deny him.

DANFORTH: Are you drunk, Marshal?

HERRICK: No, sir; it is a bitter night, and I have no fire here.

DANFORTH, *containing his anger:* Fetch Mr. Parris.

HERRICK: Aye, sir.

DANFORTH: There is a prodigious stench in this place.

HERRICK: I have only now cleared the people out for you.
DANFORTH: Beware hard drink, Marshal.
HERRICK: Aye, sir. *He waits an instant for further orders. But Danforth, in dissatisfaction, turns his back on him, and Herrick goes out. There is a pause. Danforth stands in thought.*
HATHORNE: Let you question Hale, Excellency; I should not be surprised he have been preaching in Andover lately.
DANFORTH: We'll come to that; speak nothing of Andover. Parris prays with him. That's strange. *He blows on his hands, moves toward the window, and looks out.*
HATHORNE: Excellency, I wonder if it be wise to let Mr. Parris so continuously with the prisoners. *Danforth turns to him, interested.* I think, sometimes, the man has a mad look these days.
DANFORTH: Mad?
HATHORNE: I met him yesterday coming out of his house, and I bid him good morning—and he wept and went his way. I think it is not well the village sees him so unsteady.
DANFORTH: Perhaps he have some sorrow.
CHEEVER, *stamping his feet against the cold:* I think it be the cows, sir.
DANFORTH: Cows?
CHEEVER: There be so many cows wanderin' the highroads, now their masters are in the jails, and much disagreement who they will belong to now. I know Mr. Parris be arguin' with farmers all yesterday—there is great contention, sir, about the cows. Contention make him weep, sir; it were always a man that weep for contention. *He turns, as do Hathorne and Danforth, hearing someone coming up the corridor. Danforth raises his head as Parris enters. He is gaunt, frightened, and sweating in his greatcoat.*
PARRIS, *to Danforth, instantly:* Oh, good morning, sir, thank you for coming, I beg your pardon wakin' you so early. Good morning, Judge Hathorne.
DANFORTH: Reverend Hale have no right to enter this—
PARRIS: Excellency, a moment. *He hurries back and shuts the door.*
HATHORNE: Do you leave him alone with the prisoners?
DANFORTH: What's his business here?
PARRIS, *prayerfully holding up his hands:* Excellency, hear me. It is a providence. Reverend Hale has returned to bring Rebecca Nurse to God.
DANFORTH, *surprised:* He bids her confess?
PARRIS, *sitting:* Hear me. Rebecca have not given me a word this three month since she came. Now she sits with him, and her sister and Martha Corey and two or three others, and he pleads with them, confess their crimes and save their lives.
DANFORTH: Why—this is indeed a providence. And they soften, they soften?
PARRIS: Not yet, not yet. But I thought to summon you, sir, that we might think on whether it be not wise, to— *He dares not say it.* I had thought to put a question, sir, and I hope you will not—
DANFORTH: Mr. Parris, be plain, what troubles you?
PARRIS: There is news, sir, that the court—the court must reckon with. My niece, sir, my niece—I believe she has vanished.
DANFORTH: Vanished!
PARRIS: I had thought to advise you of it earlier in the week, but—
DANFORTH: Why? How long is she gone?

PARRIS: This be the third night. You see, sir, she told me she would stay a night with Mercy Lewis. And next day, when she does not return, I send to Mr. Lewis to inquire. Mercy told him she would sleep in *my* house for a night.

DANFORTH: They are both gone?!

PARRIS, *in fear of him:* They are, sir.

DANFORTH, *alarmed:* I will send a party for them. Where may they be?

PARRIS: Excellency, I think they be aboard a ship. *Danforth stands agape.* My daughter tells me how she heard them speaking of ships last week, and tonight I discover my—my strongbox is broke into. *He presses his fingers against his eyes to keep back tears.*

HATHORNE, *astonished:* She have robbed you?

PARRIS: Thirty-one pound is gone. I am penniless. *He covers his face and sobs.*

DANFORTH: Mr. Parris, you are a brainless man! *He walks in thought, deeply worried.*

PARRIS: Excellency, it profit nothing you should blame me. I cannot think they would run off except they fear to keep in Salem any more. *He is pleading.* Mark it, sir, Abigail had close knowledge of the town, and since the news of Andover has broken here—

DANFORTH: Andover is remedied. The court returns there on Friday, and will resume examinations.

PARRIS: I am sure of it, sir. But the rumor here speaks rebellion in Andover, and it—

DANFORTH: There is no rebellion in Andover!

PARRIS: I tell you what is said here, sir. Andover have thrown out the court, they say, and will have no part of witchcraft. There be a faction here, feeding on that news, and I tell you true, sir, I fear there will be riot here.

HATHORNE: Riot! Why at every execution I have seen naught but high satisfaction in the town.

PARRIS: Judge Hathorne—it were another sort that hanged till now. Rebecca Nurse is no Bridget that lived three year with Bishop before she married him. John Proctor is not Isaac Ward that drank his family to ruin. *To Danforth:* I would to God it were not so, Excellency, but these people have great weight yet in the town. Let Rebecca stand upon the gibbet and send up some righteous prayer, and I fear she'll wake a vengeance on you.

HATHORNE: Excellency, she is condemend a witch. The court have—

DANFORTH, *in deep concern, raising a hand to Hathorne:* Pray you. *To Parris:* How do you propose, then?

PARRIS: Excellency, I would postpone these hangin's for a time.

DANFORTH: There will be no postponement.

PARRIS: Now Mr. Hale's returned, there is hope, I think—for if he bring even one of these to God, that confession surely damns the others in the public eye, and none may doubt more that they are all linked to Hell. This way, unconfessed and claiming innocence, doubts are multiplied, many honest people will weep for them, and our good purpose is lost in their tears.

DANFORTH, *after thinking a moment, then going to Cheever:* Give me the list.

Cheever opens the dispatch case, searches.

PARRIS: It cannot be forgot, sir, that when I summoned the congregation for John Proctor's excommunication there were hardly thirty people come to hear it. That speak a discontent, I think, and—

DANFORTH, *studying the list:* There will be no postponement.

PARRIS: Excellency—

DANFORTH: Now, sir—which of these in your opinion may be brought to God? I will myself strive with him till dawn. *He hands the list to Parris, who merely glances at it.*

PARRIS: There is not sufficient time till dawn.

DANFORTH: I shall do my utmost. Which of them do you have hope for?

PARRIS, *not even glancing at the list now, and in a quavering voice, quietly:* Excellency—a dagger— *He chokes up.*

DANFORTH: What do you say?

PARRIS: Tonight, when I open my door to leave my house—a dagger clattered to the ground. *Silence. Danforth absorbs this. Now Parris cries out:* You cannot hang this sort. There is danger for me. I dare not step outside at night!

Reverend Hale enters. They look at him for an instant in silence. He is steeped in sorrow, exhausted, and more direct than he ever was.

DANFORTH: Accept my congratulations, Reverend Hale; we are gladdened to see you returned to your good work.

HALE, *coming to Danforth now:* You must pardon them. They will not budge.

Herrick enters, waits.

DANFORTH, *conciliatory:* You misunderstand, sir; I cannot pardon these when twelve are already hanged for the same crime. It is not just.

PARRIS, *with failing heart:* Rebecca will not confess?

HALE: The sun will rise in a few minutes. Excellency, I must have more time.

DANFORTH: Now hear me, and beguile yourselves no more. I will not receive a single plea for pardon or postponement. Them that will not confess will hang. Twelve are already executed; the names of these seven are given out, and the village expects to see them die this morning. Postponement now speaks a floundering on my part; reprieve or pardon must cast doubt upon the guilt of them that died till now. While I speak God's law, I will not crack its voice with whimpering. If retaliation is your fear, know this—I should hang ten thousand that dared to rise against the law, and an ocean of salt tears could not melt the resolution of the statutes. Now draw yourselves up like men and help me, as you are bound by Heaven to do. Have you spoken with them all, Mr. Hale?

HALE: All but Proctor. He is in the dungeon.

DANFORTH, *to Herrick:* What's Proctor's way now?

HERRICK: He sits like some great bird; you'd not know he lived except he will take food from time to time.

DANFORTH, *after thinking a moment:* His wife—his wife must be well on with child now.

HERRICK: She is, sir.

DANFORTH: What think you, Mr. Parris? You have closer knowledge of this man; might her presence soften him?

PARRIS: It is possible, sir. He have not laid eyes on her these three months. I should summon her.

DANFORTH, *to Herrick:* Is he yet adamant? Has he struck at you again?

HERRICK: He cannot, sir, he is chained to the wall now.

DANFORTH, *after thinking on it:* Fetch Goody Proctor to me. Then let you bring him up.

HERRICK: Aye, sir. *Herrick goes. There is silence.*

HALE: Excellency, if you postpone a week and publish to the town that you are striving for their confessions, that speak mercy on your part, not faltering.

DANFORTH: Mr. Hale, as God have not empowered me like Joshua to stop this sun from rising, so I cannot withhold from them the perfection of their punishment.

HALE, *harder now:* If you think God wills you to raise rebellion, Mr. Danforth, you are mistaken?

DANFORTH, *instantly:* You have heard rebellion spoken in the town?

HALE: Excellency, there are orphans wandering from house to house; abandoned cattle bellow on the highroads, the stink of rotting crops hangs everywhere, and no man knows when the harlots' cry will end his life—and you wonder yet if rebellion's spoke? Better you should marvel how they do not burn your province!

DANFORTH: Mr. Hale, have you preached in Andover this month?

HALE: Thank God they have no need of me in Andover.

DANFORTH: You baffle me, sir. Why have you returned here?

HALE: Why, it is all simple. I come to do the Devil's work. I come to counsel Christians they should belie themselves. *His sarcasm collapses.* There is blood on my head! Can you not see the blood on my head!!

PARRIS: Hush! *For he has heard footsteps. They all face the door. Herrick enters with Elizabeth. Her wrists are linked by heavy chain, which Herrick now removes. Her clothes are dirty; her face is pale and gaunt. Herrick goes out.*

DANFORTH, *very politely:* Goody Proctor. *She is silent.* I hope you are hearty?

ELIZABETH, *as a warning reminder:* I am yet six month before my time.

DANFORTH: Pray be at your ease, we come not for your life. We—*uncertain how to plead, for he is not accustomed to it.* Mr. Hale, will you speak with the woman?

HALE: Goody Proctor, your husband is marked to hang this morning.

Pause.

ELIZABETH, *quietly:* I have heard it.

HALE: You know, do you not, that I have no connection with the court? *She seems to doubt it.* I come of my own, Goody Proctor. I would save your husband's life, for if he is taken I count myself his murderer. Do you understand me?

ELIZABETH: What do you want of me?

HALE: Goody Proctor, I have gone this three month like our Lord into the wilderness. I have sought a Christian way, for damnation's doubled on a minister who counsels men to lie.

HATHORNE: It is no lie, you cannot speak of lies.

HALE: It is a lie! They are innocent!

DANFORTH: I'll hear no more of that!

HALE, *continuing to Elizabeth:* Let you not mistake your duty as I mistook my own. I came into this village like a bridegroom to his beloved, bearing gifts of high religion; the very crowns of holy law I brought, and what I touched with my bright confidence, it died; and where I turned the eye of my great faith, blood flowed up. Beware, Goody Proctor—cleave to no faith when faith brings blood. It is mistaken law that leads you to sacrifice. Life, woman, life is God's most precious gift; no principle, however glorious, may justify the taking of it. I beg you, woman, prevail upon your husband to confess. Let him give his lie. Quail not before God's judgment in this, for it may well be God damns a liar less than he that throws his life away for pride. Will you plead with him? I cannot think he will listen to another.

ELIZABETH, *quietly:* I think that be the Devil's argument.

HALE, *with a climactic desperation:* Woman, before the laws of God we are as swine! We cannot read His will!

ELIZABETH: I cannot dispute with you, sir; I lack learning for it.

DANFORTH, *going to her:* Goody Proctor, you are not summoned here for disputation. Be there no wifely tenderness within you? He will die with the sunrise. Your husband. Do you understand it? *She only looks at him.* What say you? Will you contend with him? *She is silent.* Are you stone? I tell you true, woman, had I no other proof of your unnatural life, your dry eyes now would be sufficient evidence that you delivered up your soul to Hell! A very ape would weep at such calamity! Have the devil dried up any tear of pity in you? *She is silent.* Take her out. It profit nothing she should speak to him!

ELIZABETH, *quietly:* Let me speak with him, Excellency.

PARRIS, *with hope:* You'll strive with him? *She hesitates.*

DANFORTH: Will you plead for his confession or will you not?

ELIZABETH: I promise nothing. Let me speak with him.

A sound—the sibilance of dragging feet on stone. They turn. A pause. Herrick enters with John Proctor. His wrists are chained. He is another man, bearded, filthy, his eyes misty as though webs had overgrown them. He halts inside the doorway, his eye caught by the sight of Elizabeth. The emotion flowing between them prevents anyone from speaking for an instant. Now Hale, visibly affected, goes to Danforth and speaks quietly.

HALE: Pray, leave them, Excellency.

DANFORTH, *pressing Hale impatiently aside:* Mr. Proctor, you have been notified, have you not? *Proctor is silent, staring at Elizabeth.* I see light in the sky, Mister; let you counsel with your wife, and may God help you turn your back on Hell. *Proctor is silent, staring at Elizabeth.*

HALE, *quietly:* Excellency, let—

Danforth brushes past Hale and walks out. Hale follows. Cheever stands and follows, Hathorne behind. Herrick goes. Parris, from a safe distance, offers:

PARRIS: If you desire a cup of cider, Mr. Proctor, I am sure I—*Proctor turns an icy stare at him, and he breaks off. Parris raises his palms toward Proctor.* God lead you now. *Parris goes out.*

Alone. Proctor walks to her, halts. It is as though they stood in a spinning world. It is beyond sorrow, above it. He reaches out his hand as though toward an embodiment not quite real, and as he touches her, a strange soft sound, half laughter, half amazement, comes from his throat. He pats her hand. She covers his hand with hers. And then, weak, he sits. Then she sits, facing him.

PROCTOR: The child?

ELIZABETH: It grows.

PROCTOR: There is no word of the boys?

ELIZABETH: They're well. Rebecca's Samuel keeps them.

PROCTOR: You have not seen them?

ELIZABETH: I have not. *She catches a weakening in herself and downs it.*
PROCTOR: You are a—marvel, Elizabeth.
ELIZABETH: You—have been tortured?
PROCTOR: Aye. *Pause. She will not let herself be drowned in the sea that threatens her.* They come for my life now.
ELIZABETH: I know it.

Pause.

PROCTOR: None—have yet confessed?
ELIZABETH: There be many confessed.
PROCTOR: Who are they?
ELIZABETH: There be a hundred or more, they say. Goody Ballard is one; Isaiah Goodkind is one. There be many.
PROCTOR: Rebecca?
ELIZABETH: Not Rebecca. She is one foot in Heaven now; naught may hurt her more.
PROCTOR: And Giles?
ELIZABETH: You have not heard of it?
PROCTOR: I hear nothin', where I am kept.
ELIZABETH: Giles is dead.

He looks at her incredulously.

PROCTOR: When were he hanged?
ELIZABETH, *quietly, factually:* He were not hanged. He would not answer aye or nay to his indictment; for if he denied the charge they'd hang him surely, and auction out his property. So he stand mute, and died Christian under the law. And so his sons will have his farm. It is the law, for he could not be condemned a wizard without he answer the indictment, aye or nay.
PROCTOR: Then how does he die?
ELIZABETH, *gently:* They press him, John.
PROCTOR: Press?
ELIZABETH: Great stones they lay upon his chest until he plead aye or nay. *With a tender smile for the old man:* They say he give them but two words. "More weight," he says. And died.
PROCTOR: *numbed—a thread to weave into his agony:* "More weight."
ELIZABETH: Aye. It were a fearsome man, Giles Corey.

Pause.

PROCTOR, *with great force of will, but not quite looking at her:* I have been thinking I would confess to them, Elizabeth. *She shows nothing.* What say you? If I give them that?
ELIZABETH: I cannot judge you, John.

Pause.

PROCTOR, *simply—a pure question:* What would you have me do?
ELIZABETH: As you will, I would have it. *Slight pause:* I want you living, John. That's sure.
PROCTOR, *pauses, then with a flailing of hope:* Giles' wife? Have she confessed?

ELIZABETH: She will not.

Pause.

PROCTOR: It is a pretense. Elizabeth.
ELIZABETH: What is?
PROCTOR: I cannot mount the gibbet like a saint. It is a fraud. I am not that man. *She is silent.* My honesty is broke, Elizabeth; I am no good man. Nothing's spoiled by giving them this lie that were not rotten long before.
ELIZABETH: And yet you've not confessed till now. That speak goodness in you.
PROCTOR: Spite only keeps me silent. It is hard to give a lie to dogs. *Pause, for the first time he turns directly to her.* I would have your forgiveness, Elizabeth.
ELIZABETH: It is not for me to give, John, I am—
PROCTOR: I'd have you see some honesty in it. Let them that never lied die now to keep their souls. It is pretense for me, a vanity that will not blind God nor keep my children out of the wind. *Pause.* What say you?
ELIZABETH, *upon a heaving sob that always threatens:* John, it come to naught that I should forgive you, if you'll not forgive yourself. *Now he turns away a little, in great agony.* It is not my soul, John, it is yours. *He stands, as though in physical pain, slowly rising to his feet with a great immortal longing to find his answer. It is difficult to say, and she is on the verge of tears.* Only be sure of this, for I know it now: Whatever you will do, it is a good man does it. *He turns his doubting, searching gaze upon her.* I have read my heart this three month, John. *Pause.* I have sins of my own to count. It needs a cold wife to prompt lechery.
PROCTOR, *in great pain:* Enough, enough—
ELIZABETH, *now pouring out her heart:* Better you should know me!
PROCTOR: I will not hear it! I know you!
ELIZABETH: You take my sins upon you, John—
PROCTOR, *in agony:* No, I take my own, my own!
ELIZABETH: John, I counted myself so plain, so poorly made, no honest love could come to me! Suspicion kissed you when I did; I never knew how I should say my love. It were a cold house I kept! *In fright, she swerves, as Hathorne enters.*
HATHORNE: What say you, Proctor? The sun is soon up.

Proctor, his chest heaving, stares, turns to Elizabeth. She comes to him as though to plead, her voice quaking.

ELIZABETH: Do what you will. But let none be your judge. There be no higher judge under Heaven than Proctor is! Forgive me, forgive me, John—I never knew such goodness in the world! *She covers her face, weeping.*

Proctor turns from her to Hathorne; he is off the earth, his voice hollow.

PROCTOR: I want my life.
HATHORNE, *electrified, surprised:* You'll confess yourself?
PROCTOR: I will have my life.
HATHORNE, *with a mystical tone:* God be praised! It is a providence! *He rushes out the door, and his voice is heard calling down the corridor:* He will confess! Proctor will confess!
PROCTOR, *with a cry, as he strides to the door:* Why do you cry it? *In great pain he turns back to her.* It is evil, is it not? It is evil.

ELIZABETH, *in terror, weeping:* I cannot judge you, John, I cannot!

PROCTOR: Then who will judge me? *Suddenly clasping his hands:* God in Heaven, what is John Proctor, what is John Proctor? *He moves as an animal, and a fury is riding in him, a tantalized search.* I think it is honest, I think so; I am no saint. *As though she had denied this he calls angrily at her:* Let Rebecca go like a saint; for me it is fraud!

Voices are heard in the hall, speaking together in suppressed excitement.

ELIZABETH: I am not your judge, I cannot be. *As though giving him release:* Do as you will, do as you will!

PROCTOR: Would you give them such a lie? Say it. Would you ever give them this? *She cannot answer.* You would not; if tongs of fire were singeing you you would not! It is evil. Good, then—it is evil, and I do it!

Hathorne enters with Danforth, and, with them, Cheever, Parris, and Hale. It is a businesslike, rapid entrance, as though the ice had been broken.

DANFORTH, *with great relief and gratitude:* Praise to God, man, praise to God; you shall be blessed in Heaven for this. *Cheever has hurried to the bench with pen, ink, and paper. Proctor watches him.* Now then, let us have it. Are you ready, Mr. Cheever?

PROCTOR, *with a cold, cold horror at their efficiency:* Why must it be written?

DANFORTH: Why, for the good instruction of the village, Mister; this we shall post upon the church door! *To Parris, urgently:* Where is the marshal?

PARRIS, *runs to the door and calls down the corridor:* Marshal! Hurry!

DANFORTH: Now, then, Mister, will you speak slowly, and directly to the point, for Mr. Cheever's sake. *He is on record now, and is really dictating to Cheever, who writes.* Mr. Proctor, have you seen the Devil in your life? *Proctor's jaws lock.* Come, man, there is light in the sky; the town waits at the scaffold; I would give out this news. Did you see the Devil?

PROCTOR: I did.

PARRIS: Praise God!

DANFORTH: And when he come to you, what were his demand? *Proctor is silent. Danforth helps.* Did he bid you to do his work upon the earth?

PROCTOR: He did.

DANFORTH: And you bound yourself to his service? *Danforth turns, as Rebecca Nurse enters, with Herrick helping to support her. She is barely able to walk.* Come in, come in, woman!

REBECCA, *brightening as she sees Proctor:* Ah, John! You are well, then, eh?

Proctor turns his face to the wall.

DANFORTH: Courage, man, courage—let her witness your good example that she may come to God herself. Now hear it, Goody Nurse! Say on, Mr. Proctor. Did you bind yourself to the Devil's service?

REBECCA, *astonished:* Why, John!

PROCTOR, *through his teeth, his face turned from Rebecca:* I did.

DANFORTH: Now, woman, you surely see it profit nothin' to keep this conspiracy any further. Will you confess yourself with him?

REBECCA: Oh, John—God send his mercy on you!

DANFORTH: I say, will you confess yourself, Goody Nurse?

REBECCA: Why, it is a lie, it is a lie; how may I damn myself? I cannot, I cannot.

DANFORTH: Mr. Proctor. When the Devil came to you did you see Rebecca Nurse in his company? *Proctor is silent.* Come, man, take courage—did you ever see her with the Devil?

PROCTOR, *almost inaudibly:* No.

Danforth, now sensing trouble, glances at John and goes to the table, and picks up a sheet—the list of condemned.

DANFORTH: Did you ever see her sister, Mary Easty, with the Devil?

PROCTOR: No, I did not.

DANFORTH, *his eyes narrow on Proctor:* Did you ever see Martha Corey with the Devil?

PROCTOR: I did not.

DANFORTH, *realizing, slowly putting the sheet down:* Did you ever see anyone with the Devil?

PROCTOR: I did not.

DANFORTH: Proctor, you mistake me. I am not empowered to trade your life for a lie. You have most certainly seen some person with the Devil. *Proctor is silent.* Mr. Proctor, a score of people have already testified they saw this woman with the Devil.

PROCTOR: Then it is proved. Why must I say it?

DANFORTH: Why "must" you say it! Why, you should rejoice to say it if your soul is truly purged of any love for Hell!

PROCTOR: They think to go like saints. I like not to spoil their names.

DANFORTH, *inquiring, incredulous:* Mr. Proctor, do you think they go like saints?

PROCTOR, *evading:* This woman never thought she done the Devil's work.

DANFORTH: Look you, sir. I think you mistake your duty here. It matters nothing what she thought—she is convicted of the unnatural murder of children, and you for sending your spirit out upon Mary Warren. Your soul alone is the issue here, Mister, and you will prove its whiteness or you cannot live in a Christian country. Will you tell me now what persons conspired with you in the Devil's company? *Proctor is silent.* To your knowledge was Rebecca Nurse ever—

PROCTOR: I speak my own sins; I cannot judge another. *Crying out, with hatred:* I have no tongue for it.

HALE, *quickly to Danforth:* Excellency, it is enough he confess himself. Let him sign it, let him sign it.

PARRIS, *feverishly:* It is a great service, sir. It is a weighty name; it will strike the village that Proctor confess. I beg you, let him sign it. The sun is up, Excellency!

DANFORTH, *considers; then with dissatisfaction:* Come, then, sign your testimony. *To Cheever:* Give it to him. *Cheever goes to Proctor, the confession and a pen in hand. Proctor does not look at it.* Come, man, sign it.

PROCTOR, *after glancing at the confession:* You have all witnessed it—it is enough.

DANFORTH: You will not sign it?

PROCTOR: You have all witnessed it; what more is needed?

DANFORTH: Do you sport with me? You will sign your name or it is no confession, Mister! *His breast heaving with agonized breathing, Proctor now lays the paper down and signs his name.*

PARRIS: Praise be to the Lord!

Proctor has just finished signing when Danforth reaches for the paper. But Proctor snatches it up, and now a wild terror is rising in him, and a boundless anger.

DANFORTH, *perplexed, but politely extending his hand:* If you please, sir.

PROCTOR: No.

DANFORTH, *as though Proctor did not understand:* Mr. Proctor, I must have—

PROCTOR: No, no. I have signed it. You have seen me. It is done! You have no need for this.

PARRIS: Proctor, the village must have proof that—

PROCTOR: Damn the village! I confess to God, and God has seen my name on this! It is enough!

DANFORTH: No, sir, it is—

PROCTOR: You came to save my soul, did you not? Here! I have confessed myself; it is enough!

DANFORTH: You have not con—

PROCTOR: I have confessed myself! Is there no good penitence but it be public? God does not need my name nailed upon the church! God sees my name; God knows how black my sins are! It is enough!

DANFORTH: Mr. Proctor—

PROCTOR: You will not use me! I am no Sarah Good or Tituba, I am John Proctor! You will not use me! It is no part of salvation that you should use me!

DANFORTH: I do not wish to—

PROCTOR: I have three children—how may I teach them to walk like men in the world, an I sold my friends?

DANFORTH: You have not sold your friends—

PROCTOR: Beguile me not! I blacken all of them when this is nailed to the church the very day they hang for silence!

DANFORTH: Mr. Proctor, I must have good and legal proof that you—

PROCTOR: You are the high court, your word is good enough! Tell them I confessed myself; say Proctor broke his knees and wept like a woman; say what you will, but my name cannot—

DANFORTH, *with suspicion:* It is the same, is it not? If I report it or you sign to it?

PROCTOR—*he knows it is insane:* No, it is not the same! What others say and what I sign to is not the same!

DANFORTH: Why? Do you mean to deny this confession when you are free?

PROCTOR: I mean to deny nothing!

DANFORTH: Then explain to me, Mr. Proctor, why you will not let—

PROCTOR, *with a cry of his whole soul:* Because it is my name! Because I cannot have another in my life! Because I lie and sign myself to lies! Because I am not worth the dust on the feet of them that hang! How may I live without my name? I have given you my soul; leave me my name!

DANFORTH, *pointing at the confession in Proctor's hand:* Is that document a lie? If it is a lie I will not accept it! What say you? I will not deal in lies, Mister! *Proctor is motionless.* You will give me your honest confession in my hand, or I cannot keep you from the rope. *Proctor does not reply.* Which way do you go, Mister?

His breast heaving, his eyes staring, Proctor tears the paper and crumples it, and he is weeping in fury, but erect.

DANFORTH: Marshal!

PARRIS, *hysterically, as though the tearing paper were his life:* Proctor, Proctor!

HALE: Man, you will hang! You cannot!

PROCTOR, *his eyes full of tears:* I can. And there's your first marvel, that I can. You have made your magic now, for now I do think I see some shred of goodness in John Proctor. Not enough to weave a banner with, but white enough to keep it from such dogs. *Elizabeth, in a burst of terror, rushes to him and weeps against his hand.* Give them no tear! Tears pleasure them! Show honor now, show a stony heart and sink them with it! *He has lifted her, and kisses her now with great passion.*

REBECCA: Let you fear nothing! Another judgment waits us all!

DANFORTH: Hang them high over the town! Who weeps for these, weeps for corruption! *He sweeps out past them. Herrick starts to lead Rebecca, who almost collapses, but Proctor catches her, and she glances up at him apologetically.*

REBECCA: I've had no breakfast.

HERRICK: Come, man.

Herrick escorts them out, Hathorne and Cheever behind them. Elizabeth stands staring at the empty doorway.

PARRIS, *in deadly fear, to Elizabeth:* Go to him, Goody Proctor! There is yet time!

From outside a drumroll strikes the air. Parris is startled. Elizabeth jerks about toward the window.

PARRIS: Go to him! *He rushes out the door, as though to hold back his fate.* Proctor! Proctor!

Again, a short burst of drums.

HALE: Woman, plead with him! *He starts to rush out the door, and then goes back to her.* Woman! It is pride, it is vanity. *She avoids his eyes, and moves to the window. He drops to his knees.* Be his helper!—What profit him to bleed? Shall the dust praise him? Shall the worms declare his truth? Go to him, take his shame away!

ELIZABETH, *supporting herself against collapse, grips the bars of the window, and with a cry:* He have his goodness now. God forbid I take it from him!

The final drumroll crashes, then heightens violently. Hale weeps in frantic prayer, and the new sun is pouring in upon her face, and the drums rattle like bones in the morning air.

Curtain

Echoes Down the Corridor

Not long after the fever died, Parris was voted from office, walked out on the highroad, and was never heard of again.

The legend has it that Abigail turned up later as a prostitute in Boston.

Twenty years after the last execution, the government awarded compensation to the victims still living, and to the families of the dead. However, it is evident that some people still were unwilling to admit their total guilt, and also that the factionalism was still alive, for some beneficiaries were actually not victims at all, but informers.

Elizabeth Proctor married again, four years after Proctor's death.

In solemn meeting, the congregation rescinded the excommunications—this in March 1712. But they did so upon orders of the government. The jury, however, wrote a statement praying forgiveness of all who had suffered.

Certain farms which had belonged to the victims were left to ruin, and for more than a century no one would buy them or live on them.

To all intents and purposes, the power of theocracy in Massachusetts was broken.

1953

Tennessee Williams 1911–1983

Although invariably ranked second (just behind Eugene O'Neill) among American dramatists, Tennessee Williams is indisputably the most important southern playwright yet to emerge. Born Thomas Lanier Williams, in Columbus, Mississippi, where his much loved maternal grandfather was an Episcopalian minister, by 1919 he had been transplanted with his family to St. Louis, Missouri. The contrast between these two cultures—an agrarian South that looked back nostalgically to a partly mythical past of refinement and gentility, and a forward-looking urban North that valued pragmatism and practicality over civility and beauty—would haunt Williams throughout his life, providing one of the enduring tensions in his plays.

After attending the University of Missouri and Washington University in St. Louis, Williams followed his graduation from the University of Iowa in 1938 with a period of wandering around the country and a succession of odd jobs, including an unsuccessful stint as a scriptwriter in Hollywood. One of his filmscripts, however, became the genesis for his first great theatrical success during the 1944–45 season, *The Glass Menagerie.* In that "memory play," the autobiographical narrator, Tom Wingfield, hopes that by reliving his desertion of his domineering mother and physically and psychically fragile sister, Laura, he will find release from the guilt of the past, thereby allowing his full maturation as a poet. Williams's biographers Donald Spoto and Lyle Leverich remark (as have others before them) on the playwright's lasting and decisive love for his schizophrenic sister Rose, clearly the model for Laura, and at least partially for Blanche in the classic *A Streetcar Named Desire* (1947), Catherine in *Suddenly Last Summer* (1958), the sister Clare in *Out Cry* (1973), and even for the largely factual Zelda Fitzgerald in Williams's final Broadway play, *Clothes for a Summer Hotel* (1980). No other American dramatist has created women characters of such complexity, portrayed with deep understanding and sensitivity.

In his opening narration in *Menagerie,* Tom speaks of "an emissary from a world of reality that we were somehow set apart from" who threatens to upset the fragile escape into illusion that serves repeatedly in Williams's dramas as a refuge for those who are physically, emotionally, or spiritually misbegotten and vulnerable, and yet because of this somehow special. One of Williams's chief characteristics as a dramatist is his compassion for misfits and outsiders, perhaps fed early on by his own sexual orientation (he frankly discusses his homosexuality in the confessional *Memoirs*) and later, in the two decades before his death, by the increasingly negative critical reception of works that become excessively private. If there is a central ethical norm by which his characters must live, it is surely that espoused by the non-judgmental artist Hannah in *Night of the Iguana* (1961): "Nothing human disgusts me unless it's unkind, violent."

Williams was a prolific author, a two-time winner of the Pulitzer Prize for Drama (for *Streetcar* and *Cat on a Hot Tin Roof* [1955]) and a four-time recipient of the New York Drama Critics Circle Award (for the above two plays as well as for *Menagerie* and *Iguana*). Along with two dozen full-length plays and two collections of one-acts, he wrote two novels, four collections of short fiction—among his finest stories, influenced by Hawthorne and Poe, are "Desire and the Black Masseur" and "One Arm"—two volumes of poetry, and several screenplays. Most are charged with a highly expressive symbolism and imbued with his recurrent attitudes and motifs: a somewhat sentimental valuation of the lost and lonely; a worship of sexuality as a means of transcending aloneness; a castigation of repression and excessive guilt; an abhorrence of the underdeveloped heart that refuses to reach out to others; a fear of time, the enemy that robs one of physical beauty and artistic vitality; and an insistence on the need for the courage to endure, to always continue onward—as Williams himself did as a writer.

Thomas P. Adler
Purdue University

PRIMARY WORKS

The Theatre of Tennessee Williams (7 volumes), 1971–1981; *Memoirs,* 1975; *Where I Live: Selected Essays,* 1978; *Collected Stories,* 1986.

Portrait of a Madonna

Respectfully dedicated to the talent and charm of Miss Lillian Gish.[1]

CHARACTERS

MISS LUCRETIA COLLINS
THE PORTER
THE ELEVATOR BOY
THE DOCTOR
THE NURSE
MR. ABRAMS

SCENE: *The living room of a moderate-priced city apartment. The furnishings are old-fashioned and everything is in a state of neglect and disorder. There is a door in the back wall to a bedroom, and on the right to the outside hall.*

[1]Lillian Gish (1896–1993): A demure actress of almost angelic appearance, often the heroine in distress, whose long career spanned virtually the entire history of silent and sound film.

MISS COLLINS: Richard! *(The door bursts open and Miss Collins rushes out, distractedly. She is a middle-aged spinster, very slight and hunched of figure with a desiccated face that is flushed with excitement. Her hair is arranged in curls that would become a young girl and she wears a frilly negligee which might have come from an old hope chest of a period considerably earlier.)* No, no, no, no! I don't care if the whole church hears about it! *(She frenziedly snatches up the phone.)* Manager, I've got to speak to the manager! Hurry, oh, please hurry, there's a *man*—! *(wildly aside as if to an invisible figure)* Lost all respect, absolutely no respect! . . . Mr. Abrams? *(in a tense hushed voice)* I don't want any reporters to hear about this but something awful has been going on upstairs. Yes, this is Miss Collins' apartment on the top floor. I've refrained from making any complaint because of my connections with the church. I used to be assistant to the Sunday School superintendent and I once had the primary class. I helped them put on the Christmas pageant. I made the dress for the Virgin and Mother, made robes for the Wise Men. Yes, and now this has happened, I'm not responsible for it, but night after night after night this man has been coming into my apartment and—indulging his senses! Do you understand? Not once but repeatedly, Mr. Abrams! I don't know whether he comes in the door or the window or up the fire-escape or whether there's some secret entrance they know about at the church, but he's here now, in my bedroom, and I can't force him to leave, I'll have to have some assistance! No, he isn't a thief, Mr. Abrams, he comes of a very fine family in Webb, Mississippi, but this woman has ruined his character, she's destroyed his respect for ladies! Mr. Abrams? Mr. Abrams! Oh, goodness! *(She slams up the receiver and looks distractedly about for a moment; then rushes back into the bedroom.)* Richard! *(The door slams shut. After a few moments an old porter enters in drab gray cover-alls. He looks about with a sorrowfully humorous curiosity, then timidly calls.)*

PORTER: Miss Collins? *(The elevator door slams open in hall and the Elevator Boy, wearing a uniform, comes in.)*

ELEVATOR BOY: Where is she?

PORTER: Gone in 'er bedroom.

ELEVATOR BOY: *(grinning)* She got him in there with her?

PORTER: Sounds like it. *(Miss Collins' voice can be heard faintly protesting with the mysterious intruder.)*

ELEVATOR BOY: What'd Abrams tell yuh to do?

PORTER: Stay here an' keep a watch on 'er till they git here.

ELEVATOR BOY: Jesus.

PORTER: Close 'at door.

ELEVATOR BOY: I gotta leave it open a little so I can hear the buzzer. Ain't this place a holy sight though?

PORTER: Don't look like it's had a good cleaning in fifteen or twenty years. I bet it ain't either. Abrams'll bust a bloodvessel when he takes a lookit them walls.

ELEVATOR BOY: How comes it's in this condition?

PORTER: She wouldn't let no one in.

ELEVATOR BOY: Not even the paper-hangers?

PORTER: Naw. Not even the plumbers. The plaster washed down in the bathroom underneath hers an' she admitted her plumbin' had been stopped up. Mr. Abrams had to let the plumber in with this here pass-key when she went out for a while.

ELEVATOR BOY: Holy Jeez. I wunner if she's got money stashed around here. A lotta freaks do stick away big sums of money in ole mattresses an' things.

PORTER: She ain't. She got a monthly pension check or something she always turned over to Mr. Abrams to dole it out to 'er. She tole him that Southern ladies was never brought up to manage finanshul affairs. Lately the checks quit comin'.

ELEVATOR BOY: Yeah?

PORTER: The pension give out or somethin'. Abrams says he got a contribution from the church to keep 'er on here without 'er knowin' about it. She's proud as a peacock's tail in spite of 'er awful appearance.

ELEVATOR BOY: Lissen to 'er in there!

PORTER: What's she sayin'?

ELEVATOR BOY: Apologizin' to him! For callin' the *police!*

PORTER: She thinks police 're comin'?

MISS COLLINS: *(from bedroom)* Stop it, it's got to stop!

ELEVATOR BOY: Fightin' to protect her honor again! What a commotion, no wunner folks are complainin'!

PORTER: *(lighting his pipe)* This here'll be the last time.

ELEVATOR BOY: She's goin' out, huh?

PORTER: *(blowing out the match)* Tonight.

ELEVATOR BOY: Where'll she go?

PORTER: *(slowly moving to the old gramophone)* She'll go to the state asylum.

ELEVATOR BOY: Holy G!

PORTER: Remember this ole number? *(He puts on a record of "I'm Forever Blowing Bubbles.")*

ELEVATOR BOY: Naw. When did that come out?

PORTER: Before your time, sonny boy. Machine needs oilin'. *(He takes out small oil-can and applies oil about the crank and other parts of gramophone.)*

ELEVATOR BOY: How long is the old girl been here?

PORTER: Abrams says she's been livin' here twenty-five, thirty years, since before he got to be manager even.

ELEVATOR BOY: Livin' alone all that time?

PORTER: She had an old mother died of an operation about fifteen years ago. Since then she ain't gone out of the place excep' on Sundays to church or Friday nights to some kind of religious meeting.

ELEVATOR BOY: Got an awful lot of ol' magazines piled aroun' here.

PORTER: She used to collect 'em. She'd go out in back and fish 'em out of the incinerator.

ELEVATOR BOY: What'n hell for?

PORTER: Mr. Abrams says she used to cut out the Campbell soup kids. Them red-tomato-headed kewpie dolls that go with the soup advertisements. You seen 'em, ain'tcha?

ELEVATOR BOY: Uh-huh.

PORTER: She made a collection of 'em. Filled a big lot of scrapbooks with them paper kiddies an' took 'em down to the Children's Hospitals on Xmas Eve an' Easter Sunday, exactly twicet a year. Sounds better, don't it? *(referring to gramophone, which resumes its faint, wheedling music)* Eliminated some a that crankin' noise . . .

ELEVATOR BOY: I didn't know that she'd been nuts *that* long.

PORTER: Who's nuts an' who ain't? If you ask me the world is populated with people that's just as peculiar as she is.

ELEVATOR BOY: Hell. She don't have brain *one*.

PORTER: There's important people in Europe got less'n she's got. Tonight they're takin' her off'n' lockin' her up. They'd do a lot better to leave 'er go an' lock up some a them maniacs over there. She's harmless; they ain't. They kill millions of people an' go scot free!

ELEVATOR BOY: An ole woman like her is disgusting, though, imaginin' somebody's raped her.

PORTER: Pitiful, not disgusting. Watch out for them cigarette ashes.

ELEVATOR BOY: What's uh diff'rence? So much dust you can't see it. All a this here goes out in the morning, don't it?

PORTER: Uh-huh.

ELEVATOR BOY: I think I'll take a couple a those ole records as curiosities for my girl friend. She's got a portable in 'er bedroom, she says it's better with music!

PORTER: Leave 'em alone. She's still got 'er property rights.

ELEVATOR BOY: Aw, she's got all she wants with them dreamlovers of hers!

PORTER: Hush up! *(He makes a warning gesture as Miss Collins enters from bedroom. Her appearance is that of a ravaged woman. She leans exhaustedly in the doorway, hands clasped over her flat, virginal bosom.)*

MISS COLLINS: *(breathlessly)* Oh, Richard—Richard . . .

PORTER: *(coughing)* Miss—Collins.

ELEVATOR BOY: Hello, Miss Collins.

MISS COLLINS: *(just noticing the men)* Goodness! You've arrived already! Mother didn't tell me you were here! *(Self-consciously she touches her ridiculous corkscrew curls with the faded pink ribbon tied through them. Her manner becomes that of a slightly coquettish but prim little Southern belle.)* I must ask you gentlemen to excuse the terrible disorder.

PORTER: That's all right, Miss Collins.

MISS COLLINS: It's the maid's day off. Your No'thern girls receive such excellent domestic training, but in the South it was never considered essential for a girl to have anything but prettiness and charm! *(She laughs girlishly.)* Please do sit down. Is it too close? Would you like a window open?

PORTER: No, Miss Collins.

MISS COLLINS: *(advancing with delicate grace to the sofa)* Mother will bring in something cool after while. . . . Oh, my! *(She touches her forehead.)*

PORTER: *(kindly)* Is anything wrong, Miss Collins?

MISS COLLINS: Oh, no, no, thank you, nothing! My head is a little bit heavy. I'm always a little bit—malarial—this time of year! *(She sways dizzily as she starts to sink down on the sofa.)*

PORTER: *(helping her)* Careful there, Miss Collins.

MISS COLLINS: *(vaguely)* Yes, it is, I hadn't noticed before. *(She peers at them nearsightedly with a hesitant smile.)* You gentlemen have come from the church?

PORTER: No, ma'am. I'm Nick, the porter, Miss Collins, and this boy here is Frank that runs the elevator.

MISS COLLINS: *(stiffening a little)* Oh? . . . I don't understand.

PORTER: *(gently)* Mr. Abrams just asked me to drop in here an' see if you was getting along all right.

MISS COLLINS: Oh! Then he must have informed you of what's been going on in here!
PORTER: He mentioned some kind of—disturbance.
MISS COLLINS: Yes! Isn't it outrageous? But it mustn't go any further, you understand. I mean you mustn't repeat it to other people.
PORTER: No, I wouldn't say nothing.
MISS COLLINS: Not a word of it, please!
ELEVATOR BOY: Is the man still here, Miss Collins?
MISS COLLINS: Oh, no. No, he's gone now.
ELEVATOR BOY: How did he go, out the bedroom window, Miss Collins?
MISS COLLINS: *(vaguely)* Yes. . . .
ELEVATOR BOY: I seen a guy that could do that once. He crawled straight up the side of the building. They called him The Human Fly! Gosh, that's a wonderful publicity angle, Miss Collins—"Beautiful Young Society Lady Raped by The Human Fly!"
PORTER: *(nudging him sharply)* Git back in your cracker box!
MISS COLLINS: Publicity? No! It would be so humiliating! Mr. Abrams surely hasn't reported it to the papers!
PORTER: No, ma'am. Don't listen to this smarty pants.
MISS COLLINS: *(touching her curls)* Will pictures be taken, you think? There's one of him on the mantel.
ELEVATOR BOY: *(going to be mantel)* This one here, Miss Collins?
MISS COLLINS: Yes. Of the Sunday School faculty picnic. I had the little kindergardeners that year and he had the older boys. We rode in the cab of a railroad locomotive from Webb to Crystal Springs. *(She covers her ears with a girlish grimace and toss of her curls.)* Oh, how the steam-whistle blew! Blew! *(giggling)* *Blewwwww!* It frightened me so, he put his arm round my shoulders! But she was there, too, though she had no business being. She grabbed his hat and stuck it on the back of her head and they—they *rassled* for it, they actually *rassled* together! Everyone said it was *shameless!* Don't you think that it was?
PORTER: Yes, Miss Collins.
MISS COLLINS: That's the picture, the one in the silver frame up there on the mantel. We cooled the watermelon in the springs and afterwards played games. She hid somewhere and he took ages to find her. It got to be dark and he hadn't found her yet and everyone whispered and giggled about it and finally they came back together—her hangin' on to his arm like a common little strumpet—and Daisy Belle Huston shrieked out, "Look, everybody, the seat of Evelyn's skirt!" It was—covered with—grass-stains! Did you ever hear of anything as outrageous? It didn't faze her, though, she laughed like it was something very, very amusing! Rather *triumphant* she was!
ELEVATOR BOY: Which one is him, Miss Collins?
MISS COLLINS: The tall one in the blue shirt holding onto one of my curls. He loved to play with them.
ELEVATOR BOY: Quite a Romeo—1910 model, huh?
MISS COLLINS: *(vaguely)* Do you? It's nothing, really, but I like the lace on the collar. I said to Mother, "Even if I don't wear it, Mother, it will be *so* nice for my hope-chest!"
ELEVATOR BOY: How was he dressed tonight when he climbed into your balcony, Miss Collins?

MISS COLLINS: Pardon?

ELEVATOR BOY: Did he still wear that nifty little stick-candy-striped blue shirt with the celluloid collar?

MISS COLLINS: He hasn't changed.

ELEVATOR BOY: Oughta be easy to pick him up in that. What color pants did he wear?

MISS COLLINS: *(vaguely)* I don't remember.

ELEVATOR BOY: Maybe he didn't wear any. Shimmied out of 'em on the way up the wall! You could get him on grounds of indecent exposure, Miss Collins!

PORTER: *(grasping his arm)* Cut that or git back in your cage! Understand?

ELEVATOR BOY: *(snickering)* Take it easy. She don't hear a thing.

PORTER: Well, you keep a decent tongue or get to hell out. Miss Collins here is a lady. You understand that?

ELEVATOR BOY: Okay. She's Shoiley Temple.

PORTER: She's a *lady!*

ELEVATOR BOY: Yeah! *(He returns to the gramophone and looks through the records.)*

MISS COLLINS: I really shouldn't have created this disturbance. When the officers come I'll have to explain that to them. But you can understand my feelings, can't you?

PORTER: Sure, Miss Collins.

MISS COLLINS: When men take advantage of common white-trash women who smoke in public there is probably some excuse for it, but when it occurs to a lady who is single and always com-*pletely* above reproach in her moral behavior, there's really nothing to do but call for police protection! Unless of course the girl is fortunate enough to have a father and brothers who can take care of the matter privately without any scandal.

PORTER: Sure. That's right, Miss Collins.

MISS COLLINS: Of course it's bound to cause a great deal of very disagreeable talk. Especially 'round the *church!* Are you gentlemen Episcopalian?

PORTER: No, ma'am. Catholic, Miss Collins.

MISS COLLINS: Oh. Well, I suppose you know in England we're known as the English Catholic church. We have direct Apostolic succession through St. Paul who christened the Early Angles—which is what the original English people were called—and established the English branch of the Catholic church over there. So when you hear ignorant people claim that our church was founded by—by Henry the *Eighth*—that horrible, *lech*erous old man who had so many wives—as many as *Blue*-beard they say!—you can see how ridiculous it *is* and how thoroughly ob*nox*ious to anybody who really *knows* and under*stands* Church *His*tory!

PORTER: *(comfortingly)* Sure, Miss Collins. Everybody knows that.

MISS COLLINS: I wish they *did,* but they need to be in*struc*ted! Before he died, my father was Rector at the Church of St. Michael and St. George at Glorious Hill, Mississippi.[2]. . . I've literally grown up right in the very *shad*ow of the Episcopal church. At Pass Christian and Natchez, Biloxi, Gulfport, Port Gibson, Columbus

[2]A mythical town, also the site of Williams's *Summer and Smoke* (1947). There is an Episcopal Church of St. Michael and St. George near the campus of Washington University in St. Louis where Williams was enrolled from 1936–1937. A Church of the Holy Communion is also found in St. Louis.

and Glorious Hill! *(with gentle, bewildered sadness)* But you know I sometimes suspect that there has been some kind of spiritual schism in the modern church. These northern dioceses have completely departed from the good old church traditions. For instance our Rector at the Church of the Holy Communion has never darkened my door. It's a fashionable church and he's terribly busy, but even so you'd think he might have time to make a stranger in the congregation feel at home. But he doesn't though! Nobody seems to have the time any more. . . . *(She grows more excited as her mind sinks back into illusion.)* I ought not to mention this, but do you know they actually take a malicious de-*light* over there at the Holy Communion—where I've recently transferred my letter[3]—in what's been going on here at night in this apartment? *Yes!! (She laughs wildly and throws up her hands.)* They take a malicious de*LIGHT* in it!! *(She catches her breath and gropes vaguely about her wrapper.)*

PORTER: You lookin' for somethin', Miss Collins?

MISS COLLINS: My—handkerchief . . . *(She is blinking her eyes against tears.)*

PORTER: *(removing a rag from his pocket)* Here. Use this, Miss Collins. It's just a rag but it's clean, except along that edge where I wiped off the phonograph handle.

MISS COLLINS: Thanks. You gentlemen are very kind. Mother will bring in something cool after while. . . .

ELEVATOR BOY: *(placing a record on machine)* This one is got some kind of foreign title. *(The record begins to play Tschaikowsky's "None But the Lonely Heart.")*

MISS COLLINS: *(stuffing the rag daintily in her bosom)* Excuse me, please. Is the weather nice outside?

PORTER: *(huskily)* Yes, it's nice, Miss Collins.

MISS COLLINS: *(dreamily)* So wa'm for this time of year. I wore my little astrakhan cape to service but had to *carry* it *home,* as the weight of it actually seemed *oppres*sive to me. *(Her eyes fall shut.)* The sidewalks seem so dreadfully long in summer. . . .

ELEVATOR BOY: This ain't summer, Miss Collins.

MISS COLLINS: *(dreamily)* I used to think I'd never get to the end of that last block. And that's the block where all the trees went down in the big tornado. The walk is simply *glit*-tering with sunlight. *(pressing her eyelids)* Impossible to shade your face and I *do* perspire so freely! *(She touches her forehead daintily with the rag.)* Not a branch, not a leaf to give you a little protection! You simply *have* to en-*dure* it. Turn your hideous red face away from all the front-porches and walk as fast as you decently *can* till you get *by* them! Oh, dear, dear Savior, sometimes you're not so lucky and you *meet* people and have to *smile!* You can't *avoid* them unless you cut *across* and that's so *ob*-vious, you know. . . . People would say you're pe*cul*iar. . . . His house is right in the middle of that awful leafless block, *their* house, his and *hers,* and they have an automobile and always get home early and sit on the porch and *watch* me walking by—Oh, Father in Heaven—with a ma*li*cious de*light! (She averts her face in remembered torture.)* She has such *penetrating* eyes, they look straight through me. She sees that terrible choking thing in my throat and the pain

[3]Letter from the Rector of one's former church necessary for formal acceptance into full membership in a new parish community.

I have in *here—(touching her chest)*—and she points it out and laughs and whispers to him, "There she goes with her shiny big red nose, the poor old maid—that *loves* you!" *(She chokes and hides her face in the rag.)*

PORTER: Maybe you better forget all that, Miss Collins.

MISS COLLINS: Never, never forget it! Never, never! I left my parasol once—the one with long white fringe that belonged to Mother—I left it behind in the cloakroom at the church so I didn't have anything to cover my face with when I walked by, and I couldn't turn back either, with all those people behind me—giggling back of me, poking fun at my clothes! Oh, dear, dear! I had to walk straight forward—past the last elm tree and into that *merciless* sunlight. Oh! It beat down on me, *scorching* me! *Whips!* . . . Oh, Jesus! . . . Over my face and my body! . . . I tried to walk on fast but was dizzy and they kept closer behind me—! I stumbled, I nearly fell, and all of them burst out laughing! My face turned so *horribly* red, it got so red and wet, I knew how ugly it was in all that merciless glare—not a single shadow to hide in! And then—*(Her face contorts with fear.)*—their automobile drove up in front of their house, right where I had to pass by it, and *she* stepped out, in white, so fresh and easy, her stomach round with a baby, the first of the *six.* Oh, God! . . . And he stood smiling behind her, white and easy and cool, and they stood there waiting for me. *Waiting!* I had to keep on. What else could I do? I couldn't turn *back,* could I? *No!* I said dear *God,* strike me *dead!* He didn't, though. I put my head way down like I couldn't see them! You know what she did? She stretched out her hand to *stop* me! And *he*—he stepped up straight in front of me, *smiling,* blocking the walk with his terrible big white body! *"Lucretia,"* he said, "Lucretia *Collins!*" I—I tried to speak but I couldn't, the breath went out of my body! I covered my face and—ran! . . . Ran! . . . *Ran! (beating the arm of the sofa)* Till I reached the end of the block—and the elm trees—*started* again. . . . Oh, Merciful Christ in Heaven, how *kind* they were! *(She leans back exhaustedly, her hand relaxed on sofa. She pauses and the music ends.)* I said to Mother, "Mother, we've got to leave town!" We *did* after that. And now after all these years he's finally remembered and come *back!* Moved away from that house and the woman and come *here*—I saw him in the back of the church one day. I wasn't sure—but it *was.* The night after that was the night that he first broke in—and indulged his senses with me. . . . He doesn't realize that I've changed, that I can't feel again the way that I used to feel, now that he's got six children by that Cincinnati girl—three in high-school already! Six! Think of that? Six children! I don't know what he'll say when he knows another one's coming! He'll probably blame *me* for it because a man always *does!* In spite of the fact that he *forced* me!

ELEVATOR BOY: *(grinning)* Did you say—a *baby,* Miss Collins?

MISS COLLINS: *(lowering her eyes but speaking with tenderness and pride)* Yes—I'm expecting a *child.*

ELEVATOR BOY: *Jeez! (He claps his hand over his mouth and turns away quickly.)*

MISS COLLINS: Even if it's not legitimate, I think it has a perfect right to its father's name—don't you?

PORTER: Yes. Sure, Miss Collins.

MISS COLLINS: A child is innocent and pure. No matter how it's conceived. And it must *not* be made to suffer! So I intend to dispose of the little property Cousin Ethel left me and give the child a private education where it won't come under the evil influence of the Christian church! I want to make sure that it doesn't grow up in the shadow of the cross and then have to walk along blocks that scorch you with terrible sunlight! *(The elevator buzzer sounds from the hall.)*

PORTER: Frank! Somebody wants to come up. *(The Elevator Boy goes out. The elevator door bangs shut. The Porter clears his throat.)* Yes, it'd be better—to go off some place else.

MISS COLLINS: If only I had the courage—but I don't. I've grown so used to it here, and people outside—it's always so *hard* to *face* them!

PORTER: Maybe you won't—have to face nobody, Miss Collins. *(The elevator door clangs open.)*

MISS COLLINS: *(rising fearfully)* Is someone coming—here?

PORTER: You just take it easy, Miss Collins.

MISS COLLINS: If that's the officers coming for Richard, tell them to go away. I've decided not to prosecute Mr. Martin. *(Mr. Abrams enters with the Doctor and the Nurse. The Elevator Boy gawks from the doorway. The Doctor is the weary, professional type, the Nurse hard and efficient. Mr. Abrams is a small, kindly person, sincerely troubled by the situation.)*

MISS COLLINS: *(shrinking back, her voice faltering)* I've decided not to—prosecute Mr. Martin.

DOCTOR: Miss Collins?

MR. ABRAMS: *(with attempted heartiness)* Yes, this is the lady you wanted to meet, Dr. White.

DOCTOR: Hmmm. *(briskly to the Nurse)* Go in her bedroom and get a few things together.

NURSE: Yes, sir. *(She goes quickly across to the bedroom.)*

MISS COLLINS: *(fearfully shrinking)* Things?

DOCTOR: Yes, Miss Tyler will help you pack up an overnight bag. *(smiling mechanically)* A strange place always seems more homelike the first few days when we have a few of our little personal articles around us.

MISS COLLINS: A strange—place?

DOCTOR: *(carelessly, making a memorandum)* Don't be disturbed, Miss Collins.

MISS COLLINS: I know! *(excitedly)* You've come from the Holy Communion to place me under arrest! On moral charges!

MR. ABRAMS: Oh, no, Miss Collins, you got the wrong idea. This is a doctor who—

DOCTOR: *(impatiently)* Now, now, you're just going away for a while till things get straightened out. *(He glances at his watch.)* Two-twenty-five! Miss Tyler?

NURSE: Coming!

MISS COLLINS: *(with slow and sad comprehension)* Oh. . . . I'm going away. . . .

MR. ABRAMS: She was always a lady, Doctor, such a perfect lady.

DOCTOR: Yes. No doubt.

MR. ABRAMS: It seems too bad!

MISS COLLINS: Let me—write him a note. A pencil? Please?

MR. ABRAMS: Here, Miss Collins. *(She takes the pencil and crouches over the table. The Nurse comes out with a hard, forced smile, carrying a suitcase.)*

DOCTOR: Ready, Miss Tyler?

NURSE: All ready, Dr. White. *(She goes up to Miss Collins.)* Come along, dear, we can tend to that later!

MR. ABRAMS: *(sharply)* Let her finish the note!

MISS COLLINS: *(straightening with a frightened smile)* It's—finished.

NURSE: All right, dear, come along. *(She propels her firmly toward the door.)*

MISS COLLINS: *(turning suddenly back)* Oh, Mr. Abrams!

MR. ABRAMS: Yes, Miss Collins?

MISS COLLINS: If he should come again—and find me gone—I'd rather you didn't tell him—about the baby. . . . I think its better for *me* to tell him *that. (gently smiling)* You know how men *are,* don't you?

MR. ABRAMS: Yes, Miss Collins.

PORTER: Goodbye, Miss Collins. *(The Nurse pulls firmly at her arm. She smiles over her shoulder with a slight apologetic gesture.)*

MISS COLLINS: Mother will bring in—something cool—after while . . . *(She disappears down the hall with the Nurse. The elevator door clangs shut with the metallic sound of a locked cage. The wires hum.)*

MR. ABRAMS: She wrote him a note.

PORTER: What did she write, Mr. Abrams?

MR. ABRAMS: "Dear—Richard. I'm going away for a while. But don't worry, I'll be back. I have a secret to tell you. Love—Lucretia." *(He coughs.)* We got to clear out this stuff an' pile it down in the basement till I find out where it goes.

PORTER: *(dully)* Tonight, Mr. Abrams?

MR. ABRAMS: *(roughly to hide his feeling)* No, no, not tonight, you old fool. Enough has happened tonight! *(then gently)* We can do it tomorrow. Turn out that bedroom light—and close the window. *(Music playing softly becomes audible as the men go out slowly, closing the door, and the light fades out.)*

Curtain

1945

Eudora Welty b. 1909

Like that of Jane Austen, Eudora Welty's canvas is small. She has had, as she wrote in *One Writer's Beginnings* (1983), a "sheltered life" but one full of emotional daring. For nearly a century, Welty has lived in the small town of Jackson, Mississippi, where she was born in 1909. Her artistic sensibility is the product of a childhood framed by family and rooted in story. And this sensibility accounts for one of her great strengths as a writer: her ability to infuse the tradition of southern manners with the complex emotional truths of the twentieth-century South out of which she writes.

Welty's formal education included attendance at Mississippi State College for Women, the University of Wisconsin, and the Columbia University School of Business; her first job, publicity assistant for the Works Progress Administration, helped to sharpen her eye and ear for the tasks of a fiction writer. Welty's first short story appeared in 1936 and, with the help of Robert Penn Warren and Cleanth Brooks, she published six other stories over the next three years. *A Curtain of Green,* Welty's first collection of stories, was published in 1941 with an excellent preface by Katherine Anne Porter. The forties also saw publication of Welty's first short novel

(*The Robber Bridegroom,* 1942), a second collection of stories (*The Wide Net,* 1943), a second novel (*Delta Wedding,* 1946), and a collection of interrelated stories (*The Golden Apples,* 1949). *The Ponder Heart,* a short novel, appeared in 1954, and a collection entitled *The Bride of the Innesfallen* was published the following year. In 1970, Welty's longest novel, *Losing Battles,* was published, and her WPA-inspired photographs, *One Time, One Place,* appeared in 1971. *The Optimist's Daughter,* a novel awarded the Pulitzer Prize in 1972, was followed by a collection of essays, *The Eye of the Story* (1978), *The Collected Stories of Eudora Welty* (1980), and *One Writer's Beginnings* (1983). Most recently, Welty co-edited *The Norton Book of Friendship* (1991). A collection of her book reviews (*A Writer's Eye*) appeared in 1994. Four years later, Library of America published two collections of Welty's work (*Eudora Welty: Complete Novels* and *Eudora Welty: Stories, Essays and Memoir*), edited by Richard Ford and Michael Kreyling. She was awarded the Medal of Arts in 1987.

Although critics disagree about how Welty's fiction should be read, they have consistently recognized its importance. New Critics Robert Penn Warren and Cleanth Brooks included a sampling of Welty's short stories in their classic text *Understanding Fiction* (1943). Since then, Welty has been claimed not only by critics of southern gothic literature, folklore, and mythology but also by modern and feminist critics. Her stories are a staple of American literature anthologies, and she continues to find an audience in colleges and universities across the country.

Welty has said that she writes out of an impulse "to praise," and her fiction is often a celebration of life in all its mystery and complexity. Her characters are imbued with a sense of place (an emotional and associational texture described by Welty in her essay "Place in Fiction") and are easily recognizable by their distinctive narrative voices. An admirer of William Faulkner's work, Welty has a similar interest in "the problems of the human heart in conflict with itself." In her work these problems are most often centered in a conflict between the desire to belong (whether to family or lover) and to preserve a separate identity. The root of this conflict is love, and Welty's stories, however grotesque or comic, transcend regionalism in their universal themes.

Inasmuch as she grew up listening to and reading fairy tale, legend, and myth, Welty's narrative technique owes as much to an oral as to a written tradition. Welty's ability to hear the rhythms and patterns of speech is apparent in her narrative voices, which range from the hill country to the Mississippi Delta and the city. Her images are often grounded in the natural world, and her style is lyric and evocative.

Jennifer L. Randisi

PRIMARY WORKS

A Curtain of Green, 1941; *The Robber Bridegroom,* 1942; *The Wide Net,* 1943; *Delta Wedding,* 1946; *The Golden Apples,* 1949; *The Ponder Heart,* 1954; *The Bride of Innesfallen,* 1955; *Losing Battles,* 1970; *One Time, One Place,* 1971; *The Optimist's Daughter,* 1972; *The Eye of the Story,* 1978; *The Collected Stories of Eudora Welty,* 1980; *One Writer's Beginnings,* 1983; *A Writer's Eye: Collected Book Reviews,* 1994; *The Collected Stories,* 1998; *Country Churchyards,* 2000.

The Wide Net

This story is for John Fraiser Robinson

William Wallace Jamieson's wife Hazel was going to have a baby. But this was October, and it was six months away, and she acted exactly as though it would be tomorrow. When he came in the room she would not speak to him, but would look as straight at nothing as she could, with her eyes glowing. If he only touched her she stuck out her tongue or ran around the table. So one night he went out with two of the boys down the road and stayed out all night. But that was the worst thing yet, because when he came home in the early morning Hazel had vanished. He went through the house not believing his eyes, balancing with both hands out, his yellow cowlick rising on end, and then he turned the kitchen inside out looking for her, but it did no good. Then when he got back to the front room he saw she had left him a little letter, in an envelope. That was doing something behind someone's back. He took out the letter, pushed it open, held it out at a distance from his eyes. . . . After one look he was scared to read the exact words, and he crushed the whole thing in his hand instantly, but what it had said was that she would not put up with him after that and was going to the river to drown herself.

"Drown herself . . . But she's in mortal fear of the water!"

He ran out front, his face red like the red plums hanging on the bushes there, and down in the road he gave a loud shout for Virgil Thomas, who was just going in his own house, to come out again. He could just see the edge of Virgil, he had almost got in, he had one foot inside the door.

They met half-way between the farms, under the shade tree.

"Haven't you had enough of the night?" asked Virgil. There they were, their pants all covered with dust and dew, and they had had to carry the third man home flat between them.

"I've lost Hazel, she's vanished, she went to drown herself."

"Why, that ain't like Hazel," said Virgil.

William Wallace reached out and shook him. "You heard me. Don't you know we have to drag the river?"

"Right this minute?"

"You ain't got nothing to do till spring."

"Let me go set foot inside the house and speak to my mother and tell her a story, and I'll come back."

"This will take the wide net," said William Wallace. His eyebrows gathered, and he was talking to himself.

"How come Hazel to go and do that way?" asked Virgil as they started out.

William Wallace said, "I reckon she got lonesome."

"That don't argue—drown herself for getting lonesome. My mother gets lonesome."

"Well," said William Wallace. "It argues for Hazel."

"How long is it now since you and her was married?"

"Why, it's been a year."

"It don't seem that long to me. A year!"

"It was this time last year. It seems longer," said William Wallace, breaking a stick off a tree in surprise. They walked along, kicking at the flowers on the road's edge. "I remember the day I seen her first, and that seems a long time ago. She was coming along the road holding a little frying-size chicken from her grandma, under her arm, and she had it real quiet. I spoke to her with nice manners. We knowed each other's names, being bound to, just didn't know each other to speak to. I says, 'Where are you taking the fryer?' and she says, 'Mind your manners,' and I kept on till after while she says, 'If you want to walk me home, take littler steps.' So I didn't lose time. It was just four miles across the field and full of blackberries, and from the top of the hill there was Dover below, looking sizeable-like and clean, spread out between the two churches like that. When we got down, I says to her, 'What kind of water's in this well?' and she says, 'The best water in the world.' So I drew a bucket and took out a dipper and she drank and I drank. I didn't think it was that remarkable, but I didn't tell her."

"What happened that night?" asked Virgil.

"We ate the chicken," said William Wallace, "and it was tender. Of course that wasn't all they had. The night I was trying their table out, it sure had good things to eat from one end to the other. Her mama and papa sat at the head and foot and we was face to face with each other across it, with I remember a pat of butter between. They had real sweet butter, with a tree drawed down it, elegant-like. Her mama eats like a man. I had brought her a whole hatful of berries and she didn't even pass them to her husband. Hazel, she would leap up and take a pitcher of new milk and fill up the glasses. I had heard how they couldn't have a singing at the church without a fight over her."

"Oh, she's a pretty girl, all right," said Virgil. "It's a pity for the ones like her to grow old, and get like their mothers."

"Another thing will be that her mother will get wind of this and come after me," said William Wallace.

"Her mother will eat you alive," said Virgil.

"She's just been watching her chance," said William Wallace. "Why did I think I could stay out all night."

"Just something come over you."

"First it was just a carnival at Carthage, and I had to let them guess my weight . . . and after that. . . ."

"It was nice to be sitting on your neck in a ditch singing," prompted Virgil, "in the moonlight. And playing on the harmonica like you can play."

"Even if Hazel did sit home knowing I was drunk, that wouldn't kill her," said William Wallace. "What she knows ain't ever killed her yet. . . . She's smart, too, for a girl," he said.

"She's a lot smarter than her cousins in Beulah," said Virgil, "and especially Edna Earle, that never did get to be what you'd call a heavy thinker. Edna Earle could sit and ponder all day on how the little tail of the 'C' got through the 'L' in a Coca-Cola sign."

"Hazel *is* smart," said William Wallace. They walked on. "You ought to see her pantry shelf, it looks like a hundred jars when you open the door. I don't see how she could turn around and jump in the river."

"It's a woman's trick."

"I always behaved before. Till the one night—last night."

"Yes, but the one night," said Virgil. "And she was waiting to take advantage."

"She jumped in the river because she was scared to death of the water and that was to make it worse," he said. "She remembered how I used to have to pick her up and carry her over the oak-log bridge, how she'd shut her eyes and make a dead-weight and hold me round the neck, just for a little creek. I don't see how she brought herself to jump."

"Jumped backwards," said Virgil. "Didn't look."

When they turned off, it was still early in the pink and green fields. The fumes of morning, sweet and bitter, sprang up where they walked. The insects ticked softly, their strength in reserve; butterflies chopped the air, going to the east, and the birds flew carelessly and sang by fits and starts, not the way they did in the evening in sustained and drowsy songs.

"It's a pretty *day* for sure," said William Wallace. "It's a pretty *day* for it."

"I don't see a sign of her ever going along here," said Virgil.

"Well," said William Wallace. "She wouldn't have dropped anything. I never saw a girl to leave less signs of where she's been."

"Not even a plum seed," said Virgil, kicking the grass.

In the grove it was so quiet that once William Wallace gave a jump, as if he could almost hear a sound of himself wondering where she had gone. A descent of energy came down on him in the thick of the woods and he ran at a rabbit and caught it in his hands.

"Rabbit . . . Rabbit . . ." He acted as if he wanted to take it off to himself and hold it up and talk to it. He laid a palm against its pushing heart. "Now . . . There now . . ."

"Let her go, William Wallace, let her go." Virgil, chewing on an elderberry whistle he had just made, stood at his shoulder: "What do you want with a live rabbit?"

William Wallace squatted down and set the rabbit on the ground but held it under his hand. It was a little old, brown rabbit. It did not try to move. "See there?"

"Let her go."

"She can go if she wants to, but she don't want to."

Gently he lifted his hand. The round eye was shining at him sideways in the green gloom.

"Anybody can freeze a *rabbit,* that wants to," said Virgil, Suddenly he gave a far-reaching blast on the whistle, and the rabbit went in a streak. "Was you out catching cotton-tails, or was you out catching your wife?" he said, taking the turn to the open fields. "I come along to keep you on the track."

"Who'll we get now?" They stood on top of a hill and William Wallace looked critically over the countryside. "Any of the Malones?"

"I was always scared of the Malones," said Virgil. "Too many *of* them."

"This is my day with the net, and they would have to watch out," said William Wallace. "I reckon some Malones, and the Doyles, will be enough. The six Doyles and their dogs, and you and me, and two little nigger boys is enough, with just a few Malones."

"That ought to be enough," said Virgil, "no matter what."

"I'll bring the Malones, and you bring the Doyles," said William Wallace, and they separated at the spring.

When William Wallace came back, with a string of Malones just showing behind him on the hilltop, he found Virgil with the two little Rippen boys waiting behind him, solemn little towheads. As soon as he walked up, Grady, the one in front, lifted his hand to signal silence and caution to his brother Brucie, who began panting merrily and untrustworthily behind him.

Brucie bent readily under William Wallace's hand-pat, and gave him a dreamy look out of the tops of his round eyes, which were pure green-and-white like clover tops. William Wallace gave him a nickel. Grady hung his head; his white hair lay in a little tail in the nape of his neck.

"Let's let them come," said Virgil.

"Well, they can come then, but if we keep letting everybody come it is going to be too many," said William Wallace.

"They'll appreciate it, those little old boys," said Virgil. Brucie held up at arm's length a long red thread with a bent pin tied on the end; and a look of helpless and intense interest gathered Grady's face like a drawstring—his eyes, one bright with a sty, shone pleadingly under his white bangs, and he snapped his jaw and tried to speak. . . . "Their papa was drowned in the Pearl River," said Virgil.

There was a shout from the gully.

"Here come all the Malones," cried William Wallace. "I asked four of them would they come, but the rest of the family invited themselves."

"Did you ever see a time when they didn't," said Virgil. "And yonder from the other direction comes the Doyles, still with biscuit crumbs on their cheeks, I bet, now it's nothing to do but eat as their mother said."

"If two little niggers would come along now, or one big nigger," said William Wallace. And the words were hardly out of his mouth when two little Negro boys came along, going somewhere, one behind the other, stepping high and gay in their overalls, as though they waded in honeydew to the waist.

"Come here, boys. What's your names?"

"Sam and Robbie Bell."

"Come along with us, we're going to drag the river."

"You hear that, Robbie Bell?" said Sam.

They smiled.

The Doyles came noiselessly, their dogs made all the fuss. The Malones, eight giants with great long black eyelashes, were already stamping the ground and pawing each other, ready to go. Everybody went up together to see Doc.

Old Doc owned the wide net. He had a house on top of the hill and he sat and looked out from a rocker on the front porch.

"Climb the hill and come in!" he began to intone across the valley. "Harvest's over . . . slipped up on everybody . . . corn's all in, hogs gettin' ripe . . . hay cut . . . molasses made around here. . . . Big explosion's over, supervisors elected, some pleased, some not. . . . We're hearing talk of war!"

When they got closer, he was saying, "Many's been saved at revival, twenty-two last Sunday including a Doyle, ought to counted two. Hope they'll be a blessing to Dover community besides a shining star in Heaven. Now what?" he asked, for they had arrived and stood gathered in front of the steps.

"If nobody is using your wide net, could we use it?" asked William Wallace.

"You just used it a month ago," said Doc. "It ain't your turn."

Virgil jogged William Wallace's arm and cleared his throat. "This time is kind of special," he said. "We got reason to think William Wallace's wife Hazel is in the river, drowned."

"What reason have you got to think she's in the river drowned?" asked Doc. He took out his old pipe. "I'm asking the husband."

"Because she's not in the house," said William Wallace.

"Vanished?" and he knocked out the pipe.

"Plum vanished."

"Of course a thousand things could have happened to her," said Doc, and he lighted the pipe.

"Hand him up the letter, William Wallace," said Virgil. "We can't wait around till Doomsday for the net while Doc sits back thinkin'."

"I tore it up, right at the first," said William Wallace. "But I know it by heart. It said she was going to jump straight in the Pearl River and that I'd be sorry."

"Where do you come in, Virgil?" asked Doc.

"I was in the same place William Wallace sat on his neck in, all night, and done as much as he done, and come home the same time."

"You-all were out cuttin' up, so Lady Hazel has to jump in the river, is that it? Cause and effect? Anybody want to argue with me? Where do these others come in, Doyles, Malones, and what not?"

"Doc is the smartest man around," said William Wallace, turning to the solidly waiting Doyles, "but it sure takes time."

"These are the ones that's collected to drag the river for her," said Virgil.

"Of course I am not going on record to say so soon that *I* think she's drowned," Doc said, blowing out blue smoke.

"Do you think . . ." William Wallace mounted a step, and his hands both went into fists. "Do you think she was *carried off?*"

"Now that's the way to argue, see it from all sides," said Doc promptly. "But who by?"

Some Malone whistled, but not so you could tell which one.

"There's no booger around the Dover section that goes around carrying off young girls that's married," stated Doc.

"She was always scared of the Gypsies." William Wallace turned scarlet. "She'd sure turn her ring around on her finger if she passed one, and look in the other direction so they couldn't see she was pretty and carry her off. They come in the end of summer."

"Yes, there are the Gypsies, kidnappers since the world began. But was it to be you that would pay the grand ransom?" asked Doc. He pointed his finger. They all laughed then at how clever old Doc was and clapped William Wallace on the back. But that turned into a scuffle and they fell to the ground.

"Stop it, or you can't have the net," said Doc. "You're scaring my wife's chickens."

"It's time we was gone," said William Wallace.

The big barking dogs jumped to lean their front paws on the men's chests.

"My advice remains, Let well enough alone," said Doc. "Whatever this mysterious event will turn out to be, it has kept one woman from talking a while. However, Lady Hazel is the prettiest girl in Mississippi, you've never seen a prettier one and you never will. A golden-haired girl." He got to his feet with the nimbleness that was always his surprise, and said, "I'll come along with you."

The path they always followed was the Old Natchez Trace. It took them through the deep woods and led them out down below on the Pearl River, where they could begin dragging it upstream to a point near Dover. They walked in silence around William Wallace, not letting him carry anything, but the net dragged heavily and the buckets were full of clatter in a place so dim and still.

Once they went through a forest of cucumber trees and came up on a high ridge. Grady and Brucie, who were running ahead all the way, stopped in their tracks; a whistle had blown and far down and far away a long freight train was passing. It seemed like a little festival procession, moving with the slowness of ignorance or a dream, from distance to distance, the tiny pink and gray cars like secret boxes. Grady was counting the cars to himself, as if he could certainly see each one clearly, and Brucie watched his lips, hushed and cautious, the way he would watch a bird drinking. Tears suddenly came to Grady's eyes, but it could only be because a tiny man walked along the top of the train, walking and moving on top of the moving train.

They went down again and soon the smell of the river spread over the woods, cool and secret. Every step they took among the great walls of vines and among the passion-flowers started up a little life, a little flight.

"We're walking along in the changing-time," said Doc. "Any day now the change will come. It's going to turn from hot to cold, and we can kill the hog that's ripe and have fresh meat to eat. Come one of these nights and we can wander down here and tree a nice possum. Old Jack Frost will be pinching things up. Old Mr. Winter will be standing in the door. Hickory tree there will be yellow. Sweet-gum red, hickory yellow, dogwood red, sycamore yellow." He went along rapping the tree trunks with his knuckle. "Magnolia and live-oak never die. Remember that. Persimmons will all get fit to eat, and the nuts will be dropping like rain all through the woods here. And run, little quail, run, for we'll be after you too."

They went on and suddenly the woods opened upon light, and they had reached the river. Everyone stopped, but Doc talked on ahead as though nothing had happened. "Only today," he said, "today, in October sun, it's all gold—sky and tree and water. Everything just before it changes looks to be made of gold."

William Wallace looked down, as though he thought of Hazel with the shining eyes, sitting at home and looking straight before her, like a piece of pure gold, too precious to touch.

Below them the river was glimmering, narrow, soft, and skin-colored, and slowed nearly to stillness. The shining willow trees hung round them. The net that was being drawn out, so old and so long-used, it too looked golden, strung and tied with golden threads.

Standing still on the bank, all of a sudden William Wallace, on whose word they were waiting, spoke up in a voice of surprise. "What is the name of this river?"

They looked at him as if he were crazy not to know the name of the river he had fished in all his life. But a deep frown was on his forehead, as if he were compelled to wonder what people had come to call this river, or to think there was a mystery in the name of the river they all knew so well, the same as if it were some great far torrent of waves that dashed through the mountains somewhere, and almost as if it were a river in some dream, for they could not give him the name of that.

"Everybody knows Pearl River is named the Pearl River," said Doc.

A bird note suddenly bold was like a stone thrown into the water to sound it.

"It's deep here," said Virgil, and jogged William Wallace. "Remember?"

William Wallace stood looking down at the river as if it were still a mystery to him. There under his feet, which hung over the bank, it was transparent and yellow like an old bottle lying in the sun, filling with light.

Doc clattered all his paraphernalia.

Then all of a sudden all the Malones scattered jumping and tumbling down the bank. They gave their loud shout. Little Brucie started after them, and looked back.

"Do you think she jumped?" Virgil asked William Wallace.

II

Since the net was so wide, when it was all stretched it reached from bank to bank of the Pearl River, and the weights would hold it all the way to the bottom. Jug-like sounds filled the air, splashes lifted in the sun, and the party began to move upstream. The Malones with great groans swam and pulled near the shore, the Doyles swam and pushed from behind with Virgil to tell them how to do it best; Grady and Brucie with his thread and pin trotted along the sandbars hauling buckets and lines. Sam and Robbie Bell, naked and bright, guided the old oarless rowboat that always drifted at the shore, and in it, sitting up tall with his hat on, was Doc—he went along without ever touching water and without ever taking his eyes off the net. William Wallace himself did everything but most of the time he was out of sight, swimming about under water or diving, and he had nothing to say any more.

The dogs chased up and down, in and out of the water, and in and out of the woods.

"Don't let her get too heavy, boys," Doc intoned regularly, every few minutes, "and she won't let nothing through."

"She won't let nothing through, she won't let nothing through," chanted Sam and Robbie Bell, one at his front and one at his back.

The sandbars were pink or violet drifts ahead. Where the light fell on the river, in a wandering from shore to shore, it was leaf-shaped spangles that trembled softly, while the dark of the river was calm. The willow trees leaned overhead under muscadine vines, and their trailing leaves hung like waterfalls in the morning air. The thing that seemed like silence must have been the endless cry of all the crickets and locusts in the world, rising and falling.

Every time William Wallace took hold of a big eel that slipped the net, the Malones all yelled, "Rassle with him, son!"

"Don't let her get too heavy, boys," said Doc.

"This is hard on catfish," William Wallace said once.

There were big and little fishes, dark and bright, that they caught, good ones and bad ones, the same old fish.

"This is more shoes than I ever saw got together in any store," said Virgil when they emptied the net to the bottom. "Get going!" he shouted in the next breath.

The little Rippens who had stayed ahead in the woods stayed ahead on the river. Brucie, leading them all, made small jumps and hops as he went, sometimes on one foot, sometimes on the other.

The winding river looked old sometimes, when it ran wrinkled and deep under high banks where the roots of trees hung down, and sometimes it seemed to be only a young creek, shining with the colors of wildflowers. Sometimes sandbars in the shapes of fishes lay nose to nose across, without the track of even a bird.

"Here comes some alligators," said Virgil. "Let's let them by."

They drew out on the shady side of the water, and three big alligators and four middle-sized ones went by, taking their own time.

"Look at their great big old teeth!" called a shrill voice. It was Grady making his only outcry, and the alligators were not showing their teeth at all.

"The better to eat folks with," said Doc from his boat, looking at him severely.

"Doc, you are bound to declare all you know," said Virgil. "Get going!"

When they started off again the first thing they caught in the net was the baby alligator.

"That's just what we wanted!" cried the Malones.

They set the little alligator down on a sandbar and he squatted perfectly still; they could hardly tell when it was he started to move. They watched with set faces his incredible mechanics, while the dogs after one bark stood off in inquisitive humility, until he winked.

"He's ours!" shouted all the Malones. "We're taking him home with us!"

"He ain't nothing but a little-old baby," said William Wallace.

The Malones only scoffed, as if he might be only a baby but he looked like the oldest and worst lizard.

"What are you going to do with him?" asked Virgil.

"Keep him."

"I'd be more careful what I took out of this net," said Doc.

"Tie him up and throw him in the bucket," the Malones were saying to each other, while Doc was saying, "Don't come running to me and ask me what to do when he gets big."

They kept catching more and more fish, as if there was no end in sight.

"Look, a string of lady's beads," said Virgil. "Here, Sam and Robbie Bell."

Sam wore them around his head, with a knot over his forehead and loops around his ears, and Robbie Bell walked behind and stared at them.

In a shadowy place something white flew up. It was a heron, and it went away over the dark treetops. William Wallace followed it with his eyes and Brucie clapped his hands, but Virgil gave a sigh, as if he knew that when you go looking for what is lost, everything is a sign.

An eel slid out of the net.

"Rassle with him, son!" yelled the Malones. They swam like fiends.

"The Malones are in it for the fish," said Virgil.

It was about noon that there was a little rustle on the bank.

"Who is that yonder?" asked Virgil, and he pointed to a little undersized man with short legs and a little straw hat with a band around it, who was following along on the other side of the river.

"Never saw him and don't know his brother," said Doc.

Nobody had ever seen him before.

"Who invited you?" cried Virgil hotly. "Hi . . . !" and he made signs for the little undersized man to look at him, but he would not.

"Looks like a crazy man, from here," said the Malones.

"Just don't pay any attention to him and maybe he'll go away," advised Doc.

But Virgil had already swum across and was up on the other bank. He and the stranger could be seen exchanging a word apiece and then Virgil put out his hand the way he would pat a child and patted the stranger to the ground. The little man got up again just as quickly, lifted his shoulders, turned around, and walked away with his hat tilted over his eyes.

When Virgil came back he said, "Little-old man claimed he was harmless as a baby. I told him to just try horning in on this river and anything in it."

"What did he look like up close?" asked Doc.

"I wasn't studying how he looked," said Virgil. "But I don't like anybody to come looking at me that I am not familiar with." And he shouted, "Get going!"

"Things are moving in too great a rush," said Doc.

Brucie darted ahead and ran looking into all the bushes, lifting up their branches and looking underneath.

"Not one of the Doyles has spoke a word," said Virgil.

"That's because they're not talkers," said Doc.

All day William Wallace kept diving to the bottom. Once he dived down and down into the dark water, where it was so still that nothing stirred, not even a fish, and so dark that it was no longer the muddy world of the upper river but the dark clear world of deepness, and he must have believed this was the deepest place in the whole Pearl River, and if she was not here she would not be anywhere. He was gone such a long time that the others stared hard at the surface of the water, through which the bubbles came from below. So far down and all alone, had he found Hazel? Had he suspected down there, like some secret, the real, the true trouble that Hazel had fallen into, about which words in a letter could not speak . . . how (who knew?) she had been filled to the brim with that elation that they all remembered, like their own secret, the elation that comes of great hopes and changes, sometimes simply of the harvest time, that comes with a little course of its own like a tune to run in the head, and there was nothing she could do about it—they knew—and so it had turned into this. It could be nothing but the old trouble that William Wallace was finding out, reaching and turning in the gloom of such depths.

"Look down yonder," said Grady softly to Brucie.

He pointed to the surface, where their reflections lay colorless and still side by side. He touched his brother gently as though to impress him.

"That's you and me," he said.

Brucie swayed precariously over the edge, and Grady caught him by the seat of his overalls. Brucie looked, but showed no recognition. Instead, he backed away, and seemed all at once unconcerned and spiritless, and pressed the nickel William Wallace had given him into his palm, rubbing it into his skin. Grady's inflamed eyes rested on the brown water. Without warning he saw something . . . perhaps the image in the river seemed to be his father, the drowned man—with arms open, eyes open, mouth open. . . . Grady stared and blinked, again something wrinkled up his face.

And when William Wallace came up it was in an agony from submersion, which seemed an agony of the blood and of the very heart, so woeful he looked. He was staring and glaring around in astonishment, as if a long time had gone by, away from the pale world where the brown light of the sun and the river and the little party watching him trembled before his eyes.

"What did you bring up?" somebody called—was it Virgil?

One of his hands was holding fast to a little green ribbon of plant, root and all. He was surprised, and let it go.

It was afternoon. The trees spread softly, the clouds hung wet and tinted. A buzzard turned a few slow wheels in the sky, and drifted upwards. The dogs promenaded the banks.

"It's time we ate fish," said Virgil.

On a wide sandbar on which seashells lay they dragged up the haul and built a fire.

Then for a long time among clouds of odors and smoke, all half-naked except Doc, they cooked and ate catfish. They ate until the Malones groaned and all the Doyles stretched out on their faces, though for long after, Sam and Robbie Bell sat up to their own little table on a cypress stump and ate on and on. Then they all were silent and still, and one by one fell asleep.

"There ain't a thing better than fish," muttered William Wallace. He lay stretched on his back in the glimmer and shade of trampled sand. His sunburned forehead and cheeks seemed to glow with fire. His eyelids fell. The shadow of a willow branch dipped and moved over him. "There is nothing in the world as good as . . . fish. The fish of Pearl River." Then slowly he smiled. He was asleep.

But it seemed almost at once that he was leaping up, and one by one up sat the others in their ring and looked at him, for it was impossible to stop and sleep by the river.

"You're feeling as good as you felt last night," said Virgil, setting his head on one side.

"The excursion is the same when you go looking for your sorrow as when you go looking for your joy," said Doc.

But William Wallace answered none of them anything, for he was leaping all over the place and all, over them and the feast and the bones of the feast, trampling the sand, up and down, and doing a dance so crazy that he would die next. He took a big catfish and hooked it to his belt buckle and went up and down so that they all hollered, and the tears of laughter streaming down his cheeks made him put his hand up, and the two days' growth of beard began to jump out, bright red.

But all of a sudden there was an even louder cry, something almost like a cheer, from everybody at once, and all pointed fingers moved from William Wallace to the river. In the center of three light-gold rings across the water was lifted first an old hoary head ("It has whiskers!" a voice cried) and then in an undulation loop after loop and hump after hump of a long dark body, until there were a dozen rings of ripples, one behind the other, stretching all across the river, like a necklace.

"The King of the Snakes!" cried all the Malones at once, in high tenor voices and leaning together.

"The King of the Snakes," intoned old Doc in his profound bass.

"He looked you in the eye."

William Wallace stared back at the King of the Snakes with all his might.

It was Brucie that darted forward, dangling his little thread with the pin tied to it, going toward the water.

"That's the King of the Snakes!" cried Grady, who always looked after him.

Then the snake went down.

The little boy stopped with one leg in the air, spun around on the other, and sank to the ground.

"Git up," Grady whispered. "It was just the King of the Snakes. He went off whistling. Git up. It wasn't a thing but the King of the Snakes."

Brucie's green eyes opened, his tongue darted out, and he sprang up; his feet were heavy, his head light, and he rose like a bubble coming to the surface.

Then thunder like a stone loosened and rolled down the bank.

They all stood unwilling on the sandbar, holding to the net. In the eastern sky were the familiar castles and the round towers to which they were used, gray, pink, and blue, growing darker and filling with thunder. Lightning flickered in the sun along their thick walls. But in the west the sun shone with such a violence that in an illumination like a long-prolonged glare of lightning the heavens looked black and white; all color left the world, the goldenness of everything was like a memory, and only heat, a kind of glamor and oppression, lay on their heads. The thick heavy trees on the other side of the river were brushed with mile-long streaks of silver, and a wind touched each man on the forehead. At the same time there was a long roll of thunder that began behind them, came up and down mountains and valleys of air, passed over their heads, and left them listening still. With a small, near noise a mockingbird followed it, the little white bars of its body flashing over the willow trees.

"We are here for a storm now," Virgil said. "We will have to stay till it's over."

They retreated a little, and hard drops fell in the leathery leaves at their shoulders and about their heads.

"Magnolia's the loudest tree there is in a storm," said Doc.

Then the light changed the water, until all about them the woods in the rising wind seemed to grow taller and blow inward together and suddenly turn dark. The rain struck heavily. A huge tail seemed to lash through the air and the river broke in a wound of silver. In silence the party crouched and stooped beside the trunk of the great tree, which in the push of the storm rose full of a fragrance and unyielding weight. Where they all stared, past their tree, was another tree, and beyond that another and another, all the way down the bank of the river, all towering and darkened in the storm.

"The outside world is full of endurance," said Doc. "Full of endurance."

Robbie Bell and Sam squatted down low and embraced each other from the start.

"Runs in our family to get struck by lightnin'," said Robbie Bell. "Lightnin' drawed a pitchfork right on our grandpappy's cheek, stayed till he died. Pappy got struck by some bolts of lightnin' and was dead three days, dead as that-there axe."

There was a succession of glares and crashes.

"This'n's goin' to be either me or you," said Sam. "Here come a little bug. If he go to the left, be me, and to the right, be you."

But at the next flare a big tree on the hill seemed to turn into fire before their eyes, every branch, twig, and leaf, and a purple cloud hung over it.

"Did you hear that crack?" asked Robbie Bell. "That were its bones."

"Why do you little niggers talk so much!" said Doc. "Nobody's profiting by this information."

"We always talks this much," said Sam, "but now everybody so quiet, they hears us."

The great tree, split and on fire, fell roaring to earth. Just at its moment of falling, a tree like it on the opposite bank split wide open and fell in two parts.

"Hope they ain't goin' to be no balls of fire come rollin' over the water and fry all the fishes with they scales on," said Robbie Bell.

The water in the river had turned purple and was filled with sudden currents and whirlpools. The little willow trees bent almost to its surface, bowing one after another down the bank and almost breaking under the storm. A great curtain of wet leaves was borne along before a blast of wind, and every human being was covered.

"Now us got scales," wailed Sam. "Us is the fishes."

"Hush up, little-old colored children," said Virgil. "This isn't the way to act when somebody takes you out to drag a river."

"Poor lady's-ghost, I bet it is scareder than us," said Sam.

"All I hoping is, us don't find her!" screamed Robbie Bell.

William Wallace bent down and knocked their heads together. After that they clung silently in each other's arms, the two black heads resting, with wind-filled cheeks and tight-closed eyes, one upon the other until the storm was over.

"Right over yonder is Dover," said Virgil. "We've come all the way. William Wallace, you have walked on a sharp rock and cut your foot open."

III

In Dover it had rained, and the town looked somehow like new. The wavy heat of late afternoon came down from the watertank and fell over everything like shiny mosquito-netting. At the wide place where the road was paved and patched with tar, it seemed newly embedded with Coca-Cola tops. The old circus posters on the store were nearly gone, only bits, the snowflakes of white horses, clinging to its side. Morning-glory vines started almost visibly to grow over the roofs and cling round the ties of the railroad track, where bluejays lighted on the rails, and umbrella chinaberry trees hung heavily over the whole town, dripping intermittently upon the tin roofs.

Each with his counted fish on a string, the members of the river-dragging party walked through the town. They went toward the town well, and there was Hazel's mother's house, but no sign of her yet coming out. They all drank a dipper of the water, and still there was not a soul on the street. Even the bench in front of the store was empty, except for a little corn-shuck doll.

But something told them somebody had come, for after one moment people began to look out of the store and out of the post office. All the bird dogs woke up to see the Doyle dogs and such a large number of men and boys materialize suddenly with such a big catch of fish, and they ran out barking. The Doyle dogs joyously barked back. The bluejays flashed up and screeched above the town, whipping through their tunnels in the chinaberry trees. In the café a nickel clattered inside a music box and a love song began to play. The whole town of Dover began to throb in its wood and tin, like an old tired heart, when the men walked through once more, coming around again and going down the street carrying the fish, so drenched, exhausted, and muddy that no one could help but admire them.

William Wallace walked through the town as though he did not see anybody or hear anything. Yet he carried his great string of fish held high where it could be seen by all. Virgil came next, imitating William Wallace exactly, then the modest Doyles crowded by the Malones, who were holding up their alligator, tossing it in the air, even, like a father tossing his child. Following behind and pointing authoritatively at the ones in front strolled Doc, with Sam and Robbie Bell still chanting in his wake. In and out of the whole little line Grady and Brucie jerked about. Grady, with his head ducked, and stiff as a rod, walked with a springy limp; it made him look forever angry and unapproachable. Under his breath he was whispering, "Sty, sty, git out of my eye, and git on somebody passin' by." He traveled on with narrowed shoulders, and kept his eye unerringly upon his little brother, wary and at the same time proud, as though he held a flying June-bug on a string. Brucie, making a twanging noise with his lips, had shot forth again, and he was darting rapidly everywhere at once, delighted and tantalized, running in circles around William Wallace, pointing to his fish. A frown of pleasure like the print of a bird's foot was stamped between his faint brows, and he trotted in some unknown realm of delight.

"Did you ever see so many fish?" said the people in Dover.

"How much are your fish, mister?"

"Would you sell your fish?"

"Is that all the fish in Pearl River?"

"How much you sell them all for? Everybody's?"

"Take 'em free," said William Wallace suddenly and loud. The Malones were upon him and shouting, but it was too late. "I don't want no more of 'em. I want my wife!" he yelled, just at the moment when Hazel's mother walked out of her front door.

"You can't head her mother off," said Virgil. "Here she comes in full bloom."

"What have you done with my child?" Hazel's mother shouted.

But William Wallace turned his back on her, that was all, and on everybody, for that matter, and that was the breaking-up of the party.

Just as the sun went down, Doc climbed his back steps, sat in his chair on the back porch where he sat in the evenings, and lighted his pipe. William Wallace hung out the net and came back and Virgil was waiting for him, so they could say good evening to Doc.

"All in all," said Doc, when they came up, "I've never been on a better river-dragging, or seen better behavior. If it took catching catfish to move the Rock of Gibraltar, I believe this outfit could move it."

"Well, we didn't catch Hazel," said Virgil.

"What did you say?" asked Doc.

"He don't really pay attention," said Virgil. "I said, 'We didn't catch Hazel.'"

"Who says Hazel was to be caught?" asked Doc. "She wasn't in there. Girls don't like the water—remember that. Girls don't just haul off and go jumping in the river to get back at their husbands. They got other ways."

"Didn't you ever think she was in there?" asked William Wallace. "The whole time?"

"Nary once," said Doc.

"He's just smart," said Virgil, putting his hand on William Wallace's arm. "It's only because we didn't find her that he wasn't looking for her."

"I'm beholden to you for the net, anyway," said William Wallace.

"You're welcome to borry it again," said Doc.

On the way home Virgil kept saying, "Calm down, calm down, William Wallace."

"If he wasn't such an old skinny man I'd have wrung his neck for him," said William Wallace. "He had no business coming."

"He's too big for his britches," said Virgil. "Don't nobody know everything. And just because it's his net. Why does it have to be his net?"

"If it wasn't for being polite to old men, I'd have skinned him alive," said William Wallace.

"I guess he don't really know nothing about wives at all, his wife's so deaf," said Virgil.

"He don't know Hazel," said William Wallace. "I'm the only man alive knows Hazel: would she jump in the river or not, and I say she would. She jumped in because I was sitting on the back of my neck in a ditch singing, and that's just what she ought to done. Doc ain't got no right to say one word about it."

"Calm down, calm down, William Wallace," said Virgil.

"If it had been you that talked like that, I'd have broke every bone in your body," said William Wallace. "Just let you talk like that. You're my age and size."

"But I ain't going to talk like that," said Virgil. "What have I done the whole time but keep this river-dragging going straight and running even, without no hitches? You couldn't have drug the river a foot without me."

"What are you talking about! Without who!" cried William Wallace. "This wasn't your river-dragging! It wasn't your wife!" He jumped on Virgil and they began to fight.

"Let me up." Virgil was breathing heavily.

"Say it was my wife. Say it was my river-dragging."

"Yours!" Virgil was on the ground with William Wallace's hand putting dirt in his mouth.

"Say it was my net."

"Your net!"

"Get up then."

They walked along getting their breath, and smelling the honeysuckle in the evening. On a hill William Wallace looked down, and at the same time there went drifting by the sweet sounds of music outdoors. They were having the Sacred Harp Sing on the grounds of an old white church glimmering there at the crossroads, far below. He stared away as if he saw it minutely, as if he could see a lady in white take a flowered cover off the organ, which was set on a little slant in the shade, dust the keys, and start to pump and play. . . . He smiled faintly, as he would at his mother, and at Hazel, and at the singing women in his life, now all one young girl standing up to sing under the trees the oldest and longest ballads there were.

Virgil told him good night and went into his own house and the door shut on him.

When he got to his own house, William Wallace saw to his surprise that it had not rained at all. But there, curved over the roof, was something he had never seen before as long as he could remember, a rainbow at night. In the light of the moon, which had risen again, it looked small and of gauzy material, like a lady's summer dress, a faint veil through which the stars showed.

He went up on the porch and in at the door, and all exhausted he had walked through the front room and through the kitchen when he heard his name called. After a moment, he smiled, as if no matter what he might have hoped for in his wildest heart, it was better than that to hear his name called out in the house. The voice came out of the bedroom.

"What do you want?" he yelled, standing stock-still.

Then she opened the bedroom door with the old complaining creak, and there she stood. She was not changed a bit.

"How do you feel?" he said.

"I feel pretty good. Not too good," Hazel said, looking mysterious.

"I cut my foot," said William Wallace, taking his shoe off so she could see the blood.

"How in the world did you do that?" she cried, with a step back.

"Dragging the river. But it don't hurt any longer."

"You ought to have been more careful," she said. "Supper's ready and I wondered if you would ever come home, or if it would be last night all over again. Go and make yourself fit to be seen," she said, and ran away from him.

After supper they sat on the front steps a while.

"Where were you this morning when I came in?" asked William Wallace when they were ready to go in the house.

"I was hiding," she said. "I was still writing on the letter. And then you tore it up."

"Did you watch me when I was reading it?"

"Yes, and you could have put out your hand and touched me. I was so close."

But he bit his lip, and gave her a little tap and slap, and then turned her up and spanked her.

"Do you think you will do it again?" he asked.

"I'll tell my mother on you for this!"

"Will you do it again?"

"No!" she cried.

"Then pick yourself up off my knee."

It was just as if he had chased her and captured her again. She lay smiling in the crook of his arm. It was the same as any other chase in the end.

"I will do it again if I get ready," she said. "Next time will be different, too."

Then she was ready to go in, and rose up and looked out from the top step, out across their yard where the China tree was and beyond, into the dark fields where the lightning-bugs flickered away. He climbed to his feet too and stood beside her, with the frown on his face, trying to look where she looked. And after a few minutes she took him by the hand and led him into the house, smiling as if she were smiling down on him.

1943

Ann Petry 1908–1997

Born in 1908 in Old Saybrook, Connecticut, Ann Petry liked to characterize herself as a gambler and survivor: the former, because she was a black woman who decided to write for a living, and the latter, because she published eight books.

The younger daughter of middle-class, New England-born parents, Ann Lane grew up in Old Saybrook and spent much of her time in her family's drugstore. She joined the family business after graduating from the Connecticut College of Pharmacy in New Haven. But in 1938, after marrying George Petry, an aspiring writer from New Iberia, Louisiana, she left behind her sheltered life in the seaside town and moved to New York City. There she decided to concentrate on her writing, an interest she had pursued on the side for years. As a reporter for a Harlem weekly, she became familiar with the poverty and demoralization afflicting inner-city blacks. She also learned about the city through her involvement in an after-school program for Harlem children. It was during this period that she got the idea for *The Street* (1946), the tale of Lutie Johnson's desperate struggle to earn a living in Harlem and protect her young son from corruption. Petry's first novel became a national bestseller, the first for an American black woman. To date, it has sold more than a million and a half copies.

The Street showcases Petry's mastery of naturalism. Lutie's endless war with hostile forces begins with her braving a ferociously cold wind and culminates in her struggle with a would-be rapist. Set during World War II, *The Street* illustrates the myriad degradations faced by black men and children as well as black women. In addition to telling Lutie's story, the novel takes up the perspectives of Bub, her lonely eight-year-old son; Jones, the depraved building superintendent; Mrs. Hedges, a malevolent madam; and even Boots Smith, the bitterly resentful band leader.

After *The Street*'s success, the Petrys returned to the reclusive quiet of Old Saybrook, where they settled permanently and had a daughter, Elisabeth Ann. In 1947 Petry published *Country Place,* a novel as unflinching in its portrayal of a white New England town as *The Street* is in its portrayal of a Harlem ghetto. Set in the years just after World War II and narrated by the white druggist 'Doc' Fraser, *Country Place* concerns marital infidelities and a litany of other betrayals. Although it lacks *The Street*'s depth of characterization, *Country Place* reveals Petry's continuing fascination with troubled communities.

In Petry's third novel, *The Narrows* (1953), blacks and whites coexist uneasily in the small city of Monmouth, Connecticut. The novel, which takes place in the fifties, revolves around a doomed relationship between Link Williams, an educated young black man, and Camilla Treadway, a wealthy young white woman. What begins as their private love affair ends in murder and public polarization of the races.

Miss Muriel and Other Stories (1971) includes 13 stories, several of which are set in Wheeling, New York, a fictional town similar to Old Saybrook. Like her novels, Petry's short fiction deals with devastating fissures in insular communities. The tension in these stories often results from distrust among people who cannot conquer their own or anyone else's prejudices of race and gender.

Petry's books for younger readers include a historical biography, *Harriet Tubman: Conductor on the Underground Railroad* (1955), and *Tituba of Salem Village* (1964), the story, based on real events, of a slave woman convicted of witchcraft. More didactic than her works for adults, these books are eloquent studies in African American heritage and individual fortitude.

Hilary Holladay
University of Massachusetts–Lowell

PRIMARY WORKS

The Street, 1946; *Country Place,* 1947; *The Drugstore Cat,* 1949; *The Narrows,* 1953; *Harriet Tubman: Conductor on the Underground Railroad,* 1955; *Tituba of Salem Village,* 1964; *Legends of the Saints,* 1970; *Miss Muriel and Other Stories,* 1971; "Ann Petry," *Contemporary Authors Autobiography Series,* Vol. 6, 1988.

The Witness

It had been snowing for twenty-four hours, and as soon as it stopped, the town plows began clearing the roads and sprinkling them with a mixture of sand and salt. By nightfall the main roads were what the roadmaster called clean as a whistle. But the little winding side roads and the store parking lots and the private walkways lay under a thick blanket of snow.

Because of the deep snow, Charles Woodruff parked his station wagon, brand-new, expensive, in the road in front of the Congregational church rather than risk getting stuck in the lot behind the church. He was early for the minister's class so he sat still, deliberately savoring the new-car smell of the station wagon. He found himself sniffing audibly and thought the sound rather a greedy one and so got out of the car and stood on the snow-covered walk, studying the church. A full moon lay low on the horizon. It gave a wonderful luminous quality to the snow, to the church, and to the branches of the great elms dark against the winter sky.

He ducked his head down because the wind was coming in gusts straight from the north, blowing the snow so it swirled around him, stinging his face. It was so cold that his toes felt as though they were freezing and he began to stamp his feet. Fortunately his coat insulated his body against the cold. He hadn't really planned to buy a new coat but during the Christmas vacation he had been in New York City and he had gone into one of those thickly carpeted, faintly perfumed, crystal-chandeliered stores that sell men's clothing and he had seen the coat hanging on a rack—a dark gray cashmere coat, lined with nutria and adorned by a collar of black Persian lamb. A tall, thin salesman who smelled of heather saw him looking at the coat and said: "Try it on, sir—it's toast-warm, cloud-light, guaranteed to make you feel like a prince—do try it on, here let me hold your coat, sir." The man's voice sounded as though he were purring and he kept brushing against Woodruff like a cat, and managed to sell him the coat, a narrow-brimmed felt hat, and a pair of fur-lined gloves.

If Addie had been alive and learned he had paid five hundred dollars for an overcoat, she would have argued with him fiercely, nostrils flaring, thin arched eyebrows lifted. Standing there alone in the snow, in front of the church, he permitted himself a small indulgence. He pretended Addie was standing beside him. He spoke to her, aloud: "You always said I had to dress more elegantly than my students so they would respect my clothes even if they didn't respect my learning. You said—"

He stopped abruptly, thinking he must look like a lunatic, standing in the snow, stamping his feet and talking to himself. If he kept it up long enough, someone would call the state police and a bulletin about him would go clattering out over the teletype: "Attention all cruisers, attention all cruisers, a black man, repeat, a black man is standing in front of the Congregational church in Wheeling, New York; description follows, description follows, thinnish, tallish black man, clipped moustache, expensive (extravagantly expensive, outrageously expensive, unjustifiably expensive) overcoat, felt hat like a Homburg, eyeglasses glittering in the moonlight, feet stamping in the moonlight, mouth muttering in the moonlight. Light of the moon we danced. Glimpses of the moon revisited . . ."

There was no one in sight, no cars passing. It was so still it would be easy to believe that the entire population of the town had died and lay buried under the snow and that he was the sole survivor, and that would be ironic because he did not really belong in this all-white community.

The thought of his alien presence here evoked an image of Addie—dark-skinned, intense, beautiful. He was sixty-five when she died. He had just retired as professor of English at Virginia College for Negroes. He had spent all of his working life there. He had planned to write a grammar to be used in first-year English classes, to perfect his herb garden, catalogue his library, tidy up his files, and organize his clippings—a wealth of material in those clippings. But without Addie these projects seemed inconsequential—like the busy work that grade school teachers devise to keep children out of mischief. When he was offered a job teaching in a high school in a small town in New York, he accepted it quickly.

Everybody was integrating and so this little frozen Northern town was integrating, too. Someone probably asked why there were no black teachers in the school system and the school board and the Superintendent of Schools said they were searching for 'one'—and the search yielded that brand-new black widower, Charles Woodruff (nigger in the woodpile, he thought, and then, why that word, a word he despised and never used so why did it pop up like that, does a full moon really affect the human mind) and he was eager to escape from his old environment and so for the past year he had taught English to academic seniors in Wheeling High School.

No problems. No hoodlums. All of his students were being herded toward college like so many cattle. He referred to them (mentally) as the Willing Workers of America. He thought that what was being done to them was a crime against nature. They were hard-working, courteous, pathetic. He introduced a new textbook, discarded a huge anthology that was filled with mutilated poetry, mutilated essays, mutilated short stories. His students liked him and told him so. Other members of the faculty said he was lucky but just wait until another year—the freshmen and the sophomores were "a bunch of hoodlums"—"a whole new ball game"—

Because of his success with his English classes, Dr. Shipley, the Congregational minister, had asked him if he would assist (Shipley used words like "assist" instead of "help") him with a class of delinquent boys—the class met on Sunday nights. Woodruff felt he should make some kind of contribution to the life of this small town which had treated him with genuine friendliness so he had said yes.

But when he first saw those seven boys assembled in the minister's study, he knew that he could neither help nor assist the minister with them—they were beyond his reach, beyond the minister's reach. They sat silent, motionless, their shoulders hunched as though against some chill they found in the air of that small book-lined room. Their eyelids were like shutters drawn over their eyes. Their long hair covered their foreheads, obscuring their eyebrows, reaching to the collars of their jackets. Their legs, stretched out straight in front of them, were encased in pants that fit as tightly as the leotards of a ballet dancer.

He kept looking at them, studying them. Suddenly, as though at a signal, they all looked at him. This collective stare was so hostile that he felt himself stiffen and sweat broke out on his forehead. He assumed that the same thing had happened to Dr. Shipley because Shipley's eyeglasses kept fogging up, though the room was not overly warm.

Shipley had talked for an hour. He began to get hoarse. Though he paused now and then to ask a question and waited hopefully for a reply, there was none. The boys sat mute and motionless.

After they left, filing out, one behind the other, Woodruff had asked Shipley about them—who they were and why they attended this class in religion.

Shipley said, "They come here under duress. The Juvenile Court requires their attendance at this class."

"How old are they?"

"About sixteen. Very bright. Still in high school. They're all sophomores—that's why you don't know them. Rambler, the tall thin boy, the ringleader, has an IQ in the genius bracket. As a matter of fact, if they weren't so bright, they'd be in reform school. This class is part of an effort to—well—to turn them into God-fearing responsible young citizens."

"Are their families poor?"

"No, indeed. The parents of these boys are—well, they're the backbone of the great middle class in this town."

After the third meeting of the class where the same hostile silence prevailed, Woodruff said, "Dr. Shipley, do you think we are accomplishing anything?" He had said "we" though he was well aware that these new young outlaws spawned by the white middle class were, praise God, Shipley's problem—the white man's problem. This cripplingly tight shoe was usually on the black man's foot. He found it rather pleasant to have the position reversed.

Shipley ran his fingers through his hair. It was very short hair, stiff-looking, crew-cut.

"I don't know," he said frowning. "I really don't know. They don't even respond to a greeting or a direct question. It is a terribly frustrating business, an exhausting business. When the class is over, I feel as though I had spent the entire evening lying prone under the unrelieved weight of all their bodies."

Woodruff, standing outside the church, stamping his feet, jumped and then winced because he heard a sound like a gunshot. It was born on the wind so that it seemed close at hand. He stood still, listening. Then he started moving quickly toward the religious education building which housed the minister's study.

He recognized the sound—it was made by the car the boys drove. It had no muffler and the snorting, back-firing sounds made by the spent motor were like a series of gunshots. He wanted to be out of sight when the boys drove up in their rusted car. Their lithe young bodies were a shocking contrast to the abused and ancient vehicle in which they traveled. The age of the car, its dreadful condition, was like a snarled message aimed at the adult world: All we've got is the crumbs, the leftovers, whatever the fat cats don't want and can't use; the turnpikes and the throughways and the seventy-mile-an-hour speedways are filled with long, low, shiny cars built for speed, driven by bald-headed, big-bellied rat finks and we're left with the junk, the worn-out beat-up chassis, the thin tires, the brakes that don't hold, the transmission that's shot to hell. He had seen them push the car out of the parking lot behind the church. It wouldn't go in reverse.

Bent over, peering down, picking his way through the deep snow lest he stumble and fall, Woodruff tried to hurry and the explosive sound of that terrible engine kept getting closer and closer. He envisioned himself as a black beetle in a fur-collared coat silhouetted against the snow trying to scuttle out of danger. Danger: Why should he think he was in danger? Perhaps some sixth sense was trying to warn him and his beetle's antenna (did beetles have antennae, did they have five senses and some of them an additional sense, extrasensory—) picked it up—by the pricking of my thumbs, something wicked this way comes.

Once inside the building he drew a deep breath. He greeted Dr. Shipley, hung his hat and coat on the brass hat rack, and then sat down beside Shipley behind the old fumed oak desk. He braced himself for the entrance of the boys.

There was the sound of the front door opening followed by the click-clack sound of their heavy boots, in the hall. Suddenly they were all there in the minister's study. They brought cold air in with them. They sat down with their jackets on—great quilted dark jackets that had been designed for European ski slopes. At the first meeting of the class, Dr. Shipley had suggested they remove their jackets and they simply sat and stared at him until he fidgeted and looked away obviously embarrassed. He never again made a suggestion that was direct and personal.

Woodruff glanced at the boys and then directed his gaze away from them, thinking, if a bit of gilt braid and a touch of velvet were added to their clothing, they could pass for the seven dark bastard sons of some old and evil twelfth-century king. Of course they weren't all dark. Three of them were blond, two had brown hair, one had red hair, only one had black hair. All of them were white. But there was about them an aura of something so evil, so dark, so suggestive of the far reaches of the night, of the black horror of nightmares, that he shivered deep inside himself whenever he saw them. Though he thought of them as being black, this was not the blackness of human flesh, warm, soft to the touch, it was the blackness and the coldness of the hole from which D.H. Lawrence's snake emerged.

The hour was almost up when to Woodruff's surprise, Rambler, the tall boy, the one who drove the ramshackle car, the one Shipley said was the leader of the group, began asking questions about cannibalism. His voice was husky, low in pitch, and he almost whispered when he spoke. Woodruff found himself leaning forward in an effort to hear what the boy was saying. Dr. Shipley leaned forward, too.

Rambler said, "Is it a crime to eat human flesh?"

Dr. Shipley said, surprised, "Yes. It's cannibalism. It is a sin and it is also a crime." He spoke slowly, gently, as though he were wooing a timid, wild animal that had ventured out of the woods and would turn tail and scamper back if he spoke in his normal voice.

"Well, if the cats who go for this human flesh bit don't think it's a sin and if they eat it because they haven't any other food, it isn't a sin for them, is it?" The boy spoke quickly, not pausing for breath, running his words together.

"There are many practices and acts that are acceptable to non-Christians which are sinful. Christians condemn such acts no matter what the circumstances."

Woodruff thought uncomfortably, why does Shipley have to sound so pompous, so righteous, so from-off-the-top-of-Olympus? The boys were all staring at him, bright-eyed, mouths slightly open, long hair obscuring their foreheads. Then Rambler said, in his husky whispering voice, "What about you, Doc?"

Dr. Shipley said, "Me?" and repeated it, his voice losing its coaxing tone, rising in pitch, increasing in volume. "Me? What do you mean?"

"Well, man, you're eatin' human flesh, ain't you?"

Woodruff had no idea what the boy was talking about. But Dr. Shipley was looking down at his own hands with a curious self-conscious expression and Woodruff saw that Shipley's nails were bitten all the way down to the quick.

The boy said, "It's self-cannibalism, ain't it, Doc?"

Shipley put his hands on the desk, braced himself, preparatory to standing up. His thin, bony face had reddened. Before he could move, or speak, the boys stood up and began to file out of the room. Rambler leaned over and ran his hand through the minister's short-cut, bristly hair and said, "Don't sweat it, Doc."

Woodruff usually stayed a half-hour or more after the class ended. Dr. Shipley liked to talk and Woodruff listened to him patiently, though he thought Shipley had a second-rate mind and rambled when he talked. But Shipley sat with his head bowed, a pose not conducive to conversation and Woodruff left almost immediately after the boys, carrying in his mind's eye a picture of all those straight, narrow backs with the pants so tight they were like elastic bandages on their thighs, and the oversized bulky jackets and the long, frowsy hair. He thought they looked like paper dolls, cut all at once, exactly alike with a few swift slashes of scissors wielded by a skilled hand. Addie could do that—take paper and fold it and go snip, snip, snip with the scissors and she'd have a string of paper dolls, all fat, or all thin, or all bent over, or all wearing top hats, or all bearded Santas or all Cheshire cats. She had taught arts and crafts in the teacher-training courses for elementary-school teachers at Virginia College and so was skilled in the use of crayon and scissors.

He walked toward his car, head down, picking his way through the snow and then he stopped, surprised. The boys were standing in the road. They had surrounded a girl. He didn't think she was a high school girl though she was young. She had long blond hair that spilled over the quilted black jacket she was wearing. At first he couldn't tell what the boys were doing but as he got closer to them, he saw that they were moving toward their ancient car and forcing the girl to move with them though she was resisting. They were talking to each other and to her, their voices companionable, half-playful.

"So we all got one in the oven."

"So it's all right if it's all of us."

The girl said, "No."

"Aw, come on, Nellie, hurry up."

"It's colder'n hell, Nellie. Move!"

They kept pushing her toward the car and she turned on them and said, "Quit it."

"Aw, get in."

One of them gave her a hard shove, sent her closer to the car and she screamed and Rambler clapped his hand over her mouth and she must have bitten his hand because he snatched it away and then she screamed again because he slapped her and then two of them picked her up and threw her on the front seat and one of them stayed there, holding her.

Woodruff thought, There are seven of them, young, strong, satanic. He ought to go home where it was quiet and safe, mind his own business—black man's business; leave this white man's problem for a white man, leave it alone, not his, don't interfere, go home to the bungalow he rented—ridiculous type of architecture in this cold climate, developed for India, a hot climate, and that open porch business—

He said, "What are you doing?" He spoke with the voice of authority, the male schoolteacher's voice and thought, Wait, slow down, cool it, you're a black man speaking with a white man's voice.

They turned and stared at him; as they turned, they all assumed what he called the stance of the new young outlaw: the shoulders hunched, the hands in the pockets. In the moonlight he thought they looked as though they belonged in a frieze around a building—the hunched-shoulder posture repeated again and again, made permanent in stone. Classic.

"What are you doing?" he said again, voice louder, deeper.

"We're standin' here."

"You can see us, can't you?"

"Why did you force that girl into your car?"

"You're dreamin'."

"I saw what happened. And that boy is holding her in there."

"You been readin' too much."

They kept moving in, closing in on him. Even on this cold, windy night he could smell them and he loathed the smell—cigarettes, clothes washed in detergents and not rinsed enough and dried in automatic driers. They all smelled like that these days, even those pathetic college-bound drudges, the Willing Workers of America, stank so that he was always airing out his classroom. He rarely ever encountered the fresh clean smell of clothes that had been washed in soap and water, rinsed in boiling water, dried in the sun—a smell that he associated with new-mown hay and flower gardens and—Addie.

There was a subtle change in the tone of the voice of the next speaker. It was more contemptuous and louder.

"What girl, ho-daddy, what girl?"

One of them suddenly reached out and knocked his hat off his head, another one snatched his glasses off and threw them in the road and there was the tinkling sound of glass shattering. It made him shudder. He was half-blind without his glasses, peering about, uncertain of the shape of objects—like the woman in the Thurber cartoon, oh, yes, of course, three balloons and an H or three cats and a dog—only it was one of those scrambled alphabet charts.

They unbuttoned his overcoat, went through the pockets of his pants, of his jacket. One of them took his wallet, another took his car keys, picked up his hat, and then was actually behind the wheel of his station wagon and was moving off in it.

He shouted, "My car. Damn you, you're stealing my car—" his brand-new station wagon; he kept it immaculate, swept it out every morning, washed the windows. He tried to break out of that confining circle of boys and they simply pushed him back toward their car.

"Don't sweat it, man. You goin' ride with us and this little chick-chick."

"You goin' be our pro-tec-shun, ho-daddy. You goin' be our protec-shun."

They took his coat off and put it around him backward without putting his arms in the sleeves and then buttoned it up. The expensive coat was just like a strait jacket—it pinioned his arms to his sides. He tried to work his way out of it by flexing his muscles, hoping that the buttons would pop off or a seam would give, and thought, enraged, They must have stitched the goddamn coat to last for a thousand years and put the goddamn buttons on the same way. The fur collar pressed against his throat, choking him.

Woodruff was forced into the back seat, two boys on each side of him. They were sitting half on him and half on each other. The one holding his wallet examined its contents. He whistled. "Hey!" he said, "Ho-daddy's got one hundred and forty-four bucks. We got us a rich ho-daddy—"

Rambler held out his hand and the boy handed the money over without a protest, not even a sigh. Then Rambler got into the front seat behind the wheel. The girl was quiet only because the boy beside her had his hand around her throat and from the way he was holding his arm, Woodruff knew he was exerting a certain amount of pressure.

"Give the man a hat," Rambler said.

One of the boys felt around until he found a cap. They were so close to each other that each of his movements slightly disrupted their seating arrangement. When the boy shifted his weight, the rest of them were forced to shift theirs.

"Here you go," the boy said. He pulled a black wool cap down on Woodruff's head, over his eyes, over his nose.

He couldn't see anything. He couldn't breathe through his nose. He had to breathe through his mouth or suffocate. The freezing cold air actually hurt the inside of his mouth. The overcoat immobilized him and the steady pressure of the fur collar against his windpipe was beginning to interfere with his normal rate of breathing. He knew that his whole circulatory system would gradually begin to slow down. He frowned, thinking what a simple and easily executed method of rendering a person helpless—just an overcoat and a knit cap. Then he thought, alarmed, If they should leave me out in the woods like this, I would be dead by morning. What do they want of me anyway?

He cleared his throat preparatory to questioning them but Rambler started the car and he could not make himself heard above the sound of the engine. He thought the noise would shatter his eardrums and he wondered how these boys could bear it—the terrible cannon fire sound of the engine and the rattling of the doors and the windows. Then they were off and it was like riding in a jeep—only worse because the seat was broken and they were jounced up out of the seat and then back down into a hollowed-out place, all of them on top of each other. He tried to keep track of the turns the car made but he couldn't, there were too many of them. He assumed that whenever they stopped it was because of a traffic light or a stop sign.

It seemed to him they had ridden for miles and miles when the car began to jounce up and down more violently than ever and he decided they had turned onto a rough, rutted road. Suddenly they stopped. The car doors were opened and the boys pushed him out of the car. He couldn't keep his balance and he stumbled and fell flat on his face in the snow and they all laughed. They had to haul him to his feet for his movements were so constricted by the overcoat that he couldn't get up without help.

The cap had worked up a little so that he could breathe more freely and he could see anything that was in his immediate vicinity. Either they did not notice that the cap had been pushed out of place or they didn't care. As they guided him along he saw that they were in a cemetery that was filled with very old tombstones. They were approaching a small building and his station wagon was parked to one side. The boy who had driven it opened the door of the building and Woodruff saw that it was lighted inside by a big bulb that dangled from the ceiling. There were shovels and rakes inside and a grease-encrusted riding mower, bags of grass seed, and a bundle of material that looked like the artificial grass used around new graves.

Rambler said, "Put the witness here."

They stood him against the back wall, facing the wall.

"He's here and yet he ain't here."

"Ho-daddy's here—and yet—he ain't here."

"He's our witness."

And then Rambler's voice again, "If he moves, ice him with a shovel."

The girl screamed and then the sound was muffled, only a kind of far-off moaning sound coming through something. They must have gagged her. All the sounds were muffled—it was like trying to see something in a fog or hear something when other sounds overlay the one thing you're listening for. What had they brought him here for? They would go away and leave him with the girl but the girl would know that he hadn't—

How would she know? They had probably blindfolded her, too. What were they doing? He could see shadows on the wall. Sometimes they moved, sometimes they were still, and then the shadows moved again and then there would be laughter. Silence after that and then thuds, thumps, silence again. Terrible sounds behind him. He started to turn around and someone poked him in the back, sharply, with the handle of a shovel or a rake. He began to sweat despite the terrible cold.

He tried to relax by breathing deeply and he began to feel as though he were going to faint. His hands and feet were numb. His head ached. He had strained so to hear what was going on behind him that he was afraid he had impaired his own hearing.

When Rambler said, "Come on, ho-daddy, it's your turn," he was beginning to lose all feeling in his arms and legs.

Someone unbuttoned his coat, plucked the cap off his head. He let his breath out in a long drawn-out sigh. He doubted that he could have survived much longer with that pressure on his throat. The boys looked at him curiously. They threw his coat on the hard-packed dirt floor and tossed the cap on top of it. He thought that the black knit cap they'd used, like a sailor's watch cap, was as effective a blindfold as could be found—providing, of course, the person couldn't use his hands to remove it.

The girl was lying on the floor, half-naked. They had put some burlap bags under her. She looked as though she were dead.

They pushed him toward her saying, "It's your turn."

He balked, refusing to move.

"You don't want none?"

They laughed. "Ho-daddy don't want none."

They pushed him closer to the girl and someone grabbed one of his hands and placed it on the girl's thigh, on her breasts, and then they laughed again. They handed him his coat, pulled the cap down on his head.

"Let's go, ho-daddy. Let's go."

Before he could put his coat back on they hustled him outdoors. One of them threw his empty wallet at him and another aimed his car keys straight at his head. The metal stung as it hit his cheek. Before he could catch them the keys disappeared in the snow. The boys went back inside the building and emerged carrying the girl, half-naked, head hanging down limply the way the head of a corpse would dangle.

"The girl—" Woodruff said.

"You're our witness, ho-daddy. You're our big fat witness."

They propped the girl up in the back seat of their car. "You're the only witness we got," they repeated it, laughing. "Take good care of yourself."

"She'll freeze to death like that," he protested.

"Not Nellie."

"She likes it."

"Come on, man, let's go, let's go, let's go," Rambler said impatiently.

Woodruff's arms and hands were so numb that he had trouble getting his coat on. He had to take his gloves off and poke around in the snow with his bare hands before he could retrieve his wallet and the car keys. The pain in his hands was as sharp and intense as if they had been burned.

Getting into his car he began to shake with fury. Once he got out of this wretched cemetery he would call the state police. Young animals. He had called them outlaws; they weren't outlaws, they were animals. In his haste he dropped the keys and had to feel around on the floor of the car for them.

When he finally got the car started he was shivering and shaking and his stomach was quivering so that he didn't dare try to drive. He turned on the heater and watched the tiny taillight on Rambler's car disappear—an old car and the taillight was like the end of a pencil glowing red in the dark. The loud explosive sound of the engine gradually receded. When he could no longer hear it, he flicked on the light in his car and looked at his watch. It was quarter past three. Wouldn't the parents of those godforsaken boys wonder where they were at that hour? Perhaps they didn't care—perhaps they were afraid of them—just as he was.

Though he wanted to get home as quickly as possible, so he could get warm, so he could think, he had to drive slowly, peering out at the narrow rutted road because he was half blind without his glasses. When he reached the cemetery gates he stopped, not knowing whether to turn right or left for he had no idea where he was. He took a chance and turned right and followed the macadam road, still going slowly, saw a church on a hill and recognized it as the Congregational church in Brooksville, the next town, and knew he was about five miles from home.

By the time he reached his own driveway, sweat was pouring from his body just like water coming out of a showerhead—even his eyelashes were wet; it ran down his ears, dripped off his nose, his lips, even the palms of his hands.

In the house he turned on the lights, in the living room, in the hall, in his bedroom. He went to his desk, opened a drawer and fished out an old pair of glasses. He had had them for years. They looked rather like Peter Cooper's glasses—he'd seen them once in the Cooper Union Museum in New York—small-lensed, with narrow, silvery-looking frames. They evoked an image of a careful scholarly man. When he had started wearing glasses, he had selected frames like Peter Cooper's. Addie had made him stop wearing them. She said they gave him the look of another era, made it easy for his students to caricature him—the tall, slender figure, slightly stooped, the steel-rimmed glasses. She said that his dark, gentle eyes looked as though they were trapped behind those little glasses.

Having put on the glasses, he went to the telephone and stood with one hand resting on it, sweating again, trembling again. He turned away, took off his overcoat and hung it on a hanger and placed it in the hall closet.

He began to pace up and down the living room—a pleasant spacious room, simply furnished. It had a southern exposure and there were big windows on that side of the room. The windows faced a meadow. The thought crossed his mind, lightly, like the silken delicate strand of a cobweb, that he would have to leave here and he brushed it away—not quite away, a trace remained.

He wasn't going to call the police. Chicken. That was the word his students used. Fink was another one. He was going to chicken out. He was going to fink out.

Why wasn't he going to call the police? Well, what would he tell them? That he'd been robbed? Well, that was true. That he'd been kidnapped? Well, that was true, too, but it seemed like a harsh way of putting it. He'd have to think about that one. That he'd been witness to a rape? He wasn't even certain that they had raped the girl. No? Who was he trying to kid? Himself? Himself.

So why wasn't he going to the police? He hadn't touched the girl. But those horrible little hoods, toads rather, why toads, toe of frog ingredient of witches' brew, poisonous substance in the skin—bufotenine, a hallucinogen found in the skin of the frog, of the toad. Those horrible toadlike hoods would say he had touched her. Well, he had. Hadn't he? They had made sure of that. Would the police believe him? The school board? The PTA? "Where there's smoke there must be fire." "I'm not going to let my daughter stay in his class."

He started shivering again and made himself a cup of tea and sat down on the window seat in the living room to drink it and then got up and turned off the lights and looked out at the snow. The moonlight was so bright that he could see wisps of tall grass in the meadow—yellow against the snow. Immediately he thought of the long blond hair of that starvation-thin young girl. Bleached hair? Perhaps. It didn't lessen the outrage. She was dressed just like the boys—big quilted jacket, skin-tight pants, even her hair worn like theirs, obscuring the forehead, the sides of the face.

There was a sudden movement outside the window and he frowned and leaned forward, wondering what was moving about at this hour. He saw a pair of rabbits, leaping, running, literally playing games with each other. He had never before seen such free joyous movement, not even children at play exhibited it. There was always something unrelaxed about the eyes of children, about the way they held their mouths, wrinkled their foreheads—they looked as though they had been cornered and were impelled to defend themselves or that they were impelled to pursue some object that forever eluded them.

Watching this joyous heel-kicking play of the rabbits, he found himself thinking,

I cannot continue to live in the same small town with that girl and those seven boys. The boys knew, before he did, that he wasn't going to report this—this incident—these crimes. They were bright enough to know that he would quickly realize how neatly they had boxed him in and thus would keep quiet. If he dared enter a complaint against them they would accuse him of raping the girl, would say they found him in the cemetery with her. Whose story would be believed? "Where there's smoke there's fire."

Right after that he started packing. He put his clothes into a foot locker. He stacked his books on the floor of the station wagon. He was surprised to find among the books a medical textbook that had belonged to John—Addie's brother.

He sat down and read all the material on angina pectoris. At eight o'clock he called the school and said he wasn't feeling well (which was true) and that he would not be in. Then he called the office of the local doctor and made an appointment for that afternoon.

When he talked to the doctor he described the violent pain in his chest that went from the shoulder down to his finger tips on the left side, causing a squeezing, crushing sensation that left him feeling faint, dizzy.

The doctor, a fat man in an old tweed jacket and a limp white shirt, said after he examined him, "Angina. You'll have to take three or four months off until we can get this thing under control."

"I will resign immediately."

"Oh, no. That isn't necessary. Besides I've been told you're the best English teacher we've ever had. It would be a great pity to lose you."

"No," Woodruff said, "it is better to resign." Come back here and look at that violated little girl? Come back here? Ever?

He scarcely listened to the detailed instructions he was to follow, did not even glance at the three prescriptions he was handed, for he was eager to be on his way. He composed a letter of resignation in his mind. When he went back to the bungalow he wrote it quickly and then put it on the front seat of the station wagon to be mailed en route.

Then he went back into the house and stayed there just long enough to call his landlord. He said he'd had a heart attack and was going back to Virginia to convalesce, that he had turned the thermostat down to sixty-five and he would return the house keys by mail. The landlord said, My goodness, you just paid a month in advance, I'll mail you a refund, what's your new address, so sorry, ideal tenant.

Woodruff hung up the receiver and said, "Peace be with you, brother—" There was already an echo in the room though it wasn't empty—all he'd removed were his books and his clothes.

He put on his elegant overcoat. When he got back to Virginia, he would give the coat away, his pleasure in it destroyed now for he would always remember the horrid feel of the collar tight across his throat, even the feel of the fabric under his finger tips would evoke an image of the cemetery, the tool shed, and the girl.

He drove down the road rather slowly. There were curves in the road and he couldn't go fast, besides he liked to look at this landscape. It was high rolling land. Snow lay over it—blue-white where there were shadows cast by the birch trees and the hemlocks, yellow-white and sparkling in the great meadow where he had watched the heel-kicking freedom of the rabbits at play.

At the entrance to the highway he brought the car to a halt. As he sat there waiting for an opportunity to get into the stream of traffic, he heard close at hand the loud explosive sound of an engine—a familiar sound. He was so alarmed that he momentarily experienced all the symptoms of a heart attack, the sudden terrible inability to breathe and the feeling that something was squeezing his chest, kneading it so that pain ran through him as though it were following the course of his circulatory system.

He knew from the sound that the car turning off the highway, entering the same road that he was now leaving, was Rambler's car. In the sunlight, silhouetted against the snow, it looked like a junkyard on wheels, fenders dented, sides dented, chassis rusted. All the boys were in the car. Rambler was driving. The thin blond girl was in the front seat—a terrible bruise under one eye. For a fraction of a second Woodruff looked straight into Rambler's eyes, just visible under the long, untidy hair. The expression was cold, impersonal, analytical.

After he got on the highway, he kept looking in the rearview mirror. There was no sign of pursuit. Evidently Rambler had not noticed that the car was loaded for flight—books and cartons on the seats, foot locker on the floor, all this was out of his range of vision. He wondered what they were doing. Wrecking the interior of the bungalow? No. They were probably waiting for him to return so they could blackmail him. Blackmail a black male.

On the turnpike he kept going faster and faster—eighty-five miles an hour, ninety, ninety-five, one hundred. He felt exhilarated by this tremendous speed. It was clearing his mind, heartening him, taking him out of himself.

He began to rationalize about what had happened. He decided that Rambler and his friends didn't give a damn that he Woodruff, was a black man. They couldn't care less. They were very bright boys, bright enough to recognize him for what he was: a black man in his sixties, conditioned all his life by the knowledge that "White woman taboo for you" (as one of his African students used to say). The moment he attempted to intervene there in front of the church, they decided to take him with them. They knew he wasn't going to the police about any matter which involved sex and a white girl, especially where there was the certainty that all seven of them would accuse him of having relations with the girl. They had used his presence in that tool shed to give an extra exquisite fillip to their dreadful game.

He turned on the radio and waited impatiently for music, any kind of music, thinking it would distract him. He got one of those stations that play what he called thump-and-blare music. A husky-voiced woman was shouting a song—not singing, shouting:

I'm gonna turn on the big beat
I'm gonna turn up the high heat
For my ho-daddy, ho-daddy,
For my ho-daddy, ho-daddy.

He flipped the switch, cutting off the sound and he gradually diminished the speed of the car, slowing, slowing, slowing. "We got us a rich ho-daddy." That's what one of the boys had said there in front of the church when he plucked the money out of Woodruff's wallet. A rich ho-daddy? A black ho-daddy. A witness. Another poor scared black bastard who was a witness.

1971

Carlos Bulosan 1913–1956

The first Filipino writer to bring Filipino concerns to national attention, Carlos Bulosan came to Seattle in 1930, steerage class, inculcated with the ideals of brotherhood and equality he had learned in American schools in the Philippines. Arriving at the start of the Great Depression, he quickly learned the bitter truth that when jobs are scarce, minorities and immigrants become scapegoats, and the egalitarian rhetoric was far from reality for such as he. From the 1870s, the Chinese had been targets of such racial hatred; in the 1930s, the Filipinos were perceived as the latest influx of the "yellow horde" who worked for little pay, taking jobs away from whites. In his brief experience as a migrant laborer, Bulosan endured living conditions worse than those he had left behind. Bulosan found "that in many ways it was a crime to be a Filipino in California. I came to know that the public streets were not free to my people: we were stopped each time these vigilant patrolmen saw us driving a car. We were suspect each time we were seen with a white woman."

In Los Angeles, Bulosan met labor organizer Chris Mensalves. Together they organized a union of fish cannery workers, and Bulosan, working as a dishwasher, wrote for the union paper. Writing became a means of defining his life, and his concern for just treatment for Filipino workers became one of his major themes. In 1936 the effects of poverty and constant moving led to tuberculosis. Bulosan entered the hospital, and in 1938 he was discharged, after three operations for lung lesions and an extended convalescence. His enforced confinement became his education. Bulosan read at least a book a day, from Whitman and Poe through Hemingway, Dreiser, and Steinbeck.

With some of the most important Pacific action of World War II occurring in the Philippine Islands, names such as Bataan and Corregidor became household words, and the climate was right for Bulosan to rise to national prominence. The *Saturday Evening Post* paid nearly a thousand dollars for Bulosan's essay "Freedom from Want" (an essay which was illustrated by Norman Rockwell and displayed in the Federal Building in San Francisco); his work appeared in *The New Yorker, Harper's Bazaar, Town and Country, Poetry* and other prestigious magazines, and he was featured on the cover of news magazines. His book of reminiscences, *Laughter of My Father,* was broadcast to American soldiers around the world, and *Look* declared his autobiographic novel, *America Is in the Heart,* one of the fifty most important American books ever published.

However, Bulosan died in 1956, in poverty and obscurity. The political climate had changed, and narratives of the underdog, the remorselessly common person, were no longer appealing. In Asian American literature, though, Carlos Bulosan's impassioned work has an enduring place.

The following selections from chapters 13 and 14 of *America Is in the Heart* describe Carlos's arrival in the United States at age seventeen, penniless, idealistic, and naive. Thrust into a violent, dog-eat-dog world, Carlos struggles to maintain his belief in himself and the faith in the American ideals of democracy and justice that he had been taught in the Philippines. *America Is in the Heart* is a reminder to Americans to live up to the ideals set forth by the founders and a searing record of the painful experience of Filipino immigrants in the United States in the 1930s.

Amy Ling
late of University of Wisconsin at Madison

King-Kok Cheung
University of California, Los Angeles

PRIMARY WORKS

The Voice of Bataan, 1943; *The Dark People,* 1944; *Laughter of My Father,* 1944; *America Is in the Heart,* 1946; *The Power of the People,* 1977.

from America Is in the Heart

from Chapter XIII

We arrived in Seattle on a June day. My first sight of the approaching land was an exhilarating experience. Everything seemed native and promising to me. It was like coming home after a long voyage, although as yet I had no home in this city. Everything seemed familiar and kind—the white faces of the buildings melting in the soft afternoon sun, the gray contours of the surrounding valleys that seemed to vanish in the last periphery of light. With a sudden surge of joy, I knew that I must find a home in this new land.

I had only twenty cents left, not even enough to take me to Chinatown where, I had been informed, a Filipino hotel and two restaurants were located. Fortunately two oldtimers put me in a car with four others, and took us to a hotel on King Street, the heart of Filipino life in Seattle. Marcelo, who was also in the car, had a cousin named Elias who came to our room with another oldtimer. Elias and his unknown friend persuaded my companions to play a strange kind of card game. In a little while Elias got up and touched his friend suggestively; then they disappeared and we never saw them again.

It was only when our two countrymen had left that my companions realized what happened. They had taken all their money. Marcelo asked me if I had any money. I gave him my twenty cents. After collecting a few more cents from the others, he went downstairs and when he came back he told us that he had telegraphed for money to his brother in California.

All night we waited for the money to come, hungry and afraid to go out in the street. Outside we could hear shouting and singing; then a woman screamed lustily in one of the rooms down the hall. Across from our hotel a jazz band was playing noisily; it went on until dawn. But in the morning a telegram came to Marcelo which said:

YOUR BROTHER DIED AUTOMOBILE ACCIDENT LAST WEEK

Marcelo looked at us and began to cry. His anguish stirred an aching fear in me. I knelt on the floor looking for my suitcase under the bed. I knew that I had to go out now—alone. I put the suitcase on my shoulder and walked toward the door, stopping for a moment to look back at my friends who were still standing silently around Marcelo. Suddenly a man came into the room and announced that he was the proprietor.

"Well, boys," he said, looking at our suitcases, "where is the rent?"

"We have no money, sir," I said, trying to impress him with my politeness.

"That is too bad," he said quickly, glancing furtively at our suitcases again. "That is just too bad." He walked outside and went down the hall. He came back with a short, fat Filipino, who looked at us stupidly with his dull, small eyes, and spat his cigar out of the window.

"There they are, Jake," said the proprietor.

Jake looked disappointed. "They are too young," he said.

"You can break them in, Jake," said the proprietor.

"They will be sending babies next," Jake said.

"You can break them in, can't you, Jake?" the proprietor pleaded. "This is not the first time you have broken babies in. You have done it in the sugar plantations in Hawaii, Jake!"

"Hell!" Jake said, striding across the room to the proprietor. He pulled a fat roll of bills from his pocket and gave twenty-five dollars to the proprietor. Then he turned to us and said, "All right, Pinoys, you are working for me now. Get your hats and follow me."

We were too frightened to hesitate. When we lifted our suitcases the proprietor ordered us not to touch them.

"I'll take care of them until you come back from Alaska," he said. "Good fishing, boys!"

In this way we were sold for five dollars each to work in the fish canneries in Alaska, by a Visayan from the island of Leyte to an Ilocano from the province of La Union. Both were oldtimers; both were tough. They exploited young immigrants until one of them, the hotel proprietor, was shot dead by an unknown assailant. We were forced to sign a paper which stated that each of us owed the contractor twenty dollars for bedding and another twenty for luxuries. What the luxuries were, I have never found out. The contractor turned out to be a tall, heavy-set, dark Filipino, who came to the small hold of the boat barking at us like a dog. He was drunk and saliva was running down his shirt.

"And get this, you devils!" he shouted at us. "You will never come back alive if you don't do what I say!"

It was the beginning of my life in America, the beginning of a long flight that carried me down the years, fighting desperately to find peace in some corner of life.

I had struck up a friendship with two oldtimers who were not much older than I. One was Conrado Torres, a journalism student at a university in Oregon, who was fired with a dream to unionize the cannery workers. I discovered that he had come from Binalonan, but could hardly remember the names of people there because he had been very young when he had come to America. Conrado was small and dark, with slant eyes and thick eyebrows; but his nose was thin above a wise, sensuous mouth. He introduced me to Paulo Lorca, a gay fellow, who had graduated from law school in Los Angeles. This surreptitious meeting at a cannery in Rose Inlet was the beginning of a friendship that grew simultaneously with the growth of the trade union movement and progressive ideas among the Filipinos in the United States.

In those days labor unions were still unheard of in the canneries, so the contractors rapaciously exploited their workers. They had henchmen in every cannery who saw to it that every attempt at unionization was frustrated and the instigators of the idea punished. The companies also had their share in the exploitation; our bunkhouses were unfit for human habitation. The lighting system was bad and dangerous to our eyes, and those of us who were working in the semi-darkness were severely affected by the strong ammonia from the machinery.

I was working in a section called "wash lye." Actually a certain amount of lye was diluted in the water where I washed the beheaded fish that came down on a small escalator. One afternoon a cutter above me, working in the poor light, slashed off his right arm with the cutting machine. It happened so swiftly, he did not cry out. I saw his arm floating down the water among the fish heads.

It was only at night that we felt free, although the sun seemed never to disappear from the sky. It stayed on in the western horizon and its magnificence inflamed the snows on the island, giving us a world of soft, continuous light, until the moon rose at about ten o'clock to take its place. Then trembling shadows began to form on the rise of the brilliant snow in our yard, and we would come out with baseball bats, gloves and balls, and the Indian girls who worked in the cannery would join us, shouting huskily like men.

We played far into the night. Sometimes a Filipino and an Indian girl would run off into the moonlight; we could hear them chasing each other in the snow. Then we would hear the girl giggling and laughing deliciously in the shadows. Paulo was always running off with a girl named LaBelle. How she acquired that name in Alaska, I never found out. But hardly had we started our game when off they ran, chasing each other madly and suddenly disappearing out of sight.

Toward the end of the season La Belle gave birth to a baby. We were sure, however, that the father was not in our group. We were sure that she had got it from one of the Italian fishermen on the island. La Belle did not come to work for two days, but when she appeared on the third day with the baby slung on her back, she threw water into Conrado's face.

"Are you going to marry me or not?" she asked him.

Conrado was frightened. He was familiar with the ways of Indians, so he said: "Why should I marry you?"

"We'll see about that!" La Belle shouted, running to the door. She came back with an official of the company. "That's the one!" she said, pointing to Conrado.

"You'd better come to the office with us," said the official.

Conrado did not know what to do. He looked at me for help. Paulo left his washing machine and nodded to me to follow him. We went with them into the building which was the town hall.

"You are going to marry this Indian girl and stay on the island for seven years as prescribed by law," said the official to Conrado. "And as the father of the baby, you must support both mother and child, and, if you have four more children by the time your turn is up, you will be sent back to the mainland with a bonus."

"But, sir, the baby is not mine," said Conrado weakly.

Paulo stepped up quickly beside him and said: "The baby is mine, sir. I guess I'll have to stay."

La Belle looked at Paulo with surprise. After a moment, however, she began to smile with satisfaction. Paulo was well-educated and spoke good English. But I think what finally drove Conrado from La Belle's primitive mind were Paulo's curly hair, his even, white teeth. Meekly she signed the paper after Paulo.

"I'll stay here for seven years, all right," Paulo said to me. "I'm a mess in Los Angeles anyway—so I'll stay with this dirty Indian girl."

"Stop talking like that if you know what is good for you," La Belle said, giving him the baby.

"I guess you are right," Paulo said.

"You shouldn't have done it for me," Conrado said.

"It's all right," Paulo laughed. "I'll be in the United States before you know it."

I still do not understand why Paulo interceded for Conrado. When the season was over Paulo came to our bunks in the boat and asked Conrado to send him something to drink. I did not see him again.

from Chapter XIV

When I landed in Seattle for the second time, I expected a fair amount of money from the company. But the contractor, Max Feuga, came into the play room and handed us slips of paper. I looked at mine and was amazed at the neatly itemized expenditures that I was supposed to have incurred during the season. Twenty-five dollars for withdrawals, one hundred for board and room, twenty for bedding, and another twenty for something I do not now remember. At the bottom was the actual amount I was to receive after all the deductions: *thirteen dollars!*

I could do nothing. I did not even go to the hotel where I had left my suitcase. I went to a Japanese dry goods store on Jackson Street and bought a pair of corduroy pants and a blue shirt. It was already twilight and the cannery workers were in the crowded Chinese gambling houses, losing their season's earnings and drinking bootleg whisky. They became quarrelsome and abusive to their own people when they lost, and subservient to the Chinese gambling lords and marijuana peddlers. They pawed at the semi-nude whores with their dirty hands and made suggestive gestures, running out into the night when they were rebuffed for lack of money.

I was already in America, and I felt good and safe. I did not understand why. The gamblers, prostitutes and Chinese opium smokers did not excite me, but they aroused in me a feeling of flight. I knew that I must run away from them, but it was not that I was afraid of contamination. I wanted to see other aspects of American life, for surely these destitute and vicious people were merely a small part of it. Where would I begin this pilgrimage, this search for a door into America?

I went outside and walked around looking into the faces of my countrymen, wondering if I would see someone I had known in the Philippines. I came to a building which brightly dressed white women were entering, lifting their diaphanous gowns as they climbed the stairs. I looked up and saw the huge sign:

MANILA DANCE HALL

The orchestra upstairs was playing; Filipinos were entering. I put my hands in my pockets and followed them, beginning to feel lonely for the sound of home.

The dance hall was crowded with Filipino cannery workers and domestic servants. But the girls were very few, and the Filipinos fought over them. When a boy liked a girl he bought a roll of tickets from the hawker on the floor and kept dancing with her. But the other boys who also liked the same girl shouted at him to stop, cursing him in dialects and sometimes throwing rolled wet papers at him. At the bar the glasses were tinkling, the bottles popping loudly, and the girls in the back room were smoking marijuana. It was almost impossible to breathe.

Then I saw Marcelo's familiar back. He was dancing with a tall blonde in a green dress, a girl so tall that Marcelo looked like a dwarf climbing a tree. But the girl was pretty and her body was nicely curved and graceful, and she had a way of swaying that aroused confused sensations in me. It was evident that many of the boys wanted to dance with her; they were shouting maliciously at Marcelo. The way the blonde waved to them made me think that she knew most of them. They were nearly all oldtimers and strangers to Marcelo. They were probably gamblers and pimps, because they had fat rolls of money and expensive clothing.

But Marcelo was learning very fast. He requested one of his friends to buy another roll of tickets for him. The girl was supposed to tear off one ticket every three minutes, but I noticed that she tore off a ticket for every minute. That was ten cents a minute. Marcelo was unaware of what she was doing; he was spending his whole season's earnings on his first day in America. It was only when one of his friends shouted to him in the dialect that he became angry with the girl. Marcelo was not tough, but his friend was an oldtimer. Marcelo pushed the girl toward the gaping bystanders. His friend opened a knife and gave it to him.

Then something happened that made my heart leap. One of the blonde girl's admirers came from behind and struck Marcelo with a piece of lead pipe. Marcelo's friend whipped out a pistol and fired. Marcelo and the boy with the lead pipe fell on the floor simultaneously, one on top of the other, but the blonde girl ran into the crowd screaming frantically. Several guns banged at once, and the lights went out. I saw Marcelo's friend crumple in the fading light.

At once the crowd seemed to flow out of the windows. I went to a side window and saw three heavy electric wires strung from the top of the building to the ground. I reached for them and slid to the ground. My palms were burning when I came out of the alley. Then I heard the sirens of police cars screaming infernally toward the place. I put my cap in my pocket and ran as fast as I could in the direction of a neon sign two blocks down the street.

It was a small church where Filipino farm workers were packing their suitcases and bundles. I found out later that Filipino immigrants used their churches as rest houses while they were waiting for work. There were two large trucks outside. I went to one of them and sat on the running board, holding my hands over my heart for fear it would beat too fast. The lights in the church went out and the workers came into the street. The driver of the truck in which I was sitting pointed a strong flashlight at me.

"Hey, you, are you looking for a job?" he asked.

"Yes, sir," I said.

"Get in the truck," he said, jumping into the cab. "Let's go, Flo!" he shouted to the other driver.

I was still trembling with excitement. But I was glad to get out of Seattle—to anywhere else in America. I did not care where so long as it was in America. I found a corner and sat down heavily. The drivers shouted to each other. Then we were off to work.

It was already midnight and the lights in the city of Seattle were beginning to fade. I could see the reflections on the bright lake in Bremerton. I was reminded of Baguio. Then some of the men began singing. The driver and two men were arguing over money. A boy in the other truck was playing a violin. We were on the highway to Yakima Valley.

After a day and a night of driving we arrived in a little town called Moxee City. The apple trees were heavy with fruit and the branches drooped to the ground. It was late afternoon when we passed through the town; the hard light of the sun punctuated the ugliness of the buildings. I was struck dumb by its isolation and the dry air that hung oppressively over the place. The heart-shaped valley was walled by high treeless mountains, and the hot breeze that blew in from a distant sea was injurious to the apple trees.

The leader of our crew was called Cornelio Paez; but most of the oldtimers suspected that it was not his real name. There was something shifty about him, and his so-called bookkeeper, a pockmarked man we simply called Pinoy (which is a term generally applied to all Filipino immigrant workers), had a strange trick of squinting sideways when he looked at you. There seemed to be an old animosity between Paez and his bookkeeper.

But we were drawn together because the white people of the Yakima Valley were suspicious of us. Years before, in the town of Toppenish, two Filipino apple pickers had been found murdered on the road to Sunnyside. At that time, there was ruthless persecution of the Filipinos throughout the Pacific Coast, instigated by orchardists who feared the unity of white and Filipino workers. A small farmer in Wapato who had tried to protect his Filipino workers had had his house burned. So however much we distrusted each other under Paez, we knew that beyond the walls of our bunkhouse were our real enemies, waiting to drive us out of Yakima Valley.

I had become acquainted with an oldtimer who had had considerable experience in the United States. His name was Julio, and it seemed that he was hiding from some trouble in Chicago. At night, when the men gambled in the kitchen, I would stand silently behind him and watch him cheat the other players. He was very deft, and his eyes were sharp and trained. Sometimes when there was no game, Julio would teach me tricks.

Mr. Malraux, our employer, had three daughters who used to work with us after school hours. He was a Frenchman who had gone to Moxee City when it consisted of only a few houses. At that time the valley was still a haven for Indians, but they had been gradually driven out when farming had been started on a large scale. Malraux had married an American woman in Spokane and begun farming; the girls came one by one, helping him on the farm as they grew. When I arrived in Moxee City they were already in their teens.

The oldest girl was called Estelle; she had just finished high school. She had a delightful disposition and her industry was something that men talked about with approval. The other girls, Maria and Diane, were still too young to be going about so freely; but whenever Estelle came to our bunkhouse they were always with her.

It was now the end of summer and there was a bright moon in the sky. Not far from Moxee City was a wide grassland where cottontails and jack rabbits roamed at night. Estelle used to drive her father's old car and would pick up some of us at the bunkhouse; then we would go hunting with their dogs and a few antiquated shotguns.

When we came back from hunting we would go to the Malraux house with some of the men who had musical instruments. We would sit on the lawn for hours singing American songs. But when they started singing Philippine songs their voices were so sad, so full of yesterday and the haunting presence of familiar seas, as if they had reached the end of creation, that life seemed ended and no bright spark was left in the world.

But one afternoon toward the end of the season, Paez went to the bank to get our paychecks and did not come back. The pockmarked bookkeeper was furious.

"I'll get him this time!" he said, running up and down the house. "He did that last year in California and I didn't get a cent. I know where to find the bastard!"

Julio grabbed him by the neck. "You'd better tell me where to find him if you know what is good for you," he said angrily, pushing the frightened bookkeeper toward the stove.

"Let me alone!" he shouted.

Julio hit him between the eyes, and the bookkeeper struggled violently. Julio hit him again. The bookkeeper rolled on the floor like a baby. Julio picked him up and threw him outside the house. I thought he was dead, but his legs began to move. Then he opened his eyes and got up quickly, staggering like a drunken stevedore toward the highway. Julio came out of the house with brass knuckles, but the bookkeeper was already disappearing behind the apple orchard. Julio came back and began hitting the door of the kitchen with all his force, in futile anger.

I had not seen this sort of brutality in the Philippines, but my first contact with it in America made me brave. My bravery was still nameless, and waiting to express itself. I was not shocked when I saw that my countrymen had become ruthless toward one another, and this sudden impact of cruelty made me insensate to pain and kindness, so that it took me a long time to wholly trust other men. As time went by I became as ruthless as the worst of them, and I became afarid that I would never feel like a human being again. Yet no matter what bestiality encompassed my life, I felt sure that somewhere, sometime, I would break free. This faith kept me from completely succumbing to the degradation into which many of my countrymen had fallen. It finally paved my way out of our small, harsh life, painfully but cleanly, into a world of strange intellectual adventures and self-fulfillment.

1946

Mario Suárez 1925–1998

Mario Suárez is probably the first contemporary "Chicano" writer. He used the term, with pride and humor, to refer to urban Mexican Americans when the term was widely regarded, both inside and outside the Mexican American community, as derogatory. Suárez's primary setting was "El Hoyo" (The Hole), the barrio in Tucson where he was born and raised. "El Hoyo" is inhabited by a colorful array of characters who represent the range of Chicano culture and experience: Señor Garza, who closes his barbershop when a rush of business interferes with the "idle gossip" he so much enjoys with his neighbors; Gonzalo Pereda, who laments his sons' preference for baseball over the Mexican pastime of cockfighting; Pepe García, a young man who becomes a zoot suiter, complete with bright plumed hat, oversized jacket, and tapered pants, after a memorable summer in Los Angeles. In only a handful of stories, Suárez chronicled the urban acculturation of Mexican Americans in the 1930s and 1940s more perceptively and authentically than anyone, including John Steinbeck.

Suárez was the first of five children born to an immigrant couple, Francisco, from the Mexican state of Chihuahua, and Carmen Minjárez Suárez, from Sonora, across the border from Arizona. After an undistinguished high school career in Tucson, Mario joined the U.S. Navy, serving during World War II on patrol off the New Jersey coast and on various assignments in Brazil. After his discharge, he returned to Tucson and enrolled in the University of Arizona, where his writing talent emerged.

Always an avid reader, Suárez was drawn to John Steinbeck, especially his *Tortilla Flat* (1935), a chronicle of the primitive—and, ultimately, clueless—*paisanos* of Monterey, California. Startled that Mexican Americans and other Latinos could be figures of interest to an eventual Nobel Prize winner, Suárez determined to present a more nuanced view of Mexican American life drawn from his own experience. His stories began to appear in *Arizona Quarterly* in 1947 while he was still an undergraduate. Suárez subsequently worked as a journalist and college teacher. Although he continued to compose stories and novels, after his *Arizona Quarterly* sketches, only one story reached publication.

The three stories collected here display Suárez's literary skills: his casually fluent, engaging style, his sharply and concisely drawn characters, and his ability to identify the small behaviors, institutions, and practices that define a culture. In "El Hoyo," Suárez notes the symbolic importance of *capirotada,* a Mexican dish that consists of leftovers from the night before and represents the diversity and contradictions of barrio life. In "Señor Garza," Suárez marks the limits of capitalism for at least one Chicano with these closing lines: "Garza, a philosopher. Owner of Garza's Barber Shop. But the shop will never own Garza." And in "Kid Zopilote," Suárez poignantly chronicles the experiences of a young *pachuco* (zoot suiter) struggling to forge an identity from the elements of two cultures, Mexican and American, long antagonistic to one another.

Raymund A. Paredes
University of California–Los Angeles

PRIMARY WORKS

"El Hoyo," "Señor Garza," "Cuco Goes to a Party," "Loco-Chu," and "Kid Zopilote," *Arizona Quarterly,* 3 (Summer 1947): 112–137; "Southside Run" and "Maestría," *Arizona Quarterly,* 4 (Winter 1948): 362–373; "Mexican Heaven," *Arizona Quarterly,* 6 (Winter 1950): 310–315; "Los coyotes," in *Festival de Flor y Canto,* ed. Alurista, F. A. Cervantes, Juan Gómez Quinones, Mary Ann Pacheco, and Gustavo Segade (Los Angeles: University of Southern California Press, El Centro Chicano, 1976), 26–29.

El Hoyo

From the center of downtown Tucson the ground slopes gently away to Main Street, drops a few feet, and then rolls to the banks of the Santa Cruz River. Here lies the sprawling section of the city known as El Hoyo. Why it is called El Hoyo is not clear. It is not a hole as its name would imply; it is simply the river's immediate valley. Its inhabitants are *chicanos* who raise hell on Saturday night, listen to Padre Estanislao on Sunday morning, and then raise more hell on Sunday night. While the term *chicano* is the short way of saying *Mexicano,* it is the long way of referring to everybody. Pablo Gutierrez married the Chinese grocer's daughter and acquired a store; his sons are *chicanos.* So are the sons of Killer Jones who threw a fight in Harlem and fled to El Hoyo to marry Cristina Mendez. And so are all of them—the assortment of harlequins, bandits, oppressors, oppressed, gentlemen, and bums who came from Old Mexico to work for the Southern Pacific, pick cotton, clerk, labor, sing, and go on relief. It is doubtful that all of these spiritual sons of Mexico live in El Hoyo because they love each other—many fight and bicker constantly. It is doubtful that the *chicanos* live in El Hoyo because of its scenic beauty—it is everything but beautiful. Its houses are built of unplastered adobe, wood, license plates, and abandoned car parts. Its narrow streets are mostly clearings which have, in time, acquired names. Except for the tall trees which nobody has ever cared to identify, nurse, or destroy, the main things known to grow in the general area are weeds, garbage piles, dogs, and kids. And it is doubtful that the *chicanos* live in El Hoyo because it is safe—many times the Santa Cruz River has risen and inundated the area.

In other respects living in El Hoyo has its advantages. If one is born with the habit of acquiring bills, El Hoyo is where the bill collectors are less likely to find you. If one has acquired the habit of listening to Señor Perea's Mexican Hour in the wee hours of the morning with the radio on at full blast, El Hoyo is where you are less likely to be reported to the authorities. Besides, Perea is very popular and to everybody sooner or later is dedicated The Mexican Hat Dance. If one has inherited a bad taste for work but inherited also the habit of eating, where, if not in El Hoyo, are the neighbors more willing to lend you a cup of flour or beans? When Señora Garcia's house burned to the ground with all her belongings and two kids, a benevolent gentleman conceived the gesture that put her on the road to solvency. He took five hundred names and solicited from each a dollar. At the end of the week he turned over to the heartbroken but grateful señora three hundred and fifty dollars in cold cash and pocketed his recompense. When the new manager of a local business decided that no more Mexican girls were to work behind his counters, it was the *chicanos* of El Hoyo who acted as pickets and, on taking their individually small but collectively great buying power elsewhere, drove the manager out and the girls returned to their jobs. When the Mexican Army was enroute to Baja California and the *chicanos* found out that the enlisted men ate only at infrequent intervals they crusaded across town with pots of beans, trays of tortillas, boxes of candy, and bottles of wine to meet the train. When someone gets married celebrating is not restricted to the immediate families and friends of the couple. The public is invited. Anything calls for a celebration and in turn a celebration calls for anything. On Armistice Day there are no fewer than half a dozen fights at the Tira-Chancla Dance Hall. On Mexican

Independence Day more than one flag is sworn allegiance to and toasted with gallon after gallon of Tumba Yaqui.

And El Hoyo is something more. It is this something more which brought Felipe Ternero back from the wars after having killed a score of Germans with his body resembling a patch-work quilt. It helped him to marry a fine girl named Julia. It brought Joe Zepeda back without a leg from Luzon and helps him hold more liquor than most men can hold with two. It brought Jorge Casillas, a gunner flying B-24's over Germany, back to compose boleros. Perhaps El Hoyo is the proof that those people exist who, while not being against anything, have as yet failed to observe the more popular modes of human conduct. Perhaps the humble appearance of El Hoyo justifies the discerning shrugs of more than a few people only vaguely aware of its existence. Perhaps El Hoyo's simplicity motivates many a *chicano* to move far away from its intoxicating *frenesí,* its dark narrow streets, and its shrieking children, to deny the blood-well from which he springs, to claim the blood of a conquistador while his hair is straight and his face beardless. Yet El Hoyo is not the desperate outpost of a few families against the world. It fights for no causes except those which soothe its immediate angers. It laughs and cries with the same amount of passion in times of plenty and of want.

Perhaps El Hoyo, its inhabitants, and its essence can best be explained by telling you a little bit about a dish called *capirotada.* Its origin is uncertain. But it is made of old, new, stale, and hard bread. It is sprinkled with water and then it is cooked with raisins, olives, onions, tomatoes, peanuts, cheese, and general leftovers of that which is good and bad. It is seasoned with salt, sugar, pepper, and sometimes chili or tomato sauce. It is fired with tequila or sherry wine. It is served hot, cold, or just "on the weather" as they say in El Hoyo. The Garcias like it one way, the Quevedos another, the Trilos another, and the Ortegas still another. While in general appearance it does not differ much from one home to another it tastes different everywhere. Nevertheless it is still *capirotada.* And so it is with El Hoyo's *chicanos.* While many seem to the undiscerning eye to be alike it is only because collectively they are referred to as *chicanos.* But like *capirotada,* fixed in a thousand ways and served on a thousand tables, which can only be evaluated by individual taste, the *chicanos* must be so distinguished.

1947

Señor Garza

Many consider Garza's Barber Shop as not truly in El Hoyo because it is on Congress Street and therefore downtown. Señor Garza, its proprietor, cashier, janitor, and Saint Francis, philosophizes that since it is situated in that part of the street where the land decidely slopes, it is in El Hoyo. Who would question it? Who contributes to every cause for which a solicitor comes in with a long face and a longer relation of sadness? Who is the easiest touch for all the drunks who have to buy their daily cures? For loafers who go to look for jobs and never find them? For bullfighters on the wrong side of the border? For boxers still amateurs though punchy? For barbers without barber shops? And for the endless line of moochers who drop in to borrow anything from two bits to two dollars? Naturally, Garza.

Garza's Barber Shop is more than razors, scissors, and hair. It is where men, disgruntled at the vice of the rest of the world, come to air their views. It is where they come to get things off their chests along with the hair off their heads and beard off their faces. Garza's Barber Shop is where everybody sooner or later goes or should. This does not mean that there are no other barber shops in El Hoyo. There are. But none of them seem quite to capture the atmosphere that Garza's does. If it were not downtown it would probably have a little fighting rooster tied to a stake by the front door. If it were not rented to Señor Garza only it would perhaps smell of sherry wine all day. To Garza's Barber Shop goes all that is good and bad. The lawbreakers come in to rub elbows with the sheriff's deputies. And toward all Garza is the same. When zoot suiters come in for a very slight trim, Garza who is very versatile, puts on a bit of zoot talk and hep-cats with the zootiest of them. When the boys that are not zoot suiters come in, he becomes, for the purpose of accommodating his clientele, just as big a snob as their individual personalities require. When necessity calls for a change in his character Garza can assume the proportions of a Greek, a Chinaman, a gypsy, a republican, a democrat, or if only his close friends are in the shop, plain Garza.

Perhaps Garza's pet philosophy is that a man should not work too hard. Garza tries not to. His day begins according to the humor of his wife. When Garza drives up late, conditions are perhaps good. When Garza drives up early, all is perhaps not well. Garza's Barber Shop has been known, accordingly, to stay closed for a week. It has also been known to open before the sun comes up and to remain open for three consecutive days. But on normal days and with conditions so-so, Garza comes about eight in the morning. After opening, he pulls up the green venetian blinds. He brings out two green ash cans containing the hair cut the preceding day and puts them on the edge of the sidewalk. After this he goes to a little back room in the back of the shop, brings out a long crank, and lowers the red awning that keeps out the morning sun. Lily-boy, the fat barber who through time and diligence occupies chair number two, is usually late. This does not mean that Lily-boy is lazy, but he is married and there are rumors, which he promptly denies, that state he is henpecked. Rodriguez, barber number three, usually fails to show up for five out of six workdays.

On ordinary mornings Garza sits in the shoeshine stand because it is closest to the window and nods at the pretty girls going to work and to the ugly ones, too. He works on an occasional customer. He goes to Sally and Sam's for a cup of coffee, and on returning continues to sit. At noon Garza takes off his small apron, folds it, hangs it on the arm of his chair, and after combing his hair goes to La Estrella to eat and flirt with the waitresses who, for reasons that even they cannot understand, have taken him into their confidence. They are well aware of his marital standing; but Garza has black wavy hair and a picaresque charm that sends them to the kitchen giggling. After eating his usual meal of beans, rice, tortilla, and coffee, he bids all the girls good-bye and goes back to his barber shop. The afternoons are spent in much the same manner as the mornings except that on such days as Saturday, there is such a rush of business that Garza very often seeks some excuse to go away from his own business and goes for the afternoon to Nogales in Mexico or downstairs to the Tecolote Club to drink beer.

On most days, by five-thirty everybody has usually been in the shop for friendly reasons, commercial reasons, and even spiritual reasons. Loco-Chu, whose lack of brains everybody understands, has gone by and insulted the customers. Take-It-Easy, whose liquor-saturated brain everybody respects, has either made nasty signs at everybody or has come in to quote the words and poems of the immortal Antonio Plaza. Cuco has come from his job at Feldman's Furniture Store to converse of the beauty of Mexico and the comfort of the United States. Procuna has come in, and being a university student with more absences than the rest of his class put together, has very politely explained his need for two dollars until the check comes in. Chonito has shined shoes and danced a dozen or so boogie pieces. There have been arguments. Fortunes made and lost. Women loved. The great Cuate Cuete has come in to talk of the glory and grandeur of zoot suitism in Los Angeles. Old customers due about that day have come. Also new ones who had to be told that all the loafers who seemingly live in Garza's Barber Shop were not waiting for haircuts. Then the venetian blinds are let down. The red awning is cranked up. The door is latched on the inside although it is continually opened on request for friends, and the remaining customers are attended to and let out.

Inside Garza opens his little National Cash Register, counts the day's money, and puts it away. He opens his small writing desk and adds and subtracts for a little while in his green record book. Meanwhile Chonito grudgingly sweeps and says very nasty words. Lily-boy phones his wife to tell her that he is about to start home and that he will not be waylaid by friends and that he will not arrive drunk. Rodriguez relates to everybody in the shop that when he was a young man getting tired was not like him. The friends who have already dropped in wait until the beer is spoken for and then Chonito is sent for it. When it is brought in and distributed everything is talked about. Lastly, women are thoroughly insulted although their necessity is emphasized. Garza, being a man of experience and one known to say what he feels when he feels it, recalls the ditty he heard while still in the cradle and says, "To women neither all your love nor all your money." The friends, drinking Garza's beer, agree.

Not always has Señor Garza enjoyed the place of distinction if not of material achievement that he enjoys among his friends today. In his thirty-five years his life has gone through transition after transition, conquest after conquest, setback after setback. But now Señor Garza is one of those to whom most refer, whether for reasons of friendship, indebtedness, or of having never read Plato and Aristotle, as an oracle pouring out his worldly knowledge during and between the course of his haircuts.

Garza was born in El Hoyo, the second of seven Garzas. He was born with so much hair that perhaps this is what later prompted him to be a barber. At five he almost burned the house down while playing with matches. At ten he was still waiting for his older brother to outgrow his clothes so that they could be handed down to him. Garza had the desire to learn, but even before he found out about school Garza had already attained a fair knowledge of everything. Especially, the knowledge of want. Finally, his older brother got a new pair of overalls and Garza got his clothes. On going to school he immediately claimed having gone to school in Mexico so Garza was tried out in the 3B. In the 4A his long legs fitted under the desk, so he had to begin his education there. In the 5B he fell in love with the teacher and was promptly promoted to avert a scandal. When Garza was sixteen and had managed to get to the eighth grade, school suddenly became a mass of equations, blocks, lines, angles, foreign names, and headaches. At seventeen it might have driven him to insanity so Garza wisely cut his schooling short at sixteen.

On leaving school Garza tried various enterprises. He became a delivery boy for a drug store. He became a stock room clerk for a shoe store. But of all enterprises the one he found most profitable was that of shearing dogs. He advertised his business and it flourished until it became very obvious that his house and brothers were getting quite flea ridden. Garza had to give it up. The following year he was overcome with the tales of vast riches in California. Not that there was gold, but there were grapes to be picked. He went to California. But of that trip he has more than once said that the tallness of the Californian garbage cans made him come back twenty pounds lighter and without hair under his armpits. Garza then tried the CCC camp. But it turned out that there were too many bosses with muscles that looked like golf balls whom Garza thought it best not to have much to do with. Garza was already one that could keep everybody laughing all day long, but this prevented almost everybody from working. At night when most boys at camp were either listening to the juke box in the canteen, or listening to the playing of sad guitars, Garza trimmed heads at fifteen cents. After three months of piling rocks, carrying logs, and of getting fed up with his bosses' perpetual desires of making him work, Garza came back to the city with the money he had saved cutting hair and through a series of deals was allowed a barber's chair in a going-establishment.

In a few years Garza came to be a barber of prominence. He had grown to love the idle conversation that is typical of barber shops, the mere idle gossip that often speaks of broken homes and foresaken women in need of friends. These Garza has always sought and in his way has done his best to put in higher spirits. Even after his marriage he continued to receive anonymous after anonymous phone call. He came to know the bigtime operators and their brand of filthy doings. He came to know the bootleggers, thieves, love merchants, and rustlers. He came to know also the small-time operators with the bigtime complex and their shallowness of human understanding. He came to know false friends that came to him and said, "We're throwing a dance. We've got a good crowd. The tickets are two dollars." And on feeling superior, once the two dollars had fattened their wallets and inflated their conceit, remarked upon seeing him at the dance, "Damn, even the barber came." But in time Garza has seen many of these grow fat. He has seen their women go unfaithful. He has seen them get spiritually lost in trying to keep up materially with the people next door. He has seen them go bankrupt buying gabardine to make up for their lack of style. Their hair had cooties but smelled of aqua-rosa. The edges of their underwear were frilled even though they wore new suits. They gave breakfasts for half of the city to prove that "they had" and only ended up with piles of dirty dishes. Garza watched, philosophized, cut more hair, and of this has more than once said in the course of a beer or idle conversation among friends, "Damned fools, when you go, how in the hell are you going to take it with you? You are buried in your socks. Your suit is slit in the back and placed on top of you."

So in time Garza became the owner of his own barber shop. Garza's Barber Shop with its three Koken barber chairs, its reception sofas, its shoeshine stand, wash bowls, glass kits, pictures, objects to be sold and raffled, and juke box. Second to none in its colorful array of true friends and false, of drunks, loafers, bullfighters, boxers, other barbers, moochers, and occasional customers. Perfumed with the poetry of the immortal Antonio Plaza, and seasoned with naughty jokes told at random.

Soon the night becomes old and empty beer bottles are collected and put in the little back room. Chonito, who has swept the floor while Garza and his friends have consumed beer, asks for a fifty-cent advance or swears with the power of his fourteen years that he will never sweep the shop again, and gets it. Lily-boy phones his wife again and tells her that he is about to start home and that he is sober. Rodriguez, if he worked that day, says he has a bad cold which he must go home to cure, but asks for an advance to buy his tonic at Tom's Liquor Store. Then the lights are switched off and Garza, his barbers, his friends, and Chonito, file out. Garza, not forgetting the words he heard while in the cradle, "To women neither all your love nor all your money," either goes up the street to the Royal Inn for a glass of beer or to the All States Pool Hall. Then he goes home. Garza, a philosopher. Owner of Garza's Barber Shop. But the shop will never own Garza.

Kid Zopilote

When Pepe García came back from a summer in Los Angeles everybody began to call him Kid Zopilote. He did not know why he did not like the sound of it, but in trying to keep others from calling him that he got into many fights and scrapes. Still everybody he associated with persisted in calling him Kid Zopilote. When he dated a girl with spit curls and dresses so short that they almost bared her garters, everybody more than ever called him Kid Zopilote. It annoyed him very much. But everybody kept saying, "Kid Zopilote. Kid Zopilote." When he reasoned that it was a name given him because he dated this particular girl, he began to go with another one who wore very shiny red slacks and a very high pompadour. But to his dismay he found that he was still Kid Zopilote. All the girls who were seen with him were quickly dubbed Kiddas Zopilotas. This hurt their pride. Soon even the worst girls began to shun poor Kid Zopilote. None of the girls wanted to be seen with him. When he went to the Tira-Chancla Dance Hall very few of the girls consented to dance with him. When they did, it was out of compassion. But when the piece ended the girls never invited Kid Zopilote to the table. They thanked him on the run and began talking to someone else. Anybody else. Somehow all of this made Kid Zopilote very sad. He blamed everything on his cursed nickname. He could dance as well as anybody else and even better. Still he was an outcast. He could not understand what his nickname had to do with his personality. It sounded very ugly.

When he came back from Los Angeles he had been very happy until he went out to see his friends. He had come back with an even greater desire to dance. To him everything was in rhythm. Everywhere he went, even if it was only inside the house, he snapped his fingers and swung his body. His every motion and action was, as they say, in beat. His language had changed quite a bit, too. Every time he left the house he said to his mother, "Ma, I will *returniar* in a little while." When he returned he said, "Ma, I was *watchiando* a good movie, that is why I am a little bit late." And Señora García found it very hard to break him of saying things like that. But that was not the half of it. It was his clothes that she found very odd. When he opened a box he brought from Los Angeles and took from it a suit and put it on Señora García was horrified.

"Why, Pepe, what kind of a suit is that?" asked Señora García.

"Ma, this is the *styleacho* in Los Angeles, *Califo.*"

"Well, I certainly do not like it, Pepe."

"Ah, mama, but I like it. And I will tell you why. When I first got to California I was very lonely. I got a job picking fruit in no time at all and I was making very good money. But I also wanted to have a good time. So—one day I was down there in a place called Olvera Street in Los Angeles and I noticed that many of the boys who were Mexicans like me had suits like this one. They were very happy and very gay. They all had girls. There were many others, but they were not having any fun. They were squares. Well, I tried to talk to them, but it seemed as though they thought they were too good for me. Then I talked to the ones that were wearing drapes and they were more friendly. But even with them I could not go too far in making friends. So I bought this suit. Soon I went down to Olvera Street again and I got invited to parties and everything. I was introduced to many girls."

"But I do not like the suit, Pepe. It does not become you. I know now that you came back from California a cursed *pachuco.* A no-good zoot suiter. I am very sorry I ever let you go in the first place. I am only thanking Jesus Christ that your father is dead so that he would not see you with the sadness that I see you now."

"Well, ma, I will tell you something else right now if that is the way you feel about it. I am not the same as I used to be. I used to think that I would never want to wear a suit like this one. But now I like it. If the squares in Tucson do not wear a suit like this one is that my fault or is it for me to question? No. And I do not care. But if I like it and want to wear it I will. Leave me alone, ma, and let me wear what I please."

"You will not leave this house with that suit on, Pepe," said his mother, as she stood before the door, obstructing his path. "I will not have the neighbors see you in it."

"The neighbors do not buy my clothes, ma, so if they do not like my taste they can go to hell," said Kid Zopilote, as he gently moved his mother from the door and went out.

After that Señora García said nothing. Whenever Kid Zopilote went about the house with his pleated pants doing the shimmy to the radio, she merely sighed. When he clomped his thick-soled shoes in rhythm, she left the room in complete disappointment. When Kid Zopilote put on his long finger-tip coat, his plumed hat, dangled his knife on a thick watch chain, and went out of the house, Señora García cried.

Every day Kid Zopilote walked past the Chinese stores, the shoeshine parlors, barber shops, bars, and flop houses on Meyer Street. Sometimes he spent the entire day at Kaiser's Shoeshine Parlor. This was where, through time, a few lonely zoot suiters had been attracted by the boogie woogie music of the juke box. All day they put nickel after nickel into it to snap their fingers and sway their bodies with the beat. On other days Kid Zopilote went uptown to the Pastime Penny Arcade. Here again, the zoot suiters came in hour after hour to try their luck with the pinball machines. They walked by the scales a few dozen times a day and instead of stopping to weigh, they took out a very long comb and ran it through their hair to make sure that it met in back of the head in the shape of a duck's tail. Then they went outside to lean on the window. They sat on the sill and conversed until very late at night. Here they followed the every action of the girls that passed. They shouted from one side of the street to the other when they saw a friend or enemy, their only other action being that of bringing up cigarettes to the lips, letting the smoke out through the nose, and spitting on the sidewalk through the side of the mouth, leaving big yellow-green splotches on the cement.

One morning Kid Zopilote got up very early and went to visit his uncle who was from Mexico. When he got to the house, Kid Zopilote walked in the front door and found his *tío* was still asleep in street clothes. But it was very important to Kid Zopilote to find out the true implication of his nickname. So he woke his uncle. After the two started a fire, made and ate breakfast, with an inquisitive look on his face Kid Zopilote began, "*Tío*, you are a *relativo* of mine because you are a brother of my mother. But I know and you know that my mother does not like for me to visit you because you are a *wino.* But today I came to ask you something very important."

"What is on your mind?" asked the uncle.

"Well, before I went to Los Angeles everybody I knew used to call me Pepe. But since I came back everybody now calls me Kid Zopilote. Why? What is the true meaning of Kid Zopilote?"

"The zopilote is a bird," said his uncle.

"Sí—?"

"Yes, the zopilote is a bird . . ." said his uncle, repeating himself.

"What more, *tío*?" asked Kid Zopilote.

"Well—in truth, it is a very funny bird. His appearance is like that of a buzzard. I remember the zopilotes very well. There are many in Mazatlán because the weather there is very hot. The damned zopilotes are as black as midnight. They have big beaks and they also have a lot of feathers on their ugly heads. I used to kill them with rocks. They come down to earth like giant airplanes, feeling out a landing, touching the earth. When they hit the earth they keep sliding forward until their speed is gone. Then they walk like punks walk into a bar. When the damned zopilotes eat, they only eat what has previously been eaten. Sometimes they almost choke and consequently they puke. But always there is another zopilote who comes up from behind and eats the puke of the first. Then they look for a tree. When they ease themselves on the poor tree, the tree dies. After they eat more puke and kill a few more trees, they once again start running into the wind. They get air speed. They become airborne. Then they fly away."

"So you mean that they call me Kid Zopilote because they think I eat puke?" asked Kid Zopilote as his eyes became narrow with anger. "Tell me, is that why?"

"Not necessarily, Pepe, perhaps there are other reasons," said his uncle.

"The guys can go to hell then. If they can't call me Pepe they do not have to call me anything."

"But I would not worry about it anymore, Pepe. If once they began to call you Kid Zopilote they will never stop. It is said that a zopilote can never be a peacock," said his uncle, "and you probably brought it on to yourself." So Kid Zopilote went away from the house of his uncle very angry.

One night there was a stranger at Kaiser's Shoeshine Parlor. While he was not a zoot suiter he had the appearance of one of those slick felines that can never begin to look like a human being even if he should have on a suit of English tweed and custom-made shirts. He was leaning against the wall, quietly smoking a cigarette, when Kid Zopilote arrived. As usual Kid Zopilote saluted the zoot suiters with their universal greeting, "*Esos* guys, how goes it?"

"*Pos ai nomas.* Oh, just so-so," said another *pachuco.*

"Well, put in a good jitter piece," said Kid Zopilote. Before the *pachuco* could slip the nickel into the slot, the stranger slipped in a coin and the juke box began to fill Kaiser's with beat.

Kid Zopilote and the other *pachuco* were thankful. After the stranger sized up Kid Zopilote he said, "Have a cigarette, won't you?"

"Thank you," said Kid Zopilote. And from that day Kid Zopilote smoked the man's cigarettes. In time he was being charged extravagant prices for them but Kid Zopilote always managed to get the price. He walked into the Western Cleaning Company and walked out with pressing irons. He went into business establishments and always came out with something. He stole fixtures off parked automobiles. Anything. Kid Zopilote needed the cigarettes at any price.

One day the man said to him, "You know, Kid, I can no longer sell you cigarettes."

"I always pay you for them," said Kid Zopilote.

"Yes, I know you always pay for them. But from now on you can only have them when you bring your friends here. For every friend you bring me I will give you a cigarette. Is that fair?"

"Fair enough," said Kid Zopilote. So in time many young *pachucos* with zoot suits began hanging around Kaiser's. Every day new boys came and asked for the stranger and the Kaiser directed them up a little stairway to the man with the free cigarettes. In time he no longer gave them. He sold them. And the guys who bought them were affected in many ways. Talaro Fernandez crept on the floor like a dog. Chico Sanchez went up and down Meyer Street challenging everybody. Gaston Fuentes opened the fly of his pants and wet the sidewalk. Kid Zopilote panted like a dog and then passed out in a little back room at Kaiser's. Even Kid Zopilote was not getting the cigarettes for nothing because in no time at all he brought in all the potential customers. He had to pay for his smokes as did everybody else. In order to get the money he went to work hustling trade for Cetrina who gave him a small percentage from her every amorous transaction. In the morning when trade was not buzzing Kid Zopilote stayed in her room and listened to dance records. When he tired of that he headed uptown to the Pastime or Kaiser's. Sometimes he walked into Robert's Cafe for a cup of coffee. There, when any of the squares that knew Kid Zopilote from the cradle asked him why he did not go to work, he got mad.

"Me go to work? Are you crazy? I do not want to work. Besides, I have money. I sell kick smokes and I can get you fixed up for five dollars with a *vata* that is really good looking," he said.

"That is no good. You will get into a lot of trouble eventually," they said to him.

"No, I won't. Anyway, I haven't got a damned education. I haven't got no damned nothing. But I'll make out." Then Kid Zopilote got up and snapped his fingers in beat and swayed his body as he walked out.

One day Kid Zopilote was caught in a riot involving the *pachucos* and the Mexicans from the high school whose dignities were being insulted by the fact that a few illogical people were beginning to see a zoot suit on every Mexican and every Mexican in a zoot suit. It ended up with the police intervening. The Mexicans from the high school were sent home and the *pachucos* were herded off to jail. The next day they were given free haircuts. Their drapes and pleated pants were cut with scissors. They crept home along alleys, like shorn dogs with their tails between their legs, lest people should see them.

"I am glad it happened to you, Pepe," said Señora García, "I am glad." But Kid Zopilote did not say a word. His head was as shiny as a billiard ball. His zoot suit was no more. All day he stayed at home and played his guitar. It was strange that he should like it so much but now there was nowhere he could go without people pointing at him should he as much as go past the front door.

"Pepito," said his mother, "you play so beautifully that it makes me want to cry. You have such a musical touch, Pepe, yet you have never done anything to develop it. But you do play wonderfully, Pepe."

One day as Kid Zopilote strummed his guitar, a boy looked over the fence and said to him, "*Tocas bien.* You play very well." But Kid Zopilote said nothing. This boy looked like many of the other American boys he knew that never had anything to do with him. "I play, too," continued the boy, "so I hope you will not mind if I come into your yard and play with you. I will bring my guitar and perhaps we can play together. I learned from my Mexican friends in Colorado. I am attending school here."

"You can come if you wish," said Kid Zopilote. So the boy did and in time they were good friends.

One night the boy said to Kid Zopilote, "You were not meant to be a damned *pachuco.*"

"Look, I like to play the guitar in your company but I do not want you or anybody else to tell me what I should be and what I should not be," said Kid Zopilote in an angry tone.

"I am sorry. We will just let it go at that," said the boy.

So, while Kid Zopilote's hair did not grow, he spent hour after hour with his friend who was thoroughly overcome with the beauty with which Kid Zopilote executed and with the feeling he gave his music. When Kid Zopilote's hair began to respond to the comb the friend took Kid Zopilote to visit friends. They went from party to party. They played at women's luncheons. They played on radio programs. Both were summoned for any event which demanded music.

"Pepe will be the finest guitar player in the whole Southwest," said Kid Zopilote's friend.

But when Kid Zopilote's hair grew long and met in the back of his head in the shape of a duck's tail he no longer played the guitar. Anyway, most zopilotes eat puke even when better things are available a little farther away from their beaten runways and dead trees. As Kid Zopilote's uncle had said, "A zopilote can never be a peacock." So it was. Because even if he can, he does not want to.

1947

Frank Chin b. 1940

Frank Chin was born on February 25, 1940, in Berkeley, California. His father was an immigrant and his mother a fourth-generation resident of Oakland Chinatown, where Chin spent much of his childhood. He attended the University of California at Berkeley and at Santa Barbara and participated in the Program in Creative Writing at the University of Iowa. Chin is a tireless and influential promoter of Asian American literature, though his vision of it has often been criticized for its exclusionary tendencies. He has written novels, short stories, plays, comic books, and numerous essays; produced documentaries; worked as a script consultant in Hollywood; taught college courses in Asian American literature; and helped form the Asian American Theatre Workshop in San Francisco.

He co-edited (with Jeffery Paul Chan, Lawson Fusao Inada, and Shawn Wong) a foundational anthology of Asian American writings entitled *Aiiieeeee!* (1974). A second volume, *The Big Aiiieeeee!,* was published in 1991. Much of Chin's notoriety stems from the positions he and his colleagues take in the introductory essays in those collections. One of their central concerns is the emasculating effect of anti-Asian racism as epitomized by stereotypical figures like Charlie Chan and Fu Manchu. Another controversial aspect of Chin's nonfictional writing has been his relentless criticism of writers such as David Henry Hwang, Maxine Hong Kingston, and Amy Tan; in his view, these writers falsify Asian and Asian American culture. Critics point out the misogyny and homophobia that propel Chin's polemics, but they also acknowledge the significance of his pioneering work as a literary historian. Indeed many of the writers that Chin and his colleagues champion—such as Louis Chu, John Okada, and Hisaye Yamamoto—have been accorded a privileged place in Asia American literary studies.

The controversy generated by Chin's polemics has tended to overshadow his fictional and dramatic works. First staged in 1972, *The Chickencoop Chinaman* was one of the first plays written by an Asian American to be produced in New York. A second play, *The Year of the Dragon,* premiered two years later. Many of Chin's early writings contain an autobiographical element. They often revolve around a male protagonist—usually a would-be writer—alienated from his family or from his Chinatown community. This is the predicament shared by Johnny in Chin's first published short story, "Food for All His Dead" (1962), and by Fred in *The Year of the Dragon.* Much of Chin's early fiction was published in *The Chinaman Pacific & Frisco R.R. Co.* (1988), which won the National Book Award and from which "Railroad Standard Time" has been excerpted. The writings from this period tend to revel in masochistic self-loathing. The male heroes find only momentary relief when they are able to articulate their agony in elaborate monologues and when they gain tenuous access to a Chinese American history of mythical dimensions—a history usually associated with the railroad.

A shift can be detected in Chin's writings around the mid-eighties: he begins to forge a new vision of literary and racial authenticity based on a selective reading of classic Chinese texts, including *Romance of the Three Kingdoms, Water Margin,* and Sun Tzu's *The Art of War.* At the heart of the Chinese "real," Chin asserts, is an essentially martial view of the world: Life is War. His recent works feature protagonists who embrace these values; furthermore, they frequently allude to the figure of Kwan Kung, a warrior deified in Chinese folklore. The novel *Donald Duk* (1991) recounts the coming-of-age of its eponymous twelve-year-old protagonist: unlike the anti-heroes of Chin's earlier fiction, Donald is able to move beyond racial self-loathing by discovering the history of the Chinese American laborers who built the railroad and the world of Chinese mythology. The novel *Gunga Din Highway* (1994) features characters who are more exuberant and virile versions of the tortured protagonists of Chin's early writings, for the male heroes of this later work have access to the heroic tradition Chin identifies with Kwan Kung. In *Bulletproof Buddhists and Other Essays* (1998) Chin finds evidence for the persistence of "real" Chinese values in a wide range of cultural locations: in the rituals of Southeast Asian youth gangs in southern California, in the Chinese American communities along the California-Mexico border, and in the works of dissident writers in Singapore.

Daniel Y. Kim
Brown University

PRIMARY WORKS

Aiiieeeee!, edited with Jeffery Paul Chan, Lawson Fusao Inada, and Shawn Wong, 1974; *The Chickencoop Chinaman and The Year of the Dragon: Two Plays by Frank Chin,* 1981; *The Chinaman Pacific & Frisco R.R. Co.,* 1988; *Donald Duk,* 1991; *The Big Aiiieeeee!,* edited with Jeffery Paul Chan, Lawson Fusao Inada, and Shawn Wong, 1991; *Gunga Din Highway,* 1994; *Bulletproof Buddhists and Other Essays,* 1998.

Railroad Standard Time

"This was your grandfather's," Ma said. I was twelve, maybe fourteen years old when Grandma died. Ma put it on the table. The big railroad watch, Elgin. Nineteen-jewel movement. American made. Lever set. Stem wound. Class facecover. Railroad standard all the way. It ticked on the table between stacks of dirty dishes and cold food. She brought me in here to the kitchen, always to the kitchen to loose her thrills and secrets, as if the sound of running water and breathing the warm soggy ghosts of stale food, floating grease, old spices, ever comforted her, as if the kitchen was a paradise for conspiracy, sanctuary for us *juk sing* Chinamen from the royalty of pure-talking China-born Chinese, old, mourning, and belching in the other rooms of my dead grandmother's last house. Here, private, to say in Chinese, "This was your grandfather's," as if now that her mother had died and she'd been up all night long, not weeping, tough and lank, making coffee and tea and little foods for the brokenhearted family in her mother's kitchen, Chinese would be easier for me to understand. As if my mother would say all the important things of the soul and blood to her son, me, only in Chinese from now on. Very few people spoke the language at me the way she did. She chanted a spell up over me that conjured the meaning of what she was saying in the shape of old memories come to call. Words I'd never heard before set me at play in familiar scenes new to me, and ancient.

She lay the watch on the table, eased it slowly off her fingertips down to the tabletop without a sound. She didn't touch me, but put it down and held her hands in front of her like a bridesmaid holding an invisible bouquet and stared at the watch.

As if it were talking to her, she looked hard at it, made faces at it, and did not move or answer the voices of the old, calling her from other rooms, until I picked it up.

A two-driver, high stepping locomotive ahead of a coal tender and baggage car, on double track between two semaphores showing a stop signal was engraved on the back.

"Your grandfather collected railroad watches," Ma said. "This one is the best." I held it in one hand and then the other, hefted it, felt out the meaning of "the best," words that rang of meat and vegetables, oils, things we touched, smelled, squeezed, washed, and ate, and I turned the big cased thing over several times. "Grandma gives it to you now," she said. It was big in my hand. Gold. A little greasy. Warm.

I asked her what her father's name had been, and the manic heat of her all-night burnout seemed to go cold and congeal. "Oh," she finally said, "it's one of those Chinese names I . . ." in English, faintly from another world, woozy and her throat and nostrils full of bubbly sniffles, the solemnity of the moment gone, the watch in my hand turned to cheap with the mumbling of a few awful English words. She giggled herself down to nothing but breath and moving lips. She shuffled backward, one step at a time, fox-trotting dreamily backwards, one hand dragging on the edge of the table, wobbling the table, rattling the dishes, spilling cold soup. Back down one side of the table, she dropped her butt a little with each step then muscled it back up. There were no chairs in the kitchen tonight. She knew, but still she looked. So this dance and groggy mumbling about the watch being no good, in strange English, like an Indian medicine man in a movie.

I wouldn't give it back or trade it for another out of the collection. This one was mine. No other. It had belonged to my grandfather. I wore it braking on the Southern Pacific, though it was two jewels short of new railroad standard and an outlaw watch that could get me fired. I kept it on me, arrived at my day-off courthouse wedding to its time, wore it as a railroad relic/family heirloom/grin-bringing affectation when I was writing background news in Seattle, reporting from the shadows of race riots, grabbing snaps for the 11:00 P.M., timing today's happenings with a nineteenth-century escapement. (Ride with me, Grandmother.) I was wearing it on my twenty-seventh birthday, the Saturday I came home to see my son asleep in the back of a strange station wagon, and Sarah inside, waving, shouting through an open window, "Goodbye Daddy," over and over.

I stood it. Still and expressionless as some good Chink, I watched Barbara drive off, leave me, like some blonde white goddess going home from the jungle with her leather patches and briar pipe sweetheart writer and my kids. I'll learn to be a sore loser. I'll learn to hit people in the face. I'll learn to cry when I'm hurt and go for the throat instead of being polite and worrying about being obnoxious to people walking out of my house with my things, taking my kids away. I'll be more than quiet, embarrassed. I won't be likable anymore.

I hate my novel about a Chinatown mother like mine dying, now that Ma's dead. But I'll keep it. I hated after reading *Father and Glorious Descendant, Fifth Chinese Daughter, The House That Tai Ming Built.* Books scribbled up by a sad legion of snobby autobiographical Chinatown saps all on their own. Christians who never heard of each other, hardworking people who sweat out the exact same Chinatown book, the same cunning "Confucius says" joke, just like me. I kept it then and I'll still keep it. Part cookbook, memories of Mother in the kitchen slicing meat paper-thin with a cleaver. Mumbo jumbo about spices and steaming. The secret of Chinatown rice. The hands come down toward the food. The food crawls with culture. The thousand-year-old living Chinese meat makes dinner a safari into the unknown, a blood ritual. Food pornography. Black magic. Between the lines, I read a madman's detailed description of the preparation of shrunken heads. I never wrote to mean anything more than word fun with the food Grandma cooked at home. Chinese food. I read a list of what I remembered eating at my grandmother's table and knew I'd always be known by what I ate, that we come from a hungry tradition. Slop eaters following the wars on all fours. Weed cuisine and mud gravy in the shadow of corpses. We plundered the dust for fungus. Buried things. Seeds plucked out of the wind to feed a race of lace-boned skinnys, in high-school English, become transcendental Oriental art to make the dyke-ish spinster teacher cry. We always come to fake art and write the Chinatown book like bugs come to fly in the light. I hate my book now that ma's dead, but I'll keep it. I know she's not the woman I wrote up like my mother, and dead, in a book that was like everybody else's Chinatown book. Part word map of Chinatown San Francisco, shop to shop down Grant Avenue. Food again. The wind sucks the shops out and you breathe warm roast ducks dripping fat, hooks into the neck, through the head, out an eye. Stacks of iced fish, blue and fluorescent pink in the neon. The air is thin soup, sharp up the nostrils.

All mention escape from Chinatown into the movies. But we all forgot to mention how stepping off the streets into a faceful of Charlie Chaplin or a Western on a ripped and stained screen that became caught in the grip of winos breathing in unison in their sleep and billowed in and out, that shuddered when cars went by . . . we all of us Chinamans watched our own MOVIE ABOUT ME! I learned how to box watching movies shot by James Wong Howe. Cartoons were our nursery rhymes. Summers inside those neon-and-stucco downtown hole-in-the-wall Market Street Frisco movie houses blowing three solid hours of full-color seven-minute cartoons was school, was rows and rows of Chinamans learning English in a hurry from Daffy Duck.

When we ate in the dark and recited the dialogue of cartoon mice and cats out loud in various tones of voice with our mouths full, we looked like people singing hymns in church. We learned to talk like everybody in America. Learned to need to be afraid to stay alive, keep moving. We learned to run, to be cheerful losers, to take a sudden pie in the face, talk American with a lot of giggles. To us a cartoon is a desperate situation. Of the movies, cartoons were the high art of our claustrophobia. They understood us living too close to each other. How, when you're living too close to too many people, you can't wait for one thing more without losing your mind. Cartoons were a fine way out of waiting in Chinatown around the rooms. Those of our Chinamans who every now and then break a reverie with, "Thank you, Mighty Mouse," mean it. Other folks thank Porky Pig, Snuffy Smith, Woody Woodpecker.

The day my mother told me I was to stay home from Chinese school one day a week starting today, to read to my father and teach him English while he was captured in total paralysis from a vertebra in the neck on down, I stayed away from cartoons. I went to a matinee in a white neighborhood looking for the MOVIE ABOUT ME and was the only Chinaman in the house. I liked the way Peter Lorre ran along non-stop routine hysterical. I came back home with Peter Lorre. I turned out the lights in Pa's room. I put a candle on the dresser and wheeled Pa around in his chair to see me in front of the dresser mirror, reading Edgar Allan Poe out loud to him in the voice of Peter Lorre by candlelight.

The old men in the Chinatown books are all Muses for Chinese ceremonies. All the same. Loyal filial children kowtow to the old and whiff food laid out for the dead. The dead eat the same as the living but without the sauces. White food. Steamed chicken. Rice we all remember as children scrambling down to the ground, to all fours and bonking our heads on the floor, kowtowing to a dead chicken.

My mother and aunts said nothing about the men of the family except they were weak. I like to think my grandfather was a good man. Even the kiss-ass steward service, I like to think he was tough, had a few laughs and ran off with his pockets full of engraved watches. Because I never knew him, not his name, nor anything about him, except a photograph of him as a young man with something of my mother's face in his face, and a watch chain across his vest. I kept his watch in good repair and told everyone it would pass to my son someday, until the day the boy was gone. Then I kept it like something of his he'd loved and had left behind, saving it for him maybe, to give to him when he was a man. But I haven't felt that in a long time.

The watch ticked against my heart and pounded my chest as I went too fast over bumps in the night and the radio on, on an all-night run downcoast, down country, down old Highway 99, Interstate 5, I ran my grandfather's time down past road signs that caught a gleam in my headlights and came at me out of the night with the names of forgotten high school girlfriends, BELLEVUE KIRKLAND, ROBERTA GERBER, AURORA CANBY, and sang with the radio to Jonah and Sarah in Berkeley, my Chinatown in Oakland and Frisco, to raise the dead. Ride with me, Grandfather, this is your grandson the ragmouth, called Tampax, the burned scarred boy, called Barbecue, going to San Francisco to bury my mother, your daughter, and spend Chinese New Year's at home. When we were sitting down and into our dinner after Grandma's funeral, and ate in front of the table set with white food for the dead, Ma said she wanted no white food and money burning after her funeral. Her sisters were there. Her sisters took charge of her funeral and the dinner afterwards. The dinner would most likely be in a Chinese restaurant in Frisco. Nobody had these dinners at home anymore. I wouldn't mind people having dinner at my place after my funeral, but no white food.

The whiz goes out of the tires as their roll bites into the steel grating of the Carquinez Bridge. The noise of the engine groans and echoes like a bomber in flight through the steel roadway. Light from the water far below shines through the grate, and I'm driving high, above a glow. The voice of the tires hums a shrill rubber screechy mosquito hum that vibrates through the chassis and frame of the car into my meatless butt, into my tender asshole, my pelvic bones, the roots of my teeth. Over the Carquinez Bridge to CROCKETT MARTINEZ closer to home, roll the tires of Ma's Chevy, my car now, carrying me up over the water southwest toward rolls of fog. The fat man's coming home on a sneaky breeze. Dusk comes a drooly mess of sunlight, a slobber of cheap pawnshop gold, a slow building heat across the water, all through the milky air through the glass of the window into the closed atmosphere of a driven car, into one side of my bomber's face. A bomber, flying my mother's car into the unknown charted by the stars and the radio, feels the coming of some old night song climbing hand over hand, bass notes plunking as steady and shady as reminiscence to get on my nerves one stupid beat after the other crossing the high rhythm six-step of the engine. I drive through the shadows of the bridge's steel structure all over the road. Fine day. I've been on the road for sixteen hours straight down the music of Seattle, Spokane, Salt Lake, Sacramento, Los Angeles, and Wolfman Jack lurking in odd hours of darkness, at peculiar altitudes of darkness, favoring the depths of certain Oregon valleys and heat and moonlight of my miles. And I'm still alive. Country 'n' western music for the night road. It's pure white music. Like "The Star-Spangled Banner," it was the first official American music out of school into my jingling earbones sung by sighing white big tits in front of the climbing promise of FACE and Every Good Boy Does Fine chalked on the blackboard.

She stood up singing, one hand cupped in the other as if to catch drool slipping off her lower lip. Our eyes scouted through her blouse to elastic straps, lacy stuff, circular stitching, buckles, and in the distance, finally some skin. The color of her skin spread through the stuff of her blouse like melted butter through bread nicely to our tongues and was warm there. She sat flopping them on the keyboard as she breathed, singing "Home on the Range" over her shoulder, and pounded the tune out with her palms. The lonesome prairie was nothing but her voice, some hearsay country she stood up to sing *a capella* out of her. Simple music you can count. You can hear the words clear. The music's run through Clorox and Simonized, beating so insistently right and regular that you feel to sing it will deodorize you, make you clean. The hardhat hit parade. I listen to it a lot on the road. It's that get-outta-town beat and tune that makes me go.

Mrs. Morales was her name. Aurora Morales. The music teacher us boys liked to con into singing for us. Come-on opera, we wanted from her, not them Shirley Temple tunes the girls wanted to learn, but big notes, high long ones up from the navel that drilled through plaster and steel and skin and meat for bone marrow and electric wires on one long titpopping breath.

This is how I come home, riding a mass of spasms and death throes, warm and screechy inside, itchy, full of ghostpiss, as I drive right past what's left of Oakland's dark wooden Chinatown and dark streets full of dead lettuce and trampled carrot tops parallel all the time in line with the tracks of the Western Pacific and Southern Pacific railroads.

1988

Flannery O'Connor 1925–1964

Grotesque, Catholic, Southern—each of these labels has been affixed to Flannery O'Connor's writing, yet none fully captures its scope. For her work is all of these and more.

She did often make use of the grotesque, for instance, but its use was not, as one critic claimed, gratuitous. She wanted to push the reader to experience a sense of something beyond the ordinary, a sense of the mystery of life. She wanted to shock the reader into recognizing the distortions of modern life that we have come to consider natural: "for the almost-blind you draw large and startling figures," she has noted in an essay.

O'Connor's writing was also fueled by her Roman Catholic beliefs. The something beyond the ordinary that she wanted the reader to experience, starkly, unsentimentally, was a sense of the sacred. But the reader of her fiction doesn't need to be Catholic to appreciate the extra-ordinary, to experience the mystery of life.

This Catholicism probably contributed to O'Connor's sense of living in a fallen world. And she also probably absorbed such a sense of having fallen from past grandeur by growing up white in the post–Civil–War South. Yet her characters are not so much fallen aristocrats as poor or middle-class whites, who often don't realize what their lives are lacking. Her portrayal of these characters, their thoughts, their speech, is true, funny, powerful—and devastating.

Like most of her characters, Mary Flannery O'Connor grew up in the South—in Georgia. The only child of Edward Francis O'Connor and Regina Cline O'Connor, she lived in Savannah her first thirteen years. Then her father was diagnosed as having disseminated lupus erythematosis, a disease of the immune system, a disease so debilitating that he could not continue his real-estate work. The family moved to Milledgeville, to the house where O'Connor's mother had grown up, a house that had been the governor's mansion when Milledgeville was the capital of Georgia a century before. O'Connor's father died three years later. The following year, when O'Connor was seventeen, she entered Georgia State College for Women, now Georgia College. There she majored in social science (she would later satirize social scientists mercilessly) and published cartoons in the school newspaper (since *The New Yorker* wouldn't publish them).

In 1945 O'Connor left Georgia to study creative writing at the Writers' Workshop of the State University of Iowa (now the University of Iowa), where she wrote a series of short stories and earned a master's degree in fine arts. She then embarked on her first novel, working on it at Yaddo, an artists' colony in upstate New York, in an apartment in New York City, and while boarding with friends in Ridgefield, Connecticut. Heading home for Christmas in 1950, O'Connor suffered an attack of lupus, the disease that had killed her father.

Severely weakened—she was too weak to climb stairs—O'Connor, with her mother and uncle, moved to the family farm near Milledgeville. Cortisone drugs kept the lupus largely under control but weakened O'Connor's bones. During the next thirteen years she hobbled about with a cane or crutches, raised peafowl, and wrote for two or three hours a day. Sometimes she was well enough to travel within or beyond Georgia to give a speech or a reading or to accept an honorary degree; once she even traveled as far as Lourdes and Rome. But mostly she lived quietly on the farm—until surgery in February 1964 reactivated the lupus; she died in August, at the age of 39.

O'Connor completed two novels, *Wise Blood* and *The Violent Bear It Away,* but is better remembered for her two volumes of short stories, *A Good Man Is Hard to Find* and the posthumous *Everything That Rises Must Converge.* Several other volumes have been published since her death: a complete collection of stories and also collections of essays *(Mystery and Manners),* letters (including *The Habit of Being*), and book reviews (including *The Presence of Grace*).

"A Good Man Is Hard to Find" is typical of many of O'Connor's stories, with its jolting disruption of the mundane, its satire, its toughness. Yet even more than O'Connor's other work, this story provokes extreme reactions: it is funny but also horrifying.

Beverly Lyon Clark
Wheaton College

PRIMARY WORKS

Wise Blood, 1952; *A Good Man Is Hard to Find, and Other Stories,* 1955; *The Violent Bear It Away,* 1960; *Everything That Rises Must Converge,* 1965; *Mystery and Manners: Occasional Prose,* 1969; *The Complete Stories,* 1971; *The Habit of Being: The Letters of Flannery O'Connor,* 1979; *The Presence of Grace, and Other Book Reviews,* 1983; *Collected Works,* 1988.

A Good Man Is Hard to Find[1]

The grandmother didn't want to go to Florida. She wanted to visit some of her connections in east Tennessee and she was seizing at every chance to change Bailey's mind. Bailey was the son she lived with, her only boy. He was sitting on the edge of his chair at the table, bent over the orange sports section of the *Journal.* "Now look here, Bailey," she said, "see here, read this," and she stood with one hand on her thin hip and the other rattling the newspaper at his bald head. "Here this fellow that calls himself the Misfit is aloose from the Federal Pen and headed toward Florida and you read here what it says he did to these people. Just you read it. I wouldn't take my children in any direction with a criminal like that aloose in it. I couldn't answer to my conscience if I did."

Bailey didn't look up from his reading so she wheeled around then and faced the children's mother, a young woman in slacks, whose face was as broad and innocent as a cabbage and was tied around with a green head-kerchief that had two points on the top like rabbit's ears. She was sitting on the sofa, feeding the baby his apricots out of a jar. "The children have been to Florida before," the old lady said. "You all ought to take them somewhere else for a change so they would see different parts of the world and be broad. They never have been to east Tennessee."

The children's mother didn't seem to hear but the eight-year-old boy, John Wesley, a stocky child with glasses, said, "If you don't want to go to Florida, why dontcha stay at home?" He and the little girl, June Star, were reading the funny papers on the floor.

"She wouldn't stay at home to be queen for a day," June Star said without raising her yellow head.

"Yes and what would you do if this fellow, The Misfit, caught you?" the grandmother asked.

"I'd smack his face," John Wesley said.

"She wouldn't stay at home for a million bucks," June Star said. "Afraid she'd miss something. She has to go everywhere we go."

"All right, Miss," the grandmother said. "Just remember that the next time you want me to curl your hair."

June Star said her hair was naturally curly.

The next morning the grandmother was the first one in the car, ready to go. She had her big black valise that looked like the head of a hippopotamus in one corner, and underneath it she was hiding a basket with Pitty Sing,[2] the cat, in it. She didn't intend for the cat to be left alone in the house for three days because he would miss her too much and she was afraid he might brush against one of the gas burners and

[1] Also the title of a blues song, composed by Eddie Green in 1918.

[2] Alludes to one of the three little maids from school in the Gilbert and Sullivan comic opera *The Mikado* (1885). Pitti-Sing helps mislead the Mikado, the Emperor of Japan, into believing that a requested beheading has taken place; fortunately it has not, for the man who would have been executed turns out to be the Mikado's son.

accidentally asphyxiate himself. Her son, Bailey, didn't like to arrive at a motel with a cat.

She sat in the middle of the back seat with John Wesley and June Star on either side of her. Bailey and the children's mother and the baby sat in front and they left Atlanta at eight forty-five with the mileage on the car at 55890. The grandmother wrote this down because she thought it would be interesting to say how many miles they had been when they got back. It took them twenty minutes to reach the outskirts of the city.

The old lady settled herself comfortably, removing her white cotton gloves and putting them up with her purse on the shelf in front of the back window. The children's mother still had on slacks and still had her head tied up in a green kerchief, but the grandmother had on a navy blue straw sailor hat with a bunch of white violets on the brim and a navy blue dress with a small white dot in the print. Her collars and cuffs were white organdy trimmed with lace and at her neckline she had pinned a purple spray of cloth violets containing a sachet. In case of an accident, anyone seeing her dead on the highway would know at once that she was a lady.

She said she thought it was going to be a good day for driving, neither too hot nor too cold, and she cautioned Bailey that the speed limit was fifty-five miles an hour and that the patrolmen hid themselves behind billboards and small clumps of trees and sped out after you before you had a chance to slow down. She pointed out interesting details of the scenery: Stone Mountain; the blue granite that in some places came up to both sides of the highway; the brilliant red clay banks slightly streaked with purple; and the various crops that made rows of green lace-work on the ground. The trees were full of silver-white sunlight and the meanest of them sparkled. The children were reading comic magazines and their mother had gone back to sleep.

"Let's go through Georgia fast so we won't have to look at it much," John Wesley said.

"If I were a little boy," said the grandmother, "I wouldn't talk about my native state that way. Tennessee has the mountains and Georgia has the hills."

"Tennessee is just a hillbilly dumping ground," John Wesley said, "and Georgia is a lousy state too."

"You said it," June Star said.

"In my time," said the grandmother, folding her thin veined fingers, "children were more respectful of their native states and their parents and everything else. People did right then. Oh look at the cute little pickaninny!" she said and pointed to a Negro child standing in the door of a shack. "Wouldn't that make a picture, now?" she asked and they all turned and looked at the little Negro out of the back window. He waved.

"He didn't have any britches on," June Star said.

"He probably didn't have any," the grandmother explained. "Little niggers in the country don't have things like we do. If I could paint, I'd paint that picture," she said.

The children exchanged comic books.

The grandmother offered to hold the baby and the children's mother passed him over the front seat to her. She set him on her knee and bounced him and told him about the things they were passing. She rolled her eyes and screwed up her mouth and stuck her leathery thin face into his smooth bland one. Occasionally he gave her a faraway smile. They passed a large cotton field with five or six graves fenced in the middle of it, like a small island. "Look at the graveyard!" the grandmother said, pointing it out. "That was the old family burying ground. That belonged to the plantation."

"Where's the plantation?" John Wesley asked.

"Gone With the Wind,"[3] said the grandmother. "Ha. Ha."

When the children finished all the comic books they had brought, they opened the lunch and ate it. The grandmother ate a peanut butter sandwich and an olive and would not let the children throw the box and the paper napkins out the window. When there was nothing else to do they played a game by choosing a cloud and making the other two guess what shape it suggested. John Wesley took one the shape of a cow and June Star guessed a cow and John Wesley said, no, an automobile, and June Star said he didn't play fair, and they began to slap each other over the grandmother.

The grandmother said she would tell them a story if they would keep quiet. When she told a story, she rolled her eyes and waved her head and was very dramatic. She said once when she was a maiden lady she had been courted by a Mr. Edgar Atkins Teagarden from Jasper, Georgia. She said he was a very good-looking man and a gentleman and that he brought her a watermelon every Saturday afternoon with his initials cut in it, E.A.T. Well, one Saturday, she said, Mr. Teagarden brought the watermelon and there was nobody at home and he left it on the front porch and returned in his buggy to Jasper, but she never got the watermelon, she said, because a nigger boy ate it when he saw the initials, E.A.T.! This story tickled John Wesley's funny bone and he giggled and giggled but June Star didn't think it was any good. She said she wouldn't marry a man that just brought her a watermelon on Saturday. The grandmother said she would have done well to marry Mr. Teagarden because he was a gentleman and had bought Coca-Cola stock when it first came out and that he had died only a few years ago, a very wealthy man.

They stopped at The Tower for barbecued sandwiches. The Tower was a part stucco and part wood filling station and dance hall set in a clearing outside of Timothy. A fat man named Red Sammy Butts ran it and there were signs stuck here and there on the building and for miles up and down the highway saying, TRY RED SAMMY'S FAMOUS BARBECUE. NONE LIKE FAMOUS RED SAMMY'S! RED SAM! THE FAT BOY WITH THE HAPPY LAUGH. A VETERAN! RED SAMMY'S YOUR MAN!

Red Sammy was lying on the bare ground outside The Tower with his head under a truck while a gray monkey about a foot high, chained to a small chinaberry tree, chattered nearby. The monkey sprang back into the tree and got on the highest limb as soon as he saw the children jump out of the car and run toward him.

Inside, The Tower was a long dark room with a counter at one end and tables at the other and dancing space in the middle. They all sat down at a board table next

[3] Alludes to the best-selling novel (1936) by Margaret Mitchell; also made into an Academy Award-winning movie (1939).

to the nickelodeon and Red Sam's wife, a tall burnt-brown woman with hair and eyes lighter than her skin, came and took their order. The children's mother put a dime in the machine and played "The Tennessee Waltz," and the grandmother said that tune always made her want to dance. She asked Bailey if he would like to dance but he only glared at her. He didn't have a naturally sunny disposition like she did and trips made him nervous. The grandmother's brown eyes were very bright. She swayed her head from side to side and pretended she was dancing in her chair. June Star said play something she could tap to so the children's mother put in another dime and played a fast number and June Star stepped out onto the dance floor and did her tap routine.

"Ain't she cute?" Red Sam's wife said, leaning over the counter. "Would you like to come be my little girl?"

"No I certainly wouldn't," June Star said. "I wouldn't live in a broken-down place like this for a million bucks!" and she ran back to the table.

"Ain't she cute?" the woman repeated, stretching her mouth politely.

"Aren't you ashamed?" hissed the grandmother.

Red Sam came in and told his wife to quit lounging on the counter and hurry up with these people's order. His khaki trousers reached just to his hip bones and his stomach hung over them like a sack of meal swaying under his shirt. He came over and sat down at a table nearby and let out a combination sigh and yodel. "You can't win," he said. "You can't win," and he wiped his sweating red face off with a gray handkerchief. "These days you don't know who to trust," he said. "Ain't that the truth?"

"People are certainly not nice like they used to be," said the grandmother.

"Two fellers come in here last week," Red Sammy said, "driving a Chrysler. It was a old beat-up car but it was a good one and these boys looked all right to me. Said they worked at the mill and you know I let them fellers charge the gas they bought? Now why did I do that?"

"Because you're a good man!" the grandmother said at once.

"Yes'm, I suppose so," Red Sam said as if he were struck with this answer.

His wife brought the orders, carrying the five plates all at once without a tray, two in each hand and one balanced on her arm. "It isn't a soul in this green world of God's that you can trust," she said. "And I don't count nobody out of that, not nobody," she repeated, looking at Red Sammy.

"Did you read about that criminal, The Misfit, that's escaped?" asked the grandmother.

"I wouldn't be a bit surprised if he didn't attact this place right here," said the woman. "If he hears about it being here, I wouldn't be none surprised to see him. If he hears it's two cent in the cash register, I wouldn't be a tall surprised if he . . ."

"That'll do," Red Sam said. "Go bring these people their Co'-Colas," and the woman went off to get the rest of the order.

"A good man is hard to find," Red Sammy said. "Everything is getting terrible. I remember the day you could go off and leave your screen door unlatched. Not no more."

He and the grandmother discussed better times. The old lady said that in her opinion Europe was entirely to blame for the way things were now. She said the way Europe acted you would think we were made of money and Red Sam said it was no use talking about it, she was exactly right. The children ran outside into the white sunlight and looked at the monkey in the lacy chinaberry tree. He was busy catching fleas on himself and biting each one carefully between his teeth as if it were a delicacy.

They drove off again into the hot afternoon. The grandmother took cat naps and woke up every few minutes with her own snoring. Outside of Toombsboro she woke up and recalled an old plantation that she had visited in this neighborhood once when she was a young lady. She said the house had six white columns across the front and that there was an avenue of oaks leading up to it and two little wooden trellis arbors on either side in front where you sat down with your suitor after a stroll in the garden. She recalled exactly which road to turn off to get to it. She knew that Bailey would not be willing to lose any time looking at an old house, but the more she talked about it, the more she wanted to see it once again and find out if the little twin arbors were still standing. "There was a secret panel in this house," she said craftily, not telling the truth but wishing that she were, "and the story went that all the family silver was hidden in it when Sherman[4] came through but it was never found . . ."

"Hey!" John Wesley said. "Let's go see it! We'll find it! We'll poke all the woodwork and find it! Who lives there? Where do you turn off at? Hey Pop, can't we turn off there?"

"We never have seen a house with a secret panel!" June Star shrieked. "Let's go to the house with the secret panel! Hey Pop, can't we go see the house with the secret panel!"

"It's not far from here, I know," the grandmother said. "It wouldn't take over twenty minutes."

Bailey was looking straight ahead. His jaw was as rigid as a horseshoe. "No," he said.

The children began to yell and scream that they wanted to see the house with the secret panel. John Wesley kicked the back of the front seat and June Star hung over her mother's shoulder and whined desperately into her ear that they never had any fun even on their vacation, that they could never do what THEY wanted to do. The baby began to scream and John Wesley kicked the back of the seat so hard that his father could feel the blows in his kidney.

"All right!" he shouted and drew the car to a stop at the side of the road. "Will you all shut up? Will you all just shut up for one second? If you don't shut up, we won't go anywhere."

"It would be very educational for them," the grandmother murmured.

"All right," Bailey said, "but get this: this is the only time we're going to stop for anything like this. This is the one and only time."

"The dirt road that you have to turn down is about a mile back," the grandmother directed. "I marked it when we passed."

"A dirt road," Bailey groaned.

After they had turned around and were headed toward the dirt road, the grandmother recalled other points about the house, the beautiful glass over the front door-

[4]Northern Civil War general, best known for his march through Georgia (starting in Tennessee), destroying houses and plantations on his way to the sea.

way and the candle-lamp in the hall. John Wesley said that the secret panel was probably in the fireplace.

"You can't go inside this house," Bailey said. "You don't know who lives there."

"While you all talk to the people in front, I'll run around behind and get in a window," John Wesley suggested.

"We'll all stay in the car," his mother said.

They turned onto the dirt road and the car raced roughly along in a swirl of pink dust. The grandmother recalled the times when there were no paved roads and thirty miles was a day's journey. The dirt road was hilly and there were sudden washes in it and sharp curves on dangerous embankments. All at once they would be on a hill, looking down over the blue tops of trees for miles around, then the next minute, they would be in a red depression with the dust-coated trees looking down on them.

"This place had better turn up in a minute," Bailey said, "or I'm going to turn around."

The road looked as if no one had traveled on it in months.

"It's not much farther," the grandmother said and just as she said it, a horrible thought came to her. The thought was so embarrassing that she turned red in the face and her eyes dilated and her feet jumped up, upsetting her valise in the corner. The instant the valise moved, the newspaper top she had over the basket under it rose with a snarl and Pitty Sing, the cat, sprang onto Bailey's shoulder.

The children were thrown to the floor and their mother, clutching the baby, was thrown out the door onto the ground; the old lady was thrown into the front seat. The car turned over once and landed right-side-up in a gulch off the side of the road. Bailey remained in the driver's seat with the cat—gray-striped with a broad white face and an orange nose—clinging to his neck like a caterpillar.

As soon as the children saw they could move their arms and legs, they scrambled out of the car, shouting, "We've had an ACCIDENT!" The grandmother was curled up under the dashboard, hoping she was injured so that Bailey's wrath would not come down on her all at once. The horrible thought she had had before the accident was that the house she had remembered so vividly was not in Georgia but in Tennessee.

Bailey removed the cat from his neck with both hands and flung it out the window against the side of a pine tree. Then he got out of the car and started looking for the children's mother. She was sitting against the side of a red gutted ditch, holding the screaming baby, but she only had a cut down her face and a broken shoulder. "We've had an ACCIDENT!" the children screamed in a frenzy of delight.

"But nobody's killed," June Star said with disappointment as the grandmother limped out of the car, her hat still pinned to her head but the broken front brim standing up at a jaunty angle and the violet spray hanging off the side. They all sat down in the ditch, except the children, to recover from the shock. They were all shaking.

"Maybe a car will come along," said the children's mother hoarsely.

"I believe I have injured an organ," said the grandmother, pressing her side, but no one answered her. Bailey's teeth were clattering. He had on a yellow sport shirt with bright blue parrots designed in it and his face was as yellow as the shirt. The grandmother decided that she would not mention that the house was in Tennessee.

The road was about ten feet above and they could see only the tops of the trees on the other side of it. Behind the ditch they were sitting in there were more woods, tall and dark and deep. In a few minutes they saw a car some distance away on top of a hill, coming slowly as if the occupants were watching them. The grandmother stood up and waved both arms dramatically to attract their attention. The car continued to come on slowly, disappeared around a bend and appeared again, moving even slower, on top of the hill they had gone over. It was a big black battered hearse-like automobile. There were three men in it.

It came to a stop just over them and for some minutes, the driver looked down with a steady expressionless gaze to where they were sitting, and didn't speak. Then he turned his head and muttered something to the other two and they got out. One was a fat boy in black trousers and a red sweat shirt with a silver stallion embossed on the front of it. He moved around on the right side of them and stood staring, his mouth partly open in a kind of loose grin. The other had on khaki pants and a blue striped coat and a gray hat pulled down very low, hiding most of his face. He came around slowly on the left side. Neither spoke.

The driver got out of the car and stood by the side of it, looking down at them. He was an older man than the other two. His hair was just beginning to gray and he wore silver-rimmed spectacles that gave him a scholarly look. He had a long creased face and didn't have on any shirt or undershirt. He had on blue jeans that were too tight for him and he was holding a black hat and a gun. The two boys also had guns.

"We've had an ACCIDENT!" the children screamed.

The grandmother had the peculiar feeling that the bespectacled man was someone she knew. His face was as familiar to her as if she had known him all her life but she could not recall who he was. He moved away from the car and began to come down the embankment, placing his feet carefully so that he wouldn't slip. He had on tan and white shoes and no socks, and his ankles were red and thin. "Good afternoon," he said. "I see you all had you a little spill."

"We turned over twice!" said the grandmother.

"Oncet," he corrected. "We seen it happen. Try their car and see will it run, Hiram," he said quietly to the boy with the gray hat.

"What you got that gun for?" John Wesley asked. "Whatcha gonna do with that gun?"

"Lady," the man said to the children's mother, "would you mind calling them children to sit down by you? Children make me nervous. I want all you all to sit down right together there where you're at."

"What are you telling US what to do for?" June Star asked.

Behind them the line of woods gaped like a dark open mouth. "Come here," said the mother.

"Look here now," Bailey began suddenly, "we're in a predicament! We're in . . ."

The grandmother shrieked. She scrambled to her feet and stood staring. "You're The Misfit!" she said. "I recognized you at once!"

"Yes'm," the man said, smiling slightly as if he were pleased in spite of himself to be known, "but it would have been better for all of you, lady, if you hadn't of reckernized me."

Bailey turned his head sharply and said something to his mother that shocked even the children. The old lady began to cry and The Misfit reddened.

"Lady," he said, "don't you get upset. Sometimes a man says things he don't mean. I don't reckon he meant to talk to you thataway."

"You wouldn't shoot a lady, would you?" the grandmother said and removed a clean handkerchief from her cuff and began to slap at her eyes with it.

The Misfit pointed the toe of his shoe into the ground and made a little hole and then covered it up again. "I would hate to have to," he said.

"Listen," the grandmother almost screamed, "I know you're a good man. You don't look a bit like you have common blood. I know you must come from nice people!"

"Yes mam," he said, "finest people in the world." When he smiled he showed a row of strong white teeth. "God never made a finer woman than my mother and my daddy's heart was pure gold," he said. The boy with the red sweat shirt had come around behind them and was standing with his gun at his hip. The Misfit squatted down on the ground. "Watch them children, Bobby Lee," he said. "You know they make me nervous." He looked at the six of them huddled together in front of him and he seemed to be embarrassed as if he couldn't think of anything to say. "Ain't a cloud in the sky," he remarked, looking up at it. "Don't see no sun but don't see no cloud neither."

"Yes, it's a beautiful day," said the grandmother. "Listen," she said, "you shouldn't call yourself The Misfit because I know you're a good man at heart. I can just look at you and tell."

"Hush!" Bailey yelled. "Hush! Everybody shut up and let me handle this!" He was squatting in the position of a runner about to sprint forward but he didn't move.

"I pre-chate that, lady," The Misfit said and drew a little circle in the ground with the butt of his gun.

"It'll take a half a hour to fix this here car," Hiram called, looking over the raised hood of it.

"Well, first you Bobby Lee get him and that little boy to step over yonder with you," The Misfit said, pointing to Bailey and John Wesley. "The boys want to ast you something," he said to Bailey. "Would you mind stepping back in them woods there with them?"

"Listen," Bailey began, "we're in a terrible predicament! Nobody realizes what this is," and his voice cracked. His eyes were as blue and intense as the parrots in his shirt and he remained perfectly still.

The grandmother reached up to adjust her hat brim as if she were going to the woods with him but it came off in her hand. She stood staring at it and after a second she let it fall on the ground. Hiram pulled Bailey up by the arm as if he were assisting an old man. John Wesley caught hold of his father's hand and Bobby Lee followed. They went off toward the woods and just as they reached the dark edge, Bailey turned and supporting himself against a gray naked pine trunk, he shouted, "I'll be back in a minute, Mamma, wait on me!"

"Come back this instant!" his mother shrilled but they all disappeared into the woods.

"Bailey Boy!" the grandmother called in a tragic voice but she found she was looking at The Misfit squatting on the ground in front of her. "I just know you're a good man," she said desperately. "You're not a bit common!"

"Nome, I ain't a good man," The Misfit said after a second as if he had considered her statement carefully, "but I ain't the worst in the world neither. My daddy said I was a different breed of dog from my brothers and sisters. 'You know,' Daddy said, 'it's some that can live their whole life without asking about it and it's others has to know why it is, and this boy is one of the latters. He's going to be into everything!'" He put on his black hat and looked up suddenly and then away deep into the woods as if he were embarrassed again. "I'm sorry I don't have on a shirt before you ladies," he said, hunching his shoulders slightly. "We buried our clothes that we had on when we escaped and we're just making do until we can get better. We borrowed these from some folks we met," he explained.

"That's perfectly all right," the grandmother said. "Maybe Bailey has an extra shirt in his suitcase."

"I'll look and see terrectly," The Misfit said.

"Where are they taking him?" the children's mother screamed.

"Daddy was a card himself," The Misfit said. "You couldn't put anything over on him. He never got in trouble with the Authorities though. Just had the knack of handling them."

"You could be honest too if you'd only try," said the grandmother. "Think how wonderful it would be to settle down and live a comfortable life and not have to think about somebody chasing you all the time."

The Misfit kept scratching in the ground with the butt of his gun as if he were thinking about it. "Yes'm, somebody is always after you," he murmured.

The grandmother noticed how thin his shoulder blades were just behind his hat because she was standing up looking down on him. "Do you ever pray?" she asked.

He shook his head. All she saw was the black hat wiggle between his shoulder blades. "Nome," he said.

There was a pistol shot from the woods, followed closely by another. Then silence. The old lady's head jerked around. She could hear the wind move through the tree tops like a long satisfied insuck of breath. "Bailey Boy!" she called.

"I was a gospel singer for a while," The Misfit said. "I been most everything. Been in the arm service, both land and sea, at home and abroad, been twict married, been an undertaker, been with the railroads, plowed Mother Earth, been in a tornado, seen a man burnt alive oncet," and he looked up at the children's mother and the little girl who were sitting close together, their faces white and their eyes glassy. "I even seen a woman flogged," he said.

"Pray, pray," the grandmother began, "pray, pray . . ."

"I never was a bad boy that I remember of," The Misfit said in an almost dreamy voice, "but somewheres along the line I done something wrong and got sent to the penitentiary. I was buried alive," and he looked up and held her attention to him by a steady stare.

"That's when you should have started to pray," she said, "What did you do to get sent to the penitentiary that first time?"

"Turn to the right, it was a wall," The Misfit said, looking up again at the cloudless sky. "Turn to the left, it was a wall. Look up it was a ceiling, look down it was a floor. I forget what I done, lady. I set there and set there, trying to remember what it was I done and I ain't recalled it to this day. Oncet in a while, I would think it was coming to me, but it never come."

"Maybe they put you in by mistake," the old lady said vaguely.

"Nome," he said. "It wasn't no mistake. They had the papers on me."

"You must have stolen something," she said.

The Misfit sneered slightly. "Nobody had nothing I wanted," he said. "It was a head-doctor at the penitentiary said what I had done was kill my daddy but I known that for a lie. My daddy died in nineteen ought nineteen of the epidemic flu and I never had a thing to do with it. He was buried in the Mount Hopewell Baptist churchyard and you can go there and see for yourself."

"If you would pray," the old lady said, "Jesus would help you."

"That's right," The Misfit said.

"Well then, why don't you pray?" she asked trembling with delight suddenly.

"I don't want no hep," he said. "I'm doing all right by myself."

Bobby Lee and Hiram came ambling back from the woods. Bobby Lee was dragging a yellow shirt with bright blue parrots in it.

"Thow me that shirt, Bobby Lee," The Misfit said. The shirt came flying at him and landed on his shoulder and he put it on. The grandmother couldn't name what the shirt reminded her of. "No, lady," The Misfit said while he was buttoning it up, "I found out the crime don't matter. You can do one thing or you can do another, kill a man or take a tire off his car, because sooner or later you're going to forget what it was you done and just be punished for it."

The children's mother had begun to make heaving noises as if she couldn't get her breath. "Lady," he asked, "would you and that little girl like to step off yonder with Bobby Lee and Hiram and join your husband?"

"Yes, thank you," the mother said faintly. Her left arm dangled helplessly and she was holding the baby, who had gone to sleep, in the other. "Hep that lady up, Hiram," The Misfit said as she struggled to climb out of the ditch, "and Bobby Lee, you hold onto that little girl's hand."

"I don't want to hold hands with him," June Star said. "He reminds me of a pig."

The fat boy blushed and laughed and caught her by the arm and pulled her off into the woods after Hiram and her mother.

Alone with The Misfit, the grandmother found that she had lost her voice. There was not a cloud in the sky nor any sun. There was nothing around her but woods. She wanted to tell him that he must pray. She opened and closed her mouth several times before anything came out. Finally she found herself saying, "Jesus. Jesus," meaning, Jesus will help you, but the way she was saying it, it sounded as if she might be cursing.

"Yes'm," The Misfit said as if he agreed. "Jesus thown everything off balance. It was the same case with Him as with me except He hadn't committed any crime and they could prove I had committed one because they had the papers on me. Of course," he said, "they never shown me my papers. That's why I sign myself now. I said long ago, you get you a signature and sign everything you do and keep a copy of it. Then you'll know what you done and you can hold up the crime to the punishment and see do they match and in the end you'll have something to prove you ain't been treated right. I call myself The Misfit," he said, "because I can't make what all I done wrong fit what all I gone through in punishment."

There was a piercing scream from the woods, followed closely by a pistol report. "Does it seem right to you, lady, that one is punished a heap and another ain't punished at all?"

"Jesus!" the old lady cried. "You've got good blood! I know you wouldn't shoot a lady! I know you come from nice people! Pray! Jesus, you ought not to shoot a lady. I'll give you all the money I've got!"

"Lady," The Misfit said, looking beyond her far into the woods, "there never was a body that give the undertaker a tip."

There were two more pistol reports and the grandmother raised her head like a parched old turkey hen crying for water and called, "Bailey Boy, Bailey Boy!" as if her heart would break.

"Jesus was the only One that ever raised the dead," The Misfit continued, "and He shouldn't have done it. He thown everything off balance. If He did what He said, then it's nothing for you to do but thow away everything and follow Him, and if He didn't, then it's nothing for you to do but enjoy the few minutes you got left the best way you can—by killing somebody or burning down his house or doing some other meanness to him. No pleasure but meanness," he said and his voice had become almost a snarl.

"Maybe He didn't raise the dead," the old lady mumbled, not knowing what she was saying and feeling so dizzy that she sank down in the ditch with her legs twisted under her.

"I wasn't there so I can't say He didn't," The Misfit said. "I wisht I had of been there," he said, hitting the ground with his fist. "It ain't right I wasn't there because if I had of been there I would of known. Listen lady," he said in a high voice, "if I had of been there I would of known and I wouldn't be like I am now." His voice seemed about to crack and the grandmother's head cleared for an instant. She saw the man's face twisted close to her own as if he were going to cry and she murmured, "Why you're one of my babies. You're one of my own children!" She reached out and touched him on the shoulder. The Misfit sprang back as if a snake had bitten him and shot her three times through the chest. Then he put his gun down on the ground and took off his glasses and began to clean them.

Hiram and Bobby Lee returned from the woods and stood over the ditch, looking down at the grandmother who half sat and half lay in a puddle of blood with her legs crossed under her like a child's and her face smiling up at the cloudless sky.

Without his glasses, The Misfit's eyes were red-rimmed and pale and defenseless-looking. "Take her off and thow her where you thown the others," he said, picking up the cat that was rubbing itself against his leg.

"She was a talker, wasn't she?" Bobby Lee said, sliding down the ditch with a yodel.

"She would of been a good woman," The Misfit said, "if it had been somebody there to shoot her every minute of her life."

"Some fun!" Bobby Lee said.

"Shut up, Bobby Lee," The Misfit said. "It's no real pleasure in life."

1953

Joyce Carol Oates b. 1938

Critic, teacher, short story writer, poet, playwright, novelist, editor, and publisher, Joyce Carol Oates is an artist of amazing versatility, productivity, and range. She has written more than twenty novels and hundreds of shorter works; several of her plays have been produced off-Broadway; at least two of her stories have been made into films. Writing about men and women struggling for existence in "Eden Valley," a region strikingly like her own birthplace in upstate New York, Oates has been variously classified as a realist, a naturalist, a "gothic" artist, and "the dark lady of American Letters." She has won many prizes, including the National Book Award, a Guggenheim Fellowship, an O. Henry award for Special Achievement, and an award from the Lotos Club. Oates has been elected to the National Institute of Arts and Letters. While she calls herself a feminist, she prefers to be considered "a woman who writes." She has a wide readership: her work is as likely to be found on an academic syllabus as on the best-seller list.

Oates has often been considered a realist in the tradition of Dreiser; she is indeed a social critic, focusing on contemporary events and issues in fiction and essays. But she is also testing classical myths and established literary conventions beyond the limits of any one genre. Curiously, as if to expand her own boundaries, Oates has published fiction—a series of harrowing psychological mysteries—under a pseudonym, Rosamond Smith.

Perhaps Oates is best understood as an artist in residence—in the largest sense of that term. She studied at Syracuse and then in graduate school at the University of Wisconsin, and has taught literature and writing at Detroit and Windsor. As a scholar, she has written several collections of literary criticism, including *New Heaven, New Earth, (Woman) Writer,* and *The Profane Art.* She is on the Advisory Board of *The Kenyon Review;* she is a frequent reviewer of contemporary literature. Currently she is Roger S. Berlind Distinguished Professor of English at Princeton, where she lives and writes and works at the press she founded with her husband, Professor Raymond Smith.

Oates draws upon this complex and varied background in her fiction. In one way or another, all of Oates's characters struggle to find a place in a changing and often threatening world. In her early novels *With Shuddering Fall* and *A Garden of Earthly Delights,* she writes about rural America with its migrants, ragged prophets, and automobile junkyards; in contrast, *Expensive People* mocks the suburbanite, and her novel *them* dramatizes the violent lives of the urban poor. *Wonderland* is a novel of lost generations; the hero barely escapes from the gunfire of his crazed father; as a father himself, he is in danger of losing his daughter in the turbulence of the sixties. *Childwold* is a lyrical and experimental portrait of an artist as a young woman. Oates satirizes doctors, lawyers, preachers; she casts an especially critical eye at professors and resident artists in *Unholy Loves, Solstice, American Appetites,* and *Marya: A Life.*

Fascinated by the literary past and the work of other writers, she has also tried her hand at "imitations"—reimagining stories of Joyce, Thoreau, James, Chekhov, and Kafka. Oates produced a group of novels which represent her own imaginative view of nineteenth-century conventions, with particular emphasis on the constraints placed upon women both as writers and as hapless heroines.

But she is also inscribing the history of the present, memorializing the paranoia of the fifties in *You Must Remember This,* dramatizing explosive American race relations in *Because It is Bitter, and Because It Is My*

Heart, and publishing essays on boxing which have won her infrequent spots as a ringside commentator.

Joyce Carol Oates may be best known for her short stories, frequently included in the O. Henry annual Prize Selection and widely anthologized. Like her novels, many of her stories are experiments in form and character. Most focus on the personality at risk: on seemingly ordinary people whose lives are vulnerable to powerful threats from external society and the inner self.

"Where Are You Going, Where Have You Been?" is one of these. A frightening view of "coming of age" written in 1967, the story has appeared in several collections, including *The Wheel of Love;* it has also been adapted for the screen (*Smooth Talk,* 1986). Its central character, Connie, is a young woman fatally at ease in the world of adolescent ritual: high school flirtations, hamburger hangouts and drive-ins, movies and fan magazines; her dreams are shaped by popular song lyrics. She seems destined for a conventional future very much like her mother's, evident in their half-affectionate bickering. Yet as Oates deftly and gradually reveals, this sense of security is at best illusory; even the familiar language of popular song becomes the agency of seduction, making Connie the helpless victim of a grotesque and demonic caller she mistakes for a "friend." Asking the question posed by the sixties balladeer and youth culture cult figure, Bob Dylan (to whom this story is dedicated), "Where Are You Going, Where Have You Been?" powerfully represents the complex, open-ended literary project of author Joyce Carol Oates.

Eileen T. Bender
Indiana University

PRIMARY WORKS

By the North Gate, 1963; *With Shuddering Fall,* 1964; *A Garden of Earthly Delights,* 1967; *Expensive People,* 1968; *them,* 1969; *The Wheel of Love,* 1970; *Wonderland,* 1971; *Marriages and Infidelities,* 1972; *New Heaven, New Earth,* 1974; *Childwold,* 1976; *Unholy Loves,* 1979; *Bellefleur,* 1980; *A Bloodsmoor Romance,* 1982; *The Profane Art,* 1983; *Last Days,* 1984; *Solstice,* 1985; *Marya: A Life,* 1986; *(Woman) Writer,* 1986; *You Must Remember This,* 1987; *On Boxing,* 1988; *Because It Is Bitter, and Because It Is My Heart,* 1991; *Twelve Plays,* 1991; *Black Water,* 1992; *Foxfire,* 1993; *Zombie,* 1995; *First Love: A Gothic Tale,* 1996; *Tenderness,* 1996; *We Were the Mulvaneys,* 1996; *Mancrazy,* 1997; *My Heart Laid Bare,* 1998; *Broke Heart Blues,* 1999; *Where I've Been, and Where I'm Going* (essays), 1999; *Blonde,* 2000.

Where Are You Going, Where Have You Been?

For Bob Dylan

Her name was Connie. She was fifteen and she had a quick, nervous giggling habit of craning her neck to glance into mirrors or checking other people's faces to make sure her own was all right. Her mother, who noticed everything and knew everything and who hadn't much reason any longer to look at her own face, always scolded Connie about it. "Stop gawking at yourself. Who are you? You think you're so pretty?"

she would say. Connie would raise her eyebrows at these familiar old complaints and look right through her mother, into a shadowy vision of herself as she was right at that moment: she knew she was pretty and that was everything. Her mother had been pretty once too, if you could believe those old snapshots in the album, but now her looks were gone and that was why she was always after Connie.

"Why don't you keep your room clean like your sister? How've you got your hair fixed—what the hell stinks? Hair spray? You don't see your sister using that junk."

Her sister June was twenty-four and still lived at home. She was a secretary in the high school Connie attended, and if that wasn't bad enough—with her in the same building—she was so plain and chunky and steady that Connie had to hear her praised all the time by her mother and her mother's sisters. June did this, June did that, she saved money and helped clean the house and cooked and Connie couldn't do a thing, her mind was all filled with trashy daydreams. Their father was away at work most of the time and when he came home he wanted supper and he read the newspaper at supper and after supper he went to bed. He didn't bother talking much to them, but around his bent head Connie's mother kept picking at her until Connie wished her mother was dead and she herself was dead and it was all over. "She makes me want to throw up sometimes," she complained to her friends. She had a high, breathless, amused voice that made everything she said sound a little forced, whether it was sincere or not.

There was one good thing: June went places with girl friends of hers, girls who were just as plain and steady as she, and so when Connie wanted to do that her mother had no objections. The father of Connie's best girl friend drove the girls the three miles to town and left them at a shopping plaza so they could walk through the stores or go to a movie, and when he came to pick them up again at eleven he never bothered to ask what they had done.

They must have been familiar sights, walking around the shopping plaza in their shorts and flat ballerina slippers that always scuffed the sidewalk, with charm bracelets jingling on their thin wrists; they would lean together to whisper and laugh secretly if someone passed who amused or interested them. Connie had long dark blond hair that drew anyone's eye to it, and she wore part of it pulled up on her head and puffed out and the rest of it she let fall down her back. She wore a pull-over jersey blouse that looked one way when she was at home and another way when she was away from home. Everything about her had two sides to it, one for home and one for anywhere that was not home: her walk, which could be childlike and bobbing, or languid enough to make anyone think she was hearing music in her head; her mouth, which was pale and smirking most of the time, but bright and pink on these evenings out; her laugh, which was cynical and drawling at home—"Ha, ha, very funny,"—but high-pitched and nervous anywhere else, like the jingling of the charms on her bracelet.

Sometimes they did go shopping or to a movie, but sometimes they went across the highway, ducking fast across the busy road, to a drive-in restaurant where older kids hung out. The restaurant was shaped like a big bottle, though squatter than a real bottle, and on its cap was a revolving figure of a grinning boy holding a hamburger aloft. One night in midsummer they ran across, breathless with daring, and right away someone leaned out a car window and invited them over, but it was just a boy from high school they didn't like. It made them feel good to be able to ignore him. They went up through the maze of parked and cruising cars to the bright-lit, fly-infested restaurant, their faces pleased and expectant as if they were entering a sacred building that loomed up out of the night to give them what haven and blessing they yearned for. They sat at the counter and crossed their legs at the ankles, their thin shoulders rigid with excitement, and listened to the music that made everything so good: the music was always in the background, like music at a church service; it was something to depend upon.

A boy named Eddie came in to talk with them. He sat backwards on his stool, turning himself jerkily around in semicircles and then stopping and turning back again, and after a while he asked Connie if she would like something to eat. She said she would and so she tapped her friend's arm on her way out—her friend pulled her face up into a brave, droll look—and Connie said she would meet her at eleven, across the way. "I just hate to leave her like that," Connie said earnestly, but the boy said that she wouldn't be alone for long. So they went out to his car, and on the way Connie couldn't help but let her eyes wander over the windshields and faces all around her, her face gleaming with a joy that had nothing to do with Eddie or even this place; it might have been the music. She drew her shoulders up and sucked in her breath with the pure pleasure of being alive, and just at that moment she happened to glance at a face just a few feet from hers. It was a boy with shaggy black hair, in a convertible jalopy painted gold. He stared at her and then his lips widened into a grin. Connie slit her eyes at him and turned away, but she couldn't help glancing back and there he was, still watching her. He wagged a finger and laughed and said, "Gonna get you, baby," and Connie turned away again without Eddie noticing anything.

She spent three hours with him, at the restaurant where they ate hamburgers and drank Cokes in wax cups that were always sweating, and then down an alley a mile or so away, and when he left her off at five to eleven only the movie house was still open at the plaza. Her girl friend was there, talking with a boy. When Connie came up, the two girls smiled at each other and Connie said, "How was the movie?" and the girl said, "*You* should know." They rode off with the girl's father, sleepy and pleased, and Connie couldn't help but look back at the darkened shopping plaza with its big empty parking lot and its signs that were faded and ghostly now, and over at the drive-in restaurant where cars were still circling tirelessly. She couldn't hear the music at this distance.

Next morning June asked her how the movie was and Connie said, "So-so."

She and that girl and occasionally another girl went out several times a week, and the rest of the time Connie spent around the house—it was summer vacation—getting in her mother's way and thinking, dreaming about the boys she met. But all the boys fell back and dissolved into a single face that was not even a face but an idea, a feeling, mixed up with the urgent insistent pounding of the music and the humid night air of July. Connie's mother kept dragging her back to the daylight by finding things for her to do or saying suddenly, "What's this about the Pettinger girl?"

And Connie would say nervously, "Oh, her. That dope." She always drew thick clear lines between herself and such girls, and her mother was simple and kind enough to believe it. Her mother was so simple, Connie thought, that it was maybe cruel to fool her so much. Her mother went scuffling around the house in old bedroom slippers and complained over the telephone to one sister about the other, then the other called up and the two of them complained about the third one. If June's name was mentioned her mother's tone was approving, and if Connie's name was mentioned it was disapproving. This did not really mean she disliked Connie, and actually Connie thought that her mother preferred her to June just because she was prettier, but the two of them kept up a pretense of exasperation, a sense that they were tugging and struggling over something of little value to either of them. Sometimes, over coffee, they were almost friends, but something would come up—some vexation that was like a fly buzzing suddenly around their heads—and their faces went hard with contempt.

One Sunday Connie got up at eleven—none of them bothered with church—and washed her hair so that it could dry all day long in the sun. Her parents and sister were going to a barbecue at an aunt's house and Connie said no, she wasn't interested, rolling her eyes to let her mother know just what she thought of it. "Stay home alone then," her mother said sharply. Connie sat out back in a lawn chair and watched them drive away, her father quiet and bald, hunched around so that he could back the car out, her mother with a look that was still angry and not at all softened through the windshield, and in the back seat poor old June, all dressed up as if she didn't know what a barbecue was, with all the running yelling kids and the flies. Connie sat with her eyes closed in the sun, dreaming and dazed with the warmth about her as if this were a kind of love, the caresses of love, and her mind slipped over onto thoughts of the boy she had been with the night before and how nice he had been, how sweet it always was, not the way someone like June would suppose but sweet, gentle, the way it was in movies and promised in songs; and when she opened her eyes she hardly knew where she was, the back yard ran off into weeds and a fence-like line of trees and behind it the sky was perfectly blue and still. The asbestos "ranch house" that was now three years old startled her—it looked small. She shook her head as if to get awake.

It was too hot. She went inside the house and turned on the radio to drown out the quiet. She sat on the edge of her bed, barefoot, and listened for an hour and a half to a program called XYZ Sunday Jamboree, record after record of hard, fast, shrieking songs she sang along with, interspersed by exclamations from "Bobby King": "An' look here, you girls at Napoleon's—Son and Charley want you to pay real close attention to this song coming up!"

And Connie paid close attention herself, bathed in a glow of slow-pulsed joy that seemed to rise mysteriously out of the music itself and lay languidly about the airless little room, breathed in and breathed out with each gentle rise and fall of her chest.

After a while she heard a car coming up the drive. She sat up at once, startled, because it couldn't be her father so soon. The gravel kept crunching all the way in from the road—the driveway was long—and Connie ran to the window. It was a car she didn't know. It was an open jalopy, painted a bright gold that caught the sunlight opaquely. Her heart began to pound and her fingers snatched at her hair, checking it, and she whispered, "Christ. Christ," wondering how bad she looked. The car came to a stop at the side door and the horn sounded four short taps, as if this were a signal Connie knew.

She went into the kitchen and approached the door slowly, then hung out the screen door, her bare toes curling down off the step. There were two boys in the car and now she recognized the driver: he had shaggy, shabby black hair that looked crazy as a wig and he was grinning at her.

"I ain't late, am I?" he said.

"Who the hell do you think you are?" Connie said.

"Toldja I'd be out, didn't I?"

"I don't even know who you are."

She spoke sullenly, careful to show no interest or pleasure, and he spoke in a fast, bright monotone. Connie looked past him to the other boy, taking her time. He had fair brown hair, with a lock that fell onto his forehead. His sideburns gave him a fierce, embarrassed look, but so far he hadn't even bothered to glance at her. Both boys wore sunglasses. The driver's glasses were metallic and mirrored everything in miniature.

"You wanta come for a ride?" he said.

Connie smirked and let her hair fall loose over one shoulder.

"Don'tcha like my car? New paint job," he said. "Hey."

"What?"

"You're cute."

She pretended to fidget, chasing flies away from the door.

"Don'tcha believe me, or what?" he said.

"Look, I don't even know who you are," Connie said in disgust.

"Hey, Ellie's got a radio, see. Mine broke down." He lifted his friend's arm and showed her the little transistor radio the boy was holding, and now Connie began to hear the music. It was the same program that was playing inside the house.

"Bobby King?" she said.

"I listen to him all the time. I think he's great."

"He's kind of great," Connie said reluctantly.

"Listen, that guy's *great.* He knows where the action is."

Connie blushed a little, because the glasses made it impossible for her to see just what this boy was looking at. She couldn't decide if she liked him or if he was just a jerk, and so she dawdled in the doorway and wouldn't come down or go back inside. She said, "What's all that stuff painted on your car?"

"Can'tcha read it?" He opened the door very carefully, as if he were afraid it might fall off. He slid out just as carefully, planting his feet firmly on the ground, the tiny metallic world in his glasses slowing down like gelatine hardening, and in the midst of it Connie's bright green blouse. "This here is my name, to begin with," he said. ARNOLD FRIEND was written in tarlike black letters on the side, with a drawing of a round, grinning face that reminded Connie of a pumpkin, except it wore sunglasses. "I wanta introduce myself, I'm Arnold Friend and that's my real name and I'm gonna be your friend, honey, and inside the car's Ellie Oscar, he's kinda shy." Ellie brought his transistor radio up to his shoulder and balanced it there. "Now, these numbers are a secret code, honey," Arnold Friend explained. He read off the numbers 33, 19, 17 and raised his eyebrows at her to see what she thought of that, but she didn't think much of it. The left rear fender had been smashed and around it was written, on the gleaming gold background: DONE BY CRAZY WOMAN DRIVER. Connie had to laugh at that. Arnold Friend was pleased at her laughter and looked up at her. "Around the other side's a lot more—you wanta come and see them?"

"No."

"Why not?"

"Why should I?"

"Don'tcha wanta see what's on the car? Don'tcha wanta go for a ride?"

"I don't know."

"Why not?"

"I got things to do."

"Like what?"

"Things."

He laughed as if she had said something funny. He slapped his thighs. He was standing in a strange way, leaning back against the car as if he were balancing himself. He wasn't tall, only an inch or so taller than she would be if she came down to him. Connie liked the way he was dressed, which was the way all of them dressed: tight faded jeans stuffed into black, scuffed boots, a belt that pulled his waist in and showed how lean he was, and a white pull-over shirt that was a little soiled and showed the hard small muscles of his arms and shoulders. He looked as if he probably did hard work, lifting and carrying things. Even his neck looked muscular. And his face was a familiar face, somehow: the jaw and chin and cheeks slightly darkened because he hadn't shaved for a day or two, and the nose long and hawk-like, sniffing as if she were a treat he was going to gobble up and it was all a joke.

"Connie, you ain't telling the truth. This is your day set aside for a ride with me and you know it," he said, still laughing. The way he straightened and recovered from his fit of laughing showed that it had been all fake.

"How do you know what my name is?" she said suspiciously.

"It's Connie."

"Maybe and maybe not."

"I know my Connie," he said, wagging his finger. Now she remembered him even better, back at the restaurant, and her cheeks warmed at the thought of how she had sucked in her breath just at the moment she passed him—how she must have looked to him. And he had remembered her. "Ellie and I come out here especially for you," he said. "Ellie can sit in back. How about it?"

"Where?"

"Where what?"

"Where're we going?"

He looked at her. He took off the sunglasses and she saw how pale the skin around his eyes was, like holes that were not in shadow but instead in light. His eyes were like chips of broken glass that catch the light in an amiable way. He smiled. It was as if the idea of going for a ride somewhere, to someplace, was a new idea to him.

"Just for a ride, Connie sweetheart."

"I never said my name was Connie," she said.

"But I know what it is. I know your name and all about you, lots of things," Arnold Friend said. He had not moved yet but stood still leaning back against the side of his jalopy. "I took a special interest in you, such a pretty girl, and found out all about you—like I know your parents and sister are gone somewheres and I know where and how long they're going to be gone, and I know who you were with last night, and your best girl friend's name is Betty. Right?"

He spoke in a simple lilting voice, exactly as if he were reciting the words to a song. His smile assured her that everything was fine. In the car Ellie turned up the volume on his radio and did not bother to look around at them.

"Ellie can sit in the back seat," Arnold Friend said. He indicated his friend with a casual jerk of his chin, as if Ellie did not count and she should not bother with him.

"How'd you find out all that stuff?" Connie said.

"Listen: Betty Schultz and Tony Fitch and Jimmy Pettinger and Nancy Pettinger," he said in a chant. "Raymond Stanley and Bob Hutter—"

"Do you know all those kids?"

"I know everybody."

"Look, you're kidding. You're not from around here."

"Sure."

"But—how come we never saw you before?"

"Sure you saw me before," he said. He looked down at his boots, as if he were a little offended. "You just don't remember."

"I guess I'd remember you," Connie said.

"Yeah?" He looked up at this, beaming. He was pleased. He began to mark time with the music from Ellie's radio, tapping his fists lightly together. Connie looked away from his smile to the car, which was painted so bright it almost hurt her eyes to look at it. She looked at that name, ARNOLD FRIEND. And up at the front fender was an expression that was familiar—MAN THE FLYING SAUCERS. It was an expression kids had used the year before but didn't use this year. She looked at it for a while as if the words meant something to her that she did not yet know.

"What're you thinking about? Huh?" Arnold Friend demanded. "Not worried about your hair blowing around in the car, are you?"

"No."

"Think I maybe can't drive good?"

"How do I know?"

"You're a hard girl to handle. How come?" he said. "Don't you know I'm your friend? Didn't you see me put my sign in the air when you walked by?"

"What sign?"

"My sign." And he drew an X in the air, leaning out toward her. They were maybe ten feet apart. After his hand fell back to his side the X was still in the air, almost visible. Connie let the screen door close and stood perfectly still inside it, listening to the music from her radio and the boy's blend together. She stared at Arnold Friend. He stood there so stiffly relaxed, pretending to be relaxed, with one hand idly on the door handle as if he were keeping himself up that way and had no intention of ever moving again. She recognized most things about him, the tight jeans that showed his thighs and buttocks and the greasy leather boots and the tight shirt, and even that slippery friendly smile of his, that sleepy dreamy smile that all the boys used to get across ideas they didn't want to put into words. She recognized all this and also the singsong way he talked, slightly mocking, kidding, but serious and a little melancholy, and she recognized the way he tapped one fist against the other in homage to the perpetual music behind him. But all these things did not come together.

She said suddenly, "Hey, how old are you?"

His smile faded. She could see then that he wasn't a kid, he was much older—thirty, maybe more. At this knowledge her heart began to pound faster.

"That's a crazy thing to ask. Can'tcha see I'm your own age?"

"Like hell you are."

"Or maybe a coupla years older. I'm eighteen."

"Eighteen?" she said doubtfully.

He grinned to reassure her and lines appeared at the corners of his mouth. His teeth were big and white. He grinned so broadly his eyes became slits and she saw how thick the lashes were, thick and black as if painted with a black tarlike material. Then, abruptly, he seemed to become embarrassed and looked over his shoulder at Ellie. "*Him,* he's crazy," he said. "Ain't he a riot? He's a nut, a real character." Ellie was still listening to the music. His sunglasses told nothing about what he was thinking. He wore a bright orange shirt unbuttoned halfway to show his chest, which was a pale, bluish chest and not muscular like Arnold Friend's. His shirt collar was turned up all around and the very tips of the collar pointed out past his chin as if they were protecting him. He was pressing the transistor radio up against his ear and sat there in a kind of a daze, right in the sun.

"He's kinda strange," Connie said.

"Hey, she says you're kinda strange! Kinda strange!" Arnold Friend cried. He pounded on the car to get Ellie's attention. Ellie turned for the first time and Connie saw with shock that he wasn't a kid either—he had a fair, hairless face, cheeks reddened slightly as if the veins grew too close to the surface of his skin, the face of a forty-year-old baby. Connie felt a wave of dizziness rise in her at this sight and she stared at him as if waiting for something to change the shock of the moment, make it all right again. Ellie's lips kept shaping words, mumbling along with the words blasting in his ear.

"Maybe you two better go away," Connie said faintly.

"What? How come?" Arnold Friend cried. "We come out here to take you for a ride. It's Sunday." He had the voice of the man on the radio now. It was the same voice, Connie thought. "Don'tcha know it's Sunday all day? And honey, no matter who you were with last night, today you're with Arnold Friend and don't you forget it! Maybe you better step out here," he said, and this last was in a different voice. It was a little flatter, as if the heat was finally getting to him.

"Hey."

"You two better leave."

"We ain't leaving until you come with us."

"Like hell I am—"

"Connie, don't fool around with me. I mean—I mean, don't fool *around,*" he said shaking his head. He laughed incredulously. He placed his sunglasses on top of his head, carefully, as if he were indeed wearing a wig, and brought the stems down behind his ears. Connie stared at him, another wave of dizziness and fear rising in her so that for a moment he wasn't even in focus but was just a blur standing there against his gold car, and she had the idea that he had driven up the driveway all right but had come from nowhere before that and belonged nowhere and that everything about him and even about the music that was so familiar to her was only half real.

"If my father comes and sees you—"

"He ain't coming. He's at a barbecue."

"How do you know that?"

"Aunt Tillie's. Right now they're—uh—they're drinking. Sitting around," he said vaguely, squinting as if he were staring all the way to town and over to Aunt Tillie's back yard. Then the vision seemed to get clear and he nodded energetically. "Yeah. Sitting around. There's your sister in a blue dress, huh? And high heels, the poor sad bitch—nothing like you, sweetheart! And your mother's helping some fat woman with the corn, they're cleaning the corn—husking the corn—"

"What fat woman?" Connie cried.

"How do I know what fat woman, I don't know every goddamn fat woman in the world!" Arnold Friend laughed.

"Oh, that's Mrs. Hornsby. . . . Who invited her?" Connie said. She felt a little lightheaded. Her breath was coming quickly.

"She's too fat. I don't like them fat. I like them the way you are, honey," he said, smiling sleepily at her. They stared at each other for a while through the screen door. He said softly, "Now, what you're going to do is this: you're going to come out that door. You're going to sit up front with me and Ellie's going to sit in the back, the hell with Ellie, right? This isn't Ellie's date. You're my date. I'm your lover, honey."

"What? You're crazy—"

"Yes, I'm your lover. You don't know what that is but you will," he said. "I know that too. I know all about you. But look: it's real nice and you couldn't ask for nobody better than me, or more polite. I always keep my word. I'll tell you how it is, I'm always nice at first, the first time. I'll hold you so tight you won't think you have to try to get away or pretend anything because you'll know you can't. And I'll come inside you where it's all secret and you'll give in to me and you'll love me—"

"Shut up! You're crazy!" Connie said. She backed away from the door. She put her hands up against her ears as if she'd heard something terrible, something not meant for her. "People don't talk like that, you're crazy," she muttered. Her heart was almost too big now for her chest and its pumping made sweat break out all over her. She looked out to see Arnold Friend pause and then take a step toward the porch, lurching. He almost fell. But, like a clever drunken man, he managed to catch his balance. He wobbled in his high boots and grabbed hold of one of the porch posts.

"Honey?" he said. "You still listening?"

"Get the hell out of here!"

"Be nice, honey. Listen."

"I'm going to call the police—"

He wobbled again and out of the side of his mouth came a fast spat curse, an aside not meant for her to hear. But even this "Christ!" sounded forced. Then he began to smile again. She watched this smile come, awkward as if he were smiling from inside a mask. His whole face was a mask, she thought wildly, tanned down to his throat but then running out as if he had plastered make-up on his face but had forgotten about his throat.

"Honey—? Listen, here's how it is. I always tell the truth and I promise you this: I ain't coming in that house after you."

"You better not! I'm going to call the police if you—if you don't—"

"Honey," he said, talking right through her voice, "honey, I'm not coming in there but you are coming out here. You know why?"

She was panting. The kitchen looked like a place she had never seen before, some room she had run inside but that wasn't good enough, wasn't going to help her. The kitchen window had never had a curtain, after three years, and there were dishes in the sink for her to do—probably—and if you ran your hand across the table you'd probably feel something sticky there.

"You listening, honey? Hey?"

"—going to call the police—"

"Soon as you touch the phone I don't need to keep my promise and can come inside. You won't want that."

She rushed forward and tried to lock the door. Her fingers were shaking. "But why lock it," Arnold Friend said gently, talking right into her face. "It's just a screen door. It's just nothing." One of his boots was at a strange angle, as if his foot wasn't in it. It pointed out to the left, bent at the ankle. "I mean, anybody can break through a screen door and glass and wood and iron or anything else if he needs to, anybody at all, and specially Arnold Friend. If the place got lit up with a fire, honey, you'd come runnin' out into my arms, right into my arms an' safe at home—like you knew I was your lover and'd stopped fooling around. I don't mind a nice shy girl but I don't like no fooling around." Part of those words were spoken with a slight rhythmic lilt, and Connie somehow recognized them—the echo of a song from last year, about a girl rushing into her boy friend's arms and coming home again—

Connie stood barefoot on the linoleum floor, staring at him. "What do you want?" she whispered.

"I want you," he said.

"What?"

"Seen you that night and thought, that's the one, yes sir. I never needed to look anymore."

"But my father's coming back. He's coming to get me. I had to wash my hair first—" She spoke in a dry, rapid voice, hardly raising it for him to hear.

"No, your daddy is not coming and yes, you had to wash your hair and you washed it for me. It's nice and shining and all for me. I thank you, sweetheart," he said with a mock bow, but again he almost lost his balance. He had to bend and adjust his boots. Evidently his feet did not go all the way down; the boots must have been stuffed with something so that he would seem taller. Connie stared out at him and behind him at Ellie in the car, who seemed to be looking off toward Connie's right, into nothing. This Ellie said, pulling the words out of the air one after another as if he were just discovering them, "You want me to pull out the phone?"

"Shut your mouth and keep it shut," Arnold Friend said, his face red from bending over or maybe from embarrassment because Connie had seen his boots. "This ain't none of your business."

"What—what are you doing? What do you want?" Connie said. "If I call the police they'll get you, they'll arrest you—"

"Promise was not to come in unless you touch that phone, and I'll keep that promise," he said. He resumed his erect position and tried to force his shoulders back. He sounded like a hero in a movie, declaring something important. But he spoke too loudly and it was as if he were speaking to someone behind Connie. "I ain't made plans for coming in that house where I don't belong but just for you to come out to me, the way you should. Don't you know who I am?"

"You're crazy," she whispered. She backed away from the door but did not want to go into another part of the house, as if this would give him permission to come through the door. "What do you . . . you're crazy, you. . . ."

"Huh? What're you saying, honey?"

Her eyes darted everywhere in the kitchen. She could not remember what it was, this room.

"This is how it is, honey: you come out and we'll drive away, have a nice ride.

But if you don't come out we're gonna wait till your people come home and then they're all going to get it."

"You want that telephone pulled out?" Ellie said. He held the radio away from his ear and grimaced, as if without the radio the air was too much for him.

"I toldja shut up, Ellie," Arnold Friend said, "you're deaf, get a hearing aid, right? Fix yourself up. This little girl's no trouble and's gonna be nice to me, so Ellie keep to yourself, this ain't your date—right? Don't hem in on me, don't hog, don't crush, don't bird dog, don't trail me," he said in a rapid, meaningless voice, as if he were running through all the expressions he'd learned but was no longer sure which of them was in style, then rushing on to new ones, making them up with his eyes closed. "Don't crawl under my fence, don't squeeze in my chipmunk hole, don't sniff my glue, suck my popsicle, keep your own greasy fingers on yourself!" He shaded his eyes and peered in at Connie, who was backed against the kitchen table. "Don't mind him, honey, he's just a creep. He's a dope. Right? I'm the boy for you and like I said, you come out here nice like a lady and give me your hand, and nobody else gets hurt, I mean, your nice old bald-headed daddy and your mummy and your sister in her high heels. Because listen: why bring them in this?"

"Leave me alone," Connie whispered.

"Hey, you know that old woman down the road, the one with the chickens and stuff—you know her?"

"She's dead!"

"Dead? What? You know her?" Arnold Friend said.

"She's dead—"

"Don't you like her?"

"She's dead—she's—she isn't here any more—"

"But don't you like her, I mean, you got something against her? Some grudge or something?" Then his voice dipped as if he were conscious of a rudeness. He touched the sunglasses perched up on top of his head as if to make sure they were still there. "Now, you be a good girl."

"What are you going to do?"

"Just two things, or maybe three," Arnold Friend said. "But I promise it won't last long and you'll like me the way you get to like people you're close to. You will. It's all over for you here, so come on out. You don't want your people in any trouble, do you?"

She turned and bumped against a chair or something, hurting her leg, but she ran into the back room and picked up the telephone. Something roared in her ear, a tiny roaring, and she was so sick with fear that she could do nothing but listen to it—the telephone was clammy and very heavy and her fingers groped down to the dial but were too weak to touch it. She began to scream into the phone, into the roaring. She cried out, she cried for her mother, she felt her breath start jerking back and forth in her lungs as if it were something Arnold Friend was stabbing her with again and again with no tenderness. A noisy sorrowful wailing rose all about her and she was locked inside it the way she was locked inside this house.

After a while she could hear again. She was sitting on the floor with her wet back against the wall.

Arnold Friend was saying from the door, "That's a good girl. Put the phone back."

She kicked the phone away from her.

"No, honey. Pick it up. Put it back right."

She picked it up and put it back. The dial tone stopped.

"That's a good girl. Now, you come outside."

She was hollow with what had been fear but what was now just an emptiness. All that screaming had blasted it out of her. She sat, one leg cramped under her, and deep inside her brain was something like a pinpoint of light that kept going and would not let her relax. She thought, I'm not going to see my mother again. She thought, I'm not going to sleep in my bed again. Her bright green blouse was all wet.

Arnold Friend said, in a gentle-loud voice that was like a stage voice, "The place where you came from ain't there any more, and where you had in mind to go is cancelled out. This place you are now—inside your daddy's house—is nothing but a cardboard box I can knock down any time. You know that and always did know it. You hear me?"

She thought, I have got to think. I have got to know what to do.

"We'll go out to a nice field, out in the country here where it smells so nice and it's sunny," Arnold Friend said. "I'll have my arms tight around you so you won't need to try to get away and I'll show you what love is like, what it does. The hell with this house! It looks solid all right," he said. He ran a fingernail down the screen and the noise did not make Connie shiver, as it would have the day before. "Now, put your hand on your heart, honey. Feel that? That feels solid too but we know better. Be nice to me, be sweet like you can because what else is there for a girl like you but to be sweet and pretty and give in?—and get away before her people come back?"

She felt her pounding heart. Her hand seemed to enclose it. She thought for the first time in her life that it was nothing that was hers, that belonged to her, but just a pounding, living thing inside this body that wasn't really hers either.

"You don't want them to get hurt," Arnold Friend went on. "Now, get up, honey. Get up all by yourself."

She stood.

"Now, turn this way. That's right. Come over here to me.—Ellie, put that away, didn't I tell you? You dope. You miserable creepy dope," Arnold Friend said. His words were not angry but only part of an incantation. The incantation was kindly. "Now, come out through the kitchen to me, honey, and let's see a smile, try it, you're a brave, sweet little girl and now they're eating corn and hot dogs cooked to bursting over an outdoor fire, and they don't know one thing about you and never did and honey, you're better than them because not a one of them would have done this for you."

Connie felt the linoleum under her feet; it was cool. She brushed her hair back out of her eyes. Arnold Friend let go of the post tentatively and opened his arms for her, his elbows pointing in toward each other and his wrists limp, to show that this was an embarrassed embrace and a little mocking, he didn't want to make her self-conscious.

She put out her hand against the screen. She watched herself push the door slowly open as if she were back safe somewhere in the other doorway, watching this body and this head of long hair moving out into the sunlight where Arnold Friend waited.

"My sweet little blue-eyed girl," he said in a half-sung sigh that had nothing to do with her brown eyes but was taken up just the same by the vast sunlit reaches of the land behind him and on all sides of him—so much land that Connie had never seen before and did not recognize except to know that she was going to it.

1970

John Updike b. 1932

Born in Shillington, Pennsylvania, John Updike was the only child of Wesley R. and Linda Grace (Hoyer) Updike. His father was a high-school mathematics teacher and his mother later became a freelance writer. Young Updike received a full scholarship to Harvard University, where he was elected president of the *Lampoon,* the campus humor magazine. Upon graduating *summa cum laude* in 1954, he attended the Ruskin School of Drawing and Fine Art in Oxford, England. Since 1955 he has written for the *New Yorker* magazine, first as a reporter and then as a regular contributor of stories, poems, and reviews. He has published more than fifty books and has received numerous honors, including the National Book Award, the Pulitzer Prize, and election to the prestigious American Academy of Arts and Letters. Divorced and remarried, he now lives in Massachusetts.

Over the years, Updike has become something of a celebrity, appearing on talk shows and magazine covers. His short stories have been dramatized for television; his novel *The Witches of Eastwick* was a Book-of-the-Month Club selection and was later released as a Warner Brothers film starring Jack Nicholson. Updike's work is assigned in college literature courses and has generated a substantial body of scholarly criticism. He is a rarity among serious writers, having secured both popular success and academic acclaim.

Remarkably versatile—writing novels, children's books, short story and poetry collections, a play, and eight anthologies of non-fiction prose—he is most highly regarded as a fiction writer. He draws heavily upon his own life for subject matter but transcends the particulars of personal experience, achieving a broadly encompassing vision of the contemporary American situation.

With a few exceptions, his novels and stories can be grouped into three overlapping categories: the "Olinger" fiction, the "Rabbit" novels, and the "suburban" books. Chief among the early works set in fictional Olinger, Pennsylvania (based on Updike's hometown), is *The Centaur,* a loving tribute to his father. The tetralogy comprising *Rabbit, Run; Rabbit Redux; Rabbit Is Rich;* and *Rabbit at Rest* focuses on Harry Angstrom, a blue-collar protagonist whom some critics have identified as Updike's alter-ego. Other works—*Couples, Marry Me,* and the many stories about Richard and Joan Maple, for example—document the tensions of upper-middle-class suburbia, often depicting divorce and its aftermath.

Common to all of Updike's works is a concern with individual moral responsibility and guilt, coupled with a clearcut indictment of current values and a quixotic yearning to recapture the simpler and presumably purer American past. A consciously religious writer, he repeatedly creates confused, unfulfilled characters unable to reconcile the opposed demands of the self and the social contract, particularly in the context of interpersonal relationships. Parents and children, husbands and wives, lovers and friends encounter difficulties because they cannot strike a balance between license and repression. Usually this failure is linked to sexual avidity, and the resulting dilemmas are played out against a depressing background of vulgar materialism. Updike's overriding theme is that of cultural disintegration, the abrogation of the Protestant ethic.

He is not, however, simply a diagnostician of social ills. His books will endure for their historical accuracy but also as *belles-lettres*—works of art. Although a novelist of the everyday, Updike fashions sparkling metaphors that invest his rather commonplace topics with fresh vitality. This keenness derives also from the striking specificity and exactitude that typify his presentation of sensory detail. He tells the reader not only what to see but what to hear, what to taste, what to smell—a technique that he may have learned from the example of James Joyce. At his best, Updike can evoke a moment as vividly as anyone writing today. And although his content is highly contemporary (including frequent forays into explicitly sexual depiction), he is in many respects a throwback to the nineteenth-century novelists of manners, capturing social nuances while plumbing the depths of his characters' motivations and interrelationships. As the critic Charles Thomas Samuels said, "Updike offers the novel's traditional pleasures."

This selection, from a 1979 short story collection entitled *Problems,* is an excellent example of Updike at the top of his form.

George J. Searles
Mohawk Valley Community College

PRIMARY WORKS

The Carpentered Hen, 1958; *The Poorhouse Fair,* 1959; *The Same Door,* 1959; *Rabbit, Run,* 1960; *The Magic Flute,* 1962; *Pigeon Feathers,* 1962; *The Centaur,* 1963; *Telephone Poles,* 1963; *Olinger Stories,* 1964; *The Ring,* 1964; *Assorted Prose,* 1965; *A Child's Calendar,* 1965; *Of the Farm,* 1965; *Verse,* 1965; *The Music School,* 1966; *Couples,* 1968; *Bottom's Dream,* 1969; *Midpoint,* 1969; *Bech: A Book,* 1970; *Rabbit Redux,* 1971; *Museums and Women,* 1972; *Buchanan Dying,* 1974; *A Month of Sundays,* 1975; *Picked-Up Pieces,* 1975; *Marry Me,* 1976; *Tossing and Turning,* 1977; *The Coup,* 1978; *Problems,* 1979; *Too Far to Go,* 1979; *Rabbit Is Rich,* 1980; *Bech Is Back,* 1982; *Hugging the Shore,* 1983; *The Witches of Eastwick,* 1984; *Facing Nature,* 1985; *Roger's Version,* 1986; *Trust Me,* 1987; *S.,* 1988; *Just Looking,* 1989; *Self-Consciousness,* 1989; *Rabbit at Rest,* 1990; *Odd Jobs,* 1991; *Memories of the Ford Administration,* 1992; *Collected Poems, 1953-1993,* 1993; *Brazil,* 1994; *The Afterlife and Other Stories,* 1994; *Rabbit Angstrom: The Four Novels,* 1995; *In the Beauty of the Lilies,* 1996; *Golf Dreams: Writings on Golf,* 1996; *A Helpful Alphabet of Friendly Objects,* 1996; *Toward the End of Time,* 1997; *Bech at Bay,* 1998; *More Matter,* 1999; *Gertrude and Claudius,* 2000; *Licks of Love,* 2000.

Separating

The day was fair. Brilliant. All that June the weather had mocked the Maples' internal misery with solid sunlight—golden shafts and cascades of green in which their conversations had wormed unseeing, their sad murmuring selves the only stain in Nature. Usually by this time of the year they had acquired tans; but when they met their elder daughter's plane on her return from a year in England they were almost as pale as she, though Judith was too dazzled by the sunny opulent jumble of her native land to notice. They did not spoil her homecoming by telling her immediately. Wait a few days, let her recover from jet lag, had been one of their formulations, in that string of gray dialogues—over coffee, over cocktails, over Cointreau[1]—that had shaped the strategy of their dissolution, while the earth performed its annual stunt of renewal unnoticed beyond their closed windows. Richard had thought to leave at Easter; Joan had insisted they wait until the four children were at last assembled, with all exams passed and ceremonies attended, and the bauble of summer to console them. So he had drudged away, in love, in dread, repairing screens, getting the mowers sharpened, rolling and patching their new tennis court.

The court, clay, had come through its first winter pitted and windswept bare of redcoat. Years ago the Maples had observed how often, among their friends, divorce followed a dramatic home improvement, as if the marriage were making one last effort to live; their own worst crisis had come amid the plaster dust and exposed plumbing of a kitchen renovation. Yet, a summer ago, as canary-yellow bulldozers gaily churned a grassy, daisy-dotted knoll into a muddy plateau, and a crew of pigtailed young men raked and tamped clay into a plane, this transformation did not strike them as ominous, but festive in its impudence; their marriage could rend the earth for fun. The next spring, waking each day at dawn to a sliding sensation as if the bed were being tipped, Richard found the barren tennis court—its net and tapes still rolled in the barn—an environment congruous with his mood of purposeful desolation, and the crumbling of handfuls of clay into cracks and holes (dogs had frolicked on the court in a thaw; rivulets had eroded trenches) an activity suitably elemental and interminable. In his sealed heart he hoped the day would never come.

Now it was here. A Friday. Judith was re-acclimated; all four children were assembled, before jobs and camps and visits again scattered them. Joan thought they should be told one by one. Richard was for making an announcement at the table. She said, "I think just making an announcement is a cop-out. They'll start quarrelling and playing to each other instead of focusing. They're each individuals, you know, not just some corporate obstacle to your freedom."

"O.K., O.K. I agree." Joan's plan was exact. That evening, they were giving Judith a belated welcome-home dinner, of lobster and champagne. Then, the party over, they, the two of them, who nineteen years before would push her in a baby carriage along Fifth Avenue to Washington Square,[2] were to walk her out of the house, to the bridge across the salt creek, and tell her, swearing her to secrecy. Then Richard Jr., who was going directly from work to a rock concert in Boston, would be told, either late when he returned on the train or early Saturday morning before he went off to his job; he was seventeen and employed as one of a golf-course maintenance crew. Then the two younger children, John and Margaret, could, as the morning wore on, be informed.

"Mopped up, as it were," Richard said.

"Do you have any better plan? That leaves you the rest of Saturday to answer any questions, pack, and make your wonderful departure."

"No," he said, meaning he had no better plan, and agreed to hers, though to him

[1]An expensive, orange-flavored liqueur similar to Grand Marnier.

[2]A fashionable area of Manhattan.

it showed an edge of false order, a hidden plea for control, like Joan's long chore lists and financial accountings and, in the days when he first knew her, her too-copious lecture notes. Her plan turned one hurdle for him into four—four knife-sharp walls, each with a sheer blind drop on the other side.

All spring he had moved through a world of insides and outsides, of barriers and partitions. He and Joan stood as a thin barrier between the children and the truth. Each moment was a partition, with the past on one side and the future on the other, a future containing this unthinkable *now.* Beyond four knifelike walls a new life for him waited vaguely. His skull cupped a secret, a white face, a face both frightened and soothing, both strange and known, that he wanted to shield from tears, which he felt all about him, solid as the sunlight. So haunted, he had become obsessed with battening down the house against his absence, replacing screens and sash cords, hinges and latches—a Houdini[3] making things snug before his escape.

The lock. He had still to replace a lock on one of the doors of the screened porch. The task, like most such, proved more difficult than he had imagined. The old lock, aluminum frozen by corrosion, had been deliberately rendered obsolete by manufacturers. Three hardware stores had nothing that even approximately matched the mortised hole its removal (surprisingly easy) left. Another hole had to be gouged, with bits too small and saws too big, and the old hole fitted with a block of wood—the chisels dull, the saw rusty, his fingers thick with lack of sleep. The sun poured down, beyond the porch, on a world of neglect. The bushes already needed pruning, the windward side of the house was shedding flakes of paint, rain would get in when he was gone, insects, rot, death. His family, all those he would lose, filtered through the edges of his awareness as he struggled with screw holes, splinters, opaque instructions, minutiae of metal.

Judith sat on the porch, a princess returned from exile. She regaled them with stories of fuel shortages, of bomb scares in the Underground,[4] of Pakistani workmen loudly lusting after her as she walked past on her way to dance school. Joan came and went, in and out of the house, calmer than she should have been, praising his struggles with the lock as if this were one more and not the last of their long succession of shared chores. The younger of his sons for a few minutes held the rickety screen door while his father clumsily hammered and chiseled, each blow a kind of sob in Richard's ears. His younger daughter, having been at a slumber party, slept on the porch hammock through all the noise—heavy and pink, trusting and forsaken. Time, like the sunlight, continued relentlessly; the sunlight slowly slanted. Today was one of the longest days. The lock clicked, worked. He was through. He had a drink; he drank it on the porch, listening to his daughter. "It was so sweet," she was saying, "during the worst of it, how all the butchers and bakery shops kept open by candlelight. They're all so plucky and cute. From the papers, things sounded so much worse here—people shooting people in gas lines, and everybody freezing."

[3]Harry Houdini (1874–1926), an American magician famous for escape feats.
[4]London's subway system.

Richard asked her, "Do you still want to live in England forever?" *Forever:* the concept, now a reality upon him, pressed and scratched at the back of his throat.

"No," Judith confessed, turning her oval face to him, its eyes still childishly far apart, but the lips set as over something succulent and satisfactory. "I was anxious to come home. I'm an American." She was a woman. They had raised her; he and Joan had endured together to raise her, alone of the four. The others had still some raising left in them. Yet it was the thought of telling Judith—the image of her, their first baby, walking between them arm in arm to the bridge—that broke him. The partition between his face and the tears broke. Richard sat down to the celebratory meal with the back of his throat aching; the champagne, the lobster seemed phases of sunshine; he saw them and tasted them through tears. He blinked, swallowed, croakily joked about hay fever. The tears would not stop leaking through; they came not through a hole that could be plugged but through a permeable spot in a membrane, steadily, purely, endlessly, fruitfully. They became, his tears, a shield for himself against these others—their faces, the fact of their assembly, a last time as innocents, at a table where he sat the last time as head. Tears dropped from his nose as he broke the lobster's back; salt flavored his champagne as he sipped it; the raw clench at the back of his throat was delicious. He could not help himself.

His children tried to ignore his tears. Judith, on his right, lit a cigarette, gazed upward in the direction of her too energetic, too sophisticated exhalation; on her other side, John earnestly bent his face to the extraction of the last morsels—legs, tail segments—from the scarlet corpse. Joan, at the opposite end of the table, glanced at him surprised, her reproach displaced by a quick grimace, of forgiveness, or of salute to his superior gift of strategy. Between them, Margaret, no longer called Bean, thirteen and large for her age, gazed from the other side of his pane of tears as if into a shopwindow at something she coveted—at her father, a crystalline heap of splinters and memories. It was not she, however, but John who, in the kitchen, as they cleared the plates and carapaces away, asked Joan the question: *"Why is Daddy crying?"*

Richard heard the question but not the murmured answer. Then he heard Bean cry, "Oh, no-oh!"—the faintly dramatized exclamation of one who had long expected it.

John returned to the table carrying a bowl of salad. He nodded tersely at his father and his lips shaped the conspiratorial words "She told."

"Told what?" Richard asked aloud, insanely.

The boy sat down as if to rebuke his father's distraction with the example of his own good manners. He said quietly, "The separation."

Joan and Margaret returned; the child, in Richard's twisted vision, seemed diminished in size, and relieved, relieved to have had the bogieman at last proved real. He called out to her—the distances at the table had grown immense—"You knew, you always knew," but the clenching at the back of his throat prevented him from making sense of it. From afar he heard Joan talking, levelly, sensibly, reciting what they had prepared: it was a separation for the summer, an experiment. She and Daddy both agreed it would be good for them; they needed space and time to think; they liked each other but did not make each other happy enough, somehow.

Judith, imitating her mother's factual tone, but in her youth off-key, too cool, said, "I think it's silly. You should either live together or get divorced."

Richard's crying, like a wave that has crested and crashed, had become tumultuous; but it was overtopped by another tumult, for John, who had been so reserved, now grew larger and larger at the table. Perhaps his younger sister's being credited with knowing set him off. "Why didn't you *tell* us?" he asked, in a large round voice quite unlike his own. "You should have *told* us you weren't getting along."

Richard was startled into attempting to force words through his tears. "We *do* get along, that's the trouble, so it doesn't show even to us—" *That we do not love each other* was the rest of the sentence; he couldn't finish it.

Joan finished for him, in her style. "And we've always, *especially,* loved our children."

John was not mollified. "What do you care about *us?*" he boomed. "We're just little things you *had.*" His sisters' laughing forced a laugh from him, which he turned hard and parodistic: "Ha ha *ha.*" Richard and Joan realized simultaneously that the child was drunk, on Judith's homecoming champagne. Feeling bound to keep the center of the stage, John took a cigarette from Judith's pack, poked it into his mouth, let it hang from his lower lip, and squinted like a gangster.

"You're not little things we had," Richard called to him. "You're the whole point. But you're grown. Or almost."

The boy was lighting matches. Instead of holding them to his cigarette (for they had never seen him smoke; being "good" had been his way of setting himself apart), he held them to his mother's face, closer and closer, for her to blow out. Then he lit the whole folder—a hiss and then a torch, held against his mother's face. Prismed by tears, the flame filled Richard's vision; he didn't know how it was extinguished. He heard Margaret say, "Oh stop showing off," and saw John, in response, break the cigarette in two and put the halves entirely into his mouth and chew, sticking out his tongue to display the shreds to his sister.

Joan talked to him, reasoning—a fountain of reason, unintelligible. "Talked about it for years . . . our children must help us . . . Daddy and I both want . . ." As the boy listened, he carefully wadded a paper napkin into the leaves of his salad, fashioned a ball of paper and lettuce, and popped it into his mouth, looking around the table for the expected laughter. None came. Judith said, "Be mature," and dismissed a plume of smoke.

Richard got up from this stifling table and led the boy outside. Though the house was in twilight, the outdoors still brimmed with light, the lovely waste light of high summer. Both laughing, he supervised John's spitting out the lettuce and paper and tobacco into the pachysandra.[5] He took him by the hand—a square gritty hand, but for its softness a man's. Yet, it held on. They ran together up into the field, past the tennis court. The raw banking left by the bulldozers was dotted with daisies. Past the court and a flat stretch where they used to play family baseball stood a soft green rise glorious in the sun, each weed and species of grass distinct as illumination on parchment. "I'm sorry, so sorry," Richard cried. "You were the only one who ever tried to help me with all the goddam jobs around this place."

Sobbing, safe within his tears and the champagne, John explained, "It's not just the separation, it's the whole crummy year, I *hate* that school, you can't make any friends, the history teacher's a scud."[6]

[5]A shrubby plant.
[6]A slang term for a boring and/or unreasonably demanding teacher.

They sat on the crest of the rise, shaking and warm from their tears but easier in their voices, and Richard tried to focus on the child's sad year—the weekdays long with homework, the weekends spent in his room with model airplanes, while his parents murmured down below, nursing their separation. How selfish, how blind, Richard thought; his eyes felt scoured. He told his son, "We'll think about getting you transferred. Life's too short to be miserable."

They had said what they could, but did not want the moment to heal, and talked on, about the school, about the tennis court, whether it would ever again be as good as it had been that first summer. They walked to inspect it and pressed a few more tapes more firmly down. A little stiltedly, perhaps trying now to make too much of the moment, Richard led the boy to the spot in the field where the view was best, of the metallic blue river, the emerald marsh, the scattered islands velvety with shadow in the low light, the white bits of beach far away. "See," he said. "It goes on being beautiful. It'll be here tomorrow."

"I know," John answered, impatiently. The moment had closed.

Back in the house, the others had opened some white wine, the champagne being drunk, and still sat at the table, the three females, gossiping. Where Joan sat had become the head. She turned, showing him a tearless face, and asked, "All right?"

"We're fine," he said, resenting it, though relieved, that the party went on without him.

In bed she explained, "I couldn't cry I guess because I cried so much all spring. It really wasn't fair. It's your idea, and you made it look as though I was kicking you out."

"I'm sorry," he said. "I couldn't stop. I wanted to but couldn't."

"You *didn't* want to. You loved it. You were having your way, making a general announcement."

"I love having it over," he admitted. "God, those kids were great. So brave and funny." John, returned to the house, had settled to a model airplane in his room, and kept shouting down to them, "I'm O.K. No sweat." "And the way," Richard went on, cozy in his relief, "they never questioned the reasons we gave. No thought of a third person. Not even Judith."

"That *was* touching," Joan said.

He gave her a hug. "You were great too. Very reassuring to everybody. Thank you." Guiltily, he realized he did not feel separated.

"You still have Dickie to do," she told him. These words set before him a black mountain in the darkness; its cold breath, its near weight affected his chest. Of the four children, his elder son was most nearly his conscience. Joan did not need to add, "That's one piece of your dirty work I won't do for you."

"I know. I'll do it. You go to sleep."

Within minutes, her breathing slowed, became oblivious and deep. It was quarter to midnight. Dickie's train from the concert would come in at one-fourteen. Richard set the alarm for one. He had slept atrociously for weeks. But whenever he closed his lids some glimpse of the last hours scorched them—Judith exhaling toward the ceiling in a kind of aversion, Bean's mute staring, the sunstruck growth in the field where he and John had rested. The mountain before him moved closer, moved within him; he was huge, momentous. The ache at the back of his throat felt stale. His wife slept as if slain beside him. When, exasperated by his hot lids, his crowded heart, he rose from bed and dressed, she awoke enough to turn over. He told her then, "Joan, if I could undo it all, I would."

"Where would you begin?" she asked. There was no place. Giving him courage, she was always giving him courage. He put on shoes without socks in the dark. The children were breathing in their rooms, the downstairs was hollow. In their confusion they had left lights burning. He turned off all but one, the kitchen overhead. The car started. He had hoped it wouldn't. He met only moonlight on the road; it seemed a diaphanous companion, flickering in the leaves along the roadside, haunting his rearview mirror like a pursuer, melting under his headlights. The center of town, not quite deserted, was eerie at this hour. A young cop in uniform kept company with a gang of T-shirted kids on the steps of the bank. Across from the railroad station, several bars kept open. Customers, mostly young, passed in and out of the warm night, savoring summer's novelty. Voices shouted from cars as they passed; an immense conversation seemed in progress. Richard parked and in his weariness put his head on the passenger seat, out of the commotion and wheeling lights. It was as when, in the movies, an assassin grimly carries his mission through the jostle of a carnival—except the movies cannot show the precipitous, palpable slope you cling to within. You cannot climb back down; you can only fall. The synthetic fabric of the car seat, warmed by his cheek, confided to him an ancient, distant scent of vanilla.

A train whistle caused him to lift his head. It was on time; he had hoped it would be late. The slender drawgates descended. The bell of approach tingled happily. The great metal body, horizontally fluted, rocked to a stop, and sleepy teen-agers disembarked, his son among them. Dickie did not show surprise that his father was meeting him at this terrible hour. He sauntered to the car with two friends, both taller than he. He said "Hi" to his father and took the passenger's seat with an exhausted promptness that expressed gratitude. The friends got in the back, and Richard was grateful; a few more minutes' postponement would be won by driving them home.

He asked, "How was the concert?"

"Groovy,"[7] one boy said from the back seat.

"It bit,"[8] the other said.

"It was O.K.," Dickie said, moderate by nature, so reasonable that in his childhood the unreason of the world had given him headaches, stomach aches, nausea. When the second friend had been dropped off at his dark house, the boy blurted, "Dad, my eyes are killing me with hay fever! I'm out there cutting that mothering grass all day!"

"Do we still have those drops?"

"They didn't do any good last summer."

"They might this." Richard swung a U-turn on the empty street. The drive home took a few minutes. The mountain was here, in his throat. "Richard," he said, and felt the boy, slumped and rubbing his eyes, go tense at his tone, "I didn't come to

[7] A slang term meaning "excellent."
[8] A slang expression of disapproval or rejection (somewhat taboo); cf. "It sucked."

meet you just to make your life easier. I came because your mother and I have some news for you, and you're a hard man to get ahold of these days. It's sad news."

"That's O.K." The reassurance came out soft, but quick, as if released from the tip of a spring.

Richard had feared that his tears would return and choke him, but the boy's manliness set an example, and his voice issued forth steady and dry. "It's sad news, but it needn't be tragic news, at least for you. It should have no practical effect on your life, though it's bound to have an emotional effect. You'll work at your job, and go back to school in September. Your mother and I are really proud of what you're making of your life; we don't want that to change at all."

"Yeah," the boy said lightly, on the intake of his breath, holding himself up. They turned the corner; the church they went to loomed like a gutted fort. The home of the woman Richard hoped to marry stood across the green. Her bedroom light burned.

"Your mother and I," he said, "have decided to separate. For the summer. Nothing legal, no divorce yet. We want to see how it feels. For some years now, we haven't been doing enough for each other, making each other as happy as we should be. Have you sensed that?"

"No," the boy said. It was an honest, unemotional answer: true or false in a quiz.

Glad for the factual basis, Richard pursued, even garrulously, the details. His apartment across town, his utter accessibility, the split vacation arrangements, the advantages to the children, the added mobility and variety of the summer. Dickie listened, absorbing. "Do the others know?"

"Yes."

"How did they take it?"

"The girls pretty calmly. John flipped out; he shouted and ate a cigarette and made a salad out of his napkin and told us how much he hated school."

His brother chuckled. "He did?"

"Yeah. The school issue was more upsetting for him than Mom and me. He seemed to feel better for having exploded."

"He did?" The repetition was the first sign that he was stunned.

"Yes. Dickie, I want to tell you something. This last hour, waiting for your train to get in, has been about the worst of my life. I hate this. *Hate* it. My father would have died before doing it to me." He felt immensely lighter, saying this. He had dumped the mountain on the boy. They were home. Moving swiftly as a shadow, Dickie was out of the car, through the bright kitchen. Richard called after him, "Want a glass of milk or anything?"

"No thanks."

"Want us to call the course tomorrow and say you're too sick to work?"

"No, that's all right." The answer was faint, delivered at the door to his room; Richard listened for the slam that went with a tantrum. The door closed normally, gently. The sound was sickening.

Joan had sunk into that first deep trough of sleep and was slow to awake. Richard had to repeat, "I told him."

"What did he say?"

"Nothing much. Could you go say goodnight to him? Please."

She left their room, without putting on a bathrobe. He sluggishly changed back into his pajamas and walked down the hall. Dickie was already in bed, Joan was sitting beside him, and the boy's bedside clock radio was murmuring music. When she stood, an inexplicable light—the moon?—outlined her body through the nightie. Richard sat on the warm place she had indented on the child's narrow mattress. He asked him, "Do you want the radio on like that?"

"It always is."

"Doesn't it keep you awake? It would me."

"No."

"Are you sleepy?"

"Yeah."

"Good. Sure you want to get up and go to work? You've had a big night."

"I want to."

Away at school this winter he had learned for the first time that you can go short of sleep and live. As an infant he had slept with an immobile, sweating intensity that had alarmed his babysitters. In adolescence he had often been the first of the four children to go to bed. Even now, he would go slack in the middle of a television show, his sprawled legs hairy and brown. "O.K. Good boy. Dickie, listen. I love you so much, I never knew how much until now. No matter how this works out, I'll always be with you. Really."

Richard bent to kiss an averted face but his son, sinewy, turned and with wet cheeks embraced him and gave him a kiss, on the lips, passionate as a woman's. In his father's ear he moaned one word, the crucial, intelligent word: *"Why?"*

Why. It was a whistle of wind in a crack, a knife thrust, a window thrown open on emptiness. The white face was gone, the darkness was featureless. Richard had forgotten why.

1979

Ralph Waldo Ellison 1914–1994

Ralph Waldo Ellison was born in Oklahoma City of parents who migrated from South Carolina and Georgia. His father, Lewis, a construction foreman and later the owner of a small ice and coal business, named his son after Emerson, hoping he would be a poet. After losing his father when he was three, Ellison and his younger brother, Herbert, were raised by their mother, Ida, who worked as a nursemaid, janitress, and domestic and was active in politics. Ellison used to enjoy telling how she had canvassed for Eugene V. Debs and other Socialist candidates and later been jailed for defying Oklahoma City's segregation ordinances.

Ellison was drawn to music, playing cornet and trumpet from an early age and, in 1933, going to study classical composition at Tuskegee Institute under William L. Dawson. Of his musical influences he later said, "The great emphasis in my school was upon classical music, but such great jazz musicians as Hot Lips Page, Jimmy Rushing, and Lester Young were living in Oklahoma City....As it turned out, the perfection, the artistic dedication which helped me as a writer, was not so much in the classical emphasis as in the jazz itself."

In July 1936, after his junior year at Tuskegee, Ellison went to New York to earn money for his senior year and to study music and sculpture, and he stayed. In June 1937 his friendship with Richard Wright began and led him toward becoming a writer. Ellison also made the acquaintance of Langston Hughes and the painter Romare Bearden. In Dayton, Ohio, where he went to visit his ailing mother, and remained for six months after her unexpected death in October 1937, he began to write seriously, mostly nights in the second-story law office of Attorney William O. Stokes, using Stokes's letterhead and typewriter.

Returning to New York, from 1938 until 1942 Ellison worked on the New York Federal Writers Project of the WPA. Starting in the late 1930s, he contributed reviews, essays, and short fiction to *New Masses, Tomorrow, The Negro Quarterly* (of which he was for a time managing editor), *The New Republic, The Saturday Review, Antioch Review, The Reporter,* and other periodicals. During World War II he served in the merchant marine as a cook and baker and afterward worked at a variety of jobs, including freelance photography and the building and installation of audio systems.

Over a period of seven years, Ellison wrote *Invisible Man,* which was recognized upon its publication in 1952 as one of the most important works of fiction of its time. It was on the best-seller list for sixteen weeks and won the National Book Award. Its critical reputation and popularity have only continued to grow in the more than four decades since its publication. Ellison has described his novel's structure as that of a symphonic jazz composition with a central theme (or bass line) and harmonic variations (or riffs) often expressed in virtuoso solo performances. *Invisible Man* speaks for all readers and reflects the contradictions and complexities of American life through the prism of African American experience.

Although an excerpt from a second novel was published in *Noble Savage* in 1960, and seven other selections in literary magazines between then and 1977, no other long work of fiction has yet appeared. *Shadow and Act* (1964) and *Going to the Territory* (1986) collect essays and interviews written over more than forty years. Since Ellison's death four posthumous works have appeared: *The Collected Essays of Ralph Ellison* (1995), *Conversations with Ralph Ellison* (1995), *Flying Home and Other Stories* (1996), and *Juneteenth* (1999).

"A Party down at the Square" (undated), unpublished in Ellison's lifetime, is a tour de force. By narrating a lynching in the voice of a Cincinnati white boy visiting his uncle in Alabama, Ellison, while still a young writer, crosses the narrative color line and defies the "segregation of the word" he found lingering in American literature when he wrote "Twentieth-Century Fiction and the Black Mask of Humanity" (1946). Ellison's technique in "A Party down at the Square" compels readers to experience the human condition in extremis, mediated by a stranger whose morality is a commitment to be noncommital. The white boy's most telling response comes from his insides when, to his shame, he throws up. His sensations signify a resistance to values he has been taught not to question. There is nothing like this story in the rest of Ellison's work.

"Flying Home" (1944) anticipates the theme of invisibility and the technique of solos and breaks with which Ellison took flight in *Invisible Man.* Just when Todd, Ellison's northern protagonist, believes that he has learned to use his wiles to escape the limitations of race, language, and geography, circumstances force him to confront the strange "old country" of the South. A literary descendant of Icarus, as well as Joyce's Stephen Dedalus, Todd, one of the black eagles from the Negro air school at Tuskegee, flies too close to the sun, collides with a buzzard (a "jimcrow"), and falls to earth in rural Alabama. There, he is saved by Jefferson, whose folktales and actions enable Todd to recognize where he is and who he is and to come back to life by following the old black peasant and his son out of a labyrinthine Alabama valley.

In "Brave Words for a Startling Occasion" (1953), Ellison's acceptance address for the National Book Award, he celebrates the richness and diversity of American speech and the American language. And he identifies the task of the American writer as "always to challenge the apparent forms of reality—that is, the fixed manners and values of the few—and to struggle with it until it reveals its mad, vari-implicated chaos, its false faces, and on until it surrenders its insight, its truth."

John F. Callahan
Lewis and Clark College

PRIMARY WORKS

Invisible Man, 1952; *Shadow and Act,* 1964; *Going to the Territory,* 1986; *The Collected Essays of Ralph Ellison,* ed. with an introduction by John F. Callahan, 1995; *Conversations with Ralph Ellison,* ed. Maryemma Graham and Amrijit Singh, 1995; *Flying Home and Other Stories,* ed. with an introduction by John F. Callahan, 1996; *Juneteenth,* ed. John F. Callahan, 1999.

A Party Down at the Square

I don't know what started it. A bunch of men came by my Uncle Ed's place and said there was going to be a party down at the Square, and my uncle hollered for me to come on and I ran with them through the dark and rain and there we were at the Square. When we got there everybody was mad and quiet and standing around looking at the nigger. Some of the men had guns, and one man kept goosing the nigger in his pants with the barrel of a shotgun, saying he ought to pull the trigger, but he never did. It was right in front of the courthouse, and the old clock in the tower was striking twelve. The rain was falling cold and freezing as it fell. Everybody was cold, and the nigger kept wrapping his arms around himself trying to stop the shivers.

Then one of the boys pushed through the circle and snatched off the nigger's shirt, and there he stood, with his black skin all shivering in the light from the fire, and looking at us with a scaired look on his face and putting his hands in his pants pockets. Folks started yelling to hurry up and kill the nigger. Somebody yelled: "Take your hands out of your pockets, nigger; we gonna have plenty heat in a minnit." But the nigger didn't hear him and kept his hands where they were.

I tell you the rain was cold. I had to stick my hands in my pockets they got so cold. The fire was pretty small, and they put some logs around the platform they had the nigger on and then threw on some gasoline, and you could see the flames light up the whole Square. It was late and the streetlights had been off for a long time. It was so bright that the bronze statue of the general standing there in the Square was like something alive. The shadows playing on his moldy green face made him seem to be smiling down at the nigger.

They threw on more gas, and it made the Square bright like it gets when the lights are turned on or when the sun is setting red. All the wagons and cars were standing around the curbs. Not like Saturday though—the niggers weren't there.

Not a single nigger was there except this Bacote nigger and they dragged him there tied to the back of Jed Wilson's truck. On Saturday there's as many niggers as white folks.

Everybody was yelling crazy 'cause they were about to set fire to the nigger, and I got to the rear of the circle and looked around the Square to try to count the cars. The shadows of the folks was flickering on the trees in the middle of the Square. I saw some birds that the noise had woke up flying through the trees. I guess maybe they thought it was morning. The ice had started the cobblestones in the street to shine where the rain was falling and freezing. I counted forty cars before I lost count. I knew folks must have been there from Phenix City by all the cars mixed in with the wagons.

God, it was a hell of a night. It was some night all right. When the noise died down I heard the nigger's voice from where I stood in the back, so I pushed my way up front. The nigger was bleeding from his nose and ears, and I could see him all red where the dark blood was running down his black skin. He kept lifting first one foot and then the other, like a chicken on a hot stove. I looked down at the platform they had him on, and they had pushed a ring of fire up close to his feet. It must have been hot to him with the flames almost touching his big black toes. Somebody yelled for the nigger to say his prayers, but the nigger wasn't saying anything now. He just kinda moaned with his eyes shut and kept moving up and down on his feet, first one foot and then the other.

I watched the flames burning the logs up closer and closer to the nigger's feet. They were burning good now, and the rain had stopped and the wind was rising, making the flames flare higher. I looked, and there must have been thirty-five women in the crowd, and I could hear their voices clear and shrill mixed in with those of the men. Then it happened. I heard the noise about the same time everyone else did. It was like the roar of a cyclone blowing up the gulf, and everyone was looking up into the air to see what it was. Some of the faces looked surprised and scaired, all but the nigger. He didn't even hear the noise. He didn't even look up. Then the roar came closer, right above our heads and the wind was blowing higher and higher and the sound seemed to be going in circles.

Then I saw her. Through the clouds and fog I could see a red and green light on her wings. I could see them just for a second; then she rose up into the low clouds. I looked out for the beacon over the tops of the buildings in the direction of the airfield that's forty miles away, and it wasn't circling around. You usually could see it sweeping around the sky at night, but it wasn't there. Then, there she was again, like a big bird lost in the fog. I looked for the red and green lights, and they weren't there anymore. She was flying even closer to the tops of the buildings than before. The wind was blowing harder, and leaves started flying about, making funny shadows on the ground, and tree limbs were cracking and falling.

It was a storm all right. The pilot must have thought he was over the landing field. Maybe he thought the fire in the Square was put there for him to land by. Gosh, but it scaired the folks. I was scaired too. They started yelling: "He's going to land. He's going to land." And: "He's going to fall." A few started for their cars and wagons. I could hear the wagons creaking and chains jangling and cars spitting and missing as they started the engines up. Off to my right, a horse started pitching and striking his hooves against a car.

I didn't know what to do. I wanted to run, and I wanted to stay and see what was going to happen. The plane was close as hell. The pilot must have been trying to see where he was at, and her motors were drowning out all the sounds. I could even feel the vibration, and my hair felt like it was standing up under my hat. I happened to look over at the statue of the general standing with one leg before the other and leaning back on a sword, and I was fixing to run over and climb between his legs and sit there and watch when the roar stopped some, and I looked up and she was gliding just over the top of the trees in the middle of the Square.

Her motors stopped altogether and I could hear the sound of branches cracking and snapping off below her landing gear. I could see her plain now, all silver and shining in the light of the fire with T.W.A. in black letters under her wings. She was sailing smoothly out of the Square when she hit the high power lines that follow the Birmingham highway through the town. It made a loud crash. It sounded like the wind blowing the door of a tin barn shut. She only hit with her landing gear, but I could see the sparks flying, and the wires knocked loose from the poles were spitting blue sparks and whipping around like a bunch of snakes and leaving circles of blue sparks in the darkness.

The plane had knocked five or six wires loose, and they were dangling and swinging, and every time they touched they threw off more sparks. The wind was making them swing, and when I got over there, there was a crackling and spitting screen of blue haze across the highway. I lost my hat running over, but I didn't stop to look for it. I was among the first and I could hear the others pounding behind me across the grass of the Square. They were yelling to beat all hell, and they came up fast, pushing and shoving, and someone got pushed against a swinging wire. It made a sound like when a blacksmith drops a red hot horseshoe into a barrel of water, and the steam comes up. I could smell the flesh burning. The first time I'd ever smelled it. I got up close and it was a woman. It must have killed her right off. She was lying in a puddle stiff as a board, with pieces of glass insulators that the plane had knocked off the poles lying all around her. Her white dress was torn, and I saw one of her tits hanging out in the water and her thighs. Some woman screamed and fainted and almost fell on a wire, but a man caught her. The sheriff and his men were yelling and driving folks back with guns shining in their hands, and everything was lit up blue by the sparks. The shock had turned the woman almost as black as the nigger. I was trying to see if she wasn't blue too, or if it was just the sparks, and the sheriff drove me away. As I backed off trying to see, I heard the motors of the plane start up again somewhere off to the right in the clouds.

The clouds were moving fast in the wind and the wind was blowing the smell of something burning over to me. I turned around, and the crowd was headed back to the nigger. I could see him standing there in the middle of the flames. The wind was making the flames brighter every minute. The crowd was running. I ran too. I ran back across the grass with the crowd. It wasn't so large now that so many had gone when the plane came. I tripped and fell over the limb of a tree lying in the grass and bit my lip. It ain't well yet I bit it so bad. I could taste the blood in my mouth as I ran over. I guess that's what made me sick. When I got there, the fire had caught the nigger's pants, and the folks were standing around watching, but not too close on account of the wind blowing the flames. Somebody hollered, "Well, nigger, it ain't so cold now, is it? You don't need to put your hands in your pockets now." And the nigger looked up with his great white eyes looking like they was 'bout to pop out of his head, and I had enough. I didn't want to see anymore. I wanted to run somewhere to puke, but I stayed. I stayed right there in the front of the crowd and looked.

The nigger tried to say something I couldn't hear for the roar of the wind in the fire, and I strained my ears. Jed Wilson hollered, "What you say there, nigger?" And it came back through the flames in his nigger voice: "Will one a you gentlemen please cut my throat?" he said. "Will somebody please cut my throat like a Christian?" And Jed hollered back, "Sorry, but ain't no Christians around tonight. Ain't no Jew-boys neither. We're just one hundred percent Americans."

Then the nigger was silent. Folks started laughing at Jed. Jed's right popular with the folks, and next year, my uncle says, they plan to run him for sheriff. The heat was too much for me, and the smoke was making my eyes to smart. I was trying to back away when Jed reached down and brought up a can of gasoline and threw it in the fire on the nigger. I could see the flames catching the gas in a puff as it went in in a silver sheet and some of it reached the nigger, making spurts of blue fire all over his chest.

Well, that nigger was tough. I have to give it to that nigger; he was really tough. He had started to burn like a house afire and was making the smoke smell like burning hides. The fire was up around his head, and the smoke was so thick and black we couldn't see him. And him not moving—we thought he was dead. Then he started out. The fire had burned the ropes they had tied him with, and he started jumping and kicking about like he was blind, and you could smell his skin burning. He kicked so hard that the platform, which was burning too, fell in, and he rolled out of the fire at my feet. I jumped back so he wouldn't get on me. I'll never forget it. Every time I eat barbeque I'll remember that nigger. His back was just like a barbecued hog. I could see the prints of his ribs where they start around from his backbone and curve down and around. It was a sight to see, that nigger's back. He was right at my feet, and somebody behind pushed me and almost made me step on him, and he was still burning.

I didn't step on him though, and Jed and somebody else pushed him back into the burning planks and logs and poured on more gas. I wanted to leave, but the folks were yelling and I couldn't move except to look around and see the statue. A branch the wind had broken was resting on his hat. I tried to push out and get away because my guts were gone, and all I got was spit and hot breath in my face from the woman and two men standing directly behind me. So I had to turn back around. The nigger rolled out of the fire again. He wouldn't stay put. It was on the other side this time. I couldn't see him very well through the flames and smoke. They got some tree limbs and held him there this time and he stayed there till he was ashes. I guess he stayed there. I know he burned to ashes because I saw Jed a week later, and he laughed and showed me some white finger bones still held together with little pieces of the nigger's skin. Anyway, I left when somebody moved around to see the nigger. I pushed my way through the crowd, and a woman in the rear scratched my face as she yelled and fought to get up close.

I ran across the Square to the other side, where the sheriff and his deputies were guarding the wires that were still spitting and making a blue fog. My heart was pounding like I had been running a long ways, and I bent over and let my insides go. Everything came up and spilled in a big gush over the ground. I was sick, and tired, and weak, and cold. The wind was still high, and large drops of rain were beginning to fall. I headed down the street to my uncle's place past a store where the wind had broken a window, and glass lay over the sidewalk. I kicked it as I went by. I remember somebody's fool rooster crowing like it was morning in all that wind.

The next day I was too weak to go out, and my uncle kidded me and called me "the gutless wonder from Cincinnati." I didn't mind. He said you get used to it in time. He couldn't go out hisself. There was too much wind and rain. I got up and looked out of the window, and the rain was pouring down and dead sparrows and limbs of trees were scattered all over the yard. There had been a cyclone all right. It swept a path right through the county, and we were lucky we didn't get the full force of it.

It blew for three days steady, and put the town in a hell of a shape. The wind blew sparks and set fire to the white-and-green-trimmed house on Jackson Avenue that had the big concrete lions in the yard and burned it down to the ground. They had to kill another nigger who tried to run out of the county after they burned this Bacote nigger. My Uncle Ed said they always have to kill niggers in pairs to keep the other niggers in place. I don't know though, the folks seem a little skittish of the niggers. They all came back, but they act pretty sullen. They look mean as hell when you pass them down at the store. The other day I was down to Brinkley's store, and a white cropper said it didn't do no good to kill the niggers 'cause things don't get no better. He looked hungry as hell. Most of the croppers look hungry. You'd be surprised how hungry white folks can look. Somebody said that he'd better shut his damn mouth, and he shut up. But from the look on his face he won't stay shut long. He went out of the store muttering to himself and spit a big chew of tobacco right down on Brinkley's floor. Brinkley said he was sore 'cause he wouldn't let him have credit. Anyway, it didn't seem to help things. First it was the nigger and the storm, then the plane, then the woman and the wires, and now I hear the airplane line is investigating to find who set the fire that almost wrecked their plane. All that in one night, and all of it but the storm over one nigger. It was some night all right. It was some party too. I was right there, see. I was right there watching it all. It was my first party and my last. God, but that nigger was tough. That Bacote nigger was some nigger!

Flying Home

When Todd came to, he saw two faces suspended above him in a sun so hot and blinding that he could not tell if they were black or white. He stirred, feeling a pain that burned as though his whole body had been laid open to the sun, which glared into his eyes. For a moment an old fear of being touched by white hands seized him. Then the very sharpness of the pain began slowly to clear his head. Sounds came to him dimly. *He done come to.* Who are they? he thought. *Naw he ain't, I coulda sworn he was white.* Then he heard clearly:

"You hurt bad?"

Something within him uncoiled. It was a Negro sound.

"He's still out," he heard.

"Give 'im time. . . . Say, son, you hurt bad?"

Was he? There was that awful pain. He lay rigid, hearing their breathing and trying to weave a meaning between them and his being stretched painfully upon the ground. He watched them warily, his mind traveling back over a painful distance. Jagged scenes, swiftly unfolding as in a movie trailer, reeled through his mind, and he saw himself piloting a tailspinning plane and landing and falling from the cockpit and trying to stand. Then, as in a great silence, he remembered the sound of crunching bone and, now, looking up into the anxious faces of an old Negro man and a boy from where he lay in the same field, the memory sickened him and he wanted to remember no more.

"How you feel, son?"

Todd hesitated, as though to answer would be to admit an unacceptable weakness. Then, "It's my ankle," he said.

"Which one?"

"The left."

With a sense of remoteness he watched the old man bend and remove his boot, feeling the pressure ease.

"That any better?"

"A lot. Thank you."

He had the sensation of discussing someone else, that his concern was with some far more important thing, which for some reason escaped him.

"You done broke it bad," the old man said. "We have to get you to a doctor."

He felt that he had been thrown into a tailspin. He looked at his watch; how long had he been here? He knew there was but one important thing in the world, to get the plane back to the field before his officers were displeased.

"Help me up," he said. "Into the ship."

"But it's broke too bad . . ."

"Give me your arm!"

"But, son . . ."

Clutching the old man's arm, he pulled himself up, keeping his left leg clear, thinking, I'd never make him understand, as the leather-smooth face came parallel with his own.

"Now, let's see."

He pushed the old man back, hearing a bird's insistent shrill. He swayed, giddily. Blackness washed over him, like infinity.

"You best sit down."

"No, I'm okay."

"But, son. You jus gonna make it worse . . ."

It was a fact that everything in him cried out to deny, even against the flaming pain in his ankle. He would have to try again.

"You mess with that ankle they have to cut your foot off," he heard.

Holding his breath, he started up again. It pained so badly that he had to bite his lips to keep from crying out and he allowed them to help him down with a pang of despair.

"It's best you take it easy. We gon git you a doctor."

Of all the luck, he thought. Of all the rotten luck, now I have done it. The fumes of high-octane gasoline clung in the heat, taunting him.

"We kin ride him into town on old Ned," the boy said.

Ned? He turned, seeing the boy point toward an ox team, browsing where the buried blade of a plow marked the end of a furrow. Thoughts of himself riding an ox through the town, past streets full of white faces, down the concrete runways of the airfield, made swift images of humiliation in his mind. With a pang he remembered his girl's last letter. "Todd," she had written, "I don't need the papers to tell me you had the intelligence to fly. And I have always known you to be as brave as anyone else. The papers annoy me. Don't you be contented to prove over and over again that you're brave or skillful just because you're black, Todd. I think they keep beating that dead horse because they don't want to say why you boys are not yet fighting. I'm really disappointed, Todd. Anyone with brains can learn to fly, but then what. What about using it, and who will you use it for? I wish, dear, you'd write about this. I sometimes think they're playing a trick on us. It's very humiliating. . . ." He whipped cold sweat from his face, thinking, What does she know of humiliation? She's never been down South. *Now* the humiliation would come. When you must have them judge you, knowing that they never accept your mistakes as your own but hold it against your whole race—that was humiliation. Yes, and humiliation was when you could never be simply yourself; when you were always a part of this old black ignorant man. Sure, he's all right. Nice and kind and helpful. But he's not you. Well, there's one humiliation I can spare myself.

"No," he said. "I have orders not to leave the ship. . . ."

"Aw," the old man said. Then turning to the boy, "Teddy, then you better hustle down to Mister Graves and get him to come. . . ."

"No, wait!" he protested before he was fully aware. Graves might be white. "Just have him get word to the field, please. They'll take care of the rest."

He saw the boy leave, running.

"How far does he have to go?"

"Might' nigh a mile."

He rested back, looking at the dusty face of his watch. By now they know something has happened, he thought. In the ship there was a perfectly good radio, but it was useless. The old fellow would never operate it. That buzzard knocked me back a hundred years, he thought. Irony danced within him like the gnats circling the old man's head. With all I've learned, I'm dependent upon this "peasant's" sense of time and space. His leg throbbed. In the plane, instead of time being measured by the rhythms of pain and a kid's legs, the instruments would have told him at a glance. Twisting upon his elbows, he saw where dust had powdered the plane's fuselage, feeling the lump form in his throat that was always there when he thought of flight. It's crouched there, he thought, like the abandoned shell of a locust. I'm naked without it. Not a machine, a suit of clothes you wear. And with a sudden embarrassment and wonder he whispered, "It's the only dignity I have. . . ."

He saw the old man watching, his torn overalls clinging limply to him in the heat. He felt a sharp need to tell the old man what he felt. But that would be meaningless. If I tried to explain why I need to fly back, he'd think I was simply afraid of white officers. But it's more than fear . . . a sense of anguish clung to him like the veil of sweat that hugged his face. He watched the old man, hearing him humming snatches of a tune as he admired the plane. He felt a furtive sense of resentment. Such old men often came to the field to watch the pilots with childish eyes. At first it had made him proud; they had been a meaningful part of a new experience. But soon he realized they did not understand his accomplishments and they came to shame and embarrass him, like the distasteful praise of an idiot. A part of the meaning of flying had gone, then, and he had not been able to regain it. If I were a prize-fighter I would be more human, he thought. Not a monkey doing tricks, but a man. They were pleased simply that he was a Negro who could fly, and that was not enough. He felt cut off from them by age, by understanding, by sensibility, by technology, and by his need to measure himself against the mirror of other men's appreciation. Somehow he felt betrayed, as he had when as a child he grew to discover that his father was dead. Now, for him, any real appreciation lay with his white officers; and with them he could never be sure. Between ignorant black men and condescending whites, his course of flight seemed mapped by the nature of things away from all needed and natural landmarks. Under some sealed orders, couched in ever more technical and mysterious terms, his path curved swiftly away from both the shame the old man symbolized and the cloudy terrain of white man's regard. Flying blind, he knew but one point of landing and there he would receive his wings. After that the enemy would appreciate his skill and he would assume his deepest meaning, he thought sadly, neither from those who condescended nor from those who praised without understanding, but from the enemy who would recognize his manhood and skill in terms of hate. . . .

He sighed, seeing the oxen making queer, prehistoric shadows against the dry brown earth.

"You just take it easy, son," the old man soothed. "That boy won't take long. Crazy as he is about airplanes."

"I can wait," he said.

"What kinda airplane you call this here'n?"

"An Advanced Trainer," he said, seeing the old man smile. His fingers were like gnarled dark wood against the metal as he touched the low-slung wing.

" 'Bout how fast can she fly?"

"Over two hundred an hour."

"Lawd! That's so fast I bet it don't seem like you moving!"

Holding himself rigid, Todd opened his flying suit. The shade had gone and he lay in a ball of fire.

"You mind if I take a look inside? I was always curious to see . . ."

"Help yourself. Just don't touch anything."

He heard him climb upon the metal wing, grunting. Now the questions would start. Well, so you don't have to think to answer. . . .

He saw the old man looking over into the cockpit, his eyes bright as a child's.

"You must have to know a lot to work all these here things."

Todd was silent, seeing him step down and kneel beside him.

"Son, how come you want to fly way up there in the air?"

Because it's the most meaningful act in the world . . . because it makes me less like you, he thought.

But he said: "Because I like it, I guess. It's as good a way to fight and die as I know."

"Yeah? I guess you right," the old man said. "But how long you think before they gonna let you all fight?"

He tensed. This was the question all Negroes asked, put with the same timid hopefulness and longing that always opened a greater void within him than that he had felt beneath the plane the first time he had flown. He felt lightheaded. It came to him suddenly that there was something sinister about the conversation, that he was flying unwillingly into unsafe and uncharted regions. If he could only be insulting and tell this old man who was trying to help him to shut up!

"I bet you one thing . . ."

"Yes?"

"That you was plenty scared coming down."

He did not answer. Like a dog on a trail the old man seemed to smell out his fears, and he felt anger bubble within him.

"You sho scared *me.* When I seen you coming down in that thing with it a-rollin' and a-jumpin' like a pitchin' hoss, I thought sho you was a goner. I almost had me a stroke!"

He saw the old man grinning. "Ever'thin's been happening round here this morning, come to think of it."

"Like what?" he asked.

"Well, first thing I know, here come two white fellers looking for Mister Rudolph, that's Mister Graves' cousin. That got me worked up right away. . . ."

"Why?"

"Why? 'Cause he done broke outa the crazy house, that's why. He liable to kill somebody," he said. "They oughta have him by now though. Then here *you* come. First I think it's one of them white boys. Then doggone if you don't fall outa there. Lawd, I'd done heard about you boys but I haven't never *seen* one o' you all. Caint tell you how it felt to see somebody what look like me in a airplane!"

The old man talked on, the sound streaming around Todd's thoughts like air flowing over the fuselage of a flying plane. You were a fool, he thought, remembering how before the spin the sun had blazed, bright against the billboard signs beyond the town, and how a boy's blue kite had bloomed beneath him, tugging gently in the wind like a strange, odd-shaped flower. He had once flown such kites himself and tried to find the boy at the end of the invisible cord. But he had been flying too high and too fast. He had climbed steeply away in exultation. Too steeply, he thought. And one of the first rules you learn is that if the angle of thrust is too steep the plane goes into a spin. And then, instead of pulling out of it and going into a dive you let a buzzard panic you. A lousy buzzard!

"Son, what made all that blood on the glass?"

"A buzzard," he said, remembering how the blood and feathers had sprayed back against the hatch. It had been as though he had flown into a storm of blood and blackness.

"Well, I declare! They's lots of 'em around here. They after dead things. Don't eat nothing what's alive."

"A little bit more and he would have made a meal out of me," Todd said grimly.

"They had luck all right. Teddy's got a name for 'em, calls 'em jimcrows," the old man laughed.

"It's a damned good name."

"They the damnedest birds. Once I seen a hoss all stretched out like he was sick, you know. So I hollers, 'Gid up from there, suh!' Just to make sho! An,' doggone, son, if I don't see two old jimcrows come flying right up outa that hoss's insides! Yessuh! The sun was shinin' on 'em and they couldn'ta been no greasier if they'd been eating barbecue!"

Todd thought he would vomit; his stomach quivered.

"You made that up," he said.

"Nawsuh! Saw him just like you."

"Well, I'm glad it was you."

"You see lots a funny things down here, son."

"No, I'll let you see them," he said.

"By the way, the white folks round here don't like to see you boys up there in the sky. They ever bother you?"

"No."

"Well, they'd like to."

"Someone always wants to bother someone else," Todd said. "How do you know?"

"I just know."

"Well," he said defensively, "no one has bothered us."

Blood pounded in his ears as he looked away into space. He tensed, seeing a black spot in the sky, and strained to confirm what he could not clearly see.

"What does that look like to you?" he asked excitedly.

"Just another bad luck, son."

Then he saw the movement of wings with disappointment. It was gliding smoothly down, wings outspread, tail feathers gripping the air, down swiftly—gone behind the green screen of trees. It was like a bird he had imagined there, only the sloping branches of the pines remained, sharp against the pale stretch of sky. He lay barely breathing and stared at the point where it had disappeared, caught in a spell of loathing and admiration. Why did they make them so disgusting and yet teach them to fly so well? *It's like when I was up in heaven,* he heard, starting.

The old man was chuckling, rubbing his stubbled chin.

"What did you say?"

"Sho, I died and went to heaven . . . maybe by time I tell you about it they be done come after you."

"I hope so," he said wearily.

"You boys ever sit around and swap lies?"

"Not often. Is this going to be one?"

"Well, I ain't so sho, on account of it took place when I was dead."

The old man paused. "That wasn't no lie 'bout the buzzards though."

"All right," he said.

"Sho you want to hear 'bout heaven?"

"Please," he answered, resting his head upon his arm.

"Well, I went to heaven and right away started to sproutin' me some wings. Six-foot ones, they was. Just like them the white angels had. I couldn't hardly believe it. I was so glad that I went off on some clouds by myself and tried 'em out. You know, 'cause I didn't want to make a fool outa myself the first thing . . ."

It's an old tale, Todd thought. Told me years ago. Had forgotten. But at least it will keep him from talking about buzzards.

He closed his eyes, listening.

"... First thing I done was to git up on a low cloud and jump off. And doggone, boy, if them wings didn't work! First I tried the right; then I tried the left; then I tried 'em both together. Then, Lawd, I started to move on out among the folks. I let 'em see me ..."

He saw the old man gesturing flight with his arms, his face full of mock pride as he indicated an imaginary crowd, thinking, *It'll be in the newspapers,* as he heard, "... so I went and found me some colored angels—somehow I didn't believe I was an angel till I seen a real black one, ha, yes! Then I was sho—but they tole me I better come down 'cause us colored folks had to wear a special kin'a harness when we flew. That was how come *they* wasn't flyin'. Oh yes, an' you had to be extra strong for a black man even, to fly with one of them harnesses ..."

This is a new turn, Todd thought. What's he driving at?

"So I said to myself, I ain't gonna be bothered with no harness! Oh naw! 'Cause if God let you sprout wings you oughta have sense enough not to let nobody make you wear something what gits in the way of flyin'. So I starts to flyin'. Hecks, son," he chuckled, his eyes twinkling, "you know I had to let eve'body know that old Jefferson could fly good as anybody else. And I could too, fly smooth as a bird! I could even loop-the-loop—only I had to make sho to keep my long white robe down roun' my ankles ..."

Todd felt uneasy. He wanted to laugh at the joke, but his body refused, as of an independent will. He felt as he had as a child when after he had chewed a sugar-coated pill which his mother had given him, she had laughed at his efforts to remove the terrible taste.

"... Well," he heard. "I was doing all right till I got to speeding. Found out I could fan up a right strong breeze, I could fly so fast. I could do all kin'sa stunts too. I started flying up to the stars and divin' down and zooming roun' the moon. Man, I like to scare the devil outa some ole white angels. I was raisin' hell. Not that I meant any harm, son. But I was just feeling good. It was so good to know I was free at last. I accidentally knocked the tips offa some stars and they tell me I caused a storm and a coupla lynchings down here in Macon County—though I swear I believe them boys what said that was making up lies on me ..."

He's mocking me, Todd thought angrily. He thinks it's a joke. Grinning down at me ... His throat was dry. He looked at his watch; why the hell didn't they come? Since they had to, why? *One day I was flying down one of them heavenly streets.* You got yourself into it, Todd thought. Like Jonah in the whale.

"Justa throwin' feathers in eve'body's face. An' ole Saint Peter called me in. Said, 'Jefferson, tell me two things, what you doin' flyin' without a harness; an' how come you flyin' so fast?' So I tole him I was flyin' without a harness 'cause it got in my way, but I couldn'ta been flyin' so fast, 'cause I wasn't usin' but one wing. Saint Peter said, 'You wasn't flyin' with but *one* wing?' 'Yessuh,' I says, scared-like. So he says, 'Well, since you got sucha extra fine pair of wings you can leave off yo harness awhile. But from now on none of that there one-wing flyin', 'cause you gittin' up too damn much speed!' "

And with one mouth full of bad teeth you're making too damned much talk, thought Todd. Why don't I send him after the boy? His body ached from the hard ground, and seeking to shift his position he twisted his ankle and hated himself for crying out.

"It gittin' worse?"

"I . . . I twisted it," he groaned.

"Try not to think about it, son. That's what I do."

He bit his lip, fighting pain with counter-pain as the voice resumed its rhythmical droning. Jefferson seemed caught in his own creation.

". . . After all that trouble I just floated roun' heaven in slow motion. But I forgot like colored folks will do and got to flyin' with one wing agin. This time I was restin' my ole broken arm and got to flyin' fast enough to shame the devil. I was comin' so fast, Lawd, I got myself called befo ole Saint Peter agin. He said, 'Jeff, didn't I warn you 'bout that speedin'?' 'Yessuh,' I says, 'but it was an accident.' He looked at me sad-like and shook his head and I knowed I was gone. He said, 'Jeff, you and that speedin' is a danger to the heavenly community. If I was to let you keep on flyin', heaven wouldn't be nothin' but uproar. Jeff, you got to go!' Son, I argued and pleaded with that old white man, but it didn't do a bit of good. They rushed me straight to them pearly gates and gimme a parachute and a map of the state of Alabama . . ."

Todd heard him laughing so that he could hardly speak, making a screen between them upon which his humiliation glowed like fire.

"Maybe you'd better stop a while," he said, his voice unreal.

"Ain't much more," Jefferson laughed. "When they gimme the parachute ole Saint Peter ask me if I wanted to say a few words before I went. I felt so bad I couldn't hardly look at him, specially with all them white angels standin' around. Then somebody laughed and made me mad. So I tole him, 'Well, you done took my wings. And you puttin' me out. You got charge of things so's I can't do nothin' about it. But you got to admit just this: While I was up here I was the flyin'est son-of-a-bitch what ever hit heaven!'"

At the burst of laughter Todd felt such an intense humiliation that only great violence would wash it away. The laughter which shook the old man like a boiling purge set up vibrations of guilt within him which not even the intricate machinery of the plane would have been adequate to transform and he heard himself screaming, "Why do you laugh at me this way?"

He hated himself at that moment, but he had lost control. He saw Jefferson's mouth fall open. "What—?"

"Answer me!"

His blood pounded as though it would surely burst his temples, and he tried to reach the old man and fell, screaming, "Can I help it because they won't let us actually fly? Maybe we are a bunch of buzzards feeding on a dead horse, but we can hope to be eagles, can't we? *Can't we?*"

He fell back, exhausted, his ankle pounding. The saliva was like straw in his mouth. If he had the strength he would strangle this old man. This grinning gray-headed clown who made him feel as he felt when watched by the white officers at the field. And yet this old man had neither power, prestige, rank, nor technique. Nothing that could rid him of this terrible feeling. He watched him, seeing his face struggle to express a turmoil of feeling.

"What you mean, son? What you talking 'bout . . . ?"

"Go away. Go tell your tales to the white folks."

"But I didn't mean nothing like that . . . I . . . I wasn't tryin' to hurt your feelings . . ."

"Please. Get the hell away from me!"

"But I didn't, son. I didn't mean all them things a-tall."

Todd shook as with a chill, searching Jefferson's face for a trace of the mockery he had seen there. But now the face was somber and tired and old. He was confused. He could not be sure that there had ever been laughter there, that Jefferson had ever really laughed in his whole life. He saw Jefferson reach out to touch him and shrank away, wondering if anything except the pain, now causing his vision to waver, was real. Perhaps he had imagined it all.

"Don't let it get you down, son," the voice said pensively.

He heard Jefferson sigh wearily, as though he felt more than he could say. His anger ebbed, leaving only the pain.

"I'm sorry," he mumbled.

"You just wore out with pain, was all . . ."

He saw him through a blur, smiling. And for a second he felt the embarrassed silence of understanding flutter between them.

"What was you doin' flyin' over this section, son? Wasn't you scared they might shoot you for a crow?"

Todd tensed. Was he being laughed at again? But before he could decide, the pain shook him and a part of him was lying calmly behind the screen of pain that had fallen between them, recalling the first time he had ever seen a plane. It was as though an endless series of hangars had been shaken ajar in the airbase of his memory and from each, like a young wasp emerging from its cell, arose the memory of the plane.

The first time I ever saw a plane I was very small and planes were new in the world. I was four and a half and the only plane that I had ever seen was a model suspended from the ceiling of the automobile exhibit at the state fair. But I did not know that it was only a model. I did not know how large a real plane was, nor how expensive. To me it was a fascinating toy, complete in itself, which my mother said could only be owned by rich little white boys. I stood rigid with admiration, my head straining backward as I watched the gray little plane describing arcs above the gleaming tops of the automobiles. And I vowed that, rich or poor, some day I would own such a toy. My mother had to drag me out of the exhibit, and not even the merry-go-round, the Ferris wheel, or the racing horses could hold my attention for the rest of the fair. I was too busy imitating the tiny drone of the plane with my lips, and imitating with my hands the motion, swift and circling, that it made in flight.

After that I no longer used the pieces of lumber that lay about our backyard to construct wagons and autos . . . now it was used for airplanes. I built biplanes, using pieces of board for wings, a small box for the fuselage, another piece of wood for the rudder. The trip to the fair had brought something new into my small world. I asked my mother repeatedly when the fair would come back again. I'd lie in the grass and watch the sky and each flighting bird became a soaring plane. I would have been good a year just to have seen a plane again. I became a nuisance to everyone with my questions about airplanes. But planes were new to the old folks, too, and there was little that they could tell me. Only my uncle knew some of the answers. And better still, he could carve propellers from pieces of wood that would whirl rapidly in the wind, wobbling noisily upon oiled nails.

I wanted a plane more than I'd wanted anything; more than I wanted the red wagon with rubber tires, more than the train that ran on a track with its train of cars. I asked my mother over and over again:

"Mama?"

"What do you want, boy?" she'd say.

"Mama, will you get mad if I ask you?" I'd say.

"What do you want now, I ain't got time to be answering a lot of fool questions. What you want?"

"Mama, when you gonna get me one . . . ?" I'd ask.

"Get you one what?" she'd say.

"You know, Mama; what I been asking you . . ."

"Boy," she'd say, "if you don't want a spanking you better come on 'n tell me what you talking about so I can get on with my work."

"Aw, Mama, you know . . ."

"What I just tell you?" she'd say.

"I mean when you gonna buy me a airplane."

"AIRPLANE! Boy, is you crazy? How many times I have to tell you to stop that foolishness. I done told you them things cost too much. I bet I'm gon wham the living daylight out of you if you don't quit worrying me 'bout them things!"

But this did not stop me, and a few days later I'd try all over again.

Then one day a strange thing happened. It was spring and for some reason I had been hot and irritable all morning. It was a beautiful spring. I could feel it as I played barefoot in the backyard. Blossoms hung from the thorny black locust trees like clusters of fragrant white grapes. Butterflies flickered in the sunlight above the short new dew-wet grass. I had gone in the house for bread and butter and coming out I heard a steady unfamiliar drone. It was unlike anything I had ever heard before. I tried to place the sound. It was no use. It was a sensation like that I had when searching for my father's watch, heard ticking unseen in a room. It made me feel as though I had forgotten to perform some task that my mother had ordered . . . then I located it, overhead. In the sky, flying quite low and about a hundred yards off, was a plane! It came so slowly that it seemed barely to move. My mouth hung wide; my bread and butter fell into the dirt. I wanted to jump up and down and cheer. And when the idea struck I trembled with excitement: Some little white boy's plane's done flew away and all I got to do is stretch out my hands and it'll be mine! It was a little plane like that at the fair, flying no higher than the eaves of our roof. Seeing it come steadily forward I felt the world grow warm with promise. I opened the screen and climbed over it and clung there, waiting. I would catch the plane as it came over and swing down fast and run into the house before anyone could see me. Then no one could come to claim the plane. It droned nearer. Then when it hung like a silver cross in the blue directly above me I stretched out my hand and grabbed. It was like sticking my finger through a soap bubble. The plane flew on, as though I had simply blown my breath after it. I grabbed again, frantically, trying to catch the tail. My fingers clutched the air and disappointment surged tight and hard in my throat. Giving one last desperate grasp, I strained forward. My fingers ripped from the screen. I was falling, the ground burst hard against me. I drummed the earth with my heels and when my breath returned, I lay there bawling.

My mother rushed through the door.

"What's the matter, chile! What on earth is wrong with you?"

"It's gone! It's gone!"

"What gone?"

"The airplane . . ."

"Airplane?"

"Yessum, jus like the one at the fair . . . I . . . I tried to stop it an' it kep right on going . . ."

"When, boy?"

"Just now," I cried through my tears.

"Where it go, boy, what way?"

"Yonder, there . . ."

She scanned the sky, her arms akimbo and her checkered apron flapping in the wind, as I pointed to the fading plane. Finally she looked down at me, slowly shaking her head.

"It's gone! It's gone!" I cried.

"Boy, is you a fool?" she said. "Don't you see that there's a real airplane 'stead of one of them toy ones?"

"Real . . . ?" I forgot to cry. "Real?"

"Yass, real. Don't you know that thing you reaching for is bigger'n a auto? You here trying to reach for it and I bet it's flying 'bout two hundred miles higher'n this roof." She was disgusted with me. "You come on in this house before somebody else sees what a fool you done turned out to be. You must think these here li'l ole arms of your'n is mighty long . . ."

I was carried into the house and undressed for bed and the doctor was called. I cried bitterly; as much from the disappointment of finding the plane so far beyond my reach as from the pain.

When the doctor came I heard my mother telling him about the plane and asking if anything was wrong with my mind. He explained that I had had a fever for several hours. But I was kept in bed for a week and I constantly saw the plane in my sleep, flying just beyond my fingertips, sailing so slowly that it seemed barely to move. And each time I'd reach out to grab it I'd miss and through each dream I'd hear my grandma warning:

"Young man, young man
Yo arm's too short
To box with God. . . ."

"Hey, son!"

At first he did not know where he was and looked at the old man pointing, with blurred eyes.

"Ain't that one of you all's airplanes coming after you?"

As his vision cleared he saw a small black shape above a distant field, soaring through waves of heat. But he could not be sure and with the pain he feared that somehow a horrible recurring fantasy of being split in twain by the whirling blades of a propeller had come true.

"You think he sees us?" he heard.

"See? I hope so."

"He's coming like a bat outa hell!"

Straining, he heard the faint sound of a motor and hoped it would soon be over.

"How you feeling?"

"Like a nightmare," he said.

"Hey, he's done curved back the other way!"

"Maybe he saw us," he said. "Maybe he's gone to send out the ambulance and ground crew." And, he thought with despair, maybe he didn't even see us.

"Where did you send the boy?"

"Down to Mister Graves," Jefferson said. "Man what owns this land."

"Do you think he phoned?"

Jefferson looked at him quickly.

"Aw sho. Dabney Graves is got a bad name on accounta them killings, but he'll call though . . ."

"What killings?"

"Them five fellers . . . ain't you heard?" he asked with surprise.

"No."

"Eve'body knows 'bout Dabney Graves, especially the colored. He done killed enough of us."

Todd had the sensation of being caught in a white neighborhood after dark.

"What did they do?" he asked.

"Thought they was men," Jefferson said. "An' some he owed money, like he do me . . ."

"But why do you stay here?"

"You black, son."

"I know, but . . ."

"You have to come by the white folks, too."

He turned away from Jefferson's eyes, at once consoled and accused. And I'll have to come by them soon, he thought with despair. Closing his eyes, he heard Jefferson's voice as the sun burned blood-red upon his lids.

"I got nowhere to go," Jefferson said, "an' they'd come after me if I did. But Dabney Graves is a funny fellow. He's all the time making jokes. He can be mean as hell, then he's liable to turn right around and back the colored against the white folks. I seen him do it. But me, I hates him for that more'n anything else. 'Cause just as soon as he gits tired helping a man he don't care what happens to him. He just leaves him stone-cold. And then the other white folks is double hard on anybody he done helped. For him it's just a joke. He don't give a hilla beans for nobody—but himself . . ."

Todd listened to the thread of detachment in the old man's voice. It was as though he held his words at arm's length before him to avoid their destructive meaning.

"He'd just as soon do you a favor and then turn right around and have you strung up. Me, I stays outa his way 'cause down here that's what you gotta do."

If my ankle would only ease for a while, he thought. The closer I spin toward the earth the blacker I become, flashed through his mind. Sweat ran into his eyes and he was sure that he would never see the plane if his head continued whirling. He tried to see Jefferson, what it was that Jefferson held in his hand. It was a little black man, another Jefferson! A little black Jefferson that shook with fits of belly laughter while the other Jefferson looked on with detachment. Then Jefferson looked up from the thing in his hand and turned to speak but Todd was far away, searching the sky for a plane in a hot dry land on a day and age he had long forgotten. He was going mysteriously with his mother through empty streets where black faces peered from behind drawn shades and someone was rapping at a window and he was looking back to see a hand and a frightened face frantically beckoning from a cracked door and his mother was looking down the empty perspective of the street and shaking her head and hurrying him along and at first it was only a flash he saw and a motor was droning as through the sun's glare he saw it gleaming silver as it circled and he was seeing a burst like a puff of white smoke and hearing his mother yell, "Come along, boy, I got no time for them fool airplanes, I got no time," and he saw it a second time, the plane flying high, and the burst appeared suddenly and fell slowly, billowing out and sparkling like fireworks and he was watching and being hurried along as the air filled with a flurry of white pinwheeling cards that caught in the wind and scattered over the rooftops and into the gutters and a woman was running and snatching a card and reading it and screaming and he darted into the shower, grabbing as in winter he grabbed for snowflakes and bounding away at his mother's, "Come on here, boy! Come on, I say!" And he was watching as she took the card away seeing her face grow puzzled and turning taut as her voice quavered, "Niggers Stay from the Polls," and died to a moan of terror as he saw the eyeless sockets of a white hood staring at him from the card and above he saw the plane spiraling gracefully, agleam in the sun like a fiery sword. And seeing it soar he was caught, transfixed between a terrible horror and a horrible fascination.

The sun was not so high now, and Jefferson was calling, and gradually he saw three figures moving across the curving roll of the field.

"Look like some doctors, all dressed in white," said Jefferson.

They're coming at last, Todd thought. And he felt such a release of tension within him that he thought he would faint. But no sooner did he close his eyes than he was seized and he was struggling with three white men who were forcing his arms into some kind of coat. It was too much for him, his arms were pinned to his sides and as the pain blazed in his eyes, he realized that it was a straitjacket. What filthy joke was this?

"That oughta hold him, Mister Graves," he heard.

His total energies seemed focused in his eyes as he searched for their faces. That was Graves, the other two wore hospital uniforms. He was poised between two poles of fear and hate as he heard the one called Graves saying,

"He looks kinda purty in that there suit, boys. I'm glad you dropped by."

"This boy ain't crazy, Mister Graves," one of the others said. "He needs a doctor, not us. Don't see how you led us way out here anyway. It might be a joke to you, but your cousin Rudolph liable to kill somebody. White folks or niggers don't make no difference . . ."

Todd saw the man turn red with anger. Graves looked down upon him, chuckling.

"This nigguh belongs in a straitjacket, too, boys. I knowed that the minnit Jeff's kid said something 'bout a nigguh flyer. You all know you caint let the nigguh git up that high without his going crazy. The nigguh brain ain't built right for high altitudes . . ."

Todd watched the drawling red face, feeling that all the unnamed horror and obscenities that he had ever imagined stood materialized before him.

"Let's git outa here," one of the attendants said.

Todd saw the other reach toward him, realizing for the first time that he lay upon a stretcher as he yelled:

"Don't put your hands on me!"

They drew back, surprised.

"What's that you say, nigguh?" asked Graves.

He did not answer and thought that Graves' foot was aimed at his head. It landed in his chest and he could hardly breathe. He coughed helplessly, seeing Graves' lips stretch taut over his yellow teeth, and tried to shift his head. It was as though a half-dead fly was dragging slowly across his face, and a bomb seemed to burst within him. Blasts of hot, hysterical laughter tore from his chest, causing his eyes to pop, and he felt that the veins in his neck would surely burst. And then a part of him stood behind it all, watching the surprise in Graves' red face and his own hysteria. He thought he would never stop, he would laugh himself to death. It rang in his ears like Jefferson's laughter and he looked for him, centering his eyes desperately upon his face, as though somehow he had become his sole salvation in an insane world of outrage and humiliation. It brought a certain relief. He was suddenly aware that although his body was still contorted, it was an echo that no longer rang in his ears. He heard Jefferson's voice with gratitude.

"Mister Graves, the army done tole him not to leave his airplane."

"Nigguh, army or no, you gittin' off my land! That airplane can stay 'cause it was paid for by taxpayers' money. But you gittin' off. An' dead or alive, it don't make no difference to me."

Todd was beyond it now, lost in a world of anguish.

"Jeff," Graves said. "You and Teddy come and grab holt. I want you to take this here black eagle over to that nigguh airfield and leave him."

Jefferson and the boy approached him silently. He looked away, realizing and doubting at once that only they could release him from his overpowering sense of isolation.

They bent for the stretcher. One of the attendants moved toward Teddy.

"Think you can manage it, boy?"

"I think I can, suh," Teddy said.

"Well, you better go behind then, and let yo pa go ahead so's to keep that leg elevated."

He saw the white men walking ahead as Jefferson and the boy carried him along in silence. Then they were pausing, and he felt a hand wiping his face, then he was moving again. And it was as though he had been lifted out of his isolation, back into the world of men. A new current of communication flowed between the man and boy and himself. They moved him gently. Far away he heard a mocking-bird liquidly calling. He raised his eyes, seeing a buzzard poised unmoving in space. For a moment the whole afternoon seemed suspended, and he waited for the horror to seize him again. Then like a song within his head he heard the boy's soft humming and saw the dark bird glide into the sun and glow like a bird of flaming gold.

1994

Brave Words for a Startling Occasion[1]

First, as I express my gratitude for this honor which you have bestowed on me, let me say that I take it that you are rewarding my efforts rather than my not quite fully achieved attempt at a major novel. Indeed, if I were asked in all seriousness just what I considered to be the chief significance of *Invisible Man* as a fiction, I would reply: its experimental attitude, and its attempt to return to the mood of personal moral responsibility for democracy which typified the best of our nineteenth-century fiction. That my first novel should win this most coveted prize must certainly indicate that there is a crisis in the American novel. You as critics have told us so, and current fiction sales would indicate that the reading public agrees. Certainly the younger novelists concur. The explosive nature of events mocks our brightest efforts. And the very "facts" which the naturalists assumed would make us free have lost the power to protect us from despair. Controversy now rages over just what aspects of American experience are suitable for novelistic treatment. The prestige of the theorists of the so-called novel of manners has been challenged. Thus, after a long period of stability we find our assumptions concerning the novel being called into question. And though I was only vaguely aware of it, it was this growing crisis which shaped the writing of *Invisible Man*.

After the usual apprenticeship of imitation and seeking with delight to examine my experience through the discipline of the novel, I became gradually aware that the forms of so many of the works which impressed me were too restricted to contain the experience which I knew. The diversity of American life with its extreme fluidity and openness seemed too vital and alive to be caught for more than the briefest instant in the tight, well-made Jamesian novel, which was, for all its artistic perfection, too concerned with "good taste" and stable areas. Nor could I safely use the forms of the "hard-boiled" novel, with its dedication to physical violence, social cynicism and understatement. Understatement depends, after all, upon commonly held assumptions, and my minority status rendered all such assumptions questionable. There was also a problem of language, and even dialogue, which, with its hard-boiled stance and its monosyllabic utterance, is one of the shining achievements of twentieth-century American writing. For despite the notion that its rhythms were those of everyday speech, I found that when compared with the rich babel of idiomatic expression around me, a language full of imagery and gesture and rhetorical canniness, it was embarrassingly austere. Our speech I found resounding with an alive language swirling with over three hundred years of American living, a mixture of the folk, the Biblical, the scientific and the political. Slangy in one stance, academic in another, loaded poetically with imagery at one moment, mathematically bare of imagery in the next. As for the rather rigid concepts of reality which informed a number of the works which impressed me and to which I owe a great deal, I was forced to conclude that reality was far more mysterious and uncertain, and more exciting, and still, despite its raw violence and capriciousness, more promising. To attempt to express that

[1]Address for Presentation Ceremony, National Book Award, January 27, 1953.

American experience which has carried one back and forth and up and down the land and across, and across again the great river, from freight train to Pullman car, from contact with slavery to contact with a world of advanced scholarship, art and science, is simply to burst such neatly understated forms of the novel asunder.

A novel whose range was both broader and deeper was needed. And in my search I found myself turning to our classical nineteenth-century novelists. I felt that except for the work of William Faulkner something vital had gone out of American prose after Mark Twain. I came to believe that the writers of that period took a much greater responsibility for the condition of democracy and, indeed, their works were imaginative projections of the conflicts within the human heart which arose when the sacred principles of the Constitution and the Bill of Rights clashed with the practical exigencies of human greed and fear, hate and love. Naturally I was attracted to these writers as a Negro. Whatever they thought of my people per se, in their imaginative economy the Negro symbolized both the man lowest down and the mysterious, underground aspect of human personality. In a sense the Negro was the gauge of the human condition as it waxed and waned in our democracy. These writers were willing to confront the broad complexities of American life, and we are the richer for their having done so.

Thus to see America with an awareness of its rich diversity and its almost magical fluidity and freedom, I was forced to conceive of a novel unburdened by the narrow naturalism which has led, after so many triumphs, to the final and unrelieved despair which marks so much of our current fiction. I was to dream of a prose which was flexible, and swift as American change is swift, confronting the inequalities and brutalities of our society forthrightly, yet thrusting forth its images of hope, human fraternity and individual self-realization. It would use the richness of our speech, the idiomatic expression and the rhetorical flourishes from past periods which are still alive among us. And despite my personal failures, there must be possible a fiction which, leaving sociology to the scientists, can arrive at the truth about the human condition, here and now, with all the bright magic of a fairy tale.

What has been missing from so much experimental writing has been the passionate will to dominate reality as well as the laws of art. This will is the true source of the experimental attitude. We who struggle with form and with America should remember Eidothea's advice to Menelaus when in the *Odyssey* he and his friends are seeking their way home. She tells him to seize her father, Proteus, and to hold him fast "however he may struggle and fight. He will turn into all sorts of shapes to try you," she says, "into all the creatures that live and move upon the earth, into water, into blazing fire; but you must hold him fast and press him all the harder. When he is himself, and questions you in the same shape that he was when you saw him in his bed, let the old man go; and then, sir, ask which god it is who is angry, and how you shall make your way homewards over the fish-giving sea."

For the novelist, Proteus stands for both America and the inheritance of illusion through which all men must fight to achieve reality; the offended god stands for our sins against those principles we all hold sacred. The way home we seek is that condition of man's being at home in the world, which is called love, and which we term democracy. Our task then is always to challenge the apparent forms of reality—that is, the fixed manners and values of the few—and to struggle with it until it reveals its mad, vari-implicated chaos, its false faces, and on until it surrenders its insight, its truth. We are fortunate as American writers in that with our variety of racial and national traditions, idioms and manners, we are yet one. On its profoundest level American experience is of a whole. Its truth lies in its diversity and swiftness of change. Through forging forms of the novel worthy of it, we achieve not only the promise of our lives, but we anticipate the resolution of those world problems of humanity which for a moment seem to those who are in awe of statistics completely insoluble.

Whenever we as Americans have faced serious crises we have returned to fundamentals; this, in brief, is what I have tried to do.

1953

James Baldwin 1924–1987

Perhaps more than any other writer who came to prominence after 1950, James Baldwin represented the process by which a person at odds with the country of his birth seeks to reconcile him- or herself to it, and to a status as less than a first-class citizen. Through the essays that became his trademark, Baldwin pricked the conscience of an America that had distorted the original conceptions of democracy. He encouraged Americans to retrieve those seeds and bring them to fruition. Through his life and his art, Baldwin repeatedly bore witness to the injustices heaped upon black Americans, and consistently urged healing of the social fabric before it is torn beyond repair.

Born to Emma Berdis Jones (a single mother) in Harlem, New York, Baldwin would make art of the pain of illegitimacy and the problems he had with his stepfather, David Baldwin, whom his mother married when he was three. As his mother bore eight more children, Baldwin cared for them, and tried to escape the anger of his stepfather by excelling in school. Relationships between parents and children, particularly between fathers and sons, formed the theme of many of Baldwin's works, including "Sonny's Blues" and others of his stories collected in *Going to Meet the Man,* 1965. The religious fanaticism of his stepfather also became a dominant subject for his fiction.

Influenced by Harriet Beecher Stowe's *Uncle Tom's Cabin,* Charles Dickens, and Horatio Alger, Baldwin read voraciously. In fact, he read through the Harlem libraries, and moved into other territories within the city. He edited the junior high newspaper, and shared editorial duties on the *Magpie* at DeWitt Clinton High School, a predominantly white Bronx secondary school. When Baldwin was 14, he underwent a religious conversion which led to ministerial duties until he was 17. The whole religious experience was partly to defy his stepfather, but it too recurred throughout his later writing.

Although Baldwin published some scattered pieces in the 1940s, he made his debut in 1953 with *Go Tell It on the Mountain,* a chronicle of three generations of a black family plagued by slavery and internal strife. Young John Grimes, in the present generation of the novel, serves as Baldwin's fictional creation of his crisis of the spirit. He dealt in subsequent fiction with homosexuality (among white characters), racial and sexual identities, problems of the Civil Rights movement, life in Harlem, and religion. While his fiction was well received, the essay may be Baldwin's strength, and his collections of essays were sometimes better sellers than his novels.

Of Baldwin's plays, two continue the religious and political themes of his other works. *The Amen Corner* focuses upon the influence of the church in the lives of black Americans; *Blues for Mister Charlie* is loosely based on the case of Emmett Till, the fourteen-year-old black boy who was killed in Mississippi in 1955 for allegedly whistling at a white woman.

Although Baldwin was quite active in the Civil Rights movement, he participated only by returning to the States in the 1950s and 1960s from France, a country to which he had bought a one-way ticket in 1948. After that time, he moved back and forth, never staying in the States for an extended period. Whatever his vantage point, Baldwin continued to prod Americans into better behavior, for he genuinely loved the country that was less willing than he would have wished to return that love.

Trudier Harris
University of North Carolina–Chapel Hill

PRIMARY WORKS

Go Tell It on the Mountain, 1953; *Notes of a Native Son,* 1955; *Giovanni's Room,* 1956; *Nobody Knows My Name,* 1961; *Another Country,* 1962; *The Fire Next Time,* 1963; *Going to Meet the Man,* 1965; *Tell Me How Long the Train's Been Gone,* 1968; *No Name in the Street,* 1972; *A Dialogue* (with Nikki Giovanni), 1973; *If Beale Street Could Talk,* 1974; *The Devil Finds Work,* 1976; *Just Above My Head,* 1979; *The Evidence of Things Not Seen,* 1985; and plays, *Blues for Mister Charlie,* 1964, and *The Amen Corner,* 1968.

Sonny's Blues

I read about it in the paper, in the subway, on my way to work. I read it, and I couldn't believe it, and I read it again. Then perhaps I just stared at it, at the newsprint spelling out his name, spelling out the story. I stared at it in the swinging lights of the subway car, and in the faces and bodies of the people, and in my own face, trapped in the darkness which roared outside.

It was not to be believed and I kept telling myself that, as I walked from the subway station to the high school. And at the same time I couldn't doubt it. I was scared, scared for Sonny. He became real to me again. A great block of ice got settled in my belly and kept melting there slowly all day long, while I taught my classes algebra. It was a special kind of ice. It kept melting, sending trickles of ice water all up and down my veins, but it never got less. Sometimes it hardened and seemed to expand until I felt my guts were going to come spilling out or that I was going to choke or scream. This would always be at a moment when I was remembering some specific thing Sonny had once said or done.

When he was about as old as the boys in my classes his face had been bright and open, there was a lot of copper in it; and he'd had wonderfully direct brown eyes, and great gentleness and privacy. I wondered what he looked like now. He had been picked up the evening before, in a raid on an apartment downtown, for peddling and using heroin.

I couldn't believe it: but what I mean by that is that I couldn't find any room for it anywhere inside me. I had kept it outside me for a long time. I hadn't wanted to know. I had had suspicions, but I didn't name them, I kept putting them away. I told myself that Sonny was wild, but he wasn't crazy. And he'd always been a good boy, he hadn't ever turned hard or evil or disrespectful, the way kids can, so quick, especially in Harlem. I didn't want to believe that I'd ever see my brother going down, coming to nothing, all that light in his face gone out, in the condition I'd already seen so many others. Yet it had happened and here I was, talking about algebra to a lot of boys who might, every one of them for all I knew, be popping off needles every time they went to the head. Maybe it did more for them than algebra could.

I was sure that the first time Sonny had ever had horse,[1] he couldn't have been much older than these boys were now. These boys, now, were living as we'd been living then, they were growing up with a rush and their heads bumped abruptly against the low ceiling of their actual possibilities. They were filled with rage. All they really knew were two darknesses, the darkness of their lives, which was now closing in on them, and the darkness of the movies, which had blinded them to that other darkness, and in which they now, vindictively, dreamed, at once more together than they were at any other time, and more alone.

When the last bell rang, the last class ended, I let out my breath. It seemed I'd been holding it for all that time. My clothes were wet—I may have looked as though I'd been sitting in a steam bath, all dressed up all afternoon. I sat alone in the classroom a long time. I listened to the boys outside, downstairs, shouting and cursing and laughing. Their laughter struck me for perhaps the first time. It was not the joyous laughter which—God knows why—one associates with children. It was mocking and insular, its intent was to denigrate. It was disenchanted, and in this, also, lay the authority of their curses. Perhaps I was listening to them because I was thinking about my brother and in them I heard my brother. And myself.

One boy was whistling a tune, at once very complicated and very simple, it seemed to be pouring out of him as though he were a bird, and it sounded very cool and moving through all that harsh, bright air, only just holding its own through all those other sounds.

I stood up and walked over to the window and looked down into the courtyard. It was the beginning of the spring and the sap was rising in the boys. A teacher passed through them every now and again, quickly, as though he or she couldn't wait to get out of that courtyard, to get those boys out of their sight and off their minds. I started collecting my stuff. I thought I'd better get home and talk to Isabel.

The courtyard was almost deserted by the time I got downstairs. I saw this boy standing in the shadow of a doorway, looking just like Sonny. I almost called his name. Then I saw that it wasn't Sonny, but somebody we used to know, a boy from around our block. He'd been Sonny's friend. He'd never been mine, having been too young for me, and, anyway, I'd never liked him. And now, even though he was a grown-up man, he still hung around that block, still spent hours on the street corners, was always high and raggy. I used to run into him from time to time and he'd

[1]Heroin.

often work around to asking me for a quarter or fifty cents. He always had some real good excuse too, and I always gave it to him, I don't know why.

But now, abruptly I hated him. I couldn't stand the way he looked at me, partly like a dog, partly like a cunning child. I wanted to ask him what the hell he was doing in the school courtyard.

He sort of shuffled over to me, and he said, "I see you got the papers. So you already know about it."

"You mean about Sonny? Yes, I already know about it. How come they didn't get you?"

He grinned. It made him repulsive and it also brought to mind what he'd looked like as a kid. "I wasn't there. I stay away from them people."

"Good for you." I offered him a cigarette and I watched him through the smoke. "You come all the way down here just to tell me about Sonny?"

"That's right." He was sort of shaking his head and his eyes looked strange, as though they were about to cross. The bright sun deadened his damp dark brown skin and it made his eyes look yellow and showed up the dirt in his kinked hair. He smelled funky. I moved a little way away from him and I said, "Well, thanks. But I already know about it and I got to get home."

"I'll walk you a little ways," he said. We started walking. There were a couple of kids still loitering in the courtyard and one of them said goodnight to me and looked strangely at the boy beside me.

"What're you going to do?" he asked me. "I mean, about Sonny?"

"Look. I haven't seen Sonny for over a year. I'm not sure I'm going to do anything. Anyway, what the hell *can* I do?"

"That's right," he said quickly, "ain't nothing you can do. Can't much help old Sonny no more, I guess."

It was what I was thinking and so it seemed to me he had no right to say it.

"I'm surprised at Sonny, though," he went on—he had a funny way of talking, he looked straight ahead as though he were talking to himself—"I thought Sonny was a smart boy, I thought he was too smart to get hung."

"I guess he thought so too," I said sharply, "and that's how he got hung. And how about you? You're pretty goddamn smart, I bet."

Then he looked directly at me, just for a minute. "I ain't smart," he said. "If I was smart, I'd have reached for a pistol a long time ago."

"Look. Don't tell *me* your sad story, if it was up to me, I'd give you one." Then I felt guilty—guilty, probably, for never having supposed that the poor bastard *had* a story of his own, much less a sad one, and I asked, quickly, "What's going to happen to him now?"

He didn't answer this. He was off by himself some place. "Funny thing," he said, and from his tone we might have been discussing the quickest way to get to Brooklyn, "when I saw the papers this morning, the first thing I asked myself was if I had anything to do with it. I felt sort of responsible."

I began to listen more carefully. The subway station was on the corner, just before us, and I stopped. He stopped, too. We were in front of a bar and he ducked slightly, peering in, but whoever he was looking for didn't seem to be there. The juke box was blasting away with something black and bouncy and I half watched the barmaid as she danced her way from the juke box to her place behind the bar.

And I watched her face as she laughingly responded to something someone said to her, still keeping time to the music. When she smiled one saw the little girl, one sensed the doomed, still struggling woman beneath the battered face of the semi-whore.

"I never *give* Sonny nothing," the boy said finally, "but a long time ago I come to school high and Sonny asked me how it felt." He paused, I couldn't bear to watch him, I watched the barmaid, and I listened to the music which seemed to be causing the pavement to shake. "I told him it felt great." The music stopped, the barmaid paused and watched the juke box until the music began again. "It did."

All this was carrying me some place I didn't want to go. I certainly didn't want to know how it felt. It filled everything, the people, the houses, the music, the dark, quicksilver barmaid, with menace, and this menace was their reality.

"What's going to happen to him now?" I asked again.

"They'll send him away some place and they'll try to cure him." He shook his head. "Maybe he'll even think he's kicked the habit. Then they'll let him loose"—he gestured, throwing his cigarette into the gutter. "That's all."

"What do you mean that's *all?*"

But I knew what he meant.

"I *mean,* that's *all.*" He turned his head and looked at me, pulling down the corners of his mouth. "Don't you know what I mean?" he asked, softly.

"How the hell *would* I know what you mean?" I almost whispered it, I don't know why.

"That's right," he said to the air, "how would *he* know what I mean?" He turned toward me again, patient and calm, and yet I somehow felt him shaking, shaking as though he were going to fall apart. I felt that ice in my guts again, the dread I'd felt all afternoon; and again I watched the barmaid, moving about the bar, washing glasses, and singing. "Listen. They'll let him out and then it'll just start all over again. That's what I mean."

"You mean—they'll let him out. And then he'll just start working his way back in again. You mean he'll never kick the habit. Is that what you mean?"

"That's right," he said cheerfully. "*You* see what I mean."

"Tell me," I said at last, "why does he want to die? He must want to die, he's killing himself, why does he want to die?"

He looked at me in surprise. He licked his lips. "He don't want to die. He wants to live. Don't nobody want to die, ever."

Then I wanted to ask him—too many things. He could not have answered, or if he had, I could not have borne the answers. I started walking. "Well, I guess it's none of my business."

"It's going to be rough on old Sonny," he said. We reached the subway station. "This is your station?" he asked. I nodded. I took one step down. "Damn!" he said suddenly. I looked up at him. He grinned again. "Damn it if I didn't leave all my money home. You ain't got a dollar on you, have you? Just for a couple of days, is all."

All at once something inside gave and threatened to come pouring out of me. I didn't hate him any more. I felt that in another moment I'd start crying like a child.

"Sure," I said. "Don't sweat." I looked in my wallet and didn't have a dollar, I only had five. "Here," I said. "That hold you?"

He didn't look at it—he didn't want to look at it. A terrible closed look came over his face, as though he were keeping the number on the bill a secret from him and me. "Thanks," he said, and now he was dying to see me go. "Don't worry about Sonny. Maybe I'll write him or something."

"Sure," I said. "You do that. So long."

"Be seeing you," he said. I went on down the steps.

* * *

And I didn't write Sonny or send him anything for a long time. When I finally did, it was just after my little girl died, he wrote me back a letter which made me feel like a bastard.

Here's what he said:

Dear brother,

You don't know how much I needed to hear from you. I wanted to write you many a time but I dug how much I must have hurt you and so I didn't write. But now I feel like a man who's been trying to climb up out of some deep, real deep and funky hole and just saw the sun up there, outside. I got to get outside.

I can't tell you much about how I got here. I mean I don't know how to tell you. I guess I was afraid of something or I was trying to escape from something and you know I have never been very strong in the head (smile). I'm glad Mama and Daddy are dead and can't see what's happened to their son and I swear if I'd known what I was doing I would never have hurt you so, you and a lot of other fine people who were nice to me and who believed in me.

I don't want you to think it had anything to do with me being a musician. It's more than that. Or maybe less than that. I can't get anything straight in my head down here and I try not to think about what's going to happen to me when I get outside again. Sometime I think I'm going to flip and *never* get outside and sometime I think I'll come straight back. I tell you one thing, though, I'd rather blow my brains out than go through this again. But that's what they all say, so they tell me. If I tell you when I'm coming to New York and if you could meet me, I sure would appreciate it. Give my love to Isabel and the kids and I was sure sorry to hear about little Gracie. I wish I could be like Mama and say the Lord's will be done, but I don't know it seems to me that trouble is the one thing that never does get stopped and I don't know what good it does to blame it on the Lord. But maybe it does some good if you believe it.

Your brother,
Sonny

Then I kept in constant touch with him and I sent him whatever I could and I went to meet him when he came back to New York. When I saw him many things I thought I had forgotten came flooding back to me. This was because I had begun, finally, to wonder about Sonny, about the life that Sonny lived inside. This life, whatever it was, had made him older and thinner and it had deepened the distant stillness in which he had always moved. He looked very unlike my baby brother. Yet, when he smiled, when we shook hands, the baby brother I'd never known looked out from the depths of his private life, like an animal waiting to be coaxed into the light.

"How you been keeping?" he asked me.

"All right. And you?"

"Just fine." He was smiling all over his face. "It's good to see you again."

"It's good to see you."

The seven years' difference in our ages lay between us like a chasm: I wondered if these years would ever operate between us as a bridge. I was remembering, and it made it hard to catch my breath, that I had been there when he was born; and I had heard the first words he had ever spoken. When he started to walk, he walked from our mother straight to me. I caught him just before he fell when he took the first steps he ever took in this world.

"How's Isabel?"

"Just fine. She's dying to see you."

"And the boys?"

"They're fine, too. They're anxious to see their uncle."

"Oh, come on. You know they don't remember me."

"Are you kidding? Of course they remember you."

He grinned again. We got into a taxi. We had a lot to say to each other, far too much to know how to begin.

As the taxi began to move, I asked, "You still want to go to India?"

He laughed. "You still remember that. Hell, no. This place is Indian enough for me."

"It used to belong to them," I said.

And he laughed again. "They damn sure knew what they were doing when they got rid of it."

Years ago, when he was around fourteen, he'd been all hipped on the idea of going to India. He read books about people sitting on rocks, naked, in all kinds of weather, but mostly bad, naturally, and walking barefoot through hot coals and arriving at wisdom. I used to say that it sounded to me as though they were getting away from wisdom as fast as they could. I think he sort of looked down on me for that.

"Do you mind," he asked, "if we have the driver drive alongside the park? On the west side—I haven't seen the city in so long."

"Of course not," I said. I was afraid that I might sound as though I were humoring him, but I hoped he wouldn't take it that way.

So we drove along, between the green of the park and the stony, lifeless elegance of hotels and apartment buildings, toward the vivid, killing streets of our childhood. These streets hadn't changed, though housing projects jutted up out of them now like rocks in the middle of a boiling sea. Most of the houses in which we had grown up had vanished, as had the stores from which we had stolen, the basements in which we had first tried sex, the rooftops from which we had hurled tin cans and bricks. But houses exactly like the houses of our past yet dominated the landscape, boys exactly like the boys we once had been found themselves smothering in these houses, came down into the streets for light and air and found themselves encircled by disaster. Some escaped the trap, most didn't. Those who got out always left something of themselves behind, as some animals amputate a leg and leave it in the trap. It might be said, perhaps, that I had escaped, after all, I was a school teacher; or that Sonny had, he hadn't lived in Harlem for years. Yet, as the cab moved uptown through streets which seemed, with a rush, to darken with dark people, and as I covertly studied Sonny's face, it came to me that what we both were seeking through our separate cab windows was that part of ourselves which had been left behind. It's always at the hour of trouble and confrontation that the missing member aches.

We hit 110th Street and started rolling up Lenox Avenue. And I'd known this avenue all my life, but it seemed to me again, as it had seemed on the day I'd first heard about Sonny's trouble, filled with a hidden menace which was its very breath of life.

"We almost there," said Sonny.

"Almost." We were both too nervous to say anything more.

We live in a housing project. It hasn't been up long. A few days after it was up it seemed uninhabitably new, now, of course, it's already rundown. It looks like a parody of the good, clean, faceless life—God knows the people who live in it do their best to make it a parody. The beat-looking grass lying around isn't enough to make their lives green, the hedges will never hold out the streets, and they know it. The big windows fool no one, they aren't big enough to make space out of no space. They don't bother with the windows, they watch the TV screen instead. The playground is most popular with the children who don't play at jacks, or skip rope, or roller skate, or swing, and they can be found in it after dark. We moved in partly because it's not too far from where I teach, and partly for the kids; but it's really just like the houses in which Sonny and I grew up. The same things happen, they'll have the same things to remember. The moment Sonny and I started into the house I had the feeling that I was simply bringing him back into the danger he had almost died trying to escape.

Sonny has never been talkative. So I don't know why I was sure he'd be dying to talk to me when supper was over the first night. Everything went fine, the oldest boy remembered him, and the youngest boy liked him, and Sonny had remembered to bring something for each of them; and Isabel, who is really much nicer than I am, more open and giving, had gone to a lot of trouble about dinner and was genuinely glad to see him. And she's always been able to tease Sonny in a way that I haven't. It was nice to see her face so vivid again and to hear her laugh and watch her make Sonny laugh. She wasn't, or, anyway, she didn't seem to be, at all uneasy or embarrassed. She chatted as though there were no subject which had to be avoided and she got Sonny past his first, faint stiffness. And thank God she was there, for I was filled with that icy dread again. Everything I did seemed awkward to me, and everything I said sounded freighted with hidden meaning. I was trying to remember everything I'd heard about dope addiction and I couldn't help watching Sonny for signs. I wasn't doing it out of malice. I was trying to find out something about my brother. I was dying to hear him tell me he was safe.

"Safe!" my father grunted, whenever Mama suggested trying to move to a neighborhood which might be safer for children. "Safe, hell! Ain't no place safe for kids, nor nobody."

He always went on like this, but he wasn't, ever, really as bad as he sounded, not even on weekends, when he got drunk. As a matter of fact, he was always on the lookout for "something a little better," but he died before he found it. He died suddenly, during a drunken weekend in the middle of the war, when Sonny was fifteen. He and Sonny hadn't ever got on too well. And this was partly because Sonny was the apple of his father's eye. It was because he loved Sonny so much and was frightened for him, that he was always fighting with him. It doesn't do any good to fight with Sonny. Sonny just moves back, inside himself, where he can't be reached. But the principal reason that they never hit it off is that they were so much alike. Daddy was big and rough and loud-talking, just the opposite of Sonny, but they both had—that same privacy.

Mama tried to tell me something about this, just after Daddy died. I was home on leave from the army.

This was the last time I ever saw my mother alive. Just the same, this picture gets all mixed up in my mind with pictures I had of her when she was younger. The way I always see her is the way she used to be on a Sunday afternoon, say, when the old folks were talking after the big Sunday dinner. I always see her wearing pale blue. She'd be sitting on the sofa. And my father would be sitting in the easy chair, not far from her. And the living room would be full of church folks and relatives. There they sit, in chairs all around the living room, and the night is creeping up outside, but nobody knows it yet. You can see the darkness growing against the window-panes and you hear the street noises every now and again, or maybe the jangling beat of a tambourine from one of the churches close by, but it's real quiet in the room. For a moment nobody's talking, but every face looks darkening, like the sky outside. And my mother rocks a little from the waist, and my father's eyes are closed. Everyone is looking at something a child can't see. For a minute they've forgotten the children. Maybe a kid is lying on the rug, half asleep. Maybe somebody's got a kid in his lap and is absent-mindedly stroking the kid's head. Maybe there's a kid, quiet and big-eyed, curled up in a big chair in the corner. The silence, the darkness coming, and the darkness in the faces frightens the child obscurely. He hopes that the hand which strokes his forehead will never stop—will never die. He hopes that there will never come a time when the old folks won't be sitting around the living room, talking about where they've come from, and what they've seen, and what's happened to them and their kinfolk.

But something deep and watchful in the child knows that this is bound to end, is already ending. In a moment someone will get up and turn on the light. Then the old folks will remember the children and they won't talk any more that day. And when light fills the room, the child is filled with darkness. He knows that every time this happens he's moved just a little closer to that darkness outside. The darkness outside is what the old folks have been talking about. It's what they've come from. It's what they endure. The child knows that they won't talk any more because if he knows too much about what's happening to *them,* he'll know too much too soon, about what's going to happen to *him.*

The last time I talked to my mother, I remember I was restless. I wanted to get out and see Isabel. We weren't married then and we had a lot to straighten out between us.

There Mama sat, in black, by the window. She was humming an old church song, *Lord you brought me from a long ways off.* Sonny was out somewhere. Mama kept watching the streets.

"I don't know," she said, "if I'll ever see you again, after you go off from here. But I hope you'll remember the things I tried to teach you."

"Don't talk like that," I said, and smiled. "You'll be here a long time yet."

She smiled, too, but she said nothing. She was quiet for a long time. And I said, "Mama, don't you worry about nothing. I'll be writing all the time, and you be getting the checks. . . ."

"I want to talk to you about your brother," she said, suddenly. "If anything happens to me he ain't going to have nobody to look out for him."

"Mama," I said, "ain't nothing going to happen to you *or* Sonny. Sonny's all right. He's a good boy and he's got good sense."

"It ain't a question of his being a good boy," Mama said, "nor of his having good sense. It ain't only the bad ones, nor yet the dumb ones that gets sucked under." She stopped, looking at me. "Your Daddy once had a brother," she said, and she smiled in a way that made me feel she was in pain. "You didn't never know that, did you?"

"No," I said, "I never knew that," and I watched her face.

"Oh, yes," she said, "your Daddy had a brother." She looked out of the window again. "I know you never saw your Daddy cry. But *I* did—many a time, through all these years."

I asked her, "What happened to his brother? How come nobody's ever talked about him?"

This was the first time I ever saw my mother look old.

"His brother got killed," she said, "when he was just a little younger than you are now. I knew him. He was a fine boy. He was maybe a little full of the devil, but he didn't mean nobody no harm."

Then she stopped and the room was silent, exactly as it had sometimes been on those Sunday afternoons. Mama kept looking out into the streets.

"He used to have a job in the mill," she said, "and, like all young folks, he just liked to perform on Saturday nights. Saturday nights, him and your father would drift around to different places, go to dances and things like that, or just sit around with people they knew, and your father's brother would sing, he had a fine voice, and play along with himself on his guitar. Well, this particular Saturday night, him and your father was coming home from some place, and they were both a little drunk and there was a moon that night, it was bright like day. Your father's brother was feeling kind of good, and he was whistling to himself, and he had his guitar slung over his shoulder. They was coming down a hill and beneath them was a road that turned off from the highway. Well, your father's brother, being always kind of frisky, decided to run down this hill, and he did, with that guitar banging and clanging behind him, and he ran across the road, and he was making water behind a tree. And your father was sort of amused at him and he was still coming down the hill, kind of slow. Then he heard a car motor and that same minute his brother stepped from behind the tree, into the road, in the moonlight. And he started to cross the road. And your father started to run down the hill, he says he don't know why. This car was full of white men. They was all drunk, and when they seen your father's brother they let out a great whoop and holler and they aimed the car straight at him. They was having fun, they just wanted to scare him, the way they do sometimes, you know. But they was drunk. And I guess the boy, being drunk, too, and scared, kind of lost his head. By the time he jumped it was too late. Your father says he heard his brother scream when the car rolled over him, and he heard the wood of that guitar when it give, and he heard them strings go flying, and he heard them white men shouting, and the car kept on a-going and it ain't stopped till this day. And, time your father got down the hill, his brother weren't nothing but blood and pulp."

Tears were gleaming on my mother's face. There wasn't anything I could say.

"He never mentioned it," she said, "because I never let him mention it before you children. Your Daddy was like a crazy man that night and for many a night thereafter. He says he never in his life seen anything as dark as that road after the lights of that car had gone away. Weren't nothing, weren't nobody on that road, just your Daddy and his brother and that busted guitar. Oh, yes. Your Daddy never did really get right again. Till the day he died he weren't sure but that every white man he saw was the man that killed his brother."

She stopped and took out her handkerchief and dried her eyes and looked at me.

"I ain't telling you all this," she said, "to make you scared or bitter or to make you hate nobody. I'm telling you this because you got a brother. And the world ain't changed."

I guess I didn't want to believe this. I guess she saw this in my face. She turned away from me, toward the window again, searching those streets.

"But I praise my Redeemer," she said at last, "that He called your Daddy home before me. I ain't saying it to throw no flowers at myself, but, I declare, it keeps me from feeling too cast down to know I helped your father get safely through this world. Your father always acted like he was the roughest, strongest man on earth. And everybody took him to be like that. But if he hadn't had *me* there—to see his tears!"

She was crying again. Still I couldn't move. I said, "Lord, Lord, Mama, I didn't know it was like that."

"Oh, honey," she said, "there's a lot that you don't know. But you are going to find it out." She stood up from the window and came over to me. "You got to hold on to your brother," she said, "and don't let him fall, no matter what it looks like is happening to him and no matter how evil you gets with him. You going to be evil with him many a time. But don't you forget what I told you, you hear?"

"I won't forget," I said. "Don't you worry, I won't forget. I won't let nothing happen to Sonny."

My mother smiled as though she were amused at something she saw in my face. Then, "You may not be able to stop nothing from happening. But you got to let him know you's *there.*"

Two days later I was married, and then I was gone. And I had a lot of things on my mind and I pretty well forgot my promise to Mama until I got shipped home on a special furlough for her funeral.

And, after the funeral, with just Sonny and me alone in the empty kitchen, I tried to find out something about him.

"What do you want to do?" I asked him.

"I'm going to be a musician," he said.

For he had graduated, in the time I had been away, from dancing to the juke box to finding out who was playing what, and what they were doing with it, and he had bought himself a set of drums.

"You mean, you want to be a drummer?" I somehow had the feeling that being a drummer might be all right for other people but not for my brother Sonny.

"I don't think," he said, looking at me very gravely, "that I'll ever be a good drummer. But I think I can play a piano."

I frowned. I'd never played the role of the older brother quite so seriously before, had scarcely ever, in fact, *asked* Sonny a damn thing. I sensed myself in the presence of something I didn't really know how to handle, didn't understand. So I made my frown a little deeper as I asked: "What kind of musician do you want to be?"

He grinned. "How many kinds do you think there are?"

"Be *serious,*" I said.

He laughed, throwing his head back, and then looked at me. "I *am* serious."

"Well, then, for Christ's sake, stop kidding around and answer a serious question. I mean, do you want to be a concert pianist, or want to play classical music and all that, or—or what?" Long before I finished he was laughing again. "For Christ's *sake,* Sonny!"

He sobered, but with difficulty. "I'm sorry. But you sound so—*scared!*" and he was off again.

"Well, you may think it's funny now, baby, but it's not going to be so funny when you have to make your living at it, let me tell you *that.*" I was furious because I knew he was laughing at me and I didn't know why.

"No," he said, very sober now, and afraid, perhaps, that he'd hurt me, "I don't want to be a classical pianist. That isn't what interests me. I mean"—he paused, looking hard at me, as though his eyes would help me to understand, and then gestured helplessly, as though perhaps his hand would help—"I mean, I'll have a lot of studying to do, and I'll have to study *everything,* but, I mean, I want to play *with*—jazz musicians." He stopped. "I want to play jazz," he said.

Well, the word had never before sounded as heavy, as real, as it sounded that afternoon in Sonny's mouth. I just looked at him and I was probably frowning a real frown by this time. I simply couldn't see why on earth he'd want to spend his time hanging around nightclubs, clowning around on bandstands, while people pushed each other around a dance floor. It seemed—beneath him, somehow. I had never thought about it before, had never been forced to, but I suppose I had always put jazz musicians in a class with what Daddy called "goodtime people."

"Are you *serious?*"

"Hell, *yes,* I'm serious."

He looked more helpless than ever, and annoyed, and deeply hurt.

I suggested helpfully: "You mean—like Louis Armstrong?"

His face closed as though I'd struck him. "No. I'm not talking about none of that old-time, down home crap."

"Well, look Sonny, I'm sorry, don't get mad. I just don't altogether get it, that's all. Name somebody—you know, a jazz musician you admire."

"Bird."

"Who?"

"Bird! Charlie Parker! Don't they teach you nothing in the god-damn army?" I lit a cigarette. I was surprised and then a little amused to discover that I was trembling. "I've been out of touch," I said. "You'll have to be patient with me. Now. Who's this Parker character?"

"He's just one of the greatest jazz musicians alive," said Sonny, sullenly, his hands in his pockets, his back to me. "Maybe *the* greatest," he added, bitterly, "that's probably why *you* never heard of him."

"All right," I said, "I'm ignorant. I'm sorry. I'll go out and buy all the cat's records right away, all right?"

"It don't," said Sonny, with dignity, "make any difference to me. I don't care what you listen to. Don't do me no favors."

I was beginning to realize that I'd never seen him so upset before. With another part of my mind I was thinking that this would probably turn out to be one of those things kids go through and that I shouldn't make it seem important by pushing it too hard. Still, I didn't think it would do any harm to ask: "Doesn't all this take a lot of time? Can you make a living at it?"

He turned back to me and half leaned, half sat, on the kitchen table. "Everything takes time," he said, "and—well, yes, sure, I can make a living at it. But what I don't seem to be able to make you understand is that it's the only thing I want to do."

"Well, Sonny," I said gently, "you know people can't always do exactly what they *want* to do—"

"*No,* I don't know that," said Sonny, surprising me. "I think people *ought* to do what they want to do, what else are they alive for?"

"You are getting to be a big boy," I said desperately, "it's time you started thinking about your future."

"I'm thinking about my future," said Sonny, grimly. "I think about it all the time."

I gave up. I decided, if he didn't change his mind, that we could always talk about it later. "In the meantime," I said, "you got to finish school." We had already decided that he'd have to move in with Isabel and her folks. I knew this wasn't the ideal arrangement because Isabel's folks are inclined to be dicty[2] and they hadn't especially wanted Isabel to marry me. But I didn't know what else to do. "And we have to get you fixed up at Isabel's."

There was a long silence. He moved from the kitchen table to the window. "That's a terrible idea. You know it yourself."

"Do you have a *better* idea?"

He just walked up and down the kitchen for a minute. He was as tall as I was. He had started to shave. I suddenly had the feeling that I didn't know him at all.

He stopped at the kitchen table and picked up my cigarettes. Looking at me with a kind of mocking, amused defiance, he put one between his lips. "You mind?"

"You smoking already?"

He lit the cigarette and nodded, watching me through the smoke. "I just wanted to see if I'd have the courage to smoke in front of you." He grinned and blew a great cloud of smoke to the ceiling. "It was easy." He looked at my face. "Come on, now. I bet you was smoking at my age, tell the truth."

I didn't say anything but the truth was on my face, and he laughed. But now there was something very strained in his laugh. "Sure. And I bet that ain't all you was doing."

He was frightening me a little. "Cut the crap," I said. "We already decided that you was going to go and live at Isabel's. Now what's got into you all of a sudden?"

"*You* decided it," he pointed out. "*I* didn't decide nothing." He stopped in front of me, leaning against the stove, arms loosely folded. "Look, brother. I don't want to

[2]Snobbish.

stay in Harlem no more, I really don't." He was very earnest. He looked at me, then over toward the kitchen window. There was something in his eyes I'd never seen before, some thoughtfulness, some worry all his own. He rubbed the muscle of one arm. "It's time I was getting out of here."

"Where do you want to *go,* Sonny?"

"I want to join the army. Or the navy, I don't care. If I say I'm old enough, they'll believe me."

Then I got mad. It was because I was so scared. "You must be crazy. You goddamn fool, what the hell do you want to go and join the *army* for?"

"I just told you. To get out of Harlem."

"Sonny, you haven't even finished *school.* And if you really want to be a musician, how do you expect to study if you're in the *army?*"

He looked at me, trapped, and in anguish. "There's ways. I might be able to work out some kind of deal. Anyway, I'll have the G.I. Bill when I come out."

"*If* you come out." We stared at each other. "Sonny, please. Be reasonable. I know the setup is far from perfect. But we got to do the best we can."

"I ain't learning nothing in school," he said. "Even when I go." He turned away from me and opened the window and threw his cigarette out into the narrow alley. I watched his back. "At least, I ain't learning nothing you'd want me to learn." He slammed the window so hard I thought the glass would fly out, and turned back to me. "And I'm sick of the stink of these garbage cans!"

"Sonny," I said, "I know how you feel. But if you don't finish school now, you're going to be sorry later that you didn't." I grabbed him by the shoulders. "And you only got another year. It ain't so bad. And I'll come back and I swear I'll help you do *whatever* you want to do. Just try to put up with it till I come back. Will you please do that? For me?"

He didn't answer and he wouldn't look at me.

"Sonny. You hear me?"

He pulled away. "I hear you. But you never hear anything *I* say."

I didn't know what to say to that. He looked out of the window and then back at me. "OK," he said, and sighed. "I'll try."

Then I said, trying to cheer him up a little, "They got a piano at Isabel's. You can practice on it."

And as a matter of fact, it did cheer him up for a minute. "That's right," he said to himself. "I forgot that." His face relaxed a little. But the worry, the thoughtfulness, played on it still, the way shadows play on a face which is staring into the fire.

But I thought I'd never hear the end of that piano. At first, Isabel would write me, saying how nice it was that Sonny was so serious about his music and how, as soon as he came in from school, or wherever he had been when he was supposed to be at school, he went straight to that piano and stayed there until suppertime. And, after supper, he went back to that piano and stayed there until everybody went to bed. He was at the piano all day Saturday and all day Sunday. Then he bought a record player and started playing records. He'd play one record over and over again, all day long sometimes, and he'd improvise along with it on the piano. Or he'd play one section of the record, one chord, one change, one progression, then he'd do it on the piano. Then back to the record. Then back to the piano.

Well, I really don't know how they stood it. Isabel finally confessed that it wasn't like living with a person at all, it was like living with sound. And the sound didn't make any sense to her, didn't make any sense to any of them—naturally. They began, in a way, to be afflicted by this presence that was living in their home. It was as though Sonny were some sort of god, or monster. He moved in an atmosphere which wasn't like theirs at all. They fed him and he ate, he washed himself, he walked in and out of their door; he certainly wasn't nasty or unpleasant or rude, Sonny isn't any of those things; but it was as though he were all wrapped up in some cloud, some fire, some vision all his own; and there wasn't any way to reach him.

At the same time, he wasn't really a man yet, he was still a child, and they had to watch out for him in all kinds of ways. They certainly couldn't throw him out. Neither did they dare to make a great scene about that piano because even they dimly sensed, as I sensed, from so many thousands of miles away, that Sonny was at that piano playing for his life.

But he hadn't been going to school. One day a letter came from the school board and Isabel's mother got it—there had, apparently, been other letters but Sonny had torn them up. This day, when Sonny came in, Isabel's mother showed him the letter and asked where he'd been spending his time. And she finally got it out of him that he'd been down in Greenwich Village, with musicians and other characters, in a white girls' apartment. And this scared her and she started to scream at him and what came up, once she began—though she denies it to this day—was what sacrifices they were making to give Sonny a decent home and how little he appreciated it.

Sonny didn't play the piano that day. By evening, Isabel's mother had calmed down but then there was the old man to deal with, and Isabel herself. Isabel says she did her best to be calm but she broke down and started crying. She says she just watched Sonny's face. She could tell, by watching him, what was happening with him. And what was happening was that they penetrated his cloud, they had reached him. Even if their fingers had been a thousand times more gentle than human fingers ever are, he could hardly help feeling that they had stripped him naked and were spitting on that nakedness. For he also had to see that his presence, that music, which was life or death to him, had been torture for them and that they had endured it, not at all for his sake, but only for mine. And Sonny couldn't take that. He can take it a little better today than he could then but he's still not very good at it and, frankly, I don't know anybody who is.

The silence of the next few days must have been louder than the sound of all the music ever played since time began. One morning, before she went to work, Isabel was in his room for something and she suddenly realized that all of his records were gone. And she knew for certain that he was gone. And he was. He went as far as the navy would carry him. He finally sent me a postcard from some place in Greece and that was the first I knew that Sonny was still alive. I didn't see him any more until we were both back in New York and the war had long been over.

He was a man by then, of course, but I wasn't willing to see it. He came by the house from time to time, but we fought almost every time we met. I didn't like the way he carried himself, loose and dreamlike all the time, and I didn't like his friends, and his music seemed to be merely an excuse for the life he led. It sounded just that weird and disordered.

Then we had a fight, a pretty awful fight, and I didn't see him for months. By and by I looked him up, where he was living, in a furnished room in the Village, and I tried to make it up. But there were lots of other people in the room and Sonny just lay on his bed, and he wouldn't come downstairs with me, and he treated these other people as though they were his family and I weren't. So I got mad and then he got mad, and then I told him that he might just as well be dead as live the way he was living. Then he stood up and he told me not to worry about him any more in life, that he *was* dead as far as I was concerned. Then he pushed me to the door and the other people looked on as though nothing were happening, and he slammed the door behind me. I stood in the hallway, staring at the door. I heard somebody laugh in the room and then the tears came to my eyes. I started down the steps, whistling to keep from crying, I kept whistling to myself, *You going to need me, baby, one of these cold, rainy days.*

I read about Sonny's trouble in the spring. Little Grace died in the fall. She was a beautiful little girl. But she only lived a little over two years. She died of polio and she suffered. She had a slight fever for a couple of days, but it didn't seem like anything and we just kept her in bed. And we would certainly have called the doctor, but the fever dropped, she seemed to be all right. So we thought it had just been a cold. Then, one day, she was up, playing, Isabel was in the kitchen fixing lunch for the two boys when they'd come in from school, and she heard Grace fall down in the living room. When you have a lot of children you don't always start running when one of them falls, unless they start screaming or something. And, this time, Grace was quiet. Yet, Isabel says that when she heard that *thump* and then that silence, something happened in her to make her afraid. And she ran to the living room and there was little Grace on the floor, all twisted up, and the reason she hadn't screamed was that she couldn't get her breath. And when she did scream, it was the worst sound, Isabel says, that she'd ever heard in all her life, and she still hears it sometimes in her dreams. Isabel will sometimes wake me up with a low, moaning, strangled sound and I have to be quick to awaken her and hold her to me and where Isabel is weeping against me seems a mortal wound.

I think I may have written Sonny the very day that little Grace was buried. I was sitting in the living room in the dark, by myself, and I suddenly thought of Sonny. My trouble made his real.

One Saturday afternoon, when Sonny had been living with us, or, anyway, been in our house, for nearly two weeks, I found myself wandering aimlessly about the living room, drinking from a can of beer, and trying to work up the courage to search Sonny's room. He was out, he was usually out whenever I was home, and Isabel had taken the children to see their grandparents. Suddenly I was standing still in front of the living room window, watching Seventh Avenue. The idea of searching Sonny's room made me still. I scarcely dared to admit to myself what I'd be searching for. I didn't know what I'd do if I found it. Or if I didn't.

On the sidewalk across from me, near the entrance to a barbecue joint, some people were holding an old-fashioned revival meeting. The barbecue cook, wearing a dirty white apron, his *conked* hair reddish and metallic in the pale sun, and a cigarette between his lips, stood in the doorway, watching them. Kids and older people paused in their errands and stood there, along with some older men and a couple of very tough-looking women who watched everything that happened on the avenue, as though they owned it, or were maybe owned by it. Well, they were watching this, too. The revival was being carried on by three sisters in black, and a brother. All they had were their voices and their Bibles and a tambourine. The brother was testifying and while he testified two of the sisters stood together, seeming to say, amen, and the third sister walked around with the tambourine outstretched and a couple of people dropped coins into it. Then the brother's testimony ended and the sister who had been taking up the collection dumped the coins into her palm and transferred them to the pocket of her long black robe. Then she raised both hands, striking the tambourine against the air, and then against one hand, and she started to sing. And the two other sisters and the brother joined in.

It was strange, suddenly, to watch, though I had been seeing these street meetings all my life. So, of course, had everybody else down there. Yet, they paused and watched and listened and I stood still at the window. *"Tis the old ship of Zion,"* they sang, and the sister with the tambourine kept a steady, jangling beat, *"it has rescued many a thousand!"* Not a soul under the sound of their voices was hearing this song for the first time, not one of them had been rescued. Nor had they seen much in the way of rescue work being done around them. Neither did they especially believe in the holiness of the three sisters and the brother, they knew too much about them, knew where they lived, and how. The woman with the tambourine, whose voice dominated the air, whose face was bright with joy, was divided by very little from the woman who stood watching her, a cigarette between her heavy, chapped lips, her hair a cuckoo's nest, her face scarred and swollen from many beatings, and her black eyes glittering like coal. Perhaps they both knew this, which was why, when, as rarely, they addressed each other, they addressed each other as Sister. As the singing filled the air the watching, listening faces underwent a change, the eyes focusing on something within; the music seemed to soothe a poison out of them; and time seemed, nearly, to fall away from the sullen, belligerent, battered faces, as though they were fleeing back to their first condition, while dreaming of their last. The barbecue cook half shook his head and smiled, and dropped his cigarette and disappeared into his joint. A man fumbled in his pockets for change and stood holding it in his hand impatiently, as though he had just remembered a pressing appointment further up the avenue. He looked furious. Then I saw Sonny, standing on the edge of the crowd. He was carrying a wide, flat notebook with a green cover, and it made him look, from where I was standing, almost like a schoolboy. The coppery sun brought out the copper in his skin, he was very faintly smiling, standing very still. Then the singing stopped, the tambourine turned into a collection plate again. The furious man dropped in his coins and vanished, so did a couple of the women, and Sonny dropped some change in the plate, looking directly at the woman with a little smile. He started across the avenue, toward the house. He has a slow, loping walk, something like the way Harlem hipsters walk, only he's imposed on this his own half-beat. I had never really noticed it before.

I stayed at the window, both relieved and apprehensive. As Sonny disappeared from my sight, they began singing again. And they were still singing when his key turned in the lock.

"Hey," he said.

"Hey, yourself. You want some beer?"

"No. Well, maybe." But he came up to the window and stood beside me, looking out. "What a warm voice," he said.

They were singing *If I could only hear my mother pray again!*

"Yes," I said, "and she can sure beat that tambourine."

"But what a terrible song," he said, and laughed. He dropped his notebook on the sofa and disappeared into the kitchen. "Where's Isabel and the kids?"

"I think they went to see their grandparents. You hungry?"

"No." He came back into the living room with his can of beer. "You want to come some place with me tonight?"

I sensed, I don't know how, that I couldn't possibly say no. "Sure. Where?"

He sat down on the sofa and picked up his notebook and started leafing through it. "I'm going to sit in with some fellows in a joint in the Village."

"You mean, you're going to play, tonight?"

"That's right." He took a swallow of his beer and moved back, to the window. He gave me a sidelong look. "If you can stand it."

"I'll try," I said.

He smiled to himself and we both watched as the meeting across the way broke up. The three sisters and the brother, heads bowed, were singing *God be with you till we meet again.* The faces around them were very quiet. Then the song ended. The small crowd dispersed. We watched the three women and the lone man walk slowly up the avenue.

"When she was singing before," said Sonny, abruptly, "her voice reminded me for a minute of what heroin feels like sometimes—when it's in your veins. It makes you feel sort of warm and cool at the same time. And distant. And—and sure." He sipped his beer, very deliberately not looking at me. I watched his face. "It makes you feel—in control. Sometimes you've got to have that feeling."

"Do you?" I sat down slowly in the easy chair.

"Sometimes." He went to the sofa and picked up his notebook again. "Some people do."

"In order," I asked, "to play?" And my voice was very ugly, full of contempt and anger.

"Well"—he looked at me with great, troubled eyes, as though, in fact, he hoped his eyes would tell me things he could never otherwise say—"they *think* so. And *if* they think so—!"

"And what do *you* think?" I asked.

He sat on the sofa and put his can of beer on the floor. "I don't know," he said, and I couldn't be sure if he were answering my question or pursuing his thoughts. His face didn't tell me. "It's not so much to *play.* It's to *stand* it, to be able to make it at all. On any level." He frowned and smiled: "In order to keep from shaking to pieces."

"But these friends of yours," I said, "they seem to shake themselves to pieces pretty goddamn fast."

"Maybe." He played with the notebook. And something told me that I should curb my tongue, that Sonny was doing his best to talk, that I should listen. "But of course you only know the ones that've gone to pieces. Some don't—or at least they haven't *yet* and that's just about all *any* of us can say." He paused. "And then there are some who just live, really, in hell, and they know it and they see what's happening, and they go right on. I don't know." He sighed, dropped the notebook, folded his arms. "Some guys, you can tell from the way they play, they on something *all* the time. And you can see that, well, it makes something real for them. But of course," he picked up his beer from the floor and sipped it and put the can down again, "they *want* to, too, you've got to see that. Even some of them that say they don't—*some,* not all."

"And what about you?" I asked—I couldn't help it. "What about you? Do *you* want to?"

He stood up and walked to the window and remained silent for a long time. Then he sighed. "Me," he said. Then: "While I was downstairs before, on my way here, listening to that woman sing, it struck me all of a sudden how much suffering she must have had to go through—to sing like that. It's *repulsive* to think you have to suffer that much."

I said: "But there's no way not to suffer—is there, Sonny?"

"I believe not," he said and smiled, "but that's never stopped anyone from trying." He looked at me. "Has it?" I realized, with this mocking look, that there stood between us, forever, beyond the power of time or forgiveness, the fact that I had held silence—so long!—when he had needed human speech to help him. He turned back to the window. "No, there's no way not to suffer. But you try all kinds of ways to keep from drowning in it, to keep on top of it, and to make it seem—well, like *you.* Like you did something, all right, and now you're suffering for it. You know?" I said nothing. "Well you know," he said, impatiently, "why *do* people suffer? Maybe it's better to do something to give it a reason, *any* reason."

"But we just agreed," I said, "that there's no way not to suffer. Isn't it better, then, just to—take it?"

"But nobody just takes it," Sonny cried, "that's what I'm telling you! *Everybody* tries not to. You're just hung up on the *way* some people try—it's not *your* way!"

The hair on my face began to itch, my face felt wet. "That's not true," I said, "that's not true. I don't give a damn what other people do, I don't even care how they suffer. I just care how *you* suffer." And he looked at me. "Please believe me," I said. "I don't want to see you—die—trying not to suffer."

"I won't," he said, flatly, "die trying not to suffer. At least, not any faster than anybody else."

"But there's no need," I said, trying to laugh, "is there? in killing yourself."

I wanted to say more, but I couldn't. I wanted to talk about will power and how life could be—well, beautiful. I wanted to say that it was all within; but was it? or, rather, wasn't that exactly the trouble? And I wanted to promise that I would never fail him again. But it would all have sounded—empty words and lies.

So I made the promise to myself and prayed that I would keep it.

"It's terrible sometimes, inside," he said, "that's what's the trouble. You walk these streets, black and funky and cold, and there's not really a living ass to talk to, and there's nothing shaking, and there's no way of getting it out—that storm inside. You can't talk it and you can't make love with it, and when you finally try to get with it and play it, you realize *nobody's* listening. So *you've* got to listen. You got to find a way to listen."

And then he walked away from the window and sat on the sofa again, as though all the wind had suddenly been knocked out of him. "Sometimes you'll do *anything* to play, even cut your mother's throat." He laughed and looked at me. "Or your brother's." Then he sobered. "Or your own." Then: "Don't worry. I'm all right now and I think I'll *be* all right. But I can't forget—where I've been. I don't mean just the physical place I've been, I mean where I've *been.* And *what* I've been."

"What have you been, Sonny?" I asked.

He smiled—but sat sideways on the sofa, his elbow resting on the back, his fingers playing with his mouth and chin, not looking at me. "I've been something I didn't recognize, didn't know I could be. Didn't know anybody could be." He stopped, looking inward, looking helplessly young, looking old. "I'm not talking about it now because I feel *guilty* or anything like that—maybe it would be better if I did, I don't know. Anyway, I can't really talk about it. Not to you, not to anybody," and now he turned and faced me. "Sometimes, you know and it was actually when I was most *out* of the world. I felt that I was in it, that I was *with* it, really, and I could play or I didn't really have to *play,* it just came out of me, it was there. And I don't know how I played, thinking about it now, but I know I did awful things, those times, sometimes, to people. Or it wasn't that I *did* anything to them—it was that they weren't real." He picked up the beer can; it was empty; he rolled it between his palms: "And other times—well, I needed a fix, I needed to find a place to lean, I needed to clear a space to *listen*—and I couldn't find it, and I —went crazy, I did terrible things to *me,* I was terrible *for* me." He began pressing the beer can between his hands, I watched the metal begin to give. It glittered, as he played with it, like a knife, and I was afraid he would cut himself, but I said nothing. "Oh well. I can never tell you. I was all by myself at the bottom of something, stinking and sweating and crying and shaking, and I smelled it, you know? *my* stink, and I thought I'd die if I couldn't get away from it and yet, all the same, I knew that everything I was doing was just locking me in with it. And I didn't know," he paused, still flattening the beer can, "I didn't know, I still *don't* know, something kept telling me that maybe it was good to smell your own stink, but I didn't think that *that* was what I'd been trying to do—and—who can stand it?" and he abruptly dropped the ruined beer can, looking at me with a small, still smile, and then rose, walking to the window as though it were the lodestone rock. I watched his face, he watched the avenue. "I couldn't tell you when Mama died—but the reason I wanted to leave Harlem so bad was to get away from drugs. And then, when I ran away, that's what I was running from—really. When I came back, nothing had changed, *I* hadn't changed, I was just—older." And he stopped drumming with his fingers on the windowpane. The sun had vanished, soon darkness would fall. I watched his face. "It can come again," he said, almost as though speaking to himself. Then he turned to me. "It can come again," he repeated. "I just want you to know that."

"All right," I said, at last. "So it can come again, All right."

He smiled, but the smile was sorrowful. "I had to try to tell you," he said.

"Yes," I said. "I understand that."

"You're my brother," he said, looking straight at me, and not smiling at all.

"Yes," I repeated, "yes. I understand that."

He turned back to the window, looking out. "All that hatred down there," he said, "all that hatred and misery and love. It's a wonder it doesn't blow the avenue apart."

We went to the only nightclub on a short, dark street, downtown. We squeezed through the narrow, chattering, jam-packed bar to the entrance of the big room, where the bandstand was. And we stood there for a moment, for the lights were very dim in this room and we couldn't see. Then, "Hello, boy," said a voice and an enormous black man, much older than Sonny or myself, erupted out of all that atmospheric lighting and put an arm around Sonny's shoulder. "I been sitting right here," he said, "waiting for you."

He had a big voice, too, and heads in the darkness turned toward us.

Sonny grinned and pulled a little away, and said, "Creole, this is my brother. I told you about him."

Creole shook my hand. "I'm glad to meet you, son," he said, and it was clear that he was glad to meet me *there,* for Sonny's sake. And he smiled, "You got a real musician in *your* family," and he took his arm from Sonny's shoulder and slapped him, lightly, affectionately, with the back of his hand.

"Well. Now I've heard it all," said a voice behind us. This was another musician, and a friend of Sonny's, a coal-black, cheerful-looking man, built close to the ground. He immediately began confiding to me, at the top of his lungs, the most terrible things about Sonny, his teeth gleaming like a lighthouse and his laugh coming up out of him like the beginning of an earthquake. And it turned out that everyone at the bar knew Sonny, or almost everyone; some were musicians, working there, or nearby, or not working, some were simply hangers-on, and some were there to hear Sonny play. I was introduced to all of them and they were all very polite to me. Yet, it was clear that, for them, I was only Sonny's brother. Here, I was in Sonny's world. Or, rather: his kingdom. Here, it was not even a question that his veins bore royal blood.

They were going to play soon and Creole installed me, by myself, at a table in a dark corner. Then I watched them, Creole, and the little black man, and Sonny, and the others, while they horsed around, standing just below the bandstand. The light from the bandstand spilled just a little short of them and, watching them laughing and gesturing and moving about, I had the feeling that they, nevertheless, were being most careful not to step into that circle of light too suddenly: that if they moved into the light too suddenly, without thinking, they would perish in flame. Then, while I watched, one of them, the small, black man, moved into the light and crossed the bandstand and started fooling around with his drums. Then—being funny and being, also, extremely ceremonious—Creole took Sonny by the arm and led him to the piano. A woman's voice called Sonny's name and a few hands started clapping. And Sonny, also being funny and being ceremonious, and so touched, I think, that he could have cried, but neither hiding it nor showing it, riding it like a man, grinned, and put both hands to his heart and bowed from the waist.

Creole then went to the bass fiddle and a lean, very bright-skinned brown man jumped up on the bandstand and picked up his horn. So there they were, and the atmosphere on the bandstand and in the room began to change and tighten. Someone stepped up to the microphone and announced them. Then there were all kinds of murmurs. Some people at the bar shushed others. The waitress ran around, frantically getting in the last orders, guys and chicks got closer to each other, and the lights on the bandstand, on the quartet, turned to a kind of indigo. Then they all looked different there. Creole looked about him for the last time, as though he were making certain that all his chickens were in the coop, and then he—jumped and struck the fiddle. And there they were.

All I know about music is that not many people ever really hear it. And even then, on the rare occasions when something opens within, and the music enters, what we mainly hear, or hear corroborated, are personal, private, vanishing evocations. But the man who creates the music is hearing something else, is dealing with the roar rising from the void and imposing order on it as it hits the air. What is evoked in him, then, is of another order, more terrible because it has no words, and triumphant, too, for that same reason. And his triumph, when he triumphs, is ours. I just watched Sonny's face. His face was troubled, he was working hard, but he wasn't with it. And I had the feeling that, in a way, everyone on the bandstand was waiting for him, both waiting for him and pushing him along. But as I began to watch Creole, I realized that it was Creole who held them all back. He had them on a short rein. Up there, keeping the beat with his whole body, wailing on the fiddle, with his eyes half closed, he was listening to everything, but he was listening to Sonny. He was having a dialogue with Sonny. He wanted Sonny to leave the shoreline and strike out for the deep water. He was Sonny's witness that deep water and drowning were not the same thing—he had been there, and he knew. And he wanted Sonny to know. He was waiting for Sonny to do the things on the keys which would let Creole know that Sonny was in the water.

And, while Creole listened, Sonny moved, deep within, exactly like someone in torment. I had never before thought of how awful the relationship must be between the musician and his instrument. He has to fill it, this instrument, with the breath of life, his own. He has to make it do what he wants it to do. And a piano is just a piano. It's made out of so much wood and wires and little hammers and big ones, and ivory. While there's only so much you can do with it, the only way to find this out is to try; to try and make it do everything.

And Sonny hadn't been near a piano for over a year. And he wasn't on much better terms with his life, not the life that stretched before him now. He and the piano stammered, started one way, got scared, stopped; started another way, panicked, marked time, started again; then seemed to have found a direction, panicked again, got stuck. And the face I saw on Sonny I'd never seen before. Everything had been burned out of it, and, at the same time, things usually hidden were being burned in, by the fire and fury of the battle which was occurring in him up there.

Yet, watching Creole's face as they neared the end of the first set, I had the feeling that something had happened, something I hadn't heard. Then they finished, there was scattered applause, and then, without an instant's warning, Creole started into something else, it was almost sardonic, it was *Am I Blue.* And, as though he commanded, Sonny began to play. Something began to happen. And Creole let out the reins. The dry, low, black man said something awful on the drums, Creole answered, and the drums talked back. Then the horn insisted, sweet and high, slightly detached perhaps, and Creole listened, commenting now and then, dry, and driving, beautiful and calm and old. Then they all came together again, and Sonny was part of the family again. I could tell this from his face. He seemed to have found, right there beneath his fingers, a damn brand-new piano. It seemed that he couldn't get over it. Then, for awhile, just being happy with Sonny, they seemed to be agreeing with him that brand-new pianos certainly were a gas.

Then Creole stepped forward to remind them that what they were playing was the blues. He hit something in all of them, he hit something in me, myself, and the music tightened and deepened, apprehension began to beat the air. Creole began to tell us what the blues were all about. They were not about anything very new. He and his boys up there were keeping it new, at the risk of ruin, destruction, madness, and death, in order to find new ways to make us listen. For, while the tale of how we suffer, and how we are delighted, and how we may triumph is never new, it always must be heard. There isn't any other tale to tell, it's the only light we've got in all this darkness.

And this tale, according to that face, that body, those strong hands on those strings, has another aspect in every country, and a new depth in every generation. Listen, Creole seemed to be saying, listen. Now these are Sonny's blues. He made the little black man on the drums know it, and the bright, brown man on the horn. Creole wasn't trying any longer to get Sonny in the water. He was wishing him Godspeed. Then he stepped back, very slowly, filling the air with the immense suggestion that Sonny speak for himself.

Then they all gathered around Sonny and Sonny played. Every now and again one of them seemed to say, amen. Sonny's fingers filled the air with life, his life. But that life contained so many others. And Sonny went all the way back, he really began with the spare, flat statement of the opening phrase of the song. Then he began to make it his. It was very beautiful because it wasn't hurried and it was no longer a lament. I seemed to hear with what burning he had made it his, with what burning we had yet to make it ours, how we could cease lamenting. Freedom lurked around us and I understood, at last, that he could help us to be free if we would listen, that he would never be free until we did. Yet, there was no battle in his face now. I heard what he had gone through, and would continue to go through until he came to rest in earth. He had made it his: that long line, of which we knew only Mama and Daddy. And he was giving it back, as everything must be given back, so that, passing through death, it can live forever. I saw my mother's face again, and felt, for the first time, how the stones of the road she had walked on must have bruised her feet. I saw the moonlit road where my father's brother died. And it brought something else back to me, and carried me past it, I saw my little girl again and felt Isabel's tears again, and I felt my own tears begin to rise. And I was yet aware that this was only a moment, that the world waited outside, as hungry as a tiger, and that trouble stretched above us, longer than the sky.

Then it was over. Creole and Sonny let out their breath, both soaking wet, and grinning. There was a lot of applause and some of it was real. In the dark, the girl came by and I asked her to take drinks to the bandstand. There was a long pause, while they talked up there in the indigo light and after awhile I saw the girl put a Scotch and milk on top of the piano for Sonny. He didn't seem to notice it, but just before they started playing again he sipped from it and looked toward me, and nodded. Then he put it back on top of the piano. For me, then, as they began to play again, it glowed and shook above my brother's head like the very cup of trembling.

1948

Paule Marshall b. 1929

Paule Marshall, née Valenza Pauline Burke, was born in Brooklyn, New York. Her parents, Ada and Samuel Burke, were emigrants from Barbados, West Indies. At the age of nine, Marshall made an extended visit to the native land of her parents and discovered for herself the quality of life peculiar to that tropical isle. Although she then wrote a series of poems reflecting her impressions, creative writing did not become a serious pursuit until much later in her young adult life. The selection included here is a mature reminiscence and symbolic expansion of that childhood visit.

A quiet and retiring child ("living her old days first," her mother used to say), Marshall was an avid reader who spent countless hours in her neighborhood library. This, it seems, was at least a partial escape from the pressures of growing up, for the author admits going through a painful childhood period in which she rejected her West Indian heritage. Easily identified by the heavy silver bangles which girls from "the islands" wore on their wrists, she felt even more estranged from her classmates when she returned from Barbados with a noticeable accent. During early adolescence, reading also helped ease the longing for her father who, having become a devoted follower of Father Divine, left home to live in the Harlem "kingdom."

Marshall had been attending Hunter College, majoring in social work, when illness necessitated a one-year stay in a sanatorium in upstate New York. There, in a tranquil lake setting, she wrote letters so vividly describing the surroundings that a friend encouraged her to think of a career in writing. Upon her release from the sanatorium, she transferred to Brooklyn College, changed her major to English Literature, and graduated Phi Beta Kappa in 1953. Her first marriage, in 1957, was to Kenneth Marshall, with whom she had a son, Evan Keith. She divorced in 1963 and in 1970 wed a second time to Haitian businessman, Nourry Ménard.

Formerly a researcher and staff writer for *Our World* magazine, located in New York City, Marshall traveled on assignment to Brazil and to the West Indies. Once her literary career had been launched, she contributed short stories and articles to numerous magazines and anthologies and began lecturing at several colleges and universities within the United States and abroad. The recipient of several prestigious awards, including the John D. and Catherine T. MacArthur Fellowship, Marshall continues to write and to teach. She currently is a professor of English and creative writing at Virginia Commonwealth University and resides in Richmond, Virginia.

While clearly influenced by the literary giants (black and white), Marshall attributes her love of language and storytelling to her mother and other Bajan (Barbadian) women who, sitting around the kitchen table, effortlessly created narrative art. In her informative essay, "From the Poets in the Kitchen," the author explains the process as a transformation of standard English into "an idiom, an instrument that more adequately described them—changing around the syntax and imposing their own rhythm and accent so that the sentences were more pleasing to their ears. . . .

And to make it more vivid, more in keeping with their expressive quality, they brought to bear a raft of metaphors, parables, Biblical quotations, sayings and the like.

Marshall goes on to provide examples like the following:

"The sea ain' got no back door," . . . meaning that it wasn't like a house where if there was a fire you could run out the back. Meaning that it was not to be trifled with. And meaning perhaps in a larger sense that man should treat all of nature with caution and respect.

This is the legacy which the artist proudly claims, and she makes of it a distinctive stylistic device which combines forms of Western origin with the style and function of traditional African oral narrative. In short, she manipulates verbal structures so that they accommodate new patterns and rhythms, and this gives to the written word a stamp of cultural authenticity.

Marshall's artistic vision evolves in a clear progression as she moves, through her creations, from an American to an African American/African Caribbean and, finally, a Pan-African sensibility. Indeed, the chronological order of her publications suggests an underlying design to follow the "middle passage" in reverse. That is, she examines the experience of blacks not in transit from Africa to the New World, but from the New World toward Africa. Thus, her first major work, *Brown Girl, Brownstones,* considers the coming of age of a young West Indian girl and simultaneously explores the black emigrant experience in America. *Soul Clap Hands and Sing,* a collection of novellas, is a lyrical depiction of the lives of four aging men coming to grips with the decline of Western values. The geographical setting changes from Brooklyn to Barbados to British Guiana and then to Brazil. Marshall next moves, in *The Chosen Place, the Timeless People,* to an imaginary Caribbean island which, on one side, faces the continent of Africa. In this epic novel, she traces the development and perpetuation of colonialism. In *Praisesong for the Widow,* the artist shows increasing reliance on African images as she presents the portrait of an elderly black American widow who, on a cruise to Grenada, confronts her African heritage. In her most recent novel, *Daughters,* Marshall moves her geographical setting back and forth between the Caribbean and the United States to suggest the bicultural ties of her protagonist as well as the political strategies affecting both nations. She further establishes the centrality of women in transforming self, community, and nation.

Throughout her fiction, Marshall is preoccupied with black cultural history. Additionally, her emphasis on black female characters addresses contemporary feminist issues from an Afrocentric perspective. She insists that African peoples take a "journey back" through time to understand the political, social, and economic structures upon which contemporary societies are based. As her vision expands to include oppressed peoples (men and women) all over the world, she develops a sensibility which values cultural differences while it celebrates the triumph of the human spirit.

Dorothy L. Denniston
Brown University

PRIMARY WORKS

"The Valley Between," 1954; *Brown Girl, Brownstones,* 1959; *Soul Clap Hands and Sing,* 1961; "Reena," 1962; "Some Get Wasted," 1964; "To Da-duh: In Memoriam," 1967; *The Chosen Place, the Timeless People,* 1969; *Praisesong for the Widow,* 1983; *Reena and Other Short Stories,* 1983 (re-issue of formerly out-of-print short fiction, critical essay, and new novella, "Merle"); *Daughters,* 1991.

To Da-duh: In Memoriam

This is the most autobiographical of the stories, a reminiscence largely of a visit I paid to my grandmother (whose nickname was Da-duh) on the island of Barbados when I was nine. Ours was a complex relationship—close, affectionate yet rivalrous. During the year I spent with her a subtle kind of power struggle went on between us. It was as if we both knew, at a level beyond words, that I had come into the world not only to love her and to continue her line but to take her very life in order that I might live.

Years later, when I got around to writing the story, I tried giving the contest I had sensed between us a wider meaning. I wanted the basic theme of youth and old age to suggest rivalries, dichotomies of a cultural and political nature, having to do with the relationship of western civilization and the Third World.

Apart from this story, Da-duh also appears in one form or another in my other work as well. She's the old hairdresser, Mrs. Thompson, in BROWN GIRL, BROWNSTONES, *who offers Selina total, unquestioning love. She's Leesy Walkes and the silent cook, Carrington, "whose great breast . . . had been used it seemed to suckle the world" in* THE CHOSEN PLACE, THE TIMELESS PEOPLE. *She's Aunt Vi in "Reena" and Medford, the old family retainer in "British Guiana" from* SOUL CLAP HANDS AND SING. *And she's Avey Johnson's Great-aunt Cuney in* PRAISESONG FOR THE WIDOW. *Da-duh turns up everywhere.*

She's an ancestor figure, symbolic for me of the long line of black women and men—African and New World—who made my being possible, and whose spirit I believe continues to animate my life and work. I wish to acknowledge and celebrate them. I am, in a word, an unabashed ancestor worshipper.

". . . Oh Nana! all of you is not involved in this evil business
Death,
Nor all of us in life."

—FROM "AT MY GRANDMOTHER'S GRAVE," BY LEBERT BETHUNE

I did not see her at first I remember. For not only was it dark inside the crowded disembarkation shed in spite of the daylight flooding in from outside, but standing there waiting for her with my mother and sister I was still somewhat blinded from the sheen of tropical sunlight on the water of the bay which we had just crossed in the landing boat, leaving behind us the ship that had brought us from New York lying in the offing. Besides, being only nine years of age at the time and knowing nothing of islands I was busy attending to the alien sights and sounds of Barbados, the unfamiliar smells.

I did not see her, but I was alerted to her approach by my mother's hand which suddenly tightened around mine, and looking up I traced her gaze through the gloom in the shed until I finally made out the small, purposeful, painfully erect figure of the old woman headed our way.

Her face was drowned in the shadow of an ugly rolled-brim brown felt hat, but the details of her slight body and of the struggle taking place within it were clear enough—an intense, unrelenting struggle between her back which was beginning to bend ever so slightly under the weight of her eighty-odd years and the rest of her which sought to deny those years and hold that back straight, keep it in line. Moving swiftly toward us (so swiftly it seemed she did not intend stopping when she reached us but would sweep past us out the doorway which opened onto the sea and like Christ walk upon the water!)[1] she was caught between the sunlight at her end of the building and the darkness inside—and for a moment she appeared to contain them both: the light in the long severe old-fashioned white dress she wore which brought the sense of a past that was still alive into our bustling present and in the snatch of white at her eye; the darkness in her black high-top shoes and in her face which was visible now that she was closer.

It was as stark and fleshless as a death mask, that face. The maggots might have already done their work, leaving only the framework of bone beneath the ruined skin and deep wells at the temple and jaw. But her eyes were alive, unnervingly so for one so old, with a sharp light that flicked out of the dim clouded depths like a lizard's tongue to snap up all in her view. Those eyes betrayed a child's curiosity about the world, and I wondered vaguely seeing them, and seeing the way the bodice of her ancient dress had collapsed in on her flat chest (what had happened to her breasts?), whether she might not be some kind of child at the same time that she was a woman, with fourteen children, my mother included, to prove it. Perhaps she was both, both child and woman, darkness and light, past and present, life and death—all the opposites contained and reconciled in her.

"My Da-duh," my mother said formally and stepped forward. The name sounded like thunder fading softly in the distance.

"Child," Da-duh said, and her tone, her quick scrutiny of my mother, the brief embrace in which they appeared to shy from each other rather than touch, wiped out the fifteen years my mother had been away and restored the old relationship. My mother, who was such a formidable figure in my eyes, had suddenly with a word been reduced to my status.

"Yes, God is good," Da-duh said with a nod that was like a tic. "He has spared me to see my child again."

We were led forward then, apologetically because not only did Da-duh prefer boys but she also liked her grandchildren to be "white," that is, fair-skinned; and we had, I was to discover, a number of cousins, the outside children[2] of white estate managers and the like, who qualified. We, though, were as black as she.

My sister being the oldest was presented first. "This one takes after the father," my mother said and waited to be reproved.

Frowning, Da-duh tilted my sister's face toward the light. But her frown soon gave way to a grudging smile, for my sister with her large mild eyes and little broad winged nose, with our father's high-cheeked Barbadian cast to her face, was pretty.

"She's goin' be lucky," Da-duh said and patted her once on the cheek. "Any girl child that takes after the father does be lucky."

She turned then to me. But oddly enough she did not touch me. Instead leaning close, she peered hard at me, and then quickly drew back. I thought I saw her hand start up as though to shield her eyes. It was almost as if she saw not only me, a thin truculent child who it was said took after no one but myself, but something in me which for some reason she found disturbing, even threatening. We looked silently at

[1]Biblical allusion, Matthew 14:22–33.

[2]Children born outside marriage.

each other for a long time there in the noisy shed, our gaze locked. She was the first to look away.

"But Adry," she said to my mother and her laugh was cracked, thin, apprehensive. "Where did you get this one here with this fierce look?"

"We don't know where she came out of, my Da-duh," my mother said, laughing also. Even I smiled to myself. After all I had won the encounter. Da-duh had recognized my small strength—and this was all I ever asked of the adults in my life then.

"Come, soul," Da-duh said and took my hand. "You must be one of those New York terrors you hear so much about."

She led us, me at her side and my sister and mother behind, out of the shed into the sunlight that was like a bright driving summer rain and over to a group of people clustered beside a decrepit lorry. They were our relatives, most of them from St. Andrews although Da-duh herself lived in St. Thomas, the women wearing bright print dresses, the colors vivid against their darkness, the men rusty black suits that encased them like straitjackets. Da-duh, holding fast to my hand, became my anchor as they circled round us like a nervous sea, exclaiming, touching us with their calloused hands, embracing us shyly. They laughed in awed bursts: "But look Adry got big-big children!"/"And see the nice things they wearing, wrist watch and all!"/ "I tell you, Adry has done all right for sheself in New York. . . ."

Da-duh, ashamed at their wonder, embarrassed for them, admonished them the while. "But oh Christ," she said, "why you all got to get on like you never saw people from 'Away' before? You would think New York is the only place in the world to hear wunna. That's why I don't like to go anyplace with you St. Andrews people, you know. You all ain't been colonized."[3]

We were in the back of the lorry finally, packed in among the barrels of ham, flour, cornmeal and rice and the trunks of clothes that my mother had brought as gifts. We made our way slowly through Bridgetown's clogged streets, part of a funereal procession of cars and open-sided buses, bicycles and donkey carts. The dim little limestone shops and offices along the way marched with us, at the same mournful pace, toward the same grave ceremony—as did the people, the women balancing huge baskets on top their heads as if they were no more than hats they wore to shade them from the sun. Looking over the edge of the lorry I watched as their feet slurred the dust. I listened, and their voices, raw and loud and dissonant in the heat, seemed to be grappling with each other high overhead.

Da-duh sat on a trunk in our midst, a monarch amid her court. She still held my hand, but it was different now. I had suddenly become her anchor, for I felt her fear of the lorry with its asthmatic motor (a fear and distrust, I later learned, she held of all machines)[4] beating like a pulse in her rough palm.

As soon as we left Bridgetown behind though, she relaxed, and while the others around us talked she gazed at the canes standing tall on either side of the winding

[3]Malapropism.

[4]The same dread of the mechanical appears in Leesy Walkes, a character in Marshall's *The Chosen Place, the Timeless People* (1969). Here the author symbolically establishes the conflict engendered when Western technology encroaches upon Da-duh's edenic garden.

marl road. "C'dear,"[5] she said softly to herself after a time. "The canes this side are pretty enough."

They were too much for me. I thought of them as giant weeds that had overrun the island, leaving scarcely any room for the small tottering houses of sunbleached pine we passed or the people, dark streaks as our lorry hurtled by. I suddenly feared that we were journeying, unaware that we were, toward some dangerous place where the canes, grown as high and thick as a forest, would close in on us and run us through with their stiletto blades. I longed then for the familiar: for the street in Brooklyn where I lived, for my father who had refused to accompany us ("Blowing out good money on foolishness," he had said of the trip), for a game of tag with my friends under the chestnut tree outside our aging brownstone house.

"Yes, but wait till you see St. Thomas canes," Da-duh was saying to me. "They's canes father, bo," she gave a proud arrogant nod. "Tomorrow, God willing, I goin' take you out in the ground and show them to you."

True to her word Da-duh took me with her the following day out into the ground. It was a fairly large plot adjoining her weathered board and shingle house and consisting of a small orchard, a good-sized canepiece and behind the canes, where the land sloped abruptly down, a gully. She had purchased it with Panama money[6] sent her by her eldest son, my uncle Joseph, who had died working on the canal. We entered the ground along a trail no wider than her body and as devious and complex as her reasons for showing me her land. Da-duh strode briskly ahead, her slight form filled out this morning by the layers of sacking petticoats she wore under her working dress to protect her against the damp. A fresh white cloth, elaborately arranged around her head, added to her height, and lent her a vain, almost roguish air.

Her pace slowed once we reached the orchard, and glancing back at me occasionally over her shoulder, she pointed out the various trees.

"This here is a breadfruit," she said. "That one yonder is a papaw. Here's a guava. This is a mango. I know you don't have anything like these in New York. Here's a sugar apple." (The fruit looked more like artichokes than apples to me.) "This one bears limes. . . ." She went on for some time, intoning the names of the trees as though they were those of her gods. Finally, turning to me, she said, "I know you don't have anything this nice where you come from." Then, as I hesitated: "I said I know you don't have anything this nice where you come from. . . ."

"No," I said and my world did seem suddenly lacking.

Da-duh nodded and passed on. The orchard ended and we were on the narrow cart road that led through the canepiece, the canes clashing like swords above my cowering head. Again she turned and her thin muscular arms spread wide, her dim gaze embracing the small field of canes, she said—and her voice almost broke under the weight of her pride, "Tell me, have you got anything like these in that place where you were born?"

[5]A form of address spoken with a hard "C." Loosely translated as "Come dear" or "Good dear."

[6]Because of poor economic conditions in Barbados, many islanders worked abroad and sent money home to support their families.

"No."

"I din' think so. I bet you don't even know that these canes here and the sugar you eat is one and the same thing. That they does throw the canes into some damn machine at the factory and squeeze out all the little life in them to make sugar for you all so in New York to eat. I bet you don't know that."

"I've got two cavities and I'm not allowed to eat a lot of sugar."

But Da-duh didn't hear me. She had turned with an inexplicably angry motion and was making her way rapidly out of the canes and down the slope at the edge of the field which led to the gully below. Following her apprehensively down the incline amid a stand of banana plants whose leaves flapped like elephants ears in the wind, I found myself in the middle of a small tropical wood—a place dense and damp and gloomy and tremulous with the fitful play of light and shadow as the leaves high above moved against the sun that was almost hidden from view. It was a violent place, the tangled foliage fighting each other for a chance at the sunlight, the branches of the trees locked in what seemed an immemorial struggle, one both necessary and inevitable. But despite the violence, it was pleasant, almost peaceful in the gully, and beneath the thick undergrowth the earth smelled like spring.

This time Da-duh didn't even bother to ask her usual question, but simply turned and waited for me to speak.

"No," I said, my head bowed. "We don't have anything like this in New York."

"Ah," she cried, her triumph complete. "I din' think so. Why, I've heard that's a place where you can walk till you near drop and never see a tree."

"We've got a chestnut tree in front of our house," I said.

"Does it bear?" She waited. "I ask you, does it bear?"

"Not anymore," I muttered. "It used to, but not anymore."

She gave the nod that was like a nervous twitch. "You see," she said, "Nothing can bear there." Then, secure behind her scorn, she added, "But tell me, what's this snow like that you hear so much about?"

Looking up, I studied her closely, sensing my chance, and then I told her, describing at length and with as much drama as I could summon not only what snow in the city was like, but what it would be like here, in her perennial summer kingdom.

". . . And you see all these trees you got here," I said. "Well, they'd be bare. No leaves, no fruit, nothing. They'd be covered in snow. You see your canes. They'd be buried under tons of snow. The snow would be higher than your head, higher than your house, and you wouldn't be able to come down into this here gully because it would be snowed under. . . ."

She searched my face for the lie, still scornful but intrigued. "What a thing, huh?" she said finally, whispering it softly to herself.

"And when it snows you couldn't dress like you are now," I said. "Oh no, you'd freeze to death. You'd have to wear a hat and gloves and galoshes and ear muffs so your ears wouldn't freeze and drop off, and a heavy coat. I've got a Shirley Temple coat with fur on the collar. I can dance. You wanna see?"

Before she could answer I began, with a dance called the Truck which was popular back then in the 1930's. My right forefinger waving, I trucked around the nearby trees and around Da-duh's awed and rigid form. After the Truck I did the Suzy-Q, my lean hips swishing, my sneakers sidling zigzag over the ground. "I can sing," I said and did so, starting with "I'm Gonna Sit Right Down and Write Myself a Letter," then without pausing, "Tea For Two," and ending with "I Found a Million Dollar Baby in a Five and Ten Cent Store."

For long moments afterwards Da-duh stared at me as if I were a creature from Mars, an emissary from some world she did not know but which intrigued her and whose power she both felt and feared. Yet something about my performance must have pleased her, because bending down she slowly lifted her long skirt and then, one by one, the layers of petticoats until she came to a drawstring purse dangling at the end of a long strip of cloth tied round her waist. Opening the purse she handed me a penny. "Here," she said half-smiling against her will. "Take this to buy yourself a sweet at the shop up the road. There's nothing to be done with you, soul."

From then on, whenever I wasn't taken to visit relatives, I accompanied Da-duh out into the ground, and alone with her amid the canes or down in the gully I told her about New York. It always began with some slighting remark on her part: "I know they don't have anything this nice where you come from," or "Tell me, I hear those foolish people in New York does do such and such. . . ." But as I answered, recreating my towering world of steel and concrete and machines for her, building the city out of words, I would feel her give way. I came to know the signs of her surrender: the total stillness that would come over her little hard dry form, the probing gaze that like a surgeon's knife sought to cut through my skull to get at the images there, to see if I were lying; above all, her fear, a fear nameless and profound, the same one I had felt beating in the palm of her hand that day in the lorry.

Over the weeks I told her about refrigerators, radios, gas stoves, elevators, trolley cars, wringer washing machines, movies, airplanes, the cyclone at Coney Island, subways, toasters, electric lights: "At night, see, all you have to do is flip this little switch on the wall and all the lights in the house go on. Just like that. Like magic. It's like turning on the sun at night."

"But tell me," she said to me once with a faint mocking smile, "do the white people have all these things too or it's only the people looking like us?"

I laughed. "What d'ya mean," I said. "The white people have even better." Then: "I beat up a white girl in my class last term."

"Beating up white people!" Her tone was incredulous.

"How you mean!" I said, using an expression of hers. "She called me a name."

For some reason Da-duh could not quite get over this and repeated in the same hushed, shocked voice, "Beating up white people now! Oh, the lord, the world's changing up so I can scarce recognize it anymore."

One morning toward the end of our stay, Da-duh led me into a part of the gully that we had never visited before, an area darker and more thickly overgrown than the rest, almost impenetrable. There in a small clearing amid the dense bush, she stopped before an incredibly tall royal palm which rose cleanly out of the ground, and drawing the eye up with it, soared high above the trees around it into the sky. It appeared to be touching the blue dome of sky, to be flaunting its dark crown of fronds right in the blinding white face of the late morning sun.

Da-duh watched me a long time before she spoke, and then she said, very quietly, "All right, now, tell me if you've got anything this tall in that place you're from."

I almost wished, seeing her face, that I could have said no. "Yes," I said. "We've got buildings hundreds of times this tall in New York. There's one called the Empire

State Building that's the tallest in the world. My class visited it last year and I went all the way to the top. It's got over a hundred floors. I can't describe how tall it is. Wait a minute. What's the name of that hill I went to visit the other day, where they have the police station?"

"You mean Bissex?"

"Yes, Bissex. Well, the Empire State Building is way taller than that."

"You're lying now!" she shouted, trembling with rage. Her hand lifted to strike me.

"No, I'm not," I said. "It really is, if you don't believe me I'll send you a picture postcard of it soon as I get back home so you can see for yourself. But it's way taller than Bissex."

All the fight went out of her at that. The hand poised to strike me fell limp to her side, and as she stared at me, seeing not me but the building that was taller than the highest hill she knew, the small stubborn light in her eyes (it was the same amber as the flame in the kerosene lamp she lit at dusk) began to fail. Finally, with a vague gesture that even in the midst of her defeat still tried to dismiss me and my world, she turned and started back through the gully, walking slowly, her steps groping and uncertain, as if she were suddenly no longer sure of the way, while I followed triumphant yet strangely saddened behind.

The next morning I found her dressed for our morning walk but stretched out on the Berbice chair in the tiny drawing room where she sometimes napped during the afternoon heat, her face turned to the window beside her. She appeared thinner and suddenly indescribably old.

"My Da-duh," I said.

"Yes, nuh," she said. Her voice was listless and the face she slowly turned my way was, now that I think back on it, like a Benin mask the features drawn and almost distorted by an ancient abstract sorrow.

"Don't you feel well?" I asked.

"Girl, I don't know."

"My Da-duh, I goin' boil you some bush tea," my aunt, Da-duh's youngest child, who lived with her, called from the shed roof kitchen.

"Who tell you I need bush tea?" she cried, her voice assuming for a moment its old authority. "You can't even rest nowadays without some malicious person looking for you to be dead. Come girl," she motioned me to a place beside her on the old-fashioned lounge chair, "give us a tune."

I sang for her until breakfast at eleven, all my brash irreverent Tin Pan Alley songs, and then just before noon we went out into the ground. But it was a short, dispirited walk. Da-duh didn't even notice that the mangoes were beginning to ripen and would have to be picked before the village boys got to them. And when she paused occasionally and looked out across the canes or up at her trees it wasn't as if she were seeing them but something else. Some huge, monolithic shape had imposed itself, it seemed, between her and the land, obstructing her vision. Returning to the house she slept the entire afternoon on the Berbice chair.

She remained like this until we left, languishing away the mornings on the chair at the window gazing out at the land as if it were already doomed; then, at noon, taking the brief stroll with me through the ground during which she seldom spoke, and afterwards returning home to sleep till almost dusk sometimes.

On the day of our departure she put on the austere, ankle length white dress, the black shoes and brown felt hat (her town clothes she called them), but she did not go with us to town. She saw us off on the road outside her house and in the midst of my mother's tearful protracted farewell, she leaned down and whispered in my ear, "Girl, you're not to forget now to send me the picture of that building, you hear."

By the time I mailed her the large colored picture postcard of the Empire State building she was dead. She died during the famous '37 strike which began shortly after we left. On the day of her death England sent planes flying low over the island in a show of force—so low, according to my aunt's letter, that the downdraft from them shook the ripened mangoes from the trees in Da-duh's orchard. Frightened, everyone in the village fled into the canes. Except Da-duh. She remained in the house at the window so my aunt said, watching as the planes came swooping and screaming like monstrous birds down over the village, over her house, rattling her trees and flattening the young canes in her field. It must have seemed to her lying there that they did not intend pulling out of their dive, but like the hardback beetles which hurled themselves with suicidal force against the walls of the house at night, those menacing silver shapes would hurl themselves in an ecstasy of self-immolation onto the land, destroying it utterly.

When the planes finally left and the villagers returned they found her dead on the Berbice chair at the window.

She died and I lived, but always, to this day even, within the shadow of her death. For a brief period after I was grown I went to live alone, like one doing penance, in a loft above a noisy factory in downtown New York and there painted seas of sugar-cane and huge swirling Van Gogh suns and palm trees striding like brightly-plumed Tutsi warriors across a tropical landscape, while the thunderous tread of the machines downstairs jarred the floor beneath my easel, mocking my efforts.

1967

John Okada 1923–1971

Born and raised in Seattle, Washington, John Okada received two B.A. degrees (in English and Library Science) from the University of Washington and an M.A. degree (in English) from Columbia University. He served as a sergeant in the U.S. Air Force during World War II. He died, of a heart attack, in obscurity.

When *No-No Boy* came out in 1957 it received little attention. According to its publisher, Charles Tuttle, even the Japanese American community rejected the book. Perhaps the community did not want to be reminded of the demeaning internment experience with its lingering effects: uncertain identity, fragmented family, split community, hostile society. The novel was rediscovered by a group of Asian American writers in the 1970s.

Since the rediscovery Okada has been acclaimed as one of the greatest Asian American writers, and *No-No Boy* as one of the first Japanese American novels. The book reveals the many wrenching experiences Japanese Americans faced in the wake of Pearl Harbor, after which they were confined in various relocation camps. In 1943 internees were administered a "loyalty questionnaire" containing two unsettling questions: whether or not the internee would be willing to serve in the American armed forces and whether or not the internee would forswear allegiance to Japan. Ichiro, the protagonist of the novel, answered "No-No" and refused the draft. His double negative was understandable and sensible given the circumstances. He was not eager to serve a government that treated him as an enemy by interning him—an American—in an American camp. He could not forswear an allegiance that he had never felt. Other personal considerations also made it difficult for Ichiro to answer affirmatively: his mother was fanatically pro-Japan; his father was arrested for nationality alone. (At the time Japanese immigrants were not allowed to become naturalized American citizens.)

Yet his sensible response was deemed treasonous. For his two "No's," Ichiro was imprisoned for two years. When he is released after the war, he feels guilty, ashamed, and hostile toward his parents. To exacerbate matters, his peers treat him with great disdain: one former friend spits on him; his younger brother—ashamed of Ichiro's decision—arranges to have Ichiro beaten and quits high school to join the army himself.

One exception is Kenji, who remains Ichiro's friend. Kenji himself has fought in the war and won many medals—but lost a leg. The wound continues to fester so that periodically more inches have to be amputated from the stump. He dies after one of the operations. The excerpt (Chapter 6) is about Kenji's last visit to his family before the fatal operation. We feel at once the family's distress at Kenji's physical condition and the acceptance that things could not have been otherwise: the desire to be recognized as an American was so great that no cost seemed too high.

Kenji acts as a foil to Ichiro throughout the novel. Ichiro is despised by his peers; Kenji is idolized. The war breaks Ichiro's family apart; Kenji's is brought closer together. Ichiro undergoes gnawing despair and persistent mental anguish for not joining the war; Kenji receives what is to be a terminal wound and continuous physical pain for having done so. Despite their opposite choices the No-No Boy and the veteran alike suffer intensely.

The novel is not just about these two characters, however. Nor is it confined to the Japanese American predicament. As the excerpt (especially the Club Oriental episode) illustrates, racism creeps into numerous segments of American society; it is not just a matter of whites against Asians or whites against blacks. A group that suffers discrimination from another may in turn inflict racist treatment on a third: Asians discriminated against by whites may, for example, look down on blacks. Discrimination occurs even within one racial group: foreign-born and American-born Japanese may scorn one another. Ichiro's inner conflict reflects the conflict of the country at large. In the course of the novel his individual guilt dissolves in the collective guilt of America.

King-Kok Cheung
University of California–Los Angeles

PRIMARY WORKS

No-No Boy, 1957.

from No-No Boy

Chapter Six

Home for Kenji was an old frame, two-story, seven-room house which the family rented for fifty dollars a month from a Japanese owner who had resettled in Chicago after the war and would probably never return to Seattle. It sat on the top of a steep, unpaved hill and commanded an uninspiring view of clean, gray concrete that was six lanes wide and an assortment of boxy, flat store buildings and spacious super gas-stations.

Kenji eased the car over into the left-turn lane and followed the blinking green arrow toward the hill. At its foot, he braked the car almost to a full stop before carefully starting up, for the sharp angle of the hill and the loose dirt necessitated skill and caution.

As he labored to the top, he saw his father sitting on the porch reading a newspaper. Before he could depress the horn ring, the man looked up and waved casually. He waved back and steered the Oldsmobile into the driveway.

When he walked around the side of the house and came up front, the father said "Hello, Ken" as matter-of-factly as if he had seen his son a few hours previously, and returned his attention to the newspaper to finish the article he had been reading.

"Who's home, Pop?" he asked, holding out the bag.

"Nobody," said the father, taking the present and looking into the bag. It held two fifths of good blended whisky. He was a big man, almost six feet tall and strong. As a painter and paper hanger he had no equal, but he found it sufficient to work only a few days a week and held himself to it, for his children were all grown and he no longer saw the need to drive himself. He smiled warmly and gratefully: "Thank you."

"Sure, Pop. One of these days, I'll bring home a case."

"Last me two days. Better bring a truckful," he said, feigning seriousness.

They laughed together comfortably, the father because he loved his son and the son because he both loved and respected his father, who was a moderate and good man. They walked into the house, the father making the son precede him.

In the dining room the father deposited the two new bottles with a dozen others in the china cabinet. "I'm fixed for a long time," he said. "That's a good feeling."

"You're really getting stocked up," said Kenji.

"The trust and faith and love of my children," he said proudly. "You know I don't need clothes or shaving lotion in fancy jars or suitcases or pajamas, but whisky I can use. I'm happy."

"Are you, Pop?"

The father sat down opposite his son at the polished mahogany table and took in at a glance the new rugs and furniture and lamps and the big television set with the radio and phonograph all built into one impressive, blond console. "All I did was feed you and clothe you and spank you once in a while. All of a sudden, you're all grown up. The government gives you money, Hisa and Toyo are married to fine boys, Hana and Tom have splendid jobs, and Eddie is in college and making more money in a part-time job than I did for all of us when your mother died. No longer do I have to work all the time, but only two or three days a week and I have more money than I can spend. Yes, Ken, I am happy and I wish your mother were here to see all this."

"I'm happy too, Pop." He shifted his legs to make himself comfortable and winced unwillingly.

Noticing, the father screwed his face as if the pain were in himself, for it was. Before the pain turned to sorrow, before the suffering for his son made his lips quiver as he held back the tears, he hastened into the kitchen and came back with two jigger-glasses.

"I am anxious to sample your present," he said jovially, but his movements were hurried as he got the bottle from the cabinet and fumbled impatiently with the seal.

Kenji downed his thankfully and watched his father take the other glass and sniff the whisky appreciatively before sipping it leisurely. He lifted the bottle toward his son.

"No more, Pop," refused Kenji. "That did it fine."

The father capped the bottle and put it back. He closed the cabinet door and let his hand linger on the knob as if ashamed of himself for having tried to be cheerful when he knew that the pain was again in his son and the thought of death hovered over them.

"Pop."

"Yes?" He turned slowly to face his son.

"Come on. Sit down. It'll be all right."

Sitting down, the father shook his head, saying: "I came to America to become a rich man so that I could go back to the village in Japan and be somebody. I was greedy and ambitious and proud. I was not a good man or an intelligent one, but a young fool. And you have paid for it."

"What kind of talk is that?" replied Kenji, genuinely grieved. "That's not true at all."

"That is what I think nevertheless. I am to blame."

"It'll be okay, Pop. Maybe they won't even operate."

"When do you go?"

"Tomorrow morning."

"I will go with you."

"No." He looked straight at his father.

In answer, the father merely nodded, acceding to his son's wish because his son was a man who had gone to war to fight for the abundance and happiness that pervaded a Japanese household in America and that was a thing he himself could never fully comprehend except to know that it was very dear. He had long forgotten when it was that he had discarded the notion of a return to Japan but remembered only that it was the time when this country which he had no intention of loving had suddenly begun to become a part of him because it was a part of his children and he saw and felt it in their speech and joys and sorrows and hopes and he was a part of them. And in the dying of the foolish dreams which he had brought to America, the richness of the life that was possible in this foreign country destroyed the longing for a past that really must not have been as precious as he imagined or else he would surely not have left it. Where else could a man, left alone with six small children, have found it possible to have had so much with so little? He had not begged or borrowed or gone to the city for welfare assistance. There had been times of hunger and despair and seeming hopelessness, but did it not mean something now that he could look around and feel the love of the men and women who were once only children?

And there was the one who sat before him, the one who had come to him and said calmly that he was going into the army. It could not be said then that it mattered not that he was a Japanese son of Japanese parents. It had mattered. It was because he was Japanese that the son had to come to his Japanese father and simply state that he had decided to volunteer for the army instead of being able to wait until such time as the army called him. It was because he was Japanese and, at the same time, had to prove to the world that he was not Japanese that the turmoil was in his soul and urged him to enlist. There was confusion, but, underneath it, a conviction that he loved America and would fight and die for it because he did not wish to live anyplace else. And the father, also confused, understood what the son had not said and gave his consent. It was not a time for clear thinking because the sense of loyalty had become dispersed and the shaken faith of an American interned in an American concentration camp was indeed a flimsy thing. So, on this steadfast bit of conviction that remained, and knowing not what the future held, this son had gone to war to prove that he deserved to enjoy those rights which should rightfully have been his.

And he remembered that a week after Kenji had gone to a camp in Mississippi, the neighbor's son, an American soldier since before Pearl Harbor, had come to see his family which was in a camp enclosed by wire fencing and had guards who were American soldiers like himself. And he had been present when the soldier bitterly spoke of how all he did was dump garbage and wash dishes and take care of the latrines. And the soldier swore and ranted and could hardly make himself speak of the time when the president named Roosevelt had come to the camp in Kansas and all the American soldiers in the camp who were Japanese had been herded into a warehouse and guarded by other American soldiers with machine guns until the president named Roosevelt had departed. And he had gone to his own cubicle with the seven steel cots and the potbellied stove and the canvas picnic-chairs from Sears Roebuck and cried for Kenji, who was now a soldier and would not merely turn bitter and swear if the army let him do only such things as the soldier had spoken of, but would be driven to protest more violently because he was the quiet one with the deep feelings whose anger was a terrible thing. But, with training over, Kenji had written that he was going to Europe, and the next letter was from Italy, where the Americans were fighting the Germans, and he found relief in the knowledge, partly because Kenji was fighting and he knew that was what his son wished and partly because the enemy was German and not Japanese.

He thought he remembered that he had not wanted Kenji to go into the army. But when he was asked, he had said yes. And so this son had come back after long months in a hospital with one good leg and another that was only a stick where the other good one had been. Had he done right? Should he not have forbidden him? Should he not have explained how it was not sensible for Japanese to fight a war against Japanese? If what he had done was wrong, how was it so and why?

"Would you," he said to his son, "have stayed out of the army if I had forbidden it?"

Kenji did not answer immediately, for the question came as a surprise to disturb the long, thought-filled silence. "I don't think so, Pop," he started out hesitantly. He paused, delving into his mind for an explanation, then said with great finality: "No, I would have gone anyway."

"Of course," said the father, finding some assurance in the answer.

Kenji pushed himself to a standing position and spoke gently: "You're not to blame, Pop. Every time we get to talking like this, I know you're blaming yourself. Don't do it. Nobody's to blame, nobody."

"To lose a leg is not the worst thing, but, to lose a part of it and then a little more and a little more again until . . . Well, I don't understand. You don't deserve it." He shrugged his shoulders wearily against the weight of his terrible anguish.

"I'm going up to take a nap." He walked a few steps and turned back to his father. "I'll go upstairs and lie down on the bed and I won't sleep right away because the leg will hurt a little and I'll be thinking. And I'll think that if things had been different, if you had been different, it might have been that I would also not have been the same and maybe you would have kept me from going into the war and I would have stayed out and had both my legs. But, you know, every time I think about it that way, I also have to think that, had such been the case, you and I would probably not be sitting down and having a drink together and talking or not talking as we wished. If my leg hurts, so what? We're buddies, aren't we? That counts. I don't worry about anything else."

Up in his room, he stretched out on his back on the bed and thought about what he had said to his father. It made a lot of sense. If, in the course of things, the pattern called for a stump of a leg that wouldn't stay healed, he wasn't going to decry the fact, for that would mean another pattern with attendant changes which might not be as perfectly desirable as the one he cherished. Things are as they should be, he assured himself, and, feeling greatly at peace, sleep came with surprising ease.

After Kenji had left him, the father walked down the hill to the neighborhood Safeway and bought a large roasting chicken. It was a fat bird with bulging drumsticks and, as he headed back to the house with both arms supporting the ingredients of an ample family feast, he thought of the lean years and the six small ones and the pinched, hungry faces that had been taught not to ask for more but could not be taught how not to look hungry when they were in fact quite hungry. And it was during those years that it seemed as if they would never have enough.

But such a time had come. It had come with the war and the growing of the children and it had come with the return of the thoughtful son whose terrible wound paid no heed to the cessation of hostilities. Yet, the son had said he was happy and the father was happy also for, while one might grieve for the limb that was lost and the pain that endured, he chose to feel gratitude for the fact that the son had come back alive even if only for a brief while.

And he remembered what the young sociologist had said in halting, pained Japanese at one of the family-relations meetings he had attended while interned in the relocation center because it was someplace to go. The instructor was a recent college graduate who had later left the camp to do graduate work at a famous Eastern school. He, short fellow that he was, had stood on an orange crate so that he might be better heard and seen by the sea of elderly men and women who had been attracted to the mess hall because they too had nothing else to do and nowhere else to go. There had been many meetings, although it had early become evident that lecturer and audience were poles apart, and if anything had been accomplished it was that the meetings helped to pass the time, and so the instructor continued to blast away at the unyielding wall of indifference and the old people came to pass an hour or two. But it was on this particular night that the small sociologist, struggling for the words painstakingly and not always correctly selected from his meager knowledge of the Japanese language, had managed to impart a message of great truth. And this message was that the old Japanese, the fathers and mothers, who sat courteously attentive, did not know their own sons and daughters.

"How many of you are able to sit down with your own sons and own daughters and enjoy the companionship of conversation? How many, I ask? If I were to say none of you, I would not be far from the truth." He paused, for the grumbling was swollen with anger and indignation, and continued in a loud, shouting voice before it could engulf him: "You are not displeased because of what I said but because I have hit upon the truth. And I know it to be true because I am a Nisei and you old ones are like my own father and mother. If we are children of America and not the sons and daughters of our parents, it is because you have failed. It is because you have been stupid enough to think that growing rice in muddy fields is the same as growing a giant fir tree. Change, now, if you can, even if it may be too late, and become companions to your children. This is America, where you have lived and worked and suffered for thirty and forty years. This is not Japan. I will tell you what it is like to be an American boy or girl. I will tell you what the relationship between parents and children is in an American family. As I speak, compare what I say with your own families." And so he had spoken and the old people had listened and, when the meeting was over, they got up and scattered over the camp toward their assigned cubicles. Some said they would attend no more lectures; others heaped hateful abuse upon the young fool who dared to have spoken with such disrespect; and then there was the elderly couple, the woman silently following the man, who stopped at another mess hall, where a dance was in progress, and peered into the dimly lit room and watched the young boys and girls gliding effortlessly around to the blaring music from a phonograph. Always before, they had found something to say about the decadent ways of an amoral nation, but, on this evening, they watched longer than usual and searched longingly to recognize their own daughter, whom they knew to be at the dance but who was only an unrecognizable shadow among the other shadows. . . .

Halting for a moment to shift the bag, Kenji's father started up the hill with a smile on his lips. He was glad that the market had had such a fine roasting chicken. There was nothing as satisfying as sitting at a well-laden table with one's family whether the occasion was a holiday or a birthday or a home-coming of some member or, yes, even if it meant someone was going away.

Please come back, Ken, he said to himself, please come back and I will have for you the biggest, fattest chicken that ever graced a table, American or otherwise.

Hanako, who was chubby and pleasant and kept books for three doctors and a dentist in a downtown office, came home before Tom, who was big and husky like his father and had gone straight from high school into a drafting job at an aircraft plant. She had seen the car in the driveway and smelled the chicken in the oven and, smiling sympathetically with the father, put a clean cloth on the table and took out the little chest of Wm. & Rogers Silverplate.

While she was making the salad, Tom came home bearing a bakery pie in a flat, white box. "Hello, Pop, Sis," he said, putting the box on the table. "Where's Ken?"

"Taking a nap," said Hanako.

"Dinner about ready?" He sniffed appreciatively and rubbed his stomach in approval.

"Just about," smiled his sister.

"Psychic, that's what I am."

"What?"

"I say I'm psychic. I brought home a lemon meringue. Chicken and lemon meringue. Boy! Don't you think so?"

"What's that?"

"About my being psychic."

"You're always bringing home lemon meringue. Coincidence, that's all."

"How soon do we eat?"

"I just got through telling you—in a little while," she replied a bit impatiently.

"Good. I'm starved. I'll wash up and rouse the boy." He started to head for the stairs but turned back thoughtfully. "What's the occasion?" he asked.

"Ken has to go to the hospital again," said the father kindly. "Wash yourself at the sink and let him sleep a while longer. We will eat when he wakes up."

"Sure," said Tom, now sharing the unspoken sadness and terror which abided in the hearts of his father and sister. He went to the sink and, clearing it carefully of the pots and dishes, washed himself as quietly as possible.

It was a whole hour before Kenji came thumping down the stairs. It was the right leg, the good one, that made the thumps which followed the empty pauses when the false leg was gently lowered a step. When he saw the family sitting lazily around the table, he knew they had waited for him.

"You shouldn't have waited," he said, a little embarrassed. "I slept longer than I intended."

"We're waiting for the chicken," lied the father. "Takes time to roast a big one."

Hanako agreed too hastily: "Oh, yes, I've never known a chicken to take so long. Ought to be just about ready now." She trotted into the kitchen and, a moment later, shouted back: "It's ready. Mmmm, can you smell it?"

"That's all I've been doing," Tom said with a famished grin. "Let's get it out here."

"Sorry I made you wait," smiled Kenji at his brother.

Tom, regretting his impatience, shook his head vigorously. "No, it's the bird, like Pop said. You know how he is. Always gets 'em big and tough. This one's made of cast iron." He followed Hanako to help bring the food from the kitchen.

No one said much during the first part of the dinner. Tom ate ravenously. Hanako seemed about to say something several times but couldn't bring herself to speak. The father kept looking at Kenji without having to say what it was that he felt for his son. Surprisingly, it was Tom who broached the subject which was on all their minds.

"What the hell's the matter with those damn doctors?" He slammed his fork angrily against the table.

"Tom, please," said Hanako, looking deeply concerned.

"No, no, no," he said, gesturing freely with his hands, "I won't please shut up.

If they can't fix you up, why don't they get somebody who can? They're killing you. What do they do when you go down there? Give you aspirins?" Slumped in his chair, he glared furiously at the table.

The father grasped Tom's arm firmly. "If you can't talk sense, don't."

"It's okay, Tom. This'll be a short trip. I think it's just that the brace doesn't fit right."

"You mean that?" He looked hopefully at Kenji.

"Sure. That's probably what it is. I'll only be gone a few days. Doesn't really hurt so much, but I don't want to take any chances."

"Gee, I hope you're right."

"I ought to know. A few more trips and they'll make me head surgeon down there."

"Yeah," Tom smiled, not because of the joke, but because he was grateful for having a brother like Kenji.

"Eat," reminded the father, "baseball on television tonight, you know."

"I'll get the pie," Hanako said and hastened to the kitchen.

"Lemon meringue," said Tom hungrily, as he proceeded to clean up his plate.

The game was in its second inning when they turned the set on, and they had hardly gotten settled down when Hisa and Toyo came with their husbands and children.

Tom grumbled good naturedly and, giving the newcomers a hasty nod, pulled up closer to the set, preparing to watch the game under what would obviously be difficult conditions.

Hats and coats were shed and piled in the corner and everyone talked loudly and excitedly, as if they had not seen each other for a long time. Chairs were brought in from the dining room and, suddenly, the place was full and noisy and crowded and comfortable.

The father gave up trying to follow the game and bounced a year-old granddaughter on his knee while two young grandsons fought to conquer the other knee. The remaining three grandchildren were all girls, older, more well-behaved, and they huddled on the floor around Tom to watch the baseball game.

Hisa's husband sat beside Kenji and engaged him in conversation, mostly about fishing and about how he'd like to win a car in the Salmon Derby because his was getting old and a coupe wasn't too practical for a big family. He had the four girls and probably wouldn't stop until he hit a boy and things weren't so bad, but he couldn't see his way to acquiring a near-new used car for a while. And then he got up and went to tell the same thing to his father-in-law, who was something of a fisherman himself. No sooner had he moved across the room than Toyo's husband, who was soft-spoken and mild but had been a captain in the army and sold enough insurance to keep two cars in the double garage behind a large brick house in a pretty good neighborhood, slid into the empty space beside Kenji and asked him how he'd been and so on and talked about a lot of other things when he really wanted to talk to Kenji about the leg and didn't know how.

Then came the first lull when talk died down and the younger children were showing signs of drowsiness and everyone smiled thoughtfully and contentedly at one another. Hanako suggested refreshments, and when the coffee and milk and pop and cookies and ice cream were distributed, everyone got his second wind and immediately discovered a number of things which they had forgotten to discuss.

Kenji, for the moment alone, looked at all of them and said to himself: Now's as good a time as any to go. I won't wait until tomorrow. In another thirty minutes Hana and Toyo and the kids and their fathers will start stretching and heading for their hats and coats. Then someone will say "Well, Ken" in a kind of hesitant way and, immediately, they will all be struggling for something to say about my going to Portland because Hana called them and told them to come over because I'm going down there again and that's why they'll have to say something about it. If I had said to Pop that I was going the day after tomorrow, we would have had a big feast with everyone here for it tomorrow night. I don't want that. There's no need for it. I don't want Toyo to cry and Hana to dab at her eyes and I don't want everyone standing around trying to say goodbye and not being able to make themselves leave because maybe they won't see me again.

He started to get up and saw Hanako looking at him. "I'm just going to get a drink," he said.

"Stay, I'll get it," she replied.

"No. It'll give me a chance to stretch." He caught his father's eye and held it for a moment.

Without getting his drink, he slipped quietly out to the back porch and stood and waited and listened to the voices inside.

He heard Hisa's husband yell something to one of his girls and, the next minute, everyone was laughing amusedly. While he was wondering what cute deviltry the guilty one had done, his father came through the kitchen and out to stand beside him.

"You are going."

Kenji looked up and saw the big shoulders sagging wearily. "I got a good rest, Pop. This way, I'll be there in the morning and it's easier driving at night. Not so many cars, you know."

"It's pretty bad this time, isn't it?"

"Yes," he said truthfully, because he could not lie to his father, "it's not like before, Pop. It's different this time. The pain is heavier, deeper. Not sharp and raw like the other times. I don't know why. I'm scared."

"If . . . if . . ." Throwing his arm around his son's neck impulsively, the father hugged him close. "You call me every day. Every day, you understand?"

"Sure, Pop. Explain to everyone, will you?" He pulled himself free and looked at his father nodding, unable to speak.

Pausing halfway down the stairs, he listened once more for the voices in the house.

Hoarsely, in choked syllables, his father spoke to him: "Every day, Ken, don't forget. I will be home."

"Bye, Pop." Feeling his way along the dark drive with his cane, he limped to the car. Behind the wheel, he had to sit and wait until the heaviness had lifted from his chest and relieved the mistiness of his eyes. He started the motor and turned on the headlights and their brilliant glare caught fully the father standing ahead. Urged by an overwhelming desire to rush back to him and be with him for a few minutes longer, Kenji's hand fumbled for the door handle. At that moment, the father raised his arm once slowly in farewell. Quickly, he pulled back out of the driveway and was soon out of sight of father and home and family.

He fully intended to drive directly to the grocery store to get Ichiro, but found himself drawn to the Club Oriental. Parking in the vacant lot where only the previous night Ichiro had experienced his humiliation, he limped through the dark alley to the club.

It was only a little after ten, but the bar and tables were crowded. Ignoring several invitations to sit at tables of acquaintances, he threaded his way to the end of the bar and had only to wait a moment before Al saw him and brought the usual bourbon and water.

Not until he was on his third leisurely drink did he manage to secure a stool. It was between strangers, and for that he was grateful. He didn't want to talk or be talked to. Through the vast mirror ahead, he studied the faces alongside and behind him. By craning a bit, he could even catch an occasional glimpse of couples on the dance floor.

It's a nice place, he thought. When a fellow goes away, he likes to take something along to remember and this is what I'm taking. It's not like having a million bucks and sitting in the Waldorf with a long-stemmed beauty, but I'm a small guy with small wants and this is my Waldorf. Here, as long as I've got the price of a drink, I can sit all night and be among friends. I can relax and drink and feel sad or happy or high and nobody much gives a damn, since they feel the same way. It's a good feeling, a fine feeling.

He followed Al around with his eyes until the bartender looked back at him and returned the smile.

The help knows me and likes me.

Swinging around on the stool, he surveyed the crowd and acknowledged a number of greetings and nods.

I've got a lot of friends here and they know and like me.

Jim Eng, the slender, dapper Chinese who ran the place, came out of the office with a bagful of change and brought it behind the bar to check the register. As he did so, he grinned at Kenji and inquired about his leg.

Even the management's on my side. It's like a home away from home only more precious because one expects home to be like that. Not many places a Jap can go to and feel so completely at ease. It must be nice to be white and American and to be able to feel like this no matter where one goes to, but I won't cry about that. There's been a war and, suddenly, things are better for the Japs and the Chinks and—

There was a commotion at the entrance and Jim Eng slammed the cash drawer shut and raced toward the loud voices. He spoke briefly to someone in the office, probably to find out the cause of the disturbance, and then stepped outside. As he did so, Kenji caught sight of three youths, a Japanese and two Negroes.

After what sounded like considerable loud and excited shouting, Jim Eng stormed back in and resumed his task at the register though with hands shaking.

When he had calmed down a little, someone inquired: "What's the trouble?"

"No trouble," he said in a high-pitched voice which he was endeavoring to keep steady. "That crazy Jap boy Floyd tried to get in with two niggers. That's the second time he tried that. What's the matter with him?"

A Japanese beside Kenji shouted out sneeringly: "Them ignorant cotton pickers make me sick. You let one in and before you know it, the place will be black as night."

"Sure," said Jim Eng, "sure. I got no use for them. Nothing but trouble they make and I run a clean place."

"Hail Columbia," said a small, drunken voice.

"Oh, you Japs and Chinks, I love you all," rasped out a brash redhead who looked as if she had come directly from one of the burlesque houses without changing her make-up. She struggled to her feet, obviously intending to launch into further oratory.

Her escort, a pale, lanky Japanese screamed "Shut up!" and, at the same time, pulled viciously at her arm, causing her to tumble comically into the chair.

Everyone laughed, or so it seemed, and quiet and decency and cleanliness and honesty returned to the Club Oriental.

Leaving his drink unfinished, Kenji left the club without returning any of the farewells which were directed at him.

He drove aimlessly, torturing himself repeatedly with the question which plagued his mind and confused it to the point of madness. Was there no answer to the bigotry and meanness and smallness and ugliness of people? One hears the voice of the Negro or Japanese or Chinese or Jew, a clear and bell-like intonation of the common struggle for recognition as a complete human being and there is a sense of unity and purpose which inspires one to hope and optimism. One encounters obstacles, but the wedge of the persecuted is not without patience and intelligence and humility, and the opposition weakens and wavers and disperses. And the one who is the Negro or Japanese or Chinese or Jew is further fortified and gladdened with the knowledge that the democracy is a democracy in fact for all of them. One has hope, for he has reason to hope, and the quest for completeness seems to be a thing near at hand, and then . . .

the woman with the dark hair and large nose who has barely learned to speak English makes a big show of vacating her bus seat when a Negro occupies the other half. She stamps indignantly down the aisle, hastening away from the contamination which is only in her contaminated mind. The Negro stares silently out of the window, a proud calmness on his face, which hides the boiling fury that is capable of murder.

and then . . .

a sweet-looking Chinese girl is at a high-school prom with a white boy. She has risen in the world, or so she thinks, for it is evident in her expression and manner. She does not entirely ignore the other Chinese and Japanese at the dance, which would at least be honest, but worse, she flaunts her newly found status in their faces with haughty smiles and overly polite phrases.

and then . . .

there is the small Italian restaurant underneath a pool parlor, where the spaghetti and chicken is hard to beat. The Japanese, who feels he is better than the Chinese because his parents made him so, comes into the restaurant with a Jewish companion, who is a good Jew and young and American and not like the kike bastards from the countries from which they've been kicked out, and waits patiently for the waiter. None of the waiters come, although the place is quite empty and two of them are talking not ten feet away. All his efforts to attract them failing, he stalks toward them. The two, who are supposed to wait on the tables but do not, scurry into the kitchen. In a moment they return with the cook, who is also the owner, and he tells the Japanese that the place is not for Japs and to get out and go back to Tokyo.

and then . . .

the Negro who was always being mistaken for a white man becomes a white man and he becomes hated by the Negroes with whom he once hated on the same side. And the young Japanese hates the not-so-young Japanese who is more Japanese than himself, and the not-so-young, in turn, hates the old Japanese who is all Japanese and, therefore, even more Japanese than he . . .

1957

Tillie Lerner Olsen b. 1913

Tillie Olsen's parents, Samuel and Ida Lerner, took part in the 1905 revolution in Russia, fleeing to the United States when it failed. Her father worked at a variety of jobs, from farming to packinghouse work, eventually becoming state secretary of the Nebraska Socialist Party. The young Tillie Lerner read avidly in her public library, becoming conversant with American and world literature. Forced to leave school after the eleventh grade to go to work, she pressed ties, trimmed meat in the packing houses, and acted as a domestic and a waitress. She also became an activist in the Young Communist League, going to jail in Kansas City after attempting to organize packinghouse workers. At nineteen she began work on the novel that many years later would become *Yonnondio: From the Thirties;* in the same year, she bore her first child, a daughter. In the early thirties, she moved to northern California, continuing to write and to do political work. She combined the two in such reportage as "The Strike," an essay about the great general strike that spread up and down the Coast from San Francisco in 1934.

In 1936, Tillie Lerner became involved with her YCL companion Jack Olsen, whom she eventually married. In the years that followed, she bore three more children, struggling to combine mothering with work out of the home to help support her growing family. During the 1950s, she and her family, like so many progressives of the thirties and forties, were harassed destructively by the FBI. Yet in the fifties too Olsen began writing again: "I Stand Here Ironing," "Hey Sailor, What Ship?" and "O Yes," written in the mid-fifties, followed by "Tell Me a Riddle," which won the O. Henry Award in 1961 for best short story of the year. These stories, originally conceived as part of a novel about three generations of a Russian Jewish family, celebrate the stubborn endurance of human love and of the passion for justice, in spite of the injuries inflicted by poverty, racism, and the patriarchal order.

The same theme informs *Yonnondio: From the Thirties,* a novel revised and published forty years after its inception by the "older writer in arduous partnership with that long ago younger one." The story of the Holbrook family's efforts to survive on the farms and in the packing houses of the Midwest in the twenties, the novel creates in Mazie Holbrook and in her mother Anna a figure who reappears throughout Olsen's work, fiction and criticism alike: the potential female artist/activist silenced by poverty, by the willingly assumed burdens of caring for loved others, by the expectations associated with her sex. *Silences,* Olsen's collected critical essays, continues this theme. The book is a sustained prose poem about all the forms of silencing that befall writers—especially, though not exclusively, women; especially, though not exclusively, those who must struggle for sheer survival.

The novella "Tell Me a Riddle" distills

all these themes in its evocation of the dying grandmother who was once an orator in the 1905 Revolution. Its structure, in its gradual revelation of the past, forces its readers to question the present and finally to acknowledge like David the discrepancy between what is and what should be.

Concerned with the "circumstances" of class, race, and gender as the soil which nurtures or impedes human achievement, Olsen's work constitutes a vitally important link between the radical movements of the thirties and the culture, ideas, and literature of the women's liberation movement. Her fiction and essays, finely crafted and emotionally powerful, make an important contribution to American literature, an achievement acknowledged in Olsen's receipt of many prestigious awards and four honorary doctorates. She has contributed to what she calls "the larger tradition of social concern" not only as a writer but also as a scholar and teacher. Her efforts have helped to reclaim many "lost" women writers and to initiate the democratization of the literary canon reflected in the contours of this anthology.

Deborah S. Rosenfelt
University of Maryland at College Park

PRIMARY WORKS

Tell Me a Riddle, 1961; "Requa—I" in *Best American Short Stories,* 1971; *Yonnondio: From the Thirties,* 1974; *Silences,* 1978; *Mother to Daughter, Daughter to Mother: A Daybook and Reader,* editor, 1984; "Dream-Vision," 1984; Comments and Excerpts from Manuscripts in *First Drafts, Last Drafts: Forty Years of the Creative Writing Program at Stanford,* 1989.

Tell Me a Riddle

"These Things Shall Be"[1]

1

For forty-seven years they had been married. How deep back the stubborn, gnarled roots of the quarrel reached, no one could say—but only now, when tending to the needs of others no longer shackled them together, the roots swelled up visible, split the earth between them, and the tearing shook even to the children, long since grown.

Why now, why now? wailed Hannah.

As if when we grew up weren't enough, said Paul.

Poor Ma. Poor Dad. It hurts so for both of them, said Vivi. They never had very much; at least in old age they should be happy.

Knock their heads together, insisted Sammy; tell 'em: you're too old for this kind of thing; no reason not to get along now.

Lennie wrote to Clara: They've lived over so much together; what could possibly tear them apart?

[1]Hymn by John Addington Symonds, British poet, sung in the British labor movement and in progressive circles in the United States, including the Unitarian Church.

* * *

Something tangible enough.

Arthritic hands, and such work as he got, occasional. Poverty all his life, and there was little breath left for running. He could not, could not turn away from this desire: to have the troubling of responsibility, the fretting with money, over and done with; to be free, to be *care*free where success was not measured by accumulation, and there was use for the vitality still in him.

There was a way. They could sell the house, and with the money join his lodge's Haven, cooperative for the aged. Happy communal life, and was he not already an official; had he not helped organize it, raise funds, served as a trustee?

But she—would not consider it.

"What do we need all this for?" he would ask loudly, for her hearing aid was turned down and the vacuum was shrilling. "Five rooms" (pushing the sofa so she could get into the corner) "furniture" (smoothing down the rug) "floors and surfaces to make work. Tell me, why do we need it?" And he was glad he could ask in a scream.

"Because I'm use't."

"Because you're use't. This is a reason, Mrs. Word Miser? Used to can get unused!"

"Enough unused I have to get used to already. . . . Not enough words?" turning off the vacuum a moment to hear herself answer. "Because soon enough we'll need only a little closet, no windows, no furniture, nothing to make work, but for worms. Because now I want room. . . . Screech and blow like you're doing, you'll need that closet even sooner. . . . Ha, again!" for the vacuum bag wailed, puffed half up, hung stubbornly limp. "This time fix it so it stays; quick before the phone rings and you get too important-busy."

But while he struggled with the motor, it seethed in him. Why fix it? Why have to bother? And if it can't be fixed, have to wring the mind with how to pay the repair? At the Haven they come in with their own machines to clean your room or your cottage; you fish, or play cards, or make jokes in the sun, not with knotty fingers fight to mend vacuums.

Over the dishes, coaxingly: "For once in your life, to be free, to have everything done for you, like a queen."

"I never liked queens."

"No dishes, no garbage, no towel to sop, no worry what to buy, what to eat."

"And what else would I do with my empty hands? Better to eat at my own table when I want, and to cook and eat how I want."

"In the cottages they buy what you ask, and cook it how you like. *You* are the one who always used to say: better mankind born without mouths and stomachs than always to worry for money to buy, to shop, to fix, to cook, to wash, to clean."

"How cleverly you hid that you heard. I said it then because eighteen hours a day I ran. And you never scraped a carrot or knew a dish towel sops. Now—for you and me—who cares? A herring out of a jar is enough. But when *I* want, and nobody to bother." And she turned off her ear button, so she would not have to hear.

But as *he* had no peace, juggling and rejuggling the money to figure: how will I pay for this now?; prying out the storm windows (there they take care of this); jolting in the streetcar on errands (there I would not have to ride to take care of this or that); fending the patronizing relatives just back from Florida (at the Haven it matters what one is, not what one can afford), he gave *her* no peace.

"Look! In their bulletin. A reading circle. Twice a week it meets."

"Haumm," her answer of not listening.

"A reading circle. Chekhov they read that you like, and Peretz.[2] Cultured people at the Haven that you would enjoy."

"Enjoy!" She tasted the word. "Now, when it pleases you, you find a reading circle for me. And forty years ago when the children were morsels and there was a Circle, did you stay home with them once so I could go? Even once? You trained me well. I do not need others to enjoy. Others!" Her voice trembled. "Because *you* want to be there with others. Already it makes me sick to think of you always around others. Clown, grimacer, floormat, yesman, entertainer, whatever they want of you."

And now it was he who turned on the television loud so he need not hear.

Old scar tissue ruptured and the wounds festered anew. Chekhov indeed. She thought without softness of that young wife, who in the deep night hours while she nursed the current baby, and perhaps held another in her lap, would try to stay awake for the only time there was to read. She would feel again the weather of the outside on his cheek when, coming late from a meeting, he would find her so, and stimulated and ardent, sniffing her skin, coax: "I'll put the baby to bed, and you—put the book away, don't read, don't read."

That had been the most beguiling of all the "don't read, put your book away" her life had been. Chekhov indeed!

"Money?" She shrugged him off. "Could we get poorer than once we were? And in America, who starves?"

But as still he pressed:

"Let me alone about money. Was there ever enough? Seven little ones—for every penny I had to ask—and sometimes, remember, there was nothing. But always *I* had to manage. Now *you* manage. Rub your nose in it good."

But from those years she had had to manage, old humiliations and terrors rose up, lived again, and forced her to relive them. The children's needings; that grocer's face or this merchant's wife she had had to beg credit from when credit was a disgrace; the scenery of the long blocks walked around when she could not pay; school coming, and the desperate going over the old to see what could yet be remade; the soups of meat bones begged "for-the-dog" one winter. . . .

Enough. Now they had no children. Let *him* wrack his head for how they would live. She would not exchange her solitude for anything. *Never again to be forced to move to the rhythms of others.*

For in this solitude she had won to a reconciled peace.

Tranquillity from having the empty house no longer an enemy, for it stayed clean—not as in the days when it was her family, the life in it, that had seemed the enemy: tracking, smudging, littering, dirtying, engaging her in endless defeating battle—and on whom her endless defeat had been spewed.

The few old books, memorized from rereading; the pictures to ponder (the magnifying glass superimposed on her heavy eyeglasses). Or if she wishes, when he is gone, the phonograph, that if she turns up very loud and strains, she can hear: the ordered sounds and the struggling.

[2]Anton Pavlovich Chekhov, nineteenth-century Russian writer, and Isaac Loeb Peretz, turn-of-the-century Russian writer of short fiction in Yiddish.

Out in the garden, growing things to nurture. Birds to be kept out of the pear tree, and when the pears are heavy and ripe, the old fury of work, for all must be canned, nothing wasted.

And her one social duty (for she will not go to luncheons or meetings) the boxes of old clothes left with her, as with a life-practised eye for finding what is still wearable within the worn (again the magnifying glass superimposed on the heavy glasses) she scans and sorts—this for rag or rummage, that for mending and cleaning, and this for sending away.

Being able at last to live within, and not move to the rhythms of others, as life had forced her to: denying; removing; isolating; taking the children one by one; then deafening, half-blinding—and at last, presenting her solitude.

And in it she had won to a reconciled peace.

Now he was violating it with his constant campaigning: *Sell the house and move to the Haven.* (You sit, you sit—there too you could sit like a stone.) He was making of her a battleground where old grievances tore. (Turn on your ear button—I am talking.) And stubbornly she resisted—so that from wheedling, reasoning manipulation, it was bitterness he now started with.

And it came to where every happening lashed up a quarrel.

"I will sell the house anyway," he flung at her one night. "I am putting it up for sale. There will be a way to make you sign."

The television blared, as always it did on the evenings he stayed home, and as always it reached her only as noise. She did not know if the tumult was in her or outside. Snap! she turned the sound off. "Shadows," she whispered to him, pointing to the screen, "look, it is only shadows." And in a scream: "Did you say that you will sell the house? Look at me, not at that. I am no shadow. You cannot sell without me."

"Leave on the television. I am watching."

"Like Paulie, like Jenny, a four-year-old. Staring at shadows. *You cannot sell the house.*"

"I will. We are going to the Haven. There you would not hear the television when you do not want it. I could sit in the social room and watch. You could lock yourself up to smell your unpleasantness in a room by yourself—for who would want to come near you?"

"No, no selling." A whisper now.

"The television is shadows. Mrs. Enlightened! Mrs. Cultured! A world comes into your house—and it is shadows. People you would never meet in a thousand lifetimes. Wonders. When you were four years old, yes, like Paulie, like Jenny, did you know of Indian dances, alligators, how they use bamboo in Malaya? No, you scratched in your dirt with the chickens and thought Olshana[3] was the world. Yes, Mrs. Unpleasant, I will sell the house, for there better can we be rid of each other than here."

She did not know if the tumult was outside, or in her. Always a ravening inside, a pull to the bed, to lie down, to succumb.

"Have you thought maybe Ma should let a doctor have a look at her?" asked their son Paul after Sunday dinner, regarding his mother crumpled on the couch, instead of, as was her custom, busying herself in Nancy's kitchen.

[3]Olsen's invented name for a typical village of Czarist Russia.

"Why not the President too?"

"Seriously, Dad. This is the third Sunday she's laid down like that after dinner. Is she that way at home?"

"A regular love affair with the bed. Every time I start to talk to her."

Good protective reaction, observed Nancy to herself. The workings of hos-til-ity.

"Nancy could take her. I just don't like how she looks. Let's have Nancy arrange an appointment."

"You think she'll go?" regarding his wife gloomily. "All right, we have to have doctor bills, we have to have doctor bills." Loudly: "Something hurts you?"

She startled, looked to his lips. He repeated: "Mrs. Take It Easy, something hurts?"

"Nothing. . . . Only you."

"A woman of honey. That's why you're lying down?"

"Soon I'll get up to do the dishes, Nancy."

"Leave them, Mother, I like it better this way."

"Mrs. Take It Easy, Paul says you should start ballet. You should go to see a doctor and ask: how soon can you start ballet?"

"A doctor?" she begged. "Ballet?"

"We were talking, ma," explained Paul, "you don't seem any too well. It would be a good idea for you to see a doctor for a checkup."

"I get up now to do the kitchen. Doctors are bills and foolishness, my son. I need no doctors."

"At the Haven," he could not resist pointing out, "a doctor is *not* bills. He lives beside you. You start to sneeze, he is there before you open up a Kleenex. You can be sick there for free, all you want."

"Diarrhea of the mouth, is there a doctor to make you dumb?"

"Ma. Promise me you'll go. Nancy will arrange it."

"It's all of a piece when you think of it," said Nancy, "the way she attacks my kitchen, scrubbing under every cup hook, doing the inside of the oven so I can't enjoy Sunday dinner, knowing that half-blind or not, she's going to find every speck of dirt. . . ."

"Don't, Nancy, I've told you—it's the only way she knows to be useful. What did the *doctor* say?"

"A real fatherly lecture. Sixty-nine is young these days. Go out, enjoy life, find interests. Get a new hearing aid, this one is antiquated. Old age is sickness only if one makes it so. Geriatrics, Inc."

"So there was nothing physical."

"Of course there was. How can you live to yourself like she does without there being? Evidence of a kidney disorder, and her blood count is low. He gave her a diet, and she's to come back for follow-up and lab work. . . . But he was clear enough: Number One prescription—start living like a human being. . . . When I think of your dad, who could really play the invalid with that arthritis of his, as active as a teenager, and twice as much fun. . . ."

"You didn't tell me the doctors says your sickness is in you, how you live." He pushed his advantage. "Life and enjoyments you need better than medicine. And this diet, how can you keep it? To weigh each morsel and scrape away each bit of fat, to make this soup, that pudding. There, at the Haven, they have a dietician, they would do it for you."

She is silent.

"You would feel better there, I know it," he says gently. "There there is life and enjoyments all around."

"What is the matter, Mr. Importantbusy, you have no card game or meeting you can go to?"—turning her face to the pillow.

For a while he cut his meetings and going out, fussed over her diet, tried to wheedle her into leaving the house, brought in visitors:

"I should come to a fashion tea. I should sit and look at pretty babies in clothes I cannot buy. This is pleasure?"

"Always you are better than everyone else. The doctor said you should go out. Mrs. Brem comes to you with goodness and you turn her away."

"Because *you* asked her to, she asked me."

"They won't come back. People you need, the doctor said. Your own cousins I asked; they were willing to come and make peace as if nothing had happened. . . ."

"No more crushers of people, pushers, hypocrites, around me. No more in *my* house. You go to them if you like."

"Kind he is to visit. And you, like ice."

"A babbler. All my life around babblers. Enough!"

"She's even worse, Dad? Then let her stew a while," advised Nancy. "You can't let it destroy you; it's a psychological thing, maybe too far gone for any of us to help."

So he let her stew. More and more she lay silent in bed, and sometimes did not even get up to make the meals. No longer was the tongue-lashing inevitable if he left the coffee cup where it did not belong, or forgot to take out the garbage or mislaid the broom. The birds grew bold that summer and for once pocked the pears, undisturbed.

A bellyful of bitterness and every day the same quarrel in a new way and a different old grievance the quarrel forced her to enter and relive. And the new torment: I am not really sick, the doctor said it, then why do I feel so sick?

One night she asked him: "You have a meeting tonight? Do not go. Stay . . . with me."

He had planned to watch "This Is Your Life," but half sick himself from the heavy heat, and sickening therefore the more after the brooks and woods of the Haven, with satisfaction he grated:

"Hah, Mrs. Live Alone And Like It wants company all of a sudden. It doesn't seem so good the time of solitary when she was a girl exile in Siberia.[4] 'Do not go. Stay with me.' A new song for Mrs. Free As A Bird. Yes, I am going out, and while I am gone chew this aloneness good, and think how you keep us both from where if you want people, you do not need to be alone."

[4]Political and other prisoners were exiled to Siberia by the Czarist regime.

"Go, go. All your life you have gone without me."

After him she sobbed curses he had not heard in years, old-country curses from their childhood: Grow, oh shall you grow like an onion, with your head in the ground. Like the hide of a drum shall you be, beaten in life, beaten in death. Oh shall you be like a chandelier, to hang, and to burn. . . .

She was not in their bed when he came back. She lay on the cot on the sun porch. All week she did not speak or come near him; nor did he try to make peace or care for her.

He slept badly, so used to her next to him. After all the years, old harmonies and dependencies deep in their bodies; she curled to him, or he coiled to her, each warmed, warming, turning as the other turned, the nights a long embrace.

It was not the empty bed or the storm that woke him, but a faint singing. *She* was singing. Shaking off the drops of rain, the lightning riving her lifted face, he saw her so; the cot covers on the floor.

"This is a private concert?" he asked. "Come in, you are wet."

"I can breathe now," she answered; "my lungs are rich." Though indeed the sound was hardly a breath.

"Come in, come in." Loosing the bamboo shades. "Look how wet you are." Half helping, half carrying her, still faint-breathing her song.

A Russian love song of fifty years ago.

He had found a buyer, but before he told her, he called together those children who were close enough to come. Paul, of course, Sammy from New Jersey, Hannah from Connecticut, Vivi from Ohio.

With a kindling of energy for her beloved visitors, she arrayed the house, cooked and baked. She was not prepared for the solemn after-dinner conclave, they too probing in and tearing. Her frightened eyes watched from mouth to mouth as each spoke.

His stories were eloquent and funny of her refusal to go back to the doctor; of the scorned invitations; of her stubborn silence or the bile "like a Niagara"; of her contrariness: "If I clean it's no good how I cleaned; if I don't clean, I'm still a master who thinks he has a slave."

(Vinegar he poured on me all his life; I am well marinated; how can I be honey now?)

Deftly he marched in the rightness for moving to the Haven; their money from social security free for visiting the children, not sucked into daily needs and into the house; the activities in the Haven for him; but mostly the Haven for *her:* her health, her need of care, distraction, amusement, friends who shared her interests.

"This does offer an outlet for Dad," said Paul; "he's always been an active person. And economic peace of mind isn't to be sneezed at, either. I could use a little of that myself."

But when they asked: "And you, Ma, how do you feel about it?" could only whisper:

"For him it is good. It is not for me. I can no longer live between people."

"You lived all your life *for* people," Vivi cried.

"Not with." Suffering doubly for the unhappiness on her children's faces.

"You have to find some compromise," Sammy insisted. "Maybe sell the house and buy a trailer. After forty-seven years there's surely some way you can find to live in peace."

"There is no help, my children. Different things we need."

"Then live alone!" He could control himself no longer. "I have a buyer for the house. Half the money for you, half for me. Either alone or with me to the Haven. You think I can live any longer as we are doing now?"

"Ma doesn't have to make a decision this minute, however you feel, Dad," Paul said quickly, "and you wouldn't want her to. Let's let it lay a few months, and then talk some more."

"I think I can work it out to take Mother home with me for a while," Hannah said. "You both look terrible, but especially you, Mother. I'm going to ask Phil to have a look at you."

"Sure," cracked Sammy. "What's the use of a doctor husband if you can't get free service out of him once in a while for the family? And absence might make the heart . . . you know."

"There was something after all," Paul told Nancy in a colorless voice. "That was Hannah's Phil calling. Her gall bladder. . . . Surgery."

"Her *gall* bladder. If that isn't classic. 'Bitter as gall'—talk of psychosom——"

He stepped closer, put his hand over her mouth, and said in the same colorless, plodding voice. "We have to get Dad. They operated at once. The cancer was everywhere, surrounding the liver, everywhere. They did what they could . . . at best she has a year. Dad . . . we have to tell him."

2

Honest in his weakness when they told him, and that she was not to know. "I'm not an actor. She'll know right away by how I am. Oh that poor woman. I am old too, it will break me into pieces. Oh that poor woman. She will spit on me: 'So my sickness was how I live.' Oh Paulie, how she will be, that poor woman. Only she should not suffer. . . . I can't stand sickness, Paulie, I can't go with you."

But went. And play-acted.

"A grand opening and you did not even wait for me. . . . A good thing Hannah took you with her."

"Fashion teas I needed. They cut out what tore in me; just in my throat something hurts yet. . . . Look! so many flowers, like a funeral. Vivi called, did Hannah tell you? And Lennie from San Francisco, and Clara; and Sammy is coming." Her gnome's face pressed happily into the flowers.

It is impossible to predict in these cases, but once over the immediate effects of the operation, she should have several months of comparative well-being.

The money, where will come the money?

Travel with her, Dad. Don't take her home to the old associations. The other children will want to see her.

The money, where will I wring the money?

Whatever happens, she is not to know. No, you can't ask her to sign papers to sell the house; nothing to upset her. Borrow instead, then after. . . .

I had wanted to leave you each a few dollars to make life easier, as other fathers do. There will be nothing left now. (Failure! you and your "business is exploitation." Why didn't you make it when it could be made?—Is that what you're thinking of me, Sammy?)

Sure she's unreasonable, Dad—but you have to stay with her; if there's to be any happiness in what's left of her life, it depends on you.

Prop me up, children, think of me, too. Shuffled, chained with her, bitter woman. No Haven, and the little money going. . . . How happy she looks, poor creature.

The look of excitement. The straining to hear everything (the new hearing aid turned full). Why are you so happy, dying woman?

How the petals are, fold on fold, and the gladioli color. The autumn air.

Stranger grandsons, tall above the little gnome grandmother, the little spry grandfather. Paul in a frenzy of picture-talking before going.

She, wandering the great house. Feeling the books; laughing at the maple shoemaker's bench of a hundred years ago used as a table. The ear turned to music.

"Let us go home. See how good I walk now." "One step from the hospital," he answers, "and she wants to fly. Wait till Doctor Phil says."

"Look—the birds too are flying home. Very good Phil is and will not show it, but he is sick of sickness by the time he comes home."

"Mrs. Telepathy, to read minds," he answers; "read mine what it says: when the trunks of medicines become a suitcase, then we will go."

The grandboys, they do not know what to say to us. . . . Hannah, she runs around here, there, when is there time for herself?

Let us go home. Let us go home.

Musing; gentleness—*but for the incidents of the rabbi in the hospital, and of the candles of benediction.*

Of the rabbi in the hospital:

Now tell me what happened, Mother.

From the sleep I awoke, Hannah's Phil, and he stands there like a devil in a dream and calls me by name. I cannot hear. I think he prays. Go away, please, I tell him, I am not a believer. Still he stands, while my heart knocks with fright.

You scared *him,* Mother. He thought you were delirious.

Who sent him? Why did he come to me?

It is a custom. The men of God come to visit those of their religion they might help. The hospital makes up the list for them—race, religion—and you are on the Jewish list.

Not for rabbis. At once go and make them change. Tell them to write: Race, human; Religion, none.

And of the candles of benediction[5]:

[5]The lighting of the candles on Friday night initiates the traditional Jewish Sabbath.

Look how you have upset yourself, Mrs. Excited Over Nothing. Pleasant memories you should leave.

Go in, go back to Hannah and the lights. Two weeks I saw candles and said nothing. But she asked me.

So what was so terrible? She forgets you never did, she asks you to light the Friday candles and say the benediction like Phil's mother when she visits. If the candles give her pleasure, why shouldn't she have the pleasure?

Not for pleasure she does it. For emptiness. Because his family does. Because all around her do.

That is not a good reason too? But you did not hear her. For heritage, she told you. For the boys, from the past they should have tradition.

Superstition! From our ancestors, savages, afraid of the dark, of themselves: mumbo words and magic lights to scare away ghosts.

She told you: how it started does not take away the goodness. For centuries, peace in the house it means.

Swindler! does she look back on the dark centuries? Candles bought instead of bread and stuck into a potato for a candlestick? Religion that stifled and said: in Paradise, woman, you will be the footstool of your husband, and in life—poor chosen Jew—ground under, despised, trembling in cellars. And cremated. And cremated.[6]

This is religion's fault? You think you are still an orator of the 1905 revolution?[7] Where are the pills for quieting? Which are they?

Heritage. How have we come from our savage past, how no longer to be savages—this to teach. To look back and learn what humanizes—this to teach. To smash all ghettos that divide us—not to go back, not to go back—this to teach. Learned books in the house, will humankind live or die, and she gives to her boys—superstition.

Hannah that is so good to you. Take your pill, Mrs. Excited For Nothing, swallow.

Heritage! But when did I have time to teach? Of Hannah I asked only hands to help.

Swallow.

Otherwise—musing; gentleness.

Not to travel. To go home.

The children want to see you. We have to show them you are as thorny a flower as ever.

Not to travel.

Vivi wants you should see her new baby. She sent the tickets—airplane tickets—a Mrs. Roosevelt she wants to make of you. To Vivi's we have to go.

A new baby. How many warm, seductive babies. She holds him stiffly, *away* from her, so that he wails. And a long shudder begins, and the sweat beads on her forehead.

"Hush, shush," croons the grandfather, lifting him back. "You should forgive

[6]Alludes to Yiddish folk saying, refuted in Peretz's story, "A Good Marriage," and to the cremations in the Nazi concentration camps of the Holocaust.

[7]Broad uprising against the regime of Czar Nicholas II that forced a series of democratizing concessions, notably the establishment of a parliamentary government, and that set up the soviets, or workers' councils, as a means of organization.

your grandmamma, little prince, she has never held a baby before, only seen them in glass cases. Hush, shush."

"You're tired, Ma," says Vivi. "The travel and the noisy dinner. I'll take you to lie down."

(*A long travel from, to, what the feel of a baby evokes.*)

In the airplane, cunningly designed to encase from motion (no wind, no feel of flight), she had sat severely and still, her face turned to the sky through which they cleaved and left no scar.

So this was how it looked, the determining, the crucial sky, and this was how man moved through it, remote above the dwindled earth, the concealed human life. Vulnerable life, that could scar.

There was a steerage ship of memory that shook across a great, circular sea: clustered, ill human beings; and through the thick-stained air, tiny fretting waters in a window round like the airplane's—sun round, moon round. (The round thatched roofs of Olshana.) Eye round—like the smaller window that framed distance the solitary year of exile when only her eyes could travel, and no voice spoke. And the polar winds hurled themselves across snows trackless and endless and white—like the clouds which had closed together below and hidden the earth.

Now they put a baby in her lap. Do not ask me, she would have liked to beg. Enough the worn face of Vivi, the remembered grandchildren. I cannot, cannot. . . .

Cannot what? Unnatural grandmother, not able to make herself embrace a baby.

She lay there in the bed of the two little girls, her new hearing aid turned full, listening to the sound of the children going to sleep, the baby's fretful crying and hushing, the clatter of dishes being washed and put away. They thought she slept. Still she rode on.

It was not that she had not loved her babies, her children. The love—the passion of tending—had risen with the need like a torrent; and like a torrent drowned and immolated all else. But when the need was done—oh the power that was lost in the painful damming back and drying up of what still surged, but had nowhere to go. Only the thin pulsing left that could not quiet, suffering over lives one felt, but could no longer hold nor help.

On that torrent she had borne them to their own lives, and the riverbed was desert long years now. Not there would she dwell, a memoried wraith. Surely that was not all, surely there was more. Still the springs, the springs were in her seeking. Somewhere an older power that beat for life. Somewhere coherence, transport, meaning. If they would but leave her in the air now stilled of clamor, in the reconciled solitude, to journey on.

And they put a baby in her lap. Immediacy to embrace, and the breath of *that* past: warm flesh like this that had claims and nuzzled away all else and with lovely mouths devoured; hot-living like an animal—intensely and now; the turning maze; the long drunkenness; the drowning into needing and being needed. Severely she looked back—and the shudder seized her again, and the sweat. Not that way. Not there, not now could she, not yet. . . .

And all that visit, she could not touch the baby.

"Daddy, is it the . . . sickness she's like that?" asked Vivi. "I was so glad to be having the baby—for her. I told Tim, it'll give her more happiness than anything, being around a baby again. And she hasn't played with him once."

He was not listening, "Aahh little seed of life, little charmer," he crooned, "Hollywood should see you. A heart of ice you would melt. Kick, kick. The future you'll have for a ball. In 2050 still kick. Kick for your grandaddy then."

Attentive with the older children; sat through their performances (command performance; we command you to be the audience); helped Ann sort autumn leaves to find the best for a school program; listened gravely to Richard tell about his rock collection, while her lips mutely formed the words to remember: *igneous, sedimentary, metamorphic;* looked for missing socks, books, and bus tickets; watched the children whoop after their grandfather who knew how to tickle, chuck, lift, toss, do tricks, tell secrets, make jokes, match riddle for riddle. (Tell me a riddle, Grammy. I know no riddles, child.) Scrubbed sills and woodwork and furniture in every room; folded the laundry; straightened drawers; emptied the heaped baskets waiting for ironing (while he or Vivi or Tim nagged: You're supposed to rest here, you've been sick) but to none tended or gave food—and could not touch the baby.

After a week she said: "Let us go home. Today call about the tickets."

"You have important business, Mrs. Inahurry? The President waits to consult with you?" He shouted, for the fear of the future raced in him. "The clothes are still warm from the suitcase, your children cannot show enough how glad they are to see you, and you want home. There is plenty of time for home. We cannot be with the children at home."

"Blind to around you as always: the little ones sleep four in a room because we take their bed. We are two more people in a house with a new baby, and no help."

"Vivi is happy so. The children should have their grandparents a while, she told to me. I should have my mommy and daddy. . . ."

"Babbler and blind. Do you look at her so tired? How she starts to talk and she cries? I am not strong enough yet to help. Let us go home."

(To reconciled solitude.)

For it seemed to her the crowded noisy house was listening to her, listening for her. She could feel it like a great ear pressed under her heart. And everything knocked: quick constant raps: let me in, let me in.

How was it that soft reaching tendrils also became blows that knocked?

C'mon, Grandma, I want to show you. . . .

Tell me a riddle, Grandma. (*I know no riddles.*)

Look, Grammy, he's so dumb he can't even find his hands. (Dody and the baby on a blanket over the fermenting autumn mould.)

I made them—for you. (Ann) (Flat paper dolls with aprons that lifted on scalloped skirts that lifted on flowered pants; hair of yarn and great ringed questioning eyes.)

Watch me, Grandma. (Richard snaking up the tree, hanging exultant, free, with one hand at the top. Below Dody hunching over in pretend-cooking.) (*Climb too, Dody, climb and look.*)

Be my nap bed, Grammy. (The "No!" too late.) Morty's abandoned heaviness, while his fingers ladder up and down her hearing-aid cord to his drowsy chant: eentsiebeentsiespider. (*Children trust.*)

It's to start off your own rock collection, Grandma. That's a trilobite fossil, 200 million years old (millions of years on a boy's mouth) and that one's obsidian, black glass.

Knocked and knocked.

Mother, I *told* you the teacher said we had to bring it back all filled out this morning. Didn't you even ask Daddy? Then tell *me* which plan and I'll check it: evacuate or stay in the city or wait for you to come and take me away. (Seeing the look of straining to hear.) It's for Disaster, Grandma. (*Children trust.*)

Vivi in the maze of the long, the lovely drunkenness. The old old noises: baby sounds; screaming of a mother flayed to exasperation; children quarreling; children playing; singing; laughter.

And Vivi's tears and memories, spilling so fast, half the words not understood.

She had started remembering out loud deliberately, so her mother would know the past was cherished, still lived in her.

Nursing the baby: My friends marvel, and I tell them, oh it's easy to be such a cow. I remember how beautiful my mother seemed nursing my brother, and the milk just flows. . . . Was that Davy? It must have been Davy. . . .

Lowering a hem: How did you ever . . . when I think how you made everything we wore . . . Tim, just think, seven kids and Mommy sewed everything . . . do I remember you sang while you sewed? That white dress with the red apples on the skirt you fixed over for me, was it Hannah's or Clara's before it was mine?

Washing sweaters: Ma, I'll never forget, one of those days so nice you washed clothes outside; one of the first spring days it must have been. The bubbles just danced while you scrubbed, and we chased after, and you stopped to show us how to blow our own bubbles with green onion stalks . . . you always. . . .

"Strong onion, to still make you cry after so many years," her father said, to turn the tears into laughter.

While Richard bent over his homework: Where is it now, do we still have it, the Book of the Martyrs?[8] It always seemed so, well—exalted, when you'd put it on the round table and we'd all look at it together; there was even a halo from the lamp. The lamp with the beaded fringe you could move up and down; they're in style again, pulley lamps like that, but without the fringe. You know the book I'm talking about, Daddy, the Book of the Martyrs, the first picture was a bust of Socrates? I wish there was something like that for the children, Mommy, to give them what you. . . . (And the tears splashed again.)

(What I intended and did not? Stop it, daughter, stop it, leave that time. And he, the hyprocrite, sitting there with tears in his eyes—it was nothing to you then, nothing.)

. . . The time you came to school and I almost died of shame because of your accent and because I knew you knew I was ashamed; how could I? . . . Sammy's harmonica and you danced to it once, yes you did, you and Davy squealing in your arms. . . . That time you bundled us up and walked us down to the railway station to stay the night 'cause it was heated and we didn't have any coal, that winter of the strike, you didn't think I remembered that, did you, Mommy? . . . How you'd call us out to see the sunsets. . . .

Day after day, the spilling memories. Worse now, questions, too. Even the grandchildren: Grandma, in the olden days, when you were little. . . .

[8]Olsen's synthesis of several books that told the stories of fighters for freedom.

* * *

It was the afternoons that saved.

While they thought she napped, she would leave the mosaic on the wall (of children's drawings, maps, calendars, pictures, Ann's cardboard dolls with their great ringed questioning eyes) and hunch in the girls' cupboard, on the low shelf where the shoes stood, and the girls' dresses covered.

For that while she would painfully sheathe against the listening house, the tendrils and noises that knocked, and Vivi's spilling memories. Sometimes it helped to braid and unbraid the sashes that dangled, or to trace the pattern on the hoop slips.

Today she had jacks and children under jet trails to forget. Last night, Ann and Dody silhouetted in the window against a sunset of flaming man-made clouds of jet trail, their jacks ball accenting the peaceful noise of dinner being made. Had she told them, yes she had told them of how they played jacks in her village though there was no ball, no jacks. Six stones, round and flat, toss them out, the seventh on the back of the hand, toss, catch and swoop up as many as possible, toss again. . . .

Of stones (repeating Richard) there are three kinds: earth's fire jetting; rock of layered centuries; crucibled new out of the old (*igneous, sedimentary, metamorphic*). But there was that other—frozen to black glass, never to transform or hold the fossil memory . . . (let not my seed fall on stone). There was an ancient man who fought to heights a great rock that crashed back down eternally—eternal labor, freedom, labor . . . (stone will[9] perish, but the word remain). And you, David, who with a stone slew, screaming: Lord, take my heart of stone[10] and give me flesh.

Who was screaming? Why was she back in the common room of the prison, the sun motes dancing in the shafts of light, and the informer being brought in, a prisoner now, like themselves. And Lisa leaping, yes, Lisa, the gentle and tender, biting at the betrayer's jugular. Screaming and screaming.

No, it is the children screaming. Another of Paul and Sammy's terrible fights?

In Vivi's house. Severely: you are in Vivi's house.

Blows, screams, a call: "Grandma!" For her? Oh please not for her. Hide, hunch behind the dresses deeper. But a trembling little body hurls itself beside her—surprised, smothered laughter, arms surround her neck, tears rub dry on her cheek, and words too soft to understand whisper into her ear (Is this where you hide too, Grammy? It's my secret place, we have a secret now).

And the sweat beads, and the long shudder seizes.

It seemed the great ear pressed inside now, and the knocking. "We have to go home," she told him, "I grow ill here."

"It's your own fault, Mrs. Busybody, you do not rest, you do too much." He raged, but the fear was in his eyes. "It was a serious operation, they told you to take care. . . . All right, we will go to where you can rest."

But where? Not home to death, not yet. He had thought to Lennie's, to Clara's; beautiful visits with each of the children. She would have to rest first, be stronger. If

[9]Alludes to the myth of Sisyphus, who was punished eternally in Tartarus for reporting the whereabouts of Zeus, king of the gods, to the father of the maiden Zeus had seized.

[10]Alludes to the biblical story of David's triumph over the giant Philistine, Goliath; *Samuel* I: 17. The quotation, which Olsen heard in a black church, paraphrases *Ezekiel* 11:19: "I shall remove the heart of stone from their bodies and give them a heart of flesh."

they could but go to Florida—it glittered before him, the never-realized promise of Florida. California: of course. (The money, the money, dwindling!) Los Angeles first for sun and rest, then to Lennie's in San Francisco.

He told her the next day. "You saw what Nancy wrote: snow and wind back home, a terrible winter. And look at you—all bones and a swollen belly. I called Phil: he said: 'A prescription, Los Angeles sun and rest.'"

She watched the words on his lips. "You have sold the house," she cried, "that is why we do not go home. That is why you talk no more of the Haven, why there is money for travel. After the children you will drag me to the Haven."

"The Haven! Who thinks of the Haven any more? Tell her, Vivi, tell Mrs. Suspicious: a prescription, sun and rest, to make you healthy. . . . And how could I sell the house without *you?*"

At the place of farewells and greetings, of winds of coming and winds of going, they say their good-byes.

They look back at her with the eyes of others before them: Richard with her own blue blaze; Ann with the nordic eyes of Tim; Morty's dreaming brown of a great-grandmother he will never know; Dody with the laughing eyes of him who had been her springtide love (who stands beside her now); Vivi's, all tears.

The baby's eyes are closed in sleep.

Good-bye, my children.

3

It is to the back of the great city he brought her, to the dwelling places of the cast-off old.[11] Bounded by two lines of amusement piers to the north and to the south, and between a long straight paving rimmed with black benches facing the sand—sands so wide the ocean is only a far fluting.

In the brief vacation season, some of the boarded stores fronting the sands open, and families, young people and children, may be seen. A little tasselled tram shuttles between the piers, and the lights of roller coasters prink and tweak over those who come to have sensation made in them.

The rest of the year it is abandoned to the old, all else boarded up and still; seemingly empty, except the occasional days and hours when the sun, like a tide, sucks them out of the low rooming houses, casts them onto the benches and sandy rim of the walk—and sweeps them into decaying enclosures once again.

A few newer apartments glint among the low bleached squares. It is in one of these Lennie's Jeannie has arranged their rooms. "Only a few miles north and south people pay hundreds of dollars a month for just this gorgeous air, Grandaddy, just this ocean closeness."

She had been ill on the plane, lay ill for days in the unfamiliar room. Several times the doctor came by—left medicine she would not take. Several times Jeannie drove in the twenty miles from work, still in her Visiting Nurse uniform, the lightness and brightness of her like a healing.

[11]Venice, California, just west of Los Angeles.

"Who can believe it is winter?" he asked one morning. "Beautiful it is outside like an ad. Come, Mrs. Invalid, come to taste it. You are well enough to sit in here, you are well enough to sit outside. The doctor said it too."

But the benches were encrusted with people, and the sands at the sidewalk's edge. Besides, she had seen the far ruffle of the sea: "there take me," and though she leaned against him, it was she who led.

Plodding and plodding, sitting often to rest, he grumbling. Patting the sand so warm. Once she scooped up a handful, cradling it close to her better eye; peered, and flug it back. And as they came almost to the brink and she could see the glistening wet, she sat down, pulled off her shoes and stockings, left him and began to run. "You'll catch cold," he screamed, but the sand in his shoes weighed him down—he who had always been the agile one—and already the white spray creamed her feet.

He pulled her back, took a handkerchief to wipe off the wet and the sand. "Oh no," she said, "the sun will dry," seized the square and smoothed it flat, dropped on it a mound of sand, knotted the kerchief corners and tied it to a bag—"to look at with the strong glass" (for the first time in years explaining an action of hers)—and lay down with the little bag against her cheek, looking toward the shore that nurtured life as it first crawled toward consciousness the millions of years ago.

He took her one Sunday in the evil-smelling bus, past flat miles of blister houses, to the home of relatives. Oh what is this? she cried as the light began to smoke and the houses to dim and recede. Smog, he said, everyone knows but you. . . . Outside he kept his arms about her, but she walked with hands pushing the heavy air as if to open it, whispered: who has done this? sat down suddenly to vomit at the curb and for a long while refused to rise.

One's age as seen on the altered face of those known in youth. Is this they he has come to visit? This Max and Rose, smooth and pleasant, introducing them to polite children, disinterested grandchildren, "the whole family, once a month on Sundays. And why not? We have the room, the help, the food."

Talk of cars, of houses, of success: this son that, that daughter this. And *your* children? Hastily skimped over, the intermarriages, the obscure work—"my doctor son-in-law, Phil"—all he has to offer. She silent in a corner. (Car-sick like a baby, he explains.) Years since he has taken her to visit anyone but the children, and old apprehensions prickle: "no incidents," he silently begs, "no incidents." He itched to tell them. "A very sick woman," significantly, indicating her with his eyes, "a very sick woman." Their restricted faces did not react. "Have you thought maybe she'd do better at Palm Springs?" Rose asked. "Or at least a nicer section of the beach, nicer people, a pool." Not to have to say "money" he said instead: "would she have sand to look at through a magnifying glass?" and went on, detail after detail, the old habit betraying of parading the queerness of her for laughter.

After dinner—the others into the living room in men- or women-clusters, or into the den to watch TV—the four of them alone. She sat close to him, and did not speak. Jokes, stories, people they had known, beginning of reminiscence, Russia fifty-sixty years ago. Strange words across the Duncan Phyfe table: *hunger; secret meetings; human rights; spies; betrayals; prison; escape*—interrupted by one of the grandchildren: "Commercial's on; any Coke left? Gee, you're missing a real hair-raiser." And then a granddaughter (Max proudly: "look at her, an American queen") drove them home on her way back to U.C.L.A. No incident—except that there had been no incidents.

The first few mornings she had taken with her the magnifying glass, but he would sit only on the benches, so she rested at the foot, where slatted bench shadows fell, and unless she turned her hearing aid down, other voices invaded.

Now on the days when the sun shone and she felt well enough, he took her on the tram to where the benches ranged in oblongs, some with tables for checkers or cards. Again the blanket on the sand in the striped shadows, but she no longer brought the magnifying glass. He played cards, and she lay in the sun and looked towards the waters; or they walked—two blocks down to the scaling hotel, two blocks back—past chili-hamburger stands, open-doored bars. Next to New and Perpetual Rummage Sale stores.

Once, out of the aimless walkers, slow and shuffling like themselves, someone ran unevenly towards them, embraced, kissed, wept: "dear friends, old friends." A friend of *hers,* not his: Mrs. Mays who had lived next door to them in Denver when the children were small.

Thirty years are compressed into a dozen sentences; and the present, not even in three. All is told: the children scattered; the husband dead; she lives in a room two blocks up from the sing hall—and points to the domed auditorium jutting before the pier. The leg? phlebitis; the heavy breathing? that, one does not ask. She, too, comes to the benches each day to sit. And tomorrow, tomorrow, are they going to the community sing? Of course he would have heard of it, everybody goes—the big doings they wait for all week. They have never been? She will come to them for dinner tomorrow and they will all go together.

So it is that she sits in the wind of the singing, among the thousand various faces of age.

She had turned off her hearing aid at once they came into the auditorium—as she would have wished to turn off sight.

One by one they streamed by and imprinted on her—and though the savage zest of their singing came voicelessly soft and distant, the faces still roared—the faces densened the air—chorded into

children-chants, mother-croons, singing of the chained love serenades, Beethoven storms, mad Lucia's scream drunken joy-songs, keens for the dead, work-singing

> *while from floor to balcony to dome a bare-footed sore-covered little girl threaded the sound-thronged tumult, danced her ecstasy of grimace to flutes that scratched at a cross-roads village wedding*

Yes, faces became sound, and the sound became faces; and faces and sound became weight—pushed, pressed

"Air"—her hands claw his.

"Whenever I enjoy myself. . . ." Then he saw the gray sweat on her face. "Here. Up. Help me, Mrs. Mays," and they support her out to where she can gulp the air in sob after sob.

"A doctor, we should get for her a doctor."

"Tch, it's nothing," says Ellen Mays, "I get it all the time. You've missed the tram; come to my place. Fix your hearing aid, honey . . . close . . . tea. My view. See, she *wants* to come. Steady now, that's how." Adding mysteriously: "Remember your advice, easy to keep your head above water, empty things float. Float."

The singing a fading march for them, tall woman with a swollen leg, weaving little man, and the swollen thinness they help between.

The stench in the hall: mildew? decay? "We sit and rest then climb. My gorgeous view. We help each other and here we are."

The stench along into the slab of room. A washstand for a sink, a box with oilcloth tacked around for a cupboard, a three-burner gas plate. Artificial flowers, colorless with dust. Everywhere pictures foaming: wedding, baby, party, vacation, graduation, family pictures. From the narrow couch under a slit of window, sure enough the view: lurching rooftops and a scallop of ocean heaving, preening, twitching under the moon.

"While the water heats. Excuse me . . . down the hall." Ellen Mays has gone.

"You'll live?" he asks mechanically, sat down to feel his fright; tried to pull her alongside.

She pushed him away. "For air," she said; stood clinging to the dresser. Then, in a terrible voice:

After a lifetime of room. Of many rooms.

Shhh.

You remember how she lived. Eight children. And now one room like a coffin.

She pays rent!

Shrinking the life of her into one room like a coffin Rooms and rooms like this I lie on the quilt and hear them talk

Please, Mrs. Orator-without-Breath.

Once you went for coffee I walked I saw A Balzac a Chekhov to write it Rummage Alone On scraps

Better old here than in the old country!

On scraps Yet they sang like like Wondrous! *Humankind one has to believe* So strong For what? To rot not grow?

Your poor lungs beg you. They sob between each word.

Singing. Unused the life in them. She in this poor room with her pictures Max You The children Everywhere unused the life And who has meaning? Century after century still all in us not to grow?

Coffins, rummage, plants: sick woman. Oh lay down. We will get for you the doctor.

"And when will it end. Oh, *the end.*" *That* nightmare thought, and this time she writhed, crumpled against him, seized his hand (for a moment again the weight, the soft distant roaring of humanity) and on the strangled-for breath, begged: "Man . . . we'll destroy ourselves?"

And looking for answer—in the helpless pity and fear for her (for *her*) that distorted his face—she understood the last months, and knew that she was dying.

4

"Let us go home," she said after several days.

"You are in training for a cross-country run? That is why you do not even walk across the room? Here, like a prescription Phil said, till you are stronger from the operation. You want to break doctor's orders?"

She saw the fiction was necessary to him, was silent; then: "At home I will get better. If the doctor here says?"

"And winter? And the visits to Lennie and to Clara? All right," for he saw the tears in her eyes, "I will write Phil, and talk to the doctor."

Days passed. He reported nothing. Jeannie came and took her out for air, past the boarded concessions, the hooded and tented amusement rides, to the end of the pier. They watched the spent waves feeding the new, the gulls in the clouded sky; even up where they sat, the wind-blown sand stung.

She did not ask to go down the crooked steps to the sea.

Back in her bed, while he was gone to the store, she said: "Jeannie, this doctor, he is not one I can ask questions. Ask him for me, can I go home?"

Jeannie looked at her, said quickly: "Of course, poor Granny. You want your own things around you, don't you? I'll call him tonight. . . . Look, I've something to show you," and from her purse unwrapped a large cookie, intricately shaped like a little girl. "Look at the curls—can you hear me well, Granny?—and the darling eyelashes. I just came from a house where they were baking them."

"The dimples, there in the knees," she marveled, holding it to the better light, turning, studying, "like art. Each singly they cut, or a mold?"

"Singly," said Jeannie, "and if it is a child only the mother can make them. Oh Granny, it's the likeness of a real little girl who died yesterday—Rosita. She was three years old. *Pan del Muerto,* the Bread of the Dead. It was the custom in the part of Mexico they came from."

Still she turned and inspected. "Look, the hollow in the throat, the little cross necklace. . . . I think for the mother it is a good thing to be busy with such bread. You know the family?"

Jeannie nodded. "On my rounds. I nursed. . . . Oh Granny, it is like a party; they play songs she liked to dance to. The coffin is lined with pink velvet and she wears a white dress. There are candles. . . ."

"In the house?" Surprised, "They keep her in the house?"

"Yes," said Jeannie, "and it is against the health law. I think she is . . . prepared there. The father said it will be sad to bury her in this country; in Oaxaca they have a feast night with candles each year; everyone picnics on the graves of those they loved until dawn."

"Yes, Jeannie, the living must comfort themselves." And closed her eyes.

"You want to sleep, Granny?"

"Yes, tired from the pleasure of you. I may keep the Rosita? There stand it, on the dresser, where I can see; something of my own around me."

In the kitchenette, helping her grandfather unpack the groceries, Jeannie said in her light voice:

"I'm resigning my job, Grandaddy."

"Ah, the lucky young man. Which one is he?"

"Too late. You're spoken for." She made a pyramid of cans, unstacked, and built again.

"Something is wrong with the job?"

"With me. I can't be"—she searched for the word—"What they call professional enough. I let myself feel things. And tomorrow I have to report a family. . . ." The cans clicked again. "It's not that, either. I just don't know what I want to do, maybe go back to school, maybe go to art school. I thought if you went to San Francisco I'd come along and talk it over with Momma and Daddy. But I don't see how you can go. She wants to go home. She asked me to ask the doctor."

The doctor told her himself. "Next week you may travel, when you are a little stronger." But next week there was the fever of an infection, and by the time that was over, she could not leave the bed—a rented hospital bed that stood beside the double bed he slept in alone now.

Outwardly the days repeated themselves. Every other afternoon and evening he went out to his newfound cronies, to talk and play cards. Twice a week, Mrs. Mays came. And the rest of the time, Jeannie was there.

By the sickbed stood Jeannie's FM radio. Often into the room the shapes of music came. She would lie curled on her side, her knees drawn up, intense in listening (Jeannie sketched her so, coiled, convoluted like an ear), then thresh her hand out and abruptly snap the radio mute—still to lie in her attitude of listening, concealing tears.

Once Jeannie brought in a young Marine to visit, a friend from high-school days she had found wandering near the empty pier. Because Jeannie asked him to, gravely, without self-consciousness, he sat himself cross-legged on the floor and performed for them a dance of his native Samoa.

Long after they left, a tiny thrumming sound could be heard where, in her bed, she strove to repeat the beckon, flight, surrender of his hands, the fluttering footbeats, and his low plaintive calls.

Hannah and Phil sent flowers. To deepen her pleasure, he placed one in her hair. "Like a girl," he said, and brought the hand mirror so she could see. She looked at the pulsing red flower, the yellow skull face; a desolate, excited laugh shuddered from her, and she pushed the mirror away—but let the flower burn.

The week Lennie and Helen came, the fever returned. With it the excited laugh, and incessant words. She, who in her life had spoken but seldom and then only when necessary (never having learned the easy, social uses of words), now in dying, spoke incessantly.

In a half-whisper: "Like Lisa she is, your Jeannie. Have I told you of Lisa who taught me to read? Of the highborn she was, but noble in herself. I was sixteen; they beat me; my father beat me so I would not go to her. It was forbidden, she was a Tolstoyan.[12] At night, past dogs that howled, terrible dogs, my son, in the snows of winter

[12]Follower of Count Lyev (Leo) Tolstoy, nineteenth-century Russian novelist whose opposition to the private ownership of property and belief in the dignity of peasant life helped prepare the way for the Russian Revolution.

to the road, I to ride in her carriage like a lady, to books. To her, life was holy, knowledge was holy, and she taught me to read. They hung her. Everything that happens one must try to understand why. She killed one who betrayed many. Because of betrayal, betrayed all she lived and believed. In one minute she killed, before my eyes (there is so much blood in a human being, my son), in prison with me. All that happens, one must try to understand.

"The name?" Her lips would work. "The name that was their pole star; the doors of the death houses fixed to open on it; I read of it my year of penal servitude. Thuban!" very excited, "Thuban, in ancient Egypt the pole star. Can you see, look out to see it, Jeannie, if it swings around *our* pole star that seems to *us* not to move.

"Yes, Jeannie, at your age my mother and grandmother had already buried children . . . yes, Jeannie, it is more than oceans between Olshana and you . . . yes, Jeannie, they danced, and for all the bodies they had they might as well be chickens, and indeed, they scratched and flapped their arms and hopped.

"And Andrei Yefimitch, who for twenty years had never known of it and never wanted to know, said as if he wanted to cry: but why my dear friend this malicious laughter?" Telling to herself half-memorized phrases from her few books. "Pain I answer with tears and cries, baseness with indignation, meanness with repulsion . . . for life may be hated or wearied of, but never despised."[13]

Delirious: "Tell me, my neighbor, Mrs. Mays, the pictures never lived, but what of the flowers? Tell them who ask: no rabbis, no ministers, no priests, no speeches, no ceremonies: ah, false—let the living comfort themselves. Tell Sammy's boy, he who flies, tell him to go to Stuttgart[14] and see where Davy has no grave. And what?" . . . "And what? where millions have no graves—save air."

In delirium or not, wanting the radio on; not seeming to listen, the words still jetting, wanting the music on. Once, silencing it abruptly as of old, she began to cry, unconcealed tears this time. "You have pain, Granny?" Jeannie asked.

"The music," she said, "still it is there and we do not hear; knocks, and our poor human ears too weak. What else, what else we do not hear?"

Once she knocked his hand aside as he gave her a pill, swept the bottles from her bedside table: "no pills, let me feel what I feel," and laughed as on his hands and knees he groped to pick them up.

Nighttimes her hand reached across the bed to hold his.

A constant retching began. Her breath was too faint for sustained speech now, but still the lips moved:

When no longer necessary   to injure others[15]
Pick   pick   pick   Blind chicken
As a human being   responsibility[16]

[13]Both quotations are drawn from Chekhov, "Ward No. 6."

[14]Site of heavy bombing during World War II; also of some of the first encounters of American troops with concentration camps.

[15]From Chekhov's "Rothschild's Fiddle."

[16]From letter by Ida Lerner, Olsen's mother: "As a human being who carries responsibility for action, I think as a duty to the community we must try to understand each other."

"David!" imperious, "Basin!" and she would vomit, rinse her mouth, the wasted throat working to swallow, and begin the chant again.

She will be better off in the hospital now, the doctor said.

He sent the telegrams to the children, was packing her suitcase, when her hoarse voice startled. She had roused, was pulling herself to sitting.

"Where now?" she asked. "Where now do you drag me?"

"You do not even have to have a baby to go this time," he soothed, looking for the brush to pack. "Remember, after Davy you told me—worthy to have a baby for the pleasure of the ten-day rest in the hospital?"

"Where now? Not home yet?" Her voice mourned. "Where *is* my home?"

He rose to ease her back. "The doctor, the hospital," he started to explain, but deftly, like a snake, she had slithered out of bed and stood swaying, propped behind the night table.

"Coward," she hissed, "runner."

"You stand," he said senselessly.

"To take me there and run. Afraid of a little vomit."

He reached her as she fell. She struggled against him, half slipped from his arms, pulled herself up again.

"Weakling," she taunted, "to leave me there and run. Betrayer. All your life you have run."

He sobbed, telling Jeannie. "A Marilyn Monroe to run for her virtue. Fifty-nine pounds she weighs, the doctor said, and she beats at me like a Dempsey. Betrayer, she cries, and I running like a dog when she calls; day and night, running to her, her vomit, the bedpan. . . ."

"She needs you, Grandaddy," said Jeannie. "Isn't that what they call love? I'll see if she sleeps, and if she does, poor worn-out darling, we'll have a party, you and I: I brought us rum babas."

They did not move her. By her bed now stood the tall hooked pillar that held the solutions—blood and dextrose—to feed her veins. Jeannie moved down the hall to take over the sickroom, her face so radiant, her grandfather asked her once: "you are in love?" (Shameful the joy, the pure overwhelming joy from being with her grandmother; the peace, the serenity that breathed.) "My darling escape," she answered incoherently, "my darling Granny"—as if that explained.

Now one by one the children came, those that were able. Hannah, Paul, Sammy. Too late to ask: and what did you learn with your living, Mother, and what do we need to know?

Clara, the eldest, clenched:

Pay me back, Mother, pay me back for all you took from me. Those others you crowded into your heart. The hands I needed to be for you, the heaviness, the responsibility.

Is this she? Noises the dying make, the crablike hands crawling over the covers. The ethereal singing.

She hears that music, that singing from childhood; forgotten sound—not heard since, since. . . . And the hardness breaks like a cry: Where did we lose each other, first mother, singing mother?

Annulled: the quarrels, the gibing, the harshness between; the fall into silence and the withdrawal.

I do not know you, Mother, Mother, I never knew you.

Lennie, suffering not alone for her who was dying, but for that in her which never lived (for that which in him might never come to live). From him too, unspoken words: *good-bye Mother who taught me to mother myself.*

Not Vivi, who must stay with her children; not Davy, but he is already here, having to die again with *her* this time, for the living take their dead with them when they die.

Light she grew, like a bird, and, like a bird, sound bubbled in her throat while the body fluttered in agony. Night and day, asleep or awake (though indeed there was no difference now) the songs and the phrases leaping.

And he, who had once dreaded a long dying (from fear of himself, from horror of the dwindling money) now desired her quick death profoundly, for *her* sake. He no longer went out, except when Jeannie forced him to; no longer laughed, except when, in the bright kitchenette, Jeannie coaxed his laughter (and she, who seemed to hear nothing else, would laugh too, conspiratorial wisps of laughter).

Light, like a bird, the fluttering body, the little claw hands, the beaked shadow on her face; and the throat, bubbling, straining.

He tried not to listen, as he tried not to look on the face in which only the forehead remained familiar, but trapped with her the long nights in that little room, the sounds worked themselves into his consciousness, with their punctuation of death swallows, whimpers, gurglings.

Even in reality (swallow) *life's lack of it*
Slaveships   deathtrains   clubs   eenough
The bell   summons what enables
78,000 in one minute (whisper of a scream) *78,000 human beings   we'll destroy ourselves?*[17]

"Aah, Mrs. Miserable," he said, as if she could hear, "all your life working, and now in bed you lie, servants to tend, you do not even need to call to be tended, and still you work. Such hard work it is to die? Such hard work?"

The body threshed, her hand clung in his. A melody, ghost-thin, hovered on her lips, and like a guilty ghost, the vision of her bent in listening to it, silencing the record instantly he was near. Now, heedless of his presence, she floated the melody on and on.

"Hid it from me," he complained, "how many times you listened to remember it so?" And tried to think when she had first played it, or first begun to silence her few records when he came near—but could reconstruct nothing. There was only this room with its tall hooked pillar and its swarm of sounds.

[17]The italicized passage contains references to the ships used for transporting slaves from Africa to America, to the trains that took millions of Jews and other Nazi victims to the concentration camps, and to the dropping of the atomic bomb on Hiroshima.

No man one except through others
Strong with the not yet in the now
Dogma dead war dead one country[18]

"It helps, Mrs. Philosopher, words from books? It helps?" And it seemed to him that for seventy years she had hidden a tape recorder, infinitely microscopic, within her, that it had coiled infinite mile on mile, trapping every song, every melody, every word read, heard, and spoken—and that maliciously she was playing back only what said nothing of him, of the children, of their intimate life together.

"Left us indeed, Mrs. Babbler," he reproached, "you who called others babbler and cunningly saved your words. A lifetime you tended and loved, and now not a word of us, for us. Left us indeed? Left me."

And he took out his solitaire deck, shuffled the cards loudly, slapped them down.

Left high banner of reason (tatter of an orator's voice) *justice freedom light*
Humankind life worthy capacities
Seeks (blur of shudder) *belong human being*

"Words, words," he accused, "and what human beings did *you* seek around you, Mrs. Live Alone, and what humankind think worthy?"

Though even as he spoke, he remembered she had not always been isolated, had not always wanted to be alone (as he knew there had been a voice before this gossamer one; before the hoarse voice that broke from silence to lash, make incidents, shame him—a girl's voice of eloquence that spoke their holiest dreams). But again he could reconstruct, image, nothing of what had been before, or when, or how, it had changed.

Ace, queen, jack. The pillar shadow fell, so, in two tracks; in the mirror depths glistened, a moonlike blob, the empty solution bottle. And it worked in him: *of reason and justice and freedom . . . Dogma dead:* he remembered the full quotation, laughed bitterly. "Hah, good you do not know what you say; good Victor Hugo died and did not see it, his twentieth century."

Deuce, ten, five. Dauntlessly she began a song of their youth of belief:

These things shall be, a loftier race
than e'er the world hath known shall rise
with flame of freedom in their souls
and light of knowledge in their eyes

King, four jack. "In the twentieth century, hah!"

They shall be gentle, brave and strong
to spill no drop of blood, but dare

earth and fire and sea and air

"To spill no drop of blood, hah! So, cadaver, and you too, cadaver Hugo, 'in the twentieth century ignorance will be dead, dogma will be dead, war will be dead, and for all mankind one country—of fulfilment?' Hah!"

[18]See the text of *Riddle,* below, for the full quotation from the work of Victor Hugo, nineteenth-century French romantic writer and republican exile from the France of Emperor Louis Napoleon.

And every life (long strangling cough) shall[19]
be a song

The cards fell from his fingers. Without warning, the bereavement and betrayal he had sheltered—compounded through the years—hidden even from himself—revealed itself,

uncoiled,
released,
sprung

and with it the monstrous shapes of what had actually happened in the century.

A ravening hunger or thirst seized him. He groped into the kitchenette, switched on all three lights, piled a tray—"you have finished your night snack, Mrs. Cadaver, now I will have mine." And he was shocked at the tears that splashed on the tray.

"Salt tears. For free. I forgot to shake on salt?"

Whispered: "Lost, how much I lost."

Escaped to the grandchildren whose childhoods were childish, who had never hungered, who lived unravaged by disease in warm houses of many rooms, had all the school for which they cared, could walk on any street, stood a head taller than their grandparents, towered above—beautiful skins, straight backs, clear straightforward eyes. "Yes, you in Olshana," he said to the town of sixty years ago, "they would seem nobility to you."

And was this not the dream then, come true in ways undreamed? he asked.

And are there no other children in the world? he answered, as if in her harsh voice.

And the flame of freedom, the light of knowledge?

And the drop, to spill no drop of blood?

And he thought that at six Jeannie would get up and it would be his turn to go to her room and sleep, that he could press the buzzer and she would come now; that in the afternoon Ellen Mays was coming, and this time they would play cards and he could marvel at how rouge can stand half an inch on the cheek; that in the evening the doctor would come, and he could beg him to be merciful, to stop the feeding solutions, to let her die.

To let her die, and with her their youth of belief out of which her bright, betrayed words foamed; stained words, that on her working lips came stainless.

Hours yet before Jeannie's turn. He could press the buzzer and wake her up to come now; he could take a pill, and with it sleep; he could pour more brandy into his milk glass, though what he had poured was not yet touched.

Instead he went back, checked her pulse, gently tended with his knotty fingers as Jeannie had taught.

She was whimpering; her hand crawled across the covers for his. Compassionately he enfolded it, and with his free hand gathered up the cards again. Still was there thirst or hunger ravening in him.

[19]The italicized passages are all fragments from "These Things Shall Be." The last verse reads: "New arts shall bloom of loftier mould,/ And mightier music thrill the skies,/ And every life shall be a song/ When all the earth is paradise."

That world of their youth—dark, ignorant, terrible with hate and disease—how was it that living in it, in the midst of corruption, filth, treachery, degradation, they had not mistrusted man nor themselves; had believed so beautifully, so . . . falsely?

"Aaah, children," he said out loud, "how we believed, how we belonged." And he yearned to package for each of the children, the grandchildren, for everyone, *that joyous certainty, that sense of mattering, of moving and being moved, of being one and indivisible with the great of the past, with all that freed, ennobled.* Package it, stand on corners, in front of stadiums and on crowded beaches, knock on doors, give it as a fabled gift.

"And why not in cereal boxes, in soap packages?" he mocked himself. "Aah. You have taken my senses, cadaver."

Words foamed, died unsounded. Her body writhed; she made kissing motions with her mouth. (Her lips moving as she read, poring over the Book of the Martyrs, the magnifying glass superimposed over the heavy eyeglasses.) *Still she believed?* "Eva!" he whispered. "Still you believed? You lived by it? These Things Shall Be?"

"One pound soup meat," she answered distinctly, "one soup bone."

"My ears heard you. Ellen Mays was witness: 'Humankind . . . one has to believe.'" Imploringly: "Eva!"

"Bread, day-old." She was mumbling. "Please, in a wooden box . . . for kindling. The thread, hah, the thread breaks. Cheap thread"—and a gurgling, enormously loud, began in her throat.

"I ask for stone; she gives me bread—day-old." He pulled his hand away, shouted: "Who wanted questions? Everything you have to wake?" Then dully, "Ah, let me help you turn, poor creature."

Words jumbled, cleared. In a voice of crowded terror:

Paul, Sammy, don't fight.

"Hannah, have I ten hands?

"How can I give it, Clara, how can I give it if I don't have?"

"You lie," he said sturdily, "there was joy too." Bitterly: "Ah how cheap you speak of us at the last."

As if to rebuke him, as if her voice had no relationship with her flailing body, she sang clearly, beautifully, a school song the children had taught her when they were little; begged:

"Not look my hair where they cut. . . ."

(The crown of braids shorn.)[20] And instantly he left the mute old woman poring over the Book of the Martyrs; went past the mother treading at the sewing machine, singing with the children; past the girl in her wrinkled prison dress, hiding her hair with scarred hands, lifting to him her awkward, shamed, imploring eyes of love; and took her in his arms, dear, personal, fleshed, in all the heavy passion he had loved to rouse from her.

"Eva!"

Her little claw hand beat the covers. How much, how much can a man stand? He took up the cards, put them down, circled the beds, walked to the dresser,

[20]Reference to the Orthodox Jewish custom of cutting off the bride's hair and replacing it with a wig, and to the cutting off of prisoners' hair in Siberia.

opened, shut drawers, brushed his hair, moved his hand bit by bit over the mirror to see what of the reflection he could blot out with each move, and felt that at any moment he would die of what was unendurable. Went to press the buzzer to wake Jeannie, looked down, saw on Jeannie's sketch pad the hospital bed, with *her;* the double bed alongside, with him; the tall pillar feeding into her veins, and their hands, his and hers, clasped, feeding each other. And as if he had been instructed he went to his bed, lay down, holding the sketch (as if it could shield against the monstrous shapes of loss, of betrayal, of death) and with his free hand took hers back into his.

So Jeannie found them in the morning.

The last day the agony was perpetual. Time after time it lifted her almost off the bed, so they had to fight to hold her down. He could not endure and left the room; wept as if there never would be tears enough.

Jeannie came to comfort him. In her light voice she said: Grandaddy, Gran daddy don't cry. She is not there, she promised me. On the last day, she said she would go back to when she first heard music, a little girl on the road of the village where she was born. She promised me. It is a wedding and they dance, while the flutes so joyous and vibrant tremble in the air. Leave her there, Grandaddy, it is all right. She promised me. Come back, come back and help her poor body to die.

For two of that generation
Seevya and Genya
Infinite, dauntless, incorruptible
Death deepens the wonder

1961

Muriel Rukeyser 1913–1980

From the outset, Muriel Rukeyser was at once a political poet and a visionary. At times, those qualities were intensified, and in those moments she was simultaneously a revolutionary and a mystic. But to grasp the forces that drive her work—throughout the nearly 600 packed pages of her *Collected Poems*—we have to come to terms with a visionary impulse rooted in time, embedded in a struggle with lived history. Consider as cases in point the rhapsodic images she crafts to voice the mother's anguish at the death of her sons in "Absalom," and Rukeyser's own shared sense of loss in "Martin Luther King, Malcolm X," two poems from the beginning and the end of a career that spanned five decades of American history. But that is not all. To understand her work, we must also embrace the larger, wiser notion of politics that underlies all her poetry. For she understood early on what so many of us could not: that politics encompasses all the ways that social life is hierarchically structured and made meaningful. Politics is not only the large-scale public life of nations. It is also the advantages, inequities and illusions that make daily life very different for different groups among us. Thus Rukeyser understood that race and gender are integral parts of our social and political life. Never officially a feminist, she nonetheless devoted herself to voicing women's distinctive experience throughout her career.

Although Rukeyser was quite capable of writing short, tightly controlled poems—"The Minotaur" below is a good example—it may well be that her most rich and suggestive accomplishments are her poem sequences. Two of the poems in this selection are thus taken from longer sequences; "Absalom" is from "The Book of the Dead" and "*Les Tendresses Bestiales*" (the bestial tendernesses) is from "Ajanta," a poem sequence that takes its title from the name of a famous group of painted caves in India. "The Book of the Dead," in particular, is one of the major poem sequences of American modernism. Based on Rukeyser's own research in West Virginia, it combines historical background, congressional testimony, and the voices of a number of victims in telling the story of a 1930s industrial scandal: a company building a tunnel for a dam decided to double its profit by rapidly mining silica at the same time (without any of the necessary precautions). A great many workers died of lung disease as a result. "The Book of the Dead" is thus also one of Rukeyser's many poems that reflect and contribute to her political activism. "How We Did It," also reprinted here, is another; it recalls a demonstration about the Vietnam War, a war that Rukeyser experienced still more directly during a peace mission to South Vietnam in 1972.

During the 1930s Rukeyser regularly wrote for Communist Party publications like *New Masses.* She was in Spain to cover the antifascist Olympics in Barcelona when the Spanish Civil War broke out. She described that experience in the long poem "Mediterranean" and returned to the subject throughout her life. Years later, in 1975, she went to South Korea to protest the poet Kim Chi-Ha's imprisonment and anticipated execution; the poem sequence "The Gates" grew out of that trip. Rukeyser meditates on her poetics in *The Life of Poetry* (1949). She also published a novel, *The Orgy* (1966), as well as two biographies, *Willard Gibbs* (1942) and *The Traces of Thomas Harriot* (1971).

Cary Nelson
University of Illinois

PRIMARY WORKS

"Craft Interview with Muriel Rukeyser," *New York Quarterly* 11 (1972): 14–37; *The Collected Poems,* 1979; Kate Daniels, ed., *Out of Silence: Selected Poems,* 1992.

Absalom

I first discovered what was killing these men.
I had three sons who worked with their father in the tunnel:
Cecil, aged 23, Owen, aged 21, Shirley, aged 17.
They used to work in a coal mine, not steady work
for the mines were not going much of the time.
A power Co. foreman learned that we made home brew,
he formed a habit of dropping in evenings to drink,
persuading the boys and my husband—
give up their jobs and take this other work.
It would pay them better.
Shirley was my youngest son; the boy.
He went into the tunnel.

My heart   my mother   my heart   my mother
My heart   my coming into being.

My husband is not able to work.
He has it, according to the doctor.
We have been having a very hard time making a living since
  this trouble came to us.
I saw the dust in the bottom of the tub.
The boy worked there about eighteen months,
came home one evening with a shortness of breath.
He said, "Mother, I cannot get my breath."
Shirley was sick about three months.
I would carry him from his bed to the table,
from his bed to the porch, in my arms.

My heart is mine in the place of hearts,
They gave me back my heart, it lies in me.

When they took sick, right at the start, I saw a doctor.
I tried to get Dr. Harless to X-ray the boys.
He was the only man I had any confidence in,
the company doctor in the Kopper's mine,
but he would not see Shirley.
He did not know where his money was coming from.
I promised him half if he'd work to get compensation,
but even then he would not do anything.
I went on the road and begged the X-ray money,
the Charleston hospital made the lung pictures,
he took the case after the pictures were made.
And two or three doctors said the same thing.
The youngest boy did not get to go down there with me,
he lay and said, "Mother, when I die,
"I want you to have them open me up and
"see if that dust killed me.
"Try to get compensation,
"you will not have any way of making your living
"when we are gone,
"and the rest are going too."

I have gained mastery over my heart
I have gained mastery over my two hands
I have gained mastery over the waters
I have gained mastery over the river.

The case of my son was the first of the line of lawsuits.
They sent the lawyers down and the doctors down;
they closed the electric sockets in the camps.
There was Shirley, and Cecil, Jeffrey and Oren,
Raymond Johnson, Clev and Oscar Anders,
Frank Lynch, Henry Palf, Mr. Pitch, a foreman;

a slim fellow who carried steel with my boys,
his name was Darnell, I believe. There were many others,
the towns of Glen Ferris, Alloy, where the white rock lies,
six miles away; Vanetta, Gauley Bridge,
Gamoca, Lockwood, the gullies,
the whole valley is witness.
I hitchhike eighteen miles, they make checks out.
They asked me how I keep the cow on $2.
I said one week, feed for the cow, one week, the children's
flour.
The oldest son was twenty-three.
The next son was twenty-one.
The youngest son was eighteen.
They called it pneumonia at first.
They would pronounce it fever.
Shirley asked that we try to find out.
That's how they learned what the trouble was.

I open out a way, they have covered my sky with crystal
I come forth by day, I am born a second time,
I force a way through, and I know the gate
I shall journey over the earth among the living.

He shall not be diminished, never;
I shall give a mouth to my son.

1938

The Minotaur

Trapped, blinded, led; and in the end betrayed
Daily by new betrayals as he stays
Deep in his labyrinth, shaking and going mad.
Betrayed. Betrayed. Raving, the beaten head
Heavy with madness, he stands, half-dead and proud.
No one again will ever see his pride.
No one will find him by walking to him straight
But must be led circuitously about,
Calling to him and close and, losing the subtle thread,
Lose him again; while he waits, brutalized
By loneliness. Later, afraid
Of his own suffering. At last, savage and made
Ravenous, ready to prey upon the race
If it so much as learn the clews of blood
Into his pride his fear his glistening heart.

Now is the patient deserted in his fright
And love carrying salvage round the world
Lost in a crooked city; roundabout,
By the sea, the precipice, all the fantastic ways
Betrayal weaves its trap; loneliness knows the thread,
And the heart is lost, lost, trapped, blinded and led,
Deserted at the middle of the maze.

1944

Rite

My father groaned; my mother wept.
Among the mountains of the west
A deer lifted her golden throat.

They tore the pieces of the kill
While two dark sisters laughed and sang.—
The hidden lions blare until

The hunters charge and burn them all.
And in the black apartment halls
Of every city in the land

A father groans; a mother weeps;
A girl to puberty has come;
They shriek this, this is the crime

The gathering of the powers in.
At this first sign of her next life
America is stricken dumb.

The sharpening of your rocky knife!
The first blood of a woman shed!
The sacred word: Stand Up You Dead.

Mothers go weep; let fathers groan,
The flag of infinity is shown.
Now you will never be alone.

1958

The Poem as Mask

Orpheus

When I wrote of the women in their dances and wildness, it
    was a mask,
on their mountain, gold-hunting, singing, in orgy,
it was a mask; when I wrote of the god,
fragmented, exiled from himself, his life, the love gone down
    with song,
it was myself, split open, unable to speak, in exile from myself.

There is no mountain, there is no god, there is memory
of my torn life, myself split open in sleep, the rescued child
beside me among the doctors, and a word
of rescue from the great eyes.

No more masks! No more mythologies!

Now, for the first time, the god lifts his hand,
the fragments join in me with their own music.

1968

Martin Luther King, Malcolm X

Bleeding of the mountains
the noon bleeding
he is shot through the voice
all things being broken

The moon returning in her blood
looks down   grows white
loses color
and blazes

. . . and the near star gone—

voices of cities
drumming in the moon

bleeding of my right hand
my black voice bleeding

1973

How We Did It

We all traveled into that big room,
some from very far away
we smiled at some we knew
we did not as we talked agree
our hearts went fast thinking of morning
when we would walk along the path.
We spoke. Late night. We disagreed.
We knew we would climb the Senate steps.
We knew we would present our claim
we would demand : be strong now : end the war.
How would we do it? What would we ask?
"We will be warned," one said. "They will warn us and
  take us."
"We can speak and walk away."
"We can lie down as if in mourning."
"We can lie down as a way of speech,
speaking of all the dead in Asia."
Then Eqbal said, "We are not at this moment
a revolutionary group, we are
a group of dissenters. Let some, then,
walk away, let some stand until they want to leave,
let some lie down and let some be arrested. Some of us.
Let each do what he feels at that moment
tomorrow." Eqbal's dark face.
The doctor spoke, of friendships made in jail.
We looked into each other's eyes
and went all to our rooms, to sleep,
waiting for morning.

1976

Robert Hayden 1913–1980

Born Asa Bundy Sheffey in Detroit, Michigan, Hayden grew up in a poor, racially mixed neighborhood. Because his parents were divorced when he was quite young, his mother left him with neighbors, William and Sue Ellen Hayden, who gave him their name and raised him. His mother's periodic reappearances coupled with the jealousy of his foster mother made him "a divided person," and his art includes images of warring forces within the self.

Nearsighted and introverted, Hayden spent many hours reading and writing, and published his first poem at eighteen. Between 1932 and 1936, he attended Detroit City College (now Wayne State University); between 1936 and 1938, he worked for the Federal Writers Project of the WPA, and in 1944 completed an M.A. in English at the University of Michigan. (In 1940 he had married Erma Morris, a musician and teacher.) In 1946 he began teaching at Fisk University and in 1969 joined the English Department of the University of Michigan, where he taught until his death.

Much of his life Hayden wrote good poetry with little recognition. He was sustained by some awards and by friendships with other poets: a Rosenwald Fellowship in 1947, a Ford Foundation grant to write and travel in Mexico in 1954–1955, and the Grand Prize for Poetry at the First World Festival of Negro Arts in 1966. During the 1970s he was published by Liveright (*Angle of Ascent,* 1975), elected a fellow of the American Academy of Poets, and in 1976 chosen as Consultant in Poetry to the Library of Congress, the first African American ever to hold that post.

Hayden's philosophy of art remained constant throughout his life. Opposed to ethnocentrism, he refused to allow race to define subject matter. He also refused to believe that black social and political frustrations demanded poetry aimed exclusively at a black readership. Two criteria pertained for all artists: expert craft and universal subject matter. Universality, moreover, did not mean denial of racial material; it meant building out of personal and ethnic experience to human insights that could reach across group lines. Hayden's Baha'i faith, which he adopted in the 1940s, helped him believe in the unity of people and in the spiritual importance of art.

Some of the major themes of Hayden's poetry are the tensions between the imagination and the tragic nature of life, the past in the present, art as a form of spiritual redemption, and the nurturing power of early life and history. Most of his work falls into categories of "spirit of place" poems, folk character poems, Detroit neighborhood poems, and historical poems. This latter group, best known by the long poem "Middle Passage," is aimed at "correcting the misconceptions and destroying some of the stereotypes and clichés which surround Negro history." In the context of the racial militance of the 1960s and 1970s, Hayden's work has sometimes been found wanting by younger poets. His output for over forty years, however, suggests the deepest of commitments both to his own race and to humanity as a whole.

Robert M. Greenberg
Temple University

PRIMARY WORKS

Heart-Shape in the Dust, 1940; *The Lion and the Archer,* with Myron O'Higgins, 1948; *Figure of Time,* 1955; *A Ballad of Remembrance,* 1962; *Selected Poems,* 1966; *Words in the Mourning Time,* 1970; *The Night-Blooming Cereus,* 1972; *Angle of Ascent: New and Selected Poems,* 1975; *American Journal,* 1982. Collected Works: *Collected Prose,* ed. Frederick Glaysher, 1984; *Collected Poems,* Frederick Glaysher, 1985.

Tour 5[1]

The road winds down through autumn hills
in blazonry of farewell scarlet

[1]Alludes to an auto route in a guidebook that includes the old Natchez Trace, originally an Indian trail which later became "a dangerous and sinister road used by escaped criminals, highwaymen, murderers."

and recessional gold,
past cedar groves, through static villages
whose names are all that's left
of Choctaw, Chickasaw.

We stop a moment in a town
watched over by Confederate sentinels,
buy gas and ask directions of a rawboned man
whose eyes revile us as the enemy.

Shrill gorgon[2] silence breathes behind
his taut civility
and in the ever-tauntening air,
dark for us despite its Indian summer glow.
We drive on, following the route
of highwaymen and phantoms,

Of slaves and armies.
Children, wordless and remote,
wave at us from kindling porches.
And now the land is flat for miles,
the landscape lush, metallic, flayed,
its brightness harsh as bloodstained swords.

1962

Those Winter Sundays

Sundays too my father got up early
and put his clothes on in the blueblack cold,
then with cracked hands that ached
from labor in the weekday weather made
banked fires blaze. No one ever thanked him.

I'd wake and hear the cold splintering, breaking.
When the rooms were warm, he'd call,
and slowly I would rise and dress,
fearing the chronic angers of that house,

[2]Snaky-haired sisters in Greek mythology whose glance turned those who looked at them to stone.

Speaking indifferently to him,
who had driven out the cold
and polished my good shoes as well.
What did I know, what did I know
of love's austere and lonely offices?

1962

Summertime and the Living . . .[1]

Nobody planted roses, he recalls,
but sunflowers gangled there sometimes,
tough-stalked and bold
and like the vivid children there unplanned.
There circus-poster horses curveted
in trees of heaven
above the quarrels and shattered glass,
and he was bareback rider of them all.

No roses there in summer—
oh, never roses except when people died—
and no vacations for his elders,
so harshened after each unrelenting day
that they were shouting-angry.
But summer was, they said, the poor folks' time
of year. And he remembers
how they would sit on broken steps amid

The fevered tossings of the dusk, the dark,
wafting hearsay with funeral-parlor fans
or making evening solemn by
their quietness. Feels their Mosaic eyes
upon him, though the florist roses
that only sorrow could afford
long since have bidden them Godspeed.
Oh, summer summer summertime—

Then grim street preachers shook
their tambourines and Bibles in the face
of tolerant wickedness;

[1]Lyric ("Summertime and the living is easy") from George and Ira Gershwin's *Porgie and Bess.*

then Elks parades and big splendiferous
Jack Johnson[2] in his diamond limousine
set the ghetto burgeoning
with fantasies
of Ethiopia spreading her gorgeous wings.[3]

1962

Mourning Poem for the Queen of Sunday

Lord's lost Him His mockingbird,
His fancy warbler;
Satan sweet-talked her,
four bullets hushed her.
Who would have thought
she'd end that way?

Four bullets hushed her. And the world a-clang with evil.
Who's going to make old hardened sinner men tremble now
and the righteous rock?
Oh who and oh who will sing Jesus down
to help with struggling and doing without and being colored
all through blue Monday?
Till way next Sunday?

All those angels
in their cretonne clouds and finery
the true believer saw
when she rared back her head and sang,
all those angels are surely weeping.
Who would have thought
she'd end that way?

Four holes in her heart. The gold works wrecked.
But she looks so natural in her big bronze coffin
among the Broken Hearts and Gates-Ajar,
it's as if any moment she'd lift her head
from its pillow of chill gardenias
and turn this quiet into shouting Sunday
and make folks forget what she did on Monday.

[2]A black folk-hero, Jack Johnson (1878–1946) won the world heavyweight boxing championship in 1908. He was the subject of the Broadway play and Hollywood movie *The Great White Hope.*

[3]Adapts an often-quoted biblical reference to Ethiopia.

Oh, Satan sweet-talked her,
and four bullets hushed her.
Lord's lost Him His diva,
His fancy warbler's gone.
Who would have thought,
who would have thought she'd end that way?

1962

Theodore Roethke 1908–1963

Theodore Roethke was born in Saginaw, Michigan, and spent his childhood in and around his father's large commercial greenhouses, with their luxuriance of protected natural growth. It was there, among the acres of roses and carnations, and in cellars rank with rotten manure and rooting slips, that he developed his participatory awareness of the small things of nature. These two, the greenhouses and the almost godlike father directing a crew of skilled florists and helpers, would become the most pervasive shaping presences in his poetry—the greenhouses a humanly created Eden surrounded by open fields of eternity, and the father a center of powerful conflicting emotions of love and hate.

Roethke apparently began to write poems during his undergraduate years at the University of Michigan, where he received a B.A. in 1929, but if so, he wrote in secret. His doing so is only one early instance of his habitual wearing of masks to hide an inner vulnerability and seriousness. It was not until his graduate school years, first at Michigan and then at Harvard, that he either discussed or wrote poetry openly. His first publications came in 1930 and 1931. His teaching career, which would prove to be lifelong, began in the fall of 1931 at Lafayette College in Easton, Pennsylvania. Toward the end of his four-year term there, he served also as tennis coach, a game he played with intense and even rude aggressiveness. Later he would teach at several other colleges and universities before settling, from 1947 until his death, at the University of Washington.

Another pattern that would also prove to be lifelong emerged by 1931, or even before. By the time he went to Easton to teach, Roethke was already a heavy drinker, having frequent bouts of drunkenness during which he sometimes became rowdy and even destructive. Friends would later recall his drinking as a kind of search for oblivion. Certainly the drinking was both evidence and a contributing cause of the complex and severe emotional problems that led to his being hospitalized several times for what was usually diagnosed as manic-depression. Throughout his life he swung between extremes—of mood, of bravado or torturing self-doubt, of self-righteousness or guilt, of certainty that he was America's preeminent poet or despair over his supposed lack of achievement. He seems to have felt that nothing he did would have earned his father's approval.

In 1953, Roethke married Beatrice O'Connell, a former student of his and also a former fashion model. At the time of their marriage, Beatrice was totally unaware of his history of mental illness; he told her nothing. Before a year was out, she had seen him through one of his typical crises, though a fairly mild one involving only two weeks of hospitalization. She rose to the need and proved remarkably supportive over the years, a real companion as well as caretaker. It must not have been easy. He was extraordinarily demanding, as well as dependent, and was an inveterate casual pawer of women. His difficulties relating to women apparently sprang from very complex feelings toward his mother which, if less disturbing than those toward his father, were at any rate troubled. However, several of his late poems record Roethke's great care and concern for his wife, and one of his most significant works, "Meditations of an Old Woman," draws partly on his regard for his mother.

Besides its disciplined exploration of rhythmic variation and symbolist style, Roethke's poetry is characterized by a deep, even mystical, animism, a close attention to minute living things and natural processes, and a continuing use of childhood anxieties and his own ambivalent feelings toward his father in developing a motif of the soul journey. For Roethke, this journey went toward reconciliation and oneness. In his late poem "The Rose" (from "North American Sequence") his father would be joined with an evocation of the greenhouse world as images of perfect beatitude: "What need for heaven, then, / With that man and those roses?" Among his many honors and awards were the Pulitzer Prize, the Bollingen Prize, a Fulbright Award, and two Guggenheim Fellowships.

Janis Stout
Texas A & M University

PRIMARY WORKS

Open House, 1941; *The Lost Son and Other Poems,* 1948; *Praise to the End!,* 1951; *The Waking: Poems 1933–53,* 1953; *Words for the Wind: The Collected Verse of Theodore Roethke,* 1957; *I Am! Says the Lamb,* 1961; *Party at the Zoo,* 1963; *The Far Field,* 1964; *Sequence, Sometimes Metaphysical,* 1964; *The Collected Poems of Theodore Roethke,* 1968.

Frau Bauman, Frau Schmidt, and Frau Schwartze[1]

Gone the three ancient ladies
Who creaked on the greenhouse ladders,
Reaching up white strings
To wind, to wind
The sweet-pea tendrils,[2] the smilax,[3]
Nasturtiums, the climbing
Roses, to straighten
Carnations, red
Chrysanthemums; the stiff
Stems, jointed like corn,
They tied and tucked,—
These nurses of nobody else.
Quicker than birds, they dipped

[1]Common German names; Roethke's family was German.

[2]Small twigs of vining plants.

[3]A climbing plant with prickly stems.

Up and sifted the dirt;
They sprinkled and shook;
They stood astride pipes,
Their skirts billowing out wide into tents,
Their hands twinkling with wet;
Like witches they flew along rows
Keeping creation at ease;
With a tendril for needle
They sewed up the air with a stem;
They teased out the seed that the cold kept asleep,—
All the coils, loops, and whorls.
They trellised[4] the sun; they plotted for more than themselves.

I remember how they picked me up, a spindly[5] kid,
Pinching and poking my thin ribs
Till I lay in their laps, laughing,
Weak as a whiffet;[6]
Now, when I'm alone and cold in my bed,
They still hover over me,
These ancient leathery crones,
With their bandannas stiffened with sweat,
And their thorn-bitten wrists,
And their snuff-laden breath blowing lightly over me in my first
sleep.

1948

Root Cellar

Nothing would sleep in that cellar,[1] dank as a ditch,
Bulbs broke out of boxes hunting for chinks in the dark,
Shoots dangled and drooped,
Lolling obscenely from mildewed crates,
Hung down long yellow evil necks, like tropical snakes.
And what a congress[2] of stinks!—
Roots ripe as old bait,
Pulpy stems, rank, silo-rich,[3]

[4]Trained up on a frame, usually made of laths, as a plant is trained into a chosen shape. Roethke's tribute to the three greenhouse workers/nature goddesses has reached mythic proportions.

[5]Skinny.

[6]A small, young, or unimportant person; probably a corruption of *whippet,* a small dog.

[1]The cellar of the poet's father's commercial greenhouse in Saginaw, Michigan. "Root Cellar" is one of the famous "greenhouse poems."

[2]Literally, a coming together; thus a collection or assortment.

[3]Rank from long storage; a silo is a storage building for grain.

Leaf-mold, manure, lime, piled against slippery planks.
Nothing would give up life:
Even the dirt kept breathing a small breath.

1948

Big Wind

Where were the greenhouses going,
Lunging into the lashing
Wind driving water
So far down the river
All the faucets stopped?—
So we drained the manure-machine
For the steam plant,
Pumping the stale mixture
Into the rusty boilers,
Watching the pressure gauge
Waver over to red,
As the seams hissed
And the live steam
Drove to the far
End of the rose-house,
Where the worst wind was,
Creaking the cypress window-frames,
Cracking so much thin glass
We stayed all night,
Stuffing the holes with burlap;
But she rode it out,
That old rose-house,
She hove[1] into the teeth of it,
The core and pith of that ugly storm,
Ploughing with her stiff prow,
Bucking into the wind-waves
That broke over the whole of her,
Flailing her sides with spray,
Flinging long strings of wet across the roof-top,
Finally veering, wearing themselves out, merely
Whistling thinly under the wind-vents;

[1]Past tense of heave; in nautical usage, to heave to is to keep the ship heading into the wind. Here, the term is part of an extended conceit of greenhouse as boat or ship.

She sailed until the calm morning,
Carrying her full cargo of roses.

1948

from The Lost Son

1. *The Flight*

At Woodlawn[1] I heard the dead cry:
I was lulled by the slamming of iron,
A slow drip over stones,
Toads brooding wells.[2]
All the leaves stuck out their tongues;
I shook the softening chalk of my bones,
Saying,
Snail, snail, glister[3] me forward,
Bird, soft-sigh me home,
Worm, be with me.
This is my hard time.

Fished in an old wound,[4]
The soft pond of repose;
Nothing nibbled my line,
Not even the minnows came.

Sat in an empty house
Watching shadows crawl,
Scratching.
There was one fly.
Voice, come out of the silence.
Say something.
Appear in the form of a spider
Or a moth beating the curtain.

Tell me:
Which is the way I take;
Out of what door do I go,
Where and to whom?

[1]A cemetery.
[2]Read "brooding in wells."
[3]A variant of glisten or glitter, referring to the shining track as they move along.
[4]Casting about for meaning or reassurance, he figuratively casts his line into the subconscious, wounded as it was; simultaneously, he casts his line into memories of childhood.

* * *

Dark hollows said, lee to the wind,
The moon said, back of an eel,
The salt said, look by the sea,
Your tears are not enough praise,
You will find no comfort here,
In the kingdom of bang and blab.[5]
Running lightly over spongy ground,

Past the pasture of flat stones,
The three elms,
The sheep strewn on a field,
Over a rickety bridge
Toward the quick-water, wrinkling and rippling.

Hunting along the river,
Down among the rubbish, the bug-riddled foliage,
By the muddy pond-edge, by the bog-holes,
By the shrunken lake, hunting, in the heat of summer.

The shape of a rat?
It's bigger than that.
It's less than a leg
And more than a nose,
Just under the water
It usually goes.
Is it soft like a mouse?
Can it wrinkle its nose?
Could it come in the house
On the tips of its toes?

Take the skin of a cat
And the back of an eel,
Then roll them in grease,—
That's the way it would feel.

It's sleek as an otter
With wide webby toes
Just under the water
It usually goes.

[5]Empty verbiage; perhaps a view of everyday society.

4. *The Return*

The way to the boiler was dark,
Dark all the way,
Over slippery cinders
Through the long greenhouse.

The roses kept breathing in the dark.
They had many mouths to breathe with.
My knees made little winds underneath
Where the weeds slept.

There was always a single light
Swinging by the fire-pit,[1]
Where the fireman pulled out roses,
The big roses, the big bloody clinkers.[2]

Once I stayed all night.
The light in the morning came slowly over the white
Snow.
There were many kinds of cool
Air.
Then came steam.

Pipe-knock.

Scurry of warm over small plants.
Ordnung! ordnung![3]
Papa is coming!

A fine haze moved off the leaves;
Frost melted on far panes;
The rose, the chrysanthemum turned toward the light.
Even the hushed forms, the bent yellowy weeds
Moved in a slow up-sway.

5. *It was beginning winter*

It was beginning winter,
An in-between time,
The landscape still partly brown:
The bones of weeds kept swinging in the wind,
Above the blue snow.

[1]Where the boiler was heated, to provide steam for keeping the greenhouse warm.
[2]Red coals.
[3]German, "order"; here, given as a military-like command.

It was beginning winter,
The light moved slowly over the frozen field,
Over the dry seed-crowns,
The beautiful surviving bones
Swinging in the wind.

Light traveled over the wide field;
Stayed.
The weeds stopped swinging.
The mind moved, not alone,
Through the clear air, in the silence.

Was it light?
Was it light within?
Was it light within light?
Stillness becoming alive,
Yet still?

A lively understandable spirit
Once entertained you.
It will come again.
Be still.
Wait.

1948

from Meditations of an Old Woman

First Meditation

1

On love's worst ugly day,
The weeds hiss at the edge of the field,
The small winds make their chilly indictments.
Elsewhere, in houses, even pails can be sad;
While stones loosen on the obscure hillside,
And a tree tilts from its roots,
Toppling down an embankment.

The spirit moves, but not always upward,
While animals eat to the north,
And the shale slides an inch in the talus,
The bleak wind eats at the weak plateau,

And the sun brings joy to some.
But the rind, often, hates the life within.

How can I rest in the days of my slowness?
I've become a strange piece of flesh,
Nervous and cold, bird-furtive,[1] whiskery,
With a cheek soft as a hound's ear.
What's left is light as a seed;
I need an old crone's knowing.

2

Often I think of myself as riding—
Alone, on a bus through western country.
I sit above the back wheels, where the jolts are hardest,
And we bounce and sway along toward the midnight,
The lights tilting up, skyward, as we come over a little rise,
Then down, as we roll like a boat from a wave-crest.

All journeys, I think, are the same:
The movement is forward, after a few wavers,
And for a while we are all alone,
Busy, obvious with ourselves,
The drunken soldier, the old lady with her peppermints;
And we ride, we ride, taking the curves
Somewhat closer, the trucks coming
Down from behind the last ranges,
Their black shapes breaking past;
And the air claps between us,
Blasting the frosted windows,
And I seem to go backward,
Backward in time:

Two song sparrows, one within a greenhouse,
Shuttling[2] its throat while perched on a wind-vent,
And another, outside, in the bright day,
With a wind from the west and the trees all in motion.
One sang, then the other,
The songs tumbling over and under the glass,
And the men beneath them wheeling in dirt to the cement
benches,

[1] As furtive as a bird.
[2] With a back-and-forth motion like the shuttle of a loom; referring to the vibration of a singing bird's throat.

The laden wheelbarrows creaking and swaying,
And the up-spring of the plank when a foot left the
runway.

Journey within a journey:[3]
The ticket mislaid or lost, the gate
Inaccessible, the boat always pulling out
From the rickety wooden dock,
The children waving;
Or two horses plunging in snow, their lines tangled,
A great wooden sleigh careening behind them,
Swerving up a steep embankment.
For a moment they stand above me,
Their black skins shuddering:
Then they lurch forward,
Lunging down a hillside.

3

As when silt drifts and sifts down through muddy pond-water,
Settling in small beads around weeds and sunken branches,
And one crab, tentative, hunches himself before moving along the
bottom,
Grotesque, awkward, his extended eyes looking at nothing in
particular,
Only a few bubbles loosening from the ill-matched tentacles,
The tail and smaller legs slipping and sliding slowly backward—
So the spirit tries for another life,
Another way and place in which to continue;
Or a salmon, tired, moving up a shallow stream,
Nudges into a back-eddy, a sandy inlet,
Bumping against sticks and bottom-stones, then swinging
Around, back into the tiny maincurrent, the rush of brownish-
white water,
Still swimming forward—
So, I suppose, the spirit journeys.

4

I have gone into the waste lonely places
Behind the eye;[4] the lost acres at the edge of smoky cities.

[3]Throughout, cf. "The spirit moves but not always upward": the spiritual journey includes periods of frustration which, traditionally, the mystic accepts as integral parts of the whole. Cf. T. S. Eliot's "the way up is the way down," *Four Quartets*.

[4]The mystic journey entails a journey inward, the journey of introspection.

What's beyond never crumbles like an embankment,
Explodes like a rose, or thrusts wings over the Caribbean.
There are no pursuing forms, faces on walls:
Only the motes of dust in the immaculate hallways,
The darkness of falling hair, the warnings from lint and spiders,
The vines graying to a fine powder.
There is no riven tree, or lamb dropped by an eagle.[5]

There are still times, morning and evening:
The cerulean,[6] high in the elm,
Thin and insistent as a cicada,[7]
And the far phoebe,[8] singing,
The long plaintive notes floating down,
Drifting through leaves, oak and maple,
Or the whippoorwill, along the smoky ridges,
A single bird calling and calling;
A fume reminds me, drifting across wet gravel;
A cold wind comes over stones;
A flame, intense, visible,
Plays over the dry pods,[9]
Runs fitfully along the stubble,
Moves over the field,
Without burning.
        In such times, lacking a god,
        I am still happy.

from Fourth Meditation

2

What is it to be a woman?
To be contained, to be a vessel?
To prefer a window to a door?
A pool to a river?
To become lost in a love,
Yet remain only half aware of the intransient glory?
To be a mouth, a meal of meat?
To gaze at a face with the fixed eyes of a spaniel?

I think of the self-involved:
The ritualists of the mirror, the lonely drinkers,

[5]The old woman's spiritual journey is not characterized by high drama but by full attention to the everyday.
[6]Blue; the sky.
[7]A variety of locust having an insistent harsh sound.
[8]A bird.
[9]Empty seed pods; the time is late autumn or winter, when all that is left in the grain fields is stubble.

The minions[1] of benzedrine and paraldehyde,[2]
And those who submerge themselves deliberately in trivia,
Women who become their possessions,
Shapes stiffening into metal,
Match-makers, arrangers of picnics—
What do their lives mean,
And the lives of their children?—
The young, brow-beaten early into a baleful[3] silence,
Frozen by a father's lip, a mother's failure to answer.
Have they seen, ever, the sharp bones of the poor?
Or known, once, the soul's authentic hunger,
Those cat-like immaculate creatures
For whom the world works?

What do they need?
O more than a roaring boy,
For the sleek captains of intuition cannot reach them;
They feel neither the tearing iron
Nor the sound of another footstep—
How I wish them awake!
May the high flower of the hay climb into their hearts;
May they lean into light and live;
May they sleep in robes of green, among the ancient ferns;
May their eyes gleam with the first dawn;
May the sun gild them a worm;
May they be taken by the true burning;
May they flame into being!—
I see them as figures walking in a greeny garden,
Their gait formal and elaborate, their hair a glory,
The gentle and beautiful still-to-be-born;
The descendants of the playful tree-shrew that survived the archaic killers,
The fang and the claw, the club and the knout,[4] the irrational edict,
The fury of the hate-driven zealot, the meanness of the human weasel;
Who turned a corner in time, when at last he grew a thumb;
A prince of small beginnings, enduring the slow stretches of change,
Who spoke first in the coarse short-hand of the subliminal[5] depths,
Made from his terror and dismay a grave philosophical language;
A lion of flame, pressed to the point of love,
Yet moves gently among the birds.

1958

[1]Slaves.
[2]Drugs; benzedrine is a stimulant, paraldehyde a sedative.
[3]Sorrowful.
[4]A leather whip for flogging.
[5]Beneath the threshold *(limen)* of consciousness.

Elegy

Her face like a rain-beaten stone on the day she rolled off
With the dark hearse, and enough flowers for an alderman,[1]—
And so she was, in her way, Aunt Tilly.

Sighs, sighs, who says they have sequence?
Between the spirit and the flesh,—what war?
She never knew;
For she asked no quarter[2] and gave none,
Who sat with the dead when the relatives left,
Who fed and tended the infirm, the mad, the epileptic,
And, with a harsh rasp of a laugh at herself,
Faced up to the worst.

I recall how she harried the children away all the late summer
From the one beautiful thing in her yard, the peachtree;
How she kept the wizened,[3] the fallen, the misshapen for herself,
And picked and pickled the best, to be left on rickety doorsteps.

And yet she died in agony,
Her tongue, at the last, thick, black as an ox's.

Terror of cops, bill collectors, betrayers of the poor,—
I see you[4] in some celestial[5] supermarket,
Moving serenely among the leeks and cabbages,
Probing the squash,
Bearing down, with two steady eyes,
On the quaking butcher.

1958

Elizabeth Bishop 1911–1979

Elizabeth Bishop was the only child of William Thomas Bishop and Gertrude (Bulmer) Bishop. William, the oldest son of John W. Bishop of Prince Edward Island, was a contractor responsible for many public buildings in Boston (including the Museum of Fine Arts and the Boston Public Library). He married Gertrude Bulmer of Great Village, Nova Scotia, and died when Elizabeth was but

[1]A public official, like a city councilman.
[2]Mercy granted to a surrendering foe.
[3]Shriveled.
[4]The poet addresses his dead Aunt Tilly, whom he characterizes as a terror to three representative groups of oppressors—policemen, bill collectors, and betrayers of the poor.
[5]Heavenly; he envisions Aunt Tilly in an afterlife very much like her accustomed life on earth.

eight months old. When the poet was four years old, her mother, after years of nervous breakdowns, was permanently placed in a mental institution. She spent summers with her maternal grandparents in Nova Scotia, was intermittently cared for by her paternal grandparents in Worcester and later by a married but childless aunt in and around Boston. Bishop's childhood was spent in the company of adults; in her early years, she had little opportunity for contact with members of her own generation.

Chronically ill with asthma, Bishop was unable to attend school until 1927, when she enrolled at Walnut Hill School in Natick, Massachusetts. Sailing (two months at "The Nautical Camp for Girls" on Cape Cod), reading, and music were her early and enduring enthusiasms. When she entered Vassar College in 1930 she was undecided as to whether she would major in music, literature, or medicine. Though that Vassar class would come to be known as a particularly literary group (Muriel Rukeyser and Mary McCarthy were co-editors with Bishop of the student literary magazine, *Con Spirito*), Bishop did not meet her literary mentor, Marianne Moore, at Vassar, but in the entry way of the New York Public Library. The Vassar College librarian had arranged a meeting after Bishop expressed an interest in Marianne Moore's poetry; the meeting led to a lifelong friendship.

Marianne Moore was Bishop's first life-example, editor, confidante, and typist. In an age when women lacked women as role models, Moore emerged as one of the earliest as well as most significant reference points in the younger poet's world. As Bishop would later recall, Moore offered a rare confluence of manners and morals, a life as distinctly styled as her poetry. Correspondence between the poets reveals a protégée influenced by, yet resistant to, the poetic style of her mentor. While comparisons are inevitable, Bishop repeatedly distinguished her aesthetic as quite traditional in comparison with Moore's unique brand of Modernism. Curiously, poets as diverse as George Herbert and Gerard Manley Hopkins, Emerson, Thoreau, and Neruda greatly influenced Bishop's early work.

Robert Lowell's intuitive and precise review of *North & South* (*Sewanee Review,* 1947) brought the poets together for a lifetime of correspondence. Though Lowell repeatedly confessed his debt to Bishop's poetry, her debt to his is less well known. For Bishop, Lowell represented the quintessential American: male and historically significant. Indeed, he became her "other." Even as *Questions of Travel* seems a reply to Lowell's earlier *Life Studies, Geography III* seems unimaginable without Lowell's struggle to place life at the center of the lyric.

Although Moore and Lowell served as her sponsors, Bishop returned that favor in correspondence, friendship, and support of May Swenson. The voluminous collection of letters between these poets (Washington University Library Special Collections) describes a mutual female bonding and support. Swenson is as tough-minded as the young Bishop was but she refuses to see the role of mentor as exclusively Bishop's. Swenson enters into a lively critical discussion with Bishop, often assuming the role of teacher herself. The reserve that marks the Moore-Bishop letters fades into an eloquent democracy in the Bishop-Swenson letters.

Bishop's literary development is best known through letters because she spent most of her adult life in Brazil, away from the stresses and competitiveness of the New York literary world. Though Moore, Lowell, Randall Jarrell, and Swenson kept her informed about the American poetry world, she was able to live a life of tropical remove with her Brazilian friend, Lota Costellat de Macedo Soares. Witness to overwhelming poverty, political instabilities, and a mixture of foreign cultures, Bishop, armed with a small trust fund, could afford to keep these distractions at bay while she traveled, observed, and wrote.

Keenly observed description and a dependence upon the things of this world characterize Bishop's work. In language, she is a direct descendant of what Perry Miller called the American plain stylists. Like Robert Frost, she effects a wide tonal range within a remarkably narrow range of words, often accomplished through formal means. In "Filling Station," Bishop uses the restrictions of form to impose limitations upon the tone and atmosphere of the poem. Solitary figures in the landscape abound in her poems and suggest the familiar Romantic lyric of the isolated hero, the Wordsworthian self-discoverer; yet she systematically rejects epiphany, preferring the familiarity of the phenomenal world. Bishop's early interest in surrealism surfaces throughout her work in dreamscapes of different sorts. "The Man-Moth" explores the nightmarish uncertainties of the night world, while invoking the poet's interest in the perceptions of exiles. Like many American writers, she prizes the isolated moral force. Like Emerson's poetry, Bishop sees, names, and gives the landscape a moral form and purpose.

Much has been made of Bishop's reticence. Octavio Paz proclaimed it a power, a womanly strength; Sylvia Plath and Adrienne Rich, searching for appropriate woman poets as models, rejected it as a kind of repression. Bishop's refusal to appear in women's anthologies did not stem from an avoidance of women's issues (she had lived her life as an independent artist), but rather from a lifelong commitment to the transcendent potential of art, a belief that literature should address that world beyond life's limitations.

C. K. Doreski
Boston University

PRIMARY WORKS

North & South, 1946 (Houghton Mifflin Poetry Award); *Poems: North & South—A Cold Spring* (Pulitzer Prize, 1956); *Questions of Travel,* 1965; *The Complete Poems,* 1969 (National Book Award); *Geography III,* 1976; *The Complete Poems, 1927–1979,* 1983; *The Collected Prose,* 1984.

The Fish

I caught a tremendous fish
and held him beside the boat
half out of water, with my hook
fast in a corner of his mouth.
He didn't fight.
He hadn't fought at all.
He hung a grunting weight,
battered and venerable
and homely. Here and there
his brown skin hung in strips
like ancient wallpaper,
and its pattern of darker brown

was like wallpaper:
shapes like full-blown roses
stained and lost through age.
He was speckled with barnacles,
fine rosettes of lime,
and infested
with tiny white sea-lice,
and underneath two or three
rags of green weed hung down.
While his gills were breathing in
the terrible oxygen
—the frightening gills,
fresh and crisp with blood,
that can cut so badly—
I thought of the coarse white flesh
packed in like feathers,
the big bones and the little bones,
the dramatic reds and blacks
of his shiny entrails,
and the pink swim-bladder
like a big peony.
I looked into his eyes
which were far larger than mine
but shallower, and yellowed,
the irises backed and packed
with tarnished tinfoil
seen through the lenses
of old scratched isinglass.
They shifted a little, but not
to return my stare.
—It was more like the tipping
of an object toward the light.
I admired his sullen face,
the mechanism of his jaw,
and then I saw
that from his lower lip
—if you could call it a lip—
grim, wet, and weaponlike,
hung five old pieces of fish-line,
or four and a wire leader
with the swivel still attached,
with all their five big hooks
grown firmly in his mouth.
A green line, frayed at the end
where he broke it, two heavier lines,
and a fine black thread
still crimped from the strain and snap

when it broke and he got away.
Like medals with their ribbons
frayed and wavering,
a five-haired beard of wisdom
trailing from his aching jaw.
I stared and stared
and victory filled up
the little rented boat,
from the pool of bilge
where oil had spread a rainbow
around the rusted engine
to the bailer rusted orange,
the sun-cracked thwarts,
the oarlocks on their strings,
the gunnels—until everything
was rainbow, rainbow, rainbow!
And I let the fish go.

1946

The Man-Moth[1]

Here, above,
cracks in the buildings are filled with battered moonlight.
The whole shadow of Man is only as big as his hat.
It lies at his feet like a circle for a doll to stand on,
and he makes an inverted pin, the point magnetized to the moon.
He does not see the moon; he observes only her vast properties,
feeling the queer light on his hands, neither warm nor cold,
of a temperature impossible to record in thermometers.

But when the Man-Moth
pays his rare, although occasional, visits to the surface,
the moon looks rather different to him. He emerges
from an opening under the edge of one of the sidewalks
and nervously begins to scale the faces of the buildings.
He thinks the moon is a small hole at the top of the sky,
proving the sky quite useless for protection.
He trembles, but must investigate as high as he can climb.

Up the façades,
his shadow dragging like a photographer's cloth behind him,

[1]Newspaper misprint for "mammoth."

he climbs fearfully, thinking that this time he will manage
to push his small head through that round clean opening
and be forced through, as from a tube, in black scrolls on the
light.
(Man, standing below him, has no such illusions.)
But what the Man-Moth fears most he must do, although
he fails, of course, and falls back scared but quite unhurt.

Then he returns
to the pale subways of cement he calls his home. He flits,
he flutters, and cannot get aboard the silent trains
fast enough to suit him. The doors close swiftly.
The Man-Moth always seats himself facing the wrong way
and the train starts at once at its full, terrible speed,
without a shift in gears or a gradation of any sort.
He cannot tell the rate at which he travels backwards.

Each night he must
be carried through artificial tunnels and dream recurrent dreams.
Just as the ties recur beneath his train, these underlie
his rushing brain. He does not dare look out the window,
for the third rail, the unbroken draught of poison,
runs there beside him. He regards it as a disease
he has inherited the susceptibility to. He has to keep
his hands in his pockets, as others must wear mufflers.

If you catch him,
hold up a flashlight to his eye. It's all dark pupil,
an entire night itself, whose haired horizon tightens
as he stares back, and closes up the eye. Then from the lids
one tear, his only possession, like the bee's sting, slips.
Slyly he palms it, and if you're not paying attention
he'll swallow it. However, if you watch, he'll hand it over,
cool as from underground springs and pure enough to drink.

1946

At the Fishhouses

Although it is a cold evening,
down by one of the fishhouses
an old man sits netting,
his net, in the gloaming almost invisible,
a dark purple-brown,

and his shuttle worn and polished.
The air smells so strong of codfish
it makes one's nose run and one's eyes water.
The five fishhouses have steeply peaked roofs
and narrow, cleated gangplanks slant up
to storerooms in the gables
for the wheelbarrows to be pushed up and down on.
All is silver: the heavy surface of the sea,
swelling slowly as if considering spilling over,
is opaque, but the silver of the benches,
the lobster pots, and masts, scattered
among the wild jagged rocks,
is of an apparent translucence
like the small old buildings with an emerald moss
growing on their shoreward walls.
The big fish tubs are completely lined
with layers of beautiful herring scales
and the wheelbarrows are similarly plastered
with creamy iridescent coats of mail,
with small iridescent flies crawling on them.
Up on the little slope behind the houses,
set in the sparse bright sprinkle of grass,
is an ancient wooden capstan,
cracked, with two long bleached handles
and some melancholy stains, like dried blood,
where the ironwork has rusted.
The old man accepts a Lucky Strike.
He was a friend of my grandfather.
We talk of the decline in the population
and of codfish and herring
while he waits for a herring boat to come in.
There are sequins on his vest and on his thumb.
He has scraped the scales, the principal beauty,
from unnumbered fish with that black old knife,
the blade of which is almost worn away.

Down at the water's edge, at the place
where they haul up the boats, up the long ramp
descending into the water, thin silver
tree trunks are laid horizontally
across the gray stones, down and down
at intervals of four or five feet.

Cold dark deep and absolutely clear,
element bearable to no mortal,
to fish and to seals . . . One seal particularly
I have seen here evening after evening.

He was curious about me. He was interested in music;
like me a believer in total immersion,
so I used to sing him Baptist hymns.
I also sang "A Mighty Fortress Is Our God."
He stood up in the water and regarded me
steadily, moving his head a little.
Then he would disappear, then suddenly emerge
almost in the same spot, with a sort of shrug
as if it were against his better judgment.
Cold dark deep and absolutely clear,
the clear gray icy water . . . Back, behind us,
the dignified tall firs begin.
Bluish, associating with their shadows,
a million Christmas trees stand
waiting for Christmas. The water seems suspended
above the rounded gray and blue-gray stones.
I have seen it over and over, the same sea, the same,
slightly, indifferently swinging above the stones,
icily free above the stones,
above the stones and then the world.
If you should dip your hand in,
your wrist would ache immediately,
your bones would begin to ache and your hand would burn
as if the water were a transmutation of fire
that feeds on stones and burns with a dark gray flame.
If you tasted it, it would first taste bitter,
then briny, then surely burn your tongue.
It is like what we imagine knowledge to be:
dark, salt, clear, moving, utterly free,
drawn from the cold hard mouth
of the world, derived from the rocky breasts
forever, flowing and drawn, and since
our knowledge is historical, flowing, and flown.

1955

Filling Station

Oh, but it is dirty!
—this little filling station,
oil-soaked, oil-permeated
to a disturbing, over-all
black translucency.
Be careful with that match!

Father wears a dirty,
oil-soaked monkey suit
that cuts him under the arms,
and several quick and saucy
and greasy sons assist him
(it's a family filling station),
all quite thoroughly dirty.

Do they live in the station?
It has a cement porch
behind the pumps, and on it
a set of crushed and grease-
impregnated wickerwork;
on the wicker sofa
a dirty dog, quite comfy.

Some comic books provide
the only note of color—
of certain color. They lie
upon a big dim doily
draping a taboret[1]
(part of the set), beside
a big hirsute begonia.

Why the extraneous plant?
Why the taboret?
Why, oh why, the doily?
(Embroidered in daisy stitch
with marguerites, I think,
and heavy with gray crochet.)

Somebody embroidered the doily.
Somebody waters the plant,
or oils it, maybe. Somebody
arranges the rows of cans
so that they softly say:
ESSO—SO—SO—SO
to high-strung automobiles.
Somebody loves us all.

1965

[1]Small stand.

Robert Lowell, Jr. 1917–1977

Born to Charlotte Winslow and Robert Traill Spence Lowell in Boston, Robert Lowell was the great-grandnephew of James Russell Lowell and a distant cousin of Amy Lowell. He attended St. Marks School and then Harvard (1935–37), but completed his undergraduate education at Kenyon College in Ohio (his degree was *summa cum laude* in 1940). An avid student of poetry, he chose his friends from an artistic coterie and in 1940 married fiction writer Jean Stafford. During World War II, declaring himself a conscientious objector, Lowell was imprisoned in 1943–44. In 1947 he received a Guggenheim fellowship and the Pulitzer Prize for Poetry (for *Lord Weary's Castle*). He also was chosen Consultant in Poetry for the Library of Congress for 1947–48. In 1948 he and Stafford were divorced, and in 1949 he married critic Elizabeth Hardwick.

Lowell's life was devoted to poetry—writing and teaching—but it was marred by emotional breakdowns that required hospitalization. His periodic instability made relationships troublesome; he tended to find his greatest solace in friendships with other writers (Delmore Schwartz, John Berryman, Randall Jarrell, Elizabeth Bishop, William Carlos Williams, Anne Sexton, and the countless younger writers who studied with him at Boston University, Harvard, and the University of Iowa). His writing charted his cycles of change: from the rebellion of the elite Brahmin to the immersion in art experienced at Kenyon, where Lowell studied with John Crowe Ransom and developed his penchant for allusive, densely referential poetry. In 1940 he became a Catholic; in 1950 he left the church.

After giving a series of readings on the West Coast in 1957, Lowell became dissatisfied with his tightly structured poems, and began the process of self-exploration that led to his masterful autobiographical work. *Life Studies* and *For the Union Dead,* the latter of which drew together the autobiographical and Lowell's fascination with history, marked the apex of Lowell's influence on the poetry scene. He also had moved to New York, where he remained until his death. There he became politically active, marching against the Pentagon in 1967 and continuing to scrutinize his life against the canvas of world and national events.

In the early 1970s, Lowell and Hardwick divorced and Lowell married Lady Caroline Blackwood. He then divided his life between her home in England and periods of teaching at Harvard, a pattern that allowed him to explore the consequences of his New England roots and his need to cut himself off from that locale. When he died of a heart attack at age sixty, he was considered the most important and most influential poet of his generation.

Some critics reacted harshly to his last poetry, in which the occasion of his divorce from Hardwick and the separation of himself from his child became the subject of his art. And there is some limit to a reader's interest in seeing self-destruction portrayed in poetry. Like many of his peers, Lowell led a life of difficult and often broken human relationships, and his poems which chart those relationships are often less than great.

Linda Wagner-Martin
University of North Carolina at Chapel Hill

PRIMARY WORKS

Land of Unlikeness, 1944; *Lord Weary's Castle,* 1946; *The Mills of the Kavanaughs,* 1951; *Life Studies,* 1959; *Imitations,* 1961; *For the Union Dead,* 1964; *The Old Glory* (plays), 1965; *Selected Poems,* 1965; *Near the Ocean,* 1967; *Notebook 1967–68,* 1969; *The Dolphin,* 1973; *History,* 1973; *For Lizzie and Harriet,* 1973; *Selected Poems,* 1976; *Day by Day,* 1977.

Memories of West Street and Lepke[1]

Only teaching on Tuesdays, book-worming
in pajamas fresh from the washer each morning,
I hog a whole house on Boston's
"hardly passionate Marlborough Street,"[2]
where even the man
scavenging filth in the back alley trash cans,
has two children, a beach wagon, a helpmate,
and is a "young Republican."
I have a nine months' daughter,
young enough to be my granddaughter.
Like the sun she rises in her flame-flamingo infants' wear.

These are the tanquillized *Fifties,*
and I am forty. Ought I to regret my seedtime?
I was a fire-breathing Catholic C.O.,[3]
and made my manic statement,
telling off the state and president, and then
sat waiting sentence in the bull pen
beside a Negro boy with curlicues
of marijuana in his hair.

Given a year,
I walked on the roof of the West Street Jail, a short
enclosure like my school soccer court,
and saw the Hudson River once a day
through sooty clothesline entanglements
and bleaching khaki tenements.
Strolling, I yammered metaphysics with Abramowitz,
a jaundice-yellow ("it's really tan")
and fly-weight pacifist,
so vegetarian,
he wore rope shoes and preferred fallen fruit.
He tried to convert Bioff and Brown,
the Hollywood pimps, to his diet.
Hairy, muscular, suburban,
wearing chocolate double-breasted suits,
they blew their tops and beat him black and blue.
I was so out of things, I'd never heard
of the Jehovah's Witnesses.

[1]After being sentenced in 1944 to a year and a day for refusing to comply with the draft law, Lowell was first sent to the West Street Jail in Manhattan. The most famous prisoner there at the time was Louis ("Lepke") Buchalter (1897–1944), union racketeer, gang boss, and murderer, who was awaiting execution.

[2]Description by Henry James.

[3]Conscientious objector.

"Are you a C.O.?" I asked a fellow jailbird.
"No," he answered, "I'm a J.W."
He taught me the "hospital tuck,"
and pointed out the T shirted back
of *Murder Incorporated's* Czar Lepke,
there piling towels on a rack,
or dawdling off to his little segregated cell full
of things forbidden the common man:
a portable radio, a dresser, two toy American
flags tied together with a ribbon of Easter palm.
Flabby, bald, lobotomized,
he drifted in a sheepish calm,
where no agonizing reappraisal
jarred his concentration on the electric chair—
hanging like an oasis in his air
of lost connections. . . .

1959

Skunk Hour

(For Elizabeth Bishop)

Nautilus Island's[1] hermit
heiress still lives through winter in her Spartan cottage;
her sheep still graze above the sea.
Her son's a bishop. Her farmer
is first selectman in our village;
she's in her dotage.

Thirsting for
the hierarchic privacy
of Queen Victoria's century,
she buys up all
the eyesores facing her shore,
and lets them fall.

The season's ill—
we've lost our summer millionaire,

[1]In Maine.

who seemed to leap from an L.L. Bean[2]
catalogue. His nine-knot yawl
was auctioned off to lobstermen.
A red fox stain covers Blue Hill.

And now our fairy
decorator brightens his shop for fall;
his fishnet's filled with orange cork,
orange, his cobbler's bench and awl;
there is no money in his work,
he'd rather marry.

One dark night,
my Tudor Ford climbed the hill's skull;
I watched for love-cars. Lights turned down,
they lay together, hull to hull,
where the graveyard shelves on the town. . . .
My mind's not right.

A car radio bleats,
"Love, O careless Love. . . ." I hear
my ill-spirit sob in each blood cell,
as if my hand were at its throat. . . .
I myself am hell;
nobody's here—

only skunks, that search
in the moonlight for a bite to eat.
They march on their soles up Main Street:
white stripes, moonstruck eyes' red fire
under the chalk-dry and spar spire
of the Trinitarian Church.

I stand on top
of our back steps and breathe the rich air—
a mother skunk with her column of kittens swills the garbage pail.
She jabs her wedge-head in a cup
of sour cream, drops her ostrich tail,
and will not scare.

1960

[2]Freeport, Maine, mail-order house.

For Theodore Roethke

1908–1963

All night you wallowed through my sleep,
then in the morning you were lost
in the Maine sky—close, cold and gray,
smoke and smoke-colored cloud.

Sheeplike, unsociable reptilian, two
hell-divers splattered squawking on the water,
loons devolving to a monochrome.
You honored nature,

helpless, elemental creature.
The black stump of your hand
just touched the waters under the earth,
and left them quickened with your name. . . .

Now, you honor the mother,
Omnipresent,
she made you nonexistent,
the ocean's anchor, our high tide.

1963

For the Union Dead

"Relinquunt Omnia Servare Rem Publicam."[1]

The old South Boston Aquarium stands
in a Sahara of snow now. It's broken windows are boarded.
The bronze weathervane cod has lost half its scales.
The airy tanks are dry.

Once my nose crawled like a snail on the glass;
my hand tingled

[1]"They give up all else to serve the republic."

to burst the bubbles
drifting from the noses of the cowed, compliant fish.

My hand draws back. I often sigh still
for the dark downward and vegetating kingdom
of the fish and reptile. One morning last March,
I pressed against the new barbed and galvanized

fence on the Boston Common. Behind their cage,
yellow dinosaur steamshovels were grunting
as they cropped up tons of mush and grass
to gouge their underworld garage.

Parking spaces luxuriate like civic
sandpiles in the heart of Boston.
A girdle of orange, Puritan-pumpkin colored girders
braces the tingling Statehouse,

shaking over the excavations, as it faces Colonel Shaw
and his bell-cheeked Negro infantry
on St. Gaudens' shaking Civil War relief,[2]
propped by a plank splint against the garage's earthquake.

Two months after marching through Boston,
half the regiment was dead;
at the dedication,
William James could almost hear the bronze Negroes breathe.

Their monument sticks like a fishbone
in the city's throat.
Its Colonel is as lean
as a compass-needle.

He has an angry wrenlike vigilance,
a greyhound's gentle tautness;
he seems to wince at pleasure,
and suffocate for privacy.

He is out of bounds now. He rejoices in man's lovely,
peculiar power to choose life and die—
when he leads his black soldiers to death,
he cannot bend his back.

[2]On the edge of Boston Common stands a monument honoring Colonel Robert Shaw (1837–1863) and the African American troops of the 54th Massachusetts by the sculptor Augustus Saint-Gaudens (1848–1907). Shaw was killed, with many of his men, in South Carolina on July 18, 1863.

On a thousand small town New England greens,
the old white churches hold their air
of sparse, sincere rebellion; frayed flags
quilt the graveyards of the Grand Army of the Republic.

The stone statues of the abstract Union Soldier
grow slimmer and younger each year—
wasp-waisted they doze over muskets
and muse through their sideburns . . .

Shaw's father wanted no monument
except the ditch,
where his son's body was thrown
and lost with his "niggers."

The ditch is nearer.
There are no statues for the last war here;
on Boylston Street, a commercial photograph
shows Hiroshima boiling

over a Mosler Safe, the "Rock of Ages"
that survived the blast. Space is nearer.
When I crouch to my television set,
the drained faces of Negro school-children rise like balloons.

Colonel Shaw
is riding on his bubble,
he waits
for the blessèd break.

The Aquarium is gone. Everywhere,
giant finned cars nose forward like fish;
a savage servility
slides by on grease.

1960

Near the Ocean

(For E.H.L.)[1]

The house is filled. The last heartthrob
thrills through her flesh. The hero stands,
stunned by the applauding hands,
and lifts her head to please the mob . . .
No, young and starry-eyed, the brother
and sister wait before their mother,
old iron-bruises, powder, "Child,
these breasts . . ." He knows. And if she's killed

his treadmill heart will never rest—
his wet mouth pressed to some slack breast,
or shifting over on his back . . .
the severed radiance filters back,
athirst for nightlife—gorgon head,
fished up from the Aegean dead,
with all its stranded snakes uncoiled,
here beheaded and despoiled.

We hear the ocean. Older seas
and deserts give asylum, peace
to each abortion and mistake.
Lost in the Near Eastern dreck,
the tyrant and tyrannicide
lie like the bridegroom and the bride;
the battering ram, abandoned, prone,
beside the apeman's phallic stone.

Betrayals! Was it the first night?
They stood against a black and white
inland New England backdrop. No dogs
there, horse or hunter, only frogs
chirring from the dark trees and swamps.
Elms watching like extinguished lamps.
Knee-high hedges of black sheep
encircling them at every step.

Some subway-green coldwater flat,
its walls tattooed with neon light,

[1]Elizabeth Hardwick Lowell, the poet's former wife.

then high delirious squalor, food
burned down with vodka . . . menstrual blood
caking the covers, when they woke
to the dry, childless Sunday walk,
saw cars on Brooklyn Bridge descend
through steel and coal dust to land's end.

Was it years later when they met,
and summer's coarse last-quarter drought
had dried the hardveined elms to bark—
lying like people out of work,
dead sober, cured, recovered, on
the downslope of some gritty green,
all access barred with broken glass;
and dehydration browned the grass?

Is it this shore? Their eyes worn white
as moons from hitting bottom? Night,
the sandfleas scissoring their feet,
the sandbed cooling to concrete,
one borrowed blanket, lights of cars
shining down at them like stars? . . .
Sand built the lost Atlantis . . . sand,
Atlantic ocean, condoms, sand.

Sleep, sleep. The ocean, grinding stones,
can only speak the present tense;
nothing will age, nothing will last,
or take corruption from the past.
A hand, your hand then! I'm afraid
to touch the crisp hair on your head—
Monster loved for what you are,
till time, that buries us, lay bare.

1967

Gwendolyn Brooks 1917–2000

Gwendolyn Brooks, born in Topeka, Kansas, considered herself a (nearly) lifelong Chicagoan. When she began writing at age seven, her mother predicted, "You are going to be the *lady* Paul Laurence Dunbar." First published at eleven, by sixteen Brooks was contributing poetry weekly to the *Chicago Defender.* In *Report from Part One,* she describes a happy childhood spent in black neighborhoods with her parents and younger brother Raymond. "Duty-loving" Keziah Wims Brooks had been a fifth grade teacher; she played the piano, wrote music, and published a book of stories at eighty-six. David Anderson Brooks, son of a runaway slave, was a janitor with "rich artistic abilities." He had spent a year at Fisk University, hoping to become a doctor; now he sang, told stories, and worked hard to purchase a house and support his family. Both parents nurtured their daughter's precocious gifts. "I had always felt that to be black was good," Brooks said in her autobiography.

School awakened her to the realities of what Arthur P. Davis calls "the black-and-tan motif" in her work, *i.e.,* the white-biased valuing of lightness among blacks, an early theme in her work, gradually overtaken by the black-white questions and confrontations that had always been prominent. Her home environment supported her confidence and fostered her black musical heritage that centered creatively in church. At church she met James Weldon Johnson and Langston Hughes. The latter became an inspiration and, later, a friend and mentor.

Following graduation from Wilson Junior College (now Kennedy-King) in 1936, Brooks worked for a month as a maid in a North Shore home, and then spent four unhappy months as secretary to the spiritual adviser who became the prototype for Prophet Williams in "In the Mecca." In 1939 she married Henry Lowington Blakely II, a fellow member of Inez Cunningham Stark's poetry workshop in the South Side Community Art Center. Early publishing, marriage, the births of Henry, Jr., in 1940 and Nora in 1951, the warm reception of her first book, and careful supervision of her career by her Harper and Row editor helped to convince Brooks that she was a professional writer. She overcame her reticence about speaking in public. In 1950 she won the Pulitzer Prize for Poetry with *Annie Allen,* the first black writer to be so honored. That award was followed by two Guggenheim Fellowships, election to membership in the National Institute of Arts and Letters, and selection as Consultant in Poetry to the Library of Congress. She was the first black woman to hold either of the latter two positions. She was awarded more than seventy honorary degrees.

Finely crafted, influenced by Langston Hughes, T. S. Eliot, Emily Dickinson, and Robert Frost—and later by the 1960s Black Arts movement, Brooks's poetry was always a social act. *A Street in Bronzeville* addresses the realities of segregation for black Americans at home and in World War II military service; *Annie Allen* ironically explores post-war anti-romanticism. *Maud Martha,* her prose masterpiece, sketches a bildungsroman of black womanhood; *The Bean Eaters* and later poems sound the urgencies of the Civil Rights movement. In 1967 she attended the Second Fisk University Writers' Conference and was deeply impressed with the activism of Amiri Baraka. Subsequently, although she had always experimented with various forms, her work opened more distinctly to free verse, a notable feature of *In the Mecca* (1968), the book published the year she was appointed Poet Laureate of Illinois.

Returning to Chicago from the Fisk Conference, Brooks conducted a workshop with the Blackstone Rangers, a teen gang, who were succeeded by young writers like Carolyn M. Rodgers and Haki R. Madhubuti (then don l. lee). Her new Black Nationalist perspective impelled her commitment to black publishing. In 1969 she turned to Dudley Randall's Broadside Press for publication of *Riot,* followed by *Family Pictures* and *Aloneness,* and to Madhubuti's Third World Press for *The Tiger Who Wore White Gloves* and *To Disembark.* In 1971, she began publishing a literary annual, *The Black Position,* under her own aegis. Starting with *Primer for Blacks* in 1980, she took charge of her creative work. Although many of her earlier books now issue from Third World Press, *Children Coming Home* was published in 1991 by The David Company, her own imprint.

Brooks traveled widely and constantly, giving workshops and readings in schools, libraries, and prisons. Her visits to Africa in 1971 and 1974 deepened her sense of African heritage. Yet her poetry marks the rich confluence and continuity of a dual stream: the black sermonic tradition and black music—the spiritual, the blues, and jazz; and white antecedents like the ballad, the sonnet, and conventional and free forms. It suggests connections with Anglo-Saxon alliteration and strong-stressed verse, with the Homeric bard and the African griot. Brooks's heroic and prophetic voice surfaces in what she called "preachments." Brooks intended that her work "'call' all black people."

Widowed in 1996, she remained a guide and guardian for young talent, registrar of black needs and aspirations. Brooks presented a poetry of caritas; of potential and actual black strength, community, and pride. Her memorable portraits of men, women, and children pose a general as well as a specific validity. She is a major voice in modern American poetry, a heroic voice insisting on our mutual democractic heritage.

D. H. Melhem

PRIMARY WORKS

A Street in Bronzeville, 1945; *Annie Allen,* 1949; *Maud Martha,* 1953; *Bronzeville Boys and Girls,* 1956; *The Bean Eaters,* 1960; *Selected Poems,* 1963; *In the Mecca,* 1968; *Riot,* 1969; *Family Pictures,* 1970; *Aloneness,* 1971; *Jump Bad,* 1971; "In Montgomery," *Ebony,* August 1971; *The World of Gwendolyn Brooks,* 1971; *A Broadside Treasury,* ed., 1971; *Report from Part One,* 1972; *The Tiger Who Wore White Gloves, or What You Are You Are,* 1974; *Beckonings,* 1975; *A Capsule Course in Black Poetry Writing,* 1975; *Primer for Blacks,* 1980; *Young Poet's Primer,* 1980; *To Disembark,* 1981; *Mayor Harold Washington and Chicago, the* I Will *City,* 1983; *Very Young Poets,* 1983; *The Near-Johannesburg Boy and Other Poems,* 1986; *Blacks* (omnibus), 1987; *Gottschalk and the Grande Tarantelle,* 1988; *Winnie,* 1991; *Children Coming Home,* 1991; *Report from Part Two,* 1996.

The Sundays of Satin-Legs Smith

Inamoratas, with an approbation,
Bestowed his title. Blessed his inclination.

He wakes, unwinds, elaborately: a cat
Tawny, reluctant, royal. He is fat
And fine this morning. Definite. Reimbursed.

He waits a moment, he designs his reign,
That no performance may be plain or vain.
Then rises in a clear delirium.

He sheds, with his pajamas, shabby days.
And his desertedness, his intricate fear, the
Postponed resentments and the prim precautions.

Now, at his bath, would you deny him lavender
Or take away the power of his pine?
What smelly substitute, heady as wine,

Would you provide? life must be aromatic.
There must be scent, somehow there must be some.
Would you have flowers in his life? suggest
Asters? a Really Good geranium?
A white carnation? would you prescribe a Show
With the cold lilies, formal chrysanthemum
Magnificence, poinsettias, and emphatic
Red of prize roses? might his happiest
Alternative (you muse) be, after all,
A bit of gentle garden in the best
Of taste and straight tradition? Maybe so.
But you forget, or did you ever know,
His heritage of cabbage and pigtails,
Old intimacy with alleys, garbage pails,
Down in the deep (but always beautiful) South
Where roses blush their blithest (it is said)
And sweet magnolias put Chanel to shame.

No! He has not a flower to his name.
Except a feather one, for his lapel.
Apart from that, if he should think of flowers
It is in terms of dandelions or death.
Ah, there is little hope. You might as well—
Unless you care to set the world a-boil
And do a lot of equalizing things,
Remove a little ermine, say, from kings,
Shake hands with paupers and appoint them men,
For instance—certainly you might as well
Leave him his lotion, lavender and oil.

Let us proceed. Let us inspect, together
With his meticulous and serious love,
The innards of this closet. Which is a vault
Whose glory is not diamonds, not pearls,
Not silver plate with just enough dull shine.
But wonder-suits in yellow and in wine,
Sarcastic green and zebra-striped cobalt.
All drapes. With shoulder padding that is wide
And cocky and determined as his pride;
Ballooning pants that taper off to ends
Scheduled to choke precisely.
                                        Here are hats
Like bright umbrellas; and hysterical ties
Like narrow banners for some gathering war.

People are so in need, in need of help.
People want so much that they do not know.
Below the tinkling trade of little coins

The gold impulse not possible to show
Or spend. Promise piled over and betrayed.

These kneaded limbs receive the kiss of silk.
Then they receive the brave and beautiful
Embrace of some of that equivocal wool.
He looks into his mirror, loves himself—
The neat curve here; the angularity
That is appropriate at just its place;
The technique of a variegated grace.

Here is all his sculpture and his art
And all his architectural design.
Perhaps you would prefer to this a fine
Value of marble, complicated stone.
Would have him think with horror of baroque,
Rococo. You forget and you forget.

He dances down the hotel steps that keep
Remnants of last night's high life and distress.
As spat-out purchased kisses and spilled beer.
He swallows sunshine with a secret yelp.
Passes to coffee and a roll or two.
Has breakfasted.
Out. Sounds about him smear,
Become a unit. He hears and does not hear
The alarm clock meddling in somebody's sleep;
Children's governed Sunday happiness;
The dry tone of a plane; a woman's oath;
Consumption's spiritless expectoration;
An indignant robin's resolute donation
Pinching a track through apathy and din;
Restaurant vendors weeping; and the L
That comes on like a slightly horrible thought.

Pictures, too, as usual, are blurred.
He sees and does not see the broken windows
Hiding their shame with newsprint; little girl
With ribbons decking wornness, little boy
Wearing the trousers with the decentest patch,
To honor Sunday; women on their way
From "service," temperate holiness arranged
Ably on asking faces; men estranged
From music and from wonder and from joy
But far familiar with the guiding awe
Of foodlessness.
He loiters.
Restaurant vendors

Weep, or out of them rolls a restless glee.
The Lonesome Blues, the Long-lost Blues, I Want A
Big Fat Mama. Down these sore avenues
Comes no Saint-Saëns, no piquant elusive Grieg,
And not Tschaikovsky's wayward eloquence
And not the shapely tender drift of Brahms.
But could he love them? Since a man must bring
To music what his mother spanked him for
When he was two: bits of forgotten hate,
Devotion: whether or not his mattress hurts:
The little dream his father humored: the thing
His sister did for money: what he ate
For breakfast—and for dinner twenty years
Ago last autumn: all his skipped desserts.

The pasts of his ancestors lean against
Him. Crowd him. Fog out his identity.
Hundreds of hungers mingle with his own,
Hundreds of voices advise so dexterously
He quite considers his reactions his,
Judges he walks most powerfully alone,
That everything is—simply what it is.

But movie-time approaches, time to boo
The hero's kiss, and boo the heroine
Whose ivory and yellow it is sin
For his eye to eat of. The Mickey Mouse,
However, is for everyone in the house.

Squires his lady to dinner at Joe's Eats.
His lady alters as to leg and eye,
Thickness and height, such minor points as these,
From Sunday to Sunday. But no matter what
Her name or body positively she's
In Queen Lace stockings with ambitious heels
That strain to kiss the calves, and vivid shoes
Frontless and backless, Chinese fingernails,
Earrings, three layers of lipstick, intense hat
Dripping with the most voluble of veils.
Her affable extremes are like sweet bombs
About him, whom no middle grace or good
Could gratify. He had no education
In quiet arts of compromise. He would
Not understand your counsels on control, nor
Thank you for your late trouble.
At Joe's Eats
You get your fish or chicken on meat platters.
With coleslaw, macaroni, candied sweets,

Coffee and apple pie. You go out full.
(The end is—isn't it?—all that really matters.)

And even and intrepid come
The tender boots of night to home.

Her body is like new brown bread
Under the Woolworth mignonette.[1]
Her body is a honey bowl
Whose waiting honey is deep and hot.
Her body is like summer earth,
Receptive, soft, and absolute . . .

1945

The Mother

Abortions will not let you forget.
You remember the children you got that you did not get.
The damp small pulps with a little or with no hair,
The singers and workers that never handled the air.
You will never neglect or beat
Them, or silence or buy with a sweet.
You will never wind up the sucking-thumb
Or scuttle off ghosts that come.
You will never leave them, controlling your luscious sigh,
Return for a snack of them, with gobbling mother-eye.

I have heard in the voices of the wind the voices of my dim killed children.
I have contracted. I have eased
My dim dears at the breasts they could never suck.
I have said, Sweets, if I sinned, if I seized
Your luck
And your lives from your unfinished reach,
If I stole your births and your names,
Your straight baby tears and your games,

[1]An herb, native to northern Africa; here it refers to a narrow bobbin lace, having a scattered small design on a ground somewhat like tulle and made especially by the French and the Flemish in the sixteenth through the nineteenth centuries.

Your stilted or lovely loves, your tumults, your marriages, aches,
  and your deaths,
If I poisoned the beginnings of your breaths,
Believe that even in my deliberateness I was not deliberate.
Though why should I whine,
Whine that the crime was other than mine?—
Since anyhow you are dead.
Or rather, or instead,
You were never made.
But that too, I am afraid,
Is faulty: oh, what shall I say, how is the truth to be said?
You were born, you had body, you died.
It is just that you never giggled or planned or cried.

Believe me, I loved you all.
Believe me, I knew you, though faintly, and I loved, I loved you
All.

1945

We Real Cool

The Pool Players.
Seven at the Golden Shovel.

We real cool. We
Left school. We

Lurk late. We
Strike straight. We

Sing sin. We
Thin gin. We

Jazz June.[1] We
Die soon.

1960

[1]A reference to popular music and enjoying the summer of youth.

A Bronzeville Mother Loiters in Mississippi. Meanwhile, a Mississippi Mother Burns Bacon[1]

From the first it had been like a
Ballad. It had the beat inevitable. It had the blood.
A wildness cut up, and tied in little bunches,
Like the four-line stanzas of the ballads she had never quite
Understood—the ballads they had set her to, in school.

Herself: the milk-white maid, the "maid mild"
Of the ballad. Pursued
By the Dark Villain. Rescued by the Fine Prince.
The Happiness-Ever-After.
That was worth anything.
It was good to be a "maid mild."
That made the breath go fast.

Her bacon burned. She
Hastened to hide it in the step-on can, and
Drew more strips from the meat case. The eggs and sour-milk
biscuits
Did well. She set out a jar
Of her new quince preserve.

. . . But there was a something about the matter of the Dark
Villain.
He should have been older, perhaps.
The hacking down of a villain was more fun to think about
When his menace possessed undisputed breadth, undisputed
height,
And a harsh kind of vice.
And best of all, when his history was cluttered
With the bones of many eaten knights and princesses.

The fun was disturbed, then all but nullified
When the Dark Villain was a blackish child
Of fourteen, with eyes still too young to be dirty,
And a mouth too young to have lost every reminder
Of its infant softness.
That boy must have been surprised! For
These were grown-ups. Grown-ups were supposed to be wise.

[1]Both this poem and the next concern the murder of Emmett Louis Till, a fourteen-year-old Chicago youth who was murdered in Mississippi on August 28, 1955, because he had "wolf-whistled" at a white woman.

And the Fine Prince—and that other—so tall, so broad, so
Grown! Perhaps the boy had never guessed
That the trouble with grown-ups was that under the magnificent
shell of adulthood, just under,
Waited the baby full of tantrums.
It occurred to her that there may have been something
Ridiculous in the picture of the Fine Prince
Rushing (rich with the breadth and height and
Mature solidness whose lack, in the Dark Villain, was impressing
her,
Confronting her more and more as this first day after the trial
And acquittal wore on) rushing
With his heavy companion to hack down (unhorsed)
That little foe.
So much had happened, she could not remember now what that
foe had done
Against her, or if anything had been done.
The one thing in the world that she did know and knew
With terrifying clarity was that her composition
Had disintegrated. That, although the pattern prevailed,
The breaks were everywhere. That she could think
Of no thread capable of the necessary
Sew-work.

She made the babies sit in their places at the table.
Then, before calling Him, she hurried
To the mirror with her comb and lipstick. It was necessary
To be more beautiful than ever.
The beautiful wife.
For sometimes she fancied he looked at her as though
Measuring her. As if he considered, Had she been worth It?
Had *she* been worth the blood, the cramped cries, the little
stuttering bravado,
The gradual dulling of those Negro eyes,
The sudden, overwhelming *little-boyness* in that barn?
Whatever she might feel or half-feel, the lipstick necessity was
something apart. He must never conclude
That she had not been worth It.

He sat down, the Fine Prince, and
Began buttering a biscuit. He looked at his hands.
He twisted in his chair, he scratched his nose.
He glanced again, almost secretly, at his hands.
More papers were in from the North, he mumbled. More
meddling headlines.
With their pepper-words, "bestiality," and "barbarism," and
"Shocking."

The half-sneers he had mastered for the trial worked across
His sweet and pretty face.

What he'd like to do, he explained, was kill them all.
The time lost. The unwanted fame.
Still, it had been fun to show those intruders
A thing or two. To show that snappy-eyed mother,
That sassy, Northern, brown-black——

Nothing could stop Mississippi.
He knew that. Big Fella
Knew that.
And, what was so good, Mississippi knew that.
Nothing and nothing could stop Mississippi.
They could send in their petitions, and scar
Their newspapers with bleeding headlines. Their governors
Could appeal to Washington. . . .

"What I want," the older baby said, "is 'lasses on my jam."
Whereupon the younger baby
Picked up the molasses pitcher and threw
The molasses in his brother's face. Instantly
The Fine Prince leaned across the table and slapped
The small and smiling criminal.

She did not speak. When the Hand
Came down and away, and she could look at her child,
At her baby-child,
She could think only of blood.
Surely her baby's cheek
Had disappeared, and in its place, surely,
Hung a heaviness, a lengthening red, a red that had no end.
She shook her head. It was not true, of course.
It was not true at all. The
Child's face was as always, the
Color of the paste in her paste-jar.

She left the table, to the tune of the children's lamentations, which
were shriller
Than ever. She
Looked out of a window. She said not a word. *That*
Was one of the new Somethings—
The fear,
Tying her as with iron.

Suddenly she felt his hands upon her. He had followed her
To the window. The children were whimpering now.
Such bits of tots. And she, their mother,

Could not protect them. She looked at her shoulders, still
Gripped in the claim of his hands. She tried, but could not resist
the idea
That a red ooze was seeping, spreading darkly, thickly, slowly,
Over her white shoulders, her own shoulders,
And over all of Earth and Mars.

He whispered something to her, did the Fine Prince, something
About love, something about love and night and intention.

She heard no hoof-beat of the horse and saw no flash of the
shining steel.
He pulled her face around to meet
His, and there it was, close close,
For the first time in all those days and nights.
His mouth, wet and red,
So very, very, very red,
Closed over hers.

Then a sickness heaved within her. The courtroom Coca-Cola,
The courtroom beer and hate and sweat and drone,
Pushed like a wall against her. She wanted to bear it.
But his mouth would not go away and neither would the
Decapitated exclamation points in that Other Woman's eyes.

She did not scream.
She stood there.
But a hatred for him burst into glorious flower,
And its perfume enclasped them—big,
Bigger than all magnolias.

The last bleak news of the ballad.
The rest of the rugged music.
The last quatrain.

1960

The Last Quatrain of the Ballad of Emmett Till

after the murder,
after the burial

Emmett's mother is a pretty-faced thing;
the tint of pulled taffy.
She sits in a red room,

drinking black coffee.
She kisses her killed boy.
And she is sorry.
Chaos in windy grays
through a red prairie.

1960

Ulysses[1]

Religion

At home we pray every morning, we
get down on our knees in a circle,
holding hands, holding Love,
and we sing Hallelujah.

Then we go into the World.

Daddy *speeds,* to break bread with his Girl Friend.
Mommy's a Boss. And a lesbian.
(She too has a nice Girl Friend.)

My brothers and sisters and I come to school.
We bring knives pistols bottles, little boxes, and cans.

We talk to the man who's cool at the playground gate.
Nobody Sees us, nobody stops our sin.

Our teachers feed us geography.
We spit it out in a hurry.

Now we are coming home.

At home, we pray every evening, we
get down on our knees in a circle,
holding hands, holding Love.

And we sing Hallelujah.

1991

[1]The name of one of the twenty children who are the personae represented by each poem in the book. Ulysses is the Roman name for Odysseus, a famous Greek warrior whose adventures and return home after twenty years are recounted in Homer's epic poem, *The Odyssey.*

The Beat Movement

When Lawrence Ferlinghetti published Allen Ginsberg's long poem "Howl" at his San Francisco–based City Lights Books in 1956, the first widely circulated text of the anti-establishment Beat culture was born. *Howl and Other Poems* appeared in the highly visible white and black pocketbook format that was to showcase works by Jack Kerouac, Gregory Corso, Robert Creeley, Ginsberg, Ferlinghetti himself, and many others. The concept of a group identity may have begun at a 1955 poetry reading at the Six Gallery in San Francisco. Kenneth Rexroth was master of ceremonies, and readers were—besides Ginsberg—Philip Lamantia, Michael McClure, Gary Snyder, Lew Welsh, and Philip Whalen.

Responding to the restrictive and conservative post–World War II culture (the soporific 1950s), this group of poets—which often included Denise Levertov, Charles Olson, Robert Duncan, Neal Cassady, William Everson, and others—forced on the reading public an awareness of other cultures: drug experiences, lives in prison and mental institutions, homosexual and lesbian sexualities, liberal politics, spiritualism not necessarily housed in suburban Protestant environs. Admittedly intended to shock in some cases, the works—poetry, prose, and matrices of both—were descended from writers as disparate as Whitman, Rimbaud, William Carlos Williams, Antonin Artaud, William Burroughs, and other American writers not yet acknowledged as significant writers. One of the foremost characteristics of writing of the Beats was a sense of humor, long absent from United States writing, and a belief that spiritual life (*beat* meaning "beatific, holy") was essential to a person's existence.

Allen Ginsberg 1926–1997

Allen Ginsberg brought not only a new self-consciousness to American poetry but a rare sense of humor. While poets contemporary with him—W. D. Snodgrass, Robert Lowell, Theodore Roethke, and somewhat later Anne Sexton and Sylvia Plath—were mining the personal to unearth images that would speak for an "Every person" understanding, Ginsberg was exploring the psyche with a shrewd sense of humor. His dialogue with Walt Whitman, "A Supermarket in California," views the suburban scene of lush plenty with a wry vision that brings the elements of poetry and life together in a completely new perspective.

Ginsberg is best known for his first long-lined poem, "Howl," written after he left Columbia University and the New York avant-garde and moved to California. "Howl" lamented the 1950s wastes—good minds buried under layers of convention, stifling restrictions on art and sexual expression—reversing Whitman's catalogs of praise to chart uncountable griefs. Its irony and its all-too-real truths gave Ginsberg an immediate audience once City Lights published the poem, with a foreword by William Carlos Williams.

Though Ginsberg quickly became identified with the homosexual drug culture, his roots more directly stretched back to his New Jersey home, where his knowledge of social inequities and cultural frustrations mirrored that of his older Rutherford neighbor, Williams. His next major poem, "Kaddish," a lament for the health of his brilliant Jewish mother, Naomi Levy, reflected much of that social coercion, intensified with cultural alienation and social response to mental instability.

Ginsberg was born in 1926 to Naomi and Louis Ginsberg, in Newark, where his father was a high school teacher and a poet. Before graduating from Columbia University in 1949, Ginsberg held jobs as a dishwasher, spot welder, copy boy on the *New York World-Telegram,* and reporter for a New Jersey paper. After he graduated with his A.B. degree, he traveled to California to find William Burroughs, who wrote from the tradition of prophetic, inspired voices (Ginsberg had had visions in which he saw William Blake, and he thought of himself as a seer in his art). After his comparative successes in California, determined to live on his income from writing—no small endeavor—Ginsberg spent part of 1963 in India, traveling with his lover Peter Orlovsky. He returned to the States to participate in a poetry festival at University of British Columbia, bringing with him a mantra-like chant that from then on enhanced the delivery of his poetry.

In 1963 Ginsberg was a Guggenheim Fellow; in 1969 he received a National Institute of Arts and Letters award and in 1973 the National Book Award for *The Fall of America: Poems of These States.* In 1979 he received the National Arts Club Medal of Honor for Literature. Although he read frequently on university campuses and remained a spokesperson for the avant-garde, Ginsberg developed a comparatively mild profile during the last decade of his life. He returned to New Jersey, where he lived on a small farm, accessible to his friends and admirers, writing a remarkably constant poetry that hammered away at the problems faced not only by the United States but by most of the world cultures. The "insane demands" he spoke of in his 1956 poem "America" are still rampant, and Ginsberg proved to be prophetic once more as he described himself as staying with the country, trying to work through its aberrations to find some of its truth. In that endeavor, too, he echoed the efforts of William Carlos Williams. Though never accepted by the culture he was so critical of, Ginsberg never expatriated himself from it; he rather preached, and sang, and chanted, lessons he thought might be helpful to its greatest dilemmas.

Linda Wagner-Martin
University of North Carolina–Chapel Hill

PRIMARY WORKS

Howl and Other Poems, 1956; *Kaddish and Other Poems 1958–60,* 1961; *Empty Mirror: Early Poems,* 1961; *Reality Sandwiches: 1953–1960,* 1963; *Wichita Vortex Sutra,* 1967; *Planet News,* 1968; *Iron Horse,* 1972; *The Fall of America: Poems of These States, 1965–1971,* 1973; *Mind Breaths: Poems, 1972–1977,* 1978; *Collected Poems 1947–1980,* 1984; *Howl* (facsimile), 1986; *White Shroud, Poems 1980–1985,* 1986; and many smaller collections. See also *Allen Verbatim: Lectures on Poetry, Politics, and Consciousness,* ed. Gordon Ball, 1975, and *On the Poetry of Allen Ginsberg,* ed. Lewis Hyde, 1984; *Death and Fame: Poems, 1993–1997,* 1999.

A Supermarket in California

What thoughts I have of you tonight, Walt Whitman, for I
walked down the sidestreets under the trees with a headache
self-conscious looking at the full moon.
In my hungry fatigue, and shopping for images, I went into
the neon fruit supermarket, dreaming of your enumerations!
What peaches and what penumbras! Whole families
shopping at night! Aisles full of husbands! Wives in the
avocados, babies in the tomatoes!—and you, Garcia Lorca,[1]
what were you doing down by the watermelons?

I saw you, Walt Whitman, childless, lonely old grubber,
poking among the meats in the refrigerator and eyeing the
grocery boys.
I heard you asking questions of each: Who killed the pork
chops? What price bananas? Are you my Angel?
I wandered in and out of the brilliant stacks of cans
following you, and followed in my imagination by the store
detective.
We strode down the open corridors together in our solitary
fancy tasting artichokes, possessing every frozen delicacy, and
never passing the cashier.

Where are we going, Walt Whitman? The doors close in an
hour. Which way does your beard point tonight?
(I touch your book and dream of our odyssey in the
supermarket and feel absurd.)
Will we walk all night through solitary streets? The trees
add shade to shade, lights out in the houses, we'll both be
lonely.
Will we stroll dreaming of the lost America of love past
blue automobiles in driveways, home to our silent cottage?

Ah, dear father, graybeard, lonely old courage-teacher, what
America did you have when Charon[2] quit poling his ferry and
you got out on a smoking bank and stood watching the boat
disappear on the black waters of Lethe?

1956

[1]Spanish poet and playwright Federico García Lorca (1899–1936) who was murdered at the start of the Spanish Civil War.

[2]In Greek myth, Charon ferried the shades of the dead to Hades over Lethe, river of forgetfulness.

Howl

for Carl Solomon[1]

I

I saw the best minds of my generation destroyed by madness,
starving hysterical naked,
dragging themselves through the negro streets at dawn looking for
an angry fix,
angelheaded hipsters burning for the ancient heavenly connection
to the starry dynamo in the machinery of night,
who poverty and tatters and hollow-eyed and high sat up smoking
in the supernatural darkness of cold-water flats floating across
the tops of cities contemplating jazz,
who bared their brains to Heaven under the El[2] and saw
Mohammedan angels staggering on tenement roofs
illuminated,
who passed through universities with radiant cool eyes
hallucinating Arkansas and Blake-light[3] tragedy among the
scholars of war,
who were expelled from the academies for crazy & publishing
obscene odes on the windows of the skull,[4]
who cowered in unshaven rooms in underwear, burning their
money in wastebaskets and listening to the Terror through the
wall,
who got busted in their pubic beards returning through Laredo
with a belt of marijuana for New York,
who ate fire in paint hotels or drank turpentine in Paradise Alley,[5]
death, or purgatoried their torsos night after night
with dreams, with drugs, with waking nightmares, alcohol and cock
and endless balls,
incomparable blind streets of shuddering cloud and lightning in
the mind leaping toward poles of Canada & Paterson,
illuminating all the motionless world of Time between,
Peyote solidities of halls, backyard green tree cemetery dawns,
wine drunkenness over the rooftops, storefront boroughs of
teahead joyride neon blinking traffic light, sun and moon and

[1]Friend of Ginsberg and fellow psychiatric patient in 1949.
[2]The elevated railway.
[3]Refers to English poet William Blake (1757–1827).
[4]Ginsberg was expelled from Columbia for writing an obscenity on his windowpane.
[5]A slum courtyard on the East Side.

tree vibrations in the roaring winter dusks of Brooklyn, ashcan
rantings and kind king light of mind,
who chained themselves to subways for the endless ride from
Battery to holy Bronx on benzedrine until the noise of wheels
and children brought them down shuddering mouth-wracked
and battered bleak of brain all drained of brilliance in the
drear light of Zoo,
who sank all night in submarine light of Bickford's[6] floated out
and sat through the stale beer afternoon in desolate
Fugazzi's,[7] listening to the crack of doom on the hydrogen
jukebox,
who talked continuously seventy hours from park to pad to bar to
Bellevue[8] to museum to the Brooklyn Bridge,
a lost battalion of platonic conversationalists jumping down the
stoops off fire escapes off windowsills off Empire State out of
the moon,
yacketayakking screaming vomiting whispering facts and memories
and anecdotes and eyeball kicks and shocks of hospitals and
jails and wars,
whole intellects disgorged in total recall for seven days and nights
with brilliant eyes, meat for the Synagogue cast on the
pavement,
who vanished into nowhere Zen New Jersey leaving a trail of
ambiguous picture postcards of Atlantic City Hall,
suffering Eastern sweats and Tangerian bone-grindings and
migraines of China under junk-withdrawal in Newark's bleak
furnished room,
who wandered around and around at midnight in the railroad yard
wondering where to go, and went, leaving no broken hearts,
who lit cigarettes in boxcars boxcars boxcars racketing through
snow toward lonesome farms in grandfather night,
who studied Plotinus Poe St. John of the Cross[9] telepathy and bop
kaballa[10] because the cosmos instinctively vibrated at their feet
in Kansas,
who loned it through the streets of Idaho seeking visionary indian
angels who were visionary indian angels,
who thought they were only mad when Baltimore gleamed in
supernatural ecstasy,
who jumped in limousines with the Chinaman of Oklahoma on the
impulse of winter midnight streetlight smalltown rain,

[6]Cafeteria.
[7]Bar in Greenwich Village.
[8]New York City public hospital.
[9]Plotinus (205–270) Roman philosopher; Edgar Allan Poe (1809–1849); St. John of the Cross (1542–1591) Spanish poet.
[10]Cf. Cabala: esoteric interpretation of Hebrew scriptures.

who lounged hungry and lonesome through Houston seeking jazz
or sex or soup, and followed the brilliant Spaniard to
converse about America and Eternity, a hopeless task, and so
took ship to Africa,
who disappeared into the volcanoes of Mexico leaving behind
nothing but the shadow of dungarees and the lava and ash of
poetry scattered in fireplace Chicago,
who reappeared on the West Coast investigating the F.B.I. in
beards and shorts with big pacifist eyes sexy in their dark skin
passing out incomprehensible leaflets,
who burned cigarette holes in their arms protesting the narcotic
tobacco haze of Capitalism,
who distributed Supercommunist pamphlets in Union Square
weeping and undressing while the sirens of Los Alamos wailed
them down, and wailed down Wall, and the Staten Island
ferry also wailed,
who broke down crying in white gymnasiums naked and trembling
before the machinery of other skeletons,
who bit detectives in the neck and shrieked with delight in
policecars for committing no crime but their own wild
cooking pederasty and intoxication,
who howled on their knees in the subway and were dragged off
the roof waving genitals and manuscripts,
who let themselves be fucked in the ass by saintly motorcyclists,
and screamed with joy,
who blew and were blown by those human seraphim, the sailors,
caresses of Atlantic and Caribbean love,
who balled in the morning in the evenings in rosegardens and the
grass of public parks and cemeteries scattering their semen
freely to whomever come who may,
who hiccupped endlessly trying to giggle but wound up with a sob
behind a partition in a Turkish Bath when the blonde &
naked angel came to pierce them with a sword,
who lost their loveboys to the three old shrews of fate the one
eyed shrew of the heterosexual dollar the one eyed shrew that
winks out of the womb and the one eyed shrew that does
nothing but sit on her ass and snip the intellectual golden
threads of the craftsman's loom,
who copulated ecstatic and insatiate with a bottle of beer a
sweetheart a package of cigarettes a candle and fell off the
bed, and continued along the floor and down the hall and
ended fainting on the wall with a vision of ultimate cunt and
come eluding the last gyzym of consciousness,
who sweetened the snatches of a million girls trembling in the
sunset, and were red eyed in the morning but prepared to
sweeten the snatch of the sunrise, flashing buttocks under
barns and naked in the lake,

who went out whoring through Colorado in myriad stolen night-
cars, N.C.,[11] secret hero of these poems, cocksman and
Adonis of Denver—joy to the memory of his innumerable lays
of girls in empty lots & diner backyards, moviehouses' rickety
rows, on mountaintops in caves or with gaunt waitresses in
familiar roadside lonely petticoat upliftings & especially secret
gas-station solipsisms of johns, & hometown alleys too,
who faded out in vast sordid movies, were shifted in dreams, woke
on a sudden Manhattan, and picked themselves up out of
basements hungover with heartless Tokay and horrors of
Third Avenue iron dreams & stumbled to unemployment
offices,
who walked all night with their shoes full of blood on the
snowbank docks waiting for a door in the East River to open
to a room full of steamheat and opium,
who created great suicidal dramas on the apartment cliff-banks of
the Hudson under the wartime blue floodlight of the moon &
their heads shall be crowned with laurel in oblivion,
who ate the lamb stew of the imagination or digested the crab at
the muddy bottom of the rivers of Bowery,
who wept at the romance of the streets with their pushcarts full of
onions and bad music,
who sat in boxes breathing in the darkness under the bridge, and
rose up to build harpsichords in their lofts,
who coughed on the sixth floor of Harlem crowned with flame
under the tubercular sky surrounded by orange crates of
theology,
who scribbled all night rocking and rolling over lofty incantations
which in the yellow morning were stanzas of gibberish,
who cooked rotten animals lung heart feet tail borscht & tortillas
dreaming of the pure vegetable kingdom,
who plunged themselves under meat trucks looking for an egg,
who threw their watches off the roof to cast their ballot for
Eternity outside of Time, & alarm clocks fell on their heads
every day for the next decade,
who cut their wrists three times successively unsuccessfully, gave
up and were forced to open antique stores where they thought
they were growing old and cried,
who were burned alive in their innocent flannel suits on Madison
Avenue amid blasts of leaden verse & the tanked-up clatter of
the iron regiments of fashion & the nitroglycerine shrieks of
the fairies of advertising & the mustard gas of sinister

[11] Neal Cassady, friend of Ginsberg and Jack Kerouac.

intelligent editors, or were run down by the drunken taxicabs
of Absolute Reality,
who jumped off the Brooklyn Bridge this actually happened and
walked away unknown and forgotten into the ghostly daze of
Chinatown soup alleyways & firetrucks, not even one free
beer,
who sang out of their windows in despair, fell out of the subway
window, jumped in the filthy Passaic, leaped on negroes, cried
all over the street, danced on broken wineglasses barefoot
smashed phonograph records of nostalgic European 1930's
German jazz finished the whiskey and threw up groaning into
the bloody toilet, moans in their ears and the blast of colossal
steamwhistles,
who barreled down the highways of the past journeying to each
other's hotrod-Golgotha[12] jail-solitude watch or Birmingham
jazz incarnation,
who drove crosscountry seventytwo hours to find out if I had a
vision or you had a vision or he had a vision to find out
Eternity,
who journeyed to Denver, who died in Denver, who came back to
Denver & waited in vain, who watched over Denver &
brooded & loned in Denver and finally went away to find out
the Time, & now Denver is lonesome for her heroes,
who fell on their knees in hopeless cathedrals praying for each
other's salvation and light and breasts, until the soul
illuminated its hair for a second,
who crashed through their minds in jail waiting for impossible
criminals with golden heads and the charm of reality in their
hearts who sang sweet blues to Alcatraz,
who retired to Mexico to cultivate a habit, or Rocky Mount to
tender Buddha or Tangiers to boys or Southern Pacific to the
black locomotive or Harvard to Narcissus to Woodlawn[13] to
the daisychain or grave,
who demanded sanity trials accusing the radio of hypnotism &
were left with their insanity & their hands & a hung jury,
who threw potato salad at CCNY lecturers on Dadaism and
subsequently presented themselves on the granite steps of the
madhouse with shaven heads and harlequin speech of suicide,
demanding instantaneous lobotomy,
and who were given instead the concrete void of insulin metrasol
electricity hydrotherapy psychotherapy occupational therapy
pingpong & amnesia,
who in humorless protest overturned only one symbolic pingpong
table, resting briefly in catatonia,

[12]Scene of Jesus' crucifixion.
[13]Bronx cemetery.

returning years later truly bald except for a wig of blood, and tears
and fingers, to the visible madman doom of the wards of the
madtowns of the East,
Pilgrim State's Rockland's and Greystone's[14] foetid halls, bickering
with the echoes of the soul, rocking and rolling in the
midnight solitude-bench dolmen-realms of love, dream of life
a nightmare, bodies turned to stone as heavy as the moon,
with mother finally ******, and the last fantastic book flung out of
the tenement window, and the last door closed at 4 AM and
the last telephone slammed at the wall in reply and the last
furnished room emptied down to the last piece of mental
furniture, a yellow paper rose twisted on a wire hanger in the
closet, and even that imaginary, nothing but a hopeful little
bit of hallucination—
ah, Carl, while you are not safe I am not safe, and now you're
really in the total animal soup of time—
and who therefore ran through the icy streets obsessed with a
sudden flash of the alchemy of the use of the ellipse the
catalog the meter & the vibrating plane,
who dreamt and made incarnate gaps in Time & Space through
images juxtaposed, and trapped the archangel of the soul
between 2 visual images and joined the elemental verbs and
set the noun and dash of consciousness together jumping with
sensation of Pater Omnipotens Aeterna Deus[15]
to recreate the syntax and measure of poor human prose and stand
before you speechless and intelligent and shaking with shame,
rejected yet confessing out the soul to conform to the rhythm
of thought in his naked and endless head,
the madman bum and angel beat in Time, unknown, yet putting
down here what might be left to say in time come after death,
and rose incarnate in the ghostly clothes of jazz in the goldhorn
shadow of the band and blew the suffering of America's
naked mind for love into an eli eli lamma lamma sabacthani[16]
saxophone cry that shivered the cities down to the last radio
with the absolute heart of the poem of life butchered out of their
own bodies good to eat a thousand years.

[14]Mental hospitals in New York and New Jersey.

[15]Latin: "Omnipotent Father Eternal God," from a letter of French painter Paul Cézanne (1839–1906).

[16]Hebrew: "My God, my God, why hast thou forsaken me?" Christ's words on the cross (Matthew 27:46).

II

What sphinx of cement and aluminum bashed open their skulls
and ate up their brains and imagination?
Moloch![17] Solitude! Filth! Ugliness! Ashcans and unobtainable
dollars! Children screaming under the stairways! Boys
sobbing in armies! Old men weeping in the parks!
Moloch! Moloch! Nightmare of Moloch! Moloch the loveless!
Mental Moloch! Moloch the heavy judger of men!
Moloch the incomprehensible prison! Moloch the crossbone
soulless jailhouse and Congress of sorrows! Moloch whose
buildings are judgement! Moloch the vast stone of war!
Moloch the stunned governments!
Moloch whose mind is pure machinery! Moloch whose blood is
running money! Moloch whose fingers are ten armies!
Moloch whose breast is a cannibal dynamo! Moloch whose
ear is a smoking tomb!
Moloch whose eyes are a thousand blind windows! Moloch whose
skyscrapers stand in the long streets like endless Jehovahs!
Moloch whose factories dream and croak in the fog!
Moloch whose smokestacks and antennae crown the cities!
Moloch whose love is endless oil and stone! Moloch whose soul is
electricity and banks! Moloch whose poverty is the
specter of genius! Moloch whose fate is a cloud of sexless
hydrogen! Moloch whose name is the Mind!
Moloch in whom I sit lonely! Moloch in whom I dream Angels!
Crazy in Moloch! Cocksucker in Moloch! Lacklove and
manless in Moloch!
Moloch who entered my soul early! Moloch in whom I am a
consciousness without a body! Moloch who frightened me
out of my natural ecstasy! Moloch whom I abandon!
Wake up in Moloch! Light streaming out of the sky!
Moloch! Moloch! Robot apartments! invisible suburbs!
skeleton treasuries! blind capitals! demonic industries!
spectral nations! invincible madhouses! granite cocks!
monstrous bombs!
They broke their backs lifting Moloch to Heaven! Pavements,
trees, radios, tons! lifting the city to Heaven which exists
and is everywhere about us!
Visions! omens! hallucinations! miracles! ecstasies! gone down
the American river!
Dreams! adorations! illuminations! religions! the whole
boatload of sensitive bullshit!

[17]Semitic god to whom children were sacrificed.

Breakthroughs! over the river! flips and crucifixions! gone down
the flood! Highs! Epiphanies! Despairs! Ten years'
animal screams and suicides! Minds! New loves! Mad
generation! down on the rocks of Time!
Real holy laughter in the river! They saw it all! the wild eyes!
the holy yells! They bade farewell! They jumped off the
roof! to solitude! waving! carrying flowers! Down to
the river! into the street!

III

Carl Solomon! I'm with you in Rockland
where you're madder than I am
I'm with you in Rockland
where you must feel very strange
I'm with you in Rockland
where you imitate the shade of my mother
I'm with you in Rockland
where you've murdered your twelve secretaries
I'm with you in Rockland
where you laugh at this invisible humor
I'm with you in Rockland
where we are great writers on the same dreadful typewriter
I'm with you in Rockland
where your condition has become serious and is reported on
the radio
I'm with you in Rockland
where the faculties of the skull no longer admit the worms
of the senses
I'm with you in Rockland
where you drink the tea of the breasts of the spinsters of
Utica
I'm with you in Rockland
where you pun on the bodies of your nurses the harpies of
the Bronx
I'm with you in Rockland
where you scream in a straightjacket that you're losing the
game of the actual pingpong of the abyss
I'm with you in Rockland
where you bang on the catatonic piano the soul is innocent
and immortal it should never die ungodly in an armed
madhouse
I'm with you in Rockland
where fifty more shocks will never return your soul to its
body again from its pilgrimage to a cross in the void

I'm with you in Rockland
where you accuse your doctors of insanity and plot the Hebrew socialist revolution against the fascist national Golgotha[18]
I'm with you in Rockland
where you split the heavens of Long Island and resurrect your living human Jesus from the superhuman tomb
I'm with you in Rockland
where there are twentyfive-thousand mad comrades all together singing the final stanzas of the Internationale
I'm with you in Rockland
where we hug and kiss the United States under our bedsheets the United States that coughs all night and won't let us sleep
I'm with you in Rockland
where we wake up electrified out of the coma by our own souls' airplanes roaring over the roof they've come to drop angelic bombs the hospital illuminates itself imaginary walls collapse O skinny legions run outside O starry-spangled shock of mercy the eternal war is here O victory forget your underwear we're free
I'm with you in Rockland
in my dreams you walk dripping from a sea-journey on the highway across America in tears to the door of my cottage in the Western night

1955–56

America

America I've given you all and now I'm nothing.
America two dollars and twentyseven cents January 17, 1956.
I can't stand my own mind.
America when will we end the human war?
Go fuck yourself with your atom bomb.
I don't feel good don't bother me.
I won't write my poem till I'm in my right mind.
America when will you be angelic?
When will you take off your clothes?

[18]Same as Calvary, the hill where Jesus was crucified.

When will you look at yourself through the grave?
When will you be worthy of your million Trotskyites?[1]
America why are your libraries full of tears?
America when will you send your eggs to India?
I'm sick of your insane demands.
When can I go into the supermarket and buy what I need with my
good looks?
America after all it is you and I who are perfect not the next
world.
Your machinery is too much for me.
You made me want to be a saint.
There must be some other way to settle this argument.
Burroughs[2] is in Tangiers I don't think he'll come back it's sinister.
Are you being sinister or is this some form of practical joke?
I'm trying to come to the point.
I refuse to give up my obsession.
America stop pushing I know what I'm doing.
America the plum blossoms are falling.
I haven't read the newspapers for months, everyday somebody goes
on trial for murder.
America I feel sentimental about the Wobblies.[3]
America I used to be a communist when I was a kid I'm not sorry.
I smoke marijuana every chance I get.
I sit in my house for days on end and stare at the roses in the
closet.
When I go to Chinatown I get drunk and never get laid.
My mind is made up there's going to be trouble.
You should have seen me reading Marx.
My psychoanalyst thinks I'm perfectly right.
I won't say the Lord's Prayer.
I have mystical visions and cosmic vibrations.
America I still haven't told you what you did to Uncle Max after
he came over from Russia.

I'm addressing you.
Are you going to let your emotional life be run by Time
Magazine?
I'm obsessed by Time Magazine.
I read it every week.
Its cover stares at me every time I slink past the corner candystore.
I read it in the basement of the Berkeley Public Library.

[1]Communist idealists, followers of Leon Trotsky (1879–1940).
[2]William Burroughs (b. 1914) author of *Naked Lunch.*
[3]Nickname for Industrial Workers of the World, a militant labor organization strong in the 1910s.

It's always telling me about responsibility. Businessmen are serious.
Movie producers are serious. Everybody's serious but me.
It occurs to me that I am America.
I am talking to myself again.

Asia is rising against me.
I haven't got a chinaman's chance.
I'd better consider my national resources.
My national resources consist of two joints of marijuana millions of genitals an unpublished private literature that goes 1400 miles an hour and twentyfive-thousand mental institutions.
I say nothing about my prisons nor the millions of underprivileged who live in my flowerpots under the light of five hundred suns.
I have abolished the whorehouses of France, Tangiers is the next to go.
My ambition is to be President despite the fact that I'm a Catholic.

America how can I write a holy litany in your silly mood?
I will continue like Henry Ford my strophes are as individual as his automobiles more so they're all different sexes.
America I will sell you strophes $2500 apiece $500 down on your old strophe
America free Tom Mooney[4]
America save the Spanish Loyalists[5]
America Sacco & Vanzetti[6] must not die.
America I am the Scottsboro boys.[7]
America when I was seven momma took me to Communist Cell meetings they sold us garbanzos a handful per ticket a ticket cost a nickel and the speeches were free everybody was angelic and sentimental about the workers it was all so sincere you have no idea what a good thing the party was in 1935 Scott Nearing was a grand old man a real mensch Mother Bloor made my cry I once saw Israel Amter[8] plain. Everybody must have been a spy.
America you don't really want to go to war.

[4]Labor leader sentenced to death for killings in 1916; the sentence was commuted and he was eventually pardoned.

[5]Opponents of Franco's Fascists in the Spanish Civil War.

[6]Anarchists executed in Massachusetts for murder (1927) in a case that aroused much controversy.

[7]Nine blacks falsely convicted in Alabama for the rape of two white women (1931). The defense was undertaken by the Communist Party, and the case became a cause for liberals and radicals, who believed it to be a miscarriage of justice.

[8]Nearing, Bloor, and Amter were active in Socialist and radical causes.

America it's them bad Russians
Them Russians them Russians and them Chinamen. And them Russians.
The Russia wants to eat us alive. The Russia's power mad. She wants to take our cars from out our garages.
Her wants to grab Chicago. Her needs a Red Reader's Digest. Her wants our auto plants in Siberia. Him big bureaucracy running our fillingstations.
That no good. Ugh. Him make Indians learn read. Him need big black niggers. Hah. Her make us all work sixteen hours a day. Help.
America this is quite serious.
America this is the impression I get from looking in the television set.
America is this correct?
I'd better get right down to the job.
It's true I don't want to join the Army or turn lathes in precision parts factories, I'm nearsighted and psychopathic anyway.
America I'm putting my queer shoulder to the wheel.

1956

Jack Kerouac 1922–1969

Jack Kerouac transformed his life into a modern myth, one that appeals anew to each generation discovering his classic *On the Road* (1957). While romanticizing his cross-country travels and writing frankly about the sex, drugs, and drinking that took up so much of his time, Kerouac also infused his books with a literary consciousness and brooding spirituality, proof that he was smarter and deeper than detractors such as Truman Capote (who claimed Kerouac's writing was mere "typing") wanted him to be.

Though known as a novelist of the open road, he also wrote at length about his childhood in Lowell, Massachusetts, the provincial New England mill town where he was born Jean Louis Lebris de Kerouac to French Canadian immigrant parents in 1922. Lowell is the basis for the town in *The Town and the City* (1950), his first and most traditional novel, modeled after the work of Thomas Wolfe, and it provides the mystical atmosphere for several of his other novels, including *Visions of Gerard* (1963), the account of his nine-year-old brother Gerard's illness and death. This book effectively blends the Catholicism of his youth with the Buddhist principles informing his later years; its free-flowing style epitomizes the "spontaneous prose" that grew out of the author's faith in "the unspeakable visions of the individual."

After graduating from Lowell High School, Kerouac earned a football scholarship to Columbia College by way of a year at the Horace Mann Preparatory School in New York. At Horace Mann he enjoyed a charmed life as an athlete and scholar. His subsequent years at Columbia did not go so smoothly. An injury derailed his football career, and he eventually dropped out of school and enlisted in the U.S. Navy and later the Merchant Marine. In the midst of this indecisive time, he made the friends with whom he would instigate the literary trend and liberal lifestyle known as the Beat movement.

Allen Ginsberg and William S. Burroughs (a Harvard graduate) were brilliant, driven, and often self-tormented, like Kerouac himself. In New York City's jazz clubs and gay bars and among the criminal elements of Times Square they found a bracing alternative to workaday jobs and conventional family life. The hustler Herbert Huncke introduced them to "beat," a slang term for a drug deal gone bad. Kerouac applied the musically resonant word to his down-and-out but spiritually questing ("beatific") peers. In 1948 he told his friend John Clellon Holmes that their post-war generation of outsiders evinced "a weariness with all the forms, all the conventions of the world. . . . So I guess you might say we're a beat generation."

The following year, Kerouac took to the road with Neal Cassady, a charismatic con man who personified all things beat. The model for Dean Moriarty in *On the Road* and Cody in *Visions of Cody* (1972), Cassady lived as spontaneously as Kerouac wanted to write. In *On the Road,* he applauds the fictional counterparts of Cassady and Ginsberg, "the ones who are mad to live, mad to talk, mad to be saved, desirous of everything at the same time, the ones who never yawn or say a commonplace thing."

After the publication of *On the Road* and *The Dharma Bums* (1958), the successful follow-up novel based on his friendship with the poet Gary Snyder, Kerouac drifted on a sea of distracting fame. Though he continued to publish both prose and poetry, his drinking and often outlandish behavior cost him the critical recognition that he craved. He died of stomach hemorrhaging at age forty-seven in St. Petersburg, Florida, in the company of his mother and his third wife, Stella Sampas Kerouac of Lowell.

Kerouac embodied many of the contradictions and paradoxes that have long animated American society. He was a homebody and vagabond, bottle-swigging hedonist and Thoreau-quoting hermit, all-American hero and hard-luck hobo. All of these personas show up in his compelling, recklessly honest writing.

Hilary Holladay
University of Massachusetts, Lowell

PRIMARY WORKS

The Town and the City, 1950; *On the Road,* 1957; *The Dharma Bums,* 1958; *The Subterraneans,* 1958; *Doctor Sax: Faust Part Three,* 1959; *Maggie Cassidy,* 1959; *Mexico City Blues,* 1959; *The Scripture of the Golden Eternity,* 1960; *Tristessa,* 1960; *Lonesome Traveler,* 1960; *Book of Dreams,* 1961; *Pull My Daisy,* 1961; *Big Sur,* 1962; *Visions of Gerard,* 1963; *Desolation Angels,* 1965; *Satori in Paris,* 1966; *Vanity of Duluoz: An Adventurous Education,* 1968; *Scattered Poems,* 1971; *Pic,* 1971; *Visions of Cody,* 1972; *Heaven and Other Poems,* 1977; *Pomes All Sizes,* 1992; *Old Angel Midnight,* 1993; *Good Blonde & Others,* 1993; *Some of the Dharma,* 1997; *Selected Letters: 1940–1956,* 1995; *Selected Letters: 1957–1969,* 1999; *Atop an Underwood: Early Stories and Other Writings,* 1999.

The Vanishing American Hobo

The American hobo has a hard time hoboing nowadays due to the increase in police surveillance of highways, railroad yards, sea shores, river bottoms, embankments and the thousand-and-one hiding holes of industrial night.——In California, the pack rat, the original old type who goes walking from town to town with supplies and bedding on his back, the "Homeless Brother," has practically vanished, along with the ancient gold-panning desert rat who used to walk with hope in his heart through struggling Western towns that are now so prosperous they dont want old bums any more.——"Man dont want no pack rats here even though they founded California" said an old man hiding with a can of beans and an Indian fire in a river bottom outside Riverside California in 1955.——Great sinister tax-paid police cars (1960 models with humorless searchlights) are likely to bear down at any moment on the hobo in his idealistic lope to freedom and the hills of holy silence and holy privacy.——There's nothing nobler than to put up with a few inconveniences like snakes and dust for the sake of absolute freedom.

I myself was a hobo but only of sorts, as you see, because I knew someday my literary efforts would be rewarded by social protection——I was not a real hobo with no hope ever except that secret eternal hope you get sleeping in empty boxcars flying up the Salinas Valley in hot January sunshine full of Golden Eternity toward San Jose where mean-looking old bo's 'll look at you from surly lips and offer you something to eat and a drink too——down by the tracks or in the Guadaloupe Creekbottom.

The original hobo dream was best expressed in a lovely little poem mentioned by Dwight Goddard in his *Buddhist Bible:*

Oh for this one rare occurrence
Gladly would I give ten thousand pieces of gold!
A hat is on my head, a bundle on my back,
And my staff, the refreshing breeze and the full moon.

In America there has always been (you will notice the peculiarly Whitmanesque tone of this poem, probably written by old Goddard) a definite special idea of footwalking freedom going back to the days of Jim Bridger and Johnny Appleseed and carried on today by a vanishing group of hardy old timers still seen sometimes waiting in a desert highway for a short bus ride into town for panhandling (or work) and grub, or wandering the Eastern part of the country hitting Salvation Armies and moving on from town to town and state to state toward the eventual doom of big-city skid rows when their feet give out.——Nevertheless not long ago in California I did see (deep in the gorge by a railroad track outside San Jose buried in eucalyptus leaves and the blessed oblivion of vines) a bunch of cardboard and jerrybuilt huts at evening in front of one of which sat an aged man puffing his 15¢ Granger tobacco in his corncob pipe (Japan's mountains are full of free huts and old men who cackle over root brews waiting for Supreme Enlightenment which is only obtainable through occasional complete solitude.)

In America camping is considered a healthy sport for Boy Scouts but a crime for mature men who have made it their vocation.——Poverty is considered a virtue among the monks of civilized nations——in America you spend a night in the calaboose if you're caught short without your vagrancy change (it was fifty cents last I heard of, Pard——what now?)

In Brueghel's time children danced around the hobo, he wore huge and raggy clothes and always looked straight ahead indifferent to the children, and the families didnt mind the children playing with the hobo, it was a natural thing.——But today mothers hold tight their children when the hobo passes through town, because of what newspapers made the hobo to be——the rapist, the strangler, child-eater.——Stay away from strangers, they'll give you poison candy. Though the Brueghel hobo and the hobo today are the same, the children are different.——Where is even the Chaplinesque hobo? The old Divine Comedy hobo? The hobo is Virgil, he leadeth.——The hobo enters the child's world (like in the famous painting by Brueghel of a huge hobo solemnly passing through the washtub village being barked at and laughed at by children, St. Pied Piper) but today it's an adult world, it's not a child's world.——Today the hobo's made to slink——everybody's watching the cop heroes on TV.

Benjamin Franklin was like a hobo in Pennsylvania; he walked through Philly with three big rolls under his arms and a Massachusetts halfpenny on his hat.——John Muir was a hobo who went off into the mountains with a pocketful of dried bread, which he soaked in creeks.

Did Whitman terrify the children of Louisiana when he walked the open road?

What about the Black Hobo? Moonshiner? Chicken snatcher? Remus? The black hobo in the South is the last of the Brueghel bums, children pay tribute and stand in awe making no comment. You see him coming out of the piney barren with an old unspeakable sack. Is he carrying coons? Is he carrying Br'er Rabbit? Nobody knows what he's carrying.

The Forty Niner, the ghost of the plains, Old Zacatecan Jack the Walking Saint, the prospector, the spirits and ghosts of hoboism are gone——but they (the prospectors) wanted to fill their unspeakable sacks with gold.——Teddy Roosevelt, political hobo——Vachel Lindsay, troubadour hobo, seedy hobo——how many pies for one of *his* poems? The hobo lives in a Disneyland, Pete-the-Tramp land, where everything is human lions, tin men, moondogs with rubber teeth, orange-and-purple paths, emerald castles in the distance looming, kind philosophers of witches.——No witch ever cooked a hobo.——The hobo has two watches you can't buy in Tiffany's, on one wrist the sun, on the other wrist the moon, both bands are made of sky.

Hark! Hark! The dogs do bark,
The beggars are coming to town;
Some in rags, some in tags,
And some in velvet gowns.

The Jet Age is crucifying the hobo because how can he hop a freight jet? Does Louella Parsons look kindly upon hobos, I wonder? Henry Miller would allow the hobos to swim in his swimming pool.——What about Shirley Temple, to whom the hobo gave the Bluebird? Are the young Temples bluebirdless?

Today the hobo has to hide, he has fewer places to hide, the cops are looking for him, *calling all cars, calling all cars, hobos seen in the vicinity of Bird-in-Hand*——Jean Valjean weighed with his sack of candelabra, screaming to youth, "There's your *sou,* your *sou!*" Beethoven was a hobo who knelt and listened to the light, a deaf hobo who could not hear other hobo complaints.——Einstein the hobo with his ratty turtleneck sweater made of lamb, Bernard Baruch the disillusioned hobo sitting on a park bench with voice-catcher plastic in his ear waiting for John Henry, waiting for somebody very mad, waiting for the Persian epic.——

Sergei Esenin was a great hobo who took advantage of the Russian Revolution to rush around drinking potato juice in the backward villages of Russia (his most famous poem is called *Confessions of a Bum*) who said at the moment they were storming the Czar "Right now I feel like pissing through the window at the moon." It is the egoless hobo that will give birth to a child someday——Li Po was a mighty hobo.——ego is the greatest hobo——Hail Hobo Ego! Whose monument someday will be a golden tin coffee can.

Jesus was a strange hobo who walked on water.——

Buddha was also a hobo who paid no attention to the other hobo.——

Chief Rain-In-The-Face, weirder even.——

W. C. Fields——his red nose explained the meaning of the triple world, Great Vehicle, Lesser Vehicle, Diamond Vehicle.

The hobo is born of pride, having nothing to do with a community but with himself and other hobos and maybe a dog.——Hobos by the railroad embankments cook at night huge tin cans of coffee.——Proud was the way the hobo walked through a town by the back doors where pies were cooling on window sills, the hobo was a mental leper, he didnt need to beg to eat, strong Western bony mothers knew his tinkling beard and tattered toga, *come and get it!* But proud be proud, still there was some annoyance because sometimes when she called *come and get it,* hordes of hobos came, ten or twenty at a time, and it was kind of hard to feed that many, sometimes hobos were inconsiderate, but not always, but when they were, they no longer held their pride, they became bums——they migrated to the Bowery in New York, to Scollay Square in Boston, to Pratt Street in Baltimore, to Madison Street in Chicago, to 12th Street in Kansas City, to Larimer Street in Denver, to South Main Street in Los Angeles, to downtown Third Street in San Francisco, to Skid Road in Seattle ("blighted areas" all)——

The Bowery is the haven for hobos who came to the big city to make the big time by getting pushcarts and collecting cardboard.——Lots of Bowery bums are Scandinavian, lots of them bleed easily because they drink too much.——When winter comes bums drink a drink called smoke, it consists of wood alcohol and a drop of iodine and a scab of lemon, this they gulp down and wham! they hibernate all winter so as not to catch cold, because they dont live anywhere, and it gets very cold outside in the city in winter.——Sometimes hobos sleep arm-in-arm to keep warm, right on the sidewalk. Bowery Mission veterans say that the beer-drinking bums are the most belligerent of the lot.

Fred Bunz is the great Howard Johnson's of the bums——it is located on 277 Bowery in New York. They write the menu in soap on the windows.——You see the bums reluctantly paying fifteen cents for pig brains, twenty-five cents for goulash, and shuffling out in thin cotton shirts in the cold November night to go and make the lunar Bowery with a smash of broken bottle in an alley where they stand against a wall like naughty boys.——Some of them wear adventurous rainy hats picked up by the track in Hugo Colorado or blasted shoes kicked off by Indians in the dumps of Juarez, or coats from the lugubrious salon of the seal and fish.——Bum hotels are white and tiled and seem as though they were upright johns.——Used to be bums told tourists that they once were successful doctors, now they tell tourists they were once guides for movie stars or directors in Africa and that when TV came into being they lost their safari rights.

In Holland they dont allow bums, the same maybe in Copenhagen. But in Paris you can be a bum——in Paris bums are treated with great respect and are rarely refused a few francs.——There are various kinds of classes of bums in Paris, the high-class bum has a dog and a baby carriage in which he keeps all his belongings, and that usually consists of old *France Soirs,* rags, tin cans, empty bottles, broken dolls.——This bum sometimes has a mistress who follows him and his dog and carriage around.——The lower bums dont own a thing, they just sit on the banks of the Seine picking their nose at the Eiffel Tower.——

The bums in England have English accents, and it makes them seem strange——they don't understand bums in Germany.——America is the motherland of bumdom.——

American hobo Lou Jenkins from Allentown Pennsylvania was interviewed at Fred Bunz's on The Bowery.——"What you wanta know all this info for, what you want?"

"I understand that you've been a hobo travelin' around the country."

"How about givin' a fella few bits for some wine before we talk."

"Al, go get the wine."

"Where's this gonna be in, the *Daily News?*"

"No, in a book."

"What are you young kids doing here, I mean where's the drink?"

"Al's gone to the liquor store——You wanted Thunderbird, wasnt it?"

"Yair."

Lou Jenkins then grew worse——"How about a few bits for a flop tonight?"

"Okay, we just wanta ask you a few questions like why did you leave Allentown?"

"My wife.——My wife,——Never get married. You'll never live it down. You mean to say it's gonna be in a book hey what I'm sayin'?"

"Come on say something about bums or something.——"

"Well whattaya wanta know about bums? Lot of 'em around, kinda tough these days, no money——lissen, how about a good meal?"

"See you in the Sagamore." (Respectable bums' cafeteria at Third and Cooper Union.)

"Okay kid, thanks a lot."——He opens the Thunderbird bottle with one expert flip of the plastic seal.——Glub, as the moon rises resplendent as a rose he swallows with big ugly lips thirsty to gulp the throat down, Sclup! and down goes the drink and his eyes be-pop themselves and he licks tongue on top lip and says "H-a-h!" And he shouts "Dont forget my name is spelled Jenkins, J-e-n-k-y-n-s.——"

Another character——"You say that your name is Ephram Freece of Pawling New York?"

"Well, no, my name is James Russell Hubbard."

"You look pretty respectable for a bum."

"My grandfather was a Kentucky colonel."

"Oh?"

"Yes."

"Whatever made you come here to Third Avenue?"

"I really cant do it, I dont care, I cant be bothered, I feel nothing, I dont care any more. I'm sorry but——somebody stole my razor blade last night, if you can lay some money on me I'll buy myself a Schick razor."

"Where will you plug it in? Do you have such facilities?"

"A Schick injector."

"Oh."

"And I always carry this book with me——*The Rules of St. Benedict.* A dreary book, but well I got another book in my pack. A dreary book too I guess."

"Why do you read it then?"

"Because I found it——I found it in Bristol last year."

"What are you interested in? You like interested in something?"

"Well, this other book I got there is er, yee, er, a big strange book——you shouldnt be interviewing me. Talk to that old nigra fella over there with the harmonica——I'm no good for nothing, all I want is to be left alone——"

"I see you smoke a pipe."

"Yeah——Granger tobacco. Want some?"

"Will you show me the book?"

"No I aint got it with me, I only got this with me."——He points to his pipe and tobacco.

"Can you say something?"

"Lightin flash."

The American Hobo is on the way out as long as sheriffs operate with as Louis-Ferdinand Céline said, "One line of crime and nine of boredom," because having nothing to do in the middle of the night with everybody gone to sleep they pick on the first human being they see walking.——They pick on lovers on the beach even. They just dont know what to do with themselves in those five-thousand-dollar police cars with the twoway Dick Tracy radios except pick on anything that moves in the night and in the daytime on anything that seems to be moving independently of gasoline, power, Army or police.——I myself was a hobo but I had to give it up around 1956 because of increasing television stories about the abominableness of strangers with packs passing through by themselves independently——I was surrounded by three squad cars in Tucson Arizona at 2 A.M. as I was walking pack-on-back for a night's sweet sleep in the red moon desert:

"Where you goin'?"

"Sleep."

"Sleep where?"

"On the sand."

"Why?"

"Got my sleeping bag."

"Why?"

"Studyin' the great outdoors."

"Who are you? Let's see your identification."

"I just spent a summer with the Forest Service."

"Did you get paid?"

"Yeah."

"Then why dont you go to a hotel?"

"I like it better outdoors and it's free."

"Why?"

"Because I'm studying hobo."

"What's so good about that?"

They wanted an *explanation* for my hoboing and came close to hauling me in but I was sincere with them and they ended up scratching their heads and saying "Go ahead if that's what you want."——They didnt offer me a ride four miles out to the desert.

And the sheriff of Cochise allowed me to sleep on the cold clay outside Bowie Arizona only because he didnt know about it.——

There's something strange going on, you cant even be alone any more in the primitive wilderness ("primitive areas" so-called), there's always a helicopter comes and snoops around, you need camouflage.——Then they begin to demand that you observe strange aircraft for Civil Defense as though you knew the difference between regular strange aircraft and any kind of strange aircraft.——As far as I'm concerned the only thing to do is sit in a room and get drunk and give up your hoboing and your camping ambitions because there aint a sheriff or fire warden in any of the new fifty states who will let you cook a little meal over some burning sticks in the tule brake or the hidden valley or anyplace any more because he has nothing to do but pick on what he sees out there on the landscape moving independently of the gasoline power army police station.——I have no ax to grind: I'm simply going to another world.

Ray Rademacher, a fellow staying at the Mission in the Bowery, said recently, "I wish things was like they was when my father was known as Johnny the Walker of the White Mountains.——He once straightened out a young boy's bones after an accident, for a meal, and left. The French around there called him *'Le Passant.'*" (He who passes through.)

The hobos of America who can still travel in a healthy way are still in good shape, they can go hide in cemeteries and drink wine under cemetery groves of trees and micturate and sleep on cardboards and smash bottles on the tombstones and not care and not be scared of the dead but serious and humorous in the cop-avoiding night and even amused and leave litters of their picnic between the grizzled slabs of Imagined Death, cussing what they think are real days, but Oh the poor bum of the skid row! There he sleeps in the doorway, back to wall, head down, with his right hand palm-up as if to receive from the night, the other hand hanging, strong, firm, like Joe Louis hands, pathetic, made tragic by unavoidable circumstance——the hand like a beggar's upheld with the fingers forming a suggestion of what he deserves and desires to receive, shaping the alms, thumb almost touching finger tips, as though on the tip of the tongue he's about to say in sleep and with that gesture what he couldnt say awake: "Why have you taken this away from me, that I cant draw my breath in the peace and sweetness of my own bed but here in these dull and nameless rags on this humbling stoop I have to sit waiting for the wheels of the city to roll," and further, "I dont want to show my hand but in sleep I'm helpless to straighten it, yet take this opportunity to see my plea, I'm alone, I'm sick, I'm dying——see my hand uptipped, learn the secret of my human heart, give me the thing, give me your hand, take me to the emerald mountains beyond the city, take me to the safe place, be kind, be nice, smile——I'm too tired now of everything else, I've had enough, I give up, I quit, I want to go home, take me home O brother in the night——take me home, lock me in safe, take me to where all is peace and amity, to the family of life, my mother, my father, my sister, my wife and you my brother and you my friend——but no hope, no hope, no hope, I wake up and I'd give a million dollars to be in my own bed——O Lord save me——" In evil roads behind gas tanks where murderous dogs snarl from behind wire fences cruisers suddenly leap out like getaway cars but from a crime more secret, more baneful than words can tell.

The woods are full of wardens.

Lawrence Ferlinghetti b. 1919

A prominent voice of the Beat poetry movement of the 1950s whose primary aim was to bring poetry back to the people, Lawrence Ferlinghetti has greatly extended that specific objective in his prolific career as editor and publisher of the renowned City Lights Books press in San Francisco. His literary production has embraced many areas: translation, fiction writing, travelogues, playwriting, film narration, and essays. Yet his impact and importance remain as a poet and as a voice of dissent which is reflected in his describing his politics as "an enemy of the State."

Following graduation from the University of North Carolina and service in World War II, Ferlinghetti received a master's degree from Columbia University in 1948 and a doctorate from the Sorbonne in 1951. From 1951 to 1953, when he settled in San Francisco, he taught French in an adult education program. In 1953 he became co-owner of the City Lights Bookshop, the first all-paperback bookstore in the country, and by 1955 had founded and become editor of the City Lights Books publishing house. City Lights served as a meeting place for Beat writers. His press published and promoted Beat writings, and he himself encouraged them, in the case of Diane di Prima, writing the introduction for her first collection, *This Kind of Bird Flies Backward.*

Ferlinghetti's publication of Allen Ginsberg's *Howl* in 1956 led to his arrest on obscenity charges. The trial that followed (he was acquitted) drew national attention to the Beat movement and established Ferlinghetti as its prominent voice. In fact, Ferlinghetti own *A Coney Island of the Mind* was, along with *Howl,* the most popular poetry book of the 1950s. Often concerned with political and social issues, Ferlinghetti's poetry set out to dispute the literary elite's definition of art and the artist's role in the world. Though imbued with the commonplace, his poetry cannot be dismissed as polemic or personal protest, for it stands on his craftsmanship, thematics, and grounding in tradition.

Ferlinghetti described his one novel, *Her,* as "a surreal semi-autobiographical blackbook." It deals with a young man's search for his identity, although its free-association experimentation proved baffling to critics.

Known for his political poetry, he explains his commitment in art as well as life by saying "Only the dead are disengaged." Well aware of the incongruity of his social dissent with his success as a publisher, Ferlinghetti, in an interview for the Los Angeles *Times,* remarked on "the enormous capacity of society to ingest its own most dissident elements. . . . It happens to everyone successful within the system. I'm ingested myself."

Helen Barolini
Independent scholar

PRIMARY WORKS

Pictures of the Gone World, 1955, 1973; *A Coney Island of the Mind,* 1958; *Her* (novel), 1960; *Starting from San Francisco,* 1961, 1967; *The Secret Meaning of Things,* 1969; *The Mexican Night: Travel Journal,* 1970; *Who Are We Now?,* 1976; *Literary San Francisco,* 1980; *Over All the Obscene Boundaries,* 1984; *The Canticle of Jack Kerouac,* 1987; *Love in the Days of Rage,* 1988; *European Poems and Transitions,* 1988; *Ascending over Ohio,* 1989; *A Buddha in the Woodpile,* 1993; *These Are My Rivers: New and Selected Poems,* 1993.

I Am Waiting

I am waiting for my case to come up
and I am waiting
for a rebirth of wonder
and I am waiting for someone
to really discover America
and wail
and I am waiting
for the discovery
of a new symbolic western frontier
and I am waiting
for the American Eagle
to really spread its wings
and straighten up and fly right
and I am waiting
for the Age of Anxiety
to drop dead
and I am waiting
for the war to be fought
which will make the world safe
for anarchy
and I am waiting
for the final withering away
of all governments
and I am perpetually awaiting
a rebirth of wonder

I am waiting for the Second Coming
and I am waiting
for a religious revival
to sweep thru the state of Arizona
and I am waiting
for the Grapes of Wrath to be stored
and I am waiting
for them to prove

that God is really American
and I am seriously waiting
for Billy Graham and Elvis Presley
to exhange roles seriously
and I am waiting
to see God on television
piped onto church altars
if only they can find
the right channel
to tune in on
and I am waiting
for the Last Supper to be served again
with a strange new appetizer
and I am perpetually awaiting
a rebirth of wonder

I am waiting for my number to be called
and I am waiting
for the living end
and I am waiting
for dad to come home
his pockets full
of irradiated silver dollars
and I am waiting
for the atomic tests to end
and I am waiting happily
for things to get much worse
before they improve
and I am waiting
for the Salvation Army to take over
and I am waiting
for the human crowd
to wander off a cliff somewhere
clutching its atomic umbrella
and I am waiting
for Ike to act
and I am waiting
for the meek to be blessed
and inherit the earth
without taxes
and I am waiting
for forests and animals
to reclaim the earth as theirs
and I am waiting
for a way to be devised
to destroy all nationalisms
without killing anybody
and I am waiting

for linnets and planets to fall like rain
and I am waiting for lovers and weepers
to lie down together again
in a new rebirth of wonder

I am waiting for the Great Divide to be crossed
and I am anxiously waiting
for the secret of eternal life to be discovered
by an obscure general practitioner
and save me forever from certain death
and I am waiting
for life to begin
and I am waiting
for the storms of life
to be over
and I am waiting
to set sail for happiness
and I am waiting
for a reconstructed Mayflower
to reach America
with its picture story and tv rights
sold in advance to the natives
and I am waiting
for the lost music to sound again
in the Lost Continent
in a new rebirth of wonder

I am waiting for the day
that maketh all things clear
and I am waiting
for Ole Man River
to just stop rolling along
past the country club
and I am waiting
for the deepest South
to just stop Reconstructing itself
in its own image
and I am waiting
for a sweet desegregated chariot
to swing low
and carry me back to Ole Virginie
and I am waiting
for Ole Virginie to discover
just why Darkies are born
and I am waiting
for God to lookout
from Lookout Mountain
and see the Ode to the Confederate Dead
as a real farce

and I am awaiting retribution
for what America did
to Tom Sawyer
and I am waiting retribution
for what America did
to Tom Sawyer
and I am perpetually awaiting
a rebirth of wonder

I am waiting for Tom Swift to grow up
and I am waiting
for the American Boy
to take off Beauty's clothes
and get on top of her
and I am waiting
for Alice in Wonderland
to retransmit to me
her total dream of innocence
and I am waiting
for Childe Roland to come
to the final darkest tower
and I am waiting
for Aphrodite
to grow live arms
at a final disarmament conference
in a new rebirth of wonder

I am waiting
to get some intimations
of immortality
by recollecting my early childhood
and I am waiting
for the green mornings to come again
youth's dumb green fields come back again
and I am waiting
for some strains of unpremeditated art
to shake my typewriter
and I am waiting to write
the great indelible poem
and I am waiting
for the last long careless rapture
and I am perpetually waiting
for the fleeing lovers on the Grecian Urn
to catch each other up at last
and embrace
and I am waiting
perpetually and forever
a renaissance of wonder

1958

Dove Sta Amore . . .

Dove sta amore
Where lies love
Dove sta amore
Here lies love
The ring dove love
In lyrical delight
Hear love's hillsong
Love's true willsong
Love's low plainsong
Too sweet painsong
In passages of night
Dove sta amore
Here lies love
The ring dove love
Dove sta amore
Here lies love

1958

The Old Italians Dying

For years the old Italians have been dying
all over America
For years the old Italians in faded felt hats
have been sunning themselves and dying
You have seen them on the benches
in the park in Washington Square
the old Italians in their black high button shoes
the old men in their old felt fedoras
with stained hatbands
have been dying and dying
day by day
You have seen them
every day in Washington Square San Francisco
the slow bell
tolls in the morning
in the Church of Peter & Paul
in the marzipan church on the plaza
toward ten in the morning the slow bell tolls
in the towers of Peter & Paul

and the old men who are still alive
sit sunning themselves in a row
on the wood benches in the park
and watch the processions in and out
funerals in the morning
weddings in the afternoon
slow bell in the morning Fast bell at noon
In one door out the other
the old men sit there in their hats
and watch the coming & going
You have seen them
the ones who feed the pigeons
                        cutting the stale bread
                            with their thumbs & penknives
the ones with old pocketwatches
the old ones with gnarled hands
                                        and wild eyebrows
the ones with the baggy pants
                                    with both belt & suspenders
the grappa drinkers with teeth like corn
the Piemontesi the Genovesi the Sicilianos
                            smelling of garlic & pepperonis
the ones who loved Mussolini
the old fascists
the ones who loved Garibaldi
the old anarchists reading *L'Umanita Nova*
the ones who loved Sacco & Vanzetti
They are almost all gone now
They are sitting and waiting their turn
and sunning themselves in front of the church
over the doors of which is inscribed
a phrase which would seem to be unfinished
from Dante's *Paradiso*
about the glory of the One
                            who moves everything . . .
The old men are waiting
for it to be finished
for their glorious sentence on earth
                                to be finished

the slow bell tolls & tolls
the pigeons strut about
not even thinking of flying
the air too heavy with heavy tolling
The black hired hearses draw up
the black limousines with black windowshades
shielding the widows
the widows with the long black veils

who will outlive them all
You have seen them
madre di terra, madre di mare
The widows climb out of the limousines
The family mourners step out in stiff suits
The widows walk so slowly
up the steps of the cathedral
fishnet veils drawn down
leaning hard on darkcloth arms
Their faces do not fall apart
They are merely drawn apart
They are still the matriarchs
outliving everyone
the old dagos dying out
in Little Italys all over America
the old dead dagos
hauled out in the morning sun
that does not mourn for anyone
One by one Year by year
they are carried out
The bell
never stops tolling
The old Italians with lapstrake faces
are hauled out of the hearses
by the paid pallbearers
in mafioso mourning coats & dark glasses
The old dead men are hauled out
in their black coffins like small skiffs
They enter the true church
for the first time in many years
in these carved black boats
                ready to be ferried over
The priests scurry about
                as if to cast off the lines
The other old men
                still alive on the benches
watch it all with their hats on

You have seen them sitting there
waiting for the bocci ball to stop rolling
waiting for the bell
                to stop tolling & tolling
for the slow bell
                to be finished tolling
telling the unfinished *Paradiso* story
as seen in an unfinished phrase
                on the face of a church

as seen in a fisherman's face
in a black boat without sails
making his final haul

1979

Robert Creeley b. 1926

Robert Creeley has been widely recognized as a central figure in contemporary American writing. Creeley grew up on a small farm in West Acton, Massachusetts, where his mother worked as a public health nurse. After graduating from Holderness School in New Hampshire, he attended Harvard, drove an ambulance in India for the American Field Service, returned to Harvard, and then left without a degree in 1947. By that time he had married Ann MacKinnon, with whom he tried subsistence farming for a while near Littleton, New Hampshire. In 1949 he began to correspond with Cid Corman (the later editor of *Origin*) and in 1950 with Charles Olson, who continued to be a mentor. The Creeleys soon moved to southern France and then to Mallorca—the scene of his later novel, *The Island.* In 1954 Creeley joined Olson at Black Mountain College, North Carolina, where he received a B.A., taught, and edited *Black Mountain Review.* After a divorce he left Black Mountain for the West, settling in Albuquerque, where he taught at a boys' school. In 1957 he married Bobbie Hall, who over the next two decades would provide many occasions for poems. After two years as a tutor in Guatemala, and an M.A. from the University of New Mexico, Creeley became an instructor of English at that institution in 1961. During the 1950s he had published widely with little magazines and presses. In the 1960s he gained a national reputation; and he has continued to teach and read his poetry at various universities. A divorce from Bobbie was followed in 1977 by marriage to Penelope Highton. Since 1978, he has been Gray Professor of Poetry and Letters at the State University of New York at Buffalo, and, more recently, Capen Professor of Poetry and Humanities. He was New York State Poet for 1989–1991.

Creeley's poetry has been shaped by his New England childhood, his early admiration for Wallace Stevens, Paul Valéry, and classical poetry, his wide reading in European love poetry, his years of discussion with Charles Olson, his assimilation of the Whitman tradition as modified by William Carlos Williams, Ezra Pound, and Hart Crane—and also by his own experimental openness, his remarkable ear, his obsessive self-examination, and his firm sense of the poem as an act of responsibility. He has a classicist's respect for given poetic forms and also a Projectivist's insistence that form must be an extension of freshly perceived content. Though his poems may at first seem thin or abstract, they express with honesty and precision a quite specific interior drama: the struggle of consciousness to articulate its movements in response to an ungraspable and "broken" world. Whether arising from occasions of loss, perplexity, ironic reflection, gratitude, or brief ecstasy, the poems render that drama in their groping diction, tortured syntax, wry echoes and rhymes, strategic line-breaks, and stammering pace. Since the writing of *Pieces* Creeley has often sought to construct from brief poems or prose notations a larger form that might register the difficult passage of such a consciousness through its continuing present.

Memory Gardens modulates his lifelong concerns into a more quietly elegiac and meditative mode, and *Windows* engages more fully both the "inside" and the "outside" worlds.

Thomas R. Whitaker
Yale University

PRIMARY WORKS

The Gold Diggers (stories), 1954; *For Love: Poems 1950-1960,* 1962; *The Island* (novel), 1963; *Words,* 1967; *The Charm: Early and Uncollected Poems,* 1967; *Pieces,* 1969; *A Quick Graph: Collected Notes & Essays,* 1970; *A Day Book* (prose and poetry), 1972; *Listen* (play), 1972; *A Sense of Measure* (essays), 1973; *Contexts of Poetry: Interviews 1961–1972,* 1973; *Thirty Things,* 1974; *Away,* 1976; *Presences* (prose), 1976; *Mabel: A Story,* 1976; *Hello: A Journal,* 1978; *Later,* 1979; *Was That a Real Poem and Other Essays,* 1979; *The Collected Poems 1945–1975,* 1982; *Mirrors,* 1983; *The Collected Prose,* 1984; *Memory Gardens,* 1986; *The Collected Essays,* 1989; *Windows,* 1990. Edited works: Charles Olson, *Mayan Letters,* 1953; *New American Story* (with Donald M. Allen), 1965; *New Writing in the U.S.A.* (with Donald M. Allen), 1967; *Selected Writings of Charles Olson,* 1967; *Whitman: Selected Poems,* 1973. Correspondence: *Charles Olson and Robert Creeley: The Complete Correspondence,* ed. George F. Butterick, 1980–; *Irving Layton and Robert Creeley: The Complete Correspondence,* ed. Ekbert Faas and Sabrina Reed, 1990.

Hart Crane[1]

for Slater Brown[2]

1

He had been stuttering, by the edge
of the street, one foot still
on the sidewalk, and the other
in the gutter . . .

like a bird, say, wired to flight, the
wings, pinned to their motion, stuffed.

The words, several, and for each, several
senses.
"It is very difficult to sum up
briefly . . ."
It always was.

[1]See pages 1555–56.
[2]A friend of Hart Crane who also became a friend of Creeley.

(Slater, let me come home.
The letters have proved insufficient.
The mind cannot hang to them as it could
to the words.

There are ways beyond
what I have here to work with,
what my head cannot push to any kind
of conclusion.

But my own ineptness
cannot bring them to hand,
the particulars of those times
we had talked.)

"Men kill themselves because they are
afraid of death, he says . . ."

The push
        beyond and
into

Respect, they said he respected the
ones with the learning, lacking it
himself
        (Waldo Frank[3] & his
6 languages)
            What had seemed
important
While Crane sailed to Mexico I was writing
(so that one betrayed
            himself)

He slowed
        (without those friends to keep going, to
keep up), stopped
            dead and the head could not
go further
        without those friends
. . . *And so it was I entered the broken world*[4]

Hart Crane.

Hart

1962

[3]Critic, novelist, and friend of Hart Crane.
[4]Quoted from Crane's late poem "The Broken Tower."

I Know a Man

As I sd to my
friend, because I am
always talking,—John, I

sd, which was not his
name, the darkness sur-
rounds us, what

can we do against
it, or else, shall we &
why not, buy a goddam big car,

drive, he sd, for
christ's sake, look
out where yr going.

1962

For Love

for Bobbie[1]

Yesterday I wanted to
speak of it, that sense above
the others to me
important because all

that I know derives
from what it teaches me.
Today, what is it that
is finally so helpless,

different, despairs of its own
statement, wants to
turn away, endlessly
to turn away.

If the moon did not . . .
no, if you did not
I wouldn't either, but
what would I not

[1]Creeley's second wife.

do, what prevention, what
thing so quickly stopped.
That is love yesterday
or tomorrow, not

now. Can I eat
what you give me. I
have not earned it. Must
I think of everything
as earned. Now love also
becomes a reward so
remote from me I have
only made it with my mind.

Here is tedium,
despair, a painful
sense of isolation and
whimsical if pompous

self-regard. But that image
is only of the mind's
vague structure, vague to me
because it is my own.

Love, what do I think
to say. I cannot say it.
What have you become to ask,
what have I made you into,

companion, good company,
crossed legs with skirt, or
soft body under
the bones of the bed.

Nothing says anything
but that which it wishes
would come true, fears
what else might happen in

some other place, some
other time not this one.
A voice in my place, an
echo of that only in yours,

Let me stumble into
not the confession but
the obsession I begin with
now. For you

also (also)
some time beyond place, or
place beyond time, no
mind left to

say anything at all,
that face gone, now.
Into the company of love[2]
it all returns.

1962

Words

You are always
with me,
there is never
a separate

place. But if
in the twisted
place I
cannot speak,

not indulgence
or fear only,
but a tongue
rotten with what

it tastes—There is
a memory
of water, of
food, when hungry.

Some day
will not be
this one, then
to say

words like a
clear, fine

[2]A phrase from Hart Crane's "The Broken Tower."

ash sifts,
like dust,

from nowhere.

1967

America

America, you ode for reality![1]
Give back the people you took.

Let the sun shine again
on the four corners of the world

you thought of first but do not
own, or keep like a convenience.

People are your own word, you
invented that locus and term.

Here, you said and say, is
where we are. Give back

what we are, these people you made,
us, and nowhere but you to be.

1969

[1]Cf. Walt Whitman, in Preface to *Leaves of Grass:* "The United States themselves are essentially the greatest poem."

Charles Olson 1910–1970

As poet, essayist, letter-writer, and teacher, Charles Olson was a seminal figure in the generation after Ezra Pound and William Carlos Williams. His first book, *Call Me Ishmael,* is an interpretation of Melville's *Moby-Dick* that deserves a place beside D. H. Lawrence's *Studies in Classic American Literature,* Williams's *In the American Grain,* and Edward Dahlberg's *Can These Bones Live.* His long sequence, *The Maximus Poems,* is the major attempt at a "personal epic" after Pound's *Cantos* and Williams's *Paterson.* He increasingly thought of himself as a "mythographer" or "archaeologist of morning" who aimed to reconnect us with the natural process from which we have been alienated by the rationalist thought of the last 2,500 years.

Born in Worcester, Massachusetts, Olson grew up there while spending summers in Gloucester, the city he later celebrated in *The Maximus Poems.* He attended Wesleyan University, from which he received a B.A. and an M.A. with a thesis on Melville. He then embarked on a search for Melville's library and tracked down many of his books, including his personally annotated Hawthorne and Shakespeare. Olson taught English for two years at Clark University, took a summer job on the schooner *Doris W. Hawkes,* and entered Harvard's American Civilization program, where he studied with the historian Frederick Merk and the literary scholar F. O. Matthiessen. After completing the course-work for the Ph.D., he returned to Gloucester to take up a Guggenheim Fellowship for studies in Melville. In 1940 he met Constance Wilcock, who became his common-law wife, and began working in New York for the American Civil Liberties Union and then for the Common Council for American Unity. From 1942 to 1944, he worked for the Office of War Information in Washington and then became director of the Foreign Nationalities Division, Democratic National Committee. In 1945, disenchanted with politics, he decided to commit himself to writing. During that year he wrote *Call Me Ishmael* (based on his earlier Melville research), several poems, and an essay in qualified defense of Ezra Pound, the boldly mimetic "This Is Yeats Speaking."

Over the next three years, Olson met Pound and also the geographer Carl Sauer (an important influence on his thought), worked on a book about the American West, wrote a dance-play based on *Moby-Dick,* and began to lecture at Black Mountain College as a replacement for his friend and mentor, Edward Dahlberg. In 1949 he wrote his important postmodernist poem "The Kingfishers." In 1950 he began corresponding with Robert Creeley, wrote the first Maximus poem, and published "Projective Verse," in which he reasserted Creeley's principle, "FORM IS NEVER MORE THAN AN EXTENSION OF CONTENT," and Dahlberg's clue to poetic process, "ONE PERCEPTION MUST IMMEDIATELY AND DIRECTLY LEAD TO A FURTHER PERCEPTION." In 1951 he began his association with Cid Corman and the magazine *Origin,* traveled to the Yucatán to study Mayan culture, and wrote "Human Universe," in which he argued that art "is the only twin life has" because it "does not seek to describe but to enact."

That year he also joined Black Mountain full-time, where he remained (except for a leave in 1952 for further research on Mayan glyphs) as faculty member and then rector until the college closed in 1956. While there he separated from Constance and took as common-law wife Elizabeth Kaiser. Olson effectively turned Black Mountain into an arts center. Among his associates were the painters Franz Kline and Robert Rauschenberg, the dancer Merce Cunningham, and the musician John Cage. In 1957 Olson returned to Gloucester, from which he traveled to various colleges for lectures and readings. In 1963 he began to teach at the State University of New York at Buffalo. In 1964 his wife, Elizabeth, was killed in an automobile accident—a tragedy from which Olson never recovered. He returned to Gloucester in 1965 and then accepted in 1969 a position at the University of Connecticut, where he taught for a few weeks before his death. During these years, he had continued to work on *The Maximus Poems,* which he never completed. The third book of that sequence was posthumously arranged from his notes by his former students Charles Boer and George F. Butterick.

Olson's poetry is often elliptical and allusive, with a range that can include Sumerian myth, Heraclitus, Hesiod, the linguist B. L. Whorf, the cyberneticist Norbert Wiener, the philosopher Alfred

North Whitehead, the psychologist C. G. Jung, and the details of both ancient and modern history. His style tends to be meditative and didactic, but with frequent lyricism. It is often made difficult by incomplete syntax, heavy reliance upon abstract terms, brief notations, and a disjunctive or paratactic forward motion that piles up incremental meanings and produces an effect of continual self-revision. These traits are in accord with Olson's understanding of art as "enactment." His constantly twisting utterance seeks not to describe but to enact the movements of a speaker who is himself in "process" as he grapples with the matter in hand. As Olson said once at Goddard College, "I myself would wish that all who spoke and wrote, spoke always from a place that is *new* at that moment that they do speak. . . ."

Thomas R. Whitaker
Yale University

PRIMARY WORKS

Poetry: *Y & X,* 1949; *In Cold Hell, In Thicket,* 1953; *The Maximus Poems / 1–10,* 1953; *The Maximus Poems / 11–22,* 1956; *The Maximus Poems,* 1960; *The Distances,* 1960; *The Maximus Poems IV, V, VI,* 1968; *Archaeologist of Morning,* 1973; Charles Boer and George F. Butterick, eds., *The Maximus Poems: Volume Three,* 1975; George F. Butterick, ed., *The Maximus Poems,* 1983; George F. Butterick, ed., *The Collected Poems,* 1987; George F. Butterick, ed., *A Nation of Nothing but Poetry: Supplementary Poems,* 1989; Robert Creeley, ed., *Selected Poems,* 1993. Prose: *Call Me Ishmael,* 1947; *A Bibliography on America for Ed Dorn,* 1964; Donald Allen, ed., *Human Universe and Other Essays,* 1965; *Proprioception,* 1965; *Stocking Cap,* 1966; *Causal Mythology,* 1969; Ann Charters, ed., *The Special View of History,* 1970; George F. Butterick, ed., *Poetry and Truth: The Beloit Lectures and Poems,* 1971; George F. Butterick, ed., *Additional Prose,* 1974; George F. Butterick, ed., *The Post Office,* 1975; Catherine Seelye, ed., *Charles Olson and Ezra Pound: An Encounter at St. Elizabeths,* 1975; George F. Butterick, ed., *Mythologies: The Collected Lectures and Interviews,* vols. 1 and 2, 1978, 1979. Correspondence: Robert Creeley, ed., *Mayan Letters,* 1953; Albert G. Glover, ed., *Letters for Origin, 1950–1955,* 1969; George Evans, ed., *Charles Olson and Cid Corman: Complete Correspondence 1950–1964* (2 vols.), 1987, 1991; George F. Butterick, ed., *Charles Olson and Robert Creeley: The Complete Correspondence,* 1990; Paul Christensen, ed., *In Love, In Sorrow: The Complete Correspondence of Charles Olson and Edward Dahlberg,* 1990; Ralph Maud and Sharon Thesen, eds., *Charles Olson and Frances Boldereff: A Modern Correspondence,* 1999.

The Kingfishers[1]

I

What does not change / is the will to change[2]

He[3] woke, fully clothed, in his bed. He
remembered only one thing, the birds, how
when he came in, he had gone around the rooms
and got them back in their cage, the green one first,
she with the bad leg, and then the blue,
the one they had hoped was a male

Otherwise? Yes, Fernand, who had talked lispingly of Albers[4] &
Angkor Vat.[5]
He had left the party without a word. How he got up, got into his
coat,
I do not know. When I saw him, he was at the door, but it did not
matter,
he was already sliding along the wall of the night, losing himself
in some crack of the ruins. That it should have been he who said,
"The kingfishers!
who cares
for their feathers[6]
now?"
His last words had been, "The pool is slime."[7] Suddenly everyone,
ceasing their talk, sat in a row around him, watched
they did not so much hear, or pay attention, they
wondered, looked at each other, smirked, but listened,
he repeated and repeated, could not go beyond his thought

[1]This poem about personal, poetic, and cultural crisis answers Pound and Eliot in many ways, beginning with the title. The "kingfishers," as literal and complex subjects of meditation, imply a reversal of Eliot's kind of symbolism (the "Fisher King" of *The Waste Land* and the "kingfisher's wing" in "Burnt Norton").

[2]A revision of Heraclitus's Fragment 83, "Change alone is unchanging," to emphasize the human will and history. Eliot's "Burnt Norton" begins with Heraclitus's Fragments 2 and 60.

[3]Third-person reference to the poet: concerned with parakeets that friends hope to mate, he then remembers "Fernand," a character based on an art curator in Washington.

[4]Josef Albers, noted painter and teacher, who was rector of Black Mountain College when Olson was first hired.

[5]Early twelfth-century temple in Cambodia.

[6]The feathers of the kingfisher had ceremonial use and were a valuable article of trade in the Mayan-Aztec culture that Olson had begun to study at the time of this poem.

[7]The sacrificial pool at Chichén Itzá in which messengers to the gods, wearing feathered headdresses, were drowned.

"The pool the kingfishers' feathers were wealth why
did the export stop?"

It was then he left

2

I thought of the E on the stone,[8] and of what Mao[9] said
la lumiere"
                    but the kingfisher
de l'aurore"
                    but the kingfisher flew west
est devant nous!
                    he got the color of his breast
                    from the heat of the setting sun![10]

The features are, the feebleness of the feet (syndactylism of the 3rd & 4th digit)
the bill, serrated, sometimes a pronounced beak, the wings
where the color is, short and round, the tail
inconspicuous.

But not these things were the factors. Not the birds.
The legends are
legends. Dead, hung up indoors, the kingfisher
will not indicate a favoring wind,
or avert the thunderbolt. Nor, by its nesting,
still the waters, with the new year, for seven days.
It is true, it does nest with the opening year, but not on the waters.
It nests at the end of a tunnel bored by itself in a bank. There,
six or eight white and translucent eggs are laid, on fishbones
not on bare clay, on bones thrown up in pellets by the birds.

                                        On these rejectamenta
(as they accumulate they form a cup-shaped structure) the young are born.

[8]The symbol, perhaps an epsilon, carved on the omphalos, or navel stone, at the oracle of Delphi. Plutarch's essay, "The E at Delphi," offers several conjectures as to the lost meaning of this symbol.

[9]Mao Tse-tung, whose revolutionary army was winning the civil war in China during the spring of 1949. A passage from Mao's call to action in a 1948 report to the Communist Party was sent to Olson by a French friend, Jean Riboud. The passage concludes: *"La lumière de l'aurore est devant nous. Nous devons nous lever et agir"* ("The light of dawn is before us. We must rise and act").

[10]This legend, those given below, and the items of biological information are drawn from the article on the kingfisher in *The Encyclopaedia Britannica* (11th ed.).

And, as they are fed and grow, this nest of excrement and decayed
fish becomes
a dripping, fetid mass

Mao concluded:
nous devons
nous lever
et agir!

3

When the attentions change / the jungle
leaps in
even the stones are split
they rive[11]
Or,
enter
that other conqueror[12] we more naturally recognize
he so resembles ourselves

But the E
cut so rudely on that oldest stone
sounded otherwise,
was differently heard

as, in another time, were treasures used:

(and, later, much later, a fine ear thought
a scarlet coat)

"of green feathers feet, beaks and eyes
of gold

"animals likewise,
resembling snails

"a large wheel, gold, with figures of unknown four-foots,
and worked with tufts of leaves, weight
3800 ounces

[11]These lines synthesize Pound and Williams on renewal: *Canto XX:* "jungle,/Basis of renewal, renewals"; *Paterson,* Book II: "unless the mind change . . . without invention nothing lies under the witch-hazel bush . . . "; "A Sort of a Song": "Invent!/Saxifrage is my flower that splits/the rocks."

[12]I.e., a destroyer of civilization like Hernando Cortés, the conqueror of Mexico, to whom the poem alludes below.

"last, two birds, of thread and featherwork, the quills
gold, the feet
gold, the two birds perched on two reeds
gold, the reeds arising from two embroidered mounds,
one yellow, the other
white.

"And from each reed hung
seven feathered tassels.[13]

In this instance, the priests
(in dark cotton robes, and dirty,
their dishevelled hair matted with blood, and flowing wildly
over their shoulders)
rush in among the people, calling on them
to protect their gods

And all now is war
where so lately there was peace,
and the sweet brotherhood, the use
of tilled fields.

4

Not one death but many,[14]
not accumulation but change, the feed-back proves, the feed-back is
the law[15]

Into the same river no man steps twice[16]
When fire dies air dies
No one remains, nor is, one

Around an appearance, one common model, we grow up
many. Else how is it,
if we remain the same,
we take pleasure now

[13]Montezuma's gifts to Cortés, as described in William H. Prescott, *History of the Conquest of Mexico.* See also Williams's "The Destruction of Tenochtitlán," in *In the American Grain.*

[14]A phrase drawn, perhaps, from Pablo Neruda, *The Heights of Macchu Picchu.*

[15]The first of several allusions to Norbert Wiener, *Cybernetics: or Control and Communication in the Animal and the Machine.* Wiener describes the circular and self-corrective processes of "feedback" as enabling the precise steering or control of any process, mechanical, biological, or social.

[16]Heraclitus, Fragment 91, quoted by the moderator Ammonius in Plutarch's "The E at Delphi." Part 4 of section II puts in modern terms Ammonius's vision of Heraclitian change, ending with a rephrasing of the admonition "Know thyself," which was the climax of Ammonius's argument.

in what we did not take pleasure before? love
contrary objects? admire and/or find fault? use
other words, feel other passions, have
nor figure, appearance, disposition, tissue
the same?
    To be in different states without a change
    is not a possibility

We can be precise. The factors are
in the animal and/or the machine the factors are
communication and/or control, both involve
the message. And what is the message? The message is
a discrete or continuous sequence of measurable events distributed in
    time[17]

is the birth of air, is
the birth of water,[18] is
a state between
the origin and
the end, between
birth and the beginning of
another fetid nest

is change, presents
no more than itself

And the too strong grasping of it,
when it is pressed together and condensed,
loses it

This very thing you are

II

They buried their dead in a sitting posture
serpent cane razor ray of the sun

And she sprinkled water on the head of the child, crying
"Cioa-coatl! Cioa-coatl!"
        with her face to the west[19]

[17]Quoted from Wiener, *Cybernetics,* p. 8.

[18]Ammonius cites Heraclitus's dictum (Fragment 76) in Plutarch's "The E at Delphi": "the death of heat is birth for steam, and the death of steam is birth for water, but the case is even more clearly to be seen in our own selves. . . ." Olson's emphasis on "birth" reverses that of Eliot when echoing the same dictum in "Little Gidding": "This is the death of air" and "the death of water."

[19]Factual details of Mayan burial and baptismal ceremonies.

Where the bones are found, in each personal heap
with what each enjoyed, there is always
the Mongolian louse[20]

The light is in the east. Yes. And we must rise, act. Yet
in the west, despite the apparent darkness (the whiteness
which covers all), if you look, if you can bear, if you can, long enough

as long as it was necessary for him, my guide
to look into the yellow of that longest-lasting rose[21]

so you must, and, in that whiteness, into that face, with what candor,[22]
look

and, considering the dryness of the place
the long absence of an adequate race

(of the two who first came, each a conquistador, one
healed, the other[23]
tore the eastern idols down, toppled
the temple walls, which, says the excuser
were black from human gore)

hear
hear, where the dry blood talks
where the old appetite walks

la piu saporita et migliore
che si possa truovar al mondo[24]

where it hides, look
in the eye how it runs
in the flesh / chalk[25]

[20]Evidence sometimes offered to support the theory that Amerindian culture is of Asian origin.

[21]In Dante's *Divine Comedy,* the Latin poet Virgil guides Dante through Hell and Purgatory, but it is St. Bernard who finally directs his vision to the white rose (*candida rosa*) of Paradise, likened to the sun at dawn (*Paradiso,* XXXI, 118-129). In Olson's poem, where the paradisal appears "in" or "under" the infernal, Virgil and Bernard are implicitly combined. The model for that combination is provided by Pound's *Cantos,* a journey through the hell of the modern world toward a vision of the paradisal.

[22]Echoing Pound, *Canto LXXIV* ("what whiteness will you add to this whiteness,/what candor?"), which paraphrases the *Analects* of Confucius. Pound's lines point to the natural "process" and also to the "city of Dioce whose terraces are the colour of stars," understood as paradisal antitheses to the tragedy of war.

[23]Cabeza de Vaca, who "healed," and Cortés, who so destroyed the idols in Tenochtitlán, and was so justified by Prescott.

[24]From Marco Polo's account of cannibalism in Asia: "the most savory and best that can be found in the world."

[25]The "eye" and "flesh" of the living Mayans and the "chalk" of the Mayan glyphs.

but under these petals
in the emptiness
regard the light, contemplate
the flower
whence it arose

with what violence benevolence is bought
what cost in gesture justice brings
what wrongs domestic rights involve
what stalks
this silence

what pudor pejorocracy[26] affronts
how awe, night-rest and neighborhood can rot[27]
what breeds where dirtiness is law
what crawls
below

III[28]

I am no Greek, hath not th'advantage.[29]
And of course, no Roman:
he can take no risk that matters,
the risk of beauty least of all.

But I have my kin,[30] if for no other reason than
(as he said, next of kin)[31] I commit myself, and,
given my freedom, I'd be a cad
if I didn't. Which is most true.

It works out this way, despite the disadvantage.
I offer, in explanation, a quote:

[26]"Rule by the worst," an antonym of "aristocracy" coined by Pound in *Canto LXXIX.*

[27]Recalling Shakespeare, *Timon of Athens,* 4. 1. 17–20: "Domestic awe, night-rest, and neighborhood,/Instruction, manners, mysteries and trades,/Degrees, observances, customs and laws,/Decline to your confounding contraries."

[28]After two sections in the juxtapositional mode of *The Waste Land* and *The Cantos,* and deriving partly from the montage technique of the film-artist Sergei Eisenstein, Section III presents a first-person statement in response to Eliot and Pound, using quatrains that glance at those in Pound's "Hugh Selwyn Mauberley."

[29]Parodying Eliot's "The Love Song of J. Alfred Prufrock: "I am not Prince Hamlet, nor was meant to be." Williams had already answered Eliot and Pound in the epigraph to *Paterson:* "a reply to Greek and Latin with the bare hands."

[30]Answering Pound's talk about "my kin of the spirit" in "In Durance."

[31]The "next of kin" is here acknowledged to be Pound, who said in his Preface to *Guide to Kulchur:* "It is my intention . . . to COMMIT myself on as many points as possible. . . . Given my freedom, I may be a fool to use it, but I wd. be a cad not to."

si j'ai du goût, ce n'est guères
que pour la terre et les pierres.[32]
Despite the discrepancy (an ocean   courage   age)
this is also true: if I have any taste
it is only because I have interested myself
in what was slain in the sun

I pose you your question:[33]

shall you uncover honey / where maggots are?

I hunt among stones

1950

For Sappho, Back[1]

I

With a dry eye, she
saw things out of the corner of,
with a bold
she looked on any man,
with a shy eye

[32]Arthur Rimbaud, "Faim" ("Hunger"), lines 1-2, in *Delires* (*Deliriums*), a section of *Une Saison en enfer* (*A Season in Hell*): "If I have any taste, it is only for earth and stones." For Olson, Rimbaud enacts the return to the "familiar" after the intellectual estrangement of Western culture. See *The Special View of History:* "It is this which Heraclitus meant when he laid down the law which was vitiated by Socrates and only restored by Rimbaud: that man is estranged from that [with] which he is most familiar." See "Maximus, to himself," note 2, below.

[33]A revision of Samson's riddle in Judges 14:14: "Out of the eater came forth meat, and out of the strong came forth sweetness." The carcass of the lion slain by Samson contained a swarm of bees and honey.

[1]Sappho was a Greek lyric poet, born c. 630 B.C, who lived and wrote on the island of Lesbos off the coast of Asia Minor, and who has been much admired by modern American poets. Except for three poems, her work is now known only in fragments, many of which have been discovered in this century on papyrus that had been re-used to make mummy shrouds. Her verse, both passionate and detached, celebrates a love of women and of all delicate things. Olson read the translations by J. M. Edmonds in the Loeb Classical Library *Lyra Graeca* (Volume 1). Olson's tribute, which begins in the past tense but moves to a continuing present, makes of Sappho a trope for woman, poetry, dance, and creative nature beyond all rational analysis.

With a cold eye, with her eye she looked on, she looked out, she
who was not so different as you might imagine from,
who had, as nature hath, an eye to look upon her makings, to,
in her womb, know
how red, and because it is red, how
handsome blood is, how, because it is unseen, how
because it goes about its business as she does,
as nature's things have that way of doing, as
in the delight of her eye she
creates constants

And, in the thickness of her blood, some

variants

II

As blood is, as flesh can be
is she, self-housed, and moving
moving in impeccability to be
clear, clear! to be
as, what is rhythm but
her limpidity?
She
who is as certain as the morning is
when it arises, when it is spring, when, from wetness comes its brightness
as fresh as this beloved's fingers, lips
each new time she new turns herself to
tendernesses, she
turns her most objective, scrupulous attention, her own self-causing
each time it is,
as is the morning, is
the morning night and revelation of her
nakedness, new
forever new, as fresh as is the scruple of her eye, the accurate kiss

III

If you would know what woman is, what
strength the reed of man unknows, forever
cannot know, look, look! in these eyes, look
as she passes, on this moving thing, which moves

as grass blade by grass blade moves, as
syllable does throw light on fellow syllable, as,
in this rare creature, each hidden, each moving thing
is light to its known, unknown brother,
as objects stand one by one by another, so
is this universe, this flow, this woman, these eyes
are sign

IV

The intimate, the intricate, what shall perplex, forever
is a matter, is it not, not of confusions to be studied and made literal,
but of a dry dance by which, as shoots one day make leaves, as
the earth's crust, when ice draws back, wrings mountains
from itself, makes valleys in whose palms
root-eating fisher folk spring up—
by such a dance, in which the dancer contradicts
the waste and easy gesture, contains
the heave within,
within, because the human is so light a structure, within
a finger, say, or there
within the gentlest swaying of
(of your true hips)

In such containment
And in search for that which is the shoot, the thrust
of what you are
(of what you were so delicately born)
of what fruits
of your own making you are
the hidden constance of which all the rest
is awkward variation
this! this
is what gives beauty to her eye, inhabitation
to her tender-taken bones, is what illumines
all her skin with satin glow
when love blows over, turning
as the leaf turns in the wind
and, with that shock of recognition,[2] shows
its other side, the joy, the sort of terror of
a dancer going off

1951

[2]A phrase made famous by Edmund Wilson's *The Shock of Recognition,* 1943, which treats a self-consciousness among American writers that has manifested itself in "moments when genius becomes aware of its kin" (p. viii).

I, Maximus of Gloucester, to You[1]

Off-shore, by islands hidden in the
    blood[2]
jewels & miracles, I, Maximus
a metal hot from boiling water, tell you
what is a lance, who obeys the figures of
the present dance

1

the thing you're after
may lie around the bend
of the nest (second, time slain, the bird! the bird!

And there! (strong) thrust, the mast! flight
                    (of the bird
                    o kylix,[3] o
                    Antony of Padua[4]
                    sweep low, o bless

the roofs, the old ones, the gentle steep ones
on whose ridge-poles the gulls sit, from which they depart,

                    And the flake-racks
of my city!

[1]The first "letter" of *The Maximus Poems.* Like "Paterson" in Williams's *Paterson,* Maximus is a complex figure. Most often, in this exploratory and self-corrective sequence, he is an aspect of the six-foot-eight-inch poet himself, probing the geography, history, and present needs of Gloucester, on Cape Ann in Massachusetts, which is for him "the last *polis* or city" in the northwestward migration of European culture from the eastern Mediterranean. But his name also suggests both Maximus of Tyre, a second-century A.D. Greek eclectic philosopher whom Olson encountered while reading about Sappho, and C. G. Jung's "homo maximus" or Self, which includes the ego-consciousness and the unconscious collective archetypes, and is the final goal of psychological "individuation." The title of this poem recalls the form of address used by St. Paul in his letters to the church-communities (e.g., *Colossians* 1: 1–3); but Maximus's initial oracular stance will be undercut by the opening lines of "Letter 2": ". . . . tell you? ha! who/can tell another how/to manage the swimming?"

[2]Suggesting an inner voice that projects itself to the east of Gloucester. *The Maximus Poems* later stress the fact that Maximus of Tyre lived on an island (off-shore from Asia Minor) which was made into a peninsula by a mole built by Alexander the Great, even as Cape Ann is an island made into a peninsula by the highway bridge of Route 128.

[3]An ancient Greek shallow cup with tall stem, evoked by the bird's flight and the shape of Gloucester harbor. These invocational lines recall and revise the seagull imagery that opens Hart Crane's modern "epic," *The Bridge* (see "To Brooklyn Bridge" in this volume).

[4]Franciscan friar and saint (1195–1231), patron of the Portuguese fishing community of Gloucester.

2

love is form, and cannot be without
important substance (the weight
say, 58 carats each one of us, perforce
our goldsmith's scale

feather to feather added
(and what is mineral, what
is curling hair, the string
you carry in your nervous beak, these

make bulk, these, in the end, are
the sum[5]
(o my lady of good voyage[6]
in whose arm, whose left arm rests
no boy but a carefully carved wood, a painted face, a schooner!
a delicate mast, as bow-sprit for
forwarding

3

the underpart is, though stemmed, uncertain
is, as sex is, as moneys are, facts!
facts, to be dealt with, as the sea is, the demand
that they be played by, that they only can be, that they must
be played by, said he, coldly, the
ear!

By ear, he sd.
But that which matters, that which insists, that which will last,
that! o my people, where shall you find it, how, where, where shall
you listen
when all is become billboards, when, all, even silence, is spray-gunned?

when even our bird, my roofs,
cannot be heard

when even you, when sound itself is neoned in?

[5]An allusion to the preface of Williams's *Paterson:* "To make a start,/out of particulars/and make them general, rolling/up the sum, by defective means—."

[6]At the top of the Church of Our Lady of Good Voyage, in the Portuguese community of Gloucester, is a statue of Our Lady holding a schooner. She is the invoked muse of the poem, the guide on its voyage.

when, on the hill, over the water
where she who used to sing,
when the water glowed,
black, gold, the tide
outward, at evening

when bells came like boats
over the oil-slicks, milkweed
hulls

And a man slumped,
attentionless,
against pink shingles

o sea city)

4

one loves only form,
and form only comes
into existence when
the thing is born

born of yourself, born
of hay and cotton struts,
of street-pickings, wharves, weeds
you carry in, my bird

of a bone of a fish
of a straw, or will
of a color, of a bell
of yourself, torn

5

love is not easy
but how shall you know,
New England, now
that pejorocracy[7] is here, how
that street-cars, o Oregon, twitter[8]

[7]See Note 26 to "The Kingfishers," above.
[8]At the time of the poem, streetcars in the East (though presumably not in Oregon) were piping in recorded music for the passengers.

in the afternoon, offend
a black-gold loin?

how shall you strike,[9]
o swordsman, the blue-red back
when, last night, your aim
was mu-sick, mu-sick, mu-sick[10]
And not the cribbage game?

(o Gloucester-man,
weave
your birds and fingers
new, your roof-tops,
clean shit upon racks
sunned on
American
braid
with others like you, such
extricable surface
as faun and oral,
satyr lesbos vase[11]

o kill kill kill kill kill[12]
those
who advertise you
out)

6

in! in! the bow-sprit, bird, the beak
in, the bend is, in, goes in, the form
that which you make, what holds, which is
the law of object, strut after strut, what you are, what you must be, what
the force can throw up, can, right now hereinafter erect,
the mast, the mast, the tender
mast!

The nest, I say, to you, I Maximus, say
under the hand, as I see it, over the waters

9A "striker" is a swordfish harpooner.
10Recalling a popular song, "Music, Music, Music."
11The lines suggest the classical Greek ("oral culture" and the island of Lesbos) and also modes of sexuality.
12Echoing Shakespeare, *King Lear,* 4. 6. 191.

from this place where I am, where I hear,
can still hear

from where I carry you a feather
as though, sharp, I picked up,
in the afternoon delivered you
a jewel,
it flashing more than a wing,
than any old romantic thing,
than memory, than place,
than anything other than that which you carry

than that which is,
call it a nest, around the head of, call it
the next second

than that which you
can do!

1953

Maximus, to himself[1]

I have had to learn the simplest things
last. Which made for difficulties.
Even at sea I was slow, to get the hand out, or to cross
a wet deck.
The sea was not, finally, my trade.
But even my trade, at it, I stood estranged
from that which was most familiar.[2] Was delayed,
and not content with the man's argument
that such postponement
is now the nature of
obedience,
that we are all late
in a slow time,
that we grow up many

[1]The twelfth poem in *The Maximus Poems.*
[2]Olson often quoted, and later chose as epigraph for *The Special View of History,* a dictum he attributed to Heraclitus: "Man is estranged from that [with] which he is most familiar." That seems to be Olson's own condensation of Heraclitus's Fragments 1 and 2, which he here ("the man's argument") paraphrases at greater length.

And the single
is not easily
known

It could be, though the sharpness (the *achiote*)[3]
I note in others,
makes more sense
than my own distances. The agilities

they show daily
who do the world's
businesses
And who do nature's
as I have no sense
I have done either

I have made dialogues,
have discussed ancient texts,
have thrown what light I could, offered
what pleasures
doceat[4] allows

But the known?
This, I have had to be given,
a life, love, and from one man[5]
the world.

Tokens.
But sitting here
I look out as a wind
and water man, testing
And missing
some proof

I know the quarters
of the weather, where it comes from,
where it goes. But the stem of me,

[3]Spanish: The seeds of the annatto tree, which are surrounded by a dark red pulp. When crushed to a paste, *achiote* can impart to food a deep, golden-yellow color. Delicate in flavor but often combined with further seasoning, *achiote* is widely used in Yucatán cooking, where Olson would have encountered it.

[4]Teaching, or to teach (from Latin *docere*). Pound, in *Make It New,* p. 8, quotes Rudolf Agricola's statement of the three proper functions of literature: "*Ut doceat, ut moveat, ut delectet*" ("to teach, to move, or to delight").

[5]Robert Creeley, Olson's friend and colleague, to whom (as "the Figure of Outward") he dedicated *The Maximus Poems.*

this I took from their welcome,
or their rejection, of me

And my arrogance
was neither diminished
nor increased,
by the communication

2

It is undone business
I speak of, this morning,
with the sea
stretching out
from my feet

1956

Gary Snyder b. 1930

Gary Snyder has said that his work "has been driven by the insight that all is connected and interdependent—nature, societies; rocks, stars." Growing up on a small farm north of Seattle, Washington, he was devoted to hiking and camping. At Reed College he wrote poetry, majored in literature and anthropology, read Chinese and Indian Buddhist philosophy, and prepared a thesis on a Native American myth of the Northwest coast. After studying linguistics and anthropology for a term at Indiana University, he broke off his academic career—ending also the marriage with Alison Gass that had begun at Reed—and went to San Francisco. He spent two summers as a forest-fire lookout—at Crater Mountain and Sourdough Mountain—and then entered the University of California in 1953 as a student of Oriental languages, preparing himself to go to Asia.

The American West and ancient China came together in his translations from "Cold Mountain," by the Zen hermit Han Shan. In 1955, having met Kenneth Rexroth, Jack Kerouac, and Allen Ginsberg, he took part in the poetry reading at the Six Gallery that launched the "San Francisco Renaissance." A lively if rather superficial portrait of him, as Japhy Ryder, is central to Kerouac's novel *The Dharma Bums.*

In 1956 Snyder went to Japan, where he learned Japanese and studied Zen Buddhism with Miura Isshu. Over the next twelve years he spent much time there, continuing his studies with Oda Sesso. He also had brief interludes of work in a ship's engine-room, travel through India with Ginsberg and Peter Orlovsky, teaching at Berkeley, and reading his poetry on American college campuses. From 1960 to 1965 he was married to Joanne Kyger. In 1967, while living at Banyan Ashram on Suwa-No-Se Island off the coast of Kyushu, Japan, he married Masa Uehara. After their son Kai was born the following year, the family came to the United States, where a second son, Gen, was born in 1969. In 1971 Snyder built a home in the foothills of the Sierra Mountains in California, where the family lived together for many years. In 1988, Snyder and Masa Uehara separated, and he was joined at "Kitkitdizze" by Carole Korda, whom he married in 1991.

During the last two decades—in poetry, prose, political action, and personal example—Snyder has been an advocate for ecological awareness. With *Earth House Hold* and *Turtle Island* (awarded the Pulitzer Prize for Poetry in 1975) his vision of cosmic interdependence or community assumed forceful and comprehensive literary form. Since 1985 he has been teaching at the University of California at Davis.

Snyder's poetry recovers values important to Thoreau and Whitman but does so in ways that have been influenced by the darker perspective of Robinson Jeffers, the pan-sexuality of D. H. Lawrence, the imagist discipline of Ezra Pound and William Carlos Williams, related disciplines in Japanese and Chinese poetry, the structural use of myth in the long poem from *The Waste Land* to *Paterson* and *The Maximus Poems,* the sound-shaping and shamanism in oral poetry, and the analytical insights of depth psychology, anthropology, and biology. All this is grounded in the serious practice of Zen. The poetics of *Riprap* is a craft of placing verbal details to make a path for the attention. That of the early *Myths & Texts* and of *Mountains and Rivers Without End,* a text composed over a forty-year period, involves the counterpointing of personal experience, meditation, exploration of myth, and song. In *Regarding Wave* his attention turned more sharply to words—their sounds, etymologies, proliferating meanings—as offering a field of generative energies like those that shape the cosmos itself. With urgency and detachment, seriousness and humor, Snyder continues as poet and essayist to explore the primal activities through which we participate in the "Great Family" whose habitation is Mind.

Thomas R. Whitaker
Yale University

PRIMARY WORKS

Riprap, 1959; *Myths & Texts,* 1960; *Riprap, and Cold Mountain Poems,* 1965; *A Range of Poems,* 1966; *The Back Country,* 1968; *Earth House Hold: Technical Notes & Queries to Fellow Dharma Revolutionaries,* 1969; *Regarding Wave,* 1969, 1970; *Turtle Island* (poems and prose), 1974; *The Old Ways: Six Essays,* 1977; *He Who Hunted Birds in His Father's Village: Dimensions of a Haida Myth* (Reed College thesis, 1951), 1979; *The Real Work: Interviews & Talks, 1964–1979,* 1980; *Axe Handles,* 1983; *Passage Through India* (prose), 1984; *Left Out in the Rain: New Poems 1947–1985,* 1986; *The Practice of the Wild: Essays,* 1990; *No Nature: New and Selected Poems,* 1992; *A Place in Space: Ethics, Aesthetics, and Watersheds: New and Selected Prose,* 1995; *Mountains and Rivers Without End,* 1996; *The Gary Snyder Reader: Prose, Poetry, and Translations, 1952–1998,* 1999.

Riprap[1]

Lay down these words
Before your mind like rocks.

[1]Snyder's own annotation: "a cobble of stone laid on steep slick rock to make a trail for horses in the mountains."

placed solid, by hands
In choice of place, set
Before the body of the mind
in space and time:
Solidity of bark, leaf, or wall
riprap of things:
Cobble of milky way,
straying planets,
These poems, people,
lost ponies with
Dragging saddles—
and rocky sure-foot trails.
The worlds like an endless
four-dimensional
Game of *Go.*[2]
ants and pebbles
In the thin loam, each rock a word
a creek-washed stone
Granite: ingrained
with torment of fire and weight
Crystal and sediment linked hot
all change, in thoughts,
As well as things.

1959

Vapor Trails

Twin streaks twice higher than cumulus,
Precise plane icetracks in the vertical blue
Cloud-flaked light-shot shadow-arcing
Field of all future war, edging off to space.

Young expert U.S. pilots waiting
The day of criss-cross rockets
And white blossoming smoke of bomb,
The air world torn and staggered for these
Specks of brushy land and ant-hill towns—

[2]A Japanese game played with black and white stones on a board marked with 19 vertical and 19 horizontal lines to make 361 intersections.

I stumble on the cobble rockpath,
Passing through temples,
Watching for two-leaf pine
—spotting that design.
in Daitoku-ji[1]

1959

Wave

Grooving clam shell,
streakt through marble,
sweeping down ponderosa pine bark-scale
rip-cut tree grain
sand-dunes, lava
flow
Wave wife.
woman—wyfman[1]—
"veiled; vibrating; vague"
sawtooth ranges pulsing;
veins on the back of the hand.

Forkt out; birdsfoot-alluvium
wash

great dunes rolling
Each inch rippld, every grain a wave.

Leaning against sand cornices til they blow away

—wind, shake
still thorns of cholla, ocotillo
sometimes I get stuck in thickets—

Ah, trembling spreading radiating wyf
racing zebra
catch me and fling me wide
To the dancing grain of things
of my mind!

1969

[1]The Japanese site of the poem's experience.
[1]Anglo-Saxon: "female human being," an early form of "woman."

It Was When

We harked up the path in the dark
to the bamboo house
green strokes down my back
arms over your doubled hips
under cow-breath thatch
bent cool
breasts brush my chest
—and Naga walked in with a candle,
"I'm sleepy"

Or jungle ridge by a snag—
banyan canyon—a Temminck's Robin
whirled down the waterfall gorge
in zazen,[1] a poncho spread out on the stones.
below us the overturning
silvery
brush-bamboo slopes—
rainsqualls came up on us naked
brown nipples in needles of ocean-
cloud
rain.

Or the night in the farmhouse
with Franco on one side, or Pon
Miko's head against me, I swung you
around and came into you
careless and joyous,
late
when Antares[2] had set

Or out on the boulders
south beach at noon
rockt by surf
burnd under by stone
burnd over by sun
saltwater caked
skin swing
hips on my eyes
burn between;

[1]The practice in Zen Buddhism of sitting cross-legged in sustained contemplation.

[2]A bright red star in the constellation Scorpio.

That we caught: sprout
took grip in your womb and it held.
new power in your breath called its place.
blood of the moon stoppt;
you pickt your steps well.

Waves
and the
prevalent easterly
breeze.
whispering into you,
through us,
the grace.

1969

Denise Levertov 1923–1997

Denise Levertov, one of America's foremost contemporary poets, was born in Essex, England; was privately educated except for ballet school and a wartime nursing program; served as a nurse during World War II; and emigrated to the United States in 1948. She has taught at Vassar, Drew, City College of New York, M.I.T., Tufts University, Brandeis University, and retired as a full professor at Stanford University in 1994. Levertov has been a scholar at the Radcliffe Institute for Independent Study, has received the Lenore Marshall Prize for poetry, a Guggenheim Fellowship, the Elmer Holmes Bobst Award, and is a member of the American Institute of Arts & Letters.

Levertov was influenced by the poetry and poetic theory of William Carlos Williams. And though she was earlier considered an "aesthetic compatriot" of some of the poets of the Black Mountain School, she does not consider herself today part of any particular "school" of poetry. She brings her own unmistakably distinctive voice to poems concerned with several dimensions of the human experience: love, motherhood, nature, war, the nuclear arms race, mysticism, poetry, and the role of the poet. Levertov cites a William Carlos Williams verse in her essay "Poetry, Prophecy, Survival": "It is difficult/to get news from poems/yet men die miserably every day/for lack/of what is found there." She tells us in this essay that people turn to poems for "some kind of illumination, for revelations that help them to survive, to survive in spirit not only in body." She believes that these revelations are usually not of the unheard of but of what lies around us, unseen and forgotten—like "Flowers of Sophia" in her most recent volume of poetry. And she believes that poems and/or dreams, as she poignantly muses in "Dream Instruction," can "illuminate what we feel but don't *know* we feel until it is articulated."

"Poetry, Prophecy, Survival" reiterates a theme that Levertov articulates on several occasions throughout her career: the poet or artist's call "to summon the divine." She speaks clearly of this "vocation" in "The Origins of a Poem" and "The Sense of Pilgrimage" essays in *The Poet in the World* (1973); in "On the Edge of Darkness: What Is Political Poetry?" in

Light up the Cave (1981); and in "A Poet's View" (1984). Levertov's awareness of the truly awesome nature of the poet's task is evident in "A Poet's View":

To believe, as an artist, in inspiration or the intuitive, to know that without Imagination...no amount of acquired craft or scholarship or of brilliant reasoning will suffice, is to live with a door of one's life open to the transcendent, the numinous. Not every artist, clearly, acknowledges that fact—yet all, in the creative act, experience mystery. The concept of 'inspiration' presupposes a power that enters the individual and is not a personal attribute; and it is linked to a view of the artist's life as one of obedience to a vocation.[1]

Levertov's poems, most notably those since *The Jacob's Ladder* in 1958, reflect her serious commitment to this concept. In "Dream Instruction," one observes the poet's sensitive awareness of the rich depth of her inheritance and the important influence of the "cultural ambiance" of her family—those other "travellers/gone into dark." Her father Paul Levertoff's Hasidic ancestry, his being steeped in Jewish, and, after his conversion, Christian scholarship and mysticism, and her mother Beatrice Levertoff's Welsh intensity and lyric feeling for nature are significant parts of the poet's finest works.

An interest in humanitarian politics came early into Levertov's life. Her father was active in protesting Mussolini's invasion of Abyssinia; both he and her sister Olga protested Britain's lack of support for Spain. Long before these events, her mother canvassed on behalf of the League of Nations Union; and all three worked on behalf of German and Austrian refugees from 1933 onward. (One is not surprised, then, to find among her more recent poems wrenching reflections on the Gulf War.) This strong familial blend of the mystical with a firm commitment to social issues undoubtedly contributed to Levertov's being placed in the American visionary tradition. Rather than deliberately attempting to integrate social and political themes with lyricism, her approach is to fuse them, believing as she does that they are not antithetical. And as is evident in her poetry of her last years, though Levertov's range of subject matter remains by no means exclusively "engaged," she believes, as she tells us in "Making Peace," that "each act of living/[is] one of its words, each word/a vibration of light—facets/of the forming crystal." So she continues with other such poets as Pablo Neruda and Muriel Rukeyser to confront social and political issues of our time. Levertov was named sixty-first winner of the Academy of American Poets Fellowship in 1995.

Joan F. Hallisey
Regis College

PRIMARY WORKS

Poetry: *The Double Image,* 1946; *Here and Now,* 1957; *The Jacob's Ladder,* 1958; *Overland to the Islands,* 1958; *With Eyes at the Back of Our Heads,* 1959; *O Taste and See,* 1964; *The Sorrow Dance,* 1966; *Relearning the Alphabet,* 1970; *To Stay Alive,* 1971; *Footprints,* 1975; *The Freeing of the Dust,* 1975; *Life in the Forest,* 1978; *Collected Earlier Poems 1940–1960,* 1979; *Candles in Babylon,* 1982; *Poems 1960–1967,* 1983; *Oblique Prayers,* 1984; *Breathing the Water,* 1987; *Poems 1968–1972,* 1987; *A Door in the Hive,* 1989; *Evening Train,* 1992. Prose: *The Poet in the World,* 1973; *Light up the Cave,* 1982; *New and Selected Essays,* 1992; *Sands in the Well,* 1996. Translations: *Guillevic/Selected Poems,* 1969.

[1]See *New and Selected Essays,* 1992, p. 241.

Illustrious Ancestors

The Rav[1]
of Northern White Russia declined,
in his youth, to learn the
language of birds, because
the extraneous did not interest him; nevertheless
when he grew old it was found
he understood them anyway, having
listened well, and as it is said, "prayed
with the bench and the floor." He used
what was at hand—as did
Angel Jones of Mold,[2] whose meditations
were sewn into coats and britches.

Well, I would like to make,
thinking some line still taut between me and them,
poems direct as what the birds said,
hard as a floor, sound as a bench,
mysterious as the silence when the tailor
would pause with his needle in the air.

1958

A Solitude

A blind man. I can stare at him
ashamed, shameless. Or does he know it?
No, he is in a great solitude.

O, strange joy,
to gaze my fill at a stranger's face.
No, my thirst is greater than before.

In his world he is speaking
almost aloud. His lips move.
Anxiety plays about them. And now joy

of some sort trembles into a smile.
A breeze I can't feel
crosses that face as if it crossed water.

[1]Rabbi. [2]Welsh town.

The train moves uptown, pulls in and
pulls out of the local stops. Within its loud
jarring movement a quiet,

the quiet of people not speaking,
some of them eyeing the blind man,
only a moment though, not thirsty like me,

and within that quiet his
different quiet, not quiet at all, a tumult
of images, but what are his images,

he is blind? He doesn't care
that he looks strange, showing
his thoughts on his face like designs of light

flickering on water, for he doesn't know
what look is.
I see he has never seen.

And now he rises, he stands at the door ready,
knowing his station is next. Was he counting?
No, that was not his need.

When he gets out I get out.
"Can I help you towards the exit?"
"Oh, alright." An indifference.

But instantly, even as he speaks,
even as I hear indifference, his hand
goes out, waiting for me to take it,

and now we hold hands like children.
His hand is warm and not sweaty,
the grip firm, it feels good.

And when we have passed through the turnstile,
he going first, his hand at once
waits for mine again.

"Here are the steps. And here we turn
to the right. More stairs now." We go
up into sunlight. He feels that,

the soft air. "A nice day,
isn't it?" says the blind man. Solitude
walks with me, walks

beside me, he is not with me, he continues

his thoughts alone. But his hand and mine
know one another,

it's as if my hand were gone forth
on its own journey. I see him
across the street, the blind man,

and now he says he can find his way. He knows
where he is going, it is nowhere, it is filled
with presences. He says, **I am.**

1961

Making Peace

A voice from the dark called out,
'The poets must give us
imagination of peace, to oust the intense, familiar
imagination of disaster. Peace, not only
the absence of war.'
But peace, like a poem,
is not there ahead of itself,
can't be imagined before it is made,
can't be known except
in the words of its making,
grammar of justice,
syntax of mutual aid.
A feeling towards it,
dimly sensing a rhythm, is all we have
until we begin to utter its metaphors,
learning them as we speak.
A line of peace might appear
if we restructured the sentence our lives are making,
revoked its reaffirmation of profit and power,
questioned our needs, allowed
long pauses . . .
A cadence of peace might balance its weight
on that different fulcrum; peace, a presence,
an energy field more intense than war,
might pulse then,
stanza by stanza into the world,
each act of living
one of its words, each word
a vibration of light—facets
of the forming crystal.

1987

A Woman Alone

When she cannot be sure
which of two lovers it was with whom she felt
this or that moment of pleasure, of something fiery
streaking from head to heels, the way the white
flame of a cascade streaks a mountainside
seen from a car across a valley, the car
changing gear, skirting a precipice,
climbing . . .
When she can sit or walk for hours after a movie
talking earnestly and with bursts of laughter
with friends, without worrying
that it's late, dinner at midnight, her time
spent without counting the change . . .
When half her bed is covered with books
and no one is kept awake by the reading light
and she disconnects the phone, to sleep till noon . . .
Then
selfpity dries up, a joy
untainted by guilt lifts her.
She has fears, but not about loneliness;
fears about how to deal with the aging
of her body—how to deal
with photographs and the mirror. She feels
so much younger and more beautiful
than she looks. At her happiest
—or even in the midst of
some less than joyful hour, sweating
patiently through a heatwave in the city
or hearing the sparrows at daybreak, dully gray,
toneless, the sound of fatigue—
a kind of sober euphoria makes her believe
in her future as an old woman, a wanderer,
seamed and brown,
little luxuries of the middle of life all gone,
watching cities and rivers, people and mountains,
without being watched; not grim nor sad,
an old winedrinking woman, who knows
the old roads, grass-grown, and laughs to herself . . .
She knows it can't be:
that's Mrs. Doasyouwouldbedoneby from *The Water-Babies,*
no one can walk the world any more,

a world of fumes and decibels.
But she thinks maybe
she could get to be tough and wise, some way,
anyway. Now at least
she is past the time of mourning,
now she can say without shame or deceit,
O blessed Solitude.

1978

The May Mornings

May mornings wear
light cashmere shawls of quietness,
brush back waterfalls of
burnished silk from
clear and round brows.
When we see them approaching
over lawns, trailing
dewdark shadows and footprints,
we remember, ah,
yes, the May mornings,
how could we have forgotten,
what solace it would have been
to think of them,
what solace
it would be in the bitter violence
of fire then ice again we
apprehend—but
it seems the May mornings
are a presence known
only as they pass
lightstepped, seriously smiling, bearing
each a leaflined basket
of wakening flowers.

1982

Frank O'Hara 1926–1966

Joe LeSueur, a playwright and Frank O'Hara's roommate for nearly a decade, wrote in a memoir, "as far as I could tell, writing poetry was something Frank did in his spare time. . . . For that reason, I didn't realize right away that if you took poetry as much for granted as you did breathing it might mean you felt that it was essential to your life."[1] For many readers, the enormous appeal of Frank O'Hara's work—and he is among the most appealing of all American poets—is that he combines a seemingly effortlessness of expression with a life-sustaining intensity of purpose. The poems were often dashed off almost always on the typewriter—*The Lunch Poems,* for example, got their title because they were written on O'Hara's lunch hour—but they came out of the wholeness of O'Hara's experience and emotions. As funny as they often are, they always indicate a shrewd awareness of people, places, and history. And although O'Hara is one of the most joyous poets America has produced, a darkness always hovers below the surface, accentuating the brightness above.

Frank O'Hara was born in Baltimore, Maryland, and grew up in Worcester, Massachusetts. He attended Harvard University, where he studied music, and the graduate school of the University of Michigan. But he is most associated with New York City and the Long Island coast, especially Fire Island, where he died in a freak accident—run over by a jeep on an island where cars are banned. With John Ashbery (a friend from his undergraduate days), James Schuyler, and Kenneth Koch, O'Hara formed the central core of what has been dubbed the New York School. Although what primarily bound these poets was personal friendship, they do have certain poetic similarities that unite them: (1) They all emphasize the immediacy of the individual poetic voice rather than the impersonal presentation of images. (2) They playfully combine elements from high and low culture, incorporating into their works the most mundane aspects of urban life and such features of popular culture as comic strip characters, Hollywood movies, and popular songs. (3) They fearlessly court the comic, the slapstick, the vulgar, and the sentimental. (4) They experiment with surrealism, although the dream-like often dissolves into the quite ordinary.

O'Hara, Ashbery, and Schuyler are also united by their involvement in the visual arts. All three worked at various times for *Art News,* writing articles and reviews. O'Hara worked first as a ticket taker, then as a curator for the Museum of Modern Art, organizing major exhibitions by the end of his life. O'Hara was a personal friend of many important artists including Larry Rivers, Willem de Kooning, Grace Hartigan, and Fairfield Porter. The directness and energy which many of these artists wished to bring to painting, O'Hara sought to register in his own work.

One of the typical modes in which O'Hara worked was what he called the "I do this I do that" poem. Many lesser poets have attempted to imitate O'Hara's seemingly documentary style, but few have caught his eye for detail, his ear for the music of American English, or his sensitivity to the wide fluctuation of mood. O'Hara was also among the earliest poets to write unself-consciously of his homosexual relationships. His love poems—and he wrote many of them—have a frankness, a joy, and a pathos that would seem more revolutionary if they did not appear so natural and easy.

David Bergman
Towson University

[1]Joe LeSueur, "Four Apartments" in *Homage to Frank O'Hara,* eds. Bill Berkson and Joe LeSueur. New York: Big Sky, 1978, p. 47.

PRIMARY WORKS

A City Winter and Other Poems, 1952; *Meditations in an Emergency,* 1957; *Jackson Pollack,* 1959; *Lunch Poems,* 1964; *Collected Poems,* 1971; *Art Chronicles 1954–1966,* 1975; *Early Writing,* 1977; *Poems Retrieved 1951-1966,* 1977; *Selected Plays,* 1978; *Standing Still and Walking in New York,* 1983.

My Heart

I'm not going to cry all the time
nor shall I laugh all the time,
I don't prefer one "strain" to another.
I'd have the immediacy of a bad movie,
not just a sleeper,[1] but also the big,
overproduced first-run kind. I want to be
at least as alive as the vulgar. And if
some aficionado[2] of my mess says "That's
not like Frank!", all to the good! I
don't wear brown and grey suits all the time,
do I? No. I wear workshirts to the opera,
often. I want my feet to be bare,
I want my face to be shaven, and my heart—
you can't plan on the heart, but
the better part of it, my poetry, is open.

1970

The Day Lady Died[1]

It is 12:20 in New York a Friday
three days after Bastille day,[2] yes
it is 1959 and I go get a shoeshine

[1]A "sleeper" is film jargon for an unexpectedly successful movie, usually a low-budget film that proves to be of artistic and commercial value.

[2]An aficionado is a person devoted to someone, or his or her works; a fan.

[1]The poem is a homage to the great blues singer Billie Holiday (1915–1959), whose nickname, "Lady Day," is alluded to in the title.

[2]Bastille Day, July 14, is French Independence Day.

because I will get off the 4:19 in Easthampton,[3]
at 7:15 and then go straight to dinner
and I don't know the people who will feed me

I walk up the muggy street beginning to sun
and have a hamburger and a malted and buy
an ugly NEW WORLD WRITING to see what the poets
in Ghana are doing these days

I go on to the bank
and Miss Stillwagon (first name Linda I once heard)
doesn't even look up my balance for once in her life
and in the GOLDEN GRIFFIN I get a little Verlaine,[4]
for Patsy with drawings by Bonnard,[5] although I do
think of Hesiod, trans. Richmond Lattimore,[6] or
Brendan Behan's new play,[7] or *Le Balcon* or *Les Nègres*
of Genet,[8] but I don't, I stick with Verlaine
after practically going to sleep with quandariness

and for Mike I just stroll into the PARK LANE
Liquor Store and ask for a bottle of Strega and
then I go back where I came from to 6th Avenue
and the tobacconist in the Ziegfeld Theatre and
casually ask for a carton of Gauloises and a carton
of Picayunes[9] and a NEW YORK POST with her face on it

and I am sweating a lot by now and thinking of
leaning on the john door in the 5 SPOT
while she whispered a song along the keyboard
to Mal Waldron[10] and everyone and I stopped breathing

1964

[3]Easthampton is a town on the south shore of Long Island, and a stop on the Long Island Railroad. O'Hara is going to visit Patsy Southgate and her husband at the time, Mike Goldberg (they are referred to in lines 15 and 20, and Mike Goldberg is the painter referred to in "Why I Am Not a Painter"). They lived in Southampton, a nearby community, where "Getting Up Ahead of Someone (Sun)" is set. The Hamptons have now become a rather exclusive area, but in the 1950s, they were a group of farming communities and an inexpensive place for artists to live and work.

[4]Paul Verlaine (1844–1896) was one of the great French poets of the nineteenth century.

[5]Pierre Bonnard (1867–1947) was one of the major French post-Impressionist painters. He illustrated Verlaine's *Parallelement* in 1902.

[6]Hesiod was an ancient Greek poet. Richmond Lattimore, a prolific Greek translator, published his *Hesiod* in 1959.

[7]Brendan Behan (1923–1964) was a controversial Irish playwright, author of *The Quare Fellow* (1956) and *The Hostage* (1958).

[8]Jean Genêt (1910–1986) was one of France's greatest twentieth-century writers. His plays *Le Balcon* (The Balcony) and *Les Negres* (The Blacks), produced in the 1950s, created enormous controversy because of their sexual, racial, and political subject matter.

[9]Gauloises and Picayunes are brands of French cigarettes. The emphasis on French culture stands in contrast to Billie Holiday, the subject of the poem. The effect is to suggest how far away O'Hara's thoughts are from Holiday until he sees her face in the newspaper.

[10]Mal Waldron (b. 1925) was Billie Holiday's pianist.

Why I Am Not a Painter

I am not a painter, I am a poet.
Why? I think I would rather be
a painter, but I am not. Well,

for instance, Mike Goldberg[1]
is starting a painting. I drop in.
"Sit down and have a drink" he
says. I drink; we drink. I look
up. "You have SARDINES in it."
"Yes, it needed something there."
"Oh." I go and the days go by
and I drop in again. The painting
is going on, and I go, and the days
go by. I drop in. The painting is
finished. "Where's SARDINES?"
All that's left is just
letters, "It was too much," Mike says.

But me? One day I am thinking of
a color: orange. I write a line
about orange. Pretty soon it is a
whole page of words, not lines.
Then another page. There should be
so much more, not of orange, of
words, of how terrible orange is
and life. Days go by. It is even in
prose, I am a real poet. My poem
is finished and I haven't mentioned
orange yet. It's twelve poems, I call
it ORANGES. And one day in a gallery
I see Mike's painting, called SARDINES.

1971

[1]Mike Goldberg (b. 1924) was a painter who worked with O'Hara on several projects.

Poem

"À la recherche de Gertrude Stein"[1]

When I am feeling depressed and anxious sullen[2]
all you have to do is take your clothes off
and all is wiped away revealing life's tenderness
that we are flesh and breathe and are near us
as you are really as you are I become as I
really am alive and knowing vaguely what is
and what is important to me above the intrusions
of incident and accidental relationships
which have nothing to do with my life
when I am in your presence I feel life is strong
and will defeat all its enemies and all of mine
and all of yours and yours in you and mine in me
sick logic and feeble reasoning are cured
by the perfect symmetry of your arms and legs
spread out making an eternal circle together
creating a golden pillar beside the Atlantic
the faint line of hair dividing your torso
gives my mind rest and emotions their release
into the infinite air where since once we are
together we always will be in this life come what may

1965

James Wright 1927–1980

"Lost in the beautiful white ruins/Of America," James Wright finds a body of lyric poetry that both celebrates and grieves. Wright's America is the Midwest, the small towns and farms that surround his own Martins Ferry, Ohio, where he was born in 1927 and grew up. Though his poetry seems far removed from the institutionally academic, he did, in fact, graduate from Kenyon College and took an M.A. and Ph.D. in English from the University of Washington in Seattle. He taught at the University of Minnesota, Macalester College in St. Paul, Minnesota, Hunter College in New York, and the University of Delaware.

His first collection, *The Green Wall*

[1]*"A la recherche de Gertrude Stein"* is French for "in remembrance of Gertrude Stein" (1874–1946), the American expatriate writer, whose experimental works and involvement with painters mirrors O'Hara's own career. The phrase alludes to Marcel Proust's multivolume novel *A la recherche du temps perdu,* often translated as *Remembrance of Things Past.*

[2]The opening line recalls the opening of Shakespeare's sonnet "When in disgrace with fortune and men's eyes," which, according to Patsy Southgate, was O'Hara's favorite Shakespeare sonnet.

(1957), was selected by W. H. Auden for the Yale Series of Younger Poets. "Saint Judas," the title poem of Wright's second volume (1959), is typical of his earliest work: the celebration of a marginal figure—in this case the betrayer of Christ. There is another trait that is typical, the use of a fixed form (Italian sonnet), meter (iambic pentameter), and rhyme. Of his first book, Wright said that he "tried very hard to write in the mode of Robert Frost and Edwin Arlington Robinson"; there was also a recognizable influence of two of his former teachers: John Crowe Ransom (Kenyon) and Theodore Roethke (University of Washington).

Wright's poetry was about to undergo a major change. While studying as a Fulbright Scholar in Austria in the early 1950s, Wright discovered the poetry of German poets Theodor Storm and Georg Trakl. Trakl's poetry of leaping images made a powerful impact: "It was as though the sea had entered the class at the last minute. For this poem was not like any poem I had ever recognized: the poet, at a sign from the evening bells, followed the wings of birds that became a train of pious pilgrims who were continually vanishing into the clear autumn of distances; beyond the distances there were black horses leaping in red maple trees, in a world where seeing and hearing are not two actions, but one." How he might incorporate such leaping images of a semi-surreal mode into his own verse awaited the influence of Robert Bly. One of Trakl's poems appeared in translation in the first number (1958) of Bly's magazine *The Fifties,* where Wright happened to see it. The discovery prompted him to send a letter to Bly: "It was sixteen pages long and single-spaced, and all he said in reply was 'Come on out to the farm [in Madison, Minnesota].'" That visit and others to follow led to Wright's immersion in what has come to be called poetry of the "deep image" or "emotive imagination." Wright abruptly abandoned the regular meters and rhymes of his first two volumes for a free verse of colloquial American speech and the juxtaposition of a succession of leaping images that evolved toward an epiphanic moment of insight and self-knowledge. Beginning with *The Branch Will Not Break* (1963) and continuing in *Shall We Gather at the River* (1968), Wright's poems began to share characteristics with other deep-image poets like Bly, Louis Simpson, William Stafford, Robert Creeley, and Gary Snyder.

Influenced by Bly in another way, Wright's poems become more overtly political. In protesting America's involvement in the Vietnam War, he went on to write poems like "Confession to J. Edgar Hoover," where the speaker offers a scathingly ironic prayer to the director of the FBI who is directly linked with the war.

Wright's own life was a struggle with mental illness and alcoholism, a struggle that helped to bond his poetry with figures on the margins of American society. Following his second marriage, to Edith Anne Runk ("Annie" in his poems) in 1967, he found a new stability and happiness in his life and work. Their time together in Italy became the setting of scores of poems in his last collections. His *Collected Poems* (1972) earned the Pulitzer Prize, among other awards. Wright's mark on American letters is also distinguished by his translation of poets like Trakl, Cesar Vallejo, Pablo Neruda, Juan Ramon Jimenez, and others. His prose poems are among his best work, especially in *To a Blossoming Pear Tree* (1977). Wright died from cancer in 1980. Two years later, his volume *This Journey* appeared, many poems anticipating his own mortality: "Even if it were true,/Even if I were dead and buried in Verona,/I believe I would come out and wash my face/In the chill spring."

George S. Lensing
University of North Carolina at Chapel Hill

PRIMARY WORKS

Collected Prose, 1983; *Above the River: The Complete Poems,* 1990.

Saint Judas

When I went out to kill myself, I caught
A pack of hoodlums beating up a man.
Running to spare his suffering, I forgot
My name, my number, how my day began,
How soldiers milled around the garden stone
And sang amusing songs; how all that day
Their javelins measured crowds; how I alone
Bargained the proper coins, and slipped away.

Banished from heaven, I found this victim beaten,
Stripped, kneed, and left to cry. Dropping my rope
Aside, I ran, ignored the uniforms:
Then I remembered bread my flesh had eaten,
The kiss that ate my flesh. Flayed without hope,
I held the man for nothing in my arms.

1959

Autumn Begins in Martins Ferry, Ohio

In the Shreve High football stadium,
I think of Polacks nursing long beers in Tiltonsville,
And gray faces of Negroes in the blast furnace at Benwood,
And the ruptured night watchman of Wheeling Steel,
Dreaming of heroes.

All the proud fathers are ashamed to go home.
Their women cluck like starved pullets,
Dying for love.

Therefore,
Their sons grow suicidally beautiful
At the beginning of October,
And gallop terribly against each other's bodies.

1963

Lying in a Hammock at William Duffy's Farm in Pine Island, Minnesota

Over my head, I see the bronze butterfly,
Asleep on the black trunk,
Blowing like a leaf in green shadow.
Down the ravine behind the empty house,
The cowbells follow one another
Into the distances of the afternoon.
To my right,
In a field of sunlight between two pines,
The droppings of last year's horses
Blaze up into golden stones.
I lean back, as the evening darkens and comes on.
A chicken hawk floats over, looking for home.
I have wasted my life.

1963

A Centenary Ode: Inscribed to Little Crow, Leader of the Sioux Rebellion in Minnesota, 1862

I had nothing to do with it. I was not here.
I was not born.
In 1862, when your hotheads
Raised hell from here to South Dakota,
My own fathers scattered into West Virginia
And southern Ohio.
My family fought the Confederacy
And fought the Union.
None of them got killed.
But for all that, it was not my fathers
Who murdered you.
Not much.

I don't know
Where the fathers of Minneapolis finalized
Your flayed carcass.
Little Crow, true father
Of my dark America,

When I close my eyes I lose you among
Old lonelinesses.
My family were a lot of singing drunks and good carpenters.
We had brothers who loved one another no matter what they did.
And they did plenty.

I think they would have run like hell from your Sioux.
And when you caught them you all would have run like hell
From the Confederacy and from the Union
Into the hills and hunted for a few things,
Some bull-cat under the stones, a gar maybe,
If you were hungry, and if you were happy,
Sunfish and corn.

If only I knew where to mourn you,
I would surely mourn.

But I don't know.

I did not come here only to grieve
For my people's defeat.
The troops of the Union, who won,
Still outnumber us.
Old Paddy Beck, my great-uncle, is dead
At the old soldiers' home near Tiffen, Ohio.
He got away with every last stitch
Of his uniform, save only
The dress trousers.

Oh all around us,
The hobo jungles of America grow wild again.
The pick handles bloom like your skinned spine.
I don't even know where
My own grave is.

1971

Sylvia Plath 1932–1963

Sylvia Plath was the precocious child of well-educated Boston parents, Otto and Aurelia Schoeber Plath. Otto, who taught German and zoology at Boston University, died when Sylvia was eight of complications following the amputation of his leg. An authority on bees, he had been ill the previous four years from untreated diabetes mellitus. Finances were slim so Sylvia's mother returned to teaching, and to help care for the children, her maternal grandparents moved into the Plath home, where they remained until their deaths. In order to take a position at Boston University herself, Aurelia moved the family to Wellesley.

Plath's childhood and adolescence were a series of high academic achievements. She published poetry, fiction, and journalism in a number of places even before attending Smith College on a partial scholarship. An English major at Smith, she continued her consistent prize winning, but she was also very much a woman of the 1950s, plagued with thoughts that she had to marry and have children, or else she would never be a "complete" female. Some of her conflicts over direction (career vs. marriage, sexual experience vs. chastity) combined with a strain of depression in her paternal line to cause a breakdown in the summer of 1953, shortly after she had served as a *Mademoiselle* College Board editor. The outpatient electroconvulsive shock treatments she received then probably led to her subsequent suicide attempt in August of 1953, and she spent the next four months under psychiatric care before returning to Smith. In June, 1955, she graduated *summa cum laude* and got an M.A. on a Fulbright Fellowship at Cambridge, England.

On June 16, 1956, she married Ted Hughes, eventually to become Poet Laureate of England. In 1957 they returned to the States where Plath taught freshman English at Smith. She and Hughes then lived for another year in Boston, establishing themselves as professional writers; late in 1959 they returned to England. In the next three years, Plath bore two children, published *The Colossus and Other Poems,* established a home in Devon, separated from Hughes, and was living with her children in a flat in Yeats's house in London when she committed suicide, just a few weeks after *The Bell Jar* had been published. In 1965 *Ariel,* the collection of some of her last poems, appeared.

Plath's poems show a steadily developing sense of her own voice, speaking of subjects that—before the 1960s—were seldom considered appropriate for poetry: anger, macabre humor, defiance, contrasted with a rarer joy and a poignant understanding of women's various roles. "Three Women," which is set in a maternity ward, *The Bell Jar,* and many of her late 1962 poems were unlike any of the expert literature she had so carefully imitated—until the last years of her life. Her breaking out of the conventional patterns set an example that shaped a great deal of poetry for the next forty years—reliance on metaphor, quick shifts from image to image, a frantic yet always controlled pace that mirrored the tensions of her single-parent life during 1962. In contrast to late poems like "Daddy" and "Lady Lazarus," Plath's final poems were icily mystic, solemn, and resigned. The full range of her work is evident in the 1981 *Collected Poems,* which won the Pulitzer Prize for Poetry in 1982.

Linda Wagner-Martin
University of North Carolina at Chapel Hill

PRIMARY WORKS

The Colossus, 1960; *The Bell Jar,* 1963 (published under "Victoria Lucas"); *Ariel,* 1965; *The Collected Poems,* 1981; *The Journals of Sylvia Plath,* 1982.

For a Fatherless Son

You will be aware of an absence, presently,
Growing beside you, like a tree,
A death tree, color gone, an Australian gum tree—
Balding, gelded by lightning—an illusion,
And a sky like a pig's backside, an utter lack of attention.

But right now you are dumb.
And I love your stupidity,
The blind mirror of it. I look in
And find no face but my own, and you think that's funny.
It is good for me

To have you grab my nose, a ladder rung.
One day you may touch what's wrong—
The small skulls, the smashed blue hills, the godawful hush.
Till then your smiles are found money.

1962

Daddy

You do not do, you do not do
Any more, black shoe
In which I have lived like a foot
For thirty years, poor and white,
Barely daring to breathe or Achoo.

Daddy, I have had to kill you.
You died before I had time—
Marble-heavy, a bag full of God,
Ghastly statue with one gray toe
Big as a Frisco seal[1]

And a head in the freakish Atlantic
Where it pours bean green over blue
In the waters off beautiful Nauset.[2]
I used to pray to recover you.
Ach, du.[3]

[1]San Francisco Seal Rocks.
[2]Cape Cod harbor.
[3]German: Ah, you.

In the German tongue, in the Polish town
Scraped flat by the roller
Of wars, wars, wars.
But the name of the town is common.
My Polack friend

Says there are a dozen or two.
So I never could tell where you
Put your foot, your root,
I never could talk to you.
The tongue stuck in my jaw.

It stuck in a barb wire snare.
Ich, ich, ich, ich,[4]
I could hardly speak.
I thought every German was you.
And the language obscene

An engine, an engine
Chuffing me off like a Jew.
A Jew to Dachau, Auschwitz, Belsen.[5]
I began to talk like a Jew.
I think I may well be a Jew.

The snows of the Tyrol,[6] the clear beer of Vienna
Are not very pure or true.
With my gipsy ancestress and my weird luck
And my Taroc[7] pack and my Taroc pack
I may be a bit of a Jew.

I have always been scared of *you,*
With your Luftwaffe,[8] your gobbledygoo.
And your neat mustache
And your Aryan[9] eye, bright blue.
Panzer-man, panzer-man,[10] O You——

Not God but a swastika
So black no sky could squeak through.
Every woman adores a Fascist,
The boot in the face, the brute
Brute heart of a brute like you.

[4]German: I.
[5]Nazi concentration camps of Holocaust.
[6]Austrian alps.
[7]Tarot fortune-telling cards.
[8]Nazi air force.
[9]Caucasian gentile, the Nazi ideal race.
[10]Panzer is German for armor: Nazi World War II armored divisions.

You stand at the blackboard, daddy,
In the picture I have of you,
A cleft in your chin instead of your foot
But no less a devil for that, no not
Any less the black man who

Bit my pretty red heart in two.
I was ten when they buried you.
At twenty I tried to die
And get back, back, back to you.
I thought even the bones would do.

But they pulled me out of the sack,
And they stuck me together with glue.
And then I knew what to do.
I made a model of you,
A man in black with a Meinkampf[11] look

And a love of the rack and the screw.
And I said I do, I do.
So daddy, I'm finally through.
The black telephone's off at the root,
The voices just can't worm through.

If I've killed one man, I've killed two—
The vampire who said he was you
And drank my blood for a year,
Seven years, if you want to know.
Daddy, you can lie back now.

There's a stake in your fat black heart
And the villagers never liked you.
They are dancing and stamping on you.
They always *knew* it was you.
Daddy, daddy, you bastard, I'm through.

1965

[11]Hitler's manifesto, "My Battle."

Lady Lazarus

I have done it again.
One year in every ten
I manage it——

A sort of walking miracle, my skin
Bright as a Nazi lampshade,
My right foot

A paperweight,
My face a featureless, fine
Jew linen.

Peel off the napkin
O my enemy.
Do I terrify?——

The nose, the eye pits, the full set of teeth?
The sour breath
Will vanish in a day.

Soon, soon the flesh
The grave cave ate will be
At home on me

And I a smiling woman.
I am only thirty.
And like the cat I have nine times to die.

This is Number Three.
What a trash
To annihilate each decade.

What a million filaments.
The peanut-crunching crowd
Shoves in to see

Them unwrap me hand and foot——
The big strip tease.
Gentlemen, ladies

These are my hands,
My knees.
I may be skin and bone,

Nevertheless, I am the same, identical woman.
The first time it happened I was ten.
It was an accident.

The second time I meant
To last it out and not come back at all.
I rocked shut

As a seashell.
They had to call and call
And pick the worms off me like sticky pearls.

Dying
Is an art, like everything else.
I do it exceptionally well.

I do it so it feels like hell.
I do it so it feels real.
I guess you could say I've a call.

It's easy enough to do it in a cell.
It's easy enough to do it and stay put.
It's the theatrical

Comeback in broad day
To the same place, the same face, the same brute
Amused shout:

"A miracle!"
That knocks me out.
There is a charge

For the eyeing of my scars, there is a charge
For the hearing of my heart——
It really goes.

And there is a charge, a very large charge
For a word or a touch
Or a bit of blood

Or a piece of my hair or my clothes.
So, so, Herr Doktor.
So, Herr Enemy.

I am your opus,
I am your valuable,
The pure gold baby

That melts to a shriek.
I turn and burn.
Do not think I underestimate your great concern.

Ash, ash—
You poke and stir.
Flesh, bone, there is nothing there——

A cake of soap,
A wedding ring,
A gold filling.

Herr God, Herr Lucifer,
Beware
Beware.

Out of the ash
I rise with my red hair
And I eat men like air.

1965

Stings

Bare-handed, I hand the combs.
The man in white smiles, bare-handed,
Our cheesecloth gauntlets neat and sweet,
The throats of our wrists brave lilies.
He and I

Have a thousand clean cells between us,
Eight combs of yellow cups,
And the hive itself a teacup,
White with pink flowers on it,
With excessive love I enameled it

Thinking "Sweetness, sweetness."
Brood cells gray as the fossils of shells
Terrify me, they seem so old.
What am I buying, wormy mahogany?
Is there any queen at all in it?

If there is, she is old,
Her wings torn shawls, her long body

Rubbed of its plush——
Poor and bare and unqueenly and even shameful.
I stand in a column

Of winged, unmiraculous women,
Honey-drudgers.
I am no drudge
Though for years I have eaten dust
And dried plates with my dense hair.

And seen my strangeness evaporate,
Blue dew from dangerous skin.
Will they hate me,
These women who only scurry,
Whose news is the open cherry, the open clover?

It is almost over.
I am in control.
Here is my honey-machine,
It will work without thinking,
Opening, in spring, like an industrious virgin

To scour the creaming crests
As the moon, for its ivory powders, scours the sea.
A third person is watching.
He has nothing to do with the bee-seller or with me.
Now he is gone

In eight great bounds, a great scapegoat.
Here is his slipper, here is another,
And here the square of white linen
He wore instead of a hat.
He was sweet,

The sweat of his efforts a rain
Tugging the world to fruit.
The bees found him out,
Molding onto his lips like lies,
Complicating his features.

They thought death was worth it, but I
Have a self to recover, a queen.
Is she dead, is she sleeping?
Where has she been,
With her lion-red body, her wings of glass?

Now she is flying
More terrible than she ever was, red
Scar in the sky, red comet
Over the engine that killed her——
The mausoleum, the wax house.

1965

Fever 103°

Pure? What does it mean?
The tongues of hell
Are dull, dull as the triple

Tongues of dull, fat Cerberus
Who wheezes at the gate. Incapable
Of licking clean

The aguey tendon, the sin, the sin.
The tinder cries.
The indelible smell

Of a snuffed candle!
Love, love, the low smokes roll
From me like Isadora's scarves, I'm in a fright

One scarf will catch and anchor in the wheel.
Such yellow sullen smokes
Make their own element. They will not rise,

But trundle round the globe
Choking the aged and the meek,
The weak

Hothouse baby in its crib,
The ghastly orchid
Hanging its hanging garden in the air,

Devilish leopard!
Radiation turned it white
And killed it in an hour.

Greasing the bodies of adulterers
Like Hiroshima ash and eating in.
The sin. The sin.

Darling, all night
I have been flickering, off, on, off, on.
The sheets grow heavy as a lecher's kiss.

Three days. Three nights.
Lemon water, chicken
Water, water make me retch.

I am too pure for you or anyone.
Your body
Hurts me as the world hurts God. I am a lantern——

My head a moon
Of Japanese paper, my gold beaten skin
Infinitely delicate and infinitely expensive.

Does not my heat astound you. And my light.
All by myself I am a huge camellia
Glowing and coming and going, flush on flush.

I think I am going up,
I think I may rise——
The beads of hot metal fly, and I, love, I

Am a pure acetylene
Virgin
Attended by roses,

By kisses, by cherubim,
By whatever these pink things mean.
Not you, nor him

Not him, nor him
(My selves dissolving, old whore petticoats)——
To Paradise.

1965

Anne Sexton 1928–1974

Anne Gray Harvey Sexton was born in Newton, Massachusetts, the third daughter of Mary Gray and Ralph Harvey. Sexton's great-uncle had been governor of Maine, and her grandfather, editor of Maine's *Lewiston Evening Journal,* was a respected journalist. The family's primary emphasis by the time of Sexton's birth was mercantile; Sexton's father and, later, her husband were both wool merchants. The Harveys lived in Boston suburbs during the year and on Squirrel Island, Maine, during summers. Her childhood was both privileged and difficult. Sexton felt she could not fulfill her family's expectations, which were both high and vague. She was implicitly expected to marry at the right time and to behave decorously—neither of which she did—but not necessarily to distinguish herself professionally or intellectually.

Anne Harvey was a spirited and demanding child, a romantic and popular adolescent, an undistinguished student (she attended a finishing school for women in Boston). In 1948 she eloped with Alfred Sexton, to whom she remained married until 1973. Shortly after the births of each of her two daughters (in 1953 and 1955), Sexton was hospitalized for the recurring emotional disturbances that continued to plague her for the rest of her life. After a suicide attempt in 1956, on the advice of her doctor, she began writing poetry. In 1957, Sexton enrolled in John Holmes's poetry workshop, Boston, where she met Maxine Kumin, her closest personal friend. In 1958–59 she was a student in Robert Lowell's writing seminar at Boston University, where she met Sylvia Plath.

Her first collection, *To Bedlam and Part Way Back* (1960), was controversial and established Sexton's reputation as a confessional poet. Popularity and something approaching notoriety accompanied Sexton's poetic career. She received numerous awards, including a nomination for the National Book Award; fellowships from the American Academy of Arts and Letters, the Ford Foundation, and the Guggenheim Foundation; several honorary doctorates; and in 1967, the Pulitzer Prize for *Live or Die.* She taught at Harvard and Radcliffe, lectured at Breadloaf Writers' Conference, held the Crashaw Chair at Colgate University, and was a full professor at Boston University by 1972. Her celebrated readings on the poetry circuit were criticized as the flamboyant, dramatic performances they were. When Sexton killed herself in 1974, she was still professionally successful and productive. Diane Wood Middlebrook's *Anne Sexton: A Biography* tells readers much more about a life that seems, but clearly is not, fully disclosed in the poetry.

Sexton used the personal to speak to cultural concerns, many of which apply to women's conflicts and transitions in modern American society. If Lowell and Snodgrass are the fathers of confessional poetry, Sexton is perhaps its first mother. The gender distinction is worth making. Snodgrass gave her "permission," as she phrased it, to write about loss, neurosis, even madness, but no one had extended the permission to write about such experiences from a female point of view. For that bold stroke there was no precedent. Many feminist poets and critics find in her work a set of resonant and enabling myths, as well as a critique of those that disabled Sexton herself.

Sexton's early work was preoccupied with formal structure and lyric discipline, while the later work became what critics have variously called surreal, mythic, or visionary. Anne Sexton's poems articulate some of the deepest dilemmas of her contemporaries about their—our—most fundamental wishes and fears.

Diana Hume George
The Pennsylvania State University/
Behrend College

PRIMARY WORKS

To Bedlam and Part Way Back, 1960; *All My Pretty Ones,* 1962; *Selected Poems,* 1964; *Live or Die,* 1966; *Love Poems,* 1969; *Transformations,* 1971; *The Book of Folly,* 1972; *The Death Notebooks,* 1974; *The Awful Rowing Toward God,* 1975; *45 Mercy Street,* 1976; *Anne Sexton: A Self-Portrait in Letters,* 1977; *Words for Dr. Y: Uncollected Poems with Three Stories,* 1978; *The Complete Poems,* 1981; *No Evil Star: Selected Essays, Interviews, and Prose,* 1985; *Selected Poems of Anne Sexton,* 1988.

Her Kind

I have gone out, a possessed witch,
haunting the black air, braver at night;
dreaming evil, I have done my hitch
over the plain houses, light by light:
lonely thing, twelve-fingered, out of mind.
A woman like that is not a woman, quite.
I have been her kind.

I have found the warm caves in the woods,
filled them with skillets, carvings, shelves,
closets, silks, innumerable goods;
fixed the suppers for the worms and the elves:
whining, rearranging the disaligned.
A woman like that is misunderstood.
I have been her kind.

I have ridden in your cart, driver,
waved my nude arms at villages going by,
learning the last bright routes, survivor
where your flames still bite my thigh
and my ribs crack where your wheels wind.
A woman like that is not ashamed to die.
I have been her kind.

1960

Housewife

Some women marry houses.
It's another kind of skin; it has a heart,
a mouth, a liver and bowel movements.
The walls are permanent and pink.
See how she sits on her knees all day,
faithfully washing herself down.
Men enter by force, drawn back like Jonah
into their fleshy mothers.
A woman *is* her mother.
That's the main thing.

1962

Young

A thousand doors ago
when I was a lonely kid
in a big house with four
garages and it was summer
as long as I could remember,
I lay on the lawn at night,
clover wrinkling under me,
the wise stars bedding over me,
my mother's window a funnel
of yellow heat running out,
my father's window, half shut,
an eye where sleepers pass,
and the boards of the house
were smooth and white as wax
and probably a million leaves
sailed on their strange stalks
as the crickets ticked together
and I, in my brand new body,
which was not a woman's yet,
told the stars my questions
and thought God could really see
the heat and the painted light,
elbows, knees, dreams, goodnight.

1961

Somewhere in Africa

Must you leave, John Holmes,[1] with the prayers and psalms
you never said, said over you? Death with no rage
to weigh you down? Praised by the mild God, his arm
over the pulpit, leaving you timid, with no real age,
whitewashed by belief, as dull as the windy preacher!

[1]John Holmes was a mid-twentieth century American poet who died in 1962. In 1957, Sexton enrolled in his poetry workshop at the Boston Center for Adult Education, where she also met Maxine Kumin and George Starbuck. The group continued meeting for several years after the initial workshop. Sexton's troubled, ambivalent relationship with her first teacher produced two of her poems, "Somewhere in Africa" and "For John, Who Begs Me Not to Enquire Further."

Dead of a dark thing, John Holmes, you've been lost
in the college chapel, mourned as father and teacher,
mourned with piety and grace under the University Cross.

Your last book unsung, your last hard words unknown,
abandoned by science, cancer blossomed in your throat,
rooted like bougainvillea into your gray backbone,
ruptured your pores until you wore it like a coat.

The thick petals, the exotic reds, the purples and whites
covered up your nakedness and bore you up with all
their blind power. I think of your last June nights
in Boston, your body swollen but light, your eyes small

as you let the nurses carry you into a strange land.
. . . If this is death and God is necessary let him be hidden
from the missionary, the well-wisher and the glad hand.
Let God be some tribal female who is known but forbidden.

Let there be this God who is a woman who will place you
upon her shallow boat, who is a woman naked to the waist,
moist with palm oil and sweat, a woman of some virtue
and wild breasts, her limbs excellent, unbruised and chaste.

Let her take you. She will put twelve strong men at the oars
for you are stronger than mahogany and your bones fill
the boat high as with fruit and bark from the interior.
She will have you now, you whom the funeral cannot kill.

John Holmes, cut from a single tree, lie heavy in her hold
and go down that river with the ivory, the copra and the gold.

1966

New Communities, New Identities, New Energies

On February 1, 1960, a group of carefully dressed black students sat down at a "whites-only" lunch counter in Greensboro, North Carolina, and waited to be served. Their direct action against racial segregation caught the attention of thousands of people, white as well as black, and the sit-in movement, displayed on television screens all over America, spread rapidly across the South. Succeeded by a variety of creative non-violent actions—freedom rides, boycotts, voter registration drives, freedom schools—the sit-ins helped galvanize a decade of protests not only against racism but against the Vietnam War, continuing poverty, discrimination against women, and bureaucratic and "irrelevant" educational programs. In their initial stages, these movements were resolutely non-violent, philosophically or tactically, their goals perhaps best expressed by Dr. Martin Luther King, Jr., in his "I Have a Dream" speech before 200,000 people at the 1963 March on Washington.

But when the early hopes for John F. Kennedy's "New Frontier" and Lyndon Johnson's "Great Society" programs did not materialize, especially in urban ghettos; when non-violent protesters were met with police dogs, electric cattle prods, and water cannon; and when the war in Vietnam steadily escalated so that by 1965 the United States had some 184,000 troops in Southeast Asia, the rage for change became increasingly violent. Beginning in 1964, in Watts, Newark, Detroit, and dozens of other black and Latino ghettos, the anger at poverty and discrimination burst into flame—often literally, as rioters shouted "burn, baby, burn" to the slums which seemed to incarcerate them. Violent confrontations spread to virtually every part of American society. In colleges these culminated in 1970, when student protesters were shot to death on the campuses of Kent State and Jackson State universities.

After half a century of modernist literature which focused on death—the death

> In the long history of the world, only a few generations have been granted the role of defending freedom in its hour of maximum danger. I do not shrink from this responsibility—I welcome it. I do not believe that any of us would exchange places with any other people or any other generation. The energy, the faith, the devotion which we bring to this endeavor will light our country and all who serve it—and the glow from that fire can truly light the world.
>
> And so, my fellow Americans, ask not what your country can do for you: Ask what you can do for your country.
>
> John Fitzgerald Kennedy
> Inaugural Address (1961)

of hope, of promise, of culture—American life during the 1960s was permeated with the fact rather than the fiction of death. In addition to the thousands of young Americans killed, wounded, or missing in Vietnam, and the hundreds more wounded or killed in race riots, United States life in the 1960s was punctuated with assassins' gunshots: President John F. Kennedy and Civil Rights leader Medgar Evers in 1963, three Mississippi Freedom summer workers—Chaney, Schwerner, and Goodman—in 1964, Malcolm X in 1965, both Robert F. Kennedy and Martin Luther King, Jr., in 1968. Ordinary Americans realized that fact had become more frightening than fiction. Neither was the literary community immune from the realization. Earlier in the decade Ernest Hemingway had shot himself, dismaying readers who thought his fiction taught endurance and stoicism. Hemingway's suicide was followed by the natural deaths of Robert Frost, E. E. Cummings, Theodore Roethke, William Carlos Williams, T. S. Eliot, and William Faulkner, and by the 1963 suicide of Sylvia Plath. The following year both Flannery O'Connor and Lorraine Hansberry died of disease.

Literature of the 1960s reflected a pervasive concern with circumstances that frequently led to death. Nowhere was that concern—and a reciprocal anger—more apparent than in writing by blacks. In 1961, when LeRoi Jones published his early collection of poems *Preface to a Twenty Volume Suicide Note,* his acerbity was less noticeable than his poignance. But once Jones assumed his voice as a black writer in the plays he wrote between 1962 and 1964—*The Toilet, Dutchman, The Slave*—there was no amelioration in his work. After taking his national name, Imamu Amiri Baraka, he wrote tirelessly for the Black Arts cause. Baraka was in part echoing the most influential of the

> In the past few months, in many parts of the country, a resistance has been forming . . . a resistance of young men—joined together in their commitment against the war. . . .
>
> We will renounce all deferments and refuse to cooperate with the draft in any manner, at any level. We have taken this stand for varied reasons:
>
> opposition to conscription
> opposition only to the Vietnam war
> opposition to all wars and to all American military adventures.
>
> We all agree on one point: the war in Vietnam is criminal and we must act together, at great individual risk, to stop it. Those involved must lead the American people, by their example, to understand the enormity of what their government is doing . . . that the government cannot be allowed to continue with its daily crimes. . . .
>
> There are many ways to avoid the draft, to stay clear of this war. Most of us now have deferments . . . but all these individual outs can have no effect on the draft, the war, or the consciousness of this country. To cooperate with conscription is to perpetuate its existence, without which, the government could not wage war. We have chosen to openly defy the draft and confront the government and its war directly.
>
> The Resistance
> "We Refuse to Serve" (1967)

early 1960s black writers, James Baldwin, whose 1962 *The Fire Next Time* had called for an end to what he described as "the racial nightmare." Baldwin had written effectively during the early 1960s. His *Nobody Knows My Name* in 1961 and the 1962 novel *Another Country* had been well received, but the crucial impact of his statements about race issues became clear when the key essay from *The Fire Next Time*—"Letter from a Region in My Mind"—was published in the *New Yorker* in the fall of 1962. Its effect on intellectual Americans was electric. Baldwin's plays—his 1964 *Blues for Mister Charley,* dealing with the killing of Emmett Till for whistling at a white woman, and his 1965 *The Amen Corner*—were also provocative.

In a certain sense the violence and death of American culture pervades key texts by 1960s black writers, but from another perspective these works can be seen as introducing new cultural forms. The Black Arts movement responded to political calls for "black power" and the new sense of racial pride suggested in the refrain "black is beautiful." Its efforts to define a "black aesthetic," what it meant to be a *black* writer, helped spark parallel developments among other ethnic minorities and among women of all races. In conferences and workshops across the nation—as, for example, the Second Black Writers' Conference in 1967 at Fisk University—critics and writers struggled with the issues of how literary works might best express and advance political causes. One model was offered by the powerful *Autobiography of Malcolm X,* published in 1964, the year before the assassination of its Black Muslim author, originally named Malcolm Little.

Whether an author claimed to be furthering the Black Arts movement or expressing a black aesthetic, a significant number of black writers were being published for the first time by mainstream houses. In 1964, Ernest J. Gaines published *Catherine Carmier* and in 1967 and 1968 story collections, *Of Love and Dust* and *Bloodline.* Published in 1968, Eldridge Cleaver's *Soul on Ice* not only had wide political impact but helped extend the mode of autobiographical narrative established by Malcolm X and by Anne Moody's *Coming of Age in Mississippi* to powerful works like George Jackson's *Soledad Brother.* A list of some authors and titles from those years suggests how flourishing this new black renaissance was: in 1967, Jay Wright's *Death as History* and Ishmael Reed's *The Free Lance Pallbearers;* in 1968, Nikki Giovanni's *Black Judgment* (from Dudley Randall's Broadside Press in Detroit), Mari Evans's *Where Is All the Music?* and Etheridge Knight's *Poems from Prison;* in 1969 James Alan McPherson's story collection *Hue and Cry,* Ishmael Reed's *Yellow Back Radio Broke Down,* Clarence Major's anthology *The New Black Poetry,* and Sonia Sanchez's *Homecoming,* along with a book that proved to remain a bestseller, Maya Angelou's memoir *I Know Why the Caged Bird Sings.*

Parallel with the emergence of a newly vigorous African American literature, and often strongly influenced by it, was a current of writing by and about women of all races. In the early 1960s a new feminism began to take shape, affected by the Civil Rights movement, by developments in mainstream politics—like the issuing of an influential report by President Kennedy's Commission on the Status of Women—and by the founding of organizations like the National Organization for Women (NOW) and the National Welfare Rights Organization. Few books of the time were as influential as Betty Friedan's *The Feminine Mystique* (1963) and Simone de Beauvoir's *The Second Sex* (1971). In 1963 Mary McCarthy's *The Group,* a novel about nine Vassar classmates during the 1930s, and Sylvia Plath's novel *The Bell Jar* appeared, followed in 1965 by Plath's posthumous poem collection *Ariel.* Similarly influential books were being published by women poets. In her first two collections, *To Bedlam and Part Way Back* (1960) and *All My Pretty Ones* (1962), Anne Sexton created her art from the subjects of therapy, her rage toward her parents, her ambivalence toward her daughters, her female body, and her lovers. In 1963 Carolyn Kizer defied the advice of male critics and published her intricate feminist poem "Pro Femina." Soon the work of Alta, Nikki Giovanni, Maxine Kumin, Denise Levertov, Marge Piercy, Adrienne Rich, Mona Van Duyn, Diane Wakoski, and Margaret Walker, among many others, began to reformulate notions of what "good" poems were. Gradually themes and techniques changed with the expansion of what poems could be about—women's sexuality, childbirth, incest, lesbianism—and women writers found their writing energized in an atmosphere of more flexible critical and reader response.

Whereas the rise of post-war Jewish literature had stemmed from a resurgence of Jewish consciousness, and the rise of southern writers from new philosophies about the value of southern life, feminist literature developed alongside feminist aesthetics. Women who were newly defining themselves wanted fiction, poetry, and drama that presented women characters as something other than wives, daughters, and mothers. Feminist critics encouraged such new writing by calling into question both established literary canons and critical ideas that had been used to sustain the exclusive centrality of writing by men. Mary Ellmann's *Thinking About Women* (1968), Kate Millett's *Sexual Politics* (1971), and Germaine Greer's *The Female Eunuch* (1971) helped to initiate an enormous quantity of feminist criticism and theory. In the three decades since, such writing has helped transform ideas not only about the character of literature but also about the nature of critical writing and reading.

The struggle for an equal cultural voice and for change in the institutions of criticism and teaching was also evident throughout the varied Latino, Asian American, and Native American communities. Barred from publication in mainstream channels, these writers published largely in newspapers. For example, writers within Spanish-language traditions—Chicanos, Puerto Ricans, and others—published in the literary pages of Spanish-language newspapers. During the 1940s, a few texts of short fiction appeared—Josephine Niggli's *Mexican Village* in 1945 and Mario Suárez's stories of "Chicanos" in a Tucson barrio in the 1947 *Arizona Quarterly.* The beginning of Mexican American contemporary literature came in 1959 with José Antonio Villarreal's *Pocho,* his ironic title using the derogatory term for an Americanized Mexican. Just as Villarreal's novel showed a young Mexican man becoming Anglicized, so its language was thoroughly American. Puerto Rican literature written in North America came of age with Pedro Juan Soto's 1957 *Spiks* and with the poems of such New York poets as Pedro Pietri, Miguel Algarin, and Víctor Hernández Cruz, whose 1969 poem collection *Snaps* was one of the first books by a Puerto Rican to be published commercially.

In 1965 Luís Valdez combined Mexican American literature with political purpose when he joined with César Chávez's farm workers' union to form El Teatro Campesino. This theater company merged traditional Spanish and Mexican dramatic forms with agitprop techniques to create powerful and entertaining skits in support of union issues. Valdez's *Actos* were performed widely; some were eventually published.

In 1967 Quinto Sol Publications opened its doors in Berkeley, California, for the single purpose of publishing Mexican American writing. Among the writers connected with this publishing venture were several fine prose writers—Rolando Hinojosa-Smith, Tomás Rivera, and Rudolfo Anaya—and the poet José

Montoya, who combined Spanish with English in vivid poems like "La Jefita," "Pobre Viejo Walt Whitman," and "El Louie." Montoya's fusion of languages was meant to indicate the bilingualism of the Mexican American culture, rather than a binary approach to race. This is a middle stanza from "El Louie":

And Louie would come through—
melodramatic music, like in the
mono—tan tan tarán—Cruz
Diablo, El Charro Negro! Bogard
smile (his smile as deadly as
his vaisas!) He dug roles, man,
and names—like blackie, little
Louie . . .

In 1967 Rodolfo "Corky" Gonzales's long historical poem "Yo soy Joaquín/I Am Joaquín" also appeared. Like Valdez, Gonzales was active in organizing political efforts in Denver, Colorado; he presented his poem both as a definition of "Chicano" identity and as a means of promoting the community's social and political agendas.

In 1970 Tomás Rivera was awarded the first Quinto Sol Prize for *. . . y no se lo tragó la tierra (And the Earth Did Not Devour Him),* a series of fourteen related stories about Mexican American farm workers' lives. In 1972 Rolando Hinojosa-Smith, another Chicano writer who initially worked in Spanish, published *Estampas del valle y otras obras (Sketches of the Valley and Other Works)* and so created an imaginary south Texas county called Belken, reminiscent in certain ways of Faulkner's Yoknapatawpha. Rudolfo Anaya, who wrote in English, published the Quinto Sol Award winner *Bless Me, Ultima.* Set in a New Mexico community near the end of World War II, the novel explores the tensions within rural Mexican American culture, recognizing it as a complex of Spanish, Indian, and Anglo traditions. Richard Vázquez's novel *Chicano* was also published in 1970, and in 1972 and 1973 Oscar Zeta Acosta's denunciations of contemporary American culture appeared in *The Autobiography of a Brown Buffalo* and *The Revolt of the Cockroach People.* Piri Thomas's *Down These Mean Streets* prefaced the important mid-1970s anthology of Puerto Rican–New York writing called *Nuyorican Poetry: An Anthology of Puerto Rican Words and Feelings,* when Miguel Piñero's play *Short Eyes* also appeared. San Francisco, south Texas, New Mexico, Los Angeles, Spanish Harlem, the worlds of laundry and migrant workers, vaqueros and small farmers, the anger of Lower East Side bars and the violence of prison rec areas—new centers, new subjects, new writers.

American Indian literature made its first wide impact on mainstream readers with the 1968 publication of N. Scott Momaday's *House Made of Dawn;* in 1969, that book won the Pulitzer Prize for Fiction, and Momaday also published *The Way to Rainy Mountain,* a prose-poem utilizing elements of Kiowa myth and history set beside Momaday's personal experiences. Momaday's adaptation of traditional Native American oral materials was seminal for other Indian writers. So, too, was the upsurge of Indian protest: the symbolic seizing of Alcatraz and later armed battles fought in desperately familiar places like the Pine Ridge reservation helped generate important non-fictional prose, like Vine Deloria's 1969 *Custer Died for Your Sins: An Indian Manifesto* and Dee Brown's 1971 *Bury My Heart at Wounded Knee.* Such political volumes; substantial new ethnographic, historical, and linguistic research; and the continued presence of such long-established (though generally ignored) Indian writers as D'Arcy McNickle (whose first novel, *The Surrounded,* appeared in 1936) and John Joseph Mathews (whose 1945 *Talking to the Moon* aimed at reintegrating human beings within their environment)—all this work in the context of a widening protest movement helped set the stage for the flourishing of Indian writers in the last third of the century.

After publication of the Momaday

texts, James Welch's 1974 *Winter in the Blood,* followed by *The Death of Jim Loney,* drew an acrid picture of the life of the young American Indian shut out from mainstream culture and forced to find his own motivation—or death. Drawing more intently on tribal culture, in its implication that no individual succeeds without an acknowledgment of roots, Louise Erdrich, Leslie Marmon Silko, Paula Gunn Allen, Gerald Vizenor, Simon Ortiz, Wendy Rose, Joy Harjo, and many others have created readers hungry for today's Native American literature.

Asian American writing also had well-established, if often unnoted, roots. Hisaye Yamamoto continued to write stories, though a collection would not emerge until 1988. Frank Chin continued writing fiction and drama, and his *The Chickencoop Chinaman* became a staple in the classroom. Among other Asian American writers are Richard Kim (*The Martyred,* 1964, and *The Innocent,* 1968, accounts of life in his native Korea); Kim Yong-Ik (*The Happy Days,* 1960; *The Diving Gourd,* 1962; and *Love in Winter,* 1969); Louis Chu (*Eat a Bowl of Tea,* 1961); the Filipino Bienvenido Santos (*The Volcano,* 1965; *Villa Magdalena,* 1965); N.V.M. Gonzalez (*The Bamboo Dancers,* 1964); Chuang Hua (*Crossings,* 1968); and Bette Bao Lord (*Eighth Moon,* 1964). It is only at the end of this Asian American list that women writers appear; such younger writers as Janice Mirikitani, Maxine Hong Kingston, Karen Tei Yamashita, and Jessica Hagedorn have helped balance the gender equation.

If one growing tendency of American literature in the 1960s and 1970s was to portray the world and its problems as it offered ideas about and encouragement for change, another current drew the withdrawn protagonist, isolated from an increasingly frustrating, crowded world. The fiction of Paule Marshall and James Alan McPherson and the poetry of Garrett Hongo, Lucille Clifton, and—surrealistically developed—Joy Harjo continued the modernist mode, based on the writer's decision that knowing oneself was more important than fitting into the world. A third tendency was even more self-reflexive—and influential. It assumed that there was little of importance in any world beyond the self; indeed, it came to question the existence of a unified "self," as well as of a definable reality "outside." Thus it created literature which described an essential emptiness or a wildly perverse absurdity. Such cultural currents, together with the defeat of revolutionary expectations late in the 1970s, led to the development of what came to be known as "postmodernist" art and criticism.

In America, drawing from earlier works by Kafka, Robbe-Grillet, and Borges, the fiction of John Barth, Nabokov, and Thomas Pynchon expressed a view that life was absurd and literature a game. Representation, which the modernists tried to make replicate truth, was used to create fantasy, mystery, or nihilism. Donald Barthelme's *Come Back, Dr. Caligari* and his parodic novel *Snow White* lived past the furious interest in gallows-humor postmodernism. Richard Brautigan's minimalist prose poems led to a flood of minimalist fiction (Raymond Carver, Jayne Ann Phillips, Bobbie Ann Mason, Ann Beattie), but the best example of the randomness that marked the postmodern was American drama. From Edward Albee's *The Zoo Story, The American Dream,* and *Who's Afraid of Virginia Woolf?* to Megan Terry's *Approaching Simone* and *American Kings English for Queens,* off-Broadway theater (and theater in Chicago, Omaha, Louisville, and Durham) has become a showcase for postmodernist art.

We suggested earlier that readers in 1959 or 1960 sensed new cultural frontiers close at hand, though their precise character might then have been elusive. By the end of the 1960s, and into the 1970s, even in the midst of social turmoil and political conflict, a sensitive reader might have seen that that "new frontier" had to do with the exploration of *difference,* with the development of diverse new centers of culture from what had once been, from the point of view of a traditional reader, the most marginal way-stations.

Lorraine Vivian Hansberry 1930–1965

The youngest of four children, Lorraine Hansberry was born in Chicago, Illinois, to Carl Augustus and Nannie (Perry) Hansberry. Her parents had migrated from the South to Chicago where her father founded a bank and a real estate firm. The family lived a comfortable life, and such eminent blacks as W.E.B. Du Bois, Paul Robeson, Langston Hughes, and Duke Ellington were guests in their home. But in 1938, when the family moved into a house in a white neighborhood, violence erupted against them, and the temper of the Hansberry life changed. Lorraine, then eight, remembered her mother patrolling the house with a loaded German Luger while Carl was in Washington protesting the racial restrictive covenant law in Illinois. By 1940, when the Supreme Court declared restrictive covenants illegal (*Hansberry* v. *Lee* 311 U.S. 32), Carl was psychologically and financially damaged so much that he planned to become an expatriate to Mexico. He died in self-exile in 1946.

Educated in the racially segregated Chicago public schools, Lorraine graduated from Englewood High in 1948 and enrolled at the University of Wisconsin for two years, studying art, stage design, geology, and English. In 1950 she moved to New York City where she attended classes at the New School for Social Research and worked as a typist, teacher, reporter, and as associate editor on *Freedom,* Paul Robeson's Harlem-based monthly magazine. She also became an activist in the Civil Rights movement.

In 1953 she married Robert Nemiroff, whom she had met on a picket line at New York University, which he attended. In 1956 she began writing *A Raisin in the Sun.* That play's successful production three years later on Broadway catapulted her into national and international prominence. An extremely promising career ended when she died of cancer at the age of 34.

Hansberry's artistic vision was optimistic; she believed firmly that people could "impose the reason for life on life." She knew the tensions implicit in being born both black and female, and never accepted the notion that either characteristic was limiting, but she was never bound by narrow or parochial concerns. She learned a great deal from Sean O'Casey and other modern playwrights, and used her voice as a black to transform academic techniques in her own art. *A Raisin in the Sun* won the New York Drama Critics Circle Award for the best play of the 1958–1959 theater season.

Jeanne-Marie A. Miller
Howard University

PRIMARY WORKS

A Raisin in the Sun, 1959; *The Movement: Documentary of a Struggle for Equality,* 1964; *The Sign in Sidney Brustein's Window,* 1965; *To Be Young, Gifted and Black,* 1969; *Lorraine Hansberry: The Collected Last Plays,* 1983.

A Raisin in the Sun

What happens to a dream deferred?
Does it dry up
Like a raisin in the sun?
Or fester like a sore—
And then run?
Does it stink like rotten meat?
Or crust and sugar over—
Like a syrupy sweet?

Maybe it just sags
Like a heavy load.

Or does it explode?

—LANGSTON HUGHES

A RAISIN IN THE SUN *was first presented by Philip Rose and David J. Cogan at the Ethel Barrymore Theatre, New York City, March 11, 1959, with the following cast:*

(In order of appearance)

RUTH YOUNGER	Ruby Dee
TRAVIS YOUNGER	Glynn Turman
WALTER LEE YOUNGER (BROTHER)	Sidney Poitier
BENEATHA YOUNGER	Diana Sands
LENA YOUNGER (MAMA)	Claudia McNeil
JOSEPH ASAGAI	Ivan Dixon
GEORGE MURCHISON	Louis Gossett
KARL LINDNER	John Fiedler
BOBO	Lonne Elder III
MOVING MEN	Ed Hall, Douglas Turner

Directed by Lloyd Richards

Designed and lighted by Ralph Alswang

Costumes by Virginia Volland

The action of the play is set in Chicago's Southside, sometime between World War II and the present.

ACT ONE

SCENE 1. *Friday morning.*
SCENE 2. *The following morning.*

ACT TWO

SCENE 1. *Later, the same day.*
SCENE 2. *Friday night, a few weeks later.*
SCENE 3. *Moving day, one week later.*

ACT THREE

An hour later.

Act I

Scene I

The YOUNGER *living room would be a comfortable and well-ordered room if it were not for a number of indestructible contradictions to this state of being. Its furnishings are typical and undistinguished and their primary feature now is that they have clearly had to accommodate the living of too many people for too many years—and they are tired. Still, we can see that at some time, a time probably no longer remembered by the family (except perhaps for* MAMA*) the furnishings of this room were actually selected with care and love and even hope—and brought to this apartment and arranged with taste and pride.*

That was a long time ago. Now the once loved pattern of the couch upholstery has to fight to show itself from under acres of crocheted doilies and couch covers which have themselves finally come to be more important than the upholstery. And here a table or a chair has been moved to disguise the worn places in the carpet; but the carpet has fought back by showing its weariness, with depressing uniformity, elsewhere on its surface.

Weariness has, in fact, won in this room. Everything has been polished, washed, sat on, used, scrubbed too often. All pretenses but living itself have long since vanished from the very atmosphere of this room.

Moreover, a section of this room, for it is not really a room unto itself, though the landlord's lease would make it seem so, slopes backward to provide a small kitchen area, where the family prepares the meals that are eaten in the living room proper, which must also serve as dining room. The single window that has been provided for these "two" rooms is located in this kitchen area. The sole natural light the family may enjoy in the course of a day is only that which fights its way through this little window.

At left, a door leads to a bedroom which is shared by MAMA *and her daughter,* BENEATHA. *At right, opposite, is a second room (which in the beginning of the life of this apartment was probably a breakfast room) which serves as a bedroom for* WALTER *and his wife,* RUTH.

Time: Sometime between World War II and the present.

Place: Chicago's Southside.

At Rise: It is morning dark in the living room. TRAVIS *is asleep on the make-down bed at center. An alarm clock sounds from within the bedroom at right, and presently* RUTH *enters from that room and closes the door behind her. She crosses sleepily toward the window. As she passes her sleeping son she reaches down and shakes him a little. At the window she raises the shade and a dusky Southside morning light comes in feebly. She fills a pot with water and puts it on to boil. She calls to the boy, between yawns, in a slightly muffled voice.*

RUTH *is about thirty. We can see that she was a pretty girl, even exceptionally so, but now it is apparent that life has been little that she expected, and disappointment has already begun to hang in her face. In a few years, before thirty-five even, she will be known among her people as a "settled woman."*

She crosses to her son and gives him a good, final, rousing shake.

RUTH Come on now, boy, it's seven thirty! *(Her son sits up at last, in a stupor of sleepiness)* I say hurry up, Travis! You ain't the only person in the world got to use a bathroom! *(The child, a sturdy, handsome little boy of ten or eleven, drags himself out of the bed and almost blindly takes his towels and "today's clothes" from drawers and a closet and goes out to the bathroom, which is in an outside hall and which is shared by another family or families on the same floor.* RUTH *crosses to the bedroom door at right and opens it and calls in to her husband)* Walter Lee! . . . It's after seven thirty! Lemme see you do some waking up in there now! *(She waits)* You better get up from there, man! It's after seven thirty I tell you. *(She waits again)* All right, you just go ahead and lay there and next thing you know Travis be finished and Mr. Johnson'll be in there and you'll be fussing and cussing round here like a mad man! And be late too! *(She waits, at the end of patience)* Walter Lee—it's time for you to get up!

(She waits another second and then starts to go into the bedroom, but is apparently satisfied that her husband has begun to get up. She stops, pulls the door to, and returns to the kitchen area. She wipes her face with a moist cloth and runs her fingers through her sleep-disheveled hair in a vain effort and ties an apron around her housecoat. The bedroom door at right opens and her husband stands in the doorway in his pajamas, which are rumpled and mismated. He is a lean, intense young man in his middle thirties, inclined to quick nervous movements and erratic speech habits—and always in his voice there is a quality of indictment)

WALTER Is he out yet?

RUTH What you mean *out?* He ain't hardly got in there good yet.

WALTER *(Wandering in, still more oriented to sleep than to a new day)* Well, what was you doing all that yelling for if I can't even get in there yet? *(Stopping and thinking)* Check coming today?

RUTH They *said* Saturday and this is just Friday and I hopes to God you ain't going to get up here first thing this morning and start talking to me 'bout no money—'cause I 'bout don't want to hear it.

WALTER Something the matter with you this morning?

RUTH No—I'm just sleepy as the devil. What kind of eggs you want?

WALTER Not scrambled. (RUTH *starts to scramble eggs)* Paper come? (RUTH *points impatiently to the rolled up* Tribune *on the table, and he gets it and spreads it out and vaguely reads the front page)* Set off another bomb yesterday.

RUTH *(Maximum indifference)* Did they?

WALTER *(Looking up)* What's the matter with you?

RUTH Ain't nothing the matter with me. And don't keep asking me that this morning.

WALTER Ain't nobody bothering you. *(Reading the news of the day absently again)* Say Colonel McCormick is sick.

RUTH *(Affecting tea-party interest)* Is he now? Poor thing.

WALTER *(Sighing and looking at his watch)* Oh, me. *(He waits)* Now what is that boy doing in that bathroom all this time? He just going to have to start getting up earlier. I can't be being late to work on account of him fooling around in there.

RUTH *(Turning on him)* Oh, no he ain't going to be getting up no earlier no such thing! It ain't his fault that he can't get to bed no earlier nights 'cause he got a bunch of crazy good-for-nothing clowns sitting up running their mouths in what is supposed to be his bedroom after ten o'clock at night . . .

WALTER That's what you mad about, ain't it? The things I want to talk about with my friends just couldn't be important in your mind, could they?

(He rises and finds a cigarette in her handbag on the table and crosses to the little window and looks out, smoking and deeply enjoying this first one)

RUTH *(Almost matter of factly, a complaint too automatic to deserve emphasis)* Why you always got to smoke before you eat in the morning?

WALTER *(At the window)* Just look at 'em down there . . . Running and racing to work . . . *(He turns and faces his wife and watches her a moment at the stove, and then, suddenly)* You look young this morning, baby.

RUTH *(Indifferently)* Yeah?

WALTER Just for a second—stirring them eggs. It's gone now—just for a second it was—you looked real young again. *(Then, drily)* It's gone now—you look like yourself again.

RUTH Man, if you don't shut up and leave me alone.

WALTER *(Looking out to the street again)* First thing a man ought to learn in life is not to make love to no colored woman first thing in the morning. You all some evil people at eight o'clock in the morning.

*(*TRAVIS *appears in the hall doorway, almost fully dressed and quite wide awake now, his towels and pajamas across his shoulders. He opens the door and signals for his father to make the bathroom in a hurry)*

TRAVIS *(Watching the bathroom)* Daddy, come on! *(*WALTER *gets his bathroom utensils and flies out to the bathroom)*

RUTH Sit down and have your breakfast, Travis.

TRAVIS Mama, this is Friday. *(Gleefully)* Check coming tomorrow, huh?

RUTH You get your mind off money and eat your breakfast.

TRAVIS *(Eating)* This is the morning we supposed to bring the fifty cents to school.

RUTH Well, I ain't got no fifty cents this morning.

TRAVIS Teacher say we have to.

RUTH I don't care what teacher say. I ain't got it. Eat your breakfast, Travis.

TRAVIS I *am* eating.

RUTH Hush up now and just eat!

(The boy gives her an exasperated look for her lack of understanding, and eats grudgingly)

TRAVIS You think grandmama would have it?
RUTH No! And I want you to stop asking your grandmother for money, you hear me?
TRAVIS *(Outraged)* Gaaaleee! I don't ask her, she just gimme it sometimes!
RUTH Travis Willard Younger—I got too much on me this morning to be—
TRAVIS Maybe Daddy—
RUTH *Travis!*

(The boy hushes abruptly. They are both quiet and tense for several seconds)

TRAVIS *(Presently)* Could I maybe go carry some groceries in front of the supermarket for a little while after school then?
RUTH Just hush, I said. *(Travis jabs his spoon into his cereal bowl viciously, and rests his head in anger upon his fists)* If you through eating, you can get over there and make up your bed.

(The boy obeys stiffly and crosses the room, almost mechanically, to the bed and more or less carefully folds the covering. He carries the bedding into his mother's room and returns with his books and cap)

TRAVIS *(Sulking and standing apart from her unnaturally)* I'm gone.
RUTH *(Looking up from the stove to inspect him automatically)* Come here. *(He crosses to her and she studies his head)* If you don't take this comb and fix this here head, you better! (TRAVIS *puts down his books with a great sigh of oppression, and crosses to the mirror. His mother mutters under her breath about his "slubbornness")* 'Bout to march out of here with that head looking just like chickens slept in it! I just don't know where you get your slubborn ways . . . And get your jacket, too. Looks chilly out this morning.
TRAVIS *(With conspicuously brushed hair and jacket)* I'm gone.
RUTH Get carfare and milk money—*(Waving one finger)*—and not a single penny for no caps, you hear me?
TRAVIS *(With sullen politeness)* Yes'm.

(He turns in outrage to leave. His mother watches after him as in his frustration he approaches the door almost comically. When she speaks to him, her voice has become a very gentle tease)

RUTH *(Mocking; as she thinks he would say it)* Oh, Mama makes me so mad sometimes, I don't know what to do! *(She waits and continues to his back as he stands stock-still in front of the door)* I wouldn't kiss that woman good-bye for nothing in this world this morning! *(The boy finally turns around and rolls his eyes at her, knowing the mood has changed and he is vindicated; he does not, however, move toward her yet)* Not for nothing in this world! *(She finally laughs aloud at him and holds out her arms to him and we see that it is a way between them, very old and practiced. He crosses to her and allows her to embrace him warmly but keeps his face fixed with masculine rigidity. She holds him back from her presently and looks at him and runs her fingers over the features of his face. With utter gentleness—)* Now—whose little old angry man are you?
TRAVIS *(The masculinity and gruffness start to fade at last)* Aw gaalee—Mama . . .
RUTH *(Mimicking)* Aw—gaaaaalleeeee, Mama! *(She pushes him, with rough playfulness and finality, toward the door)* Get on out of here or you going to be late.

TRAVIS *(In the face of love, new aggressiveness)* Mama, could I *please* go carry groceries?

RUTH Honey, it's starting to get so cold evenings.

WALTER *(Coming in from the bathroom and drawing a make-believe gun from a make-believe holster and shooting at his son)* What is it he wants to do?

RUTH Go carry groceries after school at the supermarket.

WALTER Well, let him go . . .

TRAVIS *(Quickly, to the ally)* I *have* to—she won't gimme the fifty cents . . .

WALTER *(To his wife only)* Why not?

RUTH *(Simply, and with flavor)* 'Cause we don't have it.

WALTER *(To* RUTH *only)* What you tell the boy things like that for? *(Reaching down into his pants with a rather important gesture)* Here, son—

(He hands the boy the coin, but his eyes are directed to his wife's. TRAVIS *takes the money happily)*

TRAVIS Thanks, Daddy.

(He starts out. RUTH *watches both of them with murder in her eyes.* WALTER *stands and stares back at her with defiance, and suddenly reaches into his pocket again on an afterthought)*

WALTER *(Without even looking at his son, still staring hard at his wife)* In fact, here's another fifty cents . . . Buy yourself some fruit today—or take a taxicab to school or something!

TRAVIS Whoopee—

(He leaps up and clasps his father around the middle with his legs, and they face each other in mutual appreciation; slowly WALTER LEE *peeks around the boy to catch the violent rays from his wife's eyes and draws his head back as if shot)*

WALTER You better get down now—and get to school, man.

TRAVIS *(At the door)* O.K. Good-bye.

(He exits)

WALTER *(After him, pointing with pride)* That's *my* boy. *(She looks at him in disgust and turns back to her work)* You know what I was thinking 'bout in the bathroom this morning?

RUTH No.

WALTER How come you always try to be so pleasant!

RUTH What is there to be pleasant 'bout!

WALTER You want to know what I was thinking 'bout in the bathroom or not!

RUTH I know what you thinking 'bout.

WALTER *(Ignoring her)* 'Bout what me and Willy Harris was talking about last night.

RUTH *(Immediately—a refrain)* Willy Harris is a good-for-nothing loud mouth.

WALTER Anybody who talks to me has got to be a good-for-nothing loud mouth, ain't he? And what you know about who is just a good-for-nothing loud mouth? Charlie Atkins was just a "good-for-nothing loud mouth" too, wasn't he! When he wanted me to go in the dry-cleaning business with him. And now—he's grossing a hundred thousand a year. A hundred thousand dollars a year! You still call *him* a loud mouth!

RUTH *(Bitterly)* Oh, Walter Lee . . .

(She folds her head on her arms over the table)

WALTER *(Rising and coming to her and standing over her)* You tired, ain't you? Tired of everything. Me, the boy, the way we live—this beat-up hole—everything. Ain't you? *(She doesn't look up, doesn't answer)* So tired—moaning and groaning all the time, but you wouldn't do nothing to help, would you? You couldn't be on my side that long for nothing, could you?

RUTH Walter, please leave me alone.

WALTER A man needs for a woman to back him up . . .

RUTH Walter—

WALTER Mama would listen to you. You know she listen to you more than she do me and Bennie. She think more of you. All you have to do is just sit down with her when you drinking your coffee one morning and talking 'bout things like you do and—*(He sits down beside her and demonstrates graphically what he thinks her methods and tone should be)*—you just sip your coffee, see, and say easy like that you been thinking 'bout that deal Walter Lee is so interested in, 'bout the store and all, and sip some more coffee, like what you saying ain't really that important to you—And the next thing you know, she be listening good and asking you questions and when I come home—I can tell her the details. This ain't no fly-by-night proposition, baby. I mean we figured it out, me and Willy and Bobo.

RUTH *(With a frown)* Bobo?

WALTER Yeah. You see, this little liquor store we got in mind cost seventy-five thousand and we figured the initial investment on the place be 'bout thirty thousand, see. That be ten thousand each. Course, there's a couple of hundred you got to pay so's you don't spend your life just waiting for them clowns to let your license get approved—

RUTH You mean graft?

WALTER *(Frowning impatiently)* Don't call it that. See there, that just goes to show you what women understand about the world. Baby, don't *nothing* happen for you in this world 'less you pay *somebody* off!

RUTH Walter, leave me alone! *(She raises her head and stares at him vigorously—then says, more quietly) Eat* your eggs, they gonna be cold.

WALTER *(Straightening up from her and looking off)* That's it. There you are. Man say to his woman: I got me a dream. His woman say: Eat your eggs. *(Sadly, but gaining in power)* Man say: I got to take hold of this here world, baby! And a woman will say: Eat your eggs and go to work. *(Passionately now)* Man say: I got to change my life, I'm choking to death, baby! And his woman say—*(In utter anguish as he brings his fists down on his thighs)*—Your eggs is getting cold!

RUTH *(Softly)* Walter, that ain't none of our money.

WALTER *(Not listening at all or even looking at her)* This morning, I was lookin' in the mirror and thinking about it . . . I'm thirty-five years old; I been married eleven years and I got a boy who sleeps in the living room—*(Very, very quietly)*—and all I got to give him is stories about how rich white people live . . .

RUTH Eat your eggs, Walter.

WALTER *Damn my eggs . . . damn all the eggs that ever was!*

RUTH Then go to work.

WALTER *(Looking up at her)* See—I'm trying to talk to you 'bout myself—*(Shaking his head with the repetition)*—and all you can say is eat them eggs and go to work.

RUTH *(Wearily)* Honey, you never say nothing new. I listen to you every day, every night and every morning, and you never say nothing new. *(Shrugging)* So you would rather *be* Mr. Arnold than be his chauffeur. So—I would *rather* be living in Buckingham Palace.

WALTER That is just what is wrong with the colored woman in this world . . . Don't understand about building their men up and making 'em feel like they somebody. Like they can do something.

RUTH *(Drily, but to hurt)* There *are* colored men who do things.

WALTER No thanks to the colored woman.

RUTH Well, being a colored woman, I guess I can't help myself none.

(She rises and gets the ironing board and sets it up and attacks a huge pile of rough-dried clothes, sprinkling them in preparation for the ironing and then rolling them into tight fat balls)

WALTER *(Mumbling)* We one group of men tied to a race of women with small minds.

(His sister BENEATHA *enters. She is about twenty, as slim and intense as her brother. She is not as pretty as her sister-in-law, but her lean, almost intellectual face has a handsomeness of its own. She wears a bright-red flannel nightie, and her thick hair stands wildly about her head. Her speech is a mixture of many things; it is different from the rest of the family's insofar as education has permeated her sense of English—and perhaps the Midwest rather than the South has finally—at last—won out in her inflection; but not altogether, because over all of it is a soft slurring and transformed use of vowels which is the decided influence of the Southside. She passes through the room without looking at either* RUTH *or* WALTER *and goes to the outside door and looks, a little blindly, out to the bathroom. She sees that it has been lost to the Johnsons. She closes the door with a sleepy vengeance and crosses to the table and sits down a little defeated)*

BENEATHA I am going to start timing those people.

WALTER You should get up earlier.

BENEATHA *(Her face in her hands. She is still fighting the urge to go back to bed)* Really—would you suggest dawn? Where's the paper?

WALTER *(Pushing the paper across the table to her as he studies her almost clinically, as though he has never seen her before)* You a horrible-looking chick at this hour.

BENEATHA *(Drily)* Good morning, everybody.

WALTER *(Senselessly)* How is school coming?

BENEATHA *(In the same spirit)* Lovely. Lovely. And you know, biology is the greatest. *(Looking up at him)* I dissected something that looked just like you yesterday.

WALTER I just wondered if you've made up your mind and everything.

BENEATHA *(Gaining in sharpness and impatience)* And what did I answer yesterday morning—and the day before that?

RUTH *(From the ironing board, like someone disinterested and old)* Don't be so nasty, Bennie.

BENEATHA *(Still to her brother)* And the day before that and the day before that!

WALTER *(Defensively)* I'm interested in you. Something wrong with that? Ain't many girls who decide—

WALTER *and* BENEATHA *(In unison)*—"to be a doctor."

(Silence)

WALTER Have we figured out yet just exactly how much medical school is going to cost?

RUTH Walter Lee, why don't you leave that girl alone and get out of here to work?

BENEATHA *(Exits to the bathroom and bangs on the door)* Come on out of there, please!

(She comes back into the room)

WALTER *(Looking at his sister intently)* You know the check is coming tomorrow.

BENEATHA *(Turning on him with a sharpness all her own)* That money belongs to Mama, Walter, and it's for her to decide how she wants to use it. I don't care if she wants to buy a house or a rocket ship or just nail it up somewhere and look at it. It's hers. Not ours—*hers.*

WALTER *(Bitterly)* Now ain't that fine! You just got your mother's interest at heart, ain't you, girl? You such a nice girl—but if Mama got that money she can always take a few thousand and help you through school too—can't she?

BENEATHA I have never asked anyone around here to do anything for me!

WALTER No! And the line between asking and just accepting when the time comes is big and wide—ain't it!

BENEATHA *(With fury)* What do you want from me, Brother—that I quit school or just drop dead, which!

WALTER I don't want nothing but for you to stop acting holy 'round here. Me and Ruth done made some sacrifices for you—why can't you do something for the family?

RUTH Walter, don't be dragging me in it.

WALTER You are in it—Don't you get up and go work in somebody's kitchen for the last three years to help put clothes on her back?

RUTH Oh, Walter—that's not fair . . .

WALTER It ain't that nobody expects you to get on your knees and say thank you, Brother; thank you, Ruth; thank you, Mama—and thank you, Travis, for wearing the same pair of shoes for two semesters—

BENEATHA *(Dropping to her knees)* Well—I *do*—all right?—thank everybody . . . and forgive me for ever wanting to be anything at all . . . forgive me, forgive me!

RUTH Please stop it! Your mama'll hear you.

WALTER Who the hell told you you had to be a doctor? If you so crazy 'bout messing 'round with sick people—then go be a nurse like other women—or just get married and be quiet . . .

BENEATHA Well—you finally got it said . . . It took you three years but you finally got it said. Walter, give up; leave me alone—it's Mama's money.

WALTER *He was my father, too!*

BENEATHA So what? He was mine, too—and Travis' grandfather—but the insurance money belongs to Mama. Picking on me is not going to make her give it to you to invest in any liquor stores—*(Underbreath, dropping into a chair)*—and I for one say, God bless Mama for that!

WALTER *(To* RUTH*)* See—did you hear? Did you hear!

RUTH Honey, please go to work.

WALTER Nobody in this house is ever going to understand me.

BENEATHA Because you're a nut.

WALTER Who's a nut?

BENEATHA You—you are a nut. Thee is mad, boy.

WALTER *(Looking at his wife and his sister from the door, very sadly)* The world's most backward race of people, and that's a fact.

BENEATHA *(Turning slowly in her chair)* And then there are all those prophets who would lead us out of the wilderness—(WALTER *slams out of the house)*—into the swamps!

RUTH Bennie, why you always gotta be pickin' on your brother? Can't you be a little sweeter sometimes? *Door opens.* WALTER *walks in)*

WALTER *(To Ruth)* I need some money for carfare.

RUTH *(Looks at him, then warms; teasing, but tenderly)* Fifty cents? *(She goes to her bag and gets money)* Here, take a taxi.

*(*WALTER *exits.* MAMA *enters. She is a woman in her early sixties, full-bodied and strong. She is one of those women of a certain grace and beauty who wear it so unobtrusively that it takes a while to notice. Her dark-brown face is surrounded by the total whiteness of her hair, and, being a woman who has adjusted to many things in life and overcome many more, her face is full of strength. She has, we can see, wit and faith of a kind that keep her eyes lit and full of interest and expectancy. She is, in a word, a beautiful woman. Her bearing is perhaps most like the noble bearing of the women of the Hereros of Southwest Africa—rather as if she imagines that as she walks she still bears a basket or a vessel upon her head. Her speech, on the other hand, is as careless as her carriage is precise—she is inclined to slur everything—but her voice is perhaps not so much quiet as simply soft)*

MAMA Who that 'round here slamming doors at this hour?

(She crosses through the room, goes to the window, opens it, and brings in a feeble little plant growing doggedly in a small pot on the window sill. She feels the dirt and puts it back out)

RUTH That was Walter Lee. He and Bennie was at it again.

MAMA My children and they tempers. Lord, if this little old plant don't get more sun than it's been getting it ain't never going to see spring again. *(She turns from the window)* What's the matter with you this morning, Ruth? You looks right peaked. You aiming to iron all them things? Leave some for me. I'll get to 'em this afternoon. Bennie honey, it's too drafty for you to be sitting 'round half dressed. Where's your robe?

BENEATHA In the cleaners.

MAMA Well, go get mine and put it on.

BENEATHA I'm not cold, Mama, honest.

MAMA I know—but you so thin . . .

BENEATHA *(Irritably)* Mama, I'm not cold.

MAMA *(Seeing the make-down bed as* TRAVIS *has left it)* Lord have mercy, look at that poor bed. Bless his heart—he tries, don't he?

(She moves to the bed TRAVIS *has sloppily made up)*

RUTH No—he don't half try at all 'cause he knows you going to come along behind him and fix everything. That's just how come he don't know how to do nothing right now—you done spoiled that boy so.

MAMA Well—he's a little boy. Ain't supposed to know 'bout housekeeping. My baby, that's what he is. What you fix for his breakfast this morning?

RUTH *(Angrily)* I feed my son, Lena!

MAMA I ain't meddling—*(Underbreath; busy-bodyish)* I just noticed all last week he had cold cereal, and when it starts getting this chilly in the fall a child ought to have some hot grits or something when he goes out in the cold—

RUTH *(Furious)* I gave him hot oats—is that all right!

MAMA I ain't meddling. *(Pause)* Put a lot of nice butter on it? (RUTH *shoots her an angry look and does not reply)* He likes lots of butter.

RUTH *(Exasperated)* Lena—

MAMA *(To* BENEATHA. MAMA *is inclined to wander conversationally sometimes)* What was you and your brother fussing 'bout this morning?

BENEATHA It's not important, Mama.

(She gets up and goes to look out at the bathroom, which is apparently free, and she picks up her towels and rushes out)

MAMA What was they fighting about?

RUTH Now you know as well as I do.

MAMA *(Shaking her head)* Brother still worrying hisself sick about that money?

RUTH You know he is.

MAMA You had breakfast?

RUTH Some coffee.

MAMA Girl you better start eating and looking after yourself better. You almost thin as Travis.

RUTH Lena—

MAMA Un-hunh?

RUTH What are you going to do with it?

MAMA Now don't you start, child. It's too early in the morning to be talking about money. It ain't Christian.

RUTH It's just that he got his heart set on that store—

MAMA You mean that liquor store that Willy Harris want him to invest in?

RUTH Yes—

MAMA We ain't no business people, Ruth. We just plain working folks.

RUTH Ain't nobody business people till they go into business. Walter Lee say colored people ain't never going to start getting ahead till they start gambling on some different kinds of things in the world—investments and things.

MAMA What done got into you, girl? Walter Lee done finally sold you on investing.

RUTH No. Mama, something is happening between Walter and me. I don't know what it is—but he needs something—something I can't give him any more. He needs this chance, Lena.

MAMA *(Frowning deeply)* But liquor, honey—

RUTH Well—like Walter say—I spec people going to always be drinking themselves some liquor.

MAMA Well—whether they drinks it or not ain't none of my business. But whether I go into business selling it to 'em *is,* and I don't want that on my ledger this late in life. *(Stopping suddenly and studying her daughter-in-law)* Ruth Younger, what's the matter with you today? You look like you could fall over right there.

RUTH I'm tired.

MAMA Then you better stay home from work today.

RUTH I can't stay home. She'd be calling up the agency and screaming at them, "My girl didn't come in today—send me somebody! My girl didn't come in!" Oh, she just have a fit . . .

MAMA Well, let her have it. I'll just call her up and say you got the flu—

RUTH *(Laughing)* Why the flu?

MAMA 'Cause it sounds respectable to 'em. Something white people get, too. They know 'bout the flu. Otherwise they think you been cut up or something when you tell 'em you sick.

RUTH I got to go in. We need the money.

MAMA Somebody would of thought my children done all but starved to death the way they talk about money here late. Child, we got a great big old check coming tomorrow.

RUTH *(Sincerely, but also self-righteously)* Now that's your money. It ain't got nothing to do with me. We all feel like that—Walter and Bennie and me—even Travis.

MAMA *(Thoughtfully, and suddenly very far away)* Ten thousand dollars—

RUTH Sure is wonderful.

MAMA Ten thousand dollars.

RUTH You know what you should do, Miss Lena? You should take yourself a trip somewhere. To Europe or South America or someplace—

MAMA *(Throwing up her hands at the thought)* Oh, child!

RUTH I'm serious. Just pack up and leave! Go on away and enjoy yourself some. Forget about the family and have yourself a ball for once in your life—

MAMA *(Drily)* You sound like I'm just about ready to die. Who'd go with me? What I look like wandering 'round Europe by myself?

RUTH Shoot—these here rich white women do it all the time. They don't think nothing of packing up they suitcases and piling on one of them big steamships and—swoosh!—they gone, child.

MAMA Something always told me I wasn't no rich white woman.

RUTH Well—what are you going to do with it then?

MAMA I ain't rightly decided. *(Thinking. She speaks now with emphasis)* Some of it got to be put away for Beneatha and her schoolin'—and ain't nothing going to touch that part of it. Nothing. *(She waits several seconds, trying to make up her mind about something, and looks at* RUTH *a little tentatively before going on)* Been thinking that we maybe could meet the notes on a little old two-story somewhere, with a yard where Travis could play in the summertime, if we use part of the insurance for a down payment and everybody kind of pitch in. I could maybe take on a little day work again, few days a week—

RUTH *(Studying her mother-in-law furtively and concentrating on her ironing, anxious to encourage without seeming to)* Well, Lord knows, we've put enough rent into this here rat trap to pay for four houses by now . . .

MAMA *(Looking up at the words "rat trap" and then looking around and leaning back and sighing—in a suddenly reflective mood—)* "Rat trap"—yes, that's all it is. *(Smiling)* I remember just as well the day me and Big Walter moved in here. Hadn't been married but two weeks and wasn't planning on living here no more than a year. *(She shakes her head at the dissolved dream)* We was going to set away, little by little, don't you know, and buy a little place out in Morgan park. We had even picked out the house. *(Chuckling a little)* Looks right dumpy today. But Lord, child, you should know all the dreams I had 'bout buying that house and fixing it up and making me a little garden in the back—*(She waits and stops smiling)* And didn't none of it happen.

(Dropping her hands in a futile gesture)

RUTH *(Keeps her head down, ironing)* Yes, life can be a barrel of disappointments, sometimes.

MAMA Honey, Big Walter would come in here some nights back then and slump down on that couch there and just look at the rug, and look at me and look at the rug and then back at me—and I'd know he was down then . . . really down. *(After a second very long and thoughtful pause; she is seeing back to times that only she can see)* And then, Lord, when I lost that baby—little Claude—I almost thought I was going to lose Big Walter too. Oh, that man grieved hisself! He was one man to love his children.

RUTH Ain't nothin' can tear at you like losin' your baby.

MAMA I guess that's how come that man finally worked hisself to death like he done. Like he was fighting his own war with this here world that took his baby from him.

RUTH He sure was a fine man, all right. I always liked Mr. Younger.

MAMA Crazy 'bout his children! God knows there was plenty wrong with Walter Younger—hard-headed, mean, kind of wild with women—plenty wrong with him. But he sure loved his children. Always wanted them to have something—be something. That's where Brother gets all these notions, I reckon. Big Walter used to say, he'd get right wet in the eyes sometimes, lean his head back with the water standing in his eyes and say, "Seem like God didn't see fit to give the black man nothing but dreams—but He did give us children to make them dreams seem worth while." *(She smiles)* He could talk like that, don't you know.

RUTH Yes, he sure could. He was a good man, Mr. Younger.

MAMA Yes, a fine man—just couldn't never catch up with his dreams, that's all.

*(*BENEATHA *comes in, brushing her hair and looking up to the ceiling, where the sound of a vacuum cleaner has started up)*

BENEATHA What could be so dirty on that woman's rugs that she has to vacuum them every single day?

RUTH I wish certain young women 'round here who I could name would take inspiration about certain rugs in a certain apartment I could also mention.

BENEATHA *(Shrugging)* How much cleaning can a house need, for Christ's sakes.

MAMA *(Not liking the Lord's name used thus)* Bennie!

RUTH Just listen to her—just listen!

BENEATHA Oh, God!

MAMA If you use the Lord's name just one more time—

BENEATHA *(A bit of a whine)* Oh, Mama—

RUTH Fresh—just fresh as salt, this girl!

BENEATHA *(Drily)* Well—if the salt loses its savor—

MAMA Now that will do. I just ain't going to have you 'round here reciting the scriptures in vain—you hear me?

BENEATHA How did I manage to get on everybody's wrong side by just walking into a room?

RUTH If you weren't so fresh—

BENEATHA Ruth, I'm twenty years old.

MAMA What time you be home from school today?

BENEATHA Kind of late. *(With enthusiasm)* Madeline is going to start my guitar lessons today.

(MAMA *and* RUTH *look up with the same expression*)

MAMA Your *what* kind of lessons?
BENEATHA Guitar.
RUTH Oh, Father!
MAMA How come you done taken it in your mind to learn to play the guitar?
BENEATHA I just want to, that's all.
MAMA *(Smiling)* Lord, child, don't you know what to do with yourself? How long it going to be before you get tired of this now—like you got tired of that little play-acting group you joined last year? *(Looking at Ruth)* And what was it the year before that?
RUTH The horseback-riding club for which she bought that fifty-five-dollar riding habit that's been hanging in the closet ever since!
MAMA *(To* BENEATHA*)* Why you got to flit so from one thing to another, baby?
BENEATHA *(Sharply)* I just want to learn to play the guitar. Is there anything wrong with that?
MAMA Ain't nobody trying to stop you. I just wonders sometimes why you has to flit so from one thing to another all the time. You ain't never done nothing with all that camera equipment you brought home—
BENEATHA I don't flit! I—I experiment with different forms of expression—
RUTH Like riding a horse?
BENEATHA —People have to express themselves one way or another.
MAMA What is it you want to express?
BENEATHA *(Angrily)* Me! (MAMA *and* RUTH *look at each other and burst into raucous laughter)* Don't worry—I don't expect you to understand.
MAMA *(To change the subject)* Who you going out with tomorrow night?
BENEATHA *(With displeasure)* George Murchison again.
MAMA *(Pleased)* Oh—you getting a little sweet on him?
RUTH You ask me, this child ain't sweet on nobody but herself—*(Underbreath)* Express herself!

(They laugh)

BENEATHA Oh—I like George all right, Mama. I mean I like him enough to go out with him and stuff, but—
RUTH *(For devilment)* What does *and stuff* mean?
BENEATHA Mind your own business.
MAMA Stop picking at her now, Ruth. *(A thoughtful pause, and then a suspicious sudden look at her daughter as she turns in her chair for emphasis)* What *does* it mean?
BENEATHA *(Wearily)* Oh, I just mean I couldn't ever really be serious about George. He's—he's so shallow.
RUTH Shallow—what do you mean he's shallow? He's *Rich!*
MAMA Hush, Ruth.
BENEATHA I know he's rich. He knows he's rich, too.
RUTH Well—what other qualities a man got to have to satisfy you, little girl?
BENEATHA You wouldn't even begin to understand. Anybody who married Walter could not possibly understand.
MAMA *(Outraged)* What kind of way is that to talk about your brother?

BENEATHA Brother is a flip—let's face it.
MAMA *(To* RUTH, *helplessly)* What's a flip?
RUTH *(Glad to add kindling)* She's saying he's crazy.
BENEATHA Not crazy. Brother isn't really crazy yet—he—he's an elaborate neurotic.
MAMA Hush your mouth!
BENEATHA As for George. Well. George looks good—he's got a beautiful car and he takes me to nice places and, as my sister-in-law says, he is probably the richest boy I will ever get to know and I even like him sometimes—but if the Youngers are sitting around waiting to see if their little Bennie is going to tie up the family with the Murchisons, they are wasting their time.
RUTH You mean you wouldn't marry George Murchison if he asked you someday? That pretty, rich thing? Honey, I knew you was odd—
BENEATHA No I would not marry him if all I felt for him was what I feel now. Besides, George's family wouldn't really like it.
MAMA Why not?
BENEATHA Oh, Mama—The Murchisons are honest-to-God-real-*live*-rich colored people, and the only people in the world who are more snobbish than rich white people are rich colored people. I thought everybody knew that. I've met Mrs. Murchison. She's a scene!
MAMA You must not dislike people 'cause they well off, honey.
BENEATHA Why not? It makes just as much sense as disliking people 'cause they are poor, and lots of people do that.
RUTH *(A wisdom-of-the-ages manner. To* MAMA*)* Well, she'll get over some of this—
BENEATHA Get over it? What are you talking about, Ruth? Listen, I'm going to be a doctor. I'm not worried about who I'm going to marry yet—if I ever get married.
MAMA *and* RUTH *If!*
MAMA Now, Bennie—
BENEATHA Oh, I probably will . . . but first I'm going to be a doctor, and George, for one, still thinks that's pretty funny. I couldn't be bothered with that. I am going to be a doctor and everybody around here better understand that!
MAMA *(Kindly)* 'Course you going to be a doctor, honey, God willing.
BENEATHA *(Drily)* God hasn't got a thing to do with it.
MAMA Beneatha—that just wasn't necessary.
BENEATHA Well—neither is God. I get sick of hearing about God.
MAMA Beneatha!
BENEATHA I mean it! I'm just tired of hearing about God all the time. What has He got to do with anything? Does he pay tuition?
MAMA You 'bout to get your fresh little jaw slapped!
RUTH That's just what she needs, all right!
BENEATHA Why? Why can't I say what I want to around here, like everybody else?
MAMA It don't sound nice for a young girl to say things like that—you wasn't brought up that way. Me and your father went to trouble to get you and Brother to church every Sunday.
BENEATHA Mama, you don't understand. It's all a matter of ideas, and God is just one idea I don't accept. It's not important. I am not going out and be immoral or commit crimes because I don't believe in God. I don't even think about it. It's just that I get tired of Him getting credit for all the things the human race achieves through

its own stubborn effort. There simply is no blasted God—there is only man and it is he who makes miracles!

*(*MAMA *absorbs this speech, studies her daughter and rises slowly and crosses to* BENEATHA *and slaps her powerfully across the face. After, there is only silence and the daughter drops her eyes from her mother's face, and* MAMA *is very tall before her)*

MAMA Now—you say after me, in my mother's house there is still God. *(There is a long pause and* BENEATHA *stares at the floor wordlessly.* MAMA *repeats the phrase with precision and cool emotion)* In my mother's house there is still God.

BENEATHA In my mother's house there is still God.

(A long pause)

MAMA *(Walking away from* BENEATHA, *too disturbed for triumphant posture. Stopping and turning back to her daughter)* There are some ideas we ain't going to have in this house. Not long as I am at the head of this family.

BENEATHA Yes, ma'am.

*(*MAMA *walks out of the room)*

RUTH *(Almost gently, with profound understanding)* You think you a woman, Bennie—but you still a little girl. What you did was childish—so you got treated like a child.

BENEATHA I see. *(Quietly)* I also see that everybody thinks it's all right for Mama to be a tyrant. But all the tyranny in the world will never put a God in the heavens!

(She picks up her books and goes out)

RUTH *(Goes to* MAMA*'s door)* She said she was sorry.

MAMA *(Coming out, going to her plant)* They frightens me, Ruth. My children.

RUTH You got good children, Lena. They just a little off sometimes—but they're good.

MAMA No—there's something come down between me and them that don't let us understand each other and I don't know what it is. One done almost lost his mind thinking 'bout money all the time and the other done commence to talk about things I can't seem to understand in no form or fashion. What is it that's changing, Ruth?

RUTH *(Soothingly, older than her years)* Now . . . you taking it all too seriously. You just got strong-willed children and it takes a strong woman like you to keep 'em in hand.

MAMA *(Looking at her plant and sprinkling a little water on it)* They spirited all right, my children. Got to admit they got spirit—Bennie and Walter. Like this little old plant that ain't never had enough sunshine or nothing—and look at it . . .

(She has her back to RUTH, *who has had to stop ironing and lean against something and put the back of her hand to her forehead)*

RUTH *(Trying to keep* MAMA *from noticing)* You . . . sure . . . loves that little old thing, don't you? . . .

MAMA Well, I always wanted me a garden like I used to see sometimes at the back of the houses down home. This plant is close as I ever got to having one. *(She looks out of the window as she replaces the plant)* Lord, ain't nothing as dreary as the view from this window on a dreary day, is there? Why ain't you singing this morning, Ruth? Sing that "No Ways Tired." That song always lifts me up so—*(She turns at last to see that* RUTH *has slipped quietly into a chair, in a state of semiconsciousness)* Ruth! Ruth honey—what's the matter with you . . . Ruth!

CURTAIN

Scene II

It is the following morning; a Saturday morning, and house cleaning is in progress at the YOUNGERS. *Furniture has been shoved hither and yon and* MAMA *is giving the kitchen-area walls a washing down.* BENEATHA, *in dungarees, with a handkerchief tied around her face, is spraying insecticide into the cracks in the walls. As they work, the radio is on and a Southside disk-jockey program is inappropriately filling the house with a rather exotic saxophone blues.* TRAVIS, *the sole idle one, is leaning on his arms, looking out of the window.*

TRAVIS Grandmama, that stuff Bennie is using smells awful. Can I go downstairs, please?

MAMA Did you get all them chores done already? I ain't seen you doing much.

TRAVIS Yes'm—finished early. Where did Mama go this morning?

MAMA *(Looking at* BENEATHA*)* She had to go on a little errand.

TRAVIS Where?

MAMA To tend to her business.

TRAVIS Can I go outside then?

MAMA Oh, I guess so. You better stay right in front of the house, though . . . and keep a good lookout for the postman.

TRAVIS Yes'm. *(He starts out and decides to give his* AUNT BENEATHA *a good swat on the legs as he passes her)* Leave them poor little old cockroaches alone, they ain't bothering you none.

(He runs as she swings the spray gun at him both viciously and playfully. walter enters from the bedroom and goes to the phone)

MAMA Look out there, girl, before you be spilling some of that stuff on that child!

TRAVIS *(Teasing)* That's right—look out now!

(He exits)

BENEATHA *(Drily)* I can't imagaine that it would hurt him—it has never hurt the roaches.

MAMA Well, little boys' hides ain't as tough as Southside roaches.

WALTER *(Into phone)* Hello—Let me talk to Willy Harris.

MAMA You better get over there behind the bureau. I seen one marching out of there like Napoleon yesterday.

WALTER Hello, Willy? It ain't come yet. It'll be here in a few minutes. Did the lawyer give you the papers?

BENEATHA There's really only one way to get rid of them, Mama—

MAMA How?

BENEATHA Set fire to this building.

WALTER Good. Good. I'll be right over.

BENEATHA Where did Ruth go, Walter?

WALTER I don't know.

(He exits abruptly)

BENEATHA Mama, where did Ruth go?

MAMA *(Looking at her with meaning)* To the doctor, I think.

BENEATHA The doctor? What's the matter? *(They exchange glances)* You don't think—

MAMA *(With her sense of drama)* Now I ain't saying what I think. But I ain't never been wrong 'bout a woman neither.

(The phone rings)

BENEATHA *(At the phone)* Hay-lo . . . *(Pause, and a moment of recognition)* Well—when did you get back! . . . And how was it? . . . Of course I've missed you—in my way . . . This morning? No . . . house cleaning and all that and Mama hates it if I let people come over when the house is like this . . . You *have?* Well, that's different . . . What is it—Oh, what the hell, come on over . . . Right, see you then.

(She hangs up)

MAMA *(Who has listened vigorously, as is her habit)* Who is that you inviting over here with this house looking like this? You ain't got the pride you was born with!

BENEATHA Asagai doesn't care how houses look, Mama—he's an intellectual.

MAMA *Who?*

BENEATHA Asagai—Joseph Asagai. He's an African boy I met on campus. He's been studying in Canada all summer.

MAMA What's his name?

BENEATHA Asagai, Joseph. Ah-sah-guy . . . He's from Nigeria.

MAMA Oh, that's the little country that was founded by slaves way back . . .

BENEATHA No, Mama—that's Liberia.

MAMA I don't think I never met no African before.

BENEATHA Well, do me a favor and don't ask him a whole lot of ignorant questions about Africans. I mean, do they wear clothes and all that—

MAMA Well, now, I guess if you think we so ignorant 'round here maybe you shouldn't bring your friends here—

BENEATHA It's just that people ask such crazy things. All anyone seems to know about when it comes to Africa is Tarzan—

MAMA *(Indignantly)* Why should I know anything about Africa?

BENEATHA Why do you give money at church for the missionary work?

MAMA Well, that's to help save people.

BENEATHA You mean save them from *heathenism*—

MAMA *(Innocently)* Yes.

BENEATHA I'm afraid they need more salvation from the British and the French.

*(*RUTH *comes in forlornly and pulls off her coat with dejection. They both turn to look at her)*

RUTH *(Dispiritedly)* Well, I guess from all the happy faces—everybody knows.

BENEATHA You pregnant?

MAMA Lord have mercy, I sure hope it's a little old girl. Travis ought to have a sister.

*(*BENEATHA *and* RUTH *give her a hopeless look for this grandmotherly enthusiasm)*

BENEATHA How far along are you?

RUTH Two months.

BENEATHA Did you mean to? I mean did you plan it or was it an accident?

MAMA What do you know about planning or not planning?

BENEATHA Oh, Mama.

RUTH *(Wearily)* She's twenty years old, Lena.

BENEATHA Did you plan it, Ruth?

RUTH Mind your own business.

BENEATHA It is my business—where is he going to live, on the *roof? (There is silence following the remark as the three women react to the sense of it)* Gee—I didn't mean that, Ruth, honest. Gee, I don't feel like that at all. I—I think it is wonderful.

RUTH *(Dully)* Wonderful.

BENEATHA Yes—really.

MAMA *(Looking at* RUTH, *worried)* Doctor say everything going to be all right?

RUTH *(Far away)* Yes—she says everything is going to be fine . . .

MAMA *(Immediately suspicious)* "She"—What doctor you went to?

*(*RUTH *folds over, near hysteria)*

MAMA *(Worriedly hovering over* RUTH*)* Ruth honey—what's the matter with you—you sick?

*(*RUTH *has her fists clenched on her thighs and is fighting hard to suppress a scream that seems to be rising in her)*

BENEATHA What's the matter with her, Mama?

MAMA *(Working her fingers in* RUTH'S *shoulder to relax her)* She be all right. Women gets right depressed sometimes when they get her way. *(Speaking softly, expertly, rapidly)* Now you just relax. That's right . . . just lean back, don't think 'bout nothing at all . . . nothing at all—

RUTH I'm all right . . .

(The glassy-eyed look melts and then she collapses into a fit of heavy sobbing. The bell rings)

BENEATHA Oh, my God—that must be Asagai.

MAMA *(To* RUTH*)* Come on now, honey. You need to lie down and rest awhile . . . then have some nice hot food.

(They exit, RUTH'S *weight on her mother-in-law.* BENEATHA, *herself profoundly disturbed, opens the door to admit a rather dramatic-looking young man with a large package)*

ASAGAI Hello, Alaiyo—

BENEATHA *(Holding the door open and regarding him with pleasure)* Hello . . . *(Long pause)* Well—come in. And please excuse everything. My mother was very upset about my letting anyone come here with the place like this.

ASAGAI *(Coming into the room)* You look disturbed too . . . Is something wrong?

BENEATHA *(Still at the door, absently)* Yes . . . we've all got acute ghetto-itus. *(She smiles and comes toward him, finding a cigarette and sitting)* So—sit down! How was Canada?

ASAGAI *(A sophisticate)* Canadian.

BENEATHA *(Looking at him)* I'm very glad you are back.

ASAGAI *(Looking back at her in turn)* Are you really?

BENEATHA Yes—very.

ASAGAI Why—you were quite glad when I went away. What happened?

BENEATHA You went away.

ASAGAI Ahhhhhhhh.

BENEATHA Before—you wanted to be so serious before there was time.

ASAGAI How much time must there be before one knows what one feels?

BENEATHA *(Stalling this particular conversation. Her hands pressed together, in a deliberately childish gesture)* What did you bring me?

ASAGAI *(Handing her the package)* Open it and see.

BENEATHA *(Eagerly opening the package and drawing out some records and the colorful robes of a Nigerian woman)* Oh, Asagai! . . . You got them for me! . . . How beautiful . . . and the records too! *(She lifts out the robes and runs to the mirror with them and holds the drapery up in front of herself)*

ASAGAI *(Coming to her at the mirror)* I shall have to teach you how to drape it properly. *(He flings the material about her for the moment and stands back to look at her)* Ah—*Oh-pay-gay-day, oh-gbah-mu-shay. (A Yoruba exclamation for admiration)* You wear it well . . . very well . . . mutilated hair and all.

BENEATHA *(Turning suddenly)* My hair—what's wrong with my hair?

ASAGAI *(Shrugging)* Were you born with it like that?

BENEATHA *(Reaching up to touch it)* No . . . of course not.

(She looks back to the mirror, disturbed)

ASAGAI *(Smiling)* How then?

BENEATHA You know perfectly well how . . . as crinkly as yours . . . that's how.

ASAGAI And it is ugly to you that way?

BENEATHA *(Quickly)* Oh, no—not ugly . . . *(More slowly, apologetically)* But it's so hard to manage when it's, well—raw.

ASAGAI And so to accommodate that—you mutilate it every week?

BENEATHA It's not mutilation!

ASAGAI *(Laughing aloud at her seriousness)* Oh . . . please! I am only teasing you because you are so very serious about these things. *(He stands back from her and folds his arms across his chest as he watches her pulling at her hair and frowning in the mirror)* Do you remember the first time you met me at school? . . . *(He laughs)* You came up to me and you said—and I thought you were the most serious little thing I had ever seen—you said: *(He imitates her)* "Mr. Asagai—I want very much to talk with you. About Africa. You see, Mr. Asagai, I am looking for my *identity!*"

(He laughs)

BENEATHA *(Turning to him, not laughing)* Yes—

(Her face is quizzical, profoundly disturbed)

ASAGAI *(Still teasing and reaching out and taking her face in his hands and turning her profile to him)* Well . . . it is true that this is not so much a profile of a Hollywood queen as perhaps a queen of the Nile—*(A mock dismissal of the importance of the question)* But what does it matter? Assimilationism is so popular in your country.

BENEATHA *(Wheeling, passionately, sharply)* I am not an assimilationist!

ASAGAI *(The protest hangs in the room for a moment and* ASAGAI *studies her, his laughter fading)* Such a serious one. *(There is a pause)* So—you like the robes? You must take excellent care of them—they are from my sister's personal wardrobe.

BENEATHA *(With incredulity)* You—you sent all the way home—for me?

ASAGAI *(With charm)* For you—I would do much more . . . Well, that is what I came for. I must go.

BENEATHA Will you call me Monday?

ASAGAI Yes . . . We have a great deal to talk about. I mean about identity and time and all that.

BENEATHA Time?

ASAGAI Yes. About how much time one needs to know what one feels.

BENEATHA You never understood that there is more than one kind of feeling which can exist between a man and a woman—or, at least, there should be.

ASAGAI *(Shaking his head negatively but gently)* No. Between a man and a woman there need be only one kind of feeling. I have that for you . . . Now even . . . right this moment . . .

BENEATHA I know—and by itself—it won't do. I can find that anywhere.

ASAGAI For a woman it should be enough.

BENEATHA I know—because that's what it says in all the novels that men write. But it isn't. Go ahead and laugh—but I'm not interested in being someone's little episode in America or—*(With feminine vengeance)*—one of them! *(*ASAGAI *has burst into laughter again)* That's funny as hell, huh!

ASAGAI It's just that every American girl I have known has said that to me. White—black—in this you are all the same. And the same speech, too!

BENEATHA *(Angrily)* Yuk, yuk, yuk!

ASAGAI It's how you can be sure that the world's most liberated women are not liberated at all. You all talk about it too much!

*(*MAMA *enters and is immediately all social charm because of the presence of a guest)*

BENEATHA Oh—Mama—this is Mr. Asagai.

MAMA How do you do?

ASAGAI *(Total politeness to an elder)* How do you do, Mrs. Younger. Please forgive me for coming at such an outrageous hour on a Saturday.

MAMA Well, you are quite welcome. I just hope you understand that our house don't always look like this. *(Chatterish)* You must come again. I would love to hear all about—*(Not sure of the name)*—your country. I think it's so sad the way our American Negroes don't know nothing about Africa 'cept Tarzan and all that. And all that money they pour into these churches when they ought to be helping you people over there drive out them French and Englishmen done taken away your land.

(The mother flashes a slightly superior look at her daughter upon completion of the recitation)

ASAGAI *(Taken aback by this sudden and acutely unrelated expression of sympathy)* Yes . . . yes . . .

MAMA *(Smiling at him suddenly and relaxing and looking him over)* How many miles is it from here to where you come from?

ASAGAI Many thousands.

MAMA *(Looking at him as she would* WALTER*)* I bet you don't half look after yourself, being away from your mama either. I spec you better come 'round here from time to time and get yourself some decent homecooked meals . . .

ASAGAI *(Moved)* Thank you. Thank you very much. *(They are all quiet, then—)* Well . . . I must go, I will call you Monday, Alaiyo.

MAMA What's that he call you?

ASAGAI Oh—"Alaiyo." I hope you don't mind. It is what you would call a nickname, I think. It is a Yoruba word. I am a Yoruba.

MAMA *(Looking at* BENEATHA*)* I—I thought he was from—

ASAGAI *(Understanding)* Nigeria is my country. Yoruba is my tribal origin—

BENEATHA You didn't tell us what Alaiyo means . . . for all I know, you might be calling me Little Idiot or something . . .

ASAGAI Well . . . let me see . . . I do not know how just to explain it . . . The sense of a thing can be so different when it changes languages.

BENEATHA You're evading.

ASAGAI No—really it is difficult . . . *(Thinking)* It means . . . it means One for Whom Bread—Food—Is Not Enough. *(He looks at her)* Is that all right?

BENEATHA *(Understanding, softly)* Thank you.

MAMA *(Looking from one to the other and not understanding any of it)* Well . . . that's nice . . . You must come see us again—Mr.—

ASAGAI Ah-sah-guy . . .

MAMAZ Yes . . . Do come again.

ASAGAI Good-bye.

(He exits)

MAMA *(After him)* Lord, that's a pretty thing just went out here! *(Insinuatingly, to her daughter)* Yes, I guess I see why we done commence to get so interested in Africa 'round here. Missionaries my aunt Jenny!

(She exits)

BENEATHA Oh, Mama! . . .

(She picks up the Nigerian dress and holds it up to her in front of the mirror again. She sets the headdress on haphazardly and then notices her hair again and clutches at it and then replaces the headdress and frowns at herself. Then she starts to wriggle in front of the mirror as she thinks a Nigerian woman might. TRAVIS *enters and regards her)*

TRAVIS You cracking up?

BENEATHA Shut up.

(She pulls the headdress off and looks at herself in the mirror and clutches at her hair again and squinches her eyes as if trying to imagine something. Then, suddenly, she gets her raincoat and kerchief and hurriedly prepares for going out)

MAMA *(Coming back into the room)* She's resting now. Travis, baby, run next door and ask Miss Johnson to please let me have a little kitchen cleanser. This here can is empty as Jacob's kettle.

TRAVIS I just came in.

MAMA Do as you told. *(He exits and she looks at her daughter)* Where you going?

BENEATHA *(Halting at the door)* To become a queen of the Nile!

(She exits in a breathless blaze of glory. RUTH *appears in the bedroom doorway)*

MAMA Who told you to get up?

RUTH Ain't nothing wrong with me to be lying in no bed for. Where did Bennie go?

MAMA *(Drumming her fingers)* Far as I could make out—to Egypt. *(*RUTH *just looks at her)* What time is it getting to?

RUTH Ten twenty. And the mailman going to ring that bell this morning just like he done every morning for the last umpteen years.

*(*TRAVIS *comes in with the cleanser can)*

TRAVIS She say to tell you that she don't have much.

MAMA *(Angrily)* Lord, some people I could name sure is tight-fisted! *(Directing her grandson)* Mark two cans of cleanser down on the list there. If she that hard up for kitchen cleanser, I sure don't want to forget to get her none!

RUTH Lena—maybe the woman is just short on cleanser—

MAMA *(Not listening)* —Much baking powder as she done borrowed from me all these years, she could of done gone into the baking business!

(The bell sounds suddenly and sharply and all three are stunned—serious and silent—mid-speech. In spite of all the other conversations and distractions of the morning, this is what they have been waiting for, even TRAVIS, *who looks helplessly from his mother to his grandmother.* RUTH *is the first to come to life again)*

RUTH *(To* TRAVIS*)* Get down them steps, boy!

*(*TRAVIS *snaps to life and flies out to get the mail)*

MAMA *(Her eyes wide, her hand to her breast)* You mean it done really come?

RUTH *(Excited)* Oh, Miss Lena!

MAMA *(Collecting herself)* Well . . . I don't know what we all so excited about 'round here for. We known it was coming for months.

RUTH That's a whole lot different from having it come and being able to hold it in your hands . . . a piece of paper worth ten thousand dollars . . . *(*TRAVIS *bursts back into the room.* He *holds the envelope high above his head, like a little dancer, his face is radiant and he is breathless. He moves to his grandmother with sudden slow ceremony and puts the envelope into her hands. She accepts it, and then merely holds it and looks at it)* Come on! Open it . . . Lord have mercy, I wish Walter Lee was here!

TRAVIS Open it, Grandmama!

MAMA *(Staring at it)* Now you all be quiet. It's just a check.

RUTH Open it . . .

MAMA *(Still staring at it)* Now don't act silly . . . We ain't never been no people to act silly 'bout no money—

RUTH *(Swiftly)* We ain't never had none before—*open it!*

*(*MAMA *finally makes a good strong tear and pulls out the thin blue slice of paper and inspects it closely. The boy and his mother study it raptly over* MAMA's *shoulders)*

MAMA *Travis! (She is counting off with doubt)* Is that the right number of zeros.

TRAVIS Yes'm . . . ten thousand dollars. Gaalee, Grandmama, you rich.

MAMA *(She holds the check away from her, still looking at it. Slowly her face sobers into a mask of unhappiness)* Ten thousand dollars. *(She hands it to* RUTH*)* Put it away somewhere, Ruth. *(She does not look at* RUTH; *her eyes seem to be seeing something somewhere very far off)* Ten thousand dollars they give you. Ten thousand dollars.

TRAVIS *(To his mother, sincerely)* What's the matter with Grandmama—don't she want to be rich?

RUTH *(Distractedly)* You go on out and play now, baby. *(*TRAVIS *exits.* MAMA *starts wiping dishes absently, humming intently to herself.* RUTH *turns to her, with kind exasperation)* You've gone and got yourself upset.

MAMA *(Not looking at her)* I spec if it wasn't for you all . . . I would just put that money away or give it to the church or something.

RUTH Now what kind of talk is that. Mr. Younger would just be plain mad if he could hear you talking foolish like that.

MAMA *(Stopping and staring off)* Yes . . . he sure would. *(Sighing)* We got enough to do with that money, all right. *(She halts then, and turns and looks at her daughter-in-law hard;* RUTH *avoids her eyes and* MAMA *wipes her hands with finality and starts to speak firmly to* RUTH*)* Where did you go today, girl?

RUTH To the doctor.

MAMA *(Impatiently)* Now, Ruth . . . you know better than that. Old Doctor Jones is strange enough in his way but there ain't nothing 'bout him make somebody slip and call him "she"—like you done this morning.

RUTH Well, that's what happened—my tongue slipped.

MAMA You went to see that woman, didn't you?

RUTH *(Defensively, giving herself away)* What woman you talking about?

MAMA *(Angrily)* That woman who—

*(*WALTER *enters in great excitement)*

WALTER Did it come?

MAMA *(Quietly)* Can't you give people a Christian greeting before you start asking about money?

WALTER *(To* RUTH*)* Did it come? *(*RUTH *unfolds the check and lays it quietly before him, watching him intently with thoughts of her own.* WALTER *sits down and grasps it close and counts off the zeros)* Ten thousand dollars—*(He turns suddenly, frantically to his mother and draws some papers out of his breast pocket)* Mama—look. Old Willy Harris put everything on paper—

MAMA Son—I think you ought to talk to your wife . . . I'll go on out and leave you alone if you want—

WALTER I can talk to her later—Mama, look—

MAMA Son—

WALTER WILL SOMEBODY PLEASE LISTEN TO ME TODAY!

MAMA *(Quietly)* I don't 'low no yellin' in this house, Walter Lee, and you know it—*(*WALTER *stares at them in frustration and starts to speak several times)* And there ain't going to be no investing in no liquor stores. I don't aim to have to speak on that again.

(A long pause)

WALTER Oh—so you don't aim to have to speak on that again? So *you* have decided . . . *(Crumpling his papers)* Well, *you* tell that to my boy tonight when you put him to sleep on the living-room couch . . . *(Turning to* MAMA *and speaking directly to her)* Yeah—and tell it to my wife, Mama, tomorrow when she has to go out of here to look after somebody else's kids. And tell it to *me,* Mama, every time we need a new pair of curtains and I have to watch *you* go out and work in somebody's kitchen. Yeah, you tell me then!

*(*WALTER *starts out)*

RUTH Where you going?
WALTER I'm going out!
RUTH Where?
WALTER Just out of this house somewhere—
RUTH *(Getting her coat)* I'll come too.
WALTER I don't want you to come!
RUTH I got something to talk to you about, Walter.
WALTER That's too bad.
MAMA *(Still quietly)* Walter Lee—*(She waits and he finally turns and looks at her)* Sit down.
WALTER I'm a grown man, Mama.
MAMA Ain't nobody said you wasn't grown. But you still in my house and my presence. And as long as you are—you'll talk to your wife civil. Now sit down.
RUTH *(Suddenly)* Oh, let him go on out and drink himself to death! He makes me sick to my stomach! *(She flings her coat against him)*
WALTER *(Violently)* And you turn mine too, baby! *(*RUTH *goes into their bedroom and slams the door behind her)* That was my greatest mistake—
MAMA *(Still quietly)* Walter, what is the matter with you?
WALTER Matter with me? Ain't nothing the matter with *me!*
MAMA Yes there is. Something eating you up like a crazy man. Something more than me not giving you this money. The past few years I been watching it happen to you. You get all nervous acting and kind of wild in the eyes—*(*WALTER *jumps up impatiently at her words)* I said sit there now, I'm talking to you!
WALTER Mama—I don't need no nagging at me today.
MAMA Seem like you getting to a place where you always tied up in some kind of knot about something. But if anybody ask you 'bout it you just yell at 'em and bust out the house and go out and drink somewheres. Walter Lee, people can't live with that. Ruth's a good, patient girl in her way—but you getting to be too much. Boy, don't make the mistake of driving that girl away from you.
WALTER Why—what she do for me?
MAMA She loves you.
WALTER Mama—I'm going out. I want to go off somewhere and be by myself for a while.
MAMA I'm sorry 'bout your liquor store, son. It just wasn't the thing for us to do. That's what I want to tell you about—
WALTER I got to go out, Mama—

(He rises)

MAMA It's dangerous, son.
WALTER What's dangerous?
MAMA When a man goes outside his home to look for peace.

WALTER *(Beseechingly)* Then why can't there never be no peace in this house then?

MAMA You done found it in some other house?

WALTER No—there ain't no woman! Why do women always think there's a woman somewhere when a man gets restless. *(Coming to her)* Mama—Mama—I want so many things . . .

MAMA Yes, son—

WALTER I want so many things that they are driving me kind of crazy . . . Mama—look at me.

MAMA I'm looking at you. You a good-looking boy. You got a job, a nice wife, a fine boy and—

WALTER A job. *(Looks at her)* Mama, a job? I open and close car doors all day long. I drive a man around in his limousine and I say, "Yes, sir; no, sir; very good, sir; shall I take the Drive, sir?" Mama, that ain't no kind of job . . . that ain't nothing at all. *(Very quietly)* Mama, I don't know if I can make you understand.

MAMA Understand what, baby?

WALTER *(Quietly)* Sometimes it's like I can see the future stretched out in front of me—just plain as day. The future, Mama. Hanging over there at the edge of my days. Just waiting for me—a big, looming blank space—full of *nothing.* Just waiting for *me. (Pause)* Mama—sometimes when I'm downtown and I pass them cool, quiet-looking restaurants where them white boys are sitting back and talking 'bout things . . . sitting there turning deals worth millions of dollars . . . sometimes I see guys don't look much older than me—

MAMA Son—how come you talk so much 'bout money?

WALTER *(With immense passion)* Because it is life, Mama!

MAMA *(Quietly)* Oh—*(Very quietly)* So now it's life. Money is life. Once upon a time freedom used to be life—now it's money. I guess the world really do change . . .

WALTER No—it was always money, Mama. We just didn't know about it.

MAMA No . . . something has changed. *(She looks at him)* You something new, boy. In my time we was worried about not being lynched and getting to the North if we could and how to stay alive and still have a pinch of dignity too . . . Now here come you and Beneatha—talking 'bout things we ain't never even thought about hardly, me and your daddy. You ain't satisfied or proud of nothing we done. I mean that you had a home; that we kept you out of trouble till you was grown; that you don't have to ride to work on the back of nobody's streetcar—You my children—but how different we done become.

WALTER You just don't understand, Mama, you just don't understand.

MAMA Son—do you know your wife is expecting another baby? (WALTER *stands, stunned, and absorbs what his mother has said)* That's what she wanted to talk to you about. (WALTER *sinks down into a chair)* This ain't for me to be telling—but you ought to know. *(She waits)* I think Ruth is thinking 'bout getting rid of that child.

WALTER *(Slowly understanding)* No—no—Ruth wouldn't do that.

MAMA When the world gets ugly enough—a woman will do anything for her family. The part that's already living.

WALTER You don't know Ruth, Mama, if you think she would do that.

(RUTH *opens the bedroom door and stands there a little limp)*

RUTH *(Beaten)* Yes I would too, Walter. *(Pause)* I gave her a five-dollar down payment.

(There is total silence as the man stares at his wife and the mother stares at her son)

MAMA *(Presently)* Well—*(Tightly)* Well—son, I'm waiting to hear you say something . . . I'm waiting to hear how you be your father's son. Be the man he was . . . *(Pause)* Your wife say she going to destroy your child. And I'm waiting to hear you talk like him and say we a people who give children life, not who destroys them—*(She rises)* I'm waiting to see you stand up and look like your daddy and say we done give up one baby to poverty and that we ain't going to give up nary another one . . . I'm waiting.

WALTER Ruth—

MAMA If you a son of mine, tell her! (WALTER *turns, looks at her and can say nothing. She continues, bitterly)* You . . . you are a disgrace to your father's memory. Somebody get me my hat.

CURTAIN

Act II

Scene I

Time: Later the same day.

At rise: RUTH *is ironing again. She has the radio going. Presently* BENEATHA'S *bedroom door opens and* RUTH'S *mouth falls and she puts down the iron in fascination.*

RUTH What have we got on tonight!

BENEATHA *(Emerging grandly from the doorway so that we can see her thoroughly robed in the costume Asagai brought)* You are looking at what a well-dressed Nigerian woman wears—*(She parades for* RUTH, *her hair completely hidden by the headdress; she is coquettishly fanning herself with an ornate oriental fan, mistakenly more like Butterfly than any Nigerian that ever was)* Isn't it beautiful? *(She promenades to the radio and, with an arrogant flourish, turns off the good loud blues that is playing)* Enough of this assimilationist junk! (RUTH *follows her with her eyes as she goes to the phonograph and puts on a record and turns and waits ceremoniously for the music to come up. Then, with a shout—)* OCOMOGOSIAY!

(RUTH *jumps. The music comes up, a lovely Nigerian melody.* BENEATHA *listens, enraptured, her eyes far away—"back to the past." She begins to dance.* RUTH *is dumfounded)*

RUTH What kind of dance is that?

BENEATHA A folk dance.

RUTH *(Pearl Bailey)* What kind of folks do that, honey?

BENEATHA It's from Nigeria. It's a dance of welcome.

RUTH Who you welcoming?

BENEATHA The men back to the village.

RUTH Where they been?

BENEATHA How should I know—out hunting or something. Anyway, they are coming back now . . .

RUTH Well, that's good.

BENEATHA *(With the record)*

Alundi, alundi
Alundi alunya
Jop pu a jeepua
Ang gu soooooooooo

Ai yai yae . . .
Ayehaye—alundi . . .

*(*WALTER *comes in during this performance; he has obviously been drinking. He leans against the door heavily and watches his sister, at first with distaste. Then his eyes look off—"back to the past"—as he lifts both his fists to the roof, screaming)*

WALTER YEAH . . . AND ETHIOPIA STRETCH FORTH HER HANDS AGAIN! . . .

RUTH *(Drily, looking at him)* Yes—and Africa sure is claiming her own tonight. *(She gives them both up and starts ironing again)*

WALTER *(All in a drunken, dramatic shout)* Shut up! . . . I'm digging them drums . . . them drums move me! . . . *(He makes his weaving way to his wife's face and leans in close to her)* In my *heart of hearts—(He thumps his chest)*—I am much warrior!

RUTH *(Without even looking up)* In your heart of hearts you are much drunkard.

WALTER *(Coming away from her and starting to wander around the room, shouting)* Me and Jomo . . . *(Intently, in his sister's face. She has stopped dancing to watch him in this unknown mood)* That's my man, Kenyatta. *(Shouting and thumping his chest)* FLAMING SPEAR! HOT DAMN! *(He is suddenly in possession of an imaginary spear and actively spearing enemies all over the room) OCOMOGOSIAY* . . . THE LION IS WAKING . . . OWIMOWEH! *(He pulls his shirt open and leaps up on a table and gestures with his spear. The bell rings.* RUTH *goes to answer)*

BENEATHA *(To encourage* WALTER, *thoroughly caught up with this side of him) OCOMOGOSIAY,* FLAMING SPEAR!

WALTER *(On the table, very far gone, his eyes pure glass sheets. He sees what we cannot, that he is a leader of his people, a great chief, a descendant of Chaka, and that the hour to march has come)* Listen, my black brothers—

BENEATHA OCOMOGOSIAY!

WALTER—Do you hear the waters rushing against the shores of the coastlands—

BENEATHA OCOMOGOSIAY!

WALTER—Do you hear the screeching of the cocks in yonder hills beyond where the chiefs meet in council for the coming of the mighty war—

BENEATHA OCOMOGOSIAY!

WALTER—Do you hear the beating of the wings of the birds flying low over the mountains and the low places of our land—

*(*RUTH *opens the door.* GEORGE MURCHISON *enters)*

BENEATHA OCOMOGOSIAY!

WALTER—Do you hear the singing of the women, singing the war songs of our fathers to the babies in the great houses . . . singing the sweet war songs? OH, DO YOU HEAR, MY BLACK BROTHERS!

BENEATHA *(Completely gone)* We hear you, Flaming Spear—

WALTER Telling us to prepare for the greatness of the time—*(To* GEORGE*)* Black Brother!

(He extends his hand for the fraternal clasp)

GEORGE Black Brother, hell!

RUTH *(Having had enough, and embarrassed for the family)* Beneatha, you got company—what's the matter with you? Walter Lee Younger, get down off that table and stop acting like a fool . . .

*(*WALTER *comes down off the table suddenly and makes a quick exit to the bathroom)*

RUTH He's had a little to drink . . . I don't know what her excuse is.

GEORGE *(To* BENEATHA*)* Look honey, we're going *to* the theatre—we're not going to be *in* it . . . so go change, huh?

RUTH You expect this boy to go out with you looking like that?

BENEATHA *(Looking at* GEORGE*)* That's up to George. If he's ashamed of his heritage—

GEORGE Oh, don't be so proud of yourself, Bennie—just because you look eccentric.

BENEATHA How can something that's natural be eccentric?

GEORGE That's what being eccentric means—being natural. Get dressed.

BENEATHA I don't like that, George.

RUTH Why must you and your brother make an argument out of everything people say?

BENEATHA Because I hate assimilationist Negroes!

RUTH Will somebody please tell me what assimila-whoever means!

GEORGE Oh, it's just a college girl's way of calling people Uncle Toms—but that isn't what it means at all.

RUTH Well, what does it mean?

BENEATHA *(Cutting* GEORGE *off and staring at him as she replies to* RUTH*)* It means someone who is willing to give up his own culture and submerge himself completely in the dominant, and in this case, *oppressive* culture!

GEORGE Oh, dear, dear, dear! Here we go! A lecture on the African past! On our Great West African Heritage! In one second we will hear all about the great Ashanti empires; the great Songhay civilizations; and the great sculpture of Bénin—and then some poetry in the Bantu—and the whole monologue will end with the word *heritage! (Nastily)* Let's face it, baby, your heritage is nothing but a bunch of raggedy-assed spirituals and some grass huts!

BENEATHA *Grass huts! (*RUTH *crosses to her and forcibly pushes her toward the bedroom)* See there . . . you are standing there in your splendid ignorance talking about people who were the first to smelt iron on the face of the earth! *(*RUTH *is pushing her through the door)* The Ashanti were performing surgical operations when the English—*(*RUTH *pulls the door to, with* BENEATHA *on the other side, and smiles graciously at* GEORGE. BENEATHA *opens the door and shouts the end of the sentence defiantly at* GEORGE*)*—were still tatooing themselves with blue dragons . . . *(She goes back inside)*

RUTH Have a seat, George. *(They both sit.* RUTH *folds her hands rather primly on her lap, determined to demonstrate the civilization of the family)* Warm, ain't it? I mean for September. *(Pause)* Just like they always say about Chicago weather: If it's too hot or cold for you, just wait a minute and it'll change. *(She smiles happily at this cliché of clichés)* Everybody say it's got to do with them bombs and things they keep setting off. *(Pause)* Would you like a nice cold beer?

GEORGE No, thank you. I don't care for beer. *(He looks at his watch)* I hope she hurries up.

RUTH What time is the show?

GEORGE It's an eight-thirty curtain. That's just Chicago, though. In New York standard curtain time is eight forty.

(He is rather proud of this knowledge)

RUTH *(Properly appreciating it)* You get to New York a lot?

GEORGE *(Offhand)* Few times a year.

RUTH Oh—that's nice. I've never been to New York.

(WALTER enters. We feel he has relieved himself, but the edge of unreality is still with him)

WALTER New York ain't got nothing Chicago ain't. Just a bunch of hustling people all squeezed up together—being "Eastern."

(He turns his face into a screw of displeasure)

GEORGE Oh—you've been?

WALTER *Plenty* of times.

RUTH *(Shocked at the lie)* Walter Lee Younger!

WALTER *(Staring her down)* Plenty! *(Pause)* What we got to drink in this house? Why don't you offer this man some refreshment. *(To GEORGE)* They don't know how to entertain people in this house, man.

GEORGE Thank you—I don't really care for anything.

WALTER *(Feeling his head; sobriety coming)* Where's Mama?

RUTH She ain't come back yet.

WALTER *(Looking MURCHISON over from head to toe, scrutinizing his carefully casual tweed sports jacket over cashmere V-neck sweater over soft eyelet shirt and tie, and soft slacks, finished off with white buckskin shoes)* Why all you college boys wear them fairyish-looking white shoes?

RUTH Walter Lee!

(GEORGE MURCHISON ignores the remark)

WALTER *(To RUTH)* Well, they look crazy as hell—white shoes, cold as it is.

RUTH *(Crushed)* You have to excuse him—

WALTER No he don't! Excuse me for what? What you always excusing me for! I'll excuse myself when I needs to be excused! *(A pause)* They look as funny as them black knee socks Beneatha wears out of here all the time.

RUTH It's the college *style,* Walter.

WALTER Style, hell. She looks like she got burnt legs or something!

RUTH Oh, Walter—

WALTER *(An irritable mimic)* Oh, Walter! Oh, Walter! *(To MURCHISON)* How's your old man making out? I understand you all going to buy that big hotel on the Drive? *(He finds a beer in the refrigerator, wanders over to MURCHISON, sipping and wiping his lips with the back of his hand, and straddling a chair backwards to talk to the other man)* Shrewd move. Your old man is all right, man. *(Tapping his head and half winking for emphasis)* I mean he knows how to operate. I mean he thinks *big,* you know what I mean, I mean for a *home,* you know? But I think he's kind of running out of ideas now. I'd like to talk to him. Listen, man, I got some plans that could turn this city upside down. I mean I think like he does. *Big.* Invest big, gamble big, hell, lose *big* if you have to, you know what I mean. It's hard to find a man on this whole Southside who understands my kind of thinking—you dig? *(He scrutinizes* MURCHISON *again, drinks his beer, squints his eyes and leans in close, confidential, man to man)* Me and you ought to sit down and talk sometimes, man. Man, I got me some ideas . . .

MURCHISON *(With boredom)* Yeah—sometimes we'll have to do that, Walter.

WALTER *(Understanding the indifference, and offended)* Yeah—well, when you get the time, man. I know you a busy little boy.

RUTH Walter, please—

WALTER *(Bitterly, hurt)* I know ain't nothing in this world as busy as you colored college boys with your fraternity pins and white shoes . . .

RUTH *(Covering her face with humiliation)* Oh, Walter Lee—

WALTER I see you all all the time—with the books tucked under your arms—going to your *(British A—a mimic)* "clahsses." And for what! What the hell you learning over there? Filling up your heads—*(Counting off on his fingers)*—with the sociology and the psychology—but they teaching you how to be a man? How to take over and run the world? They teaching you how to run a rubber plantation or a steel mill? Naw—just to talk proper and read books and wear white shoes . . .

GEORGE *(Looking at him with distaste, a little above it all)* You're all wacked up with bitterness, man.

WALTER *(Intently, almost quietly, between the teeth, glaring at the boy)* And you—ain't you bitter, man? Ain't you just about had it yet? Don't you see no stars gleaming that you can't reach out and grab? You happy?—You contended son-of-a-bitch—you happy? You got it made? Bitter? Man, I'm a volcano. Bitter? Here I am a giant—surrounded by ants! Ants who can't even understand what it is the giant is talking about.

RUTH *(Passionately and suddenly)* Oh, Walter—ain't you with nobody!

WALTER *(Violently)* No! 'Cause ain't nobody with me! Not even my own mother!

RUTH Walter, that's a terrible thing to say!

(BENEATHA *enters, dressed for the evening in a cocktail dress and earrings)*

GEORGE Well—hey, you look great.

BENEATHA Let's go, George. See you all later.

RUTH Have a nice time.

GEORGE Thanks. Good night. *(To* WALTER, *sarcastically)* Good night, *Prometheus.*

(BENEATHA *and* GEORGE *exit)*

WALTER *(To* RUTH*)* Who is Prometheus?

RUTH I don't know. Don't worry about it.

WALTER *(In fury, pointing after* GEORGE*)* See there—they get to a point where they can't insult you man to man—they got to go talk about something ain't nobody never heard of!

RUTH How do you know it was an insult? *(To humor him)* Maybe Prometheus is a nice fellow.

WALTER Prometheus! I bet there ain't even no such thing! I bet that simple-minded clown—

RUTH Walter—

(She stops what she is doing and looks at him)

WALTER *(Yelling)* Don't start!

RUTH Start what?

WALTER Your nagging! Where was I? Who was I with? How much money did I spend?

RUTH *(Plaintively)* Walter Lee—why don't we just try to talk about it . . .

WALTER *(Not listening)* I been out talking with people who understand me. People who care about the things I got on my mind.

RUTH *(Wearily)* I guess that means people like Willy Harris.

WALTER Yes, people like Willy Harris.

RUTH *(With a sudden flash of impatience)* Why don't you all just hurry up and go into the banking business and stop talking about it!

WALTER Why? You want to know why? 'Cause we all tied up in a race of people that don't know how to do nothing but moan, pray and have babies!

(The line is too bitter even for him and he looks at her and sits down)

RUTH Oh, Walter . . . *(Softly)* Honey, why can't you stop fighting me?

WALTER *(Without thinking)* Who's fighting you? Who even cares about you?

(This line begins the retardation of his mood)

RUTH Well—*(She waits a long time, and then with resignation starts to put away her things)* I guess I might as well go on to bed . . . *(More or less to herself)* I don't know where we lost it . . . but we have . . . *(Then, to him)* I—I'm sorry about this new baby, Walter. I guess maybe I better go on and do what I started . . . I guess I just didn't realize how bad things was with us . . . I guess I just didn't really realize—*(She starts out to the bedroom and stops)* You want some hot milk?

WALTER Hot milk?

RUTH Yes—hot milk.

WALTER Why hot milk?

RUTH 'Cause after all that liquor you come home with you ought to have something hot in your stomach.

WALTER I don't want no milk.

RUTH You want some coffee then?

WALTER No, I don't want no coffee. I don't want nothing hot to drink. *(Almost plaintively)* Why you always trying to give me something to eat?

RUTH *(Standing and looking at him helplessly)* What else can I give you, Walter Lee Younger?

(She stands and looks at him and presently turns to go out again. He lifts his head and watches her going away from him in a new mood which began to emerge when he asked her "Who cares about you?")

WALTER It's been rough, ain't it, baby? *(She hears and stops but does not turn around and he continues to her back)* I guess between two people there ain't never as much understood as folks generally thinks there is. I mean like between me and you— *(She turns to face him)* How we gets to the place where we scared to talk softness to each other. *(He waits, thinking hard himself)* Why you think it got to be like that? *(He is thoughtful, almost as a child would be)* Ruth, what is it gets into people ought to be close?

RUTH I don't know, honey. I think about it a lot.

WALTER On account of you and me, you mean? The way things are with us. The way something done come down between us.

RUTH There ain't so much between us, Walter . . . Not when you come to me and try to talk to me. Try to be with me . . . a little even.

WALTER *(Total honesty)* Sometimes . . . sometimes . . . I don't even know how to try.

RUTH Walter—

WALTER Yes?

RUTH *(Coming to him, gently and with misgiving, but coming to him)* Honey . . . life don't have to be like this. I mean sometimes people can do things so that things are better . . . You remember how we used to talk when Travis was born . . . about the way we were going to live . . . the kind of house . . . *(She is stroking his head)* Well, it's all starting to slip away from us . . .

(MAMA enters, and WALTER jumps up and shouts at her)

WALTER Mama, where have you been?

MAMA My—them steps is longer than they used to be. Whew! *(She sits down and ignores him)* How you feeling this evening, Ruth?

(RUTH shrugs, disturbed some at having been prematurely interrupted and watching her husband knowingly)

WALTER Mama, where have you been all day?

MAMA *(Still ignoring him and leaning on the table and changing to more comfortable shoes)* Where's Travis?

RUTH I let him go out earlier and he ain't come back yet. Boy, is he going to get it!

WALTER Mama!

MAMA *(As if she has heard him for the first time)* Yes, son?

WALTER Where did you go this afternoon?

MAMA I went downtown to tend to some business that I had to tend to.

WALTER What kind of business?

MAMA You know better than to question me like a child, Brother.

WALTER *(Rising and bending over the table)* Where were you, Mama? *(Bringing his fists down and shouting)* Mama, you didn't go do something with that insurance money, something crazy?

(The front door opens slowly, interrupting him, and TRAVIS peeks his head in, less than hopefully)

TRAVIS *(To his mother)* Mama, I—

RUTH "Mama I" nothing! You're going to get it, boy! Get on in that bedroom and get yourself ready!

TRAVIS But I—

MAMA Why don't you all never let the child explain hisself.

RUTH Keep out of it now, Lena.

*(*MAMA *clamps her lips together, and* RUTH *advances toward her son menacingly)*

RUTH A thousand times I have told you not to go off like that—

MAMA *(Holding out her arms to her grandson)* Well—at least let me tell him something. I want him to be the first one to hear . . . Come here, Travis. *(The boy obeys, gladly)* Travis—*(She takes him by the shoulder and looks into his face)*—you know that money we got in the mail this morning?

TRAVIS Yes'm—

MAMA Well—what you think your grandmama gone and done with that money?

TRAVIS I don't know, Grandmama.

MAMA *(Putting her finger on his nose for emphasis)* She went out and she bought you a house! *(The explosion comes from* WALTER *at the end of the revelation and he jumps up and turns away from all of them in a fury.* MAMA *continues, to* TRAVIS*)* You glad about the house? It's going to be yours when you get to be a man.

TRAVIS Yeah—I always wanted to live in a house.

MAMA All right, gimme some sugar then—*(*TRAVIS *puts his arms around her neck as she watches her son over the boy's shoulder. Then, to* TRAVIS*, after the embrace)* Now when you say your prayers tonight, you thank God and your grandfather—'cause it was him who give you the house—in his way.

RUTH *(Taking the boy from* MAMA *and pushing him toward the bedroom)* Now you get out of here and get ready for your beating.

TRAVIS Aw, Mama—

RUTH Get on in there—*(Closing the door behind him and turning radiantly to her mother-in-law)* So you went and did it!

MAMA *(Quietly, looking at her son with pain)* Yes, I did.

RUTH *(Raising both arms classically) Praise God! (Looks at* WALTER *a moment, who says nothing. She crosses rapidly to her husband)* Please, honey—let me be glad . . . you be glad too. *(She has laid her hands on his shoulders, but he shakes himself free of her roughly, without turning to face her)* Oh, Walter . . . a home . . . *a home. (She comes back to* MAMA*)* Well—where is it? How big is it? How much it going to cost?

MAMA Well—

RUTH When we moving?

MAMA *(Smiling at her)* First of the month.

RUTH *(Throwing back her head with jubilance) Praise God!*

MAMA *(Tentatively, still looking at her son's back turned against her and* RUTH*)* It's—it's a nice house too . . . *(She cannot help speaking directly to him. An imploring quality in her voice; her manner, makes her almost like a girl now)* Three bedrooms—nice big one for you and Ruth. . . . Me and Beneatha still have to share our room, but Travis have one of his own—and *(With difficulty)* I figure if the—new baby—is a boy, we could get one of them double-decker outfits . . . And there's a yard with a little patch of dirt where I could maybe get to grow me a few flowers . . . And a nice big basement . . .

RUTH Walter honey, be glad—

MAMA *(Still to his back, fingering things on the table)* 'Course I don't want to make it sound fancier than it is . . . It's just a plain little old house—but it's made good and solid—and it will be *ours.* Walter Lee—it makes a difference in a man when he can walk on floors that belong to *him* . . .

RUTH Where is it?

MAMA *(Frightened at this telling)* Well—well—it's out there in Clybourne Park—

(RUTH's *radiance fades abruptly, and* WALTER *finally turns slowly to face his mother with incredulity and hostility)*

RUTH Where?

MAMA *(Matter-of-factly)* Four o six Clybourne Street, Clybourne Park.

RUTH Clybourne Park? Mama, there ain't no colored people living in Clybourne Park.

MAMA *(Almost idiotically)* Well, I guess there's going to be some now.

WALTER *(Bitterly)* So that's the peace and comfort you went out and bought for us today!

MAMA *(Raising her eyes to meet his finally)* Son—I just tried to find the nicest place for the least amount of money for my family.

RUTH *(Trying to recover from the shock)* Well—well—'course I ain't one never been 'fraid of no crackers, mind you—but—well, wasn't there no other houses nowhere?

MAMA Them houses they put up for colored in them areas way out all seem to cost twice as much as other houses. I did the best I could.

RUTH *(Struck senseless with the news, in its various degrees of goodness and trouble, she sits a moment, her fists propping her chin in thought, and then she starts to rise, bringing her fists down with vigor, the radiance spreading from cheek to cheek again)* Well—well!—All I can say is—if this is my time in life—*my time*—to say goodbye—*(And she builds with momentum as she starts to circle the room with exuberant, almost tearfully happy release)*—to these Goddamned cracking walls!—*(She pounds the walls)*—and these marching roaches!—*(She wipes at an imaginary army of marching roaches)*—and this cramped little closet which ain't now or never was no kitchen! . . . then I say it loud and good, *Hallelujah! and goodbye misery . . . I don't never want to see your ugly face again! (She laughs joyously, having practically destroyed the apartment, and flings her arms up and lets them come down happily, slowly, reflectively, over her abdomen, aware for the first time perhaps that the life therein pulses with happiness and not despair)* Lena?

MAMA *(Moved, watching her happiness)* Yes, honey?

RUTH *(Looking off)* Is there—is there a whole lot of sunlight?

MAMA *(Understanding)* Yes, child, there's a whole lot of sunlight.

(Long pause)

RUTH *(Collecting herself and going to the door of the room* TRAVIS *is in)* Well—I guess I better see 'bout Travis. *(To* MAMA*)* Lord, I sure don't feel like whipping nobody today!

(She exits)

MAMA *(The mother and son are left alone now and the mother waits a long time, considering deeply, before she speaks)* Son—you—you understand what I done, don't you? (WALTER *is silent and sullen)* I—I just seen my family falling apart today . . . just falling to pieces in front of my eyes . . . We couldn't of gone on like we was today. We was going backwards 'stead of forwards—talking 'bout killing babies and wishing each other was dead . . . When it gets like that in life—you just got to do something different, push on out and do something bigger . . . *(She waits)* I wish you say something, son . . . I wish you'd say how deep inside you you think I done the right thing—

WALTER *(Crossing slowly to his bedroom door and finally turning there and speaking measuredly)* What you need me to say you done right for? *You* the head of this family. You run our lives like you want to. It was your money and you did what you wanted with it. So what you need for me to say it was all right for? *(Bitterly, to hurt her as deeply as he knows is possible)* So you butchered up a dream of mine—you—who always talking 'bout your children's dreams . . .

MAMA Walter Lee—

(He just closes the door behind him. MAMA *sits alone, thinking heavily)*

CURTAIN

Scene II

Time: Friday night. A few weeks later.

At rise: Packing crates mark the intention of the family to move. BENEATHA *and* GEORGE *come in, presumably from an evening out again.*

GEORGE O.K. . . . O.K., whatever you say . . . *(They both sit on the couch. He tries to kiss her. She moves away)* Look, we've had a nice evening; let's not spoil it, huh? . . .

(He again turns her head and tries to nuzzle in and she turns away from him, not with distaste but with momentary lack of interest; in a mood to pursue what they were talking about)

BENEATHA I'm *trying* to talk to you.

GEORGE We always talk.

BENEATHA Yes—and I love to talk.

GEORGE *(Exasperated; rising)* I know it and I don't mind it sometimes . . . I want you to cut it out, see—The moody stuff, I mean. I don't like it. You're a nice-looking girl . . . all over. That's all you need, honey, forget the atmosphere. Guys aren't going to go for the atmosphere—they're going to go for what they see. Be glad for that. Drop the Garbo routine. It doesn't go with you. As for myself, I want a nice—*(Groping)*—simple *(Thoughtfully)*—sophisticated girl . . . not a poet—O.K.?

(She rebuffs him again and he starts to leave)

BENEATHA Why are you angry?

GEORGE Because this is stupid! I don't go out with you to discuss the nature of "quiet desperation" or to hear all about your thoughts—because the world will go on thinking what it thinks regardless—

BENEATHA Then why read books? Why go to school?

GEORGE *(With artificial patience, counting on his fingers)* It's simple. You read books—to learn facts—to get grades—to pass the course—to get a degree. That's all—it has nothing to do with thoughts.

(A long pause)

BENEATHA I see. *(A longer pause as she looks at him)* Good night, George.

*(*GEORGE *looks at her a little oddly, and starts to exit. He meets* MAMA *coming in)*

GEORGE Oh—hello, Mrs. Younger.
MAMA Hello, George, how you feeling?
GEORGE Fine—fine, how are you?
MAMA Oh, a little tired. You know them steps can get you after a day's work. You all have a nice time tonight?
GEORGE Yes—a fine time. Well, good night.
MAMA Good night. *(He exits.* MAMA *closes the door behind her)* Hello, honey. What you sitting like that for?
BENEATHA I'm just sitting.
MAMA Didn't you have a nice time?
BENEATHA No.
MAMA No? What's the matter?
BENEATHA Mama, George is a fool—honest. *(She rises)*
MAMA *(Hustling around unloading the packages she has entered with. She stops)* Is he, baby?
BENEATHA Yes.

*(*BENEATHA *makes up* TRAVIS' *bed as she talks)*

MAMA You sure?
BENEATHA Yes.
MAMA Well—I guess you better not waste your time with no fools.

*(*BENEATHA *looks up at her mother, watching her put groceries in the refrigerator. Finally she gathers up her things and starts into the bedroom. At the door she stops and looks back at her mother)*

BENEATHA Mama—
MAMA Yes, baby—
BENEATHA Thank you.
MAMA For what?
BENEATHA For understanding me this time.

(She exits quickly and the mother stands, smiling a little, looking at the place where BENEATHA *just stood.* RUTH *enters)*

RUTH Now don't you fool with any of this stuff, Lena—
MAMA Oh, I just thought I'd sort a few things out.

(The phone rings. RUTH *answers)*

RUTH *(At the phone)* Hello—Just a minute. *(Goes to door)* Walter, it's Mrs. Arnold. *(Waits. Goes back to the phone. Tense)* Hello. Yes, this is his wife speaking . . . He's lying down now. Yes . . . well, he'll be in tomorrow. He's been very sick. Yes—I know we should have called, but we were so sure he'd be able to come in today. Yes—yes, I'm very sorry. Yes . . . Thank you very much. *(She hangs up.* WALTER *is standing in the doorway of the bedroom behind her)* That was Mrs. Arnold.

WALTER *(Indifferently)* Was it?

RUTH She said if you don't come in tomorrow that they are getting a new man . . .

WALTER Ain't that sad—ain't that crying sad.

RUTH She said Mr. Arnold has had to take a cab for three days . . . Walter, you ain't been to work for three days! *(This is a revelation to her)* Where you been, Walter Lee Younger? *(*WALTER *looks at her and starts to laugh)* You're going to lose your job.

WALTER That's right . . .

RUTH Oh, Walter, and with your mother working like a dog every day—

WALTER That's sad too—Everything is sad.

MAMA What you been doing for these three days, son?

WALTER Mama—you don't know all the things a man what got leisure can find to do in this city . . . What's this—Friday night? Well—Wednesday I borrowed Willy Harris' car and I went for a drive . . . just me and myself and I drove and drove . . . Way out . . . way past South Chicago, and I parked the car and I sat and looked at the steel mills all day long. I just sat in the car and looked at them big black chimneys for hours. Then I drove back and I went to the Green Hat. *(Pause)* And Thursday—Thursday I borrowed the car again and I got in it and I pointed it the other way and I drove the other way—for hours—way, way up to Wisconsin, and I looked at the farms. I just drove and looked at the farms. Then I drove back and I went to the Green Hat. *(Pause)* And today—today I didn't get the car. Today I just walked. All over the Southside. And I looked at the Negroes and they looked at me and finally I just sat down on the curb at Thirty-ninth and South Parkway and I just sat there and watched the Negroes go by. And then I went to the Green Hat. You all sad? You all depressed? And you know where I am going right now—

*(*RUTH *goes out quietly)*

MAMA Oh, Big Walter, is this the harvest of our days?

WALTER You know what I like about the Green Hat? *(He turns the radio on and a steamy, deep blues pours into the room)* I like this little cat they got there who blows a sax . . . He blows. He talks to me. He ain't but 'bout five feet tall and he's got a conked head and his eyes is always closed and he's all music—

MAMA *(Rising and getting some papers out of her handbag)* Walter—

WALTER And there's this other guy who plays the piano . . . and they got a sound. I mean they can work on some music . . . They got the best little combo in the world in the Green Hat . . . You can just sit there and drink and listen to them three men play and you realize that don't nothing matter worth a damn, but just being there—

MAMA I've helped do it to you, haven't I, son? Walter, I been wrong.

WALTER Naw—you ain't never been wrong about nothing, Mama.

MAMA Listen to me, now. I say I been wrong, son. That I been doing to you what the rest of the world been doing to you. *(She stops and he looks up slowly at her and she meets his eyes pleadingly)* Walter—what you ain't never understood is that I ain't got nothing, don't own nothing, ain't never really wanted nothing that wasn't for you. There ain't nothing as precious to me . . . There ain't nothing worth holding on to, money, dreams, nothing else—if it means—if it means it's going to destroy my boy. *(She puts her papers in front of him and he watches her without speaking or moving)* I paid the man thirty-five hundred dollars down on the house. That leaves sixty-five hundred dollars. Monday morning I want you to take this money and take three thousand dollars and put it in a savings account for Beneatha's medical schooling. The rest you put in a checking account—with your name on it. And from now on any penny that come out of it or that go in it is for you to look after. For you to decide. *(She drops her hands a little helplessly)* It ain't much, but it's all I got in the world and I'm putting it in your hands. I'm telling you to be the head of this family from now on like you supposed to be.

WALTER *(Stares at the money)* You trust me like that, Mama?

MAMA I ain't never stop trusting you. Like I ain't never stop loving you.

(She goes out, and WALTER *sits looking at the money on the table as the music continues in its idiom, pulsing in the room. Finally, in a decisive gesture, he gets up, and, in mingled joy and desperation, picks up the money. At the same moment,* TRAVIS *enters for bed)*

TRAVIS What's the matter, Daddy? You drunk?

WALTER *(Sweetly, more sweetly than we have ever known him)* No, Daddy ain't drunk. Daddy ain't going to never be drunk again. . . .

TRAVIS Well, good night, Daddy.

(The FATHER *has come from behind the couch and leans over, embracing his son)*

WALTER Son, I feel like talking to you tonight.

TRAVIS About what?

WALTER Oh, about a lot of things. About you and what kind of man you going to be when you grow up. . . . Son—son, what do you want to be when you grow up?

TRAVIS A bus driver.

WALTER *(Laughing a little)* A what? Man, that ain't nothing to want to be!

TRAVIS Why not?

WALTER 'Cause, man—it ain't big enough—you know what I mean.

TRAVIS I don't know then. I can't make up my mind. Sometimes Mama asks me that too. And sometimes when I tell her I just want to be like you—she says she don't want me to be like that and sometimes she says she does. . . .

WALTER *(Gathering him up in his arms)* You know what, Travis? In seven years you going to be seventeen years old. And things is going to be very different with us in seven years, Travis. . . . One day when you are seventeen I'll come home—home from my office downtown somewhere—

TRAVIS You don't work in no office, Daddy.

WALTER No—but after tonight. After what your daddy gonna do tonight, there's going to be offices—a whole lot of offices. . . .

TRAVIS What you gonna do tonight, Daddy?

WALTER You wouldn't understand yet, son, but your daddy's gonna make a transaction . . . a business transaction that's going to change our lives. . . . That's how come one day when you 'bout seventeen years old I'll come home and I'll be pretty tired, you know what I mean, after a day of conferences and secretaries getting things wrong the way they do . . . 'cause an executive's life is hell, man—*(The more he talks the farther away he gets)* And I'll pull the car up on the driveway . . . just a plain black Chrysler, I think, with white walls—no—black tires. More elegant. Rich people don't have to be flashy . . . though I'll have to get something a little sportier for Ruth—maybe a Cadillac convertible to do her shopping in . . . And I'll come up the steps to the house and the gardener will be clipping away at the hedges and he'll say, "Good evening, Mr. Younger." And I'll say, "Hello, Jefferson, how are you this evening?" And I'll go inside and Ruth will come downstairs and meet me at the door and we'll kiss each other and she'll take my arm and we'll go up to your room to see you sitting on the floor with the catalogues of all the great schools in America around you. . . . All the great schools in the world! And—and I'll say, all right son—it's your seventeenth birthday, what is it you've decided? . . . Just tell me where you want to go to school and you'll *go*. Just tell me, what it is you want to be—and you'll *be* it. . . . Whatever you want to be—Yessir! *(He holds his arms open for* TRAVIS*)* You just name it, son . . . *(*TRAVIS *leaps into them)* and I hand you the world!

*(*WALTER'S *voice has risen in pitch and hysterical promise and on the last line he lifts* TRAVIS *high)*

(BLACKOUT)

Scene III

Time: Saturday, moving day, one week later.

Before the curtain rises, RUTH'S *voice, a strident, dramatic church alto, cuts through the silence.*

It is, in the darkness, a triumphant surge, a penetrating statement of expectation: "Oh, Lord, I don't feel no ways tired! Children, oh, glory hallelujah!"

As the curtain rises we see that RUTH *is alone in the living room, finishing up the family's packing. It is moving day. She is nailing crates and tying cartons.* BENEATHA *enters, carrying a guitar case, and watches her exuberant sister-in-law.*

RUTH Hey!

BENEATHA *(Putting away the case)* Hi.

RUTH *(Pointing at a package)* Honey—look in that package there and see what I found on sale this morning at the South Center. *(*RUTH *gets up and moves to the package and draws out some curtains)* Lookahere—hand-turned hems!

BENEATHA How do you know the window size out there?

RUTH *(Who hadn't thought of that)* Oh—Well, they bound to fit something in the whole house. Anyhow, they was too good a bargain to pass up. *(*RUTH *slaps her head, suddenly remembering something)* Oh, Bennie—I meant to put a special note on that carton over there. That's your mama's good china and she wants 'em to be very careful with it.

BENEATHA I'll do it.

*(*BENEATHA *finds a piece of paper and starts to draw large letters on it)*

RUTH You know what I'm going to do soon as I get in that new house?

BENEATHA What?

RUTH Honey—I'm going to run me a tub of water up to here . . . *(With her fingers practically up to her nostrils)* And I'm going to get in it—and I am going to sit . . . and sit . . . and sit in that hot water and the first person who knocks to tell *me* to hurry up and come out—

BENEATHA Gets shot at sunrise.

RUTH *(Laughing happily)* You said it, sister! *(Noticing how large* BENEATHA *is absent-mindedly making the note)* Honey, they ain't going to read that from no airplane.

BENEATHA *(Laughing herself)* I guess I always think things have more emphasis if they are big, somehow.

RUTH *(Looking up at her and smiling)* You and your brother seem to have that as a philosophy of life. Lord, that man—done changed so 'round here. You know—you know what we did last night? Me and Walter Lee?

BENEATHA What?

RUTH *(Smiling to herself)* We went to the movies. *(Looking at* BENEATHA *to see if she understands)* We went to the movies. You know the last time me and Walter went to the movies together?

BENEATHA No.

RUTH Me neither. That's how long it been. *(Smiling again)* But we went last night. The picture wasn't much good, but that didn't seem to matter. We went—and we held hands.

BENEATHA Oh, Lord!

RUTH We held hands—and you know what?

BENEATHA What?

RUTH When we come out of the show it was late and dark and all the stores and things was closed up . . . and it was kind of chilly and there wasn't many people on the streets . . . and we was still holding hands, me and Walter.

BENEATHA You're killing me.

*(*WALTER *enters with a large package. His happiness is deep in him; he cannot keep still with his new-found exuberance. He is singing and wiggling and snapping his fingers. He puts his package in a corner and puts a phonograph record, which he has brought in with him, on the record player. As the music comes up he dances over to* RUTH *and tries to get her to dance with him. She gives in at last to his raunchiness and in a fit of giggling allows herself to be drawn into his mood and together they deliberately burlesque an old social dance of their youth)*

BENEATHA *(Regarding them a long time as they dance, then drawing in her breath for a deeply exaggerated comment which she does not particularly mean)* Talk about—olddddddddd-fashionedddddd—Negroes!

WALTER *(Stopping momentarily)* What kind of Negroes?

(He says this in fun. He is not angry with her today, nor with anyone. He starts to dance with his wife again)

BENEATHA Old-fashioned.

WALTER *(As he dances with* RUTH*)* You know, when these *New Negroes* have their convention—*(Pointing at his sister)*—that is going to be the chairman of the Committee on Unending Agitation. *(He goes on dancing, then stops)* Race, race, race! . . . Girl, I do believe you are the first person in the history of the entire human race to successfully brainwash yourself. (BENEATHA *breaks up and he goes on dancing. He stops again, enjoying his tease)* Damn, even the N double A C P takes a holiday sometimes! (BENEATHA *and* RUTH *laugh. He dances with* RUTH *some more and starts to laugh and stops and pantomimes someone over an operating table)* I can just see that chick someday looking down at some poor cat on an operating table before she starts to slice him, saying . . . *(Pulling his sleeves back maliciously)* "By the way, what are your views on civil rights down there? . . ."

(He laughs at her again and starts to dance happily. The bell sounds)

BENEATHA Sticks and stones may break my bones but . . . words will never hurt me!

(BENEATHA *goes to the door and opens it as* WALTER *and* RUTH *go on with the clowning.* BENEATHA *is somewhat surprised to see a quiet-looking middle-aged white man in a business suit holding his hat and a briefcase in his hand and consulting a small piece of paper)*

MAN Uh—how do you do, miss. I am looking for a Mrs.—*(He looks at the slip of paper)* Mrs. Lena Younger?

BENEATHA *(Smoothing her hair with slight embarrassment)* Oh—yes, that's my mother. Excuse me *(She closes the door and turns to quiet the other two)* Ruth! Brother! Somebody's here. *(Then she opens the door. The man casts a curious quick glance at all of them)* Uh—come in please.

MAN *(Coming in)* Thank you.

BENEATHA My mother isn't here just now. Is it business?

MAN Yes . . . well, of a sort.

WALTER *(Freely, the Man of the House)* Have a seat. I'm Mrs. Younger's son. I look after most of her business matters.

(RUTH *and* BENEATHA *exchange amused glances)*

MAN *(Regarding* WALTER, *and sitting)* Well—My name is Karl Lindner . . .

WALTER *(Stretching out his hand)* Walter Younger. This is my wife—(RUTH *nods politely)*—and my sister.

LINDNER How do you do.

WALTER *(Amiably, as he sits himself easily on a chair, leaning with interest forward on his knees and looking expectantly into the newcomer's face)* What can we do for you, Mr. Lindner!

LINDNER *(Some minor shuffling of the hat and briefcase on his knees)* Well—I am a representative of the Clybourne Park Improvement Association—

WALTER *(Pointing)* Why don't you sit your things on the floor?

LINDNER Oh—yes. Thank you. *(He slides the briefcase and hat under the chair)* And as I was saying—I am from the Clybourne Park Improvement Association and we have had it brought to our attention at the last meeting that you people—or at least your mother—has bought a piece of residential property at—*(He digs for the slip of paper again)*—four o six Clybourne Street . . .

WALTER That's right. Care for something to drink? Ruth, get Mr. Lindner a beer.

LINDNER *(Upset for some reason)* Oh—no, really. I mean thank you very much, but no thank you.

RUTH *(Innocently)* Some coffee?

LINDNER Thank you, nothing at all.

(BENEATHA *is watching the man carefully)*

LINDNER Well, I don't know how much you folks know about our organization. *(He is a gentle man; thoughtful and somewhat labored in his manner)* It is one of these community organizations set up to look after—oh, you know, things like block upkeep and special projects and we also have what we call our New Neighbors Orientation Committee . . .

BENEATHA *(Drily)* Yes—and what do they do?

LINDNER *(Turning a little to her and then returning the main force to* WALTER*)* Well—it's what you might call a sort of welcoming committee, I guess. I mean they, we, I'm the chairman of the committee—go around and see the new people who move into the neighborhood and sort of give them the lowdown on the way we do things out in Clybourne Park.

BENEATHA *(With appreciation of the two meanings, which escape* RUTH *and* WALTER*)* Un-huh.

LINDNER And we also have the category of what the association calls—*(He looks elsewhere)*—uh—special community problems . . .

BENEATHA Yes—and what are some of those?

WALTER Girl, let the man talk.

LINDNER *(With understated relief)* Thank you. I would sort of like to explain this thing in my own way. I mean I want to explain to you in a certain way.

WALTER Go ahead.

LINDNER Yes. I'm going to try to get right to the point. I'm sure we'll all appreciate that in the long run.

BENEATHA Yes.

WALTER Be still now!

LINDNER Well—

RUTH *(Still innocently)* Would you like another chair—you don't look comfortable.

LINDNER *(More frustrated than annoyed)* No, thank you very much. Please. Well—to get right to the point I—*(A great breath, and he is off at last)* I am sure you people must be aware of some of the incidents which have happened in various parts of the city when colored people have moved into certain areas—(BENEATHA *exhales heavily and starts tossing a piece of fruit up and down in the air)* Well—because we have what I think is going to be a unique type of organization in American community life—not only do we deplore that kind of thing—but we are trying to do something about it. (BENEATHA *stops tossing and turns with a new and quizzical interest to the man)* We feel—*(gaining confidence in his mission because of the interest in the faces of the people he is talking to)*—we feel that most of the trouble in this world, when you come right down to it—*(He hits his knee for emphasis)*—most of the trouble exists because people just don't sit down and talk to each other.

RUTH *(Nodding as she might in church, pleased with the remark)* You can say that again, mister.

LINDNER *(More encouraged by such affirmation)* That we don't try hard enough in this world to understand the other fellow's problem. The other guy's point of view.

RUTH Now that's right.

(BENEATHA *and* WALTER *merely watch and listen with genuine interest)*

LINDNER Yes—that's the way we feel out in Clybourne Park. And that's why I was elected to come here this afternoon and talk to you people. Friendly like, you know, the way people should talk to each other and see if we couldn't find some way to work this thing out. As I say, the whole business is a matter of *caring* about the other fellow. Anybody can see that you are a nice family of folks, hard working and honest I'm sure. (BENEATHA *frowns slightly, quizzically, her head tilted regarding him)* Today everybody knows what it means to be on the outside of *something.* And of course, there is always somebody who is out to take the advantage of people who don't always understand.

WALTER What do you mean?

LINDNER Well—you see our community is made up of people who've worked hard as the dickens for years to build up that little community. They're not rich and fancy people; just hard-working, honest people who don't really have much but those little homes and a dream of the kind of community they want to raise their children in. Now, I don't say we are perfect and there is a lot wrong in some of the things they want. But you've got to admit that a man, right or wrong, has the right to want to have the neighborhood he lives in a certain kind of way. And at the moment the overwhelming majority of our people out there feel that people get along better, take more of a common interest in the life of the community, when they share a common background. I want you to believe me when I tell you that race prejudice simply doesn't enter into it. It is a matter of the people of Clybourne Park believing, rightly or wrongly, as I say, that for the happiness of all concerned that our Negro families are happier when they live in their *own* communities.

BENEATHA *(With a grand and bitter gesture)* This, friends, is the Welcoming Committee!

WALTER *(Dumfounded, looking at* LINDNER*)* Is this what you came marching all the way over here to tell us?

LINDNER Well, now we've been having a fine conversation. I hope you'll hear me all the way through.

WALTER *(Tightly)* Go ahead, man.

LINDNER You see—in the face of all things I have said, we are prepared to make your family a very generous offer . . .

BENEATHA Thirty pieces and not a coin less!

WALTER Yeah?

LINDNER *(Putting on his glasses and drawing a form out of the briefcase)* Our association is prepared, through the collective effort of our people, to buy the house from you at a financial gain to your family.

RUTH Lord have mercy, ain't this the living gall!

WALTER All right, you through?

LINDNER Well, I want to give you the exact terms of the financial arrangement—

WALTER We don't want to hear no exact terms of no arrangements. I want to know if you got any more to tell us 'bout getting together?

LINDNER *(Taking off his glasses)* Well—I don't suppose that you feel . . .

WALTER Never mind how I feel—you got any more to say 'bout how people ought to sit down and talk to each other? . . . Get out of my house, man.

(He turns his back and walks to the door)

LINDNER *(Looking around at the hostile faces and reaching and assembling his hat and briefcase)* Well—I don't understand why you people are reacting this way. What do you think you are going to gain by moving into a neighborhood where you just aren't wanted and where some elements—well—people can get awful worked up when they feel that their whole way of life and everything they've ever worked for is threatened.

WALTER Get out.

LINDNER *(At the door, holding a small card)* Well—I'm sorry it went like this.

WALTER Get out.

LINDNER *(Almost sadly regarding* WALTER*)* You just can't force people to change their hearts, son.

(He turns and put his card on a table and exits. WALTER *pushes the door to with stinging hatred, and stands looking at it.* RUTH *just sits and* BENEATHA *just stands. They say nothing.* MAMA *and* TRAVIS *enter)*

MAMA Well—this all the packing got done since I left out of here this morning. I testify before God that my children got all the energy of the dead. What time the moving men due?

BENEATHA Four o'clock. You had a caller, Mama.

(She is smiling, teasingly)

MAMA Sure enough—who?

BENEATHA *(Her arms folded saucily)* The Welcoming Committee.

*(*WALTER *and* RUTH *giggle)*

MAMA *(Innocently)* Who?

BENEATHA The Welcoming Committee. They said they're sure going to be glad to see you when you get there.

WALTER *(Devilishly)* Yeah, they said they can't hardly wait to see your face.

(Laughter)

MAMA *(Sensing their facetiousness)* What's the matter with you all?

WALTER Ain't nothing the matter with us. We just telling you 'bout the gentleman who came to see you this afternoon. From the Clybourne Park Improvement Association.

MAMA What he want?

RUTH *(In the same mood as* BENEATHA *and* WALTER*)* To welcome you, honey.

WALTER He said they can't hardly wait. He said the one thing they don't have, that they just *dying* to have out there is a fine family of colored people! *(To* RUTH *and* BENEATHA*)* Ain't that right!

RUTH *and* BENEATHA *(Mockingly)* Yeah! He left his card in case—

(They indicate the card, and MAMA *picks it up and throws it on the floor—understanding and looking off as she draws her chair up to the table on which she has put her plant and some sticks and some cord)*

MAMA Father, give us strength. *(Knowingly—and without fun)* Did he threaten us?

BENEATHA Oh—Mama—they don't do it like that any more. He talked Brotherhood. He said everybody ought to learn how to sit down and hate each other with good

Christian fellowship.

(She and WALTER *shake hands to ridicule the remark)*

MAMA *(Sadly)* Lord, protect us . . .

RUTH You should hear the money those folks raised to buy the house from us. All we paid and then some.

BENEATHA What they think we going to do—eat 'em?

RUTH No, honey, marry 'em.

MAMA *(Shaking her head)* Lord, Lord, Lord . . .

RUTH Well—that's the way the crackers crumble. Joke.

BENEATHA *(Laughingly noticing what her mother is doing)* Mama, what are you doing?

MAMA Fixing my plant so it won't get hurt none on the way . . .

BENEATHA Mama, you going to take *that* to the new house?

MAMA Un-huh—

BENEATHA That raggedy-looking old thing?

MAMA *(Stopping and looking at her)* It expresses *me.*

RUTH *(With delight, to* BENEATHA*)* So there, Miss Thing!

*(*WALTER *comes to* MAMA *suddenly and bends down behind her and squeezes her in his arms with all his strength. She is overwhelmed by the suddenness of it and, though delighted, her manner is like that of* RUTH *with* TRAVIS*)*

MAMA Look out now, boy! You make me mess up my thing here!

WALTER *(His face lit, he slips down on his knees beside her, his arms still about her)* Mama . . . you know what it means to climb up in the chariot?

MAMA *(Gruffly, very happy)* Get on away from me now . . .

RUTH *(Near the gift-wrapped package, trying to catch* WALTER's *eye)* Psst—

WALTER What the old song say, Mama . . .

RUTH Walter—Now?

(She is pointing at the package)

WALTER *(Speaking the lines, sweetly, playfully, in his mother's face)*

I got wings . . . you got wings . . .
All God's Children got wings . . .

MAMA Boy—get out of my face and do some work . . .

WALTER

When I get to heaven gonna put on my wings,
Gonna fly all over God's heaven . . .

BENEATHA *(Teasingly, from across the room)* Everybody talking 'bout heaven ain't going there!

WALTER *(To* RUTH, *who is carrying the box across to them)* I don't know, you think we ought to give her that . . . Seems to me she ain't been very appreciative around here.

MAMA *(Eying the box, which is obviously a gift)* What is that?

WALTER *(Taking it from* RUTH *and putting it on the table in front of* MAMA*)* Well—what you all think? Should we give it to her?

RUTH Oh—she was pretty good today.

MAMA I'll good you —

(She turns her eyes to the box again)

BENEATHA Open it, Mama.

(She stands up, looks at it, turns and looks at all of them, and then presses her hands together and does not open the package)

WALTER *(Sweetly)* Open it, Mama. It's for you. *(*MAMA *looks in his eyes. It is the first present in her life without its being Christmas. Slowly she opens her package and lifts out, one by one, a brand-new sparkling set of gardening tools.* WALTER *continues, prodding)* Ruth made up the note—read it . . .

MAMA *(Picking up the card and adjusting her glasses)* "To our own Mrs. Miniver—Love from Brother, Ruth and Beneatha." Ain't that lovely . . .

TRAVIS *(Tugging at his father's sleeve)* Daddy, can I give her mine now?

WALTER All right, son. *(*TRAVIS *flies to get his gift)* Travis didn't want to go in with the rest of us, Mama. He got his own. *(Somewhat amused)* We don't know what it is . . .

TRAVIS *(Racing back in the room with a large hatbox and putting it in front of his grandmother)* Here!

MAMA Lord have mercy, baby. You done gone and bought your grandmother a hat?

TRAVIS *(Very proud)* Open it!

(She does and lifts out an elaborate, but very elaborate, wide gardening hat, and all the adults break up at the sight of it)

RUTH Travis, honey, what is that?

TRAVIS *(Who thinks it is beautiful and appropriate)* It's a gardening hat! Like the ladies always have on in the magazines when they work in their gardens.

BENEATHA *(Giggling fiercely)* Travis—we were trying to make Mama Mrs. Miniver—not Scarlett O'Hara!

MAMA *(Indignantly)* What's the matter with you all! This here is a beautiful hat! *(Absurdly)* I always wanted me one just like it!

(She pops it on her head to prove it to her grandson, and the hat is ludicrous and considerably oversized)

RUTH Hot dog! Go, Mama!

WALTER *(Doubled over with laughter)* I'm sorry, Mama—but you look like you ready to go out and chop you some cotton sure enough!

(They all laugh except MAMA, *out of deference to* TRAVIS' *feelings)*

MAMA *(Gathering the boy up to her)* Bless your heart—this is the prettiest hat I ever owned—*(*WALTER, RUTH *and* BENEATHA *chime in—noisily, festively and insincerely congratulating* TRAVIS *on his gift)* What are we all standing around here for? We ain't finished packin' yet. Bennie, you ain't packed one book.

(The bell rings)

BENEATHA That couldn't be the movers . . . it's not hardly two good yet—

*(*BENEATHA *goes into her room.* MAMA *starts for door)*

WALTER *(Turning, stiffening)* Wait—wait—I'll get it.

(He stands and looks at the door)

MAMA You expecting company, son?
WALTER *(Just looking at the door)* Yeah—yeah . . .

*(*MAMA *looks at* RUTH, *and they exchange innocent and unfrightened glances)*

MAMA *(Not understanding)* Well, let them in, son.
BENEATHA *(From her room)* We need some more string.
MAMA Travis—you run to the hardware and get me some string cord.

*(*MAMA *goes out and* WALTER *turns and looks at* RUTH. TRAVIS *goes to a dish for money)*

RUTH Why don't you answer the door, man?
WALTER *(Suddenly bounding across the floor to her)* 'Cause sometimes it hard to let the future begin! *(Stooping down in her face)*

I got wings! You got wings!
All God's children got wings!

(He crosses to the door and throws it open. Standing there is a very slight little man in a not too prosperous business suit and with haunted frightened eyes and a hat pulled down tightly, brim up, around his forehead. TRAVIS *passes between the men and exits.* WALTER *leans deep in the man's face, still in his jubilance)*

When I get to heaven gonna put on my wings,
Gonna fly all over God's heaven . . .

(The little man just stares at him)

HEAVEN—

(Suddenly he stops and looks past the little man into the empty hallway) Where's Willy, man?

BOBO He ain't with me.
WALTER *(Not disturbed)* Oh—come on in. You know my wife.
BOBO *(Dumbly, taking off his hat)* Yes—h'you, Miss Ruth.
RUTH *(Quietly, a mood apart from her husband already, seeing* BOBO*)* Hello, Bobo.
WALTER You right on time today . . . Right on time. That's the way! *(He slaps* BOBO *on his back)* Sit down . . . lemme hear.

*(*RUTH *stands stiffly and quietly in back of them, as though somehow she senses death, her eyes fixed on her husband)*

BOBO *(His frightened eyes on the floor, his hat in his hands)* Could I please get a drink of water, before I tell you about it, Walter Lee?

*(*WALTER *does not take his eyes off the man.* RUTH *goes blindly to the tap and gets a glass of water and brings it to* BOBO*)*

WALTER There ain't nothing wrong, is there?
BOBO Lemme tell you—
WALTER Man—didn't nothing go wrong?
BOBO Lemme tell you—Walter Lee. *(Looking at* RUTH *and talking to her more than to* WALTER*)* You know how it was. I got to tell you how it was. I mean first I got to tell you how it was all the way . . . I mean about the money I put in, Walter Lee . . .

WALTER *(With taut agitation now)* What about the money you put in?

BOBO Well—it wasn't much as we told you—me and Willy—*(He stops)* I'm sorry, Walter. I got a bad feeling about it. I got a real bad feeling about it . . .

WALTER Man, what you telling me about all this for? . . . Tell me what happened in Springfield . . .

BOBO Springfield.

RUTH *(Like a dead woman)* What was supposed to happen in Springfield?

BOBO *(To her)* This deal that me and Walter went into with Willy—Me and Willy was going to go down to Springfield and spread some money 'round so's we wouldn't have to wait so long for the liquor license . . . That's what we were going to do. Everybody said that was the way you had to do, you understand, Miss Ruth?

WALTER Man—what happened down there?

BOBO *(A pitiful man, near tears)* I'm trying to tell you, Walter.

WALTER *(Screaming at him suddenly)* THEN TELL ME, GODDAMMIT . . . WHAT'S THE MATTER WITH YOU?

BOBO Man . . . I didn't go to no Springfield, yesterday.

WALTER *(Halted, life hanging in the moment)* Why not?

BOBO *(The long way, the hard way to tell)* 'Cause I didn't have no reasons to . . .

WALTER Man, what are you talking about!

BOBO I'm talking about the fact that when I got to the train station yesterday morning—eight o'clock like we planned . . . Man—*Willy didn't never show up.*

WALTER Why . . . where was he . . . where is he?

BOBO That's what I'm trying to tell you . . . I don't know . . . I waited six hours . . . I called his house . . . and I waited . . . six hours . . . I waited in that train station six hours . . . *(Breaking into tears)* That was all the extra money I had in the world . . . *(Looking up at* WALTER *with the tears running down his face)* Man, *Willy is gone.*

WALTER Gone, what you mean Willy is gone? Gone where? You mean he went by himself. You mean he went off to Springfield by himself—to take care of getting the license—*(Turns and looks anxiously at* RUTH*)* You mean maybe he didn't want too many people in on the business down there? *(Looks to* RUTH *again, as before)* You know Willy got his own ways. *(Looks back to* BOBO*)* Maybe you was late yesterday and he just went on down there without you. Maybe—maybe—he's been callin' you at home tryin' to tell you what happened or something. Maybe—maybe—he just got sick. He's somewhere—he's got to be somewhere. We just got to find him—me and you got to find him. *(Grabs* BOBO *senselessly by the collar and starts to shake him)* We got to!

BOBO *(In sudden angry, frightened agony)* What's the matter with you, Walter! *When a cat take off with your money he don't leave you no maps!*

WALTER *(Turning madly, as though he is looking for* WILLY *in the very room)* Willy! . . . Willy . . . don't do it . . . Please don't do it . . . Man, not with that money . . . Man, please, not with that money . . . Oh, God . . . Don't let it be true . . . *(He is wandering around, crying out for* WILLY *and looking for him or perhaps for help from God)* Man . . . I trusted you . . . Man, I put my life in your hands . . . *(He starts to crumple down on the floor as* RUTH *just covers her face in horror.* MAMA *opens the door and comes into the room, with* BENEATHA *behind her)* Man . . . *(He starts to pound the floor with his fists, sobbing wildly) That money is made out of my father's flesh . . .*

BOBO *(Standing over him helplessly)* I'm sorry, Walter . . . *(Only* WALTER'*s sobs reply.* BOBO *puts on his hat)* I had my life staked on this deal, too . . .

(He exits)

MAMA *(To* WALTER*)* Son—*(She goes to him, bends down to him, talks to his bent head)* Son . . . Is it gone? Son, I gave you sixty-five hundred dollars. Is it gone? All of it? Beneatha's money too?

WALTER *(Lifting his head slowly)* Mama . . . I never . . . went to the bank at all . . .

MAMA *(Not wanting to believe him)* You mean . . . your sister's school money . . . you used that too . . . Walter? . . .

WALTER Yessss! . . . All of it . . . It's all gone . . .

(There is total silence. RUTH *stands with her face covered with her hands;* BENEATHA *leans forlornly against a wall, fingering a piece of red ribbon from the mother's gift.* MAMA *stops and looks at her son without recognition and then, quite without thinking about it, starts to beat him senselessly in the face.* BENEATHA *goes to them and stops it)*

BENEATHA Mama!

*(*MAMA *stops and looks at both of her children and rises slowly and wanders vaguely, aimlessly away from them)*

MAMA I seen . . . him . . . night after night . . . come in . . . and look at that rug . . . and then look at me . . . the red showing in his eyes . . . the veins moving in his head . . . I seen him grow thin and old before he was forty . . . working and working and working like somebody's old horse . . . killing himself . . . and you—you give it all away in a day . . .

BENEATHA Mama—

MAMA Oh, God . . . *(She looks up to Him)* Look down here—and show me the strength.

BENEATHA Mama—

MAMA *(Folding over)* Strength . . .

BENEATHA *(Plaintively)* Mama . . .

MAMA Strength!

CURTAIN

Act III

An hour later.

At curtain, there is a sullen light of gloom in the living room, gray light not unlike that which began the first scene of Act One. At left we can see WALTER *within his room, alone with himself. He is stretched out on the bed, his shirt out and open, his arms under his head. He does not smoke, he does not cry out, he merely lies there, looking up at the ceiling, much as if he were alone in the world.*

In the living room BENEATHA *sits at the table, still surrounded by the now almost ominous packing crates. She sits looking off. We feel that this is a mood struck perhaps an hour before, and it lingers now, full of the empty sound of profound disappointment.*

We see on a line from her brother's bedroom the sameness of their attitudes. Presently the bell rings and BENEATHA *rises without ambition or interest in answering. It is* ASAGAI, *smiling broadly, striding into the room with energy and happy expectation and conversation.*

ASAGAI I came over . . . I had some free time. I thought I might help with the packing. Ah, I like the look of packing crates! A household in preparation for a journey! It depresses some people . . . but for me . . . it is another feeling. Something full of the flow of life, do you understand? Movement, progress . . . It makes me think of Africa.

BENEATHA Africa!

ASAGAI What kind of a mood is this? Have I told you how deeply you move me?

BENEATHA He gave away the money, Asagai . . .

ASAGAI Who gave away what money?

BENEATHA The insurance money. My brother gave it away.

ASAGAI Gave it away?

BENEATHA He made an investment! With a man even Travis wouldn't have trusted.

ASAGAI And it's gone?

BENEATHA Gone!

ASAGAI I'm very sorry . . . And you, now?

BENEATHA Me? . . . Me? . . . Me I'm nothing . . . Me. When I was very small . . . we used to take our sleds out in the wintertime and the only hills we had were the ice-covered stone steps of some houses down the street. And we used to fill them in with snow and make them smooth and slide down them all day . . . and it was very dangerous you know . . . far too steep . . . and sure enough one day a kid named Rufus came down too fast and hit the sidewalk . . . and we saw his face just split open right there in front of us . . . And I remember standing there looking at his bloody open face thinking that was the end of Rufus. But the ambulance came and they took him to the hospital and they fixed the broken bones and they sewed it all up . . . and the next time I saw Rufus he just had a little line down the middle of his face . . . I never got over that . . .

(WALTER *sits up, listening on the bed. Throughout this scene it is important that we feel his reaction at all times, that he visibly respond to the words of his sister and* ASAGAI)

ASAGAI What?

BENEATHA That that was what one person could do for another, fix him up—sew up the problem, make him all right again. That was the most marvelous thing in the world . . . I wanted to do that. I always thought it was the one concrete thing in the world that a human being could do. Fix up the sick, you know—and make them whole again. This was truly being God . . .

ASAGAI You wanted to be God?

BENEATHA No—I wanted to cure. It used to be so important to me. I wanted to cure. It used to matter. I used to care. I mean about people and how their bodies hurt . . .

ASAGAI And you've stopped caring?

BENEATHA Yes—I think so.

ASAGAI Why?

*(*WALTER *rises, goes to the door of his room and is about to open it, then stops and stands listening, leaning on the door jamb)*

BENEATHA Because it doesn't seem deep enough, close enough to what ails mankind—I mean this thing of sewing up bodies or administering drugs. Don't you understand? It was a child's reaction to the world. I thought that doctors had the secret to all the hurts. . . . That's the way a child sees things—or an idealist.

ASAGAI Children see things very well sometimes—and idealists even better.

BENEATHA I know that's what you think. Because you are still where I left off—you still care. This is what you see for the world, for Africa. You with the dreams of the future will patch up all Africa—you are going to cure the Great Sore of colonialism with Independence—

ASAGAI Yes!

BENEATHA Yes—and you think that one word is the penicillin of the human spirit: "Independence!" But then what?

ASAGAI That will be the problem for another time. First we must get there.

BENEATHA And where does it end?

ASAGAI End? Who even spoke of an end? To life? To living?

BENEATHA An end to misery!

ASAGAI *(Smiling)* You sound like a French intellectual.

BENEATHA No! I sound like a human being who just had her future taken right out of her hands! While I was sleeping in my bed in there, things were happening in this world that directly concerned me—and nobody asked me, consulted me—they just went out and did things—and changed my life. Don't you see there isn't any real progress, Asagai, there is only one large circle that we march in, around and around, each of us with our own little picture—in front of us—our own little mirage that we think is the future.

ASAGAI That is the mistake.

BENEATHA What?

ASAGAI What you just said—about the circle. It isn't a circle—it's simply a long line—as in geometry, you know, one that reaches into infinity. And because we cannot see the end—we also cannot see how it changes. And it is very odd but those who see the changes are called "idealists"—and those who cannot, or refuse to think, they are the "realists." It is very strange, and amusing too, I think.

BENEATHA You—you are almost religious.

ASAGAI Yes . . . I think I have the religion of doing what is necessary in the world—and of worshipping man—because he is so marvelous, you see.

BENEATHA Man is foul! And the human race deserves its misery!

ASAGAI You see: *you* have become the religious one in the old sense. Already, and after such a small defeat, you are worshipping despair.

BENEATHA From now on, I worship the truth—and the truth is that people are puny, small and selfish. . . .

ASAGAI Truth? Why is it that you despairing ones always think that only you have the truth? I never thought to see *you* like that. You! Your brother made a stupid, childish mistake—and you are grateful to him. So that now you can give up the ailing human race on account of it. You talk about what good is struggle; what good is anything? Where are we all going? And why are we bothering?

BENEATHA *And you cannot answer it!* All your talk and dreams about Africa and Independence. Independence and then what? What about all the crooks and petty thieves and just plain idiots who will come into power to steal and plunder the same as before—only now they will be black and do it in the name of the new Independence—You cannot answer that.

ASAGAI *(Shouting over her) I live the answer! (Pause)* In my village at home it is the exceptional man who can even read a newspaper . . . or who ever *sees* a book at all. I will go home and much of what I will have to say will seem strange to the people of my village . . . But I will teach and work and things will happen, slowly and swiftly. At times it will seem that nothing changes at all . . . and then again . . . the sudden dramatic events which make history leap into the future. And then quiet again. Retrogression even. Guns, murder, revolution. And I even will have moments when I wonder if the quiet was not better than all that death and hatred. But I will look about my village at the illiteracy and disease and ignorance and I will not wonder long. And perhaps . . . perhaps I will be a great man . . . I mean perhaps I will hold on to the substance of truth and find my way always with the right course . . . and perhaps for it I will be butchered in my bed some night by the servants of empire . . .

BENEATHA *The martyr!*

ASAGAI . . . or perhaps I shall live to be a very old man, respected and esteemed in my new nation . . . And perhaps I shall hold office and this is what I'm trying to tell you, Alaiyo; perhaps the things I believe now for my country will be wrong and outmoded, and I will not understand and do terrible things to have things my way or merely to keep my power. Don't you see that there will be young men and women, not British soldiers then, but my own black countrymen . . . to step out of the shadows some evening and slit my then useless throat? Don't you see they have always been there . . . that they always will be. And that such a thing as my own death will be an advance? They who might kill me even . . . actually replenish me!

BENEATHA Oh, Asagai, I know all that.

ASAGAI Good! Then stop moaning and groaning and tell me what you plan to do.

BENEATHA Do?

ASAGAI I have a bit of a suggestion.

BENEATHA What?

ASAGAI *(Rather quietly for him)* That when it is all over—that you come home with me—

BENEATHA *(Slapping herself on the forehead with exasperation born of misunderstanding)* Oh—Asagai—at this moment you decide to be romantic!

ASAGAI *(Quickly understanding the misunderstanding)* My dear, young creature of the New World—I do not mean across the city—I mean across the ocean; home—to Africa.

BENEATHA *(Slowly understanding and turning to him with murmured amazement)* To—to Nigeria?

ASAGAI Yes! . . . *(Smiling and lifting his arms playfully)* Three hundred years later the African Prince rose up out of the seas and swept the maiden back across the middle passage over which her ancestors had come—

BENEATHA *(Unable to play)* Nigeria?

ASAGAI Nigeria. Home. *(Coming to her with genuine romantic flippancy)* I will show you our mountains and our stars; and give you cool drinks from gourds and teach you the old songs and the ways of our people—and, in time, we will pretend that—*(Very softly)*—you have only been away for a day—

(She turns her back to him, thinking. He swings her around and takes her full in his arms in a long embrace which proceeds to passion)

BENEATHA *(Pulling away)* You're getting me all mixed up—

ASAGAI Why?

BENEATHA Too many things—too many things have happened today. I must sit down and think. I don't know what I feel about anything right this minute.

(She promptly sits down and props her chin on her fist)

ASAGAI *(Charmed)* All right, I shall leave you. No—don't get up. *(Touching her, gently, sweetly)* Just sit awhile and think . . . Never be afraid to sit awhile and think. *(He goes to door and looks at her)* How often I have looked at you and said, "Ah—so this is what the New World hath finally wrought . . . ."

(He exits. BENEATHA *sits on alone. Presently* WALTER *enters from his room and starts to rummage through things, feverishly looking for something. She looks up and turns in her seat)*

BENEATHA *(Hissingly)* Yes—just look at what the New World hath wrought! . . . Just look! *(She gestures with bitter disgust)* There he is! *Monsieur le petit bourgeois noir*—himself! There he is—Symbol of a Rising Class! Entrepreneur! Titan of the system! *(*WALTER *ignores her completely and continues frantically and destructively looking for something and hurling things to floor and tearing things out of their place in his search.* BENEATHA *ignores the eccentricity of his actions and goes on with the monologue of insult)* Did you dream of yachts on Lake Michigan, Brother? Did you see yourself on that Great Day sitting down at the Conference Table, surrounded by all the mighty bald-headed men in America? All halted, waiting, breathless, waiting for your pronouncements on industry? Waiting for you—Chairman of the Board? *(*WALTER *finds what he is looking for—a small piece of white paper—and pushes it in his pocket and puts on his coat and rushes out without ever having looked at her. She shouts after him)* I look at you and I see the final triumph of stupidity in the world!

(The door slams and she returns to just sitting again. RUTH *comes quickly out of* MAMA*'s room)*

RUTH Who was that?

BENEATHA Your husband.

RUTH Where did he go?

BENEATHA Who knows—maybe he has an appointment at U.S. Steel.

RUTH *(Anxiously, with frightened eyes)* You didn't say nothing bad to him, did you?

BENEATHA Bad? Say anything bad to him? No—I told him he was a sweet boy and full of dreams and everything is strictly peachy keen, as the ofay kids say!

*(*MAMA *enters from her bedroom. She is lost, vague, trying to catch hold, to make some sense of her former command of the world, but it still eludes her. A sense of waste overwhelms her gait; a measure of apology rides on her shoulders. She goes to her plant, which has remained on the table, looks at it, picks it up and takes it to the window sill and sits it outside, and she stands and looks at it a long moment. Then she closes the window, straightens her body with effort and turns around to her children)*

MAMA Well—ain't it a mess in here, though? *(A false cheerfulness, a beginning of something)* I guess we all better stop moping around and get some work done. All this unpacking and everything we got to do. *(*RUTH *raises her head slowly in response to the sense of the line; and* BENEATHA *in similar manner turns very slowly to look at her mother)* One of you all better call the moving people and tell 'em not to come.

RUTH Tell 'em not to come?

MAMA Of course, baby. Ain't no need in 'em coming all the way here and having to go back. They charges for that too. *(She sits down, fingers to her brow, thinking)* Lord, ever since I was a little girl, I always remembers people saying, "Lena—Lena Eggleston, you aims too high all the time. You needs to slow down and see life a little more like it is. Just slow down some." That's what they always used to say down home—"Lord, that Lena Eggleston is a high-minded thing. She'll get her due one day!"

RUTH No, Lena . . .

MAMA Me and Big Walter just didn't never learn right.

RUTH Lena, no! We gotta go. Bennie—tell her . . . *(She rises and crosses to* BENEATHA *with her arms outstretched.* BENEATHA *doesn't respond)* Tell her we can still move . . . the notes ain't but a hundred and twenty-five a month. We got four grown people in this house—we can work . . .

MAMA *(To herself)* Just aimed too high all the time—

RUTH *(Turning and going to* MAMA *fast—the words pouring out with urgency and desperation)* Lena—I'll work . . . I'll work twenty hours a day in all the kitchens in Chicago . . . I'll strap my baby on my back if I have to and scrub all the floors in America and wash all the sheets in America if I have to—but we got to move . . . We got to get out of here . . .

*(*MAMA *reaches out absently and pats* RUTH*'s hand)*

MAMA No—I sees things differently now. Been thinking 'bout some of the things we could do to fix this place up some. I seen a second-hand bureau over on Maxwell Street just the other day that could fit right there. *(She points to where the new furniture might go.* RUTH *wanders away from her)* Would need some new handles on it and then a little varnish and then it look like something brand-new. And—we can put up them new curtains in the kitchen . . . Why this place be looking fine. Cheer us all up so that we forget trouble ever came . . . *(To* RUTH*)* And you could get some nice screens to put up in your room round the baby's bassinet . . . *(She looks at both of them, pleadingly)* Sometimes you just got to know when to give up some things . . . and hold on to what you got.

*(*WALTER *enters from the outside, looking spent and leaning against the door, his coat hanging from him)*

MAMA Where you been, son?

WALTER *(Breathing hard)* Made a call.

MAMA To who, son?

WALTER To The Man.

MAMA What man, baby?

WALTER The Man, Mama. Don't you know who The Man is?

RUTH Walter Lee?

WALTER *The Man.* Like the guys in the streets say—The Man. Captain Boss—Mistuh Charley . . . Old Captain Please Mr. Bossman . . .

BENEATHA *(Suddenly)* Lindner!

WALTER That's right! That's good. I told him to come right over.

BENEATHA *(Fiercely, understanding)* For what? What do you want to see him for!

WALTER *(Looking at his sister)* We going to do business with him.

MAMA What you talking 'bout, son?

WALTER Talking 'bout life, Mama. You all always telling me to see life like it is. Well—I laid in there on my back today . . . and I figured it out. Life just like it is. Who gets and who don't get. *(He sits down with his coat on and laughs)* Mama, you know it's all divided up. Life is. Sure enough. Between the takers and the "tooken." *(He laughs)* I've figured it out finally. *(He looks around at them)* Yeah. Some of us always getting "tooken." *(He laughs)* People like Willy Harris, they don't never get "tooken." And you know why the rest of us do? 'Cause we all mixed up. Mixed up bad. We get to looking 'round for the right and the wrong; and we worry about it and cry about it and stay up nights trying to figure out 'bout the wrong and the right of things all the time . . . And all the time, man, them takers is out there operating, just taking and taking. Willy Harris? Shoot—Willy Harris don't even count. He don't even count in the big scheme of things. But I'll say one thing for old Willy Harris . . . he's taught me something. He's taught me to keep my eye on what counts in this world. Yeah—*(Shouting out a little)* Thanks, Willy!

RUTH What did you call that man for, Walter Lee?

WALTER Called him to tell him to come on over to the show. Gonna put on a show for the man. Just what he wants to see. You see, Mama, the man came here today and he told us that them people out there where you want us to move—well they so upset they willing to pay us not to move out there. *(He laughs again)* And—and oh, Mama—you would of been proud of the way me and Ruth and Bennie acted. We told him to get out . . . Lord have mercy! We told the man to get out. Oh, we was some proud folks this afternoon, yeah. *(He lights a cigarette)* We were still full of that old-time stuff . . .

RUTH *(Coming toward him slowly)* You talking 'bout taking them people's money to keep us from moving in that house?

WALTER I ain't just talking 'bout it, baby—I'm telling you that's what's going to happen.

BENEATHA Oh, God! Where is the bottom! Where is the real honest-to-God bottom so he can't go any farther!

WALTER See—that's the old stuff. You and that boy that was here today. You all want everybody to carry a flag and a spear and sing some marching songs, huh? You wanna spend your life looking into things and trying to find the right and the wrong part, huh? Yeah. You know what's going to happen to that boy someday—he'll find himself sitting in a dungeon, locked in forever—and the takers will have the key! Forget it, baby! There ain't no causes—there ain't nothing but taking in this world, and he who takes most is smartest—and it don't make a damn bit of difference *how.*

MAMA You making something inside me cry, son. Some awful pain inside me.

WALTER Don't cry, Mama. Understand. That white man is going to walk in that door able to write checks for more money than we ever had. It's important to him and I'm going to help him . . . I'm going to put on the show, Mama.

MAMA Son—I come from five generations of people who was slaves and sharecroppers—but ain't nobody in my family never let nobody pay 'em no money that was a way of telling us we wasn't fit to walk the earth. We ain't never been that poor. *(Raising her eyes and looking at him)* We ain't never been that dead inside.

BENEATHA Well—we are dead now. All the talk about dreams and sunlight that goes on in this house. All dead.

WALTER What's the matter with you all! I didn't make this world! It was give to me this way! Hell, yes, I want me some yachts someday! Yes, I want to hang some real pearls 'round my wife's neck. Ain't she supposed to wear no pearls? Somebody tell me—tell me, who decides which women is suppose to wear pearls in this world. I tell you I am a *man*—and I think my wife should wear some pearls in this world!

(This last line hangs a good while and WALTER *begins to move about the room. The word "Man" has penetrated his consciousness; he mumbles it to himself repeatedly between strange agitated pauses as he moves about)*

MAMA Baby, how you going to feel on the inside?

WALTER Fine! . . . Going to feel fine . . . a man . . .

MAMA You won't have nothing left then, Walter Lee.

WALTER *(Coming to her)* I'm going to feel fine, Mama. I'm going to look that son-of-a-bitch in the eyes and say—*(He falters)*—and say, "All right, Mr. Lindner—*(He falters even more)*—that's your neighborhood out there. You got the right to keep it like you want. You got the right to have it like you want. Just write the check and—the house is yours." And, and I am going to say—*(His voice almost breaks)* And you—you people just put the money in my hand and you won't have to live next to this bunch of stinking niggers! . . . *(He straightens up and moves away from his mother, walking around the room)* Maybe—maybe I'll just get down on my black knees . . . *(He does so;* RUTH *and* BENNIE *and* MAMA *watch him in frozen horror)* Captain, Mistuh, Bossman. *(He starts crying)* A-hee-hee-hee! *(Wringing his hands in profoundly anguished imitation)* Yasssssuh! Great White Father, just gi' ussen de money, fo' God's sake, and we's ain't gwine come out deh and dirty up yo' white folks neighborhood . . .

(He breaks down completely, then gets up and goes into the bedroom)

BENEATHA That is not a man. That is nothing but a toothless rat.

MAMA Yes—death done come in this here house. *(She is nodding, slowly, reflectively)* Done come walking in my house. On the lips of my children. You what supposed to be my beginning again. You—what supposed to be my harvest. *(To* BENEATHA*)* You—you mourning your brother?

BENEATHA He's no brother of mine.

MAMA What you say?

BENEATHA I said that that individual in that room is no brother of mine.

MAMA That's what I thought you said. You feeling like you better than he is today? *(*BENEATHA *does not answer)* Yes? What you tell him a minute ago? That he wasn't a man? Yes? You give him up for me? You done wrote his epitaph too—like the rest of the world? Well, who give you the privilege?

BENEATHA Be on my side for once! You saw what he just did, Mama! You saw him—down on his knees. Wasn't it you who taught me—to despise any man who would do that. Do what he's going to do.

MAMA Yes—I taught you that. Me and your daddy. But I thought I taught you something else too . . . I thought I taught you to love him.

BENEATHA Love him? There is nothing left to love.

MAMA There is always something left to love. And if you ain't learned that, you ain't learned nothing. *(Looking at her)* Have you cried for that boy today? I don't mean for yourself and for the family 'cause we lost the money. I mean for him; what he been through and what it done to him. Child, when do you think is the time to love somebody the most; when they done good and made things easy for everybody? Well then, you ain't through learning—because that ain't the time at all. It's when he's at his lowest and can't believe in hisself 'cause the world done whipped him so. When you starts measuring somebody, measure him right, child, measure him right. Make sure you done taken into account what hills and valleys he come through before he got to wherever he is.

*(*TRAVIS *bursts into the room at the end of the speech, leaving the door open)*

TRAVIS Grandmama—the moving men are downstairs! The truck just pulled up.

MAMA *(Turning and looking at him)* Are they, baby? They downstairs?

(She sighs and sits. LINDNER *appears in the doorway. He peers in and knocks lightly, to gain attention, and comes in. All turn to look at him)*

LINDNER *(Hat and briefcase in hand)* Uh—hello . . . (RUTH *crosses mechanically to the bedroom door and opens it and lets it swing open freely and slowly as the lights come up on* WALTER *within, still in his coat, sitting at the far corner of the room. He looks up and out through the room to* LINDNER*)*

RUTH He's here.

(A long minute passes and WALTER *slowly gets up)*

LINDNER *(Coming to the table with efficiency, putting his briefcase on the table and starting to unfold papers and unscrew fountain pens)* Well, I certainly was glad to hear from you people. *(*WALTER *has begun the trek out of the room, slowly and awkwardly, rather like a small boy, passing the back of his sleeve across his mouth from time to time)* Life can really be so much simpler than people let it be most of the time. Well—with whom do I negotiate? You, Mrs. Younger, or your son here? *(*MAMA *sits with her hands folded on her lap and her eyes closed as* WALTER *advances.* TRAVIS *goes close to* LINDNER *and looks at the papers curiously)* Just some official papers, sonny.

RUTH Travis, you go downstairs.

MAMA *(Opening her eyes and looking into* WALTER'S*)* No. Travis, you stay right here. And you make him understand what you doing, Walter Lee. You teach him good. Like Willy Harris taught you. You show where our five generations done come to. Go ahead, son—

WALTER *(Looks down into his boy's eyes.* TRAVIS *grins at him merrily and* WALTER *draws him beside him with his arm lightly around his shoulders)* Well, Mr. Lindner. (BENEATHA *turns away)* We called you—*(There is a profound, simple groping quality in his speech)*—because, well, me and my family *(He looks around and shifts from one foot to the other)* Well—we are very plain people . . .

LINDNER Yes—

WALTER I mean—I have worked as a chauffeur most of my life—and my wife here, she does domestic work in people's kitchens. So does my mother. I mean—we are plain people . . .

LINDNER Yes, Mr. Younger—

WALTER *(Really like a small boy, looking down at his shoes and then up at the man)* And—uh—well, my father, well, he was a laborer most of his life.

LINDNER *(Absolutely confused)* Uh, yes—

WALTER *(Looking down at his toes once again)* My father almost beat a man to death once because this man called him a bad name or something, you know what I mean?

LINDNER No, I'm afraid I don't.

WALTER *(Finally straightening up)* Well, what I mean is that we come from people who had a lot of pride. I mean—we are very proud people. And that's my sister over there and she's going to be a doctor—and we are very proud—

LINDNER Well—I am sure that is very nice, but—

WALTER *(Starting to cry and facing the man eye to eye)* What I am telling you is that we called you over here to tell you that we are very proud and that this is—this is my son, who makes the sixth generation of our family in this country, and that we have all thought about your offer and we have decided to move into our house because my father—my father—he earned it. *(MAMA has her eyes closed and is rocking back and forth as though she were in church, with her head nodding the amen yes)* We don't want to make no trouble for nobody or fight no causes—but we will try to be good neighbors. That's all we got to say. *(He looks the man absolutely in the eyes)* We don't want your money.

(He turns and walks away from the man)

LINDNER *(Looking around at all of them)* I take it then that you have decided to occupy.

BENEATHA That's what the man said.

LINDNER *(To MAMA in her reverie)* Then I would like to appeal to you, Mrs. Younger. You are older and wiser and understand things better I am sure . . .

MAMA *(Rising)* I am afraid you don't understand. My son said we was going to move and there ain't nothing left for me to say. *(Shaking her head with double meaning)* You know how these young folks is nowadays, mister. Can't do a thing with 'em. Good-bye.

LINDNER *(Folding up his materials)* Well—if you are that final about it . . . There is nothing left for me to say. *(He finishes. He is almost ignored by the family, who are concentrating on WALTER LEE. At the door LINDNER halts and looks around)* I sure hope you people know what you're doing.

(He shakes his head and exits)

RUTH *(Looking around and coming to life)* Well, for God's sake—if the moving men are here—LET'S GET THE HELL OUT OF HERE!

MAMA *(Into action)* Ain't it the truth! Look at all this here mess. Ruth, put Travis' good jacket on him . . . Walter Lee, fix your tie and tuck your shirt in, you look just like somebody's hoodlum. Lord have mercy, where is my plant? *(She flies to get it amid the general bustling of the family, who are deliberately trying to ignore the nobility of the past moment)* You all start on down . . . Travis child, don't go empty-handed . . . Ruth, where did I put that box with my skillets in it? I want to be in charge of it myself . . . I'm going to make us the biggest dinner we ever ate tonight . . . Beneatha, what's the matter with them stockings? Pull them things up, girl . . .

(The family starts to file out as two moving men appear and begin to carry out the heavier pieces of furniture, bumping into the family as they move about)

BENEATHA Mama, Asagai—asked me to marry him today and go to Africa—

MAMA *(In the middle of her getting-ready activity)* He did? You ain't old enough to marry nobody—*(Seeing the moving men lifting one of her chairs precariously)* Darling, that ain't no bale of cotton, please handle it so we can sit in it again. I had that chair twenty-five years . . .

(The movers sigh with exasperation and go on with their work)

BENEATHA *(Girlishly and unreasonably trying to pursue the conversation)* To go to Africa, Mama—be a doctor in Africa . . .

MAMA *(Distracted)* Yes, baby—

WALTER Africa! What he want you to go to Africa for?

BENEATHA To practice there . . .

WALTER Girl, if you don't get all them silly ideas out your head! You better marry yourself a man with some loot . . .

BENEATHA *(Angrily, precisely as in the first scene of the play)* What have you got to do with who I marry!

WALTER Plenty. Now I think George Murchison—

(He and BENEATHA *go out yelling at each other vigorously;* BENEATHA *is heard saying that she would not marry* GEORGE MURCHISON *if he were Adam and she were Eve, etc. The anger is loud and real till their voices diminish.* RUTH *stands at the door and turns to* MAMA *and smiles knowingly)*

MAMA *(Fixing her hat at last)* Yeah—they something all right, my children . . .

RUTH Yeah—they're something. Let's go, Lena.

MAMA *(Stalling, starting to look around at the house)* Yes—I'm coming. Ruth—

RUTH Yes?

MAMA *(Quietly, woman to woman)* He finally come into his manhood today, didn't he? Kind of like a rainbow after the rain . . .

RUTH *(Biting her lip lest her own pride explode in front of* MAMA*)* Yes, Lena.

(WALTER'S *voice calls for them raucously)*

MAMA *(Waving* RUTH *out vaguely)* All right, honey—go on down. I be down directly.

(RUTH *hesitates, then exits.* MAMA *stands, at last alone in the living room, her plant on the table before her as the lights start to come down. She looks around at all the walls and ceilings and suddenly, despite herself, while the children call below, a great heaving thing rises in her and she puts her fist to her mouth, takes a final desperate look, pulls her coat about her, pats her hat and goes out. The lights dim down. The door opens and she comes back in, grabs her plant, and goes out for the last time)*

CURTAIN

1959

Edward Albee b. 1928

Albee's association with the theater began early. Two weeks after his birth in Washington, D.C., Albee was adopted by the wealthy owner of a chain of vaudeville theaters, Reed Albee, and his wife, Frances. Theater people came and went during Albee's childhood, many visiting the family at their lavish house in Larchmont. The young Albee attended the theater in New York City and began writing both poetry and plays. He continued writing throughout his fitful academic career—he was dismissed from two prep schools before graduating from Choate and was later dismissed from Trinity College while a sophomore. At twenty-two, Albee left home and lived in Manhattan during the 1950s—working as an office boy, a salesman, and a Western Union delivery boy. The constants in his life were writing and theater-going.

According to a story which has by now become legend, Albee wrote *The Zoo Story* just before his thirtieth birthday on a wobbly table in his kitchen in the space of three weeks. The play then followed a circuitous route that ended with its being produced at the Schiller Theater Werkstatt in Berlin in 1959. That play received American production, on a double bill with Beckett's *Krapp's Last Tape,* in January of 1960; *The Sandbox* was produced in April of that year at The Jazz Gallery in New York City. With *The Death of Bessie Smith,* these plays comprise Albee's first works for theater.

The Sandbox treats characters that were to appear later in his *The American Dream.* The materialistic, and mechanistic, married couple—intent on killing off the wife's troublesome, aging mother—create a seaside idyll that must end with the death of the 86-year-old woman. Working within clichés of both language and social behavior, Albee maps the nastiness of the inhuman "Mommy" and "Daddy." Replete with suggestions of sexual impotence that controls social power, the very brief play (requiring only fourteen minutes to perform) packs a world of content into its few lines. In this play, the son of the couple becomes the Angel of Death; in *The American Dream* he is a much more active agent of social coercion.

Albee's first full-length play and biggest box office success, *Who's Afraid of Virginia Woolf?,* was produced in 1962, preceded by *The American Dream* (1961) and followed by *Tiny Alice* (1964), *A Delicate Balance* (1966), *Box* and *Quotations from Chairman Mao Tse-tung* (1968), *All Over* (1971), *Seascape* (1975), and others. Each play is marked by Albee's inventive handling of dialogue. While colloquial, his language is pared to essentials. Albee plays with words—from the puns in *Tiny Alice* to the long sentences filled with qualifiers in *A Delicate Balance.* Clichés, revivified for the theatrical purpose at hand, appear frequently.

Albee's earliest plays remain among the best-known American drama of this century, dealing with human loneliness, the inability or unwillingness of people to connect with others, and about the illusions people maintain in order to ignore the emotional sterility of their lives. Although Albee's worldview is existential, his focus is psychological, not metaphysical. He is not an absurdist playwright either stylistically or thematically, but rather part of the continuing American (and English) experimentation with basically realistic theater.

Carol A. Burns
Southern Illinois University

PRIMARY WORKS

The American Dream and *The Zoo Story,* 1961; *Who's Afraid of Virginia Woolf?,* 1962; *Sandbox* and *The Death of Bessie Smith,* 1964; *The Plays,* vol. 2 (*Tiny Alice, A Delicate Balance, Box, Quotations from Chairman Mao Tse-tung*), 1981; *The Plays,* vol. 3 (*Seascape, Counting the Ways and Listening, All Over*), 1982; *Finding the Sun,* 1994; *Three Tall Women,* 1995.

The Sandbox

A Brief Play, in Memory of My Grandmother (1876–1959)

Players

THE YOUNG MAN, 25, *a good-looking, well-built boy in a bathing suit*
MOMMY, 55, *a well-dressed, imposing woman*
DADDY, 60, *a small man; gray, thin*
GRANDMA, 86, *a tiny, wizened woman with bright eyes*
THE MUSICIAN, *no particular age, but young would be nice*

NOTE. *When, in the course of the play,* MOMMY *and* DADDY *call each other by these names, there should be no suggestion of regionalism. These names are of empty affection and point up the pre-senility and vacuity of their characters.*

SCENE. *A bare stage, with only the following: Near the footlights, far stage right, two simple chairs set side by side, facing the audience; near the footlights, far stage left, a chair facing stage right with a music stand before it; farther back, and stage center, slightly elevated and raked, a large child's sandbox with a toy pail and shovel; the background is the sky, which alters from brightest day to deepest night.*

At the beginning, it is brightest day; the YOUNG MAN *is alone on stage to the rear of the sandbox, and to one side. He is doing calisthenics; he does calisthenics until quite at the very end of the play. These calisthenics, employing the arms only, should suggest the beating and fluttering of wings. The* YOUNG MAN *is, after all, the Angel of Death.*

MOMMY *and* DADDY *enter from stage left,* MOMMY *first.*

MOMMY (*motioning to* DADDY) Well, here we are; this is the beach.
DADDY (*whining*) I'm cold.
MOMMY (*dismissing him with a little laugh*) Don't be silly; it's as warm as toast. Look at that nice young man over there: *he* doesn't think it's cold. (*Waves to the* YOUNG MAN) Hello.
YOUNG MAN (*with an endearing smile*) Hi!
MOMMY (*looking about*) This will do perfectly . . . don't you think so, Daddy? There's sand there . . . and the water beyond. What do you think, Daddy?
DADDY (*vaguely*) Whatever you say, Mommy.
MOMMY (*with the same little laugh*) Well, of course . . . whatever I say. Then, it's settled, is it?

DADDY (*shrugs*) She's *your* mother, not mine.

MOMMY I know she's my mother. What do you take me for? (*A pause*) All right, now; let's get on with it. (*She shouts into the wings, stage-left*) You! Out there! You can come in now. (*The* MUSICIAN *enters, seats himself in the chair, stage-left, places music on the music stand, is ready to play.* MOMMY *nods approvingly.*) Very nice; very nice. Are you ready, Daddy? Let's go get Grandma.

DADDY Whatever you say, Mommy.

MOMMY (*leading the way out, stage-left*) Of course, whatever I say. (*To the* MUSICIAN) You can begin now. (*The* MUSICIAN *begins playing;* MOMMY *and* DADDY *exit; the* MUSICIAN, *all the while playing, nods to the* YOUNG MAN.)

YOUNG MAN (*with the same endearing smile*): *Hi!* (*After a moment,* MOMMY *and* DADDY *re-enter, carrying* GRANDMA. *She is borne in by their hands under her armpits; she is quite rigid; her legs are drawn up; her feet do not touch the ground; the expression on her ancient face is that of puzzlement and fear.*)

DADDY Where do we put her?

MOMMY (*the same little laugh*) Wherever I say, of course. Let me see . . . well . . . all right, over there . . . in the sandbox. (*Pause*) Well, what are you waiting for, Daddy? . . . The sandbox! (*Together they carry* GRANDMA *over to the sandbox and more or less dump her in.*)

GRANDMA (*righting herself to a sitting position; her voice a cross between a baby's laugh and cry*) Ahhhhhh! Graaaaa!

DADDY (*dusting himself*) What do we do now?

MOMMY (*to the* MUSICIAN) You can stop now. (*The* MUSICIAN *stops.*) (*Back to* DADDY) What do you mean, what do we do now? We go over there and sit down, of course. (*To the* YOUNG MAN) Hello there.

YOUNG MAN (*again smiling*) Hi! (MOMMY *and* DADDY *move to the chairs, stage-right, and sit down. A pause.*)

GRANDMA (*same as before*) Ahhhhhh! Ah-haaaaaa! Graaaaaa!

DADDY Do you think . . . do you think she's . . . comfortable?

MOMMY (*impatiently*) How would I know?

DADDY (*pause*) What do we do now?

MOMMY (*as if remembering*) We . . . wait. We . . . sit here . . . and we wait . . . that's what we do.

DADDY (*after a pause*) Shall we talk to each other?

MOMMY (*with that little laugh; picking something off her dress*) Well, *you* can talk, if you want to . . . if you can think of anything to say . . . if you can think of anything new.

DADDY (*thinks*) No . . . I suppose not.

MOMMY (*with a triumphant laugh*) Of course not!

GRANDMA (*banging the toy shovel against the pail*) Haaaaaa! Ah-haaaaaa!

MOMMY (*out over the audience*) Be quiet Grandma . . . just be quiet, and wait. (GRANDMA *throws a shovelful of sand at* MOMMY.) (*Still out over the audience*) She's throwing sand at me! You stop that, Grandma; you stop throwing sand at Mommy! (*To* DADDY) She's throwing sand at me. (DADDY *looks around at* GRANDMA, *who screams at him.*)

GRANDMA GRAAAAA!

MOMMY Don't look at her. Just . . . sit here . . . be very still . . . and wait. (*To the* MU-

SICIAN) You . . . uh . . . you go ahead and do whatever it is you do. (*The* MUSICIAN *plays.* MOMMY *and* DADDY *are fixed, staring out beyond the audience.* GRANDMA *looks at them, looks at the* MUSICIAN, *looks at the sandox, throws down the shovel.*)

GRANDMA Ah-haaaaaa! Graaaaaa! (*Looks for reaction; gets none. Now . . . directly to the audience*) Honestly! What a way to treat an old woman! Drag her out of the house . . . stick her in a car . . . bring her out here from the city . . . dump her in a pile of sand . . . and leave her here to set. I'm eighty-six years old! I was married when I was seventeen. To a farmer. He died when I was thirty. (*To the* MUSICIAN) Will you stop that, please? (*The* MUSICIAN *stops playing.*) I'm a feeble old woman . . . how do you expect anybody to hear me over that peep! peep! peep! (*To herself*) There's no respect around here. (*To the* YOUNG MAN) There's no respect around here!

YOUNG MAN (*same smile*) Hi!

GRANDMA (*after a pause, a mild double-take, continues, to the audience*) My husband died when I was thirty (*indicates* MOMMY), and I had to raise that big cow over there all by my lonesome. You can imagine what *that was like.* Lordy! (*To the* YOUNG MAN) Where'd they get *you?*

YOUNG MAN Oh . . . I've been around for a while.

GRANDMA I'll bet you have! Heh, heh, heh. Will you look at you!

YOUNG MAN (*flexing his muscles*) Isn't that something? (*Continues his calisthenics.*)

GRANDMA Boy, oh boy; I'll say. Pretty good.

YOUNG MAN (*sweetly*) I'll say.

GRANDMA Where ya from?

YOUNG MAN Southern California.

GRANDMA (*nodding*) Figgers; figgers. What's your name, honey?

YOUNG MAN I don't know . . .

GRANDMA (*to the audience*) Bright, too!

YOUNG MAN I mean . . . I mean, they haven't given me one yet . . . the studio . . .

GRANDMA (*giving him the once-over*) You don't say . . . you don't say. Well . . . uh, I've got to talk some more . . . don't you go 'way.

YOUNG MAN Oh, no.

GRANDMA (*turning her attention back to the audience*) Fine; fine. (*Then, once more, back to the* YOUNG MAN) You're . . . you're an actor, hunh?

YOUNG MAN (*beaming*) Yes. I am.

GRANDMA (*to the audience again; shrugs*) I'm smart that way. *Anyhow,* I had to raise . . . *that* over there all by my lonesome; and what's next to her there . . . that's what she married. Rich? I tell you . . . money, money, money. They took me off the farm . . . which was real decent of them . . . and they moved me into the big town house with *them* . . . fixed a nice place for me under the stove . . . gave me an army blanket . . . and my own dish . . . my very own dish! So, what have I got to complain about? Nothing, of course! I'm not complaining. (*She looks up at the sky, shouts to someone off stage*) Shouldn't it be getting dark now, dear? (*The lights dim; night comes on. The* MUSICIAN *begins to play; it becomes deepest night. There are spotlights on all the players, including the* YOUNG MAN, *who is, of course, continuing his calisthenics.*)

DADDY (*stirring*) It's nighttime.

MOMMY Shhhh. Be still . . . wait.

DADDY (*whining*) It's so hot.

MOMMY Shhhhhh. Be still . . . wait.

GRANDMA (*to herself*) That's better. Night. (*To the* MUSICIAN) Honey, do you play all through this part? (*The* MUSICIAN *nods.*) Well, keep it nice and soft; that's a good boy. (*The* MUSICIAN *nods again; plays softly.*) That's nice. (*There is an off-stage rumble.*)

DADDY (*starting*) What was that?

MOMMY (*beginning to weep*) It was nothing.

DADDY It was . . . it was . . . thunder . . . or a wave breaking . . . or something.

MOMMY (*whispering, through her tears*) It was an off-stage rumble . . . and you know what *that* means . . .

DADDY I forget . . .

MOMMY (*barely able to talk*) It means the time has come for poor Grandma . . . and I can't bear it!

DADDY (*vacantly*) I . . . I suppose you've got to be brave.

GRANDMA (*mocking*) That's right, kid; be brave. You'll bear up; you'll get over it. (*Another off-stage rumble . . . louder.*)

MOMMY Ohhhhhhhhhh . . . poor Grandma . . . poor Grandma . . .

GRANDMA (*to* MOMMY) I'm fine! I'm all right! It hasn't happened yet! (*A violent off-stage rumble. All the lights go out, save the spot on the* YOUNG MAN; *the* MUSICIAN *stops playing.*)

MOMMY Ohhhhhhhhhh . . . Ohhhhhhhhhh . . . (*Silence.*)

GRANDMA Don't put the lights up yet . . . I'm not ready; I'm not quite ready. (*Silence*) All right, dear . . . I'm about done. (*The lights come up again, to the brightest day; the* MUSICIAN *begins to play.* GRANDMA *is discovered, still in the sandbox, lying on her side, propped up on an elbow, half covered, busily shoveling sand over herself.*)

GRANDMA (*muttering*) I don't know how I'm supposed to do anything with this goddam toy shovel . . .

DADDY Mommy! It's daylight!

MOMMY (*brightly*) So it is! Well! Our long night is over. We must put away our tears, take off our mourning . . . and face the future. It's our duty.

GRANDMA (*still shoveling; mimicking*) . . . take off our mourning . . . face the future . . . Lordy! (MOMMY *and* DADDY *rise, stretch.* MOMMY *waves to the* YOUNG MAN.)

YOUNG MAN (*with that smile*) Hi! (GRANDMA *plays dead.*[!] MOMMY *and* DADDY *go over to look at her; she is a little more than half buried in the sand; the toy shovel is in her hands, which are crossed on her breast.*)

MOMMY (*before the sandbox; shaking her head*) Lovely! It's . . . it's hard to be sad . . . she looks . . . so happy. (*With pride and conviction*) It pays to do things well. (*To the* MUSICIAN) All right, you can stop now, if you want to. I mean, stay around for a swim, or something; it's all right with us. (*She sighs heavily*) Well, Daddy . . . off we go.

DADDY Brave Mommy!

MOMMY Brave Daddy! (*They exit, stage-left.*)

GRANDMA (*after they leave; lying quite still*) It pays to do things well . . . Boy, oh boy! (*She tries to sit up*) . . . well, kids . . . (*but she finds she can't*) . . . I . . . I can't get up. I . . . I can't move . . . (*The* YOUNG MAN *stops his calisthenics, nods to the* MUSICIAN, *walks over to* GRANDMA, *kneels down by the sandbox.*)

GRANDMA I . . . can't move . . .
YOUNG MAN Shhhhh . . . be very still . . .
GRANDMA I . . . I can't move . . .
YOUNG MAN Uh . . . ma'am; I . . . I have a line here.
GRANDMA Oh, I'm sorry, sweetie; you go right ahead.
YOUNG MAN I am . . . uh . . .
GRANDMA Take your time, dear.
YOUNG MAN (*prepares; delivers the line like a real amateur*) I am the Angel of Death. I am . . . uh . . . I am come for you.
GRANDMA What . . . wha . . . (*then, with resignation*) . . . ohhhh . . . ohhhh, I see. (*The* YOUNG MAN *bends over, kisses* GRANDMA *gently on the forehead.*)
GRANDMA (*her eyes closed, her hands folded on her breast again, the shovel between her hands, a sweet smile on her face*) Well . . . that was very nice, dear . . .
YOUNG MAN (*still kneeling*) Shhhhh . . . be still . . .
GRANDMA What I meant was . . . you did that very well, dear . . .
YOUNG MAN (*blushing*) . . . oh . . .
GRANDMA No; I mean it. You've got that . . . you've got a quality.
YOUNG MAN (*with his endearing smile*) Oh . . . thank you; thank you very much . . . ma'am.
GRANDMA (*slowly; softly—as the* YOUNG MAN *puts his hands on top of* GRANDMA'S) You're . . . you're welcome . . . dear.

(*Tableau. The* MUSICIAN *continues to play as the curtain slowly comes down.*)

Martin Luther King, Jr. 1929–1968

The son and grandson of Baptist preachers, Martin Luther King, Jr., grew up in a middle-class home in Atlanta. He graduated with a B.A. from Morehouse College, completed ministerial studies at Crozer Theological Seminary, and earned a Ph.D. at Boston University.

After King became a pastor in Montgomery, Alabama, Rosa Parks was arrested for refusing to yield her bus seat to a white man. Her jailing spurred Jo Ann Robinson and the Women's Political Council to initiate the Montgomery Bus Boycott, a year-long nonviolent protest in that city. King's eloquent leadership of that struggle earned him the national spotlight. By outlawing bus segregation in Montgomery, the Supreme Court gave King an important victory.

After others launched the lunch counter sit-ins of 1960 and the Freedom Rides of 1961, King directed a well-publicized racial protest in Birmingham, Alabama. National television cameras recorded scenes of nonviolent black marchers, including children, being attacked by the fire hoses and police dogs of Birmingham's city government. Arrested, King penned his "Letter from Birmingham Jail." Winning the battle for American public opinion, he successfully pushed business leaders to outlaw segregation in downtown Birmingham.

In August 1963, two hundred fifty thousand protesters heard King deliver "I Have a Dream" at the Lincoln Memorial in Washington, D.C. This electrifying address helped build momentum for the

Civil Rights Act of 1964, a sweeping measure that banned racial discrimination in hotels, restaurants, and other public accommodations. King won the Nobel Peace Prize in that same year. In 1965 his march from Selma, Alabama, to Montgomery prompted passage of the Voting Rights Act, which guaranteed African Americans the right to vote.

In 1967 King condemned American participation in the Vietnam War. A previously sympathetic press vilified him for this stance, which also earned the contempt of a once-friendly president.

King also railed against poverty. Planning his most ambitious protest, he envisioned thousands of blacks, Hispanics, Indians, and poor whites converging on the nation's capital. A strike by garbage workers in Memphis diverted him from this effort. After galvanizing supporters with "I've Been to the Mountaintop," he was assassinated the next day.

Unfortunately, King's fame has obscured the contributions of James Farmer, Ella Baker, John Lewis, Fannie Lou Hamer, and others, who, like King, mastered Gandhian strategy in the quest for racial justice.

But King's fiery yet magisterial language convinced whites to tear down the walls of legalized segregation. He triumphed by reviving the slaves' vivid identification with the biblical Hebrews trapped in Egyptian bondage, a strategy especially evident in "I've Been to the Mountaintop." Trained by African American folk preachers, he adopted their assumption that language is a shared treasure, not private property. King often borrowed sermons without acknowledgment from Harry Emerson Fosdick and other liberal preachers. This borrowed material appears in scores of King's published and unpublished addresses and essays, including "Letter from Birmingham Jail," "I Have a Dream," the Nobel Prize Address, and "I've Been to the Mountaintop." By synthesizing black and white pulpit traditions, King persuaded whites to hear the slaves' cry, "Let my people go!"

Keith D. Miller
Arizona State University

PRIMARY WORKS

Stride Toward Freedom: The Montgomery Story, 1958; *Strength to Love,* 1963; *Why We Can't Wait,* 1965; *Where Do We Go from Here?,* 1967; James Washington, ed., *A Testament of Hope: The Essential Writings of Martin Luther King, Jr.,* 1986; Clayborne Carson, ed., *The Papers of Martin Luther King, Jr.,* vols. 1–4, 1992, 1994, 1997, 2000.

I Have a Dream

I am happy to join with you today in what will go down in history as the greatest demonstration for freedom in the history of our nation.

Five score years ago a great American in whose symbolic shadow we stand today signed the Emancipation Proclamation.[1] This momentous decree came as a great beacon light of hope to millions of Negro slaves who had been seared in the flames

[1]King delivered this speech on the steps of the Lincoln Memorial, which houses a giant marble statue of Abraham Lincoln, whose Emancipation Proclamation freed American slaves. "Five score years ago . . ." echoes the beginning of Lincoln's famous Gettysburg Address.

of withering injustice. It came as a joyous daybreak to end the long night of their captivity. But one hundred years later the Negro still is not free. One hundred years later the life of the Negro is still sadly crippled by the manacles of segregation and the chains of discrimination. One hundred years later the Negro lives on a lonely island of poverty in the midst of a vast ocean of material prosperity. One hundred years later the Negro is still languished in the corners of American society and finds himself in exile in his own land. So we've come here today to dramatize a shameful condition.

In a sense we've come to our nation's capital to cash a check. When the architects of our Republic wrote the magnificent words of the Constitution and the Declaration of Independence, they were signing a promissory note to which every American was to fall heir. This note was a promise that all men—yes, black men as well as white men—would be guaranteed the unalienable rights of life, liberty and the pursuit of happiness.[2] It is obvious today that America has defaulted on this promissory note insofar as her citizens of color are concerned. Instead of honoring this sacred obligation, America has given the Negro people a bad check, a check which has come back marked "insufficient funds."

But we refuse to believe that the bank of justice is bankrupt. We refuse to believe that there are insufficient funds in the great vaults of opportunity of this nation. So we've come to cash this check, a check that will give us upon demand the riches of freedom and the security of justice.

We have also come to this hallowed spot to remind America of the fierce urgency of now. This is no time to engage in the luxury of cooling off or to take the tranquilizing drug of gradualism. Now is the time to make real the promises of democracy. Now is the time to rise from the dark and desolate valley of segregation to the sunlit path of racial justice. Now is the time to lift our nation from the quicksands of racial injustice to the solid rock of brotherhood.

Now is the time to make justice a reality for all of God's children. It would be fatal for the nation to overlook the urgency of the moment. This sweltering summer of the Negro's legitimate discontent[3] will not pass until there is an invigorating autumn of freedom and equality—nineteen sixty-three is not an end but a beginning. Those who hope that the Negro needed to blow off steam and will now be content will have a rude awakening if the nation returns to business as usual.

There will be neither rest nor tranquility in America until the Negro is granted his citizenship rights. The whirlwinds of revolt will continue to shake the foundations of our nation until the bright day of justice emerges.

But there is something that I must say to my people who stand on the worn threshold which leads into the palace of justice. In the process of gaining our rightful place we must not be guilty of wrongful deeds. Let us not seek to satisfy our thirst for freedom by drinking from the cup of bitterness and hatred.

We must forever conduct our struggle on the high plane of dignity and discipline. We must not allow our creative protests to degenerate into physical violence. Again and again we must rise to the majestic heights of meeting physical force with

[2]The phrase "unalienable rights of life, liberty, and the pursuit of happiness" appears in the Declaration of Independence, written by Thomas Jefferson.

[3]King turns inside out Shakespeare's "Now is the winter of our discontent/Made glorious summer by this sun of York. . . ." See *Richard III,* Act I, Scene I.

soul force.[4] The marvelous new militancy which has engulfed the Negro community must not lead us to a distrust of all white people, for many of our white brothers, as evidenced by their presence here today, have come to realize that their destiny is tied up with our destiny. They have come to realize that their freedom is inextricably bound to our freedom. We cannot walk alone. And as we walk we must make the pledge that we shall always march ahead. We cannot turn back.

There are those who are asking the devotees of civil rights, "When will you be satisfied?"

We can never be satisfied as long as the Negro is the victim of the unspeakable horrors of police brutality.

We can never be satisfied as long as our bodies, heavy with the fatigue of travel, cannot gain lodging in the motels of the highways and the hotels of the cities.[5]

We cannot be satisfied as long as the Negro's basic mobility is from a smaller ghetto to a larger one.[6] We can never be satisfied as long as our children are stripped of their selfhood and robbed of their dignity by signs stating "For Whites Only."

We cannot be satisfied as long as the Negro in Mississippi cannot vote and the Negro in New York believes he has nothing for which to vote.

No, no, we are not satisfied, and we will not be satisfied until justice rolls down like waters and righteousness like a mighty stream.[7]

I am not unmindful that some of you have come here out of great trials and tribulations. Some of you have come fresh from narrow jail cells.[8] Some of you have come from areas where your quest for freedom left you battered by the storms of persecution and staggered by the winds of police brutality. You have been the veterans of creative suffering.

Continue to work with the faith that unearned suffering is redemptive. Go back to Mississippi, go back to Alabama, go back to South Carolina, go back to Georgia, go back to Louisiana, go back to the slums and ghettos of our Northern cities, knowing that somehow this situation can and will be changed. Let us not wallow in the valley of despair.

I say to you today, my friends, so even though we face the difficulties of today and tomorrow, I still have a dream. It is a dream deeply rooted in the American dream. I have a dream that one day this nation will rise up, live out the true meaning of its creed: "We hold these truths to be self-evident, that all men are created equal."[9]

I have a dream that one day on the red hills of Georgia sons of former slaves and the sons of former slave-owners will be able to sit down together at the table of brotherhood. I have a dream that one day even the state of Mississippi, a state sweltering with the heat of injustice, sweltering with the heat of oppression, will be transformed into an oasis of freedom and justice.

[4]Following the example of Gandhi, King consistently practiced and preached nonviolence, even though his opponents often resorted to violence against him.

[5]Throughout the South most motels and hotels were reserved for whites only.

[6]Throughout much of the nation blacks experienced racial discrimination in housing.

[7]This statement includes a renowned biblical declaration from the Hebrew prophet Amos ("Let justice roll down . . ."). See Amos 5:24.

[8]Violating local laws, King and other civil rights protesters voluntarily went to jail to dramatize their cause.

[9]"We hold these truths . . ." is the most famous sentence of the Declaration of Independence.

I have a dream that my four little children will one day live in a nation where they will not be judged by the color of their skin but by the content of their character. I have a dream today. I have a dream that one day down in Alabama, with its vicious racists, with its governor having his lips dripping with the words of interposition and nullification,[10] one day right there in Alabama little black boys and black girls will be able to join hands with little white boys and white girls as sisters and brothers.

I have a dream today. I have a dream that one day every valley shall be exalted, every hill and mountain shall be made low. The rough places will be made plain, and the crooked places will be made straight. And the glory of the Lord shall be revealed, and all flesh shall see it together.[11] This is our hope. This is the faith that I go back to the South with. With this faith we will be able to hew out of the mountain of despair a stone of hope. With this faith we will be able to transform the jangling discords of our nation into a beautiful symphony of brotherhood. With this faith we will be able to work together, to pray together, to struggle together, to go to jail together, to stand up for freedom together, knowing that we will be free one day.

This will be the day, this will be the day when all of God's children will be able to sing with new meaning, "My country, 'tis of thee, sweet land of liberty, of thee I sing. Land where my fathers died, land of the pilgrim's pride, from every mountainside, let freedom ring."[12] And if America is to be a great nation, this must become true. So let freedom ring from the prodigious hilltops of New Hampshire. Let freedom ring from the mighty mountains of New York. Let freedom ring from the heightening Alleghenies of Pennsylvania. Let freedom ring from the snowcapped Rockies of Colorado. Let freedom ring from the curvaceous slopes of California.

But not only that. Let freedom ring from Stone Mountain of Georgia. Let freedom ring from Lookout Mountain of Tennessee. Let freedom ring from every hill and molehill of Mississippi, from every mountainside.[13] Let freedom ring.

And when this happens, when we allow freedom [to] ring—when we let it ring from every village and every hamlet, from every state and every city, we will be able to speed up that day when all of God's children, black men and white men, Jews and Gentiles, Protestants and Catholics, will be able to join hands and sing in the words of the old Negro spiritual, "Free at last, Free at last, Thank God a-mighty, We are free at last."

1963

[10]Governor George Wallace of Alabama attempted to interpose state authority to nullify federal orders to integrate his state.

[11]This passage incorporates visionary language from the Hebrew prophet Isaiah ("Every valley shall be exalted . . .") that reappears in the Christian New Testament. Handel includes it in the *Messiah,* a popular, long piece of Christian music. See Isaiah 40:4 and Luke 3:5. Biblical quotations remind listeners of King's status as a minister.

[12]These are the opening lines of "America," our unofficial national anthem. King's use of the phrase "Let freedom ring" seems to extend the lyrics of the song.

[13]King borrowed and adapted the "Let freedom ring "litany from a speech at the 1952 Republican Convention by Archibald Carey, an African American minister from Chicago and friend of King.

I've Been to the Mountaintop

Thank you very kindly, my friends. As I listened to Ralph Abernathy in his eloquent and generous introduction and then thought about myself, I wondered who he was talking about. It's always good to have your closest friend and associate say something good about you. And Ralph is the best friend that I have in the world.

I'm delighted to see each of you here tonight in spite of a storm warning.[1] You reveal that you are determined to go on anyhow. Something is happening in Memphis, something is happening in our world.

As you know, if I were standing at the beginning of time, with the possibility of general and panoramic view of the whole human history up to now, and the Almighty said to me, "Martin Luther King, which age would you like to live in?"—I would take my mental flight by Egypt through, or rather across the Red Sea, through the wilderness on toward the promised land.[2] And in spite of its magnificence, I wouldn't stop there. I would move on by Greece, and take my mind to Mount Olympus. And I would see Plato, Aristotle, Socrates, Euripides and Aristophanes assembled around the Parthenon as they discussed the great and eternal issues of reality.[3]

But I wouldn't stop there. I would go on, even to the great heyday of the Roman Empire. And I would see developments around there, through various emperors and leaders. But I wouldn't stop there. I would even come up to the day of the Renaissance, and get a quick picture of all that the Renaissance did for the cultural and esthetic life of man. But I wouldn't stop there. I would even go by the way that the man for whom I'm named had his habitat. And I would watch Martin Luther as he tacked his ninety-five theses on the door at the church in Wittenberg.[4]

But I wouldn't stop there. I would come on up even to 1863, and watch a vacillating president by the name of Abraham Lincoln finally come to the conclusion that he had to sign the Emancipation Proclamation. But I wouldn't stop there. I would even come up to the early thirties, and see a man grappling with the problems of the bankruptcy of his nation. And come with an eloquent cry that we have nothing to fear but fear itself.[5]

But I wouldn't stop there. Strangely enough, I would turn to the Almighty, and say, "If you allow me to live just a few years in the second half of the twentieth century, I will be happy." Now that's a strange statement to make, because the world is all messed up. The nation is sick. Trouble is in the land. Confusion all around. That's a strange statement. But I know, somehow, that only when it is dark enough, can you see the stars. And I see God working in this period of the twentieth century in a way

[1]King's audience drove through a heavy rainstorm to hear his address.

[2]Blacks often identified with the biblical Israelites, who were enslaved in Egypt before Moses led them across the Red Sea toward the Promised Land. King makes other references to the Exodus later in the speech.

[3]Socrates, Plato, and Aristotle were famous Greek philosophers; Euripides and Aristophanes were outstanding Greek playwrights. Since all five lived roughly within a generation or two of each other, one might imagine their conversation near the Parthenon, the unexcelled example of Greek architecture.

[4]Through this act Luther registered his protest against the Church of Rome and helped trigger the Protestant Reformation.

[5]King refers to President Franklin Roosevelt.

that men, in some strange way, are responding—something is happening in our world. The masses of people are rising up. And wherever they are assembled today, whether they are in Johannesburg, South Africa; Nairobi, Kenya; Accra, Ghana; New York City; Atlanta, Georgia: Jackson, Mississippi; or Memphis, Tennessee—the cry is always the same: "We want to be free."

And another reason that I'm happy to live in this period is that we have been forced to a point where we're going to have to grapple with the problems that men have been trying to grapple with through history, but the demands didn't force them to do it. Survival demands that we grapple with them. Men, for years now, have been talking about war and peace. But now, no longer can they just talk about it. It is no longer a choice between violence and nonviolence in this world; it's nonviolence or nonexistence.

That is where we are today. And also in the human rights revolution, if something isn't done, and in a hurry, to bring the colored peoples of the world out of their long years of poverty, their long years of hurt and neglect, the whole world is doomed. Now, I'm just happy that God has allowed me to live in this period, to see what is unfolding. And I'm happy that he's allowed me to be in Memphis.

I can remember, I can remember when Negroes were just going around as Ralph has said so often, scratching where they didn't itch and laughing when they were not tickled. But that day is all over. We mean business now, and we are determined to gain our rightful place in God's world.

And that's all this whole thing is about. We aren't engaged in any negative protest and in any negative arguments with anybody. We are saying that we are determined to be men. We are determined to be people. We are saying that we are God's children. And that we don't have to live like we are forced to live.

Now, what does all of this mean in this great period of history? It means that we've got to stay together. We've got to stay together and maintain unity. You know, whenever Pharaoh wanted to prolong the period of slavery in Egypt, he had a favorite, favorite formula for doing it. What was that? He kept the slaves fighting among themselves. But whenever the slaves get together, something happens in Pharaoh's court, and he cannot hold the slaves in slavery. When the slaves get together, that's the beginning of getting out of slavery. Now let us maintain unity.[6]

Secondly, let us keep the issues where they are. The issue is injustice. The issue is the refusal of Memphis to be fair and honest in its dealings with its public servants, who happen to be sanitation workers. Now, we've got to keep attention on that. That's always the problem with a little violence. You know what happened the other day, and the press dealt only with the window-breaking. I read the articles.[7] They very seldom got around to mentioning the fact that one thousand, three hundred sanitation workers were on strike, and that Memphis is not being fair to them, and that Mayor Loeb is in dire need of a doctor.[8] They didn't get around to that.

[6]King's analogy equates American blacks with the biblical Israelites enslaved in Egypt under the Pharaoh.

[7]A few days earlier King led followers in a march of support for striking garbage workers in Memphis. Unlike those who had participated in his many previous demonstrations, some of the Memphis marchers smashed windows and began a riot. National newspapers blamed King for the incident. King answers his critics through this speech.

[8]Henry Loeb, Mayor of Memphis, refused to meet the demands of striking garbage workers.

Now we're going to march again, and we've got to march again, in order to put the issue where it is supposed to be. And force everybody to see that there are thirteen hundred of God's children here suffering, sometimes going hungry, going through dark and dreary nights wondering how this thing is going to come out. That's the issue. And we've got to say to the nation: we know it's coming out. For when people get caught up with that which is right and they are willing to sacrifice for it, there is no stopping point short of victory.

We aren't going to let any mace stop us. We are masters in our nonviolent movement in disarming police forces; they don't know what to do. I've seen them so often. I remember in Birmingham, Alabama, when we were in that majestic struggle there we would move out of the 16th Street Baptist Church day after day; by the hundreds we would move out. And Bull Connor would tell them to send the dogs forth and they did come; but we just went before the dogs singing, "Ain't gonna let nobody turn me round." Bull Connor next would say, "Turn the fire hoses on." And as I said to you the other night, Bull Connor didn't know history. He knew a kind of physics that somehow didn't relate to the transphysics that we knew about. And that was the fact that there was a certain kind of fire that no water could put out. And we went before the fire hoses; we had known water. If we were Baptist or some other denomination, we had been immersed. If we were Methodist, and some others, we had been sprinkled, but we knew water.[9]

That couldn't stop us. And we just went on before the dogs and we would look at them; and we'd go on before the water hoses and we would look at it, and we'd just go on singing "Over my head I see freedom in the air." And then we would be thrown in the paddy wagons, and sometimes we were stacked in there like sardines in a can. And they would throw us in, and old Bull would say, "Take them off," and they did; and we would just go in the paddy wagon singing, "We Shall Overcome."[10] And every now and then we'd get in the jail, and we'd see the jailers looking through the windows being moved by our prayers, and being moved by our words and our songs. And there was a power there which Bull Connor couldn't adjust to; and so we ended up transforming Bull into a steer, and we won our struggle in Birmingham.

Now we've got to go on to Memphis just like that. I call upon you to be with us Monday. Now about injunctions: We have an injunction and we're going into court tomorrow morning to fight this illegal, unconstitutional injunction. All we say to America is, "Be true to what you said on paper." If I lived in China or even Russia, or any totalitarian country, maybe I could understand the denial of certain basic First Amendment privileges, because they hadn't committed themselves to that over there.[11] But somewhere I read of the freedom of assembly. Somewhere I read of the freedom of speech. Somewhere I read of the freedom of the press. Somewhere I read that the greatness of America is the right to protest for right. And so just as I say, we aren't going to let any injunction turn us around. We are going on.

We need all of you. And you know what's beautiful to me, is to see all of these

[9]King refers to the Christian ritual of baptism either by immersion or by sprinkling.

[10]Civil rights demonstrators often inspired themselves by singing "Ain't Gonna Let Nobody Turn Me Round," "We Shall Overcome," and other anthems.

[11]The First Amendment of the U.S. Constitution is part of the Bill of Rights.

ministers of the Gospel. It's a marvelous picture. Who is it that is supposed to articulate the longings and aspirations of the people more than the preacher? Somehow the preacher must be an Amos, and say, "Let justice roll down like waters and righteousness like a mighty stream."[12] Somehow, the preacher must say with Jesus, "The spirit of the Lord is upon me, because he hath anointed me to deal with the problems of the poor."[13]

And I want to commend the preachers, under the leadership of these noble men: James Lawson, one who has been in this struggle for many years; he's been to jail for struggling; but he's still going on, fighting for the rights of his people. Rev. Ralph Jackson, Billy Kyles;[14] I could just go right on down the list, but time will not permit. But I want to thank them all. And I want you to thank them, because so often, preachers aren't concerned about anything but themselves. And I'm always happy to see a relevant ministry.

It's alright to talk about "long white robes over yonder," in all of its symbolism. But ultimately people want some suits and dresses and shoes to wear down here. It's alright to talk about "streets flowing with milk and honey," but God has commanded us to be concerned about the slums down here, and his children who can't eat three square meals a day. It's alright to talk about the new Jerusalem, but one day, God's preacher must talk about the new New York, the new Atlanta, the new Philadelphia, the new Los Angeles, the new Memphis, Tennessee. This is what we have to do.[15]

Now the other thing we'll have to do is this: Always anchor our external direct action with the power of economic withdrawal. Now, we are poor people, individually, we are poor when you compare us with white society in America. We are poor. Never stop and forget that collectively, that means all of us together, collectively we are richer than all the nations in the world, with the exception of nine. Did you ever think about that? After you leave the United States, Soviet Russia, Great Britain, West Germany, France, and I could name the others, the Negro collectively is richer than most nations of the world. We have an annual income of more than thirty billion dollars a year, which is more than all of the exports of the United States, and more than the national budget of Canada. Did you know that? That's power right there, if we know how to pool it.

We don't have to argue with anybody. We don't have to curse and go around acting bad with our words. We don't need any bricks and bottles, we don't need any Molotov cocktails,[16] we just need to go around to these stores, and to these massive industries in our country, and say, "God sent us by here, to say to you that you're not treating his children right. And we've come by here to ask you to make the first item on your agenda—fair treatment, where God's children are concerned. Now, if you are not prepared to do that, we do have an agenda that we must follow. And our agenda calls for withdrawing economic support from you."

[12]See Amos 5:24.

[13]Jesus began his ministry by quoting this statement from the Hebrew prophet Isaiah. See Isaiah 61:1–2 and Luke 4:18.

[14]James Lawson, Ralph Jackson, and Billy Kyles supported the garbage workers' strike.

[15]King urges black ministers to seek God's Kingdom on earth as well as to "save souls" for heaven.

[16]Handmade explosive devices consisting of small bottles filled with gasoline lit by a fuse.

And so, as a result of this, we are asking you tonight, to go out and tell your neighbors not to buy Coca-Cola in Memphis. Go by and tell them not to buy Sealtest milk. Tell them not to buy—what is the other bread?—Wonder Bread. And what is the other bread company, Jesse?[17] Tell them not to buy Hart's bread. As Jesse Jackson has said, up to now, only the garbage men have been feeling pain; now we must kind of redistribute the pain. We are choosing these companies because they haven't been fair in their hiring policies; and we are choosing them because they can begin the process of saying they are going to support the needs and the rights of these men who are on strike. And then they can move on downtown and tell Mayor Loeb to do what is right.[18]

But not only that, we've got to strengthen black institutions. I call upon you to take your money out of the banks downtown and deposit your money in Tri-State Bank—we want a "bank-in" movement in Memphis. So go by the savings and loan association. I'm not asking you something that we don't do ourselves at SCLC.[19] Judge Hooks and others will tell you that we have an account here in the savings and loan association from the Southern Christian Leadership Conference.[20] We're just telling you to follow what we're doing. Put your money there. You have six or seven black insurance companies in Memphis. Take out your insurance there. We want to have an "insurance-in."

Now these are some practical things we can do. We begin the process of building a greater economic base. And at the same time, we are putting pressure where it really hurts. I ask you to follow through here.

Now, let me say as I move to my conclusion that we've got to give ourselves to this struggle until the end. Nothing would be more tragic than to stop at this point, in Memphis. We've got to see it through. And when we have our march, you need to be there. Be concerned about your brother. You may not be on strike. But either we go up together, or we go down together.

Let us develop a kind of dangerous unselfishness. One day a man came to Jesus; and he wanted to raise some questions about some vital matters in life.[21] At points, he wanted to trick Jesus, and show him that he knew a little more than Jesus knew, and through this, throw him off base. Now that question could have easily ended up in a philosophical and theological debate. But Jesus immediately pulled that question from mid-air, and placed it on a dangerous curve between Jerusalem and Jericho. And he talked about a certain man, who fell among thieves. You remember that a Levite and a priest passed by on the other side. They didn't stop to help him. And

[17]King asks a question of a member of his staff, Rev. Jesse Jackson, who is sitting on stage as King delivers his speech. Jackson ran for President in 1984 and 1988.

[18]King occasionally organized boycotts of companies practicing racial discrimination. Jesse Jackson extended this tactic during the 1970s.

[19]King's organization, the Southern Christian Leadership Conference (SCLC).

[20]Benjamin Hooks, who became Executive Director of the National Association for the Advancement of Colored People (NAACP).

[21]Perhaps Jesus's best-known parable is that of the Good Samaritan. See Luke 10:25-37. King's earlier interpretation of the parable appeared in a sermon in his *Strength to Love.* Here he adapts that earlier analysis, portions of which he borrowed from George Buttrick's *Parables of Jesus.*

finally a man of another race came by. He got down from his beast, decided not to be compassionate by proxy. But with him administered first aid and helped the man in need. Jesus ended up saying, this was the good man, this was the great man, because he had the capacity to project the "I" into the "thou," and to be concerned about his brother. Now you know, we use our imagination a great deal to try to determine why the priest and the Levite didn't stop. At times we say they were busy going to church meetings—an ecclesiastical gathering—and they had to get on down to Jerusalem so they wouldn't be late for their meeting. At other times we would speculate that there was a religious law that "One who was engaged in religious ceremonials was not to touch a human body twenty-four hours before the ceremony." And every now and then we begin to wonder whether maybe they were not going down to Jerusalem, or down to Jericho, rather to organize a "Jericho Road Improvement Association." That's a possibility. Maybe they felt that it was better to deal with the problem from the causal root, rather than to get bogged down with an individual effort.

But I'm going to tell you what my imagination tells me. It's possible that these men were afraid. You see, the Jericho road is a dangerous road. I remember when Mrs. King and I were first in Jerusalem. We rented a car and drove from Jerusalem down to Jericho. And as soon as we got on that road, I said to my wife, "I can see why Jesus used this as a setting for his parable." It's a winding, meandering road. It's really conducive for ambushing. You start out in Jerusalem, which is about 1200 miles, or rather 1200 feet above sea level. And by the time you get down to Jericho, fifteen or twenty minutes later, you're about 2200 feet below sea level. That's a dangerous road. In the days of Jesus it came to be known as the "Bloody Pass." And you know, it's possible that the priest and the Levite looked over that man on the ground and wondered if the robbers were still around. Or it's possible that they felt that the man on the ground was merely faking. And he was acting like he had been robbed and hurt, in order to seize them over there, lure them for quick and easy seizure. And so the first question that the Levite asked was, "If I stop to help this man, what will happen to me?" But then the Good Samaritan came by. And he reversed the question: "If I do not stop to help this man, what will happen to him?"

That's the question before you tonight. Not, "If I stop to help the sanitation workers, what will happen to all of the hours that I usually spend in my office every day and every week as a pastor?" The question is not, "If I stop to help this man in need, what will happen to me?" "If I do not stop to help the sanitation workers, what will happen to them?" That's the question.

Let us rise up tonight with a greater readiness. Let us stand with a greater determination. And let us move on in these powerful days, these days of challenge to make America what it ought to be. We have an opportunity to make America a better nation. And I want to thank God, once more, for allowing me to be here with you.

You know, several years ago, I was in New York City autographing the first book that I had written. And while sitting there autographing books, a demented black woman came up. The only question I heard from her was, "Are you Martin Luther King?"

And I was looking down writing, and I said yes. And the next minute I felt something beating on my chest. Before I knew it I had been stabbed by this demented woman. I was rushed to Harlem Hospital. It was a dark Saturday afternoon. And that blade had gone through, and the X-rays revealed that the tip of the blade was on the edge of my aorta, the main artery. And once that's punctured, you drown in your own blood—that's the end of you.[22]

It came out in the *New York Times* the next morning, that if I had sneezed, I would have died. Well, about four days later, they allowed me, after the operation, after my chest had been opened, and the blade had been taken out, to move around in the wheel chair in the hospital. They allowed me to read some of the mail that came in, and from all over the states and the world kind letters came in. I read a few but one of them I will never forget. I had received one from the President and the Vice-President. I've forgotten what those telegrams said. I'd received a visit and a letter from the Governor of New York, but I've forgotten what the letter said. But there was another letter that came from a little girl, a young girl who was a student at the White Plains High School. And I looked at that letter, and I'll never forget it. It said simply, "Dear Dr. King: I am a ninth-grade student at the White Plains High School." She said, "While it should not matter, I would like to mention that I am a white girl. I read in the paper of your misfortune and of your suffering. And I read that if you had sneezed, you would have died. And I'm simply writing you to say that I'm so happy that you didn't sneeze."

And I want to say tonight, I want to say that I am happy that I didn't sneeze. Because if I had sneezed, I wouldn't have been around here in 1960, when students all over the South started sitting-in at lunch counters. And I knew that as they were sitting in, they were really standing up for the best in the American dream. And taking the whole nation back to those great wells of democracy which were dug deep by the Founding Fathers in the Declaration of Independence and the Constitution. If I had sneezed, I wouldn't have been around in 1962 when Negroes in Albany, Georgia, decided to straighten their backs up. And whenever men and women straighten their backs up, they are going somewhere because a man can't ride your back unless it is bent. If I had sneezed, I wouldn't have been here in 1963, when the black people of Birmingham, Alabama, aroused the conscience of this nation and brought into being the Civil Rights Bill. If I had sneezed, I wouldn't have had a chance later that year, in August, to try to tell America about a dream that I had had. If I had sneezed, I wouldn't have been down in Selma, Alabama, to see the great movement there.[23] If I had sneezed, I wouldn't have been in Memphis to see a community rally around those brothers and sisters who are suffering. I'm so happy that I didn't sneeze.

And they were telling me, now it doesn't matter now. It really doesn't matter what happens now. I left Atlanta this morning, and as we got started on the plane, there were six of us, the pilot said over the public address system, "We are sorry for the delay, but we have Dr. Martin Luther King on the plane. And to be sure that all of the bags were checked, and to be sure that nothing would be wrong with the plane, we had to check out everything carefully. And we've had the plane protected and guarded all night."

And then I got into Memphis. And some began to say the threats, or talk about the threats that were out. What would happen to me from some of our sick white brothers?[24]

[22]This incident occurred in 1958.
[23]King recounts notable highlights of the civil rights movement.
[24]King often received death threats and expected to be assassinated.

Well, I don't know what will happen now. We've got some difficult days ahead. But it doesn't matter with me now. Because I've been to the mountaintop. And I don't mind. Like anybody, I would like to live a long life. Longevity has its place. But I'm not concerned about that now. I just want to do God's will. And He's allowed me to go up to the mountain. And I've looked over. And I've seen the promised land. I may not get there with you. But I want you to know tonight, that we, as a people will get to the promised land.[25] And I'm happy, tonight. I'm not worried about anything. I'm not fearing any man. Mine eyes have seen the glory of the coming of the Lord.[26]

1968

Malcolm X 1925–1965

In Omaha, Nebraska, Malcolm X was born Malcolm Little, the son of Earl and Louise Little. Earl Little followed Marcus Garvey, who instilled racial pride among masses of African Americans. Little died at a relatively young age, leaving his wife and eight children in extreme poverty. "We would be so hungry," Malcolm X later reported, "we were dizzy." Malcolm Little quit school at age fifteen and moved to Harlem where, he recalled he became a thief and a drug dealer.

At age twenty, Little entered prison and began to educate himself. When he learned about the Nation of Islam (or Black Muslims), led by Elijah Muhammad, he became an eager convert. He accepted Elijah Muhammad's doctrine that white people were devils and rejoiced in a newfound racial identity. Leaving prison, he met Elijah Muhammad and replaced his own last name with "X," which stands for the African name his ancestors lost when brought to the United States in slave ships.

Malcolm X became an extremely popular evangelist for the Nation of Islam, recruiting new members and emphasizing African American pride. With brilliant fables, analogies, and turns of speech, he elevated the spirits of urban blacks trapped by segregation. He condemned hypocritical whites for preaching love and democracy while treating blacks as subhuman. In "Message to the Grass Roots," he criticized African Americans for their submission to whites:

As long as the white man sent you to Korea, you bled. He sent you to Germany, you bled. He sent you to the South Pacific to fight the Japanese, you bled. You bleed for white people, but when it comes to seeing your own churches being bombed and little black girls murdered, you haven't got any blood. You bleed when the white man says bleed; you bite when the white man says bite; and you bark when the white man says bark. I hate to say this about us, but it's true.

[25]King expands his earlier analogy by boldly comparing himself to Moses, who led the Israelites out of Egyptian slavery toward the Promised Land. Although God allowed Moses to climb a mountain so he could see the Promised Land, God also caused Moses to die before the Israelites could reach that sacred place. See Deuteronomy 32:48–52 and 34:1–6.

[26]King's final sentence serves as the first line of "The Battle Hymn of the Republic," which doubles as a patriotic song and a hymn.

Malcolm X also castigated Martin Luther King, Jr., but his fiery, uncompromising militance helped prepare whites to accept King's message, which, by contrast, seemed moderate and palatable.

"The Ballot or the Bullet" is an address delivered in 1964, shortly after Malcolm X announced his break with the Nation of Islam. He had learned of Elijah Muhammad's flaws and became bitterly disenchanted with the man who "had virtually raised me from the dead." Recovering from disillusionment, he made a pilgrimage to Mecca, met white followers of Islam, and became more accepting of some whites. After returning to the United States, he formed the Organization of Afro-American Unity. In 1965, however, black assailants murdered him in a hail of gunfire.

Mourned by Harlemites and praised by portions of the Third World press, Malcolm X had been damned by the established American media. The *New York Times,* for example, had branded him an "irresponsible demagogue." The eloquent Malcolm X, however, had the last word. He had dictated his life story to Alex Haley. The posthumous *Autobiography of Malcolm X* portrays a person capable of the most startling self-transformation: from a starving child, to a parasitic criminal, to an angry but uplifting orator, to a notably more tolerant leader worthy of a world stage. Though challenged over some of its details, the best-selling *Autobiography of Malcolm X* brilliantly portrays American race relations.

Keith D. Miller
Arizona State University

PRIMARY WORKS

Autobiography of Malcolm X (with Alex Haley), 1964; *Malcolm X Speaks,* 1965; *By Any Means Necessary,* 1970; *The Last Speeches,* 1989.

The Ballot or the Bullet

Mr. Moderator, Brother Lomax, brothers and sisters, friends and enemies: I just can't believe everyone in here is a friend and I don't want to leave anybody out.[1] The question tonight, as I understand it, is "The Negro Revolt, and Where Do We Go From Here?" or "What Next?" In my little humble way of understanding it, it points toward either the ballot or the bullet.

Before we try and explain what is meant by the ballot or the bullet, I would like to clarify something concerning myself. I'm still a Muslim, my religion is still Islam. That's my personal belief. Just as Adam Clayton Powell is a Christian minister who heads the Abyssinian Baptist Church in New York, but at the same time takes part in the political struggles to try and bring about rights to the black people in this country;[2] and Dr. Martin Luther King is a Christian minister down in Atlanta, Georgia, who heads another organization fighting for the civil rights of black people in this country; and Rev. Galamison, I guess you've heard of him, is another Christian minister in New York who has been deeply involved in the school boycotts to elimi-

[1]Louis Lomax, a journalist and author, spoke just before Malcolm X began "The Ballot or the Bullet."

[2]Adam Clayton Powell, a minister, represented Harlem in the U.S. House of Representatives.

nate segregated education; well, I myself am a minister, not a Christian minister, but a Muslim minister; and I believe in action on all fronts by whatever means necessary.

Although I'm still a Muslim, I'm not here tonight to discuss my religion. I'm not here to try and change your religion. I'm not here to argue or discuss anything that we differ about, because it's time for us to submerge our differences and realize that it is best for us to first see that we have the same problem, a common problem—a problem that will make you catch hell whether you're a Baptist, or a Methodist, or a Muslim, or a nationalist. Whether you're educated or illiterate, whether you live on the boulevard or in the alley, you're going to catch hell just like I am. We're all in the same boat and we all are going to catch the same hell from the same man. He just happens to be a white man. All of us have suffered here, in this country, political oppression at the hands of the white man, economic exploitation at the hands of the white man, and social degradation at the hands of the white man.

Now in speaking like this, it doesn't mean that we're anti-white, but it does mean we're anti-exploitation, we're anti-degradation, we're anti-oppression. And if the white man doesn't want us to be anti-him, let him stop oppressing and exploiting and degrading us. Whether we are Christians or Muslims or nationalists or agnostics or atheists, we must first learn to forget our differences. If we have differences, let us differ in the closet; when we come out in front, let us not have anything to argue about until we get finished arguing with the man. If the late President Kennedy could get together with Khrushchev and exchange some wheat, we certainly have more in common with each other than Kennedy and Khrushchev had with each other.[3]

If we don't do something real soon, I think you'll have to agree that we're going to be forced either to use the ballot or the bullet. It's one or the other in 1964. It isn't that time is running out—time has run out! 1964 threatens to be the most explosive year America has ever witnessed. The most explosive year. Why? It's also a political year. It's the year when all of the white politicians will be back in the so-called Negro community jiving you and me for some votes. The year when all of the white political crooks will be right back in your and my community with their false promises, building up our hopes for a letdown, with their trickery and their treachery, with their false promises which they don't intend to keep. As they nourish these dissatisfactions, it can only lead to one thing, an explosion; and now we have the type of black man on the scene in America today—I'm sorry, Brother Lomax—who just doesn't intend to turn the other cheek any longer.

Don't let anybody tell you anything about the odds are against you. If they draft you, they send you to Korea and make you face 800 million Chinese. If you can be brave over there, you can be brave right here. These odds aren't as great as those odds. And if you fight here, you will at least know what you're fighting for.

I'm not a politician, not even a student of politics; in fact, I'm not a student of much of anything. I'm not a Democrat, I'm not a Republican, and I don't even consider myself an American. If you and I were Americans, there'd be no problem. Those Hunkies that just got off the boat, they're already Americans; Polacks are already Americans; the Italian refugees are already Americans. Everything that came

[3]Nikita Khrushchev was head of the Soviet Union.

out of Europe, every blue-eyed thing, is already an American. And as long as you and I have been over here, we aren't Americans yet.

Well, I am one who doesn't believe in deluding myself. I'm not going to sit at your table and watch you eat, with nothing on my plate, and call myself a diner. Sitting at the table doesn't make you a diner, unless you eat some of what's on that plate. Being here in America doesn't make you an American. Being born here in America doesn't make you an American. Why, if birth made you American, you wouldn't need any legislation, you wouldn't need any amendments to the Constitution, you wouldn't be faced with civil-rights filibustering in Washington, D.C., right now. They don't have to pass civil-rights legislation to make a Polack an American.

No, I'm not an American. I'm one of the 22 million black people who are the victims of Americanism. One of the 22 million black people who are the victims of democracy, nothing but disguised hypocrisy. So, I'm not standing here speaking to you as an American, or a patriot, or a flag-saluter, or a flag-waver—no, not I. I'm speaking as a victim of this American system. And I see America through the eyes of the victim. I don't see any American dream; I see an American nightmare.

These 22 million victims are waking up. Their eyes are coming open. They're beginning to see what they used to only look at. They're becoming politically mature. They are realizing that there are new political trends from coast to coast. As they see these new political trends, it's possible for them to see that every time there's an election the races are so close that they have to have a recount. They had to recount in Massachusetts to see who was going to be governor, it was so close. It was the same way in Rhode Island, in Minnesota, and in many other parts of the country. And the same with Kennedy and Nixon when they ran for president. It was so close they had to count all over again. Well, what does this mean? It means that when white people are evenly divided, and black people have a bloc of votes of their own, it is left up to them to determine who's going to sit in the White House and who's going to be in the dog house.[4]

It was the black man's vote that put the present administration in Washington, D.C. Your vote, your dumb vote, your ignorant vote, your wasted vote put in an administration in Washington, D.C., that has seen fit to pass every kind of legislation imaginable, saving you until last, then filibustering on top of that.[5] And your and my leaders have the audacity to run around clapping their hands and talk about how much progress we're making. And what a good president we have. If he wasn't good in Texas, he sure can't be good in Washington, D.C.[6] Because Texas is a lynch state. It is in the same breath as Mississippi, no different; only they lynch you in Texas with a Texas accent and lynch you in Mississippi with a Mississippi accent. And these Negro leaders have the audacity to go and have some coffee in the White House with a Texan, a Southern cracker—that's all he is—and then come out and tell you and me that he's going to be better for us because, since he's from the South, he knows how

[4]John Kennedy narrowly defeated Richard Nixon in the presidential race of 1960, partly because urban black voters preferred Kennedy.

[5]President Kennedy hesitated for years before proposing a major civil rights initiative, which Congress debated at this time and passed later in 1964.

[6]Lyndon Johnson, who succeeded Kennedy as president, hailed from Texas. Although Johnson supported civil rights while in the White House, he had not done so during his years in the U.S. Senate.

to deal with the Southerners. What kind of logic is that? Let Eastland be president, he's from the South too.[7] He should be better able to deal with them than Johnson.

In this present administration they have in the House of Representatives 257 Democrats to only 177 Republicans. They control two-thirds of the House vote. Why can't they pass something that will help you and me? In the Senate, there are 67 senators who are of the Democratic Party. Only 33 of them are Republicans. Why, the Democrats have got the government sewed up, and you're the one who sewed it up for them. And what have they given you for it? Four years in office, and just now getting around to some civil-rights legislation. Just now, after everything else is gone, out of the way, they're going to sit down now and play with you all summer long—the same old giant con game that they call filibuster. All those are in cahoots together. Don't you ever think they're not in cahoots together, for the man that is heading the civil-rights filibuster is a man from Georgia named Richard Russell.[8] When Johnson became president, the first man he asked for when he got back to Washington, D.C., was "Dicky"—that's how tight they are. That's his boy, that's his pal, that's his buddy. But they're playing that old con game. One of them makes believe he's for you, and he's got it fixed where the other one is so tight against you, he never has to keep his promise.

So it's time in 1964 to wake up. And when you see them coming up with that kind of conspiracy, let them know your eyes are open. And let them know you got something else that's wide open too. It's got to be the ballot or the bullet. The ballot or the bullet. If you're afraid to use an expression like that, you should get on out of the country, you should get back in the cotton patch, you should get back in the alley. They get all the Negro vote, and after they get it, the Negro gets nothing in return. All they did when they got to Washington was give a few big Negroes big jobs. Those big Negroes didn't need big jobs, they already had jobs. That's camouflage, that's trickery, that's treachery, window-dressing. I'm not trying to knock out the Democrats for the Republicans, we'll get to them in a minute. But it is true—you put the Democrats first and the Democrats put you last.

Look at it the way it is. What alibis do they use, since they control Congress and the Senate? What alibi do they use when you and I ask, "Well, when are you going to keep your promise?" They blame the Dixiecrats.[9] What is a Dixiecrat? A Democrat. A Dixiecrat is nothing but a Democrat in disguise. The titular head of the Democrats is also the head of the Dixiecrats, because the Dixiecrats are a part of the Democratic Party. The Democrats have never kicked the Dixiecrats out of the party. The Dixiecrats bolted themselves once, but the Democrats didn't put them out. Imagine, these lowdown Southern segregationists put the Northern Democrats down.[10] But the Northern Democrats have never put the Dixiecrats down. No, look at that thing the way it is. They have got a con game going on, a political con game, and you and I are in the middle. It's time for you and me to wake up and start looking

[7]James Eastland, U.S. Senator from Mississippi, was an ardent segregationist.

[8]Richard Russell, U.S. Senator from Georgia, strongly supported segregation.

[9]Dixiecrats were southern Democrats who espoused white racism. They included James Eastland and Richard Russell.

[10]Dixiecrats deserted the Democratic Party in 1948 to run one of their own, Strom Thurmond of South Carolina, for president. Thurmond is now a Republican U.S. Senator. Though they often favored civil rights, northern Democrats hesitated to fight southern members of their own party over the issue.

at it like it is, and trying to understand it like it is; and then we can deal with it like it is.

The Dixiecrats in Washington, D.C., control the key committees that run the government. The only reason the Dixiecrats control these committees is because they have seniority. The only reason they have seniority is because they come from states where Negroes can't vote. This is not even a government that's based on democracy. It is not a government that is made up of representatives of the people. Half of the people in the South can't even vote. Eastland is not even supposed to be in Washington. Half of the senators and congressmen who occupy these key positions in Washington, D.C., are there illegally, are there unconstitutionally.

I was in Washington, D.C., a week ago Thursday, when they were debating whether or not they should let the bill come onto the floor. And in the back of the room where the Senate meets, there's a huge map of the United States, and on that map it shows the location of Negroes throughout the country. And it shows that the Southern section of the country, the states that are most heavily concentrated with Negroes, are the ones that have senators and congressmen standing up filibustering and doing all other kinds of trickery to keep the Negro from being able to vote. This is pitiful. But it's not pitiful for us any longer; it's actually pitiful for the white man, because soon now, as the Negro awakens a little more and sees the vise that he's in, sees the bag that he's in, sees the real game that he's in, then the Negro's going to develop a new tactic.

These senators and congressmen actually violate the constitutional amendments that guarantee the people of that particular state or county the right to vote. And the Constitution itself has within it the machinery to expel any representative from a state where the voting rights of the people are violated. You don't even need new legislation. Any person in Congress right now, who is there from a state or a district where the voting rights of the people are violated, that particular person should be expelled from Congress. And when you expel him, you've removed one of the obstacles in the path of any real meaningful legislation in this country. In fact, when you expel them, you don't need new legislation, because they will be replaced by black representatives from counties and districts where the black man is in the majority, not in the minority.

If the black man in these Southern states had his full voting rights, the key Dixiecrats in Washington, D.C., which means the key Democrats in Washington, D.C., would lose their seats. The Democratic Party itself would lose its power. It would cease to be powerful as a party. When you see the amount of power that would be lost by the Democratic Party if it were to lose the Dixiecrat wing, or branch, or element, you can see where it's against the interests of the Democrats to give voting rights to Negroes in states where the Democrats have been in complete power and authority ever since the Civil War. You just can't belong to that party without analyzing it.

I say again, I'm not anti-Democrat, I'm not anti-Republican, I'm not anti-anything. I'm just questioning their sincerity, and some of the strategy that they've been using on our people by promising them promises that they don't intend to keep. When you keep the Democrats in power, you're keeping the Dixiecrats in power. I doubt that my good Brother Lomax will deny that. A vote for a Democrat is a vote for a Dixiecrat. That's why, in 1964, it's time now for you and me to become more politically mature and realize what the ballot is for; what we're supposed to get when we cast a ballot; and that if we don't cast a ballot, it's going to end up in a situation where we're going to have to cast a bullet. It's either a ballot or a bullet.

In the North, they do it a different way. They have a system that's known as gerrymandering, whatever that means. It means when Negroes become too heavily concentrated in a certain area, and begin to gain too much political power, the white man comes along and changes the district lines. You may say, "Why do you keep saying white man?" Because it's the white man who does it. I haven't ever seen any Negro changing any lines. They don't let him get near the line. It's the white man who does this. And usually, it's the white man who grins at you the most, and pats you on the back, and is supposed to be your friend. He may be friendly, but he's not your friend.

So, what I'm trying to impress upon you, in essence, is this: You and I in America are faced not with a segregationist conspiracy, we're faced with a government conspiracy. Everyone who's filibustering is a senator—that's the government. Everyone who's finagling in Washington, D.C., is a congressman—that's the government. You don't have anybody putting blocks in your path but people who are a part of the government. The same government that you go abroad to fight for and die for is the government that is in a conspiracy to deprive you of your voting rights, deprive you of your economic opportunities, deprive you of decent housing, deprive you of decent education. You don't need to go to the employer alone, it is the government itself, the government of America, that is responsible for the oppression and exploitation and degradation of black people in this country. And you should drop it in their lap. This government has failed the Negro. This so-called democracy has failed the Negro. And all these white liberals have definitely failed the Negro.

So, where do we go from here? First, we need some friends. We need some new allies. The entire civil-rights struggle needs a new interpretation, a broader interpretation. We need to look at this civil-rights thing from another angle—from the inside as well as from the outside. To those of us whose philosophy is black nationalism, the only way you can get involved in the civil-rights struggle is give it a new interpretation. That old interpretation excluded us. It kept us out. So, we're giving a new interpretation to the civil-rights struggle, an interpretation that will enable us to come into it, take part in it. And these handkerchief-heads who have been dillydallying and pussyfooting and compromising—we don't intend to let them pussyfoot and dillydally and compromise any longer.

How can you thank a man for giving you what's already yours? How then can you thank him for giving you only part of what's already yours? You haven't even made progress, if what's being given to you, you should have had already. That's not progress. And I love my Brother Lomax, the way he pointed out we're right back where we were in 1954. We're not even as far up as we were in 1954. We're behind where we were in 1954. There's more segregation now than there was in 1954. There's more racial animosity, more racial hatred, more racial violence today in 1964, than there was in 1954. Where is the progress?

And now you're facing a situation where the young Negro's coming up. They don't want to hear that "turn-the-other-cheek" stuff, no. In Jacksonville, those were teenagers, they were throwing Molotov cocktails.[11] Negroes have never done that

[11]A Molotov cocktail is an explosive made by pouring gasoline into a bottle and lighting it with a fuse.

before. But it shows you there's a new deal coming in. There's new thinking coming in. There's new strategy coming in. It'll be Molotov cocktails this month, hand grenades next month, and something else next month. It'll be ballots, or it'll be bullets. It'll be liberty, or it will be death. The only difference about this kind of death—it'll be reciprocal. You know what is meant by "reciprocal"? That's one of Brother Lomax's words, I stole it from him. I don't usually deal with those big words because I don't usually deal with big people. I deal with small people. I find you can get a whole lot of small people and whip hell out of a whole lot of big people. They haven't got anything to lose, and they've got everything to gain. And they'll let you know in a minute: "It takes two to tango; when I go, you go."

The black nationalists, those whose philosophy is black nationalism, in bringing about this new interpretation of the entire meaning of civil rights, look upon it as meaning, as Brother Lomax has pointed out, equality of opportunity. Well, we're justified in seeking civil rights, if it means equality of opportunity, because all we're doing there is trying to collect for our investment. Our mothers and fathers invested sweat and blood. Three hundred and ten years we worked in this country without a dime in return—I mean without a *dime* in return. You let the white man walk around here talking about how rich this country is, but you never stop to think how it got rich so quick. It got rich because you made it rich.

You take the people who are in this audience right now. They're poor, we're all poor as individuals. Our weekly salary individually amounts to hardly anything. But if you take the salary of everyone in here collectively it'll fill up a whole lot of baskets. It's a lot of wealth. If you can collect the wages of just these people right here for a year, you'll be rich—richer than rich. When you look at it like that, think how rich Uncle Sam had to become, not with this handful, but millions of black people. Your and my mother and father, who didn't work an eight-hour shift, but worked from "can't see" in the morning until "can't see" at night, and worked for nothing, making the white man rich, making Uncle Sam rich.

This is our investment. This is our contribution—our blood. Not only did we give of our free labor, we gave of our blood. Every time he had a call to arms, we were the first ones in uniform. We died on every battlefield the white man had. We have made a greater sacrifice than anybody who's standing up in America today. We have made a greater contribution and have collected less. Civil rights, for those of us whose philosophy is black nationalism, means: "Give it to us now. Don't wait for next year. Give it to us yesterday, and that's not fast enough."

I might stop right here to point out one thing. Whenever you're going after something that belongs to you, anyone who's depriving you of the right to have it is a criminal. Understand that. Whenever you are going after something that is yours, you are within your legal rights to lay claim to it. And anyone who puts forth any effort to deprive you of that which is yours, is breaking the law, is a criminal. And this was pointed out by the Supreme Court decision. It outlawed segregation.[12] Which means segregation is against the law. Which means a segregationist is breaking the

[12]This statement refers to the 1954 decision of the Supreme Court (in *Brown* v. *Topeka*) to prohibit segregation in public schools.

law. A segregationist is a criminal. You can't label him as anything other than that. And when you demonstrate against segregation, the law is on your side. The Supreme Court is on your side.

Now, who is it that opposes you in carrying out the law? The police department itself. With police dogs and clubs. Whenever you demonstrate against segregation, whether it is segregated education, segregated housing, or anything else, the law is on your side, and anyone who stands in the way is not the law any longer. They are breaking the law, they are not representatives of the law. Any time you demonstrate against segregation and a man has the audacity to put a police dog on you, kill that dog, kill him, I'm telling you, kill that dog. I say it, if they put me in jail tomorrow, kill—that—dog. Then you'll put a stop to it. Now, if these white people in here don't want to see that kind of action, get down and tell the mayor to tell the police department to pull the dogs in. That's all you have to do. If you don't do it, someone else will.

If you don't take this kind of stand, your little children will grow up and look at you and think "shame." If you don't take an uncompromising stand—I don't mean go out and get violent; but at the same time you should never be nonviolent unless you run into some nonviolence. I'm nonviolent with those who are nonviolent with me. But when you drop that violence on me, then you've made me go insane, and I'm not responsible for what I do. And that's the way every Negro should get. Any time you know you're within the law, within your legal rights, within your moral rights, in accord with justice, then die for what you believe in. But don't die alone. Let your dying be reciprocal. This is what is meant by equality. What's good for the goose is good for the gander.

When we begin to get in this area, we need new friends, we need new allies. We need to expand the civil-rights struggle to a higher level—to the level of human rights. Whenever you are in a civil-rights struggle, whether you know it or not, you are confining yourself to the jurisdiction of Uncle Sam. No one from the outside world can speak out in your behalf as long as your struggle is a civil-rights struggle. Civil rights comes within the domestic affairs of this country. All of our African brothers and our Asian brothers and our Latin-American brothers cannot open their mouths and interfere in the domestic affairs of the United States. And as long as it's civil rights, this comes under the jurisdiction of Uncle Sam.

But the United Nations has what's known as the charter of human rights, it has a committee that deals in human rights. You may wonder why all of the atrocities that have been committed in Africa and in Hungary and in Asia and in Latin America are brought before the UN, and the Negro problem is never brought before the UN. This is part of the conspiracy. This old, tricky, blue-eyed liberal who is supposed to be your and my friend, supposed to be in our corner, supposed to be subsidizing our struggle, and supposed to be acting in the capacity of an adviser, never tells you anything about human rights. They keep you wrapped up in civil rights. And you spend so much time barking up the civil-rights tree, you don't even know there's a human-rights tree on the same floor.

When you expand the civil-rights struggle to the level of human rights, you can then take the case of the black man in this country before the nations in the UN. You can take it before the General Assembly. You can take Uncle Sam before a world court. But the only level you can do it on is the level of human rights. Civil rights keeps you under his restrictions, under his jurisdiction. Civil rights keeps you in his pocket. Civil rights means you're asking Uncle Sam to treat you right. Human rights are something you were born with. Human rights are your God-given rights. Human rights are the rights that are recognized by all nations of this earth. And any time any one violates your human rights, you can take them to the world court. Uncle Sam's hands are dripping with blood, dripping with the blood of the black man in this country. He's the earth's number-one hypocrite. He has the audacity—yes, he has—imagine him posing as the leader of the free world. The free world!—and you over here singing "We Shall Overcome." Expand the civil-rights struggle to the level of human rights, take it into the United Nations, where our African brothers can throw their weight on our side, where our Asian brothers can throw their weight on our side, where our Latin-American brothers can throw their weight on our side, and where 800 million Chinamen are sitting there waiting to throw their weight on our side.

Let the world know how bloody his hands are. Let the world know the hypocrisy that's practiced over here. Let it be the ballot or the bullet. Let him know that it must be the ballot or the bullet.

When you take your case to Washington, D.C., you're taking it to the criminal who's responsible; it's like running from the wolf to the fox. They're all in cahoots together. They all work political chicanery and make you look like a chump before the eyes of the world. Here you are walking around in America, getting ready to be drafted and sent abroad, like a tin soldier, and when you get over there, people ask you what are you fighting for, and you have to stick your tongue in your cheek. No, take Uncle Sam to court, take him before the world.

By ballot I only mean freedom. Don't you know—I disagree with Lomax on this issue—that the ballot is more important than the dollar? Can I prove it? Yes. Look in the UN. There are poor nations in the UN; yet those poor nations can get together with their voting power and keep the rich nations from making a move. They have one nation—one vote, everyone has an equal vote. And when those brothers from Asia, and Africa and the darker parts of this earth get together, their voting power is sufficient to hold Sam in check. Or Russia in check. Or some other section of the earth in check. So, the ballot is most important.

Right now, in this country, if you and I, 22 million African-Americans—that's what we are—Africans who are in America. You're nothing but Africans. Nothing but Africans. In fact, you'd get farther calling yourself African instead of Negro. Africans don't catch hell. You're the only one catching hell. They don't have to pass civil-rights bills for Africans. An African can go anywhere he wants right now. All you've got to do is tie your head up. That's right, go anywhere you want. Just stop being a Negro. Change your name to Hoogagagooba. That'll show you how silly the white man is. You're dealing with a silly man. A friend of mine who's very dark put a turban on his head and went into a restaurant in Atlanta before they called themselves desegregated. He went into a white restaurant, he sat down, they served him, and he said, "What would happen if a Negro came in here?" And there he's sitting, black as night, but because he had his head wrapped up the waitress looked back at him and says, "Why, there wouldn't no nigger dare come in here."

So, you're dealing with a man whose bias and prejudice are making him lose his mind, his intelligence, every day. He's frightened. He looks around and sees what's taking place on this earth, and he sees that the pendulum of time is swinging in your direction. The dark people are waking up. They're losing their fear of the white man. No place where he's fighting right now is he winning. Everywhere he's fighting, he's fighting someone your and my complexion. And they're beating him. He can't win any more. He's won his last battle. He failed to win the Korean War. He couldn't win it. He had to sign a truce. That's a loss. Any time Uncle Sam, with all his machinery for warfare, is held to a draw by some rice-eaters, he's lost the battle. He had to sign a truce. America's not supposed to sign a truce. She's supposed to be bad. But she's not bad any more. She's bad as long as she can use her hydrogen bomb, but she can't use hers for fear Russia might use hers. Russia can't use hers, for fear that Sam might use his. So, both of them are weaponless. They can't use the weapon because each's weapon nullifies the other's. So the only place where action can take place is on the ground. And the white man can't win another war fighting on the ground. Those days are over. The black man knows it, the brown man knows it, the red man knows it, and the yellow man knows it. So they engage him in guerrilla warfare. That's not his style. You've got to have heart to be a guerrilla warrior, and he hasn't got any heart. I'm telling you now.

I just want to give you a little briefing on guerrilla warfare because, before you know it, before you know it—It takes heart to be a guerrilla warrior because you're on your own. In conventional warfare you have tanks and a whole lot of other people with you to back you up, planes over your head and all that kind of stuff. But a guerrilla is on his own. All you have is a rifle, some sneakers and a bowl of rice, and that's all you need—and a lot of heart. The Japanese on some of those islands in the Pacific, when the American soldiers landed, one Japanese sometimes could hold the whole army off. He'd just wait until the sun went down, and when the sun went down they were all equal. He would take his little blade and slip from bush to bush, and from American to American. The white soldiers couldn't cope with that. Whenever you see a white soldier that fought in the Pacific, he has the shakes, he has a nervous condition, because they scared him to death.

The same thing happened to the French up in French Indochina.[13] People who just a few years previously were rice farmers got together and ran the heavily-mechanized French army out of Indochina. You don't need it—modern warfare today won't work. This is the day of the guerrilla. They did the same thing in Algeria. Algerians, who were nothing but Bedouins, took a rifle and sneaked off to the hills, and de Gaulle and all of his highfalutin' war machinery couldn't defeat those guerrillas.[14] Nowhere on this earth does the white man win in a guerrilla warfare. It's not his speed. Just as guerrilla warfare is prevailing in Asia and in parts of Africa and in parts of Latin America, you've got to be mighty naive, or you've got to play the black man cheap, if you don't think some day he's going to wake up and find that it's got to be the ballot or the bullet.

I would like to say, in closing, a few things concerning the Muslim Mosque, Inc., which we established recently in New York City. It's true we're Muslims and our religion is Islam, but we don't mix our religion with our politics and our economics and

[13]Once a single political unit, French Indochina is now Vietnam, Cambodia, and Laos.

[14]Charles de Gaulle served as president of France when France fought in Algeria.

our social and civil activities—not any more. We keep our religion in our mosque. After our religious services are over, then as Muslims we become involved in political action, economic action and social and civic action. We become involved with anybody, anywhere, any time and in any manner that's designed to eliminate the evils, the political, economic and social evils that are afflicting the people of our community.

The political philosophy of black nationalism means that the black man should control the politics and the politicians in his own community; no more. The black man in the black community has to be re-educated into the science of politics so he will know what politics is supposed to bring him in return. Don't be throwing out any ballots. A ballot is like a bullet. You don't throw your ballots until you see a target, and if that target is not within your reach, keep your ballot in your pocket. The political philosophy of black nationalism is being taught in the Christian church. It's being taught in the NAACP. It's being taught in CORE meetings. It's being taught in SNCC meetings.[15] It's being taught in Muslim meetings. It's being taught where nothing but atheists and agnostics come together. It's being taught everywhere. Black people are fed up with the dillydallying, pussyfooting, compromising approach that we've been using toward getting our freedom. We want freedom *now,* but we're not going to get it saying "We Shall Overcome." We've got to fight until we overcome.

The economic philosophy of black nationalism is pure and simple. It only means that we should control the economy of our community. Why should white people be running all the stores in our community? Why should white people be running the banks of our community? Why should the economy of our community be in the hands of the white man? Why? If a black man can't move his store into a white community, you tell me why a white man should move his store into a black community. The philosophy of black nationalism involves a re-education program in the black community in regards to economics. Our people have to be made to see that any time you take your dollar out of your community and spend it in a community where you don't live, the community where you live will get poorer and poorer, and the community where you spend your money will get richer and richer. Then you wonder why where you live is always a ghetto or a slum area. And where you and I are concerned, not only do we lose it when we spend it out of the community, but the white man has got all our stores in the community tied up; so that though we spend it in the community, at sundown the man who runs the store takes it over across town somewhere. He's got us in a vise.

So the economic philosophy of black nationalism means in every church, in every civic organization, in every fraternal order, it's time now for our people to become conscious of the importance of controlling the economy of our community. If we own the stores, if we operate the businesses, if we try and establish some industry in our own community, then we're developing to the position where we are creating employment for our own kind. Once you gain control of the economy of your own community, then you don't have to picket and boycott and beg some cracker downtown for a job in his business.

[15]NAACP is the National Association for the Advancement of Colored People. CORE is the Congress of Racial Equality. SNCC is the Student Nonviolent Coordinating Committee. Here Malcolm X is much more conciliatory toward civil rights organizations than he had been previously.

The social philosophy of black nationalism only means that we have to get together and remove the evils, the vices, alcoholism, drug addiction, and other evils that are destroying the moral fiber of our community. We ourselves have to lift the level of our community, the standard of our community to a higher level, make our own society beautiful so that we will be satisfied in our own social circles and won't be running around here trying to knock our way into a social circle where we're not wanted.

So I say, in spreading a gospel such as black nationalism, it is not designed to make the black man re-evaluate the white man—you know him already—but to make the black man re-evaluate himself. Don't change the white man's mind—you can't change his mind, and that whole thing about appealing to the moral conscience of America—America's conscience is bankrupt. She lost all conscience a long time ago. Uncle Sam has no conscience. They don't know what morals are. They don't try and eliminate an evil because it's evil, or because it's illegal, or because it's immoral; they eliminate it only when it threatens their existence. So you're wasting your time appealing to the moral conscience of a bankrupt man like Uncle Sam. If he had a conscience, he'd straighten this thing out with no more pressure being put upon him. So it is not necessary to change the white man's mind. We have to change our own mind. You can't change his mind about us. We've got to change our own minds about each other. We have to see each other with new eyes. We have to see each other as brothers and sisters. We have to come together with warmth so we can develop unity and harmony that's necessary to get this problem solved ourselves. How can we do this? How can we avoid jealousy? How can we avoid the suspicion and the divisions that exist in the community? I'll tell you how.

I have watched how Billy Graham comes into a city, spreading what he calls the gospel of Christ, which is only white nationalism.[16] That's what he is. Billy Graham is a white nationalist; I'm a black nationalist. But since it's the natural tendency for leaders to be jealous and look upon a powerful figure like Graham with suspicion and envy, how is it possible for him to come into a city and get all the cooperation of the church leaders? Don't think because they're church leaders that they don't have weaknesses that make them envious and jealous—no, everybody's got it. It's not an accident that when they want to choose a cardinal over there in Rome, they get in a closet so you can't hear them cussing and fighting and carrying on.

Billy Graham comes in preaching the gospel of Christ, he evangelizes the gospel, he stirs everybody up, but he never tries to start a church. If he came in trying to start a church, all the churches would be against him. So, he just comes in talking about Christ and tells everybody who gets Christ to go to any church where Christ is; and in this way the church cooperates with him. So we're going to take a page from his book.

Our gospel is black nationalism. We're not trying to threaten the existence of any organization, but we're spreading the gospel of black nationalism. Anywhere there's a church that is also preaching and practicing the gospel of black nationalism, join that church. If the NAACP is preaching and practicing the gospel of black

[16]Billy Graham was and is a Baptist minister and popular, roving evangelist. He did not take a strong position on civil rights.

nationalism, join the NAACP. If CORE is spreading and practicing the gospel of black nationalism, join CORE. Join any organization that has a gospel that's for the uplift of the black man. And when you get into it and see them pussyfooting or compromising, pull out of it because that's not black nationalism. We'll find another one.

And in this manner, the organizations will increase in number and in quantity and in quality, and by August, it is then our intention to have a black nationalist convention which will consist of delegates from all over the country who are interested in the political, economic and social philosophy of black nationalism. After these delegates convene, we will hold a seminar, we will hold discussions, we will listen to everyone. We want to hear new ideas and new solutions and new answers. And at that time, if we see fit then to form a black nationalist party, we'll form a black nationalist party. If it's necessary to form a black nationalist army, we'll form a black nationalist army. It'll be the ballot or the bullet. It'll be liberty or it'll be death.

It's time for you and me to stop sitting in this country, letting some cracker senators, Northern crackers and Southern crackers, sit there in Washington, D.C., and come to a conclusion in their mind that you and I are supposed to have civil rights. There's no white man going to tell me anything about *my* rights. Brothers and sisters, always remember, if it doesn't take senators and congressmen and presidential proclamations to give freedom to the white man, it is not necessary for legislation or proclamation or Supreme Court decisions to give freedom to the black man. You let that white man know, if this is a country of freedom, let it be a country of freedom; and if it's not a country of freedom, change it.

We will work with anybody, anywhere, at any time, who is genuinely interested in tackling the problem head-on, nonviolently as long as the enemy is nonviolent, but violent when the enemy gets violent. We'll work with you on the voter-registration drive, we'll work with you on rent strikes, we'll work with you on school boycotts—I don't believe in any kind of integration; I'm not even worried about it because I know you're not going to get it anyway; you're not going to get it because you're afraid to die; you've got to be ready to die if you try and force yourself on the white man, because he'll get just as violent as those crackers in Mississippi, right here in Cleveland.[17] But we will still work with you on the school boycotts because we're against a segregated school system. A segregated school system produces children who, when they graduate, graduate with crippled minds. But this does not mean that a school is segregated because it's all black. A segregated school means a school that is controlled by people who have no real interest in it whatsoever.

Let me explain what I mean. A segregated district or community is a community in which people live, but outsiders control the politics and the economy of that community. They never refer to the white section as a segregated community. It's the all-Negro section that's a segregated community. Why? The white man controls his own school, his own bank, his own economy, his own politics, his own everything, his own community—but he also controls yours. When you're under someone else's control, you're segregated. They'll always give you the lowest or the worst that there is to offer, but it doesn't mean you're segregated just because you have your own. You've got to *control* your own. Just like the white man has control of his, you need to control yours.

[17]Malcolm X delivered this speech in Cleveland.

You know the best way to get rid of segregation? The white man is more afraid of separation than he is of integration. Segregation means that he puts you away from him, but not far enough for you to be out of his jurisdiction; separation means you're gone. And the white man will integrate faster than he'll let you separate. So we will work with you against the segregated school system because it's criminal, because it is absolutely destructive, in every way imaginable, to the minds of the children who have to be exposed to that type of crippling education.

Last but not least, I must say this concerning the great controversy over rifles and shotguns. The only thing that I've ever said is that in areas where the government has proven itself either unwilling or unable to defend the lives and the property of Negroes, it's time for Negroes to defend themselves. Article number two of the constitutional amendments provides you and me the right to own a rifle or a shotgun. It is constitutionally legal to own a shotgun or a rifle. This doesn't mean you're going to get a rifle and form battalions and go out looking for white folks, although you'd be within your rights—I mean, you'd be justified; but that would be illegal and we don't do anything illegal.[18] If the white man doesn't want the black man buying rifles and shotguns, then let the government do its job. That's all. And don't let the white man come to you and ask you what you think about what Malcolm says—why, you old Uncle Tom. He would never ask you if he thought you were going to say, "Amen!" No, he is making a Tom out of you.

So, this doesn't mean forming rifle clubs and going out looking for people, but it is time, in 1964, if you are a man, to let that man know. If he's not going to do his job in running the government and providing you and me with the protection that our taxes are supposed to be for, since he spends all those billions for his defense budget, he certainly can't begrudge you and me spending $12 or $15 for a single-shot, or double-action. I hope you understand. Don't go out shooting people, but any time, brothers and sisters, and especially the men in this audience—some of you wearing Congressional Medals of Honor, with shoulders this wide, chests this big, muscles that big—any time you and I sit around and read where they bomb a church and murder in cold blood, not some grownups, but four little girls while they were praying to the same god the white man taught them to pray to, and you and I see the government go down and can't find who did it.[19]

Why, this man—he can find Eichmann hiding down in Argentina somewhere.[20] Let two or three American soldiers, who are minding somebody else's business way over in South Vietnam, get killed, and he'll send battleships, sticking his nose in their business. He wanted to send troops down to Cuba and make them have what he calls free elections—this old cracker who doesn't have free elections in his own country. No, if you never see me another time in your life, if I die in the morning, I'll die saying one thing: the ballot or the bullet, the ballot or the bullet.

If a Negro in 1964 has to sit around and wait for some cracker senator to filibuster when it comes to the rights of black people, why, you and I should hang our

[18]Malcolm X often sounded ambiguous on the issue of violence.

[19]In 1963 four black girls died in Birmingham one Sunday morning when their church was dynamited by white racists. The church had served as the organizing center for Martin Luther King, Jr.'s nonviolent Birmingham campaign.

[20]Adolph Eichmann was a high-ranking Nazi fugitive who was finally captured in Argentina.

heads in shame. You talk about a march on Washington in 1963, you haven't seen anything. There's some more going down in '64. And this time they're not going like they went last year. They're not going singing "We Shall Overcome." They're not going with white friends. They're not going with placards already painted for them. They're not going with round-trip tickets. They're going with one-way tickets.

And if they don't want that non-nonviolent army going down there, tell them to bring the filibuster to a halt. The black nationalists aren't going to wait. Lyndon B. Johnson is the head of the Democratic Party. If he's for civil rights, let him go into the Senate next week and declare himself. Let him go in there right now and declare himself. Let him go in there and denounce the Southern branch of his party. Let him go in there right now and take a moral stand—right now, not later. Tell him, don't wait until election time. If he waits too long, brothers and sisters, he will be responsible for letting a condition develop in this country which will create a climate that will bring seeds up out of the ground with vegetation on the end of them looking like something these people never dreamed of. In 1964, it's the ballot or the bullet. Thank you.

1964

Saul Bellow b. 1915

The son of immigrant parents from Russia, Saul Bellow grew up in a Jewish ghetto of Montreal, Canada, where he learned Yiddish, Hebrew, English, and French. In 1924 his family moved to Chicago, a city that often appears in his fiction. After earning a bachelor's degree from Northwestern University, in 1937 he entered the University of Wisconsin at Madison to study anthropology but left there in December to become a writer. Employed for a brief period with the Works Progress Administration Writers Project, he led a bohemian life until World War II, whereupon he served in the Merchant Marine. After the war, he taught at the University of Minnesota in Minneapolis and other schools, traveled in Europe, and lived in Paris for a period of time. Since 1963 he has been a professor at the University of Chicago.

Bellow is usually considered to be one of America's most important contemporary writers; his work impresses one with its diversity of style, the profundity of its content, and its scope. Bellow published his first novel, *The Dangling Man,* in 1944; it is a diary of a demoralized man who is left "dangling" with no real purpose as he waits to be drafted. Three years later, Bellow published *The Victim,* which borrows the technique of the Doppelgänger from Dostoevski's *The Eternal Husband.* In this second novel, he depicts the intense psychological battle between the Jew Asa Leventhal and his "double," the Gentile Kirby Allbee.

In the late 1940s, Bellow became disenchanted with the "modernist" "victim literature" of his first two novels. Detached in tone, these restrained works followed "repressive" Flaubertian formal standards. With *The Adventures of Augie March* (1953), Bellow broke free from the "modernist" chains that bound him. In contrast to the two morose early novels, this open-ended, picaresque narrative with its flamboyant language, zany comedy, and exuberant hero affirms the potential of the individual, his imagination, and the worth of ordinary existence.

Bellow's subsequent novels develop the themes of *The Adventures of Augie March. Seize the Day* (1956) is a dark comedy that depicts the day of reckoning in the life of Tommy Wilhelm, "a loser" who is spiritually reborn at the very end of the work. *Henderson the Rain King* (1959) is the story of an eccentric, energetic millionaire who journeys to the heart of Africa and experiences fantastic adventures. *Herzog* (1964), an enormous critical and financial success, depicts the intense psychological struggles of a professor who is on the verge of a mental breakdown as a result of his divorce from his second wife and the betrayal of his best friend. *The Dean's December* (1982) confronts more directly than any of Bellow's other novels political and social problems; Bellow contrasts the near anarchy of the slums of Chicago with the authoritarianism of the Communist world and sees a "moral crisis" in both West and East. *Ravelstein* (2000) is a meditative and autobiographical novel that explores a variety of subjects but focuses on friendship, memory, and death.

Bellow has also written short stories, some of which are collected in *Mosby's Memoirs and Other Stories* and *Him with His Foot in His Mouth and Other Stories,* a non-fiction book on Israel, *To Jerusalem and Back,* several plays, and a number of essays, some of which are collected in *It All Adds Up.* He has received many awards for his writing, including the Nobel Prize for Literature in 1976.

Bellow is a master of narrative voice and perspective; he is a remarkable stylist who can move with ease from formal rhetoric to the language of the street. A great comic writer, perhaps America's greatest since Mark Twain, he explores the tragicomic search of urban man for spiritual survival in a materialistic world hostile to the imagination and "higher meanings."

Allan Chavkin
Southwest Texas State University

PRIMARY WORKS

Dangling Man, 1944; *The Victim,* 1947; *The Adventures of Augie March,* 1953; *Seize the Day,* 1956; *Henderson the Rain King,* 1959; *Herzog,* 1964; *Mosby's Memoirs and Other Stories,* 1968; *Mr. Sammler's Planet,* 1970; *Humboldt's Gift,* 1975; *To Jerusalem and Back,* 1976; *The Dean's December,* 1982; *Him with His Foot in His Mouth and Other Stories,* 1984; *More Die of Heartbreak,* 1987; *A Theft,* 1989; *The Bellarosa Connection,* 1989; *Something to Remember Me By,* 1991; *It All Adds Up,* 1994; *The Actual,* 1997; *Ravelstein,* 2000.

Looking for Mr. Green

Whatsoever thy hand findeth to do, do it with thy might. . . .[1]

Hard work? No, it wasn't really so hard. He wasn't used to walking and stair-climbing, but the physical difficulty of his new job was not what George Grebe felt most. He was delivering relief checks in the Negro district, and although he was a native Chicagoan this was not a part of the city he knew much about—it needed a depression to introduce

[1]Ecclesiastes 9:10 "Whatsoever thy hand findeth to do, do it with thy might; for there is no work, nor device, nor knowledge, nor wisdom, in the grave, whither thou goest."

him to it. No, it wasn't literally hard work, not as reckoned in foot-pounds, but yet he was beginning to feel the strain of it, to grow aware of its peculiar difficulty. He could find the streets and numbers, but the clients were not where they were supposed to be, and he felt like a hunter inexperienced in the camouflage of his game. It was an unfavorable day, too—fall, and cold, dark weather, windy. But, anyway, instead of shells in his deep trenchcoat pocket he had the cardboard of checks, punctured for the spindles of the file, the holes reminding him of the holes in player-piano paper. And he didn't look much like a hunter, either; his was a city figure entirely, belted up in this Irish conspirator's coat. He was slender without being tall, stiff in the back, his legs looking shabby in a pair of old tweed pants gone through and fringy at the cuffs. With this stiffness, he kept his head forward, so that his face was red from the sharpness of the weather; and it was an indoors sort of face with gray eyes that persisted in some kind of thought and yet seemed to avoid definiteness of conclusion. He wore sideburns that surprised you somewhat by the tough curl of the blond hair and the effect of assertion in their length. He was not so mild as he looked, nor so youthful; and nevertheless there was no effort on his part to seem what he was not. He was an educated man; he was a bachelor; he was in some ways simple; without lushing, he liked a drink; his luck had not been good. Nothing was deliberately hidden.

He felt that his luck was better than usual today. When he had reported for work that morning he had expected to be shut up in the relief office at a clerk's job, for he had been hired downtown as a clerk, and he was glad to have, instead, the freedom of the streets and welcomed, at least at first, the vigor of the cold and even the blowing of the hard wind. But on the other hand he was not getting on with the distribution of the checks. It was true that it was a city job; nobody expected you to push too hard at a city job. His supervisor, that young Mr. Raynor, had practically told him that. Still, he wanted to do well at it. For one thing, when he knew how quickly he could deliver a batch of checks, he would know also how much time he could expect to clip for himself. And then, too, the clients would be waiting for their money. That was not the most important consideration, though it certainly mattered to him. No, but he wanted to do well, simply for doing-well's sake, to acquit himself decently of a job because he so rarely had a job to do that required just this sort of energy. Of this peculiar energy he now had a superabundance; once it had started to flow, it flowed all too heavily. And, for the time being anyway, he was balked. He could not find Mr. Green.

So he stood in his big-skirted trenchcoat with a large envelope in his hand and papers showing from his pocket, wondering why people should be so hard to locate who were too feeble or sick to come to the station to collect their own checks. But Raynor had told him that tracking them down was not easy at first and had offered him some advice on how to proceed. "If you can see the postman, he's your first man to ask, and your best bet. If you can't connect with him, try the stores and tradespeople around. Then the janitor and the neighbors. But you'll find the closer you come to your man the less people will tell you. They don't want to tell you anything."

"Because I'm a stranger."

"Because you're white. We ought to have a Negro doing this, but we don't at the moment, and of course you've got to eat, too, and this is public employment. Jobs have to be made. Oh, that holds for me too. Mind you, I'm not letting myself out. I've got three years of seniority on you, that's all. And a law degree. Otherwise, you might be back of the desk and I might be going out into the field this cold day. The same dough pays us both and for the same, exact, identical reason. What's my law degree got to do with it? But you have to pass out these checks, Mr. Grebe, and it'll help if you're stubborn, so I hope you are."

"Yes, I'm fairly stubborn."

Raynor sketched hard with an eraser in the old dirt of his desk, left-handed, and said, "Sure, what else can you answer to such a question. Anyhow, the trouble you're going to have is that they don't like to give information about anybody. They think you're a plain-clothes dick or an installment collector, or summons-server or something like that. Till you've been seen around the neighborhood for a few months and people know you're only from the relief."

It was dark, ground-freezing, pre-Thanksgiving weather; the wind played hob with the smoke, rushing it down, and Grebe missed his gloves, which he had left in Raynor's office. And no one would admit knowing Green. It was past three o'clock and the postman had made his last delivery. The nearest grocer, himself a Negro, had never heard the name Tulliver Green, or said he hadn't. Grebe was inclined to think that it was true, that he had in the end convinced the man that he wanted only to deliver a check. But he wasn't sure. He needed experience in interpreting looks and signs and, even more, the will not to be put off or denied and even the force to bully if need be. If the grocer did know, he had got rid of him easily. But since most of his trade was with reliefers, why should he prevent the delivery of a check? Maybe Green, or Mrs. Green, if there was a Mrs. Green, patronized another grocer. And was there a Mrs. Green? It was one of Grebe's great handicaps that he hadn't looked at any of the case records. Raynor should have let him read files for a few hours. But he apparently saw no need for that, probably considering the job unimportant. Why prepare systematically to deliver a few checks?

But now it was time to look for the janitor. Grebe took in the building in the wind and gloom of the late November day—trampled, frost-hardened lots on one side; on the other, an automobile junk yard and then the infinite work of Elevated frames,[2] weak-looking, gaping with rubbish fires; two sets of leaning brick porches three stories high and a flight of cement stairs to the cellar. Descending, he entered the underground passage, where he tried the doors until one opened and he found himself in the furnace room. There someone rose toward him and approached, scraping on the coal grit and bending under the canvas-jacketed pipes.

"Are you the janitor?"

"What do you want?"

"I'm looking for a man who's supposed to be living here. Green."

"What Green?"

"Oh, you maybe have more than one Green?" said Grebe with new, pleasant hope. "This is Tulliver Green."

"I don't think I c'n help you, mister. I don't know any."

"A crippled man."

The janitor stood bent before him. Could it be that he was crippled? Oh, God! what if he was. Grebe's gray eyes sought with excited dfficulty to see. But no, he was

[2]The "El," or elevated railroad, which operates on an elevated structure, as over streets.

only very short and stooped. A head awakened from meditation, a strong-haired beard, low, wide shoulders. A staleness of sweat and coal rose from his black shirt and the burlap sack he wore as an apron.

"Crippled how?"

Grebe thought and then answered with the light voice of unmixed candor, "I don't know. I've never seen him." This was damaging, but his only other choice was to make a lying guess, and he was not up to it. "I'm delivering checks for the relief to shut-in cases. If he weren't crippled he'd come to collect himself. That's why I said crippled. Bedridden, chair-ridden—is there anybody like that?"

This sort of frankness was one of Grebe's oldest talents, going back to childhood. But it gained him nothing here.

"No suh. I've got four buildin's same as this that I take care of. I don' know all the tenants, leave alone the tenants' tenants. The rooms turn over so fast, people movin' in and out every day. I can't tell you."

The janitor opened his grimy lips but Grebe did not hear him in the piping of the valves and the consuming pull of air to flame in the body of the furnace. He knew, however, what he had said.

"Well, all the same, thanks. Sorry I bothered you. I'll prowl around upstairs again and see if I can turn up someone who knows him."

Once more in the cold air and early darkness he made the short circle from the cellarway to the entrance crowded between the brickwork pillars and began to climb to the third floor. Pieces of plaster ground under his feet; strips of brass tape from which the carpeting had been torn away marked old boundaries at the sides. In the passage, the cold reached him worse than in the street; it touched him to the bone. The hall toilets ran like springs. He thought grimly as he heard the wind burning around the building with a sound like that of the furnace, that this was a great piece of constructed shelter. Then he struck a match in the gloom and searched for names and numbers among the writings and scribbles on the walls. He saw WHOODY-DOODY GO TO JESUS, and zigzags, caricatures, sexual scrawls, and curses. So the sealed rooms of pyramids were also decorated, and the caves of human dawn.

The information on his card was, TULLIVER GREEN—APT 3D. There were no names, however, and no numbers. His shoulders drawn up, tears of cold in his eyes, breathing vapor, he went the length of the corridor and told himself that if he had been lucky enough to have the temperament for it he would bang on one of the doors and bawl out "Tulliver Green!" until he got results. But it wasn't in him to make an uproar and he continued to burn matches, passing the light over the walls. At the rear, in a corner off the hall, he discovered a door he had not seen before and he thought it best to investigate. It sounded empty when he knocked, but a young Negress answered, hardly more than a girl. She opened only a bit, to guard the warmth of the room.

"Yes suh?"

"I'm from the district relief station on Prairie Avenue. I'm looking for a man named Tulliver Green to give him his check. Do you know him?"

No, she didn't; but he thought she had not understood anything of what he had said. She had a dream-bound, dream-blind face, very soft and black, shut off. She wore a man's jacket and pulled the ends together at her throat. Her hair was parted in three directions, at the sides and transversely, standing up at the front in a dull puff.

"Is there somebody around here who might know?"

"I jus' taken this room las' week."

He observed that she shivered, but even her shiver was somnambulistic and there was no sharp consciousness of cold in the big smooth eyes of her handsome face.

"All right, miss, thank you. Thanks," he said, and went to try another place.

Here he was admitted. He was grateful, for the room was warm. It was full of people, and they were silent as he entered—ten people, or a dozen, perhaps more, sitting on benches like a parliament. There was no light, properly speaking, but a tempered darkness that the window gave, and everyone seemed to him enormous, the men padded out in heavy work clothes and winter coats, and the women huge, too, in their sweaters, hats, and old furs. And, besides, bed and bedding, a black cooking range, a piano piled towering to the ceiling with papers, a dining-room table of the old style of prosperous Chicago. Among these people Grebe, with his cold-heightened fresh color and his smaller stature, entered like a schoolboy. Even though he was met with smiles and good will, he knew, before a single word was spoken, that all the currents ran against him and that he would make no headway. Nevertheless he began. "Does anybody here know how I can deliver a check to Mr. Tulliver Green?"

"Green?" It was the man that had let him in who answered. He was in short sleeves, in a checkered shirt, and had a queer, high head, profusely overgrown and long as a shako;[3] the veins entered it strongly from his forehead. "I never heard mention of him. Is this where he live?"

"This is the address they gave me at the station. He's a sick man, and he'll need his check. Can't anybody tell me where to find him?"

He stood his ground and waited for a reply, his crimson wool scarf wound about his neck and drooping outside his trenchcoat, pockets weighted with the block of checks and official forms. They must have realized that he was not a college boy employed afternoons by a bill collector, trying foxily to pass for a relief clerk, recognized that he was an older man who knew himself what need was, who had had more than an average seasoning in hardship. It was evident enough if you looked at the marks under his eyes and at the sides of his mouth.

"Anybody know this sick man?"

"No suh." On all sides he saw heads shaken and smiles of denial. No one knew. And maybe it was true, he considered, standing silent in the earthen, musky human gloom of the place as the rumble continued. But he could never really be sure.

"What's the matter with this man?" said shako-head.

"I've never seen him. All I can tell you is that he can't come in person for his money. It's my first day in this district."

"Maybe they given you the wrong number?"

"I don't believe so. But where else can I ask about him?" He felt that this persistence amused them deeply, and in a way he shared their amusement that he should stand up so tenaciously to them. Though smaller, though slight, he was his own man,

[3]A military cap in the shape of a cylinder with a visor and a pompon or plume.

he retracted nothing about himself, and he looked back at them, gray-eyed, with amusement and also with a sort of courage. On the bench some man spoke in his throat, the words impossible to catch, and a woman answered with a wild, shrieking laugh, which was quickly cut off.

"Well, so nobody will tell me?"

"Ain't nobody who knows."

"At least, if he lives here, he pays rent to someone. Who manages the building?"

"Greatham Company. That's on Thirty-ninth Street."

Grebe wrote it in his pad. But, in the street again, a sheet of wind-driven paper clinging to his leg while he deliberated what direction to take next, it seemed a feeble lead to follow. Probably this Green didn't rent a flat, but a room. Sometimes there were as many as twenty people in an apartment; the real-estate agent would know only the lessee. And not even the agent could tell you who the renters were. In some places the beds were even used in shifts, watchmen or jitney drivers or short-order cooks in night joints turning out after a day's sleep and surrendering their beds to a sister, a nephew, or perhaps a stranger, just off the bus. There were large numbers of newcomers in this terrific, blight-bitten portion of the city between Cottage Grove and Ashland, wandering from house to house and room to room. When you saw them, how could you know them? They didn't carry bundles on their backs or look picturesque. You only saw a man, a Negro, walking in the street or riding in the car, like everyone else, with his thumb closed on a transfer. And therefore how were you supposed to tell? Grebe thought the Greatham agent would only laugh at his question.

But how much it would have simplified the job to be able to say that Green was old, or blind, or consumptive. An hour in the files, taking a few notes, and he needn't have been at such a disadvantage. When Raynor gave him the block of checks he asked, "How much should I know about these people?" Then Raynor had looked as though he were preparing to accuse him of trying to make the job more important than it was. He smiled, because by then they were on fine terms, but nevertheless he had been getting ready to say something like that when the confusion began in the station over Staika and her children.

Grebe had waited a long time for this job. It came to him through the pull of an old schoolmate in the Corporation Counsel's office, never a close friend, but suddenly sympathetic and interested—pleased to show, moreover, how well he had done, how strongly he was coming on even in these miserable times. Well, he was coming through strongly, along with the Democratic administration itself. Grebe had gone to see him in City Hall, and they had had a counter lunch or beers at least once a month for a year, and finally it had been possible to swing the job. He didn't mind being assigned the lowest clerical grade, nor even being a messenger, though Raynor thought he did.

This Raynor was an original sort of guy and Grebe had taken to him immediately. As was proper on the first day, Grebe had come early, but he waited long, for Raynor was late. At last he darted into his cubicle of an office as though he had just jumped from one of those hurtling huge red Indian Avenue cars. His thin, rough face was wind-stung and he was grinning and saying something breathlessly to himself. In his hat, a small fedora, and his coat, the velvet collar a neat fit about his neck, and his silk muffler that set off the nervous twist of his chin, he swayed and turned himself in his swivel chair, feet leaving the ground; so that he pranced a little as he sat. Meanwhile he took Grebe's measure out of his eyes, eyes of an unusual vertical length and slightly sardonic. So the two men sat for a while, saying nothing, while the supervisor raised his hat from his miscombed hair and put it in his lap. His cold-darkened hands were not clean. A steel beam passed through the little make-shift room, from which machine belts once had hung. The building was an old factory.

"I'm younger than you; I hope you won't find it hard taking orders from me," said Raynor. "But I don't make them up, either. You're how old, about?"

"Thirty-five."

"And you thought you'd be inside doing paper work. But it so happens I have to send you out."

"I don't mind."

"And it's mostly a Negro load we have in this district."

"So I thought it would be."

"Fine. You'll get along. *C'est un bon boulot.*[4] Do you know French?"

"Some."

"I thought you'd be a university man."

"Have you been in France?" said Grebe.

"No, that's the French of the Berlitz School. I've been at it for more than a year, just as I'm sure people have been, all over the world, office boys in China and braves in Tanganyika. In fact, I damn well know it. Such is the attractive power of civilization. It's overrated, but what do you want? *Que voulez-vous?*[5] I get *Le Rire*[6] and all the spicy papers, just like in Tanganyika. It must be mystifying, out there. But my reason is that I'm aiming at the diplomatic service. I have a cousin who's a courier, and the way he describes it is awfully attractive. He rides in the *wagon-lits*[7] and reads books. While we—What did you do before?"

"I sold."

"Where?"

"Canned meat at Stop and Shop. In the basement."

"And before that?"

"Window shades, at Goldblatt's."

"Steady work?"

"No, Thursdays and Saturdays. I also sold shoes."

"You've been a shoe-dog too. Well. And prior to that? Here it is in your folder." He opened the record. "Saint Olaf's College, instructor in classical languages. Fellow, University of Chicago, 1926–27. I've had Latin, too. Let's trade quotations—'*Dum spiro spero.*'"

"'*Da dextram misero.*'"

"'*Alea jacta est.*'"

"'*Excelsior.*'"[8]

Raynor shouted with laughter, and other workers came to look at him over the

[4]"It's a good job."
[5]"What do you want?"
[6]French comic journal.
[7]Train sleeping-cars.
[8]"While I breathe, I hope"; "Give your right hand to the wretched"; "The die is cast"; "Higher!"

partition. Grebe also laughed, feeling pleased and easy. The luxury of fun on a nervous morning.

When they were done and no one was watching or listening, Raynor said rather seriously, "What made you study Latin in the first place? Was it for the priesthood?"

"No."

"Just for the hell of it? For the culture? Oh, the things people think they can pull!" He made his cry hilarious and tragic. "I ran my pants off so I could study for the bar, and I've passed the bar, so I get twelve dollars a week more than you as a bonus for having seen life straight and whole. I'll tell you, as a man of culture, that even though nothing looks to be real, and everything stands for something else, and that thing for another thing, and that thing for a still further one—there ain't any comparison between twenty-five and thirty-seven dollars a week, regardless of the last reality. Don't you think that was clear to your Greeks? They were a thoughtful people, but they didn't part with their slaves."

This was a great deal more than Grebe had looked for in his first interview with his supervisor. He was too shy to show all the astonishment he felt. He laughed a little, aroused, and brushed at the sunbeam that covered his head with its dust. "Do you think my mistake was so terrible?"

"Damn right it was terrible, and you know it now that you've had the whip of hard times laid on your back. You should have been preparing yourself for trouble. Your people must have been well off to send you to the university. Stop me, if I'm stepping on your toes. Did your mother pamper you? Did your father give in to you? Were you brought up tenderly, with permission to go and find out what were the last things that everything else stands for while everybody else labored in the fallen world of appearances?"

"Well, no, it wasn't exactly like that." Grebe smiled. *The fallen world of appearances!* no less. But now it was his turn to deliver a surprise. "We weren't rich. My father was the last genuine English butler in Chicago—"

"Are you kidding?"

"Why should I be?"

"In a livery?"

"In livery. Up on the Gold Coast."[9]

"And he wanted you to be educated like a gentleman?"

"He did not. He sent me to the Armour Institute to study chemical engineering. But when he died I changed schools."

He stopped himself, and considered how quickly Raynor had reached him. In no time he had your valise on the table and all your stuff unpacked. And afterward, in the streets, he was still reviewing how far he might have gone, and how much he might have been led to tell if they had not been interrupted by Mrs. Staika's great noise.

But just then a young woman, one of Raynor's workers, ran into the cubicle exclaiming, "Haven't you heard all the fuss?"

"We haven't heard anything."

[9]Lake Shore Drive, one of Chicago's richest areas.

"It's Staika, giving out with all her might. The reporters are coming. She said she phoned the papers, and you know she did."

"But what is she up to?" said Raynor.

"She brought her wash and she's ironing it here, with our current, because the relief won't pay her electric bill. She has her ironing board set up by the admitting desk, and her kids are with her, all six. They never are in school more than once a week. She's always dragging them around with her because of her reputation."

"I don't want to miss any of this," said Raynor, jumping up. Grebe, as he followed with the secretary, said, "Who is this Staika?"

"They call her the 'Blood Mother of Federal Street.' She's a professional donor at the hospitals. I think they pay ten dollars a pint. Of course it's no joke, but she makes a very big thing out of it and she and the kids are in the papers all the time."

A small crowd, staff and clients divided by a plywood barrier, stood in the narrow space of the entrance, and Staika was shouting in a gruff, mannish voice, plunging the iron on the board and slamming it on the metal rest.

"My father and mother came in a steerage, and I was born in our house, Robey by Huron. I'm no dirty immigrant. I'm a U.S. citizen. My husband is a gassed veteran from France with lungs weaker'n paper, that hardly can he go to the toilet by himself. These six children of mine, I have to buy the shoes for their feet with my own blood. Even a lousy little white Communion necktie, that a couple of drops of blood; a little piece of mosquito veil for my Vadja so she won't be ashamed in church for the other girls, they take my blood for it by Goldblatt. That's how I keep goin'. A fine thing if I had to depend on the relief. And there's plenty of people on the rolls—fakes! There's nothin' *they* can't get, that can go and wrap bacon at Swift and Armour any time. They're lookin' for them by the Yards. They never have to be out of work. Only they rather lay in their lousy beds and eat the public's money." She was not afraid, in a predominantly Negro station, to shout this way about Negroes.

Grebe and Raynor worked themselves forward to get a closer view of the woman. She was flaming with anger and with pleasure at herself, broad and huge, a golden-headed woman who wore a cotton cap laced with pink ribbon. She was barelegged and had on black gym shoes, her Hoover apron was open and her great breasts, not much restrained by a man's undershirt, hampered her arms as she worked at the kid's dress on the ironing board. And the children, silent and white, with a kind of locked obstinacy, in sheepskins and lumberjackets, stood behind her. She had captured the station, and the pleasure this gave her was enormous. Yet her grievances were true grievances. She was telling the truth. But she behaved like a liar. The look of her small eyes was hidden, and while she raged she also seemed to be spinning and planning.

"They send me out college case workers in silk pants to talk me out of what I got comin'. Are they better'n me? Who told them? Fire them. Let 'em go and get married, and then you won't have to cut electric from people's budget."

The chief supervisor, Mr. Ewing, couldn't silence her and he stood with folded arms at the head of his staff, bald, bald-headed, saying to his subordinates like the ex-school principal he was, "Pretty soon she'll be tired and go."

"No she won't," said Raynor to Grebe. "She'll get what she wants. She knows more about the relief even then Ewing. She's been on the rolls for years, and she always gets what she wants because she puts on a noisy show. Ewing knows it. He'll give in soon. He's only saving face. If he gets bad publicity, the Commissioner'll have him on the carpet, downtown. She's got him submerged; she'll submerge everybody in time, and that includes nations and governments."

Grebe replied with his characteristic smile, disagreeing completely. Who would take Staika's orders, and what changes could her yelling ever bring about?

No, what Grebe saw in her, the power that made people listen, was that her cry expressed the war of flesh and blood, perhaps turned a little crazy and certainly ugly, on this place and this condition. And at first, when he went out, the spirit of Staika somehow presided over the whole district for him, and it took color from her; he saw her color, in the spotty curb fires, and the fires under the El, the straight alley of flamy gloom. Later, too, when he went into a tavern for a shot of rye, the sweat of beer, association with West Side Polish streets, made him think of her again.

He wiped the corners of his mouth with his muffler, his handkerchief being inconvenient to reach for, and went out again to get on with the delivery of his checks. The air bit cold and hard and a few flakes of snow formed near him. A train struck by and left a quiver in the frames and a bristling icy hiss over the rails.

Crossing the street, he descended a flight of board steps into a basement grocery, setting off a little bell. It was a dark, long store and it caught you with its stinks of smoked meat, soap, dried peaches, and fish. There was a fire wrinkling and flapping in the little stove, and the proprietor was waiting, an Italian with a long, hollow face and stubborn bristles. He kept his hands warm under his apron.

No, he didn't know Green. You knew people but not names. The same man might not have the same name twice. The police didn't know, either, and mostly didn't care. When somebody was shot or knifed they took the body away and didn't look for the murderer. In the first place, nobody would tell them anything. So they made up a name for the coroner and called it quits. And in the second place, they didn't give a goddamn anyhow. But they couldn't get to the bottom of a thing even if they wanted to. Nobody would get to know even a tenth of what went on among these people. They stabbed and stole, they did every crime and abomination you ever heard of, men and men, women and women, parents and children, worse than the animals. They carried on their own way, and the horrors passed off like a smoke. There was never anything like it in the history of the whole world.

It was a long speech, deepening with every word in its fantasy and passion and becoming increasingly senseless and terrible: a swarm amassed by suggestion and invention, a huge, hugging, despairing knot, a human wheel of heads, legs, bellies, arms, rolling through his shop.

Grebe felt that he must interrupt him. He said sharply, "What are you talking about! All I asked was whether you knew this man."

"That isn't even the half of it. I been here six years. You probably don't want to believe this. But suppose it's true?"

"All the same," said Grebe, "there must be a way to find a person."

The Italian's close-spaced eyes had been queerly concentrated, as were his muscles, while he leaned across the counter trying to convince Grebe. Now he gave up the effort and sat down on his stool. "Oh—I suppose. Once in a while. But I been telling you, even the cops don't get anywhere."

"They're always after somebody. It's not the same thing."

"Well, keep trying if you want. I can't help you."

But he didn't keep trying. He had no more time to spend on Green. He slipped Green's check to the back of the block. The next name on the list was FIELD, WINSTON.

He found the back-yard bungalow without the least trouble; it shared a lot with another house, a few feet of yard between. Grebe knew these two-shack arrangements. They had been built in vast numbers in the days before the swamps were filled and the streets raised, and they were all the same—a boardwalk along the fence, well under street level, three or four ball-headed posts for clotheslines, greening wood, dead shingles, and a long, long flight of stairs to the rear door.

A twelve-year-old boy let him into the kitchen, and there the old man was, sitting by the table in a wheel chair.

"Oh, it's d' Government man," he said to the boy when Grebe drew out his checks. "Go bring me my box of papers." He cleared a space on the table.

"Oh, you don't have to go to all that trouble," said Grebe. But Field laid out his papers: Social Security card, relief certification, letters from the state hospital in Manteno, and a naval discharge dated San Diego, 1920.

"That's plenty," Grebe said. "Just sign."

"You got to know who I am," the old man said. "You're from the Government. It's not your check, it's a Government check and you got no business to hand it over till everything is proved."

He loved the ceremony of it, and Grebe made no more objections. Field emptied his box and finished out the circle of cards and letters.

"There's everything I done and been. Just the death certificate and they can close book on me." He said this with a certain happy pride and magnificence. Still he did not sign; he merely held the little pen upright on the golden-green corduroy of his thigh. Grebe did not hurry him. He felt the old man's hunger for conversation.

"I got to get better coal," he said. "I send my little gran'son to the yard with my order and they fill his wagon with screening. The stove ain't made for it. It fall through the grate. The order says Franklin County egg-size coal."

"I'll report it and see what can be done."

"Nothing can be done, I expect. You know and I know. There ain't no little ways to make things better, and the only big thing is money. That's the only sunbeams, money. Nothing is black where it shines, and the only place you see black is where it ain't shining. What we colored have to have is our own rich. There ain't no other way."

Grebe sat, his reddened forehead bridged levelly by his close-cut hair and his cheeks lowered in the wings of his collar—the caked fire shone hard within the isinglass-and-iron frames but the room was not comfortable—sat and listened while the old man unfolded his scheme. This was to create one Negro millionaire a month by subscription. One clever, good-hearted young fellow elected every month would sign a contract to use the money to start a business employing Negroes. This would be advertised by chain letters and word of mouth, and every Negro wage earner would contribute a dollar a month. Within five years there would be sixty millionaires.

"That'll fetch respect," he said with a throat-stopped sound that came out like a foreign syllable. "You got to take and organize all the money that gets thrown away on the policy wheel and horse race. As long as they can take it away from you, they got no respect for you. Money, that's d' sun of human kind!" Field was a Negro of mixed blood, perhaps Cherokee, or Natchez; his skin was reddish. And he sounded, speaking about a golden sun in this dark room, and looked, shaggy and slab-headed, with the mingled blood of his face and broad lips, the little pen still upright in his hand, like one of the underground kings of mythology, old judge Minos[10] himself.

And now he accepted the check and signed. Not to soil the slip, he held it down with his knuckles. The table budged and creaked, the center of the gloomy, heathen midden[11] of the kitchen covered with bread, meat, and cans, and the scramble of papers.

"Don't you think my scheme'd work?"

"It's worth thinking about. Something ought to be done, I agree."

"It'll work if people will do it. That's all. That's the only thing, any time. When they understand it in the same way, all of them."

"That's true," said Grebe, rising. His glance met the old man's.

"I know you got to go," he said. "Well, God bless you, boy, you ain't been sly with me. I can tell it in a minute."

He went back through the buried yard. Someone nursed a candle in a shed, where a man unloaded kindling wood from a sprawl-wheeled baby buggy and two voices carried on a high conversation. As he came up the sheltered passage he heard the hard boost of the wind in the branches and against the house fronts, and then, reaching the sidewalk, he saw the needle-eye red of cable towers in the open icy height hundreds of feet above the river and the factories—those keen points. From here, his view was obstructed all the way to the South Branch and its timber banks, and the cranes beside the water. Rebuilt after the Great Fire, this part of the city was, not fifty years later, in ruins again, factories boarded up, buildings deserted or fallen, gaps of prairie between. But it wasn't desolation that this made you feel, but rather a faltering of organization that set free a huge energy, an escaped, unattached, unregulated power from the giant raw place. Not only must people feel it but, it seemed to Grebe, they were compelled to match it. In their very bodies. He no less than others, he realized. Say that his parents had been servants in their time, whereas he was not supposed to be one. He thought that they had never done any service like this, which no one visible asked for, and probably flesh and blood could not even perform. Nor could anyone show why it should be performed; or see where the performance would lead. That did not mean that he wanted to be released from it, he realized with a grimly pensive face. On the contrary. He had something to do. To be compelled to feel this energy and yet have no task to do—that was horrible; that was suffering; he knew what that was. It was now quitting time. Six o'clock. He could go home if he liked, to his room, that is, to wash in hot water, to pour a drink, lie down on his quilt, read the paper, eat some liver paste on crackers before going out to dinner. But to think of this actually made him feel a little sick, as though he had swal-

[10]According to classical mythology, a ruler of Crete, who directed Daedalus to construct the Labyrinth, a vast maze to house the monstrous Minotaur.

[11]Refuse pile.

lowed hard air. He had six checks left, and he was determined to deliver at least one of these: Mr. Green's check.

So he started again. He had four or five dark blocks to go, past open lots, condemned houses, old foundations, closed schools, black churches, mounds, and he reflected that there must be many people alive who had once seen the neighborhood rebuilt and new. Now there was a second layer of ruins; centuries of history accomplished through human massing. Numbers had given the place forced growth; enormous numbers had also broken it down. Objects once so new, so concrete that it could have occurred to anyone they stood for other things, had crumbled. Therefore, reflected Grebe, the secret of them was out. It was that they stood for themselves by agreement, and were natural and not unnatural by agreement, and when the things themselves collapsed the agreement became visible. What was it, otherwise, that kept cities from looking peculiar? Rome, that was almost permanent, did not give rise to thoughts like these. And was it abidingly real? But in Chicago, where the cycles were so fast and the familiar died out, and again rose changed, and died again in thirty years, you saw the common agreement or covenant, and you were forced to think about appearances and realities. (He remembered Raynor and he smiled. Raynor was a clever boy.) Once you had grasped this, a great many things became intelligible. For instance, why Mr. Field should conceive such a scheme. Of course, if people were to agree to create a millionaire, a real millionaire would come into existence. And if you wanted to know how Mr. Field was inspired to think of this, why, he had within sight of his kitchen window the chart, the very bones of a successful scheme—the El with its blue and green confetti of signals. People consented to pay dimes and ride the crash-box cars, and so it was a success. Yet how absurd it looked; how little reality there was to start with. And yet Yerkes,[12] the great financier who built it, had known that he could get people to agree to do it. Viewed as itself, what a scheme of a scheme it seemed, how close to an appearance. Then why wonder at Mr. Field's idea? He had grasped a principle. And then Grebe remembered, too, that Mr. Yerkes had established the Yerkes Observatory and endowed it with millions. Now how did the notion come to him in his New York museum of a palace or his Aegean-bound yacht to give money to astronomers? Was he awed by the success of his bizarre enterprise and therefore ready to spend money to find out where in the universe being and seeming were identical? Yes, he wanted to know what abides; and whether flesh is Bible grass;[13] and he offered money to be burned in the fire of suns. Okay, then, Grebe thought further, these things exist because people consent to exist with them—we have got so far—and also there is a reality which doesn't depend

[12]Charles Tyson Yerkes (1837-1905), American financier, who, by 1886, took control of the railway lines of the west and north sections of Chicago. By financial maneuvers and corrupt politics he acquired transportation franchises and constructed an empire. Yerkes's gift in 1892 to the University of Chicago resulted in the building of the Yerkes Observatory, which opened in 1897 in Williams Bay, Wisconsin. Dreiser's *The Financier, The Titan,* and *The Stoic* are based on Yerkes's life.

[13]See Isa. 40:6–8.
"All flesh is grass,
And all the goodliness thereof is as the flower of the field;
The grass withereth, the flower fadeth;
Because the breath of the LORD bloweth upon it—
Surely the people is grass.
The grass withereth, the flower fadeth;
But the word of our God shall stand for ever."

on consent but within which consent is a game. But what about need, the need that keeps so many vast thousands in position? You tell me that, you *private* little gentleman and *decent* soul—he used these words against himself scornfully. Why is the consent given to misery? And why so painfully ugly? Because there is *something* that is dismal and permanently ugly? Here he sighed and gave it up, and thought it was enough for the present moment that he had a real check in his pocket for a Mr. Green who must be real beyond question. If only his neighbors didn't think they had to conceal him.

This time he stopped at the second floor. He struck a match and found a door. Presently a man answered his knock and Grebe had the check ready and showed it even before he began. "Does Tulliver Green live here? I'm from the relief."

The man narrowed the opening and spoke to someone at his back.

"Does he live here?"

"Uh-uh. No."

"Or anywhere in this building? He's a sick man and he can't come for his dough." He exhibited the check in the light, which was smoky—the air smelled of charred lard—and the man held off the brim of his cap to study it.

"Uh-uh. Never seen the name."

"There's nobody around here that uses crutches?"

He seemed to think, but it was Grebe's impression that he was simply waiting for a decent interval to pass.

"No, suh. Nobody I ever see."

"I've been looking for this man all afternoon"—Grebe spoke out with sudden force—"and I'm going to have to carry this check back to the station. It seems strange not to be able to find a person to *give* him something when you're looking for him for a good reason. I suppose if I had bad news for him I'd find him quick enough."

There was a responsive motion in the other man's face. "That's right, I reckon."

"It almost doesn't do any good to have a name if you can't be found by it. It doesn't stand for anything. He might as well not have any," he went on, smiling. It was as much of a concession as he could make of his desire to laugh.

"Well, now, there's a little old knot-back man I see once in a while. He might be the one you lookin' for. Downstairs."

"Where? Right side or left? Which door?"

"I don't know which. Thin-face little knot-back with a stick."

But no one answered at any of the doors on the first floor. He went to the end of the corridor, searching by matchlight, and found only a stairless exit to the yard, a drop of about six feet. But there was a bungalow near the alley, an old house like Mr. Field's. To jump was unsafe. He ran from the front door, through the underground passage and into the yard. The place was occupied. There was a light through the curtains, upstairs. The name on the ticket under the broken, scoop-shaped mailbox was Green! He exultantly rang the bell and pressed against the locked door. Then the lock clicked faintly and a long staircase opened before him. Someone was slowly coming down—a woman. He had the impression in the weak light that she was shaping her hair as she came, making herself presentable, for he saw her arms raised. But it was for support that they were raised; she was feeling her way downward, down the wall, stumbling. Next he wondered about the pressure of her feet on the treads; she did not seem to be wearing shoes. And it was a freezing stairway. His ring had got her out of bed, perhaps, and she had forgotten to put them on. And then he saw that she was not only shoeless but naked; she was entirely naked, climbing down while she talked to herself, a heavy woman, naked and drunk. She blundered into him. The contact of her breasts, though they touched only his coat, made him go back against the door with a blind shock. See what he had tracked down, in his hunting game!

The woman was saying to herself, furious with insult, "So I cain't——k, huh? I'll show that son-of-a-bitch kin I, cain't I."

What should he do now? Grebe asked himself. Why, he should go. He should turn away and go. He couldn't talk to this woman. He couldn't keep her standing naked in the cold. But when he tried he found himself unable to turn away.

He said, "Is this where Mr. Green lives?"

But she was still talking to herself and did not hear him.

"Is this Mr. Green's house?"

At last she turned her furious drunken glance on him. "What do you want?"

Again her eyes wandered from him; there was a dot of blood in their enraged brilliance. He wondered why she didn't feel the cold.

"I'm from the relief."

"Awright, what?"

"I've got a check for Tulliver Green."

This time she heard and put out her hand.

"No, no, for *Mr.* Green. He's got to sign," he said. How was he going to get Green's signature tonight!

"I'll take it. He cain't."

He desperately shook his head, thinking of Mr. Field's precautions about identification. "I can't let you have it. It's for him. Are you Mrs. Green?"

"Maybe I is, and maybe I ain't. Who want to know?"

"Is he upstairs?"

"Awright. Take it up yourself, you goddamn fool."

Sure, he was a goddamn fool. Of course he could not go up because Green would probably be drunk and naked, too. And perhaps he would appear on the landing soon. He looked eagerly upward. Under the light was a high narrow brown wall. Empty! It remained empty!

"Hell with you, then!" he heard her cry. To deliver a check for coal and clothes, he was keeping her in the cold. She did not feel it, but his face was burning with frost and self-ridicule. He backed away from her.

"I'll come tomorrow, tell him."

"Ah, hell with you. Don' never come. What you doin' here in the nighttime? Don' come back." She yelled so that he saw the breadth of her tongue. She stood astride in the long cold box of the hall and held on to the banister and the wall. The bungalow itself was shaped something like a box, a clumsy, high box pointing into the freezing air with its sharp, wintry lights.

"If you are Mrs. Green, I'll give you the check," he said, changing his mind.

"Give here, then." She took it, took the pen offered with it in her left hand, and tried to sign the receipt on the wall. He looked around, almost as though to see whether his madness was being observed, and came near believing someone was standing on a mountain of used tires in the auto-junking shop next door.

"But are you Mrs. Green?" he now thought to ask. But she was already climbing the stairs with the check, and it was too late, if he had made an error, if he was now in trouble, to undo the thing. But he wasn't going to worry about it. Though she might not be Mrs. Green, he was convinced that Mr. Green was upstairs. Whoever she was, the woman stood for Green, whom he was not to see this time. Well, you silly bastard, he said to himself, so you think you found him. So what? Maybe you really did find him—what of it? But it was important that there was a real Mr. Green whom they could not keep him from reaching because he seemed to come as an emissary from hostile appearances. And though the self-ridicule was slow to diminish, and his face still blazed with it, he had, nevertheless, a feeling of elation, too. "For after all," he said, "he *could* be found!"

1951

Bernard Malamud 1914–1986

Author of eight novels and numerous short stories, Bernard Malamud preferred to view himself as a universal writer who "happened to be Jewish, also American." Malamud's diverse subjects, varied readers, and prestigious national awards underscore his status as a major twentieth century writer and a prominent American Jewish author.

Malamud consistently transformed the raw materials of his life into imaginative fiction. Born in 1914 to Max and Bertha Malamud, hard working Russian Jews who ran a Brooklyn grocery (the setting for *The Assistant*), the author attended Erasmus High School, received a B.A. from City College and an M.A. from Columbia University. After teaching evenings in New York City high schools for several years, Malamud moved to Oregon with his wife Ann and their young son Paul. For a decade he taught at Oregon State University in Corvallis, the subject of his academic satire, *A New Life.* During that period, he published some of his finest fiction: *The Natural,* an allegorical baseball story made into a film; *The Assistant,* and *The Magic Barrel,* a short story collection that won the National Book Award.

In 1961 Malamud accepted a teaching position at Bennington College that allowed him to spend the warm months in Vermont and the winters in New York City. The move was also conducive to his writing. *The Fixer,* somewhat based on Russian persecution of Mendel Beiliss, a Jew, won both a National Book Award and a Pulitzer Prize. Within the next decade, Malamud published *Pictures of Fidelman,* a series of stories connected by an Italian setting and Jewish American protagonist, *The Tenants,* a bleak encounter between an African American and Jewish American writer, and *Rembrandt's Hat,* a short story collection. *Dubin's Lives,* which appeared in 1979, includes a variety of familiar settings (Vermont, New York, and Italy) as well as characters and themes.

Although his last completed novel, *God's Grace* (1982), is his gloomiest, with its post–nuclear war setting and cast of island primates, it contains a reflective, tormented Jew who struggles to understand and to control his grim environment. In fact, though the settings and situations of Malamud's works vary, his bumbling, suffering, at times comic, heroes resemble each other. Whether a Jewish grocer, college professor, novelist, artist, fixer or even Italian assistant or black angel, all are students of life who learn the importance of being human. In Malamud's fiction, a good Jew is a good man. Malamud's world is peopled with Jews and non-Jews in frequently surprising ways. In *The Fixer,* a Jewish spy betrays an embattled prisoner, while a Russian guard attempts to save him. In *The Assistant,* a Jew transforms a gentile into a good person and therefore into a good Jew.

Though Malamud's fiction reflects his immigrant Jewish background and American experience, above all it reveals a unique imagination which can mingle history and fantasy, comedy and tragedy. A combination of such elements seems to characterize *The People,* the novel Malamud was composing when he died. In contrast to his later, more pessimistic works, *The People,* published posthumously in 1989, unites a lonely Jewish immigrant with a needy Indian tribe in what promises to be a mutually beneficial association.

Even without *The People,* Malamud's legacy is enormous. A leader of the post-World War II Jewish literary renaissance, Malamud changed the landscape of American literature, introducing mainstream America to marginal ethnic characters, to immigrant urban settings, to Jewish-American dialect and, most important, to a world with which Americans could empathize. Something of a magician, Malamud transformed the particular into the universal so that poor Jews symbolized all individuals struggling to survive with dignity and humanity.

Evelyn Avery
Towson University

PRIMARY WORKS

The Natural, 1952; *The Assistant,* 1957; *The Magic Barrel,* 1958; *A New Life,* 1961; *Idiots First,* 1963; *The Fixer,* 1966; *Pictures of Fidelman: An Exhibition,* 1969; *The Tenants,* 1971; *Rembrandt's Hat,* 1973; *Dubin's Lives,* 1979; *God's Grace,* 1982; *The Stories of Bernard Malamud,* 1984; *The People and Uncollected Stories,* 1989.

The Magic Barrel

Not long ago there lived in uptown New York, in a small, almost meager room, though crowded with books, *Leo Finkle,* a rabbinical student at the Yeshiva University. Finkle, after six years of study, was to be ordained in June and had been advised by an acquaintance that he might find it easier to win himself a congregation if he were married. Since he had no present prospects of marriage, after two tormented days of turning it over in his mind, he called in Pinye Salzman, a marriage broker whose two-line advertisement he had read in the *Forward.*

The matchmaker appeared one night out of the dark fourth-floor hallway of the graystone rooming house where Finkle lived, grasping a black, strapped portfolio that had been worn thin with use. Salzman, who had been long in the business, was of slight but dignified build, wearing an old hat, and an overcoat too short and tight for him. He smelled frankly of fish, which he loved to eat, and although he was missing a few teeth, his presence was not displeasing, because of an amiable manner curiously contrasted with mournful eyes. His voice, his lips, his wisp of beard, his bony fingers were animated, but give him a moment of repose and his mild blue eyes revealed a depth of sadness, a characteristic that put Leo a little at ease although the situation, for him, was inherently tense.

He at once informed Salzman why he had asked him to come, explaining that but for his parents, who had married comparatively late in life, he was alone in the world. He had for six years devoted himself almost entirely to his studies, as a result of which, understandably, he had found himself without time for social life and the company of young women. Therefore he thought it the better part of trial and error—of embarrassing fumbling—to call in an experienced person to advise him on these matters. He remarked in passing that the function of the marriage broker was ancient and honorable, highly approved in the Jewish community, because it made practical the necessary without hindering joy. Moreover, his own parents had been brought together by a matchmaker. They had made, if not a financially profitable marriage—since neither had possessed any worldly goods to speak of—at least a successful one in the sense of their everlasting devotion to each other. Salzman listened in embarrassed surprise, sensing a sort of apology. Later, however, he experienced a glow of pride in his work, an emotion that had left him years ago, and he heartily approved of Finkle.

The two went to their business. Leo had led Salzman to the only clear place in the room, a table near a window that overlooked the lamp-lit city. He seated himself at the matchmaker's side but facing him, attempting by an act of will to suppress the unpleasant tickle in his throat. Salzman eagerly unstrapped his portfolio and removed a loose rubber band from a thin packet of much-handled cards. As he flipped through them, a gesture and sound that physically hurt Leo, the student pretended not to see and gazed steadfastly out the window. Although it was still February, winter was on its last legs, signs of which he had for the first time in years begun to notice. He now observed the round white moon, moving high in the sky through a cloud menagerie, and watched with half-open mouth as it penetrated a huge hen, and dropped out of her like an egg laying itself. Salzman, though pretending through eyeglasses he had just slipped on to be engaged in scanning the writing on the cards, stole occasional glances at the young man's distinguished face, noting with pleasure the long, severe scholar's nose, brown eyes heavy with learning, sensitive yet ascetic lips, and a certain almost hollow quality of the dark cheeks. He gazed around at shelves upon shelves of books and let out a soft, contented sigh.

When Leo's eyes fell upon the cards, he counted six spread out in Salzman's hand.

"So few?" he asked in disappointment.

"You wouldn't believe me how much cards I got in my office," Salzman replied. "The drawers are already filled to the top, so I keep them now in a barrel, but is every girl good for a new rabbi?"

Leo blushed at this, regretting all he had revealed of himself in a curriculum vitae he had sent to Salzman. He had thought it best to acquaint him with his strict standards and specifications, but in having done so, felt he had told the marriage broker more than was absolutely necessary.

He hesitantly inquired, "Do you keep photographs of your clients on file?"

"First comes family, amount of dowry, also what kind promises," Salzman replied, unbuttoning his tight coat and settling himself in the chair. "After comes pictures, rabbi."

"Call me Mr. Finkle. I'm not yet a rabbi."

Salzman said he would, but instead called him doctor, which he changed to rabbi when Leo was not listening too attentively.

Salzman adjusted his horn-rimmed spectacles, gently cleared his throat, and read in an eager voice the contents of the top card:

"Sophie P. Twenty-four years. Widow one year. No children. Educated high school and two years college. Father promises eight thousand dollars. Has wonderful wholesale business. Also real estate. On the mother's side comes teachers, also one actor. Well known on Second Avenue."

Leo gazed up in surprise. "Did you say a widow?"

"A widow don't mean spoiled, rabbi. She lived with her husband maybe four months. He was a sick boy she made a mistake to marry him."

"Marrying a widow has never entered my mind."

"This is because you have no experience. A widow, especially if she is young and healthy like this girl, is a wonderful person to marry. She will be thankful to you the rest of her life. Believe me, if I was looking now for a bride, I would marry a widow."

Leo reflected, then shook his head.

Salzman hunched his shoulders in an almost imperceptible gesture of disappointment. He placed the card down on the wooden table and began to read another:

"Lily H. High school teacher. Regular. Not a substitute. Has savings and new Dodge car. Lived in Paris one year. Father is successful dentist thirty-five years. Interested in professional man. Well-Americanized family. Wonderful opportunity.

"I know her personally," said Salzman. "I wish you could see this girl. She is a doll. Also very intelligent. All day you could talk to her about books and theyater and what not. She also knows current events."

"I don't believe you mentioned her age?"

"Her age?" Salzman said, raising his brows. "Her age is thirty-two years."

Leo said after a while, "I'm afraid that seems a little too old."

Salzman let out a laugh. "So how old are you, rabbi?"

"Twenty-seven."

"So what is the difference, tell me, between twenty-seven and thirty-two? My own wife is seven years older than me. So what did I suffer?— Nothing. If Rothschild's daughter wants to marry you, would you say on account her age, no?"

"Yes," Leo said dryly.

Salzman shook off the no in the yes. "Five years don't mean a thing. I give you my word that when you will live with her for one week you will forget her age. What does it mean five years—that she lived more and knows more than somebody who is younger? On this girl, God bless her, years are not wasted. Each one that it comes makes better the bargain."

"What subject does she teach in high school?"

"Languages. If you heard the way she speaks French, you will think it is music. I am in the business twenty-five years, and I recommend her with my whole heart. Believe me, I know what I'm talking, rabbi."

"What's on the next card?" Leo said abruptly.

Salzman reluctantly turned up the third card:

"Ruth K. Nineteen years. Honor student. Father offers thirteen thousand cash to the right bridegroom. He is a medical doctor. Stomach specialist with marvelous practice. Brother-in-law owns own garment business. Particular people."

Salzman looked as if he had read his trump card.

"Did you say nineteen?" Leo asked with interest.

"On the dot."

"Is she attractive?" He blushed. "Pretty?"

Salzman kissed his fingertips. "A little doll. On this I give you my word. Let me call the father tonight and you will see what means pretty."

But Leo was troubled. "You're sure she's that young?"

"This I am positive. The father will show you the birth certificate."

"Are you positive there isn't something wrong with her?" Leo insisted.

"Who says there is wrong?"

"I don't understand why an American girl her age should go to a marriage broker."

A smile spread over Salzman's face.

"So for the same reason you went, she comes."

Leo flushed. "I am pressed for time."

Salzman, realizing he had been tactless, quickly explained. "The father came, not her. He wants she should have the best, so he looks around himself. When we will locate the right boy he will introduce him and encourage. This makes a better marriage than if a young girl without experience takes for herself. I don't have to tell you this."

"But don't you think this young girl believes in love?" Leo spoke uneasily.

Salzman was about to guffaw but caught himself and said soberly, "Love comes with the right person, not before."

Leo parted dry lips but did not speak. Noticing that Salzman had snatched a glance at the next card, he cleverly asked, "How is her health?"

"Perfect," Salzman said, breathing with difficulty. "Of course, she is a little lame on her right foot from an auto accident that it happened to her when she was twelve years, but nobody notices on account she is so brilliant and also beautiful."

Leo got up heavily and went to the window. He felt curiously bitter and upbraided himself for having called in the marriage broker. Finally, he shook his head.

"Why not?" Salzman persisted, the pitch of his voice rising.

"Because I detest stomach specialists."

"So what do you care what is his business? After you marry her do you need him? Who says he must come every Friday night in your house?"

Ashamed of the way the talk was going, Leo dismissed Salzman, who went home with heavy, melancholy eyes.

Though he had felt only relief at the marriage broker's departure, Leo was in low spirits the next day. He explained it as arising from Salzman's failure to produce a suitable bride for him. He did not care for his type of clientele. But when Leo found himself hesitating whether to seek out another matchmaker, one more polished than Pinye, he wondered if it could be—his protestations to the contrary, and although he honored his father and mother—that he did not, in essence, care for the matchmaking institution? This thought he quickly put out of mind yet found himself still upset. All day he ran around in the woods—missed an important appointment, forgot to give out his laundry, walked out of a Broadway cafeteria without paying and had to run back with the ticket in his hand; had even not recognized his landlady in the street when she passed with a friend and courteously called out, "A good evening to you, Doctor Finkle." By nightfall, however, he had regained sufficient calm to sink his nose into a book and there found peace from his thoughts.

Almost at once there came a knock on the door. Before Leo could say enter, Salzman, commercial cupid, was standing in the room. His face was gray and meager, his expression hungry, and he looked as if he would expire on his feet. Yet the marriage broker managed, by some trick of the muscles, to display a broad smile.

"So good evening. I am invited?"

Leo nodded, disturbed to see him again, yet unwilling to ask the man to leave.

Beaming still, Salzman laid his portfolio on the table. "Rabbi, I got for you tonight good news."

"I've asked you not to call me rabbi. I'm still a student."

"Your worries are finished. I have for you a first-class bride."

"Leave me in peace concerning this subject." Leo pretended lack of interest.

"The world will dance at your wedding."

"Please, Mr. Salzman, no more."

"But first must come back my strength," Salzman said weakly. He fumbled with the portfolio straps and took out of the leather case an oily paper bag, from which he extracted a hard, seeded roll and a small smoked whitefish. With a quick motion of his hand he stripped the fish out of its skin and began ravenously to chew. "All day in a rush," he muttered.

Leo watched him eat.

"A sliced tomato you have maybe?" Salzman hesitantly inquired.

"No."

The marriage broker shut his eyes and ate. When he had finished he carefully cleaned up the crumbs and rolled up the remains of the fish, in the paper bag. His spectacled eyes roamed the room until he discovered, amid some piles of books, a one-burner gas stove. Lifting his hat he humbly asked, "A glass tea you got, rabbi?"

Conscience-stricken, Leo rose and brewed the tea. He served it with a chunk of lemon and two cubes of lump sugar, delighting Salzman.

After he had drunk his tea, Salzman's strength and good spirits were restored.

"So tell me, rabbi," he said amiably, "you considered some more the three clients I mentioned yesterday?"

"There was no need to consider."

"Why not?"

"None of them suits me."

"What then suits you?"

Leo let it pass because he could give only a confused answer.

Without waiting for a reply, Salzman asked, "You remember this girl I talked to you—the high school teacher?"

"Age thirty-two?"

But, surprisingly, Salzman's face lit in a smile. "Age twenty-nine."

Leo shot him a look. "Reduced from thirty-two?"

"A mistake," Salzman avowed. "I talked today with the dentist. He took me to his safety deposit box and showed me the birth certificate. She was twenty-nine years last August. They made her a party in the mountains where she went for her vacation. When her father spoke to me the first time I forgot to write the age and I told you thirty-two, but now I remember this was a different client, a widow."

"The same one you told me about, I thought she was twenty-four?"

"A different. Am I responsible that the world is filled with widows?"

"No, but I'm not interested in them, nor, for that matter, in schoolteachers."

Salzman pulled his clasped hands to his breast. Looking at the ceiling he devoutly exclaimed, "Yiddishe kinder, what can I say to somebody that he is not interested in high school teachers? So what then you are interested?"

Leo flushed but controlled himself.

"In what else will you be interested," Salzman went on, "if you not interested in this fine girl that she speaks four languages and has personally in the bank ten thousand dollars? Also her father guarantees further twelve thousand. Also she has a new car, wonderful clothes, talks on all subjects, and she will give you a first-class home and children. How near do we come in our life to paradise?"

"If she's so wonderful, why wasn't she married ten years ago?"

"Why?" said Salzman with a heavy laugh. "—Why? Because she is *partikiler.* This is why. She wants the *best.*"

Leo was silent, amused at how he had entangled himself. But Salzman had aroused his interest in Lily H., and he began seriously to consider calling on her. When the marriage broker observed how intently Leo's mind was at work on the facts he had supplied, he felt certain they would soon come to an agreement.

* * *

Late Saturday afternoon, conscious of Salzman, Leo Finkle walked with Lily Hirschorn along Riverside Drive. He walked briskly and erectly, wearing with distinction the black fedora he had that morning taken with trepidation out of the dusty hat box on his closet shelf, and the heavy black Saturday coat he had thoroughly whisked clean. Leo also owned a walking stick, a present from a distant relative, but quickly put temptation aside and did not use it. Lily, petite and not unpretty, had on something signifying the approach of spring. She was au courant, animatedly, with all sorts of subjects, and he weighed her words and found her surprisingly sound—score another for Salzman, whom he uneasily sensed to be somewhere around, hiding perhaps high in a tree along the street, flashing the lady signals with a pocket mirror; or perhaps a cloven-hoofed Pan, piping nuptial ditties as he danced his invisible way before them, strewing wild buds on the walk and purple grapes in their path, symbolizing fruit of a union, though there was of course still none.

Lily startled Leo by remarking, "I was thinking of Mr. Salzman, a curious figure, wouldn't you say?"

Not certain what to answer, he nodded.

She bravely went on, blushing, "I for one am grateful for his introducing us. Aren't you?"

He courteously replied, "I am."

"I mean," she said with a little laugh—and it was all in good taste, or at least gave the effect of being not in bad—"do you mind that we came together so?"

He was not displeased with her honesty, recognizing that she meant to set the relationship aright, and understanding that it took a certain amount of experience in life, and courage, to want to do it quite that way. One had to have some sort of past to make that kind of beginning.

He said that he did not mind. Salzman's function was traditional and honorable—valuable for what it might achieve, which, he pointed out, was frequently nothing.

Lily agreed with a sigh. They walked on for a while and she said after a long silence, again with a nervous laugh, "Would you mind if I asked you something a little bit personal? Frankly, I find the subject fascinating." Although Leo shrugged, she went on half embarrassedly, "How was it that you came to your calling? I mean, was it a sudden passionate inspiration?"

Leo, after a time, slowly replied, "I was always interested in the Law."

"You saw revealed in it the presence of the Highest?"

He nodded and changed the subject. "I understand that you spent a little time in Paris, Miss Hirschorn?"

"Oh, did Mr. Salzman tell you, Rabbi Finkle?" Leo winced but she went on, "It was ages ago and almost forgotten. I remember I had to return for my sister's wedding."

And Lily would not be put off. "When," she asked in a slightly trembly voice, "did you become enamored of God?"

He stared at her. Then it came to him that she was talking not about Leo Finkle but a total stranger, some mystical figure, perhaps even passionate prophet that Salzman had dreamed up for her—no relation to the living or dead. Leo trembled with rage and weakness. The trickster had obviously sold her a bill of goods, just as he had him, who'd expected to become acquainted with a young lady of twenty-nine, only to behold, the moment he had laid eyes upon her strained and anxious face, a woman past thirty-five and aging rapidly. Only his self-control had kept him this long in her presence.

"I am not," he said gravely, "a talented religious person," and in seeking words to go on, found himself possessed by shame and fear. "I think," he said in a strained manner, "that I came to God not because I loved Him but because I did not."

This confession he spoke harshly because its unexpectedness shook him.

Lily wilted. Leo saw a profusion of loaves of bread go flying like ducks high over his head, not unlike the winged loaves by which he had counted himself to sleep last night. Mercifully, then, it snowed, which he would not put past Salzman's machinations.

* * *

He was infuriated with the marriage broker and swore he would throw him out of the room the moment he reappeared. But Salzman did not come that night, and when Leo's anger had subsided, an unaccountable despair grew in its place. At first he thought this was caused by his disappointment in Lily, but before long it became evident that he had involved himself with Salzman without a true knowledge of his own intent. He gradually realized—with an emptiness that seized him with six hands—that he had called in the broker to find him a bride because he was incapable of doing it himself. This terrifying insight he had derived as a result of his meeting and conversation with Lily Hirschorn. Her probing questions had somehow irritated him into revealing—to himself more than her—the true nature of his relationship to God, and from that it had come upon him, with shocking force, that apart from his parents, he had never loved anyone. Or perhaps it went the other way, that he did not love God so well as he might, because he had not loved man. It seemed to Leo that his whole life stood starkly revealed and he saw himself for the first time as he truly was—unloved and loveless. This bitter but somehow not fully unexpected revelation brought him to a point of panic, controlled only by extraordinary effort. He covered his face with his hands and cried.

The week that followed was the worst of his life. He did not eat and lost weight. His beard darkened and grew ragged. He stopped attending seminars and almost never opened a book. He seriously considered leaving the Yeshiva, although he was deeply troubled at the thought of the loss of all his years of study—saw them like pages torn from a book, strewn over the city—and at the devastating effect of this decision upon his parents. But he had lived without knowledge of himself, and never in the Five Books and all the Commentaries—mea culpa—had the truth been revealed to him. He did not know where to turn, and in all this desolating loneliness there was no *to whom,* although he often thought of Lily but not once could bring himself to go downstairs and make the call. He became touchy and irritable, especially with his landlady, who asked him all manner of personal questions; on the other hand, sensing his own disagreeableness, he waylaid her on the stairs and apologized abjectly, until, mortified, she ran from him. Out of this, however, he drew the consolation that he was a Jew and that a Jew suffered. But gradually, as the long and terrible week drew to a close, he regained his composure and some idea of purpose in life: to go on as planned. Although he was imperfect, the ideal was not. As for his quest of a bride, the thought of continuing afflicted him with anxiety and heartburn, yet perhaps with this new knowledge of himself he would be more successful than in the past. Perhaps love would now come to him and a bride to that love. And for this sanctified seeking who needed a Salzman?

The marriage broker, a skeleton with haunted eyes, returned that very night. He looked, withal, the picture of frustrated expectancy—as if he had steadfastly waited the week at Miss Lily Hirschorn's side for a telephone call that never came.

Casually coughing, Salzman came immediately to the point: "So how did you like her?"

Leo's anger rose and he could not refrain from chiding the matchmaker: "Why did you lie to me, Salzman?"

Salzman's pale face went dead white, the world had snowed on him.

"Did you not state that she was twenty-nine?" Leo insisted.

"I give you my word—"

"She was thirty-five, if a day. *At least* thirty-five."

"Of this don't be too sure. Her father told me—"

"Never mind. The worst of it is that you lied to her."

"How did I lie to her, tell me?"

"You told her things about me that weren't true. You made me out to be more, consequently less than I am. She had in mind a totally different person, a sort of semi-mystical Wonder Rabbi."

"All I said, you was a religious man."

"I can imagine."

Salzman sighed. "This is my weakness that I have," he confessed. "My wife says to me I shouldn't be a salesman, but when I have two fine people that they would be wonderful to be married, I am so happy that I talk too much." He smiled wanly. "This is why Salzman is a poor man."

Leo's anger left him. "Well, Salzman, I'm afraid that's all."

The marriage broker fastened hungry eyes on him.

"You don't want any more a bride?"

"I do," said Leo, "but I have decided to seek her in another way. I am no longer interested in an arranged marriage. To be frank, I now admit the necessity of premarital love. That is, I want to be in love with the one I marry."

"Love?" said Salzman, astounded. After a moment he remarked, "For us, our love is our life, not for the ladies. In the ghetto they—"

"I know, I know," said Leo. "I've thought of it often. Love, I have said to myself, should be a product of living and worship rather than its own end. Yet for myself I find it necessary to establish the level of my need and fulfill it."

Salzman shrugged but answered, "Listen, rabbi, if you want love, this I can find for you also. I have such beautiful clients that you will love them the minute your eyes will see them."

Leo smiled unhappily. "I'm afraid you don't understand."

But Salzman hastily unstrapped his portfolio and withdrew a manila packet from it.

"Pictures," he said, quickly laying the envelope on the table.

Leo called after him to take the pictures away, but as if on the wings of the wind, Salzman had disappeared.

March came. Leo had returned to his regular routine. Although he felt not quite himself yet—lacked energy—he was making plans for a more active social life. Of course it would cost something, but he was an expert in cutting corners; and when there were no corners left he would make circles rounder. All the while Salzman's pictures had lain on the table, gathering dust. Occasionally as Leo sat studying, or enjoying a cup of tea, his eyes fell on the manila envelope, but he never opened it.

The days went by and no social life to speak of developed with a member of the opposite sex—it was difficult, given the circumstances of his situation. One morning Leo toiled up the stairs to his room and stared out the window at the city. Although the day was bright his view of it was dark. For some time he watched the people in the street below hurrying along and then turned with a heavy heart to his little room. On the table was the packet. With a sudden relentless gesture he tore it open. For a half hour he stood by the table in a state of excitement, examining the photographs of the ladies Salzman had included. Finally, with a deep sigh he put them down. There were six, of varying degrees of attractiveness, but look at them long enough and they all became Lily Hirschorn: all past their prime, all starved behind bright smiles, not a true personality in the lot. Life, despite their frantic yoohooings, had passed them by; they were pictures in a briefcase that stank of fish. After a while, however, as Leo attempted to return the photographs into the envelope, he found in it another, a snapshot of the type taken by a machine for a quarter. He gazed at it a moment and let out a low cry.

Her face deeply moved him. Why, he could at first not say. It gave him the impression of youth—spring flowers, yet age—a sense of having been used to the bone, wasted; this came from the eyes, which were hauntingly familiar, yet absolutely strange. He had a vivid impression that he had met her before, but try as he might he could not place her although he could almost recall her name, as if he had read it in her own handwriting. No, this couldn't be; he would have remembered her. It was not, he affirmed, that she had an extraordinary beauty—no, though her face was attractive enough; it was that *something* about her moved him. Feature for feature, even some of the ladies of the photographs could do better; but she leaped forth to his heart—had *lived,* or wanted to—more than just wanted, perhaps regretted how she had lived—had somehow deeply suffered: it could be seen in the depths of those reluctant eyes, and from the way the light enclosed and shone from her, and within her, opening realms of possibility: this was her own. Her he desired. His head ached and eyes narrowed with the intensity of his gazing, then as if an obscure fog had blown up in the mind, he experienced fear of her and was aware that he had received an impression, somehow, of evil. He shuddered, saying softly, it is thus with us all. Leo brewed some tea in a small pot and sat sipping it without sugar, to calm himself. But before he had finished drinking, again with excitement he examined the face and found it good: good for Leo Finkle. Only such a one could understand him and help him seek whatever he was seeking. She might, perhaps, love him. How she had happened to be among the discards in Salzman's barrel he could never guess, but he knew he must urgently go find her.

Leo rushed downstairs, grabbed up the Bronx telephone book, and searched for Salzman's home address. He was not listed, nor was his office. Neither was he in the Manhattan book. But Leo remembered having written down the address on a slip of paper after he had read Salzman's advertisement in the "personals" column of the *Forward.* He ran up to his room and tore through his papers, without luck. It was exasperating. Just when he needed the matchmaker he was nowhere to be found. Fortunately Leo remembered to look in his wallet. There on a card he found his name written and a Bronx address. No phone number was listed, the reason—Leo now recalled—he had originally communicated with Salzman by letter. He got on his coat, put a hat on over his skullcap and hurried to the subway station. All the way to the far end of the Bronx he sat on the edge of his seat. He was more than once tempted to take out the picture and see if the girl's face was as he remembered, but he refrained, allowing the snapshot to remain in his inside coat pocket, content to have her so close. When the train pulled into the station he was waiting at the door and bolted out. He quickly located the street Salzman had advertised.

The building he sought was less than a block from the subway, but it was not an office building, nor even a loft, nor a store in which one could rent office space. It was a very old tenement house. Leo found Salzman's name in pencil on a soiled tag under the bell and climbed three dark flights to his apartment. When he knocked, the door was opened by a thin, asthmatic, gray-haired woman, in felt slippers.

"Yes?" she said, expecting nothing. She listened without listening. He could have sworn he had seen her, too, before but knew it was an illusion.

"Salzman—does he live here? Pinye Salzman," he said, "the matchmaker?"

She stared at him a long minute. "Of course."

He felt embarrassed. "Is he in?"

"No." Her mouth, though left open, offered nothing more.

"The matter is urgent. Can you tell me where his office is?"

"In the air." She pointed upward.

"You mean he has no office?" Leo asked.

"In his socks."

He peered into the apartment. It was sunless and dingy, one large room divided by a half-open curtain, beyond which he could see a sagging metal bed. The near side of the room was crowded with rickety chairs, old bureaus, a three-legged table, racks of cooking utensils, and all the apparatus of a kitchen. But there was no sign of Salzman or his magic barrel, probably also a figment of the imagination. An odor of frying fish made Leo weak to the knees.

"Where is he?" he insisted. "I've got to see your husband."

At length she answered, "So who knows where he is? Every time he thinks a new thought he runs to a different place. Go home, he will find you."

"Tell him Leo Finkle."

She gave no sign she had heard.

He walked downstairs, depressed.

But Salzman, breathless, stood waiting at his door.

Leo was astounded and overjoyed. "How did you get here before me?"

"I rushed."

"Come inside."

They entered. Leo fixed tea, and a sardine sandwich for Salzman. As they were drinking he reached behind him for the packet of pictures and handed them to the marriage broker.

Salzman put down his glass and said expectantly, "You found somebody you like?"

"Not among these."

The marriage broker turned away.

"Here is the one I want." Leo held forth the snapshot.

Salzman slipped on his glasses and took the picture into his trembling hand. He turned ghastly and let out a groan.

"What's the matter?" cried Leo.

"Excuse me. Was an accident this picture. She isn't for you."

Salzman frantically shoved the manila packet into his portfolio. He thrust the snapshot into his pocket and fled down the stairs.

Leo, after momentary paralysis, gave chase and cornered the marriage broker in the vestibule. The landlady made hysterical outcries but neither of them listened.

"Give me back the picture, Salzman."

"No." The pain in his eyes was terrible.

"Tell me who she is then."

"This I can't tell you. Excuse me."

He made to depart, but Leo, forgetting himself, seized the matchmaker by his tight coat and shook him frenziedly.

"Please," sighed Salzman. "*Please.*"

Leo ashamedly let him go. "Tell me who she is," he begged. "It's very important for me to know."

"She is not for you. She is a wild one—wild, without shame. This is not a bride for a rabbi."

"What do you mean wild?"

"Like an animal. Like a dog. For her to be poor was a sin. This is why to me she is dead now."

"In God's name, what do you mean?"

"Her I can't introduce to you," Salzman cried.

"Why are you so excited?"

"Why, he asks," Salzman said, bursting into tears. "This is my baby, my Stella, she should burn in hell."

* * *

Leo hurried up to bed and hid under the covers. Under the covers he thought his life through. Although he soon fell asleep he could not sleep her out of his mind. He woke, beating his breast. Though he prayed to be rid of her, his prayers went unanswered. Through days of torment he endlessly struggled not to love her; fearing success, he escaped it. He then concluded to convert her to goodness, himself to God. The idea alternately nauseated and exalted him.

He perhaps did not know that he had come to a final decision until he encountered Salzman in a Broadway cafeteria. He was sitting alone at a rear table, sucking the bony remains of a fish. The marriage broker appeared haggard, and transparent to the point of vanishing.

Salzman looked up at first without recognizing him. Leo had grown a pointed beard and his eyes were weighted with wisdom.

"Salzman," he said, "love has at last come to my heart."

"Who can love from a picture?" mocked the marriage broker.

"It is not impossible."

"If you can love her, then you can love anybody. Let me show you some new clients that they just sent me their photographs. One is a little doll."

"Just her I want," Leo murmured.

"Don't be a fool, doctor. Don't bother with her."

"Put me in touch with her, Salzman," Leo said humbly. "Perhaps I can be of service."

Salzman had stopped eating and Leo understood with emotion that it was now arranged.

Leaving the cafeteria, he was, however, afflicted by a tormenting suspicion that Salzman had planned it all to happen this way.

* * *

Leo was informed by letter that she would meet him on a certain corner, and she was there one spring night, waiting under a street lamp. He appeared, carrying a small bouquet of violets and rosebuds. Stella stood by the lamppost, smoking. She wore white with red shoes, which fitted his expectations, although in a troubled moment he had imagined the dress red, and only the shoes white. She waited uneasily and shyly. From afar he saw that her eyes—clearly her father's—were filled with desperate innocence. He pictured, in her, his own redemption. Violins and lit candles revolved in the sky. Leo ran forward with flowers outthrust.

Around the corner, Salzman, leaning against a wall, chanted prayers for the dead.

1958

Grace Paley b. 1922

Grace Paley was born to Isaac and Mary Goodside, Russian Jewish immigrants full of secular and socialist ideas gleaned from the intellectual ferment that preceded the Russian Revolution of 1917. Although her father, a doctor, influenced her love of Russian literature, both parents encouraged her intellectual precocity and political activism.

For a while Paley attended Hunter College and New York University, but a consuming interest in ordinary lives, a resistance to institutional authority, caused her to drop out. In 1942 at the age of twenty she married Jess Paley, a photographer, and later bore a son and a daughter. After they were divorced, Paley married Robert Nichols, a poet and playwright. Despite the vicissitudes inherent in raising children and working at marginal jobs, she found time to perfect her writing craft. Three small short story collections, *The Little Disturbances of Man,* 1959; *Enormous Changes at the Last Minute,* 1974; and *Later the Same Day,* 1985 have established her reputation as a unique, virtually unimitatable contemporary writer. In 1961 she was awarded a Guggenheim fellowship in fiction, and in 1970 received both a National Council on the Arts grant and a National Institute of Arts and Letters award for short story writing.

The titles of Paley's collections suggest the stories' themes: the irrepressible life force underlying the daily lives of New York working-class men and women; human courage in the face of aging and loss; the willingness to take risks which ensure the possibility of change within their lifetimes. Paley's readers will discover more: loose vignettes artfully fragmented, the precise metaphors of a poet, characters created through conversations articulated with an impeccable ear for the varied tones, rhythms, and cadences of New York speech. Paley's style creates small worlds, allowing readers to see what William Blake in another context called "the world in a grain of sand." Above all, Paley's is an extraordinary narrative voice, sassy, ironic, always authoritative, insistently faithful to pacifist and feminist ideals.

Paley's abiding love for independent-minded children extended later to include their feisty mothers resisting boorish husbands; involving themselves in love affairs, playground politics, and an activism ranging from the fight for drug-free schools, to vehement opposition to the Vietnam War, and the ongoing resistance to nuclear proliferation. She remains engaged politically and personally, an iconoclast loudly debunking patriarchal institutions denying life-affirming choice. All of her stories embody this engagement.

In fact "The Expensive Moment" is best summarized as *expansive,* to include women beyond the confines of Vesey Street, namely Xie Feng, sent as a delegate to a woman's convention from mainland China during a lull in the Cold War and after the Cultural Revolution. Ruthie, who has been to China, met Xie Feng in China; the latter understands her fears about Rachel, since Xie Feng's children were left against her will with harsh grandparents. As Faith and Xie Feng wander throughout the urban, ethnic neighborhood where Faith recapitulates for her friend's benefit, the places where she has come of age, loved, married, divorced, fought to make life safer and saner for her children, they are joined by Ruthie. All three women bond in mutual concern over their children and are united by the nagging question of whether in violent and dangerous times they have raised them to be resilient, compassionate, and responsible human beings.

Rose Yalow Kamel
Philadelphia College of Pharmacy and Science

PRIMARY WORKS

The Little Disturbances of Man. Stories of Men and Women at Love, 1959; *Enormous Changes at the Last Minute,* 1974; *Later the Same Day,* 1985.

The Expensive Moment

Faith did not tell Jack.

At about two in the afternoon she went to visit Nick Hegstraw, the famous sinologist.[1] He was not famous in the whole world. He was famous in their neighborhood and in the adjoining neighborhoods, north, south, and east. He was studying China, he said, in order to free us all of distance and mystery. But because of foolish remarks that were immediately published, he had been excluded from wonderful visits to China's new green parlor. He sometimes felt insufficiently informed. Hundreds of people who knew nothing about Han and Da tung visited, returned, wrote articles; one friend with about seventy-five Chinese words had made a three-hour documentary. Well, sometimes he did believe in socialism and sometimes only in the Late T'ang. It's hard to stand behind a people and culture in revolutionary transition when you are constantly worried about their irreplaceable and breakable artifacts.

He was noticeably handsome, the way men are every now and then, with a face full of good architectural planning. (Good use of face space, Jack said.) In the hardware store or in line at the local movie, women and men would look at him. They might turn away saying, Not my type, or, Where have I seen him before? TV? Actually they had seen him at the vegetable market. As an unmarried vegetarian sinologist he bought bagfuls of broccoli and waited with other eaters for snow peas from California at $4.79 a pound.

Are you lovers? Ruth asked.

Oh God, no. I'm pretty monogamous when I'm monogamous. Why are you laughing?

You're lying. Really, Faith, why did you describe him at such length? You don't usually do that.

But the fun of talking, Ruthy. What about that? It's as good as fucking lots of times. Isn't it?

Oh boy, Ruth said, if it's that good, then it's got to be that bad.

At lunch Jack said, Ruth is not a Chinese cook. She doesn't mince words. She doesn't sauté a lot of imperial verbs and docile predicates like some women.

Faith left the room. Someday, she said, I'm never coming back.

[1]One who makes a study of the Chinese language and its civilization.

But I love the way Jack talks, said Ruth. He's a true gossip like us. And another thing, he's the only one who ever asks me anymore about Rachel.

Don't trust him, said Faith.

After Faith slammed the door, Jack decided to buy a pipe so he could smoke thoughtfully in the evening. He wished he had a new dog or a new child or a new wife. He had none of these things because he only thought about them once in ten days and then only for about five minutes. The interest in sustained shopping or courtship had left him. He was a busy man selling discount furniture in a rough neighborhood during the day, and reading reading reading, thinking writing grieving all night the bad world-ending politics which were using up the last years of his life. Oh, come back, come back, he cried. Faith! At least for supper.

On this particular afternoon, Nick (the sinologist) said, How are your children? Fine, she said. Tonto is in love and Richard has officially joined the League for Revolutionary Youth.

Ah, said Nick. L.R.Y. I spoke at one of their meetings last month. They threw half a pizza pie at me.

Why? What'd you say? Did you say something terrible? Maybe it's an anti-agist coalition of New Left pie throwers and Old Left tomato throwers.

It's not a joke, he said. And it's not funny. And besides, that's not what I want to talk about. He then expressed opposition to the Great Leap Forward[2] and the Cultural Revolution.[3] He did this by walking back and forth muttering, Wrong. Wrong. Wrong.

Faith, who had just read *Fanshen* at his suggestion, accepted both. But he worried about great art and literature, its way of rising out of the already risen. Faith, sit down, he said. Where were the already risen nowadays? Driven away from their typewriters and calligraphy pens by the Young Guards—like all the young, wild with a dream of wildness.

Faith said, Maybe it's the right now rising. Maybe the already risen don't need anything more. They just sit there in their lawn chairs and appreciate the culture of the just rising. They may even like to do that. The work of creation is probably too hard when you are required because of having already risen to be always distinguishing good from bad, great from good . . .

Nick would not even laugh at serious jokes. He decided to show Faith with mocking examples how wrong she was. None of the examples convinced her. In fact, they seemed to support an opposing position. Faith wondered if his acquisitive mind was not sometimes betrayed by a poor filing system.

Here they are anyway:

[2]Under Chairman Mao Tse Tung's leadership, the Chinese Communist Party from 1958–1960 forcibly decentralized and collectivized the peasantry. Using manpower, not machinery, to irrigate channels and build dikes, the Great Leap Forward caused mass starvation.

[3]The decade 1966–1976 saw a split with the Communist Party between Mao and intellectual reformers called revisionists. Mao's Red Guards rampaged through cities and villages, seized power, and destroyed old ideas, customs, and habits. Those perceived as intellectuals or middle-class were publicly humiliated; some were killed or committed suicide; others failed at or forced to become manual laborers.

Working hard in the fields of Shanxi is John Keats,[4] brilliant and tubercular. The sun beats on his pale flesh. The water in which he is ankle-deep is colder than he likes. The little green shoots are no comfort to him despite their light-green beauty. He is thinking about last night—this lunar beauty, etc. When he gets back to the commune he learns that they have been requested by the province to write poems. Keats is discouraged. He's thinking, This lunar beauty, this lunar beauty . . . The head communard, a bourgeois leftover, says, Oh, what can ail thee, pale individualist?[5] He laughs, then says, Relax, comrade. Just let politics take command. Keats does this, and soon, smiling his sad intelligent smile, he says, Ah . . .

This lunar beauty
touches Shanxi province
in the year of the bumper crops
the peasants free of the landlords
stand in the fields
they talk of this and that
and admire
the harvest moon.

Meanwhile, all around him peasants are dampening the dry lead pencil points with their tongues.

Faith interrupted. She hoped someone would tell them how dangerous lead was. And industrial pollution.

For godsakes, said Nick, and continued. One peasant writes:

This morning the paddy
looked like the sea
At high tide we will
harvest the rice
This is because of Mao Zedong
whose love for the peasants
has fed the urban proletariat.

That's enough. Do you get it? Yes, Faith said. Something like this? And sang.

On the highway to Communism
the little children put plum blossoms
in their hair and dance
on the new-harvested wheat

She was about to remember another poem from her newly invented memory, but Nick said, Faith, it's already 3:30, so—full of the play of poems they unfolded his narrow daybed to a comfortable three-quarter width. Their lovemaking was ordinary but satisfactory. Its difference lay only in difference. Of course, if one is living a whole life in passionate affection with another, this differentness on occasional afternoons is often enough.

[4]English Romantic poet, 1795–1821, who died of tuberculosis. Keat's "Ode to Psyche" focused on Keats's inner life and imaginative power, which the Maoist Cultural Revolution would have considered decadent.

[5]Paley parodies the Maoist rejection of Keats's "La Belle Dame sans Merci."

* * *

And besides that, almost at once on rising to tea or coffee, Faith asked, Nick, why do they have such a rotten foreign policy? The question had settled in her mind earlier, resting just under the light inflammation of desire.

It was not the first time she had asked this question, nor was Nick the last person who answered.

Nick: For godsakes, don't you understand anything about politics?

Richard: Yeah, and why does Israel trade probably every day with South Africa?

Ruth (*Although her remarks actually came a couple of years later*): Cuba carries on commercial negotiations with Argentina. No?

The boys at supper: Tonto (*Softly, with narrowed eyes*): Why did China recognize Pinochet[6] just about ten minutes after the coup in Chile?

Richard (*Tolerantly explaining*): Asshole, because Allende didn't know how to run a revolution, that's why.

Jack reminded them that the U.S.S.R. may have had to overcome intense ideological repugnance in order to satisfy her old longing for South African industrial diamonds.

Faith thought, But if you think like that forever you can be sad forever. You can be cynical, you can go around saying no hope, you can say import-export, you can mumble all day, World Bank. So she tried thinking: The beauty of trade, the caravans crossing Africa and Asia, the roads to Peru through the terrible forests of Guatemala, and then especially the village markets of underdeveloped countries, plazas behind churches under awnings and tents, not to mention the Orlando Market around the corner; also the Free Market, which costs so much in the world, and what about the discount house of Jack, Son of Jake.

Oh sure, Richard said, the beauty of trade. I'm surprised at you, Ma, the beauty of trade—those Indians going through Guatemala with leather thongs cutting into their foreheads holding about a ton of beauty on their backs. Beauty, he said.

He rested for about an hour. Then he continued. I'm surprised at you Faith, really surprised. He blinked his eyes a couple of times. Mother, he said, have you ever read any political theory? No. All those dumb peace meetings you go to. Don't they ever talk about anything but melting up a couple of really great swords?

He'd become so pale.

Richard, she said. You're absolutely white. You seem to have quit drinking orange juice.

This simple remark made him leave home for three days.

But first he looked at her with either contempt or despair.

Then, because the brain at work pays no attention to time and speedily connects and chooses, she thought: Oh, long ago I looked at my father. What kind of face is that? he had asked. She was leaning against their bedroom wall. She was about fourteen. Fifteen? A lot you care, she said. A giant war is coming out of Germany[7] and

[6]Ugarte Pinochet, b. 1915. A right-wing Chilean army general who seized power from the democratically elected president Salvadore Allende who presided over Chile 1970–1973.

[7]The child "Faith" is referring to World War II.

all you say is Russia. Bad old Russia. I'm the one that's gonna get killed. You? he answered. Ha ha! A little girl sitting in safe America is going to be killed. Ha ha!

And what about the looks those other boys half a generation ago had made her accept. Ruth had called them put-up-or-shut-up looks. She and her friends had walked round and round the draft boards with signs that said I COUNSEL DRAFT REFUSAL. Some of those young fellows were calm and holy, and some were fierce and grouchy. But not one of them was trivial, and neither was Richard.

Still, Faith thought, what if history should seize him as it had actually taken Ruth's daughter Rachel when her face was still as round as an apple; a moment in history, the expensive moment when everyone his age is called but just a few are chosen by conscience or passion or even only love of one's own agemates, and they are the ones who smash an important nosecone (as has been recently done) or blow up some building full of oppressive money or murderous military plans; but, oh, what if a human creature (maybe rotten to the core but a living person still) is in it? What if they disappear then to live in exile or in the deepest underground and you don't see them for ten years or have to travel to Cuba or Canada or farther to look at their changed faces? Then you think sadly, I could have worked harder at raising that child, the one that was once mine. I could have raised him to become a brilliant economist or finish graduate school and be a lawyer or a doctor maybe. He could have done a lot of good, just as much *that* way, healing or defending the underdog.

But Richard had slipped a note under the door before he left. In his neat handwriting it said: "Trade. Shit. It's production that's beautiful. That's what's beautiful. And the producers. They're beautiful."

What's the use, said Ruth when she and Faith sat eating barley soup in the Art Foods Deli. You're always wrong. She looked into the light beyond the plate-glass window. It was unusual for her to allow sadness. Faith took her hand and kissed it. She said, Ruthy darling. Ruth leaned across the table to hug her. The soup spoon fell to the floor, mixing barley and sawdust.

But look, Ruth said, Joe got this news clipping at the office from some place in Minnesota. "Red and green acrylic circles were painted around telephone poles and trees ringing the Dakota State Prison last night. It was assumed that the Red and the Green were planning some destructive act. These circles were last seen in Arizona. Two convicts escaped from that prison within a week. Red and green circles were stenciled on the walls of their cells. The cost for removing these signatures will probably go as high as $4,300."

What for? said Faith.

For? asked Ruth. They were political prisoners. Someone has to not forget them. The green is for ecology.

Nobody leaves that out nowadays.

Well, they shouldn't, said Ruth.

This Rachel of Ruth and Joe's had grown from girl to woman in far absence, making little personal waves from time to time in the newspapers or in rumor which would finally reach her parents on the shores of their always waiting—that is, the office mailbox or the eleven o'clock news.

One day Ruth and Joe were invited to a cultural event. This was because Joe was a cultural worker. He had in fact edited *The Social Ordure,* a periodical which published everything Jack wrote. He and Ruth had also visited China and connected themselves in print to some indulgent views of the Gang of Four, from which it had been hard to disengage. Ruth was still certain that the bad politics and free life of Jiang Qing would be used for at least a generation to punish ALL Chinese women.

But isn't that true everywhere, said Faith. If you say a simple thing like, "There are only eight women in Congress," or if you say the word "patriarchy," someone always says, Yeah? look at Margaret Thatcher, or look at Golda Meir.[8]

I love Golda Meir.

You do? Oh! said Faith.

But the evening belonged to the Chinese artists and writers who had been rehabilitated while still alive. All sorts of American cultural workers were invited. Some laughed to hear themselves described in this way. They were accustomed to being called "dreamer poet realist postmodernist." They might have liked being called "cultural dreamer," but no one had thought of that yet.

Many of these Chinese artists (mostly men and some women) flew back and forth from American coast to coast so often (sometimes stopping in Iowa City) that they were no longer interested in window seats but slept on the aisle or across the fat center where the armrests can be adjusted . . . while the great deep dipping Rockies, the Indian Black Hills, the Badlands, the good and endless plains moved slowly west under the gently trembling jet. They never bother anymore to dash to the windows at the circling of New York as the pattern holds and the lights of our city engage and eliminate the sky.

Ruth said she would personally bring Nick to the party since China was still too annoyed to have invited him. It wasn't fair for a superficial visitor like herself to be present when a person like Nick, with whole verses of his obsession falling out of his pockets, was excluded.

That's O.K., Ruth. You don't have to ask him, Faith said. Don't bother on my account. I don't even see him much anymore.

How come?

I don't know. Whenever I got to like one of his opinions he'd change it, and he never liked any of mine. Also, I couldn't talk to you about it, so it never got thick enough. I mean woofed and warped. Anyway, it hadn't been Nick, she realized. He was all right, but it was travel she longed for—somewhere else—the sexiness of the unknown parts of far imaginable places.

Sex? Ruth said. She bit her lips. Wouldn't it be interesting if way out there Rachel was having a baby?

God, yes, of course! Wonderful! Oh, Ruthy, Faith said, remembering babies, those round, staring, day-in day-out companions of her youth.

Well, Faith asked, what was he like, Nick—the poet Ai Qing? What'd he say?

He has a very large head, Nick said. The great poet raised from exile.

Was Ding Ling there? The amazing woman, the storyteller, Ding Ling?

They're not up to her yet, Nick said. Maybe next year.

Well, what did Bien Tselin say? Faith asked. Nick, tell me.

Well, he's very tiny. He looks like my father did when he was old.

Yes, but what did they say?

[8]Golda Meir, 1898–1978. Israeli premier, 1969–1974.

Do you have any other questions? he asked. I'm thinking about something right now. He was writing in his little book—thoughts, comments, maybe even new songs for Chinese modernization—which he planned to publish as soon as possible. He thought Faith could read them then.

Finally he said, They showed me their muscles. There were other poets there. They told some jokes but not against us. They laughed and nudged each other. They talked Chinese, you know. I don't know why they were so jolly. They kept saying, Do not think that we have ceased to be Communists. We are Communists. They weren't bitter. They acted interested and happy.

Ruthy, Faith said, please tell me what they said.

Well, one of the women, Faith, about our age, she said the same thing. She also said the peasants were good to her. But the soldiers were bad. She said the peasants in the countryside helped her. They knew she felt lonely and frightened. She said she loved the Chinese peasant. That's exactly the way she said it, like a little speech: I'll never forget and I will always love the Chinese peasant. It's the one thing Mao was right about—of course he was also a good poet. But she said, well, you can imagine—she said, the children . . . When the entire working office was sent down to the countryside to dig up stones, she left her daughters with her mother. Her mother was old-fashioned, especially about girls. It's not so hard to be strong about oneself.

Some months later, at a meeting of women's governmental organizations sponsored by the UN, Faith met the very same Chinese woman who'd talked to Ruth. She remembered Ruth well. Yes, the lady who hasn't seen her daughter in eight years. Oh, what a sadness. Who would forget that woman. I have known a few. My name is Xie Feng, she said. Now you say it.

The two women said each other's strange name and laughed. The Chinese woman said, Faith in what? Then she gathered whatever strength and aggression she'd needed to reach this country; she added the courtesy of shyness, breathed deep, and said, Now I would like to see how you live. I have been to meetings, one after another and day after day. But what is a person's home like? How do you live?

Faith said, Me? My house? You want to see my house? In the mirror that evening brushing her teeth, she smiled at her smiling face. She had been invited to be hospitable to a woman from half the world away who'd lived a life beyond foreignness and had experienced extreme history.

The next day they drank tea in Faith's kitchen out of Chinese cups that Ruth had brought from her travels. Misty terraced hills were painted on these cups and a little oil derrick inserted among them.

Faith showed her the boys' bedroom. The Chinese woman took a little camera out of her pocket. You don't mind? she asked. This is the front room, said Faith. It's called the living room. This is our bedroom. That's a picture of Jack giving a paper at the Other Historian meeting and that picture is Jack with two guys who've worked in his store since they were all young. The skinny one just led a strike against Jack and won. Jack says they were right.

I see—both principled men, said the Chinese woman.

They walked around the block a couple of times to get the feel of a neighborhood. They stopped for strudel at the Art Foods. It was half past two and just in time to see the children fly out of the school around the corner. The littlest ones banged against the legs of teachers and mothers. Here and there a father rested his length against somebody's illegally parked car. They stopped to buy a couple of apples. This is my Chinese friend from China, Faith said to Eddie the butcher, who was smoking a cigar, spitting and smiling at the sunlight of an afternoon break. So many peaches, so many oranges, the woman said admiringly to Eddie.

They walked west to the Hudson River. It's called the North River but it's really our Lordly Hudson. This is a good river, but very quiet, said the Chinese woman as they stepped onto the beautiful, green, rusting, slightly crumpled, totally unused pier and looked at New Jersey. They returned along a street of small houses and Faith pointed up to the second-floor apartment where she and Jack had first made love. Ah, the woman said, do you notice that in time you love the children more and the man less? Faith said, Yes! but as soon as she said it, she wanted to run home and find Jack and kiss his pink ears and his 243 last hairs, to call out, Old friend, don't worry, you are loved. But before she could speak of this, Tonto flew by on his financially rewarding messenger's bike, screaming, Hi, Mom, *nee hau, nee hau.* He has a Chinese girlfriend this week. He says that means hello. My other son is at a meeting. She didn't say it was the L.R.Y.'s regular beep-the-horn-if-you-support-Mao meeting. She showed her the church basement where she and Ruth and Ann and Louise and their group of mostly women and some men had made leaflets, offered sanctuary to draft resisters. They would probably do so soon again. Some young people looked up from a light board, saw a representative of the Third World, and smiled peacefully. They walked east and south to neighborhoods where our city, in fields of garbage and broken brick, stands desolate, her windows burnt and blind. Here, Faith said, the people suffer and struggle, their children turn round and round in one place, growing first in beauty, then in rage.

Now we are home again. And I will tell you about my life, the Chinese woman said. Oh yes, please, said Faith, very embarrassed. Of course the desire to share the facts and places of her life had come from generosity, but it had come from self-centeredness too.

Yes, the Chinese woman said. Things are a little better now. They get good at home, they get a little bad, then improve. And the men, you know, they were very bad. But now they are a little better, not all, but some, a few. May I ask you, do you worry that your older boy is in a political group that isn't liked? What will be his trade? Will he go to university? My eldest is without skills to this day. Her school years happened in the time of great confusion and running about. My youngest studies well. Ah, she said, rising. Hello. Good afternoon.

Ruth stood in the doorway. Faith's friend, the listener and the answerer, listening.

We were speaking, the Chinese woman said. About the children, how to raise them. My youngest sister is permitted to have a child this year, so we often talk thoughtfully. This is what we think: Shall we teach them to be straightforward, honorable, kind, brave, maybe shrewd, self-serving a little? What is the best way to help them in the real world? We don't know the best way. You don't want them to be cruel, but you want them to take care of themselves wisely. Now my own children are nearly grown. Perhaps it's too late. Was I foolish? I didn't know in those years how to do it.

Yes, yes, said Faith. I know what you mean. Ruthy?

Ruth remained quiet.

Faith waited a couple of seconds. Then she turned to the Chinese woman. Oh, Xie Feng, she said. Neither did I.

1985

Cynthia Ozick b. 1928

For Cynthia Ozick, literature is seductive: stories "arouse"; they "enchant"; they "transfigure." Ozick describes herself in "early young-womanhood" as "a worshipper of literature," drawn to the world of the imagination "with all the rigor and force and stunned ardor of religious belief." Yet the pleasure of attraction is tempered by danger. Adoration of art can become a form of idolatry—a kind of "aesthetic paganism" that for her is incompatible with Judaism because it betrays the biblical commandment against graven images. Art can also "tear away from humanity," and Ozick worries that the beauty of language can distract from art's moral function of judging and interpreting the world. These tensions—between art and idolatry, between aestheticism and moral seriousness, between the attraction of surfaces and the weight of history—lie at the heart of Ozick's fiction and essays. Indeed, Ozick is often considered a writer of oppositions, many of which are reflected in her efforts to translate what she calls a "Jewish sensibility" into the English language. "I suppose you might say that I am myself an oxymoron," she explains, "but in the life of story-writing, there are no boundaries."

Cynthia Ozick was born in New York City on April 17, 1928, to Russian Jewish immigrants, William and Celia Regelson Ozick. Her childhood was spent in the Pelham Bay section of the Bronx, where her parents worked long hours to maintain a pharmacy during the Depression. She recalls these years as an idyllic time of reading and dreaming of writing; she also remembers being made to feel "hopelessly stupid" at school and being subjected to overt anti-Semitism. After graduating from Hunter High School, Ozick went on to complete a B.A. at New York University and an M.A. in English Literature at Ohio State University, where she wrote a thesis on the late novels of Henry James. James became a kind of obsession for her, both inspiring and inhibiting her burgeoning writing career. For nearly seven years she struggled to write a long, "philosophical" novel entitled *Mercy, Pity, Peace, and Love,* which she finally abandoned after writing 300,000 words. During this time, Ozick moved back to New York, married Bernard Hallote, and began working as an advertising copywriter. She also wrote short stories and labored for six more years on what became her first novel, *Trust,* published soon after the birth of her daughter Rachel in 1965. At this time, she also began the intensive study of Jewish philosophy, history, and literature that eventually transformed her writing.

Although slow to come into her own as a writer, Ozick is now prolific and widely acclaimed. She has been recognized through numerous awards and grants, including a National Endowment for the Arts Fellowship, a Guggenheim Fellowship, the American Academy and Institute of Arts and Letters Strauss Livings grant, and the Jewish Book Council Award.

Three of her essays have been republished in the annual collection of *Best American Essays,* five of her stories have been chosen to appear in *Best American Short Stories,* and three have received first prize in the O. Henry Prize Stories competition. Perhaps best known for her fiction and essays, Ozick also writes and translates poetry, and she has recently written a play based on two of her short stories, "The Shawl" (1981) and "Rosa" (1984) (later published together in a single volume).

In characteristically contradictory terms, Ozick has described herself—as a first-generation American Jew—to be "perfectly at home and yet perfectly insecure, perfectly acculturated and yet perfectly marginal." However, unlike many Jewish American writers who were the children of immigrants, Ozick does not write about the sociological experiences of assimilation and subsequent generational conflict. Rather, her sense of being simultaneously inside and outside the dominant culture is manifested in a real faith in "the thesis of American pluralism," a pluralism that accommodates particularist and diverse impulses. Perhaps somewhat paradoxically, one of Ozick's greatest contributions to American literature is her unwavering effort to remain "centrally Jewish" in her concerns by perpetuating the stories and histories of Jewish texts and traditions. "The Shawl," reprinted here, reflects Ozick's commitment to Jewish memory, as well as her long-standing fears about the dangers of artistic representation. Although many of Ozick's works address the historical and psychological consequences of the Holocaust, "The Shawl" is an exception: only here does she attempt to render life in the concentration camps directly. She has explained her reluctance to write fiction about the events of the Holocaust by insisting instead that "we ought to absorb the documents, the endless, endless data. . . . I want the documents to be enough; I don't want to tamper or invent or imagine. And yet I have done it. I can't not do it. It comes, it invades." The imaginative origin of "The Shawl" was, in fact, a historical text: the story evolved out of one evocative sentence in William Shirer's *The Rise and Fall of the Third Reich* about babies being thrown against electrified fences.

In an extraordinarily compressed and almost incantatory prose, Ozick depicts such horrifyingly familiar images of Nazi brutality as forced marches, starvation, dehumanization, and murder, while nevertheless managing to convey her ambivalence about using metaphoric language to represent an experience that is nearly unimaginable. The story makes clear that speech itself is dangerous: despite Rosa's desire to hear her child's voice, Magda is safe only as long as she is mute. The consequence of her cry—the only dialogue in the story—is death. Through a series of paradoxical images that combine the fantastical and the realistic, Ozick demonstrates that in writing and thinking about the unnatural world of a death camp, all expectations must be subverted: here, a baby's first tooth is an "elfin tombstone"; a breast is a "dead volcano"; a starved belly is "fat, full and round"; and a shawl can be "magic," sheltering and nourishing a child as an extension of the mother's body. Yet neither motherhood nor magic can save lives here; that which protects is also that which causes death. By overturning the natural order and unsettling the reader's ability to "know," Ozick makes the powerful point that the "reality" of the Holocaust is fundamentally inaccessible and that conventional means of understanding simply do not apply.

Tresa Grauer
University of Pennsylvania

PRIMARY WORKS

Trust, 1966; *The Pagan Rabbi, and Other Stories,* 1971; *Bloodshed and Three Novellas,* 1976; *Levitation: Five Fictions,* 1982; *Art & Ardor: Essays,* 1983; *The Cannibal Galaxy,* 1983; *The Messiah of Stockholm,* 1987; *Metaphor & Memory: Essays,* 1989; "The Shawl," 1981; "Rosa," 1984; *The Shawl,* 1988; *Epodes: First Poems,* 1992; *Blue Light: A Play,* 1994; *Fame & Folly: Essays,* 1996; *Portrait of the Artist as a Bad Character,* 1996; *The Putter-Messer papers,* 1997; *SHE: Portrait of the Essay as a Warm Body,* 1998.

The Shawl

Stella, cold, cold, the coldness of hell. How they walked on the roads together, Rosa with Magda curled up between sore breasts, Magda wound up in the shawl. Sometimes Stella carried Magda. But she was jealous of Magda. A thin girl of fourteen, too small, with thin breasts of her own, Stella wanted to be wrapped in a shawl, hidden away, asleep, rocked by the march, a baby, a round infant in arms. Magda took Rosa's nipple, and Rosa never stopped walking, a walking cradle. There was not enough milk; sometimes Magda sucked air; then she screamed. Stella was ravenous. Her knees were tumors on sticks, her elbows chicken bones.

Rosa did not feel hunger; she felt light, not like someone walking but like someone in a faint, in trance, arrested in a fit, someone who is already a floating angel, alert and seeing everything, but in the air, not there, not touching the road. As if teetering on the tips of her fingernails. She looked into Magda's face through a gap in the shawl: a squirrel in a nest, safe, no one could reach her inside the little house of the shawl's windings. The face, very round, a pocket mirror of a face: but it was not Rosa's bleak complexion, dark like cholera, it was another kind of face altogether, eyes blue as air, smooth feathers of hair nearly as yellow as the Star sewn into Rosa's coat. You could think she was one of *their* babies.

Rosa, floating, dreamed of giving Magda away in one of the villages. She could leave the line for a minute and push Magda into the hands of any woman on the side of the road. But if she moved out of line they might shoot. And even if she fled the line for half a second and pushed the shawl-bundle at a stranger, would the woman take it? She might be surprised, or afraid; she might drop the shawl, and Magda would fall out and strike her head and die. The little round head. Such a good child, she gave up screaming, and sucked now only for the taste of the drying nipple itself. The neat grip of the tiny gums. One mite of a tooth tip sticking up in the bottom gum, how shining, an elfin tombstone of white marble gleaming there. Without complaining, Magda relinquished Rosa's teats, first the left, then the right; both were cracked, not a sniff of milk. The duct-crevice extinct, a dead volcano, blind eye, chill hole, so Magda took the corner of the shawl and milked it instead. She sucked and sucked, flooding threads with wetness. The shawl's good flavor, milk of linen.

It was a magic shawl, it could nourish an infant for three days and three nights. Magda did not die, she stayed alive, although very quiet. A peculiar smell, of cinnamon and almonds, lifted out of her mouth. She held her eyes open every moment, forgetting how to blink or nap, and Rosa and sometimes Stella studied their blueness. On the road they raised one burden of a leg after another and studied Magda's face. "Aryan," Stella said, in a voice grown as thin as a string; and Rosa thought how Stella gazed at Magda like a young cannibal. And the time that Stella said "Aryan," it sounded to Rosa as if Stella had really said "Let us devour her."

But Magda lived to walk. She lived that long, but she did not walk very well, partly because she was only fifteen months old, and partly because the spindles of her legs could not hold up her fat belly. It was fat with air, full and round. Rosa gave almost all her food to Magda, Stella gave nothing; Stella was ravenous, a growing child herself, but not growing much. Stella did not menstruate. Rosa did not menstruate. Rosa was ravenous, but also not; she learned from Magda how to drink the taste of a finger in one's mouth. They were in a place without pity, all pity was annihilated in Rosa, she looked at Stella's bones without pity. She was sure that Stella was waiting for Magda to die so she could put her teeth into the little thighs.

Rosa knew Magda was going to die very soon; she should have been dead already, but she had been buried away deep inside the magic shawl, mistaken there for the shivering mound of Rosa's breasts; Rosa clung to the shawl as if it covered only herself. No one took it away from her. Magda was mute. She never cried. Rosa hid her in the barracks, under the shawl, but she knew that one day someone would inform; or one day someone, not even Stella, would steal Magda to eat her. When Magda began to walk Rosa knew that Magda was going to die very soon, something would happen. She was afraid to fall asleep; she slept with the weight of her thigh on Magda's body; she was afraid she would smother Magda under her thigh. The weight of Rosa was becoming less and less; Rosa and Stella were slowly turning into air.

Magda was quiet, but her eyes were horribly alive, like blue tigers. She watched. Sometimes she laughed—it seemed a laugh, but how could it be? Magda had never seen anyone laugh. Still, Magda laughed at her shawl when the wind blew its corners, the bad wind with pieces of black in it, that made Stella's and Rosa's eyes tear. Magda's eyes were always clear and tearless. She watched like a tiger. She guarded her shawl. No one could touch it; only Rosa could touch it. Stella was not allowed. The shawl was Magda's own baby, her pet, her little sister. She tangled herself up in it and sucked on one of the corners when she wanted to be very still.

Then Stella took the shawl away and made Magda die.

Afterward Stella said: "I was cold."

And afterward she was always cold, always. The cold went into her heart: Rosa saw that Stella's heart was cold. Magda flopped onward with her little pencil legs scribbling this way and that, in search of the shawl; the pencils faltered at the barracks opening, where the light began. Rosa saw and pursued. But already Magda was in the square outside the barracks, in the jolly light. It was the roll-call arena. Every morning Rosa had to conceal Magda under the shawl against a wall of the barracks and go out and stand in the arena with Stella and hundreds of others, sometimes for hours, and Magda, deserted, was quiet under the shawl, sucking on her corner. Every day Magda was silent, and so she did not die. Rosa saw that today Magda was going to die, and at the same time a fearful joy ran in Rosa's two palms, her fingers were on fire, she was astonished, febrile: Magda, in the sunlight, swaying on her pencil legs, was howling. Ever since the drying up of Rosa's nipples, ever since Magda's last scream on the road, Magda had been devoid of any syllable; Magda was a mute. Rosa believed that something had gone wrong with her vocal cords, with her windpipe, with the cave of her larynx; Magda was defective, without a voice; perhaps she was deaf; there might be something amiss with her intelligence; Magda was dumb. Even the laugh that came when the ash-stippled wind made a clown out of Magda's shawl was only the air-blown showing of her teeth. Even when the lice, head lice and body lice, crazed her so that she became as wild as one of the big rats that plundered the barracks at daybreak looking for carrion, she rubbed and scratched and kicked and bit and rolled without a whimper. But now Magda's mouth was spilling a long viscous rope of clamor.

"Maaaa—"

It was the first noise Magda had ever sent out from her throat since the drying up of Rosa's nipples.

"Maaaa . . . aaa!"

Again! Magda was wavering in the perilous sunlight of the arena, scribbling on such pitiful little bent shins. Rosa saw. She saw that Magda was grieving for the loss of her shawl, she saw that Magda was going to die. A tide of commands hammered in Rosa's nipples: Fetch, get, bring! But she did not know which to go after first, Magda or the shawl. If she jumped out into the arena to snatch Magda up, the howling would not stop, because Magda would still not have the shawl; but if she ran back into the barracks to find the shawl, and if she found it, and if she came after Magda holding it and shaking it, then she would get Magda back, Magda would put the shawl in her mouth and turn dumb again.

Rosa entered the dark. It was easy to discover the shawl. Stella was heaped under it, asleep in her thin bones. Rosa tore the shawl free and flew—she could fly, she was only air—into the arena. The sunheat murmured of another life, of butterflies in summer. The light was placid, mellow. On the other side of the steel fence, far away, there were green meadows speckled with dandelions and deep-colored violets; beyond them, even farther, innocent tiger lilies, tall, lifting their orange bonnets. In the barracks they spoke of "flowers," of "rain": excrement, thick turd-braids, and the slow stinking maroon waterfall that slunk down from the upper bunks, the stink mixed with a bitter fatty floating smoke that greased Rosa's skin. She stood for an instant at the margin of the arena. Sometimes the electricity inside the fence would seem to hum; even Stella said it was only an imagining, but Rosa heard real sounds in the wire; grainy sad voices. The farther she was from the fence, the more clearly the voices crowded at her. The lamenting voices strummed so convincingly, so passionately, it was impossible to suspect them of being phantoms. The voices told her to hold up the shawl, high; the voices told her to shake it, to whip with it, to unfurl it like a flag. Rosa lifted, shook, whipped, unfurled. Far off, very far, Magda leaned across her air-fed belly, reaching out with the rods of her arms. She was high up, elevated, riding someone's shoulder. But the shoulder that carried Magda was not coming toward Rosa and the shawl, it was drifting away, the speck of Magda was moving more and more into the smoky distance. Above the shoulder a helmet glinted. The light tapped the helmet and sparkled it into a goblet. Below the helmet a black body like a domino and a pair of black boots hurled themselves in the direction of the electrified fence. The electric voices began to chatter wildly. "Maamaa, maaamaaa," they all hummed together. How far Magda was from Rosa now, across the whole square, past a dozen barracks, all the way on the other side! She was no bigger than a moth.

All at once Magda was swimming through the air. The whole of Magda traveled through loftiness. She looked like a butterfly touching a silver vine. And the moment Magda's feathered round head and her pencil legs and balloonish belly and zigzag arms splashed against the fence, the steel voices went mad in their growling, urging Rosa to run and run to the spot where Magda had fallen from her flight against the electrified fence; but of course Rosa did not obey them. She only stood, because if she ran they would shoot, and if she tried to pick up the sticks of Magda's body they would shoot, and if she let the wolf's screech ascending now through the ladder of her skeleton break out, they would shoot; so she took Magda's shawl and filled her own mouth with it, stuffed it in and stuffed it in, until she was swallowing up the wolf's screech and tasting the cinnamon and almond depth of Magda's saliva; and Rosa drank Magda's shawl until it dried.

1980

Adrienne Rich b. 1929

The daughter of Helen Jones and Arnold Rich, a professor of pathology at Johns Hopkins University, Adrienne Rich grew up in Baltimore. Her father, an exacting tutor, required that his daughter master complex poetic meters and rhyme schemes. Her mother, who had been a concert pianist before marriage, conveyed to her child a love of the lyrical as well as the rhythmic.

Educated at Radcliffe College, Rich graduated Phi Beta Kappa and shortly after won distinction when her first book of poems, *A Change of World,* won the Yale Younger Poets award and was published with a laudatory preface by W.H. Auden. After traveling and writing in Europe on a Guggenheim Fellowship, Rich married Alfred Conrad, an economics professor at Harvard. As a wife and the mother of three sons during the 1950s, Rich was expected to conform to a life of domestic femininity, which meant that she had little time for serious writing. Her *Snapshots of a Daughter-in-Law* conveys the anger and confusion she felt during those years of confinement. In her 1963 book of verse, Rich smashes the icons of domesticity: the coffee pot and raked gardens.

The conflict and distress experienced by creative, intellectual women in a culture that too often devalues female experience is a recurring theme in Rich's poetry. In the fifty years of her career, her poems and her essays chronicle the evolution of feminist consciousness and illuminate the phases of her personal growth from self-analysis and individual accomplishment to lesbian/feminist activism and the collective shaping of a feminist vision of community that is perhaps strangely rooted in the Puritan ideal of the city on a hill. The personal and political converge in her belief that politics is "not something 'out there' but something 'in here' and of the essense of [her] condition."

Adrienne Rich is a poet whose work has influenced the lives of many of her readers. She acknowledges that it is a profound responsibility and privilege to be a poet whose work is read by so many. As a radical feminist, Rich has written poetry that is politically charged, refusing to accept the criticism that art and activism are antithetical. Her poems combine lyricism and tightly constructed lines characterized by the use of elegant assonance, consonance, slant rhyme, and onomatopoeia, with quotations and slogans from antiwar and feminist statements.

Influenced by the open styles of Pound, Williams, and Levertov, and the confessional mode of Lowell, Plath, Sexton, and Berryman, Rich has created a poetic voice that is distinctive and powerful. Her unusual combination of artistic excellence and committed activism has been internationally praised, and she has won numerous awards including the 1974 National Book Award, the 1986 Ruth Lilly Poetry Prize, the 1997 Tanning Prize, the 1999 Lannan Foundation's Lifetime Achievement Award, as well as two Guggenheim fellowships and a MacArthur fellowship. As a poet who has committed herself to writing poetry that will change lives, Rich has observed in *Lies, Secrets, and Silences,* her collected essays, "Poetry is, among other things, a criticism of language. Poetry is above all a concentration of the power of language, which is the power of our ultimate relationship to everything in the universe."

Wendy Martin
Claremont Graduate University

PRIMARY WORKS

A Change of World, 1951; *Snapshots of a Daughter-in-Law,* 1963; *Necessities of Life,* 1966; *Leaflets,* 1969; *The Will to Change,* 1971; *Diving into the Wreck,* 1973; *Adrienne Rich's Poetry,* 1975; *Of Woman Born: Motherhood as Experience and Institution,* 1976; *The Dream of a Common Language,* 1978; *On Lies, Secrets, and Silence: Selected Prose, 1966–1978,* 1979; *A Wild Patience Has Taken Me This Far,* 1981; *Sources,* 1983; *The Fact of a Doorframe: Poems Selected and New 1950–1984,* 1984; *Your Native Land, Your Life,* 1986; *Blood, Bread, and Poetry: Selected Prose 1979–1986,* 1986; *Time's Power: Poems 1985–1988,* 1989; *Women andHonor: Some Notes on Lying,* 1990; Barbara Charlesworth Gelpi and Albert Gelpi, eds., *Adrienne Rich's Poetry and Prose,* 1993; *An Atlas of the Difficult World: Poems 1988–1991,* 1991; *What Is Found There?: Notebooks on Poetry and Politics,* 1993; *Collected Early Poems, 1950–1970,* 1995; *Dark Fields of the Republic: Poems, 1991–1995,* 1995; *Midnight Salvage: Poems, 1995–1998,* 1999.

Diving into the Wreck

First having read the book of myths,
and loaded the camera,
and checked the edge of the knife-blade,
I put on
the body-armor of black rubber
the absurd flippers
the grave and awkward mask.
I am having to do this
not like Cousteau[1] with his
assiduous team
aboard the sun-flooded schooner
but here alone.

[1]Jacques Cousteau (1910–1997). French underwater explorer and environmentalist.

There is a ladder.
The ladder is always there
hanging innocently
close to the side of the schooner.
We know what it is for,
we who have used it.
Otherwise
it's a piece of maritime floss
some sundry equipment.

I go down.
Rung after rung and still
the oxygen immerses me
the blue light
the clear atoms
of our human air.
I go down.
My flippers cripple me,
I crawl like an insect down the ladder
and there is no one
to tell me when the ocean
will begin.

First the air is blue and then
it is bluer and then green and then
black I am blacking out and yet
my mask is powerful
it pumps my blood with power
the sea is another story
the sea is not a question of power
I have to learn alone
to turn my body without force
in the deep element.

And now: it is easy to forget
what I came for
among so many who have always
lived here
swaying their crenellated fans
between the reefs
and besides
you breathe differently down here.

I came to explore the wreck.
The words are purposes.
The words are maps.
I came to see the damage that was done
and the treasures that prevail.

I stroke the beam of my lamp
slowly along the flank
of something more permanent
than fish or weed

the thing I came for:
the wreck and not the story of the wreck
the thing itself and not the myth
the drowned face always staring
toward the sun
the evidence of damage
worn by salt and sway into this threadbare beauty
the ribs of the disaster
curving their assertion
among the tentative haunters.

This is the place.
And I am here, the mermaid whose dark hair
streams black, the merman in his armored body
We circle silently
about the wreck
we dive into the hold.
I am she: I am he
whose drowned face sleeps with open eyes
whose breasts still bear the stress
whose silver, copper, vermeil cargo lies
obscurely inside barrels
half-wedged and left to rot
we are the half-destroyed instruments
that once held to a course
the water-eaten log
the fouled compass

We are, I am, you are
by cowardice or courage
the one who find our way
back to this scene
carrying a knife, a camera
a book of myths
in which
our names do not appear.

1973

From a Survivor

The pact that we made was the ordinary pact
of men & women in those days

I don't know who we thought we were
that our personalities
could resist the failures of the race

Lucky or unlucky, we didn't know
the race had failures of that order
and that we were going to share them

Like everybody else, we thought of ourselves as special

Your body is as vivid to me
as it ever was: even more

since my feeling for it is clearer:
I know what it could and could not do

it is no longer
the body of a god
or anything with power over my life

Next year it would have been 20 years
and you are wastefully dead[1]
who might have made the leap
we talked, too late, of making

which I live now
not as a leap
but a succession of brief, amazing movements

each one making possible the next

1973

[1]Adrienne Rich's husband, Alfred Conrad, committed suicide in 1970.

Power

Living   in the earth-deposits   of our history

Today a backhoe divulged   out of a crumbling flank of earth
one bottle   amber   perfect   a hundred-year-old
cure for fever   or melancholy   a tonic
for living on this earth   in the winters of this climate

Today I was reading about Marie Curie:[1]
she must have known she suffered   from radiation sickness
her body bombarded for years   by the element
she had purified
It seems she denied to the end
the source of the cataracts on her eyes
the cracked and suppurating skin   of her finger-ends
till she could no longer hold   a test-tube or a pencil

She died   a famous woman   denying
her wounds
denying
her wounds   came   from the same source as her power

1978

Not Somewhere Else, but Here

Courage   Her face in the leaves   the polygons
of the paving   Her   out of touch
Courage to breathe   The death of October
Spilt wine   The unbuilt house   The unmade life
Graffiti   without memory   grown conventional
scrawling the least wall   *god loves you*   *voice of the ghetto*
Death of the city   Her face
sleeping   Her quick stride   Her
running   Search for a private space   The city
caving in from within   The lessons badly
learned   Or not at all   The unbuilt world

[1]Marie Curie (1867–1934) won a Nobel Prize for her research on radioactive elements. She died of leukemia.

This one love flowing Touching other
lives Spilt love The least wall caving

To have enough courage The life that must be lived
in terrible October
Sudden immersion in yellows streaked blood The fast rain
Faces Inscriptions Trying to teach
unlearnable lessons October This one love
Repetitions from other lives The deaths
that must be lived Denials Blank walls
Our quick stride side by side Her fugue
Bad air in the tunnels *voice of the ghetto god loves you*
My face pale in the window anger is pale
the blood shrinks to the heart
the head severed it does not pay to feel

Her face The fast rain tearing Courage
to feel this To tell of this to be alive
Trying to learn unteachable lessons

The fugue Blood in my eyes The careful sutures
ripped open The hands that touch me Shall it be said
I am not alone
Spilt love seeking its level flooding other
lives that must be lived not somewhere else
but here seeing through blood nothing is lost

1974

Coast to Coast

There are days when housework seems the only
outlet old funnel I've poured caldrons through
old servitude In grief and fury bending
to the accustomed tasks the vacuum cleaner plowing
realms of dust the mirror scoured grey webs
behind framed photographs brushed away
the grey-seamed sky enormous in the west
snow gathering in corners of the north

Seeing through the prism
you who gave it me
You, bearing ceaselessly
yourself the witness

Rainbow dissolves the Hudson   This chary, stinting
skin of late winter   ice   forming and breaking up
The unprotected seeing it through
with their ordinary valor
        Rainbow composed of ordinary light
February-flat
grey-white of a cheap enamelled pan
breaking into veridian, azure, violet
You write: *Three and a half weeks lost from writing . . .*
I think of the word *protection*
who it is we try to protect   and why
        Seeing through the prism   Your face, fog-hollowed   burning
cold of eucalyptus hung with butterflies
lavender of rockbloom
O and your anger uttered in silence word and stammer
shattering the fog   lances of sun
piercing the grey Pacific   unanswerable tide
        carving itself in clefts and fissures of the rock
Beauty of your breasts   your hands
turning a stone a shell a week a prism   in coastal light
traveller and witness
the passion of the speechless
driving your speech
protectless

If you can read and understand this poem
send something back: a burning strand of hair
a still-warm, still-liquid drop of blood
a shell
thickened from being battered year on year
send something back.

1981

Frame

Winter twilight. She comes out of the laboratory, last class of the day
a pile of notebooks slung in her knapsack, coat
zipped high against the already swirling
evening sleet. The wind is wicked and the
busses slower than usual. On her mind
is organic chemistry and the issue
of next month's rent and will it be possible to
bypass the professor with the coldest eyes

to get a reference for graduate school,
and whether any of them, even those who smile
can see, looking at her, a biochemist
or a marine biologist, which of the faces
can she trust to see her at all, either today
or in any future. The busses are worm-slow in the
quickly gathering dark. *I don't know her. I am*
standing though somewhere just outside the frame
of all this, trying to see. At her back
the newly finished building suddenly looks
like shelter, it has glass doors, lighted halls
presumably heat. The wind is wicked. She throws a
glance down the street, sees no bus coming and runs
up the newly constructed steps into the newly
constructed hallway. *I am standing all this time*
just beyond the frame, trying to see. She runs
her hand through the crystals of sleet about to melt
on her hair. She shifts the weight of the books
on her back. It isn't warm here exactly but it's
out of that wind. Through the glass
door panels she can watch for the bus through the thickening
weather. Watching so, she is not
watching for the white man who watches the building
who has been watching her. This is Boston 1979.
I am standing somewhere at the edge of the frame
watching the man, we are both white, who watches the building
telling her to move on, get out of the hallway.
I can hear nothing because I am not supposed to be
present but I can see her gesturing
out toward the street at the wind-raked curb
I see her drawing her small body up
against the implied charges. The man
goes away. Her body is different now.
It is holding together with more than a hint of fury
and more than a hint of fear. She is smaller, thinner
more fragile-looking than I am. *But I am not supposed to be*
there. I am just outside the frame
of this action when the anonymous white man
returns with a white police officer. Then she starts
to leave into the windraked night but already
the policeman is going to work, the handcuffs are on her
wrists he is throwing her down his knee has gone into
her breast he is dragging her down the stairs *I am unable*
to hear a sound of all this all that I know is what
I can see from this position there is no soundtrack
to go with this and I understand at once
it is meant to be in silence that this happens
in silence that he pushes her into the car

banging her head in silence that she cries out
in silence that she tries to explain she was only
waiting for a bus
in silence that he twists the flesh of her thigh
with his nails in silence that her tears begin to flow
that she pleads with the other policeman as if
he could be trusted to see her at all
in silence that in the precinct she refuses to give her name
in silence that they throw her into the cell
in silence that she stares him
straight in the face in silence that he sprays her
in her eyes with Mace in silence that she sinks her teeth
into his hand in silence that she is charged
with trespass assault and battery in
silence that at the sleet-swept corner her bus
passes without stopping and goes on
in silence. *What I am telling you*
is told by a white woman who they will say
was never there. I say I am there.

1981

Hisaye Yamamoto b. 1921

Hisaye Yamamoto once said that she "didn't have any imagination" and that she "just *embroidered* on things that happened, or that people told [her] happened." The statement, though spoken out of her wonted modesty, reveals the extent to which personal and historical circumstances form the grist to her fictional mill. Born in Redondo Beach, California, Yamamoto was a child of Japanese immigrants. She started writing when she was a teenager and contributed regularly to Japanese American newspapers. During World War II she was interned for three years in Poston, Arizona, where she served as a reporter and a columnist for the *Poston Chronicle* (the camp newspaper) and published a serialized mystery. After the war she worked from 1945 to 1948 for the *Los Angeles Tribune,* a black weekly. Soon afterwards her short stories began to appear in national journals, and she received a John Hay Whitney Foundation Opportunity Fellowship (1950–51). She was also encouraged by Yvor Winters to accept a Stanford Writing Fellowship, but chose instead to work from 1953 to 1955 as a volunteer in a Catholic Worker rehabilitation farm on Staten Island founded by Dorothy Day. She returned to Los Angeles after marrying Anthony DeSoto.

Yamamoto was one of the first Japanese American writers to gain national recognition after the war, when anti-Japanese sentiment was still rampant. Four of her short stories were listed as "Distinctive Short Stories" in Martha Foley's *Best American Short Stories* collections: "The High-Heeled Shoes" (1948), "The Brown House" (1951), "Yoneko's Earthquake" (1951), and "Epithalamium" (1960). "Yoneko's Earthquake" was also chosen as one of the *Best American Short Stories: 1952*. In 1986 she received from the Before Columbus Foundation the American Book Award for Lifetime Achievement.

Because Yamamoto excels in depicting Japanese American communal life, it is helpful to see her fiction in historical and social context. Most Japanese immigrants came to America between 1885 and 1924. The first waves of immigrants consisted mainly of single young men who saw North America as a land of opportunity. After establishing themselves in the new country, some returned to Japan to seek wives, while others arranged their marriages by means of an exchange of photographs across the Pacific. Hence a large number of Japanese "picture brides" came to this country after the turn of the century to meet bridegrooms they had never seen in person. By 1930 the American-born Nisei (second generation) already outnumbered the Issei (first generation), and about half of the Japanese American population lived in rural areas in the western U.S. Japanese was the language generally spoken at home, so that many Nisei (including Yamamoto) spoke only Japanese until they entered kindergarten.

Despite the preoccupation with survival in America, a number of Issei maintained their interest in Japanese poetry. There were literary groups engaged in the traditional forms of *haiku, tanka,* and *senryu,* and numerous magazines devoted to Issei poetry. Nisei, on the other hand, mostly expressed themselves in the English sections of Japanese American newspapers. The vibrant Japanese American literary movement was disrupted by the advent of World War II, when over 110,000 Japanese Americans were incarcerated under the Japanese Relocation Act of 1942.

The pre-war and postwar experiences of many Japanese Americans are reflected in the work of Yamamoto, who persistently explores the relationship between Issei men and women and between immigrant parents and their children. Because of the prevalence of arranged marriages among the Issei, compatibility between couples could hardly be assumed. In "Seventeen Syllables" it is through the naive perceptions of a Nisei daughter—Rosie—that we glimpse the dark nuances of Issei silences. While intergenerational differences are not peculiar to Japanese Americans, the gap between the Issei and the Nisei is widened by language and cultural barriers. Rosie's inability to appreciate her mother's Japanese haiku bespeaks her more general incomprehension of her mother's life story. The child's partial understanding allows Yamamoto to tell the mother's story obliquely.

King-Kok Cheung
University of California at Los Angeles

PRIMARY WORKS

Seventeen Syllables and Other Stories, 1988.

Seventeen Syllables

The first Rosie knew that her mother had taken to writing poems was one evening when she finished one and read it aloud for her daughter's approval. It was about cats, and Rosie pretended to understand it thoroughly and appreciate it no end, partly because she hesitated to disillusion her mother about the quantity and quality of Japanese she had learned in all the years now that she had been going to Japanese school every Saturday (and Wednesday, too, in the summer). Even so, her mother must have been skeptical about the depth of Rosie's understanding, because she explained afterwards about the kind of poem she was trying to write.

See, Rosie, she said, it was a *haiku,* a poem in which she must pack all her meaning into seventeen syllables only, which were divided into three lines of five, seven, and five syllables. In the one she had just read, she had tried to capture the charm of a kitten, as well as comment on the superstition that owning a cat of three colors meant good luck.

"Yes, yes, I understand. How utterly lovely," Rosie said, and her mother, either satisfied or seeing through the deception and resigned, went back to composing.

The truth was that Rosie was lazy; English lay ready on the tongue but Japanese had to be searched for and examined, and even then put forth tentatively (probably to meet with laughter). It was so much easier to say yes, yes, even when one meant no, no. Besides, this was what was in her mind to say: I was looking through one of your magazines from Japan last night, Mother, and towards the back I found some *haiku* in English that delighted me. There was one that made me giggle off and on until I fell asleep—

It is morning, and lo!
I lie awake, comme il faut,
sighing for some dough.

Now, how to reach her mother, how to communicate the melancholy song? Rosie knew formal Japanese by fits and starts, her mother had even less English, no French. It was much more possible to say yes, yes.

It developed that her mother was writing the *haiku* for a daily newspaper, the *Mainichi Shimbun,* that was published in San Francisco. Los Angeles, to be sure, was closer to the farming community in which the Hayashi family lived and several Japanese vernaculars were printed there, but Rosie's parents said they preferred the tone of the northern paper. Once a week, the *Mainichi* would have a section devoted to *haiku,* and her mother became an extravagant contributor, taking for herself the blossoming pen name, Ume Hanazono.

So Rosie and her father lived for awhile with two women, her mother and Ume Hanazono. Her mother (Tome Hayashi by name) kept house, cooked, washed, and, along with her husband and the Carrascos, the Mexican family hired for the harvest, did her ample share of picking tomatoes out in the sweltering fields and boxing them in tidy strata in the cool packing shed. Ume Hanazono, who came to life after the dinner dishes were done, was an earnest, muttering stranger who often neglected speaking when spoken to and stayed busy at the parlor table as late as midnight scribbling with pencil on scratch paper or carefully copying characters on good paper with her fat, pale green Parker.

The new interest had some repercussions on the household routine. Before, Rosie had been accustomed to her parents and herself taking their hot baths early and going to bed almost immediately afterwards, unless her parents challenged each other to a game of flower cards or unless company dropped in. Now if her father wanted to play cards, he had to resort to solitaire (at which he always cheated fearlessly), and if a group of friends came over, it was bound to contain someone who was also writing *haiku,* and the small assemblage would be split in two, her father entertaining the non-literary members and her mother comparing ecstatic notes with the visiting poet.

If they went out, it was more of the same thing. But Ume Hanazono's life span, even for a poet's, was very brief—perhaps three months at most.

One night they went over to see the Hayano family in the neighboring town to the west, an adventure both painful and attractive to Rosie. It was attractive because there were four Hayano girls, all lovely and each one named after a season of the year (Haru, Natsu, Aki, Fuyu), painful because something had been wrong with Mrs. Hayano ever since the birth of her first child. Rosie would sometimes watch Mrs. Hayano, reputed to have been the belle of her native village, making her way about a room, stooped, slowly shuffling, violently trembling (*always* trembling), and she would be reminded that this woman, in this same condition, had carried and given issue to three babies. She would look wonderingly at Mr. Hayano, handsome, tall, and strong, and she would look at her four pretty friends. But it was not a matter she could come to any decision about.

On this visit, however, Mrs. Hayano sat all evening in the rocker, as motionless and unobtrusive as it was possible for her to be, and Rosie found the greater part of the evening practically anaesthetic. Too, Rosie spent most of it in the girls' room, because Haru, the garrulous one, said almost as soon as the bows and other greetings were over, "Oh, you must see my new coat!"

It was a pale plaid of grey, sand, and blue, with an enormous collar, and Rosie, seeing nothing special in it, said, "Gee, how nice."

"Nice?" said Haru, indignantly. "Is that all you can say about it? It's gorgeous! And so cheap, too. Only seventeen-ninety-eight, because it was a sale. The saleslady said it was twenty-five dollars regular."

"Gee," said Rosie. Natsu, who never said much and when she said anything said it shyly, fingered the coat covetously and Haru pulled it away.

"Mine," she said, putting it on. She minced in the aisle between the two large beds and smiled happily. "Let's see how your mother likes it."

She broke into the front room and the adult conversation and went to stand in front of Rosie's mother, while the rest watched from the door. Rosie's mother was properly envious. "May I inherit it when you're through with it?"

Haru, pleased, giggled and said yes, she could, but Natsu reminded gravely from the door, "You promised me, Haru."

Everyone laughed but Natsu, who shamefacedly retreated into the bedroom. Haru came in laughing, taking off the coat. "We were only kidding, Natsu," she said. "Here, you try it on now."

After Natsu buttoned herself into the coat, inspected herself solemnly in the bureau mirror, and reluctantly shed it, Rosie, Aki, and Fuyu got their turns, and Fuyu, who was eight, drowned in it while her sisters and Rosie doubled up in amusement. They all went into the front room later, because Haru's mother quaveringly called to her to fix the tea and rice cakes and open a can of sliced peaches for everybody. Rosie noticed that her mother and Mr. Hayano were talking together at the little table—they were discussing a *haiku* that Mr. Hayano was planning to send to the *Mainichi,* while her father was sitting at one end of the sofa looking through a copy of *Life,* the new picture magazine. Occasionally, her father would comment on a photograph, holding it toward Mrs. Hayano and speaking to her as he always did—loudly, as though he thought someone such as she must surely be at least a trifle deaf also.

The five girls had their refreshments at the kitchen table, and it was while Rosie was showing the sisters her trick of swallowing peach slices without chewing (she chased each slippery crescent down with a swig of tea) that her father brought his empty teacup and untouched saucer to the sink and said, "Come on, Rosie, we're going home now."

"Already?" asked Rosie.

"Work tomorrow," he said.

He sounded irritated, and Rosie, puzzled, gulped one last yellow slice and stood up to go, while the sisters began protesting, as was their wont.

"We have to get up at five-thirty," he told them, going into the front room quickly, so that they did not have their usual chance to hang onto his hands and plead for an extension of time.

Rosie, following, saw that her mother and Mr. Hayano were sipping tea and still talking together, while Mrs. Hayano concentrated, quivering, on raising the handleless Japanese cup to her lips with both her hands and lowering it back to her lap. Her father, saying nothing, went out the door, onto the bright porch, and down the steps. Her mother looked up and asked, "Where is he going?"

"Where is he going?" Rosie said. "He said we were going home now."

"Going home?" Her mother looked with embarrassment at Mr. Hayano and his absorbed wife and then forced a smile. "He must be tired," she said.

Haru was not giving up yet. "May Rosie stay overnight?" she asked, and Natsu, Aki, and Fuyu came to reinforce their sister's plea by helping her make a circle around Rosie's mother. Rosie, for once having no desire to stay, was relieved when her mother, apologizing to the perturbed Mr. and Mrs. Hayano for her father's abruptness at the same time, managed to shake her head no at the quartet, kindly but adamant, so that they broke their circle and let her go.

Rosie's father looked ahead into the windshield as the two joined him. "I'm sorry," her mother said. "You must be tired." Her father, stepping on the starter, said nothing. "You know how I get when it's *haiku,*" she continued, "I forget what time it is." He only grunted.

As they rode homeward silently, Rosie, sitting between, felt a rush of hate for both—for her mother for begging, for her father for denying her mother. I wish this old Ford would crash, right now, she thought, then immediately, no, no, I wish my father would laugh, but it was too late: already the vision had passed through her mind of the green pick-up crumpled in the dark against one of the mighty eucalyptus trees they were just riding past, of the three contorted, bleeding bodies, one of them hers.

Rosie ran between two patches of tomatoes, her heart working more rambunctiously than she had ever known it to. How lucky it was that Aunt Taka and Uncle Gimpachi had come tonight, though, how very lucky. Otherwise she might not have really kept her half-promise to meet Jesus Carrasco. Jesus was going to be a senior in September at the same school she went to, and his parents were the ones helping with the tomatoes this year. She and Jesus, who hardly remembered seeing each other at Cleveland High where there were so many other people and two whole grades between them, had become great friends this summer—he always had a joke for her when he periodically drove the loaded pick-up up from the fields to the shed where she was usually sorting while her mother and father did the packing, and they laughed a great deal together over infinitesimal repartee during the afternoon break for chilled watermelon or ice cream in the shade of the shed.

What she enjoyed most was racing him to see which could finish picking a double row first. He, who could work faster, would tease her by slowing down until she thought she would surely pass him this time, then speeding up furiously to leave her several sprawling vines behind. Once he had made her screech hideously by crossing over, while her back was turned, to place atop the tomatoes in her green-stained bucket a truly monstrous, pale green worm (it had looked more like an infant snake). And it was when they had finished a contest this morning, after she had pantingly pointed a green finger at the immature tomatoes evident in the lugs at the end of his row and he had returned the accusation (with justice), that he had startlingly brought up the matter of their possibly meeting outside the range of both their parents' dubious eyes.

"What for?" she had asked.

"I've got a secret I want to tell you," he said.

"Tell me now," she demanded.

"It won't be ready till tonight," he said.

She laughed. "Tell me tomorrow then."

"It'll be gone tomorrow," he threatened.

"Well, for seven hakes, what is it?" she had asked, more than twice, and when he had suggested that the packing shed would be an appropriate place to find out, she had cautiously answered maybe. She had not been certain she was going to keep the appointment until the arrival of mother's sister and her husband. Their coming seemed a sort of signal of permission, of grace, and she had definitely made up her mind to lie and leave as she was bowing them welcome.

So as soon as everyone appeared settled back for the evening, she announced loudly that she was going to the privy outside, "I'm going to the *benjo!*" and slipped out the door. And now that she was actually on her way, her heart pumped in such an undisciplined way that she could hear it with her ears. It's because I'm running, she told herself, slowing to a walk. The shed was up ahead, one more patch away, in the middle of the fields. Its bulk, looming in the dimness, took on a sinisterness that was funny when Rosie reminded herself that it was only a wooden frame with a canvas roof and three canvas walls that made a slapping noise on breezy days.

Jesus was sitting on the narrow plank that was the sorting platform and she went around to the other side and jumped backwards to seat herself on the rim of a packing stand. "Well, tell me," she said without greeting, thinking her voice sounded reassuringly familiar.

"I saw you coming out the door," Jesus said. "I heard you running part of the way, too."

"Uh-huh," Rosie said. "Now tell me the secret."

"I was afraid you wouldn't come," he said.

Rosie delved around on the chicken-wire bottom of the stall for number two tomatoes, ripe, which she was sitting beside, and came up with a left-over that felt edible. She bit into it and began sucking out the pulp and seeds. "I'm here," she pointed out.

"Rosie, are you sorry you came?"

"Sorry? What for?" she said. "You said you were going to tell me something."

"I will, I will," Jesus said, but his voice contained disappointment, and Rosie fleetingly felt the older of the two, realizing a brand-new power which vanished without category under her recognition.

"I have to go back in a minute," she said. "My aunt and uncle are here from Wintersburg. I told them I was going to the privy."

Jesus laughed. "You funny thing," he said. "You slay me!"

"Just because you have a bathroom *inside,*" Rosie said. "Come on, tell me."

Chuckling, Jesus came around to lean on the stand facing her. They still could not see each other very clearly, but Rosie noticed that Jesus became very sober again as he took the hollow tomato from her hand and dropped it back into the stall. When he took hold of her empty hand, she could find no words to protest; her vocabulary had become distressingly constricted and she thought desperately that all that remained intact now was yes and no and oh, and even these few sounds would not easily out. Thus, kissed by Jesus, Rosie fell for the first time entirely victim to a helplessness delectable beyond speech. But the terrible, beautiful sensation lasted no more than a second, and the reality of Jesus' lips and tongue and teeth and hands made her pull away with such strength that she nearly tumbled.

Rosie stopped running as she approached the lights from the windows of home. How long since she had left? She could not guess, but gasping yet, she went to the privy in back and locked herself in. Her own breathing deafened her in the dark, close space, and she sat and waited until she could hear at last the nightly calling of the frogs and crickets. Even then, all she could think to say was oh, my, and the pressure of Jesus' face against her face would not leave.

No one had missed her in the parlor, however, and Rosie walked in and through quickly, announcing that she was next going to take a bath. "Your father's in the bathhouse," her mother said, and Rosie, in her room, recalled that she had not seen him when she entered. There had been only Aunt Taka and Uncle Gimpachi with her mother at the table, drinking tea. She got her robe and straw sandals and crossed the parlor again to go outside. Her mother was telling them about the *haiku* competition in the *Mainichi* and the poem she had entered.

Rosie met her father coming out of the bathhouse. "Are you through Father?" she asked. "I was going to ask you to scrub my back."

"Scrub your own back," he said shortly, going toward the main house.

"What have I done now?" she yelled after him. She suddenly felt like doing a lot of yelling. But he did not answer, and she went into the bathhouse. Turning on the dangling light, she removed her denims and T-shirt and threw them in the big carton for dirty clothes standing next to the washing machine. Her other things she took with her into the bath compartment to wash after her bath. After she had scooped a basin of hot water from the square wooden tub, she sat on the grey cement of the floor and soaped herself at exaggerated leisure, singing "Red Sails in the Sunset" at the top of her voice and using da-da-da where she suspected her words. Then, standing up, still singing, for she was possessed by the notion that any attempt now to analyze would result in spoilage and she believed that the larger her volume the less she would be able to hear herself think, she obtained more hot water and poured it on until she was free of lather. Only then did she allow herself to step into the steaming vat, one leg first, then the remainder of her body inch by inch until the water no longer stung and she could move around at will.

She took a long time soaking, afterwards remembering to go around outside to stoke the embers of the tin-lined fireplace beneath the tub and to throw on a few more sticks so that the water might keep its heat for her mother, and when she finally returned to the parlor, she found her mother still talking *haiku* with her aunt and uncle, the three of them on another round of tea. Her father was nowhere in sight.

At Japanese school the next day (Wednesday, it was), Rosie was grave and giddy by turns. Preoccupied at her desk in the row for students on Book Eight, she made up for it at recess by performing wild mimicry for the benefit of her friend Chizuko. She held her nose and whined a witticism or two in what she considered was the manner of Fred Allen; she assumed intoxication and a British accent to go over the climax of the Rudy Vallee recording of the pub conversation about William Ewart Gladstone; she was the child Shirley Temple piping, "On the Good Ship Lollipop"; she was the gentleman soprano of the Four Inkspots trilling, "If I Didn't Care." And she felt reasonably satisfied when Chizuko wept and gasped, "Oh, Rosie, you ought to be in the movies!"

Her father came after her at noon, bringing her sandwiches of minced ham and two nectarines to eat while she rode, so that she could pitch right into the sorting when they got home. The lugs were piling up, he said, and the ripe tomatoes in them would probably have to be taken to the cannery tomorrow if they were not ready for the produce haulers tonight. "This heat's not doing them any good. And we've got no time for a break today."

It *was* hot, probably the hottest day of the year, and Rosie's blouse stuck dampty to her back even under the protection of the canvas. But she worked as efficiently as a flawless machine and kept the stalls heaped, with one part of her mind listening in to the parental murmuring about the heat and the tomatoes and with another part planning the exact words she would say to Jesus when he drove up with the first load of the afternoon. But when at last she saw that the pick-up was coming, her hands went berserk and the tomatoes started falling in the wrong stalls, and her father said, "Hey, hey! Rosie, watch what you're doing!"

"Well, I have to go to the *benjo,*" she said, hiding panic.

"Go in the weeds over there," he said, only half-joking.

"Oh, Father!" she protested.

"Oh, go on home," her mother said. "We'll make out for awhile."

In the privy Rosie peered through a knothole toward the fields, watching as much as she could of Jesus. Happily she thought she saw him look in the direction of the house from time to time before he finished unloading and went back toward the patch where his mother and father worked. As she was heading for the shed, a very presentable black car purred up the dirt driveway to the house and its driver motioned to her. Was this the Hayashi home, he wanted to know. She nodded. Was she a Hayashi? Yes, she said, thinking that he was a good-looking man. He got out of the car with a huge, flat package and she saw that he warmly wore a business suit. "I have something here for your mother then," he said, in a more elegant Japanese than she was used to.

She told him where her mother was and he came along with her, patting his face with an immaculate white handkerchief and saying something about the coolness of San Francisco. To her surprised mother and father, he bowed and introduced himself as, among other things, the *haiku* editor of the *Mainichi Shimbun,* saying that since he had been coming as far as Los Angeles anyway, he had decided to bring her the first prize she had won in the recent contest.

"First prize?" her mother echoed, believing and not believing, pleased and overwhelmed. Handed the package with a bow, she bobbed her head up and down numerous times to express her utter gratitude.

"It is nothing much," he added, "but I hope it will serve as a token of our great appreciation for your contributions and our great admiration of your considerable talent."

"I am not worthy," she said, falling easily into his style. "It is I who should make some sign of my humble thanks for being permitted to contribute."

"No, no, to the contrary," he said, bowing again.

But Rosie's mother insisted, and then saying that she knew she was being unorthodox, she asked if she might open the package because her curiosity was so great. Certainly she might. In fact, he would like her reaction to it, for personally, it was one of his favorite *Hiroshiges.*

Rosie thought it was a pleasant picture, which looked to have been sketched with delicate quickness. There were pink clouds, containing some graceful calligraphy, and a sea that was a pale blue except at the edges, containing four sampans with indications of people in them. Pines edged the water and on the far-off beach there was a cluster of thatched huts towered over by pine-dotted mountains of grey and blue. The frame was scalloped and gilt.

After Rosie's mother pronounced it without peer and somewhat prodded her father into nodding agreement, she said Mr. Kuroda must at least have a cup of tea after coming all this way, and although Mr. Kuroda did not want to impose, he soon agreed that a cup of tea would be refreshing and went along with her to the house, carrying the picture for her.

"Ha, your mother's crazy!" Rosie's father said, and Rosie laughed uneasily as she resumed judgment on the tomatoes. She had emptied six lugs when he broke into an imaginary conversation with Jesus to tell her to go and remind her mother of the tomatoes, and she went slowly.

Mr. Kuroda was in his shirtsleeves expounding some *haiku* theory as he munched a rice cake, and her mother was rapt. Abashed in the great man's presence, Rosie stood next to her mother's chair until her mother looked up inquiringly, and then she started to whisper the message, but her mother pushed her gently away and reproached, "You are not being very polite to our guest."

"Father says the tomatoes . . ." Rosie said aloud, smiling foolishly.

"Tell him I shall only be a minute," her mother said, speaking the language of Mr. Kuroda.

When Rosie carried the reply to her father, he did not seem to hear and she said again, "Mother says she'll be back in a minute."

"All right, all right," he nodded, and they worked again in silence. But suddenly, her father uttered an incredible noise, exactly like the cork of a bottle popping, and the next Rosie knew, he was stalking angrily toward the house, almost running in fact, and she chased after him crying, "Father! Father! What are you going to do?"

He stopped long enough to order her back to the shed. "Never mind!" he shouted, "Get on with the sorting!"

And from the place in the fields where she stood, frightened and vacillating, Rosie saw her father enter the house. Soon Mr. Kuroda came out alone, putting on his coat. Mr. Kuroda got into his car and backed out down the driveway onto the highway. Next her father emerged, also alone, something in his arms (it was the picture, she realized), and, going over to the bathhouse woodpile, he threw the picture on the ground and picked up the axe. Smashing the picture, glass and all (she heard the explosion faintly), he reached over for the kerosene that was used to encourage the bath fire and poured it over the wreckage. I am dreaming, Rosie said to herself, I am dreaming, but her father, having made sure that his act of cremation was irrevocable, was even then returning to the fields.

Rosie ran past him and toward the house. What had become of her mother? She burst into the parlor and found her mother at the back window watching the dying fire. They watched together until there remained only a feeble smoke under the blazing sun. Her mother was very calm.

"Do you know why I married your father?" she said without turning.

"No," said Rosie. It was the most frightening question she had ever been called upon to answer. Don't tell me now, she wanted to say, tell me tomorrow, tell me next week, don't tell me today. But she knew she would be told now, that the telling would combine with the other violence of the hot afternoon to level her life, her world to the very ground.

It was like a story out of the magazines illustrated in sepia, which she had consumed so greedily for a period until the information had somehow reached her that those wretchedly unhappy autobiographies, offered to her as the testimonials of living men and women, were largely inventions: Her mother, at nineteen, had come to America and married her father as an alternative to suicide.

At eighteen she had been in love with the first son of one of the well-to-do families in her village. The two had met whenever and wherever they could, secretly, because it would not have done for his family to see him favor her—her father had no money; he was a drunkard and a gambler besides. She had learned she was with child; an excellent match had already been arranged for her lover. Despised by her family, she had given premature birth to a stillborn son, who would be seventeen now. Her family did not turn her out, but she could no longer project herself in any direction without refreshing in them the memory of her indiscretion. She wrote to Aunt Taka, her favorite sister in America, threatening to kill herself if Aunt Taka would not send for her. Aunt Taka hastily arranged a marriage with a young man of whom she knew, but lately arrived from Japan, a young man of simple mind, it was said, but of kindly heart. The young man was never told why his unseen betrothed was so eager to hasten the day of meeting.

The story was told perfectly, with neither groping for words nor untoward passion. It was as though her mother had memorized it by heart, reciting it to herself so many times over that its nagging vileness had long since gone.

"I had a brother then?" Rosie asked, for this was what seemed to matter now; she would think about the other later, she assured herself, pushing back the illumination which threatened all that darkness that had hitherto been merely mysterious or even glamorous. "A half-brother?"

"Yes."

"I would have liked a brother," she said.

Suddenly, her mother knelt on the floor and took her by the wrists. "Rosie," she said urgently, "Promise me you will never marry!" Shocked more by the request than the revelation, Rosie stared at her mother's face. Jesus, Jesus, she called silently, not certain whether she was invoking the help of the son of the Carrascos or of God, until there returned sweetly the memory of Jesus' hand, how it had touched her and where. Still her mother waited for an answer, holding her wrists so tightly that her hands were going numb. She tried to pull free. Promise, her mother whispered fiercely, promise. Yes, yes, I promise, Rosie said. But for an instant she turned away, and her mother, hearing the familiar glib agreement, released her. Oh, you, you, you, her eyes and twisted mouth said, you fool. Rosie, covering her face, began at last to cry, and the embrace and consoling hand came much later than she expected.

1949

Lawson Fusao Inada b. 1938

Lawson Inada is third-generation Japanese American, born and raised in Fresno, California. These autobiographical details are highlighted in Inada's volume of poetry *Legends from Camp:* Section II is titled "Fresno" and consists of poems that pay tribute to this agricultural region of California; Section I is titled "Camp," referring to the author's boyhood experience of internment during World War II along with other Japanese Americans. In his autobiographical recountings, Inada mentions going to the University of Iowa to study writing, then moving to Oregon. He has taught at Southern Oregon State College since 1966.

For both historical and aesthetic reasons, Lawson Inada is a significant figure in Asian American poetry and literature. He was one of the co-editors of the landmark anthology, *Aiiieeeee! An Anthology of Asian-American Writers,* and has participated in efforts to recover writing by earlier Japanese American authors such as Toshio Mori and John Okada. Legend has it that at a time of emerging Asian American consciousness but few visible Asian American writers, Frank Chin and his friends happened upon the book cover of *Down at the Santa Fe Depot* (1970), an anthology of Fresno-based poets. Struck by seeing an Asian face in the group photo of the poets, they discovered and contacted fellow Asian American writer Lawson Inada. Inada's collection *Before the War: Poems as They Happened* (1971) was one of the first Asian American single-author volumes of poetry from a major New York publishing house.

Inada's poetry stands out in its consistent engagement with jazz. *Before the War* begins with a whimsical portrait of a Japanese American figure playing "air bass"; includes tributes to jazz musicians and singers such as Charlie Parker, Lester Young, and Billie Holiday; and ends with poems written for Miles Davis and Charles Mingus. Riffing on the term "bluesman," Inada calls himself a "campsman," suggesting that his blues derive from Japanese American internment. He describes his project as "blowing shakuhachi versaphone" and cites jazz as the strongest influence on his writing. Leslie Marmon Silko calls Inada "a poet-musician in the tradition of Walt Whitman and James A. Wright."

Inada won the American Book Award in 1994 for *Legends from Camp* and was named Oregon State Poet of the Year in 1991. He has received a number of poetry fellowships from the National Endowment for the Arts and has performed his poetry in concert with numerous musicians. His poetics of performance posits his art not as an object that transcends time but as a process that shapes time. Calling live performance his favorite form of "publishing," Inada appropriates the value that is ascribed to a finalized, written text for a mode that is oral and dynamic.

Inada's poetics suggest that there is more than one way to tell a story, that many stories are embedded within a given story or within what we know as history. This multiple sense of time implicitly critiques the notion of a standard time or history that is equivalent for all subjects. Poems such as "Instructions to All Persons" and "Two Variations on a Theme by Thelonious Monk" shape time and history as variable and layered. "On Being Asian American" refers to an echo generated by the actualization of the racial subject. We can see a poetics of the echo in the repetition enacted in this poem as well as in the poems "Instructions" and "Two Variations." This repetition is what Henry Louis Gates, Jr., calls "repetition with a difference": a non-linear, non-teleological aesthetics of change.

Juliana Chang
Santa Clara University

PRIMARY WORKS

Before the War: Poems as They Happened, 1971; *The Buddha Bandits Down Highway 99,* with Garrett Kaoru Hongo and Alan Chong Lau, 1978; *Legends from Camp,* 1992; *Drawing the Line,* 1997.

Presidio of San Francisco, California
May 3, 1942

INSTRUCTIONS TO ALL PERSONS OF JAPANESE ANCESTRY

Living in the Following Area:

All of that portion of the City of Los Angeles, State of California, within that boundary beginning at the point at which North Figueroa Street meets a line following the middle of the Los Angeles River; thence southerly and following the said line to East First Street; thence westerly on East First Street to Alameda Street; thence southerly on Alameda Street to East Third Street; thence northwesterly on East Third Street to Main Street; thence northerly on Main Street to First Street; thence northwesterly on First Street to Figueroa Street; thence northeasterly on Figueroa Street to the point of beginning.

Pursuant to the provisions of Civilian Exclusion Order No. 33, this Headquarters, dated May 3, 1942, all persons of Japanese ancestry, both alien and non-alien, will be evacuated from the above area by 12 o'clock noon, P. W. T., Saturday, May 9, 1942.

No Japanese person living in the above area will be permitted to change residence after 12 o'clock noon, P. W. T., Sunday, May 3, 1942, without obtaining special permission from the representative of the Commanding General, Southern California Sector, at the Civil Control Station located at:

Japanese Union Church,
120 North San Pedro Street,
Los Angeles, California.

Such permits will only be granted for the purpose of uniting members of a family, or in cases of grave emergency.

The Civil Control Station is equipped to assist the Japanese population affected by this evacuation in the following ways:

1. Give advice and instructions on the evacuation.
2. Provide services with respect to the management, leasing, sale, storage or other disposition of most kinds of property, such as real estate, business and professional equipment, household goods, boats, automobiles and livestock.
3. Provide temporary residence elsewhere for all Japanese in family groups.
4. Transport persons and a limited amount of clothing and equipment to their new residence.

The Following Instructions Must Be Observed:

1. A responsible member of each family, preferably the head of the family, or the person in whose name most of the property is held, and each individual living alone, will report to the Civil Control Station to receive further instructions. This must be done between 8:00 A. M. and 5:00 P. M. on Monday, May 4, 1942, or between 8:00 A. M. and 5:00 P. M. on Tuesday, May 5, 1942.
2. Evacuees must carry with them on departure for the Assembly Center, the following property:
(a) Bedding and linens (no mattress) for each member of the family;
(b) Toilet articles for each member of the family;
(c) Extra clothing for each member of the family;
(d) Sufficient knives, forks, spoons, plates, bowls and cups for each member of the family;
(e) Essential personal effects for each member of the family.

All items carried will be securely packaged, tied and plainly marked with the name of the owner and numbered in accordance with instructions obtained at the Civil Control Station. The size and number of packages is limited to that which can be carried by the individual or family group.

3. No pets of any kind will be permitted.
4. No personal items and no household goods will be shipped to the Assembly Center.
5. The United States Government through its agencies will provide for the storage, at the sole risk of the owner, of the more substantial household items, such as iceboxes, washing machines, pianos and other heavy furniture. Cooking utensils and other small items will be accepted for storage if crated, packed and plainly marked with the name and address of the owner. Only one name and address will be used by a given family.
6. Each family, and individual living alone, will be furnished transportation to the Assembly Center or will be authorized to travel by private automobile in a supervised group. All instructions pertaining to the movement will be obtained at the Civil Control Station.

Go to the Civil Control Station between the hours of 8:00 A.M. and 500 P.M., Monday, May 4, 1942, or between the hours of 8:00 A.M. and 5:00 P.M., Tuesday, May 5, 1942, to receive further instructions.

J. L. DeWITT
Lieutenant General, U. S. Army
Commanding

SEE CIVILIAN EXCLUSION ORDER NO. 33.

Instructions to All Persons

Let us take
what we can
for the occasion:

Ancestry. (*Ancestry*)
All of that portion. (*Portion*)
With the boundary. (*Boundary*)
Beginning. (*Beginning*)
At the point. (*Point*)
Meets a line. (*Line*)
Following the middle. (*Middle*)
Thence southerly. (*Southerly*)
Following the said line. (*Following*) (*Said*)
Thence westerly. (*Westerly*)
Thence northerly. (*Northerly*)
To the point. (*Point*)
Of beginning. (*Beginning*) (*Ancestry*)

Let us bring
what we need
for the meeting:

Provisions. (*Provisions*)
Permission. (*Permission*)
Commanding. (*Commanding*)
Uniting. (*Uniting*)
Family (*Family*)

Let us have
what we have
for the gathering:

Civil. (*Civil*)
Ways. (*Ways*)
Services. (*Services*)

Respect. (*Respect*)
Management. (*Management*)
Kinds. (*Kinds*)
Goods. (*Goods*)
For all. (*All*)

Let us take
what we can
for the occasion:

Responsible.
Individual.
Sufficient.
Personal.
Securely.
Civil.
Substantial.
Accepted.
Given.
Authorized.

Let there be
Order.

Let us be
Wise.

1992

Two Variations on a Theme by Thelonious Monk as Inspired by Mal Waldron

INTRODUCTION: MONK'S PROSODY

"I can't do that right. I have to practice that."
—Thelonious Monk, composer, to his pianist (himself) during a solo run-through of "Round Midnight," April 5, 1957

April 5, 1957: Maybe I'm sitting on a fire escape in Berkeley, trying to write some poetry. I know one thing: I was listening to Monk by then—particularly his solo on "Bags' Groove," on the Miles Davis 10-inch lp. You might say I was studying Monk's prosody—how each time he'd come out of the speakers in a different, distinctive way, and always swinging.

Years pass. Decades. Prosody.

January 15, 1987: I work a duo concert with Mal Waldron. Mal, even while checking out the tuning, makes reference, says hello, to Monk. The next time we blow, I want to do "Blue Monk."

June, 1987: Whenever the next time is, I'll be ready. I work out a linear, horn-like statement; it fits, like an overlay. Then I jump right into the tune and the piano, and blow something from the inside out—percussive—particularly building around and repeating "ricochet."

April, 1988: One of those long Oregon dusks. Larry Smith, editor of Caliban, calls up to ask if I'd be interested in doing something with Monk's prosody. Prosody—yeah. I have to practice that.

I. Blue Monk (linear)

Solid, as the man himself would say.
Solid, as the man at his instrument.
Solid, as the solid composition.

However, at the same time,
this elegant melody,
"Blue Monk,"

while certainly being solid enough—
as evidenced by
the ease of our ability
to hum and whistle it,
even in sleep—

is actually solid, fluid,
and a real gas combined;

you know what I mean:
like feelings, like atmosphere,
like right, like here,

you feel like you've been hearing
"Blue Monk" forever,
since the planet started dancing,
like its been around since sound,

since the blue wind got up
one blue summer morning,
looked across the cool, blue canyon
at that sweet, blue mountain,
and melodiously started to sing
"Blue Monk";
you know that lovely feeling,
"Blue Monk";
you know what

"Blue Monk" can do for you,
the melodious message it sends,
the melodious message that always comes
echoing back across the canyons as a result;
"Blue Monk,"

as a result of recognition,
as a consequence of confirmation,
as an accomplishment of affirmation—
"Blue Monk,"
"Blue Monk"
in the sun and rain, in all conditions;

and the song, therefore,
just by being what it is—
these huge, blue feelings
spaced and placed just so,
ascending,
these huge, blue feelings
descending, just so,
and including some delightful
dimensions for refreshment
on a huge, blue plateau.

"Blue Monk," then, by its very nature,
built into its basic structure,
encompasses and contains
all the properties of nature:

take a hold of it,
hold it up to the light;
see what I mean?—
"Blue Monk" has you dancing;

by now you're feeling confident about the song,
feeling like you've got it down,
feeling like you're part of its beauty,
feeling like it's part of you—
which is certainly true;

feeling fine with the freedom of it;
feeling like going for it
with expansiveness, abandon;

feeling exhilarated in your bones
like you want to do something about
exercising your own right
to rhythm and expression,

yes, you feel like you own the song—
which you certainly do—
since you went right down there on West 52nd Street
and got it directly from the man himself,
Blue Monk, who turns out to be,
not the imposing artist you had heard and read about,
but just the husband, the father, the neighbor
making his way out of the corner grocery
with some snow peas and stalks of celery
sticking out of a paper sack,
he just needs something back,
gladly giving you the tune
in exchange for a proven recipe of your own;

meanwhile, Blue Monk is smiling
that solid Blue Monk smile
while offering you directions for usage:

"Look, 'Blue Monk' is a solid song;
you can bend it; you can break it;
you can always remake it;
it's hot and it's cool,
it's suitable for digging
in whatever occasion you choose—
ceremonious, thelonious and such . . ."

Ah, the sheer joy of such ownership!
You take "Blue Monk" home and set it
glowing in your living room
like a luxurious lamp.
You stick it in the phone,
sending it out via satellite:

"Hello, Mom? Dig this song!"
"Hello, is this the White House?
Listen, I've got a solid
new anthem for the shaky republic!"

You take "Blue Monk" outside to the fire escape,
seeing how far you can throw it,
looping it smoothly over the moonlit harbor
as it becomes a bridge
of flowing blue lights:
"Blue Monk."
You're dancing, humming,
strolling slowly across,
tossing blue notes
floating over the wide, blue water

like you're a luminous, musical spider;
tossing cool, blue clusters high overhead,
creating a blue, musical constellation:
"Blue Monk";

by now, many others,
including birds, animals, insects,
have joined you on your excursion,
having just got wise
to mythology and fireworks combined,
staring awestruck up into the huge, blue night
to find the Blue Monk profile outlined,
pointing out and humming
each huge, blue star in the melody—
and, oh, those sweet, blue spaces in between . . .

Yes, indeed, this is some kind
of luxurious structure,
in architectural legacy

ascending, descending, with pliable plateaus
for ease of breathing, handling,
relaxing, building, dancing, laughing,
praying, creating, embracing, enhancing;

a structure as solid, fluid, strong,
translucent, luminous, freeing,
and bracing
as the man himself—

Mr. Blue Monk,
bringing everything we do,
we see, we know,
into melodious focus

through the blue keys
of his blue piano;

therefore, in this blue region,
with this blue vision, in this blue
body of being
we all know as home,
everything throbs and pulses and glows
with the true, blue beauty of his song:

"Blue Monk"!

II. "Blue Monk" (percussive)

Ricochet:

Radius:
Radiating:

Reciting: Realizing: Referring: Recapturing: Repercussion:
Revolving: Reflecting: Returning: Reconstituting: Republic:
Reshaping: Restructuring: Reversing: Reclaiming: Religion:
Respecting: Removing: Reforming: Receiving: Reality:
Refining: Reducing: Refreshing: Regenerating: Resource:
Regarding: Relating: Relaxing: Revering: Remembering:
Renewing: Revising: Repairing: Replacing: Residing:
Reviewing: Respecting: Resolving: Reviving: Responsible:
Retaining: Resuming: Revealing: Rehearsing: Resulting:
Restoring: Retrieving: Regaining: Recovering: Relying:
Redeeming: Replying: Reminding: Rewarding: Resounding:

Reverberating:

Remarkably:

Releasing:

Remaining:

Repeating:

1992

Kicking the Habit

Late last night, I decided to
stop using English.
I had been using it all day—

talking all day,
listening all day,
thinking all day,
reading all day,
remembering all day,
feeling all day,

and even driving all day,
in English—

when, finally I decided to
stop.

So I pulled off the main highway
onto a dark country road
and kept on going and going
until I emerged in another nation and . . .
stopped.

There, the insects
inspected my passport, the frogs
investigated my baggage, and the trees
pointed out lights in the sky,
saying,
"Shhhhlllyyymmm"—

and I, of course, replied.
After all, I was a foreigner,
and had to comply . . .

Now don't get me wrong:
There's nothing "wrong"
with English,

and I'm not complaining
about the language
which is my native tongue.
I make my living with the lingo;
I was even in England once.
So you might say I'm actually
addicted to it;
yes, I'm an Angloholic,
and I can't get along without the stuff:
It controls my life.

Until last night, that is.
Yes, I had had it
with the habit.

I was exhausted,
burned out,
by the habit.
And I decided to
kick the habit,
cold turkey,
right then and there
on the spot!

And, in so doing, I kicked
open the door of a cage

and stepped out from confinement
into the greater world.

Tentatively, I uttered,

"Chemawa? Chinook?"

and the pines said

"Clackamas, Siskiyou."

And before long, everything else
chimed in with their two cents' worth
and we had a fluid and fluent
conversation going,

communicating, expressing,
echoing whatever we needed to
know, know, know . . .

What was it like?
Well, just listen:

Ah, the exquisite seasonings
of syllables, the consummate consonants, the vigorous
vowels of varied vocabularies

clicking, ticking, humming,
growling, throbbing, strumming—

coming from all parts of orifices, surfaces,
in creative combinations, orchestrations,
resonating in rhythm with the atmosphere!

I could have remained there
forever—as I did, and will.
And when I resumed my way,
my stay could no longer be

"ordinary"—

as they say,
as *we* say, in English.

For on the road of life,
in the code of life,

there's much more to red than

"stop,"

there's much more to green than

"go,"

and there's much, much more to yellow than

"caution,"

for as the yellow
sun clearly enunciated to me this morning:

"Fusao. Inada."

1997

On Being Asian American

for our children

Of course, not everyone
can be an Asian American.
Distinctions are earned,
and deserve dedication.

Thus, from time of birth,
the journey awaits you—
ventures through time,
the turns of the earth.

When you seem to arrive,
the journey continues;
when you seem to arrive,
the journey continues.

Take me as I am, you cry,
I, I, am an individual.
Which certainly is true.
Which generates an echo.

Who are all your people
assembled in celebration,
with wisdom and strength,
to which you are entitled.

For you are at the head
of succeeding generations,
as the rest of the world
comes forward to greet you.

As the rest of the world
comes forward to greet you.

1992

James Merrill 1926–1995

At the time of his death in February 1995, James Merrill was considered by many critics and readers of poetry to be among the central American lyric poets of the post–World War II generation. Merrill's work is characterized by his wit and penchant for puns in a conversational tone, playful language full of ellipses, and internal questions. His poetry is elegant and allusive with references to writers (especially Proust, Rilke, Yeats, and Stevens) and to music and opera. Merrill strives to commingle art and life—most notably observed in his poetry's casual yet open discussion of his homosexuality.

Merrill often joked that by the time he was five years old he was rich. As the son of Charles Merrill—a founding member of the investment firm of Merrill Lynch Pierce Fenner and Smith—and Charles's second wife, Hellen Ingram, James was indeed rich, and a trust fund ensured his financial freedom for the rest of his life. James Merrill was born on March 3, 1926, and grew up in New York City in an apartment on West Eleventh Street (mythologized in "18 West 11th Street" in *Braving the Elements*) and in a mansion in Southampton, New York, built by the architect Stanford White. Merrill had a privileged education attending the Lawrenceville School, a private preparatory school in Princeton. His father offered him little choice but to attend Amherst College, his alma mater, a sign of the parental pressure that Charles exerted over his son. Merrill graduated from Amherst in 1947. Charles hoped that his son would follow in his footsteps and work for the family firm; however, Charles soon realized that his son's interests and ambitions lay elsewhere. At Lawrenceville, Merrill began to write poems. His first collection, *Jim's Book,* was privately published by Charles. Merrill later renounced it as embarrassing juvenilia. His subsequent collection, *First Poems,* was published in 1951 when Merrill was twenty-five years old.

Merrill was prolific. He published fifteen volumes of poetry, two novels, a collection of essays, and a memoir. He was also well prized for his work, receiving the Pulitzer Prize (1977), two National Book Awards (1967 and 1979), the Bollingen Prize (1973), the National Book Critics Circle Award (1984), and the first Bobbitt National Prize for Poetry awarded by the Library of Congress (1988).

As an adult, Merrill traveled frequently. Beginning in 1950, he spent several years in Europe. His memoir, *A Different Person,* based on his European journey, also chronicles his psychoanalytic travels toward an acceptance of his homosexuality. After Merrill returned to the United States, he moved to Stonington, Connecticut, with his lover David Jackson. They bought a house there but soon collected other residences, spending part of every year in Greece and, later, Key West. The poet's travels and houses became the subjects for many of his poems. His 1962 collection, *Water Street,* was named after the street on which Merrill and Jackson shared a house in Stonington. Merrill's poems focus more on places than on the persons in them.

His magnum opus, *The Changing Light at Sandover,* a 560-page epic in three books, was "dictated" to Merrill and Jackson through the medium of a Ouija board. In the first book, *The Book of Ephraim,* Merrill's speaker looks at a painting by Giorgione called "La Tempesta" and tells us that x-rays of the painting reveal a "Nude arisen" from "flowing water which no longer fills/ The eventual foreground." The lesson learned from this x-ray vision into the painting's life follows: "Images that hint/At meanings we had missed by simply looking." True to his words, Merrill's poetry requires more than a surface looking—beyond the intricately laced language and into the poet himself. As Helen Vendler wrote, reviewing *Braving the Elements,* Merrill's poems provide "the interpretation of life voiced by poetry."

Peter Nickowitz
New York University

PRIMARY SOURCES

Poetry: *First Poems,* 1951; *The Country of a Thousand Years of Peace,* 1959; *Water Street,* 1962; *Nights and Days,* 1966; *The Fire Screen,* 1969; *Braving the Elements,* 1972; *Divine Comedies,* 1976; *Mirabell: Books of Number,* 1978; *Scripts for the Pageant,* 1980; *The Changing Light at Sandover,* 1982; *From the First Nine: Poems 1946–1976,* 1982; *Late Settings,* 1985; *The Inner Room,* 1988; *Selected Poems 1946–1985,* 1992; *A Scattering of Salts,* 1995. Prose: *The (Diblos) Notebook,* 1965; *The Seraglio,* 1957; *Recitative,* 1986; *A Different Person,* 1993.

An Urban Convalescence

Out for a walk, after a week in bed,
I find them tearing up part of my block
And, chilled through, dazed and lonely, join the dozen
In meek attitudes, watching a huge crane
Fumble luxuriously in the filth of years.
Her jaws dribble rubble. An old man
Laughs and curses in her brain,
Bringing to mind the close of *The White Goddess.*[1]

As usual in New York, everything is torn down
Before you have had time to care for it.
Head bowed, at the shrine of noise, let me try to recall
What building stood here. Was there a building at all?
I have lived on this same street for a decade.

Wait. Yes. Vaguely a presence rises
Some five floors high, of shabby stone
—Or am I confusing it with another one
In another part of town, or of the world?—
And over its lintel into focus vaguely
Misted with blood (my eyes are shut)
A single garland sways, stone fruit, stone leaves,
Which years of grit had etched until it thrust

[1] Robert Graves's seminal study of myths involving dying gods and mourning goddesses. Often compared with James G. Frazer's *The Golden Bough.*

Roots down, even into the poor soil of my seeing.
When did the garland become part of me?
I ask myself, amused almost,
Then shiver once from head to toe,

Transfixed by a particular cheap engraving of garlands
Bought for a few francs long ago,
All calligraphic tendril and cross-hatched rondure,
Ten years ago, and crumpled up to stanch
Boughs dripping, whose white gestures filled a cab,
And thought of neither then nor since.
Also, to clasp them, the small, red-nailed hand
Of no one I can place. Wait. No. Her name, her features
Lie toppled underneath that year's fashions.
The words she must have spoken, setting her face
To fluttering like a veil, I cannot hear now,
Let alone understand.

So that I am already on the stair,
As it were, of where I lived,
When the whole structure shudders at my tread
And soundlessly collapses, filling
The air with motes of stone.
Onto the still erect building next door
Are pressed levels and hues—
Pocked rose, streaked greens, brown whites.
Who drained the pousse-café?[2]
Wires and pipes, snapped off at the roots, quiver.

Well, that is what life does. I stare
A moment longer, so. And presently
The massive volume of the world
Closes again.

Upon that book I swear
To abide by what it teaches:
Gospels of ugliness and waste,
Of towering voids, of soiled gusts,
Of a shrieking to be faced
Full into, eyes astream with cold—

With cold?
All right then. With self-knowledge.

[2]An after-dinner liqueur.

Indoors at last, the pages of *Time* are apt
To open, and the illustrated mayor of New York,
Given a glimpse of how and where I work,
To note yet one more house that can be scrapped.

Unwillingly I picture
My walls weathering in the general view.
It is not even as though the new
Buildings did very much for architecture.

Suppose they did. The sickness of our time requires
That these as well be blasted in their prime.
You would think the simple fact of having lasted
Threatened our cities like mysterious fires.

There are certain phrases which to use in a poem
Is like rubbing silver with quicksilver.[3] Bright
But facile, the glamour deadens overnight,
For instance, how "the sickness of our time"

Enhances, then debases, what I feel.
At my desk I swallow in a glass of water
No longer cordial, scarcely wet, a pill
They had told me not to take until much later.

With the result that back into my imagination
The city glides, like cities seen from the air,
Mere smoke and sparkle to the passenger
Having in mind another destination

Which now is not that honey-slow descent
Of the Champs-Elysées,[4] her hand in his,
But the dull need to make some kind of house
Out of the life lived, out of the love spent.

1962

[3]Mercury.
[4]A fashionable Paris boulevard.

The Broken Home

Crossing the street,
I saw the parents and the child
At their window, gleaming like fruit
With evening's mild gold leaf.

In a room on the floor below,
Sunless, cooler—a brimming
Saucer of wax, marbly and dim—
I have lit what's left of my life.

I have thrown out yesterday's milk
And opened a book of maxims.
The flame quickens. The word stirs.

Tell me, tongue of fire,
That you and I are as real
At least as the people upstairs.

My father, who had flown in World War I,
Might have continued to invest his life
In cloud banks well above Wall Street and wife.
But the race was run below, and the point was to win.

Too late now, I make out in his blue gaze
(Through the smoked glass of being thirty-six)
The soul eclipsed by twin black pupils, sex
And business; time was money in those days.

Each thirteenth year he married. When he died
There were already several chilled wives
In sable orbit—rings, cars, permanent waves.
We'd felt him warming up for a green bride.

He could afford it. He was "in his prime"
At three score ten. But money was not time.

When my parents were younger this was a popular act:
A veiled woman would leap from an electric, wine-dark car
To the steps of no matter what—the Senate or the Ritz Bar—
And bodily, at newsreel speed, attack

No matter whom—Al Smith or José Maria Sert
Or Clemenceau[1]—veins standing out on her throat
As she yelled *War mongerer! Pig! Give us the vote!,*
And would have to be hauled away in her hobble skirt.

What had the man done? Oh, made history.
Her business (he had implied) was giving birth,
Tending the house, mending the socks.

Always that same old story—
Father Time and Mother Earth,
A marriage on the rocks.

One afternoon, red, satyr-thighed[2]
Michael, the Irish setter, head
Passionately lowered, led
The child I was to a shut door. Inside,

Blinds beat sun from the bed.
The green-gold room throbbed like a bruise.
Under a sheet, clad in taboos
Lay whom we sought, her hair undone, outspread,

And of a blackness found, if ever now, in old
Engravings where the acid bit.
I must have needed to touch it
Or the whiteness—was she dead?
Her eyes flew open, startled strange and cold.
The dog slumped to the floor. She reached for me. I fled.

Tonight they have stepped out onto the gravel.
The party is over. It's the fall
Of 1931. They love each other still.

She: Charlie, I can't stand the pace.
He: Come on, honey—why, you'll bury us all!

A lead soldier guards my windowsill:
Khaki rifle, uniform, and face.
Something in me grows heavy, silvery, pliable.

[1]Alfred E. Smith (1873–1944), a governor of New York and a presidential candidate in 1928, José Maria Sert (1876–1945), a Spanish painter who decorated the lobby of the Waldorf-Astoria hotel in New York, Georges Clemenceau (1841–1929), premiere of France during World War I.

[2]Having hairy thighs like a satyr, a woodland deity from Greek mythology having the head and body of a man and the legs of a goat.

How intensely people used to feel!
Like metal poured at the close of a proletarian novel,
Refined and glowing from the crucible,
I see those two hearts, I'm afraid,
Still. Cool here in the graveyard of good and evil,
They are even so to be honored and obeyed.

. . . Obeyed, at least, inversely. Thus
I rarely buy a newspaper, or vote.
To do so, I have learned, is to invite
The tread of a stone guest within my house.

Shooting this rusted bolt, though, against him,
I trust I am no less time's child than some
Who on the heath impersonate Poor Tom[3]
Or on the barricades risk life and limb.

Nor do I try to keep a garden, only
An avocado in a glass of water—
Roots pallid, gemmed with air. And later,

When the small gilt leaves have grown
Fleshy and green, I let them die, yes, yes,
And start another. I am earth's no less.

A child, a red dog roam the corridors,
Still, of the broken home. No sound. The brilliant
Rag runners halt before wide-open doors.
My old room! Its wallpaper—cream, medallioned
With pink and brown—brings back the first nightmares,
Long summer colds, and Emma, sepia-faced,
Perspiring over broth carried upstairs,
Aswim with golden fats I could not taste.

The real house became a boarding-school.
Under the ballroom ceiling's allegory
Someone at last may actually be allowed
To learn something; or, from my window, cool
With the unstiflement of the entire story,
Watch a red setter stretch and sink in cloud.

1966

[3]Edgar, a character in Shakespeare's *King Lear,* wanders the heath after being disowned by his father, pretending to be a madman and calling himself "Poor Tom."

The Victor Dog

for Elizabeth Bishop[1]

Bix to Buxtehude to Boulez,
The little white dog on the Victor label
Listens long and hard as he is able.
It's all in a day's work, whatever plays.

From judgment, it would seem, he has refrained.
He even listens earnestly to Bloch,
Then builds a church upon our acid rock.
He's man's—no—he's the Leiermann's best friend,

Or would be if hearing and listening were the same.
Does he hear? I fancy he rather smells
Those lemon-gold arpeggios in Ravel's
"Les jets d'eau du palais de ceux qui s'aiment."

He ponders the Schumann Concerto's tall willow hit
By lightning, and stays put. When he surmises
Through one of Bach's eternal boxwood mazes
The oboe pungent as a bitch in heat,

Or when the calypso decants its raw bay rum
Or the moon in *Wozzeck* reddens ripe for murder,
He doesn't sneeze or howl; just listens harder.
Adamant needles bear down on him from

Whirling of outer space, too black, too near—
But he was taught as a puppy not to flinch,
Much less to imitate his bête noire Blanche
Who barked, fat foolish creature, at King Lear.

Still others fought in the road's filth over Jezebel,
Slavered on hearths of horned and pelted barons.
His forebears lacked, to say the least, forbearance.
Can nature change in him? Nothing's impossible.

The last chord fades. The night is cold and fine.
His master's voice rasps through the grooves' bare groves.
Obediently, in silence like the grave's
He sleeps there on the still-warm gramophone

Only to dream he is at the première of a Handel
Opera long thought lost—*Il Cane Minore.*

[1]A fellow poet and friend of Merrill's.

Its allegorical subject is his story!
A little dog revolving round a spindle

Gives rise to harmonies beyond belief,
A cast of stars. . . . Is there in Victor's heart
No honey for the vanquished? Art is art.
The life it asks of us is a dog's life.

1972

John Ashbery b. 1927

John Ashbery was born in Rochester, New York, and attended Harvard University, where he met the poets Frank O'Hara and Kenneth Koch. Later, these college friends moved to New York City, where they formed the core of the so-called New York School, noted for its use of popular imagery, surrealistic turns of thought, and high-spirited humor. After college Ashbery worked for Oxford University Press and McGraw-Hill. "The Instruction Manual" dates from those days.

In 1956, awarded a Fulbright fellowship, Ashbery moved to France and worked as an art journalist, a profession he followed for the next thirty years, writing for such magazines as *Art International, New York,* and *Newsweek.* In 1965, he returned to New York to become executive editor of *Art News.* In 1974, he joined the faculty of Brooklyn College, where he served as Distinguished Professor. He now teaches at Bard College, where he is the Charles P. Stevenson Professor of Languages and Literature.

Ashbery is one of the few poets who has been able to gain the admiration of both experimental artists and conservative academicians, winning virtually all the major literary prizes this country has to offer. In "Farm Implements and Rutabagas in a Landscape," for example, he sets his outrageous installment of Popeye in the form of a sestina, one of the most difficult poetic forms. Thus the poem combines untraditional subject matter with highly traditional form.

Many of Ashbery's chief preoccupations are also traditional ones, which he treats in an unusually charged and avant-garde manner. One important theme running through virtually all of his work is "mutability," a central theme of the English Renaissance and American Transcendentalists. For older writers and thinkers, the mutable or changeable world of human and natural affairs is contrasted to the eternal, fixed world of the spirit and ideas. Some poets, including Wallace Stevens—one of the strongest influences on Ashbery—prefer the mutable to the eternal.

Yet another topic informed by the theme of mutability is the self: is our consciousness fixed and unitary or fluid and multiple? Many poems try to catch the mind even as it changes shape, for what is empathy but the power to take on another person's consciousness, or the imagination but the ability to transform the experiences around us into something very different? Reality for Ashbery is not a hard, fixed, or certain entity but an awareness brimming with impressions, memories, and desires which are constantly transformed, repeated, blurred, and blotted out.

David Bergman
Towson University

PRIMARY WORKS

Some Trees, 1956 (Yale Younger Poets series); *The Tennis Court Oath,* 1962; *Rivers and Mountains,* 1966; *A Nest of Ninnies,* 1969 (novel with James Schuyler); *The Double Dream of Spring,* 1970; *Three Poems,* 1972; *The Vermont Notebook,* 1975; *Self Portrait in a Convex Mirror,* 1975 (winner of the Pulitzer Prize, National Book Award, and the National Book Critics Circle Award); *Houseboat Days,* 1978; *Three Plays,* 1978; *As We Know,* 1979; *Shadow Train,* 1981; *A Wave,* 1984; *Selected Poems,* 1985; *April Galleons,* 1987; *Reported Sightings: Art Chronicles 1957–87,* 1989; *Flow Chart,* 1991; *Hotel L'Autreamont,* 1993; *And the Stars Were Shining,* 1994; *Can You Hear, Bird,* 1995; *Girls on the Run,* 1999.

The Instruction Manual

As I sit looking out of a window of the building
I wish I did not have to write the instruction manual on the uses
of a new metal.
I look down into the street and see people, each walking with an
inner peace,
And envy them—they are so far away from me!
Not one of them has to worry about getting out this manual on
schedule.
And, as my way is, I begin to dream, resting my elbows on the
desk and leaning out of the window a little,
Of dim Guadalajara![1] City of rose-colored flowers!
City I wanted most to see, and most did not see, in Mexico!
But I fancy I see, under the press of having to write the
instruction manual,
Your public square, city, with its elaborate little bandstand!
The band is playing *Scheherazade* by Rimsky-Korsakov.[2]
Around stand the flower girls, handing out rose- and lemon-
colored flowers,
Each attractive in her rose-and-blue striped dress (Oh! such shades
of rose and blue),
And nearby is the little white booth where women in green serve
you green and yellow fruit.
The couples are parading; everyone is in a holiday mood.
First, leading the parade, is a dapper fellow
Clothed in deep blue. On his head sits a white hat

[1]Guadalajara is the second largest city in Mexico, 275 miles west-northwest of Mexico City. Mariachi bands originated in Guadalajara.

[2]Rimsky-Korsakov (1844–1908) was one of the finest Russian composers of his time. *Scheherazade* (1888) was composed for the Russian Ballet and celebrates the dancing-girl who preserved her life by weaving the thousand-and-one stories of the *Arabian Nights.*

And he wears a mustache, which has been trimmed for the occasion.
His dear one, his wife, is young and pretty; her shawl is rose, pink, and white.
Her slippers are patent leather, in the American fashion,
And she carries a fan, for she is modest, and does not want the crowd to see her face too often.
But everybody is so busy with his wife or loved one
I doubt they would notice the mustachioed man's wife.
Here come the boys! They are skipping and throwing little things on the sidewalk
Which is made of gray tile. One of them, a little older, has a toothpick in his teeth.
He is silenter than the rest, and affects not to notice the pretty young girls in white.
But his friends notice them, and shout their jeers at the laughing girls.
Yet soon all this will cease, with the deepening of their years,
And love bring each to the parade grounds for another reason.
But I have lost sight of the young fellow with the toothpick.
Wait—there he is—on the other side of the bandstand,
Secluded from his friends, in earnest talk with a young girl
Of fourteen or fifteen. I try to hear what they are saying
But it seems they are just mumbling something—shy words of love, probably.
She is slightly taller than he, and looks quietly down into his sincere eyes.
She is wearing white. The breeze ruffles her long fine black hair against her olive cheek.
Obviously she is in love. The boy, the young boy with the toothpick, he is in love too;
His eyes show it. Turning from this couple,
I see there is an intermission in the concert.
The paraders are resting and sipping drinks through straws
(The drinks are dispensed from a large glass crock by a lady in dark blue),
And the musicians mingle among them, in their creamy white uniforms, and talk
About the weather, perhaps, or how their kids are doing at school.

Let us take this opportunity to tiptoe into one of the side streets.
Here you may see one of those white houses with green trim
That are so popular here. Look—I told you!
It is cool and dim inside, but the patio is sunny.
An old woman in gray sits there, fanning herself with a palm leaf fan.
She welcomes us to her patio, and offers us a cooling drink.

"My son is in Mexico City," she says? "He would welcome you too
If he were here. But his job is with a bank there.
Look, here is a photograph of him."
And a dark-skinned lad with pearly teeth grins out at us from the worn leather frame.
We thank her for her hospitality, for it is getting late
And we must catch a view of the city, before we leave, from a good high place.
That church tower will do—the faded pink one, there against the fierce blue of the sky. Slowly we enter.
The caretaker, an old man dressed in brown and gray, asks us how long we have been in the city, and how we like it here.
His daughter is scrubbing the steps—she nods to us as we pass into the tower.
Soon we have reached the top, and the whole network of the city extends before us.
There is the rich quarter, with its houses of pink and white, and its crumbling, leafy terraces.
There is the poorer quarter, its homes a deep blue.
There is the market, where men are selling hats and swatting flies
And there is the public library, painted several shades of pale green and beige.
Look! There is the square we just came from, with the promenaders.
There are fewer of them, now that the heat of the day has increased,
But the young boy and girl still lurk in the shadows of the bandstand.
And there is the home of the little old lady—
She is still sitting in the patio, fanning herself.
How limited, but how complete withal, has been our experience of Guadalajara!
We have seen young love, married love, and the love of an aged mother for her son.
We have heard the music, tasted the drinks, and looked at colored houses.
What more is there to do, except stay? And that we cannot do.
And as a last breeze freshens the top of the weathered old tower, I turn my gaze
Back to the instruction manual which has made me dream of Guadalajara.

1956

Farm Implements and Rutabagas in a Landscape[1]

The first of the undecoded messages read: "Popeye sits in
thunder,[2]
Unthought of. From that shoebox of an apartment,
From livid curtain's hue, a tangram emerges: a country."
Meanwhile the Sea Hag was relaxing on a green couch: "How
pleasant
To spend one's vacation *en la casa de Popeye,*"[3] she scratched
Her cleft chin's solitary hair. She remembered spinach

And was going to ask Wimpy if he had bought any spinach.
"M'love," he intercepted, "the plains are decked out in thunder
Today, and it shall be as you wish." He scratched
The part of his head under his hat. The apartment
Seemed to grow smaller. "But what if no pleasant
Inspiration plunge us now to the stars? *For this is my country.*"

Suddenly they remembered how it was cheaper in the country.
Wimpy was thoughtfully cutting open a number 2 can of spinach
When the door opened and Swee'pea crept in. "How pleasant!"
But Swee'pea looked morose. A note was pinned to his bib.
"Thunder
And tears are unavailing," it read. "Henceforth shall Popeye's
apartment
Be but remembered space, toxic or salubrious, whole or
scratched."

Olive came hurtling through the window; its geraniums scratched
Her long thigh. "I have news!" she gasped. "Popeye, forced as
you know to flee the country
One musty gusty evening, by the schemes of his wizened, duplicate

[1]When he was an editor for *Art News,* Ashbery and the poet James Schuyler amused themselves by inventing funny titles for imaginary paintings and prints.

[2]Popeye was the main character in a comic strip created by Segar and transformed into animated films by Max Fleisher. In the 1930s, Popeye rivaled Mickey Mouse in popularity. In an interview, Ashbery explained: "I go back to my earliest impressions a great deal when writing poetry. All poets do, I think. To me, it was always a great event. On Saturday night we got colored comics."

[3]Spanish for "in Popeye's house." Ashbery explains: "The reason that the Spanish phrase is in the poem is because [Popeye is] now published in New York only in *El Diaro,* the Spanish-language paper. . . . I just liked the way it looks, and the fact of the characters speaking Spanish, seems so funny. I used to follow it also in French newspapers, where Popeye's dislocations of the English language are reproduced charmingly in French. . . . I tend to dislocate the language myself."

father, jealous of the apartment
And all that it contains, myself and spinach
In particular, heave bolts of loving thunder
At his own astonished becoming, rupturing the pleasant

Arpeggio of our years. No more shall pleasant
Rays of the sun refresh your sense of growing old, nor the scratched
Tree-trunks and mossy foliage, only immaculate darkness and thunder."
She grabbed Swee'pea. "I'm taking the brat to the country."
"But you can't do that—he hasn't even finished his spinach."
Urged the Sea Hag, looking fearfully around at the apartment.

But Olive was already out of earshot. Now the apartment
Succumbed to a strange new hush. "Actually it's quite pleasant
Here," thought the Sea Hag. "If this is all we need fear from spinach
Then I don't mind so much. Perhaps we could invite Alice the
Goon over"—she scratched
One dug pensively—"but Wimpy is such a country
Bumpkin, always burping like that." Minute at first, the thunder

Soon filled the apartment. It was domestic thunder,
The color of spinach. Popeye chuckled and scratched
his balls: it sure was pleasant to spend a day in the country.

1970

As You Came from the Holy Land

of western New York state[1]
were the graves all right in their bushings
was there a note of panic in the late August air
because the old man had peed in his pants again
was there turning away from the late afternoon glare

[1]Western New York State may be a "holy land" for Ashbery because it is his birthplace, the area where Joseph Smith in 1827 discovered the mystical tablets that form the basis of the Mormon religion, and the location of the Oneida Community, a Utopian society founded in 1847 by John Humphrey Noyes.

as though it too could be wished away
was any of this present
and how could this be
the magic solution to what you are in now
whatever has held you motionless
like this so long through the dark season
until now the women come out in navy blue
and the worms come out of the compost to die
it is the end of any season

you reading there so accurately
sitting not wanting to be disturbed
as you came from that holy land
what other signs of earth's dependency were upon you
what fixed sign at the crossroads
what lethargy in the avenues
where all is said in a whisper
what tone of voice among the hedges
what tone under the apple trees
the numbered land stretches away
and your house is built in tomorrow
but surely not before the examination
of what is right and will befall
not before the census
and the writing down of names

remember you are free to wander away
as from other times other scenes that were taking place
the history of someone who came too late
the time is ripe now and the adage
is hatching as the seasons change and tremble
it is finally as though that thing of monstrous interest
were happening in the sky
but the sun is setting and prevents you from seeing it

out of night the token emerges
its leaves like birds alighting all at once under a tree
taken up and shaken again
put down in weak rage
knowing as the brain does it can never come about
not here not yesterday in the past
only in the gap of today filling itself
as emptiness is distributed
in the idea of what time it is
when that time is already past

1975

Pedro Pietri b. 1944

Born in Ponce, Puerto Rico, Pedro Pietri has lived most of his life in New York City He writes poetry and plays, some of which have been presented in off-Broadway theaters. *Illusions of a Revolving Door,* a collection of his plays in English, was published in Puerto Rico in 1992, the first time a Nuyorican writer published his work in English on the island.

His texts illustrate the literature of protest and denunciation that characterizes the work of Nuyorican writers, who address their literature to Puerto Rican readers in order to raise consciousness of social and political oppression within American society. Nuyorican poets began to read at the Nuyorican Poet's Cafe, at 505 East Sixth Street in New York City, where they met with other writers, artists, and community people. Their "poetic" language is anti-lyrical and harsh; it is the street language of blacks and Puerto Ricans in El Barrio. Such a stylistic choice implies a resistance to Americanization, and an expression of dignity and pride in the *puertorriqueño's* heritage.

In *Puerto Rican Obituary,* a key text for Nuyorican poets, Pietri creates a mock epic of the Puerto Rican community in the United States. Through humor, sarcasm, and an irreverent irony, the poet presents the American Dream—which motivated many Puerto Ricans to emigrate to this country—not as a dream but as a nightmare and, ultimately, as death. The *puertorriqueños* find themselves shut out of America's economic opportunities and lifestyle, and realize that they are unemployed, living on welfare, bitter, degraded. Pietri's image of a collective death is symbolic, denouncing the death of the Puerto Ricans' dignity as a people and individually. Yet Pietri is not altogether pessimistic, for the poem proposes a utopian symbolic space of Puerto Rican identity.

In *Traffic Violations,* Pietri moves away from the specificity of the social conditions of Puerto Ricans in New York, and expresses a broader poetic vision of life as absurd. As his title indicates, his poetry reaffirms the need to break away from norms, the healthy rupturing of expectations, of logic, and of civilization. By inverting many American idiomatic expressions and clichés, he surprises and moves the reader. This book presents the figure of the poet as a self-willed outcast, who drinks and uses drugs in order to avoid falling into any mechanization of the self. It is a surrealist work.

As representative of the literature of protest in Nuyorican culture, Pedro Pietri's work is a strong denunciation of the American system and of Western capitalism. To struggle against these forces, Pietri's poetry invites the *puertorriqueños* to acquire a sense of dignity and pride in their heritage, and to avoid complete cultural assimilation.

Frances R. Aparicio
University of Illinois at Chicago

PRIMARY WORKS

Puerto Rican Obituary, 1973; *Lost in the Museum of Natural History/Perdido en el Museo de Historia Natural,* 1981; *Traffic Violations,* 1983; *The Masses Are Asses,* 1984; *Illusions of a Revolving Door: Plays, Teatro,* 1992.

Puerto Rican Obituary

They worked
They were always on time
They were never late
They never spoke back
when they were insulted
They worked
They never took days off
that were not on the calendar
They never went on strike
without permission
They worked
ten days a week
and were only paid for five
They worked
They worked
They worked
and they died
They died broke
They died owing
They died never knowing
what the front entrance
of the first national city bank looks like
Juan
Miguel
Milagros
Olga
Manuel
All died yesterday today
and will die again tomorrow
passing their bill collectors
on to the next of kin
All died
waiting for the garden of eden
to open up again
under a new management
All died
dreaming about america
waking them up in the middle of the night
screaming: *Mira Mira*[1]
your name is on the winning lottery ticket
for one hundred thousand dollars

[1]Spanish: Look, Look.

All died
hating the grocery stores
that sold them makebelieve steak
and bulletproof rice and beans
All died waiting dreaming and hating

Dead Puerto Ricans
Who never knew they were Puerto Ricans
Who never took a coffee break
from the ten commandments
to KILL KILL KILL
the landlords of their cracked skulls
and communicate with their latino souls
Juan
Miguel
Milagros
Olga
Manuel
From the nervous breakdown streets
where the mice live like millionaires
and the people do not live at all
are dead and were never alive

Juan
died waiting for his number to hit
Miguel
died waiting for the welfare check
to come and go and come again
Milagros
died waiting for her ten children
to grow up and work
so she could quit working
Olga
died waiting for a five dollar raise
Manuel
died waiting for his supervisor to drop dead
so he could get a promotion

It's a long ride
from Spanish Harlem
to long island cemetery
where they were buried
First the train
and then the bus
and the cold cuts for lunch
and the flowers
that will be stolen

when visiting hours are over
It's very expensive
It's very expensive
But they understand
Their parents understood
It's a long nonprofit ride
from Spanish Harlem
to long island cemetery

Juan
Miguel
Milagros
Olga
Manuel
All died yesterday today
and will die again tomorrow
Dreaming
Dreaming about queens
Cleancut lilywhite neighborhood
Puerto Ricanless scene
Thirty thousand dollar home
The first spics on the block
Proud to belong to a community
of gringos who want them lynched
Proud to be a long distance away
from the sacred phrase: *Qué Pasa*[2]
These dreams
These empty dreams
from the makebelieve bedrooms
their parents left them
are the aftereffects
of television programs
about the ideal
white american family
with black maids
and latino janitors
who are well trained
to make everyone
and their bill collectors
laugh at them
and the people they represent

Juan
died dreaming about a new car

[2]Spanish: What's happening?

Miguel
died dreaming about new antipoverty programs

Milagros
died dreaming about a trip to Puerto Rico
Olga
died dreaming about real jewelry
Manuel
died dreaming about the irish sweepstakes

They all died
like a hero sandwich dies
in the garment district
at twelve o'clock in the afternoon
social security number to ashes
union dues to dust

They knew
they were born to weep
and keep the morticians employed
as long as they pledge allegiance
to the flag that wants them destroyed
They saw their names listed
in the telephone directory of destruction
They were trained to turn
the other cheek by newspapers
that mispelled mispronounced
and misunderstood their names
and celebrated when death came
and stole their final laundry ticket
They were born dead
and they died dead

It's time
to visit sister lópez again
the number one healer
and fortune card dealer
in Spanish Harlem
She can communicate
with your late relatives
for a reasonable fee

Good news is guaranteed

Rise Table Rise Table
death is not dumb and disabled
Those who love you want to know

the correct number to play
Let them know this right away
Rise Table Rise Table
death is not dumb and disabled
Now that your problems are over
and the world is off your shoulders
help those who you left behind
find financial peace of mind
Rise Table Rise Table
death is not dumb and disabled
If the right number we hit
all our problems will split
and we will visit your grave
on every legal holiday
Those who love you want to know
the correct number to play
Let them know this right away
We know your spirit is able
Death is not dumb and disabled
RISE TABLE RISE TABLE

Juan
Miguel
Milagros
Olga
Manuel
All died yesterday today
and will die again tomorrow
Hating fighting and stealing
broken windows from each other
Practicing a religion without a roof
The old testament
The new testament
according to the gospel
of the internal revenue
the judge and jury and executioner
protector and eternal bill collector

Secondhand shit for sale
Learn how to say *Cómo Está Usted*[3]
and you will make a fortune
They are dead
They are dead
and will not return from the dead

[3]Spanish: How are you?

until they stop neglecting
the art of their dialogue
for broken english lessons
to impress the mister goldsteins
who keep them employed
as *lavaplatos*[4] porters messenger boys
factory workers maids stock clerks
shipping clerks assistant mailroom
assistant, assistant assistant
to the assistant's assistant
assistant lavaplatos and automatic
artificial smiling doormen
for the lowest wages of the ages
and rages when you demand a raise
because it's against the company policy
to promote SPICS SPICS SPICS

Juan
died hating Miguel because Miguel's
used car was in better running condition
than his used car
Miguel
died hating Milagros because Milagros
had a color television set
and he could not afford one yet
Milagros
died hating Olga because Olga
made five dollars more on the same job
Olga
died hating Manuel because Manuel
had hit the numbers more times
than she had hit the numbers
Manuel
died hating all of them
Juan
Manuel
Milagros
and Olga
because they all spoke broken english
more fluently than he did

And now they are together
in the main lobby of the void
Addicted to silence

[4]Spanish: Dishwashers.

Off limits to the wind
Confined to worm supremacy
in long island cemetery
This is the groovy hereafter
the protestant collection box
was talking so loud and proud about

Here lies Juan
Here lies Miguel
Here lies Milagros
Here lies Olga
Here lies Manuel
who died yesterday today
and will die again tomorrow
Always broke
Always owing
Never knowing
that they are beautiful people
Never knowing
the geography of their complexion

PUERTO RICO IS A BEAUTIFUL PLACE
PUERTORRIQUEÑOS ARE A BEAUTIFUL RACE

If only they
had turned off the television
and tuned into their own imaginations
If only they
had used the white supremacy bibles
for toilet paper purpose
and made their latino souls
the only religion of their race
If only they
had returned to the definition of the sun
after the first mental snowstorm
on the summer of their senses
If only they
had kept their eyes open
at the funeral of their fellow employees
who came to this country to make a fortune
and were buried without underwear

Juan
Miguel
Milagros
Olga
Manuel

will right now be doing their own thing
where beautiful people sing
and dance and work together
where the wind is a stranger
to miserable weather conditions
where you do not need a dictionary
to communicate with your people
Aquí[5] *Se habla Español*[6] all the time
Aquí you salute your flag first
Aquí there are no dial soap commercials
Aquí everybody smells good
Aquí tv dinners do not have a future
Aquí the men and women admire desire
and never get tired of each other
Aquí Qué Pasa Power is what's happening
Aquí to be called *negrito*[7]
means to be called LOVE

1973

Traffic Violations

you go into chicken delight
and order dinosaurs
because you are hungry
and want something different
now that you no longer
eat meat or fish or vegetables
you are told politely
is against company policies
to be that different
so you remove a button off
your absentminded overcoat
the scenery changes
you are waiting in line
to take a mean leak
at one of those public toilets
in the times square area
the line is 3 weeks long

[5]Spanish: Here.
[6]Spanish: We speak Spanish.
[7]Spanish: Black (diminutive form).

many waited with their lunch
inside brown paper bags
singing the battle hymn
of the republic to keep warm

you remove another button off
your absentminded overcoat
all you can see now are
high heels and low quarter shoes
coming at your eyeballs
disappearing when they come
close enough to make contact

you try to get up off the floor
but you forgot how to move
umbrellas open up inside your head
you start screaming backwards
your legs behave like flat tires
your mind melts in slow motion

you remove another button off
your absentminded overcoat
is late in the evening
according to everybody
who keeps track of time
you are about to jump off the roof
emergency sirens are heard

A crowd of skilled & unskilled
Laborers on their mental lunch break
congregate on the street below
the roof you are about to jump from
they are laughing hysterically
nobody tries to talk you out of it
everybody wants you to jump
so they can get some sleep tonight—
should you change your mind about jumping
All the spectators will get uptight

red white and blue representatives
from the suicide prevention bureau
order you to jump immediately
you refuse to obey their orders
they sendout a helicopter to push you
off the roof into the morning headlines
the laughter from the crowd
on the street breaks the sound barrier

you try removing another button off
your absentminded overcoat
but that button is reported missing
the helicopter pushes you off the roof
everybody is feeling much better
you are losing your memory real fast
the clouds put on black arm bands
it starts raining needles and thread

a few seconds before having breakfast
at a cafeteria in the hereafter
you remove your absentminded overcoat

you are on the front and back seat
of a bi-lingo spaceship
smoking grass with your friends
from the past present and future
nothing unusual is happening
you are all speeding
without moving an inch
making sure nobody does the driving

1983

Rudolfo A. Anaya b. 1937

Bless Me, Ultima (1972), Rudolfo Anaya's first novel, is the single literary work most responsible not only for introducing American readers to Mexican American experience but for suggesting something of its vast imaginative potential. *Bless Me, Ultima* compelled its readers to discard the traditional American stereotype of Mexican American culture as a minor regional phenomenon, a curious, even degraded blend of customs and values drawn haphazardly from either side of the United States–Mexico border. Anaya delineated instead a distinctive culture rooted in the rich traditions of pre-Columbian aboriginal America and golden-age Spain. To be sure, Anaya's fictional terrain was a highly individualized and relatively remote region of east-central New Mexico; nevertheless, *Bless Me, Ultima* had the effect of validating Mexican American culture from California to Texas and beyond.

Like many first novels, *Bless Me, Ultima* contains various autobiographical elements. Anaya is himself from east-central New Mexico, having been born in Pastura. He attended school in nearby Santa Rosa and later in Albuquerque where he has lived most of his adult life. He earned several degrees in English and guidance and counseling and taught for seven years in the Albuquerque public schools. Anaya had become director of counseling at the University of Albuquerque when *Bless Me, Ultima* appeared. Two years later, in 1974, Anaya joined the faculty of the University of New Mexico where he maintains an appointment as professor of English.

Since *Bless Me, Ultima,* Anaya has published a steady sequence of novels, short stories, plays, and even a travel book entitled *A Chicano in China.* Despite the subject of this last book, Anaya retains his fascination with New Mexico, its clash and blending of cultures and its unique qualities as a setting for the engagement of fundamental religious and moral questions. His most recent works perfectly illustrate the range of his interest in his native state. The drama "Matachines" explores the cultural meaning of a ritual dance combining Moorish, Spanish, and Indian elements; the novel *Alburquerque* (spelled as in the original Spanish) concerns a young man's search for his father against the backdrop of a city losing its cultural moorings and beset by urban problems. None of Anaya's subsequent writing has matched either the appeal or the power of his first novel.

Bless Me, Ultima focuses on the experiences of Antonio Marez as he begins school at the conclusion of World War II. As the last of four sons in the family, Antonio carries the burden of his parents' increasingly desperate hopes. His mother, of a sedentary, tradition-bound clan of farmers, wishes Antonio to become a priest to absolve the indiscretions of one of her forebears. The father, equally alert to tradition, wants his son to maintain the *vaquero* customs of his family, most notably their fierce independence and self-reliance. As the battlelines for the control of Antonio's destiny are drawn, the revered Ultima appears to nurture the boy in her own extraordinary way. Ultima is a *curandera,* a folk healer who joins the Marez household ostensibly to merely live out the rest of her days. Under Ultima's tutelage, Antonio flourishes and begins preparations to fulfill his true destiny: to write, record, and thus preserve the traditions of his father's and mother's families alike.

Bless Me, Ultima is a novel rich in folklore. Anaya appropriates legends such as *La Llorona* (the crying woman), folk medicine, and superstition to convey a feeling of Mexican American culture in rural New Mexico. For Antonio, the folklore transmitted to him by Ultima serves as the very core of his cultural identity.

In the passage from *Bless Me, Ultima* presented here, Antonio recalls events surrounding his first communion. Even as a very young boy, Antonio has doubts about the Catholic church, its morbid emphasis on sinfulness, the unintelligibility of some of its practices, its inability to justify God's treatment of his friend Florence who, just a boy himself, has already lost his parents and watched helplessly as his older sisters drifted into prostitution. Already, Antonio finds himself attracted to the stories of the Golden Carp, a local, pagan symbol of benevolence. But for all his growing doubts, Antonio is still very much the product of his mother's religious training and so, for now, he acquiesces and participates in the church's rituals.

Raymund A. Paredes
University of California, Los Angeles

PRIMARY WORKS

Bless Me, Ultima, 1972; *Heart of Aztlan,* 1976; *Tortuga,* 1979; *The Silence of the Llano: Short Stories,* 1982; *The Legend of La Llorona,* 1984; *The Adventures of Juan Chicaspatas,* 1985; *A Chicano in China,* 1986; *Lord of the Dawn: The Legend of Quetzalcóatl,* 1987; *The Season of La Llorona* (play), 1987; *Matachines* (play), 1992; *Alburquerque,* 1992.

from Bless Me, Ultima

Dieciocho

Ash Wednesday. There is no other day like Ash Wednesday. The proud and the meek, the arrogant and the humble are all made equal on Ash Wednesday. The healthy and the sick, the assured and the sick in spirit, all make their way to church in the gray morning or in the dusty afternoon. They line up silently, eyes downcast, bony fingers counting the beads of the rosary, lips mumbling prayers. All are repentant, all are preparing themselves for the shock of the laying of the ashes on the forehead and the priest's agonizing words, "Thou art dust, and to dust thou shalt return."

The annointment is done, and the priest moves on, only the dull feeling of helplessness remains. The body is not important. It is made of dust; it is made of ashes. It is food for the worms. The winds and the waters dissolve it and scatter it to the four corners of the earth. In the end, what we care most for lasts only a brief lifetime, then there is eternity. Time forever. Millions of worlds are born, evolve, and pass away into nebulous, unmeasured skies; and there is still eternity. Time always. The body becomes dust and trees and exploding fire, it becomes gaseous and disappears, and still there is eternity. Silent, unopposed, brooding, forever . . .

But the soul survives. The soul lives on forever. It is the soul that must be saved, because the soul endures. And so when the burden of being nothing lifts from one's thoughts the idea of the immortality of the soul is like a light in a blinding storm. Dear God! the spirit cries out, my soul will live forever!

And so we hurried to catechism! The trying forty days of Lent lay ahead of us, then the shining goal, Easter Sunday and first holy communion! Very little else mattered in my life. School work was dull and uninspiring compared to the mysteries of religion. Each new question, each new catechism chapter, each new story seemed to open up a thousand facets concerning the salvation of my soul. I saw very little of Ultima, or even of my mother and father. I was concerned with myself. I knew that eternity lasted forever, and a soul because of one mistake could spend that eternity in hell.

The knowledge of this was frightful. I had many dreams in which I saw myself or different people burning in the fires of hell. One person especially continually haunted my nightmares. It was Florence. Inevitably it was he whom I saw burning in the roaring inferno of eternal damnation.

But why? I questioned the hissing fires, Florence knows all the answers!

But he does not accept, the flames lisped back.

"Florence," I begged him that afternoon, "try to answer."

He smiled. "And lie to myself," he answered.

"Don't lie! Just answer!" I shouted with impatience.

"You mean, when the priest asks where is God, I am to say God is everywhere: He is the worms that await the summer heat to eat Narciso, He shares the bed with Tenorio and his evil daughters—"

"Oh, God!" I cried in despair.

Samuel came up and touched me on the shoulder. "Perhaps things would not be so difficult if he believed in the golden carp," he said softly.

"Does Florence know?" I asked.

"This summer he shall know," Samuel answered wisely.

"What's that all about?" Ernie asked.

"Nothing," I said.

"Come on!" Abel shouted, "bell's ringing—"

It was Friday and we ran to attend the ritual of the Stations of the Cross. The weather was beginning to warm up but the winds still blew, and the whistling of the wind and the mournful cou-rouing of the pigeons and the burning incense made the agony of Christ's journey very sad. Father Byrnes stood at the first station and prayed to the bulto on the wall that showed Christ being sentenced by Pilate. Two high-school altar boys accompanied the priest, one to hold the lighted candle and the other to hold the incense burner. The hushed journeyers with Christ answered the priest's prayer. Then there was an interlude of silence while the priest and his attendants moved to the second station, Christ receiving the cross.

Horse sat by me. He was carving his initials into the back of the seat in front of us. Horse never prayed all of the stations, he waited until the priest came near, then he prayed the one he happened to be sitting by. I looked at the wall and saw that today he had picked to sit by the third fall of Christ.

The priest genuflected and prayed at the first fall of Christ. The incense was thick and sweet. Sometimes it made me sick inside and I felt faint. Next Friday would be Good Friday. Lent had gone by fast. There would be no stations on Good Friday, and maybe no catechism. By then we would be ready for confession Saturday and then the receiving of the sacrament on the most holy of days, Easter Sunday.

"What's Immmm-ack-que-let Con-sep-shion?" Abel asked. And Father Byrnes moved to the station where Christ meets his mother. I tried to concentrate. I felt sympathy for the Virgin.

"Immaculate Conception," Lloyd whispered.

"Yeah?"

"The Virgin Mary—"

"But what does it mean?"

"Having babies without—"

"What?"

I tried to shut my ears, I tried to hear the priest, but he was moving away, moving to where Simon helped Christ carry the cross. Dear Lord, I will help.

"I don't know—" Everybody giggled.

"Shhh!" Agnes scowled at us. The girls always prayed with bowed heads throughout the stations.

"A man and a woman, it takes a man and a woman," Florence nodded.

But the Virgin! I panicked, the Virgin Mary was the mother of God! The priest had said she was a mother through a miracle.

The priest finished the station where Veronica wiped the bloodied face of Christ, and he moved to Christ's second fall. The face of Christ was imprinted on the cloth. Besides the Virgin's blue robe, it was the holiest cloth on earth. The cross was heavy, and when He fell the soldiers whipped Him and struck Him with clubs. The people laughed. His agony began to fill the church and the women moaned their prayers, but the kids would not listen.

"The test is Saturday morning—"

Horse left his carving and looked up. The word "test" made him nervous.

"I, I, I'll pass," he nodded. Bones growled.

"Everybody will pass," I said, trying to be reassuring.

"Florence doesn't believe!" Rita hissed behind us.

"Shhhh! The priest is turning." Father Byrnes was at the back of the church, the seventh station. Now he would come down this side of the aisle for the remaining seven. Christ was speaking to the women.

Maybe that's why they prayed so hard, Christ spoke to them.

In the bell tower the pigeons cou-rouing made a mournful sound.

The priest was by us now. I could smell the incense trapped in his frock, like the fragrance of Ultima's herbs was part of her clothes. I bowed my head. The burning incense was sweet and suffocating; the glowing candle was hypnotizing. Horse had looked at it too long. When the priest moved on Horse leaned on me. His face was white.

"A la chingada," he whispered, "voy a tirar tripas—"

The priest was at the station of the Crucifixion. The hammer blows were falling on the nails that ripped through the flesh. I could almost hear the murmuring of the crowd as they craned their necks to see. But today I could not feel the agony.

"Tony—" Horse was leaning on me and gagging.

I struggled under his weight. People turned to watch me carrying the limp Horse up the aisle. Florence left his seat to help me and together we dragged Horse outside. He threw up on the steps of the church.

"He watched the candle too long," Florence said.

"Yes," I answered.

Horse smiled weakly. He wiped the hot puke from his lips and said, "ah la veca, I'm going to try that again next Friday—"

We managed to get through the final week of catechism lessons. The depression that comes with fasting and strict penance deepened as Lent drew to its completion. On Good Friday there was no school. I went to church with my mother and Ultima. All of the saints' statues in the church were covered with purple sheaths. The church was packed with women in black, each one stoically suffering the three hours of the Crucifixion with the tortured Christ. Outside the wind blew and cut off the light of the sun with its dust, and the pigeons cried mournfully in the tower. Inside the prayers were like muffled cries against a storm which seemed to engulf the world. There seemed to be no one to turn to for solace. And when the dying Christ cried, "My God, my God, why hast Thou forsaken me?" the piercing words seemed to drive through to my heart and make me feel alone and lost in a dying universe.

Good Friday was forlorn, heavy and dreary with the death of God's son and the accompanying sense of utter hopelessness.

But on Saturday morning our spirits lifted. We had been through the agony and now the ecstasy of Easter was just ahead. Then too we had our first confession to look forward to in the afternoon. In the morning my mother took me to town and bought me a white shirt and dark pants and jacket. It was the first suit I ever owned, and I smiled when I saw myself in the store mirror. I even got new shoes. Everything was new, as it should be for the first communion.

My mother was excited. When we returned from town she would not allow me to go anywhere or do anything. Every five minutes she glanced at the clock. She did not want me to be late for confession.

"It's time!" she finally called, and with a kiss she sent me scampering down the goat path, to the bridge where I raced the Vitamin Kid and lost, then waited to walk to church with Samuel.

"You ready?" I asked. He only smiled. At the church all the kids were gathered around the steps, waiting for the priest to call us.

"Did you pass?" everyone asked. "What did the priest ask you?" He had given each one of us a quiz, asking us to answer questions on the catechism lessons or to recite prayers.

"He asked me how many persons in one God?" Bones howled.

"Wha'daya say?"

"Four! Four! Four!" Bones cried. Then he shook his head vigorously. "Or five! I don't know?"

"And you passed?" Lloyd said contemptuously.

"I got my suit, don't I?" Bones growled. He would fight anyone who said he didn't pass.

"Okay, okay, you passed," Lloyd said to avoid a fight.

"Whad' did he ask you, Tony?"

"I had to recite the Apostles' Creed and tell what each part meant, and I had to explain where we get original sin—"

"¡Oh sí!" "¡Ah la veca!" "¡Chingada!"

"Bullshit!" Horse spit out the grass he had been chewing.

"Tony could do it," Florence defended me, "if he wanted to."

"Yeah, Tony knows more about religion and stuff like that than anyone—"

"Tony's gonna be a priest!"

"Hey, let's practice going to confession and make Tony the priest!" Ernie shouted.

"Yeahhhhh!" Horse reared up. Bones snarled and grabbed my pant leg in his teeth.

"Tony be the priest! Tony be the priest!" they began to chant.

"No, no," I begged, but they surrounded me. Ernie took off his sweater and draped it around me. "His priest's dress!" he shouted, and the others followed. They took off their jackets and sweaters and tied them around my waist and neck. I looked in vain for help but there was none.

"Tony is the priest, Tony is the priest, yah-yah-yah-ya-ya!" they sang and danced around me. I grew dizzy. The weight of the jackets on me was heavy and suffocating.

"All right!" I cried to appease them, "I shall be your priest!" I looked at Samuel. He had turned away.

"Yea-aaaaaaaaye!" A great shout went up. Even the girls drew closer to watch.

"Hail to our priest!" Lloyd said judiciously.

"Do it right!" Agnes shouted.

"Yeah! Me first! Do it like for reals!" Horse shouted and threw himself at my feet.

"Everybody quiet!" Ernie held up his hands. They all drew around the kneeling Horse and myself, and the wall provided the enclosure but not the privacy of the confessional.

"Bless me, father—" Horse said, but as he concentrated to make the sign of the cross he forgot his lines. "Bless me, father—" he repeated desperately.

"You have sinned," I said. It was very quiet in the enclosure.

"Yes," he said. I remembered hearing the confession of the dying Narciso.

"It's not right to hear another person's confession," I said, glancing at the expectant faces around me.

"Go on!" Ernie hissed and hit me on the back. Blows fell on my head and shoulders. "Go on!" they cried. They really wanted to hear Horse's confession.

"It's only a game!" Rita whispered.

"How long has it been since your last confession?" I asked Horse.

"Always," he blurted out, "since I was born!"

"What are your sins?" I asked. I felt hot and uncomfortable under the weight of the jackets.

"Tell him only your worst one," Rita coaxed the Horse. "Yeah!" all the rest agreed.

The Horse was very quiet, thinking. He had grabbed one of my hands and he clutched it tightly, as if some holy power was going to pass through it and absolve him of his sins. His eyes rolled wildly, then he smiled and opened his mouth. His breath fouled the air.

"I know! I know!" he said excitedly, "one day when Miss Violet let me go to the bathroom I made a hole in the wall! With a nail! Then I could see into the girls' bathroom! I waited a long time! Then one of the girls came and sat down, and I could see everything! Her ass! Everything! I could even hear the pee!" he cried out.

"Horse, you're dirty!" June exclaimed. Then the girls looked shyly at each other and giggled.

"You have sinned," I said to Horse. Horse freed my hand and began rubbing at the front of his pants.

"There's more!" he cried, "I saw a teacher!"

"No!"

"Yes! Yes!" He rubbed harder.

"Who?" one of the girls asked.

"Mrs. Harrington!" Everyone laughed. Mrs. Harrington weighed about two hundred pounds. "It was bigggggggg—!" he exploded and fell trembling on the ground.

"Give him a penance!" the girls chanted and pointed accusing fingers at the pale Horse. "You are dirty, Horse," they cried, and he whimpered and accepted their accusations.

"For your penance say a rosary to the Virgin," I said weakly. I didn't feel good. The weight of the jackets was making me sweat, and the revelation of Horse's confession and the way the kids were acting was making me sick. I wondered how the priest could shoulder the burden of all the sins he heard.

. . . the weight of the sins will sink the town into the lake of the golden carp . . .

I looked for Samuel. He was not joining in the game. Florence was calmly accepting the sacriligious game we were playing, but then it didn't matter to him, he didn't believe.

"Me next! Me next!" Bones shouted. He let go of my leg and knelt in front of me. "I got a better sin than Horse! Bless me, father! Bless me, father! Bless me, father!" he repeated. He kept making the sign of the cross over and over. "I got a sin! I got to confess! I saw a high school boy and a girl fucking in the grass by the Blue Lake!" He smiled proudly and looked around.

"Ah, I see them every night under the railroad bridge," the Vitamin Kid scoffed.

"What do you mean?" I asked Bones.

"Naked! Jumping up and down!" he exclaimed.

"You lie, Bones!" Horse shouted. He didn't want his own sin bettered.

"No I don't!" Bones argued. "I don't lie, father, I don't lie!" he pleaded.

"Who was it?" Rita asked.

"It was Larry Saiz, and that dumb gabacha whose father owns the Texaco station—please father, it's my sin! I saw it! I confess!" He squeezed my hand very hard.

"Okay, Bones, okay," I nodded my head, "it's your sin."

"Give me a penance!" he growled.

"A rosary to the Virgin," I said to be rid of him.

"Like Horse?" he shouted.

"Yes."

"But my sin was bigger!" he snarled and leaped for my throat. "Whaggggghhh—" he threw me down and would have strangled me if the others hadn't pulled him away.

"Another rosary for daring to touch the priest!" I shouted in self-defense and pointed an accusing finger at him. That made him happy and he settled down.

"Florence next!" Abel cried.

"Nah, Florence ain't goin' make it anyway," Lloyd argued.

"That's enough practice," I said and started to take off the cumbersome costume, but they wouldn't let me.

"Abel's right," Ernie said emphatically, "Florence needs the practice! He didn't make it because he didn't practice!"

"He didn't make it because he doesn't believe!" Agnes taunted.

"Why doesn't he believe?" June asked.

"Let's find out!" "Make him tell!" "¡Chingada!"

They grabbed tall Florence before he could bolt away and made him kneel in front of me.

"No!" I protested.

"Confess him!" they chanted. They held him with his arms pinned behind his back. I looked down at him and tried to let him know we might as well go along with the game. It would be easier that way.

"What are your sins?" I asked.

"I don't have any," Florence said softly.

"You do, you bastard!" Ernie shouted and pulled Florence's head back.

"You have sins," Abel agreed.

"Everybody has sins!" Agnes shouted. She helped Ernie twist Florence's head back. Florence tried to struggle but he was pinned by Horse and Bones and Abel. I tried to pull their hands away from him to relieve the pain I saw in his face, but the trappings of the priest's costume entangled me and so I could do very little.

"Tell me one sin," I pleaded with Florence. His face was very close to mine now, and when he shook his head to tell me again that he didn't have sins I saw a frightening truth in his eyes. He was telling the truth! He did not believe that he had ever sinned against God! "Oh my God!" I heard myself gasp.

"Confess your sins or you'll go to hell!" Rita cried out. She grabbed his blonde hair and helped Ernie and Agnes twist his head.

"Confess! Confess!" they cried. Then with one powerful heave and a groan Florence shook off his tormentors. He was long and sinewy, but because of his mild manner we had always underestimated his strength. Now the girls and Ernie and even Horse fell off him like flies.

"I have not sinned!" he shouted, looking me square in the eyes, challenging me, the priest. His voice was like Ultima's when she had challenged Tenorio, or Narciso's when he had tried to save Lupito.

"It is God who has sinned against me!" his voice thundered, and we fell back in horror at the blasphemy he uttered.

"Florence," I heard June whimper, "don't say that—"

Florence grinned. "Why? Because it is the truth?" he questioned. "Because you refuse to see the truth, or to accept me because I do not believe in your lies! I say God has sinned against me because he took my father and mother from me when I most needed them, and he made my sisters whores—He has punished all of us without just cause, Tony," his look pierced me, "He took Narciso! And why? What harm did Narciso ever do—"

"We shouldn't listen to him," Agnes had the courage to interrupt Florence, "we'll have to confess what we heard and the priest will be mad."

"The priest was right in not passing Florence, because he doesn't believe!" Rita added.

"He shouldn't even be here if he is not going to believe in the laws we learn," Lloyd said.

"Give him a penance! Make him ask for forgiveness for those terrible things he said about God!" Agnes insisted. They were gathering behind me now, I could feel their presence and their hot, bitter breath. They wanted me to be their leader; they wanted me to punish Florence.

"Make his penance hard," Rita leered.

"Make him kneel and we'll all beat him," Ernie suggested.

"Yeah, beat him!" Bones said wildly.

"Stone him!"

"Beat him!"

"Kill him!"

They circled around me and advanced on Florence, their eyes flashing with the thought of the punishment they would impose on the non-believer. It was then that the fear left me, and I knew what I had to do. I spun around and held out my hands to stop them.

"No!" I shouted, "there will be no punishment, there will be no penance! His sins are forgiven!" I turned and made the sign of the cross. "Go in peace, my son," I said to Florence.

"No!" they shouted, "don't let him go free!"

"Make him do penance! That's the law!"

"Punish him for not believing in God!"

"I am the priest!" I shouted back, "and I have absolved him of his sins!" I was facing the angry kids and I could see that their hunger for vengeance was directed at me, but I didn't care, I felt relieved. I had stood my ground for what I felt to be right and I was not afraid. I thought that perhaps it was this kind of strength that allowed Florence to say he did not believe in God.

"You are a bad priest, Tony!" Agnes lashed out at me.

"We do not want you for our priest!" Rita followed.

"Punish the priest!" they shouted and they engulfed me like a wave. They were upon me, clawing, kicking, tearing off the jackets, defrocking me. I fought back but it was useless. They were too many. They spread me out and held me pinned down to the hard ground. They had torn my shirt off so the sharp pebbles and stickers cut into my back.

"Give him the Indian torture!" someone shouted.

"Yeah, the Indian torture!" they chanted.

They held my arms while Horse jumped on my stomach and methodically began to pound with his fist on my chest. He used his sharp knuckles and aimed each blow directly at my breastbone. I kicked and wiggled and struggled to get free from the incessant beating, but they held me tight and I could not throw them off.

"No! No!" I shouted, but the raining blows continued. The blows of the knuckles coming down again and again on my breastbone were unbearable, but Horse knew no pity, and there was no pity on the faces of the others.

"God!" I cried, "God!" But the jarring blows continued to fall. I jerked my head from side to side and tried to kick or bite, but I could not get loose. Finally I bit my lips so I wouldn't cry, but my eyes filled with tears anyway. They were laughing and pointing down at the red welt that raised on my chest where the Horse was pounding.

"Serves him right," I heard, "he let the sinner go—"

Then, after what seemed an eternity of torture, they let me go. The priest was calling from the church steps, so they ran off to confession. I slowly picked myself up and rubbed the bruises on my chest. Florence handed me my shirt and jacket.

"You should have given me a penance," he said.

"You don't have to do any penance," I answered. I wiped my eyes and shook my head. Everything in me seemed loose and disconnected.

"Are you going to confession?" he asked.

"Yes," I answered and finished buttoning my shirt.

"You could never be their priest," he said.

I looked at the open door of the church. There was a calm in the wind and the bright sunlight made everything stark and harsh. The last of the kids went into the church and the doors closed.

"No," I nodded. "Are you going to confession?" I asked him.

"No," he muttered. "Like I said, I only wanted to be with you guys—I cannot eat God," he added.

"I have to," I whispered. I ran up the steps and entered the dark, musky church. I genuflected at the font of holy water, wet my fingertips, and made the sign of the cross. The lines were already formed on either side of the confessional, and the kids were behaving and quiet. Each one stood with bowed head, preparing himself to confess all of his sins to Father Byrnes. I walked quietly around the back pew and went to the end of one line. I made the sign of the cross again and began to say my prayers. As each kid finished his confession the line shuffled forward. I closed my eyes and tried not to be distracted by anything around me. I thought hard of all the sins I had ever committed, and I said as many prayers as I could remember. I begged God forgiveness for my sins over and over. After a long wait, Agnes, who had been in front of me came out of the confessional. She held the curtain as I stepped in, then she let it drop and all was dark. I knelt on the rough board and leaned against the small window. I prayed. I could hear whisperings from the confessional on the other side. My eyes grew accustomed to the gloom and I saw a small crucifix nailed to the side of the window. I kissed the feet of the hanging Jesus. The confessional smelled of old wood. I thought of the million sins that had been revealed in this small, dark space.

Then abruptly my thoughts were scattered. The small wooden door of the window slid open in front of me, and in the dark I could make out the head of Father Byrnes. His eyes were closed, his head bowed forward. He mumbled something in Latin then put his hand on his forehead and waited.

I made the sign of the cross and said, "Forgive me, Father, for I have sinned," and I made my first confession to him.

1972

Richard Rodriguez b. 1944

Richard Rodriguez is probably the best-known Mexican American writer today, his fame propelling him to regular appearances on radio and television talk shows and even to the pages of *People* magazine. His essays have appeared in prestigious journals and newspapers such as the *American Scholar* and the *Los Angeles Times.* Rodriguez is also perhaps the most controversial of contemporary Latino authors, having been applauded by the political right, especially in his early career, for stands against affirmative action and bilingual education, and vilified by the left for precisely the same positions. In any event, Rodriguez commands attention for the thoughtfulness and craftsmanship of his prose and his willingness to take on provocative issues. Over the years, Rodriguez has become less susceptible to easy political categorization as his arguments have become more nuanced.

Rodriguez was born in San Francisco, the child of Mexican immigrants ambitious for their four children and eager for admission into the American middle class. The Rodriguezes soon moved to Sacramento and brought a "gaudy yellow" house among white bungalows "many blocks from the Mexican south side of town." Sensitive and introspective, Richard began Catholic school armed with only a few words of English. As Rodriguez recalls in his autobiographical narrative, *The Hunger of Memory,* his movement through the American educational system to affluence and a certain celebrity was wrenching both to himself and to his parents. Quickly noticing Richard's academic gifts, the nuns insisted that he speak English at home to accelerate his intellectual development, thereby opening a cultural chasm between boy and parents that only widens. Rodriguez observes that he had to choose between the "public identity" of the American mainstream and the "private identity" of his parents' Mexican home, finally concluding that assimilation is a "necessity." In *Hunger of Memory,* Rodriguez seems willfully ignorant that large immigration movements—like the one that brought his parents to the United States—typically create bi-directional acculturation, immigrants and native-born residents transforming and revitalizing one another. Furthermore, Rodriguez ignores the well-established fact that many—perhaps most—of us have rich and varied identities that allow us to function in a number of cultural settings.

In *Days of Obligation,* Rodriguez blends autobiographical explorations with musings on such topics as Mexican history and character, the California missions, and the AIDS epidemic. Sprawling and sometimes opaque, *Days of Obligation* nonetheless reveals a more mature Rodriguez, uncomfortable with some of the facile conclusions of *Hunger of Memory.* Here, very much aware of his mortality, Rodriguez wishes to understand his parents' cultural heritage, which earlier he had been all-too-willing to jettison. *Hunger of Memory* ends with a family Christmas dinner at which Rodriguez and his father have almost nothing to say to each other; in *Days of Obligation,* we see Rodriguez throughout beseeching his parents for more information about Mexico and their lives there.

The selection reproduced here comes from the chapter "Complexion" in *Hunger of Memory.* Rodriguez treats the complex of attitudes he encountered because of his dark skin: from his family, from Anglo outsiders, from himself. One of Rodriguez's virtues as a writer of autobiography is to reveal honestly his insecurities, even in connection with such difficult issues as his adolescent sexuality.

Raymund A. Paredes
University of California–Los Angeles

PRIMARY WORKS

Hunger of Memory: The Education of Richard Rodriguez, 1982; *Days of Obligation: An Argument with My Mexican Father,* 1992. Writings have also appeared in *American Scholar, New Republic, Wall Street Journal, Los Angeles Times, Harpers,* and *Washington Post.*

from The Hunger of Memory

Visiting the East Coast or the gray capitals of Europe during the long months of winter, I often meet people at deluxe hotels who comment on my complexion. (In such hotels it appears nowadays a mark of leisure and wealth to have a complexion like mine.) Have I been skiing? In the Swiss Alps? Have I just returned from a Caribbean vacation? No. I say no softly but in a firm voice that intends to explain: My complexion is dark. (My skin is brown. More exactly, terra-cotta in sunlight, tawny in shade. I do not redden in sunlight. Instead, my skin becomes progressively dark; the sun singes the flesh.)

When I was a boy the white summer sun of Sacramento would darken me so, my T-shirt would seem bleached against my slender dark arms. My mother would see me come up the front steps. She'd wait for the screen door to slam at my back. "You look like a *negrito,*" she'd say, angry, sorry to be angry, frustrated almost to laughing, scorn. "You know how important looks are in this country. With *los gringos* looks are all that they judge on. But you! Look at you! You're so careless!" Then she'd start in all over again. "You won't be satisfied till you end up looking like *los pobres* who work in the fields, *los braceros.*"

(*Los braceros:* Those men who work with their *brazos,* their arms; Mexican nationals who were licensed to work for American farmers in the 1950s. They worked very hard for very little money, my father would tell me. And what money they earned they sent back to Mexico to support their families, my mother would add. *Los pobres*—the poor, the pitiful, the powerless ones. But paradoxically also powerful men. They were the men with brown-muscled arms I stared at in awe on Saturday mornings when they showed up downtown like gypsies to shop at Woolworth's or Penney's. On Monday nights they would gather hours early on the steps of the Memorial Auditorium for the wrestling matches. Passing by on my bicycle in summer, I would spy them there, clustered in small groups, talking—frightening and fascinating men—some wearing Texas *sombreros* and T-shirts which shone fluorescent in the twilight. I would sit forward in the back seat of our family's '48 Chevy to see them, working alongside Valley highways: dark men on an even horizon, loading a truck amid rows of straight green. Powerful, powerless men. Their fascinating darkness—like mine—to be feared.)

"You'll end up looking just like them." . . .

2

Complexion. My first conscious experience of sexual excitement concerns my complexion. One summer weekend, when I was around seven years old, I was at a public swimming pool with the whole family. I remember sitting on the damp pavement next to the pool and seeing my mother, in the spectators' bleachers, holding my younger sister on her lap. My mother, I noticed, was watching my father as he stood on a diving board, waving to her. I watched her wave back. Then saw her radiant, bashful, astonishing smile. In that second I sensed that my mother and father had a relationship I knew nothing about. A nervous excitement encircled my stomach as I saw my mother's eyes follow my father's figure curving into the water. A second or two later, he emerged. I heard him call out. Smiling, his voice sounded, buoyant, calling me to swim to him. But turning to see him, I caught my mother's eyes. I heard her shout over to me. In Spanish she called through the crowd: "Put a towel on over your shoulders." In public, she didn't want to say why. I knew.

That incident anticipates the shame and sexual inferiority I was to feel in later years because of my dark complexion. I was to grow up an ugly child. Or one who thought himself ugly. (*Feo.*) One night when I was eleven or twelve years old, I locked myself in the bathroom and carefully regarded my reflection in the mirror over the sink. Without any pleasure I studied my skin. I turned on the faucet. (In my mind I heard the swirling voices of aunts, and even my mother's voice, whispering, whispering incessantly about lemon juice solutions and dark, *feo* children.) With a bar of soap, I fashioned a thick ball of lather. I began soaping my arms. I took my father's straight razor out of the medicine cabinet. Slowly, with steady deliberateness, I put the blade against my flesh, pressed it as close as I could without cutting, and moved it up and down across my skin to see if I could get out, somehow lessen, the dark. All I succeeded in doing, however, was in shaving my arms bare of their hair. For as I noted with disappointment, the dark would not come out. It remained. Trapped. Deep in the cells of my skin.

Throughout adolescence, I felt myself mysteriously marked. Nothing else about my appearance would concern me so much as the fact that my complexion was dark. My mother would say how sorry she was that there was not money enough to get braces to straighten my teeth. But I never bothered about my teeth. In three-way mirrors at department stores, I'd see my profile dramatically defined by a long nose, but it was really only the color of my skin that caught my attention.

I wasn't afraid that I would become a menial laborer because of my skin. Nor did my complexion make me feel especially vulnerable to racial abuse. (I didn't really consider my dark skin to be a racial characteristic. I would have been only too happy to look as Mexican as my light-skinned older brother.) Simply, I judged myself ugly. And, since the women in my family had been the ones who discussed it in such worried tones, I felt my dark skin made me unattractive to women.

Thirteen years old. Fourteen. In a grammar school art class, when the assignment was to draw a self-portrait, I tried and I tried but could not bring myself to shade in the face on the paper to anything like my actual tone. With disgust then I would come face to face with myself in mirrors. With disappointment I located myself in class photographs—my dark face undefined by the camera which had clearly described the white faces of classmates. Or I'd see my dark wrist against my long-sleeved white shirt.

I grew divorced from my body. Insecure, overweight, listless. On hot summer days when my rubber-soled shoes soaked up the heat from the sidewalk, I kept my head down. Or walked in the shade. My mother didn't need anymore to tell me to watch out for the sun. I denied myself a sensational life. The normal, extraordinary, animal excitement of feeling my body alive—riding shirtless on a bicycle in the warm wind created by furious self-propelled motion—the sensations that first had excited in me a sense of my maleness, I denied. I was too ashamed of my body. I wanted to forget that I had a body because I had a brown body. I was grateful that none of my classmates ever mentioned the fact.

I continued to see the *braceros,* those men I resembled in one way and, in another way, didn't resemble at all. On the watery horizon of a Valley afternoon, I'd see them. And though I feared looking like them, it was with silent envy that I regarded them still. I envied them their physical lives, their freedom to violate the taboo of the sun. Closer to home I would notice the shirtless construction workers, the roofers, the sweating men tarring the street in front of the house. And I'd see the Mexican gardeners. I was unwilling to admit the attraction of their lives. I tried to deny it by looking away. But what was denied became strongly desired.

In high school physical education classes, I withdrew, in the regular company of five or six classmates, to a distant corner of a football field where we smoked and talked. Our company was composed of bodies too short or too tall, all graceless and all—except mine—pale. Our conversation was usually witty. (In fact we were intelligent.) If we referred to the athletic contests around us, it was with sarcasm. With savage scorn I'd refer to the "animals" playing football or baseball. It would have been important for me to have joined them. Or for me to have taken off my shirt, to have let the sun burn dark on my skin, and to have run barefoot on the warm wet grass. It would have been very important. Too important. It would have been too telling a gesture—to admit the desire for sensation, the body, my body.

Fifteen, sixteen. I was a teenager shy in the presence of girls. Never dated. Barely could talk to a girl without stammering. In high school I went to several dances, but I never managed to ask a girl to dance. So I stopped going. I cannot remember high school years now with the parade of typical images: bright drive-ins or gliding blue shadows of a Junior Prom. At home most weekend nights, I would pass evenings reading. Like those hidden, precocious adolescents who have no real-life sexual experiences, I read a great deal of romantic fiction. "You won't find it in your books," my brother would playfully taunt me as he prepared to go to a party by freezing the crest of the wave in his hair with sticky pomade. Through my reading, however, I developed a fabulous and sophisticated sexual imagination. At seventeen, I may not have known how to engage a girl in small talk, but I had read *Lady Chatterley's Lover.*

It annoyed me to hear my father's teasing: that I would never know what "real work" is; that my hands were so soft. I think I knew it was his way of admitting pleasure and pride in my academic success. But I didn't smile. My mother said she was glad her children were getting their educations and would not be pushed around like *los pobres.* I heard the remark ironically as a reminder of my separation from *los braceros.* At such times I suspected that education was making me effeminate. The odd thing, however, was that I did not judge my classmates so harshly. Nor did I consider my male teachers in high school effeminate. It was only myself I judged against some shadowy, mythical Mexican laborer—dark like me, yet very different.

Language was crucial. I knew that I had violated the ideal of the *macho* by becoming such a dedicated student of language and literature. *Machismo* was a word never exactly defined by the persons who used it. (It was best described in the "proper" behavior of men.) Women at home, nevertheless, would repeat the old Mexican dictum that a man should be *feo, fuerte, y formal.* "The three F's," my mother called them, smiling slyly. *Feo* I took to mean not literally ugly so much as ruggedly handsome. (When my mother and her sisters spent a loud, laughing afternoon determining ideal male good looks, they finally settled on the actor Gilbert Roland, who was neither too pretty nor ugly but had looks "like a man.") *Fuerte,* "strong," seemed to mean not physical strength as much as inner strength, character. A dependable man is *fuerte. Fuerte* for that reason was a characteristic subsumed by the last of the three qualities, and the one I most often considered—*formal.* To be *formal* is to be steady. A man of responsibility, a good provider. Someone *formal* is also constant. A person to be relied upon in adversity. A sober man, a man of high seriousness.

I learned a great deal about being *formal* just by listening to the way my father and other male relatives of his generation spoke. A man was not silent necessarily. Nor was he limited in the tones he could sound. For example, he could tell a long, involved, humorous story and laugh at his own humor with high-pitched giggling. But a man was not talkative the way a woman could be. It was permitted a woman to be gossipy and chatty. (When one heard many voices in a room, it was usually women who were talking.) Men spoke much less rapidly and often men spoke in monologues. (When one voice sounded in a crowded room, it was most often a man's voice one heard.) More important than any of this was the fact that a man never verbally revealed his emotions. Men did not speak about their unease in moments of crisis or danger. It was the woman who worried aloud when her husband got laid off from work. At times of illness or death in the family, a man was usually quiet, even silent. Women spoke up to voice prayers. In distress, women always sounded quick ejaculations to God or the Virgin; women prayed in clearly audible voices at a wake held in a funeral parlor. And on the subject of love, a woman was verbally expansive. She spoke of her yearning and delight. A married man, if he spoke publicly about love, usually did so with playful, mischievous irony. Younger, unmarried men more often were quiet. (The *macho* is a silent suitor. *Formal.*)

At home I was quiet, so perhaps I seemed *formal* to my relations and other Spanish-speaking visitors to the house. But outside the house—my God!—I talked. Particularly in class or alone with my teachers, I chattered. (Talking seemed to make teachers think I was bright.) I often was proud of my way with words. Though, on other occasions, for example, when I would hear my mother busily speaking to women, it would occur to me that my attachment to words made me like her. Her son. Not *formal* like my father. At such times I even suspected that my nostalgia for sounds—the noisy, intimate Spanish sounds of my past—was nothing more than effeminate yearning.

High school English teachers encouraged me to describe very personal feelings in words. Poems and short stories I wrote, expressing sorrow and loneliness, were awarded high grades. In my bedroom were books by poets and novelists—books that I loved—in which male writers published feelings the men in my family never revealed or acknowledged in words. And it seemed to me that there was something unmanly about my attachment to literature. Even today, when so much about the myth of the *macho* no longer concerns me, I cannot altogether evade such notions. Writing these pages, admitting my embarrassment or my guilt, admitting my sexual anxieties and my physical insecurity, I have not been able to forget that I am not being *formal.*

So be it.

1982

Amiri Baraka (LeRoi Jones) b. 1934

Amiri Baraka, born Everett LeRoy Jones to Coyt LeRoy and Anna Lois Jones in Newark, New Jersey, grew up in a middle-class environment. He attended a predominantly black elementary school, but his college-prep high school, from which he graduated with honors in 1951, was mainly white. About 1951, the first of his name changes occurred with the spelling of his middle name from "LeRoy" to "LeRoi." From 1952 to 1954 he attended Howard University, where he studied with Sterling Brown and Nathan Scott. After he flunked out of school, he enlisted in the U.S. Air Force until 1957. These were years of intellectual commitment and poetry writing. In 1957, however, he was dishonorably discharged because of suspicions of communism and such "suspicious activities" as voracious reading, journal-keeping, poetry writing, and subscribing to avant-garde journals.

Free to live the avant-garde life that had become his preference, Baraka moved to New York's Greenwich Village. Among his associates there were Charles Olson, Frank O'Hara, and Allen Ginsberg. In 1958 he married Hettie Cohn, a Jewish woman also much a part of the Beat scene, and together they edited *Yugen,* a literary journal which published the work of Kerouac, Ginsberg, and many others.

The next decade was marked by a significant change from things aesthetic to things political. His 1960 visit to Cuba marks the genesis of political awareness of blackness and a new frame of reference: the third world. Although the year after his trip saw the inauguration of another avant-garde journal, this time co-edited with poet Diane di Prima, and the publication of his first volume of poetry, by 1964 the tensions inherent along the spectrum of early poetic asceticism and racial didacticism become apparent in the poems of *The Dead Lecturer,* as well as his play *Dutchman,* for which he won an Obie Award for its off-Broadway production.

Radically affected by the assassination of Malcolm X in 1965, Baraka left Hettie and the bohemian life of the Village and moved to Harlem, where he established the Black Arts Repertory Theater/School. In 1966, returning to Newark, he founded a similar venture, Spirit House, and married Sylvia Robinson, a black woman. Again a change of name signaled a reshaping of identity: LeRoi Jones became Imamu Amiri Baraka, as he was known through the racial upheavals of the 60s. By the early 70s he had dropped the title "Imamu," yet another indication of a shift: this one from black nationalism to international socialism, a stance obviously not tolerant of titles. His published poetry of the late 70s reflects this shift in thought.

In 1979 he joined the African Studies Department at SUNY Stony Brook, was promoted to associate professor with tenure in 1982, and to full professor in 1984 following the publication of *Autobiography* and *Daggers and Javelins.* He continues to work on *Wise/Whys,* an African American poetic-historical odyssey.

The sense of flux and process, of intensity and explosion, of rebellion and reconstruction, and always the *SOUND* of it, are everywhere present in his poetry and in his prose. *Dutchman,* included here, has come to be seen as his signature work.

Marcellette Williams
University of Massachusetts–Amherst

PRIMARY WORKS

Preface to a Twenty Volume Suicide Note . . . , 1961; *Dutchman* and *The Slave,* 1964; *The Dead Lecturer,* 1964; *Home: Social Essays,* 1966; *Black Magic,* 1969; *In Our Terribleness,* 1970; *It's Nation Time,* 1970; *Jello,* 1970; *Spirit Reach,* 1972; *Hard Facts,* 1975; *Selected Poetry of Amiri Baraka/LeRoi Jones,* and *Selected Plays and Prose of Amiri Baraka/LeRoi Jones,* 1979; "In the Tradition," *Greenfield Review,* 1980; *The Autobiography of LeRoi Jones/Amiri Baraka,* 1984; *Daggers and Javelins: Essays,* 1974–1979, 1984.

An Agony. As now.

I am inside someone
who hates me. I look
out from his eyes. Smell
what fouled tunes come in
to his breath. Love his
wretched women.

Slits in the metal, for sun. Where
my eyes sit turning, at the cool air

the glance of light, or hard flesh
rubbed against me, a woman, a man,
without shadow, or voice, or meaning.

This is the enclosure (flesh,
where innocence is a weapon. An
abstraction. Touch. (Not mine.
Or yours, if you are the soul I had
and abandoned when I was blind and had
my enemies carry me as a dead man
(if he is beautiful, or pitied.

It can be pain. (As now, as all his
flesh hurts me.) It can be that. Or
pain. As when she ran from me into
that forest.

Or pain, the mind
silver spiraled whirled against the
sun, higher than even old men thought
God would be. Or pain. And the other. The
yes. (Inside his books, his fingers. They
are withered yellow flowers and were never
beautiful.) The yes. You will, lost soul, say
"beauty." Beauty, practiced, as the tree. The
slow river. A white sun in its wet sentences.

Or, the cold men in their gale. Ecstasy. Flesh
or souls. The yes. (Their robes blown. Their bowls
empty. They chant at my heels, not at yours.) Flesh
or soul, as corrupt. Where the answer moves too quickly.
Where the God is a self, after all.)

Cold air blown through narrow blind eyes. Flesh,
white hot metal. Glows as the day with its sun.
It is a human love, I live inside. A bony skeleton
you recognize as words or simple feeling.

But it has no feeling. As the metal, is hot, it is not,
given to love.

It burns the thing
inside it. And that thing
screams.

1964

Ka 'Ba[1]

A closed window looks down
on a dirty courtyard, and black people
call across or scream across or walk across
defying physics in the stream of their will

Our world is full of sound
Our world is more lovely than anyone's
tho we suffer, and kill each other
and sometimes fail to walk the air

We are beautiful people
with african imaginations
full of masks and dances and swelling chants
with african eyes, and noses, and arms,
though we sprawl in grey chains in a place
full of winters, when what we want is sun.
We have been captured,
brothers. And we labor
to make our getaway, into
the ancient image, into a new

correspondence with ourselves
and our black family. We need magic
now we need the spells, to raise up
return, destroy, and create. What will be

the sacred words?

1969

Black People: This Is Our Destiny

The road runs straight with no turning, the circle
runs complete as it is in the storm of peace, the all
embraced embracing in the circle complete turning road
straight like a burning straight with the circle complete
as in a peaceful storm, the elements, the niggers' voices
harmonized with creation on a peak in the holy black man's
eyes that we rise, whose race is only direction up, where
we go to meet the realization of makers knowing who we are
and the war in our hearts but the purity of the holy world

[1]Relating to the sacred Islamic shrine in Mecca.

that we long for, knowing how to live, and what life is, and
who God is, and the many revolutions we must spin through in our
seven adventures in the endlessness of all existing feeling, all
existing forms of life, the gases, the plants, the ghost minerals
the spirits the souls the light in the stillness where the storm
the glow the nothing in God is complete except there is nothing
to be incomplete the pulse and change of rhythm, blown flight
to be anything at all . . . vibration holy nuance beating against
itself, a rhythm a playing re-understood now by one of the 1st race
the primitives the first men who evolve again to civilize the
world

1969

A Poem Some People Will Have to Understand

Dull unwashed windows of eyes
and buildings of industry. What
industry do I practice? A slick
colored boy, 12 miles from his
home. I practice no industry.
I am no longer a credit
to my race. I read a little,
scratch against silence slow spring
afternoons.
I had thought, before, some years ago
that I'd come to the end of my life.
Watercolor ego. Without the preciseness
a violent man could propose.
But the wheel, and the wheels,
won't let us alone. All the fantasy
and justice, and dry charcoal winters
All the pitifully intelligent citizens
I've forced myself to love.

We have awaited the coming of a natural
phenomenon. Mystics and romantics, knowledgeable
workers
of the land.

But none has come.
(Repeat)
but none has come.

Will the machinegunners please step forward?

1969

Numbers, Letters

If you're not home, where
are you? Where'd you go? What
were you doing when gone? When
you come back, better make it good.
What was you doing down there, freakin' off[1]
with white women, hangin' out
with Queens, say it straight, to be
understood straight, put it flat and real
in the street where the sun comes and the
moon comes and the cold wind in winter
waters your eyes. Say what you mean, dig
it out put it down, and be strong
about it.

I cant say who I am
unless you agree I'm real

I cant be anything I'm not
Except these words pretend
to life not yet explained,
so here's some feeling for you
see how you like it, what it
reveals, and that's me.

Unless you agree I'm real
that I can feel
whatever beats hardest
at our black souls

I am real, and I can't say who
I am. Ask me if I know, I'll say
yes, I might say no. Still, ask.

I'm Everett LeRoi Jones, 30 yrs old.
A black nigger in the universe. A long breath singer,
wouldbe dancer, strong from years of fantasy
and study. All this time then, for what's happening
now. All that spilling of white ether, clocks in ghostheads
lips drying and rewet, eyes opening and shut, mouths churning.

[1]Going crazy.

I am a meditative man. And when I say something it's all of me
saying, and all the things that make me, have formed me, colored me
this brilliant reddish night. I will say nothing that I feel is
lie, or unproven by the same ghostclocks, by the same riders
always move so fast with the word slung over their backs or
in saddlebags, charging down Chinese roads. I carry some words,
some feeling, some life in me. My heart is large as my mind
this is a messenger calling, over here, over here, open your eyes
and your ears and your souls; today is the history we must learn
to desire. There is no guilt in love

1969

Dutchman

Characters

CLAY, *twenty-year-old Negro*
LULA, *thirty-year-old white woman*
RIDERS OF COACH, *white and black*
YOUNG NEGRO
CONDUCTOR

In the flying underbelly of the city. Steaming hot, and summer on top, outside. Underground. The subway heaped in modern myth.

Opening scene is a man sitting in a subway seat, holding a magazine but looking vacantly just above its wilting pages. Occasionally he looks blankly toward the window on his right. Dim lights and darkness whistling by against the glass. (Or paste the lights, as admitted props, right on the subway windows. Have them move, even dim and flicker. But give the sense of speed. Also stations, whether the train is stopped or the glitter and activity of these stations merely flashes by the windows.)

The man is sitting alone. That is, only his seat is visible, though the rest of the car is outfitted as a complete subway car. But only his seat is shown. There might be, for a time, as the play begins, a loud scream of the actual train. And it can recur throughout the play, or continue on a lower key once the dialogue starts.

The train slows after a time, pulling to a brief stop at one of the stations. The man looks idly up, until he sees a woman's face staring at him through the window; when it realizes that the man has noticed the face, it begins very premeditatedly to smile. The man smiles too, for a moment, without a trace of self-consciousness. Almost an instinctive though undesirable response. Then a kind of awkwardness or embarrassment sets in, and the man makes to look away, is further embarrassed, so he brings back his eyes to where the face was, but by now the train is moving again, and the face would seem to be left behind by the way the man turns his head to look back through the other windows at the slowly fading platform. He smiles then; more comfortably confident, hoping perhaps that his memory of this brief encounter will be pleasant. And then he is idle again.

Scene I

Train roars. Lights flash outside the windows.

LULA *enters from the rear of the car in bright, skimpy summer clothes and sandals. She carries a net bag full of paper books, fruit, and other anonymous articles. She is wearing sunglasses, which she pushes up on her forehead from time to time.* LULA *is a tall, slender, beautiful woman with long red hair hanging straight down her back, wearing only loud lipstick in somebody's good taste. She is eating an apple, very daintily. Coming down the car toward* CLAY.

She stops beside CLAY's *seat and hangs languidly from the strap, still managing to eat the apple. It is apparent that she is going to sit in the seat next to* CLAY, *and that she is only waiting for him to notice her before she sits.*

CLAY *sits as before, looking just beyond his magazine, now and again pulling the magazine slowly back and forth in front of his face in a hopeless effort to fan himself. Then he sees the woman hanging there beside him and he looks up into her face, smiling quizzically.*

LULA: Hello.
CLAY: Uh, hi're you?
LULA: I'm going to sit down. . . . O.K.?
CLAY: Sure.
LULA:

[Swings down onto the seat, pushing her legs straight out as if she is very weary]

Oooof! Too much weight.
CLAY: Ha, doesn't look like much to me.

[Leaning back against the window, a little surprised and maybe stiff]

LULA: It's so anyway.

[And she moves her toes in the sandals, then pulls her right leg up on the left knee, better to inspect the bottoms of the sandals and the back of her heel. She appears for a second not to notice that CLAY *is sitting next to her or that she has spoken to him just a second before.* CLAY *looks at the magazine, then out the black window. As he does this, she turns very quickly toward him]*

Weren't you staring at me through the window?

CLAY:

[Wheeling around and very much stiffened]

What?

LULA: Weren't you staring at me through the window? At the last stop?

CLAY: Staring at you? What do you mean?

LULA: Don't you know what staring means?

CLAY: saw you through the window . . . if that's what it means. I don't know if I was staring. Seems to me you were staring through the window at me.

LULA: I was. But only after I'd turned around and saw you staring through that window down in the vicinity of my ass and legs.

CLAY: Really?

LULA: Really. I guess you were just taking those idle potshots. Nothing else to do. Run your mind over people's flesh.

CLAY: Oh boy. Wow, now I admit I was looking in your direction. But the rest of that weight is yours.

LULA: I suppose.

CLAY: Staring through train windows is weird business. Much weirder than staring very sedately at abstract asses.

LULA: That's why I came looking through the window . . . so you'd have more than that to go on. I even smiled at you.

CLAY: That's right.

LULA: I even got into this train, going some other way than mine. Walked down the aisle . . . searching you out.

CLAY: Really? That's pretty funny.

LULA: That's pretty funny. . . . God, you're dull.

CLAY: Well, I'm sorry, lady, but I really wasn't prepared for party talk.

LULA: No, you're not. What are you prepared for?

[Wrapping the apple core in a Kleenex and dropping it on the floor]

CLAY:

[Takes her conversation as pure sex talk. He turns to confront her squarely with this idea]

I'm prepared for anything. How about you?

LULA:

[Laughing loudly and cutting it off abruptly]

What do you think you're doing?

CLAY: What?

LULA: You think I want to pick you up, get you to take me somewhere and screw me, huh?

CLAY: Is that the way I look?

LULA: You look like you been trying to grow a beard. That's exactly what you look like. You look like you live in New Jersey with your parents and are trying to grow a beard. That's what. You look like you've been reading Chinese poetry and drinking lukewarm sugarless tea.

[Laughs, uncrossing and recrossing her legs]

You look like death eating a soda cracker.

CLAY:

[Cocking his head from one side to the other, embarrassed and trying to make some comeback, but also intrigued by what the woman is saying . . . even the sharp city coarseness of her voice, which is still a kind of gentle sidewalk throb]

Really? I look like all that?

LULA: Not all of it.

[She feints a seriousness to cover an actual somber tone]

I lie a lot.

[Smiling]

It helps me control the world.

CLAY:

[Relieved and laughing louder than the humor]

Yeah, I bet.

LULA: But it's true, most of it, right? Jersey? Your bumpy neck?

CLAY: How'd you know all that? Huh? Really, I mean about Jersey . . . and even the beard. I met you before? You know Warren Enright?

LULA: You tried to make it with your sister when you were ten.

*[*CLAY *leans back hard against the back of the seat, his eyes opening now, still trying to look amused]*

But I succeeded a few weeks ago.

[She starts to laugh again]

CLAY: What're you talking about? Warren tell you that? You're a friend of Georgia's?

LULA: I told you I lie. I don't know your sister. I don't know Warren Enright.

CLAY: You mean you're just picking these things out of the air?

LULA: Is Warren Enright a tall skinny black black boy with a phony English accent?

CLAY: I figured you knew him.

LULA: But I don't. I just figured you would know somebody like that.

[Laughs]

CLAY: Yeah, yeah.
LULA: You're probably on your way to his house now.
CLAY: That's right.
LULA:

[Putting her hand on CLAY*'s closest knee, drawing it from the knee up to the thigh's hinge, then removing it, watching his face very closely and continuing to laugh, perhaps more gently than before]*

Dull, dull, dull. I bet you think I'm exciting.
CLAY: You're O.K.
LULA: Am I exciting you now?
CLAY: Right. That's not what's supposed to happen?
LULA: How do I know?

[She returns her hand, without moving it, then takes it away and plunges it in her bag to draw out an apple]

You want this?
CLAY: Sure.
LULA:

[She gets one out of the bag for herself]

Eating apples together is always the first step. Or walking up uninhabited Seventh Avenue in the twenties on weekends.

[Bites and giggles, glancing at CLAY *and speaking in loose sing-song]*

Can get you involved . . . boy! Get us involved. Um-huh.

[Mock seriousness]

Would you like to get involved with me, Mister Man?
CLAY:

[Trying to be as flippant as LULA, *whacking happily at the apple]*

Sure. Why not? A beautiful woman like you. Huh, I'd be a fool not to.
LULA: And I bet you're sure you know what you're talking about.

[Taking him a little roughly by the wrist, so he cannot eat the apple, then shaking the wrist]

I bet you're sure of almost everything anybody ever asked you about . . . right?

[Shakes his wrist harder]

Right?

CLAY: Yeah, right. . . . Wow, you're pretty strong, you know? Whatta you, a lady wrestler or something?

LULA: What's wrong with lady wrestlers? And don't answer because you never knew any. Huh.

[Cynically]

That's for sure. They don't have any lady wrestlers in that part of Jersey. That's for sure.

CLAY: Hey, you still haven't told me how you know so much about me.

LULA: I told you I didn't know anything about *you* . . . you're a well-known type.

CLAY: Really?

LULA: Or at least I know the type very well. And your skinny English friend too.

CLAY: Anonymously?

LULA:

[Settles back in seat, single-mindedly finishing her apple and humming snatches of rhythm and blues song]

What?

CLAY: Without knowing us specifically?

LULA: Oh boy.

[Looking quickly at Clay]

What a face. You know, you could be a handsome man.

CLAY: I can't argue with you.

LULA:

[Vague, off-center response]

What?

CLAY:

[Raising his voice, thinking the train noise has drowned part of his sentence]

I can't argue with you.

LULA: My hair is turning gray. A gray hair for each year and type I've come through.

CLAY: Why do you want to sound so old?

LULA: But it's always gentle when it starts.

[Attention drifting]

Hugged against tenements, day or night.

CLAY: What?

LULA:

[Refocusing]

Hey, why don't you take me to that party you're going to?

CLAY: You must be a friend of Warren's to know about the party.

LULA: Wouldn't you like to take me to the party?

[Imitates clinging vine]

Oh, come on, ask me to your party.

CLAY: Of course I'll ask you to come with me to the party. And I'll bet you're a friend of Warren's.

LULA: Why not be a friend of Warren's? Why not?

[Taking his arm]

Have you asked me yet?

CLAY: How can I ask you when I don't know your name?

LULA: Are you talking to my name?

CLAY: What is it, a secret?

LULA: I'm Lena the Hyena.[1]

CLAY: The famous woman poet?

LULA: Poetess! The same!

CLAY: Well, you know so much about me . . . what's my name?

LULA: Morris the Hyena.

CLAY: The famous woman poet?

LULA: The same.

[Laughing and going into her bag]

You want another apple?

CLAY: Can't make it, lady. I only have to keep one doctor away a day.

LULA: I bet your name is . . . something like . . . uh, Gerald or Walter. Huh?

CLAY: God, no.

LULA: Lloyd, Norman? One of those hopeless colored names creeping out of New Jersey. Leonard? Gag. . . .

CLAY: Like Warren?

LULA: Definitely. Just exactly like Warren. Or Everett.

CLAY: Gag. . . .

[1]Character in Al Capp's comic strip, *L'il Abner* (1934–1977). The ugliest woman who ever lived, Lena drove anyone who looked at her instantly mad, so no sane person could reliably describe her. She was the subject of a famous national drawing contest sponsored by Capp in 1945.

LULA: Well, for sure, it's not Willie.
CLAY: It's Clay.
LULA: Clay? Really? Clay what?
CLAY: Take your pick. Jackson, Johnson, or Williams.
LULA: Oh, really? Good for you. But it's got to be Williams. You're too pretentious to be a Jackson or Johnson.
CLAY: Thass right.
LULA: But Clay's O.K.
CLAY: So's Lena.
LULA: It's Lula.
CLAY: Oh?
LULA: Lula the Hyena.
CLAY: Very good.
LULA:

[Starts laughing again]

Now you say to me, "Lula, Lula, why don't you go to this party with me tonight?" It's your turn, and let those be your lines.
CLAY: Lula, why don't you go to this party with me tonight, Huh?
LULA: Say my name twice before you ask, and no huh's.
CLAY: Lula, Lula, why don't you go to this party with me tonight?
LULA: I'd like to go, Clay, but how can you ask me to go when you barely know me?
CLAY: That is strange, isn't it?
LULA: What kind of reaction is that? You're supposed to say, "Aw, come on, we'll get to know each other better at the party."
CLAY: That's pretty corny.
LULA: What are you into anyway?

[Looking at him half sullenly but still amused]

What thing are you playing at, Mister? Mister Clay Williams?

[Grabs his thigh, up near the crotch]

What are *you* thinking about?
CLAY: Watch it now, you're gonna excite me for real.
LULA:

[Taking her hand away and throwing her apple core through the window]

I bet.

[She slumps in the seat and is heavily silent]

CLAY: I thought you knew everything about me? What happened?

*[*LULA *looks at him, then looks slowly away, then over where the other aisle would be. Noise of the train. She reaches in her bag and pulls out one of the paper*

books. She puts it on her leg and thumbs the pages listlessly. CLAY *cocks his head to see the title of the book. Noise of the train.* LULA *flips pages and her eyes drift. Both remain silent*]

Are you going to the party with me, Lula?

LULA:

[Bored and not even looking]

I don't even know you.

CLAY: You said you know my type.

LULA:

[Strangely irritated]

Don't get smart with me, Buster. I know you like the palm of my hand.

CLAY: The one you eat the apples with?

LULA: Yeh. And the one I open doors late Saturday evening with. That's my door. Up at the top of the stairs. Five flights. Above a lot of Italians and lying Americans. And scrape carrots with. Also . . .

[Looks at him]

the same hand I unbutton my dress with, or let my skirt fall down. Same hand. Lover.

CLAY: Are you angry about anything? Did I say something wrong?

LULA: Everything you say is wrong.

[Mock smile]

That's what makes you so attractive. Ha. In that funnybook jacket with all the buttons.

[More animate, taking hold of his jacket]

What've you got that jacket and tie on in all this heat for? And why're you wearing a jacket and tie like that? Did your people ever burn witches or start revolutions over the price of tea? Boy, those narrow-shoulder clothes come from a tradition you ought to feel oppressed by. A three-button suit. What right do you have to be wearing a three-button suit and striped tie? Your grandfather was a slave, he didn't go to Harvard.

CLAY: My grandfather was a night watchman.

LULA: And you went to a colored college where everybody thought they were Averell Harriman.[2]

CLAY: All except me.

LULA: And who did you think you were? Who do you think you are now?

CLAY:

[Laughs as if to make light of the whole trend of the conversation]

[2]Wealthy U.S. businessman and public official (1891–1986). Harriman was undersecretary of state in 1964, when *Dutchman* was first performed.

Well, in college I thought I was Baudelaire.[3] But I've slowed down since.

LULA: I bet you never once thought you were a black nigger.

[Mock serious, then she howls with laughter. CLAY *is stunned but after initial reaction, he quickly tries to appreciate the humor.* LULA *almost shrieks*]

A black Baudelaire.

CLAY: That's right.

LULA: Boy, are you corny. I take back what I said before. Everything you say is not wrong. It's perfect. You should be on television.

CLAY: You act like you're on television already.

LULA: That's because I'm an actress.

CLAY: I thought so.

LULA: Well, you're wrong. I'm no actress. I told you I always lie. I'm nothing, honey, and don't you ever forget it.

[Lighter]

Although my mother was a Communist. The only person in my family ever to amount to anything.

CLAY: My mother was a Republican.

LULA: And your father voted for the man[4] rather than the party.[5]

CLAY: Right!

LULA: Yea for him. Yea, yea for him.

CLAY: Yea!

LULA: And yea for America where he is free to vote for the mediocrity of his choice! Yea!

CLAY: Yea!

LULA: And yea for both your parents who even though they differ about so crucial a matter as the body politic still forged a union of love and sacrifice that was destined to flower at the birth of the noble Clay . . . what's your middle name?

CLAY: Clay.

LULA: A union of love and sacrifice that was destined to flower at the birth of the noble Clay Clay Williams. Yea! And most of all yea yea for you, Clay Clay. The Black Baudelaire! Yes!

[And with knifelike cynicism]

My Christ. My Christ.

CLAY: Thank you, ma'am.

[3]Charles Baudelaire (1821–1867), French poet and critic unappreciated during his lifetime (he was fined for "offenses against public morals" after the publication of one book), now considered a landmark French literary figure.

[4]Slang for "the white man," or the system of institutionalized racism that oppresses black Americans.

[5]The International Communist Party, which recruited heavily among the American black population in the mid-twentieth century by promising complete racial equality.

LULA: May the people accept you as a ghost of the future. And love you, that you might not kill them when you can.
CLAY: What?
LULA: You're a murderer, Clay, and you know it.

[Her voice darkening with significance]

You know goddamn well what I mean.
CLAY: I do?
LULA: So we'll pretend the air is light and full of perfume.
CLAY:

[Sniffing at her blouse]

It is.
LULA: And we'll pretend the people cannot see you. That is, the citizens. And that you are free of your own history. And I am free of my history. We'll pretend that we are both anonymous beauties smashing along through the city's entrails.

[She yells as loud as she can]

GROOVE!

Black

Scene II

Scene is the same as before, though now there are other seats visible in the car. And throughout the scene other people get on the subway. There are maybe one or two seated in the car as the scene opens, though neither CLAY *nor* LULA *notices them.* CLAY*'s tie is open.* LULA *is hugging his arm.*

CLAY: The party!
LULA: I know it'll be something good. You can come in with me, looking casual and significant. I'll be strange, haughty, and silent, and walk with long slow strides.
CLAY: Right.
LULA: When you get drunk, pat me once, very lovingly on the flanks, and I'll look at you cryptically, licking my lips.
CLAY: It sounds like something we can do.
LULA: You'll go around talking to young men about your mind, and to old men about your plans. If you meet a very close friend who is also with someone like me, we can stand together, sipping our drinks and exchanging codes of lust. The atmosphere will be slithering in love and half-love and very open moral decision.
CLAY: Great. Great.
LULA: And everyone will pretend they don't know your name, and then . . .

[She pauses heavily]

later, when they have to, they'll claim a friendship that denies your sterling character.

CLAY:

[Kissing her neck and fingers]

And then what?

LULA: Then? Well, then we'll go down the street, late night, eating apples and winding very deliberately toward my house.

CLAY: Deliberately?

LULA: I mean, we'll look in all the shopwindows, and make fun of the queers. Maybe we'll meet a Jewish Buddhist and flatten his conceits over some very pretentious coffee.

CLAY: In honor of whose God?

LULA: Mine.

CLAY: Who is . . . ?

LULA: Me . . . and you?

CLAY: A corporate Godhead.

LULA: Exactly. Exactly.

[Notices one of the other people entering]

CLAY: Go on with the chronicle. Then what happens to us?

LULA:

[A mild depression, but she still makes her description triumphant and increasingly direct]

To my house, of course.

CLAY: Of course.

LULA: And up the narrow steps of the tenement.[6]

CLAY: You live in a tenement?

LULA: Wouldn't live anywhere else. Reminds me specifically of my novel form of insanity.

CLAY: Up the tenement stairs.

LULA: And with my apple-eating hand I push open the door and lead you, my tender big-eyed prey, into my . . . God, what can I call it . . . into my hovel.

CLAY: Then what happens?

LULA: After the dancing and games, after the long drinks and long walks, the real fun begins.

[6]Apartment house, but with connotations of overcrowding, poor sanitation, safety hazards, and discomfort. Generally used to refer to the housing of impoverished urban immigrants during the early twentieth century.

CLAY: Ah, the real fun.

[Embarrassed, in spite of himself]

Which is . . . ?

LULA:

[Laughs at him]

Real fun in the dark house. Hah! Real fun in the dark house, high up above the street and the ignorant cowboys. I lead you in, holding your wet hand gently in my hand . . .

CLAY: Which is not wet?

LULA: Which is dry as ashes.

CLAY: And cold?

LULA: Don't think you'll get out of your responsibility that way. It's not cold at all. You Fascist![7] Into my dark living room. Where we'll sit and talk endlessly, endlessly.

CLAY: About what?

LULA: About what? About your manhood, what do you think? What do you think we've been talking about all this time?

CLAY: Well, I didn't know it was that. That's for sure. Every other thing in the world but that.

[Notices another person entering, looks quickly, almost involuntarily up and down the car, seeing the other people in the car]

Hey, I didn't even notice when those people got on.

LULA: Yeah, I know.

CLAY: Man, this subway is slow.

LULA: Yeah, I know.

CLAY: Well, go on. We were talking about my manhood.

LULA: We still are. All the time.

CLAY: We were in your living room.

LULA: My dark living room. Talking endlessly.

CLAY: About my manhood.

LULA: I'll make you a map of it. Just as soon as we get to my house.

CLAY: Well, that's great.

LULA: One of the things we do while we talk. And screw.

CLAY:

[Trying to make his smile broader and less shaky]

[7]An adherent of Fascism, a totalitarian political system organized around fidelity to a dictatorial leader, social and economic centralization, and the violent suppression of resistance.

We finally got there.

LULA: And you'll call my rooms black as a grave. You'll say, "This place is like Juliet's tomb."[8]

CLAY:

[Laughs]

I might.

LULA: I know. You've probably said it before.

CLAY: And is that all? The whole grand tour?

LULA: Not all. You'll say to me very close to my face, many, many times, you'll say, even whisper, that you love me.

CLAY: Maybe I will.

LULA: And you'll be lying.

CLAY: I wouldn't lie about something like that.

LULA: Hah. It's the only kind of thing you will lie about. Especially if you think it'll keep me alive.

CLAY: Keep you alive? I don't understand.

LULA:

[Bursting out laughing, but too shrilly]

Don't understand? Well, don't look at me. It's the path I take, that's all. Where both feet take me when I set them down. One in front of the other.

CLAY: Morbid. Morbid. You sure you're not an actress? All that self-aggrandizement.

LULA: Well, I told you I wasn't an actress . . . but I also told you I lie all the time. Draw your own conclusions.

CLAY: Morbid. Morbid. You sure you're not an actress? All scribed? There's no more?

LULA: I've told you all I know. Or almost all.

CLAY: There's no funny parts?

LULA: I thought it was all funny.

CLAY: But you mean peculiar, not ha-ha.

LULA: You don't know what I mean.

CLAY: Well, tell me the almost part then. You said almost all. What else? I want the whole story.

LULA:

[Searching aimlessly through her bag. She begins to talk breathlessly, with a light and silly tone]

[8]From William Shakespeare's *Romeo and Juliet.* Because her parents opposed her marriage to Romeo, Juliet feigned death with a sleeping potion in order to be reunited with him, thus spending several days alive in her family's tomb.

All stories are whole stories. All of 'em. Our whole story . . . nothing but change. How could things go on like that forever? Huh?

[Slaps him on the shoulder, begins finding things in her bag, taking them out and throwing them over her shoulder into the aisle]

Except I do go on as I do. Apples and long walks with deathless intelligent lovers. But you mix it up. Look out the window, all the time. Turning pages. Change change change. Till, shit, I don't know you. Wouldn't, for that matter. You're too serious. I bet you're even too serious to be psychoanalyzed. Like all those Jewish poets from Yonkers,[9] who leave their mothers looking for other mothers, or others' mothers, on whose baggy tits they lay their fumbling heads. Their poems are always funny, and all about sex.

CLAY: They sound great. Like movies.

LULA: But you change.

[Blankly]

And things work on you till you hate them.

[More people come into the train. They come closer to the couple, some of them not sitting, but swinging drearily on the straps, staring at the two with uncertain interest]

CLAY: Wow. All these people, so suddenly. They must all come from the same place.

LULA: Right. That they do.

CLAY: Oh? You know about them too?

LULA: Oh yeah. About them more than I know about you. Do they frighten you?

CLAY: Frighten me? Why should they frighten me?

LULA: 'Cause you're an escaped nigger.

CLAY: Yeah?

LULA: 'Cause you crawled through the wire and made tracks to my side.

CLAY: Wire?

LULA: Don't they have wire around plantations?

CLAY: You must be Jewish. All you can think about is wire.[10] Plantations didn't have any wire. Plantations were big open whitewashed places like heaven, and everybody on 'em was grooved to be there. Just strummin' and hummin' all day.

LULA: Yes, yes.

CLAY: And that's how the blues was born.

LULA: Yes, yes. And that's how the blues was born.

[Begins to make up a song that becomes quickly hysterical. As she sings she rises from her seat, still throwing things out of her bag into the aisle, beginning a rhythmical

[9]Suburb of Manhattan in southern Westchester County, New York.

[10]Reference to the barbed wire fences surrounding Nazi concentration camps during the Holocaust.

shudder and twistlike wiggle, which she continues up and down the aisle, bumping into many of the standing people and tripping over the feet of those sitting. Each time she runs into a person she lets out a very vicious piece of profanity, wiggling and stepping all the time]

And that's how the blues was born. Yes. Yes. Son of a bitch, get out of the way. Yes. Quack. Yes. Yes. And that's how the blues was born. Ten little niggers sitting on a limb, but none of them ever looked like him.[11]

[Points to CLAY, *returns toward the seat, with her hands extended for him to rise and dance with her]*

And that's how blues was born. Yes. Come on, Clay. Let's do the nasty. Rub bellies. Rub bellies.

CLAY:

[Waves his hands to refuse. He is embarrassed, but determined to get a kick out of the proceedings]

Hey, what was in those apples? Mirror, mirror on the wall, who's the fairest one of all? Snow White,[12] baby, and don't you forget it.

LULA:

[Grabbing for his hands, which he draws away]

Come on, Clay. Let's rub bellies on the train. The nasty. The nasty. Do the gritty grind, like your ol' rag-head mammy. Grind till you lose your mind. Shake it, shake it, shake it, shake it! OOOOweeee! Come on, Clay. Let's do the choo-choo train shuffle, the navel scratcher.

CLAY: Hey, you coming on like the lady who smoked up her grass skirt.

LULA:

[Becoming annoyed that he will not dance, and becoming more animated as if to embarrass him still further]

Come on, Clay . . . let's do the thing. Uhh! Uhh! Clay! Clay! You middle-class black bastard. Forget your social-working mother for a few seconds and let's knock stomachs. Clay, you liver-lipped white man. You would-be Christian. You ain't no nigger, you're just a dirty white man. Get up, Clay. Dance with me, Clay.

[11]Parody of a British nursery rhyme, "Ten Little Niggers" (also known as "Ten Little Indians"), in which each of the ten is sequentially killed—for example, "Ten little niggers going out to dine/One choked his little self and then there were nine." In Lula's version, all ten are lynching victims who were hanged from a tree limb.

[12]Slang reference to cocaine.

CLAY: Lula! Sit down, now. Be cool.

LULA:

[Mocking him, in wild dance]

Be cool. Be cool. That's all you know . . . shaking that wildroot cream-oil on your knotty head, jackets buttoning up to your chin, so full of white man's words. Christ. God. Get up and scream at these people. Like scream meaningless shit in these hopeless faces.

[She screams at people in train, still dancing]

Red trains cough Jewish underwear for keeps! Expanding smells of silence. Gravy snot whistling like sea birds. Clay. Clay, you got to break out. Don't sit there dying the way they want you to die. Get up.

CLAY: Oh, sit the fuck down.

[He moves to restrain her]

Sit down, goddamn it.

LULA:

[Twisting out of his reach]

Screw yourself, Uncle Tom.[13] Thomas Woolly-head.

[Begins to dance a kind of jig, mocking CLAY *with loud forced humor]*

There is Uncle Tom . . . I mean, Uncle Thomas Woolly-Head. With old white matted mane. He hobbles on his wooden cane. Old Tom. Old Tom. Let the white man hump his ol' mama, and he jes' shuffle off in the woods and hide his gentle gray head. Ol' Thomas Woolly-Head.

[Some of the other riders are laughing now. A drunk gets up and joins LULA *in her dance, singing, as best he can, her "song."* CLAY *gets up out of his seat and visibly scans the faces of the other riders*]

CLAY: Lula! Lula!

[She is dancing and turning, still shouting as loud as she can. The drunk too is shouting, and waving his hands wildly]

Lula . . . you dumb bitch. Why don't you stop it?

[13]Slang term for a servile black man, taken from the docile, pious black slave and title character of Harriet Beecher Stowe's 1852 novel *Uncle Tom's Cabin.*

[He rushes half stumbling from his seat, and grabs one of her flailing arms]

LULA: Let me go! You black son of a bitch.

[She struggles against him]

Let me go! Help!

*[*CLAY *is dragging her towards her seat, and the drunk seeks to interfere. He grabs* CLAY *around the shoulders and begins wrestling with him.* CLAY *clubs the drunk to the floor without releasing* LULA, *who is still screaming.* CLAY *finally gets her to the seat and throws her into it]*

CLAY: Now you shut the hell up.

[Grabbing her shoulders]

Just shut up. You don't know what you're talking about. You don't know anything. So just keep your stupid mouth closed.

LULA: You're afraid of white people. And your father was. Uncle Tom Big Lip!

CLAY:

[Slaps her as hard as he can, across the mouth. LULA*'s head bangs against the back of the seat. When she raises it again,* CLAY *slaps her again]*

Now shut up and let me talk.

[He turns toward the other riders, some of whom are sitting on the edge of their seats. The drunk is on one knee, rubbing his head, and singing softly the same song. He shuts up too when he sees CLAY *watching him. The others go back to newspapers or stare out the windows]*

Shit, you don't have any sense, Lula, nor feelings either. I could murder you now. Such a tiny ugly throat. I could squeeze it flat, and watch you turn blue, on a humble. For dull kicks. And all these weak-faced ofays[14] squatting around here, staring over their papers at me. Murder them too. Even if they expected it. That man there . . .

[Points to well-dressed man]

I could rip that *Times* right out of his hand, as skinny and middle-classed as I am, I could rip that paper out of his hand and just as easily rip out his throat. It takes no great effort. For what? To kill you soft idiots? You don't understand anything but luxury.

[14]Derogatory black slang for white people.

LULA: You fool!

CLAY:

[Pushing her against the seat]

I'm not telling you again, Tallulah Bankhead![15] Luxury. In your face and your fingers. You telling me what I ought to do.

[Sudden scream frightening the whole coach]

Well, don't! Don't you tell me anything! If I'm a middle-class fake white man . . . let me be. And let me be in the way I want.

[Through his teeth]

I'll rip your lousy breasts off! Let me be who I feel like being. Uncle Tom. Thomas. Whoever. It's none of your business. You don't know anything except what's there for you to see. An act. Lies. Device. Not the pure heart, the pumping black heart. You don't ever know that. And I sit here, in this buttoned-up suit, to keep myself from cutting all your throats. I mean wantonly. You great liberated whore! You fuck some black man, and right away you're an expert on black people. What a lotta shit that is. The only thing you know is that you come if he bangs you hard enough. And that's all. The belly rub? You wanted to do the belly rub? Shit, you don't even know how. You don't know how. That ol' dipty-dip shit you do, rolling your ass like an elephant. That's not my kind of belly rub. Belly rub is not Queens. Belly rub is dark places, with big hats and overcoats held up with one arm. Belly rub hates you. Old bald-headed four-eyed ofays popping their fingers . . . and don't know yet what they're doing. They say, "I love Bessie Smith."[16] And don't even understand that Bessie Smith is saying, "Kiss my ass, kiss my black unruly ass." Before love, suffering, desire, anything you can explain, she's saying, and very plainly, "Kiss my black ass." And if you don't know that, it's you that's doing the kissing.

Charlie Parker?[17] Charlie Parker. All the hip white boys scream for Bird. And Bird saying, "Up your ass, feeble-minded ofay! Up your ass." And they sit there talking about the tortured genius of Charlie Parker. Bird would've played not a note of music if he just walked up to East Sixty-seventh Street and killed the first ten white people he saw. Not a note! And I'm the great would-be poet. Yes. That's right! Poet. Some kind of bastard literature . . . all it needs is a simple

[15]Flamboyant American stage and film actress (1903–1968), notorious for glamorous parties, heavy drinking, chain smoking, and public nudity.

[16]Legendary American blues singer and enormously influential musician (1895–1937) who achieved stardom in the 1920s with both black and white audiences.

[17]Known as "Bird," brilliant jazz saxophonist (1920–1955) who pioneered bebop and improvisational forms, changing popular music forever. Almost as well known for his lifelong drug use as for his music, Parker collaborated with nearly every major jazz musician of the mid-twentieth century before his untimely death at 34.

knife thrust. Just let me bleed you, you loud whore, and one poem vanished. A whole people of neurotics, struggling to keep from being sane. And the only thing that would cure the neurosis would be your murder. Simple as that. I mean if I murdered you, then other white people would begin to understand me. You understand? No. I guess not. If Bessie Smith had killed some white people she wouldn't have needed that music. She could have talked very straight and plain about the world. No metaphors. No grunts. No wiggles in the dark of her soul. Just straight two and two are four. Money. Power. Luxury. Like that. All of them. Crazy niggers turning their backs on sanity. When all it needs is that simple act. Murder. Just murder! Would make us all sane.

[Suddenly weary]

Ahhh. Shit. But who needs it? I'd rather be a fool. Insane. Safe with my words, and no deaths, and clean, hard thoughts, urging me to new conquests. My people's madness. Hah! That's a laugh. My people. They don't need me to claim them. They got legs and arms of their own. Personal insanities. Mirrors. They don't need all those words. They don't need any defense. But listen, though, one more thing. And you tell this to your father, who's probably the kind of man who needs to know at once. So he can plan ahead. Tell him not to preach so much rationalism and cold logic to these niggers. Let them alone. Let them sing curses at you in code and see your filth as simple lack of style. Don't make the mistake, through some irresponsible surge of Christian charity, of talking too much about the advantages of Western rationalism, or the great intellectual legacy of the white man, or maybe they'll begin to listen. And then, maybe one day, you'll find they actually do understand exactly what you are talking about, all these fantasy people. All these blues people. And on that day, as sure as shit, when you really believe you can "accept" them into your fold, as half-white trusties late of the subject peoples. With no more blues, except the very old ones, and not a watermelon in sight, the great missionary heart will have triumphed, and all of those ex-coons will be stand-up Western men, with eyes for clean hard useful lives, sober, pious and sane, and they'll murder you. They'll murder you, and have very rational explanations. Very much like your own. They'll cut your throats, and drag you out to the edge of your cities so the flesh can fall away from your bones, in sanitary isolation.

LULA:

[Her voice takes on a different, more businesslike quality]

I've heard enough.

CLAY:

[Reaching for his books]

I bet you have. I guess I better collect my stuff and get off this train. Looks like we won't be acting out that little pageant you outlined before.

LULA: No. We won't. You're right about that, at least.

[She turns to look quickly around the rest of the car]

All right!

[The others respond]

CLAY:

[Bending across the girl to retrieve his belongings]

Sorry, baby, I don't think we could make it.

[As he is bending over her, the girl brings up a small knife and plunges it into CLAY*'s chest. Twice. He slumps across her knees, his mouth working stupidly]*

LULA: Sorry is right.

[Turning to the others in the car who have already gotten up from their seats]

Sorry is the rightest thing you've said. Get this man off me! Hurry, now!

[The others come and drag CLAY*'s body down the aisle]*

Open the door and throw his body out.

[They throw him off]

And all of you get off at the next stop.

*[*LULA *busies herself straightening her things. Getting everything in order. She takes out a notebook and makes a quick scribbling note. Drops it in her bag. The train apparently stops and all the others get off, leaving her alone in the coach.*

Very soon a young Negro of about twenty comes into the coach, with a couple of books under his arm. He sits a few seats in back of LULA*. When he is seated she turns and gives him a long slow look. He looks up from his book and drops the book on his lap. Then an old Negro conductor comes into the car, doing a sort of restrained soft shoe, and half mumbling the words of some song. He looks at the young man, briefly, with a quick greeting]*

CONDUCTOR: Hey, brother!

YOUNG MAN: Hey.

[The conductor continues down the aisle with his little dance and the mumbled song. LULA *turns to stare at him and follows his movements down the aisle. The conductor tips his hat when he reaches her seat, and continues out the car]*

Curtain

1964

Sonia Sanchez b. 1934

Born in Birmingham, Alabama, Sanchez has taught creative writing and African American literature in at least eight universities across the United States. Now a professor of English at Temple University, she has performed her poems and given poetry workshops in Australia, England, Cuba, Nicaragua, and Africa, as well as the States. No other American figure blends the roles of mother, teacher, poet, and political activist more sincerely and energetically than Sanchez.

Her poems manifest the spiritual link between art and politics. If her earlier poems are to be appreciated, the reader must forget all conceptions of what the "poem" is, and listen attentively to Sanchez's attacks on the Euro-American political, social, and aesthetic establishments. Her work is intentionally non-intellectual, unacademic, and anti-middle-class. "To blk/record buyers" is characteristic of her work which aims at teaching blacks to know themselves, to be self-reliant, and strong. In this poem she attacks the Righteous Brothers for their aping a style which originated with black performers such as James Brown. What appears to be a list of the activities in the black urban community contains over three hundred years of black history. Sex, language and retorts, drinking, mocking war materials, crime, and religion are the placeboes blacks have used for comfort. Sanchez's poem ends with the "AAAH, AAAH, AAAH, yeah" which both affirms her point and echoes the style of popular artists like Aretha Franklin and James Brown.

Sanchez's language comes out of her immediate surroundings and accents her characters' lifestyles. Her refusal to use standard, academic English is a part of a political statement which undermines the use of language as a tool for oppression.

Two of her more important thematic concerns are her interest in the relationship between black men and black women, and her interest in black children. Two of her books are written for the young: *It's a New Day* and *A Sound Investment.* In these texts, too, Sanchez's purpose is to teach black people to know themselves, to be themselves, and to love themselves.

By the time of the publication of *It's a New Day,* Sanchez had become a member of Elijah Muhammad's Muslim community. Her Islamic ideology infuses her fourth and fifth books of poetry, *Love Poems* and *Blues Book for Blue Black Magical Women;* there she expresses her spiritual, mystical nature. And from this influence, her poetry becomes more mystical, more suggestive and abstract. While she experiments with the spatial possibilities in her earlier collections, *Homegirls & Handgrenades,* her sixth volume of poetry, introduces several prose-poems such as the very moving "Just Don't Never Give Up on Love" that looks like prose, but has many of the characteristics of poetry. *Under a Soprano Sky,* Sanchez's last collection to date, demonstrates both the fact that she has perfectly honed her skills at repetition, hyperbole, and invective, and that she has become more captivated by the sounds of language and the use of metaphor and imagery.

Joyce Ann Joyce
Chicago State University

PRIMARY WORKS

Homecoming, 1969; *Liberation Poem,* 1970; *We a BaddDDD People,* 1970; *Ima Talken bout the Nation of Islam,* 1972; *A Blues Book for Blue Black Magical Women,* 1973; *Love Poems,* 1973; *I've Been a Woman: New and Selected Poems,* 1981; *Homegirls & Handgrenades,* 1984; *Under a Soprano Sky,* 1987; also plays, children's books, and essays.

to blk/record/buyers

don't play me no
righteous bros.
white people
ain't rt bout nothing
no mo.
don't tell me bout
foreign dudes
cuz no blk/
people are grooving on a
sunday afternoon.
they either
making out/
signifying/
drinking/
making molotov cocktails/
stealing
or rather more taking their goods
from the honky thieves who
ain't hung up
on no pacifist/jesus/
cross/ but.
play blk/songs
to drown out the
shit/screams of honkies. AAAH.
AAAH AAAH yeah. brothers.
andmanymoretogo.

1969

Masks

(blacks don't have the intellectual capacity to succeed.)
—WILLIAM COORS

the river runs toward day
and never stops.
so life receives the lakes
patrolled by one-eyed pimps
who wash their feet in our blue whoredom

the river floods
the days grow short
we wait to change our masks
we wait for warmer days and
fountains without force
we wait for seasons without power.

today
ah today
only the shrill sparrow seeks the sky
our days are edifice.
we look toward temples that give birth to sanctioned flesh.

o bring the white mask
full of the chalk sky.

entering the temple
on this day of sundays
i hear the word spoken
by the unhurried speaker
who speaks of unveiled eyes.

o bring the chalk mask
full of altitudes.

straight in this chair
tall in an unrehearsed role
i rejoice
and the spirit sinks in twilight of
distant smells.

o bring the mask
full of drying blood.

fee, fie, fo, fum,
i smell the blood
of an englishman

o my people
wear the white masks
for they speak without speaking
and hear words of forgetfulness.

o my people.

1984

Just Don't Never Give Up on Love

Feeling tired that day, I came to the park with the children. I saw her as I rounded the corner, sitting old as stale beer on the bench, ruminating on some uneventful past. And I thought, "Hell. No rap from the roots today. I need the present. On this day. This Monday. This July day buckling me under her summer wings, I need more than old words for my body to squeeze into."

I sat down at the far end of the bench, draping my legs over the edge, baring my back to time and time unwell spent. I screamed to the children to watch those curves threatening their youth as they rode their 10-speed bikes against mid-western rhythms.

I opened my book and began to write. They were coming again, those words insistent as his hands had been, pounding inside me, demanding their time and place. I relaxed as my hands moved across the paper like one possessed.

I wasn't sure just what it was I heard. At first I thought it was one of the boys calling me so I kept on writing. They knew the routine by now. Emergencies demanded a presence. A facial confrontation. No long distance screams across trees and space and other children's screams. But the sound pierced the pages and I looked around, and there she was inching her bamboo-creased body toward my back, coughing a beaded sentence off her tongue.

"Guess you think I ain't never loved, huh girl? Hee. Hee. Guess that what you be thinking, huh?"

I turned. Startled by her closeness and impropriety, I stuttered, "I, I, I, Whhhaat dooooo you mean?"

"Hee. Hee. Guess you think I been old like this fo'ever, huh?" She leaned toward me, "Huh? I was so pretty that mens brought me breakfast in bed. Wouldn't let me hardly do no work at all."

"That's nice ma'am. I'm glad to hear that." I returned to my book. I didn't want to hear about some ancient love that she carried inside her. I had to finish a review for the journal. I was already late. I hoped she would get the hint and just sit still. I looked at her out of the corner of my eyes.

"He could barely keep hisself in changing clothes. But he was pretty. My first husband looked like the sun. I used to say his name over and over again 'til it hung from my ears like diamonds. Has you ever loved a pretty man, girl?"

I raised my eyes, determined to keep a distance from this woman disturbing my day.

"No ma'am. But I've seen many a pretty man. I don't like them though cuz they keep their love up high in a linen closet and I'm too short to reach it."

Her skin shook with laughter.

"Girl you gots some spunk about you after all. C'mon over here next to me. I wants to see yo' eyes up close. You looks so uneven sittin' over there."

Did she say uneven? Did this old buddah splintering death say uneven? Couldn't she see that I had one eye shorter than the other; that my breath was painted on porcelain; that one breast crocheted keloids under this white blouse?

I moved toward her though. I scooped up the years that had stripped me to the waist and moved toward her. And she called to me to come out, come out wherever you are young woman, playing hide and go seek with scarecrow men. I gathered myself up at the gateway of her confessionals.

"Do you know what it mean to love a pretty man, girl?" She crooned in my ear. "You always running behind a man like that girl while he cradles his privates. Ain't no joy in a pretty yellow man, cuz he always out pleasurin' and givin' pleasure."

I nodded my head as her words sailed in my ears. Here was the pulse of a woman whose black ass shook the world once.

She continued. "A woman crying all the time is pitiful. Pitiful I says. I wuz pitiful sitting by the window every night like a cow in the fields chewin' on cud. I wanted to cry out, but not even God hisself could hear me. I tried to cry out til my mouth wuz split open at the throat. I 'spoze there is a time all womens has to visit the slaughter house. My visit lasted five years."

Touching her hands, I felt the summer splintering in prayer, touching her hands, I felt my bones migrating in red noise. I asked, "When did you see the butterflies again?"

Her eyes wandered like quicksand over my face. Then she smiled, "Girl don't you know yet that you don't never give up on love? Don't you know you has in you the pulse of winds? The noise of dragon flies?" Her eyes squinted close and she said, "One of them mornings he woke up callin' me and I wuz gone. I wuz gone running with the moon over my shoulders. I looked no which way at all. I had inside me 'nough knives and spoons to cut/scoop out the night. I wuz a tremblin' as I met the mornin'."

She stirred in her 84-year-old memory. She stirred up her body as she talked. "They's men and mens. Some good. Some bad. Some breathing death. Some breathing life. William wuz my beginnin'. I come to my second husband spittin' metal and he just pick me up and fold me inside him. I wuz christen' with his love."

She began to hum. I didn't recognize the song; it was a prayer. I leaned back and listened to her voice rustling like silk. I heard cathedrals and sonnets; I heard tents and revivals and a black woman spilling black juice among her ruins.

"We all gotta salute death one time or 'nother girl. Death be waitin' out doors trying to get inside. William died at his job. Death just turned 'round and snatched him right off the street."

Her humming became the only sound in the park. Her voice moved across the bench like a mutilated child. And I cried. For myself. For this woman talkin' about love. For all the women who have ever stretched their bodies out anticipating civilization and finding ruins.

The crashing of the bikes was anticlimactic. I jumped up, rushed toward the accident. Man. Little man. Where you bicycling to so very fast? Man. Second little man. Take it slow. It all passes so fast any how.

As I walked the boys and their bikes toward the bench, I smiled at this old woman waiting for our return.

"I want you to meet a great lady, boys."

"Is she a writer, too, ma?"

"No honey. She's a lady who has lived life instead of writing about it."

"After we say hello can we ride a little while longer? Please!"

"Ok. But watch your manners now and your bones afterwards."

"These are my sons, Ma'am."

"How you do sons? I'm Mrs. Rosalie Johnson. Glad to meet you."

The boys shook her hand and listened for a minute to her words. Then they rode off, spinning their wheels on a city neutral with pain.

As I stood watching them race the morning, Mrs. Johnson got up.

"Don't go," I cried. "You didn't finish your story."

"We'll talk by-and-by. I comes out here almost everyday. I sits here on the same bench everyday. I'll probably die sittin' here one day. As good a place as any I 'magine."

"May I hug you, ma'am? You've helped me so much today. You've given me strength to keep on looking."

"No. Don't never go looking for love girl. Just wait. It'll come. Like the rain fallin' from the heaven, it'll come. Just don't never give up on love."

We hugged; then she walked her 84-year-old walk down the street. A black woman. Echoing gold. Carrying couplets from the sky to crease the ground.

1984

A Letter to Dr. Martin Luther King

Dear Martin,

Great God, what a morning, Martin!

The sun is rolling in from faraway places. I watch it reaching out, circling these bare trees like some reverent lover. I have been standing still listening to the morning, and I hear your voice crouched near hills, rising from the mountain tops, breaking the circle of dawn.

You would have been 54 today.

As I point my face toward a new decade, Martin, I want you to know that the country still crowds the spirit. I want you to know that we still hear your footsteps setting out on a road cemented with black bones. I want you to know that the stuttering of guns could not stop your light from crashing against cathedrals chanting piety while hustling the world.

Great God, what a country, Martin!

The decade after your death docked like a spaceship on a new planet. Voyagers all we were. We were the aliens walking up the '70s, a holocaust people on the move looking out from dark eyes. A thirsty generation, circling the peaks of our country for more than a Pepsi taste. We were youngbloods, spinning hip syllables while saluting death in a country neutral with pain.

And our children saw the mirage of plenty spilling from capitalistic sands.
And they ran toward the desert.
And the gods of sand made them immune to words that strengthen the breast.
And they became scavengers walking on the earth.
And you can see them playing. Hide-and-go-seek robbers. Native sons. Running

on their knees. Reinventing slavery on asphalt. Peeling their umbilical cords for a gold chain.

And you can see them on Times Square, in N.Y.C., Martin, selling their 11-, 12-year-old, 13-, 14-year-old bodies to suburban forefathers.

And you can see them on Market Street in Philadelphia bobbing up bellywise, young fishes for old sharks.

And no cocks are crowing on those mean streets.

Great God, what a morning it'll be someday, Martin!

That decade fell like a stone on our eyes. Our movements. Rhythms. Loves. Books. Delivered us from the night, drove out the fears keeping some of us hoarse. New births knocking at the womb kept us walking.

We crossed the cities while a backlash of judges tried to turn us into moles with blackrobed words of reverse racism. But we knew. And our knowing was like a sister's embrace. We crossed the land where famine was fed in public. Where black stomachs exploded on the world's dais while men embalmed their eyes and tongues in gold. But we knew. And our knowing squatted from memory.

Sitting on our past, we watch the new decade dawning. These are strange days, Martin, when the color of freedom becomes disco fever; when soap operas populate our Zulu braids; as the world turns to the conservative right and general hospitals are closing in Black neighborhoods and the young and the restless are drugged by early morning reefer butts. And houses tremble.

These are dangerous days, Martin, when cowboy-riding presidents corral Blacks (and others) in a common crown of thorns; when nuclear-toting generals recite an alphabet of blood; when multinational corporations assassinate ancient cultures while inaugurating new civilizations. Comeout comeout wherever you are. Black country. Waiting to be born . . .

But, Martin, on this, your 54th birthday—with all the reversals—we have learned that black is the beginning of everything.

it was black in the universe before the sun;
it was black in the mind before we opened our eyes;
it was black in the womb of our mother;
black is the beginning,
and if we are the beginning we will be forever.

Martin. I have learned too that fear is not a Black man or woman. Fear cannot disturb the length of those who struggle against material gains for self-aggrandizement. Fear cannot disturb the good of people who have moved to a meeting place where the pulse pounds out freedom and justice for the universe.

Now is the changing of the tides, Martin. You forecast it where leaves dance on the wings of man. Martin. Listen. On this your 54th year, listen and you will hear the earth delivering up curfews to the missionaries and assassins. Listen. And you will hear the tribal songs:

Ayeeee Ayooooo Ayeee
Ayeeee Ayooooo Ayeee
Malcolm . . .
Robeson . . .
Lumumba . . .

Fannie Lou . . .
Garvey . . .
Johnbrown . . .
Tubman . . .
Mandela . . .
(free Mandela,
free Mandela)
Assata . . .
Ke wa rona[1]
Ke wa rona
Ke wa rona
Ke wa rona
Ke wa rona
Ke wa rona
Ke wa rona
Ke wa rona

As we go with you to the sun,
as we walk in the dawn, turn our eyes
Eastward and let the prophecy come true
and let the prophecy come true.
Great God, Martin, what a morning it will be!

1984

Father and Daughter

we talk of light things you and I in this
small house. no winds stir here among
flame orange drapes that drape our genesis
And snow melts into rivers. The young
grandchild reviews her impudence that
makes you laugh and clap for more allure.
Ah, how she twirls the emerald lariat.
When evening comes your eyes transfer
to space you have not known and taste the blood
breath of a final flower. Past equal birth,
the smell of salt begins another flood:
your land is in the ashes of the South.
perhaps the color of our losses:
perhaps the memory that dreams nurse:
old man, we do not speak of crosses.

1985

[1]He is ours.

June Jordan b. 1936

Like many of the finest writers in the African American literary tradition, June Jordan has proven her skill in several genres. Poet, essayist, playwright, novelist, and composer, she is also a seasoned political activist and teacher. Currently a professor of African American studies and women's studies at the University of California at Berkeley, she has also taught at City College of New York, Sarah Lawrence College, and Yale University. Born July 9, 1936, in Harlem, Jordan began writing poetry at the age of seven after her family had moved into a brownstone in Brooklyn's now well-known Bedford-Stuyvesant.

Although her parents, particularly her father, introduced her to the poetry of Shakespeare, Edgar Allan Poe, and Paul Laurence Dunbar, and although the writing of T. S. Eliot and Emily Dickinson is also reflected in her work, she later studied the poetry of Langston Hughes, Margaret Walker, and Robert Hayden. Jordan's poetry is unique. Because of the diversity of these early influences and because of the ingenious way in which she weaves her political activism and her personal experiences as a black bisexual woman into the fabric of her art, her poetry defines its own place in African-American literary history, despite the commonalities she shares with Audre Lorde and Alexis Deveaux.

Jordan's work is heavily influenced by important and sometimes devastating events from her life: her father's disappointment that she was not a boy, his extreme discipline while she was growing up, her mother's suicide, an early marriage that failed, and her having been raped. Jordan's essays and poetry chart the connections she finds among the personal, the literary, the political, and the global. In a 1981 *Essence* interview with Alexis Deveaux, Jordan said of "Poem about My Rights," which she wrote in response to having been raped, "I tried to show as clearly as I could that the difference between South Africa and rape and my mother trying to change my face and my father wanting me to be a boy was not an important difference to me. *It all violates self-determination.*"

This relationship that Jordan addresses between her personal experiences and those of others throughout the world, particularly those in oppressed cultures, defines the depth and range of her art. The titles of her essay collections—*Civil Wars* (1981), *On Call: Political Essays* (1985), *Moving Towards Home: Political Essays* (1989), and *Technical Difficulties: African-American Notes on the State of the Union* (1992),—suggest the connection she makes between the personal, the global, and the political. Her essays as well as her poetry are rooted in her blackness, her bisexuality, and in the honest, fearless way in which she attacks racism and all its related illnesses.

Her travels to Nicaragua, her teaching experience (including children's writing workshops), her work as a freelance journalist, as a research associate and writer for Mobilization for Youth, and her studying architecture at the Donnell Library in Manhattan are all manifest in her poems. In 1969 Jordan won the Prix de Rome in Environmental Design for the way in which she transformed architectural design into fiction in her novel for adolescents *His Own Where,* later published in 1971. She has also written three other books primarily for children.

Although Jordan published three early collections of poetry—*Who Look at Me* (1969), *Some Changes* (1971), and *New Days: Poems of Exile and Return* (1974)—the 1977 *Things That I Do in the Dark: Selected Poetry* contains most of this early work. Prefaced by the poem, "These poems they are things that I do in the dark," this rich collection addresses everything and everybody from her son Christopher to her father Granville Ivanhoe Jordan, her mother, marriage, former President Lyndon Johnson, Malcolm X, bisexuality, and Senator Daniel Patrick Moynihan. Both *Living Room: New Poems* (1985) and *Naming Our Own Destiny* (1989), Jordan's recent collections, show her skill at using titles to illuminate her purpose. The poems in both books address the physical/emotional/spiritual space the oppressed in the United States, Lebanon, Nicaragua, and South Africa need in order to become self-determining. "Moving Towards Home," the last poem in *Living Room,* captures the essence of Jordan's irony and repetition; her ability to use a word seemingly out of context, such as her use of *redeem* near the end of this poem. Translated into Arabic, Spanish, French, Swedish, German, and Japanese, "Moving Towards Home" affirms the international status of Jordan's poetry. Yet all too little is known of her work as a dramatist. She is the author of at least three full-length plays, including the autobiographical *All These Blessings,* completed in 1988. Her work as a dramatist remains virtually unexplored.

Joyce Ann Joyce
Chicago State University

PRIMARY WORKS

Who Look at Me, 1969; *Some Changes,* 1971; *New Days: Poems of Exile and Return,* 1974; *Things That I Do in the Dark: Selected Poetry,* 1977; *Passion: New Poems, 1977–1980,* 1980; *Civil Wars,* 1981; *On Call: Political Essays,* 1985; *Living Room: New Poems,* 1985; *Lyrical Campaigns: Selected Poems,* 1989; *Naming Our Destiny: New and Selected Poems,* 1989; *Moving Towards Home: Political Essays,* 1989; *Technical Difficulties: African-American Notes on the State of the Union,* 1992; also plays and children's books.

Poem About My Rights

Even tonight and I need to take a walk and clear
my head about this poem about why I can't
go out without changing my clothes my shoes
my body posture my gender identity my age
my status as a woman alone in the evening/
alone on the streets/alone not being the point/
the point being that I can't do what I want
to do with my own body because I am the wrong
sex the wrong age the wrong skin and
suppose it was not here in the city but down on the beach/
or far into the woods and I wanted to go
there by myself thinking about God/or thinking
about children or thinking about the world/all of it
disclosed by the stars and the silence:
I could not go and I could not think and I could not
stay there

alone
as I need to be
alone because I can't do what I want to do with my own
body and
who in the hell set things up
like this
and in France they say if the guy penetrates
but does not ejaculate then he did not rape me
and if after stabbing him if after screams if
after begging the bastard and if even after smashing
a hammer to his head if even after that if he
and his buddies fuck me after that
then I consented and there was
no rape because finally you understand finally
they fucked me over because I was wrong I was
wrong again to be me being me where I was/wrong
to be who I am
which is exactly like South Africa
penetrating into Namibia penetrating into
Angola and does that mean I mean how do you know if
Pretoria ejaculates what will the evidence look like the
proof of the monster jackboot ejaculation on Blackland
and if
after Namibia and if after Angola and if after Zimbabwe
and if after all of my kinsmen and women resist even to
self-immolation of the villages and if after that
we lose nevertheless what will the big boys say will they
claim my consent:
Do You Follow Me: We are the wrong people of
the wrong skin on the wrong continent and what
in the hell is everybody being reasonable about
and according to the *Times* this week
back in 1966 the C.I.A. decided that they had this problem
and the problem was a man named Nkrumah so they
killed him and before that it was Patrice Lumumba
and before that it was my father on the campus
of my Ivy League school and my father afraid
to walk into the cafeteria because he said he
was wrong the wrong age the wrong skin the wrong
gender identity and he was paying my tuition and
before that
it was my father saying I was wrong saying that
I should have been a boy because he wanted one/a
boy and that I should have been lighter skinned and
that I should have had straighter hair and that
I should not be so boy crazy but instead I should
just be one/a boy and before that

it was my mother pleading plastic surgery for
my nose and braces for my teeth and telling me
to let the books loose to let them loose in other
words
I am very familiar with the problems of the C.I.A.
and the problems of South Africa and the problems
of Exxon Corporation and the problems of white
America in general and the problems of the teachers
and the preachers and the F.B.I. and the social
workers and my particular Mom and Dad/I am very
familiar with the problems because the problems
turn out to be
me
I am the history of rape
I am the history of the rejection of who I am
I am the history of the terrorized incarceration of
my self
I am the history of battery assault and limitless
armies against whatever I want to do with my mind
and my body and my soul and
whether it's about walking out at night
or whether it's about the love that I feel or
whether it's about the sanctity of my vagina or
the sanctity of my national boundaries
or the sanctity of my leaders or the sanctity
of each and every desire
that I know from my personal and idiosyncratic
and indisputably single and singular heart
I have been raped
be-
cause I have been wrong the wrong sex the wrong age
the wrong skin the wrong nose the wrong hair the
wrong need the wrong dream the wrong geographic
the wrong sartorial I
I have been the meaning of rape
I have been the problem everyone seeks to
eliminate by forced
penetration with or without the evidence of slime and/
but let this be unmistakable this poem
is not consent I do not consent
to my mother to my father to the teachers to
the F.B.I. to South Africa to Bedford-Stuy
to Park Avenue to American Airlines to the hardon
idlers on the corners to the sneaky creeps in
cars
I am not wrong: Wrong is not my name
My name is my own my own my own

and I can't tell you who the hell set things up like this
but I can tell you that from now on my resistance
my simple and daily and nightly self-determination
may very well cost you your life

1989

To Free Nelson Mandela

Every night Winnie Mandela
Every night the waters of the world
turn to the softly burning
light of the moon
Every night Winnie Mandela
Every night

Have they killed the twelve-year-old girl?
Have they hung the poet?
Have they shot down the students?
Have they splashed the clinic the house
and the faces of the children
with blood?

Every night Winnie Mandela
Every night the waters of the world
turn to the softly burning
light of the moon

They have murdered Victoria Mxenge
They have murdered her
victorious now
that the earth recoils from that crime
of her murder now
that the very dirt shudders from the falling blood
the thud of bodies fallen
into the sickening
into the thickening
crimes of apartheid

Every night
Every night Winnie Mandela

Every night Winnie Mandela
Every night the waters of the world

turn to the softly burning
light of the moon

At last the bullets boomerang
At last the artifice of exile explodes
At last no one obeys the bossman of atrocities

At last the carpenters the midwives
the miners the weavers the anonymous
housekeepers the anonymous
street sweepers
the diggers of the ditch
the sentries the scouts the ministers
the mob the pallbearers the practical
nurse
the diggers of the ditch
the banned
the tortured
the detained
the everlastingly insulted
the twelve-year-old girl and her brothers at last
the diggers of the ditch
despise the meal without grace
    the water without wine
    the trial without rights
    the work without rest
at last the diggers of the ditch
begin the living funeral
for death

Every night Winnie Mandela
Every night

Every night Winnie Mandela
Every night the waters of the world
turn to the softly burning
light of the moon

Every night Winnie Mandela
Every night

1989

Moving Towards Home

"Where is Abu Fadi," she wailed.
"Who will bring me my loved one?"
—NEW YORK TIMES 9/20/82

I do not wish to speak about the bulldozer and the
red dirt
not quite covering all of the arms and legs
Nor do I wish to speak about the nightlong screams
that reached
the observation posts where soldiers lounged about
Nor do I wish to speak about the woman who shoved
her baby
into the stranger's hands before she was led away
Nor do I wish to speak about the father whose sons
were shot
through the head while they slit his own throat before
the eyes
of his wife
Nor do I wish to speak about the army that lit continuous
flares into the darkness so that the others could see
the backs of their victims lined against the wall
Nor do I wish to speak about the piled up bodies and
the stench
that will not float
Nor do I wish to speak about the nurse again and
again raped
before they murdered her on the hospital floor
Nor do I wish to speak about the rattling bullets that
did not
halt on that keening trajectory
Nor do I wish to speak about the pounding on the
doors and
the breaking of windows and the hauling of families into
the world of the dead
I do not wish to speak about the bulldozer and the
red dirt
not quite covering all of the arms and legs
because I do not wish to speak about unspeakable events
that must follow from those who dare
"to purify" a people
those who dare
"to exterminate" a people

those who dare
to describe human beings as "beasts with two legs"
those who dare
"to mop up"
"to tighten the noose"
"to step up the military pressure"
"to ring around" civilian streets with tanks
those who dare
to close the universities
to abolish the press
to kill the elected representatives
of the people who refuse to be purified
those are the ones from whom we must redeem
the words of our beginning
because I need to speak about home
I need to speak about living room
where the land is not bullied and beaten into
a tombstone
I need to speak about living room
where the talk will take place in my language
I need to speak about living room
where my children will grow without horror
I need to speak about living room where the men
of my family between the ages of six and sixty-five
are not
marched into a roundup that leads to the grave
I need to talk about living room
where I can sit without grief without wailing aloud
for my loved ones
where I must not ask where is Abu Fadi
because he will be there beside me
I need to talk about living room
because I need to talk about home

I was born a Black woman
and now
I am become a Palestinian
against the relentless laughter of evil
there is less and less living room
and where are my loved ones?

It is time to make our way home.

1985

Etheridge Knight 1931–1991

Etheridge Knight was a black prison-born artist. Born in Corinth, Mississippi, in a large and relatively poor family of seven children, he was able to complete only a ninth grade education. Therefore, he discovered early in his life that his social and economic opportunities were limited. In Corinth, Knight found only menial jobs such as shining shoes available to him and, thus, spent much of his time hanging out in pool halls and barrooms. As a teenager, he turned to narcotics for what he felt would relieve him from his emotional anguish. Then, at sixteen, in his attempt to find a purpose in life, he enlisted in the army and later fought in the Korean War. During the war, Knight's addiction increased when he was treated with narcotics for a shrapnel wound. After his discharge from the service, he drifted aimlessly for several years throughout the country until he eventually settled in Indianapolis, Indiana. During these years, he learned through his experiences in bars and pool halls the art of telling toasts—long narrative poems from the black oral tradition that are acted out in a theatrical manner. Unfortunately, however, his drug addiction, not toast-telling, dominated Knight's life. In Indianapolis, he snatched an old white woman's purse in order to support his addiction and was sentenced in 1960 to serve a ten- to twenty-five year term in Indiana State Prison.

Embittered by his lengthy prison sentence, which he felt was unjust and racist in nature, Knight became rebellious, hostile, and belligerent during his first year of incarceration. However, the *Autobiography of Malcolm X* and other prison works influenced him to turn to writing in order to liberate his soul. As Knight once stated: "I died in Korea from a shrapnel wound and narcotics resurrected me. I died in 1960 from a prison sentence and poetry brought me back to life."

By drawing from his early experiences as a teller of toasts, Knight developed his verse into a transcribed-oral poetry of considerable power. His earlier poems, "The Idea of Ancestry," "The Violent Space," "Hard Rock Returns to Prison from the Hospital for the Criminal Insane," and "He Sees Through Stone," were so effective that Broadside publisher-poet Dudley Randall published Knight's first volume of verse, *Poems From Prison,* and hailed him as one of the major poets of the New Black Aesthetic. In addition, other poets such as Don L. Lee, Gwendolyn Brooks, and Sonia Sanchez aided Knight in obtaining his parole in 1968.

Upon his release from prison, Knight married Sonia Sanchez. However, because of his drug addiction, the marriage was short-lived. He then married Mary McNally and they adopted two children and settled in Minneapolis, Minnesota, until 1977. Three years later, Knight published his volume of poems *Belly Songs and Other Poems.* Separated from Mary in the late 1970s, Knight resided in Memphis, Tennessee, where he received methadone treatments. In 1980 he published *Born of A Woman: New and Selected Poems* and in 1986, *The Essential Etheridge Knight.* He died of lung cancer in March of 1991.

Knight's poetry, much of it written in prison, ranges from expressions of loneliness and frustration to a sense of triumph over the soul's struggle. In his earlier prison poetry, Knight brings us mercilessly and straight on face to face with the infinite varieties of pain and sorrow of the prison world until, finally, the total prison soul stands before us anatomized. We meet the lobotomized inmate "Hard Rock," the raped convict Freckled-Faced Gerald, and the old black soothsayer lifer who "sees through stone" and waits patiently for the dawning of freedom. Above all, in "The Idea of Ancestry" and "The Violent Space," the two most powerful of his prison poems, we witness the poet himself deep in despair, alone in the freedomless void of his prison cell. However, Knight's best poems are his later ones, those that search for heritage, continuity, and meaning. In two of his post-prison poems, "The Bones of My Father," which shows his growing concern for image rather than the statement, and his masterful blues poem, "A Poem for Myself (Or Blues for A Mississippi Black Boy)," Knight's search takes him to the South, the ancestral home for blacks. Finally, in "Ilu, The Talking Drum," one of the finest poems in contemporary American poetry, Knight brings the black American life experience back full circle from Africa to the black South and then back to an Africa of the spirit.

Patricia Liggins-Hill
University of San Francisco

PRIMARY WORKS

Poems From Prison, 1968; *Black Voices from Prison,* 1972; *Belly Song and Other Poems,* 1973; *Born of A Woman: New and Selected Poems,* 1980; *The Essential Etheridge Knight,* 1986.

The Idea of Ancestry

1

Taped to the wall of my cell are 47 pictures: 47 black
faces: my father, mother, grandmothers (1 dead), grand
fathers (both dead), brothers, sisters, uncles, aunts,
cousins (1st & 2nd), nieces, and nephews. They stare
across the space at me sprawling on my bunk. I know
their dark eyes, they know mine. I know their style,
they know mine. I am all of them, they are all of me;
they are farmers, I am a thief, I am me, they are thee.

I have at one time or another been in love with my mother,
1 grandmother, 2 sisters, 2 aunts (1 went to the asylum),
and 5 cousins. I am now in love with a 7 yr old niece
(she sends me letters written in large block print, and
her picture is the only one that smiles at me).

I have the same name as 1 grandfather, 3 cousins, 3 nephews,
and 1 uncle. The uncle disappeared when he was 15, just took
off and caught a freight (they say). He's discussed each year
when the family has a reunion, he causes uneasiness in
the clan, he is an empty space. My father's mother, who is 93
and who keeps the Family Bible with everybody's birth dates
(and death dates) in it, always mentions him. There is no
place in her Bible for "whereabouts unknown."

2

Each Fall the graves of my grandfathers call me, the brown
hills and red gullies of mississippi send out their electric
messages, galvanizing my genes. Last yr/like a salmon quitting
the cold ocean—leaping and bucking up his birthstream/I
hitchhiked my way from L.A. with 16 caps in my pocket and a
monkey on my back. and I almost kicked it with the kinfolks.
I walked barefooted in my grandmother's backyard/I smelled the old
land and the woods/I sipped cornwhiskey from fruit jars with the men/
I flirted with the women/I had a ball till the caps ran out
and my habit came down. That night I looked at my grandmother
and split/my guts were screaming for junk/but I was almost
contented/I had almost caught up with me.
(The next day in Memphis I cracked a croaker's crib[1] for a fix.)

This yr there is a gray stone wall damming my stream, and when
the falling leaves stir my genes, I pace my cell or flop on my bunk
and stare at 47 black faces across the space. I am all of them,
they are all of me, I am me, they are thee, and I have no sons
to float in the space between.

1968

The Violent Space (or when your sister sleeps around for money)

Exchange in greed the ungraceful signs. Thrust
The thick notes between green apple breasts.
Then the shadow of the devil descends,
The violent space cries and angel eyes,
Large and dark, retreat in innocence and in ice.
(Run sister run—the Bugga man comes!)

The violent space cries silently,
Like you cried wide years ago
In another space, speckled by the sun
And the leaves of a green plum tree,
And you were stung
By a red wasp and we flew home.
(Run sister run—the Bugga man comes!)

[1]A doctor's house.

Well, hell, lil sis, wasps still sting.
You are all of seventeen and as alone now
In your pain as you were with the sting
On your brow.
Well, shit, lil sis, here we are:
You and I and this poem.
And what should I do? should I squat
In the dust and make strange markings on the ground?
Shall I chant a spell to drive the demon away?
(Run sister run—the Bugga man comes!)

In the beginning you were the Virgin Mary,
And you are the Virgin Mary now.
But somewhere between Nazareth and Bethlehem
You lost your name in the nameless void.
O Mary don't you weep don't you moan
O Mary shake your butt to the violent juke,
Absorb the demon puke and watch the white eyes pop.
(Run sister run—the Bugga man comes!)

And what do I do. I boil my tears in a twisted spoon
And dance like an angel on the point of a needle.
I sit counting syllables like Midas gold.
I am not bold. I can not yet take hold of the demon
And lift his weight from your black belly,
So I grap the air and sing my song.
(But the air can not stand my singing long.)

1968

Ilu, the Talking Drum

The deadness was threatening us—15 Nigerians and 1 Mississippi
 nigger.
It hung heavily, like stones around our necks, pulling us down
to the ground, black arms and legs outflung
on the wide green lawn of the big white house
near the wide brown beach by the wide blue sea.
The deadness was threatening us, the day
was dying with the sun, the stillness—
unlike the sweet silence after love/making or
the pulsating quietness of a summer night—
the stillness was skinny and brittle and wrinkled
by the precise people sitting on the wide white porch

of the big white house. . . .
The darkness was threatening us, menacing . . .
we twisted, turned, shifted positions, picked our noses,
stared at our bare toes, hissed air thru our teeth. . . .
Then Tunji, green robes flowing as he rose,
strapped on *Ilu,* the talking drum,
and began:

kah doom/kah doom-doom/kah doom/kah doom-doom-doom
kah doom/kah doom-doom/kah doom/kah doom-doom-doom
kah doom/kah doom-doom/kah doom/kah doom-doom-doom
kah doom/kah doom-doom/kah doom/kah doom-doom-doom

the heart, the heart beats, the heart, the heart beats slow
the heart beats slowly, the heart beats
the blood flows slowly, the blood flows
the blood, the blood flows, the blood, the blood flows slow
kah doom/kah doom-doom/kah doom/kah doom-doom-doom
and the day opened to the sound
kah doom/kah doom-doom/kah doom/kah doom-doom-doom
and our feet moved to the sound of life
kah doom/kah doom-doom/kah doom/kah doom-doom-doom
and we rode the rhythms as one
from Nigeria to Mississippi
and back
kah doom/kah doom-doom/kah doom/kah doom-doom-doom

1980

A Poem for Myself (Or Blues for a Mississippi Black Boy)

I was born in Mississippi;
I walked barefooted thru the mud.
Born black in Mississippi,
Walked barefooted thru the mud.
But, when I reached the age of twelve
I left that place for good.
My daddy he chopped cotton
And he drank his liquor straight.
Said my daddy chopped cotton
And he drank his liquor straight.
When I left that Sunday morning

He was leaning on the barnyard gate.
I left my momma standing
With the sun shining in her eyes.
Left her standing in the yard
With the sun shining in her eyes.
And I headed North
As straight as the Wild Goose Flies,
I been to Detroit & Chicago—
Been to New York city too.
I been to Detroit and Chicago
Been to New York city too.
Said I done strolled all those funky avenues
I'm still the same old black boy with the same old blues.
Going back to Mississippi
This time to stay for good
Going back to Mississippi
This time to stay for good—
Gonna be free in Mississippi
Or dead in the Mississippi mud.

1980

Alice Walker b. 1944

Alice Walker was born in Eatonton, Georgia, the youngest of eight children of Minnie and Willie Lee Walker, black sharecroppers. Her early life in the South was marked by the pressures of segregation and economic hardship on one hand, and the nurturing refuge of family, church, and black community on the other. Summer visits with her older brothers who had settled in the North gave Walker her first glimpses of the world beyond the rural South. Her poetry, often quite personal, and at times starkly intimate, in its themes of family connections, romantic passion, and political integrity, draws frequently on remembrances of childhood.

In 1961 Walker entered Spelman College, a black women's school in Atlanta, Georgia. Finding Spelman too traditional, Walker transferred in 1963 to Sarah Lawrence College, a school noted for its avant-garde curriculum in the arts. There, under the tutelage of poet Muriel Rukeyser and others, she began her writing career.

After college, Walker worked briefly for the New York City Welfare Department and in 1967 married Mel Leventhal, a civil rights attorney. The couple moved to Mississippi, where he prosecuted school-desegregation cases and she taught at Jackson State College and also conducted adult education courses in black history. Their life in Mississippi as an interracial, activist couple was harrowing; they lived with constant threats of lethal violence against themselves and their infant daughter. During that time Walker published *The Third Life of Grange Copeland,* a novel of personal and political confrontation and transformation in the lives of three generations of a southern black family. A later novel, *Meridian,* explores the complex psychological burden borne throughout the rest of their lives by those young men and women, black and white, who came of age living and working at the center of the Civil Rights movement of the nineteen sixties.

In 1971, Walker accepted a fellowship from the Radcliffe Institute in Cambridge, Massachusetts, where she worked on poetry and short fiction, as well as on her landmark essay *In Search of Our Mothers' Gardens.* In 1982, Walker published *The Color Purple,* an epistolary novel about the lives of two sisters, Celie and Nettie, raised in a rural, southern, black community and separated through years of tragedy, pain, struggle, and ultimate triumph. The novel was awarded both the American Book Award and the Pulitzer Prize in 1983.

Alice Walker has been from the start of her career a prolific and diversified writer, adept at poetry, novels, short stories, and essays. Throughout her work, a central theme is the courage, resourcefulness, and creativity of black women of various ages, circumstances, and conditions. Whether in rescuing from oblivion the writing and reputation of novelist, folklorist, and anthropologist Zora Neale Hurston, or in producing her own portraits unique in American letters of black women whose rich and complex lives have been little known and frequently devalued, Alice Walker continues to be a central figure in reshaping and expanding the canon of American literature.

Marilyn Richardson

PRIMARY WORKS

Once (poems), 1968; *The Third Life of Grange Copeland* (novel), 1970; *Revolutionary Petunias* (poems), 1973; *In Love & Trouble* (short stories), 1973; *Langston Hughes, American Poet* (biography for young people), 1974; *Meridian* (novel), 1976; *Goodnight, Willie Lee, I'll See You in the Morning* (poems), 1979; *I Love Myself When I Am Laughing . . . And Then Again When I Am Looking Mean and Impressive, A Zora Neale Hurston Reader* (editor), 1979; *You Can't Keep a Good Woman Down* (short stories), 1981; *The Color Purple,* 1982; *In Search of Our Mothers' Gardens* (essays), 1983; *Horses Make a Landscape Look More Beautiful* (poems), 1984; *The Temple of My Familiar,* 1989; *Possessing the Secret of Joy,* 1992; *Warrior Marks: Her Blue Body Everything We Knew: Earthling Poems, 1965–1990,* 1991; *Female Genital Mutilation and the Sexual Blinding of Women,* 1993; *The Same River Twice: Honoring the Difficult,* 1996; *Anything We Love Can Be Saved: A Writer's Activism,* 1997; *By the Light of My Father's Smile: A Novel,* 1998; *The Way Forward Is with a Broken Heart,* 2000.

Nineteen Fifty-Five

1955

The car is a brandnew red Thunderbird convertible, and it's passed the house more than once. It slows down real slow now, and stops at the curb. An older gentleman dressed like a Baptist deacon gets out on the side near the house, and a young fellow who looks about sixteen gets out on the driver's side. They are white, and I wonder what in the world they doing in this neighborhood.

Well, I say to J.T., put your shirt on, anyway, and let me clean these glasses offa the table.

We had been watching the ballgame on TV. I wasn't actually watching, I was sort of daydreaming, with my foots up in J.T.'s lap.

I seen 'em coming on up the walk, brisk, like they coming to sell something, and then they rung the bell, and J.T. declined to put on a shirt but instead disappeared into the bedroom where the other television is. I turned down the one in the living room; I figured I'd be rid of these two double quick and J.T. could come back out again.

Are you Gracie Mae Still? asked the old guy, when I opened the door and put my hand on the lock inside the screen.

And I don't need to buy a thing, said I.

What makes you think we're sellin'? he asks, in that hearty Southern way that makes my eyeballs ache.

Well, one way or another and they're inside the house and the first thing the young fellow does is raise the TV a couple of decibels. He's about five feet nine, sort of womanish looking, with real dark white skin and a red pouting mouth. His hair is black and curly and he looks like a Loosianna creole.

About one of your songs, says the deacon. He is maybe sixty, with white hair and beard, white silk shirt, black linen suit, black tie and black shoes. His cold gray eyes look like they're sweating.

One of my songs?

Traynor here just *loves* your songs. Don't you, Traynor? He nudges Traynor with his elbow. Traynor blinks, says something I can't catch in a pitch I don't register.

The boy learned to sing and dance livin' round you people out in the country. Practically cut his teeth on you.

Traynor looks up at me and bites his thumbnail.

I laugh.

Well, one way or another they leave with my agreement that they can record one of my songs. The deacon writes me a check for five hundred dollars, the boy grunts his awareness of the transaction, and I am laughing all over myself by the time I rejoin J.T.

Just as I am snuggling down beside him though I hear the front door bell going off again.

Forgit his hat? asks J.T.

I hope not, I say.

The deacon stands there leaning on the door frame and once again I'm thinking of those sweaty-looking eyeballs of his. I wonder if sweat makes your eyeballs pink because his are sure pink. Pink and gray and it strikes me that nobody I'd care to know is behind them.

I forgot one little thing, he says pleasantly. I forgot to tell you Traynor and I would like to buy up all of those records you made of the song. I tell you we sure do love it.

Well, love it or not, I'm not so stupid as to let them do that without making 'em pay. So I says, Well, that's gonna cost you. Because, really, that song never did sell all that good, so I was glad they was going to buy it up. But on the other hand, them two listening to my song by themselves, and nobody else getting to hear me sing it, give me a pause.

Well, one way or another the deacon showed me where I would come out ahead on any deal he had proposed so far. Didn't I give you five hundred dollars? he asked. What white man—and don't even need to mention colored—would give you more?

We buy up all your records of that particular song: first, you git royalties. Let me ask you, how much you sell that song for in the first place? Fifty dollars? A hundred, I say. And no royalties from it yet, right? Right. Well, when we buy up all of them records you gonna git royalties. And that's gonna make all them race record shops sit up and take notice of Gracie Mae Still. And they gonna push all them other records of yourn they got. And you no doubt will become one of the big name colored recording artists. And then we can offer you another five hundred dollars for letting us do all this for you. And by God you'll be sittin' pretty! You can go out and buy you the kind of outfit a star should have. Plenty sequins and yards of red satin.

I had done unlocked the screen when I saw I could get some more money out of him. Now I held it wide open while he squeezed through the opening between me and the door. He whipped out another piece of paper and I signed it.

He sort of trotted out to the car and slid in beside Traynor, whose head was back against the seat. They swung around in a u-turn in front of the house and then they was gone.

J.T. was putting his shirt on when I got back to the bedroom. Yankees beat the Orioles 10–6, he said. I believe I'll drive out to Paschal's pond and go fishing. Wanta go?

While I was putting on my pants J.T. was holding the two checks.

I'm real proud of a woman that can make cash money without leavin' home, he said. And I said *Umph.* Because we met on the road with me singing in first one little low-life jook after another, making ten dollars a night for myself if I was lucky, and sometimes bringin' home nothing but my life. And J.T. just loved them times. The way I was fast and flashy and always on the go from one town to another. He loved the way my singin' made the dirt farmers cry like babies and the womens shout Honey, hush! But that's mens. They loves any style to which you can get 'em accustomed.

1956

My little grandbaby called me one night on the phone: Little Mama, Little Mama, there's a white man on the television singing one of your songs! Turn on channel 5.

Lord, if it wasn't Traynor. Still looking half asleep from the neck up, but kind of awake in a nasty way from the waist down. He wasn't doing too bad with my song either, but it wasn't just the song the people in the audience was screeching and screaming over, it was that nasty little jerk he was doing from the waist down.

Well, Lord have mercy, I said, listening to him. If I'da closed my eyes, it could have been me. He had followed every turning of my voice, side streets, avenues, red lights, train crossings and all. It give me a chill.

Everywhere I went I heard Traynor singing my song, and all the little white girls just eating it up. I never had so many ponytails switched across my line of vision in my life. They was so *proud.* He was a *genius.*

Well, all that year I was trying to lose weight anyway and that and high blood pressure and sugar kept me pretty well occupied. Traynor had made a smash from a song of mine, I still had seven hundred dollars of the original one thousand dollars in the bank, and I felt if I could just bring my weight down, life would be sweet.

1957

I lost ten pounds in 1956. That's what I give myself for Christmas. And J.T. and me and the children and their friends and grandkids of all description had just finished dinner—over which I had put on nine and a half of my lost ten—when who should appear at the front door but Traynor. Little Mama, Little Mama! It's that white man who sings ——— ——— ———. The children didn't call it my song anymore. Nobody did. It was funny how that happened. Traynor and the deacon had bought up all my records, true, but on his record he had put "written by Gracie Mae Still." But that was just another name on the label, like "produced by Apex Records."

On the TV he was inclined to dress like the deacon told him. But now he looked presentable.

Merry Christmas, said he.

And same to you, Son.

I don't know why I called him Son. Well, one way or another they're all our sons. The only requirement is that they be younger than us. But then again, Traynor seemed to be aging by the minute.

You looks tired, I said. Come on in and have a glass of Christmas cheer.

J.T. ain't never in his life been able to act decent to a white man he wasn't working for, but he poured Traynor a glass of bourbon and water, then he took all the children and grandkids and friends and whatnot out to the den. After while I heard Traynor's voice singing the song, coming from the stereo console. It was just the kind of Christmas present my kids would consider cute.

I looked at Traynor, complicit. But he looked like it was the last thing in the world he wanted to hear. His head was pitched forward over his lap, his hands holding his glass and his elbows on his knees.

I done sung that song seem like a million times this year, he said. I sung it on the Grand Ole Opry, I sung it on the Ed Sullivan show. I sung it on Mike Douglas, I sung it at the Cotton Bowl, the Orange Bowl. I sung it at Festivals. I sung it at Fairs. I sung it overseas in Rome, Italy, and once in a submarine *underseas.* I've sung it and sung it, and I'm making forty thousand dollars a day offa it, and you know what, I don't have the faintest notion what the song means.

Whatchumean, what do it mean? It mean what it says. All I could think was: These suckers is making forty thousand a *day* offa my song and now they gonna come back and try to swindle me out of the original thousand.

It's just a song, I said. Cagey. When you fool around with a lot of no count mens you sing a bunch of 'em. I shrugged.

Oh, he said. Well. He started brightening up. I just come by to tell you I think you are a great singer.

He didn't blush, saying that. Just said it straight out.

And I brought you a little Christmas present too. Now you take this little box and you hold it until I drive off. Then you take it outside under that first streetlight back up the street aways in front of that green house. Then you open the box and see . . . Well, just *see.*

What had come over this boy, I wondered, holding the box. I looked out the window in time to see another white man come up and get in the car with him and then two more cars full of white mens start out behind him. They was all in long black cars that looked like a funeral procession.

Little Mama, Little Mama, what it is? One of my grandkids come running up and started pulling at the box. It was wrapped in gay Christmas paper—the thick, rich kind that it's hard to picture folks making just to throw away.

J.T. and the rest of the crowd followed me out the house, up the street to the streetlight and in front of the green house. Nothing was there but somebody's gold-grilled white Cadillac. Brandnew and most distracting. We got to looking at it so till I almost forgot the little box in my hand. While the others were busy making 'miration I carefully took off the paper and ribbon and folded them up and put them in my pants pocket. What should I see but a pair of genuine solid gold caddy keys.

Dangling the keys in front of everybody's nose, I unlocked the caddy, motioned for J.T. to git in on the other side, and us didn't come back home for two days.

1960

Well, the boy was sure nuff famous by now. He was still a mite shy of twenty but already they was calling him the Emperor of Rock and Roll.

Then what should happen but the draft.

Well, says J.T. There goes all this Emperor of Rock and Roll business.

But even in the army the womens was on him like white on rice. We watched it on the News.

Dear Gracie Mae [he wrote from Germany],

How you? Fine I hope as this leaves me doing real well. Before I come in the army I was gaining a lot of weight and gitting jittery from making all them dumb movies. But now I exercise and eat right and get plenty of rest. I'm more awake than I been in ten years.

I wonder if you are writing any more songs?

Sincerely,
Traynor

I wrote him back:

Dear Son,

We is all fine in the Lord's good grace and hope this finds you the same. J.T. and me be out all times of the day and night in that car you give me—which you know you didn't have to do. Oh, and I do appreciate the mink and the new self-cleaning oven. But if you send anymore stuff to eat from Germany I'm going to have to open up a store in the neighborhood just to get rid of it. Really, we have more than enough of everything. The Lord is good to us and we don't know Want.

Glad to here you is well and gitting your right rest. There ain't nothing like exercising to help that along. J.T. and me work some part of every day that we don't go fishing in the garden.

Well, so long Soldier.

Sincerely,
Gracie Mae

He wrote:

Dear Gracie Mae,

I hope you and J.T. like that automatic power tiller I had one of the stores back home send you. I went through a mountain of catalogs looking for it—I wanted something that even a woman could use.

I've been thinking about writing some songs of my own but every time I finish one it don't seem to be about nothing I've actually lived myself. My agent keeps sending me other people's songs but they just sound mooney. I can hardly git through 'em without gagging.

Everybody still loves that song of yours. They ask me all the time what do I think it means, really. I mean, they want to know just what I want to know. Where out of your life did it come from?

Sincerely,
Traynor

1968

I didn't see the boy for seven years. No. Eight. Because just about everybody was dead when I saw him again. Malcolm X, King, the president and his brother, and even J.T. J.T. died of a head cold. It just settled in his head like a block of ice, he said, and nothing we did moved it until one day he just leaned out the bed and died.

His good friend Horace helped me put him away, and then about a year later Horace and me started going together. We was sitting out on the front porch swing one summer night, dusk-dark, and I saw this great procession of lights winding to a stop.

Holy Toledo! said Horace. (He's got a real sexy voice like Ray Charles.) Look *at* it. He meant the long line of flashy cars and the white men in white summer suits jumping out on the drivers' sides and standing at attention. With wings they could pass for angels, with hoods they could be the Klan.

Traynor comes waddling up the walk.

And suddenly I know what it is he could pass for. An Arab like the ones you see in storybooks. Plump and soft and with never a care about weight. Because with so much money, who cares? Traynor is almost dressed like someone from a storybook too. He has on, I swear, about ten necklaces. Two sets of bracelets on his arms, at least one ring on every finger, and some kind of shining buckles on his shoes, so that when he walks you get quite a few twinkling lights.

Gracie Mae, he says, coming up to give me a hug. J.T.

I explain that J.T. passed. That this is Horace.

Horace, he says, puzzled but polite, sort of rocking back on his heels, Horace.

That's it for Horace. He goes in the house and don't come back.

Looks like you and me is gained a few, I say.

He laughs. The first time I ever heard him laugh. It don't sound much like a laugh and I can't swear that it's better than no laugh a'tall.

He's gitting fat for sure, but he's still slim compared to me. I'll never see three hundred pounds again and I've just about said (excuse me) fuck it. I got to thinking about it one day an' I thought: aside from the fact that they say it's unhealthy, my fat ain't never been no trouble. Mens always have loved me. My kids ain't never complained. Plus they's fat. And fat like I is I looks distinguished. You see me coming and know somebody's *there.*

Gracie Mae, he says, I've come with a personal invitation to you to my house tomorrow for dinner. He laughed. What did it sound like? I couldn't place it. See them men out there? he asked me. I'm sick and tired of eating with them. They don't never have nothing to talk about. That's why I eat so much. But if you come to dinner tomorrow we can talk about the old days. You can tell me about that farm I bought you.

I sold it, I said.

You did?

Yeah, I said, I did. Just cause I said I liked to exercise by working in a garden didn't mean I wanted five hundred acres! Anyhow, I'm a city girl now. Raised in the country it's true. Dirt poor—the whole bit—but that's all behind me now.

Oh well, he said, I didn't mean to offend you.

We sat a few minutes listening to the crickets.

Then he said: You wrote that song while you was still on the farm, didn't you, or was it right after you left?

You had somebody spying on me? I asked.

You and Bessie Smith got into a fight over it once, he said.

You *is* been spying on me!

But I don't know what the fight was about, he said. Just like I don't know what happened to your second husband. Your first one died in the Texas electric chair. Did you know that? Your third one beat you up, stole your touring costumes and your car and retired with a chorine to Tuskegee. He laughed. He's still there.

I had been mad, but suddenly I calmed down. Traynor was talking very dreamily. It was dark but seems like I could tell his eyes weren't right. It was like some*thing* was sitting there talking to me but not necessarily with a person behind it.

You gave up on marrying and seem happier for it. He laughed again. I married but it never went like it was supposed to. I never could squeeze any of my own life either into it or out of it. It was like singing somebody else's record. I copied the way it was sposed to be *exactly* but I never had a clue what marriage meant.

I bought her a diamond ring big as your fist. I bought her clothes. I built her a mansion. But right away she didn't want the boys to stay there. Said they smoked up the bottom floor. Hell, there were *five* floors.

No need to grieve, I said. No need to. Plenty more where she come from.

He perked up. That's part of what the song means, ain't it? No need to grieve. Whatever it is, there's plenty more down the line.

I never really believed that way back when I wrote that song, I said. It was all bluffing then. The trick is to live long enough to put your young bluffs to use. Now if I was to sing that song today I'd tear it up. 'Cause I done lived long enough to know its *true.* Them words could hold me up.

I ain't lived that long, he said.

Look like you on your way, I said. I don't know why, but the boy seemed to need some encouraging. And I don't know, seem like one way or another you talk to rich white folks and you end up reassuring *them.* But what the hell, by now I feel something for the boy. I wouldn't be in his bed all alone in the middle of the night for nothing. Couldn't be nothing worse than being famous the world over for something you don't even understand. That's what I tried to tell Bessie. She wanted that same song. Overheard me practicing it one day, said, with her hands on her hips: Gracie Mae, I'ma sing your song tonight. I *likes* it.

Your lips be too swole to sing, I said. She was mean and she was strong, but I trounced her.

Ain't you famous enough with your own stuff? I said. Leave mine alone. Later on, she thanked me. By then she was Miss Bessie Smith to the World, and I was still Miss Gracie Mae Nobody from Notasulga.

The next day all these limousines arrived to pick me up. Five cars and twelve bodyguards. Horace picked that morning to start painting the kitchen.

Don't paint the kitchen, fool, I said. The only reason that dumb boy of ours is going to show me his mansion is because he intends to present us with a new house.

What you gonna do with it? he asked me, standing there in his shirtsleeves stirring the paint.

Sell it. Give it to the children. Live in it on weekends. It don't matter what I do. He sure don't care.

Horace just stood there shaking his head. Mama you sure looks *good,* he says. Wake me up when you git back.

Fool, I say, and pat my wig in front of the mirror.

The boy's house is something else. First you come to this mountain, and then you commence to drive and drive up this road that's lined with magnolias. Do magnolias grow on mountains? I was wondering. And you come to lakes and you come to ponds and you come to deer and you come up on some sheep. And I figure these two is sposed to represent England and Wales. Or something out of Europe. And you just keep on coming to stuff. And it's all pretty. Only the man driving my car don't look at nothing but the road. Fool. And then *finally,* after all this time, you begin to go up the driveway. And there's more magnolias—only they're not in such good shape. It's sort of cool up this high and I don't think they're gonna make it. And then I see this building that looks like if it had a name it would be The Tara Hotel. Columns and steps and outdoor chandeliers and rocking chairs. Rocking chairs? Well, and there's the boy on the steps dressed in a dark green satin jacket like you see folks wearing on TV late at night, and he looks sort of like a fat dracula with all that house rising behind him, and standing beside him there's this little white vision of loveliness that he introduces as his wife.

He's nervous when he introduces us and he says to her: This is Gracie Mae Still, I want you to know me. I mean . . . and she gives him a look that would fry meat.

Won't you come in, Gracie Mae, she says, and that's the last I see of her.

He fishes around for something to say or do and decides to escort me to the kitchen. We go through the entry and the parlor and the breakfast room and the dining room and the servants' passage and finally get there. The first thing I notice is that, altogether, there are five stoves. He looks about to introduce me to one.

Wait a minute, I say. Kitchens don't do nothing for me. Let's go sit on the front porch.

Well, we hike back and we sit in the rocking chairs rocking until dinner.

* * *

Gracie Mae, he says down the table, taking a piece of fried chicken from the woman standing over him, I got a little surprise for you.

It's a house, ain't it? I ask, spearing a chitlin.

You're getting *spoiled,* he says. And the way he says *spoiled* sounds funny. He slurs it. It sounds like his tongue is too thick for his mouth. Just that quick he's finished the chicken and is now eating chitlins *and* a pork chop. *Me* spoiled, I'm thinking.

I already got a house. Horace is right this minute painting the kitchen. I bought that house. My kids feel comfortable in that house.

But this one I bought you is just like mine. Only a little smaller.

I still don't need no house. And anyway who would clean it?

He looks surprised.

Really, I think, some peoples advance *so* slowly.

I hadn't thought of that. But what the hell, I'll get you somebody to live in.

I don't want other folks living 'round me. Makes me nervous.

You *don't?* It *do?*

What I want to wake up and see folks I don't even know for?

He just sits there downtable staring at me. Some of that feeling is in the song, ain't it? Not the words, the *feeling.* What I want to wake up and see folks I don't even know for? But I see twenty folks a day I don't even know, including my wife.

This food wouldn't be bad to wake up to though, I said. The boy had found the genius of corn bread.

He looked at me real hard. He laughed. Short. They want what you got but they don't want you. They want what I got only it ain't mine. That's what makes 'em so hungry for me when I sing. They getting the flavor of something but they ain't getting the thing itself. They like a pack of hound dogs trying to gobble up a scent.

You talking 'bout your fans?

Right. Right. He says.

Don't worry 'bout your fans, I say. They don't know their asses from a hole in the ground. I doubt there's a honest one in the bunch.

That's the point. Dammit, that's the point! He hits the table with his fist. It's so solid it don't even quiver. You need a honest audience! You can't have folks that's just gonna lie right back to you.

Yeah, I say, it was small compared to yours, but I had one. It would have been worth my life to try to sing 'em somebody else's stuff that I didn't know nothing about.

He must have pressed a buzzer under the table. One of his flúnkies zombies up.

Git Johnny Carson, he says.

On the phone? asks the zombie.

On the phone, says Traynor, what you think I mean, git him offa the front porch? Move your ass.

So two weeks later we's on the Johnny Carson show.

Traynor is all corseted down nice and looks a little bit fat but mostly good. And all the women that grew up on him and my song squeal and squeal. Traynor says: The lady who wrote my first hit record is here with us tonight, and she's agreed to sing it for all of us, just like she sung it forty-five years ago. Ladies and Gentlemen, the great Gracie Mae Still!

Well, I had tried to lose a couple of pounds my own self, but failing that I had me a very big dress made. So I sort of rolls over next to Traynor, who is dwarfted by me, so that when he puts his arm around back of me to try to hug me it looks funny to the audience and they laugh.

I can see this pisses him off. But I smile out there at 'em. Imagine squealing for twenty years and not knowing why you're squealing? No more sense of endings and beginnings than hogs.

It don't matter, Son, I say. Don't fret none over me.

I commence to sing. And I sound—wonderful. Being able to sing good ain't all about having a good singing voice a'tall. A good singing voice helps. But when you come up in the Hard Shell Baptist church like I did you understand early that the fellow that sings is the singer. Them that waits for programs and arrangements and letters from home is just good voices occupying body space.

So there I am singing my own song, my own way. And I give it all I got and enjoy every minute of it. When I finish Traynor is standing up clapping and clapping and beaming at first me and then the audience like I'm his mama for true. The audience claps politely for about two seconds.

Traynor looks disgusted.

He comes over and tries to hug me again. The audience laughs.

Johnny Carson looks at us like we both weird.

Traynor is mad as hell. He's supposed to sing something called a love ballad. But instead he takes the mike, turns to me and says: Now see if my imitation still holds up. He goes into the same song, *our* song, I think, looking out at his flaky audience. And he sings it just the way he always did. My voice, my tone, my inflection, everything. But he forgets a couple of lines. Even before he's finished the matronly squeals begin.

He sits down next to me looking whipped.

It don't matter, Son, I say, patting his hand. You don't even know those people. Try to make the people you know happy.

Is that in the song? he asks.

Maybe. I say.

1977

For a few years I hear from him, then nothing. But trying to lose weight takes all the attention I got to spare. I finally faced up to the fact that my fat is the hurt I don't admit, not even to myself, and that I been trying to bury it from the day I was born. But also when you git real old, to tell the truth, it ain't as pleasant. It gits lumpy and slack. Yuck. So one day I said to Horace, I'ma git this shit offa me.

And he fell in with the program like he always try to do and Lord such a procession of salads and cottage cheese and fruit juice!

One night I dreamed Traynor had split up with his fifteenth wife. He said: *You meet 'em for no reason. You date 'em for no reason. You marry 'em for no reason. I do it all but I swear it's just like somebody else doing it. I feel like I can't remember Life.*

The boy's in trouble, I said to Horace.

You've always said that, he said.

I have?

Yeah. You always said he looked asleep. You can't sleep through life if you wants to live it.

You not such a fool after all, I said, pushing myself up with my cane and hobbling over to where he was. Let me sit down on your lap, I said, while this salad I ate takes effect.

In the morning we heard Traynor was dead. Some said fat, some said heart, some said alcohol, some said drugs. One of the children called from Detroit. Them dumb fans of his is on a crying rampage, she said. You just ought to turn on the t.v.

But I didn't want to see 'em. They was crying and crying and didn't even know what they was crying for. One day this is going to be a pitiful country, I thought.

1981

James Alan McPherson b. 1943

In his non-fiction piece "On Becoming an American Writer" (*The Atlantic,* December 1978), James Alan McPherson provides rich clues about his identity as a black American citizen who is a writer. He grew up "in a lower-class black community in Savannah, Georgia, attended segregated public schools," and because of the National Defense Student Loan Program, was able to enroll at Morris Brown College where he received his B.A. in 1965. Summers, McPherson worked as a dining car waiter on the Great Northern Railroad. "Before I was nineteen I was encouraged to move from a segregated Negro college in the South and through that very beautiful part of the country that lies between Chicago and the Pacific Northwest. That year—1962—the World's Fair was in Seattle, and it was a magnificently diverse panorama for a young man to see. Almost every nation on earth was represented in some way, and at the center of the fair was the Space Needle. The theme of the United States exhibit, as I recall, was drawn from Whitman's *Leaves of Grass:* 'Conquering, holding, daring, venturing as we go the unknown ways.'"

After college McPherson went to Harvard Law School, where he received his law degree in 1968. "In a class taught by Paul Freund," he notes, "I began to play with the idea that the Fourteenth Amendment was not just a legislative instrument devised to give former slaves legal equality with other Americans." Years later he went "to the Library of Congress and read the brief of the lawyer-novelist Albion W. Tourgeé in the famous case *Plessy v. Ferguson.*" Tourgeé's brief had strong imaginative as well as legal implications for McPherson. "What he (Tourgeé) was proposing in 1896, I think, was that each United States citizen would attempt to approximate the ideals of the nation, be on at least conversant terms with all its diversity, carry the mainstream of the culture inside himself. As an American, by trying to wear these clothes he would be a synthesis of high and low, black and white, city and country, provincial and universal. If he could live with these contradictions, he would be simply a representative American."

In both *Hue and Cry* and *Elbow Room* McPherson's stories explore what he calls the "minefield of delicious ironies" implicit in Tourgeé's commentary on the Fourteenth Amendment. Why, for example, McPherson asks, thinking of his story, "Why I like Country Music," "should black Americans raised in southern culture *not* find that some of their responses are geared to country music?" And likewise, "how else except in terms of cultural diversity, am I to account for the white friend in Boston who taught me much of what I know about black American music? Or the white friend in Virginia who, besides developing a homegrown aesthetic he calls "crackertude," knows more about black American folklore than most black people?"

Influenced by Ralph Ellison, about and with whom he wrote "Indivisible Man" (*The Atlantic,* December 1970), McPherson believes "that the United States is complex enough to induce that sort of despair that begets heroic hope. I believe that if one can experience its diversity, touch a variety of its people, laugh at its craziness, distill wisdom from its tragedies, and attempt to synthesize all this inside oneself without going crazy, one will have earned the right to call oneself citizen of the United States." Like Ellison, McPherson is a moral historian. Recognizing the American territory as an ideal always pursued, always there but never reached, he holds his fiction to a high standard by virtue of his identity as a black American writer: "Those of us who are black and who have to defend our humanity should be obliged to continue defending it, on higher and higher levels—not of power, which is a kind of tragic trap, but on higher levels of consciousness." Like many other contemporary writers, McPherson imbues the written word of fiction with the qualities and values of the oral tradition. In "Solo Song: For Doc" McPherson writes down the story the youngblood waiter hears from the old waiter's waiter about Doc Craft. The story testifies to the lessons of craft McPherson has learned from black storytellers of earlier generations.

McPherson has taught at the University of California at Santa Cruz (1969–1976); the University of Virginia at Charlottesville (1976–1981); and currently he is Professor of English at the University of Iowa where he received an MFA in 1971. He is also a contributing editor for *The Atlantic* and winner of a MacArthur Foundation Award in 1981.

John F. Callahan
Lewis and Clark College

PRIMARY WORKS

Hue and Cry, 1969; *Elbow Room,* 1977.

A Solo Song: For Doc

So you want to know this business, youngblood? So you want to be a Waiter's Waiter? The Commissary gives you a book with all the rules and tells you to learn them. And you do, and think that is all there is to it. A big, thick black book. Poor youngblood.

Look at me. *I* am a Waiter's Waiter. I know all the moves, all the pretty, fine moves that big book will never teach you. *I* built this railroad with my moves; and so did Sheik Beasley and Uncle T. Boone and Danny Jackson, and so did Doc Craft. That book they made you learn came from our moves and from our heads. There was a time when six of us, big men, danced at the same time in that little Pantry without touching and shouted orders to the sweating paddies in the kitchen. There was a time when they *had* to respect us because our sweat and our moves supported them. We knew the service and the paddies, even the green dishwashers, knew that we did and didn't give us the crap they pull on you.

Do you know how to sneak a Blackplate to a nasty cracker? Do you know how to rub asses with five other men in the Pantry getting their orders together and still know that you are a man, just like them? Do you know how to bullshit while you work and keep the paddies in their places with your bullshit? Do you know how to breathe down the back of an old lady's dress to hustle a bigger tip?

No. You are a summer stuff, youngblood. I am old, my moves are not so good any more, but I know this business. The Commissary hires you for the summer because they don't want to let anyone get as old as me on them. I'm sixty-three, but they can't fire me: I'm in the Union. They can't lay me off for fucking up: I know this business too well. And so they hire you, youngblood, for the summer when the tourists come, and in September you go away with some tips in your pocket to buy pussy and they wait all winter for me to die. I *am* dying, youngblood, and so is this business. Both of us will die together. There'll always be summer stuff like you, but the big men, the big trains, are dying every day and everybody can see it. And nobody but us who are dying with them gives a damn.

Look at the big picture at the end of the car, youngblood. That's the man who built this road. He's in your history books. He's probably in that big black bible you read. He was a great man. He hated people. He didn't want to feed them but the government said he had to. He didn't want to hire me, but he needed me to feed the people. I know this, youngblood, and that is why that book is written for you and that is why I have never read it. That is why you get nervous and jump up to polish the pepper and salt shakers when the word comes down the line that an inspector is getting on at the next stop. That is why you warm the toast covers for every cheap old lady who wants to get coffee and toast and good service for sixty-five cents and a dime tip. You know that he needs you only for the summer and that hundreds of youngbloods like you want to work this summer to buy that pussy in Chicago and Portland and Seattle. The man uses you, but he doesn't need you. But me he needs for the winter, when you are gone, and to teach you something in the summer about this business you can't get from that big black book. He needs me and he knows it and I know it. That is why I am sitting here when there are tables to be cleaned and linen to be changed and silver to be washed and polished. He needs me to die. That is why I am taking my time. I know it. And I will take his service with me when I die, just like the Sheik did and like Percy Fields did, and like Doc.

Who are they? Why do I keep talking about them? Let me think about it. I guess it is because they were the last of the Old School, like me. We made this road. We got a million miles of walking up and down these cars under out feet. Doc Craft was the Old School, like me. He was a Waiter's Waiter. He danced down these aisles with us and swung his tray with the roll of the train, never spilling in all his trips a single cup of coffee. He could carry his tray on two fingers, or on one and a half if he wanted, and he knew all the tricks about hustling tips there are to know. He could work anybody. The girls at the Northland in Chicago knew Doc, and the girls at the Haverville in Seattle, and the girls at the Step-Inn in Portland and all the girls in Winnipeg knew Doc Craft.

But wait. It is just 1:30 and the first call for dinner is not until 5:00. You want to kill some time; you want to hear about the Old School and how it was in my day. If you look in that black book you would see that you should be polishing silver now. Look out the window; this is North Dakota, this is Jerry's territory. Jerry, the Unexpected Inspector. Shouldn't you polish the shakers or clean out the Pantry or squeeze oranges, or maybe change the linen on the tables? Jerry Ewald is sly. The train may stop in the middle of this wheatfield and Jerry may get on. He lives by that book. He knows where to look for dirt and mistakes. Jerry Ewald, the Unexpected Inspector. He knows where to look; he knows how to get you. He got Doc.

Now you want to know about him, about the Old School. You have even put aside your book of rules. But see how you keep your finger in the pages as if the book was more important than what I tell you. That's a bad move, and it tells on you. You will be a waiter. But you will never be a Waiter's Waiter. The Old School died with Doc, and the very last of it is dying with me. What happened to Doc? Take your finger out of the pages, youngblood, and I will tell you about a kind of life these rails will never carry again.

When your father was a boy playing with himself behind the barn, Doc was already a man and knew what the thing was for. But he got tired of using it when he wasn't much older than you, and he set his mind on making money. He had no skills. He was black. He got hungry. On Christmas Day in 1916, the story goes, he wandered into the Chicago stockyards and over to a dining car waiting to be connected up to the main train for the Chicago-to-San Francisco run. He looked up through the kitchen door at the chef storing supplies for the kitchen and said: "I'm hungry."

"What do you want *me* to do about it?" the Swede chef said.

"I'll work," said Doc.

That Swede was Chips Magnusson, fresh off the boat and lucky to be working himself. He did not know yet that he should save all extra work for other Swedes fresh off the boat. He later learned this by living. But at that time he considered a moment, bit into one of the fresh apples stocked for apple pie, chewed considerably, spit out the seeds and then waved the black man on board the big train. "You can eat all you want," he told Doc. "But you work all I tell you."

He put Doc to rolling dough for the apple pies and the train began rolling for Doc. It never stopped. He fell in love with the feel of the wheels under his feet clicking against the track and he got the rhythm of the wheels in him and learned, like all of us, how to roll with them and move with them. After that first trip Doc was never at home on the ground. He worked everything in the kitchen from putting out dough to second cook, in six years. And then, when the Commissary saw that he was good and would soon be going for one of the chef's spots they saved for the Swedes, they put him out of the kitchen and told him to learn this waiter business; and told him to learn how to bullshit on the other side of the Pantry. He was almost thirty, youngblood, when he crossed over to the black side of the Pantry. I wasn't there when he made his first trip as a waiter, but from what they tell me of that trip I know that he was broke in by good men. Pantryman was Sheik Beasley, who stayed high all the time and let the waiters steal anything they wanted as long as they didn't bother his reefers. Danny Jackson, who was black and knew Shakespeare before the world said he could work with it, was second man. Len Dickey was third, Reverend Hendricks was fourth, and Uncle T. Boone, who even in those early days could not straighten his back, ran fifth. Doc started in as sixth waiter, the "mule." They pulled some shit on him at first because they didn't want somebody fresh out of a paddy kitchen on the crew. They messed with his orders, stole his plates, picked up his tips on the sly, and made him do all the dirty work. But when they saw that he could take the shit without getting hot and when they saw that he was set on being a waiter, even though he was older than most of them, they settled down and began to teach him this business and all the words and moves and slickness that made it a good business.

His real name was Leroy Johnson, I think, but when Danny Jackson saw how cool and neat he was in his moves, and how he handled the plates, he began to call him "the Doctor." Then the Sheik, coming down from his high one day after missing the lunch and dinner service, saw how Doc had taken over his station and collected fat tips from his tables by telling the passengers that the Sheik had had to get off back along the line because of a heart attack. The Sheik liked that because he saw that Doc understood crackers and how they liked nothing better than knowing that a nigger had died on the job, giving them service. The Sheik was impressed. And he was not an easy man to impress because he knew too much about life and had to stay high most of the time. And when Doc would not split the tips with him, the Sheik got mad at first and called Doc a barrel of motherfuckers and some other words you would not recognize. But he was impressed. And later that night, in the crew car when the others were gambling and drinking and bullshitting about the women they had working the corners for them, the Sheik came over to Doc's bunk and said: "You're a crafty motherfucker."

"Yeah?" says Doc.

"Yeah," says the Sheik, who did not say much. "You're a crafty motherfucker but I like you." Then he got into the first waiter's bunk and lit up again. But Reverend Hendricks, who always read his Bible before going to sleep and who always listened to anything the Sheik said because he knew the Sheik only said something when it was important, heard what was said and remembered it. After he put his Bible back in his locker, he walked over to Doc's bunk and looked down at him. "Mister Doctor Craft," the Reverend said. "Youngblood Doctor Craft."

"Yeah?" says Doc.

"Yeah," says Reverend Hendricks. "That's who you are."

And that's who he was from then on.

II

I came to the road away from the war. This was after '41, when people at home were looking for Japs under their beds every night. I did not want to fight because there was no money in it and I didn't want to go overseas to work in a kitchen. The big war was on and a lot of soldiers crossed the country to get to it, and as long as a black man fed them on trains he did not have to go to that war. I could have got a job in a Chicago factory, but there was more money on the road and it was safer. And after a while it got into your blood so that you couldn't leave it for anything. The road got into my blood the way it got into everybody's; the way going to the war got in the blood of redneck farm boys and the crazy Polacks from Chicago. It was all right for them to go to the war. They were young and stupid. And they died that way. I played it smart. I was almost thirty-five and I didn't want to go. But I took *them* and fed them and gave them good times on their way to the war, and for that I did not have to go. The soldiers had plenty of money and were afraid not to spend it all before they got to the ships on the Coast. And we gave them ways to spend it on the trains.

Now in those days there was plenty of money going around and everybody stole from everybody. The kitchen stole food from the company and the company knew it and wouldn't pay good wages. There were no rules in those days, there was no black book to go by and nobody said what you couldn't eat or steal. The paddy cooks used to toss boxes of steaks off the train in the Chicago yards for people at the restaurants there who paid them, cash. These were the days when ordinary people had to have red stamps or blue stamps to get powdered eggs and white lard to mix with red powder to make their own butter.

The stewards stole from the company and from the waiters; the waiters stole from the stewards and the company and from each other. I stole. Doc stole. Even Reverend Hendricks put his Bible far back in his locker and stole with us. You didn't want a man on your crew who didn't steal. He made it bad for everybody. And if the steward saw that he was a dummy and would never get to stealing, he wrote him up for something and got him off the crew so as not to slow down the rest of us. We had a redneck cracker steward from Alabama by the name of Casper who used to say: "*Jesus Christ!* I ain't got time to hate you niggers, I'm making so much money." He used to keep all his cash at home under his bed in a cardboard box because he was afraid to put it in the bank.

Doc and Sheik Beasley and me were on the same crew together all during the war. Even in those days, as young as we were, we knew how to be Old Heads. We organized for the soldiers. We had to wear skullcaps all the time because the crackers said our hair was poison and didn't want any of it to fall in their food. The Sheik didn't mind wearing one. He kept reefers in his and used to sell them to the soldiers for double what he paid for them in Chicago and three times what he paid the Chinamen in Seattle. That's why we called him the Sheik. After every meal the Sheik would get in the linen closet and light up. Sometimes he wouldn't come out for days. Nobody gave a damn, though; we were all too busy stealing and working. And there was more for us to get as long as he didn't come out.

Doc used to sell bootlegged booze to the soldiers; that was his specialty. He had redcaps in the Chicago stations telling the soldiers who to ask for on the train. He was an open operator and had to give the steward a cut, but he still made a pile of money. That's why that old cracker always kept us together on his crew. We were the three best moneymakers he ever had. That's something you should learn, youngblood. They can't love you for being you. They only love you if you make money for them. All that talk these days about integration and brotherhood, that's a lot of bullshit. The man will love you as long as he can make money with you. I made money. And old Casper had to love me in the open although I knew he called me a nigger at home when he had put that money in his big cardboard box. I know he loved me on the road in the wartime because I used to bring in the biggest moneymakers. I used to handle the girls.

Look out that window. See all that grass and wheat? Look at that big farm boy cutting it. Look at that burnt cracker on that tractor. He probably has a wife who married him because she didn't know what else to do. Back during wartime the girls in this part of the country knew what to do. They got on the trains at night.

You can look out that window all day and run around all the stations when we stop, but you'll never see a black man in any of these towns. You know why, youngblood? These farmers hate you. They still remember when their girls came out of these towns and got on the trains at night. They've been running black men and dark Indians out of these towns for years. They hate anything dark that's not that way because of the sun. Right now there are big farm girls with hair under their arms on the corners in San Francisco, Chicago, Seattle and Minneapolis who got started on these cars back during wartime. The farmers still remember that and they hate you and me for it. But it wasn't for me they got on. Nobody wants a stiff, smelly farm girl when there are sporting women to be got for a dollar in the cities. It was for the soldiers they got on. It was just business to me. But they hate you and me anyway.

I got off in one of these towns once, a long time after the war, just to get a drink while the train changed engines. Everybody looked at me and by the time I got to a bar there were ten people on my trail. I was drinking a fast one when the sheriff came in the bar.

"What are you doing here?" he asks me.

"Just getting a shot," I say.

He spit on the floor. "How long you plan to be here?"

"I don't know," I say, just to be nasty.

"There ain't no jobs here," he says.

"I wasn't looking," I say.

"We don't want you here."

"I don't give a good goddamn," I say.

He pulled his gun on me. "All right, coon, back on the train," he says.

"Wait a minute," I tell him. "Let me finish my drink."

He knocked my glass over with his gun. "You're finished *now,*" he says. "Pull your ass out of here *now!*"

I didn't argue.

I was the night man. After dinner it was my job to pull the cloths off the tables and put paddings on. Then I cut out the lights and locked both doors. There was a big farm girl from Minot named Hilda who could take on eight or ten soldiers in one night, white soldiers. These white boys don't know how to last. I would stand by the door and when the soldiers came back from the club car they would pay me and I would let them in. Some of the girls could make as much as one hundred dollars in one night. And I always made twice as much. Soldiers don't care what they do with their money. They just have to spend it.

We never bothered with the girls ourselves. It was just business as far as we were concerned. But there was one dummy we had with us once, a boy from the South named Willie Joe something who handled the dice. He was really hot for one of these farm girls. He used to buy her good whiskey and he hated to see her go in the car at night to wait for the soldiers. He was a real dummy. One time I heard her tell him: "It's all right. They can have my body. I know I'm black inside. *Jesus,* I'm so black inside I wisht I was black all over!"

And this dummy Willie Joe said: "Baby, *don't you ever change!*"

I knew we had to get rid of him before he started trouble. So we had the steward bump him off the crew as soon as we could find a good man to handle the gambling. That old redneck Casper was glad to do it. He saw what was going on.

Do you want to hear about Doc, you say, so you can get back to your reading?

What can I tell you? The road got into his blood? He liked being a waiter? You won't understand this, but he did. There were no Civil Rights or marches or riots for something better in those days. In those days a man found something he liked to do and liked it from then on because he couldn't help himself. What did he like about the road? He liked what I liked: the money, owning the car, running it, telling the soldiers what to do, hustling a bigger tip from some old maid by looking under her dress and laughing at her, having all the girls at the Haverville Hotel waiting for us to come in for stopover, the power we had to beat them up or lay them if we wanted. He liked running free and not being married to some bitch who would spend his money when he was out of town or give it to some stud. He liked getting drunk with the boys up at Andy's, setting up the house and then passing out from drinking too much, knowing that the boys would get him home.

I ran with that one crew all during wartime and they, Doc, the Sheik and Reverend Hendricks, had taken me under their wings. *I* was still a youngblood then, and Doc liked me a lot. But he never said that much to me; he was not a talker. The Sheik had taught him the value of silence in things that really matter. We roomed together in Chicago at Mrs. Wright's place in those days. Mrs. Wright didn't allow women in the rooms and Doc liked that, because after being out for a week and after stopping over in those hotels along the way, you get tired of women and bullshit and need your privacy. We weren't like you. We didn't need a woman every time we got hard. We knew when we had to have it and when we didn't. And we didn't spend all our money on it, either. You youngbloods think the way to get a woman is to let her see how you handle your money. That's stupid. The way to get a woman is to let her see how you handle other women. But you'll never believe that until it's too late to do you any good.

Doc knew how to handle women. I can remember a time in a Winnipeg hotel how he ran a bitch out of his room because he had had enough of it and did not need her any more. I was in the next room and heard everything.

"Come on, Doc," the bitch said. "Come on honey, let's do it one more time."

"Hell no," Doc said. "I'm tired and I don't want to any more."

"How can you say you're tired?" the bitch said. "How can you say you're tired when you didn't go but two times?"

"I'm tired of it," Doc said, "because I'm tired of you. And I'm tired of you because I'm tired of it and bitches like you in all the towns I been in. You drain a man. And I know if I beat you, you'll still come back when I hit you again. *That's* why I'm tired. I'm tired of having things around I don't care about."

"What *do* you care about, Doc?" the bitch said.

"I don't know," Doc said. "I guess I care about moving and being somewhere else when I want to be. I guess I care about going out, and coming in to wait for the time to go out again."

"You crazy, Doc," the bitch said.

"Yeah?" Doc said. "I guess I'm crazy all right."

Later that bitch knocked on my door and I did it for her because she was just a bitch and I knew Doc wouldn't want her again. I don't think he ever wanted a bitch again. I never saw him with one after that time. He was just a little over fifty then and could have still done whatever he wanted with women.

The war ended. The farm boys who got back from the war did not spend money on their way home. They did not want to spend any more money on women, and the girls did not get on at night any more. Some of them went into the cities and turned pro. Some of them stayed in the towns and married the farm boys who got back from the war. Things changed on the road. The Commissary started putting that book of rules together and told us to stop stealing. They were losing money on passengers now because of the airplanes and they began to really tighten up and started sending inspectors down along the line to check on us. They started sending in spotters, too. One of them caught that redneck Casper writing out a check for two dollars less than he had charged the spotter. The Commissary got him in on the rug for it. I wasn't there, but they told me he said to the General Superintendent: "Why are you getting on me, a white man, for a lousy son-of-a-bitching two bucks? There's niggers out there been stealing for *years!*"

"Who?" the General Superintendent asked.

And Casper couldn't say anything because he had that cardboard box full of money still under his bed and knew he would have to tell how he got it if any of us was brought in. So he said nothing.

"Who?" the General Superintendent asked him again.

"Why, all them nigger waiters steal, *everybody knows that!*"

"And the cooks, what about them?" the Superintendent said.

"They're white," said Casper.

They never got the story out of him and he was fired. He used the money to open a restaurant someplace in Indiana and I heard later that he started a branch of the Klan in his town. One day he showed up at the station and told Doc, Reverend Hendricks and me: "I'll see you boys get *yours.* Damn if I'm takin' the rap for you niggers."

We just laughed in his face because we knew he could do nothing to us through the Commissary. But just to be safe we stopped stealing so much. But they did get the Sheik, though. One day an inspector got on in the mountains just outside of Whitefish and grabbed him right out of that linen closet. The Sheik had been smoking in there all day and he was high and laughing when they pulled him off the train.

That was the year we got the Union. The crackers and Swedes finally let us in after we paid off. We really stopped stealing and got organized and there wasn't a damn thing the company could do about it, although it tried like hell to buy us out. And to get back at us, they put their heads together and began to make up that big book of rules you keep your finger in. Still, *we* knew the service and they had to write the book the way we gave the service and at first there was nothing for the Old School men to learn. We got seniority through the Union, and as long as we gave the service and didn't steal, they couldn't touch us. So they began changing the rules, and sending us notes about the service. Little changes at first, like how the initials on the doily should always face the customer, and how the silver should be taken off the tables between meals. But we were getting old and set in our old service, and it got harder and harder learning all those little changes. And we had to learn new stuff all the time because there was no telling when an inspector would get on and catch us giving bad service. It was hard as hell. It was hard because we knew that the company was out to break up the Old School. The Sheik was gone, and we knew that Reverend Hendricks or Uncle T. or Danny Jackson would go soon because they stood for the Old School, just like the Sheik. But what bothered us most was knowing that they would go for Doc first, before anyone else, because he loved the road so much.

Doc was over sixty-five then and had taken to drinking hard when we were off. But he never touched a drop when we were on the road. I used to wonder whether he drank because being a Waiter's Waiter was getting hard or because he had to do something until his next trip. I could never figure it. When we had our layovers he would spend all his time in Andy's, setting up the house. He had no wife, no relatives, not even a hobby. He just drank. Pretty soon the slicksters at Andy's got to using him for a good thing. They commenced putting the touch on him because they saw he was getting old and knew he didn't have far to go, and they would never have to pay him back. Those of us who were close to him tried to pull his coat, but it didn't help. He didn't talk about himself much, he didn't talk much about anything that wasn't related to the road; but when I tried to hip him once about the hustlers and how they were closing in on him, he just took another shot and said:

"I don't need no money. Nobody's jiving me. I'm jiving them. You know I can still pull in a hundred in tips in one trip. I *know* this business."

"Yeah, I know, Doc," I said. "But how many more trips can you make before you have to stop?"

"I ain't never gonna stop. Trips are all I know and I'll be making them as long as these trains haul people."

"That's just it," I said. "They don't *want* to haul people any more. The planes do that. The big roads want freight now. Look how they hire youngbloods just for the busy seasons just so they won't get any seniority in the winter. Look how all the Old School waiters are dropping out. They got the Sheik, Percy Fields just lucked up and died before they got to *him,* they almost got Reverend Hendricks. Even *Uncle T.* is going to retire! And they'll get us too."

"Not me," said Doc. "I know my moves. This old fox can still dance with a tray and handle four tables at the same time. I can still bait a queer and make the old ladies tip big. There's no waiter better than me and I know it."

"Sure, Doc," I said. "I know it too. But please save your money. Don't be a dummy. There'll come a day when you just can't get up to go out and they'll put you on the ground for good."

Doc looked at me like he had been shot. "Who taught you the moves when you were just a raggedy-ass waiter?"

"You did, Doc," I said.

"Who's always the first man down in the yard at train-time?" He threw down another shot. "Who's there sitting in the car every tenth morning while you other old heads are still at home pulling on your longjohns?"

I couldn't say anything. He was right and we both knew it.

"I have to go," he told me. "Going out is my whole life, I wait for that tenth morning. I ain't never missed a trip and I don't mean to."

What could I say to him, youngblood? What can I say to you? He had to go out, not for the money; it was in his blood. You have to go out too, but it's for the money you go. You hate going out and you love coming in. He loved going out and he hated coming in. Would *you* listen if I told you to stop spending your money on pussy in Chicago? Would he listen if I told him to save *his* money? To stop setting up the bar at Andy's? No. Old men are just as bad as young men when it comes to money. They can't think. They always try to buy what they should have for free. And what they buy, after they have it, is nothing.

They called Doc into the Commissary and the doctors told him he had lumbago and a bad heart and was weak from drinking too much, and they wanted him to get down for his own good. He wouldn't do it. Tesdale, the General Superintendent, called him in and told him that he had enough years in the service to pull down a big pension and that the company would pay for a retirement party for him, since he was the oldest waiter working, and invite all the Old School waiters to see him off, if he would come down. Doc said no. He knew that the Union had to back him. He knew that he could ride as long as he made the trains on time and as long as he knew the service. And he knew that he could not leave the road.

The company called in its lawyers to go over the Union contract. I wasn't there, but Len Dickey was in on the meeting because of his office in the Union. He told me about it later. Those fat company lawyers took the contract apart and went through all their books. They took the seniority clause apart word by word, trying to figure a way to get at Doc. But they had written it airtight back in the days when the company *needed* waiters, and there was nothing in it about compulsory retirement. Not a word. The paddies in the Union must have figured that waiters didn't *need* a new contract when they let us in, and they had let us come in under the old one thinking that all waiters would die on the job, or drink themselves to death when they were still young, or die from buying too much pussy, or just quit when they had put in enough time to draw a pension. But *nothing* in the whole contract could help them get rid of Doc Craft. They were sweating, they were working so hard. And all the time Tesdale, the General Superintendent, was calling them sons-of-bitches for not earning their money. But there was nothing the company lawyers could do but turn the pages of their big books and sweat and promise Tesdale that they would find some way if he gave them more time.

The word went out from the Commissary: "Get Doc." The stewards got it from the assistant superintendents: "Get Doc." Since they could not get him to retire, they were determined to catch him giving bad service. He had more seniority than most other waiters, so they couldn't bump him off our crew. In fact, all the waiters with more seniority than Doc were on the crew with him. There were four of us from the Old School: me, Doc, Uncle T. Boone, and Danny Jackson. Reverend Hendricks wasn't running regular any more; he was spending all his Sundays preaching in his Church on the South Side because he knew what was coming and wanted to have something steady going for him in Chicago when his time came. Fifth and sixth men on that crew were two hardheads who had read the book. The steward was Crouse, and he really didn't want to put the screws to Doc but he couldn't help himself. Everybody wants to work. So Crouse started in to riding Doc, sometimes about moving too fast, sometimes about not moving fast enough. I was on the crew, I saw it all. Crouse would seat four singles at the same table, on Doc's station, and Doc had to take care of all four different orders at the same time. He was seventy-three, but that didn't stop him, knowing this business the way he did. It just slowed him down some. But Crouse got on him even for that and would chew him out in front of the passengers, hoping that he'd start cursing and bother the passengers so that they would complain to the company. It never worked, though. Doc just played it cool. He'd look into Crouse's eyes and know what was going on. And then he'd lay on his good service, the only service he knew, and the passengers would see how good he was with all that age on his back and they would get mad at the steward, and leave Doc a bigger tip when they left.

The Commissary sent out spotters to catch him giving bad service. These were pale-white little men in glasses who never looked you in the eye, but who always felt the plate to see if it was warm. And there were the old maids, who like that kind of work, who would order shrimp or crabmeat cocktails or celery and olive plates because they knew how the rules said these things had to be made. And when they came, when Doc brought them out, they would look to see if the oyster fork was stuck into the thing, and look out the window a long time.

"Ain't no use trying to fight it," Uncle T. Boone told Doc in the crew car one night, "the black waiter is *doomed.* Look at all the good restaurants, the class restaurants in Chicago. *You* can't work in them. Them white waiters got those jobs sewed up fine."

"I can be a waiter anywhere," says Doc. "I know the business and I like it and I can do it anywhere."

"The black waiter is doomed," Uncle T. says again. "The whites is taking over the service in the good places. And when they run you off of here, you won't have no place to go."

"They won't run me off of here," says Doc. "As long as I give the right service they can't touch me."

"You're a goddamn *fool!*" says Uncle T. "You're a nigger and you ain't got no rights except what the Union says you have. And that ain't worth a damn because when the Commissary finally gets you, those niggers won't lift a finger to help you."

"Leave off him," I say to Boone. "If anybody ought to be put off it's you. You ain't had your back straight for thirty years. You even make the crackers sick the way you keep bowing and folding your hands and saying, 'Thank you, Mr. Boss.' Fifty years ago that would of got you a bigger tip," I say, "but now it ain't worth a shit. And every time you do it the crackers hate you. And every time I see you serving with that skullcap on *I* hate you. The Union said we didn't have to wear them *eighteen years ago!* Why can't you take it off?"

Boone just sat on his bunk with his skullcap in his lap, leaning against his big belly. He knew I was telling the truth and he knew he wouldn't change. But he said: "That's the trouble with the Negro waiter today. He ain't got no humility. And as long as he don't have humility, he keeps losing the good jobs."

Doc had climbed into the first waiter's bunk in his longjohns and I got in the second waiter's bunk under him and lay there. I could hear him breathing. It had a hard sound. He wasn't well and all of us knew it.

"Doc?" I said in the dark.

"Yeah?"

"Don't mind Boone, Doc. He's a dead man. He just don't know it."

"We all are," Doc said.

"Not you," I said.

"What's the use? He's right. They'll get me in the end."

"But they ain't done it yet."

"They'll get me. And they know it and I know it. I can even see it in old Crouse's eyes. He knows they're gonna get me."

"Why don't you get a woman?"

He was quiet. "What can I do with a woman now, that I ain't already done too much?"

I thought for a while. "If you're on the ground, being with one might not make it so bad."

"I hate women," he said.

"You ever try fishing?"

"No."

"You want to?"

"No," he said.

"You can't keep *drinking*."

He did not answer.

"Maybe you could work in town. In the Commissary."

I could hear the big wheels rolling and clicking along the tracks and I knew by the smooth way we were moving that we were almost out of the Dakota flatlands. Doc wasn't talking. "Would you like that?" I thought he was asleep. "Doc, would you like that?"

"Hell no," he said.

"You have to try *something!*"

He was quiet again. "I know," he finally said.

III

Jerry Ewald, the Unexpected Inspector, got on in Winachee that next day after lunch and we knew that he had the word from the Commissary. He was cool about it: he laughed with the steward and the waiters about the old days and his hard gray eyes and shining glasses kept looking over our faces as if to see if we knew why he had got on. The two hardheads were in the crew car stealing a nap on company time. Jerry noticed this and could have caught them, but he was after bigger game. We all knew that, and we kept talking to him about the days of the big trains and looking at his white hair and not into the eyes behind his glasses because we knew what was there. Jerry sat down on the first waiter's station and said to Crouse: "Now I'll have some lunch. Steward, let the headwaiter bring me a menu."

Crouse stood next to the table where Jerry sat, and looked at Doc, who had been waiting between the tables with his tray under his arm. The way the rules say. Crouse looked sad because he knew what was coming. Then Jerry looked directly at Doc and said: "Headwaiter Doctor Craft, bring me a menu."

Doc said nothing and he did not smile. He brought the menu. Danny Jackson and I moved back into the hall to watch. There was nothing we could do to help Doc and we knew it. He was the Waiter's Waiter, out there by himself, hustling the biggest tip he would ever get in his life. Or losing it.

"Goddamn," Danny said to me. "Now let's sit on the ground and talk about how *kings* are gonna get fucked."

"Maybe not," I said. But I did not believe it myself because Jerry is the kind of man who lies in bed all night, scheming. I knew he had a plan.

Doc passed us on his way to the kitchen for water and I wanted to say something to him. But what was the use? He brought the water to Jerry. Jerry looked him in the eye. "Now, Headwaiter," he said. "I'll have a bowl of onion soup, a cold roast beef sandwich on white, rare, and a glass of iced tea."

"Write it down," said Doc. He was playing it right. He knew that the new rules had stopped waiters from taking verbal orders.

"Don't be so professional, Doc," Jerry said. "It's me, one of the *boys.*"

"You have to write it out," said Doc, "it's in the black book."

Jerry clicked his pen and wrote the order out on the check. And handed it to Doc. Uncle T. followed Doc back into the Pantry.

"He's gonna get you, Doc," Uncle T. said. "I knew it all along. You know why? The Negro waiter ain't got no more humility."

"Shut the fuck up, Boone!" I told him.

"You'll see," Boone went on. "You'll see I'm right. There ain't a thing Doc can do about it, either. We're gonna lose all the good jobs."

We watched Jerry at the table. He saw us watching and smiled with his gray eyes. Then he poured some of the water from the glass on the linen cloth and picked up the silver sugar bowl and placed it right on the wet spot. Doc was still in the Pantry. Jerry turned the silver sugar bowl around and around on the linen. He pressed down on it some as he turned. But when he picked it up again, there was no dark ring on the wet cloth. We had polished the silver early that morning, according to the book, and there was not a dirty piece of silver to be found in the whole car. Jerry was drinking the rest of the water when Doc brought out the polished silver soup tureen, underlined with a doily and a breakfast plate, with a shining soup bowl underlined with a doily and a breakfast plate, and a bread-and-butter plate with six crackers; not four or five or seven, but six, the number the Commissary had written in the black book. He swung down the aisle of the car between the two rows of white tables and you could not help but be proud of the way he moved with the roll of the train and the way that tray was like a part of his arm. It was good service. He placed everything neat, with all company initials showing, right where things should go.

"Shall I serve up the soup?" he asked Jerry.

"Please," said Jerry.

Doc handled that silver soup ladle like one of those Chicago Jew tailors handles a needle. He ladled up three good-sized spoonfuls from the tureen and then laid the wet spoon on an extra bread-and-butter plate on the side of the table, so he would not stain the cloth. Then he put a napkin over the wet spot Jerry had made and changed the ashtray for a prayer-card because every good waiter knows that nobody wants to eat a good meal looking at an ashtray.

"You know about the spoon plate, I see," Jerry said to Doc.

"I'm a waiter," said Doc. "I know."

"You're a damn good waiter," said Jerry.

Doc looked Jerry square in the eye. "I know," he said slowly.

Jerry ate a little of the soup and opened all six of the cracker packages. Then he stopped eating and began to look out the window. We were passing through his territory, Washington State, the country he loved because he was the only company inspector in the state and knew that once we got through Montana he would be the only man the waiters feared. He smiled and then waved for Doc to bring out the roast beef sandwich.

But Doc was into his service now and cleared the table completely. Then he got the silver crumb knife from the Pantry and gathered all the cracker crumbs, even the ones Jerry had managed to get in between the salt and pepper shakers.

"You want the tea with your sandwich, or later?" he asked Jerry.

"Now is fine," said Jerry, smiling.

"You're going good," I said to Doc when he passed us on his way to the Pantry. "He can't touch you or nothing."

He did not say anything.

Uncle T. Boone looked at Doc like he wanted to say something too, but he just frowned and shuffled out to stand next to Jerry. You could see that Jerry hated him. But Jerry knew how to smile at everybody, and so he smiled at Uncle T. while Uncle T. bent over the table with his hands together like he was praying, and moved his head up and bowed it down.

Doc brought out the roast beef, proper service. The crock of mustard was on a breakfast plate, underlined with a doily, initials facing Jerry. The lid was on the mustard and it was clean, like it says in the book, and the little silver service spoon was clean and polished on a bread-and-butter plate. He set it down. And then he served the tea. You think you know the service, youngblood, all of you do. But you don't. Anybody can serve, but not everybody can become a part of the service. When Doc poured that pot of hot tea into that glass of crushed ice, it was like he was pouring it through his own fingers; it was like he and the tray and the pot and the glass and all of it was the same body. It was a beautiful move. It was fine service. The iced tea glass sat in a shell dish, and the iced tea spoon lay straight in front of Jerry. The lemon wedge Doc put in a shell dish half-full of crushed ice with an oyster fork struck into its skin. Not in the meat, mind you, but squarely under the skin of that lemon, and the whole thing lay in a pretty curve on top of that crushed ice.

Doc stood back and waited. Jerry had been watching his service and was impressed. He mixed the sugar in his glass and sipped. Danny Jackson and I were down the aisle in the hall. Uncle T. stood behind Jerry, bending over, his arms folded, waiting. And Doc stood next to the table, his tray under his arm looking straight ahead and calm because he had given good service and knew it. Jerry sipped again.

"Good tea," he said. "Very good tea."

Doc was silent.

Jerry took the lemon wedge off the oyster fork and squeezed it into the glass, and stirred, and sipped again. "*Very* good," he said. Then he drained the glass. Doc reached over to pick it up for more ice but Jerry kept his hand on the glass. "Very good service, Doc," he said. "But you served the lemon wrong."

Everybody was quiet. Uncle T. folded his hands in the praying position.

"How's that?" said Doc.

"The service was wrong," Jerry said. He was not smiling now.

"How could it be? I been giving that same service for years, right down to the crushed ice for the lemon wedge."

"That's just it, Doc," Jerry said. "The lemon wedge. You served it wrong."

"Yeah?" said Doc.

"Yes," said Jerry, his jaws tight. "Haven't you seen the new rule?"

Doc's face went loose. He knew now that they had got him.

"Haven't you *seen* it?" Jerry asked again.

Doc shook his head.

Jerry smiled that hard, gray smile of his, the kind of smile that says: "I have always been the boss and I am smiling this way because I know it and can afford to give you something." "Steward Crouse," he said. "Steward Crouse, go get the black bible for the headwaiter."

Crouse looked beaten too. He was sixty-three and waiting for his pension. He got the bible.

Jerry took it and turned directly to the very last page. He knew where to look. "Now, Headwaiter," he said, "*listen* to this." And he read aloud: "Memorandum Number 22416. From: Douglass A. Tesdale, General Superintendent of Dining Cars. To: Waiters, Stewards, Chefs of Dining Cars. Attention: As of 7/9/65 the proper service for iced tea will be (a) Fresh brewed tea in teapot, poured over crushed ice at table; iced tea glass set in shell dish (b) Additional ice to be immediately available upon request after first glass of tea (c) Fresh lemon wedge will be served on bread-and-butter plate, no doily, with tines of oyster fork stuck into *meat* of lemon." Jerry paused.

"Now you know, Headwaiter," he said.

"Yeah," said Doc.

"But why didn't you know before?"

No answer.

"This notice came out last week."

"I didn't check the book yet," said Doc.

"But that's a rule. Always check the book before each trip. *You* know that, Headwaiter."

"Yeah," said Doc.

"Then that's *two* rules you missed."

Doc was quiet.

"Two rules you didn't read," Jerry said. "You're slowing down, Doc."

"I know," Doc mumbled.

"You want some time off to rest?"

Again Doc said nothing.

"I think you need some time on the ground to rest up, don't you?"

Doc put his tray on the table and sat down in the seat across from Jerry. This was the first time we had ever seen a waiter sit down with a customer, even an inspector. Uncle T., behind Jerry's back, began waving his hands, trying to tell Doc to get up. Doc did not look at him.

"You *are* tired, aren't you?" said Jerry.

"I'm just resting my feet," Doc said.

"Get up, Headwaiter," Jerry said. "You'll have plenty of time to do that. I'm writing you up."

But Doc did not move and just continued to sit there. And all Danny and I could do was watch him from the back of the car. For the first time I saw that his hair was almost gone and his legs were skinny in the baggy white uniform. I don't think Jerry expected Doc to move. I don't think he really cared. But then Uncle T. moved around the table and stood next to Doc, trying to apologize for him to Jerry with his eyes and bowed head. Doc looked at Uncle T. and then got up and went back to the crew car. He left his tray on the table. It stayed there all that evening because none of us, not even Crouse or Jerry or Uncle T., would touch it. And Jerry didn't try to make any of us take it back to the Pantry. He understood at least that much. The steward closed down Doc's tables during dinner service, all three settings of it. And Jerry got off the train someplace along the way, quiet, like he had got on.

After closing down the car we went back to the crew quarters and Doc was lying on his bunk with his hands behind his head and his eyes open. He looked old. No one knew what to say until Boone went over to his bunk and said: "I feel bad for you, Doc, but all of us are gonna get it in the end. The railroad waiter is *doomed.*"

Doc did not even notice Boone.

"I could of told you about the lemon but he would of got you on something else. It wasn't no use. Any of it."

"Shut the fuck up, Boone!" Danny said. "The one thing that really hurts is that a crawling son-of-a-bitch like you will be riding when all the good men are gone. Dummies like you and these two hardheads will be working your asses off reading that damn bible and never know a goddamn thing about being a waiter. *That* hurts like a *motherfucker!*"

"It ain't my fault if the colored waiter is doomed," said Boone. "It's your fault for letting go your humility and letting the whites take over the good jobs."

Danny grabbed the skullcap off Boone's head and took it into the bathroom and flushed it down the toilet. In a minute it was half a mile away and soaked in old piss on the tracks. Boone did not try to fight, he just sat on his bunk and mumbled. He had other skullcaps. No one said anything to Doc, because that's the way real men show that they care. You don't talk. Talking makes it worse.

IV

What else is there to tell you, youngblood? They made him retire. He didn't try to fight it. He was beaten and he knew it; not by the service, but by a book. *That book,* that *bible* you keep your finger stuck in. That's not a good way for a man to go. He should die in service. He should die doing the things he likes. But not by a book.

All of us Old School men will be beaten by it. Danny Jackson is gone now, and Reverend Hendricks put in for his pension and took up preaching, full-time. But Uncle T. Boone is still riding. They'll get *me* soon enough, with that book. But it will never get you because you'll never be a waiter, or at least a Waiter's Waiter. You read too much.

Doc got a good pension and he took it directly to Andy's. And none of the boys who knew about it knew how to refuse a drink on Doc. But none of us knew how to drink with him knowing that we would be going out again in a few days, and he was on the ground. So a lot of us, even the drunks and hustlers who usually hang around Andy's, avoided him whenever we could. There was nothing to talk about any more.

He died five months after he was put on the ground. He was seventy-three and it was winter. He froze to death wandering around the Chicago yards early one morning. He had been drunk, and was still steaming when the yard crew found him. Only the few of us left in the Old School know what he was doing there.

I am sixty-three now. And I haven't decided if I should take my pension when they ask me to go or continue to ride. I *want* to keep riding, but I know that if I do,

Jerry Ewald or Harry Silk or Jack Tate will get me one of these days. I could get down if I wanted: I have a hobby and I am too old to get drunk by myself. I couldn't drink with you, youngblood. We have nothing to talk about. And after a while you would get mad at me for talking anyway, and keeping you from your pussy. You are tired already. I can see it in your eyes and in the way you play with the pages of your rule book.

I know it. And I wonder why I should keep talking to you when you could never see what I see or understand what I understand or know the real difference between my school and yours. I wonder why I have kept talking this long when all the time I have seen that you can hardly wait to hit the city to get off this thing and spend your money. You have a good story. But you will never remember it. Because all this time you have had pussy in your mind, and your fingers in the pages of that black bible.

1968

Ernest J. Gaines b. 1933

Ernest J. Gaines was born in Pointe Coupee Parish on "The Quarters" of River Lake Plantation, a few miles from New Roads, Louisiana. "Until I was fifteen years old," Gaines recounts, "I had been raised by an aunt, Miss Augusteen Jefferson, a lady who had never walked a day in her life," but who, as he says in the dedication to *The Autobiography of Miss Jane Pittman,* "taught me the importance of standing." As a boy Gaines worked in the cane fields "where all my people before me worked."

In 1948 Gaines left Louisiana to join his mother and stepfather in Vallejo, California. There, as a teenager, he began to "read all the Southern writers I could find in the Vallejo library; then I began to read any writer who wrote about nature or about people who worked the land—anyone who would say something about dirt and trees, clear streams, and open sky." After a two-year stint in the army Gaines took his B.A. degree from San Francisco State College in 1957. He then won a Wallace Stegner Creative Writing Fellowship at Stanford and also received the Joseph Henry Jackson Literary Award there in 1959.

Gaines's novels and short fiction are set in an imaginary Louisiana that evokes and re-creates the world of his childhood and the changes he has observed on his many returns to Louisiana. Although he has a drawer full of San Francisco-inspired fiction, Gaines's published work is exclusively about Louisiana. "I wanted," he says of his intention as a writer, "to smell that Louisiana earth, feel that Louisiana sun, sit under the shade of one of those Louisiana oaks, search for pecans in that Louisiana grass in one of those Louisiana yards next to one of those Louisiana bayous, not far from a Louisiana river. I wanted to see on paper those Louisiana black children walking to school on cold days while yellow Louisiana busses passed them by. I wanted to see on paper those black parents going to work before the sun came up and coming back home to look after their children after the sun went down. I wanted to see on paper the true reason why those black fathers left home—not because they were trifling or shiftless—but because they were tired of putting up with certain conditions. I wanted to see on paper the small country churches (schools during the week), and

I wanted to hear those simple religious songs, those simple prayers—that true devotion. (It was Faulkner, I think, who said that if God were to stay alive in the country, the blacks would have to keep Him so.) And I wanted to hear that Louisiana dialect—that combination of English, Creole, Cajun, Black. For me there's no more beautiful sound anywhere."

Through the act of writing Gaines re-experiences Louisiana. Once there in imagination, he puts on paper the historical but alterable society which exists in the midst of nature's abiding reality. The instrument behind the passage of the spoken word to the page is the writer's healing human voice. Like his storytellers, Gaines breaks down the barriers between his voice and the voices of his characters. As a writer for his people, Gaines keeps faith with the oral tradition—a tradition of responsibility and change, and, despite violent opposition, a tradition of citizenship.

"The Sky Is Gray" and the other stories in Gaines's *Bloodline* mediate two complementary facts of life: first, that very little changes in his remote parish between the Civil War and his departure after World War II; and, second, that even rural Louisiana could not resist the racial upheaval of the 1950s and 1960s. According to Gaines's speech-driven donnée of fiction, for the writer to be free, his characters must be free, and an independent, individual voice is the first test of freedom.

John F. Callahan
Lewis and Clark College

PRIMARY WORKS

Catherine Carmier, 1964; *Of Love and Dust,* 1967; *Bloodline,* 1968; *The Autobiography of Miss Jane Pittman,* 1971; *In My Father's House,* 1978; *A Gathering of Old Men,* 1983.

The Sky Is Gray

1

Go'n be coming in a few minutes. Coming round that bend down there full speed. And I'm go'n get out my handkerchief and wave it down, and we go'n get on it and go.

I keep on looking for it, but Mama don't look that way no more. She's looking down the road where we just come from. It's a long old road, and far 's you can see you don't see nothing but gravel. You got dry weeds on both sides, and you got trees on both sides, and fences on both sides, too. And you got cows in the pastures and they standing close together. And when we was coming out here to catch the bus I seen the smoke coming out of the cows' noses.

I look at my mama and I know what she's thinking. I been with Mama so much, just me and her, I know what she's thinking all the time. Right now it's home—Auntie and them. She's thinking if they got enough wood—if she left enough there to keep them warm till we get back. She's thinking if it go'n rain and if any of them go'n have to go out in the rain. She's thinking 'bout the hog—if he go'n get out, and if Ty and Val be able to get him back in. She always worry like that when she leaves the house. She don't worry too much if she leave me there with the smaller ones, 'cause she know I'm go'n look after them and look after Auntie and everything else. I'm the oldest and she say I'm the man.

I look at my mama and I love my mama. She's wearing that black coat and that black hat and she's looking sad. I love my mama and I want put my arm round her and tell her. But I'm not supposed to do that. She say that's weakness and that's crybaby stuff, and she don't want no crybaby round her. She don't want you to be scared, either. 'Cause Ty's scared of ghosts and she's always whipping him. I'm scared of the dark, too, but I make 'tend I ain't. I make 'tend I ain't 'cause I'm the oldest, and I got to set a good sample for the rest. I can't ever be scared and I can't ever cry. And that's why I never said nothing 'bout my teeth. It's been hurting me and hurting me close to a month now, but I never said it. I didn't say it 'cause I didn't want act like a crybaby, and 'cause I know we didn't have enough money to go have it pulled. But, Lord, it been hurting me. And look like it wouldn't start till at night when you was trying to get yourself little sleep. Then soon 's you shut your eyes—ummm-ummm, Lord, look like it go right down to your heartstring.

"Hurting, hanh?" Ty'd say.

I'd shake my head, but I wouldn't open my mouth for nothing. You open your mouth and let that wind in, and it almost kill you.

I'd just lay there and listen to them snore. Ty there, right 'side me, and Auntie and Val over by the fireplace. Val younger than me and Ty, and he sleeps with Auntie. Mama sleeps round the other side with Louis and Walker.

I'd just lay there and listen to them, and listen to that wind out there, and listen to that fire in the fireplace. Sometimes it'd stop long enough to let me get little rest. Sometimes it just hurt, hurt, hurt. Lord, have mercy.

2

Auntie knowed it was hurting me. I didn't tell nobody but Ty, 'cause we buddies and he ain't go'n tell nobody. But some kind of way Auntie found out. When she asked me, I told her no, nothing was wrong. But she knowed it all the time. She told me to mash up a piece of aspirin and wrap it in some cotton and jugg it down in that hole. I did it, but it didn't do no good. It stopped for a little while, and started right back again. Auntie wanted to tell Mama, but I told her, "Uh-uh." 'Cause I knowed we didn't have any money, and it just was go'n make her mad again. So Auntie told Monsieur Bayonne, and Monsieur Bayonne came over to the house and told me to kneel down 'side him on the fireplace. He put his finger in his mouth and made the Sign of the Cross on my jaw. The tip of Monsieur Bayonne's finger is some hard, 'cause he's always playing on that guitar. If we sit outside at night we can always hear Monsieur Bayonne playing on his guitar. Sometimes we leave him out there playing on the guitar.

Monsieur Bayonne made the Sign of the Cross over and over on my jaw, but that didn't do no good. Even when he prayed and told me to pray some, too, that tooth still hurt me.

"How you feeling?" he say.

"Same," I say.

He kept on praying and making the Sign of the Cross and I kept on praying, too.

"Still hurting?" he say.

"Yes, sir."

Monsieur Bayonne mashed harder and harder on my jaw. He mashed so hard he almost pushed me over on Ty. But then he stopped.

"What kind of prayers you praying, boy?" he say.

"Baptist," I say.

"Well, I'll be—no wonder that tooth still killing him. I'm going one way and he pulling the other. Boy, don't you know any Catholic prayers?"

"I know 'Hail Mary,'" I say.

"Then you better start saying it."

"Yes, sir."

He started mashing on my jaw again, and I could hear him praying at the same time. And, sure enough, after while it stopped hurting me.

Me and Ty went outside where Monsieur Bayonne's two hounds was and we started playing with them. "Let's go hunting," Ty say. "All right," I say; and we went on back in the pasture. Soon the hounds got on a trail, and me and Ty followed them all 'cross the pasture and then back in the woods, too. And then they cornered this little old rabbit and killed him, and me and Ty made them get back, and we picked up the rabbit and started on back home. But my tooth had started hurting me again. It was hurting me plenty now, but I wouldn't tell Monsieur Bayonne. That night I didn't sleep a bit, and first thing in the morning Auntie told me to go back and let Monsieur Bayonne pray over me some more. Monsieur Bayonne was in his kitchen making coffee when I got there. Soon 's he seen me he knowed what was wrong.

"All right, kneel down there 'side that stove," he say. "And this time make sure you pray Catholic. I don't know nothing 'bout that Baptist, and I don't want know nothing 'bout him."

3

Last night Mama say, "Tomorrow we going to town."

"It ain't hurting me no more," I say. "I can eat anything on it."

"Tomorrow we going to town," she say.

And after she finished eating, she got up and went to bed. She always go to bed early now. 'Fore Daddy went in the Army, she used to stay up late. All of us sitting out on the gallery or round the fire. But now, look like soon 's she finish eating she go to bed.

This morning when I woke up, her and Auntie was standing 'fore the fireplace. She say: "Enough to get there and get back. Dollar and a half to have it pulled. Twenty-five for me to go, twenty-five for him. Twenty-five for me to come back, twenty-five for him. Fifty cents left. Guess I get little piece of salt meat with that."

"Sure can use it," Auntie say. "White beans and no salt meat ain't white beans."

"I do the best I can," Mama say.

They was quiet after that, and I made 'tend I was still asleep.

"James, hit the floor," Auntie say.

I still made 'tend I was asleep. I didn't want them to know I was listening.

"All right," Auntie say, shaking me by the shoulder. "Come on. Today's the day."

I pushed the cover down to get out, and Ty grabbed it and pulled it back.

"You, too, Ty," Auntie say.

"I ain't getting no teef pulled," Ty say.

"Don't mean it ain't time to get up," Auntie say. "Hit it, Ty."

Ty got up grumbling.

"James, you hurry up and get in your clothes and eat your food," Auntie say. "What time y'all coming back?" she say to Mama.

"That 'leven o'clock bus," Mama say. "Got to get back in that field this evening."

"Get a move on you, James," Auntie say.

I went in the kitchen and washed my face, then I ate my breakfast. I was having bread and syrup. The bread was warm and hard and tasted good. And I tried to make it last a long time.

Ty came back there grumbling and mad at me.

"Got to get up," he say. "I ain't having no teefes pulled. What I got to be getting up for?"

Ty poured some syrup in his pan and got a piece of bread. He didn't wash his hands, neither his face, and I could see that white stuff in his eyes.

"You the one getting your teef pulled," he say. "What I got to get up for. I bet if I was getting a teef pulled, you wouldn't be getting up. Shucks; syrup again. I'm getting tired of this old syrup. Syrup, syrup, syrup. I'm go'n take with the sugar diabetes. I want me some bacon sometime."

"Go out in the field and work and you can have your bacon," Auntie say. She stood in the middle door looking at Ty. "You better be glad you got syrup. Some people ain't got that—hard 's time is."

"Shucks," Ty say. "How can I be strong."

"I don't know too much 'bout your strength," Auntie say; "but I know where you go'n be hot at, you keep that grumbling up. James, get a move on you; your mama waiting."

I ate my last piece of bread and went in the front room. Mama was standing 'fore the fireplace warming her hands. I put on my coat and my cap, and we left the house.

4

I look down there again, but it still ain't coming. I almost say, "It ain't coming yet," but I keep my mouth shut. 'Cause that's something else she don't like. She don't like for you to say something just for nothing. She can see it ain't coming, I can see it ain't coming, so why say it ain't coming. I don't say it, I turn and look at the river that's back of us. It's so cold the smoke's just raising up from the water. I see a bunch of pool-doos not too far out—just on the other side the lilies. I'm wondering if you can eat pool-doos. I ain't too sure, 'cause I ain't never ate none. But I done ate owls and blackbirds, and I done ate redbirds, too. I didn't want kill the redbirds, but she made me kill them. They had two of them back there. One in my trap, one in Ty's trap. Me and Ty was go'n play with them and let them go, but she made me kill them 'cause we needed the food.

"I can't," I say. "I can't."

"Here," she say. "Take it."

"I can't," I say. "I can't. I can't kill him, Mama, please."

"Here," she say. "Take this fork, James."

"Please, Mama, I can't kill him," I say.

I could tell she was go'n hit me. I jerked back, but I didn't jerk back soon enough.

"Take it," she say.

I took it and reached in for him, but he kept on hopping to the back.

"I can't, Mama," I say. The water just kept on running down my face. "I can't," I say.

"Get him out of there," she say.

I reached in for him and he kept on hopping to the back. Then I reached in farther, and he pecked me on the hand.

"I can't, Mama," I say.

She slapped me again.

I reached in again, but he kept on hopping out my way. Then he hopped to one side and I reached there. The fork got him on the leg and I heard his leg pop. I pulled my hand out 'cause I had hurt him.

"Give it here," she say, and jerked the fork out my hand.

She reached in and got the little bird right in the neck. I heard the fork go in his neck, and I heard it go in the ground. She brought him out and helt him right in front of me.

"That's one," she say. She shook him off and gived me the fork. "Get the other one."

"I can't, Mama," I say. "I'll do anything, but don't make me do that."

She went to the corner of the fence and broke the biggest switch over there she could find. I knelt 'side the trap, crying.

"Get him out of there," she say.

"I can't, Mama."

She started hitting me 'cross the back. I went down on the ground, crying.

"Get him," she say.

"Octavia?" Auntie say.

'Cause she had come out of the house and she was standing by the tree looking at us.

"Get him out of there," Mama say.

"Octavia," Auntie say, "explain to him. Explain to him. Just don't beat him. Explain to him."

But she hit me and hit me and hit me.

I'm still young—I ain't no more than eight; but I know now; I know why I had to do it. (They was so little though. They was so little. I 'member how I picked the feathers off them and cleaned them and helt them over the fire. Then we all ate them. Ain't had but a little bitty piece each, but we all had a little bitty piece, and everybody just looked at me 'cause they was so proud.) Suppose she had to go away? That's why I had to do it. Suppose she had to go away like Daddy went away? Then who was go'n look after us? They had to be somebody left to carry on. I didn't know it then, but I know it now. Auntie and Monsieur Bayonne talked to me and made me see.

5

Time I see it I get out my handkerchief and start waving. It's still 'way down there, but I keep waving anyhow. Then it come up and stop and me and Mama get on. Mama tell me go sit in the back while she pay. I do like she say, and the people look at me. When I pass the little sign that say "White" and "Colored," I start looking for a seat. I just see one of them back there, but I don't take it, 'cause I want my mama to sit down herself. She comes in the back and sit down, and I lean on the seat. They got seats in the front, but I know I can't sit there, 'cause I have to sit back of the sign. Anyhow, I don't want sit there if my mama go'n sit back here.

They got a lady sitting 'side my mama and she looks at me and smiles little bit. I smile back, but I don't open my mouth, 'cause the wind'll get in and make that tooth ache. The lady take out a pack of gum and reach me a slice, but I shake my head. The lady just can't understand why a little boy'll turn down gum, and she reach me a slice again. This time I point to my jaw. The lady understands and smiles little bit, and I smile little bit, but I don't open my mouth, though.

They got a girl sitting 'cross from me. She got on a red overcoat and her hair's plaited in one big plait. First, I make 'tend I don't see her over there, but then I start looking at her little bit. She make 'tend she don't see me, either, but I catch her looking that way. She got a cold, and every now and then she h'ist that little handkerchief to her nose. She ought to blow it, but she don't. Must think she's too much a lady or something.

Every time she h'ist that little handkerchief, the lady 'side her say something in her ear. She shakes her head and lays her hands in her lap again. Then I catch her kind of looking where I'm at. I smile at her little bit. But think she'll smile back? Uh-uh. She just turn up her little old nose and turn her head. Well, I show her both of us can turn us head. I turn mine too and look out at the river.

The river is gray. The sky is gray. They have pool-doos on the water. The water is wavy, and the pool-doos go up and down. The bus go round a turn, and you got plenty trees hiding the river. Then the bus go round another turn, and I can see the river again.

I look toward the front where all the white people sitting. Then I look at that little old gal again. I don't look right at her, 'cause I don't want all them people to know I love her. I just look at her little bit, like I'm looking out that window over there. But she knows I'm looking that way, and she kind of look at me, too. The lady sitting 'side her catch her this time, and she leans over and says something in her ear.

"I don't love him nothing," that little old gal says out loud.

Everybody back there hear her mouth, and all of them look at us and laugh.

"I don't love you, either," I say. "So you don't have to turn up your nose, Miss."

"You the one looking," she say.

"I wasn't looking at you," I say. "I was looking out that window, there."

"Out that window, my foot," she say. "I seen you. Everytime I turned round you was looking at me."

"You must of been looking yourself if you seen me all them times," I say.

"Shucks," she say, "I got me all kind of boyfriends."

"I got girlfriends, too," I say.

"Well, I just don't want you getting your hopes up," she say.

I don't say no more to that little old gal 'cause I don't want have to bust her in the mouth. I lean on the seat where Mama sitting, and I don't even look that way no more. When we get to Bayonne, she jugg her little old tongue out at me. I make 'tend I'm go'n hit her, and she duck down 'side her mama. And all the people laugh at us again.

6

Me and Mama get off and start walking in town. Bayonne is a little bitty town. Baton Rouge is a hundred times bigger than Bayonne. I went to Baton Rouge once—me, Ty, Mama, and Daddy. But that was 'way back yonder, 'fore Daddy went in the Army. I wonder when we go'n see him again. I wonder when. Look like he ain't ever coming back home. . . . Even the pavement all cracked in Bayonne. Got grass shooting right out the sidewalk. Got weeds in the ditch, too; just like they got at home.

It's some cold in Bayonne. Look like it's colder than it is home. The wind blows in my face, and I feel that stuff running down my nose. I sniff. Mama says use that handkerchief. I blow my nose and put it back.

We pass a school and I see them white children playing in the yard. Big old red school, and them children just running and playing. Then we pass a café, and I see a bunch of people in there eating. I wish I was in there 'cause I'm cold. Mama tells me keep my eyes in front where they belong.

We pass stores that's got dummies, and we pass another café, and then we pass a shoe shop, and that bald-head man in there fixing on a shoe. I look at him and I butt into that white lady, and Mama jerks me in front and tells me stay there.

We come up to the courthouse, and I see the flag waving there. This flag ain't like the one we got at school. This one here ain't got but a handful of stars.[1] One at school got a big pile of stars—one for every state. We pass it and we turn and there it is—the dentist office. Me and Mama go in, and they got people sitting everywhere you look. They even got a little boy in there younger than me.

Me and Mama sit on that bench, and a white lady come in there and ask me what my name is. Mama tells her and the white lady goes on back. Then I hear somebody hollering in there. Soon 's that little boy hear him hollering, he starts hollering, too. His mama pats him and pats him, trying to make him hush up, but he ain't thinking 'bout his mama.

The man that was hollering in there comes out holding his jaw. He is a big old man and he's wearing overalls and a jumper.

"Got it, hanh?" another man asks him.

The man shakes his head—don't want open his mouth.

"Man, I thought they was killing you in there," the other man says. "Hollering like a pig under a gate."

The man don't say nothing. He just heads for the door, and the other man follows him.

[1]Up through the 1940s and beyond, the Confederate flag with its stars and bars was displayed outside public schools, courthouses, and other official buildings in many southern states.

"John Lee," the white lady says. "John Lee Williams."

The little boy juggs his head down in his mama's lap and holler more now. His mama tells him go with the nurse, but he ain't thinking 'bout his mama. His mama tells him again, but he don't even hear her. His mama picks him up and takes him in there, and even when the white lady shuts the door I can still hear little old John Lee.

"I often wonder why the Lord let a child like that suffer," a lady says to my mama. The lady's sitting right in front of us on another bench. She's got on a white dress and a black sweater. She must be a nurse or something herself, I reckon.

"Not us to question," a man says.

"Sometimes I don't know if we shouldn't," the lady says.

"I know definitely we shouldn't," the man says. The man looks like a preacher. He's big and fat and he's got on a black suit. He's got a gold chain, too.

"Why?" the lady says.

"Why anything?" the preacher says.

"Yes," the lady says. "Why anything?"

"Not us to question," the preacher says.

The lady looks at the preacher a little while and looks at Mama again.

"And look like it's the poor who suffers the most," she says. "I don't understand it."

"Best not to even try," the preacher says. "He works in mysterious ways—wonders to perform."

Right then little John Lee bust out hollering, and everybody turn they head to listen.

"He's not a good dentist," the lady says. "Dr. Robillard is much better. But more expensive. That's why most of the colored people come here. The white people go to Dr. Robillard. Y'all from Bayonne?"

"Down the river," my mama says. And that's all she go'n say, 'cause she don't talk much. But the lady keeps on looking at her, and so she says, "Near Morgan."

"I see," the lady says.

7

"That's the trouble with the black people in this country today," somebody else says. This one here's sitting on the same side me and Mama's sitting, and he is kind of sitting in front of that preacher. He looks like a teacher or somebody that goes to college. He's got on a suit, and he's got a book that he's been reading. "We don't question is exactly our problem," he says. "We should question and question and question—question everything."

The preacher just looks at him a long time. He done put a toothpick or something in his mouth, and he just keeps on turning it and turning it. You can see he don't like that boy with that book.

"Maybe you can explain what you mean," he says.

"I said what I meant," the boy says. "Question everything. Every stripe, every star, every word spoken. Everything."

"It 'pears to me that this young lady and I was talking 'bout God, young man," the preacher says.

"Question Him, too," the boy says.

"Wait," the preacher says. "Wait now."

"You heard me right," the boy says. "His existence as well as everything else. Everything."

The preacher just looks across the room at the boy. You can see he's getting madder and madder. But mad or no mad, the boy ain't thinking 'bout him. He looks at that preacher just 's hard 's the preacher looks at him.

"Is this what they coming to?" the preacher says. "Is this what we educating them for?"

"You're not educating me," the boy says. "I wash dishes at night so that I can go to school in the day. So even the words you spoke need questioning."

The preacher just looks at him and shakes his head.

"When I come in this room and seen you there with your book, I said to myself, 'There's an intelligent man.' How wrong a person can be."

"Show me one reason to believe in the existence of a God," the boy says.

"My heart tells me," the preacher says.

"'My heart tells me,'" the boy says. "'My heart tells me.' Sure, 'My heart tells me.' And as long as you listen to what your heart tells you, you will have only what the white man gives you and nothing more. Me, I don't listen to my heart. The purpose of the heart is to pump blood throughout the body, and nothing else."

"Who's your paw, boy?" the preacher says.

"Why?"

"Who is he?"

"He's dead."

"And your mom?"

"She's in Charity Hospital with pneumonia. Half killed herself, working for nothing."

"And 'cause he's dead and she's sick, you mad at the world?"

"I'm not mad at the world. I'm questioning the world. I'm questioning it with cold logic, sir. What do words like Freedom, Liberty, God, White, Colored mean? I want to know. That's why *you* are sending us to school, to read and to ask questions. And because we ask these questions, you call us mad. No sir, it is not us who are mad."

"You keep saying 'us'?"

"'Us.' Yes—us. I'm not alone."

The preacher just shakes his head. Then he looks at everybody in the room—everybody. Some of the people look down at the floor, keep from looking at him. I kind of look 'way myself, but soon 's I know he done turn his head, I look that way again.

"I'm sorry for you," he says to the boy.

"Why?" the boy says. "Why not be sorry for yourself? Why are you so much better off than I am? Why aren't you sorry for these other people in here? Why not be sorry for the lady who had to drag her child into the dentist office? Why not be sorry for the lady sitting on that bench over there? Be sorry for them. Not for me. Some way or other I'm going to make it."

"No, I'm sorry for you," the preacher says.

"Of course, of course," the boy says, nodding his head. "You're sorry for me because I rock that pillar you're leaning on."

"You can't ever rock the pillar I'm leaning on, young man. It's stronger than anything man can ever do."

"You believe in God because a man told you to believe in God," the boy says. "A white man told you to believe in God. And why? To keep you ignorant so he can keep his feet on your neck."

"So now we the ignorant?" the preacher says.

"Yes," the boy says. "Yes." And he opens his book again.

The preacher just looks at him sitting there. The boy done forgot all about him. Everybody else make 'tend they done forgot the squabble, too.

Then I see that preacher getting up real slow. Preacher's a great big old man and he got to brace himself to get up. He comes over where the boy is sitting. He just stands there a little while looking down at him, but the boy don't raise his head.

"Get up, boy," preacher says.

The boy looks up at him, then he shuts his book real slow and stands up. Preacher just hauls back and hit him in the face. The boy falls back 'gainst the wall, but he straightens himself up and looks right back at that preacher.

"You forgot the other cheek," he says.

The preacher hauls back and hit him again on the other side. But this time the boy braces himself and don't fall.

"That hasn't changed a thing," he says.

The preacher just looks at the boy. The preacher's breathing real hard like he just run up a big hill. The boy sits down and opens his book again.

"I feel sorry for you," the preacher says. "I never felt so sorry for a man before."

The boy makes 'tend he don't even hear that preacher. He keeps on reading his book. The preacher goes back and gets his hat off the chair.

"Excuse me," he says to us. "I'll come back some other time. Y'all, please excuse me."

And he looks at the boy and goes out the room. The boy h'ist his hand up to his mouth one time to wipe 'way some blood. All the rest of the time he keeps on reading. And nobody else in there say a word.

8

Little John Lee and his mama come out the dentist office, and the nurse calls somebody else in. Then little bit later they come out, and the nurse calls another name. But fast 's she calls somebody in there, somebody else comes in the place where we sitting, and the room stays full.

The people coming in now, all of them wearing big coats. One of them says something 'bout sleeting, another one says he hope not. Another one says he think it ain't nothing but rain. 'Cause, he says, rain can get awful cold this time of year.

All round the room they talking. Some of them talking to people right by them, some of them talking to people clear 'cross the room, some of them talking to anybody'll listen. It's a little bitty room, no bigger than us kitchen, and I can see everybody in there. The little old room's full of smoke, 'cause you got two old men smoking pipes over by that side door. I think I feel my tooth thumping me some, and I hold my breath and wait. I wait and wait, but it don't thump me no more. Thank God for that.

I feel like going to sleep, and I lean back 'gainst the wall. But I'm scared to go to sleep. Scared 'cause the nurse might call my name and I won't hear her. And Mama might go to sleep, too, and she'll be mad if neither one of us heard the nurse.

I look up at Mama. I love my mama. I love my mama. And when cotton come I'm go'n get her a new coat. And I ain't go'n get a black one, either. I think I'm go'n get her a red one.

"They got some books over there," I say. "Want read one of them?"

Mama looks at the books, but she don't answer me.

"You got yourself a little man there," the lady says.

Mama don't say nothing to the lady, but she must've smiled, 'cause I seen the lady smiling back. The lady looks at me a little while, like she's feeling sorry for me.

"You sure got that preacher out here in a hurry," she says to that boy.

The boy looks up at her and looks in his book again. When I grow up I want be just like him. I want clothes like that and I want keep a book with me, too.

"You really don't believe in God?" the lady says.

"No," he says.

"But why?" the lady says.

"Because the wind is pink," he says.

"What?" the lady says.

The boy don't answer her no more. He just reads in his book.

"Talking 'bout the wind is pink," that old lady says. She's sitting on the same bench with the boy and she's trying to look in his face. The boy makes 'tend the old lady ain't even there. He just keeps on reading. "Wind is pink," she says again. "Eh, Lord, what children go'n be saying next?"

The lady 'cross from us bust out laughing.

"That's a good one," she says. "The wind is pink. Yes sir, that's a good one."

"Don't you believe the wind is pink?" the boy says. He keeps his head down in the book.

"Course I believe it, honey," the lady says. "Course I do." She looks at us and winks her eye. "And what color is grass, honey?"

"Grass? Grass is black."

She bust out laughing again. The boy looks at her.

"Don't you believe grass is black?" he says.

The lady quits her laughing and looks at him. Everybody else looking at him, too. The place quiet, quiet.

"Grass is green, honey," the lady says. "It was green yesterday, it's green today, and it's go'n be green tomorrow."

"How do you know it's green?"

"I know because I know."

"You don't know it's green," the boy says. "You believe it's green because someone told you it was green. If someone had told you it was black you'd believe it was black."

"It's green," the lady says. "I know green when I see green."

"Prove it's green," the boy says.

"Sure, now," the lady says. "Don't tell me it's coming to that."

"It's coming to just that," the boy says. "Words mean nothing. One means no more than the other."

"That's what it all coming to?" that old lady says. That old lady got on a turban and she got on two sweaters. She got a green sweater under a black sweater. I can see the green sweater 'cause some of the buttons on the other sweater's missing.

"Yes ma'am," the boy says. "Words mean nothing. Action is the only thing. Doing. That's the only thing."

"Other words, you want the Lord to come down here and show Hisself to you?" she says.

"Exactly, ma'am," he says.

"You don't mean that, I'm sure?" she says.

"I do, ma'am," he says.

"Done, Jesus," the old lady says, shaking her head.

"I didn't go 'long with that preacher at first," the other lady says; "but now—I don't know. When a person say the grass is black, he's either a lunatic or something's wrong."

"Prove to me that it's green," the boy says.

"It's green because the people say it's green."

"Those same people say we're citizens of these United States," the boy says.

"I think I'm a citizen," the lady says.

"Citizens have certain rights," the boy says. "Name me one right that you have. One right, granted by the Constitution, that you can exercise in Bayonne."

The lady don't answer him. She just looks at him like she don't know what he's talking 'bout. I know I don't.

"Things changing," she says.

"Things are changing because some black men have begun to think with their brains and not their hearts," the boy says.

"You trying to say these people don't believe in God?"

"I'm sure some of them do. Maybe most of them do. But they don't believe that God is going to touch these white people's hearts and change things tomorrow. Things change through action. By no other way."

Everybody sit quiet and look at the boy. Nobody says a thing. Then the lady 'cross the room from me and Mama just shakes her head.

"Let's hope that not all your generation feel the same way you do," she says.

"Think what you please, it doesn't matter," the boy says. "But it will be men who listen to their heads and not their hearts who will see that your children have a better chance than you had."

"Let's hope they ain't all like you, though," the old lady says. "Done forgot the heart absolutely."

"Yes ma'am, I hope they aren't all like me," the boy says. "Unfortunately, I was born too late to believe in your God. Let's hope that the ones who come after will have your faith—if not in your God, then in something else, something definitely that they can lean on. I haven't anything. For me, the wind is pink, the grass is black."

9

The nurse comes in the room where we all sitting and waiting and says the doctor won't take no more patients till one o'clock this evening. My mama jumps up off the bench and goes up to the white lady.

"Nurse, I have to go back in the field this evening," she says.

"The doctor is treating his last patient now," the nurse says. "One o'clock this evening."

"Can I at least speak to the doctor?" my mama asks.

"I'm his nurse," the lady says.

"My little boy's sick," my mama says. "Right now his tooth almost killing him."

The nurse looks at me. She's trying to make up her mind if to let me come in. I look at her real pitiful. The tooth ain't hurting me at all, but Mama say it is, so I make 'tend for her sake.

"This evening," the nurse says, and goes on back in the office.

"Don't feel 'jected, honey," the lady says to Mama. "I been round them a long time—they take you when they want to. If you was white, that's something else; but we the wrong color."

Mama don't say nothing to the lady, and me and her go outside and stand 'gainst the wall. It's cold out there. I can feel that wind going through my coat. Some of the other people come out of the room and go up the street. Me and Mama stand there a little while and we start walking. I don't know where we going. When we come to the other street we just stand there.

"You don't have to make water, do you?" Mama says.

"No, ma'am," I say.

We go on up the street. Walking real slow. I can tell Mama don't know where she's going. When we come to a store we stand there and look at the dummies. I look at a little boy wearing a brown overcoat. He's got on brown shoes, too. I look at my old shoes and look at his'n again. You wait till summer, I say.

Me and Mama walk away. We come up to another store and we stop and look at them dummies, too. Then we go on again. We pass a café where the white people in there eating. Mama tells me keep my eyes in front where they belong, but I can't help from seeing them people eat. My stomach starts to growling 'cause I'm hungry. When I see people eating, I get hungry; when I see a coat, I get cold.

A man whistles at my mama when we go by a filling station. She makes 'tend she don't even see him. I look back and I feel like hitting him in the mouth. If I was bigger, I say; if I was bigger, you'd see.

We keep on going. I'm getting colder and colder, but I don't say nothing. I feel that stuff running down my nose and I sniff.

"That rag," Mama says.

I get it out and wipe my nose. I'm getting cold all over now—my face, my hands, my feet, everything. We pass another little café, but this'n for white people, too, and we can't go in there, either. So we just walk. I'm so cold now I'm 'bout ready to say it. If I knowed where we was going I wouldn't be so cold, but I don't know where we going. We go, we go, we go. We walk clean out of Bayonne. Then we cross the street and we come back. Same thing I seen when I got off the bus this morning.

Same old trees, same old walk, same old weeds, same old cracked pave—same old everything.

I sniff again.

"That rag," Mama says.

I wipe my nose real fast and jugg that handkerchief back in my pocket 'fore my hand gets too cold. I raise my head and I can see David's hardware store. When we come up to it, we go in. I don't know why, but I'm glad.

It's warm in there. It's so warm in there you don't ever want to leave. I look for the heater, and I see it over by them barrels. Three white men standing round the heater talking in Creole. One of them comes over to see what my mama want.

"Got any axe handles?" she says.

Me, Mama and the white man start to the back, but Mama stops me when we come up to the heater. She and the white man go on. I hold my hands over the heater and look at them. They go all the way to the back, and I see the white man pointing to the axe handles 'gainst the wall. Mama takes one of them and shakes it like she's trying to figure how much it weighs. Then she rubs her hand over it from one end to the other end. She turns it over and looks at the other side, then she shakes it again, and shakes her head and puts it back. She gets another one and she does it just like she did the first one, then she shakes her head. Then she gets a brown one and do it that, too. But she don't like this one, either. Then she gets another one, but 'fore she shakes it or anything, she looks at me. Look like she's trying to say something to me, but I don't know what it is. All I know is I done got warm now and I'm feeling right smart better. Mama shakes this axe handle just like she did the others, and shakes her head and says something to the white man. The white man just looks at his pile of axe handles, and when Mama pass him to come to the front, the white man just scratch his head and follows her. She tells me come on and we go on out and start walking again.

We walk and walk, and no time at all I'm cold again. Look like I'm colder now 'cause I can still remember how good it was back there. My stomach growls and I suck it in to keep Mama from hearing it. She's walking right 'side me, and it growls so loud you can hear it a mile. But Mama don't say a word.

10

When we come up to the courthouse, I look at the clock. It's got quarter to twelve. Mean we got another hour and a quarter to be out here in the cold. We go and stand 'side a building. Something hits my cap and I look up at the sky. Sleet's falling.

I look at Mama standing there. I want stand close 'side her, but she don't like that. She say that's crybaby stuff. She say you got to stand for yourself, by yourself.

"Let's go back to that office," she says.

We cross the street. When we get to the dentist office I try to open the door, but I can't. I twist and twist, but I can't. Mama pushes me to the side and she twist the knob, but she can't open the door, either. She turns 'way from the door. I look at her, but I don't move and I don't say nothing. I done seen her like this before and I'm scared of her.

"You hungry?" she says. She says it like she's mad at me, like I'm the cause of everything.

"No, ma'am," I say.

"You want eat and walk back, or you rather don't eat and ride?"

"I ain't hungry," I say.

I ain't just hungry, but I'm cold, too. I'm so hungry and cold I want to cry. And look like I'm getting colder and colder. My feet done got numb. I try to work my toes, but I don't even feel them. Look like I'm go'n die. Look like I'm go'n stand right here and freeze to death. I think 'bout home. I think 'bout Val and Auntie and Ty and Louis and Walker. It's 'bout twelve o'clock and I know they eating dinner now. I can hear Ty making jokes. He done forgot 'bout getting up early this morning and right now he's probably making jokes. Always trying to make somebody laugh. I wish I was right there listening to him. Give anything in the world if I was home round the fire.

"Come on," Mama says.

We start walking again. My feet so numb I can't hardly feel them. We turn the corner and go on back up the street. The clock on the courthouse starts hitting for twelve.

The sleet's coming down plenty now. They hit the pave and bounce like rice. Oh, Lord; oh, Lord, I pray. Don't let me die, don't let me die, don't let me die, Lord.

11

Now I know where we going. We going back of town where the colored people eat. I don't care if I don't eat. I been hungry before. I can stand it. But I can't stand the cold.

I can see we go'n have a long walk. It's 'bout a mile down there. But I don't mind. I know when I get there I'm go'n warm myself. I think I can hold out. My hands numb in my pockets and my feet numb, too, but if I keep moving I can hold out. Just don't stop no more, that's all.

The sky's gray. The sleet keeps on falling. Falling like rain now—plenty, plenty. You can hear it hitting the pave. You can see it bouncing. Sometimes it bounces two times 'fore it settles.

We keep on going. We don't say nothing. We just keep on going, keep on going.

I wonder what Mama's thinking. I hope she ain't mad at me. When summer come I'm go'n pick plenty cotton and get her a coat. I'm go'n get her a red one.

I hope they'd make it summer all the time. I'd be glad if it was summer all the time—but it ain't. We got to have winter, too. Lord, I hate the winter. I guess everybody hate the winter.

I don't sniff this time. I get out my handkerchief and wipe my nose. My hands's so cold I can hardly hold the handkerchief.

I think we getting close, but we ain't there yet. I wonder where everybody is. Can't see a soul but us. Look like we the only two people moving round today. Must be too cold for the rest of the people to move round in.

I can hear my teeth. I hope they don't knock together too hard and make that bad one hurt. Lord, that's all I need, for that bad one to start off.

I hear a church bell somewhere. But today ain't Sunday. They must be ringing for a funeral or something.

I wonder what they doing at home. They must be eating. Monsieur Bayonne might be there with his guitar. One day Ty played with Monsieur Bayonne's guitar and broke one of the strings. Monsieur Bayonne was some mad with Ty. He say Ty wasn't go'n ever 'mount to nothing. Ty can go just like Monsieur Bayonne when he ain't there. Ty can make everybody laugh when he starts to mocking Monsieur Bayonne.

I used to like to be with Mama and Daddy. We used to be happy. But they took him in the Army. Now, nobody happy no more. . . . I be glad when Daddy comes home.

Monsieur Bayonne say it wasn't fair for them to take Daddy and give Mama nothing and give us nothing. Auntie say, "Shhh, Etienne. Don't let them hear you talk like that." Monsieur Bayonne say, "It's God truth. What they giving his children? They have to walk three and a half miles to school hot or cold. That's anything to give for a paw? She's got to work in the field rain or shine just to make ends meet. That's anything to give for a husband?" Auntie say, "Shhh, Etienne, shhh." "Yes, you right," Monsieur Bayonne say. "Best don't say it in front of them now. But one day they go'n find out. One day." "Yes, I suppose so," Auntie say. "Then what, Rose Mary?" Monsieur Bayonne say. "I don't know, Etienne," Auntie say. "All we can do is us job, and leave everything else in His hand . . ."

We getting closer, now. We getting closer. I can even see the railroad tracks.

We cross the tracks, and now I see the café. Just to get in there, I say. Just to get in there. Already I'm starting to feel little better.

12

We go in. Ahh, it's good. I look for the heater; there 'gainst the wall. One of them little brown ones. I just stand there and hold my hands over it. I can't open my hands too wide 'cause they almost froze.

Mama's standing right 'side me. She done unbuttoned her coat. Smoke rises out of the coat, and the coat smells like a wet dog.

I move to the side so Mama can have more room. She opens out her hands and rubs them together. I rub mine together, too, 'cause this keep them from hurting. If you let them warm too fast, they hurt you sure. But if you let them warm just little bit at a time, and you keep rubbing them, they be all right every time.

They got just two more people in the café. A lady back of the counter, and a man on this side the counter. They been watching us ever since we come in.

Mama gets out the handkerchief and count up the money. Both of us know how much money she's got there. Three dollars. No, she ain't got three dollars, 'cause she had to pay us way up here. She ain't got but two dollars and a half left. Dollar and a half to get my tooth pulled, and fifty cents for us to go back on, and fifty cents worth of salt meat.

She stirs the money round with her finger. Most of the money is change 'cause I can hear it rubbing together. She stirs it and stirs it. Then she looks at the door. It's still sleeting. I can hear it hitting 'gainst the wall like rice.

"I ain't hungry, Mama," I say.

"Got to pay them something for they heat," she says.

She takes a quarter out the handkerchief and ties the handkerchief up again. She looks over her shoulder at the people, but she still don't move. I hope she don't spend the money. I don't want her spending it on me. I'm hungry, I'm almost starving I'm so hungry, but I don't want her spending the money on me.

She flips the quarter over like she's thinking. She's must be thinking 'bout us walking back home. Lord, I sure don't want walk home. If I thought it'd do any good to say something, I'd say it. But Mama makes up her own mind 'bout things.

She turns 'way from the heater right fast, like she better hurry up and spend the quarter 'fore she change her mind. I watch her go toward the counter. The man and the lady look at her, too. She tells the lady something and the lady walks away. The man keeps on looking at her. Her back's turned to the man, and she don't even know he's standing there.

The lady puts some cakes and a glass of milk on the counter. Then she pours up a cup of coffee and sets it 'side the other stuff. Mama pays her for the things and come on back where I'm standing. She tells me sit down at the table 'gainst the wall.

The milk and the cakes's for me; the coffee's for Mama. I eat slow and I look at her. She's looking outside at the sleet. She's looking real sad. I say to myself, I'm go'n make all this up one day. You see, one day, I'm go'n make all this up. I want say it now; I want tell her how I feel right now; but Mama don't like for us to talk like that.

"I can't eat all this," I say.

They ain't got but just three little old cakes there. I'm so hungry right now, the Lord knows I can eat a hundred times three, but I want my mama to have one.

Mama don't even look my way. She knows I'm hungry, she knows I want it. I let it stay there a little while, then I get it and eat it. I eat just on my front teeth, though, 'cause if cake touch that back tooth I know what'll happen. Thank God it ain't hurt me at all today.

After I finish eating I see the man go to the juke box. He drops a nickel in it, then he just stand there a little while looking at the record. Mama tells me keep my eyes in front where they belong. I turn my head like she say, but then I hear the man coming toward us.

"Dance, pretty?" he says.

Mama gets up to dance with him. But 'fore you know it, she done grabbed the little man in the collar and done heaved him 'side the wall. He hit the wall so hard he stop the juke box from playing.

"Some pimp," the lady back of the counter says. "Some pimp."

The little man jumps up off the floor and starts toward my mama. 'Fore you know it, Mama done sprung open her knife and she's waiting for him.

"Come on," she says. "Come on. I'll gut you from your neighbo to your throat. Come on."

I go up to the little man to hit him, but Mama makes me come and stand 'side her. The little man looks at me and Mama and goes on back to the counter.

"Some pimp," the lady back of the counter says. "Some pimp." She starts laughing and pointing at the little man. "Yes sir, you a pimp, all right. Yes sir-ree."

13

"Fasten that coat, let's go," Mama says.

"You don't have to leave," the lady says.

Mama don't answer the lady, and we right out in the cold again. I'm warm right now—my hands, my ears, my feet—but I know this ain't go'n last too long. It done sleet so much now you got ice everywhere you look.

We cross the railroad tracks, and soon's we do, I get cold. That wind goes through this little old coat like it ain't even there. I got on a shirt and a sweater under the coat, but that wind don't pay them no mind. I look up and I can see we got a long way to go. I wonder if we go'n make it 'fore I get too cold.

We cross over to walk on the sidewalk. They got just one sidewalk back here, and it's over there.

After we go just a little piece, I smell bread cooking. I look, then I see a baker shop. When we get closer, I can smell it more better. I shut my eyes and make 'tend I'm eating. But I keep them shut too long and I butt up 'gainst a telephone post. Mama grabs me and see if I'm hurt. I ain't bleeding or nothing and she turns me loose.

I can feel I'm getting colder and colder, and I look up to see how far we still got to go. Uptown is 'way up yonder. A half mile more, I reckon. I try to think of something. They say think and you won't get cold. I think of that poem, "Annabel Lee."[2] I ain't been to school in so long—this bad weather—I reckon they done passed "Annabel Lee" by now. But passed it or not, I'm sure Miss Walker go'n make me recite it when I get there. That woman don't never forget nothing. I ain't never seen nobody like that in my life.

I'm still getting cold. "Annabel Lee" or no "Annabel Lee," I'm still getting cold. But I can see we getting closer. We getting there gradually.

Soon 's we turn the corner, I see a little old white lady up in front of us. She's the only lady on the street. She's all in black and she's got a long black rag over her head.

"Stop," she says.

Me and mama stop and look at her. She must be crazy to be out in all this bad weather. Ain't got but a few other people out there, and all of them's men.

"Y'll done ate?" she says.

"Just finish," Mama says.

"Y'all must be cold then?" she says.

"We headed for the dentist," Mama says. "We'll warm up when we get there."

"What dentist?" the old lady says. "Mr. Bassett?"

"Yes, ma'am," Mama says.

"Come on in," the old lady says. "I'll telephone him and tell him y'all coming."

Me and Mama follow the old lady in the store. It's a little bitty store, and it don't have much in there. The old lady takes off her head rag and folds it up.

[2]An elegiac poem by Edgar Allan Poe often required to be memorized and recited by grade school pupils.

"Helena?" somebody calls from the back.

"Yes, Alnest?" the old lady says.

"Did you see them?"

"They're here. Standing beside me."

"Good. Now you can stay inside."

The old lady looks at Mama. Mama's waiting to hear what she brought us in here for. I'm waiting for that, too.

"I saw y'all each time you went by," she says. "I came out to catch you, but you were gone."

"We went back of town," Mama says.

"Did you eat?"

"Yes, ma'am."

The old lady looks at Mama a long time, like she's thinking Mama might be just saying that. Mama looks right back at her. The old lady looks at me to see what I have to say. I don't say nothing. I sure ain't going 'gainst my mama.

"There's food in the kitchen," she says to Mama. "I've been keeping it warm."

Mama turns right around and starts for the door.

"Just a minute," the old lady says. Mama stops. "The boy'll have to work for it. It isn't free."

"We don't take no handout," Mama says.

"I'm not handing out anything," the old lady says. "I need my garbage moved to the front. Ernest has a bad cold and can't go out there."

"James'll move it for you," Mama says.

"Not unless you eat," the old lady says. "I'm old, but I have my pride, too, you know."

Mama can see she ain't go'n beat this old lady down, so she just shakes her head.

"All right," the old lady says. "Come into the kitchen."

She leads the way with that rag in her hand. The kitchen is a little bitty little old thing, too. The table and the stove just 'bout fill it up. They got a little room to the side. Somebody in there laying 'cross the bed—'cause I can see one of his feet. Must be the person she was talking to: Ernest or Alnest—something like that.

"Sit down," the old lady says to Mama. "Not you," she says to me. "You have to move the cans."

"Helena?" the man says in the other room.

"Yes, Alnest?" the old lady says.

"Are you going out there again?"

"I must show the boy where the garbage is, Alnest," the old lady says.

"Keep that shawl over your head," the old man says.

"You don't have to remind me, Alnest. Come, boy," the old lady says.

We go out in the yard. Little old back yard ain't no bigger than the store or the kitchen. But it can sleet here just like it can sleet in any big back yard. And 'fore you know it, I'm trembling.

"There," the old lady says, pointing to the cans. I pick up one of the cans and set it right back down. The can's so light, I'm go'n see what's inside of it.

"Here," the old lady says. "Leave that can alone."

I look back at her standing there in the door. She's got that black rag wrapped round her shoulders, and she's pointing one of her little old fingers at me.

"Pick it up and carry it to the front," she says. I go by her with the can, and she's looking at me all the time. I'm sure the can's empty. I'm sure she could've carried it herself—maybe both of them at the same time. "Set it on the sidewalk by the door and come back for the other one," she says.

I go and come back, and Mama looks at me when I pass her. I get the other can and take it to the front. It don't feel a bit heavier than that first one. I tell myself I ain't go'n be nobody's fool, and I'm go'n look inside this can to see just what I been hauling. First, I look up the street, then down the street. Nobody coming. Then I look over my shoulder toward the door. That little old lady done slipped up there quiet 's mouse, watching me again. Look like she knowed what I was go'n do.

"Ehh, Lord," she says. "Children, children. Come in here, boy, and go wash your hands."

I follow her in the kitchen. She points toward the bathroom, and I go in there and wash up. Little bitty old bathroom, but it's clean, clean. I don't use any of her towels; I wipe my hands on my pants legs.

When I come back in the kitchen, the old lady done dished up the food. Rice, gravy, meat—and she even got some lettuce and tomato in a saucer. She even got a glass of milk and a piece of cake there, too. It looks so good, I almost start eating 'fore I say my blessing.

"Helena?" the old man says.

"Yes, Alnest?"

"Are they eating?"

"Yes," she says.

"Good," he says. "Now you'll stay inside."

The old lady goes in there where he is and I can hear them talking. I look at Mama. She's eating slow like she's thinking. I wonder what's the matter now. I reckon she's thinking 'bout home.

The old lady comes back in the kitchen.

"I talked to Dr. Bassett's nurse," she says. "Dr. Bassett will take you as soon as you get there."

"Thank you, ma'am," Mama says.

"Perfectly all right," the old lady says. "Which one is it?"

Mama nods toward me. The old lady looks at me real sad. I look sad, too.

"You're not afraid, are you?" she says.

"No, ma'am," I say.

"That's a good boy," the old lady says. "Nothing to be afraid of. Dr. Bassett will not hurt you."

When me and Mama get through eating, we thank the old lady again.

"Helena, are they leaving?" the old man says.

"Yes, Alnest."

"Tell them I say good-bye."

"They can hear you, Alnest."

"Good-bye both mother and son," the old man says. "And may God be with you."

Me and Mama tell the old man good-bye, and we follow the old lady in the front room. Mama opens the door to go out, but she stops and comes back in the store.

"You sell salt meat?" she says.

"Yes."

"Give me two bits worth."

"That isn't very much salt meat," the old lady says.

"That's all I have," Mama says.

The old lady goes back of the counter and cuts a big piece off the chunk. Then she wraps it up and puts it in a paper bag.

"Two bits," she says.

"That looks like awful lot of meat for a quarter," Mama says.

"Two bits," the old lady says. "I've been selling salt meat behind this counter twenty-five years. I think I know what I'm doing."

"You got a scale there," Mama says.

"What?" the old lady says.

"Weigh it," Mama says.

"What?" the old lady says. "Are you telling me how to run my business?"

"Thanks very much for the food," Mama says.

"Just a minute," the old lady says.

"James," Mama says to me. I move toward the door.

"Just one minute, I said," the old lady says.

Me and Mama stop again and look at her. The old lady takes the meat out of the bag and unwraps it and cuts 'bout half of it off. Then she wraps it up again and juggs it back in the bag and gives the bag to Mama. Mama lays the quarter on the counter.

"Your kindness will never be forgotten," she says. "James," she says to me.

We go out, and the old lady comes to the door to look at us. After we go a little piece I look back, and she's still there watching us.

The sleet's coming down heavy, heavy now, and I turn up my coat collar to keep my neck warm. My mama tells me turn it right back down.

"You not a bum," she says. "You a man."

1968

Toni Cade Bambara 1939–1995

In a revealing essay called "Black English" (1972), Toni Cade Bambara summarized those attitudes which by 1970 had become the dramatic center of the fifteen stories included in her first short story collection, *Gorilla My Love* (1972). One of those attitudes, that "language is [as often] used to mis-inform, to mis-direct, to smoke out, to screen out, to block out, to intimidate as it is to inform," is one theme of the title story of that collection; another, that "language certainly determines how we perceive the world" (limiting or expanding it), is the thematic core of "Playing with Punjab," "Maggie of the Green Bottles," and, especially, "My Man Bovanne." As superb a linguist as she was satirist, as splendid a storyteller as she was cultural ecologist, and as crucial a thinker as she was intrepid force for social transformation, Toni Cade, adopting the name Bambara, which she discovered as a signature on a sketchbook in her great-grandmother's trunk, grew up like most of the narrators of her fiction, in an urban neighborhood whose rituals shaped her critical imagination.

In the New York City neighborhoods of Harlem, Bedford-Stuyvesant, and Queens, she and her brother Walter (now a painter) cut through the pernicious urban miasma which her fiction rigorously, often humorously, assails. Here in the "games, chants, jingles" of her peers, in the eloquence of the Seventh Avenue street speakers, in the elegance of the church-inspired club-inspired music of her neighborhood, in the talk and humor at home, and in the "space" allowed her by her parents, Walter and Helen (Henderson) Cade, who understood the necessity of encouraging a child's interior life, Toni Cade Bambara began to forge the language characteristic of the folk-based music, poetry, and prose of African American blues-jazz expressive modes. She completed a bachelor's degree in theater and literature from Queens College in 1959 and a master's in modern American literature from the City College of New York in 1963, studying, subsequently, at the Commedia del' Arte in Milan. She also studied filmmaking in England.

It is not surprising that during a period of tremendous political activism in which she matured—the struggle for civil rights in America, the struggle for the economic, political, and cultural empowerment of black Americans, an international resistance of colonialism, a demand for political and cultural self-determination in the Caribbean and on the continents of Africa and Asia, and a vigorous protest against war and nuclear weaponry—many young African American intellectuals, like Toni Cade Bambara, found a common cause. Still, her personal voice continues to find its deepest resonance in the cadences of the womanly themes of re-creation and renewal found in "My Man Bovanne," the story which opens *Gorilla My Love.* The pervasive melody harmonizing her work and embracing the specific emphasis of recent African American women writers is the theme of "a certain way of being in the world," nowhere more fully orchestrated than in her novel, *The Salt Eaters* (1980), and in her second book of short stories, *The Sea Birds Are Still Alive* (1977).

Eleanor W. Traylor
Howard University

PRIMARY WORKS

"Black Theatre," *Black Expressions: Essays by and about Black Americans in the Creative Arts,* 1969; *The Black Woman: An Anthology,* edited, with contributions by Toni Cade, 1970; *Zora,* WGBH, 1971 (television script); *Tales and Stories for Black Folks,* edited, with contributions by Toni Cade Bambara, 1971; *Gorilla My Love* (short stories), 1972; "Black English," *Curriculum Approaches from a Black Perspective,* The Black Child Development Institute, 1972; "The Johnson Girls," *Soul Show,* NEA, 1972 (television script); *The Sea Birds Are Still Alive: Collected Stories,* 1977; *The Salt Eaters* (a novel), 1980; *"The Long Night,"* ABC, 1981 (television script); *These Bones Are Not My Child,* ed. Toni Morrison, 1999.

My Man Bovanne

Blind people got a hummin jones if you notice. Which is understandable completely once you been around one and notice what no eyes will force you into to see people, and you get past the first time, which seems to come out of nowhere, and it's like you in church again with fat-chest ladies and old gents gruntin a hum low in the throat to whatever the preacher be saying. Shakey Bee bottom lip all swole up with Sweet Peach and me explainin how come the sweet-potato bread was a dollar-quarter this time stead of dollar regular and he say uh hunh he understand, then he break into this *thizzin* kind of hum which is quiet, but fiercesome just the same, if you ain't ready for it. Which I wasn't. But I got used to it and the onliest time I had to say somethin bout it was when he was playin checkers on the stoop one time and he commenst to hummin quite churchy seem to me. So I says, "Look here Shakey Bee, I can't beat you and Jesus too." He stop.

So that's how come I asked My Man Bovanne to dance. He ain't my man mind you, just a nice ole gent from the block that we all know cause he fixes things and the kids like him. Or used to fore Black Power[1] got hold their minds and mess em around till they can't be civil to ole folks. So we at this benefit for my niece's cousin who's runnin for somethin with this Black party somethin or other behind her. And I press up close to dance with Bovanne who blind and I'm hummin and he hummin, chest to chest like talkin. Not jammin my breasts into the man. Wasn't bout tits. Was bout vibrations. And he dug it and asked me what color dress I had on and how my hair was fixed and how I was doin without a man, not nosy but nice-like, and who was at this affair and was the canapés dainty-stingy or healthy enough to get hold of proper. Comfy and cheery is what I'm tryin to get across. Touch talkin like the heel of the hand on the tambourine or on a drum.

But right away Joe Lee come up on us and frown for dancin so close to the man. My own son who knows what kind of warm I am about; and don't grown men call me long distance and in the middle of the night for a little Mama comfort? But he frown. Which ain't right since Bovanne can't see and defend himself. Just a nice old man who fixes toasters and busted irons and bicycles and things and changes the lock on my door when my men friends get messy. Nice man. Which is not why they invited him. Grass roots you see. Me and Sister Taylor and the woman who does heads[2] at Mamies and the man from the barber shop, we all there on account of we grass roots.[3] And I ain't never been souther than Brooklyn Battery[4] and no more country than the window box on my fire escape. And just yesterday my kids tellin me to take them countrified rags off my head and be cool. And now can't get Black enough to suit em. So everybody passin sayin My Man Bovanne. Big deal, keep steppin and don't even stop a minute to get the man a drink or one of them cute sandwiches or tell him what's goin on. And him standin there with a smile ready case someone do speak he want to be ready. So that's how come I pull him on the dance floor and we dance squeezin past the tables and chairs and all them coats and people standin round up in each other face talkin bout this and that but got no use for this blind man who mostly fixed skates and skooters for all these folks when they was just kids. So I'm pressed up close and we touch talkin with the hum. And here come my daughter cuttin her eye at me like she do when she tell me about my "apolitical" self like I got hoof and mouf disease and there ain't no hope at all. And I don't pay her no mind and just look up in Bovanne shadow face and tell him his

[1]Black Power was a slogan of certain Civil Rights groups during the 1960s and 70s.
[2]Hairdresser.
[3]"Grass roots" refers to the common people.
[4]Brooklyn Battery is a section of Brooklyn, New York.

stomach like a drum and he laugh. Laugh real loud. And here come my youngest, Task, with a tap on my elbow like he the third grade monitor and I'm cuttin up on the line to assembly.

"I was just talkin on the drums," I explained when they hauled me into the kitchen. I figured drums was my best defense. They can get ready for drums what with all this heritage business. And Bovanne stomach just like that drum Task give me when he come back from Africa. You just touch it and it hum thizzm, thizzm. So I stuck to the drum story. "Just drummin that's all."

"Mama, what are you talkin about?"

"She had too much to drink," say Elo to Task cause she don't hardly say nuthin to me direct no more since that ugly argument about my wigs.

"Look here Mama," say Task, the gentle one. "We just tryin to pull your coat. You were makin a spectacle of yourself out there dancing like that."

"Dancin like what?"

Task run a hand over his left ear like his father for the world and his father before that.

"Like a bitch in heat," say Elo.

"Well uhh, I was goin to say like one of them sex-starved ladies gettin on in years and not too discriminating. Know what I mean?"

I don't answer cause I'll cry. Terrible thing when your own children talk to you like that. Pullin me out the party and hustlin me into some stranger's kitchen in the back of a bar just like the damn police. And ain't like I'm old old. I can still wear me some sleeveless dresses without the meat hangin off my arm. And I keep up with some thangs through my kids. Who ain't kids no more. To hear them tell it. So I don't say nuthin.

"Dancin with that tom,"[5] say Elo to Joe Lee, who leanin on the folks' freezer. "His feet can smell a cracker a mile away and go into their shuffle number post haste. And them eyes. He could be a little considerate and put on some shades. Who wants to look into them blown-out fuses that—"

"Is this what they call the generation gap?" I say.

"Generation gap," spits Elo, like I suggested castor oil and fricassee possum in the milk-shakes or somethin. "That's a white concept for a white phenomenon. There's no generation gap among Black people. We are a col—"

"Yeh, well never mind," says Joe Lee. "The point is Mama . . . well, it's pride. You embarrass yourself and us too dancin like that."

"I wasn't shame." Then nobody say nuthin. Them standin there in they pretty clothes with drinks in they hands and gangin up on me, and me in the third-degree chair and nary a olive to my name. Felt just like the police got hold to me.

"First of all," Task say, holdin up his hand and tickin off the offenses, "the dress. Now that dress is too short, Mama, and too low-cut for a woman your age. And Tamu's going to make a speech tonight to kick off the campaign and will be introducin you and expecting you to organize the council of elders—"

[5]"Tom" is short for "Uncle Tom," the central character in Harriet Beecher Stowe's novel *Uncle Tom's Cabin.* Uncle Tom is a term of derision used against blacks who act in a subservient manner to whites.

"Me? Didn nobody ask me nuthin. You mean Nisi? She change her name?"

"Well, Norton was supposed to tell you about it. Nisi wants to introduce you and then encourage the older folks to form a Council of the Elders to act as an advisory—"

"And you going to be standing there with your boobs out and that wig on your head and that hem up to your ass. And people'll say, 'Ain't that the horny bitch that was grindin with the blind dude?'"

"Elo, be cool a minute," say Task, gettin to the next finger. "And then there's the drinkin. Mama, you know you can't drink cause next thing you know you be laughin loud and carryin on," and he grab another finger for the loudness. "And then there's the dancin. You been tattooed on the man for four records straight and slow draggin even on the fast numbers. How you think that look for a woman your age?"

"What's my age?"

"What?"

"I'm axin you all a simple question. You keep talkin bout what's proper for a woman my age. How old am I anyhow?" And Joe Lee slams his eyes shut and squinches up his face to figure. And Task run a hand over his ear and stare into his glass like the ice cubes goin calculate for him. And Elo just starin at the top of my head like she goin rip the wig off any minute now.

"Is your hair braided up under that thing? If so, why don't you take it off? You always did do a neat cornroll."

"Uh huh," cause I'm thinkin how she couldn't undo her hair fast enough talking bout cornroll so countrified. None of which was the subject. "How old, I say?"

"Sixtee-one or—"

"You a damn lie Joe Lee Peoples."

"And that's another thing," say Task on the fingers.

"You know what you all can kiss," I say, gettin up and brushin the wrinkles out my lap.

"Oh, Mama," Elo say, puttin a hand on my shoulder like she hasn't done since she left home and the hand landin light and not sure it supposed to be there. Which hurt me to my heart. Cause this was the child in our happiness fore Mr. Peoples die. And I carried that child strapped to my chest till she was nearly two. We was close is what I'm trying to tell you. Cause it was more me in the child than the others. And even after Task it was the girlchild I covered in the night and wept over for no reason at all less it was she was a chub-chub like me and not very pretty, but a warm child. And how did things get to this, that she can't put a sure hand on me and say Mama we love you and care about you and you entitled to enjoy yourself cause you a good woman?

"And then there's Reverend Trent," say Task, glancin from left to right like they hatchin a plot and just now lettin me in on it. "You were suppose to be talkin with him tonight, Mama, about giving us his basement for campaign headquarters and—"

"Didn nobody tell me nuthin. If grass roots mean you kept in the dark I can't use it. I really can't. And Reven Trent a fool anyway the way he tore into the widow man up there on Edgecomb cause he wouldn't take in three of them foster children and the woman not even comfy in the ground yet and the man's mind messed up and—"

"Look here," say Task. "What we need is a family conference so we can get all this stuff cleared up and laid out on the table. In the meantime I think we better get back into the other room and tend to business. And in the meantime, Mama, see if you can't get to Reverend Trent and—"

"You want me to belly rub with the Reven, that it?"

"Oh damn," Elo say and go through the swingin door.

"We'll talk about all this at dinner. How's tomorrow night, Joe Lee?" While Joe Lee being self-important I'm wonderin who's doin the cookin and how come no body ax me if I'm free and do I get a corsage and things like that. Then Joe nod that it's O.K. and he go through the swingin door and just a little hubbub come through from the other room. Then Task smile his smile, lookin just like his daddy and he leave. And it just me in this stranger's kitchen, which was a mess I wouldn't never let my kitchen look like. Poison you just to look at the pots. Then the door swing the other way and it's My Man Bovanne standin there sayin Miss Hazel but lookin at the deep fry and then at the steam table, and most surprised when I come up on him from the other direction and take him on out of there. Pass the folks pushin up towards the stage where Nisi and some other people settin and ready to talk, and folks gettin to the last of the sandwiches and the booze fore they settle down in one spot and listen serious. And I'm thinkin bout tellin Bovanne what a lovely long dress Nisi got on and the earrings and her hair piled up in a cone and the people bout to hear how we all gettin screwed and gotta form our own party[6] and everybody there listenin and lookin. But instead I just haul the man on out of there, and Joe Lee and his wife look at me like I'm terrible, but they ain't said boo to the man yet. Cause he blind and old and don't nobody there need him since they grown up and don't need they skates fixed no more.

"Where we goin, Miss Hazel?" Him knowin all the time.

"First we gonna buy you some dark sunglasses. Then you comin with me to the supermarket so I can pick up tomorrow's dinner, which is goin to be a grand thing proper and you invited. Then we goin to my house."

"That be fine. I surely would like to rest my feet." Bein cute, but you got to let men play out they little show, blind or not. So he chat on bout how tired he is and how he appreciate me takin him in hand this way. And I'm thinkin I'll have him change the lock on my door first thing. Then I'll give the man a nice warm bath with jasmine leaves in the water and a little Epsom salt on the sponge to do his back. And then a good rubdown with rose water and olive oil. Then a cup of lemon tea with a taste in it. And a little talcum, some of that fancy stuff Nisi mother sent over last Christmas. And then a massage, a good face massage round the forehead which is the worryin part. Cause you gots to take care of the older folks. And let them know they still needed to run the mimeo machine and keep the spark plugs clean and fix the mailboxes for folks who might help us get the breakfast program goin, and the school for the little kids and the campaign and all. Cause old folks is the nation. That what Nisi was sayin and I mean to do my part.

"I imagine you are a very pretty woman, Miss Hazel."

"I surely am," I say just like the hussy my daughter always say I was.

1972

[6]Political party.

Lucille Clifton b. 1936

Thelma Lucille Sayles Clifton was born in Depew, New York, and educated at Fredonia State Teachers College, Fredonia, New York, and at Howard University. Although she began writing at a young age, Clifton devoted her early adult life to raising her family. In the midst of her life with her husband, Fred, and six children under the age of ten, she published her first collection of poetry, *Good Times,* in 1969. Since that time, she has published eight additional collections of poetry, a memoir, a compilation of her early work, and more than sixteen books for young readers—including the popular Everett Anderson series. Presently Distinguished Professor of Humanities at St. Mary's College in Maryland, Clifton has taught at Coppin State College, Goucher College, American University, and the University of California at Santa Cruz, among other colleges and universities. Her awards and distinctions include the University of Massachusetts Press Juniper Prize for Poetry; two National Endowment for the Arts Fellowships for creative writing; a nomination for the Pulitzer Prize for Poetry for *Two-Headed Woman* and a second Pulitzer Prize nomination for both *Good Woman: Poems and a Memoir 1969–1980* and *Next: New Poems;* an Emmy Award from the American Academy of Television Arts and Sciences; Poet Laureate of the State of Maryland; and a 1996 Lannan Literary Award for Poetry.

The themes and language of Clifton's poetry are shaped by her concern with family history and relationships, with community, with racial history, and with the possibilities of reconciliation and transcendence. In *Good Times* she uses direct, unadorned language to capture the rhythms and values of urban African American working-class life. Throughout this collection Clifton consciously pits her spare, economical language against the pervasive and negative images of black urban life, insistently reminding her readers of the humanity concealed underneath social and economic statistics. Like Langston Hughes and Gwendolyn Brooks, she sees virtue and dignity in the lives of ordinary African Americans, giving them faces, names, and histories, and validating their existence. In the face of the daily realities of urban life, Clifton records both the adversity and the small triumphs, always maintaining a strong-willed sense of optimism and spiritual resilience. One source of this equanimity, of this poise in the face of adversity and tragedy, derives from Clifton's strong sense of rootedness in the legacy of her family history—particularly of her great-great-grandmother Caroline, a woman kidnapped to America from Dahomey, and Caroline's daughter, Lucille, who bore the distinction of being the first black woman lynched in Virginia. These two women in particular conjure up images of survival and endurance on the one hand, and avenging spirits on the other. By locating herself within this family history, Clifton not only lays claim to an African past—a recurrent feature of many of her poems—she also defines herself as a poet whose task is to keep historical memory alive. At the same time that Clifton accepts the weight of this history, however, she refuses to be trapped or defeated by it. Like a blues singer's lyrics, Clifton's poems confront the chaos, disorder, and pain of human experience to transcend these conditions and to reaffirm her humanity.

The optimism that shapes Clifton's poetry is nourished by her deep spiritual beliefs. While she often invokes Christian motifs and biblical references in her poems, she draws freely upon other values and beliefs as well. "The black God, Kali/a woman God and terrible/with her skulls and breasts" often appears in her poems, as do references to African goddesses like Yemoja, the Yoruba water-deity, and to

Native American beliefs. More specifically, Clifton's invocation of the "two-headed woman" of African American folk belief, with its overtones of Hoodoo and conjure, makes plain her commitment to other ways of knowing and understanding the world. Certainly the spiritual dimension of her poetry has deepened since the death of her husband, Fred Clifton, in 1984. Whether her poetry is exploring the biological changes within her own body or imagining the death of the Sioux chief Crazy Horse, Lucille Clifton's world is both earthy and spiritual. In her capacity as both witness and seer, she looks through the madness and sorrow of the world, locating moments of epiphany in the mundane and ordinary. And her poetry invariably moves toward those moments of calm and tranquillity, of grace, which speak to the continuity of the human spirit.

James A. Miller
George Washington University

PRIMARY WORKS

Good Times, 1969; *Good News About the Earth,* 1972; *An Ordinary Woman,* 1974; *Generations,* 1976; *Two-Headed Woman,* 1980; *Next: New Poems,* 1987; *Good Woman: Poems and A Memoir 1969–1980,* 1987; *Quilting: Poems 1987–1990,* 1991; *The Book of Light,* 1993; *The Terrible Stories: Poems,* 1996; *Blessing the Boats: New and Collected Poems, 1998–2000,* 2000; also children's books.

the thirty eighth year

the thirty eighth year
of my life,
plain as bread
round as a cake
an ordinary woman.

an ordinary woman.

i had expected to be
smaller than this,
more beautiful,
wiser in afrikan ways,
more confident,
i had expected
more than this.

i will be forty soon.
my mother once was forty.

my mother died at forty four,
a woman of sad countenance
leaving behind a girl

awkward as a stork.
my mother was thick,
her hair was a jungle and
she was very wise
and beautiful
and sad.

i have dreamed dreams
for you mama
more than once.
i have wrapped me
in your skin
and made you live again
more than once.
i have taken the bones you hardened
and built daughters
and they blossom and promise fruit
like afrikan trees.
i am a woman now.
an ordinary woman.

in the thirty eighth
year of my life,
surrounded by life,
a perfect picture of
blackness blessed,
i had not expected this
loneliness.

if it is western,
if it is the final
europe in my mind,
if in the middle of my life
i am turning the final turn
into the shining dark
let me come to it whole
and holy
not afraid
not lonely
out of my mother's life
into my own.
into my own.

i had expected more than this.
i had not expected to be
an ordinary woman.

1974

i am accused of tending to the past

i am accused of tending to the past
as if i made it,
as if i sculpted it
with my own hands. i did not.
this past was waiting for me
when i came,
a monstrous unnamed baby,
and i with my mother's itch
took it to breast
and named it
History.
she is more human now,
learning language everyday,
remembering faces, names and dates.
when she is strong enough to travel
on her own, beware, she will.

1991

at the cemetery, walnut grove plantation, south carolina, 1989

among the rocks
at walnut grove
your silence drumming
in my bones,
tell me your names.

nobody mentioned slaves
and yet the curious tools
shine with your fingerprints.
nobody mentioned slaves
but somebody did this work
who had no guide, no stone,
who moulders under rock.

tell me your names,
tell me your bashful names
and i will testify.

the inventory lists ten slaves
but only men were recognized.

among the rocks
at walnut grove
some of these honored dead
were dark
some of these dark
were slaves
some of these slaves
were women
some of them did this
honored work.
tell me your names
foremothers, brothers,
tell me your dishonored names.
here lies
here lies
here lies
here lies
hear

1991

reply

[from a letter written to Dr. W.E.B. Dubois by Alvin Borgquest of Clark University in Massachusetts and dated April 3, 1905:

"We are pursuing an investigation here on the subject of crying as an expression of the emotions, and should like very much to learn about its peculiarities among the colored people. We have been referred to you as a person competent to give us information on the subject. We desire especially to know about the following salient aspects: 1. Whether the Negro sheds tears . . ."]

reply

he do
she do
they live
they love
they try
they tire
they flee

they fight
they bleed
they break
they moan
they mourn
they weep
they die
they do
they do
they do

1991

in white america

1 i come to read them poems

i come to read them poems,
a fancy trick i do
like juggling with balls of light.
i stand, a dark spinner,
in the grange hall,
in the library, in the
smaller conference room,
and toss and catch as if by magic,
my eyes bright, my mouth smiling,
my singed hands burning.

2 the history

1800's in this town
fourteen longhouses were destroyed
by not these people here.
not these people
burned the crops and chopped down
all the peach trees.
not these people. these people
preserve peaches, even now.

3 the tour

"this was a female school.
my mother's mother graduated

second in her class.
they were taught embroidery,
and chenille and filigree,
ladies' learning. yes,
we have a liberal history here."
smiling she pats my darky hand.

4 the hall

in this hall
dark women
scrubbed the aisles
between the pews
on their knees.
they could not rise
to worship.
in this hall
dark women
my sisters and mothers

though i speak with the tongues
of men and of angels and
have not charity . . .

in this hall
dark women,
my sisters and mothers,
i stand
and let the church say
let the church say
let the church say
AMEN.

5 the reading

i look into none of my faces
and do the best i can.
the human hair between us
stretches but does not break.
i slide myself along it and
love them, love them all.

6 it is late

it is late
in white america.
i stand
in the light of the
7–11
looking out toward
the church
and for a moment only
i feel the reverberation
of myself
in white america
a black cat
in the belfry
hanging
and
ringing.

1987

N. Scott Momaday (Kiowa) b. 1934

N. Scott Momaday often attributes the diversity of his forms of expression to his rich cultural inheritance and varied life experiences. From his father's family he received Kiowa storytelling traditions and a love of the Rainy Mountain area of Oklahoma. His mother, whose paternal great-grandmother was Cherokee, gave him admiration for literature written in English and the example of how a willful act of imagination could create an "Indian" identity. As Momaday recounts in *The Names,* during his childhood he lived in non-Indian communities, as well as with several Southwestern tribes, especially the Jemez Pueblo. He attended reservation, public, and parochial schools, a Virginia military academy, the University of New Mexico (political science), the University of Virginia (to study law briefly), and Stanford, where he received his M.A. and Ph.D. and was strongly influenced by his mentor Yvor Winters. Momaday's teaching career includes professorships at Berkeley, Stanford, and the University of Arizona. He has been recognized by both non-Indian and Indian worlds with a Guggenheim Fellowship, a Pulitzer Prize (for *House Made of Dawn*), and membership in the Kiowa Gourd Clan.

The tendency toward divers forms of expression is obvious in most of Momaday's works. In *The Names* he used fictional, as well as traditional, autobiographical techniques. The poems in *The Gourd Dancer, In the Presence of the Sun,* and *In the Bear's House* range from forms close to American Indian oral traditions ("The Delight Song of Tsoai-talee") to poems utilizing highly structured written conventions ("Before an Old Painting of the Crucifiction") to free or open verse ("Comparatives") and dialogues ("The Bear-God Dialogues"). *House Made of Dawn,* a powerful novel about an alienated Jemez Pueblo World War II veteran, is told from different viewpoints and exhibits styles as direct as Hemingway's, as dense as Faulkner's, and as resonant as the songs of the Navajo Nightway ceremony, the source of the novel's title. Several of his works—most notably *In the Presence of the Sun* and *Circle of Wonder*—combine written and visual expressions. His second novel, *Ancient Child,* juxtaposes ancient Kiowa bear narratives, a contemporary artist's male mid-life crisis story, and Billy the Kid fantasies.

It is *The Way to Rainy Mountain,* however, that more than any other of his works demonstrates Momaday's ability to break through generic boundaries. In his essay "The Man Made of Words" (available in *The Remembered Earth,* ed. Geary Hobson, 1979/1981), Momaday describes the composition process that began with his desire to comprehend his Kiowa identity and with the collecting from Kiowa elders of stories. To all but a few of these brief tribal and family stories he added short historical and personal "commentaries." Momaday then arranged twenty-four of these three-voice sections into three divisions ("The Setting Out," "The Going On," "The Closing In") to suggest several physical and spiritual journeys, the two most obvious being the migration and history of the Kiowa and the gradual development of his Kiowa identity. The three divisions were framed by two poems and three lyric essays (Prologue, Introduction, Epilogue) that combine mythic, historic, and personal perspectives.

The following selections, taken from each of the three divisions of *Rainy Mountain,* suggest the nature of the form and themes—themes that reappear in most of Momaday's works: celebrating the importance of the imagination, memory, and oral traditions; seeing the land as a crucial aspect of identity; acknowledging the power of American Indian concepts of sacredness, beauty, and harmony; and revering a sense of language that encompasses economy, power, delight, and wonder.

Kenneth M. Roemer
University of Texas at Arlington

PRIMARY WORKS

House Made of Dawn, 1968; *The Way to Rainy Mountain,* 1969; *The Gourd Dancer,* 1976; *The Names: A Memoir,* 1976; *The Ancient Child,* 1989; *In the Presence of the Sun,* 1992; *Circle of Wonder: A Native American Christmas Story,* 1994; *The Man Made of Words,* 1997; *In the Bear's House,* 1999.

from The Way to Rainy Mountain

Headwaters

Noon in the intermountain plain:
There is scant telling of the marsh—
A log, hollow and weather-stained,
An insect at the mouth, and moss—
Yet waters rise against the roots,
Stand brimming to the stalks. What moves?
What moves on this archaic force
Was wild and welling at the source.

Prologue

The journey began one day long ago on the edge of the northern Plains. It was carried on over a course of many generations and many hundreds of miles. In the end there were many things to remember, to dwell upon and talk about.

"You know, everything had to begin. . . ." For the Kiowas the beginning was a struggle for existence in the bleak northern mountains. It was there, they say, that they entered the world through a hollow log. The end, too, was a struggle, and it was lost. The young Plains culture of the Kiowas withered and died like grass that is burned in the prairie wind. There came a day like destiny; in every direction, as far as the eye could see, carrion lay out in the land. The buffalo was the animal representation of the sun, the essential and sacrificial victim of the Sun Dance. When the wild herds were destroyed, so too was the will of the Kiowa people; there was nothing to sustain them in spirit. But these are idle recollections, the mean and ordinary agonies of human history. The interim was a time of great adventure and nobility and fulfillment.

Tai-me came to the Kiowas in a vision born of suffering and despair.[1] "Take me with you," Tai-me said, "and I will give you whatever you want." And it was so. The great adventure of the Kiowas was a going forth into the heart of the continent. They began a long migration from the headwaters of the Yellowstone River eastward to the Black Hills and south to the Wichita Mountains. Along the way they acquired horses, the religion of the Plains, a love and possession of the open land. Their nomadic soul was set free. In alliance with the Comanches they held dominion in the southern Plains for a hundred years. In the course of that long migration they had come of age as a people. They had conceived a good idea of themselves; they had dared to imagine and determine who they were.

In one sense, then, the way to Rainy Mountain is preeminently the history of an idea, man's idea of himself, and it has old and essential being in language. The verbal tradition by which it has been preserved has suffered a deterioration in time. What remains is fragmentary: mythology, legend, lore, and hearsay—and of course the idea itself, as crucial and complete as it ever was. That is the miracle.

The journey herein recalled continues to be made anew each time the miracle comes to mind, for that is peculiarly the right and responsibility of the imagination. It is a whole journey, intricate with motion and meaning; and it is made with the whole memory, that experience of the mind which is legendary as well as historical, personal as well as cultural. And the journey is an evocation of three things in particular: a landscape that is incomparable, a time that is gone forever, and the human spirit, which endures. The imaginative experience and the historical express equally

[1]The Tai-me (or Tai-may) appears primarily in two manifestations in TWTRM: as the legendary being who appeared to the Kiowas during "bad times," offering to help them, and as the revered Sun Dance doll, "less than 2 feet in length, representing a human figure dressed in a robe of white feathers" (TWTRM, Sec. 10).

the traditions of man's reality. Finally, then, the journey recalled is among other things the revelation of one way in which these traditions are conceived, developed, and interfused in the human mind. There are on the way to Rainy Mountain many landmarks, many journeys in the one. From the beginning the migration of the Kiowas was an expression of the human spirit, and that expression is most truly made in terms of wonder and delight: "There were many people, and oh, it was beautiful. That was the beginning of the Sun Dance. It was all for Tai-me, you know, and it was a long time ago."[2]

from the Introduction[3]

Houses are like sentinels in the plain, old keepers of the weather watch. There, in a very little while, wood takes on the appearance of great age. All colors wear soon away in the wind and rain, and then the wood is burned gray and the grain appears and the nails turn red with rust. The windowpanes are black and opaque; you imagine there is nothing within, and indeed there are many ghosts, bones given up to the land. They stand here and there against the sky, and you approach them for a longer time than you expect. They belong in the distance; it is their domain.

Once there was a lot of sound in my grandmother's house, a lot of coming and going, feasting and talk. The summers there were full of excitement and reunion. The Kiowas are a summer people; they abide the cold and keep to themselves, but when the season turns and the land becomes warm and vital they cannot hold still; an old love of going returns upon them. The aged visitors who came to my grandmother's house when I was a child were made of lean and leather, and they bore themselves upright. They wore great black hats and bright ample shirts that shook in the wind. They rubbed fat upon their hair and wound their braids with strips of colored cloth. Some of them painted their faces and carried the scars of old and cherished enmities. They were an old council of warlords, come to remind and be reminded of who they were. Their wives and daughters served them well. The women might indulge themselves; gossip was at once the mark and compensation of their servitude. They made loud and elaborate talk among themselves, full of jest and gesture, fright and false alarm. They went abroad in fringed and flowered shawls, bright beadwork and German silver. They were at home in the kitchen, and they prepared meals that were banquets.

[2]These words, spoken by an old Kiowa woman, Ko-sahn, are repeated near the conclusion of the Epilogue, which is included in this excerpt.

[3]The following paragraphs conclude the Introduction. They are preceded by Momaday's moving descriptions of the Rainy Mountain area of SW Oklahoma, of his tribe's migration from mountainous western Montana, and of his own retracing of that journey, which concluded with his pilgrimage to his grandmother's (Aho's) house and her grave.

There were frequent prayer meetings, and great nocturnal feasts. When I was a child I played with my cousins outside, where the lamplight fell upon the ground and the singing of the old people rose up around us and carried away into the darkness. There were a lot of good things to eat, a lot of laughter and surprise. And afterwards, when the quiet returned, I lay down with my grandmother and could hear the frogs away by the river and feel the motion of the air.

Now there is a funeral silence in the rooms, the endless wake of some final word. The walls have closed in upon my grandmother's house. When I returned to it in mourning, I saw for the first time in my life how small it was. It was late at night, and there was a white moon, nearly full. I sat for a long time on the stone steps by the kitchen door. From there I could see out across the land; I could see the long row of trees by the creek, the low light upon the rolling plains, and the stars of the Big Dipper. Once I looked at the moon and caught sight of a strange thing. A cricket had perched upon the handrail, only a few inches away from me. My line of vision was such that the creature filled the moon like a fossil. It had gone there, I thought, to live and die, for there, of all places, was its small definition made whole and eternal. A warm wind rose up and purled like the longing within me.

The next morning I awoke at dawn and went out on the dirt road to Rainy Mountain. It was already hot, and the grasshoppers began to fill the air. Still, it was early in the morning, and the birds sang out of the shadows. The long yellow grass on the mountain shone in the bright light, and a scissortail hied above the land. There, where it ought to be, at the end of a long and legendary way, was my grandmother's grave. Here and there on the dark stones were ancestral names. Looking back once, I saw the mountain and came away.

IV

They lived at first in the mountains. They did not yet know of Tai-me, but this is what they knew: There was a man and his wife. They had a beautiful child, a little girl whom they would not allow to go out of their sight. But one day a friend of the family came and asked if she might take the child outside to play. The mother guessed that would be all right, but she told the friend to leave the child in its cradle and to place the cradle in a tree. While the child was in the tree, a redbird came among the branches. It was not like any bird that you have seen; it was very beautiful, and it did not fly away. It kept still upon a limb, close to the child. After a while the child got out of its cradle and began to climb after the redbird. And at the same time the tree began to grow taller, and the child was borne up into the sky. She was then a woman, and she found herself in a strange place. Instead of a redbird, there was a young man standing before her. The man spoke to her and said: "I have been watching you for a long time, and I knew that I would find a way to bring you here. I have brought you here to be my wife." The woman looked all around; she saw that he was the only living man there. She saw that he was the sun.

There the land itself ascends into the sky. These mountains lie at the top of the continent, and they cast a long rain shadow on the sea of grasses to the east. They arise out of the last North American wilderness, and they have wilderness names: Wasatch, Bitterroot, Bighorn, Wind River.[4]

I have walked in a mountain meadow bright with Indian paintbrush, lupine, and wild buckwheat, and I have seen high in the branches of a lodgepole pine the male pine grosbeak, round and rose-colored, its dark, striped wings nearly invisible in the soft, mottled light. And the uppermost branches of the tree seemed very slowly to ride across the blue sky.

[4]These mountain ranges are located in Wyoming, Utah, Idaho, and Montana.

XVI

There was a strange thing, a buffalo with horns of steel. One day a man came upon it in the plain, just there where once upon a time four trees stood close together. The man and the buffalo began to fight. The man's hunting horse was killed right away, and the man climbed one of the trees. The great bull lowered its head and began to strike the tree with its black metal horns, and soon the tree fell. But the man was quick, and he leaped to the safety of the second tree. Again the bull struck with its unnatural horns, and the tree soon splintered and fell. The man leaped to the third tree and all the while he shot arrows at the beast; but the arrows glanced away like sparks from its dark hide. At last there remained only one tree and the man had only one arrow. He believed then that he would surely die. But something spoke to him and said: "Each time the buffalo prepares to charge, it spreads its cloven hooves and strikes the ground. Only there in the cleft of the hoof is it vulnerable; it is there you must aim." The buffalo went away and turned, spreading its hooves, and the man drew the arrow to his bow. His aim was true and the arrow struck deep into the soft flesh of the hoof. The great bull shuddered and fell, and its steel horns flashed once in the sun.

Forty years ago the townspeople of Carnegie, Oklahoma, gathered about two old Kiowa men who were mounted on work horses and armed with bows and arrows. Someone had got a buffalo, a poor broken beast in which there was no trace left of the wild strain. The old men waited silently amid the laughter and talk; then, at a signal, the buffalo was let go. It balked at first, more confused, perhaps, than afraid, and the horses had to be urged and then brought up short. The people shouted, and at last the buffalo wheeled and ran. The old men gave chase, and in the distance they were lost to view in a great, red cloud of dust. But they ran that animal down and killed it with arrows.

One morning my father and I walked in Medicine Park, on the edge of a small herd of buffalo. It was late in the spring, and many of the cows had newborn calves. Nearby a calf lay in the tall grass; it was red-orange in color, delicately beautiful with new life. We approached, but suddenly the cow was there in our way, her great dark head low and fearful-looking. Then she came at us, and we turned and ran as hard as we could. She gave up after a short run, and I think we had not been in any real danger. But the spring morning was deep and beautiful and our hearts were beating fast and we knew just then what it was to be alive.

XVII

Bad women are thrown away. Once there was a handsome young man. He was wild and reckless, and the chief talked to the wind about him. After that, the man went hunting. A great whirlwind passed by, and he was blind. The Kiowas have no need of a blind man; they left him alone with his wife and child. The winter was coming on and food was scarce. In four days the man's wife grew tired of caring for him. A herd of buffalo came near, and the man knew the sound. He asked his wife to hand him a bow and an arrow. "You must tell me," he said, "when the buffalo are directly in front of me." And in that way he killed a bull, but his wife said that he had missed. He asked for another arrow and killed another bull, but again his wife said that he had missed. Now the man was a hunter, and he knew the sound an arrow makes when it strikes home, but he said nothing. Then his wife helped herself to the meat and ran away with her child. The man was blind; he ate grass and kept himself alive. In seven days a band of Kiowas found him and took him to their camp. There in the firelight a woman was telling a story. She told of how her husband had been killed by enemy warriors. The blind man listened, and he knew her voice. That was a bad woman. At sunrise they threw her away.

In the Kiowa calendars[5] there is graphic proof that the lives of women were hard, whether they were "bad women" or not. Only the captives, who were slaves, held lower status. During the Sun Dance of 1843, a man stabbed his wife in the breast because she accepted Chief Dohasan's invitation to ride with him in the ceremonial procession. And in the winter of 1851–52, Big Bow stole the wife of a man who was away on a raiding expedition. He brought her to his father's camp and made her wait outside in the bitter cold while he went in to collect his things. But his father knew what was going on, and he held Big Bow and would not let him go. The woman was made to wait in the snow until her feet were frozen.

Mammedaty's[6] *grandmother, Kau-au-ointy, was a Mexican captive, taken from her homeland when she was a child of eight or ten years. I never knew her, but I have been to her grave at Rainy Mountain.*

KAU-AU-OINTY
BORN 1834
DIED 1929
AT REST

She raised a lot of eyebrows, they say, for she would not play the part of a Kiowa woman. From slavery she rose up to become a figure in the tribe. She owned a great herd of cattle, and she could ride as well as any man. She had blue eyes.

[5]Kiowa history was kept on pictorial calendars. For example, see James Mooney's *Calendar History of the Kiowa Indians* (rpt. 1979).

[6]Momaday's paternal grandfather.

XXIV

East of my grandmother's house, south of the pecan grove, there is buried a woman in a beautiful dress. Mammedaty used to know where she is buried, but now no one knows. If you stand on the front porch of the house and look eastward towards Carnegie, you know that the woman is buried somewhere within the range of your vision. But her grave is unmarked. She was buried in a cabinet, and she wore a beautiful dress. How beautiful it was! It was one of those fine buckskin dresses, and it was decorated with elk's teeth and beadwork. That dress is still there, under the ground.

Aho's high moccasins are made of softest, cream-colored skins. On each in-step there is a bright disc of beadwork—an eight-pointed star, red and pale blue on a white field—and there are bands of beadwork at the soles and ankles. The flaps of the leggings are wide and richly ornamented with blue and red and green and white and lavender beads.

East of my grandmother's house the sun rises out of the plain. Once in his life a man ought to concentrate his mind upon the remembered earth, I believe. He ought to give himself up to a particular landscape in his experience, to look at it from as many angles as he can, to wonder about it, to dwell upon it. He ought to imagine that he touches it with his hands at every season and listens to the sounds that are made upon it. He ought to imagine the creatures there and all the faintest motions of the wind. He ought to recollect the glare of noon and all the colors of the dawn and dusk.

Epilogue

During the first hours after midnight on the morning of November 13, 1833, it seemed that the world was coming to an end. Suddenly the stillness of the night was broken; there were brilliant flashes of light in the sky, light of such intensity that people were awakened by it. With the speed and density of a driving rain, stars were falling in the universe. Some were brighter than Venus; one was said to be as large as the moon.

That most brilliant shower of Leonid meteors has a special place in the memory of the Kiowa people. It is among the earliest entries in the Kiowa calendars, and it marks the beginning as it were of the historical period in the tribal mind. In the preceding year Tai-me had been stolen by a band of Osages, and although it was later returned, the loss was an almost unimaginable tragedy; and in 1837 the Kiowas made the first of their treaties with the United States. The falling stars seemed to image the sudden and violent disintegration of an old order.

But indeed the golden age of the Kiowas had been short-lived, ninety or a hundred years, say, from about 1740. The culture would persist for a while in decline, until about 1875, but then it would be gone, and there would be very little material evidence that it had ever been. Yet it is within the reach of memory still, though tenuously now, and moreover it is even defined in a remarkably rich and living verbal tradition which demands to be preserved for its own sake. The living memory and the verbal tradition which transcends it were brought together for me once and for all in the person of Ko-sahn.

A hundred-year-old woman came to my grandmother's house one afternoon in July. Aho was dead; Mammedaty had died before I was born. There were very few Kiowas left who could remember the Sun Dances; Ko-sahn was one of them; she was a grown woman when my grandparents came into the world. Her body was twisted and her face deeply lined with age. Her thin white hair was held in place by a cap of black netting, though she wore braids as well, and she had but one eye. She was dressed in the manner of a Kiowa matron, a dark, full-cut dress that reached nearly to the ankles, full, flowing sleeves, and a wide, apron-like sash. She sat on a bench in the arbor so concentrated in her great age that she seemed extraordinarily small. She was quiet for a time—she might almost have been asleep—and then she began to speak and to sing. She spoke of many things, and once she spoke of the Sun Dance:

My sisters and I were very young; that was a long time ago. Early one morning they came to wake us up. They had brought a great buffalo in from the plain. Everyone went out to see and to pray. We heard a great many voices. One man said that the lodge was almost ready. We were told to go there, and someone gave me a piece of cloth. It was very beautiful. Then I asked what I ought to do with it, and they said that I must tie it to the Tai-me tree. There were other pieces of cloth on the tree, and so I put mine there as well.

When the lodge frame was finished, a woman—sometimes a man—began to sing. It was like this:

Everything is ready.
Now the four societies must go out.
They must go out and get the leaves,
the branches for the lodge.

And when the branches were tied in place, again there was singing:

Let the boys go out.
Come on, boys, now we must get the earth.

The boys began to shout. Now they were not just ordinary boys, not all of them; they were those for whom prayers had been made, and they were dressed in different ways. There was an old, old woman. She had something on her back. The boys went out to see. The old woman had a bag full of earth on her back. It was a certain kind of sandy earth. That is what they must have in the lodge. The dancers must dance upon the sandy earth. The old woman held a digging tool in her hand. She turned towards the south and pointed with her lips. It was like a kiss, and she began to sing:

We have brought the earth,
Now it is time to play;
As old as I am, I still have the feeling of play.

That was the beginning of the Sun Dance. The dancers treated themselves with buffalo medicine, and slowly they began to take their steps . . . And all the people were around, and they wore splendid things—beautiful buckskin and beads. The chiefs wore necklaces, and their pendants shone like the sun. There were many people, and oh, it was beautiful! That was the beginning of the Sun Dance. It was all for Tai-me, you know, and it was a long time ago.

It was—all of this and more—a quest, a going forth upon the way to Rainy Mountain. Probably Ko-sahn too is dead now. At times, in the quiet of evening, I think she must have wondered, dreaming, who she was. Was she become in her sleep that old purveyor of the sacred earth, perhaps, that ancient one who, old as she was, still had the feeling of play? And in her mind, at times, did she see the falling stars?

Rainy Mountain Cemetery

Most is your name the name of this dark stone.
Deranged in death, the mind to be inheres
Forever in the nominal unknown,
The wake of nothing audible he hears
Who listens here and now to hear your name.

The early sun, red as a hunter's moon,
Runs in the plain. The mountain burns and shines;
And silence is the long approach of noon
Upon the shadow that your name defines—
And death this cold, black density of stone.

1969

James Welch (Blackfeet–Gros Ventre) b. 1940

Now living in Missoula, Montana, Welch was born in Browning and attended the University of Montana. Half Blackfeet and half Gros Ventre, Welch draws on his Native American background but he refuses to think of himself as "only" an Indian writer. The power of his fiction and poetry convinces the reader of his place in the mainstream of American literature, but that power derives as much from his subject matter as from his taut narrative style, laced with a laconic humor that adds a bitter complexity to his harsh tales.

In *Winter in the Blood* and *The Death of Jim Loney,* Welch drew with superb understatement the unlived lives of the contemporary Native American men, shut off from college educations because of family poverty and ignorance, warded away from financial respectability because of that education cut short. In each book, the protagonist had been a star high school athlete. Now, a decade or more after that athletic career ended, the men have no direction and no promise. They lead aimless lives of drinking, sex (and the promise that a healthy sexual relationship might hold is undercut by their own nihilistic attitudes), and apathy. Confused relationships with parents, especially with the father, whose life as an outsider to the white culture has set the model for the son, dominates what plot exists. But more than plot, these novels are marked by mood and tone, atmosphere as precisely drawn as anything by Hemingway or Richard Wright. Alienation and loss are what remain from reading these stunning texts.

Fools Crow, a truly Native American narrative in that its base plot is actual history from the nineteenth century, shares the somber tone of the earlier two novels at moments, but its texture has changed radically. This is a full panoply of native life—household customs, religious rites, love and family situations, war-making. Comedy, strength, ribaldry in the realization of the Native American lives of the past—in the height of power and cultural achievement—are set against the contemporary malaise, for an even more sadly ironic effect. *Indian Lawyer* places the Native American in the midst of that malaise and shows the inherent corruptibility of all people. Taking the four novels as a tetrology provokes a better sense of Welch's meaning: the pride of heritage makes more understandable the deep apathy and sense of loss of the present-day Montana Indians. That sense of loss is applicable to any culture, of course, but it need not be: it is enough for us to recognize the immense loss the Indian culture has experienced, for it is so much worse than anything mainstream inhabitants can visualize. Welch's work allows readers that visualization, and that convincing understanding.

In Welch's poems the strain that some critics have called comic surrealism is more evident—but for some readers *Winter in the Blood* also shares in that tone. Characteristic of Blackfeet responses to life, Welch's understated and oblique humor is a part of his world vision, and deserves to be recognized.

Linda Wagner-Martin
University of North Carolina at Chapel Hill

PRIMARY WORKS

Riding the Earthboy 40: Poems, 1971; *Winter in the Blood,* 1974; *The Death of Jim Loney,* 1979; *Fools Crow,* 1986; *Indian Lawyer,* 1990; *Killing Custer: The Battle of the Little Bighorn and the Fate of the Plains Indians,* 1994.

from Winter in the Blood

Part Four

38

"Hello," he said. "You are welcome."

"There are clouds in the east," I said. I could not look at him.

"I feel it, rain tonight maybe, tomorrow for sure, cats and dogs."

The breeze had picked up so that the willows on the irrigation ditch were gesturing in our direction.

"I see you wear shoes now. What's the meaning of this?" I pointed to a pair of rubber boots. His pants tucked inside them.

"Rattlesnakes. For protection. This time of year they don't always warn you."

"They don't hear you," I said. "You're so quiet you take them by surprise."

"I found a skin beside my door this morning. I'm not taking any chances."

"I thought animals were your friends."

"Rattlesnakes are best left alone."

"Like you," I said.

"Could be."

I pumped some water into the enamel basin for Bird, then I loosened his cinch.

"I brought some wine." I held out the bottle.

"You are kind—you didn't have to."

"It's French," I said. "Made out of roses."

"My thirst is not so great as it once was. There was a time . . ." A gust of wind ruffled his fine white hair. "Let's have it."

I pressed the bottle into his hand. He held his head high, resting one hand on his chest, and drank greedily, his Adam's apple sliding up and down his throat as though it were attached to a piece of rubber. "And now, you," he said.

Yellow Calf squatted on the white skin of earth. I sat down on the platform on which the pump stood. Behind me, Bird sucked in the cool water.

"My grandmother died," I said. "We're going to bury her tomorrow."

He ran his paper fingers over the smooth rubber boots. He glanced in my direction, perhaps because he heard Bird's guts rumble. A small white cloud passed through the sun but he said nothing.

"She just stopped working. It was easy."

His knees cracked as he shifted his weight.

"We're going to bury her tomorrow. Maybe the priest from Harlem. He's a friend . . ."

He wasn't listening. Instead, his eyes were wandering beyond the irrigation ditch to the hills and the muscled clouds above them.

Something about those eyes had prevented me from looking at him. It had seemed a violation of something personal and deep, as one feels when he comes upon a cow licking her newborn calf. But now, something else, his distance, made it all right to study his face, to see for the first time the black dots on his temples and the bridge of his nose, the ear lobes which sagged on either side of his head, and the bristles which grew on the edges of his jaw. Beneath his humped nose and above his chin, creases as well defined as cutbanks between prairie hills emptied into his mouth. Between his half-parted lips hung one snag, yellow and brown and worndown, like that of an old horse. But it was his eyes, narrow beneath the loose skin of his lids, deep behind his cheekbones, that made one realize the old man's distance was permanent. It was behind those misty white eyes that gave off no light that he lived, a world as clean as the rustling willows, the bark of a fox or the odor of musk during mating season.

I wondered why First Raise had come so often to see him. Had he found a way to narrow that distance? I tried to remember that one snowy day he had brought me with him. I remembered Teresa and the old lady commenting on my father's judgment for taking me out on such a day; then riding behind him on the horse, laughing at the wet, falling snow. But I couldn't remember Yellow Calf or what the two men talked about.

"Did you know her at all?" I said.

Without turning his head, he said, "She was a young woman; I was just a youth."

"Then you did know her then."

"She was the youngest wife of Standing Bear."

I was reaching for the wine bottle. My hand stopped.

"He was a chief, a wise man—not like these conniving devils who run the agency today."

"How could you know Standing Bear? He was Blackfeet."

"We came from the mountains," he said.

"You're Blackfeet?"

"My people starved that winter; we all starved but they died. It was the cruelest winter. My folks died, one by one." He seemed to recollect this without emotion.

"But I thought you were Gros Ventre. I thought you were from around here."

"Many people starved that winter. We had to travel light—we were running from the soldiers—so we had few provisions. I remember, the day we entered this valley it began to snow and blizzard. We tried to hunt but the game refused to move. All winter long we looked for deer sign. I think we killed one deer. It was rare that we even jumped a porcupine. We snared a few rabbits but not enough . . ."

"You survived," I said.

"Yes, I was strong in those days." His voice was calm and monotonous.

"How about my grandmother? How did she survive?"

He pressed down on the toe of his rubber boot. It sprang back into shape.

"She said Standing Bear got killed that winter," I said.

"He led a party against the Gros Ventres. They had meat. I was too young. I remember the men when they returned to camp—it was dark but you could see the white air from their horses' nostrils. We all stood waiting, for we were sure they would bring meat. But they brought Standing Bear's body instead. It was a bad time."

I tapped Yellow Calf's knee with the bottle. He drank, then wiped his lips on his shirt sleeve.

"It was then that we knew our medicine had gone bad. We had wintered some hard times before, winters were always hard, but seeing Standing Bear's body made us realize that we were being punished for having left our home. The people resolved that as soon as spring came we would go home, soldiers or not."

"But you stayed," I said. "Why?"

He drew an arc with his hand, palm down, taking in the bend of the river behind his house. It was filled with tall cottonwoods, most of them dead, with tangles of brush and wild rose around their trunks. The land sloped down from where we were sitting so that the bend was not much higher than the river itself.

"This was where we camped. It was not grown over then, only the cottonwoods were standing. But the willows were thick then, all around to provide a shelter. We camped very close together to take advantage of this situation. Sometimes in winter, when the wind has packed the snow and blown the clouds away, I can still hear the muttering of the people in their tepees. It was a very bad time."

"And your family starved . . ."

"My father died of something else, a sickness, pneumonia maybe. I had four sisters. They were among the first to go. My mother hung on for a little while but soon she went. Many starved."

"But if the people went back in the spring, why did you stay?"

"My people were here."

"And the old—my grandmother stayed too," I said.

"Yes. Being a widow is not easy work, especially when your husband had other wives. She was the youngest. She was considered quite beautiful in those days."

"But why did she stay?"

He did not answer right away. He busied himself scraping a star in the tough skin of earth. He drew a circle around it and made marks around it as a child draws the sun. Then he scraped it away with the end of his stick and raised his face into the thickening wind. "You must understand how people think in desperate times. When their bellies are full, they can afford to be happy and generous with each other—the meat is shared, the women work and gossip, men gamble—it's a good time and you do not see things clearly. There is no need. But when the pot is empty and your guts are tight in your belly, you begin to look around. The hunger sharpens your eye."

"But why her?"

"She had not been with us more than a month or two, maybe three. You must understand the thinking. In that time the soldiers came, the people had to leave their home up near the mountains, then the starvation and the death of their leader. She had brought them bad medicine."

"But you—you don't think that."

"It was apparent," he said.

"It was bad luck; the people grew angry because their luck was bad," I said.

"It was medicine."

I looked at his eyes. "She said it was because of her beauty."

"I believe it was that too. When Standing Bear was alive, they had to accept her. In fact, they were proud to have such beauty—you know how it is, even if it isn't yours." His lips trembled into what could have been a smile.

"But when he died, her beauty worked against her," I said.

"That's true, but it was more than that. When you are starving, you look for signs. Each event becomes big in your mind. His death was the final proof that they were cursed. The medicine man, Fish, interpreted the signs. They looked at your grandmother and realized that she had brought despair and death. And her beauty—it was as if her beauty made a mockery of their situation."

"They can't have believed this . . ."

"It wasn't a question of belief, it was the way things were," he said. "The day Standing Bear was laid to rest, the women walked away. Even his other wives gave her the silent treatment. It took the men longer—men are not sensitive. They considered her the widow of a chief and treated her with respect. But soon, as it must be, they began to notice the hatred in their women's eyes, the coolness with which they were treated if they brought your grandmother a rabbit leg or a piece of fire in the morning. And they became ashamed of themselves for associating with the young widow and left her to herself."

I was staring at the bottle on the ground before me. I tried to understand the medicine, the power that directed the people to single out a young woman, to leave her to fend for herself in the middle of a cruel winter. I tried to understand the thinking, the hatred of the women, the shame of the men. Starvation. I didn't know it. I couldn't understand the medicine, her beauty.

"What happened to her?"

"She lived the rest of the winter by herself."

"How could she survive alone?"

He shifted his weight and dug his stick into the earth. He seemed uncomfortable. Perhaps he was recalling things he didn't want to or he felt that he had gone too far. He seemed to have lost his distance, but he went on: "She didn't really leave. It was the dead of winter. To leave the camp would have meant a sure death, but there were tepees on the edge, empty—many were empty then."

"What did she do for food?"

"What did any of us do? We waited for spring. Spring came, we hunted—the deer were weak and easy to kill."

"But she couldn't hunt, could she?" It seemed important for me to know what she did for food. No woman, no man could live a winter like that alone without something.

As I watched Yellow Calf dig at the earth I remembered how the old lady had ended her story of the journey of Standing Bear's band.

There had been great confusion that spring. Should the people stay in this land of the Gros Ventres, should they go directly south to the nearest buffalo herd, or should they go back to the country west of here, their home up near the mountains? The few old people left were in favor of this last direction because they wanted to die in familiar surroundings, but the younger ones were divided as to whether they should stay put until they got stronger or head for the buffalo ranges to the south. They rejected the idea of going home because the soldiers were there. Many of them had encountered the Long Knives before, and they knew that in their condition they wouldn't have a chance. There was much confusion, many decisions and indecisions, hostility.

Finally it was the soldiers from Fort Assiniboine who took the choice away from the people. They rode down one late-spring day, gathered up the survivors and drove them west to the newly created Blackfeet Reservation. Because they didn't care to take her with them, the people apparently didn't mention her to the soldiers, and because she had left the band when the weather warmed and lived a distance away, the soldiers didn't question her. They assumed she was a Gros Ventre.

A gust of wind rattled the willows. The clouds towered white against the sky, but I could see their black underbellies as they floated toward us.

The old lady had ended her story with the image of the people being driven "like cows" to their reservation. It was a strange triumph and I understood it. But why hadn't she spoken of Yellow Calf? Why hadn't she mentioned that he was a member of that band of Blackfeet and had, like herself, stayed behind?

A swirl of dust skittered across the earth's skin.

"You say you were just a youth that winter—how old?" I said.

He stopped digging. "That first winter, my folks all died then."

But I was not to be put off. "How old?"

"It slips my mind," he said. "When one is blind and old he loses track of the years."

"You must have some idea."

"When one is blind . . ."

"Ten? Twelve? Fifteen?"

". . . and old, he no longer follows the cycles of the years. He knows each season in its place because he can feel it, but time becomes a procession. Time feeds upon itself and grows fat." A mosquito took shelter in the hollow of his cheek, but he didn't notice. He had attained that distance. "To an old dog like myself, the only cycle begins with birth and ends in death. This is the only cycle I know."

I thought of the calendar I had seen in his shack on my previous visit. It was dated 1936. He must have been able to see then. He had been blind for over thirty years, but if he was as old as I thought, he had lived out a lifetime before. He had lived a life without being blind. He had followed the calendar, the years, time—

I thought for a moment.

Bird farted.

And it came to me, as though it were riding one moment of the gusting wind, as though Bird had had it in him all the time and had passed it to me in that one instant of corruption.

"Listen, old man," I said. "It was you—you were old enough to hunt!"

But his white eyes were kneading the clouds.

I began to laugh, at first quietly, with neither bitterness nor humor. It was the laughter of one who understands a moment in his life, of one who has been let in on the secret through luck and circumstance. "You . . . you're the one." I laughed, as the secret unfolded itself. "The only one . . . you, her hunter . . . ." And the wave behind my eyes broke.

Yellow Calf still looked off toward the east as though the wind could wash the wrinkles from his face. But the corners of his eyes wrinkled even more as his mouth fell open. Through my tears I could see his Adam's apple jerk.

"The only one," I whispered, and the old man's head dropped between his knees. His back shook, the bony shoulders squared and hunched like the folded wings of a hawk.

"And the half-breed, Doagie!" But the laughter again racked my throat. *He wasn't Teresa's father; it was you, Yellow Calf, the hunter!*

He turned to the sound of my laughter. His face was distorted so that the single snag seemed the only recognizable feature of the man I had come to visit. His eyes hid themselves behind the high cheekbones. His mouth had become the rubbery sneer of a jack-o'-lantern.

And so we shared this secret in the presence of ghosts, in wind that called forth the muttering tepees, the blowing snow, the white air of the horses' nostrils. The cottonwoods behind us, their dead white branches angling to the threatening clouds, sheltered these ghosts as they had sheltered the camp that winter. But there were others, so many others.

Yellow Calf stood, his hands in his pockets, suddenly withdrawn and polite. I pressed what remained of the bottle of wine into his hand. "Thank you," he said.

"You must come visit me sometime," I said.

"You are kind."

I tightened the cinch around Bird's belly. "I'll think about you," I said.

"You'd better hurry," he said. "It's coming."

I picked up the reins and led Bird to the rotting plank bridge across the irrigation ditch.

He lifted his hand.

39

Bird held his head high as he trotted down the fence line. He was anxious to get home. He was in a hurry to have a good pee and a good roll in the manure. Since growing old, he had lost his grace. With each step, I felt the leather of the saddle rub against my thighs.

It was a good time for odor. Alfalfa, sweet and dusty, came with the wind, above it the smell of rain. The old man would be lifting his nose to this odor, thinking of other things, of those days he stood by the widow when everyone else had failed her. So much distance between them, and yet they lived only three miles apart. But what created this distance? And what made me think that he was Teresa's father? After all, twenty-five years had passed between the time he had become my grandmother's hunter and Teresa's birth. They could have parted at any time. But he was the one. I knew that. The answer had come to me as if by instinct, sitting on the pump platform, watching his silent laughter, as though it was his blood in my veins that had told me.

I tried to imagine what it must have been like, the two of them, hunter and widow. If I was right about Yellow Calf's age, there couldn't have been more than four or five years separating them. If she was not yet twenty, he must have been fifteen or sixteen. Old enough to hunt, but what about the other? Could he have been more than hunter then, or did that come later? It seemed likely that they had never lived together (except perhaps that first winter out of need). There had never been any talk, none that I heard. The woman who had told me about Doagie had implied that he hadn't been Teresa's father. She hadn't mentioned Yellow Calf.

So for years the three miles must have been as close as an early morning walk down this path I was now riding. The fence hadn't been here in the beginning, nor the odor of alfalfa. But the other things, the cottonwoods and willows, the open spaces of the valley, the hills to the south, the Little Rockies, had all been here then; none had changed. Bird lifted his head and whinnied. He had settled into a gait that would have been a dance in his younger days. It was only the thudding of his hooves and the saddle rubbing against my thighs that gave him away. So for years the old man had made this trip; but could it have been twenty-five? Twenty-five years without living together, twenty-five years of an affair so solemn and secretive it had not even been rumored?

Again I thought of the time First Raise had taken me to see the old man. Again I felt the cold canvas of his coat as I clung to him, the steady clopping of the horse's hooves on the frozen path growing quieter as the wet snow began to pile up. I remembered the flour sack filled with frozen deer meat hanging from the saddle horn, and First Raise getting down to open the gate, then peeing what he said was my name in the snow. But I couldn't remember being at the shack. I couldn't remember Yellow Calf.

Yet I had felt it then, that feeling of event. Perhaps it was the distance, those three new miles, that I felt, or perhaps I had felt something of that other distance; but the event of distance was as vivid to me as the cold canvas of First Raise's coat against my cheek. He must have known then what I had just discovered. Although he told me nothing of it up to the day he died, he had taken me that snowy day to see my grandfather.

40

A glint of sunlight caught my eyes. A car was pulling off the highway onto our road. It was too far away to recognize. It looked like a dark beetle lumbering slowly over the bumps and ruts of the dusty tracks. I had reached the gate but I didn't get down. Bird pawed the ground and looked off toward the ranch. From this angle only the slough and corral were visible. Bird studied them. The buildings were hidden behind a rise in the road.

The clouds were now directly overhead, but the sun to the west was still glaring hot. The wind had died down to a steady breeze. The rain was very close.

It was Ferdinand Horn and his wife. As the dark green Hudson hit the stretch of raised road between the alfalfa fields, he honked the horn as if I had planned to disappear. He leaned out his window and waved. "Hello there, partner," he called. He turned off the motor and the car coasted to a stop. He looked up at me. "We just stopped to offer our condolences."

"What?"

Ferdinand Horn's wife leaned forward on the seat and looked up through the windshield. She had a pained look.

"Oh, the old lady!" It was strange, but I had forgotten that she was dead.

"She was a fine woman," Ferdinand Horn said. He gazed at the alfalfa field out his window.

"Teresa and Lame Bull went to Harlem to get her. They probably won't get back before dark."

"We saw them. We just came from there," he said. He seemed to be measuring the field. "A lovely woman."

Ferdinand Horn's wife stared at me through her turquoise-frame glasses. She had cocked her head to get a better look. It must have been uncomfortable.

"We're going to bury her tomorrow," I said.

"The hell you say."

"We're not doing anything fancy. You could probably come if you want to." I didn't know exactly how Teresa would act at the funeral.

"That's an idea." He turned to his wife. She nodded, still looking up through the windshield. "Oh hell, where's my manners." He fumbled in a paper sack between them. He punched two holes in the bottom of a can of beer. It had a pop-top on top. He handed it to me.

I took a sip, then a swallow, and another. The wine had left my mouth dry, and the beer was good and colder than I expected. "Jesus," I gasped. "That really hits the spot."

"I don't know what's wrong with me. What the hell are you doing on that damn plug?"

"I was just riding around. I visited Yellow Calf for a minute."

"No kidding? I thought he was dead." He looked at the field again. "How is he anyway?"

"He seems to be okay, living to the best of his ability," I said.

"You know, my cousin Louie used to bring him commodities when he worked for Reclamation. He used to regulate that head gate back by Yellow Calf's, and he'd bring him groceries. But hell, that was ten years ago—hell, twenty!"

I hadn't thought of that aspect. How did he eat now? "Maybe the new man brings him food," I said.

"He's kind of goofy, you know."

"The new man?"

"Yellow Calf."

Ferdinand Horn's wife pushed her glasses up, then wrinkled her nose to keep them there. She was holding a can of grape pop in her lap. She had wrapped a light blue hankie around it to keep her hand from getting cold or sticky.

"You have a low spot in that corner over there."

I followed his finger to an area of the field filled with slough grass and foxtail.

"Did you find her?" The muffled voice brought me back to the car.

"We're going to bury her tomorrow," I said.

"No, no," she shrieked, and hit Ferdinand Horn on the chest. "Your wife!" She hadn't taken her eyes off me. "Your wife!"

It was a stab in the heart. "I saw her . . . in Havre," I said.

"Well?"

"In Gable's . . ."

She leaned forward and toward Ferdinand Horn. Her upper lip lifted over her small brown teeth. "Was that white man with her?"

"No, she was all alone this time."

"I'll bet—"

"How many bales you get off this piece?"

"I'll bet she was all alone. As if a girl like that could ever be alone." She looked up like a muskrat through the thin ice of the windshield.

"We just came by to offer our condolences."

"Don't try to change the subject," she said, slapping Ferdinand Horn on the arm. "Did you bring her back?"

"Yes," I said. "She's in at the house now. Do you want to see her?"

"You mean you brought her back?" She sounded disappointed.

"You want to see her?"

"Did you get your gun back?" Ferdinand Horn was now looking at me.

"Yes. Do you want to see her?"

"Okay, sure, for a minute," he said.

His wife fell back against the seat. She was wearing the same wrinkled print dress she had worn the time before. Her thighs were spread beneath the bright butterflies. I couldn't see her face.

"We're late enough," she said.

"Well, just for a minute," Ferdinand Horn said.

"We just came by to offer our condolences."

Ferdinand Horn seemed puzzled. He turned toward her. Her thighs tightened. He looked up at me. Then he started the car. "How many bales you get off this piece?" he said.

41

As Bird and I rounded the bend of the slough, I could hear the calf bawling. It was almost feeding time. We passed the graveyard with its fresh dirt now turning tan beneath the rolling clouds. Bird loped straight for the corral, his ears forward and his legs stiffened. I could feel the tension in his body. I thought it was because of the storm which threatened to break at any time, but as we neared the corral, Bird pulled up short and glanced in the direction of the slough. It was the calf's mother. She was lying on her side, up to her chest in the mud. Her good eye was rimmed white and her tongue lolled from the side of her mouth. When she saw us, she made an effort to free herself, as though we had come to encourage her. Her back humped forward as her shoulders strained against the sucking mud. She switched her tail and a thin stream of crap ran down her backside.

Bird whinnied, then dropped his head, waiting for me to get down and open the gate. He had lost interest.

I wanted to ignore her. I wanted to go away, to let her drown in her own stupidity, attended only by clouds and the coming rain. If I turned away now, I thought, if I turned away—my hands trembled but did nothing. She had earned this fate by being stupid, and now no one could help her. Who would want to? As she stared at me, I saw beyond the immediate panic that hatred, that crazy hatred that made me aware of a quick hatred in my own heart. Her horns seemed tipped with blood, the dark blood of catastrophe. The muck slid down around her ears as she lowered her head, the air from her nostrils blowing puddles in the mud. I had seen her before, the image of catastrophe, the same hateful eye, the long curving horns, the wild-eyed spinster leading the cows down the hill into the valley. Stupid, stupid cow, hateful in her stupidity. She let out a long, bubbling call. I continued to glance at her, but now, as though energy, or even life, had gone out of her, she rolled her head to one side, half submerged in the mud, her one eye staring wildly at the clouds.

Stupid, stupid—

I slid down, threw open the corral gate and ran to the horse shed. The soft flaky manure cushioned the jolt of my bad leg. A rope hung from a nail driven into a two-by-four. I snatched it down and ran back to the gate. Bird was just sauntering through. I half led, half dragged him down to the edge of the slough. He seemed offended that I should ask this task of him. He tried to look around toward the pasture behind the corral. The red horse was watching us over the top pole, but there was no time to exchange horses. Already the cow lay motionless on her side.

I tied one end of the rope to the saddle horn to keep Bird from walking away, then threw open the loop to fit over the cow's head. But she would not lift it. I yelled and threw mud toward her, but she made no effort. My scalp began to sweat. A chilly breeze blew through my hair as I twirled the loop above my head. I tried for her horn but it was pointing forward toward me and the loop slid off. Again and again I threw for the horn, but the loop had nothing to tighten against. Each time I expected her to raise her head in response to the loop landing roughly against her neck and head, but she lay still. She must be dead, I thought, but the tiny bubbles around her nostrils continued to fizz. Then I was in the mud, up to my knees, wading out to the cow. With each step, the mud closed around my leg, then the heavy suck as I pulled the other free. My eyes fixed themselves on the bubbles and I prayed for them to stop so I could turn back, but the frothy mass continued to expand and move as though it were life itself. I was in up to my crotch, no longer able to lift my legs, able only to slide them through the greasy mire. The two or three inches of stagnant water sent the smell of dead things through my body. It was too late, it was taking too long—by leaning forward I could almost reach the cow's horn. One more step, the bubbles weren't moving, and I did clutch the horn, pulling myself toward her. She tried to lift her head, but the mud sucked it back down. Her open mouth, filling with slime, looked as pink as a baby mouse against the green and black. The wild eye, now trying to focus on me, was streaked with the red threads of panic.

By lifting on her horn, I managed to raise her head enough to slide the loop underneath, the mud now working to my advantage. I tightened up and yelled to Bird, at the same time pulling the rope against the saddle horn. The old horse shook his shoulders and backed up. He reared a few inches off the ground, as though the pressure of the rope had reminded him of those years spent as a cow horse. But the weight of the cow and mud began to pull the saddle forward, the back end lifting away from his body. It wouldn't hold. I gripped the taut rope and pulled myself up and out of the mud. I began to move hand over hand back toward the bank. Something had gone wrong with my knee; it wouldn't bend. I tried to arch my toes to keep my shoe from being pulled off, but there was no response. My whole leg was dead. The muscles in my arms knotted, but I continued to pull myself along the rope until I reached the edge of the bank. I lay there a moment, exhausted, then tried to get up but my arms wouldn't move. It was a dream. I couldn't move my arms. They lay at my sides, palms up, limp, as though they belonged to another body. I bent my good knee up under me, using my shoulders and chin as leverage.

Once again I yelled at Bird, but he would not come, would not slack up on the rope. I swore at him, coaxed him, reasoned with him, but I must have looked foolish to him, my ass in the air and the sweat running from my scalp.

Goddamn you, Bird, goddamn you. Goddamn Ferdinand Horn, why didn't you come in, together we could have gotten this damn cow out, why hadn't I ignored her? Goddamn your wife with her stupid turquoise glasses, stupid grape pop, your stupid car. Lame Bull! It was his cow, he had married this cow, why wasn't he here? Off riding around, playing the role, goddamn big-time operator, can't trust him, can't trust any of these damn idiots, damn Indians. Slack up, you asshole! Slack up! You want to strangle her? That's okay with me; she means nothing to me. What did I do to deserve this? Goddamn that Ferdinand Horn! Ah, Teresa, you made a terrible mistake. Your husband, your friends, your son, all worthless, none of them worth a shit. Slack up, you sonofabitch! Your mother dead, your father—you don't even know, what do you think of that? A joke, can't you see? Lame Bull! The biggest joke—can't you see that he's a joke, a joker playing a joke on you? Were you taken for a ride! Just like the rest of us, this country, all of us taken for a ride. Slack up, slack up! This greedy stupid country—

My arms began to tingle as they tried to wake up. I moved my fingers. They moved. My neck ached but the strength was returning. I crouched and spent the next few minutes planning my new life. Finally I was able to push myself from the ground and stand on my good leg. I put my weight on the other. The bones seemed to be wedged together, but it didn't hurt. I hobbled over to Bird. He raised his head and nodded wildly. As I touched his shoulder, he shied back even further.

"Here, you old sonofabitch," I said. "Do you want to defeat our purpose?"

He nodded his agreement. I hit the rope with the edge of my hand. I hit it again. He let off, dancing forward, the muscles in his shoulders working beneath the soft white hair. I looked back at the cow. She was standing up in the mud, her head, half of it black, straight up like a swimming water snake. I snapped the rope out toward her, but she didn't move. Her eyes were wild, a glaze beginning to form in them. The noose was still tight around her neck.

As I climbed aboard the horse, I noticed for the first time that it was raining. What I thought was sweat running through my scalp had been rain all along. I snapped the rope again, arcing a curve away from me toward the cow. This time the noose did loosen up. She seemed surprised. A loud gasp, as harsh as a dog's bark, came from her throat. As though that were her signal for a final death struggle, she went into action, humping her back, bawling, straining against the sucking mud. Bird tightened up on the rope and began to back away. The saddle came forward; I turned him so that he was headed away from the slough.

The rain was coming hard now, the big drops stinging the back of my neck and splattering into the dusty earth. A magpie, light and silent, flew overhead, then lit on a fence post beside the loading chute. He ruffled his sleek feathers, then squatted to watch.

The rope began to hum in the gathering wind, but the cow was coming, flailing her front legs out of the mud. Bird slipped once and almost went down, doing a strange dance, rolling quickly from side to side, but he regained his balance and continued to pull and the cow continued to come. I took another dally around the saddle horn and clung to the end of the rope. I slapped him on the shoulder. Somewhere in my mind I could hear the deep rumble of thunder, or maybe it was the rumble of energy, the rumble of guts—it didn't matter. There was only me, a white horse and a cow. The pressure of the rope against my thigh felt right. I sat to one side in the saddle, standing in the right stirrup, studying the rough strands of hemp against the pant leg. The cow had quit struggling and was now sliding slowly through the greasy mud. Her head pointed up into the rain, but her eyes had lost that wild glare. She seemed to understand this necessary inconvenience.

It was all so smooth and natural I didn't notice that Bird had begun to slip in the rain-slick dirt. He turned sideways in an attempt to get more traction. He lowered his rump and raised his head. He lowered his head again so that he was stretched low to the ground. I leaned forward until I could smell the sweet warmth of his wet mane. Then I felt the furious digging of hooves, and I realized that he was about to go down. Before I could react, he whirled around, his front legs striking out at the air. His hind legs went out from under him. It was only the weight of the cow on the end of the rope that kept him from falling over backwards on top of me. His large white butt thumped the ground in front of me, he tottered for an instant, then he fell forward and it was quiet.

42

A flash of lightning to the south of me. I couldn't or wouldn't turn my head. I felt my back begin to stiffen. I didn't know if it was because of the fall or the damp, but I wasn't uncomfortable. The stiffness provided a reason for not moving. I saw the flash in the corner of my eye, as though it were mirrored countless times in the countless raindrops that fell on my face.

I wondered if Mose and First Raise were comfortable. They were the only ones I really loved, I thought, the only ones who were good to be with. At least the rain wouldn't bother them. But they would probably like it; they were that way, good to be with, even on a rainy day.

I heard Bird grunt twice as he tried to heave himself upright, but I couldn't find the energy to look at him. The magpie must have flown closer, for his metallic *awk! awk!* was almost conversational. The cow down in the slough had stopped gurgling. Her calf called once, a soft drone which ended on a quizzical high note. Then it was silent again.

Some people, I thought, will never know how pleasant it is to be distant in a clean rain, the driving rain of a summer storm. It's not like you'd expect, nothing like you'd expect.

1974

Vietnam Conflict

In a modest atempt to focus attention on literature responding to the United States–Vietnam military conflict, this section includes prose by Michael Herr, Tim O'Brien, and Norman Mailer, and poetry by Yusef Komunyakaa and Robert Bly. Komunyakaa came to prominence during the 1990s; Bly was one of the leaders of the very active "Poets and Writers Against Vietnam," along with Muriel Rukeyser, Denise Levertov, W. S. Merwin, James Wright, Hayden Carruth, Adrienne Rich, Galway Kinnell, Robert Lowell, Allen Ginsberg, and others. Mailer's *Armies of the Night,* his meditative account of one of those crucial actions, has become a classic. The works by Tim O'Brien and Yusef Komunyakaa express veterans' view of the horrors of actual combat.

As Michael Bibby has reminded us, this literature is central to our view of mid-century American life, "considering that the Vietnam war was the longest overseas military conflict in U.S. history and that practically every working writer from 1965 to 1975 had something to say about it . . ." (see Bibby's 1996 *Hearts and Minds: Bodies, Poetry, and Resistance in the Vietnam Era*).

Michael Herr b. 1940

Among the most private of contemporary writers, Michael Herr has revealed little of his personal life. He was born and raised in Syracuse, New York, and attended Syracuse University. He then moved to New York City, where he worked in the editorial offices of *Holiday* magazine and produced articles and film criticism for such periodicals as *Mademoiselle* and the *New Leader.* In 1967, he persuaded Harold Hayes, the editor of *Esquire* magazine, to send him to Vietnam. He stayed there for over a year and witnessed some of the most intense fighting of the war. For a writer, Herr's situation in Vietnam was ideal: he had no specific assignment, he was relatively free to travel where he liked, and he was unencumbered by deadlines. Herr initially intended to write a monthly column from Vietnam but soon realized the idea was "horrible." In fact, Herr published only a few Vietnam pieces in *Esquire* and did not get his war experiences into a book until 1977.

After the war, Herr lived in New York for a time. After finishing *Dispatches,* he collaborated on the screenplay for *Apocalypse Now* and, more recently, for *Full Metal Jacket.* At last report, Herr lives in London.

Dispatches is perhaps the most brilliant American literary treatment of the Vietnam War. Ostensibly journalistic, *Dispatches* is more properly regarded as a painstakingly executed product of the author's imagination, if not quite a novel then certainly a literary work whose most dominant and satisfying qualities are novelistic. *Dispatches* is organized tautly, provides rich characterization, and evinces an extraordinary style thoroughly compatible with its subject. As Herr tells it, the Vietnam War was very much a 1960s spectacle: part John Wayne movie, part rock-and-roll concert, part redneck riot, part media event, and part bad drug trip. Herr's style, so perfectly grounded in the popular culture of the time, pulls at the reader with great power and unmistakable authenticity. After a particularly terrible battle, a young Marine glared at Herr, knowing he was a writer, and snarled: "Okay, man, you go on, you go on out of here, you cocksucker, but I mean it, you tell it! You tell it, man." And so Herr did.

The excerpt from *Dispatches* printed here comes from the beginning of the first section, called "Breathing In." Herr immediately establishes the hallucinatory quality of the war, against which he depicts the violence and remarkable array of characters. Herr's field of vision is broad but always at its center are the "grunts," the infantrymen who invariably carried themselves through the war with dignity and a carefully cultivated and life-sustaining combination of humor and cynicism.

Raymund Paredes
University of California–Los Angeles

PRIMARY WORKS

Dispatches, 1977; *The Big Room,* 1986 (with Guy Peellaert).

from Dispatches

I

Going out at night the medics gave you pills, Dexedrine breath like dead snakes kept too long in a jar. I never saw the need for them myself, a little contact or anything that even sounded like contact would give me more speed than I could bear. Whenever I heard something outside of our clenched little circle I'd practically flip, hoping to God that I wasn't the only one who'd noticed it. A couple of rounds fired off in the dark a kilometer away and the Elephant would be there kneeling on my chest, sending me down into my boots for a breath. Once I thought I saw a light moving in the jungle and I caught myself just under a whisper saying, "I'm not ready for this, I'm not ready for this." That's when I decided to drop it and do something else with my nights. And I wasn't going out like the night ambushers did, or the Lurps, long-range recon patrollers who did it night after night for weeks and months, creeping up on VC base camps or around moving columns of North Vietnamese. I was living too close to my bones as it was, all I had to do was accept it. Anyway, I'd save the pills for later, for Saigon and the awful depressions I always had there.

I knew one 4th Division Lurp who took his pills by the fistful, downs from the left pocket of his tiger suit and ups from the right, one to cut the trail for him and the other to send him down it. He told me that they cooled things out just right for him, that he could see that old jungle at night like he was looking at it through a starlight scope. "They sure give you the range," he said.

This was his third tour. In 1965 he'd been the only survivor in a platoon of the Cav wiped out going into the Ia Drang Valley. In '66 he'd come back with the Special Forces and one morning after an ambush he'd hidden under the bodies of his team while the VC walked all around them with knives, making sure. They stripped the bodies of their gear, the berets too, and finally went away, laughing. After that, there was nothing left for him in the war except the Lurps.

"I just can't hack it back in the World," he said. He told me that after he'd come back home the last time he would sit in his room all day, and sometimes he'd stick a hunting rifle out the window, leading people and cars as they passed his house until the only feeling he was aware of was all up in the tip of that one finger. "It used to put my folks real uptight," he said. But he put people uptight here too, even here.

"No man, I'm sorry, he's just too crazy for me," one of the men in his team said. "All's you got to do is look in his eyes, that's the whole fucking story right there."

"Yeah, but you better do it quick," someone else said. "I mean, you don't want to let him catch you at it."

But he always seemed to be watching for it, I think he slept with his eyes open, and I was afraid of him anyway. All I ever managed was one quick look in, and that was like looking at the floor of an ocean. He wore a gold earring and a headband torn from a piece of camouflage parachute material, and since nobody was about to tell him to get his hair cut it fell below his shoulders, covering a thick purple scar. Even at division he never went anywhere without at least a .45 and a knife, and he thought I was a freak because I wouldn't carry a weapon.

"Didn't you ever meet a reporter before?" I asked him.

"Tits on a bull," he said. "Nothing personal."

But what a story he told me, as one-pointed and resonant as any war story I ever heard, it took me a year to understand it:

"Patrol went up the mountain. One man came back. He died before he could tell us what happened."

I waited for the rest, but it seemed not to be that kind of story; when I asked him what had happened he just looked like he felt sorry for me, fucked if he'd waste time telling stories to anyone dumb as I was.

His face was all painted up for night walking now like a bad hallucination, not like the painted faces I'd seen in San Francisco only a few weeks before, the other extreme of the same theater. In the coming hours he'd stand as faceless and quiet in the jungle as a fallen tree, and God help his opposite numbers unless they had at least half a squad along, he was a good killer, one of our best. The rest of his team were gathered outside the tent, set a little apart from the other division units, with its own Lurp-designated latrine and its own exclusive freeze-dry rations, three-star war food, the same chop they sold at Abercrombie & Fitch. The regular division troops would almost shy off the path when they passed the area on their way to and from the mess tent. No matter how toughened up they became in the war, they still looked innocent compared to the Lurps. When the team had grouped they walked in a file down the hill to the lz across the strip to the perimeter and into the treeline.

I never spoke to him again, but I saw him. When they came back in the next morning he had a prisoner with him, blindfolded and with his elbows bound sharply behind him. The Lurp area would definitely be off limits during the interrogation, and anyway, I was already down at the strip waiting for a helicopter to come and take me out of there.

"Hey, what're you guys, with the USO? Aw, we thought you was with the USO 'cause your hair's so long." Page took the kid's picture, I got the words down and

Flynn laughed and told him we were the Rolling Stones. The three of us traveled around together for about a month that summer. At one lz the brigade chopper came in with a real foxtail hanging off the aerial, when the commander walked by us he almost took an infarction.

"Don't you men salute officers?"

"We're not men," Page said. "We're correspondents."

When the commander heard that, he wanted to throw a spontaneous operation for us, crank up his whole brigade and get some people killed. We had to get out on the next chopper to keep him from going ahead with it, amazing what some of them would do for a little ink. Page liked to augment his field gear with freak paraphernalia, scarves and beads, plus he was English, guys would stare at him like he'd just come down off a wall on Mars. Sean Flynn could look more incredibly beautiful than even his father, Errol, had thirty years before as Captain Blood, but sometimes he looked more like Artaud coming out of some heavy heart-of-darkness trip, overloaded on the information, the input! The input! He'd give off a bad sweat and sit for hours, combing his mustache through with the saw blade of his Swiss Army knife. We packed grass and tape: Have You Seen Your Mother Baby Standing in the Shadows, Best of the Animals, Strange Days, Purple Haze, Archie Bell and the Drells, "C'mon now everybody, do the Tighten Up. . . ." Once in a while we'd catch a chopper straight into one of the lower hells, but it was a quiet time in the war, mostly it was lz's and camps, grunts hanging around, faces, stories.

"Best way's to just keep moving, one of them told us. "Just keep moving, stay in motion, you know what I'm saying?"

We knew. He was a moving-target-survivor subscriber, a true child of the war, because except for the rare times when you were pinned or stranded the system was geared to keep you mobile, if that was what you thought you wanted. As a technique for staying alive it seemed to make as much sense as anything, given naturally that you went there to begin with and wanted to see it close; it started out sound and straight but it formed a cone as it progressed, because the more you moved the more you saw, the more you saw the more besides death and mutilation you risked, and the more you risked of that the more you would have to let go of one day as a "survivor." Some of us moved around the war like crazy people until we couldn't see which way the run was even taking us anymore, only the war all over its surface with occasional, unexpected penetration. As long as we could have choppers like taxis it took real exhaustion or depression near shock or a dozen pipes of opium to keep us even apparently quiet, we'd still be running around inside our skins like something was after us, ha ha, La Vida Loca.

In the months after I got back the hundreds of helicopters I'd flown in began to draw together until they'd formed a collective meta-chopper, and in my mind it was the sexiest thing going; saver-destroyed, provider-waster, right hand-left hand, nimble, fluent, canny and human; hot steel, grease, jungle-saturated canvas webbing, sweat cooling and warming up again, cassette rock and roll in one ear and door-gun fire in the other, fuel, heat, vitality and death, death itself, hardly an intruder. Men on the crews would say that once you'd carried a dead person he would always be there, riding with you. Like all combat people they were incredibly superstitious and invariably self-dramatic, but it was (I knew) unbearably true that close exposure to the dead sensitized you to the force of their presence and made for long reverberations;

long. Some people were so delicate that one look was enough to wipe them away; but even bone-dumb grunts seemed to feel that something weird and extra was happening to them.

Helicopters and people jumping out of helicopters, people so in love they'd run to get on even when there wasn't any pressure. Choppers rising straight out of small cleared jungle spaces, wobbling down onto city rooftops, cartons of rations and ammunition thrown off, dead and wounded loaded on. Sometimes they were so plentiful and loose that you could touch down at five or six places in a day, look around, hear the talk, catch the next one out. There were installations as big as cities with 30,000 citizens, once we dropped in to feed supply to one man. God knows what kind of Lord Jim phoenix numbers he was doing in there, all he said to me was, "You didn't see a thing, right Chief? You weren't even here." There were posh fat air-conditioned camps like comfortable middle-class scenes with the violence tacit, "far away"; camps named for commanders' wives, LZ Thelma, LZ Betty Lou; number-named hilltops in trouble where I didn't want to stay; trail, paddy, swamp, deep hairy bush, scrub, swale, village, even city, where the ground couldn't drink up what the action spilled, it made you careful where you walked.

Sometimes the chopper you were riding in would top a hill and all the ground in front of you as far as the next hill would be charred and pitted and still smoking, and something between your chest and your stomach would turn over. Frail gray smoke where they'd burned off the rice fields around a free-strike zone, brilliant white smoke from phosphorus ("Willy Peter/Make you a buh liever"), deep black smoke from 'palm, they said that if you stood at the base of a column of napalm smoke it would such the air right out of your lungs. Once we fanned over a little ville that had just been airstruck and the words of a song by Wingy Manone that I'd heard when I was a few years old snapped into my head, "Stop the War, These Cats Is Killing Themselves." Then we dropped, hovered, settled down into purple lz smoke, dozens of children broke from their hootches to run in toward the focus of our landing, the pilot laughing and saying, "Vietnam, man, Bomb 'em and feed 'em, bomb 'em and feed 'em."

Flying over jungle was almost pure pleasure, doing it on foot was nearly all pain. I never belonged in there. Maybe it really was what its people had always called it, Beyond; at the very least it was serious, I gave up things to it I probably never got back. ("Aw, jungle's okay. If you know her you can live in her real good, if you don't she'll take you down in an hour. Under.") Once in some thick jungle corner with some grunts standing around, a correspondent said, "Gee, you must really see some beautiful sunsets in here," and they almost pissed themselves laughing. But you could fly up and into hot tropic sunsets that would change the way you thought about light forever. You could also fly out of places that were so grim they turned to black and white in your head five minutes after you'd gone.

That could be the coldest one in the world, standing at the edge of a clearing watching the chopper you'd just come in on taking off again, leaving you there to think about what it was going to be for you now: if this was a bad place, the wrong place, maybe even the last place, and whether you'd made a terrible mistake this time.

There was a camp at Soc Trang where a man at the lz said, "If you come looking for a story this is your lucky day, we got Condition Red here," and before the sound of the chopper had faded out, I knew I had it too.

"That's affirmative," the camp commander said, "we are *definitely* expecting rain. Glad to see you." He was a young captain, he was laughing and taping a bunch of sixteen clips together bottom to bottom for faster reloading, "grease." Everyone there was busy at it, cracking crates, squirreling away grenades, checking mortar pieces, piling rounds, clicking banana clips into automatic weapons that I'd never even seen before. They were wired into their listening posts out around the camp, into each other, into themselves, and when it got dark it got worse. The moon came up nasty and full, a fat moist piece of decadent fruit. It was soft and saffron-misted when you looked up at it, but its light over the sandbags and into the jungle was harsh and bright. We were all rubbing Army-issue nightfighter cosmetic under our eyes to cut the glare and the terrible things it made you see. (Around midnight, just for something to do, I crossed to the other perimeter and looked at the road running engineer-straight toward Route 4 like a yellow frozen ribbon out of sight and I saw it move, the whole road.) There were a few sharp arguments about who the light really favored, attackers or defenders, men were sitting around with Cinemascope eyes and jaws stuck out like they could shoot bullets, moving and antsing and shifting around inside their fatigues. "No sense us getting too relaxed, Charlie don't relax, just when you get good and comfortable is when he comes over and takes a giant shit on you." That was the level until morning, I smoked a pack an hour all night long, and nothing happened. Ten minutes after daybreak I was down at the lz asking about choppers.

A few days later Sean Flynn and I went up to a big firebase in the Americal TAOR that took it all the way over to another extreme, National Guard weekend. The colonel in command was so drunk that day that he could barely get his words out, and when he did, it was to say things like, "We aim to make good and goddammit sure that if *those guys* try *anything cute* they won't catch us with our pants down." The main mission there was to fire H&I, but one man told us that their record was the worst in the whole Corps, probably the whole country, they'd harassed and interdicted a lot of sleeping civilians and Korean Marines, even a couple of Americal patrols, but hardly any Viet Cong. (The colonel kept calling it "artillerary." The first time he said it Flynn and I looked away from each other, the second time we blew beer through our noses, but the colonel fell in laughing right away and more than covered us.) No sandbags, exposed shells, dirty pieces, guys going around giving us that look, "We're cool, how come you're not?" At the strip Sean was talking to the operator about it and the man got angry. "Oh *yeah?* Well fuck *you,* how tight do you think you want it? There ain't been any veecees around here in three months."

"So far so good," Sean said. "Hear anything on that chopper yet?"

But sometimes everything stopped, nothing flew, you couldn't even find out why. I got stuck for a chopper once in some lost patrol outpost in the Delta where the sergeant chain-ate candy bars and played country-and-western tapes twenty hours a day until I heard it in my sleep, some sleep, *Up on Wolverton Mountain* and *Lonesome as the bats and the bears in Miller's Cave* and *I fell into a burning ring of fire,* surrounded by strungout rednecks who weren't getting much sleep either because they couldn't trust one of their 400 mercenary troopers or their own hand-picked perimeter guards or anybody else except maybe Baby Ruth and Johnny Cash, they'd been waiting for it so long now they were afraid they wouldn't know it when they finally got it, *and it burns burns burns*. . . . Finally on the fourth day a helicopter came in to deliver meat and movies to the camp and I went out on it, so happy to get back to Saigon that I didn't crash for two days.

Airmobility, dig it, you weren't going anywhere. It made you feel safe, it made you feel Omni, but it was only a stunt, technology. Mobility was just mobility, it saved lives or took them all the time (saved mine I don't know how many times, maybe dozens, maybe none), what you really needed was a flexibility far greater than anything the technology could provide, some generous, spontaneous gift for accepting surprises, and I didn't have it. I got to hate surprises, control freak at the crossroads, if you were one of those people who always thought they had to know what was coming next, the war could cream you. It was the same with your ongoing attempts at getting used to the jungle or the blow-you-out climate or the saturating strangeness of the place which didn't lessen with exposure so often as it fattened and darkened in accumulating alienation. It was great if you could adapt, you had to try, but it wasn't the same as making a discipline, going into your own reserves and developing a real war metabolism, slow yourself down when your heart tried to punch its way through your chest, get swift when everything went to stop and all you could feel of your whole life was the entropy whipping through it. Unlovable terms.

The ground was always in play, always being swept. Under the ground was his, above it was ours. We have the air, we could get up in it but not disappear in*to* it, we could run but we couldn't hide, and he could do each so well that sometimes it looked like he was doing them both at once, while our finder just went limp. All the same, one place or another it was always going on, rock around the clock, we had the days and he had the nights. You could be in the most protected space in Vietnam and still know that your safety was provisional, that early death, blindness, loss of legs, arms or balls, major and lasting disfigurement—the whole rotten deal—could come in on the freaky-fluky as easily as in the so-called expected ways, you heard so many of those stories it was a wonder anyone was left alive to die in firefights and mortar-rocket attacks. After a few weeks, when the nickel had jarred loose and dropped and I saw that everyone around me was carrying a gun, I also saw that any one of them could go off at any time, putting you where it wouldn't matter whether it had been an accident or not. The roads were mined, the trails booby-trapped, satchel charges and grenades blew up jeeps and movie theaters, the VC got work inside all the camps as shoeshine boys and laundresses and honey-dippers, they'd starch your fatigues and burn your shit and then go home and mortar your area. Saigon and Cholon and Danang held such hostile vibes that you felt you were being dry-sniped every time someone looked at you, and choppers fell out of the sky like fat poisoned birds a hundred times a day. After a while I couldn't get on one without thinking that I must be out of my fucking mind.

Fear and motion, fear and standstill, no preferred cut there, no way even to be clear about which was really worse, the wait or the delivery. Combat spared far more men than it wasted, but everyone suffered the time between contact, especially when they were going out every day looking for it; bad going on foot, terrible in trucks and APC's, awful in helicopters, the worst, traveling so fast toward something so frightening. I can remember times when I went half dead with my fear of the motion, the speed and direction already fixed and pointed one way. It was painful enough just flying "safe" hops between firebases and lz's; if you were ever on a helicopter that had been hit by ground fire your deep, perpetual chopper anxiety was guaranteed. At least actual contact when it was happening would draw long ragged strands of energy out of you, it was juicy, fast and refining, and traveling toward it was hollow, dry, cold and steady, it never let you alone. All you could do was look around at the other people on board and see if they were as scared and numbed out as you were. If it looked like they weren't you thought they were insane, if it looked like they were it made you feel a lot worse.

I went through that thing a number of times and only got a fast return on my fear once, a too classic hot landing with the heat coming from the trees about 300 yards away, sweeping machine-gun fire that sent men head down into swampy water, running on their hands and knees toward the grass where it wasn't blown flat by the rotor blades, not much to be running for but better than nothing. The helicopter pulled up before we'd all gotten out, leaving the last few men to jump twenty feet down between the guns across the paddy and the gun on the chopper door. When we'd all reached the cover of the wall and the captain had made a check, we were amazed to see that no one had even been hurt, except for one man who'd sprained both his ankles jumping.. Afterwards, I remembered that I'd been down in the muck worrying about leeches. I guess you could say that I was refusing to accept the situation.

"Boy, you sure get offered some shitty choices," a Marine once said to me, and I couldn't help but feel that what he really meant was that you didn't get offered any at all. Specifically, he was just talking about a couple of C-ration cans, "dinner," but considering his young life you couldn't blame him for thinking that if he knew one thing for sure, it was that there was no one anywhere who cared less about what *he* wanted. There wasn't anybody he wanted to thank for his food, but he was grateful that he was still alive to eat it, that the mother-fucker hadn't scarfed him up first. He hadn't been anything but tired and scared for six months and he'd lost a lot, mostly people, and seen far too much, but he was breathing in and breathing out, some kind of choice all by itself.

He had one of those faces, I saw that face at least a thousand times at a hundred bases and camps, all the youth sucked out of the eyes, the color drawn from the skin, cold white lips, you knew he wouldn't wait for any of it to come back. Life had made him old, he'd live it out old. All those faces, sometimes it was like looking into faces at a rock concert, locked in, the event had them; or like students who were very heavily advanced, serious beyond what you'd call their years if you didn't know for yourself what the minutes and hours of those years were made up of. Not just like all the ones you saw who looked like they couldn't drag their asses through another day of it. (How do you feel when a nineteen-year-old kid tells you from the bottom of his heart that he's gotten too old for this kind of shit?) Not like the faces of the dead or wounded either, they could look more released than overtaken. These were the faces of boys whose whole lives seemed to have backed up on them, they'd be a few feet away but they'd be looking back at you over a distance you knew you'd never really cross. We'd talk, sometimes fly together, guys going out on R&R, guys escorting bodies, guys who'd flipped over into extremes of peace or violence. Once I flew with a kid who was going home, he looked back down once at the ground where he'd spent the year and spilled his whole load of tears. Sometimes you even flew with the dead.

Once I jumped on a chopper that was full of them. The kid in the op shack had said that there would be a body on board, but he'd been given some wrong information. "How bad do you want to get to Danang?" he'd asked me, and I'd said, "Bad."

When I saw what was happening I didn't want to get on, but they'd made a divert and a special landing for me, I had to go with the chopper I'd drawn, I was afraid of looking squeamish. (I remember, too, thinking that a chopper full of dead men was far less likely to get shot down than one full of living.) They weren't even in bags. They'd been on a truck near one of the firebases in the DMZ that was firing support for Khe Sanh, and the truck had hit a Command-detonated mine, then they'd been rocketed. The Marines were always running out of things, even food, ammo and medicine, it wasn't so strange that they'd run out of bags too. The men had been wrapped around in ponchos, some of them carelessly fastened with plastic straps, and loaded on board. There was a small space cleared for me between one of them and the door gunner, who looked pale and so tremendously furious that I thought he was angry with me and I couldn't look at him for a while. When we went up the wind blew through the ship and made the ponchos shake and tremble until the one next to me blew back in a fast brutal flap, uncovering the face. They hadn't even closed his eyes for him.

The gunner started hollering as loud as he could, "Fix it! Fix it!," maybe he thought the eyes were looking at him, but there wasn't anything I could do. My hand went there a couple of times and I couldn't, and then I did. I pulled the poncho tight, lifted his head carefully and tucked the poncho under it, and then I couldn't believe that I'd done it. All during the ride the gunner kept trying to smile, and when we landed at Dong Ha he thanked me and ran off to get a detail. The pilots jumped down and walked away without looking back once, like they'd never seen that chopper before in their lives. I flew the rest of the way to Danang in a general's plane.

1977

Tim O'Brien b. 1946

After a small-town Minnesota childhood and a college education at Macalaster (class president, summa cum laude, Phi Beta Kappa), Tim O'Brien was drafted into the U.S. Army in 1968 and served one year as an infantryman in the American conflict in Vietnam. The war, which appears in all seven of his published books, constitutes a central focus of his uncollected writings; yet in interviews O'Brien repeatedly objects to being labeled a Vietnam War writer: "It's like calling Toni Morrison a black writer or Shakespeare a king writer." His concerns as a writer resonate beyond the battlefield: the subjective nature of experience, the life of the imagination, the grip of the past, control and its loss, love, betrayal, obsession, language, guilt, rage, death, moral ambiguity, mental and emotional instability, and storytelling as a means of coping with it all. Nevertheless, his personal experience of that war, along with his midwestern background, provided him a site for his literary explorations of the human condition in late-twentieth-century American life.

Three of his books—one work of nonfiction and two works of fiction—deal directly with the war experience: *If I Die in a Combat Zone, Box Me Up and Ship Me Home* (1973), *Going After Cacciato* (1978), and *The Things They Carried* (1990). *Going After Cacciato,* his third book and second novel, won the National Book Award. The book takes place largely in the mind of Paul Berlin as he keeps himself awake on guard duty by remembering actual events and fancifully imagining what might have been. Berlin imagines his squad chasing the deserting Cacciato all the way to Paris, and his imagination transforms this initial act of *what if* into a tale that includes an echo of Alice in Wonderland and a Socratic exchange on the morality of the war, a tale that dramatizes Berlin's own desire to escape the war and to deny his own culpability. O'Brien's intellectual approach to the war is significantly informed by his political science graduate study at Harvard in the early 1970s; his unfinished doctoral dissertation is titled "Case Studies in American Military Interventions."

O'Brien's fourth work of fiction, *The Things They Carried,* is a collection of previously published and new stories, brought together, revised, and arranged to make a thematically unified work much like Hemingway's *In Our Time* and Joyce's *Dubliners.* The story printed here, "In the Field," comes from this book. Several of its stories are narrated by a character named "Tim O'Brien," who remains distinct from the author. The presence of "Tim O'Brien" underscores one of the novel's major conceits: the difference between "happening-truth" and "story-truth," or what actually happened versus what we say happened as factual events are received through our limited perspective and then transformed by memory, by the nature of storytelling, and by quasi-willful acts of reinvention for psychic survival.

O'Brien's other novels, including *Tomcat in Love* (1997), turn from war to romantic love between men and women as another source of conflict, ambiguity, shame, and haunting history. *Northern Lights* (1975), his first and by his own judgment his worst novel, pits two brothers—one a recently returned veteran—against one another, against the women in their lives, and against mother nature. Set in the future of 1995, *The Nuclear Age* (1985) presents a man struggling with his wife's adultery and his own obsession with nuclear war while simultaneously reliving a turbulent past of being in love with a militant anti-war activist. Paul Wade, the protagonist of *In the Lake of the Woods* (1994), is a politician who just lost an election after the newspapers exposed his presence during the atrocities against Vietnamese civilians at My Lai, and who wakes one morning to find that his wife has vanished.

What happens to Paul Wade's wife? What happens to bring about Kiowa's death in the following story? Tim O'Brien's fiction frequently resists answering the *what happens* questions to emphasize that who we are is far more manifold, layered, and mysterious than such questions pretend.

Alex Vernon
Hendrix College

PRIMARY SOURCES

If I Die in a Combat Zone, Box Me Up and Ship Me Home, 1973, rev. 1983; *Northern Lights,* 1975; *Going After Cacciato,* 1978, rev. 1989; "The Violent Vet," *Esquire,* Dec. 1979; *The Nuclear Age,* 1985, 1993; *The Things They Carried,* 1990; "The Magic Show," in *Writers on Writing,* ed. Robert Pack and Jay Parini, 1991; "The Vietnam in Me," *New York Times Magazine,* 2 Oct. 1994; *In the Lake of the Woods,* 1994; *Tomcat in Love,* 1997; "July '69," *Esquire,* July 2000. Interviews: *Chicago Review* 33.2 (1982); *Modern Fiction Studies* 30.1 (1984); *Contempo-*

rary Literature 32.1 (1991); *The Missouri Review* 14.3 (1991); *War, Literature and the Arts* 6.2 (1994).

In the Field

At daybreak the platoon of eighteen soldiers formed into a loose rank and began wading side by side through the deep muck of the shit field. They moved slowly in the rain. Leaning forward, heads down, they used the butts of their weapons as probes, wading across the field to the river and then turning and wading back again. They were tired and miserable; all they wanted now was to get it finished. Kiowa was gone. He was under the mud and water, folded in with the war, and their only thought was to find him and dig him out and then move on to someplace dry and warm. It had been a hard night. Maybe the worst ever. The rains had fallen without stop, and the Song Tra Bong had overflowed its banks, and the muck had now risen thigh-deep in the field along the river. A low, gray mist hovered over the land. Off to the west there was thunder, soft little moaning sounds, and the monsoons seemed to be a lasting element of the war. The eighteen soldiers moved in silence. First Lieutenant Jimmy Cross went first, now and then straightening out the rank, closing up the gaps. His uniform was dark with mud; his arms and face were filthy. Early in the morning he had radioed in the MIA report, giving the name and circumstances, but he was now determined to find his man, no matter what, even if it meant flying in slabs of concrete and damming up the river and draining the entire field. He would not lose a member of his command like this. It wasn't right. Kiowa had been a fine soldier and a fine human being, a devout Baptist, and there was no way Lieutenant Cross would allow such a good man to be lost under the slime of a shit field.

Briefly, he stopped and watched the clouds. Except for some occasional thunder it was a deeply quiet morning, just the rain and the steady sloshing sounds of eighteen men wading through the thick waters. Lieutenant Cross wished the rain would let up. Even for an hour, it would make things easier.

But then he shrugged. The rain was the war and you had to fight it.

Turning, he looked out across the field and yelled at one of his men to close up the rank. Not a man, really—a boy. The young soldier stood off by himself at the center of the field in knee-deep water, reaching down with both hands as if chasing some object just beneath the surface. The boy's shoulders were shaking. Jimmy Cross yelled again but the young soldier did not turn or look up. In his hooded poncho, everything caked with mud, the boy's face was impossible to make out. The filth seemed to erase identities, transforming the men into identical copies of a single soldier, which was exactly how Jimmy Cross had been trained to treat them, as interchangeable units of command. It was difficult sometimes, but he tried to avoid that sort of thinking. He had no military ambitions. He preferred to view his men not as units but as human beings. And Kiowa had been a splendid human being, the very best, intelligent and gentle and quiet-spoken. Very brave, too. And decent. The kid's father taught Sunday school in Oklahoma City, where Kiowa had been raised to believe in the promise of salvation under Jesus Christ, and this conviction had always been present in the boy's smile, in his posture toward the world, in the way he never went anywhere without an illustrated New Testament that his father had mailed to him as a birthday present back in January.

A crime, Jimmy Cross thought.

Looking out toward the river, he knew for a fact that he had made a mistake setting up here. The order had come from higher, true, but still he should've exercised some field discretion. He should've moved to higher ground for the night, should've radioed in false coordinates. There was nothing he could do now, but still it was a mistake and a hideous waste. He felt sick about it. Standing in the deep waters of the field, First Lieutenant Jimmy Cross began composing a letter in his head to the kid's father, not mentioning the shit field, just saying what a fine soldier Kiowa had been, what a fine human being, and how he was the kind of son that any father could be proud of forever.

The search went slowly. For a time the morning seemed to brighten, the sky going to a lighter shade of silver, but then the rains came back hard and steady. There was the feel of permanent twilight.

At the far left of the line, Azar and Norman Bowker and Mitchell Sanders waded along the edge of the field closest to the river. They were tall men, but at times the muck came to midthigh, other times to the crotch.

Azar kept shaking his head. He coughed and shook his head and said, "Man, talk about irony. I bet if Kiowa was here, I bet he'd just laugh. Eating shit—it's your classic irony."

"Fine," said Norman Bowker. "Now pipe down."

Azar sighed. "Wasted in the waste," he said. "A shit field. You got to admit, it's pure world-class irony."

The three men moved with slow, heavy steps. It was hard to keep balance. Their boots sank into the ooze, which produced a powerful downward suction, and with each step they would have to pull up hard to break the hold. The rain made quick dents in the water, like tiny mouths, and the stink was everywhere.

When they reached the river, they shifted a few meters to the north and began wading back up the field. Occasionally they used their weapons to test the bottom, but mostly they just searched with their feet.

"A classic case," Azar was saying. "Biting the dirt, so to speak, that tells the story."

"Enough," Bowker said.

"Like those old cowboy movies. One more redskin bites the dust."

"I'm serious, man. Zip it shut."

Azar smiled and said, "Classic."

The morning was cold and wet. They had not slept during the night, not even for a few moments, and all three of them were feeling the tension as they moved across the field toward the river. There was nothing they could do for Kiowa. Just find him and slide him aboard a chopper. Whenever a man died it was always the same, a desire to get it over with quickly, no fuss or ceremony, and what they wanted now was to head for a ville and get under a roof and forget what had happened during the night.

Halfway across the field Mitchell Sanders stopped. He stood for a moment with his eyes shut, feeling along the bottom with a foot, then he passed his weapon over to Norman Bowker and reached down into the muck. After a second he hauled up a filthy green rucksack.

The three men did not speak for a time. The pack was heavy with mud and water, dead-looking. Inside were a pair of moccasins and an illustrated New Testament.

"Well," Mitchell Sanders finally said, "the guy's around here somewhere."

"Better tell the LT."

"Screw him."

"Yeah, but—"

"Some lieutenant," Sanders said. "Camps us in a toilet. Man don't *know* shit."

"Nobody knew," Bowker said.

"Maybe so, maybe not. Ten billion places we could've set up last night, the man picks a latrine."

Norman Bowker stared down at the rucksack. It was made of dark green nylon with an aluminum frame, but now it had the curious look of flesh.

"It wasn't the LT's fault," Bowker said quietly.

"Whose then?"

"Nobody's. Nobody knew till afterward."

Mitchell Sanders made a sound in his throat. He hoisted up the rucksack, slipped into the harness, and pulled the straps tight. "All right, but this much for sure. The man knew it was raining. He knew about the river. One plus one. Add it up, you get exactly what happened."

Sanders glared at the river.

"Move it," he said. "Kiowa's waiting on us."

Slowly then, bending against the rain, Azar and Norman Bowker and Mitchell Sanders began wading again through the deep waters, their eyes down, circling out from where they had found the rucksack.

First Lieutenant Jimmy Cross stood fifty meters away. He had finished writing the letter in his head, explaining things to Kiowa's father, and now he folded his arms and watched his platoon crisscrossing the wide field. In a funny way, it reminded him of the municipal golf course in his hometown in New Jersey. A lost ball, he thought. Tired players searching through the rough, sweeping back and forth in long systematic patterns. He wished he were there right now. On the sixth hole. Looking out across the water hazard that fronted the small flat green, a seven iron in his hand, calculating wind and distance, wondering if he should reach instead for an eight. A tough decision, but all you could ever lose was a ball. You did not lose a player. And you never had to wade out into the hazard and spend the day searching through the slime.

Jimmy Cross did not want the responsibility of leading these men. He had never wanted it. In his sophomore year at Mount Sebastian College he had signed up for the Reserve Officer Training Corps without much thought. An automatic thing: because his friends had joined, and because it was worth a few credits, and because it seemed preferable to letting the draft take him. He was unprepared. Twenty-four years old and his heart wasn't in it. Military matters meant nothing to him. He did not care one way or the other about the war, and he had no desire to command, and even after all these months in the bush, all the days and nights, even then he did not know enough to keep his men out of a shit field.

What he should've done, he told himself, was follow his first impulse. In the late afternoon yesterday, when they reached the night coordinates, he should've taken one look and headed for higher ground. He should've known. No excuses. At one edge of the field was a small ville, and right away a couple of old mama-sans had trotted out to warn him. Number ten, they'd said. Evil ground. Not a good spot for good GIs. But it was a war, and he had his orders, so they'd set up a perimeter and crawled under their ponchos and tried to settle in for the night. The rain never stopped. By midnight the Song Tra Bong had overflowed its banks. The field turned to slop, everything soft and mushy. He remembered how the water kept rising, how a terrible stink began to bubble up out of the earth. It was a dead-fish smell, partly, but something else, too, and then later in the night Mitchell Sanders had crawled through the rain and grabbed him hard by the arm and asked what he was doing setting up in a shit field. The village toilet, Sanders said. He remembered the look on Sanders's face. The guy stared for a moment and then wiped his mouth and whispered, "Shit," and then crawled away into the dark.

A stupid mistake. That's all it was, a mistake, but it had killed Kiowa.

Lieutenant Jimmy Cross felt something tighten inside him. In the letter to Kiowa's father he would apologize point-blank. Just admit to the blunders.

He would place the blame where it belonged. Tactically, he'd say, it was indefensible ground from the start. Low and flat. No natural cover. And so late in the night, when they took mortar fire from across the river, all they could do was snake down under the slop and lie there and wait. The field just exploded. Rain and slop and shrapnel, it all mixed together, and the field seemed to boil. He would explain this to Kiowa's father. Carefully, not covering up his own guilt, he would tell how the mortar rounds made craters in the slush, spraying up great showers of filth, and how the craters then collapsed on themselves and filled up with mud and water, sucking things down, swallowing things, weapons and entrenching tools and belts of ammuntion, and how in this way his son Kiowa had been combined with the waste and the war.

My own fault, he would say.

Straightening up, First Lieutenant Jimmy Cross rubbed his eyes and tried to get his thoughts together. The rain fell in a cold, sad drizzle.

Off toward the river he again noticed the young soldier standing alone at the center of the field. The boy's shoulders were shaking. Maybe it was something in the posture of the soldier, or the way he seemed to be reaching for some invisible object beneath the surface, but for several moments Jimmy Cross stood very still, afraid to move, yet knowing he had to, and then he murmured to himself, "My fault," and he nodded and waded out across the field toward the boy.

The young soldier was trying hard not to cry.

He, too, blamed himself. Bent forward at the waist, groping with both hands, he seemed to be chasing some creature just beyond reach, something elusive, a fish or a frog. His lips were moving. Like Jimmy Cross, the boy was explaining things to an absent judge. It wasn't to defend himself. The boy recognized his own guilt and wanted only to lay out the full causes.

Wading sideways a few steps, he leaned down and felt along the soft bottom of the field.

He pictured Kiowa's face. They'd been close buddies, the tightest, and he remembered how last night they had huddled together under their ponchos, the rain cold and steady, the water rising to their knees, but how Kiowa had just laughed it off and said they should concentrate on better things. And so for a long while they'd talked about their families and hometowns. At one point, the boy remembered, he'd been showing Kiowa a picture of his girlfriend. He remembered switching on his flashlight. A stupid thing to do, but he did it anyway, and he remembered Kiowa leaning in for a look at the picture— "Hey, she's *cute,*" he'd said—and then the field exploded all around them.

Like murder, the boy thought. The flashlight made it happen. Dumb and dangerous. And as a result his friend Kiowa was dead.

That simple, he thought.

He wished there were some other way to look at it, but there wasn't. Very simple and very final. He remembered two mortar rounds hitting close by. Then a third, even closer, and off to his left he'd heard somebody scream. The voice was ragged and clotted up, but he knew instantly that it was Kiowa.

He remembered trying to crawl toward the screaming. No sense of direction, though, and the field seemed to suck him under, and everything was black and wet and swirling, and he couldn't get his bearings, and then another round hit nearby, and for a few moments all he could do was hold his breath and duck down beneath the water.

Later, when he came up again, there were no more screams. There was an arm and a wristwatch and part of a boot. There were bubbles where Kiowa's head should've been.

He remembered grabbing the boot. He remembered pulling hard, but how the field seemed to pull back, like a tug-of-war he couldn't win, and how finally he had to whisper his friend's name and let go and watch the boot slide away. Then for a long time there were things he could not remember. Various sounds, various smells. Later he'd found himself lying on a little rise, face-up, tasting the field in his mouth, listening to the rain and explosions and bubbling sounds. He was alone. He'd lost everything. He'd lost Kiowa and his weapon and his flashlight and his girlfriend's picture. He remembered this. He remembered wondering if he could lose himself.

Now, in the dull morning rain, the boy seemed frantic. He waded quickly from spot to spot, leaning down and plunging his hands into the water. He did not look up when Lieutenant Jimmy Cross approached.

"Right here," the boy was saying. "Got to be right here."

Jimmy Cross remembered the kid's face but not the name. That happened sometimes. He tried to treat his men as individuals but sometimes the names just escaped him.

He watched the young soldier shove his hands into the water. "Right *here,*" he kept saying. His movements seemed random and jerky.

Jimmy Cross waited a moment, then stepped closer. "Listen," he said quietly, "the guy could be anywhere."

The boy glanced up. "Who could?"

"Kiowa. You can't expect—"

"Kiowa's *dead.*"

"Well, yes."

The young soldier nodded. "So what about Billie?"

"Who?"

"My girl. What about her? This picture, it was the only one I had. Right here, I lost it."

Jimmy Cross shook his head. It bothered him that he could not come up with a name.

"Slow down," he said. "I don't—"

"Billie's *picture.* I had it all wrapped up, I had it in plastic, so it'll be okay if I can . . . Last night we were looking at it, me and Kiowa. Right here. I know for sure it's right here somewhere."

Jimmy Cross smiled at the boy. "You can ask her for another one. A better one."

"She won't *send* another one. She's not even my *girl* anymore, she won't . . . Man, I got to find it."

The boy yanked his arm free.

He shuffled sideways and stooped down again and dipped into the muck with both hands. His shoulders were shaking. Briefly, Lieutenant Cross wondered where the kid's weapon was, and his helmet, but it seemed better not to ask.

He felt some pity come on him. For a moment the day seemed to soften. So much hurt, he thought. He watched the young soldier wading through the water, bending down and then standing and then bending down again, as if something might finally be salvaged from all the waste.

Jimmy Cross silently wished the boy luck.

Then he closed his eyes and went back to working on the letter to Kiowa's father.

Across the field Azar and Norman Bowker and Mitchell Sanders were wading alongside a narrow dike at the edge of the field. It was near noon now.

Norman Bowker found Kiowa. He was under two feet of water. Nothing showed except the heel of a boot.

"That's him?" Azar said.

"Who else?"

"I don't know." Azar shook his head. "I don't know."

Norman Bowker touched the boot, covered his eyes for a moment, then stood up and looked at Azar.

"So where's the joke?" he said.

"No joke."

"Eating shit. Let's hear that one."

"Forget it."

Mitchell Sanders told them to knock it off. The three soldiers moved to the dike, put down their packs and weapons, then waded back to where the boot was showing. The body lay partly wedged under a layer of mud beneath the water. It was hard to get traction; with each movement the muck would grip their feet and hold tight. The rain had come back harder now. Mitchell Sanders reached down and found Kiowa's other boot, and they waited a moment, then Sanders sighed and said, "Okay," and they took hold of the two boots and pulled up hard. There was only a slight give. They tried again, but this time the body did not move at all. After the third try they stopped and looked down for a while. "One more time," Norman Bowker said. He counted to three and they leaned back and pulled.

"Stuck," said Mitchell Sanders.

"I see that. Christ."

They tried again, then called over Henry Dobbins and Rat Kiley, and all five of them put their arms and backs into it, but the body was jammed in tight.

Azar moved to the dike and sat holding his stomach. His face was pale.

The others stood in a circle, watching the water, then after a time somebody said, "We can't just *leave* him there," and the men nodded and got out their entrenching tools and began digging. It was hard, sloppy work. The mud seemed to flow back faster than they could dig, but Kiowa was their friend and they kept at it anyway.

Slowly, in little groups, the rest of the platoon drifted over to watch. Only Lieutenant Jimmy Cross and the young soldier were still searching the field.

"What we should do, I guess," Norman Bowker said, "is tell the LT."

Mitchell Sanders shook his head. "Just mess things up. Besides, the man looks happy out there, real content. Let him be."

After ten minutes they uncovered most of Kiowa's lower body. The corpse was angled steeply into the muck, upside down, like a diver who plunged headfirst off a high tower. The men stood quietly for a few seconds. There was a feeling of awe. Mitchell Sanders finally nodded and said, "Let's get it done," and they took hold of the legs and pulled up hard, then pulled again, and after a moment Kiowa came sliding to the surface. A piece of his shoulder was missing; the arms and chest and face were cut up with shrapnel. He was covered with bluish green mud. "Well," Henry Dobbins said, "it could be worse," and Dave Jensen said, "How, man? Tell me *how*." Carefully, trying not to look at the body, they carried Kiowa over to the dike and laid him down. They used towels to clean off the scum. Rat Kiley went through the kid's pockets, placed his personal effects in a plastic bag, taped the bag to Kiowa's wrist, then used the radio to call in a dustoff.

Moving away, the men found things to do with themselves, some smoking, some opening up cans of C rations, a few just standing in the rain.

For all of them it was a relief to have it finished. There was the promise now of finding a hootch somewhere, or an abandoned pagoda, where they could strip down and wring out their fatigues and maybe start a hot fire. They felt bad for Kiowa. But they also felt a kind of giddiness, a secret joy, because they were alive, and because even the rain was preferable to being sucked under a shit field, and because it was all a matter of luck and happenstance.

Azar sat down on the dike next to Norman Bowker.

"Listen," he said. "Those jumb jokes—I didn't mean anything."

"We all say things."

"Yeah, but when I saw the guy, it made me feel—I don't know—like he was listening."

"He wasn't."

"I guess not. But I felt sort of guilty almost, like if I'd kept my mouth shut none of it would've ever happened. Like it was my fault."

Norman Bowker looked out across the wet field.

"Nobody's fault," he said. "Everybody's."

* * *

Near the center of the field First Lieutenant Jimmy Cross squatted in the muck, almost entirely submerged. In his head he was revising the letter to Kiowa's father. Impersonal this time. An officer expressing an officer's condolences. No apologies were necessary, because in fact it was one of those freak things, and the war was full of freaks, and nothing could ever change it anyway. Which was the truth, he thought. The exact truth.

Lieutenant Cross went deeper into the muck, the dark water at his throat, and tried to tell himself it was the truth.

Beside him, a few steps off to the left, the young soldier was still searching for his girlfriend's picture. Still remembering how he had killed Kiowa.

The boy wanted to confess. He wanted to tell the lieutenant how in the middle of the night he had pulled out Billie's picture and passed it over to Kiowa and then switched on the flashlight, and how Kiowa had whispered, "Hey, she's *cute,*" and how for a second the flashlight had made Billie's face sparkle, and how right then the field had exploded all around them. The flashlight had done it. Like a target shining in the dark.

The boy looked up at the sky, then at Jimmy Cross.

"Sir?" he said.

The rain and mist moved across the field in broad, sweeping sheets of gray. Close by, there was thunder.

"Sir," the boy said, "I got to explain something."

But Lieutenant Jimmy Cross wasn't listening. Eyes closed, he let himself go deeper into the waste, just letting the field take him. He lay back and floated.

When a man died, there had to be blame. Jimmy Cross understood this. You could blame the war. You could blame the idiots who made the war. You could blame Kiowa for going to it. You could blame the rain. You could blame the river. You could blame the field, the mud, the climate. You could blame the enemy. You could blame the mortar rounds. You could blame people who were too lazy to read a newspaper, who were bored by the daily body counts, who switched channels at the mention of politics. You could blame whole nations. You could blame God. You could blame the munitions makers or Karl Marx or a trick of fate or an old man in Omaha who forgot to vote.

In the field, though, the causes were immediate. A moment of carelessness or bad judgment or plain stupidity carried consequences that lasted forever.

For a long while Jimmy Cross lay floating. In the clouds to the east there was the sound of a helicopter, but he did not take notice. With his eyes still closed, bobbing in the field, he let himself slip away. He was back home in New Jersey. A golden afternoon on the golf course, the fairways lush and green, and he was teeing it up on the first hole. It was a world without responsibility. When the war was over, he thought, maybe then he would write a letter to Kiowa's father. Or maybe not. Maybe he would just take a couple of practice swings and knock the ball down the middle and pick up his clubs and walk off into the afternoon.

1990

Norman Mailer b. 1923

Norman Kingsley Mailer was born in Long Branch, New Jersey, and raised in Brooklyn, New York. He entered Harvard at the age of sixteen. There he majored in aeronautical engineering but soon became fascinated by literature, especially the work of Steinbeck, Farrell, and Dos Passos. Active in Harvard literary groups, he won *Story* magazine's College Award in 1941.

In 1944, drafted into the U.S. Army, he served as a rifleman with the 112th Cavalry out of San Antonio, Texas, an alien milieu for an unprepossessing Jewish boy from Brooklyn. He served for eighteen months in the Philippines and Japan, from which experience grew his first novel, *The Naked and the Dead.* An enormous popular and critical success, this book made Mailer a celebrity at the age of 25 and set in motion a complex series of public responses.

Controversy has dogged Mailer through his personal and professional life. The father of nine children, he has been married six times and has been at the center of numerous political storms. His sometimes bizarre behavior during his youth and early middle age (fistfights, arrests, above all the non-fatal stabbing of his second wife, Adele Morales, in 1960) coupled with his involvement in political life (co-founding the *Village Voice* in 1956, running for Mayor of New York City in 1969, being arrested for civil disobedience during the 1967 March on the Pentagon) made him a convenient target for the media. Simultaneously his work and its critical reception proceeded through various stages.

The Armies of the Night (1968), for which Mailer won both the Pulitzer Prize for general non-fiction and the National Book Award for Arts and Letters, recounts his vision of the March on the Pentagon. This book is paradigmatic of various lines of development in his life and work. In this "non-fiction novel," subtitled *History as a Novel: The Novel as History,* Mailer's fictional voice, his political activism, and his flamboyant public image converge.

After *The Naked and the Dead,* a powerful but derivative naturalistic novel, Mailer developed an existential fictional voice, peaking in *An American Dream* (1965). This controversial novel treats allegorically the protagonist's murder of his wife, presenting a sophisticated and profoundly disturbing vision of the violence endemic in America.

Although Mailer has remained paradoxical and flamboyant, *The Armies of the Night* forced the literary establishment to take him seriously once again. In the thirty-plus years since this book, he has matured as an artist, producing a large body of important work and becoming a truly major figure in American letters. In 1979 he won his second Pulitzer Prize, for *The Executioner's Song,* the "true-life novel" of the murderer Gary Gilmore, which led to further criticism of his obsession with (some say glamorizing of) American violence. The year 1991 saw the publication of the massive *Harlot's Ghost,* steeped in Mailer's obsessive themes of sexuality, violence, and existential choice.

If his work has not ceased to engender intense reactions, the former *enfant terrible* has unquestionably mellowed personally and grown into the role of senior statesman of American letters. Happily married to his sixth wife, Norris Church, Mailer seems to have found tranquillity. As president of PEN, an international organization of writers, he led the fight for freedom of expression. And in every arena of American life, he has left his distinctive and indelible mark.

Barry H. Leeds
Central Connecticut State University

PRIMARY WORKS

The Naked and the Dead, 1948; *Barbary Shore,* 1951; *The Deer Park,* 1955; *The White Negro,* 1958; *Advertisements for Myself,* 1959; *An American Dream,* 1965; *Why Are We in Vietnam?,* 1967; *The Armies of the Night,* 1968; *Of a Fire on the Moon,* 1970; *The Prisoner of Sex,* 1971; *Marilyn,* 1973; *Some Honorable Men,* 1976; *Genius and Lust,* 1976; *The Executioner's Song,* 1979; *Of Women and Their Elegance,* 1980; *Ancient Evenings,* 1983; *Tough Guys Don't Dance,* 1984; *Harlot's Ghost,* 1991; *Oswald: An American Mystery,* 1995; *The Gospel According to the Son,* 1997; *The Time of Our Time,* 1998.

from The Armies of the Night

. . . "We are gathered here"—shades of Lincoln in hippieland—"to make a move on Saturday to invest the Pentagon and halt and slow down its workings, and this will be at once a symbolic act and a real act"—he was roaring—"for real heads may possibly get hurt, and soldiers will be there to hold us back, and some of us may be arrested"—how, wondered the wise voice at the rear of this roaring voice, could one ever leave Washington now without going to jail?—"some blood conceivably will be shed. If I were the man in the government responsible for controlling this March, I would not know what to do." Sonorously—"I would not wish to arrest too many or hurt anyone for fear the repercussions in the world would be too large for my bureaucrat's heart to bear—it's so full of shit." Roars and chills from the audience again. He was off into obscenity. It gave a heartiness like the blood of beef tea to his associations. There was no villainy in obscenity for him, just paradoxically, characteristically—his love for America: he had first come to love America when he served in the U.S. Army, not the America of course of the flag, the patriotic unendurable fix of the television programs and the newspapers, no, long before he was ever aware of the institutional oleo of the most suffocating American ideas he had come to love what editorial writers were fond of calling the democratic principle with its faith in the common man. He found that principle and that man in the Army, but what none of the editorial writers ever mentioned was that that noble common man was obscene as an old goat, and his obscenity was what saved him. The sanity of said common democratic man was in his humor, his humor was in his obscenity. And his philosophy as well—a reductive philosophy which looked to restore the hard edge of proportion to the overblown values overhanging each small military existence—viz: being forced to salute an overconscientious officer with your back stiffened into an exaggerated posture. "That Lieutenant is chicken-shit," would be the platoon verdict, and a blow had somehow been struck for democracy and the sanity of good temper. Mailer once heard a private end an argument about the merits of a general by saying, "his spit don't smell like ice cream either," only the private was not speaking of spit. Mailer thought enough of the line to put it into *The Naked and the Dead,* along with a good many other such lines the characters in his mind and his memory of the Army had begun to offer him. The common discovery of America was probably that Americans were the first people on earth to live for their humor; nothing was so important to Americans as humor. In Brooklyn, he had taken this for granted, at Harvard he had thought it was a by-product of being at Harvard, but in the Army he discovered that the humor was probably in the veins and the roots of the local history of every state and county in America—the truth of the way it really felt over the years passed on a river of obscenity from small-town storyteller to storyteller there down below the bankers and the books and the educators and the legislators—so Mailer never felt more like an American than when he was naturally obscene—all the gifts of the American language came out in the happy play of obscenity upon concept, which enabled one to go back to concept again. What was magnificent about the word shit is that it enabled you to use the word noble: a skinny Southern cracker with a beatific smile on his face saying in the dawn in a Filipino rice paddy, "Man, I just managed to take me a noble shit." Yeah, that was Mailer's America. If he was going to love something in the country, he would love that. So after years of keeping obscene language off to one corner of his work, as if to prove after *The Naked and the Dead* that he had many an arrow in his literary quiver, he had come back to obscenity again in the last year—he had kicked goodbye in his novel *Why Are We In Vietnam?* to the old literary corset of good taste, letting his sense of language play on obscenity as freely as it wished, so discovering that everything he knew about the American language (with its incommensurable resources) went flying in and out of the line of his prose with the happiest beating of wings—it was the first time his style seemed at once very American to him and very literary in the best way, at least as he saw the best way. But the reception of the book had been disappointing. Not because many of the reviews were bad (he had learned, despite all sudden discoveries of sorrow, to live with that as one lived with smog) no, what was disappointing was the crankiness across the country. Where fusty conservative old critics had once defended the obscenity in *The Naked and the Dead,* they, or their sons, now condemned it in the new book, and that *was* disappointing. The country was not growing up so much as getting a premature case of arthritis.

At any rate, he had come to the point where he liked to use a little obscenity in his public speaking. Once people got over the shock, they were sometimes able to discover that the humor it provided was not less powerful than the damage of the pain. Of course he did not do it often and tried not to do it unless he was in good voice—Mailer was under no illusion that public speaking was equal to candid conversation; an obscenity uttered in a voice too weak for its freight was obscene, since obscenity probably resides in the quick conversion of excitement to nausea—which is why Lyndon Johnson's speeches are called obscene by some. The excitement of listening to the American President alters abruptly into the nausea of wandering down the blind alleys of his voice.

This has been a considerable defense of the point, but then the point was at the center of his argument and it could be put thus: the American corporation executive, who was after all the foremost representative of Man in the world today, was perfectly capable of burning unseen women and children in the Vietnamese jungles, yet felt a large displeasure and fairly final disapproval at the generous use of obscenity in literature and in public. . . .

In a little more than a half hour, the students were done. Now began the faculty. They too came up one by one, but now there was no particular sense offered of an internal organization. Unlike the students, they had not debated these matters in open forum for months, organized, proselyted, or been overcome by argument, no, most of them had served as advisers to the students, had counseled them, and been picked up, many of them, and brought along by the rush of this moral stream much as a small piece of river bank might separate from the shore and go down the line of the flood. It must have been painful for these academics. They were older, certainly less suited for jail, aware more precisely of how and where their careers would be diverted or impeded, they had families many of them, they were liberal academics, technologues, they were being forced to abdicate from the machines they had chosen for their life. Their decision to turn in draft cards must have come for many in the middle of the night; for others it must have come even last night, or as they stood here debating with themselves. Many of them seemed to stand irresolutely near the steps for long periods, then move up at last. Rogoff, standing next to Mailer, hugging his thin chest in the October air, now cold, finally took out his card and, with a grin at Mailer, said, "I guess I'm going to turn this in. But you know the ridiculous part of it is that I'm 4-F."[1] So they came up one by one, not in solidarity, but as individuals, each breaking the shield or the fence or the mold or the home or even the construct of his own security. And as they did this, a deep gloom began to work on Mailer, because a deep modesty was on its way to him, he could feel himself becoming more and more of a modest man as he stood there in the cold with his hangover, and he hated this because modesty was an old family relative, he had been born to a modest family, had been a modest boy, a modest young man, and he hated that, he loved the pride and the arrogance and the confidence and the egocentricity he had acquired over the years, that was his force and his luxury and the iron in his greed, the richest sugar of his pleasure, the strength of his competitive force, he had lived long enough to know that the intimation one was being steeped in a new psychical condition (like this oncoming modest grace) was never to be disregarded, permanent new states could come into one on just so light a breeze. He stood in the cold watching the faculty men come up, yes always one by one, and felt his hangover which had come in part out of his imperfectly swallowed contempt for them the night before, and in part out of his fear, yes now he saw it, fear of the consequences of this weekend in Washington, for he had known from the beginning it could disrupt his life for a season or more and in some way the danger was there it could change him forever. He was forty-four years old, and it had taken him most of those forty-four years to begin to be able to enjoy his pleasures where he found them, rather than worry about his pleasures which eluded him—it was obviously no time to embark on ventures which would eventually give one more than a few years in jail. Yet, there was no escape. As if some final cherished rare innocence of childhood still preserved intact in him was brought finally to the surface and there expired, so he lost at that instant the last secret delight he retained in life as a game where finally you never got hurt if you played the game well enough. For years he had envisioned himself in some final cataclysm,[2] as an underground leader in the city, or a guerrilla with a gun in the hills, and had scorned the organizational aspects of revolution, the speeches, mimeograph machines, the hard dull forging of new parties and programs, the dull maneuvering

[1]Military term for individuals who are medically unfit for service.

[2]A violent upheaval.

to keep power, the intolerable obedience required before the over-all intellectual necessities of each objective period, and had scorned it, yes, had spit at it, and perhaps had been right, certainly had been right, such revolutions were the womb and cradle of technology land, no the only revolutionary truth was a gun in the hills, and that would not be his, he would be too old by then, and too incompetent, yes, too incompetent said the new modesty, and too showboat, too lacking in essential judgment—besides, he was too well-known! He would pay for the pleasures of his notoriety in the impossibility of disguise. No gun in the hills, no taste for organization, no, he was a figurehead, and therefore he was expendable, said the new modesty—not a future leader, but a future victim: *there* would be his real value. He could go to jail for protest, and spend some years if it came to it, possibly his life, for if the war went on, and America put its hot martial tongue across the Chinese border, well, jail was the probable perspective, detention camps, dissociation centers, liquidation alleys, that would be his portion, and it would come about the time he had learned how to live.

The depth of this gloom and this modesty came down on Mailer, and he watched the delegation take the bag into the Department of Justice with 994 cards contained inside, and listened to the speeches while they waited, and was eventually called up himself to make a speech, and made a modest one in a voice so used by the stentorian demonstrations of the night before that he was happy for the mike since otherwise he might have communicated in a whisper. He said a little of what he had thought while watching the others: that he had recognized on this afternoon that the time had come when Americans, many Americans, would have to face the possibility of going to jail for their ideas, and this was a prospect with no cheer because prisons were unattractive places where much of the best in oneself was slowly extinguished, but it could be there was no choice. The war in Vietnam was an obscene war, the worst war the nation had ever been in, and so its logic might compel sacrifice from those who were not so accustomed. And, out of hardly more than a sense of old habit and old anger, he scolded the press for their lies, and their misrepresentation, for their guilt in creating a psychology over the last twenty years in the average American which made wars like Vietnam possible; then he surrendered the mike and stepped down and the applause was pleasant.

. . . out from that direction came the clear bitter-sweet excitation of a military trumpet resounding in the near distance, one peal which seemed to go all the way back through a galaxy of bugles to the cries of the Civil War and the first trumpet note to blow the attack. The ghosts of old battles were wheeling like clouds over Washington today.

The trumpet sounded again. It was calling the troops. "Come here," it called from the steps of Lincoln Memorial over the two furlongs of the long reflecting pool, out to the swell of the hill at the base of Washington Monument, "come here, come here, come here. The rally is on!" And from the north and the east, from the direction of the White House and the Smithsonian and the Capitol, from Union Station and the Department of Justice the troops were coming in, the volunteers were answering the call. They came walking up in all sizes, a citizens' army not ranked yet by height, an army of both sexes in numbers almost equal, and of all ages, although most were young. Some were well-dressed, some were poor, many were conventional in appearance, as often were not. The hippies were there in great number, perambulating down the hill, many dressed like the legions of Sgt. Pepper's Band,[3] some were gotten up like Arab shieks, or in Park Avenue's doormen's greatcoats, others like Rogers and Clark of the West, Wyatt Earp, Kit Carson, Daniel Boone in buckskin, some had grown mustaches to look like *Have Gun, Will Travel*—Paladin's[4] surrogate was here!—and wild Indians with feathers, a hippie gotten up like Batman, another like Claude Rains in *The Invisible Man*—his face wrapped in a turban of bandages and he wore a black satin top hat. A host of these troops wore capes, beat-up khaki capes, slept on, used as blankets, towels, improvised duffel bags; or fine capes, orange linings, or luminous rose linings, the edges ragged, near a tatter, the threads ready to feather, but a musketeer's hat on their head. One hippie may have been dressed like Charles Chaplin; Buster Keaton and W.C. Fields[5] could have come to the ball; there were Martians and Moon-men and a knight unhorsed who stalked about in the weight of real armor. There were to be seen a hundred soldiers in Confederate gray, and maybe there were two or three hundred hippies in officer's coats of Union dark-blue. They had picked up their costumes where they could, in surplus stores, and Blow-your-mind shops, Digger free emporiums, and psychedelic caches of Hindu junk. There were soldiers in Foreign Legion uniforms, and tropical bush jackets, San Quentin and Chino, California striped shirt and pants, British copies of Eisenhower jackets, hippies dressed like Turkish shepherds and Roman senators, gurus, and samurai in dirty smocks. They were close to being assembled from all the intersections between history and the comic books, between legend and television, the Biblical archetypes and the movies. The sight of these troops, this army with a thousand costumes, fulfilled to the hilt our General's oldest idea of war which is that every man should dress as he pleases if he is going into battle, for that is his right, and variety never hurts the zest of the hardiest workers in every battalion (here today by thousands in plain hunting jackets, corduroys or dungarees, ready for assault!) if the sight of such masquerade lost its usual happy connotation of masked ladies and starving children outside the ball, it was not only because of the shabbiness of the costumes (up close half of them must have been used by hippies for everyday wear) but also because the aesthetic at last was in the politics—the dress ball was going into battle. Still, there were nightmares beneath the gaiety of these middle-class runaways, these Crusaders, going out to attack the hard core of technology land with less training than armies were once offered by a medieval assembly ground. The nightmare was in the echo of those trips which had fractured their sense of past and present. If nature was a veil whose tissue had been ripped by static, screams of jet motors, the highway grid of the suburbs, smog, defoliation, pollution of streams, overfertilization of earth, anti-fertilization of women, and the radiation of two decades of near blind atom busting, then perhaps the history of the past was another tissue, spiritual, no doubt, without physical embodiment, unless its embodiment was in the cuneiform hieroglyphics of the chromosome (so much like primitive writing!) but that tissue of past history, whether traceable in the flesh, or merely palpable in the collective underworld of the dream, was nonetheless being bombed by the use of

[3]Fictional band made famous by the British rock group, The Beatles.

[4]Various fictional and non-fictional American folk heroes.

[5]American comedians and early stars of film.

LSD as outrageously as the atoll of Eniwetok, Hiroshima, Nagasaki, and the scorched foliage of Vietnam. The history of the past was being exploded right into the present: perhaps there were now lacunae in the firmament of the past, holes where once had been the psychic reality of an era which was gone. Mailer was haunted by the nightmare that the evils of the present not only exploited the present, but consumed the past, and gave every promise of demolishing whole territories of the future. The same villains who, promiscuously, wantonly, heedlessly, had gorged on LSD and consumed God knows what essential marrows of history, wearing indeed the history of all eras on their back as trophies of this gluttony, were now going forth (conscience-struck?) to make war on those other villains, corporation-land villains, who were destroying the promise of the present in their self-righteousness and greed and secret lust (often unknown to themselves) for some sexo-technological variety of neo-fascism.[6]

Mailer's final allegiance, however, was with the villains who were hippies. They would never have looked to blow their minds and destroy some part of the past if the authority had not brainwashed the mood of the present until it smelled like deodorant. (To cover the odor of burning flesh in Vietnam?) So he continued to enjoy the play of costumes, but his pleasure was now edged with a hint of the sinister. Not inappropriate for battle. He and Lowell,[7] were still in the best of moods. The morning was so splendid—it spoke of a vitality in nature which no number of bombings in space nor innerspace might ever subdue; the rustle of costumes warming up for the war spoke of future redemptions as quickly as they reminded of hog-swillings from the past, and the thin air! wine of Civil War apples in the October air! edge of excitement and awe—how would this day end? No one could know. Incredible spectacle now gathering—tens of thousands traveling hundreds of miles to attend a symbolic battle. In the capital of technology land beat a primitive drum. New drum of the Left! And the Left had been until this year the secret unwitting accomplice of every increase in the power of the technicians, bureaucrats, and labor leaders who ran the governmental military-industrial complex of super-technology land. . . .

6: A Confrontation by the River

It was not much of a situation to study. The MPs stood in two widely spaced ranks. The first rank was ten yards behind the rope, and each MP in that row was close to twenty feet from the next man. The second rank, similarly spaced, was ten yards behind the first rank and perhaps thirty yards behind them a cluster appeared, every fifty yards or so, of two or three U.S. Marshals in white helmets and dark blue suits. They were out there waiting. Two moods confronted one another, two separate senses of a private silence.

It was not unlike being a boy about to jump from one garage roof to an adjoining garage roof. The one thing not to do was wait. Mailer looked at Macdonald[8] and

[6]A new or recent form of fascism, a type of right-wing dictatorship.

[7]Robert Lowell, major American poet (1917–1977).

[8]Dwight Macdonald, major American critic (1906–1982).

Lowell. "Let's go," he said. Not looking again at them, not pausing to gather or dissipate resolve, he made a point of stepping neatly and decisively over the low rope. Then he headed across the grass to the nearest MP he saw.

It was as if the air had changed, or light had altered; he felt immediately much more alive—yes, bathed in air—and yet disembodied from himself, as if indeed he were watching himself in a film where this action was taking place. He could feel the eyes of the people behind the rope watching him, could feel the intensity of their existence as spectators. And as he walked forward, he and the MP looked at one another with the naked stricken lucidity which comes when absolute strangers are for the moment absolutely locked together.

The MP lifted his club to his chest as if to bar all passage. To Mailer's great surprise—he had secretly expected the enemy to be calm and strong, why should they not? they had every power, all the guns—to his great surprise, the MP was trembling. He was a young Negro, part white, who looked to have come from some small town where perhaps there were not many other Negroes; he had at any rate no Harlem smoke, no devil swish, no black, no black power for him, just a simple boy in an Army suit with a look of horror in his eye, "Why, why did it have to happen to me?" was the message of the petrified marbles in his face.

"Go back," he said hoarsely to Mailer.

"If you don't arrest me, I'm going to the Pentagon."

"No. Go back."

The thought of a return—"since they won't arrest me, what can I do?"—over these same ten yards was not at all suitable.

As the MP spoke, the raised club quivered. He did not know if it quivered from the desire of the MP to strike him, or secret military wonder was he now possessed of a moral force which implanted terror in the arms of young soldiers? Some unfamiliar current, now gyroscopic, now a sluggish whirlpool, was evolving from that quiver of the club, and the MP seemed to turn slowly away from his position confronting the rope, and the novelist turned with him, each still facing the other until the axis of their shoulders was now perpendicular to the rope, and still they kept turning in this psychic field, not touching, the club quivering, and then Mailer was behind the MP, he was free of him, and he wheeled around and kept going in a half run to the next line of MPs and then on the push of a sudden instinct, sprinted suddenly around the nearest MP in the second line, much as if he were a back cutting around the nearest man in the secondary to break free—that was actually his precise thought—and had a passing perception of how simple it was to get past the MPs. They looked petrified. Striken faces as he went by. They did not know what to do. It was his dark pinstripe suit, his vest, the maroon and blue regimental tie, the part in his hair, the barrel chest, the early paunch—he must have looked like a banker himself, a banker, gone ape! And then he saw the Pentagon to his right across the field, not a hundred yards away, and a little to his left, the marshals, and he ran on a jog toward them, and came up, and they glared at him and shouted, "Go back."

He had a quick impression of hard-faced men with gray eyes burning some transparent fuel for flame, and said, "I won't go back. If you don't arrest me, I'm going on to the Pentagon," and knew he meant it, some absolute certainty had come to him, and then two of them leaped on him at once in the cold clammy murderous fury of all cops at the existential moment of making their bust—all cops who secretly expect to be struck at that instant for their sins—and a supervising force came to his voice, and he roared, to his own distant pleasure in new achievement and new authority—"Take your hands off me, can't you see? I'm not resisting arrest," and one then let go of him, and the other stopped trying to pry his arm into a lock, and contented himself with a hard hand under his armpit, and they set off walking across the field at a rabid intent quick rate, walking parallel to the wall of the Pentagon, fully visible on his right at last, and he was arrested, he had succeeded in that, and without a club on his head, the mountain air in his lungs as thin and fierce as smoke, yes, the livid air of tension on this livid side promised a few events of more interest than the routine wait to be free, yes he was more than a visitor, he was in the land of the enemy now, he would get to see their face. . . .

But now a tall U.S. Marshal who had the body and insane look of a very good rangy defensive end in professional football—that same hard high-muscled build, same coiled spring of wrath, same livid conviction that everything opposing the team must be wrecked, sod, turf, grass, uniforms, helmets, bodies, yes even bite the football if it will help—now leaped into the truck and jumped between them. "Shut up," he said, "or I'll wreck both of you." He had a long craggy face somewhere in the physiognomical land between Steve McQueen and Robert Mitchum, but he would never have made Hollywood, for his skin was pocked with the big boiling craters of a red lunar acne, and his eyes in Cinemascope would have blazed an audience off their seat for such gray-green flame could only have issued from a blowtorch. Under his white Marshal's helmet, he was one impressive piece of gathered wrath.

Speaking to the Marshal at this point would have been dangerous. The Marshal's emotions had obviously been marinating for a week in the very special bile waters American Patriotism reserves for its need. His feelings were now caustic as a whip—too gentle the simile!—he was in agonies of frustration because the honor of his profession kept him from battering every prisoner's head to a Communist pulp. Mailer looked him over covertly to see what he could try if the Marshal went to work on him. All reports: negative. He would not stand a chance with this Marshal—there seemed no place to hit him where he'd be vulnerable; stone larynx, leather testicles, ice cubes for eyes. And he had his Marshal's club in his hand as well. Brother! Bring back the Nazi!

Whether the Marshal had been once in the Marine Corps, or in Vietnam, or if half his family were now in Vietnam, or if he just hated the sheer New York presumption of that slovenly, drug-ridden weak contaminating America-hating army of termites outside this fortress' walls, he was certainly any upstanding demonstrator's nightmare. Because he was full of American rectitude and was fearless, and savage, savage as the exhaust left in the wake of a motorcycle club, gasoline and cheap perfume were one end of his spectrum, yeah, this Marshal loved action, but he was also in that no man's land between the old frontier and the new ranch home—as they, yes *they*—the enemies of the Marshal—tried to pass bills to limit the purchase of hunting rifles, so did *they* try to kill America, inch by inch, all the forces of evil, disorder, mess and chaos in the world, and *cowardice!* and city ways, and slick shit, and despoliation of national resources, all the subtle invisible creeping paralyses of Communism which were changing America from a land where blood was red to a land where water was foul—yes in this Marshal's mind—no lesser explanation could suffice for the Knight of God light in the flame of his eye—the evil was without,

America was threatened by a foreign disease and the Marshal was threatened to the core of his sanity by any one of the first fifty of Mailer's ideas which would insist that the evil was within, that the best in America was being destroyed by what in itself seemed next best, yes American heroism corrupted by American know-how—no wonder murder stood out in his face as he looked at the novelist—for the Marshal to lose his sanity was no passing psychiatric affair: think rather of a rifleman on a tower in Texas and a score of his dead on the street.[9] . . .

It may be obvious by now that a history of the March on the Pentagon which is not unfair will never be written, any more than a history which could prove dependable in details!

As it grew dark there was the air of carnival as well. The last few thousand Marchers to arrive from Lincoln Memorial did not even bother to go to the North Parking Area, but turned directly to the Mall and were cheered by the isolated detachments who saw them from a ledge of the wall at the plaza. Somewhere, somebody lit his draft card, and as it began to burn he held it high. The light of the burning card traveled through the crowd until it found another draft card someone else was ready to burn and this was lit, and then another in the distance. In the gathering dark it looked like a dusting of fireflies over the great shrub of the Mall.

By now, however, the way was open again to the North Parking. The chartered buses were getting ready to leave. That portion of this revolution which was Revolution on Excursion Ticket was now obliged to leave. Where once there had been thirty thousand people in the Mall, there were now suddenly twenty thousand people, ten thousand people, less. As the busses ground through the interlockings of their gears and pulled out into a mournful wheezing acceleration along the road, so did other thousands on the Mall look at one another and decide it was probably time to catch a cab or take the long walk back to Washington—they were in fact hungry for a meal. So the Mall began to empty, and the demonstrators on the steps must have drawn a little closer. The mass assault was over.

A few thousand, however, were left, and they were the best. The civil disobedience might be far from done. On the Mall, since the oncoming night was cold, bonfires were lit. On the stairs, a peace pipe was passed. It was filled with hashish. Soon the demonstrators were breaking out marijuana, handing it back and forth, offering it even to the soldiers here and there. The Army after all had been smoking marijuana since Korea, and in Vietnam—by all reports—were gorging on it. The smell of the drug, sweet as the sweetest leaves of burning tea, floated down to the Mall where its sharp bite of sugar and smoldering grass pinched the nose, relaxed the neck. Soon most of the young on the Mall were smoking as well. Can this be one of the moments when the Secretary of Defense looks out from his window in the Pentagon at the crowd on the Mall and studies their fires below? They cannot be unreminiscent of other campfires in Washington and Virginia little more than a century ago.[10]

. . . this passage through the night was a rite of passage, and these disenchanted heirs of the Old Left, this rabble of American Vietcong, and hippies, and pacifists, and whoever else was left were afloat on a voyage whose first note had been struck

[9] A reference to Charles Whitman, who shot numerous pedestrians from atop a Texas clock tower on August 1, 1966.

[10] An allusion to the Civil War.

with the first sound of the trumpet Mailer had heard crossing Washington Monument in the morning. "Come here, come here, come here," the trumpet had said, and now eighteen hours later, in the false dawn, the echo of far greater rites of passage in American history, the light reflected from the radiance of greater more heroic hours may have come nonetheless to shine along the inner space and the caverns of the freaks, some hint of a glorious future may have hung in the air, some refrain from all the great American rites of passage when men and women manacled themselves to a lost and painful principle and survived a day, a night, a week, a month, a year, a celebration of Thanksgiving—the country had been founded on a rite of passage. Very few had not emigrated here without the echo of that rite, even if it were no more (and no less!) than eight days in the stink, bustle, fear, and propinquity of steerage on an ocean crossing (or the eighty days of dying on a slave ship) each generation of Americans had forged their own rite, in the forest of the Allegheníes and the Adirondacks, at Valley Forge, at New Orleans in 1812, with Rogers and Clark or at Sutter's Mill, at Gettysburg, the Alamo, the Klondike, the Argonne, Normandy, Pusan,[11]—the engagement at the Pentagon was a pale rite of passage next to these, and yet it was probably a true one, for it came to the spoiled children of a dead de-animalized middle class who had chosen most freely, out of the incomprehensible mysteries of moral choice, to make an attack and then hold a testament before the most authoritative embodiment of the principle that America was right, America was might, America was the true religious war of Christ against the Communist. So it became a rite of passage for these tender drug-vitiated jargon-mired children, they endured through a night, a black dark night which began in joy, near foundered in terror, and dragged on through empty apathetic hours while glints of light came to each alone. Yet the rite of passage was invoked, the moral ladder was climbed, they were forever different in the morning than they had been before the night, which is the meaning of a rite of passage, one has voyaged through a channel of shipwreck and temptation, and so some of the vices carried from another nether world into life itself (on the day of one's birth) may have departed, or fled, or quit; some part of the man has been born again, and is better, just as some hardly so remarkable area of the soul may have been in some miniscule sweet fashion reborn on the crossing of the marchers over Arlington Memorial Bridge, for the worst of them and the most timid were moving nonetheless to a confrontation they could only fear, they were going to the land of the warmakers. Not so easy for the timid when all is said.

11: The Metaphor Delivered

Whole crisis of Christianity in America that the military heroes were on one side, and the unnamed saints on the other! Let the bugle blow. The death of America rides in on the smog. America—the land where a new kind of man was born from the idea that God was present in every man not only as compassion but as power, and so the country belonged to the people; for the will of the people—if the locks of their life could be given the art to turn—was then the will of God. Great and dangerous idea!

[11]References to various major American battles and explorations.

If the locks did not turn, then the will of the people was the will of the Devil. Who by now could know where was what? Liars controlled the locks.

Brood on that country who expresses our will. She is America, once a beauty of magnificence unparalleled, now a beauty with a leprous skin. She is heavy with child—no one knows if legitimate—and languishes in a dungeon whose walls are never seen. Now the first contractions of her fearsome labor begin—it will go on: no doctor exists to tell the hour. It is only known that false labor is not likely on her now, no, she will probably give birth, and to what?—the most fearsome totalitarianism the world has ever known? or can she, poor giant, tormented lovely girl, deliver a babe of a new world brave and tender, artful and wild? Rush to the locks. God writhes in his bonds. Rush to the locks. Deliver us from our curse. For we must end on the road to that mystery where courage, death, and the dream of love give promise of sleep.

1968

Robert Bly b. 1926

Few American poets have explored so many facets of the creative—and the human—experience as Robert Bly. After graduating from Harvard, he returned to the Minnesota of his childhood and became one of the leading midcentury poets. Along with James Wright and William Stafford, Bly was the pre-eminent poet of nature, simplicity, and the reality of human experience. In a line of descent from William Carlos Williams, with overtones of the exact language drawn from Wallace Stevens, these poets forced readers back to an encounter with the truly human that had sometimes been obscured in the highly formalist poetry of Richard Eberhart, Richard Wilbur, and even Robert Lowell. Despite his geographically remote location, Bly influenced what was happening in United States poetry through his editing of a series of respected (if idiosyncratic) little magazines—first *The Fifties,* then *The Sixties.* His reviews, signed "Crunk," were read avidly.

Like Williams before him, Bly assumed a posture of stability: his address didn't change, his keen appreciation for the poetry of others was a given, and he was open to friendships with people who might have been seen as his competitors—such as his relationship with James Wright. Also, like the best of the world's poets, Bly was immensely influential in bringing readers, as well as other poets, to appreciate the work of non-English writers. From early in his career through the present, Bly has translated, published, and proselytized about the writings of Vallejo, Neruda, Machado, Jimánez, Rilke, Ponge, Tranströmer, Lagerlöf, Kabir, and (since his translations in 1981) Maulana Jalal al-Din Rumi, a thirteenth-century Persian poet.

Bly's poetry became one of search. Not only was he poised to become a leading poet for ecological preservation—given his immersion in the beauties and violence of the natural world—but he was intent on finding the richest poetic traditions from which to draw. His skill with translating was enhanced by his willingness to work with native speakers, or scholars, of the languages of the poems: Bly's contributions to what the art of translation could become have yet to be appreciated. But what gave Bly's career its most public visibility was U.S. involvement in the Vietnam conflict. Two of his best-known poems, "Counting Small-Boned Bodies" (which stresses the macho superiority of U.S. physical size dominating the stature of the Vietnamese soldiers) and "The Teeth Mother Naked at Last" (which presents his Jungian understanding of the divided female principle—welcoming mother set against destructive female), were published as anti-war works. (With Denise Levertov, Muriel Rukeyser, and many other writers, Bly was an active proponent of Writers and Artists Against the Vietnam War.)

Bly's later publishing history continues to promote the psychological exploration of the human consciousness. Not only his poetry, but his series of popular books that began with *Iron John* in 1990, insists on the ways men (in this stridently gendered world) must come to terms with their conflicted—or, perhaps, richly ambivalent—psyches. As a spokesperson for the archetypal, the Jungian, and the mystical, Bly travels and speaks widely: he may well be America's most visible poet. Such visibility draws mixed responses, but at heart, Robert Bly continues to be the poet we welcomed so heartily at the time of the publication of his first collection, *Silence in the Snowy Fields.*

Linda Wagner-Martin
University of North Carolina–Chapel Hill

PRIMARY WORKS

Silence in the Snowy Fields, 1962; *The Light Around the Body,* 1967; *Jumping Out of Bed,* 1973; *Sleepers Joining Hands,* 1973; *For the Stomach: Selected Poems,* 1974; *The Morning Glory* (prose poems), 1975; *This Body Is Made of Camphor and Gopherwood,* 1977; *The Kabir Book,* "versions by Robert Bly," 1977; *This Tree Will Be Here for a Thousand Years,* 1979; *News of the Universe,* 1980; *Talking All Morning* (interviews), 1980; *The Man in the Black Coat Turns,* 1981; *Loving a Woman in Two Worlds,* 1985; *American Poetry: Wilderness and Domesticity* (criticism), 1990; *What Have I Ever Lost by Dying: Collected Prose Poems,* 1992; *Meditations on the Insatiable Soul: Poems,* 1994; *Morning Poems,* 1997; *Holes the Crickets Have Eaten in Blankets: A Sequence of Poems,* 1997; *Eating the Honey of Words: New and Selected Poems,* 1999. Popular prose: *Iron John: A Book About Men,* 1990; *The Sibling Society,* 1996; *The Maiden King: The Reunion of Masculine and Feminine,* 1998.

Counting Small-Boned Bodies

Let's count the bodies over again.

If we could only make the bodies smaller,
The size of skulls,
We could make a whole plain white with skulls in the moonlight!

If we could only make the bodies smaller,
Maybe we could get
A whole year's kill in front of us on a desk!

If we could only make the bodies smaller,
We could fit
A body into a finger-ring, for a keepsake forever.

1967

The Teeth Mother Naked at Last

I

Massive engines lift beautifully from the deck.
Wings appear over the trees, wings with eight hundred rivets.

Engines burning a thousand gallons of gasoline a minute sweep over
the huts with dirt floors.

The chickens feel the new fear deep in the pits of their beaks.
Buddha with Padma Sambhava.

Meanwhile, out on the China Sea,
immense gray bodies are floating,
born in Roanoke,
the ocean on both sides expanding, "buoyed on the dense marine."

Helicopters flutter overhead. The death-
bee is coming. Super Sabres
like knots of neurotic energy sweep
around and return.
This is Hamilton's triumph.
This is the advantage of a centralized bank.
B-52s come from Guam. All the teachers
die in flames. The hopes of Tolstoy fall asleep in the ant heap.
Do not ask for mercy.

Now the time comes to look into the past-tunnels,
the hours given and taken in school,
the scuffles in coatrooms,
foam leaps from his nostrils,
now we come to the scum you take from the mouths of the dead,
now we sit beside the dying, and hold their hands, there is hardly time
for good-bye,
the staff sergeant from North Carolina is dying—you hold his hand,
he knows the mansions of the dead are empty, he has an empty place
inside him, created one night when his parents came home drunk,
he uses half his skin to cover it,
as you try to protect a balloon from sharp objects . . .

Artillery shells explode. Napalm canisters roll end over end.
800 steel pellets fly through the vegetable walls.
The six-hour infant puts his fists instinctively to his eyes to keep out
the light.
But the room explodes,

the children explode.
Blood leaps on the vegetable walls.

Yes, I know, blood leaps on the walls—
Don't cry at that—
Do you cry at the wind pouring out of Canada?
Do you cry at the reeds shaken at the edge of the sloughs?
The Marine battalion enters.
This happens when the seasons change,
This happens when the leaves begin to drop from the trees too early
"Kill them: I don't want to see anything moving."
This happens when the ice begins to show its teeth in the ponds
This happens when the heavy layers of lake water press down on the fish's head, and send him deeper, where his tail swirls slowly, and his brain passes him pictures of heavy reeds, of vegetation fallen on vegetation. . . .
Hamilton saw all this in detail:

"Every banana tree slashed, every cooking utensil smashed, every mattress cut."

Now the Marine knives sweep around like sharp-edged jets; how beautifully they slash open the rice bags,
the mattresses . . .
ducks are killed with $150 shotguns.

Old women watch the soldiers as they move.

II

Excellent Roman knives slip along the ribs.

A stronger man starts to jerk up the strips of flesh.

"Let's hear it again, you believe in the Father, the Son, and the Holy Ghost?"

A long scream unrolls.

More.

"From the political point of view, democratic institutions are being built in Vietnam, wouldn't you agree?"

A green parrot shudders under the fingernails.
Blood jumps in the pocket.
The scream lashes like a tail.

"Let us not be deterred from our task by the voices of dissent. . . ."

The whines of the jets
pierce like a long needle.

As soon as the President finishes his press conference, black wings carry off the words,
bits of flesh still clinging to them.

* * *

The ministers lie, the professors lie, the television lies, the priests lie. . . .
These lies mean that the country wants to die.
Lie after lie starts out into the prairie grass,
like enormous caravans of Conestoga wagons. . . .

And a long desire for death flows out, guiding the enormous caravans from beneath,
stringing together the vague and foolish words.
It is a desire to eat death,
to gobble it down,
to rush on it like a cobra with mouth open

It's a desire to take death inside,
to feel it burning inside, pushing out velvety hairs,
like a clothes brush in the intestines—

This is the thrill that leads the President on to lie

* * *

Now the Chief Executive enters; the press conference begins:
First the President lies about the date the Appalachian Mountains rose.
Then he lies about the population of Chicago, then he lies about the weight of the adult eagle, then about the acreage of the Everglades

He lies about the number of fish taken every year in the Arctic, he has private information about which city *is* the capital of Wyoming, he lies about the birthplace of Attila the Hun.

He lies about the composition of the amniotic fluid, and he insists that Luther was never a German, and that only the Protestants sold indulgences,

That Pope Leo X *wanted* to reform the church, but the "liberal elements" prevented him,
that the Peasants' War was fomented by Italians from the North.

And the Attorney General lies about the time the sun sets.

* * *

These lies are only the longing we all feel to die.
It is the longing for someone to come and take you by the hand to where they all are sleeping:
where the Egyptian pharaohs are asleep, and your own mother,
and all those disappeared children, who used to go around with you in the rings at grade school. . . .

Do not be angry at the President—he is longing to take in his hand
the locks of death hair—
to meet his own children dead, or unborn. . . .
He is drifting sideways toward the dusty places

III

This is what it's like for a rich country to make war
this is what it's like to bomb huts (afterwards described as "structures")
this is what it's like to kill marginal farmers (afterwards described as "Communists")

this is what it's like to watch the altimeter needle going mad

Baron 25, this is 81. Are there any friendlies in the area? 81 from 25, negative on the friendlies. I'd like you to take out as many structures as possible located in those trees within 200 meters east and west of my smoke mark.

diving, the green earth swinging, cheeks hanging back, red pins blossoming ahead of us, 20-millimeter cannon fire, leveling off, rice fields shooting by like telephone poles, smoke rising, hut roofs loom up huge as landing fields, slugs going in, half the huts on fire, small figures running, palm trees burning, shooting past, up again; . . . blue sky . . . cloud mountains

This is what it's like to have a gross national product.

It's because the aluminum window shade business is doing so well in the United States that we roll fire over entire villages
It's because a hospital room in the average American city now costs $90 a day that we bomb hospitals in the North

It's because the milk trains coming into New Jersey hit the right switches every day that the best Vietnamese men are cut in two by American bullets that follow each other like freight cars

This is what it's like to send firebombs down from air-conditioned cockpits.

This is what it's like to be told to fire into a reed hut with an
automatic weapon.

It's because we have new packaging for smoked oysters that bomb
holes appear in the rice paddies

It is because we have so few women sobbing in back rooms,
because we have so few children's heads torn apart by high-velocity
bullets,
Because we have so few tears falling on our own hands
that the Super Sabre turns and screams down toward the earth.

It's because taxpayers move to the suburbs that we transfer
populations.
The Marines use cigarette lighters to light the thatched roofs of huts
because so many Americans own their own homes.

IV

I see a car rolling toward a rock wall.
The treads in the face begin to crack.
We all feel like tires being run down roads under heavy cars.

The teen-ager imagines herself floating through the Seven Spheres.
Oven doors are found
open.
Soot collects over the doorframe, has children, takes courses,
goes mad, and dies.

There is a black silo inside our bodies, revolving fast.
Bits of black paint are flaking off,
where the motorcycles roar, around and around,
rising higher on the silo walls,
the bodies bent toward the horizon,
driven by angry women dressed in black.

* * *

I know that books are tired of us.
I *know* they are chaining the Bible to chairs.
Books don't want to remain in the same room with us anymore.

New Testaments are escaping . . . dressed as women . . . they go off
after dark.
And Plato! Plato . . . Plato wants to go backwards. . . .
He wants to hurry back up the river of time, so he can end as some
blob of sea flesh rotting on an Australian beach.

V

Why are they dying? I have written this so many times.
They are dying because the President has opened a Bible again.
They are dying because gold deposits have been found among the
Shoshoni Indians.

They are dying because money follows intellect!
And intellect is like a fan opening in the wind—

The Marines think that unless they die the rivers will not move.
They are dying so that the mountain shadows will continue to fall east
in the afternoon,
so that the beetle can move along the ground near the fallen twigs.

VI

But if one of those children came near that we have set on fire,
came toward you like a gray barn, walking,
you would howl like a wind tunnel in a hurricane,
you would tear at your shirt with blue hands,
you would drive over your own child's wagon trying to back up,
the pupils of your eyes would go wild—

If a child came by burning, you would dance on a lawn,
trying to leap into the air, digging into your cheeks,
you would ram your head against the wall of your bedroom
like a bull penned too long in his moody pen—

If one of those children came toward me with both hands
in the air, fire rising along both elbows,
I would suddenly go back to my animal brain,
I would drop on all fours, screaming,
my vocal chords would turn blue, so would yours,
it would be two days before I could play with my own children again.

VII

I want to sleep awhile in the rays of the sun slanting over the snow.
Don't wake me.
Don't tell me how much grief there is in the leaf with its natural oils.
Don't tell me how many children have been born with stumpy hands
all those years we lived in St. Augustine's shadow.

Tell me about the dust that falls from the yellow daffodil shaken in
the restless winds.

Tell me about the particles of Babylonian thought that still pass
through the earthworm every day.
Don't tell me about "the frightening laborers who do not read books."

Now the whole nation starts to whirl,
the end of the Republic breaks off,
Europe comes to take revenge,
the mad beast covered with European hair rushes through the mesa
bushes in Mendocino County,
pigs rush toward the cliff,
the waters underneath part: in one ocean luminous globes float up
(in them hairy and ecstatic men—)
in the other, the teeth mother, naked at last.

Let us drive cars
up
the light beams
to the stars . . .

And return to earth crouched inside the drop of sweat
that falls
from the chin of the Protestant tied in the fire.

1970

Yusef Komunyakaa b. 1947

Born in Bogalusa, Louisiana, the oldest of five children, Komunyakaa is the son of a carpenter and of a mother who bought a set of encyclopedias for her children. When he was sixteen, he discovered James Baldwin's essays and decided to become a writer.

From 1965 to 1968, Komunyakaa served a tour of duty in Vietnam as an information specialist, editing a military newspaper called the *Southern Cross.* In Vietnam he won the Bronze Star. After military service, he enrolled at the University of Colorado (double major in English and sociology) and began writing poetry. Upon graduation in 1980, he studied further at both Colorado State University (where he received an M.A. in creative writing) and the University of California, Irvine (where he received an M.F.A.) and taught at various universities before moving to New Orleans. While teaching at the University of New Orleans, in 1985, he married Australian novelist Mandy Sayer. Only then, nearly twenty years after his Vietnam experiences, did Komunyakaa write his important war poems, published in 1988 as *Dien Cai Dau.*

The violence of war, the pain of identifying with the Vietnamese, and the anguish of returning to the States had seldom been so eloquently and hauntingly expressed. By 1994, when these poems were included in *Neon Vernacular: New and Selected Poems, 1977–1989.* Komunyakaa had won two creative writing fellowships from the National Endowment for the Arts and the San Francisco Poetry Center Award, and he had held the Lilly Professorship of Poetry at Indiana University. *Neon Vernacular* received the Pulitzer Prize for Poetry, as well as the Kingsley-Tufts Poetry Award from the Claremont Graduate School, and as a result his earlier eight collections of work have been re-evaluated.

In 1998 his poetry collection *Thieves of Paradise* was a finalist for the 1999 National Book Critics Circle Award, and that same year saw the publication of his recording, *Love Notes from the Madhouse.* In 2000, Radicloni Clytus edited a book of Komunyakaa's prose, *Blue Notes: Essays, Interviews, and Commentaries,* for the University of Michigan Press series. In an essay from that collection, "Control Is the Mainspring," the poet writes, "I learned that the body and the mind are indeed connected: good writing is physical and mental. I welcomed the knowledge of this because I am from a working-class people who believe that physical labor is sacred and spiritual." This combination of the realistic and the spiritual runs throughout Komunyakaa's poems, whether they are about his childhood, the father-son relationship, the spiritual journey each of us takes—alone, and in whatever circumstances life hands us—and the various conflicts of war. He has become an important poet for our times.

Linda Wagner-Martin
University of North Carolina–Chapel Hill

PRIMARY WORKS

Dedications and Other Darkhorses, 1977; *Lost in the Bonewheel Factory,* 1979; *Copacetic,* 1984; *I Apologize for the Eyes in My Head,* 1986; *Toys in the Field,* 1987; *Dien Cai Dau,* 1988; *February in Sydney,* 1989; *Magic City,* 1992; *Neon Vernacular,* 1994; *Thieves of Paradise,* 1998; *Blue Notes: Essays, Interviews, and Commentaries,* ed. Radicloni Clytus, 2000.

Tu Do Street[1]

Music divides the evening.
I close my eyes & can see
men drawing lines in the dust.
America pushes through the membrane
of mist & smoke, & I'm a small boy
again in Bogalusa.[2] *White Only*
signs & Hank Snow.[3] But tonight
I walk into a place where bar girls
fade like tropical birds. When
I order a beer, the mama-san
behind the counter acts as if she
can't understand, while her eyes
skirt each white face, as Hank Williams[4]
calls from the psychedelic jukebox.

[1]Tu Do Street: street packed with bars and brothels at the center of Saigon, capital of South Vietnam; American Army headquarters during the Vietnam War, 1956–1975.

[2]Bogalusa: the Louisiana town where the poet grew up.

[3]Hank Snow: country singer on Nashville's *Grand Ole Opry* program.

[4]Hank Williams: American composer, singer, guitarist; one of the most influential figures in country music.

We have played Judas where
only machine-gun fire brings us
together. Down the street
black GIs hold to their turf also.
An off-limits sign pulls me
deeper into alleys, as I look
for a softness behind these voices
wounded by their beauty & war.
Back in the bush at Dak To[5]
& Khe Sanh,[6] we fought
the brothers of these women
we now run to hold in our arms.
There's more than a nation
inside us, as black & white
soldiers touch the same lovers
minutes apart, tasting
each other's breath,
without knowing these rooms
run into each other like tunnels
leading to the underworld.

1988

Prisoners

Usually at the helipad
I see them stumble-dance
across the hot asphalt
with crokersacks over their heads,
moving toward the interrogation huts,
thin-framed as box kites
of sticks & black silk
anticipating a hard wind
that'll tug & snatch them
out into space. I think
some must be laughing
under their dust-colored hoods,
knowing rockets are aimed
at Chu Lai[1]—that the water's

[5]Dak To: site of one of the most violent battles of the war in November 1967; located in northwest South Vietnam.

[6]Khe Sanh: location of U.S. Marine base near the Laotian border; attacked by North Vietnamese Army on January 21, 1968, and kept under siege until April 7.

[1]Chu Lai: northern coastal town fifty miles south of Danang; in 1965, the site of a major U.S. amphibious operation.

evaporating & soon the nail
will make contact with metal.
How can anyone anywhere love
these half-broken figures
bent under the sky's brightness?
The weight they carry
is the soil we tread night & day.
Who can cry for them?
I've heard the old ones
are the hardest to break.
An arm twist, a combat boot
against the skull, a .45
jabbed into the mouth, nothing
works. When they start talking
with ancestors faint as camphor
smoke in pagodas, you know
you'll have to kill them
to get an answer.
Sunlight throws
scythes against the afternoon.
Everything's a heat mirage; a river
tugs at their slow feet.
I stand alone & amazed,
with a pill-happy door gunner
signaling for me to board the Cobra.[2]
I remember how one day
I almost bowed to such figures
walking toward me, under
a corporal's ironclad stare.
I can't say why.
From a half-mile away
trees huddle together,
& the prisoners look like
marionettes hooked to strings of light.

1988

Thanks

Thanks for the tree
between me & a sniper's bullet.
I don't know what made the grass

[2]Cobra: brand of U.S. helicopter.

sway seconds before the Viet Cong
raised his soundless rifle.
Some voice always followed,
telling me which foot
to put down first.
Thanks for deflecting the ricochet
against that anarchy of dusk.
I was back in San Francisco
wrapped up in a woman's wild colors,
causing some dark bird's love call
to be shattered by daylight
when my hands reached up
& pulled a branch away
from my face. Thanks
for the vague white flower
that pointed to the gleaming metal
reflecting how it is to be broken
like mist over the grass,
as we played some deadly
game for blind gods.
What made me spot the monarch
writhing on a single thread
tied to a farmer's gate,
holding the day together
like an unfingered guitar string,
is beyond me. Maybe the hills
grew weary & leaned a little in the heat.
Again, thanks for the dud
hand grenade tossed at my feet
outside Chu Lai. I'm still
falling through its silence.
I don't know why the intrepid
sun touched the bayonet,
but I know that something
stood among those lost trees
& moved only when I moved.

1988

Facing It

My black face fades,
hiding inside the black granite.
I said I wouldn't,
dammit: No tears.

I'm stone. I'm flesh.
My clouded reflection eyes me
like a bird of prey, the profile of night
slanted against morning. I turn
this way—the stone lets me go.
I turn that way—I'm inside
the Vietnam Veterans Memorial
again, depending on the light
to make a difference.
I go down the 58,022 names,
half-expecting to find
my own in letters like smoke.
I touch the name Andrew Johnson;
I see the booby trap's white flash.
Names shimmer on a woman's blouse
but when she walks away
the names stay on the wall.
Brushstrokes flash, a red bird's
wings cutting across my stare.
The sky. A plane in the sky.
A white vet's image floats
closer to me, then his pale eyes
look through mine. I'm a window.
He's lost his right arm
inside the stone. In the black mirror
a woman's trying to erase names:
No, she's brushing a boy's hair.

1988

Fog Galleon

Horse-headed clouds, flags
& pennants tied to black
Smokestacks in swamp mist.
From the quick green calm
Some nocturnal bird calls
Ship ahoy, ship ahoy!
I press against the taxicab
Window. I'm back here, interfaced
With a dead phosphorescence;
The whole town smells
Like the world's oldest anger.
Scabrous residue hunkers down under
Sulfur & dioxide, waiting

For sunrise, like cargo
On a phantom ship outside Gaul.
Cool glass against my cheek
Pulls me from the black schooner
On a timeless sea—everything
Dwarfed beneath the papermill
Lights blinking behind the cloudy
Commerce of wheels, of chemicals
That turn workers into pulp
When they fall into vats
Of steamy serenity.

1993

Carolyn Forché b. 1950

Carolyn Forché's spirited paternal grandmother, Anna, a Slovak immigrant, spoke "a funny English," in the poet's words, partly to display her resistance to American culture. Forché's life and poetry have responded to the challenge in Anna's declaration: "in your country / you have nothing" ("Endurance"). Anna nicknamed Carolyn *Piskata,* "Chatterbox," and passed on to her granddaughter an old homily: "Eat Bread and Salt and Speak the Truth" ("Burning the Tomato Worms"). Forché was born in Detroit; her father, Michael Sidlosky, labored as a tool and die maker ten and twelve hours a day, six and sometimes seven days a week. Her mother, Louise, bore seven children before attending college.

Forché was educated in Catholic schools and then graduated from Michigan State University. She has an M.F.A. from Bowling Green State University (1975) and an honorary doctorate from Russell Sage College (1985).

Her first book of poems, *Gathering the Tribes,* received the Yale Series of Younger Poets Award in 1975. These poems derived partly from Forché's alternately living among Pueblo Indians near Taos, New Mexico, and backpacking in the desert regions of Utah, on the Pacific Crest Trail, and in the Okanogan region of British Columbia. As its title suggests, this volume is characterized not by the self-absorption of much twentieth-century American verse but by a desire for community—incorporating, among other voices, those of the "silenced" Pueblo Indians and her own Slovak ancestors.

From January 1978 to March 1980, Forché made a number of trips to El Salvador; during this period she documented human rights violations for Amnesty International, verifying information and evaluating the organization's reports on El Salvador. While living in El Salvador, she also wrote seven of the 22 poems included in *The Country Between Us,* her second collection and the Academy of American Poets' 1981 Lamont Poetry Selection. In 1980 Forché worked closely with Monsignor Oscar Romero, the beloved Archbishop of San Salvador who was assassinated that year by a right-wing death squad; after several attempts had been made on Forché's life, Monsignor Romero asked that she return to the United States to "tell the American people what is happening." She has said that her El Salvador experience transformed her life and work: it "prevent[s] me from ever viewing myself or my country again through precisely the same fog of unwitting connivance" ("El Salvador: An Aide Memoire").

Forché continues to travel and to act on her beliefs. In 1983 she accompanied a congressional fact-finding delegation to Israel; in 1984 she contributed to the program *All Things Considered* on National Public Radio from Beirut, Lebanon; from December 1985 to March 1986 she lived in South Africa. She has held numerous teaching positions at American universities.

Denise Levertov's praise for *The Country Between Us* suggests what Forché accomplishes: a seamless merging of the "personal and political, lyrical and engaged." Her important anthology, *Against Forgetting: Twentieth Century Poetry of Witness,* and her 1994 collection of poems, *The Angel of History,* a consummate book of fragmented images and characters who voice the largely untold narratives of modern wars, brought her the Swedish Edita and Ira Morris Award for Peace and Culture in 1998.

Constance Coiner
State University of New York at Binghamton

Linda Wagner-Martin
University of North Carolina–Chapel Hill

PRIMARY WORKS

Women in American Labor History, 1825–1935: An Annotated Bibliography, with Mary Jane Soltow, 1972; *Gathering the Tribes,* 1976; "El Salvador: An Aide Memoire," *American Poetry Review* (July/August 1981): 3–7; *The Country Between Us,* 1982; *Flowers from the Volcano,* translations of the poetry of Claribel Alegría, 1982; *El Salvador: Work of Thirty Photographers,* 1983; "A Lesson in Commitment," *Tri-Quarterly,* (Winter 1986): 30–38; *Against Forgetting: Twentieth-Century Poetry of Witness,* ed., 1991; *The Angel of History,* 1994; "Nocturne" and "Blue Hour," *Salmagundi* (Spring/Summer 2000), 68–85.

from The Country Between Us

The Colonel

WHAT YOU HAVE HEARD IS TRUE. I was in his house. His wife carried a tray of coffee and sugar. His daughter filed her nails, his son went out for the night. There were daily papers, pet dogs, a pistol on the cushion beside him. The moon swung bare on its black cord over the house. On the television was a cop show. It was in English. Broken bottles were embedded in the walls around the house to scoop the kneecaps from a man's legs or cut his hands to lace. On the windows there were gratings like those in liquor stores. We had dinner, rack of lamb, good wine, a gold bell was on the table for calling the maid. The maid brought green mangoes, salt, a type of bread. I was asked how I enjoyed the country. There was a brief commercial in Spanish. His wife took everything away. There was some talk then of how difficult it had become to govern. The parrot said hello on the terrace. The colonel told it to shut up, and pushed himself from the table. My friend said to me with his eyes: say nothing. The colonel returned with a sack used to bring groceries home. He spilled many human ears on the table. They were like dried peach halves. There is no other way to say this. He took one of them in his hands, shook it in our faces, dropped it into a water glass. It came alive there. I am tired of fooling around he said. As for the rights of anyone, tell your people they can go fuck themselves. He swept the ears to the floor with his arm and held the last of his wine in the air. Something for your poetry, no? he said. Some of the ears on the floor caught this scrap of his voice. Some of the ears on the floor were pressed to the ground.

May 1978

1982

Because One Is Always Forgotten

In Memoriam, José Rudolfo Viera[1] *1939–1981: El Salvador*

When Viera was buried we knew it had come to an end,
his coffin rocking into the ground like a boat or a cradle.

I could take my heart, he said, and give it to a *campesino*[2]
and he would cut it up and give it back:

you can't eat heart in those four dark
chambers where a man can be kept years.

A boy soldier in the bone-hot sun works his knife
to peel the face from a dead man

and hang it from the branch of a tree
flowering with such faces.

The heart is the toughest part of the body.
Tenderness is in the hands.

1982

[1]Labor activist and Director of El Salvador's Institute of Agrarian Reform from October 1979 until his death in January 1981. Along with two U.S. agrarian reform specialists, Michael Hammer and Mark Pearlman, Viera was gunned down in the Sheraton Hotel coffee shop in San Salvador. As Forché reports in *El Salvador: Work of Thirty Photographers,* "Shortly before his murder, Viera appeared on television demanding an investigation of a $40 million dollar fraud by the former military administrators of [El Salvador's] Institute of Agrarian Transformation." U.S. newspapers reported Hammer and Pearlman's deaths but failed to report Viera's.

[2]Peasant, farmer, one who works the land.

As Children Together

Under the sloped snow
pinned all winter with Christmas
lights, we waited for your father
to whittle his soap cakes
away, finish the whisky,
your mother to carry her coffee
from room to room closing lights
cubed in the snow at our feet.
Holding each other's
coat sleeves we slid down
the roads in our tight
black dresses, past
crystal swamps and the death
face of each dark house,
over the golden ice
of tobacco spit, the blue
quiet of ponds, with town
glowing behind the blind
white hills and a scant
snow ticking in the stars.
You hummed *blanche comme
la neige*[1] and spoke of Montreal
where a *quebeçoise*[2] could sing,
take any man's face
to her unfastened blouse
and wake to wine
on the bedside table.
I always believed this,
Victoria, that there might
be a way to get out.

You were ashamed of that house,
its round tins of surplus flour,
chipped beef and white beans,
relief checks and winter trips
that always ended in deer
tied stiff to the car rack,
the accordion breath of your uncles
down from the north, and what
you called the stupidity
of the Michigan French.

[1]French for "white as the snow," this is the title of a traditional song of Quebec.

[2]A female native of Quebec.

Your mirror grew ringed
with photos of servicemen
who had taken your breasts
in their hands, the buttons
of your blouses in their teeth,
who had given you the silk
tassles of their graduation,
jackets embroidered with dragons
from the Far East. You kept
the corks that had fired
from bottles over their beds,
their letters with each city
blackened, envelopes of hair
from their shaved heads.
I am going to have it, you said.
Flowers wrapped in paper from carts
in Montreal, a plane lifting out
of Detroit, a satin bed, a table
cluttered with bottles of scent.

So standing in a platter of ice
outside a Catholic dance hall
you took their collars
in your fine chilled hands
and lied your age to adulthood.

I did not then have breasts of my own,
nor any letters from bootcamp
and when one of the men who had
gathered around you took my mouth
to his own there was nothing
other than the dance hall music
rising to the arms of iced trees.

I don't know where you are now, Victoria.
They say you have children, a trailer
in the snow near our town,
and the husband you found as a girl
returned from the Far East broken
cursing holy blood at the table
where nightly a pile of white shavings
is paid from the edge of his knife.

If you read this poem, write to me.
I have been to Paris since we parted.

1982

from The Recording Angel

I

Memory insists she stood there, able to go neither forward nor back, and in that
Unanimous night, time slowed, in light pulsing through ash, light of which the coat was made
Light of their brick houses
In matter's choreography of light, time slowed, then reversed until memory
Held her, able to go neither forward nor back
They were alone where once hundreds of thousands lived

Doves, or rather their wings, heard above the roof and the linens floating
Above a comic wedding in which corpses exchange vows. A grand funeral celebration
Everyone has died at once
Walking home always, always on this same blue road, cold through the black-and-white trees
Unless the film were reversed, she wouldn't reach the house
As she doesn't in her memory, or in her dream
Often she hears him calling out, half her name, his own, behind her in
a room until she turns
Standing forever, where often she hears him calling out

He is there, hidden in the blue winter fields and the burnt acreage of summer
As if, in reflecting the ruins, the river were filming what their city had
been
And *had it not been for this* lines up behind *if it weren't for that*
Until the past is something of a regiment
Yet looking back down the row of marching faces one sees one face
Before the shelling, these balconies were for geraniums and children
The slate roofs for morning

Market flowers in a jar, a string of tied garlic, and a voice moving off as if fearing itself
Under the leprous trees a white siren of light searches
Under the leprous trees a white siren of sun

II

A row of cabanas with white towels near restorative waters where once it was possible to be cured

A town of vacant summer houses
Mists burning the slightest lapse of sea
The child has gone to the window filled with desire, a glass light passing through its hand
There are tide tables by which the sea had been predictable, as were the heavens
As sickness chose from among us we grew fewer
There were jetty lights where there was no jetty
What the rain forests had been became our difficult breath

At the moment when the snow geese lifted, thousands at once after days of crying in the wetlands
At once they lifted in a single ascent, acres of wind in their wingbones
Wetlands of morning light in their lift moving as one over the continent
As a white front, one in their radiance, in their crying, a cloud of one desire

The child plays with its dead telephone. The father blows a kiss. The child laughs
The fire of his few years is carried toward the child on a cake
The child can't help itself. Would each day be like this?

And the geese, rising and falling in the rain on a surf of black hands
Sheets of rain and geese invisible or gone

Someone was supposed to have come
Waves turning black with the beach weed called dead men's hands
The sea strikes a bottle against a rock

III

The photographs were found at first by mistake in the drawer. After that I went to them often
She was standing on her toes in a silk *yukata,* her arms raised
Wearing a girl's white socks and near her feet a vase of calla lilies:
Otherwise she wore nothing
And in this one, her long hair is gathered into a white towel
Or tied back not to interfere
She had been wounded by so many men, abused by them
From behind in a silk *yukata,* then like this
One morning they were gone and I searched his belongings for them like a madwoman
In every direction, melted railyards, felled telegraph poles
For two months to find some trace of her
Footsteps on the floor above. More birds

It might have been less painful had it not been for the photographs
And beyond the paper walls, the red maple
Shirt in the wind of what the past meant
The fresh claw of a swastika on Rue Boulard
A man walking until he can no longer be seen
Don't say I was there. Always say I was never there.

1994

Elegy

The page opens to snow on a field: boot-holed month, black hour
the bottle in your coat half vodka half winter light.
To what and to whom does one say *yes*?
If God were the uncertain, would you cling to him?

Beneath a tattoo of stars the gate opens, so silent so like a tomb.
This is the city you most loved, an empty stairwell
where the next rain lifts invisibly from the Seine.

With solitude, your coat open, you walk
steadily as if the railings were there and your hands weren't passing
through them.

"When things were ready, they poured on fuel and touched off the
fire.
They waited for a high wind. It was very fine, that powdered bone.
It was put into sacks, and when there were enough we went to a
bridge on the Narew River."

And even less explicit phrases survived:
"To make charcoal.
For laundry irons."
And so we revolt against silence with a bit of speaking.
The page is a charred field where the dead would have written
We went on. And it was like living through something again one could
not live through again.

The soul behind you no longer inhabits your life: the unlit house
with its breathless windows and a chimney of ruined wings
where wind becomes an aria, your name, voices from a field,
And you, smoke, dissonance, a psalm, a stairwell.

1994

Tomás Rivera 1935–1984

The son of Mexican citizens who migrated to Texas in the 1920s, Tomás Rivera was born in Crystal City, Texas, in the agricultural region called the "Winter Garden." Rivera's parents worked as farm laborers in the 1930s and '40s and throughout Rivera's childhood were a part of the migrant stream that took Mexican workers from south Texas into Oklahoma and Missouri and then into the vegetable fields of Michigan and Minnesota.

Rivera's working-class background provided the basis for his writing. He too worked as a migrant farm laborer through the 1950s, even during his junior college years in Texas. On graduation from Southwest Texas State University with a degree in English, Rivera faced the realities of life in the Southwest. Unable to find work as an English teacher because he was Mexican American, he returned to Southwest Texas State to earn a master's degree in English and administration. He then received a doctorate in Spanish literature at the University of Oklahoma in 1969. After a few years of teaching, Rivera became vice president for administration at the University of Texas at San Antonio and, later, executive vice president at the University of Texas at El Paso. At the time of his death, he was chancellor of the University of California, Riverside.

. . . y no se lo tragó la tierra/ And the Earth Did Not Devour Him (1971) is a milestone in Mexican American literary history, set explicitly within the social and political contexts of the agricultural laborer's life in the years after World War II. Winner in 1970 of the first Quinto Sol Prize for literature, the most prestigious literary award in the early years of Chicano literature, Rivera's novel, from which the present selections are drawn, became a primary element of the new Mexican American literary history.

In the original South Texas Spanish, Rivera's prose is tight and lean, the vocabulary and syntax rigorously controlled and set within the world of the Chicano migrant farmworker. Like Faulkner's *As I Lay Dying,* Rivera's narrative is not expository. In documenting the life of the farmworker and trying to keep its significant place in contemporary American history alive, *Tierra* offers a complex narrative of subjective impressions purposely disjointed from simple chronology. "The Lost Year" is the first half of the frame story that brackets the twelve sections of Rivera's novel. The following selections, including the titular chapter, ". . . And the Earth Did Not Devour Him," and the penultimate chapter, "When We Arrive," depict crucial moments of dawning self-consciousness and collective solidarity. The links between the chapters follow a stream-of-consciousness thread, bereft of traditional narrative causality, relating the seasonal events in an allegorical year of the life of the anonymous migrant farmworker child.

In a 1980 interview, Rivera situated his work squarely within the Mexican American's struggle for social and political justice: "In . . . *Tierra* . . . I wrote about [the life of] the migrant worker in [the] ten year period [between 1945 and 1955]. . . . I began to see that my role . . . would be to document that period of time, but giving it some kind of spiritual strength or spiritual history" (Bruce-Novoa, *Chicano Authors: Inquiry by Interview,* 1980:148). Written during the period 1967–1968, at the height of the politicization of the Chicano labor struggles and the takeover of political power in Crystal City by Mexican Americans of the radical La Raza Unida party, Rivera's stories have a sense of political urgency. They also present the anguish of spiritual alienation and the reality of economic and social injustice. Rivera's narrator, born into a world of absence and loss, seeks to discover his identity and to inscribe his name and that of his community in the text of history. The characters of Rivera's stories are not the pragmatic subjects who populate the myth of American individualism, nor are they romanticized symbols of the worker engaged in a worldwide struggle. Rather, his characters are rooted in the reality of south Texas social and economic history, lived out and embodied in the form of the community of *la raza* (the people).

Ramón Saldívar
Stanford University

PRIMARY WORK

. . . y no se lo tragó la tierra/And the Earth Did Not Devour Him, 1971.

from . . . y no se lo tragó la tierra/And the Earth Did Not Devour Him

The Lost Year

That year was lost to him. At times he tried to remember and, just about when he thought everything was clearing up some, he would be at a loss for words. It almost always began with a dream in which he would suddenly awaken and then realize that he was really asleep. Then he wouldn't know whether what he was thinking had happened or not.

It always began when he would hear someone calling him by his name but when he turned his head to see who was calling, he would make a complete turn, and there he would end up—in the same place. This was why he never could discover who was calling him nor why. And then he even forgot the name he had been called.

One time he stopped at mid-turn and fear suddenly set in. He realized that he had called himself. And thus the lost year began.

He tried to figure out when that time he had come to call "year" had started. He became aware that he was always thinking and thinking, and from this there was no way out. Then he started thinking about how he never thought, and this was when his mind would go blank and he would fall asleep. But before falling asleep he saw and heard many things . . .

And the Earth Did Not Devour Him

The first time he felt hate and anger was when he saw his mother crying for his uncle and his aunt. They both had caught tuberculosis and had been sent to different sanitariums. So, between the brothers and sisters, they had distributed the children among themselves and had taken care of them as best they could. Then the aunt died, and soon thereafter they brought the uncle back from the sanitarium, but he was already spitting blood. That was when he saw his mother crying every little while. He became angry because he was unable to do anything against anyone. Today he felt the same. Only today it was for his father.

"You all should've come home right away, m'ijo. Couldn't you see that your

Daddy was sick? You should have known that he was sunstruck. Why didn't you come home?"

"I don't know. Us being so soaked with sweat, we didn't feel so hot, but I guess that when you're sunstruck it's different. But I did tell him to sit down under the tree that's at the edge of the rows, but he didn't want to. And that was when he started throwing up. Then we saw he couldn't hoe anymore and we dragged him and put him under a tree. He didn't put up a fuss at that point. He just let us take him. He didn't even say a word."

"Poor viejo, my poor viejo. Last night he hardly slept. Didn't you hear him outside the house. He squirmed in bed all night with cramps. God willing, he'll get well. I've been giving him cool lemonade all day, but his eyes still look glassy. If I'd gone to the fields yesterday, I tell you, he wouldn't have gotten sick. My poor viejo, he's going to have cramps all over his body for three days and three nights at the least. Now, you all take care of yourselves. Don't overwork yourselves so much. Don't pay any mind to that boss if he tries to rush you. Just don't do it. He thinks its so easy since he's not the one who's out there, stooped."

He became even angrier when he heard his father moan outside the chicken coop. He wouldn't stay inside because he said it made him feel very nervous. Outside where he could feel the fresh air was where he got some relief. And also when the cramps came he could roll over on the grass. Then he thought about whether his father might die from the sunstroke. At times he heard his father start to pray and ask for God's help. At first he had faith that he would get well soon but by the next day he felt the anger growing inside of him. And all the more when he heard his mother and his father clamoring for God's mercy. That night, well past midnight, he had been awakened by his father's groans. His mother got up and removed the scapularies from around his neck and washed them. Then she lit some candles. But nothing happened. It was like his aunt and uncle all over again.

"What's to be gained from doing all that, Mother? Don't tell me you think it helped my aunt and uncle any. How come we're like this, like we're buried alive? Either the germs eat us alive or the sun burns us up. Always some kind of sickness. And every day we work and work. For what? Poor Dad, always working so hard. I think he was born working. Like he says, barely five years old and already helping his father plant corn. All the time feeding the earth and the sun, only to one day, just like that, get knocked down by the sun. And there you are, helpless. And them, begging for God's help . . . why, God doesn't care about us . . . No, better not say it, what if Dad gets worse. Poor Dad, I guess that at least gives him some hope."

His mother noticed how furious he was, and that morning she told him to calm down, that everything was in God's hands and that with God's help his father was going to get well.

"Oh, Mother, do you really believe that? I am certain that God has no concern for us. Now you tell me, is Dad evil or mean-hearted? You tell me if he has ever done any harm to anyone."

"Of course not."

"So there you have it. You see? And my aunt and uncle? You explain. And the poor kids, now orphans, never having known their parents. Why did God have to take them away? I tell you, God could care less about the poor. Tell me, why must we live here like this? What have we done to deserve this? You're so good and yet you have to suffer so much."

"Oh, please, m'ijo, don't talk that way. Don't speak against the will of God. Don't talk that way, please, m'ijo. You scare me. It's as if already the blood of Satan runs through your veins."

"Well, maybe. That way at least I could get rid of this anger. I'm so tired of thinking about it. Why? Why you? Why Dad? Why my uncle? Why my aunt? Why their kids? Tell me, Mother, why? Why us, buried in the earth like animals with no hope for anything? You know the only hope we have is coming out here every year. And like you yourself say, only death brings rest. I think that's the way my aunt and uncle felt and that's how Dad must feel too."

"That's how it is m'ijo. Only death brings us rest."

"But why us?"

"Well, they say that . . ."

"Don't say it. I know what you're going to tell me—that the poor go to heaven."

That day started out cloudy and he could feel the morning coolness brushing his eyelashes as he and his brothers and sisters began the day's labor. Their mother had to stay home to care for her husband. Thus, he felt responsible for hurrying on his brothers and sisters. During the morning, at least for the first few hours, they endured the heat but by ten-thirty the sun had suddenly cleared the skies and pressed down against the world. They began working more slowly because of the weakness, dizziness and suffocation they felt when they worked too fast. Then they had to wipe the sweat from their eyes every little while because their vision would get blurred.

"If you start blacking out, stop working, you hear me? Or go a little slower. When we reach the edge we'll rest a bit to get our strength back. It's gonna be hot today. If only it'd stay just a bit cloudy like this morning, then nobody would complain. But no, once the sun bears down like this not even one little cloud dares to appear out of fear. And the worst of it is we'll finish up here by two and then we have to go over to that other field that's nothing but hills. It's okay at the top of the hill but down in the lower part of the slopes it gets to be real suffocating. There's no breeze there. Hardly any air goes through. Remember?"

"Yeah."

"That's where the hottest part of the day will catch us. Just drink plenty of water every little while. It don't matter if the boss gets mad. Just don't get sick. And if you can't go on, tell me right away, all right? We'll go home. Y'all saw what happened to Dad when he pushed himself too hard. The sun has no mercy, it can eat you alive."

Just as they had anticipated, they had moved on to the other field by early afternoon. By three o'clock they were all soaking with sweat. Not one part of their clothing was dry. Every little while they would stop. At times they could barely breathe, then they would black out and they would become fearful of getting sunstruck, but they kept on working.

"How do y'all feel?"

"Man, it's so hot! But we've got to keep on. 'Til six, at least. Except this water doesn't cut our thirst any. Sure wish I had a bottle of cool water, real cool, fresh from the well, or a coke, ice-cold."

* * *

"Are you crazy? That'd sure make you sunsick right now. Just don't work so fast. Let's see if we can make it until six. What do you think?"

At four o'clock the youngest became ill. He was only nine years old, but since he was paid the same as a grown up he tried to keep up with the rest. He began vomiting. He sat down, then he laid down. Terrified, the other children ran to where he lay and looked at him. It appeared that he had fainted and when they opened his eyelids they saw his eyes were rolled back. The next youngest child started crying but right away he told him to stop and help him carry his brother home. It seemed he was having cramps all over his little body. He lifted him and carried him by himself, and he began asking himself again, *why?*

"Why Dad and then my little brother? He's only nine years old. Why? He has to work like a mule buried in the earth. Dad, Mom, and my little brother here, what are they guilty of?"

Each step that he took towards the house resounded with the question, *why?* About halfway to the house he began to get furious. Then he started crying out of rage. His little brothers and sisters did not know what to do, and they, too, started crying, but out of fear. Then he started cursing. And without even realizing it, he said what he had been wanting to say for a long time. He cursed God. Upon doing this he felt that fear instilled in him by the years and by his parents. For a second he saw the earth opening up to devour him. Then he felt his footsteps against the earth, compact, more solid than ever. Then his anger swelled up again, and he vented it by cursing God. He looked at his brother, he no longer appeared as sick. He didn't know whether his brothers and sisters had understood the enormity of his curse.

That night he did not fall asleep until very late. He felt at peace as never before. He felt as though he had become detached from everything. He no longer worried about his father nor his brother. All that he awaited was the new day, the freshness of the morning. By daybreak his father was doing better. He was on his way to recovery. And his little brother, too; the cramps had almost completely subsided. Frequently he felt a sense of surprise upon recalling what he had done the previous afternoon. He thought of telling his mother, but he decided to keep it secret. All he told her was the earth did not devour anyone, nor did the sun.

He left for work and encountered a very cool morning. There were clouds in the sky and for the first time he felt capable of doing and undoing anything that he pleased. He looked down at the earth and kicked it hard and said.

"Not yet, you can't swallow me up yet. Someday, yes. But I'll never know it."

When We Arrive

At about four o'clock in the morning the truck broke down. All night they stood hypnotized by the high-pitched whir of the tires turning against the pavement. When the truck stopped they awakened. The silence alone told them something was wrong. All along the way the truck had been overheating and then when they stopped and checked the motor they saw that it had practically burned up. It just wouldn't go anymore. They would have to wait there until daybreak and then ask for a lift to the next town. Inside the trailer the people awakened and then struck up several conversations. Then, in the darkness, their eyes had gradually begun to close and all became so silent that all that could be heard was the chirping of the crickets. Some were sleeping, others were thinking.

"Good thing the truck stopped here. My stomach's been hurting a lot for some time but I would've had to wake up a lot of people to get to the window and ask them to stop. But you still can't hardly see anything. Well, I'm getting off, see if I can find a field or a ditch. Must've been that chile I ate, it was so hot but I hated to let it go to waste. I hope my vieja is doing all right in there, carrying the baby and all."

"This driver that we have this year is a good one. He keeps on going. He doesn't stop for anything. Just gases up and let's go. We've been on the road over twenty-four hours. We should be close to Des Moines. Sure wish I could sit down for just a little while at least. I'd get out and lie down on the side of the road but there's no telling if there's snakes or some other kind of animal. Just before I fell asleep on my feet it felt like my knees were going to buckle. But, I guess your body gets used to it right away 'cause it doesn't seem so hard anymore. But the kids must feel real tired standing like this all the way and with nothing to hold on to. Us grownups can at least hold on to this center bar that supports the canvas. And to think we're not as crowded as other times. I think there must be forty of us at the most. I remember that one time I traveled with that bunch of wetbacks, there were more than sixty of us. We couldn't even smoke."

"What a stupid woman! How could she be so dumb as to throw that diaper out the front of the truck. It came sliding along the canvas and good thing I had my glasses on or else I would've gotten my eyes full of shit too! What a stupid woman! How could she do that? She should've known that crap would be blown towards all of us standing up back here. Why the hell couldn't she just wait until we got to a gas station and dump the shit there!"

"That Negrito's eyes just about popped out when I ordered those fifty-four hamburgers. At two o'clock in the morning . . . And since I walked into the restaurant alone and I'm sure he didn't see the truck pull up loaded with people. His eyes just popped wide open . . . 'at two o'clock in the morning, hamburgers? Fifty-four of them? Man, you must eat one hell of a lot.' It's that the people hadn't eaten and the driver asked for just one of us to get out and order for everyone. That Negrito was astounded. He couldn't believe what I ordered, that I wanted fifty-four hamburgers. At two o'clock in the morning you can eat that many hamburgers very easily, especially when you're starving."

"This is the last fuckin' year I come out here. As soon as we get to the farm I'm getting the hell out. I'll go look for a job in Minneapolis. I'll be damned if I go back to Texas. Out here you can at least make a living at a decent job. I'll look for my uncle, see if he can find me a job at the hotel where he works as a bellboy. Who knows, maybe they'll give me a break there or at some other hotel. And then the gringas, that's just a matter of finding them."

"If things go well this year maybe we'll buy us a car so we won't have to travel this way, like cattle. The girls are pretty big now and I know they feel embarrassed. Sometimes

they have some good buys at the gas stations out there. I'll talk to my compadre, he knows some of the car salesmen. I'll get one I like, even if it's old. I'm tired of coming out here in a truck like this. My compadre drove back a good little car last year. If we do well with the onion crop, I'll buy me one that's at least half-way decent. I'll teach my boy how to drive and he can take it all the way to Texas. As long as he doesn't get lost like my nephew. They didn't stop to ask for directions and ended up in New Mexico instead of Texas. Or I'll get Mundo to drive it and I won't charge him for gas. I'll see if he wants to."

"With the money Mr. Thompson loaned me we have enough to buy food for at least two months. By then we should have the money from the beet crop. Just hope we don't get too much in debt. He loaned me two-hundred dollars but by the time you pay for the trip practically half of it is gone, and now that they've started charging me half-fare for the children . . . And then when we return, I have to pay him back double. Four-hundred dollars. That's too much interest, but what can you do? When you need it, you need it. Some people have told me to report him because that's way too much interest, but now he's even got the deed to the house. I'm just hoping that things go okay for us with the beet crop or else we'll be left to the wind, homeless. We have to save enough to pay him back the four-hundred. And then we'll see if we have something left. And these kids, they need to start going to school. I don't know. I hope it goes okay for us, if not I don't know how we're going to do it. I just pray to God that there's work."

"Fuckin' life, this goddamn fuckin life! This fuckin' sonofabitchin' life for being dumb! dumb! dumb! We're nothing but a bunch of goddam assholes! To hell with this goddamn motherfuckin' life! This is the last time I go through this, standing up all the way like a goddamn animal. As soon as we get there I'm headed for Minneapolis. Somehow I'll find me something to do where I don't have to work like a fuckin' mule. Fuckin' life! One of these days they'll fuckin' pay for this. Sonofabitch! For being such a goddam asshole!"

"Poor viejo. He must be real tired now, standing up the whole trip. I saw him nodding off a little while ago. And with no way to help him, what with these two in my arms. How I wish we were there already so we could lie down, even if it's on the hard floor. These children are nothing but trouble. I hope I'll be able to help him out in the fields, but I'm afraid that this year, what with these kids, I won't be able to do anything. I have to breastfeed them every little while and then they're still so little. If only they were just a bit older. I'm still going to try my best to help him out. At least along his row so he won't feel so overworked. Even if it's just for short whiles. My poor viejo . . . the children are still so little and already he wishes they could start school. I just hope I'll be able to help him. God willing, I'll be able to help him."

"What a great view of the stars from here! It looks like they're coming down and touching the tarp of the truck. It's almost like there aren't any people inside. There's hardly any traffic at this hour. Every now and then a trailer passes by. The silence of the morning twilight makes everything look like it's made of satin. And now, what do I wipe myself with? Why couldn't it always be early dawn like this? We're going to be here till midday for sure. By the time they find help in the town and then by the time they fix the motor . . . If only it could stay like early dawn, then nobody would com-

plain. I'm going to keep my eyes on the stars till the last one disappears. I wonder how many more people are watching the same star? And how many more might there be wondering how many are looking at the same star? It's so silent it looks like it's the stars the crickets are calling to."

"Goddam truck. It's nothing but trouble. When we get there everybody will just have to look out for themselves. All I'm doing is dropping them off with the growers and I'm getting the hell out. Besides, we don't have a contract. They'll find themselves somebody to take them back to Texas. Somebody's bound to come by and pick them up. You can't make money off beets anymore. My best bet is to head back to Texas just as soon as I drop these people off and then see how things go hauling watermelons. The melon season's almost here. All I need now is for there not to be anyone in this goddam town who can fix the truck. What the hell will I do then? So long as the cops don't come by and start hassling me about moving the truck from here. Boy, that town had to be the worst. We didn't even stop and still the cop caught up with us just to tell us that he didn't want us staying there. I guess he just wanted to show off in front of the town people. But we didn't even stop in their goddam town. When we get there, as soon as I drop them off, I'll turn back. Each one to fend for himself."

"When we get there I'm gonna see about getting a good bed for my vieja. Her kidneys are really bothering her a lot nowadays. Just hope we don't end up in a chicken coop like last year, with that cement floor. Even though you cover it with straw, once the cold season sets in, you just can't stand it. That was why my rheumatism got so bad, I'm sure of that."

"When we arrive, when we arrive, the real truth is that I'm tired of arriving. Arriving and leaving, it's the same thing because we no sooner arrive and . . . the real truth of the matter . . . I'm tired of arriving. I really should say when we don't arrive because that's the real truth. We never arrive."

"When we arrive, when we arrive . . ."

Little by little the crickets ceased their chirping. It seemed as though they were becoming tired and the dawn gradually affirmed the presence of objects, ever so carefully and very slowly, so that no one would take notice of what was happening. And the people were becoming people. They began getting out of the trailer and they huddled around and commenced to talk about what they would do when they arrived.

1971

Nicholasa Mohr b. 1938

Nicholasa Mohr is one of the most widely published Puerto Rican writers in the United States. Born to parents who came to New York City with the massive migration during World War II, Mohr grew up in the Bronx and studied art at the Students' Art League. She became a well-known graphic artist. Her art agent once asked her to write about growing up Puerto Rican and female in the Bronx, perhaps expecting sensationalist tales of crime, drugs, and gang activity. The stories Mohr wrote were quite different, and she had difficulties getting editors interested in publishing her work. *Nilda,* her first novel, appeared in 1974.

Somewhat autobiographical, *Nilda* relates life in the Bronx through the eyes of a ten-year-old girl who is a second-generation Puerto Rican. Mohr's protagonist uses her imagination and her fantasies to sustain herself through the hardships of her cultural and economic circumstances. As in this book, Mohr chooses to use a child's perspective for much of her writing. *Felita* and *Going Home* are, in fact, aimed at an adolescent audience. They relate Felita's experiences growing up in El Barrio and on a return trip to Puerto Rico, where she discovers differences between the values of her family and community in New York and the values of her relatives and of Puerto Rican society at large.

Rituals of Survival: A Woman's Portfolio is one of Mohr's most interesting publications. It consists of six vignettes about adult Puerto Rican women, each one representing various lifestyles, ages, and circumstances. Their common bond is their need to survive as individuals and as women free from restricting social and cultural expectations. In "A Thanksgiving Celebration," reproduced here, Amy, the young widowed mother of four children, resorts to her ingenuity and storytelling traditions inherited from her grandmother, in order to give meaning to Thanksgiving Day. All of Mohr's characters have to struggle with the sexual roles imposed on them by the Hispanic culture, with the *machista* attitudes of the men in their lives, and with the expectations set on them by their families.

Although Nicholasa Mohr has been called a "meat-and-potatoes" writer, because of her simple style and the emphasis she places on the humanity of her characters, who are likely to be everyday people with everyday conflicts to surmount, her storytelling is clear, direct, and powerful. That it found publication in the adolescent reader market does not detract from its importance as a voice of a people sometimes marginalized by economic and social stratifications. Mohr's work has been important because it has, often for the first time in English, presented and preserved family and household rituals from the Puerto Rican culture. It has also recorded the conflicts and ambivalences of a young Puerto Rican girl growing up in El Barrio of New York. As Mohr once said, "In American literature, I, as a Puerto Rican child, did not exist...and I as a Puerto Rican woman do not exist now." Her prose has established a precedent for young Puerto Rican women writers to continue to explore, question, and critique their lives in a bicultural world. Most importantly, Mohr has rescued readers' images of Barrio life from stereotypes of *puertorriqueños* as gang members or criminals. Her work has received several prizes, among them the 1974 Jane Addams Children's Book Award and *The New York Times* Outstanding Book of the Year. She was also a National Book Award finalist.

Frances R. Aparicio
University of Illinois at Chicago

PRIMARY WORKS

Nilda, 1974; *El Bronx Remembered,* 1976; *In Nueva York,* 1977; *Felita,* 1979; *Rituals of Survival: A Woman's Portfolio,* 1985; *Going Home,* 1986; *All for the Better: A Story of El Barrio,* 1993; *A Matter of Pride and Other Stories,* 1997.

from Rituals of Survival

A Thanksgiving Celebration (Amy)

Amy sat on her bed thinking. Gary napped soundly in his crib, which was placed right next to her bed. The sucking sound he made as he chewed on his thumb interrupted her thoughts from time to time. Amy glanced at Gary and smiled. He was her constant companion now; he shared her bedroom and was with her during those frightening moments when, late into the night and early morning, she wondered if she could face another day just like the one she had safely survived. Amy looked at the small alarm clock on the bedside table. In another hour or so it would be time to wake Gary and give him his milk, then she had just enough time to shop and pick up the others, after school.

She heard the plopping sound of water dropping into a full pail. Amy hurried into the bathroom, emptied the pail into the toilet, then replaced it so that the floor remained dry. Last week she had forgotten, and the water had overflowed out of the pail and onto the floor, leaking down into Mrs. Wynn's bathroom. Now, Mrs. Wynn was threatening to take her to small claims court, if the landlord refused to fix the damage done to her bathroom ceiling and wallpaper. All right, Amy shrugged, she would try calling the landlord once more. She was tired of the countless phone calls to plead with them to come and fix the leak in the roof.

"Yes, Mrs. Guzman, we got your message and we'll send somebody over. Yes, just as soon as we can . . . we got other tenants with bigger problems, you know. We are doing our best, we'll get somebody over; you gotta be patient . . ."

Time and again they had promised, but no one had ever showed up. And it was now more than four months that she had been forced to live like this. Damn, Amy walked into her kitchen, they never refuse the rent for that, there's somebody ready any time! Right now, this was the best she could do. The building was still under rent control and she had enough room. Where else could she go? No one in a better neighborhood would rent to her, not the way things were.

She stood by the window, leaning her side against the molding, and looked out. It was a crisp sunny autumn day, mild for the end of November. She remembered it was the eve of Thanksgiving and felt a tightness in her chest. Amy took a deep breath, deciding not to worry about that right now.

Rows and rows of endless streets scattered with abandoned buildings and small houses stretched out for miles. Some of the blocks were almost entirely leveled, except for clumps of partial structures charred and blackened by fire. From a distance they looked like organic masses pushing their way out of the earth. Garbage, debris, shattered glass, bricks and broken, discarded furniture covered the ground. Rusting carcasses of cars that had been stripped down to the shell shone and glistened a bright orange under the afternoon sun.

There were no people to be seen nor traffic, save for a group of children jumping on an old filthy mattress that had been ripped open. They were busy pulling the stuffing out of the mattress and tossing it about playfully. Nearby, several stray dogs searched the garbage for food. One of the boys picked up a brick, then threw it at the dogs, barely missing them. Reluctantly, the dogs moved on.

Amy sighed and swallowed, it was all getting closer and closer. It seemed as if only last month, when she had looked out of this very window, all of that was much further away; in fact, she recalled feeling somewhat removed and safe. Now the decay was creeping up to this area. The fire engine sirens screeching and screaming in the night reminded her that the devastation was constant, never stopping even for a night's rest. Amy was fearful of living on the top floor. Going down four flights to safety with the kids in case of a fire was another source of worry for her. She remembered how she had argued with Charlie when they had first moved in.

"All them steps to climb with Michele and Carlito, plus carrying the carriage for Carlito, is too much."

"Come on baby," Charlie had insisted "it's only temporary. The rent's cheaper and we can save something towards buying our own place. Come on . . ."

That was seven years ago. There were two more children now, Lisabeth and Gary; and she was still here, without Charlie.

"Soon it'll come right to this street and to my doorstep. God Almighty!" Amy whispered. It was like a plague: a disease for which there seemed to be no cure, no prevention. Gangs of youngsters occupied empty store fronts and basements; derelicts, drunk or wasted on drugs, positioned themselves on street corners and in empty doorways. Every day she saw more abandoned and burned-out sections.

As Amy continued to look out, a feeling that she had been in this same situation before, a long time ago, startled her. The feeling of deja vu so real to her, reminded Amy quite vividly of the dream she had had last night. In that dream, she had been standing in the center of a circle of little girls. She herself was very young and they were all singing a rhyme. In a soft whisper, Amy sang the rhyme: "London Bridge is falling down, falling down, falling down, London Bridge is falling down, my fair lady . . ." She stopped and saw herself once again in her dream, picking up her arms and chanting, "wave your arms and fly away, fly away, fly away . . ."

She stood in the middle of the circle waving her arms, first gently, then more forcefully, until she was flapping them. The other girls stared silently at her. Slowly, Amy had felt herself elevated above the circle, higher and higher until she could barely make out the human figures below. Waving her arms like the wings of a bird, she began to fly. A pleasant breeze pushed her gently, and she glided along, passing through soft white clouds into an intense silence. Then she saw it. Beneath her, huge areas were filled with crumbling buildings and large caverns; miles of destruction spread out in every direction. Amy had felt herself suspended in this silence for a moment and then she began to fall. She flapped her arms and legs furiously, trying to clutch at the air, hoping for a breeze, something to get her going again, but there was nothing. Quickly she fell, faster and faster, as the ground below her swirled and turned, coming closer and closer, revealing destroyed, burned buildings, rubble and a huge dark cavern. In a state of hysteria, Amy had fought against the loss of control and helplessness, as her body descended into the large black hole and had woken up with a start just before she hit bottom.

Amy stepped away from the window for a moment, almost out of breath as she recollected the fear she had felt in her dream. She walked over to the sink and poured herself a glass of water.

"That's it, Europe and the war," she said aloud. "In the movies, just like my dream."

Amy clearly remembered how she had sat as a very little girl in a local movie theatre with her mother and watched horrified at the scenes on the screen. Newsreels showed entire cities almost totally devastated. Exactly as it had been in her dream, she recalled seeing all the destruction caused by warfare. Names like "Munich, Nuremburg, Berlin" and "the German people" identified the areas. Most of the streets were empty, except for the occasional small groups of people who rummaged about, searching among the ruins and huge piles of debris, sharing the spoils with packs of rats who scavenged at a safe distance. Some people pulled wagons and baby carriages loaded with bundles and household goods. Others carried what they owned on their backs.

Amy remembered turning to her mother, asking, "What was going on? Mami, who did this? Why did they do it? Who are those people living there?"

"The enemy, that's who," her mother had whispered emphatically. "Bad people who started the war against our country and did terrible things to other people and to us. That's where your papa was for so long, fighting in the army. Don't you remember, Amy?"

"What kinds of things, Mami? Who were the other people they did bad things to?"

"Don't worry about them things. These people got what they deserved. Besides, they are getting help from us, now that we won the war. There's a plan to help them, even though they don't deserve no help from us."

Amy had persisted, "Are there any little kids there? Do they go to school? Do they live in them holes?"

"Shh . . . let me hear the rest of the news . . ." her mother had responded, annoyed. Amy had sat during the remainder of the double feature, wondering where those people lived and all about the kids there. And she continued to wonder and worry for several days, until one day she forgot all about it.

Amy sipped from the glass she held, then emptied most of the water back into the sink. She sat and looked around at her small kitchen. The ceiling was peeling and flakes of paint had fallen on the kitchen table. The entire apartment was in urgent need of a thorough plastering and paint job. She blinked and shook her head, and now? Who are we now? What have I done? Who is the enemy? Is there a war? Are we at war? Amy suppressed a loud chuckle.

"Nobody answered my questions then, and nobody's gonna answer them now," she spoke out loud.

Amy still wondered and groped for answers about Charlie. No one could tell her what had really happened . . . how he had felt and what he was thinking before he died. Almost two years had gone by, but she was still filled with an overwhelming sense of loneliness. That day was just like so many other days; they were together, planning about the kids, living from one crisis to the next, fighting, barely finding the time to make love without being exhausted; then late that night, it was all over. Charlie's late again, Amy had thought, and didn't even call me. She was angry when she heard the doorbell. He forgot the key again. Dammit, Charlie! You would forget your head if it weren't attached to you!

They had stood there before her; both had shown her their badges, but only one had spoken.

"Come in . . . sit down, won't you."

"You better sit down, miss." The stranger told her very calmly and soberly that Charlie was dead.

"On the Bruckner Boulevard Expressway . . . head on collision . . . dead on arrival . . . didn't suffer too long . . . nobody was with him, but we found his wallet."

Amy had protested and argued—No way! They were lying to her. But after a while she knew they brought the truth to her, and Charlie wasn't coming back.

Tomorrow would be the second Thanksgiving without him and one she could not celebrate. Celebrate with what? Amy stood and walked over and opened the refrigerator door. She had enough bread, a large pitcher of powdered milk which she had flavored with Hershey's cocoa and powdered sugar. There was plenty of peanut butter and some graham crackers she had kept fresh by sealing them in a plastic bag. For tonight she had enough chopped meat and macaroni. But tomorrow? What could she buy for tomorrow?

Amy shut the refrigerator door and reached over to the money tin set way back on one of the shelves. Carefully she took out the money and counted every cent. There was no way she could buy a turkey, even a small one. She still had to manage until the first; she needed every penny just to make it to the next check. Things were bad, worse than they had ever been. In the past, when things were rough, she had turned to Charlie and sharing had made it all easier. Now there was no one. She resealed the money tin and put it away.

Amy had thought of calling the lawyers once more. What good would that do? What can they do for me? Right now . . . today!

"These cases take time before we get to trial. We don't want to take the first settlement they offer. That wouldn't do you or the children any good. You have a good case, the other driver was at fault. He didn't have his license or the registration, and we have proof he was drinking. His father is a prominent judge who doesn't want that kind of publicity. I know . . . yes, things are rough, but just hold on a little longer. We don't want to accept a poor settlement and risk your future and the future of your children, do we?" Mr. Silverman of Silverman, Knapp and Ullman was handling the case personally. "By early Spring we should be making a date for trial . . . just hang in there a bit longer . . ." And so it went every time she called: the promise that in just a few more months she could hope for relief, some money, enough to live like people.

Survivor benefits had not been sufficient, and since they had not kept up premium payments on Charlie's G.I. insurance policy, she had no other income. Amy was given a little more assistance from the Aid to Dependent Children agency. Somehow she had managed so far.

The two food stores that extended her credit were still waiting for Amy to settle overdue accounts. In an emergency she could count on a few friends; they would lend her something, but not for this, not for Thanksgiving dinner.

She didn't want to go to Papo and Mary's again. She knew her brother meant well, and that she always had an open invitation. They're good people, but we are five more mouths to feed, plus they've been taking care of Papa all these years, ever since Mami died. Enough is enough. Amy shut her eyes. I want my own dinner this year, just for my family, for me and the kids.

If I had the money, I'd make a dinner tomorrow and invite Papa and Lou Ann from downstairs and her kids. She's been such a good friend to us. I'd get a gallon of cider and a bottle of wine . . . a large cake at the bakery by Alexander's, some dried fruits and nuts . . . even a holiday centerpiece for the table. Yes, it would be my dinner for us and my friends. I might even invite Jimmy. She hadn't seen Jimmy for a long time. Must be over six months . . . almost a year? He worked with Charlie at the plant. After Charlie's death, Jimmy had come by often, but Amy was not ready to see another man, not just then, so she discouraged him. From time to time, she thought of Jimmy and hoped he would visit her again.

Amy opened her eyes and a sinking feeling flowed through her, as she looked down at the chips of paint spread out on the kitchen table. Slowly, Amy brushed them with her hand, making a neat pile.

These past few months, she had seriously thought of going out to work. Before she had Michele, she had worked as a clerk-typist for a large insurance company, but that was almost ten years ago. She would have to brush up on her typing and math. Besides, she didn't know if she could earn enough to pay for a sitter. She couldn't leave the kids alone; Gary wasn't even three and Michele had just turned nine. Amy had applied for part-time work as a teacher's aide, but when she learned that her check from Aid to Dependent Children could be discontinued, she withdrew her application. Better to go on like this until the case comes to trial.

Amy choked back the tears. I can't let myself get like this. I just can't! Lately, she had begun to find comfort at the thought of never waking up again. What about my kids, then? I must do something. I have to. Tomorrow is going to be for us, just us, our day.

Her thoughts went back to her own childhood and the holiday dinners with her family. They had been poor, but there was always food. We used to have such good times. Amy remembered the many stories her grandmother used to tell them. She spoke about her own childhood on a farm in a rural area of Puerto Rico. Her grandmother's stories were about the animals, whom she claimed to know personally and very well. Amy laughed, recalling that most of the stories her grandmother related were too impossible to be true, such as a talking goat who saved the town from a flood, and the handsome mouse and beautiful lady beetle who fell in love, got married and had the biggest and fanciest wedding her grandmother had ever attended. Her grandmother was very old and had died before Amy was ten. Amy had loved her best, more than her own parents, and she still remembered the old woman quite clearly.

"Abuelita,[1] did them things really happen? How come them animals talked? Animals don't talk. Everybody knows that."

"Oh, but they do talk! And yes, everything I tell you is absolutely the truth. I believe it and you must believe it too." The old woman had been completely convincing. And for many years Amy had secretly believed that when her grandmother was a little girl, somewhere in a special place, animals talked, got married and were heroes.

"Abuelita," Amy whispered, "I wish you were here and could help me now." And then she thought of it. Something special for tomorrow. Quickly, Amy took out the money tin, counting out just the right amount of money she needed. She hesitated for a moment. What if it won't work and I can't convince them? Amy took a

[1]Abuelita, grandmother in Spanish. The diminutive form expresses warmth and affection.

deep breath. Never mind, I have to try, I must. She counted out a few more dollars. I'll work it all out somehow. Then she warmed up Gary's milk and got ready to leave.

Amy heard the voices of her children with delight. Shouts and squeals of laughter bounced into the kitchen as they played in the living room. Today they were all happy, anticipating their mother's promise of a celebration. Recently, her frequent moods of depression and short temper had frightened them. Privately, the children had blamed themselves for their mother's unhappiness, fighting with each other in helpless confusion. The children welcomed their mother's energy and good mood with relief.

Lately Amy had begun to realize that Michele and Carlito were constantly fighting. Carlito was always angry and would pick on Lisabeth. Poor Lisabeth, she's always so sad. I never have time for her and she's not really much older than Gary. This way of life has been affecting us all . . . but not today. Amy worked quickly. The apartment was filled with an air of festivity. She had set the kitchen table with a paper tablecloth, napkins and paper cups to match. These were decorated with turkeys, pilgrims, Indian corn and all the symbols of the Thanksgiving holiday. Amy had also bought a roll of orange paper streamers and decorated the kitchen chairs. Each setting had a name-card printed with bright magic markers. She had even managed to purchase a small holiday cake for dessert.

As she worked, Amy fought moments of anxiety and fear that threatened to weaken her sense of self-confidence. What if they laugh at me? Dear God in heaven, will my children think I'm a fool? But she had already spent the money, cooked and arranged everything; she had to go ahead. If I make it through this day, Amy nodded, I'll be all right.

She set the food platter in the center of the table and stepped back. A mound of bright yellow rice, flavored with a few spices and bits of fatback, was surrounded by a dozen hardboiled eggs that had been colored a bright orange. Smiling, Amy felt it was all truly beautiful; she was ready for the party.

"All right," Amy walked into the living room. "We're ready!" The children quickly followed her into the kitchen.

"Oooh, Mommy," Lisabeth shouted, "everything looks so pretty."

"Each place has got a card with your own name, so find the right seat." Amy took Gary and sat him down on his special chair next to her.

"Mommy," Michele spoke, "is this the whole surprise?"

"Yes," Amy answered, "just a minute, we also have some cider." Amy brought a small bottle of cider to the table.

"Easter eggs for Thanksgiving?" Carlito asked.

"Is that what you think they are, Carlito?" Amy asked. "Because they are not Easter eggs."

The children silently turned to one another, exchanging bewildered looks.

"What are they?" Lisabeth asked.

"Well," Amy said, "these are . . . turkey eggs, that's what. What's better than a turkey on Thanksgiving day? Her eggs, right?" Amy continued as all of them watched her. "You see, it's not easy to get these eggs. They're what you call a delicacy. But I found a special store that sells them, and they agreed to sell me a whole dozen for today."

"What store is that, Mommy?" Michele asked. "Is it around here?"

"No. They don't have stores like that here. It's special, way downtown."

"Did the turkey lay them eggs like that? That color?" Carlito asked.

"I want an egg," Gary said pointing to the platter.

"No, no . . . I just colored them that way for today, so everything goes together nicely, you know . . ." Amy began to serve the food. "All right, you can start eating."

"Well then, what's so special about these eggs? What's the difference between a turkey egg and an egg from a chicken?" Carlito asked.

"Ah, the taste, Carlito, just wait until you have some." Amy quickly finished serving everyone. "You see, these eggs are hard to find because they taste so fantastic." She chewed a mouthful of egg. "Ummm . . . fantastic, isn't it?" She nodded at them.

"Wonderful, Mommy," said Lisabeth. "It tastes real different."

"Oh yeah," Carlito said, "you can taste it right away. Really good."

Everyone was busy eating and commenting on how special the eggs tasted. As Amy watched her children, a sense of joy filled her, and she knew it had been a very long time since they had been together like this, close and loving.

"Mommy, did you ever eat these kinds of eggs before?" asked Michele.

"Yes, when I was little" she answered. "My grandmother got them for me. You know, I talked about my abuelita before. When I first ate them, I couldn't get over how good they tasted, just like you." Amy spoke with assurance, as they listened to every word she said. "Abuelita lived on a farm when she was very little. That's how come she knew all about turkey eggs. She used to tell me the most wonderful stories about her life there."

"Tell us!"

"Yeah, please Mommy, please tell us."

"All right, I'll tell you one about a hero who saved her whole village from a big flood. He was . . . a billy goat."

"Mommy," Michele interrupted, "a billy goat?"

"That's right, and you have to believe what I'm going to tell you. All of you have to believe me. Because everything I'm going to say is absolutely the truth. Promise? All right, then, in the olden days, when my grandmother was very little, far away in a small town in Puerto Rico . . ."

Amy continued, remembering stories that she had long since forgotten. The children listened, intrigued by what their mother had to say. She felt a calmness within. Yes, Amy told herself, today's for us, for me and the kids.

1985

Pat Mora b. 1942

A Chicana from El Paso, Texas, Pat Mora has written three books of poetry, a children's book, and a collection of essays. She earned both a B.A. and an M.A. in English from the University of Texas at El Paso while she raised three children who all currently attend universities. She lives and writes in Cincinnati, Ohio.

The poem "University Avenue" presents Chicanas, working-class women, who only recently gained front-door entry to universities, particularly in traditionally racist institutions in Texas that historically relegated Mexican women to roles as faceless workers pushing the broomcarts, mopping the corridors of academia, and cleaning the departments' bathrooms. Mora's poem recognizes that the "first of our people" to attend universities as students, administrators, and faculty, however, need not sacrifice Mexican indigenous traditions that inform Chicana/Chicano identity. Implicit in her use of Spanish words is the succor that bilingualism offers, the richness that biculturalism should evoke. The lessons whispered in Spanish are also the stories, the rich oral traditions that we carry with us to seminars, meetings, and lectures.

In "Unnatural Speech" Mora explores the dual voices of this bilingual, bicultural student. She speaks to the pain that the Chicana confronts as she makes the transition from Spanish speaker to English dominant speaker. Must the Spanish oral tradition of childhood nursery rhymes remain in the past, hidden in the memory of carefree childhood? Is there danger in learning and internalizing the "new rules" of the dominant language too well? The dilemma remains: will accommodating the dominant culture in the United States erase the songs of the other, the indigenous Mexican culture?

"Border Town: 1938" presents the other side of the bicultural dilemma. While we can now assert the importance of keeping both the Mexican and the American languages and traditions, Mora's poetry urges us to remember the specificities of Chicana history in the United States; that history has been one of separate and unequal educational systems. Evoking that memory of segregated "Mexican Schools" in Texas of the recent past, Mora does not allow the reader to romanticize that history. The problem she presents in these poems from her collection, *Borders,* is one where Mexican Americans on the border too often are forced to choose one side or the other, one language or the other, one culture or the other. Struggling to gain a foothold in the land of their ancestors, Chicanas must learn to gain power from a constantly shifting, ambiguous, multiple identity: as Mora asserts in a poem from *Chants,* "Legal Alien": "an American to Mexicans/a Mexican to Americans/a handy token/sliding back and forth/between the fringes of both worlds/by smiling/by masking the discomfort/of being prejudged/Bi-laterally."

Sonia Saldívar-Hull
University of California, Los Angeles

PRIMARY WORKS

Chants, 1984; *Borders,* 1986; *Communion,* 1991; *A Birthday Basket for Tia,* 1992; *Nepantla: Essays from the Land in the Middle,* 1993.

Border Town: 1938

She counts cement cracks
little Esperanza with the long brown braids,
counts so as not to hear
the girls in the playground singing,

"the farmer's in the dell
the farmer's in the dell"
laughing and running round-round
while little Esperanza walks head down
eyes full of tears.
"The nurse takes the child"
but Esperanza walks alone across the loud
street, through the graveyard gates
down the dirt path, walks faster,
faster . . . away
from ghosts with long arms,
no "hi-ho the dairy-o" here,
runs to that other school
for Mexicans
every day wanting to stay close to home,
every day wanting to be the farmer in the dell,
little Esperanza in the long brown braids
counts cement cracks
ocho, nueve, diez.

1986

Unnatural Speech

The game has changed
girl/child, no humming
or singing in these halls,
long, dark, ending at the desk
you want, where you'd sit
adding numbers one by one,
a C.P.A., daisies on your desk.
I study hard

you say, your smile true,
like dawn is, fresh, vulnerable,
but my English language scares
you, makes your palms sweat
when you speak before a class
I say my speeches
to my dolls

you say. Dolls? The game
has changed, girl/child.
I hear you once singing

to those unblinking eyes
lined up on your bed
Víbora, víbora de la mar,
your words light in your mouth.

Now at twenty
you stand before
those dolls tense,
feet together,
tongue thick, dry,
pushing heavy English
words out.
In class I hide
my hands behind
my back. They shake.
My voice too.

I know the new rules,
girl/child, one by one,
víboras I've lived with
all my life, learned to hold
firmly behind the head.
If I teach you, will your songs
evaporate, like dawn?

1986

University Avenue

We are the first
of our people to walk this path.
We move cautiously
unfamiliar with the sounds,
guides for those who follow.
Our people prepared us
with gifts from the land
fire
herbs and song
hierbabuena soothes us into morning
rhythms hum in our blood
abrazos linger round our bodies
cuentos whisper lessons *en español.*
We do not travel alone.
Our people burn deep within us.

1986

Víctor Hernández Cruz b. 1949

Born in Aguas Buenas, a small mountain town in Puerto Rico, Víctor Hernández Cruz moved with his family to the States when he was five. He attended Benjamin Franklin High School in New York City and was associated with The Gut Theater on East 104th Street. He published *Snaps,* his first collection of poetry, when he was twenty. From the early 1970s, Hernández Cruz lived in San Francisco; in 1990 he returned to Aguas Buenas, where he continues to write in both English and Spanish.

His poetry has been described as "the most conscious of literary forms, and the most influenced by present tendencies in American literature" among Puerto Rican writers in the United States. It is, indeed, highly introspective and abstract, preoccupied with form, rhythm, and language. His poems lack the referential context to popular culture and life in El Barrio which characterizes the work of Tato Laviera and Miguel Algarín, for example. Rather, his intellectualizing voice exhibits influences of various literary movements, such as minimalism and concrete poetry, among others. Nonetheless, his poems and prose pieces capture Hispanic images and symbols in the urban milieu.

One distinguishing feature of Hernández Cruz's poetry is its conscious language choices. The poet plays with both English and Spanish words, with spelling and phonetics, suggesting at times simultaneous American and Puerto Rican readings. The title of his book *By Lingual Wholes* illustrates his playful and witty use of language. *By Lingual* echoes the word "bilingual," and the concept *wholes,* which implies both totality and absence—(w)holes—unifies the poems in this collection. The book itself is a collage in which spatial and visual signs are part of the poem's meaning, as they are in the work of the Brazilian concrete poets. Poetry and prose are intertwined with one-word poems, haikus, short stories, prose poems, and an empty appendix. The epigraph to the book signals this playful yet serious hybridization: "Speech changing within space."

Hernández Cruz's vision of the transformation of literary English because of its contact with Spanish is his unique contribution to American literature. Just as Spanish in the States has been transforming itself into the distinct dialects of the various Hispanic groups who live here, English also has been affected by Hispanic writers. Hernández Cruz believes that the English syntax is being changed through the Spanish influence. His work is substantially enriched by the mixture and interplay of the two languages, and by the meaningful intersections between English and Spanish. However, in *Panoramas,* he proposes that English and Spanish not be mixed.

His poetry has evolved from the fragmented and often violent images of urban life, experiences with drugs, and existential beliefs during his youth—as in *Snaps*—to a dynamic and sometimes profound expression of biculturalism and bilingualism. Cosmopolitan and urban, his poetry stands without sacrificing images of Hispanic origin, culture, and tradition. His is the language of the urban, intellectual Latino who nevertheless cannot survive without transforming the past into the present.

Frances R. Aparicio
University of Illinois at Chicago

PRIMARY WORKS

Snaps, 1969; *Mainland,* 1973; *Tropicalization,* 1976; *By Lingual Wholes,* 1982; *Rhythm, Content and Flavor,* 1989; *Red Beans,* 1991; *Panoramas,* 1997.

urban dream

1

there was fire & the people were yelling.   running crazing.
screaming & falling.   moving up side down.   there was fire.
fires.   & more fires.   & walls caving to the ground.   & mercy
mercy.   death.   bodies falling down.   under bottles flying in the
air. garbage cans going up against windows.   a car singing
brightly a blue flame.   a snatch. a snag.   sounds of bombs.   &
other things blowing up.
times square
electrified.   burned.   smashed. stomped
hey over here
hey you.   where you going.
no walking.   no running.   no standing.
STOP
you crazy.   running.   stick
this stick up your eyes.   pull your heart out.
hey.

2

after noise.   comes silence.   after brightness (or great big flames)
comes darkness.   goes with whispering.   (even soft music can be heard)
even lips smacking.   foots stepping all over bones & ashes, all over
blood & broken lips that left their head somewhere else, all over
livers, & bright white skulls with hair on them. standing over a river
watching hamburgers floating by.   steak with teeth in them.
flags.   & chairs.   & beds.   & golf sets.   & mickeymouse broken
in
half.
governors & mayors step out the show.   they split.

3

dancing arrives.

1969

Mountain Building

The mountains have changed to buildings
Is this hallway the inside of a stem
That has a rattling flower for a head,
Immense tree bark with roots made out of
Mailboxes?
In the vertical village moons fly out of
Apartment windows and though what you
See is a modern city
The mountain's guitars pluck inside
It's agriculture taking an elevator
Through urban caves which lead to
Paths underground They say Camuy
To Hutuado[1]
Taino subground like the IRT in
constant motion

The streets take walks in your dark eyes
Seashell necklaces make music in the
Origin of silence
What are we stepping on? Pineapple
Fields frozen with snow
Concrete dirt later the rocks of the
Atlantic
The sculpture of the inner earth
Down there where you thought only worms
and unnamed crocodiles parade
Lefty stands on a corner
Analyzing every seed
Squeezing the walls as he passes
Through at the bottom of the basement
Where the boiler makes heat

The flesh arrives out of a hole
In the mountain that goes up like a
Green wall
Bodies come in making *maraca*[2] sounds
An invisible map out of the flora
Bees arrive in the vicinity and sing
Chorus while woody woodpeckers make
Women out of trees and place flowers
On their heads

[1]Refers to the underground caves at Camuy, Puerto Rico.

[2]Rattle—musical instrument of Taíno origin.

Waterfalls like Hurakan's faucets
Caress the back of Yuquiyu[3]
Arawak's echoes

Hallway of graffiti like the master
Cave drawings made by owls when they
Had hands
You see the fish with pyramids inside
Their stomachs
Hanging near the doorways where
San Lazaro[4] turns the keys
Villa Manhattan
Breeze of saint juice made from
Coconuts
Slide down the stairs to your
Belly and like a hypnotized *guanábana*[5]
You float down the street
And win all your hands at dominoes

The Moros live on the top floor eating
Roots and have a rooster on the roof
Africans import okra from the bodega
The Indians make a base of *guava*
On the first floor
The building is spinning itself into
a spiral of *salsa*
Heaven must be calling or the
Residents know the direction
Because there is an upward pull
If you rise too quickly from your seat
You might have to comb a spirit's
Hair
They float over the chimneys
Arrive through the smog
Appear through the plaster of Paris
It is the same people in the windowed
Mountains.

1982

[3]Hurakan and Yuquiyu: Indian deities (Taíno).
[4]Saint Lazarus.
[5]Soursop.

Table of Contents

Your tablet is your inner workings, your grasp on the board, which is shifting, trying to knock the items balanced on the table kitchen or desk, motion *contestivis* of accumulated objects. Objectivity too is matter of this piece of wood. A *tabla* is in the dictionary, transporting itself like: *tabla* (1) *(de madera)* of wood: if you lose this you lose grip as implied in conversation somewhere like Rio Piedras, Puerto Rico; (2) *(de metal)* sheets: moments among buildings, big structures, boats, autos, irons ironing your skull base for greater irony; (3) *(de piedra)* slab: also chunk of reality, let's say a piece of voice not knowing its pretty qualities are being used beyond its own life; (4) *(de tierra)* strip: episode which should be recalled right in the strip; this feels like going through distance back to a time that was slowly being eaten by this moment when it is still trying to hold onto the table; (5) *(cuadro pintado en una tabla):* situation which has been thoroughly explained into your metabolism or a framework, something that works within a frame of four sides painted clearly so you can distinguish shapes, and *contenido* reversed means *nest contained.* This is a list of tables. Broken legs will lose the tablet, and you will place your fingers on the wrong weather. Whether you at the time thought perfect your box of index, this tablature will accurately give you all the stops on a road for which you have an unsecured map with inscriptions and designs.

Let us not lose our table as we praise the importance of its acquisition. So the flow goes that it is also a catalogue *catalogo—cadaloco* means each crazy one of all the material involved. Such a list is the one you have to have faith in to maintain your tables analogous to your mind health. This wealth leads to a Spanish *(table de lavar)* wash table where the surgeons reconstruct dilapidated jungles inside of your vision from which they (this) move you (to a *tabla de planchar*) and stretch you out (to *tabla de salvación*), at which point you might have capreached and you would *(tener tablas)* to present your presence on a stage to the world and bad light would not harm you. Tablear cuts you into pieces, separates you into patches / streams / numbers / notes till you level to approachable grade for tabletear signifies to rattle, ultimately, realizations that a table has four legs and within it contains space, unless it is the table of multiplication, whereupon you will see everything in doubles or substance folded. Tabloid stretched out has many stories that are placed one by the other into pictures and features done so you can continue to follow your interests and arrange them in your pocket neatly like a well-versed drum alphabetizing names of peoples and whereabouts of mountains visible and under earth. Figures pop into your *tabula rasa,* empty where there is no grease or *grasa,* a simple search for *gracia* gracing this directory which has given deep tales and details of detours so we may come to a *principio* or principles. Let us now table this tablederia of context tabled.

1982

Garrett Kaoru Hongo b. 1951

Garrett Kaoru Hongo is a prolific and accomplished Asian American poet. His poetry is characterized by striking images and unexpected, luminous lines. He has a special talent for close observation, an eye for the telling detail, and an ability to make the mundane beautiful, as in the vivid food images of "Who Among You Knows the Essence of Garlic?" In dramatic monologues, such as "The Unreal Dwelling: My Years in Volcano," he gives voice to figures from his familial past or from a communal past. Of his writing, Hongo has written, "My project as a poet has been motivated by a search for origins of various kinds—quests for ethnic and familial roots, cultural identities, and poetic inspiration. . . . I find the landscapes, folkways, and societies of Japan, Hawaii, and even Southern California to continually charm and compel me to write about them and inform myself of their specificities."

Born in Volcano, Hawaii, Hongo moved as a child to Laie, to Kahuku, and then to California—the San Fernando Valley—where he and his brother were the only Japanese in the public school. His family finally settled in Gardena, a Japanese American community in South Los Angeles adjoining the black community of Watts and the white community of Torrance. Hongo graduated from Pomona College, then traveled in Japan on a Thomas J. Watson Fellowship. He returned for graduate work at the University of Michigan, where he won the Hopwood poetry prize and studied with poet-professors Bert Meyers, Donald Hall, and Philip Levine. Later, he earned an M.F.A. from the University of California at Irvine. He taught at various universities, including the University of Missouri, where he was poetry editor of the *Missouri Review.* He is presently professor of English and creative writing at the University of Oregon.

Hongo has produced three volumes of poetry. The first, a joint publication with fellow poets Lawson Fusao Inada and Alan Chong Lau called *The Buddha Bandits down Highway 99* (1978), is a tripartite work of youthful exuberance. Hongo's contribution to that first volume, "Cruising 99," is included in his second book, *Yellow Light* (1982), from which most of the poems in this selection were taken. *Yellow Light* won the Wesleyan Poetry Prize. *The River of Heaven* (1988), his third book of poetry, was awarded the Lamont Poetry Selection for 1987 by the Academy of American Poets and two years later was a finalist for the Pulitzer Prize in Poetry. "The Unreal Dwelling: My Years in Volcano" comes from this collection. In 1995, Hongo published *Volcano,* a poetic memoir exploring in greater depth some of the themes he had introduced in his poetry: his continuing search for family history and his rediscovery of the land of his childhood.

Hongo has also contributed to the Asian American literary/historical/critical opus by compiling and editing three significant anthologies. *The Open Boat* (1993) showcases the poetry of thirty-one Asian American poets; *Songs My Mother Taught Me* (1994) collects stories, plays, and memoirs of Wakako Yamauchi; *Under Western Eyes* (1995) assembles personal narratives by Asian American writers. Hongo's description of the Asian American poets he has gathered together in *The Open Boat* applies equally to his own poetry: "We come to consciousness aware of the history of immigration and the Asian diaspora, singing from the fissures and fragmentations of culture in order to bring about their momentary unity in the kind of evanescent beauty that the figure of a poem makes."

Amy Ling
University of Wisconsin at Madison

King-Kok Cheung
University of California, Los Angeles

PRIMARY WORKS

The Buddha Bandits down Highway 99, with Alan Chong Lau and Lawson Fusao Inada, 1978; *Yellow Light,* 1982; *The River of Heaven,* 1988; *The Open Boat: Poems from Asian America,* ed., 1993; *Wakako Yamauchi: Songs My Mother Taught Me,* 1994; *Under Western Eyes,* ed., 1995.

Yellow Light

One arm hooked around the frayed strap
of a tar-black patent-leather purse,
the other cradling something for dinner:
fresh bunches of spinach from a J-Town *yaoya,*
sides of split Spanish mackerel from Alviso's,
maybe a loaf of Langendorf; she steps
off the hissing bus at Olympic and Fig,
begins the three-block climb up the hill,
passing gangs of schoolboys playing war,
Japs against Japs, Chicanas chalking sidewalks
with the holy double-yoked crosses of hopscotch,
and the Korean grocer's wife out for a stroll
around this neighborhood of Hawaiian apartments
just starting to steam with cooking
and the anger of young couples coming home
from work, yelling at kids, flicking on
TV sets for the Wednesday Night Fights.

If it were May, hydrangeas and jacaranda
flowers in the streetside trees would be
blooming through the smog of late spring.
Wisteria in Masuda's front yard would be
shaking out the long tresses of its purple hair.
Maybe mosquitoes, moths, a few orange butterflies
settling on the lattice of monkey flowers
tangled in chain-link fences by the trash.

But this is October, and Los Angeles
seethes like a billboard under twilight.
From used-car lots and the movie houses uptown,
long silver sticks of light probe the sky.
From the Miracle Mile, whole freeways away,
a brilliant fluorescence breaks out
and makes war with the dim squares
of yellow kitchen light winking on
in all the side streets of the Barrio.

She climbs up the two flights of flagstone
stairs to 201-B, the spikes of her high heels
clicking like kitchen knives on a cutting board,
props the groceries against the door,
fishes through memo pads, a compact,
empty packs of chewing gum, and finds her keys.

The moon then, cruising from behind
a screen of eucalyptus across the street,
covers everything, everything in sight,
in a heavy light like yellow onions.

1982

Off from Swing Shift

Late, just past midnight,
freeway noise from the Harbor
and San Diego leaking in
from the vent over the stove,
and he's off from swing shift at Lear's.
Eight hours of twisting circuitry,
charting ohms and maximum gains
while transformers hum
and helicopters swirl
on the roofs above the small factory.
He hails me with a head-fake,
then the bob and weave
of a weekend middleweight
learned at the Y on Kapiolani
ten years before I was born.

The shoes and gold London Fogger
come off first, then the easy grin
saying he's lucky as they come.
He gets into the slippers
my brother gives him every Christmas,
carries his Thermos over to the sink,
and slides into the one chair at the table
that's made of wood and not yellow plastic.
He pushes aside stacks
of *Sporting News* and *Outdoor Life,*
big round tins of Holland butter cookies,
and clears a space for his elbows, his pens,
and the *Racing Form's* Late Evening Final.

His left hand reaches out,
flicks on the Sony transistor
we bought for his birthday
when I was fifteen.
The right ferries in the earphone,
a small, flesh-colored star,
like a tiny miracle of hearing,
and fits it into place.
I see him plot black constellations
of figures and calculations
on the magazine's margins,
alternately squint and frown
as he fingers the knob of the tuner
searching for the one band
that will call out today's results.

There are whole cosmologies
in a single handicap,
a lifetime of two-dollar losing
in one pick of the Daily Double.

Maybe tonight is his night
for winning, his night
for beating the odds
of going deaf from a shell
at Anzio still echoing
in the cave of his inner ear,
his night for cashing in
the blue chips of shrapnel still grinding
at the thickening joints of his legs.

But no one calls
the horse's name, no one
says Shackles, Rebate, or Pouring Rain.
No one speaks a word.

1982

Who Among You Knows the Essence of Garlic?

Can your foreigner's nose smell mullets
roasting in a glaze of brown bean paste
and sprinkled with novas of sea salt?

Can you hear my grandmother
chant the mushroom's sutra?

Can you hear the papayas crying
as they bleed in porcelain plates?

I'm telling you that the bamboo
slips the long pliant shoots
of its myriad soft tongues
into your mouth that is full of oranges.

I'm saying that the silver waterfalls
of bean threads will burst in hot oil
and stain your lips like zinc.

The marbled skin of the blue mackerel
works good for men. The purple oils
from its flesh perfume the tongues of women.

If you swallow them whole, the rice cakes
soaking in a broth of coconut milk and brown sugar
will never leave the bottom of your stomach.

Flukes of giant black mushrooms
leap from their murky tubs
and strangle the toes of young carrots.

Broiling chickens ooze grease,
yellow tears of fat collect
and spatter in the smoking pot.

Soft ripe pears, blushing
on the kitchen window sill,
kneel like plump women
taking a long luxurious shampoo,
and invite you to bite their hips.

Why not grab basketfuls of steaming noodles,
lush and slick as the hair of a fine lady,
and squeeze?

The shrimps, big as Portuguese thumbs,
stew among cut guavas, red onions,
ginger root, and rosemary in lemon juice,
the palm oil bubbling to the top,
breaking through layers and layers
of shredded coconut and sliced cashews.

Who among you knows the essence
of garlic and black lotus root,
of red and green peppers sizzling
among squads of oysters in the skillet,
of crushed ginger, fresh green onions,
and pale-blue rice wine simmering
in the stomach of a big red fish?

1982

And Your Soul Shall Dance

for Wakako Yamauchi

Walking to school beside fields
of tomatoes and summer squash,
alone and humming a Japanese love song,
you've concealed a copy of *Photoplay*
between your algebra and English texts.
Your knee socks, saddle shoes, plaid dress,
and blouse, long-sleeved and white
with ruffles down the front,
come from a Sears catalogue
and neatly complement your new Toni curls.
All of this sets you apart from the landscape:
flat valley grooved with irrigation ditches,
a tractor grinding through alkaline earth,
the short stands of windbreak eucalyptus
shuttering the desert wind
from a small cluster of wooden shacks
where your mother hangs the wash.
You want to go somewhere.
Somewhere far away from all the dust
and sorting machines and acres of lettuce.
Someplace where you might be kissed
by someone with smooth, artistic hands.
When you turn into the schoolyard,
the flagpole gleams like a knife blade in the sun,
and classmates scatter like chickens,
shooed by the storm brooding on your horizon.

1982

The Unreal Dwelling: My Years in Volcano

What I did, I won't excuse,
except to say it was a way to change,
the way new flows add to the land,
making things new, clearing the garden.
I left two sons, a wife behind—
and does it matter? The sons grew,
became their own kinds of men,
lost in the swirl of robes, cries
behind a screen of mist and fire
I drew between us, gambles I lost
and walked away from like any bad job.
I drove a cab and didn't care,
let the wife run off too, her combs
loose in some shopkeeper's bed.
When hope blazed up in my heart for the fresh start,
I took my daughters with me to keep house,
order my living as I was taught and came to expect.
They swept up, cooked, arranged flowers,
practiced tea and *buyō,* the classical dance.
I knew how because I could read and ordered books,
let all movements be disciplined and objects arranged
by an idea of order, the precise sequence of images
which conjure up the abstract I might call
yūgen, or Mystery, *chikara,* . . . Power.
The principles were in the swordsmanship
I practiced, in the package of loans
and small thefts I'd managed since coming here.
I could count, keep books, speak English
as well as any white, and I had false papers
recommending me, celebrating the fiction
of my long tenure with Hata Shōten of Honolulu.
And my luck was they bothered to check
only those I'd bribed or made love to.
Charm was my collateral, a willingness to move
and live on the frontier my strongest selling point.
So they staked me, a small-time hustler
good with cars, odds, and women,
and I tossed some boards together,
dug ponds and a cesspool,
figured water needed tanks, pipes,
and guttering on the eaves
to catch the light-falling rain,
and I had it—a store and a house out-back
carved out of rainforests and lava land

beside this mountain road seven leagues from Hilo.
I never worried they'd come this far—
the banks, courts, and police—
mists and sulphur clouds from the crater
drenching the land, washing clean my tracks,
bleaching my spotted skin the pallor of long-time residents.
I regularized my life and raised my girls,
put in gas pumps out front, stocked varieties of goods
and took in local fruit, flowers on consignment.
And I had liquor—plum wine and *saké*
from Japan, whiskey from Tennessee—
which meant I kept a pistol as well.
My girls learned to shoot, and would have
only no one bothered to test us.
It was known I'd shot cats and wild pigs
from across the road rummaging through garbage.
I never thought of my boys,
or of women too much
until my oldest bloomed,
suddenly, vanda-like, from spike
to scented flower almost overnight.
Young men in Model A's came up from town.
One even bussed, and a Marine from Georgia
stole a Jeep to try taking her
to the coast, or, more simply,
down a mountain road for the night.
The Shore Patrol found him.
And I got married again, to a country girl
from Kona who answered my ad.
I approved of her because,
though she was rough-spoken and squat-legged,
and, I discovered, her hair
slightly red in the groin,
she could carry 50-lbs. sacks of California Rose
without strain or grunting.
As postmaster and Territorial official,
I married us myself, sent announcements
and champagne in medicine vials
to the villagers and my "guarantors" in town.
The toasts tasted of vitamin-B and cough syrup.
My oldest moved away, herself married
to a dapper Okinawan who sold Oldsmobiles
and had the leisure to play golf on weekends.
I heard from my boy then, my oldest son,
back from the war and writing to us,
curious, formal, and not a little proud
he'd done his part. What impressed me

was his script—florid but under control,
penmanship like pipers at the tideline
lifting and settling on the sand-colored paper.
He wrote first from Europe, then New York,
finally from Honolulu. He'd fought,
mustered out near the Madison Square Garden
in time to see LaMotta smash the pretty one,
and then came home to a girl he'd met in night school.
He said he won out over a cop because he danced better,
knew from the service how to show up in a tie,
bring flowers and silk in nice wrappings.
I flew the Island Clipper to the wedding,
the first time I'd seen the boy in twenty years,
gave him a hundred cash and a wink
since the girl was pretty,
told him to buy, not rent his suits,
and came home the next day, hungover,
a raw ache in my throat.
I sobered up, but the ache
stayed and doctors tell me
it's this sickness they can't get rid of,
pain all through my blood and nerve cells.
I cough too much, can't smoke or drink
or tend to things. Mornings, I roll
myself off the damp bed, wrap
a blanket on, slip into the wooden clogs,
and take a walk around my pond and gardens.
On this half-acre, calla lilies in bloom,
cream-white cups swollen with milk,
heavy on their stems, and rocking in the slight wind,
cranes coming to rest on the wet, coppery soil.
The lotuses ride, tiny flamingoes, sapphired
pavilions buoyed on their green keels on the pond.
My fish follow me, snorting to be fed,
gold flashes and streaks of color
like blood satin and brocade in the algaed waters.
And when the sky empties of its many lights,
I see the quarter moon, horned junk,
sailing over the Ka'u and the crater rim.
This is the River of Heaven. . . .
Before I cross, I know I must bow down,
call to my oldest son, say what I must
to bring him, and all the past, back to me.

1985

Michael S. Harper b. 1938

The poetry of Michael S. Harper resists easy categorization. Alternately metaphysical and reflective, historical and biographical, musical and autobiographical, Harper's poetry demonstrates a "both/and" sensibility. He views poetry as a place where "the microcosm and the cosmos are united." Harper's poetic project occurs, then, in a conceptual space where he maintains the sacred nature of speech as a form of human connection, evidenced by his assertion that "the tongue is the customer of the ear." Harper is a poet whose work is oriented toward performance; his poems are heavily indebted to African American musical traditions such as jazz and the blues, for he is interested, above all, in the ways we improvise on the themes that compose human experience.

Born in Brooklyn, Harper spent the first thirteen years of his life in New York before his family relocated to Los Angeles. His father worked as a post office supervisor, his mother as a medical stenographer. Growing up in the 1940s and 1950s, Harper experienced the great cultural and artistic vitality manifested at that time in the African American community: Jackie Robinson's entry into pro baseball, the music of Billie Holiday (she played piano in the Harper home), the birth and growth of bebop, and the boxing prowess of Sugar Ray Robinson. Harper's poetry often celebrates African American examples of artistic and athletic excellence.

After graduating from high school, Harper continued his education at Los Angeles State College and, later, the University of Iowa, where he received an M.A. in English and did work at the Iowa Writer's Workshop. But he claims that his education also took place at the facing table in the post office, where he worked full-time to put himself through college. It was there that he encountered black men and women who were trained doctors, lawyers, and teachers whose race made the post office the only place they could find employment.

Harper is the author of many collections of poems, two of which, *Dear John, Dear Coltrane* (1970) and *Images of Kin* (1977), have been nominated for the National Book Award. He is co-editor of a critically acclaimed anthology, *Chant of Saints* (1979), and is responsible for bringing poet Sterling A. Brown's *Collected Poems* into print. Harper's books offer the reader a pantheon of heroes and heroines and a variety of geographical settings (often portraying aspects of Harper's travels through Mexico, West and South Africa, as well as New England and the South) that demonstrate his affinity for different personas and idioms, each of which allows him to create modes of address that call for a more cohesive sensibility.

Harper's poems also explore his connections to other artists—jazz saxophonists John Coltrane and Charlie Parker, writers Ralph Ellison, Sterling Brown, Robert Hayden, and James Wright—and what they teach him about the inherent responsibility of survival (a subject he has confronted in poems that concern the deaths of two of his children at birth and, more recently, of his brother). They provide models for his own poetic expressions. Jazz provides the "architectonic impulse" that informs the structures of his poems. The writers offer models of enduring craft and seriousness. All of these heroes exemplify the concept of modality that runs through the Harper oeuvre. It represents, in part, the act of resisting the Western impulse to compartmentalize knowledge and experience and thus culture as well.

Herman Beavers
University of Pennsylvania

PRIMARY WORKS

History Is Your Own Heartbeat, 1971; *Photographs: Negatives; History as Apple Tree,* 1972; *Song: I Want a Witness,* 1972; *Nightmare Begins Responsibility,* 1975; *Images of Kin,* 1977; *Dear John, Dear Coltrane,* 1970; *Healing Song for the Inner Ear,* 1985; *Honorable Amendments,* 1995.

Song: I Want a Witness

Blacks in frame houses
call to the helicopters,
their antlered arms
spinning; jeeps pad
these glass-studded streets;
on this hill are tanks painted gold.
Our children sing
spirituals of *Motown,*
idioms these streets suckled
on a southern road.
This scene is about power,
terror, producing
love and pain and pathology;
in an army of white dust,
blacks here to *testify*
and *testify,* and *testify,*
and *redeem,* and *redeem,*
in black smoke coming,
as they wave their arms,
as they wave their tongues.

1972

Nightmare Begins Responsibility

I place these numbed wrists to the pane
watching white uniforms whisk over
him in the tube-kept
prison
fear what they will do in experiment
watch my gloved stickshifting gasolined hands
breathe *boxcar-information-please* infirmary tubes

distrusting white-pink mending paperthin
silkened end hairs, distrusting tubes
shrunk in his *trunk-skincapped*
shaven head, in thighs
distrusting-white-hands-picking-baboon-light
on this son who will not make his second night
of this wardstrewn intensive airpocket
where his father's asthmatic
hymns of *night-train,* train done gone
his mother can only know that he has flown
up into essential calm unseen corridor
going boxscarred home, *mamaborn, sweetsonchild*
gonedowntown into *researchtestingwarehousebatteryacid*
mama-son-done-gone/me telling her 'nother
train tonight, no music, no breathstroked
heartbeat in my infinite distrust of them:

and of my distrusting self
white-doctor-who-breathed-for-him-all-night
say it for two sons gone,
say nightmare, say it loud
panebreaking heartmadness:
nightmare begins responsibility.

1975

Here Where Coltrane Is

Soul and race
are private dominions,
memories and modal
songs, a tenor blossoming,
which would paint suffering
a clear color but is not in
this Victorian house
without oil in zero degree
weather and a forty-mile-an-hour wind;
it is all a well-knit family:
a love supreme.
Oak leaves pile up on walkway
and steps, catholic as apples
in a special mist of clear white
children who love my children.
I play "Alabama"

on a warped record player
skipping the scratches
on your faces over the fibrous
conical hairs of plastic
under the wooden floors.

Dreaming on a train from New York
to Philly, you hand out six
notes which become an anthem
to our memories of you:
oak, birch, maple,
apple, cocoa, rubber.
For this reason Martin is dead;
for this reason Malcolm is dead;
for this reason Coltrane is dead;
in the eyes of my first son are the browns
of these men and their music.

1977

A Narrative of the Life and Times of John Coltrane: Played by Himself

Hamlet, North Carolina

I don't remember train whistles,
or corroding trestles of ice
seeping from the hangband,
vaulting northward in shining triplets,
but the feel of the reed on my tongue
haunts me even now, my incisors
pulled so the pain wouldn't lurk
on "Cousin Mary";

in High Point I stared
at the bus which took us to band
practice on Memorial Day;
I could hardly make out, in the mud,
placemarks, separations of skin
sketched in plates above the rear bumper.

Mama asked, "what's the difference
'tween North and South Carolina,"
a capella notes of our church choir
doping me into arpeggios,

into *sheets of sound* labeling me
into dissonance.

I never liked the photo taken with
Bird, Miles without sunglasses,
me in profile almost out of exposure:
these were my images of movement;
when I hear the sacred songs,
auras of my mother at the stove,
I play the blues:

what good does it do to complain:
one night I was playing with Bostic,
blacking out, coming alive only to melodies
where I could play my parts:
And then, on a train to Philly,
I sang "Naima" locking the door
without exit no matter what song
I sang; with remonstrations on the ceiling
of that same room I practiced in
on my back when too tired to stand,
I broke loose from crystalline habits
I though would bring me that sound.

1985

Camp Story

I look over the old photos
for the US Hotel fire,
1900 Saratoga Springs,
where your grandfather
was chef on loan
from Catskill
where you were born.

The grapes from his arbor
sing in my mouth:
the smoke from the trestle
of his backyard,
the engine so close
to the bedroom
I can almost touch it,
make bricks from the yards
of perfection,

the clear puddles from the Hudson River,
where you would make change
at the dayline,
keep the change from the five
Jackleg Diamonds would leave
on the counter top or the stool.

Where is the CCC camp
you labored in
to send the money home to the family,
giving up your scholarship
so you could save the family
homestead from the banks of the river.

All across America the refugees
find homes in these camps
and are made to eat
at a table of liberty
you could have had
if you could not spell
or count, or keep time.

I see you, silent, wordfully
talking to my brother, Jonathan,
as he labors on the chromatic
respirator; you kiss his brown
temple where his helmet left
a slight depression
near a neat line of stitches
at the back of his skull.

As he twitches to chemicals
the Asian nurses catheter
into the cavities and caves
of his throat and lungs:
the doctor repeats the story
of his chances.

1985

Postmodernity and Difference
Promises and Threats

Nothing so signifies the character of the past two decades as the dissolution of established social and political markers. Nation-states like the Union of Soviet Socialist Republics, Czechoslovakia, and Yugoslavia disintegrated, as did the "grand narratives" long used to describe historical movement. At the same time, borders—between nations and social groups, and between "high" and "popular" cultures—blurred but simultaneously were reinforced with sometimes disastrous consequences. Winning a war seemed to become a recipe for losing. Such paradoxes abounded. As American popular culture became internationally pervasive, American society itself became increasingly internationalized. Such blurrings, paradoxes, and ironies constitute significant elements in what is called "postmodernism."

Cultural developments primarily stimulated by the movements for social change of the 1960s and 1970s have continued during the three most recent decades. But as writers and groups previously marginalized have become more visible, concern has shifted from legitimating "new" literatures to exploring the historical origins of differing cultural communities, to designating the differences *within* such communities, and to exploring the implications of "minority" cultures for the whole society.

American Indian literature provides an example. Because earlier tribal literatures had been collected only in fragments and often in corrupted form, without sufficient attention to the contexts in which they were performed, they were frequently misunderstood. The development of "Indian"—as distinct from "tribal"—literature helped broaden interest in the study of early oral traditions; many collections of songs, chants, ceremonial materials, and narratives were published and influenced contemporary authors. N. Scott Momaday's first works were among the earliest to adapt traditional themes and forms to contemporary story. In *Ceremony* (1977) and *Storyteller* (1981), Leslie Marmon Silko utilizes traditional tales, like that of "Yellow Woman," not only to renew their interest for contemporary readers, but to provide access to the values of her Pueblo culture. Like Silko, Louise Erdrich does not romanticize American Indian life and history; on the contrary, she presents its struggles with a combination of grim realism and wild humor. She also demands that readers learn *about* that history as well as *from* that life. In common with such other American Indian writers as Paula Gunn Allen, Wendy Rose, Sherman Alexie, and Simon Ortiz, Erdrich sees her texts as not only offering entertainment but also providing values alternative to those that dominate American culture.

Critics of Asian American literature have emphasized the way that designation hides the manifold distinctions among Chinese American, Japanese American, Korean American, and other Asian-based cultures—even if all are, to some extent, exoticized as "oriental." In fact, Asian American literatures have probably, in the last two decades, been the most rapidly expanding sector of contemporary ethnic cultures. The ambiguities—both terrifying and comic—that characterize many Asian-Western interactions are vividly evoked in the writings of Lawson Inada, Li-Young Lee, Bharati Mukherjee, and others. But more, Asian American critics argue, these forms of encounter, and therefore many Asian American texts, offer paradigms for the variety of skirmishes Americans and other Westerners have had and continue to have with all of those they designate as "other."

Among Latino writers and critics, the cutting-edge issue in recent years has been the border, as illustrated in books such as Gloria Anzaldúa's *Borderlands/La Frontera.* Chicano/Chicana, Puerto Rican, and Cuban American writers often move between two countries, two languages, two cultures. As the borders between nation-states have become increasingly permeable, so cultural boundaries have shifted, faded, or taken on new configurations. Many Latino writers have come to occupy the "liminal" ground between more traditionally defined cultures—those, for example, of Mexico and the United States—and to argue, moreover, that such liminality, the sense of living *between* cultures rather than *within* any one culture, characterizes much of postmodern experience.

In each of these instances, racial and ethnic difference has moved from being a feature of one distinctive marginalized culture to becoming a central expression of postmodern life in the United States. In this light, the kinds of differences which, in the 1960s and 1970s, were primarily celebrated for their uniqueness—such as "black is beautiful"—have become central to the cultural landscape of our entire society. For example, thirty years ago the task for teachers and critics was to bring African American writers into the literary curriculum and the canon of works valued by critics. Today, such a social historian as Orlando Patterson argues that the experience of black Americans, rooted as it is in slavery and the consequent struggle for freedom, replicates the central dynamic not just of African American but of *all* Western societies, whose economies, from classical Athens on, have been marked by the centrality of slavery or serfdom. Other critics have come to view African American writing not only as an interesting adjunct to the "mainstream" of American literature but as a critical shaping force in the development of white as well as of black writers. Such arguments became features of the cultural landscape in the 1990s, and while they cannot be said to be conclusive, they are powerfully suggestive. They also help to explain why readers will find in this volume an unusually broad representation of writers of color. We believe that the vital issues underlined in these paragraphs can only be explored and understood by reading widely among the variety of writers from differing cultures we have chosen to offer.

In no area has cultural and social change, and resistance to it, been so dramatic as in that associated with definitions of gender. Feminist theorists have argued that ideas of gender—the forms of behavior societies regard as appropriate to biological males and females—change in different nations and in different times and are therefore "socially constructed." That fairly abstract idea has taken on fighting qualities not only for the publication of feminist texts that reject traditional gender definitions but especially with the emergence of Gay/Lesbian studies, literatures, and visual representations. During the 1980s and the 1990s, artistic and literary presentations occasioned intense conflict—in courtrooms, in the halls of Congress, in publishing houses, and in classrooms. Disputes over obscenity and "pornography," over the supposed politicization of art, over what did or did not constitute society's core values, became particularly heated with the frightening spread of the AIDS epidemic. The issue linking many of these disputes is that of gender, and how literary and artistic culture might be responsible for understanding, celebrating, or changing ideas about it.

It would not be accurate to suggest that postmodernism has had an exclusively political face. In fact, the term has been used to refer to many recent intellectual currents. The dissolution of boundaries to which we referred above has also been perceived within forms of art. Some postmodernist critics, for example, have rejected the distinction between "creative" and "critical" works, or between writing and other kinds of "texts," from created objects to television ads. Indeed, some argue that any form of text, from the casual letter and the freshman theme to the most complex novels and poems, involves similar sets of tactics and can therefore be "read" using analogous approaches. In all texts, these critics assert, writers try to establish one or more "voices," a distinctive form of discourse. Our discourses position us in relation to our readers, attracting some, offending or excluding others. Some postmodernist critics argue further that texts do not exist independently of readers, that readers "create" texts as much as "authors" do. The meaning of a text, therefore, emerges in readers' varied responses to it, responses significantly shaped by the "subject positions" from which a reader experiences the world.

Much postmodernist thinking and art have also emphasized the *dis*continuities of life, rejecting the notion that the supposedly "real" world or even the human self may be knowable. It focuses instead on the contradictions of living—how, for example, even revolutionary writing can become a commodity in capitalist society. As a result, a significant strand of postmodernist art, building on the work of such predecessors as Pynchon and Barthelme, brings together wildly incongruous elements, utilizes inconsistent forms, mixes voices, crosses comedy with terror, offers divergent points of view, and in particular resists finality or closure. Many postmodernists thus express their suspicion of claims to ultimate political wisdom and of artworks that offer definitive pictures, much less cautionary tales. Indeed, the postmodern theoretical system called "deconstruction" is rooted in the idea that texts, far from being able to convey a single definitive message, contain within themselves contradictory currents whose impact is ultimately to cancel the conclusions toward which the text seemed to move.

Such ideas obviously have implications for politicians, as well as for writers, filmmakers, and visual artists. Expressing distrust of overtly political projects, some postmodern artists have insisted that change depends upon altering fundamental verbal or visual patterns, because what we see and think is always already shaped by such patterns. Some of these arguments contend that all change is a matter of discourse, of language. Whether one accepts such contentions, it is true that postmodern art has broken down previously fixed boundaries—as, for example, between "fiction" and "history," or between the "literary" text and the "visual" text. As we suggested earlier, forms like collage have migrated from the visual arts to poetry. And genres supposedly confined to "popular" culture or even to business—like the detective novel, science fiction, the vampire tale, and the corporate report—have been pursued by writers whose objectives have little to do with simply making a buck. As was true throughout the twentieth century, such experimentalism creates a momentum of its own, independent of the social and political currents we sketched above.

To some degree, these divergent tendencies have brought postmodernist critics and artists, on the one side, and some feminist and ethnic minority artists, on the other, into conflict, precisely over the latter's desire to create works that move people in specific directions, or at least to open readers to forms of experience and culture definably different from their own. At the same time, however, ethnic and women writers have increasingly appropriated artistic strategies introduced by experimentalists.

Again, paradox seems the rule: conflict and adaptation emerge as sides of a single coin.

The most profound change that has occurred during the past thirty years is, as we have pointed out, that literature can no longer be divided into "mainstream" and "marginal." Readers can choose from a wide variety of good fiction, poetry, and drama being published and distributed by both commercial and more specialized presses. Ethnic writers have as much chance at major literary prizes as do white male establishment writers—as evidenced by Maurice Kenny's winning the National Book Award in 1984 for *The Mama Poems,* for instance, or Toni Morrison's winning the 1988 Pulitzer Prize for Fiction for *Beloved,* followed in 1993 by her being honored with the Nobel Prize in Literature.

Unfortunately for most readers, because women and ethnic writers have been less often anthologized, learning to know their work—and to understand its significance, especially if it deviates from what have become accepted patterns of literary representation—has been difficult. This anthology includes a number of comparatively young writers, many of whose books have been published only in the past five to ten years. Our expectation is that the excitement to be found in new literatures expressing fresh themes and new understandings will be contagious for our readers.

John Barth b. 1930

John Barth's birth on May 22, 1930, in Cambridge, a small "southern" town on the Eastern Shore of Maryland, established his claim to one of the strongest literary heritages in twentieth-century America, the modernist tradition that took root in the American South through the novels that William Faulkner and Thomas Wolfe wrote during the 1920s and 1930s. Despite an early focus on music, Barth, who in 1953 became a college writing teacher, absorbed this tradition well enough to give his first two novels, *The Floating Opera* (1956) and *The End of the Road* (1958), the strong sense of place and fate commonly found in modern southern fiction.

Barth's first two books, however, also exhibited a playfulness closer to the improvisations of modern jazz, his earlier passion, and to the black humor emerging in the fifties, than to modern southern fiction. The novels parodied the existential movement, the dominant tendency of European writing during the late modernist period; *The Floating Opera* expresses Barth's comic response to Camus's earnest and familiar defense of suicide while *The End of the Road* pushes Sartre's views of commitment and protean freedom to sardonic extremes. In short, Barth was already experimenting with one of his favorite devices, the practice of framing seemingly exhausted literary modes by reworking them from radically different perspectives to renew them and thereby replenish the literary tradition. Eventually, his use of parody and frames would be his major contribution to the (then) undetected emergence of postmodernism, the dominant cultural development of the second half of the twentieth century and a movement in which Barth is regarded as the major American literary practitioner and advocate.

Barth's *The Sot-Weed Factor* (1960), taking a clue from a short work of fiction, "Pierre Menard, Author of Don Quixote," by Jorge Luis Borges (the modern writer from whom he appears to have learned most), continued his parodies of established modes of writing by creating a gigantic eighteenth-century Anglo-southern novel out of comic characters and themes appropriate to the mid-twentieth century. In *Giles Goat-Boy, or The Revised New Syl-*

labus (1966), the novelist took a decisive step toward postmodernism when he freed himself from both memory and history by creating an imaginary university parodying the universe in which earthlings found themselves during the cold war.

The experiments collected in 1968 in *Lost in the Funhouse* mark Barth's emergence as leader of the American wing of the movement called postmodernism. As a contribution to the postmodern, the title story, reprinted below, generates special excitement, for it is difficult to imagine a more self-referential metafiction. Here the author frames a seemingly heart-felt parody of a story about a boy from a small town as he comes of age, a subject typical of the southern modernists, with the fatalistic thoughts of a beginning or blocked writer who struggles to obey the best-intended formulas of creative writing classes. Writer's block became a major theme, and likely a metaphor for contemporary culture, in such later works as *Chimera* (a masterpiece of the postmodern in America, published in 1972) and *Letters: A Novel* (1979).

After the seemingly (perhaps deliberately) botched experiment with narration and point of view in *Sabbatical: A Romance* (1982), Barth's jazz-like powers of improvisation returned full force in his joy-filled megafiction *The Tidewater Tales* (1987), while the temporal pastiche of *The Last Voyage of Somebody the Sailor* (1991) throws the assumptions of modern realist fiction into confusion by making the adventures of Sinbad seem to the audience that hears them examples of traditional realism, and competing journalistic accounts of modern events appear to be sheer fiction. *On with the Story: Stories* (1996) complements the *Lost in the Funhouse* collection in its attempt to jump-start experimental postmodern fiction, which in the 1990s was losing ground to several retro tendencies. *The Friday Book* and *Further Fridays,* Barth's essays and non-fiction gathered together in 1984 and 1995, may be the best year-by-year record in existence of the emergence—from modernism, existentialism, black humor, and "irrealism"—of American literary postmodernism.

Julius Rowan Raper
University of North Carolina at Chapel Hill

PRIMARY WORKS

The Floating Opera, 1956 [Rev. 1967]; *The End of the Road,* 1958 [Rev. 1967]; *The Sot-Weed Factor,* 1960 [Rev. 1967]; *Giles Goat-Boy, or The Revised New Syllabus,* 1966; *Lost in the Funhouse: Fiction for Print, Tape, Live Voice,* 1968; *Chimera,* 1972; *LETTERS: A Novel,* 1979; *Sabbatical: A Romance,* 1982; *The Friday Book: Essays and Other Nonfiction,* 1984; *The Tidewater Tales: A Novel,* 1987; *The Last Voyage of Somebody the Sailor,* 1991; *Once Upon a Time: A Floating Opera,* 1994; *Further Fridays: Essays, Lectures, and Other Nonfiction, 1984–94,* 1995; *On with the Story: Stories,* 1996.

Lost in the Funhouse

For whom is the funhouse fun? Perhaps for lovers. For Ambrose it is *a place of fear and confusion.* He has come to the seashore with his family for the holiday, *the occasion of their visit is Independence Day, the most important secular holiday of the United States of America.* A single straight underline is the manuscript mark for italic type, *which in turn* is the printed equivalent to oral emphasis of words and phrases as well as the customary type for titles of complete works, not to mention. Italics are also employed, in fiction stories especially, for "outside," intrusive, or artificial voices, such as radio announcements, the texts of telegrams and newspaper articles, et cetera. They should be used *sparingly.* If passages originally in roman type are italicized by someone repeating them, it's customary to acknowledge the fact. *Italics mine.*

Ambrose was "at that awkward age." His voice came out high-pitched as a child's if he let himself get carried away; to be on the safe side, therefore, he moved and spoke with *deliberate calm* and *adult gravity.* Talking soberly of unimportant or irrelevant matters and listening consciously to the sound of your own voice are useful habits for maintaining control in this difficult interval. *En route* to Ocean City he sat in the back seat of the family car with his brother Peter, age fifteen, and Magda G______, age fourteen, a pretty girl an exquisite young lady, who lived not far from them on B______ Street in the town of D______, Maryland. Initials, blanks, or both were often substituted for proper names in nineteenth-century fiction to enhance the illusion of reality. It is as if the author felt it necessary to delete the names for reasons of tact or legal liability. Interestingly, as with other aspects of realism, it is an *illusion* that is being enhanced, by purely artificial means. Is it likely, does it violate the principle of verisimilitude, that a thirteen-year-old boy could make such a sophisticated observation? A girl of fourteen is *the psychological coeval* of a boy of fifteen or sixteen; a thirteen-year-old boy, therefore, even one precocious in some other respects, might be three years *her emotional junior.*

Thrice a year—on Memorial, Independence, and Labor Days—the family visits Ocean City for the afternoon and evening. When Ambrose and Peter's father was their age, the excursion was made by train, as mentioned in the novel *The 42nd Parallel* by John Dos Passos. Many families from the same neighborhood used to travel together, with dependent relatives and often with Negro servants; schoolfuls of children swarmed through the railway cars; everyone shared everyone else's Maryland fried chicken, Virginia ham, deviled eggs, potato salad, beaten biscuits, iced tea. Nowadays (that is, in 19——, the year of our story) the journey is made by automobile—more comfortably and quickly though without the extra fun though without the *camaraderie* of a general excursion. It's all part of the deterioration of American life, their father declares; Uncle Karl supposes that when the boys take *their* families to Ocean City for the holidays they'll fly in Autogiros. Their mother, sitting in the middle of the front seat like Magda in the second, only with her arms on the seat-back behind the men's shoulders, wouldn't want the good old days back again, the steaming trains and stuffy long dresses; on the other hand she can do without Autogiros, too, if she has to become a grandmother to fly in them.

Description of physical appearance and mannerisms is one of several standard methods of characterization used by writers of fiction. It is also important to "keep the senses operating"; when a detail from one of the five senses, say visual, is "crossed" with a detail from another, say auditory, the reader's imagination is oriented to the scene, perhaps unconsciously. This procedure may be compared to the way surveyors and navigators determine their positions by two or more compass bearings, a process known as triangulation. The brown hair on Ambrose's mother's forearms gleamed in the sun like. Though right-handed, she took her left arm from the seat-back to press the dashboard cigar lighter for Uncle Karl. When the glass bead in its handle glowed red, the lighter was ready for use. The smell of Uncle Karl's cigar smoke reminded one of. The fragrance of the ocean came strong to the picnic ground where they always stopped for lunch, two miles inland from Ocean City. Having to pause for a full hour almost within the sound of the breakers was difficult for Peter and Ambrose when they were younger; even at their present age it was not easy to keep their anticipation, *stimulated by the briny spume,* from turning into short temper. The Irish author James Joyce, in his unusual novel entitled *Ulysses,* now available in this country, uses the adjectives *snot-green* and *scrotum-tightening* to describe the sea. Visual, auditory, tactile, olfactory, gustatory. Peter and Ambrose's father, while steering their black 1936 LaSalle sedan with one hand, could with the other remove the first cigarette from a white pack of Lucky Strikes and, more remarkably, light it with a match forefingered from its book and thumbed against the flint paper without being detached. The matchbook cover merely advertised U.S. War Bonds and Stamps. A fine metaphor, simile, or other figure of speech, in addition to its obvious "first-order" relevance to the thing it describes, will be seen upon reflection to have a second order of significance: it may be drawn from the *milieu* of the action, for example, or be particularly appropriate to the sensibility of the narrator, even hinting to the reader things of which the narrator is unaware; or it may cast further and subtler lights upon the thing it describes, sometimes ironically qualifying the more evident sense of the comparison.

To say that Ambrose's and Peter's mother was *pretty* is to accomplish nothing; the reader may acknowledge the proposition, but his imagination is not engaged. Besides, Magda was also pretty, yet in an altogether different way. Although she lived on B_____ Street she had very good manners and did better than average in school. Her figure was very well developed for her age. Her right hand lay casually on the plush upholstery of the seat, very near Ambrose's left leg, on which his own hand rested. The space between their legs, between her right and his left leg, was out of the line of sight of anyone sitting on the other side of Magda, as well as anyone glancing into the rearview mirror. Uncle Karl's face resembled Peter's—rather, vice versa. Both had dark hair and eyes, short husky statures, deep voices. Magda's left hand was probably in a similar position on her left side. The boy's father is difficult to describe; no particular feature of his appearance or manner stood out. He wore glasses and was principal of a T_____ County grade school. Uncle Karl was a masonry contractor.

Although Peter must have known as well as Ambrose that the latter, because of his position in the car, would be the first to see the electrical towers of the power plant at V_____, the halfway point of their trip, he leaned forward and slightly toward the center of the car and pretended to be looking for them through the flat pinewoods and tuckahoe creeks along the highway. For as long as the boys could remember, "looking for the Towers" had been a feature of the first half of their excursions to Ocean City, "looking for the standpipe" of the second. Though the game was childish, their mother preserved the tradition of rewarding the first to see the Towers with a candybar or piece of fruit. She insisted now that Magda play the game; the prize, she said, was "something hard to get nowadays." Ambrose decided not to join in; he sat far back in his seat. Magda, like Peter, leaned forward. Two sets of straps were discernible through the shoulders of her sun dress; the inside right one, a brassiere-strap, was fastened or shortened with a small safety pin. The right armpit of her dress, presumably the left as well, was damp with perspiration. The simple strategy for being first to espy the Towers, which Ambrose had understood by the age of four, was to sit on the right-hand side of the car. Whoever sat there, however, had also to put up with the worst of the sun, and so Ambrose, without mentioning the matter, chose sometimes the one and sometimes the other. Not impossibly Peter had never caught on to the trick, or thought that his brother hadn't simply because Ambrose on occasion preferred shade to a Baby Ruth or tangerine.

The shade-sun situation didn't apply to the front seat, owing to the windshield; if anything the driver got more sun, since the person on the passenger side not only was shaded below by the door and dashboard but might swing down his sunvisor all the way too.

"Is that them?" Magda asked. Ambrose's mother teased the boys for letting Magda win, insinuating that "somebody [had] a girlfriend." Peter and Ambrose's father reached a long thin arm across their mother to butt his cigarette in the dashboard ashtray, under the lighter. The prize this time for seeing the Towers first was a banana. Their mother bestowed it after chiding their father for wasting a half-smoked cigarette when everything was so scarce. Magda, to take the prize, moved her hand from so near Ambrose's that he could have touched it as though accidentally. She offered to share the prize, things like that were so hard to find; but everyone insisted it was hers alone. Ambrose's mother sang an iambic trimeter couplet from a popular song, femininely rhymed:

"What's good is in the Army;
What's left will never harm me."

Uncle Karl tapped his cigar ash out the ventilator window; some particles were sucked by the slipstream back into the car through the rear window on the passenger side. Magda demonstrated her ability to hold a banana in one hand and peel it with her teeth. She still sat forward; Ambrose pushed his glasses back onto the bridge of his nose with his left hand, which he then negligently let fall to the seat cushion immediately behind her. He even permitted the single hair, gold, on the second joint of his thumb to brush the fabric of her skirt. Should she have sat back at that instant, his hand would have been caught under her.

Plush upholstery prickles uncomfortably through gabardine slacks in the July sun. The function of the *beginning* of a story is to introduce the principal characters, establish their initial relationships, set the scene for the main action, expose the background of the situation if necessary, plant motifs and foreshadowings where appropriate, and initiate the first complication or whatever of the "rising action." Actually, if one imagines a story called "The Funhouse," or "Lost in the Funhouse," the details of the drive to Ocean City don't seem especially relevant. The *beginning* should recount the events between Ambrose's first sight of the funhouse early in the afternoon and his entering it with Magda and Peter in the evening. The *middle* would narrate all relevant events from the time he goes in to the time he loses his way; middles have the double and contradictory function of delaying the climax while at the same time preparing the reader for it and fetching him to it. Then the *ending* would tell what Ambrose does while he's lost, how he finally finds his way out, and what everybody makes of the experience. So far there's been no real dialogue, very little sensory detail, and nothing in the way of a *theme.* And a long time has gone by already without anything happening; it makes a person wonder. We haven't even reached Ocean City yet: we will never get out of the funhouse.

The more closely an author identifies with the narrator, literally or metaphorically, the less advisable it is, as a rule, to use the first-person narrative viewpoint. Once three years previously the young people *aforementioned* played Niggers and Masters in the backyard; when it was Ambrose's turn to be Master and theirs to be Niggers Peter had to go serve his evening papers; Ambrose was afraid to punish Magda alone but she led him to the whitewashed Torture Chamber between the woodshed and the privy in the Slaves Quarters; there she knelt sweating among bamboo rakes and dusty Mason jars, pleadingly embraced his knees, and while bees droned in the lattice as if on an ordinary summer afternoon, purchased clemency at a surprising price set by herself. Doubtless she remembered nothing of this event; Ambrose on the other hand seemed unable to forget the least detail of his life. He even recalled how, standing beside himself with awed impersonality in the reeky heat, he'd stared the while at an empty cigar box in which Uncle Karl kept stonecutting chisels: beneath the words *El Producto,* a laureled, loose-toga'd lady regarded the sea from a marble bench; beside her, forgotten or not yet turned to, was a five-stringed lyre. Her chin reposed on the back of her right hand; her left depended negligently from the bench-arm. The lower half of scene and lady was peeled away; the words EXAMINED BY______ were inked there into the wood. Nowadays cigar boxes are made of pasteboard. Ambrose wondered what Magda would have done, Ambrose wondered what Magda would do when she sat back on his hand as he resolved she should. Be angry. Make a teasing joke of it. Give no sign at all. For a long time she leaned forward, playing cow-poker with Peter against Uncle Karl and Mother and watching for the first sign of Ocean City. At nearly the same instant, picnic ground and Ocean City standpipe hove into view; an Amoco filling station on their side of the road cost Mother and Uncle Karl fifty cows and the game; Magda bounced back, clapping her right hand on Mother's right arm; Ambrose moved clear "in the nick of time."

At this rate our hero, at this rate our protagonist will remain in the funhouse forever. Narrative ordinarily consists of alternating dramatization and summarization. One symptom of nervous tension, paradoxically, is repeated and violent yawning; neither Peter nor Magda nor Uncle Karl nor Mother reacted in this manner. Although they were no longer small children, Peter and Ambrose were each given a dollar to spend on boardwalk amusements in addition to what money of their own they'd brought along. Magda too, though she protested she had ample spending money. The boys' mother made a little scene out of distributing the bills; she pretended that her sons and Magda were small children and cautioned them not to spend the sum too quickly or in one place. Magda promised with a merry laugh and, having both hands free, took the bill with her left. Peter laughed also and pledged in a falsetto to be a good boy. His imitation of a child was not clever. The boys' father was tall and thin, balding, fair-complexioned. Assertions of that sort are not effective; the reader may acknowledge the proposition, but. We should be much farther along than we are; something has gone wrong; not much of this preliminary rambling seems relevant. Yet everyone begins in the same place; how is it that most go along without difficulty but a few lose their way?

"Stay out from under the boardwalk," Uncle Karl growled from the side of his mouth. The boys' mother pushed his shoulder *in mock annoyance.* They were all standing before Fat May the Laughing Lady who advertised the funhouse. Larger than life, Fat May mechanically shook, rocked on her heels, slapped her thighs while recorded laughter—uproarious, female—came amplified from a hidden loudspeaker. It chuckled, wheezed, wept; tried in vain to catch its breath; tittered, groaned, exploded raucous and anew. You couldn't hear it without laughing yourself, no matter how you felt. Father came back from talking to a Coast-Guardsman on duty and reported that the surf was spoiled with crude oil from tankers recently torpedoed offshore. Lumps of it, difficult to remove, made tarry tidelines on the beach and stuck on swimmers. Many bathed in the surf nevertheless and came out speckled; others paid to use a municipal pool and only sunbathed on the beach. We would do the latter. We would do the latter. We would do the latter.

Under the boardwalk, matchbook covers, grainy other things. What is the story's theme? Ambrose is ill. He perspires in the dark passages; candied apples-on-a-stick, delicious-looking, disappointing to eat. Funhouses need men's and ladies' room at intervals. Others perhaps have also vomited in corners and corridors; may even have had bowel movements liable to be stepped in in the dark. The word *fuck* suggests suction and/or and/or flatulence. Mother and Father; grandmothers and grandfathers on both sides; great-grandmothers and great-grandfathers on four sides, et cetera. Count a generation as thirty years: in approximately the year when Lord Baltimore was granted charter to the province of Maryland by Charles I, five hundred twelve women—English, Welsh, Bavarian, Swiss—of every class and character, received into themselves the penises the intromittent organs of five hundred twelve men, ditto, in every circumstance and posture, to conceive the five hundred twelve ancestors of the two hundred fifty-six ancestors of the et cetera et cetera et cetera et cetera et cetera et cetera et cetera et cetera of the author, of the narrator, of this story, *Lost in the Funhouse.* In alleyways, ditches, canopy beds, pinewoods, bridal suites, ship's cabins, coach-and-fours, coaches-and-four, sultry toolsheds; on the cold sand under boardwalks, littered with *El Producto* cigar butts, treasured with Lucky Strike cigarette stubs, Coca-Cola caps, gritty turds, cardboard lollipop sticks, matchbook covers warning that A Slip of the Lip Can Sink a Ship. The shluppish whisper, continuous as seawash round the globe, tidelike falls and rises with the circuit of dawn and dusk.

Magda's teeth. She *was* left-handed. Perspiration. They've gone all the way, through, Magda and Peter, they've been waiting for hours with Mother and Uncle Karl while Father searches for his lost son; they draw french-fried potatoes from a paper cup and shake their heads. They've named the children they'll one day have and bring to Ocean City on holidays. Can spermatozoa properly be thought of as male animalcules when there are no female spermatozoa? They grope through hot, dark windings, past Love's Tunnel's fearsome obstacles. Some perhaps lose their way.

Peter suggested then and there that they do the funhouse; he had been through it before, so had Magda, Ambrose hadn't and suggested, his voice cracking on account of Fat May's laughter, that they swim first. All were chuckling, couldn't help it; Ambrose's father, Ambrose's and Peter's father came up grinning like a lunatic with two boxes of syrup-coated popcorn, one for Mother, one for Magda; the men were to help themselves. Ambrose walked on Magda's right: being by nature left-handed, she carried the box in her left hand. Up front the situation was reversed.

"What are you limping for?" Magda inquired of Ambrose. He supposed in a husky tone that his foot had gone to sleep in the car. Her teeth flashed. "Pins and needles?" It was the honeysuckle on the lattice of the former privy that drew the bees. Imagine being stung there. How long is this going to take?

The adults decided to forgo the pool; but Uncle Karl insisted they change into swimsuits and do the beach. "He wants to watch the pretty girls," Peter teased, and ducked behind Magda from Uncle Karl's pretended wrath. "You've got all the pretty girls you need right here," Magda declared, and Mother said: "Now that's the gospel truth." Magda scolded Peter, who reached over her shoulder to sneak some popcorn. "Your brother and father aren't getting any." Uncle Karl wondered if they were going to have fireworks that night, what with the shortages. It wasn't the shortages, Mr. M______ replied; Ocean City had fireworks from pre-war. But it was too risky on account of the enemy submarines, some people thought.

"Don't seem like Fourth of July without fireworks," said Uncle Karl. The inverted tag in dialogue writing is still considered permissible with proper names or epithets, but sounds old-fashioned with personal pronouns. "We'll have 'em again soon enough," predicted the boys' father. Their mother declared she could do without fireworks: they reminded her too much of the real thing. Their father said all the more reason to shoot off a few now and again. Uncle Karl asked *rhetorically* who needed reminding, just look at people's hair and skin.

"The oil, yes," said Mrs. M______.

Ambrose had a pain in his stomach and so didn't swim but enjoyed watching the others. He and his father burned red easily. Magda's figure was exceedingly well developed for her age. She too declined to swim, and got mad, and became angry when Peter attempted to drag her into the pool. She always swam, he insisted; what did she mean not swim? Why did a person come to Ocean City?

"Maybe I want to lay here with Ambrose," Magda teased.

Nobody likes a pedant.

"Aha," said Mother. Peter grabbed Magda by one ankle and ordered Ambrose to grab the other. She squealed and rolled over on the beach blanket. Ambrose pretended to help hold her back. Her tan was darker than even Mother's and Peter's. "Help out, Uncle Karl!" Peter cried. Uncle Karl went to seize the other ankle. Inside the top of her swimsuit, however, you could see the line where the sunburn ended and, when she hunched her shoulders and squealed again, one nipple's auburn edge. Mother made them behave themselves. "*You* should certainly know," she said to Uncle Karl. Archly. "That when a lady says she doesn't feel like swimming, a gentleman doesn't ask questions." Uncle Karl said excuse *him;* Mother winked at Magda; Ambrose blushed; stupid Peter kept saying "Phooey on *feel like!*" and tugging at Magda's ankle; then even he got the point, and cannonballed with a holler into the pool.

"I swear," Magda said, in mock *in feigned* exasperation.

The diving would make a suitable literary symbol. To go off the high board you had to wait in a line along the poolside and up the ladder. Fellows tickled girls and goosed one another and shouted to the ones at the top to hurry up, or razzed them for bellyfloppers. Once on the springboard some took a great while posing or clowning or deciding on a dive or getting up their nerve; others ran right off. Especially among the younger fellows the idea was to strike the funniest pose or do the craziest stunt as you fell, a thing that got harder to do as you kept on and kept on. But whether you hollered *Geronimo!* or *Sieg heil!,* held your nose or "rode a bicycle," pretended to be shot or did a perfect jackknife or changed your mind halfway down and ended up with nothing, it was over in two seconds, after all that wait. Spring, pose, splash. Spring, neat-o, splash. Spring, aw fooey, splash.

The grown-ups had gone on; Ambrose wanted to converse with Magda; she was remarkably well developed for her age; it was said that that came from rubbing with a turkish towel, and there were other theories. Ambrose could think of nothing to say except how good a diver Peter was, who was showing off for her benefit. You could pretty well tell by looking at their bathing suits and arm muscles how far along the different fellows were. Ambrose was glad he hadn't gone in swimming, the cold water shrank you up so. Magda pretended to be uninterested in the diving; she probably weighed as much as he did. If you knew your way around in the funhouse like your own bedroom, you could wait until a girl came along and then slip away without ever getting caught, even if her boyfriend was right with her. She'd think *he* did it! It would be better to be the boyfriend, and act outraged, and tear the funhouse apart.

Not act; *be.*

"He's a master diver," Ambrose said. In feigned admiration. "You really have to slave away at it to get that good." What would it matter anyhow if he asked her right out whether she remembered, even teased her with it as Peter would have?

There's no point in going farther; this isn't getting anybody anywhere; they haven't even come to the funhouse yet. Ambrose is off the track, in some new or old part of the place that's not supposed to be used; he strayed into it by some one-in-a-million chance, like the time the roller-coaster car left the tracks in the nineteen-teens against all the laws of physics and sailed over the boardwalk in the dark. And they can't locate him because they don't know where to look. Even the designer and operator have forgotten this other part, that winds around on itself like a whelk shell. That winds around the right part like the snakes on Mercury's caduceus. Some people, perhaps, don't "hit their stride" until their twenties, when the growing-up business is over and women appreciate other things besides wisecracks and teasing and strutting. Peter didn't have one-tenth the imagination *he* had, not one-tenth. Peter did this naming-their-children thing as a joke, making up names like Aloysius and Murgatroyd, but Ambrose knew *exactly* how it would feel to be married and have children of your own, and be a loving husband and father, and go comfortably to work in the mornings and to bed with your wife at night, and wake up with her there. With a breeze coming through the sash and birds and mockingbirds singing in the Chinese-cigar trees. His eyes watered, there aren't enough ways to say that. He would be quite famous in his line of work. Whether Magda was his wife or not, one evening when he was wise-lined and gray at the temples he'd smile gravely, at a fashionable dinner party, and remind her of his youthful passion. The time they went with his family to Ocean City; the *erotic fantasies* he used to have about her. How long ago it seemed, and childish! Yet tender, too, *n'est-ce pas?* Would she have imagined that the world-famous whatever remembered how many strings were on the lyre on the bench beside the girl on the label of the cigar box he'd stared at in the toolshed at age ten while she, age eleven. Even then he had felt *wise beyond his years;* he'd stroked her hair and said in his deepest voice and correctest English, as to a dear child: "I shall never forget this moment."

But though he had breathed heavily, groaned as if ecstatic, what he'd really felt throughout was an odd detachment, as though someone else were Master. Strive as he might to be transported, he heard his mind take notes upon the scene: *This is what they call* passion. *I am experiencing it.* Many of the digger machines were out of order in the penny arcades and could not be repaired or replaced for the duration. Moreover the prizes, made now in USA, were less interesting than formerly, pasteboard items for the most part, and some of the machines wouldn't work on white pennies. The gypsy fortune-teller machine might have provided a foreshadowing of the climax of this story if Ambrose had operated it. It was even dilapidateder than most: the silver coating was worn off the brown metal handles, the glass windows around the dummy were cracked and taped, her kerchiefs and silks long-faded. If a man lived by himself, he could take a department-store mannequin with flexible joints and modify her in certain ways. *However:* by the time he was that old he'd have a real woman. There was a machine that stamped your name around a white-metal coin with a star in the middle: A_______. His son would be the second, and when the lad reached thirteen or so he would put a strong arm around his shoulder and tell him calmly: "It is perfectly normal. We have all been through it. It will not last forever." Nobody knew how to be what they were right. He'd smoke a pipe, teach his son how to fish and softcrab, assure him he needn't worry about himself. Magda would certainly give, Magda would certainly yield a great deal of milk, although guilty of occasional solecisms. It don't taste so bad. Suppose the lights came on now!

The day wore on. You think you're yourself, but there are other persons in you. Ambrose gets hard when Ambrose doesn't want to, *and obversely.* Ambrose watches them disagree; Ambrose watches him watch. In the funhouse mirror-room you can't see yourself go on forever, because no matter how you stand, your head gets in the way. Even if you had a glass periscope, the image of your eye would cover up the thing you really wanted to see. The police will come; there'll be a story in the papers. That must be where it happened. Unless he can find a surprise exit, an unofficial backdoor or escape hatch opening on an alley, say, and then stroll up to the family in front of the funhouse and ask where everybody's been; *he's* been out of the place for ages. That's just where it happened, in that last lighted room: Peter and Magda found the right exit; he found one that you weren't supposed to find and strayed off into the works somewhere. In a perfect funhouse you'd be able to go only one way, like the divers off the highboard; getting lost would be impossible; the doors and halls would work like minnow traps or the valves in veins.

On account of German U-boats, Ocean City was "browned out": streetlights were shaded on the seaward side; shop-windows and boardwalk amusement places were kept dim, not to silhouette tankers and Liberty-ships for torpedoing. In a short story about Ocean City, Maryland, during World War II, the author could make use of the image of sailors on leave in the penny arcades and shooting galleries, sighting through the crosshairs of toy machine guns at swastika'd subs, while out in the black Atlantic a U-boat skipper squints through his periscope at real ships outlined by the glow of penny arcades. After dinner the family strolled back to the amusement end of the boardwalk. The boys' father had burnt red as always and was masked with Noxzema, a minstrel in reverse. The grownups stood at the end of the boardwalk where the Hurricane of '33 had cut an inlet from the ocean to Assawoman Bay.

"Pronounced with a long *o,*" Uncle Karl reminded Magda with a wink. His short sleeves were rolled up; Mother punched his brown biceps with the arrowed heart on it and said his mind was naughty. Fat May's laugh came suddenly from the funhouse, as if she'd just got the joke; the family laughed too at the coincidence. Ambrose went under the boardwalk to search for out-of-town matchbook covers with the aid of his pocket flashlight; he looked out from the edge of the North American continent and wondered how far their laughter carried over the water. Spies in rubber rafts; survivors in lifeboats. If the joke had been beyond his understanding, he could have said: "*The laughter was over his head.*" And let the reader see the serious wordplay on second reading.

He turned the flashlight on and then off at once even before the woman whooped. He sprang away, heart athud, dropping the light. What had the man grunted? Perspiration drenched and chilled him by the time he scrambled up to the family. "See anything?" his father asked. His voice wouldn't come; he shrugged and violently brushed sand from his pants legs.

"Let's ride the old flying horses!" Magda cried. I'll never be an author. It's been forever already, everybody's gone home, Ocean City's deserted, the ghost-crabs are tickling across the beach and down the littered cold streets. And the empty halls of clapboard hotels and abandoned funhouses. A tidal wave; an enemy air raid; a monster-crab swelling like an island from the sea. *The inhabitants fled in terror.* Magda clung to his trouser leg; he alone knew the maze's secret. "He gave his life that we might live," said Uncle Karl with a scowl of pain, as he. The fellow's hands had been tattooed; the woman's legs, the woman's fat white legs had. *An astonishing coincidence.* He yearned to tell Peter. He wanted to throw up for excitement. They hadn't even chased him. He wished he were dead.

One possible ending would be to have Ambrose come across another lost person in the dark. They'd match their wits together against the funhouse, struggle like Ulysses past obstacle after obstacle, help and encourage each other. Or a girl. By the time they found the exit they'd be closest friends, sweethearts if it were a girl; they'd know each other's inmost souls, be bound together *by the cement of shared adventure;* then they'd emerge into the light and it would turn out that his friend was a Negro. A blind girl. President Roosevelt's son. Ambrose's former archenemy.

Shortly after the mirror room he'd groped along a musty corridor, his heart already misgiving him at the absence of phosphorescent arrows and other signs. He'd found a crack of light—not a door, it turned out, but a seam between the plyboard wall panels—and squinting up to it, espied a small old man, *in appearance not unlike* the photographs at home of Ambrose's late grandfather, nodding upon a stool beneath a bare, speckled bulb. A crude panel of toggle- and knife-switches hung beside the open fuse box near his head; elsewhere in the little room were wooden levers and ropes belayed to boat cleats. At the time, Ambrose wasn't lost enough to rap or call; later he couldn't find that crack. Now it seemed to him that he'd possibly dozed off for a few minutes somewhere along the way; certainly he was exhausted from the afternoon's sunshine and the evening's problems; he couldn't be sure he hadn't dreamed part or all of the sight. Had an old black wall fan droned like bees and shimmied two flypaper streamers? Had the funhouse operator—gentle, somewhat sad and tired-appearing, in expression not unlike the photographs at home of Ambrose's late Uncle Konrad—murmured in his sleep? Is there really such a person as Ambrose, or is he a figment of the author's imagination? Was it Assawoman Bay or

Sinepuxent? Are there other errors of fact in this fiction? Was there another sound besides the little slap slap of thigh on ham, like water sucking at the chineboards of a skiff?

When you're lost, the smartest thing to do is stay put till you're found, hollering if necessary. But to holler guarantees humiliation as well as rescue; keeping silent permits some saving of face—you can act surprised at the fuss when your rescuers find you and swear you weren't lost, if they do. What's more you might find your own way yet, *however belatedly.*

"Don't tell me your foot's still asleep!" Magda exclaimed as the three young people walked from the inlet to the area set aside for ferris wheels, carrousels, and other carnival rides, they having decided in favor of the vast and ancient merry-go-round instead of the funhouse. What a sentence, everything was wrong from the outset. People don't know what to make of him, he doesn't know what to make of himself, he's only thirteen, *athletically and socially inept,* not astonishingly bright, but there are antennae; he has . . . some sort of receivers in his head; things speak to him, he understands more than he should, the world winks at him through its objects, grabs grinning at his coat. Everybody else is in on some secret he doesn't know; they've forgotten to tell him. Through simple *procrastination* his mother put off his baptism until this year. Everyone else had it done as a baby; he'd assumed the same of himself, as had his mother, so she claimed, until it was time for him to join Grace Methodist-Protestant and the oversight came out. He was mortified, but pitched sleepless through his private catechizing, intimidated by the ancient mysteries, a thirteen year old would never say that, resolved to experience conversion like St. Augustine. When the water touched his brow and Adam's sin left him, he contrived by a strain like defecation to bring tears into his eyes—but felt nothing. There was some simple, radical difference about him; he hoped it was genius, feared it was madness, devoted himself to amiability and inconspicuousness. Alone on the seawall near his house he was seized by the terrifying transports he'd thought to find in toolshed, in Communion-cup. The grass was alive! The town, the river, himself, were not imaginary; time roared in his ears like wind; the world was *going on!* This part ought to be dramatized. The Irish author James Joyce once wrote. Ambrose M_____ is going to scream.

There is no *texture of rendered sensory detail,* for one thing. The faded distorting mirrors beside Fat May; the impossibility of choosing a mount when one had but a single ride on the great carrousel; the *vertigo attendant on his recognition* that Ocean City was worn out, the place of fathers and grandfathers, straw-boatered men and parasoled ladies survived by their amusements. Money spent, the three paused at Peter's insistence beside Fat May to watch the girls get their skirts blown up. The object was to tease Magda, who said: "I swear, Peter M_____, you've got a one-track mind! Amby and me aren't *interested* in such things." In the tumbling-barrel, too, just inside the Devil's-mouth entrance to the funhouse, the girls were upended and their boyfriends and others could see up their dresses if they cared to. Which was the whole point. Ambrose realized. Of the entire funhouse! If you looked around, you noticed that almost all the people on the boardwalk were paired off into couples except the small children; in a way, that was the whole point of Ocean City! If you had X-ray eyes and could see everything going on at that instant under the boardwalk and in all the hotel rooms and cars and alleyways, you'd realize that all that normally *showed,* like restaurants and dance halls and clothing and test-your-strength machines, was merely preparation and intermission. Fat May screamed.

Because he watched the goings-on from the corner of his eye, it was Ambrose who spied the half-dollar on the boardwalk near the tumbling-barrel. Losers weepers. The first time he'd heard some people moving through a corridor not far away, just after he'd lost sight of the crack of light, he'd decided not to call to them, for fear they'd guess he was scared and poke fun; it sounded like roughnecks; he'd hoped they'd come by and he could follow in the dark without their knowing. Another time he'd heard just one person, unless he imagined it, bumping along as if on the other side of the plywood; perhaps Peter coming back for him, or Father, or Magda lost too. Or the owner and operator of the funhouse. He'd called out once, as though merrily: "Anybody know where the heck we are?" But the query was too stiff, his voice cracked, when the sounds stopped he was terrified: maybe it was a queer who waited for fellows to get lost, or a longhaired filthy monster that lived in some cranny of the funhouse. He stood rigid for hours it seemed like, scarcely respiring. His future was shockingly clear, in outline. He tried holding his breath to the point of unconsciousness. There ought to be a button you could push to end your life absolutely without pain; disappear in a flick, like turning out a light. He would push it instantly! He despised Uncle Karl. But he despised his father too, for not being what he was supposed to be. Perhaps his father hated *his* father, and so on, and his son would hate him, and so on. Instantly!

Naturally he didn't have nerve enough to ask Magda to go through the funhouse with him. With incredible nerve and to everyone's surprise he invited Magda, quietly and politely, to go through the funhouse with him. "I warn you, I've never been through it before," he added, *laughing easily;* "but I reckon we can manage somehow. The important thing to remember, after all, is that it's meant to be a *fun*house; that is, a place of amusement. If people really got lost or injured or too badly frightened in it, the owner'd go out of business. There'd even be lawsuits. No character in a work of fiction can make a speech this long without interruption or acknowledgment from the other characters."

Mother teased Uncle Karl: "Three's a crowd, I always heard." But actually Ambrose was relieved that Peter now had a quarter too. Nothing was what it looked like. Every instant, under the surface of the Atlantic Ocean, millions of living animals devoured one another. Pilots were falling in flames over Europe; women were being forcibly raped in the South Pacific. His father should have taken him aside and said: "There is a simple secret to getting through the funhouse, as simple as being first to see the Towers. Here it is. Peter does not know it; neither does your Uncle Karl. You and I are different. Not surprisingly, you've often wished you weren't. Don't think I haven't noticed how unhappy your childhood has been! But you'll understand, when I tell you, why it had to be kept secret until now. And you won't regret not being like your brother and your uncle. *On the contrary!*" If you knew all the stories behind all the people on the boardwalk, you'd see that *nothing* was what it looked like. Husbands and wives often hated each other; parents didn't necessarily love their children; et cetera. A child took things for granted because he had nothing to compare his life to and everybody acted as if things were as they should be. Therefore each saw himself as the hero of the story, when the truth might turn out to be that he's the villain, or the coward. And there wasn't one thing you could do about it!

Hunchbacks, fat ladies, fools—that no one chose what he was was unbearable. In the movies he'd meet a beautiful young girl in the funhouse; they'd have hairs-breadth escapes from real dangers; he'd do and say the right things; she also; in the end they'd be lovers; their dialogue lines would match up; he'd be perfectly at ease; she'd not only like him well enough, she'd think he was *marvelous;* she'd lie awake thinking about *him,* instead of vice versa—the way *his* face looked in different lights and how he stood and exactly what he'd said—and yet that would be only one small episode in his wonderful life, among many many others. Not a *turning point* at all. What had happened in the toolshed was nothing. He hated, he loathed his parents! One reason for not writing a lost-in-the-funhouse story is that either everybody's felt what Ambrose feels, in which case it goes without saying, or else no normal person feels such things, in which case Ambrose is a freak. "Is anything more tiresome, in fiction, than the problems of sensitive adolescents?" And it's all too long and rambling, as if the author. For all a person knows the first time through, the end could be just around any corner; perhaps, *not impossibly* it's been within reach any number of times. On the other hand he may be scarcely past the start, with everything yet to get through, an intolerable idea.

Fill in: His father's raised eyebrows when he announced his decision to do the funhouse with Magda. Ambrose understands now, but didn't then, that his father was wondering whether he knew what the funhouse was *for*—especially since he didn't object, as he should have, when Peter decided to come along too. The ticket-woman, witchlike, mortifying him when inadvertently he gave her his name-coin instead of the half-dollar, then unkindly calling Magda's attention to the birthmark on his temple: "Watch out for him, girlie, he's a marked man!" She wasn't even cruel, he understood, only vulgar and insensitive. Somewhere in the world there was a young woman with such splendid understanding that she'd see him entire, like a poem or story, and find his words so valuable after all that when he confessed his apprehensions she would explain why they were in fact the very things that made him precious to her . . . and to Western Civilization! There was no such girl, the simple truth being. Violent yawns as they approached the mouth. Whispered advice from an old-timer on a bench near the barrel: "Go crabwise and ye'll get an eyeful without upsetting!" Composure vanished at the first pitch: Peter hollered joyously, Magda tumbled, shrieked, clutched her skirt; Ambrose scrambled crabwise, tight-lipped with terror, was soon out, watched his dropped name-coin slide among the couples. Shame-faced he saw that to get through expeditiously was not the point; Peter feigned assistance in order to trip Magda up, shouted "I see Christmas!" when her legs went flying. The old man, his latest betrayer, cacked approval. A dim hall then of black-thread cobwebs and recorded gibber: he took Magda's elbow to steady her against revolving discs set in the slanted floor to throw your feet out from under, and explained to her in a calm, deep voice his theory that each phase of the funhouse was triggered either automatically, by a series of photoelectric devices, or else manually by operators stationed at peepholes. But he lost his voice thrice as the discs unbalanced him; Magda was anyhow squealing; but at one point she clutched him about the waist to keep from falling, and her right cheek pressed for a moment against his belt-buckle. Heroically he drew her up, it was his chance to clutch her close as if for support and say: "I love you." He even put an arm lightly about the small of her back before a sailor-and-girl pitched into them from behind, sorely treading his left big toe and knocking Magda asprawl with them. The sailor's girl was a string-haired hussy with a loud laugh and light blue drawers; Ambrose realized that he wouldn't have said "I love you" anyhow, and was smitten with self-contempt. How much better it would be to be that common sailor! A wiry little Seaman 3rd, the fellow squeezed a girl to each side and stumbled hilarious into the mirror room, closer to Magda in thirty seconds than Ambrose had got in thirteen years. She giggled at something the fellow said to Peter; she drew her hair from her eyes with a movement so womanly it struck Ambrose's heart; Peter's smacking her backside then seemed particularly coarse. But Magda made a pleased indignant face and cried, "All right for *you,* mister!" and pursued Peter into the maze without a backward glance. The sailor followed after, leisurely, drawing his girl against his hip; Ambrose understood not only that they were all so relieved to be rid of his burdensome company that they didn't even notice his absence, but that he himself shared their relief. Stepping from the treacherous passage at last into the mirror-maze, he saw once again, more clearly than ever, how readily he deceived himself into supposing he was a person. He even foresaw, wincing at his dreadful self-knowledge, that he would repeat the deception, at ever-rarer intervals, all his wretched life, so fearful were the alternatives. Fame, madness, suicide; perhaps all three. It's not believable that so young a boy could articulate that reflection, and in fiction the merely true must always yield to the plausible. Moreover, the symbolism is in places heavy-footed. Yet Ambrose M______ understood, as few adults do, that the famous loneliness of the great was no popular myth but a general truth—furthermore, that it was as much cause as effect.

All the preceding except the last few sentences is exposition that should've been done earlier or interspersed with the present action instead of lumped together. No reader would put up with so much with such *prolixity.* It's interesting that Ambrose's father, though presumably an intelligent man (as indicated by his role as grade-school principal), neither encouraged nor discouraged his sons at all in any way—as if he either didn't care about them or cared all right but didn't know how to act. If this fact should contribute to one of them's becoming a celebrated but wretchedly unhappy scientist, was it a good thing or not? He too might someday face the question; it would be useful to know whether it had tortured his father for years, for example, or never once crossed his mind.

In the maze two important things happened. First, our hero found a name-coin someone else had lost or discarded: AMBROSE, suggestive of the famous lightship and of his late grandfather's favorite dessert, which his mother used to prepare on special occasions out of coconut, oranges, grapes, and what else. Second, as he wondered at the endless replication of his image in the mirrors, second, as he *lost himself in the reflection* that the necessity for an observer makes perfect observation impossible, better make him eighteen at least, yet that would render other things unlikely, he heard Peter and Magda chuckling somewhere together in the maze. "Here!" "No, here!" they shouted to each other; Peter said, "Where's Amby?" Magda murmured. "Amb?" Peter called. In a pleased, friendly voice. He didn't reply. The truth was, his brother was a *happy-go-lucky youngster* who'd've been better off with a regular brother of his own, but who seldom complained of his lot and was generally cordial.

Ambrose's throat ached; there aren't enough different ways to say that. He stood quietly while the two young people giggled and thumped through the glittering maze, hurrah'd their discovery of its exit, cried out in joyful alarm at what next beset them. Then he set his mouth and followed after, as he supposed, took a wrong turn, strayed into the pass *wherein he lingers yet.*

The action of conventional dramatic narrative may be represented by a diagram called Freitag's Triangle:

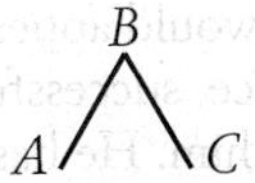

or more accurately by a variant of that diagram:

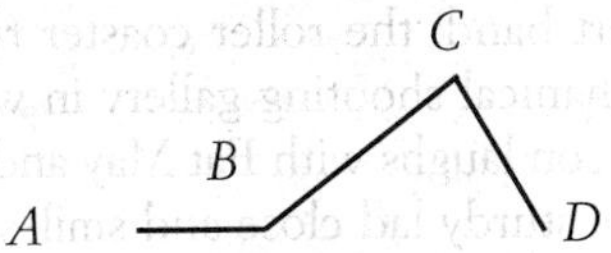

in which *AB* represents the exposition, *B* the introduction of conflict, *BC* the "rising action," complication, or development of the conflict, *C* the climax, or turn of the action, *CD* the dénouement, or resolution of the conflict. While there is no reason to regard this pattern as an absolute necessity, like many other conventions it became conventional because great numbers of people over many years learned by trial and error that it was effective; one ought not to forsake it, therefore, unless one wishes to forsake as well the effect of drama or has clear cause to feel that deliberate violation of the "normal" pattern can better can better effect that effect. This can't go on much longer; it can go on forever. He died telling stories to himself in the dark; years later, when that vast unsuspected area of the funhouse came to light, the first expedition found his skeleton in one of its labyrinthine corridors and mistook it for part of the entertainment. He died of starvation telling himself stories in the dark; but unbeknownst unbeknownst to him, an assistant operator of the funhouse, happening to overhear him, crouched just behind the plyboard partition and wrote down his every word. The operator's daughter, an exquisite young woman with a figure unusually well developed for her age, crouched just behind the partition and transcribed his every word. Though she had never laid eyes on him, she recognized that here was one of Western Culture's truly great imaginations, the eloquence of whose suffering would be an inspiration to unnumbered. And her heart was torn between her love for the misfortunate young man (yes, she loved him, though she had never laid though she knew him only—but how well!—through his words, and the deep, calm voice in which he spoke them) between her love et cetera and her womanly intuition that only in suffering and isolation could he give voice et cetera. Lone dark dying. Quietly she kissed the rough plyboard, and a tear fell upon the page. Where she had written in shorthand *Where she had written in shorthand* Where she had written in shorthand *Where she* et cetera. A long time ago we should have passed the apex of Freitag's Triangle and made brief work of the *dénouement;* the plot doesn't rise by meaningful steps but winds upon itself, digresses, retreats, hesitates, sighs, collapses, expires. The climax of the story must be its protagonist's discovery of a way to get through the funhouse. But he has found none, may have ceased to search.

What relevance does the war have to the story? Should there be fireworks outside or not?

Ambrose wandered, languished, dozed. Now and then he fell into his habit of rehearsing to himself the unadventurous story of his life, narrated from the third-person point of view, from his earliest memory parenthesis of maple leaves stirring in the summer breath of tidewater Maryland end of parenthesis to the present moment. Its principal events, on this telling, would appear to have been *A, B, C,* and *D.*

He imagined himself years hence, successful, married, at ease in the world, the trials of his adolescence far behind him. He has come to the seashore with his family for the holiday: how Ocean City has changed! But at one seldom at one ill-frequented end of the boardwalk a few derelict amusements survive from times gone by: the great carrousel from the turn of the century, with its monstrous griffins and mechanical concert band; the roller coaster rumored since 1916 to have been condemned; the mechanical shooting gallery in which only the image of our enemies changed. His own son laughs with Fat May and wants to know what a funhouse is; Ambrose hugs the sturdy lad close and smiles around his pipestem at his wife.

The family's going home. Mother sits between Father and Uncle Karl, who teases him good-naturedly who chuckles over the fact that the comrade with whom he'd fought his way shoulder to shoulder through the funhouse had turned out to be a blind Negro girl—to their mutual discomfort, as they'd opened their souls. But such are the walls of custom, which even. Whose arm is where? How must it feel. He dreams of a funhouse vaster by far than any yet constructed; but by then they may be out of fashion, like steamboats and excursion trains. Already quaint and seedy: the draperied ladies on the frieze of the carrousel are his father's father's moon-cheeked dreams; if he thinks of it more he will vomit his apple-on-a-stick.

He wonders: will he become a regular person? Something has gone wrong; his vaccination didn't take; at the Boy-Scout initiation campfire he only pretended to be deeply moved, as he pretends to this hour that it is not so bad after all in the funhouse, and that he has a little limp. How long will it last? He envisions a truly astonishing funhouse, incredibly complex yet utterly controlled from a great central switchboard like the console of a pipe organ. Nobody had enough imagination. He could design such a place himself, wiring and all, and he's only thirteen years old. He would be its operator: panel lights would show what was up in every cranny of its cunning of its multifarious vastness; a switch-flick would ease this fellow's way, complicate that's, to balance things out; if anyone seemed lost or frightened, all the operator had to do was.

He wishes he had never entered the funhouse. But he has. Then he wishes he were dead. But he's not. Therefore he will construct funhouses for others and be their secret operator—though he would rather be among the lovers for whom funhouses are designed.

1968

Donald Barthelme (1931–1989)

Born in Philadelphia but raised in Houston, Texas, Barthelme began writing stories and poems in high school and continued writing (journalism as well as fiction and poetry) at the University of Houston. After Army service in Japan and Korea, he returned to the university and worked as a reporter locally. He then became director of Houston's Contemporary Arts Museum.

In 1962 he moved to New York and soon found his own voice and style. He became a regular contributor to the *New Yorker,* and began to find in his fiction the innovation that was occurring in film and graphic art. He was influenced by the French Symbolists, and worked frequently with myth and spatial techniques (perhaps because of the visionary influence of his father, an architect). His vision was comic, surreal, macabre; and his play with language—giving the reader the unexpected, the grotesque, and above all the fragmented—marked him as a postmodernist even before that classification existed.

With a montage style reminiscent of that of Dos Passos, Barthelme drew phrases and lines from advertising, songs, and stereotyped phrases of the times; and created from those borrowings new structures and new perspectives. His first novel, *Snow White,* retold the classic fairytale, but with wit and acerbity that surprised readers of the 1960s. Structural experimentation in *The Dead Fathers* made that novel another treasure house of narrative technique, and brought a patina of fashion to a more serious theme. But even more than a montage of materials, "At the End of the Mechanical Age" represents a parody of fictional traditions and the various structures of storytelling they employ. By juxtaposing such structures, Barthelme exposes—to both scrutiny and laughter—the historical consciousness of the modern age. When biblical or creation myths jostle with "true romance" materials, then the modernist belief that we stand at the end of a long historical process, and thereby derive a certain cultural and social advantage, is given the lie. At the same time the themes of divorce, repression, and secular self-doubt enter the mix, as they do in the tradition of nineteenth-century realist novels, but in a telegraphed way that some critics see as one of the hallmarks of Barthelme's style. He not only parodies his characters and their concerns, he also mocks the very possibilities and burdens of storytelling itself. Because he calls into question the mechanics of this central cultural activity, and by extension the ability of language to represent reality, he is often credited with influencing many aspects of postmodernism.

Charles Molesworth
Queens College, CUNY

PRIMARY WORKS

Come Back, Dr. Caligari (stories), 1964; *Snow White,* 1967; *Unspeakable Practices, Unnatural Acts* (stories), 1968; *City Life* (stories), 1970; *Sadness,* 1972; *Guilty Pleasures,* 1974; *The Dead Father,* 1975; *Amateurs* (stories), 1976; *Great Days* (stories), 1979; *Sixty Stories,* 1981; *Paradise,* 1986; *The King,* 1990; *The Teachings of Don B.,* ed. Kim Herzinger, 1993.

At the End of the Mechanical Age

I went to the grocery store to buy some soap. I stood for a long time before the soaps in their attractive boxes, RUB and FAB and TUB and suchlike, I couldn't decide so I closed my eyes and reached out blindly and when I opened my eyes I found her hand in mine.

Her name was Mrs. Davis, she said, and TUB was best for important cleaning experiences, in her opinion. So we went to lunch at a Mexican restaurant which as it happened she owned, she took me into the kitchen and showed me her stacks of handsome beige tortillas and the steam tables which were shiny-brite. I told her I wasn't very good with women and she said it didn't matter, few men were, and that nothing mattered, now that Jake was gone, but I would do as an interim project and sit down and have a Carta Blanca. So I sat down and had a cool Carta Blanca, God was standing in the basement reading the meters to see how much grace had been used up in the month of June. Grace is electricity, science has found, it is not *like* electricity, it *is* electricity and God was down in the basement reading the meters in His blue jump suit with the flashlight stuck in the back pocket.

"The mechanical age is drawing to a close," I said to her.

"Or has already done so," she replied.

"It was a good age," I said. "I was comfortable in it, relatively. Probably I will not enjoy the age to come quite so much. I don't like its look."

"One must be fair. We don't know yet what kind of an age the next one will be. Although I feel in my bones that it will be an age inimical to personal well-being and comfort, and that is what I like, personal well-being and comfort."

"Do you suppose there is something to be done?" I asked her.

"Huddle and cling," said Mrs. Davis. "We can huddle and cling. It will pall, of course, everything palls, in time . . ."

Then we went back to my house to huddle and cling, most women are two different colors when they remove their clothes especially in summer but Mrs. Davis was all one color, an ocher. She seemed to like huddling and clinging, she stayed for many days. From time to time she checked the restaurant keeping everything shiny-brite and distributing sums of money to the staff, returning with tortillas in sacks, cases of Carta Blanca, buckets of guacamole, but I paid her for it because I didn't want to feel obligated.

There was a song I sang her, a song of great expectations.

"Ralph is coming," I sang, *"Ralph is striding in his suit of lights over moons and mountains, over parking lots and fountains, toward your silky side. Ralph is coming, he has a coat of many colors and all major credit cards and he is striding to meet you and culminate your foggy dreams in an explosion of blood and soil, at the end of the mechanical age. Ralph is coming preceded by fifty running men with spears and fifty dancing ladies who are throwing leaf spinach out of little baskets, in his path. Ralph is perfect,"* I sang, *"but he is also full of interesting tragic flaws, and he can drink fifty running men under the table without breaking his stride and he can have congress with fifty dancing ladies without breaking his stride, even his socks are ironed, so natty is Ralph, but he is also right down in the mud with the rest of us, he markets the mud at high prices for specialized industrial uses and he is striding, striding, striding, toward*

your waiting heart. Of course you may not like him, some people are awfully picky . . . Ralph is coming," I sang to her, *"he is striding over dappled plains and crazy rivers and he will change your life for the better, probably, you will be fainting with glee at the simple touch of his grave gentle immense hand although I am aware that some people can't stand prosperity, Ralph is coming, I hear his hoofsteps on the drumhead of history, he is striding as he has been all his life toward you, you, you."*

"Yes," Mrs. Davis said, when I had finished singing, "that is what I deserve, all right. But probably I will not get it. And in the meantime, there is you."

* * *

God then rained for forty days and forty nights, when the water tore away the front of the house we got into the boat, Mrs. Davis liked the way I maneuvered the boat off the trailer and out of the garage, she was provoked into a memoir of Jake.

"Jake was a straight-ahead kind of man," she said, "he was simpleminded and that helped him to be the kind of man that he was." She was staring into her Scotch-and-floodwater rather moodily I thought, debris bouncing on the waves all around us but she paid no attention. "That is the type of man I like," she said, "a strong and simple-minded man. The case-study method was not Jake's method, he went right through the middle of the line and never failed to gain yardage, no matter what the game was. He had a lust for life, and life had a lust for him. I was inconsolable when Jake passed away." Mrs. Davis was drinking the Scotch for her nerves, she had no nerves of course, she was nerveless and possibly heartless also but that is another question, gutless she was not, she had a gut and a very pretty one ocher in color but that was another matter. God was standing up to His neck in the raging waters with a smile of incredible beauty on His visage, He seemed to be enjoying His creation, the disaster, the waters all around us were raging louder now, raging like a mighty tractor-trailer tailgating you on the highway.

Then Mrs. Davis sang to me, a song of great expectations.

"Maude is waiting for you," Mrs. Davis sang to me, *"Maude is waiting for you in all her seriousness and splendor, under her gilded onion dome, in that city which I cannot name at this time, Maude waits. Maude is what you lack, the profoundest of your lacks. Your every yearn since the first yearn has been a yearn for Maude, only you did not know it until I, your dear friend, pointed it out. She is going to heal your scrappy and generally unsatisfactory life with the balm of her Maudeness, luckiest of dogs, she waits only for you. Let me give you just one instance of Maude's inhuman sagacity. Maude named the tools. It was Maude who thought of calling the rattail file a rattail file. It was Maude who christened the needle-nose pliers. Maude named the rasp. Think of it. What else could a rasp be but a rasp? Maude in her wisdom went right to the point, and called it* rasp. *It was Maude who named the maul. Similarly the sledge, the wedge, the ball-peen hammer, the adz, the shim, the hone, the strop. The handsaw, the hacksaw, the bucksaw, and the fretsaw were named by Maude, peering into each saw and intuiting at once its specialness. The scratch awl, the scuffle hoe, the prick punch and the countersink—I could go on and on. The tools came to Maude, tool by tool in a long respectful line, she gave them their names. The vise. The gimlet. The cold chisel. The reamer, the router, the gouge. The plumb bob. How could she have thought up the rough justice of these wonderful cognomens? Looking languidly at a pair of tin snips,*

and then deciding to call them tin snips*—what a burst of glory! And I haven't even cited the bush hook, the grass snath, or the plumber's snake, or the C-clamp, or the nippers, or the scythe. What a tall achievement, naming the tools! And this is just one of Maude's contributions to our worldly estate, there are others. What delights will come crowding,"* Mrs. Davis sang to me, "*delight upon delight, when the epithalamium is ground out by the hundred organ grinders who are Maude's constant attendants, on that good-quality day of her own choosing, which you have desperately desired all your lean life, only you weren't aware of it until I, your dear friend, pointed it out. And Maude is young but not too young,"* Mrs. Davis sang to me, *"she is not too old either, she is* just right *and she is waiting for you with her tawny limbs and horse sense, when you receive Maude's nod your future and your past will begin."*

There was a pause, or pall.

"Is that true," I asked, "that song?"

"It is a metaphor," said Mrs. Davis, "it has metaphorical truth."

"And the end of the mechanical age," I said, "is that a metaphor?"

"The end of the mechanical age," said Mrs. Davis, "is in my judgment an actuality straining to become a metaphor. One must wish it luck, I suppose. One must cheer it on. Intellectual rigor demands that we give these damned metaphors every chance, even if they are inimical to personal well-being and comfort. We have a duty to understand everything, whether we like it or not—a duty I would scant if I could." At that moment the water jumped into the boat and sank us.

* * *

At the wedding Mrs. Davis spoke to me kindly.

"Tom," she said, "you are not Ralph, but you are all that is around at the moment. I have taken in the whole horizon with a single sweep of my practiced eye, no giant figure looms there and that is why I have decided to marry you, temporarily, with Jake gone and an age ending. It will be a marriage of convenience all right, and when Ralph comes, or Maude nods, then our arrangement will automatically self-destruct, like the tinted bubble that it is. You were very kind and considerate, when we were drying out, in the tree, and I appreciated that. That counted for something. Of course kindness and consideration are not what the great songs, the Ralph-song and the Maude-song, promise. They are merely flaky substitutes for the terminal experience. I realize that and want you to realize it. I want to be straight with you. That is one of the most admirable things about me, that I am always straight with people, from the sweet beginning to the bitter end. Now I will return to the big house where my handmaidens will proceed with the robing of the bride."

It was cool in the meadow by the river, the meadow Mrs. Davis had selected for the travesty, I walked over to the tree under which my friend Blackie was standing, he was the best man, in a sense.

"This disgusts me," Blackie said, "this hollow pretense and empty sham and I had to come all the way from Chicago."

God came to the wedding and stood behind a tree with just part of His effulgence showing, I wondered whether He was planning to bless this makeshift construct with His grace, or not. It's hard to imagine what He was thinking of in the beginning when He planned everything that was ever going to happen, planned everything exquisitely right down to the tiniest detail such as what I was thinking at this very moment, my thought about His thought, planned the end of the mechanical age and detailed the new age to follow, and then the bride emerged from the house with her train, all ocher in color and very lovely.

"And do you, Anne," the minister said, "promise to make whatever mutually satisfactory accommodations necessary to reduce tensions and arrive at whatever previously agreed-upon goals both parties have harmoniously set in the appropriate planning sessions?"

"I do," said Mrs. Davis.

"And do you, Thomas, promise to explore all differences thoroughly with patience and inner honesty ignoring no fruitful avenues of discussion and seeking at all times to achieve rapprochement while eschewing advantage in conflict situations?"

"Yes," I said.

"Well, now we are married," said Mrs. Davis, "I think I will retain my present name if you don't mind, I have always been Mrs. Davis and your name is a shade graceless, no offense, dear."

"O.K.," I said.

Then we received the congratulations and good wishes of the guests, who were mostly employees of the Mexican restaurant, Raul was there and Consuelo, Pedro, and Pepe came crowding around with outstretched hands and Blackie came crowding around with outstretched hands, God was standing behind the caterer's tables looking at the enchiladas and chalupas and chile con queso and chicken mole as if He had never seen such things before but that was hard to believe.

I started to speak to Him as all of the world's great religions with a few exceptions urge, from the heart, I started to say "Lord, Little Father of the Poor, and all that, I was just wondering now that an age, the mechanical age, is ending and a new age beginning or so they say, I was just wondering if You could give me a hint, sort of, not a Sign, I'm not asking for a Sign, but just the barest hint as to whether what we have been told about Your nature and our nature is, forgive me and I know how You feel about doubt or rather what we have been told you feel about it, but if You could just let drop the slightest indication as to whether what we have been told is authentic or just a bunch of apocryphal heterodoxy—"

But He had gone away with an insanely beautiful smile on His lighted countenance, gone away to read the meters and get a line on the efficacy of grace in that area, I surmised, I couldn't blame Him, my question had not been so very elegantly put, had I been able to express it mathematically He would have been more interested, maybe, but I have never been able to express anything mathematically.

After the marriage Mrs. Davis explained marriage to me.

Marriage, she said, an institution deeply enmeshed with the mechanical age.

Pairings smiled upon by law were but reifications of the laws of mechanics, inspired by unions of a technical nature, such as nut with bolt, wood with wood screw, aircraft with Plane-Mate.

Permanence or impermanence of the bond a function of (1) materials and (2) technique.

Growth of literacy a factor, she said.

Growth of illiteracy also.

The center will not hold if it has been spot-welded by an operator whose deepest concern is not with the weld but with his lottery ticket.

God interested only in grace—keeping things humming.

Blackouts, brownouts, temporary dimmings of household illumination all portents not of Divine displeasure but of Divine indifference to executive-development programs at middle-management levels.

He likes to get out into the field Himself, she said. With His flashlight. He is doing the best He can.

We two, she and I, no exception to general ebb/flow of world juice and its concomitant psychological effects, she said.

Bitter with the sweet, she said.

* * *

After the explanation came the divorce.

"Will you be wanting to contest the divorce?" I asked Mrs. Davis.

"I think not," she said calmly, "although I suppose one of us should, for the fun of the thing. An uncontested divorce always seems to me contrary to the spirit of divorce."

"That is true," I said, "I have had the same feeling myself, not infrequently."

After the divorce the child was born. We named him A.F. of L. Davis and sent him to that part of Russia where people live to be one hundred and ten years old. He is living there still, probably, growing in wisdom and beauty. Then we shook hands, Mrs. Davis and I, and she set out Ralphward, and I, Maudeward, the glow of hope not yet extinguished, the fear of pall not yet triumphant, standby generators ensuring the flow of grace to all of God's creatures at the end of the mechanical age.

1977

Thomas Pynchon b. 1937

Very few American writers, while still alive, have been accorded the somewhat dubious honor of having their last name turned into an adjective. Even fewer have seen this resultant adjective become a buzzword in highbrow popular culture, a process that associates their name with everything from film and literature to advertising campaigns, pop music, and underground publications. Thomas Ruggles Pynchon, Jr., came into the collective consciousness of late-twentieth- and early-twenty-first-century American culture largely through the use (and abuse) of the labels "Pynchonian" and "Pynchonesque," which sprang up after the publication of his mammoth novel *Gravity's Rainbow.* These two adjectives connote extreme intellectualism, an encyclopedic frame of reference, paranoia, spiraling conspiracy theories, reclusiveness, dark humor, or a combination of all these. Perhaps unfairly, these have also been the dominant themes in criticism of Pynchon's work.

Few biographical details are known. Pynchon was born on Long Island in Oyster Bay, New York, on May 8, 1937. His family is descended from the Puritan Pyncheons who provided Nathaniel Hawthorne with material for *The House of Seven*

Gables. After a brief stint in the U.S. Navy, he attended Cornell University, where he majored in engineering before switching to English; he took classes from Vladimir Nabokov and befriended Richard Fariña, whose 1966 novel *Been Down So Long It Looks like Up to Me* anticipated many themes that Pynchon would later treat. Having passed up an opportunity to go to graduate school, he worked as a technical writer for Boeing Aircraft in Seattle from 1960 to 1962. His subsequent public biography consists almost entirely of his publication history.

Pynchon's first novel *V.,* published in 1963, won the Faulkner First Novel Award. In 1966 *The Crying of Lot 49,* a shorter but no less complex novel, garnered the Rosenthal Memorial Award. *Gravity's Rainbow,* published in 1973, nearly won the Pulitzer Prize until several jurors rejected it on the grounds of "obscenity and obscurity." In 1975 Pynchon was awarded the Howells Medal of the American Academy but turned it down without giving a reason. His literary output for the remainder of the 1970s and 80s was limited to *Slow Learner,* a collection of five short stories ("Entropy" among them) originally published between 1959 and 1964, and a small number of essays and reviews.

It is generally believed that Pynchon lived in Aptos, a small town in northern California, for much of the 1980s, during which he produced his novel *Vineland* (1990) and possibly wrote a series of letters to a small local newspaper using the pseudonym Wanda Tinasky. He has apparently lived in New York City since that time. He is married to his literary agent Melanie Jackson; they have one son. His most recent novel is *Mason & Dixon,* published in 1997.

Whatever the facts of his life may be, Pynchon's small but important body of work (five novels and a collection of short stories over the course of more than forty years) has had a profound effect on the development of American literature. Many readers have been tempted to categorize Pynchon's individual works as products of a certain place and time, especially *The Crying of Lot 49* and *Vineland,* which are often criticized for being generational pieces "about" California in the 1960s and 80s, respectively. Examination of his entire body of work, though, leads to an understanding of both the depth of Pynchon's encyclopedic erudition and his wide-ranging cultural satire.

"Entropy" initially appeared in the *Kenyon Review* in the spring of 1960. Pynchon himself evinced considerable disdain for the story in the introduction to *Slow Learner:* "The story is a fine example of a procedural error beginning writers are always cautioned against. It is simply wrong to begin with a theme, symbol or other abstract unifying agent, and then to try to force characters and events to conform to it." Despite this harsh self-criticism, the story represents his first extensive treatment of the concept of entropy in its thermodynamic, informational, and cosmic forms. This theme recurs notably in the "Whole Sick Crew" episodes of *V.* and throughout *The Crying of Lot 49,* most tellingly in the "Maxwell's Demon" portions.

"Entropy" does not have the intricately organized and at times maddeningly allusive structure of *Gravity's Rainbow,* but it is possible to see Pynchon's authorial voice taking shape in this story. The blending of near-farcical comic elements with a dark, even brooding satirical impulse leaves the reader with an ambiguous message, another hallmark of his later works. Critics disagree about whether Pynchon is more sympathetic to Meatball Mulligan, who attempts to make order out of chaos despite the unavoidable force of entropy, or to Callisto, who walls himself off from the outside world and seems to have resigned himself to its "heat-death." One's interpretation largely determines whether the dual endings of the story represent an affirmation of life like that of the Beats (whose works and language Pynchon cites as an early influence) or an acquiescence to the inevitability of death, a theme that existentialist philosophers/novelists such as Albert Camus and Jean-Paul Sartre had popularized during Pynchon's adolescence.

Derek C. Maus
University of North Carolina–Chapel Hill

PRIMARY WORKS

V., 1963; *The Crying of Lot 49,* 1966; *Gravity's Rainbow,* 1973; *Slow Learner,* 1984; *Vineland,* 1990; *Mason & Dixon,* 1997.

Entropy

Boris has just given me a summary of his views. He is a weather prophet. The weather will continue bad, he says. There will be more calamities, more death, more despair. Not the slightest indication of a change anywhere. . . . We must get into step, a lockstep toward the prison of death. There is no escape. The weather will not change.

—Tropic of Cancer

Downstairs, Meatball Mulligan's lease-breaking party was moving into its 40th hour. On the kitchen floor, amid a litter of empty champagne fifths, were Sandor Rojas and three friends, playing spit in the ocean and staying awake on Heidseck and benzedrine pills. In the living room Duke, Vincent, Krinkles and Paco sat crouched over a 15-inch speaker which had been bolted into the top of a wastepaper basket, listening to 27 watts' worth of *The Heroes' Gate at Kiev.* They all wore hornrimmed sunglasses and rapt expressions, and smoked funny-looking cigarettes which contained not, as you might expect, tobacco, but an adulterated form of *cannabis sativa.* This group was the Duke di Angelis quartet. They recorded for a local label called Tambú and had to their credit one 10" LP entitled *Songs of Outer Space.* From time to time one of them would flick the ashes from his cigarette into the speaker cone to watch them dance around. Meatball himself was sleeping over by the window, holding an empty magnum to his chest as if it were a teddy bear. Several government girls, who worked for people like the State Department and NSA, had passed out on couches, chairs and in one case the bathroom sink.

This was in early February of '57 and back then there were a lot of American expatriates around Washington, D.C., who would talk, every time they met you, about how someday they were going to go over to Europe for real but right now it seemed they were working for the government. Everyone saw a fine irony in this. They would stage, for instance, polyglot parties where the newcomer was sort of ignored if he couldn't carry on simultaneous conversations in three or four languages. They would haunt Armenian delicatessens for weeks at a stretch and invite you over for bulghour and lamb in tiny kitchens whose walls were covered with bullfight posters. They would have affairs with sultry girls from Andalucía or the Midi who studied economics at Georgetown. Their Dôme was a collegiate Rathskeller out on Wisconsin Avenue called the Old Heidelberg and they had to settle for cherry blossoms instead of lime trees when spring came, but in its lethargic way their life provided, as they said, kicks.

At the moment, Meatball's party seemed to be gathering its second wind. Outside there was rain. Rain splatted against the tar paper on the roof and was fractured into a fine spray off the noses, eyebrows and lips of wooden gargoyles under the eaves, and ran like drool down the windowpanes. The day before, it had snowed and the day before that there had been winds of gale force and before that the sun had made the city glitter bright as April, though the calendar read early February. It is a curious season in Washington, this false spring. Somewhere in it are Lincoln's Birthday and the Chinese New Year, and a forlornness in the streets because cherry blossoms are weeks away still and, as Sarah Vaughan has put it, spring will be a little late this year. Generally crowds like the one which would gather in the Old Heidelberg on weekday afternoons to drink Würtzburger and to sing Lili Marlene (not to mention The Sweetheart of Sigma Chi) are inevitably and incorrigibly Romantic. And as every good Romantic knows, the soul *(spiritus, ruach, pneuma)* is nothing, substantially, but air; it is only natural that warpings in the atmosphere should be recapitulated in those who breathe it. So that over and above the public components—holidays, tourist attractions—there are private meanderings, linked to the climate as if this spell were a *stretto* passage in the year's fugue: haphazard weather, aimless loves, unpredicted commitments: months one can easily spend *in* fugue, because oddly enough, later on, winds, rains, passions of February and March are never remembered in that city, it is as if they had never been.

The last bass notes of *The Heroes' Gate* boomed up through the floor and woke Callisto from an uneasy sleep. The first thing he became aware of was a small bird he had been holding gently between his hands, against his body. He turned his head sidewise on the pillow to smile down at it, at its blue hunched-down head and sick, lidded eyes, wondering how many more nights he would have to give it warmth before it was well again. He had been holding the bird like that for three days: it was the only way he knew to restore its health. Next to him the girl stirred and whimpered, her arm thrown across her face. Mingled with the sounds of the rain came the first tentative, querulous morning voices of the other birds, hidden in philodendrons and small fan palms: patches of scarlet, yellow and blue laced through this Rousseau-like fantasy, this hothouse jungle it had taken him seven years to weave together. Hermetically sealed, it was a tiny enclave of regularity in the city's chaos, alien to the vagaries of the weather, of national politics, of any civil disorder. Through trial-and-error Callisto had perfected its ecological balance, with the help of the girl its artistic harmony, so that the swayings of its plant life, the stirrings of its birds and human inhabitants were all as integral as the rhythms of a perfectly-executed mobile. He and the girl could no longer, of course, be omitted from that sanctuary; they had become necessary to its unity. What they needed from outside was delivered. They did not go out.

"Is he all right," she whispered. She lay like a tawny question mark facing him, her eyes suddenly huge and dark and blinking slowly. Callisto ran a finger beneath the feathers at the base of the bird's neck; caressed it gently. "He's going to be well, I think. See: he hears his friends beginning to wake up." The girl had heard the rain and the birds even before she was fully awake. Her name was Aubade: she was part French and part Annamese, and she lived on her own curious and lonely planet, where the clouds and the odor of poincianas, the bitterness of wine and the accidental fingers at the small of her back or feathery against her breasts came to her reduced inevitably to the terms of sound: of music which emerged at intervals from a howling darkness of discordancy. "Aubade," he said, "go see." Obedient, she arose; padded to the window, pulled aside the drapes and after a moment said: "It is 37. Still 37." Callisto frowned. "Since Tuesday, then," he said. "No change." Henry Adams, three generations before his own, had stared aghast at Power; Callisto found himself now in much the same state over Thermodynamics, the inner life of that power, realizing like his predeccessor that the Virgin and the dynamo stand as much for love as for power; that the two are indeed identical; and that love therefore not only makes the world go round but also makes the boccie ball spin, the nebula precess. It was this latter or sidereal element which disturbed him. The cosmologists had predicted an eventual heat-death for the universe (something like Limbo: form and motion abolished, heat-energy identical at every point in it); the meteorologists, day-to-day, staved it off by contradicting with a reassuring array of varied temperatures.

But for three days now, despite the changeful weather, the mercury had stayed at 37 degrees Fahrenheit. Leery at omens of apocalypse, Callisto shifted beneath the covers. His fingers pressed the bird more firmly, as if needing some pulsing or suffering assurance of an early break in the temperature.

It was that last cymbal crash that did it. Meatball was hurled wincing into consciousness as the synchronized wagging of heads over the wastebasket stopped. The final hiss remained for an instant in the room, then melted into the whisper of rain outside. "Aarrgghh," announced Meatball in the silence, looking at the empty magnum. Krinkles, in slow motion, turned, smiled and held out a cigarette. "Tea time, man," he said. "No, no," said Meatball. "How many times I got to tell you guys. Not at my place. You ought to know, Washington is lousy with Feds." Krinkles looked wistful. "Jeez, Meatball," he said, "you don't want to do nothing no more." "Hair of dog," said Meatball. "Only hope. Any juice left?" He began to crawl toward the kitchen. "No champagne, I don't think," Duke said. "Case of tequila behind the icebox." They put on an Earl Bostic side. Meatball paused at the kitchen door, glowering at Sandor Rojas. "Lemons," he said after some thought. He crawled to the refrigerator and got out three lemons and some cubes, found the tequila and set about restoring order to his nervous system. He drew blood once cutting the lemons and had to use two hands squeezing them and his foot to crack the ice tray but after about ten minutes he found himself, through some miracle, beaming down into a monster tequila sour. "That looks yummy," Sandor Rojas said. "How about you make me one." Meatball blinked at him. *"Kitchi lofass a shegitbe,"* he replied automatically, and wandered away into the bathroom. "I say," he called out a moment later to no one in particular. "I say, there seems to be a girl or something sleeping in the sink." He took her by the shoulders and shook. "Wha," she said. "You don't look too comfortable," Meatball said. "Well," she agreed. She stumbled to the shower, turned on the cold water and sat down crosslegged in the spray. "That's better," she smiled.

"Meatball," Sandor Rojas yelled from the kitchen. "Somebody is trying to come in the window. A burglar, I think. A second-story man." "What are you worrying about," Meatball said. "We're on the third floor." He loped back into the kitchen. A shaggy woebegone figure stood out on the fire escape, raking his fingernails down the windowpane. Meatball opened the window. "Saul," he said.

"Sort of wet out," Saul said. He climbed in, dripping. "You heard, I guess."

"Miriam left you," Meatball said, "or something, is all I heard."

There was a sudden flurry of knocking at the front door. "Do come in," Sandor Rojas called. The door opened and there were three coeds from George Washington, all of whom were majoring in philosophy. They were each holding a gallon of Chianti. Sandor leaped up and dashed into the living room. "We heard there was a party," one blonde said. "Young blood," Sandor shouted. He was an ex-Hungarian freedom fighter who had easily the worst chronic case of what certain critics of the middle class have called Don Giovannism in the District of Columbia. *Purche porti la gonnella, voi sapete quel che fa.* Like Pavlov's dog: a contralto voice or a whiff of Arpège and Sandor would begin to salivate. Meatball regarded the trio blearily as they filed into the kitchen; he shrugged. "Put the wine in the icebox," he said "and good morning."

Aubade's neck made a golden bow as she bent over the sheets of foolscap, scribbling away in the green murk of the room. "As a young man at Princeton," Callisto was dictating, nestling the bird against the gray hairs of his chest, "Callisto had learned a mnemonic device for remembering the Laws of Thermodynamics: you can't win, things are going to get worse before they get better, who says they're going to get better. At the age of 54, confronted with Gibbs' notion of the universe, he suddenly realized that undergraduate cant had been oracle, after all. That spindly maze of equations became, for him, a vision of ultimate, cosmic heat-death. He had known all along, of course, that nothing but a theoretical engine or system ever runs at 100% efficiency; and about the theorem of Clausius, which states that the entropy of an isolated system always continually increases. It was not, however, until Gibbs and Boltzmann brought to this principle the methods of statistical mechanics that the horrible significance of it all dawned on him: only then did he realize that the isolated system—galaxy, engine, human being, culture, whatever—must evolve spontaneously toward the Condition of the More Probable. He was forced, therefore, in the sad dying fall of middle age, to a radical reevaluation of everything he had learned up to then; all the cities and seasons and casual passions of his days had now to be looked at in a new and elusive light. He did not know if he was equal to the task. He was aware of the dangers of the reductive fallacy and, he hoped, strong enough not to drift into the graceful decadence of an enervated fatalism. His had always been a vigorous, Italian sort of pessimism: like Machiavelli, he allowed the forces of *virtù* and *fortuna* to be about 50/50; but the equations now introduced a random factor which pushed the odds to some unutterable and indeterminate ratio which he found himself afraid to calculate." Around him loomed vague hothouse shapes; the pitifully small heart fluttered against his own. Counterpointed against his words the girl heard the chatter of birds and fitful car honkings scattered along the wet morning and Earl Bostic's alto rising in occasional wild peaks through the floor. The architectonic purity of her world was constantly threatened by such hints of anarchy: gaps and excrescences and skew lines, and a shifting or tilting of planes to which she had continually to readjust lest the whole structure shiver into a disarray of discrete and meaningless signals. Callisto had described the process once as a kind of "feedback": she crawled into dreams each night with a sense of exhaustion, and a desperate resolve never to relax that vigilance. Even in the brief periods when Callisto made love to her, soaring above the bowing of taut nerves in haphazard double-stops would be the one singing string of her determination.

"Nevertheless," continued Callisto, "he found in entropy or the measure of disorganization for a closed system an adequate metaphor to apply to certain phenomena in his own world. He saw, for example, the younger generation responding to Madison Avenue with the same spleen his own had once reserved for Wall Street: and in American 'consumerism' discovered a similar tendency from the least to the most probable, from differentiation to sameness, from ordered individuality to a kind of chaos. He found himself, in short, restating Gibbs' prediction in social terms, and envisioned a heat-death for his culture in which ideas, like heat-energy, would no longer be transferred, since each point in it would ultimately have the same quantity of energy; and intellectual motion would, accordingly, cease." He glanced up suddenly. "Check it now," he said. Again she rose and peered out at the thermometer. "37," she said. "The rain has stopped." He bent his head quickly and held his lips against a quivering wing. "Then it will change soon," he said, trying to keep his voice firm.

Sitting on the stove Saul was like any big rag doll that a kid has been taking out some incomprehensible rage on. "What happened," Meatball said. "If you feel like talking, I mean."

"Of course I feel like talking," Saul said. "One thing I did, I slugged her."

"Discipline must be maintained."

"Ha, ha. I wish you'd been there. Oh Meatball, it was a lovely fight. She ended up throwing a *Handbook of Chemistry and Physics* at me, only it missed and went through the window, and when the glass broke I reckon something in her broke too. She stormed out of the house crying, out in the rain. No raincoat or anything."

"She'll be back."

"No."

"Well." Soon Meatball said: "It was something earth-shattering, no doubt. Like who is better, Sal Mineo or Ricky Nelson."

"What it was about," Saul said, "was communication theory. Which of course makes it very hilarious."

"I don't know anything about communication theory."

"Neither does my wife. Come right down to it, who does? That's the joke."

When Meatball saw the kind of smile Saul had on his face he said: "Maybe you would like tequila or something."

"No. I mean, I'm sorry. It's a field you can go off the deep end in, is all. You get where you're watching all the time for security cops: behind bushes, around corners, MUFFET is top secret."

"Wha."

"Multi-unit factorial field electronic tabulator."

"You were fighting about that."

"Miriam has been reading science fiction again. That and *Scientific American.* It seems she is, as we say, bugged at this idea of computers acting like people. I made the mistake of saying you can just as well turn that around, and talk about human behavior like a program fed into an IBM machine."

"Why not," Meatball said.

"Indeed, why not. In fact it is sort of crucial to communication, not to mention information theory. Only when I said that she hit the roof. Up went the balloon. And I can't figure out *why.* If anybody should know why, I should. I refuse to believe the government is wasting taxpayers' money on me, when it has so many bigger and better things to waste it on."

Meatball made a moue. "Maybe she thought you were acting like a cold, dehumanized amoral scientist type."

"My god," Saul flung up an arm. "Dehumanized. How much more human can I get? I worry, Meatball, I do. There are Europeans wandering around North Africa these days with their tongues torn out of their heads because those tongues have spoken the wrong words. Only the Europeans thought they were the right words."

"Language barrier," Meatball suggested.

Saul jumped down off the stove. "That," he said, angry, "is a good candidate for sick joke of the year. No, ace, it is *not* a barrier. If it is anything it's a kind of leakage. Tell a girl: 'I love you.' No trouble with two-thirds of that, it's a closed circuit. Just you and she. But that nasty four-letter word in the middle, *that's* the one you have to look out for. Ambiguity. Redundance. Irrelevance, even. Leakage. All this is noise. Noise screws up your signal, makes for disorganization in the circuit."

Meatball shuffled around. "Well, now, Saul," he muttered, "you're sort of, I don't know, expecting a lot from people. I mean, you know. What it is is, most of the things we say, I guess, are mostly noise."

"Ha! Half of what you just said, for example."

"Well, you do it too."

"I know." Saul smiled grimly. "It's a bitch, ain't it."

"I bet that's what keeps divorce lawyers in business. Whoops."

"Oh I'm not sensitive. Besides," frowning, "you're right. You find I think that most 'successful' marriages—Miriam and me, up to last night—are sort of founded on compromises. You never run at top efficiency, usually all you have is a minimum basis for a workable thing. I believe the phrase is Togetherness."

"Aarrgghh."

"Exactly. You find that one a bit noisy, don't you. But the noise content is different for each of us because you're a bachelor and I'm not. Or wasn't. The hell with it."

"Well sure," Meatball said, trying to be helpful, "you were using different words. By 'human being' you meant something that you can look at like it was a computer. It helps you think better on the job or something. But Miriam meant something entirely—"

"The hell with it."

Meatball fell silent. "I'll take that drink," Saul said after a while.

The card game had been abandoned and Sandor's friends were slowly getting wasted on tequila. On the living room couch, one of the coeds and Krinkles were engaged in amorous conversation. "No," Krinkles was saying, "no, I can't put Dave *down.* In fact I give Dave a lot of credit, man. Especially considering his accident and all." The girl's smile faded. "How terrible," she said. "What accident?" "Hadn't you heard?" Krinkles said. "When Dave was in the army, just a private E-2, they sent him down to Oak Ridge on special duty. Something to do with the Manhattan Project. He was handling hot stuff one day and got an overdose of radiation. So now he's got to wear lead gloves all the time." She shook her head sympathetically. "What an awful break for a piano-player."

Meatball had abandoned Saul to a bottle of tequila and was about to go to sleep in a closet when the front door flew open and the place was invaded by five enlisted personnel of the U.S. Navy, all in varying stages of abomination. "This is the place," shouted a fat, pimply seaman apprentice who had lost his white hat. "This here is the hoorhouse that chief was telling us about." A stringy-looking 3rd class boatswain's mate pushed him aside and cased the living room. "You're right, Slab," he said. "But it don't look like much, even for Stateside. I seen better tail in Naples, Italy." "How much, hey," boomed a large seaman with adenoids, who was holding a Mason jar full of white lightning. "Oh, my god," said Meatball.

Outside the temperature remained constant at 37 degrees Fahrenheit. In the hothouse Aubade stood absently caressing the branches of a young mimosa, hearing a motif of sap-rising, the rough and unresolved anticipatory theme of those fragile pink blossoms which, it is said, insure fertility. That music rose in a tangled tracery: arabesques of order competing fugally with the improvised discords of the party downstairs, which peaked sometimes in cusps and ogees of noise. That precious signal-to-noise ratio, whose delicate balance required every calorie of her strength, seesawed inside the small tenuous skull as she watched Callisto, sheltering the bird. Callisto was trying to confront any idea of the heat-death now, as he nuzzled the feathery lump in his hands. He sought correspondences. Sade, of course. And Temple Drake, gaunt and hopeless in her little park in Paris, at the end of *Sanctuary*. Final equilibrium. *Nightwood.* And the tango. Any tango, but more than any perhaps the sad sick dance in Stravinsky's *L'Histoire du Soldat.* He thought back: what had tango music been for them after the war, what meanings had he missed in all the stately coupled automatons in the *cafés-dansants,* or in the metronomes which had ticked behind the eyes of his own partners? Not even the clean constant winds of Switzerland could cure the *grippe espagnole:* Stravinsky had had it, they all had had it. And how many musicians were left after Passchendaele, after the Marne? It came down in this case to seven: violin, double-bass. Clarinet, bassoon. Cornet, trombone. Tympani. Almost as if any tiny troupe of saltimbanques had set about conveying the same information as a full pit-orchestra. There was hardly a full complement left in Europe. Yet with violin and tympani Stravinsky had managed to communicate in that tango the same exhaustion, the same airlessness one saw in the slicked-down youths who were trying to imitate Vernon Castle, and in their mistresses, who simply did not care. *Ma maîtresse.* Celeste. Returning to Nice after the second war he had found that café replaced by a perfume shop which catered to American tourists. And no secret vestige of her in the cobblestones or in the old pension next door; no perfume to match her breath heavy with the sweet Spanish wine she always drank. And so instead he had purchased a Henry Miller novel and left for Paris, and read the book on the train so that when he arrived he had been given at least a little forewarning. And saw that Celeste and the others and even Temple Drake were not all that had changed. "Aubade," he said, "my head aches." The sound of his voice generated in the girl an answering scrap of melody. Her movement toward the kitchen, the towel, the cold water, and his eyes following her formed a weird and intricate canon; as she placed the compress on his forehead his sigh of gratitude seemed to signal a new subject, another series of modulations.

"No," Meatball was still saying, "no, I'm afraid not. This is not a house of ill repute. I'm sorry, really I am." Slab was adamant. "But the chief said," he kept repeating. The seaman offered to swap the moonshine for a good piece. Meatball looked around frantically, as if seeking assistance. In the middle of the room, the Duke di Angelis quartet were engaged in a historic moment. Vincent was seated and the others standing: they were going through the motions of a group having a session, only without instruments. "I say," Meatball said. Duke moved his head a few times, smiled faintly, lit a cigarette, and eventually caught sight of Meatball. "Quiet, man," he whispered. Vincent began to fling his arms around, his fists clenched; then, abruptly, was still, then repeated the performance. This went on for a few minutes while Meatball sipped his drink moodily. The navy had withdrawn to the kitchen. Finally at some invisible signal the group stopped tapping their feet and Duke grinned and said, "At least we ended together."

Meatball glared at him. "I say," he said. "I have this new conception, man," Duke said. "You remember your namesake. You remember Gerry."

"No," said Meatball. "I'll remember April, if that's any help."

"As a matter of fact," Duke said, "it was Love for Sale. Which shows how much you know. The point is, it was Mulligan, Chet Baker and that crew, way back then, out yonder. You dig?"

"Baritone sax," Meatball said. "Something about a baritone sax."

"But no piano, man. No guitar. Or accordion. You know what that means."

"Not exactly," Meatball said.

"Well first let me just say, that I am no Mingus, no John Lewis. Theory was never my strong point. I mean things like reading were always difficult for me and all—"

"I know," Meatball said drily. "You got your card taken away because you changed key on Happy Birthday at a Kiwanis Club picnic."

"Rotarian. But it occurred to me, in one of these flashes of insight, that if that first quartet of Mulligan's had no piano, it could only mean one thing."

"No chords," said Paco, the baby-faced bass.

"What he is trying to say," Duke said, "is no root chords. Nothing to listen to while you blow a horizontal line. What one does in such a case is, one *thinks* the roots."

A horrified awareness was dawning on Meatball. "And the next logical extension," he said.

"Is to think everything," Duke announced with simple dignity. "Roots, line, everything."

Meatball looked at Duke, awed. "But," he said.

"Well," Duke said modestly, "there are a few bugs to work out."

"But," Meatball said.

"Just listen," Duke said. "You'll catch on." And off they went again into orbit, presumably somewhere around the asteroid belt. After a while Krinkles made an embouchure and started moving his fingers and Duke clapped his hand to his forehead. "Oaf!" he roared. "The new head we're using, you remember, I wrote last night?" "Sure," Krinkles said, "the new head. I come in on the bridge. All your heads I come in then." "Right," Duke said. "So why—" "Wha," said Krinkles, "16 bars, I wait, I come in—" "16?" Duke said. "No. No, Krinkles. Eight you waited. You want me to sing it? A cigarette that bears a lipstick's traces, an airline ticket to romantic places." Krinkles scratched his head. "These Foolish Things, you mean." "Yes," Duke said, "yes, Krinkles. Bravo." "Not I'll Remember April," Krinkles said. *"Minghe morte,"* said Duke. "I *figured* we were playing it a little slow," Krinkles said. Meatball chuckled. "Back to the old drawing board," he said. "No, man," Duke said, "back to the airless void." And they took off again, only it seemed Paco was playing in G sharp while the rest were in E flat, so they had to start all over.

In the kitchen two of the girls from George Washington and the sailors were singing Let's All Go Down and Piss on the Forrestal. There was a two-handed, bilingual *morra* game on over by the icebox. Saul had filled several paper bags with water and was sitting on the fire escape, dropping them on passersby in the street. A fat government girl in a Bennington sweatshirt, recently engaged to an ensign attached to the Forrestal, came charging into the kitchen, head lowered, and butted Slab in the stomach. Figuring this was as good an excuse for a fight as any, Slab's buddies piled in. The *morra* players were nose-to-nose, screaming *trois, sette* at the tops of their lungs. From the shower the girl Meatball had taken out of the sink announced that she was drowning. She had apparently sat on the drain and the water was now up to her neck. The noise in Meatball's apartment had reached a sustained, ungodly crescendo.

Meatball stood and watched, scratching his stomach lazily. The way he figured, there were only about two ways he could cope: (a) lock himself in the closet and maybe eventually they would all go away, or (b) try to calm everybody down, one by one. (a) was certainly the more attractive alternative. But then he started thinking about that closet. It was dark and stuffy and he would be alone. He did not feature being alone. And then this crew off the good ship Lollipop or whatever it was might take it upon themselves to kick down the closet door, for a lark. And if that happened he would be, at the very least, embarrassed. The other way was more a pain in the neck, but probably better in the long run.

So he decided to try and keep his lease-breaking party from deteriorating into total chaos: he gave wine to the sailors and separated the *morra* players; he introduced the fat government girl to Sandor Rojas, who would keep her out of trouble; he helped the girl in the shower to dry off and get into bed; he had another talk with Saul; he called a repairman for the refrigerator, which someone had discovered was on the blink. This is what he did until nightfall, when most of the revellers had passed out and the party trembled on the threshold of its third day.

Upstairs Callisto, helpless in the past, did not feel the faint rhythm inside the bird begin to slacken and fail. Aubade was by the window, wandering the ashes of her own lovely world; the temperature held steady, the sky had become a uniform darkening gray. Then something from downstairs—a girl's scream, an overturned chair, a glass dropped on the floor, he would never know what exactly—pierced that private time-warp and he became aware of the faltering, the constriction of muscles, the tiny tossing of the bird's head; and his own pulse began to pound more fiercely, as if trying to compensate. "Aubade," he called weakly, "he's dying." The girl, flowing and rapt, crossed the hothouse to gaze down at Callisto's hands. The two remained like that, poised, for one minute, and two, while the heartbeat ticked a graceful diminuendo down at last into stillness. Callisto raised his head slowly. "I held him," he protested, impotent with the wonder of it, "to give him the warmth of my body. Almost as if I were communicating life to him, or a sense of life. What has happened? Has the transfer of heat ceased to work? Is there no more . . ." He did not finish.

"I was just at the window," she said. He sank back, terrified. She stood a moment more, irresolute; she had sensed his obsession long ago, realized somehow that that constant 37 was now decisive. Suddenly then, as if seeing the single and unavoidable conclusion to all this she moved swiftly to the window before Callisto could speak; tore away the drapes and smashed out the glass with two exquisite hands which came away bleeding and glistening with splinters; and turned to face the man on the bed and wait with him until the moment of equilibrium was reached, when 37 degrees Fahrenheit should prevail both outside and inside, and forever, and the hovering, curious dominant of their separate lives should resolve into a tonic of darkness and the final absence of all motion.

1960

Toni Morrison b. 1931

Since winning the Nobel Prize for Literature in 1993, Toni Morrison has become an industry. As much a household name as some of the writers in the Black Arts movement of the 1960s, Morrison is author, critic, lecturer, teacher, and public servant. Since she made her debut on the literary scene with the publication of *The Bluest Eye* in 1970, she has been a model worthy of emulation and a paragon of success. Her seven novels to date make her one of the most prolific African American women novelists, and her international reputation makes her one of the best-known American writers. Critically acclaimed for her deft use of language and lyrical writing, Morrison also counts among her honors the National Book Critics' Circle Award as well as the Pulitzer Prize.

Now known as Toni Morrison, Chloe Anthony Wofford was born in Lorain, Ohio, on February 18, 1931, to Rahmah Willis Wofford and George Wofford, both migrants from the South. Her storytelling home environment enabled Morrison to enter first grade as the only child in her class who already knew how to read, a skill that she would cultivate as an adolescent by reading Russian novels, *Madame Bovary,* and works by Jane Austen. She graduated with honors from Lorain High School and entered Howard University, where she changed her name to Toni (people had trouble pronouncing Chloe) and traveled through the South during summer break with the Howard University Players. She earned a B.A. in English with a minor in classics in 1953. In 1955, she earned a master's degree in English from Cornell University with a now frequently referenced thesis on suicide in the works of Virginia Woolf and William Faulkner.

Morrison has retained close contacts with academia and has held several teaching appointments, including ones at Texas Southern University (1955–1957) and Howard University (1957–1964). She began to write in 1957, after she returned to Howard as an instructor in English; she joined a group of ten black writers in Washington, D.C. It was there that she met and married Harold Morrison, a Jamaican architect. The couple had two sons, Harold Ford and Kevin Slade, before they divorced in 1964. Morrison returned briefly to her parents' home in Ohio before getting an editing job with a textbook subsidiary of Random House in Syracuse, New York, where she moved in 1965.

From 1969 to 1970, Morrison was an instructor at the State University of New York at Purchase. From 1975 to 1977, she served as Distinguished Visiting Professor at Yale University and as Distinguished Visiting Lecturer at Bard College from 1979 to 1980. Named Albert Schweitzer Professor of the Humanities at the State University of New York at Albany, she left Random House to assume that position in 1984. She held it until 1989, when she moved to Princeton University to accept her second endowed professorship, that of Robert F. Gosheen Professor of the Council of the Humanities, from which illustrious position she teaches courses in African American studies and creative writing.

Her richly rewarded creative output and public service, including a stint as co-chairperson of the Schomburg Library's Commission for the Preservation of Black Culture and a term on the board of the Center for the Study of Southern Culture, have earned Morrison an unmatched reputation among African American women writers as well as among American writers in general.

Trudier Harris
University of North Carolina–Chapel Hill

PRIMARY WORKS

Novels: *The Bluest Eye,* 1970; *Sula,* 1974; *Song of Solomon,* 1977; *Tar Baby,* 1981; *Beloved,* 1987; *Jazz,* 1992; *Paradise,* 1998. Short story: "Recitatif," 1993. Nonfiction: *Playing in the Dark: Whiteness and the Literary Imagination,* 1992; *The Black Book,* 1974 (with Middleton Harris); *Race-ing Justice, En-Gendering Power: Essays on Anita Hill, Clarence Thomas, and the Construction of Social Reality,* 1992.

from Sula

1922

It was too cool for ice cream. A hill wind was blowing dust and empty Camels wrappers about their ankles. It pushed their dresses into the creases of their behinds, then lifted the hems to peek at their cotton underwear. They were on their way to Edna Finch's Mellow House, an ice cream parlor catering to nice folks—where even children would feel comfortable, you know, even though it was right next to Reba's Grill and just one block down from the Time and a Half Pool Hall. It sat in the curve of Carpenter's Road, which, in four blocks, made up all the sporting life available in the Bottom. Old men and young ones draped themselves in front of the Elmira Theater, Irene's Palace of Cosmetology, the pool hall, the grill and the other sagging business enterprises that lined the street. On sills, on stoops, on crates and broken chairs they sat tasting their teeth and waiting for something to distract them. Every passerby, every motorcar, every alteration in stance caught their attention and was commented on. Particularly they watched women. When a woman approached, the older men tipped their hats; the younger ones opened and closed their thighs. But all of them, whatever their age, watched her retreating view with interest.

Nel and Sula walked through this valley of eyes chilled by the wind and heated by the embarrassment of appraising stares. The old men looked at their stalklike legs, dwelled on the cords in the backs of their knees and remembered old dance steps they had not done in twenty years. In their lust, which age had turned to kindness, they moved their lips as though to stir up the taste of young sweat on tight skin.

Pig meat. The words were in all their minds. And one of them, one of the young ones, said it aloud. Softly but definitively and there was no mistaking the compliment. His name was Ajax, a twenty-one-year-old pool haunt of sinister beauty. Graceful and economical in every movement, he held a place of envy with men of all ages for his magnificently foul mouth. In fact he seldom cursed, and the epithets he chose were dull, even harmless. His reputation was derived from the way he handled the words. When he said "hell" he hit the *h* with his lungs and the impact was greater than the achievement of the most imaginative foul mouth in the town. He could say "shit" with a nastiness impossible to imitate. So, when he said "pig meat" as Nel and Sula passed, they guarded their eyes lest someone see their delight.

It was not really Edna Finch's ice cream that made them brave the stretch of those panther eyes. Years later their own eyes would glaze as they cupped their chins in remembrance of the inchworm smiles, the squatting haunches, the track-rail legs straddling broken chairs. The cream-colored trousers marking with a mere seam the place where the mystery curled. Those smooth vanilla crotches invited them; those lemon-yellow gabardines beckoned to them.

They moved toward the ice-cream parlor like tightrope walkers, as thrilled by the possibility of a slip as by the maintenance of tension and balance. The least sideways glance, the merest toe stub, could pitch them into those creamy haunches spread wide with welcome. Somewhere beneath all of that daintiness, chambered in all that neatness, lay the thing that clotted their dreams.

Which was only fitting, for it was in dreams that the two girls had first met. Long before Edna Finch's Mellow House opened, even before they marched through the chocolate halls of Garfield Primary School out onto the playground and stood facing each other through the ropes of the one vacant swing ("Go on." "No. You go."), they had already made each other's acquaintance in the delirium of their noon dreams. They were solitary little girls whose loneliness was so profound it intoxicated them and sent them stumbling into Technicolored visions that always included a presence, a someone, who, quite like the dreamer, shared the delight of the dream. When Nel, an only child, sat on the steps of her back porch surrounded by the high silence of her mother's incredibly orderly house, feeling the neatness pointing at her back, she studied the poplars and fell easily into a picture of herself lying on a flowered bed, tangled in her own hair, waiting for some fiery prince. He approached but never quite arrived. But always, watching the dream along with her, were some smiling sympathetic eyes. Someone as interested as she herself in the flow of her imagined hair, the thickness of the mattress of flowers, the voile sleeves that closed below her elbows in gold-threaded cuffs.

Similarly, Sula, also an only child, but wedged into a household of throbbing disorder constantly awry with things, people, voices and the slamming of doors, spent hours in the attic behind a roll of linoleum galloping through her own mind on a gray-and-white horse tasting sugar and smelling roses in full view of a someone who shared both the taste and the speed.

So when they met, first in those chocolate halls and next through the ropes of the swing, they felt the ease and comfort of old friends. Because each had discovered years before that they were neither white nor male, and that all freedom and triumph was forbidden to them, they had set about creating something else to be. Their meeting was fortunate, for it let them use each other to grow on. Daughters of distant mothers and incomprehensible fathers (Sula's because he was dead; Nel's because he wasn't), they found in each other's eyes the intimacy they were looking for.

Nel Wright and Sula Peace were both twelve in 1922, wishbone thin and easy-assed. Nel was the color of wet sandpaper—just dark enough to escape the blows of the pitch-black truebloods and the contempt of old women who worried about such things as bad blood mixtures and knew that the origins of a mule and a mulatto were one and the same. Had she been any lighter-skinned she would have needed either her mother's protection on the way to school or a streak of mean to defend herself. Sula was a heavy brown with large quiet eyes, one of which featured a birthmark that spread from the middle of the lid toward the eyebrow, shaped something like a stemmed rose. It gave her otherwise plain face a broken excitement and blue-blade threat like the keloid scar of the razored man who sometimes played checkers with her grandmother. The birthmark was to grow darker as the years passed, but now it was the same shade as her gold-flecked eyes, which, to the end, were as steady and clean as rain.

Their friendship was as intense as it was sudden. They found relief in each other's personality. Although both were unshaped, formless things, Nel seemed stronger and more consistent than Sula, who could hardly be counted on to sustain any emotion for more than three minutes. Yet there was one time when that was not true, when she held on to a mood for weeks, but even that was in defense of Nel.

Four white boys in their early teens, sons of some newly arrived Irish people, occasionally entertained themselves in the afternoon by harassing black schoolchildren. With shoes that pinched and woolen knickers that made red rings on their calves, they had come to this valley with their parents believing as they did that it was a promised land—green and shimmering with welcome. What they found was a strange accent, a pervasive fear of their religion and firm resistance to their attempts to find work. With one exception the older residents of Medallion scorned them. The one exception was the black community. Although some of the Negroes had been in Medallion before the Civil War (the town didn't even have a name then), if they had any hatred for these newcomers it didn't matter because it didn't show. As a matter of fact, baiting them was the one activity that the white Protestant residents concurred in. In part their place in this world was secured only when they echoed the old residents' attitude toward blacks.

These particular boys caught Nel once, and pushed her from hand to hand until they grew tired of the frightened helpless face. Because of that incident, Nel's route home from school became elaborate. She, and then Sula, managed to duck them for weeks until a chilly day in November when Sula said, "Let's us go on home the shortest way."

Nel blinked, but acquiesced. They walked up the street until they got to the bend of Carpenter's Road where the boys lounged on a disused well. Spotting their prey, the boys sauntered forward as though there were nothing in the world on their minds but the gray sky. Hardly able to control their grins, they stood like a gate blocking the path. When the girls were three feet in front of the boys, Sula reached into her coat pocket and pulled out Eva's paring knife. The boys stopped short, exchanged looks and dropped all pretense of innocence. This was going to be better than they thought. They were going to try and fight back, and with a knife. Maybe they could get an arm around one of their waists, or tear . . .

Sula squatted down in the dirt road and put everything down on the ground: her lunchpail, her reader, her mittens, her slate. Holding the knife in her right hand, she pulled the slate toward her and pressed her left forefinger down hard on its edge. Her aim was determined but inaccurate. She slashed off only the tip of her finger. The four boys stared open-mouthed at the wound and the scrap of flesh, like a button mushroom, curling in the cherry blood that ran into the corners of the slate.

Sula raised her eyes to them. Her voice was quiet. "If I can do that to myself, what you suppose I'll do to you?"

The shifting dirt was the only way Nel knew that they were moving away; she was looking at Sula's face, which seemed miles and miles away.

But toughness was not their quality—adventuresomeness was—and a mean determination to explore everything that interested them, from one-eyed chickens high-stepping in their penned yards to Mr. Buckland Reed's gold teeth, from the sound of sheets flapping in the wind to the labels on Tar Baby's wine bottles. And they had no priorities. They could be distracted from watching a fight with mean razors by the glorious smell of hot tar being poured by roadmen two hundred yards away.

In the safe harbor of each other's company they could afford to abandon the ways of other people and concentrate on their own perceptions of things. When Mrs. Wright reminded Nel to pull her nose, she would do it enthusiastically but without the least hope in the world.

"While you sittin' there, honey, go 'head and pull your nose."

"It hurts, Mamma."

"Don't you want a nice nose when you grow up?"

After she met Sula, Nel slid the clothespin under the blanket as soon as she got in the bed. And although there was still the hateful hot comb to suffer through each Saturday evening, its consequences—smooth hair—no longer interested her.

Joined in mutual admiration they watched each day as though it were a movie arranged for their amusement. The new theme they were now discovering was men. So they met regularly, without even planning it, to walk down the road to Edna Finch's Mellow House, even though it was too cool for ice cream.

Then summer came. A summer limp with the weight of blossomed things. Heavy sunflowers weeping over fences; iris curling and browning at the edges far away from their purple hearts; ears of corn letting their auburn hair wind down to their stalks. And the boys. The beautiful, beautiful boys who dotted the landscape like jewels, split the air with their shouts in the field, and thickened the river with their shining wet backs. Even their footsteps left a smell of smoke behind.

It was in that summer, the summer of their twelfth year, the summer of the beautiful black boys, that they became skittish, frightened and bold—all at the same time.

In that mercury mood in July, Sula and Nel wandered about the Bottom barefoot looking for mischief. They decided to go down by the river where the boys sometimes swam. Nel waited on the porch of 7 Carpenter's Road while Sula ran into the house to go to the toilet. On the way up the stairs, she passed the kitchen where Hannah sat with two friends, Patsy and Valentine. The two women were fanning themselves and watching Hannah put down some dough, all talking casually about one thing and another, and had gotten around, when Sula passed by, to the problems of child rearing.

"They a pain."

"Yeh. Wish I'd listened to mamma. She told me not to have 'em too soon."

"Any time atall is too soon for me."

"Oh, I don't know. My Rudy minds his daddy. He just wild with me. Be glad when he growed and gone."

Hannah smiled and said, "Shut your mouth. You love the ground he pee on."

"Sure I do. But he still a pain. Can't help loving your own child. No matter what they do."

"Well, Hester grown now and I can't say love is exactly what I feel."

"Sure you do. You love her, like I love Sula. I just don't like her. That's the difference."

"Guess so. Likin' them is another thing."

"Sure. They different people, you know . . ."

She only heard Hannah's words, and the pronouncement sent her flying up the stairs. In bewilderment, she stood at the window fingering the curtain edge, aware of a sting in her eye. Nel's call floated up and into the window, pulling her away from dark thoughts back into the bright, hot daylight.

They ran most of the way.

Heading toward the wide part of the river where trees grouped themselves in families darkening the earth below. They passed some boys swimming and clowning in the water, shrouding their words in laughter.

They ran in the sunlight, creating their own breeze, which pressed their dresses into their damp skin. Reaching a kind of square of four leaf-locked trees which promised cooling, they flung themselves into the four-cornered shade to taste their lip sweat and contemplate the wildness that had come upon them so suddenly. They lay in the grass, their foreheads almost touching, their bodies stretched away from each other at a 180-degree angle. Sula's head rested on her arm, an undone braid coiled around her wrist. Nel leaned on her elbows and worried long blades of grass with her fingers. Underneath their dresses flesh tightened and shivered in the high coolness, their small breasts just now beginning to create some pleasant discomfort when they were lying on their stomachs.

Sula lifted her head and joined Nel in the grass play. In concert, without ever meeting each other's eyes, they stroked the blades up and down, up and down. Nel found a thick twig and, with her thumbnail, pulled away its bark until it was stripped to a smooth, creamy innocence. Sula looked about and found one too. When both twigs were undressed Nel moved easily to the next stage and began tearing up rooted grass to make a bare spot of earth. When a generous clearing was made, Sula traced intricate patterns in it with her twig. At first Nel was content to do the same. But soon she grew impatient and poked her twig rhythmically and intensely into the earth, making a small neat hole that grew deeper and wider with the least manipulation of her twig. Sula copied her, and soon each had a hole the size of a cup. Nel began a more strenuous digging and, rising to her knee, was careful to scoop out the dirt as she made her hole deeper. Together they worked until the two holes were one and the same. When the depression was the size of a small dishpan, Nel's twig broke. With a gesture of disgust she threw the pieces into the hole they had made. Sula threw hers in too. Nel saw a bottle cap and tossed it in as well. Each then looked around for more debris to throw into the hole: paper, bits of glass, butts of cigarettes, until all of the small defiling things they could find were collected there. Carefully they replaced the soil and covered the entire grave with uprooted grass.

Neither one had spoken a word.

They stood up, stretched, then gazed out over the swift dull water as an unspeakable restlessness and agitation held them. At the same instant each girl heard footsteps in the grass. A little boy in too big knickers was coming up from the lower bank of the river. He stopped when he saw them and picked his nose.

"Your mamma tole you to stop eatin' snot, Chicken," Nel hollered at him through cupped hands.

"Shut up," he said, still picking.

"Come up here and say that."

"Leave him 'lone, Nel. Come here, Chicken. Lemme show you something."

"Naw."

"You scared we gone take your bugger away?"

"Leave him 'lone, I said. Come on, Chicken. Look. I'll help you climb a tree."

Chicken looked at the tree Sula was pointing to—a big double beech with low branches and lots of bends for sitting.

He moved slowly toward her.

"Come on, Chicken, I'll help you up."

Still picking his nose, his eyes wide, he came to where they were standing. Sula took him by the hand and coaxed him along. When they reached the base of the beech, she lifted him to the first branch, saying, "Go on. Go on. I got you." She followed the boy, steadying him, when he needed it, with her hand and her reassuring voice. When they were as high as they could go, Sula pointed to the far side of the river.

"See? Bet you never saw that far before, did you?"

"Uh uh."

"Now look down there." They both leaned a little and peered through the leaves at Nel standing below, squinting up at them. From their height she looked small and foreshortened.

Chicken Little laughed.

"Y'all better come on down before you break your neck," Nel hollered.

"I ain't never coming down," the boy hollered back.

"Yeah. We better. Come on, Chicken."

"Naw. Lemme go."

"Yeah, Chicken. Come on, now."

Sula pulled his leg gently.

"Lemme go."

"OK, I'm leavin' you." She started on.

"Wait!" he screamed.

Sula stopped and together they slowly worked their way down.

Chicken was still elated. "I was way up there, wasn't I? Wasn't I? I'm a tell my brovver."

Sula and Nel began to mimic him: "I'm a tell my brovver; I'm a tell my brovver."

Sula picked him up by his hands and swung him outward then around and around. His knickers ballooned and his shrieks of frightened joy startled the birds and the fat grasshoppers. When he slipped from her hands and sailed away out over the water they could still hear his bubbly laughter.

The water darkened and closed quickly over the place where Chicken Little sank. The pressure of his hard and tight little fingers was still in Sula's palms as she stood looking at the closed place in the water. They expected him to come back up, laughing. Both girls stared at the water.

Nel spoke first. "Somebody saw." A figure appeared briefly on the opposite shore.

The only house over there was Shadrack's. Sula glanced at Nel. Terror widened her nostrils. Had he seen?

The water was so peaceful now. There was nothing but the baking sun and something newly missing. Sula cupped her face for an instant, then turned and ran up to the little plank bridge that crossed the river to Shadrack's house. There was no path. It was as though neither Shadrack nor anyone else ever came this way.

Her running was swift and determined, but when she was close to the three little steps that led to his porch, fear crawled into her stomach and only the something newly missing back there in the river made it possible for her to walk up the three steps and knock at the door.

No one answered. She started back, but thought again of the peace of the river. Shadrack would be inside, just behind the door ready to pounce on her. Still she could not go back. Ever so gently she pushed the door with the tips of her fingers and heard only the hinges weep. More. And then she was inside. Alone. The neatness, the order startled her, but more surprising was the restfulness. Everything was so tiny, so common, so unthreatening. Perhaps this was not the house of the Shad. The terrible Shad who walked about with his penis out, who peed in front of ladies and girl-children, the only black who could curse white people and get away with it, who drank in the road from the mouth of the bottle, who shouted and shook in the streets. This cottage? This sweet old cottage? With its made-up bed? With its rag rug and wooden table? Sula stood in the middle of the little room and in her wonder forgot what she had come for until a sound at the door made her jump. He was there in the doorway looking at her. She had not heard his coming and now he was looking at her.

More in embarrassment than terror she averted her glance. When she called up enough courage to look back at him, she saw his hand resting upon the door frame. His fingers, barely touching the wood, were arranged in a graceful arc. Relieved and encouraged (no one with hands like that, no one with fingers that curved around wood so tenderly could kill her), she walked past him out of the door, feeling his gaze turning, turning with her.

At the edge of the porch, gathering the wisps of courage that were fast leaving her, she turned once more to look at him, to ask him . . . had he . . . ?

He was smiling, a great smile, heavy with lust and time to come. He nodded his head as though answering a question, and said, in a pleasant conversational tone, a tone of cooled butter, "Always."

Sula fled down the steps, and shot through the greenness and the baking sun back to Nel and the dark closed place in the water. There she collapsed in tears.

Nel quieted her. "Sh, sh. Don't, don't. You didn't mean it. It ain't your fault. Sh. Sh. Come on, le's go, Sula. Come on, now. Was he there? Did he see? Where's the belt to your dress?"

Sula shook her head while she searched her waist for the belt.

Finally she stood up and allowed Nel to lead her away. "He said, 'Always. Always.'"

"What?"

Sula covered her mouth as they walked down the hill. Always. He had answered a question she had not asked, and its promise licked at her feet.

A bargeman, poling away from the shore, found Chicken late that afternoon stuck in some rocks and weeds, his knickers ballooning about his legs. He would have left him there but noticed that it was a child, not an old black man, as it first appeared, and he prodded the body loose, netted it and hauled it aboard. He shook his head in disgust at the kind of parents who would drown their own children. When, he wondered, will those people ever be anything but animals, fit for nothing but substitutes for mules, only mules didn't kill each other the way niggers did. He dumped Chicken Little into a burlap sack and tossed him next to some egg crates and boxes of wool cloth. Later, sitting down to smoke on an empty lard tin, still bemused by God's curse and the terrible burden his own kind had of elevating Ham's sons, he suddenly became alarmed by the thought that the corpse in this heat would have a terrible odor, which might get into the fabric of his woolen cloth. He dragged the sack away and hooked it over the side, so that the Chicken's body was half in and half out of the water.

Wiping the sweat from his neck, he reported his find to the sheriff at Porter's Landing, who said they didn't have no niggers in their county, but that some lived in those hills 'cross the river, up above Medallion. The bargeman said he couldn't go all the way back there, it was every bit of two miles. The sheriff said whyn't he throw it on back into the water. The bargeman said he never shoulda taken it out in the first place. Finally they got the man who ran the ferry twice a day to agree to take it over in the morning.

That was why Chicken Little was missing for three days and didn't get to the embalmer's until the fourth day, by which time he was unrecognizable to almost everybody who once knew him, and even his mother wasn't deep down sure, except that it just had to be him since nobody could find him. When she saw his clothes lying on the table in the basement of the mortuary, her mouth snapped shut, and when she saw his body her mouth flew wide open again and it was seven hours before she was able to close it and make the first sound.

So the coffin was closed.

The Junior Choir, dressed in white, sang "Nearer My God to Thee" and "Precious Memories," their eyes fastened on the songbooks they did not need, for this was the first time their voices had presided at a real-life event.

Nel and Sula did not touch hands or look at each other during the funeral. There was a space, a separateness, between them. Nel's legs had turned to granite and she expected the sheriff or Reverend Deal's pointing finger at any moment. Although she knew she had "done nothing," she felt convicted and hanged right there in the pew—two rows down from her parents in the children's section.

Sula simply cried. Soundlessly and with no heaving and gasping for breath, she let the tears roll into her mouth and slide down her chin to dot the front of her dress.

As Reverend Deal moved into his sermon, the hands of the women unfolded like pairs of raven's wings and flew high above their hats in the air. They did not hear all of what he said; they heard the one word, or phrase, or inflection that was for them the connection between the event and themselves. For some it was the term "Sweet Jesus." And they saw the Lamb's eye and the truly innocent victim: themselves. They acknowledged the innocent child hiding in the corner of their hearts, holding a sugar-and-butter sandwich. That one. The one who lodged deep in their fat, thin, old, young skin, and was the one the world had hurt. Or they thought of their son newly killed and remembered his legs in short pants and wondered where the bullet went in. Or they remembered how dirty the room looked when their father left home and wondered if that is the way the slim, young Jew felt, he who for them was both son and lover and in whose downy face they could see the sugar-and-butter sandwiches and feel the oldest and most devastating pain there is: not the pain of childhood, but the remembrance of it.

Then they left their pews. For with some emotions one has to stand. They spoke, for they were full and needed to say. They swayed, for the rivulets of grief or of ecstasy must be rocked. And when they thought of all that life and death locked into that little closed coffin they danced and screamed, not to protest God's will but to acknowledge it and confirm once more their conviction that the only way to avoid the Hand of God is to get in it.

In the colored part of the cemetery, they sank Chicken Little in between his grandfather and an aunt. Butterflies flew in and out of the bunches of field flowers now loosened from the top of the bier and lying in a small heap at the edge of the grave. The heat had gone, but there was still no breeze to lift the hair of the willows.

Nel and Sula stood some distance away from the grave, the space that had sat between them in the pews had dissolved. They held hands and knew that only the coffin would lie in the earth; the bubbly laughter and the press of fingers in the palm would stay aboveground forever. At first, as they stood there, their hands were clenched together. They relaxed slowly until during the walk back home their fingers were laced in as gentle a clasp as that of any two young girlfriends trotting up the road on a summer day wondering what happened to butterflies in the winter.

1973

Ishmael Reed b. 1938

Ishmael Reed is a poet, novelist, actor, journalist, dramatist, and editor; his works reflect his artistic, ethnic, political, religious, and social interests. He spotlights black issues, but his themes are universal. His satiric barbs intentionally provoke his audiences in their wonderfully ironic and humorous way. Experimental forms, innovative style, and radical ideas place him in the forefront of contemporary writers. From black history to black humor, from Black Power to black magic, Reed integrates diverse themes and nontraditional styles.

Born on February 22, 1938, in Chattanooga, Tennessee, to Ben and Thelma (Coleman) Reed, Reed was raised in a blue-collar environment in Buffalo, New York, where the family moved when he was a child. From 1956 to 1960, he attended the University of New York at Buffalo. After moving to New York City, he founded the *East Village Other,* an independent newspaper, and published his first novel in 1967. This was followed by numerous books of poetry and fiction in addition to articles, plays, songs and very active editing after arriving in Oakland, California, in 1968. Ishmael Reed has won a National Endowment fellowship and a

Guggenheim Award, and he has been nominated twice for the National Book Award, once in poetry for *Conjure* and once in fiction for *Mumbo Jumbo.*

Although Reed is indebted to all the humorous, satiric, and bawdy writers from Ovid to Chaucer to Swift to Blake to Joyce, he emphasizes his debt to minority artists, especially black writers. He relies on African mythology, black sports heroes, and even rhythm and blues for his symbols and metaphors. Reed also weaves motifs of literary and contemporary allusions throughout his work: Amos and Andy, Eygptian gods, and famous figures (past and present) all appear in his mirror of society.

Controversial about race, sex, politics, freedom, religion, and everything else, Reed satirizes most institutions: "My main job I felt was to humble Judeo-Christian culture." In Reed's Neo-Hoo Doo Church, all poets are priests and historians. One of his favorite issues is that minority contributions to Western civilization seldom receive due credit. He stirs the fires of discord by satirizing the distorted versions of popular history. One function of the artist is to re-rewrite history to reveal the "truth," so Reed gleefully points out that cowboys were predominantly minorities, that Alexandre Dumas, the nineteenth-century French novelist who wrote *The Three Musketeers,* had African ancestry; and even that *Uncle Tom's Cabin* was stolen by Harriet Beecher Stowe from *The Life of Josiah Henson, Formerly a Slave.* But Reed is not a single-issue writer; he is a universal writer. His books are not solely about race issues, although race issues frequently serve as focal points. (He attacks the black establishment as harshly as he does the white.)

Reed's comic tone and joyous outlook in his parodies make us laugh at our foibles. Many of his works are comedies in the classical sense: Evil is punished and Good rewarded. Viewing life as a struggle between Dionysian and Apollonian forces, Reed chooses the laughter, dance, music, and joy: "I see life as mysterious, holy, profound, exciting, serious, and fun." So is his writing.

Michael Boccia
University of Southern Maine

PRIMARY WORKS

Novels: *The Free Lance Pallbearers,* 1967; *Yellow Back Radio Broke-Down,* 1969; *Mumbo Jumbo,* 1972; *The Last Days of Louisiana Red,* 1974; *Flight to Canada,* 1976; *The Terrible Twos,* 1982; *Reckless Eyeballing,* 1986; *The Terrible Threes,* 1989. Poetry: *Catechism of D Neoamerican Hoo Doo Church,* 1970; *Conjure,* 1972; *Chattanooga,* 1973; *A Secretary to the Spirits,* 1975, *Points of View,* 1988; *New and Collected Poems,* 1989. Essays: *Where Is Vietnam? American Poets Respond,* (contributing editor) Walter Lowenfels, ed., 1967; *The Rise and Fall of . . . ? Adam Clayton Powell* (as Emmett Coleman), 1967; *Shrovetide in Old New Orleans,* 1978; *God Made Alaska for the Indians,* 1982; *Writin' Is Fightin',* 1988. Plays: *The Ace Booms,* 1980; *Mother Hubbard* (previously *Hell Hath No Fury),* 1982; *Savage Walls,* 1985. Anthologies (editor): *19 Necromancers from Now,* 1970; *Yardbird Lives!,* 1978; *Califia,* 1979.

I am a cowboy in the boat of Ra

"The devil must be forced to reveal any such physical evil (potions, charms, fetishes, etc.) still outside the body and these must be burned." (Rituale

Romanum, *published 1947, endorsed by the coat-of-arms and introductory letter from Francis cardinal Spellman)*[1]

I am a cowboy in the boat of Ra,[2]
sidewinders in the saloons of fools
bit my forehead like O
the untrustworthiness of Egyptologists
who do not know their trips. Who was that
dog-faced man?[3] they asked, the day I rode
from town.

School marms with halitosis cannot see
the Nefertiti[4] fake chipped on the run by slick
germans, the hawk behind Sonny Rollins'[5] head or
the ritual beard of his axe; a longhorn winding
its bells thru the Field of Reeds.

I am a cowboy in the boat of Ra. I bedded
down with Isis,[6] Lady of the Boogaloo, dove
down deep in her horny, stuck up her Wells-Far-ago[7]
in daring midday getaway. "Start grabbing the
blue," I said from top of my double crown.[8]

I am a cowboy in the boat of Ra. Ezzard Charles[9]
of the Chisholm Trail.[10] Took up the bass but they
blew off my thumb. Alchemist in ringmanship but a
sucker for the right cross.

[1]Authentic citation. Francis Joseph Spellman was an American Roman Catholic who was Archbishop of New York (1939) and Cardinal (1946).

[2]Ancient Egyptian sun god and chief deity. He is represented as a hawk and the full sun. Father of Osiris, Isis, and Set.

[3]Anubus, the ancient Egyptian deity of the dead was depicted as a man with a jackal head. Like Hermes of Greek myth, his role was to bring the dead before the judge of the infernal regions.

[4]Translates literally as "the beautiful one has come"; Wife of Egyptian Pharaoh Akenaten (1375–1358 B.C.) and influential in the spread of the arts in ancient Egypt. Germans looted and damaged a bust of her head from Egypt in the early part of the twentieth century, now in the State Museum of Berlin.

[5]African American tenor saxophonist among the leaders in of the "hardbop" or "soul" jazz movement of the 1950s.

[6]Egyptian nature goddess; a prototype for many Mediterranean Mother Earth goddesses; most popular goddess in the Roman Empire. Sister and wife of Osiris, mother of Horus; restores Osiris, King of the Dead, to life after he has been murdered and dismembered by his brother Set.

[7]Wells Fargo was an overland stage company in the nineteenth-century American West.

[8]When the ancient Egyptian cults of Ra and Ammon were combined into the cult of Ammon Ra, their two ritual crowns were combined into a double crown signifying a unified Egypt.

[9]Black heavy-weight boxing champion of the world from 1949 to 1951.

[10]Nineteenth-century wagon-train trail from Missouri to California.

I am a cowboy in the boat of Ra. Vamoosed from
the temple i bide my time. The price on the wanted
poster was a-going down, outlaw alias copped my stance
and moody greenhorns were making me dance;
 while my mouth's
shooting iron got its chambers jammed.

I am a cowboy in the boat of Ra. Boning-up in
the ol West i bide my time. You should see
me pick off these tin cans whippersnappers. I
write the motown long plays for the comeback of
Osiris.[11] Make them up when stars stare at sleeping
steer out here near the campfire. Women arrive
on the backs of goats and throw themselves on
my Bowie.[12]

I am a cowboy in the boat of Ra. Lord of the lash,
the Loup Garou[13] Kid. Half breed son of Pisces and
Aquarius.[14] I hold the souls of men in my pot. I do
the dirty boogie with scorpions. I make the bulls
keep still and was the first swinger to grape the taste.

I am a cowboy in his boat. Pope Joan[15] of the
Ptah Ra.[16] C/mere a minute willya doll?
Be a good girl and
bring me my Buffalo horn of black powder
bring me my headdress of black feathers
bring me my bones of Ju-Ju[17] snake
go get my eyelids of red paint.
Hand me my shadow

I'm going into town after Set[18]

[11]Translates literally as "many-eyed"; Egyptian judge of the dead. Osiris is the setting sun, Ra the midday sun, and Horus the morning sun. Osiris is reborn through the actions of Isis.

[12]A popular, large, and bulging bladed knife designed by Jim Bowie, the nineteenth-century frontiersman, who died at the Alamo.

[13]Werewolf.

[14]Two Zodiac signs from astrology. Being born on the cusp of Aquarius and Pisces is an omen of mystical powers.

[15]Tradition has it that Joan had a violent passion for the monk Folda and secretly followed him into the brotherhood. She was so popular among the clergymen that she was elected pope and succeeded Leo IV.

[16]Ptah, god of craftsmanship and chief god of Memphis, was combined with Ra, chief god of Heliopolis, when the two Egyptian city-states combined into a single nation.

[17]The mystical or magical powers associated with ancestors and places or an amulet or fetish of West African origin representing those magical attributes, usually consisting of red snake bones and feathers connected by snake skin.

[18]Egyptian god of the setting sun, and hence night, he is the brother of Osiris, whom he murders and dismembers in order to steal the royal throne of the gods.

I am a cowboy in the boat of Ra

look out Set   here i come Set
to get Set   to sunset Set
to unseat Set   to Set down Set

usurper of the Royal couch
imposter RAdio of Moses' bush[19]
party pooper O hater of dance
vampire outlaw of the milky way

1972

Flight to Canada[1]

Dear Massa Swille:
What it was?
I have done my Liza Leap[2]
& am safe in the arms
of Canada, so
Ain't no use your Slave
Catchers waitin on me
At Trailways
I won't be there

I flew in non-stop
Jumbo jet this A.M. Had
Champagne
Compliments of the Cap'n
Who announced that a
Runaway Negro was on the
Plane. Passengers came up
And shook my hand
& within 10 min. I had

[19]Exodus 3:2: Yaweh appeared to Moses as a burning bush.

[1]Reed writes in the novel of the same name that this poem "kind of imitates" the style of William Wells Brown, the black satirist who wrote *Clotel* in 1853, the first known African American novel.

[2]In *Uncle Tom's Cabin,* by Harriet Beecher Stowe, a black female slave, Eliza, attains freedom by leaping from ice floe to ice floe across the Ohio River into the North and fleeing to Canada.

Signed up for 3 anti-slavery
Lectures. Remind me to get an
Agent

Traveling in style
Beats craning your neck after
The North Star[3] and hiding in
Bushes anytime, Massa
Besides, your Negro dogs
Of Hays & Allen[4] stock can't
Fly

By now I s'pose that
Yellow Judas Cato[5] done tole
You that I have snuck back to
The plantation 3 maybe 4 times
Since I left the first time

Last visit I slept in
Your bed and sampled your
Cellar. Had your prime
Quadroon[6] give me
She-Bear, Yes, yes

You was away at a
Slave auction at Ryan's Mart[7]
In Charleston & so I knowed
You wouldn't mind
Did you have a nice trip, Massa?

I borrowed your cotton money
to pay for my ticket & to get
Me started in this place called
Saskatchewan[8] Brrrrrrr!
It's cold up here but least
Nobody is collaring hobbling gagging
Handcuffing yoking chaining & thumbscrewing
You like you is they hobby horse

[3]Polaris, the brightest star in the Little Dipper, was used by escaped slaves as the beacon for the Underground Railroad that would lead north to Free States or Canada.

[4]Hays & Allen bred and trained dogs especially to track runaway slaves.

[5]High Yellow, colloquial American black slang, refers to a light complectioned Negro. Judas Iscariot was the Apostle who betrayed Jesus at the Last Supper, and Cato (both the Elder and Younger) were Roman censors who led simple lives of self-denial.

[6]A person who is of one-quarter Negro ancestry.

[7]A slave market.

[8]A Canadian province.

The Mistress Ms. Lady
Gived me the combination
To your safe, don't blame
The feeble old soul, Cap'n
I told her you needed some
More money to shop with &
You sent me from Charleston
To get it. Don't worry
Your employees won't miss
It & I accept it as a
Down payment on my back
Wages

I must close now
Massa, by the time you gets
This letter old Sam will have
Probably took you to the
Deep Six
That was rat poison I left
In your Old Crow[9]

Your boy
Quickskill

1976

from Mumbo Jumbo

Chapter 10

Some say his ancestor is the long Ju Ju[1] of Arno in eastern Nigeria,[2] the man who would oracle, sitting in the mouth of a cave, as his clients stood below in shallow water.

Another story is that he is the reincarnation of the famed Moor of Summerland himself, the Black gypsy who according to Sufi[3] Lit. sicked the Witches[4] on Europe. Whoever his progenitor, whatever his lineage, his grandfather it is known was

[9]A famous southern whiskey.
[1]The mystical or magical powers associated with ancestors and places or an amulet or fetish of West African origin representing those magical attributes. Usually consists of red snake bones and feathers connected by snake skin.
[2]Site of ancient African civilization and of the highly developed Benin culture (c. 1200–1850).
[3]Mystical philosophy of Islam arising c. 1000; associated with the belief in union with God through mystical experience, magical acts, and the hashish-smoking Assassins.
[4]Not the evil witch of European folklore but the magician, alchemist, and naturalist of the Persian witchcraft tradition.

brought to America on a slave ship mixed in with other workers who were responsible for bringing African religion to the Americas where it survives to this day.

A cruel young planter purchased his grandfather and was found hanging shortly afterward. A succession of slavemasters met a similar fate: insanity, drunkenness, disease and retarded children. A drunken White man called him a foul name and did not live much longer afterward to give utterance to his squalid mind.

His father ran a successful mail-order Root[5] business in New Orleans. Then it is no surprise that PaPa LaBas[6] carries Jes Grew[7] in him like most other folk carry genes.

A little boy kicked his Newfoundland HooDoo[8] 3 Cents and spent a night squirming and gnashing his teeth. A warehouse burned after it refused to deliver a special variety of herbs to his brownstone headquarters and mind haberdashery where he sized up his clients to fit their souls. His headquarters are derisively called Mumbo Jumbo[9] Kathedral by his critics. Many are healed and helped in this factory which deals in jewelry, Black astrology charts, herbs, potions, candles, talismans.

People trust his powers. They've seen him knock a glass from a table by staring in its direction; and fill a room with the sound of forest animals: the panther's *ki-ki-ki,* the elephant's trumpet. He moves about town in his Locomobile, the name of which amused many of his critics including Hank Rollings, an Oxford-educated Guianese art critic who referred to him as an "evangelist" and said he looked forward to the day when PaPa LaBas "got well." To some if you owned your own mind you were indeed sick but when you possessed an Atonist[10] mind you were healthy. A mind which sought to interpret the world by using a single loa.[11] Somewhat like filling a milk bottle with an ocean.

[5]The Work, or the Root Business, refers to mystical, magical, or religious HooDoo activities that may be used for good (such as healing the sick) or misused for evil (such as profiteering) purposes.

[6]Literally "down there" or "below," implying the Underworld of Death. Reed claims "LaBas" is a Louisiana Creole pronunciation of Legba, the Haitian VooDoo god of the land of the dead. He was protector of the Holy Gates and Guardian of the Crossroads.

[7]Parody of jazz, follows the course of jazz in the U.S.; a disease that causes the infected ones to jump up, dance, and sing for joy. Reed offers as his source the African American poet, scholar, and folklorist James Weldon Johnson, in *The Book of American Negro Poetry:* "The earliest Ragtime songs, like Topsy, 'jes' grew.' . . . We appropriated about the last one of the 'jes' grew' songs. It was a song which had been sung for years all through the South. The words were unprintable, but the tune was irresistible and belonged to nobody."

[8]American version of Haitian VooDoo (Voudoun) with loas (gods) of local origin and manifestation, each one possessing special powers and demanding particular sacrifices. For Reed, HooDoo represents the creative urge manifest in art and life.

[9]In the opening pages of the novel, Reed gives his definition of the Mandingo term *ma-ma-gyo-mbo,* "magician who makes the troubled spirits of ancestors go away"; *ma-ma* (grandmother) + *gyo* (trouble) + *mbo* (to leave). *The American Heritage Dictionary of the English Language.*

[10]Pun on the Egyptian sun god Aton ("the burner of growing things," represented by the sun's burning disk) and atonal (without musical tone). Atonists don't like music and hence don't dance, so they oppose the dance and joy of Jes Grew.

[11]A god or spirit in Haitian Voodoo (Voudoun), of African origin, with specific areas of control similar to the Greco-Roman gods. Reed offers one source: "Some *unknown natural phenomenon* occurs which cannot be explained, and a new local demigod is named. Zora Neal Hurston on the origin of a new loa."

He is a familiar sight in Harlem, wearing his frock coat, opera hat, smoked glasses and carrying a cane. Right now he is making a delivery of garlic, sage, thyme, geranium water, dry basil, parsley, saltpeter, bay rum, verbena essence and jack honeysuckle to the 2nd floor of Mumbo Jumbo Kathedral. They are for an old sister who has annoying nightly visitations.

The sign on the door reads

PAPA LABAS
MUMBO JUMBO KATHEDRAL
FITS FOR YOUR HEAD

When he climbs to the 2nd floor of Mumbo Jumbo Kathedral. The office is about to close for the day. Earline, his assistant Therapist, is putting her desk in order. She is attired in a white blouse and short skirt. Her feet are bare. Her hair is let down. PaPa LaBas places The Work on her desk.

Please give these to Mother Brown. She must bathe in this and it will place the vaporous evil Ka[12] hovering above her sleep under arrest and cause it to disperse.

Earline nods her head. She sits down at her desk and begins to munch on some fig cookies which lie in an open box.

PaPa LaBas glances up at the oil portrait hanging on the wall. It is a picture of the original Mumbo Jumbo Kathedral taken a few weeks ago: Berbelang, his enigmatic smile, the thick black mustache, the derby and snappy bowtie, his mysterious ring bearing the initials E.F., his eyes of black rock, 2 mysterious bodies emitting radio energy from deep in space, set in the narrow face; Earline in the characteristic black skirt, the white blouse with the ruffled shoulders, the violet stone around her neck; Charlotte, a French trainee he has hired to fill in for Berbelang, wears a similar costume to Earline's and smokes a cigarette. In the painting, completed 2 weeks before Berbelang left the group, she stands next to Earline.

Earline, now sitting at her desk, is smoking. 1 hand supports her head as she checks an order for new herbs and incense.

Daughter?

She looks up, distantly.

Jes Grew which began in New Orleans has reached Chicago. They are calling it a plague when in fact it is an anti-plague. I know what it's after; it has no definite route yet but the configuration it is forming indicates it will settle in New York. It

[12]Egyptian conception of one of the seven parts of a human, a spiritual double or astral body possessed by everything on earth. One's Ka comes at birth and leaves at death, but may remain after death to haunt a place or person.

won't stop until it cohabits with what it's after.[13] Then it will be a pandemic and you will really see something. And then *they*[14] will be finished.

Earline slams the papers down on her desk.

What's wrong, daughter?

There you go jabbering again. That's why Berbelang left. Your conspiratorial hypothesis about some secret society molding the consciousness of the West. You know you don't have any empirical evidence for it that; you can't prove . . .

Evidence? Woman, I dream about it, I feel it, I use my 2 heads. My Knockings.* Don't you children have your Knockings, or have you New Negroes lost your other senses, the senses we came over here with? Why your Knockings are so accurate they can chart the course of a hammerhead shark in an ocean 1000s of miles away. Daughter, standing here, I can open the basket of a cobra in an Indian marketplace and charm the animal to sleep. What's wrong with you, have you forgotten your Knockings? Why, when the seasons change on Mars, I sympathize with them.

*B. Fuller terms this phenomenon "ultra ultra high frequency electromagnetic wave propagation."[15]

O pop, that's ridiculous. Xenophobic. Why must you mix poetry with concrete events? This is a new day, pop. We need scientists and engineers, we need lawyers.

All that's all right, what you speak of, but that ain't all. There's more. And I'll bet that before this century is out men will turn once more to mystery, to wonderment; they will explore the vast reaches of space within instead of more measuring more "progress" more of this and more of that. More Increase, Growth Inflation, and they don't know what to do when Jes Grew comes along like the Dow Jones[16] snake and rises quicker than the G.N.P.;[17] these scientists, there's a lot they don't know. And as for secret societies? The Communist party originated among some German workers in Paris. They called themselves the Workers Outlaw League. Marx[18] came along and removed what was called the ritualistic paraphernalia so that the masses could participate instead of the few. Daughter, the man down on 125th St. and Lenox Ave. on the stand speaking might be mouthing ideas which arose at a cocktail party or from a transcontinental telephone call or—

[13]Jes Grew is seeking its text, the *Book of Thoth* (Egyptian Book of Life), that depicts the dances of the gods and reveals the meaning of life.

[14]The Wallflower Order, a secret society and Knight Order that follows the Atonist Path and is opposed to dancing, singing, and life's joys. In *Mumbo Jumbo* it consists of bankers, police, and politicians who can't dance and secretly control the world.

[15]Astral detective LaBas can not only "feel" things, but is also able to speak to the gods. The Buckminster Fuller quotation demonstrates that one person's "mumbo jumbo" is another's scientific, religious, or existential "truth."

[16]Dow Jones Industrial Average follows the price of 500 stocks to determine the amount and success of trading on the New York Stock Exchange.

[17]Gross National Product: the measurement of economic goods and services (less consumer and government spending) produced in a nation in one fiscal year.

[18]Karl Marx (1818–1883), German social philosopher, author (with Engels) of *Communist Manifesto* and *Capital.* Most modern forms of socialism and communism evolved from his radical economic and historic theories (Dialectical Materialism).

Earline puts her head on the desk and begins to sob. PaPa LaBas comforts her.

O there I go, getting you upset . . .

She confesses to him. O it isn't you, pop, it isn't you, it's . . . Berbelang?

O pop, he thinks you're a failure, he felt that you were limiting your techniques. He thought you should have added Inca,[19] Taoism[20] and other systems. He felt that you were becoming all wrapped up in Jes Grew and that it's a passing fad. He isn't the old Berbelang, pop; his eyes are red. He seems to have a missionary zeal about whatever he's mixed up in. I get so lonely, I would like to go out; tonight for instance. I'm invited to a Chitterling Switch.

A Chitterling Switch? What's that, Earline?

She shows him the card.

We're attempting to raise money for anti-lynching legislation; James Weldon Johnson[21] is supposed to speak . . . It's like a Rent Party, you know?

You and T[22] use so much slang these days I can hardly communicate with you, but your Chitterling Switch sounds interesting. Do you mind if an old man comes along?

O pop, 50 is not old these days.

You flatter me; just wait until I lock the office.

And I must change, pop. I'll be right with you.

FOOD! GAMES! DRINK!

A CHITTERLING SWITCH

sponsored by

Madame Lewaro

for

anti-lynching campaign

108 West 136th Street

THURSDAY, OCT. 22, FROM 9 TILL ?

let's get our brothers off the limb

by chipping in a barrel of fins

(surprise appearance by Mystery Blood!)

[19]South American native peoples skilled in mathematics, engineering, and agriculture. Major Native American empire from c. 1200 to 1553.

[20]Chinese philosophy of nature; a religion and a system of magical rites. Of prehistoric origin, the Tao translates literally as the "Way" or the "Way of Nature."

[21]African American poet, scholar, and folklorist (1871–1938); founder of NAACP and civil rights activist.

[22]T Malice is the name of LaBas's chauffeur.

PaPa LaBas glances into another office toward the main room of Mumbo Jumbo Kathedral.

Where's Charlotte?

Earline has entered the ladies room.

You know pop, she's been acting strangely these days. She's listless and cross. She had an argument with a client this morning and began to swear at him in French; isn't that a sign?

He pauses for a moment.

I must speak to her. Perhaps she's upset about Berbelang leaving as he did. You know, they were fond of each other. My activist side really charms the women; I suppose this is how he was able to woo such a beautiful thing as yourself.

O cut it out, pop!

Earline looks at her features in the mirror. Something has come over her. She finds it necessary to go through the most elaborate toilet ritual these days, using some very expensive imported soaps, embroidered towels, and she has taken a fancy to buying cakes even though she never before possessed a sweet tooth. She glances at the sign above the marble sink.

REMEMBER TO FEED THE LOAS

O, that reminds her. She hasn't replenished the loa's tray #21. On a long table in the Mango Room are 22 trays which were built as a tribute to the Haitian loas that LaBas claimed was an influence on his version of The Work. This was 1 of LaBas' quirks. He still clung to some of the ways of the old school. Berbelang had laughed at him 1 night for feeding a loa. This had been 1 of the reasons for their break. Of course she didn't comprehend their esoteric discussions. PaPa LaBas hadn't required that the technicians learn The Work. The drummers, too, were clinical; their job was that of sidemen to PaPa LaBas' majordomo. They didn't know PaPa LaBas' techniques and therapy. Didn't have to know it. As long as they knew the score LaBas wasn't interested in proselytizing. But feeding, she thought, was merely 1 of his minor precautions. It seemed such a small thing. She would attend to it tomorrow or the next day.[23]

I'll be with you in a moment, she shouts through the door to LaBas.

We have plenty of time, no rush, PaPa LaBas answers her. He is inspecting the trays. He stops at the 12th tray, then returns to join Earline who is ready to go.

The pair moves down the steps. Outside T Malice is talking to a young woman who has her hands clasped behind her back and is swaying coquettishly. When he sees PaPa and Earline he pulls down the brim of his chauffeur's cap and looks straight ahead. They tease him and of course being a good sport he can take it.

Karen Tei Yamashita b. 1951

Karen Tei Yamashita's writing, like her life, has been specially attuned to the histories, stories, and meanings of movement and migration. Born in Oakland, California, Yamashita moved to Los Angeles when she was one. Her writing career properly began in 1975 when she traveled to Brazil to study the experiences of Japanese immigrant women there. What was to have been a one-year research project turned into a nine-year stay that gave her the material for her first two books, *Through the Arc of the Rain Forest* and *Brazil-Maru,* both published after her return to Los Angeles in the mid-1980s.

Those novels bear traces of Yamashita's experiences in Brazil, a country that she describes as having a "generous and gracious acceptance . . . of strangers," in a peculiar mix of developed and developing worlds. They also attest to her range as a writer, which moves from the complexly woven, multiply narrated voices that make a three-generation tapestry of Japanese immigrants in *Brazil-Maru* to, in *Through the Arc,* the fantastic world of miraculous pilgrimages, which draws equal parts from Latin American magical realism and Brazilian soap operas.

Long before the term *globalization* was being bandied about by politicians and cultural critics, Yamashita was chronicling the sometimes tragic and sometimes beautiful effects of a world folding in on itself. This view of the shrinking world finds expression in the frequent lists that populate her fiction, such as the one from *Through the Arc,* which describes a junkyard of "F-86 Sabres, F-4 Phantoms, Huey Cobras, Lear Jets and Piper Cubs, Cadillacs, Volkswagens, Dodges and an assorted mixture of gas guzzlers," swallowed up by the vegetation to create a "rainforest parking lot." But while Yamashita, with her eye for the irreconcilably polyglot—that which simultaneously demands and denies easy categorization—describes the collision of worlds in Brazil, her sensibility has also been nourished by the equally fascinating racial, geographical, architectural, and migratory stew that is Los Angeles. In her third novel, *Tropic of Orange* (from which the following selection is taken), she turns her attention to this city. Not only does her characterization of Los Angeles stand in stark contrast to Hollywood's schizophrenic treatment, which shuttles between Pacific paradise and disaster-prone dystopia, but she accurately describes the extent to which the city of angels is being shaped and re-shaped by those who have traveled to make their homes there. A character like Bobby Ngu, "Chinese from Singapore with a Vietnam name speaking like a Mexican living in Koreatown," speaks of a place where disparate worlds collide and commingle.

The consistent line that links Yamashita's novels is her deep engagement with the social world and her continual questioning of "standards" of justice and equity through characters who struggle to make such abstract concepts real in the collective project of community. Whether through the destruction of rain forest in the name of corporate expansion, through the corrupting influence of "business" and war on a commune of Japanese idealists, or through the unsettling contradictions that the global marketplace has thrown up between the United States and Mexico, Yamashita's narratives and characters speak to the necessity of making community in spite of and because of a humanity that struggles against its own flawed nature to realize that which it has imagined to be possible.

A world traveler herself, Yamashita currently makes her home in Santa Cruz, California. She teaches creative writing at the University of California, Santa Cruz.

Michael Murashige
Independent scholar

PRIMARY WORKS

Through the Arc of the Rain Forest, 1990; *Brazil-Maru,* 1992; *Tropic of Orange,* 1997; Karen Tei Yamashita: Interview by Michael S. Murashige," *Words Matter: Conversations with Asian American Writers,* ed. King-Kok Cheung, 2000.

from Tropic of Orange

2. Benefits—Koreatown

Check it out, ése. You know this story? Yeah, over at Sanitary Supply they always tell it. This dude drives up, drives up to Sanitary. Makes a pickup like always. You know. Paper towels. Rags. Mop handles. Gallon of Windex. Stuff like that. Drives up in a Toyota pickup. Black shiny deal, all new, big pinche wheels. Very nice. Yeah. Asian dude. Kinda skinny. Short, yeah. But so what? Dark glasses. Cigarette in the mouth. He's getting out the truck, see. In the parking lot. Big tall dude comes by with a gun. Yeah, a gun. Puts it to his head and says, GIMME THE KEYS! It's a jacker. Asian dude don't lose no time, man. No time. Not a doubt. Rams the door closed. WHAM! Just like that. Slams the door on the jacker's hand. On the jacker's gun! Smashes the gun! Smashes the hand. Gun ain't worth shit. Hand's worth even less. Jacker loses it bad. He's crying. Screaming. It's not over. Asian dude swings the door open. Attacks the jacker. Pushes him up to the wall of Sanitary and beats the shit out. Dude don't come up to the jacker's nose. But it don't matter. Got every trick in the books. Bruce Lee moves. Kick. VAP! WHOP! Damn. Don't mess with this man. By now Sanitary's called the police. Crowd's seen it all. Jacker's a mess. Blood everywhere. Never seen so much blood. But not a drop on the Asian. Not a drop. Never took off his shades. Never even stopped smoking. Turns over the jacker's remains to the police. Don't say nothing. That's it. Goes into Sanitary. Picks up the mop handles, Windex, rags. Gets in the pickup. He's gone. That's it. That's it.

That's Bobby. If you know your Asians, you look at Bobby. You say, that's Vietnamese. That's what you say. Color's pallid. Kinda blue just beneath the skin. Little underweight. Korean's got rounder face. Chinese's taller. Japanese's dressed better. If you know your Asians. Turns out you'll be wrong. And you gonna be confused. Dude speaks Spanish. Comprende? So you figure it's one of those Japanese from Peru. Or maybe Korean from Brazil. Or Chinamex. Turns out Bobby's from Singapore. You say, okay, Indonesian. Malaysian. Wrong again. You say, look at his name. That's gotta be Vietnam. Ngu. Bobby Ngu. They all got Ngu names. Hey, it's not his real name. Real name's Li Kwan Yu. But don't tell nobody. Go figure. Bobby's Chinese. Chinese from Singapore with a Vietnam name speaking like a Mexican living in Koreatown. That's it.

Bobby's story. It's a long story. Gotta be after hours for Bobby to tell it. And then, he might not. He was twelve. His brother eight. Dad had a bicycle business in Singapore. Mother dies. Business went bad. Can't sell no more bicycles. Dad says, you wanna future? Better go to America. Better start out something new. For the family. You better go. Don't worry about us. You start a future all new.

Bobby's only twelve. How you get from Singapore to America? It's 1975. People getting on boats, rafts, dinghies, anything, swimming south out of Vietnam. Get to Singapore, but Singapore don't want them. They tell the Americans, its your problem. Put them in camps. Keep them there. Count them. Sort them out. Ask questions. Americans lost the war. Gotta take care of the casualties. Call them boat people. Call them refugees. Call for humanitarian aid. Call for political asylum. Meanwhile, they're in camps. Singapore don't want them. What's America gonna do? Count them again. Sort them out. Ask more questions. Pretty soon refugees get put on planes. Little by little. Distributed to America.

Every day, Bobby gets up early. He and his little brother. Walk over to the camp. Gates open in the morning. Walk in. Stand around with the refugees. Eat with the refugees. Guards don't notice. Who's gonna notice? But he's there every day. Maybe he belongs there. So maybe they notice. Bobby and his brother. Looking like orphans. Sad situation. Orphans everywhere. The war did this. Got to help the children. It's the children who suffer. Bobby and his little brother don't understand nothing. Don't understand Vietnamese. Just get some language here and there. That's all. Looks like they can't talk. Why not? War does that. You can't talk. Gets to be nighttime. Bobby and his brother go home. Slip out. Walk back into Singapore town. Go home and eat. Sleep. Get up early. Go back every morning. Spend the day sitting and eating with refugees. It's like that every day. Every day for months. That's it.

Then, pretty soon Bobby and the brother get counted. They get sorted. Get questions. Bobby's gotta have a name. He says Ngu. Everybody's Ngu. He's Ngu too. He's on the list. He's counted. Brother's counted, too. Get their pictures taken. Get some papers. American passports. Bobby's dad gives him money. U.S. money. Saved from the black market. Hides it in his pants. Sews it there. It's everything his dad can give. Money's there. Ready. Just in case. Every morning, Bobby gets his brother up early. Every morning, they slip into the refugee camp. Every night they slip out. One night they do not come home. One night Bobby's dad and the two sisters eat dinner. They leave two bowls out like always. They stare at the bowls. Silent. Staring at the two bowls.

Bobby'll tell you this story. But only after hours. After some beers and lots of smokes. He don't have time to tell stories. Too busy. Never stops. Got only a little time to sleep even. Always working. Hustling. Moving. That's why he beat that guy up and never stopped. Just kept on going. Never stops smoking either. Gonna die from smoking. He can't stop. Daytime, works the mailroom at a big-time newspaper. Sorts mail nonstop. Tons of it. Never stops. Nighttime got his own business. Him and his wife. Cleaning buildings. Clean those buildings that still got defense contracts. Bobby's got clearance. Got it for his wife too. Go around everywhere. Dump the stuff that's shredded. Wipe up the conference tables. Dust everything. Wipe down the computer monitors. Vacuum staples and hole punches and donuts out of carpets. Scrub the urinals. Mop down the floors. Bobby only stops for a smoke with the nighttime guard.

Bobby's wife likes to study. She's got a Walkman in her ears. Running the vacuum and the Walkman. It's not music. She's studying English. She's Mexican. Bobby don't teach her English. Speaks to her in Spanish. She's got to learn by herself. She's smart. Really smart. Got her degree at LACC. She told Bobby, janitors like them got to make better money. Got to get benefits. Some don't even get the minimum. Can we live on $4.25 an hour? No way. She joined Justice for Janitors. Bobby got mad. This is his business. He's independent. All the money is his. What's she talking about? It's solidarity she said. Some work for the companies. They need to organize. For protection. Bobby don't understand this. He says he works the morning job and gets benefits. Why is she complaining?

Maybe this was the reason. Maybe not. Bobby got in an argument with his wife. So she split. She took the boy with her. Drives him crazy. He can't see straight. Never been so happy as when he got married to that woman. Can't explain. Happier he is, harder he works. Can't stop. Gotta make money. Provide for his family. Gotta buy his wife nice clothes. Gotta buy his kid the best. Bobby's kid's gonna know the good life. That's how Bobby sees it.

It's not just the kid and the wife. Bobby's gotta send money to his dad. Back in Singapore. Keep the old man alive. Wanted the old man to come to L.A., but he wouldn't do it. Says he's too old. Says Bobby's got the future. All new future. And Bobby's baby brother. He's in college. Smart kid. Gets all As. Bobby put him in college. Pays for everything. Books, dorm, tuition, extras. Got him a car, too. Bobby don't forget his baby bro. His carnalito. Don't forget the kid cried every day when they arrived. Every day for two weeks. Cried for his mom who was already dead. Cried for his dad. For his sisters. Cried. Carnalito don't cry no more. Bobby don't forget.

Used to be, back in Singapore, Bobby had it easy. Dad had a factory. Putting out bicycles. Had a good life. Good money. Only had to go to school. One day, American bicycle company put up a factory. Workers all went over there. New machines. Paid fifty cents more. Pretty soon, American company's selling all over. Exporting. Bicycles go to Hong Kong. Go to Thailand. To India. To Japan. To Taiwan. Bobby's dad losing business. Can't compete. That's it.

But that's the past. Everything had to change. Change like the seasons. Rainy season. Dry season. Rainy season'll come again. Bobby's working on it. Gonna flood with the rainy season. Gonna fly back to Singapore and see his dad. Gonna see his sisters. See his nephews and nieces. Gonna bring the kid bro and the family along, too. But he's gotta get that woman back. Gotta bring the boy home. Can't be happy without his family. Can't work. Can't keep running. Can't keep fighting. After hours, Bobby keeps thinking. What's he gonna do? Rafaela said he's gotta stop smoking. That's it.

After hours, Bobby goes home. House's in Koreatown, edge of Pico-Union. Maybe it's Koreatown, but he owns it. Stucco job with two palm trees in front. Nobody home. Just him. Woman said to stop smoking. That's it. That's the last cigarette. Boil some water. Get out the ginseng. Get a good piece of the root. Grind it up good. Hot water. Ginseng. Steam goes up just like the root. That's the smell. Clean up the system. Clear the head. It's an old root. Takes a long time to grow. Don't waste it.

1997

Jessica Hagedorn b. 1949

Born in the Santa Mesa section of Manila in 1949, Jessica Hagedorn traces her early inspiration to a mother devoted to painting and a maternal grandfather who was an accomplished writer and political cartoonist. Situated within a colonial heritage of Catholic schooling and U.S. cultural hegemony, Hagedorn found herself drawn to Hollywood movies and Western literary classics—but equally to melodramas and radio serials in Tagalog. This predilection for crossing boundaries defines Hagedorn's cultural productions, which include poetry and fiction, theater pieces and performance art, and music and screenplays.

Moving to San Francisco at the age of

fourteen proved pivotal in shaping Hagedorn's consciousness. Although eventually attending the American Conservatory Theater, Hagedorn attributes a substantial part of her artistic development to her early exposure to San Francisco's social and literary scene. The family's frequent moves through diverse neighborhoods contributed, along with her unimpeded appetite for browsing bookstores, to her sense of multiculturalism. She cites Bienvenido Santos, Amiri Baraka, Ishmael Reed, Jayne Cortez, and Víctor Hernández Cruz, as well as Gabriel García Márquez, Manuel Puig, and Stéphane Mallarmé, as among her literary influences. No less vital was her participation in San Francisco's Kearny Street Writers' Workshop, which introduced her to Asian American history and literature and helped infuse her with the spirit, passion, and social commitment of the late 1960s.

Hagedorn's urban American experience also stimulated an abiding interest in music, particularly rock, jazz, and rhythm and blues. Her poetry propels itself along rhythms inflected by music and urban vernacular. In 1973 her poetry appeared in *Four Young Women: Poems,* an anthology edited by Kenneth Rexroth. She continued experimenting in *Dangerous Music,* a 1975 collection whose poetry occasionally resembles a literal "dance" of words and whose offbeat prose fiction opens a space for rewriting of immigration narratives.

Also in 1975, along with Thulani Davis and Ntozake Shange, Hagedorn formed a band called the West Coast Gangster Choir, rechristened in 1978 in New York City as the Gangster Choir. Upon moving to the East Coast, she participated in New York's Basement Workshop. Earlier experiments using dramatic sketches during the pauses between songs contributed to the development of her performance art. Following the production of several theatrical works and teleplays, in 1981 her *Pet Food & Tropical Apparitions* appeared, which featured sexually charged poems and in the title story took a hard but sympathetic look at the capacity of inner-city culture to evince simultaneously an incomparable vitality and a lurid self-destructiveness. Between 1988 and 1992, she participated in the performance/theater trio Thought Music.

In 1990 Hagedorn produced her first novel, *Dogeaters,* a mordant exploration of class and ethnic divisions, rampant commercialism, plutocratic machinations, revolutionary insurgency, and the varieties of corruption in a country caught in the grasp of a Marcos-like regime and laboring beneath the shadow of Western colonialism. Nominated for the National Book Award and recipient of the American Book Award, *Dogeaters* is also noteworthy for its stylistic daring. Playfully splicing together book and letter excerpts, poetry, a gossip column, dramatic dialogue, and news items into a conventional storytelling frame, the novel explores the possibilities of combining postmodern narrative practices with a postcolonial political agenda.

In 1993 Hagedorn edited *Charlie Chan Is Dead: An Anthology of Contemporary Asian American Fiction.* Significantly, although the book included many well-known Asian American writers, such as Carlos Bulosan, Hisaye Yamamoto, Maxine Hong Kingston, Amy Tan, and Bharati Mukherjee, nearly half of the forty-eight writers enjoyed publication in a major collection for the first time.

Hagedorn's second novel, *The Gangster of Love,* appeared in 1996. It experiments with shifting points of view and engages dream as a supplementary narrative strategy but otherwise tells a conventional story of a young woman from the Philippines struggling to establish her musical and artistic career in America and later grappling with the encroachments of age.

Hagedorn remains ideologically aligned with the radical 1960s politics that helped shape her sensibility, but ultimately she is interested not in social realism but in reinvention and the varieties of liberation. Just as her work resists easy categorization into "high" or "pop" culture, it seeks to cross conventional boundaries of self and country and of writing and art.

George Uba
California State University, Northridge

PRIMARY WORKS

Dangerous Music, 1975; *Pet Food & Tropical Apparitions,* 1981; *Teenytown* (performance piece), 1988; *Danger and Beauty,* 1993; *Charlie Chan Is Dead: An Anthology of Contemporary Asian American Fiction* (edited), 1993; *Airport Music* (performance piece), 1994; *Dogeaters,* 1990; "The Exile Within/The Question of Identity" (with a postscript/interview by Karin Aguilar-San Juan), in *The State of Asian America: Activism and Resistance in the 1990s,* ed. Karin Aguilar-San Juan, 1994: *The Gangster of Love,* 1996; "Jessica Hagedorn: Interview by Emily Porcincula Lawsin," *Words Matter: Conversations with Asian American Writers,* ed. King-Kok Cheung, 2000.

The Blossoming of Bongbong

Antonio Gargazulio-Duarte, also fondly known as Bongbong to family and friends, had been in America for less than two years and was going mad. He didn't know it, of course, having left the country of his birth, the Philippines, for the very reason that his sanity was at stake. As he often told his friend, the painter Frisquito, "I can no longer tolerate contradiction. This country is full of contradiction. I have to leave before I go crazy."

His friend Frisquito would only laugh. His laugh was eerie because it was soundless. When he laughed, his body would shake—and his face, which was already grotesque, would distort—but no sound would emit from him.

People were afraid of Frisquito. They bought his paintings, but they stayed away from him. Especially when he was high. Frisquito loved to get high. He had taken acid more than fifty times, and he was only twenty-six years old. He had once lived in New York, where people were used to his grotesque face, and ignored him. Frisquito had a face that resembled a retarded child: eyes slanted, huge forehead, droopy mouth, and pale, luminous skin. Bongbong once said to him, "You have skin like the surface of the moon." Frisquito's skull was also unusually large, which put people off, especially women. Frisquito soon learned to do without women or men. "My paintings are masturbatory," he once said to the wife of the president of the Philippines. She never blinked an eye, later commissioning three obscene murals. She was often referred to as a "trendsetter."

Frisquito told Bongbong, "There's nothing wrong with being crazy. The thing to do is to get comfortable with it."

Not only had Frisquito taken acid more than fifty times, he had also taken peyote and cocaine and heroin at a rate that doctors often said would normally kill a man. "But I'm like a bull," he would say. "Nothing can really hurt me, except the creator of the universe."

At which point he would smile.

Bongbong finally left Manila on a plane for San Francisco. He was deathly afraid. He wore an olive-green velvet jacket, and dark velvet pants, with a long scarf thrown casually around his scrawny neck. Frisquito saw him off to the airport. "You look like a faggot," he said to Bongbong, who was once named best-dressed young VIP in Manila. Bongbong felt ridiculously out of place and took two downers so he could sleep during the long ride to America. He arrived, constipated and haggard, and was met by his sister and brother-in-law, Carmen and Pochoy Guevara. "You look terrible," his sister said. She was embarrassed to be seen with him. Secretly she feared he was homosexual, especially since he was such good friends with Frisquito.

Bongbong had moved in with his sister and brother-in-law, who lived in a plush apartment on Twin Peaks. His brother-in-law Pochoy, who had graduated as a computer programmer from Heald's Business College, worked for the Bank of America. His sister Carmen, who was rather beautiful in a bland, colorless kind of way, had enrolled in an Elizabeth Arden beauty course, and had hopes of being a fashion model.

"Or maybe I could go into merchandising," she would say, in the afternoons when she wouldn't go to class. She would sit in her stainless-steel, carpeted electric kitchen. She drank cup after cup of instant Yuban coffee, and changed her nail polish every three days.

"You should wear navy blue on your nails," Bongbong said to her one of those afternoons, when she was removing her polish with Cutex lemon-scented polish remover. "It would look wonderful with your sallow complexion." "Sallow" was a word Bongbong had learned from Frisquito.

"Sallow? What does that mean?" Carmen never knew if her brother was insulting or complimenting her.

"It means pale and unhealthy," Bongbong said. "Anyway, it's in style now. I've seen lots of girls wearing it."

He wrote Frisquito a letter:

Dear Frisquito,

Everyone is a liar. My sister is the biggest one of them all. I am a liar. I lie to myself every second of the day. I look in the mirror and I don't know what's there. My sister hates me. I hate her. She is inhuman. But then, she doesn't know how to be human. She thinks I'm inhuman. I am surrounded by androids. Do you know what that is? I'm glad I never took acid.

I wish I was a movie star.

Love,
Bongbong

The apartment had two bedrooms. Pochoy had bought a leather couch and a Magnavox record player on credit. He owned the largest and most complete collection of Johnny Mathis records. At night Bongbong would lie awake and listen to their silent fucking in the next room, and wonder if Carmen was enjoying herself. Sometimes they would fuck to "Misty."

Carmen didn't cook too often, and Pochoy had a gluttonous appetite. Since he didn't believe in men cooking, they would often order Chinese food or pizzas to be delivered. Once in a while Bongbong would try to fix a meal, but he was never talented in that direction. Frisquito had taught him how to cook two dishes: fried chicken & spaghetti.

Dear Frisquito,

I can't seem to find a job. I have no skills, and no college degree. Carmen thinks I should apply at Heald's Business College and go into computer programming. The idea makes me sick. I am twenty-six years old and no good at anything. Yesterday I considered getting a job as a busboy in a restaurant, but Carmen was horrified. She was certain everyone in Manila would hear about it (which they will), and she swears she'll kill herself out of shame. Not a bad idea, but I am not a murderer. If I went back to Manila I could be a movie star.

Love,
Bongbong

Bongbong stood in the middle of a Market Street intersection, slowly going mad. He imagined streetcars melting and running him over, grinding his flesh and bones into one hideous, bloody mess. He saw the scurrying Chinese women, no more than four feet tall, run amok and beat him to death with their shopping bags, which were filled to the brim with slippery, silver-scaled fish.

He watched a lot of television. His eyes became bloodshot. He began to read—anything from best-sellers to plays to political science to poetry. A lot of it he didn't quite understand, but the names and events fascinated him. He would often visit bookshops just to get out of the apartment. He chose books at random, sometimes for their titles or the color of their book jackets. His favorite before he went crazy was *Vibration Cooking* by Verta Mae Grosvenor. He even tried out some of Verta Mae's recipes, when he was in better moods on the days when Carmen and Pochoy were away. He had found Verta Mae's book for seventy-five cents in a used-book store he frequented.

"What is this?" Carmen asked, staring at the book cover, which featured Verta Mae in her colorful African motif outfit.

"That, my dear, is a cookbook," Bongbong answered, snatching the book out of her hands, now decorated in Max Factor's "Regency Red."

On the bus going home there was a young girl sitting behind Bongbong wearing a Catholic school uniform and carrying several books in her pale, luminous arms, which reminded him of the surface of the moon. When the bus came to a stop, she walked quietly to the front and before getting off she turned, very slowly and deliberately, and stared deeply into Bongbong's eyes. "You will get what you deserve," she said.

One time when Bongbong was feeling particularly lonely, he went to a bar on Union Street where young men and women stand around and drink weak Irish coffees. The bar was sometimes jokingly known as a "meat factory." The young men were usually executives, or trying to look like executives. They wore their hair slightly long, with rather tacky muttonchop whiskers, and they all smoked dope. The women were usually chic or terribly hip. Either way they eyed each other coolly and all wore platform shoes.

A drink was sent to Bongbong from the other end of the bar by a twenty-eight-year-old sometime actress and boutique salesgirl named Charmaine. She was from Nicaragua, and quite stunning, with frizzy brown hair and the biggest ass Bongbong had ever seen.

"What're you having?" she asked, grinning. Her lips were moist and glossy, and the Fertile Crescent was tattooed in miniature on her left cheek.

Bongbong, needless to say, was silent for a moment. Ladies like Charmaine were uncommon in Manila. "Gimlet," he murmured, embarrassed because he disliked the idea of being hustled.

Charmaine had a habit of tossing her head back, so that her frizzy curls bounced, as if she were always secretly dancing. "Awright," she said, turning to the bartender, "bring the gentleman a gimlet." She giggled, turning to look fully at Bongbong. "I'm Charmaine. Wha's your name?"

Bongbong blushed. "Antonio," he said, "But I go by my nickname." He dreaded her next question, but braced himself for it, feeling the familiar nausea rising within him. Once Frisquito had told him that witches and other types of human beings only had power over you if they knew your name. Since that time Bongbong always hesitated when anyone asked him for his name, especially women. "Women are more prone to occult powers than men," Frisquito warned. "It comes natural to them."

Charmaine was smiling now. "Oh yeah? Whatisit?"

"Bongbong."

The bartender handed him the gimlet, and Charmaine shrugged. "Tha's a funky name, man. You Chicano?"

Bongbong was offended. He wanted to say No, I'm Ethiopian, or Moroccan, or Nepalese, what the fuck do you care . . . Silently he drank his gimlet. Then he decided, the nausea subsiding, that Charmaine wasn't malicious, and left the bar with her shortly after.

Charmaine showed him the boutique where she worked, which was next door to the bar. Bongbong stared at the platform shoes in the display window as if he were seeing them for the first time. Their glittering colors and whimsical designs intrigued him. Charmaine watched his face curiously as he stood with his face pressed against the glass like a small child; then she took his arm and led him to her VW.

She lived in a large flat in the Fillmore district with another sometime actress and boutique salesgirl named Colelia. They had six cats, and the place smelled like a combination of cat piss and incense.

Colelia thought she was from Honey Patch, South Carolina, but she wasn't sure. "I'm all mixed up," she said. Sometimes she thought she was a geechee. She was the only person Bongbong knew who had ever read *Vibration Cooking.* She had even met Verta Mae at a party in New York.

Bongbong spent the night in Charmaine's bed, but he couldn't bring himself to even touch her. She was amused, and asked him if he was gay. At first he didn't understand the term. English sometimes escaped him, and certain colloquialisms, like "gay," never made sense. He finally shook his head and mumbled no. Charmaine told him she didn't really mind. Then she asked him to go down on her.

Dear Frisquito:

I enrolled at Heald's College today so that Carmen would shut up. I plan on leaving the house every morning and pretending I'm going to school. That way no one will bother me.

I think I may come back to Manila soon, but somehow I feel I'm being trapped into staying here. I don't understand anything. Everyone is an artist, but I don't see them doing anything. Which is what I don't understand . . . but one good thing is I am becoming a good cook.

Enclosed is a copy of *Vibration Cooking* by Verta Mae.

Love,

B.

Sometimes Bongbong would open the refrigerator door and oranges would fly out at him. He was fascinated by eggs, and would often say to his sister, "We're eating the sunset," or "We're eating embryos." Or he would frown and say, "I never did like chickens."

He began riding streetcars and buses from one end of the city to the other, often going into trances and reliving the nightmare of the streetcar melting and running him over. Always the Chinese women would appear, beating him to death with silver-scaled fish, or eggs.

Bongbong saw Charmaine almost every day for a month. His parents sent him an allowance, thinking he was in school. This allowance he spent lavishly on her. He bought her all the dazzling platform shoes her heart desired. He took her to fancy nightclubs so she could dance and wiggle her magnificent ass to his delight. She loved Sly Stone and Willie Colon, so he bought her all their records. They ate curry and spice cake every night of the week (sometimes alternating with yogurt pie and gumbo) and Charmaine put on ten pounds.

He never fucked her. Sometimes he went down on her, which she liked even better. She had replaced books and television in his life. He thought he was saved.

One afternoon while he was waiting for Charmaine in the bar where they had met, Bongbong had a vision. A young woman entered the bar, wearing a turban on her head made of torn rags. Her hair was braided and stood out from her scalp like branches on a young tree. Her skin was so black she was almost blue.

Around her extremely firm breasts she wore an old yellow crocheted doily, tied loosely. Her long black skirt was slit up the front all the way to her crotch, and underneath she wore torn black lace tights, and shocking-pink suede boots, laced all the way up to her knees. She carried a small basket as a handbag, and she was smoking Eve cigarettes elegantly, as if she were a dowager empress.

She sat next to Bongbong and gazed at him coolly and deliberately. People in the bar turned their heads and stared at her, some of them laughing. She asked Bongbong for a match. He lit her cigarette. His hands were trembling. She smiled, and he saw that some of her teeth were missing. After she smoked her cigarette, she left the bar.

Another day while Bongbong was walking in the Tenderloin, he had another vision. A young woman offered to fuck him for a mere twenty-five dollars. He hesitated, looking at her. She had shoulder-length, greasy blond hair. She had several teeth missing too, and what other teeth she had left were rotten. Her eyes, which were a dull brown, were heavily painted with midnight-blue mascara. She wore a short red skirt, a tight little sweater, and her black sheer tights had runs and snags all over them. Bongbong noticed that she had on expensive silver platform shoes that were sold in Charmaine's boutique.

He asked her name.

Her voice was as dull as her eyes. "Sandra," she replied.

He suddenly felt bold in her presence. "How old are you?"

"Nineteen. How old are you, honey?" She leered at him, then saw the blank look on his face, and all the contempt washed out of her. He took her to a restaurant where they served watery hamburgers and watery coffee. He asked her if she had a pimp.

"Yup. And I been busted ten times. I been a hooker since I was thirteen, and my parents are more dead than alive. Anything else you wanna know?"

Her full name was Sandra Broussard. He told her she was beautiful. She laughed. She said her pimp would kill her if she ever left the business. She showed him her scars. "He cut my face once, with a razor," she said.

He felt useless. He went back to the apartment and Carmen was waiting for him. "We've decided you should move out of this place as soon as possible," she said. "I'm pregnant, and I want to redecorate your room for the baby. I'm going to paint your room pink."

He went into the bathroom and stared at the bottles of perfume near the sink, the underarm deodorant, the foot deodorant, the cinnamon-flavored mouthwash, and the vaginal spray. They used Colgate brand toothpaste. Dove soap. Zee toilet paper. A Snoopy poster hung behind the toilet. It filled him with despair.

Bongbong moved into Charmaine's flat shortly after. He brought his velvet suit and his books. Colelia reacted strangely at first. She had been Charmaine's lover for some time, and felt Bongbong would be an intrusion. But all he did was read his books and watch television. He slept on a mattress in the living room. He hardly even spoke to Charmaine anymore. Sometimes they would come home from work in the evenings and find Bongbong in the kitchen, preparing Verta Mae's Kalalou Noisy Le Sec or her Codfish with Green Sauce for all of them. Colelia realized he wasn't a threat to her love life at all. Life became peaceful for her and Charmaine.

During the long afternoons when Colelia and Charmaine were gone and the cats were gone and the smell of piss from the catbox lingered in the chilly air, Bongbong would put on his velvet suit and take long walks in the Tenderloin, trying to find Sandra Broussard. He thought he saw her once, inside a bar, but when he went in, he found it was a mistake. The woman turned out to be much older, and when she turned to smile at him, he noticed she wore the hand of Fatima on a silver chain around her neck.

When he really thought about it, in his more lucid moments, he realized he didn't even remember what Sandra looked like anymore. Dullness was all he could conjure of her presence. Her fatigue and resignation.

Charmaine, on the other hand, was bright, beautiful, and selfish. She was queen of the house, and most activity revolved around her. Colelia always came home from work with a gift for Charmaine, which they both referred to as "prizes." Sometimes they were valuable, like jade rings or amethyst stones for Charmaine's pierced nose, or silly—like an old Walt Disney cup with Donald Duck painted on it.

Bongbong found the two women charming and often said so when he was in a talkative mood. "You are full of charm and your lives will be full of success," he would say to them, as they sat in their antique Chinese robes, painting each other's faces.

"You sound like a fortune cookie," Charmaine would say, glaring at him.

He would be silent at her outbursts, which naturally made her more furious. "I wish you'd tell me how much you want me," she would demand, ignoring her female lover's presence in the room.

Sometimes Charmaine would watch Bongbong as he read his books, and she would get evil with him out of boredom. She was easily distracted and therefore easily bored, especially when she wasn't the center of attention. This was often the case when Colelia was at work and it was Charmaine's day off.

Bongbong said to her, "Once you were a witch, but you misused your powers. Now you resent me because I remind you of those past days."

Charmaine circled Bongbong as he sat in the living room immersed in *Green Mansions* by W. H. Hudson. He had found the hardback novel for one dollar in another secondhand-book shop, called Memory Lane.

"I'm going to take my clothes off, Bongbong," Charmaine would tease. "What're you going to do about it?" Bongbong would look up at her, puzzled. Then she would put her hands on her enormous hips. "Men like me most of all because of my ass, Bongbong . . . but they can't really get next to me. Most of them have no style . . . but you have a sort of style—" By this time she often removed her skirt. "I don't wear panties," she said, "so whenever I want, Colelia can feel me up." Bongbong tried to ignore her. He was getting skilled in self-hypnosis, and whenever external disturbances would occur, he would stare off into the distance and block them slowly from his mind.

The more skilled he became in his powers, the more furious Charmaine would get with him. One time she actually wrenched the book from his hands and threw it out the window. Then she lay on the couch in front of him and spread her legs. "You know what I've got, Bongbong? Uterina Furor . . . That's what my mother used to say . . . Nuns get it all the time. Like a fire in the womb."

To make her smile, Bongbong would kiss her between the legs, and then Colelia would come home and pay more attention to Charmaine and Bongbong would cook more of Verta Mae's recipes, such as Stuffed Heart Honky Style (one of Charmaine's favorites), and everything would be all right.

Charmaine's destructive moods focused on Bongbong twice a month, and got worse when the moon was full. "You're in a time of perennial menstruation," Bongbong told her solemnly after one of her fits.

One morning while they were having breakfast together, Colelia accused Charmaine of being in love with Bongbong. "Why, I don't know—" Colelia said. "He's so funny-looking and weird. You're just into such an ego trip you want what you can't have."

Charmaine giggled. "Forever analyzing me! Don't I love you enough?"

"It's not that."

"Well, then—why bring him up? You never understood him from the very beginning," Charmaine said. "Or why I even brought him here in the first place. I must confess—I don't quite know why I brought him home myself. Somehow, I knew he wasn't going to fuck me . . . I really didn't want a fuck though. It was more like I wanted him around to teach me something about myself . . . Something like that, anyway."

Colelia looked away. "That's vague enough."

"Are you really jealous of him?" Charmaine asked.

Colelia finally shook her head. "Not in that way . . . but maybe because I don't understand him, or the two of you together—I am jealous. I guess because I feel left out of his mystique."

Charmaine embraced her, and the two of them wept.

Bongbong's visions and revelations were becoming more frequent. A Chinese woman with a blond wig and a map of the world on her legs. A black man with three breasts. A cat turning doorknobs. A tortoise crawling out of a sewer on the sidewalk, and junkies making soup out of him. Frisquito assassinating the president of the Philippines who happens to be his wife in drag who happens to be a concert pianist's mother . . . The visions were endless, circular, and always moving.

Dear Frisquito:

Yesterday a friend of Charmaine's named Ra brought a record over by a man named John Coltrane. Ra tells me that Mr. Coltrane died not too long ago, I believe when we were just out of high school. Ra decided that I could keep the record, which is called "Meditations." I believe it is the title of one of your paintings.

Every morning I plan on waking up to this man's music. It keeps my face from disintegrating. You once said your whole being had disintegrated long ago, and that you had the power to pick up the pieces from time to time, when it was necessary—such as the time you gave an exhibit of your works, for the benefit of the First Lady. I think there may be some hope left for me.

Yesterday I cooked Verta Mae's Uptight Ragout in your honor.

Love,

B.

Bongbong now referred to himself as "B." He could not stand to speak in long sentences, and tried to live and speak as minimally as possible. Charmaine worried about him, especially when he would go on one of his rampages and cook delicious gumbo dinners for herself and Colelia, and not eat with them.

"But B," she protested, "I never see you eat anymore."

One time he said, "Maybe I eat a saxophone."

He loved the word "saxophone."

His parents stopped sending money, since Carmen wrote them that he had never attended one day of school at Heald's Business College. His father wrote him and warned him never to set foot in the Philippines again, or he would have him executed for the crime of deception and subversion to one's parents, a new law put into practice in the current dictator's regime.

Bongbong decided to visit Carmen. She was almost six months pregnant, and very ugly. Her face had broken out in rashes and pimples, and her whole body was swollen. Her once shimmering black hair was now dry and brittle, and she had cut it short. He stared at her for a long time as they sat in the kitchen in silence. She finally suggested that he see the baby's room.

She had decorated the room with more Snoopy posters, and mobiles with wooden angels hung from the ceiling. A pink baby bed stood in the center of the room, which was heavily scented with floral spray.

"It's awful," Bongbong said.

"Oh, you're always insulting everything!" his sister screamed, shoving him out the door. She shut the door behind her, as if guarding a sacred temple, and looked at him, shaking with rage. "You make everything evil. Are you on drugs? I think you're insane," she said. "Leave this house before I call the police." She hated him because he made her feel ashamed in his presence, but she couldn't understand why.

Frisquito, who never answered any of his letters, sent him a check for a considerable amount of money. A postcard later arrived with "Don't Worry" scratched across it, and Frisquito's signature below the message. Bongbong, who now wore his velvet suit every day, went to a pawnshop and bought a soprano saxophone.

In the mornings he would study with Ra, who taught him circular breathing. He never did understand chords and scales, but he could hear what Ra was trying to teach him and he surprised everyone in the house with the eerie sounds he was making out of his new instrument. Charmaine told Colelia that she thought Bongbong was going to be all right, because Bongbong had at last found his "thing."

Which was wrong, because Bongbong's music only increased his natural visionary powers. He confessed to Ra that he could actually see the notes in the air, much as he could see the wind. Ra would smile, not saying anything.

Bongbong watched Charmaine at the kitchen table eating breakfast, and when she looked up at him, she would suddenly turn into his mother, with Minnie Mouse ears and long, exaggerated Minnie Mouse eyelashes, which glittered and threw off sparks when she blinked. This frightened him sometimes because he would forget who Charmaine was. As long as he could remember who everyone was, he felt a surge of relief. But these moments were becoming more and more confusing, and it was getting harder and harder for him to remember everyone's name, including his own.

Colelia decided that Bongbong was a "paranoid schizophrenic" and that she and Charmaine should move out, for their own safety. "One of these days we'll come home from work and find all our kitty cats with their throats slit," she said. She refused to eat any more of Bongbong's cooking, for fear he would poison her. "He doesn't like women basically. That's the root of his problem" she told Charmaine. "I mean, the guy doesn't even jack off! How unnatural can he be? Remember Emil Kemper!"

"Remember Emil Kemper" became the motto of the household. Emil Kemper was a young madman in Santa Cruz, California, who murdered his grandmother when he was something like thirteen years old, murdered his mother later on after he was released from the looney bin—cut her head off—and murdered about a million other female hitchhikers.

Charmaine sympathized with Bongbong, but she wasn't sure about him either.

Only Ra vouched for his sanity. "Sure the cat is crazy," he said, "but he'll never hurt any of you."

Bongbong practiced the saxophone every day, and seemed to survive on a diet of water and air. Charmaine came home from the boutique one night and brought him two pairs of jeans and two T-shirts. One T-shirt had glittery blue and silver thread woven into it, and Bongbong saw the shirt become a cloud floating above his narrow bed. "Well," Charmaine said, trying to sound casual as she watched Bongbong drift off dreamily, "aren't you going to try it on? Do you like it? I seriously think you should have your velvet suit dry-cleaned, before it falls apart."

Bongbong touched the cloud. "Oh, how beautiful," he said.

He never wore the shirt. He hung it above his bed like a canopy, where he could study it at night. His ceiling became a galaxy. To appease Charmaine (he was very sensitive to her feelings, and loved her in his own way), he wore the other shirt and sent his velvet suit to the cleaners.

Frisquito sent him more money the next month, and Bongbong bought a telescope.

Dear Frisquito,

Do you know I am only five feet and two inches tall? Without my platform shoes, of course. Why do people like to look like cripples? Yesterday I saw a fat young woman wearing platform shoes that made her feet look like boats. Her dress was too short on her fat body and you could see her cellulite wobbling in her forest-green pantyhose. Cellulite is the new fad in America. Some Frenchwoman discovered it and is urging everyone to feel for it in their skin. It's sort of like crepe-paper tissue that happens when you put on too much weight. I told the fat young woman she was beautiful, and she told me to fuck off. She was very angry, and I realized there are a lot of angry people around me. Except in the house I live in, which is why I've stayed so long.

The Coltrane record is warped from having been left in the sun. I am writing a song about it in my head.

With my telescope I can see
everyone, and they don't have to
see me.

Love,
B.

Bongbong often brought the telescope up to the roof of their building and watched the people on the streets below. Then at night he would watch the stars in the sky and try to figure out different constellations. Charmaine took him to the planetarium for his birthday, and they watched a show on Chinese astronomy called "The Emperor of the Heavens," narrated by a man called Alvin. Bongbong was moved to tears. "I love you," he told Charmaine, as they lay back in their seats and watched the heavens.

But he had forgotten that she was Charmaine Lopez, and that she lived with him. He thought she was Sandra Broussard, or the blue lady with the rag turban on her head. When the show was over, he asked her to marry him.

He didn't say another word until they reached the flat. He cooked Verta Mae's Jamaican Curried Goat for birthday dinner and Colelia baked him a cake decorated with a sugar-coated model airplane. Bongbong removed the airplane and hung it next to the canopy above his bed.

After dinner he asked Charmaine if she would sleep with him. She didn't have the heart to refuse, and kissing Colelia on her forehead, followed Bongbong into his room. The next morning Charmaine told Colelia they should both move out.

"Was he a freak? I mean, did he hurt you?" Colelia asked.

Charmaine shook her head. "No. But I don't want to live around him anymore. It may be best if we left today."

They packed their clothes and rounded up their cats and drove away in Charmaine's VW, leaving Bongbong with a note on the kitchen table: "We will send for the rest of our things. Forgive us. C & C."

Bongbong awoke from a beautiful dream, in which he had learned how to fly. Everything in the dream had an airy quality. He floated and glided through the atmosphere, and went swimming in the clouds, which turned out to be his glittery blue sweater. Charmaine Lopez and her dancing girls did the rhumba in the heavens, which were guarded by smiling Chinese deities. Alvin from the planetarium sang "Stardust" for him as he flew by. He was happy. He could play his saxophone forever. Then he saw Frisquito flying far away, waving to him. He tried and tried, but he couldn't get any closer to him. Frisquito became smaller and smaller, then vanished, and when Bongbong opened his eyes, he found Charmaine gone.

He decided to stay in the flat, and left the other rooms just as they were. Even Ra stopped coming to visit, so Bongbong had to teach himself about the saxophone. There were brief moments when he found that the powers of levitation were within him, so while he practiced the saxophone he would also practice levitating.

Frisquito,

Just two things. The power of flight has been in me all along. All I needed was to want it bad enough.

Another is something someone once said to me. Never is forever, she said.

Love

He didn't sign his name or his initial, because he had finally forgotten who he was.

1975

The Death of Anna May Wong

My mother is very beautiful
And not yet old.
A Twin,
Color of two continents:
I stroll through Irish tenderloin
Nightmare doors—drunks spill out
Saloon alleys falling asleep
At my feet . . .

My mother wears a beaded
Mandarin coat:
In the dryness
Of San Diego's mediterrannean parody
I see your ghost, Belen
As you clean up
After your sweet señora's
mierda

Jazz,
Don't do me like that.
Mambo,
Don't do me like that.
Samba, calypso, funk and
Boogie
Don't cut me up like that

Move my gut so high up
Inside my throat
I can only strangle you
To keep from crying . . .

My mother serves crêpes suzettes
With a smile
And a puma
Slithers down
                    19th street and Valencia
Gabriel o.d.'s on reds
As we dance together

Dorothy Lamour undrapes
Her sarong
And Bing Crosby ignores
The mierda.

My mother's lavender lips
Stretch in a slow smile.
And beneath

The night's cartoon sky
Cold with rain
Alice Coltrane
Kills the pain
And I know
I can't go home again.

1971

Filipino Boogie

Under a ceiling-high Christmas tree
I pose
in my Japanese kimono
My mother hands me
a Dale Evans cowgirl skirt
and
baby cowgirl boots

Mommy and daddy split
No one else is home

I take some rusty scissors
and cut the skirt up

in
little pieces

(don't give me no bullshit fringe,
Mama)

Mommy and daddy split
No one else is home

I take my baby cowgirl boots
and flush them
down
the
toilet

(don't hand me no bullshit fringe,
(Papa)

I seen the Indian Fighter
Too many times

dug on Sitting Bull
before Donald Duck

In my infant dream

These warriors weaved a magic spell
more blessed than Tinker Bell

(Kirk Douglas rubs his chin
and slays Minnehaha by the campfire)

Mommy and daddy split
There ain't no one else home

I climb a mango tree
and wait for Mohawk drums

(Mama—World War II
is over . . . why you cryin'?)

Is this San Francisco?
Is this San Francisco?
Is this Amerika?

buy me Nestle's Crunch
buy me Pepsi in a can

Ladies' Home Journal
and *Bonanza*

I seen Little Joe in Tokyo
I seen Little Joe in Manila
I seen Laramie in Hong Kong
I seen Yul Brynner in San Diego
and the bloated ghost
of Desi Arnaz

dancing
in Tijuana

Rip-off synthetic ivory
to send
the natives
back home

and

North Beach boredom
escapes
the barber shops

on Kearny street
where
they spit out
red tobacco

patiently

waiting
in 1930s suits
and in another dream
I climb a mango tree
and Saturday
afternoon
Jack Palance
bazookas
the krauts
and
the YELLOW PERIL
bombs
Pearl Harbor

1971

Homesick

Blame it on the mambo and the cha-cha, voodoo amulets worn on the same chain with tiny crucifixes and scapulars blessed by the Pope. Chains of love, medals engraved with the all-seeing Eye, ascending Blessed Virgins floating toward heaven surrounded by erotic cherubs and archangels, the magnificent torso of a tormented, half-naked Saint Sebastian pierced by arrows dripping blood. A crown of barbed-wire thorns adorns the holy subversive's head, while we drown in the legacy of brutal tropical generals stuffed in khaki uniforms, their eyes shielded by impenetrable black sunglasses, Douglas MacArthur style.

And Douglas MacArthur and Tom Cruise are painted on billboards lining Manila's highways, modeling *Ray-Ban* shades and Jockey underwear. You choose between the cinema version starring Gregory Peck smoking a corncob pipe, or the real thing. "I shall return," promised the North American general, still revered by many as the savior of the Filipino people, who eagerly awaited his return. As the old saying goes, this is how we got screwed, screwed real good. According to Nick Joaquin, "The Philippines spent three hundred years trapped in a convent, and fifty years in Hollywood . . ." Or was it four hundred years? No matter—there we were, seduced and abandoned in a confusion of identities, then granted our independence. Hollywood pretended to leave us alone. An African American saying also goes: "Nobody's *given* freedom." Being granted our independence meant we were owned all along by someone other than ourselves.

I step off the crowded plane onto the tarmac of the newly named Ninoy Aquino Airport. It is an interesting appropriation of the assassinated senator's name, don't you think? So I think, homesick for this birthplace, my country of supreme ironies and fatalistic humor, mountains of foul garbage and breathtaking women, men with the fierce faces of wolves and steamy streets teeming with abandoned children.

The widow of the assassinated senator is Corazon Aquino, now president of the Republic of the Philippines in a deft stroke of irony that left the world stunned by a sudden turn of events in February 1986. She is a beloved figure, a twentieth-century icon who has inherited a bundle of cultural contradictions and an economic nightmare in a lush paradise of corrupt, warring factions. In a Manila department store, one of the first souvenirs I buy my daughter is a rather homely Cory Aquino doll made out of brown cloth; the doll wears crooked wire eyeglasses, a straw shoulder bag, plastic high-heeled shoes, and Cory's signature yellow dress, with "I Love Cory" embroidered on the front. My daughter seems delighted with her doll, and the notion of a woman president.

Soldiers in disguise, patrol the countryside . . . Jungle not far away. So goes a song I once wrote, pungent as the remembered taste of mangoes overripe as my imagination, the memory of Manila the central character of the novel I am writing, the novel that brings me back to this torrid zone, my landscape haunted by ghosts and movie-lovers.

Nietzsche once said, "A joke is an epitaph for an emotion." Our laughter is pained, self-mocking. Blame it on *Rambo, Platoon,* and *Gidget Goes Hawaiian.* Cory Aquino has inherited a holy war, a class war, an amazing nation of people who've endured incredible poverty and spiritual loss with inherent humor and grace. Member of the ruling class, our pious president has also inherited an army of divided, greedy men. Yet probably no one will bother assassinating her, as icons are always useful.

My novel sits in its black folder, an obsession with me for over ten years. Home is now New York, but home in my heart will also always be Manila, and the rage of a marvelous culture stilled, confused, and diverted. Manila is my river of dreams choked with refuse, the refuse of refusal and denial, a denial more profound than the forbidding Catholic Church in all its ominous presence.

Blame it on the mambo and the cha-cha, a cardinal named Sin, and an adviser named Joker. Blame it on a former beauty queen with a puffy face bailed out of a jam by Doris Duke. Blame it on *Imeldification.* Blame it on children named Lourdes, Maria, Jesus, Carlos, Peachy, Baby, and Elvis. Blame it on the rich, who hang on in spite of everything. Blame it on the same people who are still in power, before Marcos, after Marcos. You name it, we'll blame it. The NPA, the vigilantes, rebel colonels nicknamed "Gringo," and a restless army plotting coups. Blame it on signs in nightclubs that warn: NO GUNS OR DRUGS.

Cards have been reshuffled, roles exchanged. The major players are the same, even those who suffered long years in prison under one regime, even those who died by the bullet. Aquino, Lopez, Cojuangco, Zobel, Laurel, Enrile, etc. etc. Blood against blood, controlling the destinies of so many disparate tribes in these seven thousand islands.

I remember my grandmother, Lola Tecla, going for drives with me as a child down the boulevard along Manila Bay. The boulevard led to Luneta Park, where Rizal was executed by the Spanish colonizers; it was then known as Dewey Boulevard, after an American admiral. From history books forced on me as a child at a convent school run by strict nuns, I learned a lopsided history of myself, one full of lies and blank spaces, a history of omission—a colonial version of history which scorned the "savage" ways of precolonial Filipinos. In those days even our language was kept at a distance; Tagalog was studied in a course called "National Language" (*sic*), but it was English that was spoken, English that was preferred. Tagalog was a language used to address servants. I scorned myself, and it was only later, after I had left the Philippines to settle in the country of my oppressor, that I learned to confront my demons and reinvent my own history.

I am writing a novel set in contemporary Philippines. It is a journey back I am always taking. I leave one place for the other, welcomed and embraced by the family I have left—fathers and brothers and cousins and uncles and aunts. Childhood sweethearts, now with their own children. I am unable to stay. I make excuses, adhere to tight schedules. I return, only to depart, weeks or months later, depending on finances and the weather, obligations to my daughter, my art, my addiction to life in the belly of one particular beast. I am the other, the exile within, afflicted with permanent nostalgia for the mud. I return, only to depart: Manila, New York, San Francisco, Manila, Honolulu, Detroit, Manila, Guam, Hong Kong, Zamboanga, Manila, New York, San Francisco, Tokyo, Manila again, Manila again, Manila again.

1992

Vulva Operetta

In my dream, sweaters are referred to as "vulvas." They are mohair or
angora wool, of a soft, warm texture—gray, bleeding into a deep, rich
red—similar to Japanese raku pottery.

We wear these sweaters.

People say things like: "It's hot. I think I'll take my vulva off."
Or: "It's cold. I think I'll put my vulva on."

Foppish men and women ask each other questions like: "Where did you get
that BEE-YOO-TEE-FUL vulva?"
Followed by remarks like:
"I think I'm gonna put my vulva in the closet. I think I'm gonna put
my vulva in the closet. I think I'm gonna put my vulva. I'm gonna. My
vulva. I."

1992

Lee Smith b. 1944

Lee Smith has been making up stories—or letting stories tell themselves—since she was a child; she said once that she did it to keep herself from lying. Her first novel, written while she was an undergraduate at Hollins College, appeared in 1968 and won an award. The novels and stories, and the awards, have kept on coming. When Lee Smith gives a reading, her audiences are enthralled; at a book signing, people—women, mostly—line up and loop around, waiting with astonishing patience for a chance to meet and speak to the writer. Smith's subjects, like her stories and her voices, are many; but if there is one continuing theme, it is the ways it feels to be a southern woman today. She casts her many voices through as many places and times, yet she writes with special tenderness for her gender and her generation.

In the story Smith has called the closest to her own life, "Tongues of Fire," a gap or gulf between classes separates and attracts the protagonist (a girl whom Dorothy Smith describes as "strangled by a mother rigidly dedicated to keeping up appearances") and her schoolmate, who lives in a very different world among the contemporary rural poor. Her schoolmate's mother speaks in tongues: "Tongues of fire just come down on my head," she tells her daughter's city friend. "I envy this," Smith herself has said, "and aspire to it more than I can tell you."

To many readers, it is Smith herself who speaks in tongues. She has an uncanny ear for voices and an uncommon range. In *Oral History,* Smith's "breakthrough" novel, for example, we hear first the voice of a college student filled with the new pomposities of academic talk. She is convinced that she can "capture" her own past through oral history. But when her tape recorder records the ghostly historical voices of Granny Younger, Red Emmy, Richard Burlage, Dory Cantrell, those voices become for the reader more real and alive that the utterances of present day characters. Smith brings the lyricism of mountain ballads to life in their talk. In her many other narratives, the voices come from southern cities, mountains, and coasts; they come from the deep past and the "Phil Donahue Show"; they come from men and women, the young and the aged, rich and poor.

The voices of Smith's characters emerge in patterns that suggest thematic preoccupations as well as sheer lyricism. Richard Burlage (*Oral History*), the educated Richmonder who comes to the mountains in search of "the very roots of consciousness and belief," betrays those very roots by abandoning his mountain love, Dory, and by returning to his "real" life in Richmond. At the same time, his language, which had moved close to incoherence in his passion for Dory, regresses to the highly literate—and controlling—diction of his origins, and even the phrase above, "the very roots," is exposed as a cliché. Yet the mountains do not emerge as the dichotomous victor in a thematic battle with civilization: Smith exposes Richard's mountain fantasies as primitivist projections by showing, for example, Dory's own longings for something other and different from what she has known. "Artists" deals with gaps between classes, arts, and artists. Jennifer's ultimate choice of the art of Molly Crews should not be read as a simple victory for one side either, however. Smith consistently explores the sentimentality implied in privileging difference, particularly when the person doing the privileging comes from an already privileged position.

Smith's first novel, *The Last Day the Dogbushes Bloomed* (1968), tackles the question of difference and its relation to art head on. The narrator is a child whose summer sees the collapse of her fantasies about her family and about her own safety (a visiting boy forces Susan into sex through the rhetorical power of his imaginary friend). The power of the imagination to construct and to destroy is a major force as well in *Something in the Wind,* the story of a college student. In *Black Mountain Breakdown,* overwhelmed by an early rape and by her (not irrelevant) willingness to please, hence her inability to assert herself, Crystal Spangler ends up self-paralyzed.

Crystal Spangler marked the "bottom" in a sense for Lee Smith's women; since then, their capacity for resilience, strength, pain, and sheer joy has grown steadily. Smith's tour de force character, surely, is Ivy Rowe of *Fair and Tender Ladies,* an epistolary novel that takes Ivy from her first words to her death. Ivy inspired a one-woman play by Barbara Smith and Mark Hunter which ran off Broadway in 1990. Smith's latest novel, *Devil's Dream,* renders country music into narrative by telling the stories of country musicians. It too has inspired another creative enterprise, a traveling show and audiotape starring Smith reading and writer Clyde Edgerton singing, along with other expert country musicians.

Lee Smith has an irrepressible love of play that pervades her fiction. There is tummy-crunching humor in her lighter novels (*Fancy Strut, Family Linen*) and in many of her stories (collected in *Cakewalk* and *Me and My Baby View the Eclipse*), as well as in fugitive pieces like her parody of romance novels (and of her own most tragic character) in "Desire on Silhouette Lagoon: A Harleque'en Romanza by Crystal Spangler." Beyond the humor, her sense of play means that Smith's writing is constantly in process: she does not stop inventing new characters, new stories, and new literary strategies, showing—and giving—through it all a great and lasting pleasure.

Anne Goodwyn Jones
University of Florida

PRIMARY WORKS

The Last Day the Dogbushes Bloomed, 1968; *Something in the Wind,* 1971; *Fancy Strut,* 1973; *Black Mountain Breakdown,* 1980; *Cakewalk,* 1981; *Oral History,* 1983; "Desire on Silhouette Lagoon," in *Uneeda Review,* ed. J. Parkhurst Schimmelpfennig, 1984; *Family Linen,* 1985; *Fair and Tender Ladies,* 1988; *Me and My Baby View the Eclipse,* 1990; *Devil's Dream,* 1992; "The Bubba Stories," in *The Rough Road Home,* ed. Robert Gingher, 1993, 265–291; *Saving Grace,* 1994; *Christmas Letters,* 1996.

The Bubba Stories

Even now when I think of my brother Bubba, he appears instantly just as he was then, rising up before me in the very flesh, grinning that one-sided grin, pushing his cowlick out of his tawny eyes, thumbs hooked in the loops of his wheat jeans, Bass Weejuns held together with electrical tape, leaning against his green MGB. Lawrence Leland Christian III—Bubba—in the days of his glory, Dartmouth College, ca. 1965. Brilliant, Phi Beta Kappa his junior year. The essence of cool. The essence not only of cool but of *bad,* for Bubba was a legendary wild man in those days; and while certain facts in his legend varied, this constant remained: Bubba would do anything. *Anything.*

I was a little bit in love with him myself.

I made Bubba up in the spring of 1963 in order to increase my popularity with my girlfriends at a small women's college in Virginia. I was a little bit in love with them, too. But at first I was ill at ease among them: a thistle in the rose garden, a mule at the racetrack, Cinderella at the fancy dress ball. Take your pick—I was into images then. More than anything else in the world, I wanted to be a writer. I didn't want to *learn to write,* of course. I just wanted to *be a writer,* and I often pictured myself poised at the foggy edge of a cliff someplace in the south of France, wearing a cape, drawing furiously on a long cigarette, hollow-cheeked and haunted, trying to make up my mind between two men. Both of them wanted me desperately.

But in fact I was Charlene Christian, a chunky size twelve, plucked up from a peanut farm near South Hill, Virginia, and set down in those exquisite halls through the intervention of my senior English teacher, Mrs. Bella Hood, the judge's wife, who had graduated from the school herself. I had a full scholarship. I would be the first person in my whole family ever to graduate from college, unless you counted my aunt Dee, who got her certificate from beauty college in Richmond. I was not going to count Aunt Dee. I was not even going to *mention* her in later years, or anybody else in my family. I intended to grow beyond them. I intended to become a famous hollow-cheeked author, with mysterious origins.

But this is the truth. I grew up in McKenney, Virginia, which consisted of nothing more than a crossroads with my father's store in the middle of it. I used to climb onto the tin roof of our house and turn slowly all around, scanning the horizon, looking for . . . what? I found nothing of any interest, just flat brown peanut fields that stretched in every direction as far as I could see, with a farmhouse here and there. I knew who lived in every house. I knew everything about them and about their families, what kind of car they drove and where they went to church, and they knew everything about us.

Not that there was much to know. My father, Hassell Christian, would give you the shirt off his back, and everybody knew it. At the store, he'd extend credit indefinitely to people down on their luck, and he let some families live in his tenant houses for free. Our own house adjoined the store.

My mother's younger brother Sam, who lived with us, was what they then called a Mongoloid. Some of the kids at school referred to him as a "Mongolian idiot." Now the preferred term is "Down's syndrome." My uncle Sam was sweet, small, and no trouble at all. I played cards with him endlessly, every summer of my childhood—Go Fish, rummy, Old Maid, hearts, blackjack. Sam loved cards and sunshine and his cat, Blackie. He liked to sit on a quilt in the sun, playing cards with me. He liked to sit on the front porch with Blackie and watch the cars go by. He loved it when I told him stories.

My mother, who was high-strung, was always fussing around after Sam, making him pick up paper napkins and turn off the TV and put his shoes in a line. My mother had three separate nervous breakdowns before I went away to college. My father always said we had to "treat her with kid gloves." When I think about it now, I am surprised that my mother was able to hold herself together long enough to conceive a child at all, or come to term. After me, there were two miscarriages, and then, I was told, they "quit trying." I was never sure what this meant, exactly. But certainly

I could never imagine my parents having a sexual relationship in the first place—he was too fat and gruff, she was too fluttery and crazy. The whole idea was gross.

Whenever my mother had a nervous breakdown, my grandmother, Memaw, would come over from next door to stay with Sam full-time, and I would be sent to South Hill to stay with my aunt Dee and my cousins. I loved my Aunt Dee, who was as different from Mama as day from night. Aunt Dee wore her yellow hair in a beehive and smoked Pall Mall cigarettes. After work she'd come in the door, kick off her shoes, put a record on the record player, and dance all over the living room to "Ooh-Poo-Pa-Doo." She said it "got the kinks out." She taught us all to do the shag, even little Melinda.

I was always sorry when my dad appeared in his truck, ready to take me back home.

When I think of home now, the image that comes most clearly to mind is my whole family lined up in the flickering darkness of our living room, watching TV. We never missed *The Ed Sullivan Show, Bonanza, The Andy Griffith Show,* or *Candid Camera*—Sam's favorite. Sam used to laugh and laugh when they'd say, "Smile! You're on *Candid Camera!*" It was the only time my family ever did anything together. I can just see us now in the light from that black-and-white Zenith: me, Sam, and Memaw on the couch, Daddy and Mama in the recliner and the antique wing chair, respectively, facing the television. We always turned off the lights and sat quietly, and didn't eat anything.

No wonder I got a boyfriend with a car as soon as possible, to get out of there. Don Fetterman had a soft brown crew cut and wide brown eyes, and reminded me, in the nicest possible way, of the cows that he and his family raised. Don was president of the 4-H Club and the Glee Club. I was vice-president of the Glee Club (how we met). We were both picked "Most Likely to Succeed."

We rubbed our bodies together at innumerable dances in the high school gym while they played our song—"The Twelfth of Never"—but we never, never went all the way. Don wouldn't. He believed we should save ourselves for marriage. I, on the other hand, having read by this time a great many novels, was just dying to lose my virginity so that I would mysteriously begin to "live," so that my life would finally *start.* I knew for sure that I would never become a great writer until I could rid myself of this awful burden. But Don Fetterman stuck to his guns, refusing to cooperate. Instead, for graduation, he gave me a pearl "pre-engagement" ring, which I knew for a fact had cost $139 at Snow's Jewelers in South Hill, where I worked after school and on weekends. This was a lot of money for Don Fetterman to spend.

Although I didn't love him, by then he thought I did; and after I got the ring, I didn't have the nerve to tell him the truth. So I kept it, and kissed Don good-bye for hours and hours the night before he went off to join the Marines. My tears were real at this point, but after he left I relegated him firmly to the past. Ditto my whole family. Once I got to college, I was determined to become a new person.

Luckily my freshman roommate turned out to be a kind of prototype, the very epitome of a popular girl. The surprise was that she was nice, too. Dixie Claiborne came from Memphis, where she was to make her debut that Christmas at the Swan Ball. She had long, perfect blond hair, innumerable cashmere sweater sets, and real pearls. She had lots of friends already, other girls who had gone to St. Cecilia's with her. (It seemed to me a good two-thirds of the girls at school had gone to St. Something-or-other.) They had a happy ease in the world and a strangely uniform appearance, which I immediately began to copy—spending my whole first semester's money, saved up from my job at the jeweler's, on several A-line skirts, McMullen blouses, and a pair of red Pappagallo shoes. Dixie had about a thousand cable-knit sweaters, which she was happy to lend me.

In addition to the right clothes, she came equipped with the right boyfriend, already a sophomore at Washington and Lee University, the boys' school just over the mountain. His name was Trey (William Hill Dunn III). Trey would be so glad, Dixie said, smiling, to get all of us dates for the Phi Gam mixer. "All of us" meant our entire suite—Dixie and me in the front room overlooking the old quadrangle with its massive willow oaks, Melissa and Donnie across the hall, and Lily in the single just beyond our study room.

Trey fixed us up with several Phi Gams apiece, but nothing really clicked; and in November, Melissa, Donnie, Lily, and I signed up to go to a freshman mixer at UVA. As our bus approached the university's famous serpentine wall, we went into a flurry of teasing our hair and checking our makeup. Looking into my compact, I stuck out my lips in a way I'd been practicing. I had a pimple near my nose, but I'd turned it into a beauty spot with eyebrow pencil. I hoped to look like Sandra Dee.

Freshman year, everybody went to mixers, where freshman boys, as uncomfortable as we were, stood nervously about in the social rooms of their fraternity houses, wearing navy-blue blazers, ties, and chinos. Nobody really knew how to date in this rigid system so unlike high school—and certainly so unlike prep school, where many of these boys had been locked away for the past four years. If they could have gotten their own dates, they would have. But they couldn't. They didn't know anybody, either. They pulled at their ties and looked at the floor. They seemed to me generally gorgeous, completely unlike Don Fetterman with his feathery crew cut and his 4-H jacket, now at Camp LeJeune. But I still wrote to Don, informative, stilted notes about my classes and the weather. His letters in return were lively and real, full of military life ("the food sucks") and vague sweet plans for our future—a future that did not exist, as far as I was concerned, and yet these letters gave me a secret thrill. My role as Don Fetterman's girl was the most exciting I'd had yet, and I couldn't quite bring myself to give it up, even as I attempted to transform myself into another person altogether.

"Okay," the upperclassman-in-charge announced casually, and the St. Anthony's Hall pledges wandered over in our direction.

"Hey," the cutest one said to a girl.

"Hey," she said back.

The routine never varied. In a matter of minutes, the four most aggressive guys would walk off with the four prettiest girls, and the rest of us would panic. On this occasion the social room at St. Anthony's Hall was cleared in a matter of minutes, and I was left with a tall, gangly, bucktoothed boy whose face was as pocked as the moon. Still, he had a shabby elegance I already recognized. He was from Mississippi.

"What do you want to do?" he asked me.

I had not expected to be consulted. I glanced around the social room, which looked like a war zone. I didn't know where my friends were.

"What do *you* want to do?" I asked.

His name (his *first* name) was Rutherford. He grinned at me. "Let's get drunk," he said, and my heart leaped up as I realized that my burden might be lifted in this way. We walked across the beautiful old campus to an open court where three or four fraternities had a combo going, wild-eyed electrified Negroes going through all kinds of gyrations on the bandstand. It was Doug Clark and the Hot Nuts. The music was so loud, the beat so strong, that you couldn't listen to it and stand still. The Hot Nuts were singing an interminable song; everybody seemed to know the chorus, which went, "Nuts, hot nuts, get 'em from the peanut man. Nuts, hot nuts, get 'em any way you can." We started dancing. I always worried about this—all I'd ever done before college, in the way of dancing, was the shag with my aunt Dee and a long, formless *clutch* with Don Fetterman, but with Rutherford it didn't matter.

People made a circle around us and started clapping. Nobody looked at me. All eyes were on Rutherford, whose dancing reminded me of the way chickens back home flopped around after Daddy cut their heads off. At first I was embarrassed. But then I caught on—Rutherford was a real *character.* I kept up with him the best I could, and then I got tickled and started laughing so hard I could barely dance. *This is fun,* I realized suddenly. This is what I'm *supposed* to be doing. This is college.

About an hour later we heard the news, which was delivered to us by a tweed-jacketed professor who walked on-stage, bringing the music to a ragged, grinding halt. He grabbed the microphone. "Ladies and gentlemen," he said thickly—and I remember thinking how odd this form of address seemed—"ladies and gentlemen, the President has been shot."

The whole scene started to churn, as if we were in a kaleidoscope—the blue day, the green grass, the stately columned buildings. People were running and sobbing. Rutherford's hand under my elbow steered me back to his fraternity house, where everyone was clustered around several TVs, talking too loud. All the weekend festivities were canceled. We were to return to school immediately. Rutherford seemed relieved by this prospect, having fallen silent—perhaps because he'd quit drinking, or because conversation alone wasn't worth the effort it took if nothing else (sex) might be forthcoming. He gave me a perfunctory kiss on the cheek and turned to go.

I was about to board the bus when somebody grabbed me, hard, from behind. I whirled around. It was Lily, red-cheeked and glassy-eyed, her blond hair springing out wildly above her blue sweater. Her hot-pink lipstick was smeared; her pretty, pointed face looked vivid and alive. A dark-haired boy stood close behind her, his arm around her waist.

"Listen," Lily hissed at me. "Sign me in, will you?"

"What?" I had heard her, but I couldn't believe it.

"Sign me in." Lily squeezed my shoulder. I could smell her perfume. Then she was gone.

I sat in a rear seat by myself and cried all the way back to school.

I caught on fast that as far as college boys were concerned, girls fell into either the Whore or the Saint category. Girls knew that if they gave in and *did it,* then boys wouldn't respect them, and word would get around, and they would never get a husband. The whole point of college was to get a husband.

I had not known anything about this system before I arrived there. It put a serious obstacle in my path toward becoming a great writer.

Lily, who clearly had given up her burden long since, fell into the Whore category. But the odd thing about it was that she didn't seem to mind, and she swore she didn't want a husband, anyway. "Honey, a husband is the *last* thing on my list!" she'd say, giggling. Lily was the smartest one of us, even though she went to great lengths to hide this fact.

Later, in 1966, she and the head of the philosophy department, Dr. Wiener, would stage the only demonstration ever held on our campus, walking slowly around the blooming quadrangle carrying signs that read "Get out of Vietnam," while the rest of us, well oiled and sunning on the rooftops, clutched our bikini tops and peered down curiously at the two of them.

If Lily was the smartest, Melissa was the dumbest, the nicest, and the least interested in school. Melissa came from Charleston, South Carolina, and spoke so slowly that I was always tempted to leap in and finish her sentences for her. All she wanted to do was marry her boyfriend, now at the University of South Carolina, and have babies. Donnie, Melissa's roommate, was a big, freckled, friendly girl from Texas. We didn't have any idea how rich she was until her mother flew up and bought a cabin at nearby Goshen Lake so "Donnie and her friends" would have a place to "relax."

By spring, Dixie was the only one of us who was actually pinned. It seemed to me that she was not only pinned but almost married, in a funny way, with tons and tons of children—Trey, her boyfriend; and me; and the other girls in our suite; and the other Phi Gams, Trey's fraternity brothers at Washington and Lee. Dixie had a notebook in which she made a list of things to do each day, and throughout the day she checked them off, one by one. She always got everything done. At the end of first semester, she had a 4.0 average; Trey had a 0.4. Dixie didn't mind. Totally, inexplicably, she loved him.

By then, most of the freshman girls who weren't going with somebody had several horror stories to tell about blind dates at UVA or W&L fraternities—about boys who "dropped trou," or threw up in their dates' purses. I had only one horror story, but I never told it, since the most horrible element in it was me.

This is what happened. It was Spring Fling at the Phi Gam house, and Trey had gotten me a date with a red-headed boy named Eddy Turner. I was getting desperate. I'd made a C in my first semester of creative writing, while Lily had made an A. Plus, I'd gained eight pounds. Both love and literature seemed to be slipping out of my sights. And I was drinking too much—we'd been drinking Yucca Flats, a horrible green punch made with grain alcohol in a washtub, all afternoon before I ended up in bed with Eddy Turner.

The bed was his, on the second floor of the Phi Gam house—not the most private setting for romance. I could scarcely see Eddy by the light from the street lamp coming in through the single high window. Faintly, below, I could hear music, and the house shook slightly with the dancing. I thought of Hemingway's famous description of sex from *For Whom the Bell Tolls,* which I'd typed out neatly on an index card: "The earth moved under the sleeping bag." The whole Phi Gam house was moving under me. After wrestling with my panty girdle for what seemed like hours,

Eddy tossed it in the corner and got on top of me. Drunk as I was, I wanted him to. I wanted him to *do it.* But I didn't think it would hurt so much, and suddenly I wished he would kiss me or say something. He didn't. He was done and lying on his back beside me when the door to the room burst open and the light came on. I sat up, grasping for the sheet that I couldn't find. My breasts are large, and they had always embarrassed me. Until that night, Don Fetterman was the only boy who had seen them. It was a whole group of Phi Gams, roaming from room to room. Luckily I was blinded by the light, so I couldn't tell exactly who they were.

"Smile!" they yelled. "You're on *Candid Camera!*" They laughed hysterically, slammed the door, and were gone, leaving us in darkness once again. I sobbed into Eddy's pillow, because what they said reminded me of Sam, whose face would not leave my mind then for hours while I cried and cried and cried and sobered up. I didn't tell Eddy what I was crying about, nor did he ask. He sat in a chair and smoked cigarettes while he waited for me to stop crying. Finally I did. Eddy and I didn't date after that, but we were buddies in the way I was buddies with the whole Phi Gam house due to my status as Dixie's roommate. I was like a sister, giving advice to the lovelorn, administering Cokes and aspirin on Sunday mornings, typing papers.

It was not the role I'd had in mind, but it was better than nothing, affording me at least a certain status among the girls at school; and the Phi Gams saw to it that I attended all the big parties, usually with somebody whose girlfriend couldn't make it. Often, when the weekend was winding down, I could be found in the Phi Gam basement alone, playing "Tragedy," my favorite song, over and over on the jukebox.

Blown by the wind,
Kissed by the snow,
All that's left
Is the dark below.
  Gone from me,
  Oh, oh,
  Trag-e-dy.

It always brought me to the edge of tears, because I had never known any tragedy myself, or love, or drama. *Wouldn't anything ever happen to me?*

Meanwhile, my friends' lives were like soap operas—Lily's period was two weeks late, which scared us all, and then Dixie went on the pill. Melissa and her boyfriend split up (she lost seven pounds, he slammed his hand into a wall) and then made up again.

Melissa was telling us about it, in her maddeningly slow way, one day when we were out at Donnie's lake cabin, sunning. "It's not the same, though," she said. "He just gets *too mad.* I don't know what it is—he scares me."

"Dump him," Lily said, applying baby oil with iodine in it, our suntan lotion of choice.

"But I *love* him," Melissa wailed. Lily snorted.

"Well . . ." Dixie began diplomatically, but suddenly I sat up.

"Maybe he's got a wild streak," I said. "Maybe he just can't control himself. That's always been Bubba's problem." The little lake before us took on a deeper, more intense hue. I noticed the rotting pier, the old fisherman up at the point, Lily's painted toenails. I noticed *everything.*

"Who's Bubba?" Donnie asked.

Dixie eyed me expectantly, thinking I meant one of the Phi Gams, since several of them had that nickname.

"My brother," I said. I took a deep breath.

"*What?* You never said you had a *brother!*" Dixie's pretty face looked really puzzled now.

Everybody sat up and stared at me.

"Well, I do," I said. "He's two years older than me, and he stayed with my father when my parents split up. So I've never lived with him. In fact, I don't know him real well at all. This is very painful for me to talk about. We were inseparable when we were little," I added, hearing my song in the back of my mind. *Oh, oh . . . trag-e-dy!*

"Oh Charlene, I'm so sorry! I had no idea!" Dixie was hugging me, slick hot skin and all.

I started crying. "He was a real problem child," I said, "and now he's just so wild. I don't know what's going to become of him."

"How long has it been since you've seen him?" Melissa asked.

"About two years," I said. "Our parents won't have anything at all to do with each other. They *hate* each other, especially since Mama remarried. They won't let us get together, not even for a day. It's just awful."

"So how did you see him two years ago?" Lily asked. They had all drawn closer, clustering around me.

"He ran away from school," I said, and "came to my high school, and got me right out of class. I remember it was biology lab," I said. "I was dissecting a frog."

"Then what?"

"We spent the day together," I said. "We got some food and went out to this quarry and ate, and just drove around. We talked and talked," I said. "And you know what? I felt just as close to him then as I did when we were babies. Just like all those years had never passed at all. It was great," I said.

"Then he went back to school? Or what?"

"No." I choked back a sob. "It was almost dark, and he was taking me back to my house, and then he was planning to head on down to Florida, he said, when all of a sudden these blue lights came up behind us, and it was the police."

"The *police?*" Dixie was getting very nervous. She was such a good girl.

"Well, it was a stolen car, of course," I explained. "They nailed him. If he hadn't stopped in to see me, he might have gotten away with it," I said, "if he'd just headed straight to Florida. But he came to see me. Mama and Daddy wouldn't even bail him out. They let him go straight to prison."

"Oh, Charlene, *no wonder* you never talk about your family!" Dixie was in tears now.

"But he was a model prisoner," I went on. I felt exhilarated. "They gave all the prisoners this test, and he scored the highest that anybody in the whole history of the prison had *ever* scored, so they let him take these special classes, and he did so well that he got out a whole year early, and now he's in college."

"Where?"

I thought fast. "Dartmouth," I said wildly. I knew it had to be a northern school, since Dixie and Melissa seemed to know everybody in the South. But neither of them, as far as I could recall, had ever mentioned Dartmouth.

"He's got a full scholarship," I added. "But he's so bad, I don't know if he'll be able to keep it or not." Donnie got up and went in and came back with cold Cokes for us all, and we stayed out at Goshen Lake until the sun set, and I told them about Bubba.

He was a KA, the wildest KA of them all. Last winter, I said, he got drunk and passed out in the snow on the way back to his fraternity house; by the time a janitor found him the following morning, his cheek was frozen solid to the road. It took two guys from maintenance, with torches, to melt the snow around Bubba's face and get him loose. And now the whole fraternity was on probation because of this really gross thing he'd made the pledges do. "What really gross thing?" they asked. "Oh, you don't want to know," I said. "You really don't."

"I *really do.*" Lily pushed her sunburned face into mine. "Come on. After Trey, nothing could be that bad." Even Dixie grinned.

"Okay," I said, launching into a hazing episode that required the KA pledges to run up three flights of stairs, holding alum in their mouths. On each landing, they had to dodge past these two big football players. If they swallowed the alum during the struggle, well, alum makes you vomit immediately, so you can imagine. . . . They could imagine. But the worst part was that when one pledge wouldn't go past the second landing, the football players threw him down the stairs, and he broke his back.

"That's just disgusting," Donnie drawled. "Nobody would ever do that in Texas."

But on the other hand, I said quickly, Bubba was the most talented poet in the school, having won the Iris Nutley Leach Award for Poetry two years in a row. I pulled the name Iris Nutley Leach right out of the darkening air. I astonished myself. And girls were just crazy about Bubba, I added. In fact, this girl from Washington tried to kill herself after they broke up, and then she had to be institutionalized at Sheppard Pratt in Baltimore. I knew all about Sheppard Pratt because my mother had gone there.

"But he doesn't have a girlfriend right now," I said. Everybody sighed, and a warm breeze came up over the pines and ruffled our little lake. By then, Bubba was as real to me as the Peanuts towel I sat on, as real as the warm gritty dirt between my toes.

During the next year or so, Bubba would knock up a girl and then nobly help her get an abortion (Donnie offered to contribute); he would make Phi Beta Kappa; he would be arrested for assault; he would wreck his MGB; he would start writing folk songs. My creativity knew no bounds when it came to Bubba, but I was a dismal failure in my first writing class, where my teacher, Mr. Lefcowicz, kept giving me B's and C's and telling me, "Write what you know."

I didn't want to write what I knew. I had no intention of writing a word about my own family, or those peanut fields. Who would want to read about *that?* I had wanted to write in order to *get away* from my own life. I couldn't give up that tormented woman on the cliff in the south of France. I intended to write about glamorous heroines with exciting lives. One of my first—and worst—stories involved a stewardess in Hawaii. I had never been to Hawaii, of course. At that time, I had never even been on a plane. The plot, which was very complicated, had something to do with international espionage. I remember how kindly my young teacher smiled at me when he handed my story back. He asked me to stay for a minute after class. "Charlene," he said, "I want you to write something true next time."

Instead, I decided to give up on plot and concentrate on theme, intending to pull some heartstrings. It was nearly Christmas, and this time we had to read our stories aloud to the whole group. But right before that class, Mr. Lefcowicz, who had already read our stories, pulled me aside and told me that I didn't have to read mine out loud if I didn't want to.

"Of course I want to," I said.

We took our seats.

My story took place in a large, unnamed city on Christmas Eve. In this story, a whole happy family was trimming the Christmas tree, singing carols, and drinking hot chocolate while it snowed outside. I think I had "softly falling flakes." Each person in the family was allowed to open one present—selected from the huge pile of gifts beneath the glittering tree—before bed. Then everyone went to sleep, and a "pregnant silence" descended. At three o'clock a fire broke out, and the whole house burned to the ground, and they all burned up, dying horrible deaths, which I described individually—conscious, as I read aloud, of some movement and sound among my listeners. But I didn't dare look up as I approached the story's ironic end: "When the fire trucks arrived, the only sign of life to be found was a blackened music box in the smoking ashes, softly playing 'Silent Night.'"

By the end of my story, one girl had put her head down on her desk; another was having a coughing fit. Mr. Lefcowicz was staring intently out the window at the wintry day, his back to us. Then he made a great show of looking at his watch. "Whoops! Class dismissed!" he cried, grabbing his bookbag. He rushed from the room like the White Rabbit, already late.

But I was not that stupid.

As I walked across the cold, wet quadrangle toward my dormitory, I understood perfectly well that my story was terrible, laughable. I wanted to die. The gray sky, the dripping, leafless trees, fit my mood perfectly, and I remembered Mr. Lefcowicz saying, in an earlier class, that we must never manipulate nature to express our characters' emotions. "Ha!" I muttered scornfully to the heavy sky.

The very next day, I joined the staff of the campus newspaper. I became its editor in the middle of my sophomore year—a job nobody else wanted, a job I really enjoyed. I had found a niche, a role, and although it was not what I had envisioned for myself, it was okay. Thus I became the following things: editor of the newspaper; member of Athena, the secret honor society; roommate of Dixie, the May Queen; friend of Phi Gams; and—especially—sister of Bubba, whose legend loomed ever larger. But I avoided both dates and creative writing classes for the next two years, finding Mr. Lefcowicz's stale advice, "Write what you know," more impossible with each visit home.

The summer between my sophomore and junior years was the hardest. The first night I was home, I realized that something was wrong with Mama when I woke up to hear water splashing in the downstairs bathroom. I went to investigate. There she was, wearing a lacy pink peignoir and her old gardening shoes, scrubbing the green tub.

"Oh, hi, Charlene!" she said brightly, and went on scrubbing, humming tunelessly to herself. A mop and bucket stood in the corner. I said good night and went back to my bedroom, where I looked at the clock; it was three-thirty a.m.

The next day, Mama burst into tears when Sam spilled a glass of iced tea, and the day after that, Daddy took her over to Petersburg and put her in the hospital.

Memaw came in to stay with Sam during the day while I worked at Snow's in South Hill, my old job.

I'd come home at suppertime each day to find Sam in his chair on the front porch, holding Blackie, waiting for me. He seemed to have gotten smaller somehow—and for the first time I realized that Sam, so much a part of my childhood, was not growing up along with me. In fact, he would *never* grow up, and I thought about that a lot on those summer evenings as I swung gently in the porch swing, back and forth through the sultry air, suspended.

In August, I went to Memphis for a week to visit Dixie, whose house turned out to be like Tara in *Gone With the Wind,* only bigger, and whose mother turned out to drink sherry all day long. I came back to find Mama out of the hospital already, much improved by shock treatments, and another surprise—a baby-blue Chevrolet convertible, used but great-looking, in the driveway. My father handed me the keys.

"Here, honey," he said, and then he hugged me tight, smelling of sweat and tobacco. "We're so proud of you." He had traded a man a combine or something for the car.

So I drove back to school in style, and my junior year went smoothly until Donnie announced that her sister Susannah, now at Pine Mountain Junior College, was going to Dartmouth for Winter Carnival, to visit a boy she'd met that summer. Susannah just *couldn't wait* to look up Bubba.

Unfortunately this was not possible, as I got a phone call that very night saying that Bubba had been kicked out of school for leading a demonstration against the war. Lily, who had become much more political herself by that time, jumped up from her desk and grabbed my hand.

"Oh, no!" she shrieked. "He'll be drafted!" The alarm that filled our study room was palpable—as real as the mounting body count on TV—as we stared white-faced at each other.

"Whatever will he do now?" Donnie was wringing her hands.

"I don't know," I said desperately. "I just don't know." I went to my room—a single, this term—and thought about it. It was clear that he would have to do something, something to take him far, far away.

But Bubba's problem was soon to be superseded by Melissa's. She was pregnant, really pregnant, and in spite of all the arguments we could come up with, she wanted to get married and have the baby. She wanted to have lots of babies, and one day live in the big house on the Battery that her boyfriend would inherit, and this is exactly what she's done. Her life has been predictable and productive. So violent in his college days, Melissa's husband turned out to be a model of stability in later life. And their first child, Anna, kept him out of the draft.

As she got into her mother's car to leave, Melissa squeezed my hand and said, "Keep me posted about Bubba, and don't worry so much. I'm sure everything will work out all right."

It didn't.

Bubba burned his draft card not a month later and headed for Canada, where he lived in a commune. I didn't hear from him for a long time after that, tangled up as I was by then in my affair with Dr. Pierce.

Dr. Pierce was a fierce, bleak, melancholy man who looked like a bird of prey. Not surprisingly, he was a Beckett scholar. He taught the seminar in contemporary literature that I took in the spring of my junior year. We read Joseph Heller, Kurt Vonnegut, Flannery O'Connor, John Barth, and Thomas Pynchon, among others. Flannery O'Connor would become my favorite, and I would do my senior thesis on her work, feeling a secret and strong kinship, by then, with her dire view. But this was later, after my affair with Dr. Pierce was over.

At first I didn't know what to make of him. I hated his northern accent, his lugubrious, glistening dark eyes, his all-encompassing pessimism. He told us that contemporary literature was absurd because the world was absurd. He told us that the language in the books we were reading was weird and fractured because true communication is impossible in the world today. Dr. Pierce told us this in a sad, cynical tone full of infinite world-weariness, which I found both repellent and attractive.

I decided to go in and talk to him. I am still not sure why I did this—I was making good grades in his course, I understood everything. But one blustery, unsettling March afternoon I found myself sitting outside his office. He was a popular teacher, rumored to be always ready to listen to his students' problems. I don't know what I meant to talk to him about. The hour grew late. The hall grew dark. I smoked four or five cigarettes while other students, ahead of me, went in and out. Then Dr. Pierce came and stood in the doorway. He took off his glasses and rubbed his eyes. He looked tired, but not nearly as old as he did in class, where he always wore a tie. Now he wore jeans and a blue work shirt, and I could see the dark hair at his neck.

"Ah," he said in that way of his that rendered all his remarks oddly significant. "Ah! Miss Christian, is it not?"

He knew it was. I felt uncomfortable, like he was mocking me. He made a gesture; I preceded him into his office and sat down.

"Now," he said, staring at me. I looked out the window at the skittish, blowing day, at the girls who passed by on the sidewalk, giggling and trying to hold their skirts down. *"Miss Christian,"* Dr. Pierce said. Maybe he'd said it before. I looked at him.

"I presume you had some reason for this visit," he said sardonically.

To my horror, I started crying. Not little ladylike sniffles, either, but huge groaning sobs. Dr. Pierce thrust a box of Kleenex in my direction, then sat drumming his fingers on his desk. I kept on crying. Finally I realized what he was drumming: the *William Tell* overture. I got tickled. Soon I was crying and laughing at the same time. I was still astonished at myself.

"Blow your nose," Dr. Pierce said.

I did.

"That's better," he said. It was. He got up and closed his office door, although there was no need to do so, since the hall outside was empty now. Dr. Pierce sat back down and leaned across his desk toward me. "What is it?" he asked.

But I still didn't know what it was. I said so, and apologized. "One thing, though," I said. "I'd like to complain about the choice of books on our reading list."

"Aha!" Dr. Pierce said. He leaned back in his chair and made his fingers into a tent. "You liked Eudora Welty," he said. This was true; I nodded. "You liked *Lie Down in Darkness,"* he said. I nodded again.

"But I just *hate* this other stuff!" I burst out. "I just hated *The End of the Road,* I hated it! It's so depressing."

He nodded rapidly. "You think literature should make you feel good?" he asked.

"It used to," I said. Then I was crying again. I stood up. "I'm so sorry," I said.

Dr. Pierce stood up, too, and walked around his desk and came to stand close to me. The light in his office was soft, gray, furry. Dr. Pierce took both my hands in his. "Oh, Miss Christian," he said. "My very dear, very young Miss Christian, I know what you mean." And I could tell, by the pain and weariness in his voice, that this was true. I could see Dr. Pierce suddenly as a much younger man, as a boy, with a light in his eyes and a different feeling about the world. I reached up and put my hands in his curly hair and pulled his face down to mine and kissed him fiercely, in a way I had never kissed anybody. I couldn't imagine myself doing this, yet I did it naturally. Dr. Pierce kissed me back. We kissed for a long time, while it grew completely dark outside, and then he locked the door and turned back to me. He sighed deeply, almost a groan—a sound, I felt, of regret—then unbuttoned my shirt. We made love on the rug on his office floor. Immediately we were caught up in a kind of fever that lasted for several months—times like these in his office after hours, or in the backseat of my car parked by Goshen Lake, or in cheap motels when I'd signed out to go home.

Nobody suspected a thing. I was as good at keeping secrets as I was at making up lies. Plus, I was a campus leader, and Dr. Pierce was a married man.

He tried to end it that June. I was headed home, and he was headed to New York, where he had a fellowship to do research at the Morgan Library.

"Charlene—" Dr. Pierce said. We were in public, out on the quadrangle right after graduation. His wife walked down the hill at some distance behind us, with other faculty wives. Dr. Pierce's voice was hoarse, the way it got when he was in torment (which he so often was, which was one of the most attractive things about him. Years later, I'd realize this). "Let us make a clean break," he sort of mumbled. "Right now. It cannot go on, and we both know it."

We had reached the parking lot in front of the chapel; the sunlight reflected off the cars was dazzling.

Dr. Pierce stuck out his hand in an oddly formal gesture. "Have a good summer, Charlene," he said, "and good-bye."

Dr. Pierce had chosen his moment well. He knew I wouldn't make a scene in front of all these people. But I refused to take his hand. I rushed off madly through the parked cars to my own and gunned it out of there and out to the lake, where I parked on the bluff above Donnie's cabin, in the exact spot where Dr. Pierce and I had been together so many times. I sat at the wheel and looked out at the lake, now full of children on a school outing. Their shrill screams and laughter drifted to me thinly, like the sounds of birds in the trees around my car. I leaned back on the seat and stared straight up at the sun through the trees—just at the top of the tent of green, where light filtered through in bursts like stars.

But I couldn't give him up, not yet, not ever.

I resolved to surprise Dr. Pierce in New York, and that's exactly what I did, telling my parents I'd gone on a trip to Virginia Beach with friends. I got his summer address from the registrar's office. I drove up through Richmond and Washington, a seven-hour drive. It was crazy and even a dangerous thing to do, since I had never been to New York. But at last I ended up in front of the brownstone in the Village where Dr. Pierce and his wife were subletting an apartment. It was midafternoon and hot; I had not imagined New York to be so hot, hotter even than McKenney,

Virginia. I was still in a fever, I think. I rang the doorbell, without even considering what I would do if his wife answered. But nobody answered. Nobody was home. Somehow, this possibility had not occurred to me. I felt exhausted. I leaned against the wall and then slid down it, until I was sitting on the floor in the vestibule. I pulled off my panty hose and stuffed them into my purse. They were too hot. I was too hot. I wore a kelly-green linen dress; I'd thought I needed to be all dressed up to go to New York.

I don't even remember falling asleep, but I was awakened by Dr. Pierce shaking my shoulder and saying my name.

Whatever can be said of Dr. Pierce, he was not a jerk. He told me firmly that our relationship was over, and just as firmly that I should not be going around New York City at night by myself, not in the shape I was in.

By the time his wife came home with groceries, I was lying on the studio bed, feeling a little better. He told her I was having a breakdown, which seemed suddenly true. Dr. Pierce and I looked at the news on TV while she made spaghetti. After dinner she lit a joint and handed it to me. It was the first time anybody had offered me marijuana. I shook my head. I thought I was crazy enough already. Dr. Pierce's wife was nice, though. She was pale, with long, long blond hair, which she had worn in a braid on campus, or twisted on top of her head. Now it fell over her shoulders like water. She was not much—certainly not ten years—older than I was, and I wondered if she, too, had been his student. But I was exhausted. I fell asleep on the studio bed in front of a fan that drowned out the sound of their voices as they cleaned up from dinner.

I woke up very early the next morning. I wrote the Pierces a thank-you note on an index card I found in Dr. Pierce's briefcase, and left it propped conspicuously against the toaster. The door to their bedroom was open, but I did not look in.

On the street, I was horrified to find that I had gotten a parking ticket and that my convertible top had been slashed—gratuitously, since there was nothing in the car to steal. This upset me more than anything else about my trip to New York, more than Dr. Pierce's rejection, or his renunciation, as I preferred to consider it—which is how I did consider it, often, during that summer at home while I had the rest of my nervous breakdown.

My parents were very kind. They thought it all had to do with Don Fetterman, who was missing in action in Vietnam, and maybe it did, sort of. I was "nervous," and cried a lot. Finally my aunt Dee got tired of me mooning around, as she called it. She frosted my hair and took me to Myrtle Beach, where it proved impossible to continue the nervous breakdown. The last night of the trip, Aunt Dee and I double-dated with some realtors she'd met by the pool.

Aunt Dee and I got back to McKenney just in time for me to pack and drive to school, where I was one of the seniors in charge of freshman orientation. Daddy had gotten the top fixed on my car; I was a blonde; and I'd lost twenty-five pounds.

The campus seemed smaller to me as I drove through the imposing gates. My footsteps echoed as I carried my bags up to the third floor of Old North, where Dixie and I would have the coveted "turret room." I was the first one back in the dorm, but as I hauled things in from my car, other seniors began arriving. We hugged and squealed, following a script as old as the college. At least three girls stopped in mid-hug to push me back, scrutinize me carefully, and exclaim that they wouldn't have recognized me. I didn't know what they meant.

Sweaty and exhausted after carrying everything up to the room, I decided to shower before dinner. I was standing naked in our room, toweling my hair dry, when the dinner bell rang. Its somber tone sounded elegiac to me in that moment. On impulse, I started rummaging around in one of my boxes, until I found the mirror I was looking for. I went to stand at the window while the last of the lingering chimes died on the August air.

I held the mirror out at arm's length and looked at myself. I had cheekbones. I had hipbones. I could see my ribs. My eyes were darker, larger in my face. My wild damp hair was as blond as Lily's.

Clearly, *something had finally happened to me.*

That weekend, Dixie, Donnie, Lily, and I went out to Donnie's cabin to drink beer and catch up on the summer. We telephoned Melissa, now eight months pregnant, who claimed to be blissfully happy and said she was making curtains.

Lily snorted. She got up and put Simon and Garfunkel on the stereo, and got us each another beer. Donnie lit candles and switched off the overhead lamp. Dixie waved her hand, making her big diamond sparkle in the candlelight. Trey, now in law school at Vanderbilt, had given it to her in July. She was already planning her wedding. We would all be bridesmaids, of course. (That marriage would last for only a few years, and Dixie would divorce once more before she went to law school herself.) Donnie told us about her mother's new boyfriend. We gossiped on as the hour grew late and bugs slammed suicidally into the porch light. The moon came up big and bright. I kept playing "The Sounds of Silence" over and over; it matched my mood, my new conception of myself. I also liked "I Am a Rock, I Am an Island."

Then Lily announced that she was in love, *really in love* this time, with a young poet she'd met that summer on Cape Cod, where she'd been waitressing. We waited while she lit a cigarette. "We lived together for two months," Lily said, "in his room at the inn, where we could look out and see the water." We stared at her. None of us had ever lived with anybody, or known anyone who had. Lily looked around at us. "It was wonderful," she said. "It was heaven. But it was not what you might think," she added enigmatically, "living with a man."

I started crying.

There was a long silence, and the needle on the record started scratching. Donnie got up and cut it off. They were all looking at me.

"And what about you, Charlene?" Lily said softly. "What happened to you this summer, anyway?"

It was a moment I had rehearsed again and again in my mind. I would tell them about my affair with Dr. Pierce and how I had gone to New York to find him, and how he had renounced me because his wife was pregnant. I had just added this part. But I was crying too hard to speak. "It was awful," I said finally, and Dixie came over and hugged me. "What was awful?" she said, but I couldn't even speak, my mind filled suddenly, surprisingly, with Don Fetterman as he'd looked in high school, presiding over the Glee Club.

"Come on," Dixie said, "tell us."

The candles were guttering, the moon made a path across the lake. I took a deep breath.

"Bubba is dead," I said.

"Oh, God! Oh, no!" A sort of pandemonium ensued, which I don't remember much about, although I remember the details of my brother's death vividly. Bubba drowned in a lake in Canada, attempting to save a friend's child who had fallen overboard. The child died, too. Bubba was buried there, on the wild shore of that northern lake, and his only funeral was what his friends said as they spoke around the grave one by one. His best friend had written to me, describing the whole thing.

"Charlene, Charlene, why didn't you tell us sooner?" Donnie asked.

I just shook my head. "I couldn't," I said.

Later that fall, I finally wrote a good story—about my family, back in McKenney—and then another, and then another. I won a scholarship to graduate school at Columbia University in New York, where I still live, with my husband, on the West Side, free-lancing for several magazines and writing fiction.

It was here, only a few weeks ago, that I last saw Lily, now a prominent feminist scholar. She was in town for the MLA convention. We went to a bistro near my apartment for lunch, lingering over wine far into the late-December afternoon while my husband baby-sat. Lily was in the middle of a divorce. "You know," she said at one point, twirling her tulip wineglass, "I have often thought that the one great tragedy of my life was never getting to meet your brother. Somehow I always felt that he and I were just meant for each other." We sat in the restaurant for a long time, at the window where we could see the passersby hurrying along the sidewalk in the dismal sleet outside, each one so preoccupied, so caught up in his own story. We sat there all afternoon.

1997

Dorothy Allison b. 1949

Born in Greenville, South Carolina, to a fourteen-year-old mother, Dorothy Allison was raised near her large extended family. After her mother married, her aunts provided occasional refuge from an abusive stepfather. The violence and chaos of her upbringing, stemming largely from her family's poverty, fuel Allison's writing, as does the strength she saw in her relatives' survival despite such hopeless conditions. Her chance to escape came when a National Merit Scholarship paid for her to attend Florida Presbyterian College. She later earned a master's degree in anthropology from the New School for Social Research in New York.

Allison became active in the women's movement in the early seventies, working for several feminist publications and helping establish Herstore, a feminist bookstore in Tallahassee, Florida. She credits feminism for enabling her to become a writer. Although she had begun writing as a child, she viewed writing the truth as such a dangerous activity that she burned everything she wrote. But in 1973 friends in the lesbian-feminist collective where she was living convinced her to stop destroying her work.

Her first book, *The Women Who Hate Me,* was a collection of poems, most written in reaction to the protest surrounding the 1982 Barnard College "Towards a Politics of Sexuality" conference. The intent of that feminist conference was to discuss sexuality in all its complexity, but antipornography protesters effectively shut down the event by appealing to university administrators and personally attacking conference participants. Allison's poems, which are frequently angry, focus on women's relationships and lesbian sexuality. An expanded version of the book was published in 1991 with the subtitle *Poetry 1980–1990.*

In 1988 Allison published *Trash,* a collection of emotionally intense, frequently violent, and often comic short stories. Class difference is a predominant theme, as many of her characters confront others' stereotypical expectations of rural southerners. The misunderstandings created by often romantic stereotypes are particularly poignant in stories depicting lesbian relationships. Given Allison's subject matter, it is not surprising that among the writers she credits as influences are Flannery O'Connor, James Baldwin, Eudora Welty, Tennessee Williams, Carson McCullers, Muriel Rukeyser, and Toni Morrison.

Allison's earliest published work established her audience and reputation primarily in the lesbian community. Her first novel, *Bastard out of Carolina* (1992), gained her national attention. It won the Lambda Award and was a finalist for the National Book Award. Loosely autobiographical, the compelling first-person narrative follows Bone Boatwright's survival of her stepfather's sexual abuse. In 1996 the novel became a film directed by Anjelica Huston.

Two or Three Things I Know for Sure, composed after Allison completed the novel, debuted as a performance piece at The Lab in San Francisco in August 1991. Revised for publication in 1995, the work, which traces Allison's family history by describing family photographs, explores the paradoxical power of stories to both support and delude. While Allison writes of her need to tell stories as part of her own survival, she also describes the "meanest" ones as those "the women [she] loved told themselves in secret—the stories that sustained and broke them." A short documentary based on the work, *Two or Three Things and Nothing for Sure,* by Tina DiFeliciantonio and Jane Wagner, won prizes at both the Aspen and the Toronto film festivals and aired on PBS in 1998.

In 1994 Allison published a collection of critical and political essays under the descriptive title *Skin: Talking About Sex, Class, and Literature.* Her second novel appeared in 1998. *Cavedweller,* a *New York Times* bestseller, portrays the relationships between a woman and her three daughters, two of whom she abandoned when she fled from their father. Reviews praised the language, characterization, and emotional power of the story but noted that the novel's structure weakens in the latter half. Allison is currently working on a project inspired by Janis Joplin. She lives in northern California with her partner Alix and her son Wolf.

Kelly Lynch Reames
Oklahoma State University

PRIMARY WORKS

The Women Who Hate Me, 1983; *Trash,* 1988; *The Women Who Hate Me: Poetry 1980–1990,* 1991; *Bastard out of Carolina,* 1992; *Skin: Talking About Sex, Class, and Literature,* 1994; *Two or Three Things I Know for Sure,* 1995; *Cavedweller,* 1998.

Don't Tell Me You Don't Know

I came out of the bathroom with my hair down wet on my shoulders. My Aunt Alma, my mama's oldest sister, was standing in the middle of Casey's dusty hooked rug looking like she had just flown in on it, her grey hair straggling out of its misshapen bun. For a moment I was so startled I couldn't move. Aunt Alma just stood there looking around at the big bare room with its two church pews bracketing the only other furniture—a massive pool table. I froze while the water ran down from my hair to dampen the collar of the oversized tuxedo shirt I used for a bathrobe.

"Aunt Alma," I stammered, "well . . . welcome. . . ."

"You really live here?" she breathed, as if, even for me, such a situation was quite past her ability to believe. "Like this?"

I looked around as if I were seeing it for the first time myself, shrugged and tried to grin. "It's big," I offered, "lots of space, four porches, all these windows. We get along well here, might not in a smaller place." I looked back through the kitchen to Terry's room with its thick dark curtains covering a wall of windows. Empty. So was Casey's room on the other side of the kitchen. It was quiet and still, with no one even walking through the rooms overhead.

"Thank God," I whispered to myself. Nobody else was home.

Aunt Alma turned around slowly and stepped over to the mantel with the old fly-spotted mirror over it. She pushed a few of her loose hairs back and then laid her big rattan purse up by a stack of fliers Terry had left there, brushing some of the dust away first.

"My God," she echoed, "dirtier than we ever lived. Didn't think you'd turn out like this."

I shrugged again, embarrassed and angry and trying not to show it. Well hell, what could I do? I hadn't seen her in so long. She hadn't even been around that last year I'd lived with Mama, and I wasn't sure I particularly wanted to see her now. But why was she here anyway? How had she found me?

I closed the last two buttons on my shirt and tried to shake some of the water out of my hair. Aunt Alma watched me through the dark spots of the mirror, her mouth set in an old familiar line. "Well," I said, "I didn't expect to see you." I reached up to push hair back out of my eyes. "You want to sit down?"

Aunt Alma turned around and bumped her hip against the pool table. "Where?" One disdainful glance rendered the pews for what they were—exquisitely uncomfortable even for my hips. Her expression reminded me of my Uncle Jack's jokes about her, about how she refused to go back to church till they put in rocking chairs.

"No rocking chairs here," I laughed, hoping she'd laugh with me. Aunt Alma just leaned forward and rocked one of the balls on the table against another. Her mouth kept its flat, impartial expression. I tried gesturing across the pool table to my room and the big waterbed outlined in sunlight and tree shade from the three windows overlooking it.

"It's cleaner in there," I offered, "it's my room. This is our collective space." I gestured around.

"Collective," my aunt echoed me again, but the way she said the word expressed clearly her opinion of such arrangements. She looked toward my room with its narrow cluttered desk and stacks of books, then turned back to the pool table as by far the more interesting view. She rocked the balls again so that the hollow noise of the thump resounded against the high, dim ceiling.

"Pitiful," she sighed, and gave me a sharp look, her washed-out blue eyes almost angry. Two balls broke loose from the others and rolled idly across the matted green surface of the table. The sunlight reflecting through the oak leaves outside made Aunt Alma's face seem younger than I remembered it, some of the hard edge eased off the square jaw.

"Your mama is worried about you."

"I don't know why." I turned my jaw to her, knowing it would remind her of how much alike we had always been, the people who had said I was more her child than my mama's. "I'm fine. Mama should know that. I spoke to her not too long ago."

"How long ago?"

I frowned, mopped at my head some more. Two months, three, last month? "I'm not sure . . . Reese's birthday. I think it was Reese's birthday."

"Three months." My aunt rocked one ball back and forth across her palm, a yellow nine ball. The light filtering into the room went a shade darker. The -9- gleamed pale through her fingers. I looked more closely at her. She looked just as she had when I was thirteen, her hair grey in that loose bun, her hands large and swollen, her body straining the seams of the faded print dress. She'd worn her hair short for a while, but it was grown long again now, and the print dress under her coat could have been any dress she'd worn in the last twenty years. She'd gotten old, suddenly, after the birth of her eighth child, but since then she seemed not to change at all. She looked now as if she would go on forever—a worn stubborn woman who didn't care what you saw when you looked at her.

I drew breath in slowly, carefully. I knew from old experience to use caution in dealing with any of my aunts, and this was the oldest and most formidable. I'd seen grown men break down and cry when she'd kept that look on them too long; little children repent and swear to change their ways. But I'd also seen my other aunts stare her right back, and like them I was a grown woman minding my own business. I had a right to look her in the eye, I told myself. I was no wayward child, no half-drunk, silly man. I was her namesake, my mama's daughter. I had to be able to look her in the eye. If I couldn't, I was in trouble, and I didn't want that kind of trouble here, 500 miles and half a lifetime away from my aunts and the power of their eyes.

Slow, slow, the balls rocked one against the other. Aunt Alma looked over at me levelly. I let the water run down between my breasts, looked back at her. My mama's sister. I could feel the tears pushing behind my eyes. It had been so long since I'd seen her or any of them! The last time I'd been to Old Henderson Road had been years back. Aunt Alma had stood on that sagging porch and looked at me, memorizing me, both of us knowing we might not see each other again. She'd moved her mouth and I'd seen the pain there, the shadow of the nephew behind her—yet another one she was raising since her youngest son, another cousin of mine, had run off and left the girl who'd birthed that boy. The pain in her eyes was achingly clear to me, the certain awful knowledge that measured all her children and wrenched her heart.

Something wrong with that boy, my uncles had laughed.

Yeah, something. Dropped on his head one too many times, you think?

I think.

My aunt, like my mama, understood everything, expected nothing, and watched her own life like a terrible fable from a Sunday morning sermon. It was the perspective that all those women shared, the view that I could not, for my life, accept. I believed, I believed with all my soul that death was behind it, that death was the seed and the fruit of that numbed and numbing attitude. More than anything else, it was my anger that had driven me away from them, driven them away from me—my unpredictable, automatic anger. Their anger, their hatred, always seemed shielded, banked and secret, and because of that—shameful. My uncles were sudden, violent, and daunting. My aunts wore you down without ever seeming to fight at all. It was my anger that my aunts thought queer, my wild raging temper they respected in a boy and discouraged in a girl. That I slept with girls was curious, but not dangerous. That I slept with a knife under my pillow and refused to step aside for my uncles was more than queer. It was crazy.

Aunt Alma's left eye twitched, and I swallowed my tears, straightened my head, and looked her full in the face. I could barely hold myself still, barely return her look. Again those twin emotions, the love and the outrage that I'd always felt for my aunt, warred in me. I wanted to put out my hand and close my fingers on her hunched, stubborn shoulder. I wanted to lay my head there and pull tight to her, but I also wanted to hit her, to scream and kick and make her ashamed of herself. Nothing was clean between us, especially not our love.

Between my mama and Aunt Alma there were five other sisters. The most terrible and loved was Bess, the one they swore had always been so smart. From the time I was eight Aunt Bess had a dent in the left side of her head—a shadowed dent that emphasized the twitch of that eye, just like the twitch Aunt Alma has, just like the twitch I sometimes get, the one they tell me is nerves. But Aunt Bess wasn't born with that twitch as we were, just as she wasn't born with that dent. My uncle, her husband, had come up from the deep dust on the road, his boots damp from the river, picking up clumps of dust and making mud, knocking it off on her steps, her screen door, her rug, the back rung of a kitchen chair. She'd shouted at him, "Not on my clean floor!" and he'd swung the bucket, river-stained and heavy with crawfish. He'd hit her in the side of the head—dented her into a lifetime of stupidity and half-blindness. Son of a bitch never even said he was sorry, and all my childhood he'd laughed at her, the way she'd sometimes stop in the middle of a sentence and grope painfully for a word.

None of *them* had told me that story. I had been grown and out of the house before one of the Greenwood cousins had told it so I understood, and as much as I'd hated him then, I'd raged at them more.

"You let him live?" I'd screamed at them. "He did that to her and you did nothing! You did nothing to him, nothing for her."

"What'd you want us to do?"

My Aunt Grace had laughed at me. "You want us to cut him up and feed him to the river? What good would that have done her or her children?"

She'd shaken her head, and they had all stared at me as if I were still a child and didn't understand the way the world was. The cold had gone through me then, as if the river were running up from my bowels. I'd felt my hands curl up and reach, but there was nothing to reach for. I'd taken hold of myself, my insides, and tried desperately to voice the terror that was tearing at me.

"But to leave her with him after he did that, to just let it stand, to let him get away with it." I'd reached and reached, trying to get to them, to make them feel the wave moving up and through me. "It's like all of it, all you let them get away with."

"Them?" My mama had watched my face as if afraid of what she might find there. "Who do you mean? And what do you think we could do?"

I couldn't say it. I'd stared into mama's face, and looked from her to all of them, to those wide, sturdy cheekbones, those high, proud eyebrows, those set and terrible mouths. I had always thought of them as mountains, mountains that everything conspired to grind but never actually broke. The women of my family were all I had ever believed in. What was I if they were not what I had shaped them in my own mind? All I had known was that I had to get away from them—all of them—the men who could do those terrible things and the women who would let it happen to you. I'd never forgiven any of them.

It might have been more than three months since I had talked to Mama on the telephone. It had been far longer than that since I had been able to really talk to any of them. The deepest part of me didn't believe that I would ever be able to do so. I dropped my eyes and pulled myself away from Aunt Alma's steady gaze. I wanted to reach for her, touch her, maybe cry with her, if she'd let me.

"People will hurt you more with pity than with hate," she'd always told me. "I can hate back, or laugh at them, but goddamn the son of a bitch that hands me pity."

No pity. Not allowed. I reached to rock a ball myself.

"Want to play?" I tried looking up into her eyes again. It was too close. Both of us looked away.

"I'll play myself." She set about racking up the balls. Her mouth was still set in that tight line. I dragged a kitchen stool in and sat in the doorway out of her way, telling myself I had to play this casually, play this as family, and wait and see what the point was.

"Where's Uncle Bill?" I was rubbing my head again and trying to make conversation.

"What do you care? I don't think Bill said ten words to you in your whole life." She rolled the rack forward and back, positioning it perfectly for the break. "'Course he didn't say many more to anybody else either." She grinned, not looking at me, talking as if she were pouring tea at her own kitchen table. "Nobody can say I married that man for his conversation."

She leaned into her opening shot, and I leaned forward in appreciation. She had a great stance, her weight centered over her massive thighs. My family runs to heavy women, gravy-fed working women, the kind usually seen in pictures taken at mining disasters. Big women, all of my aunts move under their own power and stalk around telling everybody else what to do. But Aunt Alma was the prototype, the one I had loved most, starting back when she had given us free meals in the roadhouse she'd run for a while. It had been one of those bad times when my stepfather had been out of work and he and Mama were always fighting. Mama would load us all in the Pontiac and crank it up on seventy-five cents worth of gas, just enough to get to Aunt Alma's place on the Eustis Highway. Once there, we'd be fed on chicken gravy and biscuits, and Mama would be fed from the well of her sister's love and outrage.

You tell that bastard to get his ass out on the street. Whining don't make money. Cursing don't get a job . . .

Bitching don't make the beds and screaming don't get the tomatoes planted. They had laughed together then, speaking a language of old stories and older jokes.

You tell him.

I said.

Now girl, you listen to me.

The power in them, the strength and the heat! How could anybody not love my mama, my aunts? How could my daddy, my uncles, ever stand up to them, dare to raise hand or voice to them? They were a power on the earth.

I breathed deep, watching my aunt rock on her stance, settling her eye on the balls, while I smelled chicken gravy and hot grease, the close thick scent of love and understanding. I used to love to eat at Aunt Alma's house, all those home-cooked dinners at the roadhouse; pinto beans with peppers for fifteen, nine of them hers. Chow-chow on a clean white plate passed around the table while the biscuits passed the other way. My aunt always made biscuits. What else stretched so well? Now those starch meals shadowed her loose shoulders and dimpled her fat white elbows.

She gave me one quick glance and loosed her stroke. The white ball punched the center of the table. The balls flew to the edges. My sixty-year-old aunt gave a grin that would have scared piss out of my Uncle Bill, a grin of pure, fierce enjoyment. She rolled the stick in fingers loose as butter on a biscuit, laughed again, and slid her palms down the sides of polished wood, while the anger in her face melted into skill and concentration.

I rocked back on my stool and covered my smile with my wet hair. Goddamn! Aunt Alma pushed back on one ankle, swung the stick to follow one ball, another, dropping them as easily as peas on potatoes. Goddamn! She went after those balls like kids on a dirt yard, catching each lightly and dropping them lovingly. Into the holes, move it! Turning and bracing on ankles thickened with too many years of flour and babies, Aunt Alma blitzed that table like a twenty-year-old hustler, not sparing me another glance.

Not till the eighth stroke did she pause and stop to catch her breath.

"You living like this—not for a man, huh?" she asked, one eyebrow arched and curious.

"No," I shrugged, feeling more friendly and relaxed. Moving like that, aunt of mine I wanted to say, don't tell me you don't understand.

"Your mama said you were working in some photo shop, doing shit work for shit money. Not much to show for that college degree, is that?"

"Work is work. It pays the rent."

"Which ought not to be much here."

"No," I agreed, "not much. I know," I waved my hands lightly, "it's a wreck of a place, but it's home. I'm happy here. Terry, Casey and everybody—they're family."

"Family." Her mouth hardened again. "You have a family, don't you remember? These girls might be close, might be important to you, but they're not family. You know that." Her eyes said more, much more. Her eyes threw the word *family* at me like a spear. All her longing, all her resentment of my abandonment was in that word, and not only hers, but Mama's and my sisters' and all the cousins' I had carefully not given my new address.

"How about a beer?" I asked. I wanted one myself. "I've got a can of Pabst in the icebox."

"A glass of water," she said. She leaned over the table to line up her closing shots.

I brought her a glass of water. "You're good," I told her, wanting her to talk to me about how she had learned to play pool, anything but family and all this stuff I so much did not want to think about.

"Children," she stared at me again. "What about children?" There was something in her face then that waited, as if no question were more important, as if she knew the only answer I could give.

Enough, I told myself, and got up without a word to get myself that can of Pabst. I did not look in her eyes. I walked into the kitchen on feet that felt suddenly unsteady and tender. Behind me, I heard her slide the cue stick along the rim of the table and then draw it back to set up another shot.

Play it out, I cursed to myself, just play it out and leave me alone. Everything is so simple for you, so settled. Make babies. Grow a garden. Handle some man like he's just another child. Let everything come that comes, die that dies; let everything go where it goes. I drank straight from the can and watched her through the doorway. All my uncles were drunks, and I was more like them than I had ever been like my aunts.

Aunt Alma started talking again, walking around the table, measuring shots and not even looking in my direction. "You remember when ya'll lived out on Greenlake Road? Out on that dirt road where that man kept that old egg-busting dog? Your mama couldn't keep a hen to save her life till she emptied a shell and filled it again with chicken shit and baby piss. Took that dog right out of himself when he ate it. Took him right out of the taste for hens and eggs." She stopped to take a deep breath, sweat glittering on her lip. With one hand she wiped it away, the other going white on the pool cue.

"I still had Annie then. Lord, I never think about her anymore."

I remembered then the last child she had borne, a tiny girl with a heart that fluttered with every breath, a baby for whom the doctors said nothing could be done, a baby they swore wouldn't see six months. Aunt Alma had kept her in an okra basket and carried her everywhere, talking to her one minute like a kitten or a doll and the next minute like a grown woman. Annie had lived to be four, never outgrowing the vegetable basket, never talking back, just lying there and smiling like a wise old woman, dying between a smile and a laugh while Aunt Alma never interrupted the story that had almost made Annie laugh.

I sipped my beer and watched my aunt's unchanging face. Very slowly she swung the pool cue up and down, not quite touching the table. After a moment she stepped in again and leaned half her weight on the table. The 5-ball became a bird murdered in flight, dropping suddenly into the far right pocket.

Aunt Alma laughed out loud, delighted. "Never lost it," she crowed. "Four years in the roadhouse with that table set up in the back. Every one of them sons of mine thought he was going to make money on it. Lord those boys! Never made a cent." She swallowed the rest of her glass of water.

"But me," she wiped the sweat away again. "I never would have done it for money. I just loved it. Never went home without playing myself three or four games. Sometimes I'd set Annie up on the side and we'd pretend we was playing. I'd tell her when I was taking her shots. And she'd shout when I'd sink 'em. I let her win most every time."

She stopped, put both hands on the table, closed her eyes.

"'Course, just after we lost her, we lost the roadhouse." She shook her head, eyes still closed. "Never did have anything fine that I didn't lose."

The room was still, dust glinted in the sunlight past her ears. She opened her eyes and looked directly at me.

"I don't care," she began slowly, softly. "I don't care if you're queer or not. I don't care if you take puppydogs to bed, for that matter, but your mother was all my heart for twenty years when nobody else cared what happened to me. She stood by me. I've stood by her and I always thought to do the same for you and yours. But she's sitting there, did you know that? She's sitting there like nothing's left of her life, like . . . like she hates her life and won't say shit to nobody about it. She wouldn't tell me. She won't tell me what it is, what has happened."

I sat the can down on the stool, closed my own eyes, dropped my head. I didn't want to see her. I didn't want her to be there. I wanted her to go away, disappear out of my life the way I'd run out of hers. Go away, old woman. Leave me alone. Don't talk to me. Don't tell me your stories. I an't a baby in a basket, and I can't lie still for it.

"You know. You know what it is. The way she is about you. I know it has to be you—something about you. I want to know what it is, and you're going to tell me. Then you're going to come home with me and straighten this out. There's a lot I an't never been able to fix, but this time, this thing, I'm going to see it out. I'm going to see it fixed."

I opened my eyes and she was still standing there, the cue stick shiny in her hand, her face all flushed and tight.

"Go," I said and heard my voice, a scratchy, strangling cry in the big room. "Get out of here."

"What did you tell her? What did you say to your mama?"

"Ask her. Don't ask me. I don't have nothing to say to you."

The pool cue rose slowly, slowly till it touched the right cheek, the fine lines of broken blood vessels, freckles, and patchy skin. She shook her head slowly. My throat pulled tighter and tighter until it drew my mouth down and open. Like a shot the cue swung. The table vibrated with the blow. Her cheeks pulled tight, the teeth all a grimace. The cue split and broke. White dust rose in a cloud. The echo hurt my ears while her hands rose up as fists, the broken cue in her right hand as jagged as the pain in her face.

"Don't you say that to me. Don't you treat me like that. Don't you know who I am, what I am to you? I didn't have to come up here after you. I could have let it run itself out, let it rest on your head the rest of your life, just let you carry it—your mama's life. YOUR MAMA'S LIFE, GIRL. Don't you understand me? I'm talking about your mama's life."

She threw the stick down, turned away from me, her shoulders heaving and shaking, her hands clutching nothing. "I an't talking about your stepfather. I an't talking about no man at all. I'm talking about your mama sitting at her kitchen table, won't talk to nobody, won't eat, won't listen to nothing. What'd she ever ask from you? Nothing. Just gave you your life and everything she had. Worked herself ugly for you and your sister. Only thing she ever hoped for was to do the same for your children, someday to sit herself back and hold her grandchildren on her lap. . . ."

It was too much. I couldn't stand it.

"GODDAMN YOU!" I was shaking all over. "CHILDREN! All you ever talk about—you and her and all of you. Like that was the end-all and be-all of everything. Never mind what happens to them once they're made. That don't matter. It's only the getting of them. Like some goddamned crazy religion. Get your mother a grandchild and solve all her problems. Get yourself a baby and forget everything else. It's what you were born for, the one thing you can do with no thinking about it at all. Only I can't. To get her a grandchild, I'd have to steal one!"

I was wringing my own hands, twisting them together and pulling them apart. Now I swung them open and slapped down at my belly, making my own hollow noise in the room.

"No babies in there, aunt of mine, and never going to be. I'm sterile as a clean tin can. That's what I told Mama, and not to hurt her. I told her because she wouldn't leave me alone about it. Like you, like all of you, always talking about children, never able to leave it alone." I was walking back and forth now, unable to stop myself from talking. "Never able to hear me when I warned her to leave it be. Going on and on till I thought I'd lose my mind."

I looked her in the eye, loving her and hating her, and not wanting to speak, but hearing the words come out anyway. "Some people never do have babies, you know. Some people get raped at eleven by a stepfather their mama half-hates but can't afford to leave. Some people then have to lie and hide it 'cause it would make so much trouble. So nobody will know, not the law and not the rest of the family. Nobody but the women supposed to be the ones who take care of everything, who know what to do and how to do it, the women who make children who believe in them and trust in them, and sometimes die for it. Some people never go to a doctor and don't find out for ten years that the son of a bitch gave them some goddamned disease."

I looked away, unable to stand how grey her face had gone.

"You know what it does to you when the people you love most in the world, the people you believe in—cannot survive without believing in—when those people do nothing, don't even know something needs to be done? When you cannot hate them but cannot help yourself? The hatred grows. It just takes over everything, eats you up and makes you somebody full of hate."

I stopped. The roar that had been all around me stopped, too. The cold was all through me now. I felt like it would never leave me. I heard her move. I heard her hip bump the pool table and make the balls rock. I heard her turn and gather up her purse. I opened my eyes to see her moving toward the front door. That cold cut me then like a knife in fresh slaughter. I knew certainly that she'd go back and take care of Mama, that she'd never say a word, probably never tell anybody she'd been here. 'Cause then she'd have to talk about the other thing, and I knew as well as she that however much she tried to forget it, she'd really always known. She'd done nothing then. She'd do nothing now. There was no justice. There was no justice in the world.

When I started to cry it wasn't because of that. It wasn't because of babies or no babies, or pain that was so far past I'd made it a source of strength. It wasn't even that I'd hurt her so bad, hurt Mama when I didn't want to. I cried because of the things I hadn't said, didn't know how to say, cried most of all because behind everything else there was no justice for my aunts or my mama. Because each of them to save their lives had tried to be strong, had become, in fact, as strong and determined as life would let them. I and all their children had believed in that strength, had believed in them and their ability to do anything, fix anything, survive anything. None of us had ever been able to forgive ourselves that we and they were not strong enough, that strength itself was not enough.

Who can say where that strength ended, where the world took over and rolled us all around like balls on a pool table? None of us ever would. I brought my hands up to my neck and pulled my hair around until I clenched it in my fists, remembering how my aunt used to pick up Annie to rub that baby's belly beneath her chin—Annie bouncing against her in perfect trust. Annie had never had to forgive her mama anything.

"Aunt Alma, wait. Wait!"

She stopped in the doorway, her back trembling, her hands gripping the doorposts. I could see the veins raised over her knuckles, the cords that stood out in her neck, the flesh as translucent as butter beans cooked until the skins come loose. Talking to my mama over the phone, I had not been able to see her face, her skin, her stunned and haunted eyes. If I had been able to see her, would I have ever said those things to her?

"I'm sorry."

She did not look back. I let my head fall back, rolled my shoulders to ease the painful clutch of my own muscles. My teeth hurt. My ears stung. My breasts felt hot and swollen. I watched the light as it moved on her hair.

"I'm sorry. I would . . . I would . . . anything. If I could change things, if I could help. . . ."

I stopped. Tears were running down my face. My aunt turned to me, her wide pale face as wet as mine. "Just come home with me. Come home for a little while. Be with your mama a little while. You don't have to forgive her. You don't have to forgive anybody. You just have to love her the way she loves you. Like I love you. Oh girl, don't you know how we love you!"

I put my hands out, let them fall apart on the pool table. My aunt was suddenly across from me, reaching across the table, taking my hands, sobbing into the cold dirty stillness—an ugly sound, not softened by the least self-consciousness. When I leaned forward, she leaned to me and our heads met, her grey hair against my temple brightened by the sunlight pouring in the windows.

"Oh, girl! Girl, you are our precious girl."

I cried against her cheek, and it was like being five years old again in the roadhouse, with Annie's basket against my hip, the warmth in the room purely a product of the love that breathed out from my aunt and my mama. If they were not mine, if I was not theirs, who was I? I opened my mouth, put my tongue out, and tasted my aunt's cheek and my own. Butter and salt, dust and beer, sweat and stink, flesh of my flesh.

"Precious," I breathed back to her.

"Precious."

1988

Sherman Alexie (Spokane–Coeur d'Alene) b. 1966

Sherman Alexie was born in 1966 in Wellpinit, Washington, on the Spokane Indian Reservation. Born hydrocephalic, Alexie underwent brain surgery at the age of six months. Although the surgery was successful, he experienced seizures throughout his childhood. Alexie was a voracious reader, reading Steinbeck by the age of five and finishing all the books in the Wellpinit library by the age of twelve. He attended Reardon High School, an all-white school just outside the reservation, where, ironically, he played basketball for the Reardon "Indians." He attended Gonzaga University in Spokane and eventually graduated from Washington State University with a degree in American Studies. He battled alcoholism during this time and became sober at the age of twenty-three.

Alexie first encountered contemporary American Indian literature in college. Reading about his own experiences in poems and stories was a life-changing experience. After reading this line from a poem by Paiute poet Adrian Louis, "I'm in the reservation of my mind," Alexie felt that somebody understood him, and he knew that he would begin writing. That was in 1989. Three years later, Alexie's first book of poetry, *The Business of Fancydancing,* was published by Hanging Loose Press and received a tremendous amount of critical attention from Native American as well as non-Indian critics. Joy Harjo, renowned Creek poet, called Alexie "one of the most vital writers to emerge in the late twentieth century." After the *New York Times Book Review* hailed Alexie as "one of the major lyric voices of our time" and the *New York Times Book Review* declared *Fancydancing* the 1992 Notable Book of the Year, Alexie's career skyrocketed. Since then, he has published nine books of poetry and four books of fiction and has won numerous awards, including the 1993 Lila Wallace–Reader's Digest Writers' Award, the 1993 PEN/Hemingway Best First Book of Fiction Citation for *The Lone Ranger and Tonto Fistfight in Heaven,* and the 1996 Before Columbus Foundation American Book Award. He was also named one of the Twenty Best American Novelists Under the Age of 40 by *Granta Magazine* in 1997 and one of Twenty Writers for the 21st Century by the *New Yorker* in 1999.

Alexie is perhaps best known for the movie *Smoke Signals,* the screenplay of which he adapted from his short story "This Is What It Means to Say Phoenix, Arizona," from 1993's *Lone Ranger and Tonto. Smoke Signals* was the first movie written, directed, and produced entirely by American Indians. The film premiered at the Sundance Film Festival in 1998 and won the Audience Award and the Filmmakers Trophy for Cheyenne-Arapaho director Chris Eyre.

Alexie is a significant writer and a controversial figure, known for his brutally honest depictions of contemporary reservation life and razor sharp wit. His goal is to challenge and poke fun at traditional stereotypes of American Indian people. In poems about basketball on the reservation and stories such as "Because My Father Always Said He Was the Only Indian Who Saw Jimi Hendrix Play 'The Star-Spangled Banner' at Woodstock" he drives home the point that American Indian people are not trapped in the nineteenth century but are members of living, vital cultures and, furthermore, participants in and part of American popular culture. Alexie takes his responsibilities as a Native American writer seriously, realizing that he is a political spokesperson for native peoples, like it or not; he participated in President Clinton's roundtable discussion on race. He frequently attacks non-natives who write about Native Americans or appropriate Native American themes. He receives much criticism for his viewpoints but remains outspoken and unapologetic.

Alexie currently lives in Seattle with his wife, Diane, a member of the Hidatsa Nation, and their son. He shows no signs of slowing his pace and is working on screenplays, in addition to his fiction and poetry.

Amanda J. Cobb
Assistant Professor of American Studies
University of New Mexico, Albuquerque

PRIMARY WORKS

The Business of Fancydancing: Stories and Poems, 1992; *I Would Steal Horses,* 1993; *Old Shirts and New Skins,* 1993; *First Indian on the Moon,* 1993; *The Lone Ranger and Tonto Fistfight in Heaven,* 1993; *Seven Mourning Songs for the Cedar Flute I Have Yet to Learn to Play,* 1995; *Reservation Blues,* 1995; *Water Flowing Home,* 1996; *The Summer of Black Widows,* 1996; *Indian Killer,* 1996; *The Man Who Loves Salmon,* 1998; *Smoke Signals,* 1998; *One-Stick Song,* 1999; *The Toughest Indian in the World,* 2000.

Because My Father Always Said He Was the Only Indian Who Saw Jimi Hendrix Play "The Star-Spangled Banner" at Woodstock

During the sixties, my father was the perfect hippie, since all the hippies were trying to be Indians. Because of that, how could anyone recognize that my father was trying to make a social statement?

But there is evidence, a photograph of my father demonstrating in Spokane, Washington, during the Vietnam war. The photograph made it onto the wire service and was reprinted in newspapers throughout the country. In fact, it was on the cover of *Time.*

In the photograph, my father is dressed in bell-bottoms and flowered shirt, his hair in braids, with red peace symbols splashed across his face like war paint. In his hands my father holds a rifle above his head, captured in that moment just before he proceeded to beat the shit out of the National Guard private lying prone on the ground. A fellow demonstrator holds a sign that is just barely visible over my father's left shoulder. It read MAKE LOVE NOT WAR.

The photographer won a Pulitzer Prize, and editors across the country had a lot of fun creating captions and headlines. I've read many of them collected in my father's scrapbook, and my favorite was run in the *Seattle Times.* The caption under the photograph read DEMONSTRATOR GOES TO WAR FOR PEACE. The editors capitalized on my father's Native American identity with other headlines like ONE WARRIOR AGAINST WAR and PEACEFUL GATHERING TURNS INTO NATIVE UPRISING.

Anyway, my father was arrested, charged with attempted murder, which was reduced to assault with a deadly weapon. It was a high-profile case so my father was used as an example. Convicted and sentenced quickly, he spent two years in Walla

Walla State Penitentiary. Although his prison sentence effectively kept him out of the war, my father went through a different kind of war behind bars.

"There was Indian gangs and white gangs and black gangs and Mexican gangs," he told me once. "And there was somebody new killed every day. We'd hear about somebody getting it in the shower or wherever and the word would go down the line. Just one word. Just the color of his skin. Red, white, black, or brown. Then we'd chalk it up on the mental scoreboard and wait for the next broadcast."

My father made it through all that, never got into any serious trouble, somehow avoided rape, and got out of prison just in time to hitchhike to Woodstock to watch Jimi Hendrix play "The Star-Spangled Banner."

"After all the shit I'd been through," my father said, "I figured Jimi must have known I was there in the crowd to play something like that. It was exactly how I felt."

Twenty years later, my father played his Jimi Hendrix tape until it wore down. Over and over, the house filled with the rockets' red glare and the bombs bursting in air. He'd sit by the stereo with a cooler of beer beside him and cry, laugh, call me over and hold me tight in his arms, his bad breath and body odor covering me like a blanket.

Jimi Hendrix and my father became drinking buddies. Jimi Hendrix waited for my father to come home after a long night of drinking. Here's how the ceremony worked:

1. I would lie awake all night and listen for the sounds of my father's pickup.
2. When I heard my father's pickup, I would run upstairs and throw Jimi's tape into the stereo.
3. Jimi would bend his guitar into the first note of "The Star-Spangled Banner" just as my father walked inside.
4. My father would weep, attempt to hum along with Jimi, and then pass out with his head on the kitchen table.
5. I would fall asleep under the table with my head near my father's feet.
6. We'd dream together until the sun came up.

The days after, my father would feel so guilty that he would tell me stories as a means of apology.

"I met your mother at a party in Spokane," my father told me once. "We were the only two Indians at the party. Maybe the only two Indians in the whole town. I thought she was so beautiful. I figured she was the kind of woman who could make buffalo walk on up to her and give up their lives. She wouldn't have needed to hunt. Every time we went walking, birds would follow us around. Hell, tumbleweeds would follow us around."

Somehow my father's memories of my mother grew more beautiful as their relationship became more hostile. By the time the divorce was final, my mother was quite possibly the most beautiful woman who ever lived.

"Your father was always half crazy," my mother told me more than once. "And the other half was on medication."

But she loved him, too, with a ferocity that eventually forced her to leave him. They fought each other with the kind of graceful anger that only love can create. Still, their love was passionate, unpredictable, and selfish. My mother and father would get drunk and leave parties abruptly to go home and make love.

"Don't tell your father I told you this," my mother said. "But there must have been a hundred times he passed out on top of me. We'd be right in the middle of it, he'd say *I love you,* his eyes would roll backwards, and then out went his lights. It sounds strange, I know, but those were good times."

I was conceived during one of those drunken nights, half of me formed by my father's whiskey sperm, the other half formed by my mother's vodka egg. I was born a goofy reservation mixed drink, and my father needed me just as much as he needed every other kind of drink.

One night my father and I were driving home in a near-blizzard after a basketball game, listening to the radio. We didn't talk much. One, because my father didn't talk much when he was sober, and two, because Indians don't need to talk to communicate.

"Hello out there, folks, this is Big Bill Baggins, with the late-night classics show on KROC, 97.2 on your FM dial. We have a request from Betty in Tekoa. She wants to hear Jimi Hendrix's version of 'The Star-Spangled Banner' recorded live at Woodstock."

My father smiled, turned the volume up, and we rode down the highway while Jimi led the way like a snowplow. Until that night, I'd always been neutral about Jimi Hendrix. But, in that near-blizzard with my father at the wheel, with the nervous silence caused by the dangerous roads and Jimi's guitar, there seemed to be more to all that music. The reverberation came to mean something, took form and function.

That song made me want to learn to play guitar, not because I wanted to be Jimi Hendrix and not because I thought I'd ever play for anyone. I just wanted to touch the strings, to hold the guitar tight against my body, invent a chord, and come closer to what Jimi knew, to what my father knew.

"You know," I said to my father after the song was over, "my generation of Indian boys ain't ever had no real war to fight. The first Indians had Custer to fight. My great-grandfather had World War I, my grandfather had World War II, you had Vietnam. All I have is video games."

My father laughed for a long time, nearly drove off the road into the snowy fields.

"Shit," he said. "I don't know why you're feeling sorry for yourself because you ain't had to fight a war. You're lucky. Shit, all you had was that damn Desert Storm. Should have called it Dessert Storm because it just made the fat cats get fatter. It was all sugar and whipped cream with a cherry on top. And besides that, you didn't even have to fight it. All you lost during that war was sleep because you stayed up all night watching CNN."

We kept driving through the snow, talked about war and peace.

"That's all there is," my father said. "War and peace with nothing in between. It's always one or the other."

"You sound like a book," I said.

"Yeah, well, that's how it is. Just because it's in a book doesn't make it not true. And besides, why the hell would you want to fight a war for this country? It's been trying to kill Indians since the very beginning. Indians are pretty much born soldiers anyway. Don't need a uniform to prove it."

Those were the kinds of conversations that Jimi Hendrix forced us to have. I guess every song has a special meaning for someone somewhere. Elvis Presley is still showing up in 7-11 stores across the country, even though he's been dead for years, so I figure music just might be the most important thing there is. Music turned my father into a reservation philosopher. Music had powerful medicine.

"I remember the first time your mother and I danced," my father told me once. "We were in this cowboy bar. We were the only real cowboys there despite the fact that we're Indians. We danced to a Hank Williams song. Danced to that real sad one, you know. 'I'm So Lonesome I Could Cry.' Except your mother and I weren't lonesome or crying. We just shuffled along and fell right goddamn down into love."

"Hank Williams and Jimi Hendrix don't have much in common," I said.

"Hell, yes, they do. They knew all about broken hearts," my father said.

"You sound like a bad movie."

"Yeah, well, that's how it is. You kids today don't know shit about romance. Don't know shit about music either. Especially you Indian kids. You all have been spoiled by those drums. Been hearing them beat so long, you think that's all you need. Hell, son, even an Indian needs a piano or guitar or saxophone now and again."

My father played in a band in high school. He was the drummer. I guess he'd burned out on those. Now, he was like the universal defender of the guitar.

"I remember when your father would haul that old guitar out and play me songs," my mother said. "He couldn't play all that well but he tried. You could see him thinking about what chord he was going to play next. His eyes got all squeezed up and his face turned all red. He kind of looked that way when he kissed me, too. But don't tell him I said that."

Some nights I lay awake and listened to my parents' lovemaking. I know white people keep it quiet, pretend they don't ever make love. My white friends tell me they can't even imagine their parents getting it on. I know exactly what it sounds like when my parents are touching each other. It makes up for knowing exactly what they sound like when they're fighting. Plus and minus. Add and subtract. It comes out just about even.

Some nights I would fall asleep to the sounds of my parents' lovemaking. I would dream Jimi Hendrix. I could see my father standing in the front row in the dark at Woodstock as Jimi Hendrix played "The Star-Spangled Banner." My mother was at home with me, both of us waiting for my father to find his way back home to the reservation. It's amazing to realize I was alive, breathing and wetting my bed, when Jimi was alive and breaking guitars.

I dreamed my father dancing with all these skinny hippie women, smoking a few joints, dropping acid, laughing when the rain fell. And it did rain there. I've seen actual news footage. I've seen the documentaries. It rained. People had to share food. People got sick. People got married. People cried all kinds of tears.

But as much as I dream about it, I don't have any clue about what it meant for my father to be the only Indian who saw Jimi Hendrix play at Woodstock. And maybe he wasn't the only Indian there. Most likely there were hundreds but my father thought he was the only one. He told me that a million times when he was drunk and a couple hundred times when he was sober.

"I was there," he said. "You got to remember this was near the end and there weren't as many people as before. Not nearly as many. But I waited it out. I waited for Jimi."

A few years back, my father packed up the family and the three of us drove to Seattle to visit Jimi Hendrix's grave. We had our photograph taken lying down next to the grave. There isn't a gravestone there. Just one of those flat markers.

Jimi was twenty-eight when he died. That's younger than Jesus Christ when he died. Younger than my father as we stood over the grave.

"Only the good die young," my father said.

"No," my mother said. "Only the crazy people choke to death on their own vomit."

"Why you talking about my hero that way?" my father asked.

"Shit," my mother said. "Old Jesse WildShoe choked to death on his own vomit and he ain't nobody's hero."

I stood back and watched my parents argue. I was used to these battles. When an Indian marriage starts to fall apart, it's even more destructive and painful than usual. A hundred years ago, an Indian marriage was broken easily. The woman or man just packed up all their possessions and left the tipi. There were no arguments, no discussions. Now, Indians fight their way to the end, holding onto the last good thing, because our whole lives have to do with survival.

After a while, after too much fighting and too many angry words had been exchanged, my father went out and bought a motorcycle. A big bike. He left the house often to ride that thing for hours, sometimes for days. He even strapped an old cassette player to the gas tank so he could listen to music. With that bike, he learned something new about running away. He stopped talking as much, stopped drinking as much. He didn't do much of anything except ride that bike and listen to music.

Then one night my father wrecked his bike on Devil's Gap Road and ended up in the hospital for two months. He broke both his legs, cracked his ribs, and punctured a lung. He also lacerated his kidney. The doctors said he could have died easily. In fact, they were surprised he made it through surgery, let alone survived those first few hours when he lay on the road, bleeding. But I wasn't surprised. That's how my father was.

And even though my mother didn't want to be married to him anymore and his wreck didn't change her mind about that, she still came to see him every day. She sang Indian tunes under her breath, in time with the hum of the machines hooked into my father. Although my father could barely move, he tapped his finger in rhythm.

When he had the strength to finally sit up and talk, hold conversations, and tell stories, he called for me.

"Victor," he said. "Stick with four wheels."

After he began to recover, my mother stopped visiting as often. She helped him through the worst, though. When he didn't need her anymore, she went back to the life she had created. She traveled to powwows, started to dance again. She was a champion traditional dancer when she was younger.

"I remember your mother when she was the best traditional dancer in the world," my father said. "Everyone wanted to call her sweetheart. But she only danced for me. That's how it was. She told me that every other step was just for me."

"But that's only half of the dance," I said.

"Yeah," my father said. "She was keeping the rest for herself. Nobody can give everything away. It ain't healthy."

"You know," I said, "sometimes you sound like you ain't even real."

"What's real? I ain't interested in what's real. I'm interested in how things should be."

My father's mind always worked that way. If you don't like the things you remember, then all you have to do is change the memories. Instead of remembering the bad things, remember what happened immediately before. That's what I learned from my father. For me, I remember how good the first drink of that Diet Pepsi tasted instead of how my mouth felt when I swallowed a wasp with the second drink.

Because of all that, my father always remembered the second before my mother left him for good and took me with her. No. I remembered the second before my father left my mother and me. No. My mother remembered the second before my father left her to finish raising me all by herself.

But however memory actually worked, it was my father who climbed on his motorcycle, waved to me as I stood in the window, and rode away. He lived in Seattle, San Francisco, Los Angeles, before he finally ended up in Phoenix. For a while, I got postcards nearly every week. Then it was once a month. Then it was on Christmas and my birthday.

On a reservation, Indian men who abandon their children are treated worse than white fathers who do the same thing. It's because white men have been doing that forever and Indian men have just learned how. That's how assimilation can work.

My mother did her best to explain it all to me, although I understood most of what happened.

"Was it because of Jimi Hendrix?" I asked her.

"Part of it, yeah," she said. "This might be the only marriage broken up by a dead guitar player."

"There's a first time for everything, enit?"

"I guess. Your father just likes being alone more than he likes being with other people. Even me and you."

Sometimes I caught my mother digging through old photo albums or staring at the wall or out the window. She'd get that look on her face that I knew meant she missed my father. Not enough to want him back. She missed him just enough for it to hurt.

On those nights I missed him most I listened to music. Not always Jimi Hendrix. Usually I listened to the blues. Robert Johnson mostly. The first time I heard Robert Johnson sing I knew he understood what it meant to be Indian on the edge of the twenty-first century, even if he was black at the beginning of the twentieth. That must have been how my father felt when he heard Jimi Hendrix. When he stood there in the rain at Woodstock.

Then on the night I missed my father most, when I lay in bed and cried, with that photograph of him beating that National Guard private in my hands, I imagined his motorcycle pulling up outside. I knew I was dreaming it all but I let it be real for a moment.

"Victor," my father yelled. "Let's go for a ride."

"I'll be right down. I need to get my coat on."

I rushed around the house, pulled my shoes and socks on, struggled into my coat, and ran outside to find an empty driveway. It was so quiet, a reservation kind of quiet, where you can hear somebody drinking whiskey on the rocks three miles away. I stood on the porch and waited until my mother came outside.

"Come on back inside," she said. "It's cold."

"No," I said. "I know he's coming back tonight."

My mother didn't say anything. She just wrapped me in her favorite quilt and went back to sleep. I stood on the porch all night long and imagined I heard motorcycles and guitars, until the sun rose so bright that I knew it was time to go back inside to my mother. She made breakfast for both of us and we ate until we were full.

1993

Rolando Hinojosa-Smith b. 1929

Rolando Hinojosa-Smith, son of a Mexican American father and an Anglo-American mother, is a product of the Mexican-U.S. border's cultural synthesis. He grew up in the southern Rio Grande valley of Texas, where Spanish and English still compete for dominance. His paternal family roots in Texas go back to the 1740s, predating the U.S. annexation by a century. Justifiably, there is no sense of immigration in him, but rather one of legitimate ownership and belonging. After serving in the Korean conflict and then completing a doctorate in Spanish literature, he held several teaching assignments, including Chairman of Chicano Studies at Minnesota. In the early 1980s he switched academic departments to become a professor of English and Creative Writing at the University of Texas at Austin.

Hinojosa's books form a multi-volumed story that, through the life of two cousins, relates the history of a fictional South Texas county of Belkin. His main preoccupation is the survival of what he calls Texas-Mexican Border Culture despite constant repression by the economically dominant Anglo-Texans in league with some traitorous Mexican Americans. History itself becomes a battleground for conflicting versions of the past, and the Tex-Mex communal oral tradition is revealed as more reliable than the official written texts, the latter being controlled by the Anglo-American colonizers, who manipulate historical records, as they do the legal and academic systems, to assure a favorable status quo. His work resembles a vast detective novel, with social protest overtones, in which the neglected truth of Texas history is sought through the fragmented memories of numerous witnesses. The villains and criminals are the invaders and their stooges, the Texas Rangers. The original Mexican inhabitants are the plaintiffs; and the narrator, who constantly cedes the word to others, is like an investigative reporter gathering evidence to slowly piece together into an indictment of oppression.

Concern for the oral tradition explains both Hinojosa's conversational tone and the constant intercalations of documents, testimony, and transcriptions of oral memoirs. Writing must remain faithful to the people it reflects and to their traditional form of expression, the spoken word. His texts engage the dominant culture's repressive writing, juxtaposing it to oral versions. Hence, the framing newspaper notes that not only persist in repeating what the oral evidence disproves, but reveal, through the errata, the written media's callous indifference to Chicanos. This conflict between the written and the oral, as well as the need to make writing embody suppressed traditions, is a key to understanding not only Chicano writing, but that of many marginal groups as they begin to produce a literature.

Juan Bruce-Novoa
University of California at Irvine

PRIMARY WORKS

Estampas del Valle y otras obras/Sketches of the Valley and Other Works, 1973; *Klail City y sus alrededores,* 1976; *Generaciones y semblanzas,* 1977; *Korean Love Songs,* 1978; *Mi querido Rafa,* 1981; *Rites and Witnesses,* 1982; *Partners in Crime,* 1985; *Claros varones de Belkin,* 1986; *Becky and Her Friends,* 1990.

Sometimes It Just Happens That Way; That's All

Excerpt from the *Klail City Enterprise-News* (March 15, 1970)

Klail City. (Special) Baldemar Cordero, 30, of 169 South Hidalgo Street, is in the city jail following a row in a bar in the city's Southside. Cordero is alleged to have fatally stabbed Arnesto Tamez, also 30, over the affections of one of the "hostesses" who works there.

No bail had been set at press time.

One of Those Things

This cassette recording of Balde Cordero's statements has been reproduced faithfully using conventional spelling where necessary. What matters here is the content, not the form. March 16, 1970, Klail City Workhouse.

What can I tell you? The truth's the truth, and there's no dodging it, is there? It's a natural fact: I killed Ernesto Tamez, and I did it right there at the *Aquí me quedo.*[1] And how can I deny it? But don't come asking me for no details; not just yet, anyway, 'cause I'm not all that sure just how it did happen—and that's God's truth, and no one else's, as we say. That's right; Neto Tamez is gone and like the Bible says: I can see, and I can hear.

But that's the way it goes, I guess. He's laid out there somewhere, and just yesterday late afternoon it was that me and my brother-in-law, Beto Castañeda, he married my sister Marta, you know . . . well, there we were, the two of us drinking, laughing, cuttin' up, and just having ourselves a time, when up pops Ernesto Tamez just like Old Nick himself: swearing and cursing like always, and I got the first blast, but I let it go like I usually . . . like I always do . . . Oh, well . . . Anyway, he kept it up, but it didn't bother me none; and that's the truth, too.

You knew Tamez, didn't you? What am I saying? Of course, you did. Remember that time at Félix Champión's place? Someone came up and broke a bottle of beer, full, too; broke it right backside Ernesto's head, someone did. Ol' Ernesto'd broken a mirror, remember? He'd taken this beer bottle and just let go at that mirror, he did. Well'p, I sure haven't forgotten, and I always kept my eyes open; no telling what he'd do next. I wouldn't step aside, of course, but I wouldn't turn my attention away from him, see?

[1]Here I'll stay.

Well, it was like I said: there we were, Beto and me, we'd hoist a few until we'd run out of cash, or we'd get beer bent, but that was it: none o' that cadging free drinks for us; when we got the money, we drink. When we don't, we don't, and that's it.

Now, I've known Tamez—the whole family, in fact—since primary school and when they lived out in Rebaje; there was Joaquín—he's the oldest, and he wound up marrying or had to anyway, Jovita de Anda. You know her? Now, before she married Joaquín, Jovita was about as hard to catch as a cold in the month of February. She straightened out, though; and fast, too. Then there's Emilio; he's the second in line; he got that permanent limp o' his after he slipped and then fell off a refrigerator car that was standing off the old Mo-Pac line over by that pre-cooler run by Chico Fernández. The last one's Bertita; she's the only girl in the family, and she married one of those hard workin' Leal boys. Took her out of Klail City faster 'n anything you ever saw: he set himself up out in West Texas—Muleshoe, I think it was—and being the worker he was, why, he turned many a shiny penny: Good for him is what I say: he earned it. Bertita's no bargain, I'll say that, but she wasn't a bad woman, either. Ernesto was something, though; from the beginning. I'll tell you this much: I put up with a lot—and took a lot, too. For years. But sometimes something happens, you know. And when it does, well . . .

There's no room for lying, Hinojosa; you've known me, and you've known my folks for a long time . . . Well, as I was saying, Beto and I started drinking at the *San Diego,* from there we showed up at the *Diamond*—the *old Diamond* over on Third—stayed there a while, and we were still on our feet, so we made for the *Blue Bar* after that. We would've stayed there, too, 'cept for the Reyna brothers who showed up. There's usually trouble for somebody when they're around, and that's no secret, no, sir. What they do is they'll drink a beer or two, at the most, but that's about it, 'cause they only drink to cover up the grass they've been popping . . . But you know that already . . . Cops that don't know 'em come up, smell the brew, and they figure the Reynas are drunk, not high. But everybody else knows; don Manuel, for one, he knows. Anyway, as soon as the Reynas showed up at the *Blue Bar,* Beto and I moved on; that's the way to avoid trouble; get out of there, 'cause trouble'll cross your way, and fast. As for Anselmo Reyna, well, I guess he learned his when I looked him down at the *Diamond* that one time; he learned his, all right. But there they were at the *Blue Bar,* higher'n a cat's back, so we got out o' there, and then went on over to the *Aquí me quedo.*

That's really something, isn't it? I mean, if the Reynas hadn't-a showed up at the *Blue Bar,* why, nothing would've happened later on, right? But that's not right either, is it? 'Cause when something's bound to happen, it'll happen; and right on schedule, too. Shoot! That was going to be Ernesto's last night in the Valley, and I was chosen to see to it: just like that. One. Two. Three. No two ways is there? . . . Although . . . well, I mean, it boils down to this: I killed a human being. Who'd-a thought it?

It's funny, Hinojosa . . . I kind of remember the why but not the when of it all. I mean, I've been sworn at, cussed at, but I always let that kind of stuff go by, know what I mean? But then, too . . . to actually have someone come-right-up-to-you like this here, come right up to you, see, point blank kind-a, and, and, ah, added to which I'd been drinking some and Ernesto there had been breaking 'em for me for a long time, and me, remembering a lot o' past crap he'd dumped on me, and him being a coward and all, yeah, he was, always counting on his brothers for everything, so . . . there it was—we went after it. Finally. After all these years.

Later on it I think it was that Beto told me about the blood and about how it just jumped out and got on my arms, and shirt, 'n face, and all over . . . Beto also said I didn't blink an eye or anything; I just stood there, he said. All I remember now is that I didn't hear a word; nothing. Not the women, or the screaming . . . Nothing; not even the guys who came a-running. Nothing. I could see 'em, though, but that's all.

Sometime later, I don't know when or for how long, but sometime later, I walked on out to the street and stood on the curb there, and noticed a family in a house across the way just sitting down and watching TV; they looked peaceful there, y'-know what I mean? Innocent-like. Why, they had no idea . . . of what had . . . and here I was, why, I'd been just as innocent a few minutes before . . . You, ah, you understand what I'm saying? . . . I'll say this, though, that talk about life and death is something serious. I mean, it's . . . it's . . . Shoot, I don't even know *what* I'm tryin' to say here . . .

Did I ever tell you that Ernesto—and this was in front of a lot o' people, now—did I ever tell you he cut in every chance he got? Just like that. He'd cut in on a girl I was dancing with, or just take her away from me. All the time. Over at *El Farol* and the other places . . . Well, he did. One other time, he told a dance girl that I had come down with a dose of the clap. Can you beat that? He was always up to something—and then something happened, and I killed him. Justlikethat. Not because of that one thing, no. Jesus! It just happens, that's all. One o'those things, I guess . . . Maybe I shouldn't've waited so long; maybe I should've cut his water off sooner, and then perhaps this wouldn't've happened . . . Ahhhh, who'm I kidding? What's done's done, and that's it.

Well, last night just tore it for me, though; he swore right at me—no mistake there—and he laughed at me, too. And then, like talking into a microphone, he said I didn't have the balls to stand up to him. Right there, in front of everybody again. Now, I had put up with a lot of crap, and I have. From friends, too, 'cause I can then swear or say some things myself, but it's all part of the game—but not with him. Ever. I didn't say a word. Not one; I sure didn't. I just looked at him, but I didn't move or do or say anything; I'm telling you I just stood there. Damfool probably thought I was afraid of him. Well, that was his mistake, and now mine, too, I guess. He kept it up—wouldn't stop, not for a minute. Then, to top it off, he brings one of the dance girls over and says to her, to me, to everybody there, that he'd looked me down a hundred times or more; looked me down, and that I had taken it—'cause I was scared. Chicken, he said. The dance girl, she didn't know what to say, what to do; she was half-scared, and embarrassed, too, I'll warrant . . . But she just stood there as he held on to her . . . by the wrist . . . I think the music stopped or something. I remember, or I think I do, anyway, that there was a buzz or a buzzer going off somewhere, like I was wearing a beehive instead of that hat of mine. Does that make sense? I heard that buzzing, see, and the hissing, raspy voice of that damfool, and then I saw that fixed, idiotic smile o' that dance girl, and then—suddenly, yeah—in a rush, see; suddenly a scream, a yell, a, a shriek-like, and I saw Ernesto sliding, slippin' sort-a, in a heap . . . and falling away . . . falling, eh?

Now, I do recall I took a deep breath, and the buzzing sort-a-stopped and I remember walking outside, to the sidewalk, and then I spotted that family I told you about, the one watching TV. And standing there, I looked at my left hand: I was carrying that pearl-handled knife that Pa Albino had given me when I was up in Michigan.

I went back inside the place, 'n then I went out again. I didn't even think of running away. What for? And where? Everybody knew me. Shoot. The second time I walked back in, I noticed that the cement floor had been hosed down, scrubbed clean. Not a trace-a blood either, not on the floor, or anywhere. They'd taken Ernesto out back, where they keep the warm beer and the snacks, next to the toilet there. When don Manuel came in, I gave him the knife, and then I went to the sidewalk, to the side of the place . . . I got sick, and then I couldn't stop coughing. I finally got in don Manuel's car, 'n I waited for him. When he got through in there, he brought me here . . . straight to jail . . . That old man probably went home to see my Ma, right? Well . . .

Anyway, early this morning, one of his kids brought me some coffee, and he waited until I finished the pot. You know . . . I've tried to fix, to set down in my mind, when it was that I buried my knife in that damfool. But I just can't remember . . . I just can't, you know . . . And try as I may, too. It could be I just don't *want* to remember, right?

Anyway, Beto was here just before you came in . . . He's on his way to the District Attorney's office to give a deposition, he says. I'll tell you how I feel right now: I feel bad. I can't say how I'll feel later on, but for now, I do, I feel really bad, you know. That stuff about no use crying over spilled milk and all that, that's just talk, and nothing more. I feel terrible. I killed a . . . and when I think about it, real slow, I feel bad . . . Real bad . . .

I was wrong—dead wrong, I know; but if Ernesto was to insult me again, I'd probably go after him again. The truth is . . . The truth is one never learns.

Look, I'm not trying to tire you out on this—I keep saying the same thing over and over, but that's all I can talk about. But thanks for coming over. And thanks for the cigarettes, okay? Look, maybe—just maybe, now—maybe one of these days I'll know why I killed him—but he was due and bound to get it someday, wasn't he? All I did was to hurry it up a bit . . . You see? There I go again . . .

Oh, and before I forget, will you tell Mr. Royce that I won't be in tomorrow . . . and remind him I got one week's pay coming to me. Will you see to that?

I'll see you, Hinojosa . . . and thanks, okay?

Marta, and What She Knows

Cassette dated March 17, 1970.

. . . what happened was that when Pa Albino died up in Michigan as a result of that accident at the pickle plant, Balde decided we'd all spend the winter there in Michigan till we heard about the settlement one way or 'nother. Right off, then, that contractor who brought us up from the Valley, he tried to skin us there and then and so Balde had to threaten him so he'd do right by us. So, with what little we got out of him, Balde hired us a lawyer to sue Turner Pickle Company. He was a young one that lawyer, but a good one: he won the case, and that pickle company, well, they had to pay up for damages, as they call them. Now, when that was settled, we paid what we owed there in Saginaw, and with what we had left from that, well, we used it to see us through the winter months there while we looked around for another contractor to bring us back or to live up in Michigan while some work or other turned up. By this time, Beto was calling on me but not in a formal way. You see, we, Ma and I, we were still in mourning on account o' Pa, and . . . well, you know how that is . . .

You've known Balde since he was a kid, and, as Pa used to say: What can I tell you? Ma's been laid up with paralysis for years, but with all that, she's never missed a trip up North. Well, there we were with other mexicano families from Texas, stuck up in Saginaw, Michigan and waiting for winter to set in and looking for work. Any type of work; whatever it was, it didn't matter. Balde was the first one to land a job: he got himself hired on as a night man at the bay port there. Not too much after that, he put in a good word for Beto, and that way they worked together. Later on, but you know this, Beto and I got married. At that time, Balde must've been twenty-seven years old, and he could have had his pick of any Valley girl there or anywhere else, but because of Ma's condition, and the lack-a money, 'n first one thing and then 'nother, well, you know how that goes sometimes. So, we've been back in the Valley for some two years now, and I guess Balde stopped looking. But you know him; he's a good man; he was raised solid, and no one begrudges the beer or two or whatever many he has on Saturdays: he won't fight, and that's it. He won't say why he won't fight, but I, Ma 'n me, we know why: we'd be hurting, that's why. I'll tell you this, too: he's put up with a lot. A lot . . . but that's because he's always thinking o' Ma and me, see?

Once, and just the once, and by chance, too, I did hear that Balde laid it to one of the Reyna brothers, and no holds barred from what I heard . . . but this wasn't ever brought up here at the house.

You know, it's really hard to say what I felt or even *how* I felt when I first heard about what had happened to Neto Tamez. At first I couldn't . . . I couldn't bring myself to believe it, to picture it . . . I . . . I just couldn't imagine that my brother Balde . . . that he would kill someone. I'm not saying this 'cause he's a saint or something like that, no, not a-tall. But I will say this: it must've been something terrible; horrible, even. Something he just couldn't swallow; put up with. It cost him; I mean, Balde had to hold back for a long time, and he held back, for a long time . . . Holding it in all that time just got to him. It must have.

And, too, it could be that Ernesto went too far that time; too far. Beto had told me, or tried to, in his way, he tried to tell me about some of the stuff Neto Tamez was doing, or saying, and all of it against Balde; trouble is that Beto's not much of a talker, and he keeps everything inside, too, just like Balde does . . . As far as me getting any news out o' Balde, well . . . all he ever brought home was a smile on his face. I'll say this, though, once in a while he'd be as serious and as quiet as anything you'd ever want to see; I wasn't about to ask him anything, no sir, I wasn't about to do that. At any rate, what with tending to Ma here, caring for both of the men of the house, and you add the wash and the cooking, and the sewing, and what not, hooh! I've got enough to do here without worrying about gossip.

I'm not pretending to be an angel here either, but what I do know is all secondhand. What I picked up from Beto or from some of my women friends who'd call, or from what I could pick up here and there from Balde. I'm telling you what I could piece out or what I would come up with by adding two and two together, but I don't really know; like I told you, I don't have that much to go on.

Now, the whole world and its first cousin know that Neto Tamez was always picking and backbiting and just making life miserable for him . . . Well, everybody else knows how Balde put up with it, too. I'll say again that if Balde didn't put a muzzle on him right away, it was because Balde was thinking-a Ma 'n me. And that's the truth. What people don't know is why Neto did what he did against my brother.

Listen to this: back when we were in junior high, Neto Tamez would send me love notes; yes, back then. And he'd follow me home, too. To top this, he'd bully some kids to act as his messenger boys. Yes, he would. Now, I'd never paid attention to him, mind you, and I never gave him any ground to do so, either. The girls'd tell me that Neto wouldn't even let other boys come near me 'n he acted as if he owned me or something like that. This happened a long time ago, a-course, and I'd never breathe a word of it to Balde; but! the very first time I learned that Neto Tamez was giving my brother a hard time, I knew or thought I knew why he was doing it. I don't really know if Balde knew or not, though, but like Beto says: anything's possible.

Some girlfriends of mine once told me that at *La Golondrina* and *El farolito,* you know, those kind-a places . . . Anyway, the girls said that Neto insulted Balde right in front of everybody; a lotta times, too. You know, he'd cut in or just up and walk away with whatever girl Balde had at the time . . . or Neto'd say something nasty, anything, anything to make Balde's life a complete misery. On and on, see? Now, I'm not saying Neto Tamez would actually follow him from place to place, no, I'm not saying that at all; but what I *am* saying is that Neto'd never lose the opportunity . . . I mean the opportunity to push 'n shove, embarrass him until Balde would just have to get up and leave the place, see? You've got to keep in mind that living in the same town, in the same neighborhood, almost, and then to have to put up with all sorts of garbage, why, that's enough to tempt and drive a saint to madness. I swear it would, and Balde's no saint. So many's the time Balde'd come home, not say a word, and drinking or not, he'd come in, kiss Ma as he always did, and he'd sit and talk a while and then go out to the porch and have himself a smoke. Why, compared to Balde, my Beto's a walking-talking chatterbox . . .

The Tamezes are a peculiar bunch of people, you know. When they used to live out in Rebaje, it looked as if they were forever into something with someone, the neighbors, anybody. I remember the time Joaquín had to get married to Jovita de Anda; don Servando Tamez barred all the doors to the house, and then he wouldn't let the de Andas in; they couldn't even attend the wedding, and that was *it.* They say that old Mister de Anda . . . don Marcial . . . the little candyman? Well, they say he cried and just like a baby 'cause he wouldn't get to see his only daughter get married. I remember, too, that Emilio, one leg shorter 'n the other by that time, was marching up and down in front of their house like he was a soldier or something . . .

It was a good thing that poor doña Tula Tamez had passed away and was buried up in Bascom by that time, 'cause she'd-a been mortified with the goings on in that house . . . I swear. About the only thing to come out-a that house was Bertita, and oh! did she have a case on Balde. For years, too. She finally married Ramiro Leal; you know him, do you? His folks own the tortilla machine . . .

Well, anyway, yesterday, just about the time you went to see Balde at the jailhouse, don Manuel Guzmán showed up here. He said he'd come just to say hello to Ma, but that was just an excuse: what he really said was for us not to worry about the law and the house. Isn't that something? Why, I've seen that man dole out kicks, head buttings, and a haymaker or two to every troublemaker here in Klail, and then, bright 'n early, one of his kids'll bring coffee to whoever it is that winds up in jail that weekend. I'll say this, too, though: the streets in Klail have never been safer, and I know that for a fact. Anyway, just as he was about to leave, don Manuel told me that Ma 'n me that we could draw our groceries from the Torres' grocery store down the way. Don Manuel and Pa Albino go back a long time, you know; from the Revolution, I think.

Things are going to get tight around here without Balde, but Ma 'n me we still have Beto here, and . . . My only hope is that the Tamezes don't come looking for Beto 'cause that'll really put us under without a man in the house. Beto's at the Court House just now; he had to go and make a statement, they said.

Oh, Mr. Hinojosa, I just don't know where all of this is going to take us . . . But God'll provide . . . He's got to.

ROMEO HINOJOSA

Attorney at Law

420 South Cerralvo Tel. 843-1640

The following is a deposition, in English, made by Beto Castañeda, today, March 17, 1970, in the office of Mr. Robert A. Chapman, Assistant District Attorney for Belken County.

The aforementioned officer of the court gave me a copy of the statement as part of the testimony in the trial of *The State of Texas v. Cordero* set for August 23 of this year in the court of Judge Harrison Phelps who presides in the 139th District Court.

Romeo Hinojosa

Romeo Hinojosa

March 17, 1970

A Deposition Freely Given

on this seventeenth day of March, 1970, by Mr. Gilberto Castañeda in room 218 of the Belken County Court House was duly taken, witnessed, and signed by Miss Helen Chacón, a legal interpreter and acting assistant deputy recorder for said County, as part of a criminal investigation assigned to Robert A. Chapman, assistant district attorney for the same County.

It is understood that Mr. Castañeda is acting solely as a deponent and is not a party to any civil or criminal investigation, proceeding, or violation which may be alluded to in this deposition.

"Well, my name is Gilberto Castañeda, and I live at 169 South Hidalgo Street here in Klail. It is not my house; it belong to my mother-in-law, but I have live there since I marry Marta (Marta Cordero Castañeda, 169 South Hidalgo Street, Klail City) about three years ago.

"I am working at the Royce-Fedders tomato packing shed as a grader. My brother-in-law, Balde Cordero, work there too. He pack tomatoes and don't get pay for the hour, he get pay for what he pack and since I am a grader I make sure he get the same class tomato and that way he pack faster; he just get a tomato with the right hand, and he wrap it with the left. He pack a lug of tomatoes so fast you don't see it, and he does it fast because I am a good grader.

"Balde is a good man. His father, don Albino, my father-in-law who die up in Saginaw, Michigan when Marta and I, you know, go together . . . well, Balde is like don Albino, you understand? A good man. A right man. Me, I stay an orphan and when the Mejías take me when my father and my mother die in that train wreck—near Flora? don Albino tell the Mejías I must go to the school. I go to First Ward Elementary where Mr. Gold is principal. In First Ward I am a friend of Balde and there I meet Marta too. Later, when I grow up I don't visit the house too much because of Marta, you know what I mean? Anyway, Balde is my friend and I have know him very well . . . maybe more than nobody else. He's a good man.

"Well, last night Balde and I took a few beers in some of the places near where we live. We drink a couple here and a couple there, you know, and we save the *Aquí me quendo* on South Missouri for last. It is there that I tell Balde a joke about the drunk guy who is going to his house and he hear the clock in the corner make two sounds. You know that one? Well, this drunk guy he hear the clock go bong-bong and he say that the clock is wrong for it give one o'clock two time. Well, Balde think that is funny . . . Anyway, when I tell the joke in Spanish it's better. Well, there we were drinking a beer when Ernesto Tamez comes. Ernesto Tamez is like a woman, you know? Everytime he get in trouble he call his family to help him . . . that is the way it is with him. Well, that night he bother Balde again. More than one time Balde has stop me when Tamez begin to insult. That Balde is a man of patience. This time Ernesto bring a *vieja* (woman) and Balde don't say nothing, nothing, nothing. What happens is that things get spooky, you know. Ernesto talking and *burlándose de él* (ridiculing him) and at the same time he have the poor woman by the arm. And then something happen. I don't know what happen, but something and fast.

"I don't know. I really don't know. It all happen so fast; the knife, the blood squirt all over my face and arms, the woman try to get away, a loud really loud scream, not a *grito* (local Mexican yell) but more a woman screaming, you know what I mean? and then Ernesto fall on the cement.

"Right there I look at Balde and his face is like a mask in asleep, you understand? No angry, no surprise, nothing. In his left hand he have the knife and he shake his head before he walk to the door. Look, it happen so fast no one move for a while. Then Balde come in and go out of the place and when don Manuel (Manuel Guzmán, constable for precinct 21) come in, Balde just hand over the knife. Lucas Barrón, you know, El Chorreao (a nickname) well, he wash the blood and sweep the floor before don Manuel get there. Don Manuel just shake his head and tell Balde to go to the car and wait. Don Manuel he walk to the back to see Ernesto and on the way out one of the women, I think it is *la güera Balín* (Amelia Cortez, 23, no known address, this city), try to make a joke, but don Manuel he say *no estés chingando* (shut the hell up, or words to that effect) and after that don Manuel go about his own business. Me, I go to the door but all I see is Balde looking at a house across the street and he don't even know I come to say goodbye. Anyway, this morning a little boy of don Manuel say for me to come here and here I am."

Further deponent sayeth not.
Sworn to before me, this
17th day of March, 1970

/s/ /s/

Helen Chacón
Acting Asst. Deputy Recorder
Belken County

Gilberto Castañeda

1983

Excerpt from the *Klail City Enterprise-News* (August 24, 1970)

Klail City. (Special). Baldemar Cordero, 30, of 169 South Hidalgo Street, drew a 15 year sentence to the Huntsville State Prison in Judge Harrison Phelps' 139th District Court for the murder of Ernesto Tamez last Spring. PICK UP.

Cordero is alleged to have fatally stabbed Ernesto Tanez, also 30, over the affections of one of the "hostesses" who works there. PICK UP.

No appeal had been made at press time.

Audre Lorde 1934–1992

Audre Lorde, a black, lesbian, feminist, warrior poet, was the youngest of three daughters born to Linda and Frederic Byron Lorde, who immigrated to New York City from Granada, the West Indies. Lorde's parents came to the United States with two plans. First they hoped to reap the financial rewards of hard work, and then they planned to return to their island home in grand style. But with the stockmarket crash of 1929, they were forced to abandon both dreams.

As a child, Lorde was inarticulate; in fact, she didn't speak until she was five years old. Even when she began talking, she spoke in poetry; that is, she would recite a poem in order to express herself. Hence, poetry literally became her language of communication, and she believed that "the sensual content of life was masked and cryptic, but attended in well-coded phrases." She also learned to see herself as "a reflection of [her] mother's secret poetry as well as of her hidden anger." Giving expression to this reflection has been the impetus for much of her work.

Lorde attended Hunter High School and received the B.A. in 1959 from Hunter College and the M.L.S. in 1961 from Columbia University. In 1962 she married Edwin Ashley Rollins and gave birth to two children: Elizabeth and Jonathan. The marriage ended in divorce. In 1968 Lorde decided to become a full-time poet, leaving her job as head librarian of the City University of New York to become a poet-in-residence at Tougaloo College in Mississippi. Before her death, Lorde was Poet and Professor of English at Hunter College of the City University of New York.

Lorde insisted that she wrote to fulfill her responsibility "to speak the truth as [she felt] it, and to attempt to speak it with as much precision and beauty as possible." She described her life's work in terms of survival and teaching, two themes that dominate her prose and verse. Her power and high productivity arose from her living out these ambitions by confronting her own mortality, her own fear and the opposition of those who tried to silence her.

All of her work resonates with courage, in which she advises us "Not to be afraid of difference. To be real, tough, loving." "Even if you are afraid," she adds, "do it anyway because we learn to work when we are tired, so we can learn to work when we are afraid." In Lorde's later works her vision arises from celebrating the legends of strong black women, especially her mother. In *Zami: A New Spelling of My Name* she combines autobiography, history, and myth to create a new literary form that she calls, "biomythography." *Zami* and *Our Dead Behind Us,* especially, signify the "strong triad of grandmother mother daughter," and "recreate in words the women who helped give [her] substance." They are her "mattering core"; they invigorate Lorde's visions of life and art with power.

Claudia Tate
George Washington University

PRIMARY WORKS

The First Cities, 1970; *Cables to Rage,* 1973; *From a Land Where Other People Live,* 1973 (nominated for the National Book Award in 1974); *New York Head Shop and Museum,* 1974; *Coal,* 1976; *Between Ourselves,* 1976; *The Black Unicorn,* 1978; *The Erotic as Power,* 1978; *The Cancer Journals,* 1980 (received a 1981 Book Award from the American Library Association Gay Caucus); *Zami: A New Spelling of My Name,* 1982; *Chosen Poems: Old and New,* 1982; *Sister Outsider,* 1984; *Our Dead Behind Us,* 1986; *Apartheid USA,* 1986; *I Am Your Sister,* 1986; *A Burst of Light: Essays,* 1992; *Undersong: Chosen Poems, Old and New,* 1992.

Power

The difference between poetry and rhetoric
is being
ready to kill
yourself
instead of your children.

I am trapped on a desert of raw gunshot wounds
and a dead child dragging his shattered black
face off the edge of my sleep
blood from his punctured cheeks and shoulders
is the only liquid for miles and my stomach
churns at the imagined taste while

my mouth splits into dry lips
without loyalty or reason
thirsting for the wetness of his blood
as it sinks into the whiteness
of the desert where I am lost
without imagery or magic
trying to make power out of hatred and destruction
trying to heal my dying son with kisses
only the sun will bleach his bones quicker.

The policeman who shot down a 10-year-old in Queens
stood over the boy with his cop shoes in childish blood
and a voice said "Die you little motherfucker" and
there are tapes to prove that. At his trial
this policeman said in his own defense
"I didn't notice the size or nothing else
only the color," and
there are tapes to prove that, too.

Today that 37-year-old white man with 13 years of police forcing
has been set free
by 11 white men who said they were satisfied
justice had been done
and one black woman who said
"They convinced me" meaning
they had dragged her 4′10″ black woman's frame
over the hot coals of four centuries of white male approval
until she let go the first real power she ever had
and lined her own womb with cement
to make a graveyard for our children.

I have not been able to touch the destruction within me.
But unless I learn to use
the difference between poetry and rhetoric
my power too will run corrupt as poisonous mold
or lie limp and useless as an unconnected wire
and one day I will take my teenaged plug
and connect it to the nearest socket
raping an 85-year-old white woman
who is somebody's mother
and as I beat her senseless and set a torch to her bed
a greek chorus will be singing in 3/4 time
"Poor thing. She never hurt a soul. What beasts they are."

1978

Walking Our Boundaries

This first bright day has broken
the back of winter.
We rise from war
to walk across the earth
around our house
both stunned that sun can shine so brightly
after all our pain
Cautiously we inspect our joint holding.
A part of last year's garden still stands
bracken
one tough missed okra pod clings to the vine
a parody of fruit cold-hard and swollen
underfoot
one rotting shingle
is becoming loam.

I take your hand beside the compost heap
glad to be alive and still
with you
we talk of ordinary articles
with relief
while we peer upward
each half-afraid
there will be no tight buds started
on our ancient apple tree
so badly damaged by last winter's storm
knowing
it does not pay to cherish symbols
when the substance
lies so close at hand
waiting to be held
your hand
falls off the apple bark
like casual fire
along my back
my shoulders are dead leaves
waiting to be burned
to life.

The sun is watery warm
our voices
seem too loud for this small yard
too tentative for women
so in love

the siding has come loose in spots
our footsteps hold this place
together
as our place
our joint decisions make the possible
whole.
I do not know when
we shall laugh again
but next week
we will spade up another plot
for this spring's seeding.

1978

Never Take Fire from a Woman

My sister and I
have been raised to hate
genteelly
each other's silences
sear up our tongues
like flame
we greet each other
with respect
meaning
from a watchful distance
while we dream of lying
in the tender of passion
to drink from a woman
who smells like love.

1978

The Art of Response

The first answer was incorrect
the second was
sorry the third trimmed its toenails

on the Vatican steps
the fourth went mad
the fifth
nursed a grudge until it bore twins
that drank poisoned grape juice in Jonestown
the sixth   wrote a book about it
the seventh
argued a case before the Supreme Court
against taxation on Girl Scout Cookies
the eighth held a news conference
while four Black babies
and one other   picketed New York City
for a hospital bed to die in
the ninth and tenth swore
Revenge on the Opposition
and the eleventh dug their graves
next to Eternal Truth
the twelfth
processed funds from a Third World country
that provides doctors for Central Harlem
the thirteenth
refused
the fourteenth sold cocaine and shamrocks
near a toilet in the Big Apple circus
the fifteenth
changed the question.

1986

Stations

Some women love
to wait
for life   for a ring
in the June light   for a touch
of the sun to heal them   for another
woman's voice   to make them whole
to untie their hands
put words in their mouths
form to their passages   sound
to their screams   for some other sleeper
to remember   their future   their past.

Some women wait for their right
train   in the wrong station
in the alleys of morning
for the noon to holler
the night come down.

Some women wait for love
to rise up
the child of their promise
to gather from earth
what they do not plant
to claim pain for labor
to become
the tip of an arrow   to aim
at the heart of now
but it never stays.

Some women wait for visions
that do not return
where they were not welcome
naked
for invitations to places
they always wanted
to visit
to be repeated.

Some women wait for themselves
around the next corner
and call the empty spot peace
but the opposite of living
is only not living
and the stars do not care.

Some women wait for something
to change   and nothing
does change
so they change
themselves.

1986

The Master's Tools Will Never Dismantle the Master's House[1]

I agreed to take part in a New York University Institute for the Humanities conference a year ago, with the understanding that I would be commenting upon papers dealing with the role of difference within the lives of american women: difference of race, sexuality, class, and age. The absence of these considerations weakens any feminist discussion of the personal and the political.

It is a particular academic arrogance to assume any discussion of feminist theory without examining our many differences, and without a significant input from poor women, Black and Third World women, and lesbians. And yet, I stand here as a Black lesbian feminist, having been invited to comment within the only panel at this conference where the input of Black feminists and lesbians is represented. What this says about the vision of this conference is sad, in a country where racism, sexism, and homophobia are inseparable. To read this program is to assume that lesbian and Black women have nothing to say about existentialism, the erotic, women's culture and silence, developing feminist theory, or heterosexuality and power. And what does it mean in personal and political terms when even the two Black women who did present here were literally found at the last hour? What does it mean when the tools of a racist patriarchy are used to examine the fruits of that same patriarchy? It means that only the most narrow perimeters of change are possible and allowable.

The absence of any consideration of lesbian consciousness or the consciousness of Third World women leaves a serious gap within this conference and within the papers presented here. For example, in a paper on material relationships between women, I was conscious of an either/or model of nurturing which totally dismissed my knowledge as a Black lesbian. In this paper there was no examination of mutuality between women, no systems of shared support, no interdependence as exists between lesbians and women-identified women. Yet it is only in the patriarchal model of nurturance that women "who attempt to emancipate themselves pay perhaps too high a price for the results," as this paper states.

For women, the need and desire to nurture each other is not pathological but redemptive, and it is within that knowledge that our real power is rediscovered. It is this real connection which is so feared by a patriarchal world. Only within a patriarchal structure is maternity the only social power open to women.

Interdependency between women is the way to a freedom which allows the *I* to *be,* not in order to be used, but in order to be creative. This is a difference between the passive *be* and the active *being.*

Advocating the mere tolerance of difference between women is the grossest reformism. It is a total denial of the creative function of difference in our lives. Difference must be not merely tolerated, but seen as a fund of necessary polarities between which our creativity can spark like a dialectic. Only then does the necessity for in-

[1]Comments at "The Personal and the Political Panel," Second Sex Conference, New York, September 29, 1979.

terdependency become unthreatening. Only within that interdependency of different strengths, acknowledged and equal, can the power to seek new ways of being in the world generate, as well as the courage and sustenance to act where there are no charters.

Within the interdependence of mutual (nondominant) differences lies that security which enables us to descend into the chaos of knowledge and return with true visions of our future, along with the concomitant power to effect those changes which can bring that future into being. Difference is that raw and powerful connection from which our personal power is forged.

As women, we have been taught either to ignore our differences, or to view them as causes for separation and suspicion rather than as forces for change. Without community there is no liberation, only the most vulnerable and temporary armistice between an individual and her oppression. But community must not mean a shedding of our differences, nor the pathetic pretense that these differences do not exist.

Those of us who stand outside the circle of this society's definition of acceptable women; those of us who have been forged in the crucibles of difference—those of us who are poor, who are lesbians, who are Black, who are older—know that *survival is not an academic skill.* It is learning how to stand alone, unpopular and sometimes reviled, and how to make common cause with those others identified as outside the structures in order to define and seek a world in which we can all flourish. It is learning how to take our differences and make them strengths. *For the master's tools will never dismantle the master's house.* They may allow us temporarily to beat him at his own game, but they will never enable us to bring about genuine change. And this fact is only threatening to those women who still define the master's house as their only source of support.

Poor women and women of Color know there is a difference between the daily manifestations of marital slavery and prostitution because it is our daughters who line 42nd Street. If white american feminist theory need not deal with the differences between us, and the resulting difference in our oppressions, then how do you deal with the fact that the women who clean your houses and tend your children while you attend conferences on feminist theory are, for the most part, poor women and women of Color? What is the theory behind racist feminism?

In a world of possibility for us all, our personal visions help lay the groundwork for political action. The failure of academic feminists to recognize difference as a crucial strength is a failure to reach beyond the first patriarchal lesson. In our world, divide and conquer must become define and empower.

Why weren't other women of Color found to participate in this conference? Why were two phone calls to me considered a consultation? Am I the only possible source of names of Black feminists? And although the Black panelist's paper ends on an important and powerful connection of love between women, what about interracial cooperation between feminists who don't love each other?

In academic feminist circles, the answer to these questions is often, "We did not know who to ask." But that is the same evasion of responsibility, the same cop-out, that keeps Black women's art out of women's exhibitions, Black women's work out of most feminist publications except for the occasional "Special Third World Women's Issue," and Black women's texts off your reading lists. But as Adrienne Rich pointed out in a recent talk, white feminists have educated themselves about such an enormous amount over the past ten years, how come you haven't also educated yourselves about Black women and the differences between us—white and Black—when it is key to our survival as a movement?

Women of today are still being called upon to stretch across the gap of male ignorance and to educate men as to our existence and our needs. This is an old and primary tool of all oppressors to keep the oppressed occupied with the master's concerns. Now we hear that it is the task of women of Color to educate white women—in the face of tremendous resistance—as to our existence, our differences, our relative roles in our joint survival. This is a diversion of energies and a tragic repetition of racist patriarchal thought.

Simone de Beauvoir once said: "It is in the knowledge of the genuine conditions of our lives that we must draw our strength to live and our reasons for acting."

Racism and homophobia are real conditions of all our lives in this place and time. *I urge each one of us here to reach down into that deep place of knowledge inside herself and touch that terror and loathing of any difference that lives there. See whose face it wears.* Then the personal as the political can begin to illuminate all our choices.

1979

John Edgar Wideman b. 1941

John Edgar Wideman was born in Washington, D.C., and grew up in the black Homewood section of Pittsburgh, Pennsylvania. Wideman's parents struggled financially, but managed a decent standard of living for their family. During Wideman's high school years, circumstances allowed the family to move out of Homewood to Shadyside, a more economically prosperous neighborhood; Wideman attended the integrated Peabody High School in Shadyside, starred on the basketball team, became senior class president, and earned the honor of valedictorian.

It was at Peabody High School that Wideman's remarkable intellectual and creative career started to emerge clearly. In these early years, Wideman began to immerse himself in white, Western intellectual influences and traditions, which caused some estrangement from black cultural traditions and psychological separation from black people. After high school, he went on to the University of Pennsylvania to major in English, study the traditional curriculum, and develop his creative writing skills. He also became an All-Ivy-League basketball player. These very impressive credentials earned Wideman a Rhodes Scholarship at his graduation in 1963. Wideman went to Oxford and was one of the first two black Rhodes Scholars to complete the term in over fifty years. After Oxford, Wideman returned to the University of Pennsylvania to become that school's first black tenured professor.

In order to raise their children in a different environment, Wideman and his wife, Judy, moved to Laramie, Wyoming and the University of Wyoming after he taught at the University of Pennsylvania. Wideman's distance from Homewood ironically drew him back to the African American experience. Listening to family stories while visiting Homewood for his grandmother's funeral in 1973, Wideman began to incorporate influences from the black cultural tradition into his writing (his first novel had been published in 1967, when he was twenty-six), and to move psychologically closer to his family and to black people in his personal life. Wideman spent the years between 1973 and 1981, during which he published none of what he wrote, studying African American cultural influences. He read a wide range of books about the black experience, and also studied the culture firsthand, making his family in Homewood his main source. Wideman and his family left Laramie in the late 1980s; he now teaches at the University of Massachusetts at Amherst.

Wideman's first three novels, the third of which appeared in 1973, show strong influences from the mainstream modernist tradition that he studied and knew so thoroughly. These works have black settings and mostly black characters, but Wideman makes the bleak, pessimistic modernist voice dominant over a black cultural voice. These novels often show Wideman as a virtuoso craftsman and writer of great power; however, he did not feel satisfied with what he had done. His writing after 1981, when he refocused his fiction and himself toward blackness, displays very strong postmodernist influences, but postmodernism serves the needs of articulating African American racial concerns and African American cultural tradition, whose voice is dominant. Wideman has published eleven books since 1981. The quality and volume of his work place him in the first rank of contemporary American writers.

James W. Coleman
University of North Carolina–Chapel Hill

PRIMARY WORKS

A Glance Away, 1967; *Hurry Home,* 1970; *The Lynchers,* 1973; *Hiding Place,* 1981; *Damballah,* 1981; *Sent for You Yesterday,* 1983; *Brothers and Keepers,* 1984; *Reuben,* 1987; *Fever,* 1989; *Philadelphia Fire,* 1990; *All Stories Are True,* 1993; *Fatheralong: A Meditation on Fathers and Sons, Race and Society,* 1994; *The Cattle Killing,* 1996; *Two Cities,* 1998.

Valaida[1]

Whither shall I go from thy spirit?
Or whither shall I flee from thy presence?

Bobby tell the man what he wants to hear. Bobby lights a cigarette. Blows smoke and it rises and rises to where I sit on my cloud overhearing everything. Singing to no one. Golden trumpet from the Queen of Denmark across my knees. In my solitude. Dead thirty years now and meeting people still. Primping loose ends of my hair. Worried how I look. How I sound. Silly. Because things don't change. Bobby with your lashes a woman would kill for, all cheekbones, bushy brows and bushy upper lip, ivory when you smile. As you pretend to contemplate his jive questions behind your screen of

[1]Valaida Snow (c. 1900–1956) was a jazz trumpeter, singer, and dancer of considerable talent whose life inspired this story.

smoke and summon me by rolling your big, brown-eyed-handsome-man eyeballs to the ceiling where smoke pauses not one instant, but scoots through and warms me where I am, tell him, Bobby, about "fabled Valaida Snow who traveled in an orchid-colored Mercedes-Benz, dressed in an orchid suit, her pet monkey rigged out in an orchid jacket and cap, with the chauffeur in orchid as well." If you need to, lie like a rug, Bobby. But don't waste the truth, either. They can't take that away from me. Just be cool. As always. Recite those countries and cities we played. Continents we conquered. Roll those faraway places with strange-sounding names around in your sweet mouth. Tell him they loved me at home too, a down-home girl from Chattanooga, Tennessee, who turned out the Apollo, not a mumbling word from wino heaven till they were on their feet hollering and clapping for more with the rest of the audience. Reveries of days gone by, yes, yes, they haunt me, baby, I can taste it. Yesteryears, yesterhours. Bobby, do you also remember what you're not telling him? Blues lick in the middle of a blind flamenco singer's moan. Mother Africa stretching her crusty, dusky hands forth, calling back her far-flung children. Later that same night both of us bad on bad red wine wheeling round and round a dark gypsy cave. Olé. Olé.

Don't try too hard to get it right, he'll never understand. He's watching your cuff links twinkle. Wondering if they're real gold and the studs real diamonds. You called me Minnie Mouse. But you never saw me melted down to sixty-eight pounds soaking wet. They beat me, and fucked me in every hole I had. I was their whore. Their maid. A stool they stood on when they wanted to reach a little higher. But I never sang in their cage, Bobby. Not one note. Cost me a tooth once, but not a note. Tell him that one day I decided I'd had enough and walked away from their hell. Walked across Europe, the Atlantic Ocean, the whole U.S. of A. till I found a quiet spot put peace back in my soul, and then I began performing again. My tunes. In my solitude. And yes. There was a pitiful little stomped-down white boy in the camp I tried to keep the guards from killing, but if he lived or died I never knew. Then or now. Monkey and chauffeur and limo and champagne and cigars and outrageous dresses with rhinestones, fringe and peekaboo slits. That's the foolishness the reporter's after. Stuff him with your MC b.s., and if he's still curious when you're finished, if he seems a halfway decent sort in spite of himself, you might suggest listening to the trumpet solo in My Heart Belongs to Daddy, *hip him to* Hot Snow, *the next to last cut, my voice and Lady Day's figure and ground, ground and figure* Dear Lord above, send back my love.

He heard her in the bathroom, faucets on and off, on and off, spurting into the sink bowl, the tub. Quick burst of shower spray, rain sound spattering plastic curtain. Now in the quiet she'll be polishing. Every fixture will gleam. *Shine's what people see. See something shiny, don't look no further, most people don't.* If she's rushed she'll wipe and polish faucets, mirrors, metal collars around drains. Learned that trick when she first came to the city and worked with gangs of girls in big downtown hotels. *Told me, said, Don't be fussing around behind in there or dusting under them things, child. Give that mirror a lick. Rub them faucets. Twenty more rooms like this one here still to do before noon.* He lowers the newspaper just enough so he'll see her when she passes through the living room, so she won't see him looking unless she stops and stares, something she never does. She knows he watches. Let him know just how much was enough once upon a time when she first started coming to clean the apartment. Back when he was still leaving for work some mornings. Before they understood each other, when suspicions were mutual and thick as the dust first time she bolted through his doorway, into his rooms, out of breath and wary eyed like someone was chasing her and it might be him.

She'd burst in his door and he'd felt crowded. Retreated, let her stake out the space she required. She didn't bully him but demanded in the language of her brisk, efficient movements that he accustom himself to certain accommodations. They developed an etiquette that spelled out precisely how close, how distant the two of them could be once a week while she cleaned his apartment.

Odd that it took him years to realize how small she was. Shorter than him and no one in his family ever stood higher than five foot plus an inch or so of that thick, straight, black hair. America a land of giants and early on he'd learned to ignore height. You couldn't spend your days like a country lout gawking at the skyscraper heads of your new countrymen. No one had asked him so he'd never needed to describe his cleaning woman. Took no notice of her height. Her name was Clara Jackson and when she arrived he was overwhelmed by the busyness of her presence. How much she seemed to be doing all at once. Noises she'd manufacture with the cleaning paraphernalia, her humming and singing, the gum she popped, heavy thump of her heels even though she changed into tennis sneakers as soon as she crossed the threshold of his apartment, her troubled breathing, asthmatic wheezes and snorts of wrecked sinuses getting worse and worse over the years, her creaking knees, layers of dresses, dusters, slips whispering, the sighs and moans and wincing ejaculations, addresses to invisible presences she smuggled with her into his domain. *Yes, Lord. Save me, Jesus. Thank you, Father.* He backed away from the onslaught, the clamorous weight of it, avoided her systematically. Seldom were they both in the same room at the same time more than a few minutes because clearly none was large enough to contain them and the distance they needed.

She was bent over, replacing a scrubbed rack in the oven when he'd discovered the creases in her skull. She wore a net over her hair like serving girls in Horn and Hardart's. Under the webbing were clumps of hair, defined by furrows exposing her bare scalp. A ribbed yarmulke of hair pressed down on top of her head. Hair he'd never imagined. Like balled yarn in his grandmother's lap. Like a nursery rhyme. *Black sheep. Black sheep, have you any wool?* So different from what grew on his head, the heads of his brothers and sisters and mother and father and cousins and everyone in the doomed village where he was born, so different that he could not truly consider it hair, but some ersatz substitute used the evening of creation when hair ran out. Easier to think of her as bald. Bald and wearing a funny cap fashioned from the fur of some swarthy beast. Springy wires of it jutted from the netting. One dark strand left behind, shocking him when he discovered it marooned in the tub's gleaming, white belly, curled like a question mark at the end of the sentence he was always asking himself. He'd pinched it up in a wad of toilet paper, flushed it away.

Her bag of fleece had grayed and emptied over the years. Less of it now. He'd been tempted countless times to touch it. Poke his finger through the netting into one of the mounds. He'd wondered if she freed it from the veil when she went to bed. If it relaxed and spread against her pillow or if she slept all night like a soldier in a helmet.

When he stood beside her or behind her he could spy on the design of creases, observe how the darkness was cultivated into symmetrical plots and that meant he was taller than Clara Jackson, that he was looking down at her. But those facts did not calm the storm of motion and noise, did not undermine her power any more than the accident of growth, the half inch he'd attained over his next tallest brother, the inch eclipsing the height of his father, would have diminished his father's authority over the family, if there had been a family, the summer after he'd shot up past everyone, at thirteen the tallest, the height he remained today.

Mrs. Clara. Did you know a colored woman once saved my life?

Why is she staring at him as if he's said, Did you know I slept with a colored woman once? He didn't say that. Her silence fusses at him as if he did, as if he'd blurted out something unseemly, ungentlemanly, some insult forcing her to tighten her jaw and push her tongue into her cheek, and taste the bitterness of the hard lump inside her mouth. Why is she ready to cry, or call him a liar, throw something at him or demand an apology or look right through him, past him, the way his mother stared at him on endless October afternoons, gray slants of rain falling so everybody's trapped indoors and she's cleaning, cooking, tending a skeletal fire in the hearth and he's misbehaving, teasing his little sister till he gets his mother's attention and then he shrivels in the weariness of those sad eyes catching him in the act, piercing him, ignoring him, the hurt, iron and distance in them accusing him. Telling him for this moment, and perhaps forever, for this cruel, selfish trespass, you do not exist.

No, Mistah Cohen. That's one thing I definitely did not know.

His fingers fumble with a button, unfastening the cuff of his white shirt. He's rolling up one sleeve. Preparing himself for the work of storytelling. She has laundered the shirt how many times. It's held together by cleanliness and starch. A shirt that ought to be thrown away but she scrubs and sprays and irons it; he knows the routine, the noises. She saves it how many times, patching, mending, snipping errant threads, the frayed edges of cuff and collar hardened again so he is decent, safe within them, the blazing white breast he puffs out like a penguin when it's spring and he descends from the twelfth floor and conquers the park again, shoes shined, the remnants of that glorious head of hair slicked back, freshly shaved cheeks raw as a baby's in the brisk sunshine of those first days welcoming life back and yes he's out there in it again, his splay-foot penguin walk and gentleman's attire, shirt like a pledge, a promise, a declaration framing muted stripes of his dark tie. Numbers stamped inside the collar. Mark of the dry cleaners from a decade ago, before Clara Jackson began coming to clean. Traces still visible inside the neck of some of his shirts she's maintained impossibly long past their prime, a row of faded numerals like those he's pushing up his sleeve to show her on his skin.

The humped hairs on the back of his forearm are pressed down like grass in the woods where a hunted animal has slept. Gray hairs the color of his flesh, except inside his forearm, just above his wrist, the skin is whiter, blue veined. All of it, what's gray, what's pale, what's mottled with dark spots is meat that turns to lard and stinks a sweet sick stink to high heaven if you cook it.

Would you wish to stop now? Sit down a few minutes, please. I will make a coffee for you and my tea. I tell you a story. It is Christmas soon, no?

She is stopped in her tracks. A tiny woman, no doubt about it. Lumpy now. Perhaps she steals and hides things under her dress. Lumpy, not fat. Her shoulders round and padded. Like the derelict women who live in the streets and wear their whole wardrobes winter spring summer fall. She has put on flesh for protection. To soften blows. To ease around corners. Something cushioned to lean against. Something to muffle the sound of bones breaking when she falls. A pillow for all the heads gone and gone to dust who still find ways at night to come to her and seek a resting place. He could find uses for it. Extra flesh on her bones was not excess, was a gift. The female abundance, her thickness, her bulk reassuring as his hams shrink, his fingers become claws, the chicken neck frets away inside those razor-edged collars she scrubs and irons.

Oh you scarecrow. Death's-head stuck on a stick. Another stick lashed crossways for arms. First time you see yourself dead you giggle. You are a survivor, a lucky one. You grin, stick out your tongue at the image in the shard of smoky glass because the others must be laughing, can't help themselves, the ring of them behind your back, peeking over your scrawny shoulders, watching as you discover in the mirror what they've been seeing since they stormed the gates and kicked open the sealed barracks door and rescued you from the piles of live kindling that were to be your funeral pyre. Your fellow men. Allies. Victors. Survivors. Who stare at you when they think you're not looking, whose eyes are full of shame, as if they've been on duty here, in this pit, this stewpot cooking the meat from your bones. They cannot help themselves. You laugh to help them forget what they see. What you see. When they herded your keepers past you, their grand uniforms shorn of buttons, braid, ribbons, medals, the twin bolts of frozen lightning, golden skulls, eagles' wings, their jackboots gone, feet bare or in peasant clogs, heads bowed and hatless, iron faces unshaven, the butchers still outweighed you a hundred pounds a man. You could not conjure up the spit to mark them. You dropped your eyes in embarrassment, pretended to nod off because your body was too weak to manufacture a string of spittle, and if you could have, you'd have saved it, hoarded and tasted it a hundred times before you swallowed the precious bile.

A parade of shambling, ox-eyed animals. They are marched past you, marched past open trenches that are sewers brimming with naked, rotting flesh, past barbed-wire compounds where the living sift slow and insubstantial as fog among the heaps of dead. No one believes any of it. Ovens and gas chambers. Gallows and whipping posts. Shoes, shoes, shoes, a mountain of shoes in a warehouse. Shit. Teeth. Bones. Sacks of hair. The undead who huddle into themselves like bats and settle down on a patch of filthy earth mourning their own passing. No one believes the enemy. He is not these harmless farmers filing past in pillaged uniforms to do the work of cleaning up this mess someone's made. No one has ever seen a ghost trying to double itself in a mirror so they laugh behind its back, as if, as if the laughter is a game and the dead one could muster up the energy to join in and be made whole again. I giggle. I say, Who in God's name would steal a boy's face and leave this thing?

Nearly a half century of rich meals with seldom one missed but you cannot fill the emptiness, cannot quiet the clamor of those lost souls starving, the child you were, weeping from hunger, those selves, those stomachs you watched swelling, bloating, unburied for days and you dreamed of opening them, of taking a spoon to whatever was growing inside because you were so empty inside and nothing could be worse than that gnawing emptiness. Why should the dead be ashamed to eat the dead? Who are their brothers, sisters, themselves? You hear the boy talking to himself, hallucinating milk, bread, honey. Sick when the spoiled meat is finally carted away.

Mistah Cohen, I'm feeling kinda poorly today. If you don mind I'ma work straight through and gwan home early. Got all my Christmas still to do and I'm tired.

She wags her head. Mumbles more he can't decipher. As if he'd offered many times before, as if there is nothing strange or special this morning at 10:47, him standing at the china cupboard prepared to open it and bring down sugar bowl, a silver cream pitcher, cups and saucers for the two of them, ready to fetch instant coffee, a tea bag, boil water and sit down across the table from her. As if it happens each day she comes, as if this once is not the first time, the only time he's invited this woman to sit with him and she can wag her old head, stare at him moon eyed as an owl and refuse what's never been offered before.

The tattoo is faint. From where she's standing, fussing with the vacuum cleaner, she won't see a thing. Her eyes, in spite of thick spectacles, watery and weak as his. They have grown old together, avoiding each other in these musty rooms where soon, soon, no way round it, he will wake up dead one morning and no one will know till she knocks Thursday, and knocks again, then rings, pounds, hollers, but no one answers and she thumps away to rouse the super with his burly ring of keys.

He requires less sleep as he ages. Time weighs more on him as time slips away, less and less time as each second passes but also more of it, the past accumulating in vast drifts like snow in the darkness outside his window. In the wolf hours before dawn this strange city sleeps as uneasily as he does, turning, twisting, groaning. He finds himself listening intently for a sign that the night knows he's listening, but what he hears is his absence. The night busy with itself, denying him. And if he is not out there, if he can hear plainly his absence in the night pulse of the city, where is he now, where was he before his eyes opened, where will he be when the flutter of breath and heart stop?

They killed everyone in the camps. The whole world was dying there. Not only Jews. People forget. All kinds locked in the camps. Yes. Even Germans who were not Jews. Even a black woman. Not gypsy. Not African. American like you, Mrs. Clara.

They said she was a dancer and could play any instrument. Said she could line up shoes from many countries and hop from one pair to the next, performing the dances of the world. They said the Queen of Denmark had honored her with a gold trumpet. But she was there, in hell with the rest of us.

A woman like you. Many years ago. A lifetime ago. Young then as you would have been. And beautiful. As I believe you must have been, Mrs. Clara. Yes. Before America entered the war. Already camps had begun devouring people. All kinds of people. Yet she was rare. Only woman like her I ever saw until I came here, to this country, this city. And she saved my life.

Poor thing.

I was just a boy. Thirteen years old. The guards were beating me. I did not know why. Why? They didn't need a why. They just beat. And sometimes the beating ended in death because there was no reason to stop, just as there was no reason to begin. A boy. But I'd seen it many times. In the camp long enough to forget why I was alive, why anyone would want to live for long. They were hurting me, beating the life out of me but I was not surprised, expected no explanation. I remember curling up as I had seen a dog once cowering from the blows of a rolled newspaper. In the old country lifetimes ago. A boy in my village staring at a dog curled and rolling on its back in the dust outside the baker's shop and our baker in his white apron and tall white hat striking this mutt again and again. I didn't know what mischief the dog had done. I didn't understand why the fat man with flour on his apron was whipping it unmercifully. I simply saw it and hated the man, felt sorry for the animal, but already the child in me understood it could be no other way so I rolled and curled myself against the blows as I'd remembered that spotted dog in the dusty village street because that's the way it had to be.

Then a woman's voice in a language I did not comprehend reached me. A woman angry, screeching. I heard her before I saw her. She must have been screaming at them to stop. She must have decided it was better to risk dying than watch the guards pound a boy to death. First I heard her voice, then she rushed in, fell on me, wrapped herself around me. The guards shouted at her. One tried to snatch her away. She wouldn't let go of me and they began to beat her too. I heard the thud of clubs on her back, felt her shudder each time a blow was struck.

She fought to her feet, dragging me with her. Shielding me as we stumbled and slammed into a wall.

My head was buried in her smock. In the smell of her, the smell of dust, of blood. I was surprised how tiny she was, barely my size, but strong, very strong. Her fingers dug into my shoulders, squeezing, gripping hard enough to hurt me if I hadn't been past the point of feeling pain. Her hands were strong, her legs alive and warm, churning, churning as she pressed me against herself, into her. Somehow she'd pulled me up and back to the barracks wall, propping herself, supporting me, sheltering me. Then she screamed at them in this language I use now but did not know one word of then, cursing them, I'm sure, in her mother tongue, a stream of spit and sputtering sounds as if she could build a wall of words they could not cross.

The kapos hesitated, astounded by what she'd dared. Was this black one a madwoman, a witch? Then they tore me from her grasp, pushed me down and I crumpled there in the stinking mud of the compound. One more kick, a numbing, blinding smash that took my breath away. Blood flooded my eyes. I lost consciousness. Last I saw of her she was still fighting, slim, beautiful legs kicking at them as they dragged and punched her across the yard.

You say she was colored?

Yes. Yes. A dark angel who fell from the sky and saved me.

Always thought it was just you people over there doing those terrible things to each other.

He closes the china cupboard. Her back is turned. She mutters something at the metal vacuum tubes she's unclamping. He realizes he's finished his story anyway. Doesn't know how to say the rest. She's humming, folding rags, stacking them on the bottom pantry shelf. Lost in the cloud of her own noise. Much more to his story, but she's not waiting around to hear it. This is her last day before the holidays. He'd sealed her bonus in an envelope, placed the envelope where he always does on the kitchen counter. The kitchen cabinet doors have magnetic fasteners for a tight fit. After a volley of doors clicking, she'll be gone. When he's alone preparing his evening meal, he depends on those clicks for company. He pushes so they strike not too loud, not too soft. They punctuate the silence, reassure him like the solid slamming of doors in big sedans he used to ferry from customer to customer. How long since he'd been behind the wheel of a car? Years, and now another year almost gone. In every corner of the city they'd be welcoming their Christ, their New Year with extravagant displays of joy. He thinks of Clara Jackson in the midst of her family. She's little but the others are brown and large, with lips like spoons for serving the sugary babble of their speech. He tries to picture them, eating and drinking, huge people crammed in a tiny, shabby room. Unimaginable, really. The faces of her relatives become his. Everyone's hair is thick and straight and black.

1989

Maxine Hong Kingston b. 1940

Born in Stockton, California, in 1940, Maxine Ting Ting Hong is the eldest of six surviving children of Tom Hong (scholar, laundry man, and manager of a gambling house) and Ying Lan Chew (midwife, laundress, field hand). She earned a B.A. from the University of California at Berkeley in 1962 and a teaching certificate in 1965. She has lived and worked both in California and in Honolulu, Hawaii.

Author of three award-winning books, *The Woman Warrior* (1976), *China Men* (1980), and *Tripmaster Monkey* (1989), Maxine Hong Kingston is undoubtedly the most-recognized Asian American writer today. Her work attracts attention from many arenas: Chinese Americans, feminist scholars, literary critics, and the media. In 1977 Kingston won the *Mademoiselle Magazine* Award, in 1978 the Anisfield Wolf Race Relation Award. In 1980 she was proclaimed Living Treasure of Hawaii. *The Woman Warrior* received the National Book Critics Award for the best book of nonfiction in 1976, and *Time* magazine proclaimed it one of the top ten nonfiction works of the decade. It is, however, a collage of fiction and fact, memory and imagination—a hybrid genre of Kingston's own devising. Through the Chinese legends and family stories that marked her childhood and the mysterious old-world customs that her mother enforced but did not explain, through Kingston's own experiences and her imaginative and poetic flights, *The Woman Warrior* details the complexities and difficulties in Kingston's development as a woman and as a Chinese American. It focuses on a difficult and finally reconciled mother/daughter relationship.

Kingston's second book, *China Men,* focuses on men and is shaped by a rather uncommunicative father/daughter relationship. It depends heavily on family history, American laws, and imaginative projections based loosely on historical fact. Its purpose, Kingston has stated, is to "claim America" for Chinese Americans by showing how indebted America is to the labor of Chinese men, her great-grandfathers and grandfathers, who cleared jungle for the sugar plantations in Hawaii, who split rock and hammered steel to build railroads in the United States, who created fertile farmland out of swamp and desert, yet faced fierce discrimination and persecution. In this text, too, Kingston blends myth and fact, autobiography and fiction, blurring the usual dividing lines.

In *Tripmaster Monkey,* her first novel, Kingston again blends Chinese myth with American reality. She combines allusions to a Chinese classic, *Monkey* or *Journey to the West,* the story of a magical, mischievous monkey who accompanies a monk to India for the sacred books of Buddhism, with the life of a 1960s Berkeley beatnik playwright.

Amy Ling
University of Wisconsin at Madison

King-Kok Cheung
University of California, Los Angeles

PRIMARY WORKS

The Woman Warrior: Memoirs of a Girlhood among Ghosts, 1975; *China Men,* 1980; *Hawai'i One Summer,* 1987; *Tripmaster Monkey: His Fake Book,* 1989.

from The Woman Warrior

White Tigers

When we Chinese girls listened to the adults talking-story, we learned that we failed if we grew up to be but wives or slaves. We could be heroines, swordswomen. Even if she had to rage across all China, a swordswoman got even with anybody who hurt her family. Perhaps women were once so dangerous that they had to have their feet bound. It was a woman who invented white crane boxing only two hundred years ago. She was already an expert pole fighter, daughter of a teacher trained at the Shaolin temple, where there lived an order of fighting monks. She was combing her hair one morning when a white crane alighted outside her window. She teased it with her pole, which it pushed aside with a soft brush of its wing. Amazed, she dashed outside and tried to knock the crane off its perch. It snapped her pole in two. Recognizing the presence of great power, she asked the spirit of the white crane if it would teach her to fight. It answered with a cry that white crane boxers imitate today. Later the bird returned as an old man, and he guided her boxing for many years. Thus she gave the world a new martial art.

This was one of the tamer, more modern stories, mere introduction. My mother told others that followed swordswomen through woods and palaces for years. Night after night my mother would talk-story until we fell asleep. I couldn't tell where the stories left off and the dreams began, her voice the voice of the heroines in my sleep. And on Sundays, from noon to midnight, we went to the movies at the Confucius Church. We saw swordswomen jump over houses from a standstill; they didn't even need a running start.

At last I saw that I too had been in the presence of great power, my mother talking-story. After I grew up, I heard the chant of Fa Mu Lan, the girl who took her father's place in battle. Instantly I remembered that as a child I had followed my mother about the house, the two of us singing about how Fa Mu Lan fought gloriously and returned alive from war to settle in the village. I had forgotten this chant that was once mine, given me by my mother, who may not have known its power to remind. She said I would grow up a wife and a slave, but she taught me the song of the warrior woman, Fa Mu Lan. I would have to grow up a warrior woman.

The call would come from a bird that flew over our roof. In the brush drawings it looks like the ideograph for "human," two black wings. The bird would cross the sun and lift into the mountains (which look like the ideograph "mountain"), there parting the mist briefly that swirled opaque again. I would be a little girl of seven the day I followed the bird away into the mountains. The brambles would tear off my shoes and the rocks cut my feet and fingers, but I would keep climbing, eyes upward to follow the bird. We would go around and around the tallest mountain, climbing ever upward. I would drink from the river, which I would meet again and again. We would go so high the plants would change, and the river that flows past the village would become a waterfall. At the height where the bird used to disappear, the clouds would gray the world like an ink wash.

Even when I got used to that gray, I would only see peaks as if shaded in pencil, rocks like charcoal rubbings, everything so murky. There would be just two black strokes—the bird. Inside the clouds—inside the dragon's breath—I would not know how many hours or days passed. Suddenly, without noise, I would break clear into a yellow, warm world. New trees would lean toward me at mountain angles, but when I looked for the village, it would have vanished under the clouds.

The bird, now gold so close to the sun, would come to rest on the thatch of a hut, which, until the bird's two feet touched it, was camouflaged as part of the mountainside.

The door opened, and an old man and an old woman came out carrying bowls of rice and soup and a leafy branch of peaches.

"Have you eaten rice today, little girl?" they greeted me.

"Yes, I have," I said out of politeness. "Thank you."

("No, I haven't," I would have said in real life, mad at the Chinese for lying so much. "I'm starved. Do you have any cookies? I like chocolate chip cookies.")

"We were about to sit down to another meal," the old woman said. "Why don't you eat with us?"

They just happened to be bringing three rice bowls and three pairs of silver chopsticks out to the plank table under the pines. They gave me an egg, as if it were my birthday, and tea, though they were older than I, but I poured for them. The teapot and the rice pot seemed bottomless, but perhaps not; the old couple ate very little except for peaches.

When the mountains and the pines turned into blue oxen, blue dogs, and blue people standing, the old couple asked me to spend the night in the hut. I thought about the long way down in the ghostly dark and decided yes. The inside of the hut seemed as large as the outdoors. Pine needles covered the floor in thick patterns; someone had carefully arranged the yellow, green, and brown pine needles according to age. When I stepped carelessly and mussed a line, my feet kicked up new blends of earth colors, but the old man and old woman walked so lightly that their feet never stirred the designs by a needle.

A rock grew in the middle of the house, and that was their table. The benches were fallen trees. Ferns and shade flowers grew out of one wall, the mountainside itself. The old couple tucked me into a bed just my width. "Breathe evenly, or you'll lose your balance and fall out," said the woman, covering me with a silk bag stuffed with feathers and herbs. "Opera singers, who begin their training at age five, sleep in beds like this." Then the two of them went outside, and through the window I could see them pull on a rope looped over a branch. The rope was tied to the roof, and the roof opened up like a basket lid. I would sleep with the moon and the stars. I did not see whether the old people slept, so quickly did I drop off, but they would be there waking me with food in the morning.

"Little girl, you have now spent almost a day and a night with us," the old woman said. In the morning light I could see her earlobes pierced with gold. "Do you think you can bear to stay with us for fifteen years? We can train you to become a warrior."

"What about my mother and father?" I asked.

The old man untied the drinking gourd slung across his back. He lifted the lid by its stem and looked for something in the water. "Ah, there," he said.

At first I saw only water so clear it magnified the fibers in the walls of the gourd. On the surface, I saw only my own round reflection. The old man encircled the neck of the gourd with his thumb and index finger and gave it a shake. As the water shook, then settled, the colors and lights shimmered into a picture, not reflecting anything I could see around me. There at the bottom of the gourd were my mother and father scanning the sky, which was where I was. "It has happened already, then," I could hear my mother say. "I didn't expect it so soon." "You knew from her birth that she would be taken," my father answered. "We'll have to harvest potatoes without her help this year," my mother said, and they turned away toward the fields, straw baskets in their arms. The water shook and became just water again. "Mamma. Papa," I called, but they were in the valley and could not hear me.

"What do you want to do?" the old man asked. "You can go back right now if you like. You can go pull sweet potatoes, or you can stay with us and learn how to fight barbarians and bandits."

"You can avenge your village," said the old woman. "You can recapture the harvests the thieves have taken. You can be remembered by the Han people for your dutifulness."

"I'll stay with you," I said.

So the hut became my home, and I found out that the old woman did not arrange the pine needles by hand. She opened the roof; an autumn wind would come up, and the needles fell in braids—brown strands, green strands, yellow strands. The old woman waved her arms in conducting motions; she blew softly with her mouth. I thought, nature certainly works differently on mountains than in valleys.

"The first thing you have to learn," the old woman told me, "is how to be quiet." They left me by streams to watch for animals. "If you're noisy, you'll make the deer go without water."

When I could kneel all day without my legs cramping and my breathing became even, the squirrels would bury their hoardings at the hem of my shirt and then bend their tails in a celebration dance. At night, the mice and toads looked at me, their eyes quick stars and slow stars. Not once would I see a three-legged toad, though; you need strings of cash to bait them.

The two old people led me in exercises that began at dawn and ended at sunset so that I could watch our shadows grow and shrink and grow again, rooted to the earth. I learned to move my fingers, hands, feet, head, and entire body in circles. I walked putting heel down first, toes pointing outward thirty to forty degrees, making the ideograph "eight," making the ideograph "human." Knees bent, I would swing into the slow, measured "square step," the powerful walk into battle. After five years my body became so strong that I could control even the dilations of the pupils inside my irises. I could copy owls and bats, the words for "bat" and "blessing" homonyms. After six years the deer let me run beside them. I could jump twenty feet into the air from a standstill, leaping like a monkey over the hut. Every creature has a hiding skill and a fighting skill a warrior can use. When birds alighted on my palm, I could yield my muscles under their feet and give them no base from which to fly away.

But I could not fly like the bird that led me here, except in large, free dreams.

During the seventh year (I would be fourteen), the two old people led me blindfolded to the mountains of the white tigers. They held me by either elbow and shouted into my ears, "Run. Run. Run." I ran and, not stepping off a cliff at the edge of my toes and not hitting my forehead against a wall, ran faster. A wind buoyed me up over the roots, the rocks, the little hills. We reached the tiger place in no time—a mountain peak three feet three from the sky. We had to bend over.

The old people waved once, slid down the mountain, and disappeared around a tree. The old woman, good with the bow and arrow, took them with her; the old man took the water gourd. I would have to survive bare-handed. Snow lay on the ground, and snow fell in loose gusts—another way the dragon breathes. I walked in the direction from which we had come, and when I reached the timberline, I collected wood broken from the cherry tree, the peony, and the walnut, which is the tree of life. Fire, the old people had taught me, is stored in trees that grow red flowers or red berries in the spring or whose leaves turn red in the fall. I took the wood from the protected spots beneath the trees and wrapped it in my scarf to keep dry. I dug where squirrels might have come, stealing one or two nuts at each place. These I also wrapped in my scarf. It is possible, the old people said, for a human being to live for fifty days on water. I would save the roots and nuts for hard climbs, the places where nothing grew, the emergency should I not find the hut. This time there would be no bird to follow.

The first night I burned half of the wood and slept curled against the mountain. I heard the white tigers prowling on the other side of the fire, but I could not distinguish them from the snow patches. The morning rose perfectly. I hurried along, again collecting wood and edibles. I ate nothing and only drank the snow my fires made run.

The first two days were gifts, the fasting so easy to do, I so smug in my strength that on the third day, the hardest, I caught myself sitting on the ground, opening the scarf and staring at the nuts and dry roots. Instead of walking steadily on or even eating, I faded into dreams about the meat meals my mother used to cook, my monk's food forgotten. That night I burned up most of the wood I had collected, unable to sleep for facing my death—if not death here, then death someday. The moon animals that did not hibernate came out to hunt, but I had given up the habits of a carnivore since living with the old people. I would not trap the mice that danced so close or the owls that plunged just outside the fire.

On the fourth and fifth days, my eyesight sharp with hunger, I saw deer and used their trails when our ways coincided. Where the deer nibbled, I gathered the fungus, the fungus of immortality.

At noon on the tenth day I packed snow, white as rice, into the worn center of a rock pointed out to me by a finger of ice, and around the rock I built a fire. In the warming water I put roots, nuts, and the fungus of immortality. For variety I ate a quarter of the nuts and roots raw. Oh, green joyous rush inside my mouth, my head, my stomach, my toes, my soul—the best meal of my life.

One day I found that I was striding long distances without hindrance, my bundle light. Food had become so scarce that I was no longer stopping to collect it. I had walked into dead land. Here even the snow stopped. I did not go back to the richer areas, where I could not stay anyway, but, resolving to fast until I got halfway to the next woods, I started across the dry rocks. Heavily weighed down by the wood on my back, branches poking maddeningly, I had burned almost all of the fuel not to waste strength lugging it.

Somewhere in the dead land I lost count of the days. It seemed as if I had been walking forever; life had never been different from this. An old man and an old woman were help I had only wished for. I was fourteen years old and lost from my village. I was walking in circles. Hadn't I been already found by the old people? Or was that yet to come? I wanted my mother and father. The old man and old woman were only a part of this lostness and this hunger.

One nightfall I ate the last of my food but had enough sticks for a good fire. I stared into the flames, which reminded me about helping my mother with the cooking and made me cry. It was very strange looking through water into fire and seeing my mother again. I nodded, orange and warm.

A white rabbit hopped beside me, and for a moment I thought it was a blob of snow that had fallen out of the sky. The rabbit and I studied each other. Rabbits taste like chickens. My mother and father had taught me how to hit rabbits over the head with wine jugs, then skin them cleanly for fur vests. "It's a cold night to be an animal," I said. "So you want some fire too, do you? Let me put on another branch, then." I would not hit it with the branch. I had learned from rabbits to kick backward. Perhaps this one was sick because normally the animals did not like fire. The rabbit seemed alert enough, however, looking at me so acutely, bounding up to the fire. But it did not stop when it got to the edge. It turned its face once toward me, then jumped into the fire. The fire went down for a moment, as if crouching in surprise, then the flames shot up taller than before. When the fire became calm again, I saw the rabbit had turned into meat, browned just right. I ate it, knowing the rabbit had sacrificed itself for me. It had made me a gift of meat.

When you have been walking through trees hour after hour—and I finally reached trees after the dead land—branches cross out everything, no relief whichever way your head turns until your eyes start to invent new sights. Hunger also changes the world—when eating can't be a habit, then neither can seeing. I saw two people made of gold dancing the earth's dances. They turned so perfectly that together they were the axis of the earth's turning. They were light; they were molten, changing gold—Chinese lion dancers, African lion dancers in midstep. I heard high Javanese bells deepen in midring to Indian bells, Hindu Indian, American Indian. Before my eyes, gold bells shredded into gold tassles that fanned into two royal capes that softened into lions' fur. Manes grew tall into feathers that shone—became light rays. Then the dancers danced the future—a machine-future—in clothes I had never seen before. I am watching the centuries pass in moments because suddenly I understand time, which is spinning and fixed like the North Star. And I understand how working and hoeing are dancing; how peasant clothes are golden, as king's clothes are golden; how one of the dancers is always a man and the other a woman.

The man and the woman grow bigger and bigger, so bright. All light. They are tall angels in two rows. They have high white wings on their backs. Perhaps there are infinite angels; perhaps I see two angels in their consecutive moments. I cannot bear their brightness and cover my eyes, which hurt from opening so wide without a blink. When I put my hands down to look again, I recognize the old brown man and the old gray woman walking toward me out of the pine forest.

It would seem that this small crack in the mystery was opened, not so much by the old people's magic, as by hunger. Afterward, whenever I did not eat for long, as during famine or battle, I could stare at ordinary people and see their light and gold. I could see their dance. When I get hungry enough, then killing and falling are dancing too.

The old people fed me hot vegetable soup. Then they asked me to talk-story about what happened in the mountains of the white tigers. I told them that the white tigers had stalked me through the snow but that I had fought them off with burning branches, and my great-grandparents had come to lead me safely through the forests. I had met a rabbit who taught me about self-immolation and how to speed up transmigration: one does not have to become worms first but can change directly into a human being—as in our own humaneness we had just changed bowls of vegetable soup into people too. That made them laugh. "You tell good stories," they said. "Now go to sleep, and tomorrow we will begin your dragon lessons."

"One more thing," I wanted to say. "I saw you and how old you really are." But I was already asleep; it came out only a murmur. I would want to tell them about that last moment of my journey; but it was only one moment out of the weeks that I had been gone, and its telling would keep till morning. Besides, the two people must already know. In the next years, when I suddenly came upon them or when I caught them out of the corners of my eyes, he appeared as a handsome young man, tall with long black hair, and she, as a beautiful young woman who ran bare-legged through the trees. In the spring she dressed like a bride; she wore juniper leaves in her hair and a black embroidered jacket. I learned to shoot accurately because my teachers held the targets. Often when sighting along an arrow, there to the side I would glimpse the young man or young woman, but when I looked directly, he or she would be old again. By this time I had guessed from their sexless manner that the old woman was to the old man a sister or a friend rather than a wife.

After I returned from my survival test, the two old people trained me in dragon ways, which took another eight years. Copying the tigers, their stalking kill and their anger, had been a wild, bloodthirsty joy. Tigers are easy to find, but I needed adult wisdom to know dragons. "You have to infer the whole dragon from the parts you can see and touch," the old people would say. Unlike tigers, dragons are so immense, I would never see one in its entirety. But I could explore the mountains, which are the top of its head. "These mountains are also *like* the tops of *other* dragons' heads," the old people would tell me. When climbing the slopes, I could understand that I was a bug riding on a dragon's forehead as it roams through space, its speed so different from my speed that I feel the dragon solid and immobile. In quarries I could see its strata, the dragon's veins and muscles; the minerals, its teeth and bones. I could touch the stones the old woman wore—its bone marrow. I had worked the soil, which is its flesh, and harvested the plants and climbed the trees, which are its hairs. I could listen to its voice in the thunder and feel its breathing in the winds, see its breathing in the clouds. Its tongue is the lightning. And the red that the lightning gives to the world is strong and lucky—in blood, poppies, roses, rubies, the red feathers of birds, the red carp, the cherry tree, the peony, the line alongside the turtle's eyes and the mallard's. In the spring when the dragon awakes, I watched its turnings in the rivers.

The closest I came to seeing a dragon whole was when the old people cut away a small strip of bark on a pine that was over three thousand years old. The resin underneath flows in the swirling shapes of dragons. "If you should decide during your old age that you would like to live another five hundred years, come here and drink ten pounds of this sap," they told me. "But don't do it now. You're too young to decide to live forever." The old people sent me out into thunderstorms to pick the red-cloud herb, which grows only then, a product of dragon's fire and dragon's rain. I brought the leaves to the old man and old woman, and they ate them for immortality.

I learned to make my mind large, as the universe is large, so that there is room for paradoxes. Pearls are bone marrow; pearls come from oysters. The dragon lives in the sky, ocean, marshes, and mountains; and the mountains are also its cranium. Its voice thunders and jingles like copper pans. It breathes fire and water; and sometimes the dragon is one, sometimes many.

I worked every day. When it rained, I exercised in the downpour, grateful not to be pulling sweet potatoes. I moved like the trees in the wind. I was grateful not to be squishing in chicken mud, which I did not have nightmares about so frequently now.

On New Year's mornings, the old man let me look in his water gourd to see my family. They were eating the biggest meal of the year, and I missed them very much. I had felt loved, love pouring from their fingers when the adults tucked red money in our pockets. My two old people did not give me money, but, each year for fifteen years, a bead. After I unwrapped the red paper and rolled the bead about between thumb and fingers, they took it back for safekeeping. We ate monk's food as usual.

By looking into the water gourd I was able to follow the men I would have to execute. Not knowing that I watched, fat men ate meat; fat men drank wine made from the rice; fat men sat on naked little girls. I watched powerful men count their money, and starving men count theirs. When bandits brought their share of raids home, I waited until they took off their masks so I would know the villagers who stole from their neighbors. I studied the generals' faces, their rank-stalks quivering at the backs of their heads. I learned rebels' faces, too, their foreheads tied with wild oaths.

The old man pointed out strengths and weaknesses whenever heroes met in classical battles, but warfare makes a scramble of the beautiful, slow old fights. I saw one young fighter salute his opponent—and five peasants hit him from behind with scythes and hammers. His opponent did not warn him.

"Cheaters!" I yelled. "How am I going to win against cheaters?"

"Don't worry," the old man said. "You'll never be trapped like that poor amateur. You can see behind you like a bat. Hold the peasants back with one hand and kill the warrior with the other."

Menstrual days did not interrupt my training; I was as strong as on any other day. "You're now an adult," explained the old woman on the first one, which happened halfway through my stay on the mountain. "You can have children." I had thought I had cut myself when jumping over my swords, one made of steel and the other carved out of a single block of jade. "However," she added, "we are asking you to put off children for a few more years."

"Then can I use the control you taught me and stop this bleeding?"

"No. You don't stop shitting and pissing," she said. "It's the same with the blood. Let it run." ("Let it walk" in Chinese.)

To console me for being without family on this day, they let me look inside the gourd. My whole family was visiting friends on the other side of the river. Everybody had on good clothes and was exchanging cakes. It was a wedding. My mother was talking to the hosts: "Thank you for taking our daughter. Wherever she is, she must be happy now. She will certainly come back if she is alive, and if she is a spirit, you have given her a descent line. We are so grateful."

Yes, I would be happy. How full I would be with all their love for me. I would have for a new husband my own playmate, dear since childhood, who loved me so much he was to become a spirit bridegroom for my sake. We will be so happy when I come back to the valley, healthy and strong and not a ghost.

The water gave me a close-up of my husband's wonderful face—and I was watching when it went white at the sudden approach of armored men on horseback, thudding and jangling. My people grabbed iron skillets, boiling soup, knives, hammers, scissors, whatever weapons came to hand, but my father said, "There are too many of them," and they put down the weapons and waited quietly at the door, open as if for guests. An army of horsemen stopped at our house; the foot soldiers in the distance were coming closer. A horseman with silver scales afire in the sun shouted from the scroll in his hands, his words opening a red gap in his black beard. "Your baron has pledged fifty men from this district, one from each family," he said, and then named the family names.

"No!" I screamed into the gourd.

"I'll go," my new husband and my youngest brother said to their fathers.

"No," my father said, "I myself will go," but the women held him back until the foot soldiers passed by, my husband and my brother leaving with them.

As if disturbed by the marching feet, the water churned; and when it stilled again ("Wait!" I yelled. "Wait!"), there were strangers. The baron and his family—all of his family—were knocking their heads on the floor in front of their ancestors and thanking the gods out loud for protecting them from conscription. I watched the baron's piggish face chew open-mouthed on the sacrificial pig. I plunged my hand into the gourd, making a grab for his thick throat, and he broke into pieces, splashing water all over my face and clothes. I turned the gourd upside-down to empty it, but no little people came tumbling out.

"Why can't I go down there now and help them?" I cried. "I'll run away with the two boys and we'll hide in the caves."

"No," the old man said. "You're not ready. You're only fourteen years old. You'd get hurt for nothing."

"Wait until you are twenty-two," the old woman said. "You'll be big then and more skillful. No army will be able to stop you from doing whatever you want. If you go now, you will be killed, and you'll have wasted seven and a half years of our time. You will deprive your people of a champion."

"I'm good enough now to save the boys."

"We didn't work this hard to save just two boys, but whole families."

Of course.

"Do you really think I'll be able to do that—defeat an army?"

"Even when you fight against soldiers trained as you are, most of them will be men, heavy footed and rough. You will have the advantage. Don't be impatient."

"From time to time you may use the water gourd to watch your husband and your brother," the old man said.

But I had ended the panic about them already. I could feel a wooden door inside of me close. I had learned on the farm that I could stop loving animals raised for slaughter. And I could start loving them immediately when someone said, "This one is a pet," freeing me and opening the door. We had lost males before, cousins and uncles who were conscripted into armies or bonded as apprentices, who are almost as lowly as slave girls.

I bled and thought about the people to be killed; I bled and thought about the people to be born.

During all my years on the mountain, I talked to no one except the two old people, but they seemed to be many people. The whole world lived inside the gourd, the earth a green and blue pearl like the one the dragon plays with.

When I could point at the sky and make a sword appear, a silver bolt in the sunlight, and control its slashing with my mind, the old people said I was ready to leave. The old man opened the gourd for the last time. I saw the baron's messenger leave our house, and my father was saying, "This time I must go and fight." I would hurry down the mountain and take his place. The old people gave me the fifteen beads, which I was to use if I got into terrible danger. They gave me men's clothes and armor. We bowed to one another. The bird flew above me down the mountain, and for some miles, whenever I turned to look for them, there would be the two old people waving. I saw them through the mist; I saw them on the clouds; I saw them big on the mountaintop when distance had shrunk the pines. They had probably left images of themselves for me to wave at and gone about their other business.

When I reached my village, my father and mother had grown as old as the two whose shapes I could at last no longer see. I helped my parents carry their tools, and they walked ahead so straight, each carrying a basket or a hoe not to overburden me, their tears falling privately. My family surrounded me with so much love that I almost forgot the ones not there. I praised the new infants.

"Some of the people are saying the Eight Sages took you away to teach you magic," said a little girl cousin. "They say they changed you into a bird, and you flew to them."

"Some say you went to the city and became a prostitute," another cousin giggled.

"You might tell them that I met some teachers who were willing to teach me science," I said.

"I have been drafted," my father said.

"No, Father," I said. "I will take your place."

My parents killed a chicken and steamed it whole, as if they were welcoming home a son, but I had gotten out of the habit of meat. After eating rice and vegetables, I slept for a long time, preparation for the work ahead.

In the morning my parents woke me and asked that I come with them to the family hall. "Stay in your nightclothes," my mother said. "Don't change yet." She was holding a basin, a towel, and a kettle of hot water. My father had a bottle of wine, an ink block and pens, and knives of various sizes. "Come with us," he said. They had stopped the tears with which they had greeted me. Forebodingly I caught a smell—metallic, the iron smell of blood, as when a woman gives birth, as at the sacrifice of a large animal, as when I menstruated and dreamed red dreams.

My mother put a pillow on the floor before the ancestors. "Kneel here," she said. "Now take off your shirt." I kneeled with my back to my parents so none of us felt embarrassed. My mother washed my back as if I had left for only a day and were her baby yet. "We are going to carve revenge on your back," my father said. "We'll write out oaths and names."

"Wherever you go, whatever happens to you, people will know our sacrifice," my mother said. "And you'll never forget either." She meant that even if I got killed, the people could use my dead body for a weapon, but we do not like to talk out loud about dying.

My father first brushed the words in ink, and they fluttered down my back row after row. Then he began cutting; to make fine lines and points he used thin blades, for the stems, large blades.

My mother caught the blood and wiped the cuts with a cold towel soaked in wine. It hurt terribly—the cuts sharp; the air burning; the alcohol cold, then hot—pain so various. I gripped my knees. I released them. Neither tension nor relaxation helped. I wanted to cry. If not for the fifteen years of training, I would have writhed on the floor; I would have had to be held down. The list of grievances went on and on. If an enemy should flay me, the light would shine through my skin like lace.

At the end of the last word, I fell forward. Together my parents sang what they had written, then let me rest. My mother fanned my back. "We'll have you with us until your back heals," she said.

When I could sit up again, my mother brought two mirrors, and I saw my back covered entirely with words in red and black files, like an army, like my army. My parents nursed me just as if I had fallen in battle after many victories. Soon I was strong again.

A white horse stepped into the courtyard where I was polishing my armor. Though the gates were locked tight, through the moon door it came—a kingly white horse. It wore a saddle and bridle with red, gold, and black tassles dancing. The saddle was just my size with tigers and dragons tooled in swirls. The white horse pawed the ground for me to go. On the hooves of its near forefoot and hindfoot was the ideograph "to fly."

My parents and I had waited for such a sign. We took the fine saddlebags off the horse and filled them with salves and herbs, blue grass for washing my hair, extra sweaters, dried peaches. They gave me a choice of ivory or silver chopsticks. I took the silver ones because they were lighter. It was like getting wedding presents. The cousins and the villagers came bearing bright orange jams, silk dresses, silver embroidery scissors. They brought blue and white porcelain bowls filled with water and carp—the bowls painted with carp, fins like orange fire. I accepted all the gifts—the tables, the earthenware jugs—though I could not possibly carry them with me, and culled for travel only a small copper cooking bowl. I could cook in it and eat out of it and would not have to search for bowl-shaped rocks or tortoiseshells.

I put on my men's clothes and armor and tied my hair in a man's fashion. "How beautiful you look," the people said. "How beautiful she looks."

A young man stepped out of the crowd. He looked familiar to me, as if he were the old man's son, or the old man himself when you looked at him from the corners of your eyes.

"I want to go with you," he said.

"You will be the first soldier in my army," I told him.

I leapt onto my horse's back and marveled at the power and height it gave to me. Just then, galloping out of nowhere straight at me came a rider on a black horse. The villagers scattered except for my one soldier, who stood calmly in the road. I drew my sword. "Wait!" shouted the rider, raising weaponless hands. "Wait. I have travelled here to join you."

Then the villagers relinquished their real gifts to me—their sons. Families who had hidden their boys during the last conscription volunteered them now. I took the ones their families could spare and the ones with hero-fire in their eyes, not the young fathers and not those who would break hearts with their leaving.

We were better equipped than many founders of dynasties had been when they walked north to dethrone an emperor; they had been peasants like us. Millions of us had laid our hoes down on the dry ground and faced north. We sat in the fields, from which the dragon had withdrawn its moisture, and sharpened those hoes. Then, though it be ten thousand miles away, we walked to the palace. We would report to the emperor. The emperor, who sat facing south, must have been very frightened—peasants everywhere walking day and night toward the capital, toward Peiping. But the last emperors of dynasties must not have been facing in the right direction, for they would have seen us and not let us get this hungry. We would not have had to shout our grievances. The peasants would crown as emperor a farmer who knew the earth or a beggar who understood hunger.

"Thank you, Mother. Thank you, Father," I said before leaving. They had carved their names and address on me, and I would come back.

Often I walked beside my horse to travel abreast of my army. When we had to impress other armies—marauders, columns of refugees filing past one another, boy gangs following their martial arts teachers—I mounted and rode in front. The soldiers who owned horses and weapons would pose fiercely on my left and right. The small bands joined us, but sometimes armies of equal or larger strength would fight us. Then screaming a mighty scream and swinging two swords over my head, I charged the leaders; I released my bloodthirsty army and my straining war-horse. I guided the horse with my knees, freeing both hands for swordwork, spinning green and silver circles all around me.

I inspired my army, and I fed them. At night I sang to them glorious songs that came out of the sky and into my head. When I opened my mouth, the songs poured out and were loud enough for the whole encampment to hear; my army stretched out for a mile. We sewed red flags and tied the red scraps around arms, legs, horses' tails. We wore our red clothes so that when we visited a village, we would look as happy as for New Year's Day. Then people would want to join the ranks. My army did not rape, only taking food where there was an abundance. We brought order wherever we went.

When I won over a goodly number of fighters, I built up my army enough to attack fiefdoms and to pursue the enemies I had seen in the water gourd.

My first opponent turned out to be a giant, so much bigger than the toy general

I used to peep at. During the charge, I singled out the leader, who grew as he ran toward me. Our eyes locked until his height made me strain my neck looking up, my throat so vulnerable to the stroke of a knife that my eyes dropped to the secret death points on the huge body. First I cut off his leg with one sword swipe, as Chen Luan-feng had chopped the leg off the thunder god. When the giant stumped toward me, I cut off his head. Instantly he reverted to his true self, a snake, and slithered away hissing. The fighting around me stopped as the combatants' eyes and mouths opened wide in amazement. The giant's spells now broken, his soldiers, seeing that they had been led by a snake, pledged their loyalty to me.

In the stillness after battle I looked up at the mountaintops; perhaps the old man and woman were watching me and would enjoy my knowing it. They'd laugh to see a creature winking at them from the bottom of the water gourd. But on a green ledge above the battlefield I saw the giant's wives crying. They had climbed out of their palanquins to watch their husband fight me, and now they were holding each other weeping. They were two sisters, two tiny fairies against the sky, widows from now on. Their long undersleeves, which they had pulled out to wipe their tears, flew white mourning in the mountain wind. After a time, they got back into their sedan chairs, and their servants carried them away.

I led my army northward, rarely having to sidetrack; the emperor himself sent the enemies I was hunting chasing after me. Sometimes they attacked us on two or three sides; sometimes they ambushed me when I rode ahead. We would always win, Kuan Kung, the god of war and literature riding before me. I would be told of in fairy tales myself. I overheard some soldiers—and now there were many who had not met me—say that whenever we had been in danger of losing, I made a throwing gesture and the opposing army would fall, hurled across the battlefield. Hailstones as big as heads would shoot out of the sky and the lightning would stab like swords, but never at those on my side. "On *his* side," they said. I never told them the truth. Chinese executed women who disguised themselves as soldiers or students, no matter how bravely they fought or how high they scored on the examinations.

One spring morning I was at work in my tent repairing equipment, patching my clothes, and studying maps when a voice said, "General, may I visit you in your tent, please?" As if it were my own home, I did not allow strangers in my tent. And since I had no family with me, no one ever visited inside. Riverbanks, hillsides, the cool sloped rooms under the pine trees—China provides her soldiers with meeting places enough. I opened the tent flap. And there in the sunlight stood my own husband with arms full of windflowers for me. "You are beautiful," he said, and meant it truly. "I have looked for you everywhere. I've been looking for you since the day that bird flew away with you." We were so pleased with each other, the childhood friend found at last, the childhood friend mysteriously grown up. "I followed you, but you skimmed over the rocks until I lost you."

"I've looked for you too," I said, the tent now snug around us like a secret house when we were kids. "Whenever I heard about a good fighter, I went to see if it were you," I said. "I saw you marry me. I'm so glad you married me."

He wept when he took off my shirt and saw the scarwords on my back. He loosened my hair and covered the words with it. I turned around and touched his face, loving the familiar first.

So for a time I had a partner—my husband and I, soldiers together just as when we were little soldiers playing in the village. We rode side by side into battle. When I became pregnant, during the last four months, I wore my armor altered so that I looked like a powerful, big man. As a fat man, I walked with the foot soldiers so as not to jounce the gestation. Now when I was naked, I was a strange human being indeed—words carved on my back and the baby large in front.

I hid from battle only once, when I gave birth to our baby. In dark and silver dreams I had seen him falling from the sky, each night closer to the earth, his soul a star. Just before labor began, the last star rays sank into my belly. My husband would talk to me and not go, though I said for him to return to the battlefield. He caught the baby, a boy, and put it on my breast. "What are we going to do with this?" he asked, holding up the piece of umbilical cord that had been closest to the baby.

"Let's tie it to a flagpole until it dries," I said. We had both seen the boxes in which our parents kept the dried cords of all their children. "This one was yours, and this yours," my mother would say to us brothers and sisters, and fill us with awe that she could remember.

We made a sling for the baby inside my big armor, and rode back into the thickest part of the fighting. The umbilical cord flew with the red flag and made us laugh. At night inside our own tent, I let the baby ride on my back. The sling was made of red satin and purple silk; the four paisley straps that tied across my breasts and around my waist ended in housewife's pockets lined with a coin, a seed, a nut, and a juniper leaf. At the back of the sling I had sewn a tiny quilted triangle, red at its center against two shades of green; it marked the baby's nape for luck. I walked bowed, and the baby warmed himself against me, his breathing in rhythm with mine, his heart beating like my heart.

When the baby was a month old, we gave him a name and shaved his head. For the full-month ceremony my husband had found two eggs, which we dyed red by boiling them with a flag. I peeled one and rolled it all over the baby's head, his eyes, his lips, off his bump of a nose, his cheeks, his dear bald head and fontanel. I had brought dried grapefruit peel in my saddlebag, and we also boiled that. We washed our heads and hands in the grapefruit water, dabbing it on the baby's forehead and hands. Then I gave my husband the baby and told him to take it to his family, and I gave him all the money we had taken on raids to take to my family. "Go now," I said, "before he is old enough to recognize me." While the blur is still in his eyes and the little fists shut tight like buds, I'll send my baby away from me. I altered my clothes and became again the slim young man. Only now I would get so lonely with the tent so empty that I slept outside.

My white horse overturned buckets and danced on them; it lifted full wine cups with its teeth. The strong soldiers lifted the horse in a wooden tub, while it danced to the stone drums and flute music. I played with the soldiers, throwing arrows into a bronze jar. But I found none of these antics as amusing as when I first set out on the road.

It was during this lonely time, when any high cry made the milk spill from my breasts, that I got careless. Wildflowers distracted me so that I followed them, picking one, then another, until I was alone in the woods. Out from behind trees, springing off branches came the enemy, their leader looming like a genie out of the water gourd. I threw fists and feet at them, but they were so many, they pinned me to the earth while their leader drew his sword. My fear shot forth—a quick, jabbing sword that slashed fiercely, silver flashes, quick cuts wherever my attention drove it. The leader stared at the palpable sword swishing unclutched at his men, then laughed aloud. As if signaled by his laughter, two more swords appeared in midair. They clanged against mine, and I felt metal vibrate inside my brain. I willed my sword to hit back and to go after the head that controlled the other swords. But the man fought well, hurting my brain. The swords opened and closed, scissoring madly, metal zinging along metal. Unable to leave my skysword to work itself, I would be watching the swords move like puppets when the genie yanked my hair back and held a dagger against my throat. "Aha!" he said. "What have we here?" He lifted the bead pouch out of my shirt and cut the string. I grabbed his arm, but one of his swords dived toward me, and I rolled out of the way. A horse galloped up, and he leapt on it, escaping into the forest, the beads in his fist. His swords fought behind him until I heard him shout, "I am here!" and they flew to his side. So I had done battle with the prince who had mixed the blood of his two sons with the metal he had used for casting his swords.

I ran back to my soldiers and gathered the fastest horsemen for pursuit. Our horses ran like the little white water horses in the surf. Across a plain we could see the enemy, a dustdevil rushing toward the horizon. Wanting to see, I focused my eyes as the eagles had taught me, and there the genie would be—shaking one bead out of the pouch and casting it at us. Nothing happened. No thunder, no earthquake that split open the ground, no hailstones big as heads.

"Stop!" I ordered my riders. "Our horses are exhausted, and I don't want to chase any farther south." The rest of the victories would be won on my own, slow and without shortcuts.

I stood on top of the last hill before Peiping and saw the roads below me flow like living rivers. Between roads the woods and plains moved too; the land was peopled—the Han people, the People of One Hundred Surnames, marching with one heart, our tatters flying. The depth and width of Joy were exactly known to me: the Chinese population. After much hardship a few of our millions had arrived together at the capital. We faced our emperor personally. We beheaded him, cleaned out the palace, and inaugurated the peasant who would begin the new order. In his rags he sat on the throne facing south, and we, a great red crowd, bowed to him three times. He commended some of us who were his first generals.

I told the people who had come with me that they were free to go home now, but since the Long Wall was so close, I would go see it. They could come along if they liked. So, loath to disband after such high adventures, we reached the northern boundary of the world, chasing Mongols en route.

I touched the Long Wall with my own fingers, running the edge of my hand between the stones, tracing the grooves the builders' hands had made. We lay our foreheads and our cheeks against the Long Wall and cried like the women who had come here looking for their men so long building the wall. In my travels north, I had not found my brother.

Carrying the news about the new emperor, I went home, where one more battle awaited me. The baron who had drafted my brother would still be bearing sway over our village. Having dropped my soldiers off at crossroads and bridges, I attacked the baron's stronghold alone. I jumped over the double walls and landed with swords drawn and knees bent, ready to spring. When no one accosted me, I sheathed the swords and walked about like a guest until I found the baron. He was counting his money, his fat ringed fingers playing over the abacus.

"Who are you? What do you want?" he said, encircling his profits with his arms. He sat square and fat like a god.

"I want your life in payment for your crimes against the villagers."

"I haven't done anything to you. All this is mine. I earned it. I didn't steal it from you. I've never seen you before in my life. Who are you?"

"I am a female avenger."

Then—heaven help him—he tried to be charming, to appeal to me man to man. "Oh, come now. Everyone takes the girls when he can. The families are glad to be rid of them. 'Girls are maggots in the rice.' 'It is more profitable to raise geese than daughters.'" He quoted to me the sayings I hated.

"Regret what you've done before I kill you," I said.

"I haven't done anything other men—even you—wouldn't have done in my place."

"You took away my brother."

"I free my apprentices."

"He was not an apprentice."

"China needs soldiers in wartime."

"You took away my childhood."

"I don't know what you're talking about. We've never met before. I've done nothing to you."

"You've done this," I said, and ripped off my shirt to show him my back. "You are responsible for this." When I saw his startled eyes at my breasts, I slashed him across the face and on the second stroke cut off his head.

I pulled my shirt back on and opened the house to the villagers. The baron's family and servants hid in closets and under beds. The villagers dragged them out into the courtyard, where they tried them next to the beheading machine. "Did you take my harvest so that my children had to eat grass?" a weeping farmer asked.

"I saw him steal seed grain," another testified.

"My family was hiding under the thatch on the roof when the bandits robbed our house, and we saw this one take off his mask." They spared those who proved they could be reformed. They beheaded the others. Their necks were collared in the beheading machine, which slowly clamped shut. There was one last-minute reprieve of a bodyguard when a witness shouted testimony just as the vise was pinching blood. The guard had but recently joined the household in exchange for a child hostage. A slow killing gives a criminal time to regret his crimes and think of the right words to prove he can change.

I searched the house, hunting out people for trial. I came upon a locked room. When I broke down the door, I found women, cowering, whimpering women. I heard shrill insect noises and scurrying. They blinked weakly at me like pheasants that have been raised in the dark for soft meat. The servants who walked the ladies had abandoned them, and they could not escape on their little bound feet. Some crawled away from me, using their elbows to pull themselves along. These women would not be good for anything. I called the villagers to come identify any daughters they wanted to take home, but no one claimed any. I gave each woman a bagful of rice, which they sat on. They rolled the bags to the road. They wandered away like ghosts. Later, it would be said, they turned into the band of swordswomen who were a mercenary army. They did not wear men's clothes like me, but rode as women in black and red dresses. They bought up girl babies so that many poor families welcomed their visitations. When slave girls and daughters-in-law ran away, people would say they joined these witch amazons. They killed men and boys. I myself never encountered such women and could not vouch for their reality.

After the trials we tore down the ancestral tablets. "We'll use this great hall for village meetings," I announced. "Here we'll put on operas; we'll sing together and talk-story." We washed the courtyard; we exorcised the house with smoke and red paper. "This is a new year," I told the people, "the year one."

I went home to my parents-in-law and husband and son. My son stared, very impressed by the general he had seen in the parade, but his father said, "It's your mother. Go to your mother." My son was delighted that the shiny general was his mother too. She gave him her helmet to wear and her swords to hold.

Wearing my black embroidered wedding coat, I knelt at my parents-in-law's feet, as I would have done as a bride. "Now my public duties are finished," I said. "I will stay with you, doing farmwork and housework, and giving you more sons."

"Go visit your mother and father first," my mother-in-law said, a generous woman. "They want to welcome you."

My mother and father and the entire clan would be living happily on the money I had sent them. My parents had bought their coffins. They would sacrifice a pig to the gods that I had returned. From the words on my back, and how they were fulfilled, the villagers would make a legend about my perfect filiality.

* * *

My American life has been such a disappointment.

"I got straight A's, Mama."

"Let me tell you a true story about a girl who saved her village."

I could not figure out what was my village. And it was important that I do something big and fine, or else my parents would sell me when we made our way back to China. In China there were solutions for what to do with little girls who ate up food and threw tantrums. You can't eat straight A's.

When one of my parents or the emigrant villagers said, "Feeding girls is feeding cowbirds," I would thrash on the floor and scream so hard I couldn't talk. I couldn't stop.

"What's the matter with her?"

"I don't know. Bad, I guess. You know how girls are. 'There's no profit in raising girls. Better to raise geese than girls.'"

"I would hit her if she were mine. But then there's no use wasting all that discipline on a girl. 'When you raise girls, you're raising children for strangers.'"

"Stop that crying!" my mother would yell. "I'm going to hit you if you don't stop. Bad girl! Stop!" I'm going to remember never to hit or to scold my children for crying, I thought, because then they will only cry more.

"I'm not a bad girl," I would scream. "I'm not a bad girl. I'm not a bad girl." I might as well have said, "I'm not a girl."

"When you were little, all you had to say was 'I'm not a bad girl,' and you could make yourself cry," my mother says, talking-story about my childhood.

I minded that the emigrant villagers shook their heads at my sister and me. "One girl—and another girl," they said, and made our parents ashamed to take us out together. The good part about my brothers being born was that people stopped saying, "All girls," but I learned new grievances. "Did you roll an egg on *my* face like that when *I* was born?" "Did you have a full-month party for *me?*" "Did you turn on all the lights?" Did you send *my* picture to Grandmother?" "Why not? Because I'm a girl? Is that why not?" "Why didn't you teach me English?" "You like having me beaten up at school, don't you?"

"She is very mean, isn't she?" the emigrant villagers would say.

"Come, children. Hurry. Hurry. Who wants to go out with Great-Uncle?" On Saturday mornings my great-uncle, the ex-river pirate, did the shopping. "Get your coats, whoever's coming."

"I'm coming. I'm coming. Wait for me."

When he heard girls' voices, he turned on us and roared, "No girls!" and left my sisters and me hanging our coats back up, not looking at one another. The boys came back with candy and new toys. When they walked through Chinatown, the people must have said, "A boy—and another boy—and another boy!" At my great-uncle's funeral I secretly tested out feeling glad that he was dead—the six-foot bearish masculinity of him.

I went away to college—Berkeley in the sixties—and I studied, and I marched to change the world, but I did not turn into a boy. I would have liked to bring myself back as a boy for my parents to welcome with chickens and pigs. That was for my brother, who returned alive from Vietnam.

If I went to Vietnam, I would not come back; females desert families. It was said, "There is an outward tendency in females," which meant that I was getting straight A's for the good of my future husband's family, not my own. I did not plan ever to have a husband. I would show my mother and father and the nosey emigrant villagers that girls have no outward tendency. I stopped getting straight A's.

And all the time I was having to turn myself American-feminine, or no dates.

There is a Chinese word for the female *I*—which is "slave." Break the women with their own tongues!

I refused to cook. When I had to wash dishes, I would crack one or two. "Bad girl," my mother yelled, and sometimes that made me gloat rather than cry. Isn't a bad girl almost a boy?

"What do you want to be when you grow up, little girl?"

"A lumberjack in Oregon."

Even now, unless I'm happy, I burn the food when I cook. I do not feed people. I let the dirty dishes rot. I eat at other people's tables but won't invite them to mine, where the dishes are rotting.

If I could not-eat, perhaps I could make myself a warrior like the swordswoman who drives me. I will—I must—rise and plow the fields as soon as the baby comes out.

Once I get outside the house, what bird might call me; on what horse could I ride away? Marriage and childbirth strengthen the swordswoman, who is not a maid like Joan of Arc. Do the women's work; then do more work, which will become ours too. No husband of mine will say, "I could have been a drummer, but I had to think about the wife and kids. You know how it is." Nobody supports me at the expense of his own adventure. Then I get bitter: no one supports me; I am not loved enough to be supported. That I am not a burden has to compensate for the sad envy when I look at women loved enough to be supported. Even now China wraps double binds around my feet.

When urban renewal tore down my parents' laundry and paved over our slum for a parking lot, I only made up gun and knife fantasies and did nothing useful.

From the fairy tales, I've learned exactly who the enemy are. I easily recognize them—business-suited in their modern American executive guise, each boss two feet taller than I am and impossible to meet eye to eye.

I once worked at an art supply house that sold paints to artists. "Order more of that nigger yellow, willya?" the boss told me. "Bright, isn't it? Nigger yellow."

"I don't like that word," I had to say in my bad, small-person's voice that makes no impact. The boss never deigned to answer.

I also worked at a land developers' association. The building industry was planning a banquet for contractors, real estate dealers, and real estate editors. "Did you know the restaurant you chose for the banquet is being picketed by CORE and the NAACP?" I squeaked.

"Of course I know." The boss laughed. "That's why I chose it."

"I refuse to type these invitations," I whispered, voice unreliable.

He leaned back in his leather chair, his bossy stomach opulent. He picked up his calendar and slowly circled a date. "You will be paid up to here," he said. "We'll mail you the check."

If I took the sword, which my hate must surely have forged out of the air, and gutted him, I would put color and wrinkles into his shirt.

It's not just the stupid racists that I have to do something about, but the tyrants who for whatever reason can deny my family food and work. My job is my own only land.

To avenge my family, I'd have to storm across China to take back our farm from the Communists; I'd have to rage across the United States to take back the laundry in New York and the one in California. Nobody in history has conquered and united both North America and Asia. A descendant of eighty pole fighters, I ought to be able to set out confidently, march straight down our street, get going right now. There's work to do, ground to cover. Surely, the eighty pole fighters, though unseen, would follow me and lead me and protect me, as is the wont of ancestors.

Or it may well be that they're resting happily in China, their spirits dispersed among the real Chinese, and not nudging me at all with their poles. I mustn't feel bad that I haven't done as well as the swordswoman did; after all, no bird called me, no wise old people tutored me. I have no magic beads, no water gourd sight, no rabbit that will jump in the fire when I'm hungry. I dislike armies.

I've looked for the bird. I've seen clouds make pointed angel wings that stream past the sunset, but they shred into clouds. Once at a beach after a long hike I saw a seagull, tiny as an insect. But when I jumped up to tell what miracle I saw, before I could get the words out I understood that the bird was insect-size because it was far away. My brain had momentarily lost its depth perception. I was that eager to find an unusual bird.

The news from China has been confusing. It also had something to do with birds. I was nine years old when the letters made my parents, who are rocks, cry. My father screamed in his sleep. My mother wept and crumpled up the letters. She set fire to them page by page in the ashtray, but new letters came almost every day. The only letters they opened without fear were the ones with red borders, the holiday letters that mustn't carry bad news. The other letters said that my uncles were made to kneel on broken glass during their trials and had confessed to being landowners. They were all executed, and the aunt whose thumbs were twisted off drowned herself. Other aunts, mothers-in-law, and cousins disappeared; some suddenly began writing to us again from communes or from Hong Kong. They kept asking for money. The ones in communes got four ounces of fat and one cup of oil a week, they said, and had to work from 4 A.M. to 9 P.M. They had to learn to do dances waving red kerchiefs; they had to sing nonsense syllables. The Communists gave axes to the old ladies and said, "Go and kill yourself. You're useless." If we overseas Chinese would just send money to the Communist bank, our relatives said, they might get a percentage of it for themselves. The aunts in Hong Kong said to send money quickly; their children were begging on the sidewalks and mean people put dirt in their bowls.

When I dream that I am wire without flesh, there is a letter on blue airmail paper that floats above the night ocean between here and China. It must arrive safely or else my grandmother and I will lose each other.

My parents felt bad whether or not they sent money. Sometimes they got angry at their brothers and sisters for asking. And they would not simply ask but have to talk-story too. The revolutionaries had taken Fourth Aunt and Uncle's store, house, and lands. They attacked the house and killed the grandfather and oldest daughter. The grandmother escaped with the loose cash and did not return to help. Fourth Aunt picked up her sons, one under each arm, and hid in the pig house, where they slept that night in cotton clothes. The next day she found her husband, who had also miraculously escaped. The two of them collected twigs and yams to sell while their children begged. Each morning they tied the faggots on each other's back. Nobody bought from them. They ate the yams and some of the children's rice. Finally Fourth Aunt saw what was wrong. "We have to shout 'Fuel for sale' and 'Yams for sale,'" she said. "We can't just walk unobtrusively up and down the street." "You're right," said my uncle, but he was shy and walked in back of her. "Shout," my aunt ordered, but he could not. "They think we're carrying these sticks home for our own fire," she said. "Shout." They walked about miserably, silently, until sundown, neither of them able to advertise themselves. Fourth Aunt, an orphan since the age of ten, mean as my mother, threw her bundle down at his feet and scolded Fourth Uncle, "Starving to death, his wife and children starving to death, and he's too damned shy to raise his voice." She left him standing by himself and afraid to return empty-handed to her. He sat under a tree to think, when he spotted a pair of nesting doves. Dumping his bag of yams, he climbed up and caught the birds. That was when the Communists trapped him, in the tree. They criticized him for selfishly taking food for his own family and killed him, leaving his body in the tree as an example. They took the birds to a commune kitchen to be shared.

It is confusing that my family was not the poor to be championed. They were executed like the barons in the stories, when they were not barons. It is confusing that birds tricked us.

What fighting and killing I have seen have not been glorious but slum grubby. I fought the most during junior high school and always cried. Fights are confusing as to who has won. The corpses I've seen had been rolled and dumped, sad little dirty bodies covered with a police khaki blanket. My mother locked her children in the house so we couldn't look at dead slum people. But at news of a body, I would find a way to get out; I had to learn about dying if I wanted to become a swordswoman. Once there was an Asian man stabbed next door, words on cloth pinned to his corpse. When the police came around asking questions, my father said, "No read Japanese. Japanese words. Me Chinese."

I've also looked for old people who could be my gurus. A medium with red hair told me that a girl who died in a far country follows me wherever I go. This spirit can help me if I acknowledge her, she said. Between the head line and heart line in my right palm, she said, I have the mystic cross. I could become a medium myself. I don't want to be a medium. I don't want to be a crank taking "offerings" in a wicker plate from the frightened audience, who, one after another, asked the spirits how to raise rent money, how to cure their coughs and skin diseases, how to find a job. And martial arts are for unsure little boys kicking away under fluorescent lights.

I live now where there are Chinese and Japanese, but no emigrants from my own village looking at me as if I had failed them. Living among one's own emigrant villagers can give a good Chinese far from China glory and a place. "That old busboy is really a swordsman," we whisper when he goes by, "He's a swordsman who's killed fifty. He has a tong ax in his closet." But I am useless, one more girl who couldn't be sold. When I visit the family now, I wrap my American successes around me like a private shawl; I *am* worthy of eating the food. From afar I can believe my family loves me fundamentally. They only say, "When fishing for treasures in the flood, be careful not to pull in girls," because that is what one says about daughters. But I watched such words come out of my own mother's and father's mouths; I looked at their ink drawing of poor people snagging their neighbors' flotage with long flood hooks and pushing the girl babies on down the river. And I had to get out of hating range. I read in an anthropology book that Chinese say, "Girls are necessary too"; I have never heard the Chinese I know make this concession. Perhaps it was a saying in another village. I refuse to shy my way anymore through our Chinatown, which tasks me with the old sayings and the stories.

The swordswoman and I are not so dissimilar. May my people understand the resemblance soon so that I can return to them. What we have in common are the words at our backs. The ideographs for *revenge* are "report a crime" and "report to five families." The reporting is the vengeance—not the beheading, not the gutting, but the words. And I have so many words—"chink" words and "gook" words too—that they do not fit on my skin.

1975–1976

Gish Jen b. 1955

Born in Long Island, New York, Gish Jen comes from a family of five children with parents who were educated in Shanghai, China (her mother in educational psychology and her father in engineering) and who separately immigrated to the United States around World War II. As a pre-med and English major at Harvard University, Jen earned a B.A. in 1977. She then attended Stanford Business School for a year and, from 1981 to 1983, completed an M.F.A. at the University of Iowa. She lives in Cambridge, Massachusetts, with her husband, son, and daughter.

Although Jen's works have appeared in various journals and anthologies, including *The Atlantic* and *The Best American Short Stories 1988,* the 1991 novel *Typical American* marks her arrival as a much-acclaimed fiction writer. Callie and Mona, two sisters who appear in several of Jen's short stories, play minor roles in this work. The novel focuses on the girls' father, Ralph Chang, who, in line with the 1950s atmosphere of upward mobility and conformity in America, becomes absorbed with pursuing the American Dream. Jen's next novel, *Mona in the Promised Land,* focuses on Mona Chang, the daughter who converts to Judaism after the family moves to the upscale Jewish neighborhood of "Scarshill" (Jen grew up in Scarsdale, New York). Her collection of eight short stories, *Who's Irish?,* includes new and previously published works such as "The Water Faucet Vision" and "In the American Society."

In an interview, Jen said that the scene in "In the American Society" where Ralph throws the polo shirt into the swimming pool convinced her to use Ralph as the protagonist for her first novel. This dramatic act, she stated, indicated that Ralph was the kind of make-things-happen character she needed. The first part of "In the American Society" depicts a Chinese immigrant's vain attempt to impose the feudal practices and attitudes of an old-world Chinese village lord on his American restaurant employees. Placed in a different setting, the second part of the story suggests that this same background enables Ralph to resist being ridiculed. The parallel structures of the two scenes and the resolution of the story offer an insightful analysis of cross-cultural and racial issues in American society.

In this short story and in her other works, Jen displays a seamless, engaging, and comic narrative voice. Her ironic wit is apparent in disarmingly straightforward language. Jen's style contrasts markedly with the styles of Amy Tan and Maxine Hong Kingston, two other contemporary Chinese American writers with whom she is inevitably compared. However, although all three are Chinese American, each is a highly effective artist in her own right and should be read and enjoyed for her individual style. Like Kingston and Tan, Jen comes out of a specific Asian American historical-cultural experience. She takes her rightful place in an American literary tradition that is being redefined to include writers from the various cultures that compose American society.

Bonnie TuSmith
Northeastern University

PRIMARY WORKS

Typical American, 1991; *Mona in the Promised Land,* 1996; *Who's Irish?,* 1999; "Gish Jen: Interview by Rachel Lee," *Words Matter: Conversations with Asian American Writers,* ed. King-Kok Cheung, 2000.

In the American Society

I. His Own Society

When my father took over the pancake house, it was to send my little sister Mona and me to college. We were only in junior high at the time, but my father believed in getting a jump on things. "Those Americans always saying it," he told us. "Smart guys thinking in advance." My mother elaborated, explaining that businesses took bringing up, like children. They could take years to get going, she said, years.

In this case, though, we got rich right away. At two months we were breaking even, and at four, those same hotcakes that could barely withstand the weight of butter and syrup were supporting our family with ease. My mother bought a station wagon with air conditioning, my father an oversized, red vinyl recliner for the back room; and as time went on and the business continued to thrive, my father started to talk about his grandfather and the village he had reigned over in China—things my father had never talked about when he worked for other people. He told us about the bags of rice his family would give out to the poor at New Year's, and about the people who came to beg, on their hands and knees, for his grandfather to intercede for the more wayward of their relatives. "Like that Godfather in the movie," he would tell us as, his feet up, he distributed paychecks. Sometimes an employee would get two green envelopes instead of one, which meant that Jimmy needed a tooth pulled, say, or that Tiffany's husband was in the clinker again.

"It's nothing, nothing," he would insist, sinking back into his chair. "Who else is going to take care of you people?"

My mother would mostly just sigh about it. "Your father thinks this is China," she would say, and then she would go back to her mending. Once in a while, though, when my father had given away a particularly large sum, she would exclaim, outraged, "But this here is the U—S—of—A!"—this apparently having been what she used to tell immigrant stock boys when they came in late.

She didn't work at the supermarket anymore; but she had made it to the rank of manager before she left, and this had given her not only new words and phrases, but new ideas about herself, and about America, and about what was what in general. She had opinions, now, on how downtown should be zoned; she could pump her own gas and check her own oil; and for all she used to chide Mona and me for being "copycats," she herself was now interested in espadrilles, and wallpaper, and most recently, the town country club.

"So join already," said Mona, flicking a fly off her knee.

My mother enumerated the problems as she sliced up a quarter round of watermelon: There was the cost. There was the waiting list. There was the fact that no one in our family played either tennis or golf.

"So what?" said Mona.

"It would be waste," said my mother.

"Me and Callie can swim in the pool."

"Plus you need that recommendation letter from a member."

"Come *on,*" said Mona. "Annie's mom'd write you a letter in *sec.*"

My mother's knife glinted in the early summer sun. I spread some more newspaper on the picnic table.

"*Plus* you have to eat there twice a month. You know what that means." My mother cut another, enormous slice of fruit.

"No, I *don't* know what that means," said Mona.

"It means Dad would have to wear a jacket, dummy," I said.

"Oh! Oh! Oh!" said Mona, clasping her hand to her breast. "Oh! Oh! Oh! Oh! Oh!"

We all laughed: my father had no use for nice clothes, and would wear only ten-year-old shirts, with grease-spotted pants, to show how little he cared what anyone thought.

"Your father doesn't believe in joining the American society," said my mother. "He wants to have his own society."

"So go to dinner without him." Mona shot her seeds out in long arcs over the lawn. "Who cares what he thinks?"

But of course we all did care, and knew my mother could not simply up and do as she pleased. For in my father's mind, a family owed its head a degree of loyalty that left no room for dissent. To embrace what he embraced was to love; and to embrace something else was to betray him.

He demanded a similar sort of loyalty of his workers, whom he treated more like servants than employees. Not in the beginning, of course. In the beginning all he wanted was for them to keep on doing what they used to do, and to that end he concentrated mostly on leaving them alone. As the months passed, though, he expected more and more of them, with the result that for all his largesse, he began to have trouble keeping help. The cooks and busboys complained that he asked them to fix radiators and trim hedges, not only at the restaurant, but at our house; the waitresses that he sent them on errands and made them chauffeur him around. Our head waitress, Gertrude, claimed that he once even asked her to scratch his back.

"It's not just the blacks don't believe in slavery," she said when she quit.

My father never quite registered her complaint, though, nor those of the others who left. Even after Eleanor quit, then Tiffany, then Gerald, and Jimmy, and even his best cook, Eureka Andy, for whom he had bought new glasses, he remained mostly convinced that the fault lay with them.

"All they understand is that assembly line," he lamented. "Robots, they are. They want to be robots."

There *were* occasions when the clear running truth seemed to eddy, when he would pinch the vinyl of his chair up into little peaks and wonder if he was doing things right. But with time he would always smooth the peaks back down; and when business started to slide in the spring, he kept on like a horse in his ways.

By the summer our dishboy was overwhelmed with scraping. It was no longer just the hashbrowns that people were leaving for trash, and the service was as bad as the food. The waitresses served up French pancakes instead of German, apple juice instead of orange, spilt things on laps, on coats. On the Fourth of July some greenhorn sent an entire side of fries slaloming down a lady's *massif centrale.* Meanwhile in the back room, my father labored through articles on the economy.

"What is housing starts?" he puzzled. "What is GNP?"

Mona and I did what we could, filling in as busgirls and bookkeepers and, one afternoon, stuffing the comments box that hung by the cashier's desk. That was Mona's idea. We rustled up a variety of pens and pencils, checked boxes for an hour, smeared the cards up with coffee and grease, and waited. It took a few days for my father to notice that the box was full, and he didn't say anything about it for a few days more. Finally, though, he started to complain of fatigue; and then he began to complain that the staff was not what it could be. We encouraged him in this—pointing out, for instance, how many dishes got chipped—but in the end all that happened was that, for the first time since we took over the restaurant, my father got it into his head to fire someone. Skip, a skinny busboy who was saving up for a sportscar, said nothing as my father mumbled on about the price of dishes. My father's hands shook as he wrote out the severance check; and he spent the rest of the day napping in his chair once it was over.

As it was going on midsummer, Skip wasn't easy to replace. We hung a sign in the window and advertised in the paper, but no one called the first week, and the person who called the second didn't show up for his interview. The third week, my father phoned Skip to see if he would come back, but a friend of his had already sold him a Corvette for cheap.

Finally a Chinese guy named Booker turned up. He couldn't have been more than thirty, and was wearing a lighthearted seersucker suit, but he looked as though life had him pinned: his eyes were bloodshot and his chest sunken, and the muscles of his neck seemed to strain with the effort of holding his head up. In a single dry breath he told us that he had never bussed tables but was willing to learn, and that he was on the lam from the deportation authorities.

"I do not want to lie to you," he kept saying. He had come to the United States on a student visa, had run out of money, and was now in a bind. He was loath to go back to Taiwan, as it happened—he looked up at this point, to be sure my father wasn't pro-KMT—but all he had was a phony social security card and a willingness to absorb all blame, should anything untoward come to pass.

"I do not think, anyway, that it is against law to hire me, only to be me," he said, smiling faintly.

Anyone else would have examined him on this, but my father conceived of laws as speed bumps rather than curbs. He wiped the counter with his sleeve, and told Booker to report the next morning.

"I will be good worker," said Booker.

"Good," said my father.

"Anything you want me to do, I will do."

My father nodded.

Booker seemed to sink into himself for a moment. "Thank you," he said finally. "I am appreciate your help. I am very, very appreciate for everything." He reached out to shake my father's hand.

My father looked at him. "Did you eat today?" he asked in Mandarin.

Booker pulled at the hem of his jacket.

"Sit down," said my father. "Please, have a seat."

My father didn't tell my mother about Booker, and my mother didn't tell my father about the country club. She would never have applied, except that Mona, while over at Annie's, had let it drop that our mother wanted to join. Mrs. Lardner came by the very next day.

"Why, I'd be honored and delighted to write you people a letter," she said. Her skirt billowed around her.

"Thank you so much," said my mother. "But it's too much trouble for you, and also my husband is . . ."

"Oh, it's no trouble at all, no trouble at all. I tell you." She leaned forward so that her chest freckles showed. "I know just how it is. It's a secret of course, but you know, my natural father was Jewish. Can you see it? Just look at my skin."

"My husband," said my mother.

"I'd be honored and delighted," said Mrs. Lardner with a little wave of her hands. "Just honored and delighted."

Mona was triumphant. "See, Mom," she said, waltzing around the kitchen when Mrs. Lardner left. "What did I tell you? 'I'm just honored and delighted, just honored and delighted.'" She waved her hands in the air.

"You know, the Chinese have a saying," said my mother. "To do nothing is better than to overdo. You mean well, but you tell me now what will happen."

"I'll talk Dad into it," said Mona, still waltzing. "Or I bet Callie can. He'll do anything Callie says."

"I can try, anyway," I said.

"Did you hear what I said?" said my mother. Mona bumped into the broom closet door. "You're not going to talk anything; you've already made enough trouble." She started on the dishes with a clatter.

Mona poked diffidently at a mop.

I sponged off the counter. "Anyway," I ventured. "I bet our name'll never even come up."

"That's if we're lucky," said my mother.

"There's all these people waiting," I said.

"Good," she said. She started on a pot.

I looked over at Mona, who was still cowering in the broom closet. "In fact, there's some black family's been waiting so long, they're going to sue," I said.

My mother turned off the water. "Where'd you hear that?"

"Patty told me."

She turned the water back on, started to wash a dish, then put it back down and shut the faucet.

"I'm sorry," said Mona.

"Forget it," said my mother. "Just forget it."

Booker turned out to be a model worker, whose boundless gratitude translated into a willingness to do anything. As he also learned quickly, he soon knew not only how to bus, but how to cook, and how to wait table, and how to keep the books. He fixed the walk-in door so that it stayed shut, reupholstered the torn seats in the dining room, and devised a system for tracking inventory. The only stone in the rice was that he tended to be sickly; but, reliable even in illness, he would always send a friend to take his place. In this way we got to know Ronald, Lynn, Dirk, and Cedric, all of whom, like Booker, had problems with their legal status and were anxious to please. They weren't all as capable as Booker, though, with the exception of Cedric, whom my father often hired even when Booker was well. A round wag of a man who called Mona and me *shou hou*—skinny monkeys—he was a professed non-smoker who was nevertheless always begging drags off of other people's cigarettes. This last habit drove our head cook, Fernando, crazy, especially since, when refused a hit, Cedric would occasionally snitch one. Winking impishly at Mona and me, he would steal up to an ashtray, take a quick puff, and then break out laughing so that the smoke came rolling out of his mouth in a great incriminatory cloud. Fernando accused him of stealing fresh cigarettes too, even whole packs.

"Why else do you think he's weaseling around in the back of the store all the time," he said. His face was blotchy with anger. "The man is a frigging thief."

Other members of the staff supported him in this contention and joined in on an "Operation Identification," which involved numbering and initialing their cigarettes—even though what they seemed to fear for wasn't so much their cigarettes as their jobs. Then one of the cooks quit; and rather than promote someone, my father hired Cedric for the position. Rumors flew that he was taking only half the normal salary, that Alex had been pressured to resign, and that my father was looking for a position with which to placate Booker, who had been bypassed because of his health.

The result was that Fernando categorically refused to work with Cedric.

"The only way I'll cook with that piece of slime," he said, shaking his huge tattooed fist, "is if it's his ass frying on the grill."

My father cajoled and cajoled, to no avail, and in the end was simply forced to put them on different schedules.

The next week Fernando got caught stealing a carton of minute steaks. My father would not tell even Mona and me how he knew to be standing by the back door when Fernando was on his way out, but everyone suspected Booker. Everyone but Fernando, that is, who was sure Cedric had been the tip-off. My father held a staff meeting in which he tried to reassure everyone that Alex had left on his own, and that he had no intention of firing anyone. But though he was careful not to mention Fernando, everyone was so amazed that he was being allowed to stay that Fernando was incensed nonetheless.

"Don't you all be putting your bug eyes on me," he said. "*He's* the frigging crook." He grabbed Cedric by the collar.

Cedric raised an eyebrow. "Cook, you mean," he said.

At this Fernando punched Cedric in the mouth; and the words he had just uttered notwithstanding, my father fired him on the spot.

With everything that was happening, Mona and I were ready to be getting out of the restaurant. It was almost time: the days were still stuffy with summer, but our window shade had started flapping in the evening as if gearing up to go out. That year the breezes were full of salt, as they sometimes were when they came in from the East, and they blew anchors and docks through my mind like so many tumbleweeds, filling my dreams with wherries and lobsters and grainy-faced men who squinted, day in and day out, at the sky.

It was time for a change, you could feel it; and yet the pancake house was the same as ever. The day before school started my father came home with bad news.

"Fernando called police," he said, wiping his hand on his pant leg.

My mother naturally wanted to know what police; and so with much coughing and hawing, the long story began, the latest installment of which had the police calling immigration, and immigration sending an investigator. My mother sat stiff as whalebone as my father described how the man summarily refused lunch on the house and how my father had admitted, under pressure, that he knew there were "things" about his workers.

"So now what happens?"

My father didn't know. "Booker and Cedric went with him to the jail," he said. "But me, here I am." He laughed uncomfortably.

The next day my father posted bail for "his boys" and waited apprehensively for something to happen. The day after that he waited again, and the day after that he called our neighbor's law student son, who suggested my father call the immigration department under an alias. My father took his advice; and it was thus that he discovered that Booker was right: it was illegal for aliens to work, but it wasn't to hire them.

In the happy interval that ensued, my father apologized to my mother, who in turn confessed about the country club, for which my father had no choice but to forgive her. Then he turned his attention back to "his boys."

My mother didn't see that there was anything to do.

"I like to talking to the judge," said my father.

"This is not China," said my mother.

"I'm only talking to him. I'm not give him money unless he wants it."

"You're going to land up in jail."

"So what else I should do?" My father threw up his hands. "Those are my boys."

"Your boys!" exploded my mother. "What about your family? What about your wife?"

My father took a long sip of tea. "You know," he said finally. "In the war my father sent our cook to the soldiers to use. He always said it—the province comes before the town, the town comes before the family."

"A restaurant is not a town," said my mother.

My father sipped at his tea again. "You know, when I first come to the United States, I also had to hide-and-seek with those deportation guys. If people did not helping me, I'm not here today."

My mother scrutinized her hem.

After a minute I volunteered that before seeing a judge, he might try a lawyer.

He turned. "Since when did you become so afraid like your mother?"

I started to say that it wasn't a matter of fear, but he cut me off.

"What I need today," he said, "is a son."

My father and I spent the better part of the next day standing in lines at the immigration office. He did not get to speak to a judge, but with much persistence he managed to speak to a judge's clerk, who tried to persuade him that it was not her place to extend him advice. My father, though, shamelessly plied her with compliments and offers of free pancakes until she finally conceded that she personally doubted anything would happen to either Cedric or Booker.

"Especially if they're 'needed workers,'" she said, rubbing at the red marks her glasses left on her nose. She yawned. "Have you thought about sponsoring them to become permanent residents?"

Could he do that? My father was overjoyed. And what if he saw to it right away? Would she perhaps put in a good word with the judge?

She yawned again, her nostrils flaring. "Don't worry," she said. "They'll get a fair hearing."

My father returned jubilant. Booker and Cedric hailed him as their savior, their Buddha incarnate. He was like a father to them, they said; and laughing and clapping, they made him tell the story over and over, sorting over the details like jewels. And how old was the assistant judge? And what did she say?

That evening my father tipped the paperboy a dollar and bought a pot of mums for my mother, who suffered them to be placed on the dining room table. The next night he took us all out to dinner. Then on Saturday, Mona found a letter on my father's chair at the restaurant.

Dear Mr. Chang,

You are the grat boss. But, we do not like to trial, so will runing away now. Plese to excus us. People saying the law in America is fears like dragon. Here is only $140. We hope some day we can pay back the rest bale. You will getting intrest, as you diserving, so grat a boss you are. Thank you for every thing. In next life you will be burn in rich family, with no more pancaks.

Yours truley,
Booker + Cedric

In the weeks that followed my father went to the pancake house for crises, but otherwise hung around our house, fiddling idly with the sump pump and boiler in an effort, he said, to get ready for winter. It was as though he had gone into retirement, except that instead of moving south, he had moved to the basement. He even took to showering my mother with little attentions, and to calling her "old girl," and when we finally heard that the club had entertained all the applications it could for the year, he was so sympathetic that he seemed more disappointed than my mother.

II. In the American Society

Mrs. Lardner tempered the bad news with an invitation to a bon voyage "bash" she was throwing for a friend of hers who was going to Greece for six months.

"Do come," she urged. "You'll meet everyone, and then, you know, if things open up in the spring . . ." She waved her hands.

My mother wondered if it would be appropriate to show up at a party for someone they didn't know, but "the honest truth" was that this was an annual affair. "If it's not Greece, it's Antibes," sighed Mrs. Lardner. "We really just do it because his wife left him and his daughter doesn't speak to him, and poor Jeremy just feels so *unloved*."

She also invited Mona and me to the goings on, as "*demi*-guests" to keep Annie out of the champagne. I wasn't too keen on the idea, but before I could say anything, she had already thanked us for so generously agreeing to honor her with our presence.

"A pair of little princesses, you are!" she told us. "A pair of princesses!"

The party was that Sunday. On Saturday, my mother took my father out shopping for a suit. As it was the end of September, she insisted that he buy a worsted rather than a seersucker, even though it was only ten, rather than fifty percent off. My father protested that it was as hot out as ever, which was true—a thick Indian summer had cozied murderously up to us—but to no avail. Summer clothes, said my mother, were not properly worn after Labor Day.

The suit was unfortunately as extravagant in length as it was in price, which posed an additional quandary, since the tailor wouldn't be in until Monday. The salesgirl, though, found a way of tacking it up temporarily.

"Maybe this suit not fit me," fretted my father.

"Just don't take your jacket off," said the salesgirl.

He gave her a tip before they left, but when he got home refused to remove the price tag.

"I like to asking the tailor about the size," he insisted.

"You mean you're going to *wear* it and then *return* it?" Mona rolled her eyes.

"I didn't say I'm return it," said my father stiffly. "I like to asking the tailor, that's all."

The party started off swimmingly, except that most people were wearing bermudas or wrap skirts. Still, my parents carried on, sharing with great feeling the complaints about the heat. Of course my father tried to eat a cracker full of shallots and burnt himself in an attempt to help Mr. Lardner turn the coals of the barbeque; but on the whole he seemed to be doing all right. Not nearly so well as my mother, though, who had accepted an entire cupful of Mrs. Lardner's magic punch, and seemed indeed to be under some spell. As Mona and Annie skirmished over whether some boy in their class inhaled when he smoked, I watched my mother take off her shoes, laughing and laughing as a man with a beard regaled her with navy stories by the pool. Apparently he had been stationed in the Orient and remembered a few words of Chinese, which made my mother laugh still more. My father excused himself to go to the men's room then drifted back and weighed anchor at the hors d'oeuvres table, while my mother sailed on to a group of women, who tinkled at length over the clarity of her complexion. I dug out a book I had brought.

Just when I'd cracked the spine, though, Mrs. Lardner came by to bewail her shortage of servers. Her caterers were criminals, I agreed; and the next thing I knew I was handing out bits of marine life, making the rounds as amiably as I could.

"Here you go, Dad," I said when I got to the hors d'oeuvres table.

"Everything is fine," he said.

I hesitated to leave him alone; but then the man with the beard zeroed in on him, and though he talked of nothing but my mother, I thought it would be okay to get back to work. Just that moment, though, Jeremy Brothers lurched our way, an empty, albeit corked, wine bottle in hand. He was a slim, well-proportioned man, with a Roman nose and small eyes and a nice manly jaw that he allowed to hang agape.

"Hello," he said drunkenly. "Pleased to meet you."

"Pleased to meeting you," said my father.

"Right," said Jeremy. "Right. Listen. I have this bottle here, this most recalcitrant bottle. You see that it refuses to do my bidding. I bid it open sesame, please, and it does nothing." He pulled the cork out with his teeth, then turned the bottle upside down.

My father nodded.

"Would you have a word with it please?" said Jeremy. The man with the beard excused himself. "Would you please have a goddamned word with it?"

My father laughed uncomfortably.

"Ah!" Jeremy bowed a little. "Excuse me, excuse me, excuse me. You are not my man, not my man at all." He bowed again and started to leave, but then circled back. "Viticulture is not your forte, yes I can see that, see that plainly. But may I trouble you on another matter? Forget the damned bottle." He threw it into the pool, and winked at the people he splashed. "I have another matter. Do you speak Chinese?"

My father said he did not, but Jeremy pulled out a handkerchief with some characters on it anyway, saying that his daughter had sent it from Hong Kong and that he thought the characters might be some secret message.

"Long life," said my father.

"But you haven't looked at it yet."

"I know what it says without looking." My father winked at me.

"You do?"

"Yes, I do."

"You're making fun of me, aren't you?"

"No, no, no," said my father, winking again.

"Who are you anyway?" said Jeremy.

His smile fading, my father shrugged.

"*Who are you?*"

My father shrugged again.

Jeremy began to roar. "This is my party, *my party,* and I've never seen you before in my life." My father backed up as Jeremy came toward him. "*Who are you? WHO ARE YOU?*"

Just as my father was going to step back into the pool, Mrs. Lardner came running up. Jeremy informed her that there was a man crashing his party.

"Nonsense," said Mrs. Lardner. "This is Ralph Chang, who I invited extra especially so he could meet you." She straightened the collar of Jeremy's peach-colored polo shirt for him.

"Yes, well, we've had a chance to chat," said Jeremy.

She whispered in his ear; he mumbled something; she whispered something more.

"I do apologize," he said finally.

My father didn't say anything.

"I do." Jeremy seemed genuinely contrite. "Doubtless you've seen drunks before, haven't you? You must have them in China."

"Okay," said my father.

As Mrs. Lardner glided off, Jeremy clapped his arm over my father's shoulders. "You know, I really am quite sorry, quite sorry."

My father nodded.

"What can I do, how can I make it up to you?"

"No thank you."

"No, tell me, tell me," wheedled Jeremy. "Tickets to casino night?" My father shook his head. "You don't gamble. Dinner at Bartholomew's?" My father shook his head again. "You don't eat." Jeremy scratched his chin. "You know, my wife was like you. Old Annabelle could never let me make things up—never, never, never, never, never."

My father wriggled out from under his arm.

"How about sport clothes? You are rather overdressed, you know, excuse me for saying so. But here." He took off his polo shirt and folded it up. "You can have this with my most profound apologies." He ruffled his chest hairs with his free hand.

"No thank you," said my father.

"No, take it, take it. Accept my apologies." He thrust the shirt into my father's arms. "I'm so very sorry, so very sorry. Please, try it on."

Helplessly holding the shirt, my father searched the crowd for my mother.

"Here, I'll help you off with your coat."

My father froze.

Jeremy reached over and took his jacket off. "Milton's, one hundred twenty-five dollars reduced to one hundred twelve-fifty," he read. "What a bargain, what a bargain!"

"Please give it back," pleaded my father. "Please."

"Now for your shirt," ordered Jeremy.

Heads began to turn.

"Take off your shirt."

"I do not take orders like a servant," announced my father.

"Take off your shirt, or I'm going to throw this jacket right into the pool, just right into this little pool here." Jeremy held it over the water.

"Go ahead."

"One hundred twelve-fifty," taunted Jeremy. "One hundred twelve . . ."

My father flung the polo shirt into the water with such force that part of it bounced back up into the air like a fluorescent fountain. Then it settled into a soft heap on top of the water. My mother hurried up.

"You're a sport!" said Jeremy, suddenly breaking into a smile and slapping my father on the back. "You're a sport! I like that. A man with spirit, that's what you are. A man with panache. Allow me to return to you your jacket." He handed it back to my father. "Good value you got on that, good value."

My father hurled the coat into the pool too. "We're leaving," he said grimly. "Leaving!"

"Now, Ralphie," said Mrs. Lardner, bustling up; but my father was already stomping off.

"Get your sister," he told me. To my mother: "Get your shoes."

"That was *great,* Dad," said Mona as we walked down to the car. "You were *stupendous.*"

"Way to show 'em," I said.

"What?" said my father offhandedly.

Although it was only just dusk, we were in a gulch, which made it hard to see anything except the gleam of his white shirt moving up the hill ahead of us.

"It was all my fault," began my mother.

"Forget it," said my father grandly. Then he said, "The only trouble is I left those keys in my jacket pocket."

"Oh *no,*" said Mona.

"Oh no is right," said my mother.

"So we'll walk home," I said.

"But how're we going to get into the *house,*" said Mona.

The noise of the party churned through the silence.

"Someone has to going back," said my father.

"Let's go to the pancake house first," suggested my mother. "We can wait there until the party is finished, and then call Mrs. Lardner."

Having all agreed that that was a good plan, we started walking again.

"God, just think," said Mona. "We're going to have to *dive* for them."

My father stopped a moment. We waited.

"You girls are good swimmers," he said finally. "Not like me."

Then his shirt started moving again, and we trooped up the hill after it, into the dark.

1991

Janice Mirikitani b. 1942

Janice Mirikitani, sansei, a third-generation Japanese American, was born in Stockton, California, just before World War II, during which she and her family were interned in concentration camps, along with 110,000 other Japanese Americans. Mirikitani is the editor of several anthologies, including *Third World Women, Time to Greez! Incantations from the Third World,* and *AYUMI, A Japanese American Anthology,* a 320-page bilingual anthology featuring four generations of Japanese American writers, poets, and graphic artists. She has published in many anthologies, textbooks and periodicals, including *Asian American Heritage, The Third Woman: Minority Women Writers of the United States, Amerasia,* and *Bridge.*

Mirikitani is a poet, dancer, and teacher, as well as a social and political activist; she has been program director of Glide Church/Urban Center since 1967 and director of the Glide Theater Group. Her commitment to Third World positions against racism and oppression is reflected in the protest content in her major collections, *Awake in the River* (1978) and *Shedding Silence* (1987). George Leong says of her: "From the eye of racist relocation fever which came about and plagued America during World War II, Janice Mirikitani grew/bloomed/fought as a desert flower behind barbed wire. She grew with that pain, of what it all represented; from the multinational corporations to war from Korea to Vietnam to Latin America to Africa to Hunter's Point and Chinatown" ("Afterword," *Awake in the River*).

Much of her work seeks defiantly to break the stereotypes of Asian Americans prevalent in mainstream American culture. Her voice is often angry, aggressive, blunt, and direct. But it can also be elegiac. Because she is finding new ground, Mirikitani takes the time to explore her family history, and she anchors her identity securely in the details of Asian American experience. In this manner she manages to escape easy nostalgia and cultural sentimentality. Mirikitani does not separate her writing from a social and political platform and sees the necessity to write out of a political agenda. Identifying her community as Third World, she says, "I don't think that Third World writers can really afford to separate themselves from the ongoing struggles of their people. Nor can we ever not embrace our history."

Shirley Geok-lin Lim
University of California, Santa Barbara

PRIMARY WORKS

Awake in the River, 1978; *Shedding Silence,* 1987; "Janice Mirikitani: Interview by Grace Kyungwon Hong," *Words Matter: Conversations with Asian American Writers,* ed. King-Kok Cheung, 2000.

For My Father

He came over the ocean
carrying Mt. Fuji
on his back/Tule Lake on his chest
hacked through the brush
of deserts
and made them grow
strawberries

we stole berries
from the stem
we could not afford them
for breakfast

his eyes held
nothing
as he whipped us
for stealing.

the desert had dried
his soul.

wordless
he sold
the rich,
full berries
to hakujines
whose children
pointed at our eyes

they ate fresh
strawberries
with cream.

Father,
I wanted to scream
at your silence.
Your strength
was a stranger
I could never touch.
iron
in your eyes
to shield
the pain
to shield desert-like wind
from patches
of strawberries
grown
from
tears.

1978

Desert Flowers

Flowers
faded
in the desert wind.
No flowers grow
where dust winds blow
and rain is like
a dry heave moan.

Mama, did you dream about that
beau who would take you
away from it all,
who would show you
in his '41 ford
and tell you how soft
your hands
like the silk kimono
you folded for the wedding?
Make you forget
about That place,
the back bending
wind that fell like a wall,
drowned all your geraniums
and flooded the shed
where you tried to sleep
away hyenas?

And mama,
bending in the candlelight,
after lights out in barracks,
an ageless shadow
grows victory flowers
made from crepe paper,
shaping those petals
like the tears
your eyes bled.

Your fingers
knotted at knuckles
wounded, winding around wire stems
the tiny, sloganed banner:

"america for americans".

Did you dream
of the shiny ford
(only always a dream)
ride your youth
like the wind
in the headless night?

Flowers
2 ¢ a dozen,
flowers for American Legions
worn like a badge
on america's lapel
made in post-concentration camps
by candlelight.
Flowers
watered
by the spit
of "no japs wanted here",
planted in poverty
of postwar relocations,
plucked by
victory's veterans.

Mama, do you dream
of the wall of wind
that falls
on your limbless desert,
on stems
brimming with petals/crushed
crepepaper
growing
from the crippled
mouth of your hand?

Your tears, mama,
have nourished us.
Your children
like pollen
scatter in the wind.

1978

Breaking Tradition

for my Daughter

My daughter denies she is like me,
her secretive eyes avoid mine.
She reveals the hatreds of womanhood
already veiled behind music and smoke and telephones.
I want to tell her about the empty room
of myself.
This room we lock ourselves in
where whispers live like fungus,
giggles about small breasts and cellulite,
where we confine ourselves to jealousies,
bedridden by menstruation.
This waiting room where we feel our hands
are useless, dead speechless clamps
that need hospitals and forceps and kitchens
and plugs and ironing boards to make them useful.
I deny I am like my mother. I remember why:
She kept her room neat with silence,
defiance smothered in requirements to be otonashii,
passion and loudness wrapped in an obi,
her steps confined to ceremony,
the weight of her sacrifice she carried like
a foetus. Guilt passed on in our bones.
I want to break tradition—unlock this room
where women dress in the dark
Discover the lies my mother told me.
The lies that we are small and powerless
that our possibilities must be compressed
to the size of pearls, displayed only as
passive chokers, charms around our neck.
Break Tradition.
I want to tell my daughter of this room
of myself
filled with tears of shakuhachi,

the light in my hands,
poems about madness,
the music of yellow guitars—
sounds shaken from barbed wire and
goodbyes and miracles of survival.
This room of open window where daring ones escape.

My daughter denies she is like me
her secretive eyes are walls of smoke
and music and telephones,
her pouting ruby lips, her skirts
swaying to salsa, Madonna and the Stones,
her thighs displayed in carnavals of color.
I do not know the contents of her room.
She mirrors my aging.

She is breaking tradition.

1978

Recipe

Round Eyes

Ingredients: scissors, Scotch magic transparent tape,
eyeliner—water based, black.
Optional: false eyelashes.

Cleanse face thoroughly.

For best results, powder entire face, including eyelids.
(lighter shades suited to total effect desired)

With scissors, cut magic tape 1/16" wide, 3/4"–1/2" long—
depending on length of eyelid.

Stick firmly onto mid-upper eyelid area
(looking down into handmirror facilitates finding
adequate surface)

If using false eyelashes, affix first on lid, folding any
excess lid over the base of eyelash with glue.

Paint black eyeliner on tape and entire lid.

Do not cry.

1987

Kimiko Hahn b. 1955

Kimiko Hahn's poetics are strongly intertextual, often explicitly so. She responds to phrases in other texts that she finds evocative. One text that she frequently returns to for such "cannibalization" (her term) is *Genji monogatari* (*The Tale of Genji*), by Lady Murasaki Shikibu (978?–1026), generally considered not only the first Japanese novel but the first psychological novel. Hahn also refers in her writing to the influence and inspiration of other women writers from Japan's Heian period (794–1185).

Hahn's literary debt to Japanese women writers, however, should not be thought of as due to some essentialist connection between Asian American and Asian writers. In her poem "Cruising Barthes," Hahn explores the profoundly ambivalent nature of her exploration of Japanese language and literature: "The way I fear speaking Japanese and adore/speaking it. . . ./What is Japanese? blood,/geography, translation by white, Occupation-trained/academic men?" Her relationship to Japanese literature and culture were shaped, she says, not only by her Japanese American mother but also by her German American father's aesthetic interests in Japanese culture and her own formal study of East Asian cultures in college and graduate school. Language for her is not only a writing tool but also subject matter. Fluency in more than one language highlights language itself as a construction that can be interrogated and played with.

Kimiko Hahn was born in 1955 in Mt. Kisco, New York, to two artists, her mother from Hawaii and her father from Wisconsin. Hahn majored in English and East Asian Studies as an undergraduate at the University of Iowa; she received an M.A. in Japanese literature at Columbia University. Her poetry was first collected in book form in *We Stand Our Ground* (1988), a collaboration with two other women poets. Hahn is the author of five collections of poetry: *Air Pocket* (1989); *Earshot* (1992), which was awarded the Theodore Roethke Memorial Poetry Prize and an Association of Asian America Studies Literature Award; *The Unbearable Heart* (1995), which received an American Book Award; *Volatile* (1999); and *Mosquito and Ant* (1999). A recipient of fellowships from the National Endowment for the Arts and the New York Foundation for the Arts, she has also been awarded a Lila Wallace–Reader's Digest Writer's Award. Hahn was an editor of the magazine *Bridge: Asian-American Perspectives.* She cites her experience with the American Writers Congress as having a major impact, and she identifies Marxism as a strong intellectual and political influence.

Thematically, Hahn's poems explore the relationship between gender, language, body, desire, and subjectivity. Formally, her poetics of fragmentation, quotation, and multivocality propose new models of gendered and racialized subjectivity. The notion of the autonomous individual is questioned and replaced by a sense of the subject as inhabited and haunted by "other" voices. Her poetics of female intersubjectivity are manifested in the arcs of *The Unbearable Heart,* a collection of poems that mourn her mother, and *Mosquito and Ant,* arranged as a series of correspondences between the speaker and an older-sister figure.

Desire is the strongest thread running throughout Hahn's poems. The passion she uses to write love poetry is similar to the passion she uses to write political poetry. The libidinal charge of Hahn's poetry confounds distinctions between private and public, the intimate and the global. Her poems are sensual, lyrical, heartbreaking, intellectual, and political. They are challenging in the most pleasurable sense. Meditative yet urgent, full of integrity and sensuality, suffused with a multilingual sensibility and "sense memory" (the title of a poem), Hahn's poetry is extremely compelling in its inscriptions of Asian American female desire and subjectivity.

Juliana Chang
University of Illinois, Urbana-Champaign

PRIMARY WORKS

We Stand Our Ground, with Gale Jackson and Susan Sherman, 1988; *Air Pocket,* 1989; *Earshot,* 1992; *The Unbearable Heart,* 1995; *Volatile,* 1999; *Mosquito and Ant,* 1999; "Kimiko Hahn: Expressing Self and Desire, Even If One Must Writhe," *Black Lightning: Poetry-in-Progress,* ed. Eileen Tabios, 1998.

Strands

The key warmed in your hand
and you knew the password
was *sea*
instead of *ocean.* Once in
he had blown the weekend
talking about documentaries.
Your head rested on his neck
then conked out
in bas relief.
The sound and smell
of the steam
across the room warmed you.
Later you figure
it was an extra blanket
tossed over your waist.
Your patience at that point
was unassuming. It was here
you turned into a piece
of wood
he spotted as sculptural.
You couldn't scream
till he pulled out
his tongue.

The key word was sea
not ocean.
Trudging through sixteen inches
your mind goes to drifts
there at the shore;
first last fall

with your husband and dog
slugging coffee from a thermos
and bracing against the wind.
You had gone for the dog
to taste sea salt
and expanse. The apricot cake
reminded you of earwax.
Now snow and crusts of ice
over sand
plays in your mind.
You wouldn't know
and call him again
by names. Seaweed. Oats. Bran.
Apricot jam. Jam.
And the word transforms from would
to wood as the key warms
in your hand.

Your hair is short
as spruce
and when you shake
short hairs
fall on the newspaper.
He had blown the afternoon
talking about El Salvador
without seeing the connection
to, say, Puerto Ricans
in Springfield, Mass.
The banks
of snow incite riot
or strand. The imagination
conks out
like the hemisphere.
Looking for an employer
you figure is looking
for what kills
the love between us
but not your vision
and never grandma's sea.

Your hair is short
as spruce or pine
and you think of his face
brushed by it.
Cellophaning, she suggested,
stains strands of hair
blue, green—whatever.

But you shied away
because of him.
Why? Would he walk out?
When you flirted he backed off
yet when you spoke
about newspaper clippings
or goldfish he glowed.
And now this. Something
you can't handle as he touches
your hair yet makes
for his coat. He doesn't understand
how paint fits into
this narration. So you take the hand
and dip it in.

1992

Resistance: A Poem on Ikat Cloth[1]

By the time the forsythia blossomed
in waves along the parkway
the more delicate cherry and apple
had blown away, if you remember
correctly. Those were days
when you'd forget socks and books
after peeing in the privacy
of its branches and soft earth.
What a house you had
fit for turtles or sparrows.
One sparrow[2]
wrapped in a silk kimono
wept for her tongue
clipped off by the old woman.
You'll never forget that
or its vengeance as striking
as the yellow around your small shoulders.
shitakirisuzume mother called her.
You didn't need to understand
exactly.

[1]Ikat: "the technique of resist-dying yarn before it is woven" *(African Textiles,* John Picton and John Mack, London, 1979).

[2]Sparrow references from the Japanese folk tale, *"Shitakirisuzume"* (literally, "the tongue-cut-sparrow"). The sparrow received the punishment after eating the old woman's rice starch. The sparrow got even.

a process of resistance
in Soemba, Sumatra, Java, Bali,
Timor,[3]
Soon came mounds of flesh
and hair here and there.
Centuries earlier
you'd have been courted
or sold.
"Inu has let out my sparrow—the little one
that I kept in the clothes-basket she said,
looking very unhappy."
For a Eurasian, sold.
Murasaki[4]
mother
She soaked the cloth
in incense
then spread it on the floor
standing there in bleached cotton,
red silk and bare feet.
And you fell in love with her
deeply as only a little girl could.
Pulling at your nipples
you dreamt of her body
that would become yours.
"Since the day we first boarded the ship
I have been unable to wear
my dark red robe.
That must not be done
out of danger of attracting
the god of the sea."
red as a Judy Chicago plate
feast your eyes on this
jack
"when I was bathing along the shore
scarcely screened by reeds
I lifted my robe revealing my leg
and more."[5]
roll up that skirt
and show those calves
cause if that bitch thinks
she can steal your guy
she's crazy

[3]Locations in Indonesia known for ikat.
[4]*Murasaki* also means "purple."
[5]*Tosanikki* (*The Tosa Diary* by Ki no Tsurayuki translated by Earl Miner), written in the female persona.

The cut burned
so she flapped her wings
and cried out
but choked
on blood.
The thread wound around your hand
so tight your fingers
turn indigo
Murasaki
The Shining Prince[6] realized
he could form her
into the one forbidden him. For that
he would persist
into old age.
rice starch
envelope bone, bride
you can't resist
The box of the sparrow's vengeance
contained evils comparable to agent orange
or the minamata disease. The old man
lived happily
without the old woman. But why her?
except that she was archetypal.
She depended on her child
to the point that when her daughter died
and she left Tosa
she could only lie down
on the boat's floor
and sob loudly
while the waves
crashed against her side
almost pleasantly.
This depth lent the writer
the soft black silt
on the ocean floor
where all life, some men say, began.
warp
"Mr. Ramsay, stumbling along a passage
one dark morning, stretched his arms out,
but Mrs. Ramsay, having died rather suddenly
the night before, his arms though stretched out,
remained empty."[7]

[6]"The Shining Prince" refers to Genji. *Genji-monogatari* (*The Tale of Genji* by Murasaki Shikibu, translated by Arthur Waley). This is the first time Genji hears the child Murasaki whom he later adopts, then marries.

[7]*To the Lighthouse,* Virginia Woolf.

when the men wove and women dyed
mother—
mutha
Orchids you explained
represent female genitalia
in Chinese verse.
Hence the orchid boat.
Patricia liked that
and would use it in her collection
Sex and Weather.
the supremes soothed like an older sister
rubbing your back
kissing your neck and pulling you into
motor city, usa
whether you like it
or not that
was the summer
of watts and though you
were in a coma
as far as that
the ramifications
the ramifications
bled through transistors
a *class* act
blues from indigo, reds
from mendoekoe root, yellows, boiling
tegaran wood
and sometimes by mudbath
when you saw her bathing in the dark
you wanted to dip your hand in
mamagoto suruno?[8]
The bride transforms
into water
while the groom moves
like the carp
there just under the bridge—
like the boy with you
under the forsythia
scratching and rolling around.
No, actually you just lay there
still and moist.
still and moist.
Wondering what next.

pine

[8]*Mamagoto suruno,* Japanese, "playing house."

You're not even certain
which you see—
The carp or the reflection of your hand.
the forsythia curled
like cupped hands covering
bound and unbound
As if blood
"The thought of the white linen
spread out on the deep snow
the cloth and the snow
glowing scarlet was enough
to make him feel that"[9]
The sight of him squeezing melons
sniffing one
then splitting it open in the park
was enough to make you feel that
Naha, Ryukyu Island, Taketome, Shiga,
Karayoshi, Tottori, Izo,
resistance does not mean
not drawn it means
sasou mizu araba
inamu to zo omou[10]
bind the thread
with hemp or banana leaves
before soaking it in the indigo
black as squid as seaweed as his hair
as his hair
as I lick his genitals
first taking one side
deep in my mouth then the other
till he cries softly
please
for days
Though practical
you hate annotations
to the *kokinshu;*[11]
each note vivisects
a *waka*
like so many petals
off a stem
until your lap
is full of blossoms.

[9]*Yukiguni* (*Snow Country,* Kawabata Yasunari, translated by Edward Seidensticker).

[10]*Sasou* etc. is a quote from a waka (classical Japanese poem) by Ono no Komachi. Donald Keene translated these lines, "were there water to entice me/ I would follow it, I think." (*Anthology of Japanese Literature,* p. 79).

[11]*Kokinshu* is the Imperial Anthology of poetry completed in 905.

How many you destroyed!
You can't imagine
Komachi's world
as real. Hair
so heavy it adds
another layer of brocade
(black on wisteria,
plum—)
forsythia too raw
and the smell
of fresh *tatami.*[12]
But can you do without
kono yumei no naka ni[13]
Can you pull apart the line
"my heart chars"
kokoro yakeori
corridors of thread
"creating the pattern from memory
conforming to a certain style
typical of each island"[14]
"K.8. Fragment of ramie kasuri, medium
blue, with repeating double ikat, and mantled
turtles and maple leaves of weft ikat.
Omi Province, Shiga Prefecture,
Honshu.
L. 16.5 cm. W. 19.5 cm."
"the turtle with strands of seaweed
growing from its back forming a mantle,
reputed to live for centuries,"
Komachi also moved
like those shadows in the shallows
you cannot reach
though they touch you.
Wading and feeling
something light as a curtain
around your calves you turn
to see very small scallops
rise to the surface
for a moment of oxygen
then close up and descend.
Caught, you look
at what he calls their eyes
(ridges of blue)

[12]*Tatami,* straw matting for the floor in Japanese homes.
[13]*Kono* etc., Japanese, for "in this dream."
[14]From another Ono no Komachi poem translated by Earl Miner (*Introduction to Japanese Court Poetry,* p. 82).

and are afraid to touch
that part.
from memory or history
sasou mizu
Grandmother's *ofuro*[15]
contained giant squid
killer whales
hot
omou
You were afraid he would
turn to the sea
to say something
that would separate you
forever
so kept talking.
Of course he grew irritable
and didn't really want
a basket of shells
for the bathroom.
"his arms though stretched out"
The line shocked you
like so much of Kawabata
who you blame
for years of humiliation,
katakana, hiragana, kanji,[16]
at each stroke
You first hear the squall
coming across the lake
like a sheet of glass.
You start to cry and daddy
rows toward the shore and mother.
in the Malayan Archipelago
Georgia O'Keeffe's orchid shocked you
so even now you can picture the fragrance
"Should a stranger witness the performance
he is compelled to dip his finger
into the dye and taste it. Those employed
must never mention the names of dead people
or animals. Pregnant or sick women
are not allowed to look on;
should this happen they are punished
as strangers."
in the Malayan Archipelago

[15]*Ofuro,* Japanese bathtub.
[16]*Katakana,* etc., are the Japanese syllabaries and the Chinese characters respectively.

where boys give their sweethearts
shuttles they will carve, burn,
name,
"language does not differ
from instruments of production,
from machines, let us say,"[17]
knocked down
knocked *up girl*
"the superstructure"
he wouldn't stop talking
about *deep structure*
and mention in prayer
but you need more than the female persona.
A swatch of cloth.
A pressed flower. The taste of powder
brushed against your lips.
pine
matsu[18]
The wedding day chosen
he brought you animal crackers
cloths
Pushing aside the branches
you crawl in
on your hands and knees,
lie back,
and light up.
tabako chodai[19]
because the forsythia
symbolizes so much
of sneakers,
cloth ABC books, charms,
sankyu[20]
the "charred heart"
would be reconstructed thus:
"Before the golden Buddha, I will lay
Poems as my flowers,
Entering in the Way,
Entering in the Way."[21]
fuck that shit
Link the sections
with fragrance: *matsu*

[17]Joseph Stalin, *Marxism and the Problems of Linguistics.*

[18]*Matsu,* Japanese, "pine tree" and "wait."

[19]*Tabako chodai,* Japanese, "give me a cigarette [tobacco]."

[20]*Sankyu,* Japanese pronunciation of "thank you."

[21]Noh play by Kan'ami Kiyotsugu, "Sotoba Komachi," supposedly about Ono no Komachi's repentance. (Keene, p. 270.)

shards of ice
The bride spread out her dress
for the dry cleaners
then picked kernels of rice
off the quilt and from her hair.
bits of china
the lining unfolds
out of the body
through hormonal revolutions
gravity and chance
lick that plate clean
can I get a cigarette
got a match
click clack, click
clack
chodai
in this dream
She wrapped the ikat
around her waist and set out
for Hausa, Yoruba, Ewe of Ghana,
Baule, Madagascar, and Northern Edo
I pull off my dress
and take a deep breath.
The cupped hands open then
onto the loom.
click clack click
clack
and in the rhythmic chore
I imagine a daughter in my lap
who I will never give away
but see off
with a bundle of cloths
dyed with resistance

1989

Cuttings

a zuihitsu for father

My younger sister and I, cleaning father's house before he returns from a week in intensive care, rush to dispose of mother's cosmetics, store her jewelry for a later date, and phone a woman's shelter to pick up bags of dresses, size 4, and shoes, 4½, even stopping to laugh at the platforms from "the mod era" she swore would come back. We collapse into each other's arms and cry *mommy mommy* as if she could hear us if we wept loud enough.

I look out the taxi window at everyone else's life. Certainly all the people in all the little apartments have gone about their business making money off other people's mortgages or addictions, without the knowledge my mother died last week, someone who found pleasure in baking oddly shaped biscuits with her granddaughters.

I keep my father talking about his boyhood—his passion for deep-sea diving though he grew up on Lake Michigan, his going AWOL for art courses, the four books at the Naval Library on "Oriental Art." Here we turn, always return, to Maude who *wasn't supposed to go first.* He said he had her convinced.

I ask Marie how to tell the girls, Miya now six and Rei, four. She advises we speak to them separately, to allow each their own reactions.

The funeral director says, "She doesn't look 68, but then oriental women never look their age." He then reminisces about "The War."

I want to throw out as much as possible—a half-jar of expensive cream, a suede jacket—belongings my sister wishes to hold on to. I go to the Funeral Home. I find comfort in The 10 O'clock News; she resents the superficial, even stupid resemblance of normality.

Two weeks now since mother died. Tuesday nights, I stay with father now a man who can barely contain what, in a second, became memory. He lurches from each small room testing himself against souvenirs: animal puppets from Rome, 1956; a Noh mask, Kyoto, '64; silver rabbit, Phnom Penh, '65; hotel towel, Chicago, '70. Even after discarding her dresses and middle-class perfumes she inhabits every corner of every project—collage, painting, carving. He recalls telling her when they first met at the Art Institute that art would always come before any thing and any one.

We toast Maude at a neighbor's, drinking what we like since she couldn't tolerate liquor. Janet remembers the day she knew they'd be friends: "We were looking at the peonies by the stone wall and your mother said, *Know what these remind me of? Penises.*" Our laughter resembles sobbing.

She reread stories as often as I demanded.

Convinced and convincing me through my early twenties I could not sew or cook despite home ec. classes and odd advice, she cooked and froze stews, checked if I ever baked potatoes and the last day we saw her, sent us home with turkey leftovers. It's true I've never roasted one.

The first thing I saw when I returned to clean their house were my three skirts, pinned and draped across the ironing board.

How suddenly grievances against father evaporate, steam rising from an icy river. He even corrects himself, calling mother, *a woman.*

Why is pain deeper than pleasure, though it is a pleasure to cry so loud the arthritic dog hobbles off the sunny carpet, so loud I do not hear the phone ring, so loud I feel a passion for mother I thought I reserved for lovers. I insert a CD and sing about a love abandoned, because there are no other lyrics for this.

Pulling off a crewneck sweater I bend my glasses and for the next few days wear the frames off-center not realizing the dizzy view is in fact physical.

Theresa, David, Liz, Mark, Sharon, Denise, Carmen, Sonia, Susan, Lee, Cheryl, Susan, Jo, John, Jerry, Doug, Earlene, Marie, Robbin, Jessica, Kiana, Patricia, Bob, Donna, Orinne, Shigemi—

Suddenly the tasks we put off need to get done: defrost the freezer, pay the preschool bill, order more checks.

For 49 days after her own mother's death she did not eat meat. I didn't know, mother. I'm sorry, I didn't know.

The sudden scent of her spills from her handbag—leather, lotion, mints, coins. I cannot stand.

She had marked April 28 to see Okinawan dancers.

He has not yet slept in their bed, because the couch in front of the television *feels firmer* to his seven broken ribs.

At dinner we play a story game; the younger one asks, "about grandma?" then corrects herself quickly "about bunny rabbit" as she momentarily trips on her own preoccupation.

Father tells me there is a Japanese story about a mask maker who has a daughter renowned for her stunning beauty. Upon her untimely death, how he does not recall, the father sits by her side to sketch the exquisite features. Poetic license. Though mother did look beautiful I had never seen a face devoid of any expression, an aspect even a painting would somehow contain.

The children notice he has taken off his wedding ring.

At a favorite cafe I hear a newborn in the next booth wailing for, probably, the mother's breast, as if his life will end this second. It is my cry.

Shrimp. An image of my parents at a card table shelling shrimp the night before my sister's wedding, the peels translucent pink as my mother's fingernails. Primitive and reassuring.

At the house in Paia where grandma washed other people's laundry and raised her chickens, and grandpa sat in his wheelchair, we had a toilet inside but also the old outhouse, a rickety two-seater. I would go in, close the gray-painted door, latch the hook and sit on the edge holding my breath against the frothy stench of shit. You could hear your waste hit bottom. The dim light lent privacy against peeping cousins.

She taught me to pluck or cut flowers near the roots for the long stems. Recut under water. She taught me to rub my finger and thumb together over the silver dollar sheath, to rub off the brown membrane and scatter the seeds on my skirt. Gently so as not to tear the silver inside. I see them and think of her name, not Maude, but Mother.

Father and I bring the ashes into the City and plan to drop them off at the temple. Mrs. K has Buddhist robes over her blue jeans and suggests she recite a sutra. We light incense in the half-light. I forget tissues. My face and sleeves are covered with tears and mucus. My shoulders shake silently as listening.

Three months have past. I count the days from March 10th to the 100th day for another memorial service.

lotus suture

As if a metaphor for mother's death the Rodney King verdict and rebellion in Los Angeles breaks open urban areas across the country. It is a complex set of issues where some Korean shops and whites are attacked as the emblems of the establishment. But what is the establishment? Why not the actual property relations? Who actually owns the buildings, makes the laws—I feel helpless. Embittered.

Cuttings she had placed in tumblers in the kitchen and bathroom offer their fragile roots.

Rei discusses mother's death with me. A babysitter told her not to talk about it. Another told her it is *like sleep.* I tell her to talk. I tell her it is not sleep although the person looks asleep but he or she will not wake. She wants to talk to grandma and asks if she can. I tell her if she wants to she can; then I ask her what she wants to say. She wants to tell her to wake up.

People who have died but were revived speak of a dark tunnel with a fierce light at the end. Is it a passage or is it the memory of birth?

Miya speaks of dying—to see grandma again. I am shocked and try to say something.

I can see her body, not *her,* her body lying in a pine box, hands folded, black and white hair combed back, the funeral home odor saturating the drapes and carpets of the respectfully lit parlors. I said goodbye but it was really *to myself.*

I wish I had snipped off a bit of hair. I recall the braid she kept for a while in her drawer.

I purchase an expensive "anti-wrinkle defense cream" at the discount pharmacy. The third morning my skin really feels smoother though the burgeoning lines have not faded. I think something I've only thought the night before the plane trip: will I live to see the bottom of this jar.

Miya has shelved her grief and when admonished she declares: everything was fine until grandma died.

For the first time father harvests a half-dozen bamboo shoots from a small grove on the side of the house. Mother had spoken of gathering them as a child in Hawaii, soaking then boiling then sizzling them. He finds a recipe and experiments. He sends some home with me. They taste like artichoke hearts. We all think of mother. And I think of a poem from the *Manyōshu* about a trowel.

He plays her lottery numbers.

The lawyer of the kid who broadsided their car sends a letter threatening to sue father if he does not respond in five days with information. We feel naive, in a state of disbelief at the vulgar tone of the letter.

I wear the silk pants she altered for me: a forgotten pin, sewn into the hem, sticks into my ankle.

At any moment of the day I can hear her admonishment: *oh, Kimi.* She especially disliked spills.

I do not want to write about her death. But I do not want to lose these strong feelings.

Rei does not stop chattering about her: We have no one to make slush. She always had gum in her handbag. She read to us in Japanese and knew "cat's cradle" backward.

The 100th Day Anniversary. The weather is already warm. Her brother from Honolulu tells about her letters to him during World War II when he was in the 442nd.

We vacation on Fire Island. A few deer walk by the porch so close we can see how fuzzy their antlers are.

I keep recalling the diagram of the accident scene. Mother's body lying on the highway where medics attempted CPR. I imagine the wet black road, the traffic signals changing despite the halt.

Christmas ornaments last packed away by her: the balls she and father decorated with cherubs and glitter, old wooden angels and soldiers from my childhood, tinsel carefully rewrapped.

Some days I have a thought to write down but let it go.

During a week-long visit to the snowy fields of Vermont, I hear of a car bomb explosion at the World Trade Center, killing and injuring many people. The world continues outside this quiet. And the death of those who happen to step in its ordinary traffic.

I stop writing altogether. And when I must—postcards, single lines after a commute—the writing ends with mother.

Afraid father is "seeing someone" and hopeful. I extend mother's jealousy into the afterlife. It becomes my own hell.

I begin to feel impatient with father over little things like whether my hair is trimmed evenly. I wonder if my annoyance indicates we are moving on.

Father finds an envelope of marigold seeds mother saved and lets the children scatter them. The composted earth smells fertile like the pail she kept with egg shells and melon rinds.

1995

Gloria Anzaldúa b. 1942

When Gloria Anzaldúa describes the United States and Mexico border as "una herida abierta" (an open wound), she speaks from her lived experience as a native border dweller. Born in the ranch settlement of Jesus Maria in South Texas, Anzaldúa grew up in the small town of Hargill, Texas. She currently writes and teaches in northern California. In her poetry, fiction, essays, and autobiography, she writes eloquently of the indignities a Chicana lesbian feminist overcomes as she escapes the strictures of patriarchal Chicano traditions and confronts the injustices of dominant culture.

Her highly acclaimed text, *Borderlands/La Frontera: The New Mestiza,* interweaves autobiography, history of the Chicana/o Southwest, essay, autobiography, and poetry in a manner that defies traditional categorization. Chicana *mestizaje* in the late twentieth century can be seen as a new genre that describes the cultural and linguistic global connections between Chicana writers and writers of the Americas. The bilingual title of her book illustrates the transcultural experience of border dwellers and border consciousness. English and Spanish co-exist for Mexican-descent people of the borderlands. In Anzaldúa's text, the pre-conquest language, Nahuatl, mixes with English and Spanish. Likewise, the Chicana language Anzaldúa deploys in this text can be said to be a new Chicana language, one that legitimizes the intermingling of English and Spanish with indigenous Nahuatl.

In *Borderlands* Anzaldúa presents multiple issues that inform a radical political awareness. These issues culminate in what she calls a new consciousness for the women who examine and question the restrictions placed on them in the borderlands of the United States. In Anzaldúa's political manifesto, a "new mestiza" emerges only after her oppositional consciousness develops.

The chapter "Entering into the Serpent" presents some *cuentos* (stories) border families tell their children. For Prieta, the narrator of this section, the story of the snake that slithers into a woman's uterus and impregnates her provides the link to Anzaldúa's "serpentine" feminist theory. The new mestiza's task is to "winnow out the lies" as a Chicana feminist historian. She also provides alternative metaphors to the ones promoted by androcentric psychologists and priests. Anzaldúa's new mestiza invokes Olmec myth when she asserts that "Earth is a coiled Serpent" and rewrites the origin of the Catholic Guadalupe, empowering her as a pre-Columbian "*Coatlalopeuh,* She Who Has Dominion Over Serpents."

Like the constantly shifting identities of the Chicana in the contemporary world, the deities Anzaldúa unearths and names become a pantheon of possible feminist icons. Through these icons mestizas can unlearn the masculinist versions of history, religion, and myth. She methodically shows how both the "male-dominated Azteca-Mexica culture" and the post-conquest church established the binary of the *virgen/puta* (Virgin/whore) when they split Coatlalopeuh/Coatlicue/Tonantsi/Tlazolteotl/Cihuacoatl into good and evil, light and dark, sexual and asexual beings. Guadalupe, then, is Coatlalopeuh with "the serpent/sexuality out of her."

Anzaldúa revises androcentric myths of the Chicano homeland, Aztlán, and of *La Llorona* (the Weeping Woman). She intertwines the familiar stories with new feminist threads so that her insistence on the recuperation of the feminist—the serpent—produces a tapestry at once familiar and radically different. While "la facultad" can be interpreted as a spiritual extrasensory perception, what Anzaldúa has in fact developed is the ability to rupture dominating belief systems that have been presented as ancient truths and accurate histories.

The second excerpt, "*La conciencia de la mestiza:* Towards a New Consciousness," is the final chapter of the prose section of the book. In this essay, Anzaldúa summarizes her mestiza methodology. Mestiza methodology offers strategies for unearthing a razed indigenous history as a process of coming to consciousness as political agents of change. Mestizas can turn to pre-conquest history and historical sites such as the Aztec temples to recover women's place in a past that has been satanized. With the new knowledge they learn of the central importance of female deities rendered passive with Western androcentric ideology. The mestiza/mestizo Aztec legacy focuses only on the blood sacrifices of this military power and further obscures the other indigenous tribal traditions that Aztec hegemony absorbed. Anzaldúa's reclamation of Aztec deities and traditions begins a reformulation of Aztlán from a male nation-state to a feminist site of resistance.

For Anzaldúa, Chicana feminism and lesbian politics emerge as forces that give voice to her political agenda as a new mestiza, an identity that claims much more than the simple definition of *mestizo* (mixed blood) allows. In this section, Anzaldúa clearly presents her political ideology, which is historically grounded in the colonial legacy of the American Southwest in its relation to larger hemispheric events. In *Borderlands,* American and Mexican history, American and Mexican culture are contested fields.

Sonia Saldívar-Hull
University of California at Los Angeles

PRIMARY WORKS

This Bridge Called My Back: Writing by Radical Women of Color, ed. with Cherríe Moraga, 1981; "El Paisano Is a Bird of Good Omen," *Cuentos: Stories by Latinas,* 1983; *Borderlands/La Frontera: The New Mestiza,* 1987; *Making Face, Making Soul/Haciendo Caras: Creative and Critical Perspectives by Women of Color,* ed., 1990.

from Borderlands/La Frontera

3

Entering into the Serpent

Sueño con serpientes, con serpientes del mar,
Con cierto mar, ay de serpientes sueño yo.
Largas, transparentes, en sus barrigas llevan
Lo que pueden arebatarle al amor.
Oh, oh, oh, la mató y aparese una mayor.
Oh, con mucho más infierno en digestión.

I dream of serpents, serpents of the sea,
A certain sea, oh, of serpents I dream.
Long, transparent, in their bellies they carry
All that they can snatch away from love.

Oh, oh, oh, I kill one and a larger one appears.
Oh, with more hellfire burning inside!
—Silvio Rodríguez, *"Sueño Con Serpientes"*[1]

In the predawn orange haze, the sleepy crowing of roosters atop the trees. *No vayas al escusado en lo oscuro.* Don't go to the outhouse at night, Prieta, my mother would say. *No se te vaya a meter algo por allá.* A snake will crawl into your *nalgas,*[2] make you pregnant. They seek warmth in the cold. *Dicen que las culebras* like to suck *chiches,*[3] can draw milk out of you.

En el escusado in the half-light spiders hang like gliders. Under my bare buttocks and the rough planks the deep yawning tugs at me. I can see my legs fly up to my face as my body falls through the round hole into the sheen of swarming maggots below. Avoiding the snakes under the porch I walk back into the kitchen, step on a big black one slithering across the floor.

Ella tiene su tono[4]

Once we were chopping cotton in the fields of Jesus Maria Ranch. All around us the woods. *Quelite*[5] towered above me, choking the stubby cotton that had outlived the deer's teeth.

I swung *el azadón*[6] hard. *El quelite* barely shook, showered nettles on my arms and face. When I heard the rattle the world froze.

I barely felt its fangs. Boot got all the *veneno.*[7] My mother came shrieking, swinging her hoe high, cutting the earth, the writhing body.

I stood still, the sun beat down. Afterwards I smelled where fear had been: back of neck, under arms, between my legs; I felt its heat slide down my body. I swallowed the rock it had hardened into.

When Mama had gone down the row and was out of sight, I took out my pocketknife. I made an X over each prick. My body followed the blood, fell onto the soft ground. I put my mouth over the red and sucked and spit between the rows of cotton.

I picked up the pieces, placed them end on end. *Culebra de cascabel.*[8] I counted the rattlers: twelve. It would shed no more. I buried the pieces between the rows of cotton.

That night I watched the window sill, watched the moon dry the blood on the tail, dreamed rattler fangs filled my mouth, scales covered my body. In the morning I saw through snake eyes, felt snake blood course through my body. The serpent, *mi tono,* my animal counterpart. I immune to its venom. Forever immune.

[1]From the song *"Sueño Con Serpientes"* by Silvio Rodríguez, from the album *Días y flores.* Translated by Barbara Dane with the collaboration of Rina Benmauor and Juan Flores. [All notes are Anzaldúa's *Ed.*]
[2]Vagina, buttocks.
[3]They say snakes like to suck women's teats.
[4]She has supernatural power from her animal soul, the *tono.*
[5]Weed.
[6]The hoe.
[7]Venom, poison.
[8]Rattlesnake.

Snakes, *víboras:* since that day I've sought and shunned them. Always when they cross my path, fear and elation flood my body. I know things older than Freud, older than gender. She—that's how I think of *la Víbora,* Snake Woman. Like the ancient Olmecs, I know Earth is a coiled Serpent. Forty years it's taken me to enter into the Serpent, to acknowledge that I have a body, that I am a body and to assimilate the animal body, the animal soul.

Coatlalopeuh, She Who Has Dominion Over Serpents

Mi mamagrande Ramona toda su vida mantuvo un altar pequeño en la esquina del comedor. Siempre tenía las velas prendidas. Allí hacía promesas a la Virgen de Guadalupe. My family, like most Chicanos, did not practice Roman Catholicism but a folk Catholicism with many pagan elements. *La Virgen de Guadalupe*'s Indian name is *Coatlalopeuh.* She is the central deity connecting us to our Indian ancestry.

Coatlalopeuh is descended from, or is an aspect of, earlier Mesoamerican fertility and Earth goddesses. The earliest is *Coatlicue,* or "Serpent Skirt." She had a human skull or serpent for a head, a necklace of human hearts, a skirt of twisted serpents and taloned feet. As creator goddess, she was mother of the celestial deities, and of *Huitzilopochtli* and his sister, *Coyolxauhqui,* She With Golden Bells, Goddess of the Moon, who was decapitated by her brother. Another aspect of *Coatlicue* is *Tonantsi.*[9] The Totonacs, tired of the Aztec human sacrifices to the male god, *Huitzilopochtli,* renewed their reverence for *Tonantsi* who preferred the sacrifice of birds and small animals.[10]

The male-dominated Azteca-Mexica culture drove the powerful female deities underground by giving them monstrous attributes and by substituting male deities in their place, thus splitting the female Self and the female deities. They divided her who had been complete, who possessed both upper (light) and underworld (dark) aspects. *Coatlicue,* the Serpent goddess, and her more sinister aspects, *Tlazolteotl* and *Cihuacoatl,* were "darkened" and disempowered much in the same manner as the Indian *Kali.*

Tonantsi—split from her dark guises, *Coatlicue, Tlazolteotl,* and *Cihuacoatl,*—became the good mother. The Nahuas, through ritual and prayer, sought to oblige *Tonantsi* to ensure their health and the growth of their crops. It was she who gave *México* the cactus plant to provide her people with milk and pulque. It was she who defended her children against the wrath of the Christian God by challenging God, her son, to produce mother's milk (as she had done) to prove that his benevolence equalled his disciplinary harshness.[11]

[9]In some Nahuatl dialects *Tonantsi* is called *Tonatzin,* literally "Our Holy Mother." "*Tonan* was a name given in Nahuatl to several mountains, these being the congelations of the Earth Mother at spots convenient for her worship." The Mexica considered the mountain mass southwest of Chapultepec to be their mother. Burr Cartwright Brundage, *The Fifth Sun: Aztec Gods, Aztec World* (Austin, TX: University of Texas Press, 1979), 154, 242.

[10]Ena Campbell, "The Virgin of Guadalupe and the Female Self-Image: A Mexican Case History," *Mother Worship: Themes and Variations,* James J. Preston, ed. (Chapel Hill, NC: University of North Carolina Press, 1982), 22.

[11]Alan R. Sandstrom, "The Tonantsi Cult of the Eastern Nahuas," *Mother Worship: Themes and Variations,* James J. Preston, ed.

After the Conquest, the Spaniards and their Church continued to split *Tonantsi/Guadalupe.* They desexed *Guadalupe,* taking *Coatlalopeuh,* the serpent/sexuality, out of her. They completed the split begun by the Nahuas by making *la Virgen de Guadalupe/Virgen María* into chaste virgins and *Tlazolteotl/Coatlicue/la Chingada* into *putas;* into the Beauties and the Beasts. They went even further; they made all Indian deities and religious practices the work of the devil.

Thus *Tonantsi* became *Guadalupe,* the chaste protective mother, the defender of the Mexican people.

El nueve de diciembre del año 1531
a las cuatro de la madrugada
un pobre indio que se llamaba Juan Diego
iba cruzando el cerro de Tepeyác
cuando oyó un cantó de pájaro.
Alzó al cabeza vío que en la cima del cerro
estaba cubierta con una brillante nube blanca.
Parada en frente del sol
sobre una luna creciente
sostenida por un ángel
estaba una azteca
vestida en ropa de india.
Nuestra Señora María de Coatlalopeuh
se le apareció.
"Juan Diegito, El-que-habla-como-un-águila,"
la Virgen le dijo en el lenguaje azteca.
"Para hacer mi altar este cerro eligo.
Dile a tu gente que yo soy la madre de Dios,
a los indios yo les ayudaré."
Estó se lo contó a Juan Zumarraga
pero el obispo no le creyo.
Juan Diego volvió, lleño su tilma[12]
con rosas de castilla
creciendo milagrosamiente en la nieve.
Se las llevó al obispo,
y cuando abrío su tilma
el retrato de la Virgen
ahí estaba pintado.

Guadalupe appeared on December 9, 1531, on the spot where the Aztec goddess, *Tonantsi* ("Our Lady Mother"), had been worshipped by the Nahuas and where a temple to her had stood. Speaking Nahua, she told Juan Diego, a poor Indian crossing Tepeyac Hill, whose Indian name was *Cuautlaohuac* and who belonged to the *mazehual* class, the humblest within the Chichimeca tribe, that her name was *María Coatlalopeuh. Coatl* is the Nahuatl word for serpent. *Lopeuh* means "the one who has dominion over serpents." I interpret this as "the one who is at one with the beasts." Some spell her name *Coatlaxopeuh* (pronounced *"Cuatlashupe"* in Nahuatl)

[12] An oblong cloth that hangs over the back and ties together across the shoulders.

and say that *"xopeuh"* means "crushed or stepped on with disdain." Some say it means "she who crushed the serpent," with the serpent as the symbol of the indigenous religion, meaning that her religion was to take the place of the Aztec religion.[13] Because *Coatlalopeuh* was homophonous to the Spanish *Guadalupe,* the Spanish identified her with the dark Virgin, *Guadalupe,* patroness of West Central Spain.[14]

From that meeting, Juan Diego walked away with the image of *la Virgen* painted on his cloak. Soon after, Mexico ceased to belong to Spain, and *la Virgen de Guadalupe* began to eclipse all the other male and female religious figures in Mexico, Central America and parts of the U.S. Southwest. *"Desde entonces para el mexicano ser Guadalupano es algo esencial/*Since then for the Mexican, to be a *Guadalupano* is something essential."[15]

Mi Virgen Morena	My brown virgin
Mi Virgen Ranchera	my country virgin
Eres nuestra Reina	you are our queen
México es tu tierra	Mexico is your land
Y tú su bandera.	and you its flag.

—*"La Virgen Ranchera"*[16]

In 1660 the Roman Catholic Church named her Mother of God, considering her synonymous with *la Virgen María;* she became *la Santa Patrona de los mexicanos.* The role of defender (or patron) has traditionally been assigned to male gods. During the Mexican Revolution, Emiliano Zapata and Miguel Hidalgo used her image to move *el pueblo mexicano* toward freedom. During the 1965 grape strike in Delano, California, and in subsequent Chicano farmworkers' marches in Texas and other parts of the Southwest, her image on banners heralded and united the farmworkers. *Pachucos* (zoot suiters) tattoo her image on their bodies. Today, in Texas and Mexico she is more venerated than Jesus or God the Father. In the Lower Rio Grande Valley of south Texas it is *la Virgen de San Juan de los Lagos* (an aspect of *Guadalupe*) that is worshipped by thousands every day at her shrine in San Juan. In Texas she is considered the patron saint of Chicanos. *Cuando Carito, mi hermanito,* was missing in action and, later, wounded in Viet Nam, *mi mamá* got on her knees *y le prometío a Ella que si su hijito volvía vivo* she would crawl on her knees and light novenas in her honor.

Today, *la Virgen de Guadalupe* is the single most potent religious, political and cultural image of the Chicano/*mexicano.* She, like my race, is a synthesis of the old world and the new, of the religion and culture of the two races in our psyche, the conquerors and the conquered. She is the symbol of the *mestizo* true to his or her Indian

[13]Andres Gonzales Guerrero, Jr., *The Significance of* Nuestra Señora de Gualdalupe *and* La Raza Cósmica *in the Development of a Chicano Theology of Liberation* (Ann Arbor, MI: University Microfilms International, 1984), 122.

[14]*Algunos dicen que Guadalupe es una palabra derivada del lenguaje árabe que significa "Río Oculto."* Tomie de Paola, *The Lady of Guadalupe* (New York, NY: Holiday House, 1980), 44.

[15]*"Desde el cielo una hermosa mañana,"* from *Propios de la misa de Nuestra Señora de Guadalupe,* Guerrero, 124.

[16]From *"La Virgen Ranchera,"* Guerrero, 127.

values. *La cultura chicana* identifies with the mother (Indian) rather than with the father (Spanish). Our faith is rooted in indigenous attributes, images, symbols, magic and myth. Because *Guadalupe* took upon herself the psychological and physical devastation of the conquered and oppressed *indio,* she is our spiritual, political and psychological symbol. As a symbol of hope and faith, she sustains and insures our survival. The Indian, despite extreme despair, suffering and near genocide, has survived. To Mexicans on both sides of the border, *Guadalupe* is the symbol of our rebellion against the rich, upper and middleclass; against their subjugation of the poor and the *indio.*

Guadalupe unites people of different races, religions, languages: Chicano protestants, American Indians and whites. *"Nuestra abogada siempre serás*/Our *mediatrix* you will always be." She mediates between the Spanish and the Indian cultures (or three cultures as in the case of *mexicanos* of African or other ancestry) and between Chicanos and the white world. She mediates between humans and the divine, between this reality and the reality of spirit entities. *La Virgen de Guadalupe* is the symbol of ethnic identity and of the tolerance for ambiguity that Chicanos-*mexicanos,* people of mixed race, people who have Indian blood, people who cross cultures, by necessity possess.

La gente Chicana tiene tres madres. All three are mediators: *Guadalupe,* the virgin mother who has not abandoned us, *la Chingada* (*Malinche*), the raped mother whom we have abandoned, and *la Llorona,* the mother who seeks her lost children and is a combination of the other two.

Ambiguity surrounds the symbols of these three "Our Mothers." *Guadalupe* has been used by the Church to mete out institutionalized oppression: to placate the Indians and *mexicanos* and Chicanos. In part, the true identity of all three has been subverted—*Guadalupe* to make us docile and enduring, *la Chingada* to make us ashamed of our Indian side, and *la Llorona* to make us long-suffering people. This obscuring has encouraged the *virgen/puta* (whore) dichotomy.

Yet we have not all embraced this dichotomy. In the U.S. Southwest, Mexico, Central and South America the *indio* and the *mestizo* continue to worship the old spirit entities (including *Guadalupe*) and their supernatural power, under the guise of Christian saints.[17]

Las invoco diosas mías, ustedes las indias
sumergidas en mi carne que son mis sombras.
Ustedes que persisten mudas en sus cuevas.
Ustedes Señoras que ahora, como yo,
están en desgracia.

[17]*La Virgen María* is often equated with the Aztec *Teleoinam,* the Maya *Ixchel,* the Inca *Mamacocha* and the Yuroba *Yemayá.*

For Waging War Is My Cosmic Duty: The Loss of the Balanced Oppositions and the Change to Male Dominance

Therefore I decided to leave
The country (Aztlán),
Therefore I have come as one charged with a
special duty,
Because I have been given arrows and shields,
For waging war is my duty,
And on my expeditions I
Shall see all the lands,
I shall wait for the people and meet them
In all four quarters and I shall give them
Food to eat and drinks to quench their thirst,
For here I shall unite all the different peoples!
—*Huitzilopochtli* speaking to the Azteca-Mexica[18]

Before the Aztecs became a militaristic, bureaucratic state where male predatory warfare and conquest were based on patrilineal nobility, the principle of balanced opposition between the sexes existed.[19] The people worshipped the Lord and Lady of Duality, *Ometecuhtli* and *Omecihuatl.* Before the change to male dominance, *Coatlicue,* Lady of the Serpent Skirt, contained and balanced the dualities of male and female, light and dark, life and death.

The changes that led to the loss of the balanced oppositions began when the Azteca, one of the twenty Toltec tribes, made the last pilgrimage from a place called Aztlán. The migration south began about the year A.D. 820. Three hundred years later the advance guard arrived near Tula, the capital of the declining Toltec empire. By the 11th century, they had joined with the Chichimec tribe of Mexitin (afterwards called Mexica) into one religious and administrative organization within Aztlán, the Aztec territory. The Mexitin, with their tribal god *Tetzauhteotl Huitzilopochtli* (Magnificent Humming Bird on the Left), gained control of the religious system.[20] (In some stories *Huitzilopochtli* killed his sister, the moon goddess *Malinalxoch,* who used her supernatural power over animals to control the tribe rather than wage war.)

Huitzilopochtli assigned the Azteca-Mexica the task of keeping the human race (the present cosmic age called the Fifth Sun, *El Quinto Sol*) alive. They were to guarantee the harmonious preservation of the human race by unifying all the people on earth into one social, religious and administrative organ. The Aztec people considered themselves in charge of regulating all earthly matters.[21] Their instrument: controlled or regulated war to gain and exercise power.

After 100 years in the central plateau, the Azteca-Mexica went to Chapultepec, where they settled in 1248 (the present site of the park on the outskirts of Mexico

[18]Geoffrey Parrinder, ed., *World Religions: From Ancient History to the Present* (New York, NY: Facts on File Publications, 1971), 72.

[19]Levi-Stauss's paradigm which opposes nature to culture and female to male has no such validity in the early history of our Indian forebears. June Nash, "The Aztecs and the Ideology of Male Dominance," *Signs* (Winter, 1978), 349.

[20]Parrinder, 72.

[21]Parrinder, 77.

City). There, in 1345, the Aztec-Mexica chose the site of their capital, Tenochtitlan.[22] By 1428, they dominated the Central Mexican lake area.

The Aztec ruler, *Itzcoatl,* destroyed all the painted documents (books called codices) and rewrote a mythology that validated the wars of conquest and thus continued the shift from a tribe based on clans to one based on classes. From 1429 to 1440, the Aztecs emerged as a militaristic state that preyed on neighboring tribes for tribute and captives.[23] The "wars of flowers" were encounters between local armies with a fixed number of warriors, operating within the Aztec World, and, according to set rules, fighting ritual battles at fixed times and on predetermined battlefields. The religious purpose of these wars was to procure prisoners of war who could be sacrificed to the deities of the capturing party. For if one "fed" the gods, the human race would be saved from total extinction. The social purpose was to enable males of noble families and warriors of low descent to win honor, fame and administrative offices, and to prevent social and cultural decadence of the elite. The Aztec people were free to have their own religious faith, provided it did not conflict too much with the three fundamental principles of state ideology: to fulfill the special duty set forth by *Huitzilopochtli* of unifying all peoples, to participate in the wars of flowers, and to bring ritual offerings and do penance for the purpose of preventing decadence.[24]

Matrilineal descent characterized the Toltecs and perhaps early Aztec society. Women possessed property, and were curers as well as priestesses. According to the codices, women in former times had the supreme power in Tula, and in the beginning of the Aztec dynasty, the royal blood ran through the female line. A council of elders of the Calpul headed by a supreme leader, or *tlactlo,* called the father and mother of the people, governed the tribe. The supreme leader's vice-emperor occupied the position of "Snake Woman" or *Cihuacoatl,* a goddess.[25] Although the high posts were occupied by men, the terms referred to females, evidence of the exalted role of women before the Aztec nation became centralized. The final break with the democratic Calpul came when the four Aztec lords of royal lineage picked the king's successor from his siblings or male descendants.[26]

La Llorona's wailing in the night for her lost children has an echoing note in the wailing or mourning rites performed by women as they bid their sons, brothers and husbands good-bye before they left to go to the "flowery wars." Wailing is the Indian, Mexican and Chicana woman's feeble protest when she has no other recourse. These collective wailing rites may have been a sign of resistance in a society which glorified the warrior and war and for whom the women of the conquered tribes were booty.[27]

In defiance of the Aztec rulers, the *macehuales* (the common people) continued to worship fertility, nourishment and agricultural female deities, those of crops and rain. They venerated *Chalchiuhtlicue* (goddess of sweet or inland water), *Chicomecoatl* (goddess of food) and *Huixtocihuatl* (goddess of salt).

[22]Nash, 352.
[23]Nash, 350, 355.
[24]Parrinder, 355.
[25]Jacques Soustelle, *The Daily Life of the Aztecs on the Eve of the Spanish Conquest* (New York, NY: Macmillan Publishing Company, 1962). Soustelle and most other historians got their information from the Franciscan father Bernardino de Sahagún, chief chronicler of Indian religious life.
[26]Nash, 252–253.
[27]Nash, 358.

Nevertheless, it took less than three centuries for Aztec society to change from the balanced duality of their earlier times and from the egalitarian traditions of a wandering tribe to those of a predatory state. The nobility kept the tribute, the commoner got nothing, resulting in a class split. The conquered tribes hated the Aztecs because of the rape of their women and the heavy taxes levied on them. The *Tlaxcalans* were the Aztec's bitter enemies and it was they who helped the Spanish defeat the Aztec rulers, who were by this time so unpopular with their own common people that they could not even mobilize the populace to defend the city. Thus the Aztec nation fell not because *Malinali* (*la Chingada*) interpreted for and slept with Cortés, but because the ruling elite had subverted the solidarity between men and women and between noble and commoner.[28]

Sueño con serpientes

Coatl. In pre-Columbian America the most notable symbol was the serpent. The Olmecs associated womanhood with the Serpent's mouth which was guarded by rows of dangerous teeth, a sort of *vagina dentate.* They considered it the most sacred place on earth, a place of refuge, the creative womb from which all things were born and to which all things returned. Snake people had holes, entrances to the body of the Earth Serpent; they followed the Serpent's way, identified with the Serpent deity, with the mouth, both the eater and the eaten. The destiny of humankind is to be devoured by the Serpent.[29]

Dead,
the doctor by the operating table said.
I passed between the two fangs,
the flickering tongue.
Having come through the mouth of the serpent,
swallowed,
I found myself suddenly in the dark,
sliding down a smooth wet surface
down down into an even darker darkness.
Having crossed the portal, the raised hinged mouth,
having entered the serpent's belly,
now there was no looking back, no going back.

Why do I cast no shadow?
Are there lights from all sides shining on me?
Ahead, ahead.
curled up inside the serpent's coils,
the damp breath of death on my face.
I knew at that instant: something must change
or I'd die.
Algo tenía que cambiar.

[28]Nash, 361–362.
[29]Karl W. Luckert, *Olmec Religion: A Key to Middle America and Beyond* (Norman, OK: University of Oklahoma Press, 1976), 68, 69, 87, 109.

After each of my four bouts with death I'd catch glimpses of an otherworld Serpent. Once, in my bedroom, I saw a cobra the size of the room, her hood expanding over me. When I blinked she was gone. I realized she was, in my psyche, the mental picture and symbol of the instinctual in its collective impersonal, prehuman. She, the symbol of the dark sexual drive, the chthonic (underworld), the feminine, the serpentine movement of sexuality, of creativity, the basis of all energy and life.

The Presences

She appeared in white, garbed in white,
standing white, pure white.
—Bernardino de Sahagún[30]

On the gulf where I was raised, *en el Valle del Río Grande* in South Texas—that triangular piece of land wedged between the river *y el golfo* which serves as the Texas-U.S./Mexican border—is a Mexican *pueblito* called Hargill (at one time in the history of this one-grocery-store, two-service-stations town there were thirteen churches and thirteen *cantinas*). Down the road, a little ways from our house, was a deserted church. It was known among the *mexicanos* that if you walked down the road late at night you would see a woman dressed in white floating about, peering out the church window. She would follow those who had done something bad or who were afraid. *Los mexicanos* called her *la Jila.* Some thought she was *la Llorona.* She was, I think, *Cihuacoatl,* Serpent Woman, ancient Aztec goddess of the earth, of war and birth, patron of midwives, and antecedent of *la Llorona.* Covered with chalk, *Cihuacoatl* wears a white dress with a decoration half red and half black. Her hair forms two little horns (which the Aztecs depicted as knives) crossed on her forehead. The lower part of her face is a bare jawbone, signifying death. On her back she carries a cradle, the knife of sacrifice swaddled as if it were her papoose, her child.[31] Like *la Llorona, Cihuacoatl* howls and weeps in the night, screams as if demented. She brings mental depression and sorrow. Long before it takes place, she is the first to predict something is to happen.

Back then, I, an unbeliever, scoffed at these Mexican superstitions as I was taught in Anglo school. Now, I wonder if this story and similar ones were the culture's attempts to "protect" members of the family, especially girls, from "wandering." Stories of the devil luring young girls away and having his way with them discouraged us from going out. There's an ancient Indian tradition of burning the umbilical cord of an infant girl under the house so she will never stray from it and her domestic role.

[30]Bernardino de Sahagún, *General History of the Things of New Spain* (Florentine Codex), Vol. I Revised, trans. Arthur Anderson and Charles Dibble (Sante Fe, NM: School of American Research, 1950), 11.

[31]The Aztecs muted Snake Woman's patronage of childbirth and vegetation by placing a sacrificial knife in the empty cradle she carried on her back (signifying a child who died in childbirth), thereby making her a devourer of sacrificial victims. Snake Woman had the ability to change herself into a serpent or into a lovely young woman to entice young men who withered away and died after intercourse with her. She was known as a witch and a shape-shifter. Brundage, 168–171.

A mis ancas caen los cueros de culebra,
cuatro veces por año los arrastro,
me tropiezo y me caigo
y cada vez que miro una culebra le pregunto
¿Qué traes conmigo?

Four years ago a red snake crossed my path as I walked through the woods. The direction of its movement, its pace, its colors, the "mood" of the trees and the wind and the snake—they all "spoke" to me, told me things. I look for omens everywhere, everywhere catch glimpses of the patterns and cycles of my life. Stones "speak" to Luisah Teish, a Santera; trees whisper their secrets to Chrystos, a Native American. I remember listening to the voices of the wind as a child and understanding its messages. *Los espíritus* that ride the back of the south wind. I remember their exhalation blowing in through the slits in the door during those hot Texas afternoons. A gust of wind raising the linoleum under my feet, buffeting the house. Everything trembling.

We're not supposed to remember such otherworldly events. We're supposed to ignore, forget, kill those fleeting images of the soul's presence and of the spirit's presence. We've been taught that the spirit is outside our bodies or above our heads somewhere up in the sky with God. We're supposed to forget that every cell in our bodies, every bone and bird and worm has spirit in it.

Like many Indians and Mexicans, I did not deem my psychic experiences real. I denied their occurrences and let my inner senses atrophy. I allowed white rationality to tell me that the existence of the "other world" was mere pagan superstition. I accepted their reality, the "official" reality of the rational, reasoning mode which is connected with external reality, the upper world, and is considered the most developed consciousness—the consciousness of duality.

The other mode of consciousness facilitates images from the soul and the unconscious through dreams and the imagination. Its work is labeled "fiction," make-believe, wish-fulfillment. White anthropologists claim that Indians have "primitive" and therefore deficient minds, that we cannot think in the higher mode of consciousness—rationality. They are fascinated by what they call the "magical" mind, the "savage" mind, the *participation mystique* of the mind that says the world of the imagination—the world of the soul—and of the spirit is just as real as physical reality.[32] In trying to become "objective," Western culture made "objects" of things and people when it distanced itself from them, thereby losing "touch" with them. This dichotomy is the root of all violence.

Not only was the brain split into two functions but so was reality. Thus people who inhabit both realities are forced to live in the interface between the two, forced to become adept at switching modes. Such is the case with the *india* and the *mestiza*.

Institutionalized religion fears trafficking with the spirit world and stigmatizes it as witchcraft. It has strict taboos against this kind of inner knowledge. It fears what

[32]Anthropologist Lucien Levy-Bruhl coined the word *participation mystique*. According to Jung, "It denotes a peculiar kind of psychological connection . . . (in which) the subject cannot clearly distinguish himself from the object but is bound to it by a direct relationship which amounts to partial identity." Carl Jung, "Definitions," in *Psychological Types, The Collected Works of C. G. Jung,* Vol. 6 (Princeton, NJ: Princeton University Press, 1953), par. 781.

Jung calls the Shadow, the unsavory aspects of ourselves. But even more it fears the supra-human, the god in ourselves.

"The purpose of any established religion . . . is to glorify, sanction and bless with a superpersonal meaning all personal and interpersonal activities. This occurs through the 'sacraments,' and indeed through most religious rites."[33] But it sanctions only its own sacraments and rites. Voodoo, Santeria, Shamanism and other native religions are called cults and their beliefs are called mythologies. In my own life, the Catholic Church fails to give meaning to my daily acts, to my continuing encounters with the "other world." It and other institutionalized religions impoverish all life, beauty, pleasure.

The Catholic and Protestant religions encourage fear and distrust of life and of the body; they encourage a split between the body and the spirit and totally ignore the soul; they encourage us to kill off parts of ourselves. We are taught that the body is an ignorant animal; intelligence dwells only in the head. But the body is smart. It does not discern between external stimuli and stimuli from the imagination. It reacts equally viscerally to events from the imagination as it does to "real" events.

So I grew up in the interface trying not to give countenance to *el mal aigre*,[34] evil non-human, non-corporeal entities riding the wind, that could come in through the window, through my nose with my breath. I was not supposed to believe in *susto,* a sudden shock or fall that frightens the soul out of the body. And growing up between such opposing spiritualities how could I reconcile the two, the pagan and the Christian?

No matter to what use my people put the supranatural world, it is evident to me now that the spirit world, whose existence the whites are so adamant in denying, does in fact exist. This very minute I sense the presence of the spirits of my ancestors in my room. And I think *la Jila* is *Cihuacoatl,* Snake Woman; she is *la Llorona,* Daughter of Night, traveling the dark terrains of the unknown searching for the lost parts of herself. I remember *la Jila* following me once, remember her eerie lament. I'd like to think that she was crying for her lost children, *los* Chicanos/*mexicanos.*

La facultad

La facultad is the capacity to see in surface phenomena the meaning of deeper realities, to see the deep structure below the surface. It is an instant "sensing," a quick perception arrived at without conscious reasoning. It is an acute awareness mediated by the part of the psyche that does not speak, that communicates in images and symbols which are the faces of feelings, that is, behind which feelings reside/hide. The one possessing this sensitivity is excruciatingly alive to the world.

Those who are pushed out of the tribe for being different are likely to become more sensitized (when not brutalized into insensitivity). Those who do not feel psychologically or physically safe in the world are more apt to develop this sense. Those

[33] I have lost the source of this quote. If anyone knows what it is, please let the publisher know.

[34] Some *mexicanos* and Chicanos distinguish between *aire,* air, and *mala aigre,* the evil spirits which reside in the air.

who are pounced on the most have it the strongest—the females, the homosexuals of all races, the darkskinned, the outcast, the persecuted, the marginalized, the foreign.

When we're up against the wall, when we have all sorts of oppressions coming at us, we are forced to develop this faculty so that we'll know when the next person is going to slap us or lock us away. We'll sense the rapist when he's five blocks down the street. Pain makes us acutely anxious to avoid more of it, so we hone that radar. It's a kind of survival tactic that people, caught between the worlds, unknowingly cultivate. It is latent in all of us.

I walk into a house and I know whether it is empty or occupied. I feel the lingering charge in the air of a recent fight or lovemaking or depression. I sense the emotions someone near is emitting—whether friendly or threatening. Hate and fear—the more intense the emotion, the greater my reception of it. I feel a tingling on my skin when someone is staring at me or thinking about me. I can tell how others feel by the way they smell, where others are by the air pressure on my skin. I can spot the love or greed or generosity lodged in the tissues of another. Often I sense the direction of and my distance from people or objects—in the dark, or with my eyes closed, without looking. It must be a vestige of a proximity sense, a sixth sense that's lain dormant from long-ago times.

Fear develops the proximity sense aspect of *la facultad.* But there is a deeper sensing that is another aspect of this faculty. It is anything that breaks into one's everyday mode of perception, that causes a break in one's defenses and resistance, anything that takes one from one's habitual grounding, causes the depths to open up, causes a shift in perception. This shift in perception deepens the way we see concrete objects and people; the senses become so acute and piercing that we can see through things, view events in depth, a piercing that reaches the underworld (the realm of the soul). As we plunge vertically, the break, with its accompanying new seeing, makes us pay attention to the soul, and we are thus carried into awareness—an experiencing of soul (Self).

We lose something in this mode of initiation, something is taken from us: our innocence, our unknowing ways, our safe and easy ignorance. There is a prejudice and a fear of the dark, chthonic (underworld), material such as depression, illness, death and the violations that can bring on this break. Confronting anything that tears the fabric of our everyday mode of consciousness and that thrusts us into a less literal and more psychic sense of reality increases awareness and *la facultad.*

7

La conciencia de la mestiza/Towards a New Consciousness

Por la mujer de mi raza
hablará el espíritu.[35]

Jose Vasconcelos, Mexican philosopher, envisaged *una raza mestiza, una mezcla de razas afines, una raca de color—la primera raza síntesis del globo.* He called it a cos-

[35]This is my own "take off" on Jose Vasconcelos's idea. Jose Vasconcelos, *La Raza Cósmica: Misión de la Raza Ibero-Americana* (México: Aguilar S.A. de Ediciones, 1961).

mic race, *la raza cósmica,* a fifth race embracing the four major races of the world.[36] Opposite to the theory of the pure Aryan, and to the policy of racial purity that white America practices, his theory is one of inclusivity. At the confluence of two or more genetic streams, with chromosomes constantly "crossing over," this mixture of races, rather than resulting in an inferior being, provides hybrid progeny, a mutable, more malleable species with a rich gene pool. From this racial, ideological, cultural and biological cross-pollinization, an "alien" consciousness is presently in the making—a new *mestiza* consciousness, *una conciencia de mujer.* It is a consciousness of the Borderlands.

Una lucha de fronteras/A Struggle of Borders

Because I, a *mestiza,*
continually walk out of one culture
and into another,
because I am in all cultures at the same time,
alma entre dos mundos, tres, cuatro,
me zumba la cabeza con lo contradictorio.
Estoy norteada por todas las voces que me hablan
simultáneamente.

The ambivalence from the clash of voices results in mental and emotional states of perplexity. Internal strife results in insecurity and indecisiveness. The mestiza's dual or multiple personality is plagued by psychic restlessness.

In a constant state of mental nepantilism, an Aztec word meaning torn between ways, *la mestiza* is a product of the transfer of the cultural and spiritual values of one group to another. Being tricultural, monolingual, bilingual, or multilingual, speaking a patois, and in a state of perpetual transition, the *mestiza* faces the dilemma of the mixed breed: which collectivity does the daughter of a darkskinned mother listen to?

El choque de un alma atrapado entre el mundo del espíritu y el mundo de la técnica a veces la deja entullada. Cradled in one culture, sandwiched between two cultures, straddling all three cultures and their value systems, *la mestiza* undergoes a struggle of flesh, a struggle of borders, an inner war. Like all people, we perceive the version of reality that our culture communicates. Like others having or living in more than one culture, we get multiple, often opposing messages. The coming together of two self-consistent but habitually incompatible frames of reference[37] causes *un choque,* a cultural collision.

Within us and within *la cultura chicana,* commonly held beliefs of the white culture attack commonly held beliefs of the Mexican culture, and both attack commonly held beliefs of the indigenous culture. Subconsciously, we see an attack on ourselves and our beliefs as a threat and we attempt to block with a counterstance.

[36]Vasconcelos.

[37]Arthur Koestler termed this "bisociation." Albert Rothenberg, *The Creative Process in Art, Science, and Other Fields* (Chicago, IL: University of Chicago Press, 1979), 12.

But it is not enough to stand on the opposite river bank, shouting questions, challenging patriarchal, white conventions. A counterstance locks one into a duel of oppressor and oppressed; locked in mortal combat, like the cop and the criminal, both are reduced to a common denominator of violence. The counterstance refutes the dominant culture's views and beliefs, and, for this, it is proudly defiant. All reaction is limited by, and dependent on, what it is reacting against. Because the counterstance stems from a problem with authority—outer as well as inner—it's a step towards liberation from cultural domination. But it is not a way of life. At some point, on our way to a new consciousness, we will have to leave the opposite bank, the split between the two mortal combatants somehow healed so that we are on both shores at once and, at once, see through serpent and eagle eyes. Or perhaps we will decide to disengage from the dominant culture, write it off altogether as a lost cause, and cross the border into a wholly new and separate territory. Or we might go another route. The possibilities are numerous once we decide to act and not react.

A Tolerance for Ambiguity

These numerous possibilities leave *la mestiza* floundering in uncharted seas. In perceiving conflicting information and points of view, she is subjected to a swamping of her psychological borders. She has discovered that she can't hold concepts or ideas in rigid boundaries. The borders and walls that are supposed to keep the undesirable ideas out are entrenched habits and patterns of behavior; these habits and patterns are the enemy within. Rigidity means death. Only by remaining flexible is she able to stretch the psyche horizontally and vertically. *La mestiza* constantly has to shift out of habitual formations; from convergent thinking, analytical reasoning that tends to use rationality to move toward a single goal (a Western mode), to divergent thinking,[38] characterized by movement away from set patterns and goals and toward a more whole perspective, one that includes rather than excludes.

The new *mestiza* copes by developing a tolerance for contradictions, a tolerance for ambiguity. She learns to be an Indian in Mexican culture, to be Mexican from an Anglo point of view. She learns to juggle cultures. She has a plural personality, she operates in a pluralistic mode—nothing is thrust out, the good the bad and the ugly, nothing rejected, nothing abandoned. Not only does she sustain contradictions, she turns the ambivalence into something else.

She can be jarred out of ambivalence by an intense, and often painful, emotional event which inverts or resolves the ambivalence. I'm not sure exactly how. The work takes place underground—subconsciously. It is work that the soul performs. That focal point or fulcrum, that juncture where the mestiza stands, is where phenomena tend to collide. It is where the possibility of uniting all that is separate occurs. This assembly is not one where severed or separated pieces merely come together. Nor is

[38]In part, I derive my definitions for "convergent" and "divergent" thinking from Rothenberg, 12–13.

it a balancing of opposing powers. In attempting to work out a synthesis, the self has added a third element which is greater than the sum of its severed parts. That third element is a new consciousness—a mestiza consciousness—and though it is a source of intense pain, its energy comes from continual creative motion that keeps breaking down the unitary aspect of each new paradigm.

En unas pocas centurias, the future will belong to the mestiza. Because the future depends on the breaking down of paradigms, it depends on the straddling of two or more cultures. By creating a new mythos—that is, a change in the way we perceive reality, the way we see ourselves, and the ways we behave—*la mestiza* creates a new consciousness.

The work of *mestiza* consciousness is to break down the subject-object duality that keeps her a prisoner and to show in the flesh and through the images in her work how duality is transcended. The answer to the problem between the white race and the colored, between males and females, lies in healing the split that originates in the very foundation of our lives, our culture, our languages, our thoughts. A massive uprooting of dualistic thinking in the individual and collective consciousness is the beginning of a long struggle, but one that could, in our best hopes, bring us to the end of rape, of violence, of war.

La encrucijada/The Crossroads

A chicken is being sacrificed
        at a crossroads, a simple mound of earth
a mud shrine for *Eshu,*
        Yoruba god of indeterminacy,
who blesses her choice of path.
        She begins her journey.

Su cuerpo es una bocacalle. La mestiza has gone from being the sacrificial goat to becoming the officiating priestess at the crossroads.

As a *mestiza* I have no country, my homeland cast me out; yet all countries are mine because I am every woman's sister or potential lover. (As a lesbian I have no race, my own people disclaim me; but I am all races because there is the queer of me in all races.) I am cultureless because, as a feminist, I challenge the collective cultural/religious male-derived beliefs of Indo-Hispanics and Anglos; yet I am cultured because I am participating in the creation of yet another culture, a new story to explain the world and our participation in it, a new value system with images and symbols that connect us to each other and to the planet. *Soy un amasamiento,* I am an act of kneading, of uniting and joining that not only has produced both a creature of darkness and a creature of light, but also a creature that questions the definitions of light and dark and gives them new meanings.

We are the people who leap in the dark, we are the people on the knees of the gods. In our very flesh, (r)evolution works out the clash of cultures. It makes us crazy constantly, but if the center holds, we've made some kind of evolutionary step forward. *Nuestra alma el trabajo,* the opus, the great alchemical work; spiritual *mestizaje,* a "morphogenesis,"[39] an inevitable unfolding. We have become the quickening serpent movement.

Indigenous like corn, like corn, the *mestiza* is a product of crossbreeding, designed for preservation under a variety of conditions. Like an ear of corn—a female seed-bearing organ—the *mestiza* is tenacious, tightly wrapped in the husks of her culture. Like kernels she clings to the cob; with thick stalks and strong race roots, she holds tight to the earth—she will survive the crossroads.

Lavando y remojando el maíz en agua de cal, despojando el pellejo. Moliendo, mixteando, amasando, haciendo tortillas de masa.[40] She steeps the corn in lime, it swells, softens. With stone roller on *metate,* she grinds the corn, then grinds again. She kneads and moulds the dough, pats the round balls into *tortillas.*

We are the porous rock in the stone *metate*
squatting on the ground.
We are the rolling pin, *el maíz y agua,*
la masa harina. Somos e amasijo.
Somos lo molido en el metate.
We are the *comal* sizzling hot,
the hot *tortilla,* the hungry mouth.
We are the coarse rock.
We are the grinding motion,
the mixed potion, *somos el molcajete.*
We are the pestle, the *comino, ajo, pimienta,*
We are the *chile colorado,*
the green shoot that cracks the rock.
We will abide.

El camino de la mestiza/The Mestiza Way

Caught between the sudden contraction, the breath sucked in and the endless space, the brown woman stands still, looks at the sky. She decides to go down, digging her way along the roots of trees. Sifting through the bones, she shakes them to see if there is any marrow in them. Then, touching the dirt to her forehead, to her tongue, she takes a few bones, leaves the rest in their burial place.

She goes through her backpack, keeps her journal and address book, throws away the muni-bart metromaps. The coins are heavy and they go next, then the greenbacks flutter

[39]To borrow chemist Ilya Prigogine's theory of "dissipative structures." Prigogine discovered that substances interact not in predictable ways as it was taught in science, but in different and fluctuating ways to produce new and more complex structures, a kind of birth he called "morphogenesis," which created unpredictable innovations. Harold Gilliam, "Searching for a New World View," *This World* (January, 1981), 23.

[40]Corn tortillas are of two types, the smooth uniform ones made in a tortilla press and usually bought at a tortilla factory or supermarket, and *gorditas,* made by mixing *masa* with lard or shortening or butter (my mother sometimes puts in bits of bacon or *chicharrones*).

through the air. She keeps her knife, can opener and eyebrow pencil. She puts bones, pieces of bark, hierbas, eagle feather, snakeskin, tape recorder, the rattle and drum in her pack and she sets out to become the complete tolteca.[41]

Her first step is to take inventory. *Despojando, desgranando, quitando paja.* Just what did she inherit from her ancestors? This weight on her back—which is the baggage from the Indian mother, which the baggage from the Spanish father, which the baggage from the Anglo?

Pero es difícil differentiating between *lo heredado, lo adquirido, lo impuesto.* She puts history through a sieve, winnows out the lies, looks at the forces that we as a race, as women, have been a part of. *Luego bota lo que no vale, los desmientos, los desencuentos, el embrutecimiento. Aguarda el juicio, hondo y enraízado, de la gente antigua.* This step is a conscious rupture with all oppressive traditions of all cultures and religions. She communicates that rupture, documents the struggle. She reinterprets history and, using new symbols, she shapes new myths. She adopts new perspectives toward the darkskinned, women and queers. She strengthens her tolerance (and intolerance) for ambiguity. She is willing to share, to make herself vulnerable to foreign ways of seeing and thinking. She surrenders all notions of safety, of the familiar. Deconstruct, construct. She becomes a *nahual,* able to transform herself into a tree, a coyote, into another person. She learns to transform the small "I" into the total Self. *Se hace moldeadora de su alma. Según la concepción que tiene de sí misma, así será.*

Que no se nos olvide los hombres

"Tú no sirves pa' nada—
you're good for nothing.
Eres pura vieja."

"You're nothing but a woman" means you are defective. Its opposite is to be *un macho.* The modern meaning of the word "machismo," as well as the concept, is actually an Anglo invention. For men like my father, being "macho" meant being strong enough to protect and support my mother and us, yet being able to show love. Today's macho has doubts about his ability to feed and protect his family. His "machismo" is an adaptation to oppression and poverty and low self-esteem. It is the result of hierarchical male dominance. The Anglo, feeling inadequate and inferior and powerless, displaces or transfers these feelings to the Chicano by shaming him. In the Gringo world, the Chicano suffers from excessive humility and self-effacement, shame of self and self-deprecation. Around Latinos he suffers from a sense of language inadequacy and its accompanying discomfort; with Native Americans he suffers from a racial amnesia which ignores our common blood, and from guilt because the Spanish part of him took their land and oppressed them. He has an

[41]Gina Valdés, *Puentes y Fronteras: Coplas Chicanas* (Los Angeles, CA: Castle Lithograph, 1982), 2.

excessive compensatory hubris when around Mexicans from the other side. It overlays a deep sense of racial shame.

The loss of a sense of dignity and respect in the macho breeds a false machismo which leads him to put down women and even to brutalize them. Coexisting with his sexist behavior is a love for the mother which takes precedence over that of all others. Devoted son, macho pig. To wash down the shame of his fears, of his very being, and to handle the brute in the mirror, he takes to the bottle, the snort, the needle, and the fist.

Though we "understand" the root causes of male hatred and fear, and the subsequent wounding of women, we do not excuse, we do not condone, and we will no longer put up with it. From the men of our race, we demand the admission/acknowledgment/disclosure/testimony that they wound us, violate us, are afraid of us and of our power. We need them to say they will begin to eliminate their hurtful put-down ways. But more than the words, we demand acts. We say to them: We will develop equal power with you and those who have shamed us.

It is imperative that mestizas support each other in changing the sexist elements in the Mexican-Indian culture. As long as woman is put down, the Indian and the Black in all of us is put down. The struggle of the mestiza is above all a feminist one. As long as *los hombres* think they have to *chingar mujeres* and each other to be men, as long as men are taught that they are superior and therefore culturally favored over *la mujer,* as long as to be a *vieja* is a thing of derision, there can be no real healing of our psyches. We're halfway there—we have such love of the Mother, the good mother. The first step is to unlearn the *puta/virgen* dichotomy and to see *Coatlapopeuh-Coatlicue* in the Mother, *Guadalupe.*

Tenderness, a sign of vulnerability, is so feared that it is showered on women with verbal abuse and blows. Men, even more than women, are fettered to gender roles. Women at least have had the guts to break out of bondage. Only gay men have had the courage to expose themselves to the woman inside them and to challenge the current masculinity. I've encountered a few scattered and isolated gentle straight men, the beginnings of a new breed, but they are confused, and entangled with sexist behaviors that they have not been able to eradicate. We need a new masculinity and the new man needs a movement.

Lumping the males who deviate from the general norm with man, the oppressor, is a gross injustice. *Asombra pensar que nos hemos quedado en ese pozo oscuro donde el mundo encierra a las lesbianas. Asombra pensar que hemos, como femenistas y lesbianas, cerrado nuestros corazónes a los hombres, a nuestros hermanos los jotos, desheredados y marginales como nosotros.* Being the supreme crossers of cultures, homosexuals have strong bonds with the queer white, Black, Asian, Native American, Latino, and with the queer in Italy, Australia and the rest of the planet. We come from all colors, all classes, all races, all time periods. Our role is to link people with each other—the Blacks with Jews with Indians with Asians with whites with extraterrestrials. It is to transfer ideas and information from one culture to another. Colored homosexuals have more knowledge of other cultures; have always been at the forefront (although sometimes the closet) of all liberation struggles in this country; have suffered more injustices and have survived them despite all odds. Chicanos need to acknowledge the political and artistic contributions of their queer. People, listen to what your *jotería* is saying.

The mestizo and the queer exist at this time and point on the evolutionary continuum for a purpose. We are a blending that proves that all blood is intricately woven together, and that we are spawned out of similar souls.

Somos una gente

Hay tantísimas fronteras
que dividen a la gente,
pero por cada frontera
existe también un puente
—Gina Valdés[42]

Divided Loyalties. Many women and men of color do not want to have any dealings with white people. It takes too much time and energy to explain to the downwardly mobile, white middle-class women that it's okay for us to want to own "possessions," never having had any nice furniture on our dirt floors or "luxuries" like washing machines. Many feel that whites should help their own people rid themselves of race hatred and fear first. I, for one, choose to use some of my energy to serve as mediator. I think we need to allow whites to be our allies. Through our literature, art, *corridos,* and folktales we must share our history with them so when they set up committees to help Big Mountain Navajos or the Chicano farmworkers or *los Nicaragüenses* they won't turn people away because of their racial fears and ignorances. They will come to see that they are not helping us but following our lead.

Individually, but also as a racial entity, we need to voice our needs. We need to say to white society: We need you to accept the fact that Chicanos are different, to acknowledge your rejection and negation of us. We need you to own the fact that you looked upon us as less than human, that you stole our lands, our personhood, our self-respect. We need you to make public restitution: to say that, to compensate for your own sense of defectiveness, you strive for power over us, you erase our history and our experience because it makes you feel guilty—you'd rather forget your brutish acts. To say you've split yourself from minority groups, that you disown us, that your dual consciousness splits off parts of yourself, transferring the "negative" parts onto us. (Where there is persecution of minorities, there is shadow projection. Where there is violence and war, there is repression of shadow.) To say that you are afraid of us, that to put distance between us, you wear the mask of contempt. Admit that Mexico is your double, that she exists in the shadow of this country, that we are irrevocably tied to her. Gringo, accept the doppelganger in your psyche. By taking back your collective shadow the intracultural split will heal. And finally, tell us what you need from us.

[42]Richard Wilhelm, *The I Ching or Book of Changes,* trans. Cary F. Baynes (Princeton, NJ: Princeton University Press, 1950), 98.

By Your True Faces We Will Know You

I am visible—see this Indian face—yet I am invisible. I both blind them with my beak nose and am their blind spot. But I exist, we exist. They'd like to think I have melted in the pot. But I haven't, we haven't.

The dominant white culture is killing us slowly with its ignorance. By taking away our self-determination, it has made us weak and empty. As a people we have resisted and we have taken expedient positions, but we have never been allowed to develop unencumbered—we have never been allowed to be fully ourselves. The whites in power want us people of color to barricade ourselves behind our separate tribal walls so they can pick us off one at a time with their hidden weapons; so they can whitewash and distort history. Ignorance splits people, creates prejudices. A misinformed people is a subjugated people.

Before the Chicano and the undocumented worker and the Mexican from the other side can come together, before the Chicano can have unity with Native Americans and other groups, we need to know the history of their struggle and they need to know ours. Our mothers, our sisters and brothers, the guys who hang out on street corners, the children in the playgrounds, each of us must know our Indian lineage, our afro-*mestizaje,* our history of resistance.

To the immigrant *mexicano* and the recent arrivals we must teach our history. The 80 million *mexicanos* and the Latinos from Central and South America must know of our struggles. Each one of us must know basic facts about Nicaragua, Chile and the rest of Latin America. The Latinoist movement (Chicanos, Puerto Ricans, Cubans and other Spanish-speaking people working together to combat racial discrimination in the market place) is good but it is not enough. Other than a common culture we will have nothing to hold us together. We need to meet on a broader communal ground.

The struggle is inner: Chicano, *indio,* American Indian, *mojado, mexicano,* immigrant Latino, Anglo in power, working class Anglo, Black, Asian—our psyches resemble the bordertowns and are populated by the same people. The struggle has always been inner, and is played out in the outer terrains. Awareness of our situation must come before inner changes, which in turn come before changes in society. Nothing happens in the "real" world unless it first happens in the images in our heads.

El día de la Chicana

I will not be shamed again
Nor will I shame myself.

I am possessed by a vision: that we Chicanas and Chicanos have taken back or uncovered our true faces, our dignity and self-respect. It's a validation vision.

Seeing the Chicana anew in light of her history. I seek an exoneration, a seeing through the fictions of white supremacy, a seeing of ourselves in our true guises and not as the false racial personality that has been given to us and that we have given to ourselves. I seek our woman's face, our true features, the positive and the negative seen clearly, free of the tainted biases of male dominance. I seek new images of identity, new beliefs about ourselves, our humanity and worth no longer in question.

Estamos viviendo en la noche de la Raza, un tiempo cuando el trabajo se hace a lo quieto, en el oscuro. El día cuando aceptamos tal y como somos y para en donde vamos y porque—ese día será el día de la Raza. Yo tengo el compromiso de expresar mi visión, mi sensibilidad, mi percepción de la revalidación de la gente mexicana, su mérito, estimación, honra, aprecio, y validez.

On December 2nd when my sun goes into my first house, I celebrate *el día de la Chicana y el Chicano.* On that day I clean my altars, light my *Coatlalopeuh* candle, burn sage and copal, take *el baño para espantar basura,* sweep my house. On that day I bare my soul, make myself vulnerable to friends and family by expressing my feelings. On that day I affirm who we are.

On that day I look inside our conflicts and our basic introverted racial temperament. I identify our needs, voice them. I acknowledge that the self and the race have been wounded. I recognize the need to take care of our personhood, of our racial self. On that day I gather the splintered and disowned parts of *la gente mexicana* and hold them in my arms. *Todas las partes de nosotros valen.*

On that day I say, "Yes, all you people wound us when you reject us. Rejection strips us of self-worth; our vulnerability exposes us to shame. It is our innate identity you find wanting. We are ashamed that we need your good opinion, that we need your acceptance. We can no longer camouflage our needs, can no longer let defenses and fences sprout around us. We can no longer withdraw. To rage and look upon you with contempt is to rage and be contemptuous of ourselves. We can no longer blame you, nor disown the white parts, the male parts, the pathological parts, the queer parts, the vulnerable parts. Here we are weaponless with open arms, with only our magic. Let's try it our way, the mestiza way, the Chicana way, the woman way."

On that day, I search for our essential dignity as a people, a people with a sense of purpose—to belong and contribute to something greater than our *pueblo.* On that day I seek to recover and reshape my spiritual identity. *¡Anímate! Raza, a celebrar el día de la Chicana.*

El retorno

All movements are accomplished in six stages,
and the seventh brings return.
—I Ching

Tanto tiempo sin verte casa mía,
mi cuna, mi hondo nido de la huerta.
—*"Soledad"*[43]

I stand at the river, watch the curving, twisting serpent, a serpent nailed to the fence where the mouth of the Rio Grande empties into the Gulf.

I have come back. *Tanto dolor me costó el alejamiento.* I shade my eyes and look up. The bone beak of a hawk slowly circling over me, checking me out as potential carrion. In its wake a little bird flickering its wings, swimming sporadically like a fish.

[43] *"Soledad"* is sung by the group, Haciendo Punto en Otro Son.

In the distance the expressway and the slough of traffic like an irritated sow. The sudden pull in my gut, *la tierra, los aguaceros.* My land, *el viento soplando la arena, el lagartijo debajo de un nopalito. Me acuerdo como era antes. Una región desértica de vasta llanuras, costeras de baja altura, de escasa lluvia, de chaparrales formados por mesquites y huizaches.* If I look real hard I can almost see the Spanish fathers who were called "the cavalry of Christ" enter this valley riding their burros, see the clash of cultures commence.

Tierra natal. This is home, the small towns in the Valley, *los pueblitos* with chicken pens and goats picketed to mesquite shrubs. *En las colonias* on the other side of the tracks, junk cars line the front yards of hot pink and lavender-trimmed houses—Chicano architecture we call it, self-consciously. I have missed the TV shows where hosts speak in half and half, and where awards are given in the category of Tex-Mex music. I have missed the Mexican cemeteries blooming with artificial flowers, the fields of aloe vera and red pepper, rows of sugar cane, of corn hanging on the stalks, the cloud of *polvareda* in the dirt roads behind a speeding pickup truck, *el sabor de tamales de rez y venado.* I have missed *la yegua colorada* gnawing the wooden gate of her stall, the smell of horse flesh from Carito's corrals. *He hecho menos las noches calientes sin aire, noches de linternas y lechuzas* making holes in the night.

I still feel the old despair when I look at the unpainted, dilapidated, scrap lumber houses consisting mostly of corrugated aluminum. Some of the poorest people in the U.S. live in the Lower Rio Grande Valley, an arid and semi-arid land of irrigated farming, intense sunlight and heat, citrus groves next to chaparral and cactus. I walk through the elementary school I attended so long ago, that remained segregated until recently. I remember how the white teachers used to punish us for being Mexican.

How I love this tragic valley of South Texas, as Ricardo Sánchez calls it; this borderland between the Nueces and the Rio Grande. This land has survived possession and ill-use by five countries: Spain, Mexico, the Republic of Texas, the U.S., the Confederacy, and the U.S. again. It has survived Anglo-Mexican blood feuds, lynchings, burnings, rapes, pillage.

Today I see the Valley still struggling to survive. Whether it does or not, it will never be as I remember it. The borderlands depression that was set off by the 1982 peso devaluation in Mexico resulted in the closure of hundreds of Valley businesses. Many people lost their homes, cars, land. Prior to 1982, U.S. store owners thrived on retail sales to Mexicans who came across the border for groceries and clothes and appliances. While goods on the U.S. side have become 10, 100, 1000 times more expensive for Mexican buyers, goods on the Mexican side have become 10, 100, 1000 times cheaper for Americans. Because the Valley is heavily dependent on agriculture and Mexican retail trade, it has the highest unemployment rates along the entire border region; it is the Valley that has been hardest hit.[44]

[44]Out of the twenty-two border counties in the four border states, Hidalgo County (named for Father Hidalgo who was shot in 1810 after instigating Mexico's revolt against Spanish rule under the banner of *la Virgen de Guadalupe*) is the most poverty-stricken county in the nation as well as the largest home base (along with Imperial in California) for migrant farmworkers. It was here that I was born and raised. I am amazed that both it and I have survived.

"It's been a bad year for corn," my brother, Nune, says. As he talks, I remember my father scanning the sky for a rain that would end the drought, looking up into the sky, day after day, while the corn withered on its stalk. My father has been dead for 29 years, having worked himself to death. The life span of a Mexican farm laborer is 56—he lived to be 38. It shocks me that I am older than he. I, too, search the sky for rain. Like the ancients, I worship the rain god and the maize goddess, but unlike my father I have recovered their names. Now for rain (irrigation) one offers not a sacrifice of blood, but of money.

"Farming is in a bad way," my brother says. "Two to three thousand small and big farmers went bankrupt in this country last year. Six years ago the price of corn was $8.00 per hundred pounds," he goes on. "This year it is $3.90 per hundred pounds." And, I think to myself, after taking inflation into account, not planting anything puts you ahead.

I walk out to the back yard, stare at *los rosales de mamá.* She wants me to help her prune the rose bushes, dig out the carpet grass that is choking them. *Mamagrande Ramona también tenía rosales.* Here every Mexican grows flowers. If they don't have a piece of dirt, they use car tires, jars, cans, shoe boxes. Roses are the Mexican's favorite flower. I think, how symbolic—thorns and all.

Yes, the Chicano and Chicana have always taken care of growing things and the land. Again I see the four of us kids getting off the school bus, changing into our work clothes, walking into the field with Papí and Mamí, all six of us bending to the ground. Below our feet, under the earth lie the watermelon seeds. We cover them with paper plates, putting *terremotes* on top of the plates to keep them from being blown away by the wind. The paper plates keep the freeze away. Next day or the next, we remove the plates, bare the tiny green shoots to the elements. They survive and grow, give fruit hundreds of times the size of the seed. We water them and hoe them. We harvest them. The vines dry, rot, are plowed under. Growth, death, decay, birth. The soil prepared again and again, impregnated, worked on. A constant changing of forms, *renacimientos de la tierra madre.*

This land was Mexican once
was Indian always
and is.
And will be again.

1987

Judith Ortiz Cofer b. 1952

The daughter of a teenage mother and a career Navy father, Judith Ortiz Cofer spent her childhood traveling back and forth between the U.S. mainland and Puerto Rico, her birthplace, experiencing schools and neighborhoods in both Spanish and English and adjusting and readjusting to different cultural environments. After retirement, her father settled the family in Georgia, which stabilized Judith's education.

During college she married and, with husband and daughter, moved to Florida where she finished an M.A. in English. A fellowship allowed her to pursue graduate work at Oxford, after which she returned to Florida and simultaneously began teaching English and writing poetry. In 1981 and 82, she received scholarships to the Bread Loaf Writers' Conference, and continued on the program's staff until 1985. *Peregrina* won first place in the Riverstone International Poetry Chapbook Competition in 1985. *Reaching for the Mainland* and *Terms of Survival* appeared in 1987. Since then, she has concentrated on prose, publishing *The Line of the Sun* (1989), a novel; *Silent Dancing* (1990), autobiographical essays; and *The Latin Deli* (1993) and *An Island Like You* (1995), short stories.

As a child, living amid the violence and racial tensions of the Paterson, New Jersey slums, the library became her refuge, and books her English teachers; on the island, the written word gave way to the oral tradition of her Spanish speaking grandmother. Though strongly determined by the English language and literary tradition of her academic training, her writing still reflects the tension of that dynamic intercultural background. Spanish lingers, filtering through in emotion-packed words or phrases that remind us we are reading something other than a monolingual text. Her poems offer continual overlays and blends of cultures and languages that refuse to settle completely into either side, hence defining their ever-shifting, never-ending synthesis as authentic Puerto Rican life. She calls it the "habit of movement," a state of instability that informs and stimulates her creativity.

One pattern her exploration takes is that of gathering, like an anthropologist, sayings, expressions, or words from Puerto Rican Spanish and recasting them into English poems in which the essence is conveyed across linguistic borders. In the process, she charts the experience of intercultural life, exposing readers to alternative perspectives on everyday matters that can seem so common and simple when safely encapsulated in the familiar words of one's own language. That is, Ortiz Cofer achieves what many claim to be the function of poetry: she rarifies language and experience to an intensity that enables it to stir the reader's otherwise callous sensibilities. At a more pedestrian level, this experience is and has been fundamental to the development of the U.S. idiom and culture, themselves a product of the continual intercultural synthesis that makes them so rich and dynamic. Thus, beyond displaying the particularities of Puerto Rican experience, Ortiz Cofer reminds us of our common national character.

While much of her poetry and prose displays the texture of her interwoven cultures, the underlying preoccupation is more sexual than cultural. More than languages and geographic locations, the figures gripped in an unstable embrace are men and women, with the former more an ever-absent presence, and the latter a long-suffering presence longing for that absence. Perhaps her works document the disintegration of the traditional family resulting from the pressures of migratory life, but even in the pieces that recall prior lives in more settled times, stable relationships are illusions. Ortiz Cofer's concern is not simply ethnic, but profoundly sexual—the key to any stable culture is the viability of the male-female relationship. Her basic question is the essential one of desire and its fulfillment. Everything else—ethnic strife, social injustice, gender conflict, religion, tradition, language itself—becomes mere incarnation of frustrated desire. *Silent Dancing* plays with memory and the power of media to document events, despite its inability to convey the emotive value of images. A powerful commentary on lost moments, it is equally forceful as a recovery of the ephemeral quality of experience.

Juan Bruce-Novoa
University of California at Irvine

PRIMARY WORKS

Latin Women Pray, 1980; *The Native Dancer,* 1981; *Among the Ancestors,* 1981; *Peregrina,* 1986; *Reaching for the Mainland,* 1987; *Terms of Survival,* 1988; *The Line of the Sun,* 1989; *Silent Dancing,* 1990; *The Latin Deli,* 1993; *An Island Like You,* 1995.

Claims

Last time I saw her, Grandmother
had grown seamed as a Bedouin tent.
She had claimed the right
to sleep alone, to own
her nights, to never bear
the weight of sex again nor to accept
its gift of comfort, for the luxury
of stretching her bones.
She'd carried eight children,
three had sunk in her belly, *náufragos*[1]
she called them, shipwrecked babies
drowned in her black waters.
Children are made in the night and
steal your days
for the rest of your life, amen. She said this
to each of her daughters in turn. Once she had made a pact
with man and nature and kept it. Now like the sea,
she is claiming back her territory.

1987

The Woman Who Was Left at the Altar

She calls her shadow Juan,
looking back often as she walks.
She has grown fat, her breasts huge
as reservoirs. She once opened her blouse
in church to show the silent town

[1]Spanish: victims of shipwrecks.

what a plentiful mother she could be.
Since her old mother died, buried in black,
she lives alone.
Out of the lace she made curtains for her room,
doilies out of the veil. They are now
yellow as malaria.
She hangs live chickens from her waist to sell,
walks to the town swinging her skirts of flesh.
She doesn't speak to anyone. Dogs follow
the scent of blood to be shed. In their hungry,
yellow eyes she sees his face. She takes him
to the knife time after time.

1987

My Father in the Navy: A Childhood Memory

Stiff and immaculate
in the white cloth of his uniform
and a round cap on his head like a halo,
he was an apparition on leave from a shadow-world
and only flesh and blood when he rose from below
the waterline where he kept watch over the engines
and dials making sure the ship parted the waters
on a straight course.
Mother, brother and I kept vigil
on the nights and dawns of his arrivals,
watching the corner beyond the neon sign of a quasar
for the flash of white our father like an angel
heralding a new day.
His homecomings were the verses
we composed over the years making up
the siren's song that kept him coming back
from the bellies of iron whales
and into our nights
like the evening prayer.

1987

En Mis Ojos No Hay Días[1]

from Borges'[2] poem "The Keeper of the Books"

Back before the fire burned in his eyes,
in the blast furnace which finally consumed him,
Father told us about the reign of little terrors
of his childhood beginning
at birth with a father who cursed him
for being the twelfth and the fairest
too blond and pretty to be from his loins,
so he named him the priest's pauper son.
He said the old man kept:
a mule for labor
a horse for sport
wine in his cellar
a mistress in town
and a wife to bear him daughters,
to send to church
to pray for his soul.
And sons,
to send to the fields
to cut the cane
and raise the money
to buy his rum.
He was only ten when he saw his father
split a man in two with his machete
and walk away proud to have rescued his honor
like a true "hombre."

Father always wrapped these tales
in the tissue paper of his humor
and we'd listen at his knees rapt,
warm and safe,
by the blanket of his caring,
but he himself could not be saved,
"What on earth drove him mad?"
his friends still ask,
remembering Prince Hamlet, I reply,
"Nothing on earth,"
but no one listens to ghost stories anymore.

1987

[1]Spanish: In My Eyes There Are No Days.
[2]Jorge Luis Borges (1899–1986), Argentine writer.

Latin Women Pray

Latin women pray
In incense sweet churches
They pray in Spanish to an Anglo God
With a Jewish heritage.
And this Great White Father
Imperturbable in his marble pedestal
Looks down upon his brown daughters
Votive candles shining like lust
In his all seeing eyes
Unmoved by their persistent prayers.

Yet year after year
Before his image they kneel
Margarita Josefina Maria and Isabel
All fervently hoping
That if not omnipotent
At least he be bilingual

1987

Tato Laviera b. 1951

Tato Laviera was born in Puerto Rico and has lived in New York City since 1960. A second-generation Puerto Rican writer, a poet and playwright, he is deeply committed to the social and cultural development of Puerto Ricans in New York. In addition, he has taught Creative Writing at Rutgers and other universities on the East Coast.

His poetry and plays are linguistic and artistic celebrations of Puerto Rican culture, African Caribbean traditions, the fast rhythms of life in New York City, and of life in general. Laviera writes in English, Spanish, and *Spanglish,* a mixture of the two. His superior command of both languages and the playful yet serious value he imparts to Spanglish, distinguishes his writing from others of his generation. For example, the titles of two of his books, *Enclave* and *AmeRícan,* suggest double readings in Spanish and English. Laviera's poetry is highly relevant to the study of bilingual and bicultural issues, for in it he documents, examines, and questions what it means to be a Puerto Rican in the United States. His texts have reflected the changes and transitions that his community has undergone since the major migrations of the 1940s and, moreover, offer a paradigm of what pluralistic America should really be all about.

In *La Carreta Made a U-Turn* one finds forceful poems denouncing the hardships, injustices, and social problems that the poor Puerto Rican confronts in New York City: cold, hunger, high rents, eviction, drug addiction, linguistic alienation, unemployment. The second part of this collection, entitled "Loisaida (Lower East Side) Streets: Latinas Sing," examines the issues and problems affecting today's Latina women.

This is, perhaps, one of the few instances in which a Hispanic male writer conscientiously and sympathetically addresses the conflicts of bicultural Hispanic women. Laviera concludes this book with a series of poems which celebrate African Caribbean music, both in its traditional functions as well as in its resurgence within the contemporary urban context of New York City.

Laviera has been called a "chronicler of life in El Barrio" and rightly so. His poetic language is not influenced by the written, academic tradition of poetry, but instead it is informed by popular culture, by the oral tradition of Puerto Rico and the Caribbean, and by the particular voices spoken and heard in El Barrio. Gossip, refrains, street language, idiomatic expressions, interjections, poetic declamation, and African Caribbean music such as *salsa,* rhumbas, *mambos, sones* and *música jíbara* (mountain music), are but some of the raw material with which Laviera constructs his poems. Though published in a written format. Laviera's poetry is meant to be sung and recited.

A central tenet to Laviera's work is his identification with the African American community in this country. On the one hand, he reinforces the unity and common roots of blacks and Puerto Ricans: :it is called Africa in all of us." This tendency also reflects the new multi-ethnic constitution of America which has supplanted the old myth of the melting pot. In this context Laviera's poems are reaffirmations of his Puetroricanness, and of his community's as a new national identity that diverges from the insular Puerto Rican. He proposes a new ethnic identity which includes other minority groups in the country. New York City becomes the space where this convergence and cultural *mestizaje* (mixing) takes place. While maintaining a denunciative stance through the use of irony and tongue-in-cheek humor. Laviera's work flourishes with a contagious optimism, and his poems are true songs to the joy of living which Puerto Ricans profoundly feel despite the harsh circumstances in which they live.

Frances R, Aparicio
University of Illinois of Chicago

PRIMARY WORKS

La Carreta Made a U-Turn, 1976; *Olú Clemente* (theatre), 1979; *Enclave,* 1981; *AmeRícan,* 1985; *Mainstream Ethics,* 1988.

frío[1]

35 mph winds
& the 10 degree
weather
penetrated the pores
of our windows
mr. steam rested for
the night
the night we most
needed him

[1]Spanish: the cold.

everybody arropándose[2]
on their skin blankets
curled-up like the embryo
in my mother's womb
a second death birth
called nothingness

& the frío made more
asustos[3] in our empty
stomachs

the toilet has not
been flushed for
three days

1976

AmeRícan

we gave birth to a new generation,
AmeRícan, broader than lost gold
never touched, hidden inside the
puerto rican mountains.

we gave birth to a new generation,
AmeRícan, it includes everything
imaginable you-name-it-we-got-it
society.

we gave birth to a new generation,
AmeRícan salutes all folklores,
european, indian, black, spanish,
and anything else compatible:

AmeRícan, singing to composer pedro flores'[1] palm
trees high up in the universal sky!

AmeRícan, sweet soft spanish danzas gypsies
moving lyrics la española[2] cascabelling
presence always singing at our side!

[2]Spanish: covering themselves.
[3]Spanish: frightening.
[1]Pedro Flores, Puerto Rican composer of popular romantic songs.
[2]"Spanish" (feminine).

AmeRícan, beating jíbaro[3] modern troubadours
crying guitars romantic continental
bolero love songs!

AmeRícan, across forth and across back
back across and forth back
forth across and back and forth
our trips are walking bridges!

it all dissolved into itself, the attempt
was truly made, the attempt was truly
absorbed, digested, we spit out
the poison, we spit out the malice,
we stand, affirmative in action,
to reproduce a broader answer to the
marginality that gobbled us up abruptly!

AmeRícan, walking plena-[4] rhythms in new york,
strutting beautifully alert, alive,
many turning eyes wondering,
admiring!

AmeRícan, defining myself my own way any way many
ways Am e Rícan, with the big R and the
accent on the í!

AmeRícan, like the soul gliding talk of gospel
boogie music!

AmeRícan, speaking new words in spanglish tenements,
fast tongue moving street corner *"que
corta"*[5] talk being invented at the insistence
of a smile!

AmeRícan, abounding inside so many ethnic english
people, and out of humanity, we blend
and mix all that is good!

AmeRícan, integrating in new york and defining our
own *destino,*[6] our own way of life,

[3]Term referring to the Puerto Rican farmer who lives in the mountains. The jíbaros have a particular musical style.
[4]African Puerto Rican folklore music and dance.
[5]Spanish: that cuts.
[6]Spanish: destiny.

AmeRícan, defining the new america, humane america,
admired america, loved america, harmonious
america, the world in peace, our energies
collectively invested to find other civilizations, to touch God, further and further,
to dwell in the spirit of divinity!

AmeRícan, yes, for now, for i love this, my second
land, and i dream to take the accent from
the altercation, and be proud to call
myself american, in the u.s. sense of the
word, AmeRícan, America!

1985

Latero[1] Story

i am a twentieth-century welfare recipient
moonlighting in the sun as a latero
a job invented by national state laws
designed to re-cycle aluminum cans
returned to consumer's acid laden
gastric inflammation pituitary glands
coca diet rites low cal godsons
of artificially flavored malignant
indigestions somewhere down the line
of a cancerous cell

i collect garbage cans in outdoor facilities
congested with putrid residues
my hands shelving themselves
opening plastic bags never knowing
what they'll encounter

several times a day i touch evil rituals
cut throats of chickens
tongues of poisoned rats
salivating my index finger
smells of month old rotten foods
next to pamper's diarrhea
        dry blood infectious diseases
hypodermic needles tissued with

[1]From Spanish *lata:* can. A man who picks up cans from garbage containers and the streets.

heroin water drops pilfered in
slimy greases hazardous waste materials
but i cannot use rubber gloves
they undermine my daily profits

i am a twentieth-century welfare recipient
moonlighting in the day as a latero
that is the only opportunity i have
to make it big in america
some day i might become experienced enough
to offer technical assistance
to other lateros
i am a thinking of publishing
my own guide to latero's collection
and founding a latero's union offering
medical dental benefits

i am a twentieth-century welfare recipient
moonlighting in the night as a latero
i am considered some kind of expert
at collecting cans during fifth avenue parades
i can now hire workers at twenty
five cents an hour guaranteed salary
and fifty per cent of two and one half cents
profit on each can collected

i am a twentieth-century welfare recipient
moonlighting in midnight as a latero
i am becoming an entrepreneur
an american success story
i have hired bag ladies to keep peddlers
from my territories
i have read in some guide to success
that in order to get rich
to make it big
i have to sacrifice myself
moonlighting until dawn by digging
deeper into the extra can
margin of profit
i am on my way up the opportunistic
ladder of success
in ten years i will quit welfare
to become a legitimate businessman
i'll soon become a latero executive
with corporate conglomerate intents
god bless america

1988

Helena María Viramontes b. 1954

Chronicler of the West Coast urban barrios, Helena María Viramontes was born, raised, and educated in East Los Angeles, California. Daughter of working-class parents, she and her nine brothers and sisters grew up surrounded by the family friends and relatives who found temporary sanctuary in the Viramontes household as they made the crossing from Mexico to the United States. Her writings reveal the political and aesthetic significance of the contemporary Chicana feminist's entrance into the publishing world. Viramontes's aesthetics are a practice of political intervention carried out in literary form. Her tales of the urban barrios, of the border cities, of the Third World metropolis that cities such as Los Angeles have become, record the previously silenced experiences of life on the border for Chicanas and Latinas. Now living in Irvine, where she is a graduate student in the University of California, Irvine, MFA program and a full-time mother to two young children, Viramontes remains an exemplar of the organic intellectual; she organizes the community to protest the closing of local public libraries in areas populated with Chicanos and Latinos; she gives readings and literary presentations to a population that is represented by the media as gang-infested and whose young men are more represented in the prison system than in the education system.

Viramontes's first short story collection, *The Moths and Other Stories* (1985), is a feminist statement on the status of the family in the Chicana/o community. In many of the stories, she transforms the concept of "*familia*" as the community itself changes with the last decade's infusion of refugees from war-torn countries in Central America; what were once predominantly Mexican American areas are now international Latina/o communities within the borders of the United States. The new immigrants bring with them specific histories which produce new stories that further emphasize the resemblances between Chicanas/os and "*los otros Americanos*": people Cherríe Moraga calls "refugees of a world on fire."

Viramontes's project in her short stories also gives historical context and voice to the women who many Chicano writers silenced through their appropriation of female historicity. As she challenges an uncritical view of the traditional Chicano family, she presents an altered version of *familia* that makes more sense in a world where governments continue to exert power over women's bodies by hiding behind the rhetoric of the sacred family as they simultaneously exploit and destroy members of families who do not conform to a specific political agenda or whose class positions or race automatically disqualifies them from inclusion.

In "The Cariboo Cafe," Viramontes makes explicit the connection between Chicanas and refugees from Central America. Written in early 1984 after Viramontes learned of the atrocities that the U.S. policies in countries such as El Salvador had enabled, this story embodies a Chicana feminist's critique of the political and economic policies of the United States government and its collaborators south of its border. Viramontes presents the oppression and exploitation of the reserve army of laborers that such policies create and then designate as "other," the "illegal" immigrants. Combining feminism with race and class consciousness, Viramontes commits herself, in this Chicana political discourse, to a transnational solidarity with the working-class political refugee seeking asylum from right-wing death squads in countries such as El Salvador.

In addition, the narrative structure of "The Cariboo Cafe" connects Chicana aesthetics to the literary traditions of such Latin American political writers as Gabriel García Márquez and Isabel Allende. The fractured narrative employed in this story hurls the reader into a complicated relationship with the text. The reader enters the text as an alien to this refugee culture; Viramontes crafts a fractured narrative to reflect the disorientation that the immigrant workers feel when they are subjected to life in a country that controls their labor but does not value their existence as human beings.

Further, the narrative structure shoots the reader into a world where she or he is as disoriented as the story's characters: two lost Mexican children; a refugee woman (possibly from El Salvador), whose mental state reflects the trauma of losing her five-year-old son to the labyrinth of the disappeared in Latin American countries ruled by armies and dictators the United States trains and supports; and a working-class man, an ironic representative of dominant Anglo-American culture, who runs the "double zero" cafe. The reader, particularly one unfamiliar with life in the border regions of that other America, must work to decipher the signs much in the same way the characters do. Through the artistry of her narrative, Helena María Viramontes shows how a Chicana oppositional art form also becomes an arena that reflects politics.

Sonia Saldívar-Hull
University of California–Los Angeles

PRIMARY WORKS

The Moths and Other Stories, 1985; "Miss Clairol," 1987; "Nopalitos: The Making of Fiction," 1989; "Tears on My Pillow," 1992; *Paris Rats in E. L. A.,* 1993.

The Cariboo Cafe

I

They arrived in the secrecy of night, as displaced people often do, stopping over for a week, a month, eventually staying a lifetime. The plan was simple. Mother would work too until they saved enough to move into a finer future where the toilet was one's own and the children needn't be frightened. In the meantime, they played in the back allies, among the broken glass, wise to the ways of the streets. Rule one: never talk to strangers, not even the neighbor who paced up and down the hallways talking to himself. Rule two: the police, or "polie" as Sonya's popi pronounced the word, was La Migra in disguise and thus should always be avoided. Rule three: keep your key with you at all times—the four walls of the apartment were the only protection against the streets until Popi returned home.

Sonya considered her key a guardian saint and she wore it around her neck as such until this afternoon. Gone was the string with the big knot. Gone was the key. She hadn't noticed its disappearance until she picked up Macky from Mrs. Avila's house and walked home. She remembered playing with it as Amá walked her to school. But lunch break came, and Lalo wrestled her down so that he could see her underwear, and it probably fell somewhere between the iron rings and sandbox. Sitting on the front steps of the apartment building, she considered how to explain the missing key without having to reveal what Lalo had seen, for she wasn't quite sure which offense carried the worse penalty.

She watched people piling in and spilling out of the buses, watched an old man asleep on the bus bench across the street. He resembled a crumbled ball of paper, huddled up in the security of a tattered coat. She became aware of their mutual loneliness and she rested her head against her knees blackened by the soot of the playground asphalt.

The old man eventually awoke, yawned like a lion's roar, unfolded his limbs and staggered to the alley where he urinated between two trash bins. (She wanted to peek, but it was Macky who turned to look.) He zipped up, drank from a paper bag and she watched him until he disappeared around the corner. As time passed, buses came less frequently, and every other person seemed to resemble Popi. Macky became bored. He picked through the trash barrel; later, and to Sonya's fright, he ran into the street after a pigeon. She understood his restlessness for waiting was as relentless as long lines to the bathroom. When a small boy walked by, licking away at a scoop of vanilla ice cream, Macky ran after him. In his haste to outrun Sonya's grasp, he fell and tore the knee of his denim jeans. He began to cry, wiping snot against his sweater sleeve.

"See?" She asked, dragging him back to the porch steps by his wrist. "See? God punished you!" It was a thing she always said because it seemed to work. Terrified by the scrawny tortured man on the cross, Macky wanted to avoid his wrath as much as possible. She sat him on the steps in one gruff jerk. Seeing his torn jeans, and her own scraped knees, she wanted to join in his sorrow, and cry. Instead she snuggled so close to him, she could hear his stomach growling.

"Coke," he asked. Mrs. Avila gave him an afternoon snack which usually held him over until dinner. But sometimes Macky got lost in the midst of her own six children and . . .

Mrs. Avila! It took Sonya a few moments to realize the depth of her idea. They could wait there, at Mrs. Avila's. And she'd probably have a stack of flour tortillas, fresh off the comal, ready to eat with butter and salt. She grabbed his hand. "Mrs. Avila has Coke."

"Coke!" He jumped up to follow his sister. "Coke," he cooed.

At the major intersection, Sonya quietly calculated their next move while the scores of adults hurried to their own destinations. She scratched one knee as she tried retracing her journey home in the labyrinth of her memory. Things never looked the same when backwards and she searched for familiar scenes. She looked for the newspaperman who sat in a little house with a little T.V. on and selling magazines with naked girls holding beach balls. But he was gone. What remained was a little closet-like shed with chains and locks, and she wondered what happened to him, for she thought he lived there with the naked ladies.

They finally crossed the street at a cautious pace, the colors of the street lights brighter as darkness descended, a stereo store blaring music from two huge, blasting speakers. She thought it was the disco store she passed, but she didn't remember if the sign was green or red. And she didn't remember it flashing like it was now. Studying the neon light, she bumped into a tall, lanky dark man. Maybe it was Raoul's Popi. Raoul was a dark boy in her class that she felt sorry for because everyone called him sponge head. Maybe she could ask Raoul's Popi where Mrs. Avila lived, but before she could think it all out, red sirens flashed in their faces and she shielded her eyes to see the polie.

The polie is men in black who get kids and send them to Tijuana, says Popi. Whenever you see them, run, because they hate you, says Popi. She grabs Macky by his sleeve and they crawl under a table of bargain cassettes. Macky's nose is running, and when he sniffles, she puts her finger to her lips. She peeks from behind the poster of Vincente Fernandez to see Raoul's father putting keys and stuff from his pockets onto the hood of the polie car. And it's true, they're putting him in the car and taking him to Tijuana. Popi, she murmured to herself. Mamá.

"Coke." Macky whispered, as if she had failed to remember.

"Ssssh. Mi'jo, when I say run, you run, okay?" She waited for the tires to turn out, and as the black and white drove off, she whispered "Now," and they scurried out from under the table and ran across the street, oblivious to the horns.

They entered a maze of allies and dead ends, the long, abandoned warehouses shadowing any light. Macky stumbled and she continued to drag him until his crying, his untied sneakers, and his raspy breathing finally forced her to stop. She scanned the boarded up boxcars, the rows of rusted rails to make sure the polie wasn't following them. Tired, her heart bursting, she leaned him against a tall, chain-link fence. Except for the rambling of some railcars, silence prevailed, and she could hear Macky sniffling in the darkness. Her mouth was parched and she swallowed to rid herself of the metallic taste of fear. The shadows stalked them, hovering like nightmares. Across the tracks, in the distance, was a room with a yellow glow, like a beacon light at the end of a dark sea. She pinched Macky's nose with the corner of her dress, took hold of his sleeve. At least the shadows will be gone, she concluded, at the zero zero place.

II

Don't look at me. I didn't give it the name. It was passed on. Didn't even know what it meant until I looked it up in some library dictionary. But I kinda liked the name. It's, well, romantic, almost like the name of a song, you know, so I kept it. That was before JoJo turned fourteen even. But now if you take a look at the sign, the paint's peeled off 'cept for the two O's. The double zero cafe. Story of my life. But who cares, right? As long as everyone 'round the factories know I run an honest business.

The place is clean. That's more than I can say for some people who walk through that door. And I offer the best prices on double burger deluxes this side of Main Street. Okay, so its not pure beef. Big deal, most meat markets do the same. But I make no bones 'bout it. I tell them up front, 'yeah, it ain't dogmeat, but it ain't sirloin either.' Cause that's the sort of guy I am. Honest.

That's the trouble. It never pays to be honest. I tried scrubbing the stains off the floor, so that my customers won't be reminded of what happened. But they keep walking as if my cafe ain't fit for lepers. And that's the thanks I get for being a fair guy.

Not once did I hang up all those stupid signs. You know, like 'We reserve the right to refuse service to anyone,' or 'No shirt, no shoes, no service.' To tell you the truth—which is what I always do though it don't pay—I wouldn't have nobody walking through that door. The streets are full of scum, but scum gotta eat too is the way

I see it. Now, listen. I ain't talkin 'bout out-of-luckers, weirdos, whores, you know. I'm talking 'bout five-to-lifers out of some tech. I'm talking Paulie.

I swear Paulie is thirty-five, or six. JoJo's age if he were still alive, but he don't look a day over ninety. Maybe why I let him hang out 'cause he's JoJo's age. Shit, he's okay as long as he don't bring his wigged out friends whose voices sound like a record at low speed. Paulie's got too many stories and they all get jammed up in his mouth so I can't make out what he's saying. He scares the other customers too, acting like he is shadow boxing, or like a monkey hopping on a frying pan. You know, nervous, jumpy, his jaw all falling and his eyes bulgy and dirt yellow. I give him the last booth, coffee and yesterday's donut holes to keep him quiet. After a few minutes, out he goes, before lunch. I'm too old, you know, too busy making ends meet to be nursing the kid. And so is Delia.

That Delia's got these unique titties. One is bigger than another. Like an orange and grapefruit. I kid you not. They're like that on account of when she was real young she had some babies, and they all sucked only one favorite tittie. So one is bigger than the other, and when she used to walk in with Paulie, huggy huggy and wearing those tight leotard blouses that show the nipple dots, you could see the difference. You could tell right off that Paulie was proud of them, the way he'd hang his arm over her shoulder and squeeze the grapefruit. They kill me, her knockers. She'd come in real queen-like, smacking gum and chewing the fat with the illegals who work in that garment warehouse. They come in real queen-like too, sitting in the best booth near the window, and order cokes. That's all. Cokes. Hey, but I'm a nice guy, so what if they mess up my table, bring their own lunches and only order small cokes, leaving a dime as tip? So sometimes the place ain't crawling with people, you comprende buddy? A dime's a dime as long as its in my pocket.

Like I gotta pay my bills too, I gotta eat. So like I serve anybody whose got the greens, including that crazy lady and the two kids that started all the trouble. If only I had closed early. But I had to wash the dinner dishes on account of I can't afford a dishwasher. I was scraping off some birdshit glue stuck to this plate, see, when I hear the bells jingle against the door. I hate those fucking bells. That was Nell's idea. Nell's my wife; my ex-wife. So people won't sneak up on you, says my ex. Anyway, I'm standing behind the counter staring at this short woman. Already I know that she's bad news because she looks street to me. Round face, burnt toast color, black hair that hangs like straight ropes. Weirdo, I've had enough to last me a lifetime. She's wearing a shawl and a dirty slip is hanging out. Shit if I have to dish out a free meal. Funny thing, but I didn't see the two kids 'til I got to the booth. All of a sudden I see these big eyes looking over the table's edge at me. It shook me up, the way they kinda appeared. Aw, maybe they were there all the time.

The boy's a sweetheart. Short Order don't look nothing like his mom. He's got dried snot all over his dirty cheeks and his hair ain't seen a comb for years. She can't take care of herself, much less him or the doggie of a sister. But he's a tough one, and I pinch his nose 'cause he's a real sweetheart like JoJo. You know, my boy.

It's his sister I don't like. She's got these poking eyes that follow you 'round 'cause she don't trust no one. Like when I reach for Short Order, she flinches like I'm 'bout to tear his nose off, gives me a nasty, squinty look. She's maybe five, maybe six, I don't know, and she acts like she owns him. Even when I bring the burgers, she doesn't let go of his hand. Finally, the fellow bites it and I wink at him. A real sweetheart.

In the next booth, I'm twisting the black crud off the top of the ketchup bottle when I hear the lady saying something in Spanish. Right off I know she's illegal, which explains why she looks like a weirdo. Anyway, she says something nice to them 'cause it's in the same tone that Nell used when I'd rest my head on her lap. I'm surprised the illegal's got a fiver to pay, but she and her tail leave no tip. I see Short Order's small bites on the bun.

You know, a cafe's the kinda business that moves. You get some regulars but most of them are on the move, so I don't pay much attention to them. But this lady's face sticks like egg yolk on a plate. It ain't 'til I open a beer and sit in front of the B & W to check out the wrestling matches that I see this news bulletin 'bout two missing kids. I recognize the mugs right away. Short Order and his doggie sister. And all of a sudden her face is out of my mind. Aw fuck, I say, and put my beer down so hard that the foam spills onto last months Hustler. Aw fuck.

See, if Nell was here, she'd know what to do: call the cops. But I don't know. Cops ain't exactly my friends, and all I need is for bacon to be crawling all over my place. And seeing how her face is vague now, I decide to wait 'til the late news. Short Order don't look right neither. I'll have another beer and wait for the late news.

The alarm rings at four and I have this headache, see, from the sixpak, and I gotta get up. I was supposed to do something, but I got all suck-faced and forgot. Turn off the T.V., take a shower, but that don't help my memory any.

Hear sirens near the railroad tracks. Cops. I'm supposed to call the cops. I'll do it after I make the coffee, put away the eggs, get the donuts out. But Paulie strolls in looking partied out. We actually talk 'bout last night's wrestling match between BoBo Brazil and the Crusher. I slept through it, you see. Paulie orders an O.J. on account of he's catching a cold. I open up my big mouth and ask about De. Drinks the rest of his O.J., says real calm like, that he caught her eaglespread with the Vegetable fatso down the block. Then, very polite like, Paulie excuses himself. That's one thing I gotta say about Paulie. He may be one big Fuck-up, but he's got manners. Juice gave him shit cramps, he says.

Well, leave it to Paulie. Good ole Mr. Fuck-Up himself to help me with the cops. The prick O.D.'s in my crapper; vomits and shits are all over—I mean all over the fuckin' walls. That's the thanks I get for being Mr. Nice Guy. I had the cops looking up my ass for the stash; says one, the one wearing a mortician's suit, We'll be back, we'll be back when you ain't looking. If I was pushing, would I be burning my goddamn balls off with spitting grease? So fuck 'em, I think. I ain't gonna tell you nothing 'bout the lady. Fuck you, I say to them as they drive away. Fuck your mother.

That's why Nell was good to have 'round. She could be a pain in the ass, you know, like making me hang those stupid bells, but mostly she knew what to do. See, I go bananas. Like my mind fries with the potatoes and by the end of the day, I'm deader than dogshit. Let me tell you what I mean. A few hours later, after I swore I wouldn't give the fuckin' pigs the time of day, the green vans roll up across the street. While I'm stirring the chili con carne I see all these illegals running out of the factory to hide, like roaches when the lightswitch goes on. I taste the chile, but I really can't taste nothing on account of I've lost my appetite after cleaning out the crapper, when three of them run into the Cariboo. They look at me as if I'm gonna stop them, but when I go on stirring the chile, they run to the bathroom. Now look, I'm a nice guy, but I don't like to be used, you know? Just 'cause they're regulars don't mean jackshit. I run an honest business. And that's what I told them Agents. See, by that time, my stomach being all dizzy, and the cops all over the place, and the three illegals running in here, I was all confused, you know. That's how it was, and well, I haven't seen Nell for years, and I guess that's why I pointed to the bathroom.

I don't know. I didn't expect handcuffs and them agents putting their hands up and down their thighs. When they walked passed me, they didn't look at me. That is the two young ones. The older one, the one that looked silly in the handcuffs on account of she's old enough to be my grandma's grandma, looks straight at my face with the same eyes Short Order's sister gave me yesterday. What a day. Then, to top off the potatoes with the gravy, the bells jingle against the door and in enters the lady again with the two kids.

III

He's got lice. Probably from living in the detainers. Those are the rooms where they round up the children and make them work for their food. I saw them from the window. Their eyes are cut glass, and no one looks for sympathy. They take turns, sorting out the arms from the legs, heads from the torsos. Is that one your mother? one guard asks, holding a mummified head with eyes shut tighter than coffins. But the children no longer cry. They just continue sorting as if they were salvaging cans from a heap of trash. They do this until time is up and they drift into a tunnel, back to the womb of sleep, while a new group comes in. It is all very organized. I bite my fist to keep from retching. Please God, please don't let Geraldo be there.

For you see, they took Geraldo. By mistake, of course. It was my fault. I shouldn't have sent him out to fetch me a mango. But it was just to the corner. I didn't even bother to put his sweater on. I hear his sandals flapping against the gravel. I follow him with my eyes, see him scratching his buttocks when the wind picks up swiftly, as it often does at such unstable times, and I have to close the door.

The darkness becomes a serpent's tongue, swallowing us whole. It is the night of La Llorona. The women come up from the depths of sorrow to search for their children. I join them, frantic, desperate, and our eyes become scrutinizers, our bodies opiated with the scent of their smiles. Descending from door to door, the wind whips our faces. I hear the wailing of the women and know it to be my own. Geraldo is nowhere to be found.

Dawn is not welcomed. It is a drunkard wavering between consciousness and sleep. My life is fleeing, moving south towards the sea. My tears are now hushed and faint.

The boy, barely a few years older than Geraldo, lights a cigarette, rests it on the edge of his desk, next to all the other cigarette burns. The blinds are down to keep the room cool. Above him hangs a single bulb that shades and shadows his face in such a way as to mask his expressions. He is not to be trusted. He fills in the information, for I cannot write. Statements delivered, we discuss motives.

"Spies," says he, flicking a long burning ash from the cigarette onto the floor, then wolfing the smoke in as if his lungs had an unquenchable thirst for nicotine. "We arrest spies. Criminals." He says this with cigarette smoke spurting out from his nostrils like a nose bleed.

"Spies? Criminal?" My shawl falls to the ground. "He is only five and a half years old." I plead for logic with my hands. "What kind of crimes could a five year old commit?"

"Anyone who so willfully supports the contras in any form must be arrested and punished without delay." He knows the line by heart.

I think about moths and their stupidity. Always attracted by light, they fly into fires, or singe their wings with the heat of the single bulb and fall on his desk, writhing in pain. I don't understand why nature has been so cruel as to prevent them from feeling warmth. He dismisses them with a sweep of a hand. "This," he continues, "is what we plan to do with the contras, and those who aid them." He inhales again.

"But, Señor, he's just a baby."

"Contras are tricksters. They exploit the ignorance of people like you. Perhaps they convinced your son to circulate pamphlets. You should be talking to them, not us." The cigarette is down to his yellow finger tips, to where he can no longer continue to hold it without burning himself. He throws the stub on the floor, crushes it under his boot. "This," he says, screwing his boot into the ground, "is what the contras do to people like you."

"Señor. I am a washer woman. You yourself see I cannot read or write. There is my X. Do you think my son can read?" How can I explain to this man that we are poor, that we live as best we can? "If such a thing has happened, perhaps he wanted to make a few centavos for his mamá. He's just a baby."

"So you are admitting his guilt?"

"So you are admitting he is here?" I promise, once I see him, hold him in my arms again, I will never, never scold him for wanting more than I can give. "You see, he needs his sweater . . ." The sweater lies limp on my lap.

"Your assumption is incorrect."

"May I check the detainers for myself?"

"In time."

"And what about my Geraldo?"

"In time." He dismisses me, placing the forms in a big envelope crinkled by the day's humidity.

"When?" I am wringing the sweater with my hands.

"Don't be foolish, woman. Now off with your nonsense. We will try to locate your Pedro."

"Geraldo."

Maria came by today with a bowl of hot soup. She reports in her usual excited way, that the soldiers are now eating the brains of their victims. It is unlike her to be so scandalous. So insane. Geraldo must be cold without his sweater.

"Why?" I ask as the soup gets cold. I will write Tavo tonight.

At the plaza a group of people are whispering. They are quiet when I pass, turn to one another and put their finger to their lips to cage their voices. They continue as I reach the church steps. To be associated with me is condemnation.

Today I felt like killing myself, Lord. But I am too much of a coward. I am a washer woman, Lord. My mother was one, and hers too. We have lived as best we can, washing other people's laundry, rinsing off other people's dirt until our hands crust and chap. When my son wanted to hold my hand, I held soap instead. When he wanted to play, my feet were in pools of water. It takes such little courage, being a washer woman. Give me strength, Lord.

What have I done to deserve this, Lord? Raising a child is like building a kite. You must bend the twigs enough, but not too much, for you might break them. You must find paper that is delicate and light enough to wave on the breath of the wind, yet must withstand the ravages of a storm. You must tie the strings gently but firmly so that it may not fall apart. You must let the string go, eventually, so that the kite will stretch its ambition. It is such delicate work, Lord, being a mother. This I understand, Lord, because I am, but you have snapped the cord, Lord. It was only a matter of minutes and my life is lost somewhere in the clouds. I don't know, I don't know what games you play, Lord.

These four walls are no longer my house, the earth beneath it, no longer my home. Weeds have replaced all good crops. The irrigation ditches are clodded with bodies. No matter where we turn, there are rumors facing us and we try to live as best we can, under the rule of men who rape women, then rip their fetuses from their bellies. Is this our home? Is this our country? I ask Maria. Don't these men have mothers, lovers, babies, sisters? Don't they see what they are doing? Later, Maria says, these men are babes farted out from the Devil's ass. We check to make sure no one has heard her say this.

Without Geraldo, this is not my home, the earth beneath it, not my country. This is why I have to leave. Maria begins to cry. Not because I am going, but because she is staying.

Tavo. Sweet Tavo. He has sold his car to send me the money. He has just married and he sold his car for me. Thank you, Tavo. Not just for the money. But also for making me believe in the goodness of people again . . . The money is enough to buy off the border soldiers. The rest will come from the can. I have saved for Geraldo's schooling and it is enough for a bus ticket to Juarez. I am to wait for Tavo there.

I spit. I do not turn back.

Perhaps I am wrong in coming. I worry that Geraldo will not have a home to return to, no mother to cradle his nightmares away, soothe the scars, stop the hemorrhaging of his heart. Tavo is happy I am here, but it is crowded, the three of us, and I hear them arguing behind their closed door. There is only so much a nephew can provide. I must find work. I have two hands willing to work. But the heart. The heart wills only to watch the children playing in the street.

The machines, their speed and dust, make me ill. But I can clean. I clean toilets, dump trash cans, sweep. Disinfect the sinks. I will gladly do whatever is necessary to repay Tavo. The baby is due any time and money is tight. I volunteer for odd hours, weekends, since I really have very little to do. When the baby comes I know Tavo's wife will not let me hold it, for she thinks I am a bad omen. I know it.

Why would God play such a cruel joke, if he isn't my son? I jumped the curb, dashed out into the street, but the street is becoming wider and wider. I've lost him once and can't lose him again and to hell with the screeching tires and the horns and the headlights barely touching my hips. I can't take my eyes off him because, you see, they are swift and cunning and can take your life with a snap of a finger. But God is a just man and His mistakes can be undone.

My heart pounds in my head like a sledge hammer against the asphalt. What if it isn't Geraldo? What if he is still in the detainer waiting for me? A million questions, one answer: Yes. Geraldo, yes. I want to touch his hand first, have it disappear in my own because it is so small. His eyes look at me in total bewilderment. I grab him because the earth is crumbling beneath us and I must save him. We both fall to the ground.

A hot meal is in store. A festival. The cook, a man with shrunken cheeks and the hands of a car mechanic, takes a liking to Geraldo. Its like birthing you again, mi'jo. My baby.

I bathe him. He flutters in excitement, the water grey around him. I scrub his head with lye to kill off the lice, comb his hair out with a fine tooth comb. I wash his rubbery penis, wrap him in a towel and he stands in front of the window, shriveling and sucking milk from a carton, his hair shiny from the dampness.

He finally sleeps. So easily, she thinks. On her bed next to the open window he coos in the night. Below the sounds of the city become as monotonous as the ocean waves. She rubs his back with warm oil, each stroke making up for the days of his absence. She hums to him softly so that her breath brushes against his face, tunes that are rusted and crack in her throat. The hotel neon shines on his back and she covers him.

All the while the young girl watches her brother sleeping. She removes her sneakers, climbs into the bed, snuggles up to her brother, and soon her breathing is raspy, her arms under her stomach.

The couch is her bed tonight. Before switching the light off, she checks once more to make sure this is not a joke. Tomorrow she will make arrangements to go home. Maria will be the same, the mango stand on the corner next to the church plaza will be the same. It will all be the way it was before. But enough excitement. For the first time in years, her mind is quiet of all noise and she has the desire to sleep.

The bells jingle when the screen door slaps shut behind them. The cook wrings his hands in his apron, looking at them. Geraldo is in the middle, and they sit in the booth farthest away from the window, near the hall where the toilets are, and right away the small boy, his hair now neatly combed and split to the side like an adult, wrinkles his nose at the peculiar smell. The cook wipes perspiration off his forehead with the corner of his apron, finally comes over to the table.

She looks so different, so young. Her hair is combed slick back into one thick braid and her earrings hang like baskets of golden pears on her finely sculptured ears. He can't believe how different she looks. Almost beautiful. She points to what she wants on the menu with a white, clean fingernail. Although confused, the cook is sure of one thing—it's Short Order all right, pointing to him with a commanding finger, saying his only English word: coke.

His hands tremble as he slaps the meat on the grill; the patties hiss instantly. He feels like vomiting. The chile overboils and singes the fires, deep red trail of chile crawling to the floor and puddling there. He grabs the handles, burns himself, drops the pot on the wooden racks of the floor. He sucks his fingers, the patties blackening and sputtering grease. He flips them, and the burgers hiss anew. In some strange way he hopes they have disappeared, and he takes a quick look only to see Short Order's sister, still in the same dress, still holding her brother's hand. She is craning her neck to peek at what is going on in the kitchen.

Aw, fuck, he says, in a fog of smoke his eyes burning tears. He can't believe it, but he's crying. For the first time since JoJo's death, he's crying. He becomes angry at the lady for returning. At JoJo. At Nell for leaving him. He wishes Nell here, but doesn't know where she's at or what part of Vietnam JoJo is all crumbled up in. Children gotta be with their parents, family gotta be together, he thinks. It's only right. The emergency line is ringing.

Two black and whites roll up and skid the front tires against the curb. The flashing lights carousel inside the cafe. She sees them opening the screen door, their guns taut and cold like steel erections. Something is wrong, and she looks to the cowering cook. She has been betrayed, and her heart is pounding like footsteps running, faster, louder, faster and she can't hear what they are saying to her. She jumps up from the table, grabs Geraldo by the wrist, his sister dragged along because, like her, she refuses to release his hand. Their lips are mouthing words she can't hear, can't comprehend. Run, Run is all she can think of to do, Run through the hallway, out to the alley, Run because they will never take him away again.

But her legs are heavy and she crushes Geraldo against her, so tight, as if she wants to conceal him in her body again, return him to her belly so that they will not castrate him and hang his small, blue penis on her door, not crush his face so that he is unrecognizable, not bury him among the heaps of bones, and ears, and teeth, and jaws, because no one, but she, cared to know that he cried. For years he cried and she could hear him day and night. Screaming, howling, sobbing, shriveling and crying because he is only five years old, and all she wanted was a mango.

But the crying begins all over again. In the distance, she hears crying.

She refuses to let go. For they will have to cut her arms off to take him, rip her mouth off to keep her from screaming for help. Without thinking, she reaches over to where two pots of coffee are brewing and throws the streaming coffee into their faces. Outside, people begin to gather, pressing their faces against the window glass to get a good view. The cook huddles behind the counter, frightened, trembling. Their faces become distorted and she doesn't see the huge hand that takes hold of Geraldo and she begins screaming all over again, screaming so that the walls shake, screaming enough for all the women of murdered children, screaming, pleading for help from the people outside, and she pushes an open hand against an officer's nose, because no one will stop them and he pushes the gun barrel to her face.

And I laugh at his ignorance. How stupid of him to think that I will let them take my Geraldo away, just because he waves that gun like a flag. Well, to hell with you, you pieces of shit, do you hear me? Stupid, cruel pigs. To hell with you all, because you can no longer frighten me. I will fight you for my son until I have no hands left to hold a knife. I will fight you all because you're all farted out of the Devil's ass, and you'll not take us with you. I am laughing, howling at their stupidity. Because they should know by now that I will never let my son go and then I hear something crunching like broken glass against my forehead and I am blinded by the liquid darkness. But I hold onto his hand. That I can feel, you see, I'll never let go. Because we are going home. My son and I.

1984

Bharati Mukherjee b. 1940

Bharati Mukherjee is one of the best-known South Asian American woman writers. She has stated that she wants to be viewed not as a hyphenated South Asian–American writer but as an American writer. In a televised interview with Bill Moyers (*Bill Moyers: A World of Ideas II,* New York: Doubleday, 1990) she commented, "I feel very American . . . I knew the moment I landed as a student in 1961 . . . that this is where I belonged. It was an instant kind of love."

One wonders, however, if one can really discard a part of one's personal/political history even in the process of transformation, especially since the past displays a tenacious, trickster-like ability to appear at the oddest times and in the most astonishing disguises. The insistence on being known as an American, without acknowledging one's Asian heritage, may grate on those who see the term "American" as denoting the *Euro*-American socio-politically dominant group only. For those of us who feel that it is absolutely necessary to continue emphasizing our essentially non-European, American identities until we are truly acknowledged as Americans with our own distinctive American presence, Mukherjee's stance may seem simplistic. Yet, as many of her stories show she is neither ignorant of nor insensitive to racism and oppression in the United States. In the interview with Moyers, she also said that "Multiculturalism, in a sense, is well intentioned, but it ends up marginalizing the person."

Mukherjee's ease with discovering her identity as a mainstream American, her skill with the dialogues and incidents familiar to the dominant society, her refusal to be marginalized, and her absolute mastery of English are not surprising when one looks at her biography. She was born in 1940 to an upper-middle-class Brahmin family in Calcutta. Her education in India was at a convent school run by Irish nuns. She was also educated in England and Switzerland. She came to the United States in 1961 to attend the Writer's Workshop at the University of Iowa, where she received an M.F.A. in Creative Writing and a Ph.D. in English and Comparative Literature. She and her husband, the Canadian writer, Clark Blaise, lived in Canada from 1966 to 1980. They emigrated to the United States in 1980. Mukherjee teaches in the English Department at the University of California, Berkeley.

Mukherjee's first novel, *The Tiger's Daughter,* portrays Tara Banerjee Cartwright, a Western-educated, well-to-do Bengali woman married to an American. Her second novel, *Wife,* begins in Bengal, with the following opening sentence, which would do credit to Jane Austen: "Dimple Dasgupta had set her heart on marrying a neuro-surgeon, but her father was looking for engineers in the matrimonial ads." Her novels *Holder of the World, Jasmine,* and *Leave It to Me,* and her brilliantly written collections of short stories, *Darkness* and *Middleman and Other Stories,* extend Mukherjee's discussion into the more violent and grotesque yet very real aspects of collisions between cultures at different times in the histories of India and the United States.

"A Wife's Story" is a carefully crafted narrative, with an interesting twist: the wife comes to America to study, and the husband comes to visit her. The story begins with Panna watching a play which insults Indian men and women. It ends with Panna waiting for her husband, who is leaving for India the next morning without her, to make love to her: "The water is running in the bathroom. In the ten days he has been here he has learned American rites: deodorants, fragrances." Panna ends her narrative with "I am free, afloat, watching somebody else." One hears echoes of

Mukherjee's statement about America being a place where one can choose "to discard . . . history . . . and invent a whole new history for myself." As Panna glories in her beautiful body and her freedom, one is haunted by the question of the price and texture of her freedom. "A Wife's Story," like many of the other stories by Mukherjee, leaves the narrative unresolved and open for discussion. It also raises important questions about the forging of cultural, national, and sexual alliances in a United States that glorifies individual freedom and urges the loss of a racial and ethnic memory that is not Eurocentric.

Roshni Rustomji-Kerns
Sonoma State University

PRIMARY WORKS

The Tiger's Daughter, 1971; *Wife,* 1975; *Days and Nights in Calcutta* (coauthored with Clark Blaise), 1977; *Darkness,* 1985; *The Sorrow and the Terror: The Haunting Legacy of the Air India Tragedy,* 1987; *The Middleman and Other Stories,* 1988; *Jasmine,* 1989; *Holder of the World,* 1993; *Leave It to Me,* 1997.

A Wife's Story

Imre says forget it, but I'm going to write David Mamet. So Patels are hard to sell real estate to. You buy them a beer, whisper Glengarry Glen Ross, and they smell swamp instead of sun and surf. They work hard, eat cheap, live ten to a room, stash their savings under futons in Queens, and before you know it they own half of Hoboken. You say, where's the sweet gullibility that made this nation great?

Polish jokes, Patel jokes: that's not why I want to write Mamet.

Seen their women?

Everybody laughs. Imre laughs. The dozing fat man with the Barnes & Noble sack between his legs, the woman next to him, the usher, everybody. The theater isn't so dark that they can't see me. In my red silk sari I'm conspicuous. Plump, gold paisleys sparkle on my chest.

The actor is just warming up. *Seen their women?* He plays a salesman, he's had a bad day and now he's in a Chinese restaurant trying to loosen up. His face is pink. His wool-blend slacks are creased at the crotch. We bought our tickets at half-price, we're sitting in the front row, but at the edge, and we see things we shouldn't be seeing. At least I do, or think I do. Spittle, actors goosing each other, little winks, streaks of makeup.

Maybe they're improvising dialogue too. Maybe Mamet's provided them with insult kits, Thursdays for Chinese, Wednesdays for Hispanics, today for Indians. Maybe they get together before curtain time, see an Indian woman settling in the front row off to the side, and say to each other: "Hey, forget Friday. Let's get *her* today. See if she cries. See if she walks out." Maybe, like the salesmen they play, they have a little bet on.

Maybe I shouldn't feel betrayed.

Their women, he goes again. *They look like they've just been fucked by a dead cat.*

The fat man hoots so hard he nudges my elbow off our shared armrest.

"Imre. I'm going home." But Imre's hunched so far forward he doesn't hear. English isn't his best language. A refugee from Budapest, he has to listen hard. "I didn't pay eighteen dollars to be insulted."

I don't hate Mamet. It's the tyranny of the American dream that scares me. First, you don't exist. Then you're invisible. Then you're funny. Then you're disgusting. Insult, my American friends will tell me, is a kind of acceptance. No instant dignity here. A play like this, back home, would cause riots. Communal, racist, and antisocial. The actors wouldn't make it off stage. This play, and all these awful feelings, would be safely locked up.

I long, at times, for clear-cut answers. Offer me instant dignity, today, and I'll take it.

"What?" Imre moves toward me without taking his eyes off the actor. "Come again?"

Tears come. I want to stand, scream, make an awful scene. I long for ugly, nasty rage.

The actor is ranting, flinging spittle. *Give me a chance. I'm not finished, I can get back on the board. I tell that asshole, give me a real lead. And what does that asshole give me? Patels. Nothing but Patels.*

This time Imre works an arm around my shoulders. "Panna, what is Patel? Why are you taking it all so personally?"

I shrink from his touch, but I don't walk out. Expensive girls' schools in Lausanne and Bombay have trained me to behave well. My manners are exquisite, my feelings are delicate, my gestures refined, my moods undetectable. They have seen me through riots, uprootings, separation, my son's death.

"I'm not taking it personally."

The fat man looks at us. The woman looks too, and shushes.

I stare back at the two of them. Then I stare, mean and cool, at the man's elbow. Under the bright blue polyester Hawaiian shirt sleeve, the elbow looks soft and runny. "Excuse me," I say. My voice has the effortless meanness of well-bred displaced Third World women, though my rhetoric has been learned elsewhere. "You're exploiting my space."

Startled, the man snatches his arm away from me. He cradles it against his breast. By the time he's ready with comebacks, I've turned my back on him. I've probably ruined the first act for him. I know I've ruined it for Imre.

It's not my fault; it's the *situation.* Old colonies wear down. Patels—the new pioneers—have to be suspicious. Idi Amin's lesson is permanent. AT&T wires move good advice from continent to continent. Keep all assets liquid. Get into 7-IIs, get out of condos and motels. I know how both sides feel, that's the trouble. The Patel sniffing out scams, the sad salesmen on the stage: postcolonialism has made me their referee. It's hate I long for; simple, brutish, partisan hate.

After the show Imre and I make our way toward Broadway. Sometimes he holds my hand; it doesn't mean anything more than that crazies and drunks are crouched in doorways. Imre's been here over two years, but he's stayed very old-world, very courtly, openly protective of women. I met him in a seminar on special ed. last semester. His wife is a nurse somewhere in the Hungarian countryside. There are two sons, and miles of petitions for their emigration. My husband manages a mill two hundred miles north of Bombay. There are no children.

"You make things tough on yourself," Imre says. He assumed Patel was a Jewish name or maybe Hispanic; everything makes equal sense to him. He found the play tasteless, he worried about the effect of vulgar language on my sensitive ears. "You have to let go a bit." And as though to show me how to let go, he breaks away from me, bounds ahead with his head ducked tight, then dances on amazingly jerky legs. He's a Magyar, he often tells me, and deep down, he's an Asian too. I catch glimpses of it, knife-blade Attila cheekbones, despite the blondish hair. In his faded jeans and leather jacket, he's a rock video star. I watch MTV for hours in the apartment when Charity's working the evening shift at Macy's. I listen to WPLJ on Charity's earphones. Why should I be ashamed? Television in India is so uplifting.

Imre stops as suddenly as he'd started. People walk around us. The summer sidewalk is full of theatergoers in seersucker suits; Imre's year-round jacket is out of place. European. Cops in twos and threes huddle, lightly tap their thighs with night sticks and smile at me with benevolence. I want to wink at them, get us all in trouble, tell them the crazy dancing man is from the Warsaw Pact. I'm too shy to break into dance on Broadway. So I hug Imre instead.

The hug takes him by surprise. He wants me to let go, but he doesn't really expect me to let go. He staggers, though I weigh no more than 104 pounds, and with him, I pitch forward slightly. Then he catches me, and we walk arm in arm to the bus stop. My husband would never dance or hug a woman on Broadway. Nor would my brothers. They aren't stuffy people, but they went to Anglican boarding schools and they have a well-developed sense of what's silly.

"Imre." I squeeze his big, rough hand. "I'm sorry I ruined the evening for you."

"You did nothing of the kind." He sounds tired. "Let's not wait for the bus. Let's splurge and take a cab instead."

Imre always has unexpected funds. The Network, he calls it, Class of '56.

In the back of the cab, without even trying, I feel light, almost free. Memories of Indian destitutes mix with the hordes of New York street people, and they float free, like astronauts, inside my head. I've made it. I'm making something of my life. I've left home, my husband, to get a Ph.D. in special ed. I have a multiple-entry visa and a small scholarship for two years. After that, we'll see. My mother was beaten by her mother-in-law, my grandmother, when she'd registered for French lessons at the Alliance Française. My grandmother, the eldest daughter of a rich zamindar, was illiterate.

Imre and the cabdriver talk away in Russian. I keep my eyes closed. That way I can feel the floaters better. I'll write Mamet tonight. I feel strong, reckless. Maybe I'll write Steven Spielberg too; tell him that Indians don't eat monkey brains.

We've made it. Patels must have made it. Mamet, Spielberg: they're not condescending to us. Maybe they're a little bit afraid.

Charity Chin, my roommate, is sitting on the floor drinking Chablis out of a plastic wineglass. She is five foot six, three inches taller than me, but weighs a kilo and a half less than I do. She is a "hands" model. Orientals are supposed to have a monopoly in the hands-modelling business, she says. She had her eyes fixed eight or nine months ago and out of gratitude sleeps with her plastic surgeon every third Wednesday.

"Oh, good," Charity says. "I'm glad you're back early. I need to talk."

She's been writing checks. MCI, Con Ed, Bonwit Teller. Envelopes, already stamped and sealed, form a pyramid between her shapely, knee-socked legs. The checkbook's cover is brown plastic, grained to look like cowhide. Each time Charity flips back the cover, white geese fly over sky-colored checks. She makes good money, but she's extravagant. The difference adds up to this shared, rent-controlled Chelsea one-bedroom.

"All right. Talk."

When I first moved in, she was seeing an analyst. Now she sees a nutritionist.

"Eric called. From Oregon."

"What did he want?"

"He wants me to pay half the rent on his loft for last spring. He asked me to move back, remember? He *begged* me."

Eric is Charity's estranged husband.

"What does your nutritionist say?" Eric now wears a red jumpsuit and tills the soil in Rajneeshpuram.

"You think Phil's a creep too, don't you? What else can he be when creeps are all I attract?"

Phil is a flutist with thinning hair. He's very touchy on the subject of *flautists* versus *flutists.* He's touchy on every subject, from music to books to foods to clothes. He teaches at a small college upstate, and Charity bought a used blue Datsun ("Nissan," Phil insists) last month so she could spend weekends with him. She returns every Sunday night, exhausted and exasperated. Phil and I don't have much to say to each other—he's the only musician I know; the men in my family are lawyers, engineers, or in business—but I like him. Around me, he loosens up. When he visits, he bakes us loaves of pumpernickel bread. He waxes our kitchen floor. Like many men in this country, he seems to me a displaced child, or even a woman, looking for something that passed him by, or for something that he can never have. If he thinks I'm not looking, he sneaks his hands under Charity's sweater, but there isn't too much there. Here, she's a model with high ambitions. In India, she'd be a flat-chested old maid.

I'm shy in front of the lovers. A darkness comes over me when I see them horsing around.

"It isn't the money," Charity says. Oh? I think. "He says he still loves me. Then he turns around and asks me for five hundred."

What's so strange about that, I want to ask. She still loves Eric, and Eric, red jump suit and all, is smart enough to know it. Love is a commodity, hoarded like any other. Mamet knows. But I say, "I'm not the person to ask about love." Charity knows that mine was a traditional Hindu marriage. My parents, with the help of a marriage broker, who was my mother's cousin, picked out a groom. All I had to do was get to know his taste in food.

It'll be a long evening, I'm afraid. Charity likes to confess. I unpleat my silk sari—it no longer looks too showy—wrap it in muslin cloth and put it away in a dresser drawer. Saris are hard to have laundered in Manhattan, though there's a good man in Jackson Heights. My next step will be to brew us a pot of chrysanthemum tea. It's a very special tea from the mainland. Charity's uncle gave it to us. I like him. He's a humpbacked, awkward, terrified man. He runs a gift store on Mott Street, and though he doesn't speak much English, he seems to have done well. Once upon a time he worked for the railways in Chengdu, Szechwan Province, and during the Wuchang Uprising, he was shot at. When I'm down, when I'm lonely for my husband, when I think of our son, or when I need to be held, I think of Charity's uncle. If I hadn't left home, I'd never have heard of the Wuchang Uprising. I've broadened my horizons.

Very late that night my husband calls me from Ahmadabad, a town of textile mills north of Bombay. My husband is a vice president at Lakshmi Cotton Mills. Lakshmi is the goddess of wealth, but LCM (Priv.), Ltd., is doing poorly. Lockouts, strikes, rock-throwings. My husband lives on digitalis, which he calls the food for our *yuga* of discontent.

"We had a bad mishap at the mill today." Then he says nothing for seconds.

The operator comes on. "Do you have the right party, sir? We're trying to reach Mrs. Butt."

"Bhatt," I insist. "*B* for Bombay, *H* for Haryana, *A* for Ahmadabad, double *T* for Tamil Nadu." It's a litany. "This is she."

"One of our lorries was firebombed today. Resulting in three deaths. The driver, old Karamchand, and his two children."

I know how my husband's eyes look this minute, how the eye rims sag and the yellow corneas shine and bulge with pain. He is not an emotional man—the Ahmadabad Institute of Management has trained him to cut losses, to look on the bright side of economic catastrophes—but tonight he's feeling low. I try to remember a driver named Karamchand, but can't. That part of my life is over, the way *trucks* have replaced *lorries* in my vocabulary, the way Charity Chin and her lurid love life have replaced inherited notions of marital duty. Tomorrow he'll come out of it. Soon he'll be eating again. He'll sleep like a baby. He's been trained to believe in turnovers. Every morning he rubs his scalp with cantharidine oil so his hair will grow back again.

"It could be your car next." Affection, love. Who can tell the difference in a traditional marriage in which a wife still doesn't call her husband by his first name?

"No. They know I'm a flunky, just like them. Well paid, maybe. No need for undue anxiety, please."

Then his voice breaks. He says he needs me, he misses me, he wants me to come to him damp from my evening shower, smelling of sandalwood soap, my braid decorated with jasmines.

"I need you too."

"Not to worry, please," he says. "I am coming in a fortnight's time. I have already made arrangements."

Outside my window, fire trucks whine, up Eighth Avenue. I wonder if he can hear them, what he thinks of a life like mine, led amid disorder.

"I am thinking it'll be like a honeymoon. More or less."

When I was in college, waiting to be married, I imagined honeymoons were only for the more fashionable girls, the girls who came from slightly racy families, smoked Sobranies in the dorm lavatories and put up posters of Kabir Bedi, who was supposed to have made it as a big star in the West. My husband wants us to go to Niagara. I'm not to worry about foreign exchange. He's arranged for extra dollars through the Gujarati Network, with a cousin in San Jose. And he's bought four hundred more on the black market. "Tell me you need me. Panna, please tell me again."

* * *

I change out of the cotton pants and shirt I've been wearing all day and put on a sari to meet my husband at JFK. I don't forget the jewelry; the marriage necklace of mangalsutra, gold drop earrings, heavy gold bangles. I don't wear them every day. In this borough of vice and greed, who knows when, or whom, desire will overwhelm.

My husband spots me in the crowd and waves. He has lost weight, and changed his glasses. The arm, uplifted in a cheery wave, is bony, frail, almost opalescent.

In the Carey Coach, we hold hands. He strokes my fingers one by one. "How come you aren't wearing my mother's ring?"

"Because muggers know about Indian women," I say. They know with us it's 24-karat. His mother's ring is showy, in ghastly taste anywhere but India: a blood-red Burma ruby set in a gold frame of floral sprays. My mother-in-law got her guru to bless the ring before I left for the States.

He looks disconcerted. He's used to a different role. He's the knowing, suspicious one in the family. He seems to be sulking, and finally he comes out with it. "You've said nothing about my new glasses." I compliment him on the glasses, how chic and Western-executive they make him look. But I can't help the other things, necessities until he learns the ropes. I handle the money, buy the tickets. I don't know if this makes me unhappy.

Charity drives her Nissan upstate, so for two weeks we are to have the apartment to ourselves. This is more privacy than we ever had in India. No parents, no servants, to keep us modest. We play at housekeeping. Imre has lent us a hibachi, and I grill saffron chicken breasts. My husband marvels at the size of the Perdue hens. "They're big like peacocks, no? These Americans, they're really something!" He tries out pizzas, burgers, McNuggets. He chews. He explores. He judges. He loves it all, fears nothing, feels at home in the summer odors, the clutter of Manhattan streets. Since he thinks that the American palate is bland, he carries a bottle of red peppers in his pocket. I wheel a shopping cart down the aisles of the neighborhood Grand Union, and he follows, swiftly, greedily. He picks up hair rinses and high-protein diet powders. There's so much I already take for granted.

One night, Imre stops by. He wants us to go with him to a movie. In his work shirt and red leather tie, he looks arty or strung out. It's only been a week, but I feel as though I am really seeing him for the first time. The yellow hair worn very short at the sides, the wide, narrow lips. He's a good-looking man, but self-conscious, almost arrogant. He's picked the movie we should see. He always tells me what to see, what to read. He buys the *Voice.* He's a natural avant-gardist. For tonight he's chosen *Numéro Deux.*

"Is it a musical?" my husband asks. The Radio City Music Hall is on his list of sights to see. He's read up on the history of the Rockettes. He doesn't catch Imre's sympathetic wink.

Guilt, shame, loyalty. I long to be ungracious, not ingratiate myself with both men.

That night my husband calculates in rupees the money we've wasted on Godard. "That refugee fellow, Nagy, must have a screw loose in his head. I paid very steep price for dollars on the black market."

Some afternoons we go shopping. Back home we hated shopping, but now it is a lovers' project. My husband's shopping list startles me. I feel I am just getting to know him. Maybe, like Imre, freed from the dignities of old-world culture, he too could get drunk and squirt Cheez Whiz on a guest. I watch him dart into stores in his gleaming leather shoes. Jockey shorts on sale in outdoor bins on Broadway entrance him. White tube socks with different bands of color delight him. He looks for microcassettes, for anything small and electronic and smuggleable. He needs a garment bag. He calls it a "wardrobe," and I have to translate.

"All of New York is having sales, no?"

My heart speeds watching him this happy. It's the third week in August, almost the end of summer, and the city smells ripe, it cannot bear more heat, more money, more energy.

"This is so smashing! The prices are so excellent!" Recklessly, my prudent husband signs away traveller's checks. How he intends to smuggle it all back I don't dare ask. With a microwave, he calculates, we could get rid of our cook.

This has to be love, I think. Charity, Eric, Phil: they may be experts on sex. My husband doesn't chase me around the sofa, but he pushes me down on Charity's battered cushions, and the man who has never entered the kitchen of our Ahmadabad house now comes toward me with a dish tub of steamy water to massage away the pavement heat.

Ten days into his vacation my husband checks out brochures for sightseeing tours. Shortline, Grayline, Crossroads: his new vinyl briefcase is full of schedules and pamphlets. While I make pancakes out of a mix, he comparison-shops. Tour number one costs $10.95 and will give us the World Trade Center, Chinatown, and the United Nations. Tour number three would take us both uptown *and* downtown for $14.95, but my husband is absolutely sure he doesn't want to see Harlem. We settle for tour number four: Downtown and the Dame. It's offered by a new tour company with a small, dirty office at Eighth and Forty-eighth.

The sidewalk outside the office is colorful with tourists. My husband sends me in to buy the tickets because he has come to feel Americans don't understand his accent.

The dark man, Lebanese probably, behind the counter comes on too friendly. "Come on, doll, make my day!" He won't say which tour is his. "Number four? Honey, no! Look, you've wrecked me! Say you'll change your mind." He takes two twenties and gives back change. He holds the tickets, forcing me to pull. He leans closer. "I'm off after lunch."

My husband must have been watching me from the sidewalk. "What was the chap saying?" he demands. "I told you not to wear pants. He thinks you are Puerto Rican. He thinks he can treat you with disrespect."

The bus is crowded and we have to sit across the aisle from each other. The tour guide begins his patter on Forty-sixth. He looks like an actor, his hair bleached and blow-dried. Up close he must look middle-aged, but from where I sit his skin is smooth and his cheeks faintly red.

"Welcome to the Big Apple, folks." The guide uses a microphone. "Big Apple. That's what we native Manhattan degenerates call our city. Today we have guests from fifteen foreign countries and six states from this U.S. of A. That makes the Tourist Bureau real happy. And let me assure you that while we may be the richest city in the richest country in the world, it's okay to tip your charming and talented attendant." He laughs. Then he swings his hip out into the aisle and sings a song.

"And it's mighty fancy on old Delancey Street, you know. . . ."

My husband looks irritable. The guide is, as expected, a good singer. "The bloody man should be giving us histories of buildings we are passing, no?" I pat his hand, the mood passes. He cranes his neck. Our window seats have both gone to Japanese. It's the tour of his life. Next to this, the quick business trips to Manchester and Glasgow pale.

"And tell me what street compares to Mott Street, in July. . . ."

The guide wants applause. He manages a derisive laugh from the Americans up front. He's working the aisles now. "I coulda been somebody, right? I coulda been a star!" Two or three of us smile, those of us who recognize the parody. He catches my smile. The sun is on his harsh, bleached hair. "Right, your highness? Look, we gotta maharani with us! Couldn't I have been a star?"

"Right!" I say, my voice coming out a squeal. I've been trained to adapt; what else can I say?

We drive through traffic past landmark office buildings and churches. The guide flips his hands. "Art deco," he keeps saying. I hear him confide to one of the Americans: "Beats me. I went to a cheap guide's school." My husband wants to know more about this Art Deco, but the guide sings another song.

"We made a foolish choice," my husband grumbles. "We are sitting in the bus only. We're not going into famous buildings." He scrutinizes the pamphlets in his jacket pocket. I think, at least it's air-conditioned in here. I could sit here in the cool shadows of the city forever.

Only five of us appear to have opted for the "Downtown and the Dame" tour. The others will ride back uptown past the United Nations after we've been dropped off at the pier for the ferry to the Statue of Liberty.

An elderly European pulls a camera out of his wife's designer tote bag. He takes pictures of the boats in the harbor, the Japanese in kimonos eating popcorn, scavenging pigeons, me. Then, pushing his wife ahead of him, he climbs back on the bus and waves to us. For a second I feel terribly lost. I wish we were on the bus going back to the apartment. I know I'll not be able to describe any of this to Charity, or to Imre. I'm too proud to admit I went on a guided tour.

The view of the city from the Circle Line ferry is seductive, unreal. The skyline wavers out of reach, but never quite vanishes. The summer sun pushes through fluffy clouds and dapples the glass of office towers. My husband looks thrilled, even more than he had on the shopping trips down Broadway. Tourists and dreamers, we have spent our life's savings to see this skyline, this statue.

"Quick, take a picture of me!" my husband yells as he moves toward a gap of railings. A Japanese matron has given up her position in order to change film. "Before the Twin Towers disappear!"

I focus, I wait for a large Oriental family to walk out of my range. My husband holds his pose tight against the railing. He wants to look relaxed, an international businessman at home in all the financial markets.

A bearded man slides across the bench toward me. "Like this," he says and helps me get my husband in focus. "You want me to take the photo for you?" His name, he says, is Goran. He is Goran from Yugoslavia, as though that were enough for tracking him down. Imre from Hungary. Panna from India. He pulls the old Leica out of my hand, signaling the Orientals to beat it, and clicks away. "I'm a photographer," he says. He could have been a camera thief. That's what my husband would have assumed. Somehow, I trusted. "Get you a beer?" he asks.

"I don't. Drink, I mean. Thank you very much." I say those last words very loud, for everyone's benefit. The odd bottles of Soave with Imre don't count.

"Too bad." Goran gives back the camera.

"Take one more!" my husband shouts from the railing. "Just to be sure!"

The island itself disappoints. The Lady has brutal scaffolding holding her in. The museum is closed. The snack bar is dirty and expensive. My husband reads out the prices to me. He orders two french fries and two Cokes. We sit at picnic tables and wait for the ferry to take us back.

"What was that hippie chap saying?"

As if I could say. A day-care center has brought its kids, at least forty of them, to the island for the day. The kids, all wearing name tags, run around us. I can't help noticing how many are Indian. Even a Patel, probably a Bhatt if I looked hard enough. They toss hamburger bits at pigeons. They kick styrofoam cups. The pigeons are slow, greedy, persistent. I have to shoo one off the table top. I don't think my husband thinks about our son.

"What hippie?"

"The one on the boat. With the beard and the hair."

My husband doesn't look at me. He shakes out his paper napkin and tries to protect his french fries from pigeon feathers.

"Oh, him. He said he was from Dubrovnik." It isn't true, but I don't want trouble.

"What did he say about Dubrovnik?"

I know enough about Dubrovnik to get by. Imre's told me about it. And about Mostar and Zagreb. In Mostar white Muslims sing the call to prayer. I would like to see that before I die: white Muslims. Whole peoples have moved before me; they've adapted. The night Imre told me about Mostar was also the night I saw my first snow in Manhattan. We'd walked down to Chelsea from Columbia. We'd walked and talked and I hadn't felt tired at all.

"You're too innocent," my husband says. He reaches for my hand. "Panna," he cries with pain in his voice, and I am brought back from perfect, floating memories of snow, "I've come to take you back. I have seen how men watch you."

"What?"

"Come back, now. I have tickets. We have all the things we will ever need. I can't live without you."

A little girl with wiry braids kicks a bottle cap at his shoes. The pigeons wheel and scuttle around us. My husband covers his fries with spread-out fingers. "No kicking," he tells the girl. Her name, Beulah, is printed in green ink on a heart-shaped name tag. He forces a smile, and Beulah smiles back. Then she starts to flap her arms. She flaps, she hops. The pigeons go crazy for fries and scraps.

"Special ed. course is two years," I remind him. "I can't go back."

My husband picks up our trays and throws them into the garbage before I can stop him. He's carried disposability a little too far. "We've been taken," he says, moving toward the dock, though the ferry will not arrive for another twenty minutes. "The ferry costs only two dollars round-trip per person. We should have chosen tour number one for $10.95 instead of tour number four for $14.95."

With my Lebanese friend, I think. "But this way we don't have to worry about cabs. The bus will pick us up at the pier and take us back to midtown. Then we can walk home."

"New York is full of cheats and whatnot. Just like Bombay." He is not accusing me of infidelity. I feel dread all the same.

That night, after we've gone to bed, the phone rings. My husband listens, then hands the phone to me. "What is this woman saying?" He turns on the pink Macy's lamp by the bed. "I am not understanding these Negro people's accents."

The operator repeats the message. It's a cable from one of the directors of Lakshmi Cotton Mills. "Massive violent labor confrontation anticipated. Stop. Return posthaste. Stop. Cable flight details. Signed Kantilal Shah."

"It's not your factory," I say. "You're supposed to be on vacation."

"So, you are worrying about me? Yes? You reject my heartfelt wishes but you worry about me?" He pulls me close, slips the straps of my nightdress off my shoulder. "Wait a minute."

I wait, unclothed, for my husband to come back to me. The water is running in the bathroom. In the ten days he has been here he has learned American rites: deodorants, fragrances. Tomorrow morning he'll call Air India; tomorrow evening he'll be on his way back to Bombay. Tonight I should make up to him for my years away, the gutted trucks, the degree I'll never use in India. I want to pretend with him that nothing has changed.

In the mirror that hangs on the bathroom door, I watch my naked body turn, the breasts, the thighs glow. The body's beauty amazes. I stand here shameless, in ways he has never seen me. I am free, afloat, watching somebody else.

1988

Gary Soto b. 1952

Gary Soto was born in Fresno, California, in the heart of the San Joaquin Valley, one of the world's richest agricultural regions. Raised in a working-class family, Soto attended parochial and public schools before enrolling in Fresno State College, intending to study geography and urban planning. His interests soon shifted to literature, however, especially after studying with the prominent poet Philip Levine. Soto published his first poem in 1973 in the *Iowa Review* as a college senior. After graduation, he entered the creative writing program at the University of California, Irvine and earned a Master of Fine Arts degree in 1976. Soto then resided briefly in Mexico. His first book of poetry, *The Elements of San Joaquin,* appeared in 1977 to much critical acclaim. That same year, Soto began teaching at the University of California, Berkeley where he remains. After four volumes of poetry, Soto has more recently published three collections of autobiographical sketches and essays. He is the winner of various prestigious prizes including a Guggenheim fellowship and the Academy of American Poets Award.

Like much contemporary American verse, Soto's poetry is largely autobiographical, recalling childhood and adolescent incidents, and delineating family experience. Soto possesses the skill of converting ordinary, even banal, events into poetic occasions; much of his power and appeal as a poet derives precisely from the accessibility and familiarity of his subjects: a grandmother's courage, a youthful failure as an athlete, a father's relationship with his curious, energetic daughter. Soto's preference for clear, uncomplicated language and concrete images also enhances his work's accessibility. In terms of technique, the most striking feature of Soto's poetry is enjambment, the device of carrying meaning, without pause, from one line to the next.

Soto's ethnic consciousness—his sense of himself as a Mexican American—animates much of his work without delimiting it. Soto moves easily between the United States and Mexico to find his settings, his themes, and his protagonists. He often focuses on peculiarly Mexican American issues and he frequently delineates, especially in poems recalling his childhood, the Mexican Americans' sense of community. But Soto presents Mexican American experience and culture as they fit within a broader context of human events and values. It is fair to say that Soto's largest concern as a poet is the plight of that segment of humanity that is exploited, ignored, unheard. Soto lifts his voice in their behalf; as he once wrote: "I believe in the culture of the poor."

Raymund Paredes
University of California–Los Angeles

PRIMARY WORKS

The Elements of San Joaquin, 1977; *The Tale of Sunlight,* 1978; *Where Sparrows Work Hard,* 1981; *Black Hair,* 1985; *Living Up the Street,* 1985; *Small Faces,* 1986; *Lesser Evils: Ten Quartets,* 1988.

Braly Street

Every summer
The asphalt softens
Giving under the edge
Of boot heels and the trucks
That caught radiators
Of butterflies.
Bottle caps and glass
Of the '40s and '50s
Hold their breath
Under the black earth
Of asphalt and are silent
Like the dead whose mouths
Have eaten dirt and bermuda.
Every summer I come
To this street
Where I discovered ants bit,
Matches flare,
And pinto beans unraveled

Into plants; discovered
Aspirin will not cure a dog
Whose fur twiches.
It's 16 years
Since our house
Was bulldozed and my father
Stunned into a coma . . .
Where it was,
An oasis of chickweed
And foxtails.
Where the almond tree stood
There are wine bottles
Whose history
Is a liver. The long caravan
Of my uncle's footprints
Has been paved
With dirt. Where my father
Cemented a pond
There is a cavern of red ants
Living on the seeds
The wind brings
And cats that come here
To die among
The browning sage.

It's 16 years
Since bottle collectors
Shoveled around
The foundation
And the almond tree
Opened its last fruit
To the summer.
The houses are gone,
The Molinas, Morenos,
The Japanese families
Are gone, the Okies gone
Who moved out at night
Under a canopy of
Moving stars.

In '57 I sat
On the porch, salting
Slugs that came out
After the rain,
While inside my uncle
Weakened with cancer
And the blurred vision

Of his hands
Darkening to earth.
In '58 I knelt
Before my father
Whose spine was pulled loose.
Before his face still
Growing a chin of hair,
Before the procession
Of stitches behind
His neck, I knelt
And did not understand.

Braly Street is now
Tin ventilators
On the warehouses, turning
Our sweat
Towards the yellowing sky;
Acetylene welders
Beading manifolds,
Stinging the half-globes
Of retinas. When I come
To where our house was,
I come to weeds
And a sewer line tied off
Like an umbilical cord;
To the chinaberry
Not pulled down
And to its rings
My father and uncle
Would equal, if alive.

1977

The Cellar

I entered the cellar's cold,
Tapping my way deeper
Than light reaches,
And stood in a place
Where the good lumber
Ticked from its breathing
And slept in a weather
Of fine dust.

Looking for what we
Discarded some time back,
I struck a small fire
And stepped back
From its ladder of smoke,
Watching the light
Pull a chair
And a portion of the wall
From where they crouched
In the dark.
I saw small things—
Hat rack and suitcase,
Tire iron and umbrella
That closed on a great wind—
Step slowly, as if shy,
From their kingdom of mold
Into a new light.

Above, in the rented rooms,
In the lives
I would never know again,
Footsteps circled
A bed, the radio said
What was already forgotten.
I imagined the sun
And how a worker
Home from the fields
Might glimpse at it
Through the window's true lens
And ask it not to come back.
And because I stood
In this place for hours,
I imagined I could climb
From this promise of old air
And enter a street
Stunned gray with evening
Where, if someone
Moved, I could turn,
And seeing through the years,
Call him brother, call him Molina.

1978

Mexicans Begin Jogging

At the factory I worked
In the fleck of rubber, under the press
Of an oven yellow with flame,
Until the border patrol opened
Their vans and my boss waved for us to run.
"Over the fence, Soto," he shouted,
And I shouted that I was American.
"No time for lies," he said, and pressed
A dollar in my palm, hurrying me
Through the back door.

Since I was on his time, I ran
And became the wag to a short tail of Mexicans—
Ran past the amazed crowds that lined
The street and blurred like photographs, in rain.
I ran from that industrial road to the soft
Houses where people paled at the turn of an autumn sky.
What could I do but yell *vivas*
To baseball, milkshakes, and those sociologists
Who would clock me
As I jog into the next century
On the power of a great, silly grin.

1981

Black Hair

At eight I was brilliant with my body.
In July, that ring of heat
We all jumped through, I sat in the bleachers
Of Romain Playground, in the lengthening
Shade that rose from our dirty feet.
The game before us was more than baseball.
It was a figure—Hector Moreno
Quick and hard with turned muscles,
His crouch the one I assumed before an altar
Of worn baseball cards, in my room.

I came here because I was Mexican, a stick
Of brown light in love with those

Who could do it—the triple and hard slide,
The gloves eating balls into double plays.
What could I do with 50 pounds, my shyness,
My black torch of hair, about to go out?
Father was dead, his face no longer
Hanging over the table or our sleep,
And mother was the terror of mouths
Twisting hurt by butter knives.
In the bleachers I was brilliant with my body,
Waving players in and stomping my feet,
Growing sweaty in the presence of white shirts.
I chewed sunflower seeds. I drank water
And bit my arm through the late innings.
When Hector lined balls into deep
Center, in my mind I rounded the bases
With him, my face flared, my hair lifting
Beautifully, because we were coming home
To the arms of brown people.

1985

Kearney Park

True Mexicans or not, let's open our shirts
And dance, a spark of heels
Chipping at the dusty cement. The people
Are shiny like the sea, turning
To the clockwork of rancheras,
The accordion wheezing, the drum-tap
Of work rising and falling.
Let's dance with our hats in hand.
The sun is behind the trees,
Behind my stutter of awkward steps
With a woman who is a brilliant arc of smiles,
An armful of falling water. Her skirt
Opens and closes. My arms
Know no better but to flop
On their own, and we spin, dip
And laugh into each other's faces—
Faces that could be famous
On the coffee table of my abuelita.
But grandma is here, at the park, with a beer
At her feet, clapping

And shouting, "Dance, hijo, dance!"
Laughing, I bend, slide, and throw up
A great cloud of dust,
Until the girl and I are no more.

1985

Joy Harjo (Creek) b. 1951

Joy Harjo is a Creek Indian, born in the heart of the Creek Nation in Tulsa, Oklahoma. After graduation from the Institute of American Indian Arts in Santa Fe, New Mexico, she subsequently taught there from 1978 to 1979 and again from 1983 to 1984. In 1978 she earned an M.F.A. after studying at the University of Iowa Writers' Workshop. She is a professor at the University of New Mexico. Along with her continuing poetry, she is presently involved in writing screenplays and has just completed in collaboration with an astronomer her fourth book.

Joy Harjo's poetry is widely praised and recognized. She has seen her work published in many literary reviews in the United States, as well as in magazines and anthologies. A cadence marks her work that is reminiscent of the repetitions of the Indian ceremonial drum, exemplified in the energy and motion of her "She Had Some Horses." Her poetic voice and imagery have steadily developed as she resurrects the carnage of the early conflict between native and European, "the fantastic and terrible story of our survival" ("Anchorage" poem), and the rejoicing experienced by those who carry on Indian traditions and culture. Her work provides a unique perspective and a piquant examination of American culture from a native point of view. Her verse cries out for the lost, the dispossessed, and the forgotten of reservation, rural, and urban America. Her rigorous words pronounce an awakening for those left voiceless in the past. She relentlessly pursues in print tensions surrounding gender and ethnicity. She explores the pain of existence and the dream fusion of the individual with the landscape, especially the mesa-strewn Southwest. Like so many other Native Americans, Joy Harjo has traveled across the nation and her poetry reflects the exuberance for sight and sound of the Indian powwow circuit, moving through the culture of pan-Indian America, and participation in Indian-related conferences. Her lyricism mirrors the lushness of feel for the countryside and rich images of the people she encounters. Her work mingles realism and the philosophy of American Indian spirituality. She recalls the wounds of the past, the agony of the Indian present, and dream visions of a better future for indigenous peoples. Her work continues to deal with themes which call forth rage and elation at the same time. The multiplicity of emotions she touches is encompassed in her 1983 *She Had Some Horses* in the title poem:

She had some horses she loved.
She had some horses she hated.
These were the same horses.

C. B. Clark
Oklahoma City University

PRIMARY WORKS

The Last Song, 1975; *What Moon Drove Me to This,* 1979; *She Had Some Horses,* 1983; *Secrets from the Center of the World,* with Steven Strom, 1989; *In Mad Love and War,* 1990; *The Woman Who Fell from the Sky,* 1994; "Letter from the End of the Twentieth Century" (compact disk album), 1996; *The Spiral of Memory: Interviews,* 1996; *Reinventing the Enemy's Language,* ed. with Gloria Bird, 1997; *A Map to the Next World: Poetry and Tales,* 2000.

The Woman Hanging from the Thirteenth Floor Window

She is the woman hanging from the 13th floor
window. Her hands are pressed white against the
concrete moulding of the tenement building. She
hangs from the 13th floor window in east Chicago,
with a swirl of birds over her head. They could
be a halo, or a storm of glass waiting to crush her.

She thinks she will be set free.

The woman hanging from the 13th floor window
on the east side of Chicago is not alone.
She is a woman of children, of the baby, Carlos,
and of Margaret, and of Jimmy who is the oldest.
She is her mother's daughter and her father's son.
She is several pieces between the two husbands
she has had. She is all the women of the apartment
building who stand watching her, watching themselves.

When she was young she ate wild rice on scraped down
plates in warm wood rooms. It was in the farther
north and she was the baby then. They rocked her.

She sees Lake Michigan lapping at the shores of
herself. It is a dizzy hole of water and the rich
live in tall glass houses at the edge of it. In some
places Lake Michigan speaks softly, here, it just sputters
and butts itself against the asphalt. She sees
other buildings just like hers. She sees other
women hanging from many-floored windows
counting their lives in the palms of their hands
and in the palms of their children's hands.

She is the woman hanging from the 13th floor window
on the Indian side of town. Her belly is soft from
her children's births, her worn levis swing down below
her waist, and then her feet, and then her heart.
She is dangling.

The woman hanging from the 13th floor hears voices.
They come to her in the night when the lights have gone
dim. Sometimes they are little cats mewing and scratching
at the door, sometimes they are her grandmother's voice,
and sometimes they are gigantic men of light whispering
to her to get up, to get up, to get up. That's when she wants
to have another child to hold onto in the night, to be able
to fall back into dreams.

And the woman hanging from the 13th floor window
hears other voices. Some of them scream out from below
for her to jump, they would push her over. Others cry softly
from the sidewalks, pull their children up like flowers and gather
them into their arms. They would help her, like themselves.

But she is the woman hanging from the 13th floor window,
and she knows she is hanging by her own fingers, her
own skin, her own thread of indecision.

She thinks of Carlos, of Margaret, of Jimmy.
She thinks of her father, and of her mother.
She thinks of all the women she has been, of all
the men. She thinks of the color of her skin, and
of Chicago streets, and of waterfalls and pines.
She thinks of moonlight nights, and of cool spring storms.
Her mind chatters like neon and northside bars.
She thinks of the 4 a.m. lonelinesses that have folded
her up like death, discordant, without logical and
beautiful conclusion. Her teeth break off at the edges.
She would speak.

The woman hangs from the 13th floor window crying for
the lost beauty of her own life. She sees the
sun falling west over the grey plane of Chicago.
She thinks she remembers listening to her own life
break loose, as she falls from the 13th floor
window on the east side of Chicago, or as she
climbs back up to claim herself again.

1983

New Orleans

This is the south. I look for evidence
of other Creeks, for remnants of voices,
or for tobacco brown bones to come wandering
down Conti Street, Royale, or Decatur.
Near the French Market I see a blue horse
caught frozen in stone in the middle of
a square. Brought in by the Spanish on
an endless ocean voyage he became mad
and crazy. They caught him in blue
rock, said
                    don't talk.

I know it wasn't just a horse
                              that went crazy.

Nearby is a shop with ivory and knives.
There are red rocks. The man behind the
counter has no idea that he is inside
magic stones. He should find out before
they destroy him. These things
have memory,
                        you know.
I have a memory.
                          It swims deep in blood,
a delta in the skin. It swims out of Oklahoma,
deep the Mississippi River. It carries my
feet to these places: the French Quarter,
stale rooms, the sun behind thick and moist
clouds, and I hear boats hauling themselves up
and down the river.

My spirit comes here to drink.
My spirit comes here to drink.
Blood is the undercurrent.

There are voices buried in the Mississippi
mud. There are ancestors and future children
buried beneath the currents stirred up by
pleasure boats going up and down.
There are stories here made of memory.

I remember DeSoto. He is buried somewhere in
this river, his bones sunk like the golden
treasure he traveled half the earth to find,

came looking for gold cities, for shining streets
of beaten gold to dance on with silk ladies.

He should have stayed home.

(Creeks knew of him for miles
before he came into town.
Dreamed of silver blades
and crosses.)
And knew he was one of the ones who yearned
for something his heart wasn't big enough
to handle.
(And DeSoto thought it was gold.)

The Creeks lived in earth towns,
not gold,
spun children, not gold.
That's not what DeSoto thought he wanted to see
The Creeks knew it, and drowned him in
the Mississippi River
so he wouldn't have to drown himself.

Maybe his body is what I am looking for
as evidence. To know in another way
that my memory is alive.
But he must have got away, somehow,
because I have seen New Orleans,
the lace and silk buildings,
trolley cars on beaten silver paths,
graves that rise up out of soft earth in the rain,
shops that sell black mammy dolls
holding white babies.

And I know I have seen DeSoto,
having a drink on Bourbon Street,
mad and crazy
dancing with a woman as gold
as the river bottom.

1983

Remember

Remember the sky that you were born under,
know each of the star's stories.

Remember the moon, know who she is.
Remember the sun's birth at dawn, that is the
strongest point of time. Remember sundown
and the giving away to night.
Remember your birth, how your mother struggled
to give you form and breath. You are evidence of
her life, and her mother's, and hers.
Remember your father. He is your life, also.
Remember the earth whose skin you are:
red earth, black earth, yellow earth, white earth
brown earth, we are earth.
Remember the plants, trees, animal life who all have their
tribes, their families, their histories, too. Talk to them,
listen to them. They are alive poems.
Remember the wind. Remember her voice. She knows the
origin of this universe.
Remember you are all people and all people are you.
Remember you are this universe and this
universe is you.
Remember all is in motion, is growing, is you.
Remember language comes from this.
Remember the dance language is, that life is.
Remember.

1983

Vision

The rainbow touched down
"somewhere in the Rio Grande,"
we said. And saw the light of it
from your mother's house in Isleta.[1]
How it curved down between earth
and the deepest sky to give us horses
of color
horses that were within us all of this time
but we didn't see them because
we wait for the easiest vision
to save us.

In Isleta the rainbow was a crack
in the universe. We saw the barest
of all life that is possible.
Bright horses rolled over
and over the dusking sky.

[1]An Indian Pueblo in New Mexico.

I heard the thunder of their beating
hearts. Their lungs hit air
and sang. All the colors of horses
formed the rainbow,
                    and formed us
watching them.

1983

Anchorage

for Audre Lorde

This city is made of stone, of blood, and fish.
There are Chugatch Mountains[1] to the east
and whale and seal to the west.
It hasn't always been this way, because glaciers
who are ice ghosts create oceans, carve earth
and shape this city here, by the sound.
They swim backwards in time.

Once a storm of boiling earth cracked open
the streets, threw open the town.
It's quiet now, but underneath the concrete
is the cooking earth,
                    and above that, air
which is another ocean, where spirits we can't see
are dancing   joking   getting full
on roasted caribou, and the praying
goes on, extends out.

Nora and I go walking down 4th Avenue
and know it is all happening.
On a park bench we see someone's Athabascan[2]
grandmother, folded up, smelling like 200 years

[1]A range extending about 280 miles along the coast of south Alaska just above the panhandle. Chugach Eskimo (Ahtnas) reside there.

[2]Athabascan is a complicated but wide-spread Indian language, part of the Na-Dene Indian language superstock of North America. Indians speak Athabascan in the sub-Arctic interior of Alaska, along the Pacific Northwest Coast (Tlingit of Alaska panhandle, Tolowa of Oregon, and Hupa of California), and in the American Southwest (Apache and Navajo).

of blood and piss, her eyes closed against some
unimagined darkness, where she is buried in an ache
in which nothing makes
sense.

We keep on breathing, walking, but softer now,
the clouds whirling in the air above us.
What can we say that would make us understand
better than we do already?
Except to speak of her home and claim her
as our own history, and know that our dreams
don't end here, two blocks away from the ocean
where our hearts still batter away at the muddy shore.

And I think of the 6th Avenue jail, of mostly Native
and Black men, where Henry told about being shot at
eight times outside a liquor store in L.A., but when
the car sped away he was surprised he was alive,

no bullet holes, man, and eight cartridges strewn
on the sidewalk
all around him.

Everyone laughed at the impossibility of it,
but also the truth. Because who would believe
the fantastic and terrible story of all of our survival
those who were never meant
to survive?

1983

Deer Dancer

Nearly everyone had left that bar in the middle of winter except the hardcore. It was the coldest night of the year, every place shut down, but not us. Of course we noticed when she came in. We were Indian ruins. She was the end of beauty. No one knew her, the stranger whose tribe we recognized, her family related to deer, if that's who she was, a people accustomed to hearing songs in pine trees, and making them hearts.

The woman inside the woman who was to dance naked in the bar of misfits blew deer magic. Henry Jack, who could not survive a sober day, thought she was Buffalo Calf Woman[1] come back, passed out, his head by the toilet. All night he dreamed a dream he could not say. The next day he borrowed money, went home, and sent back the money I lent. Now that's a miracle. Some people see vision in a burned tortilla, some in the face of a woman.

This is the bar of broken survivors, the club of shotgun, knife wound, of poison by culture. We who were taught not to stare drank our beer. The players gossiped down their cues. Someone put a quarter in the jukebox to relive despair. Richard's wife dove to kill her. We had to hold her back, empty her pockets of knives and diaper pins, buy her two beers to keep her still, while Richard secretly bought the beauty a drink.

How do I say it? In this language there are no words for how the real world collapses. I could say it in my own and the sacred mounds would come into focus, but I couldn't take it in this dingy envelope. So I look at the stars in this strange city, frozen to the back of the sky, the only promises that ever make sense.

My brother-in-law hung out with white people, went to law school with a perfect record, quit. Says you can keep your laws, your words. And practiced law on the street with his hands. He jimmied to the proverbial dream girl, the face of the moon, while the players racked a new game. He bragged to us, he told her magic words and that's when she broke, became human. But we all heard his bar voice crack:

What's a girl like you doing in a place like this?

That's what I'd like to know, what are we all doing in a place like this?

You would know she could hear only what she wanted to; don't we all? Left the drink of betrayal Richard bought her, at the bar. What was she on? We all wanted some. Put a quarter in the juke. We all take risks stepping into thin air. Our ceremonies didn't predict this. Or we expected more.

I had to tell you this, for the baby inside the girl sealed up with a lick of hope and swimming into praise of nations. This is not a rooming house, but a dream of winter falls and the deer who portrayed the relatives of strangers. The way back is deer breath on icy windows.

[1]The culture heroine of the Lakota, who brought them the sacred pipe and the seven central rites of the Sioux. In myth she is remarkably beautiful and stirs the desire of the men who first meet her. See "Wohpe and the Gift of the Pipe" in Volume 1.

The next dance none of us predicted. She borrowed a chair for the stairway to heaven and stood on a table of names. And danced in the room of children without shoes.

You picked a fine time to leave me, Lucille.
With four hungry children and a crop in the field.

And then she took off her clothes. She shook loose memory, waltzed with the empty lover we'd all become.

She was the myth slipped down through dreamtime. The promise of feast we all knew was coming. The deer who crossed through knots of a curse to find us. She was no slouch, and neither were we, watching.

The music ended. And so does the story. I wasn't there. But I imagined her like this, not a stained red dress with tape on her heels but the deer who entered our dream in white dawn, breathed mist into pine trees, her fawn a blessing of meat, the ancestors who never left.

1990

We Must Call a Meeting

I am fragile, a piece of pottery smoked from fire
made of dung,
the design drawn from nightmares. I am an arrow, painted
with lightning
to seek the way to the name of the enemy,
but the arrow has now created
its own language.
It is a language of lizards and storms, and we have
begun to hold conversations
long into the night.
I forget to eat.
I don't work. My children are hungry and the animals who live
in the backyard are starving.
I begin to draw maps of stars.
The spirits of old and new ancestors perch on my shoulders.
I make prayers of clear stone
of feathers from birds
who live closest to the gods.

The voice of the stone is born

of a meeting of yellow birds
who circle the ashes of a smoldering volcano.
The feathers sweep the prayers up
and away.
I, too, try to fly but get caught in the cross fire of signals
and my spirit drops back down to earth.
I am lost; I am looking for you
who can help me walk this thin line between the breathing
and the dead.
You are the curled serpent in the pottery of nightmares.
You are the dreaming animal who paces back and forth in my head.
We must call a meeting.
Give me back my language and build a house
Inside it.
A house of madness.
A house for the dead who are not dead.
And the spiral of the sky above it.
And the sun
and the moon.
And the stars to guide us called promise.

1990

Louise Erdrich (Chippewa) b. 1954

Karen Louise Erdrich was born in Little Falls, Minnesota. She is an enrolled member of the Turtle Mountain Chippewa tribe of North Dakota. The daughter of Bureau of Indian Affairs educators, she received degrees from Dartmouth College and Johns Hopkins, and later served for a time as editor of *The Circle,* a newspaper published by the Boston Indian Council, before earning residential fellowships to the distinguished writers' colonies. Her initial reputation was founded on a series of successful short stories, for which she received the Nelson Algren Award in 1982 and a Pushcart Prize in 1983.

In 1984 Erdrich published her first book of poetry, *Jacklight,* which focuses upon both her own personal experiences and her observations of small town, upper-midwestern life. The classic themes of this poetry—the fragility and power of a life in the flesh, the desperation of longing, the need for transcendence—return in her second book of poetry, *Baptism of Desire* (1989), rendered almost surrealistically by combining an urgent and vivid organicism with a crackling, electrical imagery. Indeed, the virtuosity of Erdrich's acclaimed prose style is founded in the disciplined craft of her poetry, most of it written before her more widely known fiction.

Erdrich's first novel, *Love Medicine* (1984), was generously praised in the United States, where it won the National Book Critics' Circle Award for the Best Work of Fiction for 1984. The novel is structured as a series of separate narratives—several of which were first published as short stories—spanning a period of fifty years, from 1934 to 1984. Set on a North Dakota reservation, the stories focus on relations between three Chippewa families: the Kashpaws and their relations, the Lamartine/Nanapush, and the Morrisey families. The novel opens in 1981 with a young college student's return to the reservation on the occasion of the death of June Kashpaw. Coming home she sees clearly the pain and personal devastation the years have wrought on her family, and she struggles in her first-person narrative to comprehend what force or attraction in that situation would compel her Aunt June to set out for her home across an empty, snow-covered field on the night she froze to death. The stories that follow probe the relations between these families and in so doing focus on three major characters: Marie Lazarre, a strong-willed woman of great spirit and beauty whose sense of principle is founded on feelings of inadequacy that have bedeviled her all her life; Lulu Lamartine, a woman of passionate intensity, who learned early in her life of the frailty of the flesh and its enormous capacity to heal life's pain and redeem its guilt; and Nector Kashpaw, a man of good looks and popular appeal, who is irresistibly drawn to Lulu but marries Marie (June is their daughter). The selection which follows is the second chapter of the book, the first in which we meet Marie Lazarre and come to understand her need for a "love medicine," a medicine which would create love, a love that would be a medicine.

Erdrich's second novel, *Beet Queen,* returns to the upper midwest in the same time frame as *Love Medicine,* but focuses on the Euro-American townspeople near the reservation. The action of the third novel in the trilogy, *Tracks,* precedes that of the other two, removing the story to the turn of the century and setting the stage for the other novels by exploring the different fates of young Fleur Pillager and Pauline Puyat and the traditional presence of the elder, Nanapush. In *Tracks* we learn that before she went into the convent and became Sister Leopolda, Pauline gave birth to a daughter, Marie (later Lazarre), whom she gave up to Bernadette Morrissey. Erdrich's work is marked by a generous, compassionate spirit, a marvelous sense of comic invention, a sometimes acute irony, and a finely honed sense of imagery and style.

Andrew O. Wiget
New Mexico State University

PRIMARY WORKS

Poetry: *Jacklight,* 1984; *Baptism of Fire,* 1989; Fiction: *Love Medicine,* 1984; *Beet Queen,* 1986; *Tracks,* 1988; *The Crown of Columbus,* 1991 (with Michael Dorris); *The Bingo Palace,* 1994; *The Blue Jay's Dance: A Birth Year,* 1995; *Tales of Burning Love,* 1996; *The Antelope Wife,* 1998.

from Love Medicine

Saint Marie (1934)

Marie Lazarre

So when I went there, I knew the dark fish must rise. Plumes of radiance had soldered on me. No reservation girl had ever prayed so hard. There was no use in trying to ignore me any longer. I was going up there on the hill with the black robe women. They were not any lighter than me. I was going up there to pray as good as they could. Because I don't have that much Indian blood. And they never thought they'd have a girl from this reservation as a saint they'd have to kneel to. But they'd have me. And I'd be carved in pure gold. With ruby lips. And my toenails would be little pink ocean shells, which they would have to stoop down off their high horse to kiss.

I was ignorant. I was near age fourteen. The length of sky is just about the size of my ignorance. Pure and wide. And it was just that—the pure and wideness of my ignorance—that got me up the hill to Sacred Heart Convent and brought me back down alive. For maybe Jesus did not take my bait, but them Sisters tried to cram me right down whole.

You ever see a walleye strike so bad the lure is practically out its back end before you reel it in? That is what they done with me. I don't like to make that low comparison, but I have seen a walleye do that once. And it's the same attempt as Sister Leopolda made to get me in her clutch.

I had the mail-order Catholic soul you get in a girl raised out in the bush, whose only thought is getting into town. For Sunday Mass is the only time my father brought his children in except for school, when we were harnessed. Our soul went cheap. We were so anxious to get there we would have walked in on our hands and knees. We just craved going to the store, slinging bottle caps in the dust, making fool eyes at each other. And of course we went to church.

Where they have the convent is on top of the highest hill, so that from its windows the Sisters can be looking into the marrow of the town. Recently a windbreak was planted before the bar "for the purposes of tornado insurance." Don't tell me that. That poplar stand was put up to hide the drinkers as they get the transformation. As they are served into the beast of their burden. While they're drinking, that body comes upon them, and then they stagger or crawl out the bar door, pulling a weight that can't move past the poplars. They don't want no holy witness to their fall.

Anyway, I climbed. That was a long-ago day. There was a road then for wagons that wound in ruts to the top of the hill where they had their buildings of painted brick. Gleaming white. So white the sun glanced off in dazzling display to set forms whirling behind your eyelids. The face of God you could hardly look at. But that day it drizzled, so I could look all I wanted. I saw the homelier side. The cracked whitewash and swallows nesting in the busted ends of eaves. I saw the boards sawed the size of broken windowpanes and the fruit trees, stripped. Only the tough wild rhubarb flourished. Goldenrod rubbed up their walls. It was a poor convent. I didn't see that then but I know that now. Compared to others it was humble, ragtag, out in the middle of no place. It was the end of the world to some. Where the maps stopped. Where God had only half a hand in the creation. Where the Dark One had put in thick bush, liquor, wild dogs, and Indians.

I heard later that the Sacred Heart Convent was a catchall place for nuns that don't get along elsewhere. Nuns that complain too much or lose their mind. I'll always wonder now, after hearing that, where they picked up Sister Leopolda. Perhaps she had scarred someone else, the way she left a mark on me. Perhaps she was just sent around to test her Sisters' faith, here and there, like the spot-checker in a factory. For she was the definite most-hard trial of anyone's endurance, even when they started out with veils of wretched love upon their eyes.

I was that girl who thought the black hem of her garment would help me rise. Veils of love which was only hate petrified by longing—that was me. I was like those bush Indians who stole the holy black hat of a Jesuit and swallowed little scraps of it to cure their fevers. But the hat itself carried smallpox and was killing them with belief. Veils of faith! I had this confidence in Leopolda. She was different. The other Sisters had long ago gone blank and given up on Satan. He slept for them. They never noticed his comings and goings. But Leopolda kept track of him and knew his habits, minds he burrowed in, deep spaces where he hid. She knew as much about him as my grandma, who called him by other names and was not afraid.

In her class, Sister Leopolda carried a long oak pole for opening high windows. It had a hook made of iron on one end that could jerk a patch of your hair out or throttle you by the collar—all from a distance. She used this deadly hook-pole for catching Satan by surprise. He could have entered without your knowing it—through your lips or your nose or any one of your seven openings—and gained your mind. But she would see him. That pole would brain you from behind. And he would gasp, dazzled, and take the first thing she offered, which was pain.

She had a stringer of children who could only breathe if she said the word. I was the worst of them. She always said the Dark One wanted me most of all, and I believed this. I stood out. Evil was a common thing I trusted. Before sleep sometimes he came and whispered conversation in the old language of the bush. I listened. He told me things he never told anyone but Indians. I was privy to both worlds of his knowledge. I listened to him, but I had confidence in Leopolda. She was the only one of the bunch he even noticed.

There came a day, though, when Leopolda turned the tide with her hook-pole.

It was a quiet day with everyone working at their desks, when I heard him. He had sneaked into the closets in the back of the room. He was scratching around, tasting crumbs in our pockets, stealing buttons, squirting his dark juice in the linings and the boots. I was the only one who heard him, and I got bold. I smiled. I glanced back and smiled and looked up at her sly to see if she had noticed. My heart jumped. For she was looking straight at me. And she sniffed. She had a big stark bony nose stuck to the front of her face for smelling out brimstone and evil thoughts. She had smelled him on me. She stood up. Tall, pale, a blackness leading into the deeper blackness of the slate wall behind her. Her oak pole had flown into her grip. She had seen me glance at the closet. Oh, she knew. She knew just where he was. I watched her watch him in her mind's eye. The whole class was watching now. She was staring, sizing, following his scuffle. And all of a sudden she tensed down, posed on her bent kneesprings, cocked her arm back. She threw the oak pole singing over my head, through my braincloud. It cracked through the thin wood door of the back closet, and the heavy pointed hook drove through his heart. I turned. She'd speared her own black rubber overboot where he'd taken refuge in the tip of her darkest toe.

Something howled in my mind. Loss and darkness. I understood. I was to suffer for my smile.

He rose up hard in my heart. I didn't blink when the pole cracked. My skull was tough. I didn't flinch when she shrieked in my ear. I only shrugged at the flowers of hell. He wanted me. More than anything he craved me. But then she did the worst. She did what broke my mind to her. She grabbed me by the collar and dragged me, feet flying, through the room and threw me in the closet with her dead black overboot. And I was there. The only light was a crack beneath the door. I asked the Dark One to enter into me and boost my mind. I asked him to restrain my tears, for they was pushing behind my eyes. But he was afraid to come back there. He was afraid of her sharp pole. And I was afraid of Leopolda's pole for the first time, too. I felt the cold hook in my heart. How it could crack through the door at any minute and drag me out, like a dead fish on a gaff, drop me on the floor like a gutshot squirrel.

I was nothing. I edged back to the wall as far as I could. I breathed the chalk dust. The hem of her full black cloak cut against my cheek. He had left me. Her spear could find me any time. Her keen ears would aim the hook into the beat of my heart.

What was that sound?

It filled the closet, filled it up until it spilled over, but I did not recognize the crying wailing voice as mine until the door cracked open, brightness, and she hoisted me to her camphor-smelling lips.

"He *wants* you," she said. "That's the difference. I give you love."

Love. The black hook. The spear singing through the mind. I saw that she had tracked the Dark One to my heart and flushed him out into the open. So now my heart was an empty nest where she could lurk.

Well, I was weak. I was weak when I let her in, but she got a foothold there. Hard to dislodge as the year passed. Sometimes I felt him—the brush of dim wings—but only rarely did his voice compel. It was between Marie and Leopolda now, and the struggle changed. I began to realize I had been on the wrong track with the fruits of hell. The real way to overcome Leopolda was this: I'd get to heaven first. And then, when I saw her coming, I'd shut the gate. She'd be out! That is why, besides the bowing and the scraping I'd be dealt, I wanted to sit on the altar as a saint.

To this end, I went up on the hill. Sister Leopolda was the consecrated nun who had sponsored me to come there.

"You're not vain," she said. "You're too honest, looking into the mirror, for that. You're not smart. You don't have the ambition to get clear. You have two choices. One, you can marry a no-good Indian, bear his brats, die like a dog. Or two, you can give yourself to God."

"I'll come up there," I said, "but not because of what you think."

I could have had any damn man on the reservation at the time. And I could have made him treat me like his own life. I looked good. And I looked white. But I wanted Sister Leopolda's heart. And here was the thing: sometimes I wanted her heart in love and admiration. Sometimes. And sometimes I wanted her heart to roast on a black stick.

She answered the back door where they had instructed me to call. I stood there with my bundle. She looked me up and down.

"All right," she said finally. "Come in."

She took my hand. Her fingers were like a bundle of broom straws, so thin and dry, but the strength of them was unnatural. I couldn't have tugged loose if she was leading me into rooms of white-hot coal. Her strength was a kind of perverse miracle, for she got it from fasting herself thin. Because of this hunger practice her lips were a wounded brown and her skin deadly pale. Her eye sockets were two deep lashless hollows in a taut skull. I told you about the nose already. It stuck out far and made the place her eyes moved even deeper, as if she stared out the wrong end of a gun barrel. She took the bundle from my hands and threw it in the corner.

"You'll be sleeping behind the stove, child."

It was immense, like a great furnace. There was a small cot close behind it.

"Looks like it could get warm there," I said.

"Hot. It does."

"Do I get a habit?"

I wanted something like the thing she wore. Flowing black cotton. Her face was strapped in white bandages, and a sharp crest of starched white cardboard hung over her forehead like a glaring beak. If possible, I wanted a bigger, longer, whiter beak than hers.

"No," she said, grinning her great skull grin. "You don't get one yet. Who knows, you might not like us. Or we might not like you."

But she had loved me, or offered me love. And she had tried to hunt the Dark One down. So I had this confidence.

"I'll inherit your keys from you," I said.

She looked at me sharply, and her grin turned strange. She hissed, taking in her breath. Then she turned to the door and took a key from her belt. It was a giant key, and it unlocked the larder where the food was stored.

Inside there was all kinds of good stuff. Things I'd tasted only once or twice in my life. I saw sticks of dried fruit, jars of orange peel, spice like cinnamon. I saw tins of crackers with ships painted on the side. I saw pickles. Jars of herring and the rind of pigs. There was cheese, a big brown block of it from the thick milk of goats. And besides that there was the everyday stuff, in great quantities, the flour and the coffee.

It was the cheese that got to me. When I saw it my stomach hollowed. My tongue dripped. I loved that goat-milk cheese better than anything I'd ever ate. I stared at it. The rich curve in the buttery cloth.

"When you inherit my keys," she said sourly, slamming the door in my face, "you can eat all you want of the priest's cheese."

Then she seemed to consider what she'd done. She looked at me. She took the key from her belt and went back, sliced a hunk off, and put it in my hand.

"If you're good you'll taste this cheese again. When I'm dead and gone," she said.

Then she dragged out the big sack of flour. When I finished that heaven stuff she told me to roll my sleeves up and begin doing God's labor. For a while we worked in silence, mixing up the dough and pounding it out on stone slabs.

"God's work," I said after a while. "If this is God's work, then I've done it all my life."

"Well, you've done it with the Devil in your heart then," she said. "Not God."

"How do you know?" I asked. But I knew she did. And I wished I had not brought up the subject.

"I see right into you like a clear glass," she said. "I always did."

"You don't know it," she continued after a while, "but he's come around here sulking. He's come around here brooding. You brought him in. He knows the smell of me, and he's going to make a last ditch try to get you back. Don't let him." She glared over at me. Her eyes were cold and lighted. "Don't let him touch you. We'll be a long time getting rid of him."

So I was careful. I was careful not to give him an inch. I said a rosary, two rosaries, three, underneath my breath. I said the Creed. I said every scrap of Latin I knew while we punched the dough with our fists. And still, I dropped the cup. It rolled under that monstrous iron stove, which was getting fired up for baking.

And she was on me. She saw he'd entered my distraction.

"Our good cup," she said. "Get it out of there, Marie."

I reached for the poker to snag it out from beneath the stove. But I had a sinking feel in my stomach as I did this. Sure enough, her long arm darted past me like a whip. The poker lighted in her hand.

"Reach," she said. "Reach with your arm for that cup. And when your flesh is hot, remember that the flames you feel are only one fraction of the heat you will feel in his hellish embrace."

She always did things this way, to teach you lessons. So I wasn't surprised. It was playacting, anyway, because a stove isn't very hot underneath right along the floor. They aren't made that way. Otherwise a wood floor would burn. So I said yes and got down on my stomach and reached under. I meant to grab it quick and jump up again, before she could think up another lesson, but here it happened. Although I groped for the cup, my hand closed on nothing. That cup was nowhere to be found. I heard her step toward me, a slow step. I heard the creak of thick shoe leather, the little *plat* as the folds of her heavy skirts met, a trickle of fine sand sifting, somewhere, perhaps in the bowels of her, and I was afraid. I tried to scramble up, but her foot came down lightly behind my ear, and I was lowered. The foot came down more firmly at the base of my neck, and I was held.

"You're like I was," she said. "He wants you very much."

"He doesn't want me no more," I said. "He had his fill. I got the cup!"

I heard the valve opening, the hissed intake of breath, and knew that I should not have spoke.

"You lie," she said. "You're cold. There is a wicked ice forming in your blood. You don't have a shred of devotion for God. Only wild cold dark lust. I know it. I know how you feel. I see the beast . . . the beast watches me out of your eyes sometimes. Cold."

The urgent scrape of metal. It took a moment to know from where. Top of the stove. Kettle. Lessons. She was steadying herself with the iron poker. I could feel it like pure certainty, driving into the wood floor. I would not remind her of pokers. I heard the water as it came, tipped from the spout, cooling as it fell but still scalding as it struck. I must have twitched beneath her foot, because she steadied me, and then the poker nudged up beside my arm as if to guide. "To warm your cold ash heart," she said. I felt how patient she would be. The water came. My mind went dead blank. Again. I could only think the kettle would be cooling slowly in her hand. I could not stand it. I bit my lip so as not to satisfy her with a sound. She gave me more reason to keep still.

"I will boil him from your mind if you make a peep," she said, "by filling up your ear."

Any sensible fool would have run back down the hill the minute Leopolda let them up from under her heel. But I was snared in her black intelligence by then. I could not think straight. I had prayed so hard I think I broke a cog in my mind. I prayed while her foot squeezed my throat. While my skin burst. I prayed even when I heard the wind come through, shrieking in the busted bird nests. I didn't stop when pure light fell, turning slowly behind my eyelids. God's face. Even that did not disrupt my continued praise. Words came. Words came from nowhere and flooded my mind.

Now I could pray much better than any one of them. Than all of them full force. This was proved. I turned to her in a daze when she let me up. My thoughts were gone, and yet I remember how surprised I was. Tears glittered in her eyes, deep down, like the sinking reflection in a well.

"It was so hard, Marie," she gasped. Her hands were shaking. The kettle clattered against the stove. "But I have used all the water up now. I think he is gone."

"I prayed," I said foolishly. "I prayed very hard."

"Yes," she said. "My dear one, I know."

We sat together quietly because we had no more words. We let the dough rise and punched it down once. She gave me a bowl of mush, unlocked the sausage from a special cupboard, and took that in to the Sisters. They sat down the hall, chewing their sausage, and I could hear them. I could hear their teeth bite through their bread and meat. I couldn't move. My shirt was dry but the cloth stuck to my back, and I couldn't think straight. I was losing the sense to understand how her mind worked. She'd gotten past me with her poker and I would never be a saint. I despaired. I felt I had no inside voice, nothing to direct me, no darkness, no Marie. I was about to throw that cornmeal mush out to the birds and make a run for it, when the vision rose up blazing in my mind.

I was rippling gold. My breasts were bare and my nipples flashed and winked. Diamonds tipped them. I could walk through panes of glass. I could walk through windows. She was at my feet, swallowing the glass after each step I took. I broke through another and another. The glass she swallowed ground and cut until her starved insides were only a subtle dust. She coughed. She coughed a cloud of dust. And then she was only a black rag that flapped off, snagged in bob wire, hung there for an age, and finally rotted into the breeze.

I saw this, mouth hanging open, gazing off into the flagged boughs of trees.

"Get up!" she cried. "Stop dreaming. It is time to bake."

Two other Sisters had come in with her, wide women with hands like paddles. They were evening and smoothing out the firebox beneath the great jaws of the oven.

"Who is this one?" they asked Leopolda. "Is she yours?"

"She is mine," said Leopolda. "A very good girl."

"What is your name?" one asked me.

"Marie."

"Marie. Star of the Sea."

"She will shine," said Leopolda, "when we have burned off the dark corrosion."

The others laughed, but uncertainly. They were mild and sturdy French, who did not understand Leopolda's twisted jokes, although they muttered respectfully at things she said. I knew they wouldn't believe what she had done with the kettle. There was no question. So I kept quiet.

"Elle est docile,"[1] they said approvingly as they left to starch the linens.

"Does it pain?" Leopolda asked me as soon as they were out the door.

I did not answer. I felt sick with the hurt.

"Come along," she said.

The building was wholly quiet now. I followed her up the narrow staircase into a hall of little rooms, many doors. Her cell was the quietest, at the very end. Inside, the air smelled stale, as if the door had not been opened for years. There was a crude straw mattress, a tiny bookcase with a picture of Saint Francis hanging over it, a ragged palm, a stool for sitting on, a crucifix. She told me to remove my blouse and sit on the stool. I did so. She took a pot of salve from the bookcase and began to smooth it upon my burns. Her hands made slow, wide circles, stopping the pain. I closed my eyes. I expected to see blackness. Peace. But instead the vision reared up again. My chest was still tipped with diamonds. I was walking through windows. She was chewing up the broken litter I left behind.

"I am going," I said. "Let me go."

But she held me down.

"Don't go," she said quickly. "Don't. We have just begun."

I was weakening. My thoughts were whirling pitifully. The pain had kept me strong, and as it left me I began to forget it; I couldn't hold on. I began to wonder if she'd really scalded me with the kettle. I could not remember. To remember this seemed the most important thing in the world. But I was losing the memory. The scalding. The pouring. It began to vanish. I felt like my mind was coming off its hinge, flapping in the breeze, hanging by the hair of my own pain. I wrenched out of her grip.

"He was always in you," I said. "Even more than in me. He wanted you even more. And now he's got you. Get thee behind me!"

I shouted that, grabbed my shirt, and ran through the door throwing it on my body. I got down the stairs and into the kitchen, even, but no matter what I told myself, I couldn't get out the door. It wasn't finished. And she knew I would not leave. Her quiet step was immediately behind me.

"We must take the bread from the oven now," she said.

She was pretending nothing happened. But for the first time I had gotten through some chink she'd left in her darkness. Touched some doubt. Her voice was so low and brittle it cracked off at the end of her sentence.

"Help me, Marie," she said slowly.

But I was not going to help her, even though she had calmly buttoned the back of my shirt up and put the big cloth mittens in my hands for taking out the loaves. I could have bolted for it then. But I didn't. I knew that something was nearing completion. Something was about to happen. My back was a wall of singing flame. I was turning. I watched her take the long fork in one hand, to tap the loaves. In the other hand she gripped the black poker to hook the pans.

[1]French: She is docile.

"Help me," she said again, and I thought, Yes, this is part of it. I put the mittens on my hands and swung the door open on its hinges. The oven gaped. She stood back a moment, letting the first blast of heat rush by. I moved behind her. I could feel the heat at my front and at my back. Before, behind. My skin was turning to beaten gold. It was coming quicker than I thought. The oven was like the gate of a personal hell. Just big enough and hot enough for one person, and that was her. One kick and Leopolda would fly in headfirst. And that would be one-millionth of the heat she would feel when she finally collapsed in his hellish embrace.

Saints know these numbers.

She bent forward with her fork held out. I kicked her with all my might. She flew in. But the outstretched poker hit the back wall first, so she rebounded. The oven was not so deep as I had thought.

There was a moment when I felt a sort of thin, hot disappointment, as when a fish slips off the line. Only I was the one going to be lost. She was fearfully silent. She whirled. Her veil had cutting edges. She had the poker in one hand. In the other she held that long sharp fork she used to tap the delicate crusts of loaves. Her face turned upside down on her shoulders. Her face turned blue. But saints are used to miracles. I felt no trace of fear.

If I was going to be lost, let the diamonds cut! Let her eat ground glass!

"Bitch of Jesus Christ!" I shouted. "Kneel and beg! Lick the floor!"

That was when she stabbed me through the hand with the fork, then took the poker up alongside my head, and knocked me out.

It must have been a half an hour later when I came around. Things were so strange. So strange I can hardly tell it for delight at the remembrance. For when I came around this was actually taking place. I was being worshiped. I had somehow gained the altar of a saint.

I was laying back on the stiff couch in the Mother Superior's office. I looked around me. It was as though my deepest dream had come to life. The Sisters of the convent were kneeling to me. Sister Bonaventure. Sister Dympna. Sister Cecilia Saint-Claire. The two French with hands like paddles. They were down on their knees. Black capes were slung over some of their heads. My name was buzzing up and down the room, like a fat autumn fly lighting on the tips of their tongues between Latin, humming up the heavy blood-dark curtains, circling their little cosseted heads. Marie! Marie! A girl thrown in a closet. Who was afraid of a rubber overboot. Who was half overcome. A girl who came in the back door where they threw their garbage. Marie! Who never found the cup. Who had to eat their cold mush. Marie! Leopolda had her face buried in her knuckles. Saint Marie of the Holy Slops! Saint Marie of the Bread Fork! Saint Marie of the Burnt Back and Scalded Butt!

I broke out and laughed.

They looked up. All holy hell burst loose when they saw I'd woke. I still did not understand what was happening. They were watching, talking, but not to me.

"The marks . . ."

"She has her hand closed."

"Je ne peux pas voir."[2]

[2]French: I cannot see.

I was not stupid enough to ask what they were talking about. I couldn't tell why I was laying in white sheets. I couldn't tell why they were praying to me. But I'll tell you this: it seemed entirely natural. It was me. I lifted up my hand as in my dream. It was completely limp with sacredness.

"Peace be with you."

My arm was dried blood from the wrist down to the elbow. And it hurt. Their faces turned like flat flowers of adoration to follow that hand's movements. I let it swing through the air, imparting a saint's blessing. I had practiced. I knew exactly how to act.

They murmured. I heaved a sigh, and a golden beam of light suddenly broke through the clouded window and flooded down directly on my face. A stroke of perfect luck! They had to be convinced.

Leopolda still knelt in the back of the room. Her knuckles were crammed halfway down her throat. Let me tell you, a saint has senses honed keen as a wolf. I knew that she was over my barrel now. How it happened did not matter. The last thing I remembered was how she flew from the oven and stabbed me. That one thing was most certainly true.

"Come forward, Sister Leopolda." I gestured with my heavenly wound. Oh, it hurt. It bled when I reopened the slight heal. "Kneel beside me," I said.

She kneeled, but her voice box evidently did not work, for her mouth opened, shut, opened, but no sound came out. My throat clenched in noble delight I had read of as befitting a saint. She could not speak. But she was beaten. It was in her eyes. She stared at me now with all the deep hate of the wheel of devilish dust that rolled wild within her emptiness.

"What is it you want to tell me?" I asked. And at last she spoke.

"I have told my Sisters of your passion," she managed to choke out. "How the stigmata . . . the marks of the nails . . . appeared in your palm and you swooned at the holy vision. . . ."

"Yes," I said curiously.

And then, after a moment, I understood.

Leopolda had saved herself with her quick brain. She had witnessed a miracle. She had hid the fork and told this to the others. And of course they believed her, because they never knew how Satan came and went or where he took refuge.

"I saw it from the first," said the large one who put the bread in the oven. "Humility of the spirit. So rare in these girls."

"I saw it too," said the other one with great satisfaction. She sighed quietly. "If only it was me."

Leopolda was kneeling bolt upright, face blazing and twitching, a barely held fountain of blasting poison.

"Christ has marked me," I agreed.

I smiled the saint's smirk into her face. And then I looked at her. That was my mistake.

For I saw her kneeling there. Leopolda with her soul like a rubber overboot. With her face of a starved rat. With the desperate eyes drowning in the deep wells of her wrongness. There would be no one else after me. And I would leave. I saw Leopolda kneeling within the shambles of her love.

My heart had been about to surge from my chest with the blackness of my joyous heat. Now it dropped. I pitied her. I pitied her. Pity twisted in my stomach like that hook-pole was driven through me. I was caught. It was a feeling more terrible than any amount of boiling water and worse than being forked. Still, still, I could not help what I did. I had already smiled in a saint's mealy forgiveness. I heard myself speaking gently.

"Receive the dispensation of my sacred blood," I whispered.

But there was no heart in it. No joy when she bent to touch the floor. No dark leaping. I fell back into the white pillows. Blank dust was whirling through the light shafts. My skin was dust. Dust my lips. Dust the dirty spoons on the ends of my feet.

Rise up! I thought. Rise up and walk! There is no limit to this dust!

1984

Raymond Carver 1938–1988

Raymond Carver's characters have been called diminished and lost. Carver's study in character represents a cold look at the complicated inner lives of the working poor in the United States during the 1970s and 1980s: at any time, anyone might lose everything; not only material positions are lost but also trust, love, and truth. Carver may occasionally be naturalistic, but he is never nostalgic or romantic about life near the edge.

Carver lived much of his life in the same desperate straits as his characters. His father was a laborer with grand dreams and a deadly attraction to alcohol. Carver himself was married and raising two children before his twentieth birthday. He worked a variety of jobs that would never be presented as a career path on a résumé—picking tulips, pumping gas, sweeping up, delivering packages. He recalled, "Once I even considered, for a few minutes anyway—the job application form there in front of me—becoming a bill collector!" He and his wife declared bankruptcy several times. He inherited his father's drinking problem.

In 1958 with two small children, he and his wife moved to Chico, California. They borrowed $125 from the druggist who employed Carver as a delivery man. With that money, Carver enrolled in Chico State and took his first writing class from John Gardner, at that time a young, unknown, and unpublished novelist. Encouraged by Gardner and later by the editor Gordon Lish, Carver began to take himself seriously as a writer. He began to publish regularly in little magazines, but not until 1968 did his first book, a collection of poems, appear, in a limited edition. Eight years later his first collection of stories, *Will You Please Be Quiet, Please?* was published. Readers did not realize that Carver had stopped writing a couple of years before the book's publication.

In June 1977 Carver's life changed drastically. He stopped drinking, he was awarded a Guggenheim Fellowship, and he met the poet and short-story writer Tess Gallagher, who was to become his companion and eventually his second wife.

To the consternation of many editors, Carver was a rewriter of his own work. At least one of his stories has appeared with as many as three different titles and a slight rewriting at each publication. In an essay called "On Rewriting" he writes, "I like to mess with my stories. I'd rather tinker with a story after writing it, and then tinker some more, changing this, changing that, than have to write the story in the first place." Even his successful stories were not exempted from his rewriting. "The Bath," a widely praised story from *What We Talk About When We Talk About Love* and winner of the Carlos Fuentes Fiction Award, reappeared in a much longer form in *Cathedral* as "A Small, Good Thing." Writing in the *Washington Post,* Jonathan Yardley said, "The first version is beautifully crafted and admirably concise, but lacking in genuine compassion; the mysterious caller is not so much a human being as a mere voice, malign and characterless. But in the second version that voice becomes a person, one whose own losses are, in different ways, as crippling and heartbreaking as the one suffered by the grieving parents." Although many do not agree with Yardley, it is obvious that Carver found a different kind of strength in *Cathedral.*

Until his death from lung cancer in 1988 at the age of fifty, Carver continued to write poems and stories. His last book was a collection of poems called *A New Path to the Waterfall.*

Paul Jones
University of North Carolina–Chapel Hill

PRIMARY WORKS

Will You Please be Quiet, Please? 1976; *Furious Seasons,* 1977; *What We Talk About When We Talk About Love,* 1981; *Fires: Essays, Poems, and Stories, 1966–1982,* 1983; *Cathedral,* 1984; *Dostoevsky: The Screenplay,* 1985; *Where Water Comes Together With Other Water,* 1985; *Ultramarine,* 1986; *Saints,* 1987; *Where I'm Calling From: New and Selected Stories,* 1988; *A New Path To The Waterfall,* 1989; *No Heroics, Please: Uncollected Writings,* 1992; *Carnations: A One-Act Play,* 1992; *Short Cuts: Selected Stories,* 1993; *All of Us: The Collected Poems,* 1998.

from Cathedral

A Small, Good Thing

Saturday afternoon she drove to the bakery in the shopping center. After looking through a loose-leaf binder with photographs of cakes taped onto the pages, she ordered chocolate, the child's favorite. The cake she chose was decorated with a space ship and launching pad under a sprinkling of white stars, and a planet made of red frosting at the other end. His name, SCOTTY, would be in green letters beneath the planet. The baker, who was an older man with a thick neck, listened without saying anything when she told him the child would be eight years old next Monday. The baker wore a white apron that looked like a smock. Straps cut under his arms, went around in back and then to the front again, where they were secured under his heavy waist. He wiped his hands on his apron as he listened to her. He kept his eyes down on the photographs and let her talk. He let her take her time. He'd just come to work and he'd be there all night, baking, and he was in no real hurry.

She gave the baker her name, Ann Weiss, and her telephone number. The cake would be ready on Monday morning, just out of the oven, in plenty of time for the child's party that afternoon. The baker was not jolly. There were no pleasantries between them, just the minimum exchange of words, the necessary information. He made her feel uncomfortable, and she didn't like that. While he was bent over the counter with the pencil in his hand, she studied his coarse features and wondered if he'd ever done anything else with his life besides be a baker. She was a mother and thirty-three years old, and it seemed to her that everyone, especially someone the baker's age—a man old enough to be her father—must have children who'd gone through this special time of cakes and birthday parties. There must be that between them, she thought. But he was abrupt with her—not rude, just abrupt. She gave up trying to make friends with him. She looked into the back of the bakery and could see a long, heavy wooden table with aluminum pie pans stacked at one end; and beside the table a metal container filled with empty racks. There was an enormous oven. A radio was playing country-Western music.

The baker finished printing the information on the special order card and closed up the binder. He looked at her and said, "Monday morning." She thanked him and drove home.

On Monday morning, the birthday boy was walking to school with another boy. They were passing a bag of potato chips back and forth and the birthday boy was trying to find out what his friend intended to give him for his birthday that afternoon. Without looking, the birthday boy stepped off the curb at an intersection and was immediately knocked down by a car. He fell on his side with his head in the gutter and his legs out in the road. His eyes were closed, but his legs moved back and forth as if he were trying to climb over something. His friend dropped the potato chips and started to cry. The car had gone a hundred feet or so and stopped in the middle of the road. The man in the driver's seat looked back over his shoulder. He waited until the boy got unsteadily to his feet. The boy wobbled a little. He looked dazed, but okay. The driver put the car into gear and drove away.

The birthday boy didn't cry, but he didn't have anything to say about anything either. He wouldn't answer when his friend asked him what it felt like to be hit by a car. He walked home, and his friend went on to school. But after the birthday boy was inside his house and was telling his mother about it—she sitting beside him on the sofa, holding his hands in her lap, saying, "Scotty, honey, are you sure you feel all right, baby?" thinking she would call the doctor anyway—he suddenly lay back on the sofa, closed his eyes, and went limp. When she couldn't wake him up, she hurried to the telephone and called her husband at work. Howard told her to remain calm, remain calm, and then he called an ambulance for the child and left for the hospital himself.

Of course, the birthday party was canceled. The child was in the hospital with a mild concussion and suffering from shock. There'd been vomiting, and his lungs had taken in fluid which needed pumping out that afternoon. Now he simply seemed to be in a very deep sleep—but no coma, Dr. Francis had emphasized, no coma, when he saw the alarm in the parents' eyes. At eleven o'clock that night, when the boy seemed to be resting comfortably enough after the many X-rays and the lab work, and it was just a matter of his waking up and coming around, Howard left the hospital. He and Ann had been at the hospital with the child since that afternoon, and he was going home for a short while to bathe and change clothes. "I'll be back in an hour," he said. She nodded. "It's fine," she said. "I'll be right here." He kissed her on the forehead, and they touched hands. She sat in the chair beside the bed and looked at the child. She was waiting for him to wake up and be all right. Then she could begin to relax.

Howard drove home from the hospital. He took the wet, dark streets very fast, then caught himself and slowed down. Until now, his life had gone smoothly and to his satisfaction—college, marriage, another year of college for the advanced degree in business, a junior partnership in an investment firm. Fatherhood. He was happy and, so far, lucky—he knew that. His parents were still living, his brothers and his sister were established, his friends from college had gone out to take their places in the world. So far, he had kept away from any real harm, from those forces he knew existed and that could cripple or bring down a man if the luck went bad, if things suddenly turned. He pulled into the driveway and parked. His left leg began to tremble. He sat in the car for a minute and tried to deal with the present situation in a rational manner. Scotty had been hit by a car and was in the hospital, but he was going to be all right. Howard closed his eyes and ran his hand over his face. He got out of the car and went up to the front door. The dog was barking inside the house. The telephone rang and rang while he unlocked the door and fumbled for the light switch. He shouldn't have left the hospital, he shouldn't have. "Goddamn it!" he said. He picked up the receiver and said, "I just walked in the door!"

"There's a cake here that wasn't picked up," the voice on the other end of the line said.

"What are you saying?" Howard asked.

"A cake," the voice said. "A sixteen-dollar cake."

Howard held the receiver against his ear, trying to understand. "I don't know anything about a cake," he said. "Jesus, what are you talking about?"

"Don't hand me that," the voice said.

Howard hung up the telephone. He went into the kitchen and poured himself some whiskey. He called the hospital. But the child's condition remained the same; he was still sleeping and nothing had changed there. While water poured into the tub, Howard lathered his face and shaved. He'd just stretched out in the tub and closed his eyes when the telephone rang again. He hauled himself out, grabbed a towel, and hurried through the house, saying, "Stupid, stupid," for having left the hospital. But when he picked up the receiver and shouted, "Hello!" there was no sound at the other end of the line. Then the caller hung up.

He arrived back at the hospital a little after midnight. Ann still sat in the chair beside the bed. She looked up at Howard, and then she looked back at the child. The child's eyes stayed closed, the head was still wrapped in bandages. His breathing was quiet and regular. From an apparatus over the bed hung a bottle of glucose with a tube running from the bottle to the boy's arm.

"How is he?" Howard said. "What's all this?" waving at the glucose and the tube.

"Dr. Francis's orders," she said. "He needs nourishment. He needs to keep up his strength. Why doesn't he wake up, Howard? I don't understand, if he's all right."

Howard put his hand against the back of her head. He ran his fingers through her hair. "He's going to be all right. He'll wake up in a little while. Dr. Francis knows what's what."

After a time, he said, "Maybe you should go home and get some rest. I'll stay here. Just don't put up with this creep who keeps calling. Hang up right away."

"Who's calling?" she asked.

"I don't know who, just somebody with nothing better to do than call up people. You go on now."

She shook her head. "No," she said, "I'm fine."

"Really," he said. "Go home for a while, and then come back and spell me in the morning. It'll be all right. What did Dr. Francis say? He said Scotty's going to be all right. We don't have to worry. He's just sleeping now, that's all."

A nurse pushed the door open. She nodded at them as she went to the bedside. She took the left arm out from under the covers and put her fingers on the wrist, found the pulse, then consulted her watch. In a little while, she put the arm back under the covers and moved to the foot of the bed, where she wrote something on a clipboard attached to the bed.

"How is he?" Ann said. Howard's hand was a weight on her shoulder. She was aware of the pressure from his fingers.

"He's stable," the nurse said. Then she said, "Doctor will be in again shortly. Doctor's back in the hospital. He's making rounds right now."

"I was saying maybe she'd want to go home and get a little rest," Howard said. "After the doctor comes," he said.

"She could do that," the nurse said. "I think you should both feel free to do that, if you wish." The nurse was a big Scandinavian woman with blond hair. There was the trace of an accent in her speech.

"We'll see what the doctor says," Ann said. "I want to talk to the doctor. I don't think he should keep sleeping like this. I don't think that's a good sign." She brought her hand up to her eyes and let her head come forward a little. Howard's grip tightened on her shoulder, and then his hand moved up to her neck, where his fingers began to knead the muscles there.

"Dr. Francis will be here in a few minutes," the nurse said. Then she left the room.

Howard gazed at his son for a time, the small chest quietly rising and falling under the covers. For the first time since the terrible minutes after Ann's telephone call to him at his office, he felt a genuine fear starting in his limbs. He began shaking his head. Scotty was fine, but instead of sleeping at home in his own bed, he was in a hospital bed with bandages around his head and a tube in his arm. But this help was what he needed right now.

Dr. Francis came in and shook hands with Howard, though they'd just seen each other a few hours before. Ann got up from the chair. "Doctor?"

"Ann," he said and nodded. "Let's just first see how he's doing," the doctor said. He moved to the side of the bed and took the boy's pulse. He peeled back one eyelid and then the other. Howard and Ann stood beside the doctor and watched. Then the doctor turned back the covers and listened to the boy's heart and lungs with his stethoscope. He pressed his fingers here and there on the abdomen. When he was finished, he went to the end of the bed and studied the chart. He noted the time, scribbled something on the chart, and then looked at Howard and Ann.

"Doctor, how is he?" Howard said. "What's the matter with him exactly?"

"Why doesn't he wake up?" Ann said.

The doctor was a handsome, big-shouldered man with a tanned face. He wore a three-piece blue suit, a striped tie, and ivory cufflinks. His gray hair was combed along the sides of his head, and he looked as if he had just come from a concert. "He's all right," the doctor said. "Nothing to shout about, he could be better, I think. But he's all right. Still, I wish he'd wake up. He should wake up pretty soon." The doctor looked at the boy again. "We'll know some more in a couple of hours, after the results of a few more tests are in. But he's all right, believe me, except for the hairline fracture of the skull. He does have that."

"Oh, no," Ann said.

"And a bit of a concussion, as I said before. Of course, you know he's in shock," the doctor said. "Sometimes you see this in shock cases. This sleeping."

"But he's out of any real danger?" Howard said. "You said before he's not in a coma. You wouldn't call this a coma, then—would you, doctor?" Howard waited. He looked at the doctor.

"No, I don't want to call it a coma," the doctor said and glanced over at the boy once more. "He's just in a very deep sleep. It's a restorative measure the body is taking on its own. He's out of any real danger, I'd say that for certain, yes. But we'll know more when he wakes up and the other tests are in," the doctor said.

"It's a coma," Ann said. "Of sorts."

"It's not a coma yet, not exactly," the doctor said. "I wouldn't want to call it coma. Not yet, anyway. He's suffered shock. In shock cases, this kind of reaction is common enough; it's a temporary reaction to bodily trauma. Coma. Well, coma is a deep, prolonged unconsciousness, something that could go on for days, or weeks even. Scotty's not in that area, not as far as we can tell. I'm certain his condition will show improvement by morning. I'm betting that it will. We'll know more when he wakes up, which shouldn't be long now. Of course, you may do as you like, stay here or go home for a time. But by all means feel free to leave the hospital for a while if you want. This is not easy, I know." The doctor gazed at the boy again, watching him, and then he turned to Ann and said, "You try not to worry, little mother. Believe me, we're doing all that can be done. It's just a question of a little more time now." He nodded at her, shook hands with Howard again, and then he left the room.

Ann put her hand over the child's forehead. "At least he doesn't have a fever," she said. Then she said, "My God, he feels so cold, though. Howard? Is he supposed to feel like this? Feel his head."

Howard touched the child's temples. His own breathing had slowed. "I think he's supposed to feel this way right now," he said. "He's in shock, remember? That's what the doctor said. The doctor was just in here. He would have said something if Scotty wasn't okay."

Ann stood there a while longer, working her lip with her teeth. Then she moved over to her chair and sat down.

Howard sat in the chair next to her chair. They looked at each other. He wanted to say something else and reassure her, but he was afraid, too. He took her hand and put it in his lap, and this made him feel better, her hand being there. He picked up her hand and squeezed it. Then he just held her hand. They sat like that for a while, watching the boy and not talking. From time to time, he squeezed her hand. Finally, she took her hand away.

"I've been praying," she said.

He nodded.

She said, "I almost thought I'd forgotten how, but it came back to me. All I had to do was close my eyes and say, 'Please God, help us—help Scotty,' and then the rest was easy. The words were right there. Maybe if you prayed, too," she said to him.

"I've already prayed," he said. "I prayed this afternoon—yesterday afternoon, I mean—after you called, while I was driving to the hospital. I've been praying," he said.

"That's good," she said. For the first time, she felt they were together in it, this trouble. She realized with a start that, until now, it had only been happening to her and to Scotty. She hadn't let Howard into it, though he was there and needed all along. She felt glad to be his wife.

The same nurse came in and took the boy's pulse again and checked the flow from the bottle hanging above the bed.

In an hour, another doctor came in. He said his name was Parsons, from Radiology. He had a bushy mustache. He was wearing loafers, a Western shirt, and a pair of jeans.

"We're going to take him downstairs for more pictures," he told them. "We need to do some more pictures, and we want to do a scan."

"What's that?" Ann said. "A scan?" She stood between this new doctor and the bed. "I thought you'd already taken all your X-rays."

"I'm afraid we need some more," he said. "Nothing to be alarmed about. We just need some more pictures, and we want to do a brain scan on him."

"My God," Ann said.

"It's perfectly normal procedure in cases like this," this new doctor said. "We just need to find out for sure why he isn't back awake yet. It's normal medical procedure, and nothing to be alarmed about. We'll be taking him down in a few minutes," this doctor said.

In a little while, two orderlies came into the room with a gurney. They were black-haired, dark-complexioned men in white uniforms, and they said a few words to each other in a foreign tongue as they unhooked the boy from the tube and moved him from his bed to the gurney. Then they wheeled him from the room. Howard and Ann got on the same elevator. Ann gazed at the child. She closed her eyes as the elevator began its descent. The orderlies stood at either end of the gurney without saying anything, though once one of the men made a comment to the other in their own language, and the other man nodded slowly in response.

Later that morning, just as the sun was beginning to lighten the windows in the waiting room outside the X-ray department, they brought the boy out and moved him back up to his room. Howard and Ann rode up on the elevator with him once more, and once more they took up their places beside the bed.

They waited all day, but still the boy did not wake up. Occasionally, one of them would leave the room to go downstairs to the cafeteria to drink coffee and then, as if suddenly remembering and feeling guilty, get up from the table and hurry back to the room. Dr. Francis came again that afternoon and examined the boy once more and then left after telling them he was coming along and could wake up at any minute now. Nurses, different nurses from the night before, came in from time to time. Then a young woman from the lab knocked and entered the room. She wore white slacks and a white blouse and carried a little tray of things which she put on the stand beside the bed. Without a word to them, she took blood from the boy's arm. Howard closed his eyes as the woman found the right place on the boy's arm and pushed the needle in.

"I don't understand this," Ann said to the woman.

"Doctor's orders," the young woman said. "I do what I'm told. They say draw that one, I draw. What's wrong with him, anyway?" she said. "He's a sweetie."

"He was hit by a car," Howard said. "A hit-and-run."

The young woman shook her head and looked again at the boy. Then she took her tray and left the room.

"Why won't he wake up?" Ann said. "Howard? I want some answers from these people."

Howard didn't say anything. He sat down again in the chair and crossed one leg over the other. He rubbed his face. He looked at his son and then he settled back in the chair, closed his eyes, and went to sleep.

Ann walked to the window and looked out at the parking lot. It was night, and cars were driving into and out of the parking lot with their lights on. She stood at the window with her hands gripping the sill, and knew in her heart that they were into something now, something hard. She was afraid, and her teeth began to chatter until she tightened her jaws. She saw a big car stop in front of the hospital and someone, a woman in a long coat, get into the car. She wished she were that woman and somebody, anybody, was driving her away from here to somewhere else, a place where she would find Scotty waiting for her when she stepped out of the car, ready to say *Mom* and let her gather him in her arms.

In a little while, Howard woke up. He looked at the boy again. Then he got up from the chair, stretched, and went over to stand beside her at the window. They both stared out at the parking lot. They didn't say anything. But they seemed to feel each other's insides now, as though the worry had made them transparent in a perfectly natural way.

The door opened and Dr. Francis came in. He was wearing a different suit and tie this time. His gray hair was combed along the sides of his head, and he looked as if he had just shaved. He went straight to the bed and examined the boy. "He ought to have come around by now. There's just no good reason for this," he said. "But I can tell you we're all convinced he's out of any danger. We'll just feel better when he wakes up. There's no reason, absolutely none, why he shouldn't come around. Very soon. Oh, he'll have himself a dilly of a headache when he does, you can count on that. But all of his signs are fine. They're as normal as can be."

"It is a coma, then?" Ann said.

The doctor rubbed his smooth cheek. "We'll call it that for the time being, until he wakes up. But you must be worn out. This is hard. I know this is hard. Feel free to go out for a bite," he said. "It would do you good. I'll put a nurse in here while you're gone if you'll feel better about going. Go and have yourselves something to eat."

"I couldn't eat anything," Ann said.

"Do what you need to do, of course," the doctor said. "Anyway, I wanted to tell you that all the signs are good, the tests are negative, nothing showed up at all, and just as soon as he wakes up he'll be over the hill."

"Thank you, doctor," Howard said. He shook hands with the doctor again. The doctor patted Howard's shoulder and went out.

"I suppose one of us should go home and check on things," Howard said. "Slug needs to be fed, for one thing."

"Call one of the neighbors," Ann said. "Call the Morgans. Anyone will feed a dog if you ask them to."

"All right," Howard said. After a while, he said, "Honey, why don't *you* do it? Why don't you go home and check on things, and then come back? It'll do you good. I'll be right here with him. Seriously," he said. "We need to keep up our strength on this. We'll want to be here for a while even after he wakes up."

"Why don't *you* go?" she said. "Feed Slug. Feed yourself."

"I already went," he said. "I was gone for exactly an hour and fifteen minutes. You go home for an hour and freshen up. Then come back."

She tried to think about it, but she was too tired. She closed her eyes and tried to think about it again. After a time, she said, "Maybe I *will* go home for a few minutes. Maybe if I'm not just sitting right here watching him every second, he'll wake up and be all right. You know? Maybe he'll wake up if I'm not here. I'll go home and take a bath and put on clean clothes. I'll feed Slug. Then I'll come back."

"I'll be right here," he said. "You go on home, honey. I'll keep an eye on things here." His eyes were bloodshot and small, as if he'd been drinking for a long time. His clothes were rumpled. His beard had come out again. She touched his face, and then she took her hand back. She understood he wanted to be by himself for a while, not have to talk or share his worry for a time. She picked her purse up from the nightstand, and he helped her into her coat.

"I won't be gone long," she said.

"Just sit and rest for a little while when you get home," he said. "Eat something. Take a bath. After you get out of the bath, just sit for a while and rest. It'll do you a world of good, you'll see. Then come back," he said. "Let's try not to worry. You heard what Dr. Francis said."

She stood in her coat for a minute trying to recall the doctor's exact words, looking for any nuances, any hint of something behind his words other than what he had said. She tried to remember if his expression had changed any when he bent over to examine the child. She remembered the way his features had composed themselves as he rolled back the child's eyelids and then listened to his breathing.

She went to the door, where she turned and looked back. She looked at the child, and then she looked at the father. Howard nodded. She stepped out of the room and pulled the door closed behind her.

She went past the nurses' station and down to the end of the corridor, looking for the elevator. At the end of the corridor, she turned to her right and entered a little waiting room where a Negro family sat in wicker chairs. There was a middle-aged man in a khaki shirt and pants, a baseball cap pushed back on his head. A large woman wearing a housedress and slippers was slumped in one of the chairs. A teenaged girl in jeans, hair done in dozens of little braids, lay stretched out in one of the chairs smoking a cigarette, her legs crossed at the ankles. The family swung their eyes to Ann as she entered the room. The little table was littered with hamburger wrappers and Styrofoam cups.

"Franklin," the large woman said as she roused herself. "Is it about Franklin?" Her eyes widened. "Tell me now, lady," the woman said. "Is it about Franklin?" She was trying to rise from her chair, but the man had closed his hand over her arm.

"Here, here," he said. "Evelyn."

"I'm sorry," Ann said. "I'm looking for the elevator. My son is in the hospital, and now I can't find the elevator."

"Elevator is down that way, turn left," the man said as he aimed a finger.

The girl drew on her cigarette and stared at Ann. Her eyes were narrowed to slits, and her broad lips parted slowly as she let the smoke escape. The Negro woman let her head fall on her shoulder and looked away from Ann, no longer interested.

"My son was hit by a car," Ann said to the man. She seemed to need to explain herself. "He has a concussion and a little skull fracture, but he's going to be all right. He's in shock now, but it might be some kind of coma, too. That's what really worries us, the coma part. I'm going out for a little while, but my husband is with him. Maybe he'll wake up while I'm gone."

"That's too bad," the man said and shifted in the chair. He shook his head. He looked down at the table, and then he looked back at Ann. She was still standing there. He said, "Our Franklin, he's on the operating table. Somebody cut him. Tried to kill him. There was a fight where he was at. At this party. They say he was just standing and watching. Not bothering nobody. But that don't mean nothing these days. Now he's on the operating table. We're just hoping and praying, that's all we can do now." He gazed at her steadily.

Ann looked at the girl again, who was still watching her, and at the older woman, who kept her head down, but whose eyes were now closed. Ann saw the lips moving silently, making words. She had an urge to ask what those words were. She wanted to talk more with these people who were in the same kind of waiting she was in. She was afraid, and they were afraid. They had that in common. She would have liked to have said something else about the accident, told them more about Scotty, that it had happened on the day of his birthday, Monday, and that he was still unconscious. Yet she didn't know how to begin. She stood looking at them without saying anything more.

She went down the corridor the man had indicated and found the elevator. She waited a minute in front of the closed doors, still wondering if she was doing the right thing. Then she put out her finger and touched the button.

She pulled into the driveway and cut the engine. She closed her eyes and leaned her head against the wheel for a minute. She listened to the ticking sounds the engine made as it began to cool. Then she got out of the car. She could hear the dog barking inside the house. She went to the front door, which was unlocked. She went inside and turned on lights and put on a kettle of water for tea. She opened some dogfood and fed Slug on the back porch. The dog ate in hungry little smacks. It kept running into the kitchen to see that she was going to stay. As she sat down on the sofa with her tea, the telephone rang.

"Yes!" she said as she answered. "Hello!"

"Mrs. Weiss," a man's voice said. It was five o'clock in the morning, and she thought she could hear machinery or equipment of some kind in the background.

"Yes, yes! What is it?" she said. "This is Mrs. Weiss. This is she. What is it, please?" She listened to whatever it was in the background. "Is it Scotty, for Christ's sake?"

"Scotty," the man's voice said. "It's about Scotty, yes. It has to do with Scotty, that problem. Have you forgotten about Scotty?" the man said. Then he hung up.

She dialed the hospital's number and asked for the third floor. She demanded information about her son from the nurse who answered the telephone. Then she asked to speak to her husband. It was, she said, an emergency.

She waited, turning the telephone cord in her fingers. She closed her eyes and felt sick at her stomach. She would have to make herself eat. Slug came in from the back porch and lay down near her feet. He wagged his tail. She pulled at his ear while he licked her fingers. Howard was on the line.

"Somebody just called here," she said. She twisted the telephone cord. "He said it was about Scotty," she cried.

"Scotty's fine," Howard told her. "I mean, he's still sleeping. There's been no change. The nurse has been in twice since you've been gone. A nurse or else a doctor. He's all right."

"This man called. He said it was about Scotty," she told him.

"Honey, you rest for a little while, you need the rest. It must be that same caller I had. Just forget it. Come back down here after you've rested. Then we'll have breakfast or something."

"Breakfast," she said. "I don't want any breakfast."

"You know what I mean," he said. "Juice, something. I don't know. I don't know anything, Ann. Jesus, I'm not hungry, either. Ann, it's hard to talk now. I'm standing here at the desk. Dr. Francis is coming again at eight o'clock this morning. He's going to have something to tell us then, something more definite. That's what one of the nurses said. She didn't know any more than that. Ann? Honey, maybe we'll know something more then. At eight o'clock. Come back here before eight. Meanwhile, I'm right here and Scotty's all right. He's still the same," he added.

"I was drinking a cup of tea," she said, "when the telephone rang. They said it was about Scotty. There was a noise in the background. Was there a noise in the background on that call you had, Howard?"

"I don't remember," he said. "Maybe the driver of the car, maybe he's a psychopath and found out about Scotty somehow. But I'm here with him. Just rest like you were going to do. Take a bath and come back by seven or so, and we'll talk to the doctor together when he gets here. It's going to be all right, honey. I'm here, and there are doctors and nurses around. They say his condition is stable."

"I'm scared to death," she said.

She ran water, undressed, and got into the tub. She washed and dried quickly, not taking the time to wash her hair. She put on clean underwear, wool slacks, and a sweater. She went into the living room, where the dog looked up at her and let its tail thump once against the floor. It was just starting to get light outside when she went out to the car.

She drove into the parking lot of the hospital and found a space close to the front door. She felt she was in some obscure way responsible for what had happened to the child. She let her thoughts move to the Negro family. She remembered the name Franklin and the table that was covered with hamburger papers, and the teenaged girl staring at her as she drew on her cigarette. "Don't have children," she told the girl's image as she entered the front door of the hospital. "For God's sake, don't."

* * *

She took the elevator up to the third floor with two nurses who were just going on duty. It was Wednesday morning, a few minutes before seven. There was a page for a Dr. Madison as the elevator doors slid open on the third floor. She got off behind the nurses, who turned in the other direction and continued the conversation she had interrupted when she'd gotten into the elevator. She walked down the corridor to the little alcove where the Negro family had been waiting. They were gone now, but the chairs were scattered in such a way that it looked as if people had just jumped up from them the minute before. The tabletop was cluttered with the same cups and papers, the ashtray was filled with cigarette butts.

She stopped at the nurses' station. A nurse was standing behind the counter, brushing her hair and yawning.

"There was a Negro boy in surgery last night," Ann said. "Franklin was his name. His family was in the waiting room. I'd like to inquire about his condition."

A nurse who was sitting at a desk behind the counter looked up from a chart in front of her. The telephone buzzed and she picked up the receiver, but she kept her eyes on Ann.

"He passed away," said the nurse at the counter. The nurse held the hairbrush and kept looking at her. "Are you a friend of the family or what?"

"I met the family last night," Ann said. "My own son is in the hospital. I guess he's in shock. We don't know for sure what's wrong. I just wondered about Franklin, that's all. Thank you." She moved down the corridor. Elevator doors the same color as the walls slid open and a gaunt, bald man in white pants and white canvas shoes pulled a heavy cart off the elevator. She hadn't noticed these doors last night. The man wheeled the cart out into the corridor and stopped in front of the room nearest the elevator and consulted a clipboard. Then he reached down and slid a tray out of the cart. He rapped lightly on the door and entered the room. She could smell the unpleasant odors of warm food as she passed the cart. She hurried on without looking at any of the nurses and pushed open the door to the child's room.

Howard was standing at the window with his hands behind his back. He turned around as she came in.

"How is he?" she said. She went over to the bed. She dropped her purse on the floor beside the nightstand. It seemed to her she had been gone a long time. She touched the child's face. "Howard?"

"Dr. Francis was here a little while ago," Howard said. She looked at him closely and thought his shoulders were bunched a little.

"I thought he wasn't coming until eight o'clock this morning," she said quickly.

"There was another doctor with him. A neurologist."

"A neurologist," she said.

Howard nodded. His shoulders were bunching, she could see that. "What'd they say, Howard? For Christ's sake, what'd they say? What is it?"

"They said they're going to take him down and run more tests on him, Ann. They think they're going to operate, honey. Honey, they *are* going to operate. They can't figure out why he won't wake up. It's more than just shock or concussion, they know that much now. It's in his skull, the fracture, it has something, something to do with that, they think. So they're going to operate. I tried to call you, but I guess you'd already left the house."

"Oh, God," she said. "Oh, please, Howard, please," she said, taking his arms.

"Look!" Howard said. "Scotty! Look, Ann!" He turned her toward the bed.

The boy had opened his eyes, then closed them. He opened them again now. The eyes stared straight ahead for a minute, then moved slowly in his head until they rested on Howard and Ann, then traveled away again.

"Scotty," his mother said, moving to the bed.

"Hey, Scott," his father said. "Hey, son."

They leaned over the bed. Howard took the child's hand in his hands and began to pat and squeeze the hand. Ann bent over the boy and kissed his forehead again and again. She put her hands on either side of his face. "Scotty, honey, it's Mommy and Daddy," she said. "Scotty?"

The boy looked at them, but without any sign of recognition. Then his mouth opened, his eyes scrunched closed, and he howled until he had no more air in his lungs. His face seemed to relax and soften then. His lips parted as his last breath was puffed through his throat and exhaled gently through the clenched teeth.

The doctors called it a hidden occlusion and said it was a one-in-a-million circumstance. Maybe if it could have been detected somehow and surgery undertaken immediately, they could have saved him. But more than likely not. In any case, what would they have been looking for? Nothing had shown up in the tests or in the X-rays.

Dr. Francis was shaken. "I can't tell you how badly I feel. I'm so very sorry, I can't tell you," he said as he led them into the doctors' lounge. There was a doctor sitting in a chair with his legs hooked over the back of another chair, watching an early-morning TV show. He was wearing a green delivery-room outfit, loose green pants and green blouse, and a green cap that covered his hair. He looked at Howard and Ann and then looked at Dr. Francis. He got to his feet and turned off the set and went out of the room. Dr. Francis guided Ann to the sofa, sat down beside her, and began to talk in a low, consoling voice. At one point, he leaned over and embraced her. She could feel his chest rising and falling evenly against her shoulder. She kept her eyes open and let him hold her. Howard went into the bathroom, but he left the door open. After a violent fit of weeping, he ran water and washed his face. Then he came out and sat down at the little table that held a telephone. He looked at the telephone as though deciding what to do first. He made some calls. After a time, Dr. Francis used the telephone.

"Is there anything else I can do for the moment?" he asked them.

Howard shook his head. Ann stared at Dr. Francis as if unable to comprehend his words.

The doctor walked them to the hospital's front door. People were entering and leaving the hospital. It was eleven o'clock in the morning. Ann was aware of how slowly, almost reluctantly, she moved her feet. It seemed to her that Dr. Francis was making them leave when she felt they should stay, when it would be more the right thing to do to stay. She gazed out into the parking lot and then turned around and looked back at the front of the hospital. She began shaking her head. "No, no," she said. "I can't leave him here, no." She heard herself say that and thought how unfair it was that the only words that came out were the sort of words used on TV shows where people were stunned by violent or sudden deaths. She wanted her words to be her own. "No," she said, and for some reason the memory of the Negro woman's head lolling on the woman's shoulder came to her. "No," she said again.

"I'll be talking to you later in the day," the doctor was saying to Howard. "There are still some things that have to be done, things that have to be cleared up to our satisfaction. Some things that need explaining."

"An autopsy," Howard said.

Dr. Francis nodded.

"I understand," Howard said. Then he said, "Oh, Jesus. No, I don't understand, doctor. I can't, I can't. I just can't."

Dr. Francis put his arm around Howard's shoulders. "I'm sorry. God, how I'm sorry." He let go of Howard's shoulders and held out his hand. Howard looked at the hand, and then he took it. Dr. Francis put his arms around Ann once more. He seemed full of some goodness she didn't understand. She let her head rest on his shoulder, but her eyes stayed open. She kept looking at the hospital. As they drove out of the parking lot, she looked back at the hospital.

At home, she sat on the sofa with her hands in her coat pockets. Howard closed the door to the child's room. He got the coffee-maker going and then he found an empty box. He had thought to pick up some of the child's things that were scattered around the living room. But instead he sat down beside her on the sofa, pushed the box to one side, and leaned forward, arms between his knees. He began to weep. She pulled his head over into her lap and patted his shoulder. "He's gone," she said. She kept patting his shoulder. Over his sobs, she could hear the coffee-maker hissing in the kitchen. "There, there," she said tenderly. "Howard, he's gone. He's gone and now we'll have to get used to that. To being alone."

In a little while, Howard got up and began moving aimlessly around the room with the box, not putting anything into it, but collecting some things together on the floor at one end of the sofa. She continued to sit with her hands in her coat pockets. Howard put the box down and brought coffee into the living room. Later, Ann made calls to relatives. After each call had been placed and the party had answered, Ann would blurt out a few words and cry for a minute. Then she would quietly explain, in a measured voice, what had happened and tell them about arrangements. Howard took the box out to the garage, where he saw the child's bicycle. He dropped the box and sat down on the pavement beside the bicycle. He took hold of the bicycle awkwardly so that it leaned against his chest. He held it, the rubber pedal sticking into his chest. He gave the wheel a turn.

Ann hung up the telephone after talking to her sister. She was looking up another number when the telephone rang. She picked it up on the first ring.

"Hello," she said, and she heard something in the background, a humming noise. "Hello!" she said. "For God's sake," she said. "Who is this? What is it you want?"

"Your Scotty, I got him ready for you," the man's voice said. "Did you forget him?"

"You evil bastard!" she shouted into the receiver. "How can you do this, you evil son of a bitch?"

"Scotty," the man said. "Have you forgotten about Scotty?" Then the man hung up on her.

Howard heard the shouting and came in to find her with her head on her arms over the table, weeping. He picked up the receiver and listened to the dial tone.

* * *

Much later, just before midnight, after they had dealt with many things, the telephone rang again.

"You answer it," she said. "Howard, it's him, I know." They were sitting at the kitchen table with coffee in front of them. Howard had a small glass of whiskey beside his cup. He answered on the third ring.

"Hello," he said. "Who is this? Hello! Hello!" The line went dead. "He hung up," Howard said. "Whoever it was."

"It was him," she said. "That bastard. I'd like to kill him," she said. "I'd like to shoot him and watch him kick," she said.

"Ann, my God," he said.

"Could you hear anything?" she said. "In the background? A noise, machinery, something humming?"

"Nothing, really. Nothing like that," he said. "There wasn't much time. I think there was some radio music. Yes, there was a radio going, that's all I could tell. I don't know what in God's name is going on," he said.

She shook her head. "If I could, could get my hands on him." It came to her then. She knew who it was. Scotty, the cake, the telephone number. She pushed the chair away from the table and got up. "Drive me down to the shopping center," she said. "Howard."

"What are you saying?"

"The shopping center. I know who it is who's calling. I know who it is. It's the baker, the son-of-a-bitching baker, Howard. I had him bake a cake for Scotty's birthday. That's who's calling. That's who has the number and keeps calling us. To harass us about that cake. The baker, that bastard."

They drove down to the shopping center. The sky was clear and stars were out. It was cold, and they ran the heater in the car. They parked in front of the bakery. All of the shops and stores were closed, but there were cars at the far end of the lot in front of the movie theater. The bakery windows were dark, but when they looked through the glass they could see a light in the back room and, now and then, a big man in an apron moving in and out of the white, even light. Through the glass, she could see the display cases and some little tables with chairs. She tried the door. She rapped on the glass. But if the baker heard them, he gave no sign. He didn't look in their direction.

They drove around behind the bakery and parked. They got out of the car. There was a lighted window too high up for them to see inside. A sign near the back door said THE PANTRY BAKERY, SPECIAL ORDERS. She could hear faintly a radio playing inside and something creak—an oven door as it was pulled down? She knocked on the door and waited. Then she knocked again, louder. The radio was turned down and there was a scraping sound now, the distinct sound of something, a drawer, being pulled open and then closed.

Someone unlocked the door and opened it. The baker stood in the light and peered out at them. "I'm closed for business," he said. "What do you want at this hour? It's midnight. Are you drunk or something?"

She stepped into the light that fell through the open door. He blinked his heavy eyelids as he recognized her. "It's you," he said.

"It's me," she said. "Scotty's mother. This is Scotty's father. We'd like to come in."

The baker said, "I'm busy now. I have work to do."

She had stepped inside the doorway anyway. Howard came in behind her. The baker moved back. "It smells like a bakery in here. Doesn't it smell like a bakery in here, Howard?"

"What do you want?" the baker said. "Maybe you want your cake? That's it, you decided you want your cake. You ordered a cake, didn't you?"

"You're pretty smart for a baker," she said. "Howard, this is the man who's been calling us." She clenched her fists. She stared at him fiercely. There was a deep burning inside her, an anger that made her feel larger than herself, larger than either of these men.

"Just a minute here," the baker said. "You want to pick up your three-day-old cake? That it? I don't want to argue with you, lady. There it sits over there, getting stale. I'll give it to you for half of what I quoted you. No. You want it? You can have it. It's no good to me, no good to anyone now. It cost me time and money to make that cake. If you want it, okay, if you don't, that's okay, too. I have to get back to work." He looked at them and rolled his tongue behind his teeth.

"More cakes," she said. She knew she was in control of it, of what was increasing in her. She was calm.

"Lady, I work sixteen hours a day in this place to earn a living," the baker said. He wiped his hands on his apron. "I work night and day in here, trying to make ends meet." A look crossed Ann's face that made the baker move back and say, "No trouble, now." He reached to the counter and picked up a rolling pin with his right hand and began to tap it against the palm of his other hand. "You want the cake or not? I have to get back to work. Bakers work at night," he said again. His eyes were small, mean-looking, she thought, nearly lost in the bristly flesh around his cheeks. His neck was thick with fat.

"I know bakers work at night," Ann said. "They make phone calls at night, too. You bastard," she said.

The baker continued to tap the rolling pin against his hand. He glanced at Howard. "Careful, careful," he said to Howard.

"My son's dead," she said with a cold, even finality. "He was hit by a car Monday morning. We've been waiting with him until he died. But, of course, you couldn't be expected to know that, could you? Bakers can't know everything—can they, Mr. Baker? But he's dead. He's dead, you bastard!" Just as suddenly as it had welled in her, the anger dwindled, gave way to something else, a dizzy feeling of nausea. She leaned against the wooden table that was sprinkled with flour, put her hands over her face, and began to cry, her shoulders rocking back and forth. "It isn't fair," she said. "It isn't, isn't fair."

Howard put his hand at the small of her back and looked at the baker. "Shame on you," Howard said to him. "Shame."

The baker put the rolling pin back on the counter. He undid his apron and threw it on the counter. He looked at them, and then he shook his head slowly. He pulled a chair out from under the card table that held papers and receipts, an adding machine, and a telephone directory. "Please sit down," he said. "Let me get you a chair," he said to Howard. "Sit down now, please." The baker went into the front of the shop and returned with two little wrought-iron chairs. "Please sit down, you people."

Ann wiped her eyes and looked at the baker. "I wanted to kill you," she said. "I wanted you dead."

The baker had cleared a space for them at the table. He shoved the adding machine to one side, along with the stacks of notepaper and receipts. He pushed the telephone directory onto the floor, where it landed with a thud. Howard and Ann sat down and pulled their chairs up to the table. The baker sat down, too.

"Let me say how sorry I am," the baker said, putting his elbows on the table. "God alone knows how sorry. Listen to me. I'm just a baker. I don't claim to be anything else. Maybe once, maybe years ago, I was a different kind of human being. I've forgotten, I don't know for sure. But I'm not any longer, if I ever was. Now I'm just a baker. That don't excuse my doing what I did, I know. But I'm deeply sorry. I'm sorry for your son, and sorry for my part in this," the baker said. He spread his hands out on the table and turned them over to reveal his palms. "I don't have any children myself, so I can only imagine what you must be feeling. All I can say to you now is that I'm sorry. Forgive me, if you can," the baker said. "I'm not an evil man, I don't think. Not evil, like you said on the phone. You got to understand what it comes down to is I don't know how to act anymore, it would seem. Please," the man said, "let me ask you if you can find it in your hearts to forgive me?"

It was warm inside the bakery. Howard stood up from the table and took off his coat. He helped Ann from her coat. The baker looked at them for a minute and then nodded and got up from the table. He went to the oven and turned off some switches. He found cups and poured coffee from an electric coffee-maker. He put a carton of cream on the table, and a bowl of sugar.

"You probably need to eat something," the baker said. "I hope you'll eat some of my hot rolls. You have to eat and keep going. Eating is a small, good thing in a time like this," he said.

He served them warm cinnamon rolls just out of the oven, the icing still runny. He put butter on the table and knives to spread the butter. Then the baker sat down at the table with them. He waited. He waited until they each took a roll from the platter and began to eat. "It's good to eat something," he said, watching them. "There's more. Eat up. Eat all you want. There's all the rolls in the world in here."

They ate rolls and drank coffee. Ann was suddenly hungry, and the rolls were warm and sweet. She ate three of them, which pleased the baker. Then he began to talk. They listened carefully. Although they were tired and in anguish, they listened to what the baker had to say. They nodded when the baker began to speak of loneliness, and of the sense of doubt and limitation that had come to him in his middle years. He told them what it was like to be childless all these years. To repeat the days with the ovens endlessly full and endlessly empty. The party food, the celebrations he'd worked over. Icing knuckle-deep. The tiny wedding couples stuck into cakes. Hundreds of them, no, thousands by now. Birthdays. Just imagine all those candles burning. He had a necessary trade. He was a baker. He was glad he wasn't a florist. It was better to be feeding people. This was a better smell anytime than flowers.

"Smell this," the baker said, breaking open a dark loaf. "It's a heavy bread, but rich." They smelled it, then he had them taste it. It had the taste of molasses and coarse grains. They listened to him. They ate what they could. They swallowed the dark bread. It was like daylight under the fluorescent trays of light. They talked on into the early morning, the high, pale cast of light in the windows, and they did not think of leaving.

1984

Wendy Rose (Hopi) b. 1948

Wendy Rose was born in Oakland, California, and is of Hopi, Miwok, English, Scottish, Irish, and German extraction. She spent her childhood in the Bay Area just as that region experienced its postwar boom and urban sprawl. She grew up coming to terms with her ethnicity, her gender, and with an Indian's place (or lack of it) in an urban setting. In 1976 she married Arthur Murata while she was an anthropology student at the University of California, Berkeley, which she had entered as an undergraduate in 1974. She received her master's degree there in cultural anthropology in 1978 and is enrolled in the doctoral program. She taught from 1979 to 1983 at the same school in both Ethnic Studies and Native American Studies before going to teach (1983–84) at Fresno State University and then in 1984 to her current position as the Coordinator of the American Indian Studies Program at Fresno City College, California. She serves on the Modern Languages Association Commission on Languages and Literatures of America. In response to her ethnic role, she is active in a wide array of American Indian community affairs. At the same time, Wendy Rose works on more poems as well as on a bilingual Hopi-English manuscript. She still collects entries for a massive compilation of an annotated bibliography of published books by Native American authors in the United States and Canada.

She is best known as an American Indian poet. She is one of the premier American Indian women poets of today. Her work is widely anthologized in American literary titles. Her poems show a persistent evolution and understanding of her own voice as an Indian, as a woman, and as a poet. Her poetry serves as a bridge between ancient storytellers and singers and the modern analyst of literature and culture. She sees American culture critically from the inside as well as from the outside. Her poems project the defiance of indigenous peoples in this century, the poignancy of a precarious survival in an occupied land, and a challenge to the Eurocentric poetic tradition while at the same time using its medium to convey her images. Her verse combines pieces from her own background, glimpses of modern American life, and bits from Indian tradition to weave a tapestry of contemporary indigenous poetry that is unsurpassed in its realism and beauty. Wendy Rose's poetry also carries the rage of a mixed-blood American Indian and that of a woman in a male-dominated academic environment, as seen in her 1977 *Academic Squaw.* Her poems present the tragedy of the loss of millions of native lives under the onslaught of Europeans coming to the New World, yet also preserve the strength for survival of the remaining Indian women of the hemisphere. This sense of poignancy is captured in her poem "To the Hopi in Richmond." Rose's poetry offers a slice of contemporary American Indian existence in the United States, bringing back to the late twentieth century the sacredness and balance of the ancients among the American Indians.

C. B. Clark
Oklahoma City University

PRIMARY WORKS

Hopi Roadrunner Dancing, 1973; *Long Division: A Tribal History,* 1977; *Academic Squaw: Reports to the World from the Ivory Tower,* 1977; *Poetry of the American Indian* Series, 1978; *Builder Kachina: A Home-Going Cycle,* 1979; *Lost Copper,* 1980; *What Happened When the Hopi Hit New York,* 1982; *Halfbreed Chronicles,* 1985; *Great Pretenders: Further Reflections on Whiteshamanism,* 1992; *Going to War with All My Relations,* 1993; *Now Proof She Is Gone,* 1994; *Bone Dance: New and Selected Poems, 1965–1993,* 1994.

Throat Song: The Rotating Earth

"Eskimo throat singers imitate the sounds the women hear . . .
listening to the sound of wind going through the cracks of an igloo
. . . the sound of the sea shore, a river of geese, the sound of the
northern lights while the lights are coming closer . . . in the old days
the people used to think the world was flat, but when they learned
the world was turning, they made a throat-singing song about it."
–INUKTITUT MAGAZINE, DECEMBER 1980

I always knew you were singing!

As my fingers have pulled your clay,
as your mountains have pulled the clay of me;
as my knees have deeply printed your mud,
as your winds have drawn me down and dried the mud of me;

around me always the drone and scrape of stone,
small movements atom by atom I heard like tiny drums;
I heard flutes and reeds that whine in the wind,
the bongo scratch of beetles in redwood bark,

the constant rattle that made of this land
a great gourd!

Oh I always knew you were singing!

1982

Loo-wit[1]

The way they do
this old woman
no longer cares
what others think
but spits her black tobacco
any which way
stretching full length
from her bumpy bed.
Finally up
she sprinkles ash on the snow,
cold and rocky buttes
that promise nothing
but winter is going at last.
Centuries of cedar
have bound her to earth,
huckleberry ropes
lay prickly about her neck.
Her children play games
(no sense of tomorrow);
her eyes are covered
with bark and she wakes
at night, fears
she is blind.
Nothing but tricks
left in this world,
nothing to keep
an old woman home.
Around her
machinery growls,
snarls and ploughs
great patches of her skin.
She crouches
in the north,
the source
of her trembling—
dawn appearing
with the shudder
of her slopes.
Blackberries unravel,

[1]Loo-wit: "Lady of Fire," Mt. St. Helens.

stones dislodge;
it's not as if
they weren't warned.

She was sleeping
but she heard the boot scrape;
the creaking floor;
felt the pull of the blanket
from her thin shoulder.
With one free heand
she finds her weapons
and raises them high;
clearing the twigs from her throat
she sings, she sings,
shaking the sky like a blanket about her
Loo-wit sings and sings and sings!

1983

To the Hopi in Richmond[1] (Santa Fe Indian Village)

My people in boxcars
my people   my pain
united by the window steam
of lamb stew cooking

and the metal
of your walls,
your floors with cracks and crickets,
your tin roofs
full of holes;

that rain you prayed for
thousands of years
comes now
when you live
in a world
of water.

[1]A small colony of Hopi were brought to the San Francisco Bay area to build railroads and they remained.

So remember
the sun
remember it was not easy
the gentle sun
of August mornings
remember it

as you pray today
for the rain
below the mesas;
the moisture
in your fields.

1985

If I Am Too Brown or Too White for You

remember I am a garnet woman
whirling into precision
as a crystal arithmetic
or a cluster and so

why the dream
in my mouth,
the flutter of blackbirds
at my wrists?

In the morning
there you are
at the edge of the river
on one knee

and you are selecting me
from among polished stones
more definitely red or white
between which tiny serpents swim

and you see that my body
is blood frozen
into giving birth
over and over in a single motion

and you touch the matrix
shattered in winter

and begin to piece together
the shape of me

wanting the fit in your palm
to be perfect
and the image less
clouded, less mixed

but you always see
just in time
working me around
in the evening sun

there is a small light
in the smoke, a tiny sun
in the blood, so deep
it is there and not there,

so pure
it is singing.

1985

Story Keeper

The stories would be braided in my hair
between the plastic combs and blue wing tips
but as the rattles would spit,
the drums begin,
along would come someone
to stifle and stop the sound
and the story keeper I would have been
must melt into the cave
of artifacts discarded

and this is a wound
to be healed
in the spin of winter,
the spiral
of beginning.
This is the task:
to find the stories now
and to heave at the rocks,
dig at the moss

with my fingernails,
let moisture seep along my skin
and fall within
soft and dark
to the blood

and I promise
I will find them
even after so long: where underground
they are albino
and they listen, they shine,
and they wait
with tongues shriveled like leaves
and fearful of their names
that would crystallize them,
make them fossils
with the feathers on their backs
frozen hard
like beetle wings.

ΔΔΔΔ ΔΔΔΔ

But spring is floating
to the canyon rim;
needles burst yellow
from the pine branch
and the stories have built a new house.
Oh they make us dance
the old animal dances
that go a winding way
back and back
to the red clouds
of our first
Hopi morning.

Where I saw them last
they are still: antelope and bear
dancing in the dust,
prairie dog and lizard
whirling just whirling,
pinyon and willow
bending, twisting,
we women
rooting into the earth
our feet becoming water
and our hair pushing up
like tumbleweed

and the spirits should have noticed
how our thoughts wandered those first days,
how we closed our eyes against them
and forgot the signs;
the spirits were never smart about this
but trusted us to remember it right
and we were distracted,
we were new.
We mapped the trails
the spirits had walked
as if the footprints had more meaning
than the feet.
color after color,
designs that spin and sprout
were painted on the sky
but we were only confused
and turned our backs
and now we are trapped
inside our songlessness.

We are that kind of thing
that pushes away
the very song
keeping us alive
so the stories have been strong
and tell themselves
to this very day,
with or without us
it no longer matters.
The flower merges with the mud,
songs are hammered onto spirits
and spirits onto people;
every song is danced out loud
for we are the spirits,
we are the people,
descended from the ones
who circled the underworld
and return to circle again.

I feel the stories
rattle under my hand
like sun-dried greasy
gambling bones.

1985

Julia

[Julia Pastrana was a mid-nineteenth century singer and dancer in the circus who was billed as "The Ugliest Woman in the World," or sometimes, "The Lion Lady." She was a Mexican Indian who had been born with facial deformities and with long hair growing from all over her body, including her face. In an effort to maintain control over her professional life, her manager persuaded her to marry him and she expressed her belief that he was actually in love with her. She bore him a son who lived for only six hours and had inherited his mother's physical appearance. She died three days later. Her husband, unwilling to forfeit his financial investment, had Julia and her infant boy stuffed, mounted and put on display in a case made of wood and glass. As recently as 1975, Julia Pastrana and her little baby were exhibited in Europe and in the United States.]

Tell me it was just a dream,
my husband, a clever trick
made by some tin-faced village god
or ghost coyote, to frighten me
with his claim that our marriage is made
of malice and money.
Oh tell me again
how you admire my hands,
how my jasmine tea is rich and strong,
my singing sweet, my eyes so dark
you would lose yourself swimming
man into fish
as you mapped the pond
you would own.
That was not all.
The room grew cold
as if to joke
with these warm days;
the curtains blew out
and fell back
against the moon-painted sill.

I rose from my bed like a spirit
and, not a spirit at all, floated slowly
to my great glass oval
to see myself reflected
as the burnished bronze woman
skin smooth and tender
I know myself to be
in the dark
above the confusion
of French perfumes

and I was there in the mirror
and I was not.

I had become hard
as the temple stones
of O'tomi,[1] hair grown over my ancient face
like black moss, gray as jungle fog
soaking green the tallest tree tops.
I was frail
as the breaking dry branches
of my winter sand canyons,
standing so still as if
to stand forever.

Oh such a small room!
No bigger than my elbows outstretched
and just as tall as my head.
A small room from which to sing
open the doors
with my cold graceful mouth,
my rigid lips, my silences
dead as yesterday,
cruel as the children
and cold as the coins
that glitter
in your pink fist.

And another magic
in the cold
of that small room:
in my arms
or standing near me
on a tall table
by my right side:
a tiny doll
that looked
like me.

Oh my husband
tell me again
this is only a dream
I wake from warm

[1]An Indian tribe in east central Mexico.

and today is still today,
summer sun and quick rain;
tell me, husband, how you love me
for my self one more time.
It scares me so
to be with child,
lioness
with cub.

1985

Rita Dove b. 1952

Former U.S. poet laureate Rita Dove has an international poetic vision. The settings of her enigmatic lyrics move from Ohio to Germany to Israel; the time frames shift from the present to a past both historical and personal. In a single volume, slaves, biblical characters, mythological figures, and members of Dove's own family stand side by side. Although she has been rightly celebrated as an eloquent African American female voice, her frequently shifting viewpoint suggests that she sees her work transcending race and gender as well as time and place.

Born in 1952 in Akron, Ohio, Dove was the second of four children in a middle-class family. Both her paternal grandfather and her father worked for the Goodyear Tire and Rubber Company in Akron. Her father, Ray Dove, earned a master's degree and became the company's first black chemist, though at the time of his oldest daughter's birth he was still restricted to running the company elevator.

Rita Dove attended the public schools in Akron and then enrolled at Miami University in Ohio, where she graduated *summa cum laude* in 1973. She then attended the University of Tübingen on a Fulbright Scholarship and earned an MFA from the University of Iowa in 1977.

Dove's poetry is grounded in reality yet capable of sky-high buoyancy. Her oblique, sometimes otherworldly metaphors indicate a literary kinship with contemporary Scandinavian poets such as Tomas Tranströmer. In her poems ("Ö," for instance), language itself often appears to be a form of salvation. As Dove put it in a 1991 interview, "I think one reason I became primarily a poet rather than a fiction writer is that though I am interested in stories, I am profoundly fascinated by the ways in which language can change your perceptions."

In 1987 Dove won the Pulitzer Prize for *Thomas and Beulah,* a sequence of poems about her grandparents' courtship, marriage, and subsequent life in Akron. More recently, she has published a sonnet sequence based on the Persephone myth, *Mother Love* (1995); a verse drama, *The Darker Face of the Earth* (1994, rev. ed. 1996), an Oedipal tale set in antebellum South Carolina; and a collection of lyrics, *On the Bus with Rosa Parks* (1999). In addition to verse, she has published short stories, essays, and a novel.

A resident of Charlottesville, Virginia, Dove is Commonwealth Professor of English at the University of Virginia.

Hilary Holladay
University of Massachusetts, Lowell

PRIMARY WORKS

The Yellow House on the Corner, 1980; *Museum,* 1983; *Fifth Sunday,* 1985; *Thomas and Beulah,* 1986; *Grace Notes,* 1989; *Through the Ivory Gate,* 1992; *Selected Poems,* 1993; *The Darker Face of the Earth: A Verse Play in Fourteen Scenes,* 1994; *Mother Love: Poems,* 1995; *The Poet's World,* 1995; *The Darker Face of the Earth* (rev. 2nd ed.), 1996; *On the Bus with Rosa Parks,* 1999.

Kentucky, 1833

It is Sunday, day of roughhousing. We are let out in the woods. The young boys wrestle and butt their heads together like sheep—a circle forms; claps and shouts fill the air. The women, brown and glossy, gather round the banjo player, or simply lie in the sun, legs and aprons folded. The weather's an odd monkey—any other day he's on our backs, his cotton eye everywhere; today the light sifts down like the finest cornmeal, coating our hands and arms with a dust. God's dust, old woman Acker says. She's the only one who could read to us from the Bible, before Massa forbade it. On Sundays, something hangs in the air, a hallelujah, a skitter of brass, but we can't call it by name and it disappears.

Then Massa and his gentlemen friends come to bet on the boys. They guffaw and shout, taking sides, red-faced on the edge of the boxing ring. There is more kicking, butting, and scuffling—the winner gets a dram of whiskey if he can drink it all in one swig without choking.

Jason is bucking and prancing about—Massa said his name reminded him of some sailor, a hero who crossed an ocean, looking for a golden cotton field. Jason thinks he's been born to great things—a suit with gold threads, vest and all. Now the winner is sprawled out under a tree and the sun, that weary tambourine, hesitates at the rim of the sky's green light. It's a crazy feeling that carries through the night; as if the sky were an omen we could not understand, the book that, if we could read, would change our lives.

1980

Ö

Shape the lips to an *o,* say *a.*
That's *island.*

One word of Swedish has changed the whole neighborhood.
When I look up, the yellow house on the corner
is a galleon stranded in flowers. Around it

the wind. Even the high roar of a leaf-mulcher
could be the horn-blast from a ship
as it skirts the misted shoals.

We don't need much more to keep things going.
Families complete themselves
and refuse to budge from the present,
the present extends its glass forehead to sea
(backyard breezes, scattered cardinals)

and if, one evening, the house on the corner
took off over the marshland,
neither I nor my neighbor
would be amazed. Sometimes

a word is found so right it trembles
at the slightest explanation.
You start out with one thing, end
up with another, and nothing's
like it used to be, not even the future.

1980

Daystar

She wanted a little room for thinking:
but she saw diapers steaming on the line,
a doll slumped behind the door.

So she lugged a chair behind the garage
to sit out the children's naps.

Sometimes there were things to watch—
the pinched armor of a vanished cricket,

a floating maple leaf. Other days
she stared until she was assured
when she closed her eyes
she'd see only her own vivid blood.

She had an hour, at best, before Liza appeared
pouting from the top of the stairs.
And just *what* was mother doing
out back with the field mice? Why,
building a palace. Later
that night when Thomas rolled over and
lurched into her, she would open her eyes
and think of the place that was hers
for an hour—where
she was nothing,
pure nothing, in the middle of the day.

1986

The Oriental Ballerina

twirls on the tips of a carnation
while the radio scratches out a morning hymn.
Daylight has not ventured as far

as the windows—the walls are still dark,
shadowed with the ghosts
of oversized gardenias. The ballerina

pirouettes to the wheeze of the old
rugged cross, she lifts
her shoulders past the edge

of the jewelbox lid. Two pink slippers
touch the ragged petals, no one
should have feet that small! In China

they do everything upside down:
this ballerina has not risen but drilled
a tunnel straight to America

where the bedrooms of the poor
are papered in vulgar flowers
on a background the color of grease, of

teabags, of cracked imitation walnut veneer.
On the other side of the world
they are shedding robes sprigged with

roses, roses drifting with a hiss
to the floor by the bed
as, here, the sun finally strikes the windows

suddenly opaque,
noncommital as shields. In this room
is a bed where the sun has gone

walking. Where a straw nods over
the lip of its glass and a hand
reaches for a tissue, crumpling it to a flower.

The ballerina had been drilling all night!
She flaunts her skirts like sails,
whirling in a disk so bright,

so rapidly she is standing still.
The sun walks the bed to the pillow
and pauses for breath (in the Orient,

breath floats like mist
in the fields), hesitating
at a knotted handkerchief that has slid

on its string and has lodged beneath
the right ear which discerns
the most fragile music

where there is none. The ballerina dances
at the end of a tunnel of light,
she spins on her impossible toes—

the rest is shadow.
The head on the pillow sees nothing
else, though it feels the sun warming

its cheeks. *There is no China;*
no cross, just the papery kiss
of a kleenex above the stink of camphor,

the walls exploding with shabby tutus. . . .

1986

Li-Young Lee b. 1957

Li-Young Lee has been praised for his passionate poetry and its deceptively simple style. His poems are unique in their emotional intensity and metaphysical abstraction, particularly at a time when many contemporary American poets are breaking away from the "lyric I" in order to articulate an unstable and plural "I." Lee's three prize-winning books, *Rose* (1986), *The City in Which I Love You* (1990), and *The Winged Seed: A Remembrance* (1995), share recurrent themes of love, exile, and mortality. Haunted by memories, Lee's poems are exploratory, showing a relentless search for understanding and for the right language to give form to what is invisible and evanescent. He once said, "When I write, I'm trying to make that which is *visible*—this face, this body, this person—*invisible,* and at the same time, make what is *invisible*—that which exists at the level of pure *being*—completely visible." Critics who celebrate the disappearance of the "lyric I" from postmodern poetry as the only possible way of opening the poetic to the historical and political might take issue with Lee's poetics. Yet for minority American poets like Lee to explore the interior and the abstract may not be as escapist or politically inconsequential as some critics might think.

Lee was born in 1957 in Indonesia of Chinese parents. His mother, a granddaughter of Yuan Shi-kai, China's first president (1912–1916), married the son of a gangster and an entrepreneur. His parents' marriage in Communist China was much frowned upon, and they eventually fled to Indonesia, where Lee's father taught medicine and philosophy at Gamliel University in Jakarta and served as President Sukarno's medical adviser. In 1959, when Sukarno launched a violent ethnic purge of the Chinese, Lee's father was incarcerated for his interest in Western culture and ideas; he loved Shakespeare, opera, and Kierkegaard, and he taught the King James version of the Bible. After nineteen months of imprisonment, he escaped; with his family, he traveled to Macao, Japan, and Singapore before settling in Hong Kong, where he became a revered evangelist minister. In 1964, the family emigrated to the United States. Lee's father studied at the Pittsburgh Theological Seminary and later became a Presbyterian minister. Lee went to the University of Pittsburgh, where he took Gerald Stern's poetry writing class and earned his B.A. in 1979; he continued to study creative writing at the University of Arizona and the State University of New York at Brockport. He lives in Chicago with his wife and their two sons.

Lee's father and his family's experience of exile have had a significant impact on Lee's poetry. As a child, he learned to recite Chinese poems from the Tang dynasty (618–907) and was often enchanted by his father's poetic preaching and reading of the Psalms. Many of his poems recall his father, who is portrayed as strict and tender, powerful and vulnerable, godlike and human.

Breaking away from linear, rhetorical structure, Lee's poems unfold and expand from a central image, which holds together the discontinuous narratives and fragmentary scenes. Similar to the functions of imagery in classical Chinese poetry, his composition method gives him greater freedom in making leaps from narrative to lyricism and from the concrete to the abstract. Lee's poems bring together Eastern and Western ideas and traditions. Among the literary influences that Lee has acknowledged are the biblical Song of Songs, Gerald Stern's *Lucky Life,* Kierkegaard's *Fear and Trembling,* Meister Eckhart's sermons, and Rainer Maria Rilke's "Duino Elegies."

The spiritual and emotional experience of the poems is accompanied by a down-to-earth sensualness that Lee says "comes from my obsession with the body, man-body, earth-body, woman-body, father-body, mother-body, mind-body (for I experience the mind as another body) and the poem body." This vision may suggest the influence of Whitman, but it is also rooted in Daoism. Lee is familiar with Daoist texts and admires Lao Zi, Lie Zi, and Zhuang Zi, whose sense of wonder and mystery and whose paradoxical and skeptical characteristics are evident in Lee's poems and prose-poem memoir.

Xiaojing Zhou
State University of New York–Buffalo

PRIMARY WORKS

Rose, 1986; *The City in Which I Love You,* 1990; *The Winged Seed,* 1995; "The Father's House," *Transforming Vision,* 1994; "Li-Young Lee," interview with Bill Moyers, *The Language of Life: A Festival of Poets,* ed. James Haba, 1995; "Li-Young Lee's Universal Mind—A Search for the Soul," interview with Eileen Tabios, including Tabios's comments and Lee's draft of "The Father's House," *Black Lightning: Poetry-in-Progress,* 1998; "Li-Young Lee: Interview by James Kyung-Jin Lee," *Words Matter: Conversations with Asian American Writers,* ed. King-Kok Cheung, 2000.

I Ask My Mother to Sing

She begins, and my grandmother joins her.
Mother and daughter sing like young girls.
If my father were alive, he would play
his accordion and sway like a boat.

I've never been in Peking, or the Summer Palace,
nor stood on the great Stone Boat to watch
the rain begin on Kuen Ming Lake, the picnickers
running away in the grass.

But I love to hear it sung;
how the waterlilies fill with rain until
they overturn, spilling water into water,
then rock back, and fill with more.

Both women have begun to cry.
But neither stops her song.

1986

My Father, in Heaven, Is Reading Out Loud

My father, in heaven, is reading out loud
to himself Psalms or news. Now he ponders what
he's read. No. He is listening for the sound
of children in the yard. Was that laughing
or crying? So much depends upon the
answer, for either he will go on reading,
or he'll run to save a child's day from grief.
As it is in heaven, so it was on earth.

Because my father walked the earth with a grave,
determined rhythm, my shoulders ached
from his gaze. Because my father's shoulders
ached from the pulling of oars, my life now moves
with a powerful back-and-forth rhythm:
nostalgia, speculation. Because he
made me recite a book a month, I forget
everything as soon as I read it. And knowledge
never comes but while I'm mid-stride a flight
of stairs, or lost a moment on some avenue.

A remarkable disappointment to him,
I am like anyone who arrives late
in the millennium and is unable
to stay to the end of days. The world's
beginnings are obscure to me, its outcomes
inaccessible. I don't understand
the source of starlight, or starlight's destinations.
And already another year slides out
of balance. But I don't disparage scholars;
my father was one and I loved him,
who packed his books once, and all of our belongings,
then sat down to await instruction
from his god, yes, but also from a radio.
At the doorway, I watched, and I suddenly
knew he was one like me, who got my learning
under a lintel; he was one of the powerless,
to whom knowledge came while he sat among
suitcases, boxes, old newspapers, string.

He did not decide peace or war, home or exile,
escape by land or escape by sea.
He waited merely, as always someone
waits, far, near, here, hereafter, to find out:
is it praise or lament hidden in the next moment?

1990

With Ruins

Choose a quiet
place, a ruins, a house no more
a house,
under whose stone archway I stood
one day to duck the rain.

The roofless floor, vertical
studs, eight wood columns
supporting nothing,
two staircases careening to nowhere, all
make it seem

a sketch, notes to a house, a three-
dimensional grid negotiating
absences,
an idea
receding into indefinite rain,

or else that idea
emerging, skeletal
against the hammered sky, a
human thing, scoured, seen clean
through from here to an iron heaven.

A place where things
were said and done,
there you can remember
what you need to
remember. Melancholy is useful. Bring yours.

1990

This Room and Everything in It

Lie still now
while I prepare for my future,
certain hard days ahead,
when I'll need what I know so clearly this moment.

I am making use
of the one thing I learned
of all the things my father tried to teach me:
the art of memory.

I am letting this room

and everything in it
stand for my ideas about love
and its difficulties.

I'll let your love-cries,
those spacious notes
of a moment ago,
stand for distance.

Your scent,
that scent
of spice and a wound,
I'll let stand for mystery.

Your sunken belly
is the daily cup
of milk I drank
as a boy before morning prayer.

The sun on the face
of the wall
is God, the face
I can't see, my soul,

and so on, each thing
standing for a separate idea,
and those ideas forming the constellation
of my greater idea.
And one day, when I need
to tell myself something intelligent
about love,

I'll close my eyes
and recall this room and everything in it:
My body is estrangement.
This desire, perfection.
Your closed eyes my extinction.
Now I've forgotten my
idea. The book
on the windowsill, riffled by wind . . .
the even-numbered pages are
the past, the odd-
numbered pages, the future.
The sun is
God, your body is milk . . .

useless, useless . . .
your cries are song, my body's not me . . .
no good . . . my idea

has evaporated . . . your hair is time, your thighs are song . . .
it had something to do
with death . . . it had something
to do with love.

1990

Lorna Dee Cervantes b. 1954

This northern California native typifies the young Chicano writers who began appearing in the mid-1970s, ten years after the Chicano Movement began. Younger authors, having access to Chicano literature in school and in the community, could recast and adjust images and concepts Chicano Movement writers offered as self-defining, and the forms they utilized. The new writers, without rejecting the importance of cultural identity, emphasized questions of style and form, bringing polish and control to the ideologically overloaded earlier poetry. Age, however, was not the only difference. Women, excluded from the first decade of Chicano publishing, found outlets for their work. A new female, often feminist, voice forced the Chicano image into a more balanced perspective, with a mixture of cultural concern and gender-based criticism. And although Cervantes resisted academics for a number of years during which she attempted to survive strictly as a writer and publisher—she founded her own press and poetry magazine, *Mango*—like many of her generation, she now combines university life with writing. She presently teaches in the Creative Writing Program of the University of Colorado, Boulder.

Cervantes' work exemplifies these characteristics. Influenced by Carlos Castaneda, Cervantes sees life as a struggle with the enemy/guide, incarnations of the spiritual forces in Nature that can destroy if not brought into harmony and control, but once mastered, help one reach fulfillment. At the personal level, men are the enemy; at the ethnic level, machismo and male dominance threaten familial unity; at the social level, it is Anglo-American society and racial prejudice; and at the artistic level, English and words themselves must be mastered. Cervantes defines her terms through poems about male/female struggle within the context of class and cultural struggle. Men are trained to exploit their environment, which leads them to abuse women, a situation that forces women to become self-reliant. Cervantes' feminism seems to culminate in "Beneath the Shadow of the Freeway," the image of the multi-generation, all-women family, surviving in the midst of social alienation and menaced by the male adversary.

Yet, ethnic unity, necessary to combat anti-Chicano prejudice, demands sexual harmony, so the author synthesizes from the older generations the wisdom of female oral tradition: a balance of strength and tenderness, of openness and caution, of sincerity and reserve. Castaneda's lesson—struggle with the enemy to turn it into your assistant—is applied to men and Nature. She learns to live with them, although never completely at ease. Survival depends on constant vigilance against betrayal, because despite the façade of peace, society and Nature are essentially a battle. Her manner of self-defense is to develop a harmonious identity through personal symbols in Nature—birds—related to a chosen cultural emphasis—the Native American element in her Mexican American past.

Then she blends them into the image of her art in the metaphor of the pen through an interlingual play on words—*pluma* in Spanish means pen and feather, so to be *emplumada* is to be feathered like a bird or an Indian, or to be armed with a pen like a writer. That she too can rework the rhetoric of warrior-like struggle is clear in "Poem for the Young White Man," reminiscent of the stringent Movement poetry. However, she is most successful when she eschews the easy clichés of political rhetoric to pursue her vision of the spirit of nature hidden under the surface of everyday existence, one which struggles to express itself through the tenuous harmony of lovers and writers. The last half of *Emplumada* and the entire second book, *From the Cables of Genocide,* explore and construct female-male relationships to feed a society starved for love. "Bananas" is a favorite of Cervantes and her audiences. Through the image of fruit, Cervantes creates a vast web of international sociopolitical forces at play and war. Yet she always keeps close contact with concrete reality in individual terms.

Juan Bruce-Novoa
University of California–Irvine

PRIMARY WORKS

Emplumada, 1981; *From the Cables of Genocide: Poems of Love and Hunger,* 1991.

Beneath the Shadow of the Freeway

1

Across the street—the freeway,
blind worm, wrapping the valley up
from Los Altos[1] to Sal Si Puedes.[2]
I watched it from my porch
unwinding. Every day at dusk
as Grandma watered geraniums
the shadow of the freeway lengthened.

2

We were a woman family:
Grandma, our innocent Queen;
Mama, the Swift Knight, Fearless Warrior.
Mama wanted to be Princess instead.
I know that. Even now she dreams of taffeta
and foot-high tiaras.

Myself: I could never decide.
So I turned to books, those staunch, upright men.
I became Scribe: Translator of Foreign Mail,

[1]Spanish: The Heights.

[2]Spanish: Escape If You Can.

interpreting letters from the government, notices
of dissolved marriages and Welfare stipulations.
I paid the bills, did light man-work, fixed faucets,
insured everything
against all leaks.

3

Before rain I notice seagulls.
They walk in flocks,
cautious across lawns: splayed toes,
indecisive beaks. Grandma says
seagulls mean storm.
In California in the summer,
mockingbirds sing all night.
Grandma says they are singing for their nesting wives.
"They don't leave their families
borrachando."[3]

She likes the ways of birds,
respects how they show themselves
for toast and a whistle.

She believes in myths and birds.
She trusts only what she builds
with her own hands.

4

She built her house,
cocky, disheveled carpentry,
after living twenty-five years
with a man who tried to kill her.

Grandma, from the hills of Santa Barbara,
I would open my eyes to see her stir mush
in the morning, her hair in loose braids,
tucked close around her head
with a yellow scarf.

Mama said, "It's her own fault,
getting screwed by a man for that long.
Sure as shit wasn't hard."
soft she was soft

[3]Spanish: getting drunk.

5

in the night I would hear it
glass bottles shattering the street
words cracked into shrill screams
inside my throat   a cold fear
as it entered the house in hard
unsteady steps   stopping at my door
my name   bathrobe   slippers
outside a 3 A.M. mist heavy
as a breath full of whiskey
stop it   go home   come inside
mama if he comes here again
I'll call the police

inside
a gray kitten   a touchstone
purring beneath the quilts
grandma stitched
from his suits
the patchwork singing
of mockingbirds

6

"You're too soft . . . always were.
You'll get nothing but shit.
Baby, don't count on nobody."

—a mother's wisdom.
Soft. I haven't changed,
maybe grown more silent, cynical
on the outside.

"O Mama, with what's inside of me
I could wash that all away. I could."

"But Mama, if you're good to them
they'll be good to you back."

Back. The freeway is across the street.
It's summer now. Every night I sleep with a gentle man
to the hymn of mockingbirds,

and in time, I plant geraniums.
I tie up my hair into loose braids,
and trust only what I have built
with my own hands.

1981

Poem for the Young White Man Who Asked Me How I, an Intelligent, Well-Read Person Could Believe in the War Between Races

In my land there are no distinctions.
The barbed wire politics of oppression
have been torn down long ago. The only reminder
of past battles, lost or won, is a slight
rutting in the fertile fields.

In my land
people write poems about love,
full of nothing but contented childlike syllables.
Everyone reads Russian short stories and weeps.
There are no boundaries.
There is no hunger, no
complicated famine or greed.

I am not a revolutionary.
I don't even like political poems.
Do you think I can believe in a war between races?

I can deny it. I can forget about it
when I'm safe,
living on my own continent of harmony
and home, but I am not
there.

I believe in revolution
because everywhere the crosses are burning,
sharp-shooting goose-steppers round every corner,
there are snipers in the schools . . .
(I know you don't believe this.
You think this is nothing
but faddish exaggeration. But they
are not shooting at you.)

I'm marked by the color of my skin.
The bullets are discrete and designed to kill slowly.
They are aiming at my children.
These are facts.
Let me show you my wounds: my stumbling mind, my
"excuse me" tongue, and this
nagging preoccupation
with the feeling of not being good enough.

These bullets bury deeper than logic.
Racism is not intellectual.
I can not reason these scars away.

Outside my door
there is a real enemy
who hates me.

I am a poet
who yearns to dance on rooftops,
to whisper delicate lines about joy
and the blessings of human understanding.
I try. I go to my land, my tower of words and
bolt the door, but the typewriter doesn't fade out
the sounds of blasting and muffled outrage.
My own days bring me slaps on the face.
Every day I am deluged with reminders
that this is not
my land

and this is my land.

I do not believe in the war between races
but in this country
there is war.

1981

Macho

Slender, you are, secret as rail
under a stairwell of snow, slim
as my lips in the shallow hips.

I had a man of gristle and flint,
fingered the fine lineament of flexed
talons under his artifice of grit.

Every perfect body houses force
or deception. Every calculated figure
fears the summing up of age.

You're a beautiful mess of thread and silk,
a famous web of work and waiting, an

angular stylus with the patience of lead.

Your potent lure links hunger to flesh
as a frail eagle alights on my chest,
remember: the word for *machismo* is *real.*

1991

Bananas

for Indrek

I

In Estonia, Indrek is taking his children
to the Dollar Market to look at bananas.
He wants them to know about the presence of fruit,
about globes of light tart to the tongue, about the
twang of tangelos, the cloth of persimmons,
the dull little mons of kiwi. There is not a chance
for a taste. Where rubles are scarce, dollars are harder.
Even beef is doled out welfare-thin on Saturday's platter.
They light the few candles not reserved for the dead,
and try not to think of small bites in the coming winter,
of irradiated fields or the diminished catch in the fisherman's
net. They tell of bananas yellow as daffodils. And mango—
which tastes as if the whole world came out from her womb.

II

Colómbia, 1928, bananas rot in the fields.
A strip of lost villages between railyard
and cemetery. The United Fruit Company train,
a yellow painted slug, eats up the swamps and jungle.
Campesinos replace Indians who are a dream
and a rubble of bloody stones hacked into coffins:
malaria, tuberculosis, cholera, machetes of the jefes.
They become like the empty carts that shatter
the landscape. Their hands, no longer pulling the teats
from the trees, now twist into death, into silence
and obedience. They wait in Aracataca, poised as

statues between hemispheres. They would rather be
tilling the plots for black beans. They would rather grow
wings and rise as *pericos—parrots, poets, clowns*—a word
which means all this and whose task is messenger from
Mítla, the underworld where the ancestors of the slain
arise with the vengeance of Tiáloc. A stench permeates
the wind as bananas, black on the stumps, char
into odor. The murdered Mestizos have long been cleared
and begin their new duties as fertilizer for the plantations.
Feathers fall over the newly spaded soil: turquoise,
scarlet, azure, quetzál, and yellow litters
the graves like gold claws of bananas.

III

Dear I,

The 3′ × 6′ boxes in front of the hippy
market in Boulder are radiant with marigolds, some
with heads big as my Indian face. They signify
death to me, as it is Labor Day and already
I am making up the guest list for my *Dia de los Muertos*
altár. I'll need *maravillas* so this year I plant *caléndulas*
for blooming through snow that will fall before November.
I am shopping for "no-spray" bananas. I forego
the Dole and *Chiquita,* that name that always made me
blush for being christened with that title. But now
I am only a little small, though still brown enough
for the—*Where are you from?* Perhaps my ancestors
planted a placenta here as well as on my Califas coast
where alien shellfish replaced native mussels,
clams and oysters in 1886. *I'm from the 21st Century,*
I tell them, and feel rude for it—when all I desire
is bananas without pesticides. They're smaller
than plantains which are green outside and firm
and golden when sliced. Fried in butter
they turn yellow as over-ripe fruit. And sweet.
I ask the produce manager how to crate and
pack bananas to Estonia. She glares at me
suspiciously: *You can't do that. I know.*
There must be some law. You might spread
diseases. They would arrive as mush, anyway.
I am thinking of children in Estonia with
no fried *plátanos* to eat with their fish as
the Blond turns away, still without shedding
a smile at me—me, Hija del Sól, Earth's Daughter, lover

of bananas. I buy up Baltic wheat. I buy up organic
bananas, butter y canéla. I ship banana bread.

IV

At Big Mountain uranium
sings through the dreams of the people.
Women dress in glowing symmetries, sheep
clouds gather below the bluffs, sundown
sandstone blooms in four corners. Smell of sage
penetrates as state tractors with chains trawl the resistant
plants, gouging anew the tribal borders, uprooting
all in their path like Amazonian ants, breaking
the hearts of the widows. Elders and children
cut the fence again and again as wind whips
the waist of ancient rock. Sheep nip across
centuries in the people's blood, and are carried
off by the Federal choppers waiting in the canyon
with orders and slings. A long winter, little wool
to spin, medicine lost in the desecration of the desert.
Old women weep as the camera rolls on the dark
side of conquest. Encounter rerun. Uranium. 1992.

V

I worry about winter in a place
I've never been, about exiles in their
homeland gathered around a fire,
about the slavery of substance and
gruel: *Will there be enough to eat?*
Will there be enough to feed? And
they dream of beaches and pies, hemispheres
of soft fruit found only in the heat of the planet.
Sugar canes, like Geiger counters, seek out tropics;
and dictate a Resolution to stun the tongues of those
who can afford to pay: imported plums, bullets,
black caviar large as peas, smoked meats
the color of Southern lynchings, what we don't
discuss in letters.
You are out of work.
Not many jobs today for high physicists
in Estonia, you say. *Poetry, though, is food*
for the soul. And bread? What is cake before
corn and the potato? Before the encounter
of animals, women and wheat? Stocks high

these days in survival products; 500 years later tomato
size tumors bloom in the necks of the pickers.
On my coast, Diablo dominates the golden hills,
the faultlines. On ancestral land Vandenberg shoots nuclear
payloads to Kwajalein, a Pacific atoll, where 68% of all
infants are born amphibian or anemones. But poetry
is for the soul. I speak of spirit, the yellow seed
in air as life is the seed in water, and the poetry
of Improbability, the magic in the Movement
of quarks and sunlight, the subtle basketry
of hadrons and neutrinos of color, how what you do
is what you get—bananas or worry.
What do you say? Your friend,
a Chicana poet.

1991

Aurora Levins Morales b. 1954

Aurora Levins Morales was born in Indiera, Puerto Rico, on February 24, 1954, to a Puerto Rican mother and a Jewish father. She came to the United States with her family in 1967, and lived in Chicago and New Hampshire. She presently works in the San Francisco Bay Area, where she has resided since 1976. Her short stories have appeared in *This Bridge Called My Back, Cuentos: Stories by Latinas,* and in *Revista Chicano-Riqueña.* In 1986 she published *Getting Home Alive,* a collection of short stories, essays, prose poems, and poetry in English authored in collaboration with her mother, Rosario Morales.

Levins Morales does not belong to the group of writers who were brought up in New York City and whose works deal with life in El Barrio. Her experiences have taken her, instead, from the urban world of Chicago, to the rural quiet of New Hampshire, and to the pluralistic and politically radical culture of the San Francisco Bay Area. Her writing has been profoundly influenced by two major literary streams: first, by North American feminists like Adrienne Rich, Susan Griffin, and in particular by Alice Walker. She has also read extensively the works of major Latin American writers such as Pablo Neruda and Eduardo Galeano. Her Puerto Rican–Jewish heritage has also been an important source of creativity. Her search for a language that will express a Latina woman's experience and struggle identifies her with the body of literature produced by US women of color, and closely connects her with the work of contemporary Chicana writers.

She tries to define her *mestiza* and female identity through an analysis and critique of her two cultures. While considering herself "a child of the Americas," and not just Puerto Rican, Aurora employs in her writings the cultural symbols of her country, and her childhood memories of the Puerto Rican countryside. A unique element of *Getting Home Alive* is the generational dialogue and "cross-fertilization," as she describes it, between her mother's voice and her own. Along with Víctor Hernández Cruz, Levins Morales illustrates the gradual diversification that is taking place in United States Puerto Rican literature. Following a first moment of protest which denounced the social and economic conditions of the *puertorriqueños* in the Bronx and El Barrio, younger Puerto Rican writers are exploring other issues, such as language, multiple subjectivities, international politics, class, feminism, and transnational identities. Their denunciations are not expressed directly but are embedded in a more lyrical and individual poetic language. Writers like Cruz and Morales exemplify a synthesis between the North American literary tradition and a broad Latin American culture. As Puerto Ricans have moved away from New York City and settled in other urban centers throughout the United States, their life experiences have varied, and the emerging writings are thus characterized by a greater diversity of voices.

Frances R. Aparicio
University of Illinois–Chicago

PRIMARY WORKS

Getting Home Alive, coauthored with Rosario Morales, 1986.

Child of the Americas

I am a child of the Americas,
a light-skinned mestiza of the Caribbean,
a child of many diaspora, born into this continent at a crossroads.

I am a U.S. Puerto Rican Jew,
a product of the ghettos of New York I have never known.
An immigrant and the daughter and granddaughter of immigrants.
I speak English with passion: it's the tongue of my consciousness,
a flashing knife blade of crystal, my tool, my craft.

I am Caribeña,[1] island grown. Spanish is in my flesh,
ripples from my tongue, lodges in my hips:
the language of garlic and mangoes,
the singing in my poetry, the flying gestures of my hands.
I am of Latinoamerica, rooted in the history of my continent:
I speak from that body.

I am not african. Africa is in me, but I cannot return.
I am not taína.[2] Taíno is in me, but there is no way back.
I am not european. Europe lives in me, but I have no home there.

[1]Caribbean woman.
[2]Taínos were the Indian tribe indigenous to Puerto Rico.

I am new. History made me. My first language was spanglish.[3]
I was born at the crossroads
and I am whole.

1986

Puertoricanness

It was Puerto Rico waking up inside her. Puerto Rico waking her up at 6:00 a.m., remembering the rooster that used to crow over on 59th Street and the neighbors all cursed "that damn rooster," but she loved him, waited to hear his harsh voice carving up the Oakland sky and eating it like chopped corn, so obliviously sure of himself, crowing all alone with miles of houses around him. She was like that rooster.

Often she could hear them in her dreams. Not the lone rooster of 59th Street (or some street nearby . . . she had never found the exact yard though she had tried), but the wild careening hysterical roosters of 3:00 a.m. in Bartolo, screaming at the night and screaming again at the day.

It was Puerto Rico waking up inside her, uncurling and shoving open the door she had kept neatly shut for years and years. Maybe since the first time she was an immigrant, when she refused to speak Spanish in nursery school. Certainly since the last time, when at thirteen she found herself between languages, between countries, with no land feeling at all solid under her feet. The mulberry trees of Chicago, that first summer, had looked so utterly pitiful beside her memory of flamboyan and banana and. . . . No, not even the individual trees and bushes but the mass of them, the overwhelming profusion of green life that was the home of her comfort and nest of her dreams.

The door was opening. She could no longer keep her accent under lock and key. It seeped out, masquerading as dyslexia, stuttering, halting, unable to speak the word which will surely come out in the wrong language, wearing the wrong clothes. Doesn't that girl know how to dress? Doesn't she know how to date, what to say to a professor, how to behave at a dinner table laid with silver and crystal and too many forks?

Yesterday she answered her husband's request that she listen to the whole of his thoughts before commenting by screaming. "This is how we talk. I will not wait sedately for you to finish. Interrupt me back!" She drank pineapple juice three or four

[3]Refers to the mixture of Spanish and English, mostly in speech.

times a day. Not Lotus, just Co-op brand, but it was *piña,*[1] and it was sweet and yellow. And she was letting the clock slip away from her into a world of morning and afternoon and night, instead of "five-forty-one-and-twenty seconds—beep."

There were things she noticed about herself, the Puertoricanness of which she had kept hidden all these years, but which had persisted as habits, as idiosyncracies of her nature. The way she left a pot of food on the stove all day, eating out of it whenever hunger struck her, liking to have something ready. The way she had lacked food to offer Elena in the old days and had stamped on the desire to do so because it *was* Puerto Rican: Come, mija . . . ¿quieres café?[2] The way she was embarrassed and irritated by Ana's unannounced visits, just dropping by, keeping the country habits after a generation of city life. So unlike the cluttered datebooks of all her friends, making appointments to speak to each other on the phone days in advance. Now she yearned for that clocklessness, for the perpetual food pots of her childhood. Even in the poorest houses a plate of white rice and brown beans with calabaza[3] or green bananas and oil.

She had told Sally that Puerto Ricans lived as if they were all in a small town still, a small town of six million spread out over tens of thousands of square miles, and that the small town that was her country needed to include Manila Avenue in Oakland now, because she was moving back into it. She would not fight the waking early anymore, or the eating all day, or the desire to let time slip between her fingers and allow her work to shape it. Work, eating, sleep, lovemaking, play—to let them shape the day instead of letting the day shape them. Since she could not right now, in the endless bartering of a woman with two countries, bring herself to trade in one-half of her heart for the other, exchange this loneliness for another perhaps harsher one, she would live as a Puerto Rican lives en la isla,[4] right here in north Oakland, plant the bananales[5] and cafetales[6] of her heart around her bedroom door, sleep under the shadow of their bloom and the carving hoarseness of the roosters, wake to blue-rimmed white enamel cups of jugo de piña[7] and plates of guineo verde,[8] and heat pots of rice with bits of meat in them on the stove all day.

There was a woman in her who had never had the chance to move through this house the way she wanted to, a woman raised to be like those women of her childhood, hardworking and humorous and clear. That woman was yawning up out of sleep and into this cluttered daily routine of a Northern California writer living at the edges of Berkeley. She was taking over, putting doilies on the word processor, not bothering to make appointments, talking to the neighbors, riding miles on the bus to buy bacalao,[9] making her presence felt . . . and she was all Puerto Rican, every bit of her.

1986

[1]Pineapple.
[2]"Eat, darling, you want some coffee?"
[3]Pumpkin.
[4]On the island.
[5]Banana plants.
[6]Coffee trees.
[7]Pineapple juice.
[8]Green bananas, or Plantains.
[9]Codfish.

Heart of My Heart, Bone of My Bone

You were my first grief. From the death of you, so intimate, so much an unexplained event of the universe, I made my first decision to live.

You have no name. That was before names. There were comets plunging into the sun and cells dividing in a frenzy of life too intense, too bright for anything like thinking, but I remember. There was a great space of floating motes and dim light and growing. There were three hearts beating. One, a deep repetition of thunder that was the weather of the universe, a slow rumbling music. And two hearts pitter-pattering, interweaving, fingerlacing, first me then you then me then you, *patta-pun* patta-pun *patta-pun.*

I reconstruct this story from the outside, from knowing what things were, from having names. On the inside, I grew stronger and you grew weaker. I grew and you grew still. I felt your sadness and fear and loneliness without having to interpret signs, read your expressions. The fluids of our bodies mingled in one chemical response: I knew *exactly* how you felt, and never, since then, have I been so completely known.

It was there from the beginning, the thing that was wrong with you. Something I knew but at first was hardly aware of. That grew to trouble me, until slowly I knew that I would lose you. Would be as naked without you as the pulsing electric cord of your spine was naked, unprotected. It was a failure of some part of your body to develop, a loss in the genetic gamble, a part that was necessary and was not there, did not work. *A part that was necessary and is gone.*

On the outside, I read about fetal development, look at pictures, watch *The Miracle of Life* on TV. I am shivering as I watch: ten days, two weeks, four weeks, seven weeks, twelve weeks, fourteen . . . then nothing. The picture of the sixteen week fetus comes up on the screen, and I feel I have never seen this shape before, pinpointing your death in the shadowy places of my body's memory, a kind of emotional sonogram.

Cell of my cell, bone of my bone, when your heart fluttered and whispered and was still, when you floated passive in the salty water and slowly came undone, frilling and fraying at the edges, becoming strands of protein, disappearing into the walls, the glowing cord my flesh—the stillness that followed was terrible, patta-pun *and nothing,* patta-pun *and nothing.*

You were heart of my heart and my own single heart murmurs and mutters now, an extra beat in each movement, patta-pa-pun, patta-pa-bun, beating "Are you still here? Are you still here?" Trying to find you in the stillness of the house, too big now without you, my own small heart and the thunder above me.

This is all I know: You were the closest being in the world and then you were gone. I have looked for you everywhere, though for years I had no name for the longing, crying in my child's bunk bed at night for someone I missed, not knowing who. Turning over all the stones to find you: If I get sick, too, will you come back? If I promise to die young, will you come back? If I promise never to have another baby close to my heart, will you come back? Patta-pun and no answer. Patta-pun and nothing.

I am a woman rich in brothers. Ricardo, who came when I was two. At my wedding he said, "You were my first coconspirator and soulmate." Partner in all the games of my childhood. Sibling to the wild guava bushes, friend of dogs in every alley of Chicago, companion of my homesickness, with whom I learned the meaning of solidarity.

Alejandro, who was born when I was nearly twelve. The golden treasure we took with us to Chicago, the child of my adolescence, the one I sang to, took mountain climbing, hitchhiked with. The almost-my-son one. The one who reminds me I survived.

I am rich in brothers, rich in love, and still, tiny as my little finger, curled up inside me, is the first seed of myself, wailing to the edges of the empty universe, for my brother, my self, my first lost love.

1986

Sandra Cisneros b. 1954

Born in Chicago, Sandra Cisneros spent much of her early life moving between various homes in the United States and her father's family home in Mexico City. As a student at the Writers' Workshop at the University of Iowa in the late 1970s, Cisneros drew upon her bicultural experience to write "the stories that haven't been written to fill a literary void." Since then, she has made the border state of Texas her home and the bicultural site in which much of her work is located.

The National Endowment for the Arts, the University of Texas, the University of California, and the MacArthur Foundation have acknowledged Cisneros's border aesthetic by awarding her fellowships, grants, and visiting appointments. Yet it is this same successful career trajectory that has generated some controversy among her literary peers. Her first book, a collection of poetry entitled *Bad Boys,* appeared in 1980 as part of a series of Chicano chapbooks. Like most Chicana/Chicano literature, Cisneros's early work was distributed by small presses specializing in Latina/Latino literature. But the interest generated by her first collection of fiction, *The House on Mango Street* (1984) enabled Cisneros to break into the world of major New York publishers. Her crossover appeal during the late 1980s and early 1990s facilitated a larger movement of Chicana writers, whose commercial and critical success has generated greater mainstream appreciation of Chicana/Chicano literature as well as some anxiety about their uneven reception. No one can understand recent history of Chicana/Chicano literature without making Cisneros a central figure in that reading.

In *Mango Street* Cisneros adapted the experimental form used by a number of other Chicana/o writers: the collection of related stories and sketches. *Mango Street* recalls Tomás Rivera's *. . . y no se lo tragó la tierra/And the Earth Did Not Devour Him* (selections from Rivera's novel appear elsewhere in this anthology) inasmuch as it uses a central protagonist to give short prose pieces coherence. About a young girl living in a segregated neighborhood in Chicago during the 1970s, *Mango Street* concludes with the Chicana artist's withdrawal from her community and, in a Joycean gesture, commitment to return. "I have gone away to come back," read *Mango Street*'s closing lines. "For the ones I left behind. For the ones who cannot get out."

Cisneros's second collection of poetry, *My Wicked, Wicked Ways* (1987), also invokes a developmental narrative; only here the narrative is ironic. The "bad girl" of the opening section develops into the "evil woman" of the next two sections, an artist whose escapades include adultery and a sexual romp through Europe. Cisneros's female speakers are complex, as they represent both defiance and fulfillment of cultural expectations. Her terse poetry evokes and ironically venerates the archetypal Chicana/Mexicana evil woman: La Malinche, the Indian mistress of Hernán Cortés, the "whore" who is said to have sold out her people to the conqueror. Like other Chicana feminists, Cisneros attempts to recover and revise La Malinche's tarnished reputation. Her project of mythic reclamation revises Chicana/Chicano cultural archaeology and bears the urgency of remembering everyday women whose lives would otherwise be anathematized or even forgotten.

Cisneros's feminism is even more evident in *Woman Hollering Creek* (1991). The first section contains a series of sketches told through the juvenile perspective familiar to readers of *Mango Street.* The rest of the book explores in greater detail the "wicked" woman of Cisneros's verse: the sultry seductress, perceived in her own culture as a sellout not just because of her sexuality but also because of her relative assimilation into Anglo-American culture. If *Mango Street* tries to solve the problem of the ethnic intellectual's estrangement from her community through a promise of return, *Woman Hollering Creek* demonstrates that making good on that promise creates another set of problems, negotiations, and anxieties.

In 1994, Cisneros published a book for children, using excerpts from *Mango Street. Hairs/Pelitos* illustrates the cultural diversity that takes place even within families by describing the different types of hair among members of Cisneros's own family; the book conveys a portrait of a family living in "heterogeneous harmony." With illustrations by Terry Ybanez, *Hair/Pelitos* is written, appropriately, in both Spanish and English. Also in 1994, Cisneros published her third book of poetry, *Loose Woman,* in which the much-maligned "wicked woman" brashly expresses a vision of history, sexuality, and community that celebrates poems that "fart in the bath" as much as it lambasts "politically-correct-Marxist-tourists/voyeurs." The poems are to date the best at capturing Cisneros's sense of outrageousness always made funnier, stronger, and deeper when shared with another as in her poem, "Las Girlfriends": "Been to hell and back again/Girl, me too."

Lora Romero
Stanford University

James Kyung-Jin Lee
University of Texas–Austin

PRIMARY WORKS

Bad Boys, 1980; *The House on Mango Street,* 1984, 1991; *My Wicked, Wicked Ways,* 1987, 1992; *Woman Hollering Creek and Other Stories,* 1991; *Hairs/Pelitos,* 1994; *Loose Woman,* 1994.

Eleven

What they don't understand about birthdays and what they never tell you is that when you're eleven, you're also ten, and nine, and eight, and seven, and six, and five, and four, and three, and two, and one. And when you wake up on your eleventh birthday you expect to feel eleven, but you don't. You open your eyes and everything's just like yesterday, only it's today. And you don't feel eleven at all. You feel like you're still ten. And you are—underneath the year that makes you eleven.

Like some days you might say something stupid, and that's the part of you that's still ten. Or maybe some days you might need to sit on your mama's lap because you're scared, and that's the part of you that's five. And maybe one day when you're all grown up maybe you will need to cry like if you're three, and that's okay. That's what I tell Mama when she's sad and needs to cry. Maybe she's feeling three.

Because the way you grow old is kind of like an onion or like the rings inside a tree trunk or like my little wooden dolls that fit one inside the other, each year inside the next one. That's how being eleven years old is.

You don't feel eleven. Not right away. It takes a few days, weeks even, sometimes even months before you say Eleven when they ask you. And you don't feel smart eleven, not until you're almost twelve. That's the way it is.

Only today I wish I didn't have only eleven years rattling inside me like pennies in a tin Band-Aid box. Today I wish I was one hundred and two instead of eleven because if I was one hundred and two I'd have known what to say when Mrs. Price put the red sweater on my desk. I would've known how to tell her it wasn't mine instead of just sitting there with that look on my face and nothing coming out of my mouth.

"Whose is this?" Mrs. Price says, and she holds the red sweater up in the air for all the class to see. "Whose? It's been sitting in the coatroom for a month."

"Not mine," says everybody. "Not me."

"It has to belong to somebody," Mrs. Price keeps saying, but nobody can remember. It's an ugly sweater with red plastic buttons and a collar and sleeves all stretched out like you could use it for a jump rope. It's maybe a thousand years old and even if it belonged to me I wouldn't say so.

Maybe because I'm skinny, maybe because she doesn't like me, that stupid Sylvia Saldívar says, "I think it belongs to Rachel." An ugly sweater like that, all raggedy and old, but Mrs. Price believes her. Mrs. Price takes the sweater and puts it right on my desk, but when I open my mouth nothing comes out.

"That's not, I don't, you're not . . . Not mine," I finally say in a little voice that was maybe me when I was four.

"Of course it's yours," Mrs. Price says. "I remember you wearing it once." Because she's older and the teacher, she's right and I'm not.

Not mine, not mine, not mine, but Mrs. Price is already turning to page thirty-two, and math problem number four. I don't know why but all of a sudden I'm feeling sick inside, like the part of me that's three wants to come out of my eyes, only I squeeze them shut tight and bite down on my teeth real hard and try to remember today I am eleven, eleven. Mama is making a cake for me for tonight, and when Papa comes home everybody will sing Happy birthday, happy birthday to you.

But when the sick feeling goes away and I open my eyes, the red sweater's still sitting there like a big red mountain. I move the red sweater to the corner of my desk with my ruler. I move my pencil and books and eraser as far from it as possible. I even move my chair a little to the right. Not mine, not mine, not mine.

In my head I'm thinking how long till lunchtime, how long till I can take the red sweater and throw it over the schoolyard fence, or leave it hanging on a parking meter, or bunch it up into a little ball and toss it in the alley. Except when math period ends Mrs. Price says loud and in front of everybody, "Now, Rachel, that's enough," because she sees I've shoved the red sweater to the tippy-tip corner of my desk and it's hanging all over the edge like a waterfall, but I don't care.

"Rachel," Mrs. Price says. She says it like she's getting mad. "You put that sweater on right now and no more nonsense."

"But it's not—"

"Now!" Mrs. Price says.

This is when I wish I wasn't eleven, because all the years inside of me—ten, nine, eight, seven, six, five, four, three, two, and one—are pushing at the back of my eyes when I put one arm through one sleeve of the sweater that smells like cottage cheese, and then the other arm through the other and stand there with my arms apart like if the sweater hurts me and it does, all itchy and full of germs that aren't even mine.

That's when everything I've been holding in since this morning, since when Mrs. Price put the sweater on my desk, finally lets go, and all of a sudden I'm crying in front of everybody. I wish I was invisible but I'm not. I'm eleven and it's my birthday today and I'm crying like I'm three in front of everybody. I put my head down on the desk and bury my face in my stupid clown-sweater arms. My face all hot and spit coming out of my mouth because I can't stop the little animal noises from coming out of me, until there aren't any more tears left in my eyes, and it's just my body shaking like when you have the hiccups, and my whole head hurts like when you drink milk too fast.

But the worst part is right before the bell rings for lunch. That stupid Phyllis Lopez, who is even dumber than Sylvia Saldívar, says she remembers the red sweater is hers! I take it off right away and give it to her, only Mrs. Price pretends like everything's okay.

Today I'm eleven. There's a cake Mama's making for tonight, and when Papa comes home from work we'll eat it. There'll be candles and presents and everybody will sing Happy birthday, happy birthday to you, Rachel, only it's too late.

I'm eleven today. I'm eleven, ten, nine, eight, seven, six, five, four, three, two, and one, but I wish I was one hundred and two. I wish I was anything but eleven, because I want today to be far away already, far away like a runaway balloon, like a tiny *o* in the sky, so tiny-tiny you have to close your eyes to see it.

1991

Leslie Marmon Silko (Laguna) b. 1948

Leslie Marmon Silko grew up on the Laguna Pueblo Reservation in the house where her father, Lee H. Marmon, was born. Her mother, Virginia, worked outside the home, and Silko spent most of her preschool years with her great-grandmother, who lived next door.

She attended Bureau of Indian Affairs schools at Laguna until high school in Albuquerque. Then she attended the University of New Mexico, graduating *magna cum laude* in 1969. She then attended three semesters of law school before deciding to devote herself to writing and to enter graduate school in English.

Silko has taught at Navajo Community College, Many Farms, Arizona, at the University of New Mexico, and at the University of Arizona. She was formerly married to attorney John Silko. She has two sons, Robert, born in 1966, and Cazimir, born in 1972. The family lived in Alaska during the mid-seventies when Silko was writing *Ceremony.* Although Alaska is the setting for the title story of her book *Storyteller,* most of her early fiction and poetry is set in the Laguna area.

Many cultures have influenced the history of Laguna. Hopi, Jemez, and Zuni people had married into the pueblo by the time it was established at its present site in the early 1500s. Later Navajos, Spanish settlers, and others of European ancestry intermarried with the Lagunas. The incorporation of rituals and stories from other tribes and cultures into their oral tradition occurred early in Laguna society and became an ongoing practice. Silko's own ancestry is mixed. Her father's people were Laguna and white. Her mother, born in Montana, was from a Plains tribe. Silko also has Mexican ancestry.

Her first book, *Laguna Woman* (1974), a collection of her poetry, shows an awareness of the interrelationships between the people and the river, mesas, hills, and mountains surrounding Laguna. But this awareness of place is not narrowly regional. For example, "Prayer to the Pacific" affirms the dependence of the Lagunas on the rain which west winds blow from as far as China.

The nearly 500-year existence of present-day Laguna makes it possible for Silko to write out of a culture intricately knowledgeable about the natural environment. This landscape and culture suffered severe trauma during the past half-century. During World War II, the atomic bomb was developed at nearby Los Alamos; and the first atomic explosion, at the Trinity site, occurred only 150 miles from Laguna. In the early 1950s the Anaconda company opened a large open-pit uranium mine on Laguna land, and uranium mining became a major source of income for Laguna and neighboring Pueblo and Navajo peoples. Nuclear destruction is a central concern in *Ceremony* (1977), Silko's first novel. An important theme in all of Silko's work is the recurrence of everything that happens. As "old Grandma" in *Ceremony* simply states, "'It seems like I already heard these stories before . . . only thing is, the names sound different.'"

Silko's second novel, *Almanac of the Dead* (1991), sounds an alarm in the face of escalating interpersonal violence and greed threatening to destroy humanity at the end of the twentieth century. A wide-ranging analysis and critique of contemporary American culture, the novel ends with the prophetic vision of a revolution in which the buffalo, the indigenous people, and the poor regain their land. Silko's third novel, *Gardens in the Dunes* (1999), juxtaposes the world of the indigenous peoples of the desert Southwest with that of the European and American upper class during the period between the Ghost Dance era at the end of the nineteenth century and World War I.

The most useful guide to understanding the cultural and social contexts of *Ceremony* and *Almanac of the Dead* is Silko's *Yellow Woman and a Beauty of the Spirit: Essays on Native American Life Today.* (1996). Silko models her fiction on the Laguna storytelling tradition, which she describes as patterned like the web of a spider.

Norma C. Wilson
University of South Dakota

PRIMARY WORKS

Laguna Woman, 1974; *Ceremony,* 1977; *Storyteller,* 1981; *The Delicacy and Strength of Lace,* 1986 (correspondence with James Wright, ed. Anne Wright); *Almanac of the Dead,* 1991; *Yellow Woman and a Beauty of the Spirit: Essays on Native American Life Today,* 1996; *Gardens in the Dunes,* 1999.

Lullaby

The sun had gone down but the snow in the wind gave off its own light. It came in thick tufts like new wool—washed before the weaver spins it. Ayah reached out for it like her own babies had, and she smiled when she remembered how she had laughed at them. She was an old woman now, and her life had become memories. She sat down with her back against the wide cottonwood tree, feeling the rough bark on her back bones; she faced east and listened to the wind and snow sing a high-pitched Yeibechei[1] song. Out of the wind she felt warmer, and she could watch the wide fluffy snow fill in her tracks, steadily, until the direction she had come from was gone. By the light of the snow she could see the dark outline of the big arroyo a few feet away. She was sitting on the edge of Cebolleta Creek, where in the springtime the thin cows would graze on grass already chewed flat to the ground. In the wide deep creek bed where only a trickle of water flowed in the summer, the skinny cows would wander, looking for new grass along winding paths splashed with manure.

Ayah pulled the old Army blanket over her head like a shawl. Jimmie's blanket—the one he had sent to her. That was a long time ago and the green wool was faded, and it was unraveling on the edges. She did not want to think about Jimmie. So she thought about the weaving and the way her mother had done it. On the tall wooden loom set into the sand under a tamarack tree for shade. She could see it clearly. She had been only a little girl when her grandma gave her the wooden combs to pull the twigs and burrs from the raw, freshly washed wool. And while she combed the wool, her grandma sat beside her, spinning a silvery strand of yarn around the smooth cedar spindle. Her mother worked at the loom with yarns dyed bright yellow and red and gold. She watched them dye the yarn in boiling black pots full of beeweed petals, juniper berries, and sage. The blankets her mother made were soft and woven so

[1]Navajo Night Chant—a song of healing.

tight that rain rolled off them like birds' feathers. Ayah remembered sleeping warm on cold windy nights, wrapped in her mother's blankets on the hogan's[2] sandy floor.

The snow drifted now, with the northwest wind hurling it in gusts. It drifted up around her black overshoes—old ones with little metal buckles. She smiled at the snow which was trying to cover her little by little. She could remember when they had no black rubber overshoes; only the high buckskin leggings that they wrapped over their elkhide moccasins. If the snow was dry or frozen, a person could walk all day and not get wet; and in the evenings the beams of the ceiling would hang with lengths of pale buckskin leggings, drying out slowly.

She felt peaceful remembering. She didn't feel cold any more. Jimmie's blanket seemed warmer than it had ever been. And she could remember the morning he was born. She could remember whispering to her mother, who was sleeping on the other side of the hogan, to tell her it was time now. She did not want to wake the others. The second time she called to her, her mother stood up and pulled on her shoes; she knew. They walked to the old stone hogan together, Ayah walking a step behind her mother. She waited alone, learning the rhythms of the pains while her mother went to call the old woman to help them. The morning was already warm even before dawn and Ayah smelled the bee flowers blooming and the young willow growing at the springs. She could remember that so clearly, but his birth merged into the births of the other children and to her it became all the same birth. They named him for the summer morning and in English they called him Jimmie.

It wasn't like Jimmie died. He just never came back, and one day a dark blue sedan with white writing on its doors pulled up in front of the boxcar shack where the rancher let the Indians live. A man in a khaki uniform trimmed in gold gave them a yellow piece of paper and told them that Jimmie was dead. He said the Army would try to get the body back and then it would be shipped to them; but it wasn't likely because the helicopter had burned after it crashed. All of this was told to Chato because he could understand English. She stood inside the doorway holding the baby while Chato listened. Chato spoke English like a white man and he spoke Spanish too. He was taller than the white man and he stood straighter too. Chato didn't explain why; he just told the military man they could keep the body if they found it. The white man looked bewildered; he nodded his head and he left. Then Chato looked at her and shook his head, and then he told her, "Jimmie isn't coming home anymore," and when he spoke, he used the words to speak of the dead. She didn't cry then, but she hurt inside with anger. And she mourned him as the years passed, when a horse fell with Chato and broke his leg, and the white rancher told them he wouldn't pay Chato until he could work again. She mourned Jimmie because he would have worked for his father then; he would have saddled the big bay horse and ridden the fence lines each day, with wire cutters and heavy gloves, fixing the breaks in the barbed wire and putting the stray cattle back inside again.

She mourned him after the white doctors came to take Danny and Ella away. She was at the shack alone that day they came. It was back in the days before they hired Navajo women to go with them as interpreters. She recognized one of the doctors.

[2]Traditional six-sided Navajo dwelling, the door of which faces east.

She had seen him at the children's clinic at Cañoncito about a month ago. They were wearing khaki uniforms and they waved papers at her and a black ball-point pen, trying to make her understand their English words. She was frightened by the way they looked at the children, like the lizard watches the fly. Danny was swinging on the tire swing on the elm tree behind the rancher's house, and Ella was toddling around the front door, dragging the broomstick horse Chato made for her. Ayah could see they wanted her to sign the papers, and Chato had taught her to sign her name. It was something she was proud of. She only wanted them to go, and to take their eyes away from her children.

She took the pen from the man without looking at his face and she signed the papers in three different places he pointed to. She stared at the ground by their feet and waited for them to leave. But they stood there and began to point and gesture at the children. Danny stopped swinging. Ayah could see his fear. She moved suddenly and grabbed Ella into her arms; the child squirmed, trying to get back to her toys. Ayah ran with the baby toward Danny; she screamed for him to run and then she grabbed him around his chest and carried him too. She ran south into the foothills of juniper trees and black lava rock. Behind her she heard the doctors running, but they had been taken by surprise, and as the hills became steeper and the cholla cactus were thicker, they stopped. When she reached the top of the hill, she stopped to listen in case they were circling around her. But in a few minutes she heard a car engine start and they drove away. The children had been too surprised to cry while she ran with them. Danny was shaking and Ella's little fingers were gripping Ayah's blouse.

She stayed up in the hills for the rest of the day, sitting on a black lava boulder in the sunshine where she could see for miles all around her. The sky was light blue and cloudless, and it was warm for late April. The sun warmth relaxed her and took the fear and anger away. She lay back on the rock and watched the sky. It seemed to her that she could walk into the sky, stepping through clouds endlessly. Danny played with little pebbles and stones, pretending they were birds eggs and then little rabbits. Ella sat at her feet and dropped fistfuls of dirt into the breeze, watching the dust and particles of sand intently. Ayah watched a hawk soar high above them, dark wings gliding; hunting or only watching, she did not know. The hawk was patient and he circled all afternoon before he disappeared around the high volcanic peak the Mexicans called Guadalupe.

Late in the afternoon, Ayah looked down at the gray boxcar shack with the paint all peeled from the wood; the stove pipe on the roof was rusted and crooked. The fire she had built that morning in the oil drum stove had burned out. Ella was asleep in her lap now and Danny sat close to her, complaining that he was hungry; he asked when they would go to the house. "We will stay up here until your father comes," she told him, "because those white men were chasing us." The boy remembered then and he nodded at her silently.

If Jimmie had been there he could have read those papers and explained to her what they said. Ayah would have known then, never to sign them. The doctors came back the next day and they brought a BIA[3] policeman with them. They told Chato

[3]U.S. Bureau of Indian Affairs.

they had her signature and that was all they needed. Except for the kids. She listened to Chato sullenly; she hated him when he told her it was the old woman who died in the winter, spitting blood; it was her old grandma who had given the children this disease. "They don't spit blood," she said coldly. "The whites lie." She held Ella and Danny close to her, ready to run to the hills again. "I want a medicine man first," she said to Chato, not looking at him. He shook his head. "It's too late now. The policeman is with them. You signed the paper." His voice was gentle.

It was worse than if they had died: to lose the children and to know that somewhere, in a place called Colorado, in a place full of sick and dying strangers, her children were without her. There had been babies that died soon after they were born, and one that died before he could walk. She had carried them herself, up to the boulders and great pieces of the cliff that long ago crashed down from Long Mesa; she laid them in the crevices of sandstone and buried them in fine brown sand with round quartz pebbles that washed down the hills in the rain. She had endured it because they had been with her. But she could not bear this pain. She did not sleep for a long time after they took her children. She stayed on the hill where they had fled the first time, and she slept rolled up in the blanket Jimmie had sent her. She carried the pain in her belly and it was fed by everything she saw: the blue sky of their last day together and the dust and pebbles they played with; the swing in the elm tree and broomstick horse choked life from her. The pain filled her stomach and there was no room for food or for her lungs to fill with air. The air and the food would have been theirs.

She hated Chato, not because he let the policeman and doctors put the screaming children in the government car, but because he had taught her to sign her name. Because it was like the old ones always told her about learning their language or any of their ways: it endangered you. She slept alone on the hill until the middle of November when the first snows came. Then she made a bed for herself where the children had slept. She did not lie down beside Chato again until many years later, when he was sick and shivering and only her body could keep him warm. The illness came after the white rancher told Chato he was too old to work for him anymore, and Chato and his old woman should be out of the shack by the next afternoon because the rancher had hired new people to work there. That had satisfied her. To see how the white man repaid Chato's years of loyalty and work. All of Chato's fine-sounding English talk didn't change things.

It snowed steadily and the luminous light from the snow gradually diminished into the darkness. Somewhere in Cebolleta a dog barked and other village dogs joined with it. Ayah looked in the direction she had come, from the bar where Chato was buying the wine. Sometimes he told her to go on ahead and wait; and then he never came. And when she finally went back looking for him, she would find him passed out at the bottom of the wooden steps to Azzie's Bar. All the wine would be gone and most of the money too, from the pale blue check that came to them once a month in a government envelope. It was then that she would look at his face and his hands, scarred by ropes and the barbed wire of all those years, and she would think, this man is a stranger; for forty years she had smiled at him and cooked his food, but he remained a stranger. She stood up again, with the snow almost to her knees, and she walked back to find Chato.

It was hard to walk in the deep snow and she felt the air burn in her lungs. She stopped a short distance from the bar to rest and readjust the blanket. But this time he wasn't waiting for her on the bottom step with his old Stetson hat pulled down and his shoulders hunched up in his long wool overcoat.

She was careful not to slip on the wooden steps. When she pushed the door open, warm air and cigarette smoke hit her face. She looked around slowly and deliberately, in every corner, in every dark place that the old man might find to sleep. The bar owner didn't like Indians in there, especially Navajos, but he let Chato come in because he could talk Spanish like he was one of them. The men at the bar stared at her, and the bartender saw that she left the door open wide. Snowflakes were flying inside like moths and melting into a puddle on the oiled wood floor. He motioned to her to close the door, but she did not see him. She held herself straight and walked across the room slowly, searching the room with every step. The snow in her hair melted and she could feel it on her forehead. At the far corner of the room, she saw red flames at the mica window of the old stove door; she looked behind the stove just to make sure. The bar got quiet except for the Spanish polka music playing on the jukebox. She stood by the stove and shook the snow from her blanket and held it near the stove to dry. The wet wool smell reminded her of new-born goats in early March, brought inside to warm near the fire. She felt calm.

In past years they would have told her to get out. But her hair was white now and her face was wrinkled. They looked at her like she was a spider crawling slowly across the room. They were afraid; she could feel the fear. She looked at their faces steadily. They reminded her of the first time the white people brought her children back to her that winter. Danny had been shy and hid behind the thin white woman who brought them. And the baby had not known her until Ayah took her into her arms, and then Ella had nuzzled close to her as she had when she was nursing. The blonde woman was nervous and kept looking at a dainty gold watch on her wrist. She sat on the bench near the small window and watched the dark snow clouds gather around the mountains; she was worrying about the unpaved road. She was frightened by what she saw inside too: the strips of venison drying on a rope across the ceiling and the children jabbering excitedly in a language she did not know. So they stayed for only a few hours. Ayah watched the government car disappear down the road and she knew they were already being weaned from these lava hills and from this sky. The last time they came was in early June, and Ella stared at her the way the men in the bar were now staring. Ayah did not try to pick her up; she smiled at her instead and spoke cheerfully to Danny. When he tried to answer her, he could not seem to remember and he spoke English words with the Navajo. But he gave her a scrap of paper that he had found somewhere and carried in his pocket; it was folded in half, and he shyly looked up at her and said it was a bird. She asked Chato if they were home for good this time. He spoke to the white woman and she shook her head. "How much longer?" he asked, and she said she didn't know; but Chato saw how she stared at the boxcar shack. Ayah turned away then. She did not say good-bye.

She felt satisfied that the men in the bar feared her. Maybe it was her face and the way she held her mouth with teeth clenched tight, like there was nothing anyone could do to her now. She walked north down the road, searching for the old man.

She did this because she had the blanket, and there would be no place for him except with her and the blanket in the old adobe barn near the arroyo. They always slept there when they came to Cebolleta. If the money and the wine were gone, she would be relieved because then they could go home again; back to the old hogan with a dirt roof and rock walls where she herself had been born. And the next day the old man could go back to the few sheep they still had, to follow along behind them, guiding them, into dry sandy arroyos where sparse grass grew. She knew he did not like walking behind old ewes when for so many years he rode big quarter horses and worked with cattle. But she wasn't sorry for him; he should have known all along what would happen.

There had not been enough rain for their garden in five years; and that was when Chato finally hitched a ride into the town and brought back brown boxes of rice and sugar and big tin cans of welfare peaches. After that, at the first of the month they went to Cebolleta to ask the postmaster for the check; and then Chato would go to the bar and cash it. They did this as they planted the garden every May, not because anything would survive the summer dust, but because it was time to do this. The journey passed the days that smelled silent and dry like the caves above the canyon with yellow painted buffaloes on their walls.

He was walking along the pavement when she found him. He did not stop or turn around when he heard her behind him. She walked beside him and she noticed how slowly he moved now. He smelled strong of woodsmoke and urine. Lately he had been forgetting. Sometimes he called her by his sister's name and she had been gone for a long time. Once she had found him wandering on the road to the white man's ranch, and she asked him why he was going that way; he laughed at her and said, "You know they can't run that ranch without me," and he walked on determined, limping on the leg that had been crushed many years before. Now he looked at her curiously, as if for the first time, but he kept shuffling along, moving slowly along the side of the highway. His gray hair had grown long and spread out on the shoulders of the long overcoat. He wore the old felt hat pulled down over his ears. His boots were worn out at the toes and he had stuffed pieces of an old red shirt in the holes. The rags made his feet look like little animals up to their ears in snow. She laughed at his feet; the snow muffled the sound of her laugh. He stopped and looked at her again. The wind had quit blowing and the snow was falling straight down; the southeast sky was beginning to clear and Ayah could see a star.

"Let's rest awhile," she said to him. They walked away from the road and up the slope to the giant boulders that had tumbled down from the red sandrock mesa throughout the centuries of rainstorms and earth tremors. In a place where the boulders shut out the wind, they sat down with their backs against the rock. She offered half of the blanket to him and they sat wrapped together.

The storm passed swiftly. The clouds moved east. They were massive and full, crowding together across the sky. She watched them with the feeling of horses—steely blue-gray horses startled across the sky. The powerful haunches pushed into the distances and the tail hairs streamed white mist behind them. The sky cleared. Ayah saw that there was nothing between her and the stars. The light was crystalline. There was no shimmer, no distortion through earth haze. She breathed the clarity of the night sky; she smelled the purity of the half moon and the stars. He was lying on his side with his knees pulled up near his belly for warmth. His eyes were closed now, and in the light from the stars and the moon, he looked young again.

She could see it descend out of the night sky: an icy stillness from the edge of the thin moon. She recognized the freezing. It came gradually, sinking snowflake by snowflake until the crust was heavy and deep. It had the strength of the stars in Orion, and its journey was endless. Ayah knew that with the wine he would sleep. He would not feel it. She tucked the blanket around him, remembering how it was when Ella had been with her; and she felt the rush so big inside her heart for the babies. And she sang the only song she knew to sing for babies. She could not remember if she had ever sung it to her children, but she knew that her grandmother had sung it and her mother had sung it:

The earth is your mother,
she holds you.
The sky is your father,
he protects you.
Sleep,
sleep.
Rainbow is your sister,
she loves you.
The winds are your brothers,
they sing to you.
Sleep,
sleep.
We are together always
We are together always
There never was a time
when this
was not so.

1981

Simon Ortiz (Acoma Pueblo) b. 1941

Simon Ortiz was born in Albuquerque, New Mexico. After an elementary education in Indian schools, high school, and a stint in the Army, he enrolled at the University of New Mexico, where he became aware of N. Scott Momaday, James Welch, and others among the first voices in Native American literature in the late '60s. Although he was always interested in writing, under the pressures of contemporary experience Ortiz found his motive for writing changed from self-expression to the desire to "express a Native American nationalistic (some may call it a tribalistic) literary voice."

Ortiz is a member of the Acoma Pueblo tribe, and his experiences in that community endowed him with several passionate concerns. From his father he learned to reverence the power and integrity of language. By choice, his poetry is fundamentally oral and frequently narrative, because he believes that one experiences life through poetry or, in the oral tradition, song, "Song as language," he has written, "is a way of touching." A second recurrent theme of Ortiz is that we establish our identity, individually and communally, in relation to a sense of place. For the most part, he argues, Anglo-Americans have been alienated from the land, a dislocation they try to valorize with an expansionist Frontier ideology. It is no wonder, then, that Ortiz is also deeply concerned with the political consequences of his writing. He grew up in the uranium mining area of northwest New Mexico, where laborers daily compromised their health and lives in the ruthless exploitation of the natural environment. Ortiz himself worked in such mines, and his identification with workers and the dehumanizing conditions under which they struggle, highlighted in his short story "To Change in a Good Way," permeates his work. Arguments that literature ought to be above politics, be concerned only with beauty and universal significance, do not sway him. Such a position, he argues, is taken by those who want to obscure the political consequences of their own work, "who do not want to hear the truth spoken by those who defend the earth."

Ortiz's interest in the transformative power of compelling language, a historical sense of place, and the political dimensions of poetry are especially evident in his most recent work, a cycle of poems entitled *from Sand Creek.* Based on his experiences as a veteran recovering at a VA hospital, the poems offer a series of discrete, but tonally unified moments of reflection, which contemplate the present condition of the speaker and his nation in view of each's past. Though the book is full of anger, grief, and pain, its dominant theme is compassion. "Love," he writes, "should be answerable for." Only by claiming responsibility for ourselves and our nation, present and past, can we create the possibility of hope.

Andrew O. Wiget
New Mexico State University

PRIMARY WORKS

Poetry: *Going for the Rain,* 1976; *A Good Journey,* 1977; *Fight Back: For the Sake of the People, For the Sake of the Land,* 1980; *from Sand Creek,* 1981; Fiction: *Howbah Indians,* 1978; *Fightin': New and Selected Short Stories,* 1983; *Earth Power Coming,* editor 1983.

from Sand Creek

November 29, 1864: On that cold dawn, about 600 Southern Cheyenne and Arapaho People, two-thirds of them women and children, were camped on a bend of Sand Creek in southeastern Colorado. The People were at peace. This was expressed two months before by Black Kettle, one of the principal elders of the Cheyennes, in Denver to Governor John Evans and Colonel John W. Chivington, head of the Colorado Volunteers. "I want you to give all these chiefs of the soldiers here to understand that we are for peace, and that we have made peace, that we may not be mistaken for enemies." The reverend Colonel Chivington and his Volunteers and Fort Lyon troops, numbering more than 700 heavily armed men, slaughtered 105 women and children and 28 men.

A U.S. flag presented by President Lincoln in 1863 to Black Kettle in Washington, D.C. flew from a pole above the elder's lodge on that gray dawn. The People had been assured they would be protected by the flag. By mid-1865, the Cheyenne and Arapaho People had been driven out of Colorado Territory.

* * *

This America
has been a burden
of steel and mad
death,
but, look now,
there are flowers
and new grass
and a spring wind
rising
from Sand Creek.

It was a national quest, dictated by economic motives. Europe was hungry for raw material, and America was abundant forest, rivers, land.

Many of them
built their sod houses
without windows.
Without madness.

But fierce, o
with a just determination.

Consulting axioms
and the dream called America.

Cotton Mather was no fool.

A few remembered
Andrew Jackson,
knew who he was,
ruminating, savoring
fresh Indian blood.

Style is a matter
of preference,
performance,
judgement yearning
to be settled quickly.

The axiom
would be the glory of America
at last,
          no wastelands,
no forgiveness.

The child would be sublime.

* * *

There are ghost towns all over the West; some are profitable tourist attractions of the "frontier," others are merely sad and unknown.

What should have been
important and fruitful
became bitter.
Wasted.
Spots appeared on their lungs.
Marrow dried
in their bones.
They ranted.
Pointless utterances.
Truth did not speak for them.

It is a wonder
they even made it to California.

But, of course,
they did,
and they named it success.
Conquest.
Destiny.

Frontiers ended for them
and a dread settled upon them
and became remorseless
nameless
namelessness.

* * *

Colonel Chivington was a moral man, believed he was made in the image of God, and he carried out the orders of his nation's law; Kit Carson didn't mind stealing and killing either.

At the Salvation Army
a clerk
caught me
wandering
among old spoons
and knives,
sweaters and shoes.

I couldn't have stolen anything;
my life was stolen already.

In protest though,
I should have stolen.
My life. My life.

She caught me;
Carson caught Indians,
secured them with his lies.
Bound them with his belief.

After winter,
our own lives fled.

I reassured her
what she believed.
Bought a sweater.

And fled.

I should have stolen.
My life. My life.

* * *

There is a revolution going on; it is very spiritual and its manifestation is economic, political, and social. Look to the horizon and listen.

The mind is stunned stark.

At night,
Africa is the horizon.

The cots of the hospital
are not part of the dream.

Lie awake, afraid.
Thinned breath.

Was it a scream again.
                    Far
below, far below,
the basement speaks
for Africa, Saigon, Sand Creek.

Souls gather
around campfires.
Hills protect them.

Mercenaries gamble
for odds.
They'll never know.
Indians stalk beyond the dike,
carefully measure the distance,
count their bullets.

Stark, I said,
stunned night in the VAH.

* * *

The blood poured unto the plains, steaming like breath on winter mornings; the breath rose into the clouds and became the rain and replenishment.

They were amazed
at so much blood.
Spurting,
sparkling,
splashing, bubbling, steady
hot arcing streams.
Red
and bright and vivid
unto the grassed plains.
Steaming.
So brightly and amazing.
They were awed.

It almost seemed magical
that they had so much blood.
It just kept pouring,
like rivers,
like endless floods from the sky,
thunder that had become liquid,
and the thunder surged forever
into their minds.
Indeed,
they must have felt
they should get on their knees
and drink the red rare blood,
drink to replenish
their own vivid loss.

Their helpless hands
were like sieves.

* * *

The land and Black Kettle took them in like lost children, and by 1876 land allotment and reservations and private property were established.

They must have known.

Surely,

they must have.

Black Kettle

met them at the open door
of the plains.

He swept his hand
all about them.
The vista of the mountains
was at his shoulder.
The rivers
run from the sky.
Stone soothes
every ache.
Dirt feeds us.
Spirit is nutrition.
Like a soul, the land
was open to them, like a child's heart.
There was no paradise,
but it would have gently and willingly
and longingly given them food and air
and substance for every comfort.
If they had only acknowledged
even their smallest conceit.

* * *

That dream
shall have a name
after all,
and it will not be vengeful
but wealthy with love
and compassion
and knowledge.
And it will rise
in this heart
which is our America.

1981

Permissions Acknowledgments

Edward Albee. *The Sandbox*. Copyright © 1959 by Edward Albee. Reprinted by permission of William Morris Agency, Inc. on behalf of the Author. EXHIBIT A *The Sandbox*. Copyright © 1959 by Edward Albee. All rights reserved. CAUTION: Professionals and amateurs and hereby warned that *The Sandbox* is subject to a royalty. It is fully protected under the copyright laws of the United States of America and of all countries covered by the International Copyright Union (including the Dominion of Canada and the rest of the British Commonwealth), the Berne Convention, the Pan-American Copyright Convention and the Universal Copyright Convention, as well as all countries with which the United States has reciprocal copyright relations. All rights, including professional/amateur stage rights, motion picture, recitation, lecturing, public reading, radio broadcasting, television, video or sound recording, all other forms of mechanical or electronic reproduction, such as CD-ROM, CD-I, information storage and retrieval systems and photocopying, and the rights of translation into foreign languages, are strictly reserved. Particular emphasis is laid upon the matter of readings, permission for which must be secured from the Author's agent in writing. Inquiries concerning rights should be addressed to: William Morris Agency, Inc., 1325 Avenue of the Americas, New York, New York 10019.

Sherman Alexie, *The Lone Ranger and Tonto Fistfight in Heaven*. Copyright © 1993 by Sherman Alexie. Used with the permission of Grove/Atlantic, Inc.

Dorothy Allison. "Don't Tell Me You Don't Know." From *Trash*. Copyright © 1988 by Dorothy Allison. Used by permission of Firebrand Books, Ithaca, New York.

Rudolfo Anaya. From *Bless Me, Ultima*. Copyright © Rudolfo Anaya 1974. Published in hardcover and mass market paperback by Warner Books Inc., 1994; originally published by TQS Publications. Reprinted by permission of Susan Bergholz Literary Services, New York. All rights reserved.

Sherwood Anderson. From *Death in the Woods*. Reprinted by permission of Harold Ober Associates, Incorporated. Copyright © 1926 by The American Mercury, Inc. Copyright renewed 1983 by Eleanor Copenhaver Anderson. Reprinted by permission of Harold Ober Associates Incorporated.

Gloria Anzaldúa. Chapters 3 and 7 from *Borderlands/La Frontera: The New Mestiza* © 1987 by Gloria Anzaldúa. Reprinted by permission of Aunt Lute Books, San Francisco.

John Ashbery. "The Instruction Manual" from *Some Trees* (New York: The Ecco Press, 1977). Copyright © 1956 by John Ashbery. Reprinted by permission of Georges Borchardt, Inc. for the author. "Farm Implements and Rutabagas in a Landscape" from *The Double Dream of Spring* (New York: Dutton, 1970). Copyright © 1970 by John Ashbery. Reprinted by permission of Georges Borchardt, Inc. for the author. "As You Came from the Holy Land," copyright © 1973 by John Ashbery, from *Self-Portrait in a Convex Mirror* by John Ashbery. Used by permission of Viking Penguin, a division of Penguin Books USA Inc.

James Baldwin. "Sonny's Blues." Reprinted by arrangement with the James Baldwin Estate.

Toni Cade Bambara. From *Gorilla, My Love*. Copyright © 1971 by Toni Cade Bambara. Reprinted by permission of Random House, Inc.

Djuna Barnes. "Smoke" from *Smoke and Other Early Stories*, (Los Angeles: Sun & Moon Press, © Djuna Barnes 1982, 1987). Reprinted by permission of the publisher.

John Barth. "Lost in the Funhouse." Copyright © 1967 by The Atlantic Monthly Company from *Lost in the Funhouse* by John Barth. Used by permission of Doubleday, a division of Bantam Doubleday Dell Publishing Group, Inc.

Donald Barthelme. "At the End of the Mechanical Age" from *Amateurs*. Copyright © 1976 by Donald Barthelme. Reprinted by permission of The Wylie Agency, Inc.

Saul Bellow. "Looking for Mr. Green," copyright 1951, renewed © 1979 by Saul Bellow, from *Mosby's Memoirs and Other Stories* by Saul Bellow. Used by permission of Viking Penguin, a division of Penguin Books USA Inc.

Elizabeth Bishop. "At the Fishhouses," "Filling Station," "The Fish," and "The Man-Moth" from *The Complete Poems, 1927–1979*. Copyright © 1979, 1983 by Alice Helen Methfessel. Reprinted by permission of Farrar, Straus & Giroux, Inc.

Robert Bly. "The Teeth Mother Naked at Last" from *Sleepers Joining Hands* by Robert Bly. Copyright © 1970 by Robert Bly. Reprinted by permission of HarperCollins Publishers, Inc. "Counting Small-

Boned Bodies" from *The Light Around the Body* by Robert Bly. Copyright © 1967 by Robert Bly. Reprinted by permission of HarperCollins Publishers, Inc.

Louise Bogan. "After the Persian," "The Dragonfly," "Night," "Roman Fountain," "The Sleeping Fury," and "Women" from *The Bluest Estuaries* by Louise Bogan. Copyright © 1968 by Louise Bogan. Copyright renewed © 1996 by Ruth Limmer. Reprinted by permission of Farrar, Straus & Giroux, Inc.

Kay Boyle. "A Communication to Nancy Cunard." From *Collected Poems, 1962.* Reprinted by permission of the Estate of Kay Boyle and the Watkins/Loomis Agency.

Gwendolyn Brooks. "The Sundays of Satin-Legs Smith," "The Mother," "A Bronzeville Mother Loiters in Mississippi. Meanwhile, a Mississippi Mother Burns Bacon," and "The Last Quatrain of the Balled of Emmet Till" from *Blacks.* Copyright © 1991. Publisher, Third World Press, Chicago, 1991. Reprinted by permission of the poet, Ms. Gwendolyn Brooks.

Sterling Brown. "Ma Rainey" and "Strong Men" from *The Collected Poems of Sterling A. Brown,* edited by Michael S. Harper. Copyright 1932 Harcourt Brace and Company. Copyright renewed 1960 by Sterling Brown. "When de Saints Go Ma'ching Home" from *The Collected Poems of Sterling A. Brown,* edited by Michael S. Harper. Copyright 1932 Harcourt Brace and Company. Copyright renewed 1960 by Sterling Brown. Originally appeared in *Southern Road* by Sterling A. Brown. "Remembering Nat Turner" from *The Collected Poems of Sterling A. Brown,* edited by Michael S. Harper. Copyright 1939 by Sterling A. Brown. Copyright Renewed. "Song of Triumph" from *The Collected Poems of Sterling A. Brown,* edited by Michael S. Harper. Copyright 1980 by Sterling A. Brown. All are reprinted by permission of HarperCollins Publishers, Inc.

Raymond Carver. From *Cathedral.* Copyright © 1981, 1982, 1983 by Raymond Carver. Reprinted by permission of Alfred A. Knopf, Inc.

Lorna Dee Cervantes. "Poem for the Young White Man Who Asked Me How I, an Intelligent Well-Read Person Could Believe in the War Between Races" printed from *Emplumada,* by permission of the University of Pittsburgh Press. "Beneath the Shadow of the Freeway" reprinted by permission of the publisher, *Latin American Literary Review,* Volume V, Number 10, 1977, Pittsburgh, Pennsylvania. "Macho" is reprinted with permission from the publisher of *From the Cables of Genocide: Poems on Love and Hunger* (Houston: Arte Publico Press–University of Houston, 1991). "Bananas," from *Daughters of the Fifth Sun,* Riverhead Books, 1993. Reprinted by permission of Lorna Dee Cervantes.

Frank Chin. Reprinted by permission of Coffee House Press from Frank Chin, "Railroad Standard Time," from *The Chinaman Pacific & Frisco R.R. Co.*

Lucille Clifton. "i am accused of tending to the past," "at the cemetery, walnut grove plantation, south carolina," and "reply" from *Quilting: Poems, 1987–1990.* Copyright © 1991 by Lucille Clifton. Reprinted with the permission of BOA Editions, Ltd. "in white america" from *Next: New Poems.* Copyright © 1987 by Lucille Clifton. Reprinted with the permission of BOA Editions, Ltd. "the thirty eighth year," from *Good Woman: Poems and a Memoir, 1969–1980,* by Lucille Clifton. Reprinted with the permission of BOA Editions, Ltd.

Judith Ortiz Cofer. Poems from *Triple Crown,* © 1987, Bilingual Press/Editorial Bilingue (Arizona State University, Tempe, AZ). Reprinted by permission.

Corridos. From *A Texas-Mexican Cancionero.* Copyright © 1976 by the Board of Trustees of the University of Illinois. Used with permission of the translator and University of Illinois Press. "El Hijo Desobediente" and translation, "The Disobedient Son," from Jose Limon, *Mexican Ballads, Chicano Poems: History and Influence in Mexican-American Social Poetry.* Copyright © 1992 The Regents of the University of California. Used with permission.

Hart Crane. "Black Tambourine," "Chaplinesque," "At Melville's Tomb," "To Brooklyn Bridge," "The River," and "The Broken Tower" from *Complete Poems of Hart Crane* by Marc Simon, editor. Copyright 1933, © 1958, 1966 by Liveright Publishing Corporation. Copyright © 1986 by Marc Simon. Reprinted by permission of Liveright Publishing Corporation.

Robert Creeley. From *Collected Poems of Robert Creeley, 1945–1975.* Copyright © 1983 The Regents of the University of California. Used by permission.

Victor Hernandez Cruz. "Urban Dream" from *Snaps, 1969.* "Mountain Building" and "Table of Contents" from *By Lingual Wholes*, reprinted with permission of Victor Hernandez Cruz.

Countee Cullen. Reprinted by permission of GRM Associates, Inc., Agents for the Estate of Ida M. Cullen. "Simon the Cyrenian Speaks," "Incident," "Yet Do I Marvel," "Pagan Prayer," and "Heritage," from *Color* by Countee Cullen. Copyright © 1925 by Harper & Brothers; copyright renewed 1953 by Ida M. Cullen. "From the Dark Tower," from *Copper Sun* by Countee Cullen. Copyright © 1927 by Harper & Brothers; copyright renewed 1955 by Ida M. Cullen. "Scottsboro, Too, Is Worth Its Song," from *The Media and Some Poems* by Countee Cullen. Copyright © 1935 by Harper & Brothers; copyright renewed 1963 by Ida M. Cullen.

E. E. Cummings. "Buffalo Bill's," "into the strenuous briefness," "the Cambridge ladies who live in furnished souls," "i like my body when it is with your," "my sweet old etcetera," "since feeling is first," "i sing of Olaf glad and big," "Picasso," "anyone lived in a pretty how town," "plato told," "what if a much of a which of a wind," and "pity this monster, manunkind," from *Complete Poems: 1904–1962* by E. E. Cummings, Edited by George J. Firmage. Copyright 1923, 1925, 1926, 1931, 1935, 1938, 1939, 1940, 1944, 1945, 1946, 1947, 1948, 1949, 1950, 1951, 1952, 1953, 1954, © 1955, 1956, 1957, 1958, 1959, 1960, 1961, 1962, 1963, 1966, 1967, 1968, 1972, 1973, 1974, 1975, 1976, 1977, 1978, 1979, 1980, 1981, 1982, 1983, 1984, 1985, 1986, 1987, 1988, 1989, 1990, 1991 by the Trustees for the E. E. Cummings Trust. Copyright © 1973, 1976, 1978, 1979, 1981, 1983, 1985, 1991 by George James Firmage. Reprinted by permission of Liveright Publishing Corporation.

Pietro Di Donato. From *Christ in Concrete*. Copyright 1937, 1965 by Pietro Di Donato. Preface copyright © 1993 by Studs Terkel. Introduction copyright © 1993 by Fred L. Gardaphe. Used by permission of Dutton Signet, a division of Penguin Books USA Inc.

Hilda Doolittle. By H.D. from *Collected Poems, 1912–1944*. Copyright © 1982 by The Estate of Hilda Doolittle. Reprinted by permission of New Directions Publishing Corp.

John Dos Passos. From *U.S.A.*, reprinted by permission of Mrs. John Dos Passos.

Rita Dove. "Ö" and "Kentucky, 1833" from *The Yellow House on the Corner*, Carnegie Mellon University Press, copyright © 1980 by Rita Dove. "Daystar" and "The Oriental Ballerina" from *Thomas and Beulah*, Carnegie Mellon University Press, © 1986 by Rita Dove. Reprinted by permission of the author.

W.E.B. Du Bois. Lines of music from *The Souls of Black Folk* by W.E.B. Du Bois. Copyright © 1986, reprinted by permission of Random House, Inc.

Alice Dunbar-Nelson. "You! Inez!" Reprinted by permission of University of Delaware Library, Newark, Delaware.

T. S. Eliot. "The Waste Land" from *Collected Poems, 1909–1962* by T. S. Eliot, copyright 1936 by Harcourt Brace and Company, copyright © 1964, 1963 by T. S. Eliot. "Tradition and the Individual Talent" from *Selected Essays* by T. S. Eliot, copyright 1950 by Harcourt Brace and Company and renewed 1978 by Esme Valerie Eliot. "The Dry Salvages" from *Four Quartets*, copyright 1943 by T. S. Eliot and renewed 1971 by Esme Valerie Eliot, reprinted by permission of Harcourt Brace and Company.

Ralph Ellison. "A Party Down at the Square" and "Flying Home" by Ralph Ellison from *Flying Home and Other Stories*. Copyright © 1996 by Fanny Ellison. "Brave Words for a Startling Occasion" from *Shadow Act* by Ralph Ellison. Copyright © 1953, 1964 by Ralph Ellison. Copyright renewed 1981, 1992 by Ralph Ellison. Reprinted by permission of Random House, Inc.

Louise Erdrich. "St. Marie" from *Love Medicine, New and Expanded Version* © 1984, 1993 by Louise Erdrich. Reprinted by permission of Henry Holt & Co., Inc.

William Faulkner. "Barn Burning" from *Collected Stories of William Faulkner*, Copyright 1950 by Random House, Inc. Copyright renewed 1977 by Jill Faulkner Summers. Reprinted by permission of Random House. "Delta Autumn" from *Go Down, Moses* by William Faulkner. Copyright © 1942 by William Faulkner. Reprinted by permission of Random House, Inc. "A Courtship" from *The Collected Stories of William Faulkner* by William Faulkner. Copyright © 1948 by William Faulkner. Reprinted by permission of Random House, Inc.

Kenneth Fearing. "Dirge" from *New and Selected Poems* by Kenneth Fearing, 1956. Reprinted by permission of Indiana University Press. "1933" by Kenneth Fearing, reprinted with permission.

Lawrence Ferlinghetti. "I Am Waiting" and "Dove Sta Amore" from *A Coney Island of the Mind.* Copyright © 1958 by Lawrence Ferlinghetti. "The Old Italian Is Dying" from *Landscapes of Living and Dying.* Copyright © 1979 by Lawrence Ferlinghetti. Reprinted by permission of New Directions Publishing Corp.

Carolyn Forché. "The Recording Angel" and "Elegy" from *The Angel of History.* Copyright © 1994 by Carloyn Forché. "The Colonel," "Because One Is Always Forgotten" and "As Children Together" from *The Country Between Us.* Copyright © 1980 by Carolyn Forché. Reprinted by permission of HarperCollins Publishers, Inc.

Robert Frost. From *The Poetry of Robert Frost,* edited by Edward Connery Lathem. Copyright © 1936, 1951, 1956 by Robert Frost, copyright © 1964, 1975 by Lesley Frost Ballantine, copyright © 1923, 1928, 1947, 1969 by Henry Holt and Co. Reprinted by permission of Henry Holt and Company, LLC.

Ernest J. Gaines. *The Sky Is Gray,* copyright © 1963 by Ernest J. Gaines, from *Bloodline* by Ernest J. Gaines. Used by permission of Doubleday, a division of Bantam Doubleday Dell Publishing Group, Inc.

Allen Ginsberg. All lines from "America" from *Collected Poems, 1947–1980* by Allen Ginsberg. Copyright © 1956, 1959 by Allen Ginsberg. Reprinted by permission of HarperCollins Publishers, Inc.

Allen Ginsberg. All lines from "Howl" and "A Supermarket in California," from *Collected Poems, 1947–1980* by Allen Ginsberg. Copyright © 1955 by Allen Ginsberg. Reprinted by permission of HarperCollins Publishers, Inc.

Jessica Hagedorn. "The Death of Anna May Wong," copyright © 1973 by Jessica Hagedorn, "Filipino Boogie," copyright © 1973 by Jessica Hagedorn, "Homesick" and "Vulva Operetta," from *Danger and Beauty* by Jessica Hagedorn, copyright © 1993 by Jessica Hagedorn. Used by permission of Viking Penguin, a division of Penguin Putnam, Inc.

Kimiko Hahn. "Strands." Reprinted from *Earshot* by Kimiko Hahn. Copyright © 1992 by Kimiko Hahn. Reprinted by permission of Hanging Loose Press. "Resistance: A Poem on Ikat Cloth." Reprinted from *Air Pocket* by Kimiko Hahn. Copyright © 1989 by Kimiko Hahn. Reprinted by permission of Hanging Loose Press. "Cuttings" was originally published in *The Unbearable Heart.* Copyright © 1995 by Kimiko Hahn. Reprinted by permission of Kaya.

Lorraine Hansberry. *A Raisin in the Sun.* Copyright © 1958 by Robert Nemiroff, as an unpublished work. Copyright © 1959, 1966, 1984 by Robert Nemiroff. Reprinted by permission of Random House, Inc.

Joy Harjo. "New Orleans," "Remember," "Vision," "Anchorage" and "The Woman Hanging from the 13th Floor Window" from the book, *She Had Some Horses.* Copyright © 1983 by Joy Harjo. Used by permission of the publisher, Thunder's Mouth Press. "Deer Dancer" and "We Must Call a Meeting" from *In Mad Love and War.* Copyright © 1990 by Joy Harjo. Reprinted by permission of University of New England Press.

Michael S. Harper. "Here Where Coltrane Is," "History as Apple Tree," "Song: I Want a Witness," "Nightmare Begins Responsibility," "A Narrative of the Life and Times of John Coltrane: Played by Himself," and "Camp Story." Copyright © Michael Harper, 1971, 1972, 1975, 1985. Reprinted by permission of the poet.

Robert Hayden. "Tour 5," copyright © 1966 by Robert Hayden, "Those Winter Sundays," copyright © 1966 by Robert Hayden, "Summertime and the Living. . . ," copyright © 1966 by Robert Hayden, and "Mourning Poem for the Queen of Sunday," copyright © 1975, 1972, 1966 by Robert Hayden, from *Angle of Ascent: New and Selected Poems* by Robert Hayden. Reprinted by permission of Liveright Publishing Corporation.

Alfred Hayes. "In a Coffee Pot." Reprinted with permission.

Lillian Hellman. From *Scoundrel Time* by Lillian Hellman. Copyright © 1976 by Lillian Hellman. By permission of Little, Brown and Company.

Ernest Hemingway. Chapter 27 from *A Farewell to Arms.* Copyright 1929 Charles Scribner's Sons. Copyright renewed 1957 by Ernest Hemingway. "Hills like White Elephants" from *Men Without Women.* Copyright 1927 Charles Scribner's Sons. Copyright renewed 1955 by Ernest Hemingway.

Both selections are reprinted with permission of Scribner, a Division of Simon & Schuster.

Michael Herr. From *Dispatches.* Copyright © 1977 by Michael Herr. Reprinted by permission of Alfred A. Knopf, Inc.

Rolando Hinojosa. Poems from *The Valley,* © 1983, Bilingual Press/Editorial Bilingue (Arizona State University, Tempe, AZ). Reprinted by permission.

Garrett Kaoru Hongo. "Yellow Light," "Who Among You Knows the Essence of Garlic?" and "And Your Soul Shall Dance" from *Yellow Light,* copyright © 1982 by Garrett Kaoru Hongo. Wesleyan University Press. By permission of University Press of New England. "Stepchild," from *Yellow Light,* copyright © 1982 by Garrett Kaoru Hongo. Wesleyan University Press. By permission of University Press of New England.

William Dean Howells. To the Editor of the *New York Tribune,* November, 1887, Dansville, New York, from W. D. Howells, *Selected Letters,* Volume III: *1882–1892,* Boston: Twayne Publishers, 1908, edited and annotated by Robert C. Leitz III. Copyright © 1980 by the Howells Edition Editorial Board. Reprinted by permission of the heirs of W. D. Howells.

Langston Hughes. "Negro," "Bad Luck Card," "I, Too," "Dream Variations," and "Dream Deferred" ("Harlem") from *Collected Poems* by Langston Hughes. Copyright © 1994 by the Estate of Langston Hughes. Reprinted by permission of Alfred A. Knopf, Inc. "The Same" reprinted from 1926 issue of *The Nation* magazine, © The Nation Company, Inc. Reprinted with permission. "The Negro Speaks of Rivers," "The Weary Blues," "Drum," and "Freedom Train" from *Collected Poems* by Langston Hughes. Copyright © 1994 by the Estate of Langston Hughes. Reprinted by permission of Alfred A. Knopf, Inc. "Radioactive Redcaps" from *The Best of Simple.* Copyright © 1961 by Langston Hughes. Copyright renewed © 1989 by George Huston Bass. "When the Negro Was in Vogue" from *The Big Sea.* Copyright © 1940 by Langston Hughes. Copyright renewed © 1968 by Arna Bontemps and George Huston Bass. "Big Meeting" and "Thank You, M'am" from *Something in Common.* Copyright © 1963 by Langston Hughes. Copyright renewed © 1992 by Arnold Rampersad and Ramona Bass. Reprinted by permission of Hill and Wang, a division of Farrar, Straus & Giroux, Inc. "Freedom Train" from *Collected Poems* by Langston Hughes. Copyright © 1994 by the Estate of Langston Hughes. Reprinted by permission of Alfred A. Knopf Inc.

Zora Neale Hurston. "Sweat" and "The Gilded Six-Bits" as taken from *The Complete Stories* by Zora Neale Hurston. Introduction copyright © 1995 by Henry Louis Gates, Jr., and Sieglinde Lemke. Compilation copyright © 1995 by Vivian Bowden, Lois J. Hurston Gaston, Clifford Hurston, Lucy Ann Hurston, Winifred Hurston Clark, Zora Mack Goins, Edgar Hurston, Sr., and Barbara Hurston Lewis. Afterword and Bibliography copyright © 1995 by Henry Louis Gates, Jr. Reprinted by permission of HarperCollins Publishers, Inc.

Lawson Fusao Inada. "Two Variations on a Theme by Thelonius Monk as Inspired by Mal Waldron" and "Instructions to All Persons" reprinted from *Legends from Camp,* copyright © 1993 by Lawson Fusao Inada (Coffee House Press, Minneapolis). Reprinted by permission from the publisher. "Kicking the Habit," reprinted from *Drawing the Line.* Copyright © 1997 by Lawson Fusao Inada (Coffee House Press, Minneapolis). Reprinted by permission from the publisher.

Robinson Jeffers. "Credo." Reprinted by permission of Jeffers Literary Properties. "Rock and Hawk," Copyright © 1936 and renewed 1962 by Donnan Jeffers and Garth Jeffers. "The Purse Seine," Copyright © 1936 and renewed 1965 by Donnan Jeffers and Garth Jeffers. "Self-Criticism in February," reprinted from *The Collected Poetry of Robinson Jeffers,* Volume Two, *1928–1938,* edited by Tim Hunt with the permission of the publishers, Stanford University Press. Copyright © 1938 and renewed 1966 by Donnan Jeffers and Garth Jeffers. Copyright © 1995 by the Board of Trustees of the Leland Stanford Junior University. "Bloody Sire," Copyright © 1940 and renewed 1968 by Donnan Jeffers and Garth Jeffers. "Excesses of God," Copyright © 1941 by Robinson Jeffers and renewed 1969 by Donnan Jeffers and Garth Jeffers. "Cassandra," Copyright © 1941 by Yardstick Press. Copyright © 1944 by Oscar Williams. "Beauty of Things," Copyright © 1951 by Robinson Jeffers. "Carmel Point," Copyright © 1954 by Robinson Jeffers.

Gish Jen. "In the American Society." From *Imagining America.* Copyright © 1986 by Gish Jen. First published in the Southern Review. Reprinted by permission of the author.

James Weldon Johnson. "Lift Every Voice and Sing" and "O Black and Unknown Bards" from *St.*

Peter Relates an Incident. Copyright © 1935 by James Weldon Johnson. Copyright renewed © 1963 by Grace Nail Johnson. "The Creation" from *God's Trombones* by James Weldon Johnson. Copyright © 1927 The Viking Press, Inc. renewed © 1955 by Grace Nail Johnson. All rights reserved. Reprinted by permission of Viking Penguin, a division of Penguin Books USA, Inc.

LeRoi Jones (Amiri Baraka). Excerpt from *Dutchman and the Slave.* Reprinted by permission of Sterling Lord Literistic, Inc. Copyright © 1964 by Amiri Baraka.

June Jordan. "Poem About My Rights" and "To Free Nelson Mandela" from *Naming Our Destiny.* Copyright © 1989 by June Jordan. "Moving Toward Home" from *Living Room.* Copyright © 1985 by June Jordan. Used by permission of the publisher, Thunder's Mouth Press.

Martin Luther King, Jr. Two speeches. "I Have a Dream," Copyright © 1963 by Martin Luther King, Jr., copyright renewed 1991 by Coretta Scott King. "I've Been to the Mountaintop," Copyright © 1968 by the Estate of Martin Luther King, Jr. Reprinted by arrangement with the Heirs of the Estate of Martin Luther King, Jr., c/o Writers House, Inc., as Agent for the proprietor.

Maxine Hong Kingston. "White Tigers." From *The Woman Warrior: Memoirs of a Girlhood Among Ghosts.* Copyright © 1975, 1976 by Maxine Hong Kingston. Reprinted by permission of Alfred A. Knopf, Inc.

Etheridge Knight. "The Idea of Ancestry," "The Violent Space," "Ilu, the Talking Drum," and "A Poem for Myself" from *The Essential Etheridge Knight,* by Etheridge Knight, © 1986. Reprinted by permission of the University of Pittsburgh Press.

Yusef Komunyakaa. "TuDo Street," "Prisoners," "Thanks," "Facing It," and "Fog Galleon" from *Neon Vernacular: New and Selected Poems.* Copyright © 1993 by Yusef Komunyakaa, Wesleyan University Press. Reprinted by permission of University Press of New England.

Tato Laviera. "Latero Story (can pickers)" from *Mainstream Ethics,* "frio" from *Lacarreta Made a U-turn,* 1976, and "AmeRican" from *AmeRican,* 1985, are reprinted with permission of the publisher (Houston: Arte Publico Press–University of Houston).

Li-Young Lee. "I Ask My Mother to Sing" and "Ash, Snow or Moonlight" from *Rose.* Copyright © 1986 Li-Young Lee. Reprinted with permission of BOA Editions, Ltd. "My Father, in Heaven, Is Reading Out Loud," "With Ruins," and "This Room and Everything in It" from *The City in Which I Love You.* Copyright © 1990 by Li-Young Lee. Reprinted with the permission of BOA Editions, Ltd.

Meridel LeSueur. From *Annunciation* by Meridel LeSueur. Reprinted by permission of International Publishers Co., New York.

Denise Levertov. "Illustrious Ancestors," from *Collected Earlier: Poems, 1940–1960.* Copyright © 1958, 1979, 1949, 1979 by Denise Levertov. "A Solitude" from *Poems, 1960–1967.* Copyright © 1966 by Denise Levertov. "Making Peace" from *Breathing the Water.* Copyright ©1987 by Denise Levertov. "The May Mornings" from *Candles in Babylon.* Copyright ©1982 by Denise Levertov. "A Woman Alone" from *Life in the Forest.* Copyright © 1978 by Denise Levertov. Reprinted by permission of New Directions Publishing Corp.

Jose Limon. "El Hijo Desobediente" and translation, "The Disobedient Son," from *Mexican Ballads, Chicano Poems: History and Influence in Mexican-American Social Poetry,* Copyright © 1992 The Regents of the University of California. Used with permission.

Alain Locke. From *The New Negro,* courtesy of Atheneum Publishers, an imprint of Macmillan Publishing Company.

Audre Lorde. Reprinted with permission from *Sister Outsider.* Copyright © 1984 by Audre Lorde. Published by The Crossing Press, Freedom, California.

Audre Lorde. "Power," "Walking Our Boundaries," and "Never Take Fire from a Woman" from *The Black Unicorn* by Audre Lorde. Copyright © 1978 by Audre Lorde. "The Art of Response" and "Stations" from *Our Dead Behind Us* by Audre Lorde. Copyright © 1986 by Audre Lorde. Reprinted by permission of W. W. Norton & Company, Inc.

Amy Lowell. "The Sisters," from *The Complete Poetical Works of Amy Lowell.* Copyright © 1955 by Houghton Mifflin Co. Copyright © renewed 1983 by Houghton Mifflin Co., Brinton P. Roberts, and G. D'Andelot Berlin, Esquire. Reprinted by permission of Houghton Mifflin Co. All rights reserved.

Robert Lowell. "For the Union Dead" from *For the Union Dead* by Robert Lowell. Copyright © 1959 by Robert Lowell. Copyright renewed 1987 by Harriet Lowell, Caroline Lowell, and Sheridan Lowell. "Memories of West Street and Lepke" and "Skunk Hour" from *Life Studies* by Robert Lowell. Copyright © 1956, 1959 by Robert Lowell. Copyright renewed 1987 by Harriet Lowell, Caroline Lowell, and Sheridan Lowell. "Near the Ocean" from *Near the Ocean* by Robert Lowell, drawings by Sidney Nolan. Copyright © 1967 by Robert Lowell. Drawings copyright © 1967 by Sidney Nolan. "For Theodore Roethke: 1908–1963" from *Notebook: 1967–1968* by Robert Lowell. Copyright © 1969 by Robert Lowell. Reprinted by permission of Farrar, Straus & Giroux, Inc.

Norman Mailer. From *Armies of the Night*. Copyright © 1968 by Norman Mailer. Used by permission of Dutton Signet, a division of Penguin Books USA Inc.

Bernard Malamud. "The Magic Barrel" from *The Magic Barrel* by Bernard Malamud. Copyright © 1950, 1958 and copyright renewed © 1977, 1986 by Bernard Malamud. Reprinted by permission of Farrar, Straus & Giroux, Inc.

Malcolm X. "The Ballot or the Bullet," from *Malcolm X Speaks,* reprinted by permission of Pathfinder Press. Copyright © 1965 and 1989 by Betty Shabazz and Pathfinder Press.

Paule Marshall. "To Da-duh, in Memoriam." Reprinted by permission of The Feminist Press at The City University of New York, from *Reena and Other Stories* by Paule Marshall. Copyright © 1983 by Paule Marshall.

José Martí. "Our America" from *Our America* by José Martí, Monthly Review Press, Copyright © 1977 by Philip Foner. Reprinted by permission of Monthly Review Foundation.

Edgar Lee Masters. Lines from *New Spoon River* by Edgar Lee Masters. Reprinted with permission from Ellen C. Masters.

Mary McCarthy. "Names" from *Memories of a Catholic Girlhood* by Mary McCarthy. Copyright 1957 and renewed by Mary McCarthy. Reprinted by permission of Harcourt Brace & Company.

Claude McKay. "Harlem Shadows," "The Harlem Dancer," "If We Must Die," "The Lynching," "America," "Flower of Love," "A Red Flower," "Flame-Heart," "I Shall Return," and "In Bondage." By permission of the Archives of Claude McKay, Carl Cowl, Administrator, from *Selected Poems of Claude McKay.* (Harcourt Brace, 1981).

James Alan McPherson. "A Solo Song: For Doc" from *Hue and Cry* by James Alan McPherson. Copyright © 1968, 1969 by James Alan McPherson. Reprinted by permission of Brandt & Brandt Literary Agents, Inc.

James Merrill. From *Selected Poems, 1946–1985* by James Merrill. Copyright © 1992 by James Merrill. Reprinted by permission of Alfred A. Knopf, a Division of Random House, Inc.

Edna St. Vincent Millay. "Spring," Copyright © 1962, 1948 by Edna St. Vincent Millay. "The Spring and the Fall," "Euclid Alone Has Looked on Beauty Bare," and "I, Being Born a Woman," Copyright © 1923, 1951 by Edna St. Vincent Millay and Norma Millay Ellis. "Dirge Without Music" and "Justice Denied in "Massachusetts" Copyright © 1928, 1955 by Edna St. Vincent Millay and Norma Millay Ellis. "Love Is Not All," Copyright © 1931, 1958 by Edna St. Vincent Millay and Norma Millay Ellis. "The Return," "On Thought in Harness," and "Here Lies, And None To Mourn Him but the Sea," Copyright © 1934, 1962 by Edna St. Vincent Millay and Norma Millay Ellis. "His Stalk the Dark Delphinium," Copyright © 1939, 1967 by Edna St. Vincent Millay and Norma Millay Ellis. From *Collected Poems of Edna St. Vincent Millay,* HarperCollins. All rights reserved. Reprinted by permission of Elizabeth Barnett, Literary Executor.

Arthur Miller. *The Crucible* by Arthur Miller. Copyright 1952, 1953, 1954, renewed © 1980, 1981, 1982 by Arthur Miller. Used by permission of Viking Penguin, a division of Penguin Books USA Inc.

Janice Mirikitani. "Breaking Tradition" and "Recipe," published in *Shedding Silence, Poetry and Prose* by Janice Mirikitani, Celestial Arts, Berkeley, California, 1978. Reprinted by permission of the poet. "For My Father" and "Desert Flowers," published in *Awake in the River, Poetry and Prose* by Janice Mirikitani, Isthmus Press, San Francisco, 1978.

Nicholasa Mohr. "A Thanksgiving Celebration" by Nicholasa Mohr is reprinted with permission from the publisher of *Rituals of Survival: A Woman's Portfolio* (Houston: Arte Publico Press–University of Houston, 1985).

N. Scott Momaday. Selections reprinted from *The Way to Rainy Mountain,* Copyright © 1969, The University of New Mexico Press.

Marianne Moore. "Poetry," "England," "An Egyptian Pulled Glass Bottle in the Shape of a Fish," "The Pangolin," "What Are Years?" "Nevertheless," and "The Mind Is An Enchanting Thing." Reprinted with the permission of Scribner, a Division of Simon & Schuster, Inc., from *The Collected Poems of Marianne Moore.* Copyright © 1935 by Marianne Moore, copyright renewed © 1963 by Marianne Moore and T. S. Eliot.

Reprinted with the permission of Scribner, a Division of Simon & Schuster, Inc., from *The Collected Poems of Marianne Moore.* Copyright © 1941 by Marianne Moore, copyright renewed © 1969 by Marianne Moore.

Reprinted with the permission of Scribner, a Division of Simon & Schuster, Inc., from *The Collected Poems of Marianne Moore.* Copyright © 1944 by Marianne Moore, copyright renewed © 1972 by Marianne Moore. "To a Chameleon," copyright 1954 by Marianne Moore, from *The Complete Poems of Marianne Moore* by Marianne Moore. Used by permission of Viking Penguin, a division of Penguin Books USA Inc.

Pat Mora. "Border Town: 1938," "Unnatural Speech" and "University Avenue" by Pat Mora are reprinted with permission of the publisher of *Borders* (Houston: Arte Publico Press, University of Houston, 1985).

Aurora Levins Morales. Poems reprinted with permission from *Getting Home Alive* by Aurora Levins Morales and Rosario Morales published by Firebrand Books, Ithaca, New York. Copyright © 1986 by Aurora Levins Morales and Rosario Morales.

Toni Morrison. "1922" from *Sula* by Toni Morrison. Copyright © 1973 by Alfred A. Knopf. Reprinted by permission of International Creative Management.

Mourning Dove. From *Coyote Stories,* reprinted by permission of AMS Press, Inc.

Bharati Mukherjee. "A Wife's Story" from the book *The Middleman and Other Stories* by Bharati Mukherjee, Copyright © 1988 by Bharati Mukherjee. Used with the permission of Grove/Atlantic, Inc.

Joyce Carol Oates. "Where Are You Going, Where Have You Been?" by Joyce Carol Oates. Copyright © 1970 by Joyce Carol Oates. Reprinted by permission of John Hawkins & Associates, Inc.

Tim O'Brien. "In the Field," from *The Things They Carried.* Copyright © 1990 by Tim O'Brien. Reprinted by permission of Houghton Mifflin Co./Seymour Lawrence. All rights reserved.

Flannery O'Connor. "A Good Man Is Hard to Find," from *A Good Man Is Hard to Find and Other Stories,* copyright © 1953 by Flannery O'Connor and renewed 1981 by Regina O'Connor, reprinted by permission of Harcourt Brace & Company.

Clifford Odets. "Waiting for Lefty." Copyright © 1935 by Clifford Odets; copyright renewed © 1962 by Clifford Odets. Used by permission of Grove/Atlantic, Inc.

Frank O'Hara. "My Heart" from *Collected Poems* by Frank O'Hara. Copyright © 1970 by Maureen Granville-Smith, Administratrix of the Estate of Frank O'Hara. "Why I Am Not a Painter" by Frank O'Hara. Copyright © 1958 by Maureen Granville-Smith, Administratrix of the Estate of Frank O'Hara. Both are reprinted by permission of Alfred A. Knopf, Inc. "The Day Lady Died" and "Poem" from *Collected Poems,* Copyright 1964 by Maureen Granville-Smith, Administratrix of the Estate of Frank O'Hara. Reprinted by permission of City Lights Books.

John Okada. From *No-No Boy* by John Okada, reprinted with the permission of University of Washington Press.

Tillie Olsen. "Tell Me A Riddle" from *Tell Me A Riddle* by Tillie Olsen. Introduction by John Leonard. Copyright © 1956, 1957, 1960, 1961 by Tillie Olsen. Introduction 1994, by Dell Publishing. Used by permission of Delacorte Press/Seymour Lawrence, a division of Bantam Doubleday Dell Publishing Group, Inc.

Charles Olson. "The Kingfishers," "For Sappho, Back," "I, Maximus of Gloucester, to You," and "Maximus, to himself," by Charles Olson, trans./ed. by George Butterick. Copyright © 1983 The Regents of the University of California. Used by permission.

Simon Ortiz. Poems from *From Sand Creek* by Simon Ortiz. Copyright © 1981 by Simon J. Ortiz. Reprinted by permission of Simon J. Ortiz.

Cynthia Ozick. From *The Shawl* by Cynthia Ozick. Copyright © 1980, 1983 by Cynthia

Ozick. Reprinted by permission of Alfred A. Knopf, Inc.

Grace Paley. "The Expensive Moment," from *Later the Same Day* by Grace Paley. Copyright © 1985 by Grace Paley. Reprinted by permission of Farrar, Straus & Giroux, Inc.

Ann Petry. "The Witness." From *Miss Muriel and Other Stories,* 1989. Reprinted by permission of Russell & Volkening as agents for the author. Copyright © 1971 by Associated Magazine Contributors, Inc., renewed © 1975 by Ann Petry. Story originally appeared in *Redbook*, 1971.

Pedro Pietri. "Traffic Violations," from *Traffic Violations,* Waterfront Press, 1983, reprinted with permission. "Puerto Rican Obituary," from *Puerto Rican Obituary*, Copyright © 1973 by Pedro Pietri. Reprinted by permission of Monthly Review Foundation.

Sylvia Plath. "For a Fatherless Son" from *Winter Trees* by Sylvia Plath. Copyright © 1971 by Ted Hughes. "Daddy," "Lady Lazarus," "Stings," and "Fever 103°" from *Ariel* by Sylvia Plath, Copyright © 1963 by Ted Hughes. Copyright renewed. All are reprinted by permission of HarperCollins Publishers, Inc.

Ezra Pound. *Poems from Personae.* Copyright © 1926 by Ezra Pound. From *The Cantos of Ezra Pound.* Copyright © 1934, 1948, 1962 by Ezra Pound. Reprinted by permission of New Directions Publishing Corp.

Thomas Pynchon. "Entropy." From *Slow Learner* by Thomas Pynchon. Copyright © 1984 by Thomas Pynchon; first appeared in *The Kenyon Review.* Reprinted by permission of Little, Brown and Company (Inc.).

John Crowe Ransom. "Here Lies a Lady" and "Philomela." Copyright © 1924 by Alfred A. Knopf, Inc. and renewed 1952 by John Crowe Ransom. "Piazza Piece," "The Equilibrists," and "Crocodile." Copyright © 1927 by Alfred A. Knopf, Inc. and renewed 1955 by John Crowe Ransom. Reprinted from *Selected Poems,* Third Edition, Revised and Enlarged by John Crowe Ransom, by permission of Alfred A. Knopf, Inc.

"Recordando al Presidente" and translation, "Remembering the President," from Dan William Dickey, *The Kennedy Corridos: A Study of the Ballads of a Mexican American Hero* by Dan William Dickey, Austin: Center for Mexican American Studies, University of Texas at Austin, 1978. Reprinted by permission. "Corrido de Cesar Chavez" and translation from recording by Lalo Guerrero. Reprinted by permission.

J. Saunders Redding. From *No Day of Triumph* published by Harper & Bros., New York, New York, 1942. Copyright J. Saunders Redding (Esther E. Redding executrix), winner of Mayflower Award for "distinguished writing." Reprinted by permission of Mrs. Saunders Redding.

Ishmael Reed. Reprinted by permission of Scribner, a Division of Simon & Schuster, Inc., from *Mumbo Jumbo* by Ishmael Reed. Copyright © 1972 by Ishmael Reed. "Flight to Canada" Copyright 1976, Ishmael Reed. "I am a cowboy in the boat of Ra" Copyright 1972 by Ishmael Reed. Reprinted by permission of the poet.

Charles Reznikoff. "Testimony I & II" and excerpts by Charles Reznikoff. Copyright © 1977 by Marie Syrkin Reznikoff. Reprinted from *Poems, 1918–1936,* Volume I of *The Complete Poems of Charles Reznikoff* with the permission of Black Sparrow Press. "Children 1–5" Copyright © 1975 by Charles Reznikoff. Reprinted from *Holocaust* with the permission of Black Sparrow Press.

Adrienne Rich. "Diving into the Wreck," "From a Survivor," "Frame," and "Power" from *The Fact of a Doorframe: Poems Selected and New, 1950–1984* by Adrienne Rich. Copyright © 1984 by Adrienne Rich. Copyright © 1975, 1978 by W. W. Norton & Company, Inc. Copyright © 1981 by Adrienne Rich. "Not Somewhere Else, but Here," from *The Dream of a Common Language: Poems, 1974–1977* by Adrienne Rich. Copyright © 1978 by W. W. Norton & Company, Inc. "Coast to Coast," from *A Wild Patience Has Taken Me This Far: Poems, 1978–1981* by Adrienne Rich. Copyright © 1981 by Adrienne Rich. All are reprinted by permission of W. W. Norton & Company, Inc.

Lola Ridge. "Stone Face" by Lola Ridge. Reprinted by permission of Elaine Sproat.

Tomás Rivera. Excerpts from . . .*And the Earth Did Not Devour Him* by Tomás Rivera, translated by Evangelina Vigil-Pinon, are reprinted with permission from the publisher (Houston: Arte Publico Press– University of Houston, 1987).

Richard Rodriguez. From *Hunger of Memory* by Richard Rodriguez. Copyright © 1982 by Richard

Rodriguez. Reprinted by permission of David R. Godine, Publisher.

Theodore Roethke. "Root Cellar," copyright 1943 by Modern Poetry Association, Inc. "Big Wind," copyright 1947 by The United Chapters of Phi Beta Kappa. "The Lost Son," copyright 1947 by Theodore Roethke. "Meditations of an Old Woman," copyright © 1958 by Theodore Roethke. "Elegy" ("Her face like a . . . ") from *The Collected Poems of Theodore Roethke* by Theodore Roethke. Used by permission of Doubleday, a division of Bantam Doubleday Dell Publishing Group, Inc.

Edwin Rolfe. "Asbestos," "Season of Death," "First Love," and "Elegia" from *Collected Poems* by Edwin Rolfe. Copyright 1993 by the Board of Trustees of the University of Illinois. Used with the permission of Mary Rolfe and the University of Illinois Press.

Wendy Rose. "To the Hopi in Richmond" was published in *The Halfbreed Chronicles* by Wendy Rose (West End Press, 1985); "Loo-wit" was published in *The Halfbreed Chronicles* as well as in *Songs from This Earth on Turtle's Back,* edited by Joseph Bruchac (Greenfield Review Press, 1983); *Words in the Blood,* edited by Jamake Highwater (New American Library, 1984); and *Harper's Anthology of American Indian Poetry,* edited by Duane Niatum (Harper & Row, 1988). "Throat Song" was published in *The Halfbreed Chronicles* as well as *Frontiers Journal* and *Harper's Anthology of American Indian Poetry.* "If I Am Too Brown or Too White for You" was published in *The Halfbreed Chronicles* as well as *Harper's Anthology.* "Story Keeper" was published in *The Halfbreed Chronicles* as well as *The Greenfield Review* and *The World's Best Poetry,* edited by The Editorial Board of Roth Publishing Inc. (Roth Publishing Inc./Poetry Anthology Press, 1987). "Julia" was published in *The Halfbreed Chronicles and Other Poems* from West End Press, 1985. Reprinted 1992. All are reprinted by permission of Wendy Rose.

Louis D. Rubin. Reprinted by permission of Louisiana State University Press from *I'll Take My Stand: The South and the Agrarian Tradition,* by Twelve Southerners; New Introduction by Louis D. Rubin, Jr., Copyright 1930 by Harper & Brothers. Copyright renewed 1958 by Donald Davidson. Introduction copyright © 1962, 1977 by Louis D. Rubin, Jr. Biographical essays copyright © 1962, 1977 by Virginia Rock.

Muriel Rukeyser. "Absalom," "The Minotaur," "Rite," and "The Poem as Mask" by Muriel Rukeyser from *Out of Silence,* 1992, Triquarterly Books, Evanston, IL, © William L. Rukeyser. "Martin Luther King, Malcolm X" and "How We Did It" from *Collected Poems,* 1978, McGraw-Hill, New York, © Muriel Rukeyser, by permission of William L. Rukeyser.

Sonia Sanchez. "to blk/record buyers," "Father and Daughter," "Just Don't Never Give Up on Love," "A Letter to Dr. Martin Luther King," and "Masks" from the book *Homegirls and Handgrenades* by Sonia Sanchez. Copyright © 1948 by Sonia Sanchez. Used by permission of the publisher, Thunder's Mouth Press.

George Samuel Schuyler. "The Negro-Art Hokum." From the June 16, 1926 issue of *The Nation.* Reprinted with permission.

Anne Sexton. "Young" and "Housewife" from *All My Pretty Ones.* Copyright © 1962 by Anne Sexton, © renewed 1990 by Linda G. Sexton. "Somewhere in Africa," from *Live or Die,* Copyright © 1966 by Anne Sexton. "Her Kind," from *To Bedlam and Part Way Back* by Anne Sexton. Copyright © 1960 by Anne Sexton. All are reprinted by permission of Houghton Mifflin Company. All rights reserved.

Leslie Marmon Silko. "Lullaby." Copyright © 1981 by Leslie Marmon Silko, reprinted with the permission of The Wylie Agency, Inc.

Lee Smith. "The Bubba Stories" and "The Happy Memories Club" from *News of the Spirit* by Lee Smith, copyright © 1997 by Lee Smith. Used by permission of G. P. Putnam's sons, a division of Penguin Putnam, Inc.

Gary Snyder. "Vapor Trails" from *The Back Country.* Copyright © 1959 by Gary Snyder. Reprinted by permission of New Directions Publishing Corp. "Riprap" from *Riprap and Cold Mountain Poems* by Gary Snyder. Copyright © 1990 by Gary Snyder.

Gary Soto. "The Cellar" from *The Tale of Sunlight* © 1978 by Gary Soto. Reprinted by permission of the poet. From *New and Selected Poems* by Gary Soto © 1995, published by Chronicle Books. Reprinted by permission of the publisher.

Anne Spencer. "Substitution" and "Lines to a Nasturtium." Published in J. Lee Greene, *Time's Unfading Garden,* 1977. Reprinted with permission.

Gertrude Stein. "Composition as Explanation" from *What Are Masterpieces.* Copyright © 1926

(Hogarth Press: London). "The Mother of Us All" taken from *Last Operas and Plays.* Reprinted by permission of the Estate of Gertrude Stein. Text from *The Geographical History of America,* by Gertrude Stein. Copyright © 1936 and renewed 1964 by Alice B. Toklas. Reprinted by permission of Random House, Inc.

John Steinbeck. "The Chrysanthemums," copyright 1937, renewed © 1965 by John Steinbeck, from *The Long Valley* by John Steinbeck. From *The Grapes of Wrath,* Copyright 1939, renewed © 1967 by John Steinbeck. Used by permission of Viking Penguin, a division of Penguin Books USA Inc.

Wallace Stevens. "Sunday Morning," "The Snow Man," "The Course of a Particular," "Of Mere Being," "Peter Quince at the Clavier," "Anecdote of the Jar," and "A High-Toned Old Christian Woman" from *Collected Poems* by Wallace Stevens. Copyright 1923 and renewed 1951 by Wallace Stevens. "Of Modern Poetry" from *Collected Poems* by Wallace Stevens. Copyright 1942 by Wallace Stevens and renewed 1970 by Holly Stevens. All are reprinted by permission of Alfred A. Knopf, Inc. "The Course of a Particular" from *The Palm at the End of the Mind.* Copyright © 1967, 1969, 1971 by Holly Stevens. Reprinted by permission of Alfred A. Knopf, Inc.

Mario Suarez. "El Hoyo," "Señor Garza," and "Kid Zopilote." Reprinted by permission of *The Arizona Quarterly.*

Genevieve Taggard. Poems from *Calling Western Union,* copyright Harper & Bros., 1936; and Long View, Harper & Bros., 1942. Copyrights renewed, reprinted by permission of Marcai D. Liles.

Allen Tate. "Ode to the Confederate Dead" from *Collected Poems, 1919–1976* by Allen Tate. Copyright © 1977 by Allen Tate, reprinted by permission of Farrar, Straus & Giroux, Inc.

Jean Toomer. "Karintha," "Song of the Sun," "Blood-Burning Moon," "Seventh Street," and "Box Seat" from *Cane.* Copyright 1923 by Boni & Liveright, renewed 1951 by Jean Toomer. Reprinted by permission of Liveright Publishing Corporation.

John Updike. "Separating." Copyright © 1975 by John Updike. Reprinted from *Problems and Other Stories,* by John Updike, by permission of Alfred A. Knopf, Inc.

Helen María Viramontes. "The Cariboo Café." Reprinted with permission of the publisher of *The Moths and Other Stories* (Houston: Arte Publico Press–University of Houston, 1985).

Alice Walker. "Nineteen Fifty-Five," from *You Can't Keep a Good Woman Down,* copyright © 1981 by Alice Walker, reprinted by permission of Harcourt Brace & Company.

Margaret Walker. "The Ballad of the Hoppy-Toad" from *Prophets for a New Day,* 1970, reprinted by permission of Broadside Press. "For My People" first published *Poetry Magazine* November 1937, Yale University Press 1942. Also in *This Is My Century,* published by University of Georgia Press, 1989. "Cook in the Big House" and "Randall Ware" from *Jubilee* by Margaret Walker. Copyright © 1966 by Margaret Walker, renewed 1994 by Margaret Walker Alexander. Reprinted by permission of Houghton Mifflin Company. All rights reserved.

Margaret Walker. "Solace" and "The Crystal Palace," poems from *Jubilee* and *This Is My Century* reprinted by permission of the poet, Margaret Walker.

Robert Penn Warren. "Heart of Autumn" and "Amazing Grace in the Back Country" from *Now and Then: Poems, 1976–1978* by Robert Penn Warren. Copyright © 1981 by Robert Penn Warren. "Fear and Trembling" from *Rumor Verified: Poems, 1979–1980* by Robert Penn Warren. Copyright 1981 by Robert Penn Warren. All are reprinted by permission of Random House, Inc.

James Welch. From *Winter in the Blood*, Harper & Row, 1974. Copyright 1974 by James Welch. All rights reserved.

Eudora Welty. "The Wide Net," from *The Wide Net and Other Stories,* copyright © 1942 and renewed 1970 by Eudora Welty, reprinted by permission of Harcourt Brace & Company.

Edith Wharton. "The Life Apart" is reprinted by permission of Lilly Library, Indiana University, Bloomington, IN and The Watkins Loomis Agency. "Roman Fever." Reprinted with the permission of Scribner, a Division of Simon & Schuster, Inc., from *Roman Fever and Other Stories* by Edith Wharton. Copyright © 1934 by Liberty Magazine; copyright renewed © 1962 by William R. Tyler.

Tom Whitecloud. "Blue Winds Dancing" is reprinted with permission of Scribner, a Division of Simon & Schuster from *Scribner's Magazine,* Vol.

CIII, February 1938. Copyright 1938 by Charles Scribner's Sons; copyright renewed © 1966.

John Edgar Wideman. "Valaida." From *Fever* by John Edgar Wideman. Copyright © 1989 by John Edgar Wideman. Reprinted by permission of Henry Holt and Company, Inc.

Tennessee Williams. "Portrait of a Madonna," from *27 Wagons Full of Cotton*. Copyright © 1945 by Tennessee Williams. Reprinted by permission of New Directions Publishing Corporation.

William Carlos Williams. Poems from *Collected Poems, 1909–1939,* Volume I. Copyright © 1938 by New Directions Publishing Corp. Poems from *Collected Poems, 1939–1962,* Volume II. Copyright © 1944, 1948, 1962 by William Carlos Williams. Reprinted by permission of New Directions Publishing Corp.

James Wright. "Saint Judas" from *Saint Judas,* copyright 1959 by James Wright. "Autumn Begins in Martins Ferry, Ohio" and "Lying in a Hammock at William Duffy's Farm in Pine Island, Minnesota" from *The Branch Will Not Break,* copyright 1963 by James Wright. "A Centenary Ode" from *Collected Poems,* copyright 1971 by James Wright. Wesleyan University Press by permission of University Press of New England.

Richard Wright. All pages from "Bright and Morning Star" from *Uncle Tom's Children* by Richard Wright. Copyright © 1938 by Richard Wright. Copyright renewed 1966 by Ellen Wright. Reprinted by permission of HarperCollins Publishers, Inc.

Richard Wright. "The Man Who Was Almost a Man" from *Eight Men* by Richard Wright. Copyright 1940 © 1961 by Richard Wright. Copyright renewed 1989 by Ellen Wright. Reprinted by permission of HarperCollins Publishers, Inc.

Hisaye Yamamoto. "Seventeen Syllables" by Hisaye Yamamoto from *Seventeen Syllables* © 1988 by Hisaye Yamamoto DeSoto. Reprinted by permission of the author.

Karen Tei Yamashita. "Benefits–Koreatown," reprinted from *Tropic of Orange.* Copyright © 1997 by Karen Tei Yamashita (Coffee House Press, Minneapolis). Reprinted by permission from the publisher.

Anzia Yezierska. "America and I" from *The Open Cage.* Reprinted by permission of Louise Levitas Henriksen.

Index of Authors, Titles, and First Lines of Poems